people of the same age or those who have similar interests or do the same job. Examples are *dosh* and *dweeb*.

spoken expressions are used mainly in informal conversations, for example *Give me a break!* or *Don't ask!*

technical language is used by people who specialize in a particular subject area.

written expressions are used mainly in written language, for example *groundswell, hotfoot, vis-à-vis*.

! Taboo words are likely to be thought by many people to be obscene or shocking and you should avoid using them. Examples are *bloody* and *shit*.

The following labels show other restrictions on the use of words.

AmE describes expressions, spellings and pronunciations used in American English and not in British English, for example *bleachers, blindside, blooper*.

BrE describes expressions used in British English and not in American English, for example *jumble sale, agony aunt, chinwag*.

dialect describes expressions that are mainly used in particular regions of the British Isles, not including Scotland or Ireland, for example *beck, nowt*.

old-fashioned expressions are passing out of current use, for example *balderdash, beanfeast, blithering*.

old use describes expressions that are no longer in current use, for example *ere, hearken, perchance*.

saying describes a well-known fixed or traditional phrase, such as a proverb, that is used to make a comment, give advice, etc., for example *actions speak louder than words* and *it's all Greek to me*.

™ shows registered trademarks that belong to manufacturing companies, even though the expressions may be commonly used in speech and writing, for example *Band-Aid, Frisbee, Vegeburger*.

Key to verb patterns

Intransitive verbs

[V]   verb used alone
*A large dog **appeared**.*

[V+adv./prep.]
        verb + adverb or prepositional phrase
*A group of swans **floated by**.*

Transitive verbs

[VN]   verb + noun phrase
*Jill's behaviour **annoyed me**.*

[VN+adv./prep.]
        verb + noun phrase + adverb or prepositional phrase
*He **kicked the ball into** the net.*

Transitive verbs + two objects

[VNN]   verb + noun phrase + noun phrase
*I **gave Sue a book** for Christmas.*

Linking verbs

[V-ADJ] verb + adjective
*His voice **sounds hoarse**.*

[V-N]   verb + noun phrase
*Elena **became a doctor**.*

[VN-ADJ] verb + noun phrase + adjective
*She **considered herself lucky**.*

[VN-N] verb + noun phrase + noun phrase
*They **elected him president**.*

Verbs used with clauses or phrases

[V that]   verb + **that** clause
[V (that)] *He **said that** he would prefer to walk.*

[VN that]   verb + noun phrase + **that** clause
[VN (that)] *Can you **remind me that** I need to buy some milk?*

[V wh-]   verb + **wh-** clause
*I **wonder what** the job will be like.*

[VN wh-]   verb + noun phrase + **wh-** clause
*I **asked him where** the hall was.*

[V to]   verb + **to** infinitive
*The goldfish **need to be fed**.*

[VN to]   verb + noun phrase **to** infinitive
*He **was forced to leave** the keys.*

[VN inf]   verb + noun phrase + infinitive without 'to'
*Did you **hear the phone ring**?*

[V -ing]   verb + **-ing** phrase
*She never **stops talking**!*

[VN -ing]   verb + noun phrase + **-ing** phrase
*His comments **set me thinking**.*

Verbs + direct speech

[V speech] verb + direct speech
*'It's snowing,' she **said**.*

[VN speech] verb + noun phrase + direct speech *'Tom's coming to lunch,' she **told him**.*

For a more detailed explanation of these codes and the codes used with see Study pages **B6–11**.

Oxford Advanced Learner's Dictionary
of Current English

A S Hornby

Sixth edition

Edited by **Sally Wehmeier**

Phonetics Editor **Michael Ashby**

OXFORD
UNIVERSITY PRESS

Great Clarendon Street, Oxford OX2 6DP

Oxford University Press is a department of the University of Oxford.
It furthers the University's objective of excellence in research, scholarship, and
education by publishing worldwide in

Oxford New York

Auckland Bangkok Buenos Aires Cape Town Chennai
Dar es Salaam Delhi Hong Kong Istanbul Karachi Kolkata
Kuala Lumpur Madrid Melbourne Mexico City Mumbai Nairobi
São Paulo Shanghai Singapore Taipei Tokyo Toronto

with an associated company in Berlin

Illustrations by: Julian Baker; Lorna Barnard; Jeremy Bays; David Burroughs; Mark
Dunn; David Eaton; Gay Galsworthy; Karen Hiscock; Margaret Jones; David Marsden;
Fran Sewell; Martin Shovel; Technical Graphics Dept, Oxford University Press; Harry
Venning; Graham White; Michael Woods; Colin Woolf

Designed by Holdsworth Associates, Isle of Wight
Colour pages designed by Christopher Howson
Text capture and processing by Oxford University Press
Typesetting by Tradespools Typesetting Ltd, Frome
Printed in India by Indira Printers, New Delhi 110 020

Contents

Advisory Board

Preface

In 1998 we celebrated both the centenary of the birth of A S Hornby, the creator of the *Advanced Learner's Dictionary* and the fiftieth anniversary of the publication of the dictionary by Oxford University Press. Hornby's great contribution to lexicography was to apply his experience as a teacher of English to producing a dictionary that met the needs of learners, and his success can be measured by the fact that the *Advanced Learner's* has become one of the best-selling books of all time.

Now, in the first year of the new millennium, this edition, the sixth, breaks new ground, sharpening further the learner-centred focus of the original. We have learnt a great deal from our research into how learners use dictionaries and benefited from suggestions from very many teachers and students.

Dictionary users need to be able to find the information they need quickly, understand it once they have found it, and make use of it in their own speaking or writing. This dictionary arranges and presents information in a clear way, using **short cuts** in longer entries to help the user pinpoint the meaning they are looking for. The definitions are all written using a **defining vocabulary** of just under 3000 words, 500 fewer than in the previous edition. This defining vocabulary (listed on page 1531) includes all the items used in definitions and is not made artificially shorter by allowing prefixes and suffixes to be attached to the stem of a listed word. Learners can be sure that, if they are familiar with the words in this list, the definitions in the dictionary will pose no problems.

Our new **usage notes, word-family boxes**, **topic** and **study pages** show links between vocabulary items and, together with the user-friendly **help notes**, give invaluable guidance on usage. The **origin notes** provide fascinating insights into the etymology of some colourful words and expressions. All these features ensure that less experienced learners receive all the support they need, while the most advanced will always find something new and interesting to challenge them.

I am very grateful to all those both within and outside Oxford University Press who have helped with the writing and production of this dictionary. For this edition Michael Ashby, the Phonetics Editor, has improved our representation of the pronunciation of American English. Susan Wilkin helped with the implementation of his policy. Keith Brown gave advice on aspects of the grammatical information shown in the dictionary, especially the verb coding system. The following worked as lexicographers: Evadne Adrian-Vallance, Ruth Blackmore, Michael Britton, Alexandra Clayton, Eunice Dalleres, Margaret Jull Costa, Michael Mayor, Kate Mohideen, Allene Tuck and Annie Watson. Rosalind Combley, Stella O'Shea and Laura Wedgeworth helped with the editing in the later stages of the project. Andrew Delahunty researched and wrote the usage notes. Lisa Isenman, Diane Pecorari and Ruth Urbom were American English editors. Fran Holdsworth was responsible for the exceptionally clear and elegant page design, and for the design of the topic and study pages. Christopher Howson designed the colour pages.

In-house Sandra Pyne, Deborah Tempest and Miranda Steel worked on the dictionary in its early stages. Jane Taylor commissioned the illustrations. Our Publishing Systems Group kept the schedule on track and oversaw the capture and manipulation of data. Very many thanks are due to Anna Cotgreave, Bill Coumbe, Julie Darbyshire, Julia Hiley, Kay Pepler, Katrina Ransom and, especially, Frank Keenan. I should like to express my gratitude for their hard work and commitment to Jo Florio and Dilys Parkinson and to my senior editor, Diana Lea. Jo developed the 'short cuts', Dilys was responsible for the help and usage notes and Diana gave invaluable input into all aspects of the dictionary, particularly the topic, study and illustrations pages. Moira Runcie was unstinting in her support throughout the project. I am indebted to her. Finally, I should like to acknowledge my debt to Jonathan Crowther, whose meticulous work on the fifth edition was an inspiration to me.

Sally Wehmeier
January 2000

Key to dictionary entries

Finding the word

Information in the dictionary is given in **entries**, arranged in alphabetical order of **headwords**.

headwords

entry

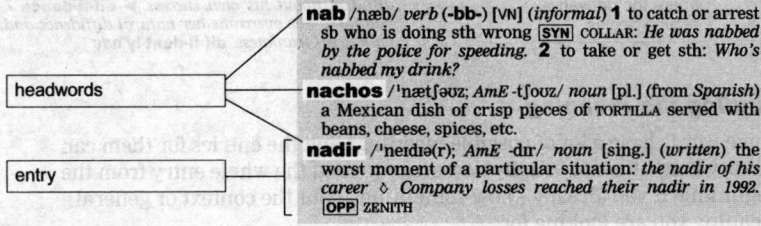

nab /næb/ *verb* (**-bb-**) [VN] (*informal*) **1** to catch or arrest sb who is doing sth wrong [SYN] COLLAR: *He was nabbed by the police for speeding.* **2** to take or get sth: *Who's nabbed my drink?*

nachos /'nætʃəʊz; *AmE* -tʃoʊz/ *noun* [pl.] (from *Spanish*) a Mexican dish of crisp pieces of TORTILLA served with beans, cheese, spices, etc.

nadir /'neɪdɪə(r); *AmE* -dɪr/ *noun* [sing.] (*written*) the worst moment of a particular situation: *the nadir of his career* ◊ *Company losses reached their nadir in 1992.* [OPP] ZENITH

Some headwords can have more than one part of speech:

headword and all possible parts of speech

Black squares show where the information on each part of speech begins.

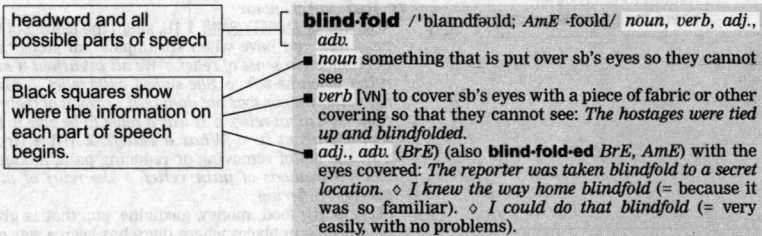

blind·fold /'blaɪndfəʊld; *AmE* -foʊld/ *noun, verb, adj., adv.*
- *noun* something that is put over sb's eyes so they cannot see
- *verb* [VN] to cover sb's eyes with a piece of fabric or other covering so that they cannot see: *The hostages were tied up and blindfolded.*
- *adj., adv.* (*BrE*) (also **blind·fold·ed** *BrE, AmE*) with the eyes covered: *The reporter was taken blindfold to a secret location.* ◊ *I knew the way home blindfold* (= because it was so familiar). ◊ *I could do that blindfold* (= very easily, with no problems).

There are some words in English that have the same spelling as each other but different pronunciations and completely different meanings:

The small **homonym number** shows that this is the first of 2 headwords spelled **punt**.

Different pronunciation is given at each headword.

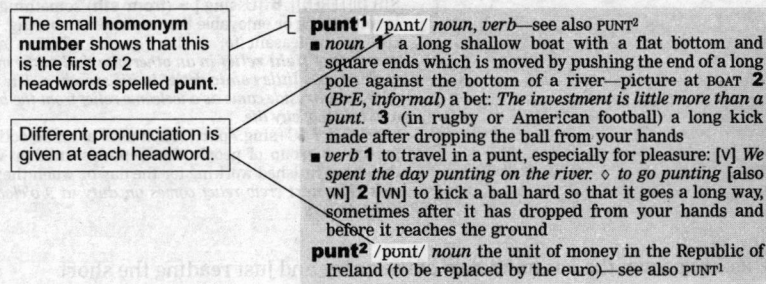

punt¹ /pʌnt/ *noun, verb*—see also PUNT²
- *noun* **1** a long shallow boat with a flat bottom and square ends which is moved by pushing the end of a long pole against the bottom of a river—picture at BOAT **2** (*BrE, informal*) a bet: *The investment is little more than a punt.* **3** (in rugby or American football) a long kick made after dropping the ball from your hands
- *verb* **1** to travel in a punt, especially for pleasure: [V] *We spent the day punting on the river.* ◊ *to go punting* [also VN] **2** [VN] to kick a ball hard so that it goes a long way, sometimes after it has dropped from your hands and before it reaches the ground

punt² /pʊnt/ *noun* the unit of money in the Republic of Ireland (to be replaced by the euro)—see also PUNT¹

There are also some words in English that have more than one possible spelling or form, when both spellings or forms are acceptable. Information about these words is given at the most frequent spelling or form:

The variant spelling is given in brackets.

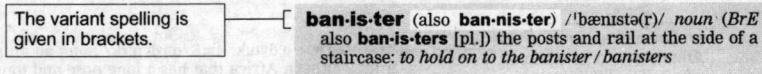

ban·is·ter (also **ban·nis·ter**) /'bænɪstə(r)/ *noun* (*BrE* also **ban·is·ters** [pl.]) the posts and rail at the side of a staircase: *to hold on to the banister / banisters*

At the entry for the less frequent spelling a cross-reference directs you to the main entry:

ban·nis·ter = BANISTER

American English variants and irregular forms of verbs are treated in the same way.

Some words that are **derivatives** of other, more frequent words, do not have their own entry in the dictionary, because they can be easily understood from the meaning of the word from which they are derived (the root word). They are given in the same entry as the root word, in a specially marked section:

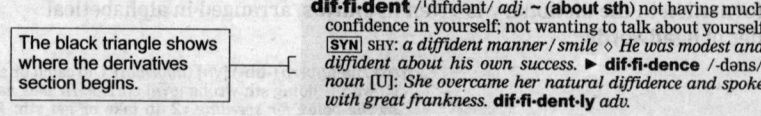

The black triangle shows where the derivatives section begins.

dif·fi·dent /'dɪfɪdənt/ adj. ~ **(about sth)** not having much confidence in yourself; not wanting to talk about yourself SYN SHY: *a diffident manner / smile* ◊ *He was modest and diffident about his own success.* ▶ **dif·fi·dence** /-dəns/ noun [U]: *She overcame her natural diffidence and spoke with great frankness.* **dif·fi·dent·ly** adv.

Finding the meaning

Some words have a lot of possible meanings and the entries for them can be very long. It is not usually necessary to read the whole entry from the beginning, if you already know something about the context or general meaning you are looking for:

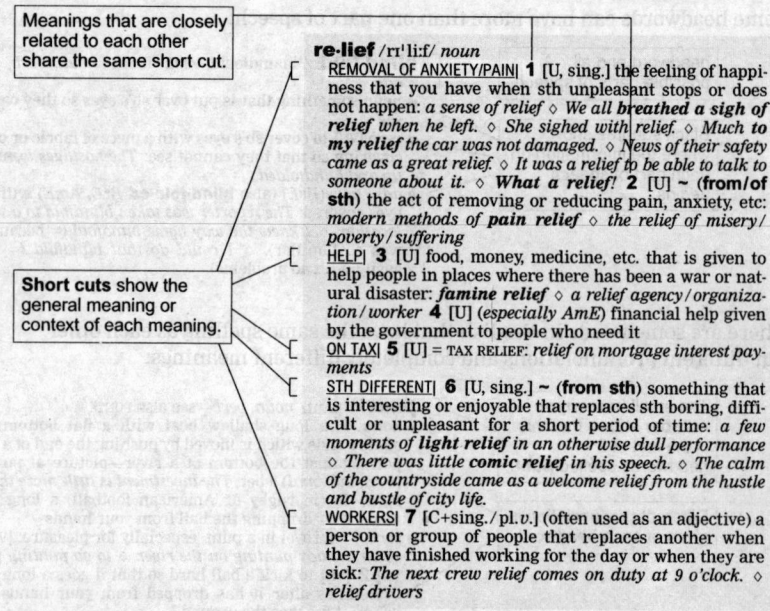

Meanings that are closely related to each other share the same short cut.

Short cuts show the general meaning or context of each meaning.

re·lief /rɪ'liːf/ noun
REMOVAL OF ANXIETY/PAIN| **1** [U, sing.] the feeling of happiness that you have when sth unpleasant stops or does not happen: *a sense of relief* ◊ *We all breathed a sigh of relief when he left.* ◊ *She sighed with relief.* ◊ *Much to my relief the car was not damaged.* ◊ *News of their safety came as a great relief.* ◊ *It was a relief to be able to talk to someone about it.* ◊ *What a relief!* **2** [U] ~ **(from/of sth)** the act of removing or reducing pain, anxiety, etc: *modern methods of pain relief* ◊ *the relief of misery / poverty / suffering*
HELP| **3** [U] food, money, medicine, etc. that is given to help people in places where there has been a war or natural disaster: *famine relief* ◊ *a relief agency / organization / worker* **4** [U] (*especially AmE*) financial help given by the government to people who need it
ON TAX| **5** [U] = TAX RELIEF: *relief on mortgage interest payments*
STH DIFFERENT| **6** [U, sing.] ~ **(from sth)** something that is interesting or enjoyable that replaces sth boring, difficult or unpleasant for a short period of time: *a few moments of light relief in an otherwise dull performance* ◊ *There was little comic relief in his speech.* ◊ *The calm of the countryside came as a welcome relief from the hustle and bustle of city life.*
WORKERS| **7** [C+sing. / pl. v.] (often used as an adjective) a person or group of people that replaces another when they have finished working for the day or when they are sick: *The next crew relief comes on duty at 9 o'clock.* ◊ *relief drivers*

By looking down the left-hand side of the entry and just reading the short cuts, you can quickly find the meaning you want.

Using the word

The entries in this dictionary contain a lot more than just the meanings of words. They show you how to use the word in your own speaking and writing.

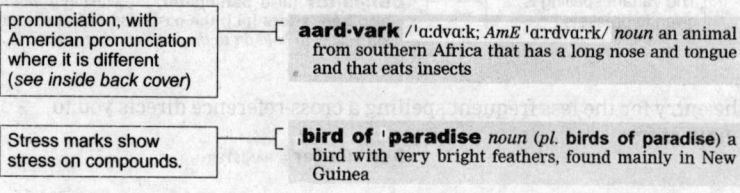

pronunciation, with American pronunciation where it is different (*see inside back cover*)

aard·vark /'ɑːdvɑːk; *AmE* 'ɑːrdvɑːrk/ noun an animal from southern Africa that has a long nose and tongue and that eats insects

Stress marks show stress on compounds.

‚bird of 'paradise noun (*pl.* **birds of paradise**) a bird with very bright feathers, found mainly in New Guinea

Irregular forms of verbs, with their pronunciation. Irregular plurals of nouns are also given.

prepositions, adverbs and structures that can be used with this word (*see Study page* B2)

examples of use in *italic type*

label giving information about usage (*see inside front cover*)

cling /klɪŋ/ *verb* (**clung, clung** /klʌŋ/) [V] **1** ~ **(on) to sb/sth** | ~ **on/together** to hold on tightly to sb/sth: *survivors clinging to a raft* ◇ *She clung onto her baby.* ◇ *Cling on tight!* ◇ *They clung together, shivering with cold.* **2** ~ **(to sth)** to stick to sth: *a dress that clings* (= fits closely and shows the shape of your body) ◇ *The wet shirt clung to his chest.* ◇ *The smell of smoke still clung to her clothes.* **3** ~ **(to sb)** (usually *disapproving*) to stay close to sb, especially because you are emotionally dependent on them: *After his mother's death, Sara clung to her aunt more than ever.* PHRV **'cling to sth** | **cling 'on to sth** to be unwilling to get rid of sth, or stop doing sth: *Throughout the trial she had clung to the belief that he was innocent.* ◇ *He had one last hope to cling on to.* ◇ *She managed to cling on to life for another couple of years.*

fixed form of noun

information on different types of noun (*see Study pages* B4–5)

common phrase in **bold type** in example, with extra explanation in brackets (*see Study page* B3)

word not in the defining vocabulary (*see Appendix 7*)

dock /dɒk; *AmE* dɑːk/ *noun, verb*
■ *noun* **1** [C] a part of a port where ships are repaired or where goods are put onto or taken off them: *dock workers* ◇ *a dock strike* ◇ *The ship was in dock.*—see also DRY DOCK **2** (**docks**) [pl.] a group of docks in a port and the buildings around them that are used for repairing ships, storing goods, etc. **3** [C] (*AmE*) = JETTY **4** [C] (*AmE*) a raised platform for loading vehicles or trains **5** [C] the part of a court of law where the person who has been accused of a crime stands or sits during a trial: *He's been in the dock* (= on trial for a crime) *several times already.* **6** [U] a wild plant of Northern Europe with large thick leaves that can be rubbed on skin that has been stung by NETTLES to make it less painful: *dock leaves*

comparatives and superlatives of adjectives given

information on usage of adjectives (*see Study pages* B4–5)

hearty /ˈhɑːti; *AmE* ˈhɑːrti/ *adj., noun*
■ *adj.* (**heart·ier, hearti·est**) **1** [usually before noun] showing friendly feelings for sb: *a hearty greeting/reception/ welcome* **2** (sometimes *disapproving*) loud, cheerful and full of energy: *a hearty and boisterous fellow* ◇ *a hearty voice/handshake* **3** [only before noun] (of a meal or sb's APPETITE) large; making you feel full: *a hearty breakfast* ◇ *to have a hearty appetite* **4** [usually before noun] showing that you feel strongly about sth: *He nodded his head in hearty agreement.* ◇ *Hearty congratulations to everyone involved.* ◇ *a hearty dislike of sth* IDM see HALE ▶ **hearti·ness** *noun* [U]

verb grammar codes (*see Study pages* B6–9.)

idioms section with special symbol IDM (*see Study page* B12)

phrasal verbs section with special symbol PHRV (*see Study pages* B10–11)

fetch /fetʃ/ *verb* **1** (especially *BrE*) to go to where sb/sth is and bring them/it back: [VN] *to fetch help/a doctor* ◇ *The inhabitants have to walk a mile to fetch water.* ◇ *She's gone to fetch the kids from school.* ◇ [VNN] *Could you fetch me my bag?* **2** [VN] to be sold for a particular price: *The painting is expected to fetch £10 000 at auction.* IDM **fetch and 'carry (for sb)** to do a lot of little jobs for sb as if you were their servant PHRV **fetch 'up** (*informal, especially BrE*) to arrive somewhere without planning to: *And then, a few years after leaving college, he somehow fetched up in Rome.*

Short notes help you to avoid common errors.

exam /ɪgˈzæm/ (also *formal* **exam·in·ation**) *noun* a formal written, spoken or practical test, especially at school or college, to see how much you know about a subject, or what you can do: *to take an exam* ◇ (*formal*) *to sit an exam* ◇ *to pass/fail an exam* ◇ (*BrE*) *to mark an exam* ◇ (*AmE*) *to grade an exam* ◇ *an exam paper* ◇ *I got my exam results today.* ◇ (*BrE*) *She did well in her exams.* ◇ (*AmE*) *She did well on her exams.* ◇ *A lot of students suffer from exam nerves.* ◇ *He's practising hard for his piano exam.* HELP Use *take/do/sit an exam* not *write an exam.*

Build your vocabulary

The dictionary also contains a lot of information that will help you increase your vocabulary and use the language productively:

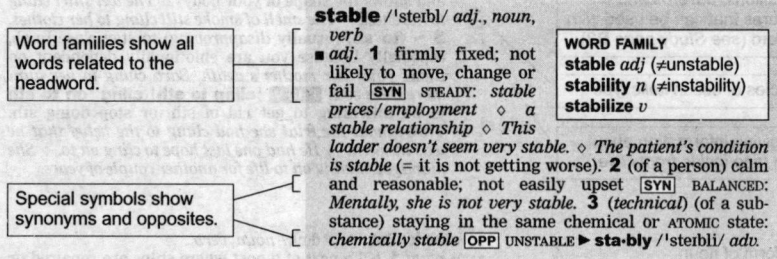

Word families show all words related to the headword.

Special symbols show synonyms and opposites.

stable /'sterbl/ *adj., noun, verb*
■ *adj.* **1** firmly fixed; not likely to move, change or fail SYN STEADY: *stable prices/employment* ◇ *a stable relationship* ◇ *This ladder doesn't seem very stable.* ◇ *The patient's condition is stable* (= it is not getting worse). **2** (of a person) calm and reasonable; not easily upset SYN BALANCED: *Mentally, she is not very stable.* **3** (*technical*) (of a substance) staying in the same chemical or ATOMIC state: *chemically stable* OPP UNSTABLE ▶ **sta·bly** /'sterbli/ *adv.*

WORD FAMILY
stable *adj* (≠unstable)
stability *n* (≠instability)
stabilize *v*

Cross-references refer you to information in other parts of the dictionary:

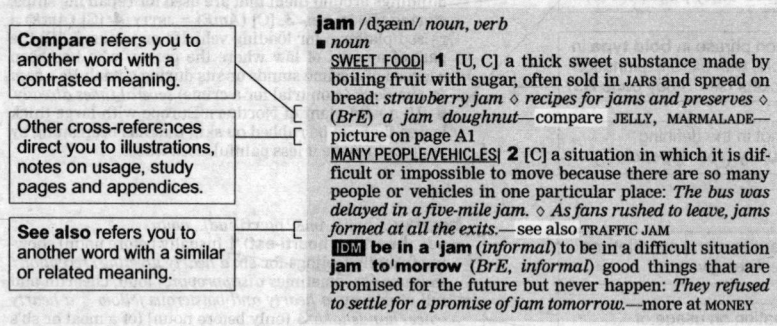

Compare refers you to another word with a contrasted meaning.

Other cross-references direct you to illustrations, notes on usage, study pages and appendices.

See also refers you to another word with a similar or related meaning.

jam /dʒæm/ *noun, verb*
■ *noun*
SWEET FOOD| **1** [U, C] a thick sweet substance made by boiling fruit with sugar, often sold in JARS and spread on bread: *strawberry jam* ◇ *recipes for jams and preserves* ◇ (*BrE*) *a jam doughnut*—compare JELLY, MARMALADE— picture on page A1
MANY PEOPLE/VEHICLES| **2** [C] a situation in which it is difficult or impossible to move because there are so many people or vehicles in one particular place: *The bus was delayed in a five-mile jam.* ◇ *As fans rushed to leave, jams formed at all the exits.*— see also TRAFFIC JAM
IDM **be in a ˈjam** (*informal*) to be in a difficult situation
jam toˈmorrow (*BrE*, *informal*) good things that are promised for the future but never happen: *They refused to settle for a promise of jam tomorrow.*—more at MONEY

Understanding definitions

All the definitions in the dictionary are written using a vocabulary of 3 000 common words. (The complete list is on pages 1531–9 at the back of the dictionary.) This makes them clear and easy to understand.

Reading through the following points before you start to use the dictionary will make understanding the definitions even simpler.

Important

The following are used a very large number of times:

sb = somebody/someone

sth = something

etc. = 'and other things of the same sort'
For example, if you say that something is 'used in books, newspapers, etc.', you mean that you are also including magazines and journals.

particular is used to emphasize that you are referring to one individual person, thing or type of thing and not others.

especially is used to give the most common or typical example of something.

For example, the meaning of the verb **to train** is shown as 'to prepare yourself for a *particular* activity, *especially* a sport'

Describing objects and substances

The definition might refer to the **shape** and or **size** of an object. Make sure that you know what the following words mean: *round, square, circular, hollow, solid, broad, narrow.*

Other **features** of the object might be mentioned:

appearance: *simple, plain, complicated, decorative, rough, smooth, pointed*

colour: *dark*, *light*, *pale*, *bright*, *coloured*, *colourless*

According to its **function**, the object might be a *container, device, instrument, machine, mechanism* or *tool*.

It might be **made of** *fabric* or *cloth* (including *cotton, wool, fur, silk*), *metal* (including *iron, steel, gold, silver*) or *glass*.

Material is a general word that means anything that something is made of. For example a **cushion** is 'a fabric bag filled with soft *material*', and **adobe** is 'mud that is ... used as a building *material*'.

Matter [U] is any substance that physically exists, used especially when defining more technical words. For example, a technical meaning of **suspension** is 'a liquid with very small pieces of solid *matter* floating in it'.

A **substance** may be *liquid* or *solid* or it may be a *gas*.

REMEMBER a **vehicle** could be a *car*, *lorry/truck/van* or *train*. An **aircraft** could be a *plane* or a helicopter.

Describing food

Food and **drink** are described as *bitter*, *sweet, salty, sour*, or *spicy*. An amount of a food prepared in a particular way and served at a meal is called a **dish**.

Describing people

People (or *human beings*) are *male* or *female*, *adults* or *children*. They, their **behaviour** or their **attitude** could be *friendly, bad-tempered, aggressive, honest, dishonest, sincere, calm, anxious, nervous, pleasant, unpleasant, intelligent, stupid, polite* or *rude*.

The **way** or **manner** in which somebody does something may be important.

People do things *deliberately* or *on purpose* (= they mean to do it) or *accidentally* or *by mistake* (= they do not mean to do it).

Somebody may *have or show* a **quality** or **feeling** such as *respect, interest, pleasure, skill, emotion, excitement, enthusiasm, sympathy, courage* or *determination*. Or they may show **a lack of** one of these qualities or **a desire to** do something.

Describing organizations

An **organization** may be a *business*, a *company*, an *institution*, a *club* or *a group of people* who work together for a particular aim. The people who lead an *organization*, a

government or *society* can be called people *in authority*.

Describing actions

An **event** may be a *ceremony*, a *festival* or a *celebration*. It could be *public, private, official* or *social*.

An **occasion** is a time when something happens. For example, a **referendum** is 'an *occasion* when all the people of a country can vote on an important issue'.

Something that somebody does, or something that happens may be described as an *act,* an *action*, an *activity* or a *process* (= a series of connected actions). When a noun is very closely linked to a verb, it may be defined in terms of the verb as *the act/action/activity/process of...* For example, one of the meanings of **achievement** is 'the *act* or *process* of achieving sth'.

Your **experience** [U] is the things you have done and the knowledge you have gained; *an* **experience** [C] is something that has happened to you. For example, **cosmopolitan** means 'having or showing wide *experience* of people and things'. **Conversion** is 'the process or *experience* of changing your religion'.

Things happen *repeatedly* (= several times, one after the other), *continuously* (= without stopping), *occasionally* or *rarely* (= not very often).

Describing situations

A **matter** [C] is a subject or situation that you must consider or deal with. For example, a **case** is 'a *matter* that is being officially investigated ...'

State and **condition** are both used to describe how something or somebody looks or is physically or mentally. A medical **condition** is a particular health problem that somebody has.

A situation that exists or a *habit* or *practice* that somebody has can be described as *the fact of...* or *the practice of...* For example, **gender** is '*the fact of* being male or female'.

Describing ideas

A strong opinion can be called a *belief*. A *set of beliefs* can be a *theory* about a particular subject. Some actions are *the expression of* particular ideas. A set of beliefs and practices can make a whole *system*, especially a *political* or *economic* system such as **capitalism**.

Numbers

1040 form /ˌten ˈfɔːti fɔːm; *AmE* ˈfɔːrti fɔːrm/ *noun* (in the US) an official document in which you give details of the amount of money that you have earned so that the government can calculate how much tax you have to pay

12 /twelv/ *noun* (in Britain) a label that is given to a film/movie to show that it can be watched legally only by people who are at least twelve years old; a film/movie that has this label: *I can take the kids too – it's a 12.*

15 /ˌfɪfˈtiːn/ *noun* (in Britain) a label that is given to a film/movie to show that it can be watched legally only by people who are at least fifteen years old; a film/movie that has this label

18 /ˌeɪˈtiːn/ *noun* (in Britain) a label that is given to a film/movie to show that it can be watched legally only by people who are at least eighteen years old; a film/movie that has this label

18-wheeler /ˌeɪtiːn ˈwiːlə(r)/ *noun* (*AmE*) a very large truck with nine wheels on each side

20/20 vision /ˌtwenti twenti ˈvɪʒn/ *noun* the ability to see perfectly without using glasses or CONTACT LENSES

2.1 /ˌtuː ˈwʌn/ *noun* the upper level of the second highest standard of degree given by a British or an Australian university: *I got a 2.1.*

2.2 /ˌtuː ˈtuː/ *noun* the lower level of the second highest standard of degree given by a British or an Australian university

24-hour clock /ˌtwenti fɔːr aʊə ˈklɒk; *AmE* aʊər ˈklɑːk/ *noun* the system of using twenty four numbers to talk about the hours of the day, instead of dividing it into two units of twelve hours

24/7 /ˌtwenti fɔː ˈsevən; *AmE* fɔːr/ *adv.* (*informal*) twenty-four hours a day, seven days a week (used to mean 'all the time'): *She's with me all the time—24/7.*

3-D (also **three-D**) /ˌθriː ˈdiː/ *noun* [U] the quality of having, or appearing to have, length, width and depth: *These glasses allow you to see the film in 3-D.*

35mm /ˌθɜːtifaɪv ˈmɪlimiːtə(r); *AmE* ˌθɜːrti-/ *noun* the size of film that is usually used in cameras for taking photographs and making films/movies

4×4 /ˌfɔː baɪ ˈfɔː; *AmE* ˌfɔːr baɪ ˈfɔːr/ *noun* a vehicle with a system in which power is applied to all four wheels, making it easier to control

911 /ˌnam wʌn ˈwʌn/ the telephone number used in the US to call the police, fire or ambulance services in an emergency: (*AmE*) *Call 911.*

99 /ˌnamtiˈnam/ *noun* (*BrE*) an ice cream in a CONE with a stick of chocolate in the top

999 /ˌnam nam ˈnam/ the telephone number used in Britain to call the police, fire or ambulance services in an emergency: (*BrE*) *Dial 999.*

Symbols

= equals; is the same as
≠ does not equal; is different from
≈ is approximately equal to
> is more than
< is less than
∵ because
∴ therefore
✓ correct
✗ incorrect
* used to mark important points (called an ASTERISK)
& and (called an AMPERSAND)
# (*BrE*) HASH (*AmE* POUND SIGN) the symbol used for example on telephones, and in addresses in the US
" DITTO; the same word as above
@ at

% (on an envelope) care of. You address a letter to a person 'care of' sb else when the place you are sending it to is not their permanent home.
£ pound sterling
$ dollar
€ euro
© copyright
ⓘ information
Ⓟ parking
♂ male
♀ female
♻ used on the packaging of products to show that they are made from recycled materials (= that have been used once then treated so that they can be used again) , or to show that they can be recycled after use

Aa

A /eɪ/ *noun, symbol, abbr.*

■ *noun* (also **a**) (*pl.* **A's, a's** /eɪz/) **1** [C, U] the first letter of the English alphabet: *'Apple' begins with (an) A/'A'.* **2** (A) [C, U] (*music*) the 6th note in the scale of C MAJOR **3** [C, U] the highest mark/grade that a student can get for a piece of work or course of study: *She got (an) A in/for Biology.* ◇ *He had* **straight A's** (= nothing but A's) *all through high school.* **4** (A) [U] used to represent the first of two or more possibilities: *Shall we go for plan A or plan B?* **5** (A) [U] used to represent a person, for example in an imagined situation or to hide their identity: *Let's assume A knows B is guilty.*—see also A-FRAME, A LEVEL, A-ROAD **IDM** **from A to B** from one place to another: *I don't care what a car looks like as long as it gets me from A to B.* **from A to Z** including everything there is to know about sth: *By the end of the week we knew the subject from A to Z.*

■ *symbol* **1** used in Britain before a number to refer to a particular important road: *the A34 to Newbury* **2** used (but not in the US) before numbers which show standard metric sizes of paper: *a sheet of A4 paper* (= 297×210mm)

■ *abbr.* (in writing) AMP(S)

a /ə; *strong form* eɪ/ (also **an** /ən; *strong form* æn/) *indefinite article* **HELP** The form **a** is used before consonant sounds and the form **an** before vowel sounds. When saying abbreviations like 'FM' or 'UN', use **a** or **an** according to how the first letter is said. For example, **F** is a consonant, but begins with the sound / e / and so you say: *an FM radio.* **U** is a vowel but begins with /j/ and so you say: *a UN declaration.* **1** used before countable or singular nouns referring to people or things that have not already been mentioned: *a man/horse/unit* ◇ *an aunt/egg/hour/ x-ray* ◇ *I can only carry two at a time.* ◇ *There's a visitor for you.* ◇ *She's a friend of my father's* (= one of my father's friends). **2** used before uncountable nouns when these have an adjective in front of them, or phrase following them: *a good knowledge of French* ◇ *a sadness that won't go away* **3** any; every: *A lion is a dangerous animal.* **4** used to show that sb/sth is a member of a group or profession: *Their new car's a BMW.* ◇ *She's a Buddhist.* ◇ *He's a teacher.* ◇ *Is that a Monet* (= a painting by Monet)*?* **5** used in front of two nouns that are seen as a single unit: *a knife and fork* **6** used instead of *one* before some numbers: *A thousand people were there.* **7** used when talking about prices, quantities and rates **SYN** PER: *They cost 50p a kilo.* ◇ *I can type 50 words a minute.* ◇ *He was driving at 50 miles an hour.* **8** a person like sb: *She's a little Hitler.* **9** used before sb's name to show that the speaker does not know the person: *There's a Mrs Green to see you.* **10** used before the names of days of the week to talk about one particular day: *She died on a Tuesday.*

a- /eɪ/ *prefix* (in nouns, adjectives and adverbs) not; without: *atheist* ◇ *atypical* ◇ *asexually*

AA /ˌeɪ 'eɪ/ *abbr.* Automobile Association (a British organization which provides services for car owners)

AAA /ˌeɪ eɪ 'eɪ/ *abbr.* American Automobile Association (an American organization which provides services for car owners)

A & E /ˌeɪ ənd 'iː/ *abbr.* ACCIDENT AND EMERGENCY

aard·vark /'ɑːdvɑːk; *AmE* 'ɑːrdvɑːrk/ *noun* an animal from southern Africa that has a long nose and tongue and that eats insects

aback /ə'bæk/ *adv.* **IDM** **be taken a'back (by sb/sth)** to be shocked or surprised by sb/sth: *She was completely taken aback by his anger.*—see also TAKE SB ABACK

aba·cus /'æbəkəs/ *noun* (*pl.* **aba·cuses** /-kəsɪz/) a frame containing rods with small balls that slide along them. It is used as a tool or toy for counting.

aban·don /ə'bændən/ *verb, noun*

■ *verb* [VN] **1 ~ sb** (**to sth**) to leave sb, especially sb you are responsible for, with no intention of returning: *The baby had been abandoned by its mother.* ◇ *People often simply abandon their pets when they go abroad.* ◇ *The study showed a deep fear among the elderly of being abandoned to the care of strangers.* **2 ~ sth** (**to sb/sth**) to leave a thing or place, especially because it is impossible or dangerous to stay: *Snow forced many drivers to abandon their vehicles.* ◇ *They had to abandon their lands and property to the invading forces.* ◇ *He gave the order to* **abandon ship** (= to leave the ship because it was sinking). **3** to stop supporting or helping sb; to stop believing in sth: *The country abandoned its political leaders after the war.* ◇ *By 1930 he had abandoned his Marxist principles.* **4** to stop doing sth, especially before it is finished; to stop having sth: *They had to abandon the match because of rain.* ◇ *I have abandoned hope of any reconciliation.* **5 ~ yourself to sth** (*literary*) to feel an emotion so strongly that you can feel nothing else: *He abandoned himself to despair.*

■ *noun* [U] (*written*) an uncontrolled way of behaving that shows that sb does not care what other people think: *He signed cheques with careless abandon.* **IDM** see GAY *adj.*

aban·doned /ə'bændənd/ *adj.* **1** left and no longer wanted, used or needed: *an abandoned car/house* ◇ *The child was found abandoned but unharmed.* **2** (*written*) (of people or their behaviour) wild; not following accepted standards

aban·don·ment /ə'bændənmənt/ *noun* [U] (*written*) **1** the act of leaving a person, thing or place with no intention of returning: *their childhood abandonment by their mother* **2** the act of giving up an idea or stopping an activity with no intention of returning to it: *the government's abandonment of its new economic policy*

abase /ə'beɪs/ *verb* [VN] **~ yourself** (*formal*) to act in a way that shows that you accept sb's power over you ▶ **abase·ment** *noun* [U]

abashed /ə'bæʃt/ *adj.* [not before noun] embarrassed and ashamed because of sth that you have done **OPP** UNABASHED

abate /ə'beɪt/ *verb* (*formal*) to become less strong; to make sth less strong: [V] *The storm showed no signs of abating.* ◇ [VN] *Steps are to be taken to abate pollution.* ▶ **abate·ment** *noun* [U]

ab·at·toir /'æbətwɑː(r)/ *noun* (*BrE*) = SLAUGHTERHOUSE

ab·bess /'æbes/ *noun* a woman who is the head of a CONVENT

abbey /'æbi/ *noun* a large church together with a group of buildings in which MONKS or NUNS live or lived in the past: *Westminster Abbey* ◇ *a ruined abbey*

abbot /'æbət/ *noun* a man who is the head of a MONASTERY or an ABBEY

ab·bre·vi·ate /ə'briːvieɪt/ *verb* [VN] [usually passive] **~ sth** (**to sth**) to make a word, phrase or name shorter by leaving out letters or using only the first letter of each word: *the Jet Propulsion Laboratory* (*usually abbreviated to JPL*) ▶ **ab·bre·vi·ated** *adj.*: *Where appropriate, abbreviated forms are used.*

ab·bre·vi·ation /əˌbriːvi'eɪʃn/ *noun* **1** [C] **~ (of/for sth)** a short form of a word, etc: *What's the abbreviation for 'Saint'?* **2** [U] the process of abbreviating sth

ABC /ˌeɪ biː 'siː/ *noun, abbr.*

■ *noun* [sing.] (*BrE*) (*AmE* **ABCs** [pl.]) **1** all the letters of the alphabet, especially as they are learnt by children: *Do*

æ	ɑː	e	ɜː	ə	ɪ	iː	i	ɒ	ɔː	ʌ	ʊ	u	uː
cat	father	ten	bird	about	sit	see	many	got	saw	cup	put	actual	too

(BrE)

you know your ABC? **2** the basic facts about a subject: *the ABC of gardening* **IDM** see EASY

■ *abbr.* American Broadcasting Company (a large national American television company)

ab·di·cate /ˈæbdɪkeɪt/ *verb* **1** to give up the position of being king or queen: [V] *He abdicated in favour of his son.* ◊ [VN] *She was forced to abdicate the throne of Spain.* **2** [VN] **~ responsibility/your responsibilities** to fail or refuse to perform a duty ▸ **ab·di·ca·tion** /ˌæbdɪˈkeɪʃn/ *noun* [U, C]

ab·do·men /ˈæbdəmən/ *noun* **1** the part of the body below the chest that contains the stomach, bowels, etc. **2** the end part of an insect's body that is attached to its THORAX—picture on page A7 ▸ **ab·dom·inal** /æbˈdɒmɪnl; *AmE* -ˈdɑːm-/ *adj.* [only before noun]: *abdominal pains*

ab·duct /æbˈdʌkt/ *verb* [VN] to take sb away illegally, especially using force [SYN] KIDNAP: *He had attempted to abduct the two children.* ▸ **ab·duc·tion** /æbˈdʌkʃn/ *noun* [U, C]: *child abduction* **ab·duct·or** *noun*

Aber·do·nian /ˌæbəˈdəʊniən; *AmE* ˌæbərˈdoʊ-/ *noun* a person from Aberdeen in Scotland ▸ **Aber·do·nian** *adj.*

ab·er·rant /æˈberənt/ *adj.* (*formal*) not usual or not socially acceptable: *aberrant behaviour*

ab·er·ra·tion /ˌæbəˈreɪʃn/ *noun* [C, U] (*formal*) a fact, an action or a way of behaving that is not usual, and that may be unacceptable

abet /əˈbet/ *verb* (**-tt-**) [VN] to help or encourage sb to do sth wrong: *He was abetted in the deception by his wife.* **IDM** see AID *v.*

abey·ance /əˈbeɪəns/ *noun* [U] **IDM** **in abeyance** (*formal*) not being used, or being stopped for a period of time

abhor /əbˈhɔː(r)/ *verb* (**-rr-**) [VN] (not used in the progressive tenses) (*formal*) to hate sth, for example a way of behaving or thinking, especially for moral reasons

ab·hor·rence /əbˈhɒrəns; *AmE* -ˈhɔːr-; -ˈhɑːr-/ *noun* [U, sing.] (*formal*) a feeling of strong hatred, especially for moral reasons

ab·hor·rent /əbˈhɒrənt; *AmE* -ˈhɔːr-; -ˈhɑːr-/ *adj.* (*formal*) **~ (to sb)** causing hatred, especially for moral reasons: *Discrimination of any sort is abhorrent to a civilized society.*

abide /əˈbaɪd/ *verb* (**abided, abided**) **HELP** In sense 2 **abode** /əˈbəʊd; *AmE* əˈboʊd/ is also used for the past tense and past participle. **1** [VN] **can't/couldn't ~ sb/sth** to dislike sb/sth so much that you hate having to be with or deal with them: *I can't abide people with no sense of humour.* ◊ *He couldn't abide the thought of being cooped up in an office.* **2** [V+adv./prep.] (*old use or formal*) to stay or live in a place: *May joy and peace abide in us all.* **PHRV** **a'bide by sth** to accept and act according to a law, an agreement, etc.: *You'll have to abide by the rules of the club.* ◊ *We will abide by their decision.*

abid·ing /əˈbaɪdɪŋ/ *adj.* (*written*) (of a feeling or belief) lasting for a long time and not changing

abil·ity /əˈbɪləti/ *noun* **1** [sing.] **~ to do sth** the fact that sb/sth is able to do sth: *The system has the ability to run more than one program at the same time.* ◊ *Everyone has the right to good medical care regardless of their ability to pay.* ◊ *A gentle form of exercise will increase your ability to relax.* [OPP] INABILITY **2** [C, U] a level of skill or intelligence: *Almost everyone has some musical ability.* ◊ *He was a man of extraordinary abilities.* ◊ *students of mixed abilities* ◊ *A woman of her ability will easily find a job.* ◊ *I try to do my job **to the best of my ability** (= as well as I can).*

-ability, -ibility ⇨ -ABLE

ab·ject /ˈæbdʒekt/ *adj.* [usually before noun] (*formal*) **1** terrible and without hope: *abject poverty/misery/failure* **2** without any pride or respect for yourself: *an abject apology* ▸ **ab·ject·ly** *adv.*

ab·jure /əbˈdʒʊə(r); *AmE* əbˈdʒʊr/ *verb* [VN] (*formal*) to promise publicly that you will give up or reject a belief or a way of behaving [SYN] RENOUNCE

ablaze /əˈbleɪz/ *adj.* [not before noun] (*written*) **1** burning quickly and strongly: *The whole building was soon ablaze.* ◊ *Cars and buses were set ablaze during the riot.* **2 ~ (with sth)** full of bright colours or light: *The trees were ablaze with the colours of autumn.* ◊ *There were lights still ablaze as they drove up to the house.* **3 ~ (with sth)** full of strong emotion or excitement: *He turned to her, his eyes ablaze with anger.*

able /ˈeɪbl/ *adj.* **1 ~ to do sth** (used as a modal verb) to have the skill, intelligence, opportunity, etc. needed to do sth: *You must be able to speak French for this job.* ◊ *A viral illness left her barely able to walk.* ◊ *I didn't feel able to disagree with him.* ◊ *Will you be able to come?* [OPP] UNABLE ⇨ note at CAN[1] **2** (**abler** /ˈeɪblə(r)/, **ablest** /ˈeɪblɪst/) intelligent; good at sth: *the ablest student in the class* ◊ *We aim to help the less able in society to lead an independent life.*—see also ABLY

> **WORD FAMILY**
> **able** *adj.* (≠ unable)
> **ability** *n.* (≠ inability)
> **disabled** *adj.*
> **disability** *n.*

-able (*BrE also* **-ible**) *suffix* (in adjectives) **1** that can or must be: *calculable* ◊ *taxable* **2** having the quality of: *fashionable* ◊ *comfortable* ◊ *changeable* ▸ **-ability, -ibility** (in nouns): *capability* ◊ *responsibility* **-ably, -ibly** (in adverbs): *noticeably* ◊ *incredibly*

able-'bodied *adj.* physically healthy, fit and strong in contrast to sb who is weak or DISABLED: *Military service is compulsory for every able-bodied male between 18 and 27.*

able 'seaman *noun* a sailor of lower rank in the British navy

ab·lu·tions /əˈbluːʃnz/ *noun* [pl.] (*formal or humorous*) the act of washing yourself

ably /ˈeɪbli/ *adv.* skilfully and well: *We were ably assisted by a team of volunteers.*—see also ABLE (2)

ab·nor·mal /æbˈnɔːml; *AmE* -ˈnɔːrml/ *adj.* different from what is usual or expected, especially in a way that is worrying, harmful or not wanted: *abnormal levels of sugar in the blood* ◊ *They thought his behaviour was abnormal.* [OPP] NORMAL ▸ **ab·nor·mal·ly** /æbˈnɔːməli; *AmE* -ˈnɔːrm-/ *adv.*: *abnormally high blood pressure*

ab·nor·mal·ity /ˌæbnɔːˈmæləti; *AmE* -nɔːrˈm-/ *noun* (*pl.* **-ies**) [C, U] a feature or characteristic in a person's body or behaviour that is not usual and may be harmful, worrying or cause illness: *abnormalities of the heart* ◊ *congenital/foetal abnormality*

aboard /əˈbɔːd; *AmE* əˈbɔːrd/ *adv., prep.* on or onto a ship, plane, bus or train: *We finally went aboard.* ◊ *He was already aboard the plane.* ◊ *The plane crashed killing all 157 passengers aboard.* ◊ ***All aboard!*** (= the bus, boat, etc. is leaving soon) ◊ ***Welcome aboard!*** (= used as a greeting to passengers or to a person joining a new organization, etc.)

abode /əˈbəʊd; *AmE* əˈboʊd/ *noun* [usually sing.] (*formal or humorous*) the place where sb lives: *homeless people of no fixed abode* (= with no permanent home) ◊ *You are most welcome to my humble abode.*—see also ABIDE *v.*, RIGHT OF ABODE

abol·ish /əˈbɒlɪʃ; *AmE* əˈbɑːl-/ *verb* [VN] to officially end a law, a system or an institution: *This tax should be abolished.*

abo·li·tion /ˌæbəˈlɪʃn/ *noun* [U] the ending of a law, a system or an institution: *the abolition of slavery/apartheid/the death penalty*

abo·li·tion·ist /ˌæbəˈlɪʃənɪst/ *noun* a person who is in favour of the abolition of sth

abom·in·able /əˈbɒmɪnəbl; *AmE* əˈbɑːm-/ *adj.* extremely unpleasant and causing disgust: *The judge described the attack as an abominable crime.* ◊ *We were served the most abominable coffee.* ▸ **abom·in·ably** /əˈbɒmɪnəbli; *AmE* əˈbɑːm-/ *adv.*: *She treated him abominably.*

A,bominable 'Snowman *noun* = YETI

abom·in·ate /əˈbɒmɪneɪt; *AmE* əˈbɑːm-/ *verb* [VN] (not used in the progressive tenses) (*formal*) to feel hatred or disgust for sth/sb

abom·in·ation /əˌbɒmɪˈneɪʃn; *AmE* əˌbɑːm-/ *noun* (*formal*) a thing that causes disgust and hatred, or is considered extremely offensive: *a concrete abomination masquerading as a hotel*

abo·ri·ginal /ˌæbəˈrɪdʒənl/ *adj., noun*

aɪ	aʊ	eɪ	əʊ	oʊ	ɔɪ	ɪə	eə	ʊə	j	w
my	now	say	go (BrE)	go (AmE)	boy	near	hair	pure	yes	wet

■ *adj.* **1** (usually **Aboriginal**) relating to the original people living in Australia: *the issue of Aboriginal land rights* **2** relating to the original people, animals, etc. of a place and to a period of time before Europeans arrived: *the aboriginal peoples of Canada* ◊ *aboriginal art/culture*

■ *noun* (usually **Aboriginal**) a member of a race of people who were the original people living in a country, especially Australia

abo·ri·gine /ˌæbəˈrɪdʒəni/ *noun* a member of a race of people who were the original people living in a country, especially Australia

abort /əˈbɔːt; *AmE* əˈbɔːrt/ *verb* **1** [VN] to end a pregnancy early in order to prevent a baby from developing and being born alive: *to abort a child/pregnancy/foetus* **2** [V] (*technical*) to give birth to a child or young animal too early for it to survive: *The virus can cause pregnant animals to abort.*—see also MISCARRY **3** [often passive] to end or cause sth to end before it has been completed, especially because it is likely to fail: [VN] *We had no option but to abort the mission.* ◊ [V] (*computing*) *If the wrong password is given the program aborts.*

abor·tion /əˈbɔːʃn; *AmE* əˈbɔːrʃn/ *noun* **1** [U] the deliberate ending of a pregnancy at an early stage: *to support/oppose abortion* ◊ *a woman's right to abortion* ◊ *abortion laws* ◊ *I've always been anti-abortion.* **2** [C] a medical operation to end an unwanted pregnancy at an early stage: *She decided to have an abortion.*—compare MISCARRIAGE

abor·tion·ist /əˈbɔːʃənɪst; *AmE* əˈbɔːrʃ-/ *noun* a person who performs abortions, especially illegally

abor·tive /əˈbɔːtɪv; *AmE* əˈbɔːrtɪv/ *adj.* (*formal*) (of an action) not successful; failed: *an abortive military coup* ◊ *abortive attempts to divert the course of the river*

abound /əˈbaʊnd/ *verb* [V] (*written*) to exist in great numbers or quantities: *Stories about his travels abound.* **PHR V** **aˈbound with/in sth** to have sth in great numbers or quantities: *The lakes abound with fish.*—see also ABUNDANCE, ABUNDANT

about /əˈbaʊt/ *adv., prep., adj.*

■ *adv.* **1** a little more or less than; a little before or after [SYN] APPROXIMATELY: *It costs about $10.* ◊ *They waited (for) about an hour.* ◊ *He arrived (at) about ten.* **2** nearly; very close to: *I'm just about ready.* ◊ *This is about the best we can hope for.* **3** (*especially BrE*) in many directions; here and there: *The children were rushing about in the garden.* **4** (*especially BrE*) in no particular order; in various places: *Her books were lying about on the floor.* **5** (*especially BrE*) doing nothing in particular: *People were standing about in the road.* **6** (*especially BrE*) able to be found in a place: *There was nobody about.* ◊ *There's a lot of flu about.* ◊ *She's somewhere about—I saw her a few minutes ago.* **7** (*technical* or *formal*) facing the opposite direction: *He brought the ship about.* ⊃ note at AROUND [IDM] **that's about 'all | that's about 'it** used to say that you have finished telling sb about sth and there is nothing to add: *'Anything else?' 'No, that's about it for now.'*—more at JUST *adv.*, OUT *adv.*

■ *prep.* **1** on the subject of sb/sth; in connection with sth: *a book about flowers* ◊ *Tell me all about it.* ◊ *What's she so angry about?* ◊ *There's something strange about him.* ◊ *I don't know what you're on about* (= talking about). ◊ *There's nothing you can do about it now.* **2** used to describe the purpose of sth: *Movies are all about making money these days.* ◊ *What was all that about?* (= what was the reason for what has just happened?) **3** busy with sth; doing sth: *Everywhere people were going about their daily business.* ◊ *And while you're about it …* (= while you're doing that) **4** (*especially BrE*) in many directions in a place; here and there: *We wandered about the town for an hour or so.* ◊ *He looked about the room.* **5** (*especially BrE*) in various parts of a place; here and there: *The papers were strewn about the room.* **6** (*especially BrE*) next to a place or person; in the area mentioned: *She's somewhere about the office.* **7** (*literary*) surrounding sb/sth: *She wore a shawl about her shoulders.* [IDM] **how/what about?** **1** used when asking for information about sb/sth: *How about Ruth? Have you heard from her?* ◊ *I'm having fish. What about you?* **2** used to make a suggestion: *How about going for a walk?* ◊ *What about a break?*

■ *adj.* [IDM] **be about to do sth** to be close to doing sth; to be going to do sth very soon: *I was just about to ask you the same thing.* **not be about to do sth** to not be willing to do sth; to not intend to do sth: *I've never done any cooking and I'm not about to start now.*

a,bout-'turn (*BrE*) (also **a,bout-'face** *AmE, BrE*) *noun* [sing.] a complete change of opinion, plan or behaviour: *The government did an about-turn over nuclear energy.*

above /əˈbʌv/ *prep., adv., adj.*

■ *prep.* **1** at or to a higher place or position than sth/sb: *The water came above our knees.* ◊ *We were flying above the clouds.* ◊ *the people in the apartment above mine* ◊ *A captain in the navy ranks above a captain in the army.* ◊ *They finished the year six places above their local rivals.* **2** more than sth; greater in number, level or age than sb/sth: *Inflation is above 6%.* ◊ *Temperatures have been above average.* ◊ *We cannot accept children above the age of 10.* **3** of greater importance or of higher quality than sb/sth: *I rate her above most other players of her age.* **4** too good or too honest to do sth: *She's not above lying when it suits her.* ◊ *He's above suspicion* (= he is completely trusted). **5** (of a sound) louder or clearer than another sound: *I couldn't hear her above the noise of the traffic.* [IDM] **above 'all** most important of all; especially: *Above all, make sure you keep in touch.* **a'bove yourself** (*disapproving*) having too high an opinion of yourself—more at OVER *prep.*

■ *adv.* **1** at or to a higher place: *Put it on the shelf above.* ◊ *Seen from above the cars looked tiny.* ◊ *They were acting on instructions from above* (= from sb in a higher position of authority). **2** greater in number, level or age: *increases of 5% or above* ◊ *A score of 70 or above will get you an 'A'.* ◊ *children aged 12 and above* **3** earlier in sth written or printed: *As was stated above …* ◊ *See above, page 97.*

■ *adj.* [only before noun] mentioned or printed previously in a letter, book, etc: *Please write to us at the above address.* ▶ **the above** *noun* [sing.+ sing./pl. *v.*]: *Please notify us if the above is not correct.* ◊ *All the above* (= people mentioned above) *have passed the exam.*

> **WHICH WORD?** (?)
> **above / over**
>
> ---
>
> **Above** and **over** can both be used to describe a position higher than something: *They built a new room above/over the garage.* When you are talking about movement from one side of something to the other, you can only use **over**: *They jumped over the stream.* **Over** can also mean 'covering': *He put a blanket over the sleeping child.*
>
> **Above** and **over** can also mean 'more than'. **Above** is used in relation to a minimum level or a fixed point: *2 000 feet above sea level* ◊ *Temperatures will not rise above zero tonight.* **Over** is used with numbers, ages, money and time: *He's over 50.* ◊ *It costs over £100.* ◊ *We waited over 2 hours.*

A

a,bove-'mentioned adj. [only before noun] (written) mentioned or named earlier in the same letter, book, etc.

abra·ca·dabra /ˌæbrəkə'dæbrə/ exclamation a word that people say when they do a magic trick, in order to make it successful

ab·rade /ə'breɪd/ verb [VN] (technical) to rub the surface of sth, such as rock or skin, and damage it or make it rough

ab·ra·sion /ə'breɪʒn/ noun (technical) **1** [C] a damaged area of the skin where it has been rubbed against sth hard and rough: He suffered cuts and abrasions to the face. **2** [U] damage to a surface caused by rubbing sth very hard against it: Diamonds have extreme resistance to abrasion.

abra·sive /ə'breɪsɪv/ adj., noun
■ adj. **1** an abrasive substance is rough and can be used to clean a surface or to make it smooth: abrasive kitchen cleaners **2** (of a person or their manner) rude and unkind; acting in a way that may hurt other people's feelings ▶ **abra·sive·ly** adv. **abra·sive·ness** noun [U]
■ noun a substance used for cleaning surfaces or for making them smooth

abreast /ə'brest/ adv. ~ (of sb/sth) next to sb/sth and facing the same way: cycling two abreast ◊ A police car drew abreast of us and signalled us to stop. **IDM** **keep abreast of sth** to make sure that you know all the most recent facts about a subject: It is almost impossible to keep abreast of all the latest developments in computing.

abridge /ə'brɪdʒ/ verb [VN] to make a book, play, etc. shorter by leaving parts out ▶ **abridged** adj.: an abridged edition/version OPP UNABRIDGED **abridge·ment** (also **abridg·ment**) noun [U, C]

abroad /ə'brɔːd/ adv. (especially BrE) **1** in or to a foreign country: to be/go/travel/live abroad ◊ She worked abroad for a year. ◊ imports of cheap food from abroad ◊ He was famous, both **at home and abroad** (= in his own country and in other countries). **2** (formal) being talked about or felt by many people: There was news abroad that a change was coming. **3** (old use) outside; outdoors

ab·ro·gate /'æbrəgeɪt/ verb [VN] (technical) to officially end a law, an agreement, etc. ▶ **ab·ro·ga·tion** /ˌæbrə'geɪʃn/ noun [U]

ab·rupt /ə'brʌpt/ adj. **1** sudden and unexpected, often in an unpleasant way: an abrupt change/halt/departure **2** speaking or acting in a way that seems unfriendly and rude; not taking time to say more than is necessary: an abrupt manner ◊ She was very abrupt with me in our meeting. ▶ **ab·rupt·ly** adv.: The interview ended abruptly. **ab·rupt·ness** noun [U]

ABS /ˌeɪ biː 'es/ abbr. anti-lock braking system

ab·scess /'æbses/ noun a swollen and infected area on your skin or in your body, full of a thick yellowish liquid (called PUS): a painful abscess on the gum

ab·scond /əb'skɒnd; AmE əb'skɑːnd/ verb [V] **1** ~ (from sth) to escape from a place that you are not allowed to leave without permission: She absconded from every children's home they placed her in. **2** ~ (with sth) to leave secretly and take with you sth, especially money, that does not belong to you: He absconded with the company funds.

ab·seil /'æbseɪl/ (BrE) (AmE **rap·pel**) verb [V] ~ (down, off, etc. sth) to go down a steep cliff or rock while attached to a rope, pushing against the slope or rock with your feet ▶ **ab·seil** (BrE) (AmE **rap·pel**) noun

ab·sence /'æbsəns/ noun **1** [U, C] ~ (from ...) the fact of sb being away from a place where they are usually expected to be; the occasion or period of time when sb is away: absence from work ◊ repeated absences from school ◊ The decision was made **in my absence** (= while I was not there). ◊ We did not receive any news during his long absence.—see also LEAVE **2** [U] the fact of sb/sth not existing or not being available; a lack of sth: The case was dismissed **in the absence** of any definite proof. ◊ the absence of any women on the board of directors OPP PRESENCE **IDM** see CONSPICUOUS

ab·sent adj., verb

■ adj. /'æbsənt/ **1** ~ (from sth) not in a place because of illness, etc: to be absent from work/school/a meeting OPP PRESENT **2** ~ (from sth) not present in sth: Love was totally absent from his childhood. OPP PRESENT **3** showing that you are not really looking at or thinking about what is happening around you: an absent expression/look/stare—see also ABSENTLY
■ verb /æb'sent/ [VN] ~ yourself (from sth) (formal) to not go to or be in a place where you are expected to be: He had absented himself from the office for the day.

ab·sen·tee /ˌæbsən'tiː/ noun a person who is not at a place where they were expected to be

absentee 'ballot noun (AmE) = POSTAL VOTE

ab·sen·tee·ism /ˌæbsən'tiːɪzəm/ noun [U] the fact of being frequently away from work or school, especially without good reasons

absentee 'landlord noun a person who rents their property to sb, but does not live in it and rarely visits it

ab·sen·tia ⇨ IN ABSENTIA

ab·sent·ly /'æbsəntli/ adv. in a way that shows you are not looking at or thinking about what is happening around you: He nodded absently, his attention absorbed by the screen.

absent-'minded adj. tending to forget things, perhaps because you are not thinking about what is around you, but about sth else: Grandpa's becoming quite absent-minded. ▶ **absent-'minded·ly** adv. **absent-'minded·ness** noun [U]

ab·so·lute /'æbsəluːt/ adj., noun
■ adj. **1** total and complete: a class for absolute beginners ◊ absolute confidence/trust/silence/truth ◊ 'You're wrong,' she said with absolute certainty. **2** [only before noun] used, especially in spoken English, to give emphasis to what you are saying: There's absolute rubbish on television tonight. ◊ He must earn an absolute fortune. **3** definite and without any doubt or uncertainty: There was no absolute proof. ◊ He taught us that the laws of physics were absolute. ◊ The divorce became absolute last week.—see also DECREE ABSOLUTE **4** not limited or restricted: absolute power/authority ◊ an absolute ruler/monarchy (= one with no limit to their power) **5** existing or measured independently and not in relation to sth else: Although prices are falling **in absolute terms**, energy is still expensive. ◊ Beauty cannot be measured by any absolute standard.—compare RELATIVE
■ noun an idea or a principle that is believed to be true or valid in all circumstances: Right and wrong are, for her, moral absolutes.

ab·so·lute·ly /'æbsəluːtli/ adv. (especially spoken) **1** used to emphasize that sth is completely true: You're absolutely right. ◊ He made it absolutely clear. **2** ~ no ... | ~ nothing used to emphasize sth negative: She did absolutely no work. ◊ There's absolutely nothing more the doctors can do. **3** used with adjectives or verbs that express strong feelings or extreme qualities to mean 'extremely': I was absolutely furious with him. ◊ She absolutely adores you. ◊ He's an absolutely brilliant cook. **4** /ˌæbsə'luːtli/ used to emphasize that you agree with sb, or to give sb permission to do sth: 'They could have told us, couldn't they?' 'Absolutely!' ◊ 'Can we leave a little early?' 'Absolutely!' **5** ~ not used to emphasize that you strongly disagree with sb, or to refuse permission: 'Was it any good?' 'No, absolutely not.'

absolute ma'jority noun (in an election) more than half of the total number of votes or winning candidates: 280 seats are needed for an absolute majority in the National Assembly.

absolute 'zero noun [U] the lowest temperature that is thought to be possible

ab·so·lu·tion /ˌæbsə'luːʃn/ noun [U] (especially in the Christian Church) a formal statement that a person is forgiven for what he or she has done wrong

ab·so·lut·ism /'æbsəluːtɪzəm/ noun [U] **1** a political system in which a ruler or government has total power at all times **2** belief in a political, religious or moral principle which is thought to be true in any circumstances ▶ **ab·so·lut·ist** noun, adj.

s	t	v	z	ʃ	ʒ	tʃ	dʒ	θ	ð	ŋ
see	tea	van	zoo	shoe	vision	chain	jam	thin	this	sing

ab·solve /əbˈzɒlv; AmE əbˈzɑːlv/ verb [VN] ~ sb (from/of sth) **1** to state formally that sb is not guilty or responsible for sth: *The court absolved him of all responsibility for the accident.* **2** to give ABSOLUTION to sb: *I absolve you from all your sins.*

ab·sorb /əbˈsɔːb; -ˈzɔːb; AmE -ˈsɔːrb; -ˈzɔːrb/ verb [VN]
LIQUID/GAS | **1** to take in a liquid, gas or other substance from the surface or space around: *Plants absorb oxygen.* ◊ *The cream is easily absorbed into the skin.*
MAKE PART OF STH LARGER | **2** [often passive] to make sth smaller become part of sth larger: *The surrounding small towns have been absorbed into the city.* ◊ *The country simply cannot absorb this influx of refugees.*
INFORMATION | **3** to take sth into the mind and learn or understand it: *It's a lot of information to absorb all at once.*
INTEREST SB | **4** to interest sb very much so that they pay no attention to anything else: *This work had absorbed him for several years.*
HEAT/LIGHT/ENERGY | **5** to take in and keep heat, light, energy, etc. instead of reflecting it: *Black walls absorb a lot of heat during the day.*
SHOCK/IMPACT | **6** to reduce the effect of a blow, hit, etc: *This tennis racket absorbs shock on impact.*—see also SHOCK ABSORBER
MONEY/TIME/CHANGES | **7** to use up a large supply of sth, especially money or time: *The new proposals would absorb $80 billion of the federal budget.* **8** to deal with changes, effects, costs, etc: *The company is unable to absorb such huge losses.*

ab·sorbed /əbˈsɔːbd; -ˈzɔːbd; AmE -ˈsɔːrbd; -ˈzɔːrbd/ adj. [not usually before noun] ~ **in sth/sb** very interested in sth/sb so that you are not paying attention to anything else: *She seemed totally absorbed in her book.*

ab·sorb·ent /əbˈsɔːbənt; -ˈzɔːb-; AmE -ˈsɔːrb-; -ˈzɔːrb-/ adj. able to take in sth easily, especially liquid: *absorbent paper/materials* ▶ **ab·sorb·ency** /-ənsi/ noun [U]

ab·sorb·ing /əbˈsɔːbɪŋ; -ˈzɔːb-; AmE -ˈsɔːrb-; -ˈzɔːrb-/ adj. interesting and enjoyable and holding your attention completely: *an absorbing book/game*

ab·sorp·tion /əbˈsɔːpʃn; -ˈzɔːp-; AmE -ˈsɔːrp-; -ˈzɔːrp-/ noun [U] **1** the process of a liquid, gas or other substance being taken in: *Vitamin D is necessary to aid the absorption of calcium from food.* **2** the process of a smaller group, country, etc. becoming part of a larger group or country: *the absorption of immigrants into the host country* **3** ~ **(in sth)** the fact of sb being very interested in sth so that it takes all their attention: *His work suffered because of his total absorption in sport.*

ab·stain /əbˈsteɪn/ verb [V] ~ **(from sth) 1** to choose not to use a vote, either in favour of or against sth: *Ten people voted in favour, five against and two abstained.* **2** to decide not to do sth, especially sth you like or enjoy, because it is bad for your health or considered morally wrong: *to abstain from alcohol/sex/drugs*—see also ABSTINENCE, ABSTENTION

ab·stain·er /əbˈsteɪnə(r)/ noun **1** a person who chooses not to vote either in favour of or against sth **2** a person who never drinks alcohol

ab·ste·mi·ous /əbˈstiːmiəs/ adj. (formal) not allowing yourself to have much food or alcohol, or to do things that are enjoyable

ab·sten·tion /əbˈstenʃn/ noun **1** [C, U] ~ **(from sth)** an act of choosing not to use a vote either in favour of or against sth: *The voting was 15 in favour, 3 against and 2 abstentions.* **2** [U] (formal) the act of not allowing yourself to have or do sth enjoyable or sth that is considered bad—see also ABSTAIN

ab·stin·ence /ˈæbstɪnəns/ noun [U] (formal) the practice of not allowing yourself sth, especially food, alcoholic drinks or sex, for moral, religious or health reasons: *total abstinence from strong drink*—see also ABSTAIN

ab·stract adj., noun, verb
■ adj. /ˈæbstrækt/ **1** based on general ideas and not on any particular real person, thing or situation: *abstract knowledge/principles* ◊ *The research shows that pre-school chil-*

dren are capable of thinking in abstract terms.*—compare CONCRETE adj. (2) **2** existing in thought or as an idea but not having a physical reality: *We may talk of beautiful things but beauty itself is abstract.* **3** (of art) not representing people or things in a realistic way, but expressing the artist's ideas about them—compare FIGURATIVE (2), REPRESENTATIONAL ▶ **ab·stract·ly** adv.
■ noun /ˈæbstrækt/ **1** an abstract work of art **2** a short piece of writing containing the main ideas in a document [SYN] SUMMARY [IDM] **in the 'abstract** in a general way, without referring to a particular real person, thing or situation: *Legal questions rarely exist in the abstract; they are based on real cases.* ◊ *I'm just talking in the abstract now.*
■ verb /æbˈstrækt/ [VN] **1** ~ **sth (from sth)** to remove sth from somewhere: *She abstracted the main points from the argument.* ◊ *a plan to abstract 8 million gallons of water from the river* **2** (technical) to make a written summary of a book, etc.

ab·stract·ed /æbˈstræktɪd/ adj. (formal) thinking deeply about sth and not paying attention to what is around you ▶ **ab·stract·ed·ly** adv.

ab·strac·tion /æbˈstrækʃn/ noun **1** [C, U] (formal) a general idea not based on any particular real person, thing or situation; the quality of being abstract: *ideological/mathematical abstractions* **2** [U] (formal) the state of thinking deeply about sth and not paying attention to what is around you: *She was gazing in abstraction at the far corner of the room.* **3** [U, C] (technical) the action of removing sth from sth else; the process of being removed from sth else: *water abstraction from rivers*

ˌabstract 'noun noun (grammar) a noun, for example *goodness* or *freedom*, that refers to an idea or a general quality, not to a physical object—compare COMMON NOUN, PROPER NOUN

ab·struse /əbˈstruːs; æb-/ adj. (formal, often disapproving) difficult to understand: *an abstruse argument*

ab·surd /əbˈsɜːd; AmE əbˈsɜːrd/ adj. **1** completely ridiculous; not logical and sensible: *That uniform makes the guards look absurd.* ◊ *Of course it's not true, what an absurd idea.* **2** (the absurd) noun [sing.] things that are or that seem to be absurd: *He has a good sense of the absurd.* ▶ **ab·surd·ity** noun [U, C] (pl. -ties): *It was only later that she could see the absurdity of the situation.* **ab·surd·ly** adv.: *The paintings were sold for absurdly high prices.*

abun·dance /əˈbʌndəns/ noun [sing., U] ~ **(of sth)** (formal) a large quantity that is more than enough [IDM] **in abundance** in large quantities: *Fruit and vegetables grew in abundance on the island.*

abun·dant /əˈbʌndənt/ adj. (formal) existing in large quantities; more than enough [SYN] PLENTIFUL: *Fish are abundant in the lake.* ◊ *We have abundant evidence to prove his guilt.*

abun·dant·ly /əˈbʌndəntli/ adv. **1** ~ **clear** very clear: *She made her wishes abundantly clear.* **2** in large quantities: *Calcium is found most abundantly in milk.*

abuse noun, verb
■ noun /əˈbjuːs/ **1** [U, sing.] ~ **(of sth)** the use of sth in a way that is wrong or harmful: *alcohol/drug/solvent abuse* ◊ *He was arrested on charges of corruption and abuse of power.* ◊ *The system of paying cash bonuses is open to abuse* (= might be used in the wrong way). ◊ *What she did was an abuse of her position as manager.* **2** [U, pl.] unfair, cruel or violent treatment of sb: *child abuse* ◊ *sexual abuse* ◊ *reported abuses by the secret police* ◊ *She suffered years of physical abuse.* **3** [U] rude and offensive remarks, usually made when sb is very angry: *to scream/hurl/shout abuse* ◊ *a stream/torrent of abuse*
■ verb /əˈbjuːz/ [VN] **1** to make bad use of sth, or to use so much of sth that it harms your health: *to abuse alcohol/drugs* ◊ *He systematically abused his body with heroin and cocaine.* **2** to use power or knowledge unfairly or wrongly: *She abused her position as principal by giving jobs to her friends.* ◊ *He felt they had abused his trust by talking about him to the press* (= deceived him, although he had trusted them). **3** to treat a person or an animal in

æ	ɑː	e	ɜː	ə	ɪ	iː	i	ɒ	ɔː	ʌ	ʊ	u	uː
cat	father	ten	bird	about	sit	see	many	got	saw	cup	put	actual	too

(BrE)

A

a cruel or violent way, especially sexually: *All the children had been physically and emotionally abused.* ◊ *He had abused his own daughter* (= had sex with her). ◊ *The boy had been viciously assaulted and sexually abused.* **4** to make rude or offensive remarks to or about sb: *Journalists covering the case have been threatened and abused.* ▶ **ab·user** *noun*: *a drug abuser* ◊ *a child abuser*

abu·sive /əˈbjuːsɪv/ *adj.* **1** (of speech or of a person) rude and offensive; criticizing rudely and unfairly: *abusive language/remarks* ◊ *He became abusive when he was drunk.* **2** (of behaviour) involving violence: *an abusive relationship* ▶ **abu·sive·ly** *adv.* (*rare*)

abut /əˈbʌt/ *verb* (**-tt-**) ~ (**on/onto sth**) (*formal*) (of land or a building) to be next to sth or to have one side touching the side of sth: [V] *His land abuts onto a road.* [also VN]

abys·mal /əˈbɪzməl/ *adj.* extremely bad or of a very low standard [SYN] TERRIBLE: *His manners are abysmal.* ▶ **abys·mal·ly** *adv.*

abyss /əˈbɪs/ *noun* [usually sing.] (*formal* or *literary*) a very deep wide space or hole that seems to have no bottom: *Ahead of them was a gaping abyss.* ◊ (*figurative*) *an abyss of ignorance/despair/loneliness* ◊ (*figurative*) *The country is stepping back from the edge of an abyss.*

AC /ˌeɪ ˈsiː/ *abbr.* **1** (also **ac, a/c**) (*especially AmE*) AIR CONDITIONING **2** ALTERNATING CURRENT (an electric current that changes direction at regular intervals many times a second)—compare DC

a/c (in writing) *abbr.* **1** account **2** AIR CONDITIONING

aca·cia /əˈkeɪʃə/ (also **aˈcacia tree**) *noun* a tree with yellow or white flowers. There are several types of acacia tree, some of which produce a sticky liquid used in making glue.

aca·demia /ˌækəˈdiːmiə/ (also *formal* or *humorous* **aca·deme** /ˈækədiːm/) *noun* [U] the world of learning, teaching, research, etc. at universities, and the people involved in it

aca·dem·ic /ˌækəˈdemɪk/ *adj., noun*
■ *adj.* **1** [usually before noun] connected with education, especially studying in schools and universities: *The students return in October for the start of the new academic year.* ◊ *high/low academic standards* ◊ *an academic career* **2** [usually before noun] involving a lot of reading and studying rather than practical or technical skills: *academic subjects/qualifications* **3** good at subjects involving a lot of reading and studying: *She wasn't very academic and hated school.* **4** not connected to a real or practical situation and therefore not important: *It is a purely academic question.* ◊ *The whole thing's academic now—we can't win anyway.* ▶ **aca·dem·ic·al·ly** /-kli/ *adv.*: *You have to do well academically to get into medical school.*
■ *noun* a person who teaches and/or does research at a university or college

acad·em·ician /əˌkædəˈmɪʃn; AmE ˌækədəˈmɪʃn/ *noun* a member of an academy (2)

acad·emy /əˈkædəmi/ (*pl.* **-ies**) **1** *noun* a school or college for special training: *the Royal Academy of Music* ◊ *a police/military academy* **2** (usually **Academy**) a type of official organization which aims to encourage and develop art, literature, science, etc: *the Royal Academy of Arts* **3** a secondary school in Scotland or a private school in the US

Aˌcademy Aˈward (also **Oscar**) *noun* one of the awards given every year by the US Academy of Motion Picture Arts and Sciences for achievement in the making of films/movies

a cap·pella /ˌæ kəˈpelə; ˌɑː/ *adj.* (of music) for singing voices alone, without musical instruments ▶ **a cap·pella** *adv.*

ACAS /ˈeɪkæs/ *abbr.* (in Britain) Advisory, Conciliation and Arbitration Service. ACAS is an organization that helps employers and employees settle disagreements.

ac·cede /əkˈsiːd/ *verb* ~ (**to sth**) (*formal*) **1** to agree to a request, proposal, etc: [V] *He acceded to demands for his resignation.* [also V speech] **2** [V] to achieve a high position, especially to become king or queen: *Queen Victoria acceded to the throne in 1837.*—see also ACCESSION

ac·cel·er·ate /əkˈseləreɪt/ *verb* **1** to happen or to make

sth happen faster or earlier than expected: [V] *Inflation continues to accelerate.* ◊ [VN] *Exposure to the sun can accelerate the ageing process.* **2** [V] (of a vehicle or person) to start to go faster: *The runners accelerated smoothly around the bend.* ◊ *The car accelerated to overtake me.* [OPP] DECELERATE

ac·cel·er·ation /əkˌseləˈreɪʃn/ *noun* **1** [U, sing.] ~ (**in sth**) an increase in how fast sth happens: *an acceleration in the rate of economic growth* **2** [U] the rate at which a vehicle increases speed: *a car with good acceleration* **3** [U] (*physics*) the rate at which the VELOCITY (= speed in a particular direction) of an object changes

ac·cel·er·ator /əkˈseləreɪtə(r)/ *noun* **1** (*BrE*) (also **ˈgas pedal** *AmE, BrE*) the PEDAL in a car or other vehicle that you press with your foot to control the speed of the engine—picture at CAR **2** (*physics*) a machine for making ELEMENTARY PARTICLES move at high speeds

ac·cent *noun, verb*
■ *noun* /ˈæksent; -sənt/ **1** [C, U] a way of pronouncing the words of a language that shows which country or area a person comes from: *a northern/Dublin/Indian accent* ◊ *a strong/broad Scottish accent* (= one that is very noticeable) ◊ *She spoke English with a faint Dutch accent.*— compare DIALECT **2** [sing.] a special importance that is given to sth: *In all our products the accent is on quality.* **3** [C] the emphasis that you should give to part of a word when saying it: *In 'today' the accent is on the second syllable.* **4** [C] a mark on a letter to show that it should be pronounced in a particular way: *Canapé has an accent on the 'e'.*
■ *verb* /ækˈsent/ [VN] (*rare*) to emphasize a part of sth: *The women accent their eyes with make-up.*

ac·cent·ed /ˈæksentɪd/ *adj.* **1** spoken with a foreign accent: *He spoke heavily accented English.* **2** (*technical*) spoken with particular emphasis: *accented vowels/syllables* **3** (*technical*) (of a letter of the alphabet) written or printed with a special mark on it to show it should be pronounced in a particular way: *accented characters*

ac·cen·tu·ate /əkˈsentʃueɪt/ *verb* [VN] to emphasize sth or make it more noticeable: *Her short hair accentuated her huge eyes.* ▶ **ac·cen·tu·ation** /əkˌsentʃuˈeɪʃn/ *noun* [U]

ac·cept /əkˈsept/ *verb*
OFFER/INVITATION | **1** to take willingly sth that is offered; to say 'yes' to an offer, invitation, etc: [V] *He asked me to marry him and I accepted.* ◊ [VN] *Please accept our sincere apologies.* ◊ *He is charged with accepting bribes from a firm of suppliers.* ◊ *It was pouring with rain so I accepted his offer of a lift.* ◊ *She's decided not to accept the job.* ◊ *She said she'd accept $15 for it.*
RECEIVE AS SUITABLE | **2** [VN] to receive sth as suitable or good enough: *My article has been accepted for publication.* ◊ *This machine only accepts coins.* ◊ *Will you accept a cheque?*
AGREE | **3** [VN] to agree to or approve of sth: *They accepted the court's decision.* ◊ *He accepted all the changes we proposed.* ◊ *She won't accept advice from anyone.*
RESPONSIBILITY | **4** [VN] to admit that you are responsible or to blame for sth: *He accepts full responsibility for what happened.* ◊ *You have to accept the consequences of your actions.*
BELIEVE | **5** ~ **sth** (**as sth**) to believe that sth is true: [VN] *I don't accept his version of events.* ◊ *Can we accept his account as the true version?* ◊ [V that] *I accept that this move will not be a popular one.* ◊ [VN that] *It is generally accepted that people are motivated by success.* ◊ [VN to inf] *The workforce is generally accepted to have the best conditions in Europe.* [HELP] This pattern is only used in the passive.
DIFFICULT SITUATION | **6** ~ **sth** (**as sth**) to continue in a difficult situation without complaining, because you realize that you cannot change it: [VN] *You just have to accept the fact that we're never going to be rich.* ◊ *Nothing will change as long as the workers continue to accept these appalling conditions.* ◊ *They accept the risks as part of the*

aɪ	aʊ	eɪ	əʊ	oʊ	ɔɪ	ɪə	eə	ʊə	j	w
my	now	say	go (BrE)	go (AmE)	boy	near	hair	pure	yes	wet

job. ◊ [V**that**] *He just refused to accept that his father was no longer there.*

WELCOME | **7** [VN] **~ sb (into sth)** | **~ sb (as sth)** to make sb feel welcome and part of a group: *It may take years to be completely accepted by the local community.* ◊ *She had never been accepted into what was essentially a man's world.* ◊ *He never really accepted her as his own child.*

ALLOW SB TO JOIN | **8 ~ sb (into sth)** | **~ sb (as sth)** to allow sb to join an organization, attend an institution, use a service, etc: [VN] *The college he applied to has accepted him.* ◊ *She was disappointed not to be accepted into the club.* ◊ *The landlord was willing to accept us as tenants.* ◊ [VN**to** inf] *She was accepted to study music.*

ac·cept·able /ək'septəbl/ *adj.* **1** agreed or approved of by most people in a society: *Children must learn socially acceptable behaviour.* **2 ~ (to sb)** that sb agrees is satisfactory or allowed: *We want a political solution that is acceptable to all parties.* ◊ *For this course a pass in English at grade B is acceptable.* ◊ *Air pollution in the city had reached four times the acceptable levels.* **3** not very good but good enough: *The food was acceptable, but no more.* ⇨ note at ENOUGH ► **ac·cept·abil·ity** /ək,septə'bɪləti/ *noun* [U] **ac·cept·ably** /-bli/ *adv.*

ac·cept·ance /ək'septəns/ *noun* **1** [U,C] the act of accepting a gift, an invitation, an offer, etc: *Please confirm your acceptance of this offer in writing.* ◊ *He made a short acceptance speech/speech of acceptance.* **2** [U] the act of agreeing with sth and approving of it: *The new laws have gained widespread acceptance.* **3** [U] the process of allowing sb to join sth or be a member of a group: *Your acceptance into the insurance plan is guaranteed.* ◊ *Social acceptance is important for most young people.* **4** [U] willingness to accept an unpleasant or difficult situation: *acceptance of death/suffering*

ac·cess /'ækses/ *noun, verb*
■ *noun* [U] **1 ~ (to sth)** a way of entering or reaching a place: *The only access to the farmhouse is across the fields.* ◊ *Disabled visitors are welcome; there is good wheelchair access to most facilities.* ◊ *The police gained access through a broken window.* **2 ~ (to sth)** the opportunity or right to use sth or to see sb/sth: *Students must have access to good resources.* ◊ *You need a password to get access to the computer system.* ◊ *access to confidential information* ◊ *Journalists were denied access to the President.* ◊ *Many divorced fathers only have access to their children at weekends* (= they are allowed by law to see them only at weekends).—compare VISITATION
■ *verb* [VN] **1** (*computing*) to open a computer file in order to get or add information **2** (*formal*) to reach, enter or use sth: *The loft can be accessed by a ladder.*

'access course *noun* (*BrE*) a course of education that prepares students without the usual qualifications, in order that they can study at university or college

ac·cess·ible /ək'sesəbl/ *adj.* **~ (to sb)** **1** that can be reached, entered, used, seen, etc: *The remote desert area is accessible only by helicopter.* ◊ *These documents are not accessible to the public.* **2** easy to understand: *Her poetry is always very accessible.* ◊ *a programme making science more accessible to young people* **3** (of a person) easy to talk to and get to know OPP INACCESSIBLE ► **ac·ces·si·bil·ity** /ək,sesə'bɪləti/ *noun* [U]

ac·ces·sion /æk'seʃn/ *noun* **~ (to sth)** **1** [U] the act of becoming a ruler of a country: *the accession of Queen Victoria to the throne*—see also ACCEDE **2** [U] the act of becoming part of an international organization: *the accession of new member states to the EU* **3** [C] (*technical*) a thing that is added to a collection of objects, paintings, etc. in a library or museum

ac·ces·sory /ək'sesəri/ *noun, adj.*
■ *noun* (*pl.* **-ies**) **1** [usually pl.] an extra piece of equipment that is useful but not essential or that can be added to sth else as a decoration: *bicycle accessories* ◊ *a range of furnishings and accessories for the home* **2** [usually pl.] a thing that you can wear or carry that matches your clothes, for example a belt or a bag: *fashion accessories to dress up your wardrobe* **3 ~ (to sth)** (*law*) a person who helps sb to commit a crime or who knows about it and

protects the person from the police: *He was charged with being an accessory to murder.* ◊ *an accessory before/ after the fact* (= before/after the crime was committed)
■ *adj.* (*technical*) not the most important when compared to others: *the accessory muscles of respiration*

'access road *noun* a road used for driving into or out of a particular place: *an access road to an industrial estate*—compare SLIP ROAD

'access time *noun* [U,C] (*computing*) the time taken to obtain data stored in a computer: *an average access time of less than 100 milliseconds*

ac·ci·dent /'æksɪdənt/ *noun* **1** [C] an unpleasant event, especially in a vehicle, that happens unexpectedly and causes injury or damage: *a car/road/traffic accident* ◊ *He was killed in an accident.* ◊ *One in seven accidents is caused by sleepy drivers.* ◊ *The accident happened at 3 p.m.* ◊ *to have an accident* ◊ *a serious/minor accident* ◊ *a fatal accident* (= in which sb is killed) ◊ *accidents in the home* ◊ *a climbing/riding accident* ◊ (*BrE*) *the hospital accident and emergency department* ◊ *Take out accident insurance before you go on your trip.* ◊ *I didn't mean to break it—it was an accident.* **2** [C,U] something that happens unexpectedly and is not planned in advance: *Their early arrival was just an accident.* ◊ *It is no accident that men fill most of the top jobs in nursing.* ◊ *an accident of birth/ fate/history* (= describing facts and events that are due to chance or circumstances) IDM **,accidents ,will 'happen** people say **accidents will happen** to tell sb who has had an accident, for example breaking sth, that it does not matter and they should not worry **by accident** in a way that is not planned or organized: *We met by accident at the airport.* ◊ *Helen got into acting purely by accident.*—more at CHAPTER, WAIT *v.*

ac·ci·den·tal /,æksɪ'dentl/ *adj.* happening by chance; not planned: *a verdict of accidental death* ◊ *I didn't think our meeting was accidental—he must have known I would be there.* ► **ac·ci·den·tal·ly** /-təli/ *adv.: As I turned around, I accidentally hit him in the face.* ◊ *The damage couldn't have been caused accidentally.*

,accident and e'mergency (*BrE*) (*abbr.* **A & E**) (*AmE* **e'mergency room**) *noun* the part of a hospital where people who need urgent treatment are taken—see also CASUALTY

'accident-prone *adj.* more likely to have accidents than other people

ac·claim /ə'kleɪm/ *verb, noun*
■ *verb* [VN] [usually passive] **~ sb/sth (as sth)** to praise or welcome sb/sth publicly: *a highly/widely acclaimed performance* ◊ *The work was acclaimed as a masterpiece.*
■ *noun* [U] praise and approval for sb/sth, especially an artistic achievement: *international/popular acclaim*

ac·clam·ation /,æklə'meɪʃn/ *noun* [U] (*formal*) **1** loud and enthusiastic approval or welcome **2** (*technical*) the act of electing sb using a spoken not written vote: *The decision was taken by acclamation.*

ac·cli·ma·tize (*BrE* also **-ise**) /ə'klaɪmətaɪz/ *verb* **~ (yourself) (to sth)** to get used to a new place, situation or climate: [V] *Arrive two days early in order to acclimatize.* ◊ [VN] *She was fine once she had acclimatized herself to the cold.* ► **ac·cli·ma·tiza·tion, -isa·tion** /ə,klaɪmətaɪ'zeɪʃn; *AmE* -tə'z-/ *noun* [U]

ac·col·ade /'ækəleɪd; ,ækə'leɪd/ *noun* (*formal*) praise or an award for an achievement that people admire

ac·com·mo·date /ə'kɒmədeɪt; *AmE* ə'kɑːm-/ *verb* **1** [VN] to provide sb with a room or place to sleep, live or sit: *The hotel can accommodate up to 500 guests.* **2** [VN] to provide enough space for sb/sth: *Over 70 minutes of music can be accommodated on one CD.* **3** [VN] (*formal*) to consider sth, such as sb's opinion or a fact, and be influenced by it when you are deciding what to do or explaining sth: *Our proposal tries to accommodate the special needs of minority groups.* **4** [VN] **~ sb (with sth)** (*formal*) to help sb by doing what they want SYN OBLIGE: *I have accommodated the press a great deal, giving numerous interviews.* **5 ~ to sth** | **~ sth/yourself to sth** (*formal*) to change your behaviour so that you can deal with a new situation

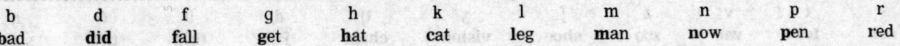

b	d	f	g	h	k	l	m	n	p	r
bad	**did**	**fall**	**get**	**hat**	**cat**	**leg**	**man**	**now**	**pen**	**red**

better: [V] *I quickly needed to accommodate to the new schedule.* [also VN]

ac·com·mo·dat·ing /əˈkɒmədeɪtɪŋ; *AmE* əˈkɑːm-/ *adj.* willing to help and do things for other people: *They are very accommodating to foreign visitors.*

ac·com·mo·da·tion /əˌkɒməˈdeɪʃn; *AmE* əˌkɑːm-/ *noun* **1** [U] (*BrE*) a place to live, work or stay in: *rented/temporary/furnished accommodation* ◊ *Hotel accommodation is included in the price of your holiday.* ◊ *The building plans include much needed new office accommodation.* ◊ *First-class accommodation is available on all flights.* **2** (**accommodations**) [pl.] (*AmE*) somewhere to live or stay, often also providing food or other services: *More and more travelers are looking for bed and breakfast accommodations in private homes.* **3** [C, U] (*formal*) a satisfactory agreement or arrangement between people or groups with different opinions; the process of reaching this agreement: *They were forced to reach an accommodation with the rebels.*

ac·com·pani·ment /əˈkʌmpənimənt/ *noun* ~ (**to sth**) **1** [C, U] music that is played to support singing or another instrument: *traditional songs with piano and flute accompaniment* **2** [C] something that you eat, drink or use together with sth else: *These wines make a good accompaniment to most fish dishes.* **3** [C] (*formal*) something that happens at the same time as another thing: *High blood pressure is a common accompaniment to this disease.* **IDM** **to the accompaniment of sth 1** while a musical instrument is being played: *They performed to the accompaniment of Spanish guitars.* **2** while sth else is happening: *She made her speech to the accompaniment of loud laughter.*

ac·com·pan·ist /əˈkʌmpənɪst/ *noun* a person who plays a musical instrument, especially a piano, while sb else plays or sings the main part of the music

ac·com·pany /əˈkʌmpəni/ *verb* (**ac·com·pan·ies**, **ac·com·pany·ing**, **ac·com·pan·ied**, **ac·com·pan·ied**) [VN] **1** (*formal*) to travel or go somewhere with sb: *His wife accompanied him on the trip.* ◊ *I must ask you to accompany me to the police station.* **2** to happen or appear with sth else: *strong winds accompanied by heavy rain* ◊ *Each pack contains a book and accompanying cassette.* **3** ~ **sb** (**at/on sth**) to play a musical instrument, especially a piano, while sb else sings or plays the main tune: *The singer was accompanied on the piano by her sister.*

ac·com·plice /əˈkʌmplɪs; *AmE* əˈkɑːm-/ *noun* a person who helps another to commit a crime or to do sth wrong

ac·com·plish /əˈkʌmplɪʃ; *AmE* əˈkɑːm-/ *verb* [VN] to succeed in doing or completing sth **SYN** ACHIEVE: *The first part of the plan has been safely accomplished.* ◊ *I don't feel I've accomplished very much today.* ◊ *That's it.* **Mission accomplished** (= we have done what we aimed to do).

ac·com·plished /əˈkʌmplɪʃt; *AmE* əˈkɑːm-/ *adj.* very good at a particular thing; having a lot of skills: *an accomplished artist/actor/chef* ◊ *She was an elegant and accomplished woman.*

ac·com·plish·ment /əˈkʌmplɪʃmənt; *AmE* əˈkɑːm-/ *noun* **1** [C] an impressive thing that is done or achieved after a lot of work: *It was one of the President's greatest accomplishments.* ◊ *The series of paintings is quite an accomplishment.* **2** [C, U] a skill or special ability: *Drawing and singing were among her many accomplishments.* ◊ *a poet of rare accomplishment* **3** [U] (*formal*) the successful completing of sth: *Money will be crucial to the accomplishment of our objectives.*

ac·cord /əˈkɔːd; *AmE* əˈkɔːrd/ *noun, verb*
▪ *noun* a formal agreement between two organizations, countries, etc: *The two sides signed a peace accord last July.* **IDM** **in accord** (**with sth/sb**) (*formal*) in agreement with: *This action would not be in accord with our policy.* **of your own ac'cord** without being asked, forced or helped: *He came back of his own accord.* ◊ *The symptoms will clear up of their own accord after a few days.* **with ˌone ac'cord** (*BrE, formal*) if people do sth **with one accord**, they do it at the same time, because they agree with each other

▪ *verb* (*formal*) **1** ~ **sth to sb/sth**| ~ **sb/sth sth** to give sb/sth authority, status or a particular type of treatment: [VN, VNN] *Our society accords great importance to the family.* ◊ *Our society accords the family great importance.* **2** [V] ~ (**with sth**) to agree with or match sth: *These results accord closely with our predictions.*

ac·cord·ance /əˈkɔːdns; *AmE* əˈkɔːrdns/ *noun* **IDM** **in accordance with sth** (*formal*) according to a rule or the way that sb says that sth should be done: *in accordance with legal requirements* ◊ *We acted in accordance with my parents' wishes.*

ac·cord·ing·ly /əˈkɔːdɪŋli; *AmE* əˈkɔːrd-/ *adv.* **1** in a way that is appropriate to what has been done or said in a particular situation: *We have to discover his plans and act accordingly.* **2** (used especially at the beginning of a sentence) for that reason; therefore: *The cost of materials rose sharply last year. Accordingly, we were forced to increase our prices.*

ac·cord·ing to /əˈkɔːdɪŋ; *AmE* əˈkɔːrdɪŋ tə/ *prep.* **1** as stated or reported by sb/sth: *According to Mick, it's a great movie.* ◊ *You've been absent six times according to our records.* **2** following or agreeing with sth: *The work was done according to her instructions.* ◊ *Everything went according to plan.* ◊ *The salary will be fixed according to qualifications and experience.*

ac·cor·dion /əˈkɔːdiən; *AmE* əˈkɔːrd-/ (*BrE* also **ˈpiano accordion**) *noun* a musical instrument that you hold in both hands to produce sounds. You press the two ends together and pull them apart and press keys and buttons to produce the different notes.

ac·cost /əˈkɒst; *AmE* əˈkɔːst; əˈkɑːst/ *verb* [VN] (*written*) to go up to sb and speak to them, especially in a way that is rude or threatening: *She was accosted in the street by a complete stranger.*

ac·count /əˈkaʊnt/ *noun, verb*
▪ *noun*
AT BANK | **1** (*abbr.* **a/c**) an arrangement that sb has with a bank, etc. to keep money there, take some out, etc: *I don't have a bank account.* ◊ *to have an account at/with a bank* ◊ *to open/close an account* ◊ *What's your account number please?* ◊ *I paid the cheque into my savings account.* ◊ *a joint account* (= one in the name of more than one person)—see also BUDGET ACCOUNT, CHECKING ACCOUNT. CURRENT ACCOUNT, DEPOSIT ACCOUNT

BUSINESS RECORDS | **2** [usually pl.] a written record of money that is owed to a business and of money that has been paid by it: *to do the accounts* ◊ *to keep the accounts up to date* ◊ *the accounts department*—see also EXPENSE ACCOUNT

WITH SHOP/STORE | **3** (*BrE* also **ˈcredit account**) (*AmE* also **ˈcharge account**) an arrangement with a shop/store or business to pay bills for goods or services at a later time, for example in regular amounts every month: *Put it on my account please.* ◊ *We have accounts with most of our suppliers.*

REGULAR CUSTOMER | **4** (*business*) a regular customer: *The advertising agency has lost several of its most important accounts.*

COMPUTING | **5** an arrangement that sb has with a company that allows them to use the Internet, send and receive messages by e-mail, etc: *an Internet/e-mail account*

DESCRIPTION | **6** a written or spoken description of sth that has happened: *She gave the police a full account of the incident.* ◊ *The diaries contained detailed accounts of the writer's experiences in China.* **7** an explanation or a description of an idea, a theory or a process: *the Biblical account of the creation of the world*

IDM **by/from all accounts** according to what other people say: *I've never been there, but it's a lovely place, by all accounts.* **by your own account** according to what you say yourself: *By his own account he had an unhappy childhood.* **give a good/poor ac'count of yourself** (*BrE*) to do sth or perform well or badly, especially in a contest: *The team gave a good account of themselves in the match on Saturday.* **of no/little ac'count** (*formal*) not important: *Emotional matters were of no account to them during the war.* **on account** if you buy sth or pay on

s	t	v	z	ʃ	ʒ	tʃ	dʒ	θ	ð	ŋ
see	tea	van	zoo	shoe	vision	chain	jam	thin	this	sing

account, you pay nothing or only a small amount immediately and the rest later **on sb's account** because of what you think sb wants: *Please don't change your plans on my account.* **on account of sth** because of sth: *She retired early on account of ill health.* **on no account | not on any account** (used to emphasize sth) not for any reason: *On no account should the house be left unlocked.* **on your own ac'count 1** for yourself: *In 1992 Smith set up in business on his own account.* **2** because you want to and you have decided, not sb else: *No one sent me, I am here on my own account.* **on this/that account** (*formal*) because of the particular thing that has been mentioned: *Weather conditions were poor, but he did not delay his departure on that account.* **put/turn sth to good ac'count** (*formal*) to use sth in a good or helpful way **take account of sth | take sth into account** to consider particular facts, circumstances, etc. when making a decision about sth: *The company takes account of environmental issues wherever possible.* ◊ *Coursework is taken into account as well as exam results.* ◊ *The defendant asked for a number of other offences to be taken into account.*—more at BLOW *n.*, CALL *v.*, SETTLE *v.*
■ *verb* [usually passive] (*formal*) to have the opinion that sb/sth is a particular thing: [VN-ADJ] *In English law a person is accounted innocent until they are proved guilty.* ◊ [VN-N] *The event was accounted a success.*
IDM **there's no accounting for 'taste** (*saying*) used to say how difficult it is to understand why sb likes sb/sth that you do not like at all: *She thinks he's wonderful—oh well, there's no accounting for taste.*
PHRV **ac'count for sth 1** to be the explanation or cause of sth: *The poor weather may have accounted for the small crowd.* ◊ *Oh well, that accounts for it* (= I understand now why it happened). **2** to give an explanation of sth: *How do you account for the show's success?* **3** to be a particular amount or part of sth: *The Japanese market accounts for 35% of the company's revenue.* **ac'count for sb/sth 1** to know where sb/sth is or what has happened to them, especially after an accident: *All passengers have now been accounted for.* **2** (*informal*) to defeat or destroy sb/sth: *Our anti-aircraft guns accounted for five enemy bombers.* **ac'count for sth (to sb)** to give a satisfactory record of how the money in your care has been spent: *We have to account for every penny we spend on business trips.*

ac·count·able /əˈkaʊntəbl/ *adj.* [not usually before noun] **~ (to sb) (for sth)** responsible for your decisions or actions and expected to explain them when you are asked: ◊ *Someone must be **held accountable** for the killings.*
▶ **ac·count·abil·ity** /əˌkaʊntəˈbɪləti/ *noun* [U]: *proposals for greater police accountability* ◊ *the accountability of a company's directors to the shareholders*

ac·count·ancy /əˈkaʊntənsi/ *noun* [U] the work or profession of an accountant

ac·count·ant /əˈkaʊntənt/ *noun* a person whose job is to keep or check financial accounts

ac·coutre·ments /əˈkuːtrəmənts/ (*AmE* also **ac·couter·ments** /əˈkuːtərmənts/) *noun* [pl.] (*formal* or *humorous*) pieces of equipment that you need for a particular activity

ac·credit /əˈkredɪt/ *verb* [VN] **1** [usually passive] **~ sth to sb| ~ sb with sth** (*formal*) to believe that sb is responsible for doing or saying sth: *The discovery of distillation is usually accredited to the Arabs of the 11th century.* ◊ *The Arabs are usually accredited with the discovery of distillation.* **2** [usually passive] **~ sb to …** (*technical*) to choose sb for an official position, especially as an AMBASSADOR: *He was accredited to Madrid.*

ac·credit·ation /əˌkredɪˈteɪʃn/ *noun* [U] official approval given by an organization stating that sb/sth has achieved a required standard: *He carried a letter of accreditation.*

ac·credit·ed /əˈkredɪtɪd/ *adj.* [usually before noun] **1** (of a person) officially recognized as sth; with official permission to be sth: *our accredited representative* ◊ *Only accredited journalists were allowed entry.* **2** officially approved as being of an accepted quality or standard: *a fully accredited school/university/course*

ac·cre·tion /əˈkriːʃn/ *noun* (*technical* or *formal*) **1** [C] a layer of a substance that is slowly added to sth **2** [U] the process of new layers being slowly added to sth: *the accretion of sand by wind action*

ac·crue /əˈkruː/ *verb* (*formal*) **1** [V] **~ (to sb) (from sth)** to increase over a period of time: *economic benefits accruing to the country from tourism* ◊ *Interest will accrue if you keep your money in a savings account.* **2** [VN] to allow a sum of money or debts to grow over a period of time [SYN] ACCUMULATE: *The firm had accrued debts of over $6m.*

ac·cu·mu·late /əˈkjuːmjəleɪt/ *verb* **1** [VN] to gradually get more and more of sth over a period of time: *I seem to have accumulated a lot of books.* ◊ *By investing wisely she accumulated a fortune.* **2** [V] to gradually increase in number or quality over a period of time [SYN] BUILD UP: *Debts began to accumulate.* ▶ **ac·cu·mu·la·tion** /əˌkjuːmjəˈleɪʃn/ *noun* [U, C]: *the accumulation of wealth* ◊ *an accumulation of toxic chemicals*

ac·cur·acy /ˈækjərəsi/ *noun* [U] the state of being exact or correct; the ability to do sth skilfully without making mistakes: *They questioned the accuracy of the information in the file.* ◊ *Candidates are judged on technical accuracy as well as artistic expression.* ◊ *She hits the ball with great accuracy.* [OPP] INACCURACY

ac·cur·ate /ˈækjərət/ *adj.* **1** correct and true in every detail: *an accurate description/account/calculation* ◊ *accurate information/data* ◊ *Accurate records must be kept.* **2** able to give completely correct information or to do sth in an exact way: *a highly accurate electronic compass* ◊ *accurate to within 3 mm* ◊ *My watch is not very accurate.* **3** an **accurate** throw, shot, weapon, etc. hits or reaches the thing that it was aimed at [OPP] INACCURATE ▶ **ac·cur·ate·ly** *adv.*: *The article accurately reflects public opinion.* ◊ *You need to hit the ball accurately.*

ac·cur·sed /əˈkɜːsɪd; *AmE* -ˈkɜːrs-/ *adj.* (*old-fashioned*) having a CURSE (= a bad magic SPELL) on it: *an accursed house*

ac·cus·ation /ˌækjuˈzeɪʃn/ *noun* [C, U] **~ (of sth) (against sb)| ~ (that…)** a statement saying that you think a person is guilty of doing sth wrong, especially of committing a crime; the fact of ACCUSING sb: *accusations of corruption/cruelty/racism* ◊ *I don't want to **make an accusation** until I have some proof.* ◊ *No one believed her wild accusations against her husband.* ◊ *He denied the accusation that he had ignored the problems.* ◊ *There was a hint of accusation in her voice.*

ac·cusa·tive /əˈkjuːzətɪv/ *noun* (*grammar*) (in some languages) the form of a noun, a pronoun or an adjective when it is the DIRECT OBJECT of a verb, or connected with the DIRECT OBJECT: *In the sentence, 'I saw him today', the word 'him' is in the accusative.*—compare DATIVE, GENITIVE, NOMINATIVE, VOCATIVE ▶ **ac·cusa·tive** *adj.*

ac·cusa·tory /əˈkjuːzətəri; ˌækjuˈzeɪtəri; *AmE* -tɔːri/ *adj.* (*formal*) suggesting that you think sb has done sth wrong

ac·cuse /əˈkjuːz/ *verb* [VN] **~ sb (of sth)** to say that sb has done sth wrong or is guilty of sth: *to accuse sb of murder/theft* ◊ *She accused him of lying.* ◊ *The government was accused of incompetence.* ◊ (*formal*) *They stand accused of crimes against humanity.* ▶ **ac·cuser** *noun*

WORD FAMILY
accuse *v.*
accusation *n.*
accusing *adj.*
accusatory *adj.*
accused *n.*

the ac·cused /əˈkjuːzd/ *noun* (*pl.* **the ac·cused**) a person who is on trial for committing a crime: *The accused was found innocent.* ◊ *All the accused have pleaded guilty.*—compare DEFENDANT

ac·cus·ing /əˈkjuːzɪŋ/ *adj.* showing that you think sb has done sth wrong: *an accusing look/finger/tone* ◊ *Her accusing eyes were fixed on him.* ▶ **ac·cus·ing·ly** *adv.*

ac·cus·tom /əˈkʌstəm/ *verb* [PHRV] **ac'custom yourself/sb to sth** to make yourself/sb familiar with sth or become used to it: *It took him a while to accustom himself to the idea.*

ac·cus·tomed /əˈkʌstəmd/ *adj.* **1 ~** to sth/to doing sth

æ	ɑː	e	ɜː	ə	ɪ	iː	i	ɒ	ɔː	ʌ	ʊ	u	uː
cat	father	ten	bird	about	sit	see	many	got	saw	cup	put	actual	too
								(BrE)					

familiar with sth and accepting it as normal or usual: *to become/get accustomed to sth* ◊ *My eyes slowly grew accustomed to the dark.* ◊ *She was a person accustomed to having eight hours' sleep a night.* **2** [usually before noun] (*formal*) usual: *He took his accustomed seat by the fire.* **OPP** UNACCUSTOMED

ace /eɪs/ *noun, adj.*
■ *noun* **1** a playing card with a large single symbol on it, which has either the highest or the lowest value in a particular card game: *the ace of spades/hearts/diamonds/clubs*—picture on page A8 **2** (*informal*) a person who is very good at doing sth: *a soccer/tennis/flying ace* ◊ *an ace pilot/marksman* **3** (in tennis) a SERVE (= the first hit) that is so good that your opponent cannot reach the ball: *He served 20 aces in the match.* **IDM an ace up your sleeve** (*BrE*) (*AmE* **an ace in the hole**) (*informal*) a secret advantage, for example a piece of information or a skill, that you are ready to use if you need to **hold all the aces** to have all the advantages in a situation **play your 'ace** to use your best argument, etc. in order to get an advantage in a situation **within an ace of sth/of doing sth** (*BrE*) very close to sth: *We came within an ace of victory.*
■ *adj.* (*informal*) very good: *We had an ace time.*

acerb·ic /əˈsɜːbɪk; *AmE* əˈsɜːrb-/ *adj.* (*formal*) (of a person or what they say) critical in a direct and rather cruel way: *The letter was written in her usual acerbic style.* ▶ **acerb·ity** /əˈsɜːbəti; *AmE* əˈsɜːrb-/ *noun* [U] (*rare*)

acet·ate /ˈæsɪteɪt/ *noun* [U] **1** a chemical compound made from acetic acid, used in making plastics, etc. **2** a type of smooth artificial fabric

acet·ic acid /əˌsiːtɪk ˈæsɪd/ *noun* [U] the acid in VINEGAR that gives it its taste and smell

acet·one /ˈæsɪtəʊn; *AmE* -toʊn/ *noun* [U] a colourless liquid with a strong smell used for cleaning things, making paint thinner and producing various chemicals

acetyl·ene /əˈsetəliːn/ *noun* [U] (*symb* C₂H₂) a gas that burns with a very hot bright flame, used for cutting or joining metal

ache /eɪk/ *verb, noun*
■ *verb* **1** [V] to feel a continuous dull pain: *I'm aching all over.* ◊ *Her eyes ached from lack of sleep.* ◊ (*figurative*) *It makes my heart ache* (= it makes me sad) *to see her suffer.* **2 ~ for sb/sth** (*written*) to have a strong desire for sb/sth or to do sth **SYN** LONG: [V] *I was aching for home.* ◊ [V to inf] *He ached to see her.*
■ *noun* (often in compounds) a continuous feeling of pain in a part of the body: *Mummy, I've got a tummy ache.* ◊ *Muscular* **aches and pains** *can be soothed by a relaxing massage.* ◊ (*figurative*) *an ache in my heart* (= a continuous sad feeling) ⇨ vocabulary notes on page 598—see also BELLYACHE, HEARTACHE ▶ **achy** *adj.* (*informal*): *I felt hot and achy all over.*

achieve /əˈtʃiːv/ *verb* **1** [VN] to succeed in reaching a particular goal, status or standard, especially by making an effort for a long time: *He had finally achieved success.* ◊ *They could not achieve their target of less than 3% inflation.* **2** [VN] to succeed in doing sth or causing sth to happen **SYN** ACCOMPLISH: *I haven't achieved very much today.* ◊ *All you've achieved is to upset my parents.* **3** [V] to be successful: *Their background gives them little chance of achieving at school.* ▶ **achiev·able** *adj.*: *Profits of $20m look achievable.* ◊ *achievable goals* **OPP** UNACHIEVABLE

achieve·ment /əˈtʃiːvmənt/ *noun* **1** [C] a thing that sb has done successfully, especially using their own effort and skill: *the greatest scientific achievement of the decade* ◊ *It was a remarkable achievement for such a young player.* ◊ *They were proud of their children's achievements.* **2** [U] the act or process of achieving sth: *the need to raise standards of achievement in education* ◊ *Even a small success gives you a sense of achievement* (= a feeling of pride).

Achil·les' heel /əˌkɪliːz ˈhiːl/ *noun* [sing.] a weak point or fault in sb's character, which can be attacked by other people **ORIGIN** Named after the Greek hero **Achilles**. When he was a small child, his mother dipped him into the river Styx, which made him invulnerable (= he could

not be injured). She held him by his heel, which therefore was not touched by the water. Achilles died after being wounded by an arrow in the heel.

A,chil·les 'ten·don (also **Achil·les**) *noun* the TENDON that connects the muscles at the back of the lower part of the leg to the heel

acid /ˈæsɪd/ *noun, adj.*
■ *noun* **1** [U, C] (*chemistry*) a chemical compound, usually a liquid, that contains HYDROGEN, and has a pH of less than seven. The HYDROGEN can be replaced by a metal to form a SALT. Acids are usually sour and can often burn holes in or damage things they touch.—compare ALKALI—see also ACETIC ACID, AMINO ACID, CITRIC ACID, HYDROCHLORIC ACID, LACTIC ACID, NITRIC ACID, NUCLEIC ACID, SULPHURIC ACID **2** [U] (*slang*) = LSD
■ *adj.* **1** (*technical*) that contains acid or has the essential characteristics of an acid; that has a pH of less than seven: *Rye is tolerant of poor, acid soils.*—compare ALKALINE **2** that has a bitter sharp taste **SYN** SOUR: *acid fruit* **3** (*written*) (of a person's remarks) critical and unkind **SYN** SARCASTIC: *an acid wit*

'acid house *noun* [U] a type of electronic music with a strong steady beat, often played at parties where some people take harmful drugs

acid·ic /əˈsɪdɪk/ *adj.* **1** very sour: *Some fruit juices are very acidic.* **2** containing acid: *acidic soil*

acid·ify /əˈsɪdɪfaɪ/ *verb* (**acid·ifies, acid·ify·ing, acid·ified, acid·ified**) [V, VN] (*technical*) to become or make sth become an acid ▶ **acid·ifi·ca·tion** *noun* [U]

acid·ity /əˈsɪdəti/ *noun* [U] the state of having a sour taste or of containing acid

acid·ly /ˈæsɪdli/ *adv.* (*written*) in an unpleasant or critical way: *'Thanks for nothing,' she said acidly.*

,acid 'rain *noun* [U] rain that contains harmful chemicals from factory gases and that damages trees, crops and buildings

,acid 'test (also **'litmus test** especially in *AmE*) *noun* [sing.] a way of deciding whether sth is successful or true: *The acid test of a good driver is whether he or she remains calm in an emergency.*

ac·know·ledge /əkˈnɒlɪdʒ; *AmE* əkˈnɑːl-/ *verb*
ADMIT | **1** to accept that sth is true: [VN] *She refuses to acknowledge the need for reform.* ◊ *a generally acknowledged fact* ◊ [V that] *I did not acknowledge that he had done anything wrong.* ◊ [VN to inf] *It is generally acknowledged to be true.* [also V -ing]
ACCEPT STATUS | **2 ~ sb/sth (as sth)** to accept that sb/sth has a particular authority or status **SYN** RECOGNIZE: [VN] *The country acknowledged his claim to the throne.* ◊ [VN, VN to inf] *He is widely acknowledged as the best player in the world.* ◊ *He is widely acknowledged to be the best player in the world.*
REPLY TO LETTER | **3** [VN] to tell sb that you have received sth that they sent to you: *All applications will be acknowledged.* ◊ *Please acknowledge receipt of this letter.*
SMILE/WAVE | **4** [VN] to show that you have noticed sb/sth by smiling, waving, etc: *I was standing right next to her, but she didn't even acknowledge me.*
EXPRESS THANKS | **5** [VN] to publicly express thanks for help you have been given: *I gratefully acknowledge financial support from several local businesses.*

ac·know·ledge·ment (also **ac·know·ledg·ment**) /əkˈnɒlɪdʒmənt; *AmE* əkˈnɑːl-/ *noun* **1** [sing., U] an act of accepting that sth exists or is true, or that sth is there: *This report is an acknowledgement of the size of the problem.* ◊ *She gave me a smile of acknowledgement* (= showed that she had seen and recognized me). **2** [C, U] an act or a statement expressing thanks to sb; something that is given to sb as thanks: *I was sent a free copy* **in acknowledgement** *of my contribution.* ◊ *The flowers were a small acknowledgement of your kindness.* **3** [C] a letter saying that sth has been received: *I didn't receive an acknowledgement of my application.* **4** [C, usually pl.] a statement, especially at the beginning of a book, in which the writer expresses thanks to the people who have helped

acme /ˈækmi/ *noun* [usually sing.] (*formal*) the highest stage of development or the most excellent example of sth

aɪ	aʊ	eɪ	əʊ	oʊ	ɔɪ	ɪə	eə	ʊə	j	w
my	now	say	go	go	boy	near	hair	pure	yes	wet
			(BrE)	(AmE)						

acne /ˈækni/ *noun* [U] a skin condition, common among young people, that produces many PIMPLES (= spots), especially on the face and neck: *to suffer from/have acne*

aco·lyte /ˈækəlaɪt/ *noun* **1** (*formal*) a person who follows and helps a leader **2** (*technical*) a person who helps a priest in some church ceremonies

acon·ite /ˈækənaɪt/ *noun* [C, U] a wild plant with yellow or blue flowers and a poisonous root that is sometimes used to make drugs

acorn /ˈeɪkɔːn; *AmE* -kɔːrn/ *noun* the small brown nut of the OAK tree, that grows in a base shaped like a cup

acous·tic /əˈkuːstɪk/ *adj.* (*AmE* also **acous·tic·al** /əˈkuːstɪkl/) **1** related to sound or to the sense of hearing **2** [usually before noun] (of a musical instrument) designed to make natural sound, not sound produced by electrical equipment ▶ **acous·tic·al·ly** *adv.*

acous·tics /əˈkuːstɪks/ *noun* **1** [pl.] (also **acous·tic** [sing.]) the shape, design, etc. of a room or theatre that make it good or bad for carrying sound: *The acoustics of the new concert hall are excellent.* **2** [U] the scientific study of sound

ac·quaint /əˈkweɪnt/ *verb* [VN] **~ sb/yourself with sth** (*formal*) to make sb/yourself familiar with or aware of sth: *Please acquaint me with the facts of the case.* ◇ *You will first need to acquaint yourself with the filing system.*

ac·quaint·ance /əˈkweɪntəns/ *noun* **1** [C] a person that you know but who is not a close friend: *He's just a business acquaintance.* ◇ *He's just a business acquaintance.* **2** [U, C] **~ (with sb)** (*formal*) slight friendship: *He hoped their acquaintance would develop further.* **3** [U, C] **~ with sth** (*formal*) knowledge of sth: *I had little acquaintance with modern poetry.* **IDM** **make sb's acquaintance | make the acquaintance of sb** (*formal*) to meet sb for the first time: *I am delighted to make your acquaintance, Mrs Baker.* ◇ *I made the acquaintance of several musicians around that time.* **of your acˈquaintance** (*formal*) that you know: *No one else of my acquaintance was as rich or successful.* **on first acˈquaintance** (*formal*) when you first meet sb: *Even on first acquaintance it was clear that he was not 'the right type'.*—more at NOD *v.*

ac·quaint·ance·ship /əˈkweɪntənsʃɪp/ *noun* [U, C, usually sing.] (*formal*) a slight friendship with sb and knowledge of sth: *It was unfair to judge her on such a brief acquaintanceship.*

ac·quaint·ed /əˈkweɪntɪd/ *adj.* [not before noun] **1 ~ with sth** (*formal*) familiar with sth, having read, seen or experienced it: *The students are already acquainted with the work of Shakespeare.* ◇ *Employees should be fully acquainted with emergency procedures.* **2 ~ with sb** not close friends with sb, but having met a few times before: *I am well acquainted with her family.* ◇ *We got acquainted at the conference* (= met and started to get to know each other).

ac·qui·esce /ˌækwiˈes/ *verb* [V] **~ (in sth)** (*formal*) to accept sth without arguing, even if you do not really agree with it: *Senior government figures must have acquiesced in the cover-up.*

ac·qui·es·cence /ˌækwiˈesns/ *noun* [U] (*formal*) the fact of being willing to do what sb wants and to accept their opinions, even if you are not sure that they are right: *There was general acquiescence in the UN sanctions.* ▶ **ac·qui·es·cent** /-ˈesnt/ *adj.*

ac·quire /əˈkwaɪə(r)/ *verb* [VN] (*formal*) **1** to gain sth by your own efforts, ability or behaviour: *She has acquired a good knowledge of English.* ◇ *He has acquired a reputation for dishonesty.* ◇ *I have recently acquired a taste for olives.* **2** to obtain sth by buying or being given it: *The company has just acquired new premises.* ◇ *I've suddenly acquired a stepbrother.* **IDM** **an acquired ˈtaste** a thing that you do not like at first but gradually learn to like: *Abstract art is an acquired taste.*

ac·qui·si·tion /ˌækwɪˈzɪʃn/ *noun* **1** [U] the act of getting sth, especially knowledge, a skill, etc: *theories of child language acquisition* **2** [C] something that sb buys to add to what they already own, usually sth valuable: *His latest acquisition is a racehorse.* ◇ *The money will be spent on*

acquisitions *for the university library.* **3** [C, U] (*business*) a company, piece of land, etc. bought by sb, especially another company; the act of buying it: *They have made acquisitions in several EU countries.* ◇ *the acquisition of shares by employees*

ac·quisi·tive /əˈkwɪzətɪv/ *adj.* (*formal, disapproving*) wanting very much to buy or get new possessions ▶ **ac·quisi·tive·ness** *noun* [U]

ac·quit /əˈkwɪt/ *verb* (**-tt-**) [VN] **1 ~ sb (of sth)** to decide and state officially in a court of law that sb is not guilty of a crime: *The jury acquitted him of murder.* ◇ *Both defendants were acquitted.* **OPP** CONVICT **2 ~ yourself well, badly, etc.** (*formal*) to perform or behave well, badly, etc: *He acquitted himself brilliantly in the exams.*

ac·quit·tal /əˈkwɪtl/ *noun* [C, U] an official decision in a court of law that a person is not guilty of a crime: *The case resulted in an acquittal.* ◇ *The jury voted for acquittal.*

acre /ˈeɪkə(r)/ *noun* a unit for measuring an area of land; 4840 square YARDS or about 4050 square metres: *3000 acres of parkland* ◇ *a three-acre wood* ◇ (*informal*) *Each house has acres of space around it* (= a lot of space).

acre·age /ˈeɪkərɪdʒ/ *noun* [U, C] an area of land measured in acres

acrid /ˈækrɪd/ *adj.* having a strong, bitter smell or taste that is unpleasant: *acrid smoke from burning tyres*

acri·mo·ni·ous /ˌækrɪˈməʊniəs; *AmE* -ˈmoʊ-/ *adj.* (*formal*) (of an argument, etc.) angry and full of strong bitter feelings and words: *His parents went through an acrimonious divorce.* ▶ **acri·mo·ni·ous·ly** *adv.*

acri·mony /ˈækrɪməni; *AmE* -moʊni/ *noun* [U] (*formal*) angry bitter feelings or words: *The dispute was settled without acrimony.*

acro·bat /ˈækrəbæt/ *noun* an entertainer who performs difficult acts such as balancing on high ropes, especially at a CIRCUS

acro·bat·ic /ˌækrəˈbætɪk/ *adj.* involving or performing difficult acts or movements with the body: *acrobatic feats* ◇ *an acrobatic dancer*

acro·bat·ics /ˌækrəˈbætɪks/ *noun* [pl.] acrobatic acts and movements: *acrobatics on the high wire* ◇ (*figurative*) *vocal acrobatics* (= performing skilfully with the voice when singing)

acro·nym /ˈækrənɪm/ *noun* a word formed from the first letters of the words that make up the name of sth, for example 'Aids' is an acronym for 'acquired immune deficiency syndrome'

across /əˈkrɒs; *AmE* əˈkrɔːs/ *adv., prep.*

▪ *adv.* **HELP** For the special uses of **across** in phrasal verbs, look at the entries for the verbs. For example **come across** is in the phrasal verb section at **come**. **1** from one side to the other side: *It's too wide. We can't swim across.* ◇ *The yard measures about 50 feet across.* **2** in a particular direction towards or at sb/sth: *When my name was called, he looked across at me.* **3** (**across from**) opposite: *There's a school just across from our house.* **4** (of an answer in a CROSSWORD) written from side to side: *I can't do 3 across.*

▪ *prep.* **1** from one side to the other side of sth: *He walked across the field.* ◇ *I drew a line across the page.* ◇ *A grin spread across her face.* ◇ *Where's the nearest bridge across the river?* **2** on the other side of sth: *There's a bank right across the street.* **3** on or over a part of the body: *He hit him across the face.* ◇ *It's too tight across the back.* **4** in every part of a place, group of people, etc. **SYN** THROUGHOUT: *Her family is scattered across the country.* ◇ *This view is common across all sections of the community.*

acryl·ic /əˈkrɪlɪk/ *adj., noun*

▪ *adj.* made of a substance or fabric produced by chemical processes from a type of acid: *acrylic paints/fibres* ◇ *an acrylic sweater*

▪ *noun* **1** [U] a type of plastic or artificial fabric produced by chemical processes **2** [C, usually pl.] a type of paint used by artists

ACT /ˌeɪ siː ˈtiː/ *abbr.* American College Test (an exam that some high school students take before they go to college)

A

act /ækt/ *noun, verb*
■ *noun*

STH THAT SB DOES | **1** [C] a particular thing that sb does: *an act of kindness/generosity* ◊ *acts of terrorism* ◊ *a serious criminal act* ◊ *The murder was the act of a psychopath.*

LAW | **2** [C] a law that has been passed by a parliament: *an Act of Congress* ◊ *the Further and Higher Education Act 1992*

PRETENDING | **3** [sing.] a way of behaving that is not sincere but is intended to have a particular effect on others: *Don't take her seriously—it's all an act.* ◊ *You could tell she was just putting on an act.*

IN PLAY/ENTERTAINMENT | **4** [C] one of the main divisions of a play, an opera, etc: *a play in five acts* ◊ *The hero dies in Act 5, Scene 3.* **5** [C] one of several short pieces of entertainment in a show: *a circus/comedy/magic act* **6** [C] a performer or group of musicians: *Oasis had a reputation as one of rock's most impressive live acts.*

IDM ,act of 'God (*law*) an event caused by natural forces beyond human control, such as a storm, a flood or an earthquake **be/get in on the act** (*informal*) to be/become involved in an activity that sb else has started, especially to get sth for yourself **do, perform, stage a disap'pearing/'vanishing act** (*informal*) to go away or be impossible to find when people need or want you **get your 'act together** (*informal*) to organize yourself and your activities in a more effective way in order to achieve sth: *He needs to get his act together if he's going to pass.* **in the act (of doing sth)** while you are doing sth: *He was caught in the act of stealing a car.*—more at CLEAN *v.*, READ *v.*

■ *verb*

DO STH | **1** [V] to do sth for a particular purpose or in order to deal with a situation: *It is vital that we act to stop the destruction of the rainforests.* ◊ *The girl's life was saved because the doctors acted so promptly.* ◊ *He claims he acted in self-defence.*

BEHAVE | **2** [V] to behave in a particular way: *John's been acting very strangely lately.* ◊ *Stop acting like spoilt children!* **HELP** In spoken English people often use **like** instead of **as if** or **as though** in this meaning, especially in AmE: *She was acting like she'd seen a ghost.* This is considered incorrect in written BrE.

PRETEND | **3** to pretend by your behaviour to be a particular type of person: [V-N] *He's been acting the devoted husband all day.* ◊ [V-ADJ] *I decided to act dumb.*

PERFORM IN PLAY/MOVIE | **4** to perform a part in a play or film/movie: [V] *Have you ever acted?* ◊ *Most of the cast act well.* ◊ [VN] *Who's acting* (= taking the part of) *Hamlet?* ◊ *She is acting the role of Juliet.* ◊ *The play was well acted.*

PERFORM FUNCTION | **5** [V] **~ as/like sth** to perform a particular role or function: *Can you act as interpreter?* ◊ *hormones in the brain that act like natural painkillers*

HAVE EFFECT | **6** [V] **~ (on sth)** to have an effect on sth: *Alcohol acts quickly on the brain.*

IDM see AGE *n.*, FOOL *n.*, OWN *v.*
PHRV 'act for/on behalf of sb to be employed to deal with sb's affairs for them, for example by representing them in a court of law 'act on/upon sth to take action as a result of advice, information, etc: *Acting on information from a member of the public, the police raided the club. Why didn't you act on her suggestion?* ,act sth↔'out **1** to perform a ceremony or show how sth happened, as if performing a play: *The ritual of the party conference is acted out in the same way every year.* ◊ *The children started to act out the whole incident.* **2** to act a part in a real situation: *She acted out the role of the wronged lover.* ,act 'up (*informal*) **1** to behave badly: *The kids started acting up.* **2** to not work as it should: *How long has your ankle been acting up?*

act·ing /'æktɪŋ/ *noun, adj.*
■ *noun* [U] the activity or profession of performing in plays, films/movies, etc.
■ *adj.* [only before noun] doing the work of another person for a short time: *the acting manager*

ac·tion /'ækʃn/ *noun, verb*
■ *noun*

WHAT SB DOES | **1** [U] the process of doing sth in order to make sth happen or to deal with a situation: *The time has come for action if these beautiful animals are to survive.* ◊ *Firefighters took action immediately to stop the blaze spreading.* ◊ *What is the best course of action in the circumstances?* ◊ *She began to explain her plan of action to the group.*—see also DIRECT ACTION, INDUSTRIAL ACTION **2** [C] a thing that sb does: *Her quick action saved the child's life.* ◊ *Each of us must take responsibility for our own actions.*

LEGAL PROCESS | **3** [C, U] a legal process to stop a person or company from doing sth, or to make them pay for a mistake, etc: *A libel action is being brought against the magazine that published the article.* ◊ *He is considering taking legal action against the hospital.*

IN WAR | **4** [U] fighting in a battle or war: *military action* ◊ *soldiers killed in action*

IN STORY/PLAY | **5** [U] the events in a story, play, etc: *The action takes place in France.*

EXCITING EVENTS | **6** [U] exciting events: *I like films with plenty of action.* ◊ *If you want to know where all the action is around here, just ask Jo.* ◊ *New York is where the action is.*

EFFECT | **7** [U] **~ of sth (on sth)** the effect that one substance or chemical has on another: *the action of sunlight on the skin*

OF PART OF THE BODY | **8** [U, C] (*technical*) the way a part of the body moves or functions: *a study of the action of the liver*

OF MACHINE | **9** [sing.] the mechanism of a piano, gun, clock, etc. or the way the parts move

IDM actions speak louder than 'words (*saying*) what a person actually does means more than what they say they will do **in 'action** if sb/sth is in action, they are doing the activity or work that is typical for them: *Just press the button to see your favourite character in action.* ◊ *I've yet to see all the players in action.* **into 'action** if you put an idea or a plan **into action**, you start making it happen or work: *The new plan for traffic control is being put into action on an experimental basis.* **out of 'action** not able to work or be used because of injury or damage: *Jon is out of action for weeks with a broken leg.* ◊ *The photocopier is out of action today.* **a piece/slice of the 'action** (*informal*) a share or role in an interesting or exciting activity, especially in order to make money: *Foreign firms will all want a piece of the action if the new airport goes ahead.*—more at EVASIVE, SPRING *v.*, SWING *v.*
■ *verb* [VN] to take appropriate steps to make sure that sth is done or dealt with: *Your request will be actioned.*

ac·tion·able /'ækʃənəbl/ *adj.* giving sb a valid reason to bring a case in a court of law

'action group *noun* (often as part of a name) a group that is formed to work for social or political change: *the Child Poverty Action Group*

'action-packed *adj.* full of exciting events and activity: *an action-packed weekend*

,action 'replay *noun* (*BrE*) **1** (*AmE* ,instant 'replay) part of sth, for example a football game on television, that is immediately repeated, often more slowly, so that you can see a goal or another exciting or important moment again **2** an event or a situation that repeats sth that has happened before: *It was an action replay of the problems of his first marriage.*

'action stations *noun* [pl.] the positions to which soldiers go to be ready for fighting

ac·ti·vate /'æktɪveɪt/ *verb* [VN] to make sth such as a device or chemical process start working: *The burglar alarm is activated by movement.* ◊ *The gene is activated by a specific protein.* ▶ **ac·ti·vation** /,æktɪ'veɪʃn/ *noun* [U]

ac·tive /'æktɪv/ *adj., noun*
■ *adj.*

BUSY | **1** always busy doing things, especially physical activities: *Although he's nearly 80, he is still very active.*

TAKING PART | **2** involved in sth; making a determined effort and not leaving sth to happen by itself: *They were both politically active.* ◊ *active involvement/participation/sup-*

s	t	v	z	ʃ	ʒ	tʃ	dʒ	θ	ð	ŋ
see	tea	van	zoo	shoe	vision	chain	jam	thin	this	sing

port/resistance ◊ She takes an **active part** in school life. ◊ The parents were active in campaigning against cuts to the education budget. ◊ They took active steps to prevent the spread of the disease.

DOING AN ACTIVITY | **3** doing sth regularly; functioning: *sexually active teenagers* ◊ *animals that are active only at night* ◊ *The virus is still active in the blood.* ◊ *an active volcano* (= likely to ERUPT)

LIVELY | **4** lively and full of ideas: *That child has a very active imagination.*

CHEMICAL | **5** having or causing a chemical effect: *What is the active ingredient in aspirin?*

GRAMMAR | **6** connected with a verb whose subject is the person or thing that performs the action: *In 'He was driving the car', the verb is active.*—compare PASSIVE

▶ **ac·tive·ly** *adv.*: *Your proposal is being actively considered.* ◊ *She was actively looking for a job.*

■ *noun* (also **'active voice**) [sing.] the form of a verb in which the subject is the person or thing that performs the action—compare PASSIVE

active 'service (*AmE* also **,active 'duty**) *noun* [U] the work of a member of the armed forces, especially during a war: *troops on active service*

ac·tiv·ist /ˈæktɪvɪst/ *noun* a person who works to achieve political or social change, especially as a member of an organization with particular aims: *gay activists* ▶ **ac·tiv·ism** /ˈæktɪvɪzəm/ *noun* [U]

ac·tiv·ity /ækˈtɪvəti/ *noun* (*pl.* **-ies**) **1** [U] a situation in which sth is happening or a lot of things are being done: *economic activity* ◊ *The streets were noisy and full of activity.* ◊ *Muscles contract and relax during physical activity.*—compare INACTIVITY **2** [C, often pl.] a thing that you do for interest or pleasure, or in order to achieve a particular aim: *leisure/outdoor/classroom activities* ◊ *The club provides a wide variety of activities including tennis, swimming and squash.* ◊ *illegal/criminal activities*

actor /ˈæktə(r)/ *noun* a person who performs on the stage, on television or in films/movies, especially as a profession

ac·tress /ˈæktrəs/ *noun* a woman who performs on the stage, on television or in films/movies, especially as a profession HELP Many women now prefer to be called **actors**, although when the context is not clear, **an actor** is usually understood to refer to a man.

ac·tual /ˈæktʃuəl/ *adj.* [only before noun] **1** used to emphasize sth that is real or exists in fact: *What were his actual words?* ◊ *The actual cost was much higher than we had expected.* ◊ *James looks younger than his wife but in actual fact* (= really) *he is several years older.* **2** used to emphasize the most important part of sth: *The wedding preparations take weeks but the actual ceremony takes less than an hour.*

WHICH WORD?
actual / current / present (?)

Actual does not mean **current** or **present**. It means 'real' or 'exact' : *I need the actual figures, not an estimate.*

Present - 'existing or happening now ': *How long have you been in your present job?*

Current also means 'existing or happening now', but can suggest that the situation is temporary: *The factory cannot continue its current level of production.*

Actually does not mean 'at the present time'. Use **currently**, **at present** or **at the moment** instead.

⇨ note at PRESENTLY

---

ac·tu·al·ity /ˌæktʃuˈæləti/ *noun* (*pl.* **-ies**) (*formal*) **1** [U] the state of sth existing in reality: *The building looked as impressive in actuality as it did in photographs.* **2** [C, usually pl.] things that exist; facts: *the grim actualities of prison life*

ac·tu·al·ly /ˈæktʃuəli/ *adv.* **1** used in speaking to emphasize a fact or a comment, or that sth is really true: *Well, what did she actually say?* ◊ *It's not actually raining at the*

moment. ◊ *That's the only reason I'm actually going.* ◊ *There are lots of people there who can actually help you.* ◊ *I didn't want to say anything without actually reading the letter first.* **2** used to show a contrast between what is true and what sb believes, and to show surprise about this contrast: *It was actually quite fun after all.* ◊ *The food was not actually all that expensive.* ◊-*Our turnover actually increased last year.* **3** used to correct sb in a polite way: *We're not American. We're Canadian.* ◊ *Actually, it would be much more sensible to do it later.* ◊ *They're not married, actually.* **4** used to get sb's attention, to introduce a new topic or to say sth that sb may not like, in a polite way: *Actually, I'll be a bit late home.* ◊ *Actually, I'm busy at the moment—can I call you back?* ⇨ note at ACTUAL

ac·tu·ary /ˈæktʃuəri; *AmE* -eri/ *noun* (*pl.* **-ies**) a person whose job involves calculating insurance risks and payments for insurance companies by studying how frequently accidents, fires, deaths, etc. happen ▶ **ac·tu·ar·ial** /ˌæktʃuˈeəriəl; *AmE* -ˈeriəl/ *adj.*

ac·tu·ate /ˈæktʃueɪt/ *verb* [VN] (*formal*) **1** to make a machine or device start to work SYN ACTIVATE: *The timer must have been actuated by radio control.* **2** [usually passive] to make sb behave in a particular way SYN MOTIVATE: *He was actuated entirely by malice.*

acu·ity /əˈkjuːəti/ *noun* [U] (*formal*) the ability to think, see or hear clearly: *a child's visual acuity*

acu·men /ˈækjəmən; əˈkjuːmən/ *noun* [U] the ability to understand and judge things quickly and clearly: *business/commercial/financial acumen*

acu·punc·ture /ˈækjupʌŋktʃə(r)/ *noun* [U] a Chinese method of treating pain and illness using special thin needles which are pushed into the skin in particular parts of the body

acu·punc·tur·ist /ˈækjupʌŋktʃərɪst/ *noun* a person who is trained to perform acupuncture

acute /əˈkjuːt/ *adj.* **1** very serious or severe: *There is an acute shortage of water.* ◊ *acute pain* ◊ *the world's acute environmental problems* ◊ *Competition for jobs is acute.* **2** an **acute** illness is one that has quickly become severe and dangerous: *acute appendicitis*—compare CHRONIC **3** (of the senses) very sensitive and well developed: *Dogs have an acute sense of smell.* **4** intelligent and quick to notice and understand things: *He is an acute observer of the social scene.* ◊ *Her judgement is acute.* **5** (*geometry*) (of an angle) less than 90° ▶ **acute·ness** *noun* [U] (*rare*)

a,cute 'accent *noun* the mark placed over a vowel to show how it should be pronounced, as over the *e* in *fiancé*—compare CIRCUMFLEX, GRAVE², TILDE, UMLAUT

a,cute 'angle *noun* an angle of less than 90°—compare OBTUSE ANGLE, REFLEX ANGLE, RIGHT ANGLE

acute·ly /əˈkjuːtli/ *adv.* **1** ~ aware/conscious noticing or feeling sth very strongly: *I am acutely aware of the difficulties we face.* **2** (describing unpleasant feelings) very; very strongly: *acutely embarrassed*

-acy ⇨ -CY

AD (*BrE*) (*AmE* **A.D.**) /ˌeɪ ˈdiː/ *abbr.* used in the Christian CALENDAR to show a particular number of years since the year when Christ was believed to have been born (from Latin 'Anno Domini'): *in (the year) AD 55* ◊ *in 55 AD* ◊ *in the fifth century AD*—compare BC, BCE, CE

ad /æd/ *noun* (*informal*) = ADVERTISEMENT: *We put an ad in the local paper.* ◊ *an ad for a new chocolate bar*

adage /ˈædɪdʒ/ *noun* a well-known phrase expressing a general truth about people or the world

ada·gio /əˈdɑːdʒiəʊ; *AmE* -dʒioʊ/ *noun* (*pl.* **-os**) (*music*) a piece of music to be played in a slow and graceful manner ▶ **ada·gio** *adj.*, *adv.*

Adam /ˈædəm/ *noun* IDM see KNOW *v.*

ad·am·ant /ˈædəmənt/ *adj.* determined not to change your mind or to be persuaded about sth: *Eva was adamant that she would not come.* ▶ **ad·am·ant·ly** *adv.*: *His family were adamantly opposed to the marriage.*

,Adam's 'apple *noun* the lump at the front of the throat that sticks out, particularly in men, and moves up and down when you swallow

---

æ	ɑː	e	ɜː	ə	ɪ	iː	i	ɒ	ɔː	ʌ	ʊ	u	uː
cat	father	ten	bird	about	sit	see	many	got	saw	cup	put	actual	too
								(BrE)					

adapt /əˈdæpt/ *verb* **1** [VN] ~ **sth (for sth)** to change sth in order to make it suitable for a new use or situation [SYN] MODIFY: *Most of these tools have been specially adapted for use by disabled people.* ◊ *These styles can be adapted to suit individual tastes.* **2** ~ **(yourself) (to sth)** to change your behaviour in order to deal more successfully with a new situation [SYN] ADJUST: [V] *We have had to adapt quickly to the new system.* ◊ *A large organization can be slow to adapt to change.* ◊ *The organisms were forced to adapt in order to survive.* ◊ *It's amazing how soon you adapt.* ◊ [VN] *It took him a while to adapt himself to his new surroundings.* **3** [VN] ~ **sth (for sth) (from sth)** to change a book or play so that it can be made into a play, film/movie, television programme, etc: *Three of her novels have been adapted for television.*

adapt·able /əˈdæptəbl/ *adj.* (*approving*) able to change or be changed in order to deal successfully with new situations: *Older workers can be as adaptable and quick to learn as anyone else.* ◊ *Successful businesses are highly adaptable to economic change.* ▶ **adapt·abil·ity** /əˌdæptəˈbɪləti/ *noun* [U]

adap·ta·tion /ˌædæpˈteɪʃn/ (also *less frequent* **adap·tion**) *noun* **1** [C] a film/movie, book or play that is based on a particular piece of work but that has been changed for a new situation: *a screen adaptation of Shakespeare's 'Macbeth'* **2** [U] the process of changing sth, for example your behaviour, to suit a new situation: *the adaptation of desert species to the hot conditions*

adap·tion /əˈdæpʃn/ *noun* (*rare*) = ADAPTATION

adap·tive /əˈdæptɪv/ *adj.* (*technical*) concerned with changing; able to change when necessary in order to deal with different situations

adap·tor (also **adap·ter**) /əˈdæptə(r)/ *noun* **1** a device for connecting pieces of electrical equipment that were not designed to fit together **2** a device for connecting more than one piece of equipment to the same SOCKET (= a place in the wall where equipment is connected to the electricity supply)

ADC /ˌeɪ diː ˈsiː/ *abbr.* AIDE-DE-CAMP

add /æd/ *verb* **1** [VN] ~ **sth (to sth)** to put sth together with sth else so as to increase the size, number, amount, etc: *A new wing was added to the building.* ◊ *Shall I add your name to the list?* ◊ *Next add the flour.* ◊ *The juice contains no added sugar.* ◊ *The plan has the added* (= extra) *advantage of bringing employment to rural areas.* **2** [VN] ~ **A to B** | ~ **A and B (together)** to put numbers or amounts together to get a total: *Add 9 to the total.* ◊ *If you add all these amounts together you get a huge figure.* [OPP] SUBTRACT **3** ~ **sth (to sth)** to say sth more; to make a further remark: [VN] *I have nothing to add to my earlier statement.* ◊ [V speech] '*And don't be late,*' *she added.* ◊ [V that] *He added that they would return a week later.* **4** [VN] ~ **sth (to sth)** to give a particular quality to an event, a situation, etc: *The suite will add a touch of class to your bedroom.* [IDM] **add ˌfuel to the ˈfire/ˈflames** to do or say sth that makes a bad situation even worse, especially by making sb more angry **add ˌinsult to ˈinjury** to make your relationship with sb even worse by offending them as well as actually harming them **ˈadded to this ...** | **ˈadd to this ...** used to introduce another fact that helps to emphasize a point you have already made: *Add to this the excellent service and you can see why it's the most popular hotel on the island.* [PHRV] **ˌadd sth↔ˈin** to include sth with sth else: *Remember to add in the cost of drinks.* **ˌadd sth↔ˈon (to sth)** to include or attach sth extra: *A service charge of 15% was added on to the bill.*—related noun ADD-ON **ˈadd to sth** to increase sth in size, number, amount, etc: *The bad weather only added to our difficulties.* ◊ *The house has been added to* (= new rooms, etc. have been built on to it) *from time to time.* **ˌadd ˈup** (*informal*) **1** (especially in negative sentences) to seem reasonable; to make sense: *His story just doesn't add up.* **2** (not used in the progressive tenses) to increase by small amounts until there is a large total: *When you're feeding a family of six the bills soon add up.* **ˌadd ˈup** | **ˌadd sth↔ˈup** to calculate the total of two or more numbers or amounts: *The waiter can't add up.* ◊ *Add up all the money I owe you.* **ˌadd ˈup to sth 1** to make a total amount of

sth: *The numbers add up to exactly 100.* **2** to lead to a particular result; to show sth: *These clues don't really add up to very much* (= give us very little information).

ad·den·dum /əˈdendəm/ *noun* (*pl.* **ad·denda** /-də/) (*formal*) a section of extra information that is added to sth, especially to a book

adder /ˈædə(r)/ *noun* a small poisonous snake, often with diamond-shaped marks on its back. Adders are the only poisonous snakes in Britain.

ad·dict /ˈædɪkt/ *noun* **1** a person who is unable to stop taking harmful drugs: *a heroin/drug/nicotine addict* **2** a person who is very interested in sth and spends a lot of their free time on it: *a video game addict*

ad·dict·ed /əˈdɪktɪd/ *adj.* [not before noun] ~ **(to sth) 1** unable to stop taking harmful drugs, or using or doing sth as a habit: *to become addicted to drugs/alcohol/gambling* **2** spending all your free time doing sth because you are so interested in it: *Her son is addicted to computer games.*

ad·dic·tion /əˈdɪkʃn/ *noun* [U, C] ~ **(to sth)** the condition of being addicted to sth: *cocaine addiction* ◊ *He is now fighting his addiction to alcohol.*

ad·dict·ive /əˈdɪktɪv/ *adj.* **1** if a drug is **addictive**, it makes people unable to stop taking it: *Heroin is highly addictive.* **2** if an activity or type of behaviour is **addictive**, people need to do it as often as possible because they enjoy it: *I find jogging very addictive.*

add·ition /əˈdɪʃn/ *noun* **1** [U] the process of adding two or more numbers together to find their total: *children learning addition and subtraction* [OPP] SUBTRACTION **2** [C] ~ **(to sth)** a thing that is added to sth else: *the latest addition to our range of cars* ◊ *an addition to the family* (= another child) ◊ *(AmE) to build a new addition onto a house* **3** [U] ~ **(of sth)** the act of adding sth to sth else: *Pasta's basic ingredients are flour and water, sometimes with the addition of eggs or oil.* [IDM] **in addition (to sb/sth)** used when you want to mention another person or thing after sth else: *In addition to these arrangements, extra ambulances will be on duty until midnight.* ◊ *There is, in addition, one further point to make.*

add·ition·al /əˈdɪʃənl/ *adj.* extra; more than was first mentioned or is usual: *additional resources/funds/security* ◊ *The government is providing an additional £25 million to expand the service.* ▶ **add·ition·al·ly** /-ʃənəli/ *adv.* (*written*): *Additionally, the bus service will run on Sundays, every two hours.*

addi·tive /ˈædətɪv/ *noun* a substance that is added in small amounts to sth, especially food, in order to improve it, give it colour, make it last longer, etc: *Food additives can cause allergies.* ◊ *additive-free orange juice* ◊ *chemical additives in petrol*

ad·dled /ˈædld/ *adj.* **1** confused; unable to think clearly: *his addled brain* **2** (of an egg) not fresh; bad to eat

ˈadd-on *noun* a thing that is added to sth else: *The company offers scuba-diving as an add-on to the basic holiday price.* ◊ *add-on software* (= added to a computer)

ad·dress *noun, verb*

■ *noun* /əˈdres; *AmE* ˈædres/ **1** [C] details of where sb lives or works and where letters, etc. can be sent: *What's your name and address?* ◊ *I'll give you my address and telephone number.* ◊ *Is that your home address?* ◊ *an address book* (= that you write addresses and phone numbers in) ◊ *an e-mail address* ◊ *Please note my change of address.* ◊ *Police found him at an address* (= a house or flat/apartment) *in West London.* ◊ *people of no fixed address* (= with no permanent home)—see also FORWARDING ADDRESS **2** [C] a formal speech that is made in front of an audience: *tonight's televised presidential address* **3** [U] **form/mode of** ~ the correct title, etc. to use when you talk to sb

■ *verb* /əˈdres/ [VN] **1** (usually passive) ~ **sth (to sb/sth)** to write on an envelope, etc. the name and address of the person, company, etc. that you are sending it to by mail: *The letter was correctly addressed, but delivered to the wrong house.* ◊ *Address your application to the Personnel Manager.*—see also SAE, SASE **2** to make a formal speech to a group of people: *to address a meeting/rally/confer-*

ence **3** ~ **sb| ~ sth to sb** (*formal*) to say sth directly to sb: *I was surprised when he addressed me in English.* ◊ *Any questions should be addressed to your teacher.* **4** ~ **sb** (**as sth**) to use a particular name or title for sb when you speak or write to them: *There are different ways in which to address a member of the royal family.* ◊ *The judge should be addressed as 'Your Honour'.* **5** ~ (**yourself to**) **sth** (*formal*) to think about a problem or a situation and decide how you are going to deal with it: *Your essay does not address the real issues.* ◊ *We must address ourselves to the problem of traffic pollution.*

ad·dress·ee /ˌædreˈsiː/ *noun* a person that a letter is addressed to

ad·duce /əˈdjuːs; *AmE* əˈduːs/ *verb* [VN] [often passive] (*formal*) to provide evidence, reasons, facts, etc. in order to explain sth or to show that sth is true: *Several factors have been adduced to explain the fall in the birth rate.*

ad·en·oids /ˈædənɔɪdz/ *noun* [pl.] pieces of soft tissue at the back of the nose and throat that can swell up and cause breathing difficulties, especially in children ▶ **ad·en·oid·al** /ˌædəˈnɔɪdl/ *adj.* [only before noun]

adept /əˈdept/ *adj.* (*written*) ~ (**at/in sth**)| ~ (**at/in doing sth**) good at doing sth that is quite difficult ▶ **adept** /ˈædept/ *noun* **adept·ly** *adv.*

ad·equate /ˈædɪkwət/ *adj.* ~ (**for sth**)| ~ (**to do sth**) enough in quantity, or good enough in quality, for a particular purpose or need: *an adequate supply of hot water* ◊ *The room was small but adequate.* ◊ *The space available is not adequate for our needs.* ◊ *There is a lack of adequate provision for disabled students.* ◊ *He didn't give an adequate answer to the question.* ◊ *training that is adequate to meet the future needs of industry* OPP INADEQUATE ⇨ note at ENOUGH ▶ **ad·equacy** /ˈædɪkwəsi/ *noun* [U]: *The adequacy of the security arrangements has been questioned.* **ad·equate·ly** *adv.*: *Are you adequately insured?*

ad·here /ədˈhɪə(r); *AmE* ədˈhɪr/ *verb* [V] ~ (**to sth**) (*formal*) to stick firmly to sth: *Once in the bloodstream, the bacteria adhere to the surface of the red cells.* PHRV **ad'here to sth** (*formal*) to behave according to a particular law, rule, set of instructions, etc.; to follow a particular set of beliefs or a fixed way of doing sth: *For ten months he adhered to a strict no-fat low-salt diet.* ◊ *She adheres to teaching methods she learned over 30 years ago.*

ad·her·ence /ədˈhɪərəns; *AmE* ədˈhɪr-/ *noun* [U] the fact of behaving according to a particular rule, etc., or of following a particular set of beliefs, or a fixed way of doing sth: *strict adherence to the rules*

ad·her·ent /ədˈhɪərənt; *AmE* ədˈhɪr-/ *noun* (*written*) a person who supports a political party or set of ideas

ad·he·sion /ədˈhiːʒn/ *noun* [U] (*technical*) the ability to stick or become attached to sth

ad·he·sive /ədˈhiːsɪv; -ˈhiːz-/ *noun, adj.*
■ *noun* [C, U] a substance that you use to make things stick together: *Use a good waterproof adhesive in addition to the screws.*
■ *adj.* that can stick to sth: *adhesive tape*—see also SELF-ADHESIVE

ad hoc /ˌæd ˈhɒk; *AmE* ˈhɑːk/ *adj.* (from *Latin*) arranged or happening when necessary and not planned in advance: *an ad hoc meeting to deal with the problem* ◊ *The meetings will be held on an ad hoc basis.* ▶ **ad hoc** *adv.*

adieu /əˈdjuː; *AmE* əˈduː/ *exclamation* (*old use* or *literary*) goodbye: *I bid you adieu.*

ad in·fin·itum /ˌæd ˌɪnfɪˈnaɪtəm/ *adv.* (from *Latin*) without ever coming to an end; again and again: *You cannot stay here ad infinitum without paying rent.* ◊ *The problem would be repeated ad infinitum.*

ad·ja·cent /əˈdʒeɪsnt/ *adj.* ~ (**to sth**) (of an area, a building, a room, etc.) situated next to or near sth: *The planes landed on adjacent runways.* ◊ *Our farm land was adjacent to the river.*

ad·jec·tive /ˈædʒɪktɪv/ *noun* (*grammar*) a word that describes a person or thing, for example *big, red* and *clever* in a *big house, red wine* and *a clever idea: 'Reliable' is not an adjective that could be applied to my car.* ▶ **ad·jec·tival** /ˌædʒekˈtaɪvl/ *adj.*: *an adjectival phrase*

ad·jec·tival·ly /-ˈtaɪvəli/ *adv.*: *In 'bread knife', the word 'bread' is used adjectivally.*

ad·join /əˈdʒɔɪn/ *verb* (*written*) to be next to or joined to sth: [VN] *A barn adjoins the farmhouse.* [also V] ▶ **ad·join·ing** *adj.* [usually before noun]: *They stayed in adjoining rooms.* ◊ *We'll have more space if we knock down the adjoining wall* (= the wall between two rooms).

ad·journ /əˈdʒɜːn; *AmE* əˈdʒɜːrn/ *verb* [often passive] to stop a meeting or an official process for a period of time, especially in a court of law: [V] *The court adjourned for lunch.* ◊ [VN] *The trial has been adjourned until next week.* ◊ *The chairman may adjourn the meeting at any time.* ▶ **ad·journ·ment** *noun* [C, U]: *The judge granted us a short adjournment.* PHRV **ad'journ to …** (*formal* or *humorous*) to go to another room or place, especially in order to relax: *I suggest we adjourn to the bar for a drink.*

ad·judge /əˈdʒʌdʒ/ *verb* [usually passive] (*formal*) to make a decision about sb/sth based on the facts that are available: [VN-ADJ] *The company was adjudged bankrupt.* ◊ [VN-N] *The tour was adjudged a great success.* ◊ [VN to inf] *The reforms were generally adjudged to have failed.* HELP This pattern is only used in the passive.

ad·ju·di·cate /əˈdʒuːdɪkeɪt/ *verb* **1** ~ (**on/upon/in sth**)| ~ (**between A and B**) to make an official decision about who is right in a disagreement between two groups or organizations: [V] *A special subcommittee adjudicates on planning applications.* ◊ [VN] *Their purpose is to adjudicate disputes between employers and employees.* **2** [V] to be a judge in a competition: *Who is adjudicating at this year's contest?* ▶ **ad·ju·di·ca·tion** /əˌdʒuːdɪˈkeɪʃn/ *noun* [U, C]: *The case was referred to a higher court for adjudication.* **ad·ju·di·ca·tor** *noun*: *You may refer your complaint to an independent adjudicator.*

ad·junct /ˈædʒʌŋkt/ *noun* **1** (*grammar*) an adverb or a phrase that adds meaning to the verb in a sentence or part of a sentence: *In 'She went home yesterday' and 'He ran away in a panic', 'yesterday' and 'in a panic' are adjuncts.* **2** (*formal*) a thing that is added or attached to sth larger or more important: *The memory expansion cards are useful adjuncts to the computer.*

ad·jure /əˈdʒʊə(r); *AmE* əˈdʒʊr/ *verb* [VN to inf] (*formal*) to ask or to order sb to do sth: *He adjured them to tell the truth.*

ad·just /əˈdʒʌst/ *verb* **1** [VN] ~ **sth** (**to sth**) to change sth slightly to make it more suitable for a new set of conditions or to make it work better: *Watch out for sharp bends and adjust your speed accordingly.* ◊ *This button is for adjusting the volume.* ◊ *Adjust your language to the age of your audience.* **2** ~ (**to sth/to doing sth**)| ~ (**yourself to sth**) to get used to a new situation by changing the way you behave and/or think: [V] *It took her a while to adjust to living alone after the divorce.* ◊ *It took several seconds for his eyes to adjust to the dark.* ◊ [VN] *You'll quickly adjust yourself to student life.* **3** [VN] to move sth slightly so that it looks neater or feels more comfortable: *He smoothed his hair and adjusted his tie.*—see also WELL ADJUSTED

ad·just·able /əˈdʒʌstəbl/ *adj.* that can be moved to different positions or changed in shape or size: *adjustable seat belts* ◊ *The height of the bicycle seat is adjustable.*

adjustable 'spanner (*BrE*) (also **monkey wrench** *AmE, BrE*) *noun* a tool that can be adjusted to hold and turn things of different widths—compare SPANNER, WRENCH—picture at TOOL

ad·just·ment /əˈdʒʌstmənt/ *noun* [C, U] **1** a small change made to sth in order to correct or improve it: *I've made a few adjustments to the design.* ◊ *Some adjustment of the lens may be necessary.* **2** a change in the way a person behaves or thinks: *She went through a period of emotional adjustment after her marriage broke up.*

ad·ju·tant /ˈædʒʊtənt/ *noun* an army officer who does office work and helps other officers

ad lib /ˌæd ˈlɪb/ *verb* (**-bb-**) to say sth in a speech or a performance that you have not prepared or practised SYN IMPROVISE: [V] *The pair have often been known to abandon their script and begin ad libbing.* ◊ [VN] *I lost my notes and had to ad lib the whole speech.* ▶ **ad lib**

A

noun: *The speech was full of ad libs and witty asides.* **ad lib** *adj.*: *an ad lib speech* **ad lib** *adv.*: *She delivered her lines ad lib.*

adman /ˈædmæn/ *noun* (*pl.* **admen** /-men/) (*informal*) a person who works in advertising

admin /ˈædmɪn/ *noun* [U] (*BrE, informal*) = ADMINISTRATION: *a few admin problems* ◇ *She works in admin.*

ad·min·is·ter /ədˈmɪnɪstə(r)/ *verb* [VN] **1** [often passive] to manage and organize the affairs of a company, an organization, a country, etc. [SYN] MANAGE: *to administer a charity/fund/school* ◇ *the high cost of administering medical services* ◇ *The pension funds are administered by commercial banks.* **2** to make sure that sth is done fairly and in the correct way: *to administer justice/the law* ◇ *The questionnaire was administered by trained interviewers.* **3 ~ sth (to sb)** (*formal*) to give or to provide sth, especially in a formal way: *The teacher has the authority to administer punishment.* **4** [often passive] **~ sth (to sb)** (*formal*) to give drugs, medicine, etc. to sb: *The dose was administered to the child intravenously.* ◇ *Police believe his wife could not have administered the poison.* **5 ~ a kick, a punch, etc. (to sb/sth)** (*formal*) to kick or to hit sb/sth: *He administered a severe blow to his opponent's head.*

ad·min·is·tra·tion /əd,mɪnɪˈstreɪʃn/ *noun* **1** (also *BrE informal* **admin**) [U] the activities that are done in order to plan, organize and run a business, school or other institution: *Administration costs are passed on to the customer.* ◇ *the day-to-day administration of a company* ◇ *I work in the Sales Administration department.* **2** [U] the process or act of organizing the way that sth is done: *the administration of justice* **3** [C] the people who plan, organize and run a business, institution, etc: *university administrations* **4** (often **Administration**) [C] the government of a country, especially the US: *This happened frequently during the Nixon Administration.* ◇ *Successive administrations have failed to solve the country's economic problems.* **5** [U] (*formal*) the act of giving a drug to sb: *the administration of antibiotics*

ad·min·is·tra·tive /ədˈmɪnɪstrətɪv; *AmE* -streɪtɪv/ *adj.* connected with organizing the work of a business or an institution: *an administrative job/assistant/error* ▶ **ad·min·is·tra·tive·ly** *adv.*

ad·min·is·tra·tor /ədˈmɪnɪstreɪtə(r)/ *noun* **1** a person whose job is to manage and organize the public or business affairs of a company or an institution: *a hospital administrator* **2** a person who is good at organizing things: *She's a brilliant organizer and administrator.*

ad·mir·able /ˈædmərəbl/ *adj.* (*formal*) having qualities that you admire and respect: *Her dedication to her work was admirable.* ◇ *He made his points with admirable clarity.* ▶ **ad·mir·ably** /-əbli/ *adv.*: *Joe coped admirably with a difficult situation.*

ad·miral /ˈædmərəl/ *noun* an officer of very high rank in the navy: *The admiral visited the ships under his command.* ◇ *Admiral Lord Nelson* ◇ *Good morning, Admiral.*—see also REAR ADMIRAL

Admiral of the ˈFleet (*BrE*) (*AmE* ˈFleet Admiral) *noun* an admiral of the highest rank in the navy

ad·mir·alty /ˈædmərəlti/ *noun* (**the Admiralty**) [sing.+ sing./pl. *v.*] (in Britain in the past) the government department controlling the navy

ad·mir·ation /,ædməˈreɪʃn/ *noun* [U] **~ (for sb/sth)** a feeling of respect and liking for sb/sth: *I have great admiration for her as a writer.* ◇ *to watch/gaze in admiration*

ad·mire /ədˈmaɪə(r)/ *verb* [VN] **1 ~ sb/sth (for sth)| ~ sb (for doing sth)** to respect sb for what they are or for what they have done: *I really admire your enthusiasm.* ◇ *The school is widely admired for its excellent teaching.* ◇ *You have to admire the way he handled the situation.* ◇ *I don't agree with her, but I admire her for sticking to her principles.* **2** to look at sth and think that it is attractive and/or impressive: *He stood back to admire his handiwork.* ◇ *I've just been admiring your new car.* ▶ **ad·mir·ing** *adj.*: *She was used to receiving admiring glances from men.* **ad·mir·ing·ly** *adv.*

ad·mirer /ədˈmaɪərə(r)/ *noun* **1 ~ of sb/sth** a person who admires sb/sth, especially a well-known person or thing: *He is a great admirer of Picasso's early paintings.* **2** a man who is attracted to a woman and admires her: *She never married but had many admirers.*

ad·mis·sible /ədˈmɪsəbl/ *adj.* that can be allowed or accepted, especially in a court of law: *Photographs are usually admissible evidence provided it can be proved that they are authentic.* [OPP] INADMISSIBLE ▶ **ad·mis·si·bil·ity** /əd,mɪsəˈbɪləti/ *noun* [U]

ad·mis·sion /ədˈmɪʃn/ *noun* **1** [U, C] **~ (to sth)** the act of accepting sb into an institution, organization, etc.; the right to enter a place or to join an institution or organization: *Hospital admission is not necessary in most cases.* ◇ *Hospital admissions for asthma attacks have doubled.* ◇ *countries applying for admission to the European Union* ◇ *the university admissions policy/office* ◇ *Last admissions to the park are at 4 p.m.* ◇ *They tried to get into the club but were refused admission.* ◇ *She failed to gain admission to the university of her choice.* ⇨ note at ENTRANCE[1] **2** [C] **~ (of sth)| ~ (that ...)** a statement in which sb admits that sth is true, especially sth wrong or bad that they have done: *an admission of guilt/failure/defeat* ◇ *The minister's resignation was an admission that she had lied.* ◇ *He is a thief by his own admission* (= he has admitted it). **3** [U] the amount of money that you pay to go into a building or to an event: *admission charges/prices* ◇ *£5 admission* ◇ *What's the admission?*

admit /ədˈmɪt/ *verb* (-tt-)

ACCEPT TRUTH | **1 ~ (to sth/to doing sth)| ~ (to sb) (that ...)** to agree, often unwillingly, that sth is true [SYN] CONFESS: [V] *She admits to being strict with her children.* ◇ *Don't be afraid to admit to your mistakes.* ◇ *It was a stupid thing to do, I admit.* ◇ [VN] *He admitted all his mistakes.* ◇ *She stubbornly refuses to admit the truth.* ◇ *Why don't you just admit defeat* (= recognize that you cannot do sth) *and let someone else try?* ◇ *Admit it! You were terrified!* ◇ [V (that)] *They freely admit (that) they still have a lot to learn.* ◇ *I couldn't admit to my parents that I was finding the course difficult.* ◇ *You must admit that it all sounds very strange.* ◇ [VN that] *It was generally admitted that the government had acted too quickly.* ◇ [V speech] *'I'm very nervous,' she admitted reluctantly.* ◇ [VN to inf] *The appointment is now generally admitted to have been a mistake.* [HELP] This pattern is only used in the passive.

ACCEPT BLAME | **2 ~ (to sth/to doing sth)** to say that you have done sth wrong or illegal [SYN] CONFESS: [V] *She admitted to having stolen the car.* ◇ *He refused to admit to the other charges.* ◇ [VN] *She admitted theft.* ◇ *He refused to admit his guilt.* ◇ [V-ing] *She admitted having driven the car without insurance.*

ALLOW TO ENTER/JOIN | **3** [VN] **~ sb/sth (to/into sth)** to allow sb/sth to enter a place: *Each ticket admits one adult and one child.* ◇ *The narrow windows admit little light into the room.* ◇ *You will not be admitted to the theatre after the performance has started.* **4** [VN] **~ sb (to/into sth)** to allow sb to become a member of a club, a school, or an organization: *The society admits all US citizens over 21.* ◇ *Women were only admitted into the club last year.*

TO HOSPITAL | **5** [VN] [often passive] **~ sb to/into a hospital, an institution, etc.** to take sb to a hospital, or other institution where they can receive special care: *Two crash victims were admitted to the local hospital.*

[PHRV] **adˈmit of sth** (*formal*) to show that sth is possible or probable as a solution, an explanation, etc.

ad·mit·tance /ədˈmɪtns/ *noun* [U] (*formal*) the right to enter or the act of entering a building, an institution, etc: *Hundreds of people were unable to gain admittance to the hall.*

ad·mit·ted·ly /ədˈmɪtɪdli/ *adv.* used, especially at the beginning of a sentence, when you are accepting that sth is true: *Admittedly, it is rather expensive but you don't need to use much.*

ad·mon·ish /ədˈmɒnɪʃ; *AmE* -ˈmɑːn-/ *verb* (*formal*) **1 ~ sb (for sth/for doing sth)** to tell sb firmly that you do not approve of sth that they have done: [VN] *She was admonished for chewing gum in class.* [also V speech, VN speech] **2** to strongly advise sb to do sth: [VN to inf] *A*

s	t	v	z	ʃ	ʒ	tʃ	dʒ	θ	ð	ŋ
see	tea	van	zoo	shoe	vision	chain	jam	thin	this	sing

warning voice admonished him not to let this happen. [also V **speech**, VN **speech**]

ad·mon·ition /ˌædməˈnɪʃn/ (also *less frequent* **ad·mon·ish·ment** /ədˈmɒnɪʃmənt; *AmE* -ˈmɑːn-/) *noun* [C, U] (*formal*) a warning to sb about their behaviour ▶ **ad·moni·tory** /ədˈmɒnɪtri; *AmE* -ˈmɑːn-/ *adj.*

ad nau·seam /ˌæd ˈnɔːziæm/ *adv.* (from *Latin*) if a person says or does sth **ad nauseam**, they say or do it again and again so that it becomes boring or annoying: *Television sports commentators repeat the same phrases ad nauseam.*

ado /əˈduː/ *noun* **IDM** **without further/more ado** (*old-fashioned*) without delaying; immediately

adobe /əˈdəʊbi; *AmE* əˈdoʊbi/ *noun* [U] mud that is dried in the sun, mixed with STRAW and used as a building material

ado·les·cence /ˌædəˈlesns/ *noun* [U] the time in a person's life when he or she develops from a child into an adult

ado·les·cent /ˌædəˈlesnt/ *noun* a young person who is developing from a child into an adult: *adolescents between the ages of 13 and 18 and the problems they face* ▶ **ado·les·cent** *adj.*: *adolescent boys/girls/experiences*

adopt /əˈdɒpt; *AmE* əˈdɑːpt/ *verb*

CHILD | **1** to take sb else's child into your family and become its legal parent(s): [V] *a campaign to encourage childless couples to adopt* ◊ [VN] *to adopt a child* ◊ *She was forced to have her baby adopted.*—compare FOSTER

METHOD | **2** [VN] to start to use a particular method or to show a particular attitude towards sb/sth: *All three teams adopted different approaches to the problem.*

SUGGESTION | **3** [VN] to formally accept a suggestion or policy by voting: *to adopt a resolution* ◊ *The council is expected to adopt the new policy at its next meeting.*

NEW NAME/COUNTRY | **4** [VN] to choose a new name, a custom, etc. and begin to use it as your own: *to adopt a name/title/language* ◊ *Early Christians in Europe adopted many of the practices of the older, pagan religions.*

WAY OF BEHAVING | **5** [VN] (*formal*) to use a particular manner, way of speaking, expression, etc: *He adopted an air of indifference.*

CANDIDATE | **6** [VN] ~ **sb** (**as sth**) (*BrE, politics*) to choose sb as a candidate in an election or as a representative: *She was adopted as parliamentary candidate for Wood Green.*

adopt·ed /əˈdɒptɪd; *AmE* əˈdɑːp-/ *adj.* **1** an **adopted** child has legally become part of a family which is not the one in which he or she was born: *Danny is their adopted son.* **2** an **adopted** country is one in which sb chooses to live although it is not the one they were born in

adop·tion /əˈdɒpʃn; *AmE* əˈdɑːpʃn/ *noun* **1** [C, U] the act of adopting a child: *She put the baby up for adoption.* **2** [U] the decision to start using sth such as an idea, a plan or a name: *the adoption of new technology* **3** [C, U] (*BrE, politics*) the act of choosing sb as a candidate for an election: *his adoption as the Labour candidate*

adop·tive /əˈdɒptɪv; *AmE* əˈdɑːp-/ *adj.* [usually before noun] an **adoptive** parent or family is one that has legally adopted a child

ador·able /əˈdɔːrəbl/ *adj.* very attractive and easy to feel love for: *What an adorable child!*

ad·or·ation /ˌædəˈreɪʃn/ *noun* [U] a feeling of great love or worship: *He gazed at her with pure adoration.* ◊ *The painting is called 'Adoration of the Infant Christ'.*

adore /əˈdɔː(r)/ *verb* (not used in the progressive tenses) **1** [VN] to love sb very much: *It's obvious that she adores him.* **2** (*informal*) to like sb very much: [VN] *I simply adore his music!* ◊ [V-ing] *She adores working with children.*

ador·ing /əˈdɔːrɪŋ/ *adj.* [usually before noun] showing much love and admiration: *her adoring grandmother* ◊ *He waved to the adoring crowds.* ▶ **ador·ing·ly** *adv.*

adorn /əˈdɔːn; *AmE* əˈdɔːrn/ *verb* [VN] [often passive] ~ **sth/sb** (**with sth**) (*formal*) to make sth/sb look more attractive by decorating it or them with sth: *The walls were adorned with paintings.* ◊ *The children adorned*

themselves with flowers. ◊ *Gold rings adorned his fingers.* ◊ (*ironic*) *Graffiti adorned the walls.* ▶ **adorn·ment** *noun* [U, C]: *A plain necklace was her only adornment.*

ad·rena·lin /əˈdrenəlɪn/ *noun* [U] a substance produced in the body when you are excited, afraid or angry. It makes the heart beat faster and increases your energy and ability to move quickly: *The excitement at the start of a race can really get the adrenalin flowing.*

adrift /əˈdrɪft/ *adj.* [not before noun] **1** if a boat or a person in a boat is **adrift**, the boat is not tied to anything or is floating without being controlled by anyone: *The survivors were adrift in a lifeboat for six days.* **2** (*BrE*) (of a person) feeling alone and without a direction or an aim in life: *young people adrift in the big city* **3** no longer attached or fixed in the right position: *I nearly suffocated when the pipe on my breathing apparatus came adrift.* ◊ (*figurative*) *She had been cut adrift from everything she had known.* ◊ (*figurative*) *Our plans had gone badly adrift.* **4** ~ (**of sb/sth**) (*BrE*) (in sport) behind the score or position of your opponents: *The team are now just six points adrift of the leaders.* **IDM** **cast/set sb adrift** (usually passive) to leave sb to be carried away on a boat that is not being controlled by anyone: (*figurative*) *Without language human beings are cast adrift.*

adroit /əˈdrɔɪt/ *adj.* (*written*) skilful and clever, especially in dealing with people: *an adroit negotiator* ▶ **adroit·ly** *adv.*: *He adroitly avoided answering my questions.* **adroit·ness** *noun* [U]

adu·la·tion /ˌædjuˈleɪʃn; *AmE* ˌædʒəˈl-/ *noun* [U] (*formal*) admiration and praise, especially when this is greater than is necessary: *The band enjoy the adulation of their fans wherever they go.* ▶ **adu·la·tory** /ˌædjuˈleɪtəri; *AmE* ˈædʒələtɔːri/ *adj.*

adult /ˈædʌlt; əˈdʌlt/ *noun, adj.*

■ *noun* **1** a fully grown person who is legally responsible for their actions: *Children must be accompanied by an adult.* ◊ *Why can't you two act like civilized adults?* **2** a fully grown animal: *The fish return to the river as adults in order to breed.*

■ *adj.* **1** fully grown or developed: *preparing young people for adult life* ◊ *the adult population* ◊ *adult monkeys* **2** behaving in an intelligent and responsible way; typical of what is expected of an adult: *When my parents split up, it was all very adult and open.* **3** [only before noun] intended for adults only, because it is about sex or contains violence: *an adult movie*—see also ADULTHOOD

adult edu·cation (also **con·tinuing edu·cation**) *noun* [U] education for adults that is available outside the formal education system, for example at evening classes

adul·ter·ate /əˈdʌltəreɪt/ *verb* [VN] [often passive] ~ **sth** (**with sth**) to make food or drink less pure by adding another substance to it—see also UNADULTERATED ▶ **adul·ter·ation** /əˌdʌltəˈreɪʃn/ *noun* [U]

adul·ter·er /əˈdʌltərə(r)/ *noun* (*formal*) a person who commits adultery

adul·ter·ess /əˈdʌltərəs/ *noun* (*formal*) a woman who commits adultery

adul·tery /əˈdʌltəri/ *noun* [U] sex between a married person and sb who is not their husband or wife: *She suspected her husband had committed adultery.* ▶ **adul·ter·ous** /əˈdʌltərəs/ *adj.*: *an adulterous relationship*

adult·hood /ˈædʌlthʊd; əˈdʌlt-/ *noun* [U] the state of being an adult: *a child reaching adulthood*

ad·um·brate /ˈædʌmbreɪt/ *verb* [VN] (*rare, formal*) to give a general idea or description of sth without details **SYN** OUTLINE

ad·vance /ədˈvɑːns; *AmE* -ˈvæns/ *noun, verb, adj.*

■ *noun*

FORWARD MOVEMENT | **1** [C] the forward movement of a group of people, especially armed forces: *We feared that an advance on the capital would soon follow.* ◊ *enemy advances*

DEVELOPMENT | **2** [C, U] ~ (**in sth**) progress or a development in a particular activity or area of understanding: *recent advances in medical science* ◊ *We live in an age of rapid technological advance.*

MONEY | **3** [C, usually sing.] money paid for work before it

æ	ɑː	e	ɜː	ə	ɪ	iː	i	ɒ	ɔː	ʌ	ʊ	u	uː
cat	father	ten	bird	about	sit	see	many	got	saw	cup	put	actual	too

(BrE)

has been done or money paid earlier than expected: *They offered an advance of £5000 after the signing of the contract.* ◊ *She asked for an advance on her salary.*

SEXUAL | **4** (**advances**) [pl.] attempts to start a sexual relationship with sb: *He had made advances to one of his students.*

PRICE INCREASE | **5** [C] ~ (**on sth**) an increase in the price or value of sth: *Share prices showed significant advances today.*

IDM **in advance (of sth) 1** before the time that is expected; before sth happens: *a week/month/year in advance* ◊ *It's cheaper if you book the tickets in advance.* ◊ *People were evacuated from the coastal regions in advance of the hurricane.* **2** more developed than sb/sth else: *Galileo's ideas were well in advance of the age in which he lived.*

■ *verb*

MOVE FORWARD | **1** [V] ~ (**on/towards sb/sth**) to move forward towards sb/sth, often in order to attack or threaten them or it: *The mob advanced on us, shouting angrily.* ◊ *The troops were finally given the order to advance.* ◊ *They had advanced 20 miles by nightfall.* ◊ *the advancing Allied troops*—compare RETREAT

DEVELOP | **2** if knowledge, technology, etc. **advances**, it develops and improves: [V] *Our knowledge of the disease has advanced considerably over recent years.* ◊ [VN] *This research has done much to advance our understanding of language learning.*

HELP TO SUCCEED | **3** [VN] to help sth to succeed **SYN** FURTHER: *Studying for new qualifications is one way of advancing your career.* ◊ *They worked together to advance the cause of democracy.*

MONEY | **4** ~ **sth (to sb)** | ~ (**sb**) **sth** to give sb money before the time it would usually be paid: [VN, VNN] *We are willing to advance the money to you.* ◊ *We will advance you the money.*

SUGGEST | **5** [VN] (*formal*) to suggest an idea, a theory, or a plan for other people to discuss **SYN** PUT FORWARD: *The article advances a new theory to explain changes in the climate.*

MAKE EARLIER | **6** [VN] (*formal*) to change the time or date of an event so that it takes place earlier **SYN** BRING FORWARD: *The date of the trial has been advanced by one week.* **OPP** POSTPONE

TO LATER PART | **7** (*formal*) to move forward to a later part of sth; to move sth forward to a later part: [V] *Users advance through the program by answering a series of questions.* ◊ [VN] *This button advances the tape to the beginning of the next track.*

INCREASE | **8** [V] (*business*) (of prices, costs, etc.) to increase in price or amount: *Inflation advanced sharply during the 1980s.*

■ *adj.* [only before noun] **1** done or given before sth is going to happen: *Please give us* **advance warning** *of any changes to the schedule.* ◊ *We need* **advance notice** *of the numbers involved.* ◊ *No* **advance booking** *is necessary on most departures.* **2** ~ **party/team** a group of people who go somewhere first, before the main group

ad·vanced /əd'vɑːnst; *AmE* -'vænst/ *adj.* **1** having the most modern and recently developed ideas, methods, etc: *advanced technology* ◊ *advanced industrial societies* **2** (of a course of study) at a high or difficult level: *There were only three of us on the advanced course.* ◊ *an advanced student of English* **3** at a late stage of development: *the advanced stages of the disease* **IDM** **of advanced 'years | sb's advanced 'age** used in polite expressions to describe sb as 'very old': *He was a man of advanced years.* ◊ (*humorous*) *Even at my advanced age I still know how to enjoy myself!*

ad'vanced level *noun* = A LEVEL: *For this course, you need two GCE Advanced Level passes.*

ad·vance·ment /əd'vɑːnsmənt; *AmE* -'væns-/ *noun* (*formal*) **1** [U, C] the process of helping sth to make progress or succeed; the progress that is made: *the advancement of knowledge/education/science* **2** [U] progress in a job, social class, etc: *There are good opportunities for advancement if you have the right skills.*

ad·van·cing /əd'vɑːnsɪŋ; *AmE* -'væns-/ *adj.* ~ **years/age** used as a polite way of referring to the fact of time passing and of sb growing older: *She is still very active, in spite of her advancing years.*

ad·van·tage /əd'vɑːntɪdʒ; *AmE* -'væn-/ *noun, verb*
■ *noun* [C, U] **1** ~ (**over sb**) a thing that helps you to be better or more successful than other people: *a big/great/definite advantage* ◊ *Being tall gave him an advantage over the other players.* ◊ *an unfair advantage* (= sth that benefits you, but not your opponents) ◊ *She had the* **advantage** *of a good education.* ◊ *Is there any advantage in getting there early?* ◊ *You will be at an advantage* (= have an advantage) *if you have thought about the interview questions in advance.* **2** a quality of sth that makes it better or more useful: *A small car has the added advantage of being cheaper to run.* ◊ *the advantages of living in a small town* ◊ *Each of these systems has its advantages and disadvantages.* **3** (in tennis) the first point scored after a score of 40–40: *Advantage Henman.* **IDM** **be/work to your ad'vantage** to give you an advantage; to change a situation in a way that gives you an advantage: *It would be to your advantage to attend this meeting.* ◊ *Eventually, the new regulations will work to our advantage.* **take ad'vantage of sth/sb 1** to make use of sth well; to make use of an opportunity: *We took full advantage of the hotel facilities.* ◊ *She took advantage of the children's absence to tidy their rooms.* **2** to make use of sb/sth in a way that is unfair or dishonest: *He took advantage of my generosity* (= for example, by taking more than I had intended to give). **to (good/best) ad'vantage** in a way that shows the best of sth: *The photograph showed him to advantage.* **turn sth to your ad'vantage** to use or change a bad situation so that it helps you
■ *verb* [VN] (*formal*) to put sb in a better position than other people or than they were in before

ad·van·taged /əd'vɑːntɪdʒd; *AmE* -'væn-/ *adj.* being in a good social or financial situation: *We aim to improve opportunities for the less advantaged in society.* **OPP** DISADVANTAGED

ad·van·ta·geous /ˌædvən'teɪdʒəs/ *adj.* ~ (**to sb**) good or useful in a particular situation: *A free trade agreement would be advantageous to both countries.* **OPP** DISADVANTAGEOUS ▶ **ad·van·ta·geous·ly** *adv.*

ad·vent /'ædvent/ *noun* **1** [sing.] (**the ~ of sth/sb**) (*written*) the coming of an important event, person, invention, etc: *the advent of new technology* **2** (**Advent**) [U] the period of four weeks before Christmas in the Christian religion

'Advent calendar *noun* a piece of stiff paper with a picture and 24 small doors with numbers on. Children open a door each day during Advent and find a picture or a piece of chocolate behind each one.

ad·ven·ti·tious /ˌædven'tɪʃəs/ *adj.* (*rare, formal*) happening accidentally; not planned

ad·ven·ture /əd'ventʃə(r)/ *noun* **1** [C] an unusual, exciting or dangerous experience, journey or series of events: *her adventures travelling in Africa* ◊ *When you're a child, life is one big adventure.* ◊ *adventure stories* **2** [U] excitement and the willingness to take risks, try new ideas, etc: *a sense/spirit of adventure*

ad,venture 'playground *noun* (*BrE*) an area where children can play, with large structures, ropes, etc. for climbing on.

ad·ven·turer /əd'ventʃərə(r)/ *noun* **1** a person who enjoys exciting new experiences, especially going to unusual places **2** (*often disapproving*) a person who is willing to take risks or act in a dishonest way in order to gain money or power

ad·ven·ture·some /əd'ventʃəsəm; *AmE* -tʃərs-/ *adj.* (*AmE*) = ADVENTUROUS

ad·ven·tur·ism /əd'ventʃərɪzəm/ *noun* [U] (*disapproving*) a willingness to take risks in business or politics in order to gain sth for yourself

ad·ven·tur·ous /əd'ventʃərəs/ *adj.* **1** (*AmE also* **ad·venture·some**) (of a person) willing to take risks and try new ideas; enjoying being in new, exciting situations: *For the more adventurous tourists, there are trips into the*

aɪ	aʊ	eɪ	əʊ	oʊ	ɔɪ	ɪə	eə	ʊə	j	w
my	now	say	go	go	boy	near	hair	pure	yes	wet
			(BrE)	(AmE)						

mountains with a local guide. ◊ Many teachers would like to be more adventurous and creative. **2** including new and interesting things, methods and ideas: The menu contained traditional favourites as well as more adventurous dishes. **3** full of new, exciting or dangerous experiences: an adventurous trip/lifestyle [OPP] UNADVENTUROUS ▶ **ad·ven·tur·ous·ly** adv. (rare)

ad·verb /ˈædvɜːb; AmE -vɜːrb/ noun (grammar) a word that adds more information about place, time, manner, cause or degree to a verb, an adjective, a phrase or another adverb: In 'speak kindly', 'incredibly deep', 'just in time' and 'too quickly', 'kindly', 'incredibly', 'just' and 'too' are all adverbs. ▶ **ad·ver·bial** /ædˈvɜːbiəl; AmE -ˈvɜːrb-/ adj.: 'Very quickly indeed' is an adverbial phrase.

ad,verbial 'particle noun (grammar) an adverb used especially after a verb to show position, direction of movement, etc: In 'come back', 'break down' and 'fall off', 'back', 'down' and 'off' are all adverbial particles.

ad·ver·sar·ial /ˌædvəˈseəriəl; AmE -ˈser-/ adj. (formal or technical) (especially of political or legal systems) involving people who are in opposition and who make attacks on each other: the adversarial nature of the two-party system ◊ an adversarial system of justice

ad·ver·sary /ˈædvəsəri; AmE -verseri/ noun (pl. -ies) (formal) a person that sb is opposed to and competing with in an argument or a battle [SYN] OPPONENT: his old political adversary

ad·verse /ˈædvɜːs; ədˈvɜːs; AmE -vɜːrs/ adj. [usually before noun] negative and unpleasant; not likely to produce a good result: adverse change/circumstances/weather conditions ◊ Lack of money will have an **adverse** effect on our research programme. ◊ They have attracted strong adverse criticism. ◊ This drug is known to have adverse side effects. ▶ **ad·verse·ly** adv.: Her health was adversely affected by the climate.

ad·ver·sity /ədˈvɜːsəti; AmE -ˈvɜːrs-/ noun [U, C] (pl. -ies) (formal) a difficult or unpleasant situation: courage in the face of adversity ◊ He overcame many personal adversities.

ad·vert /ˈædvɜːt; AmE -ˈvɜːrt/ noun (BrE) = ADVERTISEMENT: the adverts on television

ad·ver·tise /ˈædvətaɪz; AmE -vert-/ verb **1** ~ sth (as sth) to tell the public about a product or a service in order to encourage people to buy or to use it: [V] If you want to attract more customers, try advertising in the local paper. ◊ [VN] to advertise a product/a business/your services ◊ The cruise was advertised as the 'journey of a lifetime'. **2** ~ (for sb/sth) to let people know that sth is going to happen, or that a job is available by giving details about it in a newspaper, on a notice in a public place, etc: [V] We are currently advertising for a new sales manager. ◊ [VN] We should have advertised the concert much more widely. **3** [VN] to show or tell sth about yourself to other people: If I were you, I wouldn't advertise the fact that you don't have a work permit.

ad·ver·tise·ment /ədˈvɜːtɪsmənt; AmE ˌædvərˈtaɪz-/ noun **1** [C] (also informal ad) (BrE also **ad·vert**) ~ (for sth) a notice, picture or film telling people about a product, job or service: Put an advertisement in the local paper to sell your car.—see also CLASSIFIED ADVERTISEMENTS **2** [C] (BrE also **ad·vert**) ~ for sth an example of sth that shows its good qualities: Dirty streets and homelessness are no advertisement for a prosperous society. **3** [U] the act of advertising sth and making it public

ad·ver·tiser /ˈædvətaɪzə(r); AmE -vərt-/ noun a person or company that advertises

ad·ver·tis·ing /ˈædvətaɪzɪŋ; AmE -vərt-/ noun [U] the activity and industry of advertising things to people on television, in newspapers, etc: A good advertising campaign will increase our sales. ◊ Cigarette advertising has been banned. ◊ radio/TV advertising ◊ Val works for an **advertising agency** (= a company that designs advertisements). ◊ a career in advertising

ad·vice /ədˈvaɪs/ noun [U] ~ (on sth) an opinion or a suggestion about what sb should do in a particular situation: advice on road safety ◊ They **give advice** for people with HIV and Aids. ◊ You should **follow** your doctor's advice. ◊ We were advised to seek legal advice. ◊ Let me

give you **a piece of advice**. ◊ A **word** of advice—don't wear that dress. ◊ **Take my advice**—don't get married. ◊ I did it **on his advice.**

ad'vice column, ad'vice columnist noun (AmE) = AGONY COLUMN, AGONY AUNT

ad·vis·able /ədˈvaɪzəbl/ adj. [not usually before noun] ~ (to do sth) sensible and a good idea in order to achieve sth: Early booking is advisable. ◊ It is advisable to practise each exercise individually before doing the whole routine. [OPP] INADVISABLE ▶ **ad·vis·abil·ity** /ədˌvaɪzəˈbɪləti/ noun [U]

ad·vise /ədˈvaɪz/ verb **1** ~ (sb) (against/against doing sth) to tell sb what you think they should do in a particular situation: [V] I would **strongly advise** against going out on your own. ◊ [VN] Her mother was away and couldn't advise her. ◊ I'd advise extreme caution. ◊ [VN to inf] Police are advising fans without tickets to stay away. ◊ I'd advise you not to tell him. ◊ [V that] They advise that a passport be carried with you at all times. ◊ [VN that] It is strongly advised that you take out some form of medical insurance. ◊ [V -ing] I'd advise buying your tickets well in advance if you want to travel in August. ◊ [V speech, VN speech] 'Get there early,' she advised (them) —see also ILL-ADVISED, WELL ADVISED **2** ~ (sb) on sth | ~ (sb) about sth/doing sth to give sb help and information on a subject that you know a lot about: [V] We employ an expert to advise on new technology. ◊ [VN] She advises the government on environmental issues. ◊ [V wh-] The pharmacist will advise which medicines are safe to take. ◊ [VN wh-] Your lawyer can advise you whether to take any action. **3** ~ sb (of sth) (formal) to officially tell sb sth: [VN] Please advise us of any changes in your personal details. ◊ [VN wh-] I will contact you later to advise you when to come. ◊ [VN that] I regret to advise you that the course is now full.

ad·vised·ly /ədˈvaɪzədli/ adv. (formal) if you say that you are using a word **advisedly**, you mean that you have thought carefully before choosing it

ad·viser (also less frequent **ad·visor**) /ədˈvaɪzə(r)/ noun ~ (to sb) (on sth) a person who gives advice, especially sb who knows a lot about a particular subject: a financial adviser ◊ a special adviser to the President on foreign affairs

ad·vis·ory /ədˈvaɪzəri/ adj., noun
■ adj. having the role of giving professional advice: an advisory committee/body/service ◊ He acted in an advisory capacity only.
■ noun (pl. -ies) (AmE) an official warning that sth bad is going to happen: a tornado advisory

ad·vo·cacy /ˈædvəkəsi/ noun [U] **1** ~ (of sth) (formal) the giving of public support to an idea, a course of action or a belief **2** (technical) the work of lawyers who speak about cases in courts of law

ad·vo·cate verb, noun
■ verb /ˈædvəkeɪt/ (formal) to support sth publicly [SYN] RECOMMEND: [VN] The group does not advocate the use of violence. ◊ [V -ing] Many experts advocate rewarding your child for good behaviour. ◊ [V that] The report advocated that all buildings be fitted with smoke detectors. ◊ (BrE also) The report advocated that all buildings should be fitted with smoke detectors. [also VN -ing]
■ noun /ˈædvəkət/ **1** ~ (of/for sth/sb) a person who supports or speaks in favour of sb or of a public plan or action: an advocate for hospital workers ◊ a staunch advocate of free speech—see also DEVIL'S ADVOCATE **2** a person who defends sb in a court of law ⇨ note at LAWYER

adze (BrE) (AmE **adz**) /ædz/ noun a heavy tool with a curved blade at RIGHT ANGLES to the handle, used for cutting or shaping large pieces of wood

aegis /ˈiːdʒɪs/ noun [IDM] **under the aegis of sb/sth** (formal) with the protection or support of a particular organization or person

aeon (BrE) (also **eon** AmE, BrE) /ˈiːən/ noun (formal) an extremely long period of time; thousands of years: aeons of geological history

aer·ate /ˈeəreɪt; AmE ˈer-/ verb [VN] **1** to make it possible for air to become mixed with soil, water, etc: Earthworms

b	d	f	g	h	k	l	m	n	p	r
bad	did	fall	get	hat	cat	leg	man	now	pen	red

do the important job of aerating the soil. **2** to add a gas, especially CARBON DIOXIDE, to a liquid under pressure: *aerated water* ▶ **aer·ation** /eə'reɪʃn; *AmE* e'reɪ-/ *noun* [U]

aer·ial /'eəriəl; *AmE* 'er-/ *noun, adj.*
■ *noun* (*BrE*) (also **an·tenna** *AmE, BrE*) a piece of equipment made of wire or metal rods for receiving or sending radio and television signals—picture at HOUSE
■ *adj.* **1** from a plane: *aerial attacks/bombardment/photography* ◇ *an aerial view of Palm Island* **2** in the air; existing above the ground: *The banyan tree has aerial roots.*

aerie (*AmE*) = EYRIE

aero- /'eərəʊ; *AmE* 'eroʊ/ *combining form* (in nouns, adjectives and adverbs) connected with air or aircraft: *aerodynamic* ◇ *aerospace*

aero·bat·ics /ˌeərə'bætɪks; *AmE* ˌerə-/ *noun* [pl.] exciting and skilful movements performed in aircraft, such as flying upside down, especially in front of an audience ▶ **aero·batic** *adj.*: *an aerobatic display*

aer·obics /eə'rəʊbɪks; *AmE* e'roʊ-/ *noun* [U] physical exercises intended to strengthen the heart and lungs, often done in classes, with music: *to do aerobics* ▶ **aer·ob·ic** *adj.*: *aerobic exercise*

aero·drome /'eərədrəʊm; *AmE* 'erədroʊm/ (*BrE*) (*AmE* **air·drome**) *noun* (*old-fashioned*) a small airport, used mainly by private planes

aero·dy·nam·ics /ˌeərəʊdaɪ'næmɪks; *AmE* ˌeroʊ-/ *noun* **1** [pl.] the qualities of an object that affect the way it moves through the air: *Research has focused on improving the car's aerodynamics.* **2** [U] the science that deals with how objects move through air ▶ **aero·dy·nam·ic** *adj.*: *the car's aerodynamic shape* (= making it able to move faster)

aero·gramme (*BrE*) (*AmE* **aero·gram**) /'eərəgræm; *AmE* 'erə-/ (also **'air letter**) *noun* a sheet of light paper that can be folded and sent by air as a letter

aero·naut·ics /ˌeərə'nɔːtɪks; *AmE* ˌerə-/ *noun* [U] the science or practice of building and flying aircraft ▶ **aero·naut·ic·al** /-'nɔːtɪkl/ *adj.*: *an aeronautical engineer*

aero·plane /'eərəpleɪn; *AmE* 'erə-/ (*BrE*) (*AmE* **air·plane**) (also **plane** *BrE, AmE*) *noun* a flying vehicle with wings and one or more engines

aero·sol /'eərəsɒl; *AmE* 'erəsɔːl/ *noun* a metal container in which a liquid such as paint or HAIRSPRAY is kept under pressure and released as a spray: *ozone-friendly aerosols* ◇ *an aerosol can/spray*

aero·space /'eərəʊspeɪs; *AmE* 'eroʊ-/ *noun* [U] (often used as an adjective) the industry of building aircraft and vehicles and equipment to be sent into space: *jobs in aerospace and defence* ◇ *the aerospace industry*

aes·thete (*AmE* also **es·thete**) /'iːsθiːt; 'es-; *AmE* 'es-/ *noun* (*formal, sometimes disapproving*) a person who has a love and understanding of art and beautiful things

aes·thet·ic (*AmE* also **es·thet·ic**) /iːs'θetɪk; es-; *AmE* es-/ *adj., noun*
■ *adj.* **1** concerned with beauty and art and the understanding of beautiful things: *an aesthetic appreciation of the landscape* ◇ *The benefits of conservation are both financial and aesthetic.* **2** made in an artistic way and beautiful to look at: *Their furniture was more aesthetic than functional.* ▶ **aes·thet·ic·al·ly** (*AmE* also **es-**) /-kli/ *adv.*: *aesthetically pleasing colour combinations*
■ *noun* **1** [C] the aesthetic qualities and ideas of sth: *The students debated the aesthetic of the poems.* **2** (**aesthetics**) [U] the branch of philosophy that studies the principles of beauty, especially in art ▶ **aes·theti·cism** (*AmE* also **es-**) /iːs'θetɪsɪzəm; es-; *AmE* es-/ *noun* [U]

aeti·ology (*BrE*) (*AmE* **eti·ology**) /ˌiːti'ɒlədʒi; *AmE* -'aːl-/ *noun* [U] the scientific study of the causes of disease

afar /ə'fɑː(r)/ *adv.* **IDM** **from a'far** (*literary*) from a long distance away: *He loved her from afar* (= did not tell her he loved her).

af·fable /'æfəbl/ *adj.* pleasant, friendly and easy to talk to ▶ **af·fa·bil·ity** /ˌæfə'bɪləti/ *noun* [U] **af·fably** *adv.*

af·fair /ə'feə(r); *AmE* ə'fer/ *noun*
PUBLIC/POLITICAL ACTIVITIES | **1** (**affairs**) [pl.] events that are of public interest or political importance: *world/inter-*

national/business affairs ◇ *an expert on foreign affairs* (= political events in other countries) ◇ *affairs of state*—see also CURRENT AFFAIRS

EVENT | **2** [C, usually sing.] an event that people are talking about or describing in a particular way: *The newspapers exaggerated the whole affair wildly.* ◇ *The debate was a pretty disappointing affair.* ◇ *She wanted the celebration to be a simple family affair.* ◇ *the Whitewater affair*

RELATIONSHIP | **3** [C] a sexual relationship between two people, usually when one or both of them is married to sb else: *She is having an affair with her boss.*—see also LOVE AFFAIR

PRIVATE BUSINESS | **4** (**affairs**) [pl.] matters connected with a person's private business and financial situation: *I looked after my father's financial affairs.* **5** [sing.] a thing that sb is responsible for (and that other people should not be concerned with): *How I spend my money is my affair.*

OBJECT | **6** [C] (*old-fashioned*) (with an adjective) an object that is unusual or difficult to describe: *Her hat was an amazing affair with feathers and a huge brim.*

IDM see STATE *n.*

af·fect /ə'fekt/ *verb* **1** [VN] [often passive] to produce a change in sb/sth **SYN** INFLUENCE: *How will these changes affect us?* ◇ *Your opinion will not affect my decision.* ◇ *The south of the country was worst affected by the drought.* **2** [VN] [often passive] (of a disease) to attack sb or a part of the body; to make sb become ill/sick **SYN** AFFLICT: *The condition affects one in five women.* ◇ *Rub the cream into the affected areas.* **3** [VN] [often passive] to make sb have strong feelings of sadness, pity, etc. **SYN** TOUCH, MOVE: *They were deeply affected by the news of her death.* **4** (*formal*) to pretend to be feeling or thinking sth: [VN] *She affected a calmness she did not feel.* [also **v to inf**] **5** [VN] (*formal, disapproving*) to use or wear sth that is intended to impress other people **SYN** PUT ON: *I wish he wouldn't affect that ridiculous accent.*

WHICH WORD?
affect / effect (?)

- **affect** *verb* = 'to have an influence on sb/sth'. *Does television affect children's behaviour?* It is not a noun.
- **effect** *noun* = 'result, influence'. *Does television have an effect on children's behaviour?*
- **effect** *verb* is formal and means 'to achieve or produce'.

---

af·fect·ation /ˌæfek'teɪʃn/ *noun* [C, U] behaviour or an action that is not natural or sincere and that is often intended to impress other people: *His little affectations irritated her.* ◇ *Kay has no affectation at all.* ◇ *He raised his eyebrows with an affectation of surprise* (= pretending to be surprised).

af·fect·ed /ə'fektɪd/ *adj.* (of a person or their behaviour) not natural or sincere: *an affected laugh/smile* **OPP** UNAFFECTED ▶ **af·fect·ed·ly** *adv.*

af·fect·ing /ə'fektɪŋ/ *adj.* (*formal*) producing strong feelings of sadness and sympathy

af·fec·tion /ə'fekʃn/ *noun* **1** [U, sing.] ~ (**for sb/sth**) the feeling of liking or loving sb/sth very much and caring about them: *Mr Darcy's affection for his sister* ◇ *Children need lots of love and affection.* ◇ *He didn't show his wife any affection.* ◇ *She was held in deep affection by all her students.* ◇ *I have a great affection for New York.* **2** (**affections**) [pl.] (*written*) a person's feelings of love: *Anne had two men trying to win her affections.*

af·fec·tion·ate /ə'fekʃənət/ *adj.* showing caring feelings and love for sb: *He is very affectionate towards his children.* ◇ *Rosie gave her an affectionate kiss on each cheek.* ▶ **af·fec·tion·ate·ly** *adv.*: *William was affectionately known as Billy.*

af·fi·da·vit /ˌæfə'deɪvɪt/ *noun* (*law*) a written statement that you swear is true, and that can be used as evidence in a court of law

af·fili·ate *verb, noun*
■ *verb* /ə'fɪlieɪt/ **1** [VN] [usually passive] ~ **sb/sth** (**with/to sb/sth**) to link a group, a company, or an organization

A

very closely with another larger one: *The group is not affiliated to any political party.* ◊ *The hospital is affiliated with the local university.* **2 ~ (yourself) (with sb/sth)** to join, to be connected with, or to work for an organization: [VN] *The majority of people questioned affiliated themselves with a religious group.* [alsoV]

■ *noun* /ə'fɪliət/ a company, an organization, etc. that is connected with or controlled by another larger one

af·fili·ated /ə'fɪlieɪtɪd/ *adj.* [only before noun] closely connected to or controlled by a group or an organization: *All affiliated members can vote.* ◊ *a government-affiliated institute* OPP UNAFFILIATED

af·fili·ation /əˌfɪli'eɪʃn/ *noun* [U, C] (*formal*) **1** a person's connection with a political party, religion, etc: *He had been detained without trial because of his political affiliation.* **2** one group or organization's official connection with another

af·fin·ity /ə'fɪnəti/ *noun* (*pl.* -ies) (*formal*) **1** [sing.] **~ (for/ with sb/sth)| ~ (between A and B)** a strong feeling that you understand sb/sth and like them or it: *Sam was born in the country and had a deep affinity with nature.* **2** [U, C] **~ (with sb/sth)| ~ (between A and B)** a close relationship between two people or things that have similar qualities, structures or features: *There is a close affinity between Italian and Spanish.*

af·firm /ə'fɜːm; *AmE* ə'fɜːrm/ *verb* (*formal*) to state firmly or publicly that sth is true or that you support sth strongly: [VN] *Both sides affirmed their commitment to the ceasefire.* ◊ [Vthat] *I can affirm that no one will lose their job.* [alsoV**speech**] ▶ **af·firm·ation** /ˌæfə'meɪʃn; *AmE* ˌæfər'm-/ *noun* [U, C]: *She nodded her head in affirmation.*

af·firma·tive /ə'fɜːmətɪv; *AmE* ə'fɜːrm-/ *adj., noun*

■ *adj.* (*formal*) an **affirmative** word or reply means 'yes' or expresses agreement: *an affirmative response to the question* OPP NEGATIVE ▶ **af·firma·tive·ly** *adv.*: *90% voted affirmatively.*

■ *noun* (*formal*) a word or statement that means 'yes'; an agreement or a CONFIRMATION: (*formal*) *She answered* **in the affirmative** (= said 'yes'). OPP NEGATIVE

af,firmative 'action *noun* [U] (*especially AmE*) = POSITIVE DISCRIMINATION

affix *verb, noun*

■ *verb* /ə'fɪks/ [VN] [often passive] **~ sth (to sth)** (*formal*) to stick or attach sth to sth else: *The label should be firmly affixed to the package.*

■ *noun* /'æfɪks/ (*grammar*) a letter or group of letters added to the beginning or end of a word to change its meaning. The PREFIX *un-* in *unhappy* and the SUFFIX *-less* in *careless* are both affixes.

af·flict /ə'flɪkt/ *verb* [VN] [often passive] (*formal*) to affect sb/sth in an unpleasant or harmful way: *About 40% of the country's population* **is afflicted with** *the disease.* ◊ *Aid will be sent to the afflicted areas.*

af·flic·tion /ə'flɪkʃn/ *noun* [U, C] (*formal*) pain and suffering or sth that causes it

af·flu·ent /'æfluənt/ *adj.* having a lot of money and a good standard of living: *affluent Western countries* ◊ *a very affluent neighbourhood* ▶ **af·flu·ence** /'æfluəns/ *noun* [U]

af·ford /ə'fɔːd; *AmE* ə'fɔːrd/ *verb* **1** [no passive] (usually used with *can*, *could* or *be able to*, especially in negative sentences or questions) to have enough money or time to be able to buy or to do sth: [VN] *Can we afford a new car?* ◊ *None of them could afford £50 for a ticket.* ◊ *She felt she couldn't afford any more time off work.* ◊ [Vtoinf] *We can't afford to go abroad this summer.* ◊ *She never took a taxi, even though she could afford to.* ◊ [VNtoinf] *He couldn't then afford the money to go on the trip.* **2** [no passive] (usually used with *can* or *could*, especially in negative sentences and questions) if you say that you **can't afford** to do sth, you mean that you should not do it because it will cause problems for you if you do: [Vtoinf] *We cannot afford to ignore this warning.* ◊ (*formal*) *They could* **ill afford** *to lose any more staff.* ◊ [VN] *We cannot afford any more delays.* **3** (*formal*) to provide sb with sth: [VN] *The tree affords some shelter from the sun.* ◊ [VNN] *The programme affords young people the chance to gain work*

experience. ▶ **af·ford·abil·ity** /əˌfɔːdə'bɪləti; *AmE* əˌfɔːrd-/ *noun* [U] **af·ford·able** /ə'fɔːdəbl; *AmE* ə'fɔːrd-/ *adj.*: *affordable prices/housing*

af·for·est·ation /əˌfɒrɪ'steɪʃn; *AmE* əˌfɔːr-; əˌfɑːr-/ *noun* [U] the process of planting areas of land with trees in order to form a forest—compare DEFORESTATION ▶ **af·for·est** /ə'fɒrɪst; *AmE* ə'fɔːr-; ə'fɑːr-/ *verb* [VN] [usually passive]

af·fray /ə'freɪ/ *noun* [C usually sing., U] (*law*) a fight or violent behaviour in a public place

af·front /ə'frʌnt/ *noun, verb*

■ *noun* [usually sing.] **~ (to sb/sth)** a remark or an action that insults or offends sb/sth: *His speech was an affront to many in the local community.*

■ *verb* [VN] [usually passive] (*formal*) to insult or offend sb: *He hoped they would not feel affronted if they were not invited.* ◊ *an affronted expression*

Afghan hound /ˌæfgæn 'haʊnd/ *noun* a tall dog with long soft hair and a pointed nose

afi·cion·ado /əˌfɪʃə'nɑːdəʊ; *AmE* -doʊ/ *noun* (*pl.* -os) a person who likes a particular sport, activity or subject very much and knows a lot about it: *a ballet aficionado/ an aficionado of ballet*

afield /ə'fiːld/ *adv.* IDM **far/farther/further a'field** far away from home; to or in places that are not near: *You can hire a car if you want to explore further afield.* ◊ *Journalists came* **from as far afield as** *China and Brazil.*

aflame /ə'fleɪm/ *adj.* [not before noun] (*literary*) **1** burning; on fire: *The whole building was soon aflame.* **2** full of bright colours and lights: *The woods were aflame with autumn colours.* **3** showing excitement or embarrassment: *eyes/cheeks aflame*

AFL-CIO /ˌeɪ ef el eɪ siː aɪ 'əʊ; *AmE* 'oʊ/ *abbr.* American Federation of Labor and Congress of Industrial Organizations. The AFL-CIO is an organization of trade unions.

afloat /ə'fləʊt; *AmE* ə'floʊt/ *adj.* [not before noun] **1** floating on water: *Somehow we kept the boat afloat.* ◊ *He could not swim and only a life jacket kept him afloat.* **2** (of a business, etc.) having enough money to pay debts; able to survive: *They will have to borrow £10 million next year, just to* **stay afloat.**

afoot /ə'fʊt/ *adj.* [not before noun] being planned; happening: *There are plans afoot to increase taxation.* ◊ *Changes were afoot but we had no idea what they would turn out to be.*

afore·men·tioned /əˌfɔː'menʃənd; *AmE* əˌfɔːr'm-/ (also **afore·said** /ə'fɔːsed; *AmE* ə'fɔːrsed/) (also **said**) *adj.* [only before noun] (*formal* or *law*) mentioned before, in an earlier sentence: *The aforementioned person was seen acting suspiciously.*

afore·thought /ə'fɔːθɔːt; *AmE* ə'fɔːrθ-/ *adj.* IDM see MALICE

afoul /ə'faʊl/ *adv.* (*AmE*) IDM **run a'foul of sth** to do sth that is not allowed by a law or rule or sth that people in authority disapprove of: *to run afoul of the law*

afraid /ə'freɪd/ *adj.* [not before noun] **1 ~ (of sb/sth)| ~ (of doing sth)| ~ (to do sth)** feeling fear; frightened because you think that you might be hurt or suffer: *Don't be afraid. It's all over. There's nothing to be afraid of now.* ◊ *Are you afraid of spiders?* ◊ *I started to feel afraid of going out alone at night.* ◊ *She was afraid to open the door.* **2 ~ (of doing sth)| ~ (to do sth)| ~ (that ...)** worried about what might happen: *She was afraid of upsetting her parents.* ◊ *Don't be afraid to ask if you don't understand.* ◊ *We were afraid (that) we were going to capsize the boat.* **3 ~ for sb/sth** worried or frightened that sth unpleasant, dangerous, etc. will happen to a particular person or thing: *I'm not afraid for me, but for the baby.* ◊ *They had already fired three people and he was afraid for his job.* IDM **I'm afraid** (*spoken*) used as a polite way of telling sb sth that is unpleasant or disappointing, or that you are sorry about: *I can't help you, I'm afraid.* ◊ *I'm afraid we can't come.* ◊ *I'm afraid that it's not finished yet, Mr Lewis.* ◊ *'Is there any left?' ' I'm afraid not.'* ◊ *'Will it hurt?' ' I'm afraid so.'* ⇨ note on page 22

æ	ɑː	e	ɜː	ə	ɪ	iː	i	ɒ	ɔː	ʌ	ʊ	u	uː
cat	father	ten	bird	about	sit	see	many	got	saw	cup	put	actual	too
								(BrE)					

WHICH WORD?

afraid / frightened / scared

Be **afraid/frightened/scared** all mean that you feel fear: *I've never been so frightened in my life!*

Scared is very common in informal speech and is often used to describe small fears: *Dad was driving very fast and we were a bit scared.* **Afraid** is more formal and less common.

+ **of** afraid/frightened/scared **of sb/sth** means that you feel fear when you see or experience something: *I'm afraid of snakes.*

+ **for** afraid/frightened/scared **for sb/sth** means that you are worried that something unpleasant may happen to somebody: *I was frightened for his safety.*

Sometimes **about** is used with **frightened** and **scared**, but not with **afraid**: *I'm scared about going to the city again.*

You can use **very, a bit, too**, etc. with **frightened** and **scared**, but not with **afraid**.

+ **noun** *a frightened/scared child.* You cannot use **afraid** in front of a noun.

'A-frame (also ˌA-frame ˈhouse) *noun* (*especially AmE*) a house with very steep sides that meet at the top in the shape of the letter A

afresh /əˈfreʃ/ *adv.* (*written*) again, especially from the beginning or with new ideas: *He left his job to start life afresh.*

Af·ri·can /ˈæfrɪkən/ *adj., noun*
■ *adj.* of or connected with Africa
■ *noun* a person from Africa, especially a black person

ˌAfrican Aˈmerican *noun* a person from America who is a member of a race of people who have dark skin, originally from Africa ► ˌAfrican Aˈmerican *adj.*

Af·ri·kaans /ˌæfrɪˈkɑːns/ *noun* [U] a language that has developed from Dutch, spoken in South Africa

Af·ri·kaner /ˌæfrɪˈkɑːnə(r)/ *noun* a person from South Africa, usually with Dutch ancestors, whose native language is Afrikaans

Afro /ˈæfrəʊ; *AmE* ˈæfroʊ/ *noun* (*pl.* **-os**) a style of hair sometimes worn by black people and popular in the 1970s, in which the hair forms a round mass of tight curls

Afro- /ˈæfrəʊ; *AmE* ˈæfroʊ/ *combining form* (in nouns and adjectives) African: *Afro-Asian.*

aft /ɑːft; *AmE* æft/ *adv.* (*technical*) in, near or towards the back of a ship or an aircraft ► **aft** *adj.*—compare FORE

after /ˈɑːftə(r); *AmE* ˈæf-/ *prep., conj., adv., adj.*
■ *prep.* **1** later than sth; following sth in time: *We'll leave after lunch.* ◊ *They arrived shortly after 5.* ◊ *Not long after that he resigned.* ◊ *Let's meet the day after tomorrow / the week after next.* ◊ *After winning the prize she became famous overnight.* ◊ *After an hour I went home* (= when an hour had passed). ◊ (*AmE*) *It's ten after seven in the morning* (= 7.10 a.m.) **2** (...**after** ...) used to show that sth happens many times or continuously: *day after day of hot weather* ◊ *I've told you time after time not to do that.*—see also ONE AFTER ANOTHER at ONE **3** behind sb when they have left; following sb: *Shut the door after you.* ◊ *I'm always having to clean up after the children* (= clean the place after they have left it dirty and untidy). ◊ *He ran after her with the book.* ◊ *She was left staring after him.* **4** next to and following sb/sth in order or importance: *Your name comes after mine in the list.* ◊ *He's the tallest, after Richard.* ◊ *After you* (= Please go first). ◊ *After you with the paper.* (= Can I have it next?). **5** in contrast to sth: *It was pleasantly cool in the house after the sticky heat outside.* **6** as a result of or because of sth that has happened: *I'll never forgive him after what he said.* **7** in spite of sth; although sth has happened: *I can't believe she'd do that, not after all I've done for her.* **8** trying to find or catch sb/sth: *The police are after him.* ◊ *He's after a job at our place.* **9** about sb/sth: *She asked after you* (= how you were). **10** in the style of sb/sth; following the example of sb/sth: *a painting after Goya* ◊ *We named the baby 'Ena' after her grandmother.* **11** (**after-**) (used in *adjectives*) hap-

pening or done later than the time or event mentioned: *after-hours drinking* (= after closing time) ◊ *an after-school club* ◊ *after-dinner mints* **IDM** ˌafter ˈall **1** in spite of what has been said or expected: *So you made it after all!* **2** used when you are explaining sth, or giving a reason: *He should have paid. He suggested it, after all.* **be after doing sth** (*IrishE*) **1** to be going to do sth soon; to be intending to do sth soon **2** to have just done sth
■ *conj.* at a time later than sth; when sth has finished: *I'll call you after I've spoken to them.* ◊ *Several years after they'd split up they met again by chance in Paris.*
■ *adv.* later in time; afterwards: *That was in 1996.* ***Soon after**, I heard that he'd died.* ◊ *I could come next week, or the week after.* ◊ *And they all lived happily ever after.*
■ *adj.* [only before noun] (*old use*) following; later: *in after years*

after·birth /ˈɑːftəbɜːθ; *AmE* ˈæftərbɜːrθ/ *noun* (usually **the afterbirth**) [sing.] the material that comes out of a woman or female animal's body after a baby has been born, and which was necessary to feed and protect the baby **SYN** PLACENTA

after·care /ˈɑːftəkeə(r); *AmE* ˈæftərker/ *noun* [U] **1** care or treatment given to a person who has just left hospital, prison, etc: *aftercare services* **2** (*BrE*) service and advice that is offered by some companies to customers who have bought a car, washing machine, etc.

'after-effect *noun* [usually pl.] the **after-effects** of a drug, an illness or an unpleasant event are the feelings that you experience later as a result of it

after·glow /ˈɑːftəgləʊ; *AmE* ˈæftərgloʊ/ *noun* [usually sing.] (*literary*) **1** the light that is left in the sky after the sun has set **2** a warm pleasant feeling after a good experience: *He was basking in the afterglow of love.*

after·life /ˈɑːftəlaɪf; *AmE* ˈæftərl-/ *noun* [sing.] a life that some people believe exists after death

after·math /ˈɑːftəmæθ; -mɑːθ; *AmE* ˈæftərmæθ/ *noun* [usually sing.] the situation that exists as a result of an important (and usually unpleasant) event, especially a war, an accident, etc: *A lot of rebuilding took place in the aftermath of the war.* ◊ *the assassination of the Prime Minister and its immediate aftermath*

after·noon /ˌɑːftəˈnuːn; *AmE* ˌæftərˈn-/ *noun* [U, C] the part of the day from 12 midday until about 6 o'clock: *this / yesterday / tomorrow afternoon* ◊ *In the afternoon they went shopping.* ◊ *She studies art two afternoons a week.* ◊ *Are you ready for this afternoon's meeting?* ◊ *The baby always has an afternoon nap.* ◊ *Come over on Sunday afternoon.* ◊ *Where were you on the afternoon of May 21?* ◊ *Good afternoon!* (= as a formal greeting)

after·noons /ˌɑːftəˈnuːnz; *AmE* ˌæftərˈn-/ *adv.* (*especially AmE*) during the afternoon every day: *Afternoons he works at home.*

af·ters /ˈɑːftəz; *AmE* ˈæftərz/ *noun* [U] (*BrE, informal*) a sweet dish that you eat at the end of a meal: *fruit salad for afters*—see also DESSERT, PUDDING, SWEET *n.*

after·shave /ˈɑːftəʃeɪv; *AmE* ˈæftərʃ-/ *noun* [U, C] a liquid with a pleasant smell that men sometimes put on their faces after they shave

after·shock /ˈɑːftəʃɒk; *AmE* ˈæftərʃɑːk/ *noun* a small earthquake that happens after a bigger one

after·taste /ˈɑːftəteɪst; *AmE* ˈæftərt-/ *noun* [sing.] a taste (usually an unpleasant one) that stays in your mouth after you have eaten or drunk sth

after·thought /ˈɑːftəθɔːt; *AmE* ˈæftərθ-/ *noun* [usually sing.] a thing that is thought of, said or added later, and is often not carefully planned: *They only invited Jack and Sarah as an afterthought.*

after·wards /ˈɑːftəwədz; *AmE* ˈæftərwərdz/ (*especially BrE*) (*AmE* usually **after·ward**) *adv.* at a later time; after an event that has already been mentioned: *Afterwards she was sorry for what she'd said.* ◊ *Let's go to the theatre first and eat afterwards.* ◊ *Shortly afterwards he was seen in a bar in town.*

again /əˈgen; əˈgeɪn/ *adv.* **1** one more time; on another occasion: *Could you say it again, please?* ◊ *When will I see you again?* ◊ *This must never happen again.* ◊ *Once again* (= as had happened several times before), *the train was* late. ◊ *I've told you **again and again*** (= many times) *not to do that.* ◊ *I'll have to write it **all over again*** (= again from the beginning). **2** showing that sb/sth is in the same place or state that they were in originally: *He was glad to be home again.* ◊ *She spends two hours a day getting to work and **back again**.* ◊ *You'll soon feel well again.* **3** added to an amount that is already there: *The cost is about **half as much again** as it was two years ago.* ◊ *I'd like **the same again*** (= the same amount or the same thing), *please.* **4** used to show that a comment or fact is connected with what you have just said: *And again, we must think of the time involved.* **5 then/there ~** used to introduce a fact or an opinion that contrasts with what you have just said: *We might buy it but then again we might not.* **6** (*spoken*) used when you ask sb to tell you sth or repeat sth that you think they have told you already: *What was the name again?* **IDM** see NOW *adv.*, SAME *pron.*, TIME *n.*

against /ə'genst; ə'geɪnst/ *prep.* **HELP** For the special uses of **against** in phrasal verbs, look at the entries for the verbs. For example **count against sb** is in the phrasal verb section at **count**. **1** opposing or disagreeing with sb/sth: *the fight against terrorism* ◊ *We're playing against the league champions next week.* ◊ *We were rowing against the current.* ◊ *That's against the law.* ◊ *She was forced to marry against her will.* ◊ *Are you for or against the death penalty?* ◊ *She is against seeing* (= does not want to see) *him.* ◊ *I'd advise you against doing that.* **2** not to the advantage or favour of sb/sth: *The evidence is against him.* ◊ *Her age is against her.*—compare FOR *prep.* (7) **3** close to, touching or hitting sb/sth: *Put the piano there, against the wall.* ◊ *The rain beat against the windows.* **4** in order to prevent sth from happening or to reduce the harm caused by sth: *an injection against rabies* ◊ *They took precautions against fire.* ◊ *Are we insured against theft?* **5** with sth in the background, as a contrast: *His red clothes stood out clearly against the snow.* ◊ (*figurative*) *The love story unfolds against a background of civil war.* **6** used when you are comparing two things: *You must weigh the benefits against the cost.* ◊ *Check your receipts against the statement.* ◊ *What's the rate of exchange against the dollar?* **IDM** see AS *conj.*, STACKED

agape /ə'geɪp/ *adj.* [not before noun] (*written*) if a person's mouth is **agape**, it is wide open, especially because they are surprised or shocked

agate /'ægət/ *noun* [U, C] a hard stone with bands or areas of colour, used in jewellery

age /eɪdʒ/ *noun, verb*
■ *noun* **1** [C, U] the number of years that a person has lived or a thing has existed: *He left school **at the age of** 18.* ◊ *She needs to find more friends of her own age.* ◊ *children from 5–10 years of age* ◊ *Young people of all ages go there to meet.* ◊ *When I was your age I was already married.* ◊ *He started playing the piano **at an early age**.* ◊ *All ages admitted.* ◊ *Children **over the age of** 12 must pay full fare.* ◊ *She was beginning to **feel her age*** (= feel that she was getting old). ◊ *ways of calculating the age of the earth* ⇨ Appendix 3 **2** [C, U] a particular period of a person's life: *middle age* ◊ *15 is an awkward age.* ◊ *He died of old age.* **3** [C] a particular period of history: *the nuclear age* ◊ *the age of the computer*—see also BRONZE AGE, IRON AGE, NEW AGE, STONE AGE **4** [U] the state of being old: *Fine wine improves **with age**.* ◊ *The jacket was showing signs of age.* ◊ *the wisdom that comes with age* **5** (**ages**) [pl.] (also **an age** [sing.]) (*informal, especially BrE*) a very long time: *I waited **for ages**.* ◊ *It'll probably take **ages** to find a parking space.* ◊ *Carlos left **ages ago**.* ◊ *It's been **an age** since we've seen them.* **IDM** **,be/,act your 'age** to behave in a way that is suitable for sb of your age and not as though you were much younger **,come of 'age 1** when a person **comes of age**, they reach the age when they have an adult's legal rights and responsibilities **2** if sth **comes of age**, it reaches the stage of development at which people accept and value it **,look your 'age** to seem as old as you really are and not younger or older **,under 'age** not legally old enough to do a particular thing: *It is illegal to sell cigarettes to children who are under age.* ◊ *under-*

age driving/drinking/sex—more at ADVANCED, DAY, FEEL *v.*, GRAND *adj.*, RIPE, TENDER *adj.*
■ *verb* (**ag-ing**, **aged**, **aged** **HELP** In *BrE* the present participle can also be spelled **age·ing**.) **1** [V] to become older: *As he aged, his memory got worse.* ◊ *The population is aging* (= more people are living longer). **2** [VN] to make sb/sth look, feel or seem older: *The shock has aged her enormously.* ◊ *Exposure to the sun ages the skin.* **3** to develop in flavour over a period of time; to allow sth to do this: [V] *The cheese is left to age for at least a year.* ◊ [VN] *The wine is aged in oak casks.*

-age *suffix* (in nouns) **1** the action or result of: *breakage* **2** a state or condition of: *bondage* **3** a set or group of: *baggage* **4** an amount of: *mileage* **5** the cost of: *postage* **6** a place where: *anchorage*

aged *adj.* **1** /eɪdʒd/ [not before noun] of the age of: *They have two children aged six and nine.* ◊ *volunteers aged between 25 and 40* **2** /'eɪdʒɪd/ (*formal*) very old: *my aged aunt* **3** (**the aged**) /'eɪdʒɪd/ *noun* [pl.] very old people: *services for the sick and the aged*

'age group (also *less frequent* **'age bracket**) *noun* people of a similar age or within a particular range of ages: *men in the older age group* ◊ *education for the 16–18 age group* ◊ *Which age bracket are you?* (*Please tick the box*).

age·ing (*BrE*) (also **aging** *AmE, BrE*) /'eɪdʒɪŋ/ *noun, adj.*
■ *noun* [U] the process of growing old: *signs/effects of ageing*
■ *adj.* [usually before noun] becoming older and usually less useful, safe, healthy, etc: *ageing equipment* ◊ *an ageing rock star*

age·ism (*AmE* also **agism**) /'eɪdʒɪzəm/ *noun* [U] unfair treatment of people because they are considered too old ▶ **age·ist** *adj.* **age·ist** *noun*

age·less /'eɪdʒləs/ *adj.* (*literary*) **1** never looking old or never seeming to grow old: *Her beauty appeared ageless.* **2** existing for ever; impossible to give an age to: *the ageless mystery of the universe*

'age limit *noun* the oldest or youngest age at which you are allowed to do sth: *the upper/lower age limit*

agency /'eɪdʒənsi/ *noun* (*pl.* **-ies**) **1** a business or an organization that provides a particular service especially on behalf of other businesses or organizations: *an advertising/employment agency* ◊ *You can book at your local travel agency.* ◊ *international aid agencies caring for refugees*—see also DATING AGENCY, NEWS AGENCY, PRESS AGENCY **2** (*especially AmE*) a government department that provides a particular service: *the Central Intelligence Agency* (*CIA*) **IDM** **through the agency of** (*formal*) as a result of the action of sb/sth

agenda /ə'dʒendə/ *noun* a list of items to be discussed at a meeting: *The next item **on the agenda** is the publicity budget.* ◊ *For the government, education is now **at the top of the agenda*** (= most important). ◊ *In our company, quality is **high on the agenda**.* ◊ *Newspapers have been accused of trying to **set the agenda** for the government* (= decide what is important).—see also HIDDEN AGENDA

A

agent /ˈeɪdʒənt/ *noun* **1** a person whose job is to act for, or manage the affairs of, other people in business, politics, etc: *an insurance agent* ◊ *Our agent in New York deals with all US sales.*—see also ESTATE AGENT, LAND AGENT, TRAVEL AGENT **2** a person whose job is to find work for an actor, musician, etc. or to find sb who will publish a writer's work: *a theatrical/literary agent*—see also PRESS AGENT **3** = SECRET AGENT: *an enemy agent*—see also DOUBLE AGENT, SPECIAL AGENT **4** (*written*) a person or thing that has an important effect on a situation: *The charity has been an agent for social change.* **5** (*technical*) a chemical or a substance that produces an effect or a change or is used for a particular purpose: *cleaning/oxidizing agents*—see also FREE AGENT

agent pro·vo·ca·teur /ˌæʒɒ̃ prəˌvɒkəˈtɜː(r); *AmE* ˌɑːʒɑ̃ prouˌvɑːkəˈtɜːr/ *noun* (*pl.* **agents pro·vo·ca·teurs** /ˌæʒɒ̃ prəˌvɒkəˈtɜː(r); *AmE* ˌɑːʒɑ̃ prouˌvɑːkəˈtɜːr/) (from *French*) a person who is employed by a government to encourage people in political groups to do sth illegal so that they can be arrested

ˌage of conˈsent *noun* [sing.] the age at which sb is legally old enough to agree to have a sexual relationship

ˌage-ˈold *adj.* [usually before noun] having existed for a very long time: *an age-old custom/problem*

ag·glom·er·ation /əˌɡlɒməˈreɪʃn; *AmE* əˌɡlɑːm-/ *noun* [C, U] (*formal*) a group of things put together in no particular order or arrangement

ag·grand·ize·ment (*BrE* also **-ise·ment**) /əˈɡrænd-ɪzmənt/ *noun* [U] (*formal, disapproving*) an increase in the power or importance of a person or country: *Her sole aim is personal aggrandizement.*

ag·gra·vate /ˈæɡrəveɪt/ *verb* [VN] **1** to make an illness or a bad or unpleasant situation worse [SYN] WORSEN: *Pollution can aggravate asthma.* ◊ *Military intervention will only aggravate the conflict even further.* **2** (*informal*) to annoy sb, especially deliberately [SYN] IRRITATE ▶ **ag·gra·vat·ing** *adj.* **ag·gra·va·tion** /ˌæɡrəˈveɪʃn/ *noun* [U, C]: *The drug may cause an aggravation of the condition.* ◊ *I don't need all this aggravation at work.*

ag·gra·vat·ed /ˈæɡrəveɪtɪd/ *adj.* [only before noun] (*law*) an **aggravated** crime involves further unnecessary violence or unpleasant behaviour

ag·gre·gate *noun, adj., verb*
■ *noun* /ˈæɡrɪɡət/ **1** [C] a total number or amount made up of smaller amounts that are collected together: *a record aggregate of 285 points* ◊ *The three smaller parties gained an aggregate of 25 per cent of the vote.* **2** [U, C] (*technical*) sand or broken stone that is used to make CONCRETE or for building roads, etc. [IDM] **in (the) ˈaggregate** (*formal*) added together as a total or single amount **on ˈaggregate** (*BrE, sport*) when the scores of a number of games are added together: *They won 4–2 on aggregate.*
■ *adj.* /ˈæɡrɪɡət/ [only before noun] (*economics* or *sport*) made up of several amounts that are added together to form a total number: *aggregate demand/investment/turnover* ◊ *an aggregate win over their rivals*
■ *verb* /ˈæɡrɪɡeɪt/ [VN] [usually passive] ~ (**sth**) (**with sth**) (*formal* or *technical*) to combine different items, amounts, etc. into a single group or total: *The scores were aggregated with the first round totals to decide the winner.* ▶ **ag·gre·ga·tion** /ˌæɡrɪˈɡeɪʃn/ *noun* [U, C]: *the aggregation of data*

ag·gres·sion /əˈɡreʃn/ *noun* [U] **1** feelings of anger and hatred that may result in threatening or violent behaviour: *The research shows that computer games may cause aggression.* **2** a violent attack or threats by one country against another country: *unprovoked military aggression*

ag·gres·sive /əˈɡresɪv/ *adj.* **1** angry, and behaving in a threatening way; ready to attack: *As a teenager Sean was aggressive and moody.* ◊ *a dangerous aggressive dog* **2** behaving in a very determined and forceful way in order to succeed: *an aggressive advertising campaign* ◊ *A good salesperson has to be aggressive in today's competitive market.* ▶ **ag·gres·sive·ly** *adv.*: *'What do you want?'*

he demanded aggressively. ◊ *aggressively marketed products* **ag·gres·sive·ness** *noun* [U]

ag·gres·sor /əˈɡresə(r)/ *noun* a person, country, etc. that attacks first

ag·grieved /əˈɡriːvd/ *adj.* **1** (*written*) ~ (**at/by sth**) feeling that you have been treated unfairly: *He had every right to feel aggrieved at the decision.* **2** (*law*) suffering unfair or illegal treatment and making a complaint: *the aggrieved party* (= person) in the case

aggro /ˈæɡrəʊ; *AmE* ˈæɡroʊ/ *noun* [U] (*BrE, spoken, informal*) **1** violent aggressive behaviour: *Don't give me any aggro or I'll call the police.* **2** problems and difficulties that are annoying: *I had a lot of aggro at the dole office.*

aghast /əˈɡɑːst; *AmE* əˈɡæst/ *adj.* [not before noun] ~ (**at sth**) (*written*) filled with horror and surprise when you see or hear sth: *Erica looked at him aghast.* ◊ *He stood aghast at the sight of so much blood.*

agile /ˈædʒaɪl; *AmE* ˈædʒl/ *adj.* **1** able to move quickly and easily: *a strong and agile athlete* **2** able to think quickly and in an intelligent way: *an agile mind/brain* ▶ **agil·ity** /əˈdʒɪləti/ *noun* [U]: *He had the agility of a man half his age.*

aging, **agism** = AGEING, AGEISM

agi·tate /ˈædʒɪteɪt/ *verb* **1** ~ (**for/against sth**) to argue strongly for sth you want, especially for changes in a law, in social conditions, etc: [V] *political groups agitating for social change* ◊ [V toinf] *Her family are agitating to have her transferred to a prison in the UK.* **2** [VN] to make sb feel angry, anxious or nervous: *This remark seemed to agitate her guest.* **3** [VN] (*technical*) to make sth, especially a liquid, move around by stirring or shaking it: *Agitate the mixture to dissolve the powder.*

agi·tat·ed /ˈædʒɪteɪtɪd/ *adj.* showing in your behaviour that you are anxious and nervous: *Calm down! Don't get so agitated.*

agi·ta·tion /ˌædʒɪˈteɪʃn/ *noun* **1** [U] worry and anxiety that you show by behaving in a nervous way: *Dot arrived in a state of great agitation.* **2** [U, C] ~ (**for/against sth**) public protest in order to achieve political change: *widespread agitation for social reform* **3** [U] (*technical*) the act of stirring or shaking a liquid

agi·ta·tor /ˈædʒɪteɪtə(r)/ *noun* (*disapproving*) a person who tries to persuade people to take part in political protest

aglow /əˈɡləʊ; *AmE* əˈɡloʊ/ *adj.* [not before noun] (*literary*) shining with warmth and colour or happiness: *Christmas trees aglow with lights* ◊ *children's faces all aglow*

AGM /ˌeɪ dʒiː ˈem/ *abbr.* (*BrE*) the abbreviation for 'annual general meeting' (an important meeting which the members of an organization hold once a year in order to elect officers, discuss past and future activities and examine the accounts)

ag·nos·tic /æɡˈnɒstɪk; *AmE* -ˈnɑːs-/ *noun* a person who is not sure whether or not God exists or who believes that we cannot know whether God exists or not—compare ATHEIST ▶ **ag·nos·tic** *adj.* **ag·nos·ti·cism** /æɡˈnɒsti-sɪzəm; *AmE* -ˈnɑːs-/ *noun* [U]

ago /əˈɡəʊ; *AmE* əˈɡoʊ/ *adv.* used in expressions of time with the simple past tense to show how far in the past sth happened: *two weeks/months/years ago* ◊ *The letter came a few days ago.* ◊ *She was here just a minute ago.* ◊ *a short/long time ago* ◊ *How long ago did you buy it?* ◊ *It was on TV not (so) long ago.* ◊ *He stopped working some time ago* (= quite a long time ago). ◊ *They're getting married? It's not that long ago* (= it's only a short time ago) *that they met!*

agog /əˈɡɒɡ; *AmE* əˈɡɑːɡ/ *adj.* [not before noun] excited and very interested to find out sth

ag·on·ize (*BrE* also **-ise**) /ˈæɡənaɪz/ *verb* [V] ~ (**over/about sth**) to spend a long time thinking and worrying about a difficult situation or problem: *I spent days agonizing over whether to take the job or not.*

ag·on·ized (*BrE* also **-ised**) /ˈæɡənaɪzd/ *adj.* suffering or expressing severe pain or anxiety: *agonized cries*

ag·on·iz·ing (*BrE* also **-is·ing**) /ˈæɡənaɪzɪŋ/ *adj.* caus-

s	t	v	z	ʃ	ʒ	tʃ	dʒ	θ	ð	ŋ
see	tea	van	zoo	shoe	vision	chain	jam	thin	this	sing

ing great pain, anxiety or difficulty: *his father's agonizing death* ◊ *It was the most agonizing decision of her life.*

ag·on·iz·ing·ly (*BrE* also **-is·ing·ly**) /ˈægənaɪzɪŋli/ *adv.* used meaning 'extremely' to emphasize sth negative: *an agonizingly slow process*

agony /ˈægəni/ *noun* (*pl.* **-ies**) [U, C] extreme physical or mental pain: *Jack collapsed in agony on the floor.* ◊ *It was agony not knowing where the children were.* ◊ *She waited in an agony of suspense.* ◊ *The worst agonies of the war were now beginning.* **IDM** see PILE *v.*

'agony aunt (*BrE*) (*AmE* **ad'vice columnist**) *noun* a person who writes in a newspaper or magazine giving advice in reply to people's letters about their personal problems

'agony column (*BrE*) (*AmE* **ad'vice column**) *noun* part of a newspaper or magazine in which sb gives advice to readers who have sent letters about their personal problems

agora·pho·bia /ˌægərəˈfəʊbiə; *AmE* -ˈfoʊ-/ *noun* [U] (*technical*) a fear of being in public places where there are many other people—compare CLAUSTROPHOBIA

agora·pho·bic /ˌægərəˈfəʊbɪk; *AmE* -ˈfoʊ-/ *noun* a person who suffers from agoraphobia ▶ **agora·pho·bic** *adj.*

agrar·ian /əˈgreəriən; *AmE* əˈgrer-/ *adj.* [usually before noun] (*technical*) connected with farming and the use of land for farming

agree /əˈgriː/ *verb*
SHARE OPINION | **1** ~ (**with sb**) (**about/on sth**)| ~ (**with sth**) to have the same opinion as sb; to say that you have the same opinion: [V] *When he said that, I had to agree.* ◊ *He agreed with them about the need for change.* ◊ *I agree with her analysis of the situation.* ◊ *'He's a lousy cook.' 'I couldn't agree more* (= I completely agree)*!'* ◊ [V(that)] *We agreed (that) the proposal was a good one.* ◊ [V speech] *'That's true', she agreed.* **OPP** DISAGREE **2** **be agreed** (**on/about sth**)| **be agreed** (**that …**) if people are agreed or sth **is agreed**, everyone has the same opinion about sth: [VN] *Are we all agreed on this?* ◊ [VN(that)] *It was agreed (that) we should hold another meeting.*
SAY YES | **3** ~ (**to sth**) to say 'yes'; to say that you will do what sb wants or that you will allow sth to happen **SYN** CONSENT: [V] *I asked for a pay rise and she agreed.* ◊ *Do you think he'll agree to their proposal?* ◊ [V(that)] *She agreed (that) we could finish early.* ◊ [Vtoinf] *He agreed to let me go early.*
DECIDE | **4** to decide with sb else to do sth or to have sth: [VN] *They met at the agreed time.* ◊ *Can we agree a price?* ◊ *They left at ten, as agreed.* ◊ [V] *Can we agree on a date?* ◊ [Vtoinf] *We agreed to meet on Thursday.* ◊ [Vwh-] *We couldn't agree what to do.*
ACCEPT | **5** [VN] to officially accept a plan, request, etc. **SYN** APPROVE: *Next year's budget has been agreed.*
BE THE SAME | **6** [V] ~ (**with sth**) to be the same as sth **SYN** TALLY: *The figures do not agree.* ◊ *Your account of the accident does not agree with hers.* **OPP** DISAGREE
GRAMMAR | **7** [V] ~ (**with sth**) to match a word or phrase in NUMBER, GENDER or PERSON: *In 'Tom likes jazz', and 'They like rock music', the singular verb 'likes' agrees with the subject 'Tom' and the plural verb 'like' agrees with the pronoun 'they'.*
IDM **a,gree to 'differ** if two people **agree to differ**, they accept that they have different opinions about sth, but they decide not to discuss it any longer: *We must just agree to differ on this.*
PHRV **not a'gree with sb** (of food) to make you feel ill/sick: *I love strawberries, but they don't agree with me.*

agree·able /əˈgriːəbl/ *adj.* (*formal*) **1** pleasant and easy to like: *We spent a most agreeable day together.* ◊ *He seemed extremely agreeable.* **OPP** DISAGREEABLE **2** [not before noun] ~ (**to sth**) willing to do sth or allow sth: *Do you think they will be agreeable to our proposal?* **3** ~ (**to sb**) able to be accepted by sb: *The deal must be agreeable to both sides.*

agree·ably /əˈgriːəbli/ *adv.* (*formal*) in a pleasant, nice way: *an agreeably warm day* ◊ *They were agreeably surprised by the quality of the food.*

agree·ment /əˈgriːmənt/ *noun* **1** [C] ~ (**with sb**)| ~

(**between A and B**) an arrangement, a promise or a contract made with sb: *an international peace agreement* ◊ *The agreement* (= the document recording the agreement) *was signed during a meeting at the UN.* ◊ *An agreement was finally reached between management and employees.* ◊ *They had made a verbal agreement to sell.* ◊ *They had an agreement never to talk about work at home.*—see also GENTLEMAN'S AGREEMENT **2** [U] the state of sharing the same opinion or feeling: *Are we in agreement about the price?* ◊ *The two sides failed to reach agreement.* **OPP** DISAGREEMENT **3** [U] the fact of sb approving of sth and allowing it to happen: *You'll have to get your parents' agreement if you want to go on the trip.* **4** [U] ~ (**with sth**) (*grammar*) (of words in a phrase) the state of having the same NUMBER, GENDER or PERSON. **SYN** CONCORD: *In the sentence 'They live in the country', the plural form of the verb 'live' is in agreement with the plural subject 'they'.*

agri- ⇨ AGRO-

agri·busi·ness /ˈægrɪbɪznəs/ *noun* [U] (*technical*) the industry concerned with the production and sale of farm products, especially involving large companies

agri·cul·tur·al·ist /ˌægrɪˈkʌltʃərəlɪst/ *noun* an expert in agriculture who gives advice to farmers

agri·cul·ture /ˈægrɪkʌltʃə(r)/ *noun* [U] the science or practice of farming: *the Ministry of Agriculture, Farming and Fisheries* ▶ **agri·cul·tural** /ˌægrɪˈkʌltʃərəl/ *adj.*: *agricultural policy / land / production / development*

agro- /ˈægrəʊ; *AmE* ˈægroʊ/ (also **agri-** /ˈægri/) *combining form* (in nouns, adjectives and adverbs) connected with farming: *agro-industry* ◊ *agriculture*

agrono·mist /əˈgrɒnəmɪst; *AmE* əˈgrɑːn-/ *noun* a scientist who studies the relationship between crops and the environment ▶ **agron·omy** *noun* [U]

aground /əˈgraʊnd/ *adv.* if a ship **runs/goes aground**, it touches the ground in shallow water and cannot move ▶ **aground** *adj.*

ah /ɑː/ *exclamation* used to express surprise, pleasure, admiration or sympathy, or when you disagree with sb: *Ah, there you are.* ◊ *Ah, this coffee is good.* ◊ *Ah well, better luck next time.* ◊ *Ah, but that may not be true.*

aha /ɑːˈhɑː/ *exclamation* used when you are expressing pleasure that you have understood sth or found sth out: *Aha! So that's where I left it!*

ahchoo /ɑːˈtʃuː; əˈtʃuː/ *exclamation* = ATISHOO

ahead /əˈhed/ *adv.* **HELP** For the special uses of **ahead** in phrasal verbs, look at the entries for the verbs. For example **press ahead** (**with sth**) is in the phrasal verb section at **press**. **1** further forward in space or time; in front: *I'll run ahead and warn them.* ◊ *The road ahead was blocked.* ◊ *We've got a lot of hard work ahead.* ◊ *This will create problems in the months ahead.* ◊ *He was looking straight ahead* (= straight forward, in front of him). **2** earlier; in advance: *The party was planned weeks ahead.* **3** winning; further advanced: *Our team was ahead by six points.* ◊ *You need to work hard to keep ahead.*

a'head of *prep.* **1** further forward in space or time than sb/sth; in front of sb/sth: *Three boys were ahead of us.* ◊ *Ahead of us lay ten days of intensive training.* **2** earlier than sb/sth: *I finished the work several days ahead of the deadline.* **3** further advanced than sb/sth; in front of sb, for example in a race or competition: *She was always well ahead of the rest of the class.* ◊ *His ideas were way ahead of his time.*

ahem *exclamation* used in writing to show the sound of a short cough made by sb who is trying to get attention or to say sth that is difficult or embarrassing: *Ahem, can I make a suggestion?*

ahoy /əˈhɔɪ/ *exclamation* used by people in boats to attract attention: *Ahoy there!* ◊ *Ship ahoy!* (= there is a ship in sight)

AI /ˌeɪ ˈaɪ/ *abbr.* **1** ARTIFICIAL INSEMINATION: *AID or artificial insemination by a donor* **2** ARTIFICIAL INTELLIGENCE

aid /eɪd/ *noun, verb*
■ *noun* **1** [U] money, food, etc. that is sent to help countries in difficult situations: *economic / humanitarian / emergency aid* ◊ *An extra £10 million in foreign aid has been promised.* ◊ *aid agencies* (= organizations that provide

æ	ɑː	e	ɜː	ə	ɪ	iː	i	ɒ	ɔː	ʌ	ʊ	u	uː
cat	father	ten	bird	about	sit	see	many	got	saw	cup	put	actual	too

(BrE)

help) ◊ *medical aid programmes*—see also FINANCIAL AID, LEGAL AID **2** [U] help that you need to perform a particular task: *He was breathing only **with the aid of** a ventilator.* ◊ *This job would be impossible **without the aid of** a computer.* **3** [U] (*formal*) help that is given to a person: *One of the station staff saw he was in difficulty and **came to his aid** (= helped him).*—see also FIRST AID **4** [C] an object, a machine, a tool, etc. that you use to help you do sth: *a hearing aid* ◊ *Photographs make useful teaching aids.* IDM **in aid of sth/sb** (*BrE*) in order to help sb/sth: *collecting money in aid of charity* **what's ... in aid of?** (*BrE, spoken*) used to ask why sth is happening: *What's all this crying in aid of?*

■ *verb* ~ **(sb/sth) (in sth/in doing sth)| ~ sb (with sth)** (*written*) to help sb/sth to do sth, especially by making it easier: [V] *The new test should aid in the early detection of the disease.* ◊ [VN] *This feature is designed to aid inexperienced users.* ◊ *They were accused of aiding his escape.* ◊ *They were accused of aiding him in his escape.* ◊ *Aided by heat and strong winds, the fire quickly spread.* [also VN to inf] ⇨ note at HELP IDM **aid and a'bet** (*law*) to help sb to do sth illegal or wrong: *She stands accused of aiding and abetting the bombing.*

aide /eɪd/ *noun* a person who helps another person, especially a politician, in their job: *White House aides*

aide-de-camp /ˌeɪd də ˈkɒ̃; *AmE* ˈkæmp/ *noun* (*pl.* **aides-de-camp** /ˌeɪd də ˈkɒ̃; *AmE* ˈkæmp/) (*abbr.* **ADC**) an officer in the army or navy who helps a more senior officer

Aids (*BrE*) (also **AIDS** *AmE, BrE*) /eɪdz/ *noun* [U] the abbreviation for 'Acquired Immune Deficiency Syndrome' (an illness which attacks the body's ability to resist infection and which usually causes death): *Aids research/education/victims* ◊ *He developed **full-blown** Aids five years after contracting HIV.*

ail /eɪl/ *verb* [VN] **1** (*formal*) to cause problems for sb/sth: *They discussed the problems **ailing** the steel industry.* **2** (*old use*) to make sb ill/sick: *What is ailing you?*

ail·eron /ˈeɪlərɒn; *AmE* -rɑːn/ *noun* (*technical*) a part of the wing of a plane that moves up and down to control the plane's balance—picture at PLANE

ail·ing /ˈeɪlɪŋ/ *adj.* (*formal*) **1** ill and not improving: *She looked after her ailing father.* **2** (of a business, government, etc.) having problems and getting weaker: *measures to help the ailing economy*

ail·ment /ˈeɪlmənt/ *noun* an illness that is not very serious: *childhood/common/minor ailments*

aim /eɪm/ *noun, verb*
■ *noun* **1** [C] the purpose of doing sth; what sb is trying to achieve: *the aims of the lesson* ◊ *She went to London with the aim of finding a job.* ◊ *Our main aim is to increase sales in Europe.* ◊ *Bob's one aim in life is to earn a lot of money.* ◊ *Teamwork is required in order to **achieve these aims.*** ◊ *She set out the company's **aims and objectives** in her speech.* **2** [U] the action or skill of pointing a weapon at sb/sth: *Her aim was good and she hit the lion with her first shot.* ◊ *The gunman **took aim** (= pointed his weapon) and fired.* IDM **take 'aim at sb/sth** (*AmE*) to direct your criticism at sth

■ *verb* **1** ~ **(at doing sth)| ~ (at/for sth)** to try or plan to achieve sth: [V] *The government is aiming at a 50% reduction in unemployment.* ◊ *They're aiming at training everybody by the end of the year.* ◊ *We should aim for a bigger share of the market.* ◊ *He has always **aimed high** (= tried to achieve a lot).* ◊ [V to inf] *They are aiming to reduce unemployment by 50%.* ◊ *We aim to be there around six.* **2** [VN] **(be aimed at)** to have sth as an aim: *These measures are aimed at preventing violent crime.* **3** ~ **(sth) (at sb/sth)| ~ (for sb/sth)** to point or direct a weapon, a shot, a kick, etc. at sb/sth: [V] *I was aiming at the tree but hit the car by mistake.* ◊ *Aim for the middle of the target.* ◊ [VN] *The gun was aimed at her head.* **4** [VN] [usually passive] ~ **sth at sb** to say or do sth that is intended to influence or affect a particular person or group: *The book is aimed at very young children.* ◊ *My criticism wasn't aimed at you.*

aim·less /ˈeɪmləs/ *adj.* having no direction or purpose: *My life seemed aimless.* ▶ **aim·less·ly** *adv.:* *She drifted*

aimlessly from one job to another. **aim·less·ness** *noun* [U]

ain't /eɪnt/ *short form* (*non-standard* or *humorous*) **1** am not/is not/are not: *Things ain't what they used to be.* **2** has not/have not: *I ain't got no money.* ◊ *You ain't seen nothing yet.*

air /eə(r); *AmE* er/ *noun, verb*
■ *noun*
GAS | **1** [U] the mixture of gases that surrounds the earth and that we breathe: *air pollution* ◊ *Let's go out for some **fresh air**.* ◊ *I need to put some air in my tyres.* ◊ *currents of warm air*
SPACE | **2** [U] (usually **the air**) the space above the ground or that is around things: *I kicked the ball high **in/into the air.*** ◊ *Spicy smells wafted **through the air**.* ◊ *Music filled the night air.*
FOR PLANES | **3** [U] the space above the earth where planes fly: *It only takes three hours **by air** (= in a plane).* ◊ *air travel/traffic/fares* ◊ *The temple was clearly visible from the air.* ◊ *A surprise air attack (= from aircraft) was launched at night.*
IMPRESSION | **4** [sing.] the particular feeling or impression that is given by sb/sth; the way sb does sth: *The room had an **air of** luxury.* ◊ *She looked at him with a defiant air.*
TUNE | **5** [C] (*old-fashioned*) (often used in the title of a piece of music) a tune: *Bach's Air on a G string*
BEHAVIOUR | **6** (**airs**) [pl.] (*disapproving*) a way of behaving that shows that sb thinks that they are more important, educated, etc. than they really are: *I hate the way she **puts on airs**.*
IDM **ˌairs and 'graces** (*BrE, disapproving*) a way of behaving that shows that sb thinks that they are more important, educated, etc. than they really are SYN AIRS: *Even when he became a star he didn't have any airs and graces.* **float/walk on 'air** to feel very happy **in the 'air** felt by a number of people to exist or to be happening: *There's romance in the air.* **ˌon/ˌoff (the) 'air** broadcasting or not broadcasting on television or radio: *We will be back on air tomorrow morning at 7.* ◊ *The programme was taken off the air over the summer.* **up in the 'air** not yet decided: *Our travel plans are still up in the air.*—more at BREATH, CASTLE, CLEAR *v.*, NOSE *n.*, PLUCK *v.*, THIN *adj.*
■ *verb*
CLOTHES | **1** (*especially BrE*) to put clothing, etc. in a place that is warm or has plenty of air so that it dries completely and smells fresh; to be left to dry somewhere: [VN] *Air the sheets well.* ◊ [V] *Leave the towels out to air.*
A ROOM | **2** (*BrE*) (*AmE*, **ˌair** (**sth**) **'out**) to allow fresh air into a room or a building; to be filled with fresh air: [VN] *The rooms had all been cleaned and freshly aired.* [also V]
OPINIONS | **3** [VN] to express your opinions publicly: *The weekly meeting enables employees to air their grievances.*
RADIO/TV PROGRAMME | **4** (*especially AmE*) to broadcast a programme on the radio or on television; to be broadcast: [VN] *The show will be aired next Tuesday night.* ◊ [V] *The program aired last week.*
PHRV **ˌair 'out, ˌair sth↔'out** (*AmE*) = AIR (2)

'air bag *noun* a safety device in a car that fills with air if there is an accident, to protect the people in the car

air·base /ˈeəbeɪs; *AmE* ˈerb-/ *noun* a place where military aircraft fly from and are kept, and where some staff live

'air bed (*BrE*) (also **'air mattress** *AmE, BrE*) *noun* a large plastic or rubber bag that can be filled with air and used as a bed

air·borne /ˈeəbɔːn; *AmE* ˈerbɔːrn/ *adj.* **1** [not before noun] (of a plane or passengers) in the air: *Do not leave your seat until the plane is airborne.* **2** [only before noun] carried through the air: *airborne seeds/viruses*—compare WATER-BORNE **3** [only before noun] (of soldiers) trained to jump out of aircraft onto enemy land in order to fight: *an airborne division*

'air brake *noun* a BRAKE in a vehicle that is worked by air pressure

air·brush /ˈeəbrʌʃ; *AmE* ˈerb-/ *noun, verb*
■ *noun* an artist's tool for spraying paint onto a surface, that works by air pressure

A

■ *verb* [VN] **~ sth (out)** to paint sth with an airbrush; to change a detail in a photograph with an airbrush: *an airbrushed photograph of a model* ◊ *Somebody had been airbrushed out of the picture.*

air chief 'marshal *noun* an officer of very high rank in the British air force: *Air Chief Marshal Sir Robin Hall*

air 'commodore *noun* an officer of high rank in the British air force: *Air Commodore Peter Shaw*

'air conditioner *noun* a machine that cools and dries air: *a window air conditioner*

'air conditioning *noun* [U] (*abbr.* **AC, a/c**) a system that cools and dries the air in a building or car ▶ **'air-conditioned** *adj.: air-conditioned offices*

air·craft /'eəkrɑːft; *AmE* 'erkræft/ *noun* (*pl.* **air·craft**) any vehicle that can fly and carry goods or passengers: *fighter/transport/military aircraft*—see also LIGHT AIRCRAFT

'aircraft carrier *noun* a large ship that carries aircraft which use it as a base to land on and take off from

air·craft·man /'eəkrɑːftmən; *AmE* 'erkræft-/, **air·craft·woman** /'eəkrɑːftwomən; *AmE* 'erkræft-/ *noun* (*pl.* **-men** /-mən/, **-women** /-wɪmɪn/) the lowest rank in the British air force: *Aircraftman John Green*

air·crew /'eəkruː; *AmE* 'erk-/ *noun* [C+sing./pl. *v.*] the pilot and other people who fly a plane, especially in the air force: *RAF aircrew training*

air·drome /'eədrəʊm; *AmE* 'erdroʊm/ *noun* (*AmE*) = AERODROME

air·field /'eəfiːld; *AmE* 'erf-/ *noun* an area of flat ground where military or private planes can take off and land

'air force *noun* [C+sing./pl. *v.*] the part of a country's armed forces that fights using aircraft: *the US Air Force* ◊ *air-force officers*

'air gun (also **'air rifle**) *noun* a gun that uses air pressure to fire small metal balls (called PELLETS)

air·head /'eəhed; *AmE* 'erh-/ *noun* (*informal, disapproving*) a stupid person: *She's a total airhead!*

'air hostess (also **stew·ard·ess**) *noun* a woman whose job is to serve and take care of passengers on an aircraft

air·ily /'eərəli; *AmE* 'er-/ *adv.* (*written*) in a way that shows that you are not worried or that you are not treating sth as serious: *'There's nothing wrong with him,' she said airily.*

air·ing /'eərɪŋ; *AmE* 'errɪŋ/ *noun* [sing.] **1** the expression or discussion of opinions in front of a group of people: *an opportunity to give your views an airing* ◊ *The subject got a thorough airing in the British press.* **2** the act of allowing warm air to make clothes, beds, etc. fresh and dry

'airing cupboard *noun* (*BrE*) a warm cupboard in which clean sheets, clothes, etc. are put to make sure they are completely dry

air·less /'eələs; *AmE* 'erl-/ *adj.* (*written*) not having any fresh or moving air or wind, and therefore unpleasant: *a stuffy, airless room* ◊ *The night was hot and airless.*

'air letter *noun* = AEROGRAMME

air·lift /'eəlɪft; *AmE* 'erl-/ *noun, verb*
■ *noun* an operation to take people, soldiers, food, etc. to or from an area by plane, especially in an emergency or when roads are closed or dangerous
■ *verb* [VN] to take sb/sth to or from an area by plane, especially in an emergency or when roads are closed or dangerous: *Two casualties were airlifted to safety.*

air·line /'eəlaɪn; *AmE* 'erl-/ *noun* [C+sing./pl. *v.*] a company that provides regular flights to take passengers and goods to different places: *international airlines* ◊ *an airline pilot*

air·liner /'eəlaɪnə(r); *AmE* 'erl-/ *noun* a large plane that carries passengers

air·lock /'eəlɒk; *AmE* 'erlɑːk/ *noun* **1** a small room with a tightly closed door at each end, which you go through to reach another area at a different air pressure, for example on a spacecraft or SUBMARINE **2** a bubble of air that blocks the flow of liquid in a pump or pipe

air·mail /'eəmeɪl; *AmE* 'erm-/ *noun* [U] the system of sending letters, etc. by air: *Send it airmail/by airmail.*

air·man /'eəmən; *AmE* 'erm-/, **air·woman** /'eəwʊmən; *AmE* 'erw-/ *noun* (*pl.* **-men** /-mən/, *pl.* **-women** /-wɪmɪn/) **1** a member of the British air force, especially one below the rank of an officer **2** a member of one of the lowest ranks in the US air force: *Airman Brines*

air 'marshal *noun* an officer of very high rank in the British air force: *Air Marshal Gordon Black*

'air mattress *noun* (*especially AmE*) = AIR BED

air·plane /'eəpleɪn; *AmE* 'erp-/ *noun* (*AmE*) = PLANE: *They arrived in Belgium by airplane.* ◊ *an airplane crash/flight* ◊ *a commercial/jet/military airplane*

'air pocket *noun* **1** a closed area that becomes filled with air: *Make sure there are no air pockets around the roots of the plant.* **2** an area of low air pressure that makes a plane suddenly drop while flying: *The plane hit an air pocket.*

air·port /'eəpɔːt; *AmE* 'erpɔːrt/ *noun* a place where planes land and take off and that has buildings for passengers to wait in: *Gatwick Airport* ◊ *waiting in the airport lounge*

'air pump *noun* a piece of equipment for pumping air into or out of sth

'air raid *noun* an attack by a number of aircraft dropping many bombs on a place: *The family was killed in an air raid.* ◊ *an air-raid shelter/warning*

'air rifle *noun* = AIR GUN

air-sea 'rescue *noun* [U] (*especially BrE*) the process of rescuing people from the sea using aircraft

air·ship /'eəʃɪp; *AmE* 'erʃɪp/ *noun* a large aircraft without wings, filled with a gas which is lighter than air, and driven by engines

air·space /'eəspeɪs; *AmE* 'ers-/ *noun* [U] the part of the sky where planes fly, usually the part above a particular country that is legally controlled by that country: *The airspace over Europe is becoming more and more crowded.* ◊ *The jet entered Chinese airspace without permission.*

'air speed *noun* the speed at which an aircraft moves through the air

air·strip /'eəstrɪp; *AmE* 'ers-/ (also **'landing strip**) *noun* a narrow piece of cleared land that an aircraft can land on

'air terminal *noun* **1** a building at an airport that provides services for passengers travelling by plane **2** (*BrE*) an office in a city from which passengers can catch buses to the airport

air·tight /'eətaɪt; *AmE* 'ert-/ *adj.* not allowing air to get in or out: *Store the cake in an airtight container.* ◊ (*figurative*) *an airtight alibi* (= one that cannot be proved to be false)

air·time /'eətaɪm; *AmE* 'ert-/ *noun* [U] **1** the amount of time that is given to a particular subject on radio or television **2** the amount of time that is paid for when you are using a MOBILE PHONE: *This deal gives you 180 minutes free airtime a month.*

air-to-'air *adj.* [usually before noun] from one aircraft to another while they are both flying: *an air-to-air missile*

air traffic con'trol *noun* [U] **1** the activity of giving instructions by radio to pilots of aircraft so that they know when and where to take off or land **2** the group of people or the organization that provides an air traffic control service: *The pilot was given clearance to land by air traffic control.*

air traffic con'troller *noun* a person at an airport whose job is to give instructions by radio to pilots of aircraft so that they know when and where to take off or land

air vice-'marshal *noun* an officer of very high rank in the British air force: *Air Vice-Marshal Andrew Burns*

air·waves /'eəweɪvz; *AmE* 'erw-/ *noun* [pl.] radio waves that are used in broadcasting radio and television: *More and more TV and radio stations are crowding the airwaves.* ◊ *A well-known voice came over the airwaves.*

air·way /'eəweɪ; *AmE* 'erweɪ/ *noun* **1** (*medical*) the passage from the nose and throat to the lungs, through which you breathe **2** (often used in names of airlines) a route regularly used by planes: *British Airways*

air·worthy /'eəwɜːði; *AmE* 'erwɜːrði/ *adj.* (of aircraft) safe to fly ▶ **air·worthi·ness** *noun* [U]

b	d	f	g	h	k	l	m	n	p	r
bad	did	fall	get	hat	cat	leg	man	now	pen	red

A

airy /ˈeəri; *AmE* ˈeri/ *adj.* **1** with plenty of fresh air because there is a lot of space: *The office was light and airy.* **2** (*written*) acting or done in a way that shows that you are not worried or that you are not treating sth as serious: *He dismissed her with an airy wave.*—see also AIRILY **3** (*written, disapproving*) not serious or practical: *airy promises/speculation*

ˌairy-ˈfairy *adj.* (*BrE, informal, disapproving*) not clear or practical

aisle /aɪl/ *noun* a passage between rows of seats in a church, theatre, train, etc., or between rows of shelves in a SUPERMARKET: *an aisle seat* (= in a plane) ◊ *Coffee and tea are in the next aisle.*—compare GANGWAY ▣ **go/walk down the ˈaisle** (*informal*) to get married—more at ROLL *v.*

aitch /eɪtʃ/ *noun* the letter H written as a word: *He spoke with a cockney accent and **dropped his aitches** (= did not pronounce the letter H at the start of words).*

ajar /əˈdʒɑː(r)/ *adj.* [not before noun] (of a door) slightly open: *I'll leave the door ajar.*

aka /ˌeɪ keɪ ˈeɪ/ *abbr.* also known as: *Antonio Fratelli, aka 'Big Tony'*

akimbo /əˈkɪmbəʊ; *AmE* -boʊ/ *adv.* ▣ **(with) arms aˈkimbo** with your hands on your hips and your elbows pointing outwards

akin /əˈkɪn/ *adj.* **~ to sth** (*formal*) similar to: *What he felt was more akin to pity than love.*

-al *suffix* **1** (in adjectives) connected with: *magical* ◊ *verbal*—see also -ALLY **2** (in nouns) a process or state of: *survival*

à la /ˈɑː lɑː/ *prep.* (from *French*) in the same style as sb/sth else: *a new band that sings à la Beatles*

ala·bas·ter /ˈæləbɑːstə(r); *AmE* -bæs-/ *noun* [U] a type of white stone that is often carved to make statues and ornaments: *an alabaster tomb* ◊ (*literary*) *her pale, alabaster* (= white and smooth) *skin*

à la carte /ˌɑː lɑː ˈkɑːt; *AmE* ˈkɑːrt/ *adj., adv.* (from *French*) if food in a restaurant is **à la carte**, or if you eat **à la carte**, you choose from a list of dishes that have separate prices, rather than having a complete meal at a fixed price

alac·rity /əˈlækrəti/ *noun* [U] (*formal*) great willingness or enthusiasm: *They accepted the offer with alacrity.*

à la mode /ˌɑː lɑː ˈməʊd; *AmE* ˈmoʊd/ *adj., adv.* (from *French*) **1** [not before noun] (*old-fashioned*) fashionable; in the latest fashion **2** [after noun] (*AmE*) served with ice cream: *apple pie à la mode*

alarm /əˈlɑːm; *AmE* əˈlɑːrm/ *noun, verb*

■ *noun* **1** [U] fear and anxiety that sb feels when sth dangerous or unpleasant might happen: *'What have you done?' Ellie cried in alarm.* ◊ *I felt a growing sense of alarm when he did not return that night.* ◊ *The doctor said there was no **cause for alarm**.* **2** [C, usually sing.] a loud noise or a signal that warns people of danger or of a problem: *She decided to **sound the alarm** (= warn people that the situation was dangerous).* ◊ *I hammered on all the doors to **raise the alarm**.*—see also FALSE ALARM **3** [C] a device that warns people of a particular danger: *a burglar/fire/smoke alarm* ◊ *The cat **set off the alarm** (= made it start ringing).* ◊ *A car **alarm went off** in the middle of the night* (= started ringing). **4** = ALARM CLOCK: *The alarm went off at 7 o'clock.* ▣ **aˈlarm bells ring/start ringing** if you say that **alarm bells are ringing**, you mean that people are starting to feel worried and suspicious

■ *verb* **1** to make sb anxious or afraid: [VN] *The captain knew there was an engine fault but didn't want to alarm the passengers.* [also VN to inf] **2** [VN] to fit sth such as a door with a device that warns people when sb is trying to enter illegally

aˈlarm clock (also **alarm**) *noun* a clock that you can set to ring a bell, etc. at a particular time and wake you up: *I set the alarm clock for 7 o'clock.*

alarmed /əˈlɑːmd; *AmE* əˈlɑːrmd/ *adj.* [not before noun] **1 ~ (at/by sth)** anxious or afraid that sth dangerous or unpleasant might happen: *She was alarmed at the prospect of travelling alone.* **2** protected by an alarm: *This door is alarmed.*

alarm·ing /əˈlɑːmɪŋ; *AmE* əˈlɑːrm-/ *adj.* causing worry and fear: *an alarming increase in the number of cases of skin cancer* ◊ *The rainforests are disappearing **at an alarming rate**.* ▶ **alarm·ing·ly** *adv.*: *Prices have risen alarmingly.*

alarm·ist /əˈlɑːmɪst; *AmE* əˈlɑːrm-/ *adj.* (*disapproving*) causing unnecessary fear and anxiety: *A spokesperson for the food industry said the TV programme was alarmist.* ▶ **alarm·ist** *noun*

alas /əˈlæs/ *exclamation* (*old use* or *literary*) used to show you are sad or sorry: *For many people, alas, hunger is part of everyday life.*

al·ba·tross /ˈælbətrɒs; *AmE* -trɔːs; -trɑːs/ *noun* **1** a very large white seabird with long wings that lives in the Pacific and Southern Oceans **2** [usually sing.] (*written*) a thing that causes problems or prevents you from doing sth: *The national debt is an albatross around the president's neck.*—picture on page A6

al·beit /ˌɔːlˈbiːɪt/ *conj.* (*formal*) although: *He finally agreed, albeit reluctantly, to help us.*

al·bin·ism /ˈælbɪnɪzəm/ *noun* (*technical*) the condition of being an albino

al·bino /ælˈbiːnəʊ; *AmE* -ˈbaɪnoʊ/ *noun* (*pl.* **-os**) a person or an animal that is born with no colour (= PIGMENT) in the hair or skin, which are white, or in the eyes, which are pink ▶ **al·bino** *adj.* [only before noun]

album /ˈælbəm/ *noun* **1** a book in which you keep photographs, stamps, etc: *a photo album* **2** a collection of pieces of music that have been recorded on one record, CD or cassette: *the band's latest album*—compare SINGLE

al·bu·men /ˈælbjumɪn; *AmE* ælˈbjuːmən/ *noun* [U] (*technical*) the colourless inside part of an egg that is white when cooked—see also WHITE—compare YOLK

al·chem·ist /ˈælkəmɪst/ *noun* a person who studied alchemy

al·chemy /ˈælkəmi/ *noun* [U] **1** a form of chemistry studied in the Middle Ages which involved trying to discover how to change ordinary metals into gold **2** (*literary*) a mysterious power or magic that can change things

al·co·hol /ˈælkəhɒl; *AmE* -hɔːl; -hɑːl/ *noun* [U] **1** drinks such as beer, wine, etc. that can make people drunk: *He never drinks alcohol.* ◊ *alcohol abuse* **2** the colourless liquid that is found in drinks such as beer, wine, etc. and is used in medicines, cleaning products, etc: *Wine usually contains about 10% alcohol.* ◊ *levels of alcohol in the blood* ◊ *He pleaded guilty to driving with excess alcohol.* ◊ *low-alcohol beer* ◊ *Choose an alcohol-free skin toner if you have dry skin.*

al·co·hol·ic /ˌælkəˈhɒlɪk; *AmE* -ˈhɔːl-; -ˈhɑːl-/ *adj., noun*

■ *adj.* **1** connected with or containing alcohol: *alcoholic drinks* **2** caused by drinking alcohol: *The guests left in an alcoholic haze.*

■ *noun* (also *AmE informal* **lush**) a person who regularly drinks too much alcohol and cannot easily stop drinking, so that it has become an illness

al·co·hol·ism /ˈælkəhɒlɪzəm; *AmE* -hɔːl-; -hɑːl-/ *noun* [U] the medical condition caused by drinking too much alcohol regularly

al·co·pop /ˈælkəʊpɒp; *AmE* -koʊpɑːp/ *noun* (*BrE*) a sweet FIZZY drink (= with bubbles) that contains alcohol

al·cove /ˈælkəʊv; *AmE* -koʊv/ *noun* an area in a room that is formed by part of a wall being built farther back than the rest of the wall: *The bookcase fits neatly into the alcove.*

cornice

alcove

skirting board (*BrE*)/ baseboard (*AmE*)

alder /ˈɔːldə(r)/ *noun* a tree like a BIRCH that grows in northern countries, usually in wet ground

al·der·man /ˈɔːldəmən; *AmE* -dərm-/ *noun* (*pl.* **-men** /-mən/) **1** (in England and Wales in the past) a senior member of a town, BOROUGH or county

A

council, below the rank of a MAYOR, chosen by other members of the council **2** (in the US, Canada and Australia) an elected member of a town or city council: *Alderman Tim Evans*

ale /eɪl/ *noun* **1** [U, C] a type of beer, usually sold in bottles or cans. There are several kinds of ale: *brown/ pale ale* **2** [C] a glass, bottle or can of ale: *Two light ales please.* **3** [U] (*old-fashioned*) beer generally—see also GINGER ALE, REAL ALE

alec, aleck ⇨ SMART ALEC

ale·house /ˈeɪlhaʊs/ *noun* (*old-fashioned, BrE*) a place where people used to drink beer

alert /əˈlɜːt; *AmE* əˈlɜːrt/ *adj., verb, noun*
▪ *adj.* **1** able to think quickly; quick to notice things: *Suddenly he found himself awake and fully alert.* ◊ *Two alert scientists spotted the mistake.* **2 ~ to sth** aware of sth, especially a problem or danger: *We must be alert to the possibility of danger.* ▶ **alert·ly** *adj.* **alert·ness** *noun* [U]
▪ *verb* [often passive] **1** to warn sb about a dangerous or urgent situation: [VN] *Neighbours quickly alerted the emergency services.* ◊ *Alerted by a noise downstairs, he sat up and turned on the light.* [also VN (that), VN to inf] **2** [VN] **~ sb to sth** to make sb aware of sth: *They had been alerted to the possibility of further price rises.*
▪ *noun* **1** [sing., U] a situation in which people are watching for danger and ready to deal with it: *Police are warning the public to be on the alert for suspicious packages.* ◊ *More than 5000 troops have been placed on (full) alert.* **2** [C] a warning of danger or of a problem: *a bomb/fire alert*—see also RED ALERT

A level /ˈeɪ levl/ (also **ad'vanced level**) *noun* [C, U] a British exam taken in a particular subject, usually in the final year of school at the age of 18: *You need three A levels to get onto this university course.* ◊ *What A levels are you doing?* ◊ *I'm doing maths A level.* ◊ *two A level passes/two passes at A level*—compare GCE, GCSE, GNVQ

al·fal·fa /ælˈfælfə/ *noun* [U] a plant with small divided leaves and purple flowers, grown as food for farm animals and as a salad vegetable

al·fresco /ælˈfreskəʊ; *AmE* -koʊ/ *adj.* in the open air: *an alfresco lunch party* ▶ **al·fresco** *adv.*: *eating alfresco*

algae /ˈældʒiː; ˈælɡiː/ *noun* [U, pl.] (*sing.* **alga** /ˈælɡə/) *technical* very simple plants with no real leaves, stems or roots that grow in or near water, including SEAWEED ▶ **algal** /ˈælɡəl/ *adj.* [only before noun]: *algal blooms/ growth*

al·ge·bra /ˈældʒɪbrə/ *noun* [U] a type of mathematics in which letters and symbols are used to represent quantities ▶ **al·ge·bra·ic** /ˌældʒɪˈbreɪɪk/ *adj.*: *an algebraic equation*

al·go·rithm /ˈælɡərɪðəm/ *noun* (*especially computing*) a set of rules that must be followed when solving a particular problem

alias /ˈeɪliəs/ *adv., noun*
▪ *adv.* used when a person, especially a criminal or an actor, is known by two names: *Mick Clark, alias Sid Brown* ◊ *Inspector Morse, alias John Thaw* (= John Thaw plays the part of Inspector Morse) ◊ *John Thaw, alias Inspector Morse of the famous TV series*
▪ *noun* a false or different name, especially one that is used by a criminal: *He checked into the hotel under an alias.*

alibi /ˈæləbaɪ/ *noun* **1** evidence that proves that a person was in another place at the time of a crime and so could not have committed it: *The suspects all had alibis for the day of the robbery.* **2** an excuse for sth that you have done wrong

alien /ˈeɪliən/ *adj., noun*
▪ *adj.* **1 ~ (to sb/sth)** strange and frightening; different from what you are used to: *an alien environment* ◊ *In a world that had suddenly become alien and dangerous, he was her only security.* **2** (often *disapproving*) from another country or society; foreign: *an alien culture* **3 ~ to sb/sth** (*disapproving*) not usual or acceptable: *The idea is alien to our religion.* ◊ *Cruelty was quite alien to him.* **4** connected with creatures from another world: *alien beings from outer space*

▪ *noun* **1** (*AmE* also **,non-'citizen**) (*law* or *technical*) a person who is not a citizen of the country in which they live or work: *an illegal alien* **2** a creature from another world: *aliens from outer space*

alien·ate /ˈeɪliənert/ *verb* [VN] **1** to make sb less friendly or sympathetic towards you: *His comments have alienated a lot of young voters.* **2 ~ sb (from sth/sb)** to make sb feel that they do not belong in a particular group: *Very talented children may feel alienated from the others in their class.* ▶ **alien·ation** /ˌeɪliəˈneɪʃn/ *noun* [U]: *The new policy resulted in the alienation of many voters.* ◊ *Many immigrants suffer from a sense of alienation.*

alight /əˈlaɪt/ *adj., verb*
▪ *adj.* [not before noun] **1** on fire: *A cigarette set the dry grass alight.* ◊ *Her dress caught alight in the fire.* **2** (*written*) (of faces or eyes) showing a feeling of happiness or excitement **IDM** see WORLD
▪ *verb* [V] (*formal* or *literary*) **1 ~ (in/on/upon sth)** (of a bird or an insect) to land in or on sth after flying to it **2 ~ (from sth)** to get out of a bus, a train or other vehicle **SYN** GET OFF: *Do not alight from a moving bus.* **PHRV a'light on/upon sth** to think of, find or notice sth, especially by chance: *Eventually, we alighted on the idea of seeking sponsorship.* ◊ *Her eyes suddenly alighted on the bundle of documents.*

align /əˈlaɪn/ *verb* **1 ~ (sth) (with sth)** to arrange sth in the correct position, or to be in the correct position, in relation to sth else, especially in a straight line: [VN] *Make sure the shelf is aligned with the top of the cupboard.* ◊ [V] *The top and bottom line of each column on the page should align.* **2** [VN] **~ sth (with/to sth)** to change sth slightly so that it is in the correct relationship to sth else: *Domestic prices have been aligned with those in world markets.* **PHRV align yourself with sb/sth** to publicly support an organization, a set of opinions or a person that you agree with

align·ment /əˈlaɪnmənt/ *noun* [U, C] **1** arrangement in a straight line: *the alignment of the sun, moon and earth at a particular time* ◊ *A bone in my spine was out of alignment.* **2** political support given to one country or group by another: *Japan's alignment with the West*

alike /əˈlaɪk/ *adj., adv.*
▪ *adj.* [not before noun] very similar: *My sister and I do not look alike.*—compare UNLIKE
▪ *adv.* **1** in a very similar way: *They tried to treat all their children alike.* **2** used after you have referred to two people or groups, to mean 'both' or 'equally': *Good health and safety management benefits employers and employees alike.* **IDM** see SHARE *v.*

ali·men·tary canal /ˌælɪmentəri kəˈnæl/ *noun* the passage in the body that carries food from the mouth to the ANUS

ali·mony /ˈælɪməni; *AmE* -moʊni/ *noun* [U] (*especially AmE*) the money that a court of law orders sb to pay regularly to their former wife or husband when the marriage is ended—compare PALIMONY

alive /əˈlaɪv/ *adj.* [not before noun] **1** living; not dead: *We don't know whether he's alive or dead.* ◊ *Is your mother still alive?* ◊ *Doctors kept the baby alive for six weeks.* ◊ *I was glad to hear you're alive and well.* ◊ *She had to steal food just to stay alive.* ◊ *He was buried alive in the earthquake.* **2 ~ (with sth)** full of emotion, excitement, activity, etc: *Edward was alive with happiness.* **3** continuing to exist: *to keep a tradition/memory/hope alive* **4 ~ with sth** full of living or moving things: *The pool was alive with goldfish.* **5 ~ to sth** aware of sth; knowing sth exists and is important: *to be alive to the dangers/facts/ possibilities* **IDM a,live and 'kicking** very active, healthy or popular **bring sth a'live** to make sth interesting: *Maps and pictures bring the book alive.* **come a'live 1** (of a subject or an event) to become interesting and exciting: *The game came alive in the second half.* **2** (of a place) to become busy and full of activity: *The city starts to come alive after dark.* **3** (of a person) to show interest in sth and become excited about it: *She came alive as she talked about her job.*—more at EAT

æ	ɑː	e	ɜː	ə	ɪ	iː	i	ɒ	ɔː	ʌ	ʊ	u	uː
cat	father	ten	bird	about	sit	see	many	got (BrE)	saw	cup	put	actual	too

al·ka·li /ˈælkəlaɪ/ *noun* [C, U] (*chemistry*) a chemical substance that reacts with acids to form a salt and has a pH of more than seven—compare ACID

al·ka·line /ˈælkəlaɪn/ *adj.* **1** (*chemistry*) having the nature of an alkali **2** (*technical*) containing alkali: *alkaline soil*—compare ACID

al·kal·oid /ˈælkəlɔɪd/ *noun* (*biology* or *medical*) a poisonous substance found in some plants. There are many different alkaloids and some are used as the basis for drugs.

all /ɔːl/ *det., pron., adv.*
■ *det.* **1** (used with plural nouns. The noun may have *the, this, that, my, her, his*, etc. in front of it, or a number.) the whole number of: *All horses are animals, but not all animals are horses.* ◊ *Cars were coming from all directions* (= every direction). ◊ *All the people you invited are coming.* ◊ *All my plants have died.* ◊ *All five men are hard workers.* **2** (used with uncountable nouns. The noun may have *the, this, that, my, her, his*, etc. in front of it.) the whole amount of: *All wood tends to shrink.* ◊ *You've had all the fun and I've had all the hard work.* ◊ *All this mail must be answered.* ◊ *He has lost all his money.* **3** used with singular nouns showing sth has been happening for a whole period of time: *He's worked hard all year.* ◊ *She was unemployed for all that time.* **4** the greatest possible: *In all honesty* (= being as honest as I can), *I can't agree.* **5** consisting or appearing to consist of one thing only: *The magazine was all advertisements.* ◊ *She was all smiles* (= smiling a lot). **6** any whatever: *He denied all knowledge of the crime.* **IDM** **and all 'that (jazz, rubbish, etc.)** (*informal*) and other similar things: *I'm bored by history—dates and battles and all that stuff.* **not all that good, well, etc.** not particularly good, well, etc: *He doesn't sing all that well.* **not as bad(ly), etc. as all 'that** not as much as has been suggested: *They're not as rich as all that.* **of 'all people, things, etc.** (*informal*) used to express surprise because sb/sth seems the least likely person, example, etc: *I didn't think you, of all people, would become a vegetarian.* **of 'all the ...** (*informal*) used to express anger: *I've locked myself out. Of all the stupid things to do!*—more at FOR *prep.*
■ *pron.* **1** the whole number or amount: *All of the food has gone.* ◊ *They've eaten all of it.* ◊ *They've eaten it all.* ◊ *I invited some of my colleagues but not all.* ◊ *Not all of them were invited.* ◊ *All of them enjoyed the party.* ◊ *They all enjoyed it.* ◊ *His last movie was best of all.* **2** (followed by a relative clause, often without *that*) the only thing; everything: *All I want is peace and quiet.* ◊ *It was all that I had.* ⇨ note at ALTOGETHER **IDM** **all in 'all** when everything is considered: *All in all it had been a great success.* **all in 'one** having two or more uses, functions, etc: *It's a corkscrew and bottle-opener all in one.* **all or 'nothing** a situation which will end either in complete success or complete failure **and 'all 1** also; included; in addition: *She jumped into the river, clothes and all* (= with her clothes on). **2** (*spoken*) as well; too: *'I'm freezing.' 'Yeah, me and all.'* **(not) at all** in any way; to any degree: *I didn't enjoy it at all.* **in all** as a total **SYN** ALTOGETHER: *There were twelve of us in all for dinner.* ◊ *That's £25.40 in all.* **not at 'all** used as a polite reply to an expression of thanks: *'Thanks very much for your help.' 'Not at all, it was a pleasure.'* **your 'all** everything you have: *They gave their all* (= fought and died) *in the war.*—more at ABOVE *prep.*, AFTER *prep.*, END *v.*, END *n.*, FOR *prep.*, SIDE *n.*
■ *adv.* **1** completely: *She was dressed all in white.* ◊ *He lives all alone.* ◊ *The coffee went all over my skirt.* **2** (*informal*) very: *She was all excited.* ◊ *Now don't get all upset about it.* **3 ~ too ...** used to show that sth is more than you would like: *I'm all too aware of the problems.* ◊ *The end of the trip came all too soon.* **4** (in sports and games) to each side: *The score was four all.* **IDM** **all a'long** all the time; from the beginning: *I realized it was in my pocket all along.* **all a'round** ⇨ ALL ROUND **all the better, harder, etc.** so much better, harder, etc: *We'll have to work all the harder with two people off sick.* **all but 1** almost: *The party was all but over when we arrived.* ◊ *It was all but impossible to read his writing.* **2** everything or everyone except sth/sb: *All but one of the plates were damaged.* **all**

'in 1 physically tired **SYN** EXHAUSTED: *At the end of the race he felt all in.* **2** (*BrE*) including everything: *The holiday cost £250 all in.*—see also ALL-IN **all of sth** (often ironic) used to emphasize an amount, a size, etc. usually when it is very small: *It must be all of 100 metres to the car!* **all 'over 1** everywhere: *We looked all over for the ring.* **2** what you would expect of the person mentioned: *That sounds like my sister all over.* **all 'round** (*BrE*) (*AmE* **all a'round**) **1** in every way; in all respects: *a good performance all round.* **2** for each person: *She bought drinks all round.* **all 'there** (*informal*) having a healthy mind; thinking clearly: *He behaves very oddly at times—I don't think he's all quite there.* **be all about sb/sth**: *This book is all about Greece.* ◊ (*informal*) *Now then, what's this all about* (= what is the problem)? ◊ *It's all about money these days.* **be all for sth/for doing sth** to believe strongly that sth should be done: *They're all for saving money where they can.* **be all 'over sb** (*informal*) to show a lot of affection for or enthusiasm about sb: *He was all over her at the party.* **be all up (with sb)** (*old-fashioned, informal*) to be the end for sb: *It looks as though it's all up with us now* (= we are ruined, have no further chances, etc.).

all- /ɔːl/ *combining form* (in adjectives and adverbs) **1** completely: *an all-American* ◊ *an all-inclusive price* **2** in the highest degree: *all-important* ◊ *all-powerful*

Allah /ˈælə/ *noun* the name of God among Muslims

all-a'round *adj.* (*AmE*) = ALL-ROUND

allay /əˈleɪ/ *verb* [VN] (*formal*) to make sth, especially a feeling, less strong: *to allay fears/concern/suspicion*

all-'clear *noun* (**the all-clear**) [sing.] **1** if a doctor gives sb the all-clear, they tell the person that he/she does not have any health problems **2** permission to do sth: *The ship was given the all-clear to sail again.* **3** a signal (often a sound) which shows that a place or situation is no longer dangerous

al·le·ga·tion /ˌæləˈɡeɪʃn/ *noun* **~ (of sth) (against sb)** | **~ (that ...)** | **~ (about sb/sth)** a public statement that is made without giving proof, accusing sb of doing sth that is wrong or illegal: *Several newspapers made allegations of corruption in the city's police department.* ◊ *allegations of dishonesty against him* ◊ *an allegation that he had been dishonest* ◊ *to investigate/deny/withdraw an allegation*

al·lege /əˈledʒ/ *verb* [often passive] (*formal*) to state sth as a fact but without giving proof: [V (**that**)] *The prosecution alleges (that) she was driving carelessly.* ◊ [VN **that**] *It is alleged that she mistreated the prisoners.* ◊ [VN **to inf**] *He is alleged to have mistreated the prisoners.* **HELP** This pattern is only used in the passive. ◊ [VN] *This procedure should be followed in cases where dishonesty has been alleged.* [also V **speech**] ▶ **al·leged** *adj.* [only before noun] (*formal*): *the alleged attacker/victim/killer* (= that sb says is one) ◊ *the alleged attack/offence/incident* (= that sb says has happened) **al·leged·ly** /əˈledʒɪdli/ *adv.*: *crimes allegedly committed during the war*

al·le·giance /əˈliːdʒəns/ *noun* [U, C] **~ (to sb/sth)** a person's continued support for a political party, religion, ruler, etc: *to pledge/swear allegiance to sb/sth* ◊ *to switch/transfer/change allegiance* ◊ *an oath/a vow/a statement of allegiance* ◊ *People of various party allegiances joined the campaign.*

al·le·gory /ˈæləɡəri; *AmE* -ɡɔːri/ *noun* [C, U] (*pl.* **-ies**) a story, picture, etc. in which each character or event is a symbol representing an idea or a quality, such as truth, evil, death, etc.; the use of such symbols: *a political allegory* ◊ *the poet's use of allegory*—see also FABLE ▶ **al·le·gor·ic·al** /ˌæləˈɡɒrɪkl; *AmE* -ˈɡɔːr-; -ˈɡɑːr-/ *adj.*: *an allegorical figure/novel* **al·le·gor·ic·al·ly** *adv.*

al·legro /əˈleɡrəʊ; *AmE* -ɡroʊ/ *noun* (*pl.* **-os**) (*music*) a piece of music to be played in a fast and lively manner ▶ **al·legro** *adj., adv.*

al·le·luia /ˌælɪˈluːjə/ *noun, exclamation* = HALLELUJAH

all-em'bracing *adj.* (*written*) including everything: *an all-embracing theory*

Allen key™ /ˈælən kiː/ (*BrE*) (*AmE* **Allen wrench**™) *noun* a small tool used for turning an **Allen screw**

'Allen screw™ *noun* a SCREW with a hole that has six sides

al·ler·gic /əˈlɜːdʒɪk; AmE əˈlɜːrdʒɪk/ adj. **1** ~ (to sth) having an allergy to sth: *I like cats but unfortunately I'm allergic to them.* **2** caused by an allergy: *an allergic reaction/rash* **3** [not before noun] ~ to sth (*informal, humorous*) having a strong dislike of sth/sb: *You could see he was allergic to housework.*

al·lergy /ˈælədʒi; AmE ˈælərdʒi/ noun (pl. -ies) ~ (to sth) a medical condition that causes you to react badly or feel ill when you eat or touch a particular substance: *I have an allergy to animal hair.*

al·le·vi·ate /əˈliːvieɪt/ verb [VN] (*written*) to make sth less severe [SYN] EASE: *to alleviate suffering* ◊ *A number of measures were taken to alleviate the problem.* ▶ **al·le·vi·ation** /ə₁liːviˈeɪʃn/ noun [U]

alley /ˈæli/ noun **1** (also **al·ley·way** /ˈæliweɪ/) a narrow passage behind or between buildings: *a narrow/dark alley*—see also BLIND ALLEY, BOWLING ALLEY **2** (*AmE*) = TRAMLINES [IDM] **(right) up your ˈalley** (*AmE*) = (RIGHT) UP YOUR STREET at STREET

al·li·ance /əˈlaɪəns/ noun **1** ~ (with sb/sth)| ~ (between A and B) an agreement between countries, political parties, etc. to work together in order to achieve sth that they all want: *to form/make a political alliance* ◊ *The Social Democrats are now in alliance with the Greens.* **2** a group of people, political parties, etc. who work together in order to achieve sth that they all want

al·lied /ˈælaɪd; ˈælaɪd/ adj. **1** (often **Allied**) [only before noun] connected with countries that unite to fight a war together, especially the countries that fought together against Germany in the First and Second World Wars: *Italy joined the war on the Allied side in 1915.* ◊ *allied forces/troops* **2** ~ (to/with sth) (*written*) (of two or more things) similar or existing together; connected with sth: *medicine, nursing, physiotherapy and other allied professions* ◊ *In this job you will need social skills allied with technical knowledge.*—see also ALLY

al·li·ga·tor /ˈælɪɡeɪtə(r)/ noun a large reptile of the CROCODILE family, with a long tail, hard skin and very big jaws, that lives in rivers and lakes in America and China

ˌall-imˈportant adj. extremely important

ˌall-ˈin adj. [only before noun] (*BrE*) including the cost of all parts of sth: *an all-in price of £500 with no extras to pay*

ˌall-in-ˈone adj. [only before noun] (*BrE*) able to do the work of two or more things that are usually separate: *an all-in-one shampoo and conditioner*

al·lit·er·ation /ə₁lɪtəˈreɪʃn/ noun [U] (*technical*) the use of the same letter or sound at the beginning of words that are close together, as in *sing a song of sixpence* ▶ **al·lit·era·tive** /əˈlɪtrətɪv; AmE əˈlɪtəreɪtɪv/ adj.

ˈall-night adj. [only before noun] **1** (of a place) open through the night: *an all-night cafe* **2** (of an activity) continuing through the night: *an all-night party*

ˌall-ˈnighter noun (*AmE, informal*) a time when you stay awake all night studying

al·lo·cate /ˈæləkeɪt/ verb ~ sth (for sth)| ~ sth (to sb/sth)| ~ (sb/sth) sth to give sth officially to sb/sth for a particular purpose: [VN] *They intend to allocate more places to mature students this year.* ◊ *A large sum has been allocated for buying new books for the library.* ◊ [VN, VNN] *More resources are being allocated to the project.* ◊ *The project is being allocated more resources.*

al·lo·ca·tion /₁æləˈkeɪʃn/ noun **1** [C] an amount of money, space, etc. that is given to sb for a particular purpose: *We have spent our entire allocation for the year.* **2** [U] the act of giving sth to sb for a particular purpose: *the allocation of food to those who need it most*

allot /əˈlɒt; AmE əˈlɑːt/ verb (-tt-) ~ sth (to sb/sth)| ~ (sb/sth) sth to give time, money, tasks, etc. to sb/sth as a share of what is available: [VN] *I managed to complete the test within the time allotted.* ◊ [VN, VNN] *How much money has been allotted to us?* ◊ *How much money have we been allotted?*

al·lot·ment /əˈlɒtmənt; AmE əˈlɑːt-/ noun **1** [C] (*BrE*) a small area of land in a town which a person can rent in order to grow vegetables on it **2** [C, U] (*formal*) an amount of sth that sb is given or allowed to have; the process of giving sth to sb: *Water allotments to farmers were cut back*

in the drought. ◊ *the allotment of shares to company employees*

ˌall-ˈout adj. [only before noun] using or involving every possible effort and done in a very determined way: *All-out war was almost inevitable now.* ◊ *an all-out attack on the opposition* ▶ **ˌall ˈout** adv.: *We're going all out to win.*

allow /əˈlaʊ/ verb
LET SB/STH DO STH | **1** to let sb/sth do sth; to let sth happen or be done: [VN to inf] *His parents won't allow him to stay out late.* ◊ *He is not allowed to stay out late.* ◊ *They shouldn't be allowed to get away with it.* ◊ *She won't allow herself to be dictated to.* ◊ *He allowed his mind to wander.* ◊ [VN] *Smoking is not allowed in the hall.* ◊ [V-ing] *We do not allow smoking in the hall.* **2** [VNN] to let sb have sth: *You're allowed half an hour to complete the test.* ◊ *I'm not allowed visitors.* **3** [VN] [usually +adv./prep.] [usually passive] to let sb/sth go into, through, out of, etc. a place: *No dogs allowed* (= you cannot bring them in). ◊ *The prisoners are allowed out of their cells for two hours a day.* ◊ *The crowd parted to allow her through.* ◊ *You won't be allowed up* (= out of bed) *for several days.*

MAKE POSSIBLE | **4** to make sth possible: [VN] *A ramp has been installed to allow better access for wheelchairs.* [also V-ing]

TIME/MONEY/FOOD, etc. | **5** [VN] ~ sth (for sb/sth) to make sure that you have enough of sth for a particular purpose: *How much time would you allow for the trip?* ◊ *You need to allow three metres of fabric for the dress.*

ACCEPT/ADMIT | **6** (*formal*) to accept or admit sth; to agree that sth is true or correct: [VN] *The judge allowed my claim.* ◊ *'Objection!' 'I'll allow it.'* ◊ [V that] *He refuses to allow that such a situation could arise.* ◊ [VNN] *She was very helpful when my mother was ill—I'll allow you that.* [also V speech] —compare DISALLOW
[IDM] **allow ˈme** (*spoken*) used to offer help politely—more at REIN n.
[PHRV] **alˈlow for sb/sth** to include sb/sth when calculating sth: *It will take about an hour to get there, allowing for traffic delays.* ◊ *All these factors must be allowed for.* **alˈlow of sth** (*formal*) to make sth possible: *The facts allow of only one explanation.*

WHICH WORD?

allow / let / permit (?)

Let is the least formal and the most common of these verbs in spoken English. It is followed by an object and an infinitive without 'to', and is often used to give orders: *Let James sit there.* ◊ *Don't let me forget there's a cake in the oven.* ◊ *My father won't let me go out tonight.* Let is not used in the passive.

Allow is more formal than let and is more common in writing. Permit is the most formal and is used in official or technical written language. Both words can be followed by an object and a 'to' infinitive and are both often used in the passive: *I'm not allowed to smoke in the house.* ◊ *Some parents allow their children to do whatever they like.* ◊ *Photography is not permitted in the gallery.* ◊ *Customers are permitted to use the car park.*

---

al·low·able /əˈlaʊəbl/ adj. **1** that is allowed, especially by law or by a set of rules **2** (*BrE*) **allowable** amounts of money are amounts that you do not have to pay tax on

al·low·ance /əˈlaʊəns/ noun **1** an amount of money that is given to sb regularly or for a particular purpose: *an allowance of $20 a day* ◊ *a clothing/living/travel allowance* ◊ *Do you get an allowance for clothing?* **2** the amount of sth that is allowed in a particular situation: *a baggage allowance of 20 kilos* **3** (*BrE*) an amount of money that can be earned or received before you start paying tax: *personal tax allowances* **4** (*especially AmE*) = POCKET MONEY [IDM] **make allowance(s) for sth** to consider sth, for example when you are making a decision or planning sth: *The budget made allowance for inflation.* ◊ *The plan makes no allowance for people working at different rates.*
make allowances (for sb) to allow sb to behave in a

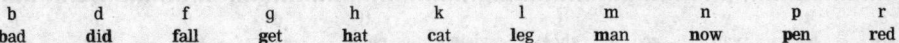

b	d	f	g	h	k	l	m	n	p	r
bad	**did**	**fall**	**get**	**hat**	**cat**	**leg**	**man**	**now**	**pen**	**red**

way that you would not usually accept, because of a problem or because there is a special reason

alloy *noun, verb*
- *noun* /'ælɔɪ/ [C, U] a metal that is formed by mixing two types of metal together, or by mixing metal with another substance: *Brass is an alloy of copper and zinc.* ◊ *alloy steel*
- *verb* /ə'lɔɪ/ [VN] ~ sth (with sth) (*technical*) to mix one metal with another, especially one of lower value

,**all-'purpose** *adj.* [only before noun] having many different uses; able to be used in many situations

all 'right (also *non-standard* or *informal* **al·right**) *adj., adv., exclamation*
- *adj., adv.* **1** satisfactory; in a satisfactory manner: *Is the coffee all right?* ◊ *Are you getting along all right in your new job?* ◊ *'They're off to Spain next week.' 'It's all right for some, isn't it?* (= some people are lucky) ' **2** safe and well: *I hope the children are all right.* ◊ *Do you feel all right?* **3** only just good enough: *Your work is all right but I'm sure you could do better.* **4** that can be allowed: *Are you sure it's all right for me to leave early?* **5** used to emphasize that there is no doubt about sth: *'Are you sure it's her?' 'Oh, it's her all right.'* **IDM** **I'm all 'right, Jack** (*BrE, informal*) used by or about sb who is happy with their own life and does not care about other people's problems **it'll be all ,right on the 'night** (*spoken*) used to say that a performance, an event, etc. will be successful even if the preparations for it have not gone well—more at BIT
- *exclamation* **1** used to check that sb agrees or understands: *We've got to get up early, all right?* **2** used to say that you agree: *'Can you do it?' 'Oh, all right.'* **3** used when accepting thanks or when sb says they are sorry: *'I'm really sorry.' 'That's all right, don't worry.'* **4** used to get sb's attention: *All right class, turn to page 20.*

,**all-'round** (*BrE*) (*AmE* ,**all-a'round**) *adj.* [only before noun] **1** including many different subjects, skills, etc: *an all-round education* **2** (of a person) with a wide range of skills or abilities: *She's a good all-round player.*

all-'rounder *noun* (*BrE*) a person who has many different skills and abilities

,**all 'singing , ,all 'dancing** *adj.* [only before noun] (*BrE, informal*) (of a machine or system) having a lot of advanced technical features and therefore able to perform many different functions

all·spice /'ɔːlspaɪs/ *noun* [U] the dried berries of a W Indian tree, used in cooking as a spice

'**all-star** *adj.* [only before noun] including many famous actors, singers, etc: *an all-star cast*

,**all-terrain 'vehicle** *noun* = ATV

'**all-time** *adj.* [only before noun] (used when you are comparing things or saying how good or bad sth is) of any time: *one of the all-time great tennis players* ◊ *my all-time favourite song* ◊ *Unemployment reached an all-time record of 3 million.* ◊ *Profits are at an all-time high/low.*

al·lude /ə'luːd/ *verb* **PHRV** **al'lude to sb/sth** (*formal*) to mention sth in an indirect way: *The problem had been alluded to briefly in earlier discussions.*—see also ALLUSION

al·lure /ə'lʊə(r); *AmE* ə'lʊr/ *noun* [U] (*written*) the quality of being attractive and exciting: *sexual allure* ◊ *the allure of the big city*

al·lur·ing /ə'lʊərɪŋ; *AmE* ə'lʊrɪŋ/ *adj.* attractive and exciting in a mysterious way: *an alluring smile* ▶ **al·lur·ing·ly** *adv.*

al·lu·sion /ə'luːʒn/ *noun* [C, U] ~ (to sb/sth) something that is said or written that refers to or mentions another person or subject in an indirect way: *His statement was seen as an allusion to the recent drug-related killings.* ◊ *Her poetry is full of obscure literary allusion.*

al·lu·sive /ə'luːsɪv/ *adj.* (*formal*) containing allusions: *an allusive style of writing*

al·lu·vial /ə'luːviəl/ *adj.* [usually before noun] (*technical*) made of sand and earth that is left by rivers or floods

ally *pl. noun, verb*
- *noun* /'ælaɪ/ (*pl.* **-ies**) **1** [C] a country that has agreed to help and support another country, especially in case of a war: *our European/NATO allies* **2** [C] a person who helps and supports sb who is in a difficult situation, especially a politician: *a close ally and friend of the prime minister* **3** (**the Allies**) [pl.] the group of countries including Britain and the US that fought together in the First and Second World Wars
- *verb* /ə'laɪ/ (**al·lies**, **ally·ing**, **al·lied**, **al·lied**) ~ **with sb/sth** (*written*) to give your support to another group or country: [VN] *The prince allied himself with the Scots.* [also V]

> **WORD FAMILY**
> ally *v., n.*
> allied *adj.*
> alliance *n.*

-ally *suffix* (makes adverbs from adjectives that end in *-al*): *magically* ◊ *sensationally*

Alma Mater (also **alma mater**) /,ælmə 'mɑːtə(r); 'meɪtə(r)/ *noun* [sing.] (*especially AmE*) the school or university that sb went to

al·manac (also *less frequent* **al·man·ack**) /'ɔːlmənæk; 'æl-/ *noun* **1** a book that is published every year giving information for that year about a particular subject or activity **2** a book that gives information about the sun, moon, times of the TIDES (= the rise and fall of the sea level), etc. for each day of the year

al·mighty /ɔːl'maɪti/ *adj.* **1** (in prayers) having complete power: *Almighty God, have mercy on us.* **2** [only before noun] (*informal*) very great or severe: *an almighty bang/crash/roar* **3** (△, *offensive*) used in the expressions shown in the example, to express surprise or anger: *Christ/God Almighty! What the hell do you think you are doing?* **4** (**the Almighty**) *noun* [sing.] God

al·mond /'ɑːmənd/ *noun* the flat pale sweet nut of the **almond tree** used in cooking and to make almond oil: *flaked/ground almonds* ◊ *blanched almonds* (= with their skins removed) ◊ *almond essence/paste* ◊ *almond eyes* .(= eyes shaped like almonds) ◊ picture at NUT

> **WHICH WORD?**
> **almost / nearly / practically**
>
> These three words have similar meanings and are used frequently with the following words:
>
> | almost ~ | nearly ~ | practically ~. |
> |---|---|---|
> | certainly | (numbers) | all |
> | all | all | every |
> | every | always | no |
> | entirely | every | nothing |
> | impossible | finished | impossible |
> | empty | died | anything |
>
> They are used in positive sentences: *She almost/nearly/practically missed her train.* They can be used before words like *all*, *every* and *everybody*: *Nearly all the students have bikes.* ◊ *I've got practically every CD they've made.* **Practically** is used more in spoken than in written English. **Nearly** is the most common with numbers: *There were nearly 200 people at the meeting.* They can also be used in negative sentences but it is more common to make a positive sentence with **only just**: *We only just got there in time.* (or: *We almost/nearly didn't get there in time.*)
>
> **Almost** and **practically** can be used before words like *any*, *anybody*, *anything*, etc.: *I'll eat almost anything.* You can also use them before *no*, *nobody*, *never*, etc. but it is much more common to use **hardly** or **scarcely** with *any*, *anybody*, *ever*, etc.: *She's hardly ever in.* (or: *She's almost never in.*)
>
> **Almost** can be used when you are saying that one thing is similar to another: *The boat looked almost like a toy.*
>
> In *BrE* you can use *very* and *so* before **nearly**: *He was very nearly caught.*
>
> ⇨ note at HARDLY

al·most /'ɔːlməʊst; *AmE* -moʊst/ *adv.* not quite; SYN NEARLY: *I like almost all of them.* ◊ *It's a mistake they always make.* ◊ *The story is almost certainly false.* ◊ *It's almost time to go.* ◊ *Dinner's almost ready.* ◊ *He slipped and almost fell.* ◊ *Their house is almost opposite ours.* ◊ *They'll eat almost anything.* ◊ *Almost no one* (hardly any-one) *believed him.* ⇨ note on page 32

alms /ɑːmz/ *noun* [pl.] (*old-fashioned*) money, clothes and food that are given to poor people

alms·house /'ɑːmzhaʊs/ *noun* (in the past in Britain) a house owned by a charity where poor people (usually the old) lived without paying rent

aloe /'æləʊ; *AmE* 'æloʊ/ *noun* a tropical plant with thick, prickly leaves that contain a lot of water. The juice of some types of aloe is used in medicine and COSMETICS.

aloft /ə'lɒft; *AmE* ə'lɔːft/ *adv.* (*formal*) high in the air: *She held the glass aloft.*

alone /ə'ləʊn; *AmE* ə'loʊn/ *adj.* [not before noun] *adv.* **1** without any other people: *I don't like going out alone at night.* ◊ *He lives alone.* ◊ *Finally the two of us were alone together.* ◊ *She was sitting all alone in the hall.* ◊ *Tom is not alone in finding Rick hard to work with.* **2** without the help of other people or things: *It's hard bringing up children alone.* ◊ *The assassin said he had acted alone.* **3** lonely and unhappy or without any friends: *Carol felt all alone in the world.* ◊ *I've been so alone since you went away.* **4** used after a noun or pronoun to show that the person or thing mentioned is the only one: *You can't blame anyone else; you alone made the decision.* **5** used after a noun or pronoun to emphasize one particular thing: *The shoes alone cost £200.* IDM **go it a'lone** to do sth without help from anyone: *Andrew decided to go it alone and start his own business.* **leave/let sb alone** to stop annoying sb or trying to get their attention: *She's asked to be left alone but the press photographers follow her everywhere.* **leave/let sth alone** to stop touching, chang-ing, or moving sth: *I've told you before—leave my things alone!* **let alone** used after a statement to emphasize that because the first thing is not true or possible, the next thing cannot be true or possible either: *There isn't enough room for us, let alone any guests.* **stand a'lone 1** to be independent or not connected with other people, organizations or ideas: *These islands are too small to stand alone as independent states.* **2** to be not near other objects or buildings: *The arch once stood alone at the entrance to the castle.*—more at TIME *n.*

> **WHICH WORD?** (?)
> **alone / lonely / lone**
>
> **Alone**, and **on your own, by yourself**, which are less formal and are the normal phrases used in spoken English, describe a person or thing that is separate from others. They do not mean that the person is unhappy: *I like being alone in the house.* ◊ *I'm going to London by myself next week.* ◊ *I want to finish this on my own* (= without anyone's help).
>
> **Lone/solitary/single** mean that there is only one person or thing there; **lone** and **solitary** may sometimes suggest that the speaker thinks the person involved is lonely: *a lone jogger in the park* ◊ *long, solitary walks.*
>
> **Lonely** (*AmE* also **lonesome**) means that you are alone and sad: *a lonely child* ◊ *Sam was very lonely when he first moved to New York.* It can also describe places or activities that make you feel lonely: *a lonely house.*

along /ə'lɒŋ; *AmE* ə'lɔːŋ/ *prep., adv.*
■ *prep.* **1** from one end to or towards the other end of sth: *They walked slowly along the road.* ◊ *I looked along the shelves for the book I needed.* **2** in a line that follows the side of sth long: *Houses had been built along both sides of the river.* **3** at a particular point on or beside sth long: *You'll find his office just along the corridor.*
■ *adv.* HELP For the special uses of **along** in phrasal verbs,

look at the entries for the verbs. For example **get along with sb** is in the phrasal verb section at **get**. **1** forward: *I was just walking along singing to myself.* ◊ *He pointed out various landmarks as we drove along.* **2** with sb: *We're going for a swim. Why don't you come along?* ◊ *I'll be along* (= I'll join you) *in a few minutes.* **3** towards a better state or position: *The book's coming along nicely.* IDM **along with sb/sth** in addition to sb/sth; in the same way as sb/sth: *She lost her job when the factory closed, along with hundreds of others.*

along·side /ə,lɒŋ'saɪd; *AmE* ə,lɔːŋ-/ *prep.* **1** next to or at the side of sth: *A police car pulled up alongside us.* **2** together with or at the same time as sth/sb: *Traditional beliefs still flourish alongside a modern urban lifestyle.* ◊
▶ **along·side** *adv.*: *Nick caught up with me and rode alongside.*

aloof /ə'luːf/ *adj.* [not usually before noun] ~ (**from sb/ sth**) not friendly or interested in other people: *He was a cold man, aloof and distant.* ▶ **aloof·ness** *noun* [U] IDM **keep/hold (yourself) aloof | remain/stand aloof** to not become involved in sth; to show no interest in people: *The Emperor kept himself aloof from the people.*

aloud /ə'laʊd/ *adv.* **1** in a voice that other people can hear: *The teacher listened to the children reading aloud.* ◊ *He read the letter aloud to us.* ◊ *'What am I going to do?' she wondered aloud.* ⇨ note at LOUD **2** in a loud voice: *She cried aloud in protest.* IDM see THINK *v.*

al·paca /æl'pækə/ *noun* **1** [C] a S American animal that is related to the LLAMA and has long hair **2** [U] a type of soft wool or fabric made from the hair of the alpaca, used especially for making expensive clothes: *an alpaca coat*

alpha /'ælfə/ *noun* the first letter of the Greek alphabet (A, α)

al·pha·bet /'ælfəbet/ *noun* a set of letters or symbols in a fixed order used for writing a language ORIGIN From *alpha* and *beta*, the first two letters of the Greek alphabet.

al·pha·bet·ic·al /,ælfə'betɪkl/ *adj.* according to the cor-rect order of the letters of the alphabet: *The names on the list are in alphabetical order.* ▶ **al·pha·bet·ic·al·ly** /-kli/ *adv.*: *arranged / listed / stored alphabetically*

al·pha·bet·ize (*BrE* also **-ise**) /'ælfəbətaɪz/ *verb* [VN] to arrange a list of words in alphabetical order

al·pine /'ælpaɪn/ *adj., noun*
■ *adj.* existing in or connected with high mountains, espe-cially the Alps in Central Europe
■ *noun* any plant that grows best on mountains

al·ready /ɔːl'redi/ *adv.* **1** before now or before a particu-lar time in the past: *'Lunch?' 'No thanks, I've already eaten.'* ◊ *We got there early but Mike had already left.* **2** used to express surprise that sth has happened so soon or so early: *Is it 10 o'clock already?* ◊ *You're not leaving already, are you?* **3** used to emphasize that a situation or problem exists: *I'm already late.* ◊ *There are far too many people already. We can't take any more.*

> **BRITISH / AMERICAN**
> **already / just / yet**
>
> **Already** and **yet** are usually used with the present perfect tense, but in *AmE* they can also be used with the simple past tense: *I already did it.* ◊ *Did you eat yet?*
>
> However, this is much more common in spoken English than in written and some Americans do not consider it acceptable, even in speech. The present perfect is more common in *AmE* and almost always used in *BrE*: *I've already done it.* ◊ *Have you eaten yet?*
>
> **Just** is mostly used with the perfect tenses in *BrE* and with the simple past in *AmE*: *I've just had some bad news.* (*BrE*) ◊ *I just got some bad news.* (*AmE*)

al·right /ɔːl'raɪt/ *adv.* (*informal*) = ALL RIGHT HELP Some people consider that this form should not be used in formal writing.

Al·sa·tian /æl'seɪʃn/ (*BrE*) (also ,**German** '**shepherd**

æ	ɑː	e	ɜː	ə	ɪ	iː	i	ɒ	ɔː	ʌ	ʊ	u	uː
cat	father	ten	bird	about	sit	see	many	got	saw	cup	put	actual	too
								(BrE)					

A

AmE, *BrE*) *noun* a large dog, often trained to help the police, to guard buildings or (especially in the US) to help blind people find their way

also /ˈɔːlsəʊ; *AmE* ˈɔːlsoʊ/ *adv.* (not used with negative verbs) in addition; too: *She's fluent in French and German. She also speaks a little Italian.* ◊ *rubella, also known as German measles* ◊ (*informal*) *I didn't like it that much. Also, it was much too expensive.* ◊ *Jake's father had also been a doctor* (= both Jake and his father were doctors). ◊ *She was **not only** extremely intelligent **but also** very practical.*

WHICH WORD?

also / as well / too

Also is more formal than **as well** and **too**, and it usually comes before the main verb or after *be*: *I went to New York last year, and I also spent some time in Washington.* In *BrE* it is not usually used at the end of a sentence. **Too** is much more common in spoken and informal English. It is usually used at the end of a sentence: *'I'm going home now.' 'I'll come too.'*. In *BrE* **as well** is used like **too**, but in *AmE* it sounds formal or old-fashioned.

When you want to add a second negative point in a negative sentence, use **not...either**: *She hasn't phoned and she hasn't written either.* If you are adding a negative point to a positive one, you can use **not...as well/too**: *You can have a burger, but you can't have fries as well.*

ˈalso-ran *noun* a person who is not successful, especially in a competition or an election or when compared with other people

altar /ˈɔːltə(r)/ *noun* a holy table in a church or TEMPLE: *the high altar* (= the most important one in a particular church) **IDM** **at/on the altar of sth** (*written*) because of sth that you think is worth suffering for: *He was willing to sacrifice his happiness on the altar of fame.*

alter /ˈɔːltə(r)/ *verb* **1** to become different; to make sb/sth different: [V] *Property prices did not significantly alter during 1999.* ◊ *He had altered so much I scarcely recognized him.* ◊ [VN] *It doesn't alter the way I feel.* ◊ *Nothing can alter the fact that we are to blame.* ◊ *The old landscape has been radically altered, severely damaging wildlife.* **2** [VN] to make changes to a piece of clothing so that it will fit you better ⇨ note at CHANGE

al·ter·ation /ˌɔːltəˈreɪʃn/ *noun* **1** [C] a change to sth that makes it different: *major/minor alterations* ◊ *They are making some **alterations** to the house.* ◊ *an **alteration in** the baby's heartbeat* **2** [U] the act of making a change to sth: *The dress will not need much alteration.*

al·ter·ca·tion /ˌɔːltəˈkeɪʃn; *AmE* -tərˈk-/ *noun* [C, U] (*formal*) a noisy argument or disagreement

alter ego /ˌæltər ˈiːɡəʊ; ˌɔːl-; *AmE* ˈiːɡoʊ/ *noun* (*pl.* **alter egos**) (from *Latin*) **1** a person whose personality is different from your own but who shows or acts as another side of your personality: *Superman's alter ego was Clark Kent.* **2** a close friend who is very like yourself

al·ter·nate *adj.*, *verb*, *noun*

■ *adj.* /ɔːlˈtɜːnət; *AmE* -ˈtɜːrn-/ [usually before noun] **1** (of two things) happening or following one after the other regularly: *alternate layers of fruit and whipped cream* **2** if sth happens on **alternate** days, nights, etc. it happens on one day, etc. but not on the next one: *John has to work on alternate Sundays.* **3** (*especially AmE*) = ALTERNATIVE ▶ **al·ter·nate·ly** *adv.*: *He felt alternately hot and cold with anxiety.*

■ *verb* /ˈɔːltəneɪt; *AmE* -tərn-/ **1** [VN] **~ A and B** | **~ A with B** to make things or people follow one after the other in a repeated pattern: *Alternate cubes of meat and slices of red pepper.* ◊ *Alternate cubes of meat with slices of red pepper.* **2** [V] **~ (with sth)** (of things or people) to follow one after the other in a repeated pattern: *alternating dark and pale stripes* ◊ *Dark stripes alternate with pale ones.* **3** [V] **~ between A and B** to keep changing from one thing to another and back again: *Her mood alternated between*

happiness and despair. ▶ **al·ter·na·tion** /ˌɔːltəˈneɪʃn; *AmE* -tərˈn-/ *noun* [U, C]: *the alternation of day and night* ■ *noun* /ˈɔːltɜːrnət; *AmE* -tərn-/ (*AmE*) a person who does a job for sb who is away

ˌalternating ˈcurrent *noun* [U, C] (*abbr.* **AC**) an electric current that changes its direction at regular intervals many times a second—compare DIRECT CURRENT

al·ter·na·tive /ɔːlˈtɜːnətɪv; *AmE* -ˈtɜːrn-/ *noun*, *adj.*

■ *noun* a thing that you can choose to do or have out of two or more possibilities: *You can be paid in cash weekly or by cheque monthly; those are the two alternatives.* ◊ *We had no alternative but to fire Gibson.* ◊ *There is a vegetarian alternative on the menu every day.*

■ *adj.* [only before noun] **1** (also **al·ter·nate** especially in *AmE*) that can be used instead of sth else: *an alternative method of doing sth* ◊ *Do you have an alternative solution to the problem?* **2** different from the usual or traditional way in which sth is done: *alternative comedy/lifestyles/values* ◊ *alternative energy* (= electricity or power that is produced using the energy from the sun, wind, water, etc.) ◊ *alternative medicine* (= any type of treatment that does not use the usual scientific methods of Western medicine, for example one using herbs instead of artificial drugs)

al·ter·na·tive·ly /ɔːlˈtɜːnətɪvli; *AmE* -ˈtɜːrn-/ *adv.* used to introduce a suggestion that is a second choice or possibility: *The agency will make travel arrangements for you. Alternatively, you can organize your own transport.*

al·ter·na·tor /ˈɔːltəneɪtə(r); *AmE* -tərn-/ *noun* a device, used especially in a car, that produces an ALTERNATING CURRENT

al·though (also *AmE informal* **altho**) /ɔːlˈðəʊ; *AmE* ɔːlˈðoʊ/ *conj.* **1** used for introducing a statement that makes the main statement in a sentence seem surprising **SYN** THOUGH: *Although the sun was shining it wasn't very warm.* ◊ *Although small, the kitchen is well designed.* **2** used to mean 'but' or 'however' when you are commenting on a statement: *I felt he was wrong, although I didn't say so at the time.*

WHICH WORD?

although / even though / though / however

You can use these words to show contrast between two clauses or two sentences. **Though** is used more in spoken English than in written. You can use **although**, **even though** and **though** at the beginning of a sentence or clause that has a verb. Notice where the commas go: *Although/Even though/Though everyone played well, we lost the game.* ◊ *We lost the game, although/even though/though everyone played well.*

You cannot use **even** on its own at the beginning of a sentence or clause instead of **although**, **even though** or **though**: ~~Even everyone played well, we lost the game.~~

Although and **though** can also mean 'but', like **however**, which is more formal. They cannot all go in the same place in a sentence. Notice where the commas go: *Everyone played well. However, we still lost the game/We still lost the game, however.* ◊ *Everyone played well. It should not be forgotten, however, that we still lost the game.* ◊ *Everyone played well, although/though we still lost the game.* ◊ *Everyone played well. We still lost the game , though.* Note that you cannot use **however** in a sentence that begins with **although**, **though** or **even though**: ~~Although everyone played well, however, we still lost the game.~~

---

al·tim·eter /ˈæltɪmiːtə(r); *AmE* ælˈtɪmətər/ *noun* an instrument for showing height above sea level, used especially in an aircraft

al·ti·tude /ˈæltɪtjuːd; *AmE* -tuːd/ *noun* **1** [C, usually sing.] the height above sea level: *We are flying **at an altitude of** 6000 metres.* ◊ *The plane made a dive to a lower altitude.* **2** [C, usually pl., U] a place that is high above sea level:

aɪ	aʊ	eɪ	əʊ	oʊ	ɔɪ	ɪə	eə	ʊə	j	w
my	now	say	go	go	boy	near	hair	pure	yes	wet
			(BrE)	(AmE)						

Snow leopards live at high altitudes. ◊ *The athletes trained at altitude in Mexico City.*

alto /ˈæltəʊ; *AmE* ˈæltoʊ/ *noun, adj.*

■ *noun* (*pl.* **-os**) **1** (also **con·tralto**) [C] a singing voice with a lower range than that of a SOPRANO; a person with an alto voice **2** [sing.] a musical part that is written for an alto voice—compare BARITONE, BASS, COUNTER-TENOR, TENOR

■ *adj.* [only before noun] (of a musical instrument) with the second highest range of notes in its group: *an alto saxophone*—compare SOPRANO, TENOR

al·together /ˌɔːltəˈɡeðə(r)/ *adv., noun*

■ *adv.* **1** (used to emphasize sth) completely; in every way: *The train went slower and slower until it stopped altogether.* ◊ *I don't altogether agree with you.* ◊ *I am not altogether happy about the decision.* ◊ *It was an altogether different situation.* **2** used to give a total number or amount: *You owe me £68 altogether.* **3** used to introduce a summary when you have mentioned a number of different things: *The food was good and we loved the atmosphere and the people. Altogether it was a great evening.*

■ *noun* **IDM** **in the alto'gether** (*old-fashioned, informal*) without any clothes on

> **WHICH WORD?**
> **altogether / all together**
>
> **Altogether** and **all together** do not mean the same thing. **Altogether** means 'in total' or (in *BrE*) 'completely': *We have invited fifty people altogether.* ◊ *I am not altogether convinced by this argument.*
>
> **All together** means 'all in one place' or 'all at once': *Can you put your books all together in this box?* ◊ *Let's sing 'Happy Birthday'. All together now!*

al·tru·ism /ˈæltruɪzəm/ *noun* [U] (*formal*) the fact of caring about the needs and happiness of other people more than your own ► **al·tru·is·tic** /ˌæltruˈɪstɪk/ *adj.*: *altruistic behaviour*

alu·min·ium /ˌæljəˈmɪniəm; ˌælə-/ (*BrE*) (*AmE* **alu·mi·num** /əˈluːmɪnəm/) *noun* [U] (*symb* Al) a chemical element. Aluminium is a light, silver-grey metal used for making pans, etc: *aluminium saucepans / window frames* ◊ *aluminium foil* (= for example, for wrapping food)

alumna /əˈlʌmnə/ *noun* (*pl.* **alum·nae** /-niː/) (*formal, especially AmE*) a former woman student of a school, college or university

alumni /əˈlʌmnaɪ/ *noun* [pl.] (*especially AmE*) the former male and female students of a school, college or university: *Harvard Alumni Association*

alum·nus /əˈlʌmnəs/ *noun* (*pl.* **alumni** /-naɪ/) (*formal, especially AmE*) a former male student of a school, college or university

al·veo·lar /ælˈviːələ(r); *BrE* also ˌælviˈəʊlə(r)/ *noun* (*phonetics*) a speech sound made with the tongue touching the part of the mouth behind the upper front teeth, for example /t/ or /d/ ► **al·veo·lar** *adj.*

al·ways /ˈɔːlweɪz/ *adv.* **1** at all times; on every occasion: *There's always somebody at home in the evenings.* ◊ *Always lock your car whenever you leave it.* ◊ *She always arrives at 7.30.* ◊ *The children always seem to be hungry.* ◊ *We're not always this busy!* **2** for a long time; since you can remember: *Pat has always loved gardening.* ◊ *This is the way we've always done it.* ◊ *This painting is very good—Ellie always was very good at art* (= so it is not very surprising). ◊ *Did you always want to be an actor?* **3** for all future time: *I'll always love you.* **4** if you say a person is **always doing** sth, or sth is **always happening**, you mean that they do it, or it happens, very often, and that this is annoying: *She's always criticizing me.* ◊ *That phone's always ringing.* **5** (**can/could always ...**, **there's always ...**) used to suggest a possible course of action: *If it doesn't fit, you can always take it back.* ◊ *If he can't help, there's always John.* **IDM** **as 'always** as usually happens or is expected: *As always, Polly was late for school.*—more at ONCE *adv.*

Alz·heim·er's dis·ease /ˈæltshaɪməz dɪziːz; *AmE* -ərz/

(also **Alz·heim·er's**) *noun* [U] a serious disease, especially affecting older people, that prevents the brain from functioning normally and causes loss of memory, loss of ability to speak clearly, etc.

AM /ˌeɪ ˈem/ *abbr.* amplitude magnification (one of the main methods of broadcasting sound by radio)

am /əm; *strong form* æm/ ⇨ BE

a.m. (*AmE* also **A.M.**) /ˌeɪ ˈem/ *abbr.* between midnight and midday (from Latin 'ante meridiem'): *It starts at 10 a.m.*—compare P.M.

amal·gam /əˈmælɡəm/ *noun* **1** [C, usually sing.] ~ (**of** sth) (*formal*) a mixture or combination of things: *The film script is an amalgam of all three books.* ◊ *an amalgam of several companies and organizations* **2** [U] (*technical*) a mixture of MERCURY and another metal, used especially to fill holes in teeth

amal·gam·ate /əˈmælɡəmeɪt/ *verb* ~ (**sth**) (**with/into** sth) **1** if two organizations **amalgamate** or **are amalgamated**, they join together to form one large organization: [V] *The company has now amalgamated with another local firm.* ◊ *A number of colleges have amalgamated to form the new university.* ◊ [VN] *The two companies were amalgamated into one.* ◊ *They decided to amalgamate the two schools.* **2** [VN] ~ **sth** (**into/with** sth) to put two or more things together so that they form one: *This information will be amalgamated with information obtained earlier* ► **amal·gam·ation** /əˌmælɡəˈmeɪʃn/ *noun* [U, C]: *the amalgamation of small farms into larger units*

amass /əˈmæs/ *verb* [VN] to collect sth, especially in large quantities: *He amassed a fortune from silver mining.*

ama·teur /ˈæmətə(r); -tʃə(r)/ *noun, adj.*

■ *noun* **1** a person who takes part in a sport or other activity for enjoyment or interest, not as a job: *The tournament is open to both amateurs and professionals.* **2** (usually *disapproving*) a person who is not skilled: *This work was done by a bunch of amateurs!* **OPP** PROFESSIONAL ► **ama·teur·ism** /ˈæmətərɪzəm; -tʃə-/ *noun* [U]: *New regulations on amateurism allow payment for promotional work.*

■ *adj.* **1** [usually before noun] doing sth for enjoyment or interest, not as a job: *an enthusiastic amateur photographer* **2** [usually before noun] done for enjoyment or interest, not as a job: *amateur athletics* **3** = AMATEURISH **OPP** PROFESSIONAL

amateur dra'matics *noun* [U] (*BrE*) the activity of producing and acting in plays for the theatre, by people who do it for enjoyment, not as a job

ama·teur·ish /ˈæmətərɪʃ; -tʃə-/ (also **ama·teur**) *adj.* (usually *disapproving*) not done or made well or with skill: *Detectives described the burglary as 'crude and amateurish'.*

amaze /əˈmeɪz/ *verb* to surprise sb very much: [VN] *Just the size of the place amazed her.* ◊ [VN **wh-**] *It never ceases to amaze me what some people will do for money.* ◊ *What amazes me is how long she managed to hide it from us.* ◊ [VN (**that**)] *It amazed her that he could be so calm at such a time.* [also VN **to** inf]

amazed /əˈmeɪzd/ *adj.* ~ (**at/by** sb/sth) | ~ (**how/that ...**) | ~ (**to see, find, learn,** etc.) very surprised: *an amazed silence* ◊ *I was amazed at her knowledge of French literature.* ◊ *We were amazed by his generosity.* ◊ *I was banging so loudly I'm amazed (that) they didn't hear me.* ◊ *She was amazed how little he had changed.* ◊ *We were amazed to find that no one was hurt.*

amaze·ment /əˈmeɪzmənt/ *noun* [U] a feeling of great surprise: *To my amazement, he was able to recite the whole poem from memory.* ◊ *She looked at him in amazement.*

amaz·ing /əˈmeɪzɪŋ/ *adj.* very surprising, especially in a way that makes you feel pleasure or admiration: *an amazing achievement / discovery / success / performance* ◊ *That's amazing, isn't it?* ◊ *It's amazing how quickly people adapt.* ► **amaz·ing·ly** *adv.*: *Amazingly, no one noticed.* ◊ *The meal was amazingly cheap.*

Amazon /ˈæməzən; *AmE* also -zɑːn/ *noun* **1** (in ancient Greek stories) a woman from a tribe of female WARRIORS (= soldiers) **2** (**amazon**) (*literary*) a tall strong woman

b	d	f	g	h	k	l	m	n	p	r
bad	did	fall	get	hat	cat	leg	man	now	pen	red

am·bas·sa·dor /æmˈbæsədə(r)/ *noun* an official who lives in a foreign country as the senior representative there of his or her own country: *the British Ambassador to Italy/in Rome* ◊ *a former ambassador to the UN* ◊ (*figurative*) *The best ambassadors for the sport are the players.* ▶ **am·bas·sa·dor·ial** /æmˌbæsəˈdɔːriəl/ *adj.*

amber /ˈæmbə(r)/ *noun* [U] **1** a hard clear yellowish-brown substance, used in making ornaments or jewellery: *amber beads* **2** a yellowish-brown colour: *The traffic lights were on amber.* ▶ **amber** *adj.*: *amber eyes/lights*

ambi- /ˈæmbi/ *prefix* (in nouns, adjectives and adverbs) referring to both of two: *ambidextrous* ◊ *ambivalent*

ambi·dex·trous /ˌæmbiˈdekstrəs/ *adj.* able to use the left hand or the right hand equally well

am·bi·ence (also **am·bi·ance**) /ˈæmbiəns/ *noun* [sing.] the character and atmosphere of a place: *the relaxed ambience of the city*

am·bi·ent /ˈæmbiənt/ *adj.* **1** [only before noun] (*technical*) relating to the surrounding area; on all sides: *ambient temperature/light/conditions* **2** (especially of music) creating a relaxed atmosphere: *a compilation of ambient electronic music* ◊ *soft, ambient lighting*

am·bi·gu·ity /ˌæmbiˈɡjuːəti/ *noun* (*pl.* **-ies**) **1** [U] the state of having more than one possible meaning: *Write clear definitions in order to avoid ambiguity.* ◊ *A lot of humour depends on ambiguity.* **2** [C] a word or statement that can be understood in more than one way: *There were several inconsistencies and ambiguities in her speech.* **3** [C, U] the state of being difficult to understand or explain because of involving many different aspects: *You must understand the ambiguity of my position.*

am·bigu·ous /æmˈbɪɡjuəs/ *adj.* **1** that can be understood in more than one way; having different meanings: *an ambiguous word/term/statement* ◊ *Her account was deliberately ambiguous.* **2** not clearly stated or defined: *His role has always been ambiguous.* [OPP] UNAMBIGUOUS ▶ **am·bigu·ous·ly** *adv.*: *an ambiguously worded agreement*

ambit /ˈæmbɪt/ *noun* [sing.] (*formal*) the range of the authority or influence of sth: *This case falls clearly within the ambit of the 1994 act.*

am·bi·tion /æmˈbɪʃn/ *noun* ~ (**to be/do sth**)| ~ (**of being/doing sth**) **1** [C] something that you want to do or achieve very much: *She never achieved her ambition of becoming a famous writer.* ◊ *His burning ambition was to study medicine.* ◊ *It had been her lifelong ambition.* ◊ *political/literary/sporting ambitions* **2** [U] the desire or determination to be successful, rich, powerful, etc: *motivated by personal ambition* ◊ *She was intelligent but suffered from a lack of ambition.*

am·bi·tious /æmˈbɪʃəs/ *adj.* **1** determined to be successful, rich, powerful, etc: *a fiercely ambitious young manager* ◊ *They were very ambitious for their children* (= they wanted them to be successful). **2** needing a lot of effort, money or time to succeed: *the government's ambitious plans for social reform* ◊ *Jogging every morning? That's very ambitious, isn't it?* [OPP] UNAMBITIOUS ▶ **am·bitious·ly** *adv.*

am·biva·lent /æmˈbɪvələnt/ *adj.* ~ (**about/towards sb/sth**) (*written*) having or showing both good and bad feelings about sb/sth: *She seems to feel ambivalent about her new job.* ◊ *He has an ambivalent attitude towards her.* ▶ **am·biva·lence** *noun* [U, sing.] ~ (**about/towards sb/sth**): *There was ambivalence among church members about women becoming priests.* ◊ *Many people feel some ambivalence towards television and its effect on our lives.*

amble /ˈæmbl/ *verb* [V+adv./prep.] to walk at a slow relaxed speed: *We ambled down to the beach.*

am·bu·lance /ˈæmbjələns/ *noun* a vehicle with special equipment, used for taking sick or injured people to a hospital: *the ambulance service* ◊ *ambulance staff* ◊ *Call an ambulance!*

ambulance chaser *noun* (*AmE, disapproving, informal*) a lawyer who earns money by encouraging people who have been in an accident to make claims in a court of law

ambulance man (also **ambulance worker**) *noun* (*BrE*) a person who drives an AMBULANCE and treats sick or injured people before they are taken to a hospital—compare PARAMEDIC

am·bush /ˈæmbʊʃ/ *noun, verb*
■ *noun* [C, U] the act of hiding and waiting for sb and then making a surprise attack on them: *Two soldiers were killed in a terrorist ambush.* ◊ *They were lying in ambush, waiting for the aid convoy.*
■ *verb* [VN] to make a surprise attack on sb/sth from a hidden position: *The guerrillas ambushed them near the bridge.* ◊ (*figurative*) *She was ambushed by reporters and cameramen.*

ameba (*AmE*) = AMOEBA

ameli·or·ate /əˈmiːliəreɪt/ *verb* [VN] (*formal*) to make sth better: *Steps have been taken to ameliorate the situation.* ▶ **ameli·or·ation** /əˌmiːliəˈreɪʃn/ *noun* [U]

amen (also **Amen**) /ɑːˈmen; eɪˈmen/ *exclamation, noun* a word used at the end of prayers and HYMNS, meaning 'may it be so': *We ask this through Christ our Lord, Amen.* ◊ *Amen to that* (= I certainly agree with that).

amen·able /əˈmiːnəbl/ *adj.* **1** ~ (**to sth**) (of people) easy to control; willing to be influenced by sb/sth: *They had three very amenable children.* ◊ *He seemed most amenable to my idea.* **2** ~ **to sth** (*formal*) that you can treat in a particular way: *'Hamlet' is the least amenable of all Shakespeare's plays to being summarized.*

amend /əˈmend/ *verb* [VN] to change a law, document, statement, etc. slightly in order to correct a mistake or to improve it: *He asked to see the amended version.*

amend·ment /əˈmendmənt/ *noun* **1** [C, U] ~ (**to sth**) a small change or improvement that is made to a law or a document; the process of changing a law or a document: *to introduce/propose/table an amendment* (= to suggest it) ◊ *She made several minor amendments to her essay.* ◊ *Parliament passed the bill without further amendment.* **2** (**Amendment**) [C] a statement of a change to the CONSTITUTION of the US: *The 19th Amendment gave women the right to vote.*

amends /əˈmendz/ *noun* [pl.] [IDM] **make amends (to sb) (for sth/for doing sth)** to do sth for sb in order to show that you are sorry for sth wrong or unfair that you have done

amen·ity /əˈmiːnəti; *AmE* əˈmenəti/ *noun* [usually pl.] (*pl.* **-ies**) a feature that makes a place pleasant, comfortable or easy to live in: *The campsite is close to all local amenities.* ◊ *Many of the houses lacked even basic amenities* (= for example, baths, showers, hot water).

Amer·asian /ˌæməˈreɪʃn; -ˈreɪʒn/ *noun* a person with one American and one Asian parent ▶ **Amer·asian** *adj.*

Ameri·can /əˈmerɪkən/ *noun, adj.*
■ *noun* **1** a person from America, especially the US—see also AFRICAN AMERICAN, NATIVE AMERICAN **2** (also **A'merican English**) the English language as spoken in the US
■ *adj.* of or connected with N or S America, especially the US: *I'm American.* ◊ *American culture/tourists* [IDM] **as A,merican as apple 'pie** used to say that sth is typical of America ⇨ note on page 37

Ameri·cana /əˌmerɪˈkɑːnə/ *noun* [pl.] things connected with the US that are thought to be typical of it

A,merican 'football *noun* [U] (*BrE*) (*AmE* **foot·ball**) an American game played by two teams of 11 players, using an OVAL ball which players kick, throw, or carry up and down the playing field. Teams try to put the ball over the other team's line.

A,merican 'Indian *noun* = NATIVE AMERICAN

Ameri·can·ism /əˈmerɪkənɪzəm/ *noun* **1** [C] a word, phrase or spelling that is typical of American English, used in another variety of English **2** [U] the essential quality of being American

Ameri·can·ize (*BrE* also **-ise**) /əˈmerɪkənaɪz/ *verb* [VN] to make sb/sth American in character ▶ **Ameri·can·iza·tion, -isa·tion** /əˌmerɪkənaɪˈzeɪʃn; *AmE* -nəˈz-/ *noun* [U]

Amer·in·dian /ˌæməˈrɪndiən/ *noun* (*old-fashioned*) = NATIVE AMERICAN

ameth·yst /ˈæməθɪst/ *noun* [C, U] a purple precious stone, used in making jewellery: *an amethyst ring*

s	t	v	z	ʃ	ʒ	tʃ	dʒ	θ	ð	ŋ
see	tea	van	zoo	shoe	vision	chain	jam	thin	this	sing

MORE ABOUT
America M**O**RE

The continent of **America** is divided into **North Amer-ica** and **South America**. The narrow region joining North and South America is **Central America**.

North America, which is a geographical term, consists of the **United States of America**, **Canada** and **Mexico**. **Latin America**, a cultural term, refers to the non-English speaking countries of Central and South America, where mainly Portuguese and Spanish are spoken. Mexico is part of Latin America.

The **United States of America** is usually shortened to the **USA**, the **US**, the **States** or simply **America**: *the US President* ◊ *Have you ever been to the States?* *She emigrated to America in 1995.* Many people from other parts of the continent dislike this use of **America** to mean just the US, but it is very common.

American is usually used to talk about somebody or something from the United States of America: *Do you have an American passport?* ◊ *American football* ◊ *I'm not American, I'm Canadian.* **Latin American** and **South American** are used to refer to other parts of the continent: *Latin American dance music* ◊ *Quite a lot of South Americans study here.*

---

ami·able /ˈeɪmiəbl/ *adj.* pleasant; friendly and easy to like: *an amiable tone of voice* ◊ *Her parents seemed very amiable.* ▶ **ami·abil·ity** /ˌeɪmiəˈbɪləti/ *noun* [U] **ami·ably** *adv.*: *'That's fine,' he replied amiably.*

am·ic·able /ˈæmɪkəbl/ *adj.* done or achieved in a polite or friendly way and without quarrelling: *an amicable relationship* ◊ *An amicable settlement was reached.* ▶ **am·ic·ably** *adv.*: *The policeman chatted amicably to the bystanders.*

amid /əˈmɪd/ (also **mid**, **amidst** /əˈmɪdst/) *prep.* (*formal*) **1** in the middle of or during sth, especially sth that causes excitement or fear: *He finished his speech amid tremendous applause.* ◊ *The firm collapsed amid allegations of fraud.* **2** surrounded by sth: *The hotel was in a beautiful position amid lemon groves.*

amid·ships /əˈmɪdʃɪps/ *adv.* (*technical*) in or near the middle part of a ship

amino acid /əˌmiːnəʊ ˈæsɪd; *AmE* -noʊ/ *noun* (*chemistry*) any of the substances which combine to form PROTEINS

amiss /əˈmɪs/ *adj.*, *adv.*
■ *adj.* [not before noun] wrong; not as it should be: *She sensed something was amiss and called the police.*
■ *adv.* **IDM** **not come/go a'miss** (*BrE*) to be useful or pleasant in a particular situation: *A little luck wouldn't go amiss right now!* **take sth a'miss** (*BrE*) to feel offended by sth, perhaps because you have understood it in the wrong way: *Would she take it amiss if I offered to help?*

amity /ˈæməti/ *noun* [U] (*rare, formal*) a friendly relationship between people or countries

am·meter /ˈæmiːtə(r)/ *noun* an instrument for measuring the strength of an electric current

ammo /ˈæməʊ; *AmE* ˈæmoʊ/ *noun* [U] (*old-fashioned, informal*) = AMMUNITION

am·mo·nia /əˈməʊniə; *AmE* əˈmoʊ-/ *noun* [U] (*symb* NH₃) a colourless gas with a strong smell; a clear liquid containing ammonia, used as a cleaning substance

am·mu·ni·tion /ˌæmjuˈnɪʃn/ *noun* **1** a supply of bullets, etc. to be fired from guns **2** information that can be used against another person in an argument: *The letter gave her all the ammunition she needed.*

am·nesia /æmˈniːziə; *AmE* -ˈniːʒə/ *noun* [U] a medical condition in which sb partly or completely loses their memory

am·nesty /ˈæmnəsti/ *noun* (*pl.* **-ies**) **1** [C usually sing, U] an official statement that allows people who have been put in prison for crimes against the state to go free: *The president granted a general amnesty for all political prisoners.* **2** [C, usually sing.] a period of time during which people can admit to a crime or give up weapons without

being punished: *2000 knives have been handed in during the month-long amnesty.*

am·nio·cen·tesis /ˌæmniəʊsenˈtiːsɪs; *AmE* -nioʊ-/ *noun* [U, sing.] a medical test that involves taking some liquid from a pregnant woman's WOMB in order to find out if the baby has particular illnesses or health problems

amoeba (*AmE* also **ameba**) /əˈmiːbə/ *noun* (*pl.* **amoe-bas** or **amoe·bae** /-biː/) a very small living creature that consists of only one cell

amok /əˈmɒk; *AmE* əˈmɑːk/ *adv.* **IDM** **run amok** to suddenly become very angry or excited and start behaving violently, especially in a public place

among /əˈmʌŋ/ (also **amongst** /əˈmʌŋst/) *prep.* **1** surrounded by sb/sth; in the middle of sb/sth: *a house among the trees* ◊ *They strolled among the crowds.* ◊ *I found the letter amongst his papers.* ◊ *It's OK, you're among friends now.* **2** being included or happening in groups of things or people: *A British woman was among the survivors.* ◊ *He was among the last to leave.* ◊ *This attitude is common among the under-25s.* ◊ *'What was wrong with the job?' 'Well, the pay wasn't good, among other things.'* ◊ *Discuss it among yourselves first* (= with each other). **3** used when you are dividing or choosing sth, and three or more people or things are involved: *They divided the money up among the children.*

amoral /ˌeɪˈmɒrəl; *AmE* -ˈmɔːr-; -ˈmɑːr-/ *adj.* not following any moral rules and not caring about right and wrong: *Guy was greedy, amoral and dishonest.*—compare IMMORAL, MORAL ▶ **amor·al·ity** /ˌeɪmɔːˈræləti/ *noun* [U]

am·or·ous /ˈæmərəs/ *adj.* showing sexual desire and love towards sb: *Mary rejected Tony's amorous advances.* ▶ **am·or·ous·ly** *adv.*

amorph·ous /əˈmɔːfəs; *AmE* -ˈmɔːrf-/ *adj.* [usually before noun] (*written*) having no definite shape, form or structure: *an amorphous mass of cells with no identity at all*

amort·ize (*BrE* also **-ise**) /əˈmɔːtaɪz; *AmE* ˈæmərtaɪz/ *verb* [VN] (*business*) to pay back a debt by making small regular payments over a period of time ▶ **amort-iza·tion**, **-isa·tion** /əˌmɔːtaɪˈzeɪʃn; *AmE* ˌæmərtəˈz-/ *noun* [U, C]

amount /əˈmaʊnt/ *noun*, *verb*
■ *noun* [C, U] **1** a sum of money: *The insurance company will refund any amount due to you.* ◊ *You will receive a bill for the full amount.* **2 ~ (of sth)** (used especially with uncountable nouns) a quantity of sth: *an amount of time/money/information* ◊ *We've had an enormous amount of help from people.* ◊ *The server is designed to store huge amounts of data.* **IDM** **any amount of sth** a large quantity of sth: *There's been any amount of research into the subject.* **no amount of sth** used for saying that sth will have no effect: *No amount of encouragement would make him jump into the pool.*
■ *verb* **PHRV** **a'mount to sth** **1** to add up to sth; to make sth as a total: *His earnings are said to amount to £300000 per annum.* ◊ *They gave me some help in the beginning but it did not amount to much* (= they did not give me much help). **2** to be equal to or the same as sth: *Her answer amounted to a complete refusal.* ◊ *Their actions amount to a breach of contract.* ◊ *We were jailed for a week—well, confined to quarters, but it amounted to the same thing.*

amp /æmp/ *noun* **1** (also **am·pere** /ˈæmpeə(r)/; *AmE* ˈæmpɪr; -per/) (*abbr.* **A**) the unit for measuring electric current: *a 13 amp fuse/plug* **2** (*informal*) = AMPLIFIER

am·per·sand /ˈæmpəsænd; *AmE* -pərs-/ *noun* the symbol (&) used to mean 'and': *She works for Bond & Green.*

am·phet·amine /æmˈfetəmiːn/ *noun* [C, U] a drug that makes you feel excited and full of energy. Amphetamines are sometimes taken illegally.

am·phib·ian /æmˈfɪbiən/ *noun* any animal that can live both on land and in water. Amphibians have cold blood and skin without scales. FROGS, TOADS and NEWTS are all amphibians.—compare REPTILE—picture on page A7

am·phibi·ous /æmˈfɪbiəs/ *adj.* **1** able to live both on land and in water **2** (of military operations) involving soldiers landing at a place from the sea **3** suitable for use on land or water: *amphibious vehicles*

amphi·theatre (*BrE*) (*AmE* **-ter**) /ˈæmfɪθɪətə(r)/; *AmE*

æ	ɑː	e	ɜː	ə	ɪ	iː	i	ɒ	ɔː	ʌ	ʊ	u	uː
cat	father	ten	bird	about	sit	see	many	got	saw	cup	put	actual	too
								(BrE)					

A

-θiːətər/ *noun* **1** a circular building without a roof and with rows of seats that rise in steps around an open space. Amphitheatres were used especially in ancient Greece and Rome for public entertainments. **2** a room, hall or theatre with rows of seats that rise in steps **3** (*technical*) an open space that is surrounded by high land in a circular slope

am·ple /ˈæmpl/ *adj.* **1** enough or more than enough: *ample opportunity/evidence/space/proof* ◊ *There was ample time to get to the airport.* ◊ *Ample free parking is available.* **2** (of a person's figure) large, often in an attractive way: *an ample bosom* ▶ **amply** /ˈæmpli/ *adv.*: *His efforts were amply rewarded.*

amp·li·fier /ˈæmplɪfaɪə(r)/ (also *informal* **amp**) *noun* an electrical device or piece of equipment that makes sounds or radio signals louder: *a 25 watt amplifier*

amp·lify /ˈæmplɪfaɪ/ *verb* (**amp·li·fies**, **amp·li·fy·ing**, **amp·li·fied**, **amp·li·fied**) **1** [VN] to increase sth in strength, especially sound: *to amplify a guitar/an electric current/a signal* **2** (*formal*) to add details to a story, statement, etc: [V] *She refused to amplify further.* ◊ [VN] *You may need to amplify this point.* ▶ **amp·li·fi·ca·tion** /ˌæmplɪfɪˈkeɪʃn/ *noun* [U]: *electronic amplification* ◊ *That comment needs some amplification.*

amp·li·tude /ˈæmplɪtjuːd; *AmE* -tuːd/ *noun* [U, C] (*physics*) the greatest distance that a wave, especially a sound or radio wave, VIBRATES (= moves up and down)—picture at WAVELENGTH

am·poule (*AmE* also **am·pule**) /ˈæmpuːl/ *noun* a small container, usually made of glass, containing a drug that will be used for an INJECTION

am·pu·tate /ˈæmpjuteɪt/ *verb* to cut off sb's arm, leg or finger in a medical operation: [VN] *He had to have both legs amputated.* ◊ [V] *They may have to amputate.* ▶ **am·pu·ta·tion** /ˌæmpjuˈteɪʃn/ *noun* [U, C]

am·pu·tee /ˌæmpjuˈtiː/ *noun* a person who has had an arm or a leg amputated

amu·let /ˈæmjʊlət/ *noun* a piece of jewellery that some people wear because they think it protects them from bad luck, illness, etc.

amuse /əˈmjuːz/ *verb* **1** [often passive] to make sb laugh or smile: [VN] *My funny drawings amused the kids.* ◊ *This will amuse you.* ◊ [VN to inf] *It amused him to think that they were probably talking about him at that very moment.* **2** [VN] to make time pass pleasantly for sb/yourself: *She suggested several ideas to help Laura amuse the twins.* ◊ *I'm sure I'll be able to amuse myself for a few hours.*

amused /əˈmjuːzd/ *adj.* **~ (at/by sth)|~ (to see, find, learn, etc.)** thinking that sb/sth is funny, so that you smile or laugh: *There was an amused look on the President's face.* ◊ *We were all amused at his stories.* ◊ *He was amused to see how seriously she took the game.* ◊ *Janet was not amused* (= she was annoyed or angry). **IDM** **keep sb a'mused** to give sb interesting things to do, or to entertain them so that they do not become bored: *Playing with water can keep children amused for hours.*

amuse·ment /əˈmjuːzmənt/ *noun* **1** [U] the feeling that you have when sth is funny or amusing, or it entertains you: *She could not hide her amusement at the way he was dancing.* ◊ *To my amusement he couldn't get the door open.* ◊ *Her eyes twinkled with amusement.* ◊ *His son was a continuous source of amusement and delight to him.* **2** [C, usually pl.] a game, an activity, etc. that provides entertainment and pleasure: *traditional seaside amusements including boats, go-karts and a funfair*

a'musement arcade (*BrE*) (also **ar·cade** *AmE, BrE*) *noun* a place where you can play games on machines which you use coins to operate

a'musement park *noun* a large park which has a lot of things that you can ride and play on and many different activities to enjoy

amus·ing /əˈmjuːzɪŋ/ *adj.* funny and enjoyable: *an amusing story/game/incident* ◊ *She writes very amusing letters.* ◊ *I didn't find the joke at all amusing.* ▶ **amus·ing·ly** *adv.*

an *indefinite article* ⇨ A

-an, -ana ⇨ -IAN, -IANA

ana·bol·ic ster·oid /ˌænəbɒlɪk ˈsterɔɪd; ˈstɪə-; *AmE* ˌænəbɑːlɪk ˈster-; ˈstɪr-/ *noun* an artificial HORMONE (= a chemical substance) that increases the size of the muscles. It is sometimes taken illegally by people who play sports.—see also STEROID

an·achron·ism /əˈnækrənɪzəm/ *noun* **1** a person, a custom or an idea that seems old-fashioned and does not belong to the present: *The monarchy is seen by many people as an anachronism in the modern world.* **2** something that is placed, for example in a book or play, in the wrong period of history: *The book is full of anachronisms which suggests there were parts rewritten in later centuries.* ▶ **ana·chron·is·tic** /əˌnækrəˈnɪstɪk/ *adj.*

ana·conda /ˌænəˈkɒndə; *AmE* -ˈkɑːn-/ *noun* a large S American snake of the BOA family, that crushes other animals to death before eating them

an·aemia (*BrE*) (*AmE* **an·e·mia**) /əˈniːmiə/ *noun* [U] a medical condition in which sb has too few red cells in their blood, making them look pale and feel weak

an·aemic (*BrE*) (*AmE* **an·emic**) /əˈniːmɪk/ *adj.* **1** suffering from anaemia: *She looks anaemic.* **2** (*written*) weak and not having much effect: *an anaemic performance*

an·aer·obic /ˌæneəˈrəʊbɪk; *AmE* ˌæneˈroʊ-/ *adj.* (*technical*) not needing OXYGEN: *anaerobic bacteria*

an·aes·the·sia /ˌænəsˈθiːziə/ (*BrE*) (*AmE* **an·es·the·sia** /-ˈθiːʒə/) *noun* [U] **1** the use of anaesthetic during medical operations **2** (*technical*) the state of being unable to feel anything, especially pain

an·aes·thet·ic (*BrE*) (*AmE* **an·es·thet·ic**) /ˌænəsˈθetɪk/ *noun, adj.*

▪ *noun* [C, U] a drug that makes a person or an animal unable to feel anything, especially pain, either in the whole body or in a part of the body: *How long will I be under the anaesthetic?* ◊ *They gave him a general anaesthetic* (= one that makes you lose consciousness). ◊ (a) *local anaesthetic* (= one that affects only a part of the body)

▪ *adj.* [only before noun] containing a substance that makes a person or an animal unable to feel pain in all or part of the body: *an anaesthetic drug/spray*

an·aes·the·tist (*BrE*) (*AmE* **an·es·the·tist**) /əˈniːsθətɪst/ *noun* a person who is trained to give anaesthetics to patients

an·aes·the·tize (*BrE* also **-ise**) (*especially BrE*) (*AmE* usually **an·es·the·tize**) /əˈniːsθətaɪz/ *verb* [VN] to make a person unable to feel pain, etc., especially by giving them an anaesthetic before a medical operation

ana·gram /ˈænəgræm/ *noun* a word or phrase that is made by arranging the letters of another word or phrase in a different order: *An anagram of 'Elvis' is 'lives'.*

anal /ˈeɪnl/ *adj.* **1** connected with the ANUS: *the anal region* **2** (also **anal-re'tentive**) (*disapproving*) caring too much about small details and about how things are organized ▶ **anal·ly** /-nəli/ *adv.*

an·al·gesia /ˌænəlˈdʒiːziə; *AmE* -ʒə/ *noun* [U] (*medical*) the loss of the ability to feel pain while still CONSCIOUS

an·al·gesic /ˌænəlˈdʒiːzɪk/ *noun* (*medical*) a substance that reduces pain **SYN** PAINKILLER: *Aspirin is a mild analgesic.* ▶ **an·al·gesic** *adj.*: *analgesic drugs/effects*

analo·gous /əˈnæləgəs/ *adj.* (*formal*) **~ (to/with sth)** similar in some way to another thing or situation and therefore able to be compared with it: *Sleep has often been thought of as being in some way analogous to death.*

ana·logue (*BrE*) (*AmE* **ana·log**) /ˈænəlɒg; *AmE* -lɔːg; -lɑːg/ *adj., noun*

▪ *adj.* (*technical*) **1** (of an electronic process) using a continuously changing range of physical quantities to measure or store data: *an analogue circuit/computer/signal* **2** (*BrE* also **ana·log**) (of a clock or watch) showing the time using hands on a DIAL and not with a display of numbers—compare DIGITAL

▪ *noun* (*formal* or *technical*) a thing that is similar to another thing: *Scientists are attempting to compare features of extinct animals with living analogues.*

ana·logy /əˈnælədʒi/ *noun* (*pl.* **-ies**) **1** [C] **~ (between A and B)|~ (with sth)** a comparison of one thing with another thing that has similar features; a feature that is similar: *The teacher* **drew an analogy** *between the human heart and a pump.* ◇ *There are no analogies with any previous legal cases.* **2** [U] the process of comparing one thing with another thing that has similar features in order to explain it: *learning* **by analogy**

,anal-re'tentive *adj.* = ANAL

ana·lyse (*BrE*) (*AmE* **ana·lyze**) /ˈænəlaɪz/ *verb* **1** to examine the nature or structure of sth, especially by separating it into its parts, in order to understand or explain it: [VN] *The job involves gathering and analysing data.* ◇ *He tried to analyse his feelings.* ◇ [Vwh-] *We need to analyse what went wrong.* **2** [VN] = PSYCHOANALYSE

ana·ly·sis /əˈnæləsɪs/ *noun* (*pl.* **ana·ly·ses** /-siːz/) **1** [U, C] the detailed study or examination of sth in order to understand more about it; the result of the study: *statistical analysis* ◇ *The book is an analysis of poverty and its causes.* **2** [U, C] a careful examination of a substance in order to find out what it consists of: *The blood samples are sent to the laboratory* **for analysis.** ◇ *You can ask for a chemical analysis of your tap water.* **3** [U] = PSYCHOANALYSIS: *In analysis the individual resolves difficult emotional conflicts.* **IDM** **in the ,final/,last a'nalysis** used to say what is most important after everything has been discussed, or considered: *In the final analysis, humour is a matter of individual interpretation.*

ana·lyst /ˈænəlɪst/ *noun* **1** a person whose job involves examining facts or materials in order to give an opinion on them: *a political/food analyst* ◇ *City analysts forecast pre-tax profits of £40 billion this year.*—see also SYSTEMS ANALYST **2** = PSYCHOANALYST

ana·lyt·ic·al /ˌænəˈlɪtɪkl/ (also **ana·lyt·ic** /ˌænəˈlɪtɪk/) *adj.* **1** using a logical method of thinking about sth in order to understand it, especially by looking at all the parts separately: *She has a clear analytical mind.* ◇ *an analytic approach to the problem* **2** using scientific analysis in order to find out about sth: *analytical methods of research* ◇ *analytical chemistry* ▶ **ana·lyt·ic·al·ly** /-kli/ *adv.*

ana·lyze (*AmE*) = ANALYSE

an·arch·ism /ˈænəkɪzəm; *AmE* ˈænərk-/ *noun* [U] the political belief that laws and governments are not necessary

an·arch·ist /ˈænəkɪst; *AmE* ˈænərk-/ *noun* a person who believes that laws and governments are not necessary ▶ **an·arch·is·tic** /ˌænəˈkɪstɪk; *AmE* ˌænərˈk-/ *adj.*

an·archy /ˈænəki; *AmE* ˈænərki/ *noun* [U] a situation in a country, an organization, etc. in which there is no government, order or control: *The overthrow of the military regime was followed by a period of anarchy.* ◇ *There was complete anarchy in the classroom when their usual teacher was away.* ▶ **an·arch·ic** /əˈnɑːkɪk; *AmE* əˈnɑːrkɪk/ (also *less frequent* **an·arch·ic·al** /-kl/) *adj.*

anath·ema /əˈnæθəmə/ *noun* [U, C, usually sing.] (*formal*) a thing or an idea which you hate because it is the opposite of what you believe: *Racial prejudice is (an) anathema to me.*

anato·mist /əˈnætəmɪst/ *noun* a scientist who studies anatomy

anat·omy /əˈnætəmi/ *noun* (*pl.* **-ies**) **1** [U] the scientific study of the structure of human or animal bodies: *the department of anatomy and physiology* **2** [C, U] the structure of an animal or a plant: *the anatomy of the horse* ◇ *human anatomy* **3** [C] (*humorous*) a person's body: *Various parts of his anatomy were clearly visible.* **4** [C] (*formal*) an examination of what sth is like, the way it works or why it happens: *an anatomy of the current recession* ▶ **ana·tom·ical** /ˌænəˈtɒmɪkl; *AmE* -ˈtɑːm-/ *adj.*: *anatomical diagrams* **ana·tom·ic·al·ly** /-kli/ *adv.*

-ance, -ence *suffix* (in nouns) the action or state of: *assistance* ◇ *confidence*

an·ces·tor /ˈænsestə(r)/ *noun* **1** a person in your family who lived a long time ago: *His ancestors had come to America from Ireland.* [SYN] FOREBEAR **2** an animal that lived in the past which a modern animal has developed from: *a reptile that was the common ancestor of lizards and turtles* **3** an early form of a machine which later

became more developed [SYN] FORERUNNER: *The ancestor of the modern bicycle was called a penny-farthing.*—compare DESCENDANT ▶ **an·ces·tral** /ænˈsestrəl/ *adj.*: *her ancestral home* (= that had belonged to her ancestors and that she had inherited from them)

an·ces·try /ˈænsestri/ *noun* [C usually sing, U] (*pl.* **-ies**) the family or the race of people that you are descended from: *to have Scottish ancestry* ◇ *He was able to trace his ancestry back over 1000 years.*

an·chor /ˈæŋkə(r)/ *noun, verb*

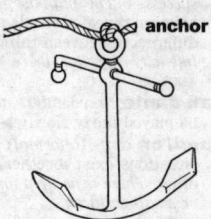
anchor

■ *noun* **1** a heavy metal object that is attached to a rope or chain and dropped over the side of a ship or boat to keep it in one place: **to drop anchor** ◇ *The ship lay* **at anchor** *two miles off the rocky coast.* ◇ *We* **weighed anchor** (= pulled it out of the water). **2** (*written*) a person or thing that gives sb a feeling of safety: *the anchor of the family* **3** (*especially AmE*) = ANCHORMAN, ANCHORWOMAN

■ *verb* **1** to lower an anchor from a boat or ship in order to prevent it from moving away: [V] *We anchored off the coast of Spain.* [also VN] **2** [VN] to fix sth firmly in position so that it cannot move: *Make sure the table is securely anchored.* **3** [VN] [usually passive] **~ sb/sth (in/to sth)** to firmly base sth on sth else: *Her novels are anchored in everyday experience.* **4** (*AmE*) to be the person who introduces reports or reads the news on television or radio: [VN] *She anchored the evening news for seven years.* [also V]

an·chor·age /ˈæŋkərɪdʒ/ *noun* [C, U] **1** a place where ships or boats can anchor **2** a place where sth can be fastened to sth else: *anchorage points for a baby's car seat*

an·chor·man /ˈæŋkəmæn; *AmE* -kɑrm-/, **an·chor·woman** /ˈæŋkəwʊmən; *AmE* -kɑrw-/ *nouns* (*pl.* **-men** /-men/) (**-women** /-wɪmɪn/) (also **an·chor** especially in *AmE*) a man or woman who presents a radio or television programme and introduces reports by other people

an·chovy /ˈæntʃəvi; *AmE* -tʃoʊvi/ *noun* [C, U] (*pl.* **-ies**) a small fish with a strong salty flavour: *a pizza topped with cheese and anchovies*

an·cient /ˈeɪnʃənt/ *adj.* **1** belonging to a period of history that is thousands of years in the past: *ancient history/civilization* ◇ *ancient Greece* **2** very old; having existed for a very long time: *an ancient oak tree* ◇ *ancient monuments* ◇ (*humorous*) *He's ancient—he must be at least fifty!* **3** (**the ancients**) *noun* [pl.] the people who lived in ancient times, especially the Egyptians, Greeks and Romans ▶ **an·cient·ly** *adv.* (*rare*): *The area where the market was anciently held* (= in ancient times).

an·cil·lary /ænˈsɪləri; *AmE* ˈænsəleri/ *adj.* **~ (to sth)** **1** providing necessary support to the main work or activities of an organization: *ancillary staff/services/equipment* ◇ *Ancillary workers in the health service such as cooks and cleaners are often badly paid.* **2** in addition to sth else but not as important: *ancillary rights under the law*

-ancy, -ency *suffix* (in nouns) the state or quality of: *expectancy* ◇ *complacency*

and /ənd; ən; also n, *especially after* t, d; *strong form* ænd/ *conj.* (used to connect words or parts of sentences) **1** also; in addition to: *bread and butter* ◇ *a table, two chairs and a desk* ◇ *Sue and I left early.* ◇ *Do it slowly and carefully.* ◇ *Can he read and write?* ◇ *I cooked lunch. And I made a cake.* (= you are emphasizing how much you have done) **HELP** When **and** is used in common phrases connecting two things or people that are closely linked, the determiner is not usually repeated before the second: *a knife and fork* ◇ *my father and mother*, but *a knife and a spoon* ◇ *my father and my uncle.* **2** added to; and: *5 and 5 makes 10.* ◇ *What's 47 and 16?* **HELP** When numbers (but not dates) are spoken, **and** is used between the hundreds and the figures that follow: *2264—two thousand, two hundred* **and** *sixty-four*, but *1964—nineteen sixty-four.* **3** then; following this: *She came in and took her coat off.* **4 go,**

A

come, try, stay, etc. ~ used before a verb instead of *to*, to show purpose: *Go and get me a pen please.* ◊ *I'll come and see you soon.* ◊ *We stopped and bought some bread.* **HELP** In this structure **try** can only be used in the infinitive or to tell somebody what to do. **5** used to introduce a comment or a question: *'We talked for hours.' 'And what did you decide?'* **6** as a result: *Miss another class and you'll fail.* **7** used between repeated words to show that sth is repeated or continuing: *He tried and tried but without success.* ◊ *The pain is getting worse and worse.* **8** used between repeated words to show that there are important differences between things or people of the same kind: *I like city life but there are cities and cities.*—see also AND/OR

an·dante /æn'dænteɪ/ *noun* (*music*) a piece of music to be played fairly slowly ▶ **an·dante** *adv.*, *adj.*

and/or *conj.* (*informal*) used when you say that two situations exist together, or as an ALTERNATIVE to each other: *There is no help for those with lots of luggage and/or small children.*

an·drogy·nous /æn'drɒdʒənəs; *AmE* -'drɑːdʒ-/ *adj.* having both male and female characteristics; looking neither strongly male nor strongly female

an·droid /'ændrɔɪd/ *noun* a ROBOT that looks like a real person

an·ec·dotal /ˌænɪk'dəʊtl; *AmE* -'doʊtl/ *adj.* based on anecdotes and possibly not true or accurate: *anecdotal evidence*

an·ec·dote /'ænɪkdəʊt; *AmE* -doʊt/ *noun* [C, U] **1** a short, interesting or amusing story about a real person or event: *amusing anecdotes about his brief career as an actor* **2** a personal account of an event: *This research is based on anecdote not fact.*

an·emia, an·emic (*AmE*) = ANAEMIA, ANAEMIC

anem·one /ə'nemənɪ/ *noun* a small plant with white, red, blue or purple flowers that are shaped like cups and have dark centres—see also SEA ANEMONE

an·es·the·sia, an·es·thet·ic, an·es·the·tist, an·es·the·tize (*AmE*) = ANAESTHESIA, ANAESTHETIC, ANAESTHETIST, ANAESTHETIZE

an·es·the·sio·logist /ˌænəsˌθiːziˈɒlədʒɪst; *AmE* -'ɑːlə-/ *noun* (*AmE*) a doctor who studies the use of anaesthetics

anew /ə'njuː; *AmE* ə'nuː/ *adv.* (*written*) if sb does sth **anew**, they do it again from the beginning or do it in a different way: *They started life anew thousands of miles away.*

angel /'eɪndʒl/ *noun* **1** a spirit who is believed to be a messenger or servant of God. Angels are often shown dressed in white, with wings.—see also GUARDIAN ANGEL **2** a person who is very good and kind; a child who behaves well: *John is no angel, believe me* (= he does not behave well). ◊ *Mary's children are little angels.* **3** (*informal*) used when you are talking to sb and you are grateful to them: *Thanks Dad, you're an angel.* ◊ *Be an angel and make me a cup of coffee.*

an·gel·ic /æn'dʒelɪk/ *adj.* good, kind or beautiful; like an angel: *an angelic smile*

an·gel·ica /æn'dʒelɪkə/ *noun* [U] pieces of a plant with a sweet smell, that have been boiled in sugar and are used to decorate cakes

an·gelus /'ændʒələs/ (also **the Angelus**) *noun* [sing.] (in the Roman Catholic Church) prayers said in the morning, at midday and in the evening; a bell rung when it is time for these prayers

anger /'æŋgə(r)/ *noun*, *verb*
- *noun* [U] ~ (at sb/sth) the strong feeling that you have when sth has happened that you think is bad and unfair: *He was filled with anger at the way he had been treated.* ◊ *Jan slammed her fist on the desk in anger.* ◊ *the growing anger and frustration of young unemployed people*
- *verb* [VN] [often passive] to make sb angry: *The question clearly angered him.*

an·gina /æn'dʒaɪnə/ *noun* [U] (*medical*) severe pain in the chest caused by a low supply of blood to the heart during exercise because the ARTERIES are partly blocked

angle /'æŋgl/ *noun*, *verb*
- *noun* **1** the space between two lines or surfaces that join, measured in degrees: *a 45° angle*—see also ACUTE ANGLE, OBTUSE ANGLE, RIGHT ANGLE, WIDE-ANGLE LENS **2** the direction that sth is leaning or pointing in when it is not in a vertical or horizontal line: *The tower of Pisa leans at an angle.* ◊ *The plane was coming in at a steep angle.* ◊ *His hair was sticking up at all angles.* **3** a position from which you look at sth: *The photo was taken from an unusual angle.* **4** a particular way of presenting or thinking about a situation, problem, etc: *We're looking for a new angle for our next advertising campaign.* ◊ *You can look at the issue from many different angles.* ◊ *The article concentrates on the human angle* (= the part that concerns people's emotions) *of the story.*
- *verb* **1** [VN] to move or place sth so that it is not straight or not directly facing sb/sth: *He angled his chair so that he could sit and watch her.* **2** [VN] to present information, a report, etc. from a particular point of view or for a particular audience: *The programme is angled towards younger viewers.* **3** (usually **go angling**) [V] to catch fish with a line and a hook **PHR V** **'angle for sth** to try to get a particular reaction or response from sb, without directly asking for what you want: *It was obvious she was angling for sympathy.*

'angle bracket *noun* [usually pl.] one of a pair of marks, < >, used to enclose words or figures to separate them from the text around them

ang·ler /'æŋglə(r)/ *noun* a person who catches fish (= goes angling) as a hobby—compare FISHERMAN

An·gli·can /'æŋglɪkən/ *noun* a member of the Church of England or of a Church connected with it in another country ▶ **An·gli·can** *adj.*: *the Anglican Church*

An·gli·cize (*BrE* also **-ise**) /'æŋglɪsaɪz/ *verb* [VN] to make sb/sth English in character: *Gutmann anglicized his name to Goodman.*

an·gling /'æŋglɪŋ/ *noun* [U] (*BrE*) the art or sport of catching fish with a fishing rod, usually in rivers and lakes rather than in the sea

Anglo- /'æŋgləʊ; *AmE* 'æŋgloʊ/ *combining form* (in nouns and adjectives) English or British: *Anglo-American* ◊ *Anglophile*

Anglo-'Catholic *noun* a member of the part of the Church of England that is most similar to the Roman Catholic Church in its beliefs and practices

Anglo·phile /'æŋgləʊfaɪl; *AmE* 'æŋgloʊ-/ *noun* a person who is not British but who likes Britain or British things very much

anglo·phone /'æŋgləʊfəʊn; *AmE* -oʊfoʊn/ *noun* a person who speaks English, especially in countries where English is not the only language that is spoken ▶ **anglo·phone** *adj.*: *anglophone communities*

Anglo-'Saxon *noun* **1** [C] a person whose ancestors were English **2** [C] an English person of the period before the Norman Conquest **3** [U] = OLD ENGLISH ▶ **Anglo-'Saxon** *adj.*: *Anglo-Saxon kings*

an·gora /æn'gɔːrə/ *noun* **1** [C] a breed of cat, goat or rabbit that has long smooth hair **2** [U] a type of soft wool or fabric made from the hair of the angora goat or rabbit: *an angora sweater*

an·gos·tura /ˌæŋgə'stjʊərə; *AmE* -'stʊrə/ *noun* [U] a bitter liquid, flavoured with the bark of a tropical tree, that is used to give flavour to alcoholic drinks

angry /'æŋgri/ *adj.* (**an·grier**, **an·gri·est**) **HELP** You can also use **more angry** and **most angry**. **1** ~ (with/at sb) (at/about sth) having strong feelings about sth that you dislike very much or about an unfair situation: *Please don't be angry with me. It wasn't my fault.* ◊ *The passengers grew angry about the delay.* ◊ *He felt angry at the injustice of the situation.* ◊ *Thousands of angry demonstrators filled the square.* ◊ *The comments provoked an angry response from union leaders.* ◊ *I was very angry with myself for making such a stupid mistake.* ◊ *Her behaviour really made me angry.* **2** (*literary*) (of the sea or the sky) dark and STORMY **3** (*literary*) (of a wound) red and infected ▶ **an·grily** /-əli/ *adv.*: *Some senators reacted angrily to the President's remarks.* ◊ *He swore angrily.*

angst /æŋst/ *noun* [U] (from *German*) a feeling of anxiety

s	t	v	z	ʃ	ʒ	tʃ	dʒ	θ	ð	ŋ
see	tea	van	zoo	shoe	vision	chain	jam	thin	this	sing

and worry about a situation, or about your life: *songs full of teenage angst*

an·guish /ˈæŋgwɪʃ/ *noun* [U] (*formal*) severe pain, mental suffering or unhappiness: *He groaned in anguish.* ◊ *Tears of anguish filled her eyes.* ▶ **an·guished** *adj.*: *anguished cries* ◊ *an anguished letter from her prison cell*

an·gu·lar /ˈæŋgjələ(r)/ *adj.* **1** (*written*) (of a person) thin and without much flesh so that the bones are noticeable: *an angular face* ◊ *a tall angular woman* **2** having angles or sharp corners: *an abstract design of large angular shapes*

ani·mal /ˈænɪml/ *noun, adj.*
■ *noun* **1** a creature that is not a bird, a fish, a reptile, an insect or a human being: *the animals and birds of South America* ◊ *a small furry animal* ◊ *Fish oils are less saturated than animal fats.* ◊ *domestic animals such as dogs and cats* **2** any living being that is not a plant or a human: *the animal kingdom* ◊ *This product has not been tested on animals.* ◊ *animal rights* (= the rights of animals to be treated well by human beings) **3** any living creature, including human beings: *Humans are the only animals to have developed speech.*—compare VEGETABLE **4** a person who behaves in a cruel or unpleasant way, or who is very dirty: *The person who did this is an animal, a brute.* **5** a particular type of person, thing, organization, etc: *She's not a political animal.* ◊ *The government which followed the election was a very different animal.*—see also DUMB ANIMALS, HIGHER ANIMALS
■ *adj.* [only before noun] relating to the physical needs and basic feelings of people: *animal desires/passion/instincts* ◊ *animal magnetism* (= a quality in sb that other people find attractive, usually in a sexual way)

ˌanimal ˈhusbandry *noun* [U] (*technical*) farming that involves keeping animals to produce food

an·im·ate *verb, adj.*
■ *verb* /ˈænɪmeɪt/ [VN] **1** to make sth more lively or full of energy: *A smile suddenly animated her face.* **2** [usually passive] to make models, toys, etc. seem to move in a film/movie by rapidly showing slightly different pictures of them in a series, one after another
■ *adj.* /ˈænɪmət/ (*formal*) living; having life: *animate beings* OPP INANIMATE

ani·mated /ˈænɪmeɪtɪd/ *adj.* **1** full of interest and energy SYN LIVELY: *an animated discussion/conversation* ◊ *Her face suddenly became animated.* **2** (of pictures, drawings, etc. in a film) made to look as if they are moving: *animated cartoons/graphics/models* ▶ **ani·mated·ly** *adv.*: *People were talking animatedly.*

ani·ma·tion /ˌænɪˈmeɪʃn/ *noun* **1** [U] energy and enthusiasm in the way you look, behave or speak: *His face was drained of all colour and animation.*—see also SUSPENDED ANIMATION **2** [U] the process of making films/movies, videos and computer games in which drawings or models of people and animals seem to move: *computer/cartoon animation* **3** [C] a film/movie in which drawings of people and animals seem to move: *The electronic dictionary included some animations.*

ani·ma·tor /ˈænɪmeɪtə(r)/ *noun* a person who makes animated films

ani·mos·ity /ˌænɪˈmɒsəti; *AmE* -ˈmɑːs-/ *noun* [U, C] (*pl.* **-ies**) ~ (**toward(s) sb/sth**)|~ (**between A and B**) a strong feeling of opposition, anger or hatred SYN HOSTILITY: *He felt no animosity towards his critics.* ◊ *personal animosities between members of the two groups*

ani·mus /ˈænɪməs/ *noun* [U, sing.] ~ (**against sb/sth**) (*formal*) a strong feeling of opposition, anger or hatred

anise /ˈænɪs/ *noun* [U] a plant with seeds that smell sweet

ani·seed /ˈænəsiːd/ *noun* [U] the dried seeds of the anise plant, used to give flavour to alcoholic drinks and sweets/candy

ankle /ˈæŋkl/ *noun* the joint connecting the foot to the leg: *to sprain/break your ankle* ◊ *My ankles have swollen.* ◊ *We found ourselves ankle-deep in water.* ◊ *ankle socks/boots* (= that cover the ankle)—picture at BODY

ank·let /ˈæŋklət/ *noun* a piece of jewellery worn around the ankle—picture at JEWELLERY

annals /ˈænlz/ *noun* [pl.] **1** an official record of events or activities year by year; historical records: *His deeds went down in the annals of British history.* **2** used in the title of academic JOURNALS: *Annals of Science, vol viii*

an·neal /əˈniːl/ *verb* [VN] (*technical*) to heat metal or glass and allow it to cool slowly, in order to make it harder

annex /əˈneks/ *verb* [VN] to take control of a country, region, etc., especially by force: *Germany annexed Austria in 1938.* ▶ **an·nex·ation** /ˌænekˈseɪʃn/ *noun* [U, C]

an·nexe (*BrE*) (also **annex** *AmE, BrE*) /ˈæneks/ *noun* **1** a building that is added to, or is near, a larger one and that provides extra living or work space: *Our rooms were in the annexe.* **2** (*formal*) an extra section of a document

an·ni·hi·late /əˈnaɪəleɪt/ *verb* [VN] **1** to destroy sb/sth completely: *The human race has enough weapons to annihilate itself.* **2** to defeat sb/sth completely: *She annihilated her opponent, who failed to win a single game.* ▶ **an·ni·hi·la·tion** /əˌnaɪəˈleɪʃn/ *noun* [U]: *the annihilation of the whole human race*

an·ni·ver·sary /ˌænɪˈvɜːsəri; *AmE* -ˈvɜːrs-/ *noun* (*pl.* **-ies**) a date that is an exact number of years after the date of an important or special event: *on the anniversary of his wife's death* ◊ *to celebrate your wedding anniversary* ◊ *the theatre's 25th anniversary celebrations*

an·no·tate /ˈænəteɪt/ *verb* [VN] to add notes to a book or text, giving explanations or comments ▶ **an·no·ta·tion** /ˌænəˈteɪʃn/ *noun* [C, U]: *It will be published with annotations and index.* **an·no·tated** *adj.*: *an annotated edition*

an·nounce /əˈnaʊns/ *verb* **1** ~ (**sth**) (**to sb**) to tell people sth officially, especially about a decision, plans, etc: [VN] *They haven't formally announced their engagement yet.* ◊ *The government yesterday announced to the media plans to create a million new jobs.* ◊ (*figurative*) *A ring at the doorbell announced the late arrival of Jack.* HELP You cannot 'announce somebody something': ~~They announced us their decision.~~ ◊ [VthatWe are pleased to announce that all five candidates were successful.* ◊ [VNthat] *It was announced that new speed restrictions would be introduced.* [also Vwh-] **2** to give information about sth in a public place, especially through a LOUDSPEAKER: [VN] *Has our flight been announced yet?* ◊ [Vthat] *They announced that the flight would be delayed.* [also Vspeech] **3** to say sth in a loud and/or serious way: [Vspeech] *'I've given up smoking,' she announced.* ◊ [Vthat] *She announced that she'd given up smoking.* [also VN] **4** [VN] ~ **yourself/sb** to tell sb your name or sb else's name when you or they arrive at a place: *Would you announce the guests as they arrive?* (= call out their names, for example at a formal party) **5** [VN] to introduce, or give information about, a programme on radio or television

an·nounce·ment /əˈnaʊnsmənt/ *noun* **1** [C] a spoken or written statement that informs people about sth: *Today's announcement of a peace agreement came after weeks of discussion.* ◊ *Announcements of births, marriages and deaths appear in some newspapers.* **2** [U] the act of publicly informing people about sth: *Announcement of the verdict was accompanied by shouts and cheers.*

an·noun·cer /əˈnaʊnsə(r)/ *noun* **1** a person who introduces, or gives information about, programmes on radio or television **2** a person who gives information about sth in a station, an airport, etc., especially through a LOUD-SPEAKER **3** (*AmE*) = PRESENTER

annoy /əˈnɔɪ/ *verb* **1** to make sb slightly angry SYN IRRITATE: [VN] *His constant joking was beginning to annoy her.* ◊ *It really annoys me when people forget to say thank you.* ◊ [VNtoinf] *It annoys me to see him getting ahead of me.* **2** [VN] to make sb uncomfortable or unable to relax SYN BOTHER: *He swatted a fly that was annoying him.*

an·noy·ance /əˈnɔɪəns/ *noun* **1** [U] the feeling of being slightly angry: *He could not conceal his annoyance at being interrupted.* ◊ *Much to our annoyance, they decided not to come after all.* ◊ *She stamped her foot in annoyance.* **2** [C] something that makes you slightly angry

annoy·ed /əˈnɔɪd/ *adj.* [not usually before noun] ~ (**with sb**) (**at/about sth**)|~ (**that …**)|~ **to find, see, etc.** slightly angry: *He was beginning to get very annoyed with me*

	æ	ɑː	e	ɜː	ə	ɪ	iː		i	ɒ	ɔː	ʌ	ʊ	u	uː
	cat	father	ten	bird	about	sit	see		many	got	saw	cup	put	actual	too
										(BrE)					

about my carelessness. ◊ *I was **annoyed with myself** for giving in so easily.* ◊ *I bet she was annoyed at having to write it out again.* ◊ *I was annoyed that they hadn't turned up.* ◊ *He was annoyed to find himself going red.*

annoy·ing /ə'nɔɪɪŋ/ *adj.* making sb feel slightly angry SYN IRRITATING: *This interruption is very annoying.* ◊ *Her most annoying habit was eating with her mouth open.* ▶ **an·noy·ing·ly** *adv.*

an·nual /'ænjuəl/ *adj., noun*
■ *adj.* [usually before noun] **1** happening or done once every year: *an annual meeting/event/report* **2** relating to a period of one year: *an annual income/subscription/budget* ◊ *an average annual growth rate of 8%* ◊ *annual rainfall*—compare BIANNUAL
■ *noun* **1** a book, especially one for children, that is published once a year, with the same title each time, but different contents **2** any plant that grows and dies within one year or season—compare BIENNIAL *n.*, PERENNIAL *n.*

an·nu·al·ized (*BrE* also **-ised**) /'ænjuəlaɪzd/ *adj.* (*technical*) calculated for a period of a year but based on the amounts for a shorter period

an·nu·al·ly /'ænjuəli/ *adv.* once a year: *The exhibition is held annually.*

an·nu·ity /ə'njuːəti; *AmE* -'nuː-/ *noun* (*pl.* **-ies**) **1** a fixed amount of money paid to sb each year, usually for the rest of their life **2** a type of insurance that pays a fixed amount of money to sb each year

annul /ə'nʌl/ *verb* (**-ll-**) [VN] to state officially that sth is no longer legally valid: *Their marriage was annulled after just six months.* ▶ **an·nul·ment** *noun* [C, U]

an·nun·ci·ation /ə,nʌnsi'eɪʃn/ *noun* [sing.] **(the Annunciation)** (in the Christian religion) the occasion when Mary was told that she was to be the mother of Christ, celebrated on 25 March

anode /'ænəʊd; *AmE* 'ænoʊd/ *noun* (*technical*) the point (or TERMINAL) in a battery or other electrical device where the electric current enters.—compare CATHODE

ano·dyne /'ænədaɪn/ *adj.* (*formal*) unlikely to cause disagreement or offend anyone; not expressing strong opinions SYN BLAND

anoint /ə'nɔɪnt/ *verb* ~ **sb/sth** (**with sth**) to put oil or water on sb's head as part of a religious ceremony: [VN] *The priest anointed her with oil.* [also VN-N]

anom·al·ous /ə'nɒmələs; *AmE* -'nɑːm-/ *adj.* (*formal*) different from what is normal or expected: *He is in an anomalous position as the only part-time worker in the firm.* ▶ **anom·al·ous·ly** *adv.*

anom·aly /ə'nɒməli; *AmE* ə'nɑːm-/ *noun* (*pl.* **-ies**) ~ (**in sth**) a thing, situation, etc. that is different from what is normal or expected: *the many anomalies in the tax system* ◊ *the apparent anomaly that those who produced the wealth, the workers, were the poorest*

anon /ə'nɒn; *AmE* ə'nɑːn/ *adv.* (*old-fashioned* or *literary*) soon: *See you anon.*

anon. /ə'nɒn; *AmE* ə'nɑːn/ *abbr.* ANONYMOUS

ano·nym·ity /,ænə'nɪməti/ *noun* [U] the state of remaining unknown to most other people: *Names of people in the documentary were changed to preserve anonymity.* ◊ *the anonymity of the big city* (= where people do not know each other) ◊ (*especially AmE*) *He agreed to give an interview on condition of anonymity* (= if his name was not mentioned).

an·onym·ous /ə'nɒnɪməs; *AmE* ə'nɑːn-/ *adj.* **1** (of a person) with a name that is not known or that is not made public: *an anonymous donor/caller/buyer/benefactor/source* ◊ *The money was donated by a local businessman who wishes to remain anonymous.* **2** (*abbr.* **anon.**) written, given, made, etc. by sb who does not want their name to be known or made public: *an anonymous letter/gift* **3** (*written*) without any unusual or interesting features: *long stretches of dull and anonymous countryside* ▶ **an·onym·ous·ly** *adv.*

ano·rak /'ænəræk/ *noun* **1** (*especially BrE*) a short coat with a HOOD that is worn as protection against rain, wind and cold—picture on page A5 **2** (*BrE, informal*) a person who spends so much of their time learning facts or

collecting things that most other people think they are boring

an·or·exia /,ænə'reksiə/ (also **an·or·exia ner·vosa** /,ænə,reksiə nɜː'vəʊsə; *AmE* nɜːr'voʊsə/) *noun* [U] an emotional disorder, especially affecting young women, in which there is an ABNORMAL fear of being fat, causing the person to stop eating, leading to dangerous weight loss—compare BULIMIA

an·or·exic /,ænə'reksɪk/ *noun* a person who is suffering from anorexia ▶ **an·or·exic** *adj.*: *She's anorexic.*

an·other /ə'nʌðə(r)/ *det., pron.* **1** one more; an extra thing or person: *Would you like another drink?* ◊ *'Finished?' 'No, I've got another three questions to do.'* ◊ *We've still got another* (= a further) *forty miles to go.* ◊ *'It's a bill.' 'Oh no, not another!'* ◊ *I got another of those calls yesterday.*—compare OTHER HELP Another can be followed by a singular noun, by **of** and a plural noun, or by a number and a plural noun. **2** different; a different person or thing: *Let's do it another time.* ◊ *We need another computer* (= a new one). ◊ *We can try that—but whether it'll work is **another matter**.* ◊ *The room's too small. Let's see if they've got **another one**.* ◊ *I don't like this room. I'm going to ask for another.* **3** a person or thing of a very similar type: *She's going to be another Kate Moss* (= as famous as her). ◊ *There'll never be another like him.*—see also ONE ANOTHER IDM **of one kind, sort, etc. or a'nother** used when you are referring to various types of a thing, without saying exactly what you mean: *We've all got problems of one kind or another.*—more at ONE

an·swer /'ɑːnsə(r); *AmE* 'æn-/ *noun, verb*
■ *noun* ~ (**to sth**) **1** something that you say, write or do to react to a question or situation: *I can't easily give an answer to your question.* ◊ *Have you had an answer to your letter?* ◊ *As if **in answer** to our prayers, she offered to lend us £10000.* ◊ *I rang the bell, but there was no answer.* ◊ *She had no answer to the accusations.* **2** something that you write or say in reply to a question in a test, an exam, an exercise, etc.; the correct reply to a question in a test, etc: *Write your answers on the sheet provided.* ◊ *Do you know the answer to question 12?* (= the right one) **3** a solution to a problem: *There is no easy answer.* ◊ *This could be the answer to all our problems.* ◊ *The obvious answer would be to cancel the party.* **4** a person or thing from one place that may be thought to be as good as a famous person or thing from another place: *The new theme park will be Britain's answer to Disneyland.* IDM **have/know all the 'answers** (*informal, often disapproving*) to be confident that you know sth, especially when you actually do not: *He thinks he knows all the answers.*—more at NO *exclam.*
■ *verb* **1** to say, write or do sth as a reaction to a question or situation SYN REPLY: [V] *I repeated the question, but she didn't answer.* ◊ [VN] *You haven't **answered my question**.* ◊ *to answer a letter/an advertisement* ◊ *to **answer the phone*** (= to pick up the phone when it rings) ◊ *to **answer the door*** (= to open the door when sb knocks/rings) ◊ *My prayers have been answered* (= I have got what I wanted). ◊ *He refused to answer the charges against him.* ◊ *Come on, answer me! Where were you?* ◊ *He answered me with a smile.* ◊ [V speech] *'I'd prefer to walk,' she answered.* ◊ [VN speech] *'I'd prefer to walk,' she answered him.* ◊ [V that] *She answered that she would prefer to walk.* ◊ [VNN] *Answer me this: how did they know we were here?* [also VN that] **2** [VN] (*formal*) to be suitable for sth; to match sth: *Does this answer your requirements?* IDM **answer to the name of sth** (especially of a pet animal) to be called sth—more at DESCRIPTION PHRV ,**answer 'back** to defend yourself against criticism: *He was given the chance to answer back in a radio interview.* ,**answer 'back**|,**answer sb 'back** to speak rudely to sb in authority, especially when they are criticizing you or telling you to do sth: *Don't answer back!* ◊ *Stop answering your mother back!* '**answer for sth 1** to accept responsibility or blame for sth: *You will have to answer for your behaviour one day.* ◊ *This government **has a lot to answer for*** (= is responsible for a lot of bad things). **2** to promise that sb has a particular quality or can be relied on to do sth:

aɪ	aʊ	eɪ	əʊ	oʊ	ɔɪ	ɪə	eə	ʊə	j	w
my	now	say	go	go	boy	near	hair	pure	yes	wet
			(BrE)	(AmE)						

I can answer for her honesty. **'answer for sb** (usually in negative sentences) to say that sb else will do sth or have a particular opinion: *I agree, but I can't answer for my colleagues.* **'answer to sb (for sth)** to have to explain your actions or decisions to sb: *All sales clerks answer to the store manager.*

WHICH WORD? ②
answer / reply

Verbs

Answer and **reply** are the most common verbs used for speaking or writing as a reaction to a question, letter, etc.

Note that you **answer** a person, question or letter, not *answer to* them, but you **reply to** somebody or something: *I'm writing to answer your questions.* ◊ *I'm writing to reply to your questions.* ◊ *I'm writing to answer to your questions.*

Although **answer** can be used with an object, it often sounds more natural without one: *I knocked on the door but nobody answered.* **Reply** is often used with the actual words spoken: *'I won't let you down,' he replied.*

Respond is less common and more formal: *The directors were unwilling to respond to questions.*

You can only **answer** a door or a phone.

— see also REJOIN, RETORT

Nouns

Note the phrases **in answer to** and **in reply to**: *I'm writing in answer to your letter.*

— see also RESPONSE, REJOINDER, RETORT

---

an·swer·able /ˈɑːnsərəbl; *AmE* ˈæn-/ *adj.* **1** [not before noun] ~ **to sb (for sth)** having to explain your actions to sb in authority over you: *She was a free agent, answerable to no one for her behaviour.* **2** [not before noun] ~ **(for sth)** responsible for sth and ready to accept punishment or criticism for it: *Ministers must be made answerable for their decisions.* **3** (of a question) that can be answered

'answering machine (*BrE* also **an·swer·phone** /ˈɑːnsəfəʊn; *AmE* ˈænsərfoʊn/) *noun* a machine which you connect to your telephone to answer your calls and record any message left by the person calling: *I called several times, but only got the answering machine.*

an·swer·phone /ˈɑːnsəfəʊn; *AmE* ˈænsərfoʊn/ *noun* (*BrE*) = ANSWERING MACHINE: *She left her name and number on his answerphone.*

ant /ænt/ *noun* a small insect that lives in highly organized groups. There are many types of ant: *an ants' nest* ◊ *an ant colony*—picture on page A7—see also ANTHILL **IDM** **have 'ants in your pants** (*informal*) to be very excited or impatient about sth and unable to stay still

-ant, -ent *suffix* **1** (in adjectives) that is or does sth: *different* ◊ *significant* **2** (in nouns) a person or thing that: *inhabitant* ◊ *deterrent*

ant·acid /ænt'æsɪd/ *noun* a medicine that prevents or corrects ACIDITY, especially in the stomach

an·tag·on·ism /æn'tægənɪzəm/ *noun* [U, pl.] ~ **(to/toward(s) sb/sth)|** ~ **(between A and B)** (*written*) feelings of hatred and opposition: *The antagonism he felt towards his old enemy was still very strong.* ◊ *the racial antagonisms in society*

an·tag·on·ist /æn'tægənɪst/ *noun* (*formal*) a person who strongly opposes sb/sth **SYN** OPPONENT

an·tag·on·is·tic /æn,tægə'nɪstɪk/ *adj.* ~ **(to/toward(s) sb/sth)** (*formal*) showing or feeling opposition **SYN** HOSTILE

an·tag·on·ize (*BrE* also **-ise**) /æn'tægənaɪz/ *verb* [VN] to do sth to make sb angry with you: *Not wishing to antagonize her further, he said no more.*

Ant·arc·tic /æn'tɑːktɪk; *AmE* -'tɑːrk-/ *noun* [sing.] (**the Antarctic**) the regions of the world around the South Pole ▶ **Ant·arc·tic** *adj.* [only before noun]: *Antarctic explorers*—compare ARCTIC

the An·tarc·tic 'Circle *noun* [sing.] the line of LATITUDE 66° 30′ South—compare ARCTIC—picture on page A7

ante /ˈænti/ *noun* [sing.] **IDM** **raise/up the 'ante** to increase the level of sth, especially demands or sums of money: *His ex-wife has upped the ante in her alimony suit against him.*

ante- /ˈænti/ *prefix* (in nouns, adjectives and verbs) before; in front of: *ante-room* ◊ *antenatal* ◊ *antedate*—compare POST-, PRE-

ant·eat·er /ˈæntiːtə(r)/ *noun* an animal with a long nose and tongue that eats ANTS

ante·ce·dent /,æntɪ'siːdnt/ *noun, adj.*
■ *noun* **1** [C] (*formal*) a thing or an event that exists or comes before another, and may have influenced it **2** (**antecedents**) [pl.] (*formal*) the people in sb's family who lived a long time ago **SYN** ANCESTORS **3** [C] (*grammar*) a word or phrase to which the following word, especially a pronoun, refers: *In 'He grabbed the ball and threw it in the air', 'ball' is the antecedent of 'it'.*
■ *adj.* (*formal*) previous: *antecedent events*

ante·cham·ber /ˈæntɪtʃeɪmbə(r)/ *noun* (*formal*) = ANTE-ROOM

ante·date /,ænti'deɪt/ *verb* [VN] = PRE-DATE

ante·di·lu·vian /,æntɪdɪ'luːviən/ *adj.* (*formal* or *humorous*) very old-fashioned

ante·lope /ˈæntɪləʊp; *AmE* -loʊp/ *noun* (*pl.* **ante·lope** or **ante·lopes**) an African animal like a deer, that runs very fast. There are many types of antelope.

ante·natal /,ænti'neɪtl/ (*BrE*) (also **pre·natal** *AmE, BrE*) *adj.* [only before noun] relating to the medical care given to pregnant women: *antenatal care/classes/screening* ◊ *an antenatal clinic*—compare POSTNATAL

an·tenna /æn'tenə/ *noun* **1** (*pl.* **an·ten·nae** /-niː/) either of the two long thin parts on the heads of some insects and some animals that live in shells, used to feel and touch things with **SYN** FEELER: (*figurative*) *The minister was praised for his acute political antennae* (= ability to understand complicated political situations).—picture on page A7 **2** (*pl.* **an·ten·nas** or **an·ten·nae**) (*especially AmE*) = AERIAL: *radio antennas*—picture at HOUSE

an·ter·ior /æn'tɪəriə(r); *AmE* -'tɪr-/ *adj.* [only before noun] (*technical*) (of a part of the body) at or near the front **OPP** POSTERIOR

'ante·room (also *formal* **ante·cham·ber**) *noun* a room where people can wait before entering a larger room, especially in a palace or an important public building

an·them /ˈænθəm/ *noun* **1** a song which has a special importance for a country or an organization and is sung on special occasions: *The European anthem was played at the opening and closing ceremonies.*—see also NATIONAL ANTHEM **2** a short religious song from a CHOIR (= a group of singers), often with an ORGAN

an·ther /ˈænθə(r)/ *noun* (*technical*) the part of a flower at the top of a STAMEN that produces POLLEN

ant·hill /ˈænthɪl/ *noun* a pile of earth formed by ANTS over their nests

an·thol·ogy /æn'θɒlədʒi; *AmE* -'θɑː-/ *noun* (*pl.* **-ies**) a collection of poems, stories, letters, etc. that are written by different people and published together in a book

an·thra·cite /ˈænθrəsaɪt/ *noun* [U] a very hard type of coal that burns slowly without producing a lot of smoke or flames

an·thrax /ˈænθræks/ *noun* [U] a serious disease that affects sheep and cows and sometimes people, and can cause death

an·thro·po- /ˈænθrəpəʊ; *AmE* -poʊ/ *combining form* (in nouns, adjectives and adverbs) connected with human beings: *anthropology*

an·thro·poid /ˈænθrəpɔɪd/ *adj., noun* (*technical*)
■ *adj.* (of an APE) looking like a human
■ *noun* any type of APE that is similar to a human

an·thro·polo·gist /,ænθrə'pɒlədʒɪst; *AmE* -'pɑːl-/ *noun* a person who studies anthropology

an·thro·pol·ogy /,ænθrə'pɒlədʒi; *AmE* -'pɑːl-/ *noun* [U] the study of the human race, especially of its origins,

A

development, customs and beliefs ▶ **an·thro·po·logic·al** /ˌænθrəpəˈlɒdʒɪkl; *AmE* -ˈlɑːdʒ-/ *adj.*

an·thro·po·morph·ic /ˌænθrəpəˈmɔːfɪk; *AmE* -ˈmɔːrf-/ *adj.* (of beliefs or ideas) treating gods, animals or objects as if they had human qualities ▶ **an·thro·po·morph·ism** /ˌænθrəpəˈmɔːfɪzəm; *AmE* -ˈmɔːrf-/ *noun* [U]

anti /ˈænti/ *prep.* (*informal*) if sb is **anti** sb/sth, they do not like or agree with that person or thing

anti- /ˈænti/ *prefix* (in nouns and adjectives) **1** opposed to; against: *anti-tank weapons* ◇ *antisocial*—compare PRO- **2** the opposite of: *anti-hero* ◇ *anticlimax* **3** preventing: *antifreeze*

anti-ˈaircraft *adj.* [only before noun] designed to destroy enemy aircraft: *anti-aircraft fire/guns/missiles*

anti·bi·ot·ic /ˌæntibaɪˈɒtɪk; *AmE* -ˈɑːtɪk/ *noun* [usually pl.] a substance, for example PENICILLIN, that can destroy or prevent the growth of bacteria and cure infections: *The doctor put her on antibiotics* (= told her to take them). ▶ **anti·bi·ot·ic** *adj.*: *an antibiotic drug* ◇ *effective antibiotic treatment*

anti·body /ˈæntibɒdi; *AmE* -bɑːdi/ *noun* (*pl.* **-ies**) a substance that the body produces in the blood to fight disease

anti-ˈchoice *adj.* (*AmE, disapproving*) against giving women the right to have an ABORTION—compare PRO-CHOICE

Anti·christ /ˈæntikraɪst/ (usually **the Antichrist**) *noun* [sing.] (in Christianity) the devil; Christ's greatest enemy

an·tici·pate /ænˈtɪsɪpeɪt/ *verb* **1** to expect sth: [VN] *We don't anticipate any major problems.* ◇ [V-ing] *They anticipate moving to bigger premises by the end of the year.* ◇ [VN-ing] *I don't anticipate it being a problem.* ◇ [Vthat] *We anticipate that sales will rise next year.* ◇ [VNthat] *It is anticipated that inflation will stabilize at 3%.* **2** to see what might happen in the future and take action to prepare for it: [VN] *We need someone who can anticipate and respond to changes in the fashion industry.* ◇ [Vwh-] *Try and anticipate what the interviewers will ask.* [alsoVthat] **3** to think with pleasure and excitement about sth that is going to happen: [VN] *We eagerly anticipated the day we would leave school.* [alsoV-ing, VN-ing] **4** (*formal*) to do sth before it can be done by sb else: [VN] *When Scott reached the South Pole he found that Amundsen had anticipated him.* [alsoVN-ing] ▶ **an·tici·pa·tory** /ænˌtɪsɪˈpeɪtəri; *AmE* ænˈtɪsəpətɔːri/ *adj.* (*formal*): *a fast anticipatory movement by the goalkeeper*

an·tici·pa·tion /ænˌtɪsɪˈpeɪʃn/ *noun* [U] **1** the fact of seeing that sth might happen in the future and perhaps doing sth about it now: *He bought extra food in anticipation of more people coming than he'd invited.* **2** a feeling of excitement about sth (usually sth good) that is going to happen: *happy/eager/excited anticipation* ◇ *The courtroom was filled with anticipation.*

anti·cli·max /ˌæntiˈklaɪmæks/ *noun* [C, U] a situation that is disappointing because it happens at the end of sth that was much more exciting, or because it is not as exciting as you expected: *Travelling in Europe was something of an anticlimax after the years he'd spent in Africa.* ◇ *a sense/feeling of anticlimax*—compare CLIMAX ▶ **anti·cli·mac·tic** /ˌæntiklaɪˈmæktɪk/ *adj.*

anti·clock·wise /ˌæntiˈklɒkwaɪz; *AmE* -ˈklɑːk-/ (*BrE*) (*AmE* **coun·ter·clock·wise**) *adv., adj.* in the opposite direction to the movement of the hands of a clock: *Turn the key anticlockwise/in an anticlockwise direction.* OPP CLOCKWISE

anti·coagu·lant /ˌæntikəʊˈægjələnt; *AmE* -koʊ-/ *noun* (*medical*) a substance that stops the blood from becoming thick and forming CLOTS

antics /ˈæntɪks/ *noun* [pl.] **1** behaviour which is silly and funny in a way that people usually like: *The bank staff got up to all sorts of antics to raise money for charity.* **2** behaviour which is ridiculous or dangerous

anti·cyc·lone /ˌæntiˈsaɪkləʊn; *AmE* -ˈkloʊn/ *noun* an area of high air pressure that produces calm weather conditions with clear skies—compare DEPRESSION

anti·depres·sant /ˌæntidɪˈpresnt/ *noun* a drug used to treat DEPRESSION ▶ **anti·depres·sant** *adj.* [only before noun]: *antidepressant drugs*

anti·dote /ˈæntidəʊt; *AmE* -doʊt/ *noun* ~ **(to sth) 1** a substance that controls the effects of a poison or disease: *There is no known antidote to the poison produced by the fish.* **2** anything that takes away the effects of sth unpleasant: *A Mediterranean cruise was the perfect antidote to a long cold winter.*

anti·freeze /ˈæntifriːz/ *noun* [U] a chemical that is added to the water in the RADIATOR of cars and other vehicles to stop it from freezing

anti·gen /ˈæntɪdʒən/ *noun* (*medical*) a substance that enters the body and can cause disease. The body then usually produces ANTIBODIES to fight the antigens.

ˈanti-hero *noun* the main character in a story, but one who does not have the qualities of a typical HERO, and is either more like an ordinary person or is very unpleasant

anti·his·ta·mine /ˌæntiˈhɪstəmiːn/ *noun* [C, U] a drug used to treat ALLERGIES, especially HAY FEVER. There are several types of antihistamine: *antihistamine cream/injections/shots*

ˈanti-lock *adj.* [only before noun] **anti-lock** BRAKES stop the wheels of a vehicle locking if you have to stop suddenly, and so make the vehicle easier to control: *an anti-lock braking system or ABS*

an·tim·ony /ˈæntɪməni; *AmE* -moʊni/ *noun* [U] (*symb* **Sb**) a chemical element. Antimony is a silver-white metal that breaks easily, used especially in making ALLOYS.

an·tip·athy /ænˈtɪpəθi/ *noun* [U, C, usually sing.] (*pl.* **-ies**) ~ **(between A and B)**| ~ **(to/toward(s) sb/sth)** (*formal*) a strong feeling of dislike: *personal/mutual/general antipathy* ◇ *a growing antipathy towards the idea* ▶ **anti·path·et·ic** /ˌæntɪpəˈθetɪk/ *adj.* ~ **(to sb/sth)**: *antipathetic to change*

anti-person'nel *adj.* [only before noun] (of weapons) designed to kill or injure people, not to destroy buildings or vehicles, etc.

anti·per·spir·ant /ˌæntiˈpɜːspərənt; *AmE* -ˈpɜːrs-/ *noun* [U, C] a substance that people use, especially under their arms, to prevent or reduce sweat—see also DEODORANT

An·tipo·des /ænˈtɪpədiːz/ *noun* (**the Antipodes**) [pl.] (*BrE*) a way of referring to Australia and New Zealand, often used in a humorous way ▶ **An·tipo·dean** /ˌæntɪpəˈdiːən/ *adj.*

anti·quar·ian /ˌæntɪˈkweəriən; *AmE* -ˈkwer-/ *adj., noun*
■ *adj.* [usually before noun] connected with the study, collection or sale of valuable old objects, especially books: *an antiquarian bookshop*
■ *noun* (also *less frequent* **anti·quary** /ˈæntɪkwəri; *AmE* -kweri/) a person who studies, collects or sells old and valuable objects

anti·quated /ˈæntɪkweɪtɪd/ *adj.* (usually *disapproving*) (of things or ideas) old-fashioned and no longer suitable for modern conditions

an·tique /ænˈtiːk/ *adj., noun*
■ *adj.* [usually before noun] (of furniture, jewellery, etc.) old and often valuable: *an antique mahogany desk*
■ *noun* an object such as a piece of furniture that is old and often valuable: *Priceless antiques were destroyed in the fire.* ◇ *an antique shop* (= one that sells antiques) ◇ *an antique dealer* (= a person who sells antiques)

an·tiquity /ænˈtɪkwəti/ *noun* (*pl.* **-ies**) **1** [U] the ancient past, especially the times of the Greeks and Romans: *The statue was brought to Rome in antiquity.* **2** [U] the state of being very old or ancient: *A number of the monuments are of considerable antiquity.* **3** [C, usually pl.] an object from ancient times: *Egyptian/Roman antiquities*

anti-Semitism /ˌænti ˈsemətɪzəm/ *noun* [U] hatred of Jews; unfair treatment of Jews ▶ **anti-Semitic** /ˌænti səˈmɪtɪk/ *adj.*: *anti-Semitic propaganda* **anti-Semite** /ˌænti ˈsiːmaɪt/ *noun*: *He was a notorious anti-Semite.*

anti·sep·tic /ˌæntiˈseptɪk/ *noun, adj.*
■ *noun* [C, U] a substance that helps to prevent infection in wounds by killing bacteria SYN DISINFECTANT
■ *adj.* **1** able to prevent infection: *antiseptic cream/lotion/wipes* ◇ *Essential oils have powerful antiseptic properties.* **2** very clean and free from bacteria SYN STERILE: *Cover the burn with an antiseptic dressing.*

s	t	v	z	ʃ	ʒ	tʃ	dʒ	θ	ð	ŋ
see	tea	van	zoo	shoe	vision	chain	jam	thin	this	sing

anti·social /ˌæntiˈsəʊʃl; AmE -ˈsoʊʃl/ adj. **1** harmful or annoying to other people, or to society in general: antisocial behaviour ◊ antisocial tendencies / activities / habits **2** not wanting to spend time with other people: They'll think you're being antisocial if you don't go.—compare SOCIABLE ⇨ note at UNSOCIABLE

an·tith·e·sis /ænˈtɪθəsɪs/ noun [C, U] (pl. an·tith·e·ses /ænˈtɪθəsiːz/) (formal) **1** the opposite of sth: Love is the antithesis of selfishness. ◊ Students finishing their education at 16 is the very antithesis of what society needs. **2** a contrast between two things: There is an antithesis between the needs of the state and the needs of the people. ▶ an·ti·thet·ic·al /ˌæntɪˈθetɪkl/ adj.

ant·ler /ˈæntlə(r)/ noun [usually pl.] one of the two horns that grow on the head of male deer—picture on page A6

ant·onym /ˈæntənɪm/ noun (technical) a word that means the opposite of another word: 'Old' has two possible antonyms: 'young' and 'new'.—compare SYNONYM

antsy /ˈæntsi/ adj. (AmE, informal) impatient; not able to keep still

anus /ˈeɪnəs/ noun (anatomy) the opening in a person's bottom through which solid waste leaves the body—see also ANAL—picture at BODY

anvil /ˈænvɪl/ noun an iron block on which a BLACKSMITH puts hot pieces of metal before shaping them with a hammer

anx·iety /æŋˈzaɪəti/ noun (pl. -ies) **1** [U] ~ (about/over sth) the state of feeling nervous or worried that sth bad is going to happen: acute / intense / deep anxiety ◊ Some hospital patients experience high levels of anxiety. **2** [C] a worry or fear about sth: If you're worried about your health, share your anxieties with your doctor. **3** [U] ~ to do sth|~ for sth a strong feeling of wanting to do sth or of wanting sth to happen: the candidate's anxiety to win the vote ◊ the people's anxiety for the war to end

anx·ious /ˈæŋkʃəs/ adj. **1** ~ (about sth)|~ (for sb) feeling worried or nervous: He seemed anxious about the meeting. ◊ Parents are naturally anxious for their children. **2** causing anxiety; showing anxiety: There were a few anxious moments in the baseball game. ◊ an anxious look / face / expression **3** ~ to do sth|~ for sth|~ for sb to do sth|~ that ... wanting sth very much: She was anxious to finish school and get a job. ◊ There are plenty of graduates anxious for work. ◊ He was anxious not to be misunderstood. ◊ I'm anxious for her to do as little as possible. ◊ She was anxious that he should meet her father. ⇨ note at WORRIED ▶ anx·ious·ly adv.: to ask / look / wait anxiously ◊ Residents are anxiously awaiting a decision.

any /ˈeni/ det., pron., adv.
■ det. **1** used with uncountable or plural nouns in negative sentences and questions, after if or whether, and after some verbs such as prevent, ban, avoid, etc. to refer to an amount or a number of sth, however large or small: I didn't eat any meat. ◊ Are there any stamps in that drawer? ◊ I've got hardly any money. ◊ You can't go out without any shoes. ◊ He forbids any talking in class. ◊ She asked if we had any questions. **HELP** In positive sentences some is usually used instead of any: I've got some paper if you want it. It is also used in questions that expect a positive answer: Would you like some milk in your tea? **2** used with singular countable nouns to refer to one of a number of things or people, when it does not matter which one: Take any book you like. ◊ Any colour will do. ◊ Any teacher will tell you that students learn at different rates.—see also IN ANY CASE at CASE n., IN ANY EVENT at EVENT, AT ANY RATE at RATE n. **3** not just ~ used to show that sb/sth is special: It isn't just any day—it's my birthday!
■ pron. **1** used in negative sentences and in questions and after if or whether to refer to an amount or a number, however large or small: We need some more paint; there isn't any left. ◊ I need some stamps. Are there any in your bag? ◊ Please let me know how many are coming, if any. ◊ She spent hardly any of the money. ◊ He returned home without any of the others. **HELP** In positive sentences some is usually used instead of any. It is also used in questions that expect a positive reply: I've got plenty of paper—would you like some? **2** one or more of a number of people or things, especially when it does not matter which: I'll take any you don't want. ◊ 'Which colour do you want?' 'Any of them will do.' **IDM** sb isn't having any (of it) (informal) sb is not interested or does not agree: I suggested sharing the cost, but he wasn't having any of it.
■ adv. **1** used to emphasize an adjective or adverb in negative sentences or questions, meaning 'at all': He wasn't any good at French. ◊ I can't run any faster. ◊ Is your father feeling any better? ◊ I don't want any more. ◊ If you don't tell them, nobody will be any the wiser. **2** (AmE, informal) used at the end of a negative sentence to mean 'at all': That won't hurt you any.

any·body /ˈenibɒdi; AmE -bʌdi; -baːdi/ pron. = ANYONE

any·how /ˈenihaʊ/ adv. **1** = ANYWAY **2** in a careless way; not arranged in an order: She piled the papers in a heap on her desk, just anyhow.

any 'more (BrE) (also any·more AmE, BrE) adv. often used at the end of negative sentences and at the end of questions, to mean 'any longer': She doesn't live here any more. ◊ Why doesn't he speak to me any more? ◊ Next year she won't have to go out to work any more. **HELP** Do not use 'no more' with this meaning: ~~She doesn't live here no more.~~

any·one /ˈeniwʌn/ (also any·body) pron. **1** used instead of someone in negative sentences and in questions after if/whether, and after verbs such as prevent, ban, avoid: Is anyone there? ◊ Does anyone else want to come? ◊ Did anyone see you? ◊ Hardly anyone came. ◊ I forbid anyone to touch that clock. **HELP** The difference between anyone and someone is the same as the difference between any and some. Look at the notes there. **2** any person at all; it does not matter who: Anybody can see that it's wrong. ◊ The exercises are so simple that almost anyone can do them. **3** (in negative sentences) an important person: She wasn't anybody before she got that job.

any·place /ˈenipleɪs/ adv. (AmE) = ANYWHERE

any·thing /ˈeniθɪŋ/ pron. **1** used instead of something in negative sentences and in questions; after if/whether; and after verbs such as prevent, ban, avoid: Would you like anything else? ◊ There's never anything worth watching on TV. ◊ If you remember anything at all, please let us know. ◊ We hope to prevent anything unpleasant from happening. **HELP** The difference between anything and something is the same as the difference between any and some. Look at the notes there. **2** any thing at all, when it does not matter which: I'm so hungry, I'll eat anything. **3** any thing of importance: Is there anything (= any truth) in these rumours? **IDM** anything but definitely not: The hotel was anything but cheap. ◊ It wasn't cheap. Anything but. as happy, quick, etc. as anything (informal) very happy, quick, etc: I felt as pleased as anything. like 'anything (BrE, informal) very much: They're always slagging me off like anything. not anything like sb (informal) not at all like; completely different from: He isn't anything like my first boss. not anything like used to emphasize that sth is not as good, not enough, etc: The book wasn't anything like as good as her first one. not for 'anything (informal) definitely not: I wouldn't give it up for anything. or anything (spoken) or another thing of a similar type: If you want to call a meeting or anything, just let me know.

'any time (BrE) (also any·time AmE, BrE) adv. at a time that is not fixed: Call me any time. **IDM** anytime 'soon (AmE) used in negative sentences and questions to refer to the near future: Do you think she'll be back anytime soon?

any·way /ˈeniweɪ/ (also any·how) adv. **1** used when adding sth to support an idea or argument **SYN** BESIDES: It's too expensive and anyway the colour doesn't suit you. ◊ It's too late now, anyway. **2** in spite of sth: The water was cold but I took a shower anyway. ◊ I'm afraid we can't come, but thanks for the invitation anyway. **3** used when changing the subject of a conversation, ending the conversation, or returning to a subject: Anyway, let's forget about that for the moment. ◊ Anyway, I'd better go now— I'll see you tomorrow. ◊ Anyhow, as I was saying ... **4** used

æ	ɑː	e	ɜː	ə	ɪ	iː	i	ɒ	ɔː	ʌ	ʊ	u	uː
cat	father	ten	bird	about	sit	see	many	got	saw	cup	put	actual	too
								(BrE)					

A

to correct or slightly change what you have said: *She works in a bank. She did when I last saw her, anyway.*

any·where /'eniweə(r); *AmE* -wer/ (*AmE* also **any-place**) *adv.* **1** used in negative sentences and in questions instead of *somewhere: I can't see it anywhere.* ◊ *Did you go anywhere interesting?* ◊ *Many of these animals are not found anywhere else.* ◊ *He's never been anywhere outside Britain.* **HELP** The difference between **anywhere** and **somewhere** is the same as the difference between **any** and **some**. Look at the notes there. **2** in, at or to any place, when it does not matter where: *Put the box down anywhere.* ◊ *An accident can happen anywhere.* ▶ **anywhere** *pron.: I don't have anywhere to stay.* ◊ *Do you know anywhere I can buy a second-hand computer?*

AOB /ˌeɪ əʊ 'biː; *AmE* oʊ/ *abbr.* any other business (the things that are discussed at the end of an official meeting that are not on the AGENDA)

aorta /eɪ'ɔːtə; *AmE* eɪ'ɔːrtə/ *noun* (*anatomy*) the main ARTERY that carries blood from the heart to the rest of the body

apace /ə'peɪs/ *adv.* (*formal*) at a fast speed; quickly: *to continue/grow/proceed/develop apace*

apart /ə'pɑːt; *AmE* ə'pɑːrt/ *adv.* **1** separated by a distance, of space or time: *The two houses stood 500 metres apart.* ◊ *Their birthdays are only three days apart.* ◊ (*figurative*) *The two sides in the talks are still a long way apart* (= are far from reaching an agreement). **2** not together; separate or separately: *We're living apart now.* ◊ *Over the years, Rosie and I had drifted apart.* ◊ *She keeps herself apart from other people.* ◊ *I can't* **tell** *the twins* **apart** (= see the difference between them). **3** into pieces: *The whole thing just came apart in my hands.* ◊ *We had to* **take** *the engine* **apart***.* ◊ *When his wife died, his world fell apart.* **4** used to say that sb/sth is not included in what you are talking about: *Colin apart, not one of them seems suitable for the job.* **IDM** see JOKE *v.*, POLE *n.*, RIP *v.*, WORLD

a'part from (also **a'side from** especially in *AmE*) *prep.* **1** except for: *I've finished apart from the last question.* **2** in addition to; as well as: *Apart from their house in London, they also have a villa in Spain.* ◊ *It was a difficult time. Apart from everything else, we had financial problems.* ◊ *You've got to help. Apart from anything else you're my brother.* ⇨ note at BESIDES

apart·heid /ə'pɑːthaɪt; -heɪt; *AmE* ə'pɑːrtaɪt-; -eɪt/ *noun* [U] the former political system in South Africa in which only white people had full political rights and other people, especially black people, were forced to live away from white people, go to separate schools, etc.

apart·ment /ə'pɑːtmənt; *AmE* ə'pɑːrt-/ *noun* **1** (especially *AmE*) a set of rooms rented for living in, usually on one floor of a building—compare CONDOMINIUM, FLAT **2** a set of rooms rented for a holiday/vacation: *self-catering holiday apartments* **3** [usually pl.] (*BrE*) a room in a house, especially a large or famous house: *You can visit the whole palace except for the private apartments.*

a'partment block (*BrE*) (*AmE* **a'partment building**) *noun* a large building with flats/apartments on each floor

a'partment house *noun* (*AmE*) a small apartment building

apa·thet·ic /ˌæpə'θetɪk/ *adj.* showing no interest or enthusiasm: *The illness made her apathetic and unwilling to meet people.* ▶ **apa·thet·ic·al·ly** /ˌæpə'θetɪkli/ *adv.*

ap·athy /'æpəθi/ *noun* [U] the feeling of not being interested in or enthusiastic about anything: *There is wide-spread apathy among the electorate.*

ape /eɪp/ *noun, verb*
■ *noun* a large animal like a monkey, with no tail. There are different types of ape: *the great apes* (for example, ORANG-UTANS or CHIMPANZEES) **IDM** **go 'ape/'apeshit** (*slang, especially AmE*) to become extremely angry or excited
■ *verb* [VN] **1** (*BrE, disapproving*) to do sth in the same way as sb else, especially when it is not done very well: *For years the British film industry merely aped Hollywood.* **2** (especially *AmE*) to copy the way sb else behaves or talks, in order to make fun of them [SYN] MIMIC: *We used to ape the teacher's southern accent.*

aperi·tif /əˌperə'tiːf/ *noun* (especially *BrE*) a drink, usually one containing alcohol, that people sometimes have just before a meal

aper·ture /'æpətʃə(r); *AmE* also -tʃʊr/ *noun* **1** (*formal*) a small opening in sth: *The soldier fired the rifle through a narrow aperture in a pile of sandbags.* **2** (*technical*) an opening that allows light to reach a LENS, especially in cameras: *For flash photography, set the aperture at f.5.6.*

ape·shit /'eɪpʃɪt/ *noun* **IDM** **go 'apeshit** = GO APE

Apex (also **APEX**) /'eɪpeks/ *abbr.* (*BrE*) Advanced Purchase Excursion (a system that offers cheaper travel tickets when they are bought in advance)

apex /'eɪpeks/ *noun* [usually sing.] (*pl.* **apexes**) the top or highest part of sth: *the apex of the roof/triangle* ◊ (*figurative*) *At 37, she'd reached the apex of her career.*

aphid /'eɪfɪd/ *noun* a very small insect that is harmful to plants. There are several types of aphid, including, for example, GREENFLY.

aph·or·ism /'æfərɪzəm/ *noun* (*formal*) a short phrase that says sth true or wise ▶ **aph·or·is·tic** /ˌæfə'rɪstɪk/ *adj.*

aph·ro·dis·iac /ˌæfrə'dɪziæk/ *noun* a food or drug that is said to give people a strong desire to have sex: *a powerful aphrodisiac* ▶ **aph·ro·dis·iac** *adj.: the aphrodisiac properties/qualities of ginseng*

apiece /ə'piːs/ *adv.* (used after a noun or number) having, costing or measuring a particular amount each: *Yorke and Cole scored a goal apiece.* ◊ *The largest stones weigh over five tonnes apiece.*

aplenty /ə'plenti/ *adv., adj.* [after noun] (*formal*) in large amounts, especially more than is needed: *Criticisms of the government were to be found aplenty.*

aplomb /ə'plɒm; *AmE* ə'plɑːm/ *noun* [U] if sb does sth **with aplomb**, they do it in a confident and successful way, often in a difficult situation: *with considerable/great/remarkable aplomb* ◊ *He delivered the speech with his usual aplomb.*

apoca·lypse /ə'pɒkəlɪps; *AmE* ə'pɑːk-/ *noun* **1** [sing., U] the destruction of the world: *Civilization is on the brink of apocalypse.* **2** (**the Apocalypse**) [sing.] the end of the world, as described in the Bible **3** [sing.] a situation causing very serious damage and destruction: *an environmental apocalypse*

apoca·lyp·tic /əˌpɒkə'lɪptɪk; *AmE* əˌpɑːk-/ *adj.* **1** describing very serious damage and destruction in past or future events: *an apocalyptic view of history* ◊ *apocalyptic warnings of the end of society* **2** like the end of the world: *an apocalyptic scene*

apoc·ryph·al /ə'pɒkrɪfl; *AmE* ə'pɑːk-/ *adj.* (of a story) well known, but probably not true: *Most of the stories about him are apocryphal.*

apo·gee /'æpədʒiː/ *noun* [sing.] **1** (*formal*) the highest point of sth, where it is greatest or most successful: *a religious community that was at its apogee in the twelfth century* **2** (*astronomy*) the point in the ORBIT of the moon, a planet or other object in space when it is furthest from the earth

apol·it·ical /ˌeɪpə'lɪtɪkl/ *adj.* **1** (of a person) not interested in politics; not thinking politics are important **2** not connected with a political party: *an apolitical organization*

apolo·get·ic /əˌpɒlə'dʒetɪk; *AmE* əˌpɑːl-/ *adj.* **~** (**about/for sth**) feeling or showing that you are sorry for doing sth wrong or for causing a problem: *'Sorry,' she said, with an apologetic smile.* ◊ *They were very apologetic about the trouble they'd caused.* ▶ **apolo·get·ic·al·ly** /əˌpɒlə'dʒetɪkli; *AmE* əˌpɑːl-/ *adv.: 'I'm sorry I'm late,' he murmured apologetically.*

apolo·gist /ə'pɒlədʒɪst; *AmE* ə'pɑːl-/ *noun* **~** (**for sb/sth**) a person who tries to explain and defend sth, especially a political system or religious ideas

apolo·gize (*BrE* also **-ise**) /ə'pɒlədʒaɪz; *AmE* ə'pɑːl-/ *verb* [V] **~** (**to sb**) (**for sth**) to say that you are sorry for doing sth wrong or causing a problem: *Why should I apologize?* ◊ *Go and apologize to her.* ◊ *We apologize for the late departure of this flight.*

apol·ogy /ə'pɒlədʒi; *AmE* ə'pɑ:l-/ *noun* (*pl.* **-ies**) **1** [C, U] ~ (**to sb**) (**for sth**) a word or statement saying sorry for sth that has been done wrong or that causes a problem: *to offer/make/demand/accept an apology* ◊ *You owe him an apology for what you said.* ◊ *We should like to offer our apologies for the delay to your flight today.* ◊ *We received a letter of apology.* **2** [C, usually pl.] information that you cannot go to a meeting or must leave early: *The meeting started with apologies* (= the names of people who said they could not go to the meeting). ◊ (*formal*) *She made her apologies and left early.* **IDM make no a'pology/ a'pologies for sth** if you say that you **make no apology/ogy/apologies** for sth, you mean that you do not feel that you have said or done sth wrong

apo·plec·tic /ˌæpə'plektɪk/ *adj.* **1** (*written*) very angry: *He was apoplectic with rage at the decision.* **2** (*old-fashioned*) connected with apoplexy: *an apoplectic attack/fit*

apo·plexy /'æpəpleksi/ *noun* [U] (*old-fashioned*) the sudden loss of the ability to feel or move caused by an injury in the brain [SYN] STROKE

apos·tate /ə'pɒsteɪt; *AmE* ə'pɑ:s-/ *noun* (*formal*) a person who has rejected their religious or political beliefs ▶ **apos·tasy** /ə'pɒstəsi; *AmE* ə'pɑ:s-/ *noun* [U]

a pos·teri·ori /ˌeɪ ˌpɒsteri'ɔ:raɪ; *AmE* ˌpɑ:s-/ *adj., adv.* (from Latin, *formal*) analysing sth by starting from known facts and then thinking about the possible causes of the facts, for example saying 'Look, the streets are wet so it must have been raining'.—compare A PRIORI

apos·tle /ə'pɒsl; *AmE* ə'pɑ:sl/ *noun* **1** (Apostle) any one of the twelve men that Christ chose to tell people about him and his teachings **2** ~ (**of sth**) (*formal*) a person who strongly believes in a policy or an idea and tries to make other people believe in it: *an apostle of free enterprise*

apos·tolic /ˌæpə'stɒlɪk; *AmE* -'stɑ:lɪk/ *adj.* (*technical*) **1** connected with the Apostles or their teaching **2** connected with the Pope or Popes, who are considered to have had authority passed down to them from Christ's Apostles

apos·tro·phe /ə'pɒstrəfi; *AmE* ə'pɑ:s-/ *noun* **1** the mark (') used to show that one or more letters or numbers have been left out, as in *she's* for *she is* and *'63* for *1963* **2** the mark (') used before or after the letter 's' to show that sth belongs to sb, as in *Sam's watch* and *the horses' tails* **3** the mark (') used before the letter 's' to show the plural of a letter or number, as in *How many 3's are there in 9?* and *There are two m's in 'comma'.* ⇨ Appendix 4

apoth·ecary /ə'pɒθəkəri; *AmE* ə'pɑ:θəkeri/ *noun* (*pl.* **-ies**) a person who made and sold medicines in the past

apothe·osis /əˌpɒθi'əʊsɪs; *AmE* əˌpɑ:θi'oʊ-/ *noun* [usually sing.] (*pl.* **apothe·oses** /-si:z/) (*formal*) **1** the highest or most perfect development of sth **2** the best time in sb's life or career **3** a formal statement that a person has become a god: *the apotheosis of a Roman Emperor*

appal (*BrE*) (*AmE* **ap·pall**) /ə'pɔ:l/ *verb* (**-ll-**) to shock sb very much: [VN] *The brutality of the crime has appalled the public.* ◊ *The idea of sharing a room appalled her.* ◊ *The thought of having to do it all again appals me.* ◊ [VN that] *It appalled me that they could simply ignore the problem.* [also VN to inf]

ap·palled /ə'pɔ:ld/ *adj.* ~ (**at sth**) feeling or showing horror or disgust at sth unpleasant or wrong: *an appalled expression/silence* ◊ *We watched appalled as the child ran in front of the car.* ◊ *They were appalled at the waste of recyclable material.*

ap·pal·ling /ə'pɔ:lɪŋ/ *adj.* **1** shocking; extremely bad: *The prisoners were living in appalling conditions.* **2** (*informal*) very bad: *The bus service is appalling now.* ▶ **ap·pal·ling·ly** *adv.*: *appallingly bad/difficult* ◊ *The essay was appallingly written.*

ap·par·at·chik /ˌæpə'rɑ:tʃɪk/ *noun* (from Russian, *disapproving* or *humorous*) an official in a large political organization: *party apparatchiks*

ap·par·atus /ˌæpə'reɪtəs; *AmE* -'rætəs/ *noun* (*pl.* **ap·par·atuses**) **1** [U] the tools or other pieces of equipment that are needed for a particular activity or task: *a piece of laboratory apparatus* ◊ *Firefighters needed breathing apparatus to enter the burning house.* **2** [C, usually sing.]

the structure of a system or an organization, particularly that of a political party or a government: *the power of the state apparatus* **3** [C, usually sing.] (*technical*) a system of organs in the body: *the sensory apparatus*

ap·parel /ə'pærəl/ *noun* [U] **1** (*especially AmE*) clothing, when it is being sold in shops/stores: *The store sells women's and children's apparel.* **2** (*old-fashioned* or *formal*) clothes, particularly those worn on a formal occasion: *lords and ladies in fine apparel*

ap·par·ent /ə'pærənt/ *adj.* **1** [not usually before noun] ~ (**from sth**) (**that …**)| ~ (**to sb**) (**that …**) easy to see or understand [SYN] OBVIOUS: *It was apparent from her face that she was really upset.* ◊ *Their devotion was apparent.* ◊ *It soon became apparent to everyone that he couldn't sing.* ◊ *Then, for no apparent reason, the train suddenly stopped.* **2** [usually before noun] that seems to be real or true but may not be: *My parents are concerned at my apparent lack of enthusiasm for school.*—see also APPEAR

ap·par·ent·ly /ə'pærəntli/ *adv.* according to what you have heard or read; according to the way sth appears: *Apparently they are getting divorced soon.* ◊ *He paused, apparently lost in thought.* ◊ *I thought she had retired, but apparently* (= in fact) *she hasn't.*

ap·par·ition /ˌæpə'rɪʃn/ *noun* a ghost or an image of a person who is dead

ap·peal /ə'pi:l/ *noun, verb*
■ *noun* **1** [C, U] ~ (**against sth**) a formal request to a court of law or to sb in authority for a judgement or a decision to be changed: (*BrE*) *to lodge an appeal* ◊ (*AmE*) *to file an appeal* ◊ (*BrE*) *an appeal court/judge* ◊ (*AmE*) *an appeals court/judge* ◊ *an appeal against the 3-match ban*—see also COURT OF APPEAL **2** [U] a quality that makes sb/sth attractive or interesting: *mass/wide/popular appeal* ◊ *The Beatles have never really lost their appeal.* ◊ *The prospect of living in a city holds little appeal for me.*—see also SEX APPEAL **3** [C, U] ~ (**to sb**) (**for sth**)| ~ **to sb to do sth** an urgent and deeply felt request for money, help or information, especially one made by a charity or by the police: *to launch a TV appeal for donations to the charity* ◊ *a look of silent appeal* ◊ *The child's mother made an emotional appeal on TV for his return.* ◊ *The police made an appeal to the public to remain calm.* **4** [C] ~ **to sth** an indirect suggestion that any good, fair or reasonable person would act in a particular way: *I relied on an appeal to his finer feelings.*

■ *verb* **1** [V] ~ (**to sb/sth**) (**against sth**) to make a formal request to a court of law or to sb in authority for a judgement or a decision to be changed: *He said he would appeal after being found guilty on four counts of murder.* ◊ *The company is appealing against the ruling.* **2** [V] ~ (**to sb**) to attract or interest sb: *The prospect of a long wait in the rain did not appeal.* ◊ *The design has to appeal to all ages and social groups.* **3** [V] ~ (**to sb**) (**for sth**) to make a serious and urgent request: *Nationalist leaders appealed for calm.* ◊ *I am appealing on behalf of the famine victims* (= asking for money). ◊ *Police have appealed for witnesses to come forward.* ◊ *Organizers appealed to the crowd not to panic.* **4** ~ (**to sth**) to try to persuade sb to do sth by suggesting that it is a fair, reasonable, or honest thing to do: [V] *They needed to appeal to his sense of justice.* [also V speech]

ap·peal·ing /ə'pi:lɪŋ/ *adj.* **1** attractive or interesting: *Spending the holidays in Britain wasn't a prospect that I found particularly appealing.* [OPP] UNAPPEALING **2** showing that you want people to help you or to show you pity or sympathy: *'Would you really help?' he said with an appealing look.* ▶ **ap·peal·ing·ly** *adv.*: *The dog looked up at her appealingly.*

ap·pear /ə'pɪə(r); *AmE* ə'pɪr/ *verb*
LOOK/SEEM **1** linking verb (not used in the progressive tenses) to give the impression of being or doing sth [SYN] SEEM: [V-ADJ] *She didn't appear at all surprised at the news.* ◊ [V-N] *He appears a perfectly normal person.* ◊ [V to inf] *She appeared to be in her late thirties.* ◊ *They appeared not to know what was happening.* ◊ *There appears to have been a mistake.* ◊ [V (that)] *It appears there has been a mistake.* ◊ *It appears unlikely that*

A

interest rates will fall further. ◊ *It would appear that this was a major problem.*

BE SEEN | **2** [V] [usually +*adv./prep.*] to start to be seen: *A bus appeared around the corner.* ◊ *Smoke appeared on the horizon.* ◊ *Three days later a rash appeared.* ◊ *Posters for the gig appeared all over town.*

BEGIN TO EXIST | **3** [V] [usually +*adv./prep.*] to begin to exist or be known or used for the first time: *When did mammals appear on the earth?* ◊ *This problem first appeared in the inner cities.*

OF BOOK/PROGRAMME | **4** [V] [usually +*adv./prep.*] to be published or broadcast: *His new book will be appearing in the spring.* ◊ *It was too late to prevent the story from appearing in the national newspapers.*

IN MOVIE/PLAY | **5** [V] [usually +*adv./prep.*] to take part in a film/movie, play, television programme, etc: *He has appeared in over 60 movies.* ◊ *She regularly appears on TV.* ◊ *Next month he will be appearing as Clinton in a new play on Broadway.*

ARRIVE | **6** [V] [usually +*adv./prep.*] to arrive at a place: *By ten o'clock Lee still hadn't appeared.*

BE WRITTEN/MENTIONED | **7** [V] [usually +*adv./prep.*] to be written or mentioned somewhere: *Your name will appear at the front of the book.*

IN COURT | **8** [V] [usually +*adv./prep.*] to be present in a court of law in order to give evidence or answer a CHARGE: *A man will appear in court today charged with the murder.* ◊ *She appeared on six charges of theft.* ◊ *They will appear before magistrates tomorrow.* ◊ *He has been asked to appear as a witness for the defence.* **9** [V] ~ **for/on behalf of sb** to act as sb's lawyer in court: *Cherie Booth is the lawyer appearing for the defendant.*—see also APPARENT—compare DISAPPEAR

ap·pear·ance /əˈpɪərəns; *AmE* əˈpɪr-/ *noun*

WAY STH LOOKS/SEEMS | **1** [C, U] the way that sb/sth looks on the outside; what sb/sth seems to be: *the physical/ outward/external appearance of sth* ◊ *She had never been greatly concerned about her appearance.* ◊ *The dog was similar in general appearance to a spaniel.* ◊ *He gave every appearance of* (= seemed very much to be) *enjoying himself.* ◊ *Judging by appearances can be misleading.* ◊ *To all appearances* (= as far as people could tell) *he was dead.* ◊ *When she lost all her money, she was determined to keep up appearances* (= hide the true situation and pretend that everything was going well).

SB/STH ARRIVING | **2** [C, usually sing.] the fact of sb/sth arriving, especially when it is not expected: *The sudden appearance of a security guard caused them to drop the money and run.* ◊ *I don't want to go to the party, but I suppose I'd better put in an appearance* (= go there for a short time). **3** [C, usually sing.] the moment at which sth begins to exist or starts to be seen or used: *the early appearance of daffodils in spring* ◊ *the appearance of organic vegetables in the supermarkets*

IN PUBLIC | **4** [C] an act of appearing in public, especially as a performer, politician, etc., or in a court of law: *The Dutch player will make his first appearance for Liverpool this Saturday.* ◊ *The singer's first public appearance was at the age of eight.* ◊ *the defendant's appearance in court*

BEING PUBLISHED/BROADCAST | **5** [C, usually sing.] an act of being published or broadcast: *the appearance of claims about the minister's private life in the press*

ap·pease /əˈpiːz/ *verb* [VN] (*formal, usually disapproving*) **1** to make sb calmer or less angry by giving them what they want: *The move was widely seen as an attempt to appease critics of the regime.* **2** to give a country what it wants in order to avoid war ▸ **ap·pease·ment** *noun* [U]: *a policy of appeasement*

ap·pel·lant /əˈpelənt/ *noun* (*law*) a person who APPEALS against a decision made in a court of law

ap·pel·late court /əˈpelət kɔːt; *AmE* kɔːrt/ *noun* (*technical*) a court of law in which people can APPEAL against decisions made in other courts of law

ap·pel·la·tion /ˌæpəˈleɪʃn/ *noun* (*formal*) a name or title

ap·pend /əˈpend/ *verb* [VN] ~ **sth (to sth)** (*formal*) to add sth to the end of a piece of writing: *Footnotes have been appended to the document.*

ap·pend·age /əˈpendɪdʒ/ *noun* (*formal*) a smaller or less important part of sth larger

ap·pend·ec·tomy /ˌæpenˈdektəmi/ *noun* [C, U] (*pl. -ies*) (*medical*) the removal of the APPENDIX by SURGERY

ap·pen·di·citis /əˌpendəˈsaɪtɪs/ *noun* [U] a painful swelling of the appendix that can be very serious

ap·pen·dix /əˈpendɪks/ *noun* (*pl.* **ap·pen·di·ces** /-dɪsiːz/) **1** a small bag of tissue that is attached to the large INTESTINE. In humans, the appendix has no real function: *He had to have his appendix out* (= removed).—picture at BODY **2** a section giving extra information at the end of a book or document: *Full details are given in Appendix 3.*

ap·per·tain /ˌæpəˈteɪn; *AmE* -pərˈt-/ *verb* PHR V **apperˈtain to sb/sth** (*formal*) to belong or refer to sb/sth: *rights appertaining to the property* ◊ *These figures appertain to last year's sales.*

ap·pe·tite /ˈæpɪtaɪt/ *noun* **1** [U, C, usually sing.] physical desire for food: *He suffered from headaches, insomnia and loss of appetite.* ◊ *The walk has given me a good appetite.* ◊ *Don't spoil your appetite by eating between meals.* **2** [C] ~ **(for sth)** a strong desire for sth: *The public have an insatiable appetite for scandal.* ◊ *sexual appetites* ◊ *The preview was intended to whet your appetite* (= make you want more).

ap·pet·izer (*BrE* also **-iser**) /ˈæpɪtaɪzə(r)/ *noun* a small amount of food or a drink that you have before a meal

ap·pe·tiz·ing (*BrE* also **-is·ing**) /ˈæpɪtaɪzɪŋ/ *adj.* (of food, etc.) that smells or looks attractive; making you feel hungry or thirsty: *the appetizing aroma of sizzling bacon* ◊ *The meals he cooked were always nourishing but never particularly appetizing.* OPP UNAPPETIZING

ap·plaud /əˈplɔːd/ *verb* **1** to show your approval of sb/ sth by CLAPPING your hands: [V] *He started to applaud and the others joined in.* ◊ [VN] *The conference rose to applaud the speaker.* ◊ *She was applauded as she came on stage.* **2** [VN] ~ **sb/sth (for sth)** (*formal*) to express praise for sb/sth because you approve of them or it: *We applaud her decision.* ◊ *His efforts to improve the situation are to be applauded.* ◊ *I applaud her for having the courage to refuse.*

ap·plause /əˈplɔːz/ *noun* [U] the noise made by a group of people CLAPPING their hands and sometimes shouting to show their approval or enjoyment: *Give her a big round of applause!* ◊ *The audience broke into rapturous applause.*

apple /ˈæpl/ *noun* a round fruit with shiny red or green skin and firm white flesh: *an apple pie* ◊ *apple sauce* ◊ *a garden with three apple trees*—picture on page A2—see also ADAM'S APPLE, BIG APPLE, COOKING APPLE, CRAB APPLE, EATING APPLE, TOFFEE APPLE IDM **the ˌapple of sb's ˈeye** a person or thing that is loved more than any other: *She is the apple of her father's eye.*—more at AMERICAN *adj.*, ROTTEN

¹**apple cart** *noun* IDM see UPSET *v.*

ap·pli·ance /əˈplaɪəns/ *noun* a machine that is designed to do a particular thing in the home, such as preparing food, heating or cleaning: *electrical/household appliances* ◊ *They sell a wide range of domestic appliances—washing machines, dishwashers and so on.*

ap·plic·able /əˈplɪkəbl; ˈæplɪkəbl/ *adj.* [not usually before noun] ~ **(to sb/sth)** that can be said to be true in the case of sb/sth SYN RELEVANT: *Much of the form was not applicable* (= did not apply) *to me.* ◊ *Give details of children where applicable* (= if you have any). ▸ **ap·plic·abil·ity** /əˌplɪkəˈbɪləti; ˌæplɪk-/ *noun* [U]: *The new approach had wide applicability to all sorts of different problems.*

ap·pli·cant /ˈæplɪkənt/ *noun* ~ **(for sth)** a person who makes a formal request for sth (= applies for it), especially for a job, a place at a college or university, etc: *There were over 500 applicants for the job.*

ap·pli·ca·tion /ˌæplɪˈkeɪʃn/ *noun*

FOR JOB/COURSE | **1** [C, U] ~ **(to sb) (for sth/to do sth)** a formal (often written) request for sth, such as a job, permission to do sth or a place at a college or university: *a planning/passport application* ◊ *His application to the court for bail has been refused.* ◊ *an application for mem-*

s	t	v	z	ʃ	ʒ	tʃ	dʒ	θ	ð	ŋ
see	tea	van	zoo	shoe	vision	chain	jam	thin	this	sing

bership/a **loan**/a **licence** ◊ an **application form** (= a piece of paper on which to apply for sth) ◊ *Further information is available* **on application** *to the principal*.

PRACTICAL USE | **2** [U, C] ~ **(of sth) (to sth)** the practical use of sth, especially a theory, discovery, etc: *the application of new technology to teaching* ◊ *The new invention would have wide application/a wide range of applications in industry*.

OF PAINT/CREAM | **3** [C, U] an act of putting or spreading sth, such as paint or medical creams, onto sth else: *lotion for external application only* (= to be put on the skin, not swallowed) ◊ *It took three applications of paint to cover the graffiti*.

OF RULE/LAW | **4** [U] the act of making a rule, etc. operate or become effective: *strict application of the law*

COMPUTING | **5** [C] a program designed to do a particular job; a piece of SOFTWARE: *a database application*—picture on page 251

HARD WORK | **6** [U] (*formal*) determination to work hard at sth; great effort: *Success as a writer demands great application*.

ap·plied /əˈplaɪd/ *adj*. [usually before noun] (especially of a subject of study) used in a practical way; not THEORETICAL: *applied mathematics* (= as used by engineers, etc.)—compare PURE (7)

ap·pli·qué /əˈpliːkeɪ; *AmE* ˌæpləˈkeɪ/ *noun* [U] a type of NEEDLEWORK in which small pieces of fabric are sewn or stuck in a pattern onto a larger piece ▶ **ap·pli·quéd** *adj*.: *appliquéd cushions*

apply /əˈplaɪ/ *verb* (**ap·plies, ap·ply·ing, ap·plied, ap·plied**)

FOR JOB/COURSE | **1** ~ **(to sb/sth) (for sth)** to make a formal request, usually in writing, for sth such as a job, a place, at college, university, etc: [V] *to apply for a job/passport/grant* ◊ *to apply to a company/university* ◊ *You should apply in person/by letter*. ◊ [Vtoinf] *He has applied to join the army*.

USE | **2** [VN] ~ **sth (to sth)** to use sth or make sth work in a particular situation: *to apply economic sanctions/political pressure* ◊ *The new technology was applied to farming*.

PAINT/CREAM | **3** [VN] ~ **sth (to sth)** to put or spread sth such as paint, cream, etc. onto a surface: *Apply the cream sparingly to your face and neck*.

BE RELEVANT | **4** (not used in the progressive tenses) ~ **(to sb/sth)** to concern or relate to sth/sth: [V] *Special conditions apply if you are under 18*. ◊ *What I am saying applies only to some of you*. ◊ [VN] *The word 'unexciting' could never be applied to her novels*.

WORK HARD | **5** [VN] ~ **yourself (to sth/to doing sth)** to work at sth or study sth very hard: *You would pass your exams if you applied yourself*. ◊ *We applied our minds to finding a solution to our problem*.

PRESS HARD | **6** [VN] to press on sth hard with your hand, foot, etc. to make sth work or have an effect on sth: *to apply the brakes (of a vehicle)* ◊ *Pressure applied to the wound will stop the bleeding*.

ap·point /əˈpɔɪnt/ *verb* **1** ~ **sb (to sth)** | ~ **sb (as) sth** to choose sb for a job or position of responsibility: [VN] *They have appointed a new head teacher at my son's school*. ◊ *She has recently been appointed to the committee*. ◊ [VN-N] *They appointed him (as) captain of the English team*. ◊ [VNtoinf] *A lawyer was appointed to represent the child*. **2** [VN] [usually passive] (*formal*) to arrange or decide on a time or place for doing sth: *A date for the meeting is still to be appointed*. ◊ *Everyone was assembled at the **appointed time**.*

ap·point·ee /əˌpɔɪnˈtiː/ *noun* a person who has been chosen for a job or position of responsibility: *the new appointee to the post*

ap·point·ment /əˈpɔɪntmənt/ *noun* **1** [C] ~ **(with sb)** a formal arrangement to meet or visit sb at a particular time, especially for a reason connected with their work: *She made an appointment for her son to see the doctor*. ◊ *I've got a **dental appointment** at 3 o'clock.* ◊ *an appointment with my lawyer* ◊ *to keep an appointment* ◊ *Viewing is **by appointment only*** (= only at a time that has been

arranged in advance). **2** [C, U] ~ **(as/to sth)** the act of choosing a person for a job or position of responsibility; the fact of being chosen for a job, etc: *Following her recent appointment to the post ...* ◊ *his appointment as principal* ◊ *the appointment of a new captain for the England team* **3** [C] (especially *BrE*) a job or position of responsibility: *a permanent/first appointment*

ap·por·tion /əˈpɔːʃn; *AmE* əˈpɔːrʃn/ *verb* [VN] ~ **sth (among/between/to sb)** (*written*) to divide sth among people; to give a share of sth to sb: *They apportioned the land among members of the family*. ◊ *The programme gives the facts but does not **apportion blame**.* ▶ **ap·por·tion·ment** *noun* [U, sing.] (*formal*): *The contract defines the apportionment of risks between employer and contractor*. ◊ *an apportionment of land*

ap·po·site /ˈæpəzɪt/ *adj*. ~ **(to sth)** (*formal*) very appropriate for a particular situation or in relation to sth: *Her remarks are extremely apposite to the present discussion*.

ap·pos·ition /ˌæpəˈzɪʃn/ *noun* [U] (*grammar*) the use of a noun phrase immediately after another noun phrase which refers to the same person or thing: *In the phrase 'Paris, the capital of France', 'the capital of France' is in apposition to 'Paris'.*

ap·prais·al /əˈpreɪzl/ *noun* [C, U] a judgement of the value, performance or nature of sb/sth: *He had read many detailed critical appraisals of her work*. ◊ *staff/performance appraisal* (= a discussion with staff members of their strengths and weaknesses in a job) ◊ *I have my appraisal today* (= a meeting to discuss my work with my manager).

ap·praise /əˈpreɪz/ *verb* [VN] **1** (*formal*) to consider or examine sb/sth and form an opinion about them or it: *an appraising glance/look* ◊ *She stepped back to appraise her workmanship*. ◊ *His eyes coolly appraised the young woman before him*. **2** to make a formal judgement about the value of a person's work, usually after a discussion with them about it: *Managers must appraise all staff*.

ap·pre·ci·able /əˈpriːʃəbl/ *adj*. large enough to be noticed or thought important SYN CONSIDERABLE: *The new regulations will not make an appreciable difference to most people*. ◊ *an appreciable effect/increase/amount* ▶ **ap·pre·ci·ably** /-əbli/ *adv*.: *The risk of infection is appreciably higher among children*.

ap·pre·ci·ate /əˈpriːʃieɪt/ *verb* **1** [VN] (not used in the progressive tenses) to recognize the good qualities of sb/sth: *You can't really appreciate foreign literature in translation*. ◊ *His talents are not fully appreciated in that company*. ◊ *Her family doesn't appreciate her*. **2** (not usually used in the progressive tenses) to be grateful for sth that sb has done; to welcome sth: [VN] *I'd appreciate some help*. ◊ *Your support is greatly appreciated*. ◊ (*spoken*) *Thanks for coming*. *I appreciate it*. ◊ *I would appreciate it if you paid in cash*. ◊ [V-ing] *I don't appreciate being treated like a second-class citizen*. ◊ [VN-ing] *We would appreciate you letting us know of any problems*. **3** (not used in the progressive tenses) to understand or realize that sth is true: [VN] *What I failed to appreciate was the distance between the two cities*. ◊ [Vwh-] *I don't think you appreciate how expensive it will be*. ◊ [Vthat] *We didn't fully appreciate that he was seriously ill*. **4** [V] to increase in value over a period of time: *Their investments have appreciated over the years*. OPP DEPRECIATE

ap·pre·ci·ation /əˌpriːʃiˈeɪʃn/ *noun* **1** [U] pleasure that you have when you recognize and enjoy the good qualities of sb/sth: *She shows little appreciation of good music*. ◊ *The crowd murmured in appreciation*. **2** [U, sing.] ~ **of sth** a full or sympathetic understanding of sth, such as a situation or a problem, and of what it involves: *I had no appreciation of the problems they faced*. **3** [U] ~ **(of/for sth)** the feeling of being grateful for sth: *Please accept this gift in appreciation of all you've done for us*. **4** [U, sing.] ~ **(in sth)** increase in value over a period of time **5** [C] ~ **(of sth)** (*formal*) a piece of writing or a speech in which the strengths and weaknesses of sb/sth, especially an artist or a work of art, are discussed and judged

ap·pre·cia·tive /əˈpriːʃətɪv/ *adj*. **1** ~ **(of sth)** feeling or

æ	ɑː	e	ɜː	ə	ɪ	iː	i	ɒ	ɔː	ʌ	ʊ	u	uː
cat	father	ten	bird	about	sit	see	many	got	saw	cup	put	actual	too
								(BrE)					

showing that you are grateful for sth: *The company was very appreciative of my efforts.* **2** showing pleasure or enjoyment: *an appreciative audience/smile* ◊ *appreciative laughter/comments* ▶ **ap·pre·cia·tive·ly** *adv.*

ap·pre·hend /ˌæprɪˈhend/ *verb* [VN] **1** (*formal*) (of the police) to catch sb and arrest them **2** (*old-fashioned*) to understand or recognize sth: *He was slow to apprehend danger.*

ap·pre·hen·sion /ˌæprɪˈhenʃn/ *noun* **1** [U, C] worry or fear that sth unpleasant may happen [SYN] ANXIETY: *There is growing apprehension that fighting will begin again.* ◊ *He watched the election results with some apprehension.* **2** [U] (*formal*) the act of capturing or arresting sb, usually by the police: *the apprehension of the terrorists in the early hours of this morning*

ap·pre·hen·sive /ˌæprɪˈhensɪv/ *adj.* ~ (**about/of** sth)| ~ (that ...) worried or frightened that sth unpleasant may happen: *I was a little apprehensive about the effects of what I had said.* ◊ *You have no reason to be apprehensive of the future.* ◊ *She was deeply apprehensive that something might go wrong.* ◊ *an apprehensive face/glance/look* ▶ **ap·pre·hen·sive·ly** *adv.*

ap·pren·tice /əˈprentɪs/ *noun, verb*
■ *noun* a young person who works for an employer for a fixed period of time in order to learn the particular skills needed in their job: *an apprentice electrician/chef*
■ *verb* [VN] [usually passive] ~ sb (**to** sb) (**as** sth) (*old-fashioned*) to make sb an apprentice

ap·pren·tice·ship /əˈprentɪʃɪp/ *noun* [C, U] a period of time working as an apprentice; a job as an apprentice: *She was in the second year of her apprenticeship as a carpenter.* ◊ *He had **served his apprenticeship** as a plumber.*

ap·prise /əˈpraɪz/ *verb* [VN] ~ sb **of** sth (*formal*) to tell or inform sb of sth

ap·proach /əˈprəʊtʃ; *AmE* əˈproʊtʃ/ *verb, noun*
■ *verb*
MOVE NEAR | **1** to come near to sb/sth in distance or time: [V] *We heard the sound of an approaching car/a car approaching* ◊ *Winter is approaching.* ◊ [VN] *As you approach the town, you'll see the college on the left.*

OFFER/ASK | **2** [VN] ~ sb (**about/for** sth)| ~ sb (**about doing** sth) to speak to sb about sth, especially to ask them for sth or to offer to do sth: *She approached the bank for a loan.* ◊ *We have been approached by a number of companies that are interested in our product.* ◊ *I'd like to ask his opinion but I find him difficult to approach* (= not easy to talk to in a friendly way).

AMOUNT/QUALITY | **3** [VN] to come close to sth in amount, level or quality: *profits approaching 30 million dollars* ◊ *Few writers approach his richness of language.*

PROBLEM/TASK | **4** [VN] to start dealing with a problem, task, etc. in a particular way: *What's the best way of approaching this problem?*
■ *noun*
TO PROBLEM/TASK | **1** [C] ~ (**to** sth) a way of dealing with sb/sth; a way of doing or thinking about sth such as a problem or a task: *The school has decided to adopt a different approach to discipline.* ◊ *She took the wrong approach in her dealings with them.*

MOVEMENT NEARER | **2** [sing.] movement nearer to sb/sth in distance or time: *She hadn't heard his approach and jumped as the door opened.* ◊ *the welcome approach of spring*

OFFER/REQUEST | **3** [C] the act of speaking to sb about sth, especially when making an offer or a request: *The club has made an approach to a local company for sponsorship.* ◊ *She resented his persistent approaches.*

PATH/ROAD | **4** [C] a path, road, etc. that leads to a place: *All the approaches to the palace were guarded by troops.* ◊ *a new approach road to the port*

OF AIRCRAFT | **5** [C] the part of an aircraft's flight immediately before landing: *to begin the final approach to the runway*

STH SIMILAR | **6** [sing.] a thing that is like sth else that is

mentioned: *That's the nearest approach to an apology you'll get from him.*

[IDM] see CARROT

ap·proach·able /əˈprəʊtʃəbl; *AmE* əˈproʊtʃ-/ *adj.* **1** friendly and easy to talk to; easy to understand: *Despite being a big star, she's very approachable.* ◊ *an approachable piece of music* [OPP] UNAPPROACHABLE **2** [not before noun] that can be reached by a particular route or from a particular direction: *The summit was approachable only from the south.*

ap·pro·ba·tion /ˌæprəˈbeɪʃn/ *noun* [U] (*formal*) approval or agreement

ap·pro·pri·ate *adj., verb*
■ *adj.* /əˈprəʊpriət; *AmE* əˈproʊ-/ ~ (**for/to** sth) suitable, acceptable or correct for the particular circumstances: *an appropriate response/measure/method* ◊ *Now that the problem has been identified, appropriate action can be taken.* ◊ *Jeans are not appropriate for a formal party.* ◊ *The book was written in a style appropriate to the age of the children.* ◊ *Is now an appropriate time to make a speech?* ◊ *Please debit my Mastercard/Visa/American Express card (delete as appropriate).* [OPP] INAPPROPRIATE ▶ **ap·pro·pri·ate·ly** *adv.*: *The government has been accused of not responding appropriately to the needs of the homeless.* ◊ *The chain of volcanoes is known, **appropriately enough**, as the 'Ring of Fire'.* **ap·pro·pri·ate·ness** *noun* [U]
■ *verb* /əˈprəʊprieɪt; *AmE* əˈproʊ-/ [VN] (*written*) **1** to take sth, sb's ideas, etc. for your own use, especially illegally or without permission: *He was accused of appropriating club funds.* ◊ *Some of the opposition party's policies have been appropriated by the government.* **2** ~ sth (**for** sth) to take or give sth, especially money for a particular purpose: *Five million dollars has been appropriated for research into the disease.*—compare MISAPPROPRIATE

ap·pro·pri·ation /əˌprəʊpriˈeɪʃn; *AmE* əˌproʊ-/ *noun* **1** [U, sing.] (*formal or law*) the act of taking sth which belongs to sb else, especially without permission: *dishonest appropriation of property*—compare MISAPPROPRIATION **2** [U, sing.] (*formal*) the act of keeping or saving money for a particular purpose: *a meeting to discuss the appropriation of funds* **3** [C] (*formal*) a sum of money to be used for a particular purpose, especially by a government or company: *an appropriation of £20 000 for payment of debts*

ap·prov·al /əˈpruːvl/ *noun* **1** [U] the feeling that sb/sth is good or acceptable; a positive opinion of sb/sth: *She desperately wanted to win her father's approval.* ◊ *Do the plans meet with your approval?* ◊ *Several people nodded **in approval**.* **2** [U, C] ~ (**for** sth) (**from** sb) agreement to, or permission for sth, especially a plan or request: *The plan will be submitted to the committee for official approval.* ◊ *parliamentary/congressional/government approval* ◊ *Senior management have given their **seal of approval** (= formal approval) to the plans.* ◊ *I can't agree to anything without my partner's approval.* ◊ *planning approvals* **3** [U] if you buy goods, or if goods are sold **on approval**, you can use them for a time without paying, until you decide if you want to buy them or not

ap·prove /əˈpruːv/ *verb* **1** [V] ~ (**of** sb/sth) to think that sb/sth is good, acceptable or suitable: *I told my mother I wanted to marry Jan but she didn't approve.* ◊ *Do you approve of my idea?* ◊ *He doesn't approve of me leaving school this year.* ◊ (*formal*) *He doesn't approve of my leaving school this year.* [OPP] DISAPPROVE **2** [VN] to officially agree to a plan, proposal, request, etc: *The committee unanimously approved the plan.* **3** [VN] [often passive] to say that sth is good enough to be used, or is correct: *The course is approved by the Department for Education.*

ap'proved school *noun* (*BrE*) a special school where young people who had committed crimes were sent in the past

ap·prov·ing /əˈpruːvɪŋ/ *adj.* showing that you believe that sb/sth is good or acceptable: *He gave me an approving nod.* ▶ **ap·prov·ing·ly** *adv.*: *She looked at him approvingly and smiled.*

approx *abbr.* APPROXIMATE, APPROXIMATELY

aɪ	aʊ	eɪ	əʊ	oʊ	ɔɪ	ɪə	eə	ʊə	j	w
my	now	say	go (BrE)	go (AmE)	boy	near	hair	pure	yes	wet

ap·proxi·mate *adj., verb*

■ *adj.* /əˈprɒksɪmət; AmE əˈprɑːk-/ (*abbr.* **approx**) almost correct or accurate, but not completely so; not exact: *an approximate number / total / cost* ◊ *The cost given is only approximate.* ◊ *Use these figures as an approximate guide in your calculations.* ▶ **ap·proxi·mate·ly** *adv.*: *The journey took approximately seven hours.* ⇨ note at ABOUT

■ *verb* /əˈprɒksɪmeɪt; AmE əˈprɑːk-/ (*written*) **1** ~ (**to**) **sth** to be similar or close to sth in nature, quality, amount, etc., but not exactly the same: [VN] *The animals were reared in conditions which approximated the wild as closely as possible.* ◊ *The total cost will approximate £15 billion.* ◊ [V] *His story approximates to the facts that we already know.* **2** [VN] to calculate or estimate sth fairly accurately: *a formula for approximating the weight of a horse*

ap·proxi·ma·tion /əˌprɒksɪˈmeɪʃn; AmE əˌprɑːk-/ *noun* **1** an estimate of a number or an amount that is almost correct, but not exact: *That's just an approximation, you understand.* **2** ~ (**of/to sth**) a thing that is similar to sth else, but is not exactly the same: *Our results should be a good approximation to the true state of affairs.*

ap·pur·ten·ance /əˈpɜːtɪnəns; AmE əˈpɜːrt-/ *noun* [usually pl.] (*formal* or *humorous*) a thing that forms a part of sth larger or more important

APR /ˌeɪ piː ˈɑː(r)/ *noun* [sing.] the abbreviation for 'annual percentage rate' (the amount of interest a bank charges on money that it lends, calculated for a period of a year): *a rate of 26.4% APR*

après-ski /ˌæpreɪ ˈskiː/ *noun* [U] (from *French*) social activities and entertainments which take place in hotels and restaurants after a day's skiing

apri·cot /ˈeɪprɪkɒt; AmE ˈæp-; -kɑːt/ *noun* **1** [C] a round fruit with yellow or orange skin and a stone/pit inside: *dried apricots* **2** [U] a yellowish-orange colour ▶ **apri·cot** *adj.*: *The room was painted apricot and white.*

April /ˈeɪprəl/ *noun* [U, C] (*abbr.* **Apr.**) the fourth month of the year, between March and May: *She was born in April.* ◊ (*BrE*) *The meeting is on the fifth of April / April the fifth.* ◊ (*AmE*) *The meeting is on April fifth.* ◊ *We went to Japan last April.* ◊ *I arrived at the end of April.* ◊ *last April's election* ◊ *April showers* ◊ *an April wedding*

April 'Fool *noun* **1** a trick that is traditionally played on sb on 1 April (called **April Fool's Day** or **All Fools' Day**) **2** a person who has a trick played on them on April Fool's Day

a pri·ori /ˌeɪ praɪˈɔːraɪ/ *adj., adv.* (from *Latin, written*) using facts or principles that are known to be true in order to decide what the probable effects or results of sth will be, for example saying 'They haven't eaten anything all day so they must be hungry.'—compare A POSTERIORI

ap·ron /ˈeɪprən/ *noun* **1** a piece of clothing worn over the front of the body, from the chest or the waist down, and tied around the waist. Aprons are worn over other clothes to keep them clean, for example when cooking.—compare PINAFORE **2** (*technical*) an area with a hard surface at an airport, where aircraft are turned around, loaded, etc. **3** (also **'apron stage**) (*technical*) (in a theatre) the part of the stage that is in front of the curtain **IDM** (**tied to) your mother's, wife's, etc. apron strings** (too much under) the influence and control of your mother, etc: *The British prime minister is too apt to cling to Washington's apron strings.*

apro·pos /ˌæprəˈpəʊ; AmE -ˈpoʊ/ (also **apro·pos of**) *prep.* concerning or related to sb/sth: *Apropos (of) what you were just saying …*

apse /æps/ *noun* a small area, often in the shape of a SEMICIRCLE, usually at the east end of a church

apt /æpt/ *adj.* **1** suitable or appropriate in the circumstances: *a particularly apt description / name / comment* ◊ *The song would have been more apt for a bass voice.* **2** ~ **to be …** | ~ **to do sth** likely or having a natural tendency to do sth: *apt to be forgetful / careless* ◊ *Babies are apt to put objects into their mouths.* **3** ~ **pupil** a person who has a natural ability to learn and understand ▶ **aptly** *adv.*: *the aptly named Grand Hotel* **apt·ness** *noun* [U]

ap·ti·tude /ˈæptɪtjuːd; AmE -tuːd/ *noun* [U, C] ~ (**for sth**) | ~ (**for doing sth**) natural ability or skill at doing sth: *She*

showed a natural aptitude for the work. ◊ *His aptitude for dealing with children got him the job.* ◊ *an* **aptitude test** (= one designed to show whether sb has the natural ability for a particular job or educational course)

aqua·mar·ine /ˌækwəməˈriːn/ *noun* **1** [C, U] a pale greenish-blue precious stone **2** [U] a pale greenish-blue colour ▶ **aqua·mar·ine** *adj.*: *an aquamarine sea*

aqua·plane /ˈækwəpleɪn/ *noun* (*BrE*) (*AmE* **hydro·plane**) *verb* [V] (of a motor vehicle) to slide out of control on a wet road

aquar·ium /əˈkweəriəm; AmE əˈkwer-/ *noun* (*pl.* **aquariums** or **aqua·ria** /-riə/) **1** a large glass container in which fish and other water creatures and plants are kept **2** a building where people can go to see fish and other water creatures

Aquar·ius /əˈkweəriəs; AmE əˈkwer-/ *noun* **1** [U] the 11th sign of the ZODIAC, the Water Carrier **2** [sing.] a person born under the influence of this sign, that is between 21 January and 19 February ▶ **Aquar·ian** *noun, adj.*

aqua·tic /əˈkwætɪk/ *adj.* [usually before noun] **1** growing or living in, on or near water: *aquatic plants* **2** connected with water: *swimming, windsurfing and other aquatic sports*

aque·duct /ˈækwɪdʌkt/ *noun* a structure for carrying water, usually one built like a bridge across a valley or low ground

aque·ous /ˈeɪkwiəs/ *adj.* (*technical*) containing water; like water

aqui·fer /ˈækwɪfə(r)/ *noun* (*geology*) a layer of rock or soil that can absorb and hold water

aquil·ine /ˈækwɪlaɪn/ *adj.* (*written*) a person with an **aquiline nose** or **aquiline features** has a nose that is thin and curved, similar to that of an EAGLE

Arab /ˈærəb/ *noun, adj.*

■ *noun* **1** a person from the Middle East or N Africa, whose ancestors lived in the Arabian Peninsula **2** a type of horse originally from Arabia

■ *adj.* of or connected with Arabia or Arabs: *Arab countries*

ar·ab·esque /ˌærəˈbesk/ *noun* **1** [C] (in ballet) a position in which the dancer balances on one leg with the other leg lifted and stretched out behind parallel to the ground **2** [C, U] (in art) a type of design where lines wind around each other

Ara·bian /əˈreɪbiən/ *adj.* of or connected with Arabia **HELP** **Arabian** is used to describe places: *the Arabian peninsula.* The people are **Arabs** and the adjective to describe them is **Arab**: *Arab children.* The language is **Arabic**: *Arabic script*

Arab·ic /ˈærəbɪk/ *noun, adj.*

■ *noun* [U] the language of the Arabs

■ *adj.* of or connected with the literature and language of Arab people: *Arabic poetry*

Arabic 'numeral *noun* any of the symbols 0, 1, 2, 3, 4, etc. used for writing numbers in many countries—compare ROMAN NUMERAL

ar·able /ˈærəbl/ *adj., noun*

■ *adj.* connected with growing crops such as wheat or corn: *arable farming / farms / crops* ◊ *arable land / fields* (= used or suitable for growing crops)

■ *noun* [U] (*technical*) arable land or crops

arach·nid /əˈræknɪd/ *noun* (*technical*) any small creature of the class that includes spiders, SCORPIONS, MITES and TICKS—compare INSECT—picture on page A7

ar·biter /ˈɑːbɪtə(r); AmE ˈɑːrb-/ *noun* ~ (**of sth**) (*written*) a person with the power or influence to make judgements and decide what will be done or accepted: *The law is the final arbiter of what is considered obscene.* ◊ *an arbiter of taste / style / fashion*

ar·bi·trage /ˈɑːbɪtrɑːʒ; -trɪdʒ; AmE ˈɑːrbətrɑːʒ/ *noun* [U] (*business*) the practice of buying sth (for example, shares or foreign money) in one place and selling it in another place where the price is higher ▶ **ar·bi·tra·geur** /ˌɑːbɪtrɑːˈʒɜː(r); AmE ˌɑːrbətrɑːˈʒɜːr/ (also **ar·bi·trager** /ˈɑːbɪtrɑːʒə(r); AmE ˈɑːrbətrɑːʒər/) *noun*

ar·bi·trary /ˈɑːbɪtrəri; AmE ˈɑːrbətreri/ *adj.* **1** (of an action, a decision, a rule, etc.) not seeming to be based on a reason, system or plan and sometimes seeming unfair: *The choice of players for the team seemed completely arbitrary.* ◇ *He makes unpredictable, arbitrary decisions.* **2** (*formal*) using power without restriction and without considering other people: *the arbitrary powers of officials* ▶ **ar·bi·trar·ily** *adv.*: *The leaders of the groups were chosen arbitrarily.* **ar·bi·trari·ness** *noun* [U]

ar·bi·trate /ˈɑːbɪtreɪt; *AmE* ˈɑːrb-/ *verb* ~ **(in/on sth)** to officially settle an argument or a disagreement between two people or groups: [V] *to arbitrate in a dispute* ◇ *A committee was created to arbitrate between management and the unions.* [also VN]

ar·bi·tra·tion /ˌɑːbɪˈtreɪʃn; *AmE* ˌɑːrb-/ *noun* [U] the official process of settling an argument or a disagreement by sb who is not involved: *Both sides in the dispute have agreed to go to arbitration.*

ar·bi·tra·tor /ˈɑːbɪtreɪtə(r); *AmE* ˈɑːrb-/ *noun* a person who is chosen to settle a dispute

ar·bor·eal /ɑːˈbɔːriəl; *AmE* ɑːrˈb-/ *adj.* (*technical*) relating to trees; living in trees

ar·bor·etum /ˌɑːbəˈriːtəm; *AmE* ˌɑːrb-/ *noun* (*pl.* **ar·bor·etums** or **ar·bor·eta** /-tə/) a garden where many different types of tree are grown, for people to look at or for scientific study

ar·bour (*BrE*) (*AmE* **arbor**) /ˈɑːbə(r); *AmE* ˈɑːrb-/ *noun* a shelter in a garden/yard for people to sit under, made by growing climbing plants over a frame

arc /ɑːk; *AmE* ɑːrk/ *noun, verb*
■ *noun* **1** (*geometry*) part of a circle or a curved line—picture at CIRCLE **2** a curved shape: *the arc of a rainbow* ◇ *The beach swept around in an arc.* **3** (*technical*) an electric current passing across a space between two TERMINALS—see also ARC LAMP
■ *verb* (**arc·ing** /ˈɑːkɪŋ; *AmE* ˈɑːrk-/, **arced**, **arced** /ɑːkt; *AmE* ɑːrkt/) [V] (*technical*) **1** to move in the shape of an arc **2** to form an electric arc

arcade

ar·cade /ɑːˈkeɪd; *AmE* ɑːrˈk-/ *noun* **1** a covered passage with arches along the side of a row of buildings (usually a row of shops/stores) **2** a covered passage between streets, with shops/stores on either side **3** (also ˈ**shopping arcade**) (both *BrE*) (also **mall**, ˈ**shopping mall** *AmE*, *BrE*) a large building with a number of shop/stores in it **4** = AMUSEMENT ARCADE: *arcade games*

ar·cane /ɑːˈkeɪn; *AmE* ɑːrˈk-/ *adj.* (*formal*) secret and mysterious and therefore difficult to understand: *the arcane rules of cricket*

arch /ɑːtʃ; *AmE* ɑːrtʃ/ *noun, verb, adj.*
■ *noun* **1** a curved structure that supports the weight of sth above it, such as a bridge or the upper part of a building: *a bridge with three arches*—picture at ARCADE **2** a structure with a curved top that is supported by straight sides, sometimes forming an entrance or built as a MONUMENT: *Go through the arch and follow the path.* ◇ *Marble Arch is a famous London landmark.* **3** the raised part of the foot formed by a curved section of bones **4** anything that forms a curved shape at the top: *the delicate arch of her eyebrows*
■ *verb* **1** if you **arch** part of your body, or if it **arches**, it moves and forms a curved shape: [VN] *The cat arched its back and hissed.* [also V] **2** [V] to be in a curved line or shape across or over sth: *Tall trees arched over the path.*

■ *adj.* [usually before noun] (often *disapproving*) an arch look, tone of voice, etc. deliberately shows amusement because the person knows more than other people or more than they pretend about a situation: *He tapped the side of his nose in an uncharacteristically arch gesture.* ▶ **arch·ly** *adv.*: *'Guess what?' she said archly.*

arch- /ɑːtʃ; *AmE* ɑːrtʃ/ *combining form* (in nouns) main; most important or most extreme: *archbishop* ◇ *archenemy*

archae·olo·gist (*AmE* also **arche·olo·gist**) /ˌɑːkiˈɒlədʒɪst; *AmE* ˌɑːrkiˈɑːl-/ *noun* a person who studies archaeology

archae·ology (*AmE* also **arche·ology**) /ˌɑːkiˈɒlədʒi; *AmE* ˌɑːrkiˈɑːl-/ *noun* [U] the study of cultures of the past, and of periods of history by examining the remains of buildings and objects found in the ground—see also INDUSTRIAL ARCHAEOLOGY ▶ **arch·aeo·logic·al** (*AmE* also **arch·eo·logic·al**) /ˌɑːkiəˈlɒdʒɪkl; *AmE* ˌɑːrkiəˈlɑːdʒ-/ *adj.*: *archaeological excavations/evidence*

ar·chaic /ɑːˈkeɪɪk; *AmE* ɑːrˈk-/ *adj.* **1** old and no longer used: *'Thou art' is an archaic form of 'you are'.* **2** very old-fashioned: *The system is archaic and unfair and needs changing.* **3** from a much earlier or ancient period of history: *archaic art*

archa·ism /ˈɑːkeɪɪzəm; *AmE* ˈɑːrk-/ *noun* (*technical*) a very old word or phrase that is no longer used

arch·an·gel /ˈɑːkeɪndʒl; *AmE* ˈɑːrk-/ *noun* an ANGEL of the highest rank: *the Archangel Gabriel*

arch·bishop /ˌɑːtʃˈbɪʃəp; *AmE* ˌɑːrtʃ-/ *noun* a BISHOP of the highest rank, responsible for all the churches in a large area: *the Archbishop of Canterbury* (= the head of the Church of England)

arch·bish·op·ric /ˌɑːtʃˈbɪʃəprɪk; *AmE* ˌɑːrtʃ-/ *noun* **1** the position of an archbishop **2** the district for which an archbishop is responsible

arch·deacon /ˌɑːtʃˈdiːkən; *AmE* ˌɑːrtʃ-/ *noun* a priest just below the rank of BISHOP, especially in the Anglican Church

arch·dio·cese /ˌɑːtʃˈdaɪəsɪs; *AmE* ˌɑːrtʃ-/ *noun* a district under the care of an ARCHBISHOP

arch·duch·ess /ˌɑːtʃˈdʌtʃəs; *AmE* ˌɑːrtʃ-/ *noun* (in the past) the wife of an archduke or a daughter of the EMPEROR of Austria

arch·duke /ˌɑːtʃˈdjuːk; *AmE* ˌɑːrtʃˈduːk/ *noun* (in the past) a son of the EMPEROR of Austria: *Archduke Franz Ferdinand*—compare GRAND DUKE

ˌ**arch-ˈenemy** *noun* a person's main enemy

arche·olo·gist, **arche·ology** (*AmE*) = ARCHAEOLO-GIST, ARCHAEOLOGY

arch·er /ˈɑːtʃə(r); *AmE* ˈɑːrtʃ-/ *noun* a person who shoots with a BOW and arrows

arch·ery /ˈɑːtʃəri; *AmE* ˈɑːrtʃ-/ *noun* [U] the art or sport of shooting arrows with a BOW

arche·typal /ˌɑːkiˈtaɪpl; *AmE* ˌɑːrki-/ *adj.* (*written*) having all the important qualities and characteristics that make sb/sth a typical example of a particular kind of person or thing: *The Beatles were the archetypal pop group.*

arche·type /ˈɑːkitaɪp/ *noun* (*written*) the most typical or perfect example of a particular kind of person or thing: *She is the archetype of an American movie star.*

archi·pel·ago /ˌɑːkɪˈpeləgəʊ; *AmE* ˌɑːrkɪˈpeləgoʊ/ *noun* (*pl.* **-os** or **-oes**) a group of islands and the sea surrounding them

archi·tect /ˈɑːkɪtekt; *AmE* ˈɑːrk-/ *noun* **1** a person whose job is designing buildings, etc. **2** a person who is responsible for planning or creating an idea, an event or a situation: *He was one of the principal architects of the revolution.*

archi·tec·tural /ˌɑːkɪˈtektʃərəl; *AmE* ˌɑːrk-/ *adj.* connected with architecture: *architectural design/features/style* ▶ **archi·tec·tur·al·ly** *adv.*: *The house is of little interest architecturally.*

archi·tec·ture /ˈɑːkɪtektʃə(r); *AmE* ˈɑːrk-/ *noun* **1** [U] the art and study of designing buildings: *to study architecture* **2** [U] the design or style of a building or buildings:

s	t	v	z	ʃ	ʒ	tʃ	dʒ	θ	ð	ŋ
see	tea	van	zoo	shoe	vision	chain	jam	thin	this	sing

the architecture of the eighteenth century ◊ *modern architecture* **3** [C, U] (*computing*) the design and structure of a computer system

arch·ive /ˈɑːkaɪv; *AmE* ˈɑːrk-/ *noun, verb*
■ *noun* (also **arch·ives** [pl.]) a collection of historical documents or records of a government, a family, a place or an organization; the place where these records are stored: *the National Sound Archive* ◊ *archive film* ◊ *The BBC's archives are bulging with material.*
■ *verb* [VN] **1** to put or store a document or other material in an archive **2** (*computing*) to move information that is not often needed to a tape or disk to store it

arch·iv·ist /ˈɑːkɪvɪst; *AmE* ˈɑːrk-/ *noun* a person whose job is to develop and manage an archive

ˌarch-ˈrival *noun* a person's main opponent

arch·way /ˈɑːtʃweɪ; *AmE* ˈɑːrtʃ-/ *noun* a passage or an entrance with an arch over it: *We went through a stone archway into the courtyard.*

ˈarc lamp (also **ˈarc light**) *noun* a lamp that gives very bright light that is produced by an electric ARC

Arc·tic /ˈɑːktɪk; *AmE* ˈɑːrk-/ *adj., noun*
■ *adj.* **1** [only before noun] related to or happening in the regions around the North Pole: *Arctic explorers*—compare ANTARCTIC **2** (**arctic**) extremely cold: *TV pictures showed the arctic conditions.*
■ *noun* [sing.] (**the Arctic**) the regions of the world around the North Pole

the ˌArctic ˈCircle *noun* [sing.] the line of LATITUDE 66° 30ʹ North—compare ANTARCTIC CIRCLE

ar·dent /ˈɑːdnt; *AmE* ˈɑːrdnt/ *adj.* [usually before noun] (*written*) very enthusiastic and showing strong feelings about sth/sb [SYN] PASSIONATE: *an ardent supporter of European unity* ▶ **ar·dent·ly** *adv.*

ar·dour (*AmE* **ardor**) /ˈɑːdə(r); *AmE* ˈɑːrdər/ *noun* [U] (*formal*) very strong feelings of enthusiasm or love [SYN] PASSION

ar·du·ous /ˈɑːdjuəs, -dʒu-; *AmE* ˈɑːrdʒuəs/ *adj.* involving a lot of effort and energy, especially over a period of time: *an arduous journey across the Andes* ◊ *The work was arduous.* ▶ **ar·du·ous·ly** *adv.* (*rare*)

are¹ /ə(r); *strong form* ɑː(r)/ ⇨ BE

are² /eə(r); ɑː(r); *AmE* er; ɑːr/ *noun* a unit for measuring an area of land; 100 square metres

area /ˈeəriə; *AmE* ˈeriə/ *noun*
PART OF PLACE | **1** [C] part of a place, town, etc., or a region of a country or the world: *mountainous/desert areas* ◊ *rural/urban/inner-city areas* ◊ *There is heavy traffic in the downtown area tonight.* ◊ *She knows the local area very well.* ◊ *John is the London area manager.* ◊ *Wreckage from the plane was scattered over a wide area.* ◊ *The farm and surrounding area was flooded.*—see also CATCHMENT AREA, CONSERVATION AREA, DEVELOPMENT AREA, NO-GO AREA **2** [C] a part of a room, building or particular space that is used for a special purpose: *the hotel reception area* ◊ *a play/parking/dining area*—see also PENALTY AREA, REST AREA, SERVICE AREA
PARTICULAR PLACE | **3** [C] a particular place on an object: *Move the cursor to a blank area of the screen and double click with the mouse.* ◊ *The tumour had not spread to other areas of the body.*
SUBJECT/ACTIVITY | **4** [C] ~ (**of sth**) a particular subject or activity, or an aspect of it: *the areas of training and development* ◊ *Finance is Mark's area.* ◊ *The big growth area of recent years has been in health clubs.*—see also GREY AREA
MEASUREMENT | **5** [C, U] the amount of space covered by a flat surface or piece of land, described as a measurement: *the area of a triangle* ◊ *The room is 12 square metres in area.*

ˈarea code *noun* (*especially AmE*) the numbers for a particular area or city, that you use when you are making a telephone call from outside the local area—compare DIALLING CODE

arena /əˈriːnə/ *noun* **1** a place with a flat open area in the middle and seats around it where people can watch

sports and entertainment: *a concert at Wembley Arena* **2** (*written*) an area of activity that concerns the public, especially one where there is a lot of opposition between different groups or countries: *the political/international arena*

aren't /ɑːnt/ *short form* **1** are not **2** (in questions) am not: *Aren't I clever?*

argon /ˈɑːɡɒn; *AmE* ˈɑːrɡɑːn/ *noun* [U] (*symb* **Ar**) a chemical element. Argon is a colourless gas that does not react with anything and is used in electric lights.

argot /ˈɑːɡəʊ; *AmE* ˈɑːrɡət; -ɡoʊ/ *noun* [sing., U] (from *French*) informal words and phrases that are used by a particular group of people and not easily understood by others

ar·gu·able /ˈɑːɡjuəbl; *AmE* ˈɑːrɡ-/ *adj.* (*formal*) **1** that you can give good reasons for: *It is arguable that giving too much detail may actually be confusing.* **2** not certain; that you do not accept without question: *It is arguable whether the case should have ever gone to trial* (= perhaps it should not have).

ar·gu·ably /ˈɑːɡjuəbli; *AmE* ˈɑːrɡ-/ *adv.* used, often before a comparative or superlative adjective, when you are stating an opinion which you believe you could give reasons to support: *He is arguably the best actor of his generation.*

argue /ˈɑːɡjuː; *AmE* ˈɑːrɡ-/ *verb* **1** [V] ~ (**with sb**) (**about/over sth**) to speak angrily to sb because you disagree with them: *My brothers are always arguing.* ◊ *We're always arguing with each other about money.* ◊ *I don't want to argue with you—just do it.* **2** ~ (**for/against sth**) | ~ (**for/against doing sth**) to give reasons why you think that sth is right/wrong, true/not true, etc., especially to persuade people that you are right: [V] *They argued for the right to strike.* ◊ [VN] *She argued the case for bringing back the death penalty.* ◊ *He was too tired to argue the point* (= discuss the matter). ◊ *a well-argued article* ◊ [V that] *He argued that they needed more time to finish the project.* ◊ [VN that] *It could be argued that laws are made by and for men.* [also V wh-] **3** [VN] (*formal*) to show clearly that sth exists or is true: *These latest developments argue a change in government policy.* [IDM] **ˌargue the ˈtoss** (*BrE, informal*) to continue to disagree about a decision, especially when it is too late to change it or it is not very important [PHRV] **ˌargue sb ˈinto/ˈout of doing sth** to persuade sb to do/not do sth by giving them reasons: *They argued him into withdrawing his complaint.* **ˈargue with sth** (usually used in negative sentences) (*informal*) to disagree with a statement: *He's a really successful man—you can't argue with that.*

ar·gu·ment /ˈɑːɡjumənt; *AmE* ˈɑːrɡ-/ *noun* **1** [C, U] ~ (**with sb**) (**about/over sth**) a conversation or discussion in which two or more people disagree, often angrily: *We had an argument with the waiter about the bill.* ◊ *She got into an argument with the teacher.* ◊ *to win/lose an argument* ◊ *After some heated argument a decision was finally taken.* **2** [C] ~ (**for/against sth**) | ~ (**that ...**) a reason or set of reasons that sb uses to show that sth is true or correct: *There are strong arguments for and against euthanasia.* ◊ *His argument was that public spending must be reduced.* ◊ *Her main argument was a moral one.* **3** [U] ~ (**about sth**) the act of disagreeing in a conversation or discussion using a reason or set of reasons: *Let's assume for the sake of argument* (= in order to discuss the problem completely) *that we can't start till March.*

ar·gu·men·ta·tive /ˌɑːɡjuˈmentətɪv; *AmE* ˌɑːrɡ-/ *adj.* a person who is **argumentative** likes arguing or often starts arguing

argy-bargy /ˌɑːdʒi ˈbɑːdʒi; *AmE* ˌɑːrdʒi ˈbɑːrdʒi/ *noun* [U] (*BrE, informal*) noisy disagreement

aria /ˈɑːriə/ *noun* a song for one voice, especially in an opera or ORATORIO

-arian *suffix* (in nouns and adjectives) believing in; practising: *humanitarian* ◊ *disciplinarian*

arid /ˈærɪd/ *adj.* **1** (of land or a climate) having little or no rain; very dry: *arid and semi-arid deserts* **2** (*formal*) with

æ	ɑː	e	ɜː	ə	ɪ	iː	i	ɒ	ɔː	ʌ	ʊ	u	uː
cat	father	ten	bird	about	sit	see	many	got	saw	cup	put	actual	too

(BrE)

nothing new or interesting in it: *an arid discussion*
▶ **arid·ity** /əˈrɪdəti/ *noun* [U]

Aries /ˈeəriːz; *AmE* ˈeriːz/ *noun* **1** [U] the first sign of the ZODIAC, the RAM **2** [sing.] a person born under the influence of this sign, that is between 21 March and 20 April

aright /əˈraɪt/ *adv.* (*old-fashioned*) correctly: *Do I hear you aright?*

arise /əˈraɪz/ *verb* (**arose** /əˈrəʊz; *AmE* əˈrouz/, **arisen** /əˈrɪzn/) [V] **1** (*rather formal*) (especially of a problem or a difficult situation) to happen; to start to exist SYN OCCUR: *A new crisis has arisen.* ◊ *We keep them informed of any changes as they arise.* ◊ *Children should be disciplined when the need arises* (= when it is necessary). ◊ *A storm arose during the night.* **2 ~** (**out of/from sth**) (*rather formal*) to happen as a result of a particular situation: *injuries arising out of a road accident* ◊ *Emotional or mental problems can arise from a physical cause.* ◊ *Are there any matters arising from the minutes of the last meeting?* **3** (*formal*) to begin to exist or develop: *Several new industries arose in the town.* **4** (*old use* or *literary*) to get out of bed; to stand up: *He arose at dawn.* **5** (*old use*) to come together to protest about sth or to fight for sth: *The peasants arose against their masters.* **6** (*literary*) (of a mountain, a tall building, etc.) to become visible gradually as you move towards it

ar·is·toc·ra·cy /ˌærɪˈstɒkrəsi; *AmE* -ˈstɑːk-/ *noun* [C+sing./pl. *v.*] (in some countries) people born in the highest social class, who have special titles: *members of the aristocracy*

ar·is·to·crat /ˈærɪstəkræt; *AmE* əˈrɪst-/ *noun* a member of the aristocracy—compare COMMONER

ar·is·to·crat·ic /ˌærɪstəˈkrætɪk; *AmE* əˌrɪstə-/ *adj.* belonging to or typical of the ARISTOCRACY: *an aristocratic name/family/lifestyle*

arith·met·ic /əˈrɪθmətɪk/ *noun* [U] **1** the type of mathematics that deals with the adding, multiplying, etc. of numbers: *He's not very good at arithmetic.* **2** sums involving the adding, multiplying, etc. of numbers: *a quick bit of mental arithmetic* ◊ *I think there's something wrong with your arithmetic.*

arith·met·ic·al /ˌærɪθˈmetɪkl/ (also **arith·met·ic**) *adj.* relating to arithmetic: *an arithmetical calculation*
▶ **arith·met·ic·al·ly** *adv.*

arithˌmetic ˈmean *noun* = MEAN

arithˌmetic proˈgression (also **arithˌmetical proˈgression**) *noun* a series of numbers that decrease or increase by the same amount each time, for example 2, 4, 6, 8—compare GEOMETRIC PROGRESSION

ark /ɑːk; *AmE* ɑːrk/ (**the ark**) (also ˌ**Noah's ˈark**) *noun* [sing.] (in the Bible) a large boat which Noah built to save his family and two of every type of animal from the flood IDM **out of the ˈark | sth went out with the ˈark** (*BrE, spoken*) if sb says that an object or a custom is **out of the ark** or **went out with the ark**, they think that it is old or old-fashioned

arm /ɑːm; *AmE* ɑːrm/ *noun, verb*
■ *noun*—see also ARMS
OF BODY | **1** either of the two long parts that stick out from the top of the body and connect the shoulders to the hands: *He escaped with only a broken arm.* ◊ *She threw her arms around his neck.* ◊ *The officer grabbed him by the arm* (= grabbed his arm). ◊ *She touched him gently on the arm.* ◊ *He held the dirty rag at arm's length* (= as far away from his body as possible). ◊ *They walked along arm in arm* (= with the arm of one person linked with the arm of the other). ◊ *She cradled the child in her arms.* ◊ *They fell asleep in each other's arms* (= holding each other). ◊ *He was carrying a number of files under his arm* (= between his arm and his body). ◊ *He walked in with a tall blonde on his arm* (= next to him and holding his arm).—picture at BODY
OF CLOTHING | **2** the part of a piece of clothing that covers the arm SYN SLEEVE: *The arms will need shortening.*
OF CHAIR | **3** the part of a chair, etc. on which you rest your arms: *She perched on the arm of his chair.*—picture at CHAIR
OF MACHINERY | **4** a long narrow part of an object or a piece

of machinery, especially one that moves, for example a record player—picture at GLASS
OF WATER/LAND | **5** a long narrow piece of water or land that is joined to a larger area: *A small bridge spans the arm of the river.*
OF ORGANIZATION | **6** [usually sing.] **~** (**of sth**) a section of a large organization that deals with one particular activity SYN WING: *the research arm of the company*
IDM **cost/pay an ˌarm and a ˈleg** (*informal*) to cost/pay a lot of money **keep sb at arm's length** to avoid having a close relationship with sb: *He keeps all his clients at arm's length.*—more at AKIMBO, BABE, BEAR *v.*, CHANCE *v.*, FOLD *v.*, LONG *adj.*, OPEN *adj.*, RIGHT *adj.*, SHOT *n.*, TWIST *v.*
■ *verb* **1 ~ yourself/sb** (**with sth**) to provide weapons for yourself/sb in order to fight a battle or a war: [VN] *The crowd armed themselves with sticks and stones.* ◊ (*figurative*) *She had armed herself for the meeting with all the latest statistics.* ◊ [V] *The country was arming against the enemy.*—see also ARMED **2** [VN] to make a bomb, etc. ready to explode—compare DISARM
IDM ˌ**armed to the ˈteeth** (*written*) having many weapons

ar·mada /ɑːˈmɑːdə; *AmE* ɑːrˈm-/ *noun* a large group of ships sailing together: *The Spanish Armada was sent to attack England in 1588.* ◊ (*figurative*) *a vast armada of football fans*

ar·ma·dillo /ˌɑːməˈdɪləʊ; *AmE* ˌɑːrməˈdɪloʊ/ *noun* (*pl.* **-os**) an American animal with a hard shell made of pieces of bone, that eats insects and rolls into a ball if sth attacks it

Ar·ma·ged·don /ˌɑːməˈɡedn; *AmE* ˌɑːrm-/ *noun* [sing., U] **1** (in the Bible) a battle between good and evil at the end of the world **2** a terrible war that could destroy the world: *nuclear Armageddon*

ar·ma·ment /ˈɑːməmənt; *AmE* ˈɑːrm-/ *noun* **1** [C, usually pl.] weapons, especially large guns, bombs, TANKS, etc: *the armaments industry* **2** [U] the process of increasing the amount of weapons an army or a country has, especially to prepare for war.—compare DISARMAMENT

arm·band /ˈɑːmbænd; *AmE* ˈɑːrm-/ *noun* **1** a band of fabric worn around the arm as a sign of sth, for example that sb has an official position: *The stewards all wore armbands.* ◊ *Many people at the funeral service were wearing black armbands.* **2** either of two plastic rings that can be filled with air and worn around the arms by sb who is learning to swim

arm·chair *noun, adj.*
■ *noun* /ˈɑːmtʃeə(r); ɑːmˈtʃeə(r); *AmE* ˈɑːrmtʃer; ɑːrmˈtʃer/ a comfortable chair with sides on which you can rest your arms: *to sit in an armchair*—picture at CHAIR
■ *adj.* /ˈɑːmtʃeə(r); *AmE* ˈɑːrmtʃer/ [only before noun] knowing about a subject through books and television, rather than by doing it for yourself: *an armchair critic/traveller*

armed /ɑːmd; *AmE* ɑːrmd/ *adj.* **1** involving the use of weapons: *an armed robbery* ◊ *an international armed conflict* (= a war) OPP UNARMED **2 ~** (**with a gun, etc.**) carrying a weapon, especially a gun: *The man is armed and dangerous.* ◊ *armed guards* ◊ *Police were heavily armed.* ◊ *He was armed with a rifle.* OPP UNARMED **3 ~** (**with sth**) knowing sth or carrying sth that you need in order to help you to perform a task: *He was armed with all the facts.* ◊ *I sat down by the lake armed with a pair of binoculars.*

the ˌarmed ˈforces (*BrE* also **the ˌarmed ˈservices**) *noun* [pl.] a country's army, navy and air force

arm·ful /ˈɑːmfʊl; *AmE* ˈɑːrm-/ *noun* a quantity that you can carry in one or both arms

arm·hole /ˈɑːmhəʊl; *AmE* ˈɑːrmhoʊl/ *noun* the place in a coat, shirt, dress, etc. that your arm goes through

ar·mis·tice /ˈɑːmɪstɪs; *AmE* ˈɑːrm-/ *noun* [sing.] a formal agreement during a war to stop fighting and discuss making peace

arm·lock /ˈɑːmlɒk; *AmE* ˈɑːrmlɑːk/ *noun* (in WRESTLING) a way of holding an opponent's arm so that they cannot move: *He had him in an armlock.*

ar·mour (*BrE*) (*AmE* **armor**) /ˈɑːmə(r); *AmE* ˈɑːrm-/ *noun* [U] **1** special metal clothing that soldiers wore in the past

aɪ	aʊ	eɪ	əʊ	oʊ	ɔɪ	ɪə	eə	ʊə	j	w
my	now	say	go	go	boy	near	hair	pure	yes	wet
			(BrE)	(AmE)						

to protect their bodies while fighting: *a suit of armour* ◇ *(figurative) Monkeys do not have any kind of protective armour and use their brains to solve problems.* **2** metal covers that protect ships and military vehicles such as TANKS **3** *(technical)* military vehicles used in war: *an attack by infantry and armour* IDM see CHINK *n.*, KNIGHT *n.*

ar·moured *(BrE)* *(AmE* **ar·mored)** /ˈɑːməd; *AmE* ˈɑːrmərd/ *adj.* **1** (especially of a military vehicle) protected by metal covers: *The cruiser was heavily armoured.* ◇ *an armoured car* **2** using armoured vehicles: *an armoured division*

ar·mour·er *(BrE)* *(AmE* **ar·mor·er)** /ˈɑːmərə(r)*; AmE* ˈɑːrm-/ *noun* a person who makes or repairs weapons and armour

armour-ˈplated *(BrE)* *(AmE* **armor-)** *adj.* (of vehicles) covered with sheets of metal to provide protection against bullets, etc.

ar·moury *(BrE)* *(AmE* **ar·mory)** /ˈɑːməri*; AmE* ˈɑːrm-/ *noun* (*pl.* **-ies**) **1** a place where weapons and armour are kept SYN ARSENAL **2** *(AmE)* a building which is the HEAD-QUARTERS for the National Guard or an Army Reserve Unit **3** *(written)* the things that sb has available to help them achieve sth: *Doctors have an armoury of drugs available.* **4** all the weapons and military equipment that a country has: *Britain's nuclear armoury*

arm·pit /ˈɑːmpɪt; *AmE* ˈɑːrm-/ (also *AmE informal* **pit**) *noun* the part of the body under the arm where it joins the shoulder—see also UNDERARM—picture at BODY

arm·rest /ˈɑːmrest; *AmE* ˈɑːrm-/ *noun* the part of some types of seat, especially in planes or cars, which supports your arm

arms /ɑːmz; *AmE* ɑːrmz/ *noun* [pl.] **1** *(formal)* weapons, especially as used by the army, navy or air force: *arms and ammunition* ◇ *Police officers in the UK do not usually carry arms.*—see also FIREARM, SMALL ARMS **2** = COAT OF ARMS: *the King's Arms* (= used as the name of a pub) IDM **be under ˈarms** to have weapons and be ready to fight in a war **lay down your ˈarms** to stop fighting **take up arms (against sb)** to prepare to fight **(be) up in ˈarms (about/over sth)** *(informal)* (of a group of people) to be very angry about sth and ready to protest strongly about it—more at BEAR *v.*, PRESENT *v.*

army /ˈɑːmi; *AmE* ˈɑːrmi/ *noun* (*pl.* **-ies**) **1** [C+sing./pl. *v.*] a large organized group of soldiers who are trained to fight on land: *The two opposing armies faced each other across the battlefield.* **2** **(the army)** [sing.+ sing./pl. *v.*] the part of a country's armed forces that fights on land: *Her husband is in the army.* ◇ *After leaving school, Mike went into the army.* ◇ *an army officer* **3** [C+sing./pl. *v.*] a large number of people or things, especially when they are organized in some way or involved in a particular activity: *an army of advisers/volunteers* ◇ *An army of ants marched across the path.*

ˈA-road *noun* (in Britain) a road that is less important than a motorway, but wider and straighter than a B-ROAD

aroma /əˈrəʊmə; *AmE* əˈroʊmə/ *noun* a pleasant, noticeable smell: *the aroma of fresh coffee*

aroma·ther·apy /əˌrəʊməˈθerəpi; *AmE* əˌroʊmə-/ *noun* [U] the use of natural oils that smell sweet for controlling pain or for rubbing into the body during MASSAGE ▶ **aroma·ther·ap·ist** *noun*

aro·mat·ic /ˌærəˈmætɪk/ *adj.* having a pleasant noticeable smell SYN FRAGRANT: *aromatic oils/herbs*

arose *pt* of ARISE

around /əˈraʊnd/ *adv., prep.*

▣ *adv.* HELP For the special uses of **around** in phrasal verbs, look at the entries for the verbs. For example **come around to sth** is in the phrasal verb section at **come. 1** approximately: *He arrived around five o'clock.* ◇ *The cost would be somewhere around £1500.* **2** on every side; surrounding sb/sth: *I could hear laughter all around.* ◇ *a yard with a fence* **all around 3** *(especially AmE)* *(BrE usually* **round)** moving in a circle: *How do you make the wheels go around?* **4** *(especially AmE)* *(BrE usually* **round)** measured in a circle: *an old tree that was at least ten feet around* **5** in or to many places: *We were all running around trying to get ready in time.* ◇ *This is our*

new office—Kay will show you around. ◇ *There were papers lying around all over the floor.* **6** used to describe activities that have no real purpose: *There were several young people sitting around looking bored.* **7** present in a place; available: *There was more money around in those days.* ◇ *I knocked but there was no one around.* ◇ *Digital television has been around for some time now.* **8** active and well known in a sport, profession, etc: *a new tennis champion who could be around for a long time* ◇ *She's been around as a film director since the 1980s.* **9** *(especially AmE)* *(BrE usually* **round)** in a circle or curve to face another way or the opposite way: *She turned the car around and drove off.* ◇ *They looked around when he called.*—see also ABOUT, ROUND IDM **have been around** to have gained knowledge and experience of the world

■ *prep.* *(especially AmE)* *(BrE usually* **round)** **1** surrounding sb/sth; on each side of sth: *The house is built around a central courtyard.* ◇ *He put his arms around her.* **2** on, to or from the other side of sb/sth: *Our house is just around the corner.* ◇ *The bus came around the bend.* ◇ *There must be a way around the problem.* **3** in a circle: *They walked around the lake.* **4** to fit in with particular people, ideas, etc: *I can't arrange everything around your timetable!* **5** in or to many places in an area: *They walked around the town looking for a place to eat.*

WHICH WORD?
around / round / about

Around and **round** can often be used with the same meaning in *BrE*, though **around** is more formal: *The earth goes round/around the sun.* ◇ *They live round/around the corner.* ◇ *We travelled round /around India.* ◇ *She turned round/around when I came in.* In *AmE* only **around** can be used in these meanings.

Around, round and **about** can also sometimes be used with the same meaning in *BrE*: *The kids were running around/round/about outside.* ◇ *I've been waiting around/round/about to see her all day.* In *AmE* only **around** can be used in these meanings. **About** or **around** can be used in both *BrE* and *AmE* to mean 'approximately': *We left around/about 8 o'clock.*

---

a,round-the-ˈclock *adj.* = ROUND-THE-CLOCK

arouse /əˈraʊz/ *verb* [VN] **1** to make sb have a particular feeling or attitude: *to arouse sb's interest/curiosity/anger* ◇ *Her strange behaviour aroused our suspicions.* **2** to make sb feel sexually excited **3** to make you feel more active and want to start doing sth: *The whole community was aroused by the crime.* **4 ~ sb (from sth)** *(formal)* to wake sb from sleep—see also ROUSE ▶ **arousal** /əˈraʊzl/ *noun* [U]: *emotional/sexual arousal*

ar·peg·gio /ɑːˈpedʒiəʊ; *AmE* ɑːrˈpedʒioʊ/ *noun* (*pl.* **-os**) *(music)* the notes of a CHORD played quickly one after the other

arr. *abbr.* **1** (in writing) arrives; ARRIVAL: *arr. London 06.00*—compare DEP. **2** *(music)* (in writing) arranged by: *Handel, arr. Mozart*

ar·raign /əˈreɪn/ *verb* [VN] [usually passive] **~ sb (for sth)** *(law)* to bring sb to court in order to formally accuse them of a crime: *He was arraigned for murder.* ◇ *He was arraigned on a charge of murder.* ▶ **ar·raign·ment** *noun* [C, U]

ar·range /əˈreɪndʒ/ *verb* **1** to plan or organize sth in advance: [VN] *The party was arranged quickly.* ◇ *She arranged a loan with the bank.* ◇ *Can I arrange an appointment for Monday? ◇ We met at six, as arranged.* ◇ [Vwh-] *We've still got to arrange how to get to the airport.* ◇ [V] *We arranged for a car to collect us from the airport.* ◇ *I've arranged with the neighbours about feeding the cat while we are away.* ◇ [Vtoinf] *Have you arranged to meet him?* ◇ [Vthat] *I've arranged that we can borrow their car.* **2** [VN] to put sth in a particular order; to make sth neat or attractive: *The books are arranged alphabetically by author.* ◇ *I must arrange my financial affairs and make a will.* ◇ *She arranged the flowers in a vase.* **3** [VN] **~ sth (for**

---

b	d	f	g	h	k	l	m	n	p	r
bad	did	fall	get	hat	cat	leg	man	now	pen	red

sth) (*abbr.* **arr.**) to write or change a piece of music so that it is suitable for a particular instrument or voice: *He arranged traditional folk songs for the piano.*

ar·ranged 'marriage *noun* a marriage in which the parents choose the husband or wife for their child

ar·range·ment /əˈreɪndʒmənt/ *noun* **1** [C, usually pl.] **~ (for sth)** a plan or preparation that you make so that sth can happen: *travel arrangements* ◇ *I'll* **make arrangements** *for you to be met at the airport.* **2** [C, usually pl.] the way things are done or organized: *She's happy with her unusual living arrangements.* ◇ *new security arrangements* ◇ *There are special arrangements for people working overseas.* **3** [C, U] **~ (with sb) (to do sth)** an agreement that you make with sb that you can both accept: *an arrangement between the school and the parents* ◇ *We can* **come to an arrangement** *over the price.* ◇ *They had an arrangement that the children would spend two weeks with each parent.* ◇ *You can cash cheques here* **by prior arrangement** *with the bank.* **4** [C, U] a group of things that are organized or placed in a particular order or position; the act of placing things in a particular order: *plans of the possible seating arrangements* ◇ *a class on the art of flower arrangement* **5** [C, U] a piece of music that has been changed, for example for another instrument to play

ar·ran·ger /əˈreɪndʒə/ *noun* **1** a person who arranges music that has been written by sb different **2** a person who arranges things: *arrangers of care services for the elderly*

ar·rant /ˈærənt/ *adj.* [only before noun] (*old-fashioned*) used to emphasize how bad sth/sb is: *arrant nonsense*

array /əˈreɪ/ *noun, verb*
▪ *noun* **1** [usually sing.] a group or collection of things or people, often one that is large or impressive: *a vast array of bottles of different shapes and sizes* ◇ *a dazzling array of talent* **2** (*computing*) a way of organizing and storing related data in a computer memory **3** (*technical*) a set of numbers, signs or values arranged in rows and columns
▪ *verb* [VN] [usually passive] (*formal*) **1** to arrange a group of things in a pleasing way or so that they are in order: *Jars of all shapes and sizes were arrayed on the shelves.* **2** to arrange soldiers in a position from which they are ready to attack

array·ed /əˈreɪd/ *adj.* [not before noun] **~ (in sth)** (*literary*) dressed in a particular way, especially in beautiful clothes: *She was arrayed in a black velvet gown.*

ar·rears /əˈrɪəz; *AmE* əˈrɪrz/ *noun* [pl.] money that sb owes that they have not paid at the right time: *rent/ mortgage/tax arrears* **IDM** **be in arrears | get/fall into arrears** to be late in paying money that you owe: *We're two months in arrears with the rent.* **in arrears** if money or a person is paid **in arrears** for work, the money is paid after the work has been done

ar·rest /əˈrest/ *verb, noun*
▪ *verb* **1** [VN] [often passive] **~ sb (for sth)** if the police **arrest** sb, the person is taken to a POLICE STATION and kept because the police believe they may be guilty of a crime: *A man has been arrested in connection with the robbery.* ◇ *Five people were arrested for drug-related offences.* ◇ *You could get arrested for doing that.* **2** [VN] (*formal*) to stop a process or a development: *They failed to arrest the company's decline.* **3** [VN] (*formal*) to make sb notice sth and pay attention to it: *An unusual noise* **arrested his attention.** **4** [V] if sb **arrests**, their heart stops beating: *He arrested in the ambulance on the way to the hospital.*
▪ *noun* [C, U] **1** the act of arresting sb: *The police made several arrests.* ◇ *a* **citizen's arrest** (= by a member of the public, not the police) ◇ *She was* **under arrest** *on suspicion of murder.* ◇ *Opposition leaders were put under* **house arrest** (= not allowed to leave their houses). **2** an act of sth stopping or being interrupted: *He died after suffering a* **cardiac arrest** (= when his heart suddenly stopped).

ar·rest·ing /əˈrestɪŋ/ *adj.* (*written*) attracting a lot of attention; very attractive

ar·rival /əˈraɪvl/ *noun* **1** [U, C] an act of coming or being brought to a place: *Guests receive dinner* **on/upon**

arrival *at the hotel.* ◇ *We apologize for the late arrival of the train.* ◇ *the arrival of the mail in the morning* ◇ *daily arrivals of refugees* ◇ *There are 120* **arrivals and departures** *every day.* **2** [C] a person or a thing that comes to a place: *The first arrivals at the concert got the best seats.* ◇ *early/late/new arrivals* ◇ *We're expecting a* **new arrival** (= a baby) *in the family soon.* **3** [U] the time when a new technology or idea is introduced: *the arrival of pay TV*

ar·rive /əˈraɪv/ *verb* [V] **1** (*abbr.* **arr.**) **~ (at/in/on ...)** to get to a place, especially at the end of a journey: *I'll wait until they arrive.* ◇ *I was pleased to hear you arrived home safely.* ◇ *to arrive early/late (for a meeting)* ◇ *She'll arrive in New York at noon.* ◇ *The train arrived at the station 20 minutes late.* ◇ *By the time I* **arrived on the scene,** *it was all over.* ◇ *We didn't arrive back at the hotel until very late.* ◇ *The police arrived to arrest him.* **2** (of things) to be brought to sb: *A letter arrived for you this morning.* ◇ *Send your application to arrive by 31 October.* ◇ *We waited an hour for our lunch to arrive.* ◇ *The new product will arrive on supermarket shelves* (= be available) *early next year.* **3** (of an event or a moment) to happen or to come, especially when you have been waiting for it: *The wedding day finally arrived.* ◇ *The baby arrived* (= was born) *early.* **IDM** **sb has ar'rived** (*informal*) somebody has become successful: *He knew he had arrived when he was short-listed for the Booker prize.* **PHRV** **ar'rive at sth** to decide on or find sth, especially after discussion and thought **SYN** REACH: *to arrive at an agreement/a decision/a conclusion* ◇ *to arrive at the truth*

ar·ro·gance /ˈærəɡəns/ *noun* [U] the behaviour of a person when they feel that they are more important than other people, so that they are rude to them or do not consider them

ar·ro·gant /ˈærəɡənt/ *adj.* behaving in a proud, unpleasant way, showing little thought for other people ▶ **ar·ro·gant·ly** *adv.*

ar·ro·gate /ˈærəɡeɪt/ *verb* **PHRV** **arrogate to yourself sth** (*formal*) to claim or take sth that you have no right to: *I do not arrogate to myself the right to decide.*

arrow /ˈærəʊ; *AmE* ˈæroʊ/ *noun* **1** a thin stick with a sharp point at one end, which is shot from a BOW: *a bow and arrow* ◇ *to fire/shoot an arrow* ◇ *The road continues as straight as an arrow.* **2** a mark or sign like an arrow (→), used to show direction or position: *Follow the arrows.* ◇ *Use the arrow keys to move the cursor.*

ar·row·head /ˈærəʊhed; *AmE* ˈæroʊ-/ *noun* the sharp pointed end of an arrow

ar·row·root /ˈærəʊruːt; *AmE* ˈæroʊ-/ *noun* [U] a powder which is prepared from the root of an American plant and used in cooking, especially to make sauces thick

arse /ɑːs; *AmE* ɑːrs/ *noun, verb*
▪ *noun* (*BrE*, △, *slang*) **1** (*AmE* **ass**) the part of the body that you sit on; your bottom: *Get off your arse* (= stop sitting around doing nothing)! **2** (usually following an adjective) a stupid person—see also SMART-ARSE **IDM** **My arse!** used by some people to show they do not believe what sb has said **work your 'arse off** to work very hard—more at KISS *v.*, KNOW *v.*, LICK *v.*, PAIN *n.*
▪ *verb* **IDM** **can't be 'arsed (to do sth)** (*BrE*, △, *slang*) to not want to do sth because it is too much trouble: *I was supposed to do some work this weekend but I couldn't be arsed.* **PHRV** **arse a'bout/a'round** (*BrE*, △, *slang*) to waste time by behaving in a silly way

arse·hole /ˈɑːshəʊl; *AmE* ˈɑːrshoʊl/ (*BrE*) (*AmE* **ass-hole**) *noun* (△, *slang*) **1** the ANUS **2** a stupid or unpleasant person: *What an arsehole!*

ar·senal /ˈɑːsənl; *AmE* ˈɑːrs-/ *noun* **1** a collection of weapons such as guns and explosives: *Britain's nuclear arsenal* **2** a building where military weapons and explosives are made or stored

ar·senic /ˈɑːsnɪk; *AmE* ˈɑːrs-/ *noun* [U] (*symb* **As**) a chemical element. Arsenic is an extremely poisonous white powder.

arson /ˈɑːsn; *AmE* ˈɑːrsn/ *noun* [U] the crime of deliberately setting fire to sth, especially a building: *to carry out an arson attack*

ar·son·ist /ˈɑːsənɪst; AmE ˈɑːrs-/ noun [U] a person who commits the crime of arson

art /ɑːt; AmE ɑːrt/ noun, verb
■ noun **1** [U] the use of the imagination to express ideas or feelings, particularly in painting, drawing or SCULPTURE: *modern/contemporary/American art* ◇ *an art critic/historian/lover* ◇ *Can we call television art?* ◇ *an art form* (= a particular type of artistic activity) ◇ *stolen works of art* ◇ *Her performance displayed great art.*—see also FINE ART **2** [U] examples of objects such as paintings, drawings or SCULPTURES: *an art gallery/exhibition* ◇ *a collection of art and antiques* **3** [U] the skill of creating objects such as paintings and drawings, especially when you study it: *She's good at art and design.* ◇ *an art teacher/student/college/class* **4** (**the arts**) [pl.] art, music, theatre, literature, etc. when you think of them as a group: *lottery funding for the arts*—see also PERFORMING ARTS **5** [C] a type of VISUAL or performing art: *Dance is a very theatrical art.* **6** [C, usually pl.] the subjects you can study at school or university which are not scientific, such as languages, history or literature: *an arts degree*—compare SCIENCE **7** [C, U] an ability or a skill that you can develop with training and practice: *a therapist trained in the art of healing* ◇ *Letter-writing is a lost art nowadays.* ◇ *Appearing confident at interviews is quite an art* (= rather difficult). IDM see FINE ART adj.
■ verb **thou art** (old use) used to mean 'you are', when talking to one person

art deco (also **Art Deco**) /ˌɑːt ˈdekəʊ; AmE ˌɑːrt ˈdekoʊ/ noun [U] a popular style of decorative art in the 1920s and 1930s that has GEOMETRIC shapes with clear outlines and bright strong colours. It was used especially on objects in the house, and in architecture.

arte·fact (also **ar·ti·fact** especially in AmE) /ˈɑːtɪfækt; AmE ˈɑːrt-/ noun (technical) an object that is made by a person, especially sth of historical or cultural interest

ar·terio·scler·osis /ɑːˌtɪəriəʊsklɪəˈrəʊsɪs; AmE ɑːrˌtɪriouskləˈrousɪs/ noun [U] (medical) a condition in which the walls of the arteries become thick and hard, making it difficult for blood to flow

ar·tery /ˈɑːtəri; AmE ˈɑːrt-/ noun (pl. **-ies**) **1** any of the tubes that carry blood from the heart to the rest of the body: *blocked arteries*—compare VEIN—see also CORONARY ARTERY **2** a large and important road, river, railway/railroad line, etc. ▶ **ar·ter·ial** /ɑːˈtɪəriəl; AmE ɑːrˈtɪr-/ adj. [only before noun]: *arterial blood/disease* ◇ *an arterial road* ◇ *arterial traffic*

ar·te·sian well /ɑːˌtiːziən ˈwel; AmE ɑːrˈtiːʒn/ noun a hole made in the ground through which water rises to the surface by natural pressure

art·ful /ˈɑːtfl; AmE ˈɑːrtfl/ adj. [usually before noun] **1** (disapproving) clever at getting what you want, sometimes by not telling the truth SYN CRAFTY **2** (of things or actions) designed or done in a clever way ▶ **art·ful·ly** /ˈɑːtfəli; AmE ˈɑːrt-/ adv.

'art gallery (also **gal·lery**) noun a building where paintings and other works of art are shown to the public

'art·house adj. art-house films/movies are usually made by small film companies and are not usually seen by a wide audience

arth·rit·ic /ɑːˈθrɪtɪk; AmE ɑːrˈθ-/ adj. suffering from or caused by arthritis: *arthritic hands/pains*

arth·ritis /ɑːˈθraɪtɪs; AmE ɑːrˈθ-/ noun [U] a disease that causes pain and swelling in one or more joints of the body—see also OSTEOARTHRITIS, RHEUMATOID ARTHRITIS

ar·ti·choke /ˈɑːtɪtʃəʊk; AmE ˈɑːrtɪtʃoʊk/ noun [C, U] **1** (also **globe 'arti·choke**) a round vegetable with a lot of thick green leaves. The bottom part of the leaves and the inside of the artichoke can be eaten when cooked.—picture on page A3 **2** (BrE) = JERUSALEM ARTICHOKE

art·icle /ˈɑːtɪkl; AmE ˈɑːrt-/ noun **1** ~ (**on/about sth**) a piece of writing about a particular subject in a newspaper or magazine: *Have you seen that article about young fashion designers?*—see also LEADING ARTICLE **2** (law) a separate item in an agreement or a contract: *The proposal breaches article 10 of the European Convention, which guarantees free speech.* **3** (formal) a particular item

or separate thing, especially one of a set: *articles of clothing* ◇ *toilet articles such as soap, toothpaste and shampoo* ◇ *The articles found in the car helped the police to identify the body.* **4** (grammar) the words *a* and *an* (**the indefinite article**) or *the* (**the definite article**)

art·icled /ˈɑːtɪkld; AmE ˈɑːrt-/ adj. (BrE) employed by a group of lawyers, ARCHITECTS or ACCOUNTANTS while training to become qualified: *an articled clerk* (= a trainee solicitor) ◇ *She was articled to a firm of solicitors.*

,article of 'faith noun (pl. **articles of faith**) something you believe very strongly, as if it were a religious belief

ar·ticu·late verb, adj.
■ verb /ɑːˈtɪkjuleɪt; AmE ɑːrˈt-/ **1** [VN] (formal) to express or explain your thoughts or feelings clearly in words: *She struggled to articulate her thoughts.* **2** to speak, pronounce or play sth in a clear way: [V] *He was too drunk to articulate properly.* ◇ [VN] *Every note was carefully articulated.* [also V speech] **3** [V] ~ (**with sth**) (written) to be related to sth so that together the two parts form a whole: [V] *These courses are designed to articulate with university degrees.* **4** (technical) ~ (**with sth**) to be joined to sth else by a joint, so that movement is possible; to join sth in this way: [V] *bones that articulate with others* ◇ [VN] *a robot with articulated limbs*
■ adj. /ɑːˈtɪkjələt; AmE ɑːrˈt-/ **1** (of a person) good at expressing ideas or feelings clearly in words: *He was unusually articulate for a ten-year-old.* **2** (of speech) clearly expressed or pronounced: *All we could hear were loud sobs, but no articulate words.* OPP INARTICULATE

ar·ticu·lated /ɑːˈtɪkjuleɪtɪd; AmE ɑːrˈt-/ adj. (BrE) (of a vehicle) with two or more sections joined together in a way that makes it easier to turn corners: *an articulated lorry/truck*—see also TRACTOR-TRAILER—picture at TRUCK

ar·ticu·la·tion /ɑːˌtɪkjuˈleɪʃn; AmE ɑːrˌt-/ noun **1** [U] (formal) the expression of an idea or a feeling in words: *the articulation and defence of his theory* **2** [U] (formal) the act of making sounds in speech or music: *The singer worked hard on the clear articulation of every note.* **3** [U, C] (technical) a joint or connection that allows movement

ar·ti·fact (especially AmE) = ARTEFACT

ar·ti·fice /ˈɑːtɪfɪs; AmE ˈɑːrt-/ noun [U, C] (formal) the clever use of tricks to deceive sb

ar·ti·fi·cial /ˌɑːtɪˈfɪʃl; AmE ˌɑːrt-/ adj. **1** made or produced to copy sth natural; not real: *an artificial limb/flower/sweetener/fertilizer* ◇ *artificial lighting/light* **2** created by people; not happening naturally: *A job interview is a very artificial situation.* ◇ *the artificial barriers of race, class and gender* **3** false; not what it appears to be: *artificial emotion* ▶ **ar·ti·fi·ci·al·ity** /ˌɑːtɪˌfɪʃiˈæləti; AmE ˌɑːrt-/ noun ◇ **ar·ti·fi·cial·ly** /ˌɑːtɪˈfɪʃəli; AmE ˌɑːrt-/ adv.: *artificially created lakes* ◇ *artificially low prices*

,artificial insemi'nation noun [U] (abbr. **AI**) the process of making a woman or female animal pregnant by an artificial method of putting male SPERM inside her, and not by sexual activity: *artificial insemination by a donor, abbreviated to 'AID'*

,artificial in'telligence noun [U] (abbr. **AI**) (computing) an area of study concerned with making computers copy intelligent human behaviour

,artificial respi'ration (BrE also **,artificial venti'lation**) noun [U] the process of helping a person who has stopped breathing begin to breathe again, usually by blowing into their mouth or nose—compare MOUTH-TO-MOUTH RESUSCITATION

ar·til·lery /ɑːˈtɪləri; AmE ɑːrˈt-/ noun **1** [U] large, heavy guns which are often moved on wheels: *The town is under heavy artillery fire.* ◇ *artillery attacks/barrages/shells* **2** (**the artillery**) [sing.] the section of an army trained to use these guns

ar·ti·san /ˌɑːtɪˈzæn; AmE ˈɑːrtəzn/ noun (formal) a person who does skilled work, making things with their hands SYN CRAFTSMAN

art·ist /ˈɑːtɪst; AmE ˈɑːrt-/ noun **1** a person who creates works of art, especially paintings or drawings: *an exhibition of work by contemporary British artists* ◇ *a graphic artist* ◇ *a make-up artist* ◇ *Police have issued an artist's*

æ	ɑː	e	ɜː	ə	ɪ	iː	i	ɒ	ɔː	ʌ	ʊ	u	uː
cat	father	ten	bird	about	sit	see	many	got	saw	cup	put	actual	too
								(BrE)					

A

impression of her attacker. ◊ (*figurative*) *Whoever made this cake is a real artist.* **2** = ARTISTE: *a recording/solo artist*

ar·tiste /ɑːˈtiːst; *AmE* ɑːrˈt-/ (also **art·ist**) *noun* (*especially BrE*) a professional entertainer such as a singer, a dancer or an actor

art·is·tic /ɑːˈtɪstɪk; *AmE* ɑːrˈt-/ *adj.* **1** connected with art or artists: *the surviving artistic works of the period* ◊ *a work of great artistic merit* ◊ *the artistic director of the theatre* **2** showing a natural skill in or enjoyment of art, especially being able to paint or draw well: *artistic abilities/achievements/skills/talent* ◊ *She comes from a very artistic family.* **3** done with skill and imagination; attractive or beautiful: *an artistic arrangement of dried flowers* IDM see LICENCE ▶ **art·is·tic·al·ly** /ɑːˈtɪstɪkli; *AmE* ɑːrˈt-/ *adv.*

art·is·try /ˈɑːtɪstri; *AmE* ˈɑːrt-/ *noun* [U] the skill of an artist: *He played the piece with effortless artistry.*

art·less /ˈɑːtləs; *AmE* ˈɑːrt-/ *adj.* (*formal*) **1** simple, natural and honest: *the artless sincerity of a young child* **2** made without skill or art

ˌarts and ˈcrafts *noun* [pl.] activities that need both artistic and practical skills, such as weaving, making jewellery and POTTERY

artsy /ˈɑːtsi; *AmE* ˈɑːrtsi/ *adj.* (*AmE*) = ARTY

art·work /ˈɑːtwɜːk; *AmE* ˈɑːrtwɜːrk/ *noun* **1** [U] photographs and pictures prepared for books, advertisements and magazines **2** [C] a work of art, especially one in a museum

arty /ˈɑːti; *AmE* ˈɑːrti/ (*BrE*) (*AmE* **artsy**) *adj.* (*informal, usually disapproving*) seeming or wanting to be very artistic or interested in the arts: *She hangs out with the arty types she met at drama school.*

aru·gula /æˈruːgjʊlə/ *noun* [U] (*AmE*) = ROCKET (4)

-ary *suffix* (in adjectives and nouns) connected with: *planetary* ◊ *budgetary*

as /əz; *strong form* æz/ *prep., adv., conj.*

■ *prep.* **1** used to describe sb/sth appearing to be sb/sth else: *They were all dressed as clowns.* ◊ *The bomb was disguised as a package.* **2** used to describe the fact that sb/sth has a particular job or function: *She works as a courier.* ◊ *Treat me as a friend.* ◊ *I respect him as a doctor.* ◊ *You can use that glass as a vase.* ◊ *The news came as a shock.* ◊ *She had been there often as a child* (= when she was a child).

■ *adv.* **1 as ... as ...** used when you are comparing two people or things, or two situations: *You're as tall as your father.* ◊ *He was as white as a sheet.* ◊ *She doesn't play as well as her sister.* ◊ *I haven't known him as long as you* (= as you have known him). ◊ *He doesn't earn as much as me.* ◊ *He doesn't earn as much as I do.* ◊ *It's not as hard as I thought.* ◊ *Run as fast as you can.* ◊ *We'd like it as soon as possible.* **2** used to say that sth happens in the same way: *As always, he said little.* ◊ *The 'h' in honest is silent, as in 'hour'.*

■ *conj.* **1** while sth else is happening: *He sat watching her as she got ready.* ◊ *As she grew older she gained in confidence.* **2** in the way in which: *They did as I had asked.* ◊ *Leave the papers as they are.* ◊ *She lost it, just as I said she would.* **3** used to state the reason for sth: *As you were out, I left a message.* ◊ *She may need some help as she's new.* **4** used to make a comment or to add information about what you have just said: *As you know, Julia is leaving soon.* ◊ *She's very tall, as is her mother.* **5** (*written*) used to say that in spite of sth being true, what follows is also true SYN THOUGH: *Happy as they were, there was something missing.* ◊ *Try as he might* (= however hard he tried), *he couldn't open the door.* IDM **as against sth** in contrast with sth: *They got 27% of the vote as against 32% at the last election.* **ˌas and ˈwhen** used to say that sth may happen at some time in the future, but only when sth else has happened: *We'll decide on the team as and when we qualify.* ◊ *I'll tell you more as and when* (= as soon as I can). **as for sb/sth** used to start talking about sb/sth SYN REGARDING: *As for Jo, she's doing fine.* ◊ *As for food for the party, that's all being taken care of.* **as from .../as of ...** used to show the time or date from which sth starts: *Our fax number is changing as from May 12.* **as if/as though** in a way that suggests sth: *He behaved as if nothing had happened.* ◊ *It sounds as though you had a good time.* ◊ *It's my birthday. As if you didn't know!* ◊ *'Don't say anything' '**As if I would!**'* (= surely you do not expect me to) **ˌas it ˈis** considering the present situation; as things are: *We were hoping to finish it by next week—as it is, it may be the week after.* ◊ *I can't help—I've got too much to do as it is* (= already). **as it ˈwere** used when a speaker is giving his or her own impression of a situation or expressing sth in a particular way: *Teachers must put the brakes on, as it were, when they notice students looking puzzled.* **as to sth | as regards sth** used when you are referring to sth: *As to tax, that will be deducted from your salary.* **as you ˈdo** used as a comment on sth that you have just said: *He smiled and I smiled back. As you do.*—more at WELL, YET

WHICH WORD?
as / like

You can use both **as** and **like** to say that things are similar.

Like is a preposition and is used before nouns and pronouns: *He has blue eyes like me.*

As is a conjunction and an adverb and is used before a clause, another adverb or a clause beginning with a preposition: *She enjoys all kinds of music, as I do.* ◊ *Repeat these five steps, as in the last exercise.*

In informal English **like** is frequently used as a conjunction or an adverb instead of **as**: *Nobody understands him like I do.* ◊ *I don't want to upset him again like before.* It is also used instead of **as if**: *It looks like we're going to be late.* These uses of **like** are common but are not considered correct in formal written English.

You will find more help on the use of **as** and **like** in the entries for particular verbs, such as *act, behave*, etc.

ASA /ˌeɪ es ˈeɪ/ *abbr.* **1** Advertising Standards Authority (an organization in Britain which controls the standard of advertising) **2** American Standards Association (used especially to show the speed of film): *a 400 ASA film*

asap /ˌeɪ es eɪ ˈpiː/ *abbr.* as soon as possible

as·bes·tos /æsˈbestəs/ *noun* [U] a soft grey mineral that does not burn, used especially in the past in building as a protection against fire or to prevent heat loss

as·cend /əˈsend/ *verb* (*formal*) **~ (to sth)** to rise; to go up; to climb up: [V] *The path started to ascend more steeply.* ◊ *Mist ascended from the valley.* ◊ *The air became colder as we ascended.* ◊ *The results, ranked **in ascending order*** (from the lowest to the highest) *are as follows:* ◊ (*figurative*) *He ascended to the peak of sporting achievement.* ◊ [VN] *Her heart was thumping as she ascended the stairs.* ◊ (*figurative*) *to ascend the throne* (= become king or queen) OPP DESCEND

as·cend·ancy (also **as·cend·ency**) /əˈsendənsi/ *noun* [U] (*formal*) **~ (over sb/sth)** the position of having power or influence over sb/sth: *moral/political/intellectual ascendancy* ◊ *The opposition party was **in the ascendancy*** (= gaining control).

as·cend·ant (also **as·cend·ent**) /əˈsendənt/ *noun* IDM **in the ascendant** (*formal*) being or becoming more powerful or popular: *British pop music is once again in the ascendant.*

as·cen·sion /əˈsenʃn/ *noun* [sing.] **1** (**the Ascension**) (in the Christian religion) the journey of Jesus from the earth into heaven **2** (*formal*) the act of moving up or of reaching a high position: *her ascension to the throne*

Asˈcension Day *noun* [U, C] (in the Christian religion) the 40th day after Easter when Christians remember when Jesus left the earth and went into heaven

as·cent /əˈsent/ *noun* **1** [C, usually sing.] the act of climbing or moving up; an upward journey: *the first ascent of Mount Everest* ◊ *The cart began its gradual ascent up the hill.* OPP DESCENT **2** [C, usually sing.] an upward path or slope: *At the other side of the valley was a* *steep ascent to the top of the hill.* OPP DESCENT **3** [U] (*formal*) the process of moving forward to a better position or of making progress: *man's ascent to civilization*

as·cer·tain /ˌæsəˈteɪn; AmE ˌæsərˈt-/ *verb* (*formal*) to find out the true or correct information about sth: [VN] *It can be difficult to ascertain the facts.* ◇ [Vthat] *I ascertained that the driver was not badly hurt.* ◇ [VNthat] *It should be ascertained that the plans comply with the law.* ◇ [Vwh-] *The police are trying to ascertain what really happened.* ◇ *Could you ascertain whether she will be coming to the meeting?* ◇ [VNwh-] *It must be ascertained if the land is still owned by the government.*

as·cet·ic /əˈsetɪk/ *adj.* [usually before noun] not allowing yourself physical pleasures, especially for religious reasons; related to a simple and strict way of living: *The monks lived a very ascetic life.* ▶ **as·cet·ic** *noun: monks, hermits and ascetics* **as·cet·i·cism** /əˈsetɪsɪzəm/ *noun* [U]

ASCII /ˈæski/ *noun* [U] (*computing*) a standard CODE used so that data can be moved between computers that use different programs (the abbreviation for 'American Standard Code for Information Interchange'): *Save the text as an ASCII file.*

ascot /ˈæskɒt; AmE ˈæskɑːt/ *noun* (*AmE*) = CRAVAT

ascribe /əˈskraɪb/ *verb* PHRV **ascribe sth to sb** to consider or state that a book, etc. was written by a particular person SYN ATTRIBUTE: *This play is usually ascribed to Shakespeare.* **ascribe sth to sb/sth** (*formal*) **1** to consider that sth is caused by a particular thing or person: *He ascribed his failure to bad luck.* **2** to consider that sb/sth has or should have a particular quality: *We ascribe great importance to these policies.* SYN ATTRIBUTE ▶ **ascrib·able** *adj.* ~ **to sb/sth**: *Their success is ascribable to the quality of their goods.* **ascrip·tion** /əˈskrɪpʃn/ *noun* [C, U] ~ **(to sb/sth)**: *the ascription of meaning to objects and events*

ASEAN /ˈæsiæn/ *abbr.* Association of South East Asian Nations

asep·tic /ˌeɪˈseptɪk/ *adj.* (*medical*) free from harmful bacteria OPP SEPTIC

asex·ual /ˌeɪˈsekʃuəl/ *adj.* **1** (*technical*) not involving sex; not having sexual organs: *asexual reproduction* **2** not having sexual qualities; not interested in sex: *the tendency to see old people as asexual*

ash /æʃ/ *noun* **1** [U] the grey or black powder that is left after sth, especially tobacco, wood or coal, has burnt: *cigarette ash* ◇ *black volcanic ash* **2** (**ashes**) [pl.] what is left after sth has been destroyed by burning: *The town was reduced to ashes in the fighting.* ◇ *the glowing ashes of the campfire* ◇ (*figurative*) *The party had risen, like a phoenix, from the ashes of electoral disaster.* **3** (**ashes**) [pl.] the powder that is left after a dead person's body has been CREMATED (= burned): *She wanted her ashes to be scattered at sea.* **4** [C, U] (also **'ash tree**) a forest tree with grey bark—see also MOUNTAIN ASH **5** [U] the hard pale wood of the ash tree IDM see SACKCLOTH

ashamed /əˈʃeɪmd/ *adj.* [not before noun] **1** ~ **(of sth/ sb/yourself)** | ~ **(that ...)** | ~ **(to be sth)** feeling shame or embarrassment about sb/sth or because of sth you have done: *She was deeply ashamed of her behaviour at the party.* ◇ *His daughter looked such a mess that he was ashamed of her.* ◇ *You should be ashamed of yourself for telling such lies.* ◇ *I feel almost ashamed that I've been so lucky.* ◇ *The football riots made me ashamed to be English.* **2** ~ **to do sth** unwilling to do sth because of shame or embarrassment: *I'm ashamed to say that I lied to her.* ◇ *I cried at the end and I'm not ashamed to admit it.*

ashen /ˈæʃn/ *adj.* (usually of sb's face) very pale; without colour because of illness or fear: *They listened ashen-faced to the news.* ◇ *His face was ashen and wet with sweat.*

ashore /əˈʃɔː(r)/ *adv.* towards, onto or on land, having come from an area of water such as the sea or a river: *to come/go ashore* ◇ *a drowned body found washed ashore on the beach* ◇ *The cruise included several days ashore.*

ash·ram /ˈæʃrəm/ *noun* a place where Hindus who wish to live apart from society live together as a group; a place where other Hindus go for a short time to say prayers before returning to society

---

WHICH WORD?

ashamed / embarrassed (?)

You feel **ashamed** when you feel guilty because of something wrong that you have deliberately done: *You should be ashamed of treating your daughter like that.* Do not use **ashamed** when you are talking about something that is not very serious or important: *I am sorry that I forgot to buy the milk.* ◇ ~~*I am ashamed that I forgot to buy the milk.*~~

You feel **embarrassed** when you have made a mistake or done something stupid or feel awkward in front of other people: *I was embarrassed about forgetting his name.*

---

ash·tray /ˈæʃtreɪ/ *noun* a container into which people who smoke put tobacco ash, cigarette ends, etc.

ˌAsh 'Wednesday *noun* [U, C] the first day of Lent—see also SHROVE TUESDAY

Asian /ˈeɪʃn; ˈeɪʒn/ *noun, adj.*
■ *noun* a person from Asia, or whose family originally came from Asia: *British Asians* HELP In *BrE* **Asian** is used especially to refer to people from India or Pakistan. In *AmE* it is used especially to refer to people from the Far East.
■ *adj.* of or connected with Asia: *Asian music*

ˌAsian A'merican *noun* a person from America whose family come from Asia, especially E Asia ▶ **ˌAsian-A'merican** *adj.*

Asi·at·ic /ˌeɪʃiˈætɪk; ˌeɪʒi-/ *adj.* (*technical*) of or connected with Asia: *the Asiatic tropics*

aside /əˈsaɪd/ *adv., noun*
■ *adv.* **1** to one side; out of the way: *She pulled the curtain aside.* ◇ *Stand aside and let these people pass.* ◇ *He took me aside* (= away from a group of people) *to give me some advice.* ◇ (*figurative*) *Leaving aside* (= not considering at this stage) *the cost of the scheme, let us examine its benefits.* ◇ *All our protests were brushed aside* (= ignored). **2** to be used later: *We set aside some money for repairs.* **3** used after nouns to say that except for one thing, sth is true: *Money worries aside, things are going well.*
■ *noun* **1** (in the theatre) something which a character in a play says to the audience, but which the other characters on stage are not intended to hear **2** a remark, often made in a low voice, which is not intended to be heard by everyone present **3** a remark that is not directly connected with the main subject that is being discussed: *I mention it only as an aside ...*

a'side from *prep.* (*especially AmE*) = APART FROM

as·in·ine /ˈæsɪnaɪn/ *adj.* (*formal*) stupid or silly SYN RIDICULOUS

ask /ɑːsk; AmE æsk/ *verb*
QUESTION | **1** ~ **(sb)** **(about sb/sth)** to say or write sth in the form of a question, in order to get information: [Vspeech] *'Where are you going?' she asked.* ◇ [VNspeech] *'Are you sure?' he asked her.* ◇ [V] *He asked about her family.* ◇ *How old are you—if you don't mind me / my asking?* ◇ [VN] *The interviewer asked me about my future plans.* ◇ *Can I ask a question?* ◇ *Did you ask the price?* ◇ [VNN] *She asked the students their names.* ◇ *I often get asked that.* ◇ [Vwh-] *He asked where I lived.* ◇ [VNwh-] *I had to ask the teacher what to do next.* ◇ *I was asked if/ whether I could drive.* HELP You cannot say 'ask to sb': ~~*I asked to my friend what had happened.*~~
REQUEST | **2** to tell sb that you would like them to do sth or that you would like sth to happen: [VNtoinf] *All the students were asked to complete a questionnaire.* ◇ *Eric asked me to marry him.* ◇ [Vwh-] *I asked whether they could change my ticket.* ◇ [VNwh-] *She asked me if I would give her English lessons.* ◇ [Vthat] (*formal*) *She asked that she be kept informed of developments.* ◇ (*BrE* also) *She asked that she should be kept informed.* **3** ~ **(sb)** **(for sth)** to say that you would like sb to give you sth: [V] *to ask for a job / a drink / an explanation* ◇ *I am writing to ask for some information about courses.* ◇ [VN] *Why don't you ask*

---

his advice? ◊ Can I ask a favour of you? ◊ [VNN] *Why don't you ask him for his advice?* ◊ *Can I ask you a favour?*

PERMISSION **|4** to request permission to do sth: [VtoInf] *Did you ask to use the car?* ◊ *I asked to see the manager.* ◊ [Vwh-] *I'll ask if it's all right to park here.* ◊ [VNwh-] *She asked her boss whether she could have the day off.*

INVITE **| 5** [usually +adv./prep.] to invite sb: [VN] *They've asked me to dinner.* ◊ *I didn't ask them in* (= to come into the house). ◊ *We must ask the neighbours round* (= to our house). ◊ [VNtoinf] *She's asked him to come to the party.*

MONEY **| 6** [VN] **~ sth (for sth)** to request a particular amount of money for sth that you are selling: *He's asking £2000 for the car.*

EXPECT/DEMAND **| 7** **~ sth (of sb)** to expect or demand sth: [VN] *I know I'm asking a great deal.* ◊ *You're asking too much of him.* ◊ [VNtoinf] *I know it's asking a lot to expect them to win again.*

IDM **'ask for it** (*informal*) to deserve sth bad that happens to you or that sb does to you **be 'asking for trouble | be 'asking for it** (*informal*) to behave in a way that is very likely to result in trouble **,don't 'ask** (*spoken, informal*) if you say **don't ask** to sb, you mean that you do not want to reply to their question, because it would be awkward, embarrassing, etc. **,don't ask 'me** (*spoken, informal*) if you say **don't ask me**, you mean that you do not know the answer to a question and are annoyed you have been asked **for the 'asking** if you can have sth **for the asking**, it is very easy for you to get it if you ask for it: *The job is yours for the asking.* **I 'ask you** (*spoken, informal*) if you say **I ask you**, you are expressing disapproval, shock or anger about sth/sb **if you ask 'me** (*spoken, informal*) in my personal opinion: *Their marriage was a mistake, if you ask me.*

PHRV **'ask after sb** (*BrE*) to say that you would like to know how sb is, what they are doing, etc: *He always asks after you in his letters.* **,ask a'round** to speak to a number of different people in order to try and get some information: *I don't know of any vacancies in the company but I'll ask around.* **,ask sb 'back** (especially *BrE*) to invite sb to come back to your house when you are both out together: *I hoped he wouldn't ask me back.* **'ask for sb/sth** to say that you want to speak to sb or be directed to a place: *When you arrive, ask for Jane.* **,ask sb 'out** to invite sb to go out with you, especially as a way of starting a romantic relationship: *He's too shy to ask her out.*

askance /əˈskæns/ *adv.* **IDM** **look askance (at sb/sth) | look (at sb/sth) askance** (*written*) to look at or react to sb/sth with suspicion or doubt, or in a critical way

askew /əˈskjuː/ *adv., adj.* [not before noun] not in a straight or level position: *Her hat was slightly askew.* ◊ *His glasses had been knocked askew by the blow.*

'asking price *noun* the price that sb wants to sell sth for—compare SELLING PRICE

asleep /əˈsliːp/ *adj.* [not before noun] sleeping: *The baby was sound asleep* (= sleeping deeply) *upstairs.* ◊ *I waited until they were all fast asleep* (= sleeping deeply). ◊ *He was so exhausted that he fell asleep at his desk.* ◊ *She was still half asleep* (= not fully awake) *when she arrived at work.* ◊ *The police found him asleep in a garage.* **IDM** see SOUND *adv.*

asp /æsp/ *noun* a small poisonous snake found especially in N Africa

as·para·gus /əˈspærəgəs/ *noun* [U] a plant whose young green or white stems are cooked and eaten as a vegetable—picture on page A3

as·pect /ˈæspekt/ *noun* **1** [C] a particular part or feature of a situation, an idea, a problem, etc.; a way in which it may be considered: *The book aims to cover all aspects of city life.* ◊ *the most important aspect of the debate* ◊ *She felt she had looked at the problem from every aspect.* ◊ *This was one aspect of her character he hadn't seen before.* **2** [U, sing.] (*formal*) the appearance of a place, a situation or a person: *Events began to take on a more sinister aspect.* **3** [C, usually sing.] (*formal*) the direction in which a building, window, piece of land, etc. faces; the side of a building which faces a particular direction **4** [U, C] (*grammar*) the form of a verb that shows, for example,

whether the action happens once or repeatedly, is completed or still continuing—see also PERFECT *adj.* (7), PROGRESSIVE *adj.*

aspen /ˈæspən/ *noun* a type of POPLAR tree, with leaves that move even when there is very little wind

as·per·ity /æˈsperəti/ *noun* [U] (*rare, formal*) the fact of being harsh or severe, especially in the way you speak to or treat sb

as·per·sions /əˈspɜːʃnz; *AmE* əˈspɜːrʒnz/ *noun* [pl.] (*formal*) critical or unpleasant remarks or judgements: *I wouldn't want to cast aspersions on your honesty.*

as·phalt /ˈæsfælt; *AmE* -fɔːlt/ *noun* [U] a thick black sticky substance used especially for making the surface of roads

as·phyxia /æsˈfɪksiə; əsˈf-/ *noun* [U] the state of being unable to breathe, causing death or loss of consciousness

as·phyxi·ate /əsˈfɪksieɪt/ *verb* [VN] to make sb become unconscious or die by preventing them from breathing **SYN** SUFFOCATE: *He was asphyxiated by the smoke.* ◊ *asphyxiating gases* ▸ **as·phyxi·ation** /əsˌfɪksiˈeɪʃn/ *noun* [U]

aspic /ˈæspɪk/ *noun* [U] clear jelly which food can be put into when it is being served cold: *chicken breast in aspic*

as·pi·dis·tra /ˌæspɪˈdɪstrə/ *noun* a plant with broad green pointed leaves, often grown indoors

as·pir·ant /əˈspaɪərənt; ˈæspərənt/ *noun* **~ (to/for sth)** (*formal*) a person with a strong desire to achieve a position of importance or to win a competition: *aspirants to the title of world champion* ▸ **as·pir·ant** *adj.* [only before noun] = ASPIRING

as·pir·ate *noun, verb*
■ *noun* /ˈæspərət/ (*phonetics*) the sound of the letter 'h': *The word 'hour' is pronounced without an initial aspirate.*
■ *verb* /ˈæspəreɪt/ [VN] **1** (*medical*) to remove liquid from a person's body with a machine **2** (*phonetics*) to pronounce sth with an 'h' sound or with a breath

as·pir·ation /ˌæspəˈreɪʃn/ *noun* **1** [C, usually pl., U] **~ (for sth) | ~ (to do sth)** a strong desire to have or do sth: *I didn't realize you had political aspirations.* ◊ *He has never had any aspiration to earn a lot of money.* **2** [U] (*phonetics*) the action of pronouncing sth with an 'h' sound

as·pire /əˈspaɪə(r)/ *verb* **~ (to sth)** to have a strong desire to achieve or to become sth: [V] *She aspired to a scientific career.* ◊ [VtoInf] *He aspired to be their next leader.*

as·pirin /ˈæsprɪn; ˈæspərɪn/ *noun* [U, C] (*pl.* **as·pirin** or **as·pir·ins**) a drug used to reduce pain, fever and INFLAMMATION: *Do you have any aspirin?* ◊ *Take two aspirin(s) for a headache.*

as·pir·ing /əˈspaɪərɪŋ/ (also *less frequent* **as·pir·ant**) *adj.* [only before noun] **1** wanting to start the career or activity that is mentioned: *Aspiring musicians need hours of practice every day.* **2** wanting to be successful in life: *He came from an aspiring working-class background.*

ass /æs/ *noun* **1** (*AmE,* △, *slang*) = ARSE **2** (*BrE, informal*) a stupid person: *Don't be such an ass!* ◊ *I made an ass of myself at the meeting—standing up and then forgetting the question.* **3** (*BrE, old use*) a DONKEY **IDM** **get your 'ass in gear | move your 'ass** (*slang, especially AmE*) a rude way of telling sb to hurry **get your ass over/in 'here,** etc. (*slang, especially AmE*) a rude way of telling sb to come here, etc.—more at KICK *v.,* KISS *v.,* PAIN *n.*

as·sail /əˈseɪl/ *verb* [VN] (*formal*) **1** to attack sb violently, either physically or with words: *He was assailed with fierce blows to the head.* ◊ *The proposal was assailed by the opposition party.* ◊ (*figurative*) *A vile smell assailed my nostrils.* **2** [usually passive] to disturb or upset sb severely: *to be assailed by worries/doubts/fears*

as·sail·ant /əˈseɪlənt/ *noun* (*formal*) a person who attacks sb, especially physically

as·sas·sin /əˈsæsɪn; *AmE* -sn/ *noun* a person who murders sb important or famous, for money or for political reasons

as·sas·sin·ate /əˈsæsɪneɪt; *AmE* -sən-/ *verb* [VN] [often passive] to murder an important or famous person, especially for political reasons: *The prime minister was assassinated by extremists.* ◊ *a plot to assassinate the president*

▶ **as·sas·sin·ation** /əˌsæsɪˈneɪʃn; *AmE* -səˈn-/ *noun* [U, C]: *The president survived a number of assassination attempts.* ◊ *the assassination of John F. Kennedy*

as·sault /əˈsɔːlt/ *noun, verb*
- *noun* **1** [U, C] **~ (on/upon sb)** the crime of attacking sb physically: *Both men were charged with assault.* ◊ *A significant number of **indecent assaults** on women go unreported.* ◊ *sexual assaults* **2** [C] **~ (on/upon/against sb/sth)** (by an army, etc.) the act of attacking a building, an area, etc. in order to take control of it: *An assault on the capital was launched in the early hours of the morning.* **3** [C] **~ (on/upon sb)** the act of trying to achieve sth that is difficult or dangerous: *The government has mounted a new assault on unemployment* (= in order to reduce it). ◊ *Three people died during an assault on the mountain* (= while trying to climb it). **4** [C] **~ (on/upon/against sb/sth)** an act of criticizing sb/sth severely: *The paper's assault on the president was totally unjustified.* ◊ *The suggested closures **came under assault** from all parties.*
- *verb* [VN] **1** to attack sb violently, especially when this is a crime: *He has been charged with assaulting a police officer.* ◊ *Four women have been **sexually assaulted** in the area recently.* **2** (*formal*) to affect your senses in a way that is very unpleasant or uncomfortable: *Loud rock music assaulted our ears.*

as·sault and ˈbattery *noun* [U] (*law*) the crime of threatening to harm sb and then attacking them physically

asˈsault course (*BrE*) (*AmE* ˈobstacle course) *noun* an area of land with many objects that are difficult to climb, jump over or go through, which is used, especially by soldiers, for improving physical skills and strength

assay /əˈseɪ/ *noun* [C, U] (*technical*) the testing of metals and chemicals for quality, often to see how pure they are ▶ **assay** *verb* [VN]

as·sem·blage /əˈsemblɪdʒ/ *noun* (*formal, technical*) a collection of things; a group of people: *Tropical rainforests have the most varied and abundant assemblage of plants in the world.*

as·sem·ble /əˈsembl/ *verb* **1** to come together as a group; to bring people or things together as a group: [V] *All the students were asked to assemble in the main hall.* ◊ *She then addressed the **assembled company** (= all the people there).* ◊ [VN] *to assemble evidence/data* ◊ *The manager has assembled a world-class team.* **2** [VN] to fit together all the separate parts of sth, for example a piece of furniture: *The shelves are easy to assemble.*

as·sem·bly /əˈsembli/ *noun* (*pl.* **-ies**) **1** (also **Assembly**) [C] a group of people who have been elected to meet together regularly and make decisions or laws for a particular region or country: *State/legislative/federal/local assemblies* ◊ *Power has been handed over to provincial and regional assemblies.* ◊ *The national assembly has voted to adopt the budget.* ◊ *the California Assembly* ◊ *the UN General Assembly* **2** [U, C] the meeting together of a group of people for a particular purpose; a group of people who meet together for a particular purpose: *They were fighting for freedom of speech and freedom of assembly.* ◊ *He was to address a public assembly on the issue.* ◊ *an assembly point* (= a place where people have been asked to meet) **3** [C, U] a meeting of the teachers and students in a school, usually at the start of the day, to give information, discuss school events or say prayers together **4** [U] the process of putting together the parts of sth such as a vehicle or piece of furniture: *Putting the bookcase together should be a simple assembly job.* ◊ *a car assembly plant*

asˈsembly line *noun* = PRODUCTION LINE: *workers on the assembly line*

as·sent /əˈsent/ *noun, verb*
- *noun* [U] **~ (to sth)** (*formal*) official agreement to or approval of sth: *The director has **given her assent** to the proposals.* ◊ *He nodded (his) assent.* ◊ *There were murmurs of both assent and dissent from the crowd.* ◊ *The bill passed in Parliament has now **received the Royal Assent** (= been approved by the king/queen).*

- *verb* **~ (to sth)** (*formal*) to agree to a request, an idea or a suggestion: [V] *Nobody would assent to the terms they proposed.* [also V **speech**]

as·sert /əˈsɜːt; *AmE* əˈsɜːrt/ *verb* **1** to state clearly and firmly that sth is true: [V **that**] *She continued to assert that she was innocent.* ◊ [VN] *She continued to assert her innocence.* ◊ [V **speech**] *'That is wrong,' he asserted.* ◊ [VN **that**] *It is commonly asserted that older people prefer to receive care from family members.* **2** [VN] **~ yourself** to behave in a confident and determined way so that other people pay attention to your opinions **3** [VN] to make other people recognize your right or authority to do sth, by behaving firmly and confidently: *to assert your independence/rights* ◊ *I was determined to **assert my authority** from the beginning.* **4** [VN] **~ itself** to start to have an effect: *Good sense asserted itself.*

as·ser·tion /əˈsɜːʃn; *AmE* əˈsɜːrʃn/ *noun* **1** [C] a statement saying that you strongly believe sth to be true SYN CLAIM: *He was correct in his assertion that the minister had been lying.* ◊ *Do you have any evidence to support your assertions?* **2** [U, C] the act of stating, using or claiming sth strongly: *the assertion of his authority* ◊ *The demonstration was an assertion of the right to peaceful protest.*

as·sert·ive /əˈsɜːtɪv; *AmE* əˈsɜːrtɪv/ *adj.* expressing opinions or desires strongly and with confidence, so that people take notice: *You should try and be more assertive.* ◊ *assertive behaviour* OPP SUBMISSIVE ▶ **as·sert·ive·ly** *adv.* **as·sert·ive·ness** *noun* [U]: *an assertiveness training course*

as·sess /əˈses/ *verb* **1** **~ sb/sth (as sth)** to make a judgement about the nature or quality of sb/sth: [VN] *It's difficult to assess the effects of these changes.* ◊ *to assess a patient's needs* ◊ *The young men were assessed as either safe or unsafe drivers.* ◊ *I'd assess your chances as low.* ◊ [V **wh-**] *The committee assesses whether a building is worth preserving.* ◊ *We are trying to assess how well the system works.* **2** [VN] **~ sth (at sth)** to calculate the amount or value of sth: *They have assessed the amount of compensation to be paid.* ◊ *Damage to the building was assessed at £40 000.*

as·sess·ment /əˈsesmənt/ *noun* **1** [C] an opinion or a judgement about sb/sth that has been thought about very carefully SYN EVALUATION: *a detailed assessment of the risks involved* ◊ *What is your assessment of the situation?* **2** [U] the act of judging or forming an opinion about sb/sth: *written and oral exams and other forms of assessment* ◊ *Objective assessment of the severity of the problem was difficult.*—see also CONTINUOUS ASSESSMENT **3** [C] an amount that has been calculated and that must be paid: *a tax assessment*

as·ses·sor /əˈsesə(r)/ *noun* **1** an expert in a particular subject who is asked by a court of law or other official group to give advice **2** a person who calculates the value or cost of sth or the amount of money to be paid: *an insurance/tax assessor* **3** a person who judges how well sb has done in an exam, a competition, etc: *College lecturers acted as external assessors of the exam results.*

asset /ˈæset/ *noun* **1** **~ (to sb/sth)** a person or thing that is valuable or useful to sb/sth: *I'm sure she'll be an asset to the team.* ◊ *In his job, patience is an invaluable asset.* **2** [usually pl.] a thing of value, especially property, that a person or company owns, which can be used or sold to pay debts: *the net **asset value** of the company* ◊ *Her assets include shares in the company and a house in France.* ◊ *asset sales/management* ◊ *income from **fixed asset investments*** ◊ *financial/capital assets*—compare LIABILITY

ˈasset-stripping *noun* [U] (*business*) (usually *disapproving*) the practice of buying a company which is in financial difficulties at a low price and then selling everything that it owns in order to make a profit

ass·hole /ˈæshəʊl; *AmE* -hoʊl/ *noun* (*AmE*, ⚠, *slang*) = ARSEHOLE

as·sidu·ous /əˈsɪdjuəs; *AmE* -dʒuəs/ *adj.* (*formal*) working very hard and taking great care that everything is done as well as it can be SYN DILIGENT: *one of the most assiduous members of the team* ▶ **as·si·du·ity** /ˌæsɪˈdjuːəti/ *noun* [U] (*rare*) **as·sidu·ous·ly** *adv.*

æ	ɑː	e	ɜː	ə	ɪ	iː	i	ɒ	ɔː	ʌ	ʊ	u	uː
cat	father	ten	bird	about	sit	see	many	got	saw	cup	put	actual	too
								(BrE)					

as·sign /əˈsaɪn/ verb **1** ~ sth (to sb)| ~ (sb) sth to give sb sth that they can use, or some work or responsibility: [VN] *The two large classrooms have been assigned to us.* ◊ *The teacher assigned a different task to each of the children.* ◊ [VNN] *We have been assigned the two large classrooms.* ◊ *The teacher assigned each of the children a different task.* **2** ~ sb (to sth/as sth) to provide a person for a particular task or position: [VN] *They've assigned their best man to the job.* ◊ [VNtoinf] *British forces have been assigned to help with peacekeeping.* **3** [VN] [usually passive] ~ sb to sb/sth to send a person to work under the authority of sb or in a particular group: *I was assigned to B platoon.* **4** ~ sth to sth to say that sth has a particular value or function, or happens at a particular time or place: [VN] *Assign a different colour to each different type of information.* ◊ [VNN] *The painting cannot be assigned an exact date.* **5** [VN] ~ sth to sb (*law*) to say that your property or rights now belong to sb else: *The agreement assigns copyright to the publisher.*

as·sig·na·tion /ˌæsɪgˈneɪʃn/ noun (*formal* or *humorous*) a meeting, especially a secret one, often with a lover

as·sign·ment /əˈsaɪnmənt/ noun **1** [C] a task or piece of work that sb is given to do, usually as part of their job or studies: *You will need to complete three written assignments per semester.* ◊ *She is in Greece on an assignment for one of the Sunday newspapers.* ◊ *one of our reporters on assignment in China* ◊ *I had set myself a tough assignment.* **2** [U] the act of giving sth to sb; the act of giving sb a particular task: *his assignment to other duties in the same company*

as·simi·late /əˈsɪmɪleɪt/ verb **1** [VN] to fully understand an idea or some information so that you are able to use it yourself: *The committee will need time to assimilate this report.* **2** ~ (sb) (into/to sth) to become, or allow sb to become, a part of a country or community rather than remaining in a separate group: [V] *New arrivals find it hard to assimilate, and may not wish to.* ◊ [VN] *Immigrants have been successfully assimilated into the community.* **3** [VN] [often passive] ~ sth into/to sth to make an idea, a person's attitude, etc. fit into sth or be acceptable: *These changes were gradually assimilated into everyday life.* ▶ **as·simi·la·tion** /əˌsɪməˈleɪʃn/ noun [U]: *the rapid assimilation of new ideas* ◊ *his assimilation into the political community*

as·sist /əˈsɪst/ verb **1** ~ (sb) (in/with sth)| ~ (sb) (in doing sth) (especially *written*) to help sb to do sth: [VN] *We'll do all we can to assist you.* ◊ *We will assist you in finding somewhere to live.* ◊ *The play was directed by Mike Johnson, assisted by Sharon Gale.* ◊ *Two men are assisting the police with their enquiries* (= are being questioned by the police). ◊ [VNtoinf] *a course to assist adults to return to the labour market* ◊ [V] *Anyone willing to assist can contact this number.* ◊ *We are looking for people who would be willing to assist in the group's work.* **2** [VN] to help sth to happen more easily: *activities that will assist the decision-making process* ⇨ note at HELP

as·sist·ance /əˈsɪstəns/ noun [U] ~ (with sth)| ~ (in doing sth/to do sth) (*formal*) help or support: *technical/ economic/military assistance* ◊ *financial assistance for people on low incomes* ◊ *Can I be of any assistance?* ◊ *Despite his cries, no one came to his assistance.* ◊ *She offered me practical assistance with my research.* ◊ *The company provides advice and assistance in finding work.* ◊ *He can walk only with the assistance of crutches.*

as·sist·ant /əˈsɪstənt/ noun, adj.
■ noun **1** a person who helps or supports sb, usually in their job: *My assistant will now demonstrate the machine in action.* ◊ *a senior research assistant*—see also PERSONAL ASSISTANT, TEACHING ASSISTANT **2** (*BrE*) = SHOP ASSISTANT: *a sales assistant in a department store*— **3** (*BrE*) a student at university or college who spends time in a foreign country teaching their language in a school
■ adj. [only before noun] (*abbr.* **Asst**) (often in titles) having a rank below a senior person and helping them in their work: *the assistant manager* ◊ *Assistant Chief Constable Ower.* ◊ *Assistant Attorney General William Weld*

as,sistant pro'fessor noun (in the US and Canada) a teacher at a college or university who has a rank just below the rank of an ASSOCIATE PROFESSOR

as·sizes /əˈsaɪzɪz/ noun a court of law in the past which travelled to each county of England and Wales ▶ **as·size** adj. [only before noun]: *the assize court*

Assoc. abbr. (in writing) Association

as·so·ci·ate verb, adj., noun
■ verb /əˈsəʊʃieɪt; AmE əˈsoʊ-/ **1** [VN] ~ sb/sth (with sb/sth) to make a connection between people or things in your mind: *I always associate the smell of baking with my childhood.* ◊ *He is closely associated in the public mind with horror movies.* **2** [V] ~ with sb to spend time with sb, especially a person or people that sb else does not approve of: *I don't like you associating with those people.* **3** [VN] ~ yourself with sth (*formal*) to show that you support or agree with sth: *May I associate myself with the Prime Minister's remarks?* (= I agree with them) OPP DISSOCIATE
■ adj. /əˈsəʊʃiət; AmE əˈsoʊ-/ [only before noun] **1** (often in titles) of a lower rank, having fewer rights in a particular profession or organization: *associate membership of the European Union* ◊ *an associate member/director/editor* **2** joined to or connected with a profession or an organization: *their dealings with an associate company in Japan*
■ noun /əˈsəʊʃiət; AmE əˈsoʊ-/ **1** a person that you work with, do business with or spend a lot of time with: *business associates* **2** (also **Associate**) an associate member **3** (**Associate**) (*AmE*) a person who has an Associate's degree (= one that is given after completing two years of study at a junior college)

as·so·ci·ated /əˈsəʊʃieɪtɪd; AmE əˈsoʊ-/ adj. **1** if one thing is **associated with** another, the two things are connected because they happen together or one thing causes the other: *the risks associated with taking drugs* ◊ *Salaries and associated costs have risen substantially.* **2** if a person is **associated with** an organization, etc. they support it: *He no longer wished to be associated with the party's policy on education.* **3** (**Associated**) used in the name of a business company that is made up of a number of smaller companies: *Associated Newspapers*

as,sociate pro'fessor noun (in the US and Canada) a teacher at a college or university who has a rank just below the rank of a PROFESSOR

as·so·ci·ation /əˌsəʊsiˈeɪʃn; AmE əˌsoʊ-/ noun **1** [C+sing./pl. v.] (*abbr.* **Assoc.**) an official group of people who have joined together for a particular purpose SYN ORGANIZATION: *Do you belong to any professional or trade associations?* ◊ *the Football Association* ◊ *a residents' association*— see also HOUSING ASSOCIATION **2** [C, U] ~ (with sb/sth) a connection or relationship between people or organizations: *his alleged association with terrorist groups* ◊ *They have maintained a close association with a college in the US.* ◊ *The book was published in association with* (= together with) *British Heritage.* ◊ *She became famous through her association with the group of poets.* **3** [C, usually pl.] an idea or a memory that is suggested by sb/sth; a mental connection between ideas: *The seaside had all sorts of pleasant associations with childhood holidays for me.* ◊ *The cat soon made the association between human beings and food.* **4** [C] a connection between things where one is caused by the other: *a proven association between passive smoking and cancer*

As,sociation 'football noun [U] (*BrE, formal*) = FOOTBALL

as·son·ance /ˈæsənəns/ noun [U] (*technical*) the effect created when two syllables in words that are close together have the same vowel sound, but different consonants, or the same consonants but different vowels, for example, *sonnet* and *porridge* or *cold* and *killed*

as·sort·ed /əˈsɔːtɪd; AmE əˈsɔːrtəd/ adj. of various different sorts: *The meat is served with salad or assorted vegetables.* ◊ *The jumper comes in assorted colours.*

as·sort·ment /əˈsɔːtmənt; AmE əˈsɔːrt-/ noun [usually sing.] a collection of different things or of different types of the same thing SYN MIXTURE: *a wide assortment of gifts*

aɪ	aʊ	eɪ	əʊ	oʊ	ɔɪ	ɪə	eə	ʊə	j	w
my	now	say	go (BrE)	go (AmE)	boy	near	hair	pure	yes	wet

to choose from ◊ *He was dressed in an odd assortment of clothes.*

Asst (also **Asst.** especially in *AmE*) *abbr.* (in writing) Assistant: *Asst Manager*

as·suage /əˈsweɪdʒ/ *verb* [VN] (*formal*) to make an unpleasant feeling less severe: *His reply did little to assuage my suspicions.*

as·sume /əˈsjuːm; *AmE* əˈsuːm/ *verb* **1** to think or accept that sth is true but without having proof of it: [V(**that**)] *It is reasonable to assume* (*that*) *the economy will continue to improve.* ◊ *Let us assume for a moment that the plan succeeds.* ◊ *I hope to go to college next year, always assuming* (*that*) *I pass my exams.* ◊ *She would, he assumed, be home at the usual time.* ◊ [VN**that**] *It is generally assumed that stress is caused by too much work.* ◊ [VN] *Don't always assume the worst* (= that sth bad has happened). ◊ *In this example we have assumed a unit price of $10.* ◊ [VN**to inf**] *I had assumed him to be a Belgian.* **2** [VN] (*formal*) to take or begin to have power or responsibility: *The court assumed responsibility for the girl's welfare.* ◊ *Rebel forces have assumed control of the capital.* **3** [VN] (*formal*) to begin to have a particular quality or appearance SYN TAKE ON: *This matter has assumed considerable importance.* ◊ *In the story the god assumes the form of an eagle.* **4** [VN] (*formal*) to pretend to have a particular feeling or quality SYN PUT ON: *He assumed an air of concern.*

as·sumed /əˈsjuːmd; *AmE* əˈsuːmd/ *adj.* [only before noun] that you suppose to be true or to exist: *the assumed differences between the two states*

as,sumed 'name *noun* a name that sb uses that is not their real name SYN PSEUDONYM: *He was living under an assumed name.*

as·sump·tion /əˈsʌmpʃn/ *noun* **1** [C] a belief or feeling that sth is true or that sth will happen, although there is no proof: *an underlying / implicit assumption* ◊ *We need to challenge some of the basic assumptions of western philosophy.* ◊ *We are working on the assumption that everyone invited will turn up.* ◊ *It was impossible to make assumptions about people's reactions.* ◊ *His actions were based on a false assumption.* **2** [C, U] ~ **of sth** (*formal*) the act of taking or beginning to have power or responsibility: *their assumption of power / control*

as·sur·ance /əˈʃʊərəns; -ˌʃɔː-; *AmE* əˈʃʊr-/ *noun* **1** [C] a statement that sth will certainly be true or will certainly happen, particularly when there has been doubt about it SYN PROMISE: *Opposition parties are calling for further assurances that the government is committed to its education policy.* ◊ *Unemployment seems to be rising, despite repeated assurances to the contrary.* **2** (also ,self-as'surance) [U] belief in your own abilities or strengths SYN CONFIDENCE: *There was an air of easy assurance and calm about him.* **3** [U] (*BrE*) a type of insurance in which money is paid out when sb dies or after an agreed period of time: *a life assurance company*—see also QUALITY ASSURANCE

as·sure /əˈʃʊə(r); -ˈʃɔː(r); *AmE* əˈʃʊr/ *verb* **1** ~ **sb** (**of sth**) to tell sb that sth is definitely true or is definitely going to happen, especially when they have doubts about it: [VN(**that**)] *I know you think I did it deliberately, but I assure you* (*that*) *I did not.* ◊ *We were assured that everything possible was being done.* ◊ [VN] *She's perfectly safe, I can assure you.* ◊ *We assured him of our loyal support.* ◊ [VN**speech**] '*He'll come back,*' *Susan assured her.* **2** ~ **yourself** (**of sth**) to make yourself certain about sth: [VN] *He assured himself of her safety.* ◊ [VN**that**] *She assured herself that the letter was still in the drawer.* **3** to make sth certain to happen SYN GUARANTEE: [VN] *Victory would assure a place in the finals.* ◊ [VNN] *Victory would assure them a place in the finals.* **4** [VN] (*BrE*) to INSURE sth, especially against sb's death: *What is the sum assured?* IDM see REST *v.*

as·sured /əˈʃʊəd; əˈʃɔːd; *AmE* əˈʃʊrd/ *adj.* **1** (also ,self-as'sured) confident in yourself and your abilities: *He spoke in a calm, assured voice.* **2** certain to happen SYN GUARANTEED: *Success seemed assured.* **3** ~ **of sth** (of a person) certain to get sth: *You are assured of a warm welcome at this hotel.*

as·sured·ly /əˈʃʊərədli; əˈʃɔːr-; *AmE* əˈʃʊr-/ *adv.* (*formal*) certainly; definitely: *Their attempts will most assuredly fail.*

aster /ˈæstə(r)/ *noun* a garden plant that has pink, purple, blue or white flowers with many long narrow PETALS around a dark centre

as·ter·isk /ˈæstərɪsk/ *noun* the symbol (✱) placed next to a particular word or phrase to make people notice it or to show that more information is given in another place: *I've placed an asterisk next to the tasks I want you to do first.* ▶ **as·ter·isk** *verb*: [VN] *I've asterisked the tasks I want you to do first.*

astern /əˈstɜːn; *AmE* əˈstɜːrn/ *adv.* (*technical*) **1** in, at or towards the back part of a ship or boat **2** if a ship or boat is moving **astern**, it is moving backwards

as·ter·oid /ˈæstərɔɪd/ *noun* any one of the many small planets which go around the sun

asthma /ˈæsmə; *AmE* ˈæzmə/ *noun* [U] a medical condition of the chest that makes breathing difficult: *a severe asthma attack*

asth·mat·ic /æsˈmætɪk; *AmE* æzˈmætɪk/ *noun* a person who suffers from asthma ▶ **asth·mat·ic** *adj.*: *asthmatic patients* ◊ *an asthmatic attack*

astig·ma·tism /əˈstɪɡmətɪzəm/ *noun* [U] a fault in the shape of a person's eye that prevents them from seeing clearly

as·ton·ish /əˈstɒnɪʃ; *AmE* əˈstɑːn-/ *verb* to surprise sb very much: [VN] *You astonish me!* ◊ *The news astonished everyone.* ◊ *She astonished us by saying she was leaving.* ◊ [VN(**that**)] *It astonishes me* (*that*) *he could be so thoughtless.*

as·ton·ished /əˈstɒnɪʃt; *AmE* əˈstɑːn-/ *adj.* ~ (**to find/ hear/learn/see sth**)| ~ (**at/by sth/sb**)| ~ (**that ...**) very surprised: *He was astonished to learn he'd won the competition.* ◊ *My parents looked astonished at my news.* ◊ *She seemed astonished* (*that*) *I had never been to Paris.* ◊ *The helicopter landed before our astonished eyes.*

as·ton·ish·ing /əˈstɒnɪʃɪŋ; *AmE* əˈstɑːn-/ *adj.* very surprising; difficult to believe: *She ran 100m in an astonishing 10.9 seconds.* ◊ *I find it absolutely astonishing that you didn't like it.* ▶ **as·ton·ish·ing·ly** *adv.*: *Jack took the news astonishingly well.* ◊ *Astonishingly, a crowd of several thousands turned out to hear him.*

as·ton·ish·ment /əˈstɒnɪʃmənt; *AmE* əˈstɑːn-/ *noun* [U] a feeling of very great surprise: *To my utter astonishment, she remembered my name.* ◊ *He stared in astonishment at the stranger.*

as·tound /əˈstaʊnd/ *verb* [VN] to surprise or shock sb very much: *His arrogance astounded her.* ◊ *She was astounded by his arrogance.*

as·tound·ed /əˈstaʊndɪd/ *adj.* ~ (**to find, learn, see, etc. sth**)| ~ (**at/by sth**)| ~ (**that ...**) very surprised or shocked by sth, because it seems very unlikely: *an astounded expression* ◊ *How can you say that? I'm absolutely astounded.* ◊ *I was astounded to see her appear from the house.* ◊ *She looked astounded at the news.* ◊ *The doctors were astounded* (*that*) *he survived.*

as·tound·ing /əˈstaʊndɪŋ/ *adj.* so surprising that it is difficult to believe: *There was an astounding 20% increase in sales.* ▶ **as·tound·ing·ly** *adv.*

as·tra·khan /ˌæstrəˈkæn; *AmE* ˈæstrəkən/ *noun* [U] a black tightly-curled fabric made from the wool of a particular type of young sheep, used especially for making coats and hats; an artificial fabric that looks like this

astray /əˈstreɪ/ *adv.* IDM **go a'stray 1** to become lost; to be stolen: *Several letters went astray or were not delivered.* ◊ *We locked up our valuables so they would not go astray.* **2** to go in the wrong direction or to have the wrong result: *Fortunately the gunman's shots went astray.* ◊ *Jack's parents thought the other boys might lead him astray* (= make him do things that are wrong).

astride /əˈstraɪd/ *prep., adv.*

■ *prep.* with one leg on each side of sth: *to sit astride a horse / bike / chair* ◊ (*figurative*) *a town astride the river*

■ *adv.* **1** with legs or feet wide apart **2** with one leg on each side

---

b	d	f	g	h	k	l	m	n	p	r
bad	did	fall	get	hat	cat	leg	man	now	pen	red

astrin·gent /əˈstrɪndʒənt/ *adj., noun*
■ *adj.* **1** (*technical*) (of a liquid or cream) able to make the skin feel less OILY or to stop a cut from bleeding **2** (*formal*) critical in a harsh or clever way: *astringent writers/comments* **3** (*formal*) (of a taste or smell) slightly bitter but fresh: *the astringent taste of lemon juice* ▶ **astrin·gency** /-ənsi/ *noun* [U]
■ *noun* a liquid or cream used in COSMETICS or medicine to make the skin less OILY or to stop a cut from bleeding

astro- /ˈæstrəʊ; *AmE* ˈæstroʊ/ *combining form* (in nouns, adjectives and adverbs) connected with the stars or outer space: *astronaut* ◊ *astrophysics*

as·trol·oger /əˈstrɒlədʒə(r); *AmE* əˈstrɑːl-/ *noun* a person who uses astrology to tell people about their character, about what might happen to them in the future, etc.

as·trol·ogy /əˈstrɒlədʒi; *AmE* əˈstrɑːl-/ *noun* [U] the study of the positions of the stars and the movements of the planets in the belief that they influence human affairs ▶ **astro·logic·al** /ˌæstrəˈlɒdʒɪkl; *AmE* -ˈlɑːdʒ-/ *adj.*: *astrological influences*

astro·naut /ˈæstrənɔːt/ *noun* a person whose job involves travelling and working in a spacecraft

as·tron·omer /əˈstrɒnəmə(r); *AmE* əˈstrɑːn-/ *noun* a scientist who studies astronomy

astro·nom·ic·al /ˌæstrəˈnɒmɪkl/ *adj.* **1** connected with ASTRONOMY: *astronomical observations* **2** (also **astro·nom·ic**) (*informal*) (of an amount, a price, etc.) very large: *the astronomical costs of land for building* ◊ *The figures are astronomical.* ▶ **astro·nom·ic·al·ly** /-kli/ *adv.*: *Interest rates are astronomically high.*

as·tron·omy /əˈstrɒnəmi; *AmE* əˈstrɑːn-/ *noun* [U] the scientific study of the sun, moon, stars, planets, etc.

astro·phys·ics /ˌæstrəʊˈfɪzɪks; *AmE* ˌæstroʊ-/ *noun* [U] the scientific study of the physical and chemical structure of the stars, planets, etc. ▶ **astro·physi·cist** /-ˈfɪzɪsɪst/ *noun*

Astro·Turf™ /ˈæstrəʊtɜːf; *AmE* ˈæstroʊtɜːrf/ *noun* [U] an artificial surface that looks like grass, for playing sports on

as·tute /əˈstjuːt; *AmE* əˈstuːt/ *adj.* very clever and quick at seeing what to do in a particular situation, especially how to get an advantage [SYN] SHREWD: *an astute businessman/politician/observer* ◊ *It was an astute move to sell the shares just then.* ▶ **as·tute·ly** *adv.* **as·tute·ness** *noun* [U]

asun·der /əˈsʌndə(r)/ *adv.* (*old-fashioned* or *literary*) into pieces; apart: *families rent/torn asunder by the revolution*

asy·lum /əˈsaɪləm/ *noun* **1** (also *formal* **po·litical asylum**) [U] protection that a government gives to people who have left their own country, usually because they were in danger for political reasons: *to seek/apply for/be granted asylum* ◊ *the rights of asylum seekers* (= people asking for political asylum) **2** [C] (*old use*) a hospital where people who were mentally ill could be cared for, often for a long time

asym·met·ric /ˌeɪsɪˈmetrɪk/ (also **asym·met·ric·al** /ˌeɪsɪˈmetrɪkl/) *adj.* **1** having two sides or parts that are not the same in size or shape: *Most people's faces are asymmetric.* [OPP] SYMMETRICAL **2** (*technical*) not equal, for example in the way each side or part behaves: *Linguists are studying the asymmetric use of Creole by parents and children* (= parents use one language and children reply in another). ▶ **asym·met·ric·al·ly** /-kli/ *adv.* **asym·met·ry** /ˌeɪˈsɪmətri/ *noun* [C, U]

at /ət/ *strong form* æt/ *prep.* **1** used to say where sth/sb is or where sth happens: *at the corner of the street* ◊ *We changed at Crewe.* ◊ *They arrived late at the airport.* ◊ *At the roundabout take the third exit.* ◊ *I'll be at home all morning.* ◊ *She's at Tom's* (= at Tom's house). ◊ *I met her at the hospital.* ◊ *How many people were there at the concert?* **2** used to say where sb works or studies: *He's been at the bank longer than anyone else.* ◊ *She's at Yale* (= Yale University). **3** used to say when sth happens: *We left at 2 o'clock.* ◊ *at the end of the week* ◊ *We woke at dawn.* ◊ *I didn't know at the time of writing* (= when I wrote). ◊ *At night you can see the stars.* ◊ (*BrE*) *What are you doing at the weekend?* **4** used to state the age at which sb does sth:

She got married at 25. ◊ *He left school at the age of 16.* **5** in the direction of or towards sb/sth: *What are you looking at?* ◊ *He pointed a gun at her.* ◊ *Somebody threw paint at the prime minister.* **6** used after a verb to show that sb tries to do sth, or partly does sth, but does not succeed or complete it: *He clutched wildly at the rope as he fell.* ◊ *She nibbled at a sandwich* (= ate only small bits of it). **7** used to state the distance away from sth: *I held it at arm's length.* ◊ *Can you read a car number plate at fifty metres?* **8** used to show the situation sb/sth is in, what sb is doing or what is happening: *The country is now at war.* ◊ *I felt at a disadvantage.* ◊ *I think Mr Harris is at lunch.* **9** used to show a rate, speed, etc: *He was driving at 70 mph.* ◊ *The noise came at two-minute intervals* (= once every two minutes). **10** ~ **sb's/sth's best/worst, etc.** used to say that sb/sth is as good, bad, etc. as they can be: *This was Henman at his best.* ◊ *The garden's at its most beautiful in June.* **11** used with adjectives to show how well sb does sth: *I'm good at French.* ◊ *She's hopeless at managing people.* **12** used with adjectives to show the cause of sth: *They were impatient at the delay.* ◊ *She was delighted at the result.* **13** (*formal*) in response to sth: *They attended the dinner at the chairman's invitation.* [IDM] **at that** used when you are giving an extra piece of information: *He managed to buy a car after all—and a nice one at that.* ,**where it's 'at** (*informal*) a place or an activity that is very popular or fashionable: *Judging by the crowds waiting to get in, this seems to be where it's at.*

at·av·is·tic /ˌætəˈvɪstɪk/ *adj.* (*formal*) related to the attitudes and behaviour of the first humans: *an atavistic urge/instinct/fear*

ate *pp of* EAT

-ate *suffix* **1** (in adjectives) full of or having the quality of: *passionate* ◊ *Italianate* **2** (in verbs) to give the thing or quality mentioned to: *hyphenate* ◊ *activate* **3** (in nouns) the status or function of: *a doctorate* **4** (in nouns) a group with the status or function of: *the electorate* **5** (in nouns) (*chemistry*) a SALT formed by the action of a particular acid: *sulphate*

atel·ier /əˈtelieɪ; *AmE* ˌætlˈjeɪ/ *noun* a room or building in which an artist works

athe·ism /ˈeɪθiɪzəm/ *noun* [U] the belief that God does not exist [OPP] THEISM ▶ **athe·is·tic** /ˌeɪθiˈɪstɪk/ *adj.*

athe·ist /ˈeɪθiɪst/ *noun* a person who believes that God does not exist—compare AGNOSTIC

ath·lete /ˈæθliːt/ *noun* **1** a person who competes in sports: *Olympic athletes* **2** (*BrE*) a person who competes in sports such as running and jumping **3** a person who is good at sports and physical exercise: *She is a natural athlete.*

,**athlete's 'foot** *noun* [U] an infectious skin disease that affects the feet, especially between the toes

ath·let·ic /æθˈletɪk/ *adj.* **1** physically strong, fit and active: *an athletic figure/build* ◊ *a tall, slim athletic girl* **2** [only before noun] (*BrE*) connected with sports such as running, jumping and throwing (= athletics): *an athletic club/coach* ▶ **ath·let·ic·al·ly** /-ɪkli/ *adv.* **ath·leti·cism** /æθˈletɪsɪzəm/ *noun* [U]: *She moved with great athleticism about the court.*

ath·let·ics /æθˈletɪks/ *noun* [U] **1** (*BrE*) (*AmE* ,**track and 'field**) sports that people compete in, such as running and jumping—picture on page 1251 **2** (*AmE*) any sports that people compete in: *students involved in all forms of college athletics*

ath'letic shoe *noun* (*AmE*) = TENNIS SHOE

ath,letic sup'porter *noun* (*especially AmE*) = JOCKSTRAP

-ation ⇨ -ION

atishoo /əˈtɪʃuː/ (*BrE*) (also **ahchoo** *AmE, BrE*) *exclamation* the word for the sound people make when they SNEEZE

-ative *suffix* (in adjectives) doing or tending to do sth: *illustrative* ◊ *talkative* ▶ **-atively** *suffix* (in adverbs): *creatively*

atlas /ˈætləs/ *noun* a book of maps: *a world atlas* ◊ *a road atlas of Europe*

A·TM /ˌeɪ tiː ˈem/ *noun* automated teller machine ⟹ CASH MACHINE

ˌAT'M card *noun* (*AmE*) = CASH CARD

at·mos·phere /ˈætməsfɪə(r), *AmE* -fɪr/ *noun* **1** (**the atmosphere**) [sing.] the mixture of gases that surrounds the earth: *the upper atmosphere* ◊ *pollution of the atmosphere* **2** [C] a mixture of gases that surrounds another planet or a star: *Saturn's atmosphere* **3** [C] the air in a room or in an enclosed space; the air around a place: *a smoky/stuffy atmosphere* ◊ *These plants grow warm, humid atmospheres.* **4** [C, U] the feeling or mood that you have in a particular place or situation; a feeling between two people or in a group of people: *a party atmosphere* ◊ *The hotel offers a friendly atmosphere and personal service.* ◊ *Use music and lighting to create a romantic atmosphere.* ◊ *There was an atmosphere of mutual trust and respect between them.* ◊ *The children grew up in an atmosphere of violence and insecurity.* ◊ *The old house is full of atmosphere* (= it's very interesting). **IDM** see HEAVY *adj.*

at·mos·pher·ic /ˌætməsˈferɪk/ *adj.* **1** [only before noun] related to the earth's atmosphere: *atmospheric pollution/conditions* ◊ *atmospheric pressure* **2** creating an exciting or emotional mood: *atmospheric music*

at·mos·pher·ics /ˌætməsˈferɪks/ *noun* [pl.] **1** qualities in sth that create a particular atmosphere **2** noises that sometimes interrupt a radio broadcast

atoll /ˈætɒl, *AmE* ˈætɔːl, -tɑːl/ *noun* an island made of CORAL and shaped like a ring with a lake of sea water (called a LAGOON) in the middle

atom /ˈætəm/ *noun* the smallest part of a chemical ELEMENT that can take part in a chemical reaction: *the splitting of the atom* ◊ *Two atoms of hydrogen combine with one atom of oxygen to form a molecule of water.*

atom·ic /əˈtɒmɪk, *AmE* əˈtɑːmɪk/ *adj.* [usually before noun] **1** connected with atoms or an atom: *atomic structure* **2** related to the energy that is produced when atoms are split; related to weapons that use this energy: *atomic energy/power* ◊ *the atomic bomb*

aˌtomic ˈnumber *noun* (*chemistry*) the number of PROTONS in the NUCLEUS (= centre) of an atom, which is characteristic of a chemical element. Elements are placed in the PERIODIC TABLE according to their atomic numbers.

aˌtomic ˈtheory *noun* (*physics*) the theory that atoms are made up of a central NUCLEUS surrounded by moving ELECTRONS

atom·ize (*BrE* also **-ise**) /ˈætəmaɪz/ *verb* [VN] to reduce sth to atoms or very small pieces

atonal /eɪˈtəʊnl, *AmE* eɪˈtoʊnl/ *adj.* (of a piece of music) not written in any particular KEY **OPP** TONAL ▶ **aton·al·ity** /ˌeɪtəʊˈnæləti, *AmE* ˌeɪtoʊˈn-/ *noun* [U]

atone /əˈtəʊn, *AmE* əˈtoʊn/ *verb* [V] ~ (**for sth**) (*formal*) to act in a way that shows you are sorry for doing sth wrong in the past: *to atone for a crime* ◊ *a desire to atone* ▶ **atone·ment** *noun* [U]: *to make atonement for his sins* ◊ *Yom Kippur, the Jewish day of atonement*

atop /əˈtɒp, *AmE* əˈtɑːp/ *prep.* (especially *AmE*) (old-fashioned or literary in *BrE*) on top of; at the top of: *a flag high atop a pole* ◊ *a scoop of ice cream atop a slice of apple pie*

-ator *suffix* (in nouns) a person or thing that does sth: *creator* ◊ *percolator*

at·rium /ˈeɪtriəm/ *noun* **1** a large high open space in the centre of a modern building: *The reception was held in the atrium.* **2** an open space in the centre of an Ancient Roman VILLA (= a large house) **3** (*anatomy*) either of the two upper spaces in the heart used to pump blood **SYN** AURICLE

atro·cious /əˈtrəʊʃəs, *AmE* əˈtroʊ-/ *adj.* **1** very bad or unpleasant **SYN** TERRIBLE: *She speaks French with an atrocious accent.* ◊ *Isn't the weather atrocious?* **2** very cruel and shocking: *atrocious acts of brutality* ▶ **atro·cious·ly** *adv.*

atro·city /əˈtrɒsəti, *AmE* əˈtrɑːs-/ *noun* [C, usually pl., U] (*pl.* **-ies**) a terrible, cruel and violent act, especially in a war

at·ro·phy /ˈætrəfi/ *noun, verb*
■ *noun* [U] (*medical*) the condition of losing flesh, muscle, strength, etc. in a part of the body because it does not have enough blood: (*figurative, formal*) *The cultural life of the country will sink into atrophy unless more writers and artists emerge.*
■ *verb* (**at·ro·phies, at·ro·phy·ing, at·ro·phied, at·ro·phied**) [V] if a part of the body **atrophies**, it becomes weak because it is not used or because it does not have enough blood: (*figurative*) *Memory can atrophy through lack of use.* ▶ **at·ro·phied** *adj.*: *atrophied muscles* ◊ *atrophied religious values*

at·tach /əˈtætʃ/ *verb* **1** [VN] ~ **sth** (**to sth**) to fasten or join one thing to another: *Attach the coupon to the front of your letter.* ◊ (*written*) *I attach a copy of my notes for your information.* ◊ (*figurative*) *They have attached a number of conditions to the agreement* (= said that the conditions must be part of the agreement).—compare DETACH **2** [VN] ~ **importance, significance, value, weight, etc.** (**to sth**) to believe that sth is important or worth thinking about: *I attach great importance to this research.* **3** [VN] ~ **yourself to sb** to join sb for a time, sometimes when you are not welcome or have not been invited: *He attached himself to me at the party and I couldn't get rid of him.* **4** ~ **to sb/sth** (*formal*) to be connected with sb/sth; to connect sth to sth: [V] *No one is suggesting that any health risks attach to this product.* ◊ *No blame attaches to you.* ◊ [VN] *This does not attach any blame to you.* **IDM** see STRING *n.*

at·taché /əˈtæʃeɪ, *AmE* ˌætəˈʃeɪ/ *noun* a person who works at an EMBASSY, usually with a special responsibility for a particular area of activity: *a cultural/military attaché*

atˈtaché case *noun* a small hard flat case used for carrying business documents—compare BRIEFCASE—picture at BAG

at·tached /əˈtætʃt/ *adj.* [not before noun] **1** ~ (**to sb/sth**) full of affection for sb/sth: *I've never seen two people so attached to each other.* ◊ *We've grown very attached to this house and would hate to move.*—compare UNATTACHED **2** [not before noun] ~ **to sth** working for or forming part of an organization: *The research unit is attached to the university.* **3** ~ (**to sth**) joined to sth: *Please complete the attached application form.*

at·tach·ment /əˈtætʃmənt/ *noun* **1** [C, U] a strong feeling of affection for sb/sth: *a child's deep attachment to its parents* **2** [C, U] belief in and continued support for an idea or a set of values: *the popular attachment to democratic government* **3** [C] an object or a device that you can fix onto a machine, to make it do another job: *an electric drill with a range of different attachments* **4** [U, C] the act of joining one thing to another; a thing that joins two things together: *All cars built since 1981 have points for the attachment of safety restraints.* ◊ *They discussed the attachment of new conditions to the peace plans.* ◊ *They had to check the strength of the seat attachments to the floor of the plane.* **5** [U, C] (*BrE*) a short time spent working with an organization such as a hospital, school or part of the armed forces: *She's on attachment to the local hospital.* ◊ *a 4-month training attachment* **6** [C] (*computing*) a document that you send to sb using e-mail—picture on page 251

at·tack /əˈtæk/ *noun, verb*
■ *noun*
VIOLENCE | **1** [C, U] ~ (**on sb**) an act of using violence to try to hurt or kill sb: *a series of racist attacks*

IN WAR | **2** [C, U] ~ (**on sb/sth**) an act of trying to kill or injure the enemy in war, using weapons such as guns and bombs: *to launch/make/mount an attack* ◊ *The patrol came under attack from all sides.*—see also COUNTER-ATTACK

CRITICISM | **3** [C, U] ~ (**on sb/sth**) strong criticism of sb/sth in speech or in writing: *a scathing attack on the government's policies* ◊ *The school has come under attack for failing to encourage bright pupils.*

ACTION TO STOP STH | **4** [C] ~ (**on sth**) an action that you take to try to stop or change sth that you feel is bad: *to*

æ	ɑː	e	ɜː	ə	ɪ	iː	i	ɒ	ɔː	ʌ	ʊ	u	uː
cat	father	ten	bird	about	sit	see	many	got	saw	cup	put	actual	too
								(BrE)					

A

launch an *all-out attack on poverty/unemployment/smoking*

OF ILLNESS | 5 [C] a sudden, short period of illness, usually severe, especially an illness that you have often: *to suffer an asthma/migraine attack* ◇ *an acute attack of food poisoning* ◇ *a panic attack* ◇ (*figurative*) *an attack of the giggles*—see also HEART ATTACK

OF EMOTION | 6 [C] a sudden period of feeling an emotion such as fear: *an attack of nerves.*

DAMAGE | 7 [U, C] the action of sth such as an insect, or a disease, that causes damage to sth/sb: *The roof timbers were affected by rot and insect attack.*

IN SPORT | 8 [sing.] (*BrE*) (*AmE* **of·fense**) the players in a team whose job is to try to score goals or points: *Germany's attack has been weakened by the loss of some key players through injury.*—compare DEFENCE **9** [C, U] the actions that players take to try to score a goal or win the game: *a sustained attack on the Arsenal goal*

■ *verb*

USE VIOLENCE | 1 to use violence to try to hurt or kill sb: [VN] [often passive] *A woman was attacked and robbed by a gang of youths.* ◇ *The man attacked him with a knife.* ◇ [V] *Most dogs will not attack unless provoked.*

IN WAR | 2 to use weapons, such as guns and bombs against an enemy in a war, etc: [VN] *At dawn the army attacked the town.* ◇ [V] *The guerrillas usually attack at night.*

CRITICIZE | 3 [VN] **~ sb/sth (for sth/for doing sth)** to criticize sb/sth severely: *a newspaper article attacking the England football manager* ◇ *She has been attacked for ignoring her own party members.*

DAMAGE | 4 [VN] to have a harmful effect on sth: *a disease that attacks the brain* ◇ *The vines had been attacked by mildew.*

DO STH WITH ENERGY | 5 [VN] to deal with sth with a lot of energy and determination: *Let's attack one problem at a time.*

IN SPORT | 6 [V] to go forward in a game in order to try to score goals or points: *Spain attacked more in the second half and deserved a goal.*

at·tack·er /əˈtækə(r)/ *noun* a person who attacks sb: *She didn't really see her attacker.*

at·tain /əˈteɪn/ *verb* [VN] **1** to succeed in getting sth, usually after a lot of effort: *Most of our students attained five 'A' grades in their exams.* **2** (*formal*) to reach a particular age, level or condition: *The cheetah can attain speeds of up to 97 kph.*

at·tain·able /əˈteɪnəbl/ *adj.* that you can achieve: *attainable goals/objectives/targets* ◇ *This standard is easily attainable by most students.* [OPP] UNATTAINABLE

at·tain·ment /əˈteɪnmənt/ *noun* (*formal*) **1** [C, usually pl.] (*BrE*) something that you learned or achieved: *a young woman of impressive educational attainments* **2** [U] success in achieving sth: *The attainment of his ambitions was still a dream.* ◇ *attainment targets* (= for example in education)

at·tempt /əˈtempt/
■ *noun* **1** [C, U] **~ (to do sth) | ~ (at sth/at doing sth)** an act of trying to do sth, especially sth difficult, often with no success: *Two factories were closed in an attempt to cut costs.* ◇ *They made no attempt to escape.* ◇ *I passed my driving test at the first attempt.* ◇ *The couple made several unsuccessful attempts at a compromise.* **2** [C] **~ (on sb/sb's life)** an act of trying to kill sb: *Someone has made an attempt on the President's life.* **3** [C] **~ (on sth)** an effort to do better than sth, such as a very good performance in sport: *the latest attempt on the world land speed record*
■ *verb* to make an effort or try to do sth, especially sth difficult: [V to inf] *I will attempt to answer all your questions.* ◇ *Do not attempt to repair this yourself.* ◇ [VN] *The prisoners attempted an escape, but failed.*

at·tempt·ed /əˈtemptɪd/ *adj.* [only before noun] (of a crime, etc.) that sb has tried to do but without success: *attempted rape/murder/robbery*

at·tend /əˈtend/ *verb* **1** to be present at an event: [VN] *The meeting was attended by 90% of shareholders.* ◇ *to attend a*

wedding/funeral ◇ [V] *We'd like as many people as possible to attend.* ⇨ note at HELP **2** [VN] to go regularly to a place: *Our children attend the same school.* ◇ *How many people attend church every Sunday?* **3** [V] **~ (to sb/sth)** (*formal*) to pay attention to what sb is saying or to what you are doing: *She hadn't been attending during the lesson.* **4** [VN] (*formal*) to happen at the same time as sth: *She dislikes the loss of privacy that attends TV celebrity.* **5** [VN] (*formal*) to be with sb and help them: *The President was attended by several members of his staff.* [PHRV] **at'tend to sb/sth** to deal with sb/sth; to take care of sb/sth: *I have some urgent business to attend to.* ◇ *A nurse attended to his needs constantly.* ◇ (*BrE, formal*) *Are you being attended to, Sir?* (= for example, in a shop).

at·tend·ance /əˈtendəns/ *noun* **1** [U, C] the act of being present at a place, for example at school: *Attendance at these lectures is not compulsory.* ◇ *Teachers must keep a record of students' attendances.* **2** [C, U] the number of people present at an organized event: *high/low/falling/poor attendances* ◇ *There was an attendance of 42 at the meeting.* [IDM] **be in at'tendance** (*formal*) to be present at a special event: *Several heads of state were in attendance at the funeral.* **be in at'tendance (on sb)** (*formal*) to be with or near sb in order to help them if necessary: *He always has at least two bodyguards in attendance.* **take at'tendance** (*AmE*) to check who is present and who is not present at a place and to mark this information on a list of names—more at DANCE *v.*

at·tend·ant /əˈtendənt/ *noun, adj.*
■ *noun* **1** a person whose job is to serve or help people in a public place: *a cloakroom/parking/museum attendant*—see also FLIGHT ATTENDANT **2** a person who takes care of and lives or travels with an important person or a sick or DISABLED person
■ *adj.* [usually before noun] **~ (upon sth)** (*formal*) closely connected with sth that has just been mentioned: *attendant problems/risks/circumstances* ◇ *We had all the usual problems attendant upon starting a new business.*

at·tend·er /əˈtendə(r)/ (*especially BrE*) (*AmE* usually **at·tend·ee**) *noun* a person who goes to a place or an event, often on a regular basis: *She's a regular attender at evening classes.*

at·ten·tion /əˈtenʃn/ *noun, exclamation*
■ *noun*
LISTENING/LOOKING CAREFULLY | 1 [U] the act of listening to, looking at or thinking about sth/sb carefully: *the report's attention to detail* ◇ *He turned his attention back to the road again.* ◇ *Small children have a very short attention span.* ◇ *Please pay attention* (= listen carefully) *to what I am saying.* ◇ *Don't pay any attention to what they say* (= don't think that it is important). ◇ *She tried to attract the waiter's attention.* ◇ *I tried not to draw attention to* (= make people notice) *the weak points in my argument.* ◇ *An article in the newspaper caught my attention.* ◇ *I couldn't give the programme my undivided attention.* ◇ (*formal*) *It has come to my attention* (= I have been informed) *that ...* ◇ (*formal*) *He called (their) attention to the fact that many files were missing.* ◇ (*formal, spoken*) *Can I have your attention please?*

INTEREST | 2 [U] interest that people show in sb/sth: *Films with big stars always attract great attention.* ◇ *As the youngest child, she was always the centre of attention.* **3** [C, usually pl.] things that sb does to try to please you or to show their interest in you: *She tried to escape the unwanted attentions of her former boyfriend.*

TREATMENT | 4 [U] special care, action or treatment: *She was in need of medical attention.* ◇ *The roof needs attention* (= needs to be repaired). ◇ *for the attention of ...* (= written on the envelope of an official letter to say who should deal with it)

SOLDIERS | 5 [U] the position soldiers take when they stand very straight with their feet together and their arms at their sides: *to stand at/to attention*—compare (STAND) AT EASE at EASE *n.*

■ *exclamation* **1** used for asking people to listen to sth that is being announced: *Attention, please! Passengers for* *flight KL412 are requested to go to gate 21 immediately.* **2** used for ordering soldiers to stand to attention

at·ten·tive /əˈtentɪv/ *adj.* **1** listening or watching carefully and with interest: *an attentive audience* **2** ~ **(to sb/sth)** helpful; making sure that people have what they need: *The hotel staff are friendly and attentive.* ◊ *Ministers should be more attentive to the needs of families.* ▶ **at·ten·tive·ly** *adv.* **at·ten·tive·ness** *noun* [U]

at·tenu·ate /əˈtenjueɪt/ *verb* [VN] (*formal*) to make sth weaker or less effective: *an attenuated strain of the virus* ▶ **at·tenu·ation** /əˌtenjuˈeɪʃn/ *noun* [U]

at·test /əˈtest/ *verb* (*formal*) **1** ~ **(to sth)** to show or prove that sth is true: [V] *Contemporary accounts attest to his courage and determination.* [also Vthat, VN] **2** to state that you believe that sth is true or genuine, for example in a court of law: [VN] *to attest a will* ◊ *The signature was attested by two witnesses.* [also Vthat]

attic /ˈætɪk/ *noun* a room or space just below the roof of a house, often used for storing things: *furniture stored in the attic* ◊ *an attic bedroom*—compare GARRET, LOFT

at·tire /əˈtaɪə(r)/ *noun* [U] (*formal*) clothes: *dressed in formal evening attire*

at·tired /əˈtaɪəd; *AmE* əˈtaɪərd/ *adj.* [not before noun] (*formal or literary*) dressed in a particular way

at·ti·tude /ˈætɪtjuːd; *AmE* ˈætɪtuːd/ *noun* **1** [C] ~ **(to/towards sb/sth)** the way that you think and feel about sb/sth; the way that you behave towards sb/sth that shows how you think and feel: *changes in public attitudes to marriage* ◊ *the government's attitude towards single parents* ◊ *to have a good/bad/positive/negative attitude towards sb/sth* ◊ *Youth is simply an attitude of mind.* ◊ *If you want to pass your exams you'd better change your attitude! You're taking a pretty selfish attitude over this, aren't you?* **2** [U] confident, sometimes aggressive behaviour that shows you do not care about other people's opinions and that you want to do things in an individual way: *a band with attitude* ◊ *You'd better get rid of that attitude and shape up, young man.* ◊ *A lot of drivers have a serious attitude problem* (= they do not behave in a way that is acceptable to other people). **3** [C] (*formal*) a position of the body: *Her hands were folded in an attitude of prayer.* **IDM** see STRIKE *v.*

at·ti·tu·din·al /ˌætɪˈtjuːdɪnl; *AmE* -ˈtuː-/ *adj.* (*formal*) related to the attitudes that people have: *attitudinal changes in society*

attn (also **attn.** especially in *AmE*) *abbr.* (*business*) (in writing) for the attention of: *Sales Dept, attn C Biggs*

at·tor·ney /əˈtɜːni; *AmE* əˈtɜːrni/ *noun* **1** (*especially AmE*) a lawyer, especially one who can act for sb in a court of law—see also DISTRICT ATTORNEY ⇨ note at LAWYER **2** a person who is given the power to act on behalf of another in business or legal matters: *She was made her father's attorney when he became ill.*—see also POWER OF ATTORNEY

At·torney-ˈGeneral *noun* (*pl.* **Attorneys General** or **Attorney Generals**) **1** the most senior legal officer in some countries or states, who advises the government or head of state on legal matters **2** (**the Attorney-General**) the head of the US Department of Justice and a member of the President's CABINET (= a group of senior politicians who advise the President)

at·tract /əˈtrækt/ *verb* [VN] **1** [usually passive] ~ **sb (to sb/sth)** if you are **attracted** by sth, it interests you and makes you want it; if you are **attracted** by sb, you like or admire them: *I had always been attracted by the idea of working abroad.* ◊ *What first attracted me to her was her sense of humour.* **2** ~ **sb/sth (to sth)** to make sb/sth come somewhere or take part in sth: *The warm damp air attracts a lot of mosquitoes.* ◊ *The exhibition has attracted thousands of visitors.* **3** to make people have a particular reaction: *This proposal has attracted a lot of interest.* ◊ *His comments were bound to attract criticism.* ◊ *She tried to attract the attention of the waiter.* **4** (*physics*) if a MAGNET or GRAVITY **attracts** sth, it makes it move towards it **OPP** REPEL **IDM** see OPPOSITE *n.*

at·trac·tion /əˈtrækʃn/ *noun* **1** [U, sing.] a feeling of liking sb, especially sexually: *She felt an immediate attraction for him.* ◊ *Sexual attraction is a large part of*

falling in love. **2** [C] an interesting or enjoyable place to go or thing to do: *Buckingham Palace is a major tourist attraction.* ◊ *The main attraction at Giverny is Monet's garden.* **3** [C, U] a feature, quality or person that makes sth seem interesting and enjoyable, and worth having or doing: *I can't see the attraction of sitting on a beach all day.* ◊ *City life holds little attraction for me.* ◊ *She is the star attraction of the show.* ◊ *And there's the added attraction of free champagne on all flights.* **4** [U] (*physics*) a force which pulls things towards each other: *gravitational/magnetic attraction*—compare REPULSION

at·tract·ive /əˈtræktɪv/ *adj.* **1** (of a person) pleasant to look at, especially in a sexual way: *an attractive woman* ◊ *I like John but I don't find him attractive physically.* **2** (of a thing or a place) pleasant to look at: *a big house with an attractive garden* **3** having features or qualities that make sth seem interesting and worth having **SYN** APPEALING: *an attractive offer/proposition* **OPP** UNATTRACTIVE ▶ **at·tract·ive·ly** *adv.*: *The room is arranged very attractively.* ◊ *attractively priced hotel rooms* **at·tract·ive·ness** *noun* [U]: *the attractiveness of travelling abroad*

at·trib·ut·able /əˈtrɪbjətəbl/ *adj.* [not before noun] ~ **to sb/sth** (*written*) probably caused by the thing mentioned: *Their illnesses are attributable to a poor diet.*

at·tri·bute *verb, noun*
■ *verb* /əˈtrɪbjuːt/ [VN] **1** ~ **sth to sth** to say or believe that sth is the result of a particular thing: *She attributes her success to hard work and a little luck.* **2** ~ **sth (to sb)** to say or believe that sb is responsible for doing sth, especially for saying, writing or painting sth: *The committee refused to attribute blame without further information.* ◊ *This play is usually attributed to Shakespeare.* ▶ **at·tri·bu·tion** /ˌætrɪˈbjuːʃn/ *noun* [U]: *The attribution of this painting to Rembrandt has never been questioned.*
■ *noun* /ˈætrɪbjuːt/ a quality or feature of sb/sth: *Patience is one of the most important attributes in a teacher.*

at·tribu·tive /əˈtrɪbjətɪv/ *adj.* (*grammar*) (of adjectives or nouns) used before a noun to describe it: *In 'the blue sky' and 'a family business', 'blue' and 'family' are attributive.*—compare PREDICATIVE ▶ **at·tribu·tive·ly** *adv.*: *Some adjectives can only be used attributively.*

at·tri·tion /əˈtrɪʃn/ *noun* [U] (*formal*) **1** a process of making sb/sth, especially your enemy, weaker by repeatedly attacking them or creating problems for them: *It was a war of attrition.* **2** (*especially AmE*) = NATURAL WASTAGE

at·tuned /əˈtjuːnd; *AmE* əˈtuːnd/ *adj.* [not before noun] ~ **(to sb/sth)** familiar with sb/sth so that you can understand or recognize them or it and act in an appropriate way: *She wasn't yet attuned to her baby's needs.*

ATV /ˌeɪ tiː ˈviː/ *noun* (*especially AmE*) the abbreviation for 'all-terrain vehicle' (a small open motor vehicle with one seat and four wheels with very thick tyres, designed especially for use on rough ground without roads)—see also FOUR-WHEEL DRIVE—picture at CAR

atyp·ical /ˌeɪˈtɪpɪkl/ *adj.* not typical or usual: *atypical behaviour* **OPP** TYPICAL

au·ber·gine /ˈəʊbəʒiːn; *AmE* ˈoʊbərʒiːn/ (*BrE*) (*AmE* **egg·plant**) *noun* [C, U] a large vegetable with shiny dark purple skin and soft white flesh—picture on page A3

au·burn /ˈɔːbən; *AmE* ˈɔːbərn/ *adj.* (of hair) reddish-brown in colour ▶ **au·burn** *noun* [U]: *the rich auburn of her hair*

auc·tion /ˈɔːkʃn; ˈɒk-; *AmE* ˈɔːk-/ *noun, verb*
■ *noun* [C, U] a public event at which things are sold to the person who offers the most money for them: *an auction of paintings* ◊ *The house is up for auction* (= will be sold at an auction). ◊ *A classic Rolls Royce fetched* (= was sold for) *£25000 at auction.*
■ *verb* [VN] [usually passive] to sell sth at an auction: *The costumes from the movie are to be auctioned for charity.* **PHRV** ˌauction sth↔ˈoff to sell sth at an auction, especially sth that is no longer needed or wanted: *The Army is auctioning off a lot of surplus equipment.*

auc·tion·eer /ˌɔːkʃəˈnɪə(r); ˌɒk-; *AmE* ˌɔːkʃəˈnɪr/ *noun* a person whose job is to direct an auction and sell the goods

b	d	f	g	h	k	l	m	n	p	r
bad	did	fall	get	hat	cat	leg	**man**	now	pen	red

A

au·da·cious /ɔːˈdeɪʃəs/ adj. (written) willing to take risks or to do sth shocking: an audacious decision ▶ **au·da·cious·ly** adv.

au·da·city /ɔːˈdæsəti/ noun [U] brave but rude or shocking behaviour: He **had the audacity** to tell me I was too fat.

aud·ible /ˈɔːdəbl/ adj. that can be heard clearly: Her voice was **barely audible** above the noise. OPP INAUDIBLE ▶ **audi·bil·ity** /ˌɔːdəˈbɪləti/ noun [U] **aud·ibly** /-əbli/ adv.

audi·ence /ˈɔːdiəns/ noun **1** [C+sing./pl. v.] the group of people who have gathered to watch or listen to sth (a play, concert, sb speaking, etc.): The audience was/were clapping for 10 minutes. ◊ an audience of 10000 ◊ The debate was televised in front of a **live audience**. **2** [C] a number of people or a particular group of people who watch, read or listen to the same thing: An audience of millions watched the wedding on TV. ◊ TV/cinema/movie audiences ◊ His book reached an even wider audience when it was made into a movie. ◊ The **target audience** for this advertisement was mainly teenagers. **3** [C] a formal meeting with an important person: an audience with the Pope

audio /ˈɔːdiəʊ; AmE ˈɔːdioʊ/ adj. [only before noun] connected with sound that is recorded: audio and video cassettes ▶ **audio** noun [U]

audio- /ˈɔːdiəʊ; AmE ˈɔːdioʊ/ combining form (in nouns, adjectives and adverbs) connected with hearing or sound: an audiobook (= a reading of a book on cassette) ◊ audiovisual

ˈaudio tape noun [U] MAGNETIC tape on which sound can be recorded

ˌaudio-ˈvisual adj. (abbr. **AV**) using both sound and pictures: audio-visual aids for the classroom

audit /ˈɔːdɪt/ noun, verb
- noun [C, U] **1** an official examination of business and financial records to see that they are true and correct: an annual audit ◊ a tax audit **2** an official examination of the quality or standard of sth
- verb [VN] **1** to officially examine the financial accounts of a company: We have just had our accounts audited. **2** (AmE) to attend a course at college or university but without taking any exams or receiving CREDIT: She audited classes at the University of California.

au·di·tion /ɔːˈdɪʃn/ noun, verb
- noun a short performance given by an actor, a singer, etc., so that sb can decide whether they are suitable to act in a play, sing in a concert, etc.
- verb **1** [V] ~ (for sth) to take part in an audition: She was auditioning for the role of Lady Macbeth. ◊ Hundreds of people auditioned. **2** [VN] ~ sb (for sth) to watch, listen to and judge sb at an audition: We auditioned over 200 children for the part.

au·dit·or /ˈɔːdɪtə(r)/ noun **1** a person who officially examines the business and financial records of a company **2** (AmE) a person who attends a college course, but without having to take exams and without receiving CREDIT

audi·tor·ium /ˌɔːdɪˈtɔːriəm/ noun (pl. **audi·tor·iums** or **audi·toria** /-riə/) **1** the part of a theatre, concert hall, etc. in which the audience sits **2** (AmE) a large building or room in which public meetings, concerts, etc. are held

audi·tory /ˈɔːdətri; AmE -tɔːri/ adj. (technical) connected with hearing: auditory stimuli

au fait /ˌəʊ ˈfeɪ; AmE ˌoʊ/ adj. [not before noun] ~ (with sth) (from French) completely familiar with sth: It's my first week here so I'm not completely au fait with the system.

aught /ɔːt/ pron. (old use) anything

aug·ment /ɔːɡˈment/ verb [VN] (formal) to increase the amount, value, size, etc. of sth ▶ **aug·men·ta·tion** /ˌɔːɡmenˈteɪʃn/ noun [U, C]

augur /ˈɔːɡə(r)/ verb [V] ~ **well/badly** (formal) to be a sign that sth will be successful or not successful in the future: Conflicts among the various groups do not augur well for the future of the peace talks.

au·gury /ˈɔːɡjʊri/ noun (pl. **-ies**) (literary) a sign of what will happen in the future SYN OMEN

Au·gust /ˈɔːɡəst/ noun [U, C] (abbr. **Aug.**) the 8th month of the year, between July and September: (BrE) August Bank Holiday (= a public holiday on the last Monday in August in Britain) HELP To see how **August** is used, look at the examples at **April**.

au·gust /ɔːˈɡʌst/ adj. [usually before noun] (formal) impressive, making you feel respect: an august group of statesmen

auk /ɔːk/ noun a northern seabird with short narrow wings

aunt /ɑːnt; AmE ænt/ noun **1** the sister of your father or mother; the wife of your uncle: Aunt Alice ◊ My aunt lives in Canada. **2** (informal) used by children, with a first name, to address a woman who is a friend of their parents—see also AGONY AUNT

aun·tie (also **aunty**) /ˈɑːnti; AmE ˈænti/ noun (informal) aunt: Auntie Mary

au pair /ˌəʊ ˈpeə(r); AmE ˌoʊ ˈper/ noun (BrE) a young person, usually a woman, who lives with a family in a foreign country in order to learn the language. An au pair helps in the house and takes care of children and receives a small wage.

aura /ˈɔːrə/ noun ~ (of sth) a feeling or particular quality that is very noticeable and seems to surround a person or place: She always has an aura of confidence.

aural /ˈɔːrəl/ adj. (technical) connected with hearing and listening: aural and visual images ◊ aural comprehension tests ▶ **aur·al·ly** adv.

aure·ole /ˈɔːriəʊl; AmE -oʊl/ noun (literary) a circle of light

au re·voir /ˌəʊ rəˈvwɑː(r); AmE ˌoʊ/ exclamation (from French) goodbye (until we meet again)

aur·icle /ˈɔːrɪkl/ noun (anatomy) **1** either of the two upper spaces in the heart used to pump blood SYN ATRIUM—compare VENTRICLE **2** the outer part of the ear

aur·ora bor·ealis /ɔːˌrɔːrə ˌbɔːriˈeɪlɪs/ noun [sing.] = THE NORTHERN LIGHTS

aus·pices /ˈɔːspɪsɪz/ noun [pl.] IDM **under the auspices of sb/sth** with the help, support or protection of sb/sth: The community centre was set up under the auspices of a government initiative.

aus·pi·cious /ɔːˈspɪʃəs/ adj. (formal) showing signs that sth is likely to be successful in the future SYN PROMISING: an auspicious start to the new school year OPP INAUSPICIOUS

Aus·sie /ˈɒzi; AmE ˈɔːzi; ˈɑːzi/ noun (informal) a person from Australia ▶ **Aus·sie** adj.

aus·tere /ɒˈstɪə(r); ɔːˈst-; AmE ɔːˈstɪr/ adj. **1** simple and plain; without any decorations: her austere bedroom with its simple narrow bed **2** (of a person) strict and serious in appearance and behaviour: My father was a distant, austere man. **3** allowing nothing that gives pleasure; not comfortable: the monks' austere way of life ▶ **aus·tere·ly** adv.

aus·ter·ity /ɒˈsterəti; AmE and BrE also ɔːˈster-/ noun (pl. **-ies**) **1** [U] a situation when people do not have much money to spend because there are bad economic conditions: War was followed by many years of austerity. **2** [U] the quality of being austere: the austerity of the monks' life **3** [C, usually pl.] something that is part of an austere way of life: the austerities of wartime Europe

Aus·tra·lian /ɒˈstreɪliən; AmE and BrE also ɔːˈstreɪ-/ adj., noun
- adj. of or connected with Australia
- noun a person from Australia

Aus·tralian ˈRules noun [U] an Australian game, similar to rugby and played by two teams of 18 players

au·then·tic /ɔːˈθentɪk/ adj. **1** known to be real and genuine and not a copy: I don't know if the painting is authentic. **2** true and accurate: an authentic account of life in the desert ◊ the authentic voice of young black Americans **3** made to be exactly the same as the original: an authentic model of the ancient town ▶ **au·then·tic·al·ly** /-kli/ adv.: authentically flavoured Mexican dishes

au·then·ti·cate /ɔːˈθentɪkeɪt/ verb [VN] ~ (sth as sth) to prove that sth is genuine, real or true: The letter has been authenticated by handwriting experts. ◊ Experts have

/s/	/t/	/v/	/z/	/ʃ/	/ʒ/	/tʃ/	/dʒ/	/θ/	/ð/	/ŋ/
see	tea	van	zoo	shoe	vision	chain	jam	thin	this	sing

authenticated the writing as that of Byron himself.
▶ **au·then·ti·ca·tion** /ɔːˌθentɪˈkeɪʃn/ *noun* [U]

au·then·ti·city /ˌɔːθenˈtɪsəti/ *noun* [U] the quality of being genuine or true: *The authenticity of the letter is beyond doubt.*

author /ˈɔːθə(r)/ *noun, verb*

■ *noun* **1** a person who writes books or the person who wrote a particular book: *Who is your favourite author?* ◇ *He is the author of three books on art.* ◇ *best-selling author Joan Collins* ◇ *Who's the author?* **2** the person who creates or starts sth, especially a plan or an idea: *As the author of the proposal I cannot agree with you.*

■ *verb* [VN] (*formal*) to be the author of a book, report, etc.

author·ess /ˈɔːθəres/ *noun* (*old-fashioned*) a woman author

au·thor·ial /ɔːˈθɔːriəl/ *adj.* [usually before noun] (*technical*) coming from or connected with the author of sth

author·ing /ˈɔːθərɪŋ/ *noun* [U] (*computing*) creating computer programs without using programming language, for use in MULTIMEDIA products

au·thori·tar·ian /ɔːˌθɒrɪˈteəriən; *AmE* əˌθɔːrəˈter-; əˈθɑːr-/ *adj.* believing that people should obey authority and rules, even when these are unfair, and even if it means that they lose their personal freedom: *an authoritarian regime/government/state* ◇ *The school was very authoritarian and exam-orientated.* ▶ **au·thori·tar·ian** *noun: Father was a strict authoritarian.* **au·thori·tar·ian·ism** *noun* [U]

au·thori·ta·tive /ɔːˈθɒrətətɪv; *AmE* əˈθɔːrəteɪtɪv; əˈθɑːr-/ *adj.* **1** showing that you expect people to obey and respect you: *an authoritative tone of voice* **2** that you can trust and respect as true and correct: *the most authoritative and up-to-date book on the subject* ▶ **au·thori·ta·tive·ly** *adv.*

au·thor·ity /ɔːˈθɒrəti; *AmE* əˈθɔːr-; əˈθɑːr-/ *noun*

POWER | **1** [U] the power to give orders to people: *in a position of authority* ◇ *She now has authority over the people who used to be her bosses.* ◇ *Nothing will be done because no one in authority* (= who has a position of power) *takes the matter seriously.* **2** [U] (**to do sth**) the power or right to do sth: *Only the manager has the authority to sign cheques.* ◇ *We have the authority to search this building.*

PERMISSION | **3** [U] official permission to do sth: *It was done without the principal's authority.* ◇ *We acted under the authority of the UN.*

ORGANIZATION | **4** [C, usually pl.] the people or an organization who have the power to make decisions or who have a particular area of responsibility in a country or region: *The health authorities are investigating the problem.* ◇ *I have to report this to the authorities.*—see also LOCAL AUTHORITY

KNOWLEDGE | **5** [U] the power to influence people because they respect your knowledge or official position: *He spoke with authority on the topic.*

EXPERT | **6** [C] ~ (**on sth**) a person with special knowledge: *She's an authority on criminal law.*

IDM **have sth on good au'thority** to be able to believe sth because you trust the person who gave you the information

au·thor·iza·tion (*BrE* also **-isa·tion**) /ˌɔːθəraɪˈzeɪʃn; *AmE* ˌɔːθərəˈzeɪʃn/ *noun* **1** [U, C] official permission or power to do sth; the act of giving permission: *You may not enter the security area without authorization.* ◇ *Who gave the authorization to release the data?* **2** [C] a document that gives sb official permission to do sth: *Can I see your authorization?*

au·thor·ize (*BrE* also **-ise**) /ˈɔːθəraɪz/ *verb* to give official permission for sth, or for sb to do sth: [VN] *I can authorize payments up to £5000.* ◇ *an authorized biography* ◇ [VN to inf] [often passive] *I have authorized him to act for me while I am away.* ◇ *The soldiers were authorized to shoot at will.*—see also UNAUTHORIZED

author·ship /ˈɔːθəʃɪp; *AmE* ˈɔːθərʃɪp/ *noun* [U] **1** the identity of the person who wrote sth, especially a book: *The authorship of the poem is unknown.* **2** the activity or fact of writing a book

aut·ism /ˈɔːtɪzəm/ *noun* [U] a mental condition in which a person is unable to communicate or form relationships with others ▶ **aut·is·tic** /ɔːˈtɪstɪk/ *adj.: autistic behaviour/children*

auto /ˈɔːtəʊ; *AmE* ˈɔːtoʊ/ *noun* (*pl.* **autos**) (*AmE*) a car: *the auto industry*

auto- /ˈɔːtəʊ; *AmE* ˈɔːtoʊ/ (also **aut-**) *combining form* (in nouns, adjectives and adverbs) **1** of or by yourself: *autobiography* **2** by itself without a person to operate it: *automatic*

auto·biog·raphy /ˌɔːtəbaɪˈɒɡrəfi; *AmE* -ˈɑːɡ-/ *noun* [C, U] (*pl.* **-ies**) the story of a person's life, written by that person; this type of writing—compare BIOGRAPHY ▶ **auto·bio·graph·ic·al** /ˌɔːtəˌbaɪəˈɡræfɪkl/ *adj.: an autobiographical novel* (= one that contains many of the writer's own experiences)

au·toc·racy /ɔːˈtɒkrəsi; *AmE* ɔːˈtɑːk-/ *noun* (*pl.* **-ies**) **1** [U] a system of government of a country in which one person has complete power **2** [C] a country that is ruled by one person who has complete power

auto·crat /ˈɔːtəkræt/ *noun* **1** a ruler who has complete power **SYN** DESPOT **2** a person who expects to be obeyed by other people and does not care about their opinions or feelings ▶ **auto·crat·ic** /ˌɔːtəˈkrætɪk/ *adj.: an autocratic manager* **auto·crat·ic·al·ly** /-kli/ *adv.*

Auto·cue™ /ˈɔːtəʊkjuː; *AmE* ˈɔːtoʊ-/ (*BrE*) (also **tele·prompt·er** *AmE, BrE*) *noun* a device used by people who are speaking in public, especially on television, which displays the words that they have to say

auto·graph /ˈɔːtəɡrɑːf; *AmE* -ɡræf/ *noun, verb*

■ *noun* a famous person's signature, especially when sb asks them to write it: *Could I have your autograph?*

■ *verb* [VN] (of a famous person) to sign your name on sth for sb to keep: *The whole team has autographed a football, which will be used as a prize.*

auto·immune /ˌɔːtəʊɪˈmjuːn; *AmE* ˌɔːtoʊ-/ *adj.* [only before noun] (*medical*) an **autoimmune** disease or medical condition is one which is caused by substances that usually prevent illness

auto·maker /ˈɔːtəʊmeɪkə(r); *AmE* ˈɔːtoʊ-/ *noun* (*AmE*) a company that makes cars

auto·mate /ˈɔːtəmeɪt/ *verb* [VN] [usually passive] to use machines and computers instead of people to do a job or task: *The entire manufacturing process has been automated.* ◇ *The factory is now fully automated.*

ˌautomated ˈteller machine *noun* (*abbr.* **ATM**) = CASH MACHINE

auto·mat·ic /ˌɔːtəˈmætɪk/ *adj., noun*

■ *adj.* **1** (of a machine, device, etc.) having controls that work without needing a person to operate them: *automatic doors* ◇ *a fully automatic driverless train* ◇ *automatic transmission* (= in a car, etc.) ◇ *an automatic rifle* (= one that continues to fire as long as the trigger is pressed) **2** done or happening without thinking **SYN** INSTINCTIVE: *Breathing is an automatic function of the body.* ◇ *My reaction was automatic.* **3** always happening as a result of a particular action or situation: *A fine for this offence is automatic.* ▶ **auto·mat·ic·al·ly** /-kli/ *adv.: The heating switches off automatically.* ◇ *I turned left automatically without thinking.* ◇ *You will automatically get free dental treatment if you are under 18.*

■ *noun* **1** a gun that can fire bullets continuously as long as the TRIGGER is pressed **2** (*BrE*) a car with a system of GEARS that operates without direct action from the driver—compare STICK SHIFT

ˌautomatic ˈpilot (also **auto·pilot**) *noun* a device in an aircraft or a ship that keeps it on a fixed course without the need for a person to control it **IDM** **be on ˌautomatic ˈpilot** to do sth without thinking because you have done the same thing many times before: *I got up and dressed on automatic pilot.*

ˌautomatic transˈmission *noun* [U, C] a system in a motor vehicle that changes the GEARS for the driver automatically

auto·ma·tion /ˌɔːtəˈmeɪʃn/ *noun* [U] the use of machines to do work that was previously done by people: *Automation meant the loss of many factory jobs.*

æ	ɑː	e	ɜː	ə	ɪ	iː	i	ɒ	ɔː	ʌ	ʊ	u	uː
cat	father	ten	bird	about	sit	see	many	got	saw	cup	put	actual	too
								(BrE)					

au·toma·ton /ɔːˈtɒmətən; AmE ɔːˈtɑːm-/ noun (pl. **au·toma·tons** or **au·tom·ata** /-tə/) **1** a person who behaves like a machine, without thinking or feeling anything SYN ROBOT **2** a machine that moves without human control; a small ROBOT

auto·mo·bile /ˈɔːtəməbiːl/ noun (AmE) a car: *the automobile industry* ◊ *an automobile accident*

auto·mo·tive /ˌɔːtəˈməʊtɪv; AmE -ˈmoʊ-/ adj. (written) connected with motor vehicles: *the automotive industry*

au·tono·mous /ɔːˈtɒnəməs; AmE ɔːˈtɑːn-/ adj. **1** (of a country, a region or an organization) able to govern itself or control its own affairs: *an autonomous republic/state/province* **2** (of a person) able to do things and make decisions without help from anyone else ▶ **au·tono·mous·ly** adv.

au·ton·omy /ɔːˈtɒnəmi; AmE ɔːˈtɑːn-/ noun [U] **1** the freedom for a country, a region or an organization to govern itself independently: *a campaign in Wales for greater autonomy* **2** the ability to act and make decisions without being controlled by anyone else: *giving individuals greater autonomy in their own lives*

auto·pilot /ˈɔːtəʊpaɪlət; AmE ˈɔːtoʊ-/ noun = AUTOMATIC PILOT

aut·opsy /ˈɔːtɒpsi; AmE ˈɔːtɑːpsi/ noun (pl. **-ies**) an official examination of a dead body by a doctor in order to discover the cause of death SYN POST-MORTEM: *an autopsy report* ◊ *to perform an autopsy*

ˌauto·suˈggestion noun [U] (psychology) a process that makes you believe sth or act in a particular way according to ideas that come from within yourself without you realizing it

au·tumn /ˈɔːtəm/ (especially BrE) (AmE usually **fall**) noun [U, C] the season of the year between summer and winter, when leaves change colour and the weather becomes colder: *in the autumn of 1995* ◊ *in early/late autumn* ◊ *the autumn term* (= for example at a school or college in Britain) ◊ *autumn colours/leaves* ◊ *It's been a very mild autumn this year.*

au·tum·nal /ɔːˈtʌmnəl/ adj. [usually before noun] like or connected with autumn: *autumnal colours*

aux·il·iary /ɔːɡˈzɪliəri/ adj., noun
■ adj. **1** (of workers) giving help or support to the main group of workers: *auxiliary nurses/workers/services* **2** (technical) (of a piece of equipment) used if there is a problem with the main piece of equipment: *an auxiliary pump*
■ noun (pl. **-ies**) **1** (also **auˌxiliary ˈverb**) (grammar) a verb such as *be, do* and *have* used with main verbs to show tense, etc. and to form questions and negatives **2** a worker who gives help or support to the main group of workers: *nursing auxiliaries*

AV /ˌeɪ ˈviː/ abbr. AUDIO-VISUAL

avail /əˈveɪl/ noun, verb
■ noun IDM **to little/no aˈvail** (formal) with little or no success: *The doctors tried everything to keep him alive but to no avail.* **of little/no aˈvail** (formal) of little or no use: *Your ability to argue is of little avail if the facts are wrong.*
■ verb [VN] (formal or old-fashioned) to be helpful or useful to sb PHRV **aˈvail yourself of sth** (formal) to make use of sth, especially an opportunity or offer: *Guests are encouraged to avail themselves of the full range of hotel facilities.*

avail·able /əˈveɪləbl/ adj. **1** (of things) that you can get, buy or find: *available resources/facilities* ◊ *readily/freely/publicly/generally available* ◊ *Tickets are available free of charge from the school.* ◊ *When will the information be made available?* ◊ *Further information is available on request.* ◊ *This was the only room available.* ◊ *We'll send you a copy as soon as it becomes available.* ◊ *Every available doctor was called to the scene.* **2** (of a person) free to see or talk to people: *Will she be available this afternoon?* ◊ *The director was not available for comment.* ▶ **avail·abil·ity** /əˌveɪləˈbɪləti/ noun [U]: *the availability of cheap flights* ◊ (BrE) *This offer is subject to availability.*

ava·lanche /ˈævəlɑːnʃ; AmE ˈævəlæntʃ/ noun a mass of snow, ice and rock that falls down the side of a mountain: *alpine villages destroyed in an avalanche* ◊ (figurative)

We received an avalanche of letters in reply to our advertisement.

avant-garde /ˌævɒ̃ ˈɡɑːd; AmE ˌævɑ̃ ˈɡɑːrd/ noun (**the avant-garde**) (from French) **1** [sing.] new and very modern ideas in art, music or literature that are sometimes surprising or shocking **2** [sing.+ sing./pl. v.] a group of artists, etc. who introduce new and very modern ideas ▶ **avant-garde** adj.

avar·ice /ˈævərɪs/ noun [U] (formal) extreme desire for wealth SYN GREED ▶ **avar·icious** /ˌævəˈrɪʃəs/ adj.

Ave. (AmE also **Av.**) abbr. (used in written addresses) Avenue: *Fifth Ave.*

avenge /əˈvendʒ/ verb [VN] ~ **sth** | ~ **yourself on sb** (formal) to punish or hurt sb in return for sth bad or wrong that they have done to you, your family or friends: *He promised to avenge his father's murder.* ◊ *She was determined to avenge herself on the man who had betrayed her.* ▶ **aven·ger** noun

> **GRAMMAR POINT**
> **avenge / revenge**
>
> People **avenge** something or **avenge** themselves **on** somebody: *She vowed to avenge her brother's death.* ◊ *He later avenged himself on his wife's killers.*
>
> People **revenge** themselves **on** somebody or **are revenged on** them: *He was later revenged on his wife's killers.* You cannot **revenge** something: ~~She vowed to revenge her brother's death.~~

av·enue /ˈævənjuː; AmE -nuː/ noun **1** (abbr. **Ave.**) a street in a town or city: *a hotel on Fifth Avenue* **2** (BrE) a wide straight road with trees on both sides, especially one leading to a big house **3** a choice or way of making progress towards sth: *Several avenues are open to us.* ◊ *We will explore every avenue until we find an answer.*

aver /əˈvɜː(r)/ verb (**-rr-**) (rare, formal) to state firmly and strongly that sth is true: [V that] *She averred that she had never seen the man before.* [also VN, V speech]

aver·age /ˈævərɪdʒ/ adj., noun, verb
■ adj. **1** [only before noun] calculated by adding several amounts together, finding a total, and dividing the total by the number of amounts: *an average rate/cost/price* ◊ *Average earnings are around £20000 per annum.* ◊ *at an average speed of 100 miles per hour* **2** typical or normal: *40 hours is a fairly average working week for most people.* ◊ *children of above/below average intelligence* ◊ *£20 for dinner is about average.* **3** ordinary; not special: *I was just an average sort of student.* ▶ **aver·age·ly** adv. (rare): *He was attractive and averagely intelligent.*
■ noun [C, U] **1** the result of adding several amounts together, finding a total, and dividing the total by the number of amounts: *The average of 4, 5 and 9 is 6.* ◊ *Parents spend an average a year on toys for their children.* ◊ *If I get an A on this essay, that will bring my average* (= average mark/grade) *up to a B+.*—see also GRADE POINT AVERAGE **2** a level which is usual: *Temperatures are above/below average for the time of year.* ◊ *400 people a year die of this disease on average.* ◊ *Class sizes in the school are below the national average.* IDM see LAW
■ verb **1** [VN] [no passive] to be equal to a particular amount as an average: *Economic growth is expected to average 2% next year.* ◊ *Drivers in London can expect to average about 12 miles per hour* (= to have that as their average speed). **2** to calculate the average of sth: [VN] *Earnings are averaged over the whole period.* [also V] PHRV ˌaverage ˈout (at sth) to result in an average amount over a period of time or when several things are considered: *The cost should average out at about £6 per person.* ◊ *Sometimes I pay, sometimes he pays—it seems to average out* (= result in us paying the same amount). ˌaverage sth↔ˈout (at sth) to calculate the average of sth

averse /əˈvɜːs; AmE əˈvɜːrs/ adj. [not before noun] **1** not ~ **to sth/to doing sth** liking sth or wanting to do sth; not opposed to doing sth: *I mentioned it to Kate and she wasn't averse to the idea.* **2** ~ **to sth/to doing sth** (formal) not

liking sth or wanting to do sth; opposed to doing sth: *He was averse to any change.*

aver·sion /əˈvɜːʃn; *AmE* əˈvɜːrʒn/ *noun* [C, U] ~ (**to sb/ sth**) a strong feeling of not liking sb/sth: *a strong aversion* ◊ *He had an aversion to getting up early.* ◊ *feelings of aversion and disgust*

avert /əˈvɜːt; *AmE* əˈvɜːrt/ *verb* [VN] (*written*) **1** to prevent sth bad or dangerous from happening: *A disaster was narrowly averted.* ◊ *He did his best to avert suspicion.* **2** ~ **your eyes, gaze, face (from sth)** to turn your eyes, etc. away from sth that you do not want to see: *She averted her eyes from the terrible scene in front of her.*

avi·ary /ˈeɪviəri; *AmE* ˈeɪvieri/ *noun* (*pl.* **-ies**) a large cage or building for keeping birds in, for example in a zoo

avi·ation /ˌeɪviˈeɪʃn/ *noun* [U] the designing, building and flying of aircraft: *civil/military aviation* ◊ *the aviation business/industry*

avi·ator /ˈeɪvieɪtə(r)/ *noun* (*old-fashioned*) a person who flies an aircraft

avid /ˈævɪd/ *adj.* **1** [usually before noun] very enthusiastic about sth (often a hobby): *an avid reader/collector* ◊ *She has taken an avid interest in the project* (= she is extremely interested in it). **2** ~ **for sth** wanting to get sth very much: *He was avid for more information.* ▶ **avid·ity** /əˈvɪdəti/ *noun* [U] (*rare*) **avid·ly** *adv.*: *She reads avidly.*

avi·on·ics /ˌeɪviˈɒnɪks; *AmE* -ˈɑːn-/ *noun* **1** [U] the science of ELECTRONICS when used in designing and making aircraft **2** [pl.] the electronic devices in an aircraft or a spacecraft ▶ **avi·on·ic** *adj.*

avo·cado /ˌævəˈkɑːdəʊ; *AmE* -ˈkɑːdoʊ/ *noun* (*pl.* **-os**) (*BrE* also ˌ**avocado** ˈ**pear**) a tropical fruit with hard, dark green skin, soft, light green flesh and a large stone/ pit inside. Avocados are not sweet and are sometimes eaten at the beginning of a meal.—picture on page A2

avoid /əˈvɔɪd/ *verb* **1** to prevent sth bad from happening: [VN] *The accident could have been avoided.* ◊ *They narrowly avoided defeat in the semi-final.* ◊ *The name was changed to avoid confusion with another firm.* ◊ [VN-ing] *They built a wall to avoid soil being washed away.* **2** to keep away from sb/sth; to try not to do sth: [VN] *He's been avoiding me all week.* ◊ *She kept avoiding my eyes* (= avoided looking at me). ◊ *I left early to avoid the rush hour.* ◊ [V-ing] *I've been avoiding getting down to work all day.* ◊ *You should avoid mentioning his divorce.* **3** [VN] to prevent yourself from hitting sth: *I had to swerve to avoid a cat.* **IDM** **avoid sb/sth like the** ˈ**plague** (*informal*) to try very hard not to meet sb, do sth, etc.—more at TRAP *n.*

avoid·able /əˈvɔɪdəbl/ *adj.* that can be prevented: *Many deaths from heart disease are actually avoidable.* **OPP** UNAVOIDABLE

avoid·ance /əˈvɔɪdəns/ *noun* [U] ~ (**of sth**) not doing sth; preventing sth from existing or happening: *A person's health improves with the avoidance of stress.*—see also TAX AVOIDANCE

avoir·du·pois /ˌævədəˈpɔɪz; ˌævwɑːdjuːˈpwɑː; *AmE* ˌævərdəˈpɔɪz/ *noun* [U] the system of weights based on the pound

avow /əˈvaʊ/ *verb* (*formal*) to say firmly and often publicly what your opinion is, what you think is true, etc: [Vthat] *An aide avowed that the President had known nothing of the deals.* [also VN, Vspeech] ▶ **avow·al** /əˈvaʊəl/ *noun* (*formal*): *an avowal of love*

avowed /əˈvaʊd/ *adj.* [only before noun] (*formal*) that has been admitted or stated in public: *an avowed anticommunist* ◊ *an avowed aim/intention/objective/purpose* ▶ **avow·ed·ly** /əˈvaʊɪdli/ *adv.*

avun·cu·lar /əˈvʌŋkjələ(r)/ *adj.* (*formal*) behaving in a kind and friendly way towards young people, similar to the way an uncle treats his NIECES or NEPHEWS

await /əˈweɪt/ *verb* [VN] (*formal*) **1** to wait for sb/sth: *He is in custody awaiting trial.* ◊ *Her latest novel is eagerly awaited.* **2** to be going to happen to sb: *A warm welcome awaits all our guests.*

awake /əˈweɪk/ *adj., verb*
■ *adj.* [not before noun] not asleep (especially immediately before or after sleeping): *to be half/fully awake* ◊ *to be*

wide awake (= fully awake) ◊ *I was still awake when he came to bed.* ◊ *The noise was keeping everyone awake.* ◊ *I was finding it hard to stay awake.* ◊ *He lies awake at night worrying about his job.* ◊ *She was awake* (= not unconscious) *during the operation on her leg.*
■ *verb* (**awoke** /əˈwəʊk; *AmE* əˈwoʊk/, **awoken** /əˈwəʊkən; *AmE* əˈwoʊkən/) (*formal*) **1** ~ (**sb**) (**from/to sth**) to wake up; to make sb wake up: [V] *I awoke from a deep sleep.* ◊ [Vtoinf] *He awoke to find her gone.* ◊ [VN] *Her voice awoke the sleeping child.* **2** if an emotion **awakes** or sth **awakes** an emotion, you start to feel that emotion: [VN] *His speech is bound to awake old fears and hostilities.* [also V] **PHRV** aˈwake to sth to become aware of sth and its possible effects or results: *It took her some time to awake to the dangers of her situation.*—compare WAKE

WHICH WORD? (?)
awake / awaken / wake up / waken

Wake (up) is the most common of these verbs. It can mean somebody has finished sleeping: *What time do you usually wake up?* or that somebody or something has disturbed your sleep: *The children woke me up.* ◊ *I was woken (up) by the telephone.*

The verb **awake** is usually only used in writing and in the past tense **awoke**: *She awoke to a day of brilliant sunshine.* **Waken** and **awaken** are much more formal. **Awaken** is used especially in literature: *The Prince awakened Sleeping Beauty with a kiss.*

Awake is also an adjective: *I was awake half the night worrying.* ◊ *Is the baby awake yet?* **Waking** is not used in this way.

Look also at ASLEEP and the verb SLEEP.

---

awaken /əˈweɪkən/ *verb* (*formal*) **1** [often passive] ~ (**sb**) (**from/to sth**) to wake up; to make sb wake up: [V] *She awakened to the sound of birds singing.* ◊ [Vtoinf] *We awakened to find the others gone.* ◊ [VN] *He was awakened at dawn by the sound of crying.* **2** if an emotion **awakens** or sth **awakens** an emotion, you start to feel that emotion: [VN] *The dream awakened terrible memories.* [also V] ▷ note at AWAKE **PHRV** aˈwaken (**sb**) to sth to become aware or to make sb aware of sth and its possible effects or results: *I gradually awakened to the realization that our marriage was over.*—compare WAKEN

awaken·ing /əˈweɪkənɪŋ/ *noun* **1** [C, usually sing.] an occasion when you realize sth or become aware of sth: *If they had expected a warm welcome, they were in for a **rude awakening*** (= they would soon realize that it would not be warm). **2** [C, U] the act of beginning to understand or feel sth; the act of sth starting or waking: *sexual awakening* ◊ *the awakening of interest in the environment*

award /əˈwɔːd; *AmE* əˈwɔːrd/ *noun, verb*
■ *noun* **1** [C] ~ (**for sth**) (often in names of particular awards) a prize such as money, etc. for sth that sb has done: *to win/receive/get an award for sth* ◊ *He was nominated for the best actor award.* ◊ *an award presentation/ceremony* ◊ *the Housing Design Award*—see also ACADEMY AWARD **2** [C] an increase in the amount of money sb earns: *an annual pay award* **3** [C, U] the amount of money that a court decides should be given to sb who has won a case; the decision to give this money: *an award of £600000 libel damages* **4** [U] the official decision to give sth (such as a DIPLOMA) to sb: *Satisfactory completion of the course will lead to the award of the Diploma of Social Work.* **5** [C] (*BrE*) money that students get to help pay for living costs while they study or do research
■ *verb* ~ (**sb**) **sth** | ~ **sth (to sb)** to make an official decision to give sth to sb as a payment, prize, etc: [VN] *He was awarded damages of £50000.* ◊ [VN, VNN] *The judges awarded equal points to both finalists.* ◊ *The judges awarded both finalists equal points.*

aˈward-winning *adj.* having won a prize: *the award-winning TV drama*

aware /əˈweə(r); *AmE* əˈwer/ *adj.* **1** [not before noun] ~ (**of sth**) | ~ (**that** ...) knowing or realizing sth: *I don't think people are really aware of just how much it costs.* ◊ *He was*

---

b	d	f	g	h	k	l	m	n	p	r
bad	did	fall	get	hat	cat	leg	**man**	now	pen	red

A

well aware of the problem. ◊ *Were you aware that something was wrong?* ◊ *Everybody should* **be made aware of** *the risks involved.* ◊ *As you're aware, this is not a new problem.* ◊ *As far as I'm aware, nobody has done anything about it.* ◊ *acutely/painfully* (= very) *aware* **2** [not before noun] ~ **(of sb/sth)** | ~ **(that ...)** noticing that sth is present, or that sth is happening: *She slipped away without him being aware of it.* ◊ *They suddenly became aware of people looking at them.* ◊ *I was aware that she was trembling.* **3** (used with an adverb) interested in and knowing about sth, and thinking it is important: *Young people are more environmentally aware than their parents.* **OPP** UNAWARE

aware·ness /ə'weənəs; *AmE* ə'wer-/ *noun* [U, sing.] ~ **(of sth)** | ~ **(that ...)** knowing sth; knowing that sth exists and is important; being interested in sth: *an awareness of the importance of eating a healthy diet* ◊ *There was an almost complete* **lack of awareness** *of the issues involved.* ◊ *It is important that students* **develop an awareness** *of how the Internet can be used.* ~ *to raise/heighten/increase public awareness of sth* ◊ *a greater/a growing/an increasing awareness of sth* ◊ *environmental awareness* (= knowing that looking after the environment is important) ◊ *Energy Awareness Week*

awash /ə'wɒʃ; *AmE* ə'wɑːʃ; ə'wɔːʃ/ *adj.* [not before noun] **1** ~ **(with water)** covered or flooded with water **2** ~ **with sth** having sth in large quantities: *The city is awash with drugs.*

away /ə'weɪ/ *adv.* **HELP** For the special uses of **away** in phrasal verbs, look at the entries for the verbs. For example **get away with sth** is in the phrasal verb section at **get**. **1** ~ **(from sb/sth)** to or at a distance from sb/sth in space or time: *The beach is a mile away.* ◊ *The station is a few minutes' walk away.* ◊ *Christmas is still months away.* **2** to a different place or in a different direction: *Go away!* ◊ *Put your toys away.* ◊ *The bright light made her look away.* **3** ~ **(from sb/sth)** not present **SYN** ABSENT: *She was away from work for a week.* ◊ *There were ten children away yesterday.* ◊ *Sorry, he's away.* **4** used after verbs to say that sth is done continuously or with a lot of energy: *She was still writing away furiously when the bell went.* ◊ *They were soon chatting away like old friends.* **5** until disappearing completely: *The water boiled away.* ◊ *The music faded away.* ◊ *They danced the night away* (= all night). **6** (*sport*) at the opponent's ground or STADIUM: *Chelsea are playing away this Saturday.* ◊ *an away match/game*—compare HOME **IDM away with ...** (*literary*) used to say that you would like to be rid of sb/sth: *Away with all these rules and regulations!*—more at COBWEBS, FAR *adv.*, DANCE *v.*, RIGHT *adv.*, STRAIGHT *adv.*

awe /ɔː/ *noun, verb*
■ *noun* [U] feelings of respect and slight fear; feelings of being very impressed by sth/sb: *awe and respect* ◊ *awe and wonder* ◊ *He speaks of her with awe.* ◊ *'It's magnificent,' she whispered in awe.* **IDM be/stand in 'awe of sb/sth** to admire sb/sth and be slightly frightened of them/it: *While Diana was in awe of her grandfather, she adored her grandmother.*
■ *verb* [VN] [usually passive] (*formal*) to fill sb with awe: *She seemed awed by the presence of so many famous people.* ▶ **awed** *adj.*: *We watched in awed silence.*

'awe-inspiring *adj.* impressive; making you feel respect and admiration: *The building was awe-inspiring in size and design.*

awe·some /'ɔːsəm/ *adj.* **1** very impressive or very difficult and perhaps rather frightening: *an awesome sight* ◊ *awesome beauty/power* ◊ *They had an awesome task ahead.* **2** (*AmE, informal*) very good, enjoyable, etc: *Hey, dudes! I just bought this awesome new CD!* ◊ *Wow! That's totally awesome!* ▶ **awe·some·ly** *adv.* (*rare*): *awesomely beautiful*

awe·struck /'ɔːstrʌk/ *adj.* (*written*) feeling very impressed by sth: *People were awestruck by the pictures the satellite sent back to earth.*

awful /'ɔːfl/ *adj., adv.*
■ *adj.* **1** (especially *spoken*) very bad or unpleasant: *That's an awful colour.* ◊ *'They didn't even offer to pay.' 'Oh that's*

awful.' ◊ *It's awful, isn't it?* ◊ *The weather last summer was awful.* ◊ *I feel awful about forgetting her birthday.* ◊ *to look/feel awful* (= to look/feel ill) ◊ *There's an awful smell in here.* ◊ *The awful thing is, it was my fault.* **2** (especially *spoken*) used to emphasize sth, especially that there is a large amount or too much of sth: *It's going to cost an awful lot of money.* ◊ *There's not an awful lot of room.* ◊ *I feel an awful lot better than I did yesterday.* ◊ (*BrE*) *I had an awful job persuading him to come* (= it was very difficult). **3** very shocking **SYN** TERRIBLE: *the awful horrors of war* ▶ **aw·ful·ness** *noun* [U]: *the sheer awfulness of the situation*
■ *adv.* (*informal, especially AmE*) very; extremely: *Clint is awful smart.*

aw·ful·ly /'ɔːfli/ *adv.* very; extremely: *I'm awfully sorry about that problem the other day.*

awhile /ə'waɪl/ *adv.* (*formal* or *literary*) for a short time

awk·ward /'ɔːkwəd; *AmE* -wərd/ *adj.* **1** making you feel embarrassed: *There was an awkward silence.* **2** difficult to deal with: *Don't ask awkward questions.* ◊ *You've put me in an awkward position.* ◊ *an awkward customer* (= a person who is difficult to deal with) ◊ *Please don't be awkward about letting him come.* **3** not convenient: *Have I come at an awkward time?* **4** difficult or dangerous because of its shape or design: *This box is very awkward for one person to carry.* **5** not graceful; not comfortable: *He tried to dance, but he was too clumsy and awkward.* ◊ *I must have slept in an awkward position—I'm aching all over.* ▶ **awk·ward·ly** *adv.*: *'I'm sorry,' he said awkwardly.* ◊ *She fell awkwardly and broke her ankle.* ◊ *an awkwardly shaped room* **awk·ward·ness** *noun* [U]: *She laughed to cover up her feeling of awkwardness.*

awn·ing /'ɔːnɪŋ/ *noun* a sheet of fabric that stretches out from above a door or window to keep off the sun or rain

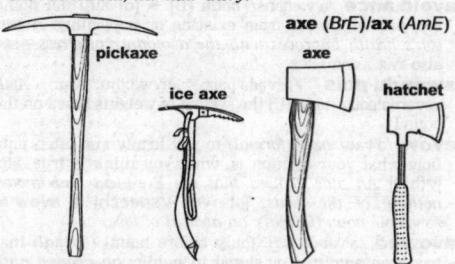

awning

awoke *pt of* AWAKE

awoken *pp of* AWAKE

AWOL /'eɪwɒl; *AmE* 'eɪwɔːl/ *abbr.* absent without leave (used especially in the armed forces when sb has left their group without permission): *He's gone AWOL from his base.* ◊ (*humorous*) *The guitarist went AWOL in the middle of the recording.*

awry /ə'raɪ/ *adv.* **1** if sth **goes awry**, it does not happen in the way that was planned: *All my plans for the party had gone awry.* **2** not in the right position **SYN** UNTIDY: *She rushed out, her hair awry.*

axe (*BrE*)/ax (*AmE*)

pickaxe   axe

ice axe   hatchet

axe /æks/ *noun, verb*
■ *noun* (especially *BrE*) (*AmE* usually **ax**) **1** a tool with a wooden handle and a heavy metal blade, used for chopping wood, cutting down trees, etc.—see also BATTLEAXE, ICE AXE, PICKAXE **2** (**the axe**) [sing.] (*informal*) if sb gets **the axe**, they lose their job; if an institution or a project gets **the axe**, it is closed or stopped, usually because of a lack of money: *Up to 300 workers are* **facing the axe** *at a struggling Merseyside firm.* ◊ *Patients are delighted their local hospital has been saved from the axe.* **IDM have an 'axe to grind** to have private reasons for being involved in sth or for arguing for a particular cause: *She had no*

axe to grind and was only acting out of concern for their safety.

■ *verb* (*BrE*) (*AmE* **ax**) [VN] [often passive] **1** to get rid of a service, system, etc. or to reduce the money spent on it by a large amount: *Other less profitable services are to be axed later this year.* **2** to remove sb from their job: *Jones has been axed from the team.* **3** to kill sb with an axe

axe·man /ˈæksmən/ *noun* (*pl.* **-men** /-men/) (*especially BrE*) (*AmE* usually **axman**) (*informal*) a man who attacks other people with an axe

axiom /ˈæksiəm/ *noun* (*formal*) a rule or principle that most people believe to be true

axio·mat·ic /ˌæksiəˈmætɪk/ *adj.* [not usually before noun] (*formal*) true in such an obvious way that you do not need to prove it: *It is axiomatic that life is not always easy.* ▶ **axio·mat·ic·al·ly** *adv.*

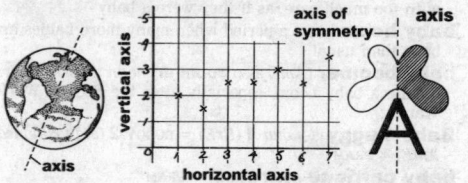

axis *pl.* /ˈæksɪs/ *noun* (*pl.* **axes** /ˈæksiːz/) **1** an imaginary line through the centre of an object, around which the object turns: *Mars takes longer to revolve on its axis than the earth.* **2** (*technical*) a fixed line against which the positions of points are measured, especially points on a GRAPH: *the vertical/horizontal axis* **3** (*geometry*) a line that divides a shape into two equal parts: *an axis of symmetry* ◊ *The axis of a circle is its diameter* **4** [usually sing.] (*formal*) an agreement or ALLIANCE between two or more countries: *the Franco-German axis*

axle /ˈæksl/ *noun* a rod that connects a pair of wheels on a vehicle: *the front/rear axle*

aya·tol·lah /ˌaɪəˈtɒlə; *AmE* -ˈtoʊlə/ *noun* a religious leader of Shiite Muslims in Iran

aye (also **ay**) /aɪ/ *exclamation* (*old use* or *dialect*) yes: *'Did you see what happened?' 'Oh aye, I was there.'*

ayes /aɪz/ *noun* [pl.] the total number of people voting 'yes' in a formal debate, for example in a parliament: *The ayes have it* (= more people have voted for sth than against it). OPP NOES

aza·lea /əˈzeɪliə/ *noun* a plant or bush with large flowers that may be pink, purple, white or yellow, grown in a pot or in a garden

azi·muth /ˈæzɪməθ/ *noun* (*astronomy*) an angle related to a distance around the earth's HORIZON, used to find out the position of a star, planet, etc.

azure /ˈæʒə(r); *BrE* also ˈæzjʊə(r)/ *adj.* (*written*) bright blue in colour like the sky: *The sun shone out of a clear azure sky.* ▶ **azure** *noun* [U]

æ	ɑː	e	ɜː	ə	ɪ	iː	i	ɒ	ɔː	ʌ	ʊ	u	uː
cat	father	ten	bird	about	sit	see	many	got	saw	cup	put	actual	too
								(BrE)					

Bb

B /biː/ *noun, symbol*

■ *noun* (also **b**) (*pl.* **B's, b's** /biːz/) **1** [C, U] the second letter of the English alphabet: *'Butter' begins with (a) B/'B'.* **2** (**B**) [C, U] (*music*) the 7th note in the scale of C MAJOR **3** (**B**) [C, U] the second highest mark/grade that a student can get for a piece of work: *She got (a) B in/for History.* **4** (**B**) [U] used to represent the second of two or more possibilities: *Shall we go for plan A or plan B?* **5** (**B**) [U] used to represent a person, for example in an imagined situation or to hide their identity: *Let's pretend A meets B in the park.*—see also B-ROAD **IDM** see A

■ *symbol* used in Britain before a number to refer to a particular secondary road: *the B1224 to York*

b. *abbr.* born: *Emily Clifton, b. 1800*

BA (*BrE*) (*AmE* **B.A.**) /ˌbiː ˈeɪ/ *noun* the abbreviation for 'Bachelor of Arts' (a first university degree in an ARTS subject): *to be/have/do a BA* ◊ (*BrE*) *Darren Green BA*

baa /bɑː/ *noun* the sound made by sheep or LAMBS ▶ **baa** *verb* [V] (**baa·ing, baaed** or **baa'd**)

bab·ble /ˈbæbl/ *noun, verb*

■ *noun* [sing.] **1** the sound of many people speaking at the same time: *a babble of voices* **2** talking that is confused or silly and is difficult to understand: *I can't listen to his constant babble.* **3** the sounds a baby makes before beginning to say actual words—see also PSYCHOBABBLE

■ *verb* **1** ~ (**away/on**) to talk in a quick and excited way that is difficult to understand: [V] *They were all babbling away in a foreign language.* ◊ *I realized I was babbling like an idiot.* [also V **speech**, VN] **2** [V] to make the sound of water flowing over rocks, like a stream: *a babbling brook*

babby /ˈbæbi/ *noun* (*pl.* **-ies**) (*BrE, dialect*) a baby

babe /beɪb/ *noun* **1** (*old use*) a baby **2** (*slang*) a word used to address a young woman, or your wife, husband or lover, usually expressing affection but sometimes considered offensive if used by a man to a woman he does not know: *What're you doing tonight, babe?* **3** (*informal*) an attractive young woman **IDM** **a ˌbabe in ˈarms** (*old-fashioned*) a very small baby that cannot yet walk—more at MOUTH *n.*

babel /ˈbeɪbl/ *noun* [sing.] (*written*) the sound of many voices talking at one time, especially when more than one language is being spoken **ORIGIN** From the Bible story in which God punished the people who were trying to build a tower to reach heaven (the **tower of Babel**) by making them unable to understand each others' languages.

ba·boon /bəˈbuːn; *AmE* bæˈb-/ *noun* a large African or Asian monkey with a long face like a dog's

baby /ˈbeɪbi/ *noun, adj., verb*

■ *noun* (*pl.* **-ies**) **1** a very young child or animal: *The baby's crying!* ◊ *a newborn baby* ◊ *My sister's expecting a baby.* ◊ *She had a baby last year.* ◊ *a baby boy/girl* ◊ *baby food/ clothes* ◊ *a baby monkey/blackbird* **2** (*informal*) the youngest member of a family or group: *He's the baby of the team.* **3** (*disapproving*) a person who behaves like a young child and is easily upset: *Stop crying and don't be such a baby.* **4** (*slang, especially AmE*) a word used to address sb, especially your wife, husband or lover, in a way that expresses affection but that can be offensive if used by a man to a woman he does not know **IDM** **be your/sb's baby** (*informal*) to be a plan or project that sb is responsible for and cares about because they have created it **leave sb holding the ˈbaby** (*informal*) to suddenly make sb responsible for sth important that is really your responsibility: *He changed to another job and we were left holding the baby.* **throw the baby out with**

the **ˈbathwater** (*informal*) to lose sth that you want at the same time as you are trying to get rid of sth that you do not want—more at SLEEP *v.*

■ *adj.* [only before noun] **baby** vegetables are a very small version of particular vegetables, or are picked when they are very small: *baby carrots*

■ *verb* (**ba·bies, baby·ing, ba·bied, ba·bied**) [VN] to treat sb with too much care, as if they were a baby

ˈbaby boom *noun* a period when many more babies are born than usual

ˈbaby boomer (*AmE also* **boom·er**) *noun* a person born during a baby boom, especially after the Second World War

ˈBaby Buggy™ *noun* **1** (*BrE*) = BUGGY **2** (*old-fashioned, AmE*) = PRAM

ˈbaby carriage *noun* (*AmE*) = PRAM

ˈbaby fat *noun* [U] (*AmE*) = PUPPY FAT

Baby·gro™ /ˈbeɪbigrəʊ; *AmE* -groʊ/ *noun* (*pl.* **-os**) (*BrE*) a piece of clothing for babies, usually covering the whole body except the head and hands, made of a fabric that stretches easily

ba·by·hood /ˈbeɪbihʊd/ *noun* [U] the period of your life when you are a baby

baby·ish /ˈbeɪbiʃ/ *adj.* (usually *disapproving*) typical of or suitable for a baby

baby·sit /ˈbeɪbisɪt/ *verb* (**baby·sit·ting, baby·sat, baby·sat**) (also **sit**) to take care of babies or children for a short time while their parents are out: [V] *She regularly babysits for us.* ◊ [VN] *He's babysitting the neighbour's children.* ▶ **baby·sit·ting** *noun* [U]

baby·sit·ter /ˈbeɪbisɪtə(r)/ (also **sit·ter** especially in *AmE*) *noun* a person who takes care of babies or children while their parents are away from home and is usually paid to do this: *I can't find a babysitter for tonight.*—see also CHILDMINDER

ˈbaby talk *noun* [U] the words or sounds a baby says when it is learning to talk; the special language adults sometimes use when talking to babies

ˈbaby tooth *noun* = MILK TOOTH

ˈbaby walker (*BrE*) (*AmE* **walk·er**) *noun* a frame with wheels and a HARNESS for a baby who can walk around a room, supported by the frame—picture at CHAIR

bac·ca·laur·eate /ˌbækəˈlɔːriət/ *noun* **1** the last secondary school exam in France and other countries, and in some international schools: *to sit/take/pass/fail your baccalaureate* **2** (in the US) a religious service or talk for students who have completed high school or college

baccy /ˈbæki/ *noun* [U] (*BrE, informal*) tobacco

bach·elor /ˈbætʃələ(r)/ *noun* **1** a man who has never been married: *an eligible bachelor* (= one that many people want to marry, especially because he is rich) ◊ *He was a confirmed bachelor* (= a person who intended never to marry; often used in newspapers to refer to a homosexual man) ◊ (*BrE*) *a bachelor flat* (= one suitable for a person living alone)—compare SPINSTER **2** (usually **Bachelor**) a person who has a Bachelor's degree (= a first university degree): *a Bachelor of Arts/Engineering/Science*—see also BA, BEd, BSc

bach·elor·hood /ˈbætʃələhʊd; *AmE* -lərh-/ *noun* [U] the time in a man's life before he is married

ˈbachelor party *noun* (*AmE*) = STAG NIGHT

ba·cil·lus /bəˈsɪləs/ *noun* (*pl.* **ba·cilli** /bəˈsɪlaɪ/) a type of bacteria. There are several types of bacillus, some of which cause disease.

back /bæk/ *noun, adj., adv., verb*

aɪ	aʊ	eɪ	əʊ	oʊ	ɔɪ	ɪə	eə	ʊə	j	w
my	now	say	go	go	boy	near	hair	pure	yes	wet
			(BrE)	(AmE)						

■ *noun*

PART OF BODY | **1** the part of the human body that is on the opposite side to the chest, between the neck and the tops of the legs; the part of an animal's body that CORRESPONDS to this: *Do you sleep on your back or your front?* ◇ *He stood with his back to the door.* ◇ *They had their hands tied behind their backs.* ◇ *back pain* ◇ *a back massage* ◇ *A small boy rode on the elephant's back.*—see also BAREBACK, HORSEBACK—picture at BODY **2** the row of bones in the middle of the back SYN BACKBONE, SPINE: *She broke her back in a riding accident.* ◇ *He put his back out* (= DISLOCATED *sth in his back) lifting the crates.*

PART FURTHEST FROM FRONT | **3** [usually sing.] **~ (of sth)** the part or area of sth that is furthest from the front: *We could only get seats at the back* (= of the room). ◇ *I found some old photos at the back of the drawer.* ◇ *He was shot in the back of the knee.* ◇ (*BrE*) *There's room for three people in the back.* ◇ (*AmE*) *There's room for three people in back.* ◇ *The house has three bedrooms at the front and two at the back.* ◇ (*BrE*) *If you'd like to come round the back* (= to the area behind the house), *I'll show you the garden.*—see also HARDBACK, PAPERBACK, SHORT BACK AND SIDES ⇨ note on page 76

OF PIECE OF PAPER | **4** [usually sing.] **~ (of sth)** the part of a piece of paper, etc. that is on the opposite side to the one that has information or the most important information on it: *Write your name on the back of the cheque.*

OF BOOK | **5** [usually sing.] **~ (of sth)** the last few pages of a book, etc: *The television guide is at the back of the paper.*

OF CHAIR | **6** the part of a chair, etc. against which you lean your back

-BACKED | **7** (in adjectives) used to describe furniture which has the type of back mentioned: *a high-backed sofa*

IN SPORT | **8** (in football, hockey, etc.) a player whose main role is to defend their team's goal—compare FORWARD *n.*—see also FULLBACK, HALFBACK

IDM **at/in the back of your mind** if a thought, etc. is at **the back of your mind**, you are aware of it but it is not what you are mainly thinking about **the ˌback of beˈyond** (*informal*) a place that is a long way from other houses, towns, etc. ˌback to ˈback **1** if two people stand **back to back**, they stand with their backs facing or touching each other—see also BACK-TO-BACK **2** if two or more things happen **back to back**, they happen one after the other ˌback to ˈfront (*BrE*) (*AmE* back-wards) if you put on a piece of clothing **back to front**, you make a mistake and put the back where the front should be: *I think you've got that sweater on back to front.*—compare INSIDE OUT at INSIDE *n.*—picture at INSIDE *n.* **be glad, etc. to see the back of sb/sth** (*informal, especially BrE*) to be happy that you will not have to deal with or see sb/sth again because you do not like them: *Was I pleased to see the back of her!* **behind sb's ˈback** without sb's knowledge or permission: *Have you been talking about me behind my back?* ◇ *They went ahead and sold it behind my back.*—compare TO SB'S FACE at FACE *n.* **be on sb's ˈback** (*informal*) to keep asking or telling sb to do sth that they do not want to do, in a way that they find annoying **break the ˈback of sth** to finish the largest or most important part of a task **get/put sb's ˈback up** (*informal*) to annoy sb: *That sort of attitude really gets my back up!* **get off sb's ˈback** (*informal*) to stop annoying sb, for example by criticizing them, or asking them to do sth: *Just get off my back, will you!* **have your ˌback to the ˈwall** (*informal*) to be in a difficult situation in which you are forced to do sth but are unable to make the choices that you would like **off the ˌback of a ˈlorry** (*BrE, informal, humorous*) goods that **fell off the back of a lorry** were probably stolen. People say or accept that they came 'off the back of a lorry' to avoid saying or asking where they really came from. **on the back of sth** as a result of an achievement or a success: *The profits growth came on the back of a 26 per cent rise in sales.* **(flat) on your back** (*informal*) in bed because you are ill/sick: *She's been flat on her back for over a week now.* ◇ (*figurative*) *The UK market was flat on its back* (= business was very bad). **put your ˈback into sth** to use a lot of effort and energy on a particular task **turn your back** to turn

so that you are facing in the opposite direction **turn your back on sb/sth 1** to move so that you are standing or sitting with your back facing sb/sth: *When on stage, try not to turn your back on the audience.* **2** to reject sb/sth that you have previously been connected with: *She turned her back on them when they needed her.*—more at EYE *n.*, KNOW *v.*, PAT *n.*, PAT *v.*, PUSH *v.*, ROD, SCRATCH *v.*, SHIRT, STAB *n.*, STAB *v.*, STRAW, WATER *n.*

■ *adj.* [only before noun]

AWAY FROM FRONT | **1** situated behind or at the back of sth: *the back door* ◇ *We were sitting in the back row.* ◇ *back teeth* ◇ *a back room* (= one at the back of a building) ◇ *the back page of a newspaper*—compare FRONT *adj.*

FROM PAST | **2** of or from a past time: *a back number of the magazine*

OWED | **3** owed for a time in the past: *back pay/taxes/rent*

IDM **by/through the back door** in an unfair or indirect way: *He used his friends to help him get into the civil service by the back door.*—see also BACK-DOOR **on the back 'burner** (*informal*) (of an idea, a plan, etc.) left for the present time, to be done or considered later—compare ON THE FRONT BURNER at FRONT *adj.*

■ *adv.* HELP For the special uses of **back** in phrasal verbs, look at the entries for the verbs. For example **pay sb back** is in the phrasal verb section at **pay.**

AWAY FROM FRONT | **1** away from the front or centre; behind you: *I stepped back to let them pass.* ◇ *Sit back and relax.* ◇ *You've combed your hair back.* ◇ *He turned and looked back.* ◇ *She fell back towards the end of the race.* OPP FORWARD

AT A DISTANCE | **2** at a distance away from sth: *The barriers failed to keep the crowds back.* ◇ *Stand back and give me some room.*

UNDER CONTROL | **3** under control; prevented from being expressed or coming out: *He could no longer hold back his tears.*

AS BEFORE | **4** to or into the place, condition, situation or activity where sb/sth was before: *Put the book back on the shelf.* ◇ *Please give me my ball back.* ◇ *He'll be back* (= will return) *on Monday.* ◇ *It takes me an hour to walk there and back.* ◇ *Could you go back to the beginning of the story?* ◇ *She woke up briefly and then went back to sleep.* ◇ *We were right back where we started, only this time without any money.*

IN PAST | **5** in or into the past; ago: *The village has a history going back to the Middle Ages.* ◇ *She left back in November.* ◇ *That was a few years back.*

AT A PREVIOUS PLACE | **6** at a place previously left or mentioned: *We should have turned left five kilometres back.* ◇ *Back at home, her parents were worried.* ◇ *I can't wait to get back home.*

IN RETURN | **7** in return or reply: *If he kicks me, I'll kick him back.* ◇ *Could you call back later, please?*

IDM ˌback and ˈforth from one place to another and back again repeatedly: *ferries sailing back and forth between the island and the mainland* **back of sth** (*AmE, informal*) behind sth: *the houses back of the church*—more at EARTH *n.*

■ *verb*

MOVE BACKWARDS | **1** [+*adv. / prep.*] to move or make sth move backwards: [V] *He backed against the wall, terrified.* ◇ [VN] *If you can't drive in forwards, try backing it in.*—compare REVERSE

SUPPORT | **2** [VN] to give help or support to sb/sth: *Her parents backed her in her choice of career.* ◇ *Doctors have backed plans to raise the tax on cigarettes.* ◇ *The programme of economic reform is backed* (= supported financially) *by foreign aid.* ◇ *a United Nations-backed peace plan*

BET MONEY | **3** [VN] to bet money on a horse in a race, a team in a competition, etc: *I backed the winner and won fifty pounds.*

MUSIC | **4** [VN] to play or sing music that supports the main singer or instrument—see also BACKING

COVER BACK | **5** [VN] **~ sth (with sth)** [usually passive] to cover the back of sth in order to support or protect it

b	d	f	g	h	k	l	m	n	p	r
bad	did	fall	get	hat	cat	leg	man	now	pen	red

B

BE BEHIND | **6** [VN] [usually passive] (*BrE*) to be situated behind sth: *The house is backed by fields.*

IDM ˌback the wrong ˈhorse (*BrE*) to support sb/sth that is not successful
PHRV ˌback aˈway (from sb/sth) to move away backwards from sth that is frightening or unpleasant; to avoid doing sth that is unpleasant ˌback ˈdown (on/from sth) (*AmE* also ˌback ˈoff) to take back a demand, an opinion, etc. that other people are strongly opposed to; to admit defeat: *She refused to back down on a point of principle.* ˌback ˈoff (from sth) to move away from sb, especially in order to stop threatening or annoying them or to avoid a difficult situation: *The government has backed off from a fundamental reform of the system.* ◇ *Back off! There's no need to yell at me.* ˌback ˈonto sth (*BrE*) (of a building) to have sth directly behind it: *Our house backs onto the river.* ˌback ˈout (of sth) to decide that you are no longer going to take part in sth that has been agreed: *He lost confidence and backed out of the deal at the last minute.* ˌback ˈup | ˌback sth↔ˈup to move backwards, especially in a vehicle: *You can back up another two feet or so.* ◇ *I backed the car up to the door.* ˌback sb/sth↔ˈup to support sb/sth; to say that what sb says, etc. is true: *I'll back you up if they don't believe you.* ˌback sth↔ˈup **1** (*computing*) to prepare a second copy of a file, program, etc. that can be used if the main one fails or needs extra support—related noun BACK-UP **2** to provide support for sb/sth: *The rebels backed up their demands with threats.* ◇ *two doctors backed up by a team of nurses*—related noun BACK-UP

WHICH WORD?
at the back / at the rear / behind (?)

At the back and **at the rear** have a similar meaning, but **at the rear** is used more in formal or official language: *What's that at the back of the fridge?* ◇ *Smoking is only allowed at the rear of the aircraft.* It is more usual to talk about the **back door** of a house but the **rear exit** of an aircraft or public building. If something is **behind** something else it is near to the back of it but not part of it. Compare: *Our room was at the back of the hotel* and *There's a lovely wood just behind our hotel.*

---

back·ache /ˈbækeɪk/ *noun* [U, C] a continuous pain in the back: (*BrE*) *to have backache/a backache* ◇ (*AmE*) *to have a backache*

ˌback ˈbench *noun* [usually pl.] (in Britain) any of the seats in the House of Commons for Members of Parliament who do not have senior positions in the government or the other parties: *He resigned as Home Secretary and returned to the back benches.* ◇ *back-bench MPs*—compare THE FRONT BENCH ▶ ˌback-ˈbencher *noun*—compare FRONTBENCHER

back·bit·ing /ˈbækbaɪtɪŋ/ *noun* [U] unpleasant and unkind talk about sb who is not present

back·board /ˈbækbɔːd; *AmE* -bɔːrd/ *noun* the board behind the basket in the game of basketball—picture on page 1250

back·bone /ˈbækbəʊn; *AmE* -boʊn/ *noun* **1** [C] the row of small bones that are connected together down the middle of the back [SYN] SPINE—picture at BODY **2** [sing.] the most important part of a system, an organization, etc. that gives it support and strength: *Agriculture forms the backbone of the rural economy.* **3** [U] the strength of character that you need to do sth difficult: *He doesn't have the backbone to face the truth.*

ˈback-breaking *adj.* (of physical work) very hard and tiring

back·chat /ˈbæktʃæt/ (*BrE*) (*AmE* ˈback talk) *noun* [U] (*informal*) a way of answering that shows no respect for sb in authority

back·cloth /ˈbækklɒθ; *AmE* -klɔːθ/ *noun* (*BrE*) = BACKDROP

back·comb /ˈbækkəʊm; *AmE* -koʊm/ (*BrE*) (*AmE* **tease**) *verb* [VN] to comb your hair in the opposite direction to the way it grows so that it looks thicker

ˌback ˈcopy *noun* (*BrE*) = BACK ISSUE

ˈback country *noun* [U] (*AmE*) an area away from roads and towns, especially in the mountains

back·date /ˌbæk'deɪt/ *verb* [VN] **1** to write a date on a cheque or other document that is earlier than the actual date—compare POST-DATE **2** (*BrE*) to make sth, especially a payment, take effect from an earlier date: *Postal workers are getting a 5.2% pay rise, backdated to February.*

ˌback-ˈdoor *adj.* [only before noun] using indirect or secret means in order to achieve sth

back·drop /ˈbækdrɒp; *AmE* -drɑːp/ (*BrE* also **back-cloth**) *noun* **1** a painted piece of fabric that is hung behind the stage in a theatre as part of the scenery **2** (*written*) the scenery surrounding an event: *The mountains provided a dramatic backdrop for our picnic.* **3** (*written*) the general conditions in which an event takes place, which sometimes help to explain that event: *It was against this backdrop of racial tension that the civil war began.*

back·er /ˈbækə(r)/ *noun* a person or company that gives support to sb/sth, especially financial support

back·fire /ˌbæk'faɪə(r)/ *verb* [V] **1** ~ (on sb) to have the opposite effect to the one intended, with bad or dangerous results: *Unfortunately the plan backfired.* **2** (of an engine or a vehicle) to make a sudden noise like an explosion—compare MISFIRE

back·gam·mon /ˈbækgæmən; ˌbæk'gæmən/ *noun* [U] a game for two people played on a board marked with long thin triangles. Players throw DICE and move pieces around the board.—picture on page A8

back·ground /ˈbækgraʊnd/ *noun*
FAMILY/EDUCATION, etc. | **1** [C] the details of a person's family, education, experience etc: *a person's family/social/cultural/educational/class background* ◇ *The job would suit someone with a business background.*

PAST | **2** [C usually sing, U] the circumstances or past events which help explain why sth is how it is; information about these: *the historical background to the war* ◇ *background information/knowledge* ◇ *The elections are taking place against a background of violence.* ◇ *Can you give me more background on the company's financial position?*

OF PICTURE/PHOTO | **3** [C, usually sing.] the part of a picture, photograph or view behind the main objects, people, etc: *a photograph with trees in the background*—compare FOREGROUND

LESS IMPORTANT POSITION | **4** [sing.] a position in which people are not paying attention to sb/sth or not as much attention as they are paying to sb/sth else: *He prefers to remain in the background and let his assistant talk to the press.* ◇ *A piano tinkled gently in the background.* ◇ *background music* ◇ *There was a lot of background noise (= that you could hear, but were not listening to).*—compare FOREGROUND

COLOUR UNDER STH | **5** [C, usually sing.] a colour or design on which sth is painted, drawn, etc: *The name of the company is written in red on a white background.*

IDM see MERGE

back·hand /ˈbækhænd/ *noun* [usually sing.] (in tennis, etc.) a stroke played with the back of the hand turned in the direction towards which the ball is hit: *He has a good backhand (= he can make good backhand strokes).* ◇ *a backhand volley/drive*—compare FOREHAND

back·han·ded /ˌbæk'hændɪd/ *adj.* having a meaning that is not directly or clearly expressed, or that is not intended **IDM** ˌbackhanded ˈcompliment (*AmE* also ˌleft-handed ˈcompliment) a remark that seems to express admiration but could also be understood as an insult

back·hand·er /ˈbækhændə(r)/ *noun* (*BrE*, *informal*) a secret and illegal payment made to sb in exchange for a favour [SYN] BRIBE

back·hoe /ˈbækhəʊ; *AmE* -hoʊ/ *noun* a large vehicle with machinery for digging, used in building roads, etc.—picture at TRUCK

back·ing /ˈbækɪŋ/ *noun* **1** [U] help; support: *financial*

---

backing ◊ *The police gave the proposals their full backing.*
2 [U] material attached to the back of sth in order to protect it or make it stronger **3** [U, C, usually sing.] (in pop songs) music that ACCOMPANIES (= is played with) the main singer or tune: *a backing group/singer/track*

,back 'issue (*BrE* also **,back 'copy**, **,back 'number**) *noun* a copy of a newspaper or magazine from a date in the past

back·lash /'bæklæʃ/ *noun* [sing.] ~ **(against sth)| ~ (from sb)** a strong negative reaction by a large number of people, for example to sth that has recently changed in society: *The government is facing an angry backlash from voters over the new tax.*

back·less /'bækləs/ *adj.* (of a dress) not covering most of the back

back·log /'bæklɒg; *AmE* -lɔːg; -lɑːg/ *noun* a quantity of work that should have been done already, but has not yet been done

,back 'number *noun* (*BrE*) = BACK ISSUE

back·pack /'bækpæk/ *noun, verb*
■ *noun* (*especially AmE*) = RUCKSACK
■ *verb* [V] (usually **go backpacking**) to travel on holiday/vacation carrying your equipment and clothes in a backpack: *They went backpacking in Spain last year.* ▶ **back·pack·er** *noun*

,back-'pedal *verb* (-ll-, *AmE* -l-) [V] **1** ~ **(on sth)** to change an earlier statement or opinion; to not do sth that you promised to do: *The protests have forced the government to back-pedal on plans to introduce a new tax.* **2** to PEDAL backwards on a bicycle; to walk or run backwards

,back 'room *noun* a room at the back of a building, away from the entrance, often where secret activities take place

'back-room boys *noun* [pl.] (*BrE*) people who do important work for a person or an organization but who are not well known themselves

back·scratch·ing /'bækskrætʃɪŋ/ *noun* [U] (*informal*, often *disapproving*) the fact of giving sb help in return for help that they have given you, often in connection with sth that might be illegal

,back 'seat *noun* a seat at the back of a vehicle **IDM** a **,back-seat 'driver 1** a passenger in a vehicle who keeps giving advice to the driver about how he or she should drive **2** a person who wants to be in control of sth that is not really their responsibility **take a back seat** to allow sb else to play a more active and important role in a particular situation than you do

back·side /'bæksaɪd/ *noun* (*informal*) the part of the body that you sit on **SYN** BEHIND, BOTTOM: *Get up off your backside and do some work!* **IDM** see PAIN *n.*

back·slap·ping /'bækslæpɪŋ/ *noun* [U] loud and enthusiastic behaviour when people are praising each other for sth good they have done ▶ **back·slap·ping** *adj.* [only before noun]: *backslapping tributes*

back·slash /'bækslæʃ/ *noun* a mark (\ ), used in computer COMMANDS

back·slid·ing /'bækslaɪdɪŋ/ *noun* [U] the situation when sb fails to do sth that they agreed to do and returns to their former bad behaviour

back·stage /,bæk'steɪdʒ/ *adv.* **1** in the part of the theatre where the actors and artists get ready and wait to perform: *After the show, we were allowed to go backstage to meet the cast.* **2** away from the attention of the public; in secret: *I'd like to know what really goes on backstage in government.* ▶ **back·stage** *adj.*

back·street /'bækstriːt/ *noun, adj.*
■ *noun* a small quiet street, usually in a poor part of a town or city, away from main roads: *He was born in the backstreets of Leeds.*
■ *adj.* [only before noun] acting or happening secretly, often dishonestly or illegally: *backstreet dealers*

back·stroke /'bækstrəʊk; *AmE* -strouk/ *noun* [U, sing.] a style of swimming in which you lie on your back: *Can you do (the) backstroke?* ◊ *He won the 100 metres backstroke* (= the race).—picture at SWIMMING

back·swing /'bækswɪŋ/ *noun* (*sport*) the backwards movement of your arm or arms before you hit the ball

'back talk *noun* [U] (*AmE*) = BACKCHAT

,back-to-'back *noun* (*BrE*) a house in a row of houses which share walls with the houses on each side and behind: *back-to-backs and tenements built for the poor in the 19th century*

back·track /'bæktræk/ *verb* [V] **1** to go back along the same route that you have just come along: *The path suddenly disappeared and we had to backtrack.* **2** to change an earlier statement, opinion or promise because of pressure from sb/sth

'back-up *noun* [U, C] **1** extra help or support that you can get if necessary: *The police had back-up from the army.* ◊ *We can use him as a back-up if one of the other players drops out.* ◊ *a back-up power supply* **2** (*computing*) a copy of a file, etc. that can be used if the original is lost or damaged: *Always make a back-up of your work.* ◊ *a back-up copy*

'backup light *noun* (*AmE*) = REVERSING LIGHT

back·ward /'bækwəd; *AmE* -wərd/ *adj.* **1** [only before noun] directed or moving towards the back: *She strode past him without a backward glance.* **2** moving in a direction that means that no progress is being made **SYN** RETROGRADE: *She felt that going back to live in her home town would be a backward step.* **3** having made less progress than normal; developing slowly: *a backward part of the country, with no paved roads and no electricity* ◊ *a backward child* ◊ (*BrE, spoken*) *She's not backward in coming forward* (= she's not shy).—compare FORWARD

back·ward·ness /'bækwədnəs; *AmE* -wərd-/ *noun* [U] the state of having made less progress than normal: *the backwardness of rural areas*

back·wards /'bækwədz; *AmE* -wərdz/ (also **back·ward** especially in *AmE*) *adv.* **1** towards a place or position that is behind: *I lost my balance and fell backwards.* ◊ *He took a step backwards.* **OPP** FORWARD **2** in the opposite direction to the usual one: *'Ambulance' is written backwards so you can read it in the mirror.* ◊ *In the movie they take a journey backwards through time.* **3** towards a worse state: *I felt that going to live with my parents would be a step backwards.* **OPP** FORWARD **4** (*AmE*) = BACK TO FRONT at BACK *n.* **IDM** **,backward(s) and 'forward(s)** from one place or position to another and back again many times: *She rocked backwards and forwards on her chair.* **bend/lean over 'backwards (to do sth)** to make a great effort, especially in order to be helpful or fair: *I've bent over backwards to help him.*—more at KNOW *v.*

back·wash /'bækwɒʃ; *AmE* -wɑːʃ; -wɔːʃ/ *noun* [sing.] **1** (*written*) the unpleasant result of an event **2** waves caused by a boat or ship moving through water; the movement of water back into the sea after a wave has hit the beach

back·water /'bækwɔːtə(r)/ *noun* **1** a part of a river away from the main part, where the water only moves slowly **2** (often *disapproving*) a place that is away from the places where most things happen, and is therefore not affected by events, progress, new ideas, etc: *a sleepy/quiet/rural backwater*

back·woods /'bækwʊdz/ *noun* [pl.] a place that is away from any big towns and from the influence of modern life

back·yard /,bæk'jɑːd; *AmE* -'jɑːrd/ *noun* **1** (*BrE*) an area with a hard surface behind a house, often surrounded by a wall **2** (*AmE*) the whole area behind and belonging to a house, including an area of grass and the garden: *a backyard barbecue*—see also YARD **IDM** **in your (own) backyard** in or near the place where you live or work: *The residents didn't want a new factory in their backyard.* ◊ *The party leader is facing opposition in his own backyard* (= from his own members).

bacon /'beɪkən/ *noun* [U] meat from the back or sides of a pig that has been CURED (= preserved using salt or smoke), usually served in thin slices: *a rasher of bacon* ◊ *bacon and eggs* ◊ *smoked/unsmoked bacon*—compare GAMMON, HAM (1), PORK **IDM** see HOME *adv.*, SAVE *v.*

bac·teria /bæk'tɪəriə; *AmE* -'tɪr-/ *noun* [pl.] (*sing.* **bacterium** /-iəm/) the simplest and smallest forms of plant life. Bacteria exist in large numbers in air, water and soil, and also in living and dead creatures and plants, and

æ	ɑː	e	ɜː	ə	ɪ	iː		i	ɒ	ɔː	ʌ	ʊ	u	uː
cat	father	ten	bird	about	sit	see		many	got	saw	cup	put	actual	too
									(BrE)					

B

are often a cause of disease ▶ **bac·ter·ial** /-riəl/ *adj.*: *bacterial infections/growth*

bac·teri·ology /bækˌtɪəriˈɒlədʒi; *AmE* -ˌtɪriˈɑːl-/ *noun* [U] the scientific study of bacteria ▶ **bac·terio·logic·al** *adj.* **bac·teri·olo·gist** /-dʒɪst/ *noun*

bad /bæd/ *adj., noun, adv.*

■ *adj.* (**worse** /wɜːs; *AmE* wɜːrs/ **worst** /wɜːst; *AmE* wɜːrst/) UNPLEASANT | **1** unpleasant; full of problems: *bad news/weather/dreams/habits* ◊ *I'm having a really bad day.* ◊ *It was the worst experience of her life.* ◊ *Smoking gives you bad breath.* ◊ *Things are **bad enough** without our own guns shelling us.*

POOR QUALITY | **2** of poor quality; below an acceptable standard: *bad conditions/driving* ◊ *a bad copy/diet* ◊ *I thought it was a very bad article.* ◊ *This isn't as bad as I thought.* ◊ *That's not a bad idea.*

NOT GOOD AT STH | **3** ~ **at sth/at doing sth** (of a person) not able to do sth well or in a satisfactory way SYN POOR: *a bad teacher* ◊ *You're a bad liar!* ◊ *He's a bad loser* (= he complains when he loses a game). ◊ *She is so bad at keeping secrets.*

SERIOUS | **4** serious; severe: *You're heading for a bad attack of sunburn.* ◊ *The engagement was a bad mistake.* ◊ *My headache is getting worse.*

NOT APPROPRIATE | **5** [only before noun] not appropriate in a particular situation: *I know that this is a bad time to ask for help.* ◊ *He now realized that it had been a bad decision on his part.*

WICKED | **6** morally unacceptable: *The hero gets to shoot all the bad guys.* ◊ *He said I must have done something bad to deserve it.*

CHILDREN | **7** [usually before noun] (especially of children) not behaving well SYN NAUGHTY: *Have you been a bad boy?*

HARMFUL | **8** [not before noun] ~ **for sb/sth** harmful; causing or likely to cause damage: *Those shoes are bad for her feet.* ◊ *Weather like this is bad for business.*

PAINFUL | **9** [usually before noun] (of parts of the body) not healthy; painful: *I've got a bad back.*

FOOD | **10** not safe to eat because it has decayed: *Put the meat in the fridge so it doesn't go bad.*

TEMPER/MOOD | **11** ~ **temper/mood** the state of feeling annoyed or angry: *It put me in a bad mood for the rest of the day.*

GUILTY/SORRY | **12** feel ~ to feel guilty or sorry about sth: *She felt bad about leaving him.* ◊ *Why should I want to make you feel bad?*

ILL/SICK | **13** feel/look ~ to feel or look ill/sick: *I'm afraid I'm feeling pretty bad.*

EXCELLENT | **14** (**bad·der, bad·dest**) (*slang, especially AmE*) good; excellent

IDM Most idioms containing **bad** are at the entries for the nouns and verbs in the idioms, for example **be bad news** (**for sb/sth**) is at **news**. **can't be bad** (*spoken*) used to try to persuade sb to agree that sth is good: *You'll save fifty dollars, which can't be bad, can it?* **not 'bad** (*spoken*) quite good; better than you expected: *'How are you?' 'Not too bad.'* ◊ *That wasn't bad for a first attempt.* **too bad** (*spoken*) **1** (*ironic*) used to say 'bad luck' or 'it's a shame' when you do not really mean it: *If sometimes they're the wrong decisions, too bad.* **2** a shame; a pity: *Too bad every day can't be as good as this.* **3** (*old-fashioned, spoken*) annoying: *Really, it was too bad of you to be so late.*

■ *noun* (**the bad**) [U] bad people, things, or events: *You will always have the bad as well as the good in the world.* IDM **go to the 'bad** (*old-fashioned*) to begin behaving in an immoral way: *I hate to see you going to the bad.* **take the ,bad with the 'good** to accept the bad aspects of sth as well as the good ones **to the 'bad** (*BrE*) used to say that sb now has a particular amount less money than they did before: *After the sale they were £300 to the bad.*

■ *adv.* (*AmE, informal*) badly: *She wanted it real bad.* ◊ *Are you hurt bad?*

,bad 'debt *noun* [C, U] a debt that is unlikely to be paid

baddy /ˈbædi/ *noun* (*pl.* **-ies**) (*BrE, informal*) a bad or evil character in a film/movie, book, play, etc: *As usual, the cops get the baddies in the end.*

bade *pt* of BID

visitor's badge — VISITOR J.E.BAYS ART.DEP

badge

badge (*BrE*)/ **button** (*AmE*)

Dr. N. Norton — name badge

police badge

badge /bædʒ/ *noun* **1** (*BrE*) a small piece of metal, fabric or plastic, with a design or words on it, that a person wears to show that they belong to an organization, support sth, have achieved sth, have a particular rank, etc: *the school badge* ◊ *She wore a badge saying 'Vote for Coates'.* ◊ *All employees have to wear name badges.*—compare BUTTON **2** a small piece of metal that you carry or wear to prove who you are, used, for example, by police officers: *He pulled out a badge and said he was a cop.* **3** (*written*) something that shows that a particular quality is present: *His gun was a badge of power for him.* **4** (*especially AmE*) = PATCH

badger /ˈbædʒə(r)/ *noun, verb*
■ *noun* an animal with grey fur and wide black and white lines on its head. Badgers are NOCTURNAL (= active mostly at night) and live in holes in the ground.
■ *verb* ~ **sb** (**into doing sth**)| ~ **sb** (**about sth**) to put pressure on sb by repeatedly asking them questions or asking them to do sth: [VN] *I finally badgered him into coming with us.* ◊ *Reporters constantly badger her about her private life.* ◊ [VN to inf] *His daughter was always badgering him to let her join the club.*

bad·in·age /ˈbædɪnɑːʒ; *AmE* ˌbædənˈɑːʒ/ *noun* [U] (from French, *literary*) friendly joking between people SYN BANTER

,bad 'language *noun* [U] words that many people find offensive SYN SWEAR WORDS

badly /ˈbædli/ *adv.* (**worse, worst**) **1** not skilfully or not carefully: *to play/sing badly* ◊ *badly designed/organized* **2** not successfully: *Things have been going badly.* ◊ *I did badly* (= was not successful) *in my exams.* **3** not in a satisfactory way: *to behave/sleep badly* ◊ *badly paid/treated* ◊ *The kids took the dog's death very badly* (= they were very unhappy). **4** in a way that makes people get a bad opinion about sth: *The economic crisis reflects badly on the government's policies.* ◊ *She's only trying to help, so don't think badly of her.* **5** used to emphasize how much you want, need, etc. sb/sth: *The building is badly in need* *of repair.* ◊ *They wanted to win so badly.* ◊ *I miss her badly.* **6** used to emphasize how serious a situation or an event is: *badly damaged / injured / hurt* ◊ *The country has been badly affected by recession.* ◊ *Everything's gone badly wrong!* **IDM** **badly 'off 1** not having much money; poor **2** not in a good situation: *I've got quite a big room so I'm not too badly off.* **be badly 'off for sth** (*BrE*) to not have enough of sth

bad·min·ton /ˈbædmɪntən/ *noun* [U] a game like tennis played by two or four people, usually indoors. Players hit a small light kind of ball, originally with feathers around it (= a SHUTTLECOCK) across a high net using a RACKET.

'bad-mouth *verb* [VN] (*informal*) to say unpleasant things about sb: *No one wants to employ somebody who bad-mouths their former employer.*

bad·ness /ˈbædnəs/ *noun* [U] the fact of being morally bad: *There was not a hint of badness in him.*

,bad-'tempered *adj.* often angry; in an angry mood: *She gets very bad-tempered when she's tired.*

baf·fle /ˈbæfl/ *verb, noun*
■ *verb* to confuse sb completely; to be too difficult or strange for sb to understand or explain: [VN] *His behaviour baffles me.* ◊ [VN, VNwh-] *I'm baffled as to why she hasn't called.* ◊ *I'm baffled why she hasn't called.* ▶ **baffle-ment** *noun* [U]: *His reaction was one of bafflement.* **baffling** *adj.*: *Some of the country's customs are baffling to outsiders.*
■ *noun* (*technical*) a screen used to control or prevent the flow of sound, light or liquid

bag /bæg/ *noun, verb*
■ *noun*
CONTAINER | **1** [C] (often in compounds) a container made of paper or plastic, that opens at the top, used especially in shops/stores: *a plastic / polythene / paper bag* ◊ *a laundry / mail bag* ◊ *a black plastic rubbish / garbage bag* **2** [C] a strong container made from cloth, plastic, leather, etc., usually with one or two handles, used to carry things in when shopping or travelling: *a shopping bag* ◊ *a make-up bag* ◊ *He's upstairs unpacking his bags.* ◊ *She opened her bag* (= her handbag) *and took out her comb.*—see also AIR BAG, BEANBAG, BUMBAG, PUNCHBAG, SANDBAG, TEA BAG
AMOUNT | **3** [C] ~ (**of sth**) the amount contained in a bag: *She ate a bag of chips.*—see also MIXED BAG, RAGBAG—picture at PACKAGING **4** (**bags** (**of sth**)) [U, pl.] (*BrE, informal*) a large amount or a large number of sth: *Get in! There's bags of room.*
UNDER EYES | **5** (**bags**) [pl.] dark circles or loose folds of skin under the eyes, because of old age or lack of sleep
UNPLEASANT WOMAN | **6** [C] (*informal, especially BrE*) an insulting word for an unpleasant or bad-tempered older woman: *Stupid old bag!*—see also RATBAG, SCUMBAG, WINDBAG
BIRDS / ANIMALS | **7** [C, usually sing.] all the birds, animals,

etc. shot or caught on one occasion: *We got a good bag today.*
HELP There are many other compounds ending in **bag.** You will find them at their place in the alphabet.
IDM **,bag and 'baggage** with all your possessions, especially secretly or suddenly: *He threw her out onto the street, bag and baggage.* **a ,bag of 'bones** (*informal*) a very thin person or animal **be in the 'bag** (*informal*) if sth is **in the bag,** it is almost certain to be won or achieved **(not) sb's 'bag** (*informal*) (not) sth that you are interested in or good at: *Poetry isn't really my bag.*—more at CAT, NERVE *n.*, PACK *v.*, TRICK *n.*
■ *verb* (**-gg-**) [VN]
PUT INTO BAGS | **1** ~ **sth** (**up**) to put sth into bags: *The fruit is washed, sorted and bagged at the farm.*
CATCH ANIMAL | **2** (*informal*) to catch or kill an animal: *We bagged ten fish in two hours.*
IN SPORT | **3** (*informal*) to score a goal, point, etc: *Dublin bagged two goals in last night's win.*
CLAIM STH | **4** (*BrE, informal*) to claim sth as yours before sb else claims it; to take sth before sb else can get it: *Sally had managed to bag the two best seats.* ◊ *Quick, bag that table over there!*
IDM **bags (I)** ... (*BrE*) (*AmE* **'dibs on ...**) used to claim sth as yours before sb else can claim it: *Bags I sit in the front seat!*

bagel /ˈbeɪgl/ *noun* a hard bread roll that is shaped like a ring—picture on page A1

bag·gage /ˈbægɪdʒ/ *noun* [U] **1** (*especially AmE*) = LUGGAGE: *excess baggage* (= weighing more than the limit allowed on a plane) ◊ *baggage handlers* (= people employed to load and unload baggage at airports) **2** the beliefs and attitudes that sb has as a result of their past experiences **IDM** see BAG *n.*

> **WHICH WORD?**
> **baggage / luggage** ②
>
> **Luggage** is the usual word in *BrE*, but **baggage** is also used, especially in the context of the bags and cases that passengers take on a flight. In *AmE* **baggage** is usually used.
> Both these words are uncountable nouns: *Do you have a lot of luggage?* ◊ *Two pieces of luggage have gone missing.* ◊ *Never leave baggage unattended.*

'baggage car *noun* (*AmE*) = LUGGAGE VAN

'baggage reclaim (*BrE*) (*AmE* **'baggage claim**) *noun* [U] the place at an airport where you get your suitcases, etc. again after you have flown

baggy /ˈbægi/ *adj.* (of clothes) fitting loosely; not tight: *a baggy T-shirt*

'bag lady *noun* a woman who has no home and who walks around carrying her possessions with her

'bag lunch *noun* (*AmE*) = PACKED LUNCH

bags

handle · handle — **suitcase** strap · pocket

backpack (*BrE also* **rucksack**)

bumbag (*BrE*)/ **fanny pack** (*AmE*)

holdall (*BrE*)/ **duffel bag** (*AmE*)

strap · buckle · **handbag** (*AmE also* **purse**)

lock · **attaché case** (*also* **briefcase**)

briefcase

carrier bag (*also* **carrier**) (*BrE*)

grocery bag (*AmE*)

pannier

b	d	f	g	h	k	l	m	n	p	r
bad	did	fall	get	hat	cat	leg	man	now	pen	red

bag·pipes /ˈbæɡpaɪps/ (also **pipes**) *noun* [pl.] (*AmE* also **bag·pipe** [sing.]) a musical instrument played especially in Scotland. The player blows air into a bag held under the arm and then slowly forces the air out through pipes to produce a noise. ▶ **bag·pipe** *adj.*: *bagpipe music*

ba·guette /bæˈɡet/ *noun* **1** (also **French ˈloaf**, **French ˈstick**) a LOAF of white bread in the shape of a long thick stick that is crisp on the outside and soft inside—picture on page A1 **2** a small baguette or part of one that is filled with food and eaten as a sandwich: *a cheese baguette*—picture on page A1

bah /bɑː/ *exclamation* used to show a sound that people make to express disapproval

bail /beɪl/ *noun*, *verb*

■ *noun* **1** [U] money that sb agrees to pay if a person accused of a crime does not appear at their trial. When bail has been arranged, the accused person is allowed to go free until the trial: *Can anyone put up bail for you?* ◇ *She was released on £2 000 bail.* ◇ *Bail was set at $1 million.* ◇ *He committed another offence while he was out on bail* (= after bail had been agreed). ◇ *The judge granted/refused bail.* ◇ *She jumped/skipped bail* (= did not appear at her trial). **2** [C, usually pl.] (in cricket) either of the two small pieces of wood on top of each set of three wooden posts (called STUMPS).

■ *verb* (*BrE* also **bale**) to release sb on bail: [VN to inf] *He was bailed to appear in court on 15 March.* [also VN] **PHRV** **ˌbail ˈout (of sth)** to jump out of a plane that is going to crash: *The pilot bailed out and parachuted into the sea.* **ˌbail ˈout**, **ˌbail sth↔ˈout** to empty water from sth by lifting it out with your hand or a container: *He had to stop rowing to bail water out of the boat.* ◇ *The boat will sink unless we bail out.* **ˌbail sb↔ˈout** to pay sb's bail for them **ˌbail sb↔ˈout (of sth)** to rescue sb from a difficult situation: *The government had to bail the company out of financial difficulty.* ◇ *Ryan's late goal bailed out his team.*

bailey /ˈbeɪli/ *noun* the open area of a castle, inside the outer wall

bail·iff /ˈbeɪlɪf/ *noun* **1** (*BrE*) a law officer whose job is to take the possessions and property of people who cannot pay their debts **2** (*BrE*) a person employed to manage land or a large farm for sb else **3** (*AmE*) an official who keeps order in a court of law, takes people to their seats, watches prisoners, etc.

bairn /beən; *AmE* bern/ *noun* (*ScotE*, *NorthE*) a child

bait /beɪt/ *noun*, *verb*

■ *noun* [U, C] **1** food put on a hook to catch fish or in nets, traps, etc. to catch animals or birds: *Live worms are used as bait.* ◇ *The fish took the bait.* **2** a person or thing that is used to catch sb or to attract them, for example to make them do what you want: *He had chosen the right bait to persuade her to go.*

■ *verb* [VN] **1** to place food on a hook, in a trap, etc. in order to attract or catch an animal: *He baited the trap with a piece of meat.* **2** to deliberately try to make sb angry by making cruel or insulting remarks **3** (- **baiting**) (in compound nouns) the activity of attacking a wild animal with dogs: *bear-baiting* ◇ *badger-baiting*

baize /beɪz/ *noun* [U] a thick woollen fabric that is usually green, used especially for covering card tables and BILLIARD, SNOOKER or POOL tables

bake /beɪk/ *verb* **1** ~ **sth (for sb)** | ~ **(sb) sth** to cook food in an oven without extra fat or liquid; to be cooked in this way: [VN] *baked potatoes* ◇ *I'm baking a birthday cake for Alex.* ◇ *I'm baking Alex a cake.* ◇ [V] *the delicious smell of baking bread* ⇨ vocabulary notes on page 274 **2** to become or to make sth become hard by heating: [V] *The bricks are left in the kiln to bake.* [VN-ADJ] *The sun had baked the ground hard.* [also VN] **3** [V] (*informal*) to be or become very hot: *We sat baking in the sun.*—see also HALF-BAKED

baked ˈbeans (*AmE* also **ˌBoston baked ˈbeans**) *noun* [pl.] small white beans cooked in a tomato sauce and usually sold in cans

Bake·lite™ /ˈbeɪkəlaɪt/ *noun* [U] a type of hard plastic, often dark brown, used in the past for electrical equipment, etc.

baker /ˈbeɪkə(r)/ *noun* **1** a person whose job is baking and selling bread and cakes **2** (**baker's**) (*pl.* **bakers**) (*BrE*) a shop that sells bread and cakes: *I'm just going to the baker's.* **IDM** **a baker's ˈdozen** (*old-fashioned*) 13

bakery /ˈbeɪkəri/ *noun* (*pl.* **-ies**) (*AmE* also **ˈbake shop**) a place where bread and cakes are made and/or sold

ˈbake shop *noun* (*AmE*) = BAKERY

bak·ing /ˈbeɪkɪŋ/ *noun*, *adj.*

■ *noun* [U] the process of cooking using dry heat in an oven: *a baking dish/sheet/tin*

■ *adj.* (also **ˌbaking ˈhot**) extremely hot

ˈbaking flour *noun* [U] (*AmE*) = SELF-RAISING FLOUR

ˈbaking powder *noun* [U] a mixture of powders that are used to make cakes rise and become light as they are baked

ˈbaking soda *noun* [U] = SODIUM BICARBONATE

ˈbaking tray *noun* a small sheet of metal used for baking food on

bala·clava /ˌbæləˈklɑːvə/ (also **ˌbalaclava ˈhelmet**) *noun* (*especially BrE*) a type of woollen hat that covers most of the head, neck and face

bala·laika /ˌbæləˈlaɪkə/ *noun* a musical instrument like a guitar with a body shaped like a triangle and two, three, or four strings, popular especially in Russia

bal·ance /ˈbæləns/ *noun*, *verb*

■ *noun*

EQUAL AMOUNTS **1** [U, sing.] ~ **(between A and B)** a situation in which different things exist in equal, correct or good amounts: *Try to keep a balance between work and relaxation.* ◇ *This newspaper maintains a good balance in its presentation of different opinions.* ◇ *Tourists often disturb the delicate balance of nature on the island.* ◇ *His wife's death disturbed the balance of his mind.*

OF BODY **2** [U] the ability to keep steady with an equal amount of weight on each side of the body: *Athletes need a good sense of balance.* ◇ *I struggled to keep my balance on my new skates.* ◇ *She cycled round the corner, lost her balance and fell off.*

MONEY **3** [C, usually sing.] the amount that is left after taking numbers or money away from a total: *to check your bank balance* (= to find out how much money there is in your account) **4** [C, usually sing.] an amount of money still owed after some payment has been made: *The balance of $500 must be paid within 90 days.*

INSTRUMENT FOR WEIGHING **5** [C] an instrument for weighing things, with a bar that is supported in the middle and has dishes hanging from each end

IDM **(on) the balance of ˈevidence/probaˈbility** (*formal*) (considering) the evidence on both sides of an argument, to find the most likely reason for or result of sth: *The balance of evidence suggests the Liberal party's decline began before the First World War.* **(be/hang) in the ˈbalance** if the future of sth/sb, or the result of sth is/hangs **in the balance**, it is uncertain: *The long-term future of the space programme hangs in the balance.* **(catch/throw sb) off ˈbalance 1** to make sb/sth unsteady and in danger of falling: *I was thrown off balance by the sudden gust of wind.* **2** to make sb surprised and no longer calm: *The senator was clearly caught off balance by the unexpected question.* **on ˈbalance** after considering all the information: *On balance, the company has had a successful year.*—more at REDRESS *v.*, STRIKE *v.*, SWING *v.*, TIP *v.*

■ *verb*

KEEP STEADY **1** ~ **(sth) (on sth)** to put your body or sth else into a position where it is steady and does not fall: [V] *How long can you balance on one leg?* ◇ [VN] *The television was precariously balanced on top of a pile of books.* ◇ *She balanced the cup on her knee.*

BE/KEEP EQUAL **2** ~ **(sth) (out)** to be equal in value, amount, etc. to sth else that has the opposite effect **SYN** OFFSET: [VN] *This year's profits will balance our previous losses.* ◇ *His lack of experience was balanced by a willingness to learn.* ◇ [V] *The good and bad effects of any decision will usually balance out.* **3** [VN] ~ **A with/and B** to give equal importance to two contrasting things or parts of sth: *She tries to balance home life and career.* COMPARE | **4 ~ A against B** to compare the relative importance of two contrasting things: *The cost of obtaining legal advice needs to be balanced against its benefits.* MONEY | **5** [VN] (*finance*) to show that in an account the total money spent is equal to the total money received; to calculate the difference between the two totals

the ˌbalance beam *noun* (*AmE*) = BEAM

bal·anced /ˈbælənst/ *adj.* [usually before noun] (*approving*) keeping or showing a balance so that different things or different parts of sth exist in equal or correct amounts: *The programme presented a balanced view of the two sides of the conflict.* ◇ *a balanced diet* (= one with the quantity and variety of food needed for good health)

ˌbalance of ˈpayments *noun* [sing.] the difference between the amount a country pays for imports and the amount it receives for exports in a particular period of time

ˌbalance of ˈpower *noun* [sing.] **1** a situation in which political or military strength is divided between two countries or groups of countries **2** the power held by a small group which can give its support to either of two larger and equally strong groups

ˌbalance of ˈtrade (also **ˌtrade ˈbalance**) *noun* [sing.] the difference in value between imports and exports: *a balance-of-trade deficit* (= when a country spends more on imports than it earns from exports)

ˈbalance sheet *noun* (*finance*) a written statement showing the amount of money and property that a company has and listing what has been received and paid out

ˈbal·an·cing act *noun* a process in which sb tries to please two or more people or groups who want different things: *The UN must perform a delicate balancing act between the different sides in the conflict.*

bal·cony /ˈbælkəni/ *noun* (*pl.* **-ies**) **1** a platform that is built on the upstairs outside wall of a building, with a wall or rail around it. You can get out onto the balcony from an upstairs room.—picture at HOUSE, MINARET **2** an area of seats upstairs in a theatre—see also CIRCLE, FIRST BALCONY

bald /bɔːld/ *adj.* **1** having little or no hair on the head: *He started going bald in his twenties.*—picture at HAIR **2** without any of the usual hair, marks, etc. covering the skin or surface of sth: *Our dog has a bald patch on its leg.* ◇ *a bald tyre* (= a tyre whose surface has become smooth) **3** without any extra explanation or detail to help you understand or accept what is being said: *The bald fact is that we don't need you any longer.* ◇ *The letter was a bald statement of our legal position.*—see also BALDLY ▶ **bald·ness** *noun* [U]

ˌbald ˈeagle *noun* a N American BIRD OF PREY (= a bird that kills other creatures for food) with a white head and white tail feathers. The bald eagle is used as a symbol of the US.

bal·der·dash /ˈbɔːldədæʃ; *AmE* -dərd-/ *noun* [U] (*old-fashioned*) nonsense

ˌbald-ˈfaced *adj.* (*disapproving, especially AmE*) making no attempt to hide your dishonest behaviour: *bald-faced lies*

bald·ing /ˈbɔːldɪŋ/ *adj.* starting to lose the hair on your head: *a short balding man with glasses*

bald·ly /ˈbɔːldli/ *adv.* in a few words with nothing extra or unnecessary: *'You're lying,' he said baldly.*

bale /beɪl/ *noun, verb*
- *noun* a large amount of a light material pressed tightly together and tied up: *bales of hay/straw/cotton/wool*
- *verb* **1** [VN] to make sth into bales: *The waste paper is baled, then sent for recycling.* **2** [VN, VN to inf] (*BrE*) = BAIL **PHRV** **ˌbale ˈout**, **ˌbale sth↔ˈout**, **ˌbale sb↔ˈout** (*BrE*) = BAIL OUT, BAIL STH OUT, BAIL SB↔OUT

bale·ful /ˈbeɪlfl/ *adj.* (*literary*) threatening evil or harm: *a baleful look/influence* ▶ **bale·ful·ly** /ˈbeɪlfəli/ *adv.*

balk (*especially AmE*) = BAULK

balky /ˈbɔːlki; ˈbɔːki/ *adj.* (*AmE*) (of a person or machine) refusing or failing to do what you want them to do

ball /bɔːl/ *noun, verb*
- *noun* **1** a round object used for throwing, hitting or kicking in games and sports: *a golf/tennis/cricket ball* ◇ *Bounce the ball and try and hit it over the net.*—picture at HOCKEY—picture on page A8 **2** a round object or a thing that has been formed into a round shape: *The sun was a huge ball of fire low on the horizon.* ◇ *a ball of string* ◇ *Some animals roll themselves into a ball for protection.* **3** a kick or hit of the ball in some sports, or (in cricket) a throw of the ball by the BOWLER to the BATSMAN: *He sent over a high ball.* **4** (in baseball) a throw by the PITCHER that the BATTER does not have to hit because it is not accurate **5 ~ of the foot/hand** the part underneath the big toe or the thumb **6** [usually pl.] (△, *informal*) a TESTICLE—see also BALLS **7** a large formal party with dancing **IDM a ˌball and ˈchain** (*BrE*) a problem that prevents you from doing what you would like to do **the ball is in your/sb's ˈcourt** it is your/sb's responsibility to take action next: *They've offered me the job, so the ball's in my court now.* **get/set/start/keep the ball ˈrolling** to make sth start happening; to make sure that sth continues to happen **have a ˈball** (*informal*) to enjoy yourself a lot **have something/a lot on the ˈball** (*AmE, informal*) to be capable of doing a job very well; to be intelligent **(be) on the ˈball** to be aware of and understand what is happening and able to react quickly: *The new publicity manager. is really on the ball.* **play ˈball (with sb)** (*informal*) to be willing to work with other people in a helpful way, especially so that sb can get what they want
- *verb* **1** to form sth into or be formed into the shape of a ball: [V] *Her hands balled into fists.* ◇ [VN] *My hands were balled into fists.* **2** [VN] (*AmE*, △, *slang*) (of a man) to have sex with a woman

bal·lad /ˈbæləd/ *noun* **1** a song or poem that tells a story: *a medieval ballad about a knight and a lady* **2** a slow popular song about love: *Her latest single is a ballad.*

bal·last /ˈbæləst/ *noun* [U] **1** heavy material placed in a ship or HOT-AIR BALLOON to make it heavier and keep it steady **2** a layer of stones that makes a strong base on which a road, railway/railroad, etc. can be built

ˌball ˈbearing *noun* a ring of small metal balls used in a machine to enable the parts to turn smoothly; one of these small metal balls

ball·boy /ˈbɔːlbɔɪ/ *noun* a boy who picks up the balls for the players in a tennis match—see also BALLGIRL

ball·cock /ˈbɔːlkɒk; *AmE* -kɑːk/ *noun* a device with a floating ball that controls the amount of water going into a container, for example the water TANK of a toilet

bal·ler·ina /ˌbæləˈriːnə/ *noun* a female dancer in ballet—see also PRIMA BALLERINA

bal·let /ˈbæleɪ/ *noun* **1** [U] a style of dancing that tells a dramatic story with music but no talking or singing: *She wants to be a ballet dancer.* ◇ *ballet shoes* **2** [C] a story or work of art performed by a group of ballet dancers: *'Swan Lake' is one of the great classical ballets.* **3** [C+sing./pl. v.] a group of dancers who work and perform ballet together: *members of the Royal Ballet*

ˈball game *noun* **1** any game played with a ball **2** (*AmE*) a game of baseball: *Are you going to the ball game?* **IDM a (whole) different/new ˈball game** (*informal*) a completely different kind of situation

ball·girl /ˈbɔːlɡɜːl; *AmE* -ɡɜːrl/ *noun* a girl who picks up the balls for the players in a tennis match—see also BALLBOY

bal·listic /bəˈlɪstɪk/ *adj.* connected with ballistics **IDM go balˈlistic** (*informal*) to become very angry: *He went ballistic when I told him.*

balˌlistic ˈmissile *noun* a MISSILE that is fired into the air at a particular speed and angle in order to fall in the right place

bal·lis·tics /bəˈlɪstɪks/ *noun* [U] the scientific study of things that are shot or fired through the air, such as bullets and MISSILES

bal·loon /bəˈluːn/ *noun, verb*
- *noun* **1** a small bag made of very thin rubber that becomes larger and rounder when you fill it with air or

æ	ɑː	e	ɜː	ə	ɪ	iː	i	ɒ	ɔː	ʌ	ʊ	u	uː
cat	father	ten	bird	about	sit	see	many	got	saw	cup	put	actual	too
								(BrE)					

gas. Balloons are brightly coloured and used as decorations or toys: *to blow up/burst/pop a balloon* ◊ *My balloon has burst!* 2 (also **hot·'air balloon**) a large balloon made of strong fabric that is filled with hot air or gas to make it rise in the air, usually carrying a basket for passengers **IDM when the bal'loon goes up** (*BrE, informal*) when the trouble that you are expecting begins—more at LEAD[2]
■ *verb* [V] 1 ~ (out/up) to suddenly swell out or get bigger: *Her skirt ballooned out in the wind.* 2 (usually **go ballooning**) to travel in a HOT-AIR BALLOON as a sport

bal·loon·ist /bəˈluːnɪst/ *noun* a person who travels in a balloon as a sport

bal·lot /ˈbælət/ *noun, verb*
■ *noun* 1 [U, C] the system of voting in writing and usually in secret; an occasion on which a vote is held: *The chairperson is chosen by secret ballot.* ◊ *The union cannot call a strike unless it holds a ballot of members.* 2 (*BrE* also **'ballot paper**) [C] the piece of paper on which sb marks who they are voting for: *What percentage of eligible voters cast their ballots?* 3 (**the ballot**) [sing.] the total number of votes in an election: *She won 58.8% of the ballot.*—see also POLL
■ *verb* 1 [VN] ~ sb (on sth) to ask sb to vote in writing and secretly about sth [SYN] POLL: *The union balloted its members on the proposed changes.* 2 [V] to vote secretly about sth: *The workers balloted for a strike.*

'ballot box *noun* 1 [C] a box in which people put their ballots after voting 2 (**the ballot box**) [sing.] the system of voting in an election: *The people make their wishes known through the ballot box.*

'ballot paper *noun* (*BrE*) = BALLOT (2)

ball·park /ˈbɔːlpɑːk; *AmE* -pɑːrk/ *noun* 1 [C] (*especially AmE*) a place where baseball is played 2 [sing.] an area or a range within which an amount is likely to be correct or within which sth can be measured: *The offers for the contract were all in the same ballpark.* ◊ *If you said two million you'd be in the ballpark.* ◊ *Give me a ballpark figure* (= a number that is approximately right).

ball·point /ˈbɔːlpɔɪnt/ (also **ballpoint 'pen**) *noun* a pen with a very small metal ball at its point, that rolls ink onto the paper—compare BIRO—picture at STATIONERY

ball·room /ˈbɔːlruːm; -rom/ *noun* a very large room used for dancing on formal occasions—compare DANCE HALL

ballroom 'dancing *noun* [U] a type of dancing done with a partner and using particular fixed steps and movements to particular types of music such as the WALTZ

balls /bɔːlz/ *noun, verb*
■ *noun* (△, *slang*) 1 [U] (*BrE*) nonsense: *That's a load of balls!* 2 [pl.] courage: *She's got balls, I'll say that for her.* ◊ *It took a lot of balls to do that.* 3 (**Balls!**) (*BrE*) exclamation used as a swear word when you are disagreeing with sth, or when you are angry about sth **HELP** Less offensive ways to express this are 'Nonsense!', or 'Come off it!'
■ *verb* **PHRV** **,balls sth↔'up** (*BrE*, △, *slang*) to spoil sth; to do sth very badly—related noun BALLS-UP **HELP** A more polite, informal way of saying this is **foul sth up**, **cock sth up** (slang), or **bungle sth**.

'balls-up *noun* (△ *slang, especially BrE*) something that has been done very badly: *I made a real balls-up of my exams.* **HELP** A more polite, informal way of saying this is **foul-up** or (*BrE*) **cock-up**.

bally·hoo /ˌbæliˈhuː; *AmE* ˈbælihuː/ *noun* [U] (*informal, disapproving*) unnecessary noise and excitement

balm /bɑːm/ *noun* [U, C, usually sing.] 1 (also **bal·sam**) oil with a pleasant smell that is obtained from some types of trees and plants, used in the past to help heal wounds, for example 2 a liquid, cream, etc. that has a pleasant smell and is used to make wounds less painful or skin softer: *He used a skin balm after shaving.* 3 (*literary*) something that makes you feel calm or relaxed: *The gentle music was a balm to his spirit.*

balmy /ˈbɑːmi/ *adj.* (*approving*) (of the air, weather, etc.) warm and pleasant: *a balmy summer evening*

ba·lo·ney /bəˈləʊni; *AmE* -ˈloʊ-/ *noun* [U] 1 (*informal,*

especially AmE) nonsense; lies: *Don't give me that baloney!* 2 (*AmE*) = BOLOGNA

balsa /ˈbɔːlsə/ (also **'balsa wood**) *noun* [U] the light wood of the tropical American **balsa tree**, used especially for making models

bal·sam /ˈbɔːlsəm/ *noun* 1 [U, C] = BALM 2 [C] any plant or tree from which BALM is obtained

bal·us·trade /ˌbæləˈstreɪd/ *noun* a row of posts, joined together at the top, built along the edge of a BALCONY, bridge, etc. to prevent people from falling off, or as a decoration

bam·boo /ˌbæmˈbuː/ *noun* [C, U] (*pl.* **-oos**) a tall tropical plant that is a member of the grass family and has hard hollow stems that are used for making furniture, poles, etc: *a bamboo grove* ◊ *a bamboo chair* ◊ *bamboo shoots* (= young bamboo plants that can be eaten)

bam·boo·zle /bæmˈbuːzl/ *verb* [VN] (*informal*) to confuse sb, especially by tricking them

ban /bæn/ *verb, noun*
■ *verb* (**-nn-**) [VN] 1 to forbid sth officially: *Chemical weapons are banned internationally.* ◊ *a campaign to ban smoking in public places* 2 [usually passive] ~ sb from sth/from doing sth to forbid sb to do sth, go somewhere, etc., especially officially: *He was banned from the meeting.* ◊ *She's been banned from leaving Greece while the allegations are investigated.* ◊ (*BrE*) *He was banned from driving for six months.*
■ *noun* ~ (on sth) an official rule that says that sth is not allowed: *There is to be a total ban on smoking in the office.* ◊ *to impose/lift a ban*

banal /bəˈnɑːl; *AmE* also ˈbeɪnl/ *adj.* (*disapproving*) very ordinary and containing nothing that is interesting or important

ban·al·ity /bəˈnæləti/ *noun* (*pl.* **-ies**) [U, C] (*disapproving*) the quality of being banal; things, remarks, etc. that are banal: *the banality of modern city life* ◊ *They exchanged banalities for a couple of minutes.*

ba·nana /bəˈnɑːnə; *AmE* bəˈnænə/ *noun* a long curved fruit with a thick yellow skin and soft flesh, that grows on trees in hot countries: *a bunch of bananas* —picture on page A2 **IDM go ba'nanas** (*slang*) to become angry, crazy or silly

ba,nana re'public *noun* (*disapproving, offensive*) a small poor country with a weak government, that depends on foreign money

ba'nana skin *noun* (*BrE, informal*) something that could cause difficulty or embarrassment, especially to sb in a public position

ba,nana 'split *noun* a cold DESSERT (= a sweet dish) made from a BANANA that is cut in half along its length and filled with ice cream, nuts, etc.

band /bænd/ *noun, verb*
■ *noun*
GROUP OF MUSICIANS 1 [C+sing./pl. *v.*] a small group of musicians who play popular music together, often with a singer or singers: *a rock/jazz band* ◊ *She's a singer with a band.* 2 [C+sing./pl. *v.*] a group of musicians who play BRASS and PERCUSSION instruments: *a military band*—see also BRASS BAND, MARCHING BAND, ONE-MAN BAND
GROUP OF PEOPLE 3 [C+sing./pl. *v.*] a group of people who do sth together or who have the same ideas: *a band of outlaws* ◊ *He persuaded a small band of volunteers to help.*
STRIP OF MATERIAL/COLOUR 4 [C] a thin flat strip or circle of any material that is put around things, for example to hold them together or to strengthen them: *She always ties her hair back in a band.* ◊ *All babies in the hospital have name bands on their wrists.* ◊ *She wore a simple band of gold on her finger.*—see also ARMBAND, HAIRBAND, HATBAND, RUBBER BAND, SWEATBAND, WAISTBAND—picture at HAT 5 [C] a strip of colour or material on sth that is different from what is around it: *a white plate with a blue band around the edge*
OF RADIO WAVES 6 (also **wave·band**) [C] a range of radio waves: *Short-wave radio uses the 20-50 metre band.*
RANGE 7 [C] a range of numbers, ages, prices, etc. within which people or things are counted or measured: *the 25-35 age band* ◊ *tax bands*

aɪ	aʊ	eɪ	əʊ	oʊ	ɔɪ	ɪə	eə	ʊə	j	w
my	now	say	go	go	boy	near	hair	pure	yes	wet
			(BrE)	(AmE)						

■ *verb* [VN] [usually passive]

WITH COLOUR/MATERIAL | **1** to put a band of a different colour or material around sth: [VN-ADJ] *Many insects are banded black and yellow.* [also VN]

PUT INTO RANGE | **2** (*BrE*) to be organized into bands of price, income, etc: *Tax is banded according to income.*

PHRV **band to'gether** to form a group in order to achieve sth: *Local people banded together to fight the drug dealers.*

ban·dage /ˈbændɪdʒ/ *noun, verb*
■ *noun* a strip of fabric used for tying around a part of the body that has been hurt in order to protect or support it—picture on page 598
■ *verb* [VN] ~ **sth** (**up**) to wrap a bandage around a part of the body in order to protect it because it is injured: *Don't bandage the wound too tightly.* ◇ *His injured leg was all bandaged up.*

'Band-Aid™ *noun* (*especially AmE*) **1** = PLASTER (3) **2** (*disapproving*) a temporary solution to a problem that does not really solve it at all

ban·danna /bænˈdænə/ *noun* a piece of brightly coloured fabric worn around the neck or head

B and B (also **b and b**) /ˌbiː ən ˈbiː/ *abbr.* (*informal, especially BrE*) bed and breakfast

ban·dit /ˈbændɪt/ *noun* a member of an armed group of thieves who attack travellers

ban·dit·ry /ˈbændɪtri/ *noun* [U] (*written*) acts of stealing and violence by bandits

ban·do·lier (also **ban·do·leer**) /ˌbændəˈlɪə(r); *AmE* -ˈlɪr/ *noun* a belt made for carrying bullets and worn over the shoulder

bands·man /ˈbændzmən/ *noun* (*pl.* **-men** /-mən/) a musician who plays in a military or BRASS band

band·stand /ˈbændstænd/ *noun* a covered platform outdoors, where musicians, especially a BRASS or military band, can stand and play

band·wagon /ˈbændwægən/ *noun* [usually sing.] an activity that more and more people are becoming involved in: *The World Cup bandwagon is starting to roll.* IDM **climb/jump on the 'bandwagon** (*informal, disapproving*) to join others in doing sth that is becoming fashionable because you hope to become popular or successful yourself: *politicians eager to jump on the environmental bandwagon*

bandy /ˈbændi/ *adj., verb*
■ *adj.* (of the legs) curving outwards so that the knees are wide apart: *to be bandy-legged*
■ *verb* (**ban·dies, bandy·ing, ban·died, ban·died**) IDM **bandy 'words (with sb)** (*old-fashioned*) to argue with sb or speak rudely to them PHRV **,bandy sth↔a'bout/a'round** [usually passive] if a name, a word, a story, etc., is **bandied about/around**, it is mentioned frequently by many people: *His name was being bandied about as a future prime minister.*

bane /beɪn/ *noun* [sing.] **the ~ of sb/sth** something that causes trouble and makes people unhappy: *The neighbours' kids are the bane of my life.*

bane·ful /ˈbeɪnfl/ *adj.* (*literary*) evil or causing evil

bang /bæŋ/ *verb, noun, adv., exclamation*
■ *verb* **1** ~ (**on**) **sth** to hit sth in a way that makes a loud noise: [VN] *The baby was banging the table with his spoon.* ◇ [V] *She banged on the door angrily.* **2** to close sth or to be closed with a loud noise: [VN] *Don't bang the door when you go out!* ◇ [V] *A window was banging somewhere* (= opening and closing noisily). ◇ [V-ADJ] *The door banged shut behind her.* **3** [VN+adv./prep.] to put sth somewhere suddenly and violently: *He banged the money down on the counter.* ◇ *She banged saucepans around irritably.* **4** [VN] to hit sth, especially a part of the body, against sth by accident: *She tripped and banged her knee on the desk.* **5** [VN] (△, *slang*) (of a man) to have sex with a woman IDM see DRUM *n.*, HEAD *n.* PHRV **,bang a'bout/a'round** to move around noisily: *We could hear the kids banging around upstairs.* **,bang 'into sth** to crash into or hit sth by mistake: *I banged into a chair and hurt my leg.* **,bang 'on about sth** (*BrE, informal*) to talk a lot about sth in a boring way: *He keeps banging on about his new job.*

■ *noun* **1** a sudden loud noise: *The door swung shut with a bang.* ◇ *Suddenly there was a loud bang and a puff of smoke.*—see also BIG BANG **2** a sudden painful blow on a part of the body: *a bang on the head* **3** (**bangs**) [pl.] (*AmE*) = FRINGE (1) IDM **with a 'bang** (*informal*) **1** very successfully: *The party went with a bang.* **2** in a way that everyone notices; with a powerful effect: *The team won their last four games, ending the season with a bang.*—more at EARTH *n.*, SLAP *adv.*

■ *adv.* (*informal, especially BrE*) exactly; completely: *Our computers are bang up to date.* ◇ *My estimate was bang on target.* ◇ *You're bang on time, as usual*—see also SLAP BANG IDM **bang goes sth** (*BrE, informal*) used when you say that sth you hoped to have or achieve is no longer possible: *Bang went my hopes of promotion.* **go 'bang** (*informal*) to burst or explode with a loud noise; to make a sudden loud noise: *A balloon suddenly went bang.* IDM see RIGHT *n.*

■ *exclamation* used to show the sound of sth loud, like a gun: *'Bang, bang, you're dead!' shouted the little boy.*

bang·er /ˈbæŋə(r)/ *noun* (*BrE, informal*) **1** a sausage: *bangers and mash* **2** (*AmE* **beat·er**) an old car that is in bad condition **3** a FIREWORK that makes a loud noise when it explodes

ban·gle /ˈbæŋgl/ *noun* a piece of jewellery in the form of a large ring of gold, silver, etc. worn loosely around the wrist—picture at JEWELLERY

'bang-up *adj.* (*AmE, informal*) very good

ban·ish /ˈbænɪʃ/ *verb* [VN] **1** [usually passive] ~ **sb** (**from …**) (**to …**) to order sb to leave a place, especially a country, as a punishment: *He was banished to Australia, where he died five years later.* ◇ *The children were banished from the dining room.* **2** ~ **sb/sth** (**from sth**) (*written*) to make sb/sth go away; to get rid of sb/sth: *The sight of food banished all other thoughts from my mind.*

ban·ish·ment /ˈbænɪʃmənt/ *noun* [U] the punishment of being sent away from a place, especially from a country

ban·is·ter (also **ban·nis·ter**) /ˈbænɪstə(r)/ *noun* (*BrE* also **ban·is·ters** [pl.]) the posts and rail at the side of a staircase: *to hold on to the banister/banisters*

banjo /ˈbændʒəʊ; *AmE* ˈbændʒoʊ/ *noun* (*pl.* **-os**) a musical instrument like a guitar, with a long neck, a round body and four or more strings

bank /bæŋk/ *noun, verb*
■ *noun*

FOR MONEY | **1** an organization that provides various financial services, for example keeping or lending money: *My salary is paid directly into my bank.* ◇ *I need to go to the bank* (= the local office of a bank). ◇ *a bank account/loan* ◇ *a bank manager*

IN GAMBLING | **2** a supply of money or things that are used as money in some games, especially those in which gambling is involved

STH COLLECTED/STORED | **3** an amount of sth that is collected; a place where sth is stored ready for use: *a bank of knowledge* ◇ *a blood/sperm bank* ◇ *a databank*

OF RIVER/CANAL | **4** the side of a river, canal, etc. and the land near it: *He jumped in and swam to the opposite bank.* ◇ *It's on the north bank of the Thames.* ◇ *They built a house on the banks of the River Severn* (= on land near the river).

SLOPE | **5** a raised area of ground that slopes at the sides, often at the edge of sth or dividing sth: *There were low banks of earth between the rice fields.* ◇ *The girls ran down the steep grassy bank.* **6** an artificial slope built at the side of a road, so that cars can drive fast around bends

OF CLOUD/SNOW, etc. | **7** a mass of cloud, snow, etc., especially one formed by the wind: *The sun disappeared behind a bank of clouds.*

OF MACHINES, etc. | **8** a row or series of similar objects, especially machines: *a bank of lights/switches/computers* IDM **not ,break the 'bank** (*informal, humorous*) if you say sth **won't break the bank**, you mean that it won't cost a lot of money, or more than you can afford—more at LAUGH *v.*

■ *verb*

MONEY | **1** [VN] to put money into a bank account: *She is*

b	d	f	g	h	k	l	m	n	p	r
bad	did	fall	get	hat	cat	leg	man	now	pen	red

believed to have banked (= been paid) £10 million in two years. **2** [V] ~ (with/at...) to have an account with a particular bank: The family had banked with Coutts for generations.

OF PLANE | **3** [V] to travel with one side higher than the other when turning: The plane banked steeply to the left.

FORM PILES | **4** [VN] ~ sth (up) to form sth into piles: They banked the earth (up) into a mound.

A FIRE | **5** [VN] ~ sth (up) to pile coal, etc. on a fire so that the fire burns slowly for a long time: The fire was banked up as high as if it were midwinter.

PHRV **'bank on sb/sth** to rely on sb/sth: I'm banking on your help. ◇ [+to inf] I'm banking on you to help me. ◇ [+ -ing] I was banking on getting something to eat on the train. **,bank 'up** to form into piles, especially because of the wind: The snow had banked up against the wall.

bank·able /ˈbæŋkəbl/ adj. (informal) likely to make money for sb: The movie's success has made her one of the world's most bankable stars.

'bank balance noun the amount of money that sb has in their bank account at a particular time

'bank card noun **1** (also **'banker's card**) (both BrE) a plastic card provided by your bank that may be used as a CHEQUE CARD or DEBIT CARD or to get money from your account out of a machine **2** (AmE) a CREDIT CARD provided by your bank, that can also be used as a DEBIT CARD and to get money from your account out of a machine

'bank draft (also **'banker's draft**) noun a cheque paid by a bank to another bank or to a particular person or organization

bank·er /ˈbæŋkə(r)/ noun **1** a person who owns a bank or has an important job at a bank: a merchant banker **2** a person who is in charge of the money in particular games

,banker's 'order noun (BrE) an instruction to your bank to pay money to sb directly from your bank account—compare STANDING ORDER

,bank 'holiday (BrE) noun a public holiday, for example Christmas Day, New Year's Day, etc: Bank Holiday Monday ◇ a bank holiday weekend (= a weekend followed by a Monday which is a holiday)—see also HOLIDAY—compare LEGAL HOLIDAY, PUBLIC HOLIDAY

bank·ing /ˈbæŋkɪŋ/ noun [U] the business activity of banks: She's thinking about a career in banking.

bank·note /ˈbæŋknəʊt; AmE -noʊt/ noun (especially BrE) = NOTE: forged (= illegally copied) banknotes

'bank rate noun the rate of interest charged by a bank for lending money, which is fixed by a central bank in a country

bank·roll /ˈbæŋkrəʊl; AmE -roʊl/ verb, noun
■ verb [VN] (informal, especially AmE) to support sb/sth financially: They claimed his campaign had been bankrolled with drug money.
■ noun (especially AmE) a supply of money: He is the candidate with the biggest campaign bankroll.

bank·rupt /ˈbæŋkrʌpt/ adj., noun, verb
■ adj. **1** without enough money to pay what you owe: They went bankrupt in 1993. ◇ The company was declared bankrupt in the High Court. **2** ~ (of sth) (formal, disapproving) completely lacking in anything that has value: a government bankrupt of new ideas ◇ a society that is morally bankrupt
■ noun (law) a person who has been judged by a court of law to be unable to pay his or her debts
■ verb [VN] to make sb bankrupt: The company was almost bankrupted by legal costs.

bank·rupt·cy /ˈbæŋkrʌptsi/ noun [U, C] (pl. -ies) the state of being bankrupt: The company filed for bankruptcy (= asked to be officially bankrupt) in 1993. ◇ moral/political bankruptcy ◇ There could be further bankruptcies among small farmers.

'bank statement (also **state·ment**) noun a printed record of all the money paid into and out of a customer's bank account within a particular period

ban·ner /ˈbænə(r)/ noun a long piece of fabric with a message on it that is carried between two poles or hung in a public place to show support for sth: A huge banner

over the street said 'Welcome home'. ◇ Protesters carried a banner reading 'Save our Wildlife'. IDM **under the ban·ner (of sth)** (written) **1** claiming to support a particular set of ideas: They fought the election under the banner of 'No new taxes'. **2** as part of a particular group or organization: Troops are in the country under the banner of the United Nations.

,banner 'headline noun a line of words printed in large letters across the front page of a newspaper

,banner 'year noun (AmE) a year in which sth is especially successful: It was a banner year for Mexico's tourist industry.

ban·nis·ter = BANISTER

banns /bænz/ noun [pl.] a public statement in church that two people intend to marry each other: to read/publish the banns

ban·quet /ˈbæŋkwɪt/ noun **1** a formal meal for a large number of people, usually for a special occasion, at which speeches are often made: a state banquet in honour of the visiting President **2** a large impressive meal

ban·quet·ing /ˈbæŋkwɪtɪŋ/ adj. connected with banquets: a banqueting hall

ban·quette /bæŋˈket/ noun a long soft seat along a wall in a restaurant, etc.

ban·shee /bænˈʃiː; ˈbænʃiː/ noun (in Irish stories) a female spirit who gives a long sad cry as a warning to people that sb in their family is going to die soon

ban·tam /ˈbæntəm/ noun a type of small chicken

ban·tam·weight /ˈbæntəmweɪt/ noun a boxer weighing between 51 and 53.5 kilograms, or a WRESTLER who weighs between 52 and 57 kilograms, heavier than a FLYWEIGHT: a bantamweight champion

ban·ter /ˈbæntə(r)/ noun, verb
■ noun [U] friendly remarks and jokes: He enjoyed exchanging banter with the customers.
■ verb [V] ~ (with sb) to joke with sb: He bantered with reporters and posed for photographers.

ban·ter·ing /ˈbæntərɪŋ/ adj. (of a way of talking) amusing and friendly: There was a friendly, bantering tone in his voice.

ban·yan /ˈbænjən/ (also **'banyan tree**) noun an Indian fruit tree with branches that grow down to the ground and form new roots

bap /bæp/ noun (BrE) a small round flat bread roll—see also BUN—picture on page A1

bap·tism /ˈbæptɪzəm/ noun a Christian ceremony in which a few drops of water are poured on sb or they are covered with water, to welcome them into the Christian Church and often to name them—compare CHRISTENING IDM **a ,baptism of 'fire** a difficult introduction to a new job or activity

bap·tis·mal /bæpˈtɪzməl/ adj. [only before noun] connected with baptism: a baptismal service/ceremony

Bap·tist /ˈbæptɪst/ noun a member of a Christian Protestant Church that believes that baptism should take place when a person is old enough to understand what it means, and not as a baby ► **Bap·tist** adj. [usually before noun]: a Baptist church

bap·tize (BrE also **-ise**) /bæpˈtaɪz/ verb [usually passive] to give sb BAPTISM: [VN-N] She was baptized Mary. ◇ I was baptized a Catholic. [also VN] —see also CHRISTEN

bar /bɑː(r)/ noun, verb, prep.
■ noun
FOR DRINKS/FOOD | **1** [C] a place where you can buy and drink alcoholic and other drinks: He's been working at a bar called the Flamingo. ◇ the island's only licensed bar (= one that is allowed to sell alcoholic drinks) ◇ a cocktail bar ◇ (BrE) I found David in the bar of the Red Lion (= a room in a pub where drinks are served).—see also BAR ROOM, LOUNGE BAR, MINIBAR, PUBLIC BAR, SALOON BAR **2** [C] a long wide wooden surface where drinks, etc. are served: She was sitting at the bar. ◇ It was so crowded I couldn't get to the bar. **3** [C] (especially in compounds) a place in which a particular kind of food or drink is the main thing

	s	t	v	z	ʃ	ʒ	tʃ	dʒ	θ	ð	ŋ
	see	tea	van	zoo	shoe	vision	chain	jam	thin	this	sing

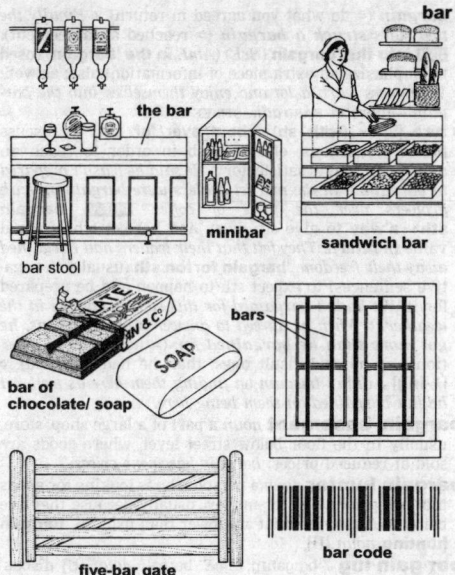

bar

the bar

minibar

sandwich bar

bar stool

bars

bar of
chocolate/ soap

five-bar gate

bar code

VOCABULARY BUILDING

a bar of chocolate

If you want to describe a whole unit of a particular
substance, or a group of things that are normally
together, for example when you buy them, you need to
use the correct word.

a **bar** of soap/chocolate; a candy **bar**
a **block** of ice/stone/wood
a **bolt/roll/length** of fabric
a **cube** of ice/sugar; an ice/sugar **cube**
a **loaf** of bread
a **roll** of film/carpet
a **slab** of marble/concrete
a **stick** of gum

a **bunch** of bananas/grapes
a **bunch/bouquet** of flowers
a **bundle** of papers/sticks
a **set/bunch** of keys
a **set** of chairs/glasses/clothes/guitar strings
⇨ note at BIT

that is served: *a sandwich bar* ◊ *a coffee bar*—see also
SNACK BAR, WINE BAR
OF CHOCOLATE/SOAP | **4** [C] a piece of sth with straight
sides: *a bar of chocolate/soap* ◊ *The kids never eat candy
bars.*
OF METAL/WOOD | **5** [C] a long straight piece of metal or
wood. Bars are often used to stop sb from getting through
a space: *He smashed the window with an iron bar.* ◊ *All
the ground floor windows were fitted with bars.* ◊ *a five-bar
gate* (= one made with five bars of wood)—see also SPACE
BAR, TOW BAR
IN ELECTRIC FIRE | **6** [C] a piece of metal with wire wrapped
around it that becomes red and hot when electricity is
passed through it: *Switch another bar on if you're cold.*
OF COLOUR/LIGHT | **7** [C] a band of colour or light: *Bars of
sunlight slanted down from the tall narrow windows.*
THAT PREVENTS STH | **8** [C, usually sing.] ~ (**to sth**) a thing
that stops sb from doing sth: *At that time being a woman
was a bar to promotion in most professions.*—see also
COLOUR BAR
IN MUSIC | **9** (*BrE*) (*AmE* **meas·ure**) [C] one of the short
sections of equal length that a piece of music is divided
into, and the notes that are in it: *four beats to the bar* ◊
Hum the opening bars of your favourite piece of music.—
picture at MUSIC
LAW | **10** (**the Bar**) [sing.] (*BrE*) the profession of BARRISTER
(= a lawyer in a higher court): *to be called to the Bar* (=
allowed to work as a qualified BARRISTER) **11** (**the Bar**)
[sing.] (*AmE*) the profession of any kind of lawyer
MEASUREMENT | **12** = MILLIBAR
—see also SCROLL BAR
IDM be,hind '**bars** (*informal*) in prison: *The murderer is
now safely behind bars.*
■ *verb* (**-rr-**) [VN]
CLOSE WITH BARS | **1** [usually passive] to close sth with a bar
or bars: *All the doors and windows were barred.*
BLOCK | **2** to block a road, path, etc. so that nobody can
pass: *Two police officers were barring her exit.* ◊ *We found
our way barred by rocks.*
PREVENT | **3** ~ **sb** (**from sth/from doing sth**) to forbid or
prevent sb from doing sth: *The players are barred from
drinking alcohol the night before a match.*
IDM see HOLD *n.*
■ *prep.* except for sb/sth: *The students all attended, bar two
who were ill.* ◊ *It's the best result we've ever had, **bar
none*** (= none was better).
IDM see SHOUTING

barb /bɑːb; *AmE* bɑːrb/ *noun* **1** the point of an arrow or a
hook that is curved backwards to make it difficult to pull
out **2** a remark that is meant to hurt sb's feelings—see
also BARBED

bar·bar·ian /bɑːˈbeəriən; *AmE* bɑːrˈber-/ *noun* **1** a person
long ago in the past who belonged to a European tribe
which was considered wild and UNCIVILIZED: *barbarian
invasions of the fifth century* **2** a person who behaves very
badly and has no respect for art, education, etc.

bar·bar·ic /bɑːˈbærɪk; *AmE* bɑːrˈb-/ *adj.* **1** cruel and violent and not as expected from people who are educated
and respect each other: *a barbaric act/custom/ritual* ◊
The way these animals are killed is barbaric. **2** connected
with a tribe of BARBARIANS (1)

bar·bar·ism /ˈbɑːbərɪzəm; *AmE* ˈbɑːrb-/ *noun* [U] (*written*) **1** a state of not having any education, respect for art,
etc. **2** cruel or violent behaviour: *the barbarism of war*

bar·bar·ity /bɑːˈbærəti; *AmE* bɑːrˈb-/ *noun* (*pl.* **-ies**) [U, C]
behaviour that deliberately causes extreme pain or suffering to others: *The barbarity of the old regime was
eventually exposed.*

bar·bar·ous /ˈbɑːbərəs; *AmE* ˈbɑːrb-/ *adj.* (*written*)
1 extremely cruel and shocking: *the barbarous treatment
of these prisoners of war* **2** showing a lack of education
and good manners ▶ **bar·bar·ous·ly** *adv.*

bar·be·cue /ˈbɑːbɪkjuː; *AmE* ˈbɑːrb-/ *noun, verb*
■ *noun* (*abbr.* **BBQ**) (also *informal* **bar·bie** *BrE*, *AustralE*)
1 a metal frame for cooking food on over an open fire
outdoors: *I put another steak on the barbecue.* ◊ *a barbecue
sausage* (= cooked in this way) ◊ *barbecue sauce* (= a spicy
sauce eaten with barbecue food) **2** an outdoor meal or
party when food is cooked in this way: *Let's have a
barbecue!*—compare COOKOUT
■ *verb* [V, VN] to cook food on a barbecue—compare BROIL—
picture on page 275

barbed /bɑːbd; *AmE* bɑːrbd/ *adj.* **1** (of an arrow or a
hook) having a point that is curved backwards (called a
BARB) **2** (of a remark or comment) meant to hurt sb's
feelings

,**barbed** '**wire** *noun* [U] strong wire with short sharp
points on it, used especially for fences: *a barbed wire
fence*

bar·bell /ˈbɑːbel; *AmE* ˈbɑːrbel/ *noun* a long metal bar
with weights at each end, used in the sport of WEIGHTLIFT-
ING and for exercise

bar·ber /ˈbɑːbə(r); *AmE* ˈbɑːrb-/ *noun* **1** a person whose
job is to cut men's hair and sometimes to shave them
2 (also **barber's**) (both *BrE*) (*pl.* **bar·bers**) a shop where
men can have their hair cut—compare HAIRDRESSER

bar·ber·shop /ˈbɑːbəʃɒp; *AmE* ˈbɑːrbərʃɑːp/ *noun*
1 (*especially AmE*) (*BrE* usually **barber's**) [C] a place
where a barber works **2** [U] a type of light music for four
parts sung by men, without instruments: *a barbershop
quartet*

æ	ɑː	e	ɜː	ə	ɪ	iː	i	ɒ	ɔː	ʌ	ʊ	u	uː
cat	father	ten	bird	about	sit	see	many	got	saw	cup	put	actual	too
									(BrE)				

bar·bie /ˈbɑːbi; AmE ˈbɑːrbi/ noun (BrE, AustralE, informal) = BARBECUE

bar·bit·ur·ate /bɑːˈbɪtʃʊrət; AmE bɑːrˈb-/ noun a powerful drug that makes you feel calm and relaxed or puts you to sleep. There are several types of barbiturate: *He died from an overdose of barbiturates.*

ˈbar chart (AmE also **ˈbar graph**) noun a diagram which uses narrow bands of different heights to show different amounts, so that they can be compared—picture at CHART

ˈbar code noun a pattern of thick and thin lines that is printed on things you buy. It contains information that a computer can read.—picture at BAR

bard /bɑːd; AmE bɑːrd/ noun (literary) a person who writes poems

bare /beə(r); AmE ber/ adj., verb
- adj. (**barer, bar·est**) **1** not covered by any clothes: *She likes to walk around in bare feet.* **2** (of trees or countryside) not covered with leaves; without plants or trees: *the bare branches of winter trees ◊ a bare mountainside* **3** (of surfaces) not covered with or protected by anything: *bare wooden floorboards ◊ Bare wires were sticking out of the cable. ◊ The walls were bare except for a clock.* **4** (of a room, cupboard, etc.) empty: *The fridge was completely bare. ◊ bare shelves* **5** [only before noun] just enough; the most basic or simple: *The family was short of even the bare necessities of life. ◊ We only had the bare essentials in the way of equipment. ◊ He did the bare minimum of work but still passed the exam. ◊ She gave me only the bare facts of the case. ◊ It was the barest hint of a smile.* ⇨ note at NAKED ▪ **bare·ness** noun [U] **IDM** **the bare ˈbones (of sth)** the basic facts: *the bare bones of the story* **with your bare ˈhands** without weapons or tools: *He was capable of killing a man with his bare hands.* **lay sth ˈbare** (written) to show sth that was covered or to make sth known that was secret: *Every aspect of their private lives has been laid bare.*—more at CUPBOARD
- verb [VN] to remove the covering from sth, especially from part of the body: *She was paid several thousand dollars to bare all* (= take all her clothes off) *for the magazine.* **IDM** **bare your ˈsoul (to sb)** to tell sb your deepest and most private feelings **bare your ˈteeth** to show your teeth in a fierce and threatening way: *The dog bared its teeth and growled.*

bare·back /ˈbeəbæk; AmE ˈberb-/ adj., adv. on a horse without a SADDLE: *a bareback rider ◊ riding bareback*

bare·faced /ˈbeəfeɪst; AmE ˈberf-/ adj. [only before noun] (disapproving) showing that you do not care about offending sb or about behaving badly: *a barefaced lie ◊ barefaced cheek*

bare·foot /ˈbeəfʊt; AmE ˈberf-/ (also less frequent **bare·foot·ed**) adj., adv. not wearing anything on your feet: *poor children going barefoot in the street*

bare·head·ed /ˌbeəˈhedɪd; AmE ˌberˈh-/ adj., adv. not wearing anything to cover your head

bare·ly /ˈbeəli; AmE ˈberli/ adv. **1** in a way that is just possible but only with difficulty: *He could barely read and write. ◊ The music was barely audible. ◊ She was barely able to stand. ◊ We barely had time to catch the train.* **2** in a way that almost does not happen or exist: *She barely acknowledged his presence. ◊ There was barely any smell.* **3** just; certainly not more than (a particular amount, age, time, etc.): *Barely 50% of the population voted. ◊ He was barely 20 years old and already running his own company. ◊ They arrived barely a minute later.* **4** only a very short time before: *I had barely started speaking when he interrupted me.* ⇨ note at HARDLY

barf /bɑːf; AmE bɑːrf/ verb [V] (AmE, informal) to VOMIT ▶ barf noun [U]

bar·gain /ˈbɑːgən; AmE ˈbɑːrgən/ noun, verb
- noun **1** a thing bought for less than the usual price: *I picked up a few good bargains in the sale. ◊ The car was a bargain at that price. ◊ bargain prices* **2** ~ (with sb) an agreement between two or more people or groups, to do sth for each other: *He and his partner had made a bargain to tell each other everything. ◊ I've done what I promised and I expect you to keep your side of the*

bargain (= do what you agreed in return). ◊ *Finally the two sides struck a bargain* (= reached an agreement). **IDM** **into the ˈbargain** (BrE) (AmE **in the ˈbargain**) (used to emphasize an extra piece of information) also; as well: *Volunteers learn a lot and enjoy themselves into the bargain.*—more at HARD adj., STRIKE v.
- verb [V] ~ (with sb) (about/over/for sth) to discuss prices, conditions, etc. with sb in order to reach an agreement that is satisfactory: *He said he wasn't prepared to bargain. ◊ In the market dealers were bargaining with growers over the price of coffee.* **PHRV** **ˌbargain sth↔aˈway** to give sth away and not get sth of equal value in return: *They felt that their leaders had bargained away their freedom.* **ˈbargain for/on sth** (usually in negative sentences) to expect sth to happen and be prepared for it: *We hadn't bargained for this sudden change in the weather. ◊ When he agreed to answer a few questions, he got more than he bargained for* (= he got more questions, or more difficult ones, than he had expected). ◊ [+ -ing] *I didn't bargain on finding them here as well. ◊ I hadn't bargained on them being here.*

ˌbargain ˈbasement noun a part of a large shop/store, usually in the floor below street level, where goods are sold at reduced prices: *bargain-basement prices*

ˈbargain hunter noun a person who is looking for goods that are good value for money, usually because they are being sold at prices that are lower than usual ▶ **ˈbargain hunting** noun [U]

bar·gain·ing /ˈbɑːgənɪŋ; AmE ˈbɑːrg-/ noun [U] discussion of prices, conditions, etc. with the aim of reaching an agreement that is satisfactory: *After much hard bargaining we reached an agreement with the finance committee. ◊ wage bargaining ◊ Exporters are in a strong bargaining position at the moment.*—see also COLLECTIVE BARGAINING, PLEA BARGAINING

ˈbargaining counter (BrE) (AmE **ˈbargaining chip**) noun a fact or a thing that a person or a group of people can use to get an advantage for themselves when they are trying to reach an agreement with another group

ˈbargaining power noun [U] the amount of control a person or group has when trying to reach an agreement with another group in a work, business or political situation

barge /bɑːdʒ; AmE bɑːrdʒ/ noun, verb
- noun a large boat with a flat bottom, used for carrying goods and people on canals and rivers—picture at BOAT
- verb [+adv./prep.] to move in an awkward way, pushing people out of the way or crashing into them: [V] *He barged past me to get to the bar.* ◊ [VN] *They barged their way through the crowds.* **PHRV** **ˌbarge ˈin (on sb/sth)** to enter a place or join a group of people rudely interrupting what sb else is doing or saying: *I hope you don't mind me barging in like this. ◊ He barged in on us while we were having a meeting.*

barge·pole /ˈbɑːdʒpəʊl; AmE ˈbɑːrdʒpoʊl/ noun **IDM** see TOUCH v.

ˈbar graph noun (AmE) = BAR CHART

bari·tone /ˈbærɪtəʊn; AmE -toʊn/ noun a man's singing voice with a range between TENOR and BASS; a man with a baritone voice—compare ALTO, BASS, TENOR

bar·ium /ˈbeəriəm; AmE ˈber-/ noun [U] (symb Ba) a chemical element. Barium is a soft silver-white metal that is often combined with other elements to form PIGMENTS.

ˌbarium ˈmeal noun a substance containing barium that a doctor gives sb to swallow before an X-RAY because it makes organs in the body easier to see

bark /bɑːk; AmE bɑːrk/ noun, verb
- noun [U, C] **1** the outer covering of a tree **2** the short loud sound made by dogs and some other animals **3** a short loud sound made by a gun or a voice: *a bark of laughter* **IDM** **sb's bark is worse than their bite** (informal) used to say that sb is not really as angry or as fierce as they sound
- verb **1** [V] ~ (at sb/sth) when a dog **barks**, it makes a short loud sound: *The dog suddenly started barking at us.* **2** ~ (out) sth to give orders, ask questions, etc. in a loud,

aɪ	aʊ	eɪ	əʊ	oʊ	ɔɪ	ɪə	eə	ʊə	j	w
my	now	say	go (BrE)	go (AmE)	boy	near	hair	pure	yes	wet

unfriendly way: [VN] *She barked out an order.* ◇ *He barked questions at her.* [also V] **speech) 3** (*especially BrE*) to rub the skin off your knee, etc. by falling or by knocking against sth [SYN] GRAZE: *I barked my shins when I fell on the steps.* [IDM] **be barking up the wrong 'tree** (*informal*) to have the wrong idea about how to get or achieve sth: *You're barking up the wrong tree if you're expecting us to lend you any money.*

bark·er /ˈbɑːkə(r); *AmE* ˈbɑːrk-/ *noun* a person who stands outside a place where there is entertainment and shouts to people to go in

,bark·ing 'mad (also **bark·ing**) *adj.* (*BrE, informal*) completely crazy

bar·ley /ˈbɑːli; *AmE* ˈbɑːrli/ *noun* [U] a plant grown for its grain that is used for making food, beer and WHISKY; the grains of this plant—picture at CEREAL

'barley sugar *noun* [U] a hard clear sweet/candy made from boiled sugar

'barley water *noun* [U] (*BrE*) a drink made by boiling BARLEY in water. It is usually flavoured with orange or lemon: *lemon barley water*

bar·maid /ˈbɑːmeɪd; *AmE* ˈbɑːrm-/ *noun* (*BrE*) (*AmE* **bartend·er**) a woman who works in a bar, serving drinks

bar·man /ˈbɑːmən; *AmE* ˈbɑːrmən/ *noun* (*pl.* **-men** /-mən/) (*especially BrE*) (*AmE* usually **bar·tend·er**) a man who works in a bar, serving drinks

bar mitz·vah /ˌbɑː ˈmɪtsvə; *AmE* ˌbɑːr/ *noun* **1** a ceremony and celebration for a Jewish boy who has reached the age of 13, at which he accepts the religious responsibilities of an adult **2** the boy who is celebrating this occasion—compare BAT MITZVAH

barmy /ˈbɑːmi; *AmE* ˈbɑːrmi/ *adj.* (*BrE, informal*) slightly crazy

barn /bɑːn; *AmE* bɑːrn/ *noun* **1** a large farm building for storing grain or keeping animals in: *a hay barn* ◇ *They live in a converted barn* (= a barn that has been turned into a house).—see also DUTCH BARN **2** a large plain ugly building: *They live in a great barn of a house.* **3** (*AmE*) a building in which buses, trucks, etc. are kept when not being used [IDM] **close, etc. the barn door after the horse has e'scaped** (*AmE*) = CLOSE, LOCK, ETC. THE STABLE DOOR AFTER THE HORSE HAS BOLTED at STABLE *n.*

bar·nacle /ˈbɑːnəkl; *AmE* ˈbɑːrn-/ *noun* a small shellfish that attaches itself to objects under water, for example to rocks and the bottoms of ships

'barn dance *noun* an informal social event at which people dance traditional COUNTRY DANCES

'barn owl *noun* a BIRD OF PREY (= a bird that kills other creatures for food) of the OWL family, that often makes its nest in BARNS and other buildings—picture on page A6

barn·storm /ˈbɑːnstɔːm; *AmE* ˈbɑːrnstɔːrm/ *verb* (*especially AmE*) to travel quickly through an area making political speeches, or getting a lot of attention for your organization, ideas, etc: [V] *He barnstormed across the southern states in an attempt to woo the voters.* [also VN]

barn·storm·ing /ˈbɑːnstɔːmɪŋ; *AmE* ˈbɑːrnstɔːrmɪŋ/ *adj.* [only before noun] a **barnstorming** performance or show of skill in a sports game, etc. is one that people find very exciting to watch

barn·yard /ˈbɑːnjɑːd; *AmE* ˈbɑːrnjɑːrd/ *noun* an area on a farm that is surrounded by farm buildings

bar·om·eter /bəˈrɒmɪtə(r); *AmE* -ˈrɑːm-/ *noun* **1** an instrument for measuring air pressure to show when the weather will change: *The barometer is falling* (= showing that it will probably rain). **2** (*written*) something that shows the changes that are happening in an economic, social or political situation: *Infant mortality is a reliable barometer of socio-economic conditions.* ▶ **baro·metric** /ˌbærəˈmetrɪk/ *adj.*: *barometric pressure*

baron /ˈbærən/ *noun* **1** a NOBLEMAN of the lowest rank. In Britain, barons use the title *Lord*; in other countries they use the title *Baron*. **2** a person who owns or controls a large part of a particular industry: *a press baron* ◇ *drug/ oil barons*

bar·on·ess /ˈbærənəs; *AmE* ˌbærəˈnes/ *noun* **1** a woman who has the same rank as a baron. In Britain, baronesses

use the title *Lady* or *Baroness*: *Baroness Thatcher* **2** the wife of a baron

bar·onet /ˈbærənət/ *noun* (*abbr.* **Bart, Bt**) (in Britain) a man who has the lowest rank of honour which can be passed from a father to his son when he dies. Baronets use the title *Sir.*—compare KNIGHT (2)

bar·on·et·cy /ˈbærənətsi/ *noun* (*pl.* **-ies**) the rank or position of a baronet

bar·on·ial /bəˈrəʊniəl; *AmE* -ˈroʊ-/ *adj.* [usually before noun] connected with or typical of a BARON: *a baronial hall*

bar·ony /ˈbærəni/ *noun* (*pl.* **-ies**) **1** the rank or position of a BARON **2** an area of land that is owned and controlled by a BARON

bar·oque (also **Bar·oque**) /bəˈrɒk; *AmE* bəˈroʊk/ *adj.* [usually before noun] used to describe European architecture, art and music of the 17th and early 18th centuries that has a grand and highly decorated style: *baroque churches/music* ◇ *the baroque period* ▶ **bar·oque** (also **Bar·oque**) *noun* [sing.]: *paintings representative of the baroque*

barque /bɑːk; *AmE* bɑːrk/ *noun* a sailing ship with three or more MASTS (= posts that support the sails)

bar·rack /ˈbærək/ *verb* [V, VN] **1** (*BrE*) to shout criticism or protests at players in a game, speakers at a meeting, performers, etc. **2** (*AustralE*) to shout encouragement to a person or team that you support ▶ **bar·rack·ing** *noun* [U]

bar·racks /ˈbærəks/ *noun* [C+sing./pl. v.] (*pl.* **bar·racks**) **1** a large building or group of buildings for soldiers to live in: *an army barracks* ◇ *The troops were ordered back to barracks.* **2** any large ugly building or buildings ▶ **bar·rack** *adj.* [only before noun]: *a barrack unit*

bar·ra·cuda /ˌbærəˈkjuːdə; *AmE* -ˈkuːdə/ *noun* a large fierce fish with sharp teeth, that lives in warm seas

bar·rage /ˈbærɑːʒ; *AmE* bəˈrɑːʒ/ *noun* **1** [C, usually sing.] the continuous firing of a large number of guns in a particular direction, especially to protect soldiers while they are attacking or moving towards the enemy **2** [sing.] ~ (**of sth**) a large number of sth, such as questions or comments, that are directed at sb very quickly, one after the other, often in an aggressive way: *a barrage of questions/criticisms/complaints* **3** /ˈbɑːrɪdʒ/ [C] a wall or barrier built across a river to store water, prevent a flood, etc.

bar·rel /ˈbærəl/ *noun, verb*
■ *noun* **1** a large round container, usually made of wood or metal, with flat ends and, usually, curved sides: *a beer/ wine barrel* **2** the contents of or the amount contained in a barrel; a unit of measurement in the oil industry equal to between 120 and 159 litres: *They got through two barrels of beer.* ◇ *Oil prices fell to $9 a barrel.* **3** the part of a gun like a tube through which the bullets are fired [IDM] **a barrel of 'laughs** (often *ironic*) very amusing; a lot of fun: *Life hasn't exactly been a barrel of laughs lately.* (**get/ have sb) over a barrel** (*informal*) (to put/have sb) in a situation in which they must accept or do what you want: *They've got us over a barrel. Either we agree to their terms or we lose the money.*—more at LOCK *n.*, SCRAPE *v.*
■ *verb* (**-l-**) [V+*adv./prep.*] (*AmE, informal*) to move very fast in a particular direction, especially in a way that you cannot control: *He came barreling down the hill and smashed into a phone booth.*

'barrel organ *noun* a musical instrument that is played by turning a handle, usually played in the streets for money—see also ORGAN-GRINDER

bar·ren /ˈbærən/ *adj.* **1** (of land or soil) not good enough for plants to grow on it: *a barren desert* ◇ *a barren landscape* (= one that is bare, with few plants) **2** (of plants or trees) not producing fruit or seeds **3** (*old-fashioned* or *formal*) (of women or female animals) not able to produce children or young animals [SYN] INFERTILE **4** [usually before noun] not producing anything useful or successful: *The team will come through this barren patch and start to win again.* ▶ **bar·ren·ness** /ˈbærənnəs/ *noun* [U]

bar·rette /bæˈret/ *noun* (*AmE*) = HAIRSLIDE

b	d	f	g	h	k	l	m	n	p	r
bad	did	fall	get	hat	cat	leg	man	now	pen	red

bar·ri·cade /ˌbærɪˈkeɪd/ *noun, verb*
■ *noun* a line of objects placed across a road, etc. to stop people from getting past: *The police stormed the barricades the demonstrators had put up.*
■ *verb* [VN] to defend or block sth by building a barricade: *They barricaded all the doors and windows.* **PHRV barricade yourself in/inside (sth)** to build a barricade in front of you in order to prevent anyone from coming in: *He had barricaded himself in his room.*

bar·rier /ˈbæriə(r)/ *noun* **1** an object like a fence that prevents people from moving forward from one place to another: *The crowd had to stand behind barriers.* ◊ *Show your ticket at the barrier.*—see also CRASH BARRIER **2** ~ **(to sth)** a problem, rule or situation that prevents sb from doing sth, or that makes sth impossible: *the removal of trade barriers* ◊ *Lack of confidence is a psychological barrier to success.* **3** ~ **(between A and B)| ~ (against sth)** something that exists between one thing or person and another and keeps them separate: *The Yangtze river is a natural barrier to the north-east.* ◊ *There was no real barrier between reality and fantasy in his mind.* ◊ *Ozone is the earth's barrier against ultra-violet radiation.* ◊ *the language barrier* (= when people cannot communicate because they do not speak the same language) **4** a particular amount, level or number which it is difficult to get past: *the first player whose earnings passed the $10 million barrier*

barrier 'reef *noun* a line of rock and CORAL in the sea, often not far from the shore

bar·ring /ˈbɑːrɪŋ/ *prep.* except for; unless there is/are: *Barring accidents, we should arrive on time.*

bar·ris·ter /ˈbærɪstə(r)/ *noun* a lawyer in Britain who has the right to argue cases in the higher courts of law ⇨ note at LAWYER

'bar room *noun* a room in which alcoholic drinks are served at a bar: *a topic much discussed in bar rooms across the country* ◊ *a bar-room brawl*

bar·row /ˈbærəʊ; *AmE* -roʊ/ *noun* **1** (*BrE*) a small open vehicle with two wheels from which fruit, vegetables, etc. are sold in the street **2** a large pile of earth built over a place where people were buried in ancient times **3** = WHEELBARROW

Bart /bɑːt; *AmE* bɑːrt/ *abbr.* BARONET

bar·tend·er /ˈbɑːtendə(r); *AmE* ˈbɑːrt-/ *noun* (*especially AmE*) = BARMAID, BARMAN

bar·ter /ˈbɑːtə(r); *AmE* ˈbɑːrt-/ *verb* ~ **sth (for sth)| ~ (with sb) (for sth)** to exchange goods, property, services, etc. for other goods, etc. without using money: [VN] *The local people bartered wheat for farm machinery.* ◊ [V] *The prisoners tried to barter with the guards for items like writing paper and books.* ▶ **bar·ter** *noun* [U]: *The islanders use a system of barter instead of money.*

bas·alt /ˈbæsɔːlt; *AmE* bəˈsɔːlt/ *noun* [U] a type of dark rock that comes from VOLCANOES

base /beɪs/ *noun, verb, adj.*
■ *noun*
  LOWEST PART | **1** [C, usually sing.] the lowest part of sth, especially the part or surface on which it rests or stands: *the base of a column/pyramid/glass* ◊ *a pain at the base of the spine* ◊ *The lamp has a heavy base.*—picture at ARCADE, BED
  ORIGINAL IDEA/SITUATION | **2** [C] an idea, a fact, a situation, etc. from which sth is developed: *She used her family's history as a base for her novel.* ◊ *His arguments have a sound economic base.*
  OF SUPPORT/INCOME/POWER | **3** [C, usually sing.] the people, activity, etc. from which sb gets most of their support, income, power, etc: *The party's main power base is in the agricultural regions.* ◊ *These policies have a broad base of support.* ◊ *an economy with a solid manufacturing base* ◊ *Our business needs to build up its customer base.*
  FIRST/MAIN SUBSTANCE | **4** [C, usually sing.] the first or main part of a substance to which other things are added: *a drink with a rum base* ◊ *Put some moisturizer on as a base before applying your make-up.*
  MAIN PLACE | **5** [C] the main place where you live or stay or

where a business operates from: *I spend a lot of time in Britain but Paris is still my base.* ◊ *The town is an ideal base for touring the area.* ◊ *The company has its base in New York, and branch offices all over the world.*
  OF ARMY/NAVY/AIR FORCE | **6** [C, U] a place where an army, a navy or an air force operates from: *a military/naval base* ◊ *an air base* ◊ *After the attack, they returned to base.*
  CHEMISTRY | **7** [C] a chemical substance, for example an ALKALI, that can combine with an acid to form a salt
  MATHEMATICS | **8** [C, usually sing.] a number on which a system of counting and expressing numbers is built up, for example 10 in the DECIMAL system and 2 in the BINARY system
  IN BASEBALL/ROUNDERS | **9** [C] one of the four positions that a player must reach in order to score points
  —see also DATABASE
  IDM off base (*AmE, informal*) completely wrong about sth: *If that's what you think, you're way off base.*—more at FIRST BASE, TOUCH *v.*
■ *verb* [VN] [usually passive] ~ **sb/sth/yourself in …** to use a particular city, town, etc. as the main place for a business, holiday/vacation, etc: *They decided to base the new company in York.* ◊ *We're going to base ourselves in Tokyo and make trips from there.*
  PHRV 'base sth on/upon sth to use an idea, a fact, a situation, etc. as the point from which sth can be developed: *What are you basing this theory on?*—see also BASED
■ *adj.* (**baser, bas·est**) (*formal*) not having moral principles or rules: *He acted from base motives.* ▶ **base·ly** *adv.*

base·ball /ˈbeɪsbɔːl/ *noun* **1** [U] a game played especially in the US by two teams of nine players, using a bat and ball. Each player tries to hit the ball and then run around four bases before the other team can return the ball: *a baseball bat/team/stadium*—compare ROUNDERS—picture on page 1250 **2** [C] the ball used in this game

'baseball cap *noun* a cap with a long PEAK (= a curved part sticking out in front), originally worn by baseball players—picture at HAT

base·board /ˈbeɪsbɔːd; *AmE* -bɔːrd/ *noun* (*AmE*) = SKIRTING BOARD

based /beɪst/ *adj.* [not before noun] **1** ~ **(on sth)** if one thing is **based** on another, it uses it or is developed from it: *The movie is based on a real-life incident.* ◊ *The report is based on figures from six different European cities.* **2** (also in compounds) if a person or business is **based** in a particular place, that is where they live or work, or where the work of the business is done: *We're based in Chicago.* ◊ *a Chicago-based company* **3** (**-based**) (in compounds) containing sth as an important part or feature: *lead-based paints* ◊ *a class-based society*—see also BROAD-BASED

'base jumping (also **'BASE jumping**) *noun* [U] the sport of jumping with a PARACHUTE from a high place such as a building or a bridge

base·less /ˈbeɪsləs/ *adj.* (*formal*) not supported by good reasons or facts: *The rumours were completely baseless.*

base·line /ˈbeɪslaɪn/ *noun* [usually sing.] **1** (*sport*) a line marking each end of the court in tennis or the edge of the area where a player can run in baseball **2** (*technical*) a line or measurement that is used as a starting point when comparing facts: *The figures for 1999 were used as a baseline for the study.*

base·ment /ˈbeɪsmənt/ *noun* a room or rooms in a building, partly or completely below the level of the ground: *Kitchen goods are sold in the basement.* ◊ *a basement flat/apartment*

base 'metal *noun* a metal that is not a precious metal such as gold

'base rate *noun* (*finance*) a rate of interest, set by a central bank, that banks in Britain use when calculating the amount of interest that they charge on money they lend—compare PRIME RATE

bases 1 *pl.* of BASIS **2** *pl.* of BASE

bash /bæʃ/ *verb, noun*
■ *verb* (*informal*) **1** ~ **(into sb/sth)** to hit sb/sth very hard: [VN] *He bashed her over the head with a hammer.* ◊ [V] *I*

braked too late and bashed into the car in front. **2** [VN] to criticize sb/sth strongly: *Bashing politicians is normal practice in the press.* ◊ *a liberal-bashing administration—* see also BASHING **PHRV** **,bash a'way (on/at sth)| ,bash 'on (with sth)** (*BrE*) to continue working hard at sth: *He sat bashing away at his essay all day.* ◊ *We'll never get finished at this rate. We'd better bash on.* **,bash sth ↔'in** to destroy sth by hitting it very hard and often: *The police bashed the door down.* ◊ *I'll bash your head in if you do that again.* **,bash sth ↔'out** to produce sth quickly and in large quantities, but not of very good quality: *She bashed out about four books a year.* **,bash sb 'up** (*BrE, informal*) to attack sb violently
■ *noun* (*informal*) **1** a hard hit: *He gave Mike a bash on the nose.* **2** a large party or celebration: *a birthday bash* **IDM** **have a bash (at sth)** (*BrE, spoken*) to try to do sth, especially when you are not sure if you will succeed: *I'm not sure I'll be any good but I'll have a bash.*

bash·ful /ˈbæʃfl/ *adj.* shy and easily embarrassed ▶ **bash·ful·ly** /-fəli/ *adv.*: *She smiled bashfully.* **bash·ful·ness** *noun* [U]

bash·ing /ˈbæʃɪŋ/ *noun* [U,C] (often in compounds) **1** (used especially in newspapers) very strong criticism of a person or group: *union-bashing* **2** a physical attack, or a series of attacks, on a person or group of people: *gay-bashing* (= attacking homosexuals) ◊ *to give sb a bashing*

BASIC /ˈbeɪsɪk/ *noun* [U] a simple language, using familiar English words, for writing computer programs

basic /ˈbeɪsɪk/ *adj.* **1 ~ (to sth)** forming the part cf sth that is most necessary and from which other things develop: *basic information/facts/ideas* ◊ *the basic principles of law* ◊ *Drums are basic to African music.* **2** of the simplest kind or at the simplest level: *The campsite provided only basic facilities.* ◊ *My knowledge of French is pretty basic.* **3** [only before noun] necessary and important to all people: *basic human rights* ◊ *the cost of basic foods* **4** before anything extra is added: *The basic pay of the average worker has risen by 3 per cent.*

ba·sic·ally /ˈbeɪsɪkli/ *adv.* **1** in the most important ways, without considering things that are less important: *Yes, that's basically correct.* ◊ *The two approaches are basically very similar.* ◊ *There have been some problems but basically it's a good system.* **2** used when you are giving your opinion or stating what is important about a situation: *Basically, there's not a lot we can do about it.* ◊ *He basically just sits there and does nothing all day.* ◊ *And that's it, basically.*

basics /ˈbeɪsɪks/ *noun* [pl.] **1 ~ (of sth)** the most important and necessary facts, skills, ideas, etc. from which other things develop: *the basics of computer programming* **2** the simplest and most important things that people need in a particular situation: *Some schools lack money for basics like books and pencils.* **IDM** **go/get back to 'basics** to think about the simple or most important ideas within a subject or an activity instead of new ideas or complicated details

basil /ˈbæzl/ *noun* [U] a plant with shiny green leaves that smell sweet and are used in cooking as a herb

ba·sil·ica /bəˈzɪlɪkə/ *noun* a large church or hall with a curved end and two rows of columns inside

basi·lisk /ˈbæzɪlɪsk/ *noun* (in ancient stories) a creature like a snake, that can kill people by looking at them or breathing on them

basin /ˈbeɪsn/ *noun* **1** (*especially BrE*) = WASHBASIN **2** a large round bowl for holding liquids or (in British English) for preparing foods in; the amount of liquid, etc. in a basin: *a pudding basin* **3** an area of land around a large river with streams running down into it: *the Amazon Basin* **4** (*technical*) a place where the earth's surface is lower than in other areas of the world: *the Pacific Basin* **5** a sheltered area of water providing a safe harbour for boats: *a yacht basin*

basis /ˈbeɪsɪs/ *noun* (*pl.* **bases** /ˈbeɪsiːz/) **1** [sing.] the reason why people take a particular action: *She was chosen for the job on the basis of her qualifications and ideas.* ◊ *Some videos have been banned on the basis that they are too violent.* **2** [sing.] the way things are organized

or arranged: *on a regular/permanent/part-time/temporary basis* ◊ *on a daily/day-to-day/weekly basis* **3** [C usually sing, U] the important facts, ideas or events that support sth and that it can develop from: *The basis of a good marriage is trust.* ◊ *This article will form the basis for our discussion.* ◊ *This theory seems to have no basis in fact.*

bask /bɑːsk; *AmE* bæsk/ *verb* [V] **~ (in sth) 1** to enjoy sitting or lying in the heat or light of sth, especially the sun: *We sat basking in the warm sunshine.* **2** to enjoy the good feelings that you have when other people praise or admire you, or when they give you a lot of attention: *He had always basked in his parents' attention, but now things were different.* ◊ *I never minded basking in my wife's reflected glory* (= enjoying the praise, attention, etc. she got).

bas·ket /ˈbɑːskɪt; *AmE* ˈbæs-/ *noun* **1** a container for holding or carrying things. Baskets are made of thin strips of material that bends and twists easily, for example plastic, wood, or wire: *a shopping basket* ◊ *a picnic basket* ◊ *a clothes/laundry basket* (= in which dirty clothes are put before being washed) ◊ *a wicker/wire basket* ◊ *a cat/dog basket* (= in which a cat or dog sleeps or is carried around)—see also WASTE-PAPER BASKET **2** the amount contained in a basket: *a basket of fruit* **3** the net and the metal ring it hangs from, high up at each end of a basketball court; a point that is scored by throwing the ball through this net: *to make/shoot a basket*—picture on page 1250 **4** (*economics*) a number of different goods or CURRENCIES: *the value of the rupee against a basket of currencies* **IDM** see EGG *n.*

bas·ket·ball /ˈbɑːskɪtbɔːl; *AmE* ˈbæs-/ *noun* **1** [U] a game played by two teams of five players, using a large ball which players try to throw into a high net hanging from a ring: *a basketball game/coach/team*—picture on page 1250 **2** [C] the ball used in this game

'basket case *noun* (*informal*) **1** a country or an organization whose economic situation is very bad **2** a person who is slightly crazy and who has problems dealing with situations

bas mitzvah /ˌbæs ˈmɪtsvə/ *noun* = BAT MITZVAH

basque /bɑːsk; bæsk/ *noun* a piece of women's underwear that covers the body from just under the arms to the tops of the legs

bass¹ /beɪs/ *noun, adj.*—see also BASS²
■ *noun* **1** [U] the lowest tone or part in music, for instruments or voices: *He always plays his stereo with the bass turned right up.* ◊ *He sings bass.* ◊ *a pounding bass line*—compare TREBLE **2** [C] a man's singing voice with a low range; a man with a bass voice—compare ALTO, BARITONE, TENOR **3** [sing.] a musical part that is written for a bass voice **4** (also ,bass gui'tar) [C] an electric guitar that plays very low notes: *a bass player* ◊ *bass and drums* ◊ *Jackie Carrera on* (= playing) *bass.* **5** [C] = DOUBLE BASS
■ *adj.* [only before noun] low in tone: *a bass drum/voice* ◊ *the bass clef* (= the symbol in music showing that the notes following it are low)—picture at MUSIC—compare TREBLE

bass² /bæs/ *noun* [C, U] (*pl.* **bass**) a sea or FRESHWATER fish that is used for food: *Fresh sea bass is a great delicacy.*—see also BASS¹

bas·set /ˈbæsɪt/ (also **'basset hound**) *noun* a dog with short legs, a long body and long ears

bas·sinet /ˌbæsɪˈnet/ *noun* a small bed for a baby, that looks like a basket

bass·ist /ˈbeɪsɪst/ *noun* a person who plays the BASS GUITAR or the DOUBLE BASS

bas·soon /bəˈsuːn/ *noun* a musical instrument of the WOODWIND group. It is shaped like a large wooden tube with a double REED that you blow into, and produces notes with a low sound.—picture on page 840

bas·soon·ist /bəˈsuːnɪst/ *noun* a person who plays the bassoon

bas·tard /ˈbɑːstəd; ˈbæs-; *AmE* ˈbæstərd/ *noun* **1** (△, *slang*) used to insult sb, especially a man, who has been rude, unpleasant or cruel: *He's a real bastard.* ◊ *You*

æ	ɑː	e	ɜː	ə	ɪ	iː	i	ɒ	ɔː	ʌ	ʊ	u	uː
cat	father	ten	bird	about	sit	see	many	got	saw	cup	put	actual	too
								(BrE)					

B

bastard! You've made her cry. **2** (*BrE, slang*) a word that some people use about or to sb, especially a man, who they feel very jealous of or sorry for: *What a lucky bastard!* ◇ *You poor bastard!* **3** (*BrE, slang*) used about sth that causes difficulties or problems: *It's a bastard of a problem.* **4** (*old-fashioned, disapproving*) a person whose parents were not married to each other when he or she was born

bas·tard·ize (*BrE* also **-ise**) /ˈbɑːstədaɪz; ˈbæs-; *AmE* ˈbæstərd-/ *verb* [VN] (*formal*) to copy sth, but change parts of it so that it is not as good as the original

baste /beɪst/ *verb* [VN] **1** to pour liquid fat or juices over meat, etc. while it is cooking **2** to sew pieces of fabric together temporarily with long loose stitches

bas·tion /ˈbæstiən/ *noun* **1** (*formal*) a group of people or a system that protects a way of life or a belief when it seems that it may disappear: *a bastion of male privilege* ◇ *a bastion of freedom* **2** a place that military forces are defending

bat /bæt/ *noun, verb*
■ *noun* **1** a piece of wood with a handle, made in various shapes and sizes, and used for hitting the ball in games such as baseball, cricket and table tennis: *a baseball/ cricket bat*—compare RACKET **2** an animal like a mouse with wings, that flies and feeds at night (= it is NOCTURNAL). There are many types of bat.—see also FRUIT BAT, OLD BAT, VAMPIRE BAT—picture on page A6 **IDM** **like a bat out of 'hell** (*informal*) very fast **off your own 'bat** (*BrE, informal*) if you do sth **off your own bat**, it is your own idea and you do it without help or encouragement from anyone else **(right) off the 'bat** (*informal, especially AmE*) immediately; without delay—more at BLIND *adj.*
■ *verb* (**-tt-**) to hit a ball with a bat, especially in a game of cricket or baseball: [V] *He bats very well.* ◇ *Who's batting first for the Orioles?* [also VN]—picture on page 1250 **IDM** ,**bat your 'eyes/'eyelashes** to open and close your eyes quickly, in a way that is supposed to be attractive **bat a 'thousand** (*AmE, informal*) to be very successful **go to 'bat for sb** (*AmE, informal*) to give sb help and support **not bat an 'eyelid** (*BrE*) (*AmE* **not bat an 'eye**) (*informal*) to show no surprise or embarrassment when sth unusual happens: *She didn't bat an eyelid when I told her my news.* **PHRV** ,**bat sth↔a'round** (*informal*) to discuss whether an idea or a plan is good or not, before deciding what to do: *It's just an idea we've been batting around.*

batch /bætʃ/ *noun, verb*
■ *noun* **1** a number of people or things that are dealt with as a group: *Each summer a new batch of students tries to find work.* ◇ *We deliver the goods in batches.* **2** an amount of food, medicine, etc. produced at one time: *a batch of cookies* **3** (*computing*) a set of jobs that are processed together on a computer: *to process a batch job* ◇ *a batch file/program*
■ *verb* to put things into groups in order to deal with them: [VN] *The service will be improved by batching and sorting enquiries.* [also V]

,**batch 'processing** *noun* [U] (*computing*) a way of running a group of programs at the same time, usually automatically

bated /ˈbeɪtɪd/ *adj.* **IDM** **with bated 'breath** (*formal*) feeling very anxious or excited: *We waited with bated breath for the winner to be announced.*

bath /bɑːθ; *AmE* bæθ/ *noun, verb*
■ *noun* (*pl.* **baths** /bɑːðz; *AmE* bæðz/) **1** [C] (*BrE*) (also **bath·tub**, *informal* **tub** *AmE, BrE*) a large, long container that you put water in and then get into to wash your whole body **2** [C] (*BrE*) the water in a bath, ready to use: *a long soak in a hot bath* ◇ *Please run a bath for me* (= fill the bath with water). **3** [C] an act of washing your whole body by sitting or lying in water: *I think I'll have a bath and go to bed.* ◇ (*especially AmE*) *to take a bath*—see also BUBBLE BATH **4** (**baths**) [pl.] (*old-fashioned, BrE*) a public building where you can go to swim—see also SWIMMING BATH, SWIMMING POOL **5** [C, usually pl.] a public place where people went in the past to wash or have a bath: *Roman villas and baths*—see also TURKISH BATH **6** [C] (*technical*) a container with a liquid such as water or a

DYE in it, in which sth is washed or placed for a period of time. Baths are used in industrial, chemical and medical processes.—see also BLOODBATH **IDM** **take a 'bath** (*AmE*) to lose money on a business agreement
■ *verb* (*BrE*) (*AmE* **bathe**) **1** [VN] to give a bath to sb: *It's your turn to bath the baby.* **2** [V] (*old-fashioned*) to have a bath

WHICH WORD?
bath / bathe / swim / sunbathe

When you wash yourself you can say that you **bath** (*BrE*) or **bathe** (*AmE*), but it is much more common to say **have a bath** (*BrE*) or **take a bath** (*AmE*).
You can also **bath** (*BrE*) or **bathe** (*AmE*) another person, for example a baby.
You **bathe** a part of your body, especially to clean a wound.
When you go swimming it is old-fashioned to say that you **bathe**, and you cannot say that you *bath* or *take a bath*. It is more common to **swim, go for a swim, have a swim** or **go swimming**: *Let's go for a quick swim in the pool.* ◇ *She goes swimming every morning before breakfast.* What you wear for this activity is usually called a **swimming costume** in *BrE* and a **bathing suit** in *AmE*.
When you lie in the sun in order to go brown you **sunbathe**. *They spent the day sunbathing and swimming. ~~take a sunbath~~.*

bathe /beɪð/ *verb, noun*
■ *verb* **1** [VN] to wash sth with water, especially a part of your body: *Bathe the wound and apply a clean dressing.* **2** (*AmE*) = BATH: [VN] *Have you bathed the baby yet?* ◇ [V] *I bathe every day.* ⇨ note at BATH **3** [V] (*old-fashioned*) to go swimming in the sea, a river, etc. for enjoyment—see also SUNBATHE **4** [VN] ~ **sth (in sth)** (*literary*) to fill or cover sth with light: *A full moon bathed the countryside in a silver light.*
■ *noun* [sing.] (*BrE, formal*) an act of swimming in the sea, a river, etc: *to go for a bathe*

bathed /beɪðd/ *adj.* ~ **in sth 1** (*literary*) covered with light: *The castle was bathed in moonlight.* **2** wet because covered with sweat or tears: *I was so nervous that I was bathed in perspiration.*

bather /ˈbeɪðə(r)/ *noun* **1** [C] (*BrE*) a person who is swimming in the sea, a river, etc. **2** (**bathers**) [pl.] (*AustralE*) = SWIMMING COSTUME, SWIMMING TRUNKS

bath·ing /ˈbeɪðɪŋ/ *noun* [U] (*BrE*) the activity of going into the sea, a river, etc. to swim: *facilities for bathing and boating* ◇ *a safe bathing beach*

'bathing cap *noun* (*especially AmE*) = SWIMMING CAP

'bathing costume *noun* (*BrE, becoming old-fashioned*) = SWIMMING COSTUME

'bathing suit *noun* (*AmE or old-fashioned*) = SWIMMING COSTUME

'bath mat *noun* **1** a piece of material that you put beside the bath to stand on when you get out **2** a piece of rubber that you put on the bottom of the bath so that you do not slip

bathos /ˈbeɪθɒs; *AmE* -θɑːs/ *noun* [U] (*formal*) (in writing or speech) a sudden change, that is not always intended, from a serious subject or feeling to sth that is silly or not important: *a serious play with moments of comic bathos*

bath·robe /ˈbɑːθrəʊb; *AmE* ˈbæθroʊb/ (also **robe**) *noun* **1** a loose piece of clothing worn before and after taking a bath **2** (*AmE*) = DRESSING GOWN

bath·room /ˈbɑːθruːm; -rʊm; *AmE* ˈbæθ-/ *noun* **1** a room in which there is a bath, a WASHBASIN and often a toilet: *Go and wash your hands in the bathroom.* **2** (*AmE*) a room in which there is a toilet, a SINK and sometimes a bath or shower: *I have to go to the bathroom* (= use the toilet). ◇ *Where's the bathroom?* (= for example in a restaurant) ⇨ note at TOILET

bath·tub /ˈbɑːθtʌb; *AmE* ˈbæθ-/ *noun* (*especially AmE*) = BATH

aɪ	aʊ	eɪ	əʊ	oʊ	ɔɪ	ɪə	eə	ʊə	j	w
my	now	say	go (BrE)	go (AmE)	boy	near	hair	pure	yes	wet

bath·water /ˈbɑːθwɔːtə(r); AmE ˈbæθwɔːtər; -wɑːt-/ noun [U] water in a bath **IDM** see BABY n.

batik /bəˈtiːk/ noun [U, C] a method of printing patterns on fabric using WAX (=a solid substance made from fat or oil) on the parts that will not have any colour; a piece of fabric printed in this way

bat·man /ˈbætmən/ noun (pl. -men /-mən/) (BrE) the personal servant of an officer in the armed forces

bat mitzvah /ˌbæt ˈmɪtsvə/ (also **bas mitzvah**) noun **1** a ceremony and celebration that is held for a Jewish girl between the ages of 12 and 14 at which she accepts the religious responsibilities of an adult **2** the girl who is celebrating this occasion—compare BAR MITZVAH

baton /ˈbætɒn; -tɒ̃; AmE bəˈtɑːn/ noun **1** (especially BrE) = TRUNCHEON: a **baton charge** (= one made by police carrying batons, to force a crowd back) **2** a thin light stick used by the person (called a CONDUCTOR) who is in control of an orchestra, etc.—picture at STICK **3** a small light stick that one member of a team in a RELAY race passes to the next person to run: to pass/hand over the baton ◊ (figurative) The President handed over the baton (= passed responsibility) to his successor.—picture on page 1251 **4** a long stick that is held and thrown in the air by a person marching in front of a band, or by a MAJORETTE

baton round noun (BrE) a rubber or plastic bullet that is fired to control a crowd that has become violent

bats·man /ˈbætsmən/ noun (pl. -men /-mən/) (in cricket) the player who is hitting the ball—picture on page 1250

bat·tal·ion /bəˈtæliən/ noun **1** (BrE) a large group of soldiers that form part of a BRIGADE **2** (written) a large group of people, especially an organized group with a particular purpose: a battalion of supporters

bat·ten /ˈbætn/ noun, verb
■ noun (technical) a long strip of wood that is used to keep other building materials in place on a wall or roof
■ verb **IDM** ˌbatten down the ˈhatches **1** to prepare yourself for a period of difficulty or trouble **2** (on a ship) to firmly shut all the entrances to the lower part, especially because a storm is expected **PHRV** ˌbatten sth↔ˈdown to fix sth firmly in position with wooden boards: He was busy battening down all the shutters and doors. ˈbatten on sb (BrE, disapproving, formal) to live well by using other people's money, etc.

bat·ter /ˈbætə(r)/ verb, noun
■ verb [often passive] ~ (at/on) sth to hit sb/sth hard many times, especially in a way that causes serious damage: [V] She battered at the door with her fists. ◊ [VN] He had been badly battered about the head and face. ◊ Somebody had battered her to death. ◊ Severe winds have been battering the north coast. **PHRV** ˌbatter sth↔ˈdown to hit sth hard many times until it breaks or comes down: The police had to batter the door down.
■ noun **1** [U, C] a mixture of eggs, milk and flour used in cooking to cover food such as fish or chicken before you fry it, or to make PANCAKES **2** [U, C] (AmE) a mixture of eggs, milk, flour, etc. used for making cakes **3** [C] (AmE) (in baseball) the player who is hitting the ball—picture on page 1250

bat·tered /ˈbætəd; AmE -tərd/ adj. **1** old, used a lot, and not in very good condition: a battered old car **2** [usually before noun] attacked violently and injured; attacked and badly damaged by weapons or by bad weather: battered women/children ◊ The child had suffered what has become known as 'battered baby syndrome.' ◊ Rockets and shells continued to hit the battered port.

bat·ter·ing /ˈbætərɪŋ/ noun [U, sing.] a violent attack that injures or damages sb/sth: wife battering ◊ (figurative) The film took a battering from critics in the US.

battering ram noun a long, heavy piece of wood used in war in the past for breaking down doors and walls

bat·tery /ˈbætri; -təri/ noun (pl. -ies) **1** [C] a device that is placed inside a car engine, clock, radio, etc. and that produces the electricity that makes it work: to replace the batteries ◊ a rechargeable battery ◊ battery-powered/-operated ◊ a car battery ◊ The battery is flat (= it is no longer producing electricity). **2** [C] ~ (of sth) (written) a large number of things or people of the same type: He faced a battery of questions. ◊ a battery of reporters **3** [C] (technical) a number of large guns that are used together **4** [C] (BrE) (often used as an adjective) a number of small cages that are joined together and are used for keeping chickens, etc. in on a farm: a battery hen ◊ battery eggs—compare FREE-RANGE **5** [U] (law) the crime of attacking sb physically—see also ASSAULT AND BATTERY **IDM** see RECHARGE

ˈ**battery farm** noun (BrE) a farm where large numbers of chickens or other animals are kept in very small cages or crowded conditions—compare FACTORY FARM, FREE-RANGE ▶ ˈ**battery farming** noun [U]

bat·tle /ˈbætl/ noun, verb
■ noun **1** [C, U] a fight between armies, ships or planes, especially during a war; a violent fight between groups of people: the battle of Waterloo ◊ to be killed **in battle** ◊ a gun battle—see also PITCHED BATTLE **2** [C] ~ (with sb) (for sth) a competition, an argument or a struggle between people or groups of people trying to win power or control: a legal battle for compensation ◊ a battle with an insurance company ◊ a **battle of wits** (= when each side uses their ability to think quickly to try to win) ◊ a **battle of wills** (= when each side is very determined to win) **3** [C, usually sing.] ~ (against/for sth) a determined effort that sb makes to solve a difficult problem or succeed in a difficult situation: her long battle against cancer ◊ to fight an uphill battle against prejudice ◊ a battle for survival **IDM** the battle lines are ˈdrawn used to say that people or groups have shown which side they intend to support in a dispute or contest that is going to begin do ˈbattle (with sb) (over sth) to fight or argue with sb half the ˈbattle the most important or difficult part of achieving sth—more at FIGHT v., JOIN v.
■ verb ~ (with/against sb/sth) (for sth) to try very hard to achieve sth difficult or to deal with sth unpleasant or dangerous: [V] She's still battling with a knee injury. ◊ Both teams battled hard. ◊ The two leaders are battling for control of the government. ◊ I had to battle hard just to stay afloat. ◊ [VN] The two sides will **battle it out** in the final next week. ◊ (AmE) He battled cancer for four years.

battle-axe (BrE) (AmE **battle-ax**) /ˈbætlæks/ noun **1** (informal, disapproving) a fierce and unpleasant older woman **2** a heavy AXE with a long handle, used in the past as a weapon

battle-cruiser /ˈbætlkruːzə(r)/ noun a large fast ship used in war in the past, faster and lighter than a BATTLE-SHIP

ˈ**battle cry** noun **1** a shout that soldiers used to give in battle to encourage their own army or to frighten the enemy **2** a word or phrase used by a group of people who work together for a particular purpose, especially a political one

battle-dress /ˈbætldres/ noun [U] (BrE) the uniform that soldiers wear for training and when they go to fight

battle-field /ˈbætlfiːld/ (also **battle-ground** /ˈbætlgraʊnd/) noun **1** a place where a battle is being fought or has been fought: heavy casualties on the battlefield **2** a subject that people feel strongly about and argue about

battle-ments /ˈbætlmənts/ noun [pl.] a low wall around the top of a castle with spaces in it that people inside could shoot through

ˈ**battle-scarred** adj. a person or place that is battle-scarred has been in a war or fight and shows the signs of injury or damage

battle-ship /ˈbætlʃɪp/ noun a very large ship used in war, with big guns and heavy ARMOUR (= metal plates that cover the ship to protect it)

batty /ˈbæti/ adj. (informal, especially BrE) (of people or ideas) slightly crazy, in a harmless way

bau·ble /ˈbɔːbl/ noun **1** a piece of jewellery that is cheap and has little artistic value **2** (BrE) a decoration for a Christmas tree in the shape of a ball

baulk (BrE) (AmE usually **balk**) /bɔːk/ verb **1** [V] ~ (at sth) to be unwilling to do sth or become involved in sth because it is difficult, dangerous, etc: Many parents may

b	d	f	g	h	k	l	m	n	p	r
bad	did	fall	get	hat	cat	leg	man	now	pen	red

baulk at the idea of paying $100 for a pair of shoes. **2** [V] **~** **(at sth)** (of a horse) to stop suddenly and refuse to jump a fence, etc. **3** [VN] **~ sb (of sth)** [usually passive] (*formal*) to prevent sb from getting sth or doing sth: *She looked like a lion baulked of its prey.*

baux·ite /ˈbɔːksaɪt/ *noun* [U] a soft mineral from which ALUMINIUM/ALUMINUM is obtained

bawdy /ˈbɔːdi/ *adj.* (**bawd·ier, bawd·iest**) (*old-fashioned*) (of songs, plays, etc.) loud, and dealing with sex in an amusing way

bawl /bɔːl/ *verb* **1 ~ (sth) (at sb)** | **~ (sth) (out)** to shout loudly, especially in an unpleasant or angry way: [V] *She bawled at him in front of everyone.* ◊ [VN] *He sat in his office bawling orders at his secretary.* ◊ [Vspeech] '*Get in here now!*' *she bawled.* **2** to cry loudly, especially in an unpleasant and annoying way: [V] *A child was bawling in the next room.* ◊ [VN] *He was bawling his eyes out* (= crying very loudly). [also Vspeech] PHRV ˌbawl sb↔ˈout (*informal*) to speak angrily to sb because they have done sth wrong: *The teacher bawled him out for being late.*

bay /beɪ/ *noun, verb, adj.*

▪ *noun* **1** a part of the sea, or of a large lake, enclosed by a wide curve of the shore: *the Bay of Bengal* ◊ *Hudson Bay* ◊ *a magnificent view across the bay*—picture at COAST **2** a marked section of ground either inside or outside a building, for example for a vehicle to park in, for storing things, etc: *a parking/loading bay* ◊ *Put the equipment in No 3 bay.*—see also SICKBAY **3** a curved area of a room or building that sticks out from the rest of the building **4** a horse of a dark brown colour: *He was riding a big bay.* **5** a deep noise, especially the noise made by dogs when hunting IDM **at ˈbay** when an animal that is being hunted is **at bay**, it must turn and face the dogs and HUNTERS because it is impossible to escape from them **hold/keep sb/sth at ˈbay** to prevent an enemy from coming close or a problem from having a bad effect: *I'm trying to keep my creditors at bay.* ◊ *Charlotte bit her lip to hold the tears at bay.*

▪ *verb* [V] **1** (of a dog or WOLF) to make a long deep sound, especially while hunting: *a pack of baying hounds* **2 ~ (for sth)** (usually used in the progressive tenses) to demand sth in a loud and angry way: *The referee's decision left the crowd baying for blood* (= threatening violence towards him).

▪ *adj.* (of a horse) dark brown in colour: *a bay mare*

ˈbay leaf *noun* the dried leaf of the BAY TREE that is used in cooking as a herb

bay·onet *noun, verb*

▪ *noun* /ˈbeɪənət/ a long, sharp knife that is fastened onto the end of a RIFLE and used as a weapon in battle

▪ *verb* /ˈbeɪənət; ˌbeɪəˈnet/ [VN] to push a bayonet into sb in order to kill them

bayou /ˈbaɪuː/ *noun* a branch of a river in the southern US that moves very slowly and has many plants growing in it

ˈbay tree *noun* a small tree with dark green leaves with a sweet smell that are used in cooking—see also BAY LEAF

ˌbay ˈwindow *noun* a large window, usually with glass on three sides, that sticks out from the outside wall of a house—picture at HOUSE

ba·zaar /bəˈzɑː(r)/ *noun* **1** (in some eastern countries) a street or an area of a town where there are many small shops **2** (in Britain, the US, etc.) a sale of goods, often items made by hand, to raise money for a charity or for people who need help

ba·zooka /bəˈzuːkə/ *noun* a long gun, shaped like a tube, which is held on the shoulder and used to fire rockets at military vehicles

BBC /ˌbiː biː ˈsiː/ *abbr.* British Broadcasting Corporation. The BBC is a national company which broadcasts television and radio programmes and which is paid for by the public and not by advertising: *The news is on BBC1 at 9.* ◊ *BBC Radio 5*

BBQ *abbr.* BARBECUE

BC (*AmE* **B.C.**) /ˌbiː ˈsiː/ *abbr.* before Christ (used in the Christian CALENDAR to show a particular number of years before the year when Christ is believed to have been born): *in* (*the year*) *2000 BC* ◊ *the third century BC*—compare AD, BCE, CE

BCE /ˌbiː siː ˈiː/ (also **B.C.E.** especially in *AmE*) *abbr.* before the Common Era (= before the birth of Christ, when the Christian CALENDAR starts counting years. BCE can be used to give dates in the same way as BC): *in* (*the year*) *2000 BCE* ◊ *the third century BCE*—compare AD, BC, CE

be /bi; *strong form* biː/ *verb, auxiliary verb* ⇨ Appendix 1

▪ *verb* **1** *linking verb* **there is/are** to exist; to be present: *Is there a God?* ◊ *Once upon a time there was a princess…* ◊ *I tried phoning but there was no answer.* ◊ *There's a bank down the road.* ◊ *Was there a pool at the hotel?* **2** [V+adv./prep.] to be situated; to be in a place: *The town is three miles away.* ◊ *If you're looking for your file, it's on the table.* ◊ *Mary's upstairs.* **3** [V+adv./prep.] to happen at a time or in a place: *The party is on Friday evening.* ◊ *The meetings are always in the main conference room.* **4** [V+adv./prep.] to remain in a place: *She has been in her room for hours.* ◊ *They're here till Christmas.* **5** [V+adv./prep.] to attend an event; to be present in a place: *I'll be at the party.* ◊ *He'll be here soon* (= will arrive soon). **6** [V+adv./prep.] (only used in the perfect tenses) to visit or call: *I've never been to Spain.* ◊ *He had been abroad many times.* ◊ (*BrE*) *Has the postman been yet?* ◊ (*AmE*) *Has the mailman come yet?* **7** [V] **~ from …** used to say what sb's native country, home town, etc. is: *She's from Italy.* **8** *linking verb* used when you are naming people or things, describing them or giving more information about them: [V-N] *Today is Monday.* ◊ '*Who is that?*' '*It's my brother.*' ◊ *She's a great beauty.* ◊ *Susan is a doctor.* ◊ *He wants to be* (= become) *a pilot when he grows up.* ◊ [V-ADJ] *It's beautiful!* ◊ *Life is unfair.* ◊ *He is ten years old.* ◊ '*How are you?*' '*I'm very well, thanks.*' ◊ *Be quick!* ◊ [V(that)] *The fact is* (*that*) *we don't have enough money.* ◊ [V-ing, V to inf] *The problem is getting it all done in the time available.* ◊ *The problem is to get it all done in the time available.* **9** *linking verb* **it is/was** used when you are describing a situation or saying what you think about it: [V-ADJ] *It was really hot in the sauna.* ◊ *It's strange how she never comes to see us any more.* ◊ *He thinks it's clever to make fun of people.* ◊ [V-N] *It would be a shame if you lost it.* ◊ *It's going to be a great match.* **10** *linking verb* **it is/was** used to talk about time: [V-N] *It's two thirty.* ◊ [V-ADJ] *It was late at night when we finally arrived.* **11** *linking verb* [V-N] used to say what sth is made of: *Is your jacket real leather?* **12** *linking verb* [V] **~ mine, yours, etc.** | **~ for me, you, etc.** used to say who sth belongs to or who it is intended for: *The money's not yours, it's John's.* ◊ *This package is for you.* **13** *linking verb* [V-N] to cost: '*How much is that dress?*' '*Eighty dollars.*' **14** *linking verb* [V-N] to be equal to: *Three and three is six.* ◊ *How much is a thousand pounds in euros?* ◊ *Let x be the sum of a and b.* ◊ *London is not England* (= do not think that all of England is like London). **15** *linking verb* [V-N] **~ everything, nothing, etc. (to sb)** used to say how important sth is to sb: *Money isn't everything* (= it is not the only important thing). ◊ *A thousand dollars is nothing to somebody as rich as he is.* IDM Most idioms containing **be** are at the entries for the nouns and adjectives in the idioms, for example **be the death of sb** is at **death**. **the ˌbe-all and ˈend-all (of sth)** (*informal*) the most important part; all that matters: *Her career is the be-all and end-all of her existence.* **as/that was** as sb/sth used to be called: *Jill Davis that was* (= before her marriage) ◊ *the Soviet Union, as was* **(he, she, etc. has) been and ˈdone sth** (*BrE, informal*) used to show that you are surprised and annoyed by sth that sb has done: *Someone's been and parked in front of the entrance!*—see also GO AND DO STH **if it wasn't/weren't for …** used to say that sb/sth stopped sb/sth from happening: *If it weren't for you, I wouldn't be alive today.* **ˌleave/ˌlet sb/sth ˈbe** to leave sb/sth alone without disturbing them or it: *Leave her be, she obviously doesn't want to talk about it.* ◊ *Let the poor dog be* (= don't annoy it). **-to-be** (in compounds) future: *his bride-to-be* ◊ *mothers-to-be* (= pregnant women)

▪ *auxiliary verb* **1** used with a past participle to form the passive: *He was killed in the war.* ◊ *Where were they made?*

s	t	v	z	ʃ	ʒ	tʃ	dʒ	θ	ð	ŋ
see	tea	van	zoo	shoe	vision	chain	jam	thin	this	sing

◇ *The house was still being built.* ◇ *You will be told what to do.* **2** used with a present participle to form progressive tenses: *I am studying Chinese.* ◇ *I'll be seeing him soon.* ◇ *What have you been doing this week?* ◇ *I'm always being criticized.* **3** used to make QUESTION TAGS (= short questions added to the end of statements): *You're not hungry, are you?* ◇ *Ben's coming, isn't he?* ◇ *The old theatre was pulled down, wasn't it?* **4** used to avoid repeating the full form of a verb in the passive or a progressive tense: *Karen wasn't beaten in any of her games, but all the others were.* ◇ *'Are you coming with us?' 'No, I'm not.'* **5 ~ to do sth** used to say what must or should be done: *I am to call them once I reach the airport.* ◇ *You are to report this to the police.* ◇ *What is to be done about this problem?* **6 ~ to do sth** used to say what is arranged to happen: *They are to be married in June.* **7 ~ to do sth** used to say what happened later: *He was to regret that decision for the rest of his life* (= he did regret it). **8 ~ not, never, etc. to be done** used to say what could not or did not happen: *Anna was nowhere to be found* (= we could not find her anywhere). ◇ *He was never to see his wife again* (= although he did not know it would be so at the time, he did not see her again). ◇ *She wanted to write a successful novel, but it was not to be* (= it turned out never to happen). **9 if sb/it were to do sth ...| were sb/it to do sth ...** (*formal*) used to express a condition: *If we were to offer you more money, would you stay?* ◇ *Were we to offer you more money, would you stay?*

be- /bɪ-/ *prefix* **1** (in verbs) to make or treat sb/sth as: *Don't belittle his achievements* (= say they are not important). ◇ *An older girl befriended me.* **2** (in adjectives ending in -ed) wearing or covered with: *heavily bejewelled fingers* ◇ *bespattered with mud* **3** (in verbs and adjectives ending in -ed) to cause sth to be: *The ship was becalmed.* ◇ *The rebels besieged the fort.* **4** used to turn INTRANSITIVE verbs (= without an object) into TRANSITIVE verbs (= with an object): *She is always bemoaning her lot.*

beach /biːtʃ/ *noun, verb*
■ *noun* an area of sand, or small stones (called SHINGLE), beside the sea or a lake: *tourists sunbathing on the beach* ◇ *a sandy/pebble/shingle beach* ◇ *a beach bar* ⇨ note and picture at COAST
■ *verb* to come or bring sth out of the water and onto the shore: [VN] *He beached the boat and lifted the boy onto the shore.* ◇ *a beached whale* (= a whale that has become stuck on the shore and cannot get back into the water) [also V]

'beach buggy (also **'dune buggy**) *noun* a small car used for driving on sand

beach·comb·er /'biːtʃkəʊmə(r); *AmE* -koʊm-/ *noun* a person who walks along beaches collecting interesting or valuable things, either for pleasure or to sell

beach·head /'biːtʃhed/ *noun* a strong position on a beach from which an army that has just landed prepares to go forward and attack—see also BRIDGEHEAD

beach·wear /'biːtʃweə(r); *AmE* -wer/ *noun* [U] (used especially in shops/stores) clothes for wearing on the beach

bea·con /'biːkən/ *noun* **1** a light that is placed somewhere to guide vehicles and warn them of danger: *a navigation beacon* ◇ (*figurative*) *He was a beacon of hope for the younger generation.*—see also BELISHA BEACON **2** a radio station whose signal helps ships and aircraft to find their position **3** (in the past) a fire lit on top of a hill as a signal

bead /biːd/ *noun* **1** [C] a small piece of glass, wood, etc. with a hole through it, that can be put on a string with others of the same type and worn as jewellery, etc: *a necklace of wooden beads* ◇ *A bead curtain separated the two rooms.*—see also WORRY BEADS—picture at JEWELLERY **2** (**beads**) [pl.] a ROSARY **3** [C] a small drop of liquid: *There were beads of sweat on his forehead.*

bead·ed /'biːdɪd/ *adj.* **1** decorated with beads: *a beaded dress* **2 ~ with sth** with small drops of a liquid on it: *His face was beaded with sweat.*

bead·ing /'biːdɪŋ/ *noun* [U] **1** a strip of wood, stone or plastic with a pattern on it, used for decorating walls,

doors and furniture **2** BEADS that are sewn together and used as a decoration on clothes

beady /'biːdi/ *adj.* (of eyes) small, round and bright; watching everything closely or with suspicion: (*BrE*) *I shall certainly keep a beady eye on his behaviour.*

bea·gle /'biːgl/ *noun* a small dog with short legs, used in hunting

beak /biːk/ *noun* **1** the hard pointed or curved outer part of a bird's mouth SYN BILL: *The gull held the fish in its beak.*—picture on page A6 **2** (*humorous*) a person's nose, especially when it is large and/or pointed **3** (*old-fashioned, BrE, slang*) a person in a position of authority, especially a judge

beaked /biːkt/ *adj.* (usually in compounds) having a beak, or the type of beak mentioned: *flat-beaked*

bea·ker /'biːkə(r)/ *noun* **1** (*BrE*) a plastic or paper cup, often without a handle, used for drinking from **2** (*BrE*) the amount contained in a beaker: *a beaker of coffee* **3** a glass cup with straight sides and a lip, used in chemistry, for example for measuring liquids—picture at LABORATORY

beam /biːm/ *noun, verb*
■ *noun* **1** a line of light, electric waves or PARTICLES: *narrow beams of light/sunlight* ◇ *the beam of a torch/flashlight* ◇ *a laser/electron beam* ◇ (*BrE*) *The approaching car's headlights were on full beam* (= shining as brightly as possible and not directed downwards). ◇ (*AmE*) *a car with its high beams on* **2** a long piece of wood, metal, etc. used to support weight, especially as part of the roof in a building: *The cottage had an original fireplace and exposed oak beams.* **3** (*especially BrE*) (*AmE* usually **the 'balance beam**) a wooden bar that is used in the sport of GYMNASTICS for people to move and balance on: *The gymnast performed a somersault on the beam.* **4** a wide and happy smile: *a beam of satisfaction* **IDM** **off 'beam** (*informal*) not correct; wrong: *Your calculation is way off beam.*
■ *verb* **1** [no passive] **~** (**sth**) (**at sb**) to have a big happy smile on your face: [V] *He beamed at the journalists.* ◇ *She was positively beaming with pleasure.* ◇ [VN] *The barman beamed a warm smile at her.* ◇ [V speech] *'I'd love to come,' she beamed* (= said with a large smile). **2** [VN+adv./ prep.] to send radio or television signals over long distances using electronic equipment: *Live pictures of the ceremony were beamed around the world.* **3** [V+adv./prep.] to produce a ray of light and/or heat: *The morning sun beamed down on us.* ◇ *Light beamed through a hole in the curtain.* **IDM** see EAR

beamed /biːmd/ *adj.* having beams of wood: *a high beamed ceiling*

bean /biːn/ *noun* **1** a seed, or POD containing seeds, of a climbing plant, eaten as a vegetable. There are several types of beans and the plants that they grow on are also called **beans**: *broad beans* ◇ *runner beans* ◇ *beans* (= BAKED BEANS) *on toast*—picture on page A3 **2** (usually in compounds) a seed from a coffee plant, or some other plants: *coffee/cocoa beans*—see also JELLY BEAN **IDM** **full of 'beans/'life** having a lot of energy **not have a 'bean** (*BrE, informal*) to have no money—more at HILL, SPILL *v.*

bean·bag /'biːnbæg/ *noun* **1** a very large bag made of fabric and filled with small pieces of plastic, used for sitting on **2** a small bag made of fabric filled with dried beans and used as a ball

'bean curd *noun* [U] = TOFU

bean·feast /'biːnfiːst/ *noun* (*old-fashioned, BrE*) a party or celebration

bean·ie /'biːni/ *noun* a small, round close-fitting hat—picture at HAT

bean·pole /'biːnpəʊl; *AmE* -poʊl/ *noun* (*informal*, usually *disapproving*) a tall thin person

'bean sprouts *noun* [pl.] bean seeds that are just beginning to grow, often eaten raw—picture on page A3

bear /beə(r); *AmE* ber/ *verb, noun*
■ *verb* (**bore** /bɔː(r)/ **borne** /bɔːn; *AmE* bɔːrn/)
‣ ACCEPT/DEAL WITH **1** (used with *can/could* in negative sentences and questions) to be able to accept and deal with sth unpleasant SYN STAND: [VN] *The pain was almost more than he could bear.* ◇ *She couldn't bear the thought*

æ	ɑː	e	ɜː	ə	ɪ	iː	i	ɒ	ɔː	ʌ	ʊ	u	uː
cat	father	ten	bird	about	sit	see	many	got	saw	cup	put	actual	too
								(BrE)					

B

of losing him. ◊ [V-ing] *I can't bear having cats in the house.* ◊ [Vtoinf] *How can you bear to eat that stuff?* ◊ [V-ing, Vtoinf] *He can't bear being laughed at.* ◊ *He can't bear to be laughed at.* [alsoVN-ing]

NOT BE SUITABLE | **2** not ~ sth/doing sth to not be suitable for sth: [VN] *Her later work does not bear comparison with her earlier novels* (= because it is not nearly as good). ◊ *The plan won't bear close inspection* (= it will be found to be not satisfactory when carefully examined). ◊ [V-ing] *The joke doesn't bear repeating* (= because it is not funny or may offend people). ◊ *His sufferings don't bear thinking about* (= because they are so terrible).

BE RESPONSIBLE FOR STH | **3** [VN] (*written*) to take responsibility for sth: *She bore the responsibility for most of the changes.* ◊ *Do parents have to bear the whole cost of tuition fees?* ◊ *You shouldn't have to bear the blame for other people's mistakes.*

NEGATIVE FEELING | **4** ~ sth (against/towards sb)| ~ sb sth (*written*) to have a feeling, especially a negative feeling: [VN] *He bears no resentment towards them.* ◊ [VNN] *She bore him no ill will.* ◊ [VN, VNN] *He's borne a grudge against me ever since that day.* ◊ *He's borne me a grudge ever since that day.*

SUPPORT WEIGHT | **5** [VN] to support the weight of sb/sth: *The ice is too thin to bear your weight.*

SHOW | **6** [VN] (*written*) to show sth; to carry sth so that it can be seen: *The document bore her signature.* ◊ *He was badly wounded in the war and still bears the scars.* ◊ *She bears little resemblance to* (= is not much like) *her mother.* ◊ *The title of the essay bore little relation to* (= was not much connected with) *the contents.*

NAME | **7** (*formal*) to have a particular name: *a family that bore an ancient and honoured name*

CARRY | **8** [VN] (*old-fashioned* or *formal*) to carry sb/sth, especially while moving: *three kings bearing gifts*

YOURSELF | **9** [VN] ~ yourself well, etc. (*written*) to move, behave or act in a particular way: *He bears himself* (= stands, walks, etc.) *proudly, like a soldier.* ◊ *She bore herself with dignity throughout the funeral.*

CHILD | **10** (*formal*) to give birth to a child: [VN] *She was not able to bear children.* ◊ [VNN] *She had borne him six sons.*

OF TREES/PLANTS | **11** [VN] (*formal*) to produce flowers or fruit

TURN | **12** [V] ~ (to the) left, north, etc. to go or turn in the direction mentioned: *When you get to the fork in the road, bear right.*

IDM **bear 'arms** (*old use*) to be a soldier; to fight **bear 'fruit** to have a successful result **bear 'hard, 'heavily, se'verely, etc. on sb** (*formal*) to be a cause of difficulty or suffering to sb: *Taxation bears heavily on us all.* **be borne 'in on sb** (*formal, especially BrE*) to be realized by sb, especially after a period of time: *It was gradually borne in on us that defeat was inevitable.* **bring sth to bear (on sb/sth)** (*formal*) to use energy, pressure, influence, etc. to try to achieve sth or make sb do sth: *We must bring all our energies to bear upon the task.* ◊ *Pressure was brought to bear on us to finish the work on time.*—more at CROSS *n.*, BRUNT, GRIN *v.*, MIND *n.*, WITNESS *n.*

PHRV ,**bear 'down on sb/sth 1** (*especially BrE*) to move quickly towards sb/sth in a determined or threatening way **2** (*especially AmE*) to press on sb/sth: *Bear down on it with all your strength so it doesn't move.* '**bear on sth** (*written*) to relate to sth **SYN** AFFECT: *These are matters that bear on the welfare of the community.* ,**bear sb/ sth↔'out** (*especially BrE*) to show that sb is right or that sth is true: *The other witnesses will bear me out.* ◊ *The other witnesses will bear out what I say.* ,**bear 'up (against/under sth)** to remain as cheerful as possible during a difficult time: *He's bearing up well under the strain of losing his job.* ◊ *'How are you?' 'Bearing up.'* '**bear with sb/sth** to be patient with sb/sth: *She's under a lot of strain. Just bear with her.* ◊ *If you will bear with me* (= be patient and listen to me) *a little longer, I'll answer your question.*

■ *noun* **1** a heavy wild animal with thick fur and sharp CLAWS (= pointed parts on the ends of its feet). There are many types of bear: *a black bear*—see also GRIZZLY BEAR,

POLAR BEAR, TEDDY BEAR **2** (*finance*) a person who sells shares in a company, etc., hoping to buy them back later at a lower price: *a bear market* (= in which share prices are falling)—compare BULL—see also BEARISH **IDM like a bear with a sore 'head** (*informal*) bad-tempered

bear·able /ˈbeərəbl; *AmE* ˈber-/ *adj.* a person or thing that is **bearable** can be accepted or dealt with: *She was the only thing that made life bearable.* **OPP** UNBEARABLE

beard /bɪəd; *AmE* bɪrd/ *noun, verb*
■ *noun* [C, U] hair that grows on the chin and cheeks of a man's face; similar hair that grows on some animals: *He has decided to grow a beard and a moustache.* ◊ *a week's growth of beard* ◊ *a goat's beard*—compare MOUSTACHE—picture at HAIR ▶ **beard·ed** *adj.*: *a bearded face/man*
■ *verb* [VN] **IDM to beard the lion in his 'den** to go to see an important or powerful person to tell them that you disagree with them, that you want sth, etc.

bear·er /ˈbeərə(r); *AmE* ˈber-/ *noun* **1** a person whose job it is to carry sth, especially at a ceremony: *coffin bearers*—see also PALL-BEARER, STANDARD-BEARER, STRETCHER-BEARER **2** a person who brings a message, a letter, etc: *I'm sorry to be the bearer of bad news.* **3** (*formal*) a person who has sth with them or is the official owner of sth, such as a document: *A pass will allow the bearer to enter the building.* **4** a person who has knowledge of sth, such as an idea or a tradition, and makes sure that it is not forgotten, by teaching others about it

'**bear hug** *noun* an act of showing affection for sb by holding them very tightly and strongly in your arms

bear·ing /ˈbeərɪŋ; *AmE* ˈber-/ *noun* **1** [U] ~ on sth the way in which sth is related to sth or influences it: *Recent events had no bearing on our decision.* ◊ *Regular exercise has a direct bearing on fitness and health.* **2** [sing.] the way in which you stand, walk or behave: *Her whole bearing was alert.* **3** [C] (*technical*) a direction measured from a fixed point using a COMPASS **4** [C] (*technical*) a part of a machine that supports a moving part, especially one that is turning—see also BALL BEARING **IDM get/find/ take your 'bearings** to make yourself familiar with your surroundings in order to find out where you are or to feel comfortable in a place **lose your 'bearings** to become lost or confused

bear·ish /ˈbeərɪʃ; *AmE* ˈber-/ *adj.* (*finance*) showing or expecting a fall in the prices of SHARES: *a bearish market* ◊ *Japanese banks remain bearish.*—compare BULLISH

bear·skin /ˈbeəskɪn; *AmE* ˈbers-/ *noun* **1** the skin and fur of a bear: *a bearskin rug* **2** a tall hat of black fur worn for special ceremonies by some British soldiers

beast /biːst/ *noun* **1** (*old-fashioned* or *formal*) an animal, especially one that is large or dangerous, or one that is unusual: *wild/savage/ferocious beasts* ◊ *mythical beasts such as unicorns and dragons* **2** a person who is cruel and whose behaviour is uncontrolled **3** (*informal*, often *humorous*) an unpleasant person or thing: *The maths exam was a real beast.* **4** (*informal*) a thing of a particular kind: *My new guitar is a very expensive beast.*

beast·ly /ˈbiːstli/ *adj.* (*old-fashioned, BrE, informal*) unpleasant **SYN** HORRIBLE, NASTY: *Don't be so beastly to him!* ▶ **beast·li·ness** *noun* [U]

,**beast of 'burden** *noun* an animal used for heavy work such as carrying or pulling things

beat /biːt/ *verb, noun, adj.*
■ *verb* (**beat, beaten** /ˈbiːtn/)
IN GAME | **1** [VN] ~ sb (at sth) to defeat sb in a game or competition: *He beat me at chess.* ◊ *Their recent wins have proved they're still the ones to beat* (= the most difficult team to beat).

CONTROL | **2** [VN] to get control of sth **SYN** DEFEAT: *The government's main aim is to beat inflation.*

BE TOO DIFFICULT | **3** to be too difficult for sb **SYN** DEFEAT: [VN] *a problem that beats even the experts* ◊ [VNwh-] *It beats me* (= I don't know) *why he did it.* ◊ *What beats me is how it was done so quickly* (= I don't understand how).

BE BETTER | **4** [VN] to do or be better than sth: *Nothing beats home cooking.* ◊ *You can't beat Italian shoes.* ◊

aɪ	aʊ	eɪ	əʊ	oʊ	ɔɪ	ɪə	eə	ʊə	j	w
my	now	say	go (BrE)	go (AmE)	boy	near	hair	pure	yes	wet

*They want to **beat** the speed record* (= go faster than anyone before).

AVOID | **5** [VN] to avoid sth: *If we go early we should beat the traffic.* ◊ *We were up and off early to **beat the heat**.*

HIT | **6** to hit sb/sth many times, usually very hard:[V, +adv. / prep.] *Somebody was beating at the door.* ◊ *Hailstones beat against the window.* ◊ [VN] [often +adv. / prep.] *Someone was beating a drum.* ◊ *She was beating dust out of the carpet* (= removing dust from the carpet by beating it). ◊ *An elderly man was found **beaten to death**.* ◊ *At that time children were regularly beaten for quite minor offences* (= a punishment). ◊ [VN-ADJ] *They beat him unconscious* (= hit him until he became unconscious).

OF HEART/DRUMS/WINGS | **7** to make, or cause sth to make, a regular sound or movement: [V] *She's alive—her heart is still beating.* ◊ *We heard the drums beating.* ◊ *The bird was **beating** its wings* (= moving them up and down) *frantically.*

MIX | **8** [VN] **~ sth (up)** | **~ A and B together** to mix sth with short quick movements with a fork, etc: *Beat the eggs up to a frothy consistency.* ◊ *Beat the flour and milk together.*

SHAPE METAL | **9 ~ sth (out) (into sth)** to change the shape of sth, especially metal, by hitting it with a hammer, etc: [VN] *beaten silver* ◊ *The gold is beaten out into thin strips.* ◊ [VN-ADJ] *The metal had been beaten flat.*

MAKE PATH | **10** [VN] **~ sth (through, across, along, etc. sth)** to make a path, etc. by walking somewhere or by pressing branches down and walking over them: *a well-beaten track* (= one that has been worn hard by much use) ◊ *The hunters beat a path through the undergrowth.*

IDM **beat about the 'bush** (*BrE*) (*AmE* **beat around the 'bush**) to talk about sth for a long time without coming to the main point: *Stop beating about the bush and tell me what you want.* **beat sb at their own 'game** to defeat or do better than sb in an activity which they have chosen or in which they think they are strong **beat your 'brains out** (*informal, especially AmE*) to think very hard about sth for a long time **beat your 'breast** to show great sadness or guilt, especially in public and in an exaggerated way **beat the 'clock** to finish a task, race, etc. before a particular time **'beat it** (*spoken, slang*) (usually used in orders) to go away immediately: *This is private land, so beat it!* **beat a path to sb's 'door** if a lot of people **beat a path to sb's 'door**, they are all interested in sth that person has to sell, or can do or tell them: *Top theatrical agents are beating a path to the teenager's door.* **beat the 'rap** (*AmE, slang*) to escape without being punished **beat a (hasty) re'treat** to go away or back quickly, especially to avoid sth unpleasant **beat 'time (to sth)** to mark or follow the rhythm of music, by waving a stick, TAPPING your foot, etc: *She beat time with her fingers.* **beat sb to the 'punch** (*informal*) to get or do sth before sb else can **can you beat that/it!** (*spoken*) used to express surprise or anger **if you can't beat them, 'join them** (*saying*) if you cannot defeat sb or be as successful as they are, then it is more sensible to join them in what they are doing and perhaps get some advantage for yourself by doing so **,off the ,beaten 'track** far away from other people, houses, etc: *They live miles off the beaten track.* **a rod/stick to 'beat sb with** a fact, an argument, etc. that is used in order to blame or punish sb **take some 'beating** to be difficult to beat: *That score is going to take some beating.* ◊ *For sheer luxury, this hotel takes some beating.*—more at BLACK *adj.*, DAYLIGHTS, DRUM *n.*, HELL

PHRV **,beat sth↔'down** to hit a door, etc. many times until it breaks open **,beat 'down (on sb/sth)** if the sun **beats down** it shines with great heat **,beat sb/sth 'down (to sth)** to persuade sb to reduce the price at which they are selling sth: *He wanted $8000 for the car but I beat him down to $6000.* ◊ *I beat down the price to $6000.* **,beat 'off** (*AmE,* ⚠, *slang*) to MASTURBATE **,beat sb/sth↔'off** to force sb/sth back or away by fighting: *The attacker was beaten off.* ◊ *She beat off a challenge to her leadership.* **,beat sth↔'out** **1** to produce a rhythm by hitting sth many times **2** to put a fire out by beating: *We beat the flames out.* **3** to remove sth by hitting it with a hammer, etc: *They can beat out the dent in the car's wing.* **'beat sb**

out of sth (*AmE, informal*) to cheat sb by taking sth from them: *Her brother beat her out of $200.* **'beat sb 'to it** to get somewhere or do sth before sb else: *She beat me to the top of the hill.* ◊ *I was about to take the last cake, but he beat me to it.* **,beat sb↔'up** to hit or kick sb hard, many times: *He was badly beaten up by a gang of thugs.* **,beat 'up on sb** (*AmE*) to hit sb hard, especially sb who is young or weak: *I've heard people say he used to beat up on his wife.*

■ *noun*

OF DRUMS/HEART/WINGS | **1** [C] a single blow to sth, such as a drum, or a movement of sth, such as your heart; the sound that this makes: *several loud beats on the drum* ◊ *His heart missed a beat when he saw her.* **2** [sing.] a series of regular blows to sth, such as a drum; the sound that this makes: *the steady beat of the drums*—see also HEART-BEAT

RHYTHM | **3** [C] the main rhythm, or a unit of rhythm, in a piece of music, a poem, etc: *This type of music has a strong beat to it.* ◊ *The piece has four beats to the bar.*

OF POLICE OFFICER | **4** [C] the area which a police officer walks around regularly and which he or she is responsible for: *More police officers out **on the beat** may help to cut crime.*

IDM see HEART, WALK *v.*

■ *adj.* [not before noun] (*informal*) = DEAD BEAT

,beaten-'up *adj.* = BEAT-UP

beat·er /'biːtə(r)/ *noun* **1** (often in compounds) a tool used for beating things: *a carpet beater* ◊ *an egg beater* **2** a person employed to drive birds and animals out of bushes, etc., into the open, so they can be shot for sport **3** (*AmE, informal*) = BANGER—see also WORLD-BEATER

bea·tif·ic /ˌbiːə'tɪfɪk/ *adj.* (*formal*) showing great joy and peace: *a beatific smile / expression*

be·atify /bi'ætɪfaɪ/ *verb* (**be·ati·fies, be·ati·fy·ing, be·ati·fied, be·ati·fied**) [VN] (of the Pope) to give a dead person a special honour by stating officially that he/she is very holy—compare BLESS, CANONIZE ▶ **be·ati·fi·ca·tion** /biˌætɪfɪk'eɪʃn/ *noun* [C, U]

beat·ing /'biːtɪŋ/ *noun* **1** [C] an act of hitting sb hard and repeatedly, as a punishment or in a fight: *to give sb a beating* **2** [C] a very heavy defeat: *The team has taken a few beatings this season.* **3** [U] a series of regular blows to sth such as a drum, or movements of sth, such as your heart; the sound that this makes: *He could hear the beating of his own heart.* ◊ *the beating of drums / wings* **IDM** **take some 'beating** (*BrE*) to be difficult to do or be better than: *As a place to live, Oxford takes some beating.*

beat·nik /'biːtnɪk/ *noun* a young person in the 1950s and early 1960s who rejected the way of life of ordinary society and showed this by behaving and dressing differently from most people

,beat-'up (also **,beaten-'up**) *adj.* [usually before noun] (*informal*) old and damaged: *a beat-up old truck*

beau /bəʊ; *AmE* boʊ/ *noun* (*pl.* **beaux** or **beaus** /bəʊz; *AmE* boʊz/) (*old-fashioned*) a woman's male lover or friend

beaut /bjuːt/ *noun, adj., exclamation*

■ *noun* (*AmE, AustralE, informal*) an excellent or beautiful person or thing

■ *adj., exclamation* (*AustralE, informal*) excellent; very good

beaut·eous /'bjuːtiəs/ *adj.* (*literary*) beautiful

beaut·ician /bjuː'tɪʃn/ *noun* a person, usually a woman, whose job is to give beauty treatments to the face and body

beau·ti·ful /'bjuːtɪfl/ *adj.* **1** having beauty; pleasing to the senses or to the mind: *a beautiful woman / face / baby / voice / poem / smell / evening* ◊ *beautiful countryside / weather / music* **2** very good or skilful: *What beautiful timing!*

beau·ti·ful·ly /'bjuːtɪfli/ *adv.* **1** in a beautiful way: *She sings beautifully.* ◊ *a beautifully decorated house* **2** very well; in a pleasing way: *It's all working out beautifully.*

beaut·ify /'bjuːtɪfaɪ/ *verb* (**beau·ti·fies, beau·ti·fy·ing,**

b	d	f	g	h	k	l	m	n	p	r
bad	did	fall	get	hat	cat	leg	man	now	pen	red

B

beau·ti·fied, beau·ti·fied) [VN] to make sb/sth beautiful or more beautiful

beauty /ˈbjuːti/ noun (pl. -ies) **1** [U] the quality of being pleasing to the senses or to the mind: *the beauty of the sunset/of poetry/of his singing* ◊ *a woman of great beauty* ◊ *The woods were designated an area of outstanding natural beauty.* ◊ *beauty products/treatment* (= intended to make a person more beautiful) **2** [C] a person or thing that is beautiful: *She had been a beauty in her day.* **3** [C] an excellent example of its type: *That last goal was a beauty!* **4** [C] a pleasing feature SYN ADVANTAGE: *One of the beauties of living here is that it's so peaceful.* ◊ *The project will require very little work to start up; that's the beauty of it.* IDM **beauty is in the eye of the ˈbeholder** (*saying*) people all have different ideas about what is beautiful **beauty is only skin-ˈdeep** (*saying*) how sb looks is less important than their character

ˈ**beauty contest** noun (*BrE*) a competition to choose the most beautiful from a group of women—compare PAGEANT

ˈ**beauty mark** noun (*AmE*) = BEAUTY SPOT

ˈ**beauty queen** noun a woman who is judged to be the most beautiful in a BEAUTY CONTEST

ˈ**beauty salon** (also ˈ**beauty parlour**) (*AmE* also ˈ**beauty shop**) noun a place where you can pay for treatment to your face, hair, nails, etc., which is intended to make you more beautiful

ˈ**beauty sleep** noun [U] (*humorous*) enough sleep at night to make sure that you look and feel healthy and beautiful

ˈ**beauty spot** noun **1** (*BrE*) a place in the countryside famous for its beautiful scenery **2** (*AmE* also ˈ**beauty mark**) a small dark spot on a woman's face, which used to be thought to make her more beautiful

beaux pl. of BEAU

bea·ver /ˈbiːvə(r)/ noun, verb

■ noun **1** [C] an animal with a wide flat tail and strong teeth. Beavers live in water and on land and can build DAMS (= barriers across rivers), made of pieces of wood and mud.—see also EAGER BEAVER—picture on page A6 **2** [U] the fur of the beaver, used in making hats and clothes

■ verb PHRV ˌbeaver aˈway (at sth) (*informal*) to work very hard at sth: *He's been beavering away at the accounts all morning.*

bebop /ˈbiːbɒp; *AmE* -baːp/ (also **bop**) noun [U] a type of jazz with complicated rhythms

be·calmed /bɪˈkɑːmd/ adj. (of a ship with a sail) unable to move because there is no wind

be·came pt of BECOME

be·cause /bɪˈkɒz; -ˈkəz; *AmE* -ˈkɔːz; -ˈkʌz/ conj. for the reason that: *I did it because he told me to.* ◊ *Just because I don't complain, people think I'm satisfied.* ▶ **because of** prep.: *They are here because of us.* ◊ *He walked slowly because of his bad leg.* ◊ *Because of his wife('s) being there, I said nothing about it.*

beck /bek/ noun (*BrE*, dialect) a small river SYN STREAM IDM **at sb's ˌbeck and ˈcall** always ready to obey sb's orders: *She is constantly at the beck and call of her invalid father.* ◊ *Don't expect to have me at your beck and call.*

beckon /ˈbekən/ verb **1** ~ **sb** (**to do sth**) to give sb a signal using your finger or hand, especially to tell them to move nearer or to follow you: [V] *He beckoned to the waiter to bring the bill.* ◊ [VN] *He beckoned her over with a wave.* ◊ *The boss beckoned him into her office.* ◊ [VN to inf] *She beckoned him to come and join them.* **2** to appear very attractive to sb: [V] *The clear blue sea beckoned.* ◊ [VN] *The prospect of a month without work was beckoning her.* **3** [V] to be sth that is likely to happen or will possibly happen to sb in the future: *For many kids leaving college the prospect of unemployment beckons.*

be·come /bɪˈkʌm/ verb (**be·came** /bɪˈkeɪm/, **be·come**) **1** linking verb to start to be sth: [V-ADJ] *It was becoming more and more difficult to live on his salary.* ◊ *It soon became apparent that no one was going to come.* ◊ *She was becoming confused.* ◊ [V-N] *She became queen in 1952.* ◊ *The bill will become law next year.* **2** [VN] [no passive] (not

used in the progressive tenses) (*formal*) to be suitable for sb: *Such behaviour did not become her.* **3** [VN] [no passive] (not used in the progressive tenses) (*formal*) to look attractive on sb SYN SUIT: *Short hair really becomes you.* IDM **what became, has become, will become of sb/sth?** used to ask what has happened or what will happen to sb/sth: *What became of that student who used to live with you?* ◊ *I dread to think what will become of them if they lose their home.*

WHICH WORD?

become / get / go / turn ❓

These verbs are used frequently with the following adjectives:

become ~	get ~	go ~	turn ~
involved	used to	wrong	blue
clear	better	right	sour
accustomed	worse	bad	bad
pregnant	pregnant	white	red
extinct	tired	crazy	cold
famous	angry	bald	
ill	dark	blind	

Become is more formal than **get**. Both describe changes in people's emotional or physical state, or natural or social changes.

Go is usually used for negative changes.

Go and **turn** are both used for changes of colour.

Turn is also used for changes in the weather.

---

be·com·ing /bɪˈkʌmɪŋ/ adj. (*formal*) **1** (of clothes, etc.) making the person wearing them look more attractive SYN FLATTERING **2** suitable or appropriate for sb or their situation SYN FITTING: *It was not very becoming behaviour for a teacher.* OPP UNBECOMING

BEd (also **B.Ed.** especially in *AmE*) /ˌbiː ˈed/ noun the abbreviation for 'Bachelor of Education' (a first university degree in education): (*BrE*) *Sarah Wells BEd*

bed /bed/ noun, verb

■ noun
FURNITURE | **1** [C, U] a piece of furniture for sleeping on: *a single/double bed* ◊ *She lay **on the bed** (= on top of the covers).* ◊ *He lay **in bed** (= under the covers).* ◊ *I'm tired—I'm going to bed.* ◊ *It's **time for bed** (= time to go to sleep).* ◊ *I'll just **put** the kids **to bed**.* ◊ *He likes to have a mug of cocoa before bed* (= before going to bed). ◊ *to **get into/out of bed** ◊ to **make the bed** (= arrange the covers in a tidy way)* ◊ *Could you give me a bed for the night* (= somewhere to sleep)? ◊ *There's a shortage of hospital beds* (= not enough room for patients to be admitted). ◊ *He has been **confined to bed** with flu for the past couple of days.*—see also AIR BED, CAMP BED, SOFA BED, TWIN BED, WATERBED

OF RIVER/LAKE/SEA | **2** [C] the bottom of a river, the sea, etc: *the ocean bed* ◊ *oyster beds* (= an area in the sea where there are many OYSTERS)

FOR FLOWERS/VEGETABLES | **3** [C] an area of ground in a garden/yard or park for growing flowers, vegetables, etc: *flower beds*—see also SEEDBED

BOTTOM LAYER | **4** [C] ~ (**of sth**) a layer of sth that other things lie or rest on: *grilled chicken, served on a bed of rice* ◊ *The blocks should be laid on a bed of concrete.*

GEOLOGY | **5** [C] a layer of clay, rock, etc. in the ground—see also BEDROCK

IDM **(not) a bed of ˈroses** (not) an easy or a pleasant situation: *Their life together hasn't exactly been a bed of roses.* **get out of bed on the wrong side** (*BrE*) (*AmE* **get up on the wrong side of the bed**) to be bad-tempered for the whole day for no particular reason **go to bed with sb** (*informal*) to have sex with sb **in bed** used to refer to sexual activity: *What's he like in bed?* ◊ *I caught them in bed together* (= having sex). **you've made your bed and you must ˈlie on it** (*saying*) you must accept the results of your actions **take to your ˈbed** to go to bed and stay there because you are ill/sick—more at DIE v., WET v.

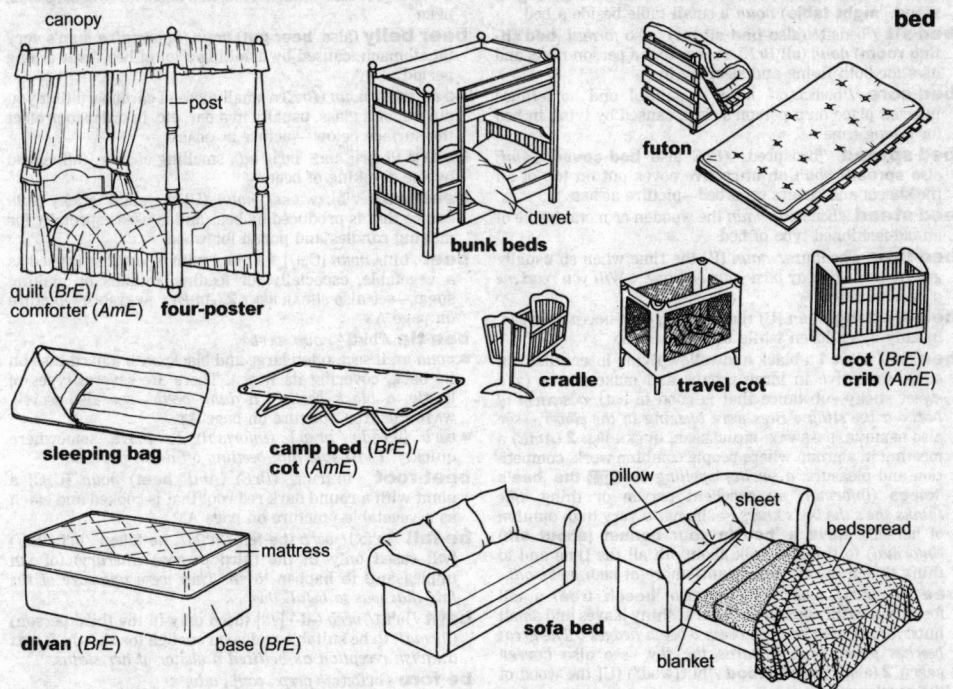

canopy
post
bed

futon

quilt (BrE)/
comforter (AmE) **four-poster**

duvet

bunk beds

cradle   **travel cot**   cot (BrE)/
crib (AmE)

sleeping bag   camp bed (BrE)/
cot (AmE)

pillow
sheet
bedspread

mattress

divan (BrE)   base (BrE)   **sofa bed**   blanket

■ *verb* (-dd-) [VN] **1 ~ sth (in sth)** to fix sth firmly in sth: *The bricks were bedded in sand to improve drainage.* ◊ *Make sure that you bed the roots firmly in the soil.* **2** (*old-fashioned*) to have sex with sb

PHR V **,bed 'down** to sleep in a place where you do not usually sleep: *You have my room and I'll bed down in the living room.*

,bed and 'board *noun* [U] (*BrE*) a room to sleep in and food

,bed and 'breakfast *noun* (*abbr.* **B and B**) **1** [U] (*BrE*) a service that provides a room to sleep in and a meal the next morning in private houses and small hotels: *Do you do bed and breakfast?* ◊ *Bed and breakfast costs £30 a night.*—compare FULL BOARD, HALF BOARD **2** [C] a place that provides this service: *There were several good bed and breakfasts in the area.*

bed·bug /'bedbʌg/ *noun* a small insect that lives in dirty houses, especially in beds, where it bites people and sucks their blood

bed·cham·ber /'bedtʃeɪmbə(r)/ *noun* (*old use*) a bedroom: *the royal bedchamber*

bed·clothes /'bedkləʊðz; *AmE* -kloʊðz/ (*BrE* also **bed-covers**) *noun* [pl.] the sheets and other covers that you put on a bed

bed·cover /'bedkʌvə(r)/ *noun* (*BrE*) **1** = BEDSPREAD **2** (**bedcovers**) = BEDCLOTHES

bed·ding /'bedɪŋ/ *noun* [U] **1** the sheets and covers that you put on a bed, often also the MATTRESS and the PILLOWS **2** STRAW, etc. for animals to sleep on

'bedding plant *noun* a plant that is planted out in a garden bed, usually just before it gets flowers. It usually grows and dies within one year.

be·deck /bɪ'dek/ *verb* [VN] [usually passive] **~ sth/sb (with/in sth)** (*literary*) to decorate sth/sb with flowers, flags, jewels, etc.

be·devil /bɪ'devl/ *verb* (**-ll-**, *AmE* **-l-**) [VN] (*formal*) to cause a lot of problems for sb/sth over a long period of time: *The expedition was bedevilled by bad weather.*

bed·fel·low /'bedfeləʊ; *AmE* -feloʊ/ *noun* a person or a thing that is connected with or related to another, often in a way that you would not expect: *strange/unlikely bedfellows*

bed·head /'bedhed/ *noun* the part of the bed which is at the end, behind the head of the person sleeping on it

bed·lam /'bedləm/ *noun* [U] a scene full of disorder and noise **SYN** CHAOS: *It was bedlam at our house on the morning of the wedding.*

bed·linen /'bedlɪnɪn/ *noun* [U] sheets and PILLOWCASES for a bed

Bed·ouin /'beduɪn/ *noun* (*pl.* **Bed·ouin**) a member of an Arab tribe that traditionally lives in tents in the desert

bed·pan /'bedpæn/ *noun* a container used as a toilet by a person who is too ill to get out of bed

bed·post /'bedpəʊst; *AmE* -poʊst/ *noun* one of the four upright supports at the corners of a bed (especially an old type of bed with a wooden or metal frame)

be·drag·gled /bɪ'drægld/ *adj.* made wet, dirty or untidy by rain, mud, etc: *bedraggled hair/clothes*

bed·rid·den /'bedrɪdn/ *adj.* having to stay in bed all the time because of illness, injury or old age

bed·rock /'bedrɒk; *AmE* -raːk/ *noun* **1** [sing.] a strong base for sth, especially the facts or the principles on which it is based: *The poor suburbs traditionally formed the bedrock of the party's support.* ◊ *Honesty is the bedrock of any healthy relationship.* **2** [U] the solid rock in the ground below the loose soil and sand

bed·room /'bedruːm; -rʊm/ *noun* **1** a room for sleeping in: *the spare bedroom* ◊ *a hotel with 20 bedrooms* **2** (**-bedroomed**) having the number of bedrooms mentioned: *a three-bedroomed house*

'bedroom community (also **'bedroom suburb**) *noun* (both *AmE*) = DORMITORY TOWN

bed·side /'bedsaɪd/ *noun* [usually sing.] the area beside a bed: *His mother has been at his bedside throughout his illness.* ◊ *a bedside lamp*

,bedside 'manner *noun* [sing.] the way in which a doctor or other person talks to sb who is ill

---

æ	ɑː	e	ɜː	ə	ɪ	iː	i	ɒ	ɔː	ʌ	ʊ	u	uː
cat	father	ten	bird	about	sit	see	many	got	saw	cup	put	actual	too
								(BrE)					

B

,bedside 'table (*especially BrE*) (*AmE* usually **night-stand**, 'night table) *noun* a small table beside a bed

bed·sit /'bedsɪt/ (also bed·sit·ter) (also *formal* ,bed'sit-ting room) *noun* (all *BrE*) a room that a person rents and uses for both living and sleeping in

bed·sore /'bedsɔ:(r)/ *noun* a painful and sometimes infected place on a person's skin, caused by lying in bed for a long time

bed·spread /'bedspred/ (*BrE* also bed·cover) (*AmE* also spread) *noun* an attractive cover put on top of all the sheets and covers on a bed—picture at BED

bed·stead /'bedsted/ *noun* the wooden or metal frame of an old-fashioned type of bed

bed·time /'bedtaɪm/ *noun* [U] the time when sb usually goes to bed: *It's way past your bedtime.* ◊ *Will you read me a bedtime story?*

'bed-wetting *noun* [U] the problem of URINATING in bed, usually by children while they are asleep

bee /bi:/ *noun* **1** a black and yellow flying insect that can sting. Bees live in large groups and make HONEY (= a sweet sticky substance that is good to eat): *a swarm of bees* ◊ *a bee sting* ◊ *Bees were buzzing in the clover.*—see also BEEHIVE, BEESWAX, BUMBLEBEE, QUEEN BEE **2** (*AmE*) a meeting in a group where people combine work, competition and pleasure: *a sewing/spelling bee* **IDM** the ,bee's 'knees (*informal*) an excellent person or thing: *She thinks she's the bee's knees* (= she has a very high opinion of herself). have a 'bee in your bonnet (about sth) (*informal*) to think or talk about sth all the time and to think that it is very important—more at BIRD, BUSY *adj.*

beech /bi:tʃ/ *noun* **1** [C, U] (also 'beech tree) a tall forest tree with smooth grey bark, shiny leaves and small nuts: *forests planted with beech* ◊ *beech hedges* ◊ *The great beeches towered up towards the sky.*—see also COPPER BEECH **2** (also 'beech·wood /'bi:tʃwʊd/) [U] the wood of the beech tree

beef /bi:f/ *noun*, *verb*
■ *noun* **1** [U] meat that comes from a cow: *roast/minced beef* ◊ *The farm has both beef and dairy cattle.*—see also CORNED BEEF **2** [C] (*informal*) a complaint: *What's his latest beef?*
■ *verb* [V] ~ (about sb/sth) (*informal*) to complain a lot about sb/sth: *Don't just beef about it—do something!* **PHRV** ,beef sth↔'up (*informal*) to make sth bigger, better, more interesting, etc.

beef·bur·ger /'bi:fbɜ:gə(r); *AmE* -bɜ:rg-/ *noun* (*BrE*) = HAMBURGER

beef·cake /'bi:fkeɪk/ *noun* [U] (*slang*) men with big muscles, especially those that appear in sex shows and magazines

beef·steak /'bi:fsteɪk/ *noun* [C, U] (*rare*) = STEAK

beefy /'bi:fi/ *adj.* (beef·ier, beefi·est) (*informal*) (of a person or their body) big or fat: *beefy men/arms/thighs*

bee·hive /'bi:haɪv/ *noun* **1** = HIVE **2** a style of hair for women, piled high on top of the head

'bee-keeper *noun* a person who owns and takes care of bees ▶ 'bee-keeping *noun* [U]

bee·line /'bi:laɪn/ *noun* **IDM** make a 'beeline for sth/sb (*informal*) to go straight towards sth/sb as quickly as you can

been /bi:n; bɪn; *AmE* bɪn/ *pp* of BE—see also GO

beep /bi:p/ *noun*, *verb*
■ *noun* a short high sound such as that made by a car horn or by electronic equipment
■ *verb* **1** [V] (of an electronic machine) to make a short high sound: *The microwave beeps to let you know when it has finished.* **2** when a car horn, etc. beeps or when you beep it, it makes a short noise: [V] *The car behind started beeping at us.* [VN] *He beeped his horn at the cyclist.* **3** [VN] (*AmE*) = BLEEP

beep·er /'bi:pə(r)/ *noun* (*especially AmE*) = BLEEPER

beer /bɪə(r); *AmE* bɪr/ *noun* **1** [U, C] a bitter alcoholic drink made from MALT and flavoured with HOPS. There are many types of beer: *a barrel/bottle/glass of beer* ◊ *beers brewed in Germany* ◊ *a beer glass* ◊ *Are you a beer drinker?* **2** [C] a glass, bottle or can of beer: *Shall we have*

a beer?—see also GINGER BEER, KEG BEER, ROOT BEER, SMALL BEER

'beer belly (also 'beer gut) *noun* (*informal*) a man's very fat stomach, caused by drinking a lot of beer over a long period

'beer mat *noun* (*BrE*) a small piece of cardboard that you put under a glass, usually in a bar, etc. in order to protect the surface below—picture at GLASS

beery /'bɪəri; *AmE* 'bɪri/ *adj.* smelling of beer; influenced by the drinking of beer

bees·wax /'bi:zwæks/ *noun* [U] a yellow sticky substance that is produced by bees and is used especially for making candles and polish for wood

beet /bi:t/ *noun* [C, U] **1** a plant with a root that is used as a vegetable, especially for feeding animals or making sugar—see also SUGAR BEET **2** (*AmE*) = BEETROOT—picture on page A3

bee·tle /'bi:tl/ *noun*, *verb*
■ *noun* an insect, often large and black, with a hard case on its back, covering its wings. There are several types of beetle: *a black beetle* ◊ *a dung beetle*—see also DEATH-WATCH BEETLE—picture on page A7
■ *verb* [V+adv. / prep.] (*informal*) to move somewhere quickly: *I last saw him beetling off down the road.*

beet·root /'bi:tru:t/ (*BrE*) (*AmE* beet) *noun* [U, C] a plant with a round dark red root that is cooked and eaten as a vegetable—picture on page A3

be·fall /bɪ'fɔ:l/ *verb* (be·fell /bɪ'fel/, be·fallen /bɪ'fɔ:lən/) [VN] (used only in the third person) (*literary*) (of sth unpleasant) to happen to sb: *They were unaware of the fate that was to befall them.*

be·fit /bɪ'fɪt/ *verb* (-tt-) [VN] (used only in the third person) (*formal*) to be suitable and good enough for sb/sth: *It was a lavish reception as befitted a visitor of her status.*

be·fore /bɪ'fɔ:(r)/ *prep.*, *conj.*, *adv.*
■ *prep.* **1** earlier than sb/sth: *before lunch* ◊ *the day before yesterday* ◊ *The year before last he won a gold medal, and the year before that he won a silver.* ◊ *She's lived there since before the war.* ◊ *He arrived before me.* ◊ *She became a lawyer as her father had before her.* ◊ *Leave your keys at reception before departure.* ◊ *Something ought to have been done before now.* ◊ *We'll know before long* (= soon). ◊ *Turn left just before* (= before you reach) *the bank.* **2** (*rather formal*) used to say that sb/sth is in a position in front of sb/sth: *They knelt before the throne.* ◊ *Before you is a list of the points we have to discuss.*—compare BEHIND **3** used to say that sb/sth is ahead of sb/sth in an order or arrangement: *Your name is before mine on the list.* ◊ *He puts his work before everything* (= regards it as more important than anything else). **4** used to say that sth is facing sb in the future: *The task before us is a daunting one.* ◊ *The whole summer lay before me.* **5** in the presence of sb who is listening, watcning, etc: *He was brought before the judge.* ◊ *She said it before witnesses.* ◊ *They had the advantage of playing before their home crowd.* **6** (*formal*) used to say how sb reacts when they have to face sb/sth: *They retreated before the enemy.*
■ *conj.* **1** earlier than the time when: *Do it before you forget.* ◊ *Did she leave a message before she went?* ◊ *Before I made a decision, I thought carefully about it.* **2** until: *It may be many years before the situation improves.* ◊ *It was some time before I realized the truth.* **3** used to warn or threaten sb that sth bad could happen: *Put that away before it gets broken.* **4** (*formal*) rather than: *I'd die before I apologized to them!*
■ *adv.* at an earlier time; in the past; already: *You should have told me so before.* ◊ *It had been fine the week before* (= the previous week). ◊ *That had happened long before* (= a long time earlier). ◊ *I think we've met before.*

be·fore·hand /bɪ'fɔ:hænd; *AmE* -'fɔ:rh-/ *adv.* earlier; before sth else happens or is done: *two weeks/three days/a few hours beforehand* ◊ *I wish we'd known about it beforehand.*

be·friend /bɪ'frend/ *verb* [VN] (usually passive) to become a friend of sb, especially sb who has just arrived in a place or who needs your help: *Shortly after my arrival at the school, I was befriended by an older girl.*

aɪ	aʊ	eɪ	əʊ	oʊ	ɔɪ	ɪə	eə	ʊə	j	w
my	now	say	go (BrE)	go (AmE)	boy	near	hair	pure	yes	wet

be·fud·dled /bɪˈfʌdld/ *adj.* confused and unable to think normally: *He was befuddled by drink.*

beg /beg/ *verb* (**-gg-**) **1 ~ (sb) (for sth)|~ (sth) (of/from sb)** to ask sb for sth especially in an anxious way because you want or need it very much: [VN] *They begged him for help.* ◊ *I managed to beg a lift from a passing motorist.* ◊ *She begged permission to leave.* ◊ [V] *He wants to see them beg for mercy.* ◊ (*formal*) *Don't leave me here, I beg of you!* ◊ [VNtoinf] *She begged him not to go.* ◊ [Vtoinf] *He begged to be told the truth.* ◊ [Vspeech] *'Give me one more chance,' he begged.* ◊ [Vthat] (*formal*) *She begged that she be allowed to go.* ◊ (*BrE* also) *She begged that she should be allowed to go.* [alsoVNspeech] **2 ~ (for sth) (from sb)| ~ sth (from sb)** to ask sb for money, food, etc., especially in the street: [V] *London is full of homeless people begging in the streets.* ◊ *The children went from door to door begging for food.* ◊ *a begging letter* (= one that asks sb for money) ◊ [VN] *We managed to beg a meal from the cafe owner.* **3** [V] if a dog **begs**, it sits on its back legs with its front legs in the air, waiting to be given sth IDM **beg 'leave to do sth** (*formal*) to ask sb for permission to do sth **be going 'begging** (*BrE, spoken*) if sth **is going begging**, it is available because nobody else wants it **beg sb's 'pardon** (*formal, especially BrE*) to ask sb to forgive you for sth you have said or done **beg the 'question 1** to make sb want to ask a question that has not yet been answered: *All of which begs the question as to who will fund the project.* **2** to talk about sth as if it were definitely true, even though it might not be: *These assumptions beg the question that children learn languages more easily than adults.* **I beg to differ** used to say politely that you do not agree with sth that has just been said **I beg your pardon** (*spoken*) **1** (*formal*) used to tell sb that you are sorry for sth you have said or done: *I beg your pardon, I thought that was my coat.* **2** used to ask sb to repeat what they have just said because you did not hear: *'It's on Duke Street.' 'I beg your pardon.' 'Duke Street.'* **3** (*especially BrE*) used to tell sb that you are offended by what they have just said or by the way that they have said it: *'Get me a drink.' 'I beg your pardon!'* PHRV **,beg 'off** to say that you are unable to do sth that you have agreed to do: *He's always begging off at the last minute.*

began *pt of* BEGIN

beget /bɪˈget/ *verb* (**be·get·ting, begot, begot** /bɪˈgɒt; *AmE* -gɑːt/ HELP In sense 1 **begat** /bɪˈgæt/ is used for the past tense, and **be·got·ten** /bɪˈgɒtn; *AmE* -ˈgɑːtn/ is used for the past participle.) [VN] **1** (old use, for example in the Bible) to become the father of a child: *Isaac begat Jacob.* **2** (*formal* or *old-fashioned*) to make sth happen: *Violence begets violence.* ▶ **be·get·ter** *noun*

beg·gar /ˈbegə(r)/ *noun, verb*
■ *noun* **1** a person who lives by asking people for money or food **2** (*BrE, spoken*) used with an adjective to describe sb in a particular way: *Aren't you dressed yet, you lazy beggar?* IDM **,beggars can't be 'choosers** (*saying*) people say **beggars can't be choosers** when there is no choice and sb must be satisfied with what is available
■ *verb* [VN] to make sb/sth very poor: *Why should I beggar myself for you?* IDM **beggar be'lief/de'scription** to be too extreme, shocking, etc. to believe/describe: *It beggars belief how things could have got this bad.*

begin /bɪˈgɪn/ *verb* (**be·gin·ning, began** /bɪˈgæn/, **begun** /bɪˈgʌn/) **1** to start doing sth; to do the first part of sth: [VN] *We began work on the project in May.* ◊ *I began* (= started reading) *this novel last month and I still haven't finished it.* ◊ *He always begins his lessons with a warm-up exercise.* ◊ *She began by thanking us all for coming.* ◊ *He began his political career as a student* (= when he was a student). ◊ [V] *Shall I begin?* ◊ *Let's begin at page 9.* ◊ [Vtoinf] *I began to feel dizzy.* ◊ *At last the guests began to arrive.* ◊ *She began to cry.* ◊ *It was beginning to snow.* ◊ *I was beginning to think you'd never come.* ◊ [V-ing] *Everyone began talking at once.* ◊ *When will you begin recruiting?* **2** [V] to start to happen or exist, especially from a particular time: *When does the concert begin?* ◊ *Work on the new bridge is due to begin in September.* ◊ *The evening began well.* **3 ~ as sth** [V] to be sth first, before becoming sth else: *He began as an actor, before starting to direct*

films. ◊ *What began as a minor scuffle turned into a full-scale riot.* **4** [V] to have sth as the first part or the point where sth starts: *Use 'an' before words beginning with a vowel.* ◊ *'I'm thinking of a country in Asia.' 'What does it begin with* (= what is the first letter)*?'* ◊ *Each chapter begins with a quotation.* ◊ *Where does Europe end and Asia begin?* ◊ *The path begins at Livingston village.* **5** [Vspeech] to start speaking: *'Ladies and gentlemen,' he began, 'welcome to the Town Hall.'* **6** to start or make sth start for the first time: [V] *The school began in 1920, with only ten pupils.* ◊ [VN] *He began a new magazine on post-war architecture.* **7** [Vtoinf] **not ~** to make no attempt to do sth or have no chance of doing sth: *I can't begin to thank you enough.* ◊ *He didn't even begin to understand my problem.* IDM **to be'gin with 1** at first: *I found it tiring to begin with but I soon got used to it.* ◊ *We'll go slowly to begin with.* **2** used to introduce the first point you want to make: *'What was it you didn't like?' 'Well, to begin with, our room was far too small.'*—more at CHARITY

be·gin·ner /bɪˈgɪnə(r)/ *noun* a person who is starting to learn sth and cannot do it very well yet: *She's in the beginners' class.* IDM **beginner's 'luck** good luck or unexpected success when you start to do sth new

be·gin·ning /bɪˈgɪnɪŋ/ *noun* **1** [C, usually sing.] **~ (of sth)** the time when sth starts; the first part of an event, a story, etc: *We're going to Japan at the beginning of July.* ◊ *She's been working there since the beginning of last summer.* ◊ *We missed the beginning of the movie.* ◊ *Let's start again from the beginning.* ◊ *The birth of their first child marked the beginning of a new era in their married life.* ◊ *I've read the whole book from beginning to end and still can't understand it.* HELP At the **beginning (of)** is used for the time and place when something begins. **In the beginning** = **at first** and suggests a contrast with a later situation. **2** (**beginnings**) [pl.] the first or early ideas, signs or stages of sth: *Did democracy have its beginnings in ancient Greece?* ◊ *He built up his multimillion pound music business from small beginnings.* IDM **the beginning of the 'end** the first sign of sth ending

be·gone /bɪˈgɒn; *AmE* -ˈgɔːn; -ˈgɑːn/ *exclamation* (*old use*) a way of telling sb to go away immediately

be·go·nia /bɪˈgəʊniə; *AmE* -ˈgoʊ-/ *noun* a plant with large shiny flowers that may be pink, red, yellow or white, grown indoors or in a garden

begot *pt of* BEGET

be·got·ten *pp of* BEGET

be·grudge /bɪˈgrʌdʒ/ *verb* (often used in negative sentences) **1** to feel unhappy that sb has sth because you do not think that they deserve it: [VNN] *You surely don't begrudge him his happiness.* ◊ [VN-ing] *I don't begrudge her being so successful.* **2** to feel unhappy about having to do, pay or give sth: [VN] *I begrudge every second I spent trying to help him.* ◊ [V-ing] *Many people begrudge paying so much money for a second-rate service.*

B

be·grudg·ing·ly /brɪˈgrʌdʒɪŋli/ adv. (rare) = GRUDGINGLY

be·guile /brɪˈgaɪl/ verb [VN] (formal) **1 ~ sb (into doing sth)** to trick sb into doing sth, especially by being nice to them: *She beguiled them into believing her version of events.* **2** to attract or interest sb: *He was beguiled by her beauty.* **3** to make time pass pleasantly by doing sth enjoyable: *They sang songs to beguile the long winter evenings.*

be·guil·ing /brɪˈgaɪlɪŋ/ adj. (formal) attractive and interesting but sometimes mysterious or trying to trick you: *beguiling advertisements* ◊ *Her beauty was beguiling.* ▶ **be·guil·ing·ly** adv.

begum /ˈbeɪgəm/ noun a title of respect used for a Muslim woman of high rank and for a married Muslim woman: *Begum Zia*

begun pp of BEGIN

be·half /brɪˈhɑːf; AmE brɪˈhæf/ noun [IDM] **in behalf of sb | in sb's behalf** (AmE) in order to help sb: *We collected money in behalf of the homeless.* **on behalf of sb | on sb's behalf** (AmE) **1** as the representative of sb or instead of them: *On behalf of the department I would like to thank you all.* ◊ *Mr Knight cannot be here, so his wife will accept the prize on his behalf.* **2** because of sb; for sb: *Don't worry on my behalf.* **3** in order to help sb: *They campaigned on behalf of asylum seekers.*

be·have /brɪˈheɪv/ verb **1** [V+adv./prep.] to do things in a particular way [SYN] ACT: *The doctor behaved very unprofessionally.* ◊ *They behaved very badly towards their guests.* ◊ *He behaved like a true gentleman.* ◊ *She behaved with great dignity.* ◊ *He behaved as if/though nothing had happened.* ◊ *They behave differently when you're not around.* [HELP] In spoken English people often use **like** instead of **as if** or **as though**, especially in AmE: *He behaved like nothing had happened.* This is considered incorrect in written BrE. **2 ~ (yourself)** to do things in a way that people think is correct or polite: [V] *Will you kids just behave!* ◊ *She doesn't know how to behave in public.* ◊ [VN] *I want you to behave yourselves while I'm away.* [OPP] MISBEHAVE **3 (-behaved)** (in adjectives) behaving in the way mentioned: *well-/badly-behaved children* **4** [V+adv./prep.] (technical) to naturally react, move, etc. in a particular way: *a study of how metals behave under pressure* [IDM] see OWN v.

be·hav·iour (BrE) (AmE **be·hav·ior**) /brɪˈheɪvjə(r)/ noun **1** [U] the way that sb behaves, especially towards other people: *good/bad behaviour* ◊ *social/sexual/criminal behaviour* ◊ *His behaviour towards her was becoming more and more aggressive.* **2** [U, C] the way a person, an animal, a plant, a chemical, etc. behaves or functions in a particular situation: *the behaviour of insects/dolphins/chromosomes* ◊ *studying human and animal behaviour* ◊ *(technical) to study learned behaviours and attitudes* ▶ **be·hav·iour·al** (BrE) (AmE **be·hav·ior·al**) /-ˈjərəl/ adj.: *children with behavioural difficulties* ◊ *behavioural science* (= the study of human behaviour) [IDM] **be on your best be'haviour** to behave in the most polite way you can

be·hav·iour·ism (BrE) (AmE **be·hav·ior·ism**) /brɪˈheɪvjərɪzəm/ noun [U] (psychology) the theory that all human behaviour is learnt by adapting to outside conditions and that learning is not influenced by thoughts and feelings ▶ **be·hav·iour·ist** (BrE) (AmE **be·hav·ior·ist**) /-jərɪst/ noun

be·head /brɪˈhed/ verb [VN] [usually passive] to cut off sb's head, especially as a punishment

be·held pt, pp of BEHOLD

be·hest /brɪˈhest/ noun [sing.] [IDM] **at sb's be'hest** (old use or formal) because sb has ordered or requested it

be·hind /brɪˈhaɪnd/ prep., adv., noun
▪ prep. **1** at or towards the back of sb/sth, and often hidden by it or them: *Who's the girl standing behind Jan?* ◊ *Stay close behind me.* ◊ *a small street behind the station* ◊ *She glanced behind her.* ◊ *Don't forget to lock the door behind you* (= when you leave). ◊ *The sun disappeared behind the clouds.*—compare IN FRONT OF ⇨ note at BACK **2** making less progress than sb/sth: *He's behind the rest of the class in reading.* ◊ *We're behind schedule* (= late). **3** giving sup-

port to or approval of sb/sth: *She knew that, whatever she decided, her family was right behind her.* **4** responsible for starting or developing sth: *What's behind that happy smile* (= what is causing it)? ◊ *He was the man behind the plan to build a new hospital.* **5** used to say that sth is in sb's past: *The accident is behind you now, so try to forget it.* ◊ *She has ten years' useful experience behind her.*
▪ adv. **1** at or towards the back of sb/sth; further back: *She rode off down the road with the dog running behind.* ◊ *The others are a long way behind.* ◊ *He was shot from behind as he ran away.* ◊ *I had fallen so far behind that it seemed pointless trying to catch up.* **2** in the place where sb/sth is or was: *I was told to* **stay behind** *after school* (= remain in school). ◊ *This bag was* **left behind** *after the class.* **3 ~ (with/in sth)** late in paying money or completing work: *She's* **fallen behind** *with the payments.* ◊ *He was terribly behind in his work.*
▪ noun (informal) a person's bottom. People often say 'behind' to avoid saying 'bottom'. [SYN] BACKSIDE: *The dog bit him on his behind.*

be·hold /brɪˈhəʊld; AmE brɪˈhoʊld/ verb (**be·held** /brɪˈheld/, **be·held**) [VN] (old use or literary) to look at or see sb/sth: *Her face was a joy to behold.* ◊ *They beheld a bright star shining in the sky.* [IDM] see LO

be·holden /brɪˈhəʊldən; AmE brɪˈhoʊld-/ adj. **~ to sb (for sth)** (formal) owing sth to sb because of sth that they have done for you: *She didn't like to be beholden to anyone.*

be·hold·er /brɪˈhəʊldə(r); AmE brɪˈhoʊld-/ noun [IDM] see BEAUTY

be·hove /brɪˈhəʊv; AmE brɪˈhoʊv/ (BrE) (AmE **be·hoove** /brɪˈhuːv/) verb [VN to inf] (**it behoves sb to do sth**) (formal) it is right or necessary for sb to do sth: *It behoves us to study these findings carefully.*

beige /beɪʒ/ adj. light yellowish-brown in colour ▶ **beige** noun [U]

being /ˈbiːɪŋ/ noun **1** [U] existence: *The Irish Free State came into being in 1922.* ◊ *A new era was brought into being by the fall of Communism.*—see also WELL-BEING **2** [C] a living creature: *human beings* ◊ *a strange being from another planet* **3** [U] (formal) your mind and all of your feelings: *I hated Stefan with my whole being.*—see also BE v.

be·jew·elled (BrE) (AmE **be·jew·eled**) /brɪˈdʒuːəld/ adj. (literary) decorated with jewels; wearing jewels

be·la·bour (BrE) (AmE **be·la·bor**) /brɪˈleɪbə(r)/ verb [VN] [IDM] **belabour the 'point** (formal) to repeat an idea, argument, etc. many times to emphasize it, especially when it has already been mentioned or understood: *I don't want to belabour the point, but it's vital you understand how important this is.*

be·lated /brɪˈleɪtɪd/ adj. coming or happening late: *a belated birthday present* ▶ **be·lated·ly** adv.

belay /ˈbiːleɪ; brɪˈleɪ/ verb [V, VN] (technical) (in climbing) to attach a rope to a rock, etc.; to make a person safe while climbing by attaching a rope to the person and to a rock, etc.

belch /beltʃ/ verb **1** [V] to let air come up noisily from your stomach and out through your mouth: *He wiped his hand across his mouth, then belched loudly.*—compare BURP **2** [V, VN] **~ (out/forth) (sth)** to send out large amounts of smoke, flames, etc.; to come out of sth in large amounts ▶ **belch** noun: *He sat back and gave a loud belch.*

be·lea·guered /brɪˈliːgəd; AmE -gərd/ adj. **1** (formal) experiencing a lot of criticism and difficulties: *The beleaguered party leader was forced to resign.* **2** surrounded by an enemy: *supplies for the beleaguered city*

bel·fry /ˈbelfri/ noun (pl. -ies) a tower in which bells hang, especially as part of a church

belie /brɪˈlaɪ/ verb (**be·lies, be·ly·ing, be·lied, be·lied**) [VN] (formal) **1** to give a false impression of sb/sth: *Her energy and youthful good looks belie her 65 years.* **2** to show that sth cannot be true or correct: *Government claims that there is no poverty are belied by the number of homeless people on the streets.*

be·lief /brɪˈliːf/ noun **1** [U] **~ (in sth/sb)** a strong feeling

s	t	v	z	ʃ	ʒ	tʃ	dʒ	θ	ð	ŋ
see	tea	van	zoo	shoe	vision	chain	jam	thin	this	sing

that sth/sb exists or is true; confidence that sth/sb is good or right: *I admire his passionate belief in what he is doing.* ◊ *belief in God/democracy* **2** [sing., U] ~ **(that …)** an opinion about sth; sth that you think is true: *She acted in the belief that she was doing good.* ◊ *Contrary to popular belief* (= in spite of what people may think)*, he was not responsible for the tragedy.* ◊ *There is a general belief that things will soon get better.* **3** [C, usually pl.] something that you believe, especially as part of your religion: *religious/political beliefs*—compare DISBELIEF, UNBELIEF **IDM** **beyond be'lief** (in a way that is) too great, difficult, etc. to be believed: *Dissatisfaction with the government has grown beyond belief.* ◊ *icy air that was cold beyond belief*—more at BEGGAR *v.*, BEST *n.*

be·liev·able /bɪˈliːvəbl/ *adj.* that can be believed **SYN** PLAUSIBLE: *Her explanation certainly sounded believable.* ◊ *a play with believable characters* **OPP** UNBELIEVABLE

be·lieve /bɪˈliːv/ *verb* (not used in the progressive tenses)
FEEL CERTAIN | **1** to feel certain that sth is true or that sb is telling you the truth: [VN] *I don't believe you!* ◊ *I believed his lies for years.* ◊ *The man claimed to be a social worker and the old woman believed him.* ◊ *I find that hard to believe.* ◊ *Believe me, she's not right for you.* ◊ *Don't believe a word of it* (= don't believe any part of what sb is saying)*.* ◊ [V(**that**)] *People used to believe (that) the earth was flat.* ◊ *He refused to believe (that) his son was involved in drugs.*
THINK POSSIBLE | **2** to think that sth is true or possible, although you are not completely certain: [V(**that**)] *Police believe (that) the man may be armed.* ◊ [VN(**that**)] *It is believed that the couple have left the country.* ◊ [VNtoinf] *The vases are believed to be worth over $20000 each.* ◊ [V] *'Where does she come from?' 'Spain, I believe.'* ◊ *'Does he still work there?' 'I believe so/not.'* ◊ [VN-ADJ] *Three sailors are missing, believed drowned.*
HAVE OPINION | **3** [V(**that**)] to have the opinion that sth is right or true: *The party believes (that) education is the most important issue facing the government.*
BE SURPRISED/ANNOYED | **4** (**don't/can't** ~ **sth**) used to say that you are surprised or annoyed at sth: [V(**that**)] *She couldn't believe (that) it was all happening again.* ◊ [Vwh-] *I can't believe how much better I feel.*
RELIGION | **5** [V] to have a religious faith: *The god appears only to those who believe.*
IDM **believe it or 'not** (*spoken*) used to introduce information that is true but that may surprise people: *Believe it or not, he asked me to marry him!* **believe (you) 'me** (*spoken*) used to emphasize that you strongly believe what you are saying: *You haven't heard the last of this, believe you me!* **don't you be'lieve it!** (*spoken*) used to tell sb that sth is definitely not true **I don't be'lieve it!** (*spoken*) used to say that you are surprised or annoyed about sth: *I don't believe it! What are you doing here?* **if you believe that, you'll believe 'anything** (*spoken*) used to say that you think sb is stupid if they believe that sth is true **make believe (that …)** to pretend that sth is true—related noun MAKE-BELIEVE **not believe your 'ears/'eyes** (*spoken*) to be very surprised at sth you hear/see: *I couldn't believe my eyes when she walked into the room.* **seeing is be'lieving** (*saying*) used to say that sb will have to believe that sth is true when they see it, although they do not think it is true now **would you be'lieve (it)?** (*spoken*) used to show that you are surprised and annoyed about sth: *And, would you believe, he didn't even apologize!* **you/you'd better be'lieve it!** (*spoken*) used to tell sb that sth is definitely true: *'He's not a bad player, is he?' 'You'd better believe it!'*—more at GIVE *v.*
PHR V **be'lieve in sb/sth** to feel certain that sb/sth exists: *Do you believe in God?* **be'lieve in sb** to feel that you can trust sb and/or that they will be successful: *They need a leader they can believe in.* **be'lieve in sth** to think that sth is good, right or acceptable: [+ -ing] *I don't believe in hitting children.* **be'lieve sth of sb** to think that sb is capable of sth: *Are you sure he was lying? I can't believe that of him.*

be·liever /bɪˈliːvə(r)/ *noun* a person who believes in the existence or truth of sth, especially sb who believes in a god or religious faith **OPP** UNBELIEVER **IDM** **be a (great/ firm) believer in sth** to believe strongly that sth is good, important or valuable

Be·li·sha bea·con /bəˌliːʃə ˈbiːkən/ *noun* (in Britain) a post with an orange flashing light on top marking a place where cars must stop to allow people to cross the road

be·lit·tle /bɪˈlɪtl/ *verb* [VN] to make sb or the things that sb does seem unimportant: *She felt her husband constantly belittled her achievements.*

bell /bel/ *noun* **1** a hollow metal object, often shaped like a cup, that makes a ringing sound when hit by a small piece of metal inside it; the sound that it makes: *A peal of church bells rang out in the distance.* ◊ *a bicycle bell* ◊ *His voice came down the line as clear as a bell.* **2** an electrical device which makes a ringing sound when a button on it is pushed; the sound that it makes, used as a signal or a warning: *Ring the bell to see if they're in.* ◊ *The bell's ringing!* ◊ *The bell went for the end of the lesson.* ◊ *An alarm bell went off.* ◊ *Warning bells started ringing in her head as she sensed that something was wrong.* **IDM** **give sb a 'bell** (*BrE*, *informal*) to call sb by telephone—more at ALARM *n.*, PULL *v.*, RING *v.*, SOUND *adj.*

bella·donna /ˌbeləˈdɒnə; *AmE* -ˈdɑːnə/ *noun* [U] **1** = DEADLY NIGHTSHADE **2** a poisonous drug made from DEADLY NIGHTSHADE

'bell-bottoms *noun* [pl.] trousers/pants with legs that become very wide below the knee

bell·boy /ˈbelbɔɪ/ (*especially AmE*) (*AmE* also **bell·hop** /ˈbelhɒp; *AmE* -hɑːp/) *noun* = PAGEBOY (1)

belle /bel/ *noun* (*old-fashioned*) a beautiful woman; the most beautiful woman in a particular place

bel·li·cose /ˈbelɪkəʊs; -kəʊz; *AmE* -koʊs; -koʊz/ *adj.* (*formal*) having or showing a desire to argue or fight **SYN** AGGRESSIVE, WARLIKE ▶ **bel·li·cos·ity** /ˌbelɪˈkɒsəti; *AmE* -ˈkɑːs-/ *noun* [U]

-bellied ⇨ BELLY

bel·liger·ent /bəˈlɪdʒərənt/ *adj.*, *noun*
■ *adj.* **1** unfriendly and aggressive **SYN** HOSTILE: *a belligerent attitude* **2** [only before noun] (*formal*) (of a country) fighting a war: *the belligerent countries/states/nations* ▶ **bel·liger·ence** /-əns/ *noun* [U] **bel·liger·ent·ly** *adv.*
■ *noun* (*formal*) a country or group that is fighting a war

bel·low /ˈbeləʊ; *AmE* -loʊ/ *verb* **1** ~ **(sth) (at sb)** to shout in a loud deep voice, especially because you are angry: [V] *They bellowed at her to stop but it was too late.* ◊ [VN] *The coach bellowed instructions from the sidelines.* [also V speech] **2** [V] when a large animal such as a BULL bellows, it makes a loud deep sound ▶ **bel·low** *noun*: *to let out a bellow of rage/pain*

bel·lows /ˈbeləʊz; *AmE* -loʊz/ *noun* [C+sing./pl. *v.*] a piece of equipment for blowing air into or through sth. Bellows are used for making a fire burn better or for producing sound in some types of musical instruments: *a pair of bellows* (= a small bellows with two handles to be pushed together)

'bell pepper *noun* (*AmE*) = PEPPER

'bell-push *noun* (*BrE*) a button that you press to make an electric bell ring

'bell-ringer (also **ringer**) *noun* a person who rings church bells as a hobby ▶ **'bell-ringing** *noun* [U] —see also CAMPANOLOGIST, CAMPANOLOGY

,bells and 'whistles *noun* [pl.] (*especially computing*) attractive extra features

belly /ˈbeli/ *noun*, *verb*
■ *noun* (*pl.* **-ies**) **1** the part of the body below the chest **SYN** STOMACH, GUT: *They crawled along on their bellies.*—see also BEER BELLY, POT BELLY **2** (*literary*) the round or curved part of an object: *the belly of a ship* **3** (*-bellied*) (in adjectives) having the type of belly mentioned: *swollen-bellied* ◊ *round-bellied*
■ *verb* (**bel·lies**, **belly·ing**, **bel·lied**, **bel·lied**) [V] ~ **(out)** (especially of sails) to fill with air and become rounder

belly·ache /ˈbeliˌeɪk/ *noun*, *verb*
■ *noun* [C, U] (*informal*) a pain in the stomach: *I've got (a) bellyache.*

æ	ɑː	e	ɜː	ə	ɪ	iː	i	ɒ	ɔː	ʌ	ʊ	u	uː
cat	father	ten	bird	about	sit	see	many	got	saw	cup	put	actual	too

(BrE)

■ *verb* [V] (*informal*) to complain a lot about sth in an annoying or unreasonable way

'belly button *noun* (*informal*) = NAVEL

'belly dance *noun* a dance, originally from the Middle East, in which a woman moves her belly and hips around ▶ **'belly dancer** *noun*

belly·flop /'belɪflɒp/ *AmE* -flɑːp/ *noun* (*informal*) a bad DIVE into water, in which the front of the body hits the water flat

belly·ful /'belɪfʊl/ *noun* **IDM** **have had a 'bellyful of sb/sth** (*informal*) to have had more than enough of sb/sth, so that you cannot deal with any more: *I've had a bellyful of your moaning.*

be·long /bɪ'lɒŋ; *AmE* -lɔːŋ/ *verb* (not used in the progressive tenses) **1** [V+*adv./prep.*] to be in the right or suitable place: *Where do these plates belong* (= where are they kept)? ◊ *Are you sure these documents belong together?* **2** [V] to feel comfortable and happy in a particular situation or with a particular group of people: *I don't feel as if I belong here.* ▶ **be·long·ing** *noun* [U]: *to feel a sense of belonging* **PHRV** **be'long to sb 1** to be owned by sb: *Who does this watch belong to?* ◊ *The islands belong to Spain.* **2** an event, a competition, etc. that **belongs to** sb is one in which they are the most successful or popular: *British actors did well at the award ceremony, but the evening belonged to the Americans.* **be'long to sth 1** to be a member of a club, an organization, etc: *Have you ever belonged to a political party?* **2** to be part of a particular group type, or system: *Lions and tigers belong to the cat family.*

be·long·ings /bɪ'lɒŋɪŋz; *AmE* -'lɔːŋ-/ *noun* [pl.] the things that you own which can be moved, for example not land or buildings: *insurance of property and personal belongings* ◊ *She packed her few belongings in a bag and left.*

be·loved *adj., noun*
■ *adj.* (*written*) **1** /bɪ'lʌvd/ ~ **by/of sb** loved very much by sb; very popular with sb: *these purple flowers so beloved by artists* **2** /bɪ'lʌvɪd/ [only before noun] loved very much: *in memory of our dearly beloved son, John*
■ *noun* /bɪ'lʌvɪd/ (*old use* or *literary*) a person who is loved very much by sb: *It was a gift from her beloved.*

below /bɪ'ləʊ; *AmE* bɪ'loʊ/ *prep., adv.*
■ *prep.* **1** at or to a lower level or position than sb/sth: *He dived below the surface of the water.* ◊ *Please do not write below this line.* ◊ *Skirts will be worn below* (= long enough to cover) *the knee.* **2** of a lower amount or standard than sb/sth: *The temperatures remained below freezing all day.* ◊ *Her work was well below average for the class.* **3** of a lower rank or of less importance than sb/sth: *A police sergeant is below an inspector.* ◊ *They're two places below Chelsea in the table.* ⇨ note at UNDER
■ *adv.* **1** at or to a lower level, position or place: *They live on the floor below.* ◊ *I could still see the airport buildings far below.* ◊ *See below* (= at the bottom of the page) *for references.* ◊ *The passengers who felt seasick stayed below* (= on a lower deck). **2** (of a temperature) lower than zero: *The thermometer had dropped to a record 40 below* (= −40 degrees). **3** at a lower rank: *This ruling applies to the ranks of Inspector and below.*

belt /belt/ *noun, verb*
■ *noun* **1** a long narrow piece of leather, fabric, etc. that you wear around the waist: *to do up/fasten/tighten a belt* ◊ *a belt buckle*—see also BLACK BELT, LIFEBELT, SEAT BELT, SUSPENDER BELT—pictures on pages A4 and A5 **2** a continuous band of material that moves round and is used to carry things along or to drive machinery—see also CONVEYOR BELT, FAN BELT **3** an area with particular characteristics or where a particular group of people live: *the country's corn/industrial belt* ◊ *We live in the commuter belt.* ◊ *a belt of rain moving across the country*—see also GREEN BELT **4** (*informal*) an act of hitting sth/sb hard: *She gave the ball a terrific belt.* **IDM** **below the 'belt** (of a remark) unfair or cruel: *That was distinctly below the belt!* **,belt and 'braces** (*informal*) taking more actions than are really necessary to make sure that sth succeeds or works as it should: *a belt-and-braces policy* **have sth**

under your 'belt (*informal*) to have already achieved or obtained sth: *She already has a couple of good wins under her belt.*—more at TIGHTEN
■ *verb* **1** [VN] (*informal*) to hit sb/sth hard: *He belted the ball right out of the park.* ◊ *I'll belt you if you do that again.* **2** [V+*adv./prep.*] (*informal, especially BrE*) to move very fast: *A truck came belting up behind us.* **3** [VN] to fasten a belt around sth: *The dress was belted at the waist.* **PHRV** **,belt sth↔'out** (*informal*) to sing a song or play music loudly: *Nobody can belt out a tune like she can.* **,belt 'up** (*BrE*) **1** (*AmE* **,buckle 'up**) (*informal*) to fasten your SEAT BELT (= a belt worn by a passenger in a vehicle) **2** (*spoken*) used to tell sb rudely to be quiet: *Just belt up, will you!*

belt·ed /'beltɪd/ *adj.* with a belt around it: *a belted jacket*

belt·way /'beltweɪ/ *noun* (*AmE*) a RING ROAD, especially the one around Washington DC

be·moan /bɪ'məʊn; *AmE* bɪ'moʊn/ *verb* [VN] (*formal*) to complain or say that you are not happy about sth: *They sat bemoaning the fact that no one would give them a chance.*

be·mused /bɪ'mjuːzd/ *adj.* showing that you are confused and unable to think clearly: *a bemused expression/ smile* ▶ **be·mus·ed·ly** *adv.*

bench /bentʃ/ *noun* **1** [C] a long seat for two or more people, usually made of wood: *a park bench*—picture at CHAIR **2** (**the bench**) [sing.] (*law*) a judge in a court of law or the seat where he/she sits; the position of being a judge or MAGISTRATE: *His lawyer turned to address the bench.* ◊ *She has recently been appointed to the bench.* **3** [C, often pl.] (in the British Parliament) a seat where a particular group of politicians sit: *There was cheering from the Opposition benches.*—see also BACK BENCH, THE FRONT BENCH **4** (**the bench**) [sing.] (*sport*) the seats where players sit when they are not playing in the game: *the substitutes' bench* **5** [C] = WORKBENCH: *a carpenter's bench*

bench·mark /'bentʃmɑːk; *AmE* -mɑːrk/ *noun* something which can be measured and used as a standard that other things can be compared with: *Tests at the age of seven provide a benchmark against which the child's progress at school can be measured.*

bend /bend/ *verb, noun*
■ *verb* (**bent, bent** /bent/) **1** [often +*adv./prep.*] (especially of sb's body or head) to lean, or make sth lean, in a particular direction: [V] *He bent and kissed her.* ◊ *fields of poppies bending in the wind* ◊ *His dark head bent over her.* ◊ *She bent forward to pick up the newspaper.* ◊ *Slowly bend from the waist and bring your head down to your knees.* ◊ [VN] *He bent his head and kissed her.* ◊ *She was bent over her desk writing a letter.* **2** if you **bend** your arm, leg, etc. or if it **bends**, you move it so that it is no longer straight: [VN] *Bend your knees, keeping your back straight.* ◊ [V] *Lie flat and let your knees bend.* **3** [VN] to force sth that was straight into an angle or a curve: *Mark the pipe where you want to bend it.* ◊ *The knives were bent out of shape.* ◊ *He bent the wire into the shape of a square.* **4** to change direction to form a curve or an angle; to make sth change direction in this way: [V] *The road bent sharply to the right.* ◊ [VN] *Glass and water both bend light.* **IDM** **bend sb's 'ear (about sth)** (*informal*) to talk to sb a lot about sth, especially about a problem that you have **bend your 'mind/'efforts to sth** (*formal*) to think very hard about or put a lot of effort into one particular thing **bend the 'truth** to say sth that is not completely true **on bended 'knee(s)** if you ask for sth **on bended knee(s)**, you ask for it in a very anxious and of HUMBLE way—more at BACKWARDS, RULE *n.* **PHRV** **'bend sb to sth** (*formal*) to force or persuade sb to do what you want or to accept your opinions: *He manipulates people and tries to bend them to his will* (= make them do what he wants).
■ *noun* **1** [C] a curve or turn, especially in a road or river: *a sharp bend in the road*—see also HAIRPIN BEND **2** (**the bends**) [pl.] severe pain and difficulty in breathing experienced by a DIVER who comes back to the surface of the water too quickly **IDM** **round the bend/twist** (*informal, especially BrE*) crazy: *She's gone completely round the bend.* ◊ *The children have been driving me round the bend today* (= annoying me very much).

bend·er /'bendə(r)/ *noun* (*slang*) a period of drinking a lot of alcohol or taking a lot of drugs: *to go on a bender*

bendy /'bendi/ *adj.* (*BrE, informal*) **1** that can be bent easily SYN FLEXIBLE **2** with many bends: *a bendy road*

be·neath /bɪ'niːθ/ *prep.* (*formal*) **1** in or to a lower position than sb/sth; under sb/sth: *They found the body buried beneath a pile of leaves.* ◊ *The boat sank beneath the waves.* **2** not good enough for sb: *He considers such jobs beneath him.* ◊ *They thought she had married beneath her* (= married a man of lower social status). ⇨ note at UNDER ▶ **be·neath** *adv.*: *Her careful make-up hid the signs of age beneath.*

Bene·dic·tine /ˌbenɪ'dɪktɪn/ *noun* a member of a Christian group of MONKS or NUNS following the rules of St Benedict ▶ **Bene·dic·tine** *adj.*: *a Benedictine monastery*

bene·dic·tion /ˌbenɪ'dɪkʃn/ *noun* [C, U] (*formal*) a Christian prayer of BLESSING

bene·fac·tion /ˌbenɪ'fækʃn/ *noun* [C] (*formal*) a gift, usually of money, that is given to a person or an organization in order to do good

bene·fac·tor /'benɪfæktə(r)/ *noun* (*formal*) a person who gives money or other help to a person or an organization such as a school or charity

bene·fice /'benɪfɪs/ *noun* the paid position of a Christian priest in charge of a PARISH

be·nefi·cent /bɪ'nefɪsnt/ *adj.* (*formal*) giving help; showing kindness SYN GENEROUS: *the beneficent powers of Nature* ▶ **be·nefi·cence** /bɪ'nefɪsns/ *noun* [U]

bene·fi·cial /ˌbenɪ'fɪʃl/ *adj.* ~ (**to sth/sb**) (*written*) improving a situation; having a helpful or useful effect SYN FAVOURABLE, ADVANTAGEOUS: *a good diet is beneficial to health*

bene·fi·ciary /ˌbenɪ'fɪʃəri; *AmE* -'fɪʃieri/ *noun* (*pl.* **-ies**) ~ (**of sth**) **1** a person who gains as a result of sth: *Who will be the main beneficiary of the cuts in income tax?* **2** a person who receives money or property when sb dies

bene·fit /'benɪfɪt/ *noun, verb*
- *noun* **1** [U, C] an advantage that sth gives you; a helpful and useful effect that sth has: *I've had the benefit of a good education.* ◊ *The new regulations will be of benefit to everyone concerned.* ◊ *It will be to your benefit to arrive early.* ◊ *He couldn't see the benefit of arguing any longer.* ◊ *the benefits of modern medicine* ◊ *It was good to see her finally reaping the benefits* (= enjoying the results) *of all her hard work.*—see also COST-BENEFIT, FRINGE BENEFIT **2** [U, C] (*BrE*) money provided by the government to people who need financial help because they are unemployed, ill, etc.—see also CHILD BENEFIT, HOUSING BENEFIT, SICKNESS BENEFIT **3** [C, usually pl.] advantages that you get from a company in addition to the money that you earn; money from an insurance company: *The insurance plan will provide substantial cash benefits to your family in case of your death.*—see also FRINGE BENEFIT **4** [C] an event such as a performance, a dinner, etc., organized in order to raise money for a particular person or charity: *a benefit match/concert* IDM **for sb's benefit** especially in order to help or be useful to sb: *I have typed out some lecture notes for the benefit of those people who were absent last week.* ◊ *Don't go to any trouble for my benefit!* **give sb the ˌbenefit of the 'doubt** to accept that sb has told the truth or has not done sth wrong because you cannot prove that they have not
- *verb* (**-t-** or **-tt-**) **1** [VN] to be useful to sb or improve their life in some way: *We should spend the money on something that will benefit everyone.* **2** [V] ~ (**from/by sth**) to be in a better position because of sth: *Who exactly stands to benefit from these changes?*

be·nevo·lent /bə'nevələnt/ *adj.* **1** (*formal*) (especially of people in authority) kind, helpful and generous: *a benevolent smile/attitude* ◊ *belief in the existence of a benevolent god* OPP MALEVOLENT **2** used in the names of some organizations that give help and money to people in need: *the RAF Benevolent Fund* ▶ **be·nevo·lence** /bə'nevələns/ *noun* [U] **be·nevo·lent·ly** *adv.*

Ben·gali /beŋ'ɡɔːli/ *noun* **1** [C] a person from Bangladesh or West Bengal **2** [U] the language of people from Bangladesh or West Bengal ▶ **Ben·gali** *adj.*

be·night·ed /bɪ'naɪtɪd/ *adj.* (*old-fashioned*) **1** (of people) without understanding **2** (of places) without the benefits of modern life

be·nign /bɪ'naɪn/ *adj.* **1** (*formal*) (of people) kind and gentle; not causing any harm **2** (*medical*) (of TUMOURS growing in the body) not dangerous or likely to cause death—compare MALIGNANT ▶ **be·nign·ly** *adv.*: *He smiled benignly.*

bent /bent/ *adj., noun*—see also BEND, BENT, BENT
- *adj.* **1** not straight: *a piece of bent wire* ◊ *Do this exercise with your knees bent* (= not with your legs straight).—picture at CURL **2** (of a person) not able to stand up straight, usually because of old age or disease: *a small bent old woman* ◊ *He was bent double with laughter.* **3** (*BrE, informal*) (of a person in authority) dishonest IDM **be 'bent on sth/on doing sth** to be determined to do sth (usually sth bad): *She seems bent on making life difficult for me.*—see also HELL-BENT
- *noun* [usually sing.] ~ (**for sth**) a natural skill or interest in sth: *She has a bent for mathematics.*

ben·zene /'benziːn/ *noun* [U] a colourless liquid obtained from PETROLEUM and COAL TAR, used in making plastics and many chemical products

be·queath /bɪ'kwiːð/ *verb* ~ **sth (to sb)**| ~ **(sb) sth** (*formal*) **1** to say in a WILL that you want sb to have your property, money, etc. after you die: [VN, VNN] *He bequeathed his entire estate to his daughter.* ◊ *He bequeathed his daughter his entire estate.* **2** [VN, VNN] to leave the results of your work, knowledge, etc. for other people to use, especially after you have died

be·quest /bɪ'kwest/ *noun* (*formal*) money or property that you ask to be given to a particular person when you die: *He left a bequest to each of his grandchildren.*

be·rate /bɪ'reɪt/ *verb* [VN] (*formal*) to criticize or speak angrily to sb because you do not approve of sth they have done

be·reave /bɪ'riːv/ *verb* [VN] (**be bereaved**) if sb is bereaved, a relative or close friend has just died: *The ceremony was an ordeal for those who had been recently bereaved.*

be·reaved /bɪ'riːvd/ *adj.* (*formal*) **1** having lost a relative or close friend who has recently died: *recently bereaved families* **2** (**the bereaved**) *noun* (*pl.* **the bereaved**) a person who is bereaved: *an organization offering counselling for the bereaved*

be·reave·ment /bɪ'riːvmənt/ *noun* **1** [U] the state of having lost a relative or close friend because they have died: *the pain of an emotional crisis such as divorce or bereavement* **2** [C] the death of a relative or close friend: *A family bereavement meant that he could not attend the conference.*

be·reft /bɪ'reft/ *adj.* [not before noun] (*formal*) **1** ~ **of sth** completely lacking sth; having lost sth: *bereft of ideas/hope* **2** (of a person) sad and lonely because you have lost sth: *He was utterly bereft when his wife died.*

beret /'bereɪ; *AmE* bə'reɪ/ *noun* a round flat cap made out of soft fabric and with a tight band around the head—picture at HAT

berk /bɜːk; *AmE* bɜːrk/ *noun* (*BrE, slang, disapproving*) a stupid person

Bermuda shorts /bə,mjuːdə 'ʃɔːts; *AmE* bər,m-; 'ʃɔːrts/ (also **Ber·mu·das** /bə'mjuːdəz; *AmE* bər'm-/) *noun* [pl.] SHORTS (= short trousers/pants) that come down to just above the knee: *a pair of Bermudas*

berry /'beri/ *noun* (*pl.* **-ies**) (often in compounds) a small fruit that grows on a bush. There are several types of berry, some of which can be eaten: *Birds feed on nuts and berries in the winter.* ◊ *blackberries/raspberries*—picture on page A2

ber·serk /bə'zɜːk; -'sɜːk; *AmE* bər'zɜːrk; -'sɜːrk/ *adj.* [not usually before noun] very angry: *He went berserk when he found out where I'd been.*

berth /bɜːθ; *AmE* bɜːrθ/ *noun, verb*
- *noun* **1** a place to sleep on a ship or train, or in a CARAVAN /CAMPER: *a cabin with three berths* **2** a place where a ship or boat can stop and stay, usually in a harbour: *a berth in dock* IDM see WIDE *adj.*

b	d	f	g	h	k	l	m	n	p	r
bad	**did**	**fall**	**get**	**hat**	**cat**	**leg**	**man**	**now**	**pen**	**red**

■ *verb* to put a ship in a berth or keep it there; to sail into a berth:[VN] *The ship is berthed at Southampton.* [also V]

be·seech /bɪ'siːtʃ/ *verb* (**be·sought**, **be·sought** /bɪ'sɔːt/) or (**be·seeched**, **be·seeched**) (*formal*) to ask sb for sth in an anxious way because you want or need it very much [SYN] IMPLORE, BEG: [VN] *Let him go, I beseech you!* [also VN to inf, V]

be·seech·ing /bɪ'siːtʃɪŋ/ *adj.* [only before noun] (*formal*) (of a look, tone of voice, etc.) showing that you want sth very much ▶ **be·seech·ing·ly** *adv.*

beset /bɪ'set/ *verb* (**be·set·ting**, **beset**, **beset**) [VN] [usually passive] (*formal*) to affect sb/sth in an unpleasant or harmful way: *The team had been beset by injury all season.* ◇ *It's one of the most difficult problems besetting our modern way of life.*

be·side /bɪ'saɪd/ *prep.* **1** next to or at the side of sb/sth: *He sat beside her all night.* ◇ *a mill beside a stream* **2** compared with sb/sth: *My painting looks childish beside yours.* [IDM] **be'side yourself (with sth)** unable to control yourself because of the strength of emotion you are feeling: *He was beside himself with rage when I told him what I had done.*

WHICH WORD?
beside / besides

The preposition **beside** usually means 'next to something/somebody' or 'at the side of something/somebody': *Sit here beside me.* **Besides** means 'in addition to something': *What other sports do you play besides hockey?* Do not use **beside** with this meaning.
The adverb **besides** is not usually used on its own with the same meaning as the preposition. It is mainly used to give another reason or argument for something: *I don't think I'll come on Saturday. I have a lot of work to do. Besides, I don't really like parties.* ◇ *She likes football. Besides, she likes tennis and basketball.*

---

be·sides /bɪ'saɪdz/ *prep., adv.*

■ *prep.* in addition to sb/sth; apart from sb/sth: *We have lots of things in common besides music.* ◇ *Besides working as a doctor, he also writes novels in his spare time.* ◇ *I've got no family besides my parents.* ⇨ note at BESIDE

■ *adv.* **1** used for making an extra comment that adds to what you have just said: *I don't really want to go. Besides, it's too late now.* ⇨ note at BESIDE **2** in addition; also: *discounts on televisions, stereos and much more besides*

WHICH WORD?
besides / apart from / except

The preposition **besides** means 'in addition to': *What other sports do you like besides football?* You use **except** when you mention the only thing that is not included in a statement: *I like all sports except football.* You can use **apart from** with both these meanings: *What other sports do you like apart from football?* ◇ *I like all sports apart from football.*
⇨ note at BESIDE

---

be·siege /bɪ'siːdʒ/ *verb* [VN] **1** to surround a building, city, etc. with soldiers until the people inside are forced to let you in: *Paris was besieged for four months and forced to surrender.* ◇ (*figurative*) *Fans besieged the box office to try and get tickets for the concert.* **2** [usually passive] (especially of sth unpleasant or annoying) to surround sb/sth in large numbers: *The actress was besieged by reporters at the airport.* **3** ~ **sb (with sth)** to send so many letters, ask so many questions, etc. that it is difficult for sb to deal with them all: *The radio station was besieged with calls from angry listeners.*

be·smirch /bɪ'smɜːtʃ; *AmE* bɪ'smɜːrtʃ/ *verb* [VN] (*formal*) to damage the opinion that people have of sb/sth [SYN] SULLY: *He had deliberately set out to besmirch her reputation.*

be·sot·ted /bɪ'sɒtɪd; *AmE* -'saːt-/ *adj.* ~ **(by/with sb/sth)** loving sb/sth so much that you do not behave in a

sensible way: *He is completely besotted with his new girlfriend.*

be·sought *pt, pp* of BESEECH

be·spec·tacled /bɪ'spektəkld/ *adj.* (*formal*) wearing SPECTACLES

be·spoke /bɪ'spəʊk; *AmE* bɪ'spoʊk/ *adj.* [usually before noun] (*especially BrE, formal*) **1** (*AmE* usually ,cus-tom-'made) (of a product) made specially, according to the needs of an individual customer: *bespoke software* ◇ *a bespoke suit* **2** making products specially, according to the needs of an individual customer: *a bespoke tailor*

best /best/ *adj., adv., noun, verb*

■ *adj.* (superlative of **good**) **1** of the most excellent type or quality: *That's the best movie I've ever seen!* ◇ *He wrote his best songs before he was 25.* ◇ *She was one of the best tennis players of her generation.* ◇ *Is that your best suit?* ◇ *They've been best friends* (= closest friends) *since they were children.* ◇ *the company's best-ever results* ◇ *We want the kids to have the best possible education.* **2** most enjoyable; happiest: *Those were the best years of my life.* **3** most suitable or appropriate: *What's the best way to cook steak?* ◇ *The best thing to do would be to apologize.* ◇ *He's the best man for the job.* ◇ *It's best if you go now.* ◇ *I'm not in the best position to advise you.* [IDM] Idioms containing **best** *adj.* are at the entries for the nouns and verbs in the idioms, for example **on your best behaviour** is at **behaviour.**

■ *adv.* (superlative of **well**, often used in adjectives) **1** most; to the greatest extent: *Which one do you like best?* ◇ *Well-drained soil suits the plant best.* ◇ *her best-known poem* **2** in the most excellent way; to the highest standard: *He works best in the mornings.* ◇ *Britain's best-dressed woman* ◇ *The beaches are beautiful, but, best of all, there are very few tourists.* **3** in the most suitable or appropriate way: *Painting is best done in daylight.* ◇ *Do as you think best* (= what you think is the most suitable thing to do). [IDM] **as ,best you 'can** not perfectly but as well as you are able: *We'll manage as best we can.*

■ *noun* [sing.] (usually **the best**) **1** the most excellent thing or person: *We all want the best for our children.* ◇ *They only buy the best.* ◇ *They're all good players, but she's the best of all.* ◇ *We're the best of friends* (= very close friends). **2** the highest standard that sb/sth can reach: *She always brings out the best in people.* ◇ *The town looks its best* (= is most attractive) *in the spring.* ◇ *Don't worry about the exam—just do your best.* ◇ *The roses are past their best now.* ◇ *I don't really feel at my best today.* **3** something that is as close as possible to what you need or want: *Fifty pounds is the best I can offer you.* ◇ *The best we can hope for in the game is a draw.* **4** the highest standard that a particular person has reached, especially in a sport: *She won the race with a personal best of 2 minutes 22.* [IDM] **all the 'best** (*informal*) used when you are saying goodbye to sb or ending a letter, to give sb your good wishes **at 'best** used for saying what is the best opinion you can have of sb/sth, or the best thing that can happen, when the situation is bad: *Their response to the proposal was, at best, cool.* ◇ *We can't arrive before Friday at best.* **be (all) for the 'best** used to say that although sth appears bad or unpleasant now, it will be good in the end: *I don't want you to leave, but perhaps it's for the best.* **the best of 'three, 'five, etc.** (especially in games and sports) up to three, five, etc. games played to decide who wins, the winner being the person who wins most of them **do, mean, etc. sth for the 'best** to do or say sth in order to achieve a good result or to help sb: *I just don't know what to do for the best.* ◇ *I'm sorry if my advice offended you—I meant it for the best.* **have/get the 'best of sth** to gain more advantage from sth than sb else: *I thought you had the best of that discussion.* **make the best of sth/it | make the best of things | make the best of a bad job** to accept a bad or difficult situation and do as well as you can **to the best of your 'knowledge/be'lief** as far as you know: *He never made a will, to the best of my knowledge.* **with the 'best (of them)** as well as anyone: *He'll be out there, dancing with the best of them.*—more at BUNCH *n.*, HOPE *v.*, LUCK *n.*, SUNDAY

---

s	t	v	z	ʃ	ʒ	tʃ	dʒ	θ	ð	ŋ
see	tea	van	zoo	shoe	vision	chain	jam	thin	this	sing

B

■ *verb* [VN] [usually passive] (*formal*) to defeat or be more successful than sb

bes·tial /ˈbestɪəl; *AmE* ˈbestʃəl/ *adj.* (*formal*) cruel and disgusting; of or like a BEAST: *bestial acts/cruelty/noises*

bes·ti·al·ity /ˌbestiˈæləti; *AmE* ˌbestʃi-/ *noun* [U] **1** (*technical*) sexual activity between a human being and an animal **2** (*formal*) cruel or disgusting behaviour

be·stir /bɪˈstɜː(r)/ *verb* (-rr-) [VN] ~ **yourself** (*formal or humorous*) to start doing things after a period during which you have been doing nothing [SYN] ROUSE

best 'man *noun* [sing.] a male friend or relative of the BRIDEGROOM at a wedding, who helps him during the wedding ceremony—compare BRIDESMAID

be·stow /bɪˈstəʊ; *AmE* bɪˈstoʊ/ *verb* [VN] ~ **sth** (**on/upon sb**) (*formal*) to give sth to sb, especially to show how much they are respected: *It was a title bestowed upon him by the king.*

best-'seller *noun* a product, usually a book, which is bought by large numbers of people: *the best-seller list* ▶ **best-'selling** *adj.*: *a best-selling novel/author*

bet /bet/ *verb, noun*
■ *verb* (**bet·ting**, **bet**, **bet**) **1** ~ (**sth**) (**on/against sth**) to risk money on a race or an event by trying to predict the result: [V] *You have to be over 16 to bet.* ◊ [VN] *He bet $2 000 on the final score of the game.* ◊ [VNN] *She bet me £20 that I wouldn't do it.* [also V that, VN that] —see also BETTING, GAMBLE **2** (*spoken*) used to say that you are almost certain that sth is true or that sth will happen: [V(that)] *I bet (that) we're too late.* ◊ *You can bet (that) the moment I sit down, the phone will ring.* ◊ [VN(that)] *I'll bet you (that) he knows all about it.* [IDM] **I/I'll bet!** (*spoken*) **1** used to show that you can understand what sb is feeling, describing, etc: *'I nearly died when he told me.' 'I bet!'* **2** used to tell sb that you do not believe what they have just said: *'I'm going to tell her what I think of her.' 'Yeah, I bet!'* I **wouldn't 'bet on it | don't 'bet on it** (*spoken*) used to say that you do not think that sth is very likely: *'She'll soon get used to the idea.' 'I wouldn't bet on it.'* **you 'bet!** (*spoken*) used instead of 'yes' to emphasize that sb has guessed sth correctly or made a good suggestion: *'Are you nervous?' 'You bet!'* **you can bet your 'life/your bottom 'dollar (on sth/(that) …)** (*spoken*) used to say that you are certain that sth will happen: *You can bet your bottom dollar that he'll be late.*
■ *noun* **1** an arrangement to risk money, etc. on the result of a particular event; the money that you risk in this way: *to win/lose a bet* ◊ *We've got a bet on who's going to arrive first.* ◊ *He had a bet on the horses.* ◊ *'Liverpool are bound to win.' 'Do you want a bet?'* (= I disagree with you, I don't think they will.) ◊ *They all put a bet on the race.* ◊ *I hear you're taking bets on whether she'll marry him.* ◊ *I did it for a bet* (= because sb had agreed to pay me money if I did). **2** (*informal*) an opinion about what is likely to happen or to have happened: *My bet is that they've been held up in traffic.* [IDM] **the/your best bet** (*informal*) used to tell sb what is the best action for them to take to get the result they want: *If you want to get around London fast, the Underground is your best bet.* **a ,good/,safe 'bet** something that is likely to happen, to succeed or to be suitable: *Clothes are a safe bet as a present for a teenager.*—more at HEDGE v.

beta /ˈbiːtə; *AmE* ˈbeɪtə/ *noun* the second letter of the Greek alphabet (Β, β)

'beta blocker *noun* a drug used to control heart rhythm, treat severe chest pain and reduce high blood pressure

betel /ˈbiːtl/ *noun* [U] the leaves of a climbing plant, also called **betel**, chewed by people in Asia

'betel nut *noun* the slightly bitter nut of a tropical Asian PALM, that is cut into small pieces, wrapped in the leaves of a plant, (called **betel**), and chewed

bête noire /ˌbet ˈnwɑː(r)/ *noun* (*pl.* **bêtes noires** /ˌbet ˈnwɑː(r)/) (from *French*) a person or thing that particularly annoys you and that you do not like

be·tide /bɪˈtaɪd/ *verb* [IDM] see WOE

be·token /bɪˈtəʊkən; *AmE* -ˈtoʊ-/ *verb* [VN] (*literary*) to be a sign of sth: *a clear blue sky betokening a fine day*

be·tray /bɪˈtreɪ/ *verb* [VN] **1** ~ **sb/sth (to sb)** to give information about sb/sth to an enemy: *For years they had been betraying state secrets to Russia.* ◊ *He was offered money to betray his colleagues.* **2** to hurt sb who trusts you, especially by not being loyal or faithful to them: *She felt betrayed when she found out the truth about him.* ◊ *She betrayed his trust over and over again.* ◊ *I have never known her to betray a confidence* (= tell other people sth that should be kept secret). **3** to ignore your principles or beliefs in order to achieve sth or gain an advantage for yourself: *He has been accused of betraying his former socialist ideals.* **4** ~ **sth/yourself** to tell sb or make them aware of a piece of information, a feeling, etc., usually without meaning to: *His voice betrayed the worry he was trying to hide.* ◊ *She was terrified of saying something that would make her betray herself* (= show her feelings or who she was).

be·tray·al /bɪˈtreɪəl/ *noun* [U, C] the act of betraying sb/sth or the fact of being betrayed: *a sense/a feeling/an act of betrayal* ◊ *I saw her actions as a betrayal of my trust.* ◊ *the many disappointments and betrayals in his life*

be·troth·al /bɪˈtrəʊðl; *AmE* -ˈtroʊ-/ *noun* ~ **(to sb)** (*formal or old-fashioned*) an agreement to marry sb [SYN] ENGAGEMENT

be·trothed /bɪˈtrəʊðd; *AmE* -ˈtroʊ-/ *adj.* (*formal or old-fashioned*) ~ **(to sb)** having promised to marry sb [SYN] ENGAGED **2** (**sb's betrothed**) *noun* [sing.] the person that sb has promised to marry

bet·ter /ˈbetə(r)/ *adj., adv., noun, verb*
■ *adj.* (comparative of *good*) **1** of a higher standard or less poor quality; not as bad as sth else: *We're hoping for better weather tomorrow.* ◊ *Her work is getting better and better.* ◊ *He is in a much better mood than usual.* ◊ *The meal couldn't have been better.* ◊ *There's nothing better than a long soak in a hot bath.* ◊ *If you can only exercise once a week, that's better than nothing* (= better than taking no exercise at all). **2** more able or skilled: *She's far better at science than her brother.* **3** more suitable or appropriate: *Can you think of a better word than 'nice'?* ◊ *It would be better for him to talk to his parents about his problems.* ◊ *You'd be better going by bus.* **4** less ill/sick or unhappy: *She's a lot better today.* ◊ *His leg was getting better.* ◊ *You'll feel all the better for a good night's sleep.* [IDM] Most idioms containing **better** are at the entries for the nouns and verbs in the idioms, for example **better luck next time** is at **luck**. **little/no better than** almost or just the same as; almost or just as bad as: *The path was no better than a sheep track.* **that's (much) 'better 1** used to give support to sb who has been upset and is trying to become calmer: *Dry your eyes now. That's better.* **2** used to praise sb who has made an effort to improve: *That's much better—you played the right notes this time.* **the ,bigger, ,smaller, ,faster, ,slower, etc. the 'better** used to say that sth should be as big, small, etc. as possible: *As far as the hard disk is concerned, the bigger the better.*—more at DISCRETION, HEAD n., PART n., PREVENTION
■ *adv.* (comparative of *well*) **1** in a more excellent or pleasant way; not as badly: *She sings much better than I do.* ◊ *Sound travels better in water than in air.* ◊ *People are better educated now.* **2** more; to a greater degree: *You'll like her when you know her better.* ◊ *A cup of tea? There's nothing I'd like better!* ◊ *Fit people are better able to cope with stress.* **3** used to suggest that sth would be a suitable or appropriate thing to do: *The money could be better spent on more urgent cases.* ◊ *Some things are better left unsaid.* ◊ *You'd do better to tell her everything before she finds out from someone else.* [IDM] Most idioms containing **better** are at the entries for the nouns, adjectives and verbs in the idioms, for example **better the devil you know** is at **devil**. **be better 'off** to have more money: *Families will be better off under the new law.* ◊ *Her promotion means she's $100 a week better off.* **be better off (doing sth)** used to say that sb is/would be happier or more satisfied if they were in a particular position or did a particular thing: *She's better off without him.* ◊ *The weather was so bad we'd have been better off staying at home.* **had better/best (do sth)** used to tell sb what you

æ	ɑː	e	ɜː	ə	ɪ	iː	i	ɒ	ɔː	ʌ	ʊ	u	uː
cat	father	ten	bird	about	sit	see	many	got	saw	cup	put	actual	too

(BrE)

think they should do: *You'd better go to the doctor about your cough.* ◇ *We'd better leave now or we'll miss the bus.* ◇ *You'd better not do that again.* ◇ *'I'll give you back the money tomorrow.' 'You'd better!'* (= as a threat) ➪ note at SHOULD
■ *noun* **1** [sing., U] something that is better: *the better of the two books* ◇ *I expected better of him* (= I thought he would have behaved better). **2 (your betters)** [pl.] (*old-fashioned*) people who are more intelligent or more important than you **IDM** **for ˌbetter or (for) ˈworse** used to say that sth cannot be changed, whether the result is good or bad **get the better of sb/sth** to defeat sb/sth or gain an advantage: *No one can get the better of her in an argument.* ◇ *She always gets the better of an argument.* ◇ *His curiosity got the better of him* (= he didn't intend to ask questions, but he wanted to know so badly that he did). **so much the ˈbetter/ˈworse** used to say that sth is even better/worse: *We don't actually need it on Tuesday, but if it arrives by then, so much the better.*—more at CHANGE *n.*, ELDER *n.*, THINK *v.*
■ *verb* [VN] **1** [often passive] to be better or do sth better than sb/sth else: *The work he produced early in his career has never really been bettered.* **2 ~ yourself** to improve your social position through education, a better job, etc: *Thousands of Victorian workers joined educational associations in an attempt to better themselves.*

bet·ter·ment /ˈbetəmənt; AmE ˈbetərm-/ *noun* [U] (*formal*) the process of becoming or making sth/sb better **SYN** IMPROVEMENT

bet·ting /ˈbetɪŋ/ *noun* [U] the act of risking money, etc. on the unknown result of an event: *illegal betting* **IDM** **What's the betting …?** | **The betting is that …** (*informal*) it seems likely that …: *What's the betting that he gets his own way?* ◇ *The betting is that he'll get his own way.*

ˈbetting shop *noun* (*BrE*) a shop where you can bet on horse races and other competitions

be·tween /bɪˈtwiːn/ *prep., adv.*
■ *prep.* **1** in or into the space separating two or more points, objects, people, etc: *Q comes between P and R in the English alphabet.* ◇ *I sat down between Jo and Diana.* ◇ *Switzerland lies between France, Germany, Austria and Italy.* ◇ *The paper had fallen down between the desk and the wall.* ◇ (*figurative*) *My job is somewhere between a secretary and a personal assistant.* **2** in the period of time that separates two days, years, events, etc: *It's cheaper between 6 p.m. and 8 a.m.* ◇ *Don't eat between meals.* ◇ *Children must attend school between the ages of 5 and 16.* ◇ *Many changes took place between the two world wars.* **3** at some point along a scale from one amount, weight, distance, etc. to another: *It weighed between nine and ten kilos.* ◇ *The temperature remained between 25° C and 30° C all week.* **4** (of a line) separating one place from another: *the border between Sweden and Norway* **5** from one place to another: *We fly between Rome and Paris twice daily.* **6** used to show a connection or relationship: *a difference/distinction/contrast between two things* ◇ *a link between unemployment and crime* ◇ *There's a lot of bad feeling between them.* ◇ *I had to choose between the two jobs.* **7** shared by two or more people or things: *We drank a bottle of wine between us.* ◇ *This is just between you and me/between ourselves* (= it is a secret). **8 ~ doing sth** used to show that several activities are involved: *Between working full-time and taking care of the kids, he didn't have much time for hobbies.*
■ *adv.* (usually **in between**) in the space or period of time separating two or more points, objects, etc. or two dates, events, etc: *The house was near a park but there was a road in between.* ◇ *I see her most weekends but not very often in between.* **IDM** see BETWIXT

be·twixt /bɪˈtwɪkst/ *adv., prep.* (*literary* or *old use*) between **IDM** **be ˌtwixt and beˈtween** (*old-fashioned*) in a middle position; neither one thing nor the other

bevel /ˈbevl/ *noun* **1** a sloping edge or surface, for example at the side of a picture frame or sheet of glass **2** a tool for making sloping edges or surfaces on wood or stone

bev·elled (*BrE*) (*AmE* **bev·eled**) /ˈbevld/ *adj.* [usually before noun] having a sloping edge or surface: *a bevelled mirror*

bev·er·age /ˈbevərɪdʒ/ *noun* (*formal*) any type of drink except water: *laws governing the sale of alcoholic beverages*

bevy /ˈbevi/ *noun* [sing.] (*informal*) a large group of people or things of the same kind: *a bevy of beauties* (= beautiful young women)

be·wail /bɪˈweɪl/ *verb* [VN] (*formal* or *humorous*) to express great sadness about sth

be·ware /bɪˈweə(r); AmE -ˈwer/ *verb* **~ (of sb/sth/of doing sth)** (used only in infinitives and in orders) if you tell sb to **beware**, you are warning them that sb/sth is dangerous and that they should be careful: [V] *Motorists have been warned to beware of icy roads.* ◇ *Beware of saying anything that might reveal where you live.* ◇ [VN] *It's a great place for swimming, but beware dangerous currents.* [also V -ing]

be·wil·der /bɪˈwɪldə(r)/ *verb* [VN] [usually passive] to confuse sb: *She was totally bewildered by his sudden change of mood.*

be·wil·der·ing /bɪˈwɪldərɪŋ/ *adj.* making you feel confused because there are too many things to choose from or because sth is difficult to understand: *a bewildering array/range* ◇ *There is a bewildering variety of software available.* ▶ **be·wil·der·ing·ly** *adv.*: *All the houses looked bewilderingly similar.*

be·wil·der·ment /bɪˈwɪldəmənt; AmE -dərm-/ *noun* [U] a feeling of being completely confused: *to look/stare in bewilderment*

be·witch /bɪˈwɪtʃ/ *verb* [VN] **1** [often passive] (*written*) to attract or impress sb so much that they cannot think in a sensible way: *He was completely bewitched by her beauty.* **2** to put a magic SPELL on sb

be·witch·ing /bɪˈwɪtʃɪŋ/ *adj.* (*written*) so beautiful or interesting that you cannot think about anything else: *a bewitching girl/smile* ◇ *a bewitching performance*

be·yond /bɪˈjɒnd; AmE bɪˈjɑːnd/ *prep., adv.*
■ *prep.* **1** on or to the further side of sth: *The road continues beyond the village up into the hills.* **2** later than a particular time: *It won't go on beyond midnight.* ◇ *I know what I'll be doing for the next three weeks but I haven't thought beyond that.* **3** more than sth: *Our success was far beyond what we thought possible.* ◇ *She's got nothing beyond her state pension.* **4** used to say that sth is not possible: *The bicycle was beyond repair* (= is too badly damaged to repair). ◇ *The situation is beyond our control.* **5** too far or too advanced for sb/sth: *The handle was just beyond my reach.* ◇ *The exercise was beyond the abilities of most of the class.* **IDM** **be beyond sb** (*informal*) to be impossible for sb to imagine, understand or do: *It's beyond me why she wants to marry Jeff.*
■ *adv.* on the other side; further on: *Snowdon and the mountains beyond were covered in snow.* ◇ *The immediate future is clear, but it's hard to tell what lies beyond.* ◇ *the year 2000 and beyond* **IDM** see BACK *n.*, DOUBT *n.*

bi- /baɪ/ *combining form* (in nouns and adjectives) two; twice; double: *bilingual* ◇ *bicentenary* **HELP** Bi- with a period of time can mean either 'happening twice' in that period of time, or 'happening once in every two' periods.

bi·an·nual /baɪˈænjuəl/ *adj.* [only before noun] happening twice a year: *a biannual meeting*—compare ANNUAL—see also BIENNIAL

bias /ˈbaɪəs/ *noun, verb*
■ *noun* **1** [U, C, usually sing.] a strong feeling in favour of or against one group of people, or one side in an argument, often not based on fair judgement: *accusations of political bias in news programmes* (= that reports are unfair and show favour to one political party) ◇ *Employers must consider all candidates impartially and without bias.* ◇ *Some institutions still have a strong bias against women.* **2** [C, usually sing.] an interest in one thing more than others; a special ability: *The course has a strong practical bias.* **3** [U, sing.] the **bias** of a piece of cloth is an edge cut DIAGONALLY across the threads: *The skirt is cut on the bias.*

■ *verb* (-s- or -ss-) [VN] ~ sb/sth (towards/against/in favour of sth) to unfairly influence sb's opinions or decisions: *The newspapers have biased people against her.*

biased (also **biassed**) /ˈbaɪəst/ *adj.* **1** ~ (toward(s)/against/in favour of sb/sth) having a tendency to show favour towards or against one group of people or one opinion for personal reasons; making unfair judgements: *biased information/sources/press reports ◊ a biased jury/witness* OPP UNBIASED **2** ~ toward(s) sth/sb having a particular interest in one thing more than others: *a school biased towards music and art*

bi·ath·lon /baɪˈæθlən/ *noun* [sing., U] a sporting event that combines CROSS-COUNTRY skiing and RIFLE shooting—compare DECATHLON, HEPTATHLON, PENTATHLON, TRIATHLON

bib /bɪb/ *noun* **1** a piece of fabric or plastic that you put under babies' chins to protect their clothes while they are eating **2** (*especially BrE*) a piece of fabric or plastic with a number or special colours on it that people wear on their chests and backs when they are taking part in a sport, for example a race or a football match, so that people know who they are IDM **your best bib and 'tucker** (*humorous*) your best clothes that you only wear on special occasions

bible /ˈbaɪbl/ *noun* **1 (the Bible)** [sing.] the holy book of the Christian religion, consisting of the Old Testament and the New Testament **2 (the Bible)** [sing.] the holy book of the Jewish religion, consisting of the Torah (or Law), the PROPHETS, and the Writings **3** [C] a copy of the holy book of the Christian or Jewish religion **4** [C] a book containing important information on a subject, that you refer to very often: *the stamp-collector's bible*

bib·lical /ˈbɪblɪkl/ (also **Biblical**) *adj.* connected with the Bible; in the Bible: *biblical scholarship/times/scenes ◊ biblical stories/passages*

biblio- /ˈbɪbliəʊ; *AmE* -liəʊ/ *combining form* (in nouns, adjectives and adverbs) connected with books: *bibliophile*

bibli·og·raphy /ˌbɪbliˈɒɡrəfi; *AmE* -ˈɑːɡ-/ *noun* (*pl.* **-ies**) **1** [C] a list of books or articles about a particular subject or by a particular author; the list of books, etc. that have been used by sb writing an article, etc: *There is a useful bibliography at the end of each chapter.* **2** [U] the study of the history of books and their production ▸ **bibli·og·raph·er** /-ˈɒɡrəfə(r); *AmE* -ˈɑːɡ-/ *noun* **bib·lio·graph·ic·al** /ˌbɪbliəˈɡræfɪkl/ *adj.*

bib·lio·phile /ˈbɪbliəfaɪl/ *noun* (*formal*) a person who loves or collects books

'bib overalls *noun* [pl.] (*AmE*) = DUNGAREES (1)

bi·cam·eral /ˌbaɪˈkæmərəl/ *adj.* (*technical*) (of a parliament) having two main parts, such as the Senate and the House of Representatives in the US, and the House of Commons and the House of Lords in Britain

bi·carb /ˈbaɪkɑːb; *AmE* -kɑːrb/ *noun* [U] (*informal*) = SODIUM BICARBONATE

bi·car·bon·ate /ˌbaɪˈkɑːbənət; *AmE* -ˈkɑːrb-/ *noun* [U] (*chemistry*) a salt containing a double amount of CARBON DIOXIDE

bi,carbonate of 'soda *noun* [U] = SODIUM BICARBONATE

bi·cen·ten·ary /ˌbaɪsenˈtiːnəri; *AmE* -ˈten-/ *noun* (*pl.* **-ies**) (*BrE*) (*AmE* **bi·cen·ten·nial**) the year, or the day, when you celebrate an important event that happened exactly 200 years earlier: *Mozart's bicentenary ◊ to celebrate/mark the bicentenary of sth/sb* ▸ **bi·cen·ten·ary** *adj.* [only before noun]: *bicentenary celebrations*

bi·cen·ten·nial /ˌbaɪsenˈtenial/ *noun* (*AmE*) = BICENTENARY ▸ **bi·cen·ten·nial** *adj.* [only before noun] (*especially AmE*): *bicentennial celebrations*

bi·ceps /ˈbaɪseps/ *noun* (*pl.* **bi·ceps**) the large muscle at the front of the top part of the arm: *He showed off his bulging biceps.*—compare TRICEPS

bicker /ˈbɪkə(r)/ *verb* [V] ~ (about/over sth) to argue about things that are not important SYN SQUABBLE: *The*

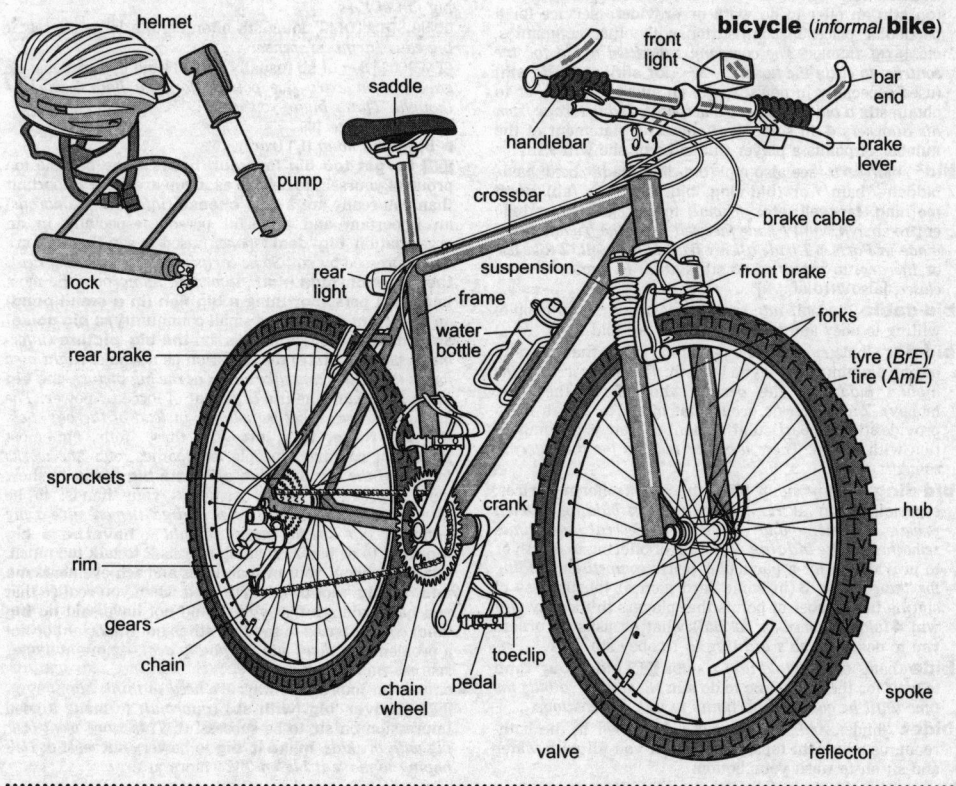

bicycle (*informal* bike)

helmet · saddle · pump · lock · rear light · handlebar · crossbar · suspension · frame · water bottle · rear brake · sprockets · rim · gears · chain · chain wheel · pedal · toeclip · crank · valve · front light · bar end · brake lever · brake cable · front brake · forks · tyre (*BrE*)/tire (*AmE*) · hub · spoke · reflector

children are always bickering about something or other.
▶ **bicker·ing** *noun* [U]

bi·cycle /ˈbaɪsɪkl/ *noun, verb*

■ *noun* (also *informal* **bike**) a road vehicle with two wheels that you ride by pushing the PEDALS with your feet: *He got on his bicycle and rode off.* ◊ *We went for a bicycle ride on Sunday.*—picture on page 107

■ *verb* [V] [usually +*adv. / prep.*] (*old-fashioned*) to go somewhere on a bicycle—compare BIKE, CYCLE

ˈbicycle clip *noun* one of the two bands that people wear around their ankles when they are riding a bicycle to stop their trousers/pants getting caught in the chain

ˈbicycle lane (also *informal* ˈbike lane) *noun* (both *AmE*) = CYCLE LANE

bi·cyc·list /ˈbaɪsɪklɪst/ *noun* (*old-fashioned* in British English, *formal* in American English) a person who rides a bicycle—compare CYCLIST

bid¹ /bɪd/ *verb, noun*—see also BID²

■ *verb* (**bid·ding, bid, bid**) **1** to offer to pay a particular price for sth, especially at an AUCTION: [VN] *I bid £2 000 for the painting.* ◊ [V] *We wanted to buy the chairs but another couple were bidding against us.* **2 ~** (**for sth**) *AmE* **~** (**on sth**) to offer to do work or provide a service for a particular price, in competition with other companies, etc. SYN TENDER: [V] *A French firm will be bidding for the contract.* [also V to inf] **3** [V to inf] (used especially in newspapers) to try to do, get or achieve sth SYN ATTEMPT: *The team is bidding to retain its place in the league.* **4** (in some card games) to say how many points you expect to win: [VN] *She bid four hearts.* [also V] IDM **what am I ˈbid?** used by an AUCTIONEER when he or she is selling sth: *What am I bid for this vase?*

■ *noun* **1 ~** (**for sth**) an offer by a person or a business company to pay a particular amount of money for sth: *Granada mounted a hostile takeover bid for Forte.* ◊ *At the auction* (= a public sale where things are sold to the person who offers most), *the highest bid for the picture was £200 000.* ◊ *Any more bids?* **2 ~** (**for sth**) | *AmE* also **~** (**on sth**) an offer to do work or provide a service for a particular price, in competition with other companies, etc. SYN TENDER: *The company submitted a bid for the contract to clean the hospital.* **3 ~** (**for sth**) | **~** (**to do sth**) (used especially in newspapers) an effort to do sth or to obtain sth: *a bid for power* ◊ *a desperate bid to escape from his attackers* **4** (in some card games) a statement of the number of points a player thinks he or she will win

bid² /bɪd/ *verb*—see also BID¹ (**bid·ding, bade, bidden** /ˈbɪdn/ or (**bid·ding, bid, bid**) **1 ~** (**sb**) **good morning, farewell,** etc. (*formal*) to say 'good morning', etc. to sb: [VN, VNN] *I bade farewell to all the friends I had made in Paris.* ◊ *I bade all my friends farewell.* **2** (*old use* or *literary*) to tell sb to do sth: [VN inf] *He bade me come closer.* [also VN to inf, VN]

bid·dable /ˈbɪdəbl/ *adj.* (*rare, especially BrE*) (of people) willing to obey and to do what they are told to

bid·der /ˈbɪdə(r)/ *noun* **1** a person or group that offers to pay an amount of money to buy sth: *The house went to the highest bidder* (= the person who offered the most money). **2** a person or group that offers to do sth or to provide sth for a particular amount of money, in competition with others: *There were six bidders for the catering contract.*

bid·ding /ˈbɪdɪŋ/ *noun* [U] **1** the act of offering prices, especially at an AUCTION: *There was fast bidding between private collectors and dealers.* ◊ *Several companies remained in the bidding.* **2** the act of offering to do sth or to provide sth for a particular price: *competitive bidding for the contract* **3** (in some card games) the process of stating the number of points that players think they will win **4** (*old-fashioned* or *formal*) what sb asks or orders you to do: *to do sb's bidding* (= to obey sb)

bide /baɪd/ *verb* [V] (*old use*) = ABIDE IDM **bide your ˈtime** to wait for the right time to do sth: *He decided to bide his time until he got an opportunity to talk to her alone.*

bidet /ˈbiːdeɪ; *AmE* bɪˈdeɪ/ *noun* a low bowl in the bathroom, usually with taps/faucets, that you fill with water and sit on to wash your bottom

bi·en·nial /baɪˈeniəl/ *adj., noun*

■ *adj.* [usually before noun] happening once every two years: *a biennial convention* ▶ **bi·en·ni·al·ly** *adv.* —see also ANNUAL, BIANNUAL

■ *noun* any plant that lives for two years, producing flowers in the second year—compare ANNUAL, PERENNIAL

bier /bɪə(r); *AmE* bɪr/ *noun* a frame on which the dead body or the COFFIN is placed or carried at a funeral

biff /bɪf/ *verb* [VN] (*old-fashioned, informal*) to hit sb hard with your FIST: *He biffed me on the nose.* ▶ **biff** *noun*

bi·focals /ˌbaɪˈfəʊklz; *AmE* -ˈfoʊ-/ *noun* [pl.] a pair of glasses with each LENS made in two parts. The upper part is for looking at things at a distance, and the lower part is for reading or for looking at things that are close to you. ▶ **bi·focal** *adj.*

bi·fur·cate /ˈbaɪfəkeɪt; *AmE* -fərk-/ *verb* [V] (*formal*) (of roads, rivers, etc.) to divide into two separate parts ▶ **bi·fur·ca·tion** /ˌbaɪfəˈkeɪʃn; *AmE* -fərˈk-/ *noun* [C, U]

big /bɪg/ *adj., adv.*

■ *adj.* (**big·ger, big·gest**)

▸ LARGE **1** large in size, degree, amount, etc: *a big man/ house/increase* ◊ *This shirt isn't big enough.* ◊ *It's the world's biggest computer company.* ◊ (*informal*) *He had this great big grin on his face.* ◊ *They were earning big money.* ◊ *The news came as a big blow.*

▸ OLDER **2** (*informal*) older: *You're a big girl now.* ◊ *my big brother*

▸ IMPORTANT **3** [only before noun] important; serious: *a big decision* ◊ *Tonight is the biggest match of his career.* ◊ *You are making a big mistake.* ◊ *She took the stage for her big moment.* ◊ (*informal*) *Do you really think we can take on the big boys* (= compete with the most powerful people)*?*

▸ AMBITIOUS **4** (*informal*) (of a plan) needing a lot of effort, money or time to succeed: *They're full of big ideas.*

▸ POPULAR **5 ~** (**in …**) (*informal*) popular with the public; successful: *Orange is the big colour this year.* ◊ *The band's very big in Japan.*

▸ ENTHUSIASTIC **6** (*informal*) enthusiastic about sb/sth: *I'm a big fan of hers.*

▸ DOING STH A LOT **7** doing sth often or to a large degree: *a big eater/drinker/spender*

▸ GENEROUS **8 ~ of sb** (usually *ironic*) kind or generous: *He gave me an extra five pounds for two hours' work. I thought 'That's big of you'.*
⇨ note on page 109
▶ **big·ness** *noun* [U] (*rare*)

IDM **be/get too big for your ˈboots** to be/become too proud of yourself; to behave as if you are more important than you really are **a ˌbig ˈcheese** (*informal, humorous*) an important and powerful person, especially in an organization **ˌbig ˈdeal** (*spoken*) used to say that you are not impressed by sth: *So he earns more than me. Big deal!* **the big enchiˈlada** (*AmE, informal, humorous*) the most important person or thing **a big fish (in a small pond)** an important person (in a small community) **a big noise/ shot/name** an important person **the big ˈpicture** (*informal, especially AmE*) the situation as a whole: *Right now forget the details and take a look at the big picture.* **the big stick** (*informal*) the use or threat of force or power: *The authorities used quiet persuasion instead of the big stick.* **the big three, four,** etc. the three, four, etc. most important countries, people, companies, etc: *She works for one of the Big Six.* **give sb/get a big ˈhand** to show your approval of sb by CLAPPING your hands; to be APPLAUDED in this way: *Ladies and gentlemen, give a big hand for our special guests tonight …* **have/be a big mouth 1** to be bad at keeping secrets **2** to talk too much, especially about your own abilities and achievements **me and my big ˈmouth** (*spoken*) used when you realize that you have said sth that you should not have said **no big ˈdeal** (*spoken*) used to say that sth is not important or not a problem: *If I don't win it's no big deal.*—more at EYE *n.*, FISH *n.*, THING, WAY *n.*

■ *adv.* in an impressive way: *We need to think big.*

IDM **go over ˈbig (with sb)** (*informal*) to make a good impression on sb; to be successful: *This story went over big with my kids.* **make it ˈbig** to be very successful: *He's hoping to make it big on TV.*—more at HIT *v.*

B

WHICH WORD? ⃝?
big / large / great

These adjectives are frequently used with the following nouns:

big ~	large ~	great ~
man	numbers	success
house	part	majority
car	area	interest
boy	room	importance
dog	company	difficulty
smile	eyes	problem
problem	family	pleasure
surprise	volume	beauty
question	population	artist
difference	problem	surprise

Large is more formal than **big** and should be used in writing unless it is in an informal style. It is not usually used to describe people, except to avoid saying 'fat'.

Great often suggests quality and not just size. Note also the phrases: *a large amount of* ◇ *a large number of* ◇ *a large quantity of* ◇ *a great deal of* ◇ *in great detail* ◇ *a person of great age*.

---

bigam·ist /ˈbɪgəmɪst/ *noun* a person who commits the crime of bigamy

big·amy /ˈbɪgəmi/ *noun* [U] the crime of marrying sb when you are still legally married to sb else—compare MONOGAMY, POLYGAMY ▶ **big·am·ous** /ˈbɪgəməs/ *adj.*: *a bigamous relationship*

the ˌBig ˈApple *noun* [sing.] (*informal*) New York City

ˈbig band *noun* a large group of musicians playing jazz or dance music: *the big-band sound*

ˌbig ˈbang *noun* [sing.] (usually **the big bang**) the single large explosion that some scientists suggest created the universe

ˌBig ˈBrother *noun* [sing.] a leader, a person in authority, or a government that tries to control people's behaviour and thoughts, but pretends to act for their benefit ORIGIN From George Orwell's novel *Nineteen Eighty-Four*, in which the leader of the government, **Big Brother**, had total control over the people. The slogan 'Big Brother is watching you' reminded people that he knew everything they did.

ˌbig ˈbucks *noun* [pl.] (*AmE, informal*) a large amount of money

ˌbig ˈbusiness *noun* [U] **1** large companies which have a lot of power and influence, considered as a group: *links between politics and big business* **2** something that has become important because people are willing to spend a lot of money on it: *Health and fitness have become big business.*

ˌbig ˈcat *noun* any large wild animal of the cat family. Lions, TIGERS and LEOPARDS are all big cats.

ˌbig ˈdipper *noun* **1** (*old-fashioned, BrE*) a small train at an AMUSEMENT PARK, which goes very quickly up and down a steep track and around bends—see also ROLLER COASTER **2** (**the ˌBig ˈDipper**) (*AmE*) = THE PLOUGH

ˌbig ˈgame *noun* [U] large wild animals that people hunt for sport, for example elephants and lions

big·gie /ˈbɪgi/ *noun* (*informal*) an important thing, person or event

ˌbig-ˈheaded *adj.* (*informal, disapproving*) having a very high opinion of how important and clever you are; too proud ▶ **ˈbig-head** *noun*

ˌbig-ˈhearted *adj.* very kind; generous

bight /baɪt/ *noun* (*rare*) a long curve in a coast: *the Great Australian Bight*

bigot /ˈbɪgət/ *noun* a person who has very strong, unreasonable beliefs or opinions about race, religion or politics and who will not listen to or accept the opinions of anyone who disagrees: *a religious/racial bigot*

big·ot·ed /ˈbɪgətɪd/ *adj.* showing strong, unreasonable beliefs or opinions and a refusal to change them

big·ot·ry /ˈbɪgətri/ *noun* [U] the state of feeling, or the act of expressing, strong, unreasonable beliefs or opinions

the ˌbig ˈscreen *noun* [sing.] the cinema (when contrasted with television): *The movie hits the big screen in July.* ◇ *her first big-screen success*

ˈbig-ticket *adj.* [only before noun] (*AmE*) costing a lot of money: *big-ticket items*

ˈbig time *noun, adv.* (*informal*)
■ *noun* (**the big time**) great success in a profession, especially the entertainment business: *a bit-part actor who finally made/hit the big time*—compare SMALL-TIME
■ *adv.* on a large scale; to a great extent: *This time they've messed up big time!*

ˌbig ˈtoe *noun* the largest toe on a person's foot—picture at BODY

ˌbig ˈtop (usually **the big top**) *noun* the large tent in which a CIRCUS gives performances

ˌbig ˈwheel *noun* **1** (usually **the Big Wheel**) (*BrE*) (also **Fer·ris wheel** *AmE, BrE*) a large upright wheel at an AMUSEMENT PARK with seats hanging at its edge for people to ride in **2** (*AmE, informal*) an important person in a company or an organization

big·wig /ˈbɪgwɪg/ *noun* (*informal*) an important person: *She had to entertain some boring local bigwigs.*

bijou /ˈbiːʒuː/ *adj.* [only before noun] (*BrE, sometimes ironic*) (of a building or a garden) small but attractive and fashionable: *The house was terribly small and cramped, but the agent described it as a bijou residence.*

bike /baɪk/ *noun, verb*
■ *noun* (*informal*) **1** a bicycle: *She got on her bike and rode off.* ◇ *I usually go to work by bike.*—see also MOUNTAIN BIKE, PUSHBIKE **2** a motorcycle IDM **on your bike!** (*BrE, informal*) a rude way of telling sb to go away
■ *verb* [V] [usually +*adv./prep.*] (*informal*) to go somewhere on a bicycle or motorcycle: *My dad bikes to work every day.* ▶ **bik·ing** *noun* [U]: *The activities on offer include horseback riding and* **mountain biking**.—compare BICYCLE, CYCLE

biker /ˈbaɪkə(r)/ *noun* **1** a person who rides a motorcycle, usually as a member of a large group: *a biker's leather jacket* **2** a person who rides a bicycle, especially a MOUNTAIN BIKE

bi·kini /bɪˈkiːni/ *noun* a piece of clothing in two pieces that women wear for swimming and lying in the sun

bi·la·bial /ˌbaɪˈleɪbial/ *noun* (*phonetics*) a speech sound made by using both lips, such as /b/, /p/ and /m/ ▶ **bi·la·bial** *adj.*

bi·lat·eral /ˌbaɪˈlætərəl/ *adj.* **1** involving two groups of people or two countries: *bilateral relations/agreements/trade/talks* **2** (*medical*) involving both of two parts or sides of the body or brain ▶ **bi·lat·eral·ly** *adv.*—compare MULTILATERAL, UNILATERAL

bil·berry /ˈbɪlbəri; *AmE* -beri/ (*pl.* **-ies**) *noun* a small dark blue berry that grows on bushes on hills and in woods in northern Europe and can be eaten. The bush is also called a **bilberry**.—compare BLUEBERRY

bile /baɪl/ *noun* [U] **1** the greenish brown liquid with a bitter unpleasant taste that is produced by the LIVER to help the body to deal with fats, and that comes into your mouth when you VOMIT with an empty stomach **2** (*written*) anger or hatred: *The critic's review of the play was just a paragraph of bile.*

bilge /bɪldʒ/ *noun* **1** [C] (also **bilges** [pl.]) the almost flat part of the bottom of a boat or a ship, inside or outside **2** (also **ˈbilge water**) [U] dirty water that collects in a ship's bilge

bil·har·zia /bɪlˈhɑːtsiə; *AmE* -ˈhɑːrt-/ *noun* [U] a serious disease, common in parts of Africa and S America, caused by small worms that get into the blood

bi·lin·gual /ˌbaɪˈlɪŋgwəl/ *adj.* **1** able to speak two languages equally well because you have used them since you were very young: *She is bilingual in English and Punjabi.* **2** using two languages; written in two languages: *bilingual education/communities* ◇ *a bilingual dictionary* ▶ **bi·lin·gual** *noun*: *Welsh/English bilinguals*—compare MONOLINGUAL, MULTILINGUAL

æ	ɑː	e	ɜː	ə	ɪ	iː	i	ɒ	ɔː	ʌ	ʊ	u	uː
cat	father	ten	bird	about	sit	see	many	got	saw	cup	put	actual	too

(BrE)

bili·ous /'bɪliəs/ *adj.* **1** feeling as if you might VOMIT soon **2** (of colours, usually green or yellow) creating an unpleasant effect: *a bilious green dress* **3** (*written*) bad-tempered; full of anger

bilk /bɪlk/ *verb* (*informal, especially AmE*) [VN] **~ sb (out of sth)**| **~ sth (from sb)** to cheat sb, especially by taking money from them: *a con man who bilked investors out of millions of dollars*

bill /bɪl/ *noun, verb*
■ *noun*
FOR PAYMENT | **1** a piece of paper that shows how much you owe sb for goods or services: *the telephone/electricity/gas bill* ◇ *We ran up a massive hotel bill.* ◇ *She always pays her bills on time.* ◇ *The bills are piling up* (= there are more and more that have still not been paid). **2** (*especially BrE*) (*AmE* usually **check**) a piece of paper that shows how much you have to pay for the food and drinks that you have had in a restaurant: *Let's ask for the bill.*
MONEY | **3** (*AmE*) = NOTE: *a ten-dollar bill*
IN PARLIAMENT | **4** a written suggestion for a new law that is presented to a country's parliament so that its members can discuss it: *to introduce/approve/reject a bill* ◇ *the Education Reform Bill*
AT THEATRE | **5** a programme of entertainment at a theatre, etc: *a horror* **double bill** (= two horror films/movies shown one after the other) ◇ *Topping the bill* (= the most important performer) *is Robbie Williams.*
ADVERTISEMENT | **6** a notice in a public place to advertise an event SYN POSTER—see also HANDBILL
OF BIRDS | **7** the hard pointed or curved outer part of a bird's mouth SYN BEAK **8** (-billed) (in adjectives) having the type of bill mentioned: *long-billed waders*
ON HAT | **9** (*AmE*) = PEAK (4)
—see also THE OLD BILL
IDM **fill/fit the 'bill** to be what is needed in a particular situation or for a particular purpose: *On paper, several of the applicants fit the bill.*—more at CLEAN *adj.*, FOOT *v.*
■ *verb*
ASK FOR PAYMENT | **1** [VN] **~ sb (for sth)** to send sb a bill for sth: *Please bill me for the books.* ◇ *You will be billed monthly for the service.*
ADVERTISE | **2** [VN] [usually passive] **~ sb/sth as sth** to advertise or describe sb/sth in a particular way: *He was billed as the new Tom Cruise.* **3** [VNtoinf] [usually passive] to advertise that sb/sth will do sth: *She was billed to speak on 'China—Yesterday and Today'.*
IDM **bill and 'coo** (*old-fashioned, informal*) if two people who are in love **bill and coo**, they kiss and speak in a loving way to each other

bill·board /'bɪlbɔːd; *AmE* -bɔːrd/ *noun* (*especially AmE*) = HOARDING

bil·let /'bɪlɪt/ *noun, verb*
■ *noun* a place, often in a private house, where soldiers live temporarily
■ *verb* [V+adv. / prep.] [usually passive] to send soldiers to live somewhere temporarily, especially in private houses during a war: *The troops were billeted in the town with local families.*

bill·fold /'bɪlfəʊld; *AmE* -foʊld/ *noun* (*AmE*) = WALLET

bill·hook /'bɪlhʊk/ *noun* a tool with a long handle and a curved blade, used for cutting the small branches off trees

bil·liards /'bɪliədz; *AmE* 'bɪljərdz/ *noun* [U] a game for two people played with CUES (= long sticks) and three balls on a long table covered with green fabric. Players try to hit the balls against each other and into pockets at the edge of the table: *a game of billiards*—compare POOL, SNOOKER ▶ **bil·liard** *adj.* [only before noun]: *a billiard cue*

bill·ing /'bɪlɪŋ/ *noun* **1** [U] the position, especially an important one, that sb is advertised or described as having in a show, etc: *to have top/star billing* **2** [U] the act of preparing and sending bills to customers **3** [C, usually pl.] the total amount of business that a company does in a particular period of time: *billings around $7 million*

bil·lion /'bɪljən/ *number* (*plural verb*) **1** (*abbr.* **bn**) 1 000 000 000; one thousand million HELP You say **a**, **one**, **two, several,** etc. **billion** without a final 's' on 'billion'. **Billions (of...)** can be used if there is no number or quantity before it. Always use a plural verb with **billion** or **billions**: *Worldwide sales reached 2.5 billion.* ◇ *half a billion dollars* ◇ *a few tens of billions of yen* ◇ *They have spent billions on the problem* (= billions of dollars, etc.). HELP There are more examples of how to use numbers at the entry for **hundred**. **2** (**a billion** or **billions**) (*informal*) a very large amount: *Our immune systems are killing billions of germs right now.* **3** (*old-fashioned, BrE*) 1 000 000 000 000; one million million SYN TRILLION

bil·lion·aire /ˌbɪljə'neə(r); *AmE* -'ner/ *noun* an extremely rich person, who has at least a thousand million pounds, dollars, etc. in money or property

bill of ex'change *noun* (*pl.* **bills of exchange**) (*business*) a written order to pay a sum of money to a particular person on a particular date

bill of 'lad·ing *noun* (*pl.* **bills of lad·ing**) (*business*) a list giving details of the goods that a ship, etc. is carrying

bill of 'rights *noun* [sing.] a written statement of the basic rights of the citizens of a country

bill of 'sale *noun* (*pl.* **bills of sale**) (*business*) an official document showing that sth has been bought

bil·low /'bɪləʊ; *AmE* -loʊ/ *verb, noun*
■ *verb* [V] **1** (of a sail, skirt, etc.) to fill with air and swell out: *The curtains billowed gently in the breeze.* **2** if smoke, cloud, etc. **billows**, it rises and moves in a large mass: *A great cloud of smoke billowed out of the chimney.*
■ *noun* [usually pl.] a moving mass or cloud of smoke, steam, etc. like a wave

billy /'bɪli/ *noun* (*pl.* **-ies**) (also **billy·can** /'bɪlikæn/) (*BrE*) a metal can with a lid and a handle used for boiling water or for cooking when you are camping

'billy club *noun* (*AmE*) a short wooden stick used as a weapon by police officers

'billy goat *noun* a male goat—compare NANNY GOAT

bimbo /'bɪmbəʊ; *AmE* -boʊ/ *noun* (*pl.* **-os**) (*informal, disapproving*) a young person, usually a woman, who is sexually attractive but not very intelligent: *He's going out with an empty-headed bimbo half his age.*

bi·month·ly /ˌbaɪ'mʌnθli/ *adj., adv.* produced or happening every two months or twice each month

bin /bɪn/ *noun, verb*
■ *noun* **1** (*BrE*) a container that you put waste in: *a rubbish bin*—see also DUSTBIN **2** a large container, usually with a lid, for storing things in: *a bread bin*
■ *verb* (**-nn-**) [VN] (*BrE, informal*) to throw sth away: *Do you need to keep these letters or shall we bin them?*

bin·ary /'baɪnəri/ *adj.* **1** (*computing, mathematics*) using only 0 and 1 as a system of numbers: *the binary system* ◇ *binary arithmetic* **2** (*technical*) based on only two numbers; consisting of two parts: *binary codes/numbers* ▶ **bin·ary** *noun* [U]: *The computer performs calculations in binary and converts the results to decimal.*

bind /baɪnd/ *verb, noun*
■ *verb* (**bound, bound** /baʊnd/)
TIE WITH ROPE/FABRIC | **1** [VN] **~ sb/sth (to sth)**| **~ sb/sth (together)** to tie sb/sth with rope, string, etc. so that they cannot move or are held together firmly: *She was bound to a chair.* ◇ *They bound his hands together.* ◇ *He was left* **bound and gagged** (= tied up and with a piece of fabric tied over his mouth). **2** [VN] **~ sth (up)** to tie a long thin piece of fabric around sth: *She bound up his wounds.*
UNITE | **3** [VN] **~ A and B (together)**| **~ A to B** to unite people, organizations, etc. so that they live or work together more happily or effectively: *Organizations such as schools, factories and clubs bind a community together.* ◇ *She thought that having his child would bind him to her forever.*
MAKE SB DO STH | **4** [usually passive] **~ sb (to sth)** to force sb to do sth by making them promise to do it or by making it their duty to do it: [VN] *He had been bound to secrecy* (= made to promise not to tell people about sth). ◇ [VNtoinf] *The agreement binds her to repay the debt in full within six months.*—see also BINDING, BOUND
STICK TOGETHER | **5** **~ (sth) (together)** to stick together or to

aɪ	aʊ	eɪ	əʊ	oʊ	ɔɪ	ɪə	eə	ʊə	j	w
my	now	say	go	go	boy	near	hair	pure	yes	wet
			(BrE)	(AmE)						

make things stick together in a solid mass: [V] *Add an egg yolk to make the mixture bind.* ◊ [VN] *Add an egg yolk to bind the mixture together.*

BOOK | **6** [VN] [usually passive] to fasten the pages of a book together and put them inside a cover: *two volumes bound in leather*

SEW EDGE | **7** [VN] [often passive] ~ **sth (with sth)** to sew the edge of sth to decorate it or to make it stronger: *The blankets were bound with satin.*

IDM see HAND *n.*
PHRV **,bind sb 'over** [usually passive] **1** (*AmE, law*) to give sb BAIL while they are waiting to go to trial: *He was bound over for trial.* **2** (*BrE, law*) to give sb a formal warning that if they break the law again they will be punished: *She was bound over to keep the peace for a year.*
■ *noun* [sing.] (*BrE, informal*) an annoying situation that is often difficult to avoid—see also DOUBLE BIND
IDM **in a 'bind** (*AmE*) in a difficult situation that you do not know how to get out of

bind·er /'baɪndə(r)/ *noun* **1** [C] a hard cover for holding sheets of paper, magazines, etc. together: *a ring binder* **2** [C] a person or machine that puts covers on books **3** [C, U] a substance that makes things stick or mix together in a solid form **4** [C] a machine that fastens corn into bunches after it has been cut

bind·ing /'baɪndɪŋ/ *adj., noun*
■ *adj.* ~ **(on/upon sb)** that must be obeyed because it is accepted in law: *a binding promise/agreement/contract*
■ *noun* **1** [C, U] the cover that holds the pages of a book together **2** [C, U] fabric that is fastened to the edge of sth to protect or decorate it **3** [C] a device on a ski that holds the heel and toe of your boot in place and releases the boot automatically if you fall—picture at SKIING

bind·weed /'baɪndwiːd/ *noun* [U] a wild plant that twists itself around other plants

binge /bɪndʒ/ *noun, verb*
■ *noun* (*informal*) a short period of time when you do too much of a particular activity, especially eating or drinking alcohol: *to go on a binge*
■ *verb* (**binge·ing** or **bin·ging**, **binged**, **binged**) [V] ~ **(on sth)** to eat or drink too much, especially without being able to control yourself: *When she's depressed she binges on chocolate.*

bingo /'bɪŋgəʊ; *AmE* -goʊ/ *noun, exclamation*
■ *noun* [U] a game in which each player has a card with numbers on. Numbers are called out in no particular order and the first player whose numbers are all called out, or who has a line of numbers called out, wins a prize: *to play bingo* ◊ *a bingo hall*
■ *exclamation* used to express pleasure and/or surprise because you have found sth that you were looking for, or done sth that you were trying to do: *The computer program searches, and bingo! We've got a match.*

'bin-liner *noun* (*BrE*) a plastic bag that is placed inside a container for holding waste

bin·man /'bɪnmæn/ *noun* (*pl.* **-men** /-men/) (*BrE, informal*) = DUSTMAN

bin·ocu·lars /bɪ'nɒkjələz; *AmE* bɪ'nɑːkjələrz/ (also **'field glasses**) *noun* [pl.] an instrument, like two small TELESCOPES fixed together, that makes objects that are far away seem nearer when you look through it: *a pair of binoculars* ◊ *We looked at the birds through binoculars.*—picture at GLASS

bi·no·mial /baɪ'nəʊmiəl; *AmE* -'noʊ-/ *noun* (*mathematics*) an expression that has two groups of numbers or letters, joined by the sign + or – ▶ **bi·no·mial** *adj.*

bio- /'baɪəʊ; *AmE* 'baɪoʊ/ *combining form* (in nouns, adjectives and adverbs) connected with living things or human life: *biodegradable* ◊ *biography*

bio·chem·ist /ˌbaɪəʊ'kemɪst; *AmE* ˌbaɪoʊ-/ *noun* a scientist who studies biochemistry

bio·chem·is·try /ˌbaɪəʊ'kemɪstri; *AmE* ˌbaɪoʊ-/ *noun* **1** [U] the scientific study of the chemistry of living things **2** [U, C] the chemical structure and behaviour of a living thing: *Your biochemistry is almost identical to that of your cat.* ▶ **bio·chem·ical** /ˌbaɪəʊ'kemɪkl; *AmE* ˌbaɪoʊ-/ *adj.*

bio·degrad·able /ˌbaɪəʊdɪ'greɪdəbl; *AmE* ˌbaɪoʊ-/ *adj.* a substance or chemical that is **biodegradable** can be changed back to a harmless natural state by the action of bacteria, and will therefore not damage the environment

bio·di·ver·sity /ˌbaɪəʊdaɪ'vɜːsəti; *AmE* ˌbaɪoʊdaɪ'vɜːrs-/ (also *less frequent* ˌ**bio,logical di'versity**) *noun* [U] the existence of a large number of different kinds of animals and plants which make a balanced environment

biog·raph·er /baɪ'ɒgrəfə(r); *AmE* -'ɑːg-/ *noun* a person who writes the story of another person's life

biog·raphy /baɪ'ɒgrəfi; *AmE* -'ɑːg-/ *noun* [C, U] (*pl.* **-ies**) the story of a person's life written by sb else; this type of writing: *Boswell's biography of Johnson*—compare AUTOBIOGRAPHY ▶ **bio·graph·ic·al** /ˌbaɪə'græfɪkl/ *adj.*

bio·logic·al /ˌbaɪə'lɒdʒɪkl; *AmE* -'lɑːdʒ-/ *adj.* **1** connected with the science of biology: *the biological sciences* **2** connected with the processes that take place within living things: *the biological effects of radiation* ◊ *the biological control of insect pests* (= using living organisms to destroy them, not chemicals) ◊ *a child's biological parents* (= natural, not adoptive parents) **3** (of washing powder, etc.) using ENZYMES (= chemical substances that are found in plants and animals) to get clothes, etc. clean: *biological and non-biological powders*

ˌ**bio,logical 'clock** *noun* (*technical*) a mechanism in plants and animals that controls regular physical activities such as sleeping: (*figurative*) *At 35, Kate's biological clock was ticking* (= she was beginning to think that she would soon be too old to have children).

ˌ**bio,logical di'versity** *noun* (*rare*) = BIODIVERSITY

ˌ**bio,logical 'warfare** (also ˌ**germ 'warfare**) *noun* [U] the use of harmful bacteria as weapons of war

biolo·gist /baɪ'ɒlədʒɪst; *AmE* -'ɑːl-/ *noun* a scientist who studies biology

biol·ogy /baɪ'ɒlədʒi; *AmE* -'ɑːl-/ *noun* [U] **1** the scientific study of the life and structure of plants and animals: *a degree in biology*—compare BOTANY, ZOOLOGY **2** the way in which the body and cells of a living thing behave: *How far is human nature determined by biology?* ◊ *the biology of marine animals*

bio·mass /'baɪəʊmæs; *AmE* 'baɪoʊ-/ *noun* [U, sing.] (*technical*) the total quantity or weight of plants and animals in a particular area or volume

bi·onic /baɪ'ɒnɪk; *AmE* -'ɑːnɪk/ *adj.* (in SCIENCE FICTION stories) having parts of the body that are electronic, and therefore able to do things that are not possible for normal human beings

bio·phys·ics /ˌbaɪəʊ'fɪzɪks; *AmE* ˌbaɪoʊ-/ *noun* [U] the science which uses the laws and methods of physics to study biology

bio·pic /'baɪəʊpɪk; *AmE* 'baɪoʊ-/ *noun* (*informal*) a film/movie about the life of a particular person

bi·opsy /'baɪɒpsi; *AmE* -ɑːpsi/ *noun* (*pl.* **-ies**) the removal and examination of tissue from the body of sb who is ill, in order to find out more about their disease

bio·sphere /'baɪəʊsfɪə(r); *AmE* 'baɪoʊsfɪr/ *noun* [sing.] (*technical*) the part of the earth's surface and atmosphere in which plants and animals can live

bio·tech·nol·ogy /ˌbaɪəʊtek'nɒlədʒi; *AmE* ˌbaɪoʊtek-'nɑːl-/ *noun* [U] (*technical*) the use of living cells and bacteria in industrial and scientific processes ▶ **bio·tech·no·logic·al** *adj.*: *biotechnological research*

bi·par·tisan /ˌbaɪpɑː'tɪzæn; *AmE* ˌbaɪ'pɑːrtɪzn/ *adj.* (*written*) involving two political parties: *a bipartisan policy*

biped /'baɪped/ *noun* (*technical*) any creature with two feet—compare QUADRUPED

bi·plane /'baɪpleɪn/ *noun* an early type of plane with two sets of wings, one above the other—compare MONOPLANE

birch /bɜːtʃ; *AmE* bɜːrtʃ/ *noun* **1** [C, U] (also **'birch tree** [C]) a tree with smooth bark and thin branches, that grows in northern countries—see also SILVER BIRCH **2** (also **birch·wood** /'bɜːtʃwʊd; *AmE* 'bɜːrtʃ-/) [U] the hard pale wood of the birch tree **3** (**the birch**) [sing.] the practice of hitting sb with a bunch of birch sticks, as a punishment

bird /bɜːd; *AmE* bɜːrd/ *noun* **1** a creature that is covered with feathers and has two wings and two legs. Most birds can fly: *a bird's nest with two eggs in it* ◊ *a species of bird* ◊ *The area has a wealth of bird life.*—see also GAME BIRD, SEABIRD, SONGBIRD, WATERBIRD—picture on page A6 **2** (*BrE, slang,* sometimes *offensive*) a way of referring to a young woman **3** (*informal*) a person of a particular type, especially sb who is strange or unusual in some way: *a wise old bird* ◊ *She is that rare bird: a politician with a social conscience.* **IDM** **be (strictly) for the birds** (*informal*) to not be important or practical **the bird has 'flown** the wanted person has escaped **a bird in the 'hand is worth two in the 'bush** (*saying*) it is better to keep sth that you already have than to risk losing it by trying to get much more **the birds and the 'bees** (*humorous*) the basic facts about sex, especially as told to children **a ˌbird's-ˌeye 'view (of sth)** a view of sth from a high position looking down **birds of a 'feather (flock to'gether)** (*saying*) people of the same sort (are found together) **give sb/get the 'bird** (*informal*) **1** (*BrE*) to shout at sb as a sign of disapproval; to be shouted at **2** (*AmE*) to make a rude sign at sb with your middle finger; to have this sign made at you—more at EARLY *adj.*, KILL *v.*, LITTLE *adj.*

bird·brain /'bɜːdbreɪn; *AmE* 'bɜːrd-/ *noun* (*especially AmE*) a stupid person

bird·cage /'bɜːdkeɪdʒ; *AmE* 'bɜːrd-/ *noun* a cage in which birds are kept, usually one in a house

bir·die /'bɜːdi; *AmE* 'bɜːrdi/ *noun* **1** (*spoken*) a child's word for a little bird **2** (in golf) a score of one stroke less than PAR (= the standard score for a hole)—compare BOGEY, EAGLE **3** (*AmE*) = SHUTTLECOCK

ˌbird of 'paradise *noun* (*pl.* **birds of paradise**) a bird with very bright feathers, found mainly in New Guinea

ˌbird of 'passage *noun* (*pl.* **birds of passage**) **1** a bird that travels regularly from one part of the world to another at different seasons of the year **2** a person who passes through a place without staying there long

ˌbird of 'prey *noun* (*pl.* **birds of prey**) a bird that hunts and kills other creatures for food. EAGLES, HAWKS and OWLS are all birds of prey.—picture on page A6

bird·song /'bɜːdsɒŋ; *AmE* 'bɜːrdsɔːŋ/ *noun* [U] the musical sounds made by birds

'bird table *noun* (*BrE*) a wooden platform in a garden on which people put food for birds

bird·watch·er /'bɜːdwɒtʃə(r); *AmE* 'bɜːrdwɑːtʃər; -wɔːtʃ-/ *noun* a person who watches birds in their natural environment and identifies different breeds ▸ **bird·watch·ing** *noun* [U]

Biro™ /'baɪrəʊ; *AmE* 'baɪroʊ/ *noun* (*pl.* **-os**) (*BrE*) a plastic pen with a metal ball at the top that rolls ink onto the paper—compare BALLPOINT—picture at STATIONERY

birth /bɜːθ; *AmE* bɜːrθ/ *noun* **1** [U, C] the time when a baby is born; the process of being born: *The baby weighed three kilos at birth.* ◊ *John was present at the birth of both his children.* ◊ *It was a difficult birth.* ◊ *a hospital/home birth* ◊ *Mark has been blind from birth.* ◊ *Please state your date of birth.* **2** [sing.] the beginning of a new situation, idea, place, etc: *the birth of a new society in South Africa* **3** [U] a person's origin or the social position of their family: *Anne was French by birth but lived most of her life in Italy.* ◊ *a woman of noble birth* **IDM** **give 'birth (to sb/sth)** to produce a baby or young animal: *She died shortly after giving birth.* ◊ *Mary gave birth to a healthy baby girl.* ◊ (*figurative*) *It was the study of history that gave birth to the social sciences.*

'birth certificate *noun* an official document that shows when and where a person was born

'birth control *noun* [U] the practice of controlling the number of children a person has, using various methods of CONTRACEPTION: *a reliable method of birth control*

birth·day /'bɜːdeɪ; *AmE* 'bɜːrð-/ *noun* the day in each year which is the same date as the one on which you were born: *Happy Birthday!* ◊ *Oliver's 13th birthday* ◊ *a birthday card/party/present* **IDM** **in your 'birthday suit** (*humorous*) not wearing any clothes

birth·ing /'bɜːθɪŋ; *AmE* 'bɜːrθ-/ *noun* [U] the action or process of giving birth: *a birthing pool*

birth·mark /'bɜːθmɑːk; *AmE* 'bɜːrθmɑːrk/ *noun* a red or brown mark on a person's skin that has been there since they were born

'birth mother *noun* the woman who gave birth to a child who has been ADOPTED

birth·place /'bɜːθpleɪs; *AmE* 'bɜːrθ-/ *noun* **1** the house or area where a person was born, especially a famous person **2** the place where sth first happened: *Hawaii was the birthplace of surfing.*

'birth rate *noun* the number of births every year for every 1000 people in the population of a place: *a low/high birth rate*

birth·right /'bɜːθraɪt/ *noun* a thing that sb has a right to because of the family or country they were born in, or because it is a basic right of all human beings: *The property is the birthright of the eldest child.* ◊ *Education is every child's birthright.*

bis·cuit /'bɪskɪt/ *noun* **1** [C] (*BrE*) a small flat dry cake for one person, usually sweet, and baked until crisp: *a packet of chocolate biscuits* ◊ *a selection of cheese biscuits*—compare COOKIE—see also DIGESTIVE BISCUIT, DOG BISCUIT **2** [C] (*AmE*) a soft bread roll, often eaten with GRAVY **3** [U] a pale yellowish-brown colour **IDM** **take the 'biscuit** (*BrE*) (also **take the 'cake** *AmE, BrE*) (*informal*) to be the most surprising, annoying, etc. thing that has happened or that sb has done: *You've done some stupid things before, but this really takes the biscuit!*

bi·sect /baɪ'sekt/ *verb* [VN] (*technical*) to divide sth into two equal parts

bi·sex·ual /ˌbaɪ'sekʃuəl/ *adj., noun*
■ *adj.* **1** sexually attracted to both men and women **2** (*biology*) having both male and female sexual organs ▸ **bi·sexu·al·ity** /ˌbaɪsekʃu'æləti/ *noun* [U]
■ *noun* a person who is bisexual—compare HETEROSEXUAL, HOMOSEXUAL

bishop /'bɪʃəp/ *noun* **1** a senior priest in charge of the work of the Church in a city or district: *the Bishop of Oxford* ◊ *Bishop Harries*—see also ARCHBISHOP **2** a piece used in the game of CHESS that is shaped like a bishop's hat and can move any number of squares in a DIAGONAL line—picture on page A8

bish·op·ric /'bɪʃəprɪk/ *noun* **1** the position of a bishop **2** the district for which a bishop is responsible **SYN** DIOCESE

bison /'baɪsn/ *noun* (*pl.* **bison**) a large hairy wild animal of the cow family. There are two types of bison, the N American (also called BUFFALO) and the European: *a herd of bison*

bis·tro /'biːstrəʊ; *AmE* -stroʊ/ *noun* (*pl.* **-os**) a small informal restaurant

bit /bɪt/ *noun*
SMALL AMOUNT **1** (**a bit**) [sing.] (used as an adverb) (*especially BrE*) rather; a little: *These trousers are a bit tight.* ◊ *'Are you tired?' 'Yes, I am a bit.'* ◊ *It costs a bit more than I wanted to spend.* ◊ *I can lend you fifty pounds, if you want. That should help a bit.* **2** (**a bit**) [sing.] (*especially BrE*) a short time or distance: *Wait a bit!* ◊ *Can you move up a bit?* ◊ *Greg thought for a bit before answering.* **3** [C] **~ of sth** (*especially BrE*) a small amount or piece of sth: *some useful bits of information* ◊ *With a bit of luck, we'll be there by 12.* ◊ *I've got a bit of shopping to do.* ◊ *a bit of cake* ◊ *bits of grass/paper*

PART OF STH **4** [C] (*especially BrE*) a part of sth larger: *The best bit of the holiday was seeing the Grand Canyon.* ◊ *The school play was a huge success—the audience roared with laughter at all the funny bits.*

LARGE AMOUNT **5** [sing.] **a ~ (of sth)** (*informal, especially BrE*) a large amount: *'How much does he earn?' 'Quite a*

s	t	v	z	ʃ	ʒ	tʃ	dʒ	θ	ð	ŋ
see	tea	van	zoo	shoe	vision	chain	jam	thin	this	sing

bit!' ◊ *The new system will* **take a bit of** *getting used to* (= it will take a long time to get used to).

COMPUTING | **6** [C] the smallest unit of information used by a computer

FOR HORSE | **7** [C] a metal bar that is put in a horse's mouth so that the rider can control it

TOOL | **8** [C] a tool or part of a tool for DRILLING (= making) holes—see also DRILL—picture at TOOL

MONEY | **9** (*AmE, informal*) an amount of money equal to 12½ cents

—see also BITE, BIT, BITTEN *v.*

IDM **the (whole)…bit** (*informal, disapproving*) behaviour or ideas that are typical of a particular group, type of person or activity: *She couldn't accept the whole drug-culture bit.* **bit by 'bit** a piece at a time; gradually: *He assembled the model aircraft bit by bit.* ◊ *Bit by bit memories of the night came back to me.* **a bit 'much** (*informal*) not fair or not reasonable: *It's a bit much calling me at three in the morning.* **a bit of a …** (*informal, especially BrE*) used when talking about unpleasant or negative things or ideas, to mean 'rather a …': *We may have a bit of a problem on our hands.* ◊ *The rail strike is a bit of a pain.* **a bit of all 'right** (*BrE, slang*) a person that you think is sexually attractive **a bit of 'rough** (*BrE, slang*) a person of a low social class who has a sexual relationship with sb of a higher class **a bit on the 'side** (*BrE, slang*) the boyfriend or girlfriend of sb who is already married or in a steady sexual relationship with sb else ,**bits and 'pieces/'bobs** (*BrE, informal*) small objects or items of various kinds: *She stuffed all her bits and pieces into a bag and left.* **do your 'bit** (*informal*) to do your share of a task: *We can finish this job on time if everyone does their bit.* **every bit as good, bad, etc. (as sb/sth)** just as good, bad, etc.; equally good, bad, etc: *Rome is every bit as beautiful as Paris.* **get the bit between your teeth** (*informal*) to become very enthusiastic about sth that you have started to do so that you are unlikely to stop until you have finished **not a 'bit | not one (little) 'bit** not at all; not in any way: *'Are you cold?' 'Not a bit.'* ◊ *It's not a bit of use* (= there's no point in) *complaining.* ◊ *I don't like that idea one bit.* **not a 'bit of it!** (*informal, BrE*) used for saying that sth that you had expected to happen did not happen: *You'd think she'd be tired after the journey but not a bit of it!* **to bits 1** into small pieces: *The book fell to bits in my hands.* ◊ *She took the engine to bits, then carefully put it together again.* **2** (*spoken, informal*) very much: *I love my kids to bits.* ◊ *She was thrilled to bits when I said I'd come.*—more at BLIND *adj.,* CHAMP *v.*

BRITISH / AMERICAN
a bit / a little

In *BrE* it is common to use **a bit** to mean 'slightly' or 'to a small extent': *These shoes are a bit tight.* ◊ *I'll be a bit later home tomorrow.* ◊ *Can you turn the volume up a bit?*

It is more common in *AmE* to say **a little**, or (*informal*) **a little bit**. You can also use these phrases in *BrE*: *These shoes are a little bit too tight.* ◊ *I'll be a little later home tomorrow.* ◊ *Can you turn the volume up a little bit?*

---

bitch /bɪtʃ/ *noun, verb*

■ *noun* **1** a female dog: *a greyhound bitch* **2** (*slang, disapproving*) an offensive way of referring to a woman, especially an unpleasant one: *You stupid little bitch!* ◊ *She can be a real bitch.* **3** (*slang*) a thing that causes problems or difficulties: *Life's a bitch.*—see also SON OF A BITCH

■ *verb* [V] ~ (**about sb/sth**) (*informal*) to make unkind and critical remarks about sb/sth, especially when they are not there

bitchy /ˈbɪtʃi/ *adj.* (*informal*) saying unpleasant and unkind things about other people: *bitchy remarks* ► **bitchi·ness** *noun* [U]

bite /baɪt/ *verb, noun*

■ *verb* (**bit** /bɪt/, **bit·ten** /ˈbɪtn/)

USE TEETH | **1** ~ (**into/through/off sth**) to use your teeth to

---

cut into or through sth: [VN] *She was bitten by the family dog.* ◊ *Stop biting your nails!* ◊ [V] *She bit into a ripe juicy pear.* ◊ *Does your dog bite?* ◊ (*spoken*) *Come here! I won't bite!* (= you don't need to be afraid) ◊ *He bit off a large chunk of bread/He bit a large chunk of bread off.*

OF INSECT/SNAKE | **2** to wound sb by making a small hole or mark in their skin: [VN] *We were badly bitten by mosquitoes.* ◊ [V] *Most European spiders don't bite.*

OF FISH | **3** [V] if a fish **bites**, it takes food from the hook of a FISHING LINE and may get caught

HAVE EFFECT | **4** [V] to have an unpleasant effect: *The recession is beginning to bite.*

IDM **be bitten by sth** to develop a strong interest in or enthusiasm for sth: *He's been bitten by the travel bug.* **bite the 'bullet** (*informal*) to start to deal with an unpleasant or difficult situation which cannot be avoided **ORIGIN** From the custom of giving soldiers a bullet to bite on during a medical operation without anaesthetic. **bite the 'dust** (*informal*) **1** to fail, or to be defeated or destroyed: *Thousands of small businesses bite the dust every year.* **2** (*humorous*) to die **bite the hand that 'feeds you** to harm sb who has helped you or supported you **bite your 'lip** to stop yourself from saying sth or from showing an emotion **bite off more than you can 'chew** to try to do too much, or sth that is too difficult **bite your 'tongue** to stop yourself from saying sth that might upset sb or cause an argument, although you want to speak: *I didn't believe her explanation but I bit my tongue.* **I, etc. could have bitten my/his/her 'tongue out/off** used when sb says sth stupid or embarrassing and immediately wishes they had not said it—more at HEAD *n.,* ONCE *adv.*

PHRV ,**bite 'back (at sb/sth)** to react angrily, especially when sb has criticized or harmed you: *The election was a chance for the people to bite back at the government.* ,**bite sth↔'back** to stop yourself from saying sth or from showing your feelings: *She bit back her anger.* ,**bite 'into sth** to cut into the surface of sth: *The horses' hooves bit deep into the soft earth.*

■ *noun*

USING TEETH | **1** [C] an act of biting: *The dog gave me a playful bite.* ◊ *He has to wear a brace to correct his bite* (= the way the upper and lower teeth fit together).

FOOD | **2** [C] a small piece of food that you can bite from a larger piece: *She took a couple of bites of the sandwich.* ◊ *He didn't eat a bite of his dinner* (= he ate nothing). **3 a** ~ (**to eat**) [sing.] (*informal*) a small amount of food; a small meal: *How about a bite of lunch?* ◊ *We just have time for a bite to eat before the movie.*

OF INSECT/ANIMAL | **4** [C] a wound made by an animal or insect: *Dog bites can get infected.* ◊ *a mosquito/snake bite*

STRONG TASTE | **5** [U] a pleasant strong taste: *Cheese will add extra bite to any pasta dish.*

COLD | **6** [sing.] a sharp cold feeling: *There's a bite in the air tonight.*

POWERFUL EFFECT | **7** [U] a quality that makes sth effective or powerful: *The performance had no bite to it.*

OF FISH | **8** [C] the act of a fish biting food on a hook

—see also FROSTBITE, LOVE BITE, SOUND BITE

IDM **a bite at/of the 'cherry** (*BrE*) an opportunity to do sth: *They were eager for a second bite of the cherry.*—more at BARK *n.*

'**bite-sized** (also '**bite-size**) *adj.* [usually before noun] small enough to put into the mouth and eat: *Cut the meat into bite-sized pieces.*

bit·ing /ˈbaɪtɪŋ/ *adj.* **1** (of a wind) very cold and unpleasant **2** (of remarks) cruel and critical: *biting sarcasm/wit* ► **bit·ing·ly** *adv.*

bit·map /ˈbɪtmæp/ *noun* (*computing*) a way in which an image is stored with a fixed number of BITS (= units of information) for each unit of the image ► **bit·map** *verb* (-pp-) [VN]

'**bit part** *noun* a small part in a film/movie

bit·ten *pp of* BITE

bit·ter /ˈbɪtə(r)/ *adj., noun*

■ *adj.* **HELP** **more bitter** and **most bitter** are the usual comparative and superlative forms, but **bitterest** can

| æ | ɑː | e | ɜː | ə | ɪ | iː | i | ɒ | ɔː | ʌ | ʊ | u | uː |
| cat | father | ten | bird | about | sit | see | many | got | saw | cup | put | actual | too |

(BrE)

B

also be used. **1** (of arguments, disputes, etc.) very fierce and unpleasant, with a lot of anger and hatred involved: *a long and bitter dispute* **2** (of people) feeling angry and unhappy because you feel that you have been treated unfairly: *She is very bitter about losing her job.* **3** [usually before noun] making you feel very unhappy; caused by great unhappiness: *to weep/shed bitter tears* ◊ *Losing the match was a bitter disappointment for the team.* ◊ *I've learnt from bitter experience not to trust what he says.* **4** (of food, etc) having a strong, unpleasant taste; not sweet: *Black coffee leaves a bitter taste in the mouth.*—compare SWEET **5** (of weather conditions) extremely cold and unpleasant: *bitter cold* ◊ *a bitter wind* ◊ *It's really bitter out today.* ▶ **bit·ter·ness** *noun* [U]: *The pay cut caused bitterness among the staff.* ◊ *The flowers of the hop plant add bitterness to the beer.* **IDM** **a bitter 'pill (for sb) (to swallow)** a fact or an event that is unpleasant and difficult to accept **to/until the bitter 'end** continuing until you have done everything you can, or until sth is completely finished, in spite of difficulties and problems: *They were prepared to fight to the bitter end for their rights.*

■ *noun* (*BrE*) **1** [U, C] a type of beer with a dark colour and a strong bitter taste, that is very popular in Britain: *A pint of bitter, please.*—compare MILD **2** (**bitters**) [U+sing./ pl. *v.*] a strong bitter alcoholic liquid that is made from plants and added to other alcoholic drinks to give flavour: *gin with a dash of bitters*

bitter 'lemon *noun* [U] (*BrE*) a FIZZY drink (= with bubbles) that tastes of lemon and is slightly BITTER

bit·ter·ly /'bɪtəli; *AmE* -tərli/ *adv.* **1** in a way that shows feelings of sadness or anger: *She wept bitterly.* ◊ *They complained bitterly.* ◊ *The development was bitterly opposed by the local community.* **2** (describing unpleasant or sad feelings) extremely: *bitterly disappointed/ashamed* **3**—cold very cold

bitter-'sweet *adj.* (*BrE*) **1** bringing pleasure mixed with sadness: *bitter-sweet memories* **2** (of tastes or smells) bitter and sweet at the same time

bitty /'bɪti/ *adj.* (*BrE, informal*) made up of many small separate parts, which do not seem to fit together well

bitu·men /'bɪtʃəmən; *AmE* bə'tu:mən/ *noun* [U] a black sticky substance obtained from oil, used for covering roads or roofs

bi·tu·min·ous /bɪ'tju:mɪnəs; *AmE* -bə'tu:-/ *adj.* containing bitumen

bi·valve /'baɪvælv/ *noun* (*technical*) any shellfish with a shell in two parts, for example a MUSSEL—compare MOLLUSC

biv·ouac /'bɪvuæk/ *noun, verb*
■ *noun* a temporary camp or shelter, without using a tent, that is made and used especially by people climbing mountains or by soldiers
■ *verb* (-ck-) [V] to spend the night in a bivouac

bi·zarre /bɪ'zɑː(r)/ *adj.* very strange or unusual **SYN** WEIRD: *a bizarre situation/incident/story* ◊ *bizarre behaviour* ▶ **bi·zarre·ly** *adv.*: *bizarrely dressed*

blab /blæb/ *verb* (-bb-) ~ (to sb) (about sth) (*informal*) to tell sb information that should be kept secret: [V] *Someone must have blabbed to the police.* [also VN]

blab·ber /'blæbə(r)/ *verb* [V] ~ (on) (about sth) (*informal*) to talk in a way that other people think is silly and annoying: *What was she blabbering on about this time?*

black /blæk/ *adj., noun, verb*
■ *adj.* (**black·er, black·est**)
COLOUR **1** having the very darkest colour, like night or coal: *a shiny black car* ◊ *black storm clouds*
WITH NO LIGHT **2** without light; completely dark: *a black night*
PEOPLE **3** (also **Black**) belonging to a race of people who have dark skin; connected with black people: *a black woman writer* ◊ *black culture* **HELP** **Black** is the word most widely used and generally accepted in Britain.

In the US the currently accepted term is **African American**.
TEA/COFFEE **4** without milk: *Two black coffees, please.*—compare WHITE
DIRTY **5** very dirty; covered with dirt: *chimneys black with smoke* ◊ *Go and wash your hands; they're absolutely black!*
ANGRY **6** full of anger or hatred: *She's been in a really black mood all day.* ◊ *Rory shot her a black look.*
DEPRESSING **7** without hope; very depressing: *The future looks pretty black, I'm afraid.* ◊ *It's been another black day for the north-east with the announcement of further job losses.*
EVIL **8** (*literary*) evil or wicked: *black deeds/lies*
HUMOUR **9** dealing with unpleasant or terrible things, such as murder, in a humorous way: *'Good place to bury the bodies,' she joked with black humour.* ◊ *The play is a black comedy.*
▶ **black·ness** *noun* [U, sing.]: *She peered out into the blackness of the night.*
IDM **(beat sb) black and 'blue** (to hit sb until they are) covered with BRUISES (= blue, brown or purple marks on the body) **not as black as he/she/it is 'painted** not as bad as people say he/she/it is: *He's not very friendly, but he's not as black as he's painted.*—more at POT *n.*
■ *noun*
COLOUR **1** [U] the very darkest colour, like night or coal: *the black of the night sky* ◊ *Everyone at the funeral was dressed in black.*
PEOPLE **2** (also **Black**) [C, usually pl.] a member of a race of people who have dark skin **HELP** In this meaning **black** is more common in the plural. It can sound offensive in the singular. Instead, you can use the adjective ('a black man/woman') or, in the US, **African American**.
IDM **be in the 'black** to have money, for example in your bank account: *The company has managed to stay in the black for the year ending December 31.*—compare (BE IN) THE RED at RED **,black and 'white** having no colours except black, white and shades of grey (in photographs, on television, etc.): *a film made in black and white* ◊ *black-and-white photos* **in black and white** in writing or in print: *I never thought they'd put it in black and white on the front page.* **(in) black and white** in a way that makes people or things seem completely bad or good, or completely right or wrong: *It's a complex issue, but he only sees it in black and white.* ◊ *This is not a black-and-white decision* (= where the difference between two choices is completely clear).
■ *verb* [VN] **1** (*BrE*) to refuse to deal with goods or to do business with sb as a political protest **SYN** BOYCOTT: *The unions have blacked all imports from the country.* **2** (*rare*) to make sth black **SYN** BLACKEN
PHRV **,black 'out** to lose consciousness for a short time: *The driver had probably blacked out at the wheel.*—related noun BLACKOUT **,black sth↔'out 1** to make a place dark by turning off lights, covering windows, etc: *A power failure blacked out the city last night.* ◊ *a house with blacked out windows*—related noun BLACKOUT **2** to prevent sth such as a piece of writing or a television broadcast from being read or seen: *Some lines of the document have been blacked out for security reasons.*

the ,black 'arts *noun* [pl.] = BLACK MAGIC

black·ball /'blækbɔːl/ *verb* [VN] to prevent sb from joining a club or a group by voting against them

,black 'belt *noun* **1** a belt that you can earn in a sport such as JUDO or KARATE which shows that you have reached a very high standard **2** a person who has gained a black belt

black·berry /'blækbəri; *AmE* -beri/ (*pl.* **-ies**) (*BrE* also **bram·ble**) *noun* a small soft black fruit that grows on a prickly bush in gardens/yards or in the countryside. The bush is also called a **blackberry/bramble**: *blackberry and apple pie*—picture on page A2

black·berry·ing /'blækbəriɪŋ; *AmE* -beriɪŋ/ *noun* [U] the act of picking blackberries: *Shall we go blackberrying?*

black·bird /'blækbɜːd; *AmE* -bɜːrd/ *noun* **1** a European

aɪ	aʊ	eɪ	əʊ	oʊ	ɔɪ	ɪə	eə	ʊə	j	w
my	now	say	go (BrE)	go (AmE)	boy	near	hair	pure	yes	wet

bird: the male is black with a yellow beak and the female is brown with a brown beak **2** a black N American bird, larger than the European blackbird, related to the STARLING

black·board /ˈblækbɔːd; *AmE* -bɔːrd/ (also **chalk·board** especially in *AmE*) *noun* a large board with a smooth black or dark green surface that teachers write on with a piece of chalk: *to write on the blackboard*—compare WHITEBOARD

black 'box *noun* **1** (also **'flight recorder**) a small machine in a plane that records all the details of each flight and is useful for finding out the cause of an accident **2** [usually sing.] (*technical*) a complicated piece of equipment, usually electronic, that you know produces particular results, but that you do not completely understand

black·cur·rant /ˌblækˈkʌrənt; *AmE* -ˈkɜːr-/ *noun* a small black berry that grows in bunches on a garden bush and can be eaten: *blackcurrant jam* ◊ *a blackcurrant bush*

the ˌblack eˈconomy *noun* [sing.] (*BrE*) business activity or work that is done without the knowledge of the government or other officials so that people can avoid paying tax on the money they earn

black·en /ˈblækən/ *verb* **1** to make sth black; to become black: [VN] *Their faces were blackened with soot.* ◊ *Smoke had blackened the walls.* [alsoV] **2** [VN] ~ **sb's name/reputation/character** to say unpleasant things that give people a bad opinion of sb: *He accused the newspaper of trying to blacken his name.*

black 'eye *noun* an area of dark skin (called a BRUISE), that can form around sb's eye when they receive a blow on it

black·guard /ˈblægɑːd; *AmE* -gɑːrd/ *noun* (*old-fashioned, BrE*) a man who is dishonest and has no sense of what is right and what is wrong

black·head /ˈblækhed/ *noun* a small spot on the skin, often on the face, with a black top

black 'hole *noun* an area in space that nothing, not even light, can escape from, because GRAVITY (= the force that pulls objects in space towards each other) is so strong there: (*figurative*) *The company viewed the venture as a financial black hole* (= it would use a lot of the company's money with no real result).

black 'ice *noun* [U] ice in a thin layer on the surface of a road

black·jack /ˈblækdʒæk/ *noun* **1** (*BrE* also **pon·toon**) [U] a card game in which players try to collect cards with a total value of 21 **2** (*especially AmE*) a type of CLUB used as a weapon, especially a metal pipe covered with leather

black·leg /ˈblækleg/ *noun* (*BrE, disapproving*) a person who continues to work when the people they work with are on strike; a person who is employed to work instead of those who are on strike—compare STRIKE-BREAKER—see also SCAB

black·list /ˈblæklɪst/ *noun, verb*

▪ *noun* a list of the names of people, companies, products or countries that an organization or a government considers unacceptable and that must be avoided

▪ *verb* [VN] to put the name of a person, a company, a product or a country on a blacklist: *She was blacklisted by all the major Hollywood studios because of her political views.*

black 'magic *noun* [U] (also **the black 'arts** [pl.]) a type of magic which is believed to use the power of the Devil in order to do evil

black·mail /ˈblækmeɪl/ *noun, verb*

▪ *noun* [U] **1** the crime of demanding money from a person by threatening to tell sb else a secret about them **2** the act of putting pressure on a person or a group to do sth they do not want to do, for example by making threats or by making them feel guilty: *emotional/moral blackmail*

▪ *verb* [VN] ~ **sb** (**into doing sth**) to force sb to give you money or do sth for you by threatening them, for example by saying you will tell people a secret about them: *She blackmailed him for years by threatening to tell the newspapers about their affair.* ◊ *The President said he*

wouldn't be blackmailed into agreeing to the terrorists' demands.

black·mail·er /ˈblækmeɪlə(r)/ *noun* a person who commits blackmail

Black Maria /ˌblæk məˈraɪə/ *noun* (*old-fashioned, BrE*) a police van for transporting prisoners

black 'mark *noun* (*BrE*) a note, either in writing on an official record, or in sb's mind, of sth you have done or said that makes people think badly of you: *She earned a black mark for opposing company policy.* ◊ *The public scandal was a black mark against him.*

black 'market *noun* [usually sing.] an illegal form of trade in which foreign money, or goods that are difficult to obtain, are bought and sold: *to buy/sell goods on the black market* ◊ *a flourishing black market in foreign currency*

black marke'teer *noun* a person who sells goods on the black market

Black 'Muslim *noun* a member of a group of black people, especially in the US, who follow the religion of Islam and want a separate black society

black·out /ˈblækaʊt/ *noun* **1** a period of darkness caused by an electrical power failure **2** a situation when the government or the police will not allow any news or information on a particular subject to be given to the public **3** (*especially BrE*) a period of time during a war when all lights must be put out or covered at night, so that they cannot be seen by an enemy attacking by air **4** [usually pl.] (*BrE*) a covering for windows that stops light being seen from outside, or light from outside from coming into a room **5** a temporary loss of consciousness, sight or memory: *She had a blackout and couldn't remember anything about the accident.*

black 'pudding (*BrE*) (*AmE* **'blood sausage**) *noun* [U, C] a type of large dark sausage made from pig's blood, fat and grain

black 'sheep *noun* [usually sing.] a person who is different from the rest of their family or another group, and who is considered bad or embarrassing: *the black sheep of the family*

black·smith /ˈblæksmɪθ/ (also **smith**) *noun* a person whose job is to make and repair things made of iron, especially HORSESHOES—compare FARRIER

ˈblack spot *noun* (*BrE*) a place, a situation or an event that is a problem or that causes a lot of problems: *an environmental black spot* ◊ *That corner is a notorious accident black spot* (= a lot of accidents happen there).

black·thorn /ˈblækθɔːn; *AmE* -θɔːrn/ *noun* [U] a prickly bush with black branches, white flowers and sour purple fruit called SLOES: *a blackthorn bush/hedge*

black 'tie *noun* a black BOW TIE worn with a DINNER JACKET ▶ **black 'tie** *adj.*: *The party is black tie* (= dinner jackets should be worn). ◊ *a black-tie dinner*

black·top /ˈblæktɒp; *AmE* -tɑːp/ *noun, verb* (*AmE*) = TARMAC

black 'widow *noun* a poisonous American spider. The female black widow often eats the male.

blad·der /ˈblædə(r)/ *noun* **1** an organ that is shaped like a bag in which liquid waste (= URINE) collects before it is passed out of the body—see also GALL BLADDER—picture at BODY **2** a bag made of rubber, leather, etc. that can be filled with air or liquid, such as the one inside a football

blade /bleɪd/ *noun* **1** the flat part of a knife, tool or machine, which has a sharp edge or edges for cutting—see also RAZOR BLADE, SWITCHBLADE—picture at CUTLERY, SCISSORS **2** one of the flat parts that turn around in an engine or on a HELICOPTER: *the blades of a propeller* ◊ *rotor blades on a helicopter* **3** the flat wide part of an OAR (= one of the long poles that are used to row a boat) that goes in the water—picture at BOAT **4** a single flat leaf of grass—see also SHOULDER BLADE

blah /blɑː/ *noun, adj.*

▪ *noun* [U] (*spoken*) people say **blah, blah, blah**, when they do not want to give the exact words that sb has said or written because they think they are not important or are boring: *They said, 'Come in, sit down, blah, blah, blah, sign here'.*

■ *adj.* (*AmE, informal*) **1** not interesting: *The movie was pretty blah.* **2** not feeling well; feeling slightly unhappy: *I don't know what's wrong with me; I just feel kind of blah.*

blame /bleɪm/ *verb, noun*

■ *verb* [VN] ~ **sb/sth (for sth)**| ~ **sth on sb/sth** to think or say that sb/sth is responsible for sth bad: *She doesn't blame anyone for her father's death.* ◊ *A dropped cigarette is being blamed for the fire.* ◊ *Police are blaming the accident on dangerous driving.* **IDM be to blame (for sth)** to be responsible for sth bad: *If anyone's to blame, it's me.* ◊ *Which driver was to blame for the accident?* **don't blame 'me** (*spoken*) used to advise sb not to do sth, when you think they will do it despite your advice: *Call her if you like, but don't blame me if she's angry.* **I don't 'blame you/her, etc. (for doing sth)** (*spoken*) used to say that you think that what sb did was reasonable and the right thing to do: *'I just slammed the phone down when he said that.' 'I don't blame you!'* **only have yourself to 'blame** used to say that you think sth is sb's own fault: *If you lose your job, you'll only have yourself to blame.*

■ *noun* [U] ~ **(for sth)** responsibility for doing sth badly or wrongly; saying that sb is responsible for sth: *to lay/put the blame for sth on sb* ◊ *The government will have to take the blame for the riots.* ◊ *Why do I always get the blame for everything that goes wrong?*—compare CREDIT *n.* (7)

blame·less /ˈbleɪmləs/ *adj.* (*written*) doing no wrong; free from responsibility for doing sth bad **SYN** INNOCENT: *to lead a blameless life* ◊ *None of us is entirely blameless in this matter.* ► **blame·less·ly** *adv.*

blame·worthy /ˈbleɪmwɜːði; *AmE* -wɜːrði/ *adj.* (*formal*) deserving disapproval and criticism; responsible for doing sth wrong

blanch /blɑːntʃ; *AmE* blæntʃ/ *verb* **1** [V] ~ **(at sth)** (*written*) to become pale because you are shocked or frightened: *He blanched visibly when he heard the news.* **2** [VN] to prepare food, especially vegetables, by putting it into boiling water for a short time

blanc·mange /bləˈmɒnʒ; *AmE* -ˈmɑːnʒ/ *noun* [C, U] (*BrE*) a cold DESSERT (= a sweet dish) that looks like jelly, made with milk and flavoured with fruit

bland /blænd/ *adj.* (**bland·er, bland·est**) **1** with little colour, excitement or interest; without anything to attract attention: *bland background music* **2** not having a strong or interesting taste: *a rather bland diet of soup, fish and bread* **3** showing no strong emotions or excitement; not saying anything very interesting: *a bland expression/smile* ◊ *After the meeting, a bland statement was issued.* ► **bland·ly** *adv.* **bland·ness** *noun* [U]

bland·ish·ments /ˈblændɪʃmənts/ *noun* [pl.] (*formal*) pleasant things that you say to sb or do for them to try to persuade them to do sth

blank /blæŋk/ *adj., noun, verb*

■ *adj.* **1** empty, with nothing written, printed or recorded on it: *Sign your name in the blank space below.* ◊ *a blank cassette* ◊ *Write on one side of the paper and leave the other side blank.* ◊ *She turned to a blank page in her notebook.* **2** (of a wall or screen) empty; with no pictures, marks or decoration: *blank whitewashed walls* ◊ *Suddenly the screen went blank.* **3** showing no feeling, understanding or interest: *She stared at me with a blank expression on her face.* ◊ *Steve looked blank and said he had no idea what I was talking about.* ◊ *Suddenly my mind went blank* (= I could not remember anything). **4** [only before noun] (of negative items) complete and total: *a blank refusal/denial*—see also POINT-BLANK ► **blank·ly** *adv.*: *She stared blankly into space, not knowing what to say next.* **blank·ness** *noun* [U]

■ *noun* **1** [C] an empty space on a printed form or document for you to write answers, information, etc. in: *Please fill in the blanks with a black pen.* ◊ *If you can't answer the question, leave a blank.* **2** [sing.] a state of not being able to remember anything: *My mind was a blank and I couldn't remember her name.* **3** [C] (also ˌblank 'cartridge) a CARTRIDGE in a gun that contains an explosive but no bullet: *The troops fired blanks in the air.* **IDM** see DRAW *v.*

■ *verb* **1** [VN] (*BrE, informal*) to ignore sb completely: *I saw her on the bus this morning, but she totally blanked me.* **2** [V] (*AmE*) to be suddenly unable to remember or think of sth: *I knew the answer, but I totally blanked during the test.* **PHRV** ˌblank 'out to suddenly become empty: *The screen blanked out.* ˌblank sth↔'out **1** to cover sth completely so that it cannot be seen: *All the names in the letter had been blanked out.* **2** to deliberately forget sth unpleasant: *She had tried to blank out the whole experience.*

ˌblank 'cheque (*BrE*) (*AmE* ˌblank 'check) *noun* **1** a cheque that is signed but which does not have the amount of money to be paid written on it **2** permission or authority to do sth that is necessary in a particular situation: *The President was given a blank check by Congress to continue the war.*

blan·ket /ˈblæŋkɪt/ *noun, adj., verb*

■ *noun* **1** a large cover, often made of wool, used especially on beds to keep people warm—see also ELECTRIC BLANKET—picture at BED **2** [usually sing.] ~ **of sth** a thick layer or covering of sth: *a blanket of fog/snow/cloud* ◊ (*figurative*) *The trial was conducted under a blanket of secrecy.*—see also WET BLANKET

■ *adj.* [only before noun] including or affecting all possible cases, situations or people: *a blanket ban on tobacco advertising* ◊ *a blanket refusal*

■ *verb* [VN] [often passive] (*written*) to cover sth completely with a thick layer: *Snow soon blanketed the frozen ground.*

blankety-blank /ˌblæŋkəti ˈblæŋk/ *adj.* [only before noun] (*spoken*) used in place of a rude word that the speaker does not want to say: *It's not my blankety-blank fault!*

ˌblank 'verse *noun* [U] (*technical*) poetry that has a regular rhythm, usually with ten syllables and five stresses in each line, but which does not RHYME—compare FREE VERSE

blare /bleə(r); *AmE* bler/ *verb, noun*

■ *verb* ~ **(sth) (out)** to make a loud unpleasant noise: [V] *police cars with lights flashing and sirens blaring* ◊ *Music blared out from the open window.* ◊ [VN] *The radio was blaring (out) rock music.*

■ *noun* [sing.] a loud unpleasant noise: *the blare of car horns*

blar·ney /ˈblɑːni; *AmE* ˈblɑːrni/ *noun* [U] (*informal*) talk that is friendly and amusing but probably not true, and which may be used to persuade or trick you **ORIGIN** From *Blarney*, a castle in Ireland where there is a stone which is said to have magical powers: anyone who kisses the 'Blarney stone' is given the gift of speaking persuasively ('the gift of the gab').

blasé /ˈblɑːzeɪ; *AmE* blɑːˈzeɪ/ *adj.* ~ **(about sth)** not impressed, excited or worried about sth, because you have seen or experienced it many times before

blas·pheme /blæsˈfiːm/ *verb* [V, VN] to speak about God or the holy things of a particular religion in an offensive way; to swear using the names of God or holy things ► **blas·phemer** *noun*

blas·phemy /ˈblæsfəmi/ *noun* (*pl.* **-ies**) [U, C] behaviour or language that insults or shows a lack of respect for God or religion ► **blas·phem·ous** /ˈblæsfəməs/ *adj.*: *Many people found the film blasphemous.* **blas·phem·ous·ly** *adv.*

blast /blɑːst; *AmE* blæst/ *noun, verb, exclamation*

■ *noun*

EXPLOSION | **1** [C] an explosion or a powerful movement of air caused by an explosion: *a bomb blast* ◊ *27 schoolchildren were injured in the blast.*

OF AIR | **2** [C] a sudden strong movement of air: *A blast of hot air hit us as we stepped off the plane.* ◊ *the wind's icy blasts*

LOUD NOISE | **3** [C] a sudden loud noise, especially one made by a musical instrument that you blow, or by a whistle or a car horn: *three short blasts on the ship's siren*

CRITICISM | **4** [C] (used especially in newspapers) strong criticism: *Blast for prison governors in judge's report.*

FUN | **5** [sing.] (*AmE*) a very enjoyable experience that is a

s	t	v	z	ʃ	ʒ	tʃ	dʒ	θ	ð	ŋ
see	tea	van	zoo	shoe	vision	chain	jam	thin	this	sing

lot of fun: *The party was a blast.* ◇ *We had a blast at the party.*

IDM **(at) full ˈblast** with the greatest possible volume or power: *She had the car stereo on at full blast.*

■ *verb*

EXPLODE | **1** to violently destroy or break sth into pieces, using explosives: [VN] *They blasted a huge crater in the runway.* ◇ *Builders had to blast a tunnel through the mountain.* ◇ *All the windows were blasted inwards with the force of the explosion.* ◇ *The jumbo jet was blasted out of the sky.* ◇ [V] *Danger! Blasting in Progress!* [also VN-ADJ]

MAKE LOUD NOISE | **2** ~ (sth) (out) to make a loud unpleasant noise, especially music: [V] *Music suddenly blasted out from the speakers.* ◇ [VN] *The radio blasted out rock music at full volume.*

CRITICIZE | **3** [VN] ~ sb/sth (for sth/for doing sth) (*informal*) to criticize sb/sth severely: *The movie was blasted by all the critics.*

HIT/KICK | **4** [VN] (*informal*) to hit or kick sb/sth with a lot of force: *He blasted the ball past the goalie.* ◇ *He blasted the policeman right between the eyes.*

AIR/WATER | **5** [VN] to direct air, water, etc. at sb/sth with a lot of force: *Police blasted the demonstrators with water cannons.*

DESTROY WITH DISEASE, etc. | **6** [VN] [usually passive] to destroy sth such as a plant with disease, cold, heat, etc: *Their whole crop had been blasted by a late frost.*

PHRV ˌblast aˈway if a gun or sb using a gun **blasts away**, the gun fires continuously and loudly: *The machine guns blasted away non-stop.* ˌblast ˈoff (of spacecraft) to leave the ground; to take off—related noun BLAST-OFF

■ *exclamation* (*informal*) people sometimes say **Blast!** when they are annoyed about sth: *Oh blast! The car won't start.*

blast·ed /ˈblɑːstɪd; AmE ˈblæs-/ adj. [only before noun] (*spoken*) used when you are very annoyed about sth: *Make your own blasted coffee!*

ˈblast furnace *noun* a large structure like an oven in which iron ORE (= rock containing iron) is melted in order to take out the metal

ˈblast-off *noun* [U] the moment when a spacecraft leaves the ground

bla·tant /ˈbleɪtnt/ adj. (*disapproving*) (of actions that are considered bad) done in an obvious and open way without caring if people object or are shocked SYN FLAGRANT: *a blatant attempt to buy votes* ◇ *It was a blatant lie.* ► **bla·tant·ly** adv.: *a blatantly unfair decision*

blather /ˈblæðə(r)/ (also **bleth·er** /ˈbleðə(r)/) verb [V] ~ (on) (about sth) (*informal, especially BrE*) to talk continuously about things that are silly or unimportant: *What are you blathering on about now?* ► **blather** (also **blether**) *noun* [U]

blaze /bleɪz/ verb, noun

■ *verb* **1** [V] to burn brightly and strongly: *A huge fire was blazing in the fireplace.* ◇ *Within minutes the whole building was blazing.* ◇ *He rushed back into the blazing house.* **2** [V] to shine brightly: *The sun blazed down from a clear blue sky.* ◇ *The garden blazed with colour.* **3** [V] ~ (with sth) (*written*) if sb's eyes **blaze**, they look extremely angry: *Her eyes were blazing with fury.* **4** (also **blazon**) [VN] [usually passive] ~ sth (across/all over sth) to make news or information widely known by telling people about it in a way they are sure to notice: *The story was blazed all over the daily papers.* **5** ~ (away) if a gun or sb using a gun **blazes**, the gun fires continuously: *In the distance machine guns were blazing.* **IDM** **blaze a ˈtrail** to be the first to do or to discover sth that others follow: *The department is blazing a trail in the field of laser surgery.*—compare TRAILBLAZER **PHRV** ˌblaze ˈup **1** to suddenly start burning very strongly **2** to suddenly become very angry

■ *noun* **1** [C] (used especially in newspapers) a very large fire, especially a dangerous one: *Five people died in the blaze.* **2** [sing.] strong bright flames in a fire: *Dry wood makes a good blaze.* **3** [sing.] **a ~ of sth** a very bright show of lights or colour; an impressive or noticeable

show of sth: *The gardens in summer are a blaze of colour.* ◇ *a blaze of lights in the city centre* ◇ *the bright blaze of the sun* ◇ *a blaze of glory* ◇ *They got married in a blaze of publicity.* **4** [sing.] **(a) ~ of sth** a sudden show of very strong feeling: *a blaze of anger/passion/hate* **5** [C, usually sing.] a white mark on an animal's face **IDM** **what/where/who the ˈblazes …?** (*old-fashioned, spoken*) used to emphasize that you are annoyed and surprised, to avoid using the word 'hell': *What the blazes have you done?* **like blazes** (*old-fashioned, spoken*) very hard; very fast

blazer /ˈbleɪzə(r)/ *noun* a jacket, not worn with matching trousers/pants, often showing the colours or BADGE of a club, school, team, etc.

blaz·ing /ˈbleɪzɪŋ/ adj. [only before noun] **1** (also ˌblaz·ing ˈhot) extremely hot: *blazing heat* ◇ *a blazing hot day* **2** extremely angry or full of strong emotion: *She had a blazing row with Eddie and stormed out of the house.*

blazon /ˈbleɪzn/ *verb* [VN] **1** [usually passive] ~ sth (on/across/over sth) = EMBLAZON: *He had the word 'Cool' blazoned across his chest.* **2** = BLAZE (4)

bleach /bliːtʃ/ verb, noun

■ *verb* to make sth white or pale by a chemical process or by the effect of sunlight; to become white or pale in this way: [VN] ◇ *His hair was bleached by the sun.* ◇ *bleached cotton/paper* ◇ [VN-ADJ] *She bleached her hair blonde.* [V] *bones of animals bleaching in the sun*

■ *noun* [U, C] a chemical that is used to make sth become white or pale and as a DISINFECTANT (= to prevent infection from spreading)

bleach·ers /ˈbliːtʃəz; AmE -tʃərz/ *noun* [pl.] (*AmE*) cheap seats at a sports ground

bleak /bliːk/ adj. (**bleak·er**, **bleak·est**) **1** (of a situation) not hopeful or encouraging: *a bleak outlook/prospect* ◇ *The future looks bleak for the fishing industry.* ◇ *The medical prognosis was bleak.* **2** (of the weather) cold and unpleasant: *a bleak winter's day* **3** (of a place) bare, empty or with no pleasant features: *a bleak landscape/hillside/moor* ◇ *bleak concrete housing* ► **bleak·ly** adv.: *'There seems no hope,' she said bleakly.* ◇ *bleakly lit corridors* ◇ *It was a bleakly impressive coastline.* **bleak·ness** *noun* [U]

blear·ily /ˈblɪərəli; AmE ˈblɪr-/ adv. with bleary eyes; in a tired way: *'I was asleep,' she explained blearily.*

bleary /ˈblɪəri; AmE ˈblɪri/ adj. (of eyes) not able to see clearly, especially because you are tired: *She had bleary red eyes from lack of sleep.*

ˌbleary-ˈeyed adj. with bleary eyes and seeming tired: *He appeared at breakfast bleary-eyed and with a hangover.*

bleat /bliːt/ verb **1** [V] to make the sound that sheep and goats make **2** ~ (on) (about sth) to speak in a weak or complaining voice: [V speech] *'But I've only just got here,' he bleated feebly.* [also V that, V] ► **bleat** *noun*: *The lamb gave a faint bleat.* **bleat·ing** *noun* [U, C]: *the distant bleating of sheep*

bleed /bliːd/ verb (**bled**, **bled** /bled/) **1** [V] to lose blood, especially from a wound or an injury: *My finger's bleeding.* ◇ *She slowly bled to death.* ◇ *He was bleeding from a gash on his head.* **2** [VN] (in the past) to take blood from sb as a way of treating disease **3** [VN] ~ sb (for sth) (*informal*) to force sb to pay a lot of money over a period of time: *My ex-wife is bleeding me for every penny I have.* **4** [VN] to remove air or liquid from sth so that it works correctly **5** [V] to spread from one area of sth to another area: *Keep the paint fairly dry so that the colours don't bleed into each other.* **IDM** **bleed sb ˈdry** (*disapproving*) to take away all sb's money: *The big corporations are bleeding some of these small countries dry.*—more at HEART

bleed·er /ˈbliːdə(r)/ *noun* (*old-fashioned, BrE, spoken*) a rude way of referring to a person

bleed·ing /ˈbliːdɪŋ/ adj., noun

■ *adj.* [only before noun] (*BrE, slang*) = BLOODY

■ *noun* [U] the process of losing blood from the body: *Press firmly on the wound to stop the bleeding.*

ˌbleeding ˈheart *noun* (*disapproving*) a person who is too kind and sympathetic towards people that other people think do not deserve kindness: *a bleeding-heart liberal*

æ	ɑː	e	ɜː	ə	ɪ	iː	i	ɒ	ɔː	ʌ	ʊ	u	uː
cat	father	ten	bird	about	sit	see	many	got	saw	cup	put	actual	too
							(BrE)						

bleep /bliːp/ *noun, verb*
- *noun* a short high sound made by a piece of electronic equipment
- *verb* **1** [V] to make a short high electronic sound: *The microwave will bleep when your meal is ready.* **2** (*BrE*) (*AmE* **beep**) [VN] to call sb on their bleeper: *Please bleep the doctor on duty immediately.*—see also PAGE

bleep·er /ˈbliːpə(r)/ (*AmE* **beep·er**) *noun* a small electronic device that you carry around with you and that lets you know when sb is trying to contact you, by making a sound: *All the doctors in the hospital carry a bleeper.*

blem·ish /ˈblemɪʃ/ *noun, verb*
- *noun* a mark on the skin or on an object that spoils it and makes it look less beautiful or perfect: *make-up to cover blemishes* ◊ (*figurative*) *His reputation is without a blemish.*
- *verb* [VN] [usually passive] (*formal*) to spoil sth that is beautiful or perfect in all other ways

blench /blentʃ/ *verb* [V] (*BrE, formal*) to react to sth in a way that shows you are frightened: *He blenched when he heard her name announced.*

blend /blend/ *verb, noun*
- *verb* **1** [VN] **~ A with B** | **~ A and B (together)** to mix two or more substances together: *Blend the flour with the milk to make a smooth paste.* ◊ *Blend together the eggs, sugar and flour.* **2** [V] **~ (with sth)** | **~ (together)** to form a mixture with sth: *Oil does not blend with water.* ◊ *Oil and water do not blend.* **3 ~ (with sth)** | **~ (together)** to combine with sth in an attractive or effective way; to combine sth in this way: [V] *The old and new buildings blend together perfectly.* ◊ [VN] *Their music blends traditional and modern styles.* **4** [VN] [usually passive] to produce sth by mixing different types together: *blended whisky/tea* IDM see WOODWORK PHRV **blend 'in (with sth/sb)** if sth blends in, it is similar to its surroundings or matches its surroundings: *Choose curtains that blend in with your decor.* **blend sth↔'in** (in cooking) to add another substance and mix it in with the others: *Beat the butter and sugar; then blend in the egg.* **blend 'into sth** to look so similar to the background that it is difficult for you to see it separately: *He blended into the crowd.*
- *noun* **1** a mixture of different types of the same thing: *a blend of tea/coffee/whisky* **2** [usually sing.] a pleasant or useful combination of different things: *a blend of youth and experience*

blend·er /ˈblendə(r)/ (*BrE* also **li·quid·izer**) *noun* an electric machine for mixing soft food or liquid—picture at MIXER

bless /bles/ *verb* (**blessed, blessed** /blest/) [VN] **1** to ask God for protection for sb/sth: *They brought the children to Jesus and he blessed them.* ◊ *God bless you!*—compare BEATIFY **2** to make sth holy by saying a prayer over it: *The priest blessed the bread and wine.* **3** (*formal*) to call God holy; to praise God: *We bless your holy name, O Lord.* **4** (*old-fashioned, spoken*) used to express surprise: *Bless my soul! Here comes Bill!* ◊ *'Where's Joe?' 'I'm blessed if I know* (= I don't know)*!'* IDM **be blessed with sth/sb** to have sth good such as ability, great happiness, etc: *She's blessed with excellent health.* ◊ *We're blessed with five lovely grandchildren.* **'bless you, her, him, etc.** (*spoken*) used to show that you are pleased with sb, especially because of sth they have done: *Sarah, bless her, had made a cup of tea.* **'bless you** (*spoken*) said to sb after they have SNEEZED—more at GOD

blessed /ˈblesɪd/ *adj.* **1** holy: *the Blessed Virgin Mary* **2** (in religious language) lucky: *Blessed are the poor.* **3** [only before noun] enjoyable in a way that gives you a sense of peace or RELIEF from anxiety or pain: *a moment of blessed calm* **4** [only before noun] (*old-fashioned, informal*) used to express mild anger: *I can't see a blessed thing without my glasses.* ▶ **bless·ed·ly** *adv.*: *The kitchen was warm and blessedly familiar.* **bless·ed·ness** /ˈblesɪdnəs/ *noun* [U]

bless·ing /ˈblesɪŋ/ *noun* **1** [usually sing.] God's help and protection, or a PRAYER asking for this: *to pray for God's blessing* ◊ *The bishop said the blessing.* **2** [usually sing.]

approval of or permission for sth: *The government gave its blessing to the new plans.* ◊ *He went with his parents' blessing.* **3** something that is good or helpful: *Lack of traffic is one of the blessings of country life.* ◊ *It's a blessing that nobody was in the house at the time.*—see also MIXED BLESSING IDM **a blessing in dis'guise** something that seems to be a problem at first, but that has good results in the end—more at COUNT *v.*

blether /ˈbleðə(r)/ *verb, noun* = BLATHER

blew *pt of* BLOW

blight /blaɪt/ *verb, noun*
- *verb* [VN] to spoil or damage sth, especially by causing a lot of problems: *His career has been blighted by injuries.* ◊ *an area blighted by unemployment*
- *noun* **1** [U, C] any disease that kills plants, especially crops: *potato blight* **2** [sing., U] **~ (on sb/sth)** something that has a bad effect on a situation, a person's life or the environment: *His death cast a blight on the whole of that year.* ◊ *urban blight* (= ugly or neglected areas in a city)

blight·er /ˈblaɪtə(r)/ *noun* (*old-fashioned, BrE, informal*) a way of referring to a person (usually a man) that you either find unpleasant or that you feel some sympathy or ENVY for

bli·mey /ˈblaɪmi/ (also **cor blimey** /ˌkɔː ˈblaɪmi; *AmE* ˌkɔːr/) *exclamation* (*BrE, informal, slang*) used to express surprise or anger: *Blimey, it's hot today.*

blimp /blɪmp/ *noun* **1** (*especially AmE*) a small AIRSHIP (= an aircraft without wings) **2** (also **Colonel 'Blimp**) (*old-fashioned, BrE, disapproving*) an older person, especially an old army officer, with very old-fashioned political opinions ▶ **blimp·ish** *adj.*

blind /blaɪnd/ *adj., verb, noun, adv.*
- *adj.* (**blind·er, blind·est**) **1** not able to see: *Doctors think he will go blind.* ◊ *blind and partially sighted people* ◊ *One of her parents is blind.* **2** (**the blind**) *noun* [pl.] people who are blind: *recorded books for the blind* ◊ *guide dogs for the blind* **3 ~ (to sth)** not noticing or realizing sth: *She is blind to her husband's faults.* ◊ *I must have been blind not to realize the danger we were in.* **4** [usually before noun] (of strong feelings) seeming to be unreasonable, and accepted without question; seeming to be out of control: *blind faith/obedience* ◊ *blind panic* **5** [usually before noun] (of a situation or an event) that cannot be controlled by reason: *blind chance* ◊ *the blind force of nature* **6** that a driver in a car cannot see, or cannot see around: *a blind driveway* ◊ *a blind bend/corner* ▶ **blind·ness** *noun* [U]: *total/temporary/partial blindness*—see also BLINDLY IDM **(as) blind as a 'bat** (*humorous*) not able to see well **the blind leading the 'blind** a situation in which people with almost no experience or knowledge give advice to others who also have no experience or knowledge **not a blind bit/the blindest bit of ...** (*BrE, spoken*) not any: *He didn't take a blind bit of notice of me* (= he ignored me). ◊ *It won't make the blindest bit of difference* (= it will make no difference at all). **turn a blind 'eye (to sth)** to pretend not to notice sth bad that is happening, so you do not have to do anything about it
- *verb* [VN] **1** to permanently destroy sb's ability to see: *She was blinded in the explosion.* **2** to make it difficult for sb to see for a short time: *When she went outside she was temporarily blinded by the sun.* **3 ~ sb (to sth)** to make sb no longer able to think clearly or behave in a sensible way: *His sense of loyalty blinded him to the truth.* IDM **blind sb with science** to confuse sb by using technical or complicated language that they do not understand—more at EFF

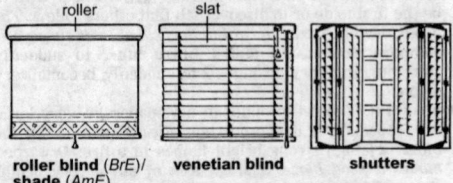

roller blind (*BrE*)/ **venetian blind** **shutters**
shade (*AmE*)

aɪ	aʊ	eɪ	əʊ	oʊ	ɔɪ	ɪə	eə	ʊə	j	w
my	now	say	go	go	boy	near	hair	pure	yes	wet
			(BrE)	(AmE)						

■ *noun* **1** (*AmE* also **shade**, **'window shade**) [C] a covering for a window, especially one made of a roll of fabric that is fixed at the top of the window and can be pulled up and down—see also VENETIAN BLIND **2** [sing.] something people say or do to hide the truth about sth in order to deceive other people

■ *adv.* (in connection with flying) without being able to see; using instruments only **IDM** **blind 'drunk** extremely drunk—more at ROB, SWEAR

WHICH WORD?
blind / blindly

There are two adverbs that come from the adjective **blind**. **Blindly** means 'not being able to see what you are doing' or 'not thinking about something'. The adverb **blind** is mainly used in the context of flying and means 'without being able to see', 'using instruments only'.

,**blind 'alley** *noun* a way of doing sth that seems useful at first, but does not produce useful results, like following a path that suddenly stops

,**blind 'date** *noun* a meeting between two people who have not met each other before. The meeting is usually organized by their friends because they want them to develop a romantic relationship.

blind·er /'blaɪndə(r)/ *noun* **1** [C, usually sing.] (*BrE*, *informal*) something which is excellent, especially in sport: *United are playing a blinder of a game.* **2** (**blinders**) [pl.] (*AmE*) = BLINKERS

blind·fold /'blaɪndfəʊld; *AmE* -foʊld/ *noun, verb, adj., adv.*

■ *noun* something that is put over sb's eyes so they cannot see

■ *verb* [VN] to cover sb's eyes with a piece of fabric or other covering so that they cannot see: *The hostages were tied up and blindfolded.*

■ *adj., adv.* (*BrE*) (also **blind·fold·ed** *BrE, AmE*) with the eyes covered: *The reporter was taken blindfold to a secret location.* ◊ *I knew the way home blindfold* (= because it was so familiar). ◊ *I could do that blindfold* (= very easily, with no problems).

blind·ing /'blaɪndɪŋ/ *adj.* [usually before noun] **1** very bright; so strong that you cannot see: *a blinding flash of light* ◊ *blinding rain/snow* ◊ (*figurative*) *a blinding* (= very bad) *headache* **2** (*BrE*, *spoken*) very good or enjoyable

blind·ing·ly /'blaɪndɪŋli/ *adv.* very; extremely: *The reason is blindingly obvious.* ◊ *The latest computers can work at a blindingly fast speed.*

blind·ly /'blaɪndli/ *adv.* **1** without being able to see what you are doing: *She groped blindly for the light switch in the dark room.* **2** without thinking about what you are doing: *He wanted to decide for himself instead of blindly following his parents' advice.* ⇨ note at BLIND

,**blind man's 'buff** (*BrE*) (*AmE* ,**blind man's 'bluff**) *noun* [U] a children's game in which a player whose eyes are covered with a piece of fabric tries to catch and identify the other players

blind·side /'blaɪndsaɪd/ *verb* [VN] (*AmE*) **1** to attack sb from the direction where they cannot see you coming **2** [usually passive] to give sb an unpleasant surprise that leaves them in a state of shock: *Just when it seemed life was going well, she was blindsided by a devastating illness.*

'**blind spot** *noun* **1** an area that sb cannot see, especially an area of the road when they are driving a car **2** if sb has a **blind spot** about sth, they ignore it or they are unwilling or unable to understand it **3** the part of the RETINA in the eye that is not sensitive to light

blink /blɪŋk/ *verb, noun*

■ *verb* **1** when you **blink** or **blink your eyes** or your **eyes blink**, you shut and open your eyes quickly: [V] *He blinked in the bright sunlight.* ◊ *I'll be back before you can blink* (= very quickly). ◊ *When I told him the news he didn't even blink* (= showed no surprise at all). [also VN] —compare WINK **2** [V] to shine with an unsteady light; to

flash on and off: *Suddenly a warning light blinked.* **PHR V** ,**blink sth↔a'way/'back** to try to control tears or clear your eyes by blinking: *She bravely blinked back her tears.*

■ *noun* [usually sing.] the act of shutting and opening your eyes very quickly **IDM** **in the blink of an 'eye** very quickly; in a short time **on the 'blink** (*informal*) (of a machine) no longer working correctly

blink·er /'blɪŋkə(r)/ *noun* **1** [C] (*informal*) = INDICATOR **2** (**blinkers**) (*AmE* also **blind·ers**) [pl.] pieces of leather that are placed at the side of a horse's eyes to stop it from looking sideways: (*figurative*) *We need to have a fresh look at the plan, without blinkers* (= we need to consider every aspect of it).

blink·ered /'blɪŋkəd; *AmE* -kərd/ *adj.* (*disapproving*) not aware of every aspect of a situation; not willing to accept different ideas about sth **SYN** NARROW-MINDED: *a blinkered policy/attitude/approach*

blink·ing /'blɪŋkɪŋ/ *adj., adv.* (*BrE*, *spoken*) a mild swear word that some people use when they are annoyed, to avoid saying 'bloody': *Shut the blinking door!*

blip /blɪp/ *noun* **1** a bright light flashing on the screen of a piece of equipment, sometimes with a short high sound **2** a change in a process or situation, usually when it gets worse for a short time before it gets better; a temporary problem: *a temporary blip*

bliss /blɪs/ *noun* [U] extreme happiness; joy: *married/ wedded/domestic bliss* ◊ *My idea of bliss is a month in the Bahamas.* **IDM** see IGNORANCE

bliss·ful /'blɪsfl/ *adj.* extremely happy; showing happiness: *We spent three blissful weeks away from work.* ◊ *a blissful smile* ◊ *We preferred to remain in blissful ignorance of what was going on* (= not to know). ▶ **bliss·ful·ly** /-fəli/ *adv.*: *blissfully happy* ◊ *blissfully ignorant/ unaware*

blis·ter /'blɪstə(r)/ *noun, verb*

■ *noun* a swelling on the surface of the skin that is filled with liquid and is caused, for example, by rubbing or burning

■ *verb* **1** to form blisters; to make sth form blisters: [V] *His skin was beginning to blister.* ◊ [VN] *Her face had been blistered by the sun.* **2** [V, VN] when a surface **blisters** or sth **blisters** it, it swells and cracks ▶ **blis·tered** *adj.*: *cracked and blistered skin* ◊ *blistered paintwork*

blis·ter·ing /'blɪstərɪŋ/ *adj.* [usually before noun] **1** (describing actions in sport) done very fast or with great energy: *The runners set off at a blistering pace.* **2** extremely hot in a way that is uncomfortable: *a blistering July day* ◊ *blistering heat* **3** very critical: *a blistering attack* ▶ **blis·ter·ing·ly** *adv.*

blithe /blaɪð/ *adj.* [usually before noun] **1** (*disapproving*) showing you do not care or are not anxious about what you are doing: *He drove with blithe disregard for the rules of the road.* **2** (*literary*) happy; not anxious: *a blithe and carefree girl* ▶ **blithe·ly** *adv.*: *He was blithely unaware of the trouble he'd caused.* ◊ *'It'll be easy,' she said blithely.*

blitz /blɪts/ *noun, verb*

■ *noun* **1** [C, usually sing.] something which is done with a lot of energy: *an advertising/a media blitz* (= a lot of information about sth on television, in newspapers, etc.) **2** [C, usually sing.] **~** (**on sth**) a sudden attack: *Five shops were damaged in a firebomb blitz.* ◊ (*figurative*) *a blitz on passengers who avoid paying fares* ◊ (*figurative*) *I've had a blitz on the house* (= cleaned it very thoroughly). **3** (**the Blitz**) [sing.] the German air attacks on Britain in 1940

■ *verb* [VN] to attack or damage a city by dropping a large number of bombs on it in a short time

blitz·krieg /'blɪtskriːɡ/ *noun* (from *German*) a sudden military attack intended to win a quick victory

bliz·zard /'blɪzəd; *AmE* -zərd/ *noun* **1** a SNOWSTORM with very strong winds: *blizzard conditions* **2** (*written*) a large quantity of things that may seem to be attacking you: *a blizzard of documents*

bloat /bləʊt; *AmE* bloʊt/ *verb* to swell or make sth swell, especially in an unpleasant way: [VN] *Her features had been bloated by years of drinking and drug-taking.* [also V]

bloat·ed /'bləʊtɪd; *AmE* 'bloʊ-/ *adj.* **1** full of liquid or gas and therefore bigger than normal, in a way that is

B

unpleasant: *a bloated body floating in the canal* ◊ *(figurative) a bloated organization* (= with too many people in it) **2** full of food and feeling uncomfortable: *I felt bloated after the huge meal they'd served.*

blob /blɒb; *AmE* blɑːb/ *noun* a small amount or drop of sth, especially a liquid; a small area of colour: *a blob of ink* ◊ *a pink blob*

bloc /blɒk; *AmE* blɑːk/ *noun* a group of countries that work closely together because they have similar political interests: *the former Soviet bloc*—see also EN BLOC

block /blɒk; *AmE* blɑːk/ *noun, verb*
■ *noun*
SOLID MATERIAL | **1** [C] a large piece of a solid material that is square in shape and usually has flat sides: *a block of ice/concrete/stone* ◊ *a chopping block* (= for cutting food on)—see also BREEZE BLOCK, BUILDING BLOCK, CINDER BLOCK
FOR PUNISHMENT | **2 (the block)** [sing.] (in the past) the piece of wood on which a person's head was cut off as a punishment
BUILDING | **3** [C] (*BrE*) a tall building that contains flats or offices; buildings that form part of a school, hospital, etc. which are used for a particular purpose: *a tower block* ◊ *a block of flats* ◊ *an office block* ◊ *the university's science block*
STREETS | **4** [C] a group of buildings with streets on all sides: *She took the dog for a walk around the block.* **5** [C] (*AmE*) the length of one side of a piece of land or group of buildings, from the place where one street crosses it to the next: *His apartment is three blocks away from the police station.*
AREA OF LAND | **6** [C] (*especially AmE*) a large area of land
AMOUNT | **7** [C] a quantity of sth or an amount of time that is considered as a single unit: *a block of shares* ◊ *a block of text in a document* ◊ (*BrE*) *The theatre gives discounts for block bookings* (= a large number of tickets bought at the same time). ◊ *The three-hour class is divided into four blocks of 45 minutes each.*
THAT STOPS PROGRESS | **8** [C, usually sing.] something that makes movement or progress difficult or impossible [SYN] OBSTACLE: *Lack of training acts as a block to progress in a career.* ◊ *Tony had writer's block for two years* (= he couldn't write anything).—see also ROADBLOCK, STUMBLING BLOCK
IN SPORT | **9** [C] a movement that stops another player from going forward **10 (the blocks)** [pl.] = STARTING BLOCKS
[IDM] **go on the ˈblock** to be sold, especially at an AUCTION (= a sale in which items are sold to the person who offers the most money) **put/lay your head/neck on the block** to risk your job, damaging your reputation, etc. by doing or saying sth: *It's not a matter that I'm prepared to put my head on the block for.*—more at CHIP *n.*, KNOCK *v.*
■ *verb* [VN] **1** to stop sth from moving or flowing through a pipe, a passage, a road, etc. by putting sth in it or across it: *After today's heavy snow, many roads are still blocked.* ◊ *a blocked sink* **2 ~ sb's way, exit, view, etc.** to stop sb from going somewhere or seeing sth by standing in front of them or in their way: *One of the guards moved to block her path.* ◊ *An ugly new building blocked the view from the window.* **3** to prevent sth from happening, developing or making progress: *The proposed merger has been blocked by the government.* **4** to stop a ball, blow, etc. from reaching somewhere by moving in front of it: *Zola's shot was blocked by the goalie.*
[PHRV] **ˌblock sb/sth↔ˈin** to prevent a car from being able to be driven away by parking too close to it **ˌblock sth↔ˈin** to draw or paint sth roughly, without showing any detail: *I have blocked in the shapes of the larger buildings.* **ˌblock sth↔ˈoff** to close a road or an opening by placing a barrier at one end or in front of it: *The main roads of the city have been blocked off.* **ˌblock sth↔ˈout 1** to stop light or noise from coming in: *Black clouds blocked out the sun.* **2** to stop yourself from thinking about or remembering sth unpleasant: *Over the years she had tried to block out that part of her life.* **ˌblock sth↔ˈup** to completely fill a hole or an opening and so

prevent anything from passing through it: *One door had been blocked up.* ◊ *My nose is blocked up.*

block·ade /blɒˈkeɪd; *AmE* blɑːˈk-/ *noun, verb*
■ *noun* **1** the action of surrounding or closing a place, especially a port, in order to stop people or goods from coming in or out: *a naval blockade* ◊ *to impose/lift a blockade* ◊ *an economic blockade* (= stopping goods from entering or leaving a country) **2** a barrier that stops people or vehicles from entering or leaving a place: *The police set up blockades on highways leading out of the city.*
■ *verb* [VN] to surround a place, especially a port, in order to stop people or goods from coming in or out

block·age /ˈblɒkɪdʒ; *AmE* ˈblɑːk-/ *noun* **1** a thing that blocks flow or movement, for example of a liquid in a narrow place: *a blockage in an artery/a pipe/a drain* **2** the state of being blocked: *to cause/clear the blockage*

ˌblock and ˈtackle *noun* [sing.] a piece of equipment for lifting heavy objects, which works by a system of ropes and PULLEYS (= small wheels around which the ropes are stretched)

block·bust·er /ˈblɒkbʌstə(r); *AmE* ˈblɑːk-/ *noun* (*informal*) something very successful, especially a very successful book or film/movie: *the latest Hollywood blockbuster* ▶ **block·bust·ing** *adj.*: *a blockbusting performance*

ˌblock ˈcapitals (also **ˌblock ˈletters**) *noun* [pl.] separate capital letters: *Please fill out the form in block capitals.*

block·head /ˈblɒkhed; *AmE* ˈblɑːk-/ *noun* (*informal*) a very stupid person

ˌblock ˈvote *noun* a voting system in which each person who votes represents a number of people

bloke /bləʊk; *AmE* bloʊk/ *noun* (*BrE, informal*) a man: *He seemed like a nice bloke.*

blonde /blɒnd; *AmE* blɑːnd/ *adj., noun*
■ *adj.* (also **blond**) **1** (of hair) pale gold in colour **2** (of a person) having blonde hair: *a small, blond boy*
■ *noun* a woman with hair that is pale gold in colour: *Is she a natural blonde* (= Is her hair naturally blonde)?

blood /blʌd/ *noun, verb*
■ *noun* **1** [U] the red liquid that flows through the bodies of humans and animals: *He lost a lot of blood in the accident.* ◊ *Blood was pouring out of a cut on her head.* ◊ *to give blood* (= to have blood taken from you so that it can be used in the medical treatment of other people) ◊ *to draw blood* (= to make a person bleed) ◊ *a blood cell/sample* **2 (-blooded)** (in adjectives) having the type of blood mentioned: *cold-blooded reptiles*—see also BLUE-BLOODED, HOT-BLOODED, RED-BLOODED **3** [U] (*formal*) family origins: *She is of noble blood.* **4** [C] (*old-fashioned, BrE*) a rich and fashionable man [IDM] **bad ˈblood (between A and B)** (*old-fashioned*) feelings of hatred or strong dislike **be after/out for sb's ˈblood** (*informal, often humorous*) to be angry with sb and want to hurt or punish them **be/run in your ˈblood** to be a natural part of your character and of the character of other members of your family **blood is thicker than ˈwater** (*saying*) family relationships are stronger than any others **sb's ˈblood is up** (*BrE*) somebody is very angry and ready to argue or fight **blood, sweat and ˈtears** very hard work; a lot of effort: *The only way to succeed is through old-fashioned blood, sweat and tears.* **have sb's ˈblood on your hands** to be responsible for sb's death: *a dictator with the blood of thousands on his hands* **like getting blood out of/from a ˈstone** almost impossible to obtain: *Getting an apology from him was like getting blood from a stone.* **make sb's ˈblood boil** to make sb extremely angry **make sb's ˈblood run cold** to make sb very frightened or fill them with horror **new/fresh ˈblood** new members or employees, especially young ones, with new ideas, skills or ways of doing things—more at COLD *adj.*, FLESH *n.*, FREEZE *v.*, SPILL *v.*, SPIT *v.*, SWEAT *v.*
■ *verb* [VN] (*especially BrE*) to give sb their first experience of an activity

ˈblood bank *noun* a place where blood is kept for use in hospitals, etc.

blood·bath /ˈblʌdbɑːθ; *AmE* -bæθ/ *noun* [sing.] a situa-

B

ation in which many people are killed violently SYN MASSACRE

'blood brother *noun* a man who has promised to treat another man as his brother, usually in a ceremony in which their blood is mixed together

'blood clot (also **clot**) *noun* a lump that is formed when blood dries or becomes thicker: *a blood clot on the brain*

'blood count *noun* the number of red and white cells in sb's blood; a medical test to count these

'blood-curdling *adj.* (of a sound or a story) filling you with horror; extremely frightening: *a blood-curdling scream/story*

'blood donor *noun* a person who gives some of his or her blood to be used in the medical treatment of other people

'blood group (also **'blood type** especially in *AmE*) *noun* any of the different types that human blood is separated into for medical purposes: *(BrE) What blood group are you?* ◊ *(AmE) What blood type do you have?* ◊ *blood group/ type O*

'blood heat *noun* [U] the normal temperature of a human body

blood·hound /ˈblʌdhaʊnd/ *noun* a large dog with a very good sense of smell, used to follow or look for people

blood·ied /ˈblʌdid/ *adj.* covered in blood: *his bruised and bloodied nose*

blood·less /ˈblʌdləs/ *adj.* **1** without any killing: *a bloodless coup/revolution* **2** (of a person or a part of the body) very pale: *bloodless lips* **3** lacking human emotion SYN COLD, UNEMOTIONAL

blood·let·ting /ˈblʌdletɪŋ/ *noun* [U] **1** (*formal*) the killing or wounding of people SYN BLOODSHED **2** a medical treatment used in the past in which some of a patient's blood was removed

blood·lust /ˈblʌdlʌst/ *noun* [U] a strong desire to kill or be violent

'blood money *noun* [U] (*disapproving*) **1** money paid to a person who is hired to murder sb **2** money paid to the family of a murdered person

'blood orange *noun* a type of orange with red flesh

'blood poisoning *noun* an illness where the blood becomes infected with harmful bacteria, especially because of a cut or a wound

'blood pressure *noun* [U] the pressure of blood as it travels around the body: *to have high/low blood pressure* ◊ *to take* (= measure) *sb's blood pressure*

blood-'red *adj.* bright red in colour, like fresh blood

'blood relation (also **'blood relative**) *noun* a person related to sb by birth rather than by marriage

'blood sausage *noun* [U, C] (*AmE*) = BLACK PUDDING

blood·shed /ˈblʌdʃed/ *noun* [U] the killing or wounding of people, usually during fighting or a war: *The two sides called a truce to avoid further bloodshed.*

blood·shot /ˈblʌdʃɒt; *AmE* -ʃɑːt/ *adj.* (of eyes) with the part that is usually white full of red lines because of lack of sleep, etc.

'blood sport *noun* [usually pl.] a sport in which animals or birds are killed

blood·stain /ˈblʌdsteɪn/ *noun* a mark or spot of blood on sth ▶ **blood·stained** *adj.*: *a bloodstained shirt*

blood·stock /ˈblʌdstɒk; *AmE* -stɑːk/ *noun* [U] horses of pure breed, bred especially for racing

blood·stream /ˈblʌdstriːm/ *noun* [sing.] the blood flowing through the body: *They injected the drug directly into her bloodstream.*

'blood test *noun* an examination of a small amount of your blood by doctors in order to make judgements about your medical condition

blood·thirsty /ˈblʌdθɜːsti; *AmE* -θɜːrsti/ *adj.* **1** wanting to kill or wound; enjoying seeing or hearing about killing and violence **2** (of a book, film/movie, etc.) describing or showing killing and violence

'blood transfusion (also **transfusion**) *noun* [C, U] the process of putting new blood into the body of a person or an animal: *He was given a blood transfusion.*

'blood type *noun* (*especially AmE*) = BLOOD GROUP

'blood vessel *noun* any of the tubes through which blood flows through the body—see also ARTERY, VEIN

bloody¹ /ˈblʌdi/ *adj.* [only before noun] *adv.*—see also BLOODY² (*BrE*, △, *spoken*) a swear word that many people find offensive that is used to emphasize a comment or an angry statement: *Don't be such a bloody fool.* ◊ *That was a bloody good meal!* ◊ *What bloody awful weather!* ◊ *She did bloody well to win that race.* ◊ *He doesn't bloody care about anybody else.* ◊ *'Will you apologize?' 'Not bloody likely* (= Certainly not).*'* IDM **bloody well** (*BrE*, △, *spoken*) used to emphasize an angry statement or an order: *You can bloody well keep your job—I don't want it!*

bloody² /ˈblʌdi/ *adj.*—see also BLOODY¹ (**blood·ier**, **bloodi·est**) **1** involving a lot of violence and killing: *a bloody battle* ◊ *The terrorists have halted their bloody campaign of violence.* **2** covered with blood; bleeding: *to give sb a bloody nose* (= in a fight) ▶ **blood·ily** *adv.* IDM see SCREAM *v.*

bloody-'minded *adj.* (*BrE*, *informal*) behaving in a way that makes things difficult for other people; refusing to be helpful ▶ **bloody-'minded·ness** *noun* [U]

bloom /bluːm/ *noun, verb*

■ *noun* (*written or technical*) **1** [C] a flower (usually one on a plant that people admire for its flowers): *the exotic blooms of the orchid* **2** [sing., U] a healthy fresh appearance: *the bloom in her cheeks* IDM **in (full) bloom** (of trees, plants, gardens, etc.) with the flowers fully open

■ *verb* [V] **1** to produce flowers: *Most roses will begin to bloom from late May.* **2** to become healthy, happy or confident: *The children had bloomed during their stay on the farm.*

bloom·er /ˈbluːmə(r)/ *noun* (*old-fashioned, BrE, informal*) a mistake

bloom·ers /ˈbluːməz; *AmE* -ərz/ *noun* [pl.] **1** (*informal*) an old-fashioned piece of women's underwear like long loose UNDERPANTS **2** short loose trousers/pants that fit tightly at the knee, worn in the past by women for games, riding bicycles, etc: *a pair of bloomers*

bloom·ing /ˈbluːmɪŋ; ˈblʊm-/ *adj.* [only before noun] *adv.* (*BrE, spoken*) a mild swear word, used to emphasize a comment or a statement, especially an angry one: *What blooming awful weather!*

bloop·er /ˈbluːpə(r)/ *noun* (*AmE*) an embarrassing mistake that you make in public

blos·som /ˈblɒsəm; *AmE* ˈblɑːs-/ *noun, verb*

■ *noun* [C, U] a flower or a mass of flowers, especially on a fruit tree or bush: *cherry/orange/apple blossom* ◊ *The trees are in blossom.*

■ *verb* [V] **1** (of a tree or bush) to produce blossom **2** ~ (into sth) to become more healthy, confident or successful: *She has visibly blossomed over the last few months.* ◊ *Their friendship blossomed into love.*

blot /blɒt; *AmE* blɑːt/ *verb, noun*

■ *verb* (-tt-) [VN] **1** to remove liquid from a surface by pressing soft paper or cloth on it **2** to make a spot or spots of ink fall on paper IDM **blot your 'copybook** (*old-fashioned, informal*) to do sth to spoil the opinion that other people have of you PHRV **blot sth↔'out 1** to cover or hide sth completely: *Clouds blotted out the sun.* **2** to deliberately try to forget an unpleasant memory or thought: *He tried to blot out the image of Helen's sad face.*

■ *noun* **1** a spot or dirty mark on sth, made by ink, etc. **2** ~ (on sth) something that spoils the opinion that other people have of you, or your happiness: *Her involvement in the fraud has left a serious blot on her character.* IDM **a blot on the 'landscape** an object, especially an ugly building, that spoils the beauty of a place

blotch /blɒtʃ; *AmE* blɑːtʃ/ *noun* a mark, usually not regular in shape, on skin, plants, material, etc: *Overnight he had come out in* (= become covered in) *dark red blotches.*

blotchy /ˈblɒtʃi; *AmE* ˈblɑː-/ (*BrE* also **blotched**) *adj.* covered in blotches: *her blotchy and swollen face*

blot·ter /ˈblɒtə(r); *AmE* ˈblɑːt-/ *noun* **1** a large piece of blotting paper in a cover with a stiff back which is kept

æ	ɑː	e	ɜː	ə	ɪ	iː	i	ɒ	ɔː	ʌ	ʊ	u	uː
cat	father	ten	bird	about	sit	see	many	got	saw	cup	put	actual	too
								(BrE)					

on a desk **2** (*AmE*) the record of ARRESTS in a police district

'blotting paper *noun* [U] soft thick paper used for drying ink after you have written sth on a piece of paper

blotto /'blɒtəʊ; *AmE* 'blɑːtoʊ/ *adj.* [not before noun] (*old-fashioned, informal*) very drunk

blouse /blaʊz; *AmE* blaʊs/ *noun* a piece of clothing like a shirt, worn by women—picture on page A4

blow /bləʊ; *AmE* bloʊ/ *verb, noun, exclamation*

■ *verb* (**blew** /bluː/ **blown** /bləʊn; *AmE* bloʊn/ **HELP** In sense 13 **blowed** /bləʊd; *AmE* bloʊd/ is used for the past participle.)

FROM MOUTH | **1** [+*adv. / prep.*] to send out air from the mouth: [V] *You're not blowing hard enough!* ◊ *The policeman asked me to blow into the breathalyser.* ◊ [VN] *He drew on his cigarette and blew out a stream of smoke.*

OF WIND | **2** when the wind or a current of air **blows**, it is moving; when it **blows**, the wind is blowing: [V, often +*adv. / prep.*] *A cold wind blew from the east.* ◊ *It was blowing hard.* ◊ [VN] *It was blowing a gale* (= there was a strong wind).

MOVE WITH WIND/BREATH | **3** [+*adv. / prep.*] to be moved by the wind, sb's breath, etc.; to move sth in this way: [V] *My hat blew off.* ◊ [V-ADJ] *The door blew open.* ◊ [VN] *I was almost blown over by the wind.* ◊ *She blew the dust off the book.* ◊ *The ship was blown onto the rocks.* [also VN-ADJ]

WHISTLE / INSTRUMENT | **4** if you **blow** a whistle, musical instrument, etc. or if a whistle, etc. **blows**, you produce a sound by blowing into the whistle, etc: [VN] *The referee blew his whistle.* ◊ [V] *the sound of trumpets blowing*

YOUR NOSE | **5** [VN] **~ your nose** to clear your nose by blowing strongly through it into a HANDKERCHIEF

A KISS | **6** [VN, VNN] **~ (sb) a kiss** to kiss your hand and then pretend to blow the kiss towards sb

SHAPE STH | **7** [VN] to make or shape sth by blowing: *to blow smoke rings* ◊ *to blow bubbles* (= for example, by blowing onto a thin layer of water mixed with soap) ◊ *to blow glass* (= to send a current of air into melted glass to shape it)

ELECTRICITY | **8** [V, VN] if a FUSE **blows** or you **blow** a FUSE, the electricity stops flowing suddenly because the FUSE (= a thin wire) has melted because the current was too strong

WITH EXPLOSIVES | **9** [VN] to break sth open with explosives: *The safe had been blown by the thieves.*

SECRET | **10** [VN] (*informal*) to make known sth that was secret: *One mistake could blow your cover* (= make your real name, job, intentions, etc. known).

MONEY | **11** [VN] **~ sth (on sth)** (*informal*) to spend or waste a lot of money on sth: *He inherited over a million dollars and blew it all on drink and gambling.*

OPPORTUNITY | **12** [VN] (*informal*) to waste an opportunity: *She blew her chances by arriving late for the interview.* ◊ *You had your chance and you blew it.*

EXCLAMATION | **13** [VN] (*BrE, informal*) used to show that you are annoyed, surprised or do not care about sth: *Blow it! We've missed the bus.* ◊ *Well, blow me down! I never thought I'd see you again.* ◊ *I'm blowed if I'm going to* (= I certainly will not) *let him treat you like that.* ◊ *Let's take a taxi and blow* (= never mind) *the expense.*

LEAVE SUDDENLY | **14** (*AmE, slang*) to leave a place suddenly: [VN] *Let's blow this joint.* [also V]

IDM **blow your/sb's 'brains out** to kill yourself/sb by shooting yourself/them in the head **blow a 'fuse** (*informal*) to get very angry **blow the 'gaff (on sb/sth)** (*BrE, informal*) to tell sth secret, especially by mistake **blow hot and 'cold (about sth)** (*informal*) to change your opinion about sth often **blow your 'mind** (*informal*) to produce a very strong pleasant or shocking feeling: *Wait till you hear this. It'll blow your mind.*—see also MIND-BLOWING **blow your own 'trumpet** (*especially BrE*) (*AmE usually* **blow/toot your own 'horn**) (*informal*) to praise your own abilities and achievements **SYN** BOAST **blow your 'top** (*BrE*) (*AmE also* **blow your 'stack**) (*informal*) to get very angry **blow up in sb's 'face** if a plan, etc. **blows up in your face**, it goes wrong in a way that causes you

damage, embarrassment, etc. **blow the 'whistle on sb/sth** (*informal*) to tell sb in authority about sth wrong or illegal that sb is doing—see also WHISTLE-BLOWER **IDM** see COBWEB, ILL *adj.*, LARK *n.*, LID, PUFF *v.*, SOCK *n.*, WAY *n.*

PHRV **,blow sb↔'a'way** (*informal, especially AmE*) **1** to kill sb by shooting them **2** to impress sb a lot or to make them very happy **,blow 'in| ,blow 'into sth** (*informal*) to arrive or enter a place suddenly: *Look who's just blown in!* **,blow sb↔'off** (*AmE*) to deliberately not meet sb when you said you would **SYN** STAND UP **,blow 'out 1** if a flame, etc. **blows out**, it is put out by the wind, etc: *Somebody opened the door and the candle blew out.* **2** if an oil or gas WELL **blows out**, it sends out gas suddenly and forcefully—related noun BLOW-OUT **,blow itself 'out** when a storm **blows itself out**, it finally loses its force **,blow sb↔'out** (*AmE, informal*) to defeat sb easily **,blow sth↔'out** to put out a flame, etc. by blowing **,blow 'over** to go away without having a serious effect: *The storm blew over in the night.* ◊ *The scandal will soon blow over.* **,blow 'up 1** to explode; to be destroyed by an explosion: *The bomb blew up.* ◊ *A police officer was killed when his car blew up.* **2** to start suddenly and with force: *A storm was blowing up.* ◊ *A crisis has blown up over the President's latest speech.* **,blow sth↔'up 1** to destroy sth by an explosion: *The police station was blown up by terrorists.* **2** to fill sth with air or gas so that it becomes firm: *The tyres on my bike need blowing up.* **3** to make a photograph bigger **SYN** ENLARGE—related noun BLOW-UP **4** to make sth seem more important, better, worse, etc. than it really is: *The whole affair was blown up out of all proportion.* **,blow 'up (at sb)** (*informal*) to get angry with sb: *I'm sorry I blew up at you.*—related noun BLOW-UP

■ *noun* **1** a hard hit with the hand, a weapon, etc: *She received a severe blow on the head.* ◊ *He was knocked out by a single blow to the head.* ◊ *The two men were yelling at each other and exchanging blows.* ◊ *He landed a blow on Hill's nose.* **2 ~ (to sb/sth)** a sudden event which has damaging effects on sb/sth, causing sadness or disappointment: *Losing his job came as a terrible blow to him.* ◊ *It was a shattering blow to her pride.*—see also BODY BLOW **3** the action of blowing: *Give your nose a good blow* (= clear it completely).

IDM **a ,blow-by-,blow ac'count, de'scription, etc. (of sth)** (*informal*) a description of an event which gives you all the details in the order in which they happen **come to 'blows (over sth)** to start fighting because of sth **soften/ cushion the 'blow** to make sth unpleasant seem less unpleasant and easier to accept—more at DEAL *v.*, STRIKE *v.*

■ *exclamation* (*old-fashioned, BrE*) used to show that you are annoyed about sth: *Blow! I forgot to tell them I'd be late.*

'blow-dry *verb* [VN] to dry hair with a HAIRDRYER and shape it into a particular style ▶ **'blow-dry** *noun*: *a cut and blow-dry*

blow·er /'bləʊə(r); *AmE* 'bloʊ-/ *noun* **1** [C] a device that produces a current of air: *a hot-air blower* **2** (**the blower**) [sing.] (*old-fashioned, BrE, informal*) the telephone—see also WHISTLE-BLOWER

blow·hard /'bləʊhɑːd; *AmE* 'bloʊhɑːrd/ *noun* (*AmE, informal, disapproving*) a person who talks too proudly about sth they own or sth they have done

blow·hole /'bləʊhəʊl; *AmE* 'bloʊhoʊl/ *noun* **1** a hole in the top of a WHALE's head through which it breathes—picture on page A6 **2** a hole in a large area of ice, through which SEALS, etc. breathe

'blow job *noun* (⚠, *slang*) the act of touching a man's PENIS with the tongue and lips to give sexual pleasure **SYN** FELLATIO

blow·lamp /'bləʊlæmp; *AmE* 'bloʊ-/ (*BrE*) (*AmE* **torch**, **'blow-torch**) *noun* a tool for directing a very hot flame onto part of a surface, for example to remove paint—picture at TORCH

blown *pp* of BLOW

'blow-out *noun* **1** an occasion when a tyre suddenly bursts on a motor vehicle while it is moving: *to have a*

blow-out **2** [usually sing.] (*informal*) a large meal at which people eat too much **3** (*AmE, informal*) a large party or social occasion **4** (*AmE, informal*) an easy victory **5** a sudden escape of oil or gas from an OIL WELL

blowsy (also **blowzy**) /ˈblaʊzi/ *adj.* (*BrE, disapproving*) a woman who is blowsy is big and fat and looks untidy

blow·torch /ˈbləʊtɔːtʃ; *AmE* ˈbloʊtɔːrtʃ/ *noun* (*AmE*) = BLOWLAMP

ˈ**blow-up** *noun* **1** an ENLARGEMENT of a photograph, picture or design: *Can you do me a blow-up of his face?* **2** (*AmE*) an occasion when sb suddenly becomes angry

BLT /ˌbiː el ˈtiː/ *abbr.* bacon, lettuce and tomato, (used to refer to a sandwich filled with this): *I'll have a BLT with extra mayonnaise.*

blub·ber /ˈblʌbə(r)/ *noun, verb*
- *noun* [U] the fat of WHALES and other sea animals
- *verb* (*informal, disapproving*) to cry noisily: [V] *There he sat, blubbering like a baby.* [also V speech]

bludg·eon /ˈblʌdʒən/ *verb* [VN] (*written*) **1** to hit sb several times with a heavy object **2** ~ (**into sth/into doing sth**) to force sb to do sth, especially by arguing with them: *They tried to bludgeon me into joining their protest.*

blue /bluː/ *adj., noun*
- *adj.* (**bluer, blu·est**) **1** having the colour of a clear sky or the sea/ocean on a clear day: *piercing blue eyes* ◇ *a blue shirt* **2** (of a person or part of the body) looking slightly blue in colour because the person is cold or cannot breathe easily: *Her hands were blue with cold.* **3** (*informal*) sad; depressed: *He'd been feeling blue all week.* **4** films/movies, jokes or stories that are blue are about sex: *a blue movie*—see also TRUE-BLUE ▶ **blue·ness** *noun* [U, sing.]: *the blueness of the water* IDM **sb's ,blue-eyed** ˈ**boy** (*BrE, informal, often disapproving*) a person treated with special favour by sb: *He's the manager's blue-eyed boy.* **do sth till you are blue in the** ˈ**face** (*informal*) to try to do sth as hard and as long as you possibly can but without success: *You can argue till you're blue in the face, but you won't change my mind.*—more at BLACK *adj.*, DEVIL, EYE *n.*, ONCE *adv.*, SCREAM *v.*
- *noun*—see also BLUES **1** [C, U] the colour of a clear sky or the sea/ocean on a clear day: *bright/dark/light/pale blue* ◇ *The room was decorated in vibrant blues and yellows.* ◇ *She was dressed in blue.* **2** (*BrE*) a person who has played a particular sport for Oxford or Cambridge University; a title given to them IDM **out of the** ˈ**blue** unexpectedly; without warning: *His resignation came right out of the blue.*—more at BOLT *n.*, BOY *n.*

,**blue** ˈ**baby** *noun* a baby whose skin is slightly blue at birth because there is sth wrong with its heart

blue·bell /ˈbluːbel/ *noun* **1** a garden or wild flower with a short stem and small blue or white flowers shaped like bells **2** (*ScotE*) = HAREBELL

blue·berry /ˈbluːbəri; *AmE* -beri/ *noun* (*pl.* **-ies**) a dark blue berry that grows on bushes in N America and can be eaten—compare BILBERRY

blue·bird /ˈbluːbɜːd; *AmE* -bɜːrd/ *noun* a small N American bird with blue feathers on its back or head

,**blue-**ˈ**blooded** *adj.* from a royal or NOBLE family ▶ ,**blue** ˈ**blood** *noun* [U]

blue·bot·tle /ˈbluːbɒtl; *AmE* -bɑːtl/ *noun* a large fly with a blue body

,**blue** ˈ**cheese** *noun* [U, C] cheese with lines of blue MOULD in it

,**blue-**ˈ**chip** *adj.* [only before noun] (*finance*) a **blue-chip** INVESTMENT is thought to be safe and likely to make a profit: *blue-chip companies/stocks*

,**blue-**ˈ**collar** *adj.* [only before noun] connected with people who do physical work in industry: *blue-collar workers/voters/votes*—compare WHITE-COLLAR

,**blue** ˈ**funk** *noun* = FUNK

blue·grass /ˈbluːɡrɑːs; *AmE* -ɡræs/ *noun* [U] a type of traditional American country music played on guitars and BANJOS

blue·jay /ˈbluːdʒeɪ/ *noun* a large N American bird with blue feathers on its back and a row of feathers (called a CREST) standing up on its head

blue·print /ˈbluːprɪnt/ *noun* **1** a photographic print of a plan for a building or a machine, with white lines on a blue background: *blueprints of a new aircraft* **2** ~ (**for sth**) a plan which shows what can be achieved and how it can be achieved: *a blueprint for the privatization of health care* **3** (*technical*) the pattern in every living cell, which decides how the plant, animal or person will develop and what it will look like: *DNA carries the genetic blueprint which tells any organism how to build itself.*

blue riband /ˌbluː ˈrɪbənd/ (*BrE*) (also ,**blue** ˈ**ribbon** *AmE, BrE*) *noun* an honour (sometimes in the form of a piece of blue RIBBON) given to the winner of the first prize in a competition: *a blue-riband event* (= a very important one)

blues /bluːz/ *noun* **1** (often **the blues**) [U] a type of slow sad music with strong rhythms, developed by African American musicians in the southern US: *a blues band/singer* **2** [C] (*pl.* **blues**) a blues song **3** (**the blues**) [pl.] feelings of deep sadness: *the Monday morning blues*

blue·stock·ing /ˈbluːstɒkɪŋ; *AmE* -stɑːk-/ *noun* (*old-fashioned, BrE, sometimes disapproving*) a well-educated woman who is more interested in ideas and studying than in traditional FEMININE things

bluesy /ˈbluːzi/ *adj.* having the slow strong rhythms and sad mood of blues music: *a bluesy sound/voice*

ˈ**blue tit** *noun* a small European bird of the TIT family, with a blue head, wings and tail and yellow parts underneath

,**blue** ˈ**whale** *noun* a type of WHALE that is the largest known living animal

bluff /blʌf/ *verb, noun, adj.*
- *verb* to try to make sb believe that you will do sth that you do not really intend to do, or that you know sth that you do not really know: [V] *I don't think he'll shoot—I think he's just bluffing.* [also VN] PHRV ˈ**bluff sb into doing sth** to make sb do sth by tricking them, especially by pretending you have more experience, knowledge, etc. than you really have ,**bluff it** ˈ**out** to get out of a difficult situation by continuing to deceive sb, especially when they suspect you are not being honest ,**bluff your way** ˈ**in/** ˈ**out/** ˈ**through|** ,**bluff your way** ˈ**into/** ˈ**out of/** ˈ**through sth** to succeed in dealing with a difficult situation by deceiving other people: *She successfully bluffed her way through the interview.*
- *noun* **1** [U, C] an attempt to trick sb by making them believe that you will do sth when you really have no intention of doing it, or that you know sth when you do not, in fact, know it: *It was just a game of bluff.* ◇ *He said he would resign if he didn't get more money, but it was only a bluff.*—see also DOUBLE BLUFF **2** [C] a steep cliff or slope, especially by the sea or a river IDM see CALL *v.*
- *adj.* (of people or their manner) very direct and cheerful, with good intentions, although not always very polite: *Beneath his bluff exterior he was really quite a sensitive man.*

blu·ish /ˈbluːɪʃ/ *adj.* fairly blue in colour: *a bluish-green carpet*

blun·der /ˈblʌndə(r)/ *noun, verb*
- *noun* a stupid or careless mistake: *to make a terrible blunder* ◇ *a series of political blunders*
- *verb* [V] to make a stupid or careless mistake: *The government had blundered in its handling of the affair.* PHRV ,**blunder a**ˈ**bout, a**ˈ**round, etc.** to move around in an awkward way, knocking into things, as if you cannot see where you are going: *I could hear him blundering around the bathroom in the dark.* ,**blunder** ˈ**into sth 1** to knock into sth because you are awkward or are not able to see **2** to accidentally find yourself in a difficult or unpleasant situation: *She realized that she had blundered into a trap.* ,**blunder** ˈ**on** to continue doing sth in a careless or stupid way

blun·der·buss /ˈblʌndəbʌs; *AmE* -dərb-/ *noun* an old type of gun with a wide end

blunt /blʌnt/ *adj., verb*
- *adj.* (**blunt·er, blunt·est**) **1** without a sharp edge or point: *a blunt knife* ◇ *This pencil's blunt!* ◇ *The police said he had been hit with a blunt instrument.* OPP SHARP **2** (of a

B

person or remark) very direct; saying exactly what you think without trying to be polite: *She has a reputation for blunt speaking.* ◊ *To be blunt, your work is appalling.* ▶ **blunt·ness** *noun* [U]

■ *verb* [VN] **1** to make sth weaker or less effective: *Age hadn't blunted his passion for adventure.* **2** to make a point or an edge less sharp

blunt·ly /ˈblʌntli/ *adv.* in a very direct way, without trying to be polite or kind: *To put it bluntly, I want a divorce.* ◊ *'Is she dead?' he asked bluntly.*

blur /blɜː(r)/ *noun, verb*

■ *noun* [usually sing.] **1** a shape that you cannot see clearly, often because it is moving too fast: *His arm was a rapid blur of movement as he struck.* ◊ *Everything is a blur when I take my glasses off.* **2** something that you cannot remember clearly: *The events of that day were just a blur.*

■ *verb* (-rr-) **1** if the shape or outline of sth **blurs**, or if sth **blurs** it, it becomes less clear and sharp: [V] *The writing blurred and danced before his eyes.* ◊ [VN] *The mist blurred the edges of the buildings.* **2** if sth **blurs** your eyes or vision, or your eyes or vision **blur**, you cannot see things clearly: [VN] *Tears blurred her eyes.* [also V] **3** to become or make sth become difficult to distinguish clearly: [V] *The differences between art and life seem to have blurred.* ◊ [VN] *She tends to blur the distinction between her friends and her colleagues.*

blurb /blɜːb; *AmE* blɜːrb/ *noun* a short description of a book, a new product, etc., written by the people who have produced it, that is intended to attract your attention and make you want to buy it

blurred /blɜːd; *AmE* blɜːrd/ *adj.* **1** not clear; without a clear outline or shape: *She suffered from dizziness and blurred vision.* ◊ *a blurred image/picture* **2** difficult to remember clearly: *blurred memories* **3** difficult to distinguish, so that differences are not clear: *blurred distinctions/boundaries*

blurry /ˈblɜːri/ *adj.* (*informal*) without a clear outline; not clear: *blurry, distorted photographs* ◊ (*figurative*) *a blurry policy*

blurt /blɜːt; *AmE* blɜːrt/ *verb* ~ **sth (out)** to say sth suddenly and without thinking carefully enough: [VN] *She blurted it out before I could stop her.* ◊ [V speech] *'She's pregnant,' Jack blurted.* [also V that, V wh-]

blush /blʌʃ/ *verb, noun*

■ *verb* **1** ~ **(with sth) (at sth)** to become red in the face because you are embarrassed or ashamed: [V] *to blush with embarrassment/shame* ◊ *She blushed furiously at the memory of the conversation.* ◊ [V-ADJ] *He blushed scarlet at the thought.* [also V-N] **2** [V to inf] to be ashamed or embarrassed about sth: *I blush to admit it, but I quite like her music.*

■ *noun* **1** the red colour that spreads over your face when you are embarrassed or ashamed: *She felt a warm blush rise to her cheeks.* ◊ *He turned away to hide his blushes.* **2** (*AmE*) = BLUSHER **IDM** see SPARE *v.*

blush·er /ˈblʌʃə(r)/ (*AmE* also **blush**) *noun* [U, C] a coloured cream or powder that some people put on their cheeks to give them more colour

blus·ter /ˈblʌstə(r)/ *verb* **1** to talk in an aggressive or threatening way, but with little effect: [V speech] *'I don't know what you're talking about,' he blustered.* ◊ [V] *a blustering bully* **2** [V] (of the wind) to blow violently ▶ **blus·ter** *noun* [U]: *I wasn't frightened by what he said—it was all bluster.*

blus·tery /ˈblʌstəri/ *adj.* (of weather) with strong winds: *blustery winds/conditions/weather* ◊ *The day was cold and blustery.*

Blu-tack™ /ˈbluː tæk/ *noun* [U] (*BrE*) a blue sticky material used to attach paper to walls

Blvd. *abbr.* (used in written addresses) BOULEVARD

bn *abbr.* (*BrE*) (in writing) BILLION

BO /ˌbiː ˈəʊ; *AmE* ˈoʊ/ *noun* [U] an unpleasant smell from a person's body, especially of sweat (the abbreviation for 'body odour'): *She's got BO.*

boa /ˈbəʊə; *AmE* ˈboʊə/ *noun* **1** = BOA CONSTRICTOR **2** = FEATHER BOA

boa constrictor /ˈbəʊə kənstrɪktə(r); *AmE* ˈboʊə/ (also

boa) *noun* a large S American snake that kills animals for food by winding its long-body around them and crushing them

boar /bɔː(r)/ *noun* (*pl.* **boar** or **boars**) **1** (also ˌ**wild** ˈ**boar**) a wild pig **2** a male pig that has not been CASTRATED—compare HOG, SOW

board /bɔːd; *AmE* bɔːrd/ *noun, verb*

■ *noun*

PIECE OF WOOD ▏ **1** [C, U] a long thin piece of strong hard material, especially wood, used, for example, for making floors, building walls and roofs and making boats: *He had ripped up the carpet, leaving only the bare boards.*—see also CHIPBOARD, FLOORBOARD, HARDBOARD, SKIRTING BOARD **2** [C] (especially in compounds) a piece of wood, or other strong material, that is used for a special purpose: *a blackboard* ◊ *I'll write it up on the board.* ◊ (*BrE*) *a noticeboard* ◊ (*AmE*) *a bulletin board* ◊ *The exam results went up on the board.* ◊ *a diving board* ◊ *She jumped off the top board.* ◊ *a chessboard* ◊ *He removed the figure from the board.*

IN WATER SPORTS ▏ **3** [C] = SAILBOARD, SURFBOARD

GROUP OF PEOPLE ▏ **4** [C+sing./pl. *v.*] a group of people who have power to make decisions and control a company or other organization: *She has a seat on the board of directors.* ◊ *The board is/are unhappy about falling sales.* ◊ *members of the board* ◊ *discussions at board level* ◊ *the academic board* (= for example, of a British university) ◊ (*AmE*) *the Board of Education* (= a group of elected officials who are in charge of all the public schools in a particular area)

ORGANIZATION ▏ **5** [C] used in the name of some organizations: *the Welsh Tourist Board* (= responsible for giving tourist information) ◊ *the Cambridge Examination Board* (= responsible for organizing some public exams)

MEALS ▏ **6** [U] the meals that are provided when you stay in a hotel, GUEST HOUSE, etc.; what you pay for the meals: *He pays £90 a week board and lodging.*—see also BED AND BOARD, FULL BOARD, HALF BOARD

EXAMS ▏ **7** (**boards**) [pl.] (*old-fashioned, AmE*) exams that you take when you apply to go to college in the US

IN THEATRE ▏ **8** (**the boards**) [pl.] (*old-fashioned, informal*) the STAGE in a theatre: *His play is on the boards on Broadway.* ◊ *She's treading the boards* (= working as an actress).

HELP There are many other compounds ending in **board**. You will find them at their place in the alphabet.

IDM a·**cross the** ˈ**board** involving everyone or everything in a company, an industry, etc: *The industry needs more investment across the board.* ◊ *an across-the-board wage increase* **be above** ˈ**board** (especially of a business arrangement) to be honest and open: *Don't worry; the deal was completely above board.* ˌ**go by the** ˈ**board** (*BrE*) (of plans or principles) to be rejected or ignored; to be no longer possible: *All her efforts to be polite went by the board and she started to shout.* **on** ˈ**board** on or in a ship, an aircraft or a train: *Have the passengers gone on board yet?* ◊ (*figurative*) *It's good to have you on board* (= working with us) *for this project.* **take sth on** ˈ**board** to accept and understand an idea or a suggestion: *I told her what I thought, but she didn't take my advice on board.*—more at SWEEP *v.*

■ *verb*

GET ON PLANE/SHIP, etc. ▏ **1** to get on a ship, train, plane, bus, etc: [VN] *The ship was boarded by customs officials.* ◊ [V] *Passengers are waiting to board.* **2** [V] (**be boarding**) when a plane or ship **is boarding**, it is ready for passengers to get on: *Flight BA193 for Paris is now boarding at Gate 37.*

LIVE SOMEWHERE ▏ **3** [V] ~ **at.../with sb** to live and take meals in sb's home, in return for payment: *She always had one or two students boarding with her.* **4** [V] to live at a school during the TERM/SEMESTER

PHRV ˌ**board sb** ˈ**out** to arrange for sb to live somewhere away from their place of work, school, etc. in return for payment ˌ**board sth**↔ˈ**up** to cover a window, door, etc. with wooden boards

board·er /ˈbɔːdə(r); *AmE* ˈbɔːrd-/ *noun* (*especially BrE*) **1** a child who lives at school and goes home for the

s	t	v	z	ʃ	ʒ	tʃ	dʒ	θ	ð	ŋ
see	tea	van	zoo	shoe	vision	chain	jam	thin	this	sing

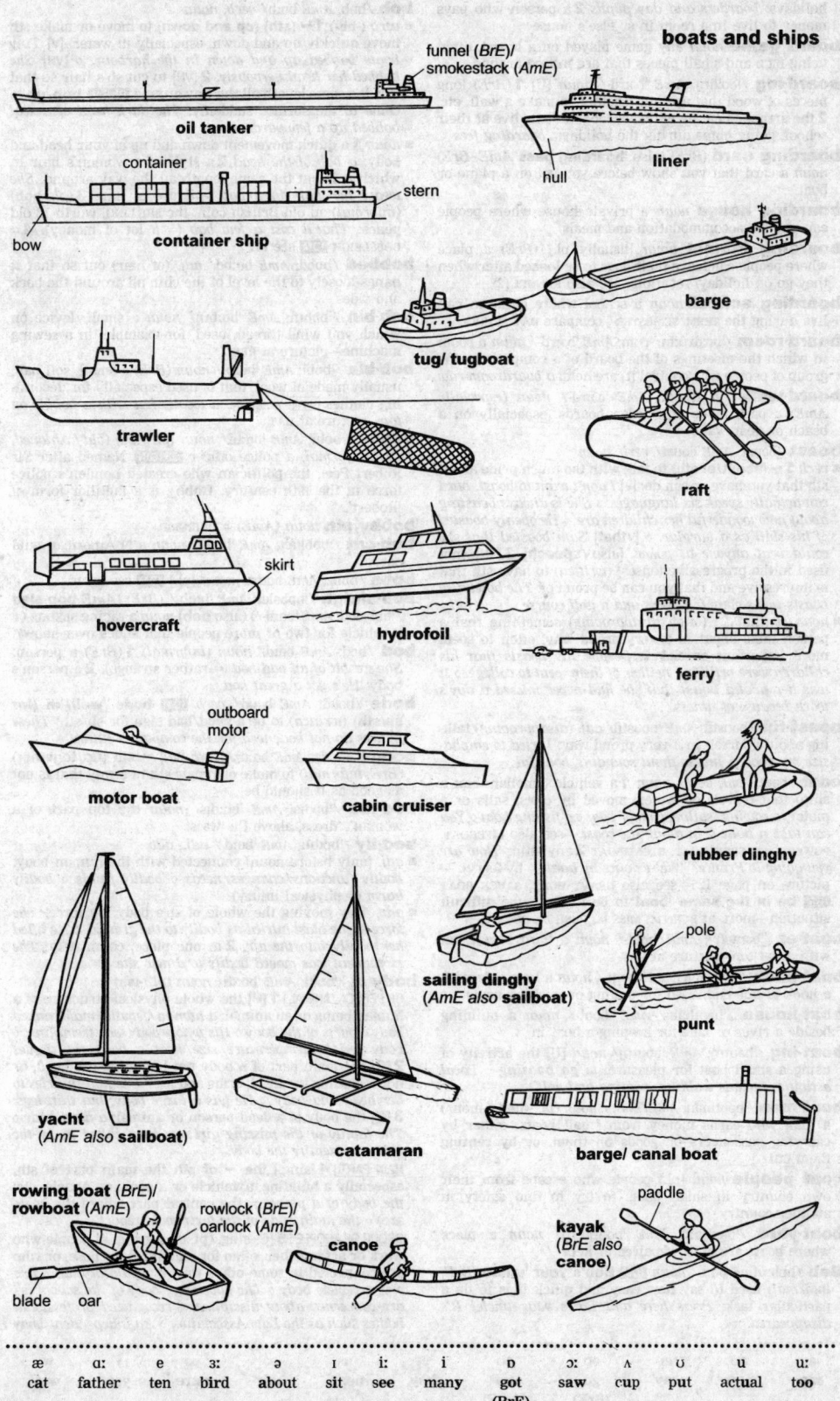

boats and ships

B

funnel (*BrE*)/ smokestack (*AmE*)

oil tanker

container

stern

bow

container ship

liner

hull

barge

tug/ tugboat

trawler

raft

skirt

hovercraft

hydrofoil

ferry

outboard motor

motor boat

cabin cruiser

rubber dinghy

pole

sailing dinghy
(*AmE also* **sailboat**)

punt

yacht
(*AmE also* **sailboat**)

catamaran

barge/ canal boat

rowing boat (*BrE*)/
rowboat (*AmE*)

rowlock (*BrE*)/
oarlock (*AmE*)

paddle

canoe

kayak
(*BrE also*
canoe)

blade   oar

æ	ɑː	e	ɜː	ə	ɪ	iː	i	ɒ	ɔː	ʌ	ʊ	u	uː
cat	father	ten	bird	about	sit	see	many	got	saw	cup	put	actual	too
								(BrE)					

B

holidays: *boarders and day pupils* **2** a person who pays money to live in a room in sb else's house

'board game *noun* any game played on a board, often using DICE and small pieces that are moved around

board·ing /'bɔːdɪŋ; *AmE* 'bɔːrd-/ *noun* [U] **1** (*BrE*) long pieces of wood that are put together to make a wall, etc. **2** the arrangement by which school students live at their school, going home during the holidays: *boarding fees*

'boarding card (*BrE*) (also **'boarding pass** *AmE, BrE*) *noun* a card that you show before you get on a plane or boat

'boarding house *noun* a private house where people can pay for accommodation and meals

'boarding kennel *noun* [usually pl.] (*BrE*) a place where people can leave their dogs to be looked after when they go on holiday/vacation—see also KENNEL (2)

'boarding school *noun* a school where children can live during the TERM/SEMESTER—compare DAY SCHOOL

board·room /'bɔːdruːm; -rʊm; *AmE* 'bɔːrd-/ *noun* a room in which the meetings of the board of a company (= the group of people who control it) are held: *a boardroom row*

board·walk /'bɔːdwɔːk; *AmE* 'bɔːrd-/ *noun* (*especially AmE*) a path made of wooden boards, especially on a beach or near water

boast /bəʊst; *AmE* boʊst/ *verb, noun*
■ *verb* **1** ~ (**about/of sth**) to talk with too much pride about sth that you have or can do: [V] *I don't want to boast, but I can actually speak six languages.* ◇ *She is always boasting about how wonderful her children are.* ◇ *He openly boasted of his skill as a burglar.* ◇ [V that] *Sam boasted that she could beat anyone at poker.* [also V speech] **2** [VN] (not used in the progressive tenses) (*written*) to have sth that is impressive and that you can be proud of: *The hotel also boasts two swimming pools and a golf course.*
■ *noun* ~ (**that ...**) (often *disapproving*) something that a person talks about in a very proud way, often to seem more important or clever: *Despite his boasts that his children were brilliant, neither of them went to college.* ◇ *It was her proud boast that she had never missed a day's work because of illness.*

boast·ful /'bəʊstfl; *AmE* 'boʊstfl/ *adj.* (*disapproving*) talking about yourself in a very proud way: *I tried to emphasize my good points without sounding boastful.*

boat /bəʊt; *AmE* boʊt/ *noun* **1** a vehicle (smaller than a ship) that travels on water, moved by OARS, sails or a motor: *a rowing/sailing/motor boat* ◇ *a fishing boat* ◇ *You can take a boat trip along the coast.*—see also LIFEBOAT, POWERBOAT, SPEEDBOAT, STEAMBOAT **2** any ship: *'How are you going to France?' 'We're going by boat* (= by ferry).'—picture on page 125—see also GRAVY BOAT, SAUCE BOAT **IDM** **be in the same 'boat** to be in the same difficult situation—more at BURN *v.*, MISS *v.*, PUSH *v.*, ROCK *v.*

boat·er /'bəʊtə(r); *AmE* 'boʊt-/ *noun* a hard STRAW hat with a flat top—picture at HAT

boat·hook /'bəʊthʊk; *AmE* 'boʊt-/ *noun* a long pole with a hook at one end, used for pulling or pushing boats

boat·house /'bəʊthaʊs; *AmE* 'boʊt-/ *noun* a building beside a river or lake for keeping a boat in

boat·ing /'bəʊtɪŋ; *AmE* 'boʊtɪŋ/ *noun* [U] the activity of using a small boat for pleasure: *to go boating* ◇ *Local activities include walking, boating and golf.*

boat·man /'bəʊtmən; *AmE* 'boʊt-/ *noun* (*pl.* **-men** /-mən/) a man who earns money from small boats, either by carrying passengers or goods on them, or by renting them out

'boat people *noun* [pl.] people who escape from their own country in small boats to try to find safety in another country

boat·yard /'bəʊtjɑːd; *AmE* 'boʊtjɑːrd/ *noun* a place where boats are built, repaired or kept

Bob /bɒb; *AmE* bɑːb/ *noun* **IDM** **Bob's your 'uncle** (*BrE, informal*) used to say how easy and quick it is to do a particular task: *Press here and Bob's your uncle! It's disappeared.*

bob /bɒb; *AmE* bɑːb/ *verb, noun*
■ *verb* (**-bb-**) **1** ~ (**sth**) (**up and down**) to move or make sth move quickly up and down, especially in water: [V] *Tiny boats bobbed úp and down in the harbour.* ◇ [VN] *She bobbed her head nervously.* **2** [VN] to cut sb's hair so that it is the same length all the way around **PHRV** **bob 'up** to come to the surface suddenly: *The dark head of a seal bobbed up a few yards away.*
■ *noun* **1** a quick movement down and up of your head and body: *a bob of the head* **2** a style of a woman's hair in which it is cut the same length all the way around: *She wears her hair in a bob.*—picture at HAIR **3** (*pl.* **bob**) (*informal*) an old British coin, the SHILLING, worth 12 old pence: *That'll cost a few bob* (= a lot of money). **4** = BOBSLEIGH **IDM** see BIT

bobbed /bɒbd; *AmE* bɑːbd/ *adj.* (of hair) cut so that it hangs loosely to the level of the chin all around the back and sides

bob·bin /'bɒbɪn; *AmE* 'bɑːbɪn/ *noun* a small device on which you wind thread, used, for example, in a sewing machine—picture at REEL

bob·ble /'bɒbl; *AmE* 'bɑːbl/ *noun* (*BrE*) a small, soft ball, usually made of wool, that is used especially for decorating clothes [SYN] POMPOM: *a woolly hat with a bobble on top*—picture at HAT

bobby /'bɒbi; *AmE* 'bɑːbi/ *noun* (*pl.* **-ies**) (*old-fashioned, BrE, informal*) a police officer **ORIGIN** Named after Sir Robert Peel, the politician who created London's police force in the 19th century. **Bobby** is a familiar form of 'Robert'.

'bobby pin *noun* (*AmE*) = HAIRGRIP

bob·cat /'bɒbkæt; *AmE* 'bɑːb-/ *noun* a N American wild cat

bobs /bɒbz; *AmE* bɑːbz/ *noun* [pl.] **IDM** see BIT *n.*

bob·sleigh /'bɒbsleɪ; *AmE* 'bɑːb-/ (*BrE*) (*AmE* **bob·sled** /'bɒbsled; *AmE* 'bɑːb-/) (also **bob**) *noun* a racing SLEDGE (= a vehicle for two or more people that slides over snow)

bod /bɒd; *AmE* bɑːd/ *noun* (*informal*) **1** (*BrE*) a person: *She's a bit of an odd bod* (= rather strange). **2** a person's body: *He's got a great bod.*

bode /bəʊd; *AmE* boʊd/ *verb* **IDM** **bode 'well/'ill (for sb/sth)** (*written*) to be a good/bad sign for sb/sth: *These figures do not bode well for the company's future.*

bodge /bɒdʒ; *AmE* bɑːdʒ/ *verb* [VN] ~ **sth** (**up/together**) (*BrE, informal*) to make or repair sth in a way that is not as good as it should be

bod·ice /'bɒdɪs; *AmE* 'bɑːdɪs/ *noun* the top part of a woman's dress, above the waist

bod·ily /'bɒdɪli; *AmE* 'bɑːd-/ *adj., adv.*
■ *adj.* [only before noun] connected with the human body: *bodily functions/changes/needs* ◇ *bodily fluids* ◇ *bodily harm* (= physical injury)
■ *adv.* **1** by moving the whole of sb's body; by force: *The force of the blast hurled us bodily to the ground.* ◇ *He lifted her bodily into the air.* **2** in one piece; completely: *The monument was moved bodily to a new site.*

body *pl.* /'bɒdi; *AmE* 'bɑːdi/ *noun* (*pl.* **-ies**)
OF PERSON/ANIMAL | **1** [C] the whole physical structure of a human being or an animal: *a human/female/male/naked body* ◇ *parts of the body* ◇ *His whole body was trembling.* ◇ *body weight/temperature/size/heat* ◇ *body fat/tissues* **2** [C] the main part of a body not including the head, or not including the head, arms and legs: *She had injuries to her head and body.* ◇ *He has a large body, but thin legs.* **3** [C] the body of a dead person or animal: *a dead body* ◇ *The family of the missing girl has been called in by the police to identify the body.*

MAIN PART | **4** [sing.] **the ~ of sth** the main part of sth, especially a building, a vehicle or a book, an article, etc: *the body of a plane* (= the central part where the seats are) ◇ *the main body of the text/book/report*

GROUP OF PEOPLE | **5** [C+sing./pl. *v.*] a group of people who work or act together, often for an official purpose, or who are connected in some other way: *a regulatory/an advisory/a review body* ◇ *The governing body of the school is/are concerned about discipline.* ◇ *recognized professional bodies such as the Law Association* ◇ *An independent body*

aɪ	aʊ	eɪ	əʊ	oʊ	ɔɪ	ɪə	eə	ʊə	j	w
my	now	say	go	go	boy	near	hair	pure	yes	wet
			(BrE)	(AmE)						

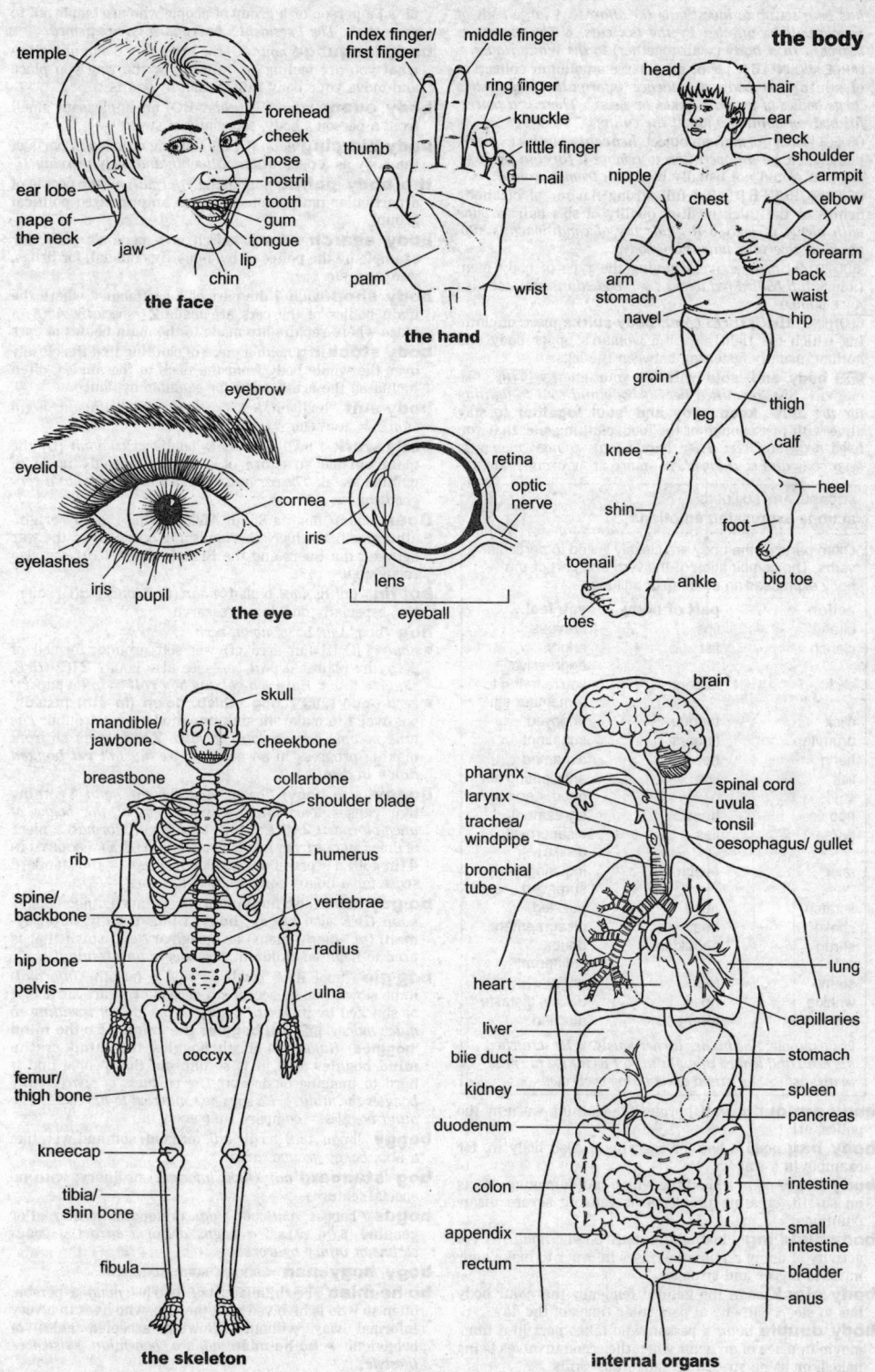

the face

temple
forehead
cheek
nose
nostril
tooth
gum
tongue
lip
ear lobe
nape of
the neck
jaw
chin

the hand

index finger/
first finger
middle finger
ring finger
knuckle
thumb
little finger
nail
palm
wrist

the body

head
hair
ear
neck
shoulder
armpit
elbow
nipple
chest
forearm
arm
back
stomach
waist
navel
hip
groin
thigh
leg
calf
knee
heel
shin
foot
toenail
ankle
big toe
toes

the eye

eyebrow
retina
optic
nerve
eyelid
cornea
iris
eyelashes
iris
pupil
lens
eyeball

the skeleton

skull
mandible/
jawbone
cheekbone
breastbone
collarbone
shoulder blade
rib
humerus
spine/
backbone
vertebrae
radius
hip bone
pelvis
ulna
coccyx
femur/
thigh bone
kneecap
tibia/
shin bone
fibula

internal organs

brain
pharynx
spinal cord
larynx
uvula
trachea/
windpipe
tonsil
oesophagus/ gullet
bronchial
tube
lung
heart
capillaries
liver
stomach
biie duct
spleen
kidney
pancreas
duodenum
colon
intestine
appendix
small
intestine
rectum
bladder
anus

b	d	f	g	h	k	l	m	n	p	r
bad	**did**	**fall**	**get**	**hat**	**cat**	**leg**	**man**	**now**	**pen**	**red**

B

has been set up to *investigate the affair.* ◊ *A large body of people will be affected by the tax cuts.* ◊ *The protesters marched* **in a body** (= all together) *to the White House.*

LARGE AMOUNT | **6** [C] **~ of sth** a large amount or collection of sth: *a vast body of evidence/information/research* ◊ *large bodies of water* (= lakes or seas) ◊ *There is a powerful body of opinion against the ruling.*

OBJECT | **7** [C] (*formal*) an object: *heavenly bodies* (= stars, planets, etc.) ◊ *an operation to remove a foreign body* (= sth that would not usually be there) *from a wound*

OF DRINK/HAIR | **8** [U] the full strong flavour of alcoholic drinks or the thick healthy quality of sb's hair: *a wine with plenty of body* ◊ *Regular use of conditioner is supposed to give your hair more body.*

-BODIED | **9** (in adjectives) having the type of body mentioned: *full-bodied red wines* ◊ *soft-bodied insects*—see also ABLE-BODIED

CLOTHING | **10** [C] (*BrE*) (*AmE* **body-suit**) a piece of clothing which fits tightly over a woman's upper body and bottom, usually fastening between the legs

IDM **body and 'soul** with all your energy **SYN** COMPLETELY: *She committed herself body and soul to fighting for the cause.* **keep body and 'soul together** to stay alive with just enough of the food, clothing, etc. that you need **SYN** SURVIVE: *They barely have enough money to keep body and soul together.*—more at DEAD *adj.*, SELL *v.*

VOCABULARY BUILDING
actions expressing emotions

Often parts of the body are closely linked to particular verbs. The combination of the verb and part of the body expresses an emotion or attitude.

action	part of body	you feel...
bite	lips	nervous
clench	fist	angry, aggressive
click	fingers	you're trying to remember sth
click	tongue	annoyed
drum/tap	fingers	impatient
hang	head	ashamed
lick	lips	anticipating sth good, nervous
nod	head	agreement
purse	lips	disapproval, dislike
raise	eyebrows	inquiring, surprised
scratch	head	puzzled
shake	head	disagreement
shrug	shoulders	doubt, indifferent
stamp	foot	angry
wrinkle	nose	dislike, distaste
wrinkle	forehead	puzzled

For example: *She bit her lip nervously.* ◊ *He scratched his head and looked thoughtful.* ◊ *I wrinkled my nose in disgust.* ◊ *She raised questioning eyebrows.*

'body armour *noun* [U] protective clothing worn by the police, etc.

'body bag *noun* a bag for carrying a dead body in, for example in a war

'body blow *noun* something which has damaging effects on sb/sth, creating problems or causing severe disappointment

body·build·ing /'bɒdibɪldɪŋ; *AmE* 'bɑːdi-/ *noun* [U] the activity of doing regular exercises in order to make your muscles bigger and stronger

'body clock *noun* the natural tendency that your body has to sleep, eat, etc. at particular times of the day

'body double *noun* a person who takes part in a film/movie in place of an actor when the scene involves being naked, or using special or dangerous skills

body·guard /'bɒdigɑːd; *AmE* 'bɑːdigɑːrd/ *noun* [C+sing./ pl. *v.*] a person or a group of people who are employed to protect sb: *The President's bodyguard is/are armed.*

'body language *noun* [U] the process of communicating what you are feeling or thinking by the way you place and move your body rather than by words

'body odour *noun* [U] (*abbr.* **BO**) an unpleasant smell from a person's body, especially of sweat

'body piercing *noun* [U] the making of holes in parts of the body as a decoration: *tattooing and body piercing*

the ,body 'politic *noun* [sing.] (*formal*) all the people of a particular nation considered as an organized political group

'body search *noun* a search of a person's body, for example by the police or by a CUSTOMS official, for drugs, weapons, etc.

'body shop *noun* **1** the part of a car factory where the main bodies of the cars are made **2** (*especially AmE*) a place where repairs are made to the main bodies of cars

'body stocking *noun* a piece of clothing that fits closely over the whole body from the neck to the ankles, often including the arms, worn for example by dancers

body·suit /'bɒdisuːt; *BrE* also -sjuːt; *AmE* 'bɑːdisuːt/ *noun* (*AmE*) = BODY (10)

body·work /'bɒdiwɜːk; *AmE* 'bɑːdiwɜːrk/ *noun* [U] the main outside structure of a vehicle, usually made of painted metal: *The car had damaged bodywork but a very good engine.*

Boer /bɔː(r)/ *noun* a South African whose family originally came from the Netherlands: *the Boer War* (= the war between the Boers and the British (1899-1902))—see also AFRIKANER

bof·fin /'bɒfɪn; *AmE* 'bɑːfən/ *noun* (*BrE*, *informal*) a scientist, especially one doing research

bog /bɒg; *AmE* bɔːg/ *noun, verb*
- *noun* **1** [C, U] (an area of) wet soft ground, formed of decaying plants: *a peat bog*—see also BOGGY **2** [C] (*BrE*, *slang*) a toilet: *Have you got any bog roll* (= toilet paper)?
- *verb* (-gg-) **PHRV** **,bog sth/sb 'down (in sth)** [usually passive] **1** to make sth sink into mud or wet ground: *The tank became bogged down in mud.* **2** to prevent sb from making progress in an activity: *We mustn't get bogged down in details.*

bogey (also **bogy**) /'bəʊgi; *AmE* 'boʊgi/ *noun* **1** a thing that causes fear, often without reason: *the bogey of unemployment* **2** (*BrE*) (*AmE* **boo·ger**) (*informal*) a piece of dried MUCUS from inside your nose **3** (*BrE*) = BOGEYMAN **4** (in golf) a score of one stroke over PAR (= the standard score for a hole)—compare BIRDIE, EAGLE

bo·gey·man (also **bogy·man**) /'bəʊgimæn; *AmE* 'boʊgi-/ *noun* (*BrE* also **bogey**, **bogy**) (*AmE* usually **boo·gey·man**) (*pl.* -men /-mən/) an imaginary evil spirit that is used to frighten children: *The bogeyman's coming!*

bog·gle /'bɒgl; *AmE* 'bɔːgl/ *verb* [V] **~ (at sth)** (*informal*) to be slow to do or accept sth because you are surprised or shocked by it: *Even I boggle at the idea of spending so much money.* **IDM** **sth boggles the 'mind** (also **the mind 'boggles**) (*informal*) if sth boggles the mind or the mind boggles at it, it is so unusual that people find it hard to imagine or accept: *The vastness of space really boggles the mind.* ◊ *'He says he's married to his cats!' 'The mind boggles!'*—compare MIND-BOGGLING

boggy /'bɒgi; *AmE* 'bɔːgi/ *adj.* (of land) soft and wet, like a BOG: *boggy ground/areas*

,bog 'standard *adj.* (*BrE*, *informal*) ordinary; with no special features

bogus /'bəʊgəs; *AmE* 'boʊ-/ *adj.* pretending to be real or genuine **SYN** FALSE: *a bogus doctor/contract* ◊ *bogus claims of injury by workers*

bogy, **bogy·man** = BOGEY, BOGEYMAN

bo·he·mian /bəʊ'hiːmiən; *AmE* boʊ'h-/ *noun* a person, often sb who is involved with the arts, who lives in a very informal way without following accepted rules of behaviour ▶ **bo·he·mian** *adj.*: *a bohemian existence/ lifestyle*

boil /bɔɪl/ *verb, noun*

s	t	v	z	ʃ	ʒ	tʃ	dʒ	θ	ð	ŋ
see	tea	van	zoo	shoe	vision	chain	jam	thin	this	sing

■ *verb* **1** when a liquid **boils** or when you **boil** it, it is heated to the point where it forms bubbles and turns to steam or VAPOUR: [V] *The water was bubbling and boiling away.* ◊ [VN] *Boil plenty of salted water, then add the spaghetti.* ⇨ vocabulary notes on page 274 **2** when a KETTLE, pan, etc. **boils** or when you **boil** a KETTLE, etc., it is heated until the water inside it **boils**: [VN] *I'll boil the kettle and make some tea.* ◊ [V] (*BrE*) *The kettle's boiling.* ◊ [V-ADJ] *She left the gas on by mistake and the pan boiled dry* (= the water boiled until there was none left). **3** to cook or wash sth in boiling water; to be cooked or washed in boiling water: [V] *She put some potatoes on to boil.* ◊ [VN] *boiled carrots/cabbage* ◊ [VN, VNN] *to boil an egg for sb* ◊ *to boil sb an egg* **4** [V] (*written*) if you **boil** with anger, etc. or anger, etc. **boils** inside you, you are very angry: *He was boiling with rage.* **IDM** see BLOOD *n.* **PHRV** **,boil 'down | ,boil sth↔'down** to be reduced or to reduce sth by boiling **,boil sth 'down (to sth)** to make sth, especially information, shorter by leaving out the parts that are not important: *The original speech I had written got boiled down to about ten minutes.* **,boil 'down to sth** (not used in the progressive tenses) (of a situation, problem, etc.) to have sth as a main or basic part: *In the end, what it all boils down to is money, or the lack of it.* **,boil 'over 1** (of liquid) to boil and flow over the top of a pan, etc: *The milk is boiling over.* **2** (*informal*) to become very angry **3** (of a situation, an emotion, etc.) to change into sth more dangerous or violent **SYN** EXPLODE: *Racial tension finally boiled over in the inner city riots.* **,boil 'up** if a situation or an emotion **boils up**, it becomes dangerous, worrying, etc: *I could feel anger boiling up inside me.* **,boil sth↔'up** to heat a liquid or some food until it boils
■ *noun* **1** [sing.] a period of boiling; the point at which liquid boils: (*BrE*) *Bring the soup to the boil, then allow it to simmer for five minutes.* ◊ (*AmE*) *Bring the soup to a boil.* **2** [C] a painful infected swelling under the skin which is full of a thick yellow liquid (called PUS) **IDM off the 'boil** (*BrE*) less good than before: *The second series of the show really went off the boil.* **on the 'boil** very active: *We have several projects all on the boil at once.*

,boiled 'sweet (*BrE*) (*AmE* **,hard 'candy** [U]) *noun* a hard sweet/candy made from boiled sugar, often with fruit flavours

boil·er /'bɔɪlə(r)/ (also **fur·nace** especially in *AmE*) *noun* a container in which water is heated to provide hot water and heating in a building or to produce steam in an engine

'boiler suit *noun* (*especially BrE*) (*AmE* usually **cov·er·alls**) a piece of clothing like trousers/pants and a jacket in one piece, worn for doing dirty work—compare OVERALLS

boil·ing /'bɔɪlɪŋ/ (also **,boiling 'hot**) *adj.* very hot: *You must be boiling in that sweater!* ◊ *a boiling hot day*

'boiling point *noun* **1** the temperature at which a liquid starts to boil **2** the point at which a person becomes very angry, or a situation is likely to become violent: *Racial tension has reached boiling point.*

bois·ter·ous /'bɔɪstərəs/ *adj.* (of people, animals or behaviour) noisy and full of life and energy: *It was a challenge, keeping ten boisterous seven-year-olds amused.* ▶ **bois·ter·ous·ly** *adv.*

bok choy /ˌbɒk 'tʃɔɪ; *AmE* ˌbaːk/ *noun* [U] (*AmE*) = CHINESE CABBAGE

bold /bəʊld; *AmE* boʊld/ *adj.* (**bold·er**, **bold·est**) **1** (of people or behaviour) brave and confident; not afraid to say what you feel or to take risks: *It was a bold move on their part to open a branch of the business in France.* ◊ *The wine made him bold enough to approach her and introduce himself.* **2** (of shape, colour, lines, etc.) that can be easily seen; having a strong clear appearance: *the bold outline of a mountain against the sky* ◊ *She paints with bold strokes of the brush.* **3** (*technical*) (of printed words or letters) in a thick, dark TYPE: *Highlight the important words in bold* (*type*). ◊ *bold lettering* ▶ **bold·ly** *adv.* **bold·ness** *noun* [U] **IDM be/make so bold (as to do sth)** (*formal*) used especially when politely asking a question or making a suggestion which you hope will not offend anyone (although it may criticize them slightly): *If I may be so bold as to suggest that he made a mistake in his calculations …* **(as) bold as 'brass** (*BrE, informal*) without showing any respect, shame or fear: *She marched in here, bold as brass, and demanded a pay rise.*

bole /bəʊl; *AmE* boʊl/ *noun* (*rare*) the main stem of a tree **SYN** TRUNK

bol·ero /bə'leərəʊ; *AmE* bə'leroʊ/ *noun* (*pl.* **-os**) **1** a traditional Spanish dance; a piece of music for this dance **2** / also 'bɒlərəʊ; *AmE* bə'leroʊ/ a women's short jacket that is not fastened at the front

boll /bəʊl; *AmE* boʊl/ *noun* the part of the cotton plant that contains the seeds

bol·lard /'bɒlɑːd; *AmE* 'baːlərd/ *noun* **1** (*BrE*) a short thick post that is used to stop motor vehicles from going on to a road or part of a road **2** a short thick post on a ship, or on land close to water, to which a ship's rope may be tied

bol·lock·ing /'bɒləkɪŋ; *AmE* 'baː-/ *noun* (*BrE*, ⚠) an occasion when sb tells you that they are very angry with you, often by shouting at you: *to give sb a bollocking* ◊ *to get a bollocking* **HELP** There are more polite ways to express this, for example **to give sb/to get a rocket**, or **to tear a strip off sb.**

bol·locks /'bɒləks; *AmE* 'baː-/ *noun* (*BrE*, ⚠, slang) **1** [U] nonsense: *You're talking a load of bollocks!* **2** [pl.] a man's TESTICLES **3** (**Bollocks!**) *exclamation* used as a swear word when sb is disagreeing with sth, or when they are angry about sth: *Bollocks! He never said that!*

bol·ogna /bə'ləʊnjə; bə'lɒnjə; *AmE* -'loʊ-/ (also **ba·lo·ney**) *noun* [U] (*AmE*) a type of sausage that is put in sandwiches, made of a mixture of meats

bolo tie /'bəʊləʊ taɪ; *AmE* 'boʊloʊ/ *noun* (*AmE*) a string worn around the neck and fastened with a decorative CLASP or bar

bol·shie (also **bol·shy**) /'bɒlʃi; *AmE* 'boʊl-/ *adj.* (*BrE, informal, disapproving*) (of a person) creating difficulties or arguments deliberately, and refusing to be helpful: *She was in a bolshie mood.*

bol·ster /'bəʊlstə(r); *AmE* 'boʊl-/ *verb, noun*
■ *verb* [VN] **~ sb/sth (up)** to improve sth or make it stronger: *to bolster sb's confidence/courage/morale* ◊ *Falling interest rates may help to bolster up the economy.*
■ *noun* a long thick PILLOW that is placed across the top of a bed under the other pillows

bolt /bəʊlt; *AmE* boʊlt/ *noun, verb, adv.*
■ *noun* **1** a long, narrow piece of metal that you slide across the inside of a door or window in order to lock it **2** a piece of metal like a screw without a point which is used with a circular piece of metal (= a NUT) to fasten things together: *nuts and bolts*—picture at TOOL **3** **~ of lightning** a sudden flash of LIGHTNING in the sky, appearing as a line **4** a short heavy arrow shot from a CROSSBOW **5** a long piece of fabric wound in a roll around a piece of cardboard **IDM a ,bolt from the 'blue** an event or a piece of news which is sudden and unexpected; a complete surprise: *Her dismissal came as a bolt from the blue.* **make a 'bolt for sth | make a 'bolt for it** to run away very fast, in order to escape—more at NUT *n.*, SHOT *v.*
■ *verb* **1** to fasten sth such as a door or window by sliding a bolt across; to be able to be fastened in this way: [VN] *Don't forget to bolt the door.* ◊ [V] *The gate bolts on the inside.* **2** [VN] **~ A to B | ~ A and B together** to fasten things together with a bolt: *The vice is bolted to the workbench.* ◊ *The various parts of the car are then bolted together.* **3** [V] if an animal, especially a horse, **bolts**, it suddenly runs away because it is frightened **4** [V] [usually + *adv./prep.*] (of a person) to run away, especially in order to escape: *When he saw the police arrive, he bolted down an alley.* **5** [VN] **~ sth (down)** to eat sth very quickly: *Don't bolt your food!* **6** (*AmE*) to stop supporting a particular group or political party: [VN] *Many Democrats bolted the party to vote Republican.* [also V] **7** [V] (of a plant, especially a vegetable) to grow too quickly and start producing seeds and so become less good to eat **IDM** see STABLE *n.*

æ　　ɑː　　e　　ɜː　　ə　　ɪ　　iː　　　i　　ɒ　　ɔː　　ʌ　　ʊ　　u　　uː
cat　father　ten　bird　about　sit　see　many　got　saw　cup　put　actual　too
　　　　　　　　　　　　　　　　　　　　　　　(BrE)

■ *adv.* **IDM** **sit/stand bolt 'upright** to sit or stand with your back straight

'bolt-hole *noun* (*BrE*) a place that you can escape to, for example when you are in a difficult situation

bomb /bɒm; *AmE* bɑːm/ *noun, verb*

■ *noun* **1** [C] a weapon designed to explode at a particular time or when it is dropped or thrown: *a bomb attack/ blast/explosion* ◊ *a bomb goes off/explodes* ◊ *extensive bomb damage* ◊ *Hundreds of bombs were dropped on the city.* **2 (the bomb)** [sing.] nuclear weapons (ATOMIC or HYDROGEN bombs): *countries which have the bomb* **3** (a bomb) [sing.] (*BrE, informal*) a lot of money: *That dress must have cost a bomb!* **4 (a bomb)** [sing.] (*AmE, informal*) a complete failure: *The musical was a complete bomb on Broadway.* **IDM** **go down a 'bomb | go (like) a 'bomb** (*BrE*) to be very successful: *Our performance went down a bomb.* ◊ *The party was really going (like) a bomb.* **go like a 'bomb** (*BrE*) (of a vehicle) to go very fast

■ *verb* **1** [VN] to attack sb/sth by leaving a bomb in a place or by dropping bombs from a plane: *Terrorists bombed several army barracks.* ◊ *Coventry was heavily bombed during the last war.* **2** [V+adv./prep.] (*BrE, informal*) to move very fast, especially in a vehicle, in a particular direction: *They were bombing down the road at about 80 miles an hour.* **3** [VN] (*AmE, informal*) to fail a test or an exam very badly: [VN] *The exam was impossible! I definitely bombed it.* [alsoV] **4** [V] (*informal*) (of a play, show, etc.) to fail very badly: *His latest musical bombed and lost thousands of dollars.* **PHRV** **be ,bombed 'out (of sth) 1** if you are **bombed out**, your home is destroyed by bombs. **2** if a building is **bombed out**, it has been destroyed by bombs

'bomb alert *noun* (*BrE*) = BOMB SCARE

bom·bard /bɒm'bɑːd; *AmE* bɑːm'bɑːrd/ *verb* [VN] ~ **sb/ sth (with sth) 1** to attack a place by firing large guns at it or dropping bombs on it continuously: *Madrid was heavily bombarded for several months.* **2** to attack sb with a lot of questions, criticisms, etc. or by giving them too much information: *We have been bombarded with letters of complaint.* ► **bom·bard·ment** *noun* [U, C]: *The city came under heavy bombardment.*

bom·bard·ier /ˌbɒmbə'dɪə(r); *AmE* ˌbɑːmbər'dɪr/ *noun* **1** the person on a military plane in the US air force who is responsible for aiming and dropping bombs **2** a member of a low rank in the Royal Artillery (= a part of the British army that uses large guns)

bom·bast /'bɒmbæst; *AmE* 'bɑːm-/ *noun* [U] (*formal*) words which sound important but have little meaning, used to impress people ► **bom·bas·tic** /bɒm'bæstɪk; *AmE* bɑːm-/ *adj.*: *a bombastic speaker*

'bomb disposal *noun* [U] the job of removing or exploding bombs in order to make an area safe: *a bomb disposal expert/squad/team*

bomb·er /'bɒmə(r); *AmE* 'bɑːm-/ *noun* **1** a plane that carries and drops bombs **2** a person who puts a bomb somewhere illegally

'bomber jacket *noun* a short jacket that fits tightly around the waist and fastens with a ZIP/ZIPPER

bomb·ing /'bɒmɪŋ; *AmE* 'bɑːm-/ *noun* [C, U] an occasion when a bomb is dropped or left somewhere; the act of doing this: *recent bombings in major cities* ◊ *enemy bombing*

'bomb scare (also **'bomb threat** especially in *AmE*) (*BrE* also **'bomb alert**) *noun* an occasion when sb says that they have put a bomb somewhere and everyone has to leave the area

bomb·shell /'bɒmʃel; *AmE* 'bɑːm-/ *noun* [usually sing.] (*informal*) **1** an event or a piece of news which is unexpected and usually unpleasant: *The news of his death came as a bombshell.* ◊ *She dropped a bombshell at the meeting and announced that she was leaving.* **2** (a blond(e) bombshell) (*informal*) a very attractive woman with BLONDE hair

'bomb site *noun* an area where all the buildings have been destroyed by bombs

bona fide /ˌbəʊnə 'faɪdi; *AmE* ˌboʊnə 'faɪd/ *adj.* [usually before noun] (from *Latin*) genuine, real or legal; not false: *a*

bona fide reason ◊ *Is it a bona fide, reputable organization?*

bona fides /ˌbəʊnə 'faɪdiːz; *AmE* ˌboʊnə/ *noun* [pl.] (from *Latin*) evidence that sb is who they say that they are; evidence that sb/sth is honest

bon·anza /bə'nænzə/ *noun* [sing.] **1** a situation in which people can make a lot of money or be very successful: *a cash bonanza for investors* ◊ *a bonanza year for the computer industry* **2** a situation where there is a large amount of sth pleasant: *the usual bonanza of sport in the summer*

bon·bon /'bɒnbɒn; *AmE* 'bɑːnbɑːn/ *noun* a sweet/candy, especially one with a soft centre

bonce /bɒns; *AmE* bɑːns/ *noun* (*BrE, informal*) a person's head

bond /bɒnd; *AmE* bɑːnd/ *noun, verb*

■ *noun*

STRONG CONNECTION | **1** [C] ~ **(between A and B)** something that forms a connection between people or groups, such as a feeling of friendship or shared ideas and experiences: *A bond of friendship had been forged between them.* ◊ *The agreement strengthened the bonds between the two countries.* ◊ *the special bond between mother and child*

MONEY | **2** [C] an agreement by a government or a company to pay you interest on the money you have lent; a document containing this agreement: *government bonds*—see also JUNK BOND **3** [U] (*law*) (*especially AmE*) a sum of money that is paid as BAIL: *He was released on $5000 bond.*

ROPES/CHAINS | **4** (bonds) [pl.] (*formal*) the ropes or chains keeping sb prisoner; anything that stops you from being free to do what you want: *to release sb from their bonds* ◊ *the bonds of oppression/injustice*

LEGAL AGREEMENT | **5** [C] (*formal*) a legal written agreement or promise: *We entered into a solemn bond.*

JOIN | **6** [C] the way in which two things are joined together: *a firm bond between the two surfaces*

CHEMISTRY | **7** [C] the way in which ATOMS are held together in a chemical compound

IDM see WORD *n.*

■ *verb*

JOIN FIRMLY | **1** ~ **(A and B) (together)** | ~ **(A) to B** to join two things firmly together; to join firmly to sth else: [VN] *This new glue bonds a variety of surfaces in seconds.* ◊ *It cannot be used to bond wood to metal.* ◊ [V] *The atoms bond together to form a molecule.*

DEVELOP RELATIONSHIP | **2** ~ **(with sb)** to develop or create a relationship of trust and affection with sb: *Mothers who are depressed sometimes fail to bond with their children.* [alsoVN]

bond·age /'bɒndɪdʒ; *AmE* 'bɑːn-/ *noun* **1** (*old-fashioned* or *formal*) the state of being a slave or prisoner: (*figurative*) *women's liberation from the bondage of domestic life* **2** the practice of being tied with ropes, chains, etc. in order to gain sexual pleasure

bond·ing /'bɒndɪŋ; *AmE* 'bɑːn-/ *noun* [U] **1** the process of forming a special relationship with sb or with a group of people: *mother-child bonding* ◊ *male bonding* **2** (*chemistry*) the process of atoms joining together: *hydrogen bonding*

bone /bəʊn; *AmE* boʊn/ *noun, verb*

■ *noun* **1** [C] any of the hard parts that form the SKELETON of the body of a human or an animal: *He survived the accident with no broken bones.* ◊ *This fish has a lot of bones in it.* **2** [U] the hard substance that bones are made of: *knives with bone handles* **3** (-boned) (in adjectives) having bones of the type mentioned: *fine-boned* **IDM** **a bone of con'tention** a subject which causes disagreement and arguments between people **close to the 'bone** (*BrE, informal*) (of a remark, joke, story, etc.) so honest or clearly expressed that it is likely to cause offence to some people: *His comments about her size were a bit close to the bone.* **cut, pare, etc. sth to the 'bone** to reduce sth, such as costs, as much as you possibly can **have a 'bone to pick with sb** (*spoken*) to be angry with sb about sth and want to discuss it with them **make no bones about (doing) sth** to be honest and open about sth; to not hesitate to do sth: *She made no bones about telling him*

aɪ	aʊ	eɪ	əʊ	oʊ	ɔɪ	ɪə	eə	ʊə	j	w
my	now	say	go	go	boy	near	hair	pure	yes	wet
			(BrE)	(AmE)						

exactly what she thought of him. **to the 'bone** affecting you very strongly: *His threats chilled her to the bone.*—more at BAG *n.*, BARE *adj.*, FEEL *v.*, FINGER *n.*, FLESH *n.*, SKIN *n.*

■ *verb* [VN] to take the bones out of fish or meat PHRV ,**bone 'up on sth** (*informal*) to try to learn about sth or to remind yourself of what you already know about it: *She had boned up on the city's history before the visit.*

,**bone 'china** *noun* [U] thin delicate CHINA made of clay mixed with crushed bone; cups, plates, etc. made of this

,**bone 'dry** *adj.* [not usually before noun] completely dry

,**bone 'idle** *adj.* (*old-fashioned, BrE, informal*) very lazy

'**bone marrow** (also **mar·row**) *noun* [U] a soft substance that fills the hollow parts of bones: *a bone marrow transplant*

bone-meal /'bəʊnmiːl; *AmE* 'boʊn-/ *noun* [U] a substance made from crushed animal bones which is used to make soil richer

boner /'bəʊnə(r); *AmE* 'boʊn-/ *noun* (*AmE, informal*) **1** (⚠) an ERECTION of the PENIS **2** an embarrassing mistake

bon·fire /'bɒnfaɪə(r); *AmE* 'bɑːn-/ *noun* a large outdoor fire for burning waste or as part of a celebration

'**Bonfire Night** (also ,**Guy 'Fawkes night**) *noun* [U, C] (in Britain) the night of 5 November when people light bonfires and have FIREWORKS to celebrate the failure of the plan in 1605 to destroy the parliament buildings with explosives

bongo /'bɒŋgəʊ; *AmE* 'bɑːŋgoʊ/ (*pl.* -os) (also '**bongo drum**) *noun* a small drum, usually one of a pair, that you play with your fingers

bon·homie /'bɒnəmi; *AmE* ,bɑːnə'miː/ *noun* [U] (from French, *formal*) a feeling of cheerful friendship

bonk /bɒŋk; *AmE* bɑːŋk/ *noun, verb*

■ *noun* (*BrE, informal*) **1** [sing.] an act of having sex with sb **2** [C] the act of hitting sb on the head or of hitting your head on sth

■ *verb* (*BrE, informal*) **1** to have sex with sb: [VN] *He's been bonking one of his students.* [also V] **2** [VN] to hit sb lightly on the head or to hit yourself by mistake: *I bonked my head on the doorway.*

bonk·ers /'bɒŋkəz; *AmE* 'bɑːŋkərz/ *adj.* [not before noun] (*informal*) completely crazy and silly: *I'll go bonkers if I have to wait any longer.* IDM see RAVING *adv.*

bon mot /,bɒn 'məʊ; *AmE* ,bɑːn 'moʊ/ *noun* (*pl.* **bons mots** /,bɒn 'məʊ; *AmE* ,bɑːn 'moʊ/) (from French, *formal*) a funny and clever remark

bon·net /'bɒnɪt; *AmE* 'bɑːnət/ *noun* **1** a hat tied with strings under the chin, worn by babies and, especially in the past, by women **2** (*BrE*) (*AmE* **hood**) the metal part over the front of a motor vehicle, usually covering the engine—picture at CAR IDM see BEE

bonny (also **bonnie**) /'bɒni; *AmE* 'bɑːni/ *adj.* (**bon·nier**, **bon·ni·est**) (*dialect*, especially *ScotE*) very pretty; attractive: *a bonny baby/lass*

bon·sai /'bɒnsaɪ; *AmE* 'bɑːn-/ *noun* (*pl.* **bonsai**) **1** [C] a small tree that is grown in a pot and prevented from reaching its normal size **2** [U] the Japanese art of growing bonsai

bonus /'bəʊnəs; *AmE* 'boʊ-/ *noun* (*pl.* -es) **1** an extra amount of money that is added to a payment, especially to sb's wages as a reward: *All employees received a £100 Christmas bonus.* ◊ *productivity bonuses* **2** anything pleasant that is extra and more or better than you were expecting: *Being able to walk to work is an **added bonus** of the new job.*—see also NO-CLAIMS BONUS

bony /'bəʊni; *AmE* 'boʊni/ *adj.* **1** (of a person or part of the body) very thin so that the bones can be seen under the skin **2** (of fish) full of small bones **3** consisting of or like bone

boo /buː/ *exclamation, noun, verb*

■ *exclamation, noun* **1** a sound that people make to show that they do not like an actor, speaker, etc: *'Boo!' they shouted, 'Get off!'.* ◊ *The speech was greeted with loud boos from the audience.* **2** people shout **Boo!** when they want to surprise or frighten sb

■ *verb* to show that you do not like a person, performance, idea, etc. by shouting 'boo': [V] *The audience booed as she started her speech.* ◊ [VN] *He was booed off the stage.*

boob /buːb/ *noun, verb*

■ *noun* **1** (*slang*) a woman's breast **2** (*BrE*) (also **boo·boo** /'buːbuː/, *AmE, BrE*) (*informal*) a stupid mistake: *I made a bit of a boob throwing that file away.* **3** (*AmE*) a stupid person

■ *verb* [V] (*informal*) to make a stupid mistake

'**boob tube** *noun* **1** (*BrE, informal*) (*AmE* '**tube top**) a piece of women's clothing that is made of fabric that stretches and covers the chest **2** (*AmE, informal, disapproving*) the television

booby prize /'buːbi praɪz/ *noun* a prize that is given as a joke to the person who is last in a competition

'**booby trap** *noun* **1** a hidden bomb that explodes when the object that it is connected to is touched **2** a hidden device that is meant as a joke to surprise sb, for example an object placed above a door so that it will fall on the first person who opens the door

'**booby-trap** *verb* (-pp-) [VN] to place a booby trap in or on sth

boo·ger /'buːgə(r)/ *noun* (*AmE*) = BOGEY (2)

boo·gey·man /'buːgimæn/ *noun* (*AmE*) = BOGEYMAN

boo·gie /'buːgi; *AmE* 'bʊgi/ *noun, verb*

■ *noun* (also ,**boogie-'woogie** /-'wuːgi; *AmE* -'wʊgi/) [U] a type of blues music played on the piano, with a fast strong rhythm

■ *verb* [V] (*informal*) to dance to fast pop music

boo-hoo /'buːhuː; ,buː'huː/ *exclamation* used in written English to show the sound of sb crying

book /bʊk/ *noun, verb*

■ *noun*

PRINTED WORK | **1** [C] a set of printed pages that are fastened inside a cover so that you can turn them and read them: *a pile of books* ◊ *hardback/paperback books* **2** [C] a written work published in printed or electronic form: *She's reading a book by Stephen King.* ◊ *a book about/on wildlife* ◊ *reference/children's/library books*

FOR WRITING IN | **3** [C] a set of sheets of paper that are fastened together inside a cover and used for writing in: *an exercise book* ◊ *an address book* ◊ *a notebook*

OF STAMPS/TICKETS/MATCHES, etc. | **4** [C] a set of things that are fastened together like a book: *a book of stamps/tickets/matches* ◊ *a chequebook*

ACCOUNTS | **5** (**books**) [pl.] the written records of the financial affairs of a business SYN ACCOUNTS: *to do the books* (= to check the accounts)

SECTION OF BIBLE, etc. | **6** [C] a section of a large written work: *the books of the Bible*

IDM **be in sb's good/bad 'books** (*informal*) used to say that sb is pleased/annoyed with you: *I'm in her good books at the moment because I cleared up the kitchen.* **bring sb to 'book (for sth)** (*formal, especially BrE*) to punish sb for doing sth wrong and make them explain their behaviour **by the 'book** following rules and instructions in a very strict way: *She always does everything by the book.* **in my 'book** (*spoken*) used when you are giving your opinion: *That's cheating in my book.* **(be) on sb's 'books** (to be) on an organization's list, for example of people who are available for a particular type of work: *We have very few nurses on our books at the moment.* ◊ *Most of the houses on our books are in the north of the city.* **throw the 'book at sb** (*informal*) to punish sb who has committed an offence as severely as possible—more at CLOSE[1] *v.*, CLOSED, COOK *v.*, HISTORY, JUDGE *v.*, LEAF *n.*, OPEN *adj.*, READ *v.*, SUIT *n.*, TRICK *n.*

■ *verb* **1** (*especially BrE*) to arrange with a hotel, restaurant, theatre, etc. to have a room, table, seat, etc. on a particular date: [V] *Book early to avoid disappointment.* ◊ [VN] *I'd like to book a table for two for 8 o'clock tonight.* ◊ *The performance is booked up* (= there are no more tickets available). ◊ *I'm sorry—we're fully booked.*—compare RESERVE **2** [VN] to arrange for sb to have a seat on a plane, etc: *I've booked you on the 10 o'clock flight.* **3** [VN] to arrange for a singer, etc. to perform on a particular date:

b	d	f	g	h	k	l	m	n	p	r
bad	**did**	**fall**	**get**	**hat**	**cat**	**leg**	**man**	**now**	**pen**	**red**

We've booked a band for the wedding reception. **4** [VN] (informal) to write down sb's name and address because they have committed a crime or an offence: He was booked for possession of cannabis. **5** [VN] (BrE, informal) (of a referee) to write down in an official book the name of a player who has broken the rules of the game

PHR V ,book 'in/'into sth to arrive at a hotel, etc. and arrange to stay there: I got in at ten and booked straight into a hotel. ,book sb 'in/'into sth to arrange for sb to have a room at a hotel, etc.

book·able /'bʊkəbl/ adj. **1** tickets, etc. that are **bookable** can be ordered in advance **2** (BrE) if an offence in football is **bookable**, the name of the player responsible is written down in a book by the REFEREE as a punishment **3** (AmE) if a crime is a **bookable** offence, the person responsible can be arrested

book·bind·er /'bʊkbaɪndə(r)/ noun a person whose job is fastening the pages of books together and putting covers on them ▶ **book·bind·ing** noun [U]

book·case /'bʊkkeɪs/ noun a piece of furniture with shelves for keeping books on

'**book club** noun an organization that sells books cheaply to its members

book·end /'bʊkend/ noun [usually pl.] one of a pair of objects used to keep a row of books upright

bookie /'bʊki/ noun (informal) = BOOKMAKER

book·ing /'bʊkɪŋ/ noun **1** [C, U] (especially BrE) an arrangement that you make in advance to buy a ticket to travel somewhere, go to the theatre, etc: a booking form/ office/hall/clerk ◇ Can I make a booking for Friday afternoon? ◇ Early booking is strongly recommended. ◇ No advance booking is necessary. ◇ We can't take any more bookings.—compare BOOKING **2** [C] an arrangement for sb to perform at a theatre, in a concert, etc. **3** [C] (BrE) (in football) an act of the REFEREE writing a player's name in a book, as a punishment because an offence has been committed

book·ish /'bʊkɪʃ/ adj. (often disapproving) interested in reading and studying, rather than in more active or practical things

book·keep·er /'bʊkkiːpə(r)/ noun a person whose job is to keep an accurate record of the accounts of a business ▶ **book·keep·ing** noun [U]

book·let /'bʊklət/ noun a small thin book with a paper cover that contains information about a particular subject

book·maker /'bʊkmeɪkə(r)/ (also informal **bookie**) (also BrE formal '**turf accountant**) noun a person whose job is to take bets on the result of horse races, etc. and pay out money to people who win ▶ **book·mak·ing** noun [U]

book·mark /'bʊkmɑːk; AmE -mɑːrk/ noun **1** a strip of paper, etc. that you put between the pages of a book when you finish reading so that you can easily find the place again **2** (computing) a record of the address of a file, a page on the Internet, etc. that enables you to find it quickly ▶ **book·mark** verb: [VN] Do you want to bookmark this site?

book·plate /'bʊkpleɪt/ noun a decorative piece of paper that is stuck in a book to show the name of the person who owns it

book·sel·ler /'bʊkselə(r)/ noun a person whose job is selling books

book·shop /'bʊkʃɒp; AmE -ʃɑːp/ (especially BrE) (AmE usually **book·store** /'bʊkstɔː(r)/) noun a shop/store that sells books

book·stall /'bʊkstɔːl/ (especially BrE) (AmE usually **news-stand**) noun a small shop/store that is open at the front, where you can buy books, newspapers or magazines, for example at a station or an airport

'**book token** noun (BrE) a card, usually given as a gift, that you can exchange for books of a particular value

book·worm /'bʊkwɜːm; AmE -wɜːrm/ noun a person who likes reading very much

boom /buːm/ noun, verb
■ noun
IN BUSINESS/ECONOMY | **1** ~ (in sth) a sudden increase in trade and economic activity; a period of wealth and success: a boom in car sales ◇ Living standards improved rapidly during the post-war boom. ◇ a boom year (for trade, exports, etc.)—compare SLUMP—see also BABY BOOM

POPULAR PERIOD | **2** [usually sing.] a period when sth such as a sport or a type of music suddenly becomes very popular and successful: The only way to satisfy the golf boom was to build more courses.

ON BOAT | **3** a long pole that the bottom of a sail is attached to and that you move to change the position of the sail—picture at YACHT

SOUND | **4** [usually sing.] a loud deep sound: the distant boom of the guns
—see also SONIC BOOM

IN RIVER/HARBOUR | **5** a floating barrier that is placed across a river or the entrance to a harbour to prevent ships or other objects from coming in or going out

FOR MICROPHONE | **6** a long pole that carries a MICROPHONE or other equipment
■ verb
MAKE LOUD SOUND | **1** [V] to make a loud deep sound: Outside, thunder boomed and crashed. **2** ~ (out) to say sth in a loud deep voice: [V speech] 'Get out of my sight!' he boomed. ◇ [V] A voice boomed out from the darkness.

OF BUSINESS/ECONOMY | **3** [V] to have a period of rapid growth; to become bigger, more successful, etc: By the 1980s, the computer industry was booming. ◇ Business is booming!

'**boom box** noun (especially AmE) = GHETTO BLASTER

boom·er /'buːmə(r)/ noun (AmE) = BABY BOOMER

boom·er·ang /'buːməræŋ/ noun, verb
■ noun a curved flat piece of wood that you throw and that can fly in a circle and come back to you. Boomerangs were first used by Australian ABORIGINES as weapons when they were hunting.
■ verb [V] if a plan **boomerangs** on sb, it hurts them instead of the person it was intended to hurt [SYN] BACK-FIRE

'**boom town** noun a town that has become rich and successful because trade and industry has developed there

boon /buːn/ noun ~ (to/for sb) something that is very helpful and makes life easier for you: The new software will prove a boon to home computer users.

,**boon com'panion** noun (literary) a very good friend

boon·docks /'buːndɒks; AmE -dɑːks/ (also **boon·ies**) noun [pl.] (AmE, informal, disapproving) an area far away from cities or towns

boon·dog·gle /'buːndɒgl; AmE -dɑːgl; -dɔːgl/ noun (AmE, informal) a piece of work that is unnecessary and that wastes time and/or money

boon·ies /'buːniz/ noun = BOONDOCKS

boor /bʊə(r); bɔː(r); AmE bʊr/ noun (old-fashioned) a rude unpleasant person

boor·ish /'bʊərɪʃ; 'bɔːr-; AmE 'bʊr-/ adj. (of people and their behaviour) very unpleasant and rude

boost /buːst/ verb, noun
■ verb [VN] to make sth increase, or become better or more successful: to boost exports/profits ◇ The movie helped boost her screen career. ◇ to boost sb's confidence/morale ◇ Getting that job did a lot to boost his ego (= make him feel more confident).
■ noun [usually sing.] **1** something that helps or encourages sb/sth: a great/tremendous/welcome boost ◇ The tax cuts will give a much needed boost to the economy. ◇ Winning the competition was a wonderful boost for her morale. **2** an increase in sth: a boost in car sales **3** an increase in power in an engine or a piece of electrical equipment **4** (especially AmE) an act of pushing sb up from behind: He gave her a boost over the fence.

boost·er /'buːstə(r)/ noun **1** (also '**booster rocket**) a rocket that gives a spacecraft extra power when it leaves the earth, or that makes a MISSILE go further **2** a device that gives extra power to a piece of electrical equipment **3** an extra small amount of a drug that is given to increase the effect of one given earlier, for example to protect you from a disease for longer: *a tetanus booster* **4** a thing that helps, encourages or improves sb/sth: *a morale/confidence booster* **5** (*especially AmE*) a person who gives their support to sb/sth, especially in politics: *a meeting of Republican boosters*

'booster seat *noun* a seat that you put on a car seat, or on a chair at a table, so that a small child can sit higher

boot /buːt/ *noun, verb*
■ *noun* **1** a strong shoe that covers the foot and ankle and often the lower part of the leg: (*BrE*) *walking boots* ◊ (*AmE*) *hiking boots* ◊ *a pair of black leather boots* ◊ *cowboy boots*—see also DESERT BOOT, FOOTBALL BOOT, WELLINGTON—picture at SHOE **2** (*BrE*) (*AmE* **trunk**) the enclosed space at the back of a car that you put bags, cases, etc. in: *I'll put the luggage in the boot.*—see also CAR BOOT SALE—picture at CAR **3** [usually sing.] (*informal*) a quick hard kick: *He gave the ball a tremendous boot.* **4** (*AmE*) = CLAMP **IDM** **be given the 'boot | get the 'boot** (*informal*) to be told that you must leave your job or that a relationship you are having with sb is over **the boot is on the other 'foot** (*BrE*) (*AmE* **the shoe is on the other 'foot**) used to say that a situation has changed so that sb now has power or authority over the person who used to have power or authority over them **put/stick the 'boot in** (*BrE, informal*) **1** to kick sb very hard, especially when they are on the ground **2** to attack sb by criticizing them when they are in a difficult situation **to boot** (*old-fashioned* or *humorous*) used to add a comment to sth that you have said: *He was a vegetarian, and a fussy one to boot.*—more at BIG *adj.*, FILL *v.*, LICK *v.*, TOUGH *adj.*
■ *verb* **1** [VN+*adv./prep.*] to kick sb/sth hard with your foot: *He booted the ball clear of the goal.* **2** [V, VN] ~ **(sth) (up)** (*computing*) to prepare a computer for use by loading its OPERATING SYSTEM **3** [VN] **(be/get booted)** (*AmE, informal*) if you or your car is **booted**, a piece of equipment is fixed to the car's wheel so that you cannot drive it away, usually because the car is illegally parked—see also CLAMP **PHRV** **,boot sb↔'out (of sth)** (*informal*) to force sb to leave a place or job

'boot camp *noun* **1** a training camp for new members of the armed forces, where they have to work hard **2** a type of prison for young criminals where there is strict discipline

boot·ee /buːˈtiː/ (also **bootie**) *noun* **1** a baby's sock, worn instead of shoes: *a pair of pink bootees* **2** a woman's short boot

booth /buːð; *AmE* buːθ/ *noun* **1** a small enclosed place where you can do sth privately, for example make a telephone call, or vote: *a phone booth* ◊ *a polling/voting booth*—see also PHOTO BOOTH, TOLLBOOTH **2** a small tent or temporary structure at a market, an EXHIBITION or a FAIRGROUND, where you can buy things, get information or watch sth: *The stalls and booths were doing a brisk trade.* **3** a place to sit in a restaurant which consists of two long seats with a table between them

boot·lace /ˈbuːtleɪs/ *noun* [usually pl.] a long thin piece of leather or string used to fasten boots or shoes

boot·leg /ˈbuːtleg/ *adj., verb*
■ *adj.* [only before noun] made and sold illegally: *a bootleg cassette* (= for example, one recorded illegally at a concert)—see also PIRATE ▶ **boot·leg** *noun*: *a bootleg of the concert*
■ *verb* (-gg-) [VN] to make or sell goods, especially alcohol, illegally ▶ **boot·leg·ger** *noun* **boot·leg·ging** *noun* [U]

boot·strap /ˈbuːtstræp/ *noun* **IDM** **pull/drag yourself up by your (own) 'bootstraps** (*informal*) to improve your situation yourself, without help from other people

booty /ˈbuːti/ *noun* [U] valuable things that are stolen, especially by soldiers in a time of war **SYN** LOOT

booze /buːz/ *noun, verb*
■ *noun* [U] (*informal*) alcoholic drink
■ *verb* [V] (*informal*) (usually used in the progressive tenses) to drink alcohol, especially in large quantities: *He's out boozing with his mates.*

boozer /ˈbuːzə(r)/ *noun* (*informal*) **1** (*BrE*) a pub **2** a person who drinks a lot of alcohol

'booze-up *noun* (*BrE, informal*) an occasion when people drink a lot of alcohol

boozy /ˈbuːzi/ *adj.* (*informal*) liking to drink a lot of alcohol; involving a lot of alcoholic drink: *one of my boozy friends* ◊ *a boozy lunch*

bop /bɒp; *AmE* baːp/ *noun, verb*
■ *noun* **1** [C] (*BrE, informal*) a dance to pop music; a social event at which people dance to pop music: *Fancy a bop?* ◊ *There's a bop on in the village hall tonight.* **2** [U] = BEBOP
■ *verb* (-pp-) **1** [V] (*BrE, informal*) to dance to pop music **2** [VN] to hit sb lightly

bor·age /ˈbɒrɪdʒ; *AmE* ˈbɔːrɪdʒ/ *noun* [U] a Mediterranean plant with blue flowers that are shaped like stars, and hairy leaves that are eaten raw as a salad vegetable

borax /ˈbɔːræks/ *noun* [U] a white mineral, usually in powder form, used in making glass and as an ANTISEPTIC (= a substance that helps to prevent infection in wounds)

bor·dello /bɔːˈdeləʊ; *AmE* bɔːrˈdeloʊ/ *noun* (*pl.* **-os**) (*especially AmE*) = BROTHEL

bor·der /ˈbɔːdə(r); *AmE* ˈbɔːrd-/ *noun, verb*
■ *noun* **1** the line that divides two countries or areas; the land near this line: *a national park on the border between Kenya and Tanzania* ◊ *Denmark's border with Germany* ◊ *in the US, near the Canadian border* ◊ *Nevada's northern border* ◊ *to cross the border* ◊ *to flee across/over the border* ◊ *border guards/controls* ◊ *a border dispute/incident* ◊ *a border town/state* ◊ (*figurative*) *It is difficult to define the border between love and friendship.* **2** a strip around the edge of sth such as a picture or a piece of fabric: *a pillowcase with a lace border* **3** (in a garden) a strip of soil which is planted with flowers, along the edge of the grass—picture at HOUSE
■ *verb* [VN] **1** (of a country or an area) to share a border with another country or area: *the countries bordering the Baltic* **2** (*written*) to form a line along or around the edge of sth: *Meadows bordered the path to the woods.* ◊ *The large garden is bordered by a stream.* **PHRV** **'border on sth 1** to come very close to being sth, especially a strong or unpleasant emotion or quality: *She felt an anxiety bordering on hysteria.* **2** to be next to sth: *areas bordering on the Black Sea*

bor·der·land /ˈbɔːdəlænd; *AmE* ˈbɔːrdər-/ *noun* **1** [C] an area of land close to a border between two countries **2** [sing.] an area between two qualities, ideas or subjects that has features of both but is not clearly one or the other: *the murky borderland between history and myth*

bor·der·line /ˈbɔːdəlaɪn; *AmE* ˈbɔːrdər-/ *adj., noun*
■ *adj.* not clearly belonging to a particular condition or group; not clearly acceptable: *In doubtful and **borderline** cases teachers will take the final decision, based on the student's previous work.* ◊ *a borderline pass/fail in an exam*
■ *noun* the division between two qualities or conditions: *This biography sometimes crosses the borderline between fact and fiction.*

bore /bɔː(r)/ *verb, noun*—see also BEAR, BORE, BORNE *v.*
■ *verb* **1** [VN] to make sb feel bored, especially by talking too much: *I'm not boring you, am I?* ◊ *Has he been boring you with his stories about China?* **2** ~ **(into/through sth)** to make a long deep hole with a tool or by digging: [V] *The drill is strong enough to bore through solid rock.* ◊ [VN] *to bore a hole in sth* **3** [V] ~ **into sb/sth** (of eyes) to stare in a way that makes sb feel uncomfortable: *His blue eyes seemed to bore into her.*
■ *noun* **1** [C] a person who is very boring, usually because they talk too much **2** [sing.] a situation or thing that is boring or that annoys you: *It's such a bore having to stay late this evening.* **3** (also **gauge** especially in *AmE*) (especially in compounds) the hollow inside of a tube, such as a pipe or a gun; the width of the hole: *a tube with a wide/narrow bore* ◊ *a twelve-bore shotgun* **4** a strong, high wave that rushes along a river from the sea at particular times of the year **5** (also **bore-hole**) a deep hole made in the ground, especially to find water or oil **IDM** see CRASH *v.*

bored /bɔːd; *AmE* bɔːrd/ *adj.* ~ **(with sb/sth)** | ~ **(with doing sth)** feeling tired and impatient because you have

æ	ɑː	e	ɜː	ə	ɪ	iː	i	ɒ	ɔː	ʌ	ʊ	uː
cat	father	ten	bird	about	sit	see	many	got	saw	cup	put	actual	too

(BrE)

B

lost interest in sb/sth or because you have nothing to do: *The children quickly got **bored** with staying indoors.* ◊ *There was a **bored** expression on her face.* **IDM** **bored 'stiff | bored to 'death/'tears | bored out of your 'mind** extremely bored—more at WITLESS

bore·dom /'bɔːdəm; *AmE* 'bɔːrdəm/ *noun* [U] the state of feeling bored; the quality of being very boring: *I started to eat too much out of sheer boredom.* ◊ *Television helps to relieve the boredom of the long winter evenings.*

bore·hole /'bɔːhəʊl; *AmE* 'bɔːrhəʊl/ *noun* = BORE (5)

bor·ing /'bɔːrɪŋ/ *adj.* not interesting; making you feel tired and impatient: *He's such a boring man!* ◊ *a boring job/book/evening* ▶ **bor·ing·ly** *adv.*: *boringly normal*

born /bɔːn; *AmE* bɔːrn/ *verb, adj.*
■ *verb* (**be born**) (used only in the passive, without *by*) **1** (*abbr.* **b.**) to come out of your mother's body at the beginning of your life: [VN] *I was born in 1976.* ◊ *She was **born into** a very musical family.* ◊ *He was **born of/to** German parents.* ◊ *She was born with a weak heart.* ◊ [VN-ADJ] *Her brother was **born blind** (= was blind when he was born).* ◊ [VN-N] *John Wayne was born Marion Michael Morrison (= that was his name at birth).* **2** [VN] (of an idea, an organization, a feeling, etc.) to start to exist: *'Solidarity' was born as a protest movement, not a political party.* ◊ *She acted with a courage **born (out) of** desperation.* **3** (**-born**) (in compounds) born in the order, way, place, etc. mentioned: *firstborn* ◊ *nobly-born* ◊ *French-born*—see also NEWBORN **IDM** **be 'born to be/do sth** to have sth as your DESTINY (= what is certain to happen to you) from birth: *He was born to be a great composer.* **born and 'bred** born and having grown up in a particular place with a particular background and education: *He was born and bred in Boston.* ◊ *I'm a Londoner, born and bred.* **born with a silver 'spoon in your mouth** (*saying*) having rich parents **in all my born 'days** (*old-fashioned, informal*) used when you are very surprised at sth you have never heard or seen before: *I've never heard such nonsense in all my born days.* **not be born 'yesterday** (*spoken*) used to say that you are not stupid enough to believe what sb is telling you: *Oh yeah? I wasn't born yesterday, you know.* **there's one born every 'minute** (*saying*) used to say that sb is very stupid—more at KNOW *v.*, MANNER, WAY *n.*
■ *adj.* [only before noun] having a natural ability or skill for a particular activity or job: *a born athlete/writer/leader* ◊ *a born loser (= a person who always loses or is unsuccessful)*

born-a'gain *adj.* [usually before noun] having come to have a strong belief in a particular religion (especially EVANGELICAL Christianity) or idea, and wanting other people to have the same belief: *a born-again Christian* ◊ *a born-again vegetarian*

borne /bɔːn; *AmE* bɔːrn/ **1** *pp* of BEAR **2** (**-borne**) (in compounds) carried by: *water-borne diseases*

bor·ough /'bʌrə; *AmE* 'bɜːroʊ/ *noun* a town or part of a city that has its own local government: *the London borough of Westminster* ◊ *The Bronx is one of the five boroughs of New York.* ◊ *a borough council*

bor·row /'bɒrəʊ; *AmE* 'bɑːroʊ; 'bɔːr-/ *verb* **1** [VN] ~ **sth (from sb/sth)** to take and use sth that belongs to sb else, and return it to them at a later time: *Can I borrow your umbrella?* ◊ *Members can borrow up to ten books from the library at any one time.*—compare LEND **2** ~ **(sth) (from sb/sth)** to take money from a person or bank and agree to pay it back to them at a later time: [VN] *How much did you have to borrow to pay for this?* ◊ *She borrowed £2000 from her parents.* ◊ [V] *I don't like to borrow from friends.*—compare LEND **3** ~ **(sth) (from sb/sth)** to take words, ideas, etc. from another language, person, etc. and use them, as your own: [V] *The author borrows heavily from Henry James.* ◊ [VN] *Some musical terms are borrowed from Italian.* **IDM** **be (living) on borrowed 'time 1** to still be alive after the time when you were expected to die **2** to be doing sth that other people are likely to soon stop you from doing

bor·row·er /'bɒrəʊə(r); *AmE* 'bɑːroʊ-; 'bɔːr-/ *noun* a person or an organization that borrows money, especially from a bank—compare LENDER

bor·row·ing /'bɒrəʊɪŋ; *AmE* 'bɑːroʊɪŋ; 'bɔːr-/ *noun* **1** [C, U] the money that a company, an organization or a person borrows; the act of borrowing money: *an attempt to reduce bank borrowings* ◊ *High interest rates help to keep borrowing down.* **2** [C] a word, a phrase or an idea that sb has taken from another person's work or from another language and used in their own

bor·stal /'bɔːstl; *AmE* 'bɔːrstl/ *noun* [C, U] (in Britain in the past) a type of prison for young criminals—see also YOUTH CUSTODY

bosom /'bʊzəm/ *noun* **1** [C] a woman's chest or breasts: *her ample bosom* ◊ *She pressed him to her bosom.* **2** [C] the part of a piece of clothing that covers a woman's bosom: *a rose pinned to her bosom* **3** the ~ of sth [sing.] a situation in which you are with people who love and protect you: *to live in the bosom of your family*

bosom 'friend (*AmE* also **bosom 'buddy**) *noun* a very close friend

boss /bɒs; *AmE* bɔːs/ *noun, verb, adj.*
■ *noun* **1** a person who is in charge of other people at work and tells them what to do: *I'll ask my boss if I can have the day off.* ◊ *I like being my own boss (= working for myself and making my own decisions).* ◊ *Who's the boss (= who's in control) in this house?* **2** (*informal*) a person who is in charge of a large organization: *the new boss at IBM* ◊ *Hospital bosses protested at the decision.* **IDM** see SHOW *v.*
■ *verb* [VN] ~ **sb (about/around)** to tell sb what to do in an aggressive and/or annoying way: *I'm sick of you bossing me around!*
■ *adj.* (*slang, especially BrE*) very good

bossy /'bɒsi; *AmE* 'bɔːsi/ *adj.* (*disapproving*) always telling people what to do ▶ **boss·ily** *adv.* **bossi·ness** *noun* [U]

Boston baked 'beans *noun* [pl.] (*AmE*) = BAKED BEANS

bo·tan·ic·al /bə'tænɪkl/ *adj.* connected with the science of botany

bo·tanical 'garden (also **bo·tanic 'garden**) *noun* [usually pl.] a park where plants, trees and flowers are grown for scientific study

bot·an·ist /'bɒtənɪst; *AmE* 'bɑːt-/ *noun* a scientist who studies botany

bot·any /'bɒtəni; *AmE* 'bɑːt-/ *noun* [U] the scientific study of plants and their structure—compare BIOLOGY, ZOOLOGY

botch /bɒtʃ; *AmE* bɑːtʃ/ *verb, noun*
■ *verb* [VN] ~ **sth (up)** (*informal*) to spoil sth by doing it badly: *He completely botched up the interview.* ◊ *The work they did on the house was a botched job.*
■ *noun* (also **'botch-up**) (*BrE, informal*) a piece of work or a job that has been done badly: *I've made a real botch of the decorating.*

both /bəʊθ; *AmE* boʊθ/ *det., pron.* **1** used with plural nouns to mean 'the two' or 'the one as well as the other': *Both women were French.* ◊ *Both the women were French.* ◊ *Both of the women were French.* ◊ *I talked to the women. Both of them were French/They were both French.* ◊ *I liked them both.* ◊ *We were both tired.* ◊ *Both of us were tired.* ◊ *We have both seen the movie.* ◊ *I have two sisters. Both of them live in London/They both live in London.* ◊ *Both (my) sisters live in London.* **2** both ...and ... not only ...but also ...: *Both his mother and his father will be there.* ◊ *For this job you will need a good knowledge of both Italian and Spanish.*

bother /'bɒðə(r); *AmE* 'bɑːð-/ *verb, noun, exclamation*
■ *verb* **1** (often used in negative sentences and questions) ~ **(with/about sth)** to spend time and/or energy doing sth: [V] *'Shall I wait?' 'No, don't bother'.* ◊ *It's not worth*

bothering with (= using) *an umbrella—the car's just out-side.* ◇ *I don't know why I bother! Nobody ever listens!* ◇ *I don't know why you bother with that crowd* (= why you spend time with them). ◇ [vtoinf] *He didn't even bother to let me know he was coming.* ◇ [v-ing] *Why bother asking if you're not really interested?* **2 ~ sb (about/with sth)** to annoy, worry or upset sb; to cause sb trouble or pain: [VN] *The thing that bothers me is …* ◇ *You don't sound too bothered about it.* ◇ *I don't want to bother her with my problems at the moment.* ◇ *That sprained ankle is still bothering her* (= hurting). ◇ *I'm sorry he was so rude to you.' 'It doesn't bother me.'* ◇ [VNthat] *Does it bother you that she earns more than you?* ◇ [VNtoinf] *It bothers me to think of her alone in that big house.* **3** [VN] to interrupt sb; to talk to sb when they do not want to talk to you: *Stop bothering me when I'm working.* ◇ *Let me know if he bothers you again.* ◇ *Sorry to bother you, but there's a call for you on line two.* **IDM** **be bothered (about sb/sth)** (*especially BrE*) to think that sb/sth is important: *I'm not bothered about what he thinks.* ◇ *'Where shall we eat?' 'I'm not bothered.'* (= I don't mind where we go). **can't be bothered (to do sth)** used to say that you do not want to spend time and/or energy doing sth: *I should really do some work this weekend but I can't be bothered.* ◇ *All this has happened because you couldn't be bothered to give me the message.* **not bother yourself/your head with/about sth** (*especially BrE*) to not spend time/effort on sth, because it is not important or you are not interested in it—more at HOT *adj.*
- *noun* **1** [U] trouble or difficulty: *You seem to have got yourself into a spot of bother.* ◇ *I don't want to put you to any bother* (= cause you any trouble). ◇ *Don't go to the bother of tidying up on my account* (= don't make the effort to do it). ◇ *'Thanks for your help!' 'It was no bother.'* ◇ *Call them and save yourself the bother of going round.* **2 (a bother)** [sing.] (*BrE*) an annoying situation, thing or person SYN NUISANCE: *I hope I haven't been a bother.*
- *exclamation* (*BrE*) used to express the fact that you are annoyed about sth/sb: *Bother! I've left my wallet at home.* ◇ *Oh, bother him! He's never around when you need him.*

both·er·some /ˈbɒðəsəm; *AmE* ˈbɑːðərsəm/ *adj.* (*old-fashioned*) causing trouble or difficulty SYN ANNOYING

bothy /ˈbɒθi; *AmE* ˈbɔːθi/ *noun* (*pl.* **-ies**) a mountain hut in Scotland built for farm workers to live in or for people to shelter in

bot·tle /ˈbɒtl; *AmE* ˈbɑːtl/ *noun, verb*
- *noun* **1** [C] a glass or plastic container, usually round with straight sides and a narrow neck, used especially for storing liquids: *a wine/beer/milk bottle* ◇ *Put the top back on the bottle.*—picture at PACKAGING **2** [C] (*also* **bottle·ful** /-fʊl/) the amount contained in a bottle: *We drank a whole bottle of wine.* **3 (the bottle)** [sing.] (*informal*) alcoholic drink: *After his wife died, he really hit the bottle* (= started drinking heavily). **4** [C, usually sing.] a bottle used to give milk to a baby; the milk from such a bottle (used instead of mother's milk): *It's time for her bottle.* **5** [U] (*BrE, informal*) courage or confidence, for example to do sth that is dangerous or unpleasant: *It took a lot of bottle to do that.* ◇ *I didn't think she'd have the bottle to ask him.*
- *verb* [VN] **1** to put a liquid into a bottle: *The wines are bottled after three years.* **2** to put fruit or vegetables into glass containers in order to preserve them ▶ **bot·tled** *adj.*: *bottled beer/water/pickles* ◇ *bottled gas* (= sold in metal containers for use in heating and cooking). **IDM** **bottle it** (*BrE, informal*) to not do sth, or not finish sth, because you are frightened **PHRV** **,bottle 'out (of sth/doing sth)** (*BrE, informal*) to not do sth that you had intended to do because you are too frightened **,bottle sth↔'up** to not allow other people to see that you are unhappy, angry, etc., especially when this happens over a long period of time: *Try not to bottle up your emotions.*

'bottle bank *noun* (*BrE*) a large container in a public place where people can leave their empty bottles so that the glass can be used again (= RECYCLED); a public place with several of these containers

'bottle-feed *verb* [VN, V] to feed a baby with artificial milk from a bottle—compare BREASTFEED

,bottle-'green *adj.* (*especially BrE*) dark green in colour: *a bottle-green coat* ▶ **,bottle 'green** *noun* [U]

bottle·neck /ˈbɒtlnek; *AmE* ˈbɑːtl-/ *noun* **1** a narrow or busy section of road where the traffic often slows down and stops **2** anything that slows down development or progress, particularly in business or industry

'bottle-opener *noun* a small tool for opening bottles with metal tops, for example beer bottles—picture at KITCHEN

bot·tom /ˈbɒtəm; *AmE* ˈbɑːtəm/ *noun, adj., verb*
- *noun*
  LOWEST PART | **1** [C, usually sing.] **~ (of sth)** the lowest part of sth: *Footnotes are given at the bottom of each page.* ◇ *I waited for them at the bottom of the hill.* ◇ *The book I want is right at the bottom* (= of the pile). **2** [C, usually sing.] **~ (of sth)** the part of sth that faces downwards and is not usually seen: *The manufacturer's name is on the bottom of the plate.*
  OF CONTAINER | **3** [C, usually sing.] **~ (of sth)** the lowest surface on the inside of a container: *I found some French coins at the bottom of my bag.*
  OF RIVER/POOL | **4** [sing.] the ground below the water in a lake, river, swimming pool, etc: *He dived in and hit his head on the bottom.*
  END OF STH | **5 the ~ (of sth)** [sing.] (*especially BrE*) the part of sth that is furthest from you, your house, etc: *I went to the school at the bottom of our street.* ◇ *There was a stream at the bottom of the garden.*
  LOWEST POSITION | **6 ~ (of sth)** [sing.] the lowest position in a class, on a list, etc.; a person, team, etc. that is in this position: *a battle between the teams at the bottom of the league* ◇ *You have to be prepared to start at the bottom and work your way up.* ◇ *I was always bottom of the class in math.*
  PART OF BODY | **7** [C] (*especially BrE*) the part of the body that you sit on: *I'll smack your bottom if you do that again!* SYN BACKSIDE, BEHIND—picture at BODY
  CLOTHING | **8** [C, usually pl.] the lower part of a set of clothes that consists of two pieces: *a bikini bottom* ◇ *a pair of pyjama/tracksuit bottoms*
  OF SHIP | **9** [C] the lower part of a ship that is below the surface of the water SYN HULL
  -BOTTOMED | **10** (in adjectives) having the type of bottom mentioned: *a flat-bottomed boat*
  —see also ROCK-BOTTOM
  IDM **at bottom** used to say what sb/sth is really like: *Their offer to help was at bottom self-centred.* **be/lie at the bottom of sth** to be the original cause of sth, especially sth unpleasant **the bottom drops/falls out (of sth)** people stop buying or using the products of a particular industry: *The bottom has fallen out of the travel market.* **bottoms 'up!** (*spoken*) used to express good wishes when drinking alcohol, or to tell sb to finish their drink **get to the bottom of sth** to find out the real cause of sth, especially sth unpleasant—more at HEAP *n.*, HEART, PILE *n.*, SCRAPE *v.*, TOP *n.*, TOUCH *v.*
- *adj.* [only before noun] in the lowest, last or furthest place or position: *the bottom line (on a page)* ◇ *your bottom lip* ◇ *the bottom step (of a flight of stairs)* ◇ *on the bottom shelf* ◇ *Put your clothes in the bottom drawer.* ◇ *Their house is at the bottom end of Bury Road* (= the end furthest from where you enter the road). ◇ *Sign in the bottom right-hand corner of the page.* ◇ *the bottom end of the price range* ◇ *to go up a hill in bottom gear* **IDM** see BET *v.*
- *verb*
  PHRV **,bottom 'out** (of prices, a bad situation, etc.) to stop getting worse: *The recession is finally beginning to show signs of bottoming out.*

bot·tom·less /ˈbɒtəmləs; *AmE* ˈbɑːt-/ *adj.* (*formal*) very deep; seeming to have no bottom or limit: *a bottomless abyss* **IDM** **a bottomless 'pit (of sth)** a thing or situation which seems to have no limits or seems never to end: *There isn't a bottomless pit of money for public spending.* ◇ *the bottomless pit of his sorrow*

,bottom 'line *noun* [sing.] **1 (the bottom line)** the most important thing that you have to consider or accept; the essential point in a discussion, etc: *The bottom line is that we have to make a decision today.* **2** (*business*) the amount of money that is a profit or a loss after everything has been calculated: *The bottom line for 1999 was a pre-tax profit of £85 million.* **3** the lowest price that sb will accept: *Two thousand—and that's my bottom line!*

botu·lism /ˈbɒtjuliːzəm; *AmE* ˈbɑːtʃə-/ *noun* [U] a serious illness caused by bacteria in badly preserved food

bou·doir /ˈbuːdwɑː(r)/ *noun* (*old-fashioned*) a woman's small private room or bedroom

bouf·fant /ˈbuːfɒ; *AmE* buːˈfɑːnt/ *adj.* (of a person's hair) in a style that raises it up and back from the head in a high round shape

bou·gain·vil·lea (also **bou·gain·vil·laea**) /ˌbuːgənˈvɪliə/ *noun* a tropical climbing plant with red, purple, white or pink flowers

bough /baʊ/ *noun* (*formal* or *literary*) a large branch of a tree

bought *pt, pp* of BUY

bouil·lon /ˈbuːjɒn; *AmE* -jɑːn/ *noun* [U, C] a liquid made by boiling meat or vegetables in water, used for making clear soups or sauces

boul·der /ˈbəʊldə(r); *AmE* ˈboʊl-/ *noun* a very large rock which has been shaped by water or the weather

boule·vard /ˈbuːləvɑːd; *AmE* ˈbʊləvɑːrd/ *noun* **1** (*BrE*) a wide city street, often with trees on either side **2** (*abbr.* **Blvd.**) (*AmE*) a wide main road (often used in the name of streets): *Sunset Boulevard*

bounce /baʊns/ *verb, noun*

■ *verb*

MOVE OFF SURFACE | **1** if sth **bounces** or you **bounce** it, it moves quickly away from a surface it has just hit or you make it do this: [V] *The ball bounced twice before he could reach it.* ◊ *Short sound waves bounce off even small objects.* ◊ *The light bounced off the river and dazzled her.* ◊ [VN] *She bounced the ball against the wall.*

MOVE UP AND DOWN | *noun* **2** [V] (of a person) to jump up and down on sth: *She bounced up and down excitedly on the bed.* **3** [VN] to move a child up and down while he or she is sitting on your knee in order to entertain him or her **4** to move up and down; to move sth up and down: [V] *Her hair bounced from side to side as she walked.* [also VN] **5** [V+*adv./prep.*] to move up and down in a particular direction: *The bus bounced down the hill.*

MOVE WITH ENERGY | **6** [V+*adv./prep.*] (of a person) to move somewhere in a lively and cheerful way: *He bounced across the room to greet them.*

CHEQUE | **7** [V, VN] (*informal*) if a cheque **bounces**, or a bank **bounces** it, the bank refuses to accept it because there is not enough money in the account

IDEAS | **8** [VN] ~ **ideas** (off sb)/(around) to tell sb your ideas in order to find out what they think about them: *He bounced ideas off colleagues everywhere he went.*

COMPUTING | **9** [V, VN] ~ (sth) (back) if an e-mail **bounces** or the system **bounces** it, it returns to the person who sent it because the system cannot deliver it

PHR V ,bounce ˈback to become healthy, successful or confident again after being ill/sick or having difficulties **SYN** RECOVER: *He's had a lot of problems, but he always seems to bounce back pretty quickly.* ,bounce sb ˈinto sth (*BrE*) to make sb do sth without giving them enough time to think about it

■ *noun*

MOVEMENT | **1** [C] the action of bouncing: *one bounce of the ball* ◊ (*AmE*) *a bounce* (= increase) *in popularity* **2** [U] the ability to bounce or to make sth bounce: *There's not much bounce left in these balls.* ◊ *Players complained about the uneven bounce of the tennis court.*

ENERGY | **3** [U, C] the energy that a person has: *All her old bounce was back.* ◊ *There was a bounce to his step which I hadn't seen before.*

OF HAIR | **4** [U] the quality in a person's hair that shows that it is in good condition and means that it does not lie flat: *thin fine hair, lacking in bounce*

boun·cer /ˈbaʊnsə(r)/ *noun* **1** a person employed to stand at the entrance to a club, pub, etc. to stop people

who are not wanted from going in, and to throw out people who are causing trouble inside **2** (in cricket) a ball thrown very fast that rises high after it hits the ground

boun·cing /ˈbaʊnsɪŋ/ *adj.* ~ (with sth) healthy and full of energy: *a bouncing baby boy* ◊ *He was bouncing with health.*

boun·cy /ˈbaʊnsi/ *adj.* **1** that bounces well or that has the ability to make sth bounce: *a very bouncy ball* ◊ *his bouncy blond curls* ◊ (*BrE*) *a bouncy castle* (= a plastic castle or other shape which is filled with air and which children can jump and play on) **2** lively and full of energy

bound /baʊnd/ *adj., verb, noun*—see also BIND, BOUND, BOUND *v.*

■ *adj.* [not before noun] **1** ~ **to do/be sth** certain or likely to happen, or to do or be sth: *There are bound to be changes when the new system is introduced.* ◊ *It's bound to be sunny again tomorrow.* ◊ *You've done so much work—you're bound to pass the exam.* ◊ *It was bound to happen sooner or later* (= we should have expected it). ◊ *You're bound to be nervous the first time* (= it's understandable). **2** ~ (by sth)| ~ (by sth) (to do sth) forced to do sth by law, duty or a particular situation: *We are not bound by the decision.* ◊ *You are bound by the contract to pay before the end of the month.* ◊ (*BrE, formal*) *I am bound to say I disagree with you on this point.* **3** (in compounds) prevented from going somewhere or from working normally by the conditions mentioned: *Strike-bound travellers face long delays.* ◊ *fogbound airports* **4** ~ (for …) (also in compounds) travelling, or ready to travel, in a particular direction or to a particular place: *homeward bound* (= going home) ◊ *a plane bound for Dublin* ◊ *Paris-bound* ◊ *northbound/southbound/eastbound/westbound* **IDM** be bound toˈgether by/in sth to be closely connected: *communities bound together by customs and traditions* be bound ˈup in sth very busy with sth; very interested or involved in sth: *He's too bound up in his work to have much time for his children.* bound ˈup with sth closely connected with sth: *From that moment my life became inextricably bound up with hers.* ˈI'll be bound (*old-fashioned, BrE, informal*) I feel sure—more at HONOUR *n.*

■ *verb* **1** [V+*adv./prep.*] to run with long steps, especially in an enthusiastic way: *The dogs bounded ahead.* **2** [VN] [usually passive] (*formal*) to form the edge or limit of an area: *The field was bounded on the left by a wood.*

■ *noun* (*written*) a high or long jump—see also BOUNDS **IDM** see LEAP *n.*

bound·ary /ˈbaʊndri/ *noun* (*pl.* **-ies**) **1** a real or imagined line that marks the limits or edges of sth and separates it from other things or places; a dividing line: *national boundaries* ◊ (*BrE*) *county boundaries* ◊ *boundary changes/disputes* ◊ *The fence marks the boundary between my property and hers.* ◊ *Scientists continue to push back the boundaries of human knowledge.* ◊ *the boundary between acceptable and unacceptable behaviour* **2** (in cricket) a hit of the ball that crosses the boundary of the playing area and scores extra points

bound·en /ˈbaʊndən/ *adj.* **IDM** aˈyour bounden ˈduty (*old-fashioned, formal*) something that you feel you must do; a responsibility which cannot be ignored

bound·less /ˈbaʊndləs/ *adj.* (*written*) without limits; seeming to have no end: *boundless energy/enthusiasm*

bounds /baʊndz/ *noun* [pl.] the accepted or furthest limits of sth: *beyond/outside/within the bounds of decency* ◊ *Public spending must be kept within reasonable bounds.* ◊ *It was not beyond the bounds of possibility that they would meet again one day.* ◊ *His enthusiasm knew no bounds* (= was very great). **IDM** out of ˈbounds (to/for sb) (*especially BrE*) (*AmE usually* ,off ˈlimits) if a place is out of bounds or off limits, people are not allowed to go there out of ˈbounds **1** (in some sports) outside the area of play which is allowed: *His shot went out of bounds.* **2** (*AmE*) not reasonable or acceptable: *His demands were out of bounds.*—more at LEAP *n.*

boun·teous /ˈbaʊntiəs/ *adj.* (*formal* or *literary*) giving very generously

boun·ti·ful /ˈbaʊntɪfl/ *adj.* (*formal* or *literary*) **1** in large

B

quantities; large: *a bountiful supply of food* **2** giving generously SYN GENEROUS: *belief in a bountiful god*

bounty /ˈbaʊnti/ *noun* (*pl.* **-ies**) **1** [U, C] (*literary*) generous actions; sth provided in large quantities: *to thank the Lord for his bounty* **2** [C] money given as a reward: *a bounty hunter* (= sb who catches criminals or kills people for a reward)

bou·quet /buˈkeɪ/ *noun* **1** [C] a bunch of flowers arranged in an attractive way so that it can be carried in a ceremony or presented as a gift **2** [C, U] the pleasant smell of a type of food or drink, especially of wine

bou·quet garni /ˌbuːkeɪ ɡɑːˈniː; *AmE* ɡɑːrˈniː/ *noun* (*pl.* **bou·quets gar·nis** /ˌbuːkeɪ ɡɑːˈniː; *AmE* ɡɑːrˈniː/) (from *French*) a bunch of different herbs in a small bag, used in cooking to give extra flavour to food

bour·bon /ˈbɜːbən; *AmE* ˈbɜːrbən/ *noun* **1** [U, C] a type of American whisky made with MAIZE and RYE **2** [C] a glass of bourbon

bour·geois /ˈbʊəʒwɑː; ˌbʊəˈʒwɑː; *AmE* ˌbʊrˈʒ-; ˈbʊrʒ-/ *adj.* **1** belonging to the middle class: *a traditional bourgeois family*—see also PETIT BOURGEOIS **2** (*disapproving*) interested mainly in possessions and social status and supporting traditional values: *bourgeois attitudes/tastes ◊ They've become very bourgeois since they got married.* **3** (*politics*) supporting the interests of CAPITALISM: *bourgeois ideology* ▶ **bour·geois** *noun* (*pl.* **bour·geois**)

bour·geoi·sie /ˌbʊəʒwɑːˈziː; *AmE* ˌbʊrʒ-/ *noun* (**the bourgeoisie**) [sing.+ sing./pl. *v.*] **1** the middle classes in society: *the rise of the bourgeoisie in the nineteenth century* **2** (*politics*) the CAPITALIST class: *the proletariat and the bourgeoisie*

bout /baʊt/ *noun* **1** ~ (**of sth/of doing sth**) a short period of great activity; a short period during which there is a lot of a particular thing, usually sth unpleasant: *They had been fighting after a drinking bout. ◊ the latest bout of inflation* **2** ~ (**of sth**) an attack or period of illness: *a severe bout of flu/coughing ◊ He suffered occasional bouts of depression. ◊* (*AmE*) *a bout with the flu* **3** a boxing or WRESTLING match

bou·tique /buːˈtiːk/ *noun* a small shop/store that sells fashionable clothes or expensive gifts

bou·ton·nière /ˌbuːtɒnˈjeə(r); *AmE* ˌbuːtnˈɪr; -tənˈjer/ *noun* (*AmE*) = BUTTONHOLE (2)

bo·vine /ˈbəʊvaɪn; *AmE* ˈboʊ-/ *adj.* [usually before noun] **1** (*technical*) connected with cows: *bovine diseases* **2** (*written, disapproving*) (of a person) stupid and slow

bow¹ /baʊ/ *verb, noun*—see also BOW²
- *verb* **1** [V] ~ (**down**) (**to/before sb/sth**) to move your head or the top half of your body forwards and downwards as a sign of respect or as a greeting: *He bowed low to the assembled crowd. ◊ The people all bowed down before the Emperor.* **2** [VN] to move your head forwards and downwards: *She bowed her head in shame. ◊ They stood in silence with their heads bowed.* **3** to bend or make sth bend: [V] *The pines bowed in the wind. ◊* [VN] *Their backs were bowed under the weight of their packs.* IDM ˌbow and ˈscrape (*disapproving*) to be too polite to an important person in order to gain their approval—more at SHOT *n*. PHRV ˌbow ˈdown to sb/sth (*disapproving*) to allow sb to tell you what to do ˌbow ˈout (of sth) to stop taking part in an activity, especially one in which you have been successful in the past: *She has finally decided it's time to bow out of international tennis.* ˈbow to sth to agree unwillingly to do sth because other people want you to: *They finally bowed to pressure from the public. ◊ She bowed to the inevitable* (= accepted a situation in which she had no choice) *and resigned.*
- *noun* **1** the act of bending your head or the upper part of your body forwards in order to greet sb or to show respect **2** (also **bows** [pl.]) the front part of a boat or ship—compare STERN *n*.—picture at BOAT, YACHT IDM take a/ your ˈbow (of a performer) to bow to the audience as they are APPLAUDING you—more at SHOT

bow² /bəʊ; *AmE* boʊ/ *noun, verb*—see also BOW¹
- *noun* **1** a weapon used for shooting arrows, consisting of a long curved piece of wood with a tight string joining its ends: *He was armed with a bow and arrow.* **2** a knot

with two LOOPS and two loose ends which is used for decoration on clothes, in hair, etc. or for tying shoes: *to tie your shoelaces in a bow ◊ Her hair was tied back in a neat bow.* **3** a long thin piece of wood with thin string stretched along it, used for playing musical instruments such as the violin—picture on page 840 IDM see STRING *n*.
- *verb* [V, VN] to use a bow to play a musical instrument that has strings

bowd·ler·ize (*BrE* also **-ise**) /ˈbaʊdləraɪz/ *verb* [VN] (usually *disapproving*) to remove the parts of a book, play, etc. that you think are likely to shock or offend people SYN EXPURGATE ORIGIN Named after Dr Thomas Bowdler, who in 1818 produced a version of Shakespeare from which he had taken out all the material which he considered unsuitable for family use.

bowel /ˈbaʊəl/ *noun* **1** [C, usually pl.] one of a system of tubes below the stomach in which solid waste collects before it is passed out of the body: (*medical*) *to empty/ move/open your bowels* (= to pass solid waste out of the body) *◊ bowel cancer/cancer of the bowel* **2** (**the bowels of sth**) [pl.] (*literary*) the part that is deepest inside sth: *A rumble came from the bowels of the earth* (= deep underground).

ˈ**bowel movement** (also **movement**) *noun* (*medical*) an act of emptying waste material from the bowels; the waste material that is emptied

bower /ˈbaʊə(r)/ *noun* (*literary*) a pleasant place in the shade under trees or climbing plants in a wood or garden/yard

bowl /bəʊl; *AmE* boʊl/ *noun, verb*
- *noun*
CONTAINER | **1** [C] (especially in compounds) a deep round dish with a wide open top, used especially for holding food or liquid: *a salad/fruit/sugar bowl ◊ a washing-up bowl*
AMOUNT | **2** [C] (also **bowl·ful** /-fʊl/) the amount contained in a bowl: *a bowl of soup*
SHAPE | **3** [C] the part of some objects that is shaped like a bowl: *the bowl of a spoon ◊ a toilet/lavatory bowl*
THEATRE | **4** [C] (*especially AmE*) (in names) a large round theatre without a roof, used for concerts, etc. in the open air SYN STADIUM: *the Hollywood Bowl*
BALL | **5** [C] a heavy wooden ball that is used in the game of **bowls**
GAME | **6** (**bowls**) [U] (*AmE* also ˈ**lawn bowling**) a game played on an area of very smooth grass, in which players take turns to roll bowls as near as possible to a small ball
FOOTBALL GAME | **7** [C] (*AmE*) (in names) a football game played after the main season between the best teams: *the Super Bowl*
- *verb*
ROLL BALL | **1** [V, VN] to roll a ball in the games of bowls and BOWLING
IN CRICKET | **2** [V, VN] to throw a ball to the BATSMAN (= the person who hits the ball)—picture on page 1250 **3** [VN] ~ sb (**out**) to make the BATSMAN have to leave the field by throwing a ball that hits the WICKET
MOVE QUICKLY | **4** [V+*adv./prep.*] (*BrE, written*) to move quickly in a particular direction, especially in a vehicle: *Soon we were bowling along the country roads.*
PHRV ˌbowl sb ˈover **1** to run into sb and knock them down **2** to surprise or impress sb a lot

bow legs /ˌbəʊ ˈleɡz; *AmE* ˌboʊ/ *noun* [pl.] legs that curve out at the knees ▶ **bow-legged** /ˌbəʊ ˈleɡɪd; *AmE* ˌboʊ/ *adj.*

bowl·er /ˈbəʊlə(r); *AmE* ˈboʊ-/ *noun* **1** (in cricket) a player who throws the ball at the BATSMAN—picture on page 1250 **2** (also ˌbowler ˈhat) (both *especially BrE*) (*AmE* usually **derby**) a hard black hat with a curved BRIM and round top, worn, for example, in the past by men in business in Britain—picture at HAT

bowl·ing /ˈbəʊlɪŋ; *AmE* ˈboʊ-/ *noun* [U] a game in which players roll heavy balls (called BOWLS) along a special track towards a group of PINS (= bottle-shaped objects) and try to knock over as many of them as possible

ˈ**bowling alley** *noun* a building or part of a building where people can go bowling

bowling green *noun* an area of grass that has been cut short on which the game of BOWLS is played

bow·man /'bəʊmən; *AmE* 'boʊ-/ *noun* (*pl.* **-men** /-mən/) (*old-fashioned*) = ARCHER

bow tie /ˌbəʊ 'taɪ; *AmE* ˌboʊ/ *noun* a man's tie that is tied in the shape of a bow and that does not hang down—picture on page A4

bow-wow /'baʊ waʊ/ *noun* a child's word for a dog

box /bɒks; *AmE* bɑːks/ *noun, verb*

■ *noun*

CONTAINER | **1** [C] (especially in compounds) a container made of wood, cardboard, metal, etc. with a flat stiff base and sides and often a lid, used especially for holding solid things: *She kept all the letters in a box.* ◊ *a money box* ◊ *cardboard boxes* ◊ *a toolbox* ◊ *a matchbox*—picture at PACKAGING **2** [C] a box and its contents: *a box of chocolates/matches*—picture at PACKAGING

IN THEATRE/COURT | **3** [C] a small area in a theatre or court of law separated off from where other people sit: *a box at the opera* ◊ *the witness/jury box*

HUT | **4** [C] a small hut used for a particular purpose: *a sentry/signal box* ◊ (*BrE*) *a telephone box* ◊ *I called him from the phone box on the corner.*

SHAPE | **5** [C] a small square or RECTANGLE drawn on a page for people to write information in: *Put a cross in the appropriate box.* ◊ *to tick/check a box*

TELEVISION | **6** (**the box**) [sing.] (*informal*) the television: *What's on the box tonight?*

ON ROAD | **7** [C] (*BrE*) = BOX JUNCTION: *Only traffic turning right may enter the box.*

IN SPORT | **8** [C] an area on a sports field that is marked by lines and used for a particular purpose: (*BrE*) *He was fouled in the box* (= the penalty box).

FOR MAIL | **9** [C] = BOX NUMBER—see also PO Box

PROTECTION | **10** [C] (*BrE*) a piece of plastic that a man wears over his sex organs to protect them while he is playing a sport, especially cricket

TREE/WOOD | **11** [C, U] a small EVERGREEN tree or bush with thick dark leaves, used especially for garden HEDGES **12** (also **box·wood**) [U] the hard wood of this bush

IDM **give sb a box on the 'ears** (*old-fashioned*) to hit sb with your hand on the side of their head as a punishment—more at TRICK *n.*

■ *verb*

FIGHT | **1** [V, VN] to fight sb in the sport of boxing

PUT IN CONTAINER | **2** [VN] ~ **sth** (**up**) to put sth in a box

IDM **box sb's 'ears** (*old-fashioned*) to hit sb with your hand on the side of their head as a punishment

PHR V ˌ**box sb/sth 'in 1** to prevent sb/sth from being able to move to by surrounding them with people, vehicles, etc: *Someone had parked behind us and boxed us in.* **2** [usually passive] (of a situation) to prevent sb from doing what they want by creating unnecessary problems: *She felt boxed in by all their petty rules.*

box·car /'bɒkskɑː(r); *AmE* 'bɑːks-/ *noun* (*especially AmE*) a closed railway carriage with a sliding door, used for carrying goods

boxed /bɒkst; *AmE* bɑːkst/ *adj.* put and/or sold in a box: *a boxed set of original recordings*

boxer /'bɒksə(r); *AmE* 'bɑːk-/ *noun* **1** a person who boxes, especially as a job: *a professional/amateur/heavyweight boxer* **2** a large dog with smooth hair, a short flat nose and a tail that has usually been cut very short

'**boxer shorts** (also **boxers**) (*AmE* also **shorts**) *noun* [pl.] men's UNDERPANTS similar to the SHORTS worn by boxers: *a pair of boxer shorts*

box·ful /'bɒksfʊl; *AmE* 'bɑːksfʊl/ *noun* a full box (of sth)

box·ing /'bɒksɪŋ; *AmE* 'bɑːks-/ *noun* [U] a sport in which two people fight each other with their hands, while wearing very large thick gloves (called **boxing gloves**): *a boxing champion/match* ◊ *heavyweight boxing*

'**Box·ing Day** *noun* [U, C] (*BrE*) the first day after Christmas Day that is not a Sunday. Boxing Day is an official holiday in Britain.

'**box junction** (also **box**) *noun* (*BrE*) a place where two roads cross or join, marked with a pattern of yellow lines to show that vehicles must not stop

'**box number** (also **box**) *noun* a number used as an address, especially one given in newspaper advertisements to which replies can be sent

'**box office** *noun* the place at a theatre, cinema/movie theater, etc. where the tickets are sold: *The movie has been a huge box-office success* (= many people have been to see it).

box·room /'bɒksruːm; -rʊm; *AmE* 'bɑːks-/ *noun* (*BrE*) a small room in a house for storing things in

box·wood /'bɒkswʊd; *AmE* 'bɑːks-/ *noun* [U] = BOX (12)

boy /bɔɪ/ *noun, exclamation*

■ *noun* **1** [C] a male child or a young male person: *a little/small/young boy* ◊ *I used to play here as a boy.* ◊ *The older boys at school used to tease him.* ◊ *Now she's a teenager, she's starting to be interested in boys.*—see also OLD BOY **2** [C] a young son: *They have two boys and a girl.* ◊ *Her eldest boy is at college.* **3** [C] (in compounds; offensive when used of an older man) a boy or young man who does a particular job: *a delivery boy*—see also BACK-ROOM BOYS **4** [C] a way of talking about sb who comes from a particular place, etc: *He's a local boy.* ◊ *a city/country boy* **5** (**the boys**) [pl.] (*informal*) a group of male friends who often go out together: *a night out with the boys* **6** (**our boys**) [pl.] a way of talking with affection about your country's soldiers **7** (*AmE*, ⚠) used as an offensive way of addressing a black man IDM **the boys in 'blue** (*informal*) the police ˌ**boys ˌwill be 'boys** (*saying*) you should not be surprised when boys or men behave in a noisy or rough way as this is part of typical male behaviour—more at BLUE, JOB *n.*, MAN *n.*

■ *exclamation* (*informal, especially AmE*) used to express feelings of surprise, pleasure, pain, etc: *Boy, it sure is hot!* ◊ *Oh boy! That's great!*

boy·cott /'bɔɪkɒt; *AmE* -kɑːt/ *verb, noun*

■ *verb* [VN] to refuse to buy, use or take part in sth as a way of protesting: *We are asking people to boycott goods from companies that use child labour.*

■ *noun* ~ (**of/on sth**) an act of boycotting sb/sth: *a trade boycott of British goods* ◊ *a boycott on the use of tropical wood*

boy·friend /'bɔɪfrend/ *noun* a man or boy that sb has a romantic or sexual relationship with

boy·hood /'bɔɪhʊd/ *noun* [U] (becoming *old-fashioned*) the time in a man's life when he is a boy: *boyhood days/memories/friends*

boy·ish /'bɔɪɪʃ/ *adj.* (*approving*) looking or behaving like a boy, in a way that is attractive: *boyish charm/enthusiasm* ◊ *her slim boyish figure* ▶ **boy·ish·ly** *adv.*

ˌ**Boy 'Scout** *noun* (*AmE* or *old-fashioned*) a boy who is a member of THE SCOUTS

bozo /'bəʊzəʊ; *AmE* 'boʊzoʊ/ *noun* (*pl.* **-os**) (*informal, especially AmE*) a stupid person

Br. *abbr.* (in writing) British

bra /brɑː/ (also *formal* **brassière**) *noun* a piece of women's underwear worn to cover and support the breasts

brace /breɪs/ *noun, verb*

■ *noun* **1** [C] a device that holds things firmly together or holds and supports them in position: *a neck brace* (= worn to support the neck after an injury) **2** [C] (*AmE* **braces** [pl.]) a metal device that children wear inside the mouth to help their teeth grow straight **3** (**braces**) (*BrE*) (*AmE* **sus·pend·ers**) [pl.] straps for holding trousers/pants up. They are fastened to the top of the trousers/pants at the front and back and passed over the shoulders: *a pair of braces*—picture on page A4 **4** [C, usually pl.] (*AmE*) = CALLIPER **5** [C] either of the two marks, {}, used to show that the words, etc. between them are connected—compare BRACKET **6** [C] (*pl.* **brace**) a pair of birds or animals that have been killed in hunting: *two brace of partridge(s)* IDM see BELT *n.*

■ *verb* **1** ~ **sb/yourself** (**for sth**) to prepare sb/yourself for sth difficult or unpleasant that is going to happen: [VN] *UN troops are braced for more violence.* ◊ *They are bracing* themselves for a long legal battle. [also VN to inf] **2** [VN] ~ **sth/yourself (against sth)** to press your body or part of your body firmly against sth in order to stop yourself from falling: *They braced themselves against the wind.* **3** [VN] to tighten the muscles in your body or part of your body before doing sth that is physically difficult: *He stood with his legs and shoulders braced, ready to lift the weights.* **4** [VN] (*technical*) to make sth stronger or more solid by supporting it with sth: *The roof was braced by lengths of timber.*

brace·let /ˈbreɪslət/ *noun* a piece of jewellery worn around the wrist or arm—picture at JEWELLERY

brac·ing /ˈbreɪsɪŋ/ *adj.* (especially of weather) making you feel full of energy because it is cold: *bracing sea air*

bracken /ˈbrækən/ *noun* [U] a wild plant with large leaves that grows thickly on hills and in woods and turns brown in the autumn/fall

bracket /ˈbrækɪt/ *noun, verb*
- *noun* **1** (also **ˈround bracket**) (both *BrE*) (also **par·en·thesis** *AmE* or *formal*) [usually pl.] either of a pair of marks, ( ) placed around extra information in a piece of writing or part of a problem in mathematics: *Publication dates are given in brackets after each title.* ◇ *Add the numbers in brackets first.*—see also ANGLE BRACKET—compare BRACE ⇨ Appendix 4 **2** [usually pl.] (*AmE*) = SQUARE BRACKET **3** price, age, income, etc. ~ prices, etc. within a particular range: *people in the lower income bracket* ◇ *Most of the houses are out of our price bracket.* ◇ *the 30–34 age bracket* (= people aged between 30 and 34) **4** a piece of wood, metal or plastic fixed to the wall to support a shelf, lamp, etc.
- *verb* [VN] **1** to put words, information, etc. between brackets **2** ~ **A and B (together)** | ~ **A (together) with B** [often passive] to consider people or things to be similar or connected in some way: *It is unfair to bracket together those who cannot work with those who will not.*

brack·ish /ˈbrækɪʃ/ *adj.* (of water) salty in an unpleasant way: *brackish lakes/lagoons/marshes*

brae /breɪ/ *noun* (*ScotE*) (often in place names) a steep slope or hill

brag /bræg/ *verb* (-gg-) ~ **to sb (about/of sth)** (*disapproving*) to talk too proudly about sth you own or sth you have done [SYN] BOAST: *He bragged to his friends about the crime.* [also V that, V speech]

brag·gart /ˈbrægət/ *AmE* -gərt/ *noun* (*old-fashioned*) a person who brags

Brah·man /ˈbrɑːmən/ *noun* (also **Brah·min** /-ɪn/) a Hindu who belongs to the highest CASTE (= division of society), in which all the members are priests

braid /breɪd/ *noun, verb*
- *noun* **1** [U] thin coloured rope that is used to decorate furniture and military uniforms: *The general's uniform was trimmed with gold braid.*—picture at TASSEL **2** [C] (*especially AmE*) = PLAIT: *She wears her hair in braids.*
- *verb* [VN] (*especially AmE*) = PLAIT: *She'd braided her hair.*

Braille (also **braille**) /breɪl/ *noun* [U] a system of printing for blind people in which the letters of the alphabet and the numbers are printed as raised dots that can be read by touching them

brain /breɪn/ *noun, verb*
- *noun*
  IN HEAD | **1** [C] the organ inside the head that controls movement, thought, memory and feeling: *damage to the brain* ◇ *brain cells* ◇ *She died of a brain tumour.* ◇ *a device to measure brain activity during sleep*—picture at BODY
  FOOD | **2** (**brains**) [pl.] the brain of an animal, eaten as food: *sheep's brains*
  INTELLIGENCE | **3** [U, C, usually pl.] the ability to learn quickly and think about things in a logical and intelligent way: *It doesn't take much brain to work out that both stories can't be true.* ◇ *Teachers spotted that he had a good brain at an early age.* ◇ *You need brains as well as brawn* (= intelligence as well as strength) *to do this job.*
  INTELLIGENT PERSON | **4** [C, usually pl.] (*informal*) an intelligent person: *We have the best scientific brains in the country working on this.* **5** (**the brains**) [sing.] the most intelligent person in a particular group; the person who

is responsible for thinking of and organizing sth: *He's always been the brains of the family.* ◇ *The band's drummer is the brains behind their latest venture.*
[IDM] **have sth on the brain** (*informal*) to think about sth all the time, especially in a way that is annoying: *He has sex on the brain.*—more at BEAT *v.*, BLOW *v.*, CUDGEL *v.*, PICK *v.*, RACK *v.*
- *verb* [VN] (*informal*) to kill a person or an animal by hitting them very hard on the head: *I nearly brained myself on that low beam.*

brain·child /ˈbreɪntʃaɪld/ *noun* [sing.] **the ~ (of sb)** an idea or invention of one person or a small group of people

ˈbrain damage *noun* [U] permanent damage to the brain caused by illness or an accident ▶ **ˈbrain-dam·aged** *adj.*

ˈbrain-dead *adj.* **1** suffering from serious damage to the brain and needing machines to stay alive **2** (*humorous*) very stupid and boring; not thinking in an intelligent way

ˈbrain death *noun* [U] very serious damage to the brain that cannot be cured. A person who is suffering from brain death needs machines to keep them alive, even though their heart is still beating.

ˈbrain drain *noun* [sing.] (*informal*) the movement of highly skilled and qualified people to a country where they can work in better conditions and earn more money

brain·less /ˈbreɪnləs/ *adj.* stupid; not able to think or talk in an intelligent way

brain·power /ˈbreɪnpaʊə(r)/ *noun* [U] the ability to think; intelligence

brain·storm /ˈbreɪnstɔːm/ *AmE* -stɔːrm/ *noun* [sing.] **1** (*BrE*) a sudden inability to think clearly which causes unusual behaviour: *She had a brainstorm in the exam and didn't answer a single question.* **2** (*AmE*) = BRAINWAVE

brain·storm·ing /ˈbreɪnstɔːmɪŋ/ *AmE* -stɔːrm-/ *noun* [U] a way of making a group of people all think about sth at the same time, often in order to solve a problem or to create good ideas: *a brainstorming session* ▶ **brain·storm** *verb*: [VN] *Brainstorm as many ideas as possible.* [also V]

ˈbrain-teaser *noun* a problem that is difficult but fun to solve

brain·wash /ˈbreɪnwɒʃ/ *AmE* -wɑːʃ; -wɔːʃ/ *verb.* ~ **sb (into doing sth)** to force sb to accept your ideas or beliefs, for example by repeating the same thing many times or by preventing the person from thinking clearly: [VN] *The group is accused of brainwashing its young members.* ◇ *Women have been brainwashed into thinking that they must go out to work in order to fulfil themselves.* [also VN, VN to inf] ▶ **brain·wash·ing** *noun* [U]: *the victims of brainwashing and torture*

brain·wave /ˈbreɪnweɪv/ *noun* **1** (*AmE* also **brainstorm**) a sudden good idea: *I've had a brainwave that might help.* **2** an electrical signal in the brain

brainy /ˈbreɪni/ *adj.* (*old-fashioned, informal*) very intelligent

braise /breɪz/ *verb* [VN] to cook meat or vegetables very slowly with a little liquid in a closed container: *braising steak* (= that is suitable for braising)

brake /breɪk/ *noun, verb*
- *noun* **1** a device for slowing or stopping a vehicle: *to put/slam on the brakes* ◇ *the brake pedal*—see also AIR BRAKE, DISC BRAKE, HANDBRAKE—picture at BICYCLE, CAR **2** ~ (**on sth**) a thing that stops sth or makes it difficult: *High interest rates are a brake on the economy.* [IDM] see JAM *v.*
- *verb* to slow down or make a vehicle slow down using the brake: [V] *The car braked and swerved.* ◇ *The truck braked to a halt.* ◇ *You don't need to brake at every bend.* ◇ *She had to brake hard to avoid running into the car in front.* ◇ [VN] *He braked the car and pulled in to the side of the road.*

ˈbrake light (*AmE* also **ˈstop light**) *noun* a red light on the back of a vehicle that comes on when the brakes are used

bram·ble /ˈbræmbl/ *noun* **1** (*especially BrE*) a prickly wild bush on which BLACKBERRIES grow **2** (*BrE*) = BLACKBERRY

b	d	f	g	h	k	l	m	n	p	r
bad	did	fall	get	hat	cat	leg	man	now	pen	red

B

B

bran /bræn/ *noun* [U] the outer covering of grain which is left when the grain is made into flour

branch /brɑːntʃ; *AmE* bræntʃ/ *noun, verb*

■ *noun*

OF TREE | **1** a part of a tree that grows out from the main stem and on which leaves, flowers and fruit grow: *She climbed the tree and hid in the branches.*

OF COMPANY | **2** a local office or shop/store belonging to a large company or organization: *The bank has branches all over the country.* ◊ *Our New York branch is dealing with the matter.*

OF GOVERNMENT | **3** a part of a government or other large organization that deals with one particular aspect of its work [SYN] DEPARTMENT: *the anti-terrorist branch*

OF KNOWLEDGE | **4** a division of an area of knowledge or a group of languages: *the branch of computer science known as 'artificial intelligence'*

OF RIVER/ROAD | **5** a smaller or less important part of a river, road, railway/railroad, etc. that leads away from the main part: *a branch of the Rhine* ◊ *a branch line* (= a small line off a main railway line, often in country areas)

OF FAMILY | **6** a group of members of a family who all have the same ancestors: *My uncle's branch of the family emigrated to Canada.*

IDM see ROOT *n.*

■ *verb* [V] to divide into two or more parts, especially smaller or less important parts: *The accident happened where the road branches.*

PHR V ,branch 'off **1** (of a road or river) to be joined to another road or river but lead in a different direction: *Just after the lake, the path branches off to the right.* **2** (of a person) to leave a road or path and travel in a different direction ,branch 'out (into sth) to start to do an activity that you have not done before, especially in your work or business: *The company has now branched out into selling insurance.* ◊ *I decided to branch out on my own.*

brand /brænd/ *noun, verb*

■ *noun* **1** a type of product made by a particular company: *Which brand of toothpaste do you use?* ◊ (*BrE*) *You pay less for the supermarket's own brand.* ◊ (*AmE*) *You pay less for the store brand.* ◊ *brand loyalty* (= the tendency of customers to continue buying the same brand) ◊ *Champagne houses owe their success to brand image.* ◊ *the leading brand of detergent*—see also OWN-BRAND **2** a particular type or kind of sth: *an unorthodox brand of humour* **3** a mark made with a piece of hot metal, especially on farm animals to show who owns them

■ *verb* [often passive] **1** ~ sb (as) sth to describe sb as being sth bad or unpleasant, especially unfairly: [VN] *They were branded as liars and cheats.* ◊ [VN-N] *The newspapers branded her a hypocrite.* [also VN-ADJ] **2** [VN] ~ sth (with sth) to mark an animal with a brand to show who owns it

brand·ed /'brændɪd/ *adj.* [only before noun] (of a product) made by a well-known company and having that company's name on it: *branded drugs/goods/products*

'branding iron *noun* a metal tool that is heated and used for marking farm animals by branding them

bran·dish /'brændɪʃ/ *verb* [VN] (*written*) to hold or wave sth, especially a weapon, in an aggressive or threatening way

'brand name (also **'trade name**) *noun* the name given to a product by the company that produces it

,brand 'new *adj.* completely new: *a brand new computer* ◊ *She bought her car brand new.*

brandy /'brændi/ *noun* (*pl.* -ies) **1** [U, C] a strong alcoholic drink made from wine. There are several types of brandy: *The finest brandies are made in Cognac.* **2** [C] a glass of brandy

'brandy snap *noun* (*especially BrE*) a thin crisp biscuit/cookie in the shape of a tube, flavoured with GINGER and often filled with cream

brash /bræʃ/ *adj.* (*disapproving*) **1** confident in an aggressive way: *Beneath his brash exterior, he's still a little boy inside.* **2** (*BrE*) (of things and places) too bright or too noisy in a way that is not attractive ► **brash·ly** *adv.* **brash·ness** *noun* [U]

brass /brɑːs; *AmE* bræs/ *noun*

METAL | **1** [U] a bright yellow metal made by mixing COPPER and ZINC; objects made of brass: *solid brass fittings/door handles* ◊ *a brass plate* (= a sign outside a building giving the name and profession of the person who works there) ◊ *to clean/polish the brass*

MUSICAL INSTRUMENTS | **2** [U+sing./pl. *v.*] the musical instruments made of metal, such as TRUMPETS or FRENCH HORNS, that form a band or section of an orchestra; the people who play them: *music for piano, strings and brass*—compare PERCUSSION, STRINGS, WOODWIND, WIND INSTRUMENT—picture on page 840

ORNAMENT | **3** [C] (*BrE*) a decorated piece of brass used as an ornament, especially a round flat piece attached to a horse's HARNESS

IN CHURCH | **4** [C] (*especially BrE*) a flat piece of brass with words or a picture on it, fixed to the floor or wall of a church in memory of sb who has died: *a memorial brass*

IMPORTANT PEOPLE | **5** [U+sing./pl. *v.*] (*especially AmE*) = TOP BRASS

MONEY | **6** [U] (*old-fashioned, BrE, informal*) money

—see also BRASSY

IDM **,brass 'monkeys | ,brass 'monkey weather** (*BrE, slang*) if you say that it is **brass monkeys** or **brass monkey weather**, you mean that it is very cold weather **,brass 'neck/'nerve** (*BrE, informal*) a combination of confidence and lack of respect: *I didn't think she would have the brass neck to do that.* **(get down to) brass 'tacks** (*informal*) (to start to consider) the basic facts or practical details of sth—more at BOLD, MUCK *n.*

,brass 'band *noun* a group of musicians who play brass instruments

,brassed 'off *adj.* (*BrE, slang*) annoyed

bras·serie /'bræsəri; *AmE* ˌbræsə'riː/ *noun* a type of restaurant, often one that serves both food and drinks or drinks alone

brass·ière /'bræziə(r); *AmE* brə'zɪr/ *noun* (*formal*) = BRA

,brass 'knuckles *noun* [pl.] (*AmE*) = KNUCKLEDUSTER

'brass rubbing *noun* [U, C] the art of rubbing a soft pencil or chalk on a piece of paper placed over a BRASS in a church; the pattern you get by doing this

brassy /'brɑːsi; *AmE* 'bræsi/ *adj.* **1** (sometimes *disapproving*) (of music) loud and harsh **2** (*informal, disapproving*) (of a woman) dressing in a way that makes her sexual attraction obvious, but without style: *the brassy blonde behind the bar* **3** like BRASS(1) in colour; too yellow and bright **4** (*AmE, informal*) saying what you think, without caring about other people

brat /bræt/ *noun* (*informal, disapproving*) a person, especially a child, who behaves badly: *a spoiled/spoilt brat*

bra·vado /brə'vɑːdəʊ; *AmE* -doʊ/ *noun* [U] a confident way of behaving that is intended to impress people, sometimes as a way of hiding a lack of confidence: *an act of sheer bravado*

brave /breɪv/ *adj., verb, noun*

■ *adj.* (**braver, brav·est**) **1** (of a person) willing to do things which are difficult, dangerous or painful; not afraid [SYN] COURAGEOUS: *brave men and women* ◊ *Be brave!* ◊ *I wasn't brave enough to tell her what I thought of her.* **2** (of an action) requiring or showing courage: *a brave decision* ◊ *She died after a brave fight against cancer.* ◊ *He felt homesick, but made a brave attempt to appear cheerful.* **3** ~ new (sometimes *ironic*) new in an impressive way: *a vision of a brave new Britain* ► **brave·ly** *adv.* **bravery** /'breɪvəri/ *noun* [U]: *an award for outstanding bravery* ◊ *acts of skill and bravery* IDM **(a) ,brave new 'world** a situation or society that changes in a way that is meant to improve people's lives but is often a source of extra problems: *the brave new world of technology* **put on a brave 'face | put a brave 'face on sth** to pretend that you feel confident and happy when you do not

■ *verb* [VN] to have to deal with sth difficult or unpleasant in order to achieve sth: *He did not feel up to braving the journalists at the airport.* ◊ *Over a thousand people braved the elements* (= went outside in spite of the bad weather) *to attend the march.*

s	t	v	z	ʃ	ʒ	tʃ	dʒ	θ	ð	ŋ
see	tea	van	zoo	shoe	vision	chain	jam	thin	this	sing

■ *noun* **1** (**the brave**) [pl.] people who are brave: *America—the land of the free and the home of the brave* **2** [C] (*old-fashioned*) a Native American WARRIOR

bravo /ˌbrɑːˈvəʊ; *AmE* -ˈvoʊ/ *exclamation* (becoming *old-fashioned*) people say **Bravo!** at the end of sth they have enjoyed, such as a play at the theatre

bra·vura /brəˈvjʊərə; *AmE* -ˈvjʊrə/ *noun* [U] (*formal*) great skill and enthusiasm in doing sth artistic: *a bravura performance*

brawl /brɔːl/ *noun, verb*
■ *noun* a noisy and violent fight involving a group of people, usually in a public place: *a drunken brawl*
■ *verb* [V] to take part in a noisy and violent fight, usually in a public place: *They were arrested for brawling in the street.* ▶ **brawl·er** *noun*

brawn /brɔːn/ *noun* [U] **1** physical strength: *In this job you need brains as well as brawn.* **2** (*BrE*) (*AmE* **head-cheese**) meat made from the head of a pig or CALF that has been boiled and pressed into a container, served cold in thin slices

brawny /ˈbrɔːni/ *adj.* (*informal*) having strong muscles: *He was a great brawny brute of a man.*

bray /breɪ/ *verb* **1** [V] when a DONKEY **brays**, it makes a loud harsh sound **2** (of a person) to talk or laugh in a loud unpleasant voice: [V] *He brayed with laughter.* ◊ *a braying voice* [also V **speech**] ▶ **bray** *noun*

bra·zen /ˈbreɪzn/ *adj., verb*
■ *adj.* **1** (*disapproving*) open and without SHAME, usually about sth that people find shocking: *She had become brazen about the whole affair.* ◊ *his brazen admission that he was cheating* **2** made of, or the colour of, BRASS (1) ▶ **brazen·ly** *adv.*: *She had brazenly admitted allowing him back into the house.*
■ *verb* PHRV ˌbrazen it ˈout to behave as if you are not ashamed or embarrassed about sth even though you should be: *Now that everyone knew the truth, the only thing to do was to brazen it out.*

bra·zier /ˈbreɪziə(r)/ *noun* a large metal container that holds a fire and is used to keep people warm when they are outside

bra·zil /brəˈzɪl/ (also **braˈzil nut**) *noun* the curved nut of a large S American tree. It has a hard shell with three sides.—picture at NUT

breach /briːtʃ/ *noun, verb*
■ *noun* **1** [C, U] ~ **of sth** a failure to do sth that must be done by law: *a breach of contract/copyright/warranty* ◊ *They are in breach of Article 119.* ◊ (*BrE*) (a) **breach of the peace** (= the crime of behaving in a noisy or violent way in public) **2** [C, U] ~ **of sth** an action that breaks an agreement to behave in a particular way: *a breach of confidence/trust* ◊ *a breach of security* (= when sth that is normally protected is no longer secure) **3** [C] a break in a relationship between people or countries: *a breach in Franco-German relations* **4** [C] an opening that is created during a military attack or by strong winds or seas: *They escaped through a breach in the wire fence.* IDM see STEP *v.*
■ *verb* [VN] **1** to not keep to an agreement or not keep a promise: *The government is accused of breaching the terms of the treaty.* **2** to make a hole in a wall, fence, etc. so that sb/sth can go through it: *The dam had been breached.* ◊ *Demonstrators breached police lines around the embassy.*

bread /bred/ *noun* [U] **1** a type of food made from flour, water and usually YEAST mixed together and baked: *a loaf/slice/piece of bread* ◊ *white/brown/wholemeal bread*—see also CRISPBREAD, FRENCH BREAD, GINGER-BREAD—picture on page A1 **2** (*old-fashioned, slang*) money IDM **take the bread out of sb's ˈmouth** to take away sb's job so that they are no longer able to earn enough money to live—more at DAILY *adj.*, KNOW *v.*, THING

ˌbread and ˈbutter *noun* [U] **1** slices of bread that have been spread with butter: *a piece of bread and butter* **2** (*informal*) a person or company's main source of income

ˌbread-and-ˈbutter *adj.* [only before noun] basic; very important: *Employment and taxation are the bread-and-butter issues of politics.*

bread·bas·ket /ˈbredbɑːskɪt; *AmE* -bæs-/ *noun* [sing.] (*especially AmE*) the part of a country or region that produces large amounts of food, especially grain, for the rest of the country or region

bread·board /ˈbredbɔːd; *AmE* -bɔːrd/ *noun* a flat board used for cutting bread on

bread·crumbs /ˈbredkrʌmz/ *noun* [pl.] very small pieces of bread that can be used in cooking

bread·ed /ˈbredɪd/ *adj.* covered in breadcrumbs: *breaded cod*

bread·fruit /ˈbredfruːt/ *noun* [C, U] (*pl.* **bread·fruit**) a large tropical fruit with a thick skin, that tastes and feels like bread when it is cooked

bread·line /ˈbredlaɪn/ *noun* (**the breadline**) [sing.] (*BrE*) the level of income of very poor people: *Many people without jobs are living on the breadline* (= are very poor).

ˌbread ˈroll *noun* = ROLL

breadth /bredθ/ *noun* [U, C] **1** (also **broad·ness**) the distance or measurement from one side to the other; how BROAD or wide sth is [SYN] WIDTH: *She estimated the breadth of the lake to be 500 metres.*—compare LENGTH **2** a wide range (of knowledge, interests, etc.): *He was surprised at her breadth of reading.* ◊ *The curriculum needs breadth and balance.* ◊ *a new political leader whose breadth of vision* (= willingness to accept new ideas) *can persuade others to change* IDM SEE LENGTH

bread·win·ner /ˈbredwɪnə(r)/ *noun* a person who supports their family with the money they earn: *When the baby was born, I became the sole breadwinner.*

break /breɪk/ *verb, noun*
■ *verb* (**broke** /brəʊk; *AmE* broʊk/ **broken** /ˈbrəʊkən; *AmE* ˈbroʊkən/)

IN PIECES | **1** ~ (**sth**) (**in/into sth**) to be damaged and separated into two or more parts, as a result of force; to damage sth in this way: [V] *All the windows broke with the force of the blast.* ◊ *She dropped the plate and it broke into pieces.* ◊ [VN] *to break a cup/window* ◊ *She fell off a ladder and broke her arm.* ◊ *He broke the chocolate in two.*

STOP WORKING | **2** to stop working as a result of being damaged; to damage sth and stop it from working: [V] *My watch has broken.* ◊ [VN] *I think I've broken the washing machine.*

SKIN | **3** [VN] to cut the surface of the skin and make it bleed: *The dog bit me but didn't break the skin.*

LAW/PROMISE | **4** [VN] to do sth that is against the law; to not keep a promise, etc: *to break the law/rules/conditions* ◊ *to break an agreement/a contract/a promise/your word* ◊ *to break an appointment* (= not to come to it) ◊ *He was breaking the speed limit* (= travelling faster than the law allows).

STOP FOR SHORT TIME | **5** ~ (**for sth**) to stop doing sth for a while, especially when it is time to eat or have a drink: [V] *Let's break for lunch.* ◊ [VN] *a broken night's sleep* (= a night during which you often wake up) ◊ (*especially BrE*) *We broke our journey at Oxford* (= stopped in Oxford on the way to the place we were going to).

END STH | **6** [VN] to interrupt sth so that it ends suddenly: *She broke the silence by coughing.* ◊ *A tree broke his fall* (= stopped him as he was falling). ◊ *The phone rang and broke my train of thought.* **7** [VN] to make sth end by using force or strong action: *an attempt to break the year-long siege* ◊ *Management has not succeeded in breaking the strike.* **8** [VN] to end a connection with sth or a relationship with sb: *He broke all links with the Communist party.*

ESCAPE | **9** [V+*adv. / prep.*] ~ **free** (**from sb/sth**) (of a person or an object) to get away from or out of a position in which they are stuck or trapped: *He finally managed to break free from his attacker.*

DESTROY | **10** to destroy sth or make sb/sth weaker; to become weak or be destroyed: [VN] *to break sb's morale/resistance/resolve/spirit* ◊ *The government was determined to break the power of the trade unions.* ◊ *The scandal broke him* (= ruined his reputation and destroyed his confidence). ◊ [V] *She broke under questioning* (= was no longer able to bear it) *and confessed to everything.*

MAKE SB FEEL BAD | **11** [VN] to make sb feel so sad, lonely,

æ	ɑː	e	ɜː	ə	ɪ	iː	i	ɒ	ɔː	ʌ	ʊ	u	uː
cat	father	ten	bird	about	sit	see	many	got	saw	cup	put	actual	too

(BrE)

etc. that they cannot live a normal life: *The death of his wife broke him completely.*

OF WEATHER | **12** [V] to change suddenly, usually after a period when it has been fine

SHOW OPENING | **13** [V] to show an opening: *The clouds broke and the sun came out.*

OF DAY/DAWN/STORM | **14** [V] when the day or DAWN or a storm **breaks**, it begins: *Dawn was breaking when they finally left.*—see also DAYBREAK

OF NEWS | **15** [V] if a piece of news **breaks**, it becomes known: *There was a public outcry when the scandal broke.*

OF VOICE | **16** [V] if sb's voice **breaks**, it changes its tone because of emotion: *Her voice broke as she told us the dreadful news.* **17** [V] when a boy's voice **breaks**, it becomes permanently deeper at about the age of 13 or 14

A RECORD | **18** [VN] to do sth better, faster, etc. than anyone has ever done it before: *She had broken the world 100 metres record.* ◊ *The movie broke all box-office records.*

OF WAVES | **19** [V] when waves **break**, they fall and are dissolved into FOAM, usually near the shore: *the sound of waves breaking on the beach* ◊ *The sea was breaking over the wrecked ship.*

STH SECRET | **20** [VN] to find the meaning of sth secret: *to break a code*

MONEY | **21** [VN] (*especially AmE*) to change a BANKNOTE for coins: *Can you break a twenty dollar bill?*

VOCABULARY BUILDING
words that mean **'break'**

burst	*The balloon hit a tree and burst.*
crack	*The ice started to crack.*
crumble	*Crumble the cheese into a bowl.*
cut	*Now cut the wire in two.*
fracture	*He fell and fractured his hip.*
shatter	*The vase hit the floor and shattered.*
smash	*Vandals had smashed two windows.*
snap	*I snapped the pencil in half.*
split	*The bag had split open on the way home.*
tear	*She tore the letter into pieces.*

All these verbs, except *cut*, can be used with or without an object.

IDM Idioms containing **break** are at the entries for the nouns and adjectives in the idioms, for example **break sb's heart** is at **heart**.

PHR V ,break a'way (from sb/sth) **1** to escape suddenly from sb who is holding you or keeping you prisoner: *The prisoner broke away from his guards.* **2** to leave a political party, state, etc., especially to form a new one: *The people of the province wished to break away and form a new state.*—related noun BREAKAWAY **3** to move away from a crowd or group, especially in a race: *She broke away from the pack and opened up a two second lead.*

,break 'down **1** (of a machine or vehicle) to stop working because of a fault: *The telephone system has broken down.* ◊ *We* (= the car) *broke down on the freeway.*—related noun BREAKDOWN **2** to fail: *Negotiations between the two sides have broken down.*—related noun BREAKDOWN **3** to become very bad: *Her health broke down under the pressure of work.*—see also NERVOUS BREAKDOWN **4** to lose control of your feelings and start crying: *He broke down and wept when he heard the news.* **5** to divide into parts to be analysed: *Expenditure on the project breaks down as follows: wages $10m, plant $4m, raw materials $5m.* ,break sth↔'down **1** to make sth fall down, open, etc. by hitting it hard: *Firefighters had to break the door down to reach the people trapped inside.* **2** to destroy sth or make it disappear, especially a particular feeling or attitude that sb has: *to break down resistance/opposition* ◊ *to break down sb's reserve/shyness* ◊ *Attempts must be made to break down the barriers of fear and hostility which divide the two communities.* **3** to divide sth into parts in order to analyse it or make it easier to do: *Break your expenditure down into bills, food and other.* ◊ *Each lesson is broken down into several units.*—related noun BREAKDOWN **4** to make a substance separate into parts or change into a different form in a chemical process: *Sugar and starch are*

broken down in the stomach.—related noun BREAKDOWN
'break for sth to suddenly run towards sth when you are trying to escape: *She had to hold him back as he tried to break for the door.*

,break 'in to enter a building by force: *Burglars had broken in while we were away.*—related noun BREAK-IN ,break sb/sth 'in **1** to train sb/sth in sth new that they must do: *to break in new recruits* ◊ *The young horse was not yet broken in* (= trained to carry a rider). **2** to wear sth, especially new shoes, until they become comfortable ,break 'in (on sth) to interrupt or disturb sth: *She longed to break in on their conversation but didn't want to appear rude.* ◊*'I didn't do it!' she broke in.*

,break 'into sth **1** to enter a building by force; to open a car, etc. by force: *We had our car broken into last week.*—related noun BREAK-IN **2** to begin laughing, singing, etc. suddenly: *As the President's car drew up, the crowd broke into loud applause.* **3** to suddenly start running; to start running faster than before: *He broke into a run when he saw the police.* ◊ *Her horse broke into a trot.* **4** (*BrE*) to use a BANKNOTE of high value to buy sth that costs less: *I had to break into a £20 to pay the bus fare.* **5** to open and use sth that has been kept for an emergency: *They had to break into the emergency food supplies.* **6** to be successful when you get involved in sth: *The company is having difficulty breaking into new markets.*

,break 'off **1** to become separated from sth as a result of force: *The back section of the plane had broken off.* **2** to stop speaking or stop doing sth for a time: *He broke off in the middle of a sentence.* ,break sth↔'off **1** to separate sth, using force: *She broke off a piece of chocolate and gave it to me.* **2** to end sth suddenly: *Britain threatened to break off diplomatic relations.* ◊ *They've broken off their engagement.*

,break 'out (of war, fighting or other unpleasant events) to start suddenly: *They had escaped to America shortly before war broke out in 1939.* ◊ *Fighting had broken out between rival groups of fans.* ◊ *Fire broke out during the night.*—related noun OUTBREAK ,break 'out (of sth) to escape from a place or situation: *Several prisoners broke out of the jail.* ◊ *She needed to break out of her daily routine and do something exciting.*—related noun BREAKOUT ,break 'out in sth to suddenly become covered in sth: *Her face broke out in a rash.* ◊ *He broke out in a cold sweat* (= for example, through fear).

,break 'through to make new and important discoveries: *Scientists think they are beginning to break through in the fight against cancer.*—related noun BREAKTHROUGH ,break 'through | ,break 'through sth **1** to make a way through sth using force: *Demonstrators broke through the police cordon.* **2** (of the sun or moon) to appear from behind clouds: *The sun broke through at last in the afternoon.* 'break through sth to succeed in dealing with an attitude that sb has and the difficulties it creates **SYN** OVERCOME: *He had finally managed to break through her reserve.*

,break 'up **1** to separate into smaller pieces: *The ship broke up on the rocks.* **2** to come to an end: *Their marriage has broken up.*—related noun BREAK-UP **3** to go away in different directions: *The meeting broke up at eleven o'clock.* **4** (*especially BrE*) to begin the holidays when school closes at the end of a TERM: *When do you break up for Christmas?* **5** (*BrE*) to become very weak: *He was breaking up under the strain.* **6** (*AmE*) to laugh very hard: *Woody Allen makes me just break up.* ,break sth↔'up **1** to make sth separate into smaller pieces; to divide sth into smaller parts: *The ship was broken up for scrap metal.* ◊ *Sentences can be broken up into clauses.* **2** to end a relationship, a company, etc: *They decided to break up the partnership.*—related noun BREAK-UP **3** to make people leave sth or stop doing sth, especially by using force: *Police were called in to break up the fight.* ,break 'up (with sb) to end a relationship with sb: *She's just broken up with her boyfriend.*—related noun BREAK-UP
'break with sth to end a connection with sth: *to break with tradition/old habits/the past*

■ *noun*

SHORT STOP/PAUSE | **1** [C] a short period of time when you stop what you are doing and rest, eat, etc: *a coffee/lunch/*

tea break ◊ Let's take a break. ◊ a break for lunch ◊ She worked all day without a break. **2** (also **'break time**) (both BrE) (AmE **re·cess**) [U] a period of time between lessons at school: Come and see me at break. **3** [C] a pause or period of time when sth stops before starting again: a break in my daily routine ◊ She wanted to take a career break in order to have children. **4** [C] a pause for advertisements in the middle of a television or radio programme: More news after the break.

HOLIDAY/VACATION | **5** [C] a short holiday/vacation: We had a weekend break in New York. ◊ a well-earned break

CHANGE IN SITUATION | **6** [sing.] ~ (in sth) | ~ (with sb/sth) the moment when a situation that has existed for a time changes, ends or is interrupted: He needed to make a complete break with the past. ◊ a break with tradition/convention (= a change from what is accepted, in sth such as art, behaviour, etc.) ◊ a **break in the weather** (= a change from one type of weather to a different one) ◊ a break in diplomatic relations

OPENING/SPACE | **7** [C] ~ (in sth) a space or an opening between two or more things: We could see the moon through a break in the clouds.

OPPORTUNITY | **8** [C] (informal) an opportunity to do sth, usually to get sth that you want or to achieve success: I got my **lucky** break when I won a 'Young Journalist of the Year' competition. ◊ We've had a few bad breaks (= pieces of bad luck) along the way.

OF BONE | **9** [C] a place where sth, especially a bone in your body, has broken: The X-ray showed there was no break in his leg.

IN TENNIS | **10** (also **break of 'serve**) [C] a win in a game in which your opponent is SERVING: It was her second break in the set. ◊ **break point** (= a situation in which, if you win the next point, you win the game)

IN BILLIARDS/SNOOKER | **11** [C] a series of successful shots by one player; the number of points scored in a series of successful shots: He's put together a magnificent break. ◊ a 147 break (= the highest possible break in SNOOKER)

IDM **break of 'day** / **'dawn** (literary) the moment in the early hours of the morning when it begins to get light **give me a 'break!** (spoken) used when sb wants sb else to stop doing or saying sth that is annoying, or to stop saying sth that is not true **give sb a 'break** to give sb a chance; to not judge sb too harshly: Give the lad a break—it's only his second day on the job. **make a 'break for sth/for it** to run towards sth in order to try and escape: He suddenly leapt up and made a break for the door. ◊ They decided to make a break for it (= to try and escape) that night.—more at CLEAN adj.

WHICH WORD? (?)
break / recess / interval / intermission / interlude / pause

All these words mean the short time when an activity stops before it starts again, but they are used in different situations.

A **break** is a rest during the working day: a lunch / coffee break ◊ I'm exhausted – I need a break.

At school, children have **break** [U] (BrE) or **recess** [U] (AmE): Come and see me at break/recess.

Recess is also the time when Parliament or Congress is officially not working, or when work stops in a court of law.

An **interval** (BrE) or **intermission** [C,U] (AmE) is the period between the parts of a play, concert, etc: We had a quick drink in the interval.

An **interlude** may be a short space of time between the parts of a play, etc., or a period of time during a longer activity when something different happens: Her time in Paris was a happy interlude in a difficult career.

Pause is often applied to speech: a pause for breath ◊ After a pause, she said 'Yes.'

---

break·able /'breɪkəbl/ adj. likely to break; easily broken

break·age /'breɪkɪdʒ/ noun **1** [C, usually pl.] an object that has been broken: The last time we moved house there were very few breakages. **2** [U, C] the act of breaking sth: Wrap it up carefully to protect against breakage.

break·away /'breɪkəweɪ/ adj., noun
■ adj. [only before noun] (of a political group, an organization, or a part of a country) having separated from a larger group or country: a breakaway faction/group/section ◊ a breakaway republic
■ noun [sing.] **1** an occasion when members of a political party or an organization leave it in order to form a new party, etc. **2** a change from an accepted style: a breakaway from his earlier singing style

'break-dancing noun [U] a style of dancing with ACROBATIC movements, often performed in the street ▶ **'break-dance** verb [V] **'break-dancer** noun

break·down /'breɪkdaʊn/ noun **1** [C] an occasion when a vehicle or machine stops working: a breakdown on the motorway ◊ a breakdown recovery service **2** [C, U] a failure of a relationship, discussion or system: the breakdown of a marriage ◊ marriage breakdown ◊ a breakdown in communications ◊ The breakdown of the negotiations was not unexpected. ◊ the breakdown of law and order **3** [C, usually sing.] detailed information that you get by studying a set of figures: First, let's look at a breakdown of the costs. **4** [U] (technical) the breaking of a substance into the parts of which it is made: the breakdown of proteins in the digestive system **5** [C] = NERVOUS BREAKDOWN: She's still recovering from her breakdown.

'breakdown lane noun (AmE) = HARD SHOULDER

'breakdown truck (BrE) (AmE **'tow truck**) noun a truck that is used for taking cars away to be repaired when they have had a breakdown—picture at TRUCK

break·er /'breɪkə(r)/ noun a large wave covered with white bubbles that is moving towards the shore—see also CIRCUIT-BREAKER, ICE-BREAKER, HOUSEBREAKER, LAW-BREAKER, RECORD-BREAKER, STRIKE-BREAKER, TIEBREAKER

break·fast /'brekfəst/ noun, verb
■ noun [C, U] the first meal of the day: a big/hearty/light breakfast ◊ (especially BrE) a cooked breakfast ◊ Do you want bacon and eggs for breakfast? ◊ They were having breakfast when I arrived. ◊ She doesn't eat much breakfast.—see also BED AND BREAKFAST, CONTINENTAL BREAKFAST, ENGLISH BREAKFAST, WEDDING BREAKFAST **IDM** see DOG n.
■ verb [V] ~ (on sth) (formal) to eat breakfast

'break-in noun an entry into a building using force, usually to steal sth

breaking and 'entering noun [U] (AmE or old-fashioned) the crime of entering a building illegally and using force

'breaking point noun [U] the time when problems become so great that a person, an organization or a system can no longer deal with them: to be at/to reach breaking point ◊ to be stretched to breaking point

break·neck /'breɪknek/ adj. [only before noun] very fast and dangerous: to drive/travel/do sth **at breakneck speed**

break·out /'breɪkaʊt/ noun an escape from prison, usually by a group of prisoners: a mass breakout from a top security prison

break·through /'breɪkθruː/ noun an important development that may lead to an agreement or achievement: to make/achieve a breakthrough ◊ a significant breakthrough in negotiations ◊ a major breakthrough in cancer research

'break time noun [U] (BrE) = BREAK

'break-up noun **1** the ending of a relationship or an association: He did nothing to stop the break-up of their marriage. ◊ family break-ups **2** the division of a large organization or country into smaller parts: the break-up of the company

break·water /'breɪkwɔːtə(r)/ noun a wall built out into

b	d	f	g	h	k	l	m	n	p	r
bad	did	fall	get	hat	cat	leg	man	now	pen	red

B

the sea to protect the shore or harbour from the force of the waves

bream /briːm/ *noun* (*pl.* **bream**) a FRESHWATER or sea fish that is used for food

breast /brest/ *noun, verb*

■ *noun*

PART OF BODY | **1** [C] either of the two round soft parts at the front of a woman's body that produce milk when she has had a baby: *She put the baby to her breast.* ◇ *breast cancer* ◇ *breast milk* **2** [C] the similar, smaller part on a man's body, which does not produce milk **3** [C] (*literary*) the top part of the front of your body, below your neck [SYN] CHEST: *She cradled the child against her breast.*

CLOTHING | **4** [C] the part of a piece of clothing that covers your chest: *A row of medals was pinned to the breast of his coat.*

OF BIRD | **5** [C] the front part of a bird's body: *breast feathers* ◇ *The robin has a red breast.*

MEAT | **6** [C, U] meat from the front part of the body of a bird or an animal: *chicken/turkey breasts* ◇ *breast of lamb*

-BREASTED | **7** (in adjectives) having the type of chest or breasts mentioned: *a small-breasted/full-breasted woman* ◇ *bare-breasted* ◇ *the yellow-breasted male of the species*—see also DOUBLE-BREASTED, SINGLE-BREASTED

HEART | **8** [C] (*literary*) the part of the body where the feelings and emotions are thought to be: *a troubled breast* —see also CHIMNEY BREAST [IDM] see BEAT *v.*, CLEAN *adj.*

■ *verb* [VN] (*formal*) **1** to reach the top of a hill, etc: *As they breasted the ridge, they saw the valley and lake before them.* **2** to push through sth, touching it with your chest: *He strode into the ocean, breasting the waves.*

breast·bone /ˈbrestbəʊn; *AmE* -boʊn/ *noun* the long flat bone in the chest that the seven top pairs of RIBS are connected to [SYN] STERNUM—picture at BODY

breast·feed /ˈbrestfiːd/ *verb* (**breast·fed, breast·fed** /-fed/) [V, VN] when a woman **breastfeeds**, she feeds her baby with milk from her breasts.—compare BOTTLE-FEED, NURSE *v.* (6)

breast·plate /ˈbrestpleɪt/ *noun* a piece of ARMOUR worn by soldiers in the past to protect the upper front part of the body

breast ˈpocket *noun* a pocket on a shirt, or on the outside or inside of the part of a jacket that covers the chest—picture on page A4

breast·stroke /ˈbreststrəʊk; *AmE* -stroʊk/ *noun* [U, sing.] a style of swimming that you do on your front, moving your arms and legs away from your body and then back towards it in a circular movement—picture at SWIMMING

breath /breθ/ *noun* **1** [U] the air that you take into your lungs and send out again: *His breath smelt of garlic.* ◇ *bad breath* (= that smells bad) ◇ *We had to stop for breath before we got to the top.* ◇ *She was very short of breath* (= had difficulty breathing). **2** [C] an amount of air that enters the lungs at one time: *to take a deep breath* ◇ *He recited the whole poem in one breath.* **3~ of sth** [sing.] (*formal*) a small amount of sth; slight evidence of sth: *a breath of suspicion/scandal* **4 a ~ of air, wind** [sing.] (*literary*) a slight movement of air: *there wasn't a breath of air* ◇ **a breath of (fresh) ˈair** clean air breathed in after being indoors or in a dirty atmosphere: *We'll get a breath of fresh air at lunchtime.* **a breath of fresh ˈair** a person, thing or place that is new and different and therefore interesting and exciting ◇ **the breath of ˈlife to/for sb** (*literary*) an essential part of a person's existence ◇ **get your ˈbreath (again/back)** (*BrE*) (also **catch your ˈbreath** *AmE, BrE*) to breathe normally again after running or doing some tiring exercise ◇ **hold your ˈbreath 1** to stop breathing for a short time: *Hold your breath and count to ten.* **2** to be anxious while you are waiting for sth that you are worried about: *He held his breath while the results were read out.* **3** (*informal*) people say **don't hold your breath!** to emphasize that sth will take a long time or may not happen: *She said she'd do it this week, but don't hold your breath!* ◇ **in the same ˈbreath** immediately after saying sth that suggests the opposite intention or meaning: *He praised my work and in the same breath told me I would*

have to leave. ◇ **his/her last/dying ˈbreath** the last moment of a person's life ◇ **out of ˈbreath** having difficulty breathing after exercise: *We were out of breath after only five minutes.* ◇ **say sth, speak, etc. under your ˈbreath** to say sth quietly so that people cannot hear: *'Rubbish!' he murmured under his breath.* ◇ **take sb's ˈbreath away** to be very surprising or beautiful: *My first view of the island from the air took my breath away.*—more at BATED, CATCH *v.*, DRAW *v.*, SAVE *v.*, WASTE *v.*

breath·able /ˈbriːðəbl/ *adj.* (*technical*) (of fabric used in making clothes) allowing air to pass through: *Breathable, waterproof clothing is essential for most outdoor sports.*

breath·alyse (*BrE*) (*AmE* **breath·alyze**) /ˈbreθəlaɪz/ *verb* [VN] [usually passive] to check how much alcohol a driver has drunk by making him or her breathe into a breathalyser: *Both drivers were breathalysed at the scene of the accident.*

breath·alyser (*BrE*) (*AmE* **Breath·alyzer**™) /ˈbreθəlaɪzə(r)/ *noun* a device used by the police to measure the amount of alcohol in a driver's breath

breathe /briːð/ *verb*

AIR/BREATH | **1** to take air into your lungs and send it out again through your nose or mouth: [V] *He breathed deeply before speaking again.* ◇ *The air was so cold we could hardly breathe.* ◇ *She was beginning to breathe more easily.* ◇ [VN] *Most people don't realize that they are breathing polluted air.* **2** [VN] to send air, smoke or a particular smell out of your mouth: *He came up close, breathing alcohol fumes all over me.*

SAY QUIETLY | **3** (*literary*) to say sth quietly: [V speech] *'I'm over here,' she breathed.* [also VN]

OF WINE | **4** [V] if you allow wine to **breathe**, you open the bottle and let air get in before you drink it

OF FABRIC/SKIN | **5** [V] if fabric, leather, skin, etc. can **breathe**, air can move around or through it: *Cotton clothing allows your skin to breathe.*

FEELING/QUALITY | **6** [VN] (*formal*) to be full of a particular feeling or quality: *Her performance breathed wit and charm.*

[IDM] **breathe (easily/freely) again** to feel calm again after sth unpleasant or frightening has ended ◇ **breathe down sb's ˈneck** (*informal*) to watch closely what sb is doing in a way that makes them feel anxious and/or annoyed ◇ **breathe (new) ˈlife into sth** to improve sth by introducing new ideas and making people more interested in it ◇ **breathe your ˈlast** (*literary*) to die—more at LIVE[1]

[PHRV] **breathe ˈin** to take air into your lungs through your nose or mouth ◇ **breathe sth↔ˈin** to take air, smoke, etc. into your lungs through your nose or mouth: *His illness is a result of breathing in paint fumes over many years.* ◇ **breathe ˈout** to send air out of your lungs through your nose or mouth ◇ **breathe sth↔ˈout** to send air, smoke, etc. out of your lungs through your nose or mouth: *Humans take in oxygen and breathe out carbon dioxide.*

breather /ˈbriːðə(r)/ *noun* (*informal*) a short pause for rest or to relax: *Tell me when you need a breather.* ◇ *to take/have a five-minute breather*—see also HEAVY BREATHER

breath·ing /ˈbriːðɪŋ/ *noun* [U] the action of taking air into the lungs and sending it out again: *Her breathing became steady and she fell asleep.* ◇ *Deep breathing exercises will help you relax.* ◇ *Heavy* (= loud) *breathing was all I could hear.*

ˈbreathing space *noun* [C, U] a short rest in the middle of a period of mental or physical effort

breath·less /ˈbreθləs/ *adj.* **1** having difficulty in breathing; making it difficult for sb to breathe: *He arrived breathless at the top of the stairs.* ◇ *They maintained a breathless* (= very fast) *pace for half an hour.* **2 ~ (with sth)** (*written*) experiencing, or making sb experience, a strong emotional reaction: *breathless with terror* ◇ *the breathless excitement of seeing each other again* **3** (*written*) with no air or wind: *the breathless heat of a summer afternoon* ▶ **breath·less·ly** *adv.* **breath·less·ness** *noun* [U]

s	t	v	z	ʃ	ʒ	tʃ	dʒ	θ	ð	ŋ
see	tea	van	zoo	shoe	vision	chain	jam	thin	this	sing

breath·tak·ing /ˈbreθteɪkɪŋ/ *adj.* very exciting or impressive (usually in a pleasant way); very surprising: *a breathtaking view of the mountains* ◊ *The scene was one of breathtaking beauty.* ◊ *He spoke with breathtaking arrogance.* ▶ **breath·tak·ing·ly** *adv.*: *a breathtakingly expensive diamond*

'**breath test** *noun* a test used by the police to show the amount of alcohol in a driver's breath

breathy /ˈbreθi/ *adj.* speaking or singing with a noticeable sound of breathing

bred *pt, pp* of BREED

breech /briːtʃ/ *noun* the part of a gun at the back where the bullets are loaded

'**breech birth** (also ,**breech de·livery**) *noun* a birth in which the baby's bottom or feet come out of the mother first

breeches /ˈbrɪtʃɪz/ *noun* [pl.] short trousers/pants fastened just below the knee: *a pair of breeches* ◊ *riding breeches*

breed /briːd/ *verb, noun*
■ *verb* (**bred, bred** /bred/) **1** [V] (of animals) to have sex and produce young: *Many animals breed only at certain times of the year.*—see also INTERBREED **2** [VN] ~ **sth** (**for/as sth**) to keep animals or plants in order to produce young ones in a controlled way: *The rabbits are bred for their long coats.*—see also CROSS-BRED, PURE-BRED, THOROUGHBRED **3** [VN] to be the cause of sth: *Nothing breeds success like success.* **4** [VN] [usually passive] ~ **sth into sb** to educate sb in a particular way as they are growing up: *Fear of failure was bred into him at an early age.*—see also WELL BRED IDM see BORN *v.*, FAMILIARITY
■ *noun* **1** a particular type of animal that has been developed by people in a controlled way, especially a type of dog, cat or farm animal: *Labradors and other large breeds of dog* ◊ *a breed of cattle/sheep* **2** [usually sing.] a type of person: *He represents a new breed of politician.* ◊ *Players as skilful as this are **a rare breed**.*

breed·er /ˈbriːdə(r)/ *noun* a person who breeds animals: *a dog/horse/cattle breeder*

breed·ing /ˈbriːdɪŋ/ *noun* [U] **1** the keeping of animals in order to breed from them: *the breeding of horses* **2** the producing of young animals, plants, etc: *the breeding season* **3** the family or social background that is thought to result in good manners: *a sign of good breeding*

'**breeding ground** *noun* **1** [usually pl.] a place where wild animals go to produce their young **2** ~ (**for sth**) [usually sing.] a place where sth, especially sth bad, is able to develop: *This area of the city has become a breeding ground for violent crime.*

breeze /briːz/ *noun, verb*
■ *noun* **1** [C] a light wind: *a sea breeze* ◊ *The flowers were gently swaying **in the breeze**.* ◊ *A light breeze was blowing.* **2** [sing.] (*informal*) a thing that is easy to do: *It was a breeze.* IDM see SHOOT *v.*
■ *verb* [V+*adv./prep.*] to move in a cheerful and confident way in a particular direction: *She just breezed in and asked me to help.* PHRV ,**breeze 'through sth** to do sth successfully and easily: *He breezed through the tests.*

'**breeze block** (*BrE*) (*AmE* '**cinder block**) *noun* a light building block, made of sand, coal ashes and CEMENT

breezy /ˈbriːzi/ *adj.* **1** with the wind blowing quite strongly: *It was a bright, breezy day.* ◊ *the breezy east coast* **2** having or showing a cheerful and relaxed manner: *You're very bright and breezy today!* ▶ **breez·ily** /ˈbriːzɪli/ *adv.*: *'Hi folks,' he said breezily.* **breezi·ness** /ˈbriːzinəs/ *noun* [U]

breth·ren /ˈbreðrən/ *noun* [pl.] (*old-fashioned*) **1** used to talk to people in church or to talk about the members of a male religious group: *Let us pray, brethren.* **2** people who are part of the same society as yourself: *We should do all we can to help our less fortunate brethren.*

brev·ity /ˈbrevəti/ *noun* [U] (*formal*) **1** the quality of using few words when speaking or writing: *The report is a masterpiece of brevity.* **2** the fact of lasting a short time: *the brevity of human life*—see also BRIEF

brew /bruː/ *verb, noun*

■ *verb* **1** to make beer: [VN] *The beer is brewed in the Czech Republic.* [alsoV] **2** [VN] to make a hot drink of tea or coffee: *freshly brewed coffee* **3** [V] (*especially BrE*) (of tea or coffee) to mix with hot water and become ready to drink: *Always let tea brew for a few minutes.* **4** [V] ~ (**up**) (usually used in the progressive tenses) if sth unpleasant is **brewing** or **brewing up**, it seems likely to happen soon PHRV ,**brew 'up**|,**brew sth**↔'**up** (*BrE, informal*) to make a hot drink of tea or coffee: *Whose turn is it to brew up?*—related noun BREW-UP
■ *noun* **1** [C, U] a type of beer, especially one made in a particular place: *I thought I'd try the local brew.* ◊ *home brew* (= beer made at home) **2** [C, usually sing.] (*BrE, informal*) an amount of tea made at one time: *I'll make a fresh brew.* ◊ *Let's have a brew.* **3** [C, usually sing.] a mixture of different ideas, circumstances, events, etc: *The movie is a potent brew of adventure, sex and comedy.* ◊ *His music is **a heady brew** (= a powerful mixture) of heavy metal and punk.* IDM **a witch's/an evil 'brew** (*BrE*) an unpleasant drink that is a mixture of different things

brew·er /ˈbruːə(r)/ *noun* a person or company that makes beer

brew·ery /ˈbruːəri/ *noun* (*pl.* **-ies**) a factory where beer is made; a company that makes beer

'**brew-up** *noun* (*BrE, informal*) an act of making tea: *We always have a brew-up at 11 o'clock.*

briar (also **brier**) /ˈbraɪə(r)/ *noun* **1** any prickly wild bush, especially a wild rose bush **2** a bush with a hard root that is used for making tobacco pipes; a tobacco pipe made from this root

bribe /braɪb/ *noun, verb*
■ *noun* a sum of money or sth valuable that you give or offer to sb to persuade them to help you, especially by doing sth dishonest: *It was alleged that he had **taken bribes** while in office.* ◊ *She had been **offered** a $50000 bribe to drop the charges.*
■ *verb* ~ **sb** (**with sth**)| ~ **sb** (**into doing sth**) to give sb money or sth valuable in order to persuade them to help you, especially by doing sth dishonest: [VN] *They bribed the guards with cigarettes.* ◊ *She was bribed into handing over secret information.* ◊ *He managed to **bribe his way** onto the ship.* [alsoVN to inf]

brib·ery /ˈbraɪbəri/ *noun* [U] the giving or taking of bribes: *She was arrested on bribery charges.* ◊ *allegations of bribery and corruption*

bric-a-brac /ˈbrɪk ə bræk/ *noun* [U] ornaments and other small decorative objects of little value: *market stalls selling cheap bric-a-brac*

brick /brɪk/ *noun, verb*
■ *noun* **1** [C, U] baked clay used for building walls, houses and other buildings; an individual block of this: *The school is built of brick.* ◊ *a pile of bricks* ◊ *a brick wall*—see also RED-BRICK—picture at HOUSE **2** [C] a plastic or wooden block, used as a toy for young children to build things with **3** [C, usually sing.] (*old-fashioned, BrE, informal*) a friend that you can rely on when you need help IDM **be up against a brick 'wall** to be unable to make any progress because there is a difficulty that stops you **bricks and 'mortar** a building, when you are thinking of it in connection with how much it cost to build or how much it is worth: *A home isn't just bricks and mortar.* **make bricks without 'straw** (*BrE*) to try to work without the necessary material, money, information, etc.—more at CAT *n.*, DROP *v.*, HEAD *n.*, TON *n.*
■ *verb* PHRV ,**brick sth**↔'**in/'up** to fill an opening in a wall with bricks: *The windows had been bricked up.*

brick·bat /ˈbrɪkbæt/ *noun* [usually pl.] an insulting remark made in public

brick·lay·er /ˈbrɪkleɪə(r)/ (also *BrE informal* **brickie**) *noun* a person whose job is to build walls, etc. with bricks ▶ **brick·lay·ing** *noun* [U]

brick·work /ˈbrɪkwɜːk; *AmE* -wɜːrk/ *noun* **1** [U] the bricks in a wall, building, etc: *Plaster had fallen away in places, exposing the brickwork.* **2** (**brick·works**) [C] (*pl.* **brick·works**) (*BrE*) a place where bricks are made

bri·dal /ˈbraɪdl/ *adj.* [only before noun] connected with a

æ	ɑː	e	ɜː	ə	ɪ	iː	i	ɒ	ɔː	ʌ	ʊ	u	uː
cat	father	ten	bird	about	sit	see	many	got	saw	cup	put	actual	too
								(BrE)					

BRIDE or a wedding: *a bridal gown* ◊ *the bridal party* (= the bride and the people helping her at her wedding) ◊ *a bridal suite* (= a set of rooms in a hotel for a couple who have just got married) ◊ *(AmE) a bridal shower* (= a party for a woman who will get married soon)

bride /braɪd/ *noun* a woman on her wedding day, or just before or just after it: *a toast to the **bride and groom*** ◊ *He introduced his new bride.*

bride·groom /ˈbraɪdgruːm/ (also **groom**) *noun* a man on his wedding day, or just before or just after it

brides·maid /ˈbraɪdzmeɪd/ *noun* a young woman or girl who helps a BRIDE before and during the marriage ceremony: *Jo asked her sister to be (a) bridesmaid.*—compare BEST MAN, PAGEBOY

bridge /brɪdʒ/ *noun, verb*
■ *noun*
OVER ROAD/RIVER | **1** [C] a structure that is built over a road, railway/railroad, river, etc. so that people or vehicles can cross from one side to the other: *We crossed the bridge over the river Windrush.*—see also SUSPENSION BRIDGE, SWING BRIDGE
CONNECTION | **2** [C] a thing that provides a connection or contact between two different things: *Cultural exchanges are a way of **building bridges** between countries.*
OF SHIP | **3** (usually **the bridge**) the part of a ship where the captain and other officers stand when they are controlling and steering the ship: *Who was on the bridge when the collision took place?*
CARD GAME | **4** [U] a card game for two pairs of players who have to predict how many cards they will win. They score points if they succeed in winning that number of cards and lose points if they fail.
OF NOSE | **5 the ~ of sb's nose** [sing.] the hard part at the top of the nose, between the eyes
OF GLASSES | **6** [C] the part of a pair of glasses that rests on your nose—picture at GLASS
OF GUITAR/VIOLIN | **7** [C] a small piece of wood on a guitar, violin, etc. over which the strings are stretched.
FALSE TEETH | **8** [C] a false tooth or false teeth that are held permanently in place by being fastened to natural teeth on either side
IDM see BURN *v.*, CROSS *v.*, WATER *n.*
■ *verb*
BUILD/FORM BRIDGE | [VN] to build or form a bridge over sth: *The valley was originally bridged by the Romans.* ◊ *A plank of wood bridged the stream.*
IDM **bridge the ˈgap/ˈgulf/diˈvide (between A and B)** to reduce or get rid of the differences that exist between two things or groups of people

bridge·head /ˈbrɪdʒhed/ *noun* **1** a strong position that an army has captured in enemy land, from which it can go forward or attack the enemy **2** [usually sing.] (*written*) a good position from which to make progress: *This agreement will be a bridgehead for further talks.*

ˈbridging loan *noun* (*BrE*) an amount of money that a bank lends you for a short time, especially so that you can buy a new house while you are waiting to sell your old one

bridle /ˈbraɪdl/ *noun, verb*
■ *noun* a set of leather bands, attached to REINS, which is put around a horse's head and used for controlling it
■ *verb* **1** [VN] to put a bridle on a horse **2** [V] **~ (at sth)** (*literary*) to show that you are annoyed and/or offended at sth, especially by moving your head up and backwards in a proud way: *She bridled at the suggestion that she was lying.*

ˈbridle path (*BrE* also **bridle·way**) *noun* a rough path that is suitable for people riding horses or walking, but not for cars

Brie /briː/ *noun* [U, C] a type of soft French cheese

brief /briːf/ *adj., noun, verb*
■ *adj.* (**brief·er, brief·est**) **1** lasting only a short time; short: *a brief visit/meeting/conversation* ◊ *a brief pause/silence* ◊ *Mozart's life was brief.* **2** using few words: *a brief description/summary/account* ◊ *Please be brief* (= say what you want to say quickly). **3** (of clothes) short and

not covering much of the body: *a brief skirt*—see also BREVITY, BRIEFLY **IDM in brief** in a few words, without details: *In brief, the meeting was a disaster.* ◊ *Now the rest of the news in brief.*
■ *noun*—see also BRIEFS **1** (*BrE*) the instructions that a person is given explaining what their job is and what their duties are: *It wasn't part of his brief to speak to the press.* ◊ *I was given the brief of reorganizing the department.* ◊ *to stick to your brief* (= to only do what you are asked to do) ◊ *to prepare/produce a brief for sb* **2** (*BrE, law*) a legal case that is given to a lawyer to argue in court; a piece of work for a BARRISTER **3** (*AmE, law*) a written summary of the facts that support one side of a legal case, that will be presented to a court **4** (*BrE, informal*) a SOLICITOR or a defence lawyer: *I want to see my brief.* **IDM hold no brief for sb/sth** (*BrE, formal*) to not support or be in favour of sb/sth: *I hold no brief for either side in this war.*
■ *verb* **1 ~ sb (on/about sth)** to give sb information about sth so that they are prepared to deal with it: [VN] *The officer briefed her on what to expect.* ◊ *I expect to be kept fully briefed at all times.* [also VN to inf] —compare DEBRIEF **2** [VN, VN to inf] (*BrE, law*) to give a lawyer, especially a BARRISTER, the main facts of a legal case so that it can be argued in a court of law

brief·case /ˈbriːfkeɪs/ *noun* a flat case used for carrying papers and documents—compare ATTACHÉ CASE—picture at BAG

brief·ing /ˈbriːfɪŋ/ *noun* **1** [C] a meeting in which people are given instructions or information: *a press briefing* **2** [C, U] the detailed instructions or information that are given at such a meeting: *Captain Trent gave his men a full briefing.* ◊ *a briefing session/paper*

brief·ly /ˈbriːfli/ *adv.* **1** for a short time: *He had spoken to Emma only briefly.* **2** in few words: *Briefly, the argument is as follows ...* ◊ *Let me tell you briefly what happened.*

briefs /briːfs/ *noun* [pl.] men's UNDERPANTS or women's KNICKERS: *a pair of briefs*

brier = BRIAR

brig /brɪg/ *noun* **1** a ship with two MASTS (= posts that support the sails) and square sails **2** (*AmE*) a prison, especially one on a WARSHIP

Brig. *abbr.* (in writing) BRIGADIER

bri·gade /brɪˈgeɪd/ *noun* **1** a large group of soldiers that forms a unit of an army **2** [usually sing.] (often *disapproving*) used, always with a word or phrase in front of it, to describe a group of people who share the same opinions or are similar in some other way: *the anti-smoking brigade*—see also FIRE BRIGADE **IDM** see HEAVY *adj.*

briga·dier /ˌbrɪgəˈdɪə(r)/; *AmE* -ˈdɪr/ *noun* (*abbr.* **Brig.**) an officer of high rank in the British army: *Brigadier Michael Swift*

ˌbrigadier ˈgeneral *noun* an officer of high rank in the US army, air force and MARINES

brig·and /ˈbrɪgənd/ *noun* (*old-fashioned*) a member of a group of criminals that robs people, especially one that attacks travellers

bright /braɪt/ *adj., adv.*
■ *adj.* (**bright·er, bright·est**) **1** full of light; shining strongly: *bright light/sunshine* ◊ *a bright room* ◊ *Her eyes were bright with tears.* ◊ *a bright morning* (= with the sun shining) **2** (of a colour) strong and easy to see: *I like bright colours.* ◊ *a bright yellow dress* ◊ *Jack's face turned bright red.* **3** cheerful and lively: *His eyes were bright and excited.* ◊ *She gave me a bright smile.* ◊ *Why are you so bright and cheerful today?* ◊ *His face was bright with excitement.* **4** intelligent; quick to learn: *the brightest pupil in the class* ◊ *Do you have any bright ideas* (= clever ideas)? **5** hopeful; likely to be successful: *This young musician has a bright future.* ◊ *Prospects for the coming year look bright.* ◊ *a bright start to the week* ▶ **bright·ly** *adv.*: *a brightly lit room* ◊ *'Hi!' she called brightly.* **brightness** *noun* [U] **IDM bright and ˈearly** very early in the morning: *You're up bright and early today!* **(as) bright as a ˈbutton** (*BrE*) intelligent and quick to understand **the bright ˈlights** the excitement of city life: *Although he grew up in the country, he's always had a taste for the*

bright lights. **a bright ˈspark** (*BrE, informal,* often *ironic*) a lively and intelligent person, especially sb young: *Some bright spark* (= stupid person) *left the tap running all night*. **a/the ˈbright spot** a good or pleasant part of sth that is unpleasant or bad in all other ways: *The win last week was the only bright spot in their last ten games*. **look on the ˈbright side** to be cheerful or hopeful about a bad situation, for example by thinking only of the advantages and not the disadvantages

▪ *adv.* (**bright·er, bright·est**) (*literary*) (usually with the verbs *burn* and *shine*) brightly: *The stars were shining bright*.

bright·en /ˈbraɪtn/ *verb* **1** to become or make sth lighter or brighter in colour: [V] *In the distance, the sky was beginning to brighten.* ◊ [VN] *a shampoo to brighten and condition your hair* **2** ~ (**sth**) (**up**) to become, feel or look happier; to make sb look happier: [V] *Her eyes brightened.* ◊ *He brightened up at their words of encouragement.* ◊ [VN] *A smile brightened her face.* **3** ~ (**sth**) (**up**) to become or make sth become more pleasant, enjoyable or hopeful: [VN] *A personal letter will usually brighten up a person's day.* [alsoV] **4** [VN] ~ **sth** (**up**) to make sth look more colourful and attractive: *Fresh flowers will brighten up any room in the house.* **5** [V] ~ (**up**) (of the weather) to improve and become brighter: *According to the forecast, it should brighten up later.*

ˌbright-ˈeyed (also *less frequent* ˌbright-eyed and ˌbushy-ˈtailed) *adj.* (of a person) full of interest and enthusiasm

brill /brɪl/ *adj.* (*BrE, informal*) very good

bril·liant /ˈbrɪliənt/ *adj.* **1** extremely clever or impressive: *What a brilliant idea!* ◊ *a brilliant performance/invention* **2** very successful: *a brilliant career* ◊ *The play was a brilliant success.* **3** very intelligent or skilful: *a brilliant young scientist* ◊ *She has one of the most brilliant minds in the country.* **4** (of light or colours) very bright: *brilliant sunshine* ◊ *brilliant blue eyes* **5** (*BrE, spoken*) very good; excellent: *'How was it?' 'Brilliant!'* ◊ *Thanks. You've been brilliant* (= very kind). ▶ **bril·liance** /ˈbrɪliəns/ *noun* [U] **bril·li·ant·ly** *adv.: The plan worked brilliantly.* ◊ *It was brilliantly sunny.*

brim /brɪm/ *noun, verb*

▪ *noun* **1** the top edge of a cup, bowl, glass, etc: *two wine glasses, filled to the brim* **2** the flat edge around the bottom of a hat that sticks out—picture at HAT **3** (**-brimmed**) (in adjectives) having the type of brim mentioned: *a wide-brimmed hat*

▪ *verb* (**-mm-**) [V] ~ (**with sth**) to be full of sth; to fill sth: *Her eyes brimmed with tears.* ◊ *Tears brimmed in her eyes.* ◊ *The team were brimming with confidence before the game.*
PHRV ˌbrim ˈover (**with sth**) (of a cup, container, etc.) to be so full of a liquid that it flows over the edge **SYN** OVERFLOW: (*figurative*) *Her heart was brimming over with happiness.*

brim·ful /ˈbrɪmfʊl/ *adj.* (*especially BrE*) ~ **of sth** completely full of sth: *She's certainly brimful of energy.* ◊ *a jug brimful of cream*

brim·stone /ˈbrɪmstəʊn; *AmE* -stoʊn/ *noun* (*old use*) the chemical element SULPHUR

brin·dle /ˈbrɪndl/ (also **brin·dled** /ˈbrɪndld/) *adj.* (of dogs, cats and cows) brown with bands or marks of another colour

brine /braɪn/ *noun* [U] very salty water, used especially for preserving food—see also BRINY

bring /brɪŋ/ *verb* (**brought, brought** /brɔːt/)
COME WITH SB/STH | **1** ~ **sb/sth** (**with you**)| ~ **sth** (**for sb**)| ~ (**sb**) **sth** to come to a place with sb/sth: [VN] *Don't forget to bring your books with you.* ◊ *She brought her boyfriend to the party.* ◊ [VN, VNN] *Bring a present for Helen.* ◊ *Bring Helen a present.*
PROVIDE | **2** ~ **sb/sth sth**| ~ **sth to sb/sth** to provide sb/sth with sth: [VNN] *His writing brings him $10000 a year.* ◊ [VN] *The team's new manager brings ten years' experience to the job.*
CAUSE | **3** [VN] to cause sth: *The revolution brought many changes.* ◊ *The news brought tears to his eyes* (= made him cry). ◊ *Retirement usually brings with it a massive*

drop in income. **4** [VN+*adv./prep.*] to cause sb/sth to be in a particular condition or place: *to bring a meeting to an end/a close/a conclusion* ◊ *Bring the water to the boil.* ◊ *The article brought her into conflict with the authorities.* ◊ *Hello Simon! What brings you here?*
MAKE SB/STH MOVE | **5** to make sb/sth move in a particular direction or way: [VN+*adv./prep.*] *The judge brought his hammer down on the table.* ◊ [VN-*ing*] *Her cries brought the neighbours running* (= made them run to her).
ACCUSATION | **6** [VN] ~ **sth** (**against sb**) to officially accuse sb of a crime: *to bring a charge/a legal action/an accusation against sb*
FORCE YOURSELF | **7** [VNtoinf] ~ **yourself to do sth** to force yourself to do sth: *She could not bring herself to tell him the news.*
IDM Idioms containing **bring** are at the entries for the nouns and adjectives in the idioms, for example **bring sb/sth to heel** is at **heel**.
PHRV ˌbring sth↔aˈbout to make sth happen **SYN** CAUSE: *What brought about the change in his attitude?*
ˌbring sb aˈround (*AmE*) = BRING SB ROUND ˌbring sth aˈround (*AmE*) = BRING STH ROUND
ˌbring sb/sth↔ˈback to return sb/sth: *Please bring back all library books by the end of the week.* ◊ *He brought me back* (= gave me a ride home) *in his car.* ˌbring sth↔ˈback **1** to make sb remember sth or think about it again: *The photographs brought back many pleasant memories.* **2** to make sth that existed before be introduced again **SYN** REINTRODUCE: *Most people are against bringing back the death penalty.* ˌbring sb sth↔ˈback| ˌbring sth↔ˈback (**for sb**) to return with sth for sb: *What did you bring the kids back from Italy?* ◊ *I brought a T-shirt back for Mark.*
ˈbring sb/sth before sb (*formal*) to present sb/sth for discussion or judgement: *The matter will be brought before the committee.* ◊ *He was brought before the court and found guilty.*
ˌbring sb↔ˈdown **1** to make sb lose power or be defeated: *The scandal may bring down the government.* **2** (in football and rugby) to make sb fall over: *He was brought down in the penalty area.* ˌbring sth↔ˈdown **1** to lower or reduce sth: *We aim to bring down prices on all our computers.* **2** to land an aircraft: *The pilot managed to bring the plane down in a field.* **3** to make an aircraft fall out of the sky: *Twelve enemy fighters had been brought down.* **4** to make an animal or a bird fall down or fall out of the sky by killing or wounding it: *He brought down the bear with a single shot.*
ˌbring sb/sth↔ˈforth (*old use* or *formal*) to give birth to sb; to produce sth: *She brought forth a son.* ◊ *trees bringing forth fruit*
ˌbring sth↔ˈforward **1** to move sth to an earlier date or time: *The meeting has been brought forward from 10 May to 3 May.* **2** to suggest sth for discussion: *Please bring the matter forward at the next meeting.* **3** to move a total sum from the bottom of one page or column of numbers to the top of the next: *A credit balance of $50 was brought forward from his September account.*
ˌbring sb↔ˈin **1** to ask sb to do a particular job or to be involved in sth: *Local residents were angry at not being brought in on* (= asked for their opinion about) *the new housing proposal.* ◊ [+toinf] *Experts were brought in to advise the government.* **2** (of the police) to bring sb to a police station in order to ask them questions or arrest them: *Two men were brought in for questioning.* ˌbring sth↔ˈin **1** to introduce a new law: *They want to bring in a bill to limit arms exports.* **2** to attract sb/sth to a place or business: *We need to bring in a lot more new business.* **3** to give a decision in a court of law: *The jury brought in a verdict of guilty.* ˌbring sb ˈin sth| ˌbring ˈin sth to make or earn a particular amount of money: *His freelance work brings him in about $20000 a year.* ◊ *How much does she bring in now?*
ˌbring sth↔ˈoff to succeed in doing sth difficult: *It was a difficult task but we brought it off.* ◊ *The goalie brought off a superb save.*
ˌbring sb↔ˈon to help sb develop or improve while they are learning to do sth ˌbring sth↔ˈon **1** to make sth

B

develop, usually sth unpleasant $\boxed{\text{SYN}}$ CAUSE: *He was suffering from stress brought on by overwork.* **2** to make crops, fruit, etc. grow well ,bring sth 'on yourself/sb to be responsible for sth unpleasant that happens to you/sb: *I have no sympathy—you brought it all on yourself.* ,bring sb↔'out (*BrE*) to make people go on strike ,bring sb 'out of himself, herself, etc. to help sb to feel more confident: *She's a shy girl who needs friends to bring her out of herself.* ,bring sth↔'out **1** to make sth appear: *A crisis brings out the best in her.* **2** to make sth easy to see or understand: *That dress really brings out the colour of your eyes.* **3** to produce sth; to publish sth: *The band have just brought out their second album.* ,bring sth 'out in sth to make sb's skin be covered in spots, etc: *The heat brought him out in a rash.*
,bring sb 'round (*BrE*) (*AmE* ,bring sb a'round) (also ,bring sb 'to) to make sb who is unconscious become conscious again ,bring sb 'round (to ...) (*BrE*) (*AmE* ,bring sb a'round) to bring sb to sb's house: *Bring the family round one evening; we'd love to meet them.* ,bring sb 'round (to sth) (*BrE*) (*AmE* ,bring sb a'round) to persuade sb to agree to sth: *He didn't like the plan at first, but we managed to bring him round.* ,bring sth 'round to sth (*BrE*) (*AmE* ,bring sth a'round to sth) to direct a conversation to a particular subject
,bring sb 'to = BRING SB ROUND
,bring A and B to'gether to help two people or groups to end a quarrel: *The loss of their son brought the two of them together.*
,bring sb↔'up **1** [often passive] to care for a child, teaching him or her how to behave, etc: *She brought up five children.* ◊ *He was brought up by his aunt.* ◊ *a well/badly brought up child* ◊[+to inf] *They were brought up to (= taught as children to) respect authority.* ◊[+N] *I was brought up a Catholic.*—compare RAISE—related noun UPBRINGING **2** (*law*) to make sb appear for trial: *He was brought up on a charge of drunken driving.* ,bring sth↔'up **1** to mention a subject or start to talk about it $\boxed{\text{SYN}}$ RAISE: *Bring it up at the meeting.* **2** (*BrE*) to VOMIT: *to bring up your lunch* **3** to make sth appear on a computer screen: *Click with the right mouse button to bring up a new menu.* ,bring sb 'up against sth to force sb to know about sth and have to deal with it: *Working in the slums brought her up against the realities of poverty.*

,bring-and-'buy sale *noun* (*BrE*) ·a sale, usually for charity, at which people bring things for sale and buy those brought by others

brink /brɪŋk/ *noun* [sing.] **1 the ~ (of sth)** if you are on the **brink** of sth, you are almost in a very new, dangerous or exciting situation: *on the brink of collapse/war/death/disaster* ◊ *Scientists are on the brink of making a major new discovery.* ◊ *He's pulled the company **back from the brink** (= he has saved it from disaster).* **2** (*literary*) the extreme edge of land, for example at the top of a cliff or by a river: *the brink of the precipice* $\boxed{\text{IDM}}$ see TEETER

brink·man·ship /'brɪŋkmənʃɪp/ (*AmE* also **brinks·man·ship** /'brɪŋks-/) *noun* [U] the activity, especially in politics, of getting into a situation that could be very dangerous in order to frighten people and make them do what you want

briny /'braɪni/ *adj.* (of water) containing a lot of salt—see also BRINE

brio /'briːəʊ; *AmE* 'briːoʊ/ *noun* [U] (*written*) enthusiasm and individual style

bri·quette /brɪ'ket/ *noun* a small hard block made from coal dust and used as fuel

brisk /brɪsk/ *adj.* (*comparative* **brisk·er** no *superlative*) **1** quick; busy: *a brisk walk* ◊ *to set off at a brisk pace* ◊ *Ice-cream vendors were doing a brisk trade* (= selling a lot of ice cream). **2** (of a person, their voice or manner) practical and confident; showing a desire to get things done quickly: *His tone became brisk and businesslike.* **3** (of wind and the weather) cold but pleasantly fresh: *a brisk wind/breeze* ▶ **brisk·ly** *adv.* **brisk·ness** *noun* [U]

bris·ket /'brɪskɪt/ *noun* [U] meat that comes from the chest of an animal, especially a cow

bris·tle /'brɪsl/ *noun, verb*

■ *noun* **1** a short stiff hair: *the bristles on his chin* **2** one of the short stiff hairs or wires in a brush
■ *verb* [V] **1 ~ (with sth) (at sth)** to suddenly become very annoyed or offended at what sb says or does: *His lies made her bristle with rage.* **2** (of an animal's fur) to stand up on the back and neck because the animal is frightened or angry $\boxed{\text{PHR V}}$ 'bristle with sth (*written*) to contain a large number of sth: *The whole subject bristles with problems.*

brist·ly /'brɪsli/ *adj.* like or full of bristles; rough: *a bristly chin/moustache*

Brit /brɪt/ *noun* (*informal*) a person from Britain ⇨ note at BRITISH

Brit·ish /'brɪtɪʃ/ *adj.* **1** (*abbr.* **Br.**) connected with the United Kingdom of Great Britain and Northern Ireland or the people who live there: *the British Government* ◊ *He was born in France but his parents are British.* ◊ *British-based/British-born/British-made* **2 (the British)** *noun* [pl.] the people of the United Kingdom ▶ **Brit·ish·ness** *noun* [U]

> **WHICH WORD?**
> **British / English / Briton / Brit**
>
> There is no noun which is commonly used to refer to the people of Britain. Instead the adjective **British** is used: *She's British.* ◊ *The British have a very odd sense of humour.* The adjective **English** refers only to people from England, not the rest of the United Kingdom.
> The noun **Briton** is used mainly in newspapers: *The survivors of the avalanche included 12 Britons.* It also describes the early inhabitants of Britain: *the ancient Britons.* **Brit** is informal and can sound negative. **Britisher** is now very old-fashioned.
>
> ⇨ note at SCOTTISH

,British 'English *noun* [U] the English language as spoken in Britain

Brit·ish·er /'brɪtɪʃə(r)/ *noun* (*AmE, informal*) a person from Britain

Briton /'brɪtn/ *noun* (*formal*) a person from Britain: *the ancient Britons* ◊ *the first Briton to climb Everest without oxygen* ⇨ note at BRITISH

Brit·pop /'brɪtpɒp; *AmE* -pɑːp/ *noun* [U] a type of popular music played by British groups in the 1990s, influenced by a variety of British musical traditions

brit·tle /'brɪtl/ *adj.* **1** hard but easily broken: *brittle bones/nails* **2** a **brittle** mood or state of mind is one that appears to be happy or strong but is actually nervous and easily damaged: *brittle confidence/gaiety* ◊ *a brittle temperament* **3** (of a sound) hard and sharp in an unpleasant way: *a brittle laugh* ▶ **brittle·ness** *noun* [U]

bro /brəʊ; *AmE* broʊ/ *noun* (*pl.* **bros**) (*spoken*) **1** a brother **2** (*especially AmE*) a friendly way of addressing a male person: *Thanks, bro!*

broach /brəʊtʃ; *AmE* broʊtʃ/ *verb* [VN] **~ (sth) (to/with sb)** to begin talking about a subject that is difficult to discuss, especially because it is embarrassing or because people disagree about it: *She was dreading having to broach the subject of money to her father.*

,**B-road** *noun* (in Britain) a road that is less important than an A-ROAD and usually joins small towns and villages

broad /brɔːd/ *adj., noun*
■ *adj.* (**broad·er, broad·est**)
▸ WIDE ◂ **1** wide: *a broad street/avenue/river* ◊ *broad shoulders* ◊ *He is tall, broad and muscular.* ◊ *a broad smile/grin* (= one in which your mouth is stretched very wide because you are very pleased or amused) $\boxed{\text{OPP}}$ NARROW (1) **2** used after a measurement of distance to show how wide sth is: *two metres broad and one metre high*
▸ WIDE RANGE ◂ **3** including a great variety of people or things: *a broad range of products* ◊ *a broad spectrum of interests* ◊ *There is broad support for the government's policies.* ◊ *She took a broad view of the duties of being a*

teacher (= she believed her duties included a wide range of things). OPP NARROW

GENERAL | **4** [only before noun] general; not detailed: *the broad outline of a proposal* ◇ *The negotiators were in broad agreement on the main issues.* ◇ *She's a feminist, in the broadest sense of the word.* ◇ *In broad terms, the paper argues that each country should develop its own policy.* OPP NARROW

LAND/WATER | **5** covering a wide area: *a broad expanse of water*

ACCENT | **6** if sb has a **broad accent**, you can hear very easily which area they come from: *a broad Yorkshire accent*

HINT | **7** if sb gives a **broad hint**, they make it very clear what they are thinking or what they want

—see also BREADTH, BROADLY ⇨ note at WIDE

IDM **a broad 'church** (*BrE*) an organization that accepts a wide range of opinions **(in) broad 'daylight** (in) the clear light of day, when it is easy to see: *The robbery occurred in broad daylight, in a crowded street.* **it's as ˌbroad as it's 'long** (*BrE, spoken*) it makes no real difference which of two possible choices you make—more at PAINT *v.*

■ *noun* (*old-fashioned, AmE, slang*) an offensive way of referring to a woman

ˌbroad-'based (also ˌbroadly-'based) *adj.* based on a wide variety of people, things or ideas; not limited: *broad-based support*

ˌbroad 'bean *noun* (*BrE*) a type of round, pale green bean. Several broad beans grow together inside a fat POD.

'broad-brush *adj.* [only before noun] dealing with a subject or problem in a general way rather than considering details: *a broad-brush approach*

broad·cast /'brɔ:dka:st; *AmE* -kæst/ *verb, noun*

■ *verb* (broad·cast, broad·cast) **1** to send out programmes on television or radio: [VN] *The concert will be broadcast live* (= at the same time as it takes place) *tomorrow evening.* ◇ [V] *They began broadcasting in 1922.* **2** [VN] to tell a lot of people about sth: *I don't like to broadcast the fact that my father owns the company.*

■ *noun* a radio or television programme: (*BrE*) *a party political broadcast* (= for example, before an election) ◇ *We watched a live broadcast of the speech* (= one shown at the same time as the speech was made).

broad·cast·er /'brɔ:dka:stə(r); *AmE* -kæst-/ *noun* **1** a person whose job is presenting or talking on television or radio programmes **2** a company that sends out television or radio programmes: *the new Australian rugby broadcaster, Channel Ten*

broad·cast·ing /'brɔ:dka:stɪŋ; *AmE* -kæst-/ *noun* [U] the business of making and sending out radio and television programmes: *to work in broadcasting* ◇ *the British Broadcasting Corporation* (= the BBC)

broad·en /'brɔ:dn/ *verb* **1** [V] to become wider: *Her smile broadened.* **2** to affect or make sth affect more people or things: [VN] *a promise to broaden access to higher education* ◇ *The party needs to broaden its appeal to voters.* [also V] **3** [VN] to increase your experience, knowledge, etc: *Few would disagree that travel broadens the mind* (= helps you to understand other people's beliefs, customs, etc.) ◇ *Spending a year working in the city helped to broaden his horizons.* PHRV ˌbroaden 'out (of a road, river, etc.) to become wider

the 'broad jump *noun* [sing.] (*AmE*) = THE LONG JUMP

broad·leaved /'brɔ:dli:vd/ (also *less frequent* broad·leaf /'brɔ:dli:f/) *adj.* (*technical*) (of plants) having broad flat leaves

broad·ly /'brɔ:dli/ *adv.* **1** generally, without considering details: *Broadly speaking, I agree with you.* ◇ *broadly similar/comparable/equivalent/consistent* **2** if you smile broadly, you smile with your mouth stretched very wide because you are very pleased or amused

ˌbroad-'minded *adj.* willing to listen to other people's opinions and accept behaviour that is different from your own SYN TOLERANT OPP NARROW-MINDED ▶ ˌbroad-'minded·ness *noun* [U]

broad·ness /'brɔ:dnəs/ *noun* [U] = BREADTH

broad·sheet /'brɔ:dʃi:t/ *noun* **1** a newspaper printed on a large size of paper, generally considered more serious than smaller newspapers—compare TABLOID **2** a large piece of paper printed on one side only with information or an advertisement

broad·side /'brɔ:dsaɪd/ *noun, adv., verb*

■ *noun* a fierce attack in words, whether written or spoken: *The prime minister fired a broadside at his critics.*

■ *adv.* with one side facing sth SYN SIDEWAYS: *The car skidded and crashed broadside into another car.* ◇ (*BrE*) *The boat swung broadside on to the current of the river.*

■ *verb* [VN] (*AmE*) to crash into the side of sth: *The driver ran a stop light and broadsided the truck.*

broad·sword /'brɔ:dsɔ:d; *AmE* -sɔ:rd/ *noun* a large SWORD with a broad flat blade

bro·cade /brə'keɪd/ *noun* [U, C] a thick heavy fabric with a raised pattern woven especially from gold or silver silk thread: *brocade curtains* ◇ *rich velvets and brocades*

broc·coli /'brɒkəli; *AmE* 'brɑ:k-/ *noun* [U] a vegetable with a thick green stem and several dark green or purple flower heads—picture on page A3

bro·chure /'brəʊʃə(r); *AmE* broʊ'ʃʊr/ *noun* a small magazine or book containing pictures and information about sth or advertising sth: *a travel brochure*

brogue /brəʊg; *AmE* broʊg/ *noun* **1** [usually pl.] a strong shoe which usually has a pattern in the leather: *a pair of brogues* **2** [usually sing.] the ACCENT that sb has when they are speaking, especially the accent of Irish or Scottish speakers of English

broil /brɔɪl/ *verb* **1** [VN] (*AmE*) to cook meat or fish under direct heat or over heat on metal bars: *broiled chicken*—compare BARBECUE, GRILL—picture on page 275 **2** to become or make sb become very hot: [V] *They lay broiling in the sun.* [also VN]

broil·er /'brɔɪlə(r)/ *noun* **1** (also 'broiler chicken) (*especially AmE*) a young chicken suitable for broiling or ROASTING **2** (*AmE*) the part inside the oven of a cooker/stove that directs heat downwards to cook food that is placed underneath it—compare GRILL

broke /brəʊk; *AmE* broʊk/ *adj.* [not before noun] (*informal*) having no money: *I'm always broke by the end of the month.* ◇ *During the recession thousands of small businesses went broke* (= had to stop doing business). ◇ *flat/stony broke* (= completely broke) —see also BREAK *v.* IDM **go for 'broke** (*informal*) to risk everything in one determined effort to do sth

broken /'brəʊkən; *AmE* 'broʊ-/ *adj.*

DAMAGED | **1** that has been damaged or injured; no longer whole or working correctly: *a broken window/plate* ◇ *a broken leg/arm* ◇ *pieces of broken glass* ◇ *How did this dish get broken?* ◇ *The TV's broken.*—see also BROKEN HEART

RELATIONSHIP | **2** [usually before noun] ended or destroyed: *a broken marriage/engagement*—see also BROKEN HOME

PROMISE/AGREEMENT | **3** [usually before noun] not kept

NOT CONTINUOUS | **4** [usually before noun] not continuous; disturbed or interrupted: *a night of broken sleep* ◇ *a single broken white line across the road*

PERSON | **5** [only before noun] made weak and tired by illness or difficulties: *He was a broken man after the failure of his business.*

LANGUAGE | **6** [only before noun] (of a language that is not your own) spoken slowly and with a lot of mistakes; not FLUENT: *to speak in broken English*

GROUND | **7** having a rough surface: *an area of broken, rocky ground*

—see also BREAK, BROKE, BROKEN *v.*

ˌbroken-'down *adj.* [usually before noun] in a very bad condition; not working correctly; very tired and sick: *a broken-down old car/horse*

ˌbroken 'heart *noun* a feeling of great sadness, especially when sb you love has died or left you: *No one ever died of a broken heart.* ▶ ˌbroken-'hearted *adj.*: *He was broken-hearted when his wife died.*—compare HEART-BROKEN

broken 'home *noun* a family in which the parents are divorced or separated: *She comes from a broken home.*

broken·ly /'brəʊkənli; *AmE* 'broʊ-/ *adv.* (*formal*) (of sb's manner of speaking) in phrases that are very short or not complete, with a lot of pauses; not FLUENTLY

broker /'brəʊkə(r); *AmE* 'broʊ-/ *noun, verb*
■ *noun* **1** a person who buys and sells things, for example, shares in a business, for other people: *an insurance broker* **2** = STOCKBROKER—see also HONEST BROKER, PAWN-BROKER, POWER BROKER
■ *verb* [VN] to arrange the details of an agreement, especially between different countries: *a peace plan brokered by the UN*

broker·age /'brəʊkərɪdʒ; *AmE* 'broʊ-/ *noun* [U] **1** the business of being a broker: *a brokerage firm/house* **2** an amount of money charged by a broker for work that he/she does

brolly /'brɒli; *AmE* 'brɑːli/ *noun* (*pl.* **-ies**) (*BrE, informal*) = UMBRELLA

brom·ide /'brəʊmaɪd; *AmE* 'broʊ-/ *noun* [C, U] a chemical compound used in medicine to make people feel calm

bron·chial /'brɒŋkiəl; *AmE* 'brɑːŋ-/ *adj.* [usually before noun] (*medical*) of or affecting the two main branches of the WINDPIPE (called **bronchial tubes**) leading to the lungs: *bronchial pneumonia*—picture at BODY

bron·chitis /brɒŋ'kaɪtɪs; *AmE* brɑːŋ-/ *noun* [U] an illness that affects the bronchial tubes leading to the lungs: *He was suffering from chronic bronchitis.* ▶ **bron·chit·ic** /brɒŋ'kɪtɪk; *AmE* brɑːŋ-/ *adj.*: *a bronchitic cough*

bronco /'brɒŋkəʊ; *AmE* 'brɑːŋkoʊ/ *noun* (*pl.* **-os**) a wild horse of the western US: *a bucking bronco in the rodeo*

bron·to·saurus /ˌbrɒntə'sɔːrəs; *AmE* ˌbrɑːn-/ *noun* a very large DINOSAUR (= a reptile that lived millions of years ago) with a long neck and tail

Bronx cheer /ˌbrɒŋks 'tʃɪə(r); *AmE* ˌbrɑːŋks 'tʃɪr/ *noun* (*AmE, informal*) = RASPBERRY (2)

bronze /brɒnz; *AmE* brɑːnz/ *noun, adj.*
■ *noun* **1** [U] a dark reddish-brown metal made by mixing COPPER and tin: *a bronze statue* ◇ *a figure cast in bronze* **2** [U] a dark reddish-brown colour, like bronze **3** [C] a work of art made of bronze, for example a statue: *a fine collection of bronzes* **4** [C, U] = BRONZE MEDAL
■ *adj.* dark reddish-brown in colour: *bronze skin*

the 'Bronze Age *noun* [sing.] the period in history between the Stone Age and the Iron Age when people used tools and weapons made of bronze

bronzed /brɒnzd; *AmE* brɑːnzd/ *adj.* having skin that has been turned brown in an attractive way by the sun: *strong bronzed arms*

bronze 'medal (also **bronze**) *noun* [C, U] a medal given as third prize in a competition or race: *an Olympic bronze medal winner* ◇ *She won (a) bronze at the Olympics.*—compare GOLD MEDAL, SILVER MEDAL ▶ **bronze 'medallist** (*BrE*) (*AmE* **bronze 'medalist**) *noun*: *She's an Olympic bronze medallist.*

brooch /brəʊtʃ; *AmE* broʊtʃ/ (*especially BrE*) (*AmE* usually **pin**) *noun* a piece of jewellery with a pin on the back of it, that can be fastened to your clothes—picture at JEWELLERY

brood /bruːd/ *verb, noun*
■ *verb* **1** [V] ~ (**over/on/about sth**) to think a lot about sth that makes you annoyed, anxious or upset: *You're not still brooding over what he said, are you?* **2** [V, VN] if a bird **broods**, or broods its eggs, it sits on the eggs in order to HATCH them (= make the young come out of them)
■ *noun* [C+sing./pl. v.] **1** all the young birds or creatures that a mother produces at one time **2** (*humorous*) a large family of children: *She grew up amidst a lively brood of brothers and sisters.*

brood·ing /'bruːdɪŋ/ *adj.* (*literary*) sad and mysterious or threatening: *dark, brooding eyes* ◇ *a brooding silence* ◇ *Ireland's brooding landscape*

'brood mare *noun* a female horse kept for breeding

broody /'bruːdi/ *adj.* **1** (of a woman) wanting very much to have a baby: *I reached the age of 27 and suddenly started to feel broody.* **2** (of a female bird) wanting to lay

eggs and sit on them: *a broody hen* **3** silent and thinking about sth because you are unhappy or disappointed ▶ **broodi·ness** *noun* [U]

brook /brʊk/ *noun, verb*
■ *noun* a small stream
■ *verb* (**not brook sth/brook no**) (*formal*) to not allow sth [SYN] TOLERATE: [VN] *The tone in his voice brooked no argument.* [also VN -ing]

broom /bruːm/ *noun* **1** [C] a brush on the end of a long handle, used for SWEEPING floors—see also NEW BROOM **2** [U] a wild bush with small yellow flowers

'broom cupboard *noun* (*BrE*) **1** a large built-in cupboard used for keeping cleaning equipment, etc. in **2** (often *humorous*) a very small room: *I couldn't afford more than a broom cupboard to set up office in.*

broom·stick /'bruːmstɪk/ *noun* a broom with a long handle and small thin sticks at the end, or the handle of a broom. In stories WITCHES (= women with evil magic powers) ride through the air on broomsticks.

Bros (also **Bros.** especially in *AmE*) *abbr.* (used in the name of a company) Brothers: *Warner Bros*

broth /brɒθ; *AmE* brɔːθ/ *noun* [U, C] thick soup made by boiling meat or fish and vegetables in water: *chicken broth* [IDM] see COOK *n.*

brothel /'brɒθl; *AmE* 'brɑːθl; 'brɔːθl/ (also **bor·dello** especially in *AmE*) *noun* a house where people pay to have sex with prostitutes

brother /'brʌðə(r)/ *noun, exclamation*
■ *noun*
IN FAMILY **1** a boy or man who has the same mother and father as another person: *We're brothers.* ◇ *He's my brother.* ◇ *an older/younger brother* ◇ *a twin brother* ◇ *Does she have any brothers and sisters?* ◇ *Edward was the youngest of the Kennedy brothers.* ◇ *He was like a brother to me* (= very close).—see also HALF-BROTHER, STEPBROTHER

OTHER MEN **2** (*pl.* **brothers** or *old-fashioned* **brethren**) used for talking to or talking about other male members of an organization or other men who have the same ideas, purpose, etc. as yourself: *We must work together, brothers!* ◇ *We are all brothers in the fight against injustice.* ◇ *He was greatly respected by his brother officers.* ◇ *We must support our weaker brethren.*

IN RELIGIOUS GROUP **3** (also **Brother**) (*pl.* **brethren** or **brothers**) a male member of a religious group, especially a MONK: *Brother Luke* ◇ *The Brethren meet regularly for prayer.*

FORM OF ADDRESS **4** (*AmE, informal*) used by black people as a form of address for a black man

AT COLLEGE/UNIVERSITY **5** (in the US) a member of a FRA-TERNITY (= a club for a group of male students at a college or university)
■ *exclamation* (*old-fashioned, especially AmE*) used to express the fact that you are annoyed or surprised: *Oh brother!*

brother·hood /'brʌðəhʊd; *AmE* -ðərh-/ *noun* **1** [U] friendship and understanding between people: *to live in peace and brotherhood* **2** [C+sing./pl. v.] an organization formed for a particular purpose, especially a religious society or political organization: *the Russian Orthodox Brotherhood* **3** [U] the relationship of brothers: *the ties of brotherhood*

brother-in-law (*pl.* **brothers-in-law**) *noun* the brother of your husband or wife; your sister's husband; the husband of your sister or wife's sister—compare SISTER-IN-LAW

brother·ly /'brʌðəli; *AmE* -ðərli/ *adj.* [usually before noun] showing feelings of affection and kindness that you would expect a brother to show: *brotherly love/advice* ◇ *He gave her a brotherly kiss on the cheek.*

brougham /'bruːəm/ *noun* a type of carriage used in the past, which had a closed roof and four wheels and was pulled by one horse

brought *pt, pp* of BRING [IDM] see LOW *adj.*

brow /braʊ/ *noun* **1** the part of the face above the eyes and below the hair [SYN] FOREHEAD: *The nurse mopped his*

aɪ	aʊ	eɪ	əʊ	oʊ	ɔɪ	ɪə	eə	ʊə	j	w
my	now	say	go	go	boy	near	hair	pure	yes	wet
				(BrE)	(AmE)					

fevered brow. ◊ *Her* **brow** *furrowed in concentration.*
2 [usually pl.] = EYEBROW: *One dark brow rose in surprise.*
3 [usually sing.] the top part of a hill: *The path disappeared over the brow of the hill.*—see also HIGHBROW, MIDDLEBROW, LOWBROW IDM see KNIT *v.*

brow·beat /ˈbraʊbiːt/ *verb* (**brow·beat, brow·beat·en** /ˈbraʊbiːtn/) [VN] **~ sb** (**into doing sth**) to frighten or threaten sb in order to make them do sth SYN INTIMIDATE: *They were browbeaten into accepting the offer.*

brown /braʊn/ *adj., noun, verb*
■ *adj.* (**brown·er, brown·est**) **1** having the colour of earth, or coffee mixed with milk: *brown eyes ◊ brown bread ◊ dark brown shoe polish ◊ a package wrapped in brown paper* **2** (*especially BrE*) having skin that is naturally brown or has been made brown by the sun: *I don't go brown very easily. ◊ After the summer in Spain, the children were brown as berries.*
■ *noun* [U, C] the colour of earth, or coffee mixed with milk: *leaves of various shades of brown ◊ Brown doesn't* (= brown clothes don't) *suit you.*
■ *verb* to become brown; to make sth brown: [V] *Heat the butter until it browns. ◊ The grass was browning in patches.* ◊ [VN] *Brown the onions before adding the meat.*
IDM **,browned ˈoff** (**with sb**) (*BrE, informal*) bored, unhappy and/or annoyed: *By now the passengers were getting browned off with the delay.*

brown·field /ˈbraʊnfiːld/ *adj.* [only before noun] (*BrE*) used to describe an area of land in a city that was used by industry or for offices in the past and that may now be cleared for new building development: *a brownfield site*

brownie /ˈbraʊni/ *noun* **1** [C] a thick soft flat cake made with chocolate and sometimes nuts: *a fudge brownie* **2** (**the Brownies**) [pl.] a branch of the SCOUT ASSOCIATION for girls between the ages of seven and ten or eleven: *to join the Brownies* **3** [C] (**Brownie**) (*BrE also* **Brownie Guide**) a member of the Brownies—compare CUB, GUIDE, SCOUT

ˈbrownie point *noun* [usually pl.] (*informal*) if sb does sth to earn **brownie points**, they do it to make sb in authority have a good opinion of them

brown·ish /ˈbraʊnɪʃ/ (*also less frequent* **browny** /ˈbraʊni/) *adj.* fairly brown in colour: *You can't see in this light, but my new coat is a sort of brownish colour.*

ˈbrown-nose *verb* [V] (*slang, disapproving*) to treat sb in authority with special respect in order to make them approve of you or treat you better

brown·stone /ˈbraʊnstəʊn/; *AmE* -stoʊn/ *noun* (*AmE*) a house built of, or with a front made of, a type of reddish-brown stone, which is also called **brownstone**: *New York brownstones*

,brown ˈsugar *noun* [U] sugar that has a brown colour and has only been partly REFINED (= it is not completely pure)

browse /braʊz/ *verb* **1** to look at a lot of things in a shop/store rather than looking for one particular thing: [V] *You are welcome to come in and browse. ◊* [VN] *She browsed the shelves for something interesting to read.* **2 ~ (through sth)** to look through the pages of a book, newspaper, etc. without reading everything: [V] *I found the article while I was browsing through some old magazines.* [also VN] **3** [V, VN] (*computing*) to look for information on a computer **4** [V] **~ (on sth)** (of cows, goats, etc.) to eat leaves, etc. that are growing high up ▸ **browse** *noun* [sing.]: *The gift shop is well worth a browse.*

browser /ˈbraʊzə(r)/ *noun* **1** (*computing*) a program that lets you look at or read documents on the Internet: *a Web browser*—picture on page 251 **2** a person who looks through books, magazines, etc. or at things for sale, but may not seriously intend to buy anything

bruise /bruːz/ *verb, noun*
■ *verb* **1** to develop a bruise, or make a bruise or bruises appear on the skin of sb/sth: [V] *Strawberries bruise easily. ◊* [VN] *She had slipped and badly bruised her face.* **2** [VN] [usually passive] to affect sb badly and make them feel unhappy and less confident: *They had been badly bruised by the defeat.* ▸ **bruised** *adj.*: *He suffered badly bruised ribs in the crash. ◊ bruised fruit ◊ a bruised ego*

bruis·ing *noun* [U]: *She suffered severe bruising, but no bones were broken. ◊ internal bruising*—see also BRUISING *adj.*
■ *noun* **1** a blue, brown or purple mark that appears on the skin after sb has fallen, been hit, etc: *to be covered in bruises ◊ cuts and bruises* **2** a mark on a fruit or vegetable where it is damaged

bruiser /ˈbruːzə(r)/ *noun* (*informal*) a large strong aggressive man

bruis·ing /ˈbruːzɪŋ/ *adj.* difficult and unpleasant, making you feel tired or weak: *a bruising meeting/experience*

Brum·mie /ˈbrʌmi/ *noun* (*BrE, informal*) a person from the city of Birmingham in England ▸ **Brum·mie** *adj.*: *a Brummie accent*

brunch /brʌntʃ/ *noun* [C, U] (*informal*) a meal that you eat in the late morning as a combination of breakfast and lunch

bru·nette /bruːˈnet/ *noun* a white-skinned woman with dark brown hair

brunt /brʌnt/ *noun* IDM **bear, take, etc. the ˈbrunt of sth** to receive the main force of sth unpleasant: *Schools will bear the brunt of cuts in government spending.*

brush /brʌʃ/ *noun, verb*
■ *noun* **1** [C] an object made of short stiff hairs (called BRISTLES) or wires set in a block of wood or plastic, usually attached to a handle. Brushes are used for many different jobs, such as cleaning, painting and tidying your hair: *a paintbrush ◊ a hairbrush ◊ a toothbrush ◊ brush strokes* (= the marks left by a brush when painting) *◊ a dustpan and brush ◊ Apply the paint with a fine brush.* **2** [sing.] an act of brushing: *to give your hair/teeth a good brush* **3** [sing.] a light touch made in passing sth/sb: *the brush of his lips on her cheek* **4** [C] **~ with sth/sb** a short unfriendly meeting with sb; an occasion when you nearly experience sth unpleasant: *She had a nasty brush with her boss this morning. ◊ In his job he's had frequent brushes with death. ◊ a brush with the law* **5** [U] land covered by small trees or bushes: *a brush fire* **6** [C] the tail of a FOX IDM see DAFT *adj.*, PAINT *v.*, TAR *v.*
■ *verb* **1** to clean, polish, or make smooth with a brush: [VN] *to brush your hair/teeth/shoes ◊* [VN-ADJ] *A tiled floor is easy to brush clean.* **2** [VN] **~ A with B | ~ B over A** to put sth, for example oil, milk or egg, on sth using a brush: *Brush the pastry with beaten egg. ◊ Brush beaten egg over the pastry.* **3** [VN+adv./prep.] to remove sth from a surface with a brush or with your hand: *He brushed the dirt off his jacket. ◊ She brushed the fly away.* **4 ~ (against/by/past) sb/sth** to touch sb/sth lightly while moving close to them/it: [V] *She brushed past him. ◊ His hand accidentally brushed against hers. ◊* [VN] *The leaves brushed her cheek. ◊ He brushed her lips with his.* PHRV **,brush sb/sth↔ˈaside** to ignore sb/sth; to treat sb/sth as unimportant SYN DISMISS: *He brushed aside my fears.* **,brush sb/yourself ˈdown** (*BrE*) = BRUSH SB/YOURSELF OFF **,brush sth↔ˈdown** to clean sth by brushing it: *to brush a coat/horse down* **,brush ˈoff** to be removed by brushing: *Mud brushes off easily when it is dry.* **,brush sb↔ˈoff** to rudely ignore sb or refuse to listen to them: *She brushed him off impatiently.*—related noun BRUSH-OFF **,brush sb/yourself ˈoff** to make sb/yourself tidy, especially after you have fallen, by brushing your clothes, etc. with your hands **,brush sth↔ˈup| ,brush ˈup on sth** to quickly improve a skill, especially when you have not used it for a time: *I must brush up on my Spanish before I go to Seville.*

ˈbrush-off *noun* [sing.] (*informal*) rude or unfriendly behaviour that shows that a person is not interested in sb: *Paul asked Tara out to dinner but she gave him the brush-off.*

brush·wood /ˈbrʌʃwʊd/ *noun* [U] small broken or dead branches of trees, often used to make fires

brush·work /ˈbrʌʃwɜːk/; *AmE* -wɜːrk/ *noun* [U] the particular way in which an artist uses a brush to paint

brusque /bruːsk; brʊsk; *AmE* brʌsk/ *adj.* using very few words and sounding rude: *The doctor spoke in a brusque tone.* ▸ **brusque·ly** *adv.*: *'What's your name?' he asked brusquely.* **brusque·ness** *noun* [U]

B

b	d	f	g	h	k	l	m	n	p	r
bad	did	fall	get	hat	cat	leg	man	now	pen	red

Brus·sels sprout /ˌbrʌslz 'spraʊt/ (also **Brussel sprout, sprout**) *noun* a small round green vegetable like a very small CABBAGE—picture on page A3

bru·tal /'bruːtl/ *adj.* **1** violent and cruel: *a brutal attack/murder/rape/killing* **2** direct and clear about sth unpleasant; not thinking of people's feelings: *With brutal honesty she told him she did not love him.* ▶ **bru·tal·ity** /bruː'tæləti/ *noun* [U, C] (*pl.* **-ies**): *police brutality* ◊ *the brutalities of war* **bru·tal·ly** /-təli/ *adv.*: *He was brutally assaulted.* ◊ *Let me be brutally frank about this.*

brutalize (*BrE* also **-ise**) /'bruːtəlaɪz/ *verb* [VN] **1** (usually passive) to make sb unable to feel normal human emotions such as pity: *soldiers brutalized by war* **2** to treat sb in a cruel or violent way

brute /bruːt/ *noun, adj.*
■ *noun* **1** (sometimes *humorous*) a man who treats people in an unkind, cruel way: *His father was a drunken brute.* ◊ *You've forgotten my birthday again, you brute!* **2** a large strong animal
■ *adj.* [only before noun] **1** involving physical strength only and not thought or intelligence: *brute force/strength* **2** basic, simple and unpleasant: *the brute facts of inequality*

bru·tish /'bruːtɪʃ/ *adj.* unkind and violent and not showing thought or intelligence ▶ **bru·tish·ness** *noun* [U]

BS (*BrE*) (*AmE* **B.S.**) /ˌbiː 'es/ *abbr.* **1** (*AmE*) = BSc **2** (*BrE*) the abbreviation for 'Bachelor of Surgery' (a university degree in medicine) **3** British Standard (used on labels, etc. showing a number given by the British Standards Institution which controls the quality of products): *produced to BS4353* **4** (*AmE*, ⚠, *slang*) BULLSHIT: *That guy's full of BS.*

BSc /ˌbiː es 'siː/ (*BrE*) (*AmE* **B.S.**) *noun* the abbreviation for 'Bachelor of Science' (a first university degree in science): *to be/have/do a BSc in Zoology* ◊ (*BrE*) *Jill Ayres BSc*

BSE /ˌbiː es 'iː/ (also *informal* ˌmad 'cow disease) *noun* [U] the abbreviation for 'bovine spongiform encephalopathy' (a brain disease of cows that causes death)

BST /ˌbiː es 'tiː/ *noun* [U] the abbreviation for 'British Summer Time'

BTEC /'biːtek/ *noun* used to refer to any of a large group of British qualifications that can be taken in many different subjects at several levels (the abbreviation for 'Business and Technician Education Council'): *a BTEC Higher National Diploma in Public Service Studies*

btw *abbr.* used in writing to mean 'by the way'

bub·ble /'bʌbl/ *noun, verb*
■ *noun* **1** a ball of air or gas in a liquid, or a ball of air inside a solid substance such as glass: *champagne bubbles* ◊ *a bubble of oxygen* ◊ *blowing bubbles into water through a straw* **2** a round ball of liquid, containing air, produced by soap and water: *The children like to have bubbles in their bath.* **3** a small amount of a feeling that sb wants to express: *a bubble of laughter/hope/enthusiasm*—see also SPEECH BUBBLE **IDM** **the bubble 'bursts** there is a sudden end to a good or lucky situation: *When the bubble finally burst, hundreds of people lost their jobs.*—more at BURST *v.*
■ *verb* [V] **1** to form bubbles: *The water in the pan was beginning to bubble.* ◊ *Add the white wine and let it **bubble up**.* **2** [usually+adv./prep.] to make a bubbling sound, especially when moving in the direction mentioned: *I could hear the soup bubbling away.* ◊ *A stream came bubbling between the stones.* **3** ~ (**over**) **with** sth to be full of a particular feeling: *She was bubbling over with excitement.* **4** [+adv./prep.] (of a feeling) to be felt strongly by a person; to be present in a situation: *Laughter bubbled up inside him.* ◊ *the anger that bubbled beneath the surface*

ˌbubble and 'squeak *noun* [U] a type of British food made from cold cooked potatoes and CABBAGE that are mixed together and fried

ˈbubble bath *noun* **1** [U] a liquid soap that smells pleasant and makes a lot of bubbles when it is added to bath water **2** [C] a bath with bubble bath in the water

bubble·gum /'bʌblɡʌm/ *noun* [U] a type of CHEWING GUM that can be blown into bubbles

bubble·jet printer /'bʌbldʒet prɪntə(r)/ *noun* a type of printer that uses bubbles of air to blow small dots of ink in order to form letters, numbers, etc. on paper

bubb·ly /'bʌbli/ *adj., noun*
■ *adj.* **1** full of bubbles **2** (of a person) always cheerful, friendly and enthusiastic
■ *noun* [U] (*informal*) CHAMPAGNE

bu·bon·ic plague /bjuːˌbɒnɪk 'pleɪɡ; *AmE* -ˌbɑːnɪk/ (also **the plague**) *noun* [U] a disease spread by rats that causes fever, swellings on the body and usually death

buc·can·eer /ˌbʌkə'nɪə(r); *AmE* -'nɪr/ *noun* **1** (in the past) a sailor who attacked and robbed ships at sea [SYN] PIRATE **2** (especially in business) a person who achieves success in a skilful but not always honest way

buck /bʌk/ *noun, verb*
■ *noun* **1** [C] (*informal, especially AmE*) a US or an Australian dollar: *They cost ten bucks.* ◊ *We're talking big bucks* (= a lot of money) *here.* **2** [C] a male deer, HARE or rabbit (also called a **buck rabbit**)—compare DOE, HART, STAG **3** [C] (*old-fashioned, informal*) a young man **4** (**the buck**) [sing.] used in some expressions to refer to the responsibility or blame for sth: *It was my decision. The buck stops here* (= nobody else can be blamed). ◊ *I was tempted to **pass the buck*** (= make sb else responsible). **ORIGIN** From **buck**, an object which in a poker game is placed in front of the player whose turn it is to deal. **IDM** **make a fast/quick buck** (*informal*, often *disapproving*) to earn money quickly and easily—more at MILLION
■ *verb* **1** [V] (of a horse) to jump with the two back feet or all four feet off the ground **2** [V] to move up and down suddenly or in a way that is not controlled: *The boat bucked and heaved beneath them.* **3** [VN] (*informal*) to resist or oppose sth: *One or two companies have managed to buck the trend of the recession.* ◊ *He admired her willingness to **buck the system*** (= oppose authority or rules). **IDM** **buck your i'deas up** (*BrE, informal*) to start behaving in a more acceptable way, so that work gets done better, etc. **PHRV** ˌbuck 'up (*informal*) **1** (often in orders) to become more cheerful: *Buck up kid! It's not the end of the game.* **2** (**buck up!**) (*old-fashioned*) used to tell sb to hurry ˌbuck sb 'up (*BrE, informal*) to make sb more cheerful: *The good news bucked us all up.*

bucket /'bʌkɪt/ *noun, verb*
■ *noun* **1** (*AmE* also **pail**) [C] a round open container with a handle, used for carrying or holding liquids, sand, etc: *a plastic bucket* ◊ *They were playing on the beach with their buckets and spades.* **2** (also **bucket·ful** /-fʊl/) (*AmE* also **pail, pail·ful**) [C] the amount contained in a bucket: *two buckets/bucketfuls of water* ◊ *They used to drink tea by the bucket/bucketful* (= in large quantities). **3** (**buckets**) [pl.] (*informal*) a large amount: *To succeed in show business, you need buckets of confidence.* ◊ *We wept buckets.* ◊ *He was sweating buckets by the end of the race.* ◊ *The rain was coming down **in buckets*** (= it was raining very heavily). **IDM** see DROP *n.*, KICK *v.*
■ *verb* **PHRV** ˈbucket down (*BrE, informal*) to rain heavily: *It's bucketing down.*

ˈbucket seat *noun* a seat with a curved back for one person, especially in a car

ˈbucket shop *noun* (*informal, especially BrE*) a place that sells cheap plane tickets

buckle /'bʌkl/ *verb, noun*
■ *verb* **1** ~ (**sth on/up**) to fasten sth or be fastened with a buckle: [VN] *She buckled her belt.* ◊ *He buckled on his sword.* ◊ [V] *These shoes buckle at the side.*—picture on page A5 **2** to become crushed or bent under a weight or force; to crush or bend sth in this way: [V] *The steel frames began to buckle under the strain.* ◊ (*figurative*) *A weaker man would have buckled under the pressure.* ◊ [VN] *The crash buckled the front of my car.* **3** [V] when your knees or legs **buckle** or when you **buckle** at the knees, your knees become weak and you start to fall **PHRV** ˌbuckle 'down (to sth) (*informal*) to start to do sth seriously: *I'd better buckle down to those reports.* ˌbuckle 'up (*AmE*) = BELT UP at BELT *v.*

s	t	v	z	ʃ	ʒ	tʃ	dʒ	θ	ð	ŋ
see	tea	van	zoo	shoe	vision	chain	jam	thin	this	sing

■ *noun* a piece of metal or plastic used for joining the ends of a belt or for fastening a strap on a bag, shoe, etc.—picture at FASTENER

buck 'naked adj. (*AmE, informal*) (of a person) not wearing any clothes at all

buck·ram /ˈbʌkrəm/ noun [U] a stiff fabric made especially from cotton or LINEN, used in the past for covering books and for making clothes stiffer

buck·shot /ˈbʌkʃɒt; *AmE* -ʃɑːt/ noun [U] balls of LEAD that are fired from a SHOTGUN

buck·skin /ˈbʌkskɪn/ noun [U] soft leather made from the skin of deer or goats, used for making gloves, bags, etc.

buck-'teeth noun [pl.] top teeth that stick forward ▶ **buck-'toothed** adj.

buck·wheat /ˈbʌkwiːt/ noun [U] small dark grain that is grown as food for animals and for making flour

bu·col·ic /bjuːˈkɒlɪk; *AmE* -ˈkɑːlɪk/ adj. (*literary*) connected with the countryside or country life

bud /bʌd/ noun, verb
■ *noun* **1** a small lump that grows on a plant and from which a flower, leaf or stem develops: *the first buds appearing in spring* ◊ *The magnolia tree is in bud already.*—picture at PLANT **2** a flower or leaf that is not fully open = BUDDY: *Listen, bud, enough of the wisecracks, OK?*—see also COTTON BUD, ROSEBUD, TASTE BUD **IDM** see NIP v.
■ *verb* [V] to produce buds

Bud·dhism /ˈbʊdɪzəm/ noun [U] an Asian religion based on the teaching of Gautama Siddhartha (or Buddha) ▶ **Bud·dhist** /ˈbʊdɪst/ noun: *a devout Buddhist* **Bud·dhist** /ˈbʊdɪst/ adj. [usually before noun]: *a Buddhist monk / temple*

bud·ding /ˈbʌdɪŋ/ adj. [only before noun] beginning to develop or become successful: *a budding artist / writer* ◊ *our budding romance*

buddy /ˈbʌdi/ noun, verb
■ *noun* (pl. -ies) **1** (*AmE* also **bud**) (*informal*) a friend: *an old college buddy of mine* **2** (*esp AmE*) used to speak to a man you do not know: *'Where to, buddy?' the driver asked.* **3** (*especially AmE*) a partner who does an activity with you so that you can each help each other: *The school uses a buddy system to pair newcomers with older students.* ◊ *Her driving buddy was in trouble.*
■ *verb* (bud·dies, buddy·ing, bud·died, bud·died) **PHR V** **,buddy 'up (to/with sb)** (*AmE*) **1** = PAL UP (WITH SB): *You and your neighbour might want to buddy up to make the trip more enjoyable.* **2** to become friendly with sb in order to get an advantage for yourself

budge /bʌdʒ/ verb (usually used in negative sentences) **1** to move slightly; to make sth/sb move slightly: [V] *She pushed at the door but it wouldn't budge.* ◊ *The dog refused to budge.* ◊ [VN] *I heaved with all my might but still couldn't budge it.* **2** to change your opinion about sth; to make sb change their opinion: [V] *He won't budge an inch on the issue.* ◊ [VN] *He was not to be budged on the issue.* **PHR V** **,budge 'up** (*BrE, informal*) to move, so that there is room for other people: *Budge up a bit!*

budg·eri·gar /ˈbʌdʒərɪɡɑː(r)/ noun (also *informal* **budgie**) (both *BrE*) a small bird of the PARROT family, often kept in a cage as a pet

budget /ˈbʌdʒɪt/ noun, verb, adj.
■ *noun* **1** [C, U] the money that is available to a person or an organization and a plan of how it will be spent over a period of time: *a monthly / an annual / a family budget* ◊ *the education / defence budget* (= the amount of money that can be spent on this) ◊ *an advertising budget of $2 million* ◊ *a big-budget movie* ◊ *We decorated the house on a tight budget* (= without much money to spend). ◊ *The work was finished on time and within budget* (= did not cost more money than was planned). ◊ *They went over budget* (= spent too much money). ◊ *budget cuts* **2** (*BrE* also **Budget**) an official statement by the government of a country's income from taxes, etc. and how it will be spent: *tax cuts in this year's budget* ◊ *a budget deficit* (= when the government spends more money than it earns)

■ *verb* ~ (**sth**) (**for sth**)| ~ **sth** (**at sth**) to be careful about the amount of money you spend; to plan to spend an amount of money for a particular purpose: [V] *If we budget carefully we'll be able to afford the trip.* ◊ *I've budgeted for two new members of staff.* ◊ [VN] *Ten million francs has been budgeted for the project.* ◊ *The project has been budgeted at ten million francs.* ▶ **budget·ing** noun [U]
■ *adj.* [only before noun] (used in advertising, etc.) low in price: *a budget flight / hotel*

'budget account noun (*BrE*) an arrangement with a shop/store or company to pay your bills in fixed regular amounts and not as one large payment

budget·ary /ˈbʌdʒɪtəri; *AmE* -teri/ adj. connected with a budget: *budgetary control / policies / reform*

budgie /ˈbʌdʒi/ noun (*BrE, informal*) = BUDGERIGAR

buff /bʌf/ noun, adj., verb
■ *noun* **1** [C] (used in compounds) a person who is very interested in a particular subject or activity and knows a lot about it: *a computer / opera / wine buff* **2** [U] a pale yellow-brown colour **3** [U] soft strong yellowish-brown leather made especially from the skin of BUFFALO and OXEN—see also BLIND MAN'S BUFF **IDM** **in the 'buff** (*informal*) wearing no clothes
■ *adj.* pale yellow-brown in colour: *a buff envelope*
■ *verb* [VN] ~ **sth** (**up**) to polish sth with a soft cloth

buf·falo /ˈbʌfələʊ; *AmE* -loʊ/ noun (pl. **buf·falo** or **buf·faloes**) **1** a large animal of the cow family. There are two types of buffalo, the African and the Asian, which has wide, curved horns. **2** = BISON—see also WATER BUFFALO

buf·fer /ˈbʌfə(r)/ noun, verb
■ *noun* **1** ~ (**against sth**)| ~ (**between sth and sth**) a thing or person that reduces a shock or protects sb/sth against difficulties: *Support from family and friends acts as a buffer against stress.* ◊ *She often had to act as a buffer between father and son.* ◊ *a buffer state* (= a small country between two powerful states that helps keep peace between them) ◊ *a buffer zone* (= an area of land between two opposing armies or countries) **2** (*BrE*) one of two round metal devices on the front or end of a train, or at the end of a railway track, that reduce the shock if the train hits sth **3** (also **old buffer**) (*old-fashioned, BrE*) a silly old man **IDM** see HIT v.
■ *verb* [VN] **1** to reduce the harmful effects of sth: *to buffer the effects of stress on health* **2** ~ **sb** (**against sth**) to protect sb from sth: *They tried to buffer themselves against problems and uncertainties.*

buf·fet¹ /ˈbʊfeɪ; ˈbʌfeɪ; *AmE* bəˈfeɪ/ noun—see also BUFFET² **1** a meal at which people serve themselves from a table and then stand or sit somewhere else to eat: *a buffet lunch / supper* ◊ *Dinner will be a cold buffet, not a sit-down meal.* **2** a place, for example in a train or bus station, where you can buy food and drinks to eat or drink there, or to take away **3** (*BrE*) = BUFFET CAR **4** (*especially AmE*) = SIDEBOARD (1)

buf·fet² /ˈbʌfɪt/ verb [VN] [often passive] to knock or push sb/sth roughly from side to side: *to be buffeted by the wind* ◊ (*figurative, formal*) *The nation had been buffeted by a wave of strikes.*—see also BUFFET¹ ▶ **buf·fet·ing** noun [U, C, usually sing.]

buffet car /ˈbʊfeɪ kɑː(r); ˈbʌfeɪ; *AmE* bəˈfeɪ/ (also **buffet**) noun (*BrE*) the part of a train where you can buy sth to eat and drink

buf·foon /bəˈfuːn/ noun (*old-fashioned*) a person who does silly but amusing things ▶ **buf·foon·ery** /-əri/ noun [U]

bug /bʌɡ/ noun, verb
■ *noun* **1** [C] (*especially AmE*) any small insect **2** [C] (*informal*) an infectious illness that is usually fairly mild: *a flu bug* ◊ *There's a stomach bug going round* (= people are catching it from each other). ◊ *I picked up a bug in the office.* **3** (usually **the ... bug**) [sing.] (*informal*) an enthusiastic interest in sth such as a sport or a hobby: *the travel bug* ◊ *She was never interested in fitness before but now she's been bitten by the bug.* **4** [C] (*informal*) a small

æ	ɑː	e	ɜː	ə	ɪ	iː	i	ɒ	ɔː	ʌ	ʊ	u	uː
cat	father	ten	bird	about	sit	see	many	got	saw	cup	put	actual	too
								(BrE)					

hidden device for listening to other people's conversations **5** [C] a fault in a machine, especially in a computer system or program—see also THE MILLENNIUM BUG

■ verb (-gg-) [VN] **1** to put a special device (= a bug) somewhere in order to listen secretly to other people's conversations: *They bugged her hotel room.* ◊ *They were bugging his telephone conversations.* ◊ *a bugging device* **2** (*informal*) to annoy or irritate sb: *Stop bugging me!* ◊ *It's something that's been bugging me a lot recently.* ◊ *She's really beginning to bug me.* **IDM** **bug 'off!** (*AmE, spoken*) a rude way of telling sb to go away

bug·bear /ˈbʌɡbeə(r); *AmE* -ber/ *noun* (*especially BrE*) a thing that annoys people and that they worry about: *Inflation is the government's main bugbear.*

'bug-eyed *adj.* (*informal*) having eyes that stick out

bug·ger /ˈbʌɡə(r)/ *noun, verb*

■ *noun* (*BrE*, △, *slang*) **1** an offensive word used to insult sb, especially a man, and to show anger or dislike: *Come here, you little bugger!* ◊ *You stupid bugger! You could have run me over!* **2** used to refer to a person, especially a man, that you like or feel sympathy for: *Poor bugger! His wife left him last week.* ◊ *He's a tough old bugger.* **3** a thing that is difficult or causes problems: *This door's a bugger to open.* ◊ *Question 6 is a real bugger.* **IDM** see SILLY *adj.*

■ *verb* **1** (*BrE*, △, *slang*) used as a swear word when sb is annoyed about sth or to show that they do not care about sth at all: [V] *Bugger! I've left my keys at home.* ◊ [VN] *Bugger it! I've burnt the toast.* ◊ *Oh, bugger the cost! Let's get it anyway.* **2** [VN] (*BrE*, △, *slang*) to break or ruin sth: *I think I've buggered the computer.* **3** [VN] (△ or *law*) to have ANAL sex with sb **IDM** ,**bugger 'me** (*BrE*, △, *spoken*) used to express surprise: *Bugger me! Did you see that?* **PHRV** ,**bugger a'bout/a'round** (*BrE*, △, *slang*) to waste time by behaving in a silly way or with no clear purpose: *Stop buggering about and get back to work.* **HELP** A more polite, informal way of saying this is **mess about** (*BrE*) or **mess around** (*AmE, BrE*). ,**bugger sb a'bout/ a'round** (*BrE*, △, *slang*) to treat sb in a way that is deliberately not helpful to them or wastes their time: *I'm sick of being buggered about by the company.* **HELP** A more polite, informal way of saying this is **mess sb about/around** (*BrE*). ,**bugger 'off** (*BrE*, △, *slang*) (often used in orders) to go away: *Bugger off and leave me alone.* ◊ *Where is everyone? They've all buggered off.* ,**bugger sth↔'up** (*BrE*, △, *slang*) to do sth badly or spoil sth: *I buggered up the exam.* ◊ *Sorry for buggering up your plans.* **HELP** A more polite, informal way of saying this is **foul sth up, cock sth up** (*slang*), **mess sth up** or **bungle sth**.

,**bugger 'all** *noun* [U] (*BrE*, △, *slang*) nothing at all; none at all: *There's bugger all on TV tonight.* ◊ *Well, she was bugger all help* (= no help at all).

bug·gered /ˈbʌɡəd; *AmE* -ɡərd/ *adj.* [not before noun] (*BrE*, △, *slang*) **1** very tired **2** broken or ruined: *Oh no, the TV's buggered.* **IDM** **I'll be buggered** (*BrE*, △, *slang*) used to express surprise: *Well, I'll be buggered! Look who's here.* **I'm 'buggered if ...** (*BrE*, △, *spoken*) used to say that you do not know sth or to refuse to do sth: *'What's this meeting all about?' 'I'm buggered if I know.'* ◊ *Well I'm buggered if I'm going to help her after what she said to me.*

bug·gery /ˈbʌɡəri/ *noun* [U] (*BrE*, △, *slang* or *law*) ANAL sex

buggy /ˈbʌɡi/ *noun* (*pl.* **-ies**) **1** (*BrE*) (*AmE* **cart**) a small car, often without a roof or doors, used for a particular purpose: *a garden/golf buggy*—see also BEACH BUGGY **2** (also **'Baby Buggy™**) (*both BrE*) (*AmE* **strol·ler**) a type of light folding chair on wheels in which a baby or small child is pushed along—compare PUSHCHAIR **3** a light carriage for one or two people, pulled by one horse

bugle /ˈbjuːɡl/ *noun* a musical instrument like a small TRUMPET, used in the army for giving signals

bu·gler /ˈbjuːɡlə(r)/ *noun* a person who plays the bugle

build /bɪld/ *verb, noun*

■ *verb* (**built**, **built** /bɪlt/) **1** ~ sth (*of/in/from* sth)| ~ sth (*for* sb)| ~ sb sth to make sth, especially a building, by putting parts together: [VN] *They have permission to build 200 new houses.* ◊ *Robins build nests almost anywhere.* ◊ *a*

house built of stone ◊ *They had a house built for them.* ◊ [VNN] *David built us a shed in the back yard.* ◊ [V] *They're going to build on the site of the old power station.* **2** [VN] to create or develop sth: *She's built a new career for herself.* ◊ *We want to build a better life.* ◊ *This information will help us build a picture of his attacker.* **3** [V] (*written*) (of a feeling) to become gradually stronger: *The tension and excitement built gradually all day.* **IDM** see CASTLE, ROME **PHRV** ,**build sth a'round sth** [usually passive] to create sth, using sth else as a basis: *The story is built around a group of high school dropouts.* ,**build sth↔'in**| ,**build sth 'into sth** [often passive] **1** to make sth a permanent part of a larger structure: *We're having new wardrobes built in.* ◊ *The pipes were built into the concrete.* **2** to make sth a permanent part of a system, plan, etc: *A certain amount of flexibility is built into the system.*—see also BUILT-IN '**build on sth** to use sth as a basis for further progress: *This study builds on earlier work.* '**build sth on sth** [usually passive] to base sth on sth: *an argument built on sound logic.* ,**build sth↔'on**| ,**build sth 'onto sth** to add sth (for example, an extra room) to an existing structure by building: *They've built an extension on.* ◊ *The new wing was built onto the hospital last year.* ,**build 'up (to sth)** to become greater, more powerful or larger in number: *All the pressure built up and he was off work for weeks with stress.* ◊ *The music builds up to a rousing climax.*—related noun BUILD-UP (1) ,**build 'up to sth**| ,**build yourself 'up to sth** to prepare for a particular moment or event: *Build yourself up to peak performance on the day of the exam.*—related noun BUILD-UP (2) ,**build sb/sth 'up** [usually passive] to give a very positive and enthusiastic description of sb/sth, often exaggerating your claims: *The play was built up to be a masterpiece but I found it very disappointing.*—related noun BUILD-UP (3) ,**build sb/yourself↔'up** to make sb/yourself healthier or stronger: *You need more protein to build you up.* ,**build sth↔'up 1** to create or develop sth: *She's built up a very successful business.* ◊ *These finds help us build up a picture of life in the Middle Ages.* ◊ *I am anxious not to build up false hopes* (= to encourage people to hope for too much). **2** to make sth higher or stronger than it was before

■ *noun* [U, C, usually sing.] the shape and size of the human body: *a man of average build*

build·er /ˈbɪldə(r)/ *noun* **1** a person or company whose job is to build or repair houses or other buildings **2** (*usually in compounds*) a person or thing that builds, creates or develops sth: *a shipbuilder* ◊ *a confidence builder* ◊ *a bodybuilder*

build·ing /ˈbɪldɪŋ/ *noun* **1** [C] a structure such as a house or school that has a roof and walls: *tall/old/historic buildings* **2** [U] the process and work of building: *the building of the Channel Tunnel* ◊ *There's building work going on next door.* ◊ *the building trade* ◊ *building materials/costs/regulations*

'building block *noun* **1** [C] a piece of wood or plastic used as a toy for children to build things with—picture on page A8 **2** (**building blocks**) [pl.] parts that are joined together in order to make a large thing exist: *Single words are the building blocks of language.*

'building site *noun* (*especially BrE*) an area of land where sth is being built

'building society *noun* (*BrE*) (*AmE* ,**savings and 'loan association**) an organization like a bank that lends money to people who want to buy a house. People also save money with a building society.

'build-up *noun* **1** [sing., U] an increase in the amount of sth over a period of time: *a steady build-up of traffic in the evenings* **2** [C, usually sing.] ~ (**to sth**) the time before an important event, when people are preparing for it: *the build-up to the President's visit* **3** [C, usually sing.] a very positive and enthusiastic description of sth that is going to happen, and that is intended to make people excited about it: *The media has given the show a huge build-up.*

built /bɪlt/ *combining form* (*after adverbs and in compound adjectives*) made in the particular way that is mentioned: *a newly built station* ◊ *American-built cars*—see also PURPOSE-BUILT, WELL BUILT

aɪ	aʊ	eɪ	əʊ	oʊ	ɔɪ	ɪə	eə	ʊə	j	w
my	now	say	go	go	boy	near	hair	pure	yes	wet
			(BrE)	(AmE)						

‚built-'in (also *less frequent* ‚**in-'built**) *adj.* [only before noun] included as part of sth and not separate from it: *built-in cupboards*—compare INBUILT

‚built-'up *adj.* [usually before noun] (*especially BrE*) (of an area of land) covered in buildings, roads, etc: *to reduce the speed limit in built-up areas*

bulb /bʌlb/ *noun* **1** (also **'light bulb**) the glass part that fits into an electric lamp, etc. to give light when it is switched on: *a 60-watt bulb* ◊ *a room lit by bare bulbs* (= with no decorative cover) **2** the round underground part of some plants, shaped like an onion, that grows into a new plant every year: *daffodil bulbs*—picture at PLANT **3** an object shaped like a bulb, for example the end of a THERMOMETER

bulb·ous /'bʌlbəs/ *adj.* (*written*) shaped like a bulb; round and fat in an ugly way: *a bulbous red nose*

bulge /bʌldʒ/ *verb, noun*
■ *verb* [V] **1** ~ (**with sth**) (usually used in the progressive tenses) to be completely full (of sth): *Her pockets were bulging with presents.* ◊ *a bulging briefcase* **2** to stick out from sth in a round shape: *His eyes bulged.* IDM see SEAM
■ *noun* **1** a lump that sticks out from sth in a round shape: *the bulge of a gun in his pocket* **2** (*informal*) fat on the body that sticks out in a round shape: *That skirt's too tight. It shows all your bulges.* **3** a sudden temporary increase in the amount of sth: *After the war there was a bulge in the birth rate.*

bu·limia /buˈlɪmiə; bjuː-; -ˈliːmiə/ (also **bulimia nervosa** /bʊˌlɪmiə nɜːˈvəʊsə; AmE nɜːrˈvoʊsə/) *noun* [U] an emotional disorder in which a person repeatedly eats too much and then forces him- or herself to VOMIT—compare ANOREXIA ▶ **bu·lim·ic** /buˈlɪmɪk; bjuː-; -ˈliːmɪk/ *adj.* **bu·lim·ic** *noun*

bulk /bʌlk/ *noun, verb*
■ *noun* **1** [sing.] **the ~ (of sth)** the main part of sth; most of sth: *The bulk of the population lives in cities.* **2** [U] the (large) size or quantity of sth: *Despite its bulk and weight, the car is extremely fast.* ◊ *a bulk order* (= one for a large number of similar items) ◊ *bulk buying* (= buying in large amounts, often at a reduced price) ◊ *It's cheaper to buy in bulk.* **3** [sing.] the weight or shape of sb/sth large: *She heaved her bulk out of the chair.*
■ *verb* [V] IDM **bulk 'large** (*BrE, formal*) to be the most important part of sth PHRV ‚**bulk sth↔'out/'up** to make sth bigger, thicker or heavier

bulk·head /'bʌlkhed/ *noun* (*technical*) a wall that divides a ship or an aircraft into separate parts

bulky /'bʌlki/ *adj.* (**bulk·ier, bulki·est**) **1** (of a thing) large and difficult to move or carry: *Bulky items will be collected separately.* **2** (of a person) tall and heavy: *The bulky figure of Inspector Jones appeared at the door.*

bull /bʊl/ *noun* **1** [C] the male of any animal in the cow family: *a bull neck* (= a short thick neck like a bull's)—compare BULLOCK, COW, OX, STEER **2** [C] the male of the elephant, WHALE and some other large animals—compare COW **3** [C] (*finance*) a person who buys shares in a company, hoping to sell them soon afterwards at a higher price: *a bull market* (= a situation in which share prices are rising)—compare BEAR **4** [C] an official order or statement from the POPE (= the head of the Roman Catholic Church): *a papal bull* **5** [U] (*slang*) = BULLSHIT: *That's a load of bull!* **6** [C] = BULLSEYE—see also COCK AND BULL STORY IDM **a bull in a 'china shop** a person who is careless, or who moves or acts in a rough or awkward way, in a place or situation where skill and care are needed **take the bull by the 'horns** to face a difficult or dangerous situation directly and with courage—more at RED *adj.,* SHOOT *v.*

bull·dog /'bʊldɒg; AmE -dɔːg/ *noun* a short strong dog with a large head, a short flat nose and a short thick neck

'Bulldog clip™ *noun* (*BrE*) a metal device for holding papers together—picture at STATIONERY

bull·doze /'bʊldəʊz; AmE -doʊz/ *verb* **1** [VN] to destroy buildings, trees, etc. with a bulldozer: *The trees are being bulldozed to make way for a new superstore.* **2** [+*adv./prep.*] to force your way somewhere; to force sth somewhere: [V] *Andy Roland bulldozed through to score.* ◊ [VN]

He bulldozed his way to victory. ◊ *They bulldozed the tax through Parliament.* **3** [VN] ~ **sb (into doing sth)** to force sb to do sth: *They bulldozed him into selling.*

bull·dozer /'bʊldəʊzə(r); AmE -doʊz-/ *noun* a powerful motor vehicle with a broad steel blade in front, used for moving earth or knocking down buildings—picture at TRUCK

bul·let /'bʊlɪt/ *noun* a small metal object that is fired from a gun: *bullet wounds* ◊ *There were bullet holes in the door.* ◊ *He was killed by a bullet in the head.*—see also PLASTIC BULLET, RUBBER BULLET IDM see BITE *v.*

bul·letin /'bʊlətɪn/ *noun* **1** a short news report on the radio or television **2** an official statement about sth important: *a medical bulletin on the President's health* **3** a printed report that gives news about an organization or a group

'bulletin board *noun* **1** (*AmE*) = NOTICEBOARD **2** (*computing*) a place in a computer system where any user can write or read messages

bul·let·proof /'bʊlɪtpruːf/ *adj.* that can stop bullets from passing through it: *a bulletproof vest*

bull·fight /'bʊlfaɪt/ *noun* a traditional public entertainment, popular especially in Spain, in which BULLS are fought and usually killed ▶ **bull·fight·er** *noun* **bull·fight·ing** *noun* [U] —see also MATADOR

bull·finch /'bʊlfɪntʃ/ *noun* a small European bird of the FINCH family, with a strong curved beak and a pink breast

bull·frog /'bʊlfrɒg; AmE -frɔːg; -frɑːg/ *noun* a large American FROG with a loud CROAK

bull·horn /'bʊlhɔːn; AmE -hɔːrn/ *noun* (*AmE*) = LOUDHAILER

bul·lion /'bʊliən/ *noun* [U] gold or silver in large amounts or in the form of bars: *gold bullion*

bull·ish /'bʊlɪʃ/ *adj.* **1** confident and hopeful about the future: *in a bullish mood* **2** (*finance*) causing, or connected with, an increase in the price of shares: *a bullish market*—compare BEARISH

bul·lock /'bʊlək/ *noun* a young BULL (= a male cow) that has been CASTRATED (= had part of its sex organs removed)—compare OX, STEER

bull·ring /'bʊlrɪŋ/ *noun* the large circular area, like an outdoor theatre, where BULLFIGHTS take place

'bull session *noun* (*AmE, informal*) an occasion when people meet and talk in an informal way

bulls·eye /'bʊlzaɪ/ (also **bull**) *noun* [usually sing.] the centre of the TARGET that you shoot or throw at in shooting, ARCHERY or DARTS; a shot or throw that hits this: *He scored a bullseye.*

bull·shit /'bʊlʃɪt/ *noun, verb*
■ *noun* [U] (⚠, *slang*) (also *informal* **bull**) (*abbr.* **BS**) nonsense: *That's just bullshit.*
■ *verb* (-**tt**-) (⚠, *slang*) to say things that are not true, especially in order to deceive sb: [V] *She's just bullshitting.* ◊ [VN] *Don't try to bullshit me!* ▶ **bull·shit·ter** *noun*

‚bull 'terrier *noun* a strong dog with short hair, a thick neck and a long nose—see also PIT BULL TERRIER

bully /'bʊli/ *noun, verb, exclamation*
■ *noun* (*pl.* -**ies**) a person who uses their strength or power to frighten or hurt weaker people: *the school bully*
■ *verb* (**bul·lies, bully·ing, bul·lied, bul·lied**) [VN] ~ **sb (into sth/into doing sth)** to frighten or hurt a weaker person; to use your strength or power to make sb do sth: *My son is being bullied at school.* ◊ *I won't be bullied into signing anything.* ▶ **bully·ing** *noun* [U]: *Bullying is a problem in many schools.* ◊ *He refused to give in to bullying and threats.* ◊ *bullying behaviour/tactics*
■ *exclamation* IDM **bully for you, etc.** (*spoken*) used to show that you do not think that what sb has said or done is very impressive: *He's got a job in New York? Well, bully for him!*

'bully boy *noun* (*BrE, informal*) an aggressive violent man: *The group have frequently used bully-boy tactics.*

bul·rush /'bʊlrʌʃ/ *noun* a tall plant with long narrow leaves and a long brown head of flowers, that grows in or near water

b	d	f	g	h	k	l	m	n	p	r
bad	did	fall	get	hat	cat	leg	man	now	pen	red

B

bul·wark /ˈbʊlwək; AmE -wɜːrk/ noun **1** ~ (against sth) (formal) a person or thing that protects or defends sth: a bulwark against communism **2** a wall built as a defence **3** [usually pl.] the part of a ship's side that is above the level of the DECK

bum /bʌm/ noun, verb, adj.
■ noun (informal) **1** (BrE) the part of the body that you sit on SYN BACKSIDE, BEHIND, BOTTOM **2** (especially AmE) a person who has no home or job and who asks other people for money or food: a beach bum (= sb who spends all their time on the beach, without having a job) **3** a lazy person who does nothing for other people or for society: He's nothing but a no-good bum! IDM **bums on 'seats** (BrE, informal) used to refer to the number of people who attend a show, talk, etc., especially when emphasizing the need or desire to attract a large number: They're not bothered about attracting the right audience—they just want bums on seats.
■ verb (-mm-) [VN] **1** ~ sth (off sb) (informal) to get sth from sb by asking: Can I bum a cigarette off you? **2** ~ sb (out) (AmE, informal) to make sb feel upset or disappointed PHRV **bum a'round/a'bout** (informal) to travel around or spend your time with no particular plans: He bummed around the world for a year.
■ adj. [only before noun] (informal) of bad quality; wrong or useless: He didn't play one bum note. ◊ a bum deal (= a situation where you do not get what you deserve or have paid for)

bum·bag /ˈbʌmbæg/ (BrE) (AmE 'fanny pack) noun (informal) a small bag attached to a belt and worn around the waist, to keep money, etc. in—picture at BAG

bum·ble /ˈbʌmbl/ verb [V+adv./prep.] to act or move in an awkward or confused way: I could hear him bumbling around in the kitchen.

bumble·bee /ˈbʌmblbiː/ noun a large hairy bee that makes a loud noise as it flies—picture on page A7

bum·bling /ˈbʌmblɪŋ/ adj. [only before noun] behaving in an awkward confused way, often making careless mistakes

bumf (also **bumph**) /bʌmf/ noun [U] (BrE, informal) written information, especially advertisements, official documents, forms, etc., that seem boring or unnecessary: He threw away my letter, thinking it was just more election bumf.

bum·mer /ˈbʌmə(r)/ noun (a bummer) [sing.] (informal) a disappointing or unpleasant situation: It's a real bummer that she can't come.

bump /bʌmp/ verb, noun
■ verb **1** [V] ~ against/into sb/sth to hit sb/sth accidentally: In the dark I bumped into a chair. ◊ The car bumped against the kerb. **2** [VN] ~ sth (against/on sth) to hit sth, especially a part of your body, against or on sth: Be careful not to bump your head on the beam when you stand up. **3** [+adv./prep.] to move across a rough surface: [V] The jeep bumped along the dirt track. ◊ [VN] The car bumped its way slowly down the drive. PHRV **bump 'into sb** (informal) to meet sb by chance **bump sb↔'off** (informal) to murder sb **bump sth↔'up** (informal) to increase or raise sth
■ noun **1** [C] the action or sound of sth hitting a hard surface: He fell to the ground with a bump. ◊ We could hear loud bumps from upstairs where the children were playing. **2** [C] a swelling on the body, often caused by a blow SYN LUMP: She was covered in bumps and bruises. ◊ How did you get that bump on your forehead? **3** [C] a part of a flat surface that is not even, but raised above the rest of it: a bump in the road—see also BUMPY **4** [C] a slight accident in which your vehicle hits sth **5** (the bumps) [pl.] (BrE) (on a child's birthday) the act of lifting the child in the air and then putting them down on the ground, once for every year of their age: We gave her the bumps. IDM see EARTH n., THING

bump·er /ˈbʌmpə(r)/ noun, adj.
■ noun a bar fixed to the front and back of a car, etc. to reduce the effect if it hits anything: a bumper sticker (= a sign that people stick on the bumper of their cars with a message on it) ◊ The cars were bumper to bumper on the road to the coast (= so close that their bumpers were nearly touching).—picture at CAR
■ adj. [only before noun] (approving) unusually large; producing an unusually large amount: a bumper issue (= of a magazine, etc.) ◊ a bumper crop/harvest/season/year

'bumper car noun (especially AmE) = DODGEM

bumph = BUMF

bump·kin /ˈbʌmpkɪn/ noun = COUNTRY BUMPKIN

bump·tious /ˈbʌmpʃəs/ adj. (disapproving) showing that you think that you are very important; often giving your opinions in a loud, confident and annoying way

bumpy /ˈbʌmpi/ adj. (bump·ier, bumpi·est) **1** (of a surface) not even; with a lot of bumps: a bumpy road/track ◊ bumpy ground **2** (of a journey) uncomfortable with a lot of sudden unpleasant movements caused by the road surface, weather conditions, etc: a bumpy ride/flight IDM **have/give sb a bumpy 'ride** to have a difficult time; to make a situation difficult for sb

bun /bʌn/ noun **1** [C] (BrE) a small round sweet cake: an iced bun—see also HOT CROSS BUN **2** [C] (BrE also **bap**) a small round flat bread roll: a hamburger bun—compare ROLL—picture on page A1 **3** [C] long hair that has been twisted into a round shape and is worn on top or at the back of the head: She wore her hair in a bun.—picture at HAIR **4** (buns) [pl.] (slang, especially AmE) the two sides of a person's bottom IDM **have a 'bun in the oven** (informal, humorous) to be pregnant

bunch /bʌntʃ/ noun, verb
■ noun **1** [C] ~ of sth a number of things of the same type which are growing or fastened together: a bunch of bananas/grapes ◊ a bunch of keys ◊ She picked me a bunch of flowers.—picture on page A2 **2** [sing.] a ~ (of sth) (especially AmE) a large amount of sth; a large number of things or people: I have a whole bunch of stuff to do this morning. **3** [sing.] (informal) a group of people: The people that I work with are a great bunch. **4** (bunches) [pl.] (BrE) long hair that is divided in two and tied at each side of the head: She wore her hair in bunches.—picture at HAIR IDM **the best/pick of the 'bunch** the best out of a group of people or things
■ verb ~ (sth) (up) to become tight or to form tight folds; to make sth do this: [V] His muscles bunched under his shirt. ◊ Her skirt had bunched up round her waist. ◊ [VN] His forehead was bunched in a frown. PHRV **bunch 'up/ to'gether| bunch sb/sth 'up/to'gether** to move closer and form into a group; to make people or things do this: The sheep bunched together as soon as they saw the dog.

bun·dle /ˈbʌndl/ noun, verb
■ noun **1** [C] a number of things tied or wrapped together; sth that is wrapped up: a bundle of rags/papers/firewood ◊ She held her little bundle (= her baby) tightly in her arms. **2** [C] a number of things that belong, or are sold together: a bundle of ideas/considerations ◊ a bundle of graphics packages for your PC **3** [sing.] a ~ of laughs, fun, joy, etc. (informal) a person or thing that makes you laugh: He wasn't exactly a bundle of laughs (= a happy person to be with) last night. **4** (a bundle) [sing.] (informal) a large amount of money: That car must have cost a bundle. IDM **not go a bundle on sb/sth** (BrE, informal) to not like sb/sth very much—more at NERVE n.
■ verb **1** [VN+adv./prep.] to push or send sb somewhere quickly and not carefully: They bundled her into the back of a car. ◊ He was bundled off to boarding school. **2** [V+adv./prep.] to move somewhere quickly in a group: We bundled out onto the street. **3** [VN] ~ sth (with sth) to supply extra equipment, especially SOFTWARE when selling a new computer, at no extra cost: A further nine applications are bundled with the system. PHRV **bundle sth↔'up| bundle sth↔to'gether** to make or tie sth into a bundle: He bundled up the dirty clothes and stuffed them into the bag. ◊ The papers were all bundled together, ready to be thrown out. **bundle sb 'up (in sth)** to put warm clothes or coverings on sb: I bundled her up in a blanket and gave her a hot drink.

bung /bʌŋ/ verb, noun
■ verb [VN+adv./prep.] (BrE, informal) to put or throw sth somewhere, carelessly and quickly: Bung this in the bin,

s	t	v	z	ʃ	ʒ	tʃ	dʒ	θ	ð	ŋ
see	tea	van	zoo	shoe	vision	chain	jam	thin	this	sing

can you? **PHRV** ˌbung sth ˈup (with sth) [usually passive] to block sth: *My nose is all bunged up.* ◊ *The drains are bunged up with dead leaves.*
- *noun* **1** a round piece of wood, rubber, etc. used for closing the hole in a container such as a BARREL or JAR **2** (*BrE, informal*) an amount of money that is given to sb to persuade them to do sth illegal

bun·ga·low /ˈbʌŋɡələʊ; *AmE* -loʊ/ (*BrE*) *noun* a house built all on one level, without stairs—compare RANCH HOUSE

bun·gee jump·ing /ˈbʌndʒi dʒʌmpɪŋ/ *noun* [U] a sport in which a person jumps from a high place, such as a bridge or a cliff, with a long elastic rope (called a **bungee**) tied to their feet: *to go bungee jumping* ▶ **bun·gee jump** *noun*: *to do/make a bungee jump*

bun·gle /ˈbʌŋɡl/ *verb, noun*
- *verb* to do sth badly or without skill; to fail at sth: [VN] *They bungled the job.* ◊ *a bungled robbery/raid/attempt* [also V] ▶ **bun·gler** /ˈbʌŋɡlə(r)/ *noun* **bun·gling** *adj.*: *bungling incompetence*
- *noun* [usually sing.] something that is done badly and that causes problems: *Their pay was late because of a computer bungle.*

bun·ion /ˈbʌnjən/ *noun* a painful swelling on the foot, usually on the big toe

bunk /bʌŋk/ *noun, verb*
- *noun* **1** [C] a narrow bed that is fixed to a wall, especially on a ship or train **2** [C] (also **ˈbunk bed**) one of two beds that are fixed together, one above the other, especially for children—picture at BED **3** [U] (*old-fashioned, informal*) nonsense **IDM** **do a ˈbunk** (*BrE, informal*) to run away from a place without telling anyone
- *verb* **PHRV** ˌbunk ˈoff| ˌbunk off ˈschool/ˈwork (*BrE, informal*) to stay away from school or work when you should be there; to leave school or work early **SYN** SKIVE

bun·ker /ˈbʌŋkə(r)/ *noun, verb*
- *noun* **1** a strongly built shelter for soldiers or guns, usually underground: *a concrete/underground/secret bunker* **2** a container for storing coal, especially on a ship or outside a house: *a coal bunker* **3** (*AmE* also **ˈsand trap, trap**) a small area filled with sand on a golf course—picture at GOLF
- *verb* [VN] (**be bunkered**) (in golf) to have hit your ball into a bunker (and therefore to be in a difficult position)

bunk·house /ˈbʌŋkhaʊs/ *noun* a building for workers to sleep in

bun·kum /ˈbʌŋkəm/ *noun* [U] (*old-fashioned, informal*) nonsense

bunny /ˈbʌni/ *noun* (*pl.* **-ies**) (also **ˈbunny rabbit**) a child's word for a rabbit

ˈbunny slope *noun* (*AmE*) = NURSERY SLOPE

Bun·sen burn·er /ˌbʌnsn ˈbɜːnə(r); *AmE* ˈbɜːrn-/ *noun* an instrument used in scientific work that produces a hot gas flame—picture at LABORATORY

bunt /bʌnt/ *verb* [VN,V] (*AmE*) (in baseball) to deliberately hit the ball only a short distance ▶ **bunt** *noun*

bunt·ing /ˈbʌntɪŋ/ *noun* **1** [U] coloured flags or paper used for decorating streets and buildings in celebrations **2** [C] a small bird related to the FINCH and SPARROW families. There are several types of bunting: *a corn/reed/snow bunting*

buoy /bɔɪ; *AmE* also ˈbuːi/ *noun, verb*
- *noun* an object which floats on the sea or a river to mark the places where it is dangerous and where it is safe for boats to go—see also LIFEBUOY
- *verb* [VN] [usually passive] **1** ~ sb (up) to make sb feel cheerful or confident: *Buoyed by their win yesterday the team feel confident of further success.* **2** ~ sb/sth (up) to keep sb/sth floating on water **3** ~ sth (up) to keep prices at a high or satisfactory level

buoy·ant /ˈbɔɪənt; *AmE* ˈbuːjənt/ *adj.* **1** (of prices, business activity, etc.) tending to increase or stay at a high level, usually showing financial success: *a buoyant economy/market* ◊ *buoyant sales/prices* ◊ *a buoyant demand for homes* **2** cheerful and feeling sure that things will be successful: *They were all in buoyant mood.* **3** floating, able to float or able to keep things floating: *The boat bobbed*

like a cork on the waves: light and buoyant. ◊ *Salt water is more buoyant than fresh water.* ▶ **buoy·ancy** /-ənsi/ *noun* [U]: *the buoyancy of the market* ◊ *a mood of buoyancy* ◊ *a buoyancy aid* (= sth to help you float)

bur = BURR

bur·ble /ˈbɜːbl; *AmE* ˈbɜːrbl/ *verb* **1** ~ (on) (about sth) (*BrE, disapproving*) to speak in a confused or silly way that is difficult to hear or understand: [V] *What's he burbling about?* [also V **speech**] **2** [V] to make the gentle sound of a stream flowing over stones

burbs /bɜːbz; *AmE* bɜːrbz/ *noun* (**the burbs**) [pl.] (*AmE, informal*) = SUBURBS

bur·den /ˈbɜːdn; *AmE* ˈbɜːrdn/ *noun, verb*
- *noun* **1** the ~ (of sth)| a ~ (on/to sb) a duty, responsibility, etc. that causes worry, difficulty or hard work: *to bear/carry/ease/reduce/share the burden* ◊ *The main burden of caring for old people falls on the state.* ◊ *the heavy tax burden on working people* ◊ *I don't want to become a burden to my children when I'm old.* **2** (*formal*) a heavy load that is difficult to carry—see also BEAST OF BURDEN
- *verb* [VN] **1** ~ sb/yourself (with sth) to give sb a duty, responsibility, etc. that causes worry, difficulty or hard work: *They have burdened themselves with a high mortgage.* ◊ *I don't want to burden you with my worries.* ◊ *to be burdened by high taxation* **OPP** UNBURDEN **2** (**be burdened with sth**) to be carrying sth heavy: *She got off the bus, burdened with two heavy suitcases.*

the ˌburden of ˈproof *noun* [sing.] (*law*) the task or responsibility of proving that sth is true

bur·den·some /ˈbɜːdnsəm; *AmE* ˈbɜːrd-/ *adj.* (*formal*) causing worry, difficulty or hard work

bur·eau /ˈbjʊərəʊ; *AmE* ˈbjʊroʊ/ *noun* (*pl.* **bur·eaux** or **bur·eaus** /-rəʊz; *AmE* -roʊz/) **1** (*BrE*) a desk with drawers and usually a top that opens down to make a table to write on **2** (*AmE*) = CHEST OF DRAWERS **3** an office or organization that provides information on a particular subject: *an employment bureau* **4** (in the US) a government department or part of a government department: *the Federal Bureau of Investigation*

bur·eau·cracy /bjʊəˈrɒkrəsi; *AmE* bjʊˈrɑːk-/ *noun* (*pl.* **-ies**) **1** [U] (*often disapproving*) the system of official rules and ways of doing things that a government or an organization has, especially when these seem to be too complicated: *unnecessary/excessive bureaucracy* **2** [U,C] a system of government in which there are a large number of state officials who are not elected; a country with such a system: *the power of the state bureaucracy* ◊ *living in a modern bureaucracy*

bur·eau·crat /ˈbjʊərəkræt; *AmE* ˈbjʊr-/ *noun* (*often disapproving*) an official working in an organization or a government department, especially one who follows the rules of the department too strictly

bur·eau·crat·ic /ˌbjʊərəˈkrætɪk; *AmE* ˌbjʊr-/ *adj.* (*often disapproving*) connected with a bureaucracy or bureaucrats and involving complicated official rules which may seem unnecessary: *bureaucratic power/control/procedures/organizations* ◊ *The report revealed a great deal of bureaucratic inefficiency.* ▶ **bur·eau·crat·ic·al·ly** /-ɪkli/ *adv.*

bur·ette (*AmE* also **buret**) /bjuˈret/ *noun* a glass tube with measurements on it and a tap/faucet at one end, used, for example, in chemical experiments for measuring out amounts of a liquid—picture at LABORATORY

bur·geon /ˈbɜːdʒən; *AmE* ˈbɜːrdʒən/ *verb* [V] (*formal*) to begin to grow or develop rapidly ▶ **bur·geon·ing** *adj.*: *a burgeoning population* ◊ *burgeoning demand*

bur·ger /ˈbɜːɡə(r); *AmE* ˈbɜːrɡ-/ *noun* **1** = HAMBURGER **2** (**-bur·ger**) (in compounds) finely chopped fish, vegetables, nuts, etc. made into flat round shapes like HAMBURGERS: *a spicy beanburger*—see also CHEESEBURGER, VEGGIE BURGER

burgh /ˈbʌrə/ *noun* (*old-fashioned* or *ScotE*) a town or district which is an administrative unit

bur·gher /ˈbɜːɡə(r); *AmE* ˈbɜːrɡ-/ *noun* (*old use* or *humorous*) a citizen of a particular town

burg·lar /ˈbɜːɡlə(r); *AmE* ˈbɜːrɡ-/ *noun* a person who

æ	ɑː	e	ɜː	ə	ɪ	iː	i	ɒ	ɔː	ʌ	ʊ	u	uː
cat	father	ten	bird	about	sit	see	many	got	saw	cup	put	actual	too

(BrE)

enters a building illegally in order to steal ⇨ note at STEAL

'burglar alarm *noun* an electronic device, often fixed to a wall, that rings a loud bell if sb tries to enter a building by force

burg·lary /'bɜːgləri; *AmE* 'bɜːrg-/ *noun* [U, C] (*pl.* **-ies**) the crime of entering a building illegally and stealing things from it SYN HOUSEBREAKING: *The youth was charged with three counts of burglary.* ◊ *a rise in the number of burglaries committed in the area*—compare ROBBERY, THEFT

bur·gle /'bɜːgl; *AmE* 'bɜːrgl/ (*BrE*) (*AmE* **burg·lar·ize** /'bɜːgləraɪz; *AmE* 'bɜːrg-/) *verb* [VN] to enter a building illegally, usually using force, and steal from it: *We were burgled while we were away* (= our house was burgled). ◊ *The house next door has been burgled three times.* ⇨ note at STEAL

bur·gundy /'bɜːgəndi; *AmE* 'bɜːrg-/ *noun* **1** (**Burgundy**) [U, C] (*pl.* **-ies**) a red or white wine from the Burgundy area of eastern France. There are several types of Burgundy. **2** [U] a dark red colour ▶ **bur·gundy** *adj.*: *a burgundy leather briefcase*

bur·ial /'beriəl/ *noun* [U, C] the act or ceremony of burying a dead body: *a burial place/mound/site* ◊ *Her body was sent home for burial.* ◊ *His family insisted he should be given a proper burial.*

'burial ground *noun* a place where dead bodies are buried, especially an ancient place

bur·lap /'bɜːlæp; *AmE* 'bɜːrl-/ *noun* [U] (*especially AmE*) = HESSIAN

bur·lesque /bɜː'lesk; *AmE* bɜːr'l-/ *noun* **1** [C] a performance or piece of writing which tries to make sth look ridiculous by representing it in a humorous way SYN PARODY: *a burlesque of literary life* **2** [U] (*AmE*) a type of entertainment, popular in the past in the US, involving humorous acts, singing, dancing, etc. and often including STRIPTEASE ▶ **bur·lesque** *adj.* [usually before noun]

burly /'bɜːli; *AmE* 'bɜːrli/ *adj.* (of a man or a man's body) big, strong and heavy

burn /bɜːn; *AmE* bɜːrn/ *verb, noun*

■ *verb* (**burnt**, **burnt** /bɜːnt; *AmE* bɜːrnt/) or (**burned**, **burned** /bɜːnd; *AmE* bɜːrnd/)

FIRE | **1** [V] to produce flames and heat: *A welcoming fire was burning in the fireplace.* ◊ *Fires were burning all over the city.* **2** [V] (used especially in the progressive tenses) to be on fire: *By nightfall the whole city was burning.* ◊ *Two children were rescued from the burning car.* ◊ *The smell of burning rubber filled the air.* **3** to destroy, damage, injure or kill sb/sth by fire; to be destroyed, etc. by fire: [VN] *to burn waste paper/dead leaves* ◊ *All his belongings were burnt in the fire.* ◊ *The cigarette burned a hole in the carpet.* ◊ *The house was burnt to the ground* (= completely destroyed) *by protesters.* ◊ [VN-ADJ] *His greatest fear is of being burnt alive.* ◊ [V] *The house burned to the ground.* ◊ *Ten people burned to death in the hotel fire.*

FUEL | **4** if you **burn** a fuel, or a fuel **burns**, it produces heat, light or energy: [VN] *a furnace that burns gas/oil/coke* ◊ (*figurative*) *Some people burn calories* (= use food to produce energy) *faster than others.* ◊ [V] *Which fuel burns most efficiently?*

FOOD | **5** if food **burns**, or if you **burn** it, it is spoiled because it gets too hot: [V] *I can smell something burning in the kitchen.* ◊ [VN] *Sorry—I burnt the toast.*

SUN/HEAT/ACID | **6** to be damaged or injured by the sun, heat, acid, etc.; to damage or injure sb/sth in this way: [V] *My skin burns easily* (= in the sun). ◊ [VN] *I got badly burned by the sun yesterday.* ◊ *The soup's hot. Don't burn your mouth.* ◊ *I burned myself on the stove.*

OF PART OF BODY | **7** [V] if part of your body **burns** or is **burning**, it feels very hot and painful: *Your forehead's burning. Have you got a fever?* ◊ *Her cheeks burned with embarrassment.*

OF A LIGHT | **8** [V] to produce light: *Lights were burning upstairs, but no one answered the door.*

FEEL EMOTION/DESIRE | **9** ~ (**with sth**) (*written*) to feel a very strong emotion or desire: [V] *to be burning with rage/*

ambition/love ◊ [V to inf] *He was burning to go climbing again.*

IDM **burn your 'bridges** (*BrE* also **burn your 'boats**) to do sth that makes it impossible to return to the previous situation later: *Think carefully before you resign—you don't want to burn your bridges.* **burn the candle at both 'ends** to become very tired by trying to do too many things and going to bed late and getting up early **burn your 'fingers | get your 'fingers burnt** to suffer as a result of doing sth without realizing the possible bad results, especially in business: *He got his fingers badly burnt dabbling in the stock market.* **burn a 'hole in your pocket** if money **burns a hole in your pocket**, you want to spend it as soon as you have it **burn the midnight 'oil** to study or work until late at night **burn sth to a 'cinder/'crisp** to cook sth for too long or with too much heat, so that it becomes badly burnt—more at EAR, MONEY

PHRV **,burn a'way | ,burn sth↔a'way** to disappear as a result of burning; to make sth do this: *Half the candle had burnt away.* ◊ *The clothing on his back got burnt away in the fire.* **,burn 'down** if a fire **burns down**, it becomes weaker and has smaller flames **,burn 'down | ,burn sth↔'down** to be destroyed, or to destroy sth, by fire: *The house burned down in 1995.* **,burn sth↔'off 1** to remove sth by burning: *Burn off the old paint before repainting the door.* **2** to use energy by doing exercise: *This workout helps you to burn off fat and tone muscles.* **,burn 'out | ,burn itself 'out** (of a fire) to stop burning because there is nothing more to burn: *The fire had burnt (itself) out before the fire engines arrived.* **,burn 'out | ,burn sth↔'out** to stop working or to make sth stop working because it gets too hot or is used too much: *The clutch has burnt out.* **,burn 'out | ,burn yourself/sb 'out** to become extremely tired or sick by working too hard over a period of time: *If he doesn't stop working so hard, he'll burn himself out.* ◊ *By the age of 25 she was completely burned out and retired from the sport.*—related noun BURNOUT **,burn sth 'out** [usually passive] to destroy sth completely by fire so that only the outer frame remains: *The hotel was completely burnt out.* ◊ *the burnt-out wreck of a car* **,burn 'up 1** to be destroyed by heat:. *The spacecraft burned up as it entered the earth's atmosphere.* **2** (usually used in the progressive tenses) (*informal*) to have a high temperature: *You're burning up—have you seen a doctor?* **3** (of a fire) to burn more strongly and with larger flames **,burn sb 'up** (*AmE, informal*) to make sb very angry **,burn sth↔'up 1** to get rid of or destroy sth by burning: *The fire burned up 1500 acres of farmland.* **2** to use CALORIES or energy by doing exercise: *Which burns up more calories—swimming or cycling?*

■ *noun*

INJURY | **1** [C] an injury or a mark caused by fire, heat or acid: *minor/severe/third-degree burns* ◊ *cigarette burns on the furniture* ◊ *burn marks* ◊ *a specialist burns unit in a hospital*

IN MUSCLES | **2** (**the burn**) [sing.] the feeling that you get in your muscles when you have done a lot of exercise: *Feel the burn!*

RIVER | **3** [C] (*ScotE*) a small river SYN STREAM

IDM see SLOW *adj.*

burn·er /'bɜːnə(r); *AmE* 'bɜːrn-/ *noun* **1** the part of a cooker/stove, etc. that produces a flame—picture at RING **2** a large, solid, metal piece of equipment for burning wood or coal, used for heating a room: *a wood burner*—see also BUNSEN BURNER IDM see BACK *adj.*, FRONT *adj.*

burn·ing /'bɜːnɪŋ; *AmE* 'bɜːrn-/ *adj., adv.*

■ *adj.* [only before noun] **1** (of feelings, etc.) very strong; extreme: *a burning desire to win* ◊ *He's always had a burning ambition to start his own business.* **2 a** ~ **issue/question** a very important and urgent problem: *one of the burning issues of the day* **3** (of pain, etc.) very strong and giving a feeling of burning **4** very hot; looking and feeling very hot: *the burning sun* ◊ *her burning face* **5** ~ **eyes** (*literary*) eyes that seem to be staring at you very hard

■ *adv.* (**burning hot**) very hot

bur·nish /'bɜːnɪʃ; *AmE* 'bɜːrnɪʃ/ *verb* [VN] (*formal*) to polish metal until it is smooth and shiny ▶ **bur·nished** *adj.* [usually before noun]: *burnished gold / copper*

burn·out /'bɜːnaʊt; *AmE* 'bɜːrn-/ *noun* [C, U] **1** the state of being extremely tired or ill, either physically or mentally, because you have worked too hard **2** the point at which a rocket has used all of its fuel and has no more power

burnt /bɜːnt; *AmE* bɜːrnt/ *adj.* damaged or injured by burning: *burnt toast* ◇ *Your hand looks badly burnt.*

burp /bɜːp; *AmE* bɜːrp/ *verb* (*informal*) **1** [V] to let out air from the stomach through the mouth, making a noise—compare BELCH **2** [VN] to make a baby bring up air from the stomach, especially by rubbing or PATTING its back ▶ **burp** *noun*

burr /bɜː(r)/ *noun* **1** [usually sing.] a strong pronunciation of the 'r' sound, typical of some ACCENTS in English; an ACCENT with this type of pronunciation: *She speaks with a soft West Country burr.* **2** [usually sing.] the soft regular noise made by parts of a machine moving quickly **3** (also **bur**) the seed container of some plants which is covered in very small hooks that stick to clothes or fur

bur·rito /bʊ'riːtəʊ; *AmE* -toʊ/ *noun* (*pl.* **-os**) (from *Spanish*) a Mexican dish consisting of a TORTILLA filled with meat or beans

bur·row /'bʌrəʊ; *AmE* 'bʌroʊ/ *verb, noun*
■ *verb* **1** to make a hole or a tunnel in the ground by digging: [V, usually +*adv./prep.*] *Earthworms burrow deep into the soil.* ◇ [VN+*adv./prep.*] *The rodent burrowed its way into the sand.* **2** [+*adv./prep.*] to press yourself close to sb or under sth: [V] *He burrowed down beneath the blankets.* ◇ [VN] *She burrowed her face into his chest.* **3** [V+*adv./prep.*] to search for sth under or among things: *She burrowed in the drawer for a pair of socks.* ◇ *He was afraid that they would burrow into his past.*
■ *noun* a hole or tunnel in the ground made by animals such as rabbits for them to live in

bur·sar /'bɜːsə(r); *AmE* 'bɜːrs-/ *noun* (*especially BrE*) a person whose job is to manage the financial affairs of a school or college

bur·sary /'bɜːsəri; *AmE* 'bɜːrs-/ *noun* (*pl.* **-ies**) (*BrE*) an amount of money that is given to sb so that they can study, usually at a college or university [SYN] SCHOLAR-SHIP, GRANT

burst /bɜːst; *AmE* bɜːrst/ *verb, noun*
■ *verb* (**burst**, **burst**) **1** to break open or apart, especially because of pressure from inside; to make sth break in this way: [V] *That balloon will burst if you blow it up any more.* ◇ *The dam burst under the weight of water.* ◇ *Shells were bursting* (= exploding) *all around us.* ◇ (*figurative*) *He felt he would burst with anger and shame.* ◇ *a burst pipe* ◇ [VN] *Don't burst that balloon!* ◇ *The river burst its banks and flooded nearby towns.* **2** [V+*adv./prep.*] to go or move somewhere suddenly with great force; to come from somewhere suddenly with great force: *He burst into the room without knocking.* ◇ *The sun burst through the clouds.* ◇ *The words burst from her in an angry rush.* **3** [V] **be bursting (with sth)** to be very full of sth; to be very full and almost breaking open: *The roads are bursting with cars.* ◇ *to be bursting with ideas / enthusiasm.* ◇ *The hall was filled to bursting point.* ◇ *The hall was full to bursting.* ◇ (*informal*) *I'm bursting* (*for a pee*)! (= I need to use the toilet right now). [IDM] **be bursting to do sth** to want to do sth so much that you can hardly stop yourself: *She was bursting to tell him the good news.* **,burst sb's 'bubble** to bring an end to sb's hopes, happiness, etc. **,burst 'open** | **,burst (sth) 'open** to open suddenly or violently; to make sth open in this way: *The door burst open.* ◇ *Firefighters burst the door open and rescued them.*—more at BUBBLE *n.*, SEAM [PHR V] **,burst 'in** | **,burst into a 'room, 'building, etc.** to enter a room or building suddenly and noisily **,burst 'in on sb/sth** to interrupt sb/sth by entering a place suddenly and noisily: *He burst in on the meeting.* **'burst into sth** to start producing sth suddenly and with great force: *The aircraft crashed and burst into flames* (= suddenly began to burn). ◇ *She burst into tears* (= suddenly began to cry). **'burst on/onto sth** to appear somewhere suddenly in a way that is very noticeable: *A*

major new talent has **burst onto the literary scene.** **,burst 'out 1** to speak suddenly, loudly and with strong feeling: [+speech] *'For heavens' sake!' he burst out.*—related noun OUTBURST **2** to begin doing sth suddenly: [+-ing] *Karen burst out laughing.*
■ *noun* **1** a short period of a particular activity or strong emotion that often starts suddenly: *a sudden burst of activity / energy / anger / enthusiasm* ◇ *Her breath was coming in short bursts.* ◇ *I tend to work in bursts.* ◇ *spontaneous bursts of applause* **2** an occasion when sth bursts; the hole left where sth has burst: *a burst in a water pipe* **3** a short series of shots from a gun: *frequent bursts of machine-gun fire*

bur·ton /'bɜːtn; *AmE* 'bɜːrtn/ *noun* [IDM] **gone for a 'burton** (*old-fashioned, BrE, informal*) lost or destroyed

bury /'beri/ *verb* (**bur·ies**, **bury·ing**, **bur·ied**, **bur·ied**)
DEAD PERSON | **1** [VN] to place a dead body in a grave: *He was buried in Highgate Cemetery.* ◇ (*figurative*) *Their ambitions were finally dead and buried.* **2** [VN] (*old-fashioned*) to lose sb by death: *She's 85 and has buried three husbands.*
HIDE IN GROUND | **3** [VN] to hide sth in the ground: *buried treasure* ◇ *The dog had buried its bone in the garden.*
COVER | **4** [often passive] to cover sb/sth with soil, rocks, leaves, etc: [VN] *The house was buried under ten feet of snow.* ◇ [VN-ADJ] *The miners were buried alive when the tunnel collapsed.* **5** [VN] to cover sth so that it cannot be seen: *Your letter got buried under a pile of papers.* ◇ *He buried his face in his hands and wept.*
HIDE FEELING | **6** [VN] to ignore or hide a feeling, a mistake, etc: *She had learnt to bury her feelings.*
PUT DEEPLY INTO STH | **7** [VN] **~ sth (in sth)** to put sth deeply into sth else: *He walked slowly, his hands buried in his pockets.* ◇ *She always has her head buried in a book.*
[IDM] **,bury the 'hatchet** | **,bury your 'differences** to stop being unfriendly and become friends again—more at HEAD *n.*
[PHR V] **'bury yourself in sth 1** to give all your attention to sth: *Since she left, he's buried himself in his work.* **2** to go to or be in a place where you will not meet many people: *She buried herself in the country to write a book.*

bus /bʌs/ *noun, verb*

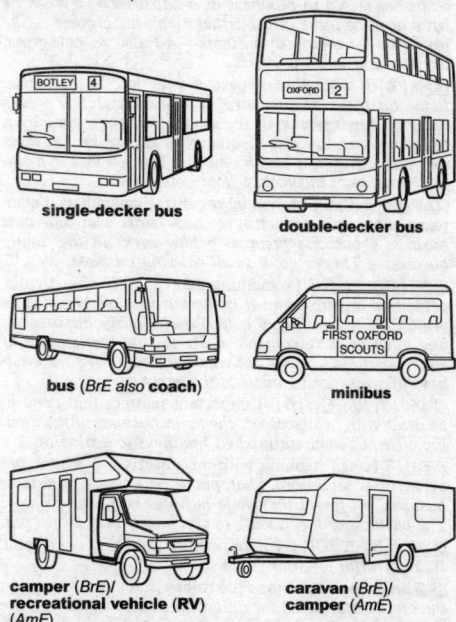

single-decker bus

double-decker bus

bus (*BrE also* **coach**)

minibus

camper (*BrE*)/ **recreational vehicle** (**RV**) (*AmE*)

caravan (*BrE*)/ **camper** (*AmE*)

■ *noun* (*pl.* **buses**, *AmE also* **busses**) a large road vehicle that carries passengers, especially one that travels along a fixed route and stops regularly to let people get on and

B

off: *Shall we walk or go by bus?* ◊ *A regular bus service connects the train station with the town centre.* ◊ *a bus company/driver* ◊ *a school bus*—compare COACH—see also BUS LANE, BUS SHELTER, BUS STATION, BUS STOP, MINIBUS, TROLLEY BUS

■ *verb* (**-s-** or **-ss-**) [VN] **1 ~ sb (from/to …)** to transport sb by bus: *We were bussed from the airport to our hotel.* **2** (*AmE*) to transport young people by bus to another area so that students of different races can be educated together **3** (*AmE*) to take the dirty plates, etc. off the tables in a restaurant, as a job

bus·boy /'bʌsbɔɪ/ *noun* (*AmE*) a person who works in a restaurant and whose job is to clear the dirty dishes, etc.

busby /'bʌzbi/ *noun* (*pl.* **-ies**) a tall fur hat worn by some British soldiers for special ceremonies

bush /bʊʃ/ *noun* **1** [C] a plant that grows thickly with several hard stems coming up from the root: *a rose bush* ◊ *holly bushes*—compare TREE **2** [C] a thing that looks like a bush, especially an area of thick hair or fur **3** (often **the bush**) [U] an area of wild land that has not been cleared, especially in Africa and Australia **IDM** see BEAT *v.*, BIRD

bushed /bʊʃt/ *adj.* [not before noun] (*informal*) very tired

bushel /'bʊʃl/ *noun* **1** [C] a unit for measuring grain and fruit (equal in volume to 8 GALLONS) **2** (**bushels**) [pl.] **~ (of sth)** (*AmE, informal*) a large amount of sth **IDM** see HIDE *v.*

bush-league *adj.* (*AmE, informal*) of very low quality

Bush·man /'bʊʃmən/ *noun* (*pl.* **-men** /-mən/) a member of one of the races of people from southern Africa who live and hunt in the African BUSH

bushy /'bʊʃi/ *adj.* **1** (of hair or fur) growing thickly: *a bushy beard/tail* ◊ *bushy eyebrows* **2** (of plants) growing thickly, with a lot of leaves

bushy-'tailed *adj.* ⊳ BRIGHT-EYED

busily ⊳ BUSY

busi·ness /'bɪznəs/ *noun*

TRADE | **1** [U] the activity of making, buying, selling or supplying goods or services for money [SYN] COMMERCE, TRADE: *business contacts/affairs/interests* ◊ *a business investment* ◊ *It's been a pleasure to do business with you.* ◊ *She has set up in business as a hairdresser.* ◊ *When he left school, he went into business with his brother.* ◊ *She works in the computer business.*—see also AGRIBUSINESS, BIG BUSINESS, SHOW BUSINESS

WORK | **2** [U] work that is part of your job: *Is the trip to Rome business or pleasure?* ◊ *a business lunch* ◊ *He's away on business.* **3** [U] the amount of work done by a company, etc.; the rate or quality of this work: *Business was bad.* ◊ *Business was booming.* ◊ *Her job was to drum up* (= increase) *business.* ◊ *How's business?*

COMPANY | **4** [C] a commercial organization such as a company, shop/store or factory: *to have/start/run your own business* ◊ *business premises* ◊ *She works in the family business.* ◊ *They've got a small catering business.*

RESPONSIBILITY | **5** [U] something that concerns a particular person or organization: *It is the business of the police to protect the community.* ◊ *I shall make it my business to find out who is responsible.* ◊ *My private life is none of your business* (= does not concern you). ◊ *It's no business of yours who I invite to the party.*

IMPORTANT MATTERS | **6** [U] important matters that need to be dealt with or discussed: *the main business of the meeting* ◊ *He has some unfinished business to deal with.*

EVENT | **7** [sing.] (usually with an adjective) a matter, an event or a situation: *That plane crash was a terrible business.* ◊ *I found the whole business very depressing.* ◊ *The business of the missing tickets hasn't been sorted out.*

BEING A CUSTOMER | **8** [U] (*especially AmE*) = CUSTOM (3): *We're grateful for your business.*

IDM **any other 'business** the things that are discussed at the end of an official meeting that do not appear on the AGENDA: *I think we've finished item four. Now is there any other business?*—see also AOB **be in 'business** (*informal*) to have everything that you need in order to be able to start sth immediately: *All we need is a car and we'll be in*

business. **be the 'business** (*spoken, slang*) to be very good **business as 'usual** a way of saying that things will continue as normal in spite of a difficult situation ,**busi·ness is 'business** a way of saying that financial and commercial matters are the important things to consider and you should not be influenced by friendship, etc. **get down to 'business** to start dealing with the matter that needs to be dealt with, or doing the work that needs to be done: *Let's get down to business right away—we'll stop for coffee later.* **go about your 'business** to do the things that you normally do: *streets filled with people going about their daily business* **have no business doing sth | have no business to do sth** to have no right to do sth: *You have no business being here.* **like 'nobody's business** (*BrE, spoken*) very much, very fast, very well, etc: *I've been working like nobody's business to get it finished in time.* **not be in the business of doing sth** not intending to do sth (which it would be surprising for you to do): *I'm not in the business of getting other people to do my work for me.* **out of 'business** having stopped operating as a business because there is no more money or work available: *The new regulations will put many small businesses out of business.* ◊ *Some small companies will probably go out of business this summer.*—more at MEAN *v.*, MIND *v.*, PLY *v.*

'**business card** (also **card**) *noun* a small card printed with sb's name and details of their job and company—compare VISITING CARD

the 'business end *noun* [sing.] **~ (of sth)** (*informal*) the end of a tool or weapon which performs its main function: *Never hold a gun by the business end.*

'**business hours** *noun* [pl.] the hours in a day that a shop/store or company is open

busi·ness·like /'bɪznəslaɪk/ *adj.* (of a person) working in an efficient and organized way and not wasting time or thinking about personal things: *Wearing a suit made him feel more businesslike.* ◊ *She adopted a brisk businesslike tone.*

busi·ness·man /'bɪznəsmæn; -mən/, **busi·ness·woman** /'bɪznəswʊmən/ *noun* (*pl.* **-men** /-mən/, **-women** /-wɪmɪn/) **1** a person who works in business, especially at a high level **2** a person who is skilful in business and financial matters: *I should have got a better price for the car, but I'm not much of a businessman.*

'**business park** *noun* an area of land that is specially designed for offices and small factories

'**business studies** *noun* [U+sing./pl. *v.*] the study of subjects connected with money and managing a business: *a degree in business studies*

busk /bʌsk/ *verb* [V] (*informal, especially BrE*) to perform music in a public place and ask for money from people passing by ▸ **busk·er** *noun* **busk·ing** *noun* [U]

'**bus lane** *noun* a part of a road that only buses are allowed to use

bus·load /'bʌsləʊd; *AmE* -loʊd/ *noun* (*especially AmE*) a large group of people on a bus

,**bus·man's 'holi·day** *noun* [sing.] a holiday that is spent doing the same thing that you do at work

'**bus shelter** *noun* a structure with a roof where people can stand while they are waiting for a bus

'**bus station** *noun* the place in a town or city where buses (especially to or from other towns) leave and arrive

'**bus stop** *noun* a place at the side of a road that is marked with a sign, where buses stop

bust /bʌst/ *verb, noun, adj.*

■ *verb* (**bust, bust**) or (**bust·ed, bust·ed**) [VN] (*informal*) **1** to break sth: *I bust my camera.* ◊ *The lights are busted.* ◊ *Come out, or I'll bust the door down!* **2 ~ sb/sth (for sth)** (of the police) to suddenly enter a place and search it or arrest sb: *He's been busted for drugs.* **3** (*especially AmE*) to make sb lower in military rank as a punishment **IDM** **bust a 'gut (doing sth/to do sth)** (*informal*) to make a great effort to do sth: *It's a problem which nobody is going to bust a gut trying to solve.* **…or 'bust** (*informal*) used to say that you will try very hard to get somewhere or achieve sth: *For him it's the Olympics or bust.* **PHRV** ,**bust 'up** (*informal*) (of a couple, friends, partners, etc.) to

s	t	v	z	ʃ	ʒ	tʃ	dʒ	θ	ð	ŋ
see	tea	van	zoo	shoe	vision	chain	jam	thin	this	sing

quarrel and separate: *They bust up after five years of marriage.*—related noun BUST-UP ,**bust sth**↔'**up** (*informal*) to make sth end by disturbing or ruining it: *It was his drinking that bust up his marriage.*

■ *noun* **1** a stone or metal model of a person's head, shoulders and chest **2** (used especially when talking about clothes or measurements) a woman's breasts or the measurement around the breasts and back: *What is your bust measurement, Madam?* **3** (*informal*) an unexpected visit made by the police in order to arrest people for doing sth illegal: *a drug bust*

■ *adj.* [not usually before noun] (*informal*) **1** (*BrE*) broken: *My watch is bust.* **2** (of a person or business) failed because of a lack of money: *We're bust!* ◇ *We lost our money when the travel company went bust.*

bus·ter /'bʌstə(r)/ *noun* **1** (*AmE, informal*) used to speak to a man you do not like: *Get lost, buster!* **2** (usually in compounds; often used in newspapers) a person or thing that stops or gets rid of sth: *crime busters*

bus·tier /'bʌstieɪ/ *noun* a woman's tight top without sleeves or shoulder straps

bus·tle /'bʌsl/ *verb, noun*

■ *verb* [+*adv./prep.*] to move around in a busy way or to hurry sb in a particular direction: [V] *She bustled around in the kitchen.* ◇ [VN] *The nurse bustled us out of the room.*

■ *noun* **1** [U] busy and noisy activity: *the hustle and bustle of city life* **2** [C] a frame that was worn under a skirt by women in the past in order to hold the skirt out at the back

bust·ling /'bʌslɪŋ/ *adj.* ~ **(with sth)** full of people moving about in a busy way: *a bustling city/port* ◇ *The market was bustling with life.*

'**bust-up** *noun* (*informal, especially BrE*) **1** a bad argument or very angry disagreement: *Sue and Tony had a bust-up and aren't speaking to each other.* **2** the end of a relationship: *the final bust-up of their marriage*

busty /'bʌsti/ *adj.* (*informal*) (of a woman) having large breasts

busy /'bɪzi/ *adj., verb*

■ *adj.* (**busier, busi·est**)

DOING STH | **1** ~ **(with sth/sb)** having a lot to do; perhaps not free to do sth else because you are working on sth: *Are you busy tonight?* ◇ *Kate's busy with her homework.* ◇ *I'm afraid the doctor is busy at the moment. Can he call you back?* ◇ *I'll be too busy to come to the meeting.* ◇ *The principal is a very busy woman.* ◇ *She was always too busy to listen.* ◇ *a very busy life* **2** ~ **(doing sth)** spending a lot of time on sth: *James is busy practising for the school concert.* ◇ *Let's get busy with the clearing up.*

PLACE | **3** full of people, activity, vehicles, etc: *a busy main road* ◇ *Victoria is one of London's busiest stations.*

PERIOD OF TIME | **4** full of work and activity: *Have you had a busy day?* ◇ *This is one of the busiest times of the year for the department.*

TELEPHONE | **5** (*especially AmE*) being used SYN ENGAGED: *The line is busy—I'll try again later.* ◇ *the busy signal*

PATTERN/DESIGN | **6** too full of small details

▶ **busily** *adv.*: *He was busily engaged repairing his bike.* IDM **as busy as a** '**bee** very busy **keep yourself** '**busy** to find enough things to do: *Since she retired she's kept herself very busy.*

■ *verb* (**busies, busy·ing, busied, busied**) ~ **yourself (with sth)** | ~ **yourself (in/with) doing sth** to fill your time doing an activity or a task: [VN-*ing*] *While we talked, Bill busied himself fixing lunch.* ◇ [VN] *She busied herself with the preparations for the party.*

busy·body /'bɪzibɒdi; *AmE* -baːdi/ *noun* (*pl.* -**ies**) (*disapproving*) a person who is too interested in what other people are doing: *He's an interfering old busybody!*

busy Lizzie /,bɪzi 'lɪzi/ *noun* a small plant with a lot of red, pink or white flowers, often grown indoors or in gardens

busy·work /'bɪziwɜːk; *AmE* -wɜːrk/ *noun* [U] (*AmE*) work that is given to sb to keep them busy, without really being useful

but /bət; *strong form* bʌt/ *conj., prep., adv., noun*

■ *conj.* **1** used to introduce a word or phrase that contrasts with what was said before: *I got it wrong. It wasn't the red one but the blue one.* ◇ *His mother won't be there, but his father might.* ◇ *It isn't that he lied exactly, but he did tend to exaggerate.* **2** however; in spite of this: *I'd asked everybody but only two people came.* ◇ *By the end of the day we were tired but happy.* **3** used when you are saying sorry about sth: *I'm sorry but I can't stay any longer.* **4** used to introduce a statement that shows that you are surprised or annoyed, or that you disagree: *But that's not possible!* ◇ *'Here's the money I owe you.' 'But that's not right—it was only £10.'* **5** except: *I had no choice but to sign the contract.* **6** used before repeating a word in order to emphasize it: *Nothing, but nothing would make him change his mind.* **7** (*literary*) used to emphasize that sth is always true: *She never passed her old home but she thought of the happy years she had spent there* (= she always thought of them). IDM **but then (again)** **1** however; on the other hand: *He might agree. But then again he might have a completely different opinion.* **2** used before a statement that explains or gives a reason for what has just been said: *She speaks very good Italian. But then she did live in Rome for a year* (= so it's not surprising). **you cannot/could not but ...** (*formal*) used to show that everything else is impossible except the thing that you are saying: *What could he do but forgive her?* (= that was the only thing possible)

■ *prep.* except; apart from: *We've had nothing but trouble with this car.* ◇ *The problem is anything but easy.* ◇ *Who but Rosa could think of something like that?* ◇ *Everyone was there but him.* ◇ *I came last but one in the race* (= I wasn't last but next to last). ◇ *Take the first turning but one* (= not the first one but the one after it).

■ *adv.* only: *I don't think we'll manage it. Still, we can but try.* ◇ *There were a lot of famous people there: Tom Hanks and Julia Roberts, to name but two.*

■ *noun* /bʌt/ [usually pl.] a reason that sb gives for not doing sth or not agreeing: *'Let us have no buts,' he said firmly. 'You are coming.'*

bu·tane /'bjuːteɪn/ *noun* [U] a gas produced from PETROLEUM, used in liquid form as a fuel for cooking, heating, etc.

butch /bʊtʃ/ *adj.* (*informal*) **1** (of a woman) behaving or dressing like a man **2** (of a man) big, and often behaving in an aggressive way

butcher /'bʊtʃə(r)/ *noun, verb*

■ *noun* **1** a person whose job is cutting up and selling meat in a shop/store or killing animals for this purpose **2** (**butcher's**) (*pl.* **butchers**) a shop/store that sells meat: *He owns the butcher's in the main street.* **3** a person who kills people in a cruel and violent way IDM **have/take a** '**butcher's** (*BrE, slang*) to have a look at sth ORIGIN From rhyming slang, in which **butcher's hook** stands for 'look'.

■ *verb* [VN] **1** to kill people in a very cruel and violent way **2** to kill animals and cut them up for use as meat **3** (*especially AmE*) to spoil sth by doing it very badly: *The script was good, but those guys butchered it.*

butch·ery /'bʊtʃəri/ *noun* [U] **1** cruel, violent and unnecessary killing **2** the work of preparing meat to be sold

but·ler /'bʌtlə(r)/ *noun* the main male servant in a large house

butt /bʌt/ *verb, noun*

■ *verb* [VN] **1** to hit or push sb/sth hard with your head **2** if an animal **butts** sth/sb, it hits them or it hard with its horns and head PHRV ,**butt** '**in (on sb/sth)** **1** to interrupt a conversation rudely: *How can I explain if you keep butting in?* ◇ [+ *speech*] *'Is that normal?' Josie butted in.* **2** (*informal*) to become involved in a situation that does not concern you: *I didn't ask you to butt in on my private business.* ,**butt** '**out** (*spoken, especially AmE*) used to tell sb rudely to go away or to stop interfering in sth that does not concern them: *Butt out, Neil! This is none of your business.*

■ *noun* **1** the thick end of a weapon or tool: *a rifle butt* **2** the part of a cigarette or CIGAR that is left after it has been smoked **3** (*BrE*) a large round container for storing or collecting liquids: *a water butt* **4** (*informal, especially*

æ	ɑː	e	ɜː	ə	ɪ	iː	i	ɒ	ɔː	ʌ	ʊ	u	uː
cat	father	ten	bird	about	sit	see	many	got	saw	cup	put	actual	too
								(BrE)					

AmE) the part of the body that you sit on SYN BUTTOCKS: *Get off your butt and do some work!* ◊ *Get your butt over here!* (= Come here!) **5** the act of hitting sb with your head: *a head butt* IDM **be the butt of sth** to be the person or thing that other people often joke about or criticize: *She was the butt of some very unkind jokes.*—more at PAIN *n.*

but·ter /ˈbʌtə(r)/ *noun, verb*
- *noun* [U] a soft yellow food made from cream or milk, used in cooking and for spreading on bread: *Fry the onions in butter.*—see also BREAD AND BUTTER, PEANUT BUTTER IDM **butter wouldn't melt in sb's ˈmouth** (*spoken*) used to say that sb seems to be innocent, kind, etc. when they are not really—more at KNIFE *v.*
- *verb* [VN] to spread or put butter on sth: *She buttered four thick slices of bread.* IDM see KNOW *v.* PHRV **ˌbutter sb↔ˈup** (*informal*) to say nice things to sb so that they will help you or give you sth

ˈbutter bean *noun* (*BrE*) a large pale yellow bean. Butter beans are often sold dried.

but·ter·cup /ˈbʌtəkʌp; *AmE* -tərk-/ *noun* a wild plant with small shiny yellow flowers that are shaped like cups

but·ter·fin·gers /ˈbʌtəfɪŋgəz; *AmE* ˈbʌtərfɪŋgərz/ *noun* [sing.] (*informal*) a person who often drops things

but·ter·fly /ˈbʌtəflaɪ; *AmE* -tərf-/ *noun* (*pl.* -ies) **1** [C] a flying insect with a long thin body and four large, usually brightly coloured, wings: *butterflies and moths* ◊ *She's like a butterfly. She flits in and out of people's lives.*—picture on page A7 **2** [U] a swimming stroke in which you swim on your front and lift both arms forward at the same time while your legs move up and down together: *She was third in the 200m butterfly* (= a swimming race).—picture at SWIMMING IDM **have ˈbutterflies (in your stomach)** (*informal*) to have a nervous feeling in your stomach before doing sth

but·ter·milk /ˈbʌtəmɪlk; *AmE* -tərm-/ *noun* [U] the liquid that remains after butter has been separated from milk, used in cooking or as a drink

but·ter·scotch /ˈbʌtəskɒtʃ; *AmE* ˈbʌtərskɑːtʃ/ *noun* [U] **1** a type of hard pale brown sweet/candy made by boiling butter and brown sugar together **2** (*especially AmE*) a sauce flavoured with butterscotch, used for pouring on ice cream, etc.

but·tery /ˈbʌtəri/ *adj.* like, containing or covered with butter

but·tock /ˈbʌtək/ *noun* [usually pl.] either of the two round soft parts at the top of a person's legs: *The beating had left red weals on his buttocks* (= on his bottom).—picture at BODY

but·ton /ˈbʌtn/ *noun, verb*
- *noun* **1** a small round piece of metal, plastic, etc. that is sewn onto a piece of clothing and used for fastening two parts together: (*BrE*) *to do up/undo your buttons* ◊ (*AmE*) *to button/unbutton your buttons* ◊ *to sew on a button* ◊ *shirt buttons*—picture at FASTENER **2** a small part of a machine that you press to make it work: *the play/stop/rewind button* ◊ *Adam pressed a button and waited for the lift.* ◊ *Choose 'printer' from the menu and click with the right mouse button.* ◊ *The windows slide down at the touch of a button.*—see also PUSH-BUTTON **3** (*especially AmE*) a BADGE, especially one with a message printed on it—picture at BADGE—see also BELLY BUTTON IDM see BRIGHT *adj.*
- *verb* **1** [VN] ~ **sth (up)** to fasten sth with buttons: *She hurriedly buttoned (up) her blouse.* **2** [V] ~ **(up)** to be fastened with buttons: *The dress buttons (up) at the back.* IDM **ˈbutton it!** (*BrE, spoken*) used to tell sb rudely to be quiet

ˌbutton-ˈdown *adj.* a button-down collar, shirt, etc. has the ends of the collar fastened to the shirt with buttons—picture on page A4

but·ton·hole /ˈbʌtnhəʊl; *AmE* -hoʊl/ *noun, verb*
- *noun* **1** a hole on a piece of clothing for a button to be put through—picture at FASTENER **2** (*BrE*) (*AmE* **bou·ton·nière**) a flower that is worn in the buttonhole of a coat or jacket

- *verb* (*informal*) [VN] to make sb stop and listen to you, especially when they do not want to

ˌbutton ˈmushroom *noun* a small young MUSHROOM used in cooking

but·tress /ˈbʌtrəs/ *noun, verb*
- *noun* a stone or brick structure that supports a wall
- *verb* [VN] (*formal*) to support or give strength to sb/sth: *The sharp increase in crime seems to buttress the argument for more police officers on the street.*

butty /ˈbʌti/ *noun* (*pl.* -ies) (*BrE, informal*) a sandwich: *a jam butty*

buxom /ˈbʌksəm/ *adj.* (of a woman) large in an attractive way, and with large breasts

buy /baɪ/ *verb, noun*
- *verb* (**bought, bought** /bɔːt/)
  WITH MONEY | **1** ~ **sb sth** | ~ **sth (for sb)** to obtain sth by paying money for it: [VNN, VN] *He bought me a new coat.* ◊ *He bought a new coat for me.* ◊ [VN] *Where did you buy that dress?* ◊ *I bought it from a friend for £10.* ◊ [V] *If you're thinking of getting a new car, now is a good time to buy.* ◊ [VN-ADJ] *I bought my car second-hand.* **2** [VN] (of money) to be enough to pay for sth: *He gave his children the best education that money can buy.* ◊ *Five pounds doesn't buy much nowadays.* **3** [VN] to persuade sb to do sth dishonest in return for money SYN BRIBE: *He can't be bought* (= he's too honest to accept money in this way).
  OBTAIN | **4** [VN] [usually passive] to obtain sth by losing sth else of great value: *Her fame was bought at the expense of her marriage.*
  BELIEVE | **5** [VN] (*informal*) to believe that sth is true, especially sth that is not very likely: *You could say you were ill but I don't think they'd buy it* (= accept the explanation).
  IDM **(have) ˈbought it** (*BrE, informal*) to be killed, especially in an accident or a war **buy ˈtime** to do sth in order to delay an event, a decision, etc.—more at PIG *n.*, PUP PHRV **ˌbuy sb↔ˈin** (*BrE*) to buy sth in large quantities **ˌbuy ˈinto sth 1** to buy shares in a company, especially in order to gain some control over it **2** (*informal*) to believe sth, especially an idea that many other people believe in: *She had never bought into the idea that to be attractive you have to be thin.* **ˌbuy sb↔ˈoff** to pay sb money, especially dishonestly, to prevent them from doing sth you do not want them to do **ˌbuy sb↔ˈout 1** to pay sb for their share in a business, usually in order to get total control of it for yourself—related noun BUYOUT **2** to pay money so that sb can leave an organization, especially the army, before the end of an agreed period **ˌbuy sth↔ˈup** to buy all or as much as possible of sth: *Developers are buying up all the land on the island.*
- *noun*
  STH BOUGHT | **1** a good, better, etc. ~ a thing that is worth the money that you pay for it: *That jacket was a really good buy.* ◊ *Best buys this week are carrots and cabbages.* **2** something that is bought or that is for sale; the act of buying sth: *Computer games are a popular buy this Christmas.*

buyer /ˈbaɪə(r)/ *noun* **1** a person who buys sth, especially sth expensive: *Have you found a buyer for your house?*—compare PURCHASER **2** a person whose job is to choose goods that will be sold in a large shop/store IDM **a ˌbuyer's ˈmarket** a situation in which there is a lot of a particular item for sale, so that prices are low and people buying have a choice

buy·out /ˈbaɪaʊt/ *noun* a situation in which a person or group gains control of a company by buying all or most of its shares: *a management buyout*

buzz /bʌz/ *verb, noun*
- *verb* **1** [V] (of a bee) to make a continuous low sound: *Bees buzzed lazily among the flowers.* **2** [V] to make a sound like a bee buzzing: *The doorbell buzzed loudly.* ◊ *My ears were buzzing* (= were filled with a continuous sound). **3** [V] ~ **(with sth)** to be full of excitement, activity, etc: *The place was buzzing with journalists.* ◊ *New York buzzes from dawn to dusk.* ◊ *My head was still buzzing after the day's events.* **4** ~ **(for sb/sth)** to call sb to come by pressing a BUZZER: [V] *The doctor buzzed for the next*

aɪ	aʊ	eɪ	əʊ	oʊ	ɔɪ	ɪə	eə	ʊə	j	w
my	now	say	go	go	boy	near	hair	pure	yes	wet
			(BrE)	(AmE)						

patient to come in. [also VN] **5** [VN] (*informal*) to fly very close to sb/sth, especially as a warning or threat PHRV **,buzz a'bout/a'round** to move around quickly, especially because you are very busy: *I've been buzzing around town all day sorting out my trip.* **,buzz 'off** (*informal*) used to tell sb rudely to go away: *Just buzz off and let me get on with my work.*
■ *noun* **1** [C, usually sing.] (also **buzz·ing** [U, sing.]) a continuous sound like the one that a bee, a BUZZER or other electronic device makes: *the buzz of bees hunting nectar* ◊ *The buzz of the Entryphone interrupted our conversation.* ◊ *hums and buzzes from the amplifier* **2** [sing.] the sound of people talking, especially in an excited way: *The buzz of conversation suddenly stopped when she came into the room.* **3** [sing.] (*informal*) a strong feeling of pleasure, excitement or achievement: *a buzz of excitement/expectation* ◊ *She gets a buzz out of her work.* ◊ *Flying gives me a real buzz.* ◊ *You can sense the creative buzz in the city.* **4** (**the buzz**) [sing.] (*informal*) news that people tell each other that may or may not be true SYN RUMOUR IDM **give sb a 'buzz** (*informal*) to telephone sb: *I'll give you a buzz on Monday, OK?*

buz·zard /'bʌzəd; AmE -zərd/ *noun* **1** (*BrE*) a large European BIRD OF PREY (= a bird that kills other creatures for food) of the HAWK family **2** (*AmE*) a large American bird like a VULTURE that eats the flesh of animals that are already dead

buzz·er /'bʌzə(r)/ *noun* an electrical device that produces a BUZZING sound as a signal

buzz·word /'bʌzwɜːd; AmE -wɜːrd/ *noun* a word or phrase, especially one connected with a particular subject, that has become fashionable and popular and is used a lot in newspapers, etc: *Digital is the buzzword of the moment in communications technology.*

by /baɪ/ *prep., adv.*
■ *prep.* **1** near sb/sth; at the side of sb/sth; beside sb/sth: *a house by the river* ◊ *The telephone is by the window.* ◊ *Come and sit by me.* **2** used, usually after a passive verb, to show who or what does, creates or causes sth: *He was knocked down by a bus.* ◊ *a play by Ibsen* ◊ *Who's that book by?* ◊ *I was frightened by the noise.* **3** used for showing how or in what way sth is done: *The house is heated by gas.* ◊ *May I pay by cheque?* ◊ *I will contact you by letter.* ◊ *to travel by boat/bus/car/plane* ◊ *to travel by air/land/sea* ◊ *Switch it on by pressing this button.* **4** used before particular nouns without *the*, to say that sth happens as a result of sth: *They met by chance.* ◊ *I did it by mistake.* ◊ *The coroner's verdict was 'death by misadventure'.* **5** not later than the time mentioned; before: *Can you finish the work by five o'clock?* ◊ *I'll have it done by tomorrow.* ◊ *By this time next week we'll be in New York.* ◊ *He ought to have arrived by now/by this time.* ◊ *By the time (that) this letter reaches you I will have left the country.* **6** past sb/sth: *He walked by me without speaking.* **7** during sth; in a particular situation: *to travel by day/night* ◊ *We had to work by candlelight.* **8** used to show the degree or amount of sth: *The bullet missed him by two inches.* ◊ *House prices went up by 10%.* ◊ *It would be better by far* (= much better) *to ...* **9** from what sth shows or says; according to sth: *By my watch it is two o'clock.* ◊ *I could tell by the look on her face that something terrible had happened.* ◊ *By law, you are a child until you are 18.* **10** used to show the part of sb/sth that sb touches, holds, etc: *I took him by the hand.* ◊ *She seized her by the hair.* ◊ *Pick it up by the handle!* **11** used with *the* to show the period or quantity used for buying, selling or measuring sth: *We rented the car by the day.* ◊ *They're paid by the hour.* ◊ *We only sell it by the metre.* **12** used to state the rate at which sth happens: *They're improving day by day.* ◊ *We'll do it bit by bit.* ◊ *The children came in two by two* (= in groups of two). **13** used for giving more information about where sb comes from, what sb does, etc: *He's German by birth.* ◊ *They're both doctors by profession.* **14** used when swearing to mean 'in the name of': *I swear by Almighty God ...* **15** used to show the measurements of sth: *The room measures fifteen feet by twenty feet.* **16** used when multiplying or dividing: *6 multiplied by 2 equals 12.*

◊ *6 divided by 2 equals 3.* IDM **by the 'by/'bye** = BY THE WAY at WAY
■ *adv.* **1** past: *Just drive by. Don't stop.* ◊ *He hurried by without speaking to me.* ◊ *Excuse me, I can't get by.* ◊ *Time goes by so quickly.* **2** used to say that sth is saved so that it can be used in the future: *I've put some money by for college fees.* **3** in order to visit sb for a short time: *I'll come by this evening and pick up the books.* IDM **by and 'by** (*old-fashioned*) before long; soon: *By and by she met an old man with a beard.*

by- (also **bye-**) /baɪ/ *prefix* (in nouns and verbs) **1** less important: *a by-product* **2** near: *a bystander*

bye /baɪ/ *exclamation, noun*
■ *exclamation* (also **,bye-'bye**, **'bye-bye**) (*informal*) goodbye: *Bye! See you next week.* ◊ *She waved bye-bye and got into the car.* ◊ *Bye for now Dad!*
■ *noun* (*sport*) a situation in which a player or team does not have an opponent in one part of the competition and continues to the next part as if they had won IDM see BY

'by-election *noun* (*BrE*) an election of a new Member of Parliament to replace sb who has died or left parliament—compare GENERAL ELECTION

by·gone /'baɪɡɒn; AmE -ɡɔːn; -ɡɑːn/ *adj.* [only before noun] happening or existing a long time ago: *a bygone age/era*

by·gones /'baɪɡɒnz; AmE -ɡɔːnz; -ɡɑːnz/ *noun* [pl.] IDM **let ,bygones be 'bygones** to decide to forget about disagreements that happened in the past

'by-law (also **'bye-law**) *noun* **1** (*BrE*) a law that is made by a local authority and that applies only to that area **2** (*AmE*) a law or rule of a club or company

by·line /'baɪlaɪn/ *noun* a line at the beginning or end of a piece of writing in a newspaper or magazine that gives the writer's name

by·pass /'baɪpɑːs/ *noun, verb*
■ *noun* **1** (*especially BrE*) a road that passes around a town or city rather than through the centre **2** a medical operation on the heart in which blood is directed along a different route so that it does not flow through a part that is damaged or blocked; the new route that the blood takes: *heart bypass surgery* ◊ *a triple bypass operation*
■ *verb* [VN] **1** to go around or avoid a place: *A new road now bypasses the town.* **2** to ignore a rule, an official system or sb in authority, especially in order to get sth done quickly

'by-product *noun* **1** a substance that is produced during the process of making or destroying sth else: *When burnt, plastic produces dangerous by-products.* **2** a thing that happens, often unexpectedly, as the result of sth else: *One of the by-products of unemployment is an increase in crime.*

byre /'baɪə(r)/ *noun* (*old-fashioned, BrE*) a farm building in which cows are kept

by·stand·er /'baɪstændə(r)/ *noun* a person who sees sth that is happening but is not involved SYN ONLOOKER: *innocent bystanders at the scene of the accident*

byte /baɪt/ *noun* a unit of information stored in a computer, equal to 8 BITS. A computer's memory is measured in bytes.

byway /'baɪweɪ/ *noun* **1** [C] a small road that is not used very much **2** (**byways**) [pl.] the less important areas of a subject

by·word /'baɪwɜːd; AmE -wɜːrd/ *noun* [usually sing.] **1** **a ~ for sth** a person or thing that is a well-known or typical example of a particular quality: *The name Chanel became a byword for elegance.* **2** (*especially AmE*) a word or phrase that is well known or often used

By·zan·tine /baɪ'zæntaɪn; bɪ-; -tiːn; AmE 'bɪzəntiːn/ *adj.* [usually before noun] **1** connected with Byzantium or the Eastern Roman Empire **2** used to describe architecture of the 5th to the 15th centuries in the Byzantine Empire, especially churches with high central DOMES and MOSAICS **3** (also **byzantine**) (*formal*) (of an idea, a system, etc.) complicated, secret and difficult to change: *an organization of byzantine complexity*

b	d	f	g	h	k	l	m	n	p	r
bad	did	fall	get	hat	cat	leg	man	now	pen	red

Cc

C /siː/ *noun, abbr., symbol*

■ *noun* (also **c**) [C, U] (*pl.* **C's, c's** /siːz/) **1** the third letter of the English alphabet: *'Cat' begins with (a) C/'C'.* **2** (**C**) (*music*) the first note in the scale of C MAJOR—see also MIDDLE C **3** (**C**) the third highest mark/grade that a student can get for a piece of work: *She got (a) C/'C' in/for Physics.*

■ *abbr.* **1** (**C.**) CAPE: *C. Horn* (= for example, on a map) **2** CELSIUS, CENTIGRADE: *Water freezes at 0° C.* **3** (also ©) (*AmE* also **C.**) COPYRIGHT: © *Oxford University Press 1999*—see also C. OF E., C. & W.

■ *symbol* (also **c**) the number 100 in ROMAN NUMERALS

c (*BrE*) (also **c.** *AmE, BrE*) *abbr.* **1** (in writing) CENT(S) **2** (also **C**) (in writing) century: *in the 19th c* ◊ (*AmE*) *a C19th church*—see also CENT. **3** (also **ca**) (especially before dates) about; approximately (from Latin *circa*): *c1890* **4** (*AmE*) (in cooking) cup: *add 2c. flour*

cab /kæb/ *noun* **1** a taxi **2** the place where the driver sits in a bus, train or lorry/truck

cabal /kəˈbæl/ *noun* (*formal*, usually *disapproving*) a small group of people who are involved in secret plans to get political power

caba·ret /ˈkæbəreɪ; *AmE* ˌkæbəˈreɪ/ *noun* **1** [C, U] entertainment with singing and dancing that is performed in restaurants or clubs in the evenings: *a cabaret act/singer/band* **2** [C] a restaurant or club where cabaret entertainment is performed

cab·bage /ˈkæbɪdʒ/ *noun* **1** [U, C] a round vegetable with large green, purplish-red or white leaves that can be eaten raw or cooked: *Do you like cabbage?* ◊ *two cabbages* ◊ *white/red cabbage* **2** (*BrE*) = VEGETABLE (2)—picture on page A3

cabby (also **cab·bie**) /ˈkæbi/ *noun* (*pl.* **-ies**) (*informal*) a person who drives a taxi

caber /ˈkeɪbə(r)/ *noun* a long heavy wooden pole that is thrown into the air as a test of strength in the traditional Scottish sport of **tossing the caber**

cabin /ˈkæbɪn/ *noun* **1** a small room on a ship in which you live or sleep—picture at YACHT **2** one of the areas for passengers to sit in a plane—picture at PLANE **3** a small house or shelter, usually made of wood: *a log cabin*

'cabin boy *noun* a boy or young man who works as a servant on a ship

'cabin crew *noun* [C+sing./pl. *v.*] the people whose job is to take care of passengers on a plane

'cabin cruiser *noun* = CRUISER

cab·inet /ˈkæbɪnət/ *noun* **1** (usually **the Cabinet**) [C+sing./pl. *v.*] a group of the most important government ministers, or ADVISERS to a president, responsible for advising and deciding on government policy: *a cabinet meeting* ◊ (*BrE*) *a cabinet minister* ◊ (*BrE*) *the shadow Cabinet* (= the most important members of the opposition party) **2** [C] a piece of furniture with doors, drawers and/or shelves, that is used for storing or showing things: *kitchen cabinets* ◊ *a medicine cabinet* ◊ *The china was displayed in a glass cabinet.*—see also FILING CABINET

cab·inet·maker /ˈkæbɪnətmeɪkə(r)/ *noun* a person who makes fine wooden furniture, especially as a job

cable /ˈkeɪbl/ *noun, verb*

■ *noun* **1** [U, C] thick strong metal rope used on ships, for supporting bridges, etc.—picture at ROPE **2** [C, U] a set of wires, covered in plastic or rubber, that carries electricity, telephone signals, etc: *overhead/underground cables* ◊ *a 10000 volt cable* ◊ *fibre-optic cable* **3** [U] = CABLE TELEVISION: *We can receive up to 500 cable channels.* **4** [C] (*old-fashioned*) a message sent by electrical signals and printed out

■ *verb* [V, VN] (*old-fashioned*) to send sb a message by cable

'cable car *noun* **1** a vehicle that hangs from and is pulled by a moving cable and that carries passengers up and down a mountain **2** (*especially AmE*) a vehicle that runs on tracks and is pulled by a moving cable

ˌcable 'television (also **cable**, **ˌcable T'V**) *noun* [U] a system of broadcasting television programmes along wires rather than by radio waves

cab·ling /ˈkeɪblɪŋ/ *noun* [U] all the cables that are required for particular equipment or a particular system

ca·boo·dle /kəˈbuːdl/ *noun* **IDM** **the whole (kit and) ca'boodle** everything: *I had new clothes, a new hairstyle—the whole caboodle.*

ca·boose /kəˈbuːs/ *noun* (*AmE*) the part at the back of a train where the person who is in charge of the train rides

cache /kæʃ/ *noun* **1** a hidden store of things such as weapons: *an arms cache* **2** (*computing*) a part of a computer's memory that stores copies of data that is often needed while a program is running. This data can be ACCESSED very quickly.

cachet /ˈkæʃeɪ; *AmE* kæˈʃeɪ/ *noun* [U, sing.] (*formal*) if sth has **cachet**, it has a special quality that people admire and approve of: *No other brand name has quite the same cachet.*

cack-handed /ˌkæk ˈhændɪd/ *adj.* (*BrE, informal, disapproving*) a **cack-handed** person often drops or breaks things or does things badly

cackle /ˈkækl/ *verb, noun*

■ *verb* **1** [V] (of a chicken) to make a loud unpleasant noise **2** to laugh in a loud unpleasant way: [V] *They all cackled with delight.* [also V **speech**]

■ *noun* **1** the loud noise that a HEN makes **2** a harsh unpleasant laugh

cac·oph·ony /kəˈkɒfəni; *AmE* -ˈkɑːf-/ *noun* [U, sing.] (*formal*) a mixture of loud unpleasant sounds ▶ **cac·oph·on·ous** /-nəs/ *adj.*

cac·tus /ˈkæktəs/ *noun* (*pl.* **cac·tuses** or **cacti** /ˈkæktaɪ/) a plant that grows in hot dry regions, especially one with thick stems covered in SPINES but without leaves. There are many different types of cactus.

CAD /kæd; ˌsiː eɪ ˈdiː/ *noun* [U] the abbreviation for 'computer-aided design' (the use of computers to design machines, buildings, vehicles, etc.)

cad /kæd/ *noun* (*old-fashioned*) a man who behaves in a dishonest or unfair way

ca·da·ver /kəˈdævə(r)/ *noun* (*technical*) a dead human body **SYN** CORPSE

ca·da·ver·ous /kəˈdævərəs/ *adj.* (*literary*) (of a person) extremely pale, thin and looking ill/sick

cad·die (also **caddy**) /ˈkædi/ *noun, verb*

■ *noun* (*pl.* **-ies**) (in the game of golf) a person who helps a player by carrying his or her CLUBS and equipment during a game

■ *verb* (**cad·dies, caddy·ing, cad·died, cad·died**) [V] to act as a caddie in the game of golf

caddy /ˈkædi/ *noun* (*pl.* **-ies**) **1** (*especially BrE*) = TEA CADDY **2** (*AmE*) a small bag for storing or carrying small objects: *a sewing/make-up caddy* **3** = CADDIE

ca·dence /ˈkeɪdns/ *noun* **1** (*formal*) the rise and fall of the voice in speaking: *He delivered his words in slow, measured cadences.* **2** the end of a musical phrase

ca·denza /kəˈdenzə/ *noun* (*music*) a short passage, usually near the end of a piece of classical music, which is played or sung by the SOLOIST alone, and intended to show the performer's skill

cadet /kəˈdet/ *noun* a young person who is training to

become an officer in the police or armed forces: *army cadets*

cadge /kædʒ/ *verb* ~ (sth) (from/off sb) (*BrE, informal*) to ask sb for food, money, etc. especially because you cannot or do not want to pay for sth yourself: [VN] *I managed to cadge some money off my dad.* [also V] ▶ **cadger** *noun*

cad·mium /'kædmiəm/ *noun* [U] (*symb* Cd) a chemical element. Cadmium is a soft poisonous bluish-white metal that is used in batteries and nuclear REACTORS.

cadre /'kɑːdə(r); *AmE* 'kædri/ *noun* (*formal*) **1** [C+sing./ pl. *v.*] a small group of people who are specially chosen and trained for a particular purpose **2** [C] a member of this kind of group: *They were to become the cadres of the new Communist party.*

Cae·sar·ean /si'zeəriən; *AmE* -'zer-/ (also **Cae·sar·ian**, **Cae,sarean 'section**, **Cae,sarian 'section**) (*AmE* also **ce·sar·ean**, **'C-section**, **ce·sar·ian**) *noun* [C,U] a medical operation in which an opening is cut in a woman's body in order to take out a baby: *an emergency Caesarean* ◇ *The baby was born by Caesarean section.* ◇ *She had to have a Caesarean.*

cae·sium (*BrE*) (*AmE* **ces·ium**) /'siːziəm/ *noun* [U] (*symb* Cs) a chemical element. Caesium is a soft silver-white metal, used in PHOTOELECTRIC CELLS.

caes·ura /si'zjʊərə; *AmE* si'zjʊrə/ *noun* (*technical*) a pause near the middle of a line of poetry—compare ENJAMBEMENT

cafe /'kæfeɪ; *AmE* kæ'feɪ/ *noun* a place where you can buy drinks and simple meals. Alcohol is not usually served in British or American cafes.—compare RESTAURANT

cafe·teria /ˌkæfə'tɪəriə; *AmE* -'tɪr-/ *noun* a restaurant where you choose and pay for your meal at a COUNTER and carry it to a table. Cafeterias are often found in factories, colleges, hospitals, etc.

cafe·tière /ˌkæfə'tjeə(r); *AmE* -'tjer/ *noun* a special glass container for making coffee with a metal FILTER that you push down

cafetière
plunger—
—filter

caff /'kæf/ *noun* (*BrE, informal*) a cafe serving simple, basic food: *a transport caff*

caf·feine /'kæfiːn/ *noun* [U] a drug found in coffee and tea that makes you feel more active—see also DECAFFEINATED

caffè latte /ˌkæfeɪ 'lɑːteɪ/ (also **latte**) *noun* (from Italian) a drink made by adding a small amount of strong coffee to a glass or cup of FROTHY steamed milk

caf·tan *noun* = KAFTAN

cage /keɪdʒ/ *noun, verb*
■ *noun* a structure made of metal bars or wire in which animals or birds are kept: *a birdcage*—see also RIBCAGE **IDM** see RATTLE *v.*
■ *verb* ~ sth (up) [VN] [usually passive] to put or keep an animal in a cage: *The dogs are caged (up) at night.* ▶ **caged** *adj.*: *He paced the room like a caged animal.*

cagey /'keɪdʒi/ *adj.* (**cagi·er**, **cagi·est**) ~ (about sth) (*informal*) not wanting to give sb information **SYN** SECRETIVE: *Tony is very cagey about his family.* ▶ **cagi·ly** *adv.*

ca·goule /kə'guːl/ *noun* (*BrE*) a long light jacket with a HOOD, worn to give protection from wind and rain—picture on page A5

ca·hoots /kə'huːts/ *noun* **IDM** **be in cahoots (with sb)** (*informal*) to be planning or doing sth dishonest with sb else

cai·man = CAYMAN

cairn /keən; *AmE* kern/ *noun* a pile of stones which mark a special place such as the top of a mountain or a place where sb is buried

ca·jole /kə'dʒəʊl; *AmE* kə'dʒoʊl/ *verb* ~ sb (into sth/into doing sth) | ~ sth out of sb to make sb do sth by talking to them and being very nice to them **SYN** COAX: [VN] *He cajoled me into agreeing to do the work.* ◇ *I managed to cajole his address out of them.* ◇ [V] *Her voice was soft and cajoling.* [also V speech]

Cajun /'keɪdʒn/ *noun, adj.*
■ *noun* **1** [C] a person from Louisiana whose ancestors were French and who speaks an old form of French, also called **Cajun 2** [U] a type of music originally played by Cajuns, that is a mixture of BLUES and FOLK MUSIC
■ *adj.* connected with the Cajuns, their language, music or spicy cooking: *Cajun chicken/cuisine*

cake /keɪk/ *noun, verb*
■ *noun* **1** [C, U] a sweet food made from a mixture of flour, eggs, butter, sugar, etc. that is baked in an oven. Cakes are made in various shapes and sizes and are often decorated, for example with cream or ICING: *a piece/slice of cake* ◇ *to make/bake a cake* ◇ *a chocolate cake* ◇ *a birthday cake* ◇ (*BrE*) *a cake tin* (= for cooking a cake in) ◇ (*AmE*) *a cake pan*—see also CHRISTMAS CAKE, FRUIT CAKE, SPONGE CAKE, WEDDING CAKE—picture on page A1 **2** [C] a food mixture that is cooked in a round flat shape: *potato cakes*—see also FISH CAKE **IDM** **have your cake and 'eat it** (*BrE*) (also **have your cake and eat it too** *AmE, BrE*) to have the advantages of sth without its disadvantages; to have both things that are available **a slice/share of the 'cake** (*BrE*) (*AmE* **a piece/slice/share of the 'pie**) a share of the available money or benefits that you believe you have a right to **take the 'cake** (*especially AmE*) = TAKE THE BISCUIT at BISCUIT—more at HOT *adj.*, ICING, PIECE *n.*
■ *verb* **1** [VN] [usually passive] ~ sth (in/with sth) to cover sth with a thick layer of sth soft that becomes hard when it dries: *Her shoes were caked with mud.* **2** [V] if a substance **cakes**, it becomes hard when it dries ▶ **caked** *adj.*: *caked blood*

CAL /kæl/ *abbr.* computer assisted learning—compare CALL

cala·mine /'kæləmaɪn/ (also **'calamine lotion**) *noun* [U] a pink liquid that you put on burnt or sore skin to make it less painful

ca·lami·t·ous /kə'læmɪtəs/ *adj.* (*formal*) causing great harm or damage **SYN** DISASTROUS

ca·lam·ity /kə'læməti/ *noun* (*pl.* **-ies**) an event that causes great harm or damage **SYN** DISASTER

cal·cify /'kælsɪfaɪ/ *verb* (**cal·ci·fies**, **cal·ci·fy·ing**, **cal·ci·fied**, **cal·ci·fied**) [V, VN] (*technical*) to become hard or make sth hard by adding CALCIUM salts

cal·cium /'kælsiəm/ *noun* [U] (*symb* Ca) a chemical element. Calcium is a soft silver-white metal that is found as a compound in bones, teeth and chalk.

cal·cul·able /'kælkjələbl/ *adj.* that can be calculated: *a calculable risk*—compare INCALCULABLE

cal·cu·late /'kælkjuleɪt/ *verb* **1** to use numbers to find out a total number, amount, distance, etc: [VN] *Use the formula to calculate the volume of the container.* ◇ *Benefit is calculated on the basis of average weekly earnings.* ◇ *We haven't really calculated the cost of the vacation yet.* ◇ [V wh-] *You'll need to calculate how much time the assignment will take.* ◇ [VN that] *It has been calculated that at least 47000 jobs were lost last year.* **2** to guess sth or form an opinion by using all the information available: [V that] *Conservationists calculate that hundreds of species could be lost in this area.* ◇ [V wh-] *It is impossible to calculate what influence he had on her life.*

cal·cu·lated /'kælkjuleɪtɪd/ *adj.* [usually before noun] carefully planned to get what you want: *a calculated insult* ◇ *He took a calculated risk* (= a risk that you decide is worth taking even though you know it might have bad results). **IDM** **be calculated to do sth** to be intended to do sth; to be likely to do sth: *Her latest play is calculated to shock.* ◇ *This sort of life is not calculated to appeal to a young man of 20.*

cal·cu·lat·ing /'kælkjuleɪtɪŋ/ *adj.* (*disapproving*) good at planning things so that you have an advantage, without caring about other people: *a cold and calculating killer* ◇ *I never realized you could be so calculating.*

cal·cu·la·tion /ˌkælkju'leɪʃn/ *noun* **1** [C,U] the act or

æ	ɑː	e	ɜː	ə	ɪ	iː	i	ɒ	ɔː	ʌ	ʊ	u	uː
cat	father	ten	bird	about	sit	see	many	got	saw	cup	put	actual	too

(BrE)

process of using numbers to find out an amount: *Cathy did a rough calculation.* ◊ *By my calculation(s), we made a profit of £20000 last year.* ◊ *Our guess was confirmed by calculation.* **2** [C, U] the process of using your judgement to decide what the results would be of doing sth **3** [U] (*disapproving*) careful planning for yourself without caring about other people: *an act of cold calculation*

cal·cu·la·tor /ˈkælkjuleɪtə(r)/ *noun* a small electronic device for calculating with numbers: *a pocket calculator*

cal·cu·lus /ˈkælkjələs/ *noun* [U] the type of mathematics that deals with rates of change, for example in the slope of a curve or the speed of a falling object

cal·dron (*AmE*) = CAULDRON

cal·en·dar /ˈkælɪndə(r)/ *noun* **1** a page or series of pages showing the days, weeks and months of a particular year, especially one that you hang on a wall: *a calendar for 2001*—see also ADVENT CALENDAR **2** (*AmE*) a record of what you have to do each day; the book in which you write this down **3** [usually sing.] a list of important events or dates of a particular type during the year: *This is one of the biggest weeks in the racing calendar.* **4** a system by which time is divided into fixed periods, showing the beginning and end of a year: *the Islamic calendar*

ˌcalendar ˈmonth *noun* (*technical*) **1** one of the twelve months of the year—compare LUNAR MONTH **2** a period of time from a particular date in one month to the same date in the next one

ˌcalendar ˈyear *noun* (*technical*) the period of time from 1 January to 31 December in the same year

calf /kɑːf; *AmE* kæf/ *noun* (*pl.* **calves** /kɑːvz; *AmE* kævz/) **1** [C] the back part of the leg between the ankle and the knee: *I've torn a calf muscle.*—picture at BODY **2** [C] a young cow **3** [C] a young animal of some other type such as a young elephant or WHALE **4** [U] = CALFSKIN **IDM in/with ˈcalf** (of a cow) pregnant

calf·skin /ˈkɑːfskɪn; *AmE* ˈkæf-/ (also **calf**) *noun* [U] soft thin leather made from the skin of calves, used especially for making shoes and clothing

cali·brate /ˈkælɪbreɪt/ *verb* [VN] (*technical*) to mark units of measurement on an instrument such as a THERMOMETER so that it can be used for measuring sth accurately

cali·bra·tion /ˌkælɪˈbreɪʃn/ *noun* (*technical*) **1** [U] the act of calibrating: *a calibration error* **2** [C] the units of measurement marked on a THERMOMETER or other instrument

cali·bre (*especially BrE*) (*AmE* usually **cali·ber**) /ˈkælɪbə(r)/ *noun* **1** [U] the quality of sth, especially a person's ability: *He was impressed by the high calibre of applicants for the job.* ◊ *The firm needs more people of your calibre.* **2** [C] the width of the inside of a tube or gun; the width of a bullet

cal·ico /ˈkælɪkəʊ; *AmE* -koʊ/ *noun* [U] **1** (*especially BrE*) a heavy cotton fabric that is usually plain white **2** (*especially AmE*) a rough cotton fabric that has a pattern printed on it

ˈcalico cat *noun* (*AmE*) = TORTOISESHELL (2)

cali·per (*especially AmE*) = CALLIPER

ca·liph /ˈkeɪlɪf/ *noun* a title used by Muslim rulers, especially in the past

ca·liph·ate /ˈkælɪfeɪt/ *noun* **1** the position of a caliph **2** an area of land that is ruled over by a caliph

cal·is·then·ics *noun* (*AmE*) = CALLISTHENICS

CALL /kɔːl/ *abbr.* computer assisted language learning—compare CAL

call /kɔːl/ *verb, noun*

■ *verb*

GIVE NAME | **1** to give sb/sth a particular name; to use a particular name or title when you are talking to sb: [VN-N] *They decided to call the baby Brooklyn.* ◊ *His name's Hiroshi but everyone calls him Hiro.* ◊ *What do they call that new fabric?* ◊ [VN] *They called their first daughter after her grandmother.* ◊ *We call each other by our first names here.*—see also CALLED

DESCRIBE | **2** to describe sb/sth in a particular way; to consider sb/sth to be sth: [VN-N] *I wouldn't call German*

an easy language. ◊ *Are you calling me a liar?* ◊ *He was in the front room, or the lounge or whatever you want to call it.* ◊ [VN-ADJ] *Would you call it blue or green?* ◊ [VN-N] *I make it ten pounds forty-three you owe me. Let's call it ten pounds.*

SHOUT | **3** ~ (**sth**) (**out**) | ~ (**out**) **to sb** (**for sth**) to shout or say sth loudly to attract sb's attention: [V] *I thought I heard somebody calling.* ◊ *She called out to her father for help.* ◊ [VN] *Did somebody call my name?* ◊ *He called out a warning from the kitchen.* ◊ [V speech] *'See you later!' she called.* **4** to ask sb to come by shouting or speaking loudly: [VN] *Will you call the kids in for lunch?* ◊ [V] *Did you call?*

TELEPHONE | **5** to ask sb/sth to come quickly to a particular place by telephoning: [VN] *to call the fire department / the police / a doctor / an ambulance* ◊ *The doctor has been called to an urgent case.* ◊ [VN, VNN] *I'll call a taxi for you.* ◊ *I'll call you a taxi.* **6** to telephone sb: [V] *I'll call again later.* ◊ [VN] *I called the office to tell them I'd be late.* ◊ *My brother called me from Germany last night.* ⇨ note at PHONE

ORDER SB TO COME | **7** [VN+adv. / prep.] [usually passive] (*formal*) to order sb to come to a place: *Several candidates were called for a second interview.* ◊ *The ambassador was called back to London by the prime minister.* ◊ *He felt called to the priesthood* (= had a strong feeling that he must become a priest).

VISIT | **8** (*especially BrE*) to make a short visit to a person or place: [V] *Let's call on John.* ◊ *I'll call round and see you on my way home.* ◊ *He was out when I called to see him.*

MEETING / STRIKE, etc. | **9** [VN] to order sth to happen; to announce that sth will happen: *to call a meeting / an election / a strike*

OF BIRD / ANIMAL | **10** [V] to make the cry that is typical for it

IN GAMES | **11** to say which side of a coin you think will face upwards after it is thrown: [VN] *to call heads / tails* [also V]

IDM **call sb's ˈbluff** to tell sb to do what they are threatening to do, because you believe that they will not be cruel or brave enough to do it **call sth into ˈplay** (*written*) to make use of sth: *Chess is a game that calls into play all your powers of concentration.* **call sth into ˈquestion** to doubt sth or make others doubt sth: *His honesty has never been called into question.* **call it a ˈday** (*informal*) to decide or agree to stop doing sth: *After forty years in politics I think it's time for me to call it a day* (= to retire). **call it ˈquits** (*informal*) **1** to agree to stop a contest, quarrel, etc. because both sides seem equal **2** to decide to stop doing sth **call sb ˈnames** to use insulting words about sb **call the ˈshots / ˈtune** (*informal*) to be the person who controls a situation **call a spade a ˈspade** to say exactly what you think without trying to hide your opinion **call ˈtime (on sth)** (*BrE*) to say or decide that it is time for sth to finish **call sb to acˈcount (for / over sth)** to make sb explain a mistake, etc. because they are responsible for it **call sb/sth to ˈorder** to ask people in a meeting to be silent so that the meeting can start or continue—more at CARPET *n.*, MIND *n.*, PAY *v.*, POT *n.*, WHAT

PHR V **ˈcall at …** (*BrE*) (of a train, etc.) to stop at a place for a short time: *This train calls at Didcot and Reading.* **ˌcall sb aˈway** to ask sb to stop what they are doing and to go somewhere else: *She was called away from the meeting to take an urgent phone call.* **ˌcall ˈback | ˌcall sb ˈback** to telephone sb again or to telephone sb who telephoned you earlier: *She said she'd call back.* ◊ *I'm waiting for someone to call me back with a price.* **ˈcall for sb** (*especially BrE*) to collect sb in order to go somewhere: *I'll call for you at 7 o'clock.* **ˈcall for sth** to need sth: *The situation calls for prompt action.* ◊ *'I've been promoted.' 'This calls for a celebration!'*—see also UNCALLED FOR **2** to publicly ask for sth to happen: *They called for the immediate release of the hostages.* ◊ *The opposition have called for him to resign.* **ˌcall sth ↔ ˈforth** (*formal*) to produce a particular reaction: *His speech called forth an angry response.* **ˌcall ˈin** to telephone a place, especially the place where you work: *Several people have called in sick today.* **ˌcall sb ↔ ˈin** to ask for the services of sb: *to*

aɪ	aʊ	eɪ	əʊ	oʊ	ɔɪ	ɪə	eə	ʊə	j	w
my	now	say	go	go	boy	near	hair	pure	yes	wet
			(BrE)	(AmE)						

calm

call in a doctor / the police ,**call** sth ↔ **in** to order or ask for the return of sth: *Cars with serious faults have been called in by the manufacturers.* ,**call** sb/sth ↔ **off** to order a dog or a person to stop attacking, searching, etc. ,**call** sth ↔ **off** to cancel sth; to decide that sth will not happen: *to call off a deal / trip / strike* ◊ *They have called off their engagement* (= decided not to get married). ◊ *The game was called off because of bad weather.* '**call on/upon** sb (*formal*) **1** to formally invite or ask sb to speak, etc: *I now call upon the chairman to address the meeting.* **2** to ask or demand that sb do sth: *I feel called upon* (= feel that I ought) *to warn you that …* ,**call** sb '**out 1** to ask sb to come, especially to an emergency: *to call out an engineer / a plumber / the troops* **2** to order or advise workers to stop work as a protest—related noun CALL-OUT ,**call** sb ↔ '**up 1** (*especially AmE*) to make a telephone call to sb **2** to make sb do their training in the army, etc. or fight in a war SYN CONSCRIPT, DRAFT **3** to give sb the opportunity to play in a sports team, especially for their country— related noun CALL-UP ,**call** sth ↔ '**up 1** to bring sth back to your mind SYN RECALL: *The smell of the sea called up memories of her childhood.* **2** to use sth that is stored or kept available: *I called his address up on the computer.* ◊ *She called up her last reserves of strength.*

■ *noun*

ON TELEPHONE | **1** [C] (also '**phone call**) the act of speaking to sb on the telephone: *to get / have / receive a call from sb* ◊ *to give sb / to make a call* ◊ *Were there any calls for me while I was out?* ◊ *I'll take* (= answer) *the call upstairs.* ◊ *I left a message but he didn't return my call.* ◊ *a local call* ◊ *a long-distance call* ⇨ note at PHONE

LOUD SOUND | **2** [C] a loud sound made by a bird or an animal, or by a person to attract attention: *the distinctive call of the cuckoo* ◊ *a call for help*

VISIT | **3** [C] a short visit to sb's house: *The doctor has five calls to make this morning.* ◊ (*old-fashioned*) *to pay a call on an old friend*

REQUEST / DEMAND | **4** [C] ~ (**for** sth) a request, an order or a demand for sb to do sth or to go somewhere: *calls for the minister to resign* ◊ *calls for national unity* ◊ *This is the last call for passengers travelling on British Airways flight 199 to Rome.* ◊ (*formal*) *a call to arms* (= a strong request to fight in the army, etc.)—see also CURTAIN CALL **5** [U] no ~ **for** sth | no ~ (**for** sb) **to do** sth no demand for sth; no reason for sb's behaviour: *There isn't a lot of call for small specialist shops nowadays.* **6** [C] ~ **on** sb/sth a demand or pressure placed on sb/sth: *She is a busy woman with many calls on her time.*

OF A PLACE | **7** [sing.] ~ (**of** sth) (*literary*) a strong feeling of attraction that a particular place has for you: *the call of the sea / your homeland*

TO A PARTICULAR JOB | **8** [sing.] ~ (**to do** sth) a strong feeling to do sth, especially a particular job

DECISION | **9** [C] (*informal*) a decision: *It's your call!*

IN TENNIS | **10** [C] a decision made by the UMPIRE: *There was a disputed call in the second set.*

IN CARD GAMES | **11** [C] a player's BID or turn to BID

IDM **the call of** '**nature** (*humorous*) the need to go to the toilet **have first** '**call (on** sb/sth) to be the most important person or thing competing for sb's time, money, etc. and to be dealt with or paid for before other people or things: *The children always have first call on her time.* (**be) on** '**call** (of a doctor, police officer, etc.) available for work if necessary, especially in an emergency: *I'll be on call the night of the party.*—more at BECK, CLOSE² *adj.*

'**call box** *noun* **1** (*BrE*) = PHONE BOX **2** (*AmE*) a small box beside a road, with a telephone in it, to call for help after an accident, etc.

'**call centre** (*BrE*) (*AmE* '**call center**) *noun* an office in which a large number of people work using telephones, for example arranging insurance for people, or taking customers' orders and answering questions

called /kɔːld/ *adj.* [not before noun] to have a particular name: *What's their son called?* ◊ *I don't know anyone called Scott.* ◊ *I've forgotten what the firm he works for is called.* ◊ *What's it called again? Yeah, that's right. A modem.*—see also SO-CALLED

call·er /ˈkɔːlə(r)/ *noun* **1** a person who is making a telephone call: *The caller hung up.* ◊ *an anonymous caller* **2** a person who goes to a house or a building

'**call girl** *noun* a prostitute who makes her arrangements by telephone

cal·lig·ra·phy /kəˈlɪɡrəfi/ *noun* [U] beautiful HANDWRITING that you do with a special pen or brush; the art of producing this: *I'm teaching myself calligraphy.* ▶ **cal·lig·raph·er** *noun*

'**call-in** *noun* (*AmE*) = PHONE-IN

call·ing /ˈkɔːlɪŋ/ *noun* **1** a strong desire or feeling of duty to do a particular job, especially one in which you help other people SYN VOCATION : *He realized that his calling was to preach the gospel.* **2** (*formal*) a profession or career

'**calling card** *noun* (*AmE*) = VISITING CARD

cal·li·per (*BrE*) (also **cali·per** *AmE*, *BrE*) /ˈkælɪpə(r)/ **1** (**callipers**) [pl.] an instrument with two long thin parts joined at one end, used for measuring the DIAMETER of tubes and round objects (= the distance across them): *a pair of callipers* **2** (*BrE*) (*AmE* **brace**) [C, usually pl.] a metal support for weak or injured legs

cal·lis·then·ics (*BrE*) (*AmE* **cal·is·then·ics**) /ˌkælɪsˈθenɪks/ *noun* [U+sing. / pl. v.] physical exercises intended to develop a strong and graceful body

'**call letters** *noun* [pl.] (*AmE*) the letters that are used to identify a radio or television station: *the call letters WNBC*

cal·lous /ˈkæləs/ *adj.* not caring about other people's feelings or suffering: *a callous killer / attitude / act* ◊ *a callous disregard for the feelings of others* ▶ **cal·lous·ly** *adv.* **cal·lous·ness** *noun* [U]

cal·loused /ˈkæləst/ *adj.* (of the skin) made rough and hard, usually by hard work: *calloused hands*

'**call-out** *noun* an occasion when sb is called to do repairs, rescue sb, etc: *a call-out charge* ◊ *ambulance call-outs*

cal·low /ˈkæləʊ; *AmE* -loʊ/ *adj.* (*formal*, *disapproving*) young and without experience: *a callow youth*

'**call sign** *noun* the letters and numbers used in radio communication to identify the person who is sending a message

'**call-up** (*BrE*) *noun* **1** [U, C, usually sing.] an order to join the armed forces SYN CONSCRIPTION, THE DRAFT: *to receive your call-up papers* **2** [C] the opportunity to play in a sports team, especially for your country: *Fowler's recent form has earned him a call-up to the England squad.*

cal·lus /ˈkæləs/ *noun* an area of thick hard skin on a hand or foot, usually caused by rubbing

calm /kɑːm/ *adj.*, *verb*, *noun*

■ *adj.* (**calm·er**, **calm·est**) **1** not excited, nervous or upset: *It is important to keep calm in an emergency.* ◊ *Try to remain calm.* ◊ *Her voice was surprisingly calm.* ◊ *The city is calm again* (= free from disorder and fighting) *after yesterday's riots.* **2** (of the sea) without large waves **3** (of the weather) without wind: *a calm, cloudless day* ▶ **calm·ly** *adv.*: '*I'll call the doctor,' he said calmly.* **calm·ness** *noun* [U]

■ *verb* [VN] to make sb/sth become quiet and more relaxed, especially after strong emotion or excitement: *Have some brandy; it'll calm your nerves.* ◊ *His presence had a calming influence.*—see also TRAFFIC CALMING PHRV ,**calm** '**down** | ,**calm** sb/sth ↔ '**down** to become calm or make sb become calm: *Look, calm down! We'll find her.* ◊ *We waited inside until things calmed down.* ◊ *He took a few deep breaths to calm himself down.*

■ *noun* [C, U] **1** a quiet and peaceful time or situation: *the calm of a summer evening* ◊ *The police appealed for calm.* **2** a quiet and relaxed manner: *Her previous calm gave way to terror.* IDM **the calm before the storm** a calm time immediately before an expected period of violent activity or argument ⇨ note on page 168

b	d	f	g	h	k	l	m	n	p	r
bad	did	fall	get	hat	cat	leg	man	now	pen	red

C

Calor gas™ /ˈkælə gæs; *AmE* ˈkælər/ (*BrE*) (*AmE* **cooking gas**) *noun* [U] a type of gas stored as a liquid under pressure in metal containers and used for heating and cooking in places where there is no gas supply

cal·orie /ˈkæləri/ *noun* **1** a unit for measuring how much energy food will produce: *No sugar for me, thanks—I'm counting my calories.* ◊ *a low-calorie drink/diet* **2** (*technical*) a unit for measuring a quantity of heat; the amount of heat needed to raise the temperature of a gram of water by one degree Celsius

cal·or·if·ic /ˌkæləˈrɪfɪk/ *adj.* [usually before noun] (*technical*) connected with or producing heat: *the calorific value of food* (= the quantity of heat or energy produced by a particular amount of food)

cal·umny /ˈkæləmni/ *noun* (*pl.* **-ies**) (*formal*) **1** [C] a false statement about a person that is made to damage their reputation **2** [U] the act of making such a statement

calve /kɑːv; *AmE* kæv/ *verb* [V] (of a cow) to give birth to a CALF

calves *pl.* of CALF

Cal·vin·ist /ˈkælvɪnɪst/ *adj., noun*
- *adj.* (also **Cal·vin·is·tic**) **1** connected with Calvinism **2** having very strict moral attitudes
- *noun* a member of a Church that follows the teaching of the French Protestant John Calvin ► **Cal·vin·ism** *noun* [U]

ca·lypso /kəˈlɪpsəʊ; *AmE* -soʊ/ *noun* [C, U] (*pl.* **-os**) a Caribbean song about a subject of current interest; this type of music

calyx /ˈkeɪlɪks/ *noun* (*pl.* **ca·lyxes** or **ca·ly·ces** /ˈkeɪlɪsiːz/) (*technical*) the ring of small green leaves, (called SEPALS), that protect a flower before it opens

CAM /kæm/ *abbr.* computer aided manufacturing

cam /kæm/ *noun* a part on a wheel that sticks out and changes the circular movement of the wheel into up-and-down or backwards-and-forwards movement

cama·rad·erie /ˌkæməˈrɑːdəri; *AmE* ˌkɑːməˈrɑːdəri/ *noun* [U] (*written*) a feeling of friendship and trust among people who work or spend a lot of time together

cam·ber /ˈkæmbə(r)/ *noun* a slight downward curve from the middle of a road to each side

cam·bric /ˈkæmbrɪk/ *noun* [U] a thin white fabric made from cotton or LINEN

cam·cord·er /ˈkæmkɔːdə(r); *AmE* -kɔːrd-/ *noun* a video camera that records pictures and sound and that can be carried around

came *pt* of COME

camel /ˈkæml/ *noun* **1** [C] an animal with a long neck and one or two HUMPS on its back, used in desert countries for riding on or for carrying goods—compare DROMEDARY **2** [U] = CAMEL HAIR: *a camel coat* **SEE** STRAW

'camel hair *noun* [U] **1** (also **camel**) a thick soft pale brown fabric made from camel's hair or a mixture of camel's hair and wool, used especially for making coats: *a camel-hair coat* **2** the fine soft hair from a SQUIRREL'S tail, used for making artists' PAINTBRUSHES

cam·el·lia /kəˈmiːliə/ *noun* a bush with shiny leaves and white, red or pink flowers that look like roses and are also called **camellias**

Cam·em·bert /ˈkæməmbeə(r); *AmE* -ber/ *noun* [U, C] a type of soft French cheese with a strong flavour

cameo /ˈkæmiəʊ; *AmE* -mioʊ/ *noun* (*pl.* **-os**) **1** a small part in a film/movie or play for a famous actor: *a cameo role/appearance* **2** a short piece of writing that gives a good description of sb/sth **3** a piece of jewellery that consists of a raised design, often of a head, on a background of a different colour: *a cameo brooch/ring*

cam·era /ˈkæmərə/ *noun* a piece of equipment for taking photographs, moving pictures or television pictures: *Just point the camera and press the button.* ◊ *Cameras started clicking as soon as she stepped out of the car.* ◊ *a TV/video camera* ◊ *a camera crew* **IDM** **in 'camera** (*law*) in a judge's private room, without the press or the public being present: *The trial was held in camera.* **on 'camera** being filmed or shown on television: *Are you prepared to tell your story on camera?*

cam·era·man /ˈkæmrəmæn/, **came·ra·woman** /ˈkæmrəwʊmən/ *noun* (*pl.* **-men** /-men/) (*pl.* **-women** /-wɪmɪn/) a person whose job is operating a camera for making films/movies or television programmes

cam·era·work /ˈkæmrəwɜːk; *AmE* -wɜːrk/ *noun* [U] the style in which sb takes photographs or uses a film camera

cami·sole /ˈkæmɪsəʊl; *AmE* -soʊl/ *noun* a short piece of women's underwear that is worn on the top half of the body and has thin shoulder straps

camo·mile = CHAMOMILE

cam·ou·flage /ˈkæməflɑːʒ/ *noun, verb*
- *noun* **1** [U] a way of hiding soldiers and military equipment, using paint, leaves or nets, so that they look like part of their surroundings: *a camouflage jacket* (= covered with green and brown marks and worn by soldiers) ◊ *troops dressed in camouflage* **2** [U, sing.] the way in which an animal's colour or shape matches its surroundings and makes it difficult to see **3** [U, sing.] behaviour that is deliberately meant to hide the truth: *Her angry words were camouflage for the way she felt.*
- *verb* [VN] **~ sth (with sth)** to hide sb/sth by making them or it look like the things around, or like sth else: *The soldiers camouflaged themselves with leaves and twigs.* ◊ *Her size was camouflaged by the long loose dark dress she wore.*

camp /kæmp/ *noun, verb, adj.*
- *noun*

IN TENTS | **1** [C, U] a place where people live temporarily in tents or huts: *Let's return to camp.* ◊ *to pitch/make camp* (= put up tents) ◊ *to break camp* (= to take down tents)—see also HOLIDAY CAMP

HOLIDAY/VACATION | **2** [C, U] a place where young people go on holiday/vacation and take part in various activities or a particular activity: *a tennis camp* ◊ *He spent two weeks at camp this summer.* ◊ *summer camp*

PRISON, etc. | **3** [C] (used in compounds) a place where people are kept in huts or tents, especially by a government and often for long periods: *a refugee camp* ◊ *a camp guard*—see also CONCENTRATION CAMP, PRISON CAMP, TRANSIT CAMP

ARMY | **4** [C, U] a place where soldiers live while they are training or fighting: *an army camp*

GROUP OF PEOPLE | **5** [C] a group of people who have the same ideas about sth and oppose people with other ideas: *the socialist camp* ◊ *We were in opposing camps.* **6** [C] one of the sides in a competition and the people connected with it: *There was an air of confidence in the England camp.*

IDM see FOOT *n.*
- *verb*

LIVE IN TENT | **1** [V] to put up a tent and live in it for a short time: *I camped overnight in a field.* **2** [V] **(go camping)** to stay in a tent, especially while you are on holiday/vacation: *They go camping in France every year.*

STAY FOR SHORT TIME | **3** [V] **~ (out)** to live in sb's house for a short time, especially when you do not have a bed there: *I'm camping out at a friend's apartment at the moment.*

PHR V **ˌcamp 'out** to live outside for a short time: *Dozens of reporters camped out on her doorstep.* ◊ **ˌcamp it 'up** (*BrE, informal*) to behave in a very exaggerated manner, especially to attract attention to yourself or to make people laugh
- *adj.* **1** (*BrE*) (of a man or his manner) deliberately behaving in a way that some people think is typical of a HOMOSEXUAL **SYN** EFFEMINATE **2** exaggerated in style, especially in a deliberately amusing way: *The movie is a camp celebration of the fashion industry.*

cam·paign /kæmˈpeɪn/ *noun, verb*

■ **noun 1** ~ **(against/for sth)** a series of planned activities that are intended to achieve a particular social, commercial or political aim: *to conduct a campaign* ◇ *a campaign against ageism in the workplace* ◇ *the campaign for parliamentary reform* ◇ *an anti-smoking campaign* ◇ *Today police launched* (= began) *a campaign to reduce road accidents.* ◇ *an advertising campaign* ◇ *an election campaign* ◇ *the President's campaign team/manager* **2** a series of attacks and battles that are intended to achieve a particular military aim during a war

■ **verb** ~ **(for/against sb/sth)** to take part in or lead a campaign, for example to achieve political change or in order to win an election: [V] *We have campaigned against whaling for the last 15 years.* ◇ *The party* **campaigned vigorously** *in the north of the country.* ◇ [V to inf] *They are campaigning to save the area from building development.*
► **cam·paign·ing** *noun* [U]

cam·paign·er /kæmˈpeɪnə(r)/ *noun* a person who leads or takes part in a campaign, especially one for political or social change: *a leading human rights campaigner* ◇ *a campaigner on environmental issues* ◇ *a campaigner for women priests* ◇ *an old/veteran/seasoned campaigner* (= a person with a lot of experience of a particular activity) ◇ (*especially AmE*) *Bush campaigners* (= people working for Bush in a campaign)

cam·pa·nile /ˌkæmpəˈniːli/ *noun* a tower that contains a bell, especially one that is not part of another building

cam·pan·ology /ˌkæmpəˈnɒlədʒi; AmE -ˈnɑːl-/ *noun* [U] (*formal*) the study of bells and the art of ringing bells
► **cam·pan·olo·gist** /-ədʒɪst/ *noun*—see also BELL-RINGER

camp ˈbed (*BrE*) (*AmE* **cot**) *noun* a light narrow bed that you can fold up and carry easily—picture at BED

camp·er /ˈkæmpə(r)/ *noun* **1** a person who spends a holiday/vacation living in a tent or at a holiday camp **2** (also **ˈcamper van**) (both *BrE*) (*AmE* **RV**, **recre·ational ˈvehicle**) (also **motor·home** *AmE, BrE*) a large motor vehicle designed for people to live and sleep in when they are travelling—picture at BUS **3** (*AmE*) = CARAVAN

camp·fire /ˈkæmpfaɪə(r)/ *noun* an outdoor fire made by people who are sleeping outside or living in a tent

camp ˈfollower *noun* **1** a person who supports a particular group or political party but is not a member of it **2** (in the past) a person who was not a soldier but followed an army from place to place to sell goods or services

camp·ground /ˈkæmpɡraʊnd/ *noun* (*AmE*) = CAMPSITE

cam·phor /ˈkæmfə(r)/ *noun* [U] a white substance with a strong smell, used in medicine, for making plastics and to keep insects away from clothes

camp·ing /ˈkæmpɪŋ/ *noun* [U] living in a tent, etc. on holiday/vacation: *Do you go camping?* ◇ *a camping trip*

camp·site /ˈkæmpsaɪt/ *noun* **1** (also **ˈcamping site**) (both *BrE*) (*AmE* **ˈcamp-ground**) a place where people on holiday/vacation can put up their tents, park their CARAVAN, CAMPER, etc., often with toilets, water, etc. **2** (*AmE*) a place in a campground where you can put up one tent or park one CAMPER, etc.

cam·pus /ˈkæmpəs/ *noun* the buildings of a university or college and the land around them: *She lives* **on campus** (= within the main university area). ◇ *campus life*

cam·shaft /ˈkæmʃɑːft; AmE -ʃæft/ *noun* a rod with a CAM on it joining parts of machinery, especially in a motor vehicle

can¹ /kən; kæn/ *modal verb*—see also CAN² (*negative* **cannot** /ˈkænɒt; AmE -nɑːt/, *short form* **can't** /kɑːnt; AmE kænt/, *pt* **could** /kəd; strong form* kʊd/, *negative* **could not**, *short form* **couldn't** /ˈkʊdnt/) **1** used to say that it is possible for sb/sth to do sth, or for sth to happen: *I can run fast.* ◇ *Can you call back tomorrow?* ◇ *He couldn't answer the question.* ◇ *The stadium can be emptied in four minutes.* ◇ *I can't promise anything, but I'll do what I can.* **2** used to say that sb knows how to do sth: *She can speak Spanish.* ◇ *Can he cook?* ◇ *I could drive a car before I left school.* **3** used with the verbs 'feel', 'hear', 'see', 'smell', 'taste': *She could feel a lump in her breast.* ◇ *I can hear music.* **4** used to show that sb is allowed to do sth: *You*

can take the car, if you want. ◇ *We can't wear jeans at work.* **5** (*spoken*) used to ask permission to do sth: *Can I read your newspaper?* ◇ *Can I take you home?* **6** (*spoken*) used to ask sb to help you: *Can you help me with this box?* ◇ *Can you feed the cat, please?* **7** used in the negative for saying that you are sure sth is not true: *That can't be Mary—she's in New York.* ◇ *He can't have slept through all that noise.* **8** used to express doubt or surprise: *What can they be doing?* ◇ *Can he be serious?* ◇ *Where can she have put it?* **9** used to say what sb/sth is often like: *He can be*

> **WHICH WORD?**
> **can / may** (?)
>
> **Can** and **cannot** (or **can't**) are the most common words used for asking for, giving or refusing permission: *Can I borrow your calculator?* ◇ *You can come with us if you want to.* ◇ *You can't park your car there.*
>
> **May** (negative **may not**) is used as a polite and fairly formal way to ask for or give permission: *May I borrow your newspaper?* ◇ *You may come if you wish.* It is often used in official signs and rules: *Visitors may use the swimming pool between 7 a.m. and 7 p.m.* ◇ *Students may not use the college car park.* The form **mayn't** is almost never used in modern English.

very tactless sometimes. ◇ *It can be quite cold here in winter.* **10** used to make suggestions: *We can eat in a restaurant, if you like.* ◇ *I can take the car if necessary.* **11** (*spoken*) used to say that sb must do sth, usually when you are angry: *You can shut up or get out!* ⇨ note at MODAL **IDM** **can't be doing with sth** (*informal*) used to say that you do not like sth and are unwilling to accept it: *I can't be doing with people who complain all the time.*

> **GRAMMAR POINT**
> **can / could / be able to / manage**
>
> **Can** is used to say that somebody knows how to do something: *Can you play the piano?* It is also used with verbs of seeing, noticing, etc.: *I can hear someone calling*, and with passive infinitives: *The video can be rented from your local store.*
>
> **Can** or **be able to** are used to say that something is possible or that somebody has the opportunity to do something: *Can you/are you able to come on Saturday?*
>
> You use **be able to** to form the future and perfect tenses and the infinitive: *You'll be able to get a taxi outside the station.* ◇ *I haven't been able to get much work done today.* ◇ *She'd love to be able to play the piano.*
>
> **Could** is used to talk about what someone was generally able to do in the past: *Our daughter could walk when she was nine months old.*
>
> You use **was/were able to** or **manage** (but not **could**) when you are saying that something was possible on a particular occasion in the past: *I was able to/ managed to find some useful books in the library.* ◇ ~~I could find some useful books in the library.~~ In negative sentences, **could not** can also be used: *We weren't able to / didn't manage to / couldn't get there in time.* **Could** is also used with this meaning with verbs of seeing, noticing, understanding, etc.: *I could see there was something wrong.*
>
> **Could have** is used when you are saying that it was possible for somebody to do something in the past but they did not try: *I could have won the game but decided to let her win.*
>
> ⇨ note at MAY

can² /kæn/ *noun, verb*—see also CAN¹
■ **noun 1** (*BrE* also **tin**) [C] a metal container in which food and drink is sold: *a can of beans* ◇ *a beer/paint can*—picture at PACKAGING **HELP** In *AmE* **can** is the usual word used for both food and drink. In *BrE* **can** is always used

æ	ɑː	e	ɜː	ə	ɪ	iː	i	ɒ	ɔː	ʌ	ʊ	u	uː
cat	father	ten	bird	about	sit	see	many	got	saw	cup	put	actual	too

(BrE)

for drink, but **tin** or **can** can be used for food, paint, etc. **2** [C] the amount contained in a can: *We drank a can of Coke each.* **3** [C] a metal or plastic container for holding or carrying liquids: *an oil can* ◊ *a watering can* **4** [C] a metal container in which liquids are kept under pressure and let out in a fine spray when you press a button on the lid: *a can of hairspray*—picture at PACKAGING **5** (**the can**) [sing.] (*AmE, slang*) prison **6** (**the can**) [sing.] (*AmE, slang*) the toilet **IDM a can of ˈworms** (*informal*) if you open up a **can of worms**, you start doing sth that will cause a lot of problems and be very difficult **be in the ˈcan** (*informal*) (especially of filmed or recorded material) to be completed and ready for use—more at CARRY
■ *verb* (**-nn-**) [VN] **1** (*especially AmE*) to preserve food by putting it in a can **2** (*AmE, informal*) to dismiss sb from their job

canal /kəˈnæl/ *noun* **1** a long straight passage dug in the ground and filled with water for boats and ships to travel along; a smaller passage used for carrying water to fields, crops, etc: *the Panama/Suez Canal* ◊ *an irrigation canal* **2** a tube inside the body through which air or food passes—see also ALIMENTARY CANAL

can·al·ize (*BrE* also **-ise**) /ˈkænəlaɪz/ *verb* [VN] **1** (*technical*) to make a river wider, deeper or straighter; to make a river into a canal **2** (*formal*) to control an emotion, activity, etc. so that it is aimed at a particular purpose SYN CHANNEL ▶ **can·al·iza·tion**, **-isa·tion** /ˌkænəlaɪˈzeɪʃn; *AmE* -nələˈz-/ *noun* [U]

can·apé /ˈkænəpeɪ; *AmE* ˌkænsəˈpeɪ/ *noun* [usually pl.] a small biscuit or piece of bread with cheese, meat, fish, etc. on it, usually served with drinks at a party—picture on page A1

can·ard /kæˈnɑːd; ˈkænɑːd; *AmE* kəˈnɑːrd; ˈkænɑːrd/ *noun* (*formal*) a false report or piece of news

can·ary /kəˈneəri; *AmE* -ˈneri/ *noun* (*pl.* **-ies**) a small yellow bird with a beautiful song, often kept in a cage as a pet

can·can /ˈkænkæn/ *noun* (often **the cancan**) [sing.] a fast dance in which a line of women kick their legs high in the air

can·cel /ˈkænsl/ *verb* (**-ll-**, *AmE* **-l-**) **1** [VN] to decide that sth that has been arranged will not now take place: *All flights have been cancelled because of bad weather.* ◊ *Don't forget to cancel the newspaper* (= arrange for it not to be delivered) *before going away.*—compare POSTPONE **2** to say that you no longer want to continue with an agreement, especially one that has been legally arranged: [VN] *to cancel a policy/subscription* ◊ *Is it too late to cancel my order?* ◊ *The US has agreed to cancel debts* (= say that they no longer need to be paid) *totalling $10 million.* ◊ [V] *No charge will be made if you cancel within 10 days.* **3** [VN] to mark a ticket or stamp so that it cannot be used again PHRV ˌcancel ˈout; ˌcancel sth↔ˈout if two or more things **cancel out** or one **cancels out** the other, they are equally important but have an opposite effect on a situation so that the situation does not change: *Recent losses have cancelled out any profits made at the start of the year.* ◊ *The advantages and disadvantages would appear to cancel each other out.*

can·cel·la·tion /ˌkænsəˈleɪʃn/ (*AmE* also **can·cel·ation**) *noun* **1** [U, C] a decision to stop sth that has already been arranged from happening; a statement that sth will not happen: *We need at least 24 hours' notice of cancellation.* ◊ *a cancellation fee/charge* ◊ *Heavy seas can cause cancellation of ferry services.* ◊ *Cancellations must be made in writing.* **2** [C] something that has been cancelled: *Are there any cancellations for this evening's performance?* (= tickets that have been returned) **3** [U] the fact of making sth no longer valid: *the cancellation of the contract*

Can·cer /ˈkænsə(r)/ *noun* **1** [U] the fourth sign of the ZODIAC, the CRAB **2** [sing.] a person born under the influence of this sign, who was born between 22 June and 22 July, approximately ▶ **Can·cer·ian** /kænˈsɪəriən; *AmE* -ˈsɪr-/ *noun, adj.*

can·cer /ˈkænsə(r)/ *noun* **1** [U, C] a serious disease in which growths of cells, also called cancers, form in the body and kill normal body cells. The disease often causes death: *lung/breast cancer* ◊ *cancer of the bowel/stomach* ◊ *Most skin cancers are completely curable.* ◊ *The cancer has spread to his stomach.* ◊ *cancer patients* ◊ *cancer research* **2** [C] (*literary*) an evil or dangerous thing that spreads quickly: *Violence is a cancer in our society.* ▶ **can·cer·ous** /ˈkænsərəs/ *adj.*: *to become cancerous* ◊ *cancerous cells/growths/tumours*

can·de·la·bra /ˌkændəˈlɑːbrə/ (also less frequent **can·de·la·brum** /ˌkændəˈlɑːbrəm/) *noun* (*pl.* **can·de·la·bra**, **can·de·la·bras**, *AmE* also **can·de·la·brums**) an object with several branches for holding candles or lights

can·did /ˈkændɪd/ *adj.* **1** saying what you think openly and honestly; not hiding your thoughts: *a candid statement/interview* ◊ *You must be absolutely honest and candid.*—see also CANDOUR **2** a **candid** photograph is one that is taken without the person in it knowing that they are being photographed ▶ **can·did·ly** *adv.*

can·di·dacy /ˈkændɪdəsi/ *noun* [C, U] (*pl.* **-ies**) (also **can·di·da·ture** especially in *BrE*) the fact of being a candidate in an election: *to announce/declare/withdraw your candidacy for the post*

can·di·date /ˈkændɪdət; -deɪt/ *noun* **1** ~ (**for sth**) a person who is trying to be elected or is applying for a job: *one of the leading candidates for the presidency* ◊ *a presidential candidate* ◊ (*BrE*) *He stood as a candidate in the local elections.* ◊ *There were a large number of candidates for the job.* **2** (*BrE*) a person taking an exam: *a candidate for the degree of MPhil* **3** ~ (**for sth**) a person or group that is considered suitable for sth or that is likely to get sth or to be sth: *Our team is a prime candidate for relegation this year.* ◊ *Your father is an obvious candidate for a heart attack.*

can·di·da·ture /ˈkændɪdətʃə(r)/ *noun* (*especially BrE*) = CANDIDACY

can·died /ˈkændid/ *adj.* [only before noun] (of fruit or other food) preserved by boiling in sugar; cooked in sugar: *candied fruit*

can·dle /ˈkændl/ *noun* a round stick of WAX with a piece of string (called a WICK) through the middle which is lit to give light as it burns **IDM cannot hold a candle to sb/sth** is not as good as sb or sth else: *His singing can't hold a candle to Pavarotti's.*—more at BURN *v.*, WORTH *adj.*

candle·light /ˈkændllaɪt/ *noun* [U] the light that a candle produces: *to read by candlelight*

candle·lit /ˈkændllɪt/ *adj.* [only before noun] lit by candles: *a romantic candlelit dinner*

candle·stick /ˈkændlstɪk/ *noun* an object for holding a candle

candle·wick /ˈkændlwɪk/ *noun* [U] a soft cotton fabric with a raised pattern of threads, used especially for making BEDSPREADS

ˌcan-ˈdo *adj.* [only before noun] (*informal*) willing to try new things and expecting that they will be successful: *a can-do attitude/spirit*

cand·our (*BrE*) (*AmE* **can·dor**) /ˈkændə(r)/ *noun* [U] the quality of saying what you think openly and honestly: *'I don't trust him,' he said, in a rare moment of candour.*—see also CANDID

C & W *abbr.* COUNTRY AND WESTERN

candy /ˈkændi/ *noun* [U, C] (*pl.* **-ies**) (*AmE*) sweet food made of sugar and/or chocolate, eaten between meals; a piece of this SYN SWEET: *a box of candy* ◊ *a candy store* ◊ *candy ˌbar* ◊ *Who wants the last piece of candy?*

ˈcandy apple *noun* (*AmE*) = TOFFEE APPLE

candy·floss /ˈkændiflɒs; *AmE* -flɔːs; -flɑːs/ (*BrE*) (*AmE* ˌcotton ˈcandy) *noun* [U] a type of sweet/candy in the form of a mass of sticky threads made from melted sugar and served on a stick, especially at FAIRGROUNDS

cane /keɪn/ *noun, verb*
■ *noun* **1** [C] the hard hollow stem of some plants, for example BAMBOO or sugar: *bean plants supported by bamboo canes* **2** [U] these stems used as a material for making furniture, etc: *a cane chair* **3** [C] a piece of cane or a thin rod, used to help sb to walk—see also WALKING STICK **4** [C] a piece of cane or a thin rod, used in the past in some schools for beating children as a punishment: *to get the cane* (= be punished with a cane)

■ *verb* [VN] to hit a child with a cane as a punishment
▶ **can·ing** *noun* [U, C]: *the abolition of caning in schools*

'cane sugar *noun* [U] sugar obtained from the juice of SUGAR CANE

ca·nine /'keɪnaɪn/ *adj., noun*
■ *adj.* connected with dogs
■ *noun* **1** (also **'canine tooth**) one of the four pointed teeth in the front of a human being's mouth—compare INCISOR, MOLAR **2** (*formal*) a dog

can·is·ter /'kænɪstə(r)/ *noun* **1** a container with a lid for holding tea, coffee, etc. **2** a strong metal container containing gas or a chemical substance, especially one that bursts when it is fired from a gun or thrown: *tear-gas canisters* **3** a flat round metal container used for storing film: *a film canister*

can·ker /'kæŋkə(r)/ *noun* **1** [U] a disease that destroys the wood of plants and trees **2** [U] a disease that causes sore areas in the ears of animals, especially dogs and cats **3** [C] (*literary*) an evil or dangerous influence that spreads and affects people's behaviour

'canker sore *noun* (*AmE*) = MOUTH ULCER

can·na·bis /'kænəbɪs/ *noun* [U] a drug made from the dried leaves and flowers or RESIN of the HEMP plant, which gives a feeling of being relaxed when it is smoked or eaten. Use of the drug is illegal in many countries.

canned /kænd/ *adj.* **1** (*BrE* also **tinned**) (of food) preserved in a can: *canned food/soup* **2** ~ **laughter/music** laughter or music that has been previously recorded and used in television and radio programmes

can·nery /'kænəri/ *noun* (*pl.* **-ies**) a factory where food is put into cans

can·ni·bal /'kænɪbl/ *noun* **1** a person who eats human flesh: *a tribe of cannibals* **2** an animal that eats the flesh of other animals of the same kind ▶ **can·ni·bal·ism** /'kænɪbəlɪzəm/ *noun* [U]: *to practise cannibalism* **can·ni·bal·is·tic** /ˌkænɪbə'lɪstɪk/ *adj.*

can·ni·bal·ize (*BrE* also **-ise**) /'kænɪbəlaɪz/ *verb* [VN] to take the parts of a machine, vehicle, etc. and use them to repair or build another ▶ **can·ni·bal·iza·tion, -isa·tion** /ˌkænɪbəlaɪ'zeɪʃn; *AmE* -lə'z-/ *noun* [U]

can·non /'kænən/ *noun, verb*
■ *noun* (*pl.* **can·non** or **can·nons**) **1** an old type of large heavy gun, usually on wheels, that fires solid metal or stone balls—see also LOOSE CANNON, WATER CANNON **2** an AUTOMATIC gun that is fired from an aircraft
■ *verb* [V+*adv./prep.*] to hit sb/sth with a lot of force while you are moving: *He ran around the corner, cannoning into a group of kids.*

can·non·ade /ˌkænə'neɪd/ *noun* a continuous firing of large guns

can·non·ball /'kænənbɔːl/ *noun* a large metal or stone ball that is fired from a CANNON

'cannon fodder *noun* [U] soldiers who are thought of not as people whose lives are important, but as material to be used up in war

can·not /'kænɒt; *AmE* -nɑːt/ = CAN NOT

canny /'kæni/ *adj.* intelligent, careful and showing good judgement, especially in business or politics: *a canny politician* ◊ *a canny money move* ▶ **can·nily** *adv.*

canoe /kə'nuː/ *noun, verb*
■ *noun* a light narrow boat which you move along in the water with a PADDLE—see also KAYAK—picture at BOAT
■ *verb* (**ca·noe·ing, ca·noed, ca·noed**) [V] (often **go canoe·ing**) to travel in a canoe

ca·noe·ing /kə'nuːɪŋ/ *noun* [U] the sport of travelling in or racing a canoe: *to go canoeing*

ca·noe·ist /kə'nuːɪst/ *noun* a person travelling in a canoe

canon /'kænən/ *noun* **1** a Christian priest with special duties in a CATHEDRAL **2** (*formal*) a generally accepted rule, standard or principle by which sth is judged: *the canons of good taste* **3** a list of the books or other works that are generally accepted as the genuine work of a particular writer or as being important: *the Shakespeare canon* ◊ *'Wuthering Heights' is a central book in the canon of English literature.* **4** a piece of music in which singers

or instruments take it in turns to repeat the MELODY (= tune)

ca·non·ic·al /kə'nɒnɪkl; *AmE* -'nɑːn-/ *adj.* **1** included in a list of holy books that are accepted as genuine; connected with works of literature that are highly respected **2** according to the law of the Christian Church **3** (*technical*) in the simplest accepted form in mathematics

can·on·ize (*BrE* also **-ise**) /'kænənaɪz/ *verb* [VN] [usually passive] (of the POPE) to state officially that sb is now a saint—compare BEATIFY ▶ **can·on·iza·tion, -isa·tion** /ˌkænənaɪ'zeɪʃn; *AmE* -nə'z-/ *noun* [C, U]

ˌcanon 'law *noun* [U] the law of the Christian church

ca·noo·dle /kə'nuːdl/ *verb* [V] (*BrE, informal*) (of two people) to kiss and touch each other in a sexual way

'can-opener *noun* (*especially AmE*) = TIN-OPENER

can·opy /'kænəpi/ *noun* (*pl.* **-ies**) **1** a cover that is fixed or hangs above a bed, seat, etc. as a shelter or decoration—picture at BED, PUSHCHAIR **2** a layer of sth that spreads over an area like a roof, especially branches of trees in a forest: *a canopy of leaves* ◊ *a glorious canopy of stars* **3** a cover for the COCKPIT of an aircraft

cant /kænt/ *noun, verb*
■ *noun* [U] statements, especially about moral or religious issues, that are not sincere and that you cannot trust SYN HYPOCRISY
■ *verb* [V, VN] (*formal*) to be or put sth in a sloping position

can't *short form* cannot

Cantab /'kæntæb/ *abbr.* (used after degree titles) of Cambridge University: *James Cox MA (Cantab)*

can·tan·ker·ous /kæn'tæŋkərəs/ *adj.* bad-tempered and always complaining: *a cantankerous old man*

can·tata /kæn'tɑːtə/ *noun* a short musical work, often on a religious subject, sung by SOLO singers, often with a CHOIR and orchestra—compare ORATORIO, MOTET

can·teen /kæn'tiːn/ *noun* **1** (*especially BrE*) a place where food and drink are served in a factory, a school, etc. **2** a small container used by soldiers, travellers, etc. for carrying water or other liquid **3** ~ **of cutlery** (*BrE*) a box containing a set of knives, forks and spoons

can·ter /'kæntə(r)/ *noun, verb*
■ *noun* [usually sing.] a movement of a horse at a speed that is fairly fast but not very fast; a ride on a horse moving at this speed: *She set off across the field at a canter.*
■ *verb* (of a horse or rider) to move or make a horse move at a canter: [V] *We cantered along the beach.* [alsoVN] —compare GALLOP, TROT

can·ticle /'kæntɪkl/ *noun* a religious song with words taken from the Bible

can·ti·lever /'kæntɪliːvə(r)/ *noun* a long piece of metal or wood that sticks out from a wall to support the end of a bridge or other structure

canto /'kæntəʊ; *AmE* -toʊ/ *noun* (*pl.* **-os**) one of the sections of a long poem

can·ton /'kæntɒn; *AmE* -tən; -tɑːn/ *noun* one of the official regions which some countries, such as Switzerland, are divided into

can·tor /'kæntɔː(r)/ *noun* the person who leads the singing in a SYNAGOGUE or in a church CHOIR

can·vas /'kænvəs/ *noun* **1** [U] a strong heavy rough fabric used for making tents, sails, etc. and by artists for painting on **2** [C] a piece of canvas used for painting on; a painting done on a piece of canvas, using oil paints: *a sale of the artist's early canvases* IDM **under 'canvas** in a tent: *They spent the night under canvas.*

can·vass /'kænvəs/ *verb* **1** ~ (sb) (for sth) to ask sb to support a particular person, political party, etc., especially by going around an area and talking to people: [V] *He spent the whole month canvassing for votes.* ◊ [VN] *Party workers are busy canvassing local residents.* **2** [VN] to ask people about sth in order to find out what they think about it: *He has been canvassing opinion on the issue.* ◊ *People are being canvassed for their views on the proposed new road.* **3** [VN] ~ **support** to try and get support from a group of people **4** [VN] to discuss an idea thoroughly: *The* proposal is currently being canvassed. ▶ **can·vass** noun: to carry out a canvass **can·vass·er** noun

can·yon /ˈkænjən/ noun a deep valley with steep sides of rock

can·yon·ing /ˈkænjənɪŋ/ noun [U] a sport in which you jump into a mountain stream and allow yourself to be carried down at high speed

CAP /ˌsi: eɪ ˈpi:/ abbr. Common Agricultural Policy (of the European Union)

cap /kæp/ noun, verb
■ noun
HAT | **1** a type of soft flat hat with a PEAK (= a hard curved part sticking out in front). Caps are worn especially by men and boys, often as part of a uniform: *a school cap*—see also BASEBALL CAP, CLOTH CAP, MOB CAP—picture at HAT **2** (usually in compounds) a soft hat that fits closely and is worn for a particular purpose: *a shower cap* **3** a soft hat with a square flat top worn by some university teachers and students at special ceremonies—compare MORTAR BOARD
IN SPORT | **4** (*BrE*) a cap given to sb who is chosen to play for a school, country, etc.; a player chosen to play for their country, etc: *He won his first cap* (= was first chosen to play) *for England against France.* ◊ *There are three new caps in the side.*
ON PEN/BOTTLE | **5** a protective cover or top for a pen, bottle, etc: *a lens cap*—see also FILLER CAP, HUBCAP—picture at PACKAGING
LIMIT ON MONEY | **6** an upper limit on an amount of money that can be spent or borrowed by a particular institution or in a particular situation: *The government has placed a cap on local council spending.*
IN TOY GUNS | **7** a small paper container with explosive powder inside it, used especially in toy guns
FOR WOMAN | **8** (*BrE*) = DIAPHRAGM (2)
—see also ICE CAP, THINKING CAP
IDM **go cap in ˈhand (to sb)** (*BrE*) (*AmE* **go hat in ˈhand**) to ask sb for sth, especially money, in a very polite way that makes you seem less important: *There's no way he'll go cap in hand to his brother.* **if the cap fits (ˌwear it)** (*BrE*) (*AmE* **if the shoe fits (ˌwear it)**) (*spoken*) if you feel that a remark applies to you, you should accept it and take it as a warning or criticism: *I didn't actually say that you were lazy, but if the cap fits …*—more at FEATHER *n.*
■ verb (-pp-) [VN]
COVER TOP | **1** [usually passive] ~ **sth (with sth)** to cover the top or end of sth with sth: *mountains capped with snow* ◊ *snow-capped mountains*
LIMIT MONEY | **2** [often passive] (*especially BrE*) to limit the amount of money that can be charged for sth or spent on sth: *a capped mortgage*
BEAT | **3** (*especially BrE*) to say or do sth that is funnier, more impressive, etc. than sth that has been said or done before: *What an amazing story. Can anyone cap that?*
TOOTH | **4** [usually passive] to put an artificial covering on a tooth to make it look more attractive: *He's had his front teeth capped.* **SYN** CROWN
IN SPORT | **5** [usually passive] (*BrE*) to choose sb to play football, cricket, etc. in their country's national team: *He has been capped more than 30 times for Wales.*
IDM **to cap/top it ˈall** (*spoken*) used to introduce the final piece of information that is worse than the other bad things that you have just mentioned

cap·abil·ity /ˌkeɪpəˈbɪləti/ noun [C, U] (*pl.* **-ies**) **1** ~ (**to do sth/of doing sth**) the ability or qualities necessary to do sth: *Animals in the zoo have lost the capability to catch/of catching food for themselves.* ◊ *beyond/within the capabilities of current technology* ◊ *Age affects the range of a person's capabilities.* **2** the power or weapons that a country has for war or for military action: *Britain's nuclear/military capability*

cap·able /ˈkeɪpəbl/ adj. **1** ~ **of sth/of doing sth** having the ability or qualities necessary for doing sth: *He's quite capable of lying to get out of trouble.* ◊ *I'm perfectly capable of doing it myself, thank you.* ◊ *You are capable of*

better work than this. **2** having the ability to do things well **SYN** SKILLED, COMPETENT: *She's a very capable teacher.* ◊ *I'll leave the organization in your capable hands.* **OPP** INCAPABLE ▶ **cap·ably** adv.

cap·acious /kəˈpeɪʃəs/ adj. (*formal*) having a lot of space to put things in **SYN** ROOMY: *capacious pockets*

cap·acity /kəˈpæsəti/ noun (*pl.* **-ies**)
OF CONTAINER | **1** [U, C, usually sing.] the number of things or people that a container or space can hold: *The theatre has a seating capacity of 2000.* ◊ *a fuel tank with a capacity of 50 litres* ◊ *The hall was filled to capacity* (= was completely full). ◊ *They played to a capacity crowd* (= one that filled all the space or seats).
ABILITY | **2** [C usually sing, U] ~ (**for sth/for doing sth**) | ~ (**to do sth**) the ability to understand or to do sth: *She has an enormous capacity for hard work.* ◊ *His capacity for learning languages astonished me.* ◊ *your capacity to enjoy life* ◊ *intellectual capacity* ◊ *Limited resources are restricting our capacity for developing new products.*
ROLE | **3** [C, usually sing.] the official position or function that sb has: *acting in her capacity as manager/in her managerial capacity*
OF FACTORY/MACHINE | **4** [sing., U] the quantity that a factory, machine, etc. can produce: *The factory is working at full capacity.*
OF ENGINE | **5** [C, U] the size or power of a piece of equipment, especially the engine of a vehicle: *an engine with a capacity of 1600 ccs*

cape /keɪp/ noun **1** a loose outer piece of clothing that has no sleeves, fastens at the neck and hangs from the shoulders, like a CLOAK but shorter: *a bullfighter's cape* **2** (*abbr.* **C.**) (often in place names) a piece of high land that sticks out into the sea: *Cape Horn*

caped /keɪpt/ adj. wearing a cape

caper /ˈkeɪpə(r)/ noun, verb
■ noun **1** [usually pl.] the small green flower BUD of a Mediterranean bush, preserved in VINEGAR and used to flavour dishes and sauces **2** (*informal*) an activity, especially one that is illegal or dangerous: *A call to the police should put an end to their little caper.* **3** a short jump or dance: *He cut a little celebratory caper* (= jumped or danced a few steps) *in the middle of the road.*
■ verb [V] [usually +adv./prep.] (*written*) to run or jump around in a happy and excited way

ca·pil·lary /kəˈpɪləri; AmE ˈkæpəleri/ noun (*pl.* **-ies**) (*anatomy*) any of the smallest tubes in the body that carry blood—picture at BODY

ca·ˈpillary action noun [U] (*technical*) the force that makes a liquid move up a narrow tube

cap·ital /ˈkæpɪtl/ noun, adj.
■ noun
CITY | **1** (also ˌcapital ˈcity) [C] the most important town or city of a country, usually where the central government operates from: *Cairo is the capital of Egypt.* ◊ (*figurative*) *Paris, the fashion capital of the world*
MONEY | **2** [sing.] a large amount of money that is invested or is used to start a business: *to set up a business with a starting capital of £100000* **3** [U] wealth or property that is owned by a business or a person: *capital assets* ◊ *capital expenditure* (= money that an organization spends on buildings, equipment, etc.) **4** [U] (*technical*) people who use their money to start businesses, considered as a group: *capital and labour*
LETTER | **5** (also ˌcapital ˈletter) [C] a letter of the form and size that is used at the beginning of a sentence or a name (= A,B,C rather than a,b,c): *Use block capitals* (= separate capital letters). ◊ *Please write in capitals/in capital letters.*
ARCHITECTURE | **6** the top part of a column—picture at ARCADE
IDM **make capital (out) of sth** to use a situation for your own advantage: *The opposition parties are all making political capital out of the disagreements within the government.*
■ adj.
PUNISHMENT | **1** [only before noun] involving punishment by death: *a capital offence*

s	t	v	z	ʃ	ʒ	tʃ	dʒ	θ	ð	ŋ
see	tea	van	zoo	shoe	vision	chain	jam	thin	this	sing

LETTER | **2** [only before noun] (of letters of the alphabet) having the form and size used at the beginning of a sentence or a name: *English is written with a capital 'E'.*—compare LOWER CASE

EXCELLENT | **3** (*old-fashioned*, *BrE*) excellent

IDM **with a capital A, B, etc.** used to emphasize that a word has a stronger meaning than usual in a particular situation: *He was romantic with a capital R.*

,**capital 'gains** *noun* [pl.] profits that you make from selling sth, especially property: *to pay **capital gains tax***

'**capital goods** *noun* [pl.] (*business*) goods such as factory machines that are used for producing other goods—compare CONSUMER GOODS

,**capital-in'tensive** *adj.* (of a business, an industry, etc.) needing large amounts of money in order to operate well—compare LABOUR-INTENSIVE

cap·it·al·ism /ˈkæpɪtəlɪzəm/ *noun* [U] an economic system in which a country's businesses and industry are controlled and run for profit by private owners rather than by the government: *the growth of industrial capitalism in the West*—compare SOCIALISM

cap·it·al·ist /ˈkæpɪtəlɪst/ *noun*, *adj.*
■ *noun* **1** a person who supports capitalism **2** a person who owns or controls a lot of wealth and uses it to produce more wealth
■ *adj.* (also *less frequent* **cap·it·al·is·tic** /ˌkæpɪtəˈlɪstɪk/) based on the principles of capitalism: *a capitalist society/ system/economy*

cap·it·al·ize (*BrE* also **-ise**) /ˈkæpɪtəlaɪz/ *verb* [VN] **1** to write or print a letter of the alphabet as a CAPITAL; to begin a word with a capital letter **2** (*business*) to sell possessions in order to change them into money **3** [usually passive] (*business*) to provide a company etc. with the money it needs to function ► **cap·it·al·iza·tion**, **-isa·tion** /ˌkæpɪtəlaɪˈzeɪʃn; *AmE* -ləˈz-/ *noun* [U, sing.] **PHRV** '**capitalize on/upon sth** to gain a further advantage for yourself from a situation **SYN** TAKE ADVANTAGE OF STH: *The team failed to capitalize on their early lead.*

,**capital 'pun·ish·ment** *noun* [U] punishment by death

,**capital 'sum** *noun* a single payment of money that is made to sb, for example by an insurance company

capi·ta·tion /ˌkæpɪˈteɪʃn/ *noun* [C, U] (*technical*) a tax or payment of an equal amount for each person; the system of payments of this kind: *a capitation fee for each pupil*

ca·pitu·late /kəˈpɪtʃuleɪt/ *verb* [V] ~ (**to sb/sth**) **1** to agree to do sth that you have been refusing to do for a long time **SYN** YIELD: *They were finally forced to capitulate to the terrorists' demands.* **2** to stop resisting an enemy and accept that you are defeated **SYN** SURRENDER: *The town capitulated after a three-week siege.* ► **ca·pitu·la·tion** /kəˌpɪtʃuˈleɪʃn/ *noun* [C, U]

capon /ˈkeɪpɒn; ˈkeɪpən; *AmE* -pɑːn/ *noun* a male chicken that has been CASTRATED (= had part of its sex organs removed) and made fat for eating

cap·pella ⇨ A CAPPELLA

cap·puc·cino /ˌkæpuˈtʃiːnəʊ; *AmE* -noʊ/ *noun* (*pl.* **-os**) **1** [U] a type of coffee made with hot FROTHY milk and sometimes with chocolate powder on the top **2** [C] a cup of cappuccino

ca·price /kəˈpriːs/ *noun* (*formal*) **1** [C] a sudden change in attitude or behaviour for no obvious reason **SYN** WHIM **2** [U] the tendency to change your mind suddenly or behave unexpectedly

ca·pri·cious /kəˈprɪʃəs/ *adj.* (*formal*) **1** showing sudden changes in attitude or behaviour: *a movie star who was capricious and difficult to please* **2** changing suddenly and quickly: *a capricious climate* ► **ca·pri·cious·ly** *adv.* **ca·pri·cious·ness** *noun* [U]

Cap·ri·corn /ˈkæprɪkɔːn; *AmE* -kɔːrn/ *noun* **1** [U] the 10th sign of the ZODIAC, the Goat **2** [C] a person born under the influence of this sign, that is between 21 December and 20 January, approximately

cap·sicum /ˈkæpsɪkəm/ *noun* (*technical*) a type of PEPPER (= a hollow fruit, which may be green, red or yellow, eaten as a vegetable raw or cooked)

cap·size /kæpˈsaɪz; *AmE* ˈkæpsaɪz/ *verb* [V, VN] if a boat **capsizes** or sth **capsizes** it, it turns over in the water

cap·stan /ˈkæpstən/ *noun* **1** a thick CYLINDER that winds up a rope, used for lifting heavy objects such as an ANCHOR on a ship **2** the round bar on a TAPE RECORDER that guides the tape at a speed that does not change

cap·sule /ˈkæpsjuːl; *AmE* also ˈkæpsl/ *noun* **1** a small container which has a measured amount of a medicine inside and which dissolves when you swallow it—picture on page 599 **2** a small plastic container with a substance or liquid inside **3** the part of a spacecraft in which people travel and that often separates from the main rocket **4** (*technical*) a shell or container for seeds or eggs in some plants and animals—see also TIME CAPSULE

Capt. *abbr.* captain (not used for captains in sports teams)

cap·tain /ˈkæptɪn/ *noun*, *verb*
■ *noun* **1** the person in charge of a ship or commercial aircraft: *Captain Cook* ◇ *The captain gave the order to abandon ship.* ◇ *Captain Jones and his co-pilot* **2** an officer of fairly high rank in the navy, the army and the US air force: *Captain Lance Price*—see also GROUP CAPTAIN **3** the leader of a group of people, especially a sports team: *She was captain of the hockey team at school.* **4** an officer of high rank in a US police or fire department
■ *verb* [VN] to be a captain of a sports team or a ship

cap·tain·cy /ˈkæptənsi/ *noun* [C usually sing, U] (*pl.* **-ies**) the position of captain of a team; the period during which sb is captain

,**captain of 'industry** *noun* (*pl.* **captains of industry**) used in newspapers, etc. to describe a person who manages a large business company

cap·tion /ˈkæpʃn/ *noun*, *verb*
■ *noun* words that are printed underneath a picture, CARTOON, etc. that explain or describe it—see also CLOSED-CAPTIONED
■ *verb* [VN] [usually passive] to write a caption for a picture, photograph, etc.

cap·tiv·ate /ˈkæptɪveɪt/ *verb* [VN] [often passive] (*written*) to keep sb's close attention by being extremely interesting, attractive, etc: *The children were captivated by her stories.*

cap·tiv·at·ing /ˈkæptɪveɪtɪŋ/ *adj.* (*written*) taking all your attention; very attractive and interesting: *He found her captivating.*

cap·tive /ˈkæptɪv/ *adj.*, *noun*
■ *adj.* **1** kept as a prisoner or in an enclosed space; unable to escape: *captive animals* ◇ *They were **taken captive** by masked gunmen.* ◇ *captive breeding* (= the catching and breeding of wild animals) **2** [only before noun] not free to leave a particular place or to choose what you want do to: *A salesman loves to have a **captive audience*** (= listening because they have no choice).
■ *noun* a person who is kept as a prisoner, especially in a war

cap·tiv·ity /kæpˈtɪvəti/ *noun* [U] the state of being kept as a prisoner or in an enclosed space: *He was held **in captivity** for three years.* ◇ *The bird had escaped from captivity.*

cap·tor /ˈkæptə(r)/ *noun* (*written*) a person who captures a person or an animal and keeps them as a prisoner: *The hostages were treated well by their captors.*

cap·ture /ˈkæptʃə(r)/ *verb*, *noun*
■ *verb* [VN]
CATCH | **1** to catch a person or an animal and keep them as a prisoner or in an enclosed space: *Allied troops captured over 300 enemy soldiers.* ◇ *The animals are captured in nets and sold to local zoos.*
TAKE CONTROL | **2** to take control of a place, building, etc. using force: *The city was captured in 1941.* **3** to succeed in getting control of sth that other people are also trying to control: *The company has now captured almost 90% of the market.*
MAKE SB INTERESTED | **4** ~ sb's attention/imagination/interest to make sb interested in sth: *They use puppets to capture the imagination of younger audiences.*

æ	ɑː	e	ɜː	ə	ɪ	iː	i	ɒ	ɔː	ʌ	ʊ	u	uː
cat	father	ten	bird	about	sit	see	many	got	saw	cup	put	actual	too

(BrE)

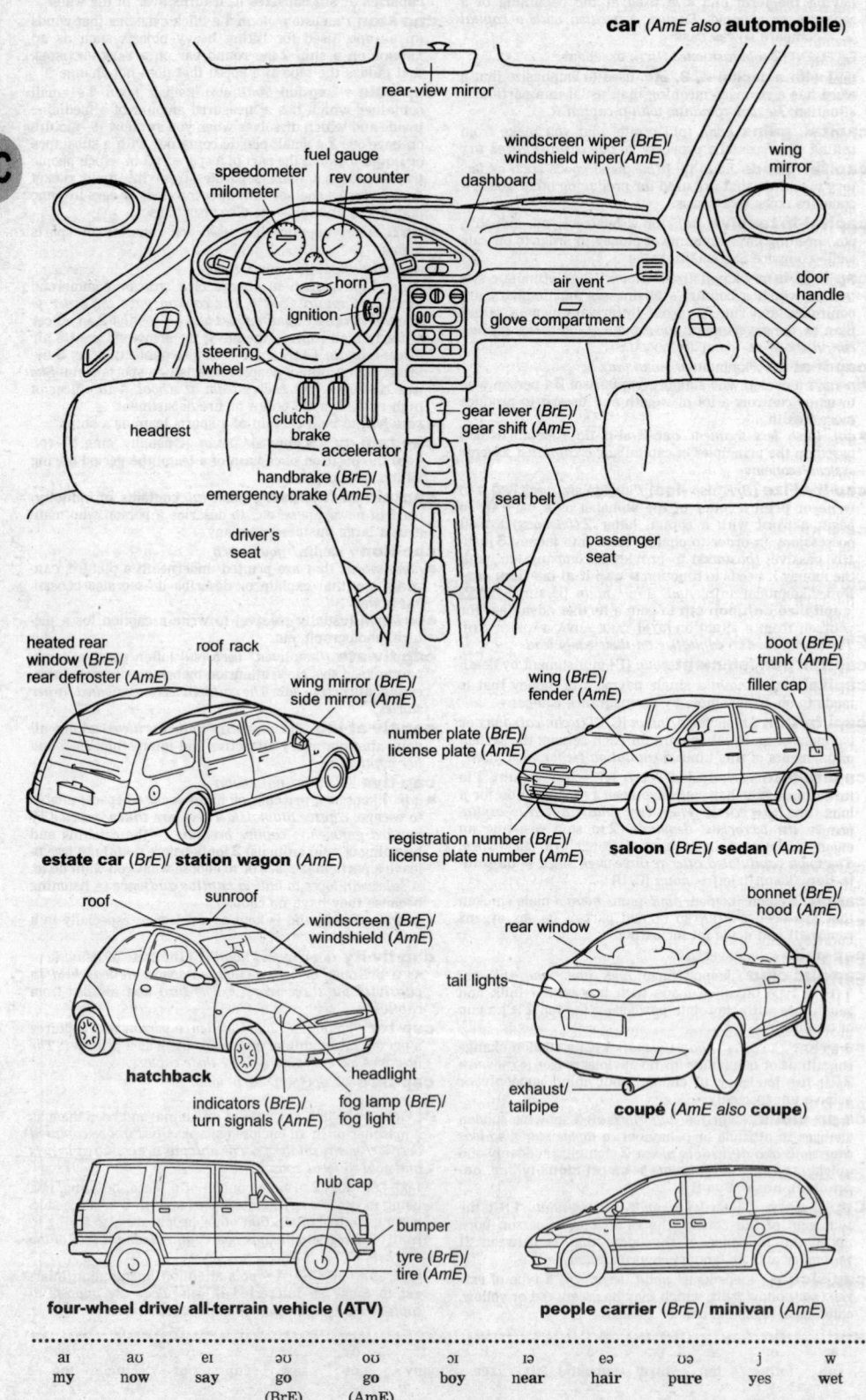

car (*AmE* also **automobile**)

rear-view mirror

windscreen wiper (*BrE*)/
windshield wiper(*AmE*)

wing
mirror

fuel gauge

speedometer
milometer

rev counter

dashboard

air vent

door
handle

horn

ignition

glove compartment

steering
wheel

clutch
brake

accelerator

gear lever (*BrE*)/
gear shift (*AmE*)

headrest

handbrake (*BrE*)/
emergency brake (*AmE*)

seat belt

driver's
seat

passenger
seat

heated rear
window (*BrE*)/
rear defroster (*AmE*)

roof rack

wing mirror (*BrE*)/
side mirror (*AmE*)

boot (*BrE*)/
trunk (*AmE*)

wing (*BrE*)/
fender (*AmE*)

filler cap

number plate (*BrE*)/
license plate (*AmE*)

registration number (*BrE*)/
license plate number (*AmE*)

estate car (*BrE*)/ **station wagon** (*AmE*)

saloon (*BrE*)/ **sedan** (*AmE*)

roof

sunroof

windscreen (*BrE*)/
windshield (*AmE*)

bonnet (*BrE*)/
hood (*AmE*)

rear window

tail lights

hatchback

headlight

indicators (*BrE*)/
turn signals (*AmE*)

fog lamp (*BrE*)/
fog light

exhaust/
tailpipe

coupé (*AmE* also **coupe**)

hub cap

bumper

tyre (*BrE*)/
tire (*AmE*)

four-wheel drive/ all-terrain vehicle (ATV)

people carrier (*BrE*)/ **minivan** (*AmE*)

aɪ	aʊ	eɪ	ɔː	oʊ	ɔɪ	ɪə	eə	ʊə	j	w
my	now	say	go	go	boy	near	hair	pure	yes	wet
			(BrE)	(AmE)						

C

FEELING/ATMOSPHERE | **5** to succeed in accurately expressing a feeling, an atmosphere, etc. in a picture, piece of writing, film/movie, etc: *The article captured the mood of the nation.*

FILM/RECORD/PAINT | **6** [often passive] ~ *sb/sth* **on film/ tape/canvas, etc.** to film/record/paint, etc. sb/sth: *The attack was captured on film by security cameras.*

SB'S HEART | **7** ~ *sb's* **heart** to make sb love you

COMPUTING | **8** to put sth into a computer in a form it can use

■ *noun* [U] the act of capturing sb/sth or of being captured: *the capture of enemy territory* ◊ *He evaded capture for three days.* ◊ *data capture*

car /kɑː(r)/ (also *BrE formal* **'motor car**) (*AmE* also **auto·mo·bile**) *noun* **1** a road vehicle with an engine and four wheels that can carry a small number of passengers: *Paula got into the car and drove off.* ◊ *'How did you come?' 'By car.'* ◊ *Are you going* **in the car?** ◊ *a car driver/ manufacturer/dealer* ◊ *a car accident/crash* ◊ *Where can I park the car?* **2** (*AmE*) any carriage on a train: *Several cars went off the rails.* **3** (*BrE*) (in compounds) a railway carriage of a particular type: *a sleeping/dining car*

ca·rafe /kəˈræf/ *noun* a glass container with a wide neck in which wine or water is served at meals; the amount contained in a carafe

cara·mel /ˈkærəməl/ *noun* **1** [U, C] a type of hard sticky sweet/candy made from butter, sugar and milk; a small piece of this **2** [U] burnt sugar used for adding colour and flavour to food: *ice cream with caramel sauce*—see also CRÈME CARAMEL **3** [U] a light brown colour

cara·mel·ize (*BrE* also **-ise**) /ˈkærəməlaɪz/ *verb* **1** [V] (of sugar) to turn into caramel **2** [VN] to cook sth, especially fruit, with sugar so that it is covered with caramel

cara·pace /ˈkærəpeɪs/ *noun* (*technical*) the hard shell on the back of some animals such as CRABS, that protects them

carat /ˈkærət/ *noun* (*abbr.* **ct**) **1** a unit for measuring the weight of diamonds and other precious stones, equal to 200 MILLIGRAMS **2** (*especially BrE*) (*AmE* usually **karat**) [usually sing.] a unit for measuring how pure gold is. The purest gold is 24 carats: *an 18-carat gold ring*

cara·van /ˈkærəvæn/ *noun* **1** (*BrE*) (*AmE* **camp·er**) a road vehicle without an engine that is pulled by a car, designed for people to live and sleep in, especially when they are on holiday/vacation: *a caravan site/park*—picture at BUS **2** (*BrE*) a covered vehicle that is pulled by a horse and used for living in: *a gypsy caravan* **3** a group of people with vehicles or animals who are travelling together, especially across the desert

cara·van·ning /ˈkærəvænɪŋ/ *noun* [U] (*BrE*) the activity of spending a holiday/vacation in a caravan: *Camping and caravanning attract people of all ages.*

cara·way /ˈkærəweɪ/ *noun* [U] the dried seeds of the caraway plant, used to give flavour to food: *caraway seeds*

car·bine /ˈkɑːbaɪn; *AmE* ˈkɑːrb-/ *noun* a short light RIFLE

carbo·hy·drate /ˌkɑːbəʊˈhaɪdreɪt; *AmE* ˌkɑːrboʊ-/ *noun* **1** [C, U] a substance such as sugar or STARCH that consists of CARBON, HYDROGEN and OXYGEN. Carbohydrates in food provide the body with energy and heat. **2** (**carbohydrates**) [pl.] foods such as bread, potatoes and rice that contain a lot of carbohydrate: *I'm trying to cut down on carbohydrates.*

car·bol·ic /kɑːˈbɒlɪk; *AmE* kɑːrˈbɑːlɪk/ (also **car,bolic 'acid**) *noun* [U] a chemical that kills bacteria, used as an ANTISEPTIC and as a DISINFECTANT (= to prevent infection from spreading): *carbolic soap*

'car bomb *noun* a bomb hidden inside or under a parked car

car·bon /ˈkɑːbən; *AmE* ˈkɑːrb-/ *noun* **1** [U] (*symb* **C**) a chemical element. Carbon is found in all living things, existing in a pure state as diamond and GRAPHITE: *carbon fibre* **2** [C] = CARBON COPY **3** [C] a piece of CARBON PAPER

car·bon·ated /ˈkɑːbəneɪtɪd; *AmE* ˈkɑːrb-/ *adj.* (*technical*) (of a drink) containing small bubbles of CARBON DIOXIDE [SYN] FIZZY: *carbonated mineral water*

,carbon 'copy (also **car·bon**) *noun* **1** a copy of a document, letter, etc. made with CARBON PAPER—see also CC **2** a person or thing that is very similar to sb/sth else: *She is a carbon copy of her sister.*

,carbon 'dating (also *formal* **,radiocarbon 'dating**) *noun* a method of calculating the age of very old objects by measuring the amounts of different forms of carbon in them

,carbon di'oxide *noun* [U] (*symb* CO_2) a gas breathed out by people and animals from the lungs or produced by burning CARBON

car·bon·ifer·ous /ˌkɑːbəˈnɪfərəs; *AmE* ˌkɑːrb-/ *adj.* (*geology*) **1** producing or containing coal **2** (**Carboniferous**) of the period in the earth's history when layers of coal were formed underground

,carbon mon'oxide *noun* [U] (*symb* **CO**) a poisonous gas formed when CARBON burns partly but not completely. It is produced when petrol/gas is burnt in car engines.

'carbon paper *noun* thin paper with a dark substance on one side, that is used between two sheets of paper for making copies of written or typed documents

,car 'boot sale *noun* (*BrE*) an outdoor sale where people sell things that they no longer want from the backs of their cars

car·boy /ˈkɑːbɔɪ; *AmE* ˈkɑːrbɔɪ/ *noun* a large round glass or plastic bottle, usually protected by an outer frame of wood and used for storing and transporting dangerous liquids

car·bun·cle /ˈkɑːbʌŋkl; *AmE* ˈkɑːrb-/ *noun* **1** a large painful swelling under the skin **2** a bright red jewel, usually cut into a round shape

car·bur·et·tor /ˌkɑːbəˈretə(r)/ (*BrE*) (*AmE* **car·bur·etor** /ˈkɑːrbəreɪtər/) *noun* the part of an engine, for example in a car, where petrol/gas and air are mixed together and burn to provide power

car·cass (*BrE* also *less frequent* **car·case**) /ˈkɑːkəs; *AmE* ˈkɑːrkəs/ *noun* the dead body of an animal, especially of a large one or of one that is ready for cutting up as meat

car·cino·gen /kɑːˈsɪnədʒən; *AmE* kɑːrˈs-/ *noun* a substance that can cause CANCER: *exposure to chemical carcinogens in cigarette smoke*

car·cino·gen·ic /ˌkɑːsɪnəˈdʒenɪk; *AmE* ˌkɑːrs-/ *adj.* likely to cause CANCER: *the carcinogenic effects of some pesticides used on fruit*

card /kɑːd; *AmE* kɑːrd/ *noun, verb*
■ *noun*
PAPER | **1** [U] (*BrE*) thick stiff paper: *a piece of card* ◊ *The model of the building was made of card.*

WITH INFORMATION | **2** [C] a small piece of stiff paper or plastic with information on it, especially information about sb's identity: *a membership card* ◊ *an appointment card*—see also GREEN CARD, IDENTITY CARD, RED CARD, REPORT CARD, YELLOW CARD **3** [C] = BUSINESS CARD: *Here's my card if you need to contact me again.* **4** [C] = VISITING CARD

FOR MONEY | **5** [C] a small piece of plastic, especially one given by a bank or shop/store, used for buying things or obtaining money: *I put the meal on* (= paid for it using) *my card.* ◊ *a phone card*—see also CASH CARD, CHARGE CARD, CHEQUE CARD, CREDIT CARD, SMART CARD, SWIPE CARD

WITH GREETINGS | **6** [C] a piece of stiff paper that is folded in the middle and has a picture on the front of it, used for sending sb a greeting, an invitation, etc: *a birthday/ get-well/good luck card* ◊ *a card shop/store*—see also CHRISTMAS CARD, GREETINGS CARD **7** [C] = POSTCARD: *Did you get my card from Italy?*

IN GAMES | **8** [C] = PLAYING CARD: *Let's have a game of cards.* ◊ (*BrE*) *a pack of cards* ◊ (*AmE*) *a deck of cards*—see also TRUMP CARD, WILD CARD—picture on page A8 **9** (**cards**) [pl.] a game or games in which playing cards are used: *Who wants to play cards?* ◊ *I've never been very good at cards. She won £20 at cards.*

COMPUTING | **10** [C] a small device containing an electronic CIRCUIT that is part of a computer or added to it, enabling it to perform particular functions: *a printed circuit card* ◊ *a graphics/network/sound card*

b	d	f	g	h	k	l	m	n	p	r
bad	did	fall	get	hat	cat	leg	man	now	pen	red

PERSON | **11** [C] (*old-fashioned, informal*) an unusual or amusing person

HORSE RACES | **12** [C] a list of all the races at a particular RACE MEETING (= a series of horse races): *a race card*

FOR WOOL/COTTON | **13** [C] (*technical*) a machine or tool used for cleaning and combing wool or cotton before it is spun

IDM **sb's best/strongest/winning 'card** something that gives sb an advantage over other people in a particular situation **get your 'cards** (*BrE, informal*) to be told to leave a job **give sb their 'cards** (*BrE, informal*) to make sb leave their job **have a card up your 'sleeve** to have an idea, a plan, etc. that will give you an advantage in a particular situation and that you keep secret until it is needed **hold all the 'cards** (*informal*) to be able to control a particular situation because you have an advantage over other people **hold/keep/play your cards close to your 'chest** to keep your ideas, plans, etc. secret **lay/put your cards on the 'table** to tell sb honestly what your plans, ideas, etc. are **on the 'cards** (*BrE*) (*AmE* **in the 'cards**) (*informal*) likely to happen: *The merger has been on the cards for some time now.* **play your 'cards right** to deal successfully with a particular situation so that you achieve some advantage or sth that you want—more at SHOW v., STACKED

■ *verb* [VN] **1** (*technical*) to clean wool using a wire instrument **2** (*AmE, informal*) to ask a person to show their identity card as a means of checking how old they are, for example if they want to buy alcohol

car·da·mom /'kɑːdəməm; *AmE* 'kɑːrd-/ *noun* [U] the dried seeds of a SE Asian plant, used in cooking as a spice: *cardamom pods*

card·board /'kɑːdbɔːd; *AmE* 'kɑːrdbɔːrd/ *noun, adj.*
■ *noun* [U] stiff material like very thick paper, often used for making boxes: *a cardboard box* ◊ *a piece of cardboard* ◊ *a model made out of cardboard*
■ *adj.* [only before noun] not seeming real or genuine: *With its superficial cardboard characters, the novel was typical of her work.*

cardboard 'city *noun* an area of a city where people who have nowhere to live sleep outside, protected only by cardboard boxes

'card-carrying *adj.* [only before noun] known to be an official and usually active member of a political organization: *a card-carrying member of the Conservative party*

'card catalog *noun* (*AmE*) = CARD INDEX

'card game *noun* a game in which playing cards are used

card·hold·er /'kɑːdhəʊldə(r); *AmE* 'kɑːrdhoʊl-/ *noun* a person who has a CREDIT CARD from a bank, etc.

car·diac /'kɑːdiæk; *AmE* 'kɑːrd-/ *adj.* [only before noun] (*medical*) connected with the heart or heart disease: *cardiac disease/failure/surgery* ◊ *to suffer cardiac arrest* (= an occasion when a person's heart stops temporarily or permanently)

car·di·gan /'kɑːdɪgən; *AmE* 'kɑːrd-/ (*AmE* also **cardigan 'sweater**) *noun* a knitted woollen jacket, usually with no collar and fastened with buttons at the front—picture on page A5

car·din·al /'kɑːdɪnl; *AmE* 'kɑːrd-/ *noun, adj.*
■ *noun* **1** a priest of the highest rank in the Roman Catholic Church. Cardinals elect and advise the POPE: *Cardinal Hume* **2** (also **cardinal 'number**) a number, such as 1, 2 and 3, used to show quantity rather than order—compare ORDINAL **3** a N American bird. The male cardinal is bright red.
■ *adj.* [only before noun] (*formal*) most important; having other things based on it: *Respect for life is a cardinal principle of English law.*

cardinal 'points *noun* [pl.] (*technical*) the four main points (North, South, East and West) of the COMPASS

cardinal 'sin *noun* **1** (sometimes *humorous*) an action that is a serious mistake or that other people disapprove of: *He committed the cardinal sin of criticizing his teammates.* **2** a serious SIN in the Christian Church

'card index (also **index**) (both *BrE*) (*AmE* **'card catalog**) *noun* a box of cards with information on them, arranged in alphabetical order—picture at STATIONERY

cardio- /'kɑːdiəʊ; *AmE* 'kɑːrdioʊ/ *combining form* (in nouns, adjectives and adverbs) connected with the heart: *cardiogram*

car·di·olo·gist /ˌkɑːdi'ɒlədʒɪst; *AmE* ˌkɑːrdi'ɑːl-/ *noun* a doctor who studies and treats heart diseases ► **car·di·ology** /-dʒi/ *noun* [U]

'card table *noun* a small table for playing card games on, especially one that you can fold

care /keə(r); *AmE* ker/ *noun, verb*
■ *noun* **1** [U] the process of caring for sb/sth and providing what they need for their health or protection: *medical/patient care* ◊ *How much do men share housework and the care of the children?* ◊ *the provision of care for the elderly* ◊ *skin/hair care products*—see also DAY CARE, HEALTH CARE, INTENSIVE CARE **2** [U] attention or thought that you give to sth that you are doing so that you will do it well and avoid mistakes or damage: *She chose her words with care.* ◊ *Great care is needed when choosing a used car.* ◊ *Fragile—handle with care* (= written on a container holding sth which is easily broken or damaged) **3** [C, usually pl., U] (*formal*) a feeling of worry or anxiety; something that causes problems or anxiety: *I felt free from the cares of the day as soon as I left the building.* ◊ *Sam looked as if he didn't have a care in the world.* **IDM** **'care of sb** (*AmE* also **in 'care of sb**) (*abbr.* **c/o**) used when writing to sb at another person's address: *Write to him care of his lawyer.* **in 'care** (*BrE*) (of children) living in an institution run by the local authority rather than with their parents: *The two girls were taken into care after their parents were killed.* **in the care of sb/in sb's care** being cared for by sb: *The child was left in the care of friends.* ◊ *You won't come to any harm while you're in their care.* **take 'care** (*spoken*) used when saying goodbye: *Bye! Take care!* **take care (that.../to do sth)** to be careful: *Take care (that) you don't drink too much!* ◊ *Care should be taken to close the lid securely.* **take care of sb/sth/yourself 1** to care for sb/sth/yourself; to be careful about sth: *Who's taking care of the children while you're away?* ◊ *She takes great care of her clothes.* ◊ *He's old enough to take care of himself.* **2** to be responsible for or to deal with a situation or task: *Don't worry about the travel arrangements. They're all being taken care of.* ◊ *Celia takes care of the marketing side of things.* **under the care of sb** receiving medical care from sb: *He's under the care of Dr Parks.*
■ *verb* (not used in the progressive tenses) **1** ~ (about sth) to feel that sth is important and worth worrying about: [V] *She cares deeply about environmental issues.* ◊ *I don't care* (= I will not be upset) *if I never see him again!* ◊ *He threatened to fire me, as if I cared!.* ◊ [Vwh-] *I don't care what he thinks.* ◊ [Vthat] *She doesn't seem to care that he's been married four times before.* **2** [V] ~ (about sb) to like or love sb and worry about what happens to them: *He genuinely cares about his employees.* **3** [VtoInf] to make the effort to do sth: *I've done this job more times than I care to remember.* **IDM** **couldn't care 'less** (*informal*) used to say, often rudely, that you do not think that sb/sth is important or worth worrying about: *Quite honestly, I couldn't care less what they do.* **for all you, I, they, etc. care** (*spoken*) used to say that a person is not worried about or interested in what happens to sb/sth: *I could be dead for all he cares!* **who 'cares?** | **What do I, you, etc. care?** (*spoken*) used to say, often rudely, that you do not think that sth is important or interesting: *Who cares what she thinks?* **would you care for...** | **would you care to...** (*formal*) used to ask sb politely if they would like sth or would like to do sth, or if they would be willing to do sth: *Would you care for another drink?* ◊ *If you'd care to follow me, I'll show you where his office is.* ⇨ note at WANT—more at DAMN n., FIG n., HOOT n., TUPPENCE

PHRV **'care for sb 1** to look after sb who is sick, very old, very young, etc: *She moved back home to care for her elderly parents.*—see also UNCARED FOR **2** to love or like sb very much: *He cared for her more than she realized.* **not 'care for sb/sth** (*formal*) to not like sb/sth: *He didn't much care for her friends.* ⇨ note on page 177

WHICH WORD?
take care of / look after / care for

You can **take care of** or, especially in *BrE*, **look after** someone who is very young, very old, or sick, or something that needs keeping in good condition: *We've asked my mother to take care of/look after the kids while we're away.* ◇ *You can borrow my camera if you promise to take care of/look after it.*
In more formal language you can also **care for** someone: *She does some voluntary work, caring for the elderly*, but **care for** is more commonly used to mean 'like': *I don't really care for spicy food.*

'care assistant *noun* (*BrE*) = CARE WORKER

car·een /kəˈriːn/ *verb* [V+*adv./prep.*] (*especially AmE*) (of a person or vehicle) to move forward very quickly especially in a way that is dangerous or uncontrolled SYN HURTLE

car·eer /kəˈrɪə(r); *AmE* kəˈrɪr/ *noun, verb*
■ *noun* **1** the series of jobs that a person has in a particular area of work, usually involving more responsibility as time passes: *a career in medicine/politics* ◇ *a teaching/academic career* ◇ *What made you decide on a career as a vet?* ◇ *She has been concentrating on her career.* ◇ *a change of career* ◇ *a career soldier/diplomat* (= a professional one) ◇ (*BrE*) *a careers adviser/officer* (= a person whose job is to give people advice and information about jobs) **2** the period of time that you spend in your life working or doing a particular thing: *She started her career as an English teacher.* ◇ *He is playing the best tennis of his career.* ◇ *My school career was not very impressive.*
■ *verb* [V+*adv./prep.*] (of a person or vehicle) to move forward very quickly, especially in an uncontrolled way SYN HURTLE: *The vehicle careered across the road and hit a cyclist.*

ca'reer break *noun* a period of time when you do not do your usual job, for example because you have children to care for

car·eer·ist /kəˈrɪərɪst; *AmE* -ˈrɪr-/ *noun* (often *disapproving*) a person whose career is more important to them than anything else ▶ **car·eer·ism** *noun* [U]

ca'reer woman *noun* a woman whose career is more important to her than getting married and having children

care·free /ˈkeəfriː; *AmE* ˈkerf-/ *adj.* having no worries or responsibilities: *He looked happy and carefree.* ◇ *a carefree attitude/life*

care·ful /ˈkeəfl; *AmE* ˈkerfl/ *adj.* **1** [not before noun] ~ (**to do sth**)| ~ (**not to do sth**)| ~ (**when/what/how, etc.**)| ~ (**of/about/with sth**) giving attention or thought to what you are doing so that you avoid hurting yourself, damaging sth or doing sth wrong: *Be careful!* ◇ *He was careful to keep out of sight.* ◇ *Be careful not to wake the baby.* ◇ *You must be careful when handling chemicals.* ◇ *Be careful of the traffic.* ◇ *Please be careful with my glasses* (= Don't break them). ◇ *Be careful you don't bump your head.* **2** giving a lot of attention to details: *a careful piece of work* ◇ *a careful examination of the facts* ◇ *After careful consideration we have decided to offer you the job.* ▶ **care·ful·ly** /ˈkeəfəli; *AmE* ˈker-/ *adv.*: *Please listen carefully.* ◇ *She put the glass down carefully.* ◇ *Drive carefully.* **care·ful·ness** *noun* [U] IDM **you can't be too 'careful** (*spoken*) used to warn sb that they should take care to avoid danger or problems: *Don't stay out in the sun for too long—you can't be too careful.* **careful with money** not spending money on unimportant things

care·giver /ˈkeəɡɪvə(r); *AmE* ˈkerɡ-/ *noun* (*AmE*) = CARER

care·less /ˈkeələs; *AmE* ˈkerləs/ *adj.* **1** not giving enough attention and thought to what you are doing, so that you make mistakes: *It was careless of me to leave the door open.* ◇ *Don't be so careless about/with spelling.* ◇ *a careless worker/driver* **2** resulting from a lack of attention and thought: *a careless mistake/error* **3** ~ **of sth** (*formal*) not at all worried about sth: *He seemed careless of his own safety.* **4** not showing interest or effort SYN CASUAL: *She gave a careless shrug.* ◇ *a careless laugh/smile* ▶ **care-**

less·ly *adv.*: *Someone had carelessly left a window open.* ◇ *She threw her coat carelessly onto the chair.* ◇ *'I don't mind,' he said carelessly.* **care·less·ness** *noun* [U]: *a moment of carelessness*

carer /ˈkeərə(r); *AmE* ˈker-/ (*BrE*) (*AmE* **care·giver**) *noun* a person who looks after a sick or old person at home

ca·ress /kəˈres/ *verb, noun*
■ *verb* [VN] to touch sb/sth gently, especially in a sexual way or in a way that shows affection: *His fingers caressed the back of her neck.*
■ *noun* a gentle touch or kiss to show you love sb

care·taker /ˈkeəteɪkə(r); *AmE* ˈkert-/ *noun, adj.*
■ *noun* **1** (*BrE*) (*AmE, ScotE* **jani·tor**) (*AmE also* **cus·to·dian**) a person whose job is to take care of a building such as a school or a block of flats or an apartment building **2** (*especially AmE*) a person who takes care of a house or land while the owner is away **3** (*especially AmE*) a person such as a teacher, parent, nurse, etc., who takes care of other people
■ *adj.* [only before noun] in charge for a short time, until a new leader or government is chosen: *a caretaker manager/government*

'care worker (*also* **'care assistant**) (*both BrE*) *noun* a person whose job is to help and take care of people who are mentally ill, sick or DISABLED, especially those who live in special homes or hospitals

care·worn /ˈkeəwɔːn; *AmE* ˈkerwɔːrn/ *adj.* (*written*) looking tired because you have a lot of worries

cargo /ˈkɑːɡəʊ; *AmE* ˈkɑːrɡoʊ/ *noun* [C, U] (*pl.* **-oes**, *AmE also* **-os**) the goods carried in a ship or plane: *The tanker began to spill its cargo of oil.* ◇ *a cargo ship*

cari·bou /ˈkærɪbuː/ *noun* (*pl.* **cari·bou**) a N American REINDEER

cari·ca·ture /ˈkærɪkətʃʊə(r); *AmE* -tʃər; -tʃʊr/ *noun, verb*
■ *noun* **1** [C] a funny drawing or picture of sb that exaggerates some of their features **2** [C] a description of a person or thing that makes them seem ridiculous by exaggerating some of their characteristics: *He had unfairly presented a caricature of my views.* **3** [U] the art of drawing or writing caricatures ▶ **cari·ca·tur·ist** *noun*
■ *verb* [VN] [often passive] ~ **sb/sth** (**as sth**) to produce a caricature of sb; to describe or present sb as a type of person you would laugh at or not respect: *She was unfairly caricatured as a dumb blonde.*

car·ies /ˈkeəriːz; *AmE* ˈker-/ *noun* [U] (*medical*) decay in teeth or bones: *dental caries*

car·il·lon /kəˈrɪljən; *AmE* ˈkærələn/ *noun* **1** a set of bells on which tunes can be played, sometimes using a piano keyboard **2** a tune played on bells

car·ing /ˈkeərɪŋ; *AmE* ˈker-/ *adj.* [usually before noun] kind, helpful and showing that you care about other people: *He's a very caring person.* ◇ *Children need a caring environment.* ◇ (*BrE*) *a caring profession* (= a job that involves looking after or helping other people)

car·jack·ing /ˈkɑːdʒækɪŋ; *AmE* ˈkɑːrdʒ-/ *noun* [U, C] (*especially AmE*) the crime of forcing the driver of a car to take you somewhere or give you their car, using threats and violence—compare HIJACKING ▶ **car·jack** *verb* [VN] **car·jack·er** *noun*

car·load /ˈkɑːləʊd; *AmE* ˈkɑːrloʊd/ *noun* the number of people or things that a car is carrying or is able to carry

car·mine /ˈkɑːmaɪn; *AmE* ˈkɑːrm-/ *adj.* (*rare, formal*) dark red in colour ▶ **car·mine** *noun* [U]

carn·age /ˈkɑːnɪdʒ; *AmE* ˈkɑːrn-/ *noun* [U] the violent killing of a large number of people: *a scene of carnage*

car·nal /ˈkɑːnl; *AmE* ˈkɑːrnl/ *adj.* [usually before noun] (*formal or law*) connected with the body or with sex: *carnal desires/appetites* ▶ **car·nal·ly** /ˈkɑːnəli; *AmE* ˈkɑːrn-/ *adv.*

carnal 'knowledge *noun* [U] (*old-fashioned or law*) = SEXUAL INTERCOURSE

car·na·tion /kɑːˈneɪʃn; *AmE* kɑːrˈn-/ *noun* a white, pink or red flower, often worn as a decoration on formal occasions: *He was wearing a carnation in his buttonhole.*

car·ni·val /ˈkɑːnɪvl; *AmE* ˈkɑːrn-/ *noun* **1** [C, U] a public festival, usually one that happens at a regular time each

æ	ɑː	e	ɜː	ə	ɪ	iː	i	ɒ	ɔː	ʌ	ʊ	u	uː
cat	father	ten	bird	about	sit	see	many	got	saw	cup	put	actual	too
								(BrE)					

C

year, that involves music and dancing in the streets, for which people wear colourful clothes: *There is a local carnival every year.* ◊ *the carnival in Rio* ◊ *a carnival atmosphere* **2** [C] (*AmE*) = FAIR *n.* (1) **3** [C] (*AmE*) = FÊTE **4** [sing.] **~ of sth** (*written*) an exciting or colourful mixture of things: *this summer's carnival of sport*

car·ni·vore /ˈkɑːnɪvɔː(r); *AmE* ˈkɑːrn-/ *noun* any animal that eats meat—compare HERBIVORE, INSECTIVORE, OMNIVORE ▶ **car·ni·vor·ous** /kɑːˈnɪvərəs; *AmE* kɑːrˈn-/ *adj.*: *a carnivorous diet*—compare OMNIVOROUS

carob /ˈkærəb/ (also **ˈcarob tree**) *noun* a southern European tree with dark brown fruit that can be made into a powder that tastes like chocolate

carol /ˈkærəl/ *noun, verb*
■ *noun* (also ˌChristmas ˈcarol) a Christian religious song sung at Christmas
■ *verb* (-ll-, *AmE* -l-) [V, VN, Vspeech] (*written*) to sing sth in a cheerful way

ca·rotid ar·tery /kəˈrɒtɪd ɑːtəri; *AmE* -ˈrɑːt- ɑːrt-/ *noun* (*anatomy*) either of the two large ARTERIES in the neck that carry blood to the head

ca·rouse /kəˈraʊz/ *verb* [V] (*literary*) to spend time drinking alcohol, laughing and enjoying yourself in a noisy way with other people

car·ou·sel /ˌkærəˈsel/ *noun* **1** (*especially AmE*) = MERRY-GO-ROUND (1) **2** a moving belt from which you collect your bags at an airport

carp /kɑːp; *AmE* kɑːrp/ *noun, verb*
■ *noun* [C, U] (*pl.* **carp**) a large FRESHWATER fish that is used for food
■ *verb* [V] **~ (at sb) (about sth)** to keep complaining about sb/sth in an annoying way

car·pal tun·nel syn·drome /ˌkɑːpl ˈtʌnl sɪndrəʊm; *AmE* ˌkɑːrpl ˈtʌnl sɪndroʊm/ *noun* [U] (*medical*) a painful condition of the hand and fingers caused by pressure on a nerve because of repeated movements over a long period

ˈcar park *noun* (*BrE*) an area or a building where people can leave their cars—see also GARAGE, MULTI-STOREY CAR PARK—compare PARKING LOT·

car·pen·ter /ˈkɑːpəntə(r); *AmE* ˈkɑːrp-/ *noun* a person whose job is making and repairing wooden objects and structures—compare JOINER

car·pen·try /ˈkɑːpəntri; *AmE* ˈkɑːrp-/ *noun* [U] **1** the work of a carpenter **2** things made by a carpenter

car·pet /ˈkɑːpɪt; *AmE* ˈkɑːrpɪt/ *noun, verb*
■ *noun* **1** [U] thick woollen or artificial fabric for covering floors or stairs: *a roll of carpet* **2** [C] a piece of carpet used as a floor covering, especially when shaped to fit a room: *to lay a carpet* ◊ *a bedroom carpet* ◊ (*BrE*) *We have fitted carpets* (= carpets from wall to wall) *in our house.*—see also CARPETING, RED CARPET, RUG **3** [C] **~ (of sth)** (*written*) a thick layer of sth on the ground: *a carpet of snow* **IDM (be/ get called) on the ˈcarpet** (*informal, especially AmE*) called to see sb in authority because you have done sth wrong: *I got called on the carpet for being late.*—more at SWEEP *v.*
■ *verb* [VN] [usually passive] **1** to cover the floor of a room with a carpet: *The hall was carpeted in blue.* **2 ~ sth (with/in sth)** (*written*) to cover sth with a thick layer of sth: *The forest floor was carpeted with wild flowers.* **3** (*informal, especially BrE*) to speak angrily to sb because they have done sth wrong [SYN] REPRIMAND: *Senior officials were carpeted for leaking information to the press.*

car·pet·bag·ger /ˈkɑːpɪtbægə(r); *AmE* ˈkɑːrp-/ *noun* **1** (*disapproving*) a politician who tries to be elected in an area where he or she is not known and is therefore not welcome **2** a person from the northern states of the US who went to the South after the Civil War in order to make money or get political power

car·pet·ing /ˈkɑːpɪtɪŋ; *AmE* ˈkɑːrp-/ *noun* **1** [U] carpets in general or the material used for carpets: *new offices with wall-to-wall carpeting* ◊ (*AmE*) *We need new carpeting* (= a new carpet) *in the living room.* **2** [C] (*BrE, informal*) an act of speaking angrily to sb because they have done sth wrong

ˈcarpet slipper *noun* [usually pl.] (*old-fashioned, BrE*) a type of SLIPPER (= a shoe that you wear in the house), with the upper part made of fabric

ˈcarpet sweeper *noun* a simple machine for cleaning carpets, with a long handle and brushes that go round

ˈcar phone *noun* a radio telephone for use in a car

ˈcar pool *noun* **1** a group of car owners who take turns to drive everyone in the group to work, so that only one car is used at a time (*BrE*) (also **ˈmotor pool** *AmE, BrE*) a group of cars owned by a company or an organization, that its staff can use

car·port /ˈkɑːpɔːt; *AmE* ˈkɑːrpɔːrt/ *noun* a shelter for a car, usually built beside a house and consisting of a roof supported by posts

car·rel /ˈkærəl/ *noun* a small enclosed area with a desk, where one person can work in a library

car·riage /ˈkærɪdʒ/ *noun* **1** (also **coach**) (both *BrE*) (*AmE* **car**) [C] a separate section of a train for carrying passengers: *a railway carriage* **2** [C] a road vehicle, usually with four wheels, that is pulled by one or more horses and was used in the past to carry people: *a horse-drawn carriage* **3** (*BrE*) (also **hand·ling** *AmE, BrE*) [U] (*formal*) the act or cost of transporting goods from one place to another: *£16.95 including VAT and carriage* **4** [C] a moving part of a machine that supports or moves another part, for example on a TYPEWRITER: *a carriage return* (= the act of starting a new line when typing) **5** [sing.] (*old-fashioned*) the way in which sb holds and moves their head and body—see also BABY CARRIAGE, UNDERCARRIAGE

ˈcarriage house *noun* (*AmE*) = MEWS HOUSE

car·riage·way /ˈkærɪdʒweɪ/ *noun* (*BrE*) **1** one of the two sides of a motorway or other large road, intended for traffic moving in one direction: *the eastbound carriageway of the M50 motorway*—see also DUAL CARRIAGEWAY **2** the part of a road intended for vehicles, not people walking, etc.

car·rier /ˈkæriə(r)/ *noun* **1** a company that carries goods or passengers from one place to another, especially by air **2** a military vehicle or ship that carries soldiers or equipment from one place to another: *an armoured personnel carrier*—see also AIRCRAFT CARRIER, PEOPLE CARRIER **3** a person who passes a disease to other people but does not suffer from it **4** a metal frame that is fixed to a bicycle and used for carrying bags **5** a person or thing that carries sth: *Aquarius, the Water Carrier* ◊ *a baby carrier* (= for carrying a baby on your back or in front of you)—picture at PUSHCHAIR **6** (*BrE*) = CARRIER BAG

ˈcarrier bag (also **car·rier**) *noun* (*BrE*) a paper or plastic bag for carrying shopping—picture at BAG

ˈcarrier pigeon *noun* a PIGEON (= a type of bird) that has been trained to carry messages tied to its leg or neck

car·rion /ˈkæriən/ *noun* [U] the decaying flesh of dead animals: *crows feeding on carrion*—picture on page A6

car·rot /ˈkærət/ *noun* **1** [U, C] a long pointed orange root vegetable: *grated carrot* ◊ *a pound of carrots*—picture on page A3 **2** [C] a reward promised to sb in order to persuade them to do sth: *They are holding out a carrot of $120 million in economic aid.* **IDM the carrot and (the) stick (approach)** if you use **the carrot and stick approach**, you persuade sb to try harder by offering them a reward if they do, or a punishment if they do not

car·roty /ˈkærəti/ *adj.* (sometimes *disapproving*) (of hair) orange in colour

carry /ˈkæri/ *verb* (**car·ries, carry·ing, car·ried, car·ried**) **TAKE WITH YOU 1** [VN] to support the weight of sb/sth and take them or it from place to place; to take sb/sth from one place to another: *He was carrying a suitcase.* ◊ *She carried her baby in her arms.* ◊ *The injured were carried away on stretchers.* ◊ *a train carrying commuters to work* **2** [VN] to have sth with you and take it wherever you go: *Police in many countries carry guns.* ◊ *I never carry much money on me.* ⇨ note at WEAR

OF PIPES/WIRES 3 [VN] to contain and direct the flow of water, electricity, etc: *a pipeline carrying oil* ◊ *The veins carry blood to the heart.*

aɪ	aʊ	eɪ	əʊ	oʊ	ɔɪ	ɪə	eə	ʊə	j	w
my	now	say	go	go	boy	near	hair	pure	yes	wet
			(BrE)	(AmE)						

<u>DISEASE</u> | **4** if a person, an insect, etc. **carries** a disease, they are infected with it and might spread it to others although they might not become sick themselves: *Ticks can carry a nasty disease which affects humans.*

<u>REMEMBER</u> | **5** [VN+*adv./prep.*] **~ sth in your head/mind** to be able to remember sth

<u>SUPPORT WEIGHT</u> | **6** [VN] to support the weight of sth: *A road bridge has to carry a lot of traffic.*

<u>RESPONSIBILITY</u> | **7** [VN] to accept responsibility for sth; to suffer the results of sth: *He is carrying the department* (= it is only working because of his efforts). ◊ *Their group was targeted to carry the burden of job losses.*

<u>HAVE AS QUALITY/FEATURE</u> | **8** [VN] to have sth as a quality or feature: *Her speech carried the ring of authority.* ◊ *My views don't carry much weight* with (= have much influence on) *the boss.* ◊ *Each bike carries a ten-year guarantee.* **9** [VN] to have sth as a result: *Crimes of violence carry heavy penalties.* ◊ *Being a combat sport, karate carries with it the risk of injury.*

<u>OF THROW/KICK</u> | **10** [VN+*adv./prep.*] if sth that is thrown, kicked, etc. **carries** a particular distance, it travels that distance before stopping: *The fullback's kick carried 50 metres into the crowd.*

<u>OF SOUND</u> | **11** [V] [often +*adv./prep.*] if a sound **carries**, it can be heard a long distance away

<u>TAKE TO PLACE/POSITION</u> | **12** [VN] **~ sth/sb to/into sth** to take sth/sb to a particular point or in a particular direction: *The war was carried into enemy territory.* ◊ *Her abilities carried her to the top of her profession.*

<u>APPROVAL/SUPPORT</u> | **13** [VN] [usually passive] to approve of sth by more people voting for it than against it: *The resolution was carried by 340 votes to 210.* **14** [VN] to win the support or sympathy of sb; to persuade people to accept your argument: *His moving speech was enough to carry the audience.* ◊ *She nodded in agreement, and he saw he had carried his point.*

<u>HAVE LABEL</u> | **15** [VN] to have a particular label or piece of information attached: *Cigarettes must carry a health warning.*

<u>NEWS STORY</u> | **16** [VN] if a newspaper or broadcast **carries** a particular story, it publishes or broadcasts it

<u>ITEM IN STORE</u> | **17** [VN] if a shop/store **carries** a particular item, it has it for sale: *We carry a range of educational software.*

<u>BABY</u> | **18** [VN] (**be carrying sb**) to be pregnant with sb: *She was carrying twins.*

<u>YOURSELF</u> | **19** [VN+*adv./prep.*] to hold or move your head or body in a particular way: *to carry yourself well/proudly*

IDM **be/get carried a'way** to get very excited or lose control of your feelings: *I got carried away and started shouting at the television.* **carry all/everything be'fore you** (*written*) to be completely successful **carry the 'can (for sb/sth)** (*BrE, informal*) to accept the blame for sth, especially when it is not your fault **carry a torch for sb** to be in love with sb, especially sb who does not love you in return—more at DAY, FAST *adv.*, FETCH

PHRV ,**carry sb 'back (to sth)** to make sb remember a time in the past: *The smell of the sea carried her back to her childhood.* ,**carry sth↔'forward** (also ,**carry sth↔'over**) to move a total amount from one column or page to the next ,**carry sth↔'off 1** to win sth: *He carried off most of the prizes.* **2** to succeed in doing sth that most people would find difficult: *She's had her hair cut really short, but she can carry it off.* ,**carry 'on 1** (*especially BrE*) to continue moving: *Carry on until you get to the junction, then turn left.* **2** (*informal*) to argue or complain noisily: *He was shouting and carrying on.*—related noun CARRY-ON ,**carry 'on (with sth)** | ,**carry sth↔'on** to continue doing sth: *Carry on with your work while I'm away.* ◊ *After he left I just tried to carry on as normal* (= do the things I usually do). ◊ *Carry on the good work!* ◊ [+-ing] *He carried on peeling the potatoes.* ,**carry 'on (with sb)** (*old-fashioned*) to have a sexual relationship with sb when you should not: *His wife found out he'd been carrying on with another woman.* ,**carry sth↔'out 1** to do sth that you have said you will do or have been asked to do:

to carry out a promise/a threat/a plan/an order **2** to do and complete a task: *to carry out an inquiry/an investigation/a survey* ◊ *Extensive tests have been carried out on the patient.* ,**carry 'over** to continue to exist in a different situation: *Attitudes learned at home carry over into the playground.* ,**carry sth↔'over 1** to keep sth from one situation and use it or deal with it in a different situation **2** to delay sth until a later time: *The match had to be carried over until Sunday.* **3** = CARRY STH FORWARD ,**carry sb 'through** | ,**carry sb 'through sth** to help sb to survive a difficult period: *His determination carried him through the ordeal.* ,**carry sth 'through** to complete sth successfully: *It's a difficult job but she's the person to carry it through.* ,**carry 'through (on/with sth)** (*AmE*) to do what you have said you will do: *He has proved he can carry through on his promises.*

carry·cot /'kærikɒt; *AmE* -kɑːt/ *noun* (*BrE*) a small bed for a baby, with handles at the sides so you can carry it—picture at PUSHCHAIR

'carry-on *noun* **1** [usually sing.] (*BrE, informal*) a display of excitement, anger or silly behaviour over sth unimportant: *What a carry-on!* **2** (*AmE*) a small bag or case that you carry onto a plane with you: *Only one carry-on is allowed.* ◊ *carry-on baggage*

'carry-out *noun* (*AmE, ScotE*) = TAKEAWAY: *Let's get a carry-out.* ◊ *carry-out coffees*

'car seat *noun* **1** (also **'child seat**) a special safety seat for a child, that can be fitted into a car—picture at CHAIR **2** a seat in a car

car·sick /'kɑːsɪk; *AmE* 'kɑːrsɪk/ *adj.* [not usually before noun] feeling ill/sick because you are travelling in a car: *Do you get carsick?* ▶ **car·sick·ness** *noun* [U]

cart /kɑːt; *AmE* kɑːrt/ *noun, verb*
■ *noun* **1** a vehicle with two or four wheels that is pulled by a horse and used for carrying loads: *a horse and cart* **2** (also **hand·cart**) a light vehicle with wheels that you pull or push by hand **3** (*AmE*) = TROLLEY: *a shopping/ baggage cart* ◊ *a serving cart* **4** (*AmE*) = BUGGY: *a golf cart* **IDM** **put the ,cart before the 'horse** to put or do things in the wrong order
■ *verb* [VN] **1** [usually +*adv./prep.*] to carry sth in a cart or other vehicle: *The rubbish is then carted away for recycling.* **2** [+*adv./prep.*] (*informal*) to carry sth that is large, heavy or awkward in your hands: *We had to cart our luggage up six flights of stairs.* **3** [+*adv./prep.*] (*informal*) to take sb somewhere, especially with difficulty: *The demonstrators were carted off to the local police station.*

carte blanche /,kɑːt 'blɑːnʃ; *AmE* ,kɑːrt/ *noun* [U] (from French) **~ (to do sth)** the complete freedom or authority to do whatever you like: *He was given carte blanche to say what he liked in the report.*

car·tel /kɑːˈtel; *AmE* kɑːrˈtel/ *noun* [C+sing./pl. *v.*] a group of separate companies that agree to increase profits by fixing prices and not competing with each other

cart·horse /'kɑːtɔːs; *AmE* 'kɑːrthɔːrs/ *noun* a large strong horse used especially in the past for heavy work on farms

car·til·age /'kɑːtɪlɪdʒ; *AmE* 'kɑːrt-/ *noun* [U, C] the strong white FLEXIBLE substance found between the joints in the body; a piece of this: *I've damaged the cartilage in my knee.*

cart·load /'kɑːtləʊd; *AmE* 'kɑːrtloʊd/ *noun* **1** the amount of sth that fills a CART **2** [usually pl.] (*informal*) a large amount of sth

car·tog·raph·er /kɑːˈtɒɡrəfə(r); *AmE* kɑːrˈtɑːɡ-/ *noun* a person who draws or makes maps

car·tog·raphy /kɑːˈtɒɡrəfi; *AmE* kɑːrˈtɑːɡ-/ *noun* [U] the art or process of drawing or making maps ▶ **carto·graph·ic** /,kɑːtəˈɡræfɪk; *AmE* ,kɑːrt-/ *adj.*

car·ton /'kɑːtn; *AmE* 'kɑːrtn/ *noun* **1** a light cardboard or plastic box or pot for holding goods, especially food or liquid; the contents of a carton: *a milk carton/a carton of milk*—picture at PACKAGING **2** (*AmE*) a large container in which goods are packed in smaller containers: *a carton of cigarettes*

car·toon /kɑːˈtuːn; *AmE* kɑːrˈt-/ *noun* **1** an amusing drawing in a newspaper or magazine, especially one

b	d	f	g	h	k	l	m	n	p	r
bad	**did**	**fall**	**get**	**hat**	**cat**	**leg**	**man**	**now**	**pen**	**red**

about politics or events in the news **2** = COMIC STRIP **3** (also ˌanimated carˈtoon) a film/movie made by photographing a series of gradually changing drawings or models, so that they look as if they are moving: *a Walt Disney cartoon* ◇ *a cartoon character* **4** (*technical*) a drawing made by an artist as a preparation for a painting

car·toon·ist /kɑːˈtuːnɪst; *AmE* kɑːrˈt-/ *noun* a person who draws cartoons

cart·ridge /ˈkɑːtrɪdʒ; *AmE* ˈkɑːrt-/ *noun* **1** (*AmE* also **shell**) a tube or case containing explosive and a bullet or SHOT, for shooting from a gun **2** a case containing sth that is used in a machine, for example photographic film for a camera, ink for a printer, etc. Cartridges are put into the machine and can be removed and replaced when they are finished or empty. **3** a thin tube containing ink which you put inside a pen

ˈ**cartridge paper** *noun* [U] (*BrE*) thick strong paper for drawing on

ˈ**cart track** *noun* (*BrE*) a rough track that is not suitable for ordinary motor vehicles

cart·wheel /ˈkɑːtwiːl; *AmE* ˈkɑːrt-/ *noun* **1** a fast physical movement in which you turn in a circle sideways by putting your hands on the ground and bringing your legs, one at a time, over your head: *to do/turn cartwheels* **2** the wheel of a CART ▶ **cart·wheel** *verb* [V]

carve /kɑːv; *AmE* kɑːrv/ *verb* **1** to make objects, patterns, etc. by cutting away material from wood or stone: [VN] *a richly carved doorway* ◇ *The statue was carved out of a single piece of stone.* ◇ *The piece of wood had been carved into the shape of a flower.* ◇ [V] *She carves in both stone and wood.* **2** [VN] to write sth on a surface by cutting into it: *They carved their initials on the desk.* **3** to cut a large piece of cooked meat into smaller pieces for eating: [VN] *Who's going to carve the turkey?* [alsoV, VNN] **4** [VN] [no passive] ~ sth (out) (for yourself) to work hard in order to have a successful career, reputation, etc: *She has carved a place for herself in the fashion world.* ◇ *Against all odds, he succeeded in carving out a career in the media.* **IDM** **carved in ˈstone** (of a decision, plan, etc.) unable to be changed: *People should remember that our proposals aren't carved in stone.* **PHRV** ˌ**carve sth**↔**up** (*disapproving*) to divide a company, an area of land, etc. into smaller parts in order to share it between people: *They have been accused of carving up the industry for their own benefit.*

car·very /ˈkɑːvəri; *AmE* ˈkɑːrv-/ *noun* (*pl.* **-ies**) (*BrE*) a restaurant that serves ROAST meat

carv·ing /ˈkɑːvɪŋ; *AmE* ˈkɑːrvɪŋ/ *noun* **1** [C, U] an object or a pattern made by cutting away material from wood or stone **2** [U] the art of making objects in this way

ˈ**carving knife** *noun* a large sharp knife for cutting cooked meat—picture at CUTLERY

ˈ**car wash** *noun* a place with special equipment, where you can pay to have your car washed

Casa·nova /ˌkæsəˈnəʊvə; ˌkæzə-; *AmE* -ˈnoʊvə/ *noun* a man who has a lot of lovers

cas·cade /kæˈskeɪd/ *noun, verb*
■ *noun* **1** a small WATERFALL, especially one of several falling down a steep rocky slope with rocks **2** a large amount of water falling or pouring down: *a cascade of rainwater* **3** (*written*) a large amount of sth hanging down: *Her hair tumbled in a dark brown cascade down her back.* **4** (*written*) a large number of things falling or coming quickly at the same time: *He crashed to the ground in a cascade of oil cans.*
■ *verb* [V+adv./prep.] **1** to flow downwards in large amounts: *Water cascaded down the mountainside.* **2** (*written*) to fall or hang in large amounts: *Blonde hair cascaded over her shoulders.* ▶ **cas·cad·ing** *adj.* [only before noun]: *cascading waterfalls/hair*

case /keɪs/ *noun, verb*
■ *noun*
SITUATION | **1** [C] a particular situation or a situation of a particular type: *In some cases people have had to wait several weeks for an appointment.* ◇ *The company only dismisses its employees in cases of gross misconduct.* ◇ *It's a classic case* (= a very typical case) *of bad planning.*—see

also WORST-CASE **2** (**the case**) [sing.] ~ (**that**…) the true situation: *If that is the case* (= if the situation described is true), *we need more staff.* ◇ *It is simply not the case that prison conditions are improving.* **3** [C, usually sing.] a situation that relates to a particular person or thing: *In your case, we are prepared to be lenient.* ◇ *I cannot make an exception in your case* (= for you and not for others).

POLICE INVESTIGATION | **4** [C] a matter that is being officially investigated, especially by the police: *a murder case* ◇ *a case of theft*

IN COURT OF LAW | **5** [C] a question to be decided in a court of law: *The case will be heard next week.* ◇ *a court case* ◇ *to win/lose a case*—see also TEST CASE

ARGUMENTS | **6** [C, usually sing.] ~ (**for/against sth**) a set of facts or arguments that support one side in a court of law, discussion, etc: *the case for the defence/prosecution* ◇ *Our lawyer didn't think we had a case* (= had enough good arguments to win in a court of law). ◇ *the case for/against private education* ◇ *The report makes out a strong case* (= gives good arguments) *for spending more money on hospitals.*

CONTAINER | **7** [C] (often in compounds) a container or covering used to protect or store things; a container with its contents or the amount that it contains: *a pencil case* ◇ *a jewellery case* ◇ *a packing case* (= a large wooden box for packing things in) ◇ *The museum was full of stuffed animals in glass cases.* ◇ *a case* (= 12 bottles) *of champagne*—picture at GRANDFATHER CLOCK **8** [C] = SUITCASE: *Let me carry your case for you.*

OF DISEASE | **9** [C] the fact of sb having a disease or an injury; a person suffering from a disease or an injury: *a severe case of typhoid* ◇ *The most serious cases were treated at the scene of the accident.*

PERSON | **10** [C] a person who needs, or is thought to need, special treatment or attention: *He's a hopeless case.*

GRAMMAR | **11** [C, U] the form of a noun, an adjective or a pronoun in some languages, that shows its relationship to another word: *the nominative/accusative/genitive case* ◇ *Latin nouns have case, number and gender.*

IDM **as the ˌcase may ˈbe** used to say that one of two or more possibilities is true, but which one is true depends on the circumstances: *There may be an announcement about this tomorrow—or not, as the case may be.* **be on sb's ˈcase** (*informal*) to criticize sb all the time: *She's always on my case about cleaning my room.* **be on the ˈcase** to be dealing with a particular matter, especially a criminal investigation: *We have two agents on the case.* **get off my ˈcase** (*spoken*) used to tell sb to stop criticizing you **a case in ˈpoint** a clear example of the problem, situation, etc. that is being discussed **in ˈany case** whatever happens or may have happened: *There's no point complaining now—we're leaving tomorrow in any case.* **(just) in case (…)** because of the possibility of sth happening: *You'd better take the keys in case I'm out.* ◇ *You probably won't need to call—but take my number, just in case.* ◇ *In case* (= if it is true that) *you're wondering why Jo's here—let me explain …* **in case of sth** (often on official notices) if sth happens: *In case of fire, ring the alarm bell.* **in ˈthat case** if that happens or has happened; if that is the situation: *'I've made up my mind.' 'In that case, there's no point discussing it'*—more at REST *v.*
■ *verb* [VN]
IDM **case the joint** (*informal*) to look carefully around a building so that you can plan how to steal things from it at a later time

case·book /ˈkeɪsbʊk/ *noun* a written record kept by doctors, lawyers, etc. of cases they have dealt with

cased /keɪst/ *adj.* ~ **in sth** completely covered with a particular material: *The towers are made of steel cased in granite.*—see also CASING

ˌ**case ˈhistory** *noun* a record of a person's background, past illnesses, etc. that a doctor or SOCIAL WORKER studies

ˈ**case law** *noun* [U] (*law*) law based on decisions made by judges in earlier cases—compare COMMON LAW, STATUTE LAW—see also TEST CASE

case·load /ˈkeɪsləʊd; *AmE* -loʊd/ *noun* all the people that

s	t	v	z	ʃ	ʒ		tʃ	dʒ	θ	ð	ŋ
see	tea	van	zoo	shoe	vision		chain	jam	thin	this	sing

C

a doctor, SOCIAL WORKER, etc. is responsible for at one time: *a heavy caseload*

case·ment /ˈkeɪsmənt/ (also ˌcasement ˈwindow) *noun* a window that opens on HINGES like a door—picture at HOUSE

ˈ**case study** *noun* a detailed account of the development of a person, a group of people or a situation over a period of time

case·work /ˈkeɪswɜːk; *AmE* -wɜːrk/ *noun* [U] social work (= work done to help people in the community with special needs) involving the study of a particular person's family and background

case·work·er /ˈkeɪswɜːkə(r); *AmE* -wɜːrk-/ *noun* (*especially AmE*) a SOCIAL WORKER who helps a particular person or family in the community with special needs

cash /kæʃ/ *noun, verb*
■ *noun* [U] **1** money in the form of coins or notes/bills: *How much cash do you have on you?* ◊ *Payments can be made by cheque or* **in cash.** ◊ *Customers are offered a 10% discount if they* **pay cash.** ◊ *The thieves stole £500 in cash.*—see also HARD CASH, PETTY CASH **2** (*informal*) money in any form: *The museum needs to find ways of raising cash.* ◊ *I'm short of cash right now.* ◊ *I'm constantly* **strapped for cash** (= without enough money). **IDM** **cash** ˈ**down** (*BrE*) (also ˌcash up ˈfront *AmE, BrE*) with immediate payment of cash: *to pay for sth cash down* ˌcash in ˈhand (*BrE, informal*) if you pay for goods and services **cash in hand,** you pay in cash, especially so that the person being paid can avoid paying tax on the amount ˌcash on deˈlivery (*abbr.* **COD**) a system of paying for goods when they are delivered
■ *verb* [VN] **~ a cheque/check** to exchange a cheque/check for the amount of money that it is worth **PHRV** ˌcash ˈin (**on sth**) (*disapproving*) to gain an advantage for yourself from a situation, especially in a way that other people think is wrong or immoral: *The film studio is being accused of cashing in on the singer's death.* ˌcash sth↔ˈin to exchange sth, such as an insurance policy, for money before the date on which it would normally end ˌcash ˈup (*BrE*) (*AmE* ˌcash ˈout) to add up the amount of money that has been received in a shop/store, club, etc., especially at the end of the day

ˌ**cash and** ˈ**carry** *noun* [C, U] a large WHOLESALE shop/store that sells goods in large quantities at low prices to customers from other businesses who pay in cash and take the goods away themselves; the system of buying and selling goods in this way

ˈ**cash card** *noun* (*BrE*) (*AmE* **AT**ˈ**M card**) a plastic card used to get money from a CASH DISPENSER (= a machine in or outside a bank)—compare CHEQUE CARD, DEBIT CARD

ˈ**cash cow** *noun* (*business*) the part of a business that always makes a profit and that provides money for the rest of the business

ˈ**cash crop** *noun* a crop grown for selling, rather than for use by the person who grows it—compare SUBSISTENCE

ˈ**cash desk** *noun* (*BrE*) the place in a shop/store where you pay for goods that you have bought

ˈ**cash dispenser** *noun* (*BrE*) = CASH MACHINE

cashew /ˈkæʃuː; kæˈʃuː/ (also ˈcashew nut) *noun* the small curved nut of the tropical American **cashew tree,** used in cooking and often eaten salted with alcoholic drinks—picture at NUT

ˈ**cash flow** *noun* [C, U] the movement of money into and out of a business as goods are bought and sold: *a healthy cash flow* (= having enough money to make payments when necessary) ◊ *cash-flow problems*

cash·ier /kæˈʃɪə(r); *AmE* -ˈʃɪr/ *noun, verb*
■ *noun* a person whose job is to receive and pay out money in a bank, shop/store, hotel, etc.
■ *verb* [VN] [usually passive] to make sb leave the army, navy or air force because they have done sth wrong

cash·less /ˈkæʃləs/ *adj.* done or working without using cash: *We are moving towards the cashless society.*

ˈ**cash machine** (*BrE* also ˈcash dispenser, ˈcashpoint) (also **ATM** *AmE, BrE*) *noun* a machine in or outside a bank, etc., from which you can get money from your bank account using a special plastic card

cash·mere /ˈkæʃmɪə(r); ˌkæʃˈm-; *AmE* ˈkæʒmɪr; ˈkæʃ-/ *noun* [U] fine soft wool made from the long hair of a type of goat, used especially for making expensive clothes: *a cashmere sweater* ◊ *The scarf is 70% cashmere.*

ˈ**cash register** (*BrE* also **till**) (*AmE* also **regis·ter**) *noun* a machine used in shops/stores, restaurants, etc. that has a drawer for keeping money in, and that shows and records the amount of money received for each thing that is sold

ˈ**cash-starved** *adj.* [only before noun] without enough money, usually because another organization, such as the government, has failed to provide it: *cash-starved public services*

ˈ**cash-strapped** *adj.* [only before noun] without enough money: *cash-strapped governments/shoppers*

cas·ing /ˈkeɪsɪŋ/ *noun* [C, U] a covering that protects sth

ca·sino /kəˈsiːnəʊ; *AmE* -noʊ/ *noun* (*pl.* **-os**) a public building or room where people play gambling games for money

cask /kɑːsk; *AmE* kæsk/ *noun* a small wooden BARREL used for storing liquids, especially alcoholic drinks; the amount contained in a cask: *a wine cask/a cask of wine*

cas·ket /ˈkɑːskɪt; *AmE* ˈkæs-/ *noun* **1** a small decorated box for holding jewels or other valuable things, especially in the past **2** (*AmE*) = COFFIN

cas·sava /kəˈsɑːvə/ *noun* [U] a type of flour made from the thick roots of a tropical plant

cas·ser·ole /ˈkæsərəʊl; *AmE* -roʊl/ *noun* **1** [C, U] a hot dish made with meat, vegetables, etc. that are cooked slowly in liquid in an oven: *a chicken casserole* ◊ *Is there any casserole left?* **2** [C] (also ˈ**casserole dish**) a container with a lid used for cooking meat, etc. in liquid in an oven—picture at PAN ▶ **cas·ser·ole** *verb* [VN] —picture on page 275

cas·sette /kəˈset/ *noun* **1** a small flat plastic case containing tape for playing or recording music or sound: *a cassette recorder/player* ◊ *available* **on cassette** ◊ *a video cassette* (= for recording sound and pictures) **2** a plastic case containing photographic film that can be put into a camera

cas·sock /ˈkæsək/ *noun* a long piece of clothing, usually black or red, worn by some Christian priests and other people with special duties in a church

cast /kɑːst; *AmE* kæst/ *verb, noun*
■ *verb* (**cast, cast**)
A LOOK/GLANCE/SMILE **1** to look, smile, etc. in a particular direction: [VN] *She cast a welcoming smile in his direction.* [also VNN]
LIGHT/A SHADOW **2** [VN] to make light, a shadow, etc. appear in a particular place: *The setting sun cast an orange glow over the mountains.* ◊ (*figurative*) *The sad news cast a shadow over the proceedings* (= made people feel unhappy).
DOUBT **3** [VN] **~ doubt/aspersions** (**on/upon sth**) to say, do or suggest sth that makes people doubt sth or think that sb is less honest, good, etc: *This latest evidence casts serious doubt on his version of events.*
FISHING LINE **4** [V, VN] to throw one end of a FISHING LINE into a river, etc.
THROW **5** [VN] (*literary*) to throw sb/sth somewhere, especially using force: *The priceless treasures had been cast into the Nile.* ◊ *They cast anchor at nightfall.*
SKIN **6** [VN] when a snake **casts** its skin, the skin comes off as part of a natural process **SYN** SHED
SHOE **7** [VN] if a horse **casts** a shoe, the shoe comes off by accident
ACTORS **8 ~ sb** (**as sb**) to choose actors to play the different parts in a film/movie, play, etc.; to choose an actor to play a particular role: [VN] *The play is being cast in both the US and Britain.* ◊ *He has cast her as an ambitious lawyer in his latest movie.* [also V]
DESCRIBE **9** [VN] **~ sb** (**as sth**) | **~ sb** (**in sth**) to describe or present sb in a particular way: *He cast himself as the innocent victim of a hate campaign.* ◊ *The press were quick to cast her in the role of 'the other woman'.*

æ	ɑː	e	ɜː	ə	ɪ	iː	i	ɒ	ɔː	ʌ	ʊ	u	uː
cat	father	ten	bird	about	sit	see	many	got (BrE)	saw	cup	put	actual	too

C

VOTE | **10** [VN] ~ a/your vote/ballot (for sb/sth) to vote for sb/sth

SHAPE METAL | **11** [VN] ~ sth (in sth) to shape hot liquid metal, etc. by pouring it into a hollow container (called a MOULD): *a statue cast in bronze* ◊ *(figurative) an artist cast in the mould of* (= very similar to) *Miro*

IDM **cast your mind back (to sth)** to make yourself think about sth that happened in the past: *I want you to cast your minds back to the first time you met.* **cast your net wide** to consider a lot of different people, activities, possibilities, etc. when you are looking for sth: *It's worth casting your net wide when applying for your first job.* **cast a 'spell (on sb/sth)** to use words that are thought to be magic and have the power to change or influence sb/sth—more at ADRIFT, CAUTION *n.*, DIE *n.*, EYE *n.*, LIGHT *n.*, LOT *n.*

PHRV **,cast a'bout/a'round for sth** (*written*) to try hard to think of or find sth, especially when this is difficult: *She cast around desperately for a safe topic of conversation.* **,cast sb/sth ◂▸a'side** (*formal*) to get rid of sth because you no longer want or need them SYN DISCARD **be ,cast a'way** to be left somewhere after a SHIPWRECK—related noun CASTAWAY **be ,cast 'down (by sth)** (*literary*) to be sad or unhappy about sth—see also DOWNCAST **,cast 'off| ,cast sth ◂▸'off 1** to undo the ropes that are holding a boat in a fixed position, in order to sail away **2** (in knitting) to remove stitches from the needles in a way that forms an edge that will not come undone **,cast sth ◂▸'off** (*written*) to get rid of sth because you no longer want or need it: *The town is still trying to cast off its dull image.* **,cast 'on| ,cast sth ◂▸'on** (in knitting) to put the first row of stitches on a needle **,cast sb/sth ◂▸'out** (*literary*) to get rid of sb/sth, especially by using force: *He claimed to have the power to cast out demons.*—related noun OUTCAST

■ *noun*

ACTORS | **1** [C+sing./pl. *v.*] all the people who act in a play or film/movie: *The whole cast performs/perform brilliantly.* ◊ *members of the cast* ◊ *an all-star cast* (= including many well-known actors) ◊ *the supporting cast* (= not the main actors, but the others) ◊ *a cast list*

IN SHAPING METAL | **2** [C] an object that is made by pouring hot liquid metal, etc. into a MOULD (= a specially shaped container) **3** [C] a shaped container used to make an object SYN MOULD

APPEARANCE | **4** [sing.] (*BrE, formal*) the way that a person or a thing is or appears: *He has an unusual cast of mind.* ◊ *I disliked the arrogant cast to her mouth.*

THROW | **5** [C] an act of throwing sth, especially a fishing line

ON ARM/LEG | **6** [C] = PLASTER CAST: *Her leg's in a cast.*
—see also OPENCAST

cas·ta·nets /ˌkæstəˈnets/ *noun* [pl.] a musical instrument that consists of two small round pieces of wood that you hold in the hand and hit together with the fingers to make a noise. Castanets are used especially by Spanish dancers.

cast·away /ˈkɑːstəweɪ; *AmE* ˈkæst-/ *noun* a person whose ship has sunk (= who has been SHIPWRECKED) and who has had to swim to a lonely place, usually an island

caste /kɑːst; *AmE* kæst/ *noun* **1** [C] any of the four main divisions of Hindu society, originally those made according to functions in society: *the caste system* ◊ *high-caste Brahmins* **2** [C] a social class, especially one whose members do not allow others to join it: *the ruling caste* **3** [U] the system of dividing society into classes based on differences in family origin, rank or wealth

cas·tel·lated /ˈkæstəleɪtɪd/ *adj.* (*architecture*) built in the style of a castle with BATTLEMENTS

cas·ter (*AmE*) = CASTOR

,caster 'sugar (also **,castor 'sugar**) *noun* [U] (*BrE*) white sugar in the form of very fine grains, used in cooking

cas·ti·gate /ˈkæstɪgeɪt/ *verb* [VN] ~ sb/sth (for sth) (*formal*) to criticize sb/sth severely: *He castigated himself for being so stupid.* ▶ **cas·ti·ga·tion** /ˌkæstɪˈgeɪʃn/ *noun* [U]

cast·ing /ˈkɑːstɪŋ; *AmE* ˈkæst-/ *noun* **1** [U] the process of choosing actors for a play or film/movie **2** [C] an object made by pouring hot liquid metal, etc. into a MOULD (= a specially shaped container)

,casting 'vote *noun* [usually sing.] the vote given by the person in charge of an official meeting to decide an issue when votes on each side are equal

,cast 'iron *noun* [U] a hard type of iron that does not bend easily and is shaped by pouring the hot liquid metal into a MOULD (= a specially shaped container)—compare WROUGHT IRON

,cast-'iron *adj.* **1** made of cast iron: *a cast-iron bridge* **2** very strong or certain; that cannot be broken or fail: *a cast-iron guarantee/promise* ◊ *a cast-iron excuse/alibi*

cas·tle /ˈkɑːsl/ *noun* **1** a large strong building with thick high walls and towers, built in the past by kings or queens, or other important people, to defend themselves against attack: *Windsor Castle* ◊ *a medieval castle*—see also SANDCASTLE **2** (also **rook**) (in the game of CHESS) any of the four pieces placed in the corner squares of the board at the start of the game, usually made to look like a castle—picture on page A8 **IDM** **(build) castles in the 'air** (*BrE*) (to have) plans or dreams that are not likely to happen or come true—more at ENGLISHMAN

'cast-off (*BrE*) (also **hand-me-down** *AmE*, *BrE*) *noun* [usually pl.] a piece of clothing that the original owner no longer wants to wear ▶ **'cast-off** (*BrE*) (also **hand-me-down** *AmE*, *BrE*) *adj.*: *a cast-off overcoat*

cas·tor (*BrE*) (*AmE* **cas·ter**) /ˈkɑːstə(r); *AmE* ˈkæs-/ *noun* one of the small wheels fixed to the bottom of a piece of furniture so that it can be moved easily—picture at CHAIR

,castor 'oil *noun* [U] a thick yellow oil obtained from a tropical plant and used in the past as a type of medicine, usually as a LAXATIVE

,castor 'sugar *noun* [U] = CASTER SUGAR

cas·trate /kæˈstreɪt; *AmE* ˈkæstreɪt/ *verb* [VN] to remove the TESTICLES of a male animal or person ▶ **cas·tra·tion** /kæˈstreɪʃn/ *noun* [U, C]

cas·ual /ˈkæʒuəl/ *adj., noun*

■ *adj.*

WITHOUT CARE/ATTENTION | **1** [usually before noun] not showing much care or thought; seeming not to be worried; not wanting to show that sth is important to you: *a casual manner* ◊ *It was just a casual remark—I wasn't really serious.* ◊ *He tried to sound casual, but I knew he was worried.* ◊ *They have a casual attitude towards safety* (= they don't care enough). **2** [usually before noun] without paying attention to detail: *a casual glance* ◊ *It's obvious even to the casual observer.*

NOT FORMAL | **3** not formal: *casual clothes* (= comfortable clothes that you choose to wear in your free time) ◊ *family parties and other casual occasions*

WORK | **4** [usually before noun] (*BrE*) not permanent; not done, or doing sth regularly: *casual workers/labour* ◊ *Students sometimes do casual work in the building or tourist trades.* ◊ *They are employed on a casual basis* (= they do not have a permanent job with the company).

RELATIONSHIP | **5** [usually before noun] without deep affection: *a casual acquaintance* ◊ *a casual friendship* ◊ *to have casual sex* (= to have sex without having a steady relationship with that partner)

BY CHANCE | **6** [only before noun] happening by chance; doing sth by chance: *a casual encounter/meeting* ◊ *a casual passer-by* ◊ *The exhibition is interesting to both the enthusiast and the casual visitor.* ◊ *The disease is not spread by casual contact.*

▶ **cas·ual·ly** *adv.*: *'What did he say about me?' she asked as casually as she could.* ◊ *They chatted casually on the phone.* ◊ *dressed casually in jeans and T-shirt* **cas·ual·ness** *noun* [U]: *He was sure that the casualness of the gesture was deliberate.*

■ *noun* (*BrE*)

CLOTHES | **1** (**casuals**) [pl.] informal clothes or shoes: *dressed in casuals*

WORKER | **2** [C] a casual worker (= one who does not work permanently for a company)

aɪ	aʊ	eɪ	əʊ	oʊ	ɔɪ	ɪə	eə	ʊə	j	w
my	now	say	go (BrE)	go (AmE)	boy	near	hair	pure	yes	wet

casu·alty /ˈkæʒuəlti/ *noun* (*pl.* **-ies**) **1** [C] a person who is killed or injured in war or in an accident: *road casualties* ◊ *Both sides had suffered **heavy casualties*** (= many people had been killed). **2** [C] a person that suffers or a thing that is destroyed when sth else takes place: *She became a casualty of the reduction in part-time work* (= she lost her job). ◊ *Small shops have been a casualty of the recession.* **3** [U] (*also* **ˈcasualty department**, **ˌaccident and eˈmergency**) (*all BrE*) (*AmE* **eˈmergency room**) the part of a hospital where people who need urgent treatment are taken: *The victims were rushed to casualty in an ambulance.*

casu·is·try /ˈkæʒuɪstri/ *noun* [U] (*formal, disapproving*) a way of solving moral or legal problems by using clever arguments that may be false

cat /kæt/ *noun* **1** a small animal with soft fur that people often keep as a pet. Cats catch and kill birds and mice: *cat food*—see also KITTEN, TOMCAT **2** a wild animal of the cat family: *the big cats* (= lions, TIGERS, etc.)—see also FAT CAT, WILDCAT **IDM** **be the cat's ˈwhiskers/pyˈjamas** (*informal*) to be the best thing, person, idea, etc: *He thinks he's the cat's whiskers* (= he has a high opinion of himself). **let the ˈcat out of the bag** to tell a secret carelessly or by mistake: *I wanted it to be a surprise, but my sister let the cat out of the bag.* **like a ˌcat on hot ˈbricks** (*BrE*) very nervous: *She was like a cat on hot bricks before her driving test.* **like a cat that's got the ˈcream** very pleased with yourself [SYN] SMUG **look like sth the ˈcat brought in** (*informal*) (of a person) to look dirty and untidy **not have/stand a cat in ˈhell's chance (of doing sth)** to have no chance at all **play (a game of) ˌcat and ˈmouse with sb | play a ˌcat-and-ˈmouse game with sb** to play a cruel game with sb in your power by changing your behaviour very often, so that they become nervous and do not know what to expect **put/set the cat among the ˈpigeons** (*BrE*) to say or do sth that is likely to cause trouble **when the cat's aˈway the mice will ˈplay** (*saying*) people enjoy themselves more and behave with greater freedom when the person in charge of them is not there—more at RAIN *v.*, ROOM *n.*

cata·clysm /ˈkætəklɪzəm/ *noun* (*formal*) a sudden disaster or a violent event that causes change, for example a flood or a war ▶ **cata·clys·mic** /ˌkætəˈklɪzmɪk/ *adj.* [usually before noun]

cata·combs /ˈkætəkuːmz; *AmE* -koumz/ *noun* [pl.] a series of underground tunnels used for burying dead people, especially in ancient times

cata·logue (*AmE also* **cata·log**) /ˈkætəlɒg; *AmE* -lɔːg; -lɑːg/ *noun, verb*
▪ *noun* **1** a complete list of items, for example of things that people can look at or buy: *a mail-order catalogue* (= a book showing goods for sale to be sent to people's homes) ◊ *to consult the library catalogue* ◊ *An illustrated catalogue accompanies the exhibition.* ◊ *an online catalogue* **2** a long series of things that happen (usually bad things): *a catalogue of disasters/errors/misfortunes*
▪ *verb* [VN] **1** to arrange a list of things in order in a catalogue; to record sth in a catalogue **2** to give a list of things connected with a particular person, event, etc: *Interviews with the refugees catalogue a history of discrimination and violence.*

cata·lyse (*BrE*) (*AmE* **cata·lyze**) /ˈkætəlaɪz/ *verb* [VN] (*chemistry*) to make a chemical reaction happen faster

cata·lyst /ˈkætəlɪst/ *noun* **1** (*chemistry*) a substance that makes a chemical reaction happen faster without being changed itself **2** ~ **(for sth)** a person or thing that causes a change: *I see my role as being a catalyst for change.*

cata·lyt·ic con·vert·er /ˌkætəˈlɪtɪk kənˈvɜːtə(r); *AmE* -ˈvɜːrt-/ *noun* a device used in the EXHAUST system of motor vehicles to reduce the damage caused to the environment

cata·ma·ran /ˌkætəməˈræn/ *noun* a fast sailing boat with two HULLS—picture at BOAT—compare TRIMARAN

cata·pult /ˈkætəpʌlt/ *noun, verb*
▪ *noun* **1** (*BrE*) (*AmE* **sling·shot**) a stick shaped like a Y with a rubber band attached to it, used by children for shooting stones **2** a weapon used in the past to throw heavy stones **3** a machine used for sending planes up into the air from a ship
▪ *verb* [+*adv.*/*prep.*] to throw sb/sth or be thrown suddenly and violently through the air: [VN] *She was catapulted out of the car as it hit the wall.* ◊ (*figurative*) *The movie catapulted him to international stardom.* [also V]

cat·ar·act /ˈkætərækt/ *noun* **1** a medical condition that affects the LENS of the eye and causes a gradual loss of sight **2** (*literary*) a large steep WATERFALL

ca·tarrh /kəˈtɑː(r)/ *noun* [U] thick liquid (called PHLEGM) that you have in your nose and throat because, for example, you have a cold

ca·tas·trophe /kəˈtæstrəfi/ *noun* **1** a sudden disaster that causes many people to suffer: *Early warnings of rising water levels prevented another major catastrophe.* **2** an event that causes one person or a group of people personal suffering, or that makes difficulties: *The attempt to expand the business was a catastrophe for the firm.* ◊ *We've had a few catastrophes with the food for the party.* ▶ **cata·stroph·ic** /ˌkætəˈstrɒfɪk; *AmE* -ˈstrɑː-/ *adj.*: *catastrophic effects/losses/results* ◊ (*AmE*) *a catastrophic illness* (= one that costs a very large amount to treat) **cata·stroph·ic·al·ly** *adv.*

cata·ton·ic /ˌkætəˈtɒnɪk; *AmE* -ˈtɑːnɪk/ *adj.* (*medical*) not able to move or show any reaction to things because of illness, shock, etc: *a catatonic trance*

ˈcat burglar *noun* a thief who climbs up the outside of a building in order to enter it and steal sth

cat·call /ˈkætkɔːl/ *noun* [usually pl.] a noise or shout expressing anger at or disapproval of sb who is speaking or performing in public

catch /kætʃ/ *verb, noun*
▪ *verb* (**caught, caught** /kɔːt/)
HOLD | **1** [VN] to stop and hold a moving object, especially in your hands: *She managed to catch the keys as they fell.* ◊ *'Throw me over that towel, will you?' 'OK. Catch!'* ◊ *The dog caught the stick in its mouth.* **2** [VN] to hold a liquid when it falls: *The roof was leaking and I had to use a bucket to catch the drips.* **3** [VN] [usually +*adv.*/*prep.*] to take hold of sb/sth: *He **caught hold of** her arm as she tried to push past him.*
CAPTURE | **4** [VN] to capture a person or an animal that tries or would try to escape: *The murderer was never caught.* ◊ *Our cat is hopeless at catching mice.* ◊ *How many fish did you catch?*
SB DOING STH | **5** to find or discover sb doing sth, especially sth wrong: [VN-ing] *I caught her smoking in the bathroom.* ◊ ***You wouldn't catch me** working* (= I would never work) *on a Sunday!* ◊ *She **caught herself** wondering whether she had made a mistake.* ◊ [VN+*adv.*/*prep.*] *He was caught with bomb-making equipment in his home.* ◊ *Mark walked in and **caught them at it*** (= in the act of doing sth wrong). ◊ *thieves **caught in the act*** ◊ *You've caught me at a bad time* (= at a time when I am busy).
BE IN TIME | **6** [VN] to be in time to do sth, talk to sb, etc: *I caught him just as he was leaving the building.* ◊ *I was hoping to catch you at home* (= to telephone you at home when you were there). ◊ *The illness can be treated provided it's caught* (= discovered) *early enough.* ◊ (*BrE*) *to **catch the post*** (= post letters before the box is emptied) ◊ (*BrE, spoken*) *Bye for now! I'll **catch you later*** (= speak to you again later).
BUS/TRAIN/PLANE | **7** [VN] to be in time for a bus, train, plane, etc. and get on it: *We caught the 12.15 from Oxford.* ◊ *I must go—I have a train to catch.*
HAPPEN UNEXPECTEDLY | **8** [VN] to happen unexpectedly and put sb in a difficult situation: *His arrival **caught me by surprise**.* ◊ *She got **caught in** a thunderstorm.*
SEE/HEAR | **9** [VN] (*informal, especially AmE*) to see or hear sth; to attend sth: *Let's eat now and maybe we could catch a movie later.*
ILLNESS | **10** [VN] to get an illness: *to catch measles* ◊ *I think I must have caught this cold from you.*
BECOME STUCK | **11** ~ **(sth) (in/on sth)** to become stuck in or on sth; to make sth become stuck: [V] *Her dress caught on a nail.* ◊ [VN] *He caught his thumb in the door.*
HIT | **12** [+*adv.*/*prep.*] to hit sb/sth: [VN] *The stone caught*

him on the side of the head. ◊ [VNN] *She caught him a blow on the chin.*

NOTICE | **13** [VN] to notice sth only for a moment: *She caught sight of a car in the distance.* ◊ *He caught a glimpse of himself in the mirror.* ◊ *I caught a look of surprise on her face.* ◊ *He caught a whiff of her perfume.*

HEAR/ UNDERSTAND | **14** [VN] to hear or understand sth: *Sorry, I didn't quite catch what you said.*

INTEREST | **15** [VN] ~ sb's interest, imagination, attention, etc. if sth **catches** your interest, etc., you notice it and feel interested in it

SHOW ACCURATELY | **16** [VN] to show or describe sth accurately: *The artist has caught her smile perfectly.*

LIGHT | **17** [VN] if sth **catches** the light or the light **catches** it, the light shines on it and makes it shine too: *The knife gleamed as it caught the light.*

THE SUN | **18** [VN] (*informal*) if you **catch the sun**, you become red or brown because of spending time in the sun

BURN | **19** to begin to burn: [VN] *The wooden rafters caught fire.* ◊ [V] *These logs are wet: they won't catch.*

IN CRICKET | **20** [VN] to make a player unable to continue BATTING by catching the ball they have hit before it touches the ground

IDM **catch your 'breath 1** to stop breathing for a moment because of fear, shock, etc. **2** to breathe normally again after running or doing some tiring exercise **catch your 'death (of 'cold)** (*old-fashioned, informal*) to catch a very bad cold **catch sb's 'eye** to attract sb's attention: *Can you catch the waiter's eye?* **'catch it** (*BrE*) (*AmE* **catch 'hell, 'get it**) (*spoken*) to be punished or spoken to angrily about sth: *If your dad finds out you'll really catch it!* **catch sb 'napping** (*BrE*) to get an advantage over sb by doing sth when they are not expecting it and not ready for it **catch sb on the 'hop** (*BrE, informal*) to surprise sb by doing sth when they are not expecting it and not ready for it **catch sb red-'handed** to catch sb in the act of doing sth wrong or committing a crime **catch sb with their 'pants down** (*BrE* also **catch sb with their 'trousers down**) (*informal*) to arrive or do sth when sb is not expecting it and not ready, especially when they are in an embarrassing situation—more at BALANCE *n.*, CLEFT *adj.*, FANCY *n.*, RAW *n.*, ROCK *n.*, SHORT *adj.*

PHRV **'catch at sth** = CLUTCH AT STH **,catch 'on** to become popular or fashionable: *He invented an electric car, but it never really caught on.* **,catch 'on (to sth)** (*informal*) to understand sth: *He is very quick to catch on to things.* **,catch sb 'out 1** to surprise sb and put them in a difficult position: *Many investors were caught out by the fall in share prices.* **2** to show that sb does not know much or is doing sth wrong: *They tried to catch her out with a difficult question.* **,catch 'up on sth 1** to spend extra time doing sth because you have not done it earlier: *I have a lot of work to catch up on.* **2** to find out about things that have happened: *We spent the evening catching up on each other's news.* **be/ get ,caught 'up in sth** to become involved in sth, especially when you do not want to be: *Innocent passers-by got caught up in the riots.* **,catch 'up (with sb)** (*BrE* also **,catch sb 'up**) **1** to reach sb who is ahead by going faster: *Go on ahead. I'll catch up with you.* ◊ *I'll catch you up.* **2** to reach the same level or standard as sb who was better or more advanced: *After missing a term through illness he had to work hard to catch up with the others.* **,catch 'up with sb 1** to finally start to cause problems for sb after they have managed to avoid this for some time: *She was terrified that one day her past problems would catch up with her.* **2** if the police or authorities **catch up with** sb, they find and punish them after some time: *The law caught up with him years later when he had moved to Spain.*

■ *noun*

OF BALL | **1** [C] an act of catching sth, for example a ball: *to make a catch*

AMOUNT CAUGHT | **2** [C] the total amount of things that are caught: *a huge catch of fish*

FASTENING | **3** [C] a device used for fastening sth: *a catch on the door* ◊ *safety catches for the windows*

DIFFICULTY | **4** [C, usually sing.] a hidden difficulty or disad-

vantage: *All that money for two hours' work—what's the catch?*

CHILD'S GAME | **5** [U] a child's game in which two people throw a ball to each other

PERSON | **6** [sing.] (*old-fashioned*) a person that other people see as a good person to marry, employ, etc.

IDM **(a) catch-22 | a catch-22 situation** (*informal*) a difficult situation from which there is no escape because you need to do one thing before doing a second, and you cannot do the second thing before doing the first: *I can't get a job because I haven't got anywhere to live but I can't afford a place to live until I get a job—it's a catch-22 situation.*

'catch-all *noun* **1** (*especially AmE*) a thing for holding many small objects **2** a group or a description that includes different things and that does not state clearly what is included or not ▶ **'catch-all** *adj.* [only before noun]: *a catch-all phrase/ term*

catch-er /'kætʃə(r)/ *noun* **1** (in baseball) the player who stands behind the BATTER and catches the ball if he or she does not hit it—picture on page 1250 **2** (usually in compounds) a person or thing that catches sth: *a rat catcher*

catch-ing /'kætʃɪŋ/ *adj.* [not before noun] **1** (of a disease) easily caught by one person from another SYN INFECTIOUS **2** (of an emotion or a mood) passing quickly from one person to another SYN INFECTIOUS: *Try to be as enthusiastic as possible (enthusiasm is catching).*

catch-ment area /'kætʃmənt eəriə; *AmE* eriə/ *noun* **1** (*BrE*) the area from which a school takes its students, a hospital its patients, etc. **2** (also **catch-ment**) (*technical*) the area from which rain flows into a particular river or lake

catch-phrase /'kætʃfreɪz/ *noun* a popular phrase that is connected with the politician or entertainer who used it and made it famous

catchy /'kætʃi/ *adj.* (*informal*) (of music or the words of an advertisement) pleasing and easily remembered: *a catchy tune/ slogan*

cat-ech-ism /'kætəkɪzəm/ *noun* [usually sing.] a set of questions and answers that are used for teaching people about the beliefs of the Christian religion

cat-egor-ic-al /,kætə'gɒrɪkl; *AmE* -'gɔːr-/ *adj.* [usually before noun] (*formal*) expressed clearly and in a way that shows that you are very sure about what you are saying: *to make a categorical statement* ◊ *to give a categorical assurance* ▶ **cat-egor-ic-al-ly** /-kli/ *adv.*: *He categorically rejected our offer.*

cat-egor-ize (*BrE* also **-ise**) /'kætəgəraɪz/ *verb* [VN] ~ sb/sth (as sth) to put people or things into groups according to what type they are SYN CLASSIFY: *Participants were categorized according to age and sex.* ◊ *His latest work cannot be categorized as either a novel or an autobiography.*

cat-egory /'kætəgəri; *AmE* -gɔːri/ *noun* (*pl.* **-ies**) a group of people or things with particular features in common: *Students over 25 fall into a different category.* ◊ *The results of this survey can be divided into three main categories.*

cater /'keɪtə(r)/ *verb* ~ (for sb/sth) to provide food and drinks for a social event: [V] (*BrE*) *Most of our work now involves catering for weddings.* ◊ [VN] (*AmE*) *Who will be catering the wedding?* **PHRV** **'cater for sb/sth** to provide the things that a particular person or situation needs or wants: *The class caters for all ability ranges.* **'cater to sb/sth** to provide the things that a particular type or person wants, especially things that you do not approve of: *They only publish novels which cater to the mass market.*

cater-er /'keɪtərə(r)/ *noun* a person or company whose job is to provide food and drinks at a business meeting or for a special occasion such as a wedding

cater-ing /'keɪtərɪŋ/ *noun* [U] the work of providing food and drinks for meetings or social events: *Who did the catering for your son's wedding?*

cat-er-pil-lar /'kætəpɪlə(r); *AmE* -tərp-/ *noun* a small creature like a worm with legs, that develops into a

s	t	v	z	ʃ	ʒ	tʃ	dʒ	θ	ð	ŋ
see	tea	van	zoo	shoe	vision	chain	jam	thin	this	sing

BUTTERFLY or MOTH (= flying insects with large, sometimes colourful, wings). Caterpillars eat the leaves of plants.—picture on page A7

cat·er·waul /ˈkætəwɔːl; *AmE* ˈkætər-/ *verb* [V] to make the loud unpleasant noise that is typical of a cat

cat·fish /ˈkætfɪʃ/ *noun* (*pl.* **cat·fish**) a large fish with long stiff hairs, like a cat's WHISKERS, around its mouth. There are several types of catfish, most of which are FRESH-WATER fish.

'cat flap (*BrE*) (*AmE* **'cat door**) *noun* a hole cut in the bottom of the door to a house, covered by a piece of plastic that swings, so a pet cat can go in and out

cat·gut /ˈkætgʌt/ (also **gut**) *noun* [U] thin strong twisted string made from the INTESTINES of sheep and used in making musical instruments

cath·ar·sis /kəˈθɑːsɪs; *AmE* -ˈθɑːrs-/ *noun* [U, C] (*pl.* **cath-arses** /-siːz/) (*technical*) the process of releasing strong feelings, for example through plays or other artistic activities, as a way of providing RELIEF from anger, suffering, etc. ▶ **cath·ar·tic** /kəˈθɑːtɪk; *AmE* -ˈθɑːrt-/ *adj.*: *It was a cathartic experience.*

cath·edral /kəˈθiːdrəl/ *noun* the main church of a district, under the care of a BISHOP (= a priest of high rank): *St Paul's Cathedral* ◊ (*BrE*) *a cathedral city*

Cath·er·ine wheel /ˈkæθrɪn wiːl/ (*especially BrE*) (*AmE* usually **pin·wheel**) *noun* a flat, circular FIREWORK that spins around when lit

cath·eter /ˈkæθɪtə(r)/ *noun* a thin tube that is put into the body in order to remove liquid such as URINE

cath·ode /ˈkæθəʊd; *AmE* -oʊd/ *noun* (*technical*) the point (or TERMINAL) in a battery or other electrical device where the electric current leaves—compare ANODE

,cathode 'ray tube *noun* a VACUUM tube inside a television or computer screen, etc. from which a beam of ELECTRONS produces images on the screen

Cath·olic /ˈkæθlɪk/ *noun* = ROMAN CATHOLIC: *They're Catholics.* ▶ **Cath·oli·cism** /kəˈθɒləsɪzəm; *AmE* -θɑːlə-/ *noun* [U] = ROMAN CATHOLICISM

cath·olic /ˈkæθlɪk/ *adj.* **1** (**Catholic**): *Are they Catholic or Protestant?* ◊ *a Catholic church* = ROMAN CATHOLIC **2** (*often* **Catholic**) (*technical*) connected with all Christians or the whole Christian Church **3** (*formal*) including many or most things: *to have catholic tastes* (= like many different things)

cat·kin /ˈkætkɪn/ *noun* a long thin hanging bunch, or short upright group, of soft flowers on the branches of trees such as the WILLOW

cat·mint /ˈkætmɪnt/ (*BrE*) (also **cat·nip** /ˈkætnɪp/ *AmE, BrE*) *noun* [U] a plant that has white flowers with purple spots, hairy leaves and a smell that is attractive to cats

cat·nap /ˈkætnæp/ *noun* a short sleep ▶ **cat·nap** *verb* (**-pp-**) [V]

,cat's 'cradle *noun* **1** [U] a game in which you wrap string around the fingers of both hands to make different patterns **2** [C] a pattern made with string in a game of cat's cradle

Cats·eye™ /ˈkætsaɪ/ *noun* (*BrE*) one of a line of small objects that are fixed into a road and that reflect a car's lights in order to guide traffic at night

cat·suit /ˈkætsuːt; *BrE* also -sjuːt/ *noun* a piece of women's clothing that fits closely and covers the body and legs

cat·tery /ˈkætəri/ *noun* (*pl.* **-ies**) (*BrE*) a place where people can pay to leave their cats to be cared for while they are away

cat·tle /ˈkætl/ *noun* [pl.] cows and BULLS that are kept as farm animals for their milk or meat: *a herd of cattle* ◊ *twenty head of cattle* (= twenty cows) ◊ *dairy/beef cattle*

'cattle grid (*BrE*) (*AmE* **'cattle guard**) *noun* metal bars that are placed over a hole that has been made in the road. Cars can pass over the metal bars but animals such as sheep and cows cannot.

catty /ˈkæti/ *adj.* (*informal*) (of a woman) saying unkind things about other people SYN BITCHY, SPITEFUL: *a catty comment* ▶ **cat·ti·ness** *noun* [U]

,catty-'corner(ed) (also **,kitty-'corner(ed)**) *adj., adv.* (*AmE, informal*) opposite and at a DIAGONAL angle from sth/sb: *a restaurant catty-corner from the theater* ◊ *Motorcyclists cut catty-cornered across his yard.*

cat·walk /ˈkætwɔːk/ *noun* **1** (*BrE*) (*AmE* **run·way**) the long stage that models walk on during a fashion show **2** a narrow platform for people to walk on, for example along the outside of a building or a bridge

Cau·ca·sian /kɔːˈkeɪziən; kɔːˈkeɪʒn/ *noun* a member of any of the races of people who have pale skin ▶ **Cau·casian** *adj.*: *The police are looking for a Caucasian male in his forties.*

cau·cus /ˈkɔːkəs/ *noun* **1** (*especially AmE*) a meeting of the members or leaders of a political party to choose candidates or to decide policy; the members or leaders of a political party as a group: *20 states will hold precinct caucuses on Tuesday to choose delegates to the parties' national conventions.* **2** a group of people with similar interests, often within a larger organization or political party: *the Congressional Black Caucus*

caught *pt, pp* of CATCH

caul·dron (*AmE* also **cal·dron**) /ˈkɔːldrən/ *noun* a large deep pot for boiling liquids or cooking food over a fire: *a witch's cauldron* ◊ (*figurative*) *The stadium was a seething cauldron of emotion.*

cauli·flower /ˈkɒliflaʊə(r); *AmE* ˈkɔːli-; ˈkɑːli-/ *noun* [U, C] a vegetable with green leaves around a large hard white head of flowers: *Do you like cauliflower?* ◊ *two cauliflowers*—picture on page A3

,cauliflower 'cheese (*BrE*) (*AmE* **,cauliflower with 'cheese**) *noun* [U] a hot dish of cauliflower cooked and served in a cheese sauce

,cauliflower 'ear *noun* an ear that is permanently SWOLLEN because it has been hit many times

caulk /kɔːk/ *verb* [VN] to fill the holes or cracks in sth, especially a ship, with a substance that keeps out water

causal /ˈkɔːzl/ *adj.* **1** (*formal*) connected with the relationship between two things, where one causes the other to happen: *the causal relationship between poverty and disease* **2 ~ conjunction/connective** (*grammar*) a word such as *because* that introduces a statement about the cause of sth

caus·al·ity /kɔːˈzæləti/ (also **caus·ation**) *noun* [U] (*formal*) the relationship between sth that happens and the reason for it happening; the principle that nothing can happen without a cause

caus·ation /kɔːˈzeɪʃn/ *noun* [U] (*formal*) **1** the process of one event causing or producing another event **2** = CAUS-ALITY

causa·tive /ˈkɔːzətɪv/ *adj.* **1** (*formal*) acting as the cause of sth: *Smoking is a causative factor in several major diseases.* **2** (*grammar*) a **causative verb** expresses a cause, for example *blacken* which means 'to cause to become black'

cause /kɔːz/ *noun, verb*

■ *noun* **1** [C] the person or thing that makes sth happen: *Unemployment is a major cause of poverty.* ◊ *There was discussion about the fire and its likely cause.* ◊ *Drinking and driving is one of the most common causes of traffic accidents.* **2** [U] **~ (for sth)** a reason for having particular feelings or behaving in a particular way: *There is no cause for concern.* ◊ *The food was excellent—I had no cause for complaint.* ◊ *with/without good cause* (= with/without a good reason) **3** [C] an organization or idea that people support or fight for: *Animal welfare campaigners raised £70000 for their cause last year.* ◊ *a good cause* (= an organization that does good work, such as a charity) ◊ *fighting for the Republican cause*—see also LOST CAUSE **4** [C] (*law*) a case that goes to a court of law ▯▯▯ **be for/ in a good 'cause** worth doing, because it is helping other people—more at COMMON *adj.*

■ *verb* to make sth happen, especially sth bad or unpleasant: [VN] *Do they know what caused the fire?* ◊ *Are you causing trouble again?* ◊ *The bad weather is causing problems for many farmers.* ◊ *deaths caused by dangerous*

æ	ɑː	e	ɜː	ə	ɪ	iː	i	ɒ	ɔː	ʌ	ʊ	u	uː
cat	father	ten	bird	about	sit	see	many	got	saw	cup	put	actual	too

(BrE)

driving ◇ [VN **to** inf] *The poor harvest caused prices to rise sharply.* ◇ [VNN] *The project is still causing him a lot of problems.*

The **cause** of something is what makes it happen: *We do not yet know the cause of the accident.*

A **reason** explains something: *He has given no reasons for his decision.* ◇ *There are several reasons why this is my favourite book.* You talk about the **reason for** (not *the reason of*) something, but the **cause of** (not *the cause for*) something.

The **purpose** of something you do is the reason for doing it, the thing that you hope to achieve: *The purpose of the trip is to raise funds for the election campaign.*

---

cause·way /ˈkɔːzweɪ/ *noun* a raised road or path across water or wet ground: *The islands are linked by causeways and bridges.*

caus·tic /ˈkɔːstɪk/ *adj.* **1** (of a chemical substance) able to destroy or dissolve other substances **2** critical in a bitter or SARCASTIC way: *caustic comments/wit* ▶ **caus·tic·al·ly** /-kli/ *adv.*

ˌcaustic ˈsoda *noun* [U] a chemical used in making paper and soap

caut·er·ize (*BrE* also **-ise**) /ˈkɔːtəraɪz/ *verb* [VN] (*medical*) to burn a wound, using a chemical or heat, in order to stop it from bleeding or becoming infected

cau·tion /ˈkɔːʃn/ *noun, verb*
■ *noun* **1** [U] care that you take in order to avoid danger or mistakes; not taking any risks: *extreme/great caution* ◇ *Statistics should be treated with caution.* **2** [C] (*BrE*) a warning that is given by the police to sb who has committed a crime that is not too serious: *As a first offender, she got off with a caution.* **3** [U, C] (*formal*) a warning or a piece of advice about a possible danger or risk: *a word/note of caution* ◇ *Some cautions must be mentioned—for example good tools are essential to do the job well.* IDM **throw/cast caution to the ˈwind(s)** to stop caring about how dangerous sth might be; to start taking risks: *He threw caution to the wind and dived into the water after the child.*
■ *verb* **1** ~ (sb) **against sth**| ~ **sb about sth** to warn sb about the possible dangers or problems of sth: [V] *I would caution against getting too involved.* ◇ [VN] *Sam cautioned him against making a hasty decision.* ◇ [V that] *The government cautioned that pay increases could lead to job losses.* [also VN to inf, V speech, VN speech] **2** [VN] (*BrE, law*) to warn sb officially that anything they say may be used as evidence against them in a court of law: *Suspects must be cautioned before any questions are asked.* **3** [VN] [usually passive] ~ **sb (for sth)** to warn sb officially that they will be punished if they do sth wrong or illegal again: *She wasn't sent to the juvenile court; instead she was cautioned.*

cau·tion·ary /ˈkɔːʃənəri; *AmE* -neri/ *adj.* giving advice or a warning: *a cautionary tale about the problems of buying a computer* ◇ *In her conclusion, the author sounds a cautionary note.*

cau·tious /ˈkɔːʃəs/ *adj.* ~ (**about sb/sth**)| ~ (**about doing sth**) being careful about what you say or do, especially to avoid danger or mistakes; not taking any risks: *He was very cautious about committing himself to anything.* ◇ *The government has been cautious in its response to the report.* ◇ *They've taken a very cautious approach.* ◇ *They expressed cautious optimism about a solution to the crisis.* ▶ **cau·tious·ly** *adv.*: *She looked cautiously around and then walked away from the house.* **cau·tious·ness** *noun* [U]

cav·al·cade /ˌkævlˈkeɪd/ *noun* a line of people on horses or in vehicles forming part of a ceremony

cava·lier /ˌkævəˈlɪə(r); *AmE* -ˈlɪr/ *adj.* [usually before noun] not caring enough about sth important or about the feelings of other people: *The government takes a cavalier attitude to the problems of prison overcrowding.*

A **cautious** person is nervous that something may be dangerous or unwise, so they only do it very slowly or after a lot of thought. (opposite = **rash**)

A **careful** person is not nervous but does take extra care to make sure that everything is correct or nothing goes wrong. (opposite = **careless**)
*People are now more **cautious about** buying luxuries.* ◇ *I should be very **careful not to** annoy her.*

Notice also:
*Be **careful** / **Take care** when you drive on icy roads.*
***Caution** / **Warning** – thin ice.*

---

cav·alry /ˈkævlri/ *noun* (usually **the cavalry**) [sing.+ sing./pl. *v.*] (in the past) the part of the army that fought on horses; the part of the modern army that uses ARMOURED vehicles

cave /keɪv/ *noun, verb*
■ *noun* a large hole in the side of a hill or under the ground: *the mouth* (= the entrance) *of the cave* ◇ *The area contains vast underground cave systems.*—picture at COAST
■ *verb* PHRV **ˌcave ˈin (on sb/sth)** (of a roof, wall, etc.) to fall down and inwards: *The ceiling suddenly caved in on top of them.*—related noun CAVE-IN **ˌcave ˈin (to sth)** to finally do what sb wants after you have been strongly opposing them: *The President is unlikely to cave in to demands for a public inquiry.*—see also CAVING

cav·eat /ˈkæviæt/ *noun* (*formal, from Latin*) a warning that particular things need to be considered before sth can be done

cav·eat emp·tor /ˌkæviæt ˈemptɔː(r)/ *noun* (from *Latin*) the principle that a person who buys sth is responsible for finding any faults in the thing they buy

ˈcave-in *noun* the fact of sth suddenly falling inwards or of COLLAPSING

cave·man /ˈkeɪvmæn/ *noun* (*pl.* **-men** /-men/) **1** a person who lived in a CAVE thousands of years ago **2** (*informal*) a man who behaves in an aggressive way

caver /ˈkeɪvə(r)/ (also **pot·holer**) (both *BrE*) (*AmE* **spe·lunk·er** /spɪˈlʌŋkə(r)/) *noun* a person who goes into CAVES under the ground as a sport or hobby—compare SPELEOLOGIST

cav·ern /ˈkævən; *AmE* -vərn/ *noun* a CAVE, especially a large one

cav·ern·ous /ˈkævənəs; *AmE* -vərn-/ *adj.* (*written*) (of a room or space) very large and often empty and/or dark; like a CAVE: *the vast, cavernous space of the empty concert hall*

cav·iar (also **cavi·are**) /ˈkæviɑː(r)/ *noun* [U] the eggs of some types of fish, especially the STURGEON, that are preserved using salt and eaten as a very special and expensive type of food

cavil /ˈkævl/ *verb* (**-ll-**, *AmE* **-l-**) [V] ~ (**at sth**) (*rare, formal*) to make unnecessary complaints about sth SYN QUIBBLE

cav·ing /ˈkeɪvɪŋ/ (also **pot·hol·ing**) (both *BrE*) (*AmE* **spe·lunk·ing**) *noun* [U] the sport or activity of going into CAVES under the ground: *He had always wanted to go caving.*

cav·ity /ˈkævəti/ *noun* (*pl.* **-ies**) **1** a hole or empty space inside sth solid: *the abdominal cavity* **2** a hole in a tooth

ˌcavity ˈwall *noun* a wall consisting of two walls with a space between them, designed to prevent heat from escaping: *cavity wall insulation*

ca·vort /kəˈvɔːt; *AmE* kəˈvɔːrt/ *verb* [V+adv./prep.] to jump or move around in a noisy, excited and often sexual way: *The photos showed her cavorting on the beach with her new lover.*

caw /kɔː/ *noun* the harsh sound that is made by birds such as CROWS and ROOKS ▶ **caw** *verb* [V]

cay·enne /keɪˈen/ (also **ˌcayenne ˈpepper**) *noun* [U] a type of red pepper used in cooking to give a hot flavour to food

---

aɪ	aʊ	eɪ	əʊ	oʊ	ɔɪ	ɪə	eə	ʊə	j	w
my	now	say	go (BrE)	go (AmE)	boy	near	hair	pure	yes	wet

cay·man (also **cai·man**) /ˈkeɪmən/ noun (pl. **-mans**) a N American reptile similar to an ALLIGATOR

CB /ˌsiː ˈbiː/ noun [U] the abbreviation for 'Citizens' Band' (a range of waves on a radio on which people can talk to each other over short distances, especially when driving): *A truck driver used his CB radio to call for help.*

CBE /ˌsiː biː ˈiː/ noun the abbreviation for 'Commander (of the Order) of the British Empire' (an award given in Britain to some people for a special achievement): *He was made a CBE in 1995.* ◊ *Jon Adams CBE*

CBI /ˌsiː biː ˈaɪ/ abbr. Confederation of British Industry (an important organization to which businesses and industries belong)

CBS /ˌsiː biː ˈes/ abbr. Columbia Broadcasting System (an American recording and broadcasting company that produces records, television programmes, etc.)

cc /ˌsiː ˈsiː/ abbr. **1** carbon copy (to) (used on business letters and e-mails to show that a copy is being sent to another person): *to Luke Peters, cc Janet Gold*—picture on page 251 **2** cubic centimetre(s): *an 850cc engine*

CCTV /ˌsiː siː tiː ˈviː/ abbr. CLOSED-CIRCUIT TELEVISION

CD /ˌsiː ˈdiː/ (also **disc**) noun a small disc on which sound or information is recorded. CDs are played on a special machine called a **CD player**. CD is an abbreviation for 'compact disc'.

Cdr (also **Cdr.** especially in AmE) abbr. (in writing) COMMANDER: *Cdr (John) Stone*

CD-ROM (AmE **CD/ROM**) /ˌsiː diː ˈrɒm; AmE ˈrɑːm/ noun [C, U] a CD on which large amounts of information, sound and pictures can be stored, for use on a computer (an abbreviation for 'compact disc read-only memory'): *The software package contains 5 CD-ROMs.* ◊ *The encyclopedia is available on CD-ROM.* ◊ *a CD-ROM drive* (= in a computer)—compare ROM—picture on page 251

CE /ˌsiː ˈiː/ abbr. **1** (in Britain) Church of England **2** (also **C.E.** especially in AmE) Common Era (= the period since the birth of Christ when the Christian CALENDAR starts counting years). CE can be used to give dates in the same way as AD.—compare AD, BC, BCE

cease /siːs/ verb (formal) to stop happening or existing; to stop sth from happening or existing: [V] *Welfare payments cease as soon as an individual starts a job.* ◊ [V to inf] *You never cease to amaze me!* ◊ [VN] *They voted to cease strike action immediately.* ◊ *He ordered his men to cease fire* (= stop shooting). ◊ [V -ing] *The company ceased trading in June.*—see also CESSATION ▪ IDM see WONDER n.

cease·fire /ˈsiːsfaɪə(r)/ noun a time when enemies agree to stop fighting, usually while a way is found to end the fighting permanently SYN TRUCE: *a call for an immediate ceasefire* ◊ *Observers have reported serious violations of the ceasefire.*

cease·less /ˈsiːsləs/ adj. (formal) not stopping; seeming to have no end: *the ceaseless rain* ▶ **cease·less·ly** adv.

cedar /ˈsiːdə(r)/ noun **1** [C] a tall EVERGREEN tree with wide spreading branches **2** (also **cedar·wood**) [U] the hard red wood of the cedar tree, that has a sweet smell

cede /siːd/ verb [VN] **~ sth (to sb)** (formal) to give sb control of sth or give them power, a right, etc., especially unwillingly: *Cuba was ceded by Spain to the US in 1898.*—see also CESSION

ce·dilla /sɪˈdɪlə/ noun the mark placed under the letter *c*, especially in French, to show that it is pronounced like an *s* rather than a *k* (as in façade); a similar mark under *s* in Turkish and other eastern languages

cei·lidh /ˈkeɪli/ noun a social occasion with music and dancing, especially in Scotland and Ireland

ceil·ing /ˈsiːlɪŋ/ noun **1** the top inside surface of a room: *She lay on her back staring up at the ceiling.* ◊ *a large room with a high ceiling* **2** the highest limit or amount of sth: *price ceilings*—compare FLOOR **3** (technical) the greatest height at which a particular aircraft is able to fly—see also GLASS CEILING ▪ IDM see HIT v.

'ceiling rose (also **rose**) noun (technical) a circular object that is fixed to the ceiling of a room for the wires of an electric light to go through

celeb /səˈleb/ noun (informal) = CELEBRITY

cele·brant /ˈselɪbrənt/ noun **1** a priest who leads a church service, especially the COMMUNION service; a person who attends a service **2** (AmE) a person who is celebrating sth, for example at a party

cele·brate /ˈselɪbreɪt/ verb **1** to show that a day or an event is important by doing sth special on it: [V] *Jake's passed his exams. We're going out to celebrate.* ◊ [VN] *We celebrated our 25th wedding anniversary in Florence.* ◊ *How do people celebrate New Year in your country?* **2** [VN] to perform a religious ceremony, especially the Christian COMMUNION service **3** [VN] (formal) to praise sb/sth: *a movie celebrating the life and work of Martin Luther King*

cele·brated /ˈselɪbreɪtɪd/ adj. famous for having good qualities: *a celebrated painter*

cele·bra·tion /ˌselɪˈbreɪʃn/ noun **1** [C, often pl.] a special event that people organize in order to celebrate sth: *birthday/wedding celebrations* **2** [U, C] the act of celebrating sth: *Her triumph was a cause for celebration.* ◊ *a party in celebration of their fiftieth wedding anniversary* ◊ *The service was a celebration of his life* (= praised what he had done in his life).

cele·bra·tory /ˌseləˈbreɪtəri; AmE ˈseləbrətɔːri/ adj. celebrating sth or marking a special occasion: *a celebratory drink/dinner*

ce·leb·rity /səˈlebrəti/ noun (pl. **-ies**) **1** (also informal **celeb**) [C] a famous person: *TV celebrities* **2** [U] the state of being famous SYN FAME: *Does he find his new celebrity intruding on his private life?*

cel·eri·ac /səˈleriæk/ noun [U] a large white root vegetable which is a type of CELERY and which is eaten raw or cooked

cel·ery /ˈseləri/ noun [U] a vegetable with long crisp light green stems that are often eaten raw: *a stick of celery*—picture on page A3

ce·les·tial /səˈlestiəl; AmE -tʃl/ adj. [usually before noun] (formal or literary) of the sky or of heaven: *celestial bodies* (= the sun, moon, stars, etc.) ◊ *celestial light/music*—compare TERRESTRIAL

celi·bate /ˈselɪbət/ adj., noun
▪ adj. **1** not married and not having sex, especially for religious reasons: *celibate priests* **2** not having sex: *I've been celibate for the past six months.* ▶ **celi·bacy** /ˈselɪbəsi/ noun [U]: *a vow of celibacy*
▪ noun (formal) a person who has chosen not to marry; a person who never has sex

cell /sel/ noun **1** a room for one or more prisoners in a prison or police station—see also PADDED CELL **2** a small room without much furniture in which a MONK or NUN lives **3** the smallest unit of living matter that can exist on its own. All plants and animals are made up of cells: *red blood cells* ◊ *the nucleus of a cell* **4** each of the small sections that together form a larger structure, for example a HONEYCOMB **5** a device for producing an electric current, for example by the action of chemicals or light: *a photoelectric cell* **6** a small group of people who work as part of a larger political organization, especially secretly: *a terrorist cell*

cel·lar /ˈselə(r)/ noun **1** an underground room often used for storing things: *a coal cellar* **2** = WINE CELLAR—see also SALT CELLAR

cell·ist /ˈtʃelɪst/ noun a person who plays the CELLO

cell·mate noun /ˈselmeɪt/ a prisoner with whom another prisoner shares a cell

cello /ˈtʃeləʊ; AmE -loʊ/ noun (pl. **-os**) a musical instrument with strings, shaped like a large violin. The player sits down and holds the cello between his or her knees.—picture on page 840

Cel·lo·phane™ /ˈseləfeɪn/ noun [U] a thin transparent plastic material used for wrapping things: *a cellophane wrapper/bag*

cell·phone /ˈselfəʊn; AmE -foʊn/ noun (especially AmE) = MOBILE PHONE

cel·lu·lar /ˈseljələ(r)/ adj. **1** connected with or consisting of the cells of plants or animals: *cellular structure/processes* **2** connected with a telephone system that works by radio instead of wires: *a cellular network* ◊ *cellular radio*

C

b	d	f	g	h	k	l	m	n	p	r
bad	did	fall	get	hat	cat	leg	man	now	pen	red

3 (*BrE*) (of fabric) loosely woven for extra warmth: *cellular blankets*

,cellular 'phone (also **cell·phone**) *noun* (*especially AmE*) = MOBILE PHONE

cel·lu·lite /'seljulaɪt/ *noun* [U] a type of fat that some people get below their skin, which stops the surface of the skin looking smooth

cel·lu·loid /'seljulɔɪd/ *noun* [U] **1** a thin transparent plastic material made in sheets, used in the past for photographic film **2** (*old-fashioned*) used as a way of referring to films/movies

cel·lu·lose /'seljuləʊs; *AmE* -loʊs/ *noun* [U] **1** a natural substance that forms the cell walls of all plants and trees and is used in making plastics, paper, etc. **2** any compound of cellulose used in making paint, LACQUER, etc.

Cel·sius /'selsiəs/ (also **centi·grade**) *adj.* (*abbr.* **C**) of or using a scale of temperature in which water freezes at 0° and boils at 100°: *It will be a mild night, around nine degrees Celsius.* ◊ *the Celsius Scale* ⇨ Appendix 3 ▶ **Celsius** *noun* [U]: *temperatures in Celsius and Fahrenheit*

Celt /kelt; selt/ *noun* **1** a member of a race of people from western Europe who settled in Ancient Britain before the Romans came **2** a person whose ancestors were Celts, especially one from Ireland, Wales, Scotland, Cornwall or Brittany

Cel·tic /'keltɪk; 'seltɪk/ *adj.* connected with the Celts or their language: *Celtic history*

ce·ment /sɪ'ment/ *noun, verb*
■ *noun* [U] **1** a grey powder made by burning clay and LIME that sets hard when it is mixed with water. Cement is used in building to stick bricks together and to make very hard surfaces. **2** the hard substance that is formed when cement becomes dry and hard: *a floor of cement* ◊ *a cement floor*—see also CONCRETE, MORTAR **3** a soft substance that becomes hard when dry and is used for sticking things together or filling in holes: *dental cement* (= for filling holes in teeth) **4** something that unites people in a common interest: *values which are the cement of society*
■ *verb* [VN] **1** [often passive] **~ A and B** (**together**) to join two things together using cement, glue, etc. **2** to make a relationship, an agreement, etc. stronger: *The President's visit was intended to cement the alliance between the two countries.*

ce'ment mixer (also ¦**concrete mixer**) *noun* a machine with a drum that holds sand, water and cement and turns to mix them together—picture at TRUCK

cem·et·ery /'semətri; *AmE* -teri/ *noun* (*pl.* **-ies**) an area of land used for burying dead people, especially one that is not beside a church—compare CHURCHYARD, GRAVEYARD

ceno·taph /'senətɑːf; *AmE* -tæf/ *noun* a MONUMENT built in memory of soldiers killed in war who are buried somewhere else

cen·sor /'sensə(r)/ *noun, verb*
■ *noun* a person whose job is to examine books, films/movies, etc. and remove parts which are considered offensive, immoral or politically dangerous
■ *verb* [VN] to remove the parts of a book, film/movie, etc. that are considered offensive, immoral or politically dangerous: *The news reports had been heavily censored.*

cen·sori·ous /sen'sɔːriəs/ *adj.* (*formal*) tending to criticize people or things a lot

cen·sor·ship /'sensəʃɪp; *AmE* -sərʃ-/ *noun* [U] the act or policy of CENSORING books, etc: *press censorship* ◊ *The decree imposed strict censorship of the media.*

cen·sure /'senʃə(r)/ *noun, verb*
■ *noun* [U] (*formal*) strong criticism: *a vote of censure on the government's foreign policy*
■ *verb* [VN] **~ sb** (**for sth**) (*formal*) to criticize sb severely, and often publicly, because of sth they have done: *He was censured by the council for leaking information to the press.*

cen·sus /'sensəs/ *noun* (*pl.* **cen·suses**) the process of officially counting sth, especially a country's population, and recording various facts

cent /sent/ *noun* (*abbr.* **c**, **ct**) a coin and unit of money

worth 1% of the main unit of money in many countries, for example of the US dollar—see also PER CENT, RED CENT

cent. *abbr.* century: *in the 20th cent.*

cen·taur /'sentɔː(r)/ *noun* (in ancient Greek stories) a creature with a man's head, arms and upper body on a horse's body and legs

cen·ten·ar·ian /ˌsentɪ'neəriən; *AmE* -'ner-/ *noun* a person who is 100 years old or more

cen·ten·ary /sen'tiːnəri; *AmE* -'tenəri/ (*pl.* **-ies**) (*BrE*) (also **cen·ten·nial** *AmE*, *BrE*) *noun* the 100th anniversary of an event: *The club will celebrate its centenary next year.* ◊ *the centenary year*—see also BICENTENARY, TERCENTENARY

cen·ten·nial /sen'teniəl/ *noun* (*especially AmE*) = CENTENARY—see also BICENTENNIAL

cen·ter (*AmE*) = CENTRE

centi- /'senti-/ *combining form* (in nouns) **1** hundred: *centipede* **2** (often used in units of measurement) one HUNDREDTH: *centimetre*

centi·grade /'sentɪgreɪd/ *adj.* = CELSIUS (*abbr.* **C**): *a temperature of 40 degrees centigrade* ▶ **centi·grade** *noun* [U]: *temperatures in centigrade and Fahrenheit*

centi·gram (also **centi·gramme**) /'sentɪgræm/ *noun* a unit for measuring weight. There are 100 centigrams in a gram.

centi·litre (*BrE*) (*AmE* **centi·liter**) /'sentiliːtə(r)/ *noun* (*abbr.* **cl**) a unit for measuring liquids. There are 100 centilitres in a litre.

centi·metre (*BrE*) (*AmE* **centi·meter**) /'sentimiːtə(r)/ *noun* (*abbr.* **cm**) a unit for measuring length. There are 100 centimetres in a metre.

centi·pede /'sentɪpiːd/ *noun* a small creature like an insect, with a long thin body and many legs

cen·tral /'sentrəl/ *adj.* **1** most important; main: *The central issue is that of widespread racism.* ◊ *She has been a central figure in the campaign.* ◊ *Prevention also plays a central role in traditional medicine.* ◊ *Reducing inflation is* **central to** (= is an important part of) *the government's economic policy.* **2** having power or control over other parts: *the central committee* (= of a political party) ◊ *The organization has a central office in York.* ◊ *The car has power steering and a central locking system.* **3** in the centre of an area or object: *central London* ◊ *Central America/Europe/Asia* ◊ *the central area of the brain* **4** easily reached from many areas: *The flat is very central—just five minutes from Princes Street.* ◊ *a central location* ▶ **cen·tral·ity** /sen'trælətɪ/ *noun* [U] (*formal*): *the centrality of the family as a social institution* **cen·tral·ly** /'sentrəli/ *adv.*: *The hotel is centrally located for all major attractions.* ◊ *a centrally planned economy* ◊ *Is the house centrally heated* (= does it have central heating)?

,central 'bank *noun* a national bank that does business with the government and other banks, and ISSUES the country's coins and paper money

,central 'government *noun* [U, C] the government of a whole country, rather than LOCAL GOVERNMENT which is concerned with smaller areas

,central 'heating *noun* [U] a system for heating a building from one source which then pumps the hot water or hot air through pipes all around the building

the ,Central In'telligence Agency = CIA

cen·tral·ism /'sentrəlɪzəm/ *noun* [U] a way of organizing sth, such as government or education, that involves one central group of people controlling the whole system ▶ **cen·tral·ist** *adj.*: *centralist control of schools*

cen·tral·ize (*BrE* also **-ise**) /'sentrəlaɪz/ *verb* [VN] to give the control of a country or an organization to a group of people in one particular place: *a highly centralized system of government* ▶ **cen·tral·iza·tion, -isa·tion** /ˌsentrəlaɪ'zeɪʃn; *AmE* -lə'z-/ *noun* [U]: *the centralization of political power*

,central 'nervous system *noun* (*anatomy*) the part of the system of nerves in the body that consists of the brain and the SPINAL CORD—see also NERVOUS SYSTEM

,central 'processing unit *noun* (*computing*) (*abbr.* **CPU**) the part of a computer that controls all the other parts of the system

s	t	v	z	ʃ	ʒ	.	tʃ	dʒ	θ	ð	ŋ
see	tea	van	zoo	shoe	vision		chain	jam	thin	this	sing

¦central reser'vation (*BrE*) (*AmE* **me·dian**, **¦median strip**) *noun* a narrow strip of land that separates the two sides of a motorway/freeway

centre (*BrE*) (*AmE* **cen·ter**) /'sentə(r)/ *noun, verb*
■ *noun* [VN]
MIDDLE | **1** [C] the middle point or part of sth: *the centre of a circle* ◊ *a long table in the centre of the room* ◊ *chocolates with soft centres*—picture at CIRCLE

TOWN/CITY | **2** [C] (*especially BrE*) (*AmE* usually **down·town** [usually *sing.*]) the main part of a town or city where there are a lot of shops/stores and offices: *in the town/city centre* ◊ *the centre of town* ◊ *a town centre car park* **3** [C] a place or an area where a lot of people live; a place where a lot of business or cultural activity takes place: *major urban/industrial centres* ◊ *a centre of population* ◊ *Small towns in South India serve as economic and cultural centres for the surrounding villages.*

BUILDING | **4** [C] a building or place used for a particular purpose or activity: *a shopping/sports/leisure/community centre* ◊ *the Centre for Policy Studies*

OF EXCELLENCE | **5** [C] ~ **of excellence** a place where a particular kind of work is done extremely well

OF ATTENTION | **6** [C, usually *sing.*] the point towards which people direct their attention: *Children like to be the centre of attention.* ◊ *The prime minister is at the centre of a political row over leaked Cabinet documents.*

-CENTRED | **7** (in adjectives) having the thing mentioned as the most important feature or FOCUS (= point) of attention: *a child-centred approach to teaching*—see also SELF-CENTRED

IN POLITICS | **8** (usually **the centre**) [*sing.*] a MODERATE (= middle) political position or party, between the extremes of LEFT-WING and RIGHT-WING parties: *a party of the centre*

IN SPORT | **9** [C] = CENTRE FORWARD

IDM see FRONT *n.*, LEFT *adv.*
■ *verb* [VN] to move sth so that it is in the centre of sth else: *Carefully centre the photograph on the page and stick it in place.*
PHRV **¦centre around/on/round/upon sb/sth** | **¦centre sth around/on/round/upon sb/sth** to be or make sb/sth become the person or thing around which most activity, etc. takes place: *State occasions always centred around the king himself.* ◊ *Discussions were centred on developments in Eastern Europe.* **¦centre sth in ...** [usually *passive*] to make somewhere the place where an activity or event takes place: *Most of the fighting was centred in the north of the capital.*

¦centre 'back (*BrE*) (*AmE* **¦center 'back**) *noun* (in football and some other sports) a player or position in the middle of the back line of players

centre·board (*BrE*) (*AmE* **center·board**) /'sentəbɔːd; *AmE* 'sentərbɔːrd/ *noun* a board that can be lowered through a hole in the bottom of a sailing boat to keep it steady when sailing

centre·fold (*BrE*) (*AmE* **cen·ter·fold**) /'sentəfəʊld; *AmE* -tərfoʊld/ *noun* **1** a large picture, often of a young woman with few or no clothes on, folded to form the middle pages of a magazine **2** a person whose picture is the centrefold of a magazine

¦centre 'forward (also **centre**) (both *BrE*) (*AmE* **¦center 'forward**, **cen·ter**) *noun* (in football and some other sports) a player or position in the middle of the front line of players

¦centre 'half (*BrE*) (*AmE* **¦center 'half**) *noun* (in football and some other sports) a player or position in the middle of the HALFBACK line of players

¦centre of 'gravity *noun* (*pl.* **centres of gravity**) the point in an object around which its MASS (= weight) is evenly DISTRIBUTED (= spread)

centre·piece (*BrE*) (*AmE* **cen·ter·piece**) /'sentəpiːs; *AmE* -tərp-/ *noun* **1** [*sing.*] the most important item: *This treaty is the centrepiece of the government's foreign policy.* **2** an ornament or a decoration for the centre of a table

¦centre 'spread *noun* the two facing middle pages of a newspaper or magazine

¦centre 'stage (*BrE*) (*AmE* **¦center 'stage**) *noun* [U] an important position where sb/sth can easily get people's attention: *Education is taking centre stage in the government's plans.* ◊ *The Balkans continue to occupy centre stage in world affairs.* ▶ **¦centre 'stage** *adv.*: *The minister said, 'We are putting full employment centre stage'.*

cen·tri·fu·gal /ˌsentrɪ'fjuːgl; sen'trɪfjəgl/ *adj.* (*technical*) moving or tending to move away from a centre

cen¦trifugal 'force *noun* (*physics*) a force that appears to cause an object travelling around a centre to fly outwards and away from its circular path

cen·tri·fuge /'sentrɪfjuːdʒ/ *noun* a machine with a part that spins around to separate substances, for example liquids from solids, by forcing the heavier substance to the outer edge

cen·tri·pet·al /sen'trɪpɪtl; ˌsentrɪ'piːtl/ *adj.* (*technical*) moving or tending to move towards a centre

cen·trist /'sentrɪst/ *noun* a person with political views that are not extreme **SYN** MODERATE ▶ **cen·trist** *adj.*: *a centrist politician*

cen·tur·ion /sen'tjʊəriən; *AmE* -'tʃʊr-/ *noun* (in ancient Rome) an army officer who commanded 100 soldiers

cen·tury /'sentʃəri/ *noun* (*pl.* **-ies**) **1** a period of 100 years **2** (*abbr.* **c**, **cent.**) any of the periods of 100 years before or after the birth of Christ: *the 20th century* (= AD1901–2000 or 1900–1999) ◊ *eighteenth-century writers* **3** (in cricket) a score of 100 RUNS by one player in one INNINGS **IDM** see TURN *n.*

CEO /ˌsiː iː 'əʊ; *AmE* 'oʊ/ *abbr.* chief executive officer (the person with the highest rank in a business company)

cer·am·ic /sə'ræmɪk/ *noun* **1** [C, usually *pl.*] a pot or other object made of clay that has been made permanently hard by heat: *an exhibition of ceramics by Picasso* **2** (**ceramics**) [U] the art of making and decorating ceramics ▶ **cer·am·ic** *adj.*: *ceramic tiles*

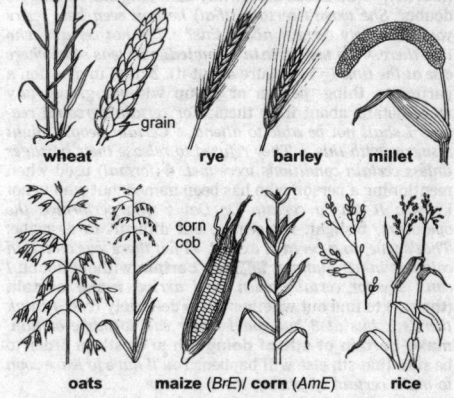

cereals

an ear of wheat

grain

wheat   **rye**   **barley**   **millet**

corn cob

oats   **maize** (*BrE*)/**corn** (*AmE*)   **rice**

cer·eal /'sɪəriəl; *AmE* 'sɪr-/ *noun* **1** [C] one of various types of grass that produce grains that can be eaten or are used to make flour or bread. Wheat, BARLEY and RYE are all cereals: *cereal crops* **2** [U] the grain produced by cereal crops **3** [C, U] food made from the grain of cereals, often eaten for breakfast with milk: *breakfast cereals* ◊ *a bowl of cereal*

ce·re·bel·lum /ˌserə'beləm/ *noun* (*pl.* **ce·re·bel·lums** or **cere·bella** /-'belə/) (*anatomy*) the part of the brain at the back of the head that controls the activity of the muscles

cere·bral /'serəbrəl; *AmE* sə'riːbrəl/ *adj.* **1** relating to the brain: *a cerebral haemorrhage* **2** (*formal*) relating to the mind rather than the feelings **SYN** INTELLECTUAL: *His poetry is very cerebral.*

¦cerebral 'palsy *noun* [U] a medical condition usually caused by brain damage before or at birth that causes the loss of control of movement of the limbs

cere·brum /sə'riːbrəm; 'serəbrəm/ *noun* (*pl.* **ce·re·bra**

/-brə/) (*anatomy*) the front part of the brain, responsible for thoughts, emotions and personality

cere·mo·nial /ˌserɪˈməʊniəl; *AmE* -ˈmoʊ-/ *adj., noun*
■ *adj.* relating to or used in a ceremony: *ceremonial occasions* ◊ *a ceremonial sword* ▶ **cere·mo·ni·al·ly** /-niəli/ *adv.*
■ *noun* [U, C] the system of rules and traditions that states how things should be done at a ceremony or formal occasion: *The visit was conducted with all due ceremonial.*

cere·mo·ni·ous /ˌserəˈməʊniəs; *AmE* -ˈmoʊ-/ *adj.* (*written*) behaving or performed in an extremely formal way [OPP] UNCEREMONIOUS ▶ **cere·mo·ni·ous·ly** *adv.*: *Dr North ceremoniously raised his glass to offer a toast.*

cere·mony /ˈserəməni; *AmE* -moʊni/ *noun* (*pl.* -ies) **1** [C] a public or religious occasion that includes a series of formal or traditional actions: *an awards/opening ceremony* ◊ *a wedding/marriage ceremony* **2** [U] formal behaviour; traditional actions and words used on particular formal occasions [IDM] **stand on ˈceremony** (*BrE*) to behave formally: *Please don't stand on ceremony* (= Please be natural and relaxed) *with me.* **without ˈceremony** in a very rough or informal way: *He found himself pushed without ceremony out of the house and the door slammed in his face.*—see also MASTER OF CEREMONIES

cer·ise /səˈriːz; səˈriːs/ *adj.* pinkish-red in colour ▶ **cerise** *noun* [U]

cert /sɜːt; *AmE* sɜːrt/ *noun* (*BrE, informal*) a thing that is sure to happen or be successful [SYN] CERTAINTY: *That horse is a **dead cert** for* (= is sure to win) *the next race.*

cert. *abbr.* **1** CERTIFICATE **2** CERTIFIED

cer·tain /ˈsɜːtn; *AmE* ˈsɜːrtn/ *adj., pron.*
■ *adj.* **1** ~ (that ...)| ~ (to do sth)| ~ (of sth/of doing sth) that you can rely on to happen or to be true: *It is certain that they will agree/They are certain to agree.* ◊ *She looks certain to win an Oscar.* ◊ *The climbers face certain death if the rescue today is unsuccessful.* ◊ *If you want to be certain of getting a ticket, book now.* ⇨ note at SURE **2** ~ (that ...)| ~ (of/about sth) firmly believing sth; having no doubts: *She wasn't certain (that) he had seen her.* ◊ *Are you absolutely certain about this?* ◊ *I'm not certain who was there.* ◊ **To my certain knowledge** *he was somewhere else at the time* (= I am sure about it). **3** used to mention a particular thing, person or group without giving any more details about it or them: *For certain personal reasons I shall not be able to attend.* ◊ *Certain people might disagree with this.* ◊ *They refused to release their hostages unless certain conditions were met.* **4** (*formal*) used when mentioning a person who has been named, but who is not known: *It was a certain Dr Davis who performed the operation.* **5** slight; noticeable, but difficult to describe: *That's true,* **to a certain extent.** ◊ *I felt there was a certain coldness in her manner.* [IDM] **for ˈcertain** without doubt: *I can't say for certain when we'll arrive.* **make certain (that ...)** to find out whether sth is definitely true: *I think there's a bus at 8 but you'd better call to make certain.* **make certain of sth/of doing sth** to do sth in order to be sure that sth else will happen: *You'll have to leave soon to make certain of getting there on time.*
■ *pron.* (**certain of ...**) (*formal*) used for talking about some members of a group of people or things without giving any of their names: *Certain of those present were unwilling to discuss the matter further.*

cer·tain·ly /ˈsɜːtnli; *AmE* ˈsɜːrtnli/ *adv.* **1** without doubt; definitely: *Without treatment, she will almost certainly die.* ◊ *Certainly, the early learning years are crucial to a child's educational development.* ◊ *I'm certainly never going there again.* ⇨ note at SURELY **2** (used in answer to questions) of course: *'May I see your passport, Mr Scott?' 'Certainly.'* ◊ *'Do you think all this money will change your life?' 'Certainly not.'*

cer·tainty /ˈsɜːtnti; *AmE* ˈsɜːrtnti/ *noun* (*pl.* -ies) **1** [C] a thing that is certain: *political/moral certainties* ◊ *Her return to the team now seems a certainty.* **2** [U] the state of being certain: *There is no certainty that the president's removal would end the civil war.* ◊ *I can't say **with any certainty** where I'll be next week.*

cer·ti·fi·able /ˈsɜːtɪfaɪəbl; *AmE* ˈsɜːrt-/ *adj.* **1** (*BrE*) a per-

son who is **certifiable** can or should be officially stated to be INSANE: (*informal*) *He's certifiable* (= he's crazy). **2** (*especially AmE*) good enough to be officially accepted or recommended

cer·tifi·cate *noun, verb*
■ *noun* /səˈtɪfɪkət; *AmE* sərˈt-/ (*abbr.* **cert.**) **1** an official document that may be used to prove that the facts it states are true: *a birth/marriage/death certificate* **2** an official document proving that you have completed a course of study or passed an exam; a qualification obtained after a course of study or an exam: *a Postgraduate Certificate in Education* (= a British qualification for teachers) ⇨ note at DEGREE
■ *verb* /səˈtɪfɪkeɪt; *AmE* sərˈt-/ [VN, VN to inf] (*BrE*) to give sb an official document proving that they have successfully completed a training course, especially for a particular profession

cer·tifi·cated /səˈtɪfɪkeɪtɪd; *AmE* sərˈt-/ *adj.* (*BrE*) having the certificate which shows that the necessary training for a particular job has been done

cer·ti·fi·ca·tion /ˌsɜːtɪfɪˈkeɪʃn; *AmE* ˌsɜːrt-/ *noun* [U] (*technical*) **1** the act of CERTIFYING sth: *the medical certification of the cause of death* **2** the process of giving CERTIFICATES for a course of education: *the certification of the exam modules*

ˌcertified ˈcheque (*BrE*) (*AmE* ˌcertified ˈcheck) *noun* a cheque that a bank GUARANTEES

ˌcertified ˈmail *noun* [U] (*AmE*) = RECORDED DELIVERY

ˌcertified ˌpublic acˈcountant *noun* (*AmE*) = CHARTERED ACCOUNTANT

cer·tify /ˈsɜːtɪfaɪ; *AmE* ˈsɜːrt-/ *verb* (**cer·ti·fies, cer·ti·fy·ing, cer·ti·fied, cer·ti·fied**) **1** ~ sb/sth (as) sth to state officially, especially in writing, that sth is true: [V(that)] *He handed her a piece of paper certifying (that) she was in good health.* ◊ *This* (= this document) *is to certify that ...* ◊ [VN-ADJ] *He was certified dead on arrival.* ◊ *The accounts were certified (as) correct by the finance department.* [also VN to inf] **2** [VN] [usually passive] ~ sb (as sth) to give sb an official document proving that they are qualified to work in a particular profession **3** [usually passive] (*BrE, law*) to officially state that sb is mentally ill, so that they can be given medical treatment: [VN] *Patients must be certified before they can be admitted to the hospital.* [also VN-ADJ]

cer·ti·tude /ˈsɜːtɪtjuːd; *AmE* ˈsɜːrtɪtuːd/ *noun* [U, C] (*formal*) a feeling of being certain; a thing about which you are certain: *'You will like Rome,' he said, with absolute certitude.* ◊ *the collapse of moral certitudes*

cer·vical /ˈsɜːvɪkl; səˈvaɪkl; *AmE* ˈsɜːrvɪkl/ *adj.* [only before noun] (*anatomy*) **1** connected with the cervix: *cervical cancer* **2** connected with the neck: *the cervical spine*

ˌcervical ˈsmear *noun* (*BrE*) = SMEAR TEST

cer·vix /ˈsɜːvɪks; *AmE* ˈsɜːrv-/ *noun* (*pl.* **cer·vi·ces** /-vɪsiːz/ or **cer·vi·xes** /-vɪksɪz/) (*anatomy*) the narrow passage at the opening of a woman's WOMB

ce·sar·ean, ce·sar·ian (*AmE*) = CAESAREAN

ces·ium (*AmE*) = CAESIUM

ces·sa·tion /seˈseɪʃn/ *noun* [U, C] (*formal*) the stopping of sth; a pause in sth: *Mexico called for an immediate cessation of hostilities.*

ces·sion /ˈseʃn/ *noun* [U, C] (*formal*) the act of giving up land or rights, especially to another country after a war—see also CEDE

cess·pit /ˈsespɪt/ (also **cess·pool** /ˈsespuːl/) *noun* **1** a covered hole or container in the ground for collecting waste from a building, especially from the toilets **2** a place where dishonest or immoral people gather: *a cesspit of corruption*

cf. *abbr.* (in writing) compare

CFC /ˌsiː ef ˈsiː/ *noun* [C, U] a type of gas used especially in AEROSOLS (= types of container that release liquid in the form of a spray). CFCs are harmful to the layer of the gas OZONE in the earth's atmosphere. (abbreviation for 'chlorofluorocarbon')

cha-cha /ˈtʃɑː tʃɑː/ (also **ˈcha-cha-cha**) *noun* a S American dance with small fast steps: *to dance/do the cha-cha*

C

aɪ	aʊ	eɪ	əʊ	oʊ	ɔɪ	ɪə	eə	ʊə	j	w
my	now	say	go	go	boy	near	hair	pure	yes	wet
			(BrE)	(AmE)						

chafe /tʃeɪf/ *verb* **1** if skin **chafes**, or if sth **chafes** it, it becomes sore because the thing is rubbing against it: [V] *Her wrists chafed where the rope had been.* ◊ [VN] *The collar was far too tight and chafed her neck.* **2** [V] ~ **(at/ under sth)** (*formal*) to feel annoyed and impatient about sth, especially because it limits what you can do: *He soon chafed at the restrictions of his situation.*

chaff /tʃɑːf; *AmE* tʃæf/ *noun, verb*
■ *noun* [U] **1** the outer covering of the seeds of grain such as wheat, which is separated from the grain before it is eaten **2** STRAW (= the dried stems of wheat) and HAY (= dried grass) cut up as food for cows **IDM** see WHEAT
■ *verb* [VN] (*old-fashioned* or *formal*) to make jokes about sb in a friendly way **SYN** TEASE

chaf·finch /ˈtʃæfɪntʃ/ *noun* a small European bird of the FINCH family

chag·rin /ˈʃæɡrɪn; *AmE* ʃəˈɡrɪn/ *noun* [U] (*formal*) a feeling of being disappointed or annoyed ▶ **chag·rined** *adj.*

chain /tʃeɪn/ *noun, verb*

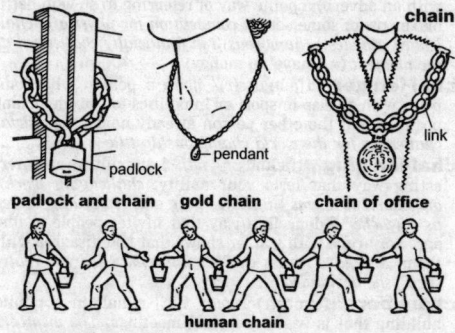

padlock and chain   gold chain   chain of office

human chain

■ *noun*
METAL RINGS | **1** [C, U] a series of connected metal rings, used for pulling or fastening things; a length of chain used for a particular purpose: *a short length of chain* ◊ *She wore a heavy gold chain around her neck.* ◊ *The mayor wore his chain of office.* ◊ *a bicycle chain* ◊ *The prisoners were kept in chains* (= with chains around their arms and legs, to prevent them from escaping).—picture at BICYCLE
CONNECTED THINGS | **2** [C] a series of connected things or people: *to set in motion a chain of events* ◊ *a chain of command* (= a system in an organization by which instructions are passed from one person to another) ◊ *mountain/island chains* ◊ *Volunteers formed a* **human chain** *to rescue precious items from the burning house.*—see also FOOD CHAIN
OF SHOPS/HOTELS | **3** [C] a group of shops/stores or hotels owned by the same company: *a chain of supermarkets/a supermarket chain*
RESTRICTION | **4** [C, usually pl.] (*formal or literary*) a thing that restricts sb's freedom or ability to do sth: *the chains of fear/misery*
IN HOUSE BUYING | **5** [C, usually sing.] (*BrE*) a situation in which a number of people selling and buying houses must each complete the sale of their house before buying from the next person
IDM see BALL *n.*, LINK *n.*, WEAK
■ *verb* [VN] [often passive] ~ **sb/sth (to sb/sth)** | ~ **sb/sth (up)** to fasten sth with a chain; to fasten sb/sth to another person or thing with a chain, so that they do not escape or get stolen: *The doors were always locked and chained.* ◊ *She chained her bicycle to the gate.* ◊ *The dog was chained up for the night.* ◊ (*figurative*) *I've been chained to my desk all week* (= because there was so much work).

'chain gang *noun* a group of prisoners chained together and forced to work

'chain letter *noun* a letter sent to several people asking them to make copies of the letter and send them on to more people

,chain-,link 'fence *noun* a fence made of wire in a diamond pattern—picture at HOUSE

'chain mail (also **mail**) *noun* [U] ARMOUR (= protective covering for the body worn when fighting) made of small metal rings linked together

,chain re'action *noun* **1** (*chemistry*) a chemical change that forms products which themselves cause more changes and new products **2** a series of events, each of which causes the next: *It set off a chain reaction in the international money markets.*

chain·saw /ˈtʃeɪnsɔː/ *noun* a tool made of a chain with sharp teeth set in it, that is driven by a motor and used for cutting wood

'chain-smoke *verb* [V, VN] to smoke cigarettes continuously, lighting the next one from the one you have just smoked ▶ **'chain-smoker** *noun*

'chain store (*BrE* also **mul·tiple**, **,multiple 'store**) *noun* a shop/store that is one of a series of similar shops/stores owned by the same company

chair /tʃeə(r); *AmE* tʃer/ *noun, verb*
■ *noun* **1** [C] a piece of furniture for one person to sit on, with a back, a seat and four legs: *a table and chairs* ◊ *Sit*

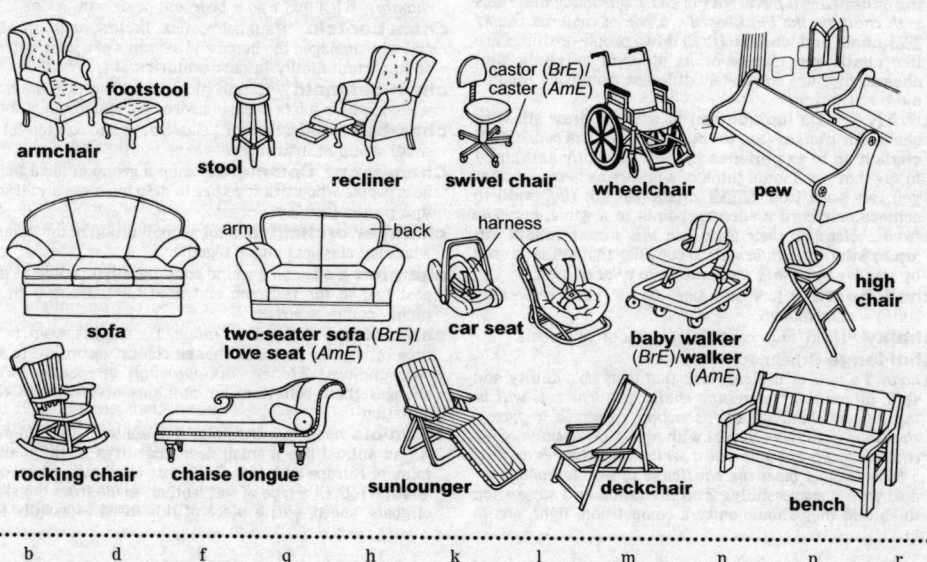

footstool

armchair

stool

recliner

castor (*BrE*)/ caster (*AmE*)

swivel chair

wheelchair

pew

arm   back

harness

sofa

two-seater sofa (*BrE*)/ love seat (*AmE*)

car seat

baby walker (*BrE*)/walker (*AmE*)

high chair

rocking chair   chaise longue

sunlounger

deckchair

bench

C

on your chair! ◊ *an old man asleep in a chair* (= an armchair)—see also ARMCHAIR, DECKCHAIR, EASY CHAIR, HIGH CHAIR, MUSICAL CHAIRS, ROCKING CHAIR, WHEELCHAIR **2 (the chair)** [sing.] the position of being in charge of a meeting or committee; the person who holds this position: *She takes the chair in all our meetings.* ◊ *Who is in the chair today?* ◊ *He was elected chair of the city council.* **3** [C] the position of being in charge of a department in a university: *He holds the chair of philosophy at Oxford.* **4 (the chair)** [sing.] (*AmE, informal*) = THE ELECTRIC CHAIR
■ *verb* [VN] to act as the CHAIRPERSON of a meeting, discussion, etc: *Who's chairing the meeting?*

chair·lift /'tʃeəlɪft; *AmE* 'tʃer-/ *noun* a series of chairs hanging from a moving cable, for carrying people up and down a mountain

chair·man /'tʃeəmən; *AmE* 'tʃer-/ *noun* (*pl.* **-men** /-mən/) **1** the person in charge of a meeting, who tells people when they can speak, etc: *Sir Herbert took it upon himself to act as chairman.* **2** the person in charge of a committee, a company, etc: *the chairman of the board of governors* (= of a school) ◊ *The chairman of the company presented the annual report.* ⇨ note at GENDER

chair·man·ship /'tʃeəmənʃɪp; *AmE* 'tʃer-/ *noun* **1** [C] the position of a CHAIRMAN or CHAIRWOMAN: *the chairmanship of the committee* **2** [U] the state of being a CHAIRMAN or CHAIRWOMAN: *under her skilful chairmanship*

chair·per·son /'tʃeəpɜːsn; *AmE* 'tʃerpɜːrsn/ *noun* (*pl.* **-per·sons**) a CHAIRMAN or CHAIRWOMAN—see also CHAIR (2)

chair·woman /'tʃeəwʊmən; *AmE* 'tʃer-/ *noun* (*pl.* **-women** /-wɪmɪn/) a woman in charge of a meeting, a committee or an organization ⇨ note at GENDER

chaise longue /,ʃeɪz 'lɒŋ; *AmE* 'lɔːŋ/ *noun* (*pl.* **chaises longues** /,ʃeɪz 'lɒŋ; *AmE* 'lɔːŋ/) (from *French*) **1** a long low seat with a back and one arm, on which the person sitting can stretch out their legs **2** (*AmE*) (also *informal* **chaise lounge**) a long chair with a back that can be upright for sitting on or flat for lying on outdoors—picture at CHAIR

cha·let /'ʃæleɪ/ *noun* **1** a wooden house with a roof that slopes steeply down over the sides, usually built in mountain areas, especially in Switzerland **2** (*BrE*) a small house or HUT, especially one used by people on holiday/vacation at the sea

chal·ice /'tʃælɪs/ *noun* a large cup for holding wine, especially one from which wine is drunk in the Christian COMMUNION service **IDM** see POISON *v.*

chalk /tʃɔːk/ *noun, verb*
■ *noun* [U] **1** a type of soft white stone: *the chalk cliffs of southern England* **2** (also **chalks** [pl.]) a substance similar to chalk made into white or coloured sticks for writing or drawing: *a piece/stick of chalk* ◊ *drawing diagrams with chalk on the blackboard* ◊ *a box of coloured chalks* **IDM** ,**chalk and 'cheese** (*BrE*) if two people or things are like **chalk and cheese** or as different as **chalk and cheese**, they are completely different from each other—more at LONG *adj.*
■ *verb* [VN] ~ **sth (up) (on sth)** to write or draw sth with chalk: *She chalked (up) the day's menu on the board.* **IDM** **chalk it up to ex'perience** (*spoken, especially AmE*) used to say that you should think of a failure as being sth that you can learn from **PHRV** ,**chalk 'up sth** (*informal*) to achieve or record a success, points in a game, etc: *The team chalked up their tenth win this season.* ,**chalk sth 'up to sth** (*AmE, informal*) to consider that sth is caused by sth: *We can chalk that win up to a lot of luck.*

chalk·board /'tʃɔːkbɔːd; *AmE* -bɔːrd/ *noun* (*especially AmE*) = BLACKBOARD

chalky /'tʃɔːki/ *adj.* containing chalk or like chalk

chal·lenge /'tʃælɪndʒ/ *noun, verb*
■ *noun* **1** a new or difficult task that tests sb's ability and skill: *an exciting/interesting challenge* ◊ *The role will be the biggest challenge of his acting career.* ◊ *to face a challenge* (= to have to deal with one) ◊ *Destruction of the environment is one of the most serious challenges we face.* ◊ *Schools must meet the challenge of new technology* (= deal with it successfully). **2** an invitation or a suggestion to sb that they should enter a competition, fight, etc: *to*

accept/take up a challenge ◊ *to mount a challenge* **3** ~ **(to sth)** a statement or an action that shows that sb refuses to accept sth and questions whether it is right, legal, etc: *It was a direct challenge to the president's authority.* ◊ *Their legal challenge was unsuccessful.*
■ *verb* **1** [VN] to question whether a statement or an action is right, legal, etc.; to refuse to accept sth: *The story was completely untrue and was successfully challenged in court.* ◊ *She does not like anyone challenging her authority.* ◊ *This discovery challenges traditional beliefs.* **2** ~ **sb (to sth)** to invite sb to enter a competition, fight, etc.; to suggest strongly that sb should do sth (especially when you think that they might be unwilling to do it): [VN] *Mike challenged me to a game of chess.* ◊ [VN to inf] *The opposition leader challenged the prime minister to call an election.* **3** [VN] to test sb's ability and skills, especially in an interesting way: *The job doesn't really challenge her.* **4** [VN] to order sb to stop and say who they are or what they are doing: *We were challenged by police at the border.*

chal·lenged /'tʃælɪndʒd/ *adj.* (*especially AmE*) (used with an adverb) a polite way of referring to sb who has a DISABILITY of some sort: *a competition for physically challenged athletes* ◊ (*humorous*) *I'm financially challenged at the moment* (= I have no money).

chal·len·ger /'tʃælɪndʒə(r)/ *noun* a person who competes with sb else in sport or in politics for an important position that the other person already holds: *the official challenger for the world championship title*

chal·len·ging /'tʃælɪndʒɪŋ/ *adj.* **1** difficult in an interesting way that tests your ability: *challenging work/questions/problems* ◊ *a challenging and rewarding career as a teacher* **2** done in a way that invites people to disagree or argue with you, or shows that you disagree with them: *She gave him a challenging look. 'Are you really sure?' she demanded.*

cham·ber /'tʃeɪmbə(r)/ *noun* **1** [C] a hall in a public building that is used for formal meetings: *The members left the council chamber.* ◊ *the Senate/House chamber*—see also CHAMBER OF COMMERCE **2** [C+sing./pl. *v.*] one of the parts of a parliament: *the Lower/Upper Chamber* (= in Britain, the House of Commons/House of Lords) ◊ *the Chamber of Deputies in the Italian parliament* ◊ *Under Senate rules, the chamber must vote on the bill by this Friday.* **3** [C] (in compounds) a room used for the particular purpose that is mentioned: *a burial chamber* ◊ *Divers transfer from the water to a decompression chamber.*—see also GAS CHAMBER **4** [C] an enclosed space in the body, in a plant or in a machine: *the chambers of the heart* ◊ *the rocket's combustion chamber* ◊ *the chamber of a gun* (= the part that holds the bullets) **5** [C] an enclosed space under the ground: *They found themselves in a vast underground chamber.* **6** [C] (*old use*) a bedroom or private room

cham·ber·lain /'tʃeɪmbəlɪn; *AmE* -bərlɪn/ *noun* an official who managed the home and servants of a king, queen or important family in past centuries

cham·ber·maid /'tʃeɪmbəmeɪd; *AmE* -bərm-/ *noun* a woman whose job is to clean bedrooms, usually in a hotel

'**chamber music** *noun* [U] classical music written for a small group of instruments

,**Chamber of 'Commerce** *noun* a group of local business people who work together to help business and trade in a particular town

'**chamber orchestra** *noun* a small group of musicians who play classical music together

'**chamber pot** *noun* a round container that people in the past had in the bedroom and used for URINATING in at night—compare POTTY

cha·meleon /kə'miːliən/ *noun* **1** a small LIZARD (= a type of reptile) that can change colour according to its surroundings **2** (often *disapproving*) a person who changes their behaviour or opinions according to the situation

cham·ois *noun* (*pl.* **chamois**) **1** /'ʃæmwɑː; *AmE* 'ʃæmi/ [C] an animal like a small deer, that lives in the mountains of Europe and Asia **2** /'ʃæmi/ (*BrE* also ,**chamois 'leather**) [U, C] a type of soft leather, made from the skin of goats, sheep, etc.; a piece of this, used especially for

s	t	v	z	ʃ	ʒ	tʃ	dʒ	θ	ð	ŋ
see	tea	van	zoo	shoe	vision	chain	jam	thin	this	sing

cleaning windows **3** /ˈʃæmi/ [U] (*AmE*) a soft thick cotton fabric, used especially for making shirts

chamo·mile (also **camo·mile**) /ˈkæməmaɪl/ *noun* [U] a plant with a sweet smell and small white and yellow flowers. Its dried leaves and flowers are used to make tea, medicine, etc: *chamomile tea*

champ /tʃæmp/ *verb, noun*
- *verb* [V, VN] (especially of horses) to bite or eat sth noisily **IDM** ˌchamping at the ˈbit (*informal*) impatient to do or start doing sth
- *noun* an informal way of referring to a CHAMPION, often used in newspapers: *Scottish champs celebrate victory!*

cham·pagne /ʃæmˈpeɪn/ *noun* [U, C] a French SPARK-LING white wine (= one with bubbles) that is drunk on special occasions: *a glass of champagne*

cham·pers /ˈʃæmpəz; *AmE* -pərz/ *noun* [U] (*BrE*, *informal*) = CHAMPAGNE

cham·pion /ˈtʃæmpiən/ *noun, verb*
- *noun* **1** a person, team, etc. that has won a competition, especially in a sport: *the world basketball champions ◊ a champion jockey/boxer/swimmer ◊ the reigning champion* (= the person who is champion now) **2 ~ (of sth)** a person who fights for, or speaks in support of, a group of people or a belief: *She was a champion of the poor all her life.*
- *verb* [VN] to fight for or speak in support of a group of people or a belief: *He has always championed the cause of gay rights.*

cham·pion·ship /ˈtʃæmpiənʃɪp/ *noun* **1** (also **cham-pion·ships** [pl.]) a competition to find the best player or team in a particular sport: *the National Basketball Association Championship ◊ He won a silver medal at the Euro-pean Championships.* **2** the position of being a champion: *They've held the championship for the past two years.*

chance /tʃɑːns; *AmE* tʃæns/ *noun, verb, adj.*
- *noun* **1** [C, U] **~ of doing sth | ~ that ... | ~ of sth happen-ing | ~ of sth** a possibility of sth happening, especially sth that you want: *Is there any chance of getting tickets for tonight? ◊ She has only a slim chance of passing the exam. ◊ There's a slight chance that he'll be back in time. ◊ There is no chance that he will change his mind. ◊ What chance is there of anybody being found alive? ◊ Nowadays a premature baby has a very good chance of survival. ◊ The operation has a fifty-fifty chance of success. ◊ The chances are a million to one against being struck by lightning. ◊ an outside chance* (= a very small one) ⇨ note at POSSIBILITY **2** [C] **~ (of sth) | ~ (to do sth) | ~ (for sb to do sth)** a suitable time or situation when you have the opportunity to do sth: *We won't get another chance of a holiday this year. ◊ Please give me a chance to explain. ◊ It was the chance she had been waiting for. ◊ There will be a chance for parents to look around the school. ◊ Jeff deceived me once already—I won't give him a second chance. ◊ This is your big chance* (= opportunity for success). *◊ Tonight is your last chance to catch the play at your local theatre.* **3** [C] an unpleasant or danger-ous possibility: *When installing electrical equipment don't take any chances. A mistake could kill.* **4** [U] the way that some things happen without any cause that you can see or understand **SYN** LUCK: *I met her by chance* (= without planning to) *at the airport. ◊ Chess is not a game of chance. ◊ It was pure chance that we were both there. ◊ We'll plan everything very carefully and leave nothing to chance.* **IDM** as ˌchance would ˈhave it happening in a way that was lucky, although it was not planned: *As chance would have it, John was going to London too, so I went with him.* **by ˈany chance** used especially in ques-tions, to ask whether sth is true, possible, etc: *Are you in love with him, by any chance?* **the chances ˈare (that) ...** (*informal*) it is likely that ...: *The chances are you won't have to pay.* **ˈchance would be a fine thing** (*BrE*, *spoken*) people say **chance would be a fine thing** to show that they would like to do or have the thing that sb has mentioned, but that they do not think that it is very likely **give sb/sth half a ˈchance** to give sb/sth some opportunity to do sth: *That dog will give you a nasty bite, given half a chance.* **ˈno chance** (*spoken*) there is no possibility: *'Do you think he'll do it?' 'No chance.'* **on the ˈoff chance (that)** because of the possibility of sth hap-

pening, although it is unlikely: *I didn't think you'd be at home but I just called by on the off chance.* **stand a ˈchance (of doing sth)** to have the possibility of succeed-ing or achieving sth: *The driver didn't stand a chance of stopping in time.* **take a ˈchance (on sth)** to decide to do sth, knowing that it might be the wrong choice: *We took a chance on the weather and planned to have the party outside.* **take your ˈchances** to take a risk or to use the opportunities that you have and hope that things will happen in the way that you want: *He took his chances and jumped into the water.*—more at CAT, DOG *n.*, EVEN *adj.*, EYE *n.*, FAT *adj.*, FIGHT *v.*, SNOWBALL *n.*, SPORTING
- *verb* **1** (*informal*) to risk sth, although you know the result may not be successful: [VN] *She was chancing her luck driving without a licence. ◊ 'Take an umbrella.' 'No, I'll chance it '* (= take the risk that it may rain). ◊ [V-ing] *I stayed hidden; I couldn't chance coming out.* **2** (*written* or *formal*) to happen or to do sth by chance: [V to inf] *If I do chance to find out where she is, I'll inform you immedi-ately. ◊ They chanced to be staying at the same hotel. ◊* [V (that)] *It chanced (that) they were staying at the same hotel.* **IDM** ˌchance your ˈarm (*BrE*, *informal*) to take a risk although you will probably fail **PHRV** ˈchance on/ upon sb/sth (*formal*) to find or meet sb/sth unexpectedly or by chance: *One day he chanced upon Emma's diary and began reading it.*
- *adj.* [only before noun] not planned: *a chance meeting/ encounter*

chan·cel /ˈtʃɑːnsl; *AmE* ˈtʃænsl/ *noun* the part of a church near the ALTAR, where the priests and the CHOIR (= singers) sit during services

chan·cel·lery /ˈtʃɑːnsələri; *AmE* ˈtʃæn-/ *noun* (*pl.* -ies) **1** [C, usually sing.] the position that a chancellor has in his or her office **2** [sing.+ sing./pl. *v.*] the staff in the depart-ment of a chancellor

chan·cel·lor (also **Chan·cel·lor**) /ˈtʃɑːnsələ(r); *AmE* ˈtʃæns-/ *noun* (often used in a title) **1** the head of govern-ment in Germany or Austria: *Chancellor Schröder* **2** (*BrE*) = CHANCELLOR OF THE EXCHEQUER: *MPs waited for the chancellor's announcement. ◊ the Shadow Chancellor Francis Maude* **3** the official head of a university in Brit-ain. Chancellor is an HONORARY title.—compare VICE CHANCELLOR **4** the head of some American universities **5** used in the titles of some senior state officials in Brit-ain: *the Lord Chancellor* (= a senior law official)

ˌChancellor of the Exˈchequer *noun* (in Britain) the government minister who is responsible for financial affairs

chan·cery /ˈtʃɑːnsəri; *AmE* ˈtʃæns-/ *noun* [sing.] **1 (Chancery)** (*law*) a division of the High Court in Brit-ain **2** (*especially BrE*) an office where public records are kept **3** (also **ˈchancery court**) a court of law in the US that decides legal cases based on the principle of EQUITY **4** the offices where the official representative of a country works, in another country

chancy /ˈtʃɑːnsi; *AmE* ˈtʃænsi/ *adj.* (*informal*) involving risks and uncertainty **SYN** RISKY

chan·de·lier /ˌʃændəˈlɪə(r); *AmE* -ˈlɪr/ *noun* a large round frame with branches that hold lights or candles. Chandeliers are decorated with many small pieces of glass and hang from the ceiling.

chand·ler /ˈtʃɑːndlə(r); *AmE* ˈtʃænd-/ (also **ˈship's chandler**) *noun* a person or shop/store that sells equip-ment for ships

change /tʃeɪndʒ/ *verb, noun*
- *verb*
  BECOME/MAKE DIFFERENT **1** [V] to become different: *Rick hasn't changed. He looks exactly the same as he did at school. ◊ changing attitudes towards education ◊ Her life changed completely when she won the lottery.* **2** [VN] to make sb/sth different: *Fame hasn't really changed him. ◊ Information technology has changed the way people work.* **3 ~ (sb/sth) (from A) to/into B** to pass or make sb/sth pass from one state or form into another: [V] *Caterpillars change into butterflies. ◊ Wait for the traffic lights to change. ◊ The lights changed from red to green. ◊* [VN] *With a wave of her magic wand, she changed the frog into a*

æ	ɑː	e	ɜː	ə	ɪ	iː	i	ɒ	ɔː	ʌ	ʊ	u	uː
cat	father	ten	bird	about	sit	see	many	got	saw	cup	put	actual	too

(BrE)

C

handsome prince. **4** [VN] to stop having one state, position or direction and start having another: *Leaves change colour in autumn.* ◊ *The wind has changed direction.* ◊ *Our ship changed course.*

REPLACE | **5** [VN] ~ **sb/sth (for sb/sth)** | ~ **sth (to sth)** to replace one thing, person, service, etc. with sth new or different: *I want to change my doctor.* ◊ *We change our car every two years.* ◊ *We changed the car for a bigger one.* ◊ *Marie changed her name when she got married.* ◊ *She changed her name to his.* ◊ *That back tyre needs changing.*

EXCHANGE | **6** [VN] ~ **sth (with sb)** (used with a plural object) to exchange positions, places, etc. with sb else, so that you have what they have, and they have what you have: *At half-time the teams change ends.* ◊ *Can we change seats?* ◊ *Can I change seats with you?*

CLOTHES | **7** ~ **(into sth)** | ~ **(out of sth)** to put on different or clean clothes: [V] *I went into the bedroom to change.* ◊ *She changed into her swimsuit.* ◊ *You need to change out of those wet things.* ◊ [VN] *(especially BrE) I didn't have time to get changed before the party* (= to put different clothes on). ◊ *(especially AmE) I didn't have time to change clothes before the party.*

BABY | **8** [VN] to put clean clothes or a clean NAPPY/DIAPER on a baby: *She can't even change a nappy.* ◊ *The baby needs changing.* ◊ *There are baby changing facilities in all our stores.*

BED | **9** [VN] to put clean sheets, etc. on a bed: *to change the sheets* ◊ *Could you help me change the bed?*

MONEY | **10** [VN] ~ **sth (into sth)** to exchange money into the money of another country: *Where can I change my traveller's cheques?* ◊ *to change dollars into yen* **11** [VN] ~ **sth (for/into sth)** to exchange money for the same amount in different coins or notes: *Can you change a £20 note?* ◊ *to change a dollar bill for four quarters*

GOODS | **12** [VN] ~ **sth (for sth)** (BrE) to exchange sth that you have bought for sth else, especially because there is sth wrong with it; to give a customer a new item because there is sth wrong with the one they have bought: *This shirt I bought's too small—I'll have to change it for a bigger one.* ◊ *Of course we'll change it for a larger size, Madam.*

BUS/TRAIN/PLANE | **13** to go from one bus, train, etc. to another in order to continue a journey: [V] *Where do I have to change?* ◊ *Change at Reading (for London).* ◊ [VN] *I stopped in Moscow only to change planes.*
—see also UNCHANGING

IDM **change 'hands** to pass to a different owner: *The house has changed hands several times.* **change horses in mid'stream** to change to a different or new activity while you are in the middle of sth else; to change from supporting one person or thing to another **change your/ sb's 'mind** to change a decision or an opinion: *Nothing will make me change my mind.* **change your 'tune** (informal) to express a different opinion or behave differently when your situation changes: *Wait until it happens to him—he'll soon change his tune.* **change your 'ways** to start to live or behave in a different way from before—more at CHOP v., LEOPARD, PLACE n.

PHRV **,change 'back (into sb/sth)** to return to a previous situation, form, etc. **,change 'back (into sth)** to take off your clothes and put on what you were wearing earlier: *She changed back into her work clothes.* **,change sth 'back (into sth)** to exchange an amount of money into the CURRENCY that it was in before: *You can change back unused dollars into pounds at the bank.* **,change 'down** (BrE) to start using a lower GEAR when you are driving a car, etc: *Change down into second.* **,change 'over (from sth) (to sth)** to change from one system or position to another: *The farm has changed over to organic methods.*—related noun CHANGEOVER **,change 'up** (BrE) to start using a higher GEAR when driving a car, etc: *Change up into fifth.*

■ *noun*

DIFFERENCE | **1** [C, U] ~ **(in/to sth)** the act or result of sth becoming different: *a change in the weather* ◊ *important changes to the tax system* ◊ *There was no change in the*

patient's condition overnight. ◊ *She is someone who hates change.* ◊ *social/political/economic change*

STH NEW AND INTERESTING | **2 (a change)** [sing.] ~ **(from sth)** the fact of a situation, a place or an experience being different from what is usual and therefore likely to be interesting, enjoyable, etc: *Finishing early was a welcome change.* ◊ *Let's stay in tonight for a change.* ◊ *Can you just listen for a change?* ◊ *It makes a change to read some good news for once.*

REPLACING STH | **3** [C] ~ **(of sth)** | ~ **(from sth to sth)** the process of replacing sth with sth new or different; a thing that is used to replace sth: *a change of address* ◊ *The country needs a change of government.* ◊ *a change from agriculture to industry* ◊ *There will be a crew change when we land at Dubai.* ◊ *(BrE) Let's get away for the weekend. A change of scene* (= time in a different place) *will do you good.*

OF CLOTHES | **4** ~ **of clothes, etc.** [C] an extra set of clothes, etc: *She packed a change of clothes for the weekend.* ◊ *I keep a change of shoes in the car.*

MONEY | **5** [U] the money that you get back when you have paid for sth giving more money than the amount it costs: *Don't forget your change!* ◊ *That's 40p change.* ◊ *The ticket machine gives change.* **6** [U] coins rather than paper money: *Do you have any change for the phone?* ◊ *a pound/ dollar in change* (= coins that together are worth one pound/dollar) ◊ *I didn't have any small change* (= coins of low value) *to leave as a tip.* ◊ *He puts his loose change in a money box for the children.* ◊ *Could you give me change for a ten pound note* (= coins or notes that are worth this amount)?

OF BUS/TRAIN/PLANE | **7** [C] an occasion when you go from one bus, train or plane to another during a journey: *The journey involved three changes.*

IDM **a change for the 'better/'worse** a person, thing, situation, etc. that is better/worse than the previous or present one **a ,change of 'heart** if you have **a change of heart**, your attitude towards sth changes, usually making you feel more friendly, helpful, etc. **the ,change of 'life** (informal) = MENOPAUSE **a ,change of 'mind** an act of changing what you think about a situation, etc. **get no change out of sb** (BrE, spoken) to get no help or information from sb—more at RING v., WIND¹ n.

> **WHICH WORD?** (?)
> **change / alter / modify / vary**
>
> **Change** has the most general use and describes any act of making something different: *Marriage has changed her.* ◊ *The rules are always being changed.*
>
> **Alter** can be used instead of **change**, especially when you are talking about the differences between one time and another. It can sound more formal: *Marriage has altered her.* ◊ *The rules are always being altered.*
>
> You also **alter** something by making a difference in its appearance, character or use: *Some of my old dresses will have to be altered to fit me now.* You cannot use **change** here.
>
> **Modify** is more formal than **change** and suggests making something more suitable for a particular situation: *Adults often modify their language when talking to young children.* It is also the word you use when you are talking about making changes to the design of something: *The design of the car has been modified for racing.*
>
> **Vary** describes something that changes often, especially so that it remains interesting and effective: *I think you need to vary your diet a little more.*
>
> **Change**, **alter** and **vary** can also be used without an object: *You never change/alter.* ◊ *Opinions on this vary quite a lot.*

change·able /ˈtʃeɪndʒəbl/ *adj.* likely to change; often changing: *The weather is very changeable at this time of year.*—compare UNCHANGEABLE ▶ **change·abil·ity** /ˌtʃeɪndʒəˈbɪləti/ *noun* [U]

aɪ	aʊ	eɪ	əʊ	oʊ	ɔɪ	ɪə	eə	ʊə	j	w
my	now	say	go	go	boy	near	hair	pure	yes	wet
			(BrE)	(AmE)						

changed /tʃeɪndʒd/ adj. [only before noun] (of people or situations) very different from what they were before: *She's a changed woman since she got that job.* ◊ *This will not be possible in the changed economic climate.* OPP UNCHANGED

change·less /ˈtʃeɪndʒləs/ adj. (formal) never changing

change·ling /ˈtʃeɪndʒlɪŋ/ noun (literary) a child who is believed to have been secretly left in exchange for another, especially (in stories) by FAIRIES

change·over /ˈtʃeɪndʒəʊvə(r); AmE -oʊv-/ noun a change from one system, or method of working to another: *the changeover from a manual to a computerized system* ◊ *a changeover period*

'change purse noun (AmE) a small bag made of leather, plastic, etc. for carrying coins—compare PURSE—picture at MONEY

'changing room noun (BrE) a room for changing clothes in, especially before playing sports—compare LOCKER ROOM

chan·nel /ˈtʃænl/ noun, verb
■ noun
ON TELEVISION/RADIO | **1** [C] a television station: *What's on Channel 4 tonight?* ◊ *a movie/sports channel* ◊ *to change/switch channels* **2** [C] a band of radio waves used for broadcasting television or radio programmes: *terrestrial/satellite channels*
FOR COMMUNICATING | **3** [C] (also **chan·nels** [pl.]) a method or system that people use to get information, to communicate, or to send sth somewhere: *Complaints must be made through the proper channels.* ◊ *The newsletter is a useful channel of communication between teacher and students.* ◊ *The company has worldwide distribution channels.*
FOR IDEAS/FEELINGS | **4** [C] a way of expressing ideas and feelings: *The campaign provided a channel for protest against the war.* ◊ *Music is a great channel for releasing your emotions.*
WATER | **5** [C] a passage that water can flow along, especially in the ground, on the bottom of a river, etc: *drainage channels in the rice fields* **6** [C] a deep passage of water in a river or near the coast that can be used as route for ships **7** [C] a passage of water that connects two areas of water, especially two seas: *the Bristol Channel* **8** (the Channel) [sing.] the area of sea between England and France, also known as **the English Channel**: *the Channel Tunnel* ◊ *cross-Channel ferries*
■ verb (-ll-, AmE usually -l-) [VN]
IDEAS/FEELINGS | **1** ~ sth (into sth) to direct money, feelings, ideas, etc. towards a particular thing or purpose: *He channels his aggression into sport.*
MONEY/HELP | **2** ~ sth (through sth) to send money, help, etc. using a particular route: *Money for the project will be channelled through local government.*
WATER/LIGHT | **3** to carry or send water, light, etc. through a passage: *A sensor channels the light signal along an optical fibre.*

chant /tʃɑːnt; AmE tʃænt/ noun, verb
■ noun **1** [C] words or phrases that a group of people shout or sing again and again: *The crowd broke into chants of 'Out! Out!'* ◊ *football chants* **2** [C,U] a religious song or prayer or a way of singing, using only a few notes that are repeated many times: *a Buddhist chant*—see also GREGORIAN CHANT
■ verb **1** to sing or shout the same words or phrases many times: [VN] *The crowd chanted their hero's name.* ◊ [V] *A group of protesters, chanting and carrying placards, waited outside.* ◊ [V+speech] *'Resign! Resign!' they chanted.* **2** [V, VN] to sing or say a religious song or prayer using only a few notes that are repeated many times
▶ **chant·ing** noun [U]: *The chanting rose in volume.*

chanty, chantey (AmE) = SHANTY (2)
Cha·nuk·kah = HANUKKAH
chaos /ˈkeɪɒs; AmE ˈkeɪɑːs/ noun [U] a state of complete confusion and disorder: *economic/political/domestic chaos* ◊ *Heavy snow has caused total chaos on the roads.* ◊ *The house was in chaos after the party.*

'chaos theory noun [U] (mathematics) the study of a group of connected things that are very sensitive so that small changes in conditions affect them very much

cha·ot·ic /keɪˈɒtɪk; AmE -ˈɑːtɪk/ adj. in a state of complete confusion and disorder: *The traffic in the city is chaotic in the rush hour.* ▶ **cha·ot·ic·al·ly** /keɪˈɒtɪkli; AmE -ˈɑːtɪk-/ adv.

chap /tʃæp/ noun (BrE, informal, becoming old-fashioned) used to talk about a man in a friendly way: *He isn't such a bad chap really.*

chap. abbr. (in writing) chapter

chap·ar·ral /ˌʃæpəˈræl/ noun [U] (AmE) an area of dry land that is covered with small bushes

cha·patti (also **cha·pati**) /tʃəˈpæti; -ˈpɑːti/ noun a type of flat round Indian bread

chapel /ˈtʃæpl/ noun **1** [C] a small building or room used for Christian worship in a school, prison, large private house, etc: *a college chapel* **2** [C] a separate part of a church or CATHEDRAL, with its own ALTAR, used for some services and private prayer **3** [C,U] (BrE) the word for a church used in some Christian DENOMINATIONS, for example by Nonconformists in Britain: *a Methodist chapel* ◊ *a Mormon chapel* ◊ *She always went to chapel on Sundays.* **4** [C] a small church: *a tiny chapel in the mountains* **5** [C] a small building or room used for funeral services, especially at a CEMETERY or CREMATORIUM: *a chapel of rest*

chap·er·one (BrE also **chap·eron**) /ˈʃæpərəʊn; AmE -oʊn/ noun, verb
■ noun **1** (in the past) an older woman who, on social occasions, took care of a young woman who was not married **2** a person who takes care of children in public, especially when they are working, for example as actors **3** (AmE) a person, such as a parent or a teacher, who goes with a group of young people on a trip or to a dance to encourage good behaviour
■ verb [VN] to act as a chaperone for sb, especially a woman

chap·lain /ˈtʃæplɪn/ noun a priest or other Christian minister who is responsible for the religious needs of people in a prison, hospital, etc. or in the armed forces—compare PADRE, PRIEST

chap·lain·cy /ˈtʃæplɪnsi/ noun (pl. -ies) the position or work of a chaplain; the place where a chaplain works

chapped /tʃæpt/ adj. (of the skin or lips) rough, dry and sore, especially because of wind or cold weather

chaps /tʃæps/ noun [pl.] protective leather coverings worn over trousers/pants by COWBOYS, etc. when riding a horse: *a pair of chaps*

chap·ter /ˈtʃæptə(r)/ noun **1** (abbr. **chap.**) [C] a separate section of a book, usually with a number or title: *I've just finished Chapter 3.* ◊ *in the previous/next/last chapter* ◊ *Have you read the chapter on the legal system?* **2** [C] a period of time in a person's life or in history: *a difficult chapter in our country's history* **3** [C+sing./pl. v.] all the priests of a CATHEDRAL or members of a religious community: *a meeting of the dean and chapter* **4** [C] (especially AmE) a local branch of a society, club, etc: *the local chapter of the Rotary club* IDM **,chapter and 'verse** the exact details of sth, especially the exact place where particular information may be found: *I can't give chapter and verse, but that's the rough outline of our legal position.* **a ,chapter of 'accidents** (BrE, written) a series of unfortunate events

'chapter house noun a building where all the priests of a CATHEDRAL or members of a religious community meet

char /tʃɑː(r)/ verb, noun
■ verb (-rr-) **1** [V, VN] to become black by burning; to make sth black by burning it—see also CHARRED **2** [V] (old-fashioned, BrE) to work as a cleaner in a house
■ noun (old-fashioned, BrE) **1** [C] = CHARWOMAN **2** [U] (informal) tea: *a cup of char*

chara·banc /ˈʃærəbæŋ/ noun (old-fashioned, BrE) an early type of bus, used in the past especially for pleasure trips

char·ac·ter /ˈkærəktə(r)/ noun
QUALITIES/FEATURES | **1** [C, usually sing.] all the qualities and features that make a person, groups of people, and

C

places different from others: *to have a strong/weak character* ◊ *character traits/defects* ◊ *The book gives a fascinating insight into Mrs Blair's character.* ◊ *Generosity is part of the American character.* ◊ *The character of the neighbourhood hasn't changed at all.* **2** [C usually sing, U] the way that sth is, or a particular quality or feature that a thing, an event or a place has: *the delicate character of the light in the evening* ◊ *buildings that are very simple in character* **3** [U] (*approving*) strong personal qualities such as the ability to deal with difficult or dangerous situations: *Everyone admires her strength of character and determination.* ◊ *He showed great character returning to the sport after his accident.* ◊ *Adventure camps are considered to be character-building* (= meant to improve sb's strong qualities). **4** [U] (usually *approving*) the interesting or unusual quality that a place or a person has: *The modern hotels here have no real character.* ◊ *a face with a lot of character*

STRANGE/INTERESTING PERSON | **5** [C] (*informal*) (used with an adjective) a person, particularly an unpleasant or strange one: *There were some really strange characters hanging around the bar.* **6** [C] (*informal*) an interesting or unusual person: *She's a character!*

REPUTATION | **7** [C, U] (*formal*) the opinion that people have of you, particularly of whether you can be trusted or relied on: *a man of good character and integrity* ◊ *She was a victim of character assassination* (= an unfair attack on the good opinion people had of her). ◊ *a slur/attack on his character*

IN BOOK/PLAY/MOVIE | **8** [C] a person or an animal in a book, play or film/movie: *a major/minor character in the book* ◊ *cartoon characters*

SYMBOL/LETTER | **9** [C] a letter, sign, mark or symbol used in writing, printing or on computers: *Chinese characters* ◊ *a line 30 characters long*

IDM ˌin ˈcharacter | ˌout of ˈcharacter typical/not typical of a person's character: *Her behaviour last night was completely out of character.* ˌin ˈcharacter (with sth) in the same style as sth: *The new wing of the museum was not really in character with the rest of the building.*

ˈcharacter actor *noun* an actor who always takes the parts of interesting or unusual people

char·ac·ter·ful /ˈkærəktəfl; *AmE* -tərfl/ *adj.* (*written*) very interesting and unusual

char·ac·ter·is·tic /ˌkærəktəˈrɪstɪk/ *adj., noun*
■ *adj.* ~ (of sth/sb) very typical of sth or of sb's character: *She spoke with characteristic enthusiasm.* **OPP** UNCHARACTERISTIC ▸ **char·ac·ter·is·tic·al·ly** *adv.*: *Characteristically, Helen paid for everyone.*
■ *noun* ~ (of sth/sb) a typical feature or quality that sth/sb has: *The need to communicate is a key characteristic of human society.* ◊ *The two groups of children have quite different characteristics.* ◊ *Personal characteristics, such as age, sex and marital status are taken into account.* ◊ *genetic characteristics*

char·ac·ter·iza·tion (*BrE* also **-isa·tion**) /ˌkærəktəraɪˈzeɪʃn/ *noun* [U, C] **1** the way that a writer makes characters in a book or play seem real **2** (*formal*) the way in which sb/sth is described or defined: *the characterization of physics as the study of simplicity*

char·ac·ter·ize (*BrE* also **-ise**) /ˈkærəktəraɪz/ *verb* [VN] (*formal*) **1** to be typical of a person, place or thing: *the rolling hills that characterize this part of England* **2** [often passive] to give sth its typical or most noticeable qualities or features: *The city is characterized by tall modern buildings in steel and glass.* **3** ~ sb/sth (as sth) to describe or show the qualities of sb/sth in a particular way: *activities that are characterized as 'male' or 'female' work* ◊ *How would you characterize the mood of the 1990s?*

char·ac·ter·less /ˈkærəktələs; *AmE* -tərləs/ *adj.* having no interesting qualities

cha·rade /ʃəˈrɑːd; *AmE* ʃəˈreɪd/ *noun* **1** [C] a situation in which people pretend that sth is true when it clearly is not: *Their whole marriage had been a charade—they had never loved each other.* **2** (**charades**) [U] a game in which one player acts out the syllables of a word or title and the other players try to guess what it is: *Let's play charades.*

char·coal /ˈtʃɑːkəʊl; *AmE* ˈtʃɑːrkoʊl/ *noun* [U] **1** a black substance made by burning wood slowly in an oven with little air. Charcoal is used as a fuel or for drawing: *charcoal grilled steaks* ◊ *a charcoal drawing* **2** (also ˌcharcoal ˈgrey) a very dark grey colour

chard /tʃɑːd; *AmE* tʃɑːrd/ (also ˌSwiss ˈchard) *noun* [U] a vegetable with thick white stems and large leaves

charge /tʃɑːdʒ; *AmE* tʃɑːrdʒ/ *noun, verb*
■ *noun*
MONEY | **1** [C, U] ~ (for sth) the amount of money that sb asks for goods and services: *We have to make a small charge for refreshments.* ◊ *admission charges* ◊ *Delivery is free of charge.* ⇨ note at PRICE **2** [C, U] (*AmE, informal*) CHARGE ACCOUNT, CREDIT ACCOUNT: *Would you like to put that on your charge?* '*Are you paying cash?*' '*No, it'll be a charge.*'

OF CRIME/STH WRONG | **3** [C, U] an official claim made by the police that sb has committed a crime: *criminal charges* ◊ *a murder/assault charge* ◊ *He will be sent back to England to face a charge of* (= to be on trial for) *armed robbery.* ◊ *They decided to* **drop the charges** *against the newspaper and settle out of court.* ◊ *After being questioned by the police, she was released* **without charge.** **4** [C] a statement accusing sb of doing sth wrong or bad: *She rejected the charge that the story was untrue.* ◊ *Be careful you don't* **leave yourself open to charges** *of political bias.*

RESPONSIBILITY | **5** [U] a position of having control over sb/sth; responsibility for sb/sth: *She has charge of the day-to-day running of the business.* ◊ *They left the au pair* **in charge of** *the children for a week.* ◊ *He* **took charge of** *the farm after his father's death.* ◊ *I'm leaving the school in your charge.* **6** [C] (*formal* or *humorous*) a person that you have responsibility for and care for

ELECTRICITY | **7** [C, U] the amount of electricity that is put into a battery or carried by a substance: *a positive/negative charge*

RUSH/ATTACK | **8** [C] a sudden rush or violent attack, for example by soldiers, wild animals or players of a game such as football: *He led the charge down the field.*

EXPLOSIVE | **9** [C] the amount of explosive material needed to fire a gun or make an explosion—see also DEPTH CHARGE

STRONG FEELING | **10** [sing.] the power to cause strong feelings: *the emotional charge of the piano piece*

TASK | **11** [sing.] (*formal*) a task or duty: *His charge was to obtain specific information.*

IDM **bring/press/prefer ˈcharges against sb** (*law*) to accuse sb formally of a crime so that there can be a trial in a court of law **get a ˈcharge out of sth** (*AmE*) to get a strong feeling of excitement or pleasure from sth—more at REVERSE *v.*

■ *verb*
MONEY | **1** ~ (sb/sth) for sth | ~ (sb) sth (for sth) to ask an amount of money for goods or a service: [VN] *What did they charge for the repairs?* ◊ *The restaurant charged £20 for dinner.* ◊ *We won't charge you for delivery.* ◊ *They're charging £3 for the catalogue.* ◊ [VNN] *He only charged me half price.* ◊ [V] *Do you think museums should charge for admission?* [also V to inf, VN to inf] **2** [VN] ~ sth to sth to record the cost of sth as an amount that sb has to pay: *They charge the calls to their credit-card account.* ◊ (*AmE*) *Don't worry. I'll charge it* (= pay by credit card).

WITH CRIME/STH WRONG | **3** [VN] ~ sb (with sth/with doing sth) to accuse sb formally of a crime so that there can be a trial in a court of law: *He was charged with murder.* ◊ *Several people were arrested but nobody was charged.* **4** [VN] ~ sb (with sth/with doing sth) (*formal*) to accuse sb publicly of doing sth wrong or bad: *Opposition MPs charged the minister with neglecting her duty.*

RUSH/ATTACK | **5** to rush forward and attack sb/sth: [V] *The bull put its head down and charged.* ◊ *We charged at the enemy.* [also VN] **6** [V+adv./prep.] to rush in a particular direction: *The children charged down the stairs.* ◊ *He came charging into my room and demanded to know what was going on.*

WITH RESPONSIBILITY/TASK | **7** [VN] (usually passive) ~ sb with sth (*formal*) to give sb a responsibility or task: *The*

s	t	v	z	.	ʃ	ʒ		tʃ	dʒ	θ	ð	ŋ
see	tea	van	zoo		shoe	vision		chain	jam	thin	this	sing

committee has been charged with the development of sport in the region. ◊ *The governing body is charged with managing the school within its budget.*

WITH ELECTRICITY | **8** [VN] **~ (sth) (up)** to pass electricity through sth so that it is stored there: *Before use, the battery must be charged.* ◊ *The shaver can be charged up and used when travelling.*

WITH STRONG FEELING | **9** [VN] (usually passive) **~ sth (with sth)** (*written*) to fill sb with an emotion: *The room was charged with hatred.* ◊ *a highly charged atmosphere*

GLASS | **10** [VN] (*BrE, formal*) to fill a glass: *Please charge your glasses and drink a toast to the bride and groom!*

GUN | **11** [VN] (*old use*) to load a gun

charge·able /ˈtʃɑːdʒəbl; *AmE* ˈtʃɑːrdʒ-/ *adj.* **~ (to sb/ sth) 1** (of a sum of money) that must be paid by sb: *Any expenses you may incur will be chargeable to the company.* **2** (of income or other money that you earn) that you must pay tax on: *chargeable earnings/income*

ˈ**charge account** *noun* (*AmE*) = ACCOUNT *n* (3)

ˈ**charge capping** *noun* [U] (*BrE*) the act of setting a limit on the amount of money that the local government of an area can charge people in order to pay for public services

ˈ**charge card** *noun* a small plastic card provided by a shop/store which you use to buy goods there, paying for them later—see also CREDIT CARD

chargé d'af·faires /ˌʃɑːʒeɪ dæˈfeə(r); *AmE* ˌʃɑːrʒeɪ dæˈfer/ *noun* (*pl.* **chargés d'af·faires** /ˌʃɑːʒeɪ dæˈfeə(r); *AmE* ˌʃɑːrʒeɪ dæˈfer/) (from *French*) **1** an official who takes the place of an AMBASSADOR in a foreign country when he or she is away **2** an official below the rank of AMBASSADOR who acts as the senior representative of his or her country in a foreign country where there is no AMBASSADOR

charge·hand /ˈtʃɑːdʒhænd; *AmE* ˈtʃɑːrdʒ-/ *noun* (*BrE*) a worker in charge of others on a particular job, but below the rank of a FOREMAN

ˈ**charge nurse** *noun* (*BrE*) a nurse, especially a man, who is in charge of a hospital WARD

char·ger /ˈtʃɑːdʒə(r); *AmE* ˈtʃɑːrdʒ-/ *noun* **1** a piece of equipment for loading a battery with electricity **2** (*old use*) a horse that a soldier or KNIGHT rode in battle in the past

ˈ**charge sheet** *noun* (*BrE*) a record kept in a police station of the names of people that the police have stated to be guilty of a crime (= that they have charged)

char·iot /ˈtʃæriət/ *noun* an open vehicle with two wheels, pulled by horses, used in ancient times in battle and for racing

char·iot·eer /ˌtʃæriəˈtɪə(r); *AmE* -ˈtɪr/ *noun* the driver of a chariot

cha·ris·ma /kəˈrɪzmə/ *noun* [U] the powerful personal quality that some people have to attract and impress other people: *The President has great personal charisma.* ◊ *a lack of charisma*

cha·ris·mat·ic /ˌkærɪzˈmætɪk/ *adj., noun*
■ *adj.* **1** having charisma: *a charismatic figure/leader/personality* **2** (of a Christian religious group) believing in special gifts from God; worshipping in a very enthusiastic way: *the charismatic movement*
■ *noun* (often **Charismatic**) a charismatic Christian

char·it·able /ˈtʃærətəbl/ *adj.* **1** connected with a charity or charities: *a charitable institution/foundation/trust* ◊ *a charitable donation/gift* ◊ (*BrE*) *to have charitable status* (= to be an official charity) **2** helping people who are poor or in need: *His later years were devoted largely to charitable work.* **3** kind in your attitude to other people, especially when you are judging them: *Let's be charitable and assume she just made a mistake.* OPP UNCHARITABLE
► **char·it·ably** /-bli/ *adv.*: *Try to think about him a little more charitably.*

char·ity /ˈtʃærəti/ *noun* (*pl.* **-ies**) **1** [C] an organization for helping people in need: *Many charities sent money to help the victims of the famine.* ◊ *The concert will raise money for local charities.* **2** [U] the aim of giving money, food, help, etc. to people who are in need: *Most of the*

runners in the London Marathon are **raising money for charity**. ◊ *Do you give much to charity?* ◊ *a charity concert* (= organized to get money for charity) ◊ *to live on/off charity* (= to live on money which other people give you because you are poor) **3** [U] (*formal*) kindness and sympathy towards other people, especially when you are judging them: *Her article showed no charity towards her former friends.* IDM **charity begins at ˈhome** (*saying*) you should help and care for your own family, etc. before you start helping other people

ˈ**charity shop** *noun* (*BrE*) a shop that sells clothes and other goods given by people to raise money for a charity

char·lady /ˈtʃɑːleɪdi; *AmE* ˈtʃɑːr-/ *noun* (*pl.* **-ies**) (*old-fashioned, BrE*) = CHARWOMAN

char·la·tan /ˈʃɑːlətən; *AmE* ˈʃɑːrl-/ *noun* a person who claims to have knowledge or skills that they do not really have

Charles·ton /ˈtʃɑːlstən; *AmE* ˈtʃɑːrl-/ *noun* (usually **the Charleston**) [sing.] a fast dance that was popular in the 1920s

char·ley horse /ˈtʃɑːli hɔːs; *AmE* ˈtʃɑːrli hɔːrs/ *noun* [usually sing.] (*AmE, informal*) = CRAMP: *Ow! I just got a charley horse in my leg.*

char·lie /ˈtʃɑːli; *AmE* ˈtʃɑːrli/ *noun* (*old-fashioned, BrE, spoken*) a silly person: *You must have felt a proper charlie!*

charm /tʃɑːm; *AmE* tʃɑːrm/ *noun, verb*
■ *noun* **1** [U] the power of pleasing or attracting people: *a man of great charm* ◊ *The hotel is full of charm and character.* **2** [C] a feature or quality that is pleasing or attractive: *her physical charms* (= her beauty) **3** [C] a small object worn on a chain or BRACELET, that is believed to bring good luck: *a lucky charm* ◊ *a charm bracelet*—picture at JEWELLERY **4** [C] an act or words believed to have magic power SYN SPELL IDM **¡work like a ˈcharm** to be immediately and completely successful—more at THIRD
■ *verb* **1** to please or attract sb in order to make them like you or do what you want: [VN] *He was charmed by her beauty and wit.* ◊ [V] *Her words had lost their power to charm.* **2** [VN] to control or protect sb/sth using magic, or as if using magic: *He has led a charmed life* (= he has been lucky even in dangerous or difficult situations). PHRV **¡charm sth ˈout of sb** to obtain sth such as information, money, etc. from sb by using charm

¡charmed ˈcircle *noun* [sing.] (*written*) a group of people who have special influence

charm·er /ˈtʃɑːmə(r); *AmE* ˈtʃɑːrm-/ *noun* a person who acts in a way that makes them attractive to other people, sometimes using this to influence others—see also SNAKE CHARMER

charm·ing /ˈtʃɑːmɪŋ; *AmE* ˈtʃɑːrmɪŋ/ *adj.* **1** very pleasant or attractive: *The cottage is tiny, but it's charming.* ◊ *She's a charming person.* **2** (*ironic, spoken*) used to show that you have a low opinion of sb's behaviour: *They left me to tidy it all up myself. Charming, wasn't it?* ► **charm·ing·ly** *adv.*

charm·less /ˈtʃɑːmləs; *AmE* ˈtʃɑːrm-/ *adj.* (*written*) not at all pleasant or interesting: *a charmless industrial town*

ˈ**charm offensive** *noun* a situation in which a person, for example a politician, is especially friendly and pleasant in order to get other people to like them and to support their point of view

char·nel house /ˈtʃɑːnl haʊs; *AmE* ˈtʃɑːrnl/ *noun* a place used in the past for keeping dead human bodies or bones

charred /tʃɑːd; *AmE* tʃɑːrd/ *adj.* [usually before noun] burnt and black: *the charred remains of a burnt-out car*

chart /tʃɑːt; *AmE* tʃɑːrt/ *noun, verb*

bar chart   flow chart   pie chart

æ	ɑː	e	ɜː	ə	ɪ	iː	i	ɒ	ɔː	ʌ	ʊ	u	uː
cat	father	ten	bird	about	sit	see	many	got	saw	cup	put	actual	too

(BrE)

C

■ noun **1** [C] a page or sheet of information in the form of diagrams, lists of figures, etc: *a weather chart* ◊ *a sales chart* (= showing the level of a company's sales)—see also BAR CHART, FLOW CHART, PIE CHART **2** [C] a detailed map of the sea: *a naval chart* **3** (**the charts**) [pl.] (*especially BrE*) a list, produced each week, of the pop music records that have sold the most copies: *'Two Tribes' went straight into the charts at number 1.* ◊ *to top the charts* (= to be the record that has sold more copies than all the others)
■ verb [VN] **1** to record or follow the progress or development of sb/sth: *The exhibition charts the history of the palace.* **2** to plan a course of action: *She had carefully charted her route to the top of her profession.* **3** to make a map of an area [SYN] MAP: *Cook charted the coast of New Zealand in 1768.*

char·ter /ˈtʃɑːtə(r); *AmE* ˈtʃɑːrt-/ *noun, verb*
■ noun **1** [C] a written statement describing the rights that a particular group of people should have: *the European Union's Social Charter of workers' rights* **2** [C] a written statement of the principles and aims of an organization [SYN] CONSTITUTION: *the United Nations Charter* **3** [C] an official document stating that a ruler or government allows a new organization, town or university to be established and gives it particular rights and privileges: *The Royal College received its charter as a university in 1967.* **4** [sing.] (~ **for sth**) (*BrE*) a law or policy that seems likely to help criminals: *The new law will be a charter for unscrupulous financial advisers.* ◊ *a blackmailer's charter* **5** [U] the hiring of a plane, boat, etc: *a yacht available for charter*
■ verb [VN] **1** to hire/rent a plane, boat, etc. for your own use: *a chartered plane* **2** to state officially that a new organization, town or university has been established and has special rights and privileges

char·tered /ˈtʃɑːtəd; *AmE* ˈtʃɑːrtərd/ *adj.* [only before noun] **1** (*BrE*) qualified according to the rules of a professional organization that has a royal charter: *a chartered surveyor/engineer* **2** (of an aircraft, a ship or a boat) hired for a particular purpose: *a chartered plane*

chartered ac'countant (*BrE*) (*AmE* **certified public ac'countant**) *noun* a fully trained and qualified ACCOUNTANT

'charter flight *noun* a flight in an aircraft in which all the seats are paid for by a travel company and then sold to their customers, usually at a lower cost than that of a SCHEDULED FLIGHT

charter 'member *noun* (*AmE*) = FOUNDER MEMBER

char·treuse /ʃɑːˈtrɜːz; *AmE* ʃɑːrˈtruːz/ *noun* [U] **1** a green or yellow LIQUEUR (= a strong sweet alcoholic drink) **2** a pale yellow or pale green colour

char·woman /ˈtʃɑːwʊmən; *AmE* ˈtʃɑːr-/ *noun* (*pl.* **-women** /-wɪmɪn/) (*BrE also* **char**, **char·lady**) (*old-fashioned*) a woman whose job is to clean a house, an office building, etc.

chary /ˈtʃeəri; *AmE* ˈtʃeri/ *adj.* ~ **of sth/of doing sth** not willing to risk doing sth; fearing possible problems if you do sth [SYN] WARY

chase /tʃeɪs/ *verb, noun*
■ verb
RUN/DRIVE AFTER | **1** [VN] ~ (**after**) **sb/sth** to run, drive, etc. after sb/sth in order to catch them: [VN] *My dog likes chasing rabbits.* ◊ *The kids chased each other around the kitchen table.* ◊ [V] *He chased after the burglar but couldn't catch him.*
MONEY/WORK/SUCCESS | **2** [VN] to try to obtain or achieve sth, for example money, work or success: *Too many people are chasing too few jobs nowadays.* ◊ *The team is chasing its first win in five games.*
MAN/WOMAN | **3** ~ (**after**) **sb** (*informal*) to try to persuade sb to have a sexual relationship with you: [V] *Kevin's been chasing after Jan for months.* ◊ [VN] *Girls are always chasing him.*
REMIND SB | **4** [VN] (*informal*) to persuade sb to do sth that they should have done already: *I need to chase him about organizing the meeting.*
RUSH | **5** [V+*adv.*/*prep.*] (*informal*) to rush or hurry some-

where: *I've been chasing around town all morning looking for a present for Sharon.*
METAL | **6** [VN] (*technical*) to cut patterns or designs on metal: *chased silver*
[PHRV] **chase sb/sth ⟨‣a'way, 'off, 'out, etc.** to force sb/sth to run away: *Chase the cat out—we don't want her in the kitchen.* **chase sb ⟨‣'up 1** to remind sb to do sth that they should have done already: *We need to chase up all members who have not yet paid.* **2** (*BrE*) (*AmE* **chase sth ⟨‣'down**) to find sth that is needed; to deal with sth that has been forgotten: *My job was to chase up late replies.*
■ noun
RUNNING/DRIVING AFTER | **1** [C] (often used with *the*) an act of running or driving after sb/sth in order to catch them: *The thieves were caught by police after a short chase.* ◊ *a high-speed car chase* ◊ *We lost him in the narrow streets and had to give up the chase* (= stop chasing him). ◊ *to take up the chase* (= start chasing sb)
FOR SUCCESS/MONEY/WORK | **2** [sing.] a process of trying hard to get sth: *Three teams are involved in the chase for the championship.*
IN SPORT | **3** (**the chase**) [sing.] hunting animals as a sport **4** [C] = STEEPLECHASE—see also WILD GOOSE CHASE
[IDM] **give 'chase** to begin to run after sb/sth in order to catch them: *We gave chase along the footpath.*

chaser /ˈtʃeɪsə(r)/ *noun* **1** a drink that you have after another of a different kind, for example a stronger alcoholic drink after a weak one: *a beer with a whisky chaser* **2** a horse for STEEPLECHASE racing (= in which horses must jump over a series of fences)

chasm /ˈkæzəm/ *noun* **1** [C] (*literary*) a deep crack or opening in the ground **2** [sing.] ~ (**between A and B**) (*formal*) a very big difference between two people or groups, for example because they have different attitudes

chas·sis /ˈʃæsi/ *noun* (*pl.* **chas·sis**) the frame that a vehicle is built on

chaste /tʃeɪst/ *adj.* **1** (*old-fashioned*) not having sex with anyone; only having sex with the person that you are married to: *to remain chaste* **2** (*formal*) not expressing sexual feelings: *She gave him a chaste kiss on the cheek.* **3** (*formal*) simple and plain in style; not decorated: *the cool, chaste interior of the hall* ◊ *She wore a chaste gold chain around her neck.* ▶ **chaste·ly** *adv.*: *He kissed her chastely on the cheek.*

chas·ten /ˈtʃeɪsn/ *verb* [VN] [usually passive] (*formal*) to make sb feel sorry for sth they have done: *He felt suitably chastened and apologized.* ◊ *She gave them a chastening lecture.*

chas·tise /tʃæˈstaɪz/ *verb* [VN] **1** ~ **sb** (**for sth/for doing sth**) (*formal*) to criticize sb for doing sth wrong: *He chastised the team for their lack of commitment.* **2** (*old-fashioned*) to punish sb physically ▶ **chas·tise·ment** /tʃæˈstaɪzmənt; ˈtʃæstɪzmənt/ *noun* [U]

chas·tity /ˈtʃæstəti/ *noun* [U] the state of not having sex with anyone or only having sex with the person you are married to; being CHASTE: *vows of chastity* (= those taken by some priests)

chat /tʃæt/ *verb, noun*
■ verb (**-tt-**) [V] ~ (**away**) (**to/with sb**)| ~ (**about sth/sb**) to talk in a friendly informal way to sb: *My kids spend hours chatting on the phone to their friends.* ◊ *Within minutes of being introduced they were chatting away like old friends.* ◊ *What were you chatting about?* [PHRV] **chat sb ⟨‣'up** (*BrE, informal*) to talk in a friendly way to sb you are sexually attracted to: *She went straight over and tried to chat him up.*
■ noun **1** [C] (*especially BrE*) a friendly informal conversation: *I just called in for a chat.* ◊ *I had a long chat with her.* **2** [U] talking, especially informal conversation: *That's enough chat from me—on with the music!*

cha·teau (*also* **châ·teau**) /ˈʃætəʊ; *AmE* ʃæˈtoʊ/ *noun* (*pl.* **cha·teaux** *or* **cha·teaus** /-təʊz; *AmE* -ˈtoʊz/) (from *French*) a castle or large country house in France

chat·line /ˈtʃætlaɪn/ *noun* a telephone service which allows a conversation among a number of people who call in separately

aɪ	aʊ	eɪ	əʊ	oʊ	ɔɪ	ɪə	eə	ʊə	j	w
my	now	say	go (BrE)	go (AmE)	boy	near	hair	pure	yes	wet

'chat room *noun* an area on the Internet where people can communicate with each other, usually about one particular topic

'chat show (*BrE*) (also **'talk show** *AmE*, *BrE*) *noun* a television or radio programme in which people are asked questions and talk in an informal way about their work and opinions on various topics: *a chat-show host*

chat·tel /'tʃætl/ *noun* [C, U] (*law* or *old-fashioned*) something that belongs to you: *Women are now considered as equal partners, not as chattels or housekeepers.*—see also GOODS AND CHATTELS

chat·ter /'tʃætə(r)/ *verb, noun*
■ *verb* [V] **1 ~ (away/on) (to sb) (about sth)** to talk quickly and continuously, especially about things that are not important: *They chattered away happily for a while.* ◇ *The children chattered to each other excitedly about the next day's events.* **2** (of teeth) to knock together continuously because you are cold or frightened **3** (of birds or monkeys) to make a series of short high sounds **IDM** **the 'chattering classes** (*BrE*) the people in society who like to give their opinions on political or social issues
■ *noun* [U] **1** continuous rapid talk about things that are not important: *Jane's constant chatter was beginning to annoy him.* ◇ *idle chatter* **2** a series of quick short high sounds that some animals make: *the chatter of monkeys* **3** a series of short sounds made by things knocking together: *the chatter of teeth*

chat·ter·box /'tʃætəbɒks; *AmE* 'tʃætərbɑːks/ *noun* (*informal*) a person who talks a lot, especially a child

chatty /'tʃæti/ *adj.* (*informal, especially BrE*) **1** talking a lot in a friendly way: *You're very chatty today, Alice.* **2** having a friendly informal style: *a chatty letter*

chauf·feur /'ʃəʊfə(r); *AmE* ʃoʊ'fɜːr/ *noun, verb*
■ *noun* a person whose job is to drive a car, especially for sb rich or important
■ *verb* [VN] to drive sb in a car, usually as your job: *He was chauffeured to all his meetings.* ◇ *a chauffeured limousine*

chau·vin·ism /'ʃəʊvɪnɪzəm; *AmE* 'ʃoʊ-/ *noun* [U] (*disapproving*) **1** an aggressive and unreasonable belief that your own country is better than all others: *It was a typical case of British chauvinism and insularity.* **2** = MALE CHAUVINISM

chau·vin·ist /'ʃəʊvɪnɪst; *AmE* 'ʃoʊ-/ *noun* **1** = MALE CHAUVINIST **2** a person who has an aggressive and unreasonable belief that their own country is better than all others ▶ **chau·vin·is·tic** /ˌʃəʊvɪ'nɪstɪk; *AmE* ˌʃoʊ-/ (also *less frequent* **chau·vin·ist**) *adj.* **chau·vin·is·tic·al·ly** /-kli/ *adv.*

ChB /ˌsi: eɪtʃ 'biː/ *abbr.* (*BrE*) Bachelor of Surgery

cheap /tʃiːp/ *adj., adv.*
■ *adj.* (**cheap·er, cheap·est**)
LOW PRICE | **1** costing little money or less money than you expected: *cheap fares* ◇ *Personal computers are cheap and getting cheaper.* ◇ *Cycling is a cheap way to get around.* ◇ (*BrE*) *The printer isn't exactly cheap at £200.* ◇ *immigrant workers, used as a source of* **cheap labour** (= workers who are paid very little, especially unfairly)—see also DIRT CHEAP **2** charging low prices: *a cheap restaurant/hotel* ◇ (*BrE*) *We found a* **cheap and cheerful** *cafe* (= one that is simple and charges low prices but is pleasant).
POOR QUALITY | **3** (*disapproving*) low in price and quality: *cheap perfume/jewellery/shoes* ◇ (*BrE*) *a* **cheap and nasty** *bottle of wine*
UNKIND | **4** unpleasant or unkind and rather obvious: *I was tired of his cheap jokes at my expense.*
LOW STATUS | **5** (*disapproving*) having a low status and therefore not deserving respect: *He's just a cheap crook.* ◇ *His treatment of her made her* **feel cheap** (= ashamed, because she had lost her respect for herself).
NOT GENEROUS | **6** (*AmE*) (*BrE* **mean**) (*informal, disapproving*) not liking to spend money: *Don't be so cheap!*
▶ **cheap·ness** *noun* [U]
IDM **cheap at the 'price** (*BrE*) (*AmE* **cheap at 'twice the price**) so good or useful that the cost does not seem too much **on the 'cheap** spending less money than you usually need to spend to do sth: *a guide to decorating your house on the cheap*—more at LIFE

■ *adv.* (*comparative* **cheap·er** no *superlative*) (*informal*) for a low price: *I got this dress cheap in a sale.*
IDM **be ˌgoing 'cheap** to be offered for sale at a lower price than usual **sth does not come 'cheap** something is expensive: *Violins like this don't come cheap.*

cheap·en /'tʃiːpən/ *verb* [VN] **1** to make sb lose respect for himself or herself **SYN** DEGRADE: *She never cheapened herself by lowering her standards.* **2** to make sth lower in price: *to cheapen the cost of raw materials* **3** to make sth appear to have less value: *The movie was accused of cheapening human life.*

cheap·ly /'tʃiːpli/ *adv.* without spending or costing much money: *I'm sure I could buy this more cheaply somewhere else.* ◇ *a cheaply made movie*

cheapo /'tʃiːpəʊ; *AmE* -poʊ/ *adj.* [only before noun] (*informal, disapproving*) cheap and often of poor quality

cheap·skate /'tʃiːpskeɪt/ *noun* (*informal, disapproving*) a person who does not like to spend money

cheat /tʃiːt/ *verb, noun*
■ *verb* **1** [VN] to trick or deceive sb, especially when they trust you: *She is accused of attempting to cheat the taxman.* ◇ *Many people* **feel cheated** *by the government's refusal to hold a referendum.* ◇ *He* **cheated his way** *into the job.* **2** [V] **~ (at sth)** to act in a dishonest way in order to gain an advantage, especially in a game, a competition, an exam, etc: *He cheats at cards.* ◇ *You're not allowed to look at the answers—that's cheating.* **3** [V] **~ (on sb)** (of sb who is married or who has a regular sexual partner) to have a secret sexual relationship with sb else **IDM** **cheat 'death** (often used in newspapers) to survive in a situation where you could have died **PHRV** **ˌcheat sb ('out) of sth** to prevent sb from having sth, especially in a way that is not honest or fair: *They cheated him out of his share of the profits.*
■ *noun* (*especially BrE*) **1** (also **cheat·er** especially in *AmE*) [C] a person who cheats, especially in a game: *You little cheat!* **2** [sing.] something that seems unfair or dishonest, for example a way of doing sth with less effort than it usually needs: *It's really a cheat, but you can use ready-made pastry if you want.*

check /tʃek/ *verb, noun, exclamation*
■ *verb*
EXAMINE | **1** [VN] **~ sth (for sth)** to examine sth to see if it is correct, safe or satisfactory: *Check the container for cracks or leaks.* ◇ *She gave me the minutes of the meeting to read and check.* ◇ *Check the oil and water before setting off.* ◇ *Check your work before handing it in.*
MAKE SURE | **2 ~ (with sb)** to find out if sth is correct or true or if sth is how you think it is: [V(**that**)] *Go and check (that) I've locked the windows.* ◇ [V] *'Is Mary in the office?' 'Just a moment. I'll go and check.'* ◇ [V**wh-**] *You'd better check with Jane what time she's expecting us tonight.*—see also CROSS-CHECK, DOUBLE-CHECK
CONTROL | **3** [VN] to control sth; to stop sth from increasing or getting worse: *The government is determined to check the growth of public spending.* **4** [VN] to stop yourself from saying or doing sth or from showing a particular emotion: *to check your anger/laughter/tears* ◇ *She wanted to tell him the whole truth but she checked herself—it wasn't the right moment.*
COATS/BAGS/CASES | **5** [VN] (*AmE*) to leave coats, bags, etc. in an official place (called a CHECKROOM) while you are visiting a club, restaurant, etc: *Do you want to check your coats?* **6** [VN] (*AmE*) to leave bags or cases with an official so that they can be put on a plane or train
MAKE MARK | **7** [VN] (*AmE*) = TICK: *Check the box next to the right answer.*
PHRV **ˌcheck 'in (at …)** | **'check into …** to go to a desk in a hotel, an airport, etc. and tell an official there that you have arrived: *Please check in at least an hour before departure.*—related noun CHECK-IN **ˌcheck sth↔'in** to leave bags or cases with an official to be put on a plane or train: *We checked in our luggage and went through to the departure lounge.*—related noun CHECK-IN **ˌcheck sb/ sth↔'off** (*AmE*) = TICK SB/STH OFF: *Check the names off as the guests arrive.* **'check on sb/sth** to make sure that there is nothing wrong with sb/sth: *I'll just go and check*

b	d	f	g	h	k	l	m	n	p	r
bad	did	fall	get	hat	cat	leg	man	now	pen	red

C

on the children. ,**check** '**out (of ...)** to pay your bill and leave a hotel, etc: *Guests should check out of their rooms by noon.*—related noun CHECKOUT (2) ,**check sth↔**'**out 1** to find out if sth is correct, true or acceptable: *The police are checking out his alibi.* **2** (*informal*) to look at or examine sth that seems interesting or attractive: *Check out the prices at our new store!* ◊ *Hey, check out that car!* **3** to borrow sth from an official place, for example a book from a library: *The book has been checked out in your name.* ,**check** '**over/**'**through↔sth** to examine sth carefully to make sure that it is correct or acceptable: *Check over your work for mistakes.* ,**check** '**up on sb** to make sure that sb is doing what they should be doing: *My parents are always checking up on me.* ,**check** '**up on sth** to find out if sth is true or correct: *I need to check up on a few things before I can decide.*

■ *noun*

EXAMINATION | **1** [C] ~ (**on sth**) an act of making sure that sth is safe, correct or in good condition by examining it: *Could you give the tyres a check?* ◊ *a health check* ◊ *The drugs were found in their car during a routine check by police.* ◊ *I'll just have a quick check to see if the letter's arrived yet.* ◊ *It is vital to keep a check on your speed* (= look at it regularly in order to control it).

INVESTIGATION | **2** [C] ~ (**on sth**) an investigation to find out more information about sth: *The police ran a check on the registration number of the car.* ◊ *Was any check made on Mr Morris when he applied for the post?*

CONTROL | **3** [C] ~ (**on/to sth**) (*formal*) something that slows down the progress of sth else or stops it from getting worse: *A cold spring will provide a natural check on the number of insects.*

PATTERN | **4** [C, U] a pattern of squares, usually of two colours: *Do you prefer checks or stripes?* ◊ *a check shirt/suit* ◊ *a yellow and red check skirt*—see also CHECKED

MONEY | **5** [C] (*AmE*) = CHEQUE **6** [C] (*AmE*) = BILL: *Can I have the check, please?*

FOR COATS/BAGS | **7** [C] (*AmE*) **coat** ~ a place in a club, restaurant, etc. where you can leave your coat or bag **8** [C] (*AmE*) a ticket that you get when you leave your coat, bag, etc. in, for example, a restaurant or theatre

IN GAME | **9** [U] (in the game of CHESS) a position in which a player's king (= the most important piece) can be directly attacked by the other player's pieces: *There, you're in check.*—see also CHECKMATE

MARK | **10** (also '**check mark**) [C] (*AmE*) = TICK

IDM **hold/keep sth in** '**check** to keep sth under control so that it does not spread or get worse—more at RAIN CHECK

■ *exclamation* used to show that you agree with sb or that sth on a list has been dealt with: '*Do you have your tickets?' 'Check.' 'Passport?' 'Check.'*

check·book = CHEQUEBOOK

checked /tʃekt/ *adj.* having a pattern of squares, usually of two colours: *checked material*—see also CHECK

check·er /'tʃekə(r)/ *noun*—see also CHECKERS **1** (*AmE*) a person who works at the CHECKOUT in a supermarket **2** (in compounds) a computer program that you use to check sth, for example the spelling and grammar of sth you have written: *a spelling/grammar/virus checker* **3** a person who checks things: *a quality control checker*

check·er·board /'tʃekəbɔːd; *AmE* 'tʃekərbɔːrd/ *noun* (*AmE*) = DRAUGHTBOARD

check·ered *adj.* (*especially AmE*) = CHEQUERED

check·ers /'tʃekəz; *AmE* -ərz/ *noun* [U] (*AmE*) = DRAUGHTS

'**check-in** *noun* **1** [C, U] the place where you go first when you arrive at an airport, to show your ticket, etc: *The airline apologizes for long delays at check-ins today.* **2** [U] the act of showing your ticket, etc. when you arrive at an airport: *Do you know your check-in time?* ◊ (*BrE*) *the check-in desk* ◊ (*AmE*) *the check-in counter*

'**checking account** *noun* (*AmE*) = CURRENT ACCOUNT

check·list /'tʃeklɪst/ *noun* a list of the things that you must remember to do, to take with you or to find out

check·mate /ˌtʃek'meɪt/ (also **mate**) *noun* [U] **1** (in the

game of CHESS) a position in which one player cannot prevent his or her king (= the most important piece) being captured and therefore loses the game—see also CHECK—compare STALEMATE **2** a situation in which sb has been completely defeated ► **check·mate** (also **mate**) *verb*: [VN] *His king had been checkmated.* ◊ *She hoped the plan would checkmate her opponents.*

check·out /'tʃekaʊt/ *noun* **1** [C] the place where you pay for the things that you are buying in a supermarket: *a checkout assistant/operator* **2** [U] the time when you leave a hotel at the end of your stay: *At checkout, your bill will be printed for you.*

check·point /'tʃekpɔɪnt/ *noun* a place, especially on a border between two countries, where people have to stop so their vehicles and documents can be checked: *There are border guards at the checkpoint crossing.*

check·room /'tʃekruːm; -rʊm/ *noun* (*AmE*) = CLOAK-ROOM

'**check-up** *noun* an examination of sth, especially a medical one to make sure that you are healthy: *to go for/to have a check-up* ◊ *a medical/dental/routine/thorough check-up*

Ched·dar /'tʃedə(r)/ (also ˌ**Cheddar** '**cheese**) *noun* [U] a type of hard yellow cheese

cheek /tʃiːk/ *noun, verb*

■ *noun* **1** [C] either side of the face below the eyes: *chubby/rosy/pink cheeks* ◊ *He kissed her on both cheeks.* ◊ *Couples were dancing* **cheek to cheek**.—picture at BODY **2** (**-cheeked**) (in adjectives) having the type of cheeks mentioned: *chubby-cheeked/rosy-cheeked/hollow-cheeked* **3** [C] (*informal*) either of the BUTTOCKS **4** [U, sing.] (*BrE*) talk or behaviour that people think is annoying, rude or lacking in respect: *What a cheek!* ◊ *He* **had the cheek** *to ask his ex-girlfriend to babysit for them.* ◊ *I think they've* **got a cheek** *making you pay to park the car.* **IDM** ,**cheek by** '**jowl (with sb/sth)** very close to sb/sth **turn the other** '**cheek** to make a deliberate decision to remain calm and not to act in an aggressive way when sb has hurt you or made you angry—more at ROSE *n.*, TONGUE *n.*

■ *verb* [VN] (*BrE, informal*) to speak to sb in a rude way that shows a lack of respect

cheek·bone /'tʃiːkbəʊn; *AmE* -boʊn/ *noun* the bone below the eye—picture at BODY

cheeky /'tʃiːki/ *adj.* (**cheek·ier**, **cheeki·est**) (*BrE*, especially *spoken*) rude in an amusing or an annoying way: *You cheeky monkey!* ◊ *a cheeky grin* ◊ *You're getting far too cheeky!* ► **cheek·ily** *adv.* **cheeki·ness** *noun* [U]

cheep /tʃiːp/ *verb* [V] (of young birds) to make short high sounds ► **cheep** *noun*

cheer /tʃɪə(r); *AmE* tʃɪr/ *noun, verb*

■ *noun* **1** [C] a shout of joy, support or praise: *A great cheer went up from the crowd.* ◊ *cheers of encouragement* ◊ **Three cheers for the winners!** (= used when you are asking a group of people to cheer three times, in order to congratulate sb, etc.) **2** [C] (*AmE*) a special song or poem used by CHEERLEADERS **3** [U] (*formal* or *literary*) an atmosphere of happiness: *Christmas and New Year are a time of* **good cheer** *in the company of family and friends.*

■ *verb* **1** to shout loudly, to show support or praise for sb, or to give them encouragement: [V] *We all cheered as the team came on to the field.* ◊ *Cheering crowds greeted their arrival.* ◊ [VN] *The crowd cheered the President as he drove slowly by.* **2** [VN] [usually passive] to give hope, comfort or encouragement to sb: *She was cheered by the news from home.* ► **cheer·ing** *noun* [U]: *He came on stage amid clapping and cheering.* **cheer·ing** *adj.*: *The results of the test were very cheering.* **PHRV** ,**cheer sb↔**'**on** to give shouts of encouragement to sb in a race, competition, etc: *The spectators cheered the runners on.* ,**cheer** '**up |** ,**cheer sb/sth↔**'**up** to become more cheerful; to make sb/sth more cheerful: *Oh, come on—cheer up!* ◊ *Give Mary a call; she needs cheering up.* ◊ *Bright curtains can cheer up a dull room.*

cheer·ful /'tʃɪəfl; *AmE* 'tʃɪrfl/ *adj.* **1** happy, and showing it by the way that you behave: *You're not your usual cheerful self today.* ◊ *He felt bright and cheerful and full of energy.* ◊ *a cheerful, hard-working employee* ◊ *a cheerful*

s	t	v	z	ʃ	ʒ	tʃ	dʒ	θ	ð	ŋ
see	tea	van	zoo	shoe	vision	chain	jam	thin	this	sing

C

smile/voice **2** giving you a feeling of happiness: *a bright, cheerful restaurant* ◊ *walls painted in cheerful* (= light and bright) *colours* ◊ *a chatty, cheerful letter* ▶ **cheer·ful·ly** /-fəli/ *adv.*: *to laugh/nod/whistle cheerfully* ◊ *I could cheerfully have killed him when he said that* (= I would have liked to). ◊ *She cheerfully admitted that she had no experience at all* (= she wasn't afraid to do so). **cheer·ful·ness** *noun* [U]

cheerio /ˌtʃɪəriˈəʊ; *AmE* ˌtʃɪriˈoʊ/ *exclamation* (*BrE, informal*) goodbye: *Cheerio! I'll see you later.*

cheer·lead·er /ˈtʃɪəliːdə(r); *AmE* ˈtʃɪrl-/ *noun* **1** (in the US) one of the members of a group of young people (usually women) wearing special uniforms, who encourage the crowd to CHEER for their team at a sports event **2** a person who supports a particular politician, idea, or way of doing sth: *one of the leading cheerleaders for the President's welfare policies*

cheer·less /ˈtʃɪələs; *AmE* ˈtʃɪrl-/ *adj.* (*written*) (of a place, etc.) without warmth or colour so it makes you feel depressed SYN GLOOMY: *a dark and cheerless room* ◊ *a damp and cheerless December afternoon*

cheers /tʃɪəz; *AmE* tʃɪrz/ *exclamation* **1** a word that people say to each other as they lift up their glasses to drink **2** (*BrE, informal*) goodbye: *Cheers then. See you later.* **3** (*BrE, informal*) thank you

cheery /ˈtʃɪəri; *AmE* ˈtʃɪri/ *adj.* (**cheer·ier, cheeri·est**) (*informal*) (of a person or their behaviour) happy and cheerful: *a cheery remark/smile/wave* ◊ *He left with a cheery 'See you again soon'.* ▶ **cheer·ily** *adv.*

cheese /tʃiːz/ *noun* **1** [U, C] a type of food made from milk that can be either soft or hard and is usually white or yellow in colour; a particular type of this food: *Cheddar cheese* ◊ *goat's cheese* (= made from the milk of a goat) ◊ *a cheese sandwich/salad* ◊ *a chunk/piece/slice of cheese* ◊ *a selection of French cheeses* ◊ *a cheese knife* (= a knife with a special curved blade with two points on the end, used for cutting and picking up pieces of cheese)—picture at CUTLERY—see also BLUE CHEESE, CAULIFLOWER CHEESE, COTTAGE CHEESE, CREAM CHEESE, MACARONI CHEESE **2 cheese!** what you ask sb to say before you take their photograph IDM see BIG *adj.*, CHALK *n.*, HARD *adj.*

cheese·board /ˈtʃiːzbɔːd; *AmE* -bɔːrd/ *noun* (*BrE*) **1** a board that is used to cut cheese on **2** a variety of cheeses that are served at the end of a meal

cheese·bur·ger /ˈtʃiːzbɜːgə(r); *AmE* -bɜːrg-/ *noun* a hamburger with a slice of cheese on top of the meat

cheese·cake /ˈtʃiːzkeɪk/ *noun* [C, U] a cold DESSERT (= a sweet dish) made from a soft mixture of CREAM CHEESE, sugar, eggs, etc. on a base of cake or crushed biscuits/cookies, sometimes with fruit on top: *a strawberry cheesecake* ◊ *Is there any cheesecake left?*—picture on page A1

cheese·cloth /ˈtʃiːzklɒθ; *AmE* -klɔːθ/ *noun* [U] a loosely-woven cotton fabric used especially for making shirts

cheesed 'off *adj.* [not before noun] **~ (with/about sb/sth)** (*BrE, informal*) annoyed or bored: *I was extremely cheesed off to be woken so early.*

cheesy /ˈtʃiːzi/ *adj.* **1** (*slang*) of low quality and without style SYN CORNY, TACKY: *an incredibly cheesy love song* **2** smelling or tasting of cheese

chee·tah /ˈtʃiːtə/ *noun* a wild animal of the cat family, with black spots, that runs very fast

chef /ʃef/ *noun* a professional cook, especially the most senior cook in a restaurant, hotel, etc.

chef-d'oeuvre /ˌʃeɪ ˈdɜːvrə/ *noun* (*pl.* **chefs-d'oeuvre** /ˌʃeɪ ˈdɜːvrə/) (from *French, formal*) a very good piece of work, especially the best work by a particular artist, writer, etc. SYN MASTERPIECE

chem·ical /ˈkemɪkl/ *adj., noun*

■ *adj.* **1** connected with chemistry: *a chemical element* ◊ *the chemical industry* **2** produced by or using processes which involve changes to atoms or MOLECULES: *chemical reactions/processes* ▶ **chem·ic·al·ly** /-kli/ *adv.*: *The raw sewage is chemically treated.*

■ *noun* a substance obtained by or used in a chemical process

chemical engi'neering *noun* [U] the study of the design and use of machines in industrial chemical processes ▶ **chemical engi'neer** *noun*

chemical 'war·fare *noun* [U] the use of poisonous gases and chemicals as weapons in a war

che·mise /ʃəˈmiːz/ *noun* a loose dress or piece of women's underwear that hangs straight from the shoulders

chem·ist /ˈkemɪst/ *noun* **1** (also **dis'pensing chemist**) (both *BrE*) (*AmE* **drug·gist**) a person whose job is to prepare and sell medicines, and who works in a shop—compare PHARMACIST **2** (**chemist's**) (*pl.* **chem·ists**) (*BrE*) a shop/store that sells medicines and usually also soap, MAKE-UP, etc: *You can obtain the product from all good chemists.* ◊ *Take this prescription to the chemist's.* ◊ *I'll get it at the chemist's.* ◊ *a chemist's/chemist shop*—see also DRUGSTORE—compare PHARMACY **3** a scientist who studies chemistry: *a research chemist*

chem·is·try /ˈkemɪstri/ *noun* [U] **1** the scientific study of the structure of substances, how they react when combined or in contact with one another, and how they behave under different conditions: *a degree in chemistry* ◊ *the university's chemistry department* ◊ *inorganic/organic chemistry*—see also BIOCHEMISTRY **2** (*technical*) the chemical structure and behaviour of a particular substance: *the chemistry of copper* ◊ *The patient's blood chemistry was monitored regularly.* **3** the relationship between two people, usually a strong sexual attraction: *sexual chemistry* ◊ *The chemistry just wasn't right.*

chemo·ther·apy /ˌkiːməʊˈθerəpi; *AmE* -moʊ-/ *noun* [U] the treatment of disease, especially CANCER, with the use of chemical substances—compare RADIATION, RADIOTHERAPY

che·nille /ʃəˈniːl/ *noun* [U] a type of thick, soft thread; fabric made from this: *a chenille sweater*

cheque (*BrE*) (*AmE* **check**) /tʃek/ *noun* a printed form that you can write on and sign as a way of paying for sth instead of using money: *a cheque for £50* ◊ *to write a cheque* ◊ *to make a cheque out to sb* ◊ *to pay by cheque* ◊ *to cash a cheque* (= to get or give money for a cheque)—see also BLANK CHEQUE, TRAVELLER'S CHEQUE—picture at MONEY

cheque·book (*BrE*) (*AmE* **check·book**) /ˈtʃekbʊk/ *noun* a book of printed cheques

chequebook 'journalism *noun* [U] (*BrE, disapproving*) the practice of journalists paying people large amounts of money to give them personal or private information for a newspaper story

'cheque card (also **cheque guaran'tee card**) *noun* (both *BrE*) a card that you must show when you pay by cheque to prove that the bank you have an account with will pay the money on the cheque—compare CASH CARD

che·quered (*BrE*) (also **check·ered** *AmE, BrE*) /ˈtʃekəd; *AmE* -kərd/ *adj.* **1 ~ past/history/career** a person's past, etc. that contains both successful and not successful periods **2** having a pattern of squares of different colours

the chequered 'flag (*BrE*) (also **check·ered flag** *AmE, BrE*) *noun* a flag with black and white squares that is waved when a driver has finished a motor race

cher·ish /ˈtʃerɪʃ/ *verb* [VN] (*written*) **1** to love sb/sth very much and want to protect them or it: *Children need to be cherished.* ◊ *her most cherished possession* **2** to keep an idea, a hope or a pleasant feeling in your mind for a long time: *Cherish the memory of those days in Paris.*

che·root /ʃəˈruːt/ *noun* a type of CIGAR with two open ends

cherry /ˈtʃeri/ *noun, adj.*

■ *noun* (*pl.* **-ies**) **1** [C] a small soft round fruit with shiny red or black skin and a stone/pit inside—picture on page A2 **2** (also **'cherry tree**) [C] a tree on which cherries grow, or a similar tree, grown for its flowers: *cherry blossom* ◊ *a winter-flowering cherry* **3** (also **cherry·wood** /ˈtʃeriwʊd/) [U] the wood of the cherry tree **4** (also **cherry 'red**) [U] a bright red colour IDM see BITE *n.*

■ *adj.* (also **cherry 'red**) bright red in colour: *cherry lips*

æ	ɑː	e	ɜː	ə	ɪ	iː	i	ɒ	ɔː	ʌ	ʊ	u	uː
cat	father	ten	bird	about	sit	see	many	got	saw	cup	put	actual	too
								(BrE)					

'cherry-pick verb [VN, V] to choose the best people or things from a group and leave those which are not so good

cherub /'tʃerəb/ noun **1** (in art) a type of ANGEL, shown as a small fat, usually male, child with wings—compare SERAPH **2** (informal) a pretty child; a child who behaves well ▸ **cher·ub·ic** /tʃə'ruːbɪk/ adj. (formal): a cherubic face (= plump, and with the innocence of a small child)

cher·vil /'tʃɜːvɪl; AmE 'tʃɜːrvɪl/ noun [U] a plant with leaves that are used in cooking as a herb and to decorate food

chess /tʃes/ noun [U] a game for two people played on a board marked with black and white squares on which each playing piece (representing a king, queen, castle, etc.) is moved according to special rules. The aim is to put the other player's king in a position from which it cannot escape (= to CHECKMATE it).—picture on page A8

chess·board /'tʃesbɔːd; AmE -bɔːrd/ noun a board with 64 black and white squares that chess is played on—picture on page A8

chess·man /'tʃesmæn/ noun (pl. **-men** /-men/) any of the 32 pieces used in the game of chess—picture on page A8

chest /tʃest/ noun **1** the top part of the front of the body, between the neck and the stomach: The bullet hit him in the chest. ◇ She gasped for breath, her chest heaving. ◇ a chest infection ◇ chest pains ◇ a hairy chest—picture at BODY **2** (-chested) (in adjectives) having the type of chest mentioned: flat-chested ◇ broad-chested **3** a large strong box, usually made of wood, used for storing things in and/or moving them from one place to another: a medicine chest ◇ a treasure chest—see also TEA CHEST—see also WAR CHEST **IDM** **get sth off your 'chest** to talk about sth that has been worrying you for a long time so that you feel less anxious—more at CARD n.

chest·nut /'tʃesnʌt/ noun, adj.
■ noun **1** (also **'chestnut tree**) [C] a large tree with spreading branches, that produces smooth brown nuts inside prickly cases. There are several types of chestnut tree.—see also HORSE CHESTNUT **2** [C] a smooth brown nut of a chestnut tree, some types of which can be eaten: roast chestnuts—see also WATER CHESTNUT—compare CONKER—picture at NUT **3** [U] a deep reddish-brown colour **4** [C] a horse of a reddish-brown colour **5** [C] (informal) an old joke or story that has been told so many times that it is no longer amusing or interesting
■ adj. reddish-brown in colour

‚chest of 'drawers noun (pl. **chests of drawers**) (AmE also **bur·eau, dresser**) a piece of furniture with drawers for keeping clothes in

chesty /'tʃesti/ adj. (informal, especially BrE) suffering from or showing signs of chest disease

chev·ron /'ʃevrən/ noun **1** a line or pattern in the shape of a V **2** a piece of fabric in the shape of a V which soldiers and police officers wear on their uniforms to show their rank

chew /tʃuː/ verb, noun
■ verb **1** ~ (at/on/through sth)|~ sth (up) to bite food into small pieces in your mouth with your teeth to make it easier to swallow: [V] After the operation you may find it difficult to chew and swallow. ◇ [VN] teeth designed for chewing meat ◇ He is always chewing gum. **2** ~ (on sth) to bite sth continuously, for example because you are nervous or to taste it: [V] Rosa chewed on her lip and stared at the floor. ◇ The dog was chewing on a bone. ◇ [VN] to chew your nails **IDM** **‚chew the 'fat** (informal) to have a long friendly talk with sb about sth—more at BITE v. **PHRV** **‚chew sth↔'over** to think about or discuss sth slowly and carefully
■ noun **1** an act of chewing sth **2** a type of sweet/candy that you chew **3** a piece of tobacco that you chew

'chewing gum (also **gum**) noun [U] a sweet/candy that you chew but do not swallow

chewy /'tʃuːi/ adj. (of food) needing to be chewed a lot before it can be swallowed

chic /ʃiːk/ adj. very fashionable and elegant: She is always so chic, so elegant. ◇ a chic new restaurant ▸ **chic** noun [U]: a perfectly dressed woman with an air of chic that was unmistakably French

chi·cane /ʃɪ'keɪn/ noun (BrE) a sharp double bend, either on a track where cars race, or on an ordinary road to stop vehicles from going too fast

chi·can·ery /ʃɪ'keɪnəri/ noun [U] (rare, formal) the use of complicated plans and clever talk in order to deceive people

Chi·cano /tʃɪ'kɑːnəʊ; ʃɪ-; 'keɪn-; AmE tʃɪ'kɑːnoʊ; ʃɪ-/ noun (pl. **-os**) (especially AmE) a N American person whose family came from Mexico—compare LATINO

chick /tʃɪk/ noun **1** a baby bird, especially a baby chicken **2** (old-fashioned, sometimes offensive) a way of referring to a young woman

chicka·dee /'tʃɪkədiː; ˌtʃɪkə'diː/ noun a small N American bird of the TIT family. There are many types of chickadee.

chick·en /'tʃɪkɪn/ noun, verb, adj.
■ noun **1** [C] a large bird that is often kept for its eggs or meat: They keep chickens in the back yard. ◇ free-range chickens—compare COCK, HEN—picture on page A6 **2** [U] meat from a chicken: fried/roast chicken ◇ chicken stock/soup ◇ chicken breasts/livers/thighs ◇ chicken and chips—see also SPRING CHICKEN **IDM** **a ‚chicken-and-'egg situation, problem, etc.** a situation in which it is difficult to tell which one of two things was the cause of the other—more at COUNT v., HEADLESS, HOME adv.
■ verb **PHRV** **‚chicken 'out (of sth/of doing sth)** (informal) to decide not to do sth because you are afraid: You're not going to chicken out, are you?
■ adj. [not before noun] (informal) not brave; afraid to do sth **SYN** COWARDLY

'chicken feed noun [U] (informal) an amount of money that is not large enough to be important

chick·en·pox /'tʃɪkɪnpɒks; AmE -pɑːks/ noun [U] a disease, especially of children, that causes a slight fever and many spots on the skin: to catch/get chickenpox

chick·en·shit /'tʃɪkɪnʃɪt/ noun, adj.
■ noun [U] (AmE, slang) nonsense
■ adj. (AmE, slang) (of a person) not brave **SYN** COWARDLY

chick·pea /'tʃɪk piː/ noun (especially BrE) (AmE usually **gar·ban·zo, gar'banzo bean**) a hard round seed, like a light brown pea, that is cooked and eaten as a vegetable

chic·ory /'tʃɪkəri/ noun [U] **1** (BrE) (AmE **en·dive**) [C, U] a small pale green plant with bitter leaves that are eaten raw or cooked as a vegetable. The root can be dried and used with or instead of coffee. **2** (AmE) = ENDIVE (1)

chide /tʃaɪd/ verb ~ sb (for sth/for doing sth) (formal) to criticize or blame sb because they have done sth wrong: [VN] She chided herself for being so impatient with the children. ◇ [V speech] 'Isn't that a bit selfish?' he chided. [also VN speech]

chief /tʃiːf/ adj., noun
■ adj. [only before noun] **1** most important; main: the chief cause/problem/reason ◇ one of the President's chief rivals **2** (often **Chief**) highest in rank: the Chief Education Officer ◇ the chief financial officer of the company ◇ Detective Chief Inspector Williams **3** (-'n-'chief) (in nouns) of the highest rank: commander-in-chief—see also CHIEFLY
■ noun **1** a person with a high rank or the highest rank in a company or an organization: army/industry/police chiefs **2** (often as a title) a leader or ruler of a tribe: Chief Buthelezi ◇ Chief Crazy Horse **IDM** **there are too many chiefs and not enough Indians** (BrE, informal) used to describe a situation in which there are too many people telling other people what to do, and not enough people to do the work

‚chief 'constable noun (in Britain) a senior police officer who is in charge of the police force in a particular area: Chief Constable Brian Turner

‚chief e'xecutive noun **1** the person with the highest rank in a company or an organization: The chief executive addressed the board. **2** (Chief Executive) the President of the US

‚chief e'xecutive officer noun (abbr. CEO) the person in a company who has the most power and authority

aɪ	aʊ	eɪ	əʊ	oʊ	ɔɪ	ɪə	eə	ʊə	j	w
my	now	say	go	go	boy	near	hair	pure	yes	wet
			(BrE)	(AmE)						

C

,chief in'spector *noun* (in Britain) a police officer above the rank of an INSPECTOR

,chief 'justice (also Chief Justice) *noun* the most important judge in a court of law, especially the US Supreme Court

chief·ly /'tʃiːfli/ *adv.* not completely, but as a most important part SYN PRIMARILY, MAINLY: *We are chiefly concerned with improving educational standards.* ◊ *He's travelled widely, chiefly in Africa and Asia.*

,chief of 'staff *noun* (*pl.* ,chiefs of 'staff) an officer of very high rank, responsible for advising the person who commands each of the armed forces—see also JOINT CHIEFS OF STAFF

,chief superin'tendent *noun* (in Britain) a police officer above the rank of SUPERINTENDENT

chief·tain /'tʃiːftən/ *noun* the leader of a tribe or a CLAN in Scotland

chif·fon /'ʃɪfɒn; *AmE* ʃɪ'fɑːn/ *noun* [U] a fine transparent silk or NYLON fabric, used especially for making clothes

chi·gnon /'ʃiːnjɒn; *AmE* -jɑːn/ *noun* (from *French*) a style for women's hair in which the hair is pulled back and twisted into a smooth knot at the back

chi·hua·hua /tʃɪ'wɑːwə; *AmE* -'wɑːwɑː/ *noun* a very small dog with smooth hair

chil·blain /'tʃɪlbleɪn/ *noun* [usually pl.] a painful red swelling on the hands or feet that is caused by cold or bad CIRCULATION of the blood

child /tʃaɪld/ *noun* (*pl.* chil·dren /'tʃɪldrən/) **1** a young human being who is not yet an adult: *a child of three* ◊ *a three-year-old child* ◊ *men, women and children* ◊ *an unborn child* ◊ *not suitable for young children* ◊ *I lived in London as a child.* ◊ *a child star*—see also BRAINCHILD, LATCHKEY CHILD, SCHOOLCHILD **2** a son or daughter of any age: *They have three grown-up children.* ◊ *a support group for adult children of alcoholics*—see also GODCHILD, GRANDCHILD, LOVE CHILD, ONLY CHILD, STEPCHILD—compare KID **3** a person who is strongly influenced by the ideas and attitudes of a particular time or person: *a child of the 90s* **4** (*disapproving*) an adult who behaves like a child and is not MATURE or responsible IDM be with 'child (*old-fashioned*) to be pregnant be 'child's play (*informal*) to be very easy to do, so not even a child would find it difficult

'child abuse *noun* [U] the crime of harming a child in a physical, sexual or emotional way: *victims of child abuse*

child·bear·ing /'tʃaɪldbeərɪŋ; *AmE* -ber-/ *noun* [U] the process of giving birth to children: *women of childbearing age*

,child 'bene·fit *noun* [U] (in Britain) money that the government regularly pays to parents of children up to a particular age

child·birth /'tʃaɪldbɜːθ; *AmE* -bɜːrθ/ *noun* [U] the process of giving birth to a baby: *pregnancy and childbirth* ◊ *His wife died in childbirth.*

child·care /'tʃaɪldkeə(r); *AmE* -ker-/ *noun* [U] the care of children, especially while parents are at work: *childcare facilities for working parents*

child·hood /'tʃaɪldhʊd/ *noun* [U, C] the period of sb's life when they are a child: *childhood, adolescence and adulthood* ◊ *in early childhood* ◊ *childhood memories/experiences* ◊ *She had a happy childhood.* ◊ *childhood cancer* IDM a/sb's second 'childhood a time in the life of an adult person when they behave like a child again

child·ish /'tʃaɪldɪʃ/ *adj.* **1** connected with or typical of a child: *childish handwriting* **2** (*disapproving*) (of an adult) behaving in a stupid or silly way SYN IMMATURE: *Don't be so childish!*—compare CHILDLIKE ▶ child·ish·ly *adv.*: *to behave childishly* child·ish·ness *noun* [U]

child·less /'tʃaɪldləs/ *adj.* having no children: *a childless couple/marriage*

child·like /'tʃaɪldlaɪk/ *adj.* (usually *approving*) having the qualities that children usually have, especially INNOCENCE: *childlike enthusiasm/simplicity/delight*—compare CHILDISH

child·mind·er /'tʃaɪldmaɪndə(r)/ *noun* (*BrE*) a person, usually a woman, who is paid to care for children while their parents are at work. A childminder usually does this in his or her own home.—see also BABYSITTER

child·proof /'tʃaɪldpruːf/ *adj.* designed so that young children cannot open, use, or damage it: *childproof containers for medicines*

'child restraint *noun* a belt, or small seat with a belt, that is used in a car to control and protect a child

'child seat *noun* = CAR SEAT

chili (*AmE*) **1** = CHILLI **2** = CHILLI CON CARNE

chill /tʃɪl/ *noun, verb, adj.*
■ *noun* **1** [sing.] a feeling of being cold: *There's a chill in the air this morning.* ◊ *A small fire was burning to take the chill off the room.* **2** [C] an illness caused by being cold and wet, causing fever and SHIVERING (= shaking of the body) **3** [sing.] a feeling of fear: *a chill of fear/apprehension* ◊ *His words sent a chill down her spine.*
■ *verb* **1** [VN] [usually passive] to make sb very cold: *They were chilled by the icy wind.* ◊ *Let's go home, I'm chilled to the bone* (= very cold). **2** when food or a drink chills or when sb chills it, it is made very cold but it does not freeze: [V] *Let the pudding chill for an hour until set.* ◊ [VN] *This wine is best served chilled.* ◊ *chilled foods* (= for example in a supermarket) **3** [VN] [usually passive]: (*literary*) to frighten sb: *His words chilled her.* ◊ *We were chilled at the prospect of war.* ◊ *What he saw chilled his blood.* PHRV ,chill 'out (*informal*) to relax and stop feeling angry or nervous about sth: *They sometimes meet up to chill out and drink a few beers.* ◊ *Sit down and chill out!*
■ *adj.* (*formal*) (especially of weather and the wind) cold, in an unpleasant way: *the chill grey dawn* ◊ *a chill wind*

chilli (*BrE*) (*AmE* chili) /'tʃɪli/ *noun* (*pl.* chil·lies, *AmE* chilies) **1** (*AmE* also 'chili pepper) [C, U] the small green or red fruit of a type of pepper plant that is used in cooking to give a hot taste to food, often dried or made into powder, also called chilli or chilli powder **2** [U] = CHILLI CON CARNE

chilli con carne /,tʃɪli kɒn 'kɑːni; *AmE* kɑːn 'kɑːrni/ (*especially BrE*) (*BrE* also chilli) (*AmE* also chili) *noun* [U] a hot spicy Mexican dish made with meat, beans and chillies

chill·ing /'tʃɪlɪŋ/ *adj.* frightening, usually because it is connected with sth violent or cruel: *a chilling story* ◊ *The film evokes chilling reminders of the war.*

chilly /'tʃɪli/ *adj.* **1** (especially of the weather or a place, but also of people) too cold to be comfortable: *It's chilly today.* ◊ *I was feeling chilly.* **2** not friendly: *The visitors got a very chilly reception.* ▶ chil·li·ness *noun* [U]

chime /tʃaɪm/ *verb, noun*
■ *verb* (of a bell or a clock) to ring; to show the time by making a ringing sound: [V] *I heard the clock chime.* ◊ *Eight o'clock had already chimed.* ◊ [VN] *The clock chimed midday.* PHRV ,chime 'in (with sth) to join or interrupt a conversation: *He kept chiming in with his own opinions.* ◊ [+ speech] 'And me!' she chimed in. chime (in) with sth (*written*) (of plans, ideas, etc.) to agree with sth; to be similar to sth: *His opinions chimed in with the mood of the nation.*
■ *noun* a ringing sound, especially one that is made by a bell: *door chimes*

chi·mera (also chi·maera) /kaɪ'mɪərə; *AmE* -'mɪrə/ *noun* **1** (in ancient Greek stories) a creature with a lion's head, a goat's body and a snake's tail, that can breathe out fire **2** (*formal*) an impossible idea or hope

chim·ney /'tʃɪmni/ *noun* **1** a structure through which smoke or steam is carried up away from a fire, etc. and through the roof of a building; the part of this that is above the roof: *He threw the paper onto the fire and it flew up the chimney.* ◊ *the factory chimneys of an industrial landscape*—picture at HOUSE **2** (*technical*) a narrow opening in an area of rock that a person can climb up

'chim·ney breast *noun* (*BrE*) the wall around the bottom part of a chimney, above a FIREPLACE

'chim·ney piece *noun* (*BrE*) a brick or stone structure that is built over a FIREPLACE

'chim·ney pot *noun* (*BrE*) a short wide pipe that is placed on top of a chimney—picture at HOUSE

b	d	f	g	h	k	l	m	n	p	r
bad	did	fall	get	hat	cat	leg	man	now	pen	red

C

'chim·ney stack *noun* (*BrE*) **1** the part of the chimney that is above the roof of a building **2** (*AmE* **smoke-stack**) a very tall chimney, especially one in a factory

'chimney sweep (also **sweep**) *noun* a person whose job is to clean the inside of chimneys

chim·pan·zee /ˌtʃɪmpænˈziː/ (also *informal* **chimp**) *noun* a small intelligent African APE (= an animal like a large monkey without a tail)—picture on page A6

chin /tʃɪn/ *noun* the part of the face below the mouth and above the neck: *A strap fastens under the chin to keep the helmet in place.*—picture at BODY—see also DOUBLE CHIN **IDM** (**keep your**) **'chin up** (*spoken*) used to tell sb to try to stay cheerful even though they are in a difficult or unpleasant situation: *Chin up! Only two exams left.* **take sth on the 'chin** (*informal*) to accept a difficult or unpleasant situation without complaining, trying to make excuses, etc.—more at CHUCK *v.*

china /ˈtʃaɪnə/ *noun* [U] **1** white clay which is baked and used for making delicate cups, plates, etc: *a china vase*—see also BONE CHINA **2** cups, plates, etc. that are made of china: *She got out the best china.* **IDM** see BULL, TEA

china 'clay *noun* [U] = KAOLIN

Chinese 'cabbage *noun* [U] (*BrE* also **Chinese 'leaf**, **pak 'choi** [U], **Chinese 'leaves** [pl.]) a vegetable like CABBAGE with long, pale green leaves

Chinese 'chequers (*BrE*) (*AmE* **Chinese 'checkers**) *noun* [U] a game for two to six players who try to move the playing pieces from one corner to the opposite corner of the board, which is shaped like a star

Chinese 'whispers *noun* [U] (*BrE*) the situation when information is passed from one person to another and gets slightly changed each time

Chink /tʃɪŋk/ *noun* (⚠, *slang*) a very offensive word for a Chinese person

chink /tʃɪŋk/ *noun, verb*
■ *noun* **1** a narrow opening in sth, especially one that lets light through: *a chink in the curtains* **2 ~ of light** a small area of light shining through a narrow opening **3** [usually sing.] the light ringing sound that is made when glass objects or coins touch: *the chink of glasses* **IDM** **a chink in sb's 'armour** a weak point in sb's argument, character, etc., that can be used in an attack
■ *verb* when glasses, coins or other glass or metal objects **chink** or when you **chink** them, they make a light ringing sound: [V] *the sound of bottles chinking* ◇ [VN] *We chinked glasses and drank to each other's health.*

chinos /ˈtʃiːnəʊz; *AmE* -noʊz/ *noun* [pl.] informal trousers/pants made from strong woven cotton: *a pair of chinos*

chintz /tʃɪnts/ *noun* [U, C] a shiny cotton fabric with a printed design, especially of flowers, used for making curtains, covering furniture, etc.

chintzy /ˈtʃɪntsi/ *adj.* **1** (*BrE*) covered in or decorated with chintz **2** (*AmE*, *informal*) cheap and not attractive **3** (*AmE*, *humorous*) not willing to spend money [SYN] CHEAP, STINGY

'chin-up *noun* (*especially AmE*) = PULL-UP

chin·wag /ˈtʃɪnwæɡ/ *noun* [sing.] (*BrE*, *spoken*) a friendly, informal conversation with sb that you know well

chip /tʃɪp/ *noun, verb*
■ *noun* **1** the place from which a small piece of wood, glass, etc. has broken from an object: *This mug has a chip in it.* **2** a small piece of wood, glass, etc. that has broken off an object: *chips of wood* ◇ *chocolate chip cookies* (= biscuits containing small pieces of chocolate) **3** (*BrE*) (also **French 'fry, fry** *AmE*, *BrE*) [usually pl.] a long thin piece of potato fried in oil or fat: *All main courses are served with chips or baked potato.*—see also FISH AND CHIPS **4** (*AmE*) = CRISP: *potato chips* **5** = MICROCHIP: *chip technology* **6** a small flat piece of plastic used to represent a particular amount of money in some types of gambling: (*figurative*) *The release of prisoners was used as a bargaining chip.* **7** (also **'chip shot**) (in golf, football, etc.) an act of hitting or kicking a ball high in the air so that it lands within a short distance: *She left herself with a short chip to the green.*—see also BLUE-CHIP **IDM** **a 'chip off the**

old 'block (*informal*) a person who is very similar to their mother or father in the way that they look or behave **have a 'chip on your shoulder** (**about sth**) (*informal*) to be sensitive about sth that happened in the past and become easily offended if it is mentioned because you think that you were treated unfairly **have had your 'chips** (*BrE*, *informal*) to be in a situation in which you are certain to be defeated or killed **when the chips are 'down** (*informal*) used to refer to a difficult situation in which you are forced to decide what is important to you: *I'm not sure what I'll do when the chips are down.*
■ *verb* (**-pp-**) **1** to damage sth by breaking a small piece off it; to become damaged in this way: [VN] *a badly chipped saucer* ◇ *She chipped one of her front teeth.* ◇ [V] *These plates chip easily.* **2** [VN+adv. / prep.] to cut or break small pieces off sth with a tool: *Chip away the damaged area.* ◇ *The fossils had been chipped out of the rock.* **3** [VN, V] (especially in golf and football) to hit or kick the ball so that it goes high in the air and then lands within a short distance **4** [VN] **~ potatoes** (*BrE*) to cut potatoes into long thin pieces and fry them in deep oil **PHRV** **chip a'way at sth** to keep breaking small pieces off sth: *He was chipping away at the stone.* ◇ (*figurative*) *They chipped away at the power of the government* (= gradually made it weaker). **chip 'in** (**with sth**) (*informal*) **1** to join in or interrupt a conversation; to add sth to a conversation or discussion: *Pete and Anne chipped in with suggestions.* ◇ [+speech] *'That's different,' she chipped in.* **2** (also **chip 'in sth**) to give some money so that a group of people can buy sth together: *If everyone chips in we'll be able to buy her a really nice present.* ◇ *We each chipped in (with) £5.* **chip 'off, chip sth ↔ 'off** to damage sth by breaking a small piece off it; to be damaged in this way: *He chipped off a piece of his tooth.* ◇ *Use a good varnish that will not chip off.*

chip·board /ˈtʃɪpbɔːd; *AmE* -bɔːrd/ *noun* [U] a type of board that is used for building, made of small pieces of wood that are pressed together and stuck with glue

chip·munk /ˈtʃɪpmʌŋk/ *noun* a small N American animal of the SQUIRREL family, with light and dark marks on its back

chipo·lata /ˌtʃɪpəˈlɑːtə/ *noun* (*especially BrE*) a small thin sausage

chip·pings /ˈtʃɪpɪŋz/ *noun* [pl.] (*BrE*) small pieces of stone or wood

chippy /ˈtʃɪpi/ *noun, adj.*
■ *noun* (also **chip·pie**) (*pl.* **-ies**) (*BrE*, *informal*) **1** = CHIP SHOP **2** = CARPENTER
■ *adj.* (*informal*) (of a person) getting annoyed or offended easily

'chip shop (also *informal* **chip·py, chip·pie**) *noun* (in Britain) a shop that cooks and sells fish and chips and other fried food for people to take home and eat

chir·opo·dist /kɪˈrɒpədɪst; *AmE* kɪˈrɑːp-/ (*especially BrE*) (*AmE* usually **po·dia·trist**) *noun* a person whose job is the care and treatment of people's feet

chir·opody /kɪˈrɒpədi; *AmE* kɪˈrɑːp-/ (*especially BrE*) (*AmE* usually **po·dia·try**) *noun* [U] the work of a chiropodist

chiro·prac·tic /ˌkaɪərəʊˈpræktɪk; *AmE* -roʊ-/ *noun* [U] the work of a chiropractor

chiro·prac·tor /ˈkaɪərəʊpræktə(r); *AmE* -roʊ-/ *noun* a person whose job involves treating some diseases and physical problems by pressing and moving the bones in a person's SPINE or joints—compare OSTEOPATH

chirp /tʃɜːp; *AmE* tʃɜːrp/ (also **chir·rup** /ˈtʃɪrəp/) *verb* **1** [V] (of small birds and some insects) to make short high sounds **2** [V, V speech] to speak in a lively and cheerful way ► **chirp** (also **chir·rup**) *noun*

chirpy /ˈtʃɜːpi; *AmE* ˈtʃɜːrpi/ *adj.* (*informal*) lively and cheerful; in a good mood ► **chirp·ily** *adv.* **chirpi·ness** *noun* [U]

chisel /ˈtʃɪzl/ *noun, verb*
■ *noun* a tool with a sharp flat edge at the end, used for shaping wood, stone or metal—picture at TOOL

s	t	v	z	ʃ	ʒ	tʃ	dʒ	θ	ð	ŋ
see	tea	van	zoo	shoe	vision	chain	jam	thin	this	sing

C

■ *verb* (**-ll-**, *AmE* usually **-l-**) [often+*adv.*/*prep.*] to cut or shape wood or stone with a chisel: [VN] *A name was chiselled into the stone.* ◇ *She was chiselling some marble.* [also V]

chis·elled (*BrE*) (*AmE* **chis·eled**) /ˈtʃɪzld/ *adj.* (of a person's face) having clear strong features

chit /tʃɪt/ *noun* (*BrE*) **1** a short written note, signed by sb, showing an amount of money that is owed, or giving sb permission to do sth **2** (*old-fashioned, disapproving*) a young woman or girl, especially one who is thought to have no respect for older people

chit-chat *noun* [U] (*informal*) conversation about things that are not important [SYN] CHAT

chiv·al·rous /ˈʃɪvlrəs/ *adj.* (of men) polite, kind and behaving with honour, especially towards women ▶ **chiv·al·rous·ly** *adv.*

chiv·alry /ˈʃɪvəlri/ *noun* [U] **1** polite and kind behaviour that shows a sense of honour, especially by men towards women **2** (in the Middle Ages) the religious and moral system of behaviour which the perfect KNIGHT was expected to follow: *the age of chivalry*

chives /tʃaɪvz/ *noun* [pl.] the long thin leaves of a plant with purple flowers. Chives taste like onions and are used to give flavour to food. ▶ **chive** *adj.* [only before noun]: *a chive and garlic dressing*

chivvy /ˈtʃɪvi/ *verb* (**chiv·vies, chivvy·ing, chiv·vied, chiv·vied**) ~ **sb (into sth)**| ~ **sb (along)** (*BrE*) to try and make sb hurry or do sth quickly, especially when they do not want to do it: [VN] *He chivvied them into the car.* [also VN to inf]

chlor·ide /ˈklɔːraɪd/ *noun* [U, C] (*chemistry*) a compound of CHLORINE and another chemical element—see also SODIUM CHLORIDE

chlor·in·ate /ˈklɔːrɪneɪt/ *verb* [VN] to put chlorine in sth, especially water ▶ **chlor·in·ation** /ˌklɔːrɪˈneɪʃn/ *noun* [U]: *a chlorination plant*

chlor·ine /ˈklɔːriːn/ *noun* [U] (*symb* **Cl**) a chemical element. Chlorine is a poisonous greenish-yellow gas with a strong smell. It is often used in swimming pools to keep the water clean.

chloro·fluoro·car·bon /ˌklɔːrəʊˈflʊərəʊkɑːbən; *AmE* ˌklɔːroʊˈflʊroʊkɑːrbən/ *noun* (*chemistry*) a CFC

chloro·form /ˈklɒrəfɔːm; *AmE* ˈklɔːrəfɔːrm/ *noun* [U] (*symb* **CHCl₃**) a colourless liquid used in the past in medicine, etc. to make people unconscious, for example before an operation

chloro·phyll /ˈklɒrəfɪl; *AmE* ˈklɔːr-/ *noun* [U] the green substance in plants that absorbs light from the sun to help them grow—see also PHOTOSYNTHESIS

choc /tʃɒk; *AmE* tʃɑːk/ *noun* (*BrE, informal*) a chocolate: *a box of chocs*

choca·hol·ic = CHOCOHOLIC

choc ice *noun* (*BrE*) a small block of ice cream covered with chocolate

chock-a-block /ˌtʃɒk ə ˈblɒk; *AmE* ˌtʃɑːk ə ˈblɑːk/ *adj.* [not before noun] ~ **(with sth/sb)** (*BrE, informal*) very full of things or people pressed close together: *The shelves were chock-a-block with souvenirs and ornaments.* ◇ *It was chock-a-block in town today* (= full of people).

chock-full /ˌtʃɒk ˈful; *AmE* tʃɑːk/ *adj.* [not before noun] ~ **(of sth/sb)** (*informal*) completely full

choco·hol·ic (also **choca·hol·ic**) /ˌtʃɒkəˈhɒlɪk; *AmE* ˌtʃɑːkəˈhɑːlɪk; -ˈhɔːlɪk/ *noun* (*informal*) a person who likes chocolate very much and eats a lot of it

choc·olate /ˈtʃɒklət; *AmE* ˈtʃɑːk-/ *noun* **1** [U] a hard brown sweet food made from COCOA beans, used in cooking to add flavour to cakes, etc. or eaten as a sweet/candy: *a bar/piece of chocolate* ◇ *a chocolate cake* ◇ *a chocolate factory*—see also MILK CHOCOLATE, PLAIN CHOCOLATE **2** [C] a sweet/candy that is made of or covered with chocolate: *a box of chocolates* **3** [U, C] (*BrE*) = HOT CHOCOLATE: *a mug of drinking chocolate*—compare COCOA **4** [U] a dark brown colour

chocolate-box *adj.* [only before noun] (*BrE*) (especially of places) very pretty, but in a way that does not seem real: *a chocolate-box village*

choice /tʃɔɪs/ *noun, adj.*

■ *noun* **1** [C] ~ **(between A and B)** an act of choosing between two or more possibilities; something that you can choose: *women forced to make a choice between family and career* ◇ *We are faced with a difficult choice.* ◇ *We aim to help students make more informed career choices.* ◇ *There is a wide range of choices open to you.* **2** [U, sing.] the right to choose or the possibility of choosing: *If I had the choice, I would stop working tomorrow.* ◇ *He had no choice but to leave* (= this was the only thing he could do). ◇ *She's going to do it. She doesn't have much choice, really, does she?* ◇ *This government is committed to extending parental choice in education.* **3** [C] a person or thing that is chosen: *She's the obvious choice for the job.* ◇ *Hawaii remains a popular choice for winter vacation travel.* ◇ *This colour wasn't my first choice.* ◇ *She wouldn't be my choice as manager.* **4** [sing., U] the number or range of different things from which to choose: *The menu has a good choice of desserts.* ◇ *There wasn't much choice of colour.*—see also HOBSON'S CHOICE, MULTIPLE-CHOICE [IDM] **by ˈchoice** because you have chosen: *I wouldn't go there by choice.* **of ˈchoice (for sb/sth)** (used after a noun) that is chosen by a particular group of people or for a particular purpose: *It's the software of choice for business use.* **of your ˈchoice** that you choose yourself: *First prize will be a meal for two at the restaurant of your choice.*—more at SPOILT

■ *adj.* (**choicer, choicest**) [only before noun] **1** (especially of food) of very good quality **2** (*AmE*) (of meat) of very good, but not the highest, quality **3** ~ **words/phrases** carefully chosen words or phrases: *She summed up the situation in a few choice phrases.* ◇ (*humorous*) *He used some pretty choice* (= rude or offensive) *language.*

choir /ˈkwaɪə(r)/ *noun* **1** [C+sing./pl. v.] a group of people who sing together, especially in church services or public performances: *She sings in the school choir.* **2** [C] the part of a church where the choir sits during services

choir·boy /ˈkwaɪəbɔɪ; *AmE* ˈkwaɪərbɔɪ/, **choir·girl** /ˈkwaɪəgɜːl; *AmE* ˈkwaɪərgɜːrl/ *noun* a boy or girl who sings in the choir of a church or CATHEDRAL—see also CHORISTER

choir·mas·ter /ˈkwaɪəmɑːstə(r); *AmE* ˈkwaɪərmæstər/ *noun* a person who trains a CHOIR to sing

choke /tʃəʊk; *AmE* tʃoʊk/ *verb, noun*

■ *verb* **1** ~ **(on sth)** to be unable to breathe because the passage to your lungs is blocked or you cannot get enough air; to make sb unable to breathe: [V] *He was choking on a piece of toast.* ◇ *She almost choked to death in the thick fumes.* ◇ [VN] *Very small toys can choke a baby.* **2** [VN] to make sb stop breathing by squeezing their throat [SYN] STRANGLE: *He may have been choked or poisoned.* **3** ~ **(with sth)** to be unable to speak normally especially because of strong emotion; to make sb feel too emotional to speak normally: [V] *His voice was choking with rage.* ◇ [VN] *Despair choked her words.* ◇ *'I can't bear it,' he said in a choked voice.*—see also CHOKED **4** [VN] ~ **sth (up) (with sth)** to block or fill a passage, space, etc. so that movement is difficult: *The pond was choked with rotten leaves.* ◇ *The roads are choked up with traffic.* **5** [V] (*AmE, informal*) to fail at sth, for example because you are nervous [PHRV] **ˌchoke sth↔ˈback** to try hard to prevent your feelings from showing: *to choke back tears/anger/sobs* **ˌchoke sth↔ˈdown** to swallow sth with difficulty **ˌchoke sth↔ˈoff 1** to prevent or limit sth: *High prices have choked off demand.* **2** to interrupt sth; to stop sth: *Her screams were suddenly choked off.* **ˌchoke ˈout**| **choke out sth** to say sth with great difficulty because you feel a strong emotion: *He choked out a reply.* ◇ [+speech] *'I hate you!' she choked out.* **ˌchoke ˈup** (*AmE*) to find it difficult to speak, because of the strong emotion that you are feeling: *She choked up when she began to talk about her mother.*

■ *noun* **1** a device that controls the amount of air flowing into the engine of a vehicle **2** an act or the sound of choking

choked /tʃəʊkt; *AmE* tʃoʊkt/ *adj.* [not before noun] ~ **up (about sth)**| (*BrE* also) ~ **(about sth)** (*informal*) upset or angry about sth, so that you find it difficult to speak

æ ɑː e ɜː ə ɪ iː i ɒ ɔː ʌ ʊ u uː
cat father ten bird about sit see many got saw cup put actual too
(BrE)

chok·er /'tʃəʊkə(r); *AmE* 'tʃoʊ-/ *noun* a piece of jewellery or narrow band of fabric worn closely around the neck: *a pearl choker*

chol·era /'kɒlərə; *AmE* 'kɑːl-/ *noun* [U] a disease caught from infected water that causes severe DIARRHOEA and VOMITING and often causes death

chol·er·ic /'kɒlərɪk; *AmE* 'kɑːl-/ *adj.* (*rare, formal*) easily made angry; bad-tempered

chol·es·terol /kə'lestərɒl; *AmE* -rɔːl/ *noun* [U] a substance found in blood, fat and most tissues of the body. Too much cholesterol can cause heart disease: *a high cholesterol level*

chomp /tʃɒmp; *AmE* tʃɑːmp; tʃɔːmp/ *verb* ~ (**on/through sth**) to eat or bite food noisily: [VN] *He chomped his way through two hot dogs.* ◊ [V] *She was chomping away on a bagel.*

choose /tʃuːz/ *verb* (**chose** /tʃəʊz; *AmE* tʃoʊz/, **chosen** /'tʃəʊzn; *AmE* 'tʃoʊzn/) **1** ~ (**between A and/or B**)|~ (**A**) (**from B**)|~ **sb/sth as sth** to decide which thing or person you want out of the ones that are available: [V] *You choose, I can't decide.* ◊ *There are plenty of restaurants to choose from.* ◊ *She had to choose between giving up her job or hiring a nanny.* ◊ [VN] *Sarah chose her words carefully.* ◊ *We have to choose a new manager from a shortlist of five candidates.* ◊ *This site has been chosen for the new school.* ◊ *He chose banking as a career.* ◊ *We chose Paul Stubbs as/for chairperson.* ◊ [Vwh-] *You'll have to choose whether to buy it or not.* ◊ [VtoINF] *We chose to go by train.* ◊ [VNtoINF] *We chose Paul Stubbs to be chairperson.* **2** to prefer or decide to do sth: [V] *Employees can retire at 60 if they choose.* ◊ [VtoINF] *Many people choose not to marry.*—see also CHOICE *n.* **IDM there is nothing/not much/little to choose between A and B** there is very little difference between two or more things or people—more at PICK *v.*

chooser /'tʃuːzə(r)/ *noun* **IDM** see BEGGAR *n.*

choosy /'tʃuːzi/ *adj.* (*informal*) careful in choosing; difficult to please **SYN** PICKY: *I'm very choosy about my clothes.*

chop /tʃɒp; *AmE* tʃɑːp/ *verb, noun*
■ *verb* (**-pp-**) **1** ~ **sth** (**up**) (**into sth**) to cut sth into pieces with a sharp tool such as a knife: [VN] *Chop the carrots up into small pieces.* ◊ *Add the finely chopped onions.* ◊ *He was chopping logs for firewood.* ◊ (*figurative*) *The country was chopped up into small administrative areas.* **2** [VN] [usually passive] (*informal*) to reduce sth by a large amount; to stop sth **SYN** CUT: *The share price was chopped from 50 pence to 20 pence.* **3** [VN] to hit sth with a short downward stroke or blow **IDM** ˌchop and ˈchange (*BrE, informal*) to keep changing your mind or what you are doing **PHRV** ˈchop (**away**) **at sth** to aim blows at sth with a heavy sharp tool such as an AXE ˌchop **sth↔ˈdown** to make sth, such as a tree, fall by cutting it at the base with a sharp tool ˌchop **sth↔ˈoff** (**sth**) to remove sth by cutting it with a sharp tool: *He chopped a branch off the tree.* ◊ (*informal*) *Anne Boleyn had her head chopped off.*
■ *noun* **1** [C] A thick slice of meat with a bone attached to it, especially from a pig or sheep: *a pork/lamb chop* **2** [C] an act of cutting sth with a quick downward movement using an AXE or a knife **3** [C] an act of hitting sth with the side of your hand in a quick downward movement: *a karate chop* **4** (**chops**) [pl.] (*informal*) the part of a person's or an animal's face around the mouth: *The dog sat licking its chops.* **IDM** **get/be given the ˈchop** (*BrE, informal*) **1** (of a person) to be dismissed from a job: *The whole department has been given the chop.* **2** (of a plan, project, etc.) to be stopped or ended: *Three more schemes have got the chop.* **be for the ˈchop** (*BrE, informal*) **1** (of a person) to be likely to be dismissed from a job: *Who's next for the chop?* **2** (of a plan, project, etc.) to be likely to be stopped or ended

ˌchop-ˈchop *exclamation* (*BrE, informal*) hurry up!: *Chop-chop! We haven't got all day!* **ORIGIN** From pidgin English based on a Chinese dialect word for 'quick'.

chop·per /'tʃɒpə(r); *AmE* 'tʃɑːp-/ *noun* **1** (*informal*) = HELICOPTER **2** a large heavy knife or small AXE **3** (*AmE*) a type of motorcycle with a long piece of metal connecting the front wheel to the HANDLEBARS

ˈchopping board (*BrE*) (*AmE* **ˈcutting board**) *noun* a board made of wood or plastic used for cutting meat or vegetables on

choppy /'tʃɒpi; *AmE* 'tʃɑːpi/ *adj.* **1** (of the sea, etc.) with a lot of small waves; not calm: *choppy waters* **2** (*AmE, disapproving*) (of a style of writing) containing a lot of short sentences and changing topics too often

chop·stick /'tʃɒpstɪk; *AmE* 'tʃɑːp-/ *noun* [usually pl.] either of a pair of thin sticks that are used for eating with, especially in Asian countries—picture at CUTLERY, STICK

chop suey /ˌtʃɒp 'suːi; *AmE* ˌtʃɑːp/ *noun* [U] a Chinese-style dish of small pieces of meat fried with vegetables and served with rice

choral /'kɔːrəl/ *adj.* connected with, written for or sung by a CHOIR (= a group of singers): *choral music*

chor·ale /kɒ'rɑːl; *AmE* kə'ræl; -'rɑːl/ *noun* **1** a piece of church music with an impressive but simple tune **2** (*especially AmE*) a group of singers; a CHOIR

chord /kɔːd; *AmE* kɔːrd/ *noun* **1** (*music*) two or more notes played together **2** (*mathematics*) a straight line that joins two points on a curve—picture at CIRCLE—see also VOCAL CORDS **IDM** **strike/touch a ˈchord (with sb)** to say or do sth that makes people feel sympathy or enthusiasm: *The speaker had obviously struck a chord with his audience.*

chore /tʃɔː(r)/ *noun* **1** a task that you do regularly: *doing the household/domestic chores* **2** an unpleasant or boring task: *Shopping's a real chore for me.*

choreo·graph /'kɒriəɡrɑːf; -ɡræf; *AmE* 'kɔːriəɡræf/ *verb* [VN] to design and arrange the steps and movements for dancers in a ballet or a show: (*figurative*) *There was some carefully choreographed flag-waving as the President drove by.*

chore·og·raphy /ˌkɒri'ɒɡrəfi; *AmE* ˌkɔːri'ɑːɡ-/ *noun* [U] the art of designing and arranging the steps and movements in dances, especially in ballet; the steps and movements in a particular ballet or show ▶ **chore·og·raph·er** /ˌkɒri'ɒɡrəfə(r); *AmE* ˌkɔːri'ɑːɡ-/ *noun* **choreo·graph·ic** /ˌkɒriə'ɡræfɪk; *AmE* ˌkɔːriə-/ *adj.*

chor·is·ter /'kɒrɪstə(r); *AmE* 'kɔːr-/ *noun* a person, especially a boy, who sings in the CHOIR of a church

chor·tle /'tʃɔːtl; *AmE* 'tʃɔːrtl/ *verb* to laugh loudly with pleasure or amusement: [V] *Gill chortled with delight.* [also Vspeech] ▶ **chor·tle** *noun*

chorus /'kɔːrəs/ *noun, verb*
■ *noun* **1** [C] part of a song that is sung after each verse **SYN** REFRAIN: *Everyone joined in the chorus.* **2** [C] a piece of music, usually part of a larger work, that is written for a CHOIR (= a group of singers): *the Hallelujah Chorus* **3** [C+sing./pl. v.] (often in names) a large group of singers **SYN** CHOIR: *the Bath Festival Chorus* **4** [C+sing./pl. v.] a group of performers who sing and dance in a musical show: *the chorus line* (= a line of singers and dancers performing together) **5 a** ~ **of sth** [sing.] the sound of a lot of people expressing approval or disapproval at the same time: *a chorus of praise/complaint* ◊ *a chorus of voices calling for her resignation*—see also DAWN CHORUS **6** [sing.+ sing. v.] (in ancient Greek drama) a group of performers who comment together on the events of the play **7** [sing.] (especially in 16th century drama) an actor who speaks the opening and closing words of the play **IDM** **in chorus** all together **SYN** IN UNISON: *'Thank you,' they said in chorus.*
■ *verb* to sing or say sth all together: [Vspeech] *'Hello, Paul,' they chorused.* [also VN]

ˈchorus girl *noun* a girl or young woman who is a member of the chorus in a musical show, etc.

chose *pt* of CHOOSE

chosen *pp* of CHOOSE

chow /tʃaʊ/ *noun* **1** [U] (*slang*) food **2** (also **ˈchow chow**) [C] a dog with long thick hair, a curled tail and a blue-black tongue, originally from China

chow·der /'tʃaʊdə(r)/ *noun* [U] a thick soup made with fish and vegetables: *clam chowder*

aɪ	aʊ	eɪ	əʊ	oʊ	ɔɪ	ɪə	eə	ʊə	j	w
my	now	say	go (BrE)	go (AmE)	boy	near	hair	pure	yes	wet

Christ /kraɪst/ (also **Jesus, ˌJesus ˈChrist**) *noun, exclamation*
- *noun* the man that Christians believe is the son of God and on whose teachings the Christian religion is based
- *exclamation* (⚠, *informal*) a swear word that many people find offensive, used to show that you are angry, annoyed or surprised: *Christ! Look at the time—I'm late!*

chris·ten /ˈkrɪsn/ *verb* (*informal*) **1** to give a name to a baby at his or her baptism to welcome him or her into the Christian Church: [VN-N] *The child was christened Mary.* ◊ [VN] *Did you have your children christened?* **2** to give a name to sb/sth: [VN-N] *This area has been christened 'Britain's last wilderness'.* ◊ *They christened the boat 'Oceania'.* [also VN] **3** [VN] (*informal*) to use sth for the first time: *Let's have a drink to christen our new wine glasses.*

Chris·ten·dom /ˈkrɪsndəm/ *noun* [U] (*old-fashioned*) all the Christian people and countries of the world

chris·ten·ing /ˈkrɪsnɪŋ/ *noun* a Christian ceremony in which a baby is officially named and welcomed into the Christian Church—compare BAPTISM

Chris·tian /ˈkrɪstʃən/ *adj., noun*
- *adj.* **1** based on or believing the teachings of Jesus Christ: *the Christian Church/faith/religion* ◊ *She had a Christian upbringing.* ◊ *a Christian country* **2** connected with Christians: *the Christian sector of the city* **3** (also **christian**) showing the qualities that are thought of as typical of a Christian; good and kind
- *noun* a person who believes in the teachings of Jesus Christ or has been BAPTIZED in a Christian church: *Only 10% of the population are now practising Christians.*

Chris·tian·ity /ˌkrɪsti'ænəti/ *noun* [U] the religion that is based on the teachings of Jesus Christ and the belief that he was the son of God

ˈChristian name *noun* (*BrE*) (in western countries) a name given to sb when they are born or when they are CHRISTENED; a personal name, not a family name: *We're all on Christian name terms here.*

Christ·mas /ˈkrɪsməs/ *noun* [U,C] **1** (also **ˌChristmas ˈDay**) 25 December, the day when Christians celebrate the birth of Christ: *Christmas dinner/presents*—see also BOXING DAY **2** (also **Christ·mas·time**) the period that includes Christmas Day and the days close to it: *the Christmas holidays/vacation* ◊ *Are you spending Christmas with your family?* ◊ *Happy Christmas!* ◊ *Merry Christmas and a Happy New Year!*

ˈChristmas box *noun* (*BrE, old-fashioned*) a small gift, usually of money, given at Christmas to sb who provides a service during the year, for example a POSTMAN

ˈChristmas cake *noun* [C, U] a fruit cake covered with MARZIPAN and ICING, traditionally eaten in Britain at Christmas

ˈChristmas card *noun* a card with a picture on it that you send to friends and relatives at Christmas with your good wishes

ˌChristmas ˈcracker *noun* = CRACKER

ˌChristmas ˈEve *noun* [U, C] the day before Christmas Day, 24 December; the evening of this day

ˌChristmas ˈpudding *noun* [C, U] a hot PUDDING (= a sweet dish) like a dark fruit cake, traditionally eaten in Britain at Christmas—picture on page A1

ˌChristmas ˈstocking (also **stock·ing**) *noun* a long sock which children leave out when they go to bed on Christmas Eve so that it can be filled with presents

Christ·massy /ˈkrɪsməsi/ *adj.* (*informal*) typical of Christmas: *We put up the decorations and the tree and started to feel Christmassy at last.*

Christ·mas·time /ˈkrɪsməstaɪm/ *noun* [U, C] = CHRISTMAS (2)

ˈChristmas tree *noun* an EVERGREEN tree, or an artificial tree that looks similar, that people decorate with coloured lights and ornaments and have in their homes or outside at Christmas

chro·mat·ic /krə'mætɪk/ *adj.* (*music*) of the **chromatic scale**, a series of musical notes that rise and fall in SEMITONES/HALF-TONES—compare DIATONIC

chrome /krəʊm; *AmE* kroʊm/ *noun* [U] a hard shiny metal used especially as a protective covering for other metals; chromium or an ALLOY of chromium and other metals: *glittering modern buildings of chrome, steel and glass*

chro·mium /ˈkrəʊmiəm; *AmE* ˈkroʊ-/ *noun* [U] (*symb* **Cr**) a chemical element. Chromium is a hard grey metal that shines brightly when polished and is often used to cover other metals in order to prevent them from RUSTING: *chromium-plated steel*

chromo·some /ˈkrəʊməsəʊm; *AmE* ˈkroʊməsoʊm/ *noun* (*biology*) one of the very small parts like threads in the NUCLEI (= central parts) of animal and plant cells, that carry the GENES—see also SEX CHROMOSOME, X CHROMOSOME, Y CHROMOSOME ▶ **chromo·somal** /-əl/ *adj.*: *chromosomal abnormalities/DNA*

chron·ic /ˈkrɒnɪk; *AmE* ˈkrɑːn-/ *adj.* **1** (especially of a disease) lasting for a long time; difficult to cure or get rid of: *chronic bronchitis/arthritis/asthma* ◊ *the country's chronic unemployment problem* ◊ *a chronic shortage of housing in rural areas*—compare ACUTE **2** having had a disease for a long time: *a chronic alcoholic/depressive* **3** (*BrE, informal*) very bad: *The film was just chronic.* ▶ **chron·ic·al·ly** /ˈkrɒnɪkli; *AmE* ˈkrɑːn-/ *adv.*: *a hospital for the chronically ill*

ˌchronic fa'tigue syndrome *noun* [U] = ME

chron·icle /ˈkrɒnɪkl; *AmE* ˈkrɑːn-/ *noun, verb*
- *noun* a written record of events in the order in which they happened: *the Anglo-Saxon Chronicle* ◊ *Her latest novel is a chronicle of life in a Devon village.*
- *verb* [VN] (*written*) to record events in the order in which they happened: *Her achievements are chronicled in a new biography out this week.* ▶ **chron·ic·ler** /ˈkrɒnɪklə(r); *AmE* ˈkrɑːn-/ *noun*

chrono- /ˈkrɒnəʊ; *AmE* ˈkrɑːnoʊ/ *combining form* (in nouns, adjectives and adverbs) connected with time: *chronological*

chrono·logic·al /ˌkrɒnə'lɒdʒɪkl; *AmE* ˌkrɑːnə'lɑːdʒ-/ *adj.* **1** (of a number of events) arranged in the order in which they happened: *The facts should be presented clearly and in chronological order.* **2** ~ **age** (*formal*) the number of years a person has lived as opposed to their level of physical, mental or emotional development—compare MENTAL AGE ▶ **chrono·logic·al·ly** /-kli/ *adv.*

chron·ology /krə'nɒlədʒi; *AmE* -'nɑːl-/ *noun* (*pl.* **-ies**) [U, C] the order in which a series of events happened; a list of these events in order: *Historians seem to have confused the chronology of these events.* ◊ *a problem of chronology* ◊ *a chronology of Mozart's life*

chron·om·eter /krə'nɒmɪtə(r); *AmE* -'nɑːm-/ *noun* a very accurate clock, especially one used at sea

chrys·alis /ˈkrɪsəlɪs/ *noun* (also **chrys·alid**) the form of an insect, especially a BUTTERFLY or MOTH, while it is changing into an adult inside a hard case, also called a chrysalis—compare PUPA—picture on page A7

chrys·an·the·mum /krɪ'sænθəməm; -'zæn-/ *noun* a large, brightly coloured garden flower that is shaped like a ball and made up of many long narrow PETALS

chub /tʃʌb/ *noun* (*pl.* **chub**) a FRESHWATER fish with a thick body

chubby /ˈtʃʌbi/ *adj.* slightly fat in a way that people usually find attractive: *chubby cheeks/fingers/hands* ▶ **chub·bi·ness** *noun* [U]

chuck /tʃʌk/ *verb, noun*
- *verb* (*informal*) **1** (*especially BrE*) to throw sth carelessly or without much thought: [VN, usually +*adv./prep.*] *He chucked the paper in a drawer.* ◊ [VNN] *Chuck me the newspaper, would you?* [also VN] **2** [VN] ~ **sth (in/up)** to give up or stop doing sth: *You haven't chucked your job?* ◊ *I'm going to chuck it all in* (= give up my job) *and go abroad.* **3** [VN] (*BrE*) to leave your boyfriend or girlfriend and stop having a relationship with him or her: *Has he chucked her?* **4** [VN] (*spoken*) to throw sth away: *That's no good—just chuck it.* IDM **chuck sb under the chin** (*old-fashioned, BrE*) to touch sb gently under the chin in a friendly way **it's 'chucking it down** (*BrE, spoken*) it's raining heavily PHRV **ˌchuck sth↔a'way**| **ˌchuck sth↔'out** to throw sth away: *Those old clothes can be*

chucked out. ,chuck sb '**off (sth)**| ,chuck sb '**out (of sth)** to force sb to leave a place or a job: *They got chucked off the bus.* ◇ *You can't just chuck him out.*

■ *noun* **1** [C] a part of a tool such as a DRILL that can be adjusted to hold sth tightly—picture at TOOL **2** [sing.] (*NorthE, informal*) a friendly way of addressing sb: *What's up with you, chuck?* **3** (also ,chuck '**steak**) [U] meat from the shoulder of a cow

chuckle /'tʃʌkl/ *verb* ~ (**at/about sth**) to laugh quietly: [V] *She chuckled at the memory.* [also V speech] ▶ **chuckle** *noun*: *She gave a chuckle of delight.*

chuffed /tʃʌft/ *adj.* [not before noun] ~ (**about sth**) (*BrE, informal*) very pleased

chug /tʃʌɡ/ *verb, noun*
■ *verb* (**-gg-**) **1** [V] [usually +*adv./prep.*] to move making the sound of an engine running slowly: *The boat chugged down the river.* **2** [VN] (*AmE, slang*) to drink all of sth quickly without stopping
■ *noun* the sound made by a chugging engine

chum /tʃʌm/ *noun* (*old-fashioned, informal*) a friend: *an old school chum*

chummy /'tʃʌmi/ *adj.* (*old-fashioned, informal*) very friendly ▶ **chum·mily** *adv.* **chum·mi·ness** *noun* [U]

chump /tʃʌmp/ *noun* (*old-fashioned, informal*) a stupid person: *Don't be such a chump!*

chun·der /'tʃʌndə(r)/ *verb* [V] (*AustralE, informal*) to VOMIT ▶ **chun·der** *noun* [U]

chunk /tʃʌŋk/ *noun* **1** a thick solid piece that has been cut or broken off sth: *a chunk of cheese/masonry* **2** (*informal*) a fairly large amount of sth: *I've already written a fair chunk of the article.*

chunky /'tʃʌŋki/ *adj.* **1** thick and heavy: *a chunky gold bracelet* ◇ (*BrE*) *a chunky sweater* **2** having a short strong body: *a squat chunky man* **3** (of food) containing thick pieces: *chunky marmalade*

chun·ter /'tʃʌntə(r)/ *verb* [V] ~ (**on**) (**about sth**) (*BrE, informal*) to talk or complain about sth in a way that other people think is boring or annoying: *He's always chuntering on about something or other.*

church /tʃɜːtʃ; *AmE* tʃɜːrtʃ/ *noun* **1** [C] a building where Christians go to worship: *a church tower* ◇ *The procession moved into the church.* ◇ *church services* **2** [U] a service or services in a church: *How often do you go to church?* ◇ (*BrE*) *They're at church* (= attending a church service). ◇ (*AmE*) *They're in church.* ◇ *Church is at 9 o'clock.* ⇨ note at SCHOOL **3** (**Church**) [C] a particular group of Christians: *the Anglican Church* ◇ *the Catholic Church* ◇ *the Free Churches*—see also DENOMINATION **4** (**the**) **Church** [sing.] the ministers of the Christian religion; the institution of the Christian religion: *The Church has a duty to condemn violence.* ◇ *the conflict between Church and State* ◇ *to go into the Church* (= to become a Christian minister) IDM see BROAD *adj.*

church·goer /'tʃɜːtʃɡəʊə(r); *AmE* 'tʃɜːrtʃɡoʊər/ *noun* a person who goes to church services regularly ▶ **church-going** *noun* [U]

church·man /'tʃɜːtʃmən; *AmE* 'tʃɜːrtʃ-/, **church-woman** /'tʃɜːtʃwʊmən; *AmE* 'tʃɜːrtʃ-/ *noun* (*pl.* **-men** /-mən/, **-women** /-wɪmɪn/) = CLERGYMAN, CLERGYWOMAN

the ,Church of 'England *noun* (*abbr.* **CE, C. of E.**) [sing.] the official Church in England, whose leader is the Queen or King

church·war·den /ˌtʃɜːtʃ'wɔːdn; *AmE* ˌtʃɜːrtʃ'wɔːrdn/ *noun* (in the Anglican Church) a person who is chosen by the members of a church to take care of church property and money

church·yard /'tʃɜːtʃjɑːd; *AmE* 'tʃɜːrtʃjɑːrd/ *noun* an enclosed area of land around a church, often used for burying people—compare CEMETERY, GRAVEYARD

churl·ish /'tʃɜːlɪʃ; *AmE* 'tʃɜːrlɪʃ/ *adj.* (*formal*) rude or bad-tempered: *It would be churlish to refuse such a generous offer.* ▶ **churl·ish·ly** *adv.* **churl·ish·ness** *noun* [U]

churn /tʃɜːn; *AmE* tʃɜːrn/ *verb, noun*
■ *verb* **1** ~ (**sth**) (**up**) if water, mud, etc. **churns**, or if sth **churns it** (**up**), it moves or is moved around violently: [V] *The water churned beneath the huge ship.* ◇ [VN] *Vast crowds had churned the field into a sea of mud.* **2** if your stomach **churns** or if sth **churns** your stomach, you feel a strong, unpleasant feeling of worry, disgust or fear: [V] *My stomach churned as the names were read out.* [also VN] **3** ~ (**sb**) (**up**) to feel or to make sb feel upset or emotionally confused: [V] *Conflicting emotions churned inside him.* [also VN] **4** [VN] to turn and stir milk in a special container in order to make butter PHRV ,churn sth↔'out (*informal, often disapproving*) to produce sth quickly and in large amounts: *She churns out novels at the rate of three a year.*
■ *noun* **1** a machine in which milk or cream is shaken to make butter **2** (*BrE*) a large metal container in which milk was carried from a farm in the past

chute /ʃuːt/ *noun* **1** a tube or passage down which people or things can slide: *a water chute* (= at a swimming pool) ◇ *a laundry/rubbish/garbage chute* (= from the upper floors of a high building) **2** (*informal*) = PARACHUTE

,**Chutes and 'Ladders**™ *noun* [U] (*AmE*) = SNAKES AND LADDERS

chut·ney /'tʃʌtni/ *noun* [U] a cold thick sauce made from fruit, sugar, spices, and VINEGAR, eaten with cold meat, cheese, etc.

chutz·pah /'xʊtspə; 'hʊ-/ *noun* [U] (*often approving*) behaviour, or a person's attitude, that is rude or shocking but so confident that people may feel forced to admire it SYN NERVE

CIA /ˌsiː aɪ 'eɪ/ *abbr.* Central Intelligence Agency. The CIA is a department of the US government which collects information about other countries, often secretly.

ciao /tʃaʊ/ *exclamation* (from *Italian, informal*) goodbye

ci·cada /sɪ'kɑːdə; *AmE* sɪ'keɪdə/ *noun* a large insect with transparent wings, common in hot countries, that makes a continuous high sound by rubbing its legs together: *Cicadas buzzed in the heat of the day.*

CID /ˌsiː aɪ 'diː/ *abbr.* Criminal Investigation Department. The CID is the department of the British police force that is responsible for solving crimes.

-cide *combining form* (in nouns) **1** the act of killing: *suicide* ◇ *genocide* **2** a person or thing that kills: *insecticide* ▶ **-cidal** (in adjectives): *homicidal*

cider /'saɪdə(r)/ *noun* **1** (*BrE*) (*AmE* '**hard cider**) [U, C] an alcoholic drink made from the juice of apples: *dry/sweet cider* ◇ *cider apples* ◇ *a cider press* (= for squeezing the juice from apples) **2** (*AmE*) [U, C] a drink made from the juice of apples that does not contain alcohol **3** [C] a glass of cider—compare PERRY

cigar /sɪ'ɡɑː(r)/ *noun* a roll of dried tobacco leaves that people smoke, like a cigarette but bigger and without paper around it: *cigar smoke*

cig·ar·ette /ˌsɪɡə'ret; *AmE* 'sɪɡəret/ *noun* a thin tube of paper filled with tobacco, for smoking: *a packet/pack of cigarettes* ◇ *to light a cigarette*

ciga'rette end (*BrE*) (also **ciga'rette butt** *AmE, BrE*) *noun* the part of a cigarette that is left when sb has finished smoking it

ciga'rette holder *noun* a narrow tube for holding a cigarette in while you are smoking

ciga'rette lighter *noun* = LIGHTER

ciga'rette paper *noun* a thin piece of paper in which people roll tobacco to make their own cigarettes

ciggy /'sɪɡi/ *noun* (*pl.* **-ies**) (*informal*) a cigarette

ci·lan·tro /sɪ'læntrəʊ; *AmE* -troʊ/ *noun* [U] (*AmE*) the leaves of the CORIANDER plant, used in cooking as a herb

C.-in-C. /ˌsiː ɪn 'siː/ *abbr.* COMMANDER-IN-CHIEF

cinch /sɪntʃ/ *noun, verb*
■ *noun* [sing.] (*informal*) **1** something that is very easy: *The first question is a cinch.* **2** (*especially AmE*) a thing that is certain to happen; a person who is certain to do sth: *He's a cinch to win the race.*
■ *verb* [VN] **1** (*especially AmE*) to fasten sth tightly around your waist; to be fastened around sb's waist **2** (*AmE*) to fasten a GIRTH around a horse **3** (*AmE, informal*) to make sth certain

cin·der /'sɪndə(r)/ *noun* [usually pl.] a small piece of ash or partly burnt coal, wood, etc. that is no longer burning but may still be hot: *a cinder track* (= a track for runners made with finely crushed cinders) **IDM** see BURN *v*.

'cinder block *noun* (*AmE*) = BREEZE BLOCK

Cin·der·ella /ˌsɪndə'relə/ *noun* [usually sing.] a person or thing that has been ignored and deserves to receive more attention: *For years radio has been the Cinderella of the media world.* **ORIGIN** From the European fairy tale about a beautiful girl, **Cinderella**, who was treated harshly by her two ugly sisters. She had to do all the work and received no reward or thanks until she met and married Prince Charming.

cine /'sɪni/ *adj.* [only before noun] (*BrE*) connected with films/movies and the film/movie industry: *a cine cam-era/film/photographer*

cin·ema /'sɪnəmə/ *noun* 1 (*BrE*) (*AmE* **'movie theater, theater**) [C] a building in which films/movies are shown: *the local cinema* 2 (**the cinema**) [sing.] (*BrE*) (*AmE* **the movies** [pl.]) when you go to **the cinema** or to **the movies**, you go to a cinema/movie theater to see a film/movie: *I used to go to the cinema every week.* 3 [U, sing.] (*especially BrE*) (*AmE* usually **the movies** [pl.]) films/movies as an art or an industry: *one of the great successes of British cinema*

'cinema-goer *noun* (*BrE*) = FILM-GOER

cine·mat·ic /ˌsɪnə'mætɪk/ *adj.* (*technical*) connected with films/movies and how they are made: *cinematic effects/techniques*

cine·ma·tog·raphy /ˌsɪnəmə'tɒɡrəfi; *AmE* -'tɑːɡ-/ *noun* [U] (*technical*) the art or process of making films/movies ▶ **cine·ma·tog·raph·er** /ˌsɪnəmə'tɒɡrəfə(r); *AmE* -'tɑːɡ-/ *noun*

cin·na·mon /'sɪnəmən/ *noun* [U] the inner bark of a SE Asian tree, used in cooking as a spice, especially to give flavour to sweet foods

ci·pher (also **cy·pher**) /'saɪfə(r)/ *noun* 1 [U, C] a secret way of writing, especially one in which a set of letters or symbols is used to represent others: *a message in cipher*—see also DECIPHER 2 [C] (*formal, disapproving*) a person or thing of no importance: *To her employers she was a mere cipher, with no human feelings at all.* 3 (*BrE*) the first letters of sb's name combined in a design and used to mark things

circa /'sɜːkə; *AmE* 'sɜːrkə/ *prep.* (from *Latin*) (*abbr.* **c**) (used with dates) about: *born circa 150 BC*

cir·ca·dian /sɜː'keɪdiən; *AmE* sɜːr'k-/ *adj.* [only before noun] (*technical*) connected with the changes in the bodies of people or animals over each period of 24 hours

cir·cle /'sɜːkl; *AmE* 'sɜːrkl/ *noun, verb*

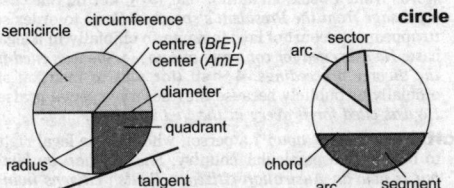

circle

semicircle — circumference — arc — sector
centre (*BrE*)/center (*AmE*)
diameter
quadrant
radius
tangent — chord — arc — segment

■ *noun* 1 a completely round flat shape: *Cut out two circles of paper.*—see also SEMICIRCLE 2 the line that encloses a circle: *Draw a circle.* ◊ *She walked the horse round in a circle.*—see also ANTARCTIC CIRCLE, ARCTIC CIRCLE, TURN-ING CIRCLE 3 a thing or a group of people or things shaped like a circle: *a circle of trees/chairs* ◊ *The children stood in a circle.*—see also CORN CIRCLE, CROP CIRCLE 4 (*BrE*) (also **bal·cony** *AmE, BrE*) an upper floor of a theatre or cinema/movie theater where the seats are arranged in curved rows: *We had seats in the circle.*—see also DRESS CIRCLE 5 a group of people who are connected because they have the same interests, jobs, etc: *the family circle* ◊ *She's well known in theatrical circles.* ◊ *a large/wide circle of friends*—see also CHARMED CIRCLE, INNER CIRCLE, VICIOUS CIRCLE **IDM** **come, turn, etc. full 'circle** to return to the situation in which you started, after a series of events or experiences **go round in 'circles** to work hard at sth or discuss sth without making any progress **run**

round in 'circles (*informal*) to be busy doing sth without achieving anything important or making progress

■ *verb* 1 ~ (**around**) (**above/over sb/sth**) to move in a circle, especially in the air: [V] *Seagulls circled around above his head.* ◊ [VN] *The plane circled the airport to burn up excess fuel.* 2 [VN] to draw a circle around sth: *Spelling mistakes are circled in red ink.*

circ·let /'sɜːklət; *AmE* 'sɜːrk-/ *noun* a circular band made of precious metal, flowers, etc., worn around the head as an ornament

cir·cuit /'sɜːkɪt; *AmE* 'sɜːrkɪt/ *noun* 1 a line, route, or journey around a place: *The race ended with eight laps of a city centre circuit.* ◊ *The earth takes a year to make a circuit of* (= go around) *the sun.* 2 the complete path of wires and equipment along which an electric current flows: *an electrical circuit* ◊ *a circuit diagram* (= one showing all the connections in the different parts of the circuit)—see also INTEGRATED CIRCUIT, PRINTED CIRCUIT, SHORT CIRCUIT 3 (in sport) a series of games or matches in which the same players regularly take part: *the women's tennis circuit* 4 a track for cars or motorcycles to race around 5 a series of places or events of a particular kind at which the same people appear or take part: *the lecture/cabaret circuit*—see also CLOSED-CIRCUIT TELEVISION 6 a regular journey made by a judge to hear court cases in each of the courts of law in a particular area: *a circuit judge*

'circuit board *noun* a board that holds electrical circuits inside a piece of electrical equipment

'circuit-breaker *noun* a device that can automatically stop an electric current if it becomes dangerous

cir·cu·it·ous /sə'kjuːɪtəs; *AmE* sɜːr'k-/ *adj.* (*formal*) (of a route or journey) long and not direct: *He took us on a circuitous route to the hotel.* ▶ **cir·cu·it·ous·ly** *adv.*

cir·cuit·ry /'sɜːkɪtri; *AmE* 'sɜːrk-/ *noun* [U] a system of electrical CIRCUITS or the equipment that forms this

'circuit training *noun* [U] (*BrE*) a type of training in sport in which different exercises are each done for a short time

cir·cu·lar /'sɜːkjələ(r); *AmE* 'sɜːrk-/ *adj., noun*
■ *adj.* 1 shaped like a circle; round: *a circular building* 2 moving around in a circle: *a circular tour of the city on an open-topped bus* 3 (of an argument or a theory) using an idea or a statement to prove sth which is then used to prove the idea or statement at the beginning 4 (of a letter) sent to a large number of people ▶ **cir·cu·lar·ity** /ˌsɜːkjə'lærəti; *AmE* ˌsɜːrk-/ *noun* [U]: *There is a danger-ous circularity about this argument.*
■ *noun* a printed letter, notice or advertisement that is sent to a large number of people at the same time

ˌcircular 'saw *noun* a SAW in the form of a metal disc that turns quickly, driven by a motor, and is used for cutting wood, etc.

cir·cu·late /'sɜːkjəleɪt; *AmE* 'sɜːrk-/ *verb* 1 when a liquid, gas, or air **circulates** or **is circulated**, it moves continu-ously around a place or system: [V] *The condition prevents the blood from circulating freely.* ◊ [VN] *Cooled air is circulated throughout the building.* 2 if a story, an idea, information, etc. **circulates** or if you **circulate** it, it spreads or it is passed from one person to another: [V] *Rumours began to circulate about his financial problems.* [also VN] 3 [VN] ~ **sth** (**to sb**) to send goods or information to all the people in a group: *The document will be circu-lated to all members.* 4 [V] to move around a group, espe-cially at a party, talking to different people

cir·cu·la·tion /ˌsɜːkjə'leɪʃn; *AmE* ˌsɜːrk-/ *noun* 1 the movement of blood around the body: *Regular exercise will improve blood circulation.* ◊ *to have good/bad circulation* 2 [U] the passing or spreading of sth from one person or place to another: *the circulation of money/information/ideas* ◊ *A number of forged tickets are in circulation.* ◊ *The coins were taken out of circulation.* ◊ *Copies of the magazine were withdrawn from circulation.* 3 [U] the fact that sb takes part in social activities at a particular time: *Anne has been ill but now she's back in circulation.* ◊ *I was out of circulation for months after the baby was born.* 4 [C, usually sing.] the usual number of copies of a

æ ɑː e ɜː ə ɪ iː i ɒ ɔː ʌ ʊ u uː
cat father ten bird about sit see many got saw cup put actual too
(BrE)

newspaper or magazine that are sold each day, week, etc: *a daily circulation of more than one million* **5** [U, C] the movement of sth (for example air, water, gas, etc.) around an area or inside a system or machine

cir·cu·la·tory /ˌsɜːkjəˈleɪtəri; *AmE* ˈsɜːrkjələtɔːri/ *adj.* relating to the circulation of the blood: *the circulatory system*

cir·cum·cise /ˈsɜːkəmsaɪz; *AmE* ˈsɜːrk-/ *verb* [VN] **1** to remove the FORESKIN of a boy or man for religious or medical reasons **2** to cut off part of the sex organs of a girl or woman

cir·cum·ci·sion /ˌsɜːkəmˈsɪʒn; *AmE* ˌsɜːrk-/ *noun* [U, C] the act of circumcising sb; the religious ceremony when sb, especially a baby, is circumcised

cir·cum·fer·ence /səˈkʌmfərəns; *AmE* sərˈk-/ *noun* [C, U] a line that goes around a circle or any other curved shape; the length of this line: *the circumference of the earth* ◇ *The earth is almost 25000 miles* **in circumference.**—compare PERIMETER—picture at CIRCLE

cir·cum·flex /ˈsɜːkəmfleks; *AmE* ˈsɜːrk-/ (also **circumflex ˈaccent**) *noun* the mark placed over a vowel in some languages to show how it should be pronounced, as over the *o* in *rôle*—compare ACUTE ACCENT, GRAVE², TILDE, UMLAUT

cir·cum·lo·cu·tion /ˌsɜːkəmləˈkjuːʃn; *AmE* ˌsɜːrk-/ *noun* [U, C] (*formal*) using more words than are necessary, instead of speaking or writing in a clear, direct way ▶ **cir·cum·lo·cu·tory** /ˌsɜːkəmˈlɒkjutəri; ˌsɜːkəmləˈkjuːtəri; *AmE* ˌsɜːrkəmˈlɑːkjətɔːri/ *adj.*

cir·cum·navi·gate /ˌsɜːkəmˈnævɪgeɪt; *AmE* ˌsɜːrk-/ *verb* [VN] (*formal*) to sail all the way around sth, especially all the way around the world ▶ **cir·cum·navi·ga·tion** /ˌsɜːkəmˌnævɪˈgeɪʃn; *AmE* ˌsɜːrk-/ *noun* [U]: *the circumnavigation of the globe*

cir·cum·scribe /ˈsɜːkəmskraɪb; *AmE* ˈsɜːrk-/ *verb* [VN] **1** [often passive] (*formal*) to limit sb/sth's freedom, rights, power, etc: *The power of the monarchy was circumscribed by the new law.* **2** (*technical*) to draw a circle around another shape ▶ **cir·cum·scrip·tion** /ˌsɜːkəmˈskrɪpʃn; *AmE* ˌsɜːrk-/ *noun* [U]

cir·cum·spect /ˈsɜːkəmspekt; *AmE* ˈsɜːrk-/ *adj.* (*formal*) thinking very carefully about sth before doing it, because there may be risks involved [SYN] CAUTIOUS ▶ **cir·cum·spec·tion** /ˌsɜːkəmˈspekʃn; *AmE* ˌsɜːrk-/ *noun* [U] **cir·cum·spect·ly** *adv.*

cir·cum·stance /ˈsɜːkəmstəns; -stɑːns; -stæns; *AmE* ˈsɜːrkəmstæns/ *noun* **1** [C, usually pl.] the conditions and facts that are connected with and affect a situation, an event or an action: *The company reserves the right to cancel this agreement in certain circumstances.* ◇ *changing social and political circumstances* ◇ *I know I can trust her in any circumstance.* ◇ *Police said there were no* **suspicious circumstances** *surrounding the boy's death.* ◇ *The ship sank in mysterious circumstances.* ◇ *She never discovered the true circumstances of her birth.* **2** (**circumstances**) [pl.] the conditions of a person's life, especially the money they have: *Grants are awarded according to your financial circumstances.* ◇ *family / domestic / personal circumstances* **3** [U] (*formal*) situations and events that affect and influence your life and that are not in your control: *a* **victim of circumstance** (= a person who has suffered because of a situation that they cannot control) ◇ *He had to leave the country through* **force of circumstance** (= events or the situation made it necessary). [IDM] **in / under the ˈcircumstances** used before or after a statement to show that you have thought about the conditions that affect a situation before making a decision or a statement: *Under the circumstances, it seemed better not to tell him about the accident.* ◇ *She did the job very well in the circumstances.* **in / under no circumstances** used to emphasize that sth should never happen or be allowed: *Under no circumstances should you lend Paul any money.* ◇ *Don't open the door, in any circumstances.*—more at POMP, REDUCE

cir·cum·stan·tial /ˌsɜːkəmˈstænʃl; *AmE* ˌsɜːrk-/ *adj.* **1** (*law*) containing information and details that strongly suggest that sth is true but do not prove it: *circumstantial*

evidence ◇ *The case against him was largely circumstantial.* **2** (*formal*) connected with particular circumstances: *Their problems were circumstantial rather than personal.*

cir·cum·vent /ˌsɜːkəmˈvent; *AmE* ˌsɜːrk-/ *verb* [VN] (*formal*) **1** to find a way of avoiding a difficulty or a rule: *They found a way of circumventing the law.* **2** to go or travel around sth that is blocking your way ▶ **cir·cum·ven·tion** /ˌsɜːkəmˈvenʃn; *AmE* ˌsɜːrk-/ *noun* [U]

cir·cus /ˈsɜːkəs; *AmE* ˈsɜːrkəs/ *noun* **1** [C] a group of entertainers, sometimes with trained animals, who perform skilful or amusing acts in a show that travels around to different places: *circus acrobats / clowns / elephants* **2** (**the circus**) [sing.] a show performed by circus entertainers, usually in a large tent called a BIG TOP: *We took the children to the circus.* **3** [sing.] (*informal, disapproving*) a group of people or an event that attracts a lot of attention: *A media circus surrounded the royal couple wherever they went.* ◇ *the American electoral circus* **4** [C] (*BrE*) (used in some place names) a round open area in a town where several streets meet: *Piccadilly Circus* **5** [C] (in ancient Rome) a place like a big round outdoor theatre for public games, races, etc.

cir·rho·sis /səˈrəʊsɪs; *AmE* -ˈroʊ-/ *noun* a serious disease of the LIVER, caused especially by drinking too much alcohol

cir·rus /ˈsɪrəs/ *noun* [U] (*technical*) a type of light cloud that forms high in the sky

cissy (*BrE*) = SISSY

cis·tern /ˈsɪstən; *AmE* -tərn/ *noun* (*BrE*) a container in which water is stored in a building, especially one in the roof or connected to a toilet

cita·del /ˈsɪtədəl; -del/ *noun* (in the past) a castle on high ground in or near a city where people could go when the city was being attacked: (*figurative*) *citadels of private economic power*

cit·ation /saɪˈteɪʃn/ *noun* **1** [C] words or lines taken from a book or a speech [SYN] QUOTATION **2** [C] an official statement about sth special that sb has done, especially about acts of courage in a war: *a citation for bravery* **3** [U] (*formal*) an act of citing or being cited: *Space does not permit the citation of the examples.* **4** [C] (*AmE*) = SUMMONS: *The judge issued a contempt citation against the woman for violating a previous court order.*

cite /saɪt/ *verb* [VN] (*formal*) **1** ~ sth (as sth) to mention sth as a reason or an example, or in order to support what you are saying: *He cited his heavy workload as the reason for his breakdown.* **2** to speak or write the exact words from a book, an author, etc. [SYN] QUOTE: *She cited a passage from the President's speech.* **3** (*law*) to order sb to appear in a court of law; to name sb officially in a legal case: *He was cited for contempt of court.* ◇ *She was cited in the divorce proceedings.* **4** ~ sb (for sth) to mention sb officially or publicly because they deserve special praise: *He was cited for bravery in the Vietnam War.*

citi·zen /ˈsɪtɪzn/ *noun* **1** a person who has the legal right to belong to a particular country: *She's Italian by birth but is now an Australian citizen.* ◇ *British citizens living in other parts of the European Union* **2** a person who lives in a particular place: *the citizens of Budapest* ◇ *When you're old, people treat you like a* **second-class citizen.**—see also SENIOR CITIZEN—compare SUBJECT (6)

WHICH WORD?

citizen / subject / national

These words all mean a person who has the rights given by a country or state to the people, for example the rights to vote and to live there permanently. **Citizen** is the most general word: *American citizens living and working abroad* ◇ *After living in France for years, she eventually became a French citizen.* **Subject** can be used when the state is ruled by a king or queen: *a British subject.* **National** is most often used when somebody is living in another country: *diplomats and foreign nationals.*

---

aɪ	aʊ	eɪ	əʊ	oʊ	ɔɪ	ɪə	eə	ʊə	j	w
my	now	say	go	go	boy	near	hair	pure	yes	wet
			(BrE)	(AmE)						

citi·zen·ry /'sɪtɪzənri/ *noun* [sing.+ sing./pl. *v.*] (*formal*) (less *formal* in *AmE*) all the citizens of a particular town, country, etc.

'Citizens' Band *noun* [U] = CB

citi·zen·ship /'sɪtɪzənʃɪp/ *noun* [U] **1** the legal right to belong to a particular country: *French citizenship* ◇ *You can apply for citizenship after five years' residency.* **2** the state of being a citizen and accepting the responsibilities of it: *educational methods that prepare young people for citizenship*

cit·ric acid /ˌsɪtrɪk 'æsɪd/ *noun* [U] a weak acid found in the juice of oranges and other sour fruits

cit·rus /'sɪtrəs/ *noun* [U] fruit belonging to the group of fruit that includes oranges, lemons, LIMES and GRAPE-FRUIT: *citrus fruit/trees/growers* ◇ *fabric in bright citrus shades* (= orange, yellow or green)—picture on page A2

city /'sɪti/ *noun* (*pl.* -**ies**) **1** [C] a large and important town: *We live ten minutes from the city centre by bus.* ◇ *one of the world's most beautiful cities*—see also INNER CITY **2** [C] (*BrE*) a town that has been given special rights by a king or queen, usually one that has a CATH-EDRAL: *the city of York* **3** [C] (*AmE*) a town that has been given special rights by the state government **4** [sing.+ sing./pl. *v.*] all the people who live in a city: *The city turned out to welcome the victorious team home.* **5** (**the City**) [sing.] (*BrE*) Britain's financial and business centre, in the oldest part of London: *a City stockbroker* ◇ *What is the City's reaction to the cut in interest rates?* **6** [U] (*informal*) used after other nouns to say that a place is full of a particular thing: *It's not exactly fun city here is it?* IDM see FREEDOM

'city desk *noun* **1** (*BrE*) the department of a newspaper that deals with financial news **2** (*AmE*) the department of a newspaper that deals with local news

'city editor *noun* **1** (*BrE*) a journalist who is responsible for financial news in a newspaper or magazine **2** (*AmE*) a journalist who is responsible for local news in a newspaper or magazine

city 'hall *noun* [C, U] (*AmE*) the local government of a city and the offices it uses

city 'slicker *noun* (*informal*, often *disapproving*) a person who behaves in a way that is typical of people who live in big cities

city 'state *noun* (especially in the past) an independent state consisting of a city and the area around it (for example, Athens in ancient times)

civet /'sɪvɪt/ *noun* **1** [C] a wild animal like a cat, that lives in central Africa and S Asia **2** [U] a substance with a strong smell, obtained from a civet, and used in making PERFUME

civic /'sɪvɪk/ *adj.* [usually before noun] **1** officially connected with a town or city: *civic buildings/leaders* **2** connected with the people who live in a town or city: *a sense of civic pride* (= pride that people feel for their town or city) ◇ *civic duties/responsibilities*

civic 'centre *noun* **1** (*BrE*) the area where the public buildings are, in a town **2** (**civic center**) (*AmE*) a large building where public entertainments and meetings are held: *Atlanta Civic Center*

civ·ics /'sɪvɪks/ *noun* [U] (*especially AmE*) the school subject which studies the way government works and deals with the rights and duties that you have as a citizen and a member of a particular society

civil /'sɪvl/ *adj.* **1** [only before noun] connected with the people who live in a country: *civil unrest* (= that is caused by groups of people within a country)—see also CIVIL WAR **2** [only before noun] connected with the state rather than with religion or with the armed forces: *a civil marriage ceremony* **3** [only before noun] involving personal legal matters and not criminal law: *a civil court*—compare CRIMINAL—see also CIVIL LAW **4** polite in a formal way but possibly not friendly: *The less time I have to spend being civil to him the better!* OPP UNCIVIL ▶ **civ·il·ly** /'sɪvəli/ *adv.*: *She greeted him civilly but with no sign of affection.*

civil de'fence (*BrE*) (*AmE* **civil de'fense**) *noun* [U] the organization and training of ordinary people to protect themselves from attack during a war or, in the US, from natural disasters such as HURRICANES

civil diso'bedience *noun* [U] refusal by a large group of people to obey particular laws or pay taxes, usually as a form of peaceful political protest

civil engi'neering *noun* [U] the design, building and repair of roads, bridges, canals, etc.; the study of this as a subject ▶ **civil engi'neer** *noun*

ci·vil·ian /sə'vɪliən/ *noun* a person who is not a member of the armed forces or the police ▶ **ci·vil·ian** *adj.* [usually before noun]: *He left the army and returned to civilian life.*—compare MILITARY

ci·vil·ity /sə'vɪləti/ *noun* (*formal*) **1** [U] polite behaviour: *Staff members are trained to treat customers with civility at all times.* **2** (**civilities**) [pl.] remarks that are said only in order to be polite

civ·il·iza·tion (*BrE* also **-isa·tion**) /ˌsɪvəlaɪ'zeɪʃn; *AmE* -lə'z-/ *noun* **1** [U] a state of human society that is very developed and organized: *the technology of modern civilization* ◇ *The Victorians regarded the railways as bringing progress and civilization.* **2** [U, C] a society, its culture and its way of life during a particular period of time or in a particular part of the world: *the civilizations of ancient Greece and Rome* ◇ *diseases that are common in Western civilization* **3** [U] all the people in the world and the societies they live in, considered as a whole: *Environmental damage threatens the whole of civilization.* **4** [U] (often *humorous*) a place that offers you the comfortable way of life of a modern society: *It's good to be back in civilization after two weeks in a tent!*

civ·il·ize (*BrE* also **-ise**) /'sɪvəlaɪz/ *verb* [VN] to educate and improve a person or a society; to make sb's behaviour or manners better: *The girls in a class tend to have a civilizing influence on the boys.*

civ·il·ized (*BrE* also **-ised**) /'sɪvəlaɪzd/ *adj.* **1** well-organized socially with a very developed culture and way of life: *the civilized world* ◇ *rising crime in our so-called civilized societies* ◇ *civilized peoples* **2** having laws and customs that are fair and morally acceptable: *No civilized country should allow such terrible injustices.* **3** having or showing polite and reasonable behaviour: *We couldn't even have a civilized conversation any more.* **4** typical of a comfortable and pleasant way of life: *Breakfast on the terrace—how civilized!* OPP UNCIVILIZED

civil 'law *noun* [U] law that deals with the rights of private citizens rather than with crime

civil 'liberty *noun* [C, usually pl., U] the right of people to be free to say or do what they want while respecting others and staying within the law

the 'Civil List *noun* [sing.] a sum of money that is given to the British royal family each year by Parliament

civil 'rights *noun* [pl.] the rights that every person in a society has, for example to be treated equally, to be able to vote, work, etc. whatever their sex, race or religion: *the civil rights leader Martin Luther King*

civil 'servant *noun* a person who works in the civil service

the ˌcivil 'service *noun* [sing.] the government departments in a country, except the armed forces, and the people who work for them

civil 'war *noun* [C, U] a war between groups of people in the same country: *the Spanish Civil War* ◇ *30 years of bitter civil war*

civ·vies /'sɪviz/ *noun* [pl.] (*slang*) (used by people in the armed forces) ordinary clothes, not military uniform

Civvy Street /'sɪvi striːt/ *noun* [U] (*old-fashioned*, *BrE*, *slang*) ordinary life outside the armed forces

CJD /ˌsiː dʒeɪ 'diː/ *abbr.* CREUTZFELDT-JAKOB DISEASE

cl *abbr.* (*pl.* **cl** or **cls**) CENTILITRE: *75cl*

clack /klæk/ *verb* [V] if two hard objects **clack**, they make a short loud sound when they hit each other: *Her heels clacked on the marble floor.* ▶ **clack** *noun* [sing.]: *the clack of high heels on the floor* ◇ *the click-clack of her knitting needles*

clad /klæd/ *adj.* (usually *written*) **1** ~ (**in sth**) (often used after an adverb or in compounds) wearing a particular

b	d	f	g	h	k	l	m	n	p	r
bad	did	fall	get	hat	cat	leg	man	now	pen	red

type of clothing: *She was clad in blue velvet.* ◊ *warmly/ scantily clad* ◊ *leather-clad motorcyclists* **2** (**-clad**) (in compounds) covered in a particular thing: *snow-clad hills*

clad·ding /ˈklædɪŋ/ *noun* [U] a protective covering of a hard material: *metal/plastic cladding*—picture at HOUSE

claim /kleɪm/ *verb, noun*

▪ *verb*

SAY STH IS TRUE | **1** to say that sth is true although it has not been proved and other people may not believe it: [V(**that**)] *He claims (that) he was not given a fair hearing.* ◊ [V to inf] *I don't claim to be an expert.* ◊ [VN] *Scientists are claiming a major breakthrough in the fight against cancer.* ◊ [VN that] *It was claimed that some doctors were working 80 hours a week.* [also V speech, VN to inf]

DEMAND LEGAL RIGHT | **2** [VN] to demand or ask for sth because you believe it is your legal right to own or to have it: *A lot of lost property is never claimed.* ◊ *The family arrived in the UK in the 1990s and claimed political asylum.*

MONEY | **3** to ask for money from the government or a company because you have a right to it: [VN] *He's not entitled to claim unemployment benefit.* ◊ *She claimed damages from the company for the injury she had suffered.* ◊ *You could have claimed the cost of the hotel room from your insurance.* ◊ [V] *You can claim on your insurance for that coat you left on the train.*

ATTENTION/THOUGHT | **4** [VN] to get or take sb's attention: *A most unwelcome event claimed his attention.*

GAIN/WIN | **5** [VN] (*written*) to gain, win or achieve sth: *She has finally claimed a place on the team.*

CAUSE DEATH | **6** [VN] (*written*) (of a disaster, an accident, etc.) to cause sb's death: *The car crash claimed three lives.*

PHRV ˌclaim sth↔ˈback to ask or demand to have sth returned because you have a right to it: *You can claim back the tax on your purchases.*

▪ *noun*

SAYING STH IS TRUE | **1** [C] ~ (that ...) a statement that sth is true although it has not been proved and other people may not agree with or believe it: *The singer has denied the magazine's claim that she is leaving the band.*

LEGAL RIGHT | **2** [C, U] ~ (on/to sth) a right that sb believes they have to sth, especially property, land, etc: *They had no claim on the land, which was believed to be rich in oil.* ◊ *She has more claim to the book's success than anybody* (= she deserves to be praised for it).

FOR MONEY | **3** [C] ~ (for sth) a request for a sum of money that you believe you have a right to, especially from a company, the government, etc: *You can make a claim on your insurance policy.* ◊ *to put in a claim for an allowance* ◊ *a claim for £2000* ◊ *Make sure your claims for expenses are submitted by the end of the month.* ◊ *a three per cent pay claim* ◊ *Complete a claim form* (= an official document which you must use in order to request money from an organization).

IDM ˌclaim to ˈfame (often *humorous*) one thing that makes a person or place important or interesting: *His main claim to fame is that he went to school with the Prime Minister.* **have a claim on sb** to have the right to demand time, attention, etc. from sb **lay claim to sth** to state that you have a right to own sth **make no claim** used when you are saying that you cannot do sth: *I make no claim to understand modern art.*—more at STAKE *v.*

claim·ant /ˈkleɪmənt/ *noun* **1** a person who claims sth because they believe they have a right to it: *a claimant to the throne* **2** (*BrE*) a person who is receiving money from the state because they are unemployed, etc.

clair·voy·ance /kleəˈvɔɪəns; *AmE* klerˈv-/ *noun* [U] the power that some people are believed to have to be able to see future events or to communicate with people who are dead or far away ▶ **clair·voy·ant** /kleəˈvɔɪənt; *AmE* klerˈv-/ *noun*: *to consult a clairvoyant* **clair·voy·ant** *adj.*

clam /klæm/

▪ *noun* a large shellfish that can be eaten. It has a shell in two parts that can open and close: *clam chowder/soup*

▪ *verb* (**-mm-**) **PHRV** ˌclam ˈup (on sb) (*informal*) to refuse to speak, especially when sb asks you about sth

clam·bake /ˈklæmbeɪk/ *noun* (*AmE*) an outdoor party, especially for eating clams and other SEAFOOD

clam·ber /ˈklæmbə(r)/ *verb* [V+adv./prep.] to climb or move with difficulty or a lot of effort, using your hands and feet: *The children clambered up the steep bank.*

clammy /ˈklæmi/ *adj.* damp and sticky in an unpleasant way: *His skin felt cold and clammy.* ◊ *clammy hands*

clam·our (*BrE*) (*AmE* **clamor**) /ˈklæmə(r)/ *verb, noun*

▪ *verb* **1** ~ (for sth) (*written*) to demand sth loudly: [V] *People began to clamour for his resignation.* ◊ [V to inf] *Everyone was clamouring to know how much they would get.* ◊ [V speech] *'Play with us!' the children clamoured.* **2** [V] (of many people) to shout loudly, especially in a confused way: *A crowd of reporters clamoured around the car.*

▪ *noun* [sing., U] (*formal*) **1** a loud noise especially one that is made by a lot of people or animals: *the clamour of the market* **2** ~ (for sth) a demand for sth made by a lot of people: *The clamour for her resignation grew louder.* ▶ **clam·or·ous** /ˈklæmərəs/ *adj.*

clamp /klæmp/ *verb, noun*

▪ *verb* **1** ~ A to B | ~ A and B (**together**) to hold sth tightly, or fasten two things together, with a clamp: [VN] *Clamp one end of the plank to the edge of the table.* ◊ *Clamp the two halves together until the glue dries.* [also VN-ADJ] **2** [+adv./prep.] to hold or fasten sth very tightly so that it does not move; to be held tightly: [VN] *He had a cigar clamped between his teeth.* ◊ *She clamped a pair of headphones over her ears.* ◊ *I clamped a hand on his shoulder.* ◊ [V] *Her lips clamped tightly together.* **3** [VN] [often passive] (*BrE*) to fix a clamp to a car's wheel so that the car cannot be driven away **PHRV** ˌclamp ˈdown (on sb/sth) to take strict action in order to prevent sth, especially crime: *a campaign by police to clamp down on street crime*—related noun CLAMPDOWN ˈclamp sth on sb (*especially AmE*) to force sb to accept sth such as a restriction or law: *The army clamped a curfew on five towns.*

▪ *noun* **1** a tool for holding things tightly together, usually by means of a screw—picture at VICE, LABORATORY **2** (also ˈwheel clamp) (both *BrE*) (*AmE* ˌDenver ˈBoot, boot) a device that is attached to the wheel of a car that has been parked illegally, so that it cannot be driven away

clamp·down /ˈklæmpdaʊn/ *noun* [usually sing.] sudden action that is taken in order to stop an illegal activity: *a clampdown on drinking and driving*

clan /klæn/ *noun* [C+sing./pl. *v.*] **1** a group of families who are related to each other, especially in Scotland: *the Macleod clan* ◊ *clan warfare* **2** (*informal*, sometimes *humorous*) a very large family, or a group of people who are connected because of a particular thing: *one of a growing clan of stars who have left Hollywood*

clan·des·tine /klænˈdestɪn; ˈklændestaɪn/ *adj.* (*formal*) done secretly or kept secret: *a clandestine meeting/relationship*

clang /klæŋ/ *verb* [usually+adv./prep.] to make a loud ringing sound like that of metal being hit; to cause sth to make this sound: [V] *Bells were clanging in the tower.* ◊ [V-ADJ] *The gates clanged shut.* ◊ [VN] *The trams clanged their way along the streets.* ▶ **clang** (also **clang·ing**) *noun* [usually sing.]

clang·er /ˈklæŋə(r)/ *noun* (*BrE, informal*) an obvious and embarrassing mistake: *Mentioning her ex-husband was a bit of a clanger.* **IDM** see DROP *v.*

clank /klæŋk/ *verb* to make a loud sound like pieces of metal hitting each other; to cause sth to make this sound: [V] *clanking chains* ◊ [V-ADJ] *I heard a door clank shut.* ◊ [VN] *The guard clanked his heavy ring of keys.* ▶ **clank** (also **clank·ing**) *noun* [usually sing.]

clan·nish /ˈklænɪʃ/ *adj.* (often *disapproving*) (of members of a group) not showing interest in people who are not in a CLAN

clans·man /ˈklænzmən/ *noun* (*pl.* -men /-mən/) a member of a CLAN

clap /klæp/ *verb, noun*

▪ *verb* (**-pp-**) **1** to hit your open hands together several times to show that you approve of or have enjoyed sth: [V] *The audience cheered and clapped.* ◊ [VN] *Everyone clapped* *us when we went up to get our prize.* **2 ~ (your hands)** to hit your open hands together: [VN] *She **clapped** her* **hands** *in delight.* ◊ *He clapped his hands for silence.* ◊ [V] *Everyone clapped in time to the music.* **3** [VN] **~ sb on the back/shoulder** to lightly hit sb with your open hand, usually in a friendly way **4** [VN+*adv./prep.*] to put sth/sb somewhere quickly and suddenly: *'Oh dear!' she cried,* **clapping a hand** *over her mouth.* ◊ *to clap sb in irons/ jail/prison* **IDM** see EYE *n.*

■ *noun* **1** [sing.] an act of clapping the hands; the sound this makes: *Give him a clap!* (= to praise sb at the end of a performance) **2** [C] a sudden loud noise: *a clap of thunder* **3** (also **the clap**) [U] (*slang*) a disease of the sexual organs, caught by having sex with an infected person **SYN** GONORRHOEA

clap·board /ˈklæpbɔːd; *AmE* ˈklæbərd/ *noun* [U] (*especially AmE*) = WEATHERBOARD

clapped 'out *adj.* (*BrE, informal*) (of a car or machine) old and in bad condition: *The van's totally clapped out.* ◊ *a clapped-out old Mini*

clap·per /ˈklæpə(r)/ *noun* the piece of metal inside a bell that hits the sides and makes the bell ring **IDM** **like the** ˈ**clappers** (*BrE, informal*) extremely fast: *to run/ride/ drive like the clappers*

clap·per·board /ˈklæpəbɔːd; *AmE* ˈklæpərbɔːrd/ *noun* a device that is used when making films/movies. It consists of two connected boards that are hit together at the start of a scene, and its purpose is to help to match the pictures with the sound.

clap·trap /ˈklæptræp/ *noun* [U] (*informal*) stupid talk that has no value

claret /ˈklærət/ *noun* **1** [U, C] a dry red wine, especially from the Bordeaux area of France. There are several types of claret. **2** [U] a dark red colour

clar·ify /ˈklærəfaɪ/ *verb* (clari·fies, clari·fy·ing, clari·fied, clari·fied) **1** (*formal*) to make sth clearer or easier to understand: [VN] *to clarify a situation/problem/issue* ◊ *I hope this* **clarifies my position.** ◊ [V wh-] *She asked him to clarify what he meant.* **2** [VN] to make sth, especially butter, pure by heating it: *clarified butter* ▶ **clari·fi·ca·tion** /ˌklærəfɪˈkeɪʃn/ *noun* [U, C]: *I am* **seeking clarification** *of the regulations.*

clari·net /ˌklærəˈnet/ *noun* a musical instrument of the WOODWIND group. It is shaped like a pipe and has a REED and a MOUTHPIECE at the top that you blow into.—picture on page 840

cla·ri·net·tist (also **cla·ri·net·ist**) /ˌklærəˈnetɪst/ *noun* a person who plays the clarinet

clar·ion call /ˈklæriən kɔːl/ *noun* [sing.] (*formal*) a clear message or request for people to do sth

clar·ity /ˈklærəti/ *noun* [U] **1** the quality of being expressed clearly: *a lack of clarity in the law* **2** the ability to think about or understand sth clearly: *clarity of thought/purpose/vision* **3** if a picture, substance or sound has **clarity**, you can see or hear it very clearly, or see through it easily: *the clarity of sound on a compact disc*

clash /klæʃ/ *noun, verb*
■ *noun*
FIGHT | **1 ~ (with sb)** | **~ (between A and B)** a short fight between two groups of people: *Clashes broke out between police and demonstrators.*
ARGUMENT | **2 ~ (with sb) (over sth)** | **~ (between A and B) (over sth)** an argument between two people or groups of people who have different beliefs and ideas: *a head-on clash between the two leaders over education policy*
DIFFERENCE | **3** the difference that exists between two things that are opposed to each other: *a clash of interests/ opinions/cultures* ◊ *a* **personality clash** *with the boss*
OF TWO EVENTS | **4** a situation in which two events happen at the same time so that you cannot go to or see them both: *a clash in the timetable/schedule*
OF COLOURS | **5** the situation when two colours, designs, etc. look ugly when they are put together
LOUD NOISE | **6** a loud noise made by two metal objects being hit together: *a clash of cymbals/swords*

IN SPORT | **7** (used in newspapers, about sports) an occasion when two teams or players compete against each other: *Bayern's clash with Real Madrid in the European Cup*
■ *verb*
FIGHT/COMPETE | **1** [V] **~ (with sb)** to come together and fight or compete in a contest: *The two sets of supporters clashed outside the stadium.* ◊ *The two teams clash in tomorrow's final.*
ARGUE | **2** [V] **~ (with sb) (over/on sth)** to argue or disagree seriously with sb about sth, and to show this in public: *The leaders clashed with party members on the issue.* ◊ *The leaders and members clashed on the issue.*
BE DIFFERENT | **3** [V] **~ (with sth)** (of beliefs, ideas or personalities) to be very different and opposed to each other: *His left-wing views clashed with his father's politics.* ◊ *His views and his father's clashed.* ◊ *They have clashing personalities.*
OF TWO EVENTS | **4** [V] **~ (with sth)** (of events) to happen at the same time so that you cannot go to or see them both: *Unfortunately your party clashes with a wedding I'm going to.* ◊ *There are two good movies on TV tonight, but they clash.*
OF COLOURS | **5** [V] **~ (with sth)** (of colours, patterns or styles) to look ugly when put together: *The wallpaper clashes with the carpet.* ◊ *The wallpaper and the carpet clash.*
MAKE LOUD NOISE | **6 ~ (sth) (together)** to hit together and make a harsh ringing noise; to make two metal objects do this: [V] *The long blades clashed together.* ◊ [VN] *She clashed the cymbals.*

clasp /klɑːsp; *AmE* klæsp/ *verb, noun*
■ *verb* [VN] **1** to hold sth tightly in your hand: *He leaned forward, his* **hands clasped** *tightly together.* ◊ *They* **clasped hands** (= held each other's hands). ◊ *I stood there, clasping the door handle.* **2** to hold sb/sth tightly with your arms around them: *She clasped the children in her arms.* ◊ *He* **clasped** *her* **to him.** **3** to fasten sth with a clasp: *She clasped the bracelet around her wrist.*
■ *noun* **1** [C] a device that fastens sth, such as a bag or the ends of a belt or a piece of jewellery: *the clasp of a necklace/handbag*—picture at JEWELLERY **2** [sing.] a tight hold with your hand or in your arms: *He took her hand in his firm warm clasp.*

class /klɑːs; *AmE* klæs/ *noun, verb, adj.*
■ *noun*
IN EDUCATION | **1** [C+sing./pl. *v.*] a group of students who are taught together: *We were in the same class at school.* ◊ *She is the youngest in her class.* ◊ *He came* **top of the class.** ◊ *The whole class was/were told to stay behind after school.* **2** [C, U] an occasion when a group of students meets to be taught **SYN** LESSON: *I was late for a class.* ◊ *See me after class.* ◊ *She works hard* **in class** (= during the class). ◊ *I have a history class at 9 o'clock.* **3** [C] (also **classes** [pl.]) a series of classes on a particular subject **SYN** COURSE: *I've been* **taking classes** *in pottery.* ◊ *Are you still doing your French evening class?* **4** [C+sing./pl. *v.*] (*especially AmE*) a group of students who finish their studies at school, college or university in a particular year: *the class of 98*
IN SOCIETY | **5** [C+sing./pl. *v.*] one of the groups of people in a society that are thought of as being at the same social or economic level: *the working/middle/upper class* ◊ *The party tries to appeal to all classes of society.* ◊ *the professional classes* **6** [U] the way that people are divided into different social and economic groups: *differences of class, race or gender* ◊ *the class system* ◊ *a society in which class is more important than ability*
GROUP OF PEOPLE/ANIMALS | **7** [C] a group of people, animals or things that have similar characteristics or qualities: *It was good accommodation for a hotel of this class.* ◊ *different classes of drugs* ◊ *Dickens was* **in a different class** *from* (= was much better than) *most of his contemporaries.* ◊ *As a jazz singer she's* **in a class of her own** (= better than most others).—see also FIRST-CLASS, HIGH-CLASS, LOW-CLASS, SECOND-CLASS
SKILL/STYLE | **8** [U] an elegant quality or a high level of skill

æ	ɑː	e	ɜː	ə	ɪ	iː	i	ɒ	ɔː	ʌ	ʊ	u	uː
cat	father	ten	bird	about	sit	see	many	got	saw	cup	put	actual	too
								(BrE)					

C

that is impressive: *She has class all right—she looks like a model.* ◊ *There's a real touch of class about this team.*

IN TRAIN/PLANE | **9** [C] (especially in compounds) each of several different levels of comfort that are available to travellers in a plane, etc: *He always travels business class.* ◊ *The first-class compartment is situated at the front of the train.*—see also SECOND-CLASS, THIRD-CLASS, TOURIST CLASS

OF UNIVERSITY DEGREE | **10** [C] (especially in compounds) one of the levels of achievement in a British university degree exam: *a first-/second-/third-class degree*

BIOLOGY | **11** [C] a group into which animals, plants, etc. that have similar characteristics are divided, below a PHYLUM—compare FAMILY, GENUS, SPECIES

IDM see CHATTER *v.*

■ *verb* [VN] [often passive] **~ sb/sth (as sth)**

PUT INTO GROUP | to think or decide that sb/sth is a particular type of person or thing: *Immigrant workers were classed as aliens.* ◊ *One in five people in the country are classed as poor.*

■ *adj.* [only before noun] (*informal*)

WITH SKILL/STYLE | very good: *a class player/performer* ◊ *She's a real class act.*

,class 'action *noun* (*AmE*) a type of LAWSUIT that is started by a group of people who have a problem in common

'class-conscious *adj.* very aware of belonging to a particular social class and of the differences between social classes ▶ 'class-consciousness *noun* [U]

clas·sic /ˈklæsɪk/ *adj., noun*

■ *adj.* [usually before noun] **1** accepted or deserving to be accepted as one of the best or most important of its kind: *a classic novel/study/goal* **2** (also **clas·sic·al**) with all the features you would expect to find; very typical: *a* **classic example** *of poor communication* ◊ *She displayed the classic symptoms of depression.* ◊ *I made the classic mistake of clapping in a pause in the music!* **3** elegant, but simple and traditional in style or design; not affected by changes in fashion: *a classic grey suit* ◊ *classic design* ◊ *classic cars* (= cars which are no longer made, but which are still popular) **4** (*informal*) people say **That's classic!** when they find sth very amusing, when they think sb has been very stupid or when sth annoying, but not surprising, happens: *She's not going to be!? Oh, that's classic!*

■ *noun* **1** [C] a book, film/movie or song which is well known and considered to be of very high quality, setting standards for other books, etc: *English classics such as 'Alice in Wonderland'* ◊ *The novel may become a modern classic.* **2** [C] a thing that is an excellent example of its kind: *That match was a classic.* **3** (**Classics**) [U] the study of ancient Greek and Roman culture, especially their languages and literature: *a degree in Classics*

WHICH WORD?
classic / classical
....

These adjectives are frequently used with the following nouns:

classic ~	classical ~
example	music
case	ballet
novel	architecture
work	scholar
car	period

Classic describes something that is accepted as being of very high quality and one of the best of its kind: *a classic movie/work*. It is also used to describe a typical example of something: *a classic example/mistake*, or something elegant but simple and traditional: *classic design*.

Classical describes a form of traditional Western music and other things that are traditional in style: *a classical composer* ◊ *a classical theory*. It is also used to talk about things that are connected with the culture of Ancient Greece and Rome: *a classical scholar* ◊ *classical mythology*.

---

clas·sic·al /ˈklæsɪkl/ *adj.* [usually before noun] **1** widely accepted and used for a long time; traditional in style or idea: *the classical economics of Smith and Ricardo* ◊ *the classical theory of unemployment* ◊ *classical and modern ballet/dance* **2** connected with or influenced by the culture of ancient Greece and Rome: *classical studies* ◊ *a classical scholar* (= an expert in Latin and Greek) **3** (of music) written in a Western musical tradition, usually using an established form (for example a SYMPHONY) and not played on electronic instruments. Classical music is generally considered to be serious and to have a lasting value: *He plays classical music, as well as pop and jazz.* ◊ *a classical album/composer/violinist* **4** = CLASSIC: *These are classical examples of food allergy.* **5** (of a language) ancient in its form and no longer used in a spoken form: *classical Arabic* **6** simple and attractive: *the classical elegance of the design* ▶ **clas·sic·al·ly** /ˈklæsɪkli/ *adv.*: *Her face is classically beautiful.* ◊ *a classically educated reader* ◊ *classically trained singers/dancers*

clas·si·cism /ˈklæsɪsɪzəm/ *noun* [U] **1** a style of art and literature that is simple and elegant and is based on the styles of ancient Greece and Rome. Classicism was popular in Europe in the 18th century. **2** a style or form that has simple, natural qualities and pleasing combinations of parts

clas·si·cist /ˈklæsɪsɪst/ *noun* **1** a person who studies ancient Greek or Latin **2** a person who follows classicism in art or literature

clas·si·fi·able /ˈklæsɪfaɪəbl/ *adj.* that you can or should CLASSIFY: *The information was not easily classifiable.* ◊ *top-secret or classifiable information*

clas·si·fi·ca·tion /ˌklæsɪfɪˈkeɪʃn/ *noun* **1** [U] the act or process of putting people or things into a group or class (= of CLASSIFYING them): *a style of music that defies classification* (= is like no other) **2** [C] a group, class, division, etc. into which sb or sth is put **3** [U] (*biology*) the act of putting animals, plants, etc. into groups, classes or divisions according to their characteristics: *The classification of bony fish is extremely complicated.* **4** [C] (*technical*) a system of arranging books, tapes, magazines, etc. in a library into groups according to their subject

clas·si·fied /ˈklæsɪfaɪd/ *adj.* [usually before noun] **1** (of information) officially secret and available only to particular people: *classified information/documents/material* **OPP** UNCLASSIFIED **2** with information arranged in groups according to subjects: *a classified catalogue* **3** (**classi-fieds**) *noun* [pl.] = CLASSIFIED ADVERTISEMENTS

,classified ad'vertisements (also ,classified 'ads, 'classifieds) (*BrE* also 'small ads) (*AmE* also 'want ads) *noun* [pl.] the section in a newspaper with small advertisements arranged in groups according to their subject, that are placed by people or small companies who want to buy or sell sth, find or offer a job, etc.

clas·sify /ˈklæsɪfaɪ/ *verb* (**clas·si·fies, clas·si·fy·ing, clas·si·fied, clas·si·fied**) [VN] **1** to arrange sth in groups according to features that they have in common: *The books in the library* **are classified according to** *subject.* ◊ *Patients* **are classified into** *three categories.* **2 ~ sth as sth** to decide which type or group sb/sth belongs to: *Only eleven of these accidents were classified as major.* ◊ *Would you classify it as a hard drug or a soft drug?*

class·less /ˈklɑːsləs; *AmE* ˈklæs-/ *adj.* **1** (*approving*) with no divisions into social classes: *Will Britain ever become a classless society?* **2** not clearly belonging to a particular social class: *a classless accent* ▶ **class·less·ness** *noun* [U]

class·mate /ˈklɑːsmeɪt; *AmE* ˈklæs-/ *noun* a person who is or was in the same class as you at school or college

class·room /ˈklɑːsruːm; -rʊm; *AmE* ˈklæs-/ *noun* a room where a class of children or students is taught: *classroom activities* ◊ *the use of computers in the classroom*

,class 'struggle (also ,class 'war) *noun* [U, sing.] (*politics*) opposition between the different social classes in society, especially that described in Marxist theory

classy /ˈklɑːsi; *AmE* ˈklæsi/ *adj.* (**class·ier, classi·est**) (*informal*) of high quality; expensive and/or fashionable: *a classy player* ◊ *a classy hotel/restaurant*

---

aɪ	aʊ	eɪ	əʊ	oʊ	ɔɪ	ɪə	eə	ʊə	j	w
my	now	say	go	go	boy	near	hair	pure	yes	wet
			(BrE)	(AmE)						

clat·ter /ˈklætə(r)/ verb **1** [V] if hard objects **clatter**, they knock together and make a loud noise: *He dropped the knife and it clattered on the stone floor.* ◊ *Her cup clattered in the saucer.* **2** [V+adv. / prep.] to move making a loud noise like hard objects knocking together: *The cart clattered over the cobbles.* ◊ *She heard him clattering around downstairs.* ▶ **clat·ter** (also **clat·ter·ing**) noun [sing.]: *the clatter of horses' hoofs*

clause /klɔːz/ noun **1** (*grammar*) a group of words that includes a subject and a verb, and forms a sentence or part of a sentence: *In the sentence 'They often go to Italy because they love the food', 'They often go to Italy' is the main clause and 'because they love the food' is a subordinate clause.* **2** an item in a legal document that says that a particular thing must or must not be done

claus·tro·pho·bia /ˌklɔːstrəˈfəʊbiə; AmE -ˈfoʊ-/ noun [U] an extreme fear of being in a small enclosed place; the unpleasant feeling that a person gets in a situation which restricts them: *to suffer from claustrophobia* ◊ *She felt she had to escape from the claustrophobia of suburban family life.*—compare AGORAPHOBIA

claus·tro·pho·bic /ˌklɔːstrəˈfəʊbɪk; AmE -ˈfoʊ-/ adj. giving you claustrophobia; suffering from claustrophobia: *the claustrophobic atmosphere of the room* ◊ *to feel claustrophobic*

clavi·chord /ˈklævɪkɔːd; AmE -kɔːrd/ noun an early type of musical instrument, like a piano with a very soft tone

clav·icle /ˈklævɪkl/ noun (anatomy) the COLLARBONE

claw /klɔː/ noun, verb
■ noun **1** one of the sharp curved nails on the end of an animal's or a bird's foot: *The cat lashed out with its claws.*—pictures on pages A6, A7 **2** a long, sharp curved part of the body of some types of SHELLFISH, used for catching and holding things: *the claws of a crab* **3** part of a tool or machine, like a claw, used for holding, pulling or lifting things: *a claw hammer* (= used for pulling out nails)—picture at TOOL **IDM** **get your claws into sb 1** (*disapproving*) if a woman **gets her claws** into a man, she tries hard to make him marry her or to have a relationship with her **2** to criticize sb severely: *Wait until the media gets its claws into her.*—more at RED adj.
■ verb ~ (**at**) **sb/sth** to scratch or tear sb/sth with claws or with your fingernails:[V] *The cat was clawing at the leg of the chair.* ◊ [VN] *She had clawed Stephen across the face.* ◊ (*figurative*) *His hands clawed the air.* **IDM** **claw your way back, into sth, out of sth, to sth, etc.** to gradually achieve sth or move somewhere by using a lot of determination and effort: *She clawed her way to the top of her profession.* ◊ *Slowly, he clawed his way out from under the collapsed building.* **PHRV** **claw sth↔back 1** to get sth back that you have lost, usually by using a lot of effort **2** (of a government) to get back money that has been paid to people, usually by taxing them—related noun CLAW-BACK

claw·back /ˈklɔːbæk/ noun (*BrE, business*) the act of getting money back from people it has been paid to; the money that is paid back

clay /kleɪ/ noun [U] a type of heavy, sticky earth that becomes hard when it is baked and is used to make things such as pots and bricks—picture at POT **IDM** see FOOT n.

clay court noun a tennis court that has a surface made of clay

clay·more /ˈkleɪmɔː(r)/ noun a large SWORD with a broad blade with two sharp edges that was used in Scotland in the past

clay pigeon shooting (*BrE*) (*AmE* **skeet shooting**) noun a sport in which a disc of baked clay (called a **clay pigeon**) is thrown into the air for people to shoot at

clean /kliːn/ adj., verb, adv., noun
■ adj. (**clean·er, clean·est**)
NOT DIRTY | **1** not dirty: *Are your hands clean?* ◊ *to wipe / brush sth clean* ◊ *The hotel was spotlessly* (= extremely) *clean.* ◊ (*BrE*) *It is your responsibility to keep the room clean and tidy.* ◊ (*AmE*) *Keep your room neat and clean.* ◊ *I can't find a clean shirt* (= one I haven't worn since it

was washed). **2** having a clean appearance and clean surroundings: *Cats are very clean animals.*

NOT HARMFUL | **3** free from harmful or unpleasant substances: *clean drinking water* ◊ *clean air* ◊ *the cleaner cars of the future* (= not producing so many harmful substances)

PAPER | **4** [usually before noun] with nothing written on it: *a clean sheet of paper*

NOT OFFENSIVE | **5** not offensive or referring to sex; not doing anything that is considered immoral or bad: *The entertainment was good clean fun for the whole family.* ◊ *Keep the jokes clean please!* ◊ *The sport has a very clean image.*

NOT ILLEGAL | **6** not showing or having any record of doing sth that is against the law: *a clean driving licence / driver's license* ◊ *a clean police record* **7** (*slang*) not owning or carrying anything illegal such as drugs or weapons: *The police searched her but she was clean.*

FAIR | **8** played or done in a fair way and within the rules: *It was a tough but clean game.*

SMOOTH/SIMPLE | **9** having a smooth edge, surface or shape; simple and regular: *A sharp knife makes a clean cut.* ◊ *a modern design with clean lines and a bright appearance*

ACCURATE | **10** done in a skilful and accurate way: *The plane made a clean take-off.*

TASTE/SMELL | **11** tasting, smelling or looking pleasant and fresh: *The wine has a clean taste and a lovely golden colour.*

—compare UNCLEAN

IDM **as clean as a whistle** (*informal*) very clean **a clean bill of health** a report that says sb is healthy or that sth is in good condition **a clean break 1** a complete separation from a person, an organization, a way of life, etc: *She wanted to make a clean break with the past.* **2** a break in a bone in one place **a clean sheet/slate** a record of your work or behaviour that does not show any mistakes or bad things that you have done: *No government operates with a completely clean sheet.* ◊ *They kept a clean sheet in the match* (= no goals were scored against them). **make a clean breast of sth** to tell the truth about sth so that you no longer feel guilty **make a clean sweep (of sth) 1** to remove all the people or things from an organization that are thought to be unnecessary or need changing **2** to win all the prizes or parts of a game or competition: *China made a clean sweep of the medals in the gymnastics events.* ◊ *The opinion poll suggests a clean sweep for the Democrats.*—more at NOSE n., WIPE v.
■ verb **1** to make sth free from dirt or dust by washing or rubbing it: [VN] *to clean the windows / bath / floor* ◊ *to clean a wound* ◊ *Have you cleaned your teeth?* ◊ *The villa is cleaned twice a week.* ◊ [V] *I spent all day cooking and cleaning.*—see also DRY-CLEAN, SPRING-CLEAN **2** [V] to become clean: *This oven cleans easily* (= is easy to clean). **3** [VN] = DRY-CLEAN: *This coat is filthy. I'll have it cleaned.* **4** [VN] to remove the inside parts of a fish, chicken, etc. before you cook it **IDM** **clean house** (*AmE*) **1** to remove people or things that are not necessary or wanted: *The new manager said he wanted to clean house.* **2** to make your house clean **clean up your act** (*informal*) to start behaving in a moral or responsible way: *He cleaned up his act and came off drugs.* **PHRV** **clean sth↔down** to clean sth thoroughly: *All the equipment should be cleaned down regularly.* **clean sth off/from sth | clean sth↔off** to remove sth from sth by brushing, rubbing, etc: *I cleaned the mud off my shoes.* **clean sth↔out** to clean the inside of sth thoroughly: *I must clean the fish tank out.* **clean sb out** (*informal*) to use all of sb's money: *Paying for all those drinks has cleaned me out.* **clean sb/sth out** (*informal*) to steal everything from a person or place: *The burglars totally cleaned her out.* **clean (yourself) up** (*informal*) to make yourself clean, usually by washing: *I need to change and clean up.* ◊ *Go and clean yourself up.* ◊ *You'd better get cleaned up.*—related noun CLEAN-UP **clean up | clean sth↔up 1** to remove dirt, etc. from somewhere: *He*

b	d	f	g	h	k	l	m	n	p	r
bad	**did**	**fall**	**get**	**hat**	**cat**	**leg**	**man**	**now**	**pen**	**red**

always expected other people to **clean up after** him (= when he had made the place dirty or untidy). ◇ *Who's going to clean up this mess?* ◇ *to clean up beaches after an oil spillage*—related noun CLEAN-UP **2** (*informal*) to win or make a lot of money: *This film should clean up at the box offices.* ◇ **,clean sth↔'up** to remove crime and immoral behaviour from a place or an activity: *The new mayor is determined to clean up the city.* ◇ *Soccer needs to* **clean up** *its image.*—related noun CLEAN-UP

■ *adv.* (*informal*) used to emphasize that an action takes place completely: *The thief got clean away.* ◇ *I clean forgot about calling him.*

IDM **come clean (with sb) (about sth)** to admit and explain sth that you have kept as a secret: *Isn't it time the government came clean about their plans for education?*

■ *noun* [sing.] the act or process of cleaning sth: *The house needed a good clean.*

,clean-'cut *adj.* (especially of a young man) looking neat and clean and therefore socially acceptable: *Simon's clean-cut good looks*

clean-er /'kli:nə(r)/ *noun* **1** a person whose job is to clean other people's houses or offices, etc: *an office cleaner* **2** a machine or substance that is used for cleaning: *a vacuum cleaner* ◇ *a bottle of kitchen cleaner* **3** (**cleaner's**) (*pl.* **cleaners**) (also **,dry-'cleaner's**) a shop/store where clothes and fabrics are cleaned, especially with chemicals: *Can you pick up my suit from the cleaner's?* **IDM** **take sb to the 'cleaners** (*informal*) **1** to rob or cheat sb of all their money, etc. **2** to defeat sb completely: *Our team got taken to the cleaners.*

clean-ing /'kli:nɪŋ/ *noun* [U] the work of making the inside of a house, etc. clean: *They pay someone to* **do the cleaning**.

'cleaning lady (also **'cleaning woman**) *noun* a woman whose job is to clean the rooms and furniture in an office, a house, etc.

clean-li-ness /'klenlinəs/ *noun* [U] the state of being clean or the habit of keeping things clean: *Some people are obsessive about cleanliness.*

clean-ly /'kli:nli/ *adv.* **1** easily and smoothly in one movement: *The boat moved cleanly through the water.* **2** in a clean way: *fuel that burns cleanly*

cleanse /klenz/ *verb* [VN] **1** to clean your skin or a wound: *a cleansing cream* **2** ~ **sb** (**of/from sth**) (*literary*) to make sb free from guilt or SIN—see also ETHNIC CLEANSING

cleans-er /'klenzə(r)/ *noun* **1** a liquid or cream for cleaning your face, especially for removing MAKE-UP **2** a substance that contains chemicals and is used for cleaning things

,clean-'shaven *adj.* a man who is **clean-shaven** does not have a BEARD or MOUSTACHE (= hair that is allowed to grow on the face)

'clean-up *noun* [usually sing.] the process of removing dirt, POLLUTION, or things that are considered bad or immoral from a place: *The clean-up of the river is going to take months.* ◇ *a clean-up campaign/operation/programme*

clear /klɪə(r); *AmE* klɪr/ *adj., verb, adv.*

WORD FAMILY
clear *adj.*
clarity *n.*
clarify *v.*

■ *adj.* (**clear-er, clear-est**)

WITHOUT CONFUSION/DOUBT | **1** easy to understand and not causing any confusion: *She gave me clear and precise directions.* ◇ *Are these instructions clear enough?* ◇ *You'll do as you're told, is that clear?* ◇ *This behaviour must stop—do I* **make myself clear** (= express myself clearly so there is no doubt about what I mean)? ◇ *I hope I* **made it clear** *to him that he was no longer welcome here.* **2** ~ (**to sb**) (**that**)| ~ **what, how, whether, etc.** obvious and leaving no doubt at all: *This is a clear case of fraud.* ◇ *She won the election by a clear majority.* ◇ *His height gives him a clear advantage.* ◇ *It was quite clear to me that she was lying.* ◇ *It is not clear what they want us to do.* **3** ~ (**about/on sth**)| ~ **what, how, whether, etc.** having or feeling no doubt or confusion: *Are you clear about the arrangements for tomorrow?* ◇ *My memory is not clear on that point.* ◇

I'm still not clear what the job involves. ◇ *We need a* **clear understanding** *of the problems involved.*

MIND | **4** thinking in a sensible and logical way, especially in a difficult situation: *a clear thinker* ◇ *You'll need to* **keep a clear head** *for your interview.*

EASY TO SEE/HEAR | **5** easy to see or hear: *The photo wasn't very clear.* ◇ *The voice on the phone was clear and strong.* ◇ *She was in Australia but I could hear her voice* **as clear as a bell**.

TRANSPARENT | **6** that you can see through: *The water was so clear we could see the bottom of the lake.* ◇ *clear glass* ◇ *a clear colourless liquid*

SKY/WEATHER | **7** without cloud or MIST: *a clear blue sky* ◇ *On a clear day you can see France.*

SKIN | **8** without spots or marks: *clear skin* ◇ *a clear complexion*

EYES | **9** bright and lively

NOT BLOCKED | **10** ~ (**of sth**) free from things that are blocking the way or covering the surface of sth: *The road was clear and I ran over.* ◇ *All exits must be kept clear of baggage.* ◇ *You won't get a clear view of the stage from here.* ◇ *I always leave a clear desk at the end of the day.*

CONSCIENCE | **11** if you have a **clear** CONSCIENCE or your CONSCIENCE is **clear**, you do not feel guilty

FREE FROM STH BAD | **12** ~ **of sth** free from sth that is unpleasant: *They were still not clear of all suspicion.* ◇ *We are finally clear of debt.*

NOT TOUCHING/NEAR | **13** [not before noun] ~ (**of sb/sth**) not touching sth; a distance away from sth: *The plane climbed until it was clear of the clouds.* ◇ *Make sure you park your car clear of the entrance.*

PERIOD OF TIME | **14** [only before noun] whole or complete: *Allow three clear days for the letter to arrive.*

SUM OF MONEY | **15** [only before noun] remaining when taxes, costs, etc. have been taken away; [SYN] NET: *They had made a clear profit of £2 000.*

IDM **be clear 'sailing** (*AmE*) = BE PLAIN SAILING at PLAIN *adj.* (**as) clear as 'day** easy to see or understand (**as) clear as 'mud** (*spoken*) not clear at all; not easy to understand: *Oh well, that's all as clear as mud, then.* **in the 'clear** (*informal*) no longer in danger or thought to be guilty of sth: *It seems that the original suspect is in the clear.*—more at FIELD *n.*, HEAD *n.*, LOUD *adv.*

■ *verb*

REMOVE STH/SB | **1** [VN] ~ **A (of B)**| ~ **B (from/off A)** to remove sth that is not wanted or needed from a place: *I cleared my desk of papers and got down to work.* ◇ *Clear all those papers off the desk.* ◇ *I had cleared my desk before I left.* ◇ *It's your turn to* **clear the table** (= to take away the dirty plates, etc. after a meal). ◇ *She cleared a space on the sofa for him to sit down.* ◇ *The streets had been cleared of snow.* ◇ *The remains of the snow had been cleared from the streets.* ◇ *It was several hours before the road was cleared after the accident.*—see also CLEAR AWAY **2** [VN] to make people leave a place: *After the bomb warning, police cleared the streets.*

NOT BE BLOCKED | **3** [V] to move freely again; to no longer be blocked: *The traffic took a long time to clear after the accident.* ◇ *The boy's lungs cleared and he began to breathe more easily.*

OF SKY/WEATHER | **4** [V] when the sky or the weather **clears**, it becomes brighter and free of cloud or rain: *The sky cleared after the storm.* ◇ *The rain is clearing slowly.*

OF LIQUID | **5** [V] when a liquid **clears**, it becomes transparent and you can see through it: *The muddy water slowly cleared.*

OF SMOKE, etc. | **6** [V] ~ (**away**) when smoke, FOG, etc. **clears**, it disappears so that it is easier to see things: *The mist will clear by mid-morning.*

YOUR HEAD/MIND | **7** if your head or mind **clears**, or you **clear** it, you become free of thoughts that worry or confuse you or the effects of alcohol, a blow, etc. and you are able to think clearly: [V] *As her mind cleared, she remembered what had happened.* ◇ [VN] *I went for a walk to clear my head.*

	s	t	v	z	ʃ	ʒ	tʃ	dʒ	θ	ð	ŋ
	see	tea	van	zoo	shoe	vision	chain	jam	thin	this	sing

OF FACE/EXPRESSION | **8** [V] if your face or expression **clears**, you stop looking angry or worried

PROVE SB INNOCENT | **9** [VN] **~ sb (of sth)** to prove that sb is innocent: *She was cleared of all charges against her.* ◊ *Throughout his years in prison, he fought to clear his name.*

GIVE OFFICIAL PERMISSION | **10** [VN] **~ sth (with sb/sth)** to give or get official approval for sth to be done: *His appointment had been cleared by the board.* ◊ *I'll have to clear it with the manager before I can refund your money.* **11** [VN] to give official permission for a person, a ship, a plane or goods to leave or enter a place: *The plane had been cleared for take-off.* ◊ *to clear goods through customs* **12** [VN] to decide officially, after finding out information about sb, that they can be given special work or allowed to see secret papers: *She hasn't been cleared by security.*

MONEY | **13** if a cheque that you pay into your bank account **clears**, or a bank **clears** it, the money is available for you to use: [V] *Cheques usually take three working days to clear.* [also VN] **14** [VN] to gain or earn a sum of money as profit: *She cleared £1000 on the deal.* **15** [VN] if you **clear** a debt or a LOAN (= money you have borrowed), you pay all the money back

GET OVER/PAST | **16** [VN] to jump over or get past sth without touching it: *The horse cleared the fence easily.* ◊ *The car only just cleared* (= avoided hitting) *the gatepost.*

IN SPORT | **17** [V, VN] (in football and some other sports) if you **clear** a ball, or a ball **clears**, it is kicked or hit away from the area near your own goal

IDM **clear the 'air** to improve a difficult or tense situation by talking about worries, doubts, etc. **clear the 'decks** (*informal*) to prepare for an activity, event, etc. by removing anything that is not essential to it **clear your 'throat** to cough so that you can speak clearly **clear the way (for sth/for sth to happen)** to remove things that are stopping the progress or movement of sth: *The ruling could clear the way for extradition proceedings.*—more at COAST *n.*, COBWEB

PHRV **ˌclear aˈway | ˌclear sth↔aˈway** to remove sth because it is not wanted or needed, or in order to leave a clear space: *He cleared away and made coffee.* ◊ *It's time your toys were cleared away.* **ˌclear 'off** (*informal*) to go or run away: *He cleared off when he heard the police siren.* ◊ (*spoken*) *You've no right to be here. Clear off!* **ˌclear 'out (of …)** (*informal*) to leave a place quickly: *He cleared out with all the money and left her with the kids.* **ˌclear 'out | ˌclear sth↔'out** to make sth empty and clean by removing things or throwing things away: *to clear out a drawer/room* ◊ *We cleared out all our old clothes.* ◊ *I found the letters when I was clearing out after my father died.*—related noun CLEAR-OUT **ˌclear 'up 1** (of the weather) to become fine or bright: *I hope it clears up this afternoon.* **2** (of an illness, infection, etc.) to disappear: *Has your rash cleared up yet?* **ˌclear 'up | ˌclear sth↔'up** to make sth clean and neat: *It's time to clear up.* ◊ *I'm fed up with clearing up after you!* ◊ *Clear up your own mess!* **ˌclear sth↔'up** to solve or explain sth: *to clear up a mystery/ difficulty/misunderstanding*

■ *adv.*

NOT NEAR/TOUCHING | **1 ~ (of sth)** away from sth; not near or touching sth: *Stand clear of the train doors.* ◊ *He injured his arm as he jumped clear of the car.* ◊ *By the end of the first lap Walker was two metres clear of the rest of the runners.*

ALL THE WAY | **2** (*especially AmE*) all the way to sth that is far away: *She could see clear down the highway into the town.*

IDM **keep/stay/steer clear (of sb/sth)** to avoid a person or thing because it may cause problems: *Steer clear of the centre of town at this time of the evening.*—more at WAY *n.*

clear·ance /ˈklɪərəns; *AmE* ˈklɪr-/ *noun* **1** [C, U] the removal of things that are not wanted: *There were forest clearances in Java thousands of years ago.* ◊ *slum clearance* (= the removal of houses that are in very bad condition in an area of a town) ◊ *a clearance sale* (= in a shop/store, when goods are sold cheaply to get rid of them quickly) **2** [U, C] the amount of space or distance that is needed between two objects so that they do not touch each other: *There is not much clearance for vehicles passing under this bridge.* ◊ *a clearance of one metre* **3** [U, C] official permission that is given to sb before they can work somewhere, have particular information, or do sth they want to do: *I'm waiting for clearance from headquarters.* ◊ *All employees at the submarine base require security clearance.* **4** [U] official permission for a person or vehicle to enter or leave an airport or a country: *The pilot was waiting for clearance for take-off.* **5** [U, C] the process of a cheque being paid by a bank **6** [C] a **clearance** in football and some other sports is when a player kicks or hits the ball away from the goal of his or her own team

ˌclear-ˈcut *adj.* definite and easy to see or identify: *There is no clear-cut answer to this question.* ◊ *a clear-cut distinction*

ˌclear-ˈheaded *adj.* able to think in a clear and sensible way, especially in a difficult situation

clear·ing /ˈklɪərɪŋ; *AmE* ˈklɪrɪŋ/ *noun* an open space in a forest where there are no trees

ˈclearing bank *noun* (in Britain) a bank that uses a clearing house when dealing with other banks

ˈclearing house *noun* **1** a central office that banks use in order to pay each other money and exchange cheques, etc. **2** an organization that collects and exchanges information on behalf of people or other organizations: *a clearing house for applications to universities*

clear·ly /ˈklɪəli; *AmE* ˈklɪrli/ *adv.* **1** in a way that is easy to see or hear: *Please speak clearly after the tone.* **2** in a way that is sensible and easy to understand: *She explained everything very clearly.* **3** used to emphasize that what you are saying is obvious and true: *Clearly, this will cost a lot more than we realized.*

clear·ness /ˈklɪənəs; *AmE* ˈklɪrnəs/ *noun* [U] (much less frequent than *clarity*) the state of being clear

ˈclear-out *noun* [usually sing.] (*informal, especially BrE*) a process of getting rid of things or people that you no longer want: *If you are really living in a mess, have a grand clear-out and put the whole place straight.*

ˌclear-ˈsighted *adj.* understanding or thinking clearly; able to make good decisions and judgements

clear·way /ˈklɪəweɪ; *AmE* ˈklɪrweɪ/ *noun* (in Britain) a road on which vehicles must not stop

cleat /kliːt/ *noun* **1** [C] a small wooden or metal bar fastened to sth, on which ropes may be fastened by winding **2** [C] a piece of rubber on the bottom of a shoe, etc. to stop it from slipping—picture at SHOE **3** (**cleats**) [pl.] (*AmE*) shoes with cleats, often worn for playing sports—compare FOOTBALL BOOT, SPIKE (2), STUD (3)—picture at SHOE

cleav·age /ˈkliːvɪdʒ/ *noun* **1** [C, U] the space between a woman's breasts that can be seen above a dress that does not completely cover them **2** [C] (*formal*) a difference or division between people or groups: *a deep cleavage between rich and poor in society*

cleave /kliːv/ *verb* (**cleaved**, **cleaved** **HELP** Less commonly, **cleft** /kleft/ and **clove** /kləʊv; *AmE* kloʊv/ are used for the past tense, and **cleft** for the past participle.) **1** [VN] (*old-fashioned* or *literary*) to split or cut sth in two using sth sharp and heavy: *She cleaved his skull in two with an axe.* ◊ (*figurative*) *His skin was cleft with deep lines.* **2 ~ (through) sth** (*old-fashioned* or *literary*) to move quickly through sth: [V] *a ship cleaving through the water* ◊ [VN] *The huge boat cleaved the darkness.* **3 ~ to sb/sth** [V] (*literary*) to stick close to sth/sb: *Her tongue clove to the roof of her mouth.* **4** (**cleaved**, **cleaved**) [V] (*formal*) to continue to believe in or be loyal to sth: *to cleave to a belief/idea* **IDM** see CLEFT

cleav·er /ˈkliːvə(r)/ *noun* a heavy knife with a broad blade, used for cutting large pieces of meat

clef /klef/ *noun* (*music*) a symbol at the beginning of a line of printed music (called a STAVE or STAFF) that shows the PITCH of the notes on it: *the treble/bass clef*

cleft /kleft/ *noun, adj.*—see also CLEAVE *v.*

æ	ɑː	e	ɜː	ə	ɪ	iː	i	ɒ	ɔː	ʌ	ʊ	u	uː
cat	father	ten	bird	about	sit	see	many	got	saw	cup	put	actual	too

(BrE)

C

■ *noun* a natural opening or crack, for example in the ground or in rock, or in a person's chin: *a cleft in the rocks*

■ *adj.* IDM **be (caught) in a cleft ˈstick** to be in a difficult situation when any action you take will have bad results

ˌcleft ˈlip *noun* a condition in which sb is born with their upper lip split

ˌcleft ˈpalate *noun* a condition in which sb is born with the roof of their mouth split, making them unable to speak clearly

cle·ma·tis /ˈklemətɪs; kləˈmeɪtɪs/ *noun* [C, U] a climbing plant with large white, purple or pink flowers

clem·ency /ˈklemənsi/ *noun* [U] (*formal*) kindness shown to sb when they are being punished; willingness not to punish sb so severely SYN MERCY: *a plea for clemency*

clem·ent /ˈklemənt/ *adj.* (*formal*) **1** (especially of weather) mild and pleasant OPP INCLEMENT **2** showing kindness and MERCY to sb who is being punished

clem·en·tine /ˈkleməntiːn/ *noun* a fruit like a small orange

clench /klentʃ/ *verb* **1** when you **clench** your hands, teeth, etc., or when they **clench**, you press or squeeze them together tightly, usually showing that you are angry, determined or upset: [VN] *He clenched his fists in anger.* ◊ *Through clenched teeth she told him to leave.* ◊ [V] *His fists clenched slowly until his knuckles were white.* **2** [VN] **~ sth (in/between sth)** to hold sth tightly and firmly: *She sat at the desk, her pen clenched between her teeth.*

clergy /ˈklɜːdʒi; AmE ˈklɜːrdʒi/ *noun* (often **the clergy**) *noun* [pl.] the priests or ministers of a religion, especially of the Christian Church: *All the local clergy were asked to attend the ceremony.* ◊ *The new proposals affect both clergy and laity.*—compare LAITY

cler·gy·man /ˈklɜːdʒimən; AmE ˈklɜːrdʒ-/ (also **church-man**) *noun* (*pl.* **-men** /-mən/) a male priest or minister in the Christian Church—compare PRIEST

cler·gy·wo·man /ˈklɜːdʒiwʊmən; AmE ˈklɜːrdʒ-/ *noun* (*pl.* **-women** /-wɪmɪn/) a female priest or minister in the Christian Church

cler·ic /ˈklerɪk/ *noun* **1** (*old-fashioned* or *formal*) a clergyman **2** a religious leader in any religion: *Muslim clerics*

cler·ic·al /ˈklerɪkl/ *adj.* **1** connected with office work: *clerical workers/staff/assistants* ◊ *a clerical error* (= one made in copying or calculating sth) **2** connected with the CLERGY (= priests): *a clerical collar* (= one that fastens at the back, worn by some priests)

clerk /klɑːk; AmE klɜːrk/ *noun, verb*

■ *noun* **1** a person whose job is to keep the records or accounts in an office, shop/store etc: *an office clerk*—see also FILING CLERK **2** an official in charge of the records of a council, court, etc: *the Town Clerk* ◊ *the Clerk of the Court*—see also COUNTY CLERK, PARISH CLERK, CLERK OF WORKS **3** (also **ˈsales clerk**) (both *AmE*) = SHOP ASSISTANT **4** (also **ˈdesk clerk**) (both *AmE*) a person whose job is dealing with people arriving at or leaving a hotel SYN RECEPTIONIST

■ *verb* (*AmE*) [V] to work as a clerk: *a clerking job*

ˌclerk of ˈworks *noun* (*BrE*) a person whose job is to be in charge of repairs to buildings or of building works, for an organization or institution

clever /ˈklevə(r)/ *adj.* (**clever·er, clever·est**) HELP You can also use **more clever** and **most clever. 1** (*especially BrE*) quick at learning and understanding things SYN INTELLIGENT: *a clever child* ◊ *Clever girl!* ◊ *How clever of you to work it out!* ◊ *He's too clever by half, if you ask me* (= it annoys me or makes me suspicious). **2 ~ (at sth)** (*especially BrE*) skilful: *She's clever at getting what she wants.* ◊ *He's clever with his hands.* **3** showing intelligence or skill, for example in the design of an object, in an idea or sb's actions: *a clever little gadget* ◊ *What a clever idea!* ◊ *That* (= what you just did) *wasn't very clever, was it?* (= it wasn't sensible) **4** (*BrE, informal, disapproving*) quick with words in a way that annoys people or does not show respect: *Don't you get clever with me!* ▶ **clev·er·ly** *adv.* **clev·er·ness** *noun* [U]

ˈclever Dick (also ˈclever clogs) *noun* (both *BrE, informal, disapproving*) a person who thinks they are always right or that they know everything

cli·ché (also **cliche**) /ˈkliːʃeɪ; AmE kliːˈʃeɪ/ *noun* (*disapproving*) **1** [C] a phrase or an idea that has been used so often that it no longer has much meaning and is not interesting: *She trotted out the old cliché that 'a trouble shared is a trouble halved.'* **2** [U] the use of clichés in writing or speaking ▶ **cli·ché·d** (also **cli·ché'd, cliched**) /ˈkliːʃeɪd; AmE kliːˈʃeɪd/ *adj.*: *a clichéd view of upper-class life*

click /klɪk/ *verb, noun*

■ *verb* **1** to make or cause sth to make a short sharp sound: [V] *The cameras clicked away.* ◊ *The bolt clicked into place.* ◊ [V-ADJ] *The door clicked shut.* ◊ [VN] *He clicked his fingers at the waiter.* ◊ *Polly clicked her tongue in annoyance.* **2 ~ (on sth)** to choose a particular function or item on a computer screen, etc., by pressing one of the buttons on a mouse: [VN] *Click the OK button to start.* ◊ [V] *I clicked on the link to the next page of the website.* ◊ *To run a window, just double-click on the icon.* **3** [V] (*informal*) to suddenly become clear or understood: *Suddenly it clicked—we'd been talking about different people.* ◊ *It all clicked into place.* **4** [V] (*informal*) to become friends with sb at once; to become popular with sb: *We met at a party and clicked immediately.* ◊ *He's never really clicked with his students.* **5** [V] (*informal*) to work well together: *The team don't seem to have clicked yet.*

■ *noun* **1** a short sharp sound: *The front door closed with a click.* **2** the act of pressing the button on a computer mouse

clicking his fingers

cli·ent /ˈklaɪənt/ *noun* **1** a person who uses the services or advice of a professional person or organization: *a well-known lawyer with many famous clients* ◊ *to act on behalf of a client* ◊ *Social workers must consider the best interests of their clients in every situation.* ⇨ note at CUSTOMER **2** (*computing*) a computer that is linked to a SERVER

cli·en·tele /ˌkliːənˈtel; AmE ˌklaɪənˈtel/ *noun* [sing.+ sing./pl. *v.*] all the customers or clients of a shop/store, restaurant, organization, etc: *an international clientele*

ˌclient-ˈserver *adj.* [only before noun] (*computing*) (of a computer system) in which a central SERVER provides data to a number of computers connected together in a NETWORK

ˌclient ˈstate *noun* a country which depends on a larger and more powerful country for support and protection

cliff /klɪf/ *noun* a high area of rock with a very steep side, often at the edge of the sea or ocean: *the cliff edge/top* ◊ *the chalk cliffs of Southern England* ◊ *a castle perched high on the cliffs above the river*—picture at COAST

cliff·hang·er /ˈklɪfhæŋə(r)/ *noun* a situation in a story, film/movie, competition, etc. that is very exciting because you cannot guess what will happen next, or you do not find out immediately what happens next: *The first part of the serial ended with a real cliffhanger.* ▶ **cliff·hang·ing** *adj.*

cliff·top /ˈklɪftɒp; AmE -tɑːp/ *noun* the area of land at the top of a cliff

cli·mac·tic /klaɪˈmæktɪk/ *adj.* (*written*) (of an event or a point in time) very exciting, most important: *The play builds up to a final climactic scene between father and daughter.*

cli·mate /ˈklaɪmət/ *noun* **1** [C, U] the regular pattern of weather conditions of a particular place: *a mild/temperate/warm/wet climate* ◊ *the threat of global climate change* **2** [C] an area with particular weather conditions: *They wanted to move to a warmer climate.* **3** [C] a general attitude or feeling; an atmosphere or a situation which

aɪ	aʊ	eɪ	əʊ	oʊ	ɔɪ	ɪə	eə	ʊə	j	w
my	now	say	go (BrE)	go (AmE)	boy	near	hair	pure	yes	wet

exists in a particular place: *the present political climate* ◊ *the current climate of opinion* (= what people generally are thinking about a particular issue) ◊ *a climate of suspicion/violence* ◊ *We need to create a climate in which business can prosper.*

cli·mat·ic /klaɪˈmætɪk/ *adj.* [only before noun] connected with the weather of a particular area: *climatic changes/conditions* ► **cli·mat·ic·al·ly** /-kli/ *adv.*

cli·mat·ology /ˌklaɪmətˈtɒlədʒi; *AmE* -ˈtɑːl-/ *noun* [U] the scientific study of climate ► **cli·ma·to·logic·al** /ˌklaɪmətəˈlɒdʒɪkl; *AmE* -ˈlɑːdʒ-/ *adj.* **cli·mat·olo·gist** /ˌklaɪmətˈtɒlədʒist; *AmE* -ˈtɑːl-/ *noun*

cli·max /ˈklaɪmæks/ *noun, verb*
■ *noun* **1** the most exciting or important event or point in time: *to come to/reach a climax* ◊ *the climax of his political career* **2** the most exciting part of a play, piece of music, etc. that usually happens near the end: *The book's powerful climax is the murder of Nancy by her lover Bill Sikes.* **3** the highest point of sexual pleasure SYN ORGASM—compare ANTICLIMAX
■ *verb* (*written*) **1** ~ **with/in** sth to come to or form the best, most exciting, or most important point in sth: [V] *The festival will climax on Sunday with a gala concert.* ◊ [VN] (*especially AmE*) *The sensational verdict climaxed a six-month trial.* **2** [V] to have an ORGASM

climb /klaɪm/ *verb, noun*
■ *verb*
GO UP | **1** ~ **(up)** (sth) to go up sth towards the top: [VN] *to climb a mountain/hill/tree/wall* ◊ *She climbed up the stairs.* ◊ *The car slowly climbed the hill.* ◊ [V] *As they climbed higher, the air became cooler.*
GO THROUGH/DOWN/OVER | **2** [V+adv./prep.] to move somewhere, especially with difficulty or effort: *I climbed through the window.* ◊ *Sue climbed into bed.* ◊ *Can you climb down?* ◊ *The boys climbed over the wall.*
MOUNTAIN/ROCK, etc. | **3** (**go climbing**) to go up mountains or climb rocks as a hobby or sport: *He likes to go climbing most weekends.*
AIRCRAFT/SUN, etc. | **4** [V] to go higher in the sky: *The plane climbed to 33 000 feet.*
SLOPE UP | **5** [V] to slope upwards: *From here the path climbs steeply to the summit.*
OF PLANTS | **6** [V] to grow up a wall or frame: *a climbing rose*
INCREASE | **7** [V] (of temperature, a country's money, etc.) to increase in value or amount: *The dollar has been climbing all week.* ◊ *The paper's circulation continues to climb.*
IMPROVE POSITION/STATUS | **8** [V] to move to a higher position or social rank by your own effort: *In a few years he had climbed to the top of his profession.* ◊ *The team has now climbed to fourth in the league.*
IDM see BANDWAGON
PHRV ˌclimb ˈdown (over sth) to admit that you have made a mistake or that you were wrong—related noun CLIMBDOWN
■ *noun*
MOUNTAIN/STEPS | **1** an act of climbing up a mountain, rock or large number of steps; a period of time spent climbing: *an exhausting climb* ◊ *It's an hour's climb to the summit.* **2** a mountain or rock which people climb up for sport: *Titan's Wall is the mountain's hardest rock climb.*
INCREASE | **3** [usually sing.] an increase in value or amount: *the dollar's climb against the euro*
TO A HIGHER POSITION OR STATUS | **4** [usually sing.] progress to a higher status, standard or position: *a rapid climb to stardom* ◊ *the long slow climb out of the recession*

climb·down /ˈklaɪmdaʊn/ *noun* an act of admitting that you were wrong, or of changing your position in an argument: *The Chancellor was forced into a humiliating climbdown on his economic policies.*

climb·er /ˈklaɪmə(r)/ *noun* **1** a person who climbs (especially mountains) or an animal that climbs: *climbers and hill walkers* ◊ *Monkeys are efficient climbers.* **2** a climbing plant—see also SOCIAL CLIMBER

climb·ing /ˈklaɪmɪŋ/ *noun* [U] the sport or activity of

climbing rocks or mountains: *to go climbing* ◊ *a climbing accident* ◊ *a climbing wall* (= one that is especially made to practise climbing on)

ˈclimbing frame (*BrE*) (*AmE* **ˈjungle gym**) *noun* a structure made of metal bars joined together for children to climb and play on—picture at FRAME

clime /klaɪm/ *noun* [usually pl.] (*literary* or *humorous*) a country with a particular kind of climate: *I'm heading for sunnier climes next month.*

clinch /klɪntʃ/ *verb, noun*
■ *verb* [VN] **1** to succeed in achieving or winning sth: *to clinch an argument/a deal/a victory* **2** to provide the answer to sth; to settle sth that was not certain: *'I'll pay your air fare.' 'Okay, that clinches it—I'll come with you.'* ◊ *a clinching argument*
■ *noun* **1** (*informal*) a position in which two lovers hold each other tightly SYN EMBRACE **2** a position in a fight in which two opponents hold each other tightly with the arms

clinch·er /ˈklɪntʃə(r)/ *noun* [usually sing.] (*informal*) a fact, a remark or an event that settles an argument, a decision or a competition

cline /klaɪn/ *noun* a series of similar items in which each is almost the same as the ones next to it, but the last is very different from the first SYN CONTINUUM

cling /klɪŋ/ *verb* (**clung, clung** /klʌŋ/) [V] **1** ~ **(on) to sb/sth** | ~ **on/together** to hold on tightly to sb/sth: *survivors clinging to a raft* ◊ *She clung on to her baby.* ◊ *Cling on tight!* ◊ *They clung together, shivering with cold.* **2** ~ **(to sth)** to stick to sth: *a dress that clings* (= fits closely and shows the shape of your body) ◊ *The wet shirt clung to his chest.* ◊ *The smell of smoke still clung to her clothes.* **3** ~ **(to sb)** (usually *disapproving*) to stay close to sb, especially because you are emotionally dependent on them: *After her mother's death, Sara clung to her aunt more than ever.* PHRV ˈcling to sth | ˌcling ˈon to sth to be unwilling to get rid of sth, or stop doing sth: *Throughout the trial she had clung to the belief that he was innocent.* ◊ *He had one last hope to cling on to.* ◊ *She managed to cling on to life for another couple of years.*

ˈcling film (*BrE*) (*AmE* **ˈplastic wrap**) *noun* [U] a thin transparent plastic material that sticks to a surface and to itself, used especially for wrapping food

cling·ing /ˈklɪŋɪŋ/ (also **clingy** /ˈklɪŋi/) *adj.* **1** (of clothes or fabric) sticking to the body and showing its shape **2** (usually *disapproving*) too dependent on another person: *a clinging child*

clin·ic /ˈklɪnɪk/ *noun* **1** a building or part of a hospital where people can go for special medical treatment or advice: *the local family planning clinic* **2** (*especially BrE*) a period of time during which doctors give special medical treatment or advice: *The antenatal clinic is on Wednesdays.* **3** (*especially BrE*) a private hospital or one that treats health problems of a particular kind: *He is being treated at the London clinic.* ◊ *a rehabilitation clinic for alcoholics* **4** (*AmE*) a building where visiting patients can get medical treatment; a building shared by a group of doctors who work together **5** an occasion in a hospital when medical students learn by watching a specialist examine and treat patients **6** an occasion at which a professional person, especially a SPORTSMAN or SPORTSWOMAN gives advice and training: *a coaching clinic for young tennis players*

clin·ic·al /ˈklɪnɪkl/ *adj.* **1** [only before noun] relating to the examination and treatment of patients and their illnesses: *clinical research* (= done on patients, not just considering theory) ◊ *clinical training* (= the part of a doctor's training done in a hospital) ◊ *clinical trials of a drug* **2** (*disapproving*) cold and calm and without feeling or sympathy: *He watched her suffering with clinical detachment.* **3** (*disapproving*) (of a room, building, etc.) very plain; without decoration ► **clin·ic·al·ly** *adv.*: *clinically dead* (= judged to be dead from the condition of the body) ◊ *clinically depressed*

clin·ician /klɪˈnɪʃn/ *noun* a doctor, PSYCHOLOGIST, etc. who has direct contact with patients

b	d	f	g	h	k	l	m	n	p	r
bad	did	fall	get	hat	cat	leg	man	now	pen	red

clink /klɪŋk/ *verb, noun*

■ *verb* to make or cause sth to make a sharp ringing sound, like that of glasses being hit against each other: [V] *clinking coins* ◊ [VN] *They clinked glasses and drank to each other's health.*

They clinked their glasses.

■ *noun* [sing.] **1** (also **clinking**) a sharp ringing sound like the sound made by glasses being hit against each other **2** (*old-fashioned, slang*) prison

clink·er /ˈklɪŋkə(r)/ *noun* **1** [U, C] the hard rough substance left after coal has burnt at a high temperature; a piece of this substance **2** [sing.] (*AmE*) a wrong musical note: *The singer hit a clinker.*

clip /klɪp/ *noun, verb*

■ *noun* **1** [C] (often in compounds) a small metal or plastic object used for holding things together or in place: *a hair clip* ◊ *toe clips on a bicycle*—see also BICYCLE CLIP, BULLDOG CLIP, PAPER CLIP—picture at BICYCLE, STATIONERY **2** [C] a piece of jewellery that fastens to your clothes: *a diamond clip* **3** [sing.] the act of cutting sth to make it shorter: *He gave the hedge a clip.* **4** [C] a short part of a film/movie that is shown separately: *Here is a clip from her latest movie.* **5** [C] (*BrE, informal*) a quick hit with your hand: *She gave him **a clip round the ear** for being cheeky.* **6** [C] a set of bullets in a metal container that is placed in or attached to a gun for firing IDM **at a fast, good, steady, etc. 'clip** (*especially AmE*) quickly: *Land prices will rise at a healthy clip.*

■ *verb* (**-pp-**) **1** [+*adv./prep.*] to fasten sth to sth else with a clip; to be fastened with a clip: [VN] *He **clipped** the microphone (**on) to his collar.* ◊ **Clip** *the pages **together**.* ◊ [V] *Do those earrings clip on?* **2** [VN] ~ **sth (off/from sth)** to cut sth with scissors or SHEARS, in order to make it shorter; to remove sth from somewhere by cutting it off: *to clip a hedge* ◊ *He clipped off a length of wire.* **3** [VN] to hit the edge or side of sth: *The car clipped the kerb as it turned.* ◊ *She clipped the ball into the net.* **4** [VN] ~ **sth (out of/from sth)** to cut sth out of sth else using scissors: *to clip a coupon (out of the paper)* IDM **clip sb's 'wings** to restrict a person's freedom or power PHRV **,clip sth 'off sth** (*informal*) to reduce the time that it takes to do sth by a particular length of time: *She clipped two seconds off her previous best time.*

clip·board /ˈklɪpbɔːd; *AmE* -bɔːrd/ *noun* **1** a small board with a clip at the top for holding papers, used by sb who wants to write while standing or moving around—picture at STATIONERY **2** (*computing*) a place where information from a computer file is stored temporarily until it is added to another file

clip-clop /ˈklɪp klɒp; *AmE* klɑːp/ *noun* a sound like the sound of a horse's HOOVES on a hard surface

'clip joint *noun* (*informal, disapproving*) a NIGHTCLUB which charges prices that are too high

'clip-on *adj.* [only before noun] fastened to sth with a CLIP: *clip-on earrings*—picture at JEWELLERY

clipped /klɪpt/ *adj.* (of a person's way of speaking) clear and fast but not very friendly: *his clipped military tones*

clip·per /ˈklɪpə(r)/ *noun* **1** (**clippers**) [pl.] a tool for cutting small pieces off things: *a pair of clippers* ◊ *nail clippers* **2** a fast sailing ship, used in the past

clip·ping /ˈklɪpɪŋ/ *noun* **1** [usually pl.] a piece cut off sth: *hedge/nail clippings* **2** (*especially AmE*) = CUTTING

clique /kliːk/ *noun* [C+sing./pl. v.] (*often disapproving*) a small group of people who spend their time together and do not allow others to join them

cliquey /ˈkliːki/ (also **cliqu·ish** /ˈkliːkɪʃ/) *adj.* (*disapproving*) tending to form a clique; controlled by cliques: *He found the school very cliquey and elitist.*

clit·oris /ˈklɪtərɪs/ *noun* the small sensitive organ just above the opening of a woman's VAGINA which becomes larger when she is sexually excited ▶ **clit·or·al** /ˈklɪtərəl/ *adj.* [only before noun]

Cllr *abbr.* (*BrE*) (used before names in writing) COUNCILLOR: *Cllr Michael Booth*

cloak /kləʊk; *AmE* kloʊk/ *noun, verb*

■ *noun* **1** [C] a type of coat that has no sleeves, fastens at the neck and hangs loosely from the shoulders, worn especially in the past **2** [sing.] (*literary*) a thing that hides or covers sb/sth: *They left under the cloak of darkness.*

■ *verb* [VN] ~ **sth (in sth)** [often passive] (*written*) to cover or hide sth: *The hills were cloaked in thick mist.* ◊ *The meeting was cloaked in mystery.* ▶ **cloaked** *adj.*: *a tall cloaked figure* (= a person wearing a cloak)

,cloak-and-'dagger *adj.* [only before noun] **cloak-and-dagger** activities are secret and mysterious, sometimes in a way that people think is unnecessary or ridiculous

cloak·room /ˈkləʊkruːm; -rʊm; *AmE* ˈkloʊk-/ *noun* **1** (*especially BrE*) (*AmE* usually **check·room**, **'coat check**, **coat·room**) a room in a public building where people can leave coats, bags, etc. for a time **2** (*BrE*) a room in a public building where there are toilets: *the ladies' cloakroom*

clob·ber /ˈklɒbə(r); *AmE* ˈklɑːb-/ *verb, noun*

■ *verb* [VN] (*informal*) **1** to hit sb very hard: *If you do that again, I'll clobber you!* **2** [often passive] to affect sb badly or to punish them, especially by making them lose money: *The paper got clobbered with libel damages of half a million pounds.* **3** [usually passive] to defeat sb completely: *We got clobbered in the game on Saturday.*

■ *noun* [U] (*BrE, informal*) a person's clothes or equipment

cloche /klɒʃ; *AmE* kloʊʃ/ *noun* **1** (also **,cloche 'hat**) a woman's hat, shaped like a bell, and fitting close to the head, worn especially in the 1920s **2** a glass or plastic cover placed over young plants to protect them from cold weather

clock /klɒk; *AmE* klɑːk/ *noun, verb*

■ *noun* **1** [C] an instrument for measuring and showing time, in a room or on the wall of a building (not worn or carried like a watch): *It was ten past six by the kitchen clock.* ◊ *The clock struck twelve/midnight.* ◊ *The clock is fast/slow.* ◊ *The clock has stopped.* ◊ *the clock face* (= the front part of a clock with the numbers on) ◊ *The hands of the clock crept slowly around.* ◊ *Ellen heard the loud ticking of the clock in the hall.*—see also ALARM CLOCK, BIOLOGICAL CLOCK, BODY CLOCK, CUCKOO CLOCK, GRANDFATHER CLOCK, O'CLOCK, TIME CLOCK **2** (**the clock**) [sing.] (*informal*) = MILOMETER: *a used car with 20 000 miles on the clock* IDM **against the clock** if you do sth **against the clock**, you do it fast in order to finish before a particular time **around/round the 'clock** all day and all night without stopping **put the clocks forward/back** (*BrE*) (*AmE* **set/move the clocks ahead/back**) to change the time shown by clocks, usually by one hour, when the time changes officially, for example at the beginning and end of summer **put/turn the 'clock back 1** to return to a situation that existed in the past; to remember a past age: *I wish we could turn the clock back two years and give the marriage another chance.* **2** (*disapproving*) to return to old-fashioned methods or ideas: *The new censorship law will turn the clock back 50 years.* **run out the clock** (*AmE*) if a sports team tries to **run out the clock** at the end of a game, it stops trying to score and just tries to keep hold of the ball to stop the other team from scoring **the clocks go forward/back** the time changes officially, for example at the beginning and end of summer—more at BEAT *v.*, RACE *n.*, STOP *v.*, WATCH *v.*

■ *verb* **1** [VN] to reach a particular time or speed: *He clocked 10.09 seconds in the 100 metres final.* **2** ~ **sb/sth (at sth)** to measure the speed at which sb/sth is travelling: [VN-ING] *The police clocked him doing over 100 miles an hour.* ◊ [VN] *Wind gusts at 80 m.p.h. were clocked at Rapid City.* **3** (*BrE, informal*) to notice or recognize sb: [VN] *I clocked her in the driving mirror.* [also V wh-, V that] PHRV **,clock 'in/ 'on** (*BrE*) (*AmE* **,punch 'in**) to record the time at which you arrive at work, especially by putting a card into a machine **,clock 'out/'off** (*BrE*) (*AmE* **,punch 'out**) to record the time at which you leave work, especially by putting a card into a machine **,clock 'up sth** to reach a particular amount or number: *On the trip we clocked up*

s	t	v	z	ʃ	ʒ	tʃ	dʒ	θ	ð	ŋ
see	tea	van	zoo	shoe	vision	chain	jam	thin	this	sing

over 1 800 miles. ◊ He has clocked up more than 25 years on the committee.

‚clock 'radio noun a clock combined with a radio that can be set to come on at a particular time in order to wake sb up

'clock tower noun a tall tower, usually part of another building, with a clock at the top

'clock-watcher noun (disapproving) a worker who is always checking the time to make sure that they do not work longer than they need to

clock·wise /'klɒkwaɪz; AmE 'klɑːk-/ adv., adj. moving around in the same direction as the hands of a clock: Turn the key clockwise. ◊ a clockwise direction OPP ANTICLOCKWISE, COUNTERCLOCKWISE

clock·work /'klɒkwɜːk; AmE 'klɑːkwɜːrk/ noun [U] machinery with wheels and SPRINGS like that inside a clock: clockwork toys (= toys that you wind up with a key) ◊ He is home by six every day regular as clockwork. IDM go/run like 'clockwork to happen according to plan; to happen without difficulties or problems

clod /klɒd; AmE klɑːd/ noun 1 [usually pl.] a lump of earth or clay 2 (informal) a stupid person

clod·hop·per /'klɒdhɒpə(r); AmE 'klɑːdhɑːp-/ noun (informal) 1 [usually pl.] a large heavy shoe 2 (disapproving) an awkward or CLUMSY person

clog /klɒg; AmE klɑːg/ verb, noun
■ verb (-gg-) ~ (up) (with sth) | ~ sth (up) (with sth) to block sth or to become blocked: [VN] [often passive] The narrow streets were clogged with traffic. ◊ Tears clogged her throat. ◊ [V] Within a few years the pipes began to clog up.
■ noun a shoe that is completely made of wood or one that has a thick wooden sole and a leather top—picture at SHOE IDM see POP v.

clois·ter /'klɔɪstə(r)/ noun 1 [C, usually pl.] a covered passage with arches around a square garden, usually forming part of a CATHEDRAL, CONVENT or MONASTERY 2 [sing.] life in a CONVENT or MONASTERY: the calm of the cloister

clois·tered /'klɔɪstəd; AmE -tərd/ adj. (formal) protected from the problems and dangers of normal life: a cloistered life ◊ the cloistered world of the university

clone /kləʊn; AmE kloʊn/ noun, verb
■ noun 1 (biology) a plant or an animal that is produced artificially from the cells of another plant or animal and is therefore exactly the same as it 2 (sometimes disapproving) a person or thing that seems to be an exact copy of another 3 (computing) a computer designed to work in exactly the same way as another, usually one made by a different company and more expensive
■ verb [VN] to produce an exact copy of an animal or a plant from its cells: A team from the UK were the first to successfully clone an animal. ◊ Dolly, the cloned sheep ▶ **clon·ing** noun [U]

clonk /klɒŋk; AmE klɑːŋk/ noun (BrE, informal) a short loud sound of heavy things hitting each other ▶ **clonk** verb [V, VN]

close¹ /kləʊz; AmE kloʊz/ verb, noun—see also CLOSE²
■ verb
WINDOW/DOOR, etc. | 1 to put sth into a position so that it covers an opening; to get into this position SYN SHUT: [VN] Would anyone mind if I closed the window? ◊ She closed the gate behind her. ◊ It's dark now—let's close the curtains. ◊ [V] I closed my eyes against the bright light. ◊ [V] The doors open and close automatically. OPP OPEN
BOOK/UMBRELLA, etc. | 2 [VN] ~ sth (up) to move the parts of sth together so that it is no longer open SYN SHUT: to close a book/an umbrella OPP OPEN
SHOP/STORE/BUSINESS | 3 ~ (sth) (to sb/sth) to make the work of a shop/store, etc. stop for a period of time; to not be open for people to use: [VN] [often passive] The museum has been closed for renovation. ◊ The road was closed to traffic for two days. ◊ [V] What time does the bank close? ◊ We close for lunch between twelve and two. OPP OPEN
4 (also ‚close 'down, ‚close sth↔'down) if a company, shop/store, etc. closes, or if you close it, it stops operating as a business: [VN] The club was closed by the police. ◊

[V] The hospital closed at the end of last year. ◊ The play closed after just three nights. OPP OPEN
END | 5 to end or make sth end: [VN] to close a meeting/debate ◊ to close a case/an investigation ◊ to close an account (= to stop keeping money in a bank account) ◊ The subject is now closed (= we will not discuss it again). ◊ [V] The meeting will close at 10.00 p.m. ◊ The offer closes at the end of the week. OPP OPEN
FINANCE | 6 [V] to be worth a particular amount at the end of the day's business: Shares in the company closed at 265p. ◊ closing prices [also V-ADJ]
DISTANCE/DIFFERENCE | 7 to make the distance or difference between two people or things smaller; to become smaller or narrower: [VN] These measures are aimed at closing the gap between rich and poor. ◊ [V] The gap between the two top teams is closing all the time.
HOLD FIRMLY | 8 ~ (sth) about/around/over sb/sth to hold sth/sb firmly: [VN] She closed her hand over his. [also V]

> **WHICH WORD?**
> **close / shut**
>
> You can **close** and **shut** doors, windows, your eyes, mouth, etc.
>
> **Shut** can suggest more noise and is often found in phrases such as slammed shut, banged shut, snapped shut.
>
> **Shut** is also usually used for containers such as boxes, suitcases, etc.
>
> To talk about the time when shops, offices, etc. are not open, use **close** or **shut**: What time do the banks close/shut? ◊ A strike has shut the factory. You can also use **closed** or **shut** (AmE usually **closed**): The store is closed/shut today. Especially in AmE, **shut** can sound less polite.
>
> **Closed** is used in front of a noun, but **shut** is not: a closed window.
>
> We usually use **closed** about roads, airports, etc.: The road is closed because of the snow.
>
> **Close** is also used in formal English to talk about ending a meeting or conversation.

IDM **close the book on sth** to stop doing sth because you no longer believe you will be successful or will find a solution: The police have closed the book on the case (= they have stopped trying to solve it). **close its doors** (of a business, etc.) to stop trading: The factory closed its doors for the last time in 1997. **close your 'mind to sth** to refuse to think about sth as a possibility **close 'ranks 1** if a group of people **close ranks**, they work closely together to defend themselves, especially when they are being criticized: It's not unusual for the police to close ranks when one of their officers is being investigated. **2** if soldiers **close ranks**, they move closer together in order to defend themselves—more at DOOR, EAR, EYE n.
PHRV ‚close 'down (BrE) when a radio or television station **closes down**, it stops broadcasting at the end of the day—related noun CLOSE-DOWN ‚close 'down| ‚close sth↔'down = CLOSE(4): All the steelworks around here were closed down in the 1980s.—related noun CLOSE-DOWN OPP OPEN UP ‚close 'in 1 when the days **close in**, they become gradually shorter during the autumn/fall 2 if the weather **closes in**, it gets worse 3 when the night **closes in**, it gets darker: They huddled around the fire as the night closed in. ‚close 'in (on sb/sth) to move nearer to sb/sth, especially in order to attack them: The lions closed in on their prey. ‚close sth↔'off to separate sth from other parts so that people cannot use it: The entrance to the train station was closed off following the explosion. ‚close 'out sth (AmE) 1 to sell goods very cheaply in order to get rid of them quickly—related noun CLOSEOUT 2 to finish or settle sth: A rock concert closed out the festivities. ‚close 'over sb/sth to surround and cover sb/sth: The water closed over his head. ‚close 'up 1 when a wound **closes up**, it heals 2 to hide your thoughts or emotions: She closed up when I asked about her family. ‚close 'up| ‚close sth↔'up 1 to shut and lock sth such as a shop/store or a building, especially for a short

æ	ɑː	e	ɜː	ə	ɪ	iː	i	ɒ	ɔː	ʌ	ʊ	u	uː
cat	father	ten	bird	about	sit	see	many	got	saw	cup	put	actual	too
								(BrE)					

period of time: *Why don't we close up and go out for lunch?* ◊ *Can the last one out close up the office?* OPP OPEN UP **2** to come closer together; to bring people or things closer together: *Traffic was heavy and cars were closing up behind each other.* **3** to become narrower and less open: *Every time he tried to speak, his throat closed up with fear.* OPP OPEN UP

■ *noun* [sing.] (*formal*) the end of a period of time or an activity: *at the close of the 17th century* ◊ *His life was drawing to a close.* ◊ *Can we bring this meeting to a close?*

close² /kləʊs; *AmE* kloʊs/ *adj., adv., noun*—see also CLOSE¹

■ *adj.* (**closer**, **clos·est**)
NEAR | **1** [not usually before noun] ~ **(to sb/sth)**| ~ **(together)** near in space or time: *Our new house is close to the school.* ◊ *I had no idea the beach was so close.* ◊ *The two buildings are* **close together**. ◊ *This is the closest we can get to the beach by car.* ◊ *We all have to work in close proximity* (= near each other). ◊ *The President was shot at close range* (= from a short distance away). ◊ *The children are close to each other in age.* ◊ *Their birthdays are very close together.* ⇨ note at NEAR

ALMOST/LIKELY | **2** [not before noun] ~ **(to sth)**| ~ **(to doing sth)** almost in a particular state; likely to do sth soon: *He was close to tears.* ◊ *The new library is close to completion.* ◊ *She knew she was close to death.* ◊ *We are close to signing the agreement.*

RELATIONSHIP | **3** ~ **(to sb)** knowing sb very well and liking them very much: *Jo is a very close friend.* ◊ *She is very close to her father.* ◊ *She and her father are very close.* ◊ *We're a very close family.* **4** near in family relationship: *close relatives, such as your mother and father, and brothers and sisters* ◊ *The groom and his close family took their places.* **5** very involved in the work or activities of sb else, usually seeing and talking to them regularly: *He is one of the prime minister's closest advisers.* ◊ *The college has close links with many other institutions.* ◊ *She has kept in close contact with the victims' families.* ◊ *We keep in close touch with the police.*

CAREFUL | **6** [only before noun] careful and thorough: *Take a close look at this photograph.* ◊ *On closer examination the painting proved to be a fake.* ◊ *Pay close attention to what I am telling you.*

SIMILAR | **7** ~ **(to sth)** very similar to sth else or to an amount: *There's a close resemblance* (= they are very much alike). ◊ *His feeling for her was close to hatred.* ◊ *The unemployment total was close to 20% of the workforce.* ◊ *We tried to match the colours, but this is the closest we could get.*

COMPETITION/ELECTION, etc. | **8** won by only a small amount or distance: *a close contest/match/election* ◊ *It was a very close finish.* ◊ *I think it's going to be close.* ◊ *The game was closer than the score suggests.* ◊ *The result is going to be too close to call* (= either side may win).

ALMOST BAD RESULT | **9** used to describe sth, usually a dangerous or unpleasant situation, that nearly happens: *Phew! That was close—that car nearly hit us.* ◊ *We caught the bus in the end but it was close* (= we nearly missed it).

WITHOUT SPACE | **10** with little or no space in between: *over 1000 pages of close print* ◊ *The soldiers advanced in close formation.*

CUT SHORT | **11** cut very short, near to the skin: *a close haircut/shave*

GUARDED | **12** [only before noun] carefully guarded: *The donor's identity is a close secret.* ◊ *She was kept under close arrest.*

WEATHER/ROOM | **13** warm in an uncomfortable way because there does not seem to be enough fresh air SYN STUFFY: *It's very close today—I think there's going to be a storm.*

PRIVATE | **14** [not before noun] ~ **(about sth)** not willing to give personal information about yourself: *He was close about his past.*

MEAN | **15** [not before noun] (*BrE*) not liking to spend money: *She's always been very close with her money.*

PHONETICS | **16** (of vowels) pronounced with the tongue raised near to the top of the mouth

▶ **close·ly** *adv.*: *I sat and watched everyone very closely* (= carefully). ◊ *He walked into the room, closely followed by the rest of the family.* ◊ *a closely contested election* ◊ *She closely resembled her mother at the same age.* ◊ *The two events are closely connected.* **close·ness** *noun* [U]

IDM **at/from ˌclose ˈquarters** very near: *fighting at close quarters* **a ˌclose ˈcall/ˈshave** (*informal*) a situation in which you only just manage to avoid an accident, etc. **a close ˈthing** a situation in which success or failure is equally possible: *We got him out in the end, but it was a close thing.* **close to ˈhome** if a remark or topic of discussion is **close to home**, it is accurate or connected with you in a way that makes you uncomfortable or embarrassed: *Her remarks about me were embarrassingly close to home.* **keep a close ˈeye/ˈwatch on sb/sth** to watch sb/sth carefully: *Over the next few months we will keep a close eye on sales.*—more at HEART

■ *adv.* (**closer**, **clos·est**) near; not far away: *They sat close together.* ◊ *Don't come too close!* ◊ *She held Tom close and pressed her cheek to his.* ◊ *I couldn't get close enough to see.* ◊ *A second police car followed close behind.*

IDM **close at ˈhand** near; in a place where sb/sth can be reached easily: *There are good cafes and a restaurant close at hand.* **close ˈby (sb/sth)** at a short distance (from sb/sth): *Our friends live close by.* ◊ *The route passes close by the town.* **close on | close to** almost; nearly: *She is close on sixty.* ◊ *It is close on midnight.* ◊ *a profit close to £200 million* **a close run ˈthing** a situation in which sb only just wins or loses, for example in a competition or an election: *Mr Taylor's election defeat was a close run thing.* **close ˈto | close ˈup** in a position very near to sth: *The picture looks very different when you see it close to.* **close up to sb/sth** very near in space to sb/sth: *She snuggled close up to him.* **come close (to sth/to doing sth)** to almost reach or do sth: *He'd come close to death.* ◊ *We didn't win but we came close.* **run sb/sth ˈclose** (*BrE*) to be nearly as good, fast, successful, etc. as sb/sth else: *Germany ran Argentina very close in the final.*—more at CARD *n.*, MARK *n.*, SAIL *v.*

■ *noun* **1** (*BrE*) (especially in street names) a street that is closed at one end: *Brookside Close* **2** the grounds and buildings that surround and belong to a CATHEDRAL

close-cropped /ˌkləʊs ˈkrɒpt; *AmE* ˌkloʊs ˈkrɑːpt/ *adj.* (of hair, grass, etc.) cut very short

closed /kləʊzd; *AmE* kloʊzd/ *adj.* **1** [not before noun] shut: *Keep the door closed.* **2** [not before noun] shut, especially of a shop/store or public building that is not open for a period of time: *The museum is closed on Mondays.* ◊ *This road is closed to traffic.* **3** not willing to accept outside influences or new ideas: *a closed society* ◊ *He has a closed mind.* **4** [usually before noun] limited to a particular group of people; not open to everyone: *a closed membership* OPP OPEN ⇨ note at CLOSE¹ IDM **behind closed ˈdoors** without the public being allowed to attend or know what is happening; in private **a closed ˈbook (to sb)** a subject or person that you know nothing about

ˌclosed-ˈcaptioned *adj.* (*AmE*) (of a TV programme) having CAPTIONS that can only be read if you have a special machine (= a DECODER)

ˌclosed-ˌcircuit ˈtelevision *noun* [U] (*abbr.* CCTV) a television system that works within a limited area, for example a public building, to protect it from crime

close-down /ˈkləʊz daʊn; *AmE* ˈkloʊz/ *noun* [U, sing.] **1** the stopping of work, especially permanently, in an office, a factory, etc. **2** (*BrE*) the end of broadcasting on television or radio at the end of a day

ˈclosed season *noun* [sing.] = CLOSE SEASON

ˌclosed ˈshop *noun* a factory, business, etc. in which employees must all be members of a particular TRADE/LABOR UNION

close-fitting /ˌkləʊs ˈfɪtɪŋ; *AmE* ˌkloʊs/ *adj.* (of clothes) fitting tightly, showing the shape of the body

close-knit /ˌkləʊs ˈnɪt; *AmE* ˌkloʊs/ (also *less frequent* **ˌclosely-ˈknit**) *adj.* (of a group of people) having strong relationships with each other and taking a close, friendly

aɪ	aʊ	eɪ	əʊ	oʊ	ɔɪ	ɪə	eə	ʊə	j	w
my	now	say	go (BrE)	go (AmE)	boy	near	hair	pure	yes	wet

interest in each other's activities and problems: *the close-knit community of a small village*

close-mouthed /ˌkləʊs ˈmaʊðd; *AmE* ˌkloʊs/ *adj.* [not usually before noun] not willing to say much about sth because you want to keep a secret

close-out /ˈkləʊzaʊt; *AmE* ˈkloʊz-/ *noun* (*AmE*) an occasion when goods are sold cheaply in order to get rid of them quickly

close-range /ˌkləʊs ˈreɪndʒ; *AmE* ˌkloʊs/ *adj.* [only before noun] at or from a short distance: *The close-range shot was blocked by the goalkeeper.*

close-run /ˌkləʊs ˈrʌn; *AmE* ˌkloʊs/ *adj.* [usually before noun] (of a race or competition) won by a very small amount or distance: *The election was a close-run thing.*

close season /ˈkləʊz siːzn; *AmE* ˈkloʊz/ *noun* [sing.] (*BrE*) **1** (also **closed season** *AmE, BrE*) the time of year when it is illegal to kill particular kinds of animal, bird and fish because they are breeding OPP OPEN SEASON **2** (*AmE* **ˈoff season**) (in sport) the time during the summer when teams do not play important games

close-set /ˌkləʊs ˈset; *AmE* ˌkloʊs/ *adj.* very close together: *close-set eyes*

closet /ˈklɒzɪt; *AmE* ˈklɑːzət/ *noun, adj., verb*
■ *noun* (especially *AmE*) a small room or a space in a wall with a door that reaches the floor, used for storing things: *a walk-in closet*—compare CUPBOARD, WARDROBE—see also WATER CLOSET IDM **come out of the closet** to admit sth openly that you kept secret before, especially because of shame or embarrassment: *Homosexuals in public life are now coming out of the closet.*—more at SKELETON
■ *adj.* [only before noun] used to describe people who want to keep some fact about themselves secret: *closet gays* ◊ *I suspect he's a closet fascist.*
■ *verb* [VN] to put sb in a room away from other people, especially so that they can talk privately with sb, or so that they can be alone: *He was closeted with the President for much of the day.* ◊ *She had closeted herself away in her room.*

close-up /ˈkləʊs ʌp; *AmE* ˈkloʊs/ *noun* [C, U] a photograph, or picture in a film/movie, taken very close to sb/sth so that it shows a lot of detail: *a close-up of a human eye* ◊ *It was strange to see her own face in close-up on the screen.* ◊ *close-up pictures of the planet*

clos·ing /ˈkləʊzɪŋ; *AmE* ˈkloʊzɪŋ/ *adj., noun*
■ *adj.* [only before noun] coming at the end of a speech, a period of time or an activity: *his closing remarks* ◊ *the closing stages of the game* OPP OPENING
■ *noun* [U] the act of shutting sth such as a factory, hospital, school, etc. permanently: *the closing of the local school* OPP OPENING

ˈclosing date *noun* the last date by which sth must be done, such as applying for a job or entering a competition: *The closing date for applications is 25 May.*

ˈclosing time *noun* [C, U] the time when a pub, shop/store, bar, etc. ends business for the day and people have to leave

clos·ure /ˈkləʊʒə(r); *AmE* ˈkloʊ-/ *noun* [C, U] **1** the situation when a factory, school, hospital, etc. shuts permanently: *factory closures* ◊ *The hospital has been threatened with closure.* **2** the temporary closing of a road or bridge: *There will be road closures and diversions in the area from 8 p.m.*

clot /klɒt; *AmE* klɑːt/ *noun, verb*
■ *noun* **1** = BLOOD CLOT: *They removed a clot from his brain.* **2** (*old-fashioned, BrE, informal*) a stupid person
■ *verb* (-tt-) when blood or cream **clots** or when sth **clots** it, it forms thick lumps or clots: [V] *a drug that stops blood from clotting during operations* ◊ [VN] *the blood clotting agent, Factor 8*

cloth /klɒθ; *AmE* klɔːθ/ *noun* (*pl.* **cloths** /klɒθs; *AmE* klɔːðz/) **1** [U] fabric made by weaving or knitting cotton, wool, silk, etc: *woollen/cotton cloth* ◊ *bandages made from strips of cloth* ◊ *the cloth industry/trade* ◊ *a cloth bag* **2** [C] (often in compounds) a piece of cloth, often used for a special purpose, especially cleaning things or covering a table: *Wipe the surface with a damp cloth.* ◊ *a floor cloth* —see also DISHCLOTH, TABLECLOTH **3** (**the cloth**) [sing.]

(*literary*) used to refer to Christian priests as a group: *a man of the cloth* IDM see COAT *n.*

ˌcloth ˈcap (also ˌflat ˈcap) (both *BrE*) *noun* a soft cap, normally made of wool, traditionally a symbol of working men: *The party has successfully shed its cloth cap image* (= it is not just a working-class party any more).—picture at HAT

clothe /kləʊð; *AmE* kloʊð/ *verb* [VN] **1** ~ sb/yourself (in sth) (*formal*) to dress sb/yourself: *They clothe their children in the latest fashions.* ◊ (*figurative*) *Climbing plants clothed the courtyard walls.* **2** to provide clothes for sb to wear: *the costs of feeding and clothing a family*

clothed /kləʊðd; *AmE* kloʊðd/ *adj.* [not usually before noun] ~ (in sth) dressed in a particular way: *a man clothed in black* ◊ *She jumped fully clothed into the water.* ◊ (*figurative*) *The valley was clothed in trees and shrubs.*

clothes /kləʊðz; kləʊz; *AmE* kloʊðz; kloʊz/ *noun* [pl.] the things that you wear, such as trousers/pants, dresses and jackets: *I bought some new clothes for the trip.* ◊ *to put on/take off your clothes* ◊ *Bring a change of clothes with you.* ◊ *She has no clothes sense* (= she does not know what clothes look attractive).—picture on page A4, A5

WHICH WORD?
clothes / clothing

You use **clothes** [pl] to talk about the things that you wear: *I'll just put on some clean clothes.* You use **clothing** [U] to talk about clothes in general or a particular type of clothes: *the clothing industry* ◊ *protective clothing.*

Note that there is no singular form of **clothes**. You can, however, talk about *a piece/an item/an article of clothing.* Note also the expression: *I haven't got anything to wear* (= any suitable clothes) *for the party tonight.*

⇨ note at WEAR

ˈclothes-hanger *noun* = HANGER

ˈclothes horse *noun* **1** (*BrE*) a wooden or plastic folding frame that you put clothes on to dry after you have washed them **2** (*disapproving*) a person, especially a woman, who is too interested in fashionable clothes

ˈclothes line (*BrE*) (also **line** *AmE, BrE*) (*BrE* also **ˈwashing line**) *noun* a piece of thin rope or wire, attached to posts, that you hang clothes on to dry outside after you have washed them

ˈclothes peg (*BrE*) (*AmE* **ˈclothes-pin**) *noun* = PEG (3)

cloth·ing /ˈkləʊðɪŋ; *AmE* ˈkloʊðɪŋ/ *noun* [U] clothes, especially a particular type of clothes: *protective/warm clothing* ◊ *the high cost of food, clothing and shelter* ◊ *an item/article of clothing* ⇨ note at CLOTHES IDM see WOLF *n.*

ˌclot·ted ˈcream *noun* [U] a very thick type of cream made by slowly heating milk, made and eaten especially in Britain: *scones and jam with clotted cream*—picture on page A1

cloud /klaʊd/ *noun, verb*
■ *noun* **1** [C, U] a grey or white mass made of very small drops of water, that floats in the sky: *The sun went behind a cloud.* ◊ *The plane was flying in cloud most of the way.*—see also STORM CLOUD, THUNDERCLOUD **2** [C] a large mass of sth in the air, for example dust or smoke, or a number of insects flying all together **3** [C] something that makes you feel sad or anxious: *Her father's illness cast a cloud over her wedding day.* ◊ *The only dark cloud on the horizon was that they might have to move house.* ◊ *He still has a cloud of suspicion hanging over him.* IDM **every cloud has a silver ˈlining** (*saying*) every sad or difficult situation has a positive or hopeful side **on cloud ˈnine** (*old-fashioned, informal*) extremely happy **under a ˈcloud** if sb is under a cloud, other people think that they have done sth wrong and are suspicious of them—more at HEAD *n.*
■ *verb* **1** [VN] if sth **clouds** your judgement, memory, etc., it makes it difficult for you to understand or remember sth clearly: *Doubts were beginning to cloud my mind.* ◊ *His*

C

judgement was clouded by jealousy. **2 ~** (**over**) (*written*) (of sb's face) to show sadness, fear, anger, etc.; to make sb look sad, afraid, angry, etc: [V] *Her face clouded over with anger.* ◊ [VN] *Suspicion clouded his face.* **3** [VN] **~ the issue** to make sth you are discussing or considering less clear, especially by introducing subjects that are not connected with it **4** [V] **~** (**over**) (of the sky) to fill with clouds: *It was beginning to cloud over.* **5** [VN] to make sth less pleasant or enjoyable: *His last years were clouded by financial worries.* **6** if glass, water, etc. **clouds**, or if sth **clouds** it, it becomes less transparent: [V] *Her eyes clouded with tears.* ◊ [VN] *Steam had clouded the mirror.*

cloud·burst /ˈklaʊdbɜːst; *AmE* -bɜːrst/ *noun* a sudden very heavy fall of rain

cloud-ˈcuckoo-land (*BrE*) (*AmE* **cloud·land**, **ˈla-la land**) *noun* [U] (*informal, disapproving*) if you say that sb is living **in cloud-cuckoo-land**, you mean that they do not understand what a situation is really like, but think it is much better than it is

cloud·less /ˈklaʊdləs/ *adj.* (*written*) clear; with no clouds: *a cloudless sky*

cloudy /ˈklaʊdi/ *adj.* **1** (of the sky or the weather) covered with clouds; with a lot of clouds: *a grey, cloudy day* **2** (of liquids) not clear or transparent ▶ **cloudi·ness** *noun* [U]

clout /klaʊt/ *noun, verb*
■ *noun* **1** [U] power and influence: *political/financial clout* ◊ *The World Bank can use its clout with poorer countries to insist on reforms.* ◊ *I knew his opinion carried a lot of clout.* **2** [C, usually sing.] (*informal*) a blow with the hand or a hard object
■ *verb* [VN] (*informal*) to hit sb hard, especially with your hand

clove /kləʊv; *AmE* kloʊv/ *noun* **1** [C, U] the dried flower of a tropical tree, used in cooking as a spice, especially to give flavour to sweet foods. Cloves look like small nails. **2** [C] **a garlic ~** | **a ~ of garlic** one of the small separate sections of a BULB (= the round underground part) of GARLIC—picture on page A3—see also CLEAVE *v.*

cloven ˈhoof *noun* the foot of an animal such as a cow, a sheep, or a goat, that is divided into two parts

clo·ver /ˈkləʊvə(r); *AmE* ˈkloʊ-/ *noun* [U] a small wild plant that usually has three leaves on each stem and purple, pink or white flowers that are shaped like balls: *a four-leaf clover* (= one with four leaves instead of three, thought to bring good luck) **IDM** **be/live in clover** (*informal*) to have enough money to be able to live a very comfortable life

clown /klaʊn/ *noun, verb*
■ *noun* **1** an entertainer who wears funny clothes and a large red nose and does silly things to make people laugh: (*figurative*) *Robert was always the class clown* (= he did silly or funny things to make the other students laugh). **2** (*disapproving*) a person that you disapprove of because they act in a stupid way: *What do those clowns in the government think they are doing?*
■ *verb* [V] **~** (**around**) (often *disapproving*) to behave in a silly way, especially in order to make other people laugh

clown·ish /ˈklaʊnɪʃ/ *adj.* like a clown; silly

cloy·ing /ˈklɔɪɪŋ/ *adj.* (*formal*) **1** (of food, a smell, etc.) so sweet that it is unpleasant **2** using emotion in a very obvious way, so that the result is unpleasant: *His acting was passionate, but never cloying or sentimental.* ▶ **cloying·ly** *adv.*

cloze test /ˈkləʊz test; *AmE* ˈkloʊz/ *noun* a type of test in which you have to put suitable words in spaces in a text where words have been left out

club /klʌb/ *noun, verb*
■ *noun*
FOR ACTIVITY/SPORT | **1** [C+sing./pl. *v.*] (especially in compounds) a group of people who meet together regularly, for a particular activity, sport, etc: *a golf/tennis club* ◊ *a chess/film/movie club* ◊ *to join/belong to a club* ◊ *The club has/have voted to admit 50 new members.*—see also FAN CLUB, YOUTH CLUB **2** [C] the building or rooms that a particular club uses: *We had lunch at the golf club.* ◊ *the club bar*—see also COUNTRY CLUB, HEALTH CLUB

3 [C+sing./pl. *v.*] (*BrE*) a professional sports organization that includes the players, managers, owners and members: *Manchester United Football Club*

MUSIC/DANCING | **4** [C] a place where people, especially young people, go and listen to music, dance, etc: *a jazz club* ◊ *the club scene in Newcastle*—see also CLUBBING, NIGHTCLUB, STRIP CLUB

SOCIAL | **5** [C+sing./pl. *v.*] (especially in Britain) an organization and a place where people, usually men only, can meet together socially or stay: *He's a member of several London clubs.*

SELLING BOOKS/CDS | **6** [C] an organization that sells books, CDs, etc. cheaply to its members: *a music/record club*—see also BOOK CLUB

WEAPON | **7** [C] a heavy stick with one end thicker than the other, that is used as a weapon—see also BILLY CLUB

IN GOLF | **8** [C] = GOLF CLUB

IN CARD GAMES | **9** (**clubs**) [pl., U] one of the four set of cards (called SUITS) in a pack/deck of cards. The clubs have a black design shaped like three black leaves on a short stem: *the five/queen/ace of clubs*—picture on page A8 **10** [C] one card from the SUIT called clubs: *I played a club.* **IDM** **be in the club** (*BrE, informal*) to be pregnant—more at JOIN *v.*
■ *verb* (**-bb-**) **1** [VN] to hit a person or an animal with a heavy stick or similar object: *The victim was clubbed to death with a baseball bat.* **2** [V] (**go clubbing**) (*BrE, informal*) to spend time dancing and drinking in NIGHTCLUBS **PHRV** **club toˈgether** (*BrE*) if two or more people **club together**, they each give an amount of money and the total is used to pay for sth: *We clubbed together to buy them a new television.*

club·bing /ˈklʌbɪŋ/ *noun* [U] the activity of going to NIGHTCLUBS regularly: *They go clubbing most weekends.* ▶ **club·ber** *noun: The venue was packed with 3000 clubbers.*

club ˈfoot *noun* [C, U] a foot that has been DEFORMED (= badly shaped) since birth ▶ **club-ˈfooted** *adj.*

club·house /ˈklʌbhaʊs/ *noun* the building used by a club, especially a sports club

club·land /ˈklʌblænd/ *noun* [U] (*BrE*) popular NIGHTCLUBS in general and the people who go to them; an area of a town where there are a lot of NIGHTCLUBS: *modern clubland* ◊ *London's clubland*

club ˈsandwich *noun* a sandwich consisting of three slices of bread with two layers of food between them—picture on page A1

cluck /klʌk/ *verb, noun*
■ *verb* **1** [V] when a chicken **clucks**, it makes a series of short low sounds **2** to make a short low sound with your tongue to show that you feel sorry for sb or that you disapprove of sth: [V] *The teacher clucked sympathetically at the child's story.* [also VN, Vspeech]
■ *noun* the low, short sounds that a chicken makes: (*figurative*) *a cluck of impatience/annoyance*

clue /kluː/ *noun, verb*
■ *noun* **1 ~** (**to sth**) an object, a piece of evidence or some information that helps the police solve a crime: *The police think the videotape may hold some vital clues to the identity of the killer.* **2 ~** (**to sth**) a fact or a piece of evidence that helps you discover the answer to a problem: *Diet may hold the clue to the causes of migraine.* **3** some words or a piece of information that helps you find the answers to a CROSSWORD, a game or a question: *'You'll never guess who I saw today!' 'Give me a clue.'* **IDM** **not have a ˈclue** (*informal*) **1** to know nothing about sth or about how to do sth: *I don't have a clue where she lives.* **2** (*disapproving*) to be very stupid: *Don't ask him to do it—he doesn't have a clue!*
■ *verb* **PHRV** **clue sb ˈin** (**on sth**) (*informal*) to give sb the most recent information about sth: *He's just clued me in on the latest developments.*

clued-ˈup (*BrE*) (*AmE* **clued-ˈin**) *adj.* **~** (**on sth**) (*informal*) knowing a lot about sth; having a lot of information about sth

clue·less /ˈkluːləs/ *adj.* (*informal, disapproving*) very stupid; not able to understand or to do sth: *He's completely clueless about computers.*

clump /klʌmp/ *noun, verb*
■ *noun* **1** a small group of things or people very close together, especially trees or plants; a bunch of sth such as grass or hair: *a clump of trees/bushes* **2** the sound made by sb putting their feet down very heavily
■ *verb* **1** [V+adv./prep.] (*especially BrE*) to put your feet down noisily and heavily as you walk: *The children clumped down the stairs.* **2 ~ (together)| ~ A and B (together)** to come together or be brought together to form a tight group: [V] *Galaxies tend to clump together in clusters.* [also VN]

clumpy /klʌmpi/ *adj.* (*BrE*) (of shoes and boots) big, thick and heavy

clumsy /ˈklʌmzi/ *adj.* (**clum·sier, clum·si·est**) **1** (of people and animals) moving or doing things in a very awkward way: *I spilt your coffee. Sorry—that was clumsy of me.* ◇ *His clumsy fingers couldn't untie the knot.* **2** (of actions and statements) done without skill or in a way that offends people: *She made a clumsy attempt to apologize.* **3** (of objects) difficult to move or use easily; not well designed **4** (of processes) awkward; too complicated to understand or use easily: *The complaints procedure is clumsy and time-consuming.* ▶ **clum·si·ly** *adv.* **clum·si·ness** *noun* [U]

clung *pt, pp* of CLING

clunk /klʌŋk/ *noun* a dull sound made by two heavy objects hitting each other: *the clunk of a car door being shut* ▶ **clunk** *verb* [V]

clunk·er /ˈklʌŋkə(r)/ *noun* (*AmE, informal*) **1** an old car in bad condition **2** a serious mistake

clunky /ˈklʌŋki/ *adj.* (*informal, especially AmE*) heavy and awkward: *clunky leather shoes*

clus·ter /ˈklʌstə(r)/ *noun, verb*
■ *noun* **1** a group of things of the same type that grow or appear close together: *a cluster of stars* ◇ *The plant bears its flowers in clusters.* ◇ *a leukaemia cluster* (= an area where there are more cases of the disease than you would expect) **2** a group of people, animals or things close together: *a cluster of spectators* ◇ *a little cluster of houses*
■ *verb* [V+adv./prep.] **~ (together)** to come together in a small group or groups: *The children clustered together in the corner of the room.* ◇ *The doctors clustered anxiously around his bed.*

'cluster bomb *noun* a type of bomb that throws out smaller bombs when it explodes

clutch /klʌtʃ/ *verb, noun*
■ *verb* **1** to hold sb/sth tightly: [VN] *He clutched the child to him.* ◇ *She stood there, the flowers still clutched in her hand.* ◇ [V+adv./prep.] *I clutched on to the chair for support* **2 ~ (at) sb/sth** to take hold of sth suddenly, because you are afraid or in pain: [VN] *He gasped and clutched his stomach.* ◇ (*figurative*) [V] *Fear clutched at her heart.* **IDM** see STRAW **PHRV 'clutch/'catch at sth/sb** to try to quickly get hold of sth/sb
■ *noun* **1** [C] the PEDAL in a car or other vehicle that you press with your foot so that you can change GEAR: *Put your foot on the clutch.* **2** [C] a device in a machine that connects and DISCONNECTS working parts, especially the engine and the GEARS: *The car needs a new clutch.*—picture at CAR **3 a ~ of sth** [sing.] (*BrE*) a group of people, animals or things: *He's won a whole clutch of awards.* **4** (**clutches**) [pl.] (*informal*) power or control: *He managed to escape from their clutches.* ◇ *Now that she had him in her clutches, she wasn't going to let go.* **5** [C, usually sing.] a tight hold on sb/sth: (*figurative*) *She felt the sudden clutch of fear.* **6** [C] a group of eggs that a bird lays at one time; the young birds that come out of a group of eggs at the same time **7** [C] (*AmE*) = CLUTCH BAG

'clutch bag (*AmE also* **clutch**) *noun* a small, flat bag that women carry in their hands, especially on formal occasions

clut·ter /ˈklʌtə(r)/ *verb, noun*
■ *verb* [VN] **~ sth (up) (with sth/sb)** to fill a place with too many things, so that it is untidy: *Don't clutter the page with too many diagrams.* ◇ *I don't want all these files*

cluttering up my desk. ◇ (*figurative*) *Try not to clutter your head with trivia.*
■ *noun* [U, sing.] (*disapproving*) a lot of things in an untidy state, especially things that are not necessary or are not being used; a state of disorder: *There's always so much clutter on your desk!* ◇ *There was a clutter of bottles and tubes on the shelf.*

clut·tered /ˈklʌtəd; *AmE* -tərd/ *adj.* **~ (up) (with sb/sth)** covered with, or full of, a lot of things or people, in a way that is untidy: *a cluttered room/desk* ◇ (*figurative*) *a cluttered mind* **OPP** UNCLUTTERED

cm *abbr.* (*pl.* **cm** *or* **cms**) CENTIMETRE

CNN /ˌsiː en ˈen/ *abbr.* Cable News Network (an American broadcasting company that sends television news programmes all over the world)

CO /ˌsiː ˈəʊ; *AmE* ˈoʊ/ *abbr.* Commanding Officer (an officer who commands a group of soldiers, sailors, etc.)

Co. /kəʊ; *AmE* koʊ/ *abbr.* **1** (*business*) company: *Pitt, Briggs & Co.* **2** (in writing) county **3** (**and co.**) (*BrE, spoken*) and other members of a group of people: *Were Jane and co. at the party?*

co- /kəʊ; *AmE* koʊ/ *prefix* (used in adjectives, adverbs, nouns and verbs) together with: *co-produced* ◇ *cooperatively* ◇ *co-author* ◇ *coexist*

c/o /ˌsiː ˈəʊ; *AmE* ˈoʊ/ *abbr.* (used on letters to a person staying at sb else's house) care of: *Mr P Brown, c/o Ms M Jones*

coach /kəʊtʃ; *AmE* koʊtʃ/ *noun, verb*
■ *noun* **1** [C] somebody who trains a person or team in sport: *a basketball/football/tennis coach* ◇ *Italy's national coach* **2** [C] (*BrE*) a person who gives private lessons to sb, often to prepare them for an exam: *a maths coach* **3** [C] (*BrE*) a comfortable bus for carrying passengers over long distances: *They went to Italy on a coach tour.* ◇ *Travel is by coach overnight to Berlin.* ◇ *a coach station* (= where coaches start and end their journey) ◇ *a coach party* (= a group of people travelling together on a coach)—picture at BUS **4** [C] (*BrE*) = CARRIAGE: *a railway coach* **5** [C] a large carriage with four wheels, pulled by horses, used in the past for carrying passengers—see also STAGECOACH **6** [U] (*AmE*) the cheapest seats in a plane: *to fly coach* ◇ *coach fares/passengers/seats* **IDM** see DRIVE *v.*
■ *verb* **~ sb (in/for sth)** **1** to train sb to play a sport, to do a job better, or to improve a skill: [VN] *Her father coached her for the Olympics.* ◇ *She has coached hundreds of young singers.* ◇ *He coaches basketball and soccer.* [also VN to inf] **2** [VN] (*especially BrE*) to give a student extra teaching in a particular subject especially so that they will pass an exam **3 ~ sb (in/on sth)** to give sb special instructions for what they should do or say in a particular situation: [VN] *They believed the witnesses had been coached on what to say.* [also VN to inf]

'coach house *noun* a building where carriages pulled by horses are or were kept

coach·ing /ˈkəʊtʃɪŋ; *AmE* ˈkoʊtʃ-/ *noun* [U] **1** the process of training sb to play a sport, to do a job better or to improve a skill: *a coaching session* **2** (*especially BrE*) the process of giving a student extra teaching in a particular subject

coach·load /ˈkəʊtʃləʊd; *AmE* ˈkoʊtʃloʊd/ *noun* (*BrE*) a group of people travelling together in a coach: *Tourists were arriving by the coachload.*

coach·man /ˈkəʊtʃmən; *AmE* ˈkoʊtʃ-/ *noun* (*pl.* **-men** /-mən/) (in the past) a man who drove a carriage pulled by horses

'coach station *noun* (*BrE*) a place where coaches start and finish their journeys

co·agu·late /kəʊˈægjuleɪt; *AmE* koʊ-/ *verb* if a liquid **coagulates** or sth **coagulates** it, it becomes thick and partly solid: [V] *Blood began to coagulate around the edges of the wound.* [also VN] ▶ **co·agu·la·tion** /kəʊˌægjuˈleɪʃn; *AmE* koʊ-/ *noun* [U]

coal /kəʊl; *AmE* koʊl/ *noun* **1** [U] a hard black mineral that is found below the ground and burnt to produce heat: *I put more coal on the fire.* ◇ *a lump of coal* ◇ *a coal fire* ◇ *a coal mine* ◇ *the coal industry* **2** [C] a piece of coal, especially one that is burning: *A hot coal fell out of the fire*

C

æ	ɑː	e	ɜː	ə	ɪ	iː	i	ɒ	ɔː	ʌ	ʊ	u	uː
cat	father	ten	bird	about	sit	see	many	got	saw	cup	put	actual	too

(BrE)

and burnt the carpet. **IDM** **carry, take, etc. coals to 'Newcastle** (*BrE*) to take goods to a place where there are already plenty of them; to supply sth where it is not needed—more at HAUL *v.*, RAKE *v.*

,coal-'black *adj.* very dark in colour: *coal-black eyes*

co·alesce /ˌkəʊəˈles; *AmE* ˌkoʊə-/ *verb* [V] **~ (into/with sth)** (*formal*) to come together to form one larger group, substance, etc. **SYN** AMALGAMATE: *The puddles had coalesced into a small stream.* ▶ **co·ales·cence** /ˌkəʊə-ˈlesns; *AmE* ˌkoʊə-/ *noun* [U]

coal·face /ˈkəʊlfeɪs; *AmE* ˈkoʊl-/ (also **face**) *noun* the place deep inside a mine where the coal is cut out of the rock **IDM** **at the 'coalface** (*BrE*) where the real work is done, not just where people talk about it: *Many of the best ideas come from doctors at the coalface.*

coal·field /ˈkəʊlfiːld; *AmE* ˈkoʊl-/ *noun* a large area where there is a lot of coal under the ground

,coal-'fired *adj.* using coal as fuel: *a coal-fired power station*

'coal gas *noun* [U] a mixture of gases produced from coal, that can be used for electricity and heating

co·ali·tion /ˌkəʊəˈlɪʃn; *AmE* ˌkoʊə-/ *noun* **1** [C+sing./pl. *v.*] a government formed by two or more political parties working together: *to form a coalition* ◊ *a two-party coalition* ◊ *a coalition government* **2** [C+sing./pl. *v.*] a group formed by people from several different groups, especially political ones, agreeing to work together for a particular purpose: *a coalition of environmental and consumer groups* **3** [U] the act of two or more groups joining together: *They didn't rule out coalition with the Social Democrats.*

'coal mine (also **pit**) *noun* a place underground where coal is dug

'coal miner *noun* a person whose job is digging coal in a coal mine

'coal scuttle (also **scuttle**) *noun* a container with a handle, used for carrying coal and usually kept beside the FIREPLACE

'coal tar *noun* [U] a thick black sticky substance produced when gas is made from coal

coarse /kɔːs; *AmE* kɔːrs/ *adj.* (**coars·er**, **coars·est**) **1** (of skin or fabric) rough; not soft: *coarse hands/linen* **2** consisting of relatively large pieces; not fine: *coarse sand/ salt/hair* **3** rude and offensive, especially about sex **SYN** VULGAR: *coarse manners/laughter* ▶ **coarse·ly** *adv.*: *coarsely chopped onions* (= cut into large pieces) ◊ *He laughed coarsely at her embarrassment.* **coarse·ness** *noun* [U]

,coarse 'fish *noun* (*pl.* **coarse fish**) (*BrE*) any fish, except SALMON and TROUT, that lives in rivers and lakes rather than in the sea

,coarse 'fishing *noun* [U] (*BrE*) the sport of catching coarse fish: *to go coarse fishing*

coars·en /ˈkɔːsn; *AmE* ˈkɔːrsn/ *verb* **1** to become or make sth become thicker and/or rougher: [V] *Her hair gradually coarsened as she grew older.* ◊ [VN] *His features had been coarsened by the weather.* **2** to become or make sb become less polite and often offensive in the way they behave: [VN] *The six long years in prison had coarsened him.* [also V]

coast /kəʊst; *AmE* koʊst/ *noun, verb*

■ *noun* [C, U] the land beside or near to the sea or ocean: *a town on the south coast of England* ◊ *islands off the west coast of Ireland* ◊ *a trip to the coast* ◊ *We walked along the coast for five miles.* ◊ *a mountainous area near the Welsh coast* ◊ *a pretty stretch of coast* ◊ *the coast road* **IDM** **the ,coast is 'clear** (*informal*) there is no danger of being seen or caught: *As soon as the coast was clear he climbed in through the window.*

■ *verb* [V] **1** [usually +*adv./prep.*] (of a car or a bicycle) to move, especially down a hill, without using any power: *The car coasted along until it stopped.* ◊ *She took her feet off the pedals and coasted downhill.* **2** [usually +*adv./ prep.*] (of a vehicle) to move quickly and smoothly, without using much power: *The plane coasted down the runway.* **3 ~ (through/to sth)** to be successful at sth without having to try hard: *He coasted through his final exams.* **4 ~ (along)** (*disapproving*) to put very little effort into sth: *You're just coasting—it's time to work hard now.* **5** (of

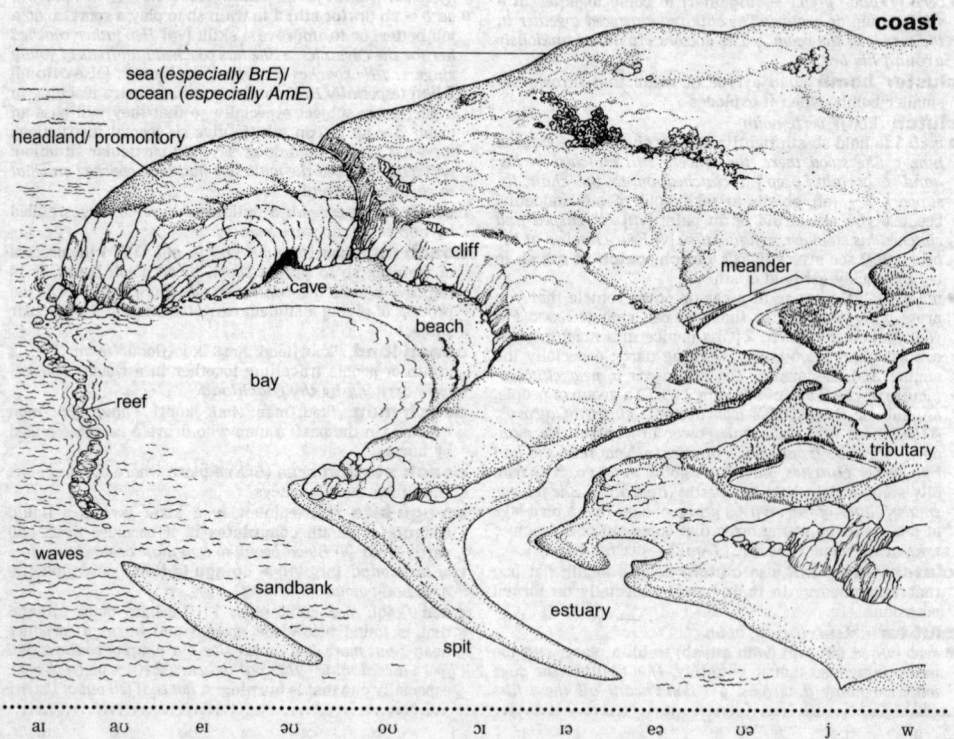

coast

sea (*especially BrE*)/
ocean (*especially AmE*)

headland/ promontory

cliff

meander

cave

beach

bay

reef

tributary

waves

sandbank

estuary

spit

aɪ	aʊ	eɪ	əʊ	oʊ	ɔɪ	ɪə	eə	ʊə	j	w
my	now	say	go	go	boy	near	hair	pure	yes	wet
			(BrE)	(AmE)						

a ship) to stay close to land while sailing around the coast

WHICH WORD?
coast / shore / beach / seaside

The **coast** is usually a long stretch of land next to the sea, for example the part of a country that is next to the sea: *We live on the coast.*

The **shore** is the land at the edge of the sea or a lake: *We camped on the north shore of Lake Michigan.* ◇ *The survivors swam to shore.*

The **beach** is the part of the shore which is often covered with sand and is where people go to enjoy themselves or to relax: *We went for a walk along the beach.* ◇ *She took the kids to the beach for the day.*

In *BrE*, the **seaside** is sometimes used to mean an area on the coast where people go on holiday / vacation, but **sea** is now much more common for this. In both *BrE* and *AmE* **seaside** can be used in front of a noun: *a seaside resort.*

---

coast·al /ˈkəʊstl; *AmE* ˈkoʊstl/ *adj.* [usually before noun] of or near a coast: *coastal waters / resorts / scenery* ◇ *a coastal path* (= one that follows the line of the coast)—compare INLAND

coast·er /ˈkəʊstə(r); *AmE* ˈkoʊst-/ *noun* **1** a small flat object which you put under a glass to protect the top of a table **2** a ship that sails from port to port along a coast—see also ROLLER COASTER

coast·guard /ˈkəʊstɡɑːd; *AmE* ˈkoʊstɡɑːrd/ *noun* **1** (usually **the coastguard**) [sing.] an official organization (in the US a branch of the armed forces) whose job is to watch the sea near a coast in order to help ships and people in trouble, and to stop people from breaking the law: *The coastguard was alerted.* ◇ *They radioed Dover Coastguard.* ◇ *a coastguard station* **2** [C] (*especially BrE*) (*AmE* usually **coast·guard·man**) a member of this organization

coast·line /ˈkəʊstlaɪn; *AmE* ˈkoʊst-/ *noun* the land along a coast, especially when you are thinking of its shape or appearance: *a rugged / rocky / beautiful coastline* ◇ *to protect the coastline from oil spillage*

coat /kəʊt; *AmE* koʊt/ *noun, verb*
■ *noun* **1** a piece of outdoor clothing that is worn over other clothes to keep warm or dry. Coats have sleeves and may be long or short: *a fur / leather coat* ◇ *a long winter coat* ◇ *to put on / take off your coat*—see also DUFFEL COAT, GREAT-COAT, HOUSECOAT, OVERCOAT, PETTICOAT, RAINCOAT, TRENCH COAT—picture on page A5 **2** (*AmE*) (*old-fashioned in BrE*) a jacket that is worn as part of a suit—see also FROCK COAT, MORNING COAT, TAILCOAT, WAISTCOAT **3** the fur, hair or wool that covers an animal's body: *a dog with a smooth / shaggy coat*—picture on page A6 **4** a layer of paint or some other substance that covers a surface: *to give the walls a second coat of paint*—see also TOPCOAT, UNDERCOAT **IDM** **cut your ˈcoat acˌcording to your ˈcloth** (*saying*) to do only what you have enough money to do and no more
■ *verb* [VN] (often passive) **~ sth (with/in sth)** to cover sth with a layer of a substance: *cookies thickly coated with chocolate* ◇ *A film of dust coated the table.* ◇ *The mask was coated in gold leaf.*—see also SUGAR-COATED

ˈcoat check *noun* (*AmE*) = CLOAKROOM

ˈcoat hanger *noun* = HANGER

coat·ing /ˈkəʊtɪŋ; *AmE* ˈkoʊt-/ *noun* a thin layer of a substance covering a surface: *a thin coating of chocolate* ◇ *magnetic coating on a floppy disk*

ˌcoat of ˈarms *noun* (*pl.* **coats of arms**) (also **arms** [pl.]) a design or a SHIELD that is a special symbol of a family, city or other organization: *the royal coat of arms*

coat·room /ˈkəʊtruːm; -rʊm; *AmE* ˈkoʊt-/ *noun* (*AmE*) = CLOAKROOM (1)

ˈcoat-tails *noun* [pl.] **IDM** **on sb's coat-tails** using the success and influence of another person to help yourself become successful: *She got where she is today on her brother's coat-tails.*

ˌco-ˈauthor *noun* a person who writes a book or an article with sb else ▶ **ˌco-ˈauthor** *verb* [VN] **ˌco-ˈauthor·ship** *noun* [U]

coax /kəʊks; *AmE* koʊks/ *verb* **~ sb (into doing sth)** | **~ sb (into/out of sth)** to persuade sb to do sth by talking to them in a kind and gentle way: [VN] *She coaxed the horse into coming a little closer.* ◇ *He was coaxed out of retirement to help the failing company.* ◇ *She had to coax the car along.* ◇ [V speech] *'Nearly there,' she coaxed.* [also VN speech] **PHRV** **coax sth out of/from sb** to gently persuade sb to do sth or give you sth: *The director coaxed a brilliant performance out of the cast.*

coax·ing /ˈkəʊksɪŋ; *AmE* ˈkoʊ-/ *noun* [U] gentle attempts to persuade sb to do sth or to get a machine to start: *No amount of coaxing will make me change my mind.* ▶ **coax·ing** *adj.* **coax·ing·ly** *adv.*

cob /kɒb; *AmE* kɑːb/ *noun* **1** = CORN COB: *corn on the cob* **2** a strong horse with short legs **3** (*BrE*) a round LOAF of bread: *a crusty cob*

co·balt /ˈkəʊbɔːlt; *AmE* ˈkoʊ-/ *noun* [U] **1** (*symb* Co) a chemical element. Cobalt is a hard silver-white metal, often mixed with other metals and used to give a deep blue-green colour to glass. **2** (also **ˌcobalt ˈblue**) a deep blue-green colour

cob·ber /ˈkɒbə(r); *AmE* ˈkɑːb-/ *noun* (*AustralE, informal*) (used especially by a man addressing another man) a friend

cob·ble /ˈkɒbl; *AmE* ˈkɑːbl/ *verb* [VN] (*old-fashioned*) to make or repair shoes **PHRV** **ˌcobble sth↔toˈgether** to produce sth quickly and without great care or effort, so that it can be used but is not perfect: *The essay was cobbled together from some old notes.*

cob·bled /ˈkɒbld; *AmE* ˈkɑːbld/ *adj.* (of streets and roads) having a surface that is made of COBBLES

cob·bler /ˈkɒblə(r); *AmE* ˈkɑːb-/ *noun* **1** [C] (*especially AmE*) a type of fruit pie with thick pastry on top: *peach cobbler* **2** [C] (*old-fashioned*) a person who repairs shoes—compare SHOEMAKER **3** [U] (*BrE, spoken*) nonsense: *He said it was all a load of cobblers.*

cob·bles /ˈkɒblz; *AmE* ˈkɑːblz/ (also **cobble·stones**) *noun* [pl.] small round stones used to make the surfaces of roads, especially in the past: *a cart clattering over the cobbles*

cobble·stones /ˈkɒblstəʊnz; *AmE* ˈkɑːblstoʊnz/ *noun* [pl.] = COBBLES ▶ **cobble·stone** *adj.*

cobra /ˈkəʊbrə; *AmE* ˈkoʊ-/ *noun* a poisonous snake that can spread the skin at the back of its neck to make itself look bigger. Cobras live in India and Africa.—picture on page A7

cob·web /ˈkɒbweb; *AmE* ˈkɑːb-/ *noun* a fine net of threads made by a spider to catch insects; a single thread of this net (usually used when it is old and covered with dirt): *Thick cobwebs hung in the dusty corners.* ◇ *He brushed a cobweb out of his hair.*—see also WEB, SPIDER'S WEB ▶ **cob·webbed** /ˈkɒbwebd; *AmE* ˈkɑːb-/ *adj.*: *cobwebbed corners* **IDM** **blow/clear the ˈcobwebs away** to help sb start sth in a fresh, lively state of mind: *A brisk walk should blow the cobwebs away.*

Coca-Cola™ /ˌkəʊkə ˈkəʊlə; *AmE* ˌkoʊkə ˈkoʊlə/ (also informal **Coke**™) *noun* **1** [U, C] a popular type of COLA drink **2** [C] a glass, bottle or can of Coca-Cola

co·caine /kəʊˈkeɪn; *AmE* koʊ-/ (also informal **coke**) *noun* [U] a powerful drug that some people take illegally for pleasure and can become ADDICTED to. Doctors sometimes use it as an ANAESTHETIC.

coc·cyx /ˈkɒksɪks; *AmE* ˈkɑːk-/ *noun* (*pl.* **coc·cyxes** or **coc·cy·ges** /ˈkɒksɪdʒiːz; *AmE* ˈkɑːk-/) (*anatomy*) the small bone at the bottom of the SPINE **SYN** TAILBONE—picture at BODY

coch·in·eal /ˌkɒtʃɪˈniːl; *AmE* ˈkɑːtʃəniːl/ *noun* [U] a bright red substance used to give colour to food

cock /kɒk; *AmE* kɑːk/ *noun, verb*
■ *noun* **1** (*BrE*) (also **roost·er** *AmE, BrE*) [C] an adult male chicken: *The cock crowed.*—compare HEN **2** [C] (*especially in compounds*) a male of any other bird: *a cock pheasant*—see also PEACOCK **3** [C] (△, *slang*) a PENIS **4** [C] =

C

STOPCOCK—see also BALLCOCK **5** [sing.] (*old-fashioned, BrE, slang*) used as a friendly form of address between men—see also HALF-COCK

■ *verb* [VN] **1** to raise a part of your body so that it is upright or at an angle: *The dog cocked its leg by every tree on our route* (= in order to urinate). ◇ *He cocked an inquisitive eyebrow at her.* ◇ *She cocked her head to one side and looked at me.* ◇ *The dog stood listening, its ears cocked.* **2 ~ a gun/pistol/rifle** to raise the HAMMER on a gun so that it is ready to fire [IDM] **cock an ear/eye at sth/sb** to look at or listen to sb/sth carefully and with a lot of attention **cock a snook at sb/sth** (*BrE*) to say or do sth that clearly shows you do not respect sb/sth: *to cock a snook at authority* [PHRV] **,cock sth↔'up** (*BrE, slang*) to ruin sth by doing it badly, or by making a careless or stupid mistake [SYN] BUNGLE: *I really cocked that exam up!* ◇ *She cocked up all the arrangements for the party.*—related noun COCK-UP

cock-a-doodle-doo /ˌkɒk ə ˌduːdl ˈduː; AmE ˌkɑːk/ *noun* the word for the sound that a COCK/ ROOSTER makes

,cock-a-'hoop *adj.* [not usually before noun] **~ (about/ at/ over sth)** (*informal*) very pleased and excited, especially about achieving sth

cock-ama-mie (also **cock-ama-my**) /ˈkɒkəmeɪmi; AmE ˈkɑːk-/ *adj.* (*AmE, informal*) (of an idea, a story, etc.) silly; not to be believed

,cock and 'bull story *noun* a story that is unlikely to be true but is used as an explanation or excuse

cocka-too /ˌkɒkəˈtuː; AmE ˈkɑːkətuː/ *noun* (*pl.* **-oos**) an Australian bird of the PARROT family, with a large row of feathers (called a CREST) standing up on its head

,cocked 'hat *noun* [IDM] see KNOCK *v.*

cock-erel /ˈkɒkərəl; AmE ˈkɑːk-/ *noun* a young male chicken

'cock-eyed *adj.* (*informal*) **1** not level or straight [SYN] CROOKED: *Doesn't that picture look cock-eyed to you?* **2** not practical; not likely to succeed: *a cock-eyed scheme to make people use less water*

cock-fight /ˈkɒkfaɪt; AmE ˈkɑːk-/ *noun* a fight between two adult male chickens, watched as a sport and illegal in many countries ▶ **cock-fight-ing** *noun* [U]

cockle /ˈkɒkl; AmE ˈkɑːkl/ *noun* a small shellfish that can be eaten [IDM] see WARM *v.*

cock-ney /ˈkɒkni; AmE ˈkɑːkni/ *noun* **1** [C] a person from the East End of London **2** [U] the way of speaking that is typical of cockneys: *a cockney accent*

cock-pit /ˈkɒkpɪt; AmE ˈkɑːk-/ *noun* an enclosed area in a plane, boat or racing car where the pilot or driver sits

cock-roach /ˈkɒkrəʊtʃ; AmE ˈkɑːkrəʊtʃ/ (also AmE informal **roach**) *noun* a large brown insect with wings, that lives in houses, especially where there is dirt: *The kitchens were discovered to be infested with cockroaches.*

cock-sure /ˌkɒkˈʃʊə(r); -ˈʃɔː(r); AmE ˌkɑːkˈʃʊr/ *adj.* (*old-fashioned, informal*) confident in a way that is annoying to other people and that they might find offensive

cock-tail /ˈkɒkteɪl; AmE ˈkɑːk-/ *noun* **1** [C] a drink usually made from a mixture of one or more SPIRITS (= strong alcoholic drinks) and fruit juice. It can also be made without alcohol: *a cocktail bar/cabinet/lounge* **2** [C, U] a dish of small pieces of food, usually served cold: *a prawn cocktail* ◇ *fruit cocktail* **3** [C] a mixture of different substances, usually ones that do not mix together well: *a lethal cocktail of drugs*—see also MOLOTOV COCKTAIL

'cocktail dress *noun* a dress that is suitable for formal social occasions

'cocktail party *noun* a formal social occasion, usually in the early evening, when people drink COCKTAILS or other alcoholic drinks

'cocktail stick *noun* (*BrE*) a small, sharp piece of wood on which small pieces of food are placed, for guests to eat at parties

'cock-up *noun* (*BrE, informal, spoken*) a mistake that spoils people's arrangements; sth that has been spoilt because it was badly organized: *There's been a bit of a cock-up over the travel arrangements.*

cocky /ˈkɒki; AmE ˈkɑːki/ *adj.* (*informal*) too confident

about yourself in a way that annoys other people: *For a young man on his first day at work he's remarkably cocky.* ▶ **cocki-ness** *noun* [U]

cocoa /ˈkəʊkəʊ; AmE ˈkoʊkoʊ/ *noun* **1** [U] dark brown powder made from the crushed seeds (called **cocoa beans**) of a tropical tree **2** [U] a hot drink made by mixing cocoa powder with milk and/or water and usually sugar: *a mug of cocoa* **3** [C] a cup of cocoa—compare CHOCOLATE, DRINKING CHOCOLATE

'cocoa butter *noun* [U] fat that is obtained from cocoa beans and used in making chocolate and COSMETICS

co-co-nut /ˈkəʊkənʌt; AmE ˈkoʊ-/ *noun* **1** [C] the large nut of a tropical tree called a **coconut palm**. It has a hard hairy shell containing a soft white substance that can be eaten and juice that can be drunk: *coconut milk*—picture at NUT **2** [U] the soft white substance inside a coconut, used in cooking: *desiccated coconut* ◇ *coconut biscuits/ cookies* ◇ *coconut oil*

,coconut 'matting *noun* [U] (*BrE*) a material used to cover floors that is made from the hair on the shells of coconuts

'coconut shy *noun* (*pl.* **coconut shies**) (*BrE*) an outdoor entertainment in which people try to knock coconuts off stands by throwing balls at them

co-coon /kəˈkuːn/ *noun, verb*

■ *noun* **1** a covering of silk threads that some insects make to protect themselves before they become adults **2** a soft covering that wraps all around a person or thing and forms a protection: (*figurative*) *the cocoon of a caring family*

■ *verb* [VN] [usually passive] **~ sb/sth (in sth)** to protect sb/sth by surrounding them or it completely with sth: *We were warm and safe, cocooned in our sleeping bags.*

cod /kɒd; AmE kɑːd/ *noun* [C, U] (*pl.* **cod**) a large sea fish with white flesh that is used for food: *fishing for cod* ◇ *cod fillets* ◇ *cod and parsley sauce*

COD /ˌsi: əʊ ˈdi:; AmE oʊ/ *abbr.* cash on delivery or (in American English) collect on delivery (payment for goods will be made when the goods are delivered)

coda /ˈkəʊdə; AmE ˈkoʊdə/ *noun* the final passage of a piece of music: (*figurative*) *The final two months were a miserable coda to de Gaulle's first period in office.*

cod-dle /ˈkɒdl; AmE ˈkɑːdl/ *verb* [VN] **1** (*often disapproving*) to treat sb with too much care and attention: *She coddles him like a child.*—compare MOLLYCODDLE **2** to cook eggs in water slightly below boiling point

code /kəʊd; AmE koʊd/ *noun, verb*

■ *noun* **1** [C, U] (often in compounds) a system of words, letters, numbers or symbols that represent a message or record information secretly or in a shorter form: *to break/crack a code* (= to understand and read the message) ◇ *It's written in code.* ◇ *Tap your code number into the machine.* ◇ *In the event of the machine not operating correctly, an error code will appear.*—see also AREA CODE, BAR CODE, MORSE CODE, POSTCODE, ZIP CODE **2** [C] = DIALLING CODE: *There are two codes for London.* **3** [U] (*computing*) a system of computer PROGRAMMING instructions—see also MACHINE CODE, SOURCE CODE **4** [C] a set of moral principles or rules of behaviour that are generally accepted by society or a social group: *a strict code of conduct* **5** [C] a system of laws or written rules that state how people in an institution or a country should behave: *the penal code*—see also HIGHWAY CODE

■ *verb* [VN] **1** to write or print words, letters, numbers, etc. on sth so that you know what it is, what group it belongs to, etc: *Each order is coded separately.* **2** to put a message into code so that it can only be understood by a few people **3** (*computing*) to write a computer program by putting one system of numbers, words and symbols into another system [SYN] ENCODE

coded /ˈkəʊdɪd; AmE ˈkoʊ-/ *adj.* **1** [only before noun] a **coded** message or **coded** information is written or sent using a special system of words, letters, numbers, etc. that can only be understood by a few other people or by a computer: *a coded warning of a bomb at the airport* **2** expressed in an indirect way: *There was coded criticism of the government from some party members.*

s	t	v	z	ʃ	ʒ	tʃ	dʒ	θ	ð	ŋ
see	tea	van	zoo	shoe	vision	chain	jam	thin	this	sing

C

co·deine /ˈkəʊdiːn; AmE ˈkoʊ-/ noun [U] a drug used to reduce pain

code name noun a name used for a person or thing in order to keep the real name secret ▶ **code-named** adj. [not before noun]: a drug investigation, code-named Snoopy

code of practice noun (pl. **codes of practice**) a set of standards that members of a particular profession agree to follow in their work

cod·ger /ˈkɒdʒə(r); AmE ˈkɑːdʒ-/ noun (informal) (**old codger**) an informal way of referring to an old man that shows that you do not respect him

co·di·cil /ˈkəʊdɪsɪl; AmE ˈkɑːdəsl/ noun (law) an instruction that is added later to a WILL, usually to change a part of it

co·dify /ˈkəʊdɪfaɪ; AmE ˈkɑːd-/ verb (**co·di·fies, co·di·fy·ing, co·di·fied, co·di·fied**) [VN] (technical) to arrange laws, rules, etc. into a system ▶ **co·difi·ca·tion** /ˌkəʊdɪfɪˈkeɪʃn; AmE ˌkɑːd-/ noun [U]

cod liver oil noun [U] a thick yellow oil from the LIVER of COD (= a type of fish), containing a lot of VITAMINS A and D and often given as a medicine, especially to children

cods·wal·lop /ˈkɒdzwɒləp; AmE ˈkɑːdzwɑːləp/ noun [U] (old-fashioned, BrE, informal) nonsense: I've never heard such a load of old codswallop in my life.

coed /ˌkəʊˈed; AmE ˌkoʊ-/ noun (old-fashioned, AmE) a female student at a co-educational school or college

co-edu·cational (also informal **coed**) adj. (of a school or an EDUCATIONAL system) where girls and boys are taught together ▶ **co-edu·cation** noun [U]

co·ef·fi·cient /ˌkəʊɪˈfɪʃnt; AmE ˌkoʊ-/ noun **1** (mathematics) a number which is placed before another quantity and which multiplies it, for example 3 in the quantity 3x **2** (physics) a number that measures a particular PROPERTY (= characteristic) of a substance: the coefficient of friction / expansion

co·erce /kəʊˈɜːs; AmE koʊˈɜːrs/ verb ~ sb (into sth/into doing sth) (formal) to force sb to do sth by using threats: [VN] They were coerced into negotiating a settlement. [also VN to inf]

co·er·cion /kəʊˈɜːʃn; AmE koʊˈɜːrʒn/ noun [U] (formal) the action of making sb do sth that they do not want to do, using force or threatening to use force: He claimed he had only acted under coercion.

co·er·cive /kəʊˈɜːsɪv; AmE koʊˈɜːrsɪv/ adj. (formal) using force or the threat of force: coercive measures / powers

co·ex·ist /ˌkəʊɪgˈzɪst; AmE ˌkoʊ-/ verb [V] ~ (with sb/sth) (formal) to exist together in the same place or at the same time, especially in a peaceful way: The illness frequently coexists with other chronic diseases. ◇ English speakers now coexist peacefully with their Spanish-speaking neighbours. ◇ Different traditions coexist successfully side by side.

co·ex·ist·ence /ˌkəʊɪgˈzɪstəns; AmE ˌkoʊ-/ noun [U] the state of being together in the same place at the same time: to live in uneasy / peaceful coexistence within one nation

C. of E. /ˌsiː əv ˈiː/ abbr. Church of England—see also CE

cof·fee /ˈkɒfi; AmE ˈkɔː-; ˈkɑː-/ noun **1** [U, C] the ROASTED seeds (called **coffee beans**) of a tropical bush; a powder made from them: decaffeinated / instant coffee ◇ ground / real coffee ◇ a jar of coffee ◇ a blend of Brazilian and Colombian coffees ◇ coffee ice cream **2** [U] a hot drink made from coffee powder and boiling water. It may be drunk with milk and/or sugar added: black / white coffee (= without / with milk) ◇ Tea or coffee? ◇ I'll just make the coffee. ◇ Let's talk over coffee (= while drinking coffee). ◇ a coffee machine **3** [C] a cup of coffee: Two strong black coffees, please. **4** [U] the colour of coffee mixed with milk; light brown

coffee bar noun **1** (BrE) (also **coffee shop** AmE, BrE) a small restaurant, often in a store, hotel, etc., where coffee, tea, other drinks without alcohol and simple food are served **2** (AmE) a small restaurant that sells special sorts of coffee and cakes

coffee break noun a short period of rest when you stop working and drink coffee: to have a coffee break

coffee house noun **1** a restaurant serving coffee, etc., especially one of a type popular in Britain in the 18th century or one in a city in Central Europe: the coffee houses of Vienna **2** (AmE) a restaurant serving coffee, etc. where people go to listen to music, poetry, etc.

coffee morning noun (BrE) a social event held in the morning, often at a person's house, where money is usually given to help a charity

coffee shop noun (especially AmE) = COFFEE BAR

coffee table noun a small low table for putting magazines, cups, etc. on, usually in front of a SOFA

coffee-table book noun a large expensive book containing many pictures or photographs, that is designed for people to look through rather than to read carefully

cof·fer /ˈkɒfə(r); AmE ˈkɔːf-; ˈkɑːf-/ noun **1** [C] a large strong box, used in the past for storing money or valuable objects **2** (also **cof·fers**) [pl.] (written) a way of referring to the money that a government, an organization, etc. has available to spend: The nation's coffers are empty.

cof·fin /ˈkɒfɪn; AmE ˈkɔːfɪn/ (especially BrE) (AmE usually **cas·ket**) noun a box in which a dead body is buried or CREMATED **IDM** see NAIL n.

cog /kɒg; AmE kɑːg/ noun **1** one of a series of teeth on the edge of a wheel that fit between the teeth on the next wheel and cause it to move **2** = COGWHEEL **IDM** **a cog in the maˈchine / ˈwheel** (informal) a person who is a small part of a large organization

cog

cogwheel   cog

co·gent /ˈkəʊdʒənt; AmE ˈkoʊ-/ adj. (formal) strongly and clearly expressed in a way that influences what people believe: She put forward some cogent reasons for abandoning the plan. ▶ **co·gency** /ˈkəʊdʒənsi; AmE ˈkoʊ-/ noun [U] **co·gent·ly** adv.

cogi·tate /ˈkɒdʒɪteɪt; AmE ˈkɑːdʒ-/ verb [V] ~ (about/on sth) (formal) to think carefully about sth ▶ **cogi·ta·tion** /ˌkɒdʒɪˈteɪʃn; AmE ˌkɑːdʒ-/ noun [U, C]

co·gnac /ˈkɒnjæk; AmE ˈkoʊn-/ noun **1** [U, C] a type of fine BRANDY made in western France **2** [C] a glass of cognac: Would you like a cognac with your coffee?

cog·nate /ˈkɒɡneɪt; AmE ˈkɑːg-/ adj., noun
■ adj. **1** (linguistics) having the same origin as another word or language: 'Haus' in German is cognate with 'house' in English. ◇ German and Dutch are cognate languages. **2** (formal) related in some way and therefore similar: a cognate development / field / group
■ noun (linguistics) a word that has the same origin as another: 'Haus' and 'house' are cognates.

cog·ni·tion /kɒgˈnɪʃn; AmE kɑːg-/ noun [U] (psychology) the process by which knowledge and understanding is developed in the mind: child studies centring on theories of cognition

cog·ni·tive /ˈkɒgnətɪv; AmE ˈkɑːg-/ adj. [usually before noun] connected with mental processes of understanding: a child's cognitive abilities / behaviour / development ◇ cognitive psychology

cog·ni·zance (BrE also **-i·sance**) /ˈkɒgnɪzəns; AmE ˈkɑːg-/ noun [U] (formal) knowledge or understanding of sth ▶ **cog·ni·zant, -i·sant** adj. [not before noun]: cognizant of the importance of the case **IDM** **take cognizance of sth** (law) to understand or consider sth; to take notice of sth

co·gnos·centi /ˌkɒnjəˈʃenti; AmE ˌkɑːn-/ noun [pl.] (**the cognoscenti**) (from Italian, formal) people with a lot of knowledge about a particular subject

cog·wheel /ˈkɒgwiːl; AmE ˈkɑːg-/ (also **cog**) noun a wheel with a series of teeth on the edge that fit between the teeth on the next wheel and cause it to move—picture at COG

co·habit /kəʊˈhæbɪt; AmE koʊ-/ verb [V] ~ (with sb) (formal) (usually of a man and a woman) to live together

| æ | ɑː | e | ɜː | ə | ɪ | iː | i | ɒ | ɔː | ʌ | ʊ | u | uː |
| cat | father | ten | bird | about | sit | see | many | got | saw | cup | put | actual | too |

(BrE)

C

and have a sexual relationship without being married: *cohabiting couples* ◊ *She refused to cohabit with him before the wedding.* ▶ **co·hab·it·ation** /ˌkəʊˌhæbɪˈteɪʃn; *AmE* ˌkoʊ-/ *noun* [U]

co·here /kəʊˈhɪə(r); *AmE* koʊˈhɪr/ *verb* [V] ~ (**with sth**) (*formal*) **1** (of different ideas, arguments, sentences, etc.) to have a clear logical connection so that together they make a whole: *This view does not cohere with their other beliefs.* **2** (of people) to work closely together: *It can be difficult to get a group of people to cohere.*

co·her·ence /kəʊˈhɪərəns; *AmE* koʊˈhɪr-/ *noun* [U] the situation in which all the parts of sth fit together well: *The points you make are fine, but the whole essay lacks coherence.* OPP INCOHERENCE

co·her·ent /kəʊˈhɪərənt; *AmE* koʊˈhɪr-/ *adj.* **1** (of ideas, thoughts, arguments, etc.) logical and well organized; easy to understand and clear: *a coherent narrative/ account/explanation* ◊ *a coherent policy for the transport system* **2** (of a person) able to talk and express yourself clearly: *She only became coherent again two hours after the attack.* OPP INCOHERENT ▶ **co·her·ent·ly** *adv.*: *to express yourself coherently*

co·he·sion /kəʊˈhiːʒn; *AmE* koʊ-/ *noun* [U] **1** (*formal*) the act or state of sticking together SYN UNITY: *the cohesion of the nuclear family* ◊ *social/political/economic cohesion* **2** (*physics, chemistry*) the force causing MOLECULES of the same substance to stick together

co·he·sive /kəʊˈhiːsɪv; *AmE* koʊ-/ *adj.* (*formal*) **1** forming a united whole: *a cohesive group* **2** causing people or things to become united: *the cohesive power of shared suffering* ◊ *well-structured sentences illustrating the use of cohesive markers such as 'nevertheless' and 'however'* ▶ **co·he·sive·ness** *noun* [U]: *a strong sense of cohesiveness within the family*

co·hort /ˈkəʊhɔːt; *AmE* ˈkoʊhɔːrt/ *noun* [C+sing./pl. *v.*] **1** (*technical*) a group of people who share a common feature or aspect of behaviour: *the 1989 birth cohort* (= all those born in 1989) **2** (*disapproving*) a member of a group of people who support another person: *Robinson and his cohorts were soon ejected from the hall.*

coif·fure /kwɑːˈfjʊə(r); *AmE* -ˈfjʊr/ *noun* (from *French, formal* or *humorous*) the way in which a person's hair is arranged SYN HAIRSTYLE

coil /kɔɪl/ *verb, noun*
■ *verb* ~ (**sth**) **round, around, etc. sth** | ~ (**sth**) **up** to wind into a series of circles; to make sth do this: [V, +*adv./prep.*] *The snake coiled up, ready to strike.* ◊ *Mist coiled around the tops of the hills.* ◊ [VN] *to coil a rope into a loop* ◊ *Her hair was coiled on top of her head.* ◊ *a coiled spring*

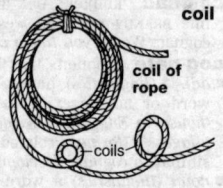

coil

coil of rope

coils

■ *noun* **1** a series of circles formed by winding up a length of rope, wire, etc: *a coil of wire* **2** one circle of rope, wire, etc. in a series: *Shake the rope and let the coils unwind.* ◊ *a snake's coils* **3** a length of wire, wound into circles, that can carry electricity **4** = IUD

coin /kɔɪn/ *noun, verb*
■ *noun* **1** [C] a small flat piece of metal used as money: *a pound coin*—picture at MONEY **2** [U] money made of metal: *notes and coin* IDM see SIDE *n.*, TWO
■ *verb* [VN] **1** to invent a new word or phrase that other people then begin to use: *The term 'cardboard city' was coined to describe communities of homeless people living in cardboard boxes.* **2** to make coins out of metal IDM be **'coining it (in)** | be ˌcoining **'money** (*BrE, informal*) to earn a lot of money quickly or easily SYN RAKE IN **to coin a 'phrase 1** used to show that you are aware that you are using an expression that is not new: *Oh well, no news is good news, to coin a phrase.* **2** used to introduce a well-known expression that you have changed slightly in order to be funny

coin·age /ˈkɔɪnɪdʒ/ *noun* **1** [U] the coins used in a particular place or at a particular time; coins of a particular type: *Roman coinage* ◊ *gold/silver/bronze coinage* **2** [U]

the system of money used in a particular country: *decimal coinage* **3** [C, U] a word or phrase that has been invented recently; the process of inventing a word or phrase: *new coinages*

co·in·cide /ˌkəʊɪnˈsaɪd; *AmE* ˌkoʊ-/ *verb* [V] ~ (**with sth/ sb**) **1** (of two or more events) to take place at the same time: *It's a pity our trips to New York don't coincide.* ◊ *The strike was timed to coincide with the party conference.* **2** (of ideas, opinions, etc.) to be the same or very similar: *The interests of employers and employees do not always coincide.* ◊ *Her story coincided exactly with her brother's.* **3** (*formal*) (of objects or places) to meet; to share the same space: *At this point the two paths coincide briefly.* ◊ *The present position of the house coincides with that of an earlier dwelling.*

co·in·ci·dence /kəʊˈɪnsɪdəns; *AmE* koʊ-/ *noun* **1** [C, U] the fact of two things happening at the same time by chance, in a surprising way: *a strange/an extraordinary/ a remarkable coincidence* ◊ **What a coincidence!** *I wasn't expecting to see you here.* ◊ *It's not a coincidence that none of the directors are women* (= it did not happen by chance). ◊ **By** (**sheer**) **coincidence**, *I met the person we'd been discussing the next day.* **2** [sing.] (*formal*) the fact of things being present at the same time: *the coincidence of inflation and unemployment* **3** [sing.] (*formal*) the fact of two or more opinions, etc. being the same: *a coincidence of interests between the two partners*

co·in·ci·dent /kəʊˈɪnsɪdənt; *AmE* koʊ-/ *adj.* ~ (**with sth**) (*formal*) happening in the same place or at the same time

co·in·ci·dent·al /ˌkəʊˌɪnsɪˈdentl; *AmE* koʊ-/ *adj.* [not usually before noun] happening by chance; not planned: *I suppose your presence here today is not entirely coincidental.* ◊ *It's purely coincidental that we both chose to call our daughters Emma.* ▶ **co·in·ci·den·tal·ly** *adv.*: *Coincidentally, they had both studied in Paris.*

coir /ˈkɔɪə(r)/ *noun* [U] rough material made from the shells of COCONUTS, used for making ropes, for covering floors, etc.

co·itus /ˈkɔɪtəs; ˈkəʊɪtəs; *AmE* ˈkoʊ-/ *noun* [U] (*medical* or *formal*) = SEXUAL INTERCOURSE

coitus interruptus /ˌkɔɪtəs ɪntəˈrʌptəs; ˌkəʊɪtəs; *AmE* ˌkoʊ-/ *noun* [U] an act of SEXUAL INTERCOURSE in which the man removes his PENIS from the woman's body before he EJACULATES, in order to prevent the woman from becoming pregnant

Coke™ /kəʊk; *AmE* koʊk/ *noun* [C, U] (*informal*) = COCA-COLA: *Can I have a Diet Coke?*

coke /kəʊk; *AmE* koʊk/ *noun* [U] **1** (*informal*) = COCAINE **2** a black substance that is produced from coal and burnt to provide heat

cola /ˈkəʊlə; *AmE* ˈkoʊlə/ *noun* **1** [U, C] a sweet brown, FIZZY drink (= with bubbles) that does not contain alcohol. Its flavour comes from the seeds of a W African tree and other substances. **2** [C] a glass, can or bottle of cola—see also COCA-COLA, COKE

Col. *abbr.* (in writing) COLONEL: *Col. Stewart*

col /kɒl; *AmE* kɑːl/ *noun* (*technical*) a low point between two higher points in a mountain range SYN PASS

col. *abbr.* (in writing) COLUMN

col·an·der /ˈkʌləndə(r); *AmE* ˈkɑːl-/ *noun* a metal or plastic bowl with a lot of small holes in it, used for DRAINING water from vegetables, etc. after washing or cooking—picture at KITCHEN

cold /kəʊld; *AmE* koʊld/ *adj., noun, adv.*
■ *adj.* (**cold·er, cold·est**)
LOW TEMPERATURE | **1** having a lower than usual temperature; having a temperature lower than the human body: *I'm cold. Turn the heating up.* ◊ *to feel/look cold* ◊ *cold hands and feet* ◊ *a cold room/house* ◊ *hot and cold water in every room* ◊ *Isn't it cold today?* ◊ *It's freezing cold.* ◊ *to get/turn colder* ◊ *bitterly cold weather* ◊ *the coldest May on record* ◊ (*BrE*) *The water has gone cold.*

FOOD/DRINK | **2** not heated; cooled after being cooked: *a cold drink* ◊ *Hot and cold food is available in the cafeteria.* ◊ *cold chicken for lunch*

UNFRIENDLY | **3** (of a person) without emotion; unfriendly:

to give sb a cold look/stare/welcome ◇ *Her manner was* **cold and distant.** ◇ *He was staring at her with* **cold eyes.**

LIGHT/COLOURS | **4** seeming to lack warmth, in an unpleasant way: *clear cold light* ◇ *cold grey skies*

ROUTE | **5** not easy to find: *The police followed the robbers to the airport but then the* **trail went cold.**

IN GAMES | **6** used in children's games to say that the person playing is not close to finding a person or thing, or to guessing the correct answer

UNCONSCIOUS | **7** (**out** ~) [not before noun] (*informal*) unconscious: *He was knocked out cold in the second round.*

FACTS | **8** (**the** ~ **facts/truth**) facts with nothing added to make them more interesting or pleasant—see also COLDLY, COLDNESS

IDM a cold 'fish a person who seems unfriendly and without strong emotions **get/have cold 'feet** (*informal*) to suddenly become nervous about doing sth that you had planned to do: *He was going to ask her but he got cold feet and said nothing.* **give sb the cold 'shoulder** (*informal*) to treat sb in an unfriendly way—see also COLD-SHOULDER **in cold 'blood** acting in a way that is deliberately cruel; with no pity: *to kill/murder/shoot sb in cold blood* **in the cold light of day** when you have had time to think calmly about sth; in the morning when things are clearer: *These things always look different in the cold light of day.* **leave sb 'cold** to fail to affect or interest sb: *Most modern art leaves me cold.* **pour/throw cold 'water on sth** to give reasons for not being in favour of sth; to criticize sth: *She immediately poured cold water on his plans to expand the business.*—more at BLOOD, BLOW *v.*, HOT *adj.*

■ *noun*
LOW TEMPERATURE | **1** [U] a lack of heat or warmth; a low temperature, especially in the atmosphere: *He shivered with cold.* ◇ *Don't stand outside in the cold.* ◇ *She doesn't seem to feel the cold.* ◇ *You'll catch your death of cold* (= used to warn sb they could become very ill if they do not keep warm in cold weather).

ILLNESS | **2** [C] (also *less frequent* **the ‚common 'cold** [sing.]) a common illness that affects the nose and/or throat, making you cough, SNEEZE, etc: *I've got a cold.* ◇ *a bad/heavy/slight cold* ◇ *to catch a cold*

IDM come in from the 'cold to become accepted or included in a group, etc. after a period of being outside it **leave sb ‚out in the 'cold** to not include sb in a group or an activity—more at CATCH *v.*

■ *adv.* **1** (*AmE*) suddenly and completely: *His final request stopped her cold.* **2** without preparing: *I can't just walk in there cold and give a lesson on the passive!*

‚**cold-'blooded** *adj.* **1** (of people and their actions) showing no feelings or pity for other people: *a cold-blooded killer* ◇ *cold-blooded murder* **2** (*biology*) (of animals, for example fish or snakes) having a body temperature that depends on the temperature of the surrounding air or water—compare WARM-BLOODED ▶ ‚**cold-'bloodedly** *adv.*

‚**cold-'calling** *noun* [U] the practice of telephoning sb that you do not know, in order to sell them sth ▶ ‚**cold 'call** *noun*

‚**cold 'cash** *noun* [U] (*AmE*) = HARD CASH

‚**cold 'comfort** *noun* [U] the fact that sth that would normally be good does not make you happy because the whole situation is bad: *A small drop in the inflation rate was cold comfort for the millions without a job.*

'**cold cream** *noun* [U] a thick white cream that people use for cleaning their face or making their skin soft

'**cold cuts** *noun* [pl.] (*especially AmE*) slices of cooked meat that are served cold

'**cold frame** (also **frame**) *noun* a small wooden or metal frame covered with glass that you grow seeds or small plants in to protect them from cold weather

‚**cold-'hearted** *adj.* not showing any love or sympathy for other people; unkind—compare WARM-HEARTED

cold·ly /'kəʊldli; *AmE* 'koʊld-/ *adv.* without any emotion or warm feelings; in an unfriendly way: *to stare/smile/reply coldly*

cold·ness /'kəʊldnəs; *AmE* 'koʊld-/ *noun* [U] **1** the lack

of warm feelings; unfriendly behaviour: *She was hurt by the coldness in his voice.* **2** the state of being cold: *the icy coldness of the water*

‚**cold-'shoulder** *verb* [VN] to treat sb in an unfriendly way—see also GIVE SB THE COLD SHOULDER at COLD *adj.*

'**cold snap** *noun* (*informal*) a sudden short period of very cold weather

'**cold sore** *noun* a small painful spot on the lips or inside the mouth that is caused by a VIRUS

'**cold spell** *noun* a period when the weather is colder than usual

‚**cold 'storage** *noun* [U] a place where food, etc. can be kept fresh or frozen until it is needed; the storing of sth in such a place: (*figurative*) *I've had to put my plans into cold storage* (= I've decided not to carry them out immediately but to keep them for later).

'**cold store** *noun* a room where food, etc. can be kept at a low temperature in order to keep it in good condition

‚**cold 'sweat** *noun* [usually sing.] a state when you have sweat on your face or body but still feel cold, usually because you are very frightened or anxious: *to break out into a cold sweat* ◇ *I woke up in a cold sweat about the interview.*

‚**cold 'turkey** *noun* [U] the unpleasant state that drug ADDICTS experience when they suddenly stop taking a drug; a way of treating drug ADDICTS that makes them experience this state ▶ ‚**cold 'turkey** *adv.*: *I quit smoking cold turkey.*

‚**cold 'war** *noun* (sing., U] (often **Cold War**) a very unfriendly relationship between two countries who are not actually fighting each other, usually used about the situation between the US and the Soviet Union after the Second World War

cole·slaw /'kəʊlslɔː; *AmE* 'koʊl-/ *noun* [U] finely chopped pieces of raw CABBAGE, CARROT, onion, etc., mixed with MAYONNAISE and eaten with meat or salads

colic /'kɒlɪk; *AmE* 'kɑːlɪk/ *noun* [U] severe pain in the stomach and bowels, suffered especially by babies ▶ **col·icky** *adj.*

col·itis /kə'laɪtɪs/ *noun* [U] (*medical*) a disease that causes pain and swelling in the COLON (= part of the bowels)

col·lab·or·ate /kə'læbəreɪt/ *verb* [V] **1** ~ (**with sb**) (**on sth**) | ~ (**with sb**) (**in sth/in doing sth**) to work together with sb in order to produce or achieve sth: [V] *We have collaborated on many projects over the years.* ◇ *She agreed to collaborate with him in writing her biography.* ◇ *Researchers around the world are collaborating to develop a new vaccine.* **2** ~ (**with sb**) (*disapproving*) to help the enemy who has taken control of your country during a war: *He was accused of collaborating with the enemy.*

col·lab·or·ation /kə‚læbə'reɪʃn/ *noun* **1** [U, C] ~ (**with sb**) (**on sth**) | ~ (**between A and B**) the act of working with another person or group of people to create or produce sth: *She wrote the book in collaboration with one of her students.* ◇ *The government worked in close collaboration with teachers on the new curriculum.* ◇ *collaboration between the teachers and the government* ◇ *It was a collaboration that produced extremely useful results.* **2** [C] a piece of work produced by two or more people or groups of people working together **3** [U] (*disapproving*) the act of helping the enemy during a war when they have taken control of your country

col·lab·ora·tive /kə'læbərətɪv; *AmE* -reɪtɪv/ *adj.* [only before noun] (*formal*) involving, or done by, several people or groups of people working together: *collaborative projects/studies/research* ◇ *a collaborative effort/venture* ▶ **col·lab·ora·tive·ly** *adv.*

col·lab·or·ator /kə'læbəreɪtə(r)/ *noun* **1** a person who works with another person to create or produce sth such as a book **2** (*disapproving*) a person who helps the enemy in a war, when they have taken control of the person's country

col·lage /'kɒlɑːʒ; *AmE* kə'lɑːʒ/ *noun* **1** [U, C] the art of making a picture by sticking pieces of coloured paper, fabric, or photographs onto a surface; a picture that you

b	d	f	g	h	k	l	m	n	p	r
bad	did	fall	get	hat	cat	leg	man	now	pen	red

make by doing this **2** [C] a collection of things, which may be similar or different: *an interesting collage of 1960s songs*

col·lapse /kəˈlæps/ *verb, noun*

■ *verb*

OF BUILDING | **1** [V] to fall down or fall in suddenly, often after breaking apart SYN GIVE WAY: *The roof collapsed under the weight of snow.*

OF SICK PERSON | **2** [V] to fall down (and usually become unconscious), especially because you are very ill/sick: *He collapsed in the street and died two hours later.*

RELAX | **3** [V] (*informal*) to sit or lie down and relax, especially after working hard: *When I get home I like to collapse on the sofa and listen to music.*

FAIL | **4** [V] to fail suddenly or completely SYN BREAK DOWN: *Talks between management and unions have collapsed.* ◇ *All opposition to the plan has collapsed.*

OF PRICES/ CURRENCIES | **5** [V] to decrease suddenly in amount or value: *Share prices collapsed after news of poor trading figures.*

FOLD | **6** to fold sth into a shape that uses less space; to be able to be folded in this way: [V] *The table collapses for easy storage.* [also VN]

MEDICAL | **7** [V, VN] if a lung or BLOOD VESSEL **collapses** or is **collapsed**, it falls inwards and becomes flat and empty

▶ **col·lapsed** *adj.*: *collapsed buildings* ◇ *a collapsed investment bank* ◇ *a collapsed lung*

■ *noun*

FAILURE | **1** [C usually sing, U] a sudden failure of sth, such as an institution, a business or a course of action: *the collapse of law and order in the area* ◇ *The peace talks were on the verge of collapse.*

OF BUILDING | **2** [U] the action of a building suddenly falling: *The walls were strengthened to protect them from collapse.*

ILLNESS | **3** [U, C, usually sing.] a medical condition when a person suddenly becomes very ill/sick, or when sb falls because they are ill/sick or weak: *a state of mental/ nervous collapse* ◇ *She was taken to hospital after her collapse at work.*

OF PRICES/CURRENCIES | **4** [C, usually sing.] a sudden fall in value: *the collapse of share prices/the dollar/the market*

col·laps·ible /kəˈlæpsəbl/ *adj.* that can be folded flat or made into a smaller shape that uses less space: *a collapsible chair/boat/bicycle*

col·lar /ˈkɒlə(r); AmE ˈkɑːl-/ *noun, verb*

■ *noun* **1** the part around the neck of a shirt, jacket or coat that usually folds down: *a coat with a fur collar* ◇ *I turned up my collar against the wind* (= to keep warm). ◇ *He always wears a collar and tie for work.*—see also BLUE-COLLAR, DOG COLLAR, WHITE-COLLAR, WING COLLAR—picture on page A4 **2** a band of leather or plastic put around the neck of an animal, especially a dog: *a collar and lead/ leash* **3** (*technical*) a band made of a strong material that is put round sth, such as a pipe or a piece of machinery, to strengthen it or to join two parts together IDM see HOT *adj.*

■ *verb* [VN] (*informal*) **1** to capture sb and hold them tightly so that they cannot escape from you: *Police collared the culprit as he was leaving the premises.* **2** to stop sb in order to talk to them: *I was collared in the street by a woman doing a survey.*

col·lar·bone /ˈkɒləbəʊn; AmE ˈkɑːlərbəʊn/ *noun* either of the two bones that go from the base of the neck to the shoulders SYN CLAVICLE—picture at BODY

col·lard greens /ˈkɒlɑːd griːnz; AmE ˈkɑːlərd/ *noun* [pl.] (*AmE*) = KALE

col·lar·less /ˈkɒlələs; AmE ˈkɑːlərləs/ *adj.* with no collar: *a collarless shirt*

col·late /kəˈleɪt/ *verb* [VN] **1** to collect information together from different sources in order to examine and compare it: *to collate data/information/figures* **2** to collect pieces of paper or the pages of a book, etc. and arrange them in the correct order ▶ **col·la·tion** /kəˈleɪʃn/ *noun* [U]: *the collation of information*

col·lat·eral /kəˈlætərəl/ *noun, adj.*

■ *noun* [U] (*finance*) property or sth valuable that you promise to give to sb if you cannot pay back money that you borrow

■ *adj.* (*formal*) **1** connected with sth else, but in addition to it and less important: *collateral benefits* ◇ *The government denied that there had been any collateral damage* (= injury to ordinary people or buildings) *during the bombing raid.* **2** (*technical*) (of people) in the same family, but not closely related

col·league /ˈkɒliːɡ; AmE ˈkɑː-/ *noun* a person that you work with, especially in a profession or a business: *a colleague of mine from the office* ◇ *We were friends and colleagues for more than 20 years.* ◇ *the Prime Minister and his Cabinet colleagues*

col·lect /kəˈlekt/ *verb, adj, adv.*

■ *verb*

BRING TOGETHER | **1** [VN] ~ sth (from sb/sth) to bring things together from different people or places SYN GATHER: *to collect data/evidence/information* ◇ *We're collecting signatures for a petition.* ◇ *Samples were collected from over 200 patients.*

AS HOBBY | **2** [VN] to buy or find things of a particular type and keep them as a hobby: *to collect stamps/postcards/ fossils*—see also STAMP COLLECTING

OF PEOPLE | **3** [V] to come together in one place to form a larger group SYN GATHER: *A crowd began to collect in front of the embassy.*

INCREASE IN AMOUNT | **4** to gradually increase in amount in a place; to gradually obtain more and more of sth in a place SYN ACCUMULATE: [V] *Dirt had collected in the corners of the room.* ◇ [VN] *We seem to have collected an enormous number of boxes* (= without intending to). ◇ *That guitar's been sitting collecting dust* (= not being used) *for years now.*

TAKE AWAY | **5** [VN] ~ sb/sth (from …) to go somewhere in order to take sb/sth away: *What day do they collect the rubbish/garbage?* ◇ *The package is waiting to be collected.* ◇ (*BrE*) *She's gone to collect her son from school.*

MONEY | **6** ~ (sth) (for sth) to ask people to give you money for a particular purpose: [V] *We're collecting for local charities.* ◇ [VN] *We collected over £300 for the appeal.* **7** [VN] to obtain the money, etc. that sb owes, for example by going to their house to get it: *to collect rent/debts/tax*

RECEIVE/WIN | **8** to receive sth; to win sth: *to collect a prize/a medal* ◇ *She collected £25 000 in compensation.* ◇ *She collected $50 000 on her husband's life insurance policies.* [also V]

IDM **collect yourself/your thoughts 1** to try to control your emotions and become calm: *I'm fine—I just need a minute to collect myself.* **2** to prepare yourself mentally for sth: *She paused to collect her thoughts before entering the interview room.*

PHRV **col,lect sth↔ˈup** to bring together things that are no longer being used: *Would somebody collect up all the dirty glasses?*

■ *adj.* (*AmE*) (of a telephone call) paid for by the person who receives the call: *to make a collect call*—see also REVERSE *v.* (7) ▶ **col·lect** *adv.*: *to call sb collect*

col·lect·able (also **col·lect·ible**) /kəˈlektəbl/ *adj.* worth collecting because it is beautiful or may become valuable ▶ **col·lect·able** (also **col·lect·ible**) *noun* [usually pl.]

col·lect·ed /kəˈlektɪd/ *adj.* [not before noun] **1** very calm and in control of yourself: *She always stays cool, calm and collected in a crisis.* **2** ~ works, papers, poems, etc. all the books, etc. written by one author, published in one book or in a set: *the collected works of Edgar Allan Poe*

col·lec·tion /kəˈlekʃn/ *noun*

GROUP OF OBJECTS/PEOPLE | **1** [C] a group of objects, often of the same sort, that have been collected: *a stamp/coin collection* ◇ *The painting comes from his private collection.* **2** [C] a group of objects or people: *There was a collection of books and shoes on the floor.* ◇ *There is always a strange collection of runners in the London Marathon.*

TAKING AWAY/BRINGING TOGETHER | **3** [C, U] an act of taking sth away from a place; an act of bringing things together into one place: *refuse/garbage collection* ◇ *The last collec-*

tion from this postbox is at 5.15. ◊ *Your suit will be ready for collection on Tuesday.* ◊ *The first stage in research is data collection.*—compare PICKUP

POEMS/STORIES/MUSIC | **4** [C] a group of poems, stories or pieces of music published together as one book or disc: *a collection of stories by women writers*

MONEY | **5** [C] an act of collecting money to help a charity or during a church service; the money collected: *a house-to-house collection for Cancer Research* ◊ *The total collection last week amounted to £250.*

NEW CLOTHES | **6** [C] a range of new clothes or items for the home that are designed, made and offered for sale, often for a particular season: *Armani's stunning new autumn collection*

col·lect·ive /kəˈlektɪv/ *adj., noun*

■ *adj.* [usually before noun] **1** done or shared by all members of a group of people; involving a whole group or society: *collective leadership/decision-making* ◊ *collective responsibility* ◊ *collective consciousness/memory* (= things that a group of people or a community know or remember, that are often passed from parents to children) **2** used to refer to all members of a group: *The collective name for mast, boom and sails on a boat is the 'rig'.* ▶ **col·lect·ive·ly** *adv.*: *the collectively agreed rate* ◊ *We have had a successful year, both collectively and individually.* ◊ *rain, snow and hail, collectively known as 'precipitation'* (= as a group)

■ *noun* a group of people who own a business or a farm and run it together; the business that they run: *an independent collective making films for television*

col,lective ˈbargaining *noun* [U] discussions between a TRADE/LABOR UNION and an employer about the pay and working conditions of the union members

col,lective ˈfarm *noun* a large farm, or a group of farms, owned by the government and run by a group of people

col,lective ˈnoun *noun* (*grammar*) a singular noun, such as *committee* or *team*, that refers to a group of people, animals or things and, in British English, can be used with either a singular or a plural verb. In American English it must be used with a singular verb.

col·lect·iv·ism /kəˈlektɪvɪzəm/ *noun* [U] the political system in which all farms, businesses and industries are owned by the government or by all the people ▶ **col·lect·iv·ist** *adj.*: *collectivist ideology*

col·lect·iv·ize (*BrE* also **-ise**) /kəˈlektɪvaɪz/ *verb* [VN] [often passive] to join several private farms, industries, etc. together so that they are controlled by the community or by the government ▶ **col·lect·iv·iza·tion, -isa·tion** /kəˌlektɪvaɪˈzeɪʃn; *AmE* -vəˈz-/ *noun* [U]

col·lect·or /kəˈlektə(r)/ *noun* (especially in compounds) a person who collects things, either as a hobby, or as a job: *an art/a stamp collector* ◊ *ticket/tax/debt collectors*

colˈlector's item *noun* a thing that is valued because it is very old or rare, or because it has some special interest

col·leen /kɒˈliːn; *AmE* kɑːˈl-/ *noun* **1** (*IrishE*) a girl or young woman **2** a girl or young woman from Ireland

col·lege /ˈkɒlɪdʒ; *AmE* ˈkɑːl-/ *noun* **1** [C, U] (often in names) (in Britain) a place where students go to study or to receive training after they have left school: *a college of further education* (= providing education and training for people over 16) ◊ *a technical/secretarial college* ◊ *the Royal College of Art* ◊ *a college course/library/student* ◊ *She's at college.*—see also COMMUNITY COLLEGE (1), SIXTH-FORM COLLEGE **2** [C, U] (often in names) (in the US) a university where students can study for a degree after they have left school: *Carleton College* ◊ *a college campus/student* ◊ *a private college* ◊ *He got interested in politics when he was in college.* ◊ *She's away at college in California.*—see also COMMUNITY COLLEGE (2) **3** [C, U] one of the separate institutions that some British universities, such as Oxford and Cambridge, are divided into: *King's College, Cambridge* ◊ *a tour of Oxford colleges* ◊ *Most students live in college.* **4** (in the US) one of the main divisions of some large universities: *The history department is part of the College of Arts and Sciences.* **5** [C+sing./pl. *v.*] the teach-

ers and/or students of a college **6** [C] (especially in names, in Britain and some other countries) a secondary school, especially one where you must pay: *Eton College* **7** [C] (*formal*) (usually in names) an organized group of professional people with special interests, duties or powers: *the Royal College of Physicians* ◊ *the American College of Cardiology*—see also ELECTORAL COLLEGE

BRITISH / AMERICAN
college / university

In both *BrE* and *AmE* a **college** is a place where you can go to study after you leave secondary school. In Britain you can go to a **college** to study or to receive training in a particular skill. In the USA you can study for your first degree at a **college**. A **university** offers more advanced degrees in addition to first degrees.

In *AmE* **college** is often used to mean a **university**, especially when talking about people who are studying for their first degree. **The** is not used when you are talking about someone studying there: *My son has gone away to college.* ◊ *'Where did you go to college?' 'Ohio State University.'*

In *BrE* you can say: *My daughter is at college* ◊ *My daughter is at university.* In *AmE* you cannot use **university** in this way. You use it with **a** or **the** to mean a particular university. *My daughter is at college.* ◊ *I didn't want to go to a large university.*

---

col·le·gi·ate /kəˈliːdʒiət/ *adj.* **1** relating to a college or its students: *collegiate life* **2** (*BrE*) divided into a number of colleges: *a collegiate university*

col·lide /kəˈlaɪd/ *verb* [V] **~** (**with sth/sb**) **1** if two people, vehicles, etc. **collide**, they crash into each other; if a person, vehicle, etc. **collides** with another, or with sth that is not moving, they crash into it: *The car and the van collided head-on in thick fog.* ◊ *The car collided head-on with the van.* ◊ *As he fell, his head collided with the table.* **2 ~** (**with sb**) (**over sth**) (*written*) (of people, their opinions, etc.) to disagree strongly: *They regularly collide over policy decisions.*—see also COLLISION

col·lie /ˈkɒli; *AmE* ˈkɑːli/ *noun* a dog of which there are several types. Those with long pointed noses and long thick hair are popular as pets. Smaller collies with shorter hair are often trained to help control sheep on a farm.

col·lier /ˈkɒliə(r); *AmE* ˈkɑːl-/ *noun* **1** (*old-fashioned, especially BrE*) = COAL MINER **2** a ship that carries coal

col·liery /ˈkɒliəri; *AmE* ˈkɑːl-/ *noun* (*pl.* **-ies**) (*BrE*) a coal mine with its buildings and equipment

col·li·sion /kəˈlɪʒn/ *noun* [C, U] **~** (**with sb/sth**)| **~** (**between/of A and B**) **1** an accident in which two vehicles or people crash into each other: *a collision between two trains* ◊ *Stewart was injured in a collision with another player.* ◊ *a head-on collision* (= between two cars that are moving towards each other) ◊ *a mid-air collision* (= between two aircraft while they are flying) ◊ *His car was in collision with a motorbike.* **2** (*written*) a strong disagreement between two people or between opposing ideas, opinions, etc.; the meeting of two things that are very different: *a collision between two opposing points of view* ◊ *In his work we see the collision of two different traditions.* **IDM** **be on a colˈlision course** (**with sb/sth**) **1** to be in a situation which is almost certain to cause a disagreement or dispute: *I was on a collision course with my boss over the sales figures.* **2** to be moving in a direction in which it is likely that you will crash into sb/sth: *A giant iceberg was on a collision course with the ship.*

col·lo·cate /ˈkɒləkeɪt; *AmE* ˈkɑːl-/ *verb* [V] (*linguistics*) **~** (**with sth**) (of words) to be often used together in a language: *'Bitter' collocates with 'tears' but 'sour' does not.* ◊ *'Bitter' and 'tears' collocate.* ▶ **col·lo·cate** /ˈkɒləkət; *AmE* ˈkɑːl-/ *noun*: *'Bitter' and 'tears' are collocates.*

col·lo·ca·tion /ˌkɒləˈkeɪʃn; *AmE* ˌkɑːl-/ *noun* (*linguistics*) **1** [C] a combination of words in a language, that happens very often and more frequently than would happen by

æ	ɑː	e	ɜː	ə	ɪ	iː	i	ɒ	ɔː	ʌ	ʊ	u	uː
cat	father	ten	bird	about	sit	see	many	got	saw	cup	put	actual	too

(BrE)

chance: *'Resounding success' and 'crying shame' are English collocations.* **2** [U] the fact of two or more words often being used together, in a way that happens more frequently than would happen by chance: *Advanced students need to be aware of the importance of collocation.* ⇨ Study page B3

col·lo·quial /kəˈləʊkwiəl; *AmE* -ˈloʊ-/ *adj.* (of words and language) used in conversation but not in formal speech or writing ▶ **col·lo·qui·al·ly** /-kwiəli/ *adv.*

col·lo·qui·al·ism /kəˈləʊkwiəlɪzəm; *AmE* -ˈloʊ-/ *noun* a word or phrase that is used in conversation but not in formal speech or writing

col·lo·quium /kəˈləʊkwiəm; *AmE* -ˈloʊ-/ *noun* (*pl.* **col·lo·quia** /kəˈləʊkwiə; *AmE* -ˈloʊ-/) a formal academic SEMINAR or CONFERENCE

col·lo·quy /ˈkɒləkwi; *AmE* ˈkɑːl-/ *noun* (*pl.* **-ies**) (*rare, formal*) a conversation

col·lude /kəˈluːd/ *verb* [V] ~ (**with sb**) (**in sth/in doing sth**)| ~ (**with sb**) (**to do sth**) (*formal, disapproving*) to work together secretly or illegally in order to deceive other people: *Several people had colluded in the murder.* ◊ *They colluded with terrorists to overthrow the government.*

col·lu·sion /kəˈluːʒn/ *noun* [U] (*formal, disapproving*) secret agreement especially in order to do sth dishonest or to deceive people: *The police were operating in collusion with the drug dealers.* ◊ *There was collusion between the two witnesses* (= they gave the same false evidence). ▶ **col·lu·sive** /kəˈluːsɪv/ *adj.*

co·logne /kəˈləʊn; *AmE* kəˈloʊn/ (also **eau de cologne**) *noun* [U] a type of light PERFUME

colon /ˈkəʊlən; *AmE* ˈkoʊ-/ *noun* **1** the mark (:) used to introduce a list, a summary, an explanation, etc. or before reporting what sb has said—compare SEMICOLON ⇨ Appendix 4 **2** (*anatomy*) the lower part of the large INTESTINE (= part of the bowels)—picture at BODY

col·onel /ˈkɜːnl/ *noun* (*abbr.* **Col.**) an officer of high rank in the army, the Marines, or the US air force: *Colonel Jim Edge*

Colonel 'Blimp *noun* = BLIMP

co·lo·nial /kəˈləʊniəl; *AmE* -ˈloʊ-/ *adj., noun*
■ *adj.* **1** connected with or belonging to a country that controls another country: *a colonial power* ◊ *Tunisia achieved independence from French colonial rule in 1956.* ◊ *Western colonial attitudes*—see also COLONY **2** (often **Colonial**) typical or connected with the US at the time when it was still a British COLONY: *life in colonial times* ◊ *the Colonial government of Vermont*
■ *noun* a person who lives in a COLONY and who comes from the country that controls it: *British colonials in India*

co·lo·ni·al·ism /kəˈləʊniəlɪzəm; *AmE* -ˈloʊ-/ *noun* [U] the practice by which a powerful country controls another country or other countries: *European colonialism* ▶ **co·lo·ni·al·ist** *adj., noun*: *colonialist laws*

co·lon·ic /kəˈlɒnɪk; *AmE* -ˈlɑːn-/ *adj.* (*anatomy*) connected with the COLON (= part of the bowels): *colonic irrigation* (= the process of washing out the COLON *with water*)

col·on·ist /ˈkɒlənɪst; *AmE* ˈkɑːl-/ *noun* a person who settles in an area that has become a COLONY

col·on·ize (*BrE* also **-ise**) /ˈkɒlənaɪz; *AmE* ˈkɑː-/ *verb* [VN] **1** to take control of an area or a country that is not your own, especially using force, and send people from your own country to live there: *The area was colonized by the Vikings.* **2** (*biology*) (of animals or plants) to live or grow in large numbers in a particular area: *The lower slopes are colonized by flowering plants.* ◊ *Thousands of bats had colonized the ruins.* ▶ **col·on·iza·tion, -isa·tion** /ˌkɒlənaɪˈzeɪʃn; *AmE* ˌkɑːlənəˈz-/ *noun* [U]: *the colonization of the 'New World'* ◊ *plant colonization* **col·on·izer, -iser** *noun*

col·on·nade /ˌkɒləˈneɪd; *AmE* ˌkɑːl-/ *noun* a row of stone columns with equal spaces between them, usually supporting a roof ▶ **col·on·naded** /ˌkɒləˈneɪdɪd; *AmE* ˌkɑːl-/ *adj.*

col·ony /ˈkɒləni; *AmE* ˈkɑːl-/ *noun* (*pl.* **-ies**) **1** [C] a country or an area that is governed by people from another, more powerful, country: *former British colonies* **2** [sing.+

sing./pl. *v.*] a group of people who go to live permanently in a colony **3** [C+sing./pl. *v.*] a group of people from the same place or with the same work or interests who live in a particular city or country or who live together: *the American colony in Paris* ◊ *an artists' colony* **4** [C+sing./pl. *v.*] (*biology*) a group of plants or animals that live together or grow in the same place: *a colony of ants* ◊ *a bird colony*

color (*AmE*) = COLOUR **HELP** You will find most words formed with **color** at the spelling **colour**.

col·or·ation (*BrE* also **col·our·ation**) /ˌkʌləˈreɪʃn/ *noun* [U] (*technical*) the natural colours and patterns on a plant or an animal

col·ora·tura /ˌkɒlərəˈtʊərə; *AmE* ˌkʌlərəˈtʊrə/ *noun* [U] (*music*) complicated passages for a singer, for example in opera: *a coloratura soprano* (= one who often sings coloratura passages)

'color guard *noun* (*AmE*) a small group of people who carry official flags in a ceremony

col·or·ist (*AmE*) = COLOURIST

col·or·ize (*BrE* also **col·our·ize**) /ˈkʌləraɪz/ *verb* [VN] (*technical*) to add colour to a black and white film/movie, using a computer process

'color line *noun* (*AmE*) = COLOUR BAR

col·os·sal /kəˈlɒsl; *AmE* kəˈlɑːsl/ *adj.* extremely large: *a colossal statue* ◊ *The singer earns a colossal amount of money.*

col·os·sus /kəˈlɒsəs; *AmE* -ˈlɑːs-/ *noun* **1** [sing.] (*formal*) a person or thing that is extremely important or large in size **2** [C] (*pl.* **co·lossi** /kəˈlɒsaɪ; *AmE* -ˈlɑːs-/) an extremely large statue

col·our (*BrE*) (*AmE* **color**) /ˈkʌlə(r)/ *noun, verb*
■ *noun*
RED, GREEN, etc. | **1** [C, U] the appearance that things have that results from the way in which they reflect light. Red, orange and green are colours: *What's your favourite colour?* ◊ *bright/dark/light colours* ◊ *available in 12 different colours* ◊ *the colour of the sky* ◊ *Her hair is a reddish-brown colour.* ◊ *to add/give/lend colour to sth* (= make it more colourful) ◊ *Foods which go through a factory process lose much of their colour, flavour and texture.* ◊ *The garden was a mass of colour.* **2** [U] (usually before another noun) the use of all the colours, not only black and white: *a colour TV in every room* ◊ *colour photography/printing* ◊ *a full-colour brochure* ◊ *Do you dream in colour?*
OF FACE | **3** [U] a red or pink colour in sb's face, especially when it shows that they look healthy or that they are embarrassed: *The fresh air brought colour to their cheeks.* ◊ *Colour flooded her face when she thought of what had happened.* ◊ *His face was drained of colour* (= he looked pale and ill).
OF SKIN | **4** [U, C] the colour of a person's skin, when it shows the race they belong to: *discrimination on the grounds of race, colour or religion* ◊ (*especially AmE*) *a person/man/woman of colour* (= who is not white)
SUBSTANCE | **5** [C, U] a substance that is used to give colour to sth: *a semi-permanent hair colour that lasts six to eight washes*—see also WATERCOLOUR
INTERESTING DETAILS | **6** [U] interesting and exciting details or qualities: *The old town is full of colour, character and attractions.* ◊ *Her acting added warmth and colour to the production.*—see also LOCAL COLOUR
OF TEAM/COUNTRY, etc. | **7** (**colours**) [pl.] the particular colours that are used on clothes, flags, etc. to represent a team, school, political party or country: *Red and white are the team colours.* ◊ *Spain's national colours* ◊ (*figurative*) *There are people of different political colours on the committee.* **8** (**colours**) [pl.] (*especially BrE*) a flag, BADGE, etc. that represents a team, country, ship, etc: *Most buildings had a flagpole with the national colours flying.* ◊ *sailing under the French colours*
IDM **off 'colour** [not before noun] (*BrE, informal*) **1** not in good health; looking or feeling ill: *Jo seems a little off colour today.* **2** (usually before noun) (*especially AmE*) an **off-colour** joke is one that people think is rude, usually because it is about sex **see the colour of sb's 'money**

aɪ	aʊ	eɪ	əʊ	oʊ	ɔɪ	ɪə	eə	ʊə	j	w
my	now	say	go	go	boy	near	hair	pure	yes	wet
			(BrE)	(AmE)						

(especially *spoken*) to make sure that sb has enough money to pay for sth—more at NAIL *v.*, TRUE *adj.*, FLYING *adj.*

■ *verb*

PUT COLOUR ON STH | **1** to put colour on sth using paint, coloured pencils, etc: [V] *The children love to draw and colour.* ◊ *a colouring book* (= with pictures that you can add colour to) ◊ [VN] *How long have you been colouring* (= dying) *your hair?* ◊ [VN-ADJ] *He drew a monster and coloured it red.*

OF FACE | **2** [V] ~ (**at sth**) (*written*) (of a person or their face) to become red with embarrassment SYN BLUSH: *She coloured at his remarks.*

AFFECT | **3** [VN] to affect sth, especially in a negative way: *This incident coloured her whole life.* ◊ *Don't let your judgement be coloured by personal feelings.*

PHRV **,colour sth ↔ 'in** to put colour inside a particular area, shape, etc. using coloured pencils, CRAYONS, etc: *I'll draw a tree and you can colour it in.*

col·our·ant /ˈkʌlərənt/ (*BrE*) (*AmE* **col·or·ant**) *noun* a substance that is used to put colour in sth, especially a person's hair

col·our·ation (*BrE*) = COLORATION

'colour bar (*BrE*) (*AmE* **'color bar, color line**) *noun* [usually sing.] a social system which does not allow black people the same rights as white people

'colour-blind (*BrE*) (*AmE* **'color-blind**) *adj.* **1** unable to see the difference between some colours, especially red and green **2** treating people with different coloured skin in exactly the same way ▶ **'colour-blindness** (*BrE*) (*AmE* **'color-blindness**) *noun* [U]

'colour code (*BrE*) (*AmE* **'color code**) *noun* a system of marking things with different colours so that you can easily identify them ▶ **'colour-coded** (*BrE*) (*AmE* **'color-coded**) *adj.*: *The files have labels that are colour-coded according to subject.*

col·oured (*BrE*) (*AmE* **col·ored**) /ˈkʌləd; *AmE* -ərd/ *adj., noun*

■ *adj.* **1** (often in compounds) having a particular colour or different colours: *brightly coloured balloons* ◊ *coloured lights/glass/paper* ◊ *She was wearing a cream-coloured suit.* **2** (*old-fashioned* or *offensive*) (of a person) from a race that does not have white skin **3** (**Coloured**) (in South Africa) having parents who are of different races

■ *noun* **1** (*old-fashioned* or *offensive*) a person who does not have white skin **2** (**Coloured**) (in South Africa) a person whose parents are of different races

'colour fast (*BrE*) (*AmE* **'color·fast**) *adj.* fabric that is **colour fast** will not change or lose colour when it is washed

col·our·ful (*BrE*) (*AmE* **col·or·ful**) /ˈkʌləfl; *AmE* -ərfl/ *adj.* **1** full of bright colours or having a lot of different colours: *colourful shop windows* ◊ *The male birds are more colourful than the females.* **2** interesting or exciting; full of variety, sometimes in a way that is slightly shocking: *a colourful history/past/career* ◊ *one of the book's most colourful characters*

col·our·ing (*BrE*) (*AmE* **col·or·ing**) /ˈkʌlərɪŋ/ *noun* **1** [U, C] a substance that is used to give a particular colour to food: *red food colouring* **2** [U] the colour of a person's skin, eyes and hair: *Blue suited her fair colouring.* **3** [U] the colours that exist in sth, especially a plant or an animal: *insects with vivid yellow and black colouring*

col·our·ist (*BrE*) (*AmE* **col·or·ist**) /ˈkʌlərɪst/ *noun* a person who uses colour, especially an artist or a HAIR-DRESSER

col·our·ize (*BrE*) = COLORIZE

col·our·less (*BrE*) (*AmE* **col·or·less**) /ˈkʌlələs; *AmE* -lərl-/ *adj.* **1** without colour or very pale: *a colourless liquid like water* ◊ *colourless lips* **2** not interesting SYN DULL: *a colourless personality/world*

'colour scheme (*BrE*) (*AmE* **'color scheme**) *noun* the way in which colours are arranged, especially in the furniture and decoration of a room

'colour supplement *noun* (*BrE*) a magazine printed in colour and forming an extra part of a newspaper, particularly on Saturdays or Sundays

col·our·way /ˈkʌləweɪ; *AmE* -lərw-/ *noun* (*BrE*) a colour or combination of colours which a piece of clothing, etc. is available in: *The designs are available in two colourways: red/grey or blue/grey.*

colt /kəʊlt; *AmE* koʊlt/ *noun* **1** a young male horse up to the age of four or five—compare FILLY, STALLION **2** (*BrE*) a member of a sports team consisting of young players

col·umn /ˈkɒləm; *AmE* ˈkɑːləm/ *noun* **1** a tall, solid, vertical post, usually round and made of stone, which supports or decorates a building or stands alone as a MONUMENT: *The temple is supported by marble columns.* ◊ *Nelson's Column in London*—picture at ARCADE **2** a thing shaped like a column: *a column of smoke* (= smoke rising straight up)—see also SPINAL COLUMN, STEERING COLUMN **3** (*abbr.* **col.**) one of the vertical sections into which the printed page of a book, newspaper, etc. is divided: *a column of text* ◊ *a dictionary with two columns per page* ◊ *Put a mark in the appropriate column.* ◊ *Their divorce filled a lot of column inches in the national papers* (= got a lot of attention). **4** a part of a newspaper or magazine which appears regularly and deals with a particular subject or is written by a particular writer: *the gossip/financial column* ◊ *I always read her column in the local paper.*—see also AGONY COLUMN, PERSONAL COLUMN **5** a series of numbers or words arranged one under the other down a page: *to add up a column of figures* **6** a long, moving line of people or vehicles: *a long column of troops and tanks*—see also FIFTH COLUMN

col·um·nist /ˈkɒləmnɪst; *AmE* ˈkɑːl-/ *noun* a journalist who writes regular articles, usually on a particular topic, for a newspaper or magazine

coma /ˈkəʊmə; *AmE* ˈkoʊmə/ *noun* a deep unconscious state, usually lasting a long time and caused by serious illness or injury: *to go into/be in a coma*

co·ma·tose /ˈkəʊmətəʊs; *AmE* ˈkoʊmətoʊs/ *adj.* **1** (*medical*) deeply unconscious; in a coma **2** (*humorous*) extremely tired and lacking in energy; sleeping deeply

comb /kəʊm; *AmE* koʊm/ *noun, verb*

■ *noun* **1** [C] a flat piece of plastic or metal with a row of thin teeth along one side, used for making your hair neat; a smaller version of this worn by women in their hair to hold it in place or as an ornament **2** [C, usually sing.] the act of using a comb on your hair: *Your hair needs a good comb.* **3** [C, U] = HONEYCOMB **4** [C] the soft, red piece of flesh on the head of a male chicken IDM see FINE-TOOTH COMB *adj.*

■ *verb* **1** [VN] to pull a comb through your hair in order to make it neat: *Don't forget to comb your hair!* ◊ *Her hair was neatly combed back.* **2** ~ (**through**) **sth** (**for sb/sth**) to search sth carefully in order to find sth or sb/sth: [VN] *The police combed the area for clues.* ◊ *I combed the shops looking for something to wear.* ◊ [V] *They combed through the files for evidence of fraud.* **3** [VN] (*technical*) to make wool, cotton, etc. clean and straight using a special comb so that it can be used to make fabric PHRV **,comb sth ↔ 'out** to pull a comb through hair in order to make it neat or to remove knots from it

com·bat /ˈkɒmbæt; *AmE* ˈkɑːm-/ *noun, verb*

■ *noun* [U, C] fighting or a fight, especially during a time of war: *armed/unarmed combat* (= with/without weapons) ◊ *combat troops/aircraft/uniform* ◊ *He was killed in combat.*—see also SINGLE COMBAT

■ *verb* (**-t-** or **-tt-**) [VN] **1** to stop sth unpleasant or harmful from happening or from getting worse: *measures to combat crime/inflation/unemployment/disease* **2** (*formal*) to fight against an enemy

com·bat·ant /ˈkɒmbətənt; *AmE* ˈkɑːm-/ *noun* a person or group involved in fighting in a war or battle—compare NON-COMBATANT

com·bat·ive /ˈkɒmbətɪv; *AmE* ˈkɑːm-/ *adj.* ready and willing to fight or argue: *in a combative mood/spirit*

com·bin·ation /ˌkɒmbɪˈneɪʃn; *AmE* ˌkɑːm-/ *noun* **1** [C] two or more things joined or mixed together to form a single unit: *His treatment was a combination of surgery,*

b	d	f	g	h	k	l	m	n	p	r
bad	did	fall	get	hat	cat	leg	man	now	pen	red

C

radiation and drugs. ◊ *What an unusual combination of flavours!* ◊ *Technology and good management:a winning combination* (= one that will certainly be successful). **2** [U] the act of joining or mixing together two or more things to form a single unit: *The firm is working on a new product in combination with several overseas partners.* ◊ *These paints can be used individually or in combination.* **3** [C] a series of numbers or letters used to open a combination lock: *I can't remember the combination.* **4** (**combinations**) (*BrE*) [pl.] a piece of underwear covering the body and legs, worn in the past

combi·nation lock *noun* a type of lock which can only be opened by using a particular series of numbers or letters

com·bine *verb, noun*
■ *verb* /kəm'baɪn/ **1** ~ (**sth**) (**with sth**)| ~ **A and B** (**together**) to come together to form a single thing or group; to join two or more things or groups together to form a single one: [V] *Hydrogen and oxygen combine to form water.* ◊ *Hydrogen combines with oxygen to form water.* ◊ *Several factors had combined to ruin our plans.* ◊ [VN] *Combine all the ingredients in a bowl.* ◊ *Combine the eggs with a little flour and heat the mixture gently.* ◊ *The German team scored a combined total of 652 points.* **2** [VN] ~ **A and/with B** to have two or more different features or characteristics; to put two or more different things, features or qualities together: *The hotel combines comfort with convenience.* ◊ *This model combines a telephone and fax machine.* ◊ *a kitchen and dining-room combined* ◊ *We are still looking for someone who combines all the necessary qualities.* ◊ *They have successfully combined the old with the new in this room.* **3** [VN] ~ **A and/with B** to do two or more things at the same time: *The trip will combine business with pleasure.* ◊ *She has successfully combined a career and bringing up a family.* **4** to come together in order to work or act together; to put two things or groups together so that they work or act together: [V] *The gangs combined against a common enemy.* ◊ [VN] *the combined effects of the two drugs* ◊ *You should try to combine exercise with a healthy diet.* ◊ *It took the combined efforts of both the press and the public to bring about a change in the law.* **IDM** see FORCE *n.*
■ *noun* /'kɒmbaɪn; *AmE* 'kɑːm-/ **1** (*BrE* also ,**combine 'harvester**) a large farm machine which cuts a crop and separates the grains from the rest of the plant **2** a group of people or organizations acting together in business

com·bining form *noun* (*grammar*) a form of a word that can combine with another word or another combining form to make a new word, for example *techno-* and *-phobe* in *technophobe*

combo /'kɒmbəʊ; *AmE* 'kɑːmboʊ/ *noun* (*pl.* **-os**) **1** a small band that plays jazz or dance music **2** (*AmE, informal*) a number of different things combined together, especially different types of food: *I'll have the steak and chicken combo platter.*

com·bust·ible /kəm'bʌstəbl/ *adj.* able to begin burning easily: *combustible material/gases*

com·bus·tion /kəm'bʌstʃən/ *noun* [U] **1** the process of burning **2** (*technical*) a chemical process in which substances combine with the OXYGEN in the air to produce heat and light

com'bustion chamber *noun* an enclosed space in which combustion takes place, for example in an engine

come /kʌm/ *verb, exclamation, noun*
■ *verb* (**came** /keɪm/ **come**)
TO A PLACE | **1** to move to or towards a person or place: [V, usually +*adv./prep.*] *He came into the room and shut the door.* ◊ *She comes to work by bus.* ◊ *My son is coming home soon.* ◊ *Come here!* ◊ *Come and see us soon!* ◊ *Here comes Jo* (= Jo is coming)*!* ◊ *He has come all the way from Tokyo.* ◊ *There's a storm coming.* ◊ [V to inf] *They're coming to stay for a week.* **HELP** In spoken English **come** can be used with **and** plus another verb, instead of with **to** and the infinitive, to show purpose or to tell sb what to do: *When did she last come and see you?* ◊ *Come and have your dinner.* The **and** is sometimes left out, especially in *AmE*: *Come have your dinner.* **2** [V] ~ (**to** …) to arrive at or

reach a place: *They continued until they came to a river.* ◊ *What time did you come* (= to my house)*?* ◊ *Spring came late this year.* ◊ *Your breakfast is coming soon.* ◊ *Have any letters come for me?* ◊ *Help came at last.* ◊ *The CD comes complete with all the words of the songs.* ◊ *The time has come* (= now is the moment) *to act.* **3** ~ **for/about sth** | ~ **to do sth** to arrive somewhere in order to do sth or get sth: [V] *I've come for my book.* ◊ *I've come about my book.* ◊ *I've come to get my book.* ◊ [V -ing] *He came looking for me.* **4** ~ (**to sth**) (**with sb**) to move or travel, especially with sb else, to a particular place or in order to be present at an event: [V] *I've only come for an hour.* ◊ *Are you coming to the club with us tonight?* ◊ *Thanks for coming* (= to my house, party, etc.)*.* ◊ [V -ing] *Why don't you come skating tonight?*

RUNNING/HURRYING etc. | **5** [V -ing, usually +*adv./prep.*] to move in a particular way or while doing sth else: *The children came running into the room.*

TRAVEL | **6** [VN] to travel a particular distance: *We've come 50 miles this morning.* ◊ (*figurative*) *The company has come a long way* (= made lot of progress) *in the last 5 years.*

HAPPEN | **7** [V] to happen: *The agreement came after several hours of negotiations.* ◊ *The rains came too late to do any good.* ◊ *Her death came as a terrible shock to us.* ◊ *His resignation came as no surprise.* **8** [V to inf] used in questions to talk about how or why sth happened: *How did he come to break his leg?* ◊ *How do you come to be so late?*—see also HOW COME?

TO A POSITION/STATE | **9** [V +*adv./prep.*] (not used in the progressive tenses) to have a particular position: *That comes a long way down my list of priorities.* ◊ *His family comes first* (= is the most important thing in his life). ◊ *She came second* (= received the second highest score) *in the exam.* **10** [V] ~ **to/into sth** used in many expressions to show that sth has reached a particular state: *At last winter came to an end.* ◊ *He came to power in 1959.* ◊ *When will they come to a decision?* ◊ *The trees are coming into leaf.* **11** ~ (**in sth**) (not used in the progressive tenses) (of goods, products, etc.) to be available or to exist in a particular way: [V] *This dress comes in black, brown and red.* ◊ [V-ADJ] (*informal*) *New cars don't come cheap* (= they are expensive). **12** to become: [V-ADJ] *The buttons on her blouse had come undone.* ◊ *The handle came loose.* ◊ *Everything will come right in the end.* ◊ [V to inf] *This design came to be known as the Oriental style.* **13** [V to inf] to reach a point where you realize, understand or believe sth: *In time she came to love him.* ◊ *She had come to see the problem in a new light.* ◊ *I've come to expect this kind of behaviour from him.*

TIME | **14** (**come**) [VN] (*old-fashioned, informal*) when the time mentioned comes: *They would have been married forty years come this June.*

SEX | **15** [V] (*slang*) to have an ORGASM

IDM Most idioms containing **come** are at the entries for the nouns or adjectives in the idioms, for example **come a cropper** is at **cropper**. **be as ,clever, ,stupid, etc. as they 'come** (*informal*) to be very clever, stupid, etc. ,**come a'gain?** (*spoken, informal*) used to ask sb to repeat sth: *'She's an entomologist.' 'Come again?' 'An entomologist—she studies insects.'* ,**come and 'go 1** to arrive and leave; to move freely: *They had a party next door—we heard people coming and going all night.* **2** to be present for a short time and then go away: *The pain in my leg comes and goes.* **come 'easily, 'naturally, etc. to sb** (of an activity, a skill, etc.) to be easy, natural, etc. for sb to do: *Acting comes naturally to her.* ,**come over (all) 'faint, 'dizzy, 'giddy, etc.** (*old-fashioned, BrE, informal*) to suddenly feel ill/sick or FAINT **come to 'nothing | not 'come to anything** to be unsuccessful; to have no successful result: *How sad that all his hard work should come to nothing.* ◊ *Her plans didn't come to anything.* **come to 'that | if it comes to 'that** (*informal, especially BrE*) used to introduce sth extra that is connected with what has just been said: *I don't really trust him—nor his wife, come to that.* ,**come what 'may** in spite of any problems or difficulties you may have: *He promised to support her come what may.* **how come (…)?** (*spoken*) used to say

s	t	v	z	ʃ	ʒ	tʃ	dʒ	θ	ð	ŋ
see	tea	van	zoo	shoe	vision	chain	jam	thin	this	sing

you do not understand how sth can happen and would like an explanation: *If she spent five years in Paris, how come her French is so bad?* **not 'come to much** to not be important or successful **to 'come** (used after a noun) in the future: *They may well regret the decision in years to come.* ◊ *This will be a problem for some time to come* (= for a period of time in the future). **when it comes to sth/to doing sth** when it is a question of sth: *When it comes to getting things done, he's useless.* **where sb is 'coming from** (*informal, spoken*) somebody's ideas, beliefs, personality, etc. that makes them say what they have said: *I see where you're coming from* (= I understand what you mean).

PHRV ,**come a'bout (that …)** to happen: *Can you tell me how the accident came about?*

,**come a'cross** (also ,**come 'over**) **1** to be understood: *He spoke for a long time but his meaning didn't really come across.* **2** to make a particular impression: *She comes across well in interviews.* ◊ *He came over as a sympathetic person.* '**come across sb/sth** [no passive] to meet or find sb/sth by chance: *I came across children sleeping under bridges.* ◊ *She came across some old photographs in a drawer.* ,**come a'cross (with sth)** [no passive] to provide or supply sth when you need it: *I hoped she'd come across with some more information.*

,**come 'after sb** [no passive] to chase or follow sb

,**come a'long 1** to arrive; to appear: *When the right opportunity comes along, she'll take it.* **2** to go somewhere with sb: *I'm glad you came along.* **3** to improve or develop in the way that you want: *Your French has come along a lot recently.* **4** used in orders to tell sb to hurry, or to try harder: *Come along! We're late already.* ◊ *Come along! It's easy!*

,**come a'part** to break into pieces: *The book just came apart in my hands.* ◊ (*figurative*) *My whole life had come apart at the seams.*

,**come a'round/'round 1** (also ,**come 'to**) to become conscious again: *Your mother hasn't yet come round from the anaesthetic.* **2** (of a date or a regular event) to happen again: *My birthday seems to come around quicker every year.* ,**come a'round/'round (to …)** to come to a place, especially sb's house, to visit for a short time: *Do come around and see us some time.* ,**come a'round/'round (to sth)** to change your mood or your opinion: *He'll never come round to our way of thinking.*

'**come at sb** [no passive] to move towards sb as though you are going to attack them: *She came at me with a knife.* ◊ (*figurative*) *The noise came at us from all sides.* '**come at sth** to think about a problem, question, etc. in a particular way: *We're getting nowhere—let's come at it from another angle.*

,**come a'way (from sth)** to become separated from sth: *The plaster had started to come away from the wall.* ,**come a'way with sth** [no passive] to leave a place with a particular feeling or impression: *We came away with the distinct impression that all was not well with their marriage.*

,**come 'back 1** to return: *You came back* (= came home) *very late last night.* ◊ *The colour was coming back to her cheeks.* ◊ (*figurative*) *United came back from being two goals down to win 3–2.* **2** to become popular or successful again: *Long hair for men seems to be coming back in.*— related noun COMEBACK (2) ,**come 'back (at sb) (with sth)** to reply to sb forcefully or angrily: *She came back at the speaker with some sharp questions.*—related noun COMEBACK (3) ,**come 'back (to sb)** to return to sb's memory: *It's all coming back to me now.* ◊ *Once you've been in France a few days, your French will soon come back.* ,**come 'back to sth** [no passive] to return to a subject, an idea, etc: *Let's come back to the point at issue.* ◊ *It all comes back to a question of money.*

'**come before sb/sth** [no passive] (*formal*) to be presented to sb/sth for discussion or a decision: *The case comes before the court next week.*

,**come be'tween sb and sb** [no passive] to damage a relationship between two people: *I'd hate anything to come between us.*

,**come 'by** (*AmE*) to make a short visit to a place, in order to see sb: *She came by the house.* '**come by sth 1** to manage to get sth: *Jobs are hard to come by these days.* **2** to receive sth: *How did you come by that scratch on your cheek?*

,**come 'down 1** to break and fall to the ground: *The ceiling came down with a terrific crash.* **2** (of rain, snow, etc.) to fall: *The rain came down in torrents.* **3** (of an aircraft) to land or fall from the sky: *We were forced to come down in a field.* **4** if a price, a temperature, a rate, etc. **comes down**, it gets lower: *The price of gas is coming down.* ◊ *Gas is coming down in price.* **5** to decide and say publicly that you support or oppose sb: *The committee came down in support of his application.* **6** to reach as far down as a particular point: *Her hair comes down to her waist.* ,**come 'down (from …)** (*BrE, formal*) to leave a university, especially Oxford or Cambridge, at the end of a TERM or after finishing your studies OPP COME UP (TO …) ,**come 'down (from …) (to …)** to come from one place to another, usually from the north of a country to the south, or from a larger place to a smaller one ,**come 'down on sb** [no passive] (*informal*) to criticize sb severely or punish sb: *Don't come down too hard on her.* ◊ *The courts are coming down heavily on young offenders.* ,**come 'down (to sb)** to have come from a long time in the past: *The name has come down from the last century.* ,**come 'down to sth** [no passive] to be able to be explained by a single important point: *What it comes down to is, either I get more money or I leave.* ,**come 'down with sth** [no passive] to get an illness that is not very serious: *I think I'm coming down with flu.*

,**come 'forward** to offer your help, services, etc: *Several people came forward with information.* ◊ *Police have asked witnesses of the accident to come forward.*

'**come from …** (not used in the progressive tenses) to have as your place of birth or the place where you live: *She comes from London.* ◊ *Where do you come from?* '**come from sth 1** to start in a particular place or be produced from a particular thing: *Much of our butter comes from New Zealand.* ◊ *This wool comes from goats, not sheep.* ◊ *This poem comes from his new book.* ◊ *Where does her attitude come from?* ◊ *Where's that smell coming from?* ◊ *He comes from a family of actors.* ◊ *'She doesn't try hard enough.' 'That's rich, coming from you* (= you do not try hard either).*' 2* = COME OF STH

,**come 'in 1** when the TIDE **comes in**, it moves towards the land OPP GO OUT **2** to finish a race in a particular position: *My horse came in last.* **3** to become fashionable: *Long hair for men came in in the sixties.* **4** to become available: *We're still waiting for copies of the book to come in.* **5** to have a part in sth: *I understand the plan perfectly, but I can't see where I come in.* **6** to arrive somewhere; to be received: *The train is coming in now.* ◊ *News is coming in of a serious plane crash in France.* ◊ *She has over a thousand pounds a month coming in from her investments.* **7** to take part in a discussion: *Would you like to come in at this point, Susan?* **8** (of a law or rule) to be introduced; to begin to be used ,**come 'in for sth** [no passive] to receive sth, especially sth unpleasant: *The government's economic policies have come in for a lot of criticism.* ,**come 'in (on sth)** to become involved in sth: *If you want to come in on the deal, you need to decide now.*

,**come 'into sth** [no passive] **1** to be left money by sb who has died: *She came into a fortune when her uncle died.* **2** to be important in a particular situation: *I've worked very hard to pass this exam—luck doesn't come into it.*

'**come of/from sth** to be the result of sth: *I made a few enquiries, but nothing came of it in the end.* ◊ [+ -ing] *That comes of eating too much!*

,**come 'off 1** to be able to be removed: *Does this hood come off?* ◊ *That mark won't come off.* **2** (*informal*) to take place; to happen: *Did the trip to Rome ever come off?* **3** (*informal*) (of a plan, etc.) to be successful; to have the intended effect or result: *They had wanted it to be a surprise but the plan didn't come off.* **4 ~ well, badly, etc.** (*informal*) to be successful/not successful in a fight, contest, etc: *I thought they came off very well in the debate.* ,**come 'off (sth) 1** to fall from sth: *to come off your bicycle/horse* **2** to become separated from sth: *When I*

æ	ɑː	e	ɜː	ə	ɪ	iː	i	ɒ	ɔː	ʌ	ʊ	u	uː
cat	father	ten	bird	about	sit	see	many	got	saw	cup	put	actual	too

(BrE)

C

tried to lift the jug, the handle came off in my hand. ◇ *A button had come off my coat.* **come 'off it** (*spoken*) used to disagree with sb rudely: *Come off it! We don't have a chance.* **come 'off sth** [no passive] to stop taking medicine, a drug, alcohol, etc: *I've tried to get him to come off the tranquillizers.*

come 'on 1 (of an actor) to walk onto the stage **2** (of a player) to join a team during a game: *Owen came on for Fowler ten minutes before the end of the game.* **3** to improve or develop in the way you want: *The project is coming on fine.* **4** used in orders to tell sb to hurry or to try harder: *Come on! We don't have much time.* ◇ *Come on! Try once more.* **5** used to show that you know what sb has said is not correct: *Oh, come on—you know that isn't true!* **6** (usually used in the progressive tenses) (of an illness or a mood) to begin: *I can feel a cold coming on.* ◇ *I think there's rain coming on.* ◇[+**to** inf] *It came on to rain.* **7** (of a TV programme, etc.) to start: *What time does the news come on?* **8** to begin to operate: *Set the oven to come on at six.* ◇ *When does the heating come on?* **'come on/upon sb/sth** [no passive] (*formal*) to meet or find sb/sth by chance **come 'on to sb** (*informal*) to behave in a way that shows sb that you want to have a sexual relationship with them—related noun COME-ON **come 'on to sth** [no passive] to start talking about a subject: *I'd like to come on to that question later.*

come 'out 1 when the sun, moon or stars **come out**, they appear: *The rain stopped and the sun came out.* **2** (of flowers) to open: *The daffodils came out early this year.* **3** to be produced or published: *When is her new novel coming out?* **4** (of news, the truth, etc.) to become known: *The full story came out at the trial.* ◇[+**that**] *It came out that he'd been telling lies.* **5** if a photograph **comes out**, it is a clear picture when it is developed and printed: *The photos from our trip didn't come out.* **6** to be shown clearly: *Her best qualities come out in a crisis.* **7** when words **come out**, they are spoken: *I tried to say 'I love you,' but the words wouldn't come out.* **8** to say publicly whether you agree or disagree with sth: *He came out against the plan.* ◇ *In her speech, the senator came out in favour of a change in the law.* **9** (*BrE*) to stop work and go on strike **10** to no longer hide the fact that you are HOMOSEXUAL **11** (of a young UPPER-CLASS girl, especially in the past) to be formally introduced into society **come 'out (of sth) 1** (of an object) to be removed from a place where it is fixed: *This nail won't come out.* **2** (of dirt, a mark, etc.) to be removed from sth by washing or cleaning: *These ink stains won't come out of my dress.* ◇ *Will the colour come out* (= fade or disappear) *if I wash it?* **come 'out at sth** [no passive] to add up to a particular cost or sum: *The total bill comes out at £500.* **come 'out in sth** [no passive] (of a person) to become covered in spots, etc. on the skin: *Hot weather makes her come out in a rash.* **come 'out of yourself** to relax and become more confident and friendly with other people: *It was when she started drama classes that she really came out of herself.* **come 'out of sth** [no passive] to develop from sth: *The book came out of his experiences in India.* ◇ *Rock music came out of the blues.* **come 'out with sth** [no passive] to say sth, especially sth surprising or rude: *He came out with a stream of abuse.* ◇ *She sometimes comes out with the most extraordinary remarks.*

come 'over 1 (*BrE, informal*) to suddenly feel sth: [+ADJ] *I suddenly came over all shy.* **2** = COME ACROSS: *He came over well in the interview.* **come 'over (to ...)** to come to a place, especially sb's house, to visit for a short time **come 'over (to ...) (from ...)** to travel from one place to another, usually over a long distance: *Why don't you come over to England in the summer?* ◇ *Her grandparents came over from Ireland during the famine.* **come 'over (to sth)** to change from one side, opinion, etc. to another **come 'over sb** [no passive] to affect sb: *A fit of dizziness came over her.* ◇ *I can't think what came over me* (= I do not know what caused me to behave in that way).

come 'round | come 'round (to sth) (*BrE*) = COME AROUND

come 'through (of news or a message) to arrive by telephone, radio, etc. or through an official organization: *A message is just coming through.* **come 'through (sth)**

to get better after a serious illness or to avoid serious injury: *With such a weak heart she was lucky to come through the operation.* **come 'through (with sth)** to successfully do or complete sth that you have promised to do: *We were worried she wouldn't be able to handle it, but she came through in the end.* ◇ *The bank finally came through with the money.*

come 'to = COME AROUND (1) **come to your'self** (*old-fashioned*) to return to your normal state **'come to sb** [no passive] (of an idea) to enter your mind: *The idea came to me in the bath.* ◇[+**that**] *It suddenly came to her that she had been wrong all along.* **'come to sth** [no passive] **1** to add up to sth: *The bill came to $30.* ◇ *I never expected those few items to come to so much.* **2** to reach a particular situation, especially a bad one: *The doctors will operate if it proves necessary—but it may not come to that.* ◇ *Who'd have thought things would come to this* (= become so bad or unpleasant)?

come to'gether if two or more different people or things **come together**, they form a united group: *Three colleges have come together to create a new university.* ◇ *Bits and pieces of things he'd read and heard were coming together, and he began to understand.*

'come under sth [no passive] **1** to be included in a particular group: *What heading does this come under?* **2** to be a person that others are attacking or criticizing: *The head teacher came under a lot of criticism from the parents.* **3** to be controlled or influenced by sth: *All her students came under her spell.*

come 'up 1 (of plants) to appear above the soil: *The daffodils are just beginning to come up.* **2** (of the sun) to rise: *We watched the sun come up.* **3** to happen: *I'm afraid something urgent has come up.* ◇ *We'll let you know if any vacancies come up.* **4** to be mentioned or discussed: *The subject came up in conversation.* ◇ *The question is bound to come up at the meeting.* **5** (of an event or a time) to be going to happen very soon: *Her birthday is coming up soon.* **6** to be dealt with by a court of law: *Her divorce case comes up next month.* **7** if your number, name, ticket, etc. **comes up** in a betting game, it is chosen and you win sth **8** (*spoken, informal*) (usually used in the progressive tenses) to arrive; to be ready soon: *'Is lunch ready?' 'Coming up!'* **come 'up (to ...)** (*BrE, formal*) to arrive at a university, especially Oxford or Cambridge, at the beginning of a TERM or in order to begin your studies OPP COME DOWN (FROM ...) **come 'up (to ...) (from ...)** to come from one place to another, especially from the south of a country to the north or from a smaller place to a larger one: *Why don't you come up to Scotland for a few days?* **come 'up (to sb)** to move towards sb, in order to talk to them: *He came up to me and asked for a light.* **come 'up against sb/sth** [no passive] to be faced with or opposed by sb/sth: *We expect to come up against a lot of opposition to the plan.* **come 'up for sth** [no passive] **1** to be considered for a job, an important position, etc: *She comes up for re-election next year.* **2** to be reaching the time when sth must be done: *His contract is coming up for renewal.* **come 'up to sth** [no passive] **1** to reach as far as a particular point: *The water came up to my neck.* **2** to reach an acceptable level or standard: *His performance didn't really come up to his usual high standard.* ◇ *Their trip to France didn't come up to expectations.* **come 'up with sth** [no passive] to find or produce an answer, a sum of money, etc: *She came up with a new idea for increasing sales.* ◇ *How soon can you come up with the money?* **'come upon sb/sth** = COME ON SB/STH

■ *exclamation* (*old-fashioned*) used when encouraging sb to be sensible or reasonable, or when showing slight disapproval: *Oh come now, things aren't as bad as all that.* ◇ *Come, come, Miss Jones, you know perfectly well what I mean.*

■ *noun* [U] (*slang*) SEMEN

come·back /ˈkʌmbæk/ *noun* **1** [usually sing.] if a person in public life makes a **comeback**, they start doing sth again which they had stopped doing, or they become popular again: *an ageing pop star trying to stage a comeback* **2** if a thing makes a **comeback**, it becomes popular and fashionable or successful again **3** (*informal*) a quick reply to a critical remark **4** a way of holding sb responsible for sth wrong which has been done to you: *You agreed to the contract in writing, so now you have no comeback.*

com·edian /kəˈmiːdiən/ *noun* an entertainer who makes people laugh by telling jokes or funny stories: *a stand-up comedian*

com·edi·enne /kəˌmiːdiˈen/ *noun* (*old-fashioned*) a female entertainer who makes people laugh by telling jokes or funny stories

come·down /ˈkʌmdaʊn/ *noun* [usually sing.] (*informal*) a situation in which a person is not as important as before, or does not get as much respect from other people

com·edy /ˈkɒmədi; *AmE* ˈkɑːm-/ *noun* (*pl.* **-ies**) **1** [C, U] a play or film/movie that is intended to be funny, usually with a happy ending; plays and films/movies of this type: *a romantic comedy*—compare TRAGEDY **2** [U] an amusing aspect of sth **SYN** HUMOUR: *He didn't appreciate the comedy of the situation.* ◇ *slapstick comedy*—see also BLACK *adj.* (9), SITUATION COMEDY

come·ly /ˈkʌmli/ *adj.* (*literary*) (especially of a woman) pleasant to look at **SYN** ATTRACTIVE

ˈcome-on *noun* [usually sing.] (*informal*) an object or action which is intended to attract sb or to persuade them to do sth: *She was definitely giving him the come-on* (= trying to attract him sexually).

comer /ˈkʌmə(r)/ *noun* **1** (**all comers**) [pl.] anyone who is interested in, or comes forward for, sth, especially a competition: *The event is open to all comers.* **2** (with adjectives) a person who arrives somewhere—see also LATECOMER, NEWCOMER **3** (*AmE, informal*) a person who is likely to be successful

comet /ˈkɒmɪt; *AmE* ˈkɑːmət/ *noun* a mass of ice and dust that moves around the sun and looks like a bright star with a tail: *Halley's Comet*

come·up·pance /kʌmˈʌpəns/ *noun* [sing.] (*informal*) a punishment for sth bad that you have done, that other people feel you really deserve: *I was glad to see that the bad guy got his comeuppance at the end of the movie.*

com·fort /ˈkʌmfət; *AmE* -fərt/ *noun, verb*
■ *noun* **1** [U] the state of being physically relaxed and free from pain; the state of having a pleasant life, with everything that you need: *These tennis shoes are designed for comfort and performance.* ◇ *With video, you can watch the latest movies in the comfort of your own home.* ◇ *The hotel offers a high standard of comfort and service.* ◇ *They had enough money to live in comfort in their old age.* **2** [U] a feeling of not suffering or worrying so much; a feeling of being less unhappy **SYN** CONSOLATION: *to take/draw comfort from sb's words* ◇ *I tried to offer a few words of comfort.* ◇ *The sound of gunfire was too close for comfort.* ◇ *If it's any comfort to you, I'm in the same situation.* ◇ *His words were of little comfort in the circumstances.* ◇ *comfort food* (= food that makes you feel better) **3** [sing.] a person or thing that helps you when you are suffering, worried or unhappy: *The children have been a great comfort to me through all of this.* ◇ *It's a comfort to know that she is safe.*—see also COLD COMFORT **4** [C, usually pl.] a thing that makes your life easier or more comfortable: *The hotel has all modern comforts/every modern comfort.* ◇ *material comforts* (= money and possessions)—see also CREATURE COMFORTS
■ *verb* to make sb who is worried or unhappy feel better by being kind and sympathetic towards them: [VN] *The victim's widow was today being comforted by family and friends.* ◇ *She comforted herself with the thought that it would soon be spring.* ◇ [VN to inf] *It comforted her to feel his arms around her.*

com·fort·able /ˈkʌmftəbl; *BrE* also -fət-; *AmE* also -fərt-/ *adj.*
CLOTHES/FURNITURE | **1** (of clothes, furniture, etc.) making you feel physically relaxed; pleasant to wear, sit on, etc: *It's such a comfortable bed.* ◇ *These new shoes are not very comfortable.* ◇ *a warm comfortable house* **OPP** UNCOMFORTABLE
PHYSICALLY RELAXED | **2** feeling pleasantly physically relaxed; warm enough, without pain, etc: *Are you comfort-*

able? ◇ *She shifted into a more comfortable position on the chair.* ◇ *Please make yourself comfortable while I get some coffee.* ◇ *The patient is comfortable* (= not in pain) *after his operation.* **OPP** UNCOMFORTABLE
CONFIDENT | **3** confident and not worried or afraid: *He's more comfortable with computers than with people.* ◇ *I never feel very comfortable in her presence.* **OPP** UNCOMFORTABLE
HAVING MONEY | **4** having enough money to buy what you want without worrying about the cost: *They're not millionaires, but they're certainly very comfortable.*
VICTORY | **5** quite large; allowing you to win easily: *The party won with a comfortable majority.* ◇ *a comfortable 2–0 win*

com·fort·ably /ˈkʌmftəbli; -fət-; *AmE* -fərt-/ *adv.* **1** in a comfortable way: *All the rooms were comfortably furnished.* ◇ *If you're all sitting comfortably, then I'll begin.* **2** with no problem **SYN** EASILY: *He can comfortably afford the extra expense.* ◇ *They are comfortably ahead in the opinion polls.* **IDM** ˌcomfortably ˈoff having enough money to buy what you want without worrying about the cost

com·fort·er /ˈkʌmfətə(r); *AmE* -fərt-/ *noun* **1** a person or thing that makes you feel calmer or less worried **2** (*AmE*) a type of thick cover for a bed—picture at BED—compare QUILT

com·fort·ing /ˈkʌmfətɪŋ; *AmE* -fərt-/ *adj.* making you feel calmer and less worried or unhappy: *her comforting words* ◇ *It's comforting to know that you'll be there.* ▶ **com·fort·ing·ly** *adv.*

com·fort·less /ˈkʌmfətləs; *AmE* -fərt-/ *adj.* (*formal*) without anything to make a place more comfortable

comfy /ˈkʌmfi/ *adj.* (**com·fier**, **com·fi·est**) (*informal*) comfortable: *a comfy armchair/bed* **HELP** more comfy is also common as a comparative.

comic /ˈkɒmɪk; *AmE* ˈkɑːmɪk/ *adj., noun*
■ *adj.* **1** amusing and making you laugh: *a comic monologue/story* ◇ *The play is both comic and tragic.* ◇ *She can always be relied on to provide comic relief* (= sth to make you relax and laugh) *at a boring party.* **2** [only before noun] connected with COMEDY (= entertainment that is funny and that makes people laugh): *a comic opera* ◇ *a very fine comic actor*
■ *noun* **1** an entertainer who makes people laugh by telling jokes or funny stories **SYN** COMEDIAN **2** (*AmE* also ˈcomic book) a magazine, especially for children, that tells stories through pictures **3** (**the comics**) [pl.] (*AmE*) the section of a newspaper that contains COMIC STRIPS

com·ic·al /ˈkɒmɪkl; *AmE* ˈkɑːm-/ *adj.* (*old-fashioned*) funny or amusing because of being strange or unusual ▶ **com·ic·al·ly** /-kli/ *adv.*

ˈcomic strip (also ˈcar·toon) (*BrE* also ˌstrip carˈtoon) (*AmE* also **strip**) *noun* a series of drawings inside boxes that tell a story and are often printed in newspapers

com·ing /ˈkʌmɪŋ/ *noun, adj.*
■ *noun* [sing.] **the ~ of sth** the time when sth new begins: *With the coming of modern technology, many jobs were lost.* **IDM** ˌcomings and ˈgoings (*informal*) the movement of people arriving at and leaving a particular place: *It's hard to keep track of the children's comings and goings.*
■ *adj.* [only before noun] happening soon; next: *in the coming months* ◇ *This coming Sunday is her birthday.*

comma /ˈkɒmə; *AmE* ˈkɑːmə/ *noun* the mark (,) used to separate the items in a list or to show where there is a slight pause in a sentence—see also INVERTED COMMAS ⇨ Appendix 4

com·mand /kəˈmɑːnd; *AmE* kəˈmænd/ *noun, verb*
■ *noun*
ORDER | **1** [C] an order given to a person or an animal: *Begin when I give the command.* ◇ *You must obey the captain's commands.*
FOR COMPUTER | **2** [C] an instruction given to a computer
CONTROL | **3** [U] control and authority over a situation or a group of people: *He has 1200 men under his command.* ◇ *He has command of 1200 men.* ◇ *The police arrived and*

C

took command of the situation. ◊ *For the first time in years, she felt in command of her life.* ◊ *He looked relaxed and totally in command of himself.* ◊ *Who is in command here?*—see also SECOND IN COMMAND

IN ARMED FORCES | **4** (**Command**) [C] a part of an army, air force, etc. that is organized and controlled separately; a group of officers who give orders: *Bomber Command*

KNOWLEDGE | **5** [U, sing.] **~ (of sth)** your knowledge of sth; your ability to do or use sth, especially a language: *Applicants will be expected to have (a) good command of English.*

IDM **at your com'mand** if you have a skill or an amount of sth **at your command**, you are able to use it well and completely **be at sb's com'mand** (*formal*) to be ready to obey sb: *I'm at your command—what would you like me to do?*—more at WISH *n.*

■ *verb*

ORDER | **1** (of sb in a position of authority) to tell sb to do sth **SYN** ORDER: [VN **to** inf] *He commanded his men to retreat.* ◊ [VN] *She commanded the release of the prisoners.* ◊ [V **that**] (*formal*) *The commission intervened and commanded that work on the building cease.* ◊ (*BrE* also) *The commission commanded that work on the building should cease.* [also V **speech**, VN **speech**, V] ⇨ note at ORDER

IN ARMED FORCES | **2** to be in charge of a group of people in the army, navy or air force: [VN] *The troops were commanded by General Haig.* [also V]

DESERVE AND GET | **3** [VN] [no passive] (not used in the progressive tenses) to deserve and get sth because of the special qualities you have: *to command sympathy/support* ◊ *She was able to command the respect of the class.* ◊ *The headlines commanded her attention.* ◊ *As a top lawyer, he can expect to command a six-figure salary.*

VIEW | **4** [VN] [no passive] (not used in the progressive tenses) (*formal*) to be in a position from where you can see or control sth: *The hotel commands a fine view of the valley.*

CONTROL | **5** [VN] [no passive] (not used in the progressive tenses) (*formal*) to have control of sth; to have sth available for use: *The party was no longer able to command a majority in Parliament.* ◊ *the power and finances commanded by the police*

com·mand·ant /ˈkɒmandænt; *AmE* ˈkɑːm-/ *noun* the officer in charge of a particular military group or institution

com·man·deer /ˌkɒmənˈdɪə(r); *AmE* ˌkɑːmənˈdɪr/ *verb* [VN] to take control of a building, a vehicle, etc. for military purposes during a war, or by force for your own use **SYN** REQUISITION

com·mand·er /kəˈmɑːndə(r); *AmE* -ˈmæn-/ *noun* **1** a person who is in charge of sth, especially an officer in charge of a particular group of soldiers or a military operation: *military/allied/field/flight commanders* ◊ *the commander of the expedition* **2** (*abbr.* **Cdr**) an officer of fairly high rank in the British or American navy **3** (*abbr.* **Cdr**) (in Britain) a London police officer of high rank

com,mander-in-'chief (*abbr.* **C.-in-C.**) *noun* (*pl.* **com-manders-in-chief**) the officer who commands all the armed forces of a country or all its forces in a particular area

com·mand·ing /kəˈmɑːndɪŋ; *AmE* -ˈmæn-/ *adj.* **1** [only before noun] in a position of authority that allows you to give formal orders: *Who is your commanding officer?* **2** [usually before noun] if you are in a **commanding position** or have a **commanding lead**, you are likely to win a race or competition **3** [usually before noun] powerful and making people admire and obey you: *a commanding figure/presence/tone/voice* **4** [only before noun] if a building is in a **commanding position** or has a **commanding view**, you can see the area around very well from it: *The castle occupies a commanding position on a hill.*

com·mand·ment /kəˈmɑːndmənt; *AmE* -ˈmæn-/ *noun* a law given by God, especially any of **the Ten Commandments** given to the Jews in the Bible

com·mando /kəˈmɑːndəʊ; *AmE* kəˈmændoʊ/ *noun* (*pl.* -os) a soldier or a group of soldiers who are trained to make quick attacks in enemy areas

com,mand per'formance *noun* [usually sing.] a special performance, for example at a theatre, that is given for a head of state

com·mem·or·ate /kəˈmeməreɪt/ *verb* [VN] to remind people of an important person or event from the past with a special action or object; to exist to remind people of a person or an event from the past: *A series of movies will be shown to commemorate the 30th anniversary of his death.* ◊ *Many of the people and places in the book have been commemorated in the names of streets.* ◊ *A plaque commemorates the battle.*

com·mem·or·ation /kəˌmeməˈreɪʃn/ *noun* [U, C] an action, or a ceremony, etc. that makes people remember and show respect for an important person or event in the past: *a commemoration service* ◊ *a statue in commemoration of a national hero*

com·mem·ora·tive /kəˈmemərətɪv; *AmE* -əreɪt-/ *adj.* intended to help people remember and respect an important person or event in the past: *commemorative stamps/medals*

com·mence /kəˈmens/ *verb* **~ (with sth)** (*formal*) to begin to happen; to begin sth **SYN** START: [V] *The meeting is scheduled to commence at noon.* ◊ *The day commenced with a welcome from the principal.* ◊ *I will be on leave during the week commencing 15 February.* ◊ [VN] *She commenced her medical career in 1956.* ◊ [V-ing] *We commence building next week.* [also V **to** inf]

com·mence·ment /kəˈmensmənt/ *noun* [U, C, usually sing.] **1** (*formal*) beginning: *the commencement of the financial year* **2** (*AmE*) a ceremony at which students receive their academic degrees or DIPLOMAS **SYN** GRADUATION

com·mend /kəˈmend/ *verb* [VN] **1 ~ sb (for sth/for doing sth)** | **~ sb (on sth/on doing sth)** to praise sb/sth, especially publicly: *She was commended on her handling of the situation.* ◊ *His designs were highly commended by the judges* (= they did not get a prize but they were especially praised). **2 ~ sb/sth (to sb)** (*formal*) to recommend sb/sth to sb: *She is an excellent worker and I commend her to you without reservation.* ◊ *The movie has little to commend it* (= it has few good qualities). **3** (*formal*) if sth **commends** itself to sb, they approve of it: *His outspoken behaviour did not commend itself to his colleagues.* **4 ~ sb/sth to sb** (*formal*) to give sb/sth to sb in order to be taken care of: *We commend her soul to God.*

com·mend·able /kəˈmendəbl/ *adj.* (*formal*) deserving praise and approval: *commendable honesty* ▶ **com·mend·ably** /-əbli/ *adv.*

com·men·da·tion /ˌkɒmenˈdeɪʃn; *AmE* ˌkɑːm-/ *noun* **1** [U] (*formal*) praise; approval **2** [C] **~ (for sth)** an award or official statement giving public praise for sb/sth: *a commendation for bravery*

com·men·sur·ate /kəˈmenʃərət/ *adj.* **~ (with sth)** (*formal*) matching sth in size, importance, quality, etc: *Salary will be commensurate with experience.* ▶ **com·men·sur·ate·ly** *adv.*

com·ment /ˈkɒment; *AmE* ˈkɑːm-/ *noun, verb*

■ *noun* **1** [C, U] **~ (about/on sth)** something that you say or write which gives an opinion on or explains sb/sth: *Have you any comment to make about the cause of the disaster?* ◊ *She made helpful comments on my work.* ◊ *The director was not available for comment.* ◊ *He handed me the document without comment.* ◊ (*especially BrE*) *What she said was fair comment* (= a reasonable criticism). **2** [sing., U] criticism that shows the faults of sth: *The results are a clear comment on government education policy.* ◊ *There was a lot of comment about his behaviour.* **IDM** **,no 'comment** (said in reply to a question, usually from a journalist) I have nothing to say about that: *'Will you resign, sir?' 'No comment!'*

■ *verb* **~ (on/upon sth)** to express an opinion about sth: [V] *I don't feel I can comment on their decision.* ◊ *He refused to comment until after the trial.* ◊ [V **that**] *A spokesperson commented that levels of carbon dioxide were very high.* ◊

s	t	v	z	ʃ	ʒ	tʃ	dʒ	θ	ð	ŋ
see	tea	van	zoo	shoe	vision	chain	jam	thin	this	sing

[v **speech**] *'Not his best performance,' she commented to the woman sitting next to her.*

com·men·tary /ˈkɒməntri; *AmE* ˈkɑːmənteri/ *noun* (*pl.* **-ies**) ~ **(on sth)** **1** [C, U] a spoken description of an event that is given while it is happening, especially on the radio or television: *a sports commentary* ◊ *Our reporters will give a running commentary* (= a continuous one) *on the election results as they are announced.* ◊ *He kept up a running commentary on everyone who came in or went out.* **2** [C] a written explanation or discussion of sth such as a book or a play: *a critical commentary on the final speech of the play* **3** [C, U] a criticism or discussion of sth: *The petty quarrels were a sad commentary on the state of the government.* ◊ *political/social commentary*

com·men·tate /ˈkɒməntert; *AmE* ˈkɑːm-/ *verb* [V] ~ **(on sth)** to give a spoken description of an event as it happens, especially on television or radio: *Who will be commentating on the game?*

com·men·ta·tor /ˈkɒmənteɪtə(r); *AmE* ˈkɑːm-/ *noun* ~ **(on sth)** **1** a person who is an expert on a particular subject and talks or writes about it on television or radio, or in a newspaper: *a political commentator* **2** a person who describes an event while it is happening, especially on television or radio: *a television/radio/sports commentator*

com·merce /ˈkɒmɜːs; *AmE* ˈkɑːmɜːrs/ *noun* [U] trade, especially between countries; the buying and selling of goods and services: *leaders of industry and commerce*—see also CHAMBER OF COMMERCE

com·mer·cial /kəˈmɜːʃl; *AmE* kəˈmɜːrʃl/ *adj., noun*
■ *adj.* **1** [usually before noun] connected with the buying and selling of goods and services: *the commercial heart of the city* ◊ *a commercial vehicle* (= one that is used for carrying goods or passengers who pay) ◊ *commercial baby foods* ◊ *the first commercial flights across the Atlantic* **2** [only before noun] making or intended to make a profit: *The movie was not a commercial success* (= did not make money). **3** (*disapproving*) more concerned with profit and being popular than with quality: *Their more recent music is far too commercial.* **4** (of television or radio) paid for by the money charged for broadcasting advertisements: *a commercial radio station/TV channel* ► **com·mer·cial·ly** /-ʃəli/ *adv.*: *commercially produced/grown/developed* ◊ *The product is not yet commercially available.* ◊ *His invention was not commercially successful.*
■ *noun* an advertisement on the radio or on television: *a commercial break* (= a time during or between programmes when advertisements are broadcast)

com·mer·cial·ism /kəˈmɜːʃəlɪzəm; *AmE* -ˈmɜːrʃl-/ *noun* [U] (*disapproving*) the fact of being more interested in making money than in the value or quality of things

com·mer·cial·ize (*BrE* also **-ise**) /kəˈmɜːʃəlaɪz; *AmE* -ˈmɜːrʃl-/ *verb* [VN] [often passive] to use sth to try to make a profit, especially in a way that other people do not approve of: *Their music has become very commercialized in recent years.* ► **com·mer·cial·iza·tion, -isa·tion** /kəˌmɜːʃəlaɪˈzeɪʃn; *AmE* -ˌmɜːrʃləˈz-/ *noun* [U]

com,mercial ˈtraveller *noun* (*old-fashioned, BrE*) = SALES REPRESENTATIVE

com·mie /ˈkɒmi; *AmE* ˈkɑːmi/ *noun* (*especially AmE*) an insulting way of referring to sb that you think has ideas similar to those of COMMUNISTS or SOCIALISTS, or who is a member of a COMMUNIST or SOCIALIST party

com·mis·er·ate /kəˈmɪzəreɪt/ *verb* ~ **(with sb) (on/about/for/over sth)** to show sb sympathy when they are upset or disappointed about sth: [V] *She commiserated with the losers on their defeat.* [also V **speech**]

com·mis·er·ation /kəˌmɪzəˈreɪʃn/ *noun* [U, C] (*formal*) an expression of sympathy for sb who has had sth unpleasant happen to them, especially not winning a competition: *I offered him my commiseration.* ◊ *Commiserations to the losing team.*

com·mis·sary /ˈkɒmɪsəri; *AmE* ˈkɑːmɪseri/ *noun* (*pl.* **-ies**) (*AmE*) **1** a shop/store that sells food, etc. in a military base, a prison, etc. **2** a restaurant for people working in a large organization, especially a film STUDIO

com·mis·sion /kəˈmɪʃn/ *noun, verb*

■ *noun*
OFFICIAL GROUP | **1** (often **Commission**) [C] an official group of people who have been given responsibility to control sth, or to find out about sth, usually for the government: *the European Commission* ◊ (*BrE*) *The government has set up a commission of inquiry into the disturbances at the prison.* ◊ *a commission on human rights*
MONEY | **2** [U, C] an amount of money that is paid to sb for selling goods and which increases with the amount of goods that are sold: *You get a 10% commission on everything you sell.* ◊ *He earned £2 000 in commission last month.* ◊ *In this job you work on commission* (= are paid according to the amount you sell). **3** [U] an amount of money that is charged by a bank, etc. for providing a particular service: *One per cent commission is charged for cashing traveller's cheques.*
FOR ART/MUSIC, etc. | **4** [C] a formal request to sb to design or make a piece of work such as a building or a painting: *a commission to design the new parliament building*
IN ARMED FORCES | **5** [C] an officer's position in the armed forces: *He resigned his commission when he got married.*
OF CRIME | **6** [U] (*formal*) the act of doing sth wrong or illegal: *the commission of a crime*
IDM **in/out of com'mission** available/not available to be used: *Several of the airline's planes are temporarily out of commission and undergoing safety checks.*
■ *verb*
PIECE OF ART/MUSIC, etc. | **1** to officially ask sb to write, make or create sth or to do a task for you: [VN to inf] *She has been commissioned to write a new national anthem.* ◊ [VN] *Publishers have commissioned a French translation of the book.* ◊ *The survey on consumer taste was commissioned by local stores.*
IN ARMED FORCES | **2** [usually passive] ~ **sb (as) sth** to choose sb as an officer in one of the armed forces: [VN] *She was commissioned in 1992.* ◊ [VN-N] *He has just been commissioned (as a) pilot officer.*

com·mis·sion·aire /kəˌmɪʃəˈneə(r); *AmE* -ˈner/ *noun* (*BrE, becoming old-fashioned*) a person in uniform whose job is to stand at the entrance to a hotel, theatre, cinema/movie theater, etc. and open the door for visitors, find them taxis, etc.—see also DOORMAN

com,missioned ˈofficer *noun* an officer in the armed forces who has a higher rank, such as a captain or a GENERAL—compare NON-COMMISSIONED OFFICER

com·mis·sion·er /kəˈmɪʃənə(r)/ *noun* **1** (usually **Com·missioner**) a member of a COMMISSION (= an official group of people who are responsible for controlling or finding out about sth): *the Church Commissioners* (= the group of people responsible for controlling the financial affairs of the Church of England) ◊ *European Commissioners* **2** (also **po'lice commissioner** especially in *AmE*) the head of a particular police force in some countries: *the Metropolitan Police Commissioner* (= in London) **3** the head of a government department in some countries: *the agriculture/health commissioner* ◊ *Commissioner Rhodes was unavailable for comment.*—see also HIGH COMMISSIONER **4** (in the US) an official chosen by a sports association to control it: *the baseball commissioner*

com,missioner for ˈoaths *noun* (*BrE*) a lawyer who has official authority to be present when sb makes a formal promise that a written statement that they will use as evidence in a court of law is true

com·mit /kəˈmɪt/ *verb* (**-tt-**)
CRIME | **1** [VN] ~ **a crime, etc.** to do sth wrong or illegal: *to commit murder/adultery, etc.* ◊ *Most crimes are committed by young men.* ◊ *appalling crimes committed against innocent children*
SUICIDE | **2** [VN] ~ **suicide** to kill yourself deliberately
PROMISE/SAY DEFINITELY | **3** ~ **sb/yourself (to sth/to doing sth)** [often passive] to promise sincerely that you will definitely do sth, keep to an agreement or arrangement, etc: [VN] *The President is committed to reforming health care.* ◊ *Borrowers should think carefully before committing themselves to taking out a loan.* ◊ [VN to inf] *Both sides committed themselves to settle the dispute peacefully.* **4** [VN] ~ **yourself (to sth)** to give an opinion or make a decision

---

æ	ɑː	e	ɜː	ə	ɪ	iː	i	ɒ	ɔː	ʌ	ʊ	u	uː
cat	father	ten	bird	about	sit	see	many	got	saw	cup	put	actual	too

(BrE)

C

openly so that it is then difficult to change it: *You don't have to commit yourself now, just think about it.*—see also NON-COMMITTAL

BE LOYAL | **5** [V] **~ (to sb/sth)** to be completely loyal to one person, organization, etc. or give all your time and effort to your work, an activity, etc: *Why are so many men scared to commit?* (= say they will be loyal to one person) .—see also COMMITTED

MONEY/TIME | **6** [VN] to spend money or time on sth/sb: *The council has committed large amounts of money to housing projects.*

TO HOSPITAL/PRISON | **7** [VN] [often passive] **~ sb to sth** to order sb to be sent to a hospital, prison, etc: *She was committed to a psychiatric hospital.*

SB FOR TRIAL | **8** [VN] to send sb for trial in a court of law

STH TO MEMORY | **9** [VN] to learn sth well enough to remember it exactly: *She committed the instructions to memory.*

STH TO PAPER/WRITING | **10** [VN] to write sth down

com·mit·ment /kə'mɪtmənt/ *noun* **1** [C, U] **~ (to sb/sth)** | **~ to do sth** a promise to do sth or to behave in a particular way; a promise to support sb/sth; the fact of committing yourself: *She doesn't want to make a big emotional commitment to Steve at the moment.* ◊ *The company's commitment to providing quality at a reasonable price has been vital to its success.* ◊ *the government's commitment to public services* **2** [U] **~ (to sb/sth)** the willingness to work hard and give your energy and time to a job or an activity: *A career as an actor requires one hundred per cent commitment.* **3** [C] a thing that you have promised or agreed to do, or that you have to do: *He's busy for the next month with filming commitments.* ◊ *Women very often have to juggle work with their family commitments.* **4** [C] the fact of having to pay an amount of money regularly: *Buying a house is a big financial commitment.* **5** [U, C] **~ (of sth) (to sth)** agreeing to use money, time or people in order to achieve sth: *the commitment of resources to education* ◊ *Achieving success at this level requires a commitment of time and energy.*

com·mit·tal /kə'mɪtl/ *noun* [U] (*technical*) the official process of sending sb to prison or to a mental hospital: *He was released on bail pending committal proceedings.*

com·mit·ted /kə'mɪtɪd/ *adj.* (*approving*) willing to work hard and give your time and energy to sth; believing strongly in sth: *a committed member of the team* ◊ *They are committed socialists.* OPP UNCOMMITTED

com·mit·tee /kə'mɪti/ *noun* [C+sing./pl. *v.*] a group of people who are chosen, usually by a larger group, to make decisions or to deal with a particular subject: *She's on the management committee.* ◊ *The committee has/have decided to close the restaurant.* ◊ *a committee member/a member of the committee* ◊ *a committee meeting* ◊ *The player was fined by the disciplinary committee.*

com·mode /kə'məʊd; *AmE* kə'moʊd/ *noun* **1** a piece of furniture that looks like a chair but has a toilet under the seat **2** a piece of furniture, especially an old or ANTIQUE one, with drawers for storing things in

com·modi·ous /kə'məʊdiəs; *AmE* -'moʊ-/ *adj.* (*formal*) having a lot of space

com·mod·ity /kə'mɒdəti; *AmE* -'mɑːd-/ *noun* (*pl.* -ies) **1** (*economics*) a product or a raw material that can be bought and sold, especially between countries: *rice, flour and other basic commodities* ◊ *a drop in commodity prices* ◊ *Crude oil is the world's most important commodity.* **2** a thing that is useful or has a useful quality: *Water is a precious commodity that is often taken for granted in the West.*

com·mo·dore /'kɒmədɔː(r); *AmE* 'kɑːm-/ *noun* (*abbr.* **Cdre**) an officer of high rank in the navy: *Commodore John Barry*

com·mon /'kɒmən; *AmE* 'kɑːmən/ *adj., noun*

■ *adj.* (**com·mon·er, com·mon·est**) HELP more common and most common are more frequent **1** happening often; existing in large numbers or in many places: *Jackson is a common English name.* ◊ *Breast cancer is the most common form of cancer among women in this country.* ◊ *Some kinds of birds which were once a common sight are now becoming rare.* ◊ *a common spelling mistake* ◊ *Allergies to*

milk are quite common in childhood. OPP UNCOMMON **2** [usually before noun] **~ (to sb/sth)** shared by or belonging to two or more people or by the people in a group: *They share a common interest in photography.* ◊ *basic features which are common to all human languages* ◊ *We are working together for a common purpose.* ◊ *common ownership of the land* ◊ *This decision was taken for the common good* (= the advantage of everyone). ◊ *It is, by common consent, Scotland's prettiest coast* (= everyone agrees that it is). **3** [only before noun] ordinary; not unusual or special: *the common garden frog* ◊ *Shakespeare's work was popular among the common people in his day.* ◊ *In most people's eyes she was nothing more than a common criminal.* ◊ *You'd think he'd have the common courtesy to apologize* (= this would be the polite behaviour that people would expect). ◊ *It's only common decency to let her know what's happening* (= people would expect it). **4** (*BrE, disapproving*) typical of sb from a low social class and not having good manners: *She thought he was very common and uneducated.* IDM **,common or 'garden** (*BrE*) (*AmE* **'garden-variety**) (*informal*) ordinary; with no special features—**the ,common 'touch** the ability of a powerful or famous person to talk to and understand ordinary people **make common 'cause with sb** (*formal*) to be united with sb about sth that you both agree on, believe in or wish to achieve—more at KNOWLEDGE

■ *noun* **1** [C] an area of open land in a town or village that anyone may use: *We went for a walk on the common.* ◊ *Wimbledon Common* **2** (**commons**) [sing.] (*AmE*) a large room where students can eat in a school, college, etc: *The commons is next to the gym.* IDM **have sth in common (with sb)** (of people) to have the same interests, ideas, etc. as sb else: *Jane and I have nothing in common.* / *I have nothing in common with Jane.* **have sth in common (with sth)** (of things, places, etc.) to have the same features, characteristics, etc: *The two cultures have a lot in common.* **in common** (*technical*) by everyone in a group: *They hold the property as tenants in common.* **in common with sb/sth** (*formal*) in the same way as sb/sth: *Britain, in common with many other industrialized countries, has experienced major changes over the last 100 years.*

the ,common 'cold *noun* [sing.] = COLD

,common de'nominator *noun* **1** (*mathematics*) a number that can be divided exactly by all the numbers below the line in a set of FRACTIONS—compare DENOMINATOR **2** an idea, attitude or experience that is shared by all the members of a group—see also LOWEST COMMON DENOMINATOR

com·mon·er /'kɒmənə(r); *AmE* 'kɑːm-/ *noun* a person who does not come from a NOBLE family: *It was not acceptable for royalty to marry commoners in those days.*—compare ARISTOCRAT

,common 'ground *noun* [U] opinions, interests and aims that you share with sb, although you may not agree with them about other things: *Despite our disagreements, we have been able to find some common ground.*

'common land *noun* [U] (*BrE*) land that belongs to or may be used by the local community

,common 'law *noun* [U] (in England) a system of laws that have been developed from customs and from decisions made by judges, not created by Parliament—compare CASE LAW, STATUTE LAW

,common-law 'husband, **,common-law 'wife** *noun* a person that a woman or man has lived with for a long time and who is recognized as a husband or wife, without a formal marriage ceremony

com·mon·ly /'kɒmənli; *AmE* 'kɑːm-/ *adv.* usually; very often; by most people: *Christopher is commonly known as Kit.* ◊ *commonly held opinions* ◊ *This is one of the most commonly used methods.*

,common 'noun *noun* (*grammar*) a word such as *table*, *cat*, or *sea*, that refers to an object or a thing but is not the name of a particular person, place or thing—compare ABSTRACT NOUN, PROPER NOUN

com·mon·place /'kɒmənpleɪs; *AmE* 'kɑːm-/ *adj., noun*

aɪ	aʊ	eɪ	əʊ	oʊ	ɔɪ	ɪə	eə	ʊə	j	w
my	now .	say	go (BrE)	go (AmE)	boy	near	hair	pure	yes	wet

■ *adj.* done very often, or existing in many places, and therefore not unusual: *Computers are now commonplace in primary classrooms.*

■ *noun (formal)* **1** [usually sing.] an event, etc. that happens very often and is not unusual **2** a remark, etc. that is not new or interesting: *The speech was full of commonplaces.*

'common room *noun (especially BrE)* a room used by the teachers or students of a school, college, etc. when they are not teaching or studying

Com·mons /'kɒmənz; *AmE* 'kɑːm-/ *noun* (**the Commons**) [pl.] = THE HOUSE OF COMMONS—compare THE LORDS

,common 'sense *noun* [U] the ability to think about things in a practical way and make sensible decisions: *For goodness' sake, just use your common sense!* ◇ *a common-sense approach to a problem*

com·mon·wealth /'kɒmənwelθ; *AmE* 'kɑːm-/ *noun* [sing.] **1** (**the Commonwealth**) an organization consisting of the United Kingdom and most of the countries that used to be part of the British Empire: *a member of the Commonwealth* ◇ *Commonwealth countries* **2** (usually **the Commonwealth**) used in the official names of, and to refer to, some states of the US (Kentucky, Massachusetts, Pennsylvania and Virginia): *the Commonwealth of Virginia* ◇ *The city and the Commonwealth have lost a great leader.* **3** (*AmE*) an independent country that is strongly connected to the US: *Puerto Rico remains a US commonwealth, not a state.* **4** (usually **Commonwealth**) used in the names of some groups of countries or states that have chosen to be politically linked with each other: *the Commonwealth of Independent States* (*CIS*)

com·mo·tion /kə'məʊʃn; *AmE* -'moʊ-/ *noun* [C usually sing, U] sudden noisy confusion or excitement: *I heard a commotion and went to see what was happening.* ◇ *The crowd waiting outside was causing a commotion.*

com·mu·nal /kə'mjuːnl; 'kɒmjənl; *AmE* 'kɑːm-/ *adj.* **1** shared by, or for the use of, a number of people, especially people who live together: *a communal kitchen/garden* ◇ *As a student he tried communal living for a few years.* **2** involving different groups of people in a community: *communal violence between religious groups* ▶ **com·mu·nal·ly** *adv.*: *The property was owned communally.*

com·mune *noun, verb*
■ *noun* /'kɒmjuːn; *AmE* 'kɑːm-/ [C+sing./pl. *v.*] **1** a group of people who live together and share responsibilities, possessions, etc: *a 1970s hippy commune* **2** the smallest division of local government in France and some other countries
■ *verb* /kə'mjuːn/ PHRV **com'mune with sb/sth** (*formal*) to share your emotions and feelings with sb/sth without speaking: *He spent much of this time communing with nature.*

com·mu·nic·able /kə'mjuːnɪkəbl/ *adj.* (*formal*) that sb can pass on to other people or communicate to sb else: *communicable diseases*

com·mu·ni·cant /kə'mjuːnɪkənt/ *noun* a person who receives COMMUNION in a Christian church service

com·mu·ni·cate /kə'mjuːnɪkeɪt/ *verb*
EXCHANGE INFORMATION | **1** ~ (**with sb**) to exchange information, news, ideas, etc. with sb: [V] *We only communicate by e-mail.* ◇ *They communicated in sign language.* ◇ *Dolphins use sound to communicate with each other.* ◇ [VN] *to communicate information/a message to sb*

SHARE IDEAS/FEELINGS | **2** to make your ideas, feelings, thoughts, etc. known to other people so that they understand them: [VN] *He was eager to communicate his ideas to the group.* ◇ *Her nervousness was communicating itself to the children.* ◇ [V] *Candidates must be able to communicate effectively.* [also V wh-] **3** [V] ~ (**with sb**) to have a good relationship because you are able to understand and talk about your own and other people's thoughts, feelings, etc: *The novel is about a family who can't communicate with each other.*

DISEASE | **4** [VN] [usually passive] to pass a disease from one person, animal, etc. to another: *The disease is communicated through dirty drinking water.*

OF TWO ROOMS | **5** [V] if two rooms **communicate**, they are next to each other and you can get from one to the other: *a communicating door* (= one that connects two rooms)

com·mu·ni·ca·tion /kə,mjuːnɪ'keɪʃn/ *noun* **1** [U] the activity or process of expressing ideas and feelings or of giving people information: *Speech is the fastest method of communication between people.* ◇ *All channels of communication need to be kept open.* ◇ *Doctors do not always have good communication skills.* ◇ *non-verbal communication* ◇ *We are in regular communication by letter.* **2** [U] (also **com·mu·ni·ca·tions** [pl.]) methods of sending information, especially telephones, radio, computers, etc. or roads and railways: *communication systems/links/technology* ◇ *The new airport will improve communications between the islands.* ◇ *Snow has prevented communication with the outside world for three days.* **3** [C] (*formal*) a message, letter or telephone call: *a communication from the leader of the party*

com·mu·ni·ca·tive /kə'mjuːnɪkətɪv; *AmE* -keɪtɪv/ *adj.* **1** able and willing to talk and give information to other people: *I don't find him very communicative.* OPP UNCOMMUNICATIVE **2** connected with the ability to communicate in a language, especially a foreign language: *communicative skills*

com·mu·ni·ca·tor /kə'mjuːnɪkeɪtə(r)/ *noun* a person who is able to describe their ideas and feelings clearly to others: *an effective/skilled/successful communicator*

com·mu·nion /kə'mjuːniən/ *noun* **1** (also **Com·mu·nion**, **,Holy Com'munion**) [U] a ceremony in the Christian Church during which people eat bread and drink wine in memory of the last meal that Christ had with his DISCIPLES: *to go to Communion* (= attend church for this celebration) ◇ *to take/receive communion* (= receive the bread and wine)—see also EUCHARIST, MASS **2** [U] ~ (**with sb/sth**) (*formal*) the state of sharing or exchanging thoughts and feelings; the feeling of being part of sth: *poets living in communion with nature* **3** [C] (*technical*) a group of people with the same religious beliefs: *the Anglican communion*

com·mu·ni·qué /kə'mjuːnɪkeɪ; *AmE* kə,mjuːnə'keɪ/ *noun* an official statement or report, especially to newspapers

com·mun·ism /'kɒmjunɪzəm; *AmE* 'kɑːm-/ *noun* [U] **1** a political movement that believes in an economic system in which the state controls the means of producing everything on behalf of the people. It aims to create a society in which everyone is treated equally. **2** (**Communism**) the system of government by a ruling Communist Party, such as in the former Soviet Union—compare CAPITALISM

com·mun·ist /'kɒmjənɪst; *AmE* 'kɑːm-/ *noun* **1** a person who believes in or supports communism **2** (**Communist**) a member of a Communist Party ▶ **com·mun·ist** (also **Com·mun·ist**) *adj.*: *communist ideology* ◇ *a Communist country/government/leader*

the 'Communist Party *noun* a political party that supports COMMUNISM or rules in a COMMUNIST country

com·mu·nity /kə'mjuːnəti/ *noun* (*pl.* **-ies**) **1** [sing.] all the people who live in a particular area, country, etc. when talked about as a group: *The local community was shocked by the murders.* ◇ *health workers based in the community* (= working with people in a local area) ◇ *the international community* (= the countries of the world as a group) ◇ *good community relations with the police* ◇ (*AmE*) *community parks/libraries* (= paid for by the local town/city) **2** [C+sing./pl. *v.*] a group of people who share the same religion, race, job, etc: *the Polish community in London* ◇ *ethnic communities* ◇ *the farming community* **3** [U] the feeling of sharing things and belonging to a group in the place where you live: *There is a strong sense of community in this town.* ◇ *community spirit* **4** [C] (*biology*) a group of animals or plants living or growing in the same place

com'munity centre (*BrE*) (*AmE* **com'munity center**) *noun* a place where people from the same area can meet for social events or sports or to take classes

com'munity college *noun* **1** (also **com'munity school**) (in Britain) a secondary school that is open to adults from the local community as well as to its own

b	d	f	g	h	k	l	m	n	p	r
bad	**did**	**fall**	**get**	**hat**	**cat**	**leg**	**man**	**now**	**pen**	**red**

C

C

students **2** (in the US) a college that is mainly for students from the local community and that offers programmes that are two years long, including programmes in practical skills. Some students go to a university or college offering four-year programmes after they have finished studying at a community college.

com,munity 'service noun work helping people in the local community that sb does without being paid, either because they want to, or because they have been ordered to by a court of law as a punishment

com·mu·ta·tion /ˌkɒmjuˈteɪʃn; AmE ˌkɑːm-/ noun [C, U] **1** (law) the act of making a punishment less severe: He appealed for a commutation of the death sentence to life imprisonment. **2** (finance) the act of replacing one method of payment with another; a payment that is replaced with another .

com·mute /kəˈmjuːt/ verb, noun
■ verb **1** [V] to travel regularly by bus, train, car, etc. between your place of work and your home: She commutes from Oxford to London every day. ◊ He spent that year commuting between New York and Chicago. ◊ I live within commuting distance of Dublin. ◊ People are prepared to commute long distances if they are desperate for work. **2** [VN] ~ sth (to sth) (law) to replace one punishment with another that is less severe: The death sentence was commuted to life imprisonment. **3** [VN] ~ sth (for/into sth) (finance) to exchange one form of payment, for sth else
■ noun (especially AmE) the journey that a person makes when they commute to work: a two-hour commute into downtown Washington ◊ I have only a short commute to work. ◊ I plan my day's work during the morning commute.

com·muter /kəˈmjuːtə(r)/ noun a person who travels into a city to work each day, usually from quite far away: (BrE) the commuter belt (= the area around a city where people live and from which they travel to work in the city)

com·pact adj., noun, verb
■ adj. /kəmˈpækt/ **1** small and easy to carry: a compact camera **2** using or filling only a small amount of space: The kitchen was compact but well equipped. **3** closely and firmly packed: a compact mass of earth **4** (of a person or an animal) small and strong: He had a compact and muscular body. ▶ **com·pact·ly** adv. **com·pact·ness** noun [U]
■ noun /ˈkɒmpækt; AmE ˈkɑːm-/ **1** (AmE) a small car—compare SUBCOMPACT **2** a small flat box with a mirror, containing powder that women use on their faces **3** (formal) a formal agreement between two or more people or countries
■ verb /kəmˈpækt/ [VN] [usually passive] to press sth together firmly: a layer of compacted snow

,compact 'disc noun = CD

com·pan·ion /kəmˈpæniən/ noun **1** a person or an animal that travels with you or spends a lot of time with you: travelling companions ◊ Geoff was my companion on the journey. ◊ (figurative) Fear was the hostages' constant companion. **2** a person who has similar tastes, interests, etc. to your own and whose company you enjoy: She was a charming dinner companion. ◊ His younger brother is not much of a companion for him. ◊ They're drinking companions (= they go out drinking together). **3** a person who shares in your work, pleasures, sadness, etc: We became companions in misfortune. **4** a person, usually a woman, employed to live with and help sb, especially sb old or ill/sick **5** one of a pair of things that go together or can be used together: A companion volume is soon to be published. **6** used in book titles to describe a book giving useful facts and information on a particular subject: A Companion to French Literature—see also BOON COMPANION

com·pan·ion·able /kəmˈpæniənəbl/ adj. (written) friendly ▶ **com·pan·ion·ably** /-əbli/ adv.

com·pan·ion·ship /kəmˈpæniənʃɪp/ noun [U] the pleasant feeling that you have when you have a friendly relationship with sb and are not alone: They meet at the club for companionship and advice. ◊ She had only her cat for companionship.

com·pan·ion·way /kəmˈpæniənweɪ/ noun (technical) a staircase on a ship

com·pany /ˈkʌmpəni/ noun (pl. -ies)
BUSINESS | **1** [C+sing./pl. v.] (often in names) a business organization that makes money by producing or selling goods or services: one of the largest computer companies in the world ◊ the National Bus Company ◊ She joined the company in 1992. ◊ Mike gets a company car with his new job. ◊ Company profits were 5% lower than last year.
THEATRE/DANCE | **2** (often in names) [C+sing./pl. v.] a group of people who work or perform together: a theatre/dance company ◊ the Royal Shakespeare Company
BEING WITH SB | **3** [U] the fact of being with sb else and not alone: I enjoy Jo's company (= I enjoy being with her). ◊ She enjoys her own company (= being by herself) when she is travelling. ◊ The children are very good company (= pleasant to be with) at this age. ◊ a pleasant evening in the company of friends ◊ He's coming with me for company.
GUESTS | **4** [U] (formal) guests in your house: I didn't realize you had company.
GROUP OF PEOPLE | **5** [U] (formal) a group of people together: She told the assembled company what had happened. ◊ It is bad manners to whisper in company (= in a group of people).
SOLDIERS | **6** [C+sing./pl. v.] a group of soldiers that is part of a BATTALION
IDM the 'company sb keeps the people that sb spends time with: Judging by the company he kept, Mark must have been a wealthy man. get into/keep bad 'company to be friends with people that others disapprove of in company with sb/sth (formal) together with or at the same time as sb/sth: She arrived in company with the ship's captain. ◊ The US dollar went through a difficult time, in company with the oil market. in good 'company if you say that sb is in good company, you mean that they should not worry about a mistake, etc. because sb else, especially sb more important, has done the same thing keep sb 'company to stay with sb so that they are not alone: I'll keep you company while you're waiting. two's 'company (, three's a 'crowd) (saying) used to suggest that it is better to be in a group of only two people than have a third person with you as well—more at PART v., PRESENT adj.

com·par·able /ˈkɒmpərəbl; AmE ˈkɑːm-/ adj. ~ (to/with sb/sth) similar to sb/sth else and able to be compared: A comparable house in the south of the city would cost twice as much. ◊ The situation in the US is not directly comparable to that in the UK. ◊ Inflation is now at a rate comparable with that in other European countries. ▶ **com·par·abil·ity** /ˌkɒmpərəˈbɪləti; AmE ˌkɑːm-/ noun [U]: Each group will have the same set of questions, in order to ensure comparability.

com·para·tive /kəmˈpærətɪv/ adj., noun
■ adj. **1** connected with studying things to find out how similar or different they are: comparative linguistics ◊ a comparative study of the educational systems of two countries **2** measured or judged by how similar or different it is to sth else: Then he was living in comparative comfort (= compared with others or with his own life at a previous time). ◊ The company is a comparative newcomer to the software market (= other companies have been in business much longer). **3** (grammar) relating to adjectives or adverbs that express more in amount, degree or quality, for example better, worse, slower and more difficult—compare SUPERLATIVE
■ noun (grammar) the form of an adjective or adverb that expresses more in amount, degree or quality: 'Better' is the comparative of 'good' and 'more difficult' is the comparative of 'difficult'.—compare SUPERLATIVE

com·para·tive·ly /kəmˈpærətɪvli/ adv. as compared to sth/sb else: The unit is comparatively easy to install and cheap to operate. ◊ We prefer to work with a comparatively small number of clients. ◊ He died comparatively young (=

at a younger age than most people die). ◊ *comparatively few/low/rare/recent*

com·pare /kəmˈpeə(r); AmE -ˈper/ *verb, noun*

■ *verb* **1** (*abbr.* **cf., cp.**) [VN] ~ **A and B** | ~ **A with/to B** to examine people or things to see how they are similar and how they are different: *It is interesting to compare their situation and ours.* ◊ *We compared the two reports carefully.* ◊ *We carefully compared the first report with the second.* ◊ *My own problems seem insignificant compared with other people's.* ◊ *Standards in health care have improved enormously compared to 40 years ago.* **2** [V] ~ **with/to sb/sth** to be similar to sb/sth else, either better or worse: *This school compares with the best in the country* (= it is as good as them). ◊ *This house doesn't compare with our previous one* (= it is not as good). ◊ *I've had some difficulties, but they were nothing compared to yours* (= they were not nearly as bad as yours). ◊ *Their prices compare favourably with those of their competitors.* **3** [VN] ~ **A to B** to show or state that sb/sth is similar to sb/sth else: *The critics compared his work to that of Martin Amis.* **IDM** **compare ˈnotes (with sb)** if two or more people **compare notes**, they each say what they think about the same event, situation, etc.

■ *noun* **IDM** **beyond/without comˈpare** (*literary*) better than anything else of the same kind: *a diamond beyond compare*

com·pari·son /kəmˈpærɪsn/ *noun* **1** [U] ~ **(with sb/sth)** the process of comparing two or more people or things: *Comparison with other oil-producing countries is extremely interesting.* ◊ *I enclose the two plans for comparison.* ◊ *The education system bears/stands no comparison with that in many Eastern European countries* (= it is not as good). **2** [C] ~ **(of A and/to/with B)** | ~ **(between A and B)** an occasion when two or more people or things are compared: *a comparison of the rail systems in Britain and France* ◊ *comparisons between Britain and the rest of Europe* ◊ *a comparison of men's salaries with those of women* ◊ *It is difficult to make a comparison with her previous book—they are completely different.* ◊ *You can draw comparisons with the situation in Ireland* (= say how the two situations are similar). ◊ *a comparison of the brain to a computer* (= showing similarities). **IDM** **by comparison** (*written*) used especially at the beginning of a sentence when the next thing that is mentioned is compared with sth in the previous sentence: *By comparison, expenditure on education increased last year.* **by/in comparison (with sb/sth)** when compared with sb/sth: *The second half of the game was dull by comparison with the first.* ◊ *The tallest buildings in London are small in comparison with New York's skyscrapers.* **there's no comˈparison** used to emphasize the difference between two people or things that are being compared: *In terms of price there's no comparison* (= one thing is much more expensive than the other).—more at PALE *v.*

com·part·ment /kəmˈpɑːtmənt; AmE -ˈpɑːrt-/ *noun* **1** one of the separate sections which a railway carriage is divided into **2** one of the separate sections that sth such as a piece of furniture or equipment has for keeping things in: *The desk has a secret compartment.* ◊ *There is a handy storage compartment beneath the oven.*—see also GLOVE COMPARTMENT·

com·part·men·tal·ize (*BrE* also **-ise**) /ˌkɒmpɑːtˈmentəlaɪz; AmE kəmˌpɑːrt-ˈ-/ *verb* [VN] ~ **sth (into sth)** (*written*) to divide sth into separate sections, especially so that one thing does not affect the other: *Life today is rigidly compartmentalized into work and leisure.*

com·pass /ˈkʌmpəs/ *noun* **1** (also **magˌnetic ˈcompass**) [C] an instrument for finding direction, with a needle that always points to the north: *a map and compass* ◊ *the points of the compass* (= N, S, E, W, etc.) **2** [C] (also **com·passes** [pl.]) an instrument with two long thin parts joined together at the top, used for drawing circles and measuring distances on a map: *a pair of compasses* **3** [sing.] (*formal*) a range or an extent, especially of what can be achieved in a particular situation: *We need to bring research techniques within the compass of normal teaching.* ◊ *the compass of a singer's voice* (= the range from the lowest to the highest note that he or she can sing)

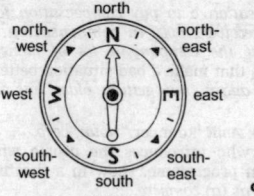
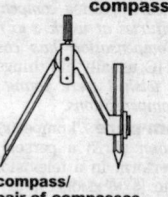

compass

compass

compass/
pair of compasses

com·pas·sion /kəmˈpæʃn/ *noun* [U] ~ **(for sb)** a strong feeling of sympathy for people who are suffering and a desire to help them: *to feel/show compassion*

com·pas·sion·ate /kəmˈpæʃənət/ *adj.* feeling or showing sympathy for people who are suffering: *He was allowed to go home on compassionate grounds* (= because he was suffering). ► **com·pas·sion·ate·ly** *adv.*

comˌpassionate ˈleave *noun* [U] (*BrE*) time that you are allowed to be away from work because sb in your family is ill/sick or has died, or for other personal reasons

com·pati·bil·ity /kəmˌpætəˈbɪləti/ *noun* [U] ~ **(with sb/sth)** | ~ **(between A and B)** **1** the ability of people or things to live together without problems **2** the ability of machines, especially computers, and computer programs to be used together

com·pat·ible /kəmˈpætəbl/ *adj.* ~ **(with sb/sth)** **1** (of machines, especially computers) able to be used together: *compatible software* ◊ *The new system will be compatible with existing equipment.* **2** (of ideas, methods or things) able to exist or be used together without causing problems: *Are measures to protect the environment compatible with economic growth?* ◊ *compatible blood groups* **3** if two people are **compatible**, they can have a good relationship because they have similar ideas, interests, etc. ► **com·pat·ibly** /-əbli/ *adv.*

com·pat·riot /kəmˈpætriət; AmE -ˈpeɪt-/ *noun* a person who was born in, or is a citizen of, the same country as sb else [SYN] COUNTRYMAN: *He played against one of his compatriots in the semi-final.*

com·pel /kəmˈpel/ *verb* (**-ll-**) (*formal*) **1** to force sb to do sth; to make sth necessary: [VNtoinf] *The law can compel fathers to make regular payments for their children.* ◊ *I feel compelled to write and tell you how much I enjoyed your book.* ◊ [VN] *Last year ill health compelled his retirement.* **2** [VN] (not used in the progressive tenses) to cause a particular reaction: *He spoke with an authority that compelled the attention of the whole crowd.*—see also COMPULSION

com·pel·ling /kəmˈpelɪŋ/ *adj.* (*written*) **1** that makes you pay attention to it because it is so interesting and exciting: *Her latest book makes compelling reading.* **2** so strong that you must do sth about it: *a compelling need/desire* **3** that makes you think it is true: *There is no compelling reason to believe him.* ◊ *compelling evidence* ► **com·pel·ling·ly** *adv.: compellingly attractive*

com·pen·dium /kəmˈpendiəm/ *noun* (*pl.* **com·pen·dia** /-diə/ or **com·pen·diums**) a collection of facts, drawings and photographs on a particular subject, especially in a book: *a compendium of natural history*

com·pen·sate /ˈkɒmpenseɪt; AmE ˈkɑːm-/ *verb* **1** [V] ~ **(for sth)** to provide sth good to balance or reduce the bad effects of damage, loss, etc. [SYN] MAKE UP FOR: *Nothing can compensate for the loss of a loved one.* **2** [VN] ~ **sb (for sth)** to pay sb money because they have suffered some damage, loss, injury, etc: *Her lawyers say she should be compensated both for her injuries and for the suffering she had been caused.* ► **com·pen·sa·tory** /ˌkɒmpenˈseɪtəri; AmE kəmˈpensətɔːri/ *adj.: He received a compensatory payment of $20000.*

com·pen·sa·tion /ˌkɒmpenˈseɪʃn; AmE ˌkɑːm-/ *noun* ~ **(for sth)** **1** [U, C] something, especially money, that sb gives you because they have hurt you, or damaged sth that you own; the act of giving this to sb: *to claim/*

æ	ɑː	e	ɜː	ə	ɪ	iː	i	ɒ	ɔː	ʌ	ʊ	u	uː
cat	father	ten	bird	about	sit	see	many	got	saw	cup	put	actual	too
								(BrE)					

award / receive compensation ◊ to pay compensation for injuries at work ◊ to receive £10000 **in compensation**. ◊ Compensation has cost the company a lot of money. **2** [C, usually pl.] things that make a bad situation better: I wish I were young again, but getting older has its compensations.

com·père /ˈkɒmpeə(r); AmE ˈkɑːmper/ noun, verb
■ noun (BrE) a person who introduces the people who perform in a television programme, show in a theatre, etc. [SYN] EMCEE: to act as (a) compère
■ verb [VN, V] (BrE) to act as a compère for a show

com·pete /kəmˈpiːt/ verb **1** ~ (with/against sb) (for sth) to try to be more successful or better than sb else who is trying to do the same as you: [V] Several companies are competing for the contract. ◊ We can't compete with them on price. ◊ Young children will usually compete for their mother's attention. ◊ Small traders cannot compete in the face of cheap foreign imports. [also V to inf] **2** [V] ~ (in sth) (against sb) to take part in a contest or game: He's hoping to compete in the London marathon.

com·pe·tence /ˈkɒmpɪtəns; AmE ˈkɑːm-/ noun **1** (also less frequent **com·pe·ten·cy**) [U, C] ~ (in sth) | ~ (in doing sth) the ability to do sth well: to gain a high level of competence in English ◊ professional / technical competence **2** [U] (law) the power that a court, an organization or a person has to deal with sth: The judge has to act within the competence of the court. ◊ outside sb's area of competence **3** [C] (also less frequent **com·pe·ten·cy** technical) a skill that you need in a particular job or for a particular task: The syllabus lists the knowledge and competences required at this level.

com·pe·tency /ˈkɒmpɪtənsi; AmE ˈkɑːm-/ noun (pl. -ies) = COMPETENCE

com·pe·tent /ˈkɒmpɪtənt; AmE ˈkɑːm-/ adj. ~ (to do sth) **1** having enough skill or knowledge to do sth well or to the necessary standard: Make sure the firm is competent to carry out the work. ◊ He's very competent in his work. ◊ a highly confident and competent teacher [OPP] INCOMPETENT **2** having the power to decide sth: the case was referred to a competent authority ▶ **com·pe·tent·ly** adv.: to perform competently

com·pe·ti·tion /ˌkɒmpəˈtɪʃn; AmE ˌkɑːm-/ noun **1** ~ (between/with sb) | ~ (for sth) [U] a situation in which people or organizations compete with each other for sth that not everyone can have: There is now intense competition between schools to attract students. ◊ We are **in competition with** four other companies for the contract. ◊ We won the contract in the face of **stiff competition**. **2** [C] an event in which people compete with each other to find out who is the best at sth: a music / photo / swimming competition ◊ to enter / win / lose a competition **3** (**the competition**) [sing. + sing./pl. v.] the people who are competing against sb: We'll be able to assess the competition at the conference.

com·peti·tive /kəmˈpetətɪv/ adj. **1** used to describe a situation in which people or organizations compete against each other: competitive games / sports ◊ Graduates have to fight for jobs in a highly competitive market. **2** ~ (with sb/sth) as good as or better than others: a shop selling clothes at competitive prices (= as low as any other shop) ◊ We need to work harder to remain competitive with other companies. ◊ to gain a competitive advantage over rival companies [OPP] UNCOMPETITIVE **3** (of a person) trying very hard to be better than others: You have to be highly competitive to do well in sport these days. ▶ **com·peti·tive·ly** adv.: competitively priced goods **com·peti·tive·ness** noun: an attempt to improve the competitiveness of British industry

com·peti·tor /kəmˈpetɪtə(r)/ noun [C] **1** a person or an organization that competes against others, especially in business: our main / major / nearest competitor ◊ We produce cheaper goods than our competitors. **2** a person who takes part in a competition: Over 200 competitors entered the race.

com·pil·ation /ˌkɒmpɪˈleɪʃn; AmE ˌkɑːm-/ noun **1** [C] a collection of items, especially pieces of music or writing, taken from different places and put together: Her latest CD is a compilation of all her best singles. ◊ a compilation album **2** [U] the process of compiling sth: the compilation of a dictionary

com·pile /kəmˈpaɪl/ verb [VN] **1** to produce a book, list, report, etc. by bringing together different items, articles, songs, etc: We are trying to compile a list of suitable people for the job. ◊ The album was compiled from live recordings from last year's tour. **2** (computing) to translate instructions from one computer language into another so that a particular computer can understand them

com·piler /kəmˈpaɪlə(r)/ noun **1** a person who compiles sth **2** (computing) a program that translates instructions from one computer language into another for a computer to understand

com·pla·cency /kəmˈpleɪsnsi/ noun [U] (usually disapproving) a feeling of satisfaction with yourself or with a situation, so that you do not think any change is necessary; the state of being complacent: His early success as a writer led to complacency and arrogance. ◊ Despite signs of an improvement in the economy, there is no room for complacency.

com·pla·cent /kəmˈpleɪsnt/ adj. ~ (about sb/sth) (usually disapproving) too satisfied with yourself or with a situation, so that you do not feel that any change is necessary; showing or feeling complacency: a complacent smile ◊ a dangerously complacent attitude to the increase in unemployment ◊ We must not become complacent about progress. ▶ **com·pla·cent·ly** adv.: to nod / smile / speak complacently

com·plain /kəmˈpleɪn/ verb ~ (to sb) (about/of sth) to say that you are annoyed, unhappy or not satisfied about sb/sth: [V] I'm going to complain to the manager about this. ◊ She never complains, but she's obviously exhausted. ◊ The defendant complained of intimidation during the investigation. ◊ (spoken) 'How are you?' 'Oh, I can't complain (= I'm all right).' ◊ [V (that)] He complained bitterly that he had been unfairly treated. ◊ [V speech] 'It's not fair,' she complained. [PHRV] **comˈplain of sth** to say that you feel ill or are suffering from a pain: She left early, complaining of a headache.

com·plain·ant noun (BrE) = PLAINTIFF

com·plaint /kəmˈpleɪnt/ noun **1** [C] ~ (about/against sb/sth) | ~ (that…) a reason for not being satisfied; a statement that sb makes saying that they are not satisfied: The most common complaint is about poor service. ◊ We received a number of complaints from customers about the lack of parking facilities. ◊ I believe you have a complaint against one of our nurses. ◊ I'd like to **make a complaint** about the noise. ◊ a **formal complaint** ◊ a complaint that he had been unfairly treated ◊ (formal) to file / lodge (= make) a complaint **2** [U] the act of complaining: I can see no **grounds for complaint**. ◊ a letter of complaint **3** [C] an illness, especially one that is not serious, and often one that affects a particular part of the body: a skin complaint

com·plai·sant /kəmˈpleɪzənt/ adj. (old-fashioned) ready to accept other people's actions and opinions and to do what other people want ▶ **com·plai·sance** /kəmˈpleɪzəns/ noun [U]

com·plect·ed /kəmˈplektɪd/ adj. (AmE, informal) (used with adjectives) with skin and a COMPLEXION of the type mentioned: fair / dark complected

com·ple·ment verb, noun
■ verb /ˈkɒmplɪment; AmE ˈkɑːm-/ [VN] to add to sth in a way that improves it or makes it more attractive: The excellent menu is complemented by a good wine list. ◊ The team needs players who complement each other. ⇨ note at COMPLIMENT
■ noun /ˈkɒmplɪmənt; AmE ˈkɑːm-/ **1** ~ (to sth) a thing that adds new qualities to sth in a way that improves it or makes it more attractive **2** the complete number or quantity needed or allowed: We've taken our full complement of trainees this year. **3** (grammar) a word or words, especially an adjective or a noun, that is used after linking verbs such as be and become, and describes the subject of the verb: In the sentences 'I'm angry' and 'He became a politician.', 'angry' and 'politician' are complements.

com·ple·men·tary /ˌkɒmplɪˈmentri; AmE ˌkɑːm-/ adj.

aɪ	aʊ	eɪ	əʊ	oʊ	ɔɪ	ɪə	eə	ʊə	j	w
my	now	say	go	go	boy	near	hair	pure	yes	wet
			(BrE)	(AmE)						

~ (to sth) two people or things that are **complementary** are different but together form a useful or attractive combination of skills, qualities or physical features: *The school's approach must be complementary to that of the parents.* ⇨ note at COMPLIMENT

ˌcomplementary ˈangle *noun* (*geometry*) either of two angles which together make 90°

ˌcomplementary ˈmedicine *noun* [U] (*BrE*) medical treatment that is not part of the usual scientific treatment used in Western countries, for example ACUPUNCTURE

com·plete /kəmˈpliːt/ *adj., verb*
■ *adj.* **1** [usually before noun] used when you are emphasizing sth, to mean 'to the greatest degree possible' [SYN] TOTAL: *We were in complete agreement.* ◊ *a complete change* ◊ *in complete silence* ◊ *a complete stranger* ◊ *It came as a complete surprise.* ◊ *I felt a complete idiot.* **2** including all the parts, etc. that are necessary; whole: *I've collected the complete set.* ◊ *a complete guide to events in Oxford* ◊ *the* **complete works** *of Tolstoy* ◊ *You will receive payment for each complete day that you work.* [OPP] INCOMPLETE **3 ~ with sth** [not before noun] including sth as an extra part or feature: *The furniture comes complete with tools and instructions for assembly.* ◊ *The book, complete with cassette, costs £35.* **4** [not before noun] finished: *Work on the office building will be complete at the end of the year.* [OPP] INCOMPLETE ▶ **com·plete·ness** *noun* [U]: *the accuracy and completeness of the information* ◊ *For the sake of completeness, all names are given in full.*
■ *verb* [VN] **1** [often passive] to finish making or doing sth: *She's just completed a master's degree in Law.* ◊ *The project should be completed within a year.* **2** to write all the information you are asked for on a form: *2000 shoppers completed our questionnaire.* **3** to make sth whole or perfect: *I only need one more card to complete the set.*

com·plete·ly /kəmˈpliːtli/ *adv.* (used to emphasize the following word or phrase) in every way possible [SYN] TOTALLY: *completely different* ◊ *completely and utterly broke* ◊ *I've completely forgotten her name.* ◊ *The explosion completely destroyed the building.*

com·ple·tion /kəmˈpliːʃn/ *noun* **1** [U] the act or process of finishing sth; the state of being finished and complete: *the completion of the new hospital building* ◊ *Satisfactory completion of the course does not ensure you a job.* ◊ *The project is* **due for completion** *in the spring.* ◊ *The road is* **nearing completion** (= it is nearly finished). ◊ *the date of completion / the completion date* **2** [U, C] (*BrE*) the formal act of completing the sale of property, for example the sale of a house

com·plex *adj., noun*
■ *adj.* /ˈkɒmpleks; *AmE* kəmˈpleks; ˈkɑːm-/ **1** made of many different things or parts that are connected; difficult to understand: *complex machinery* ◊ *the complex structure of the human brain* ◊ *a complex argument / problem / subject* **2** (*grammar*) (of a word or sentence) containing one main part (= the ROOT of a word or MAIN CLAUSE of a sentence) and one or more other parts (AFFIXES or SUBORDINATE CLAUSES)—compare COMPOUND *adj.*
■ *noun* /ˈkɒmpleks; *AmE* ˈkɑːm-/ **1** a group of buildings of a similar type together in one place: *a sports complex* ◊ *an apartment complex* ◊ *an industrial complex* (= a site with many factories) **2** a group of things that are connected: *This is just one of a whole complex of issues.* **3** (especially in compounds) a mental state that is not normal: *to suffer from a guilt complex*—see also INFERIORITY COMPLEX, OEDIPUS COMPLEX, PERSECUTION COMPLEX **4** if sb has a **complex** about sth, they are worried about it in way that is not normal

com·plex·ion /kəmˈplekʃn/ *noun* **1** the natural colour and condition of the skin on a person's face: *a pale / bad complexion* **2** [usually sing.] the general character of sth: *a move which changed the political complexion of the northern states* [IDM] **put a new / different ˈcomplexion on sth** to change the way that a situation appears

com·plex·ity /kəmˈpleksəti/ *noun* **1** [U] the state of being formed of many parts; the state of being difficult to understand: *the increasing complexity of modern telecom-*

munication systems ◊ *I was astonished by the size and complexity of the problem.* **2** (**complexities**) [pl.] the features of a problem or situation that are difficult to understand: *the complexities of the system*

com·pli·ance /kəmˈplaɪəns/ *noun* [U] **~ (with sth)** (*written*) the practice of obeying rules or requests made by people in authority: *procedures that must be followed to ensure full compliance with the law* ◊ *Safety measures were carried out* **in compliance with** *paragraph 6 of the building regulations.* [OPP] NON-COMPLIANCE—see also COMPLY

com·pli·ant /kəmˈplaɪənt/ *adj.* (*written*) **1** (usually *disapproving*) willing to agree with other people or to obey rules: *By then, Henry seemed less compliant with his wife's wishes than he had six months before.* ◊ *We should not be producing compliant students who do not dare to criticize.* **2** in agreement with a set of rules: *computer software that is year 2000 compliant*—see also COMPLY

com·pli·cate /ˈkɒmplɪkeɪt; *AmE* ˈkɑːm-/ *verb* [VN] to make sth more difficult to do, understand or deal with: *I do not wish to complicate the task more than is necessary.* ◊ **To complicate matters** *further, there will be no transport available till 8 o'clock.* ◊ *The issue* **is complicated by the fact that** *a vital document is missing.*

com·pli·cated /ˈkɒmplɪkeɪtɪd; *AmE* ˈkɑːm-/ *adj.* made of many different things or parts that are connected; difficult to understand: *a complicated system* ◊ *The instructions look very complicated.* ◊ *The story is extremely complicated.* ◊ *It's all very complicated—but I'll try and explain.*

com·pli·ca·tion /ˌkɒmplɪˈkeɪʃn; *AmE* ˌkɑːm-/ *noun* **1** [C, U] a thing that makes a situation more complicated or difficult: *The bad weather added a further complication to our journey.* **2** [C, usually pl.] (*medical*) a new problem or illness that makes treatment of a previous one more complicated or difficult: *She developed complications after the surgery.*

com·pli·city /kəmˈplɪsəti/ *noun* [U] **~ (in sth)** (*formal*) the act of taking part with another person in a crime [SYN] COLLUSION: *to be guilty of complicity in the murder* ◊ *evident complicity between the two brothers*

com·pli·ment *noun, verb*
■ *noun* /ˈkɒmplɪmənt; *AmE* ˈkɑːm-/ **1** [C] a remark that expresses praise or admiration of sb: **to pay sb a compliment** (= to praise them for sth) ◊ *'You understand the problem because you're so much older.' 'I'll* **take that as a compliment!'** ◊ *It's a great compliment to be asked to do the job.* ◊ **to return the compliment** (= to treat sb in the same way as they have treated you) **2** (**compliments**) [pl.] (*formal*) greetings, especially when used to express praise and admiration: *My compliments to the chef!* ◊ (*BrE*) *Compliments of the season!* (= for Christmas or the New Year) ◊ *Please accept these flowers* **with the compliments of** (= as a gift from) *the manager.* [IDM] see BACKHANDED
■ *verb* /ˈkɒmplɪment; *AmE* ˈkɑːm-/ [VN] **~ sb (on sth)** to tell sb that you like or admire sth they have done, their appearance, etc: *She complimented him on his excellent German.*

> **WHICH WORD?**
> **compliment / complement**
>
> These words have similar spellings but completely different meanings. If you **compliment** someone, you say something very nice to them: *She complimented me on my English.* If one thing **complements** another, the two things work or look better because they are together: *The different flavours complement each other perfectly.*
> The adjectives are also often confused.
> **Complimentary**: *She made some very complimentary remarks about my English.* It can also mean 'free': *There was a complimentary basket of fruit in our room.* **Complementary**: *The team members have different but complementary skills.*

com·pli·men·tary /ˌkɒmplɪˈmentri; *AmE* ˌkɑːm-/ *adj.* **1** given free of charge: *complimentary tickets for the show* **2 ~ (about sth)** expressing admiration, praise, etc: *a* *complimentary remark* ◊ *She was extremely complimentary about his work.*—compare UNCOMPLIMENTARY ⇨ note at COMPLIMENT

'compliments slip *noun* a small piece of paper printed with the name of a company, that is sent out together with information, goods, etc.·

com·ply /kəm'plaɪ/ *verb* (**com·plies, com·ply·ing, com·plied, com·plied**) [V] **~ (with sth)** to obey a rule, an order, etc: *They refused to comply with the UN resolution.*—see also COMPLIANCE

com·pon·ent /kəm'pəʊnənt; AmE -'poʊ-/ *noun* one of several parts of which sth is made: *the components of a machine* ◊ *the car component industry* ◊ *Key components of the government's plan are ...* ◊ *Trust is a vital component in any relationship.* ▶ **com·pon·ent** *adj.* [only before noun]: *to break sth down into its component parts*

com·port /kəm'pɔːt; AmE -'pɔːrt/ *verb* [VN+*adv./prep.*] (**~ yourself**) (*formal*) to behave in a particular way: *She always comports herself with great dignity.*

com·pose /kəm'pəʊz; AmE -'poʊz/ *verb* **1** [VN] [no passive] (not used in the progressive tenses) (*formal*) to combine together to form a whole: *Ten men compose the committee.*—see also COMPOSED ⇨ note at COMPRISE **2** to write music: [VN] *Mozart composed his last opera shortly before he died.* [also V] **3** [VN] **~ a letter/speech/poem** to write a letter, etc. usually with a lot of care and thought: *She composed a letter of protest.* **4** [VN] [no passive] (*formal*) to manage to control your feelings or expression: *Emma frowned, making an effort to **compose herself.*** ◊ *I was so confused that I could hardly compose my thoughts.*—see also COMPOSURE

com·posed /kəm'pəʊzd; AmE -'poʊzd/ *adj.* **1** (**be composed of sth**) to be made or formed from several parts, things or people: *The committee is composed mainly of lawyers.* **2** [not usually before noun] calm and in control of your feelings: *She seemed outwardly composed.*

com·poser /kəm'pəʊzə(r); AmE -'poʊz-/ *noun* a person who writes music, especially classical music

com·pos·ite /'kɒmpəzɪt; AmE kəm'pɑːzət/ *adj., noun*
■ *adj.* [only before noun] made of different parts or materials: *a composite picture* (= one made from several pictures)
■ *noun* **1** something made by putting together different parts or materials: *The document was a composite of information from various sources.* **2** (*AmE*) = IDENTIKIT

com·pos·ition /ˌkɒmpə'zɪʃn; AmE ˌkɑːm-/ *noun* **1** [U] the different parts which sth is made of; the way in which the different parts are organized: *the chemical composition of the soil* ◊ *the composition of the board of directors* ◊ *the size and composition of an average class* **2** [C] a piece of music or art, or a poem: *one of Beethoven's finest compositions* **3** [U] the act of COMPOSING sth: *pieces performed in the order of their composition* **4** [U] the art of writing music: *to study composition* **5** [C] a short text that is written as a school exercise; a short ESSAY **6** [U] (*art*) the arrangement of people or objects in a painting or photograph

com·pos men·tis /ˌkɒmpəs 'mentɪs; AmE ˌkɑːm-/ *adj.* [not before noun] (from *Latin, formal* or *humorous*) having full control of your mind: *Are you sure she was fully compos mentis when she said it?*

com·post /'kɒmpɒst; AmE 'kɑːmpoʊst/ *noun, verb*
■ *noun* [U, C] a mixture of decayed plants, food, etc. that can be added to soil to help plants grow: *potting compost* (= a mixture of soil and compost that you can buy to grow new plants in) ◊ *a compost heap* (= a place in the garden where leaves, plants, etc. are piled, to make compost)
■ *verb* [VN] **1** to make sth into compost **2** to put compost on or in sth

com·pos·ure /kəm'pəʊʒə(r); AmE -'poʊ-/ *noun* [U] the state of being calm and in control of your feelings or behaviour: *to keep/lose/recover/regain your composure*

com·pote /'kɒmpɒt; AmE 'kɑːmpoʊt/ *noun* [C, U] a cold DESSERT (= a sweet dish) made of fruit that has been cooked slowly with sugar

com·pound *noun, adj., verb*

■ *noun* /'kɒmpaʊnd; AmE 'kɑːm-/ **1** a thing consisting of two or more separate things combined together **2** (*chemistry*) a substance formed by a chemical reaction of two or more elements in fixed amounts relative to each other: *Common salt is a compound of sodium and chlorine.*—compare ELEMENT, MIXTURE **3** (*grammar*) a noun, an adjective or a verb made of two or more words or parts of words, written as one or more words, or joined by a HYPHEN. *Travel agent, dark-haired* and *bathroom* are all compounds. **4** an area surrounded by a fence or wall in which a factory or other group of buildings stands: *a prison compound*
■ *adj.* /'kɒmpaʊnd; AmE 'kɑːm-/ [not before noun] (*technical*) formed of two or more parts: *a compound adjective, such as fair-skinned* ◊ *A compound sentence contains two or more clauses.* ◊ *the compound eye of a wasp*
■ *verb* /kəm'paʊnd/ [VN] **1** [often passive] (*written*) to make sth bad become even worse by causing further harm: *The problems were compounded by severe food shortages.* **2** (**be compounded of/from sth**) (*formal*) to be formed from sth: *The DNA molecule is compounded from many smaller molecules.* **3** [often passive] (*formal* or *technical*) to mix sth together: *liquid soaps compounded with disinfectant* **4** (*finance*) to pay or charge interest on an amount of money that includes any interest already earned or charged

ˌcompound 'fracture *noun* an injury in which a bone in the body is broken and part of the bone comes through the skin—compare SIMPLE FRACTURE

ˌcompound 'interest *noun* [U] interest that is paid both on the original amount of money saved and on the interest that has been added to it—compare SIMPLE INTEREST

com·pre·hend /ˌkɒmprɪ'hend; AmE ˌkɑːm-/ *verb* (often used in negative sentences) (*formal*) to understand sth fully: [VN] *The infinite distances of space are too great for the human mind to comprehend.* ◊ [V wh-] *She could not comprehend how someone would risk people's lives in that way.* ◊ [V] *He stood staring at the dead body, unable to comprehend.* [also V that]

com·pre·hen·sible /ˌkɒmprɪ'hensəbl; AmE ˌkɑːm-/ *adj.* **~ (to sb)** (*formal*) that can be understood by sb: *easily/readily comprehensible to the average reader* ▶ **com·pre·hen·sib·il·ity** /ˌkɒmprɪˌhensə'bɪləti; AmE ˌkɑːm-/ *noun* [U]

com·pre·hen·sion /ˌkɒmprɪ'henʃn; AmE ˌkɑːm-/ *noun* [U, C] **1** [U] (especially *written*) the ability to understand: *speech and comprehension* ◊ *The task requires a good comprehension of complex instructions.* ◊ *His behaviour was completely beyond comprehension* (= impossible to understand). ◊ *She had no comprehension of what was involved.* **2** an exercise that trains students to understand a language: *listening comprehension* ◊ *a reading comprehension*

com·pre·hen·sive /ˌkɒmprɪ'hensɪv; AmE ˌkɑːm-/ *adj., noun*
■ *adj.* **1** including all, or almost all, the items, details, facts, information, etc., that may be concerned: *a comprehensive list of addresses* ◊ *a comprehensive report/study/survey* ◊ *comprehensive insurance* (= covering all risks) **2** (*BrE*) (of education) designed for students of all abilities in the same school ▶ **com·pre·hen·sive·ness** *noun* [U]
■ *noun* (also **compre'hensive school**) (in Britain) a secondary school for young people of all levels of ability

com·pre·hen·sive·ly /ˌkɒmprɪ'hensɪvli; AmE ˌkɑːm-/ *adv.* completely; thoroughly: *They were comprehensively beaten in the final.* ◊ *The matter has been comprehensively discussed.*

com·press *verb, noun*
■ *verb* /kəm'pres/ **1 ~ (sth) (into sth)** to press or squeeze sth together or into a smaller space; to be pressed or squeezed in this way: [VN] *compressed air/gas* ◊ [V] *Her lips compressed into a thin line.* **2** [VN] **~ sth (into sth)** to reduce sth and fit it into a smaller space or amount of time [SYN] CONDENSE: *The main arguments were compressed into one chapter.* **3** [VN] (*computing*) to make com-

puter files, etc. smaller so that they use less space on a disk, etc. OPP DECOMPRESS ► **com·pres·sion** /kəmˈpreʃn/ *noun* [U]: *the compression of air* ◊ *data compression*

■ *noun* /ˈkɒmpres; *AmE* ˈkɑːm-/ a cloth that is pressed onto a part of the body to stop bleeding, reduce pain, etc.: *to apply a cold compress*

com·pres·sor /kəmˈpresə(r)/ *noun* a machine that compresses air or other gases

com·prise /kəmˈpraɪz/ *verb* [VN] (not used in the progressive tenses) **1** (also **be comprised of**) to have sb/sth as parts or members; to consist of sb/sth: *The collection comprises 327 paintings.* ◊ *The committee is comprised of representatives from both the public and private sectors.* **2** to be the parts or members that form sth SYN MAKE STH UP: *Older people comprise a large proportion of those living in poverty.*

┌───┐
│ **WHICH WORD?**   (?) │
│ **comprise / compose / consist of /**   │
│ **constitute / make up / include**   │
├───┤
│ When you want to mention the different parts that│
│ something is formed from, you can say that   │
│ something **comprises, consists of, is composed**│
│ **of** or **is made up of** a number of different│
│ things: *The committee comprises/consists of two*│
│ *lawyers, two journalists and a teacher.* You can│
│ also say **is comprised of**, though this use is │
│ often avoided in written English. It is not   │
│ correct to use *comprises of* or *is composed by/*│
│ *from.*   │
│ When you mention first all the parts that together│
│ form the whole, **constitute, compose** and **make**│
│ **up** are used. *Two lawyers, two journalists and*│
│ *a head teacher compose/constitute the committee.*│
│ **Comprise** can be used in this way but is less │
│ common.   │
│ You use **include** if you only mention some of │
│ the parts: *The committee includes two lawyers.* │
│ These verbs are not used in the progressive   │
│ tenses.   │
└───┘

com·prom·ise /ˈkɒmprəmaɪz; *AmE* ˈkɑːm-/ *noun, verb*
■ *noun* **1** [C] an agreement made between two people or groups in which each side gives up some of the things they want so that both sides are happy at the end: *After lengthy talks the two sides finally reached a compromise.* ◊ *In any relationship, you have to make compromises.* ◊ *a compromise solution/agreement/candidate* **2** [C] ~ **(between A and B)** a solution to a problem in which two or more things cannot exist together as they are, in which each thing is reduced or changed slightly so that they can exist together: *This model represents the best compromise between price and quality.* **3** [U] the act of reaching a compromise: *Compromise is an inevitable part of life.* ◊ *There is no prospect of compromise in sight.*
■ *verb* **1** [V] ~ **(with sb) (on sth)** to give up some of your demands after a dispute with sb, in order to reach an agreement: *Neither side is prepared to compromise.* ◊ *After much argument, the judges finally compromised on (= agreed to give the prize to) the 18-year old pianist.* ◊ *They were unwilling to compromise with the Communists.* **2** ~ **(on sth)** to do sth that is against your principles or does not reach standards that you have set: [VN] *I refuse to compromise my principles.* ◊ [V] *We are not prepared to compromise on safety standards.* **3** [VN] ~ **sb/sth/yourself** to bring sb/sth/yourself into danger or under suspicion, especially by acting in a way that is not very sensible: *She had already compromised herself by accepting his invitation.* ◊ *Defeat at this stage would compromise their chances (= reduce their chances) of reaching the finals of the competition.*

com·prom·is·ing /ˈkɒmprəmaɪzɪŋ; *AmE* ˈkɑːm-/ *adj.* if sth is **compromising**, it shows or tells people sth that you want to keep secret, because it is wrong or embarrassing: *compromising photos/circumstances*

comp·trol·ler /kənˈtrəʊlə(r); *AmE* -ˈtroʊ-/ *noun* = CONTROLLER

com·pul·sion /kəmˈpʌlʃn/ *noun* ~ **(to do sth)** **1** [U, C] strong pressure that makes sb do sth that they do not

want to do: *You are under no compulsion to pay immediately.* ◊ *There are no compulsions on students to attend classes.* **2** [C] a strong desire to do sth, especially sth that is wrong, silly or dangerous: *He felt a great compulsion to drive too fast.* ◊ *Obsessions and compulsions often develop in people who live stressful lives.*—see also COMPEL

com·pul·sive /kəmˈpʌlsɪv/ *adj.* **1** (of behaviour) that is difficult to stop or control: *compulsive eating/spending/gambling* **2** (of people) not being able to control their behaviour: *a compulsive drinker/gambler/liar* **3** that makes you pay attention to it because it is so interesting and exciting: *The programme made compulsive viewing.* ► **com·pul·sive·ly** *adv.*: *She watched him compulsively.* ◊ *a compulsively readable book*

com·pul·sory /kəmˈpʌlsəri/ *adj.* that must be done because of a law or a rule: *It is compulsory for all motorcyclists to wear helmets.* ◊ *English is a compulsory subject at this level.* ◊ *compulsory education/schooling* ◊ *compulsory redundancies* OPP VOLUNTARY ► **com·pul·sor·ily** /kəmˈpʌlsərəli/ *adv.*: *Over 600 workers were made compulsorily redundant.*

com·punc·tion /kəmˈpʌŋkʃn/ *noun* [U] (also [C] in *AmE*) ~ **(about doing sth)** (*formal*) a feeling of guilt about doing sth: *She felt no compunction about leaving her job.* ◊ *He had lied to her without compunction.* ◊ (*AmE*) *She has no compunctions about rejecting the plan.*

com·pu·ta·tion /ˌkɒmpjuˈteɪʃn; *AmE* ˌkɑːm-/ *noun* [C, U] (*formal*) an act or the process of calculating sth: *All the statistical computations were performed by the new software system.* ◊ *an error in the computation*

com·pu·ta·tion·al /ˌkɒmpjuˈteɪʃənl; *AmE* ˌkɑːm-/ *adj.* [usually before noun] using or connected with computers: *computational linguistics/theory/methods/skills* ◊ *a computational approach*

com·pute /kəmˈpjuːt/ *verb* [VN] (*formal*) to calculate sth: *The losses were computed at £5 million.*

com·puter /kəmˈpjuːtə(r)/ *noun* an electronic machine that can store, organize and find information, do calculations and control other machines: *a personal computer* ◊ *Our sales information is processed by computer.* ◊ *a computer program* ◊ *computer software/hardware/graphics* ◊ *a computer error* ◊ *computer-aided design*—see also DESKTOP COMPUTER, MICROCOMPUTER, PERSONAL COMPUTER, SUPERCOMPUTER—picture on page 250

comˈputer game *noun* a game played on a computer

com·pu·ter·ize (*BrE* also **-ise**) /kəmˈpjuːtəraɪz/ *verb* [VN] **1** to provide a computer or computers to do the work of sth: *The factory has been fully computerized.* **2** to store information on a computer: *computerized databases/information* ◊ *The firm has computerized its records.* ► **com·pu·ter·iza·tion, -isa·tion** /kəmˌpjuːtəraɪˈzeɪʃn; *AmE* -rəˈz-/ *noun* [U]

comˌputer-ˈliterate *adj.* able to use computers well ► **comˌputer ˈliteracy** *noun* [U]

comˌputer ˈscience *noun* [U] the study of computers and how they can be used: *a degree in computer science* ► **comˌputer ˈscientist** *noun*

com·put·ing /kəmˈpjuːtɪŋ/ *noun* [U] the fact of using computers: *to work in computing* ◊ *to study computing* ◊ *educational/network/scientific computing* ◊ *computing power/services/skills/systems*—picture on pages 250, 251

com·rade /ˈkɒmreɪd; *AmE* ˈkɑːmræd/ *noun* **1** a person who is a member of the same COMMUNIST or SOCIALIST political party as the person speaking: *We must fight for our rights, comrades!* **2** (*BrE* also ˌ**comrade-in-ˈarms**) (*old-fashioned*) a friend or other person that you work with, especially as soldiers during a war: *They were old army comrades.* ► **com·rade·ly** /ˈkɒmreɪdli; *AmE* ˈkɑːmrædli/ *adj.* **com·rade·ship** /ˈkɒmreɪdʃɪp; *AmE* ˈkɑːmræd-/ *noun* [U]: *There was a sense of comradeship between them.*

Con *abbr.* (in British politics) CONSERVATIVE: *Jim Crofton (Con)*

con /kɒn/ *noun, verb*
■ *noun* (*informal*) **1** [sing.] (also *BrE formal* ˈ**confidence trick**) (also *AmE formal* ˈ**confidence game**) a trick; an act of cheating sb: *The so-called bargain was just a big*

Computing

Equipment

- This computer has a **processor speed** of *450 MHz* (= megahertz), *256 Mb* (= megabytes) of **RAM** (= **random access memory**) and a **hard disk capacity** of *13 Gb* (= gigabytes).
- It comes with a *56K* **modem** and a **speech recognition** system.
- The **multimedia** system includes a **sound card** with 3D stereo sound and a **graphics card** with 8 Mb of **video RAM** for a **high resolution** colour **display**.
- With **DVD** (= **digital videodisc** or **digital versatile disk**) you can view photographic quality images.
- You pay extra for the **laser printer, scanner** and other **peripherals**.
- The new **operating system** should be **compatible with** existing **hardware**.

monitor
screen
floppy disk drive
CD-ROM/
DVD-ROM drive
hard disk
(also hard drive)
speaker
floppy disk (also diskette)
CD-ROM/
DVD-ROM
mouse
keyboard
mouse mat (BrE)/
mouse pad (AmE)

Getting started

- **PC users** should **log on** to the **network** by entering their **user name** and **password**.
- **Load** the **program** into the computer.
- **Save** your **files** onto your **hard disk** and **back** them **up** onto **floppies**.
- Important **data** is **stored** on the central **file server**.

When things go wrong

- I can't **log in** – the **server** is **down**.
- The **system** keeps **crashing** – I've lost all my files.
- You'll have to switch off and **reboot**.
- **Error**. User name contains **invalid character**.
- My computer can't **read** this disk.
- The **virus** in the **software** was **programmed** to **corrupt** the hard disk.

User interface

- **Click on** the **window** to make it **active**.
- You can **run** several **applications** at the same time.
- To **create** a new document, **select** New from the File **menu**.
- **Insert** the **cursor** at the beginning of the line.
- Use the **mouse** to **drag** the **icon** to a new position.
- **Scroll** up or down the text by clicking on the **scroll bar**.

- Search and replace **options** are **activated** from the command **prompt**.
- **Interactive** computer **terminals** allow visitors to take an 'electronic walk' through a **virtual** Pompeii.

The Internet

- There is a wide range of **Internet service providers**.
- My free time is spent **surfing the net**.
- It's a **software package** that helps you **browse the Web**.
- This **search engine** indexes over a million **websites**.
- **Do a search on** language schools in the UK.
- When you have found what you want **download** it to your PC.
- Brief summaries are **hyperlinked to** the complete texts.
- The site's **webmaster** says it has over 100 000 **hits** a day.
- This **chat room** is a forum for debating civil liberties issues **online**.
- Are you **online**?
- Do you **have access to** the net?
- Are you contactable **by/via e-mail**?
- Do you have an **e-mail address** / a **web page**?
- My **e-mail address** is 'smithj@oup.co.uk' (said 'Smith J at O-U-P dot co (/kəʊ; AmE koʊ/) dot U-K').
- The **web address** is 'www.oup.com' (said 'double-U, double-U, double-U dot o-u-p dot com /kɒm; AmE kɑːm/).

printer

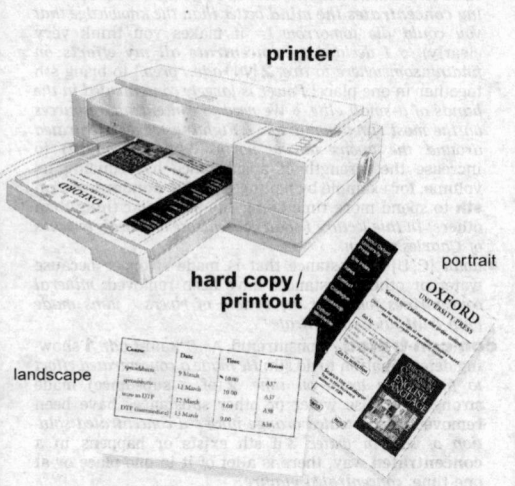

hard copy / printout

portrait

landscape

in box

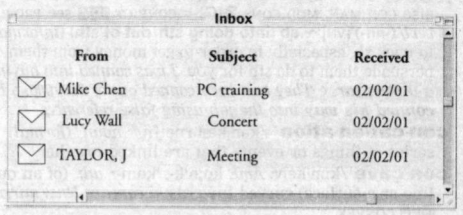

Inbox		
From	**Subject**	**Received**
Mike Chen	PC training	02/02/01
Lucy Wall	Concert	02/02/01
TAYLOR, J	Meeting	02/02/01

CC (= carbon copy: a copy of this message has been sent to:)   address

e-mail

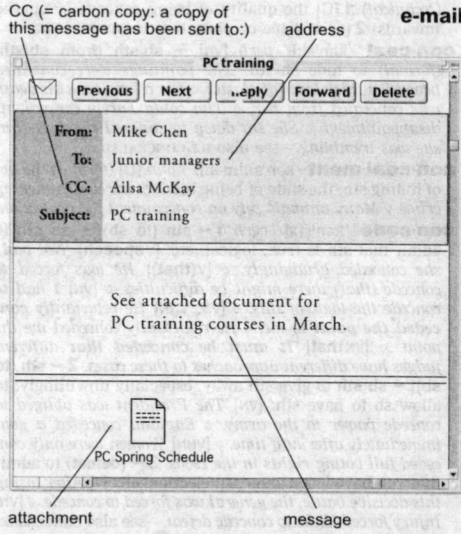

PC training

Previous   Next   Reply   Forward   Delete

From: Mike Chen
To: Junior managers
CC: Ailsa McKay
Subject: PC training

See attached document for
PC training courses in March.

PC Spring Schedule

attachment   message

screen

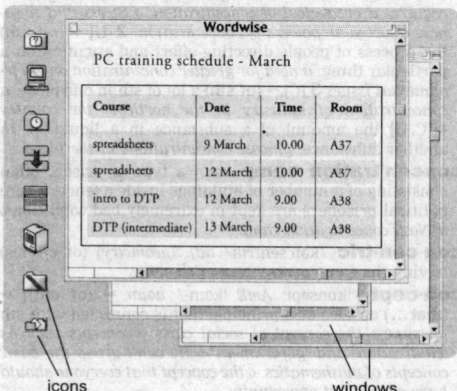

Wordwise

PC training schedule - March

Course	Date	Time	Room
spreadsheets	9 March	10.00	A37
spreadsheets	12 March	10.00	A37
intro to DTP	12 March	9.00	A38
DTP (intermediate)	13 March	9.00	A38

icons   windows

contents   website   web browser   **home page**

application (= a word-processing, database, spreadsheet, etc. program)

pull-down menu   **window**

document   dialog box

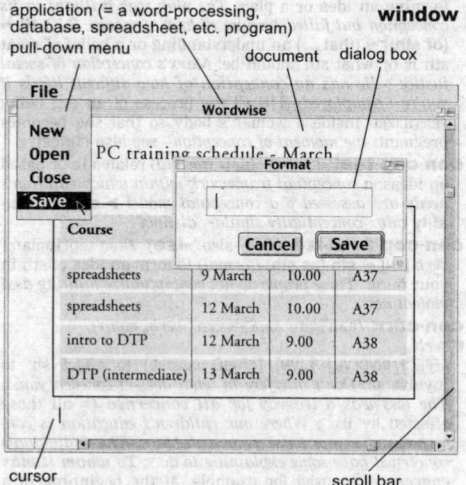

File
New
Open
Close
Save

Wordwise
PC training schedule - March

Format

Cancel   Save

Course			
spreadsheets	9 March	10.00	A37
spreadsheets	12 March	10.00	A37
intro to DTP	12 March	9.00	A38
DTP (intermediate)	13 March	9.00	A38

cursor   scroll bar

Wordwise

Back Forward Print Home Images Stop
Website http://www.oup.com

About Oxford University Press
Site Index
News
Contact
Catalogue
Bookshop
Oxford Worldwide
Oxford English Dictionary

OXFORD
UNIVERSITY PRESS

Search our catalogue and order online

Click here for more details of our online shopping basket and secure credit card payment system

Go to...
Academic and Professional
Children's and School Books
College
Dictionaries and Reference
Electronic Publishing

Go to selection

Search the catalogue
Type in title keyword, author, or ISBN

Search   Help

THE OXFORD COMPANION TO THE ENGLISH LANGUAGE
EDITED BY TOM McARTHUR

link   index

con! ◊ *(BrE) a con trick* ◊ *(AmE) a con game* ◊ *He's a real* **con artist** (= a person who regularly cheats others).—see also CON MAN, MOD CONS **2** [C] = CONVICT **IDM** see PRO *n.*

■ *verb* (-nn-) [VN] ~ **sb** (**into doing sth/out of sth**) (*informal*) to trick sb, especially in order to get money from them or persuade them to do sth for you: *I was conned into buying a useless car.* ◊ *They had been conned out of £100000.* ◊ *He* **conned his way** *into the job using false references.*

con·cat·en·ation /kənˌkætəˈneɪʃn/ *noun* (*formal*) a series of things or events that are linked together

con·cave /kɒnˈkeɪv; *AmE* kɑːnˈk-; ˈkɑːn-/ *adj.* (of an outline or a surface) curved inwards: *a concave lens/mirror* **OPP** CONVEX

con·cav·ity /ˌkɒnˈkævəti; *AmE* ˌkɑːn-/ *noun* (*pl.* -ies) (*technical*) **1** [U] the quality of being concave (= curved inwards) **2** [C] a shape or place that is curved inwards

con·ceal /kənˈsiːl/ *verb* [VN] ~ **sb/sth** (**from sb/sth**) (*formal*) to hide sb/sth: *The paintings were concealed beneath a thick layer of plaster.* ◊ *For a long time his death was concealed from her.* ◊ *Tim could barely conceal his disappointment.* ◊ *She sat down to* **conceal the fact that** *she was trembling.*—see also ILL-CONCEALED

con·ceal·ment /kənˈsiːlmənt/ *noun* [U] (*formal*) the act of hiding sth; the state of being hidden: *the concealment of crime* ◊ *Many animals rely on concealment for protection.*

con·cede /kənˈsiːd/ *verb* **1** ~ **sth** (**to sb**) | ~ **sb sth** to admit that sth is true, logical, etc: [V speech] *'Not bad,'* *she conceded grudgingly.* ◊ [V(**that**)] *He was forced to concede (that) there might be difficulties.* ◊ [VN] *I had to concede the logic of this.* ◊ [VN, VNN] *He reluctantly* **conceded the point** *to me.* ◊ *He reluctantly conceded me the point.* ◊ [VNthat] *It must be conceded that different judges have different approaches to these cases.* **2** ~ **sth** (**to sb**) | ~ **sb sth** to give sth away, especially unwillingly; to allow sb to have sth: [VN] *The President was obliged to concede power to the army.* ◊ *England conceded a goal immediately after half-time.* ◊ [VNN] *Women were only conceded full voting rights in the 1950s.* **3** ~ (**defeat**) to admit that you have lost a game, an election, etc: [V] *After losing this decisive battle, the general was forced to concede.* ◊ [VN] *Injury forced Hicks to concede defeat.*—see also CONCESSION

con·ceit /kənˈsiːt/ *noun* **1** [U] (*disapproving*) too much pride in yourself and what you do **2** [C] (*formal*) an artistic effect or device, especially one that is very clever or tries to be very clever but does not succeed: *The ill-advised conceit of the guardian angel dooms the film from the start.* **3** (*technical*) a clever or FANCIFUL expression in writing or speech that involves a comparison between two things [SYN] METAPHOR: *The idea of the wind singing is a romantic conceit.*

con·ceit·ed /kənˈsiːtɪd/ *adj.* (*disapproving*) having too much pride in yourself and what you do: *a very conceited person* ◊ *It's very conceited of you to assume that your work is always the best.* ▶ **con·ceit·ed·ly** /-li/ *adv.*

con·ceiv·able /kənˈsiːvəbl/ *adj.* that you can imagine or believe [SYN] POSSIBLE: *It is conceivable that I'll see her tomorrow.* ◊ *a beautiful city with buildings of every conceivable age and style* **OPP** INCONCEIVABLE ▶ **con·ceiv·ably** /-əbli/ *adv.*: *The disease could conceivably be transferred to humans.*

con·ceive /kənˈsiːv/ *verb*
1 ~ (**of**) **sth** (**as sth**) (*formal*) to form an idea, a plan, etc. in your mind; to imagine sth: [VN] *He conceived the idea of transforming the old power station into an arts centre.* ◊ *God is often conceived of as male.* ◊ [V(**that**)] *I cannot conceive* (= I do not believe) (*that*) *he would wish to harm us.* ◊ [Vwh-] *I cannot conceive what it must be like.* **2** when a woman **conceives** or **conceives a child**, she becomes pregnant: [V] *She is unable to conceive.* ◊ [VN] *Their first child was conceived on their wedding night.*—see also CONCEPTION

WORD FAMILY
conceive *v.*
concept *n.*
conception *n.*
conceivable *adj.* (≠ inconceivable)
conceptual *adj.*

con·cen·trate /ˈkɒnsntreɪt; *AmE* ˈkɑːn-/ *verb, noun*
■ *verb* **1** ~ (**sth**) (**on sth/on doing sth**) to give all your attention to sth and not think about anything else: [V] *I can't concentrate with all that noise going on.* ◊ [VN] *Nothing concentrates the mind better than the knowledge that you could die tomorrow* (= it makes you think very clearly). ◊ *I decided to* **concentrate** *all my efforts on finding somewhere to live.* **2** [VN+adv./prep.] to bring sth together in one place: *Power is largely concentrated in the hands of a small elite.* ◊ *We need to concentrate resources on the most run-down areas.* ◊ *Fighting was concentrated around the towns to the north.* **3** [VN] (*technical*) to increase the strength of a substance by reducing its volume, for example by boiling it **PHRV** **ˈconcentrate on sth** to spend more time doing one particular thing than others: *In this lecture I shall concentrate on the early years of Charles's reign.*
■ *noun* [C, U] a substance that is made stronger because water or other substances have been removed: *mineral concentrates found at the bottom of rivers* ◊ *jams made with fruit juice concentrate*

con·cen·trated /ˈkɒnsntreɪtɪd; *AmE* ˈkɑːn-/ *adj.* **1** showing determination to do sth: *He made a concentrated effort to finish the work on time.* **2** (of a substance) made stronger because water or other substances have been removed: *concentrated orange juice* ◊ *a concentrated solution of salt in water* **3** if sth exists or happens in a **concentrated** way, there is a lot of it in one place or at one time: *concentrated gunfire*

con·cen·tra·tion /ˌkɒnsnˈtreɪʃn; *AmE* ˌkɑːn-/ *noun* **1** [U] the ability to direct all your effort and attention on one thing, without thinking of other things: *This book requires a great deal of concentration.* ◊ *Stress and tiredness affect your powers of concentration.* **2** [U] ~ (**on sth**) the process of people directing effort and attention on a particular thing: *a need for greater concentration on environmental issues* **3** [C] ~ (**of sth**) a lot of sth in one place: *a concentration of industry in the north of the country* **4** [C, U] the amount of a substance in a liquid or in another substance: *glucose concentrations in the blood*

concenˈtration camp *noun* a type of prison, often consisting of a number of buildings inside a fence, where political prisoners are kept in extremely bad conditions: *a Nazi concentration camp*

con·cen·tric /kənˈsentrɪk/ *adj.* (*geometry*) (of circles) having the same centre: *concentric rings*

con·cept /ˈkɒnsept; *AmE* ˈkɑːn-/ *noun* ~ (**of sth**) | ~ (**that...**) an idea or a principle that is connected with sth ABSTRACT: *the concept of social class* ◊ *concepts such as 'civilization' and 'government'* ◊ *He can't grasp the basic concepts of mathematics.* ◊ *the concept that everyone should have equality of opportunity*

con·cep·tion /kənˈsepʃn/ *noun* **1** [U] the process of forming an idea or a plan: *The plan was brilliant in its conception but failed because of lack of money.* **2** [C, U] ~ (**of sth**) | ~ (**that...**) an understanding or a belief of what sth is or what sth should be: *Marx's conception of social justice* ◊ *He has* **no conception** *of how difficult life is if you're unemployed.* **3** [U, C] the process of an egg being FERTILIZED inside a woman's body so that she becomes pregnant: *the moment of conception*—see also CONCEIVE

con·cep·tual /kənˈseptʃuəl/ *adj.* (*formal*) related to or based on ideas: *a conceptual framework within which children's needs are assessed* ◊ *a conceptual model* ▶ **con·cep·tu·al·ly** *adv.*: *conceptually similar/distinct*

con·cep·tu·al·ize (*BrE* also **-ise**) /kənˈseptʃuəlaɪz/ *verb* [VN] ~ **sth** (**as sth**) (*formal*) to form an idea of sth in your mind: *These people do not conceptualize hunting as a violent act.*

con·cern /kənˈsɜːn; *AmE* -ˈsɜːrn/ *verb, noun*
■ *verb*
AFFECT/INVOLVE **1** [VN] [often passive] to affect sb; to involve sb: *Don't interfere in what doesn't concern you.* ◊ *The loss was a tragedy for* **all concerned** (= all those affected by it). ◊ *Where our children's education is concerned, no compromise is acceptable.* ◊ *The individuals concerned have some explaining to do.* ◊ **To whom it may concern** ... (= used for example, at the beginning of a

public notice or of a job reference about sb's character and ability) ◊ *Everyone who was directly concerned in* (= had some responsibility for) *the incident has now resigned.*

BE ABOUT | **2** [VN] (also **be concerned with sth**) to be about sth: *The story concerns the prince's efforts to rescue Pamina.* ◊ *The book is primarily concerned with Soviet-American relations during the Cold War.* ◊ *This chapter concerns itself with the historical background.* ◊ *One major difference between these computers concerns the way in which they store information.*

WORRY SB | **3** to worry sb: [VN] *What concerns me is our lack of preparation for the change.* ◊ [VN that] *It concerns me that you no longer seem to care.*—see also CONCERNED

TAKE AN INTEREST | **4** [VN] **~ yourself with/about sth** to take an interest in sth: *He didn't concern himself with the details.*

CONSIDER IMPORTANT | **5** [VN to inf] (**be concerned to do sth**) (*formal*) to think it is important to do sth: *She was concerned to write about situations that everybody could identify with.*
IDM see FAR *adv.*

■ *noun*

WORRY | **1** [U, C] **~ (about/for/over sth/sb)| ~ (that …)** a feeling of worry, especially one that is shared by many people: *There is growing concern about violence on television.* ◊ *She hasn't been seen for four days and there is concern for her safety.* ◊ *The report expressed concern over continuing high unemployment.* ◊ *There is widespread concern that new houses will be built on protected land.* ◊ *Stress at work is **a matter of concern** to staff and management.* ◊ *The President's health was giving serious **cause for concern**.* ◊ *Don't hesitate to ask if you have any queries or concerns about this work.* ◊ *In the meeting, voters raised concerns about health care.*—compare UNCONCERN

DESIRE TO PROTECT | **2** [U] a desire to protect and help sb/sth: *parents' concern for their children*

STH IMPORTANT | **3** [C] something that is important to a person, an organization, etc: *What are your main concerns as a writer?* ◊ *The government's primary concern is to reduce crime.*

RESPONSIBILITY | **4** [C, usually sing.] (*formal*) something that is your responsibility or that you have a right to know about: *This matter is their concern.* ◊ *How much money I make is none of your concern.*

COMPANY | **5** [C] a company or business: *a major publishing concern*
IDM see GOING *adj.*

con·cerned /kənˈsɜːnd; *AmE* -ˈsɜːrnd/ *adj.* **1 ~ (about/ for sth)| ~ (that …)** worried and feeling concern about sth: *Concerned parents held a meeting.* ◊ *The President is deeply concerned about this issue.* ◊ *He didn't seem in the least concerned for her safety.* ◊ *She was concerned that she might miss the turning and get lost.* ⇨ note at WORRIED **2 ~ (about/with sth)** interested in sth: *They were more concerned with how the other women had dressed than in what the speaker was saying.* **OPP** UNCONCERNED **IDM** see FAR *adv.*

con·cern·ing /kənˈsɜːnɪŋ; *AmE* -ˈsɜːrn-/ *prep.* (*formal*) about sth; involving sb/sth: *He asked several questions concerning the future of the company.* ◊ *All cases concerning children are dealt with in a special children's court.*

con·cert /ˈkɒnsət; *AmE* ˈkɑːnsərt/ *noun* a public performance of music: *a concert of music by Bach* ◊ *a rock/pop concert* ◊ *Oasis in concert at Wembley Arena* ◊ *a concert hall/pianist* **IDM** **in concert with sb/sth** (*formal*) working together with sb/sth

con·cert·ed /kənˈsɜːtɪd; *AmE* -ˈsɜːrt-/ *adj.* [only before noun] done in a planned and determined way, especially by more than one person, government, country, etc: *a concerted approach/attack/campaign* ◊ *She has begun to **make a concerted effort** to find a job.*

ˈconcert-goer *noun* a person who regularly goes to concerts, especially of classical music

con·cer·tina /ˌkɒnsəˈtiːnə; *AmE* ˌkɑːnsərˈt-/ *noun, verb*

■ *noun* a musical instrument like a small ACCORDION, that you hold in both hands. You press the ends together and pull them apart to produce sounds.
■ *verb* (**con·cer·tina·ing, con·cer·tinaed, con·cer·tinaed**) [V] (*BrE*) to fold up like a concertina: *The truck crashed into the tree and concertinaed.*

con·cert·mas·ter /ˈkɒnsətmɑːstə(r); *AmE* ˈkɑːnsərt-mæs-/ *noun* (*especially AmE*) = LEADER (3)

con·certo /kənˈtʃɜːtəʊ; *AmE* -ˈtʃɜːrtoʊ/ *noun* (*pl.* **-os**) a piece of music for one or more SOLO instruments playing with an orchestra: *a piano concerto* ◊ *a concerto for flute and harp*

con·ces·sion /kənˈseʃn/ *noun* **1** [C, U] something that you allow or do, or allow sb to have, in order to end an argument or to make a situation less difficult: *The firm will be forced to **make concessions** if it wants to avoid a strike.* ◊ *to win a concession from sb* ◊ *a major/an important concession* ◊ *She **made no concession** to his age; she expected him to work as hard as she did.*—see also CONCEDE **2** [U] the act of giving sth or allowing sth; the act of CONCEDING: *the concession of university status to some colleges* ◊ (*especially AmE*) *Dole's concession speech* (= when he admitted that he had lost the election) **3** [C, usually pl.] (*BrE*) a reduction in an amount of money that has to be paid; a ticket that is sold at a reduced price to a particular group of people: *tax concessions* ◊ *Tickets are £3; there is a £1 concession for students.* ◊ *Adults £2.50, concessions £2, family £5* **4** [C] a right or an advantage that is given to a group of people, an organization, etc., especially by a government or an employer: *The Bolivian government has granted logging concessions covering 22 million hectares.* **5** [C] (*especially AmE*) the right to sell sth in a particular place; the place where you sell it, sometimes an area which is part of a larger building or store: *the burger concessions at the stadium* ◊ *They went to the concession stand to get a hot dog.*

con·ces·sion·aire /kənˌseʃəˈneə(r); *AmE* -ˈner/ *noun* (*especially BrE*) a person or a business that has been given a concession to sell sth

con·ces·sion·ary /kənˈseʃənəri; *AmE* -neri/ *adj.* [usually before noun] (*BrE*) costing less money for people in particular situations; given as a CONCESSION (2): *concessionary rates/fares/travel*

conch /kɒntʃ; *AmE* kɑːntʃ/ *noun* the shell of a sea creature which is also called a **conch**

con·cili·ate /kənˈsɪlieɪt/ *verb* (*formal*) to make sb less angry or more friendly, especially by being kind and pleasant or by giving them sth ▶ **con·cili·ation** /kənˌsɪliˈeɪʃn/ *noun* [U]: *A conciliation service helps to settle disputes between employers and workers.*

con·cili·ator /kənˈsɪlieɪtə(r)/ *noun* a person or an organization that tries to make angry people calm so that they can discuss or solve their problems successfully

con·cili·atory /kənˈsɪliətəri; *AmE* -tɔːri/ *adj.* having the intention or effect of making angry people calm: *a conciliatory approach/attitude/gesture/move*

con·cise /kənˈsaɪs/ *adj.* **1** giving only the information that is necessary and important, using few words: *a concise statement/summary* ◊ *clear and concise instructions* **2** [only before noun] (of a book) shorter than the original book, on which it was based: *a concise dictionary* ▶ **con·cise·ly** *adv.* **con·cise·ness** *noun* [U]

con·clave /ˈkɒŋkleɪv; *AmE* ˈkɑːŋ-/ *noun* (*formal*) a meeting to discuss sth in private; the people at this meeting

con·clude /kənˈkluːd/ *verb* **1** (not used in the progressive tenses) **~ sth (from sth)| ~ (from sth) that …** to decide or believe sth as a result of what you have heard or seen: [VN] *What do you conclude from that?* ◊ [V (that)] *The report concluded (that) the cheapest option was to close the laboratory.* ◊ [V that] *He concluded from their remarks that they were not in favour of the plan.* ◊ [VN that] *It was concluded that the level of change necessary would be low.* [also V speech] **2 ~ (sth) (with sth)** (*formal*) to come to an end; to bring sth to an end: [V] *Let me make just a few concluding remarks.* ◊ *The programme concluded with Stravinsky's 'Rite of Spring'.* ◊ *He concluded by wishing everyone a safe trip home.* ◊ [VN] *The commission concluded*

æ	ɑː	e	ɜː	ə	ɪ	iː	i	ɒ	ɔː	ʌ	ʊ	u	uː
cat	father	ten	bird	about	sit	see	many	got	saw	cup	put	actual	too
								(BrE)					

its investigation last month. ◇ [Vspeech] *'Anyway, she should be back soon,' he concluded.* **3** [VN] **~ sth (with sb)** to arrange and settle an agreement with sb formally and finally: *They concluded a treaty with Turkey.* ◇ *A trade agreement was concluded between the two countries.*

con·clu·sion /kənˈkluːʒn/ *noun* **1** [C] something that you decide when you have thought about all the information connected with the situation: *I've come to the conclusion that he's not the right person for the job.* ◇ *It took the jury some time to reach the conclusion that she was guilty.* ◇ *New evidence might lead to the conclusion that we are wrong.* ◇ *We can safely draw some conclusions from our discussion.* **2** [C, usually sing.] the end of sth such as a speech or a piece of writing: *The conclusion of the book was disappointing.* ◇ *In conclusion,* (= finally) *I would like to thank...* ◇ *If we took this argument to its logical conclusion ...* **3** [U] the formal and final arrangement of sth official: *the successful conclusion of a trade treaty* **IDM** **jump/leap to con'clusions | jump/leap to the con'clusion that ...** to make a decision about sb/sth too quickly, before you know or have thought about all the facts: *There I go again—jumping to conclusions.*—more at FOREGONE

con·clu·sive /kənˈkluːsɪv/ *adj.* proving sth, and allowing no doubt or uncertainty: *conclusive evidence/proof/results* **OPP** INCONCLUSIVE ▶ **con·clu·sive·ly** *adv.*: *to demonstrate/establish/prove/show sth conclusively*

con·coct /kənˈkɒkt; *AmE* -ˈkɑːkt/ *verb* [VN] **1** to make sth, especially food or drink, by mixing different things: *The soup was concocted from up to a dozen different kinds of fish.* **2** to invent a story, an excuse, etc. **SYN** COOK UP: *She concocted some elaborate story to explain her absence.*

con·coc·tion /kənˈkɒkʃn; *AmE* -ˈkɑːkʃn/ *noun* a strange or unusual mixture of things, especially drinks or medicines: *a concoction of cream and rum*

con·comi·tant /kənˈkɒmɪtənt; *AmE* -ˈkɑːm-/ *adj., noun*
■ *adj.* (*formal*) happening at the same time as sth else, especially because one thing is related to or causes the other: *an increase in student numbers and the concomitant increase in class size*
■ *noun* (*formal*) a thing that happens at the same time as sth else

con·cord /ˈkɒŋkɔːd; *AmE* ˈkɑːŋkɔːrd/ *noun* [U] **1 ~ (with sb)** (*formal*) peace and agreement **SYN** HARMONY: *living in concord with neighbouring states* **OPP** DISCORD **2** [U] **~ (with sth)** (*grammar*) (of words in a phrase) the fact of having the same NUMBER, GENDER or PERSON **SYN** AGREEMENT

con·cord·ance /kənˈkɔːdəns; *AmE* -ˈkɔːrd-/ *noun* **1** [C] an alphabetical list of the words used in a book, etc. showing where and how often they are used: *a Bible concordance* **2** [C] a list produced by a computer that shows all the examples of an individual word in a book, etc. **3** [U] (*technical*) the state of being similar to sth or CONSISTENT with it: *There is reasonable concordance between the two sets of results.*

con·cordat /kənˈkɔːdæt; *AmE* -ˈkɔːrd- Br also* kɒn-/ *noun* an agreement, especially between the Roman Catholic Church and the state

con·course /ˈkɒŋkɔːs; *AmE* ˈkɑːŋkɔːrs/ *noun* **1** a large, open part of a public building, especially an airport or a train station: *the station concourse* **2** (*formal*) a large group of people; a crowd

con·crete /ˈkɒŋkriːt; *AmE* ˈkɑːŋ-/ *adj., noun, verb*
■ *adj.* **1** made of concrete: *a concrete floor/wall/building* **2** based on facts, not on ideas or guesses: *concrete evidence/proposals/proof* ◇ *'It's only a suspicion,' she said, 'nothing concrete.'* ◇ *It is easier to think in concrete terms rather than in the abstract.*—compare ABSTRACT (1) **3** a concrete object is one that you can see and feel ▶ **con·crete·ly** *adv.*
■ *noun* [U] building material that is made by mixing together CEMENT, sand, small stones and water: *a slab of concrete*
■ *verb* [VN] **~ sth (over)** to cover sth with concrete: *The garden had been concreted over.*

con·crete ˈjungle *noun* [usually sing.] a way of describing a city or an area that is unpleasant because it has many large modern buildings and no trees or parks

ˈconcrete mixer *noun* = CEMENT MIXER

con·cu·bine /ˈkɒŋkjubaɪn; *AmE* ˈkɑːŋ-/ *noun* (especially in some societies in the past) a woman who lives with a man, often in addition to his wife or wives, but who is less important than they are

con·cur /kənˈkɜː(r)/ *verb* (**-rr-**) **~ (with sb) (in sth)| ~ (with sth)** (*formal*) to agree: [V] *Historians have concurred with each other in this view.* ◇ *The coroner concurred with this assessment.* [also Vthat, Vspeech]

con·cur·rence /kənˈkʌrəns; *AmE* -ˈkɜːr-/ *noun* (*formal*) **1** [U, sing.] agreement: *The doctor may seek the concurrence of a relative before carrying out the procedure.* **2** [sing.] an example of two or more things happening at the same time: *an unfortunate concurrence of events*

con·cur·rent /kənˈkʌrənt; *AmE* -ˈkɜːr-/ *adj.* **~ (with sth)** existing or happening at the same time: *He was imprisoned for two concurrent terms of 30 months and 18 months.* ▶ **con·cur·rent·ly** *adv.*: *The prison sentences will run concurrently.*

con·cuss /kənˈkʌs/ *verb* [VN] [usually passive] to hit sb on the head, making them become unconscious or confused for a short time: *She was concussed after being thrown from her horse.*

con·cus·sion /kənˈkʌʃn/ *noun* [U] (This word is only [C] in *AmE.*) a temporary loss of consciousness caused by a blow to the head; the effects of a severe blow to the head such as confusion and temporary loss of physical and mental abilities: (*BrE*) *He was taken to hospital with concussion.* ◇ (*AmE*) *He was taken to the hospital with a concussion.*

con·demn /kənˈdem/ *verb*
EXPRESS DISAPPROVAL | **1** [VN] **~ sb/sth (for/as sth)** to express very strong disapproval of sb/sth, usually for moral reasons: *The government issued a statement condemning the killings.* ◇ *The editor of the newspaper was condemned as lacking integrity.*
SB TO PUNISHMENT | **2** [usually passive] **~ sb (to sth)** to say what sb's punishment will be **SYN** SENTENCE: [VN] *He was condemned to death for murder and later hanged.* ◇ [VN to inf] *She was condemned to hang for killing her husband.*
SB TO DIFFICULT SITUATION | **3** [VN] [usually passive] **~ sb to sth** to force sb to accept a difficult or unpleasant situation **SYN** DOOM: *They were condemned to a life of hardship.* ◇ *He was condemned to spend the rest of the football season on the bench.*
STH DANGEROUS | **4** [VN] [usually passive] **~ sth (as sth)** to say officially that sth is not safe enough to be used: *a condemned building* ◇ *The meat was condemned as unfit to eat.*
SHOW GUILT | **5** [VN] to show or suggest that sb is guilty of sth: *She is condemned out of her own mouth* (= her own words show her guilt).

con·dem·na·tion /ˌkɒndemˈneɪʃn; *AmE* ˌkɑːn-/ *noun* [U, C] **~ (of sb/sth)** an expression of very strong disapproval: *There was widespread condemnation of the invasion.*

con,demned ˈcell *noun* (*BrE*) a prison cell where a person who is going to be punished by death is kept

con·den·sa·tion /ˌkɒndenˈseɪʃn; *AmE* ˌkɑːn-/ *noun* **1** [U] drops of water that form on a cold surface when warm water VAPOUR becomes cool **2** [U] the process of a gas changing to a liquid **3** [C usually sing, U] (*formal*) the process of making a book, etc. shorter by taking out anything that is not necessary

con·dense /kənˈdens/ *verb* **1 ~ (sth) (into sth)** to change from a gas into a liquid; to make a gas change into a liquid: *Steam condenses into water when it cools.* ◇ [VN] *The steam was condensed rapidly by injecting cold water into the cylinder.* **2** if a liquid **condenses** or you **condense** it, it becomes thicker and stronger because it has lost some of its water: [VN] *Condense the soup by boiling it for several minutes.* [also V] **3** [VN] **~ sth (into**

aɪ	aʊ	eɪ	əʊ	oʊ	ɔɪ	ɪə	eə	ʊə	j	w
my	now	say	go (BrE)	go (AmE)	boy	near	hair	pure	yes	wet

sth) to put sth such as a piece of writing into fewer words; to put a lot of information into a small space: *The article was condensed into just two pages.* ◊ *The author has condensed a great deal of material into just 100 pages.*

con·densed 'milk *noun* [U] a type of thick sweet milk that is sold in cans

con·dens·er /kən'densə(r)/ *noun* **1** a device that cools gas in order to change it into a liquid **2** a device that receives or stores electricity, especially in a car engine

con·des·cend /ˌkɒndɪ'send/ *verb* **1** [VtoINF] (often *disapproving*) to do sth that you think it is below your social or professional position to do SYN DEIGN: *We had to wait almost an hour before he condescended to see us.* **2** [V] ~ **to sb** to behave towards sb as though you are more important and more intelligent than they are: *When giving a talk, be careful not to condescend to your audience.* ▶ **con·des·cen·sion** /ˌkɒndɪ'senʃn; *AmE* ˌkɑːn-/ *noun* [U]: *Her smile was a mixture of pity and condescension.*

con·des·cend·ing /ˌkɒndɪ'sendɪŋ; *AmE* ˌkɑːn-/ *adj.* behaving as though you are more important and more intelligent than other people: *He has a condescending attitude towards women.* ▶ **con·des·cend·ing·ly** *adv.*

con·di·ment /'kɒndɪmənt; *AmE* 'kɑːn-/ *noun* [usually pl.] **1** (*BrE*) a substance such as salt or pepper that is used to give flavour to food **2** (*especially AmE*) a sauce, etc. that is used to give flavour to food, or that is eaten with food: *hot condiments made from a variety of chili peppers*

con·di·tion /kən'dɪʃn/ *noun, verb*
■ *noun*
‾STATE OF STH‾ **1** [U, sing.] the state that sth is in: *to be in bad / good / excellent condition* ◊ *a used car in perfect condition*
‾MEDICAL‾ **2** [U, sing.] the state of sb's health or how fit they are: *He is overweight and out of condition* (= not physically fit). ◊ *You are in no condition* (= too ill, etc.) *to go anywhere.* ◊ *The motorcyclist was in a critical condition in hospital last night.* **3** [C] an illness or a medical problem that you have for a long time because it is not possible to cure it: *a medical condition* ◊ *He suffers from a serious heart condition.* ⇨ vocabulary notes on page 599
‾CIRCUMSTANCES‾ **4** (**conditions**) [pl.] the circumstances or situation in which people live, work or do things: *living / housing / working conditions* ◊ *changing economic conditions* ◊ *neglected children living under the most appalling conditions* ◊ *a strike to improve pay and conditions* **5** (**conditions**) [pl.] the physical situation that affects how sth happens: *The plants grow best in cool, damp conditions.* ◊ *freezing / icy / humid conditions* ◊ *Conditions are ideal* (= the weather is very good) *for sailing today.* ◊ *treacherous driving conditions*
‾RULE‾ **6** [C] a rule or decision that you must agree to, sometimes forming part of a contract or an official agreement: *the terms and conditions of employment* ◊ *The offer is subject to certain conditions.* ◊ *They agreed to lend us the car on condition that* (= only if) *we returned it before the weekend.* ◊ *They will give us the money on one condition—that we pay it back within six months.* ◊ (*especially AmE*) *They agreed under the condition that the matter be dealt with promptly.* ◊ *Congress can impose strict conditions on the bank.* ◊ *They have agreed to the ceasefire provided their conditions are met.*
‾NECESSARY SITUATION‾ **7** [C] a situation that must exist in order for sth else to happen: *a necessary condition for economic growth* ◊ *A good training programme is one of the conditions for successful industry.*
‾STATE OF GROUP‾ **8** [sing.] (*formal*) the state of a particular group of people because of their situation in life, their problems, etc: *He spoke angrily about the condition of the urban poor.* ◊ *Work is basic to the human condition* (= the fact of being alive).
IDM on 'no condition (*AmE also* **under 'no condition**) (*formal*) not in any situation; never: *You must on no condition tell them what happened.*—more at MINT *n.*
■ *verb* **1** [usually passive] ~ **sb/sth (to sth/to do sth)** to train sb/sth to behave in a particular way or to become

used to a particular situation: [VN] *the difference between inborn and conditioned reflexes* (= reactions that are learned / not natural) ◊ *Patients can become conditioned to particular forms of treatment.* ◊ [VNtoINF] *The rats had been conditioned to ring a bell when they wanted food.* **2** [VN] to have an important effect on sb/sth; to influence the way that sth happens: *Gender roles are often conditioned by cultural factors.* **3** [VN] to keep sth such as your hair or skin healthy: *a shampoo that cleans and conditions hair* ◊ *a polish for conditioning leather*

WHICH WORD?	
condition / state	

The following adjectives are frequently used with these nouns:

~ condition	~ state
good	present
excellent	current
physical	mental
poor	solid
human	no
perfect	emotional
no	physical
better	natural

State is a more general word than **condition** and is used for the condition that something is in at a particular time. It can be used without an adjective: *the present state of medical knowledge* ◊ *We're worried about his mental state.* ◊ *What a state this room is in* (= very bad).

Condition is used with an adjective and refers especially to the appearance, quality or working order of somebody or something: *The car is in excellent condition.*

con·di·tion·al /kən'dɪʃənl/ *adj., noun*
■ *adj.* **1** ~ (**on/upon sth**) depending on sth: *conditional approval / acceptance* ◊ *Payment is conditional upon delivery of the goods* (= if the goods are not delivered the money will not be paid) ◊ *He was found guilty and given a conditional discharge* (= allowed to go free on particular conditions). ◊ *a conditional offer* (= that depends on particular conditions being fulfilled) **2** [only before noun] (*grammar*) expressing sth that must happen or be true if another thing is to happen or be true: *a conditional sentence / clause* ▶ **con·di·tion·al·ly** /-ʃənəli/ *adv.*: *The offer was made conditionally.*
■ *noun* (*grammar*) **1** [C] a sentence or CLAUSE that begins with *if* or *unless* and expresses a condition **2** (**the conditional**) [sing.] the form of a verb that expresses a conditional action, for example *should* in *If I should die ...*: *the present / past / perfect conditional* ◊ *the first / second / third conditional*

con·di·tion·er /kən'dɪʃənə(r)/ *noun* [C, U] **1** a liquid that makes hair soft and shiny after washing: *shampoo and conditioner* **2** a liquid, used after washing clothes, that makes them softer: *fabric conditioner*

con·di·tion·ing /kən'dɪʃənɪŋ/ *noun* [U] the training or experience that an animal or a person has that makes them behave in a particular way in a particular situation: *Is personality the result of conditioning from parents and society, or are we born with it?*—see also AIR CONDITIONING

condo /'kɒndəʊ; *AmE* 'kɑːndoʊ/ *noun* (*pl.* **-os**) (*AmE, informal*) = CONDOMINIUM

con·dol·ence /kən'dəʊləns; *AmE* -'doʊ-/ *noun* [C, usually pl., U] sympathy that you feel for sb when a person in their family or that they know well has died; an expression of this sympathy: *to give / offer / express your condolences* ◊ *Our condolences go to his wife and family.* ◊ *a letter of condolence*

con·dom /'kɒndɒm; *AmE* 'kɑːndəm/ *noun* **1** (*BrE. also* **sheath**) (*also AmE formal or technical* **prophy·lac·tic**) a thin rubber covering that a man wears over his PENIS during sex to stop a woman from becoming pregnant or to protect against disease **2 (female condom)** a thin rubber device that a woman wears inside her VAGINA during sex to prevent herself from becoming pregnant

con·do·min·ium /ˌkɒndəˈmɪniəm; AmE ˌkɑːn-/ (also informal **condo**) noun (especially AmE) an apartment building in which each flat/apartment is owned by the person living in it but the building and shared areas are owned by everyone together; a flat/apartment in such a building

con·done /kənˈdəʊn; AmE -ˈdoʊn/ verb to accept behaviour that is morally wrong or to treat it as if it were not serious: [VN] *Terrorism can never be condoned.* [also V-ing, VN-ing]

con·dor /ˈkɒndɔː(r); AmE ˈkɑːn-/ noun a large bird of the VULTURE family, that lives mainly in S America

con·du·cive /kənˈdjuːsɪv; AmE -ˈduːs-/ adj. ~ to sth (written) making it easy, possible or likely for sth to happen: *Chairs in rows are not as conducive to discussion as chairs arranged in a circle.*

con·duct verb, noun
■ verb /kənˈdʌkt/ **1** [VN] to organize and/or do a particular activity: *to conduct an experiment/an inquiry/a survey* ◊ *The negotiations have been conducted in a positive manner.* **2** to direct a group of people who are singing or playing music: [VN] *a concert by the Philharmonic Orchestra, conducted by Sir Colin Davis* [also V] **3** [VN+adv./prep.] to lead or guide sb through or around a place: *a conducted tour of Athens* (= one with a guide, giving information about it) ◊ *The guide conducted us around the ruins of the ancient city.* **4** [VN+adv./prep.] ~ yourself ... (formal) to behave in a particular way: *He conducted himself far better than expected.* **5** [VN] (physics) (of a substance) to allow heat or electricity to pass along or through it: *Copper conducts electricity better than other materials do.*
■ noun /ˈkɒndʌkt; AmE ˈkɑːn-/ [U] (formal) **1** a person's behaviour in a particular place or in a particular situation: *The sport has a strict code of conduct.* ◊ *improving standards of training and professional conduct* **2** ~ of sth the way in which a business or an activity is organized and managed: *There was growing criticism of the government's conduct of the war.*—see also SAFE CONDUCT

con·duc·tion /kənˈdʌkʃn/ noun [U] (physics) the process by which heat or electricity passes through a material

con·duct·ive /kənˈdʌktɪv/ adj. (physics) able to CONDUCT electricity, heat, etc. ▶ **con·duct·iv·ity** /ˌkɒndʌkˈtɪvəti; AmE ˌkɑːn-/ noun [U]

con·duct·or /kənˈdʌktə(r)/ noun **1** a person who stands in front of an orchestra, a group of singers etc., and directs their performance, especially sb who does this as a profession **2** (BrE also **guard**) a person who is in charge of a train and travels with it, but does not drive it **3** (BrE) a person whose job is to collect money from passengers on a bus or check their tickets: *a bus conductor* **4** (physics) a substance that allows electricity or heat to pass along it or through it: *Wood is a poor conductor.*—see also LIGHTNING CONDUCTOR

con·duc·tress /kənˈdʌktrəs/ noun (BrE, old-fashioned) a woman who collects money from passengers on a bus or checks their tickets

con·duit /ˈkɒndjuːt; AmE ˈkɑːnduːɪt/ noun **1** (technical) a pipe, channel or tube which liquid, gas or electrical wire can pass through **2** (formal) a person, an organization or a country that is used to pass things or information to other people or places: *The organization had acted as a conduit for money from the arms industry.*

cone /kəʊn; AmE koʊn/ noun, verb
■ noun **1** a solid or hollow object with a round flat base and sides that slope up to a point—see also CONICAL—picture at SOLID **2 a** solid or hollow object that is shaped like a cone: *a paper cone full of popcorn* ◊ *the cone of a volcano*—see also

cone (BrE also **fir cone**)

NOSE-CONE **3** (also ˈ**traffic cone**) a plastic object shaped like a cone and often red and white, or yellow, in colour, used on roads to show where vehicles are not allowed to go, for example while repairs are being done **4** (also old-fashioned **cornet**) a piece of thin crisp biscuit shaped like a cone, which you can put ice cream in to eat it **5** the hard dry fruit of a PINE or FIR tree: *a pine cone*—see also FIR CONE
■ verb PHRV ˌ**cone sth↔ˈoff** to close a road or part of a road by putting a line of cones across it

con·fec·tion /kənˈfekʃn/ noun **1** (formal) a cake or other sweet food that looks very attractive **2** (written) a thing such as a building or piece of clothing, that is made in a skilful or complicated way: *Her hat was an elaborate confection of satin and net.*

con·fec·tion·er /kənˈfekʃənə(r)/ noun a person or a business that makes or sells cakes and sweets/candy

conˈfectioners' sugar noun [U] (AmE) = ICING SUGAR

con·fec·tion·ery /kənˈfekʃənəri; AmE -ʃəneri/ noun [U] (written) sweets/candy, chocolate, etc: *Confectionery is a multi-million-pound business.*

con·fed·er·acy /kənˈfedərəsi/ noun [sing.] a union of states, groups of people or political parties with the same aim

con·fed·er·ate /kənˈfedərət/ noun, adj.
■ noun a person who helps sb, especially to do sth illegal or secret SYN ACCOMPLICE
■ adj. belonging to a confederacy

con·fed·er·ation /kənˌfedəˈreɪʃn/ noun an organization consisting of countries, businesses, etc. that have joined together in order to help each other: *the Confederation of British Industry*

con·fer /kənˈfɜː(r)/ verb (-rr-) (formal) **1** [V] ~ (with sb) (on/about sth) to discuss sth with sb, especially in order to exchange opinions or get advice: *He wanted to confer with his colleagues before reaching a decision.* **2** [VN] ~ sth (on/upon sb) to give sb an award, a university degree or a particular honour or right: *An honorary degree was conferred on him by Oxford University in 1995.*

con·fer·ence /ˈkɒnfərəns; AmE ˈkɑːn-/ noun **1** a large official meeting, usually lasting for a few days, at which people with the same work or interests come together to discuss their views: *The hotel is used for exhibitions, conferences and social events.* ◊ *a conference room/centre/hall* ◊ *She is attending a three-day conference on Aids education.* ◊ *The Aids conference will be held in Glasgow.* ◊ *delegates to the Labour Party's annual conference* **2** a meeting at which people have formal discussions: *Ministers from all four countries involved will meet at the conference table this week.* ◊ *He was in conference with his lawyers all day.*—see also PRESS CONFERENCE **3** (especially AmE) a group of sports teams that play against each other in a LEAGUE: *Southeast Conference football champions*

ˈ**conference call** noun a telephone call in which three or more people take part

con·fer·ment /kənˈfɜːmənt; AmE -ˈfɜːrm-/ noun [U, C] (formal) the action of giving sb an award, a university degree or a particular honour or right

con·fess /kənˈfes/ verb **1** ~ (to sth/to doing sth) to admit, especially formally or to the police, that you have done sth wrong or illegal: [V] *She confessed to the murder.* ◊ *After hours of questioning, the suspect confessed.* ◊ [V (that)] *He confessed that he had stolen the money.* ◊ [VN] *We persuaded her to confess her crime.* **2** ~ (to sth/to doing sth) to admit sth that you feel ashamed or embarrassed about: [VN] *She was reluctant to confess her ignorance.* ◊ [V] *I must confess to knowing nothing about computers.* ◊ [VN-ADJ] (formal) *I confess myself bewildered by their explanation.* [also V (that), V speech] —see also SELF-CONFESSED **3** [V, VN] ~ (sth) (to sb) (especially in the Roman Catholic Church) to tell God or a priest about the bad things you have done so that you can say that you are sorry and be forgiven **4** [VN] (of a priest) to hear sb confess their SINS (= the bad things they have done)

con·fes·sion /kənˈfeʃn/ noun **1** [C, U] a statement that a person makes, admitting that they are guilty of a crime;

the act of making such a statement: *After hours of questioning by police, she made a full confession.* **2** [C, U] a statement admitting sth that you are ashamed or embarrassed about; the act of making such a statement: *I've a confession to make—I lied about my age.* **3** [U, C] (especially in the Roman Catholic Church) a private statement to a priest about the bad things that you have done: *to go to confession* ◊ *to hear sb's confession* **4** [C] (*formal*) a statement of your religious beliefs, principles, etc: *a confession of faith*

con·fes·sion·al /kən'feʃənl/ *noun* a private enclosed place in a church where a priest listens to people making confessions

con·fes·sor /kən'fesə(r)/ *noun* a Roman Catholic priest who listens to CONFESSIONS

con·fetti /kən'feti/ *noun* [U] small pieces of coloured paper that people often throw over a man and woman who have just been married or (in the US) at other special events

con·fi·dant (*feminine also* **con·fi·dante**) /'kɒnfɪdænt; ˌkɒnfɪ'dɑːnt; *AmE* 'kɑːnfɪdænt/ *noun* a person that you trust and who you talk to about private or secret things: *a close/trusted confidant of the President*

con·fide /kən'faɪd/ *verb* ~ (**sth**) (**to sb**) to tell sb secrets and personal information that you do not want other people to know: [VN] *She confided all her secrets to her best friend.* ◊ [V that] *He confided to me that he had applied for another job.* [also V speech] **PHRV** **con'fide in sb** to tell sb secrets and personal information because you feel you can trust them: *It is important to have someone you can confide in.*

con·fi·dence /'kɒnfɪdəns; *AmE* 'kɑːn-/ *noun*
BELIEF IN OTHERS **1** [U] ~ (**in sb/sth**) the feeling that you can trust, believe in and be sure about the abilities or good qualities of sb/sth: *The players all have confidence in their manager.* ◊ *A fall in unemployment will help to restore consumer confidence.* ◊ *a lack of confidence in the government* ◊ *The new contracts have undermined the confidence of employees.* ◊ *She has every confidence in her students' abilities.*—see also VOTE OF CONFIDENCE, VOTE OF NO CONFIDENCE
BELIEF IN YOURSELF **2** [U] a belief in your own ability to do things and be successful: *He answered the questions with confidence.* ◊ *Women often lose confidence when they stop work to have a baby.* ◊ *He gained confidence when he went to college.* ◊ *She suffers from a lack of confidence.* ◊ *While girls lack confidence, boys often overestimate their abilities.* ◊ *I didn't have any confidence in myself at school.*
FEELING CERTAIN **3** [U] the feeling that you are certain about sth: *They could not say with confidence that he would be able to walk again after the accident.* ◊ *He expressed his confidence that they would win.*
TRUST **4** [U] a feeling of trust that sb will keep information private: *Eva told me about their relationship in confidence.* ◊ *This is in the strictest confidence.* ◊ *It took a long time to gain her confidence* (= make her feel she could trust me).
A SECRET **5** [C] (*formal*) a secret that you tell sb: *The girls exchanged confidences.* ◊ *I could never forgive Mike for betraying a confidence.*
IDM **be in sb's confidence** to be trusted with sb's secrets: *He is said to be very much in the President's confidence.* **take sb into your confidence** to tell sb secrets and personal information about yourself: *She took me into her confidence and told me about the problems she was facing.*

'confidence trick (*BrE*) (*AmE* **'confidence game**) *noun* (*formal*) = CON

con·fi·dent /'kɒnfɪdənt; *AmE* 'kɑːn-/ *adj.* **1** feeling sure about your own ability to do things and be successful: *She was in a relaxed, confident mood.* ◊ *The teacher wants the children to feel confident about asking questions when they don't understand.*—see also SELF-CONFIDENT **2** ~ **of sth** | ~ **that ...** feeling certain that sth will happen in the way that you want or expect: *I'm confident that you will get the job.* ◊ *The team feels confident of winning.* ▶ **con·fi·dent·ly** *adv.*

con·fi·den·tial /ˌkɒnfɪ'denʃl; *AmE* ˌkɑːn-/ *adj.* **1** meant to be kept secret and not told to or shared with other people: *confidential information/documents* ◊ *Your medical records are strictly confidential* (= completely secret). **2** (of a way of speaking) showing that what you are saying is private or secret: *He spoke in a confidential tone, his voice low.* **3** [only before noun] trusted with private or secret information: *a confidential secretary* ▶ **con·fi·den·tial·ly** /-ʃəli/ *adv.*: *She told me confidentially that she is going to retire early.*

con·fi·den·ti·al·ity /ˌkɒnfɪˌdenʃi'æləti; *AmE* ˌkɑːn-/ *noun* [U] a situation in which you expect sb to keep information secret: *They signed a confidentiality agreement.* ◊ *All letters will be treated with complete confidentiality.*

con·fid·ing /kən'faɪdɪŋ/ *adj.* [usually before noun] showing trust; showing that you want to tell sb a secret: *a confiding relationship* ▶ **con·fid·ing·ly** *adv.*

con·fig·ur·ation /kənˌfɪɡə'reɪʃn; *AmE* -ˌfɪɡjə'r-/ *noun* **1** (*formal or technical*) an arrangement of the parts of sth or a group of things; the form or shape that this arrangement produces **2** (*computing*) the equipment and programs that form a computer system and the way that these are set up to run

con·fig·ure /kən'fɪɡə(r); *AmE* -'fɪɡjər/ *verb* [VN] [usually passive] (*technical*) to arrange sth in a particular way, especially computer equipment; to make equipment or SOFTWARE work in the way that the user prefers

con·fine /kən'faɪn/ *verb* [VN] **1** ~ **sb/sth to sth** [often passive] to keep sb/sth inside the limits of a particular activity, subject, area, etc. **SYN** RESTRICT: *The work will not be confined to the Glasgow area.* ◊ *I will confine myself to looking at the period from 1900 to 1916.* **2** ~ **sb/sth (in sth)** [usually passive] to keep a person or an animal in a small or closed space: *Keep the dog confined in a suitable travelling cage.* ◊ *Here the river is confined in a narrow channel.* ◊ *The soldiers concerned were confined to barracks* (= had to stay in the barracks, as a punishment) **3 be confined to bed, a wheelchair, etc.** to have to stay in bed, in a WHEELCHAIR, etc: *She was confined to bed with the flu.* ◊ *He was confined to a wheelchair after the accident.*

con·fined /kən'faɪnd/ *adj.* [usually before noun] (of a space or an area) small and enclosed by walls or sides: *It is cruel to keep animals in confined spaces.*

con·fine·ment /kən'faɪnmənt/ *noun* **1** [U] the state of being forced to stay in a closed space, prison, etc., the act of putting sb there: *her confinement to a wheelchair* ◊ *years of confinement as a political prisoner*—see also SOLITARY CONFINEMENT **2** [U, C] (*formal* or *old-fashioned*) the time when a woman gives birth to a baby: *the expected date of confinement* ◊ *a hospital/home confinement*

con·fines /'kɒnfaɪnz; *AmE* 'kɑːn-/ *noun* [pl.] (*formal*) limits or borders: *It is beyond the confines of human knowledge.* ◊ *the confines of family life*

con·firm /kən'fɜːm; *AmE* -'fɜːrm/ *verb* **1** to state or show that sth is definitely true or correct, especially by providing evidence: [VN] *Rumours of job losses were later confirmed* ◊ *His guilty expression confirmed my suspicions.* ◊ *Please write to confirm your reservation* (= say that it is definite). ◊ [V (that)] *Has everyone confirmed (that) they're coming?* ◊ [V wh-] *Can you confirm what happened?* ◊ [VN that] *It has been confirmed that Lewis's next fight will be against Bruno.* **2** [VN] ~ **sth** | ~ **sb (in sth)** to make sb feel or believe sth even more strongly: *The walk in the mountains confirmed his fear of heights.* **3** [VN] to make a position, an agreement, etc. more definite or official; to establish sb/sth firmly: *After a six-month probationary period, her position was confirmed.* ◊ *He was confirmed as captain for the rest of the season.* **4** [VN] [usually passive] to make sb a full member of the Christian Church: *She was baptized when she was a month old and confirmed when she was thirteen.*

con·firm·ation /ˌkɒnfə'meɪʃn; *AmE* ˌkɑːnfər'm-/ *noun* [U, C] **1** a statement, letter, etc. that shows that sth is true, correct or definite: *I'm still waiting for confirmation of the test results.* **2** a ceremony at which a person

æ	ɑː	e	ɜː	ə	ɪ	iː	i	ɒ	ɔː	ʌ	ʊ	u	uː
cat	father	ten	bird	about	sit	see	many	got	saw	cup	put	actual	too

(BrE)

becomes a full member of the Christian Church: *a confirmation service*

con·firmed /kənˈfɜːmd; *AmE* -ˈfɜːrmd/ *adj.* [only before noun] having a particular habit or way of life and not likely to change: *a confirmed bachelor* (= a man who is not likely to get married, often used in newspapers to refer to a HOMOSEXUAL man)

con·fis·cate /ˈkɒnfɪskeɪt; *AmE* ˈkɑːn-/ *verb* [VN] to officially take sth away from sb, especially as a punishment: *Their land was confiscated after the war.* ◇ *The teacher threatened to confiscate their Yo Yos if they kept playing in class.* ▸ **con·fis·ca·tion** /ˌkɒnfɪˈskeɪʃn; *AmE* ˌkɑːn-/ *noun* [U, C]

con·flag·ra·tion /ˌkɒnfləˈɡreɪʃn; *AmE* ˌkɑːn-/ *noun* (*formal*) a very large fire that destroys a lot of land or buildings

con·flate /kənˈfleɪt/ *verb* [VN] (*formal*) to put two or more things together to make one new thing: *The issues of race and class are separate and should not be conflated.* ▸ **con·fla·tion** /kənˈfleɪʃn/ *noun* [U, C]

con·flict *noun, verb*
■ *noun* /ˈkɒnflɪkt; *AmE* ˈkɑːn-/ [C, U] **~ (between A and B)** | **~ (over sth)** **1** a situation in which people, groups or countries are involved in a serious disagreement or argument: *a conflict between two cultures* ◇ *The violence was the result of political and ethnic conflicts.* ◇ *She found herself* **in conflict with** *her parents over her future career.* ◇ *John often* **comes into conflict with** *his boss.* ◇ *The government has done nothing to* **resolve the conflict** *over nurses' pay.* **2** a violent situation or period of fighting between two countries: *armed/military conflict* **3** a situation in which there are opposing ideas, opinions, feelings or wishes; a situation in which it is difficult to choose: *The story tells of a classic conflict between love and duty.* ◇ *Her diary was a record of her inner conflict.* ◇ *Many of these ideas appear to be* **in conflict with** *each other.* **IDM** **conflict of ˈinterest(s)** a situation in which there are two jobs, aims, roles, etc. and it is not possible for both of them to be treated equally and fairly at the same time: *There was a conflict of interest between his business dealings and his political activities.*
■ *verb* /kənˈflɪkt/ [V] **~ (with sth)** if two ideas, beliefs, stories, etc. **conflict**, it is not possible for them to exist together or for them both to be true [SYN] CLASH: *conflicting emotions/interests/loyalties* ◇ *These results conflict with earlier findings.* ◇ *Reports conflicted on how much of the aid was reaching the famine victims.*

con·flu·ence /ˈkɒnfluəns; *AmE* ˈkɑːn-/ *noun* [usually sing.] **1** (*technical*) the place where two rivers flow together and become one **2** (*formal*) the fact of two or more things becoming one: *a confluence of social factors*

con·form /kənˈfɔːm; *AmE* -ˈfɔːrm/ *verb* [V] **1 ~ (to sth)** to behave and think in the same way as most other people in a group or society: *There is considerable pressure on teenagers to conform.* ◇ *He refused to conform to the local customs.* **2 ~ to/with sth** to obey a rule, law, etc. [SYN] COMPLY: *The building does not conform with safety regulations.* **3 ~ to sth** to agree with or match sth: *It did not conform to the usual stereotype of an industrial city.*

con·form·ation /ˌkɒnfɔːˈmeɪʃn; *AmE* ˌkɑːnfɔːrˈm-/ *noun* [U, C] (*formal*) the way in which sth is formed; the structure of sth, especially an animal

con·form·ist /kənˈfɔːmɪst; *AmE* -ˈfɔːrm-/ *noun* (often *disapproving*) a person who behaves and thinks in the same way as most other people and who does not want to be different ▸ **con·form·ist** *adj.*: *Boys tend to be less conformist than girls.*—see also NONCONFORMIST

con·form·ity /kənˈfɔːməti; *AmE* -ˈfɔːrm-/ *noun* [U] **~ (to/with sth)** (*formal*) behaviour or actions that follow the accepted rules of society **IDM** **in conˈformity with sth** following the rules of sth; conforming to sth: *regulations that are in conformity with European law*

con·found /kənˈfaʊnd/ *verb* [VN] (*formal*) **1** to confuse and surprise sb: *The sudden rise in share prices has confounded economists.* **2** to prove sb/sth wrong: *to confound expectations/an argument/expert opinion* ◇ *She confounded her critics and proved she could do the job.*

3 (*old-fashioned*) to defeat an enemy **IDM** **conˈfound it/ you!** (*old-fashioned*) used to show that you are angry about sth/with sb

con·found·ed /kənˈfaʊndɪd/ *adj.* [only before noun] (*old-fashioned*) used when describing sth to show that you are annoyed

con·front /kənˈfrʌnt/ *verb* [VN] **1** (of problems or a difficult situation) to appear and need to be dealt with by sb: *the economic problems confronting the country* ◇ *The government found itself confronted by massive opposition.* **2** to deal with a problem or difficult situation: *She knew that she had to confront her fears.* **3** to face sb so that they cannot avoid seeing and hearing you, especially in an unfriendly or dangerous situation: *This was the first time he had confronted an armed robber.* **4 ~ sb with sb/sth** to make sb face or deal with an unpleasant or difficult person or situation: *He confronted her with a choice between her career or their relationship.* **5** (**be confronted with sth**) to have sth in front of you that you have to deal with or react to: *Most people when confronted with a horse will pat it.*

con·fron·ta·tion /ˌkɒnfrʌnˈteɪʃn; *AmE* ˌkɑːnfrən-/ *noun* [U, C] **~ (with sb)** | **~ (between A and B)** a situation in which there is an angry disagreement between people or groups who have different opinions: *She wanted to avoid another confrontation with her father.* ◇ *confrontation between employers and unions*

con·fuse /kənˈfjuːz/ *verb* [VN] **1** to make sb unable to think clearly or understand sth: *They confused me with conflicting accounts of what happened.* **2 ~ A and/with B** to think wrongly that sb/sth is sb/sth else [SYN] MIX UP: *People often confuse me and my twin sister.* ◇ *Be careful not to confuse quantity with quality.* **3** to make a subject more difficult to understand: *His comments only served to confuse the issue further.*

con·fused /kənˈfjuːzd/ *adj.* **1** unable to think clearly or to understand what is happening or what sb is saying: *People are confused about all the different labels on food these days.* ◇ *He was depressed and in a confused state of mind.* ◇ *I'm confused—say all that again.* **2** not clear or easy to understand: *The children gave a confused account of what had happened.* ▸ **con·fused·ly** /-ədli/ *adv.*

con·fus·ing /kənˈfjuːzɪŋ/ *adj.* difficult to understand; not clear: *The instructions on the box are very confusing.* ◇ *a very confusing experience* ▸ **con·fus·ing·ly** *adv.*

con·fu·sion /kənˈfjuːʒn/ *noun* **1** [U, C] **~ (about/over sth)** | **~ (as to sth)** a state of uncertainty about what is happening, what you should do, what sth means, etc: *There is some confusion about what the correct procedure should be.* ◇ *a confusion as to what to do next* **2** [U, C] **~ (between A and B)** the fact of making a mistake about who sb is or what sth is: *To avoid confusion, please write the children's names clearly on all their school clothes.* ◇ *confusion between letters of the alphabet like 'o' or 'a'* **3** [U] a feeling of embarrassment when you do not understand sth and are not sure what to do in a situation: *He looked at me in confusion and did not answer the question.* ◇ *Sacha felt confusion sweeping over her as she read the letter.* **4** [U] a situation of disorder in which people do not know what action to take: *Fighting had broken out and all was chaos and confusion.* ◇ *Her unexpected arrival threw us into total confusion.*

con·fute /kənˈfjuːt/ *verb* [VN] (*rare, formal*) to prove a person or an argument to be wrong

conga /ˈkɒŋɡə; *AmE* ˈkɑːŋɡə/ *noun* a fast dance in which the dancers follow a leader in a long winding line, with each person holding on to the person in front; a piece of music for this dance

con·geal /kənˈdʒiːl/ *verb* [V] (of blood, fat, etc.) to become thick or solid: *congealed blood* ◇ *The cold remains of supper had congealed on the plate.* ◇ (*figurative*) *The bitterness and tears had congealed into hatred.*

con·gen·ial /kənˈdʒiːniəl/ *adj.* (*formal*) **1** (of a person) pleasant to spend time with because their interests and character are similar to your own: *a congenial colleague* **2 ~ (to sb)** (of a place, job, etc.) pleasant because it suits your character: *a congenial working environment* **3 ~ (to**

aɪ	aʊ	eɪ	əʊ	oʊ	ɔɪ	ɪə	eə	ʊə	j	w
my	now	say	go	go	boy	near	hair	pure	yes	wet
			(BrE)	(AmE)						

C

sth) (*formal*) suitable for sth: *a situation that was congenial to the expression of nationalist opinions*

con·gen·i·tal /kən'dʒenɪtl/ *adj.* **1** (of a disease or medical condition) existing since or before birth: *congenital abnormalities* **2** [only before noun] existing as part of a person's character and not likely to change: *a congenital inability to tell the truth* **3** [only before noun] (of a person) born with a particular illness: (*figurative*) *a congenital liar* (= one who will not change)

con·ger /'kɒŋgə(r); *AmE* 'kɑːŋ-/ (also ˌconger 'eel) *noun* a large EEL (= a long thin fish) that lives in the sea

con·gest·ed /kən'dʒestɪd/ *adj.* **1 ~ (with sth)** crowded; full of vehicles or traffic: *congested city streets* ◊ *Many of Europe's airports are heavily congested.* **2** (*medical*) (of a part of the body) blocked with blood or MUCUS ▶ **con·ges·tion** /kən'dʒestʃən/ *noun* [U]: *traffic congestion and pollution* ◊ *congestion of the lungs* ◊ *medicine to relieve nasal congestion*

con·glom·er·ate /kən'glɒmərət; *AmE* -'glɑː-/ *noun* **1** [C] (*business*) a large company formed by joining together different firms: *a media conglomerate* **2** [sing.] (*written*) a number of things or parts that are put together to form a whole **3** [U] (*geology*) a type of rock made of small stones held together by dried clay

con·glom·er·ation /kən,glɒmə'reɪʃn; *AmE* -,glɑːm-/ *noun* [C, usually sing.] **1 ~ (of sth)** (*formal*) a mixture of different things that are found all together: *a conglomeration of buildings of different sizes and styles* **2** [U] the process of forming a conglomerate or the state of being a conglomerate

con·gratu·late /kən'grætʃuleɪt/ *verb* [VN] **1 ~ sb (on sth)** to tell sb that you are pleased about their success or achievements: *I congratulated them all on their results.* ◊ *The authors are to be congratulated on producing such a clear and authoritative work.* **2 ~ yourself (on sth)** to feel pleased and proud because you have achieved sth or been successful at sth: *You can congratulate yourself on having done an excellent job.*

con·gratu·la·tion /kən,grætʃu'leɪʃn/ *noun* **1** (**congratulations**) [pl.] a message congratulating sb (= saying that you are happy about their good luck or success): *to offer / send your congratulations to sb* **2** (**Congratulations!**) used when you want to congratulate sb: *'We're getting married!' 'Congratulations!'* ◊ *Congratulations on your exam results!* **3** [U] the act of congratulating sb: *a letter of congratulation*

con·gratu·la·tory /kən,grætʃu'leɪtəri; *AmE* kən-'grætʃələtɔːri/ *adj.* expressing congratulations: *a congratulatory message*

con·gre·gate /'kɒŋgrɪgeɪt; *AmE* 'kɑːŋ-/ *verb* [V] to come together in a group: *Young people often congregate in the main square in the evenings.*

con·gre·ga·tion /,kɒŋgrɪ'geɪʃn; *AmE* ,kɑːŋ-/ *noun* [C+sing./pl. *v.*] **1** a group of people who are gathered together in a church to worship God, not including the priest and CHOIR: *The congregation stood to sing the hymn.* **2** the group of people who belong to a particular church and go there regularly to worship ▶ **con·gre·ga·tion·al** /,kɒŋgrɪ'geɪʃnl; *AmE* ,kɑːŋ-/ *adj.*: *congregational singing*

Con·gre·ga·tion·al·ism /,kɒŋgrɪ'geɪʃnəlɪzəm; *AmE* ,kɑːŋ-/ *noun* a type of Christianity in which the congregation of each church is responsible for its own affairs ▶ **Con·gre·ga·tion·al** *adj.* **Con·gre·ga·tion·al·ist** *noun*

con·gress /'kɒŋgres; *AmE* 'kɑːŋgrəs/ *noun* [C+sing./pl. *v.*] **1** a large formal meeting or series of meetings where representatives from different groups discuss ideas, make decisions, etc: *an international congress of trades unions* **2** (**Congress**) (in the US and some other countries) the name of the group of people who are elected to make laws, in the US consisting of the SENATE and the HOUSE OF REPRESENTATIVES: *Congress will vote on the proposals tomorrow.* **3** used in the names of political parties in some countries: *the African National Congress*

con·gres·sion·al /kən'greʃənl/ *adj.* [only before noun] related to or belonging to a congress or the Congress in the US: *a congressional committee / bill* ◊ *the midterm Congressional elections*

Con·gress·man /'kɒŋgresmən; *AmE* 'kɑːŋgrəs-/, **Con·gress·woman** /'kɒŋgreswʊmən; *AmE* 'kɑːŋgrəs-/ *noun* (*pl.* **-men** /-mən/ **-women** /-wɪmɪn/) (also **Con·gress·person** /-pɜːsn; *AmE* -pɜːrsn/) a member of Congress in the US, especially the House of Representatives

con·gru·ent /'kɒŋgruənt; *AmE* 'kɑːŋ-/ *adj.* **1** (*geometry*) having the same size and shape: *congruent triangles* **2 ~ (with sth)** (*formal*) suitable for sth; appropriate in a particular situation ▶ **con·gru·ence** /'kɒŋgruəns; *AmE* 'kɑːŋ-/ *noun* [U]

con·ic·al /'kɒnɪkl; *AmE* 'kɑːn-/ *adj.* shaped like a CONE

con·ifer /'kɒnɪfə(r); 'kəʊn-; *AmE* 'kɑːn-; 'koʊn-/ *noun* any tree that produces hard dry fruit called CONES. Most conifers are EVERGREEN (= have leaves that stay on the tree all year). ▶ **con·ifer·ous** /kə'nɪfərəs/ *adj.*: *coniferous trees / forests*

con·jec·ture /kən'dʒektʃə(r)/ *noun, verb*

■ *noun* (*formal*) **1** [C] an opinion or idea that is not based on definite knowledge and is formed by guessing SYN GUESS: *The truth of his conjecture was confirmed by the newspaper report.* **2** [U] the forming of an opinion or idea that is not based on definite knowledge SYN GUESS: *What was going through the killer's mind is a matter for conjecture.* ▶ **con·jec·tural** /kən'dʒektʃərəl/ *adj.*

■ *verb* (*formal*) to form an opinion about sth even though you do not have much information on it SYN GUESS: [V] *We can only conjecture about what was in the killer's mind.* ◊ [Vthat] *He conjectured that the population might double in ten years.* ◊ [VN] *She conjectured the existence of a completely new species.* [also V wh-, VN to inf]

con·join /kən'dʒɔɪn/ *verb* [V, VN] (*formal*) to join together; to join two or more things together

con,joined 'twin *noun* (*technical*) = SIAMESE TWIN

con·ju·gal /'kɒndʒəgl; *AmE* 'kɑːn-/ *adj.* [only before noun] (*formal*) connected with marriage and the sexual relationship between a husband and wife: *conjugal love / rights*

con·ju·gate /'kɒndʒəgeɪt; *AmE* 'kɑːn-/ *verb* (*grammar*) **1** [VN] to give the different forms of a verb, as they vary according to NUMBER, PERSON, tense, etc. **2** [V] (of a verb) to have different forms, showing NUMBER, PERSON, tense, etc: *How does this verb conjugate?*—compare DECLINE

con·ju·ga·tion /,kɒndʒu'geɪʃn; *AmE* ,kɑːndʒə-/ *noun* (*grammar*) **1** [C, U] the way in which a verb conjugates: *a verb with an irregular conjugation* **2** [C] a group of verbs that conjugate in the same way: *Latin verbs of the second conjugation*

con·junc·tion /kən'dʒʌŋkʃn/ *noun* **1** [C] (*grammar*) a word that joins words, phrases or sentences, for example 'and', 'but', 'or' **2** [C] (*formal*) a combination of events, etc., that causes a particular result: *The conjunction of low inflation and low unemployment came as a very pleasant surprise.* **3** [C, U] (*astronomy*) the fact of stars, planets, etc. passing close together as seen from the earth ⏺ **in con'junction with** (*formal*) together with: *The police are working in conjunction with tax officers on the investigation.* ◊ *The system is designed to be used in conjunction with a word processing program.*

con·junc·tiv·itis /kən,dʒʌŋktɪ'vaɪtɪs/ *noun* [U] an infectious eye disease that causes pain and swelling in part of the eye

con·jure /'kʌndʒə(r)/ *verb* to do clever tricks such as making things seem to appear or disappear as if by magic: [V] *Her grandfather taught her to conjure.* ◊ [VN+adv. / prep.] *He could conjure coins from behind people's ears.* PHRV ˌconjure sth↔'up **1** to make sth appear as a picture in your mind SYN EVOKE: *That smell always conjures up memories of holidays in France.* **2** to ask the spirit of a dead person to appear by using special words **conjure sth from / out of sth** to create sth or make sth appear in a surprising or unexpected way: *He conjured a delicious meal out of a few leftovers.*

con·jur·ing /'kʌndʒərɪŋ/ *noun* [U] entertainment in the form of magic tricks, especially ones which seem to make things appear or disappear: *a conjuring trick*

con·juror (also **con·jurer**) /'kʌndʒərə(r)/ *noun* a person who performs conjuring tricks

b	d	f	g	h	k	l	m	n	p	r
bad	did	fall	get	hat	cat	leg	man	now	pen	red

conk /kɒŋk; *AmE* kɑːŋk; kɔːŋk/ *verb, noun*
■ *verb* [VN] (*informal, especially AmE*) to hit sb hard on their head **PHRV** ,conk 'out (*informal*) **1** (of a machine, etc.) to stop working: *The car conked out halfway up the hill.* **2** (*especially AmE*) (of a person) to fall asleep because you are very tired
■ *noun* (*BrE, slang*) a person's nose

conk·er /'kɒŋkə(r); *AmE* 'kɑːŋ-/ *noun* (*informal, especially BrE*) **1** [C] the smooth shiny brown nut of the HORSE CHESTNUT tree—compare CHESTNUT, HORSE CHESTNUT **2** (**conkers**) [U] (*BrE*) a children's game played with conkers on strings, in which two players take turns to try to hit and break each other's conker

'**con man** *noun* (*informal*) a man who tricks others into giving him money, etc.

con·nect /kə'nekt/ *verb*
JOIN | **1** ~ **A to/with B** | ~ **A and B** to join together two or more things; to be joined together: [VN] *The towns are connected by train and bus services.* ◇ *The canal was built to connect Sheffield with the Humber estuary.* ◇ *a connecting door* (= one that connects two rooms) ◇ [V] *The rooms on this floor connect.*
ELECTRICITY/GAS/WATER | **2** [VN] ~ **sth** (**to sth**) to join sth to the main supply of electricity, gas, water, etc. or to another piece of equipment: *First connect the printer to the computer.* ◇ *We're waiting for the telephone to be connected.* **OPP** DISCONNECT
LINK | **3** [VN] [usually passive] ~ **sb/sth** (**with sb/sth**) to have a link with sb/sth: *They are connected by marriage.* ◇ *The two subjects are closely connected.* ◇ *jobs connected with the environment*—see also UNCONNECTED, WELL CON-NECTED **4** [VN] ~ **sb/sth** (**with sb/sth**) to notice or make a link between people, things, events, etc. **SYN** ASSOCIATE: *There was nothing to connect him with the crime.* ◇ *I was surprised to hear them mentioned together; I had never connected them before.*
OF TRAIN/BUS/PLANE | **5** [V] ~ (**with sth**) to arrive just before another one leaves so that passengers can change from one to the other: *His flight to Amsterdam connects with an afternoon flight to New York.* ◇ *There's a connecting flight at noon.*
TELEPHONE LINES | **6** [VN] to join telephone lines so that people can speak to each other **SYN** PUT THROUGH: *Hold on please, I'm trying to connect you.* **OPP** DISCONNECT
FORM RELATIONSHIP | **7** [V] ~ (**with sb**) (*especially AmE*) to form a good relationship with sb so that you like and understand each other: *They met a couple of times but they didn't really connect.*
HIT | **8** [V] (*especially AmE*) ~ (**with sb/sth**) (*informal*) to hit sb/sth: *The blow connected and she felt a surge of pain.* **PHRV** con,nect sth↔'up (**to sth**) | con,nect 'up (**to sth**) to join sth to a supply of electricity, gas, etc. or to another piece of equipment; to be joined in this way: *She connected up the two computers.* **OPP** DISCONNECT

con·nec·tion (*BrE* also *less frequent* **con·nex·ion**) /kə'nekʃn/ *noun*
LINK | **1** [C] ~ (**between A and B**) | ~ (**with sth**) something that connects two facts, ideas, etc: *Scientists have estab-lished a connection between cholesterol levels and heart disease.* ◇ *His resignation must have some connection with the recent scandal.* ◇ *a direct/close/strong connection with sth* ◇ *How did you make the connection* (= realize that there was a connection between two facts that did not seem to be related)?
BEING CONNECTED | **2** [U] ~ (**to sth**) the act of connecting or the state of being connected: *Connection to the gas supply was delayed for three days.*
IN ELECTRICAL SYSTEM | **3** [C] a point, especially in an elec-trical system, where two parts connect: *A faulty con-nection caused the machine to stop.*
TRAIN/BUS/PLANE | **4** [C] a train, bus or plane at a station or an airport that a passenger can take soon after getting off another in order to continue their journey: *We arrived in good time for the connection to Paris.* **5** [C, usually pl.] a means of travelling to another place: *There are good bus and train connections between the resort and major cities.*
PERSON/ORGANIZATION | **6** [C, usually pl.] a person or an

organization that you know and that can help or advise you in your social or professional life: *One of my business connections gave them my name.*
DISTANT RELATIVES | **7** (**connections**) [pl.] people who are your relatives, but not members of your close family: *She is British and also has German connections.*
IDM **in con nection with sb/sth** (*written*) for reasons connected with sb/sth: *A man has been arrested in con-nection with the murder of the teenager.* ◇ *I am writing to you in connection with your recent job application.* **in this/ that connection** (*formal*) for reasons connected with sth recently mentioned

con·nect·ive /kə'nektɪv/ *adj., noun*
■ *adj.* (especially *medical*) that connects things: *connective tissue*
■ *noun* (*grammar*) a word that connects two parts of a sentence: *Don't overuse a causal connective like 'because'.*

con·niv·ance /kə'naɪvəns/ *noun* [U] (*disapproving*) help in doing sth wrong; the failure to stop sth wrong from happening: *The crime was committed with the connivance of a police officer.*

con·nive /kə'naɪv/ *verb* [V] (*disapproving*) **1** ~ **at/in sth** to seem to allow sth wrong to happen: *She knew that if she said nothing she would be conniving in an injustice.* **2** ~ (**with sb**) (**to do sth**) to work together with sb to do sth wrong or illegal **SYN** CONSPIRE: *The government was accused of having connived with the security forces to permit murder.*

con·niv·ing /kə'naɪvɪŋ/ *adj.* (*disapproving*) behaving in a way that secretly harms others or deliberately fails to prevent harm to others

con·nois·seur /ˌkɒnə'sɜː(r); *AmE* ˌkɑːnə'sɜːr; -'sʊr/ *noun* an expert on matters involving the judgement of beauty, quality or skill in art, food or music: *a connoisseur of Italian painting* ◇ *a wine connoisseur*

con·no·ta·tion /ˌkɒnə'teɪʃn; *AmE* ˌkɑːn-/ *noun* an idea suggested by a word in addition to its main meaning: *The word 'professional' has connotations of skill and excel-lence.* ◇ *negative connotations*

con·note /kə'nəʊt; *AmE* kə'noʊt/ *verb* [VN] (*formal*) (of a word) to suggest a feeling, an idea, etc. as well as the main meaning: *Very soon 'Third World' came to connote poverty.*—compare DENOTE

con·quer /'kɒŋkə(r); *AmE* 'kɑːŋ-/ *verb* [VN] **1** to take con-trol of a country or city and its people by force: *The Normans conquered England in 1066.* ◇ *conquered peoples/ races/territories* **2** to defeat sb, especially in a competi-tion, race, etc: *The world champion conquered yet another challenger last night.* ◇ *The team members were greeted like conquering heroes.* **3** to succeed in dealing with or controlling sth: *The only way to conquer a fear is to face it.* ◇ *Mount Everest was conquered* (= successfully climbed) *in 1953.* **4** to become very popular or successful in a place: *The band is now setting out to conquer the world.*

con·queror /'kɒŋkərə(r); *AmE* 'kɑːŋ-/ *noun* a person who conquers: *William the Conqueror* (= King William I of England)

con·quest /'kɒŋkwest; *AmE* 'kɑːŋ-/ *noun* **1** [sing., U] the act of taking control of a country, city, etc. by force: *the Norman Conquest* (= in 1066) **2** [C] an area of land taken by force: *the Spanish conquests in South Amer-ica* **3** [C] (usually *humorous*) a person that sb has per-suaded to love them or to have sex with them: *I'm just one of his many conquests.* **4** [U] the act of gaining control over sth that is difficult or dangerous: *the conquest of inflation*

con·san·guin·ity /ˌkɒnsæŋ'gwɪnəti; *AmE* ˌkɑːn-/ *noun* [U] (*formal*) relationship by birth in the same family

con·science /'kɒnʃəns; *AmE* 'kɑːn-/ *noun* **1** [C, U] the part of your mind that tells you whether your actions are right or wrong: *to have a clear/guilty conscience* (= to feel that you have done right/wrong) ◇ *This is a matter of individual conscience* (= everyone must make their own judgement about it). ◇ *He won't let it trouble his conscience.*—see also SOCIAL CONSCIENCE **2** [U,C] a feeling of guilt about sth you have done or failed to do: *She was seized by a sudden pang of conscience.* ◇ *I have a terrible* *conscience about it.* **3** [U] the fact of behaving in a way that you feel is right even though this may cause problems: *freedom of conscience* (= the freedom to do what you believe to be right) ◊ *Emilia is the voice of conscience in the play.*—see also PRISONER OF CONSCIENCE **IDM in (all/good) conscience** (*formal*) believing your actions to be fair [SYN] HONESTLY: *We cannot in all conscience refuse to help.* **on your 'conscience** making you feel guilty for doing or failing to do sth: *I'll write and apologize. I've had it on my conscience for weeks.*—more at PRICK *v.*

'conscience-stricken *adj.* feeling guilty about sth you have done or failed to do

con·scien·tious /ˌkɒnʃiˈenʃəs; *AmE* ˌkɑːn-/ *adj.* taking care to do things carefully and correctly: *a conscientious student/teacher* ▶ **con·scien·tious·ly** *adv.*: *She performed all her duties conscientiously.* **con·scien·tious·ness** *noun* [U]

ˌconscientious ob'jector *noun* a person who refuses to serve in the armed forces for moral reasons—compare DRAFT DODGER, PACIFIST

con·scious /ˈkɒnʃəs; *AmE* ˈkɑːn-/ *adj.* **1** [not before noun] ~ **of (doing) sth|** ~ **that** aware of sth; noticing sth: *She's very conscious of the problems involved.* ◊ *He became acutely conscious of having failed his parents.* ◊ *I was vaguely conscious that I was being watched.* [OPP] UNCONSCIOUS—see also SELF-CONSCIOUS **2** able to use your senses and mental powers to understand what is happening: *A patient who is not fully conscious should never be left alone.* [OPP] UNCONSCIOUS **3** (of actions, feelings, etc.) deliberate or controlled: *to make a conscious decision* ◊ *I made a conscious effort to get there on time.* ◊ *a conscious act of cruelty* [OPP] UNCONSCIOUS—compare SUBCONSCIOUS **4** being particularly interested in sth: *environmentally-conscious* ◊ *They have become increasingly health-conscious.* ▶ **con·scious·ly** *adv.*: *Whether consciously or unconsciously, you made a choice.*

con·scious·ness /ˈkɒnʃəsnəs; *AmE* ˈkɑːn-/ *noun* [U] **1** the state of being able to use your senses and mental powers to understand what is happening: *I can't remember any more—I must have lost consciousness.* ◊ *She did not regain consciousness and died the next day.* **2** the state of being aware of sth: *his consciousness of the challenge facing him* ◊ *surviving traces of class-consciousness* (= consciousness of different classes in society) **3** the ideas and opinions of a person or group: *her newly-developed political consciousness*—see also STREAM OF CONSCIOUSNESS

'consciousness-raising *noun* [U] the process of making people aware of important social and political issues

con·script *verb, noun*
■ *verb* /kənˈskrɪpt/ [VN] [usually passive] ~ **sb (into sth)** (*especially BrE*) (*AmE* usually **draft**) to make sb join the armed forces [SYN] CALL UP: *He was conscripted into the army in 1939.*
■ *noun* /ˈkɒnskrɪpt; *AmE* ˈkɑːn-/ (*especially BrE*) (*AmE* usually **draft·ee**) a person who has been conscripted to join the armed forces: *young army conscripts* ◊ *conscript soldiers/armies*—compare VOLUNTEER

con·scrip·tion /kənˈskrɪpʃn/ *noun* [U] (*especially BrE*) (*AmE* usually **the draft** [sing.]) the practice of ordering people by law to serve in the armed forces [SYN] CALL-UP

con·se·crate /ˈkɒnsɪkreɪt; *AmE* ˈkɑːn-/ *verb* **1** [VN] to state officially in a religious ceremony that sth is holy and can be used for religious purposes: *The church was consecrated in 1853.* ◊ *consecrated ground* **2** [VN] (in Christian belief) to make bread and wine into the body and blood of Christ **3** ~ **sb (as) (sth)** to state officially in a religious ceremony that sb is now a priest, etc: [VN-N] *He was consecrated (as) bishop last year.* [also VN] **4** [VN] ~ **sth/sb/yourself to sth** (*formal*) to give sth/sb or yourself to a special purpose, especially a religious one ▶ **con·se·cra·tion** /ˌkɒnsɪˈkreɪʃn; *AmE* ˌkɑːn-/ *noun* [C, U]: *the consecration of a church/bishop*

con·secu·tive /kənˈsekjətɪv/ *adj.* [usually before noun] following one after another in a series, without interruption: *She was absent for nine consecutive days.* ◊ *He is*

beginning his fourth consecutive term of office. ▶ **con·secu·tive·ly** *adv.*

con·sen·su·al /kənˈsenʃuəl/ *adj.* (*formal*) **1** which people in general agree with: *a consensual approach* **2** (of an activity) which the people taking part have agreed to: *consensual sex*

con·sen·sus /kənˈsensəs/ *noun* [sing., U] ~ **(among sb)|** ~ **(about sth)|** ~ **(that ...)** an opinion that all members of a group agree with: *There is a general consensus among teachers about the need for greater security in schools.* ◊ *There seems to be a consensus that the plan should be rejected.* ◊ *There is a growing consensus of opinion on this issue.* ◊ *an attempt to reach a consensus* ◊ *She is skilled at achieving consensus on sensitive issues.*

con·sent /kənˈsent/ *noun, verb*
■ *noun* **1** [U] ~ **(to sth)** permission to do sth, especially given by sb in authority: *Children under 16 cannot give consent to medical treatment.* ◊ *The written consent of a parent is required.* ◊ *to refuse/withhold your consent* ◊ *He is charged with taking a car without the owner's consent.*—see also AGE OF CONSENT **2** [U] agreement about sth: *She was chosen as leader by common consent* (= everyone agreed to the choice). ◊ *By mutual consent they didn't go out* (= they both agreed not to). **3** [C] an official document giving permission for sth
■ *verb* ~ **(to sth)** (rather *formal*) to agree to sth or give your permission for sth: [V] *When she told them what she intended they readily consented.* ◊ *He reluctantly consented to his daughter's marriage.* ◊ [V to inf] *She finally consented to answer our questions.*

con,senting 'adult *noun* a person who is considered old enough, by law, to decide whether they should agree to have sex; a person who has agreed to have sex

con·se·quence /ˈkɒnsɪkwəns; *AmE* ˈkɑːnsəkwens/ *noun* **1** [C, often pl.] ~ **(for sb/sth)** a result of sth that has happened: *This decision could have serious consequences for the future of the industry.* ◊ *Two hundred people lost their jobs as a direct consequence of the merger.* ◊ *He drove too fast with tragic consequences.* ◊ *to suffer/face/take the consequences of your actions* **2** [U] (*formal*) importance: *Don't worry. It's of no consequence.* **IDM in consequence (of sth)** (*formal*) as a result of sth: *The child was born deformed in consequence of an injury to its mother.*

con·se·quent /ˈkɒnsɪkwənt/ *adj.* ~ **(on/upon sth)** (*formal*) happening as a result of sth: *the lowering of taxes and the consequent increase in spending* ◊ *the responsibilities consequent upon the arrival of a new child*

con·se·quen·tial /ˌkɒnsɪˈkwenʃl; *AmE* ˌkɑːnsəˈk-/ *adj.* (*formal*) **1** happening as a result or an effect of sth: *retirement and the consequential reduction in income* **2** important; that will have important results: *The report discusses a number of consequential matters that are yet to be decided.* [OPP] INCONSEQUENTIAL ▶ **con·se·quen·tial·ly** /-ʃəli/ *adv.*

con·se·quent·ly /ˈkɒnsɪkwəntli; *AmE* ˈkɑːnsəkwentli/ *adv.* (*written*) as a result; therefore: *This poses a threat to agriculture and the food chain, and consequently to human health.*

con·ser·vancy /kənˈsɜːvənsi; *AmE* -ˈsɜːrv-/ *noun* **1** (**Conservancy**) [sing.+ sing./pl. *v.*] a group of officials who control the use of a port, a river, an area of land, etc: *the Thames Conservancy* ◊ *Texas Nature Conservancy* **2** [U] (*formal*) the protection of the natural environment [SYN] CONSERVATION: *nature conservancy*

con·ser·va·tion /ˌkɒnsəˈveɪʃn; *AmE* ˌkɑːnsərˈv-/ *noun* [U] **1** the protection of the natural environment: *to be interested in wildlife conservation* **2** the act of preventing sth from being lost, wasted, damaged or destroyed: *to encourage the conservation of water/fuel* ◊ *energy conservation*—see also CONSERVE

conser'vation area *noun* (*BrE*) an area where the natural environment or the buildings are protected by law from being damaged or changed

con·ser·va·tion·ist /ˌkɒnsəˈveɪʃənɪst; *AmE* ˌkɑːnsərˈv-/ *noun* a person who takes an active part in the protection of the environment: *a meeting of local conservationists*

C

æ	ɑː	e	ɜː	ə	ɪ	iː	i	ɒ	ɔː	ʌ	ʊ	u	uː
cat	father	ten	bird	about	sit	see	many	got	saw	cup	put	actual	too
								(BrE)					

con·ser·va·tism /kənˈsɜːvətɪzəm; *AmE* -ˈsɜːrv-/ *noun* [U] **1** the tendency to resist great or sudden change: *the innate conservatism of older people* **2** (also **Conservatism**) the political belief that society should change as little as possible: *an examination of the political theories of conservatism and liberalism* **3** (usually **Conservatism**) the principles of the Conservative Party in British politics

con·ser·va·tive /kənˈsɜːvətɪv; *AmE* -ˈsɜːrv-/ *adj., noun*
■ *adj.* **1** opposed to great or sudden social change; showing that you prefer traditional styles and values: *the conservative views of his parents* ◊ *Her style of dress was never conservative.* **2** (usually **Conservative**) connected with the British Conservative Party: *Conservative members/supporters* **3** (of an estimate) lower than what is probably the real amount or number: *At a conservative estimate, he'll be earning £50000.* ▶ **con·ser·va·tive·ly** *adv.*
■ *noun* **1** (usually **Conservative**) (*abbr.* **Con**) a member or supporter of the British Conservative Party **2** a conservative person

the Con·serv·a·tive Party *noun* [sing.+ sing./pl. *v.*] one of the main British political parties, on the political right, which especially believes in FREE ENTERPRISE and that industry should be privately owned

con·ser·va·toire /kənˈsɜːvətwɑː(r); *AmE* -ˈsɜːrv-/ (*BrE*) (*AmE* **con·ser·va·tory**) *noun* a school or college at which people are trained in music and theatre

con·ser·va·tory /kənˈsɜːvətri; *AmE* -ˈsɜːrvətɔːri/ *noun* (*pl.* **-ies**) **1** (*BrE*) a room with glass walls and a glass roof that is built on the side of a house. Conservatories are used for sitting in to enjoy the sun, and to protect plants from cold weather. **2** (*AmE*) = CONSERVATOIRE

con·serve *verb, noun*
■ *verb* /kənˈsɜːv; *AmE* -ˈsɜːrv/ [VN] **1** to use as little of sth as possible so that it lasts a long time: *Help to conserve energy by insulating your home.* **2** to protect sth and prevent it from being changed or destroyed: *new laws to conserve wildlife in the area*—see also CONSERVATION—compare PRESERVE
■ *noun* /ˈkɒnsɜːv; *AmE* ˈkɑːnsɜːrv/ [C, U] jam containing large or whole pieces of fruit: *a strawberry conserve*

con·sider /kənˈsɪdə(r)/ *verb* **1** to think about sth carefully, especially in order to make a decision: [VN] *She considered her options.* ◊ *a carefully considered response/decision* ◊ *The company is being actively considered as a potential partner* (= it is thought possible that it could become one). ◊ [V-ing] *We're considering buying a new car.* ◊ [V**wh-**] *We need to consider how the law might be reformed.* ◊ *He was considering what to do next.* ◊ [V] *I'd like some time to consider.* **2** ~ **sb/sth** (**as**) **sth** to think of sb/sth in a particular way: [VN-N] *This award is considered (to be) a great honour.* ◊ *He considers himself an expert on the subject.* ◊ *These workers are considered (as) a high-risk group.* ◊ [VN-ADJ] *Who do you consider (to be) responsible for the accident?* ◊ *Consider yourself lucky you weren't fired.* ◊ [V(**that**)] *She considers that it is too early to form a definite conclusion.* ◊ [VN**to**inf] *He's generally considered to have the finest tenor voice in the country.* [also VN**that**] **3** [VN] to think about sth, especially the feelings of other people, and be influenced by it when making a decision, etc: *You should consider other people before you act.* **4** [VN] (*formal*) to look carefully at sb/sth: *He stood there, considering the painting.* **IDM your con‚sidered o'pinion** your opinion that is the result of careful thought

con·sid·er·able /kənˈsɪdərəbl/ *adj.* (*formal*) great in amount, size, importance, etc: *The project wasted a considerable amount of time and money.* ◊ *Damage to the building was considerable.*

con·sid·er·ably /kənˈsɪdərəbli/ *adv.* (*formal*) much; a lot: *The need for sleep varies considerably from person to person.*

con·sid·er·ate /kənˈsɪdərət/ *adj.* always thinking of other people's wishes and feelings; careful not to hurt or upset others [SYN] THOUGHTFUL: *She is always polite and considerate towards her employees.* ◊ *It was very considerate of him to wait.* [OPP] INCONSIDERATE ▶ **con·sid·er·ate·ly** *adv.*

con·sid·er·ation /kənˌsɪdəˈreɪʃn/ *noun* **1** [U, C] (*formal*) the act of thinking carefully about sth: *Careful consideration should be given to issues of health and safety.* ◊ *The proposals are currently **under consideration*** (= being discussed). ◊ *After a few moments' consideration, he began to speak.* ◊ *a consideration of the legal issues involved* **2** [C] something that must be thought about when you are planning or deciding sth: *economic/commercial/environmental/practical considerations* ◊ *Time is another important consideration.* **3** [U] ~ (**for sb/sth**) the quality of being sensitive towards others and thinking about their wishes and feelings: *They showed no consideration whatsoever for my feelings.* ◊ *Journalists stayed away from the funeral **out of consideration** for the bereaved family.* ◊ *Their kindness and consideration will not be forgotten.* **4** [C] (*formal*) a reward or payment for a service [IDM] **in consideration of sth** (*formal*) as payment for sth: *a small sum in consideration of your services* **take sth into consideration** to think about and include a particular thing or fact when you are forming an opinion or making a decision: *The candidates' experience and qualifications will be taken into consideration when the decision is made.* ◊ *Taking everything into consideration, the event was a great success.*—more at MATURE *adj.*

con·sid·er·ing /kənˈsɪdərɪŋ/ *prep., conj.* used to show that you are thinking about a particular fact, and are influenced by it, when you make a statement about sth: *She's very active, considering her age.* ◊ *Considering he's only just started, he knows quite a lot about it.* ◊ *You've done very well, considering* (= in the difficult circumstances).

con·sign /kənˈsaɪn/ *verb* [VN] (*formal*) **1** ~ **sb/sth to sth** to put sb/sth somewhere in order to get rid of them: *I consigned her letter to the waste basket.* ◊ *What I didn't want was to see my mother consigned to an old people's home.* **2** ~ **sb/sth to sth** to put sb/sth in an unpleasant situation: *The decision to close the factory has **consigned** 6000 people to the scrap heap.* ◊ *A car accident consigned him to a wheelchair for the rest of his life.* **3** to give or send sth to sb

con·sign·ment /kənˈsaɪnmənt/ *noun* **1** [C] a quantity of goods that are sent or delivered somewhere: *a consignment of medicines* **2** [U] the act of sending or delivering sb/sth

con'signment store *noun* (*AmE*) a shop/store where people take their old clothes, etc. to be sold to sb else. The consignment store keeps part of the money after an item is sold and gives the other part to the person who brought it in.

con·sist /kənˈsɪst/ *verb* (not used in the progressive tenses) [PHRV] **con'sist in sth** (*formal*) to have sth as the main or only part or feature: *The beauty of the city consists in its magnificent buildings.* ◊ [+ -ing] *True education does not consist in simply being taught facts.* **con'sist of sth** to be formed from the things or people mentioned: *The committee consists of ten members.* ◊ *Their diet consisted largely of vegetables.* ◊ [+ -ing] *Most of the fieldwork consisted of making tape recordings.* ⇨ note at COMPRISE

con·sist·ency /kənˈsɪstənsi/ *noun* (*pl.* **-ies**) **1** [U] (*approving*) the quality of always behaving in the same way or of having the same opinions, standard, etc.; the quality of being consistent: *She has played with great consistency all season.* ◊ *We need to ensure the consistency of service to our customers.* [OPP] INCONSISTENCY **2** [C, U] the consistency of a mixture or a liquid substance is how thick, smooth, etc. it is: *Beat the ingredients together to a creamy consistency.* ◊ *The cement should have the consistency of wet sand.*

con·sist·ent /kənˈsɪstənt/ *adj.* **1** (*approving*) always behaving in the same way, or having the same opinions, standards, etc: *She's not very consistent in the way she treats her children.* ◊ *He has been Milan's most consistent player this season.* ◊ *We must be consistent in applying the rules.* ◊ *a consistent approach to the problem* ◊ *We need results that are consistent* (= of the same standard) *throughout the year.* **2** happening in the same way and continuing for a period of time: *the party's consistent failure to come up with any new policies* ◊ *a pattern of*

aɪ	aʊ	eɪ	ɔʊ	oʊ	ɔɪ	ɪə	eə	ʊə	j	w
my	now	say	go	go	boy	near	hair	pure	yes	wet
			(BrE)	(AmE)						

consistent growth in the economy **3** ~ **with sth** in agreement with sth; not CONTRADICTING sth: *The results are entirely consistent with our earlier research.* ◊ *injuries consistent with a fall from an upper storey* (= similar to those such a fall would have caused) **4** (of an argument or a set of ideas) having different parts that all agree with each other: *a well-thought-out and consistent argument* OPP INCONSISTENT ▶ **con·sist·ent·ly** *adv.*: *Her work has been of a consistently l.igh standard.* ◊ *We have argued consistently for a change in the law.*

con·sola·tion /ˌkɒnsəˈleɪʃn; *AmE* ˌkɑːn-/ *noun* [U, C] a person or thing that makes you feel better when you are unhappy or disappointed SYN COMFORT: *a few words of consolation* ◊ *If it's any consolation, she didn't get the job, either.* ◊ *The children were a great consolation to him when his wife died.*

conso'lation prize *noun* a small prize given to sb who has not won a competition

con·sola·tory /kənˈsɒlətəri; *AmE* kənˈsəʊlətɔːri; -ˈsɑːlə-/ *adj.* (*formal*) intended to make sb who is unhappy or disappointed feel better

con·sole¹ /kənˈsəʊl; *AmE* -ˈsoʊl/ *verb* ~ **sb/yourself** (**with sth**) to give comfort or sympathy to sb who is unhappy or disappointed: [VN] *Nothing could console him when his wife died.* ◊ *She put a consoling arm around his shoulders.* ◊ *Console yourself with the thought that you did your best.* ◊ [VN **that**] *I didn't like lying but I consoled myself that it was for a good cause.* ◊ [VN **speech**] *'Never mind,' Anne consoled her.*

con·sole² /ˈkɒnsəʊl; *AmE* ˈkɑːnsoʊl/ *noun* a flat surface which contains all the controls and switches for a machine, a piece of electronic equipment, etc.—picture on page A8

con·soli·date /kənˈsɒlɪdeɪt; *AmE* -ˈsɑːl-/ *verb* **1** to make a position of power or success stronger so that it is more likely to continue: [VN] *With this new movie he has consolidated his position as the country's leading director.* ◊ *Italy consolidated their lead with a second goal.* [also V] **2** (*technical*) to join things together into one; to be joined into one: [VN] *All the debts have been consolidated.* ◊ *consolidated accounts* ◊ [V] *The two companies consolidated for greater efficiency.* ▶ **con·soli·da·tion** /kənˌsɒlɪˈdeɪʃn; *AmE* -ˌsɑːl-/ *noun* [U]: *the consolidation of power/authority/democracy* ◊ *the consolidation of Japan's banking industry*

con·sommé /kənˈsɒmeɪ; *AmE* ˌkɑːnsəˈmeɪ/ *noun* [U] a clear soup made with the juices from meat

con·son·ance /ˈkɒnsənəns; *AmE* ˈkɑːn-/ *noun* **1** [U] ~ (**with sth**) (*formal*) agreement: *a policy that is popular because of its consonance with traditional party doctrine* **2** [U, C] (*music*) a combination of musical notes that sound pleasing together OPP DISSONANCE

con·son·ant /ˈkɒnsənənt; *AmE* ˈkɑːn-/ *noun, adj.*
▪ *noun* (*phonetics*) **1** a speech sound made by completely or partly stopping the flow of air being breathed out through the mouth **2** a letter of the alphabet that represents a consonant sound, for example 'b', 'c', 'd', 'f', etc.—compare VOWEL
▪ *adj.* ~ **with sth** (*formal*) agreeing with or being the same as sth else

con·sort *noun, verb*
▪ *noun* /ˈkɒnsɔːt; *AmE* ˈkɑːnsɔːrt/ **1** the husband or wife of a ruler: *the prince consort* (= the queen's husband) **2** a group of old-fashioned musical instruments, or a group of musicians who play music from several centuries ago
▪ *verb* /kənˈsɔːt; *AmE* -ˈsɔːrt/ [V] ~ **with sb** (*formal*) to spend time with sb that other people do not approve of: *He is known to have consorted with prostitutes.*

con·sor·tium /kənˈsɔːtiəm; *AmE* -ˈsɔːrt-/ *noun* (*pl.* **con·sor·tiums** or **con·sor·tia** /-tiə/) a group of people, countries, companies, etc. who are working together on a particular project: *the Anglo-French consortium that built the Channel Tunnel*

con·spicu·ous /kənˈspɪkjuəs/ *adj.* easy to see or notice; likely to attract attention: *Mary's red hair always made her conspicuous at school.* ◊ *I felt very conspicuous in my new car.* ◊ *The advertisements were all posted in a con-*

spicuous place. ◊ *The event was a conspicuous success* (= a very great one). OPP INCONSPICUOUS ▶ **con·spicu·ous·ly** *adv.*: *Women were conspicuously absent from the planning committee.* **con·spicu·ous·ness** *noun* [U] IDM **con,spicu·ous by your ¹absence** not present in a situation or place, when it is obvious that you should be there: *When it came to cleaning up afterwards, Anne was conspicuous by her absence.*

con,spicuous con'sumption *noun* [U] the buying of expensive goods in order to impress people and show them how rich you are

con·spir·acy /kənˈspɪrəsi/ *noun* [C, U] (*pl.* **-ies**) ~ (**to do sth**)|~ (**against sb/sth**) a secret plan by a group of people to do sth harmful or illegal: *a conspiracy to overthrow the government* ◊ *conspiracies against the president* ◊ *a conspiracy of silence* (= an agreement not to talk publicly about sth which should not remain secret) ◊ *They were charged with conspiracy to murder.* ◊ *a conspiracy theory* (= the belief that a secret plan is responsible for a particular event)

con·spir·ator /kənˈspɪrətə(r)/ *noun* a person who is involved in a conspiracy

con·spira·tor·ial /kənˌspɪrəˈtɔːriəl/ *adj.* **1** connected with, or like, a conspiracy **2** (of a person's behaviour) suggesting that a secret is being shared: *'I know you understand,' he said and gave a conspiratorial wink.*

con·spire /kənˈspaɪə(r)/ *verb* **1** [V] ~ (**with sb**) (**against sb**)|~ (**together**) to secretly plan with other people to do sth illegal or harmful: *They were accused of conspiring against the king.* ◊ *They deny conspiring together to smuggle drugs.* ◊ *She admitted conspiring with her lover to murder her husband.* **2** ~ **against sb/sth**|~ **to do sth** (*written*) (of events) to seem to work together to make sth bad happen: [V] *Circumstances had conspired against them.* ◊ [V **to inf**] *Everything conspired to make her life a misery.*

con·stable /ˈkʌnstəbl; *AmE* ˈkɑːn-/ *noun* (used especially when talking to a police officer of the lowest rank) = POLICE CONSTABLE: *Have you finished your report, Constable?*—see also CHIEF CONSTABLE

con·stabu·lary /kənˈstæbjələri; *AmE* -leri/ *noun* [C+sing./pl. *v.*] (*pl.* **-ies**) (in Britain) the police force of a particular area or town

con·stancy /ˈkɒnstənsi; *AmE* ˈkɑːn-/ *noun* [U] (*formal*) **1** the quality of staying the same and not changing: *the constancy of temperature inside the plane* **2** (*approving*) the quality of being faithful SYN FIDELITY: *He admired her courage and constancy.*

con·stant /ˈkɒnstənt; *AmE* ˈkɑːn-/ *adj., noun*
▪ *adj.* **1** [usually before noun] happening all the time or repeatedly: *constant interruptions* ◊ *a constant stream of visitors all day* ◊ *Babies need constant attention.* ◊ *This entrance is in constant use.* **2** that does not change SYN FIXED: *travelling at a constant speed of 50 m.p.h.*
▪ *noun* (*mathematics, physics*) a number or quantity that does not vary SYN VARIABLE

con·stant·ly /ˈkɒnstəntli; *AmE* ˈkɑːn-/ *adv.* all the time; repeatedly: *Fashion is constantly changing.* ◊ *Heat the sauce, stirring constantly.*

con·stel·la·tion /ˌkɒnstəˈleɪʃn; *AmE* ˌkɑːn-/ *noun* **1** a group of stars that forms a shape in the sky and has a name **2** (*written*) a group of related ideas, things or people: *a constellation of Hollywood talent*

con·ster·na·tion /ˌkɒnstəˈneɪʃn; *AmE* ˌkɑːnstərˈn-/ *noun* [U] (*formal*) a feeling of great surprise, shock or anxiety SYN DISMAY: *The announcement of her retirement caused consternation among tennis fans.*

con·sti·pated /ˈkɒnstɪpeɪtɪd; *AmE* ˈkɑːn-/ *adj.* unable to get rid of waste material from the bowels easily

con·sti·pa·tion /ˌkɒnstɪˈpeɪʃn; *AmE* ˌkɑːn-/ *noun* [U] the condition of being unable to get rid of waste material from the bowels easily (= being constipated)

con·stitu·ency /kənˈstɪtjuənsi; *AmE* -tʃu-/ *noun* (*pl.* **-ies**) **1** [C] (in Britain) a district that elects its own representative to parliament: *Unemployment is high in her constituency.* ◊ *He owns a house in his Darlington constituency.* **2** [C+sing./pl. *v.*] (in Britain) the people

b	d	f	g	h	k	l	m	n	p	r
bad	**did**	**fall**	**get**	**hat**	**cat**	**leg**	**man**	**now**	**pen**	**red**

C

who live in and vote in a particular district: *constituency opinion* **3** [C+sing./pl. *v.*] a particular group of people in society who are likely to support sb politically: *the Labour party's traditional constituency among trade unions*

con·stitu·ent /kənˈstɪtjuənt; *AmE* -tʃu-/ *noun, adj.*

■ *noun* **1** a person who lives, and can vote in a constituency: *She has the full support of her constituents.* **2** one of the parts of sth that combine to form the whole

■ *adj.* [only before noun] (*formal*) forming or helping to make a whole: *to break something up into its constituent parts/elements*

con·stituent as·sembly *noun* [C+sing./pl. *v.*] a group of elected representatives with the power to make or change a country's CONSTITUTION

con·sti·tute /ˈkɒnstɪtjuːt; *AmE* ˈkɑːnstətuːt/ *verb* (*written*) **1** *linking verb* [V-N] (not used in the progressive tenses) to be considered as sth: *Does such an activity constitute a criminal offence?* ◇ *The increase in racial tension constitutes a threat to our society.* ◇ *His action was interpreted as constituting a threat to the community.* **2** *linking verb* [V-N] (not used in the progressive tenses) to be the parts that together form sth SYN MAKE UP: *Female workers constitute the majority of the labour force.* ⇨ note at COMPRISE **3** [VN] [usually passive] to form a group legally or officially: *The committee was constituted in 1974 by an Act of Parliament.*

con·sti·tu·tion /ˌkɒnstɪˈtjuːʃn; *AmE* ˌkɑːnstəˈtuːʃn/ *noun* **1** [C] the system of laws and basic principles that a state, a country or an organization is governed by: *your right to vote under the constitution* ◇ *According to the constitution ...* ◇ *to propose a new amendment to the Constitution* (= of the US) ◇ *the South African Constitution* **2** [C] the condition of a person's body and how healthy it is: *to have a healthy/strong/weak constitution* **3** [U, C] (*formal*) the way sth is formed or organized SYN STRUCTURE: *the genetic constitution of cells* **4** [U] (*formal*) the act of forming sth: *He recommended the constitution of a review committee.*

con·sti·tu·tion·al /ˌkɒnstɪˈtjuːʃənl; *AmE* ˌkɑːnstəˈtuː-/ *adj., noun*

■ *adj.* **1** [only before noun] connected with the constitution of a country or an organization: *constitutional government/reform* ◇ *a constitutional amendment* **2** allowed or limited by the constitution of a country or an organization: *They can't pass this law. It's not constitutional.* ◇ *constitutional rights* ◇ *a constitutional monarchy* (= a country with a king or queen, whose power is controlled by a set of laws and basic principles) OPP UNCONSTITUTIONAL **3** [usually before noun] related to the body's ability to stay healthy, be strong and fight illness ▶ **con·sti·tu·tion·al·ly** /-ʃənəli/ *adv.*: *constitutionally guaranteed rights*

■ *noun* (*old-fashioned* or *humorous*) a short walk that people take because it is good for their health

con·sti·tu·tion·al·ism /ˌkɒnstɪˈtjuːʃənəlɪzəm; *AmE* ˌkɑːnstəˈtuː-/ *noun* [U] a belief in constitutional government

con·sti·tu·tion·al·ity /ˌkɒnstɪtjuːʃəˈnæləti; *AmE* ˌkɑːnstətuː-/ *noun* [U] (*technical*) the fact that sth is acceptable according to a CONSTITUTION: *They questioned the constitutionality of the law.*

con·strain /kənˈstreɪn/ *verb* (*formal*) **1** [VN to inf] [usually passive] to force sb to do sth or behave in a particular way: *The evidence was so compelling that he felt constrained to accept it.* **2** [VN] [often passive] ~ **sb** (**from doing sth**) to restrict or limit sb/sth: *Research has been constrained by a lack of funds.* ◇ *She felt constrained from continuing by the threat of losing her job.*

con·strained /kənˈstreɪnd/ *adj.* (*formal*) not natural; forced or too controlled: *constrained emotions*

con·straint /kənˈstreɪnt/ *noun* **1** [C] ~ (**on sth**) a thing that limits or restricts sth, or your freedom to do sth SYN RESTRICTION: *constraints of time/money/space* ◇ *financial/economic/legal/political constraints* ◇ *This decision will impose serious constraints on all schools.* ◇ *Magistrates are under a constraint not to send young*

people to prison. **2** [U] strict control over the way that you behave or are allowed to behave: *At last we could relax and talk without constraint.*

con·strict /kənˈstrɪkt/ *verb* **1** to become tighter or narrower; to make sth tighter or narrower: [V] *Her throat constricted and she swallowed hard.* ◇ [VN] *a drug that constricts the blood vessels.* **2** [VN] to limit or restrict what sb is able to do: *Film-makers of the time were constricted by the censors.* ◇ *constricting rules and regulations* ▶ **con·strict·ed** *adj.*: *Her throat felt dry and constricted.* ◇ *a constricted vision of the world* **con·stric·tion** /kənˈstrɪkʃn/ *noun* [U, C]: *a feeling of constriction in the throat/chest* ◇ *political constrictions*

con·struct *verb, noun*

■ *verb* /kənˈstrʌkt/ [VN] **1** [often passive] ~ **sth** (**from/out of/of sth**) to build or make sth such as a road, building or machine: *When was the bridge constructed?* ◇ *They constructed a shelter out of fallen branches.* **2** to form sth by putting different things together: *You must learn how to construct a logical argument.* ◇ *to construct a theory/diagram/plan* ◇ *a well-constructed novel* **3** (*geometry*) to draw a line or shape according to the rules of mathematics: *to construct a triangle*

■ *noun* /ˈkɒnstrʌkt; *AmE* ˈkɑːn-/ (*formal*) **1** an idea or a belief that is based on various pieces of evidence which are not always true: *a contrast between lived reality and the construct held in the mind* **2** (*linguistics*) a group of words that form a phrase **3** a thing that is built or made

con·struc·tion /kənˈstrʌkʃn/ *noun*

OF ROADS/BUILDINGS | **1** [U] the process or method of building or making sth, especially roads, buildings, bridges, etc: *the construction industry* ◇ *road construction* ◇ *Work has been begun on the construction of the new airport.* ◇ *Our new offices are still under construction* (= being built). ◇ *the construction of a new database* **2** [U] the way that sth has been built or made: *light/strong/weak in construction* ◇ *ships of steel construction*

BUILDING/STRUCTURE | **3** [C] (*formal*) a thing that has been built or made: *The summer house was a simple wooden construction.*

GRAMMAR | **4** [C] the way in which words are used together and arranged to form a sentence, phrase, etc: *grammatical constructions*

OF THEORY, etc. | **5** [U, C] the creating of sth from ideas, opinions and knowledge: *the construction of a new theory*

MEANING | **6** [C] (*formal*) the way in which words, actions, statements, etc. are understood by sb SYN INTERPRETATION: *What construction do you put on this letter* (= what do you think it means)?

con·struc·tion·al /kənˈstrʌkʃənl/ *adj.* connected with the making or building of things

con·struction paper *noun* [U] (*AmE*) thick coloured paper that people cut out to make designs, models, etc.

con·struct·ive /kənˈstrʌktɪv/ *adj.* having a useful and helpful effect rather than being negative or with no purpose: *constructive criticism/suggestions/advice* ◇ *His work involved helping hyperactive children to use their energy in a constructive way.* ◇ *The government is encouraging all parties to play a constructive role in the reform process.*—compare DESTRUCTIVE ▶ **con·struct·ive·ly** *adv.*

con·struct·or /kənˈstrʌktə(r)/ *noun* a person or company that builds things, especially cars or aircraft

con·strue /kənˈstruː/ *verb* [VN] [usually passive] ~ **sth** (**as sth**) (*formal*) to understand the meaning of a word, a sentence, or an action in a particular way: *He considered how the remark was to be construed.* ◇ *Her words could hardly be construed as an apology.*

con·sul /ˈkɒnsl; *AmE* ˈkɑːnsl/ *noun* a government official who is the representative of his or her country in a foreign city: *the British consul in Miami* ▶ **con·su·lar** /ˈkɒnsjələ(r); *AmE* ˈkɑːnsəl-/ *adj.*: *consular officials*

con·sul·ate /ˈkɒnsjələt; *AmE* ˈkɑːnsəl-/ *noun* the building where a consul works: *the American consulate in Marseilles*—compare EMBASSY

con·sult /kənˈsʌlt/ *verb* **1** ~ **sb** (**about sth**) to go to sb for information or advice: [VN] *If the pain continues, consult your doctor.* ◇ *Have you consulted your lawyer about this?* ◇

s	t	v	z	ʃ	ʒ	tʃ	dʒ	θ	ð	ŋ
see	tea	van	zoo	shoe	vision	chain	jam	thin	this	sing

[V] *a consulting engineer* (= one who has expert knowledge and gives advice) **2 ~ (with) sb (about/on sth)** to discuss sth with sb to get their permission for sth, or to help you make a decision: [VN] *You shouldn't have done it without consulting me.* ◇ *I expect to be consulted about major issues.* ◇ [V] *I need to consult with my colleagues on the proposals.* **3** [VN] to look in or at sth to get information SYN REFER TO: *He consulted the manual.*

con·sult·ancy /kən'sʌltənsi/ *noun (pl. -ies)* **1** [C] a company that gives expert advice on a particular subject to other companies, people or organizations: *a management/design/computer consultancy* **2** [U] expert advice that a company or person is paid to provide on a particular subject: *consultancy fees*

con·sult·ant /kən'sʌltənt/ *noun* **1 ~ (on sth)** a person who knows a lot about a particular subject and is employed to give advice about it to other people: *a firm of management consultants* ◇ *the President's consultant on economic affairs* **2** (*BrE*) a hospital doctor of the highest rank who is a specialist in a particular area of medicine: *a consultant in obstetrics* ◇ *a consultant surgeon*—compare REGISTRAR

con·sult·ation /ˌkɒnsl'teɪʃn; *AmE* ˌkɑːn-/ *noun* **1** [U] the act of discussing sth with sb or with a group of people before making a decision about it: *a consultation document/paper/period/process* ◇ *acting in consultation with all the departments involved* ◇ *The decision was taken after close consultation with local residents.* **2** [C] a formal meeting to discuss sth: *extensive consultations between the two countries* **3** [C] a meeting with an expert, especially a doctor, to get advice or treatment **4** the act of looking for information in a book, etc: *There is a large collection of texts available for consultation on-screen.*

con·sulta·tive /kən'sʌltətɪv/ *adj.* giving advice or making suggestions SYN ADVISORY: *a consultative committee/body/document*

con'sulting room *noun* a room where a doctor talks to and examines patients

con·sume /kən'sjuːm; *AmE* -'suːm/ *verb* [VN] (*written*) **1** to use sth, especially fuel, energy or time: *The electricity industry consumes large amounts of fossil fuels.* **2** to eat or drink sth: *Before he died he had consumed a large quantity of alcohol.* **3 ~ sb (with sth)** [usually passive] to fill sb with a strong feeling: *Carolyn was consumed with guilt.* ◇ *Rage consumed him.* **4** (of fire) to completely destroy sth: *The hotel was quickly consumed by fire.*—see also CONSUMING, CONSUMPTION, TIME-CONSUMING

con·sumer /kən'sjuːmə(r); *AmE* -'suː-/ *noun* a person who buys goods or uses services: *consumer demand/choice/rights* ◇ *Health-conscious consumers want more information about the food they buy.* ◇ *a consumer society* (= one where buying and selling is considered to be very important) ◇ *Tax cuts will boost consumer confidence after the recession.*—compare PRODUCER

con,sumer 'durables (*BrE*) (*AmE* **'durable goods**) *noun* [pl.] (*business*) goods which are expected to last for a long time after they have been bought, such as cars, televisions, etc.

con'sumer goods *noun* [pl.] goods such as food, clothing, etc. bought by individual customers—compare CAPITAL GOODS

con·sumer·ism /kən'sjuːmərɪzəm; *AmE* -'suː-/ *noun* [U] (sometimes *disapproving*) the buying and using of goods and services; the belief that it is good for a society or an individual person to buy and use a large quantity of goods and services ▶ **con·sumer·ist** *adj.*: *consumerist values*

,consumer 'price index *noun* [sing.] (*abbr.* **CPI**) (in the US) a list of the prices of some ordinary goods and services which shows how much these prices change each month—see also RETAIL PRICE INDEX

con·sum·ing /kən'sjuːmɪŋ; *AmE* -'suː-/ *adj.* [only before noun] (of a feeling, an interest, etc.) so strong or important that it takes up all your time and energy: *Basketball is his consuming passion.*—see also TIME-CONSUMING

con·sum·mate¹ /kən'sʌmət; 'kɒnsəmət; *AmE* 'kɑːn-/ *adj.* [usually before noun] (*formal*) extremely skilled; perfect: *She was a consummate performer.* ◇ *He played the shot with consummate skill.* ◇ (*disapproving*) *a consummate liar* ▶ **con·sum·mate·ly** *adv.*

con·sum·mate² /'kɒnsəmeɪt; *AmE* 'kɑːn-/ *verb* [VN] (*formal*) **1** to make a marriage or a relationship complete by having sex: *The marriage lasted only a week and was never consummated.* **2** to make sth complete or perfect

con·sum·ma·tion /ˌkɒnsə'meɪʃn; *AmE* ˌkɑːn-/ *noun* [C, U] **1** the act of making a marriage or relationship complete by having sex **2** the fact of making sth complete or perfect: *The paintings are the consummation of his life's work.*

con·sump·tion /kən'sʌmpʃn/ *noun* [U] **1** the act of using energy, food or materials; the amount used: *the production of fuel for domestic consumption* (= to be used in the country where it is produced) ◇ *Gas and oil consumption always increases in cold weather.* ◇ *The meat was declared unfit for human consumption.* ◇ *He was advised to reduce his alcohol consumption.* ◇ *Her speech to party members was not intended for public consumption* (= to be heard by the public).—see also CONSUME **2** the act of buying and using products: *Consumption rather than saving has become the central feature of contemporary societies.*—see also CONSPICUOUS CONSUMPTION, CONSUME **3** (*old-fashioned*) a serious infectious disease of the lungs SYN TUBERCULOSIS

con·sump·tive /kən'sʌmptɪv/ *noun* (*old-fashioned*) a person who suffers from consumption (= a disease of the lungs) ▶ **con·sump·tive** *adj.*

cont. (also **contd**) *abbr.* continued: *cont. on p74*

con·tact /'kɒntækt; *AmE* 'kɑːn-/ *noun, verb*
■ *noun*
  ACT OF COMMUNICATING | **1** [U] **~ (with sb)** | **~ (between A and B)** the act of communicating with sb, especially regularly: *I don't have much contact with my uncle.* ◇ *There is little contact between the two organizations.* ◇ *Have you kept in contact with any of your friends from college* (= do you still see them or speak or write to them)*?* ◇ *She's lost contact with* (= no longer sees or writes to) *her son.* ◇ *I finally made contact with* (= succeeded in speaking to or meeting) *her in Paris.* ◇ *The organization put me in contact with other people in a similar position* (= gave me their addresses or telephone numbers). ◇ *two people avoiding eye contact* (= avoiding looking directly at each other) ◇ *Here's my contact number* (= temporary telephone number) *while I'm away.*
  TOUCHING SB/STH | **2** [U] the state of touching sth: *His fingers were briefly in contact with the ball.* ◇ *This substance should not come into contact with food.* ◇ *a fear of physical contact* ◇ *This pesticide kills insects on contact* (= as soon as it touches them).
  MEETING SB/STH | **3** [U] the state of meeting sb or having to deal with sth: *In her job she often comes into contact with* (= meets) *lawyers.* ◇ *Children should be brought into contact with poetry at an early age.*
  RELATIONSHIP | **4** [C, usually pl.] an occasion on which you meet or communicate with sb; a relationship with sb: *We have good contacts with the local community.* ◇ *The company has maintained trade contacts with India.*
  PERSON | **5** [C] a person that you know, especially sb who can be helpful to you in your work: *social/personal contacts* ◇ *I've made some useful contacts in journalism.*
  ELECTRICAL | **6** [C] an electrical connection: *The switches close the contacts and complete the circuit.*
  FOR EYES | **7** (**contacts**) [pl.] (*informal*) = CONTACT LENSES
  MEDICAL | **8** [C] a person who may be infectious because he or she has recently been near to sb with a CONTAGIOUS disease
  IDM see POINT *n.*
■ *verb* [VN] to communicate with sb, for example by telephone or letter: *I've been trying to contact you all day.*

'contact lens (also *informal* **con·tact**, **lens**) *noun* a small round piece of thin plastic that you put on your eye to help you see better

con·ta·gion /kən'teɪdʒən/ *noun* **1** [U] the spreading of a disease by people touching each other: *There is no risk of contagion.* **2** [C] (*old use*) a disease that can be spread by

æ	ɑː	e	ɜː	ə	ɪ	iː	i	ɒ	ɔː	ʌ	ʊ	u	uː
cat	father	ten	bird	about	sit	see	many	got	saw	cup	put	actual	too
								(BrE)					

people touching each other. **3** [C] (*formal*) something bad that spreads quickly by being passed from person to person: *the contagion of political extremism*—compare INFECTION

con·ta·gious /kənˈteɪdʒəs/ *adj.* **1** a **contagious** disease spreads by people touching each other: *Scarlet fever is highly contagious.* ◇ (*figurative*) *His enthusiasm was contagious* (= spread quickly to other people). ◇ *a contagious laugh* **2** [not usually before noun] if a person is **contagious**, they have a disease that can be spread to other people by touch—compare INFECTIOUS ▶ **con·ta·gious·ly** *adv.*

con·tain /kənˈteɪn/ *verb* [VN] (not used in the progressive tenses) **1** if sth **contains** sth else, it has that thing inside it or as part of it: *This drink doesn't contain any alcohol.* ◇ *Her statement contained one or two inaccuracies.* ◇ *a brown envelope containing a hundred dollar bills* ◇ *The bottle contains* (= can hold) *two litres.* **2** (*written*) to keep your feelings under control: *She was unable to contain her excitement.* ◇ *I was so furious I just couldn't contain myself* (= I had to express my feelings). **3** (*written*) to prevent sth harmful from spreading or getting worse: *to contain an epidemic* ◇ *Government forces have failed to contain the rebellion.*

con·tain·er /kənˈteɪnə(r)/ *noun* **1** a box, bottle, etc. in which sth can be stored or transported: *Food will last longer if kept in an airtight container.* **2** a large metal or wooden box of a standard size in which goods are packed so that they can easily be lifted onto a ship, train, etc. to be transported: *a container ship* (= one designed to transport such containers)—picture at BOAT

con·tain·ment /kənˈteɪnmənt/ *noun* [U] (*formal*) **1** the act of keeping sth under control so that it cannot spread in a harmful way: *the containment of the epidemic/rebellion* **2** the act of keeping another country's power within limits so that it does not become too powerful: *a policy of containment*

con·tam·in·ant /kənˈtæmɪnənt/ *noun* (*technical*) a substance that makes sth IMPURE: *Filters do not remove all contaminants from water.*

con·tam·in·ate /kənˈtæmɪneɪt/ *verb* [VN] **1** ~ sth (with sth) to make a substance or place dirty or no longer pure by adding a substance that is dangerous or carries disease: *The drinking water has become contaminated with lead.* ◇ *contaminated blood/food/soil* **2** (*formal*) to influence people's ideas or attitudes in a bad way: *They were accused of contaminating the minds of our young people.*—see also UNCONTAMINATED ▶ **con·tam·in·ation** /kən-ˌtæmɪˈneɪʃn/ *noun* [U]: *radioactive contamination*

contd *abbr.* = CONT.

con·tem·plate /ˈkɒntəmpleɪt; *AmE* ˈkɑːn-/ *verb* **1** to think about whether you should do sth, or how you should do sth [SYN] CONSIDER, THINK ABOUT/OF: [VN] *You're too young to be contemplating retirement.* ◇ [V-ing] *I have never contemplated living abroad.* [also V wh-, VN-ing] **2** to think carefully about and accept the possibility of sth happening: [VN] *The thought of war is too awful to contemplate.* ◇ [V wh-] *I can't contemplate what it would be like to be alone.* [also V that] **3** (*formal*) to think deeply about sth for a long time: [VN] *to contemplate your future* ◇ [V] *She lay in bed, contemplating.* **4** [VN] (*formal*) to look at sth in a careful way for a long time: *She contemplated him in silence.*

con·tem·pla·tion /ˌkɒntəmˈpleɪʃn; *AmE* ˌkɑːn-/ *noun* [U] (*formal*) **1** the act of thinking deeply about sth: *He sat there deep in contemplation.* ◇ *a few moments of quiet contemplation* ◇ *a life of prayer and contemplation* **2** the act of looking at sth in a calm and careful way: *She turned from her contemplation of the photograph.* [IDM] **in contemˈplation** (*formal*) being considered: *By 1613 even more desperate measures were in contemplation.*

con·tem·pla·tive /kənˈtemplətɪv/ *adj.*, *noun*
▪ *adj.* (*formal*) **1** thinking quietly and seriously about sth: *She was in contemplative mood.* **2** spending time thinking deeply about religious matters: *the contemplative life* (= life in a religious community)

▪ *noun* (*formal*) a person who spends their life thinking deeply about religious matters

con·tem·por·an·eous /kənˌtempəˈreɪniəs/ *adj.* ~ (with sb/sth) (*formal*) happening or existing at the same time: *How do we know that the signature is contemporaneous with the document?* ◇ *contemporaneous events/accounts* ▶ **con·tem·por·an·eous·ly** *adv.*

con·tem·por·ary /kənˈtemprəri; *AmE* -pəreri/ *adj.*, *noun*
▪ *adj.* **1** ~ (with sb/sth) belonging to the same time: *We have no contemporary account of the battle* (= written near the time that it happened). ◇ *He was contemporary with the dramatist Congreve.* **2** belonging to the present time [SYN] MODERN: *life in contemporary Britain* ◇ *contemporary fiction/music/dance*
▪ *noun* (*pl.* -**ies**) a person who lives or lived at the same time as sb else, especially sb who is about the same age: *She and I were contemporaries at college.* ◇ *He was a contemporary of Freud and may have known him.*

con·tempt /kənˈtempt/ *noun* [U, sing.] **1** ~ (for sb/sth) the feeling that sb/sth is without value and deserves no respect at all: *She looked at him with contempt.* ◇ *I shall treat that suggestion with the contempt it deserves.* ◇ *His treatment of his children is beneath contempt* (= so unacceptable that it is not even worth feeling contempt for). ◇ *Politicians seem to be generally held in contempt by the police.* ◇ *They had shown a contempt for the values she thought important.* **2** ~ for sth a lack of worry or fear about rules, danger, etc: *The firefighters showed a contempt for their own safety.* ◇ *His remarks betray a staggering contempt for the truth* (= are completely false). **3** = CONTEMPT OF COURT: *He could be jailed for two years for contempt.* ◇ *She was held in contempt for refusing to testify.* [IDM] see FAMILIARITY

con·tempt·ible /kənˈtemptəbl/ *adj.* (*formal*) not deserving any respect at all: *mean and contemptible behaviour*

con·ˌtempt of ˈcourt (also **con·tempt**) *noun* [U] the crime of refusing to obey an order made by a court of law; not showing respect for a court or judge: *Any person who disregards this order will be in contempt of court.* ◇ *to be guilty of contempt of court*

con·temp·tu·ous /kənˈtemptʃuəs/ *adj.* ~ (of sb/sth) feeling or showing that you have no respect for sb/sth: *She gave him a contemptuous look.* ◇ *You're contemptuous of everything I do.* ▶ **con·temp·tu·ous·ly** *adv.*: *to laugh contemptuously*

con·tend /kənˈtend/ *verb* (*formal*) **1** to say that sth is true, especially in an argument: [V that] *I would contend that the minister's thinking is flawed on this point.* [also V N] **2** [V] ~ (for sth) to compete against sb in order to gain sth: *Three armed groups were contending for power.* [PHRV] **conˈtend with sth** to have to deal with a problem or difficult situation: *Nurses often have to contend with violent or drunken patients.*

con·tend·er /kənˈtendə(r)/ *noun* a person who takes part in a competition or tries to win sth: *Peter is a contender for a gold medal in the Olympics.* ◇ *a leading/serious/strong contender for the party leadership*

con·tent[1] /ˈkɒntent; *AmE* ˈkɑːn-/ *noun*—see also CONTENT[2] **1** (**contents**) [pl.] the things that are contained in sth: *He tipped the contents of the bag onto the table.* ◇ *Fire has caused severe damage to the contents of the building.* ◇ *She hadn't read the letter and so was unaware of its contents.* **2** (**contents**) [pl.] the different sections that are contained in a book: *a table of contents* (= the list at the front of a book) ◇ *a contents page* **3** [sing.] the subject matter of a book, speech, programme, etc: *Your tone of voice is as important as the content of what you have to say.* ◇ *The content of the course depends on what the students would like to study.* ◇ *Her poetry has a good deal of political content.* **4** [sing.] (following a noun) the amount of a substance that is contained in sth else: *food with a high fat content* ◇ *the alcohol content of a drink*

con·tent[2] /kənˈtent/ *adj.*, *verb*, *noun*—see also CONTENT[1]
▪ *adj.* [not before noun] **1** ~ (with sth) happy and satisfied with what you have: *Not content with stealing my boy-*

friend (= not thinking that this was enough), *she has turned all my friends against me.* ◊ *He seemed more content, less bitter.* ◊ *He had to be content with third place.* **2 ~ to do sth** willing to do sth: *I was content to wait.*—compare CONTENTED

■ *verb* [VN] **1 ~ yourself with sth** to accept and be satisfied with sth and not try to have or do sth better: *Martina contented herself with a single glass of wine.* **2** (*formal*) to make sb feel happy or satisfied: *My apology seemed to content him.*

■ *noun* = CONTENTMENT **IDM** see HEART

con·tent·ed /kən'tentɪd/ *adj.* [usually before noun] showing or feeling happiness or satisfaction, especially because your life is good: *a contented smile* ◊ *He was a contented man.*—compare CONTENT² *adj.* **OPP** DISCONTENTED ▶ **con·tent·ed·ly** *adv.*: *She smiled contentedly.*

con·ten·tion /kən'tenʃn/ *noun* **1** [U] (*formal*) angry disagreement between people: *One area of contention is the availability of nursery care.* ◊ *a point of contention* **2** [C] **~ (that ...)** (*formal*) a belief or an opinion that you express, especially in an argument: *It is our client's contention that the fire was an accident.* ◊ *I would reject that contention.* **IDM in con'tention (for sth)** with a chance of winning sth: *Only three teams are now in contention for the title.* **out of con'tention (for sth)** without a chance of winning sth: *to slip/drop out of contention*—more at BONE *n.*

con·ten·tious /kən'tenʃəs/ *adj.* (*formal*) **1** likely to cause disagreement between people: *a contentious issue/topic/subject* ◊ *Both views are highly contentious.* ◊ *Try to avoid any contentious wording.* **OPP** UNCONTENTIOUS **2** liking to argue; involving a lot of arguing: *a contentious meeting*

con·tent·ment /kən'tentmənt/ (also *less frequent* **content**) *noun* [U] a feeling of happiness or satisfaction: *He has found contentment at last.* ◊ *a sigh of contentment*—compare DISCONTENT

con·test *noun, verb*
■ *noun* /'kɒntest; AmE 'kɑːn-/ **1** a competition in which people try to win sth: *a singing/writing/beauty contest* ◊ *to enter a contest* **2 ~ (for sth)** a struggle to gain control or power: *a contest for the leadership of the party* **IDM be ,no 'contest** used to say that one side in a competition is so much stronger or better than the other that it is sure to win easily

■ *verb* /kən'test/ [VN] **1** to take part in a competition, election, etc. and try to win it: *Three candidates contested the leadership.* ◊ *a hotly/fiercely/keenly contested game* (= one in which the players try very hard to win and the scores are close) **2** to formally oppose a decision or statement because you think it is wrong: *to contest a will* (= try to show that it was not correctly made in law) ◊ *The divorce was not contested.*

con·test·ant /kən'testənt/ *noun* a person who takes part in a contest: *Please welcome our next contestant.*

con·text /'kɒntekst; AmE 'kɑːn-/ *noun* [C, U] **1** the situation in which sth happens and that helps you to understand it: *This speech needs to be set in the context of Britain in the 1960s.* ◊ *His decision can only be understood in context.* **2** the words that come just before and after a word, phrase or statement and help you to understand its meaning: *You should be able to guess the meaning of the word from the context.* ◊ *This quotation has been taken out of context* (= repeated without giving the circumstances in which it was said).

con·text·ual /kən'tekstʃuəl/ *adj.* (*written*) connected with a particular context: *contextual factors/information* ◊ *contextual clues to the meaning* ▶ **con·text·ual·ly** *adv.*

con·text·ual·ize (*BrE* also **-ise**) /kən'tekstʃuəlaɪz/ *verb* [VN] (*formal*) to consider sth in relation to the situation in which it happens or exists ▶ **con·text·ual·iza·tion, -isa·tion** /kən,tekstʃuəlaɪz'eɪʃn/ *noun* [U]

con·tigu·ous /kən'tɪgjuəs/ *adj.* **~ (with/to)** (*formal or technical*) touching or next to sth: *The two countries are contiguous.* ◊ *The bruising was not contiguous to the wound.* ▶ **con·tigu·ity** /,kɒntɪ'gjuːəti; AmE ,kɑːn-/ *noun* [U]

con·tin·ence /'kɒntɪnəns; AmE 'kɑːn-/ *noun* [U]

1 (*formal*) the control of your feelings, especially your desire to have sex **2** the ability to control the BLADDER and bowels **OPP** INCONTINENCE ▶ **con·tin·ent** /'kɒntɪnənt; AmE 'kɑːn-/ *adj.*

con·tin·ent /'kɒntɪnənt; AmE 'kɑːn-/ *noun* **1** [C] one of the large land masses of the earth such as Europe, Asia or Africa: *the continent of Africa* ◊ *the African continent* **2 (the Continent)** [sing.] (*BrE*) the main part of the continent of Europe, not including Britain or Ireland: *We're going to spend a weekend on the Continent.*

con·tin·en·tal /,kɒntɪ'nentl; AmE ,kɑːn-/ *adj., noun*
■ *adj.* **1** (also **Continental**) [only before noun] (*BrE*) of or in the continent of Europe, not including Britain and Ireland: *a popular continental holiday resort* ◊ *Britain's continental neighbours* **2** (*BrE*) following the customs of countries in western and southern Europe: *a continental lifestyle* ◊ *The shutters and the balconies make the street look almost continental.* **3** [only before noun] connected with the main part of the N American continent: *Prices are often higher in Hawaii than in the continental United States.* **4** forming part of, or typical of, any of the seven main land masses of the earth: *continental Antarctica/Asia/Europe* ◊ *to study continental geography*
■ *noun* (*BrE*, often *disapproving*) a person who lives in the continent of Europe: *The continentals have never understood our preference for warm beer.*

,continental 'breakfast *noun* a light breakfast, usually consisting of coffee and bread rolls with butter and jam—compare ENGLISH BREAKFAST

,continental 'drift *noun* [U] (*geology*) the slow movement of the continents towards and away from each other during the history of the earth—see also PLATE TECTONICS

,continental 'quilt *noun* (*BrE*) = DUVET

,continental 'shelf *noun* [usually sing.] (*technical*) the area of land on the edge of a continent that slopes into the ocean

con·tin·gency /kən'tɪndʒənsi/ *noun* (*pl.* **-ies**) an event that may or may not happen **SYN** POSSIBILITY: *We must consider all possible contingencies.* ◊ *to make contingency plans* (= plans for what to do if a particular event happens or does not happen) ◊ *a contingency fund* (= to pay for sth that might happen in the future)

con'tingency fee *noun* (in the US) an amount of money that is paid to a lawyer only if the person he or she is advising wins in court

con·tin·gent /kən'tɪndʒənt/ *noun, adj.*
■ *noun* [C+sing./pl. *v.*] **1** a group of people at a meeting or an event who have sth in common, especially the place they come from, that is not shared by other people at the event: *The largest contingent was from the United States.* ◊ *A strong contingent of local residents were there to block the proposal.* **2** a group of soldiers that are part of a larger force: *the French contingent in the UN peacekeeping force*
■ *adj.* **~ (on/upon sth)** (*formal*) dependent on sth that may or may not happen: *Any further payments are contingent upon satisfactory completion dates.* ▶ **con·tin·gent·ly** *adv.*

con·tin·ual /kən'tɪnjuəl/ *adj.* [only before noun] **1** repeated many times in a way that is annoying: *continual complaints/interruptions* ◊ *Prisoners' families face continual harassment and attack.* **2** continuing without interruption **SYN** CONTINUOUS: *He was in a continual process of rewriting his material.* ◊ *We lived in continual fear of being discovered.* ◊ *Her daughter was a continual source of delight to her.* ⇨ note at CONTINUOUS ▶ **con·tinu·al·ly** /-juəli/ *adv.*: *They argue continually about money.* ◊ *the need to adapt to new and continually changing circumstances* ◊ *New products are continually being developed.*

con·tinu·ance /kən'tɪnjuəns/ *noun* [U, sing.] (*formal*) the state of continuing to exist or function: *We can no longer support the President's continuance in office.*

con·tinu·ation /kən,tɪnju'eɪʃn/ *noun* **~ (of/ in sth) 1** [U, sing.] an act or the state of continuing: *They are anxious to ensure the continuation of the economic reform programme.* ◊ *This year saw a continuation in the upward trend in sales.* **2** [C] something that continues or follows

b	d	f	g	h	k	l	m	n	p	r
bad	did	fall	get	hat	cat	leg	man	now	pen	red

sth else: *Her new book is a continuation of her autobiography.* **3** [C] something that is joined on to sth else and forms a part of it: *There are plans to build a continuation of the by-pass next year.*

con·tinue /kən'tɪnjuː/ *verb* **1** to keep existing or happening without stopping: [V] *The exhibition continues until 25 July.* ◊ *The trial is expected to continue for three months.* ◊ [V**to**inf] *The rain continued to fall all afternoon.* ◊ [V**-ing**] *The rain continued falling all afternoon.* **2 ~ (with sth)** to keep doing sth without stopping: [V**-ing**] *She wanted to continue working after she was married.* ◊ [V**to**inf] *He continued to ignore everything I was saying.* ◊ [VN] *The board of inquiry is continuing its investigations.* ◊ [V] *Are you going to continue with the project?* **3** [V] [usually +*adv./prep.*] to go or move further in the same direction: *The path continued over rough, rocky ground.* ◊ *He continued on his way.* **4** [V] **~ (as sth)** to remain in a particular job or condition: *I want you to continue as project manager.* ◊ *She will continue in her present job until a replacement can be found.* **5** (*abbr.* **cont.**) to start or start sth again after stopping for a time [SYN] RESUME: [V] *The story continues in our next issue.* ◊ [VN] *The story will be continued in our next issue.* **6** to start speaking again after stopping: [V] *Please continue—I didn't mean to interrupt.* ◊ [V**speech**] *'In fact,' he continued, 'I'd like to congratulate you.'*

con·tinued /kən'tɪnjuːd/ (also **con·tinu·ing** /kən'tɪnjuɪŋ/) *adj.* [only before noun] existing in the same state without change or interruption: *We are grateful for your continued/continuing support.* ◊ *continued fighting/interest* ◊ *continuing involvement/opposition*

con,tinuing edu'cation *noun* [U] = ADULT EDUCATION

con·tinu·ity /ˌkɒntɪ'njuːəti; *AmE* ˌkɑːntə'nuː-/ *noun* (*pl.* **-ies**) **1** [U] the fact of not stopping or not changing: *to ensure/provide/maintain continuity of fuel supplies* [OPP] DISCONTINUITY **2** [U,C] a logical connection between the parts of sth, or between two things: *The novel fails to achieve narrative continuity.* ◊ *There are obvious continuities between diet and health.* [OPP] DISCONTINUITY **3** [U] (*technical*) the organization of a film/movie or television programme, especially making sure that people's clothes, objects, etc. are the same from one scene to the next

con·tinu·ous /kən'tɪnjuəs/ *adj.* **1** happening or existing for a period of time without interruption: *Recovery after the accident will be a continuous process that may take several months.* ◊ *She was in continuous employment until the age of sixty-five.* ◊ *The rain has been continuous since this morning.* **2** spreading in a line or over an area without any spaces: *a continuous line of traffic* **3** (*informal*) repeated many times [SYN] CONTINUAL: *For four days the town suffered continuous attacks.* [HELP] Continual is much more frequent in this meaning. **4** (*grammar*) = PROGRESSIVE: *the continuous tenses* ▶ **con·tinu·ous·ly** *adv.*: *He has lived and worked in France almost continuously since 1961.*

con,tinuous as'sessment *noun* [U] (*BrE*) a system of giving a student a final mark/grade based on work done during a course of study rather than on one exam

con·tinuum /kən'tɪnjuəm/ *noun* (*pl.* **con·tinua** /-juə/) a series of similar items in which each is almost the same as the ones next to it but the last is very different from the first [SYN] CLINE: *It is impossible to say at what point along the continuum a dialect becomes a separate language.*

con·tort /kən'tɔːt; *AmE* -'tɔːrt/ *verb* to become twisted or make sth twisted out of its natural or normal shape: [V] *His face contorted with anger.* ◊ [VN] *Her mouth was contorted in a snarl.* ▶ **con·tort·ed** *adj.*: *contorted limbs/bodies* ◊ (*figurative*) *It was a contorted version of the truth.*

con·tor·tion /kən'tɔːʃn; *AmE* -'tɔːrʃn/ *noun* **1** [U] the state of the face or body being twisted out of its natural shape: *Their bodies had suffered contortion as a result of malnutrition.* **2** [C] a movement which twists the body out of its natural shape: *His facial contortions amused the audience of schoolchildren.* ◊ (*figurative*) *We had to go through all the usual contortions to get a ticket* (= a difficult series of actions).

WHICH WORD?
continuous / continual

These adjectives are frequently used with the following nouns:

continuous ~	**continual ~**
process	change
employment	problems
flow	updating
line	questions
speech	pain
supply	fear

Continuous describes something that continues without stopping.

Continual usually describes an action that is repeated again and again.

The difference between these two words is now disappearing. In particular, **continual** can also mean the same as **continuous** and is used especially about undesirable things: *Life was a continual struggle for them.* However, **continuous** is much more frequent in this sense.

con·tor·tion·ist /kən'tɔːʃənɪst; *AmE* -'tɔːrʃ-/ *noun* a performer who does contortions of their body to entertain others

con·tour /'kɒntʊə(r); *AmE* 'kɑːntʊr/ *noun* **1** the outer edges of sth; the outline of its shape or form: *The road follows the natural contours of the coastline.* ◊ *She traced the contours of his face with her finger.* **2** (also **'contour line**) a line on a map showing points that are the same height above sea level: *a contour map* (= a map that includes these lines)

con·toured /'kɒntʊəd; *AmE* 'kɑːntʊrd/ *adj.* **1** with a specially designed outline that makes sth attractive or comfortable: *It is smoothly contoured to look like a racing car.* **2** having or showing contours (2): *contoured hills/maps*

contra- /'kɒntrə; *AmE* 'kɑːntrə/ *combining form* **1** (in nouns, verbs and adjectives) against; opposite: *contraflow* ◊ *contradict* **2** (in nouns) (*music*) having a PITCH an OCTAVE below: *a contra-bassoon*

con·tra·band /'kɒntrəbænd; *AmE* 'kɑːn-/ *noun* [U] goods that are illegally taken into or out of a country: *contraband goods* ◊ *to smuggle contraband*

con·tra·cep·tion /ˌkɒntrə'sepʃn; *AmE* ˌkɑːn-/ *noun* [U] the practice of preventing a woman from becoming pregnant; the methods of doing this: *to give advice about contraception*

con·tra·cep·tive /ˌkɒntrə'septɪv; *AmE* ˌkɑːn-/ *noun* a drug, device or practice used to prevent a woman becoming pregnant: *oral contraceptives* ▶ **con·tra·cep·tive** *adj.* [only before noun]: *a contraceptive pill* ◊ *contraceptive advice/precautions/methods*

con·tract *noun*, *verb*

■ *noun* /'kɒntrækt; *AmE* 'kɑːn-/ **1 ~ (with sb)** | **~ (between A and B)** | **~ (for sth/to do sth)** an official written agreement: *to enter into/make/sign a contract with the supplier* ◊ *a contract for the supply of vehicles* ◊ *to win/be awarded a contract to build a new school* ◊ *These clauses form part of the contract between buyer and seller.* ◊ *a contract of employment* ◊ *a research contract* ◊ *a contract worker* (= one employed on a contract for a fixed period of time) ◊ *I was on a three-year contract that expired last week.* ◊ ***Under the terms of the contract** the job should have been finished yesterday.* ◊ *She is **under contract to** (= has a contract to work for) a major American computer firm.* ◊ *The offer has been accepted, **subject to contract** (= the agreement is not legally binding before contracts are signed).* ◊ *They were sued for **breach of contract** (= not keeping to a contract).* **2 ~ (on sb)** (*informal*) an agreement to kill sb for money: *to take out a contract on sb*

■ *verb* /kən'trækt/ **1** to become less or smaller; to make sth become less or smaller: [V] *Glass contracts as it cools.* ◊ *a contracting market* ◊ *The heart muscles contract to expel the blood.* ◊ [VN] *'I will' and 'I shall' are usually contracted* to 'I'll' (= made shorter). ◊ *The exercise consists of stretching and contracting the leg muscles.* <u>OPP</u> EXPAND **2** [VN] *(written)* to get an illness: *to contract Aids/a virus/a disease* **3 ~ sb (to sth)** to make a legal agreement with sb for them to work for you or provide you with a service: [VNtoinf] *The player is contracted to play until August.* ◊ [VN] *Several computer engineers have been contracted to the finance department.* **4** [Vtoinf] to make a legal agreement to work for sb or provide them with a service: *She has contracted to work 20 hours a week.* **5** [VN] **~ a marriage/an alliance (with sb)** *(formal)* to formally agree to marry sb/form an ALLIANCE with sb <u>PHRV</u> con,tract **'in (to sth)** *(BrE)* to formally agree that you will take part in sth con,tract **'out (of sth)** *(BrE)* to formally agree that you will not take part in sth: *Many employees contracted out of the pension plan.* **con,tract sth ↔ 'out (to sb)** to arrange for work to be done by another company rather than your own

con·trac·tion /kən'trækʃn/ *noun* **1** [U] the process of becoming smaller: *the expansion and contraction of the metal* ◊ *The sudden contraction of the markets left them with a lot of unwanted stock.* **2** [C, U] a sudden and painful tightening of muscles, especially the tightening of the muscles around a woman's WOMB that happen when she is giving birth to a child: *The contractions started coming every five minutes.* **3** [C] *(linguistics)* a short form of a word: *'He's' may be a contraction of 'he is' or 'he has'.*

con·tract·or /kən'træktə(r)/ *noun* a person or company that has a contract to do work or provide goods or services for another company: *a building/haulage contractor* ◊ *to employ an independent/outside contractor*

con·tract·ual /kən'træktʃuəl/ *adj.* connected with the conditions of a legal written agreement; agreed in a CONTRACT

con·tra·dict /ˌkɒntrə'dɪkt; *AmE* ˌkɑːn-/ *verb* **1** to say that sth that sb else has said is wrong, and that the opposite is true: [VN] *All evening her husband contradicted everything she said.* ◊ *You've just contradicted yourself* (= said the opposite of what you said before). [alsoVspeech, VNspeech] **2** [VN] (of statements or pieces of evidence) to be so different from each other that one of them must be wrong: *The two stories contradict each other.*

con·tra·dic·tion /ˌkɒntrə'dɪkʃn; *AmE* ˌkɑːn-/ *noun* **1** [C, U] **~ (between A and B)** a lack of agreement between facts, opinions, actions, etc: *There is a contradiction between the two sets of figures.* ◊ *His public speeches are in direct contradiction to his personal lifestyle.* ◊ *How can we resolve this apparent contradiction?* **2** [U, C] the act of saying that sth that sb else has said is wrong or not true; an example of this: *I think I can say, without fear of contradiction, that ...* ◊ *Now you say you both left at ten—that's a contradiction of your last statement.* <u>IDM</u> **a ,contradiction in 'terms** a statement containing two words that contradict each other's meaning: *A 'nomad settlement' is a contradiction in terms.*

con·tra·dict·ory /ˌkɒntrə'dɪktəri; *AmE* ˌkɑːn-/ *adj.* containing or showing a contradiction: *We are faced with two apparently contradictory statements.* ◊ *The advice I received was often contradictory.*

con·tra·dis·tinc·tion /ˌkɒntrədɪ'stɪŋkʃn; *AmE* ˌkɑːn-/ *noun* <u>IDM</u> **in contradistinction to sth/sb** *(formal)* in contrast with sth/sb

con·tra·flow /'kɒntrəfləʊ; *AmE* 'kɑːntrəfloʊ/ *noun (BrE)* a system that is used when one half of a large road is closed for repairs, and the traffic going in both directions has to use the other half: *A contraflow system is in operation on this section of the motorway.*

con·tra·indi·ca·tion /ˌkɒntrəˌɪndɪ'keɪʃn; *AmE* ˌkɑːn-/ *noun (medical)* a possible reason for not giving sb a particular drug or medical treatment

con·tralto /kən'træltəʊ; *AmE* -toʊ/ *noun (pl.* **-os)** = ALTO

con·trap·tion /kən'træpʃn/ *noun* a machine or piece of equipment that looks strange: *She showed us a strange contraption that looked like a satellite dish.*

con·tra·pun·tal /ˌkɒntrə'pʌntl; *AmE* ˌkɑːn-/ *adj. (music)* having two or more tunes played together to form a whole—see also COUNTERPOINT

con·trari·wise /'kɒntreəriwaɪz; *AmE* -trer-/ *adv.* *(formal)* **1** used at the beginning of a sentence or CLAUSE to introduce a contrast **2** in the opposite way: *It worked contrariwise—first you dialled the number, then you put the money in.*

con·trary¹ /'kɒntrəri; *AmE* 'kɑːntreri/ *adj., noun*—see also CONTRARY²

■ *adj.* **1 ~ to sth** different from sth; against sth: *Contrary to popular belief, many cats dislike milk.* ◊ *The government has decided that the publication of the report would be 'contrary to the public interest'.* **2** [only before noun] completely different in nature or direction <u>SYN</u> OPPOSITE: *contrary advice/opinions/arguments* ◊ *The contrary view is that prison provides an excellent education—in crime.*

■ *noun* **(the contrary)** [sing.] the opposite fact, event or situation: *In the end the contrary was proved true: he was innocent and she was guilty.* <u>IDM</u> **on the 'contrary** used to introduce a statement that says the opposite of the last one: *'It must have been terrible.' 'On the contrary, I enjoyed every minute.'* **,quite the 'contrary** used to emphasize that the opposite of what has been said is true: *I don't find him funny at all. Quite the contrary.* **to the 'contrary** showing or proving the opposite: *Show me some evidence to the contrary* (= proving that sth is not true). ◊ *I will expect to see you on Sunday unless I hear anything to the contrary* (= that you are not coming).

con·trary² /kən'treəri; *AmE* -'treri/ *adj. (formal, disapproving)* (usually of children) behaving badly; choosing to do or say the opposite of what is expected: *She was such a contrary child—it was impossible to please her.*—see also CONTRARY¹ ▶ **con·trar·ily** *adv.* **con·trari·ness** *noun* [U]

con·trast *noun, verb*

■ *noun* /'kɒntrɑːst; *AmE* 'kɑːntræst/ **1** [C, U] **~ (between A and B)** | **~ (to/with sb/sth)** a difference between two or more people or things that you can see clearly when they are compared or put close together; the fact of comparing two or more things in order to show the differences between them: *There is an obvious contrast between the cultures of East and West.* ◊ *The company lost $7 million this quarter in contrast to a profit of $6.2 million a year earlier.* ◊ *When you look at their new system, ours seems very old-fashioned by contrast.* ◊ *The situation when we arrived was in marked contrast to the news reports.* ◊ *to show a sharp/stark/striking contrast with sth* ◊ *The poverty of her childhood stands in total contrast to her life in Hollywood.* ◊ *A wool jacket complements the silk trousers and provides an interesting contrast in texture.* ◊ *Careful contrast of the two plans shows some important differences.* **2** [C] **~ (to sb/sth)** a person or thing that is clearly different from sb/sth else: *The work you did today is quite a contrast to* (= very much better/worse than) *what you did last week.* **3** [U] differences in colour or in light and dark, used in photographs and paintings to create a special effect: *The artist's use of contrast is masterly.* **4** [U] the amount of difference between light and dark in a picture on a television screen: *Use this button to adjust the contrast.*

■ *verb* /kən'trɑːst; *AmE* -'træst/ **1** [VN] **~ (A and/with B)** to compare two things in order to show the differences between them: *It is interesting to contrast the British legal system with the American one.* ◊ *The poem contrasts youth and age.* **2** [V] **~ (with sth)** to show a clear difference when close together or when compared: *Her actions contrasted sharply with her promises.* ◊ *Her actions and her promises contrasted sharply.*

con·trast·ing /kən'trɑːstɪŋ; *AmE* -'træs-/ *adj.* [usually before noun] very different in style, colour or attitude: *bright, contrasting colours* ◊ *The book explores contrasting views of the poet's early work.*

con·tra·vene /ˌkɒntrə'viːn; *AmE* ˌkɑːn-/ *verb* [VN] *(written)* to do sth that is not allowed by a law or rule: *The company was found guilty of contravening safety regulations.* ▶ **con·tra·ven·tion** /ˌkɒntrə'venʃn; *AmE* ˌkɑːn-/ *noun* [U, C]: *These actions are in contravention of European law.*

con·tre·temps /'kɒntrətɒŋ; *AmE* 'kɑːntrətɑː/ *noun (pl.* **con·tre·temps)** (from *French, formal* or *humorous*) an

æ	ɑː	e	ɜː	ə	ɪ	iː	i	ɒ	ɔː	ʌ	ʊ	u	uː
cat	father	ten	bird	about	sit	see	many	got (BrE)	saw	cup	put	actual	too

unfortunate event or embarrassing disagreement with another person: *They have been ignoring me since our last contretemps.*

con·trib·ute /kənˈtrɪbjuːt; *BrE* also /ˈkɒntrɪbjuːt/ *verb* **1 ~ (sth) (to/towards sth)** to give sth, especially money or goods, to help sb/sth: [VN] *The writer personally contributed £5000 to the earthquake fund.* ◊ [V] *Would you like to contribute to our collection?* ◊ *Do you wish to contribute?* **2** [V] **~ (to sth)** to be one of the causes of sth: *Medical negligence was said to have contributed to her death.* ◊ *Human error may have been a **contributing factor**.* **3 ~ (sth) to sth** to increase, improve or add to sth: [V] *Immigrants have contributed to British culture in many ways.* ◊ [VN] *This book contributes little to our understanding of the subject.* **4 ~ (sth) (to sth)** to write things for a newspaper, magazine, or a radio or television programme; to speak during a meeting or conversation, especially to give your opinion: [VN] *She contributed a number of articles to the magazine.* ◊ [V] *He contributes regularly to the magazine 'New Scientist'.* ◊ *We hope everyone will contribute to the discussion.*

con·tri·bu·tion /ˌkɒntrɪˈbjuːʃn; *AmE* ˌkɑːn-/ *noun* **~ (to sth)** | **~ (towards(s) sth/doing sth) 1** [C] a sum of money that is given to a person or an organization in order to help pay for sth: *to make a major/substantial contribution to charity* ◊ *All contributions will be gratefully received.* ◊ *valuable contributions towards the upkeep of the cathedral* **2** [C] a sum of money that you pay regularly to your employer or the government in order to pay for benefits such as health insurance, a PENSION, etc: *You can increase your monthly contributions to the pension scheme.* **3** [C, usually sing.] an action or a service that helps to cause or increase sth: *He made a very positive contribution to the overall success of the project.* ◊ *These measures would make a valuable contribution towards reducing industrial accidents.* ◊ *the car's contribution to the greenhouse effect* **4** [C] an item that forms part of a book, magazine, broadcast, discussion, etc: *an important contribution to the debate* ◊ *All contributions for the May issue must be received by Friday.* **5** [U] the act of giving sth, especially money, to help a person or an organization: *We rely entirely on voluntary contribution.*

con·tribu·tor /kənˈtrɪbjətə(r)/ *noun* **~ (to sth) 1** a person who writes articles for a magazine or a book, or who talks on a radio or television programme or at a meeting **2** a person or a thing that provides money to help pay for sth, or support for a project: *Older people are important contributors to the economy.* **3** something that helps to cause sth: *Sulphur dioxide is a pollutant and a major contributor to acid rain.*

con·tribu·tory /kənˈtrɪbjətəri; *AmE* -tɔːri/ *adj.* [usually before noun] **1** helping to cause sth: *Alcohol is a contributory factor in 10% of all road accidents.* **2** involving payments from the people who will benefit: *a contributory pension scheme/plan* (= paid for by both employers and employees) [OPP] NON-CONTRIBUTORY

con·trite /ˈkɒntraɪt; kənˈtraɪt; *AmE* ˈkɑːntraɪt/ *adj.* (*formal*) very sorry for sth bad that you have done ▶ **con·trite·ly** *adv.* **con·tri·tion** /kənˈtrɪʃn/ *noun* [U]: *a look of contrition*

con·triv·ance /kənˈtraɪvəns/ *noun* (*formal*) **1** [C, U] (usually *disapproving*) something that sb has done or written that does not seem natural; the fact of seeming artificial: *The film is spoilt by unrealistic contrivances of plot.* ◊ *The story is told with a complete absence of contrivance.* **2** [C] a clever or complicated device or tool made for a particular purpose **3** [C, U] a clever plan or trick; the act of using a clever plan or trick: *an ingenious contrivance to get her to sign the document without reading it*

con·trive /kənˈtraɪv/ *verb* (*formal*) **1** [V to inf] to manage to do sth in spite of difficulties: *She contrived to spend a couple of hours with him every Sunday evening.* **2** [VN] to succeed in making sth happen in spite of difficulties: *I decided to contrive a meeting between the two of them.* **3** [VN] to think of or make sth, for example a plan or a machine, in a clever way: *They contrived a plan to defraud the company.*

con·trived /kənˈtraɪvd/ *adj.* (*disapproving*) planned in advance and not natural or genuine; written or arranged in a way that is not natural or realistic: *a contrived situation* ◊ *The book's happy ending seemed contrived.*

con·trol /kənˈtrəʊl; *AmE* -ˈtroʊl/ *noun, verb*
■ *noun*
POWER | **1** [U] **~ (of/over sb/sth)** the power to make decisions about how a country, an area, an organization, etc. is run: *The party is expecting to gain control of the council in the next election.* ◊ *The Democrats will probably lose control of Congress.* ◊ *A military junta took control of the country.* ◊ *The city is in the control of enemy forces.* ◊ *The city is under enemy control.* ◊ *The family has sold most of its shares and will lose control of the company.* **2** [U] **~ (of/over sb/sth)** the ability to make sb/sth do what you want: *The teacher had no control over the children.* ◊ *She struggled to keep control of her voice.* ◊ *She lost control of her car on the ice.* ◊ *He got so angry he lost control* (= shouted and said or did things he would not normally do). ◊ *Owing to circumstances beyond our control, the flight to Rome has been cancelled.* ◊ *The coach made the team work hard on ball control* (= in a sport such as football).—see also SELF-CONTROL
LIMITING/MANAGING | **3** [U, C] **~ (of/on sth)** (often in compounds) the act of restricting, limiting or managing sth; a method of doing this: *traffic control* ◊ *talks on arms control* ◊ *government controls on trade and industry* ◊ *A new advance has been made in the control of malaria.* ◊ *Price controls on food were ended.* ◊ *a pest control officer*—see also BIRTH CONTROL, QUALITY CONTROL
IN MACHINE | **4** [C, usually pl.] the switches and buttons, etc. that you use to operate a machine or a vehicle: *the controls of an aircraft* ◊ *the control panel* ◊ *the volume control of a CD player* ◊ *The co-pilot was at the controls when the plane landed.*—see also REMOTE CONTROL
IN EXPERIMENT | **5** [C] (*technical*) a person, thing or group used as a standard of comparison for checking the results of a scientific experiment; an experiment whose result is known, used for checking working methods: *One group was treated with the new drug, and the control group was given a sugar pill.*
PLACE | **6** [sing.] a place where orders are given or where checks are made; the people who work in this place: *air traffic control* ◊ *We went through passport control and into the departure lounge.* ◊ *This is Mission Control calling the space shuttle Discovery.*
ON COMPUTER | **7** [U] (also **conˈtrol key** [sing.]) (on a computer keyboard) a key that you press when you want to perform a particular operation
[IDM] **be in control (of sth) 1** to direct or manage an organization, an area or a situation: *He's reached retiring age, but he's still firmly in control.* ◊ *There has been some violence after the match, but the police are now in control of the situation.* **2** to be able to organize your life well and keep calm: *In spite of all her family problems, she's really in control.* **be/get/run/etc. out of conˈtrol** to be or become impossible to manage or to control: *The children are completely out of control since their father left.* ◊ *A truck ran out of control on the hill.* **be under conˈtrol** to be being dealt with successfully: *Don't worry—everything's under control!* **bring/get/keep sth under conˈtrol** to succeed in dealing with sth so that it does not cause any harm: *It took two hours to bring the fire under control.* ◊ *Please keep your dog under control!*
■ *verb* (-ll-)
HAVE POWER | **1** [VN] to have power over a person, company, country, etc. so that you are able to decide what they must do or how it is run: *By the age of 21 he controlled the company.* ◊ *The whole territory is now controlled by the army.* ◊ *Can't you control your children?*
LIMIT/MANAGE | **2** to limit sth or make it happen in a particular way: [VN] *government attempts to control immigration* ◊ *Many biological processes are controlled by hormones.* ◊ [Vwh-] *Parents should control what their kids watch on television.* **3** [VN] to stop sth from spreading or getting worse: *Firefighters are still trying to control the blaze.* ◊ *She was given drugs to control the pain.*

MACHINE | **4** [VN] to make sth, such as a machine or system, work in the way that you want it to: *This knob controls the volume.* ◊ *The traffic lights are controlled by a central computer.*

STAY CALM | **5** [VN] to manage to make yourself remain calm, even though you are upset or angry: *I was so furious I couldn't **control myself** and I hit him.* ◊ *He was finding it difficult to control his feelings.*

con·trol freak *noun* (*informal, disapproving*) a person who always wants to be in control of their own and others' lives, and to organize how things are done

con·trol·lable /kənˈtrəʊləbl; *AmE* -ˈtroʊ-/ *adj.* that can be controlled: *Cooking with gas is fast, controllable and clean.*

con·trolled /kənˈtrəʊld; *AmE* -ˈtroʊld/ *adj.* **1** done or arranged in a very careful way: *a controlled explosion* ◊ *a controlled environment* **2** limited, or managed by law or by rules: *controlled airspace* **3** (**-controlled**) (in compounds) managed by a particular group, or in a particular way: *a British-controlled company* ◊ *computer-controlled systems* **4** remaining calm and not getting angry or upset: *She remained quiet and controlled.*—compare UNCONTROLLED

ˌcontrolled ˈsubstance *noun* (*technical*) an illegal drug: *to be arrested for possession of a controlled substance*

con·trol·ler /kənˈtrəʊlə(r); *AmE* -ˈtroʊ-/ *noun* **1** a person who manages or directs sth, especially a large organization or part of an organization: *the controller of BBC Radio 4*—see also AIR TRAFFIC CONTROLLER **2** (*technical*) a device that controls or REGULATES a machine or part of a machine: *a temperature controller* **3** (also **comp·trol·ler**) a person who is in charge of the financial accounts of a business company

conˌtrolling ˈinterest *noun* [usually sing.] the fact of owning enough shares in a company to be able to make decisions about what the company should do

con·trol tower *noun* a building at an airport from which the movements of aircraft are controlled

con·tro·ver·sial /ˌkɒntrəˈvɜːʃl; *AmE* ˌkɑːntrəˈvɜːrʃl/ *adj.* causing a lot of angry public discussion and disagreement: *a highly controversial issue / topic / decision / book* ◊ *a controversial plan to build a new road* ◊ *Winston Churchill and Richard Nixon were both controversial figures.* NON-CONTROVERSIAL, UNCONTROVERSIAL ▶ **con·tro·ver·sial·ly** /-ʃəli/ *adv.*

con·tro·versy /ˈkɒntrəvɜːsi; *BrE* also kənˈtrɒvəsi; *AmE* ˈkɑːntrəvɜːrsi/ *noun* [U, C] (*pl.* **-ies**) **~** (**over / about / surrounding sb / sth**) public discussion and argument about sth that many people strongly disagree about, disapprove of, or are shocked by: *to arouse / cause controversy* ◊ *a bitter controversy over / about the site of the new airport* ◊ *the controversy surrounding his latest movie* ◊ *The President resigned amid considerable controversy.*

con·tro·vert /ˌkɒntrəˈvɜːt; *AmE* ˈkɑːntrəvɜːrt/ *verb* [VN] (*formal*) to say or prove that sth is not true SYN REFUTE—see also INCONTROVERTIBLE

con·tu·sion /kənˈtjuːʒn; *AmE* -ˈtuː-/ *noun* [C, U] (*medical*) an injury to part of the body that does not break the skin SYN BRUISE

con·un·drum /kəˈnʌndrəm/ *noun* **1** a confusing problem or question that is very difficult to solve **2** a question, usually involving a trick with words, that you ask for fun SYN RIDDLE

con·ur·ba·tion /ˌkɒnɜːˈbeɪʃn; *AmE* ˌkɑːnɜːrˈb-/ *noun* (*formal, especially BrE*) a large area where towns have grown and joined together, often around a city

con·va·lesce /ˌkɒnvəˈles; *AmE* ˌkɑːn-/ *verb* [V] to spend time getting your health and strength back after an illness SYN RECUPERATE: *She is convalescing at home after her operation.*

con·va·les·cence /ˌkɒnvəˈlesns; *AmE* ˌkɑːn-/ *noun* [sing., U] a period of time when you get well again after an illness or a medical operation; the process of getting well: *You need four to six weeks' convalescence.*

con·va·les·cent /ˌkɒnvəˈlesnt; *AmE* ˌkɑːn-/ *adj.* connected with convalescence; in the process of convalescence: *a convalescent home* (= a type of hospital where people go to get well after an illness) ◊ *a convalescent child* ▶ **con·va·les·cent** *noun*: *I treated him as a convalescent, not as a sick man.*

con·vec·tion /kənˈvekʃn/ *noun* (*technical*) the process in which heat moves through a gas or a liquid as the hotter part rises and the cooler, heavier part sinks: *convection currents*

con·vect·or /kənˈvektə(r)/ (also **conˌvector ˈheater**) *noun* a device for heating the air in a room using convection

con·vene /kənˈviːn/ *verb* (*formal*) **1** [VN] to arrange for people to come together for a formal meeting: *to convene a meeting / conference* ◊ *A Board of Inquiry was convened immediately after the accident.* **2** [V] to come together for a formal meeting: *The committee will convene at 11.30 next Thursday.*

con·vener (also **con·venor**) /kənˈviːnə(r)/ *noun* **1** a person who arranges meetings of groups or committees **2** (*BrE*) a senior official of a trade union at a factory or other place of work

con·veni·ence /kənˈviːniəns/ *noun* **1** [U] the quality of being useful, easy or suitable for sb: *We have provided seats for the convenience of our customers.* ◊ **For** (**the sake of**) **convenience**, *the two groups have been treated as one in this report.* ◊ *The position of the house combines quietness and convenience.* ◊ *In this resort you can enjoy all the comfort and convenience of modern tourism.*—see also FLAG OF CONVENIENCE, MARRIAGE OF CONVENIENCE **2** [C] something that is useful and can make things easier or quicker to do, or more comfortable: *It was a great convenience to have the school so near.* ◊ *The house had all the modern conveniences* (= central heating, hot water, etc.) *that were unusual at that time.*—see also PUBLIC CONVENIENCE IDM **at sb's conˈvenience** (*formal*) at a time or a place which is suitable for sb: *Can you telephone me at your convenience to arrange a meeting?*—more at EARLY *adj.*

conˈvenience food *noun* [C, U] food that you buy frozen or in a box or can, that you can prepare and cook very quickly and easily

conˈvenience store *noun* (*especially AmE*) a shop / store that sells food, newspapers, etc. and sometimes gas / petrol and often stays open 24 hours a day

con·veni·ent /kənˈviːniənt/ *adj.* **1 ~** (**for sb / sth**) useful, easy or quick to do; not causing problems: *It is very convenient to pay by credit card.* ◊ *You'll find these meals quick and convenient to prepare.* ◊ *Fruit is a convenient source of vitamins and energy.* ◊ *A bicycle is often more convenient than a car in towns.* ◊ *I can't see him now—it isn't convenient.* ◊ *I'll call back at a more convenient time.* ◊ (*disapproving*) *He used his wife's birthday as a convenient excuse for not going to the meeting.* **2 ~** (**for sth**) near to a particular place; easy to get to: *The house is very convenient for several schools.* OPP INCONVENIENT ▶ **con·veni·ent·ly** *adv.*: *The report can be conveniently divided into three main sections.* ◊ *The hotel is conveniently situated close to the beach and the shops.* ◊ *She conveniently forgot to mention that her husband would be at the party, too* (= because it suited her not to say).

con·venor = CONVENER

con·vent /ˈkɒnvənt; *AmE* ˈkɑːnvent; -vənt/ *noun* **1** a building in which NUNS (= members of a female religious community) live together **2** (also **ˈconvent school**) a school run by NUNS

con·ven·tion /kənˈvenʃn/ *noun* **1** [C, U] the way in which sth is done that most people in a society expect and consider to be polite or the right way to do it: *social conventions* ◊ **By convention** *the deputy leader is always a woman.* ◊ *She is a young woman who enjoys flouting conventions.* **2** [C] a large meeting of the members of a profession, a political party, etc. SYN CONFERENCE: *to hold a convention* ◊ *the Democratic Party Convention* (= to elect a candidate for president) **3** [C] an official agreement between countries or leaders: *the Geneva convention* ◊ *the United Nations convention on the rights of the child* **4** [C, U] a traditional method or style in literature, art or the theatre: *the conventions of Greek tragedy*

b	d	f	g	h	k	l	m	n	p	r
bad	did	fall	get	hat	cat	leg	man	now	pen	red

con·ven·tion·al /kən'venʃənl/ *adj.* **1** (often *disapproving*) tending to follow what is done or considered acceptable by society in general; normal and ordinary, and perhaps not very interesting: *conventional behaviour / morality* ◊ *She's very conventional in her views.* OPP UNCONVENTIONAL **2** [usually before noun] following what is traditional or the way sth has been done for a long time: *conventional methods / approaches* ◊ *It's not a hotel, in the conventional sense, but rather a whole village turned into a hotel.* OPP UNCONVENTIONAL **3** [usually before noun] (especially of weapons) not nuclear: *conventional forces / weapons* ◊ *a conventional power station* (= using oil or coal as fuel, rather than nuclear power) ▶ **con·ven·tion·al·ity** /kən,venʃə'næləti/ *noun* [U] **con·ven·tion·al·ly** /-ʃənəli/ *adv.*: *conventionally dressed* ◊ *conventionally grown food* (= grown according to conventional methods) IDM see WISDOM

con·ven·tion·eer /kən,venʃə'nɪə(r); *AmE* -'nɪr/ *noun* (*AmE*) a person who is attending a CONVENTION

con·verge /kən'vɜːdʒ; *AmE* -'vɜːrdʒ/ *verb* [V] **1** ~ (on ...) (of people or vehicles) to move towards a place from different directions and meet to form a large crowd: *Thousands of supporters converged on London for the rally.* **2** (of two or more lines, paths, etc.) to move towards each other and meet at a point: *There was a signpost where the two paths converged.* **3** if ideas, policies, aims, etc. converge, they become very similar or the same OPP DIVERGE ▶ **con·ver·gent** /-dʒənt/ *adj.*: *convergent lines / opinions* **con·ver·gence** *noun* [U]

con·ver·sant /kən'vɜːsnt; *AmE* -'vɜːrs-/ *adj.* (*formal*) ~ with sth knowing about sth; familiar with sth: *You need to become fully conversant with the company's procedures.*

con·ver·sa·tion /,kɒnvə'seɪʃn; *AmE* ,kɑːnvər'-/ *noun* [C, U] ~ (with sb) (about sth) an informal talk involving a small group of people or only two; the activity of talking in this way: *a telephone conversation* ◊ *I had a long conversation with her the other day.* ◊ *The main topic of conversation was the likely outcome of the election.* ◊ *Don was deep in conversation with the girl on his right.* ◊ (*BrE*) *to get into conversation with sb* ◊ (*AmE*) *to get into a conversation with sb* ◊ *The conversation turned to gardening.* ◊ *I tried to make polite conversation* (= to speak in order to appear polite).

con·ver·sa·tion·al /,kɒnvə'seɪʃənl; *AmE* ,kɑːnvər'-/ *adj.* **1** not formal; as used in conversation SYN COLLOQUIAL: *a casual and conversational tone* ◊ *I learnt conversational Spanish at evening classes.* **2** [only before noun] connected with conversation: *Men have a more direct conversational style.* ▶ **con·ver·sa·tion·al·ly** *adv.*: *'Have you been here long?' he asked conversationally.*

con·ver·sa·tion·al·ist /,kɒnvə'seɪʃənəlɪst; *AmE* ,kɑːnvər'-/ *noun* a person who is good at talking to others, especially in an informal way

con·verse¹ /kən'vɜːs; *AmE* -'vɜːrs/ *verb* [V] ~ (with sb) (*formal*) to have a conversation with sb

con·verse² /'kɒnvɜːs; *AmE* 'kɑːnvɜːrs/ *noun* (the con·verse) [sing.] (*formal*) the opposite or REVERSE of a fact or statement: *Building new roads increases traffic and the converse is equally true: reducing the number and size of roads means less traffic.* ▶ **con·verse** *adj.*: *the converse effect*

con·verse·ly /'kɒnvɜːsli; *AmE* 'kɑːnvɜːrs-/ *adv.* (*formal*) in a way that is the opposite or REVERSE of sth: *You can add the fluid to the powder, or, conversely, the powder to the fluid.*

con·ver·sion /kən'vɜːʃn; *AmE* -'vɜːrʒn; -ʃn/ *noun* **1** [U, C] ~ (from sth) (into/to sth) the act or process of changing sth from one form, use or system to another: *the conversion of farm buildings into family homes* ◊ *Conversion to gas central heating will save you a lot of money.* ◊ *No conversion from analogue to digital data is needed.* ◊ *a metric conversion table* (= showing how to change metric amounts into or out of another system) ◊ *a firm which specializes in house conversions* (= turning large houses into several smaller flats / apartments) **2** [U, C] ~ (from sth) (to sth) the process or experience of changing your religion or beliefs: *the conversion of the Anglo-Saxons by*

Christian missionaries ◊ *his conversion from Judaism to Christianity* **3** [C] (in rugby) a way of scoring extra points by kicking the ball over the goal after scoring a TRY **4** [C] **barn / loft** ~ a building or room that has been changed so that it can be used for a different purpose, especially for living in

con'version van (also **'van conversion**) *noun* (*AmE*) a motor vehicle in which the back part behind the driver has been arranged as a living space

con·vert *verb, noun*
■ *verb* /kən'vɜːt; *AmE* -'vɜːrt/ **1** ~ (sth) (from sth) (into/to sth) to change or make sth change from one form, purpose, system, etc. to another: [VN] *The hotel is going to be converted into a nursing home.* ◊ *What rate will I get if I convert my dollars into euros?* ◊ [V] *We've converted from coal to gas central heating.* **2** [V] ~ into/to sth to be able to be changed from one form, purpose, or system to another: *a sofa that converts into a bed* **3** ~ (sb) (from sth) (to sth) to change or make sb change their religion or beliefs: [V] *He converted from Christianity to Islam.* ◊ [VN] *She was soon converted to the socialist cause.* **4** ~ (sb) (from sth) (to sth) to change an opinion, a habit, etc: [V] *I've converted to organic food.* ◊ [VN] *I didn't use to like opera but my husband has converted me.* **5** [VN] ~ a try (in rugby) to gain extra points by kicking the ball over the goal IDM see PREACH
■ *noun* /'kɒnvɜːt; *AmE* 'kɑːnvɜːrt/ ~ (from sth) (to sth) a person who has changed their religion, beliefs or opinions: *a convert to Islam* ◊ *converts from other faiths*

con·vert·er (also **con·ver·tor**) /kən'vɜːtə(r); *AmE* -'vɜːrt-/ *noun* **1** a person or thing that converts sth: *a catalytic converter* **2** (*physics*) a device for converting ALTERNATING CURRENT into DIRECT CURRENT or the other way around **3** (*physics*) a device for converting a radio signal from one FREQUENCY to another **4** (*technical*) a container used in turning liquid metal into steel

con·vert·ible /kən'vɜːtəbl; *AmE* -'vɜːrt-/ *adj., noun*
■ *adj.* ~ (into/to sth) that can be changed to a different form or use: *a convertible sofa* (= one that can be used as a bed) ◊ *convertible currencies* (= ones that can be exchanged for those of other countries) ◊ *The bonds are convertible into ordinary shares.* ▶ **con·vert·ibil·ity** /kən,vɜːtə'bɪləti; *AmE* -,vɜːrt-/ *noun* [U]
■ *noun* a car with a roof that can be folded down or taken off

con·vex /'kɒnveks; *AmE* 'kɑːn-/ *adj.* (of an outline or a surface) curved outwards: *a convex lens / mirror* OPP CONCAVE ▶ **con·vex·ity** /kɒn'veksəti; *AmE* kɑːn'v-/ *noun* [U]

con·vey /kən'veɪ/ *verb* **1** ~ sth (to sb) to make ideas, feelings, etc. known to sb SYN COMMUNICATE: [VN] *Colours like red convey a sense of energy and strength.* ◊ (*formal*) *Please convey my apologies to your wife.* ◊ [V wh-] *He tried desperately to convey how urgent the situation was.* ◊ [V that] *She did not wish to convey that they were all at fault.* **2** [VN] ~ sb/sth (from ...) (to ...) (*formal*) to take, carry or transport sb/sth from one place to another: *Pipes convey hot water from the boiler to the radiators.*

con·vey·ance /kən'veɪəns/ *noun* **1** [U] (*formal*) the process of taking sb/sth from one place to another: *the conveyance of goods by rail* **2** [C] (*formal*) a vehicle: *horse-drawn conveyances* **3** [C] (*law*) a legal document that moves property from one owner to another: *to draw up a conveyance*

con·vey·an·cer /kən'veɪənsə(r)/ *noun* a lawyer who is an expert in conveyancing

con·vey·an·cing /kən'veɪənsɪŋ/ *noun* [U] (*law*) the branch of law concerned with moving property from one owner to another

con·vey·or /kən'veɪə(r)/ *noun* **1** = CONVEYOR BELT **2** (also **con·vey·er**) (*formal*) a person or thing that carries sth or makes sth known

con'veyor belt (also **con·vey·or**) *noun* a continuous moving band used for transporting goods from one part of a building to another, for example products in a factory or suitcases in an airport

con·vict *verb, noun*

■ verb /kən'vɪkt/ [VN] [often passive] ~ **sb** (**of sth**) to decide and state officially in a court of law that sb is guilty of a crime: *a convicted murderer* ◊ *He was convicted of fraud.* OPP ACQUIT

■ noun /'kɒnvɪkt; AmE 'kɑːn-/ (also *informal* **con**) a person who has been found guilty of a crime and sent to prison: *an escaped convict*

con·vic·tion /kən'vɪkʃn/ noun **1** [C, U] ~ (**for sth**) the act of finding sb guilty of a crime in a court of law; the fact of having been found guilty: *She has six previous convictions for theft.* ◊ *He plans to appeal against his conviction.* ◊ *an offence which carries, on conviction, a sentence of not more than five years' imprisonment* **2** [C, U] ~ (**that …**) a strong opinion or belief: *strong political/ moral convictions* ◊ *She was motivated by deep religious conviction.* ◊ *a conviction that all would be well in the end* **3** [U] the feeling or appearance of believing sth strongly and of being sure about it: *'Not true!' she said with conviction.* ◊ *He said he agreed but his voice lacked conviction.* ◊ *The leader's speech in defence of the policy didn't carry much conviction.* IDM see COURAGE

con·vince /kən'vɪns/ verb **1** ~ **sb/yourself** (**of sth**) to make sb/yourself believe that sth is true: [VN] *You'll need to convince them of your enthusiasm for the job.* ◊ [VN(that)] *I'd convinced myself (that) I was right.* **2** [VN to inf] to persuade sb to do sth: *I've been trying to convince him to see a doctor.* ⇨ note at PERSUADE

con·vinced /kən'vɪnst/ adj. **1** [not before noun] ~ (**of sth/that …**) completely sure about sth: *I am convinced of her innocence.* ◊ *I am convinced that she is innocent.* ◊ *Sam nodded but he didn't look convinced.* OPP UNCONVINCED **2** [only before noun] believing strongly in a particular religion or set of political ideas: *a convinced Christian*

con·vin·cing /kən'vɪnsɪŋ/ adj. that makes sb believe that sth is true: *a convincing argument/explanation/case* ◊ *She sounded very convincing to me* (= I believed what she said). ◊ *a convincing victory/win* (= an easy one) OPP UNCONVINCING ▶ **con·vin·cing·ly** adv.: *Her case was convincingly argued.* ◊ *They won convincingly.*

con·viv·ial /kən'vɪviəl/ adj. (especially *formal*) cheerful and friendly in atmosphere or character: *a convivial evening/atmosphere* ◊ *convivial company* ▶ **con·vivi·al·ity** /kən,vɪvi'æləti/ noun [U]

con·vo·ca·tion /ˌkɒnvə'keɪʃn; AmE ˌkɑːn-/ noun (*formal*) **1** [C] a large formal meeting, especially of Church officials or members of a university **2** [U] the act of calling together a convocation **3** [C] a ceremony held in a university or college when students receive their degrees

con·vo·luted /'kɒnvəluːtɪd; AmE 'kɑːn-/ adj. **1** extremely complicated and difficult to follow: *a convoluted argument/explanation* ◊ *a book with a convoluted plot* **2** (*formal*) having many twists or curves: *a convoluted coastline*

con·vo·lu·tion /ˌkɒnvə'luːʃn; AmE ˌkɑːn-/ noun [usually pl.] (*formal*) **1** a thing that is very complicated and difficult to follow: *the bizarre convolutions of the story* **2** a twist or curve, especially one of many: *the convolutions of the left hemisphere of the brain*

con·voy /'kɒnvɔɪ; AmE 'kɑːn-/ noun a group of vehicles or ships travelling together, especially when soldiers or other vehicles travel with them for protection: *a convoy of trucks/lorries/freighters* ◊ *A United Nations aid convoy loaded with food and medicine finally got through to the besieged town.* IDM **in 'convoy** (of travelling vehicles) as a group; together: *We drove in convoy because I didn't know the route.*

con·vulse /kən'vʌls/ verb **1** ~ (**sb**) (**with sth**) to cause a sudden shaking movement in sb's body; to make this movement: [VN] *A violent shiver convulsed him.* ◊ [V] *His whole body convulsed.* **2** [VN] (**be convulsed with laughter, anger,** etc.) to be laughing so much, so angry, etc. that you cannot control your movements

con·vul·sion /kən'vʌlʃn/ noun [usually pl.] **1** a sudden shaking movement of the body that cannot be controlled: *The child went into convulsions.* **2** a sudden important change that happens to a country or an organization:

political convulsions threatening the stability of new democracies

con·vul·sive /kən'vʌlsɪv/ adj. (of movements or actions) sudden and impossible to control: *a convulsive movement/attack/fit* ◊ *Her breath came in convulsive gasps.* ▶ **con·vul·sive·ly** adv.: *weeping convulsively*

coo /kuː/ verb, exclamation
■ verb (**coo·ing, cooed, cooed**) **1** [V] when a DOVE or a PIGEON **coos**, it makes a soft low sound **2** [V, V speech] to say sth in a soft quiet voice, especially to sb you love IDM see BILL v. ▶ **coo** noun
■ exclamation (*BrE, informal*) used to show that you are surprised: *Coo, look at him!*

cook /kʊk/ verb, noun
■ verb **1** to prepare food by heating it, for example by boiling, baking or frying it: [V] *Where did you learn to cook?* ◊ [VN] *What's the best way to cook trout?* ◊ *Who's going to cook supper?* ◊ [VNN, VN] *He cooked me lunch.* ◊ *He cooked lunch for me.* ⇨ vocabulary notes on page 274 **2** [V] (of food) to be prepared by boiling, baking, frying, etc: *While the pasta is cooking, prepare the sauce.* **3** [V] (**be cooking**) (*informal*) to be planned secretly: *Everyone is being very secretive—there's something cooking.* IDM **be cooking with 'gas** (*AmE, informal*) to be doing sth very well and successfully ,**cook the 'books** (*informal*) to change facts or figures dishonestly or illegally: *His accountant had been cooking the books for years.* **cook sb's 'goose** (*informal*) to ruin sb's chances of success PHR V ,**cook sth↔'up** (*informal*) to invent sth, especially in order to deceive sb SYN CONCOCT: *to cook up a story*
■ noun a person who cooks food or whose job is cooking: *John is a very good cook* (= he cooks well). ◊ *Who was the cook* (= who cooked the food)*?* ◊ *She was employed as a cook in a hotel.*—compare CHEF IDM **too many cooks spoil the 'broth** (*saying*) if too many people are involved in doing sth, it will not be done well

cook·book /'kʊkbʊk/ (*BrE* also **'cookery book**) noun a book that gives instructions on cooking and how to cook individual dishes

'cook-chill adj. [only before noun] (*BrE*) food prepared by the **cook-chill** method is cooked, kept at a low temperature and then heated again

cook·er /'kʊkə(r)/ (*BrE*) (*AmE* **range, stove**) noun a large piece of equipment for cooking food, containing an oven and gas or electric rings on top: *a gas cooker* ◊ *an electric cooker*—see also PRESSURE COOKER—picture on page 274

cook·ery /'kʊkəri/ noun [U] the art or activity of preparing and cooking food: *a cookery course* ◊ *Italian cookery*

'cookery book noun (*BrE*) = COOKBOOK

cook·house /'kʊkhaʊs/ noun an outdoor kitchen, for example in a military camp

cookie /'kʊki/ noun (*pl.* **-ies**) **1** (*especially AmE*) a small flat sweet cake for one person, usually baked until crisp: *chocolate chip cookies* ◊ *a cookie jar*—compare BISCUIT, CRACKER—see also FORTUNE COOKIE **2 smart/tough** ~ (*AmE, informal*) a SMART/TOUGH person IDM see WAY n.

cook·ing /'kʊkɪŋ/ noun, adj.
■ noun [U] **1** the process of preparing food: *My husband does all the cooking.* ◊ *a book on Indian cooking* ⇨ vocabulary notes on pages 274, 275 **2** food that has been prepared in a particular way: *The restaurant offers traditional home cooking* (= food similar to that cooked at home). ◊ *They serve good French cooking.*
■ adj. suitable for cooking rather than eating raw or drinking: *cooking oil/sherry*

'cooking apple noun (*BrE*) any type of apple that is suitable for cooking, rather than eating raw—compare EATING APPLE

'cooking gas noun [U] (*AmE*) = CALOR GAS™

cook·out /'kʊkaʊt/ noun (*AmE, informal*) a meal or party when food is cooked over an open fire outdoors, for example at a beach—compare BARBECUE

cook·ware /'kʊkweə(r); AmE -wer/ noun [U] pots and containers used in cooking

cool /kuːl/ adj., verb, noun
■ adj. (**cool·er, cool·est**)

Cooking

Cook

When talking generally about preparing meals, use the verb **to cook**:

- *Do you like cooking?*
- *She still hasn't learned how to cook.*

You can **cook** food or a meal:

gas ring (*BrE*)/ burner (*AmE*)

oven

cooker (*BrE*)/ stove (*AmE*)

- *He's cooking dinner.*
- *Add the onion and cook gently (= cook the onion gently) for five minutes.*

or the meal can **cook**:

- *Dinner won't be long. It's cooking now.*
- *Add the meat and let it cook for ten minutes.*

There are different verbs for particular ways of cooking: with water, oil or in dry heat.

Boil

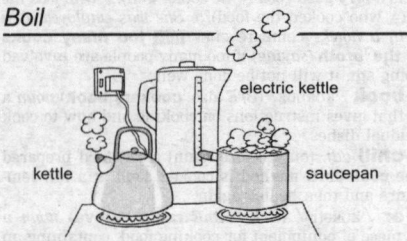

electric kettle

kettle

saucepan

You can **boil** vegetables, eggs, rice, etc. by covering them with water and heating to the **boiling point** (=100°C):

- *boiled potatoes / rice*

You can also just **boil** the water:

- *I'm boiling the water for the pasta now.*

or the container the water is in:

- *Boil a large pan of salted water.*

or the vegetables, the water or (in British English) the container can **boil**:

- *The potatoes were boiling away merrily.*
- *Make sure the water is really boiling.*
- *The kettle's boiled! Do you want some tea? (BrE)*

If you **bring something to the boil** (*BrE*)/ **a boil** (*AmE*) you heat it until it boils; you can then **simmer** it or let it **simmer** by letting it boil gently for a period of time:

- *Simmer the carrots in a large pan of water.*
- *Bring to the boil and let it simmer for five minutes.*

Steam

You can **steam** fish, vegetables, etc. by placing the food above boiling water in a container with holes so that the steam reaches it, and covering it:

- *Chinese rice is always white and usually prepared by steaming.*

steamer

Bake

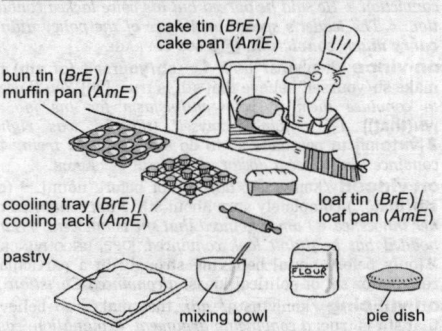

cake tin (*BrE*)/ cake pan (*AmE*)

bun tin (*BrE*)/ muffin pan (*AmE*)

cooling tray (*BrE*)/ cooling rack (*AmE*)

loaf tin (*BrE*)/ loaf pan (*AmE*)

pastry

mixing bowl

FLOUR

pie dish

You can **bake** bread, cakes, potatoes, etc. in the dry heat of an oven or a fire:

- *He baked a cake for her birthday.*

or the bread, cakes, etc. can **bake**:

- *While the cake is baking, avoid opening the oven door.*

Baking can be used for things that are baked or the activity of baking them:

- *A nice smell of baking came from the kitchen.*
- *My grandmother always used to bake / do the baking on Saturdays.*

Fry

 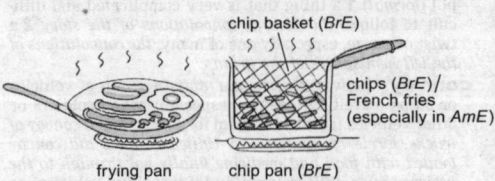

chip basket (*BrE*)

chips (*BrE*)/ French fries (especially in *AmE*)

frying pan

chip pan (*BrE*)

You can **fry** meat, fish, eggs, etc. in a shallow pan of hot oil, or the meat, fish, eggs, etc. can **fry**:

- *Fry the onion and garlic for five minutes.*
- *The smell of frying bacon made her mouth water.*

Chips (*BrE*)/ Fries (*AmE*), etc. can be completely covered in very hot oil and **deep-fried**.

Roast

You can **roast** large pieces of meat, potatoes, etc. by covering the surface of the food with oil in the heat of an oven.

roasting tin (BrE)/ roasting pan (AmE)

Microwave

microwave (also microwave oven)

You can talk about cooking food in a **microwave** or **microwave oven** in two ways:

- **Microwave** the contents of the package for three minutes.
- I usually just **heat** something **up** in the microwave for dinner.

Grill (BrE)/Broil (AmE)

grill pan (BrE)/ broiler pan (AmE)

Casserole

oven gloves

casserole

Flambé

For more cooking equipment see the illustrations at KITCHEN, MIXER, PAN and POT.

Barbecue

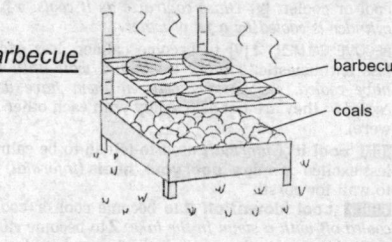

barbecue

coals

Stir-fry

spatula

wok

Toast

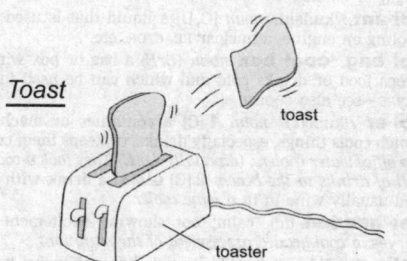

toast

toaster

C

FAIRLY COLD | **1** fairly cold; not hot or warm: *a cool breeze/ drink/climate* ◇ *Cooler weather is forecast for the weekend.* ◇ *Let's sit in the shade and keep cool.* ◇ *Store lemons in a cool dry place.*

COLOURS | **2** making you feel pleasantly cool: *a room painted in cool greens and blues*

CALM | **3** calm; not excited, angry or emotional: *Keep cool!* ◇ *She tried to remain cool, calm and collected* (= calm). ◇ *He has a cool head* (= he stays calm in an emergency).

NOT FRIENDLY/ENTHUSIASTIC | **4** not friendly, interested or enthusiastic: *She was decidedly cool about the proposal.* ◇ *He has been cool towards me ever since we had that argument.* ◇ *They gave the Prime Minister a cool reception.*

APPROVING | **5** (*informal*) used to show that you admire or approve of something because it is fashionable, attractive and often different: *You look pretty cool with that new haircut.* ◇ *It's a cool movie.* **6** (*spoken*) people say **Cool!** or **That's cool** to show that they approve of sth or agree to a suggestion: *'We're meeting Jake for lunch and we can go on the yacht in the afternoon.' 'Cool!'*

CONFIDENT | **7** (*informal*) calm and confident in a way that lacks respect for other people, but makes people admire you as well as disapprove: *She just took his keys and walked out with them, cool as you please.*

MONEY | **8** [only before noun] used about a sum of money to emphasize how large it is: *The car cost a cool thirty thousand.*

FINE | **9** used to say that sth is acceptable and not a problem for you: *'Can you come at 10.30 tomorrow?' 'That's cool.'* ◇ (*especially AmE, spoken*) *I was surprised by her promotion, but I'm cool with it.*

—see also COOLLY, COOLNESS

IDM (**as**) ˌcool as a ˈcucumber very calm and controlled, especially in a difficult situation **play it ˈcool** (*informal*) to deal with a situation in a calm way: *For once I felt uncertain about blurting out my real feelings. I decided to play it cool.*

■ *verb*

BECOME COLDER | **1** to become or to make sb/sth become cool or cooler: [V] *Glass contracts as it cools.* ◇ [VN] *The cylinder is cooled by a jet of water.*

BECOME CALMER | **2** [V] to become calmer, less excited or less enthusiastic: *I think we should wait until tempers have cooled.* ◇ *Relations between them have definitely cooled* (= they are not as friendly with each other as they were).

IDM ˈcool it! (*informal*) used to tell sb to be calmer and less excited or angry ˌcool your ˈheels (*informal*) to have to wait for sb/sth

PHRV ˌcool ˈdown/ˈoff **1** to become cool or cooler: *We cooled off with a swim in the lake.* **2** to become calm, less excited or less enthusiastic: *I think you should wait until she's cooled down a little.* ˌcool sb↔ˈdown/ˈoff **1** to make sb feel cooler: *Drink plenty of cold water to cool yourself down.* **2** to make sb calm, less excited or less enthusiastic: *A few hours in a police cell should cool him off.* ˌcool sth↔ˈdown/ˈoff to make sth cool or cooler

■ *noun* (**the cool**) [sing.] cool air or a cool place: *the cool of the evening*

IDM keep your cool (*informal*) to remain calm in a difficult situation **lose your cool** (*informal*) to become angry or excited

cool·ant /ˈkuːlənt/ *noun* [C, U] a liquid that is used for cooling an engine, a nuclear REACTOR, etc.

ˈcool bag, ˈcool box *noun* (*BrE*) a bag or box which keeps food or drinks cold and which can be used for a PICNIC—see also COOLER

cool·er /ˈkuːlə(r)/ *noun* **1** [C] a container or machine which cools things, especially drinks, or keeps them cold: *the office water cooler* ◇ (*especially AmE*) *They took a cooler full of drinks to the beach.* **2** [C] (*AmE*) a drink with ice and usually wine in it: *a wine cooler*

ˌcool-ˈheaded *adj.* calm; not showing excitement or nerves: *a cool-headed assessment of the situation*

coolie /ˈkuːli/ *noun* (*old-fashioned*, ⚠) an offensive word

for a worker in Eastern countries with no special skills or training

ˌcooling-ˈoff period *noun* **1** a period of time during which two sides in a dispute try to reach an agreement before taking further action, for example by going on strike **2** a period of time after sb has agreed to buy sth, such as an insurance plan, during which they can change their mind

ˈcooling tower *noun* a large high round building used in industry for cooling water before it is used again

cool·ly /ˈkuːlli/ *adv.* in a way that is not friendly, interested or enthusiastic: *'We're just good friends,' she said coolly.* ◇ *He received my suggestion coolly.*

cool·ness /ˈkuːlnəs/ *noun* [U] the quality of being cool: *the delicious coolness of the water* ◇ *I admire her coolness under pressure.* ◇ *I noticed a certain coolness* (= lack of friendly feeling) *between them.*

coon /kuːn/ *noun* (⚠, *slang*) a very offensive word for a black person

coop /kuːp/ *noun, verb*
■ *noun* a cage for chickens, etc. **IDM** see FLY *v.*
■ *verb* **PHRV** ˌcoop sb/sth ˈup [usually passive] to keep a person or an animal inside a building or in a small space

ˈco-op *noun* (*informal*) a COOPERATIVE shop/store, society or business: *a food/housing co-op*

coop·er /ˈkuːpə(r)/ *noun* a person who makes BARRELS

co·oper·ate (*BrE also* **co-operate**) /kəʊˈɒpəreɪt; *AmE* koʊˈɑːp-/ *verb* [V] ~ (**with sb**) (**in/on sth**) **1** to work together with sb else in order to achieve sth: *The two groups agreed to cooperate with each other.* ◇ *They had cooperated closely in the planning of the project.* **2** to be helpful by doing what sb asks you to do: *Their captors told them they would be killed unless they cooperated.*

co·oper·ation (*BrE also* **co-operation**) /kəʊˌɒpəˈreɪʃn; *AmE* koʊˌɑːp-/ *noun* [U] **1** ~ (**with sb**) (**in doing sth**)| ~ (**between A and B**) the fact of doing sth together or of working together towards a shared aim: *a report produced by the government in cooperation with the chemical industry* ◇ *We would like to see close cooperation between colleges and schools in developing computer use.* **2** willingness to be helpful and do as you are asked: *We would be grateful for your cooperation in clearing the hall as quickly as possible.*

co·opera·tive (*BrE also* **co-operative**) /kəʊˈɒpərətɪv; *AmE* koʊˈɑːp-/ *adj., noun*
■ *adj.* **1** [usually before noun] involving doing sth together or working together with others towards a shared aim: *Cooperative activity is essential to effective community work.* **2** helpful by doing what you are asked to do: *Employees will generally be more cooperative if their views are taken seriously.* **OPP** UNCOOPERATIVE **3** [usually before noun] (*business*) owned and run by the people involved, with the profits shared by them: *a cooperative farm* ◇ *The cooperative movement started in Britain in the 19th century.* ▶ **co·opera·tive·ly** (*BrE also* **co-operatively**) *adv.*
■ *noun* a cooperative business or other organization: *agricultural cooperatives in India and China* ◇ *The factory is now a workers' cooperative.*

ˌco-ˈopt *verb* [VN] ~ **sb** (**onto/into sth**) **1** to make sb a member of a group, committee, etc. by the agreement of all the other members: *She was co-opted onto the board.* **2** to include sb in sth, often when they do not want to be part of it

co·ord·in·ate (*BrE also* **co-ordinate**) *verb, noun*
■ *verb* /kəʊˈɔːdɪneɪt; *AmE* koʊˈɔːrd-/ **1** [VN] to organize the different parts of an activity and the people involved in it so that it works well: *They appointed a new manager to coordinate the work of the team.* ◇ *We need to develop a coordinated approach to the problem.* **2** [VN] to make the different parts of your body work well together—see also UNCOORDINATED **3** ~ (**sth**) (**with sth**) if you **coordinate** clothes, fabrics, etc. or if they **coordinate**, they look nice together: [V] *This shade coordinates with a wide range of other colours.* [also VN] ▶ **co·ord·in·ator** (*BrE also* **co-ordinator**) *noun*: *The campaign needs an effective coordinator.*

s	t	v	z	ʃ	ʒ	tʃ	dʒ	θ	ð	ŋ
see	tea	van	zoo	shoe	vision	chain	jam	thin	this	sing

■ noun /kəʊˈɔːdɪnət; *AmE* koʊˈɔːrd-/ **1** [C] either of two numbers or letters used to fix the position of a point on a map or GRAPH: *the x, y coordinates of any point on a line* **2 (coordinates)** [pl.] (used in shops/stores etc.) pieces of clothing that can be worn together because, for example, the colours look good together

coordinate clause /kəʊˌɔːdɪnət ˈklɔːz; *AmE* koʊˌɔːrd-/ *noun* (*grammar*) each of two or more parts of a sentence, often joined by *and*, *or*, *but*, etc. that make separate statements that each have an equal importance—compare SUBORDINATE CLAUSE

co·ord·in·ation (*BrE* also **co-ordination**) /kəʊˌɔːdɪˈneɪʃn; *AmE* koʊˌɔːrd-/ *noun* [U] **1** the act of making parts of sth, groups of people, etc. work together in an efficient and organized way: *We have improved the coordination of services.* ◊ *a need for greater coordination between departments* ◊ *a lack of coordination in conservation policy* ◊ *a pamphlet produced by the government in coordination with* (= working together with) *the Sports Council* ◊ *advice on colour coordination* (= choosing colours that look nice together, for example in clothes or furniture) **2** the ability to control your movements well: *You need good hand-eye coordination to play ball games.*

coot /kuːt/ *noun* **1** a black bird with a white spot on its forehead that lives on or near water **2** old **~** (*AmE*, *informal*) a stupid person

cop /kɒp; *AmE* kɑːp/ *noun, verb*

■ noun (*informal*) a police officer: *Somebody call the cops!* ◊ *children playing cops and robbers* ◊ *a TV cop show* **IDM** **not much ˈcop** (*BrE*, *slang*) not very good: *He's not much cop as a singer.*—more at FAIR *adj*.

■ verb (**-pp-**) [VN] (*informal*) **1** to receive or suffer sth unpleasant: *He copped all the hassle after the accident.* **2** to notice sth: *Cop a load of this* (= Listen to this)*!* **IDM** **cop hold of sth** (*BrE*, *informal*) to take hold of sth **cop a ˈplea** (*AmE*, *informal*) to admit in a court of law to being guilty of a small crime in the hope of receiving less severe punishment for a more serious crime—compare PLEA BARGAINING **ˈcop it** (*BrE*, *slang*) **1** to be punished **2** to be killed **PHRV** **ˌcop ˈoff (with sb)** (*BrE*, *slang*) to start a sexual or romantic experience with sb: *Who did he cop off with at the party?* **ˌcop ˈout (of sth)** (*informal*) to avoid or stop doing sth that you should do because you are afraid, lazy, etc: *You're not going to cop out at the last minute, are you?*—related noun COP-OUT

cope /kəʊp; *AmE* koʊp/ *verb, noun*

■ verb [V] **~ (with sth)** to deal successfully with sth difficult **SYN** MANAGE: *I got to the stage where I wasn't coping any more.* ◊ *He wasn't able to cope with the stresses and strains of the job.* ◊ *Desert plants are adapted to cope with extreme heat.*

■ noun a long loose piece of clothing worn by priests on special occasions

copier /ˈkɒpiə(r); *AmE* ˈkɑːp-/ *noun* (*especially AmE*) = PHOTOCOPIER

ˈco-pilot *noun* a second pilot who helps the main pilot in an aircraft

cop·ing /ˈkəʊpɪŋ; *AmE* ˈkoʊpɪŋ/ *noun* (*architecture*) the top row of bricks or stones, usually sloping, on a wall

co·pi·ous /ˈkəʊpiəs; *AmE* ˈkoʊ-/ *adj.* in large amounts **SYN** ABUNDANT: *copious* (= large) *amounts of water* ◊ *I took copious notes.* ◊ *She supports her theory with copious evidence.* ▶ **co·pi·ous·ly** *adv.*: *bleeding copiously*

ˈcop-out *noun* (*informal, disapproving*) a way of avoiding doing sth that you should do, or an excuse for not doing it: *The ending of the film is a cop-out—the director didn't really want to face up to the racial issues involved.*

cop·per /ˈkɒpə(r); *AmE* ˈkɑːp-/ *noun* **1** [U] (*symb* Cu) a chemical element. Copper is a soft reddish-brown metal used for making electric wires, pipes and coins: *a copper mine* ◊ *copper wire/pipes* ◊ *copper-coloured hair* **2** (**coppers**) [pl.] (*BrE*) brown coins that do not have much value: *I only paid a few coppers for it.* **3** [C] (*BrE*, *informal*) a police officer

ˌcopper ˈbeech *noun* a tall type of BEECH tree with smooth bark and reddish-brown leaves

cop·per·plate /ˈkɒpəpleɪt; *AmE* ˈkɑːpər-/ *noun* [U] a neat old-fashioned way of writing with sloping letters joined together

cop·pery /ˈkɒpəri; *AmE* ˈkɑːp-/ *adj.* similar to or having the colour of COPPER: *coppery hair*

cop·pice /ˈkɒpɪs; *AmE* ˈkɑːp-/ *verb* [VN, V] (*technical*) to cut back young trees in order to make them grow faster

copra /ˈkɒprə; *AmE* ˈkoʊprə/ *noun* [U] the dried white flesh of COCONUTS

copse /kɒps; *AmE* kɑːps/ (also **cop·pice** /ˈkɒpɪs; *AmE* ˈkɑːpəs/) *noun* a small area of trees or bushes growing together

ˈcop shop *noun* (*BrE*, *informal*) a police station

cop·ter /ˈkɒptə(r); *AmE* ˈkɑːp-/ *noun* (*informal*) = HELICOPTER

cop·ula /ˈkɒpjələ; *AmE* ˈkɑːp-/ *noun* (*grammar*) = LINKING VERB

copu·late /ˈkɒpjuleɪt; *AmE* ˈkɑːp-/ *verb* [V] **~ (with sb/sth)** (*technical*) to have sex: *Some animals perform elaborate mating rituals before they copulate.* ▶ **copu·la·tion** /ˌkɒpjuˈleɪʃn; *AmE* ˌkɑːp-/ *noun* [U]

copy /ˈkɒpi; *AmE* ˈkɑːp-/ *noun, verb*

■ noun (*pl.* **-ies**) **1** [C] **~ (of sth)** a thing that is made to look like sth else, especially a document or a work of art: *I will send you a copy of the report.* ◊ *The thieves replaced the original painting with a copy.* ◊ *You should make a copy of the disk as a back-up.*—see also HARD COPY **2** [C] a single example of a book, newspaper, etc. of which many have been made: *a copy of 'The Times'* ◊ *The book sold 20000 copies within two weeks.*—see also BACK COPY **3** [U] written material that is to be printed in a newspaper, magazine, etc.; news or information that can be used in a newspaper article or advertisement: *The subeditors prepare the reporters' copy for the paper and write the headlines.* ◊ *This will make great copy for the advertisement.* **4** = PHOTOCOPY: *Could I have ten copies of this page, please?*

■ verb (**cop·ies, copy·ing, cop·ied, cop·ied**) **1** [VN] to make sth that is exactly like sth else: *They copied the designs from those on Greek vases.* ◊ *Everything in the computer's memory can be copied onto diskettes.* **2** [VN] **~ sth (from sth into/onto sth)** **~ sth (down/out)** to write sth exactly as it is written somewhere else: *She copied the phone number into her address book.* ◊ *I copied out several poems.* **3** [VN] to behave or do sth in the same way as sb else **SYN** IMITATE: *She copies everything her sister does.* ◊ *Their tactics have been copied by other terrorist organizations.* **4** [V] **~ (from/off sb)** to cheat in an exam, school work, etc. by writing what sb else has written and pretending it is your own work **5** [VN] (*especially AmE*) = PHOTOCOPY

copy·book /ˈkɒpibʊk; *AmE* ˈkɑːp-/ *noun, adj.*

■ noun a book, used in the past by children in school, containing examples of writing which school students had to copy **IDM** See BLOT *v.*

■ adj. [only before noun] (*BrE*) done exactly how it should be done: *It was a copybook operation by the police.*

copy·cat /ˈkɒpikæt; *AmE* ˈkɑːp-/ *noun, adj.*

■ noun (*informal, disapproving*) used especially by children about and to a person who copies what sb else does because they have no ideas of their own

■ adj. [only before noun] (*of crimes*) similar to and seen as copying an earlier well-known crime

ˈcopy editor *noun* a person whose job is to correct and prepare a text for printing ▶ **ˈcopy-edit** *verb* [VN]

copy·ist /ˈkɒpiɪst; *AmE* ˈkɑːp-/ *noun* a person who makes copies of written documents or works of art

copy·right /ˈkɒpiraɪt; *AmE* ˈkɑːp-/ *noun, adj., verb*

■ noun [U, C] **~ (in/on sth)** if a person or an organization holds the **copyright** on a piece of writing, music, etc., they are the only people who have the legal right to publish, broadcast, perform it etc., and other people must ask their permission to use it or any part of it: *Who owns the copyright on this song?* ◊ *Copyright expires seventy years after the death of the author.* ◊ *They were sued for breach/infringement of copyright.*

■ adj. (*abbr.* C) protected by copyright; not allowed to be copied without permission: *copyright material*

■ verb [VN] to get the copyright for sth

æ	ɑː	e	ɜː	ə	ɪ	iː	i	ɒ	ɔː	ʌ	ʊ	u	uː
cat	father	ten	bird	about	sit	see	many	got	saw	cup	put	actual	too
								(BrE)					

copy·writer /ˈkɒpɪraɪtə(r); AmE ˈkɑːp-/ noun a person whose job is to write the words for advertising material

co·quet·ry /ˈkɒkɪtri; AmE ˈkoʊk-/ noun [U] (literary) behaviour that is typical of a coquette

co·quette /kɒˈket; AmE koʊˈket/ noun (literary, often disapproving) a woman who behaves in a way that is intended to attract men SYN FLIRT ▶ **co·quet·tish** /kɒˈketɪʃ; AmE koʊˈk-/ adj.: a coquettish smile **co·quet·tish·ly** adv.

cor /kɔː(r)/ (also ˌcor ˈbli·mey) exclamation (BrE, informal) used when you are surprised, pleased or impressed by sth: Cor! Look at that!

cor·acle /ˈkɒrəkl; AmE ˈkɔːr-; ˈkɑːr-/ noun a small round boat with a wooden frame, used in Wales and Ireland by people catching fish

coral /ˈkɒrəl; AmE ˈkɔːrəl; ˈkɑːrəl/ noun, adj.
■ noun **1** [U] a hard substance that is red, pink or white in colour, and that forms on the bottom of the sea from the bones of very small creatures. Coral is often used in jewellery: coral reefs/islands ◇ a coral necklace **2** [C] a creature that produces coral
■ adj. pink or red in colour, like coral: coral lipstick

cor ang·lais /ˌkɒr ˈɒŋgleɪ; AmE ɔːn ˈgleɪ/ noun (pl. **cors anglais** /ˌkɒr ˈɒŋgleɪ; AmE ɔːn ˈgleɪ/) (also ˌEnglish ˈhorn especially in AmE) a musical instrument of the WOODWIND group, like an OBOE but larger and playing lower notes

cord /kɔːd; AmE kɔːrd/ noun **1** [U, C] strong thick string or thin rope; a piece of this: a piece/length of cord ◇ picture cord (= used for hanging pictures) ◇ a silk bag tied with a gold cord—picture at ROPE, TASSEL **2** [C, U] (especially AmE) = FLEX: an electrical cord ◇ telephone cord—see also CORDLESS—picture at ROPE **3** [U] = CORDUROY: a cord jacket **4** (**cords**) (also old-fashioned **corduroys**) [pl.] trousers/pants made of CORDUROY: a pair of cords—picture on page A4—see also SPINAL CORD, UMBILICAL CORD, VOCAL CORDS

cord·ed /ˈkɔːdɪd; AmE ˈkɔːrd-/ adj. **1** (of fabric) having raised lines SYN RIBBED **2** (of a muscle) tense and standing out so that it looks like a piece of cord **3** that has a cord attached: a corded phone OPP CORDLESS

cor·dial /ˈkɔːdiəl; AmE ˈkɔːrdʒəl/ adj., noun
■ adj. (formal) pleasant and friendly: a cordial atmosphere/meeting/relationship ▶ **cor·di·al·ity** /ˌkɔːdiˈæləti; AmE ˌkɔːrdʒi-/ noun [U]: I was greeted with a show of cordiality.
■ noun **1** (BrE) [U, C] a sweet drink that does not contain alcohol, made from fruit juice. It is drunk with water added: blackcurrant cordial **2** [U, C] (AmE) = LIQUEUR **3** [C] a glass of cordial

cor·di·al·ly /ˈkɔːdiəli; AmE ˈkɔːrdʒəli/ adv. **1** (formal) in a pleasant and friendly manner: You are cordially invited to a celebration for Mr Michael Brown on his retirement. **2** (formal) (used with verbs showing dislike) very much: They cordially detest each other.

cord·ite /ˈkɔːdaɪt; AmE ˈkɔːrd-/ noun [U] an explosive used in bullets, bombs, etc.

cord·less /ˈkɔːdləs; AmE ˈkɔːrd-/ adj. (of a telephone or an electrical tool) not connected to its power supply by wires: a cordless phone/drill OPP CORDED

cor·don /ˈkɔːdn; AmE ˈkɔːrdn/ noun, verb
■ noun a line or ring of police officers, soldiers, etc. guarding sth or stopping people from entering or leaving a place: Demonstrators tried to break through the police cordon.
■ verb PHRV ˌcordon sth ↔ ˈoff to stop people from getting into an area by surrounding it with police, soldiers, etc: Police cordoned off the area until the bomb was made safe.

cor·don bleu /ˌkɔːdɒ̃ ˈblɜː; AmE ˌkɔːrdɑː-/ adj. [usually before noun] (from French) of the highest standard of skill in cooking: a cordon bleu chef ◇ cordon bleu cuisine

cor·du·roy /ˈkɔːdərɔɪ; AmE ˈkɔːrd-/ noun **1** (also **cord**) [U] a strong soft cotton fabric with a pattern of raised parallel lines on it, used for making clothes: a corduroy jacket **2** (**cor·du·roys**) [pl.] (old-fashioned) = CORDS—picture on page A4

core /kɔː(r)/ noun, verb

■ noun **1** the hard central part of a fruit such as an apple, that contains the seeds—picture on page A2 **2** the central part of an object: the earth's core ◇ the core of a nuclear reactor ◇ (figurative) Concern for the environment is at the core of our policies. **3** the most important part of sth: the core of the argument ◇ core subjects (= subjects that all the students have to do) ◇ the core curriculum ◇ the core activities of the job **4** a small group of people who take part in a particular activity: He gathered a small core of advisers around him.—see also HARD CORE IDM **to the ˈcore** so that the whole of a thing or a person is affected: She was shaken to the core by the news. ◇ He's a politician to the core (= in all his attitudes, beliefs and actions).
■ verb [VN] to take out the core of a fruit

ˌco-reˈspond·ent noun (law) a person who is said to have committed ADULTERY with the husband or wife of sb who is trying to get divorced

corgi /ˈkɔːgi; AmE ˈkɔːrgi/ noun a small dog with short legs and a pointed nose

cori·an·der /ˌkɒriˈændə(r); AmE ˌkɔːr-/ noun [U] a plant whose leaves are used in cooking as a herb and whose seeds are used in cooking as a spice—compare CILANTRO

cork /kɔːk; AmE kɔːrk/ noun, verb
■ noun **1** [U] a light, soft material that is the thick bark of a type of Mediterranean OAK tree: a cork mat ◇ cork tiles **2** [C] a small round object made of cork or plastic, that is used for closing bottles, especially wine bottles.—picture at PACKAGING
■ verb [VN] to close a bottle with a cork OPP UNCORK

corked /kɔːkt; AmE kɔːrkt/ adj. (of wine) with a bad taste because the cork has decayed

cork·er /ˈkɔːkə(r); AmE ˈkɔːrk-/ noun [usually sing.] (old-fashioned, BrE, informal) a person or thing that is extremely good, beautiful or amusing

cork·screw /ˈkɔːkskruː; AmE ˈkɔːrk-/ noun, verb
■ noun a tool for pulling CORKS from bottles. Most corkscrews have a handle and a twisted metal rod for pushing into the cork.—picture at KITCHEN
■ verb [V] [usually +adv./prep.] to make a series of circular movements in a particular direction

corm /kɔːm; AmE kɔːrm/ noun the small round underground part of some plants, from which the new plant grows every year

cor·mor·ant /ˈkɔːmərənt; AmE ˈkɔːrm-/ noun a large black seabird with a long neck

corn /kɔːn; AmE kɔːrn/ noun **1** (BrE) [U] any plant that is grown for its grain, such as wheat; the grain of these plants: a field of corn ◇ ears/sheaves of corn ◇ corn-fed chicken—picture at CEREAL **2** [U] (AmE) = MAIZE—see also CORN COB, CORN ON THE COB **3** [U] (AmE) = SWEETCORN **4** [C] a small area of hard skin on the foot, especially the toe, that is sometimes painful

ˈcorn circle noun = CROP CIRCLE

ˈcorn cob (especially BrE) (also **cob** AmE, BrE) noun the long hard part of the MAIZE plant that the rows of yellow grains grow on—picture at CEREAL

cor·nea /ˈkɔːniə; AmE ˈkɔːrniə/ noun (anatomy) the transparent protective layer covering the outer part of the eye—picture at BODY ▶ **cor·neal** /ˈkɔːniəl; AmE ˈkɔːrniəl/ adj. [only before noun]: a corneal transplant

corned beef /ˌkɔːnd ˈbiːf; AmE ˌkɔːrnd/ noun [U] beef that has been cooked and preserved using salt, often sold in cans

cor·ner /ˈkɔːnə(r); AmE ˈkɔːrn-/ noun, verb
■ noun
OF BUILDING/OBJECT/SHAPE **1** a part of sth where two or more sides, lines or edges join: the four corners of a square ◇ Write your address in the top right-hand corner of the letter. ◇ I hit my knee on the corner of the table. ◇ A smile lifted the corner of his mouth. ◇ a speck of dirt in the corner of her eye
-CORNERED **2** (in adjectives) with the number of corners mentioned; involving the number of groups mentioned: a three-cornered hat ◇ a three-cornered contest
OF ROOM/BOX **3** the place inside a room or a box where two sides join; the area around this place: There was a

aɪ	aʊ	eɪ	əʊ	oʊ	ɔɪ	ɪə	eə	ʊə	j	w
my	now	say	go	go	boy	near	hair	pure	yes	wet
			(BrE)	(AmE)						

C

television in the far corner of the room. ◊ a corner table/seat/cupboard

OF ROADS | **4** a place where two streets join: *There was a large group of youths standing on the street corner.* ◊ *Turn right at the corner of Sunset and Crescent Heights Boulevards.* ◊ *There's a hotel on/at the corner of my street.* ◊ *The wind hit him as he **turned the corner**.* **5** a sharp bend in a road: *The car was taking the corners too fast.*

AREA/REGION | **6** a region or an area of a place (sometimes used for one that is far away or difficult to reach): *She lives in a quiet corner of rural Yorkshire.* ◊ *Students come here from the four corners of the world.* ◊ *He knew every corner of the old town.*

DIFFICULT SITUATION | **7** [usually sing.] a difficult situation: *to back/drive/force sb into a corner* ◊ *They had got her in a corner, and there wasn't much she could do about it.* ◊ *He was used to talking his way out of **tight corners**.*

IN SPORT | **8** (in sports such as football and hockey) a free kick or hit that you take from the corner of your opponent's end of the field: *to take a corner* ◊ *The referee awarded a corner.*—see also CORNER KICK **9** (in boxing and WRESTLING) any of the four corners of a RING; the supporters who help in the corner

IDM **(just) around/round the 'corner** very near: *Her house is just around the corner.* ◊ (*figurative*) *There were good times around the corner* (= they would soon come). **cut 'corners** (*disapproving*) to do sth in the easiest, cheapest or quickest way, often by ignoring rules or leaving sth out **cut the 'corner** (also **cut off the 'corner** especially in *BrE*) to go across the corner of an area and not around the sides of it, because it is quicker **see sth out of the corner of your 'eye** to see sth accidentally or not very clearly because you see it from the side of your eye and are not looking straight at it: *Out of the corner of her eye, she saw him coming closer.* **turn the 'corner** to pass a very important point in an illness or a difficult situation and begin to improve—more at TIGHT

■ *verb*

TRAP SB | **1** [VN] [often passive] to get a person or an animal into a place or situation from which they cannot escape: *The man was finally cornered by police in a garage.* ◊ *If disturbed or cornered, the snake will defend itself.* **2** [VN] to go towards sb in a determined way, because you want to speak to them: *I found myself cornered by her on the stairs.*

THE MARKET | **3** [VN] ~ **the market (in sth)** to get control of the trade in a particular type of goods: *They've cornered the market in silver.*

OF VEHICLE/DRIVER | **4** [V] (*BrE*) to go around a corner

'corner kick (also **cor·ner**) *noun* (in football) a free kick that you take from the corner of your opponent's end of the field

'corner shop *noun* (*BrE*) a small shop that sells food, newspapers, cigarettes, etc., especially one near people's houses

cor·ner·stone /ˈkɔːnəstəʊn; *AmE* ˈkɔːrnərstoʊn/ *noun* **1** (*especially AmE*) a stone at the corner of the base of a building, often laid in a special ceremony **2** the most important part of sth that the rest depends on: *This study is the cornerstone of the whole research programme.*

cor·net /ˈkɔːnɪt; *AmE* ˈkɔːrnɪt/ *noun* **1** a BRASS musical instrument like a small TRUMPET **2** (*BrE, old-fashioned*) = CONE: *an ice-cream cornet*

'corn exchange *noun* (*BrE*) a building where corn used to be bought and sold

corn-flakes /ˈkɔːnfleɪks; *AmE* ˈkɔːrn-/ *noun* [pl.] small crisp yellow pieces of crushed MAIZE, usually eaten with milk and sugar for breakfast

corn·flour /ˈkɔːnflaʊə(r); *AmE* ˈkɔːrn-/ (*BrE*) (*AmE* **cornstarch**) *noun* [U] fine white flour made from MAIZE, used especially for making sauces thicker

corn·flower /ˈkɔːnflaʊə(r); *AmE* ˈkɔːrn-/ *noun* a small wild plant with bluish-purple flowers: *cornflower-blue eyes*

cor·nice /ˈkɔːnɪs; *AmE* ˈkɔːrnɪs/ *noun* (*architecture*) a decorative border around the top of the walls in a room or on the outside walls of a building—picture at ALCOVE

Cornish pasty /ˌkɔːnɪʃ ˈpæsti; *AmE* ˌkɔːrnɪʃ/ *noun* (*BrE*) a small pie in the shape of a half circle, containing meat and vegetables

corn·meal /ˈkɔːnmiːl; *AmE* ˈkɔːrn-/ *noun* [U] flour made from MAIZE

,corn on the 'cob *noun* [U] corn that is cooked with all the grains still attached to the inner part and eaten as a vegetable—picture on page A3

'corn pone (also **pone**) (both *AmE*) *noun* [U] a type of bread made from MAIZE and water

corn·rows /ˈkɔːnrəʊz; *AmE* ˈkɔːrnroʊz/ *noun* [pl.] a hairstyle worn especially by black women, in which the hair is put into lines of PLAITS along the head—picture at HAIR

corn·starch /ˈkɔːnstɑːtʃ; *AmE* ˈkɔːrnstɑːrtʃ/ *noun* [U] (*AmE*) = CORNFLOUR

,corn 'syrup *noun* [U] a thick sweet liquid made from MAIZE and used in cooking

cor·nu·co·pia /ˌkɔːnjuˈkəʊpiə; *AmE* ˌkɔːrnjuˈkoʊpiə/ *noun* **1** (also **,horn of 'plenty**) a decorative object shaped like an animal's horn, shown in art as full of fruit and flowers **2** (*written*) something that is or contains a large supply of good things: *The book is a cornucopia of good ideas.*

corny /ˈkɔːni; *AmE* ˈkɔːrni/ *adj.* (**corn·ier**, **corni·est**) (*informal*) not original; used too often to be interesting or to sound sincere: *a corny joke/song* ◊ *I know it sounds corny, but it really was love at first sight!*

cor·ol·lary /kəˈrɒləri; *AmE* ˈkɔːrəleri; ˈkɑːr-/ *noun* (*pl.* **-ies**) ~ **(of/to sth)** (*formal* or *technical*) a situation, an argument or a fact that is the natural and direct result of another one

cor·ona /kəˈrəʊnə; *AmE* -ˈroʊ-/ *noun* (*pl.* **co·ro·nae** /-niː/) (*astronomy*) (also *informal* **halo**) a ring of light seen around the sun or moon, especially during an ECLIPSE

cor·on·ary /ˈkɒrənri; *AmE* ˈkɔːrəneri/ *adj.* (*medical*) connected with the heart, particularly the ARTERIES that take blood to the heart: *coronary (heart) disease* ◊ *a coronary patient* (= sb suffering from coronary disease).

,coronary 'artery *noun* (*anatomy*) either of the two ARTERIES that supply blood to the heart

,coronary throm'bosis (also *informal* **cor·on·ary**) *noun* (*medical*) a blocking of the flow of blood by a blood CLOT in an ARTERY supplying blood to the heart—compare HEART ATTACK

cor·on·ation /ˌkɒrəˈneɪʃn; *AmE* ˌkɔːr-/ *noun* a ceremony at which a CROWN is formally placed on the head of a new king or queen

cor·on·er /ˈkɒrənə(r); *AmE* ˈkɔːr-/ *noun* an official whose job is to discover the cause of any sudden, violent or suspicious death by holding an INQUEST

cor·onet /ˈkɒrənet; *AmE* ˌkɔːrəˈnet; ˌkɑːr-/ *noun* **1** a small CROWN worn on formal occasions by princes, princesses, LORDS, etc. **2** a circular decoration for the head, especially one made of flowers

Corp. *abbr.* CORPORATION

cor·poral /ˈkɔːpərəl; *AmE* ˈkɔːrp-/ *noun* (*abbr.* **Cpl**) a member of one of the lower ranks in the army, the MARINES or the British air force: *Corporal Masters*

,corporal 'punishment *noun* [U] the physical punishment of people, especially by hitting or beating them

cor·por·ate /ˈkɔːpərət; *AmE* ˈkɔːrp-/ *adj.* [only before noun] **1** connected with a corporation: *corporate finance/planning/strategy* ◊ *corporate identity* (= the image of a company, that all its members share) ◊ *corporate hospitality* (= when companies entertain customers to help develop good business relationships) **2** (*technical*) forming a CORPORATION: *The BBC is a corporate body.* ◊ *The law applies to both individuals and corporate bodies.* **3** involving or shared by all the members of a group: *corporate responsibility*

cor·por·ation /ˌkɔːpəˈreɪʃn; *AmE* ˌkɔːrp-/ *noun* **1** (*abbr.* **Corp.**) a large business company: *multinational corporations* ◊ *the Chrysler corporation* **2** an organization or a group of organizations that is recognized by law as a single unit: *urban development corporations* **3** (*BrE*) a

b	d	f	g	h	k	l	m	n	p	r
bad	did	fall	get	hat	cat	leg	man	now	pen	red

group of people elected to govern a large town or city and provide public services

corpo'ration tax *noun* [U] (*BrE*) a tax that companies pay on their profits

cor·por·at·ism /'kɔːpərətɪzəm; *AmE* 'kɔːrp-/ *noun* [U] the control of a country, etc. by large groups, especially businesses

cor·por·eal /kɔː'pɔːriəl; *AmE* kɔːr'p-/ *adj.* (*formal*) **1** that can be touched; physical rather than spiritual: *his corporeal presence* **2** of or for the body: *corporeal needs*

corps /kɔː(r)/ *noun* (*pl.* **corps** /kɔːz; *AmE* kɔːrz/) [C+sing./pl. *v.*] **1** a large unit of an army, consisting of two or more DIVISIONS: *the commander of the third army corps* **2** one of the groups of an army with a special responsibility: *the Royal Army Medical Corps* ◊ *the Army Corps of Engineers* **3** a group of people involved in a particular job or activity: *a corps of trained and experienced doctors*—see also DIPLOMATIC CORPS, PRESS CORPS

corps de bal·let /ˌkɔː də 'bæleɪ; *AmE* ˌkɔːr də bæ'leɪ/ *noun* [C+sing./pl. *v.*] (from *French*) dancers in a ballet company who dance together as a group

corpse /kɔːps; *AmE* kɔːrps/ *noun* a dead body, especially of a human being: *The corpse was barely recognizable.*

cor·pu·lent /'kɔːpjələnt; *AmE* 'kɔːrp-/ *adj.* (*formal*) (of a person) fat. People say 'corpulent' to avoid saying 'fat'.

cor·pus /'kɔːpəs; *AmE* 'kɔːrpəs/ *noun* (*pl.* **cor·pora** /'kɔːpərə; *AmE* 'kɔːrp-/ or **cor·puses** /-sɪz/) (*technical*) a collection of written or spoken texts: *a corpus of 100 million words of spoken English* ◊ *the whole corpus of Renaissance poetry*—see also HABEAS CORPUS

cor·puscle /'kɔːpʌsl; *AmE* 'kɔːrp-/ *noun* (*anatomy*) any of the red or white cells found in blood: *red/white corpuscles*

cor·ral /kə'rɑːl; *AmE* -'ræl/ *noun, verb*
■ *noun* (in N America) a fenced area for horses, cows etc. on a farm or RANCH: *They drove the ponies into a corral.*
■ *verb* [VN] (**-ll-**, *AmE* also **-l-**) **1** to force horses or cows into a corral **2** to gather a group of people together and keep them in a particular place

cor·rect /kə'rekt/ *adj., verb*
■ *adj.* **1** accurate or true, without any mistakes SYN RIGHT: *Do you have the correct time?* ◊ *the correct answer* ◊ *Please check that these details are correct.* ◊ *'Are you in charge here?' 'That's correct.'* ◊ *Am I correct in saying that you know a lot about wine?* OPP INCORRECT **2** right and suitable, so that sth is done as it should be done: *Do you know the correct way to shut the machine down?* ◊ *I think you've made the correct decision.* **3** taking care to speak or behave in a way that follows the accepted standards or rules: *a correct young lady* ◊ *He is always very correct in his speech.* OPP INCORRECT—see also POLITICALLY CORRECT ▶ **cor·rect·ly** *adv.*: *Have you spelled it correctly?* ◊ *They reasoned, correctly, that she was away for the weekend.* ◊ *He was looking correctly grave.* **cor·rect·ness** *noun* [U]: *The correctness of this decision may be doubted.*—see also POLITICAL CORRECTNESS IDM see PRESENT *adj.*
■ *verb* **1** [VN] to make sth right or accurate, for example by changing it or removing mistakes: *Read through your work and correct any mistakes that you find.* ◊ *Their eyesight can be corrected in just a few minutes by the use of a laser.* ◊ *They issued a statement correcting the one they had made earlier.* **2** [VN] (of a teacher) to mark the mistakes in a piece of work (and sometimes give a mark/grade to the work): *I spent all evening correcting essays.* **3** to tell sb that they have made a mistake: [VN] *Correct me if I'm wrong, but isn't this last year's brochure?* ◊ *Yes, you're right—I stand corrected* (= I accept that I made a mistake). ◊ [VN **speech**] *'It's Yates, not Wates,' she corrected him.* [also V **speech**]

cor·rec·tion /kə'rekʃn/ *noun, exclamation*
■ *noun* **1** [C] a change that makes sth more accurate than it was before: *I've made a few small corrections to your report.* ◊ *The paper had to publish a correction to the story.* **2** [U] the act or process of correcting sth: *There are some programming errors that need correction.* **3** [U] (*old-fashioned*) punishment: *the correction of young offenders*

■ *exclamation* (*informal*) used when you want to correct sth that you have just said: *I don't know. Correction—I do know, but I'm not going to tell you.*

cor·rec·tion·al /kə'rekʃənl/ *adj.* [only before noun] (*especially AmE*) concerned with improving the behaviour of criminals, usually by punishing them: *a correctional center/institution/facility* (= a prison)

cor'rection fluid *noun* [U] a white liquid that you use to cover mistakes that you make when you are writing or typing, and that you can write on top of—see also TIPP-EX, WITEOUT—picture at STATIONERY

cor·rect·ive /kə'rektɪv/ *adj., noun*
■ *adj.* (*written*) designed to make sth right that was wrong before: *We need to take corrective action to halt this country's decline.* ◊ *corrective measures* ◊ *corrective surgery/glasses*
■ *noun* **~ (to sth)** (*formal*) something that helps to give a more accurate or fairer view of sb/sth: *I should like to add a corrective to what I have written previously.*

cor·rel·ate /'kɒrəleɪt; *AmE* 'kɔːr-; 'kɑːr-/ *verb* **1** [V] if two or more facts, figures, etc. **correlate** or if a fact, figure, etc. **correlates with** another, the facts are closely connected and affect or depend on each other: *The figures do not seem to correlate.* ◊ *A high-fat diet correlates with a greater risk of heart disease.* **2** [VN] to show that there is a close connection between two or more facts, figures, etc: *Researchers are trying to correlate the two sets of figures.* ▶ **cor·rel·ate** /'kɒrələt; *AmE* 'kɔːr-; 'kɑːr-/ *noun*

cor·rel·ation /ˌkɒrə'leɪʃn; *AmE* ˌkɔːr-; ˌkɑːr-/ *noun* [C, U] **~ (between A and B)** | **~ (of A with B)** a connection between two things in which one thing changes as the other does: *There is a direct correlation between exposure to sun and skin cancer.* ◊ *the correlation of social power with wealth*

cor·rela·tive /kə'relətɪv/ *noun* (*formal*) a fact or an idea that is closely related to or depends on another fact or idea: *The child's right to education is a correlative of the parent's duty to send the child to school.* ▶ **cor·rela·tive** *adj.*

cor·res·pond /ˌkɒrə'spɒnd; *AmE* ˌkɔːrə'spɑːnd; ˌkɑː-/ *verb* [V] **1 ~ (to/with sth)** to be the same as or match sth: *Your account of events does not correspond with hers.* ◊ *Your account and hers do not correspond.* ◊ *The written record of the conversation doesn't correspond to* (= is different from) *what was actually said.* **2 ~ (to sth)** to be similar to or the same as sth else: *The British job of Lecturer corresponds roughly to the US Associate Professor.* **3 ~ (with sb)** (*formal*) to write letters to sb and receive letters from them

cor·res·pond·ence /ˌkɒrə'spɒndəns; *AmE* ˌkɔːrə'spɑːn-; ˌkɑː-/ *noun* **1** [U] **~ (with sb)** the letters a person sends and receives: *personal/private correspondence* ◊ *The editor welcomes correspondence from readers on any subject.* ◊ *the correspondence column/page* (= in a newspaper) **2** [U, C] **~ (with sb)** the activity of writing letters: *I refused to enter into any correspondence* (= to exchange letters) *with him about it.* ◊ *We have been in correspondence for months.* ◊ *We kept up a correspondence for many years.* **3** [C, U] **~ (between A and B)** a connection between two things; the fact of two things being similar: *There is a close correspondence between the two extracts.*

corre'spondence course *noun* a course of study that you do at home, using books and exercises sent to you by post/mail

cor·res·pond·ent /ˌkɒrə'spɒndənt; *AmE* ˌkɔːrə'spɑːn-; ˌkɑː-/ *noun* **1** a person who reports news from a particular country or on a particular subject for a newspaper or a television or radio station: *the BBC's political correspondent* ◊ *a foreign/war/sports correspondent* ◊ *our Hong Kong correspondent* **2** (used with an adjective) a person who writes letters to another person: *She's a poor correspondent* (= she does not write regularly).

cor·res·pond·ing /ˌkɒrə'spɒndɪŋ; *AmE* ˌkɔːrə'spɑːn-; ˌkɑː-/ *adj.* **~ (to sth)** matching or connected with sth that you have just mentioned: *A change in the money supply brings a corresponding change in expenditure.* ◊ *Profits have risen by 15 per cent compared with the corresponding* period last year. ◊ *Give each picture a number corresponding to its position on the page.* ◊ *The Redskins lost to the Cowboys in the corresponding game last year.* ▶ **cor·res·pond·ing·ly** *adv.*: *a period of high demand and correspondingly high prices*

cor·ri·dor /ˈkɒrɪdɔː(r); *AmE* ˈkɔːr-; ˈkɑːr-/ *noun* **1** (*AmE* also **hall·way**) a long narrow passage in a building or train, with doors that open into rooms on either side: *Go along the corridor, turn left, and you'll see his office in front of you.* **2** a long narrow strip of land belonging to one country that passes through the land of another country: *the Polish corridor* IDM **the corridors of ˈpower** (sometimes *humorous*) the higher levels of government, where important decisions are made

cor·rie /ˈkɒri; *AmE* ˈkɔːri; ˈkɑːri/ *noun* a round hollow area in the side of a mountain

cor·rob·or·ate /kəˈrɒbəreɪt; *AmE* -ˈrɑːb-/ *verb* [VN] [often passive] (*formal*) to provide evidence or information that supports a statement, theory, etc: *The evidence was corroborated by two independent witnesses.* ◊ *corroborating evidence* ▶ **cor·rob·or·ation** /kəˌrɒbəˈreɪʃn; *AmE* -ˌrɑːbə-/ *noun* [U]

cor·rob·ora·tive /kəˈrɒbərətɪv; *AmE* kəˈrɑːbəˌreɪtɪv/ *adj.* (*formal*) [usually before noun] giving support to a statement or theory: *Is there any corroborative evidence for this theory?*

cor·rode /kəˈrəʊd; *AmE* kəˈroʊd/ *verb* to destroy sth slowly, especially by chemical action; to be destroyed in this way: [VN] *Acid corrodes metal.* ◊ (*figurative*) *Corruption corrodes public confidence in a political system.* ◊ [V] *The copper pipework has corroded in places.* ▶ **cor·ro·sion** /kəˈrəʊʒn; *AmE* -ˈroʊ-/ *noun* [U]: *Look for signs of corrosion.* ◊ *Clean off any corrosion before applying the paint.*

cor·ro·sive /kəˈrəʊsɪv; *AmE* -ˈroʊ-/ *adj.* **1** tending to destroy sth slowly by chemical action: *the corrosive effects of salt water* ◊ *corrosive acid* **2** (*written*) tending to damage sth gradually: *Unemployment is having a corrosive effect on our economy.*

cor·ru·gated /ˈkɒrəgeɪtɪd; *AmE* ˈkɔːr-; ˈkɑːr-/ *adj.* shaped into a series of regular folds that look like waves: *a corrugated iron roof* ◊ *corrugated cardboard*

corrugated

cor·rupt /kəˈrʌpt/ *adj., verb*

■ *adj.* **1** (of people) willing to use their power to do dishonest or illegal things in return for money or to get an advantage: *a corrupt regime* ◊ *corrupt officials accepting bribes* **2** (of behaviour) dishonest or immoral: *corrupt practices* ◊ *The whole system is inefficient and corrupt.* **3** (*computing*) containing changes or faults, and no longer in the original state: *corrupt software* ◊ *The text on the disk seems to be corrupt.* ▶ **cor·rupt·ly** *adv.*

■ *verb* **1** [VN] to have a bad effect on sb and make them behave in an immoral or dishonest way: *He was corrupted by power and ambition.* ◊ *the corrupting effects of great wealth* **2** [VN] [often passive] to change the original form of sth, so that it is damaged or spoiled in some way: *a corrupted form of Buddhism* **3** (*computing*) to cause mistakes to appear in a computer file, etc. with the result that the information in it is no longer correct: [VN] *The program has somehow corrupted the system files.* ◊ *corrupted data* ◊ [V] *The disk will corrupt if it is overloaded.*

cor·rupt·ible /kəˈrʌptəbl/ *adj.* that can be corrupted OPP INCORRUPTIBLE

cor·rup·tion /kəˈrʌpʃn/ *noun* **1** [U] dishonest or illegal behaviour, especially of people in authority: *allegations of bribery and corruption* ◊ *The new district attorney has promised to fight police corruption.* **2** [U] the act or effect of making sb change from moral to immoral standards of behaviour: *He claimed that sex and violence on TV led to the corruption of young people.* **3** [C, usually sing.] the form of a word or phrase that has become changed from

its original form in some way: *The word 'holiday' is a corruption of 'holy day'.*

cor·sage /kɔːˈsɑːʒ; *AmE* kɔːrˈsɑːʒ/ *noun* a small bunch of flowers that is worn on a woman's dress, for example at a wedding

cor·set /ˈkɔːsɪt; *AmE* ˈkɔːrsɪt/ *noun* a piece of women's underwear, fitting the body tightly, worn especially in the past to make the waist look smaller

cor·tège (also **cor·tege** especially in *AmE*) /kɔːˈteʒ; -ˈteɪʒ; *AmE* kɔːrˈteʒ/ *noun* a line of cars or people moving along slowly at a funeral

cor·tex /ˈkɔːteks; *AmE* ˈkɔːrt-/ *noun* (*pl.* **cor·ti·ces** /ˈkɔːtɪsiːz; *AmE* ˈkɔːrt-/) (*anatomy*) the outer layer of an organ in the body, especially the brain: *the cerebral/renal cortex* (= around the brain/kidney) ▶ **cor·tic·al** /ˈkɔːtɪkl; *AmE* ˈkɔːrt-/ *adj.*

cor·ti·sone /ˈkɔːtɪzəʊn; -səʊn; *AmE* ˈkɔːrtəsoʊn; -zoʊn/ *noun* [U] (*medical*) a HORMONE used in the treatment of diseases such as ARTHRITIS, to reduce swelling

cor·vette /kɔːˈvet; *AmE* kɔːrˈvet/ *noun* a small fast ship used in war to protect other ships from attack

cos¹ (also **'cos**) /kɒz; *AmE* kəz/ *conj.* (*BrE*, *spoken*) because: *I can't see her at all, cos it's too dark.*

cos² *abbr.* (in writing) COSINE

cosh /kɒʃ; *AmE* kɑːʃ/ *noun, verb*
■ *noun* (*especially BrE*) a short thick heavy piece of metal or solid rubber that is used as a weapon
■ *verb* [VN] (*especially BrE*) to hit sb hard with a cosh or sth similar

co-'signatory *noun* one of two or more people who sign a formal document: *co-signatories of/to the treaty*

co·sine /ˈkəʊsaɪn; *AmE* ˈkoʊ-/ *noun* (*abbr.* **cos**) (*mathematics*) the RATIO of the length of the side next to an ACUTE ANGLE in a RIGHT-ANGLED triangle to the length of the longest side (= the HYPOTENUSE)—compare SINE, TANGENT

cos lettuce /ˌkɒs ˈletɪs; ˌkɒz; *AmE* ˌkɑːs; ˌkɔːs/ (*BrE*) (*AmE* **ro·maine**) *noun* [C, U] a type of LETTUCE with long crisp leaves

cos·met·ic /kɒzˈmetɪk; *AmE* kɑːz-/ *noun, adj.*
■ *noun* [usually pl.] a substance that you put on your face or body to make it more attractive: *the cosmetics industry* ◊ *a cosmetic company* ◊ *cosmetic products*
■ *adj.* **1** improving only the outside appearance of sth and not its basic character: *These reforms are not merely cosmetic.* ◊ *She dismissed the moves as a cosmetic exercise to win votes.* **2** connected with medical treatment that is intended to improve a person's appearance: *cosmetic surgery* ◊ *cosmetic dental work* ▶ **cos·met·ic·al·ly** /-kli/ *adv.*

cos·mic /ˈkɒzmɪk; *AmE* ˈkɑːz-/ *adj.* [usually before noun] **1** connected with the whole universe: *Do you believe in a cosmic plan?* ◊ *cosmic dust* **2** very great and important: *This was disaster on a cosmic scale.*

cosmic 'rays *noun* [pl.] rays that reach the earth from outer space

cos·mol·ogy /kɒzˈmɒlədʒi; *AmE* kɑːzˈmɑːl-/ *noun* [U] the scientific study of the universe and its origin and development ▶ **cosmo·logic·al** /ˌkɒzməˈlɒdʒɪkl; *AmE* ˌkɑːzməˈlɑːdʒ-/ *adj.* **cos·molo·gist** /kɒzˈmɒlədʒɪst; *AmE* kɑːzˈmɑːl-/ *noun*

cosmo·naut /ˈkɒzmənɔːt; *AmE* ˈkɑːz-/ *noun* an ASTRONAUT from the former Soviet Union

cosmo·pol·itan /ˌkɒzməˈpɒlɪtən; *AmE* ˌkɑːzməˈpɑːl-/ *adj., noun*
■ *adj.* (*approving*) **1** containing people of different types or from different countries, and influenced by their culture: *a cosmopolitan city/resort* ◊ *The club has a cosmopolitan atmosphere.* **2** having or showing a wide experience of people and things from many different countries: *people with a truly cosmopolitan outlook* ◊ *cosmopolitan young people*
■ *noun* a person who has experience of many different parts of the world: *She's a real cosmopolitan.*

cos·mos /ˈkɒzmɒs; *AmE* ˈkɑːzmoʊs; -məs/ (**the cosmos**) *noun* [sing.] the universe, especially when it is thought of

æ	ɑː	e	ɜː	ə	ɪ	iː	i	ɒ	ɔː	ʌ	ʊ	u	uː
cat	father	ten	bird	about	sit	see	many	got	saw	cup	put	actual	too
								(BrE)					

as an ordered system: *the structure of the cosmos* ◊ *our place in the cosmos*

cos·set /ˈkɒsɪt; *AmE* ˈkɑːs-/ *verb* [VN] (*often disapproving*) to treat sb with a lot of care and give them a lot of attention, sometimes too much SYN PAMPER: *As a child, she had been spoiled and cosseted.*

cost /kɒst; *AmE* kɔːst/ *noun, verb*

▪ *noun* **1** [C, U] the amount of money that you need in order to buy, make or do sth: *the high/low cost of housing* ◊ *A new computer system has been installed at a cost of £80000.* ◊ *The plan had to be abandoned on grounds of cost.* ◊ *We did not even make enough money to cover the cost of the food.* ◊ *Consumers will have to bear the full cost of these pay increases.* ◊ *The total cost to you* (= the amount you have to pay) *is £3000.* **2** (**costs**) [pl.] the total amount of money that needs to be spent by a business: *The use of cheap labour helped to keep costs down.* ◊ *to cut/reduce costs* ◊ *running/operating/labour costs* ◊ *We have had to raise our prices because of rising costs.* **3** [U, sing.] the effort, loss or damage that is involved in order to do or achieve sth: *the terrible cost of the war in death and suffering* ◊ *the environmental cost of nuclear power* ◊ *She saved him from the fire but at the cost of her own life* (= she died). ◊ *He worked non-stop for three months, at considerable cost to his health.* ◊ *I felt a need to please people, whatever the cost in time and energy.* **4** (**costs**) (*AmE* also **ˈcourt costs**) [pl.] the sum of money that sb is ordered to pay for lawyers, etc. in a legal case: *He was ordered to pay £2000 costs.* ⇨ note at PRICE IDM **at ˈall cost/costs** whatever is needed to achieve sth: *You must stop the press from finding out at all costs.* **at ˈany cost** under any circumstances: *He is determined to win at any cost.* **at ˈcost** for only the amount of money that is needed to make or get sth, without any profit being added on: *goods sold at cost* **know/learn/find sth to your ˈcost** to know sth because of sth unpleasant that has happened to you: *He's a ruthless businessman, as I know to my cost.*—more at COUNT *v.*

▪ *verb* (**cost, cost**) HELP In sense 4 **costed** is used for the past tense and past participle. **1** if sth **costs** a particular amount of money, you need to pay that amount in order to buy, make or do it: [VN] *How much did it cost?* ◊ *I didn't get it because it cost too much.* ◊ *Tickets cost ten dollars each.* ◊ *Calls to the helpline cost 38p per minute.* ◊ *Don't use too much of it—it cost a lot of money.* ◊ *All these reforms will cost money* (= be expensive). ◊ *Good food need not cost a fortune* (= cost a lot of money). ◊ [VNN] *The meal cost us about £40.* ◊ *This is costing the taxpayer £10 billion a year.* ◊ [VN to inf] *The hospital will cost an estimated £2 million to build.* ◊ *It costs a fortune to fly first class.* **2** to cause the loss of sth: [VNN] *That one mistake almost cost him his life.* ◊ *A late penalty cost United the game* (= meant that they did not win the game). ◊ [VN] *The closure of the factory is likely to cost 1000 jobs.* **3** [VNN] to involve you in making an effort or doing sth unpleasant: *The accident cost me a visit to the doctor.* ◊ *Financial worries cost her many sleepless nights.* **4** (**costed, costed**) [VN] [usually passive] **~ sth (out)** to estimate how much money will be needed for sth or the price that should be charged for sth: *The project needs to be costed in detail.* ◊ *Their accountants have costed the project at $8.1 million.* ◊ *Have you costed out these proposals yet?*—see also COSTING IDM **cost sb ˈdear** to make sb suffer a lot: *That one mistake has cost him dear over the years.* **it will ˈcost you** (*spoken*) used to say that sth will be expensive: *There is a de luxe model available, but it'll cost you.*—more at ARM *n.*

ˈcost accounting *noun* [U] (*business*) the process of recording and analysing the costs involved in running a business

ˈco-star *noun, verb*

▪ *noun* one of two or more famous actors who appear together in a film/movie or play

▪ *verb* (**-rr-**) **1** [V] **~ (with sb)** to appear as one of the main actors with sb in a play or film/movie: *a new movie in which Johnny Depp co-stars with Winona Ryder* **2** [VN] (of a film/movie or play) to have two or more famous actors acting in it: *a new movie co-starring Johnny Depp and Winona Ryder*

ˈcost-benefit *noun* [U] (*economics*) the relationship between the cost of doing sth and the value of the benefit that results from it: *cost-benefit analysis*

ˈcost-cutting *noun* [U] the reduction of the amount of money spent on sth, especially because of financial difficulty: *Deliveries of mail could be delayed because of cost-cutting.* ◊ *a cost-cutting exercise/measure/programme*

ˌcost-efˈfective *adj.* giving the best possible profit or benefits in comparison with the money that is spent: *a cost-effective way to fight crime* ▶ **ˌcost-efˈfectiveness** *noun* [U]

cost·ing /ˈkɒstɪŋ; *AmE* ˈkɔːst-/ *noun* an estimate of how much money will be needed for sth: *Here is a detailed costing of our proposals.* ◊ *You'd better do some costings.*

cost·ly /ˈkɒstli; *AmE* ˈkɔːst-/ *adj.* (**cost·lier, cost·li·est**) HELP You can also use **more costly** and **most costly**. **1** costing a lot of money, especially more than you want to pay: *Buying new furniture may prove too costly.* **2** causing problems or the loss of sth: *a costly mistake/failure* ◊ *Mining can be costly in terms of lives* (= too many people can die). ▶ **cost·li·ness** *noun* [U]

the ˌcost of ˈliving *noun* [sing.] the amount of money that people need to pay for food, clothing and somewhere to live: *a steady rise in the cost of living* ◊ *the high cost of living in London*

ˌcost ˈprice *noun* [U] the cost of producing sth or the price at which it is sold without profit: *Copies of the CD can be purchased at cost price.*—compare SELLING PRICE

cos·tume /ˈkɒstjuːm; *AmE* ˈkɑːstuːm/ *noun* **1** [C, U] the clothes worn by people from a particular place or during a particular historical period: *Some of the singers wore the Welsh national costume.* **2** [C, U] the clothes worn by actors in a play or film/movie, or worn by sb to make them look like sth else: *The actors were still in costume and make-up.* ◊ *She has four costume changes during the play.* ◊ *He went to the party in a giant chicken costume.* ◊ *a costume designer* **3** [C] (*BrE, informal*) = SWIMMING COSTUME

cos·tumed /ˈkɒstjuːmd; *AmE* ˈkɑːstuːmd/ *adj.* [usually before noun] wearing a costume

ˈcostume drama *noun* [C, U] a play or film/movie set in the past

ˈcostume jewellery *noun* [U] large heavy jewellery that can look expensive but is made with cheap materials

cos·tu·mier /kɒsˈtjuːmiə(r); *AmE* kɑːsˈtuːmier/ (*BrE*) (*AmE* **ˈcos·tu·mer**) *noun* a person or company that makes COSTUMES or has COSTUMES to hire, especially for the theatre: *a firm of theatrical costumiers*

cosy (*BrE*) (*AmE* **cozy**) /ˈkəʊzi; *AmE* ˈkoʊzi/ *adj.* (**cosi·er, cosi·est**) **1** warm, comfortable and safe, especially because of being small or enclosed: *a cosy little room* ◊ *a cosy feeling* ◊ *I felt warm and cosy sitting by the fire.* **2** friendly and private: *a cosy chat with a friend* **3** (*often disapproving*) easy and convenient, but not always honest or right: *The firm has a cosy relationship with the Ministry of Defence.* ◊ *The danger is that things get too cosy.* ▶ **cosi·ly** (*BrE*) (*AmE* **cozi·ly**) *adv.*: *sitting cosily by the fire* **cosi·ness** (*BrE*) (*AmE* **cozi·ness**) *noun* [U]: *the warmth and cosiness of the kitchen*

cot /kɒt; *AmE* kɑːt/ *noun* **1** (*BrE*) (*AmE* **crib**) a small bed with high sides for a baby or young child: *a travel cot* (= one that can be moved around easily, used when travelling)—see also CARRYCOT—picture at BED **2** (*AmE*) = CAMP BED

ˈcot death (*BrE*) (*AmE* **ˈcrib death**) *noun* [U, C] the sudden death while sleeping of a baby which appears to be healthy

co·terie /ˈkəʊtəri; *AmE* ˈkoʊ-/ *noun* [C+sing./pl. *v.*] (*formal, often disapproving*) a small group of people who have the same interests and do things together but do not like to include others

co·ter·min·ous /kəʊˈtɜːmɪnəs; *AmE* koʊˈtɜːrm-/ *adj.* [not usually before noun] **~ (with sth)** (*formal*) **1** (of countries or areas) sharing a border **2** (of things or ideas) having so much in common that they are almost the same as each other

cot·tage /ˈkɒtɪdʒ; *AmE* ˈkɑːt-/ *noun* a small house, especially in the country: *a charming country cottage with roses around the door* ◊ *(BrE) a holiday cottage*

,cottage 'cheese *noun* [U] soft white cheese with small lumps in it

,cottage 'hospital *noun (BrE)* a small hospital in a country area

cot·tage 'in·dus·try *noun* a small business in which the work is done by people in their homes: *Weaving and knitting are traditional cottage industries.*

,cottage 'pie *noun* [C, U] = SHEPHERD'S PIE

cot·tager /'kɒtɪdʒə(r); AmE 'kɑːt-/ *noun (BrE)* (especially in the past) a person who lives in a small house or COTTAGE in the country

cot·ta·ging /'kɒtɪdʒɪŋ; AmE 'kɑːt-/ *noun* [U] *(BrE, slang)* the practice of HOMOSEXUAL men looking for sexual partners in a public toilet

cot·ton /'kɒtn; AmE 'kɑːtn/ *noun, verb*
- *noun* [U] **1** a plant grown in warm countries for the soft white hairs around its seeds that are used to make fabric and thread: *cotton fields/plants* ◊ *bales of cotton* **2** the fabric made from the cotton plant: *The sheets are 100% pure cotton.* ◊ *a cotton shirt/skirt* ◊ *printed cotton fabric* ◊ *the cotton industry* ◊ *a cotton mill* **3** *(especially BrE)* thread that is used for sewing: *sewing cotton* ◊ *a cotton reel* **4** *(AmE)* = COTTON WOOL: *Use a cotton ball to apply the lotion.*
- *verb* PHRV ,cotton 'on (to sth) *(informal)* to begin to understand or realize sth without being told: *I suddenly cottoned on to what he was doing.* 'cotton (up) to sb/sth *(AmE, informal)* to make an attempt to be friendly to sb

,cotton 'bud *(BrE)* (also Q-Tip™ *AmE, BrE*) *noun* a small stick with COTTON WOOL at each end, used for cleaning inside the ears, etc.

,cotton 'candy *noun* [U] *(AmE)* = CANDYFLOSS

cot·ton·wood /'kɒtnwʊd; AmE 'kɑːtn-/ (also 'cotton-wood tree) *noun* a type of N American POPLAR tree, with seeds that are covered in hairs that look like white cotton

,cotton 'wool *(BrE) (AmE* cot·ton) *noun* [U] a soft mass of white material that is used for cleaning the skin or a wound: *cotton wool balls/pads*—picture on page 598

couch /kaʊtʃ/ *noun, verb*
- *noun* **1** a long comfortable seat for two or more people to sit on SYN SETTEE, SOFA **2** a long piece of furniture like a bed, especially in a doctor's office: *on the psychiatrist's couch*
- *verb* [VN] [usually passive] **~ sth (in sth)** *(formal)* to say or write words in a particular style or manner: *The letter was deliberately couched in very vague terms.*

couch·ette /kuː'ʃet/ *noun* a narrow bed on a train, that folds down from the wall

'couch potato *noun (informal, disapproving)* a person who spends a lot of time sitting and watching television

cou·gar /'kuːɡə(r)/ *noun (especially AmE)* = PUMA

cough /kɒf; AmE kɔːf/ *verb, noun*
- *verb* **1** [V] to force out air suddenly and noisily through your throat, for example when you have a cold: *I couldn't stop coughing.* ◊ *to cough nervously/discreetly*—picture on page 599 **2** [VN] **~ sth (up)** to force sth out of your throat or lungs by coughing: *Sometimes she coughed (up) blood.* **3** [V] (of an engine) to make a sudden harsh noise PHRV ,cough 'up | ,cough sth↔'up *(informal)* to give sth, especially money, unwillingly: *Steve finally coughed up the money he owed us.*
- *noun* **1** an act or a sound of coughing: *She gave a little cough to attract my attention.* **2** an illness or infection that makes you cough often: *to have a dry/persistent/ hacking cough* ◊ *My cold's better, but I can't seem to shake off this cough.*—see also WHOOPING COUGH

cough·ing *noun* [U] the action of coughing: *Another fit of coughing seized him.*

'cough mixture *(BrE)* (also 'cough syrup, 'cough medicine *BrE, AmE) noun* [U] liquid medicine that you take for a cough

could /kəd; *strong form* kʊd/ *modal verb (negative* could not, *short form* couldn't /'kʊdnt/) **1** used as the past tense of 'can': *She said that she couldn't come.* ◊ *I couldn't hear what they were saying.* ◊ *Sorry, I couldn't get any more.* ⇨ note at CAN[1] **2** used to ask if you can do sth: *Could I use your phone, please?* ◊ *Could we stop by next week?* **3** used to politely ask sb to do sth for you: *Could you babysit for us on Friday?* **4** used to show that sth is or might be possible: *I could do it now, if you like.* ◊ *Don't worry—they could have just forgotten to call.* ◊ *You couldn't have left it on the bus, could you?* ◊ *'Have some more cake.' 'Oh, I couldn't, thank you* (= I'm too full).*'* **5** used to suggest sth: *We could write a letter to the director.* ◊ *You could always try his home number.* **6** used to show that you are annoyed that sb did not do sth: *They could have let me know they were going to be late!* **7** *(informal)* used to emphasize how strongly you want to express your feelings: *I'm so fed up I could scream!* ⇨ note at MODAL IDM could do with sth *(spoken)* used to say that you need or would like to have sth: *I could do with a drink!* ◊ *Her hair could have done with a wash.*

cou·lis /'kuːli; AmE kuː'liː/ *noun (pl.* cou·lis) (from *French*) a thin fruit sauce

coun·cil /'kaʊnsl/ *noun* [C+sing./pl. *v.*] **1** a group of people who are elected to govern an area such as a city or county: *a city/county/borough/district council* ◊ *She's on the local council.* ◊ *a council member/meeting* **2** *(BrE)* the organization that provides services in a city or county, for example education, houses, libraries, etc: *council workers/services* **3** a group of people chosen to give advice, make rules, do research, provide money, etc: *the Medical Research Council* ◊ *In Britain, the Arts Council gives grants to theatres.* **4** *(formal)* (especially in the past) a formal meeting to discuss what action to take in a particular situation: *The King held a council at Notting-ham from 14 to 19 October 1330.*—see also PRIVY COUNCIL

'council chamber *noun (BrE)* a large room in which a council meets

'council estate *noun (BrE)* a large group of houses built by a local council

'council house, 'council flat *noun (BrE)* a house or flat rented from the local council

coun·cil·lor *(AmE also* coun·cil·or) /'kaʊnsələ(r)/ *noun (abbr.* Cllr) a member of a council: *Councillor Ann Jones* ◊ *Talk to your local councillor about the problem.*—see also COUNCILMAN, COUNCILWOMAN

coun·cil·man /'kaʊnslmən/ *noun (pl.* -men /-mən/) *(AmE)* = COUNCILLOR

,council of 'war *noun (pl.* councils of war) *(BrE)* a meeting to discuss how to deal with an urgent and diffi-cult situation: *She called together senior managers for a council of war.*

'council tax *noun* (often the council tax) [sing., U] (in Britain) a tax charged by local councils, based on the value of a person's home

coun·cil·woman /'kaʊnslwʊmən/ *noun (pl.* -women /-wɪmɪn/) *(AmE)* = COUNCILLOR

coun·sel /'kaʊnsl/ *noun, verb*
- *noun* [U, C] **1** *(formal)* advice, especially given by older people or experts; a piece of advice: *Listen to the counsel of your elders.* ◊ *In the end, wiser counsels prevailed.* **2** *(law)* a lawyer or group of lawyers representing sb in a court of law: *to be represented by counsel* ◊ *the counsel for the defence/prosecution* ◊ *defence/prosecuting counsel* ◊ *The court then heard counsel for the dead woman's father.*—see also KING'S/QUEEN'S COUNSEL ⇨ note at LAW-YER IDM a counsel of des'pair *(formal)* advice not to try to do sth because it is too difficult a counsel of per'fec-tion *(formal)* advice that is good but that is difficult or impossible to follow keep your own 'counsel *(formal)* to keep your opinions, plans, etc. secret
- *verb* (-ll-, *AmE* -l-) **1** [VN] to listen to and give support or professional advice to sb who needs help: *Therapists were brought in to counsel the bereaved.* **2** *(formal)* to advise sb to do sth: [VN] *Most experts counsel caution in such cases.* ◊ [VN to inf] *He counselled them to give up the plan.*

coun·sel·ling *(BrE) (AmE* coun·sel·ing) /'kaʊnsəlɪŋ/ *noun* [U] professional advice about a problem: *marriage guidance counselling* ◊ *a student counselling service*

coun·sel·lor *(especially BrE) (AmE usually* coun·sel·or)

C

b	d	f	g	h	k	l	m	n	p	r
bad	did	fall	get	hat	cat	leg	man	now	pen	red

/'kaʊnsələ(r)/ *noun* **1** a person who has been trained to advise people with problems, especially personal problems: *a marriage guidance counsellor* **2** (*AmE, IrishE*) a lawyer **3** (*AmE*) a person who is in charge of young people at a summer camp

count /kaʊnt/ *verb, noun*

▪ *verb*

SAY NUMBERS ┃ **1** [V] **~ (from sth) (to/up to sth)** to say numbers in the correct order: *Billy can't count yet.* ◊ *She can count up to 10 in Italian.* ◊ *to count from 1 to 10*

FIND TOTAL ┃ **2 ~ (sth) (up)** to calculate the total number of people, things, etc. in a particular group: [VN] *The diet is based on counting calories.* ◊ [V**wh-**] *She began to count up how many guests they had to invite.* ◊ [V] *There are 12 weeks to go, counting from today.*

INCLUDE ┃ **3** [VN] to include sb/sth when you calculate a total: *We have invited 50 people, not counting the children.*

MATTER ┃ **4** [V] **~ (for sth)** (not used in the progressive tenses) to be important: *Every point in this game counts.* ◊ *The fact that she had apologized counted for nothing with him.* ◊ *It's the thought that counts* (= used about a small but kind action or gift).

ACCEPT OFFICIALLY ┃ **5** to be officially accepted; to accept sth officially: [V] *Don't go over that line or your throw won't count.* ◊ [VN] *Applications received after 1 July will not be counted.*

CONSIDER ┃ **6 ~ sb/sth (as) sb/sth | ~ as sb/sth** to consider sb/sth in a particular way; to be considered in a particular way: [V, VN] *For tax purposes that money counts/is counted as income.* ◊ [VN] *I count him among my closest friends.* ◊ [VN-ADJ] *I count myself lucky to have known him.* ◊ [VN] *She counts herself one of the lucky ones.*

IDM **be able to count sb/sth on (the fingers of) one 'hand** used to say that the total number of sb/sth is very small: *She could count on the fingers of one hand the people she actually enjoyed being with.* **count your 'blessings** to be grateful for the good things in your life **don't count your 'chickens (before they are 'hatched)** (*saying*) you should not be too confident that sth will be successful, because sth may still go wrong **count the cost (of sth)** to feel the bad effects of a mistake, an accident, etc: *The town is now counting the cost of its failure to provide adequate flood protection.* **count 'sheep** to imagine that sheep are jumping over a fence and to count them, as a way of getting to sleep **stand up and be 'counted** to say publicly that you support sb or you agree with sth **Who's 'counting?** (*informal*) used to say that you do not care how many times sth happens

PHR V **,count a'gainst sb | ,count sth a'gainst sb** to be considered or to consider sth as a disadvantage in sb: *For that job her lack of experience may count against her.* **,count 'down (to sth)** to think about a future event with pleasure or excitement and count the minutes, days, etc. until it happens: *She's already counting down to the big day.*—related noun COUNTDOWN **,count sb 'in** to include sb in an activity: *I hear you're organizing a trip to the game next week? Count me in!* **'count on sb/sth** to trust sb to do sth or to be sure that sth will happen: *'I'm sure he'll help.' 'Don't count on it.'* ◊ [+ to inf] *I'm counting on you to help me.* ◊ [+ -ing] *Few people can count on having a job for life.* ◊ *We can't count on this warm weather lasting.* **,count sb/sth↔'out** to count things one after the other as you put them somewhere: *She counted out £70 in £10 notes.* **,count sb 'out** to not include sb in an activity: *If you're going out tonight you'll have to count me out.* **,count to'wards/to'ward sth** to be included as part of sth that you hope to achieve in the future: *Students gain college credits which count towards their degree.*

▪ *noun*

TOTAL ┃ **1** [usually sing.] an act of counting to find the total number of sth; the total number that you find: *The bus driver did a quick count of the empty seats.* ◊ *If the election result is close, there will be a second count.* ◊ *The body count* (= the total number of people who have died) *stands at 24.*—see also HEADCOUNT

SAYING NUMBERS ┃ **2** [usually sing.] an act of saying num-

bers in order beginning with 1: *Raise your leg and hold for a count of ten.* ◊ *He was knocked to the ground and stayed down for a count of eight* (= in boxing).

MEASUREMENT ┃ **3** [usually sing.] (*technical*) a measurement of the amount of sth contained in a particular substance or area: *a raised white blood cell count*—see also BLOOD COUNT, POLLEN COUNT

CRIME ┃ **4** (*law*) a crime that sb is accused of committing: *They were found guilty on all counts.* ◊ *She appeared in court on three counts of fraud.*

IN DISCUSSION/ARGUMENT ┃ **5** [usually pl.] a point made during a discussion or an argument: *I disagree with you on both counts.*

RANK/TITLE ┃ **6** (in some European countries) a NOBLEMAN of high rank, similar to an EARL in Britain: *Count Tolstoy*—see also COUNTESS

IDM **at the last 'count** according to the latest information about the numbers of sth: *She'd applied for 30 jobs at the last count.* **keep (a) count (of sth)** to remember or keep a record of numbers or amounts of sth over a period of time: *Keep a count of your calorie intake for one week.* **lose count (of sth)** to forget the total of sth before you have finished counting it: *I lost count and had to start again.* ◊ *She had lost count of the number of times she'd told him to be careful* (= she could not remember because there were so many). **,out for the 'count** (*BrE*) (*AmE* **,down for the 'count**) **1** (of a boxer) unable to get up again within ten seconds after being knocked down **2** in a deep sleep

count·able /'kaʊntəbl/ *adj.* (*grammar*) a noun that is **countable** can be used in the plural or with *a* or *an*, for example *table, cat* and *idea* **OPP** UNCOUNTABLE

count·down /'kaʊntdaʊn/ *noun* **~ (to sth)** **1** [sing., U] the action of counting seconds backwards to zero, for example before a spacecraft is LAUNCHED (= sent into space) **2** [sing.] the period of time just before sth important happens: *the countdown to the wedding*

coun·ten·ance /'kaʊntənəns/ *noun, verb*

▪ *noun* (*formal* or *literary*) a person's face or their expression

▪ *verb* (*formal*) to support sth or agree to sth happening: [VN] *The committee refused to countenance his proposals.* [also V -ing, VN -ing]

coun·ter /'kaʊntə(r)/ *noun, verb, adv.*

▪ *noun* **1** a long flat surface over which goods are sold or business is done in a shop/store, bank, etc: *I asked the woman behind the counter if they had any postcards of the church.* **2** (*especially AmE*) = WORKTOP **3** a small disc used for playing or scoring in some board games—see also BARGAINING COUNTER—picture on page A8 **4** (especially in compounds) an electronic device for counting sth: *The needle on the rev counter soared.*—see also GEIGER COUNTER **5** [usually sing.] **~ (to sb/sth)** (*formal*) a response to sb/sth that opposes their ideas, position, etc: *The employers' association was seen as a counter to union power.* **IDM** **over the 'counter** goods, especially medicines, for sale **over the counter** can be bought without a PRESCRIPTION (= written permission from a doctor to buy a medicine) or special LICENCE (= written permission): *These tablets are available over the counter.*—see also OVER-THE-COUNTER **under the 'counter** goods that are bought or sold **under the counter** are sold secretly and sometimes illegally

▪ *verb* **1** **~ (sb/sth) (with sth)** to reply to sb by trying to prove that what they said is not true: [VN] *Such arguments are not easily countered.* ◊ [V that] *I tried to argue but he countered that the plans were not yet finished.* [also V speech, V] **2** [VN] to do sth to reduce or prevent the bad effects of sth: *Businesses would like to see new laws to counter late payments of debts.*

▪ *adv.* **~ to sth** in the opposite direction to sth; in opposition to sth: *The government's plans run counter to agreed European policy on this issue.*

counter- /'kaʊntə(r)/ *combining form* (in nouns, verbs, adjectives and adverbs) **1** against; opposite: *counterterrorism* ◊ *counter-argument* **2** CORRESPONDING: *counterpart*

coun·ter·act /ˌkaʊntər'ækt/ *verb* [VN] to do sth to

s	t	v	z	ʃ	ʒ	tʃ	dʒ	θ	ð	ŋ
see	tea	van	zoo	shoe	vision	chain	jam	thin	this	sing

reduce or prevent the bad or harmful effects of sth SYN COUNTER: *These exercises aim to counteract the effects of stress and tension.*

counter-attack *noun, verb*
■ *noun* an attack made in response to the attack of an enemy or opponent in war, sport or an argument: *Loyal armed forces launched a counter-attack against the rebels.* ◇ *The Inter player was swift to respond with a counter-attack.*
■ *verb* [V, VN] to make an attack in response to the attack of an enemy or opponent in war, sport or an argument SYN RETALIATE

coun·ter·bal·ance *verb, noun*
■ *verb* /ˌkaʊntəˈbæləns; AmE ˌkaʊntərˈb-/ [VN] (*formal*) to have an equal but opposite effect to sth else SYN OFFSET: *Parents' natural desire to protect their children should be counterbalanced by the child's need for independence.*
■ *noun* /ˈkaʊntəbæləns; AmE ˈkaʊntərb-/ (also **coun·ter·weight**) [usually sing.] ~ (to sth) a thing that has an equal but opposite effect to sth else and can be used to limit the bad effects of sth: *The accused's right to silence was a vital counterbalance to the powers of the police.*

coun·ter·claim /ˈkaʊntəkleɪm; AmE -tərk-/ *noun* a claim made in reply to another claim and different from it: *Amid all the claims and counterclaims it was hard to say who was telling the truth.*

coun·ter·clock·wise /ˌkaʊntəˈklɒkwaɪz; AmE -tərˈklɑːk-/ *adv., adj.* (*AmE*) = ANTICLOCKWISE OPP CLOCKWISE

coun·ter·cul·ture /ˈkaʊntəkʌltʃə(r); AmE -tərk-/ *noun* [C, U] a way of life and set of ideas that are opposed to those accepted by most of society; a group of people who share such a way of life and such ideas: *the anti-military counterculture of the 1960s*

counter-espionage *noun* [U] secret action taken by a country to prevent an enemy country from finding out its secrets

coun·ter·feit /ˈkaʊntəfɪt; AmE -tərf-/ *adj., verb*
■ *adj.* (of money and goods for sale) made to look exactly like sth in order to trick people into thinking that they are getting the real thing; not genuine: *counterfeit watches* ◇ *Are you aware these notes are counterfeit?* ► **coun·ter·feit** *noun*—compare FORGERY
■ *verb* [VN] to make an exact copy of sth in order to trick people into thinking that it is the real thing—compare FORGE ► **coun·ter·feit·ing** *noun* [U]

coun·ter·feit·er /ˈkaʊntəfɪtə(r); AmE -tərf-/ *noun* a person who counterfeits money or goods—compare FORGER

coun·ter·foil /ˈkaʊntəfɔɪl; AmE -tərfɔɪl-/ *noun* (*BrE*) the part of a cheque, ticket, etc. that you keep when you give the other part to sb else

counter-insurgency *noun* [U] action taken against a group of people who are trying to take control of a country by force: *counter-insurgency operations*

counter-intelligence *noun* [U] secret action taken by a country to prevent an enemy country from finding out its secrets, for example by giving them false information; the department of a government, etc. that is responsible for this

coun·ter·mand /ˌkaʊntəˈmɑːnd; AmE ˈkaʊntərmænd/ *verb* [VN] (*formal*) to cancel an order that has been given, especially by giving a different order

coun·ter·meas·ure /ˈkaʊntəmeʒə(r); AmE -tərm-/ *noun* [often pl.] a course of action taken to protect against sth that is considered bad or dangerous: *countermeasures to neutralize the threat of terrorism*

coun·ter·of·fen·sive /ˈkaʊntərəfensɪv/ *noun* an attack made in order to defend against enemy attacks

coun·ter·pane /ˈkaʊntəpeɪn; AmE -tərp-/ *noun* (*old-fashioned, BrE*) = BEDSPREAD

coun·ter·part /ˈkaʊntəpɑːt; AmE -tərpɑːrt/ *noun* a person or thing that has the same position or function as sb/sth else in a different place or situation: *The Foreign Minister held talks with his Chinese counterpart.* ◇ *The women's shoe, like its male counterpart, is specifically designed for the serious tennis player.*

coun·ter·point /ˈkaʊntəpɔɪnt; AmE -tərp-/ *noun, verb*
■ *noun* **1** [U] (*music*) the combination of two or more tunes played together to form a single piece of music SYN POLYPHONY: *The two melodies are played in counterpoint.*—see also CONTRAPUNTAL **2** [C] ~ (to sth) (*music*) a tune played in combination with another one **3** [U, C] (*written*) a pleasing or interesting contrast: *This work is in austere counterpoint to that of Gaudi.*
■ *verb* [VN] ~ sth (with/against sth) (*formal*) to contrast sth with sth else; to form a contrast with sth

coun·ter·pro·duct·ive /ˌkaʊntəprəˈdʌktɪv; AmE -tərp-/ *adj.* [not usually before noun] having the opposite effect to the one which was intended: *Increases in taxation would be counterproductive.*—compare PRODUCTIVE

counter-revolution *noun* [C, U] opposition to or violent action against a government that came to power as a result of a revolution, in order to destroy and replace it: *to stage a counter-revolution* ◇ *the forces of counter-revolution*

counter-revolutionary *noun* a person involved in a counter-revolution ► **counter-revolutionary** *adj.*

coun·ter·sign /ˈkaʊntəsaɪn; AmE -tərs-/ *verb* [VN] (*technical*) to sign a document that has already been signed by another person, especially in order to show that it is valid

counter-tenor *noun* a man who is trained to sing with a very high voice; a male ALTO—compare ALTO

counter-terrorism *noun* [U] action taken to prevent the activities of political groups who use violence to try to achieve their aims ► **counter-terrorist** *adj.*

coun·ter·vail·ing /ˈkaʊntəveɪlɪŋ; AmE -tərv-/ *adj.* [only before noun] (*formal*) having an equal but opposite effect

coun·ter·weight /ˈkaʊntəweɪt; AmE -tərw-/ *noun* [usually sing.] = COUNTERBALANCE

count·ess /ˈkaʊntəs; -es/ *noun* **1** a woman who has the rank of a COUNT or an EARL **2** the wife of a COUNT or an EARL: *the Earl and Countess of Rosebery*

count·less /ˈkaʊntləs/ *adj.* [usually before noun] very many; too many to be counted or mentioned: *I've warned her countless times.* ◇ *The new treatment could save Emma's life and the lives of countless others.*—compare UNCOUNTABLE

count noun *noun* (*grammar*) a COUNTABLE noun

coun·tri·fied /ˈkʌntrifaɪd/ *adj.* (often *disapproving*) like the countryside or the people who live there

---

WHICH WORD?
country / state

Country is the most usual, neutral word for a geographical area that has or used to have its own government.
State emphasizes the political organization of an area under an independent government. Especially in *BrE*, it can also mean the government: *the member states of the EU* ◇ *The state provides free education.* In *AmE* **the state** usually refers to one of the 50 states of the US, not to the government of the country as a whole.

---

coun·try /ˈkʌntri/ *noun* (*pl.* **-ies**) **1** [C] an area of land that has or used to have its own government and laws: *European countries* ◇ *leading industrial countries* ◇ *She didn't know what life in a foreign country would be like.* ◇ *It's good to meet people from different parts of the country.* **2** [U] (often following an adjective) an area of land, especially with particular physical features, suitable for a particular purpose or connected with a particular person or people: *open/wooded country* ◇ *superb walking country* ◇ *Explore Thomas Hardy country.* **3** (**the country**) [sing.] the people of a country; the nation as a whole: *They have the support of most of the country.* ◇ *The rich benefited from the reforms, not the country as a whole.*—see also MOTHER COUNTRY, THE OLD COUNTRY, UP-COUNTRY **4** (**the country**) [sing.] any area outside towns and cities, with fields, woods, farms, etc: *to live in the country* ◇ *We spent a pleasant day in the country.* ◇ *a country lane* ⇨ note at LANDSCAPE **5** [U] = COUNTRY-AND-WESTERN:

C

æ	ɑː	e	ɜː	ə	ɪ	iː	i	ɒ	ɔː	ʌ	ʊ	u	uː
cat	father	ten	bird	about	sit	see	many	got	saw	cup	put	actual	too
(BrE)

pop, folk and country **IDM** **across country** directly across fields, etc.; not by a main road: *riding across country*—see also CROSS-COUNTRY **go to the ˈcountry** (*BrE*) (of a government) to hold an election to choose a new parliament—more at FREE *adj.*

ˌcountry and ˈwestern (*abbr.* C & W) (also ˈcountry music, country, hill·billy) *noun* [U] a type of music in the style of the traditional music of the southern and western US: *a country and western singer*

ˌcountry ˈbumpkin (also bump·kin) *noun* (*disapproving*) a person from the countryside who seems stupid

ˈcountry club *noun* a club in the country, or on the edge of a town, where people can play sports and go to social events

ˌcountry ˈdance *noun* (*BrE*) a type of traditional dance, especially one in which couples dance in long lines or circles

ˌcountry ˈhouse *noun* (*BrE*) a large house in the country, especially one that belongs or used to belong to a rich important family

coun·try·man /ˈkʌntrimən/ *noun* (*pl.* -men /-mən/) **1** a person born in or living in the same country as sb else **SYN** COMPATRIOT: *Sampras looks set to play his fellow countryman Agassi in the final.* **2** a man living or born in the country, not in the town

ˈcountry music *noun* [U] = COUNTRY AND WESTERN

ˌcountry ˈseat *noun* (*BrE*) = SEAT (7)

coun·try·side /ˈkʌntrisaɪd/ *noun* [U] land outside towns and cities, with fields, woods, etc: *The surrounding countryside is windswept and rocky.* ◇ *magnificent views over open countryside* ◇ *Everyone should enjoy the right of access to the countryside.* ⇨ note at LANDSCAPE

coun·try·wide /ˌkʌntriˈwaɪd/ *adj.* over the whole of a country: *a countrywide mail-order service* ▶ coun·try·wide *adv.*: *The film will be released in London in March and countrywide in May.*

coun·try·woman /ˈkʌntriwʊmən/ *noun* (*pl.* -women /-wɪmɪn/) **1** a woman living or born in the country, not the town **2** (*rare*) a woman born or living in the same country as sb else

county /ˈkaʊnti/ *noun, adj.*
■ *noun* (*pl.* -ies) (*abbr.* Co.) an area of Britain, Ireland or the US that has its own government: *the southern counties* ◇ *county boundaries* ◇ *Orange County*—see also THE HOME COUNTIES
■ *adj.* (*BrE*, usually *disapproving*) typical of English upper-class people

ˌcounty ˈclerk *noun* (in the US) an elected county official who is responsible for elections and who keeps records of who owns buildings in the county, etc.

ˌcounty ˈcouncil *noun* [C+sing./pl. *v.*] (in Britain) a group of people elected to the local government of a county: *a member of Lancashire County Council* ▶ ˌcounty ˈcouncillor *noun*

ˌcounty ˈcourt *noun* a local court of law. In Britain county courts only deal with private disputes but in the US they also deal with criminal cases.—compare CROWN COURT

ˌcounty ˈtown (*BrE*) (*AmE* ˌcounty ˈseat) *noun* the main town of a county, where its government is

coun·ty·wide /ˌkaʊntiˈwaɪd/ *adj.* over the whole of a county ▶ coun·ty·wide *adv.*

coup /kuː/ *noun* (*pl.* coups /kuːz/) **1** (also coup d'état) a sudden, illegal and often violent, change of government: *He seized power in a military coup in 1981.* ◇ *to stage/ mount a coup* ◇ *an attempted coup* ◇ *a failed/an abortive coup* ◇ *She lost her position in a boardroom coup* (= a sudden change of power among senior managers in a company). **2** the fact of achieving sth that was difficult to do: *Getting this contract has been quite a coup for us.*

coup de grâce /ˌkuː də ˈɡrɑːs/ *noun* [sing.] (from *French, formal*) **1** an action or event that finally ends sth that has been getting weaker or worse: *My disastrous exam results dealt the coup de grâce to my university career.* **2** a hit or shot that finally kills a person or an

animal, especially to put an end to their suffering **SYN** DEATH BLOW

coup d'état /ˌkuː deɪˈtɑː/ *noun* (*pl.* coups d'état /ˌkuː deɪˈtɑː/) = COUP

coupé /ˈkuːpeɪ; *AmE* kuːˈpeɪ/ (*AmE* also coupe /kuːp/) *noun* a car with two doors and usually a sloping back—picture at CAR

couple /ˈkʌpl/ *noun, verb*
■ *noun* **1** [sing.+ sing./pl. *v.*] ~ (of sth) two people or things: *I saw a couple of men get out.* **HELP** In *BrE* a plural verb is usually used in all 3 senses. **2** [sing.+ sing./pl. *v.*] ~ (of sth) a small number of people or things **SYN** A FEW: *a couple of minutes* ◇ *We went there a couple of years ago.* ◇ *I've seen her a couple of times before.* ◇ *I'll be with you in a minute. There are a couple of things I have to do first.* ◇ *There are a couple more files to read first.* ◇ *We can do it in the next couple of weeks.* ◇ *The last couple of years have been difficult.* **3** [C+sing./pl. *v.*] two people who are seen together, especially if they are married or in a romantic or sexual relationship: *married couples* ◇ *a young/an elderly couple* ◇ *Several couples were on the dance floor.* ◇ *The couple was/were married in 1976.* **IDM** see SHAKE *n.* ▶ **a couple** *pron.*: *Do you need any more glasses? I've got a couple I can lend you.* **couple** *det.* (*AmE*): *It's only a couple blocks away.*
■ *verb* **1** [VN] [usually passive] ~ A (to B)| ~ A and B **together** to join together two parts of sth, for example two vehicles or pieces of equipment: *The two train cars had been coupled together.* ◇ *CDTV uses a CD-ROM system that is coupled to a powerful computer.* **2** [V] (*formal*) (of two people or animals) to have sex **PHRV** ˈcouple sb/sth **with sb/sth** [usually passive] to link one thing, situation, etc. to another: *Overproduction, coupled with falling sales, has led to huge losses for the company.*

coup·let /ˈkʌplət/ *noun* two lines of poetry of equal length one after the other: *a poem written in rhyming couplets*

coup·ling /ˈkʌplɪŋ/ *noun* **1** [usually sing.] an action of joining or combining two things: *a coupling of Mozart's Prague Symphony and Schubert's Unfinished Symphony* (= for example, on the same CD) **2** (*formal*) an act of having sex: *illicit couplings* **3** (*technical*) a thing that joins together two parts of sth, two vehicles or two pieces of equipment

cou·pon /ˈkuːpɒn; *AmE* -pɑːn; ˈkjuː-/ *noun* **1** a small piece of printed paper that you can exchange for sth or that gives you the right to buy sth at a cheaper price than normal: *money-off coupons* ◇ *clothing/petrol coupons* ◇ *Enclose a stamped addressed envelope or an international reply coupon.* ⇨ note at VOUCHER **2** a printed form, often cut out from a newspaper, that is used to enter a competition, order goods, etc: *Fill in and return the attached coupon.*

cour·age /ˈkʌrɪdʒ; *AmE* ˈkɜːr-/ *noun* [U] the ability to do sth dangerous, or to face pain or opposition, without showing fear **SYN** BRAVERY: *He showed great courage and determination.* ◇ *I haven't yet plucked up the courage to ask her.* ◇ *moral/physical courage* ◇ *courage in the face of danger*—see also DUTCH COURAGE **IDM** **have/lack the courage of your conˈvictions** to be/not be brave enough to do what you feel to be right **take courage (from sth)** to begin to feel happier and more confident because of sth **take your ˌcourage in both ˈhands** to make yourself do sth that you are afraid of: *Taking her courage in both hands, she opened the door and walked in.*—more at SCREW *v.*

cour·age·ous /kəˈreɪdʒəs/ *adj.* showing courage **SYN** BRAVE: *a very courageous decision* ◇ *I hope people will be courageous enough to speak out against this injustice.* ▶ cour·age·ous·ly *adv.*

cour·gette /kʊəˈʒet; kɔːˈʒet; *AmE* kʊrˈʒet/ (*BrE*) (*AmE* zuc·chini) *noun* a long vegetable with dark green skin and white flesh—picture on page A3

cour·ier /ˈkʊriə(r)/ *noun* **1** a person or company whose job is to take packages or important papers somewhere: *We sent the documents by courier.* **2** (*BrE*) a person who is employed by a travel company to give advice and help to

aɪ	aʊ	eɪ	əʊ	oʊ	ɔɪ	ɪə	eə	ʊə	j	w
my	now	say	go (BrE)	go (AmE)	boy	near	hair	pure	yes	wet

a group of tourists on holiday ▶ **cour·ier** *verb*: [VN] *Courier that letter—it needs to get there today* (= send it by courier).

course /kɔːs; *AmE* kɔːrs/ *noun, verb*

■ *noun*

EDUCATION | **1** [C] ~ **(in/on sth)** a series of lessons or LECTURES on a particular subject: *a French/chemistry course* ◊ *to take/do a course in art and design* ◊ *to go on a management training course* ◊ *The college runs specialist language courses.*—see also CORRESPONDENCE COURSE, CRASH *adj.*, FOUNDATION COURSE, INDUCTION COURSE, REFRESHER COURSE, SANDWICH COURSE **2** [C] (*especially BrE*) a period of study at a college or university that leads to an exam or a qualification: *a degree course* ◊ *a two-year postgraduate course leading to a master's degree*—compare PROGRAMME *n.* (5)

DIRECTION | **3** [U, C, usually sing.] a direction or route followed by a ship or an aircraft: *The plane was on/off course* (= going/not going in the right direction). ◊ *He radioed the pilot to change course.* ◊ *They set a course for the islands.* **4** [C, usually sing.] the general direction in which sb's ideas or actions are moving: *The president appears likely to change course on some key issues.* ◊ *Politicians are often obliged to steer a course between incompatible interests.*

ACTION | **5** (also ,course of 'action) [C] a way of acting in or dealing with a particular situation: *There are various courses open to us.* ◊ *What course of action would you recommend?* ◊ *The wisest course would be to say nothing.*

DEVELOPMENT | **6** [sing.] ~ **of sth** the way sth develops or should develop: *an event that changed the course of history* ◊ *The unexpected course of events aroused considerable alarm.*

PART OF MEAL | **7** [C] any of the separate parts of a meal: *a four-course dinner* ◊ *The main course was roast duck.*

FOR GOLF | **8** [C] = GOLF COURSE: *He set a new course record.*

FOR RACES | **9** [C] an area of land or water where races are held: *She was overtaken on the last stretch of the course.*—see also ASSAULT COURSE, RACECOURSE

OF RIVER | **10** [C, usually sing.] the direction a river moves in: *The path follows the course of the river.*

MEDICAL TREATMENT | **11** [C] ~ **(of sth)** a series of medical treatments, PILLS, etc: *to prescribe a course of antibiotics*

IN WALL | **12** [C] a continuous layer of bricks, stone, etc. in a wall: *A new damp-proof course could cost £1000 or more.*

IDM **in course of sth** (*formal*) going through a particular process: *The new textbook is in course of preparation.* **in/over the course of ...** (used with expressions for periods of time) during: *He's seen many changes in the course of his long life.* ◊ *The company faces major challenges over the course of the next few years.* **in the course of 'time** when enough time has passed SYN EVENTUALLY: *It is possible that in the course of time a cure for cancer will be found.* **in the ordinary, normal, etc. course of events, things, etc.** as things usually happen SYN NORMALLY: *In the normal course of things we would not treat her disappearance as suspicious.* **of course 1** (also *informal* **course**) (*spoken*) used to emphasize that what you are saying is true or correct: *'Don't you like my mother?' 'Of course I do!'* ◊ *'Will you be there?' 'Course I will.'* **2** (also *informal* **course**) (*spoken*) used as a polite way of giving sb permission to do sth: *'Can I come, too?' 'Course you can.'* ◊ *'Can I have one of those pens?' 'Of course—help yourself.'* **3** (*spoken*) used as a polite way of agreeing with what sb has just said: *'I did all I could to help.' 'Of course,'* he murmured gently. **4** used to show that what you are saying is not surprising or is generally known or accepted: *Ben, of course, was the last to arrive.* ◊ *Of course, there are other ways of doing this.* **of 'course not** (also *informal* **'course not**) used to emphasize the fact that you are saying 'no': *'Are you going?' 'Of course not.'* ◊ *'Do you mind?' 'No, of course not.'* **on 'course for sth/to do sth** likely to achieve or do sth because you have already started to do it: *The American economy is on course for higher inflation than Britain by the end of the year.* **run/take its 'course** to develop in the usual way and come to the usual end: *When her tears had run their course, she*

felt calmer and more in control. ◊ *With minor ailments the best thing is often to let nature take its course.*—more at COLLISION, DUE *adj.*, HORSE *n.*, MATTER *n.*, MIDDLE *adj.*, PAR, PERVERT *v.*, STAY *v.*

BRITISH / AMERICAN
course / program

In *BrE* **course** is used for a series of lessons or lectures on a particular subject: *a physics course* ◊ *a course of ten lectures.* In *AmE* you would say: *a physics course/program* ◊ *a program of ten lectures.*

In *AmE* a **course** is usually an individual unit that forms part of a longer period of study: *I have to take a physics course/class.* This is called a **module** in Britain, especially in a college or university.

In *BrE* **course** can also mean a period of study at a college or university: *a two-year college course.* In *AmE* you would say: *a two-year college program.*

■ *verb* [V+adv./prep.] (*literary*) (of liquid) to move or flow quickly

---

MORE ABOUT
of course

Of course is often used to show that what you are saying is not surprising or is generally known or accepted. For this reason, and because it can be difficult to get the right intonation, you may not sound polite if you use **of course** or **of course not** when you answer a request for information or permission. It can be safer to use a different word or phrase.

'Is this the right room for the English class?' 'Yes, it is.' ◊ ~~'Of course.'~~ or ~~'Of course it is.'~~

'Can I borrow your dictionary?' 'Certainly.' (*formal*) ◊ *'Sure.'* (*informal*)

'Do you mind if I borrow your dictionary?' 'Not at all.' ◊ *'Go ahead.'* (*informal*).

If you say **of course/of course not** it may sound as though you think the answer to the question is obvious and that the person should not ask. In the same way, **of course** should not be used as a reply to a statement of fact or when someone expresses an opinion: *'It's a lovely day.' 'It certainly is.'/'Yes it is.'* ◊ ~~'Of course it is.'~~ ◊ *'I think you'll enjoy that play.' 'I'm sure I will.'/'Yes, it sounds really good.'* ◊ ~~Of course.~~

---

course·book /'kɔːsbʊk; *AmE* 'kɔːrs-/ *noun* (*BrE*) a book for studying from, used regularly in class

,**course of** 'action *noun* (*pl.* ,courses of 'action) = COURSE (5)

course·work /'kɔːswɜːk; *AmE* 'kɔːrswɜːrk/ *noun* [U] work that students do during a course of study, not in exams, that is included in their final mark/grade: *Coursework accounts for 40% of the final marks.*

court /kɔːt; *AmE* kɔːrt/ *noun, verb*

■ *noun*

LAW | **1** [C, U] the place where legal trials take place and where crimes, etc. are judged: *the civil/criminal courts* ◊ *Her lawyer made a statement outside the court.* ◊ *She will appear in court tomorrow.* ◊ *They took their landlord to court for breaking the contract.* ◊ *The case took five years to come to court* (= to be heard by the court). ◊ *There wasn't enough evidence to bring the case to court* (= start a trial). ◊ *He won the court case and was awarded damages.* ◊ *She can't pay her tax and is facing court action.* ◊ *The case was settled out of court* (= a decision was reached without a trial).—see also COURTHOUSE, COURTROOM ⇨ note at SCHOOL **2 (the court)** [sing.] the people in a court, especially those who make the decisions, such as the judge and JURY: *Please tell the court what happened.*—see also CONTEMPT OF COURT, COUNTY COURT, CROWN COURT, HIGH COURT, JUVENILE COURT, SUPREME COURT

FOR SPORT | **3** [C] a place where games such as tennis are played: *a tennis/squash/badminton court* ◊ *He won after*

---

b	d	f	g	h	k	l	m	n	p	r
bad	**did**	**fall**	**get**	**hat**	**cat**	**leg**	**man**	**now**	**pen**	**red**

only 52 minutes on court.—see also CLAY COURT, GRASS COURT—picture on page 1250

KINGS/QUEENS | 4 [C, U] the official place where kings and queens live: *the court of Queen Victoria* 5 (**the court**) [sing.] the king or queen, their family, and the people who work for them and/or give advice to them

BUILDINGS | 6 [C] = COURTYARD 7 (*abbr.* **Ct**) [C] used in the names of blocks of flats or apartment buildings, or of some short streets; (in Britain) used in the name of some large houses 8 [C] a large open section of a building, often with a glass roof: *the food court at the shopping mall*

IDM **hold 'court (with sb)** to entertain people by telling them interesting or funny things **rule/throw sth out of 'court** to say that sth is completely wrong or not worth considering, especially in a court of law: *The charges were thrown out of court.* ◇ *Well that's my theory ruled out of court.*—more at BALL *n.*, LAUGH *v.*, PAY *v.*

■ *verb*

TRY TO PLEASE | 1 [VN] to try to please sb in order to get sth you want, especially the support of a person, an organization, etc. **SYN** CULTIVATE: *The company is courting French distributors with a view to selling its products in France.*

TRY TO GET | 2 [VN] (*formal*) to try to obtain sth: *He has never courted popularity.*

INVITE STH BAD | 3 [VN] (*formal*) to do sth that might result in sth unpleasant happening: *to court danger/death/disaster* ◇ *As a politician he has often courted controversy.*

HAVE RELATIONSHIP | 4 [VN] (*old-fashioned*) if a man **courts** a woman, he spends time with her and tries to make her love him, so that they can get married 5 [V] (**be courting**) (*old-fashioned*) (of a man and a woman) to have a romantic relationship before getting married: *At that time they had been courting for several years.*—see also COURTSHIP

> **WHICH WORD?** (?)
> **court / law court / court of law**
>
> All these words can be used to refer to a place where legal trials take place. **Court** and (*formal*) **court of law** usually refer to the actual room where cases are judged. **Courtroom** is also used for this. **Law court** (*BrE*) is more often used to refer to the building: *The prison is opposite the law court.* **Courthouse** is used for this in *AmE*.

'court card (*BrE*) (also **'face card** *AmE, BrE*) *noun* a playing card with a picture of a king, queen or JACK on it—picture on page A8

'court costs *noun* [pl.] (*AmE*) = COSTS at COST *n.*

cour·te·ous /'kɜːtiəs; *AmE* 'kɜːrt-/ *adj.* polite, especially in a way that shows respect: *a courteous young man* ◇ *The hotel staff are friendly and courteous.* **OPP** DISCOURTEOUS
► **cour·te·ous·ly** *adv.*

cour·tesan /ˌkɔːtɪ'zæn; *AmE* 'kɔːrtɪzn/ *noun* (in the past) a prostitute, especially one with rich customers

cour·tesy /'kɜːtəsi; *AmE* 'kɜːrt-/ *noun, adj.*

■ *noun* (*pl.* **-ies**) 1 [U] polite behaviour that shows respect for other people: *I was treated with the utmost courtesy by the staff.* ◇ *It's only **common courtesy** to tell the neighbours that we'll be having a party* (= the sort of behaviour that people would expect). 2 [C, usually pl.] (*formal*) a polite thing that you say or do when you meet people in formal situations: *an exchange of courtesies before the meeting* **IDM** **courtesy of sb/sth** 1 (also **by courtesy of sb/sth**) with the official permission of sb/sth and as a favour: *The pictures have been reproduced by courtesy of the British Museum.* 2 given as a prize or provided free by a person or an organization: *Win a weekend in Rome, courtesy of Fiat.* 3 as the result of a particular thing or situation: *Viewers can see the stadium from the air, courtesy of a camera fastened to the plane.* **do sb the courtesy of doing sth** to be polite by doing the thing that is mentioned: *Please do me the courtesy of listening to what I'm saying.* **have the courtesy to do sth** to know when you should do sth in order to be polite: *You think he'd at least have the courtesy to call to say he'd be late.*

■ *adj.* [only before noun] (of a bus, car, etc.) provided free, at no cost to the person using it: *A courtesy bus operates between the hotel and the town centre.* ◇ *The dealer will provide you with a courtesy car while your vehicle is being repaired.*

'courtesy call (also **'courtesy visit**) *noun* a formal or official visit, usually by one important person to another, just to be polite, not to discuss important business

'courtesy title *noun* a title that sb is allowed to use but which has no legal status

court·house /'kɔːthaʊs; *AmE* 'kɔːrt-/ *noun* 1 (*especially AmE*) a building containing courts of law ⇨ note at COURT 2 (in the US) a building containing the offices of a county government

court·ier /'kɔːtiə(r); *AmE* 'kɔːrt-/ *noun* (especially in the past) a person who is part of the COURT of a king or queen

court·ly /'kɔːtli; *AmE* 'kɔːrt-/ *adj.* (*formal or literary*) extremely polite and full of respect, especially in a old-fashioned way

court 'martial *noun* [C, U] (*pl.* **courts martial**) a military court that deals with members of the armed forces who break military law; a trial at such a court: *He was convicted at a court martial.* ◇ *All the men now face court martial.*

court-'mar·tial *verb* (**-ll-**, *AmE* **-l-**) [VN] [often passive] to hold a trial of sb in a military court: *He was court-martialled for desertion.*

court of ap'peal *noun* 1 (*pl.* **courts of appeal**) a court of law that people can go to in order to try and change decisions that have been made by a lower court—see also APPELLATE COURT 2 (ˌCourt of Ap'peal) [sing.] (*BrE*) the highest court in Britain (apart from the HOUSE OF LORDS), that can change decisions made by a lower court 3 (ˌCourt of Ap'peals) [C] (*AmE*) one of the courts of law in the US that can change decisions made by a lower court

court of en'quiry (also **ˌcourt of in'quiry**) *noun* (*pl.* **courts of enquiry/inquiry**) (*BrE*) a special official group of people that investigates a particular problem

court of 'law *noun* (*pl.* **courts of law**) (also **law court**) a room or building where legal cases are judged ⇨ note at COURT

court 'order *noun* a decision that is made in a court of law about what must happen in a particular situation

court·room /'kɔːtruːm; -rʊm; *AmE* 'kɔːrt-/ *noun* a room in which trials or other legal cases are held ⇨ note at COURT

court·ship /'kɔːtʃɪp; *AmE* 'kɔːrt-/ *noun* 1 [C, U] (*old-fashioned*) the time when two people have a romantic relationship before they get married; the process of developing this relationship: *They married after a short courtship.* ◇ *Mr Elton's courtship of Harriet* 2 [U] the special way animals behave in order to attract a MATE for producing young animals: *courtship displays* 3 ~ (**of sb/sth**) (*written*) the process or act of attracting a business partner, etc: *the company's courtship by the government*

court shoe (*BrE*) (*AmE* **pump**) *noun* a woman's formal shoe that is plain and does not cover the top part of the foot—picture at SHOE

court·yard /'kɔːtjɑːd; *AmE* 'kɔːrtjɑːrd/ (also **court**) *noun* an open space that is partly or completely surrounded by buildings and is usually part of a castle, a large house, etc: *the central/inner courtyard*

cous·cous /'kʊskʊs; 'kuːskuːs/ *noun* [U] a type of N African food made from crushed wheat; a dish of meat and/or vegetables with couscous

cousin /'kʌzn/ *noun* 1 (also **ˌfirst 'cousin**) a child of your aunt or uncle: *She's my cousin.* ◇ *We're cousins.*—see also SECOND COUSIN, REMOVE 2 a person who is in your wider family but who is not closely related to you: *He's a distant cousin of mine.* 3 [usually pl.] a way of describing people from another country who are similar in some way to people in your own country: *our American cousins*

cou·ture /ku'tjʊə(r); *AmE* -'tʊr/ *noun* [U] (from *French*) the design and production of expensive and fashionable clothes; these clothes: *a couture evening dress*—see also HAUTE COUTURE

cou·tur·ier /kuˈtjʊəriei; *AmE* -ˈtʊr-/ *noun* (from *French*) a person who designs, makes and sells expensive, fashionable clothes, especially for women

cove /kəʊv; *AmE* koʊv/ *noun* **1** a small BAY (= an area of sea that is partly enclosed by land): *a secluded cove* **2** (*old-fashioned*, *BrE*, *slang*) a man

coven /ˈkʌvn/ *noun* a group or meeting of WITCHES

cov·en·ant /ˈkʌvənənt/ *noun* a promise to sb, or a legal agreement, especially one to pay a regular amount of money to sb/sth: *God's covenant with Abraham* ◇ *a covenant to a charity* ▶ **cov·en·ant** *verb*: [VN] *All profits are covenanted to medical charities.*

Cov·en·try /ˈkʌvəntri; *BrE* also ˈkɒv-; *AmE* also ˈkɑːv-/ *noun* IDM **send sb to 'Coventry** (*BrE*) to refuse to speak to sb, as a way of punishing them for sth that they have done

cover /ˈkʌvə(r)/ *verb, noun*

■ *verb*

HIDE/PROTECT | **1** [VN] ~ **sth** (**with sth**) to place sth over or in front of sth in order to hide or protect it: *Cover the chicken loosely with foil.* ◇ *She covered her face with her hands.* ◇ (*figurative*) *He laughed to cover* (= hide) *his nervousness.*

SPREAD OVER SURFACE | **2** [VN] to lie or spread over the surface of sth: *Snow covered the ground.* ◇ *Much of the country is covered by forest.* **3** [VN] ~ **sb/sth in/with sth** to put or spread a layer of liquid, dust, etc. on sb/sth: *The players were soon covered in mud.* ◇ *The wind blew in from the desert and covered everything with sand.*

INCLUDE | **4** [VN] to include sth; to deal with sth: *The survey covers all aspects of the business.* ◇ *The lectures covered a lot of ground* (= a lot of material, subjects, etc.). ◇ *the sales team covering the northern part of the country* (= selling to people in that area) ◇ *Do the rules cover* (= do they apply to) *a case like this?*

MONEY | **5** [VN] to be or provide enough money for sth: *$100 should cover your expenses.* ◇ *Your parents will have to cover your tuition fees.* ◇ *The show barely covered its costs.*

DISTANCE/AREA | **6** [VN] to travel the distance mentioned: *By sunset we had covered thirty miles.* ◇ *They walked for a long time and covered a good deal of ground.* **7** [VN] to spread over the area mentioned: *The reserve covers an area of some 1140 square kilometres.*

REPORT NEWS | **8** [VN] to report on an event for television, a newspaper, etc.; to show an event on television: *She's covering the party's annual conference.* ◇ *The BBC will cover all the major games of the tournament.*

FOR SB | **9** [V] ~ **for sb** to do sb's work or duties while they are away: *I'm covering for Jane while she's on leave.* **10** [V] ~ **for sb** to invent a lie or an excuse that will stop sb from getting into trouble: *I have to go out for a minute—will you cover for me if anyone asks where I am?*

WITH INSURANCE | **11** ~ **sb/sth** (**against/for sth**) to protect sb against loss, injury, etc. by insurance: [VN] *Are you fully covered for fire and theft?* ◇ [VN to inf] *Does this policy cover my husband to drive?*

AGAINST BLAME | **12** [VN] ~ **yourself** (**against sth**) to take action in order to protect yourself against being blamed for sth: *One reason doctors take temperatures is to cover themselves against negligence claims.*

WITH GUN | **13** [VN] to protect sb by threatening to shoot at anyone who tries to attack them: *Cover me while I move forward.* **14** [VN] to aim a gun at a place or person so that nobody can escape or shoot: *The police covered the exits to the building.* ◇ *Don't move—we've got you covered!*

SONG | **15** [VN] to record a new version of a song that was originally recorded by another band or singer: *They've covered an old Rolling Stones number.*

IDM **cover your 'tracks** to try and hide what you have done, because you do not want other people to find out about it: *He had attempted to cover his tracks by making her death appear like suicide.*—more at MULTITUDE

PHR V **,cover sth↔'in** to put a covering or roof over an open space **,cover sth↔'over** to cover sth completely so that it cannot be seen: *The Roman remains are now covered over by office buildings.* **,cover 'up** | **,cover yourself 'up** to put on more clothes **,cover sth↔'up 1** to cover sth completely so that it cannot be seen: *He covered up the body with a sheet.* **2** (*disapproving*) to try to stop people from knowing the truth about a mistake, a crime, etc.—related noun COVER-UP

■ *noun*

cover

dust cover

PROTECTION/SHELTER | **1** [C] a thing that is put over or on another thing, usually to protect it or to decorate it: *a cushion cover* ◇ *a plastic waterproof cover for the stroller*—see also DUST COVER, LOOSE COVER—picture at LABORATORY **2** [U] a place that provides shelter from bad weather or protection from an attack: *Everyone ran for cover when it started to rain.* ◇ *The climbers took cover from the storm in a cave.* ◇ *After the explosion the street was full of people running for cover.*

OF BOOK | **3** [C] the outside of a book or a magazine: *the front/back cover* ◇ *Her face was on the cover* (= the front cover) *of every magazine.* ◇ *He always reads the paper from cover to cover* (= everything in it).

INSURANCE | **4** (*BrE*) (*AmE* **cov·er·age**) [U] ~ (**against sth**) protection that an insurance company provides by promising to pay you money if a particular event happens: *accident cover* ◇ *cover against accidental damage*

WITH WEAPONS | **5** [U] support and protection that is provided when sb is attacking or in danger of being attacked: *The ships needed air cover* (= protection by military planes) *once they reached enemy waters.*

TREES/PLANTS | **6** [U] trees and plants that grow on an area of land: *The total forest cover of the earth is decreasing.*

CLOUD/SNOW | **7** [U] the fact of the sky being covered with cloud or the ground with snow: *Fog and low cloud cover are expected this afternoon.* ◇ *In this area there is snow cover for six months of the year.*

ON BED | **8** (**the covers**) [pl.] the sheets BLANKETS, etc. on a bed: *She threw back the covers and leapt out of bed.*

SONG | **9** [C] = COVER VERSION

HIDING STH | **10** [C, usually sing.] ~ (**for sth**) activities or behaviour that seem honest or true but that hide sb's real identity or feelings, or that hide sth illegal: *His work as a civil servant was a cover for his activities as a spy.* ◇ *Her over-confident attitude was a cover for her nervousness.* ◇ *It would only take one phone call to blow their cover* (= make known their true identities and what they were really doing).

FOR SB'S WORK | **11** [U] the fact of sb doing another person's job when they are away or when there are not enough staff: *It's the manager's job to organize cover for staff who are absent.* ◇ *Ambulance drivers provided only emergency cover during the dispute.*

IDM **break 'cover** to leave a place that you have been hiding in, usually at a high speed **under 'cover 1** pretending to be sb else in order to do sth secretly: *a police officer working under cover* **2** under a structure that gives protection from the weather **under (the) cover of sth** hidden or protected by sth: *Later, under cover of darkness, they crept into the house.* **under separate 'cover** (*business*) in a separate envelope: *The information you requested is being forwarded to you under separate cover.*—more at JUDGE *v.*

cov·er·age /ˈkʌvərɪdʒ/ *noun* [U] **1** the reporting of news and sport in newspapers and on the radio and television: *media/newspaper/press coverage* ◇ *tonight's live coverage of the hockey game* **2** the range or quality of information that is included in a book or course of study, on television, etc: *magazines with extensive coverage of diet and health topics* **3** the amount of sth that sth provides; the amount or way that sth covers an area: *Immunization coverage against fatal diseases has increased to 95% in*

æ	ɑː	e	ɜː	ə	ɪ	iː	i	ɒ	ɔː	ʌ	ʊ	u	uː
cat	father	ten	bird	about	sit	see	many	got	saw	cup	put	actual	oo
													(BrE)

some countries. **4** (*AmE*) = COVER (3): *insurance coverage* ◊ *Medicaid health coverage for low-income families*

cov·er·alls /ˈkʌvərɔːlz/ *noun* [pl.] (*AmE*) = OVERALLS

'cover charge *noun* [usually sing.] an amount of money that you pay in some restaurants or clubs in addition to the cost of the food and drink

covered /ˈkʌvəd; *AmE* -vərd/ *adj.* **1** [not before noun] ~ in/with sth having a layer or amount of sth on it: *His face was covered in blood.* ◊ *The walls were covered with pictures.* **2** having a roof over it: *a covered area of the stadium with seats*

,covered 'wagon *noun* a large wooden vehicle with a curved roof made of cloth, that is pulled by horses, used especially in the past in N America by people travelling across the land to the west

'cover girl *noun* a young woman whose photograph is on the front of a magazine

cov·er·ing /ˈkʌvərɪŋ/ *noun* **1** a layer of sth that covers sth else: *a thick covering of snow on the ground* **2** a layer of material such as carpet or WALLPAPER, used to cover, decorate and protect floors, walls, etc: *floor/wall coverings* **3** a piece of material that covers sth: *He pulled the plastic covering off the dead body.*

,covering 'letter (*BrE*) (*AmE* **'cover letter**) *noun* a letter containing extra information that you send with sth

cov·er·let /ˈkʌvələt; *AmE* -vərl-/ *noun* (*old-fashioned*) a type of BEDSPREAD to cover a bed

'cover story *noun* **1** the main story in a magazine especially one that goes with the picture shown on the front cover **2** a story that is invented in order to hide sth, especially a person's identity or their reasons for doing sth

cov·ert /ˈkʌvət; *AmE* -vərt/ *adj.*, *noun*
■ *adj.* /ˈkʌvət; ˈkəʊvɜːt; *AmE* ˈkoʊvɜːrt/ (*formal*) secret or hidden, making it difficult to notice: *covert operations/surveillance* ◊ *He stole a covert glance at her across the table.*—compare OVERT ▶ **cov·ert·ly** *adv.*: *He watched her covertly in the mirror.*
■ *noun* /ˈkʌvət; *AmE* -vərt/ an area of thick low bushes and trees where animals can hide

'cover-up *noun* [usually sing.] action that is taken to hide a mistake or illegal activity from the public: *Government sources denied there had been a deliberate cover-up.*

'cover version (also **cover**) *noun* a new recording of an old song by a different band or singer

covet /ˈkʌvət/ *verb* [VN] (*formal*) to want sth very much, especially sth that belongs to sb else: [VN] *He had long coveted the chance to work with a famous musician.* ◊ *They are this year's winners of the coveted trophy* (= that everyone would like to win).

cov·et·ous /ˈkʌvətəs/ *adj.* (*formal*) having a strong desire for the things that other people have ▶ **cov·et·ous·ness** *noun* [U]

cow /kaʊ/ *noun*, *verb*
■ *noun* **1** a large female animal kept on farms to produce milk or beef: *cow's milk* ◊ *a herd of dairy cows* (= cows kept for their milk)—compare BULL, CALF, HEIFER—see also CATTLE **2** the female of the elephant, WHALE and some other large animals—compare BULL **3** (*slang, disapproving*) an offensive word for a woman: *You stupid cow!* ◊ *That interfering old cow has never liked me.*—see also CASH COW, SACRED COW **IDM** **till the 'cows come home** (*informal*) for a very long time; for ever
■ *verb* [VN] [usually passive] to frighten sb in order to make them obey you **SYN** INTIMIDATE: *She was easily cowed by people in authority.*

cow·ard /ˈkaʊəd; *AmE* -ərd/ *noun* (*disapproving*) a person who is not brave or who does not have the courage to do things that other people do not think are especially difficult: *You coward! What are you afraid of?* ◊ *I'm a real coward when it comes to going to the dentist.* ▶ **cow·ard·ly** *adj.*: *a cowardly attack on a defenceless man*

cow·ard·ice /ˈkaʊədɪs; *AmE* -ərd-/ *noun* [U] fear or lack of courage

cow·boy /ˈkaʊbɔɪ/ *noun* **1** a man who rides a horse and whose job is to take care of CATTLE in the western parts of the US: *cowboy boots/hats* **2** a man like this as a character in a film/movie about the American West: *children playing a game of cowboys and Indians* **3** (*BrE, informal, disapproving*) a dishonest person in business, especially sb who produces work of bad quality or charges too high a price

'cowboy hat *noun* a hat with a wide BRIM, worn by American cowboys—picture at HAT

cow·catch·er /ˈkaʊkætʃə(r)/ *noun* (*AmE*) a pointed metal structure at the front of a train that is used for pushing things off the track

cowed /kaʊd/ *adj.* made to feel afraid and that you are not as good as sb else—see also COW *v*.

cower /ˈkaʊə(r)/ *verb* [V] to bend low and/or move backwards because you are frightened: *A gun went off and people cowered behind walls and under tables.*

cow·girl /ˈkaʊgɜːl; *AmE* -gɜːrl/ *noun* a female cowboy in the American West

cow·hand /ˈkaʊhænd/ *noun* a person whose job is taking care of cows

cowl /kaʊl/ *noun* **1** a large loose covering for the head, worn especially by MONKS **2** a cover for a chimney, etc., usually made of metal. Cowls often turn with the wind and are designed to improve the flow of air or smoke.

cowl·ing /ˈkaʊlɪŋ/ *noun* (*technical*) a metal cover for an engine, especially on an aircraft—picture at PLANE

'co-worker *noun* a person that sb works with, doing the same kind of job

'cow parsley *noun* [U] a European wild plant with a lot of very small white flowers that look like LACE

cow·pat /ˈkaʊpæt/ (*BrE*) *noun* a round flat piece of solid waste from a cow

cow·poke /ˈkaʊpəʊk; *AmE* -poʊk/ *noun* (*AmE, old-fashioned* or *humorous*) = COWBOY

cow·rie /ˈkaʊri/ *noun* a small shiny shell that was used as money in the past in parts of Africa and Asia

cow·shed /ˈkaʊʃed/ *noun* (*BrE*) a farm building in which cows are kept

cow·slip /ˈkaʊslɪp/ *noun* a small wild plant with yellow flowers with a sweet smell

cox /kɒks; *AmE* kɑːks/ *noun*, *verb*
■ *noun* (also **cox·swain**) the person who controls the direction of a ROWING BOAT while other people are rowing
■ *verb* [VN, V] to control the direction of a ROWING BOAT while other people are rowing; to act as a COX

cox·swain /ˈkɒksn; *AmE* ˈkɑːksn/ *noun* **1** the person who is in charge of a LIFEBOAT and who controls its direction **2** = COX

coy /kɔɪ/ *adj.* **1** shy or pretending to be shy and innocent, especially about love or sex and sometimes in order to make people more interested in you: *She gave me a coy smile.* **2** ~ (about sth) not willing to give information about sth, or answer questions that tell people too much about you **SYN** RETICENT: *She was a little coy about how much her dress cost.* ▶ **coyly** *adv.* **coy·ness** *noun* [U]

coy·ote /kaɪˈəʊti; *BrE* also kɔɪ-; *AmE* -ˈoʊti; ˈkaɪoʊt/ *noun* a N American wild animal of the dog family

cozy (*AmE*) = COSY

cp. *abbr.* (in writing) compare

CPI /ˌsiː piː ˈaɪ/ *abbr.* CONSUMER PRICE INDEX

Cpl (*BrE*) (*AmE* **Cpl.**) *abbr.* (in writing) CORPORAL

CPU /ˌsiː piː ˈjuː/ *abbr.* (*computing*) the abbreviation for 'central processing unit' (the part of a computer that controls all the other parts of the system)

crab /kræb/ *noun* **1** [C] a sea creature with a hard shell, eight legs and two PINCERS (= curved and pointed limbs for catching and holding things). Crabs move sideways on land.—see also HERMIT CRAB—picture on page A7 **2** [U] meat from a crab, used for food: *dressed crab* **3** (**crabs**) (*informal*) the condition caused by having LICE (called **crab lice**) in the hair around the GENITALS

'crab apple *noun* a tree that produces fruit like small hard sour apples, also called **crab apples** : *crab-apple jelly*

a	aʊ	eɪ	əʊ	oʊ	ɔɪ	ɪə	eə	ʊə	j	w
my	now	say	go	go	boy	near	hair	pure	yes	wet
			(BrE)	(AmE)						

crabbed /'kræbɪd; kræbd/ *adj.* **1** (*rare* or *literary*) (of sb's writing) small and difficult to read **2** (*old-fashioned*) = CRABBY

crabby /'kræbi/ *adj.* (*informal*) (of people) bad-tempered and unpleasant

crab·grass /'kræbgrɑːs; *AmE* -græs/ *noun* [U] (*especially AmE*) a type of grass that grows where it is not wanted, spreads quickly and is hard to get rid of

crack /kræk/ *verb, noun, adj.*

■ *verb*

BREAK | **1** to break without dividing into separate parts; to break sth in this way: [V] *The ice cracked as I stepped onto it.* ◊ [VN] *He has cracked a bone in his arm.* ◊ *Her lips were dry and cracked.* **2** to break open or into pieces; to break sth in this way: [V, +*adv./prep.*] *A chunk of the cliff had cracked off in a storm.* ◊ (*figurative*) *His face cracked into a smile.* ◊ [VN] *to crack a nut* ◊ *She cracked an egg into the pan.*

HIT | **3** [VN] ~ *sth/sb* (**on/against** *sth*) to hit sth/sb with a short hard blow: *I cracked my head on the low ceiling.* ◊ *He cracked me on the head with a ruler.*

MAKE SOUND | **4** to make a sharp sound; to make sth do this: [V] *A shot cracked across the ridge.* ◊ [VN] [no passive] *He cracked his whip and galloped away.*

OF VOICE | **5** [V] if your voice **cracks**, it changes in depth, volume, etc. suddenly and in a way that you cannot control: *In a voice cracking with emotion, he told us of his son's death.*

UNDER PRESSURE | **6** [V] to no longer be able to function normally because of pressure: *Things are terrible at work and people are cracking under the strain.* ◊ *They questioned him for days before he cracked.* ◊ *The old institutions are cracking.*

FIND SOLUTION | **7** [VN] to find the solution to a problem, etc.; to find the way to do sth difficult: *to crack the enemy's code* ◊ (*spoken*) *After a year in this job I think I've got it cracked!*

STOP SB/STH | **8** [VN] to find a way of stopping or defeating a criminal or an enemy: *Police have cracked a major drugs ring.*

OPEN BOTTLE | **9** [VN] ~ (**open**) **a bottle** (*informal*) to open a bottle, especially of wine, and drink it

A JOKE | **10** [VN] ~ **a joke** (*informal*) to tell a joke

IDM **get 'cracking** (*informal*) to begin immediately and work quickly: *There's a lot to be done, so let's get cracking.* **not all, everything, etc. sb's cracked 'up to be** (*informal*) not as good as people say: *He's not nearly such a good writer as he's cracked up to be.*—more at SLEDGEHAMMER

PHRV **,crack 'down (on** *sb/sth*) to try harder to prevent an illegal activity and deal more severely with those who are caught doing it: *Police are cracking down on drug dealers.*—related noun CRACKDOWN **,crack 'on (with** *sth*) (*BrE, informal*) to work hard at sth so that you finish it quickly; to pass or continue quickly: *If we crack on with the painting we should finish it today.* ◊ *Time was cracking on and we were nowhere near finished.* **,crack 'up** (*informal*) **1** to become ill, either physically or mentally, because of pressure: *You'll crack up if you carry on working like this.* **2** to start laughing a lot: *He walked in and everyone just cracked up.* **,crack** *sb* **'up** (*informal*) to make sb laugh a lot: *Gill's so funny, she just cracks me up.*

■ *noun*

BREAK | **1** [C] ~ (**in** *sth*) a line on the surface of sth where it has broken but not split into separate parts: *This cup has a crack in it.* ◊ *Cracks began to appear in the walls.* ◊ (*figurative*) *The cracks* (= faults) *in the government's economic policy are already beginning to show.*

NARROW OPENING | **2** [C] a narrow space or opening: *She peeped through the crack in the curtains.* ◊ *The door opened a crack* (= a small amount).

SOUND | **3** [C] a sudden loud noise: *a crack of thunder* ◊ *the sharp crack of a rifle shot*

HIT | **4** [C] ~ (**on** *sth*) a sharp blow that can be heard: *She fell over and got a nasty crack on the head.*

ATTEMPT | **5** [C] ~ (**at** *sth*)| ~ (**at doing** *sth*) (*informal*) an occasion when you try to do sth: *She hopes to have another crack at the world record this year.*

DRUG | **6** (also ,crack co'caine) [U] a powerful, illegal drug that is a form of COCAINE: *a crack addict*

JOKE | **7** [C] (*informal*) a joke, especially a critical one: *He made a very unfair crack about her looks.*

CONVERSATION | **8** (also **craic**) [U, sing.] (*IrishE, spoken*) a good time; friendly, enjoyable talk: *Where's the crack tonight?* ◊ *He's a person who enjoys a drink and a bit of crack.*

IDM **at the crack of 'dawn** (*informal*) very early in the morning—more at FAIR *adj.*

■ *adj.* [only before noun] expert and highly trained; excellent at sth: *crack troops* ◊ *He's a crack shot* (= accurate and skilled at shooting).

crack·down /'krækdaʊn/ *noun* ~ (**on** *sb/sth*) severe action taken to restrict the activities of criminals or of people opposed to the government or authorities: *a military crackdown on student protesters* ◊ *Police officers are confident their successful crackdown on crime will continue.*

cracked /krækt/ *adj.* **1** damaged with lines in its surface but not completely broken: *a cracked mirror/mug* ◊ *He suffered cracked ribs and bruising.* ◊ *She passed her tongue over her cracked lips and tried to speak.* **2** (of sb's voice) sounding rough with sudden changes in how loud or high it is, because the person is upset: *'I'm just fine,' she said in a cracked voice.* **3** [not before noun] (*informal*) crazy: *I think he must be cracked, don't you?*

crack·er /'krækə(r)/ *noun*
1 a thin dry biscuit that is often salty and usually eaten with cheese **2** (also ,Christmas 'cracker) a tube of coloured paper that makes a loud explosive sound when it is pulled open by two people. Crack-

cracker   cracker

ers usually contain a paper hat, a small present and a joke, and are used in Britain at Christmas parties and meals: *Who wants to pull this cracker with me?*—see also FIRECRACKER **3** (*BrE, informal*) something that you think is very good, funny, etc: *It was a cracker of a goal.* ◊ *I've got a joke for you. It's a real cracker!* **4** (*old-fashioned, BrE, informal*) an attractive woman **5** (*AmE, slang*) an offensive word for a poor white person with little education from the southern US

crack·er·jack /'krækədʒæk; *AmE* -kərdʒæk/ *noun* (*AmE, informal*) an excellent person or thing ▶ **crack·er·jack** *adj.*

crack·ers /'krækəz; *AmE* -kərz/ *adj.* [not before noun] (*BrE, informal*) crazy: *That noise is driving me crackers.* ◊ *You must be absolutely crackers even to think of it.*

crack·ing /'krækɪŋ/ *noun, adj.*
■ *noun* [U] **1** lines on a surface where it is damaged or beginning to break: *All planes are being inspected for possible cracking and corrosion.* **2** the sound of sth cracking: *the cracking of thunder/twigs*
■ *adj.* [usually before noun] (*BrE, informal*) excellent: *That was a cracking goal.* ◊ *She's in cracking form at the moment.* ◊ *We set off at a cracking pace* (= very quickly) ▶ **crack·ing** *adv.*: *a cracking good* (= extremely good) *dinner*

crackle /'krækl/ *verb, noun*
■ *verb* [V] to make short sharp sounds like sth that is burning in a fire: *A log fire crackled in the hearth.* ◊ *The radio crackled into life.* ◊ (*figurative*) *The atmosphere crackled with tension.*
■ *noun* [U, C] a series of short sharp sounds: *the distant crackle of machine-gun fire* ▶ **crack·ly** /'krækli/ *adj.*: *She picked up the phone and heard a crackly voice saying: 'Pat here.'*

crack·ling /'kræklɪŋ/ *noun* **1** [U, sing.] a series of sharp sounds: *He could hear the crackling of burning trees.* **2** [U] (*BrE*) (*AmE* **crack·lings** [pl.]) the hard skin of PORK = meat from a pig) that has been cooked in the oven

crack·pot /'krækpɒt; AmE -pɑːt/ noun (informal) a person with strange or crazy ideas ▶ **crack·pot** adj. [only before noun]: *crackpot ideas/theories*

-cracy combining form (in nouns) the government or rule of: *democracy* ◊ *bureaucracy*

cra·dle /'kreɪdl/ noun, verb
■ noun **1** a small bed for a baby which can be pushed gently from side to side: *She rocked the baby to sleep in its cradle.*—picture at BED **2** [usually sing.] **~ of sth** the place where sth important began: *Greece, the cradle of Western civilization* **3** (BrE) a small platform that can be moved up and down the outside of a high building, used by people cleaning windows, etc. **4** the part of a telephone on which the RECEIVER rests **IDM** **from the ˌcradle to the ˈgrave** a way of referring to the whole of a person's life, from birth until death
■ verb [VN] to hold sb/sth gently in your arms or hands: *The old man cradled the tiny baby in his arms.*

craft /krɑːft; AmE kræft/ noun, verb
■ noun **1** [C, U] an activity involving a special skill at making things with your hands: *traditional crafts like basket-weaving* ◊ *a craft fair/workshop* ◊ *Craft, Design and Technology* (= a subject in some British schools)—see also ARTS AND CRAFTS **2** [sing.] all the skills needed for a particular activity: *chefs who learned their craft in top hotels* ◊ *the writer's craft* **3** [U] (formal, disapproving) skill in making people believe what you want them to believe: *He knew how to win by craft and diplomacy what he could not gain by force.* **4** [C] (pl. **craft**) a boat or ship: *Hundreds of small craft bobbed around the liner as it steamed into the harbour.* ◊ *a landing/pleasure craft* **5** [C] (pl. **craft**) an aircraft or spacecraft
■ verb [VN] [usually passive] to make sth using special skills, especially with your hands: *All the furniture is crafted from natural materials.* ◊ *a carefully crafted speech*

ˈcraft knife noun (BrE) a very sharp knife used for cutting paper or thin pieces of wood

crafts·man /'krɑːftsmən; AmE 'kræf-/ (also **crafts·person**) noun (pl. **-men** /-mən/) a skilled person, especially one who makes beautiful things by hand: *rugs handmade by local craftsmen* ◊ *It is clearly the work of a master craftsman.*—see also CRAFTSWOMAN

crafts·man·ship /'krɑːftsmənʃɪp; AmE 'kræf-/ noun [U] **1** the level of skill shown by sb in making sth beautiful with their hands: *The whole house is a monument to her craftsmanship.* **2** the quality of design and work shown by sth that has been made by hand: *the superb craftsmanship of the carvings*

crafts·person /'krɑːftspɜːsn; AmE 'kræftspɜːrsn/ noun (pl. **-people** /-piːpl/) = CRAFTSMAN

crafts·woman /'krɑːftswʊmən; AmE 'kræf-/ noun (pl. **-women** /-wɪmɪn/) a skilled woman, especially one who makes beautiful things by hand

craft·work /'krɑːftwɜːk; AmE 'kræftwɜːrk/ noun [U] work done by a CRAFTSMAN

crafty /'krɑːfti; AmE 'kræfti/ adj. (**craft·ier**, **crafti·est**) (usually disapproving) clever at getting what you want, especially by indirect or dishonest methods: *He's a crafty old devil.* ◊ *one of the party's craftiest political strategists* ▶ **craft·ily** adv. **crafti·ness** noun [U]

crag /kræg/ noun a high steep rough mass of rock: *a castle set on a crag above the village*

craggy /'krægi/ adj. **1** having many crags: *a craggy coastline* **2** (usually approving) (of a man's face) having strong features and deep lines

craic noun = CRACK (8)

cram /kræm/ verb (**-mm-**) **1** **~** (sth) **into/onto sth** | **~** (sth) **in** to push or force sb/sth into a small space; to move into a small space with the result that it is full: [VN] *He crammed eight people into his car.* ◊ *I could never cram in all that she does in a day.* ◊ *I managed to cram down a few mouthfuls of food.* ◊ *Supporters crammed the streets.* ◊ [V] *We all managed to cram into his car.* [also VN-ADJ] **2** [V] **~ (for sth)** (rather old-fashioned) to learn a lot of things in a short time, in preparation for an exam: *He's been cramming for his exams all week.*

crammed /kræmd/ adj. **~ (with sb/sth)** **1** full of things

or people: *All the shelves were crammed with books.* ◊ *The room was crammed full of people.* ◊ *The article was crammed full of ideas.* **2** [not before noun] if people are crammed into a place, there is not much room for them in it: *We were crammed four to an office.*

cram·mer /'kræmə(r)/ noun (BrE) a school or book that prepares people quickly for exams

cramp /kræmp/ noun, verb
■ noun **1** [U, C] (AmE also **ˈcharley horse** [C]) a sudden pain that you get when the muscles in a particular part of your body tighten, usually caused by cold or too much exercise: (BrE) *to get cramp in your leg* ◊ (AmE) *to get a cramp in your leg*—see also WRITER'S CRAMP **2** (**cramps**) [pl.] severe pain in the stomach
■ verb [VN] to prevent the development or progress of sb/sth: *Tighter trade restrictions might cramp economic growth.* **IDM** **cramp sb's ˈstyle** (informal) to stop sb from behaving in the way they want to: *She didn't want me to go with her to the party in case I cramped her style.*

cramped /kræmpt/ adj. **1** a cramped room, etc. does not have enough space for the people in it: *working in cramped conditions* **2** (of people) not having room to move freely **3** (of sb's writing) with small letters close together and therefore difficult to read

cram·pon /'kræmpɒn; AmE -pɑːn/ noun [usually pl.] a metal plate with pointed pieces of metal underneath, worn on sb's shoes when they are walking or climbing on ice and snow

cran·berry /'krænbəri; AmE -beri/ noun (pl. **-ies**) a small sour red berry that grows on a small bush and is used in cooking: *cranberry sauce*

crane /kreɪn/ noun, verb
■ noun **1** a tall machine with a long arm, used to lift and move building materials and other heavy objects **2** a large bird with long legs and a long neck
■ verb [V] [usually +adv./prep.] to lean or stretch over sth in order to see sth better; to stretch your neck: [V] *People were craning out of the windows and waving.* ◊ [VN] *She craned her neck to get a better view of the stage.*

ˈcrane fly (also informal ˌdaddy-ˈlong-legs) noun a flying insect with very long legs

cra·nium /'kreɪniəm/ noun (pl. **cra·ni·ums** or **cra·nia** /'kreɪniə/) (anatomy) the bone structure that forms the head and surrounds and protects the brain **SYN** SKULL ▶ **cra·nial** /'kreɪniəl/ adj. [only before noun]: *cranial nerves/injuries*

crank /kræŋk/ noun, verb
■ noun **1** (disapproving) a person with ideas that other people find strange: *Vegetarians are no longer dismissed as cranks.* **2** (AmE) a person who easily gets angry or annoyed **3** a bar and handle in the shape of an L that you pull or turn to produce movement in a machine, etc.—picture at BICYCLE
■ verb [VN] **~ sth (up)** to make sth turn or move by using a crank: *to crank an engine* ◊ (figurative) *He has a limited time to crank the reforms into action.* **PHRV** ˌcrank sth↔ˈout (AmE, informal) to produce a lot of sth quickly, especially things of low quality **SYN** TURN OUT ˌcrank sth↔ˈup (informal) **1** to make a machine, etc. work or work at a higher level **2** to make music, etc. louder **SYN** TURN UP: *Crank up the volume!*

crank·shaft /'kræŋkʃɑːft; AmE -ʃæft/ noun (technical) a metal rod in a vehicle that connects the engine to the wheels and helps turn the engine's power into movement

cranky /'kræŋki/ adj. (informal) **1** (BrE) strange **SYN** ECCENTRIC: *cranky ideas/schemes* **2** (especially AmE) bad-tempered: *The kids were getting tired and a little cranky.*

cranny /'kræni/ noun (pl. **-ies**) a very small hole or opening, especially in a wall **IDM** see NOOK

crap /kræp/ noun, adj., verb
■ noun (⚠, slang) **1** [U] nonsense: *He's so full of crap.* ◊ *Let's cut the crap and get down to business.* ◊ (BrE) *You're talking a load of crap!* ◊ (AmE) *What a bunch of crap!* **2** [U] something of bad quality: *This work is complete crap.* ◊ (BrE) *Her latest film is a load of crap.* ◊ (AmE) *Her latest movie is a bunch of crap.* **HELP** More acceptable words are **rubbish**, **garbage**, **trash** or **junk**. **3** [U] criti-

s	t	v	z	ʃ	ʒ	tʃ	dʒ	θ	ð	ŋ
see	tea	van	zoo	shoe	vision	chain	jam	thin	this	sing

cism or unfair treatment: *I'm not going to take this crap any more.* **4** [U] solid waste matter from the bowels SYN EXCREMENT **5** [sing.] an act of emptying solid waste matter from the bowels: *to have a crap*
■ *adj.* (*BrE*, △, *slang*) bad; of very bad quality: *a crap band* ◇ *The concert was crap.* ▶ **crap** *adv.*: *The team played crap yesterday.*
■ *verb* (**-pp-**) [V] (△, *slang*) to empty solid waste from the bowels SYN DEFECATE HELP A more polite way of expressing this is 'to go to the toilet/lavatory' (*BrE*), 'to go to the bathroom' (*AmE*), or 'to go'. A more formal expression is 'to empty the bowels'.

crappy /ˈkræpi/ *adj.* [usually before noun] (*slang*) of very bad quality: *a crappy novel*

craps /kræps/ *noun* [U] (*AmE*) a gambling game played with two DICE: *to shoot craps* (= play this game) ▶ **crap** *adj.* [only before noun]: *a crap game*

crash /kræʃ/ *noun, verb, adj.*
■ *noun*
VEHICLE ACCIDENT | **1** (*AmE* also **wreck**) an accident in which a vehicle hits sth, for example another vehicle, usually causing damage and often injuring or killing the passengers: *A girl was killed yesterday in a crash involving a stolen car.* ◇ *a car/plane crash*
LOUD NOISE | **2** [usually sing.] a sudden loud noise made, for example, by sth falling or breaking: *The tree fell with a great crash.* ◇ *The first distant crash of thunder shook the air.*
IN FINANCE/BUSINESS | **3** a sudden serious fall in the price or value of sth; the occasion when a business, etc. fails: *the 1987 stock market crash*
COMPUTING | **4** a sudden failure of a machine or system, especially of a computer or computer system
■ *verb*
OF VEHICLE | **1** ~ (sth) (into sth) if a vehicle **crashes** or the driver **crashes** it, it hits an object or another vehicle, causing damage: [V] *I was terrified that the plane would crash.* ◇ *We're going to crash, aren't we?* ◇ *A truck went out of control and crashed into the back of a bus.* ◇ [VN] *He crashed his car into a wall.*
HIT HARD/LOUD NOISE | **2** [+*adv./prep.*] to hit sth hard while moving, causing noise and/or damage; to make sth hit sb/sth in this way: [V] *A brick crashed through the window.* ◇ *With a sweep of his hand he sent the glasses crashing to the floor.* ◇ [V-ADJ] *The door crashed open.* ◇ [VN-ADJ] *She stormed out of the room and crashed the door shut behind her.* **3** [V] to make a loud noise: *Thunder crashed overhead.*
IN FINANCE/BUSINESS | **4** [V] (of prices, a business, shares, etc.) to lose value or fail suddenly and quickly: *Share prices crashed to an all-time low yesterday.* ◇ *The company crashed with debts of £50 million.*
COMPUTING | **5** if a computer **crashes** or you **crash** a computer, it stops working suddenly: [V] *Files can be lost if the system suddenly crashes.* [also VN]
PARTY | **6** [VN] (*informal*) = GATECRASH
IN SPORT | **7** [V] [usually +*adv./prep.*] (*especially BrE*) to lose very badly in a sports game: *The team crashed to their worst defeat this season.*
SLEEP | **8** [V] ~ (out) (*informal*) to fall asleep; to sleep somewhere you do not usually sleep: *I was so tired I crashed out on the sofa.* ◇ *I've come to crash on your floor for a couple of nights.*
MEDICAL | **9** [V] if sb **crashes**, their heart stops beating
IDM **a crashing** ˈbore (*old-fashioned, BrE*) a very boring person
■ *adj.* [only before noun] involving hard work or a lot of effort over a short period of time in order to achieve quick results: *a crash course in computer programming* ◇ *a crash diet*

ˈ**crash barrier** (*BrE*) (*AmE* ˈ**guard rail**) *noun* a strong low fence or wall at the side of a road or between the two halves of a motorway/freeway, designed to prevent accidents

ˈ**crash helmet** *noun* a hat made of very strong material and worn when riding a motorcycle to protect the head—picture at HAT

ˈ**crash-land** *verb* [V, VN] if a plane **crash-lands** or a pilot **crash-lands** it, the pilot lands it roughly in an emergency, usually because it is damaged and cannot land normally ▶ ˌ**crash** ˈ**landing** *noun*: *to make a crash landing*

crass /kræs/ *adj.* very stupid and showing no sympathy or understanding: *the crass questions all disabled people get asked* ◇ *an act of crass* (= great) *stupidity* ▶ **crass·ly** *adv.* **crass·ness** *noun* [U]

-crat *combining form* (in nouns) a member or supporter of a particular type of government or system: *democrat* ◇ *bureaucrat* ▶ **-cratic** (in adjectives): *aristocratic*

crate /kreɪt/ *noun, verb*
■ *noun* **1** a large wooden container for transporting goods: *a crate of bananas* **2** a container made of plastic or metal divided into small sections, for transporting or storing bottles: *a beer crate* **3** the amount of sth contained in a crate: *They drank two crates of beer.*
■ *verb* [VN] ~ sth (up) to pack sth in a crate

crater /ˈkreɪtə(r)/ *noun* **1** a large hole in the top of a VOLCANO—picture at VOLCANO **2** a large hole in the ground caused by the explosion of a bomb or by sth large hitting it: *a meteorite crater*

cra·vat /krəˈvæt/ (*AmE* also **ascot**) *noun* a short wide strip of fabric worn by men around the neck, folded inside the collar of a shirt—picture on page A4

crave /kreɪv/ *verb* **1** (*written*) to have a very strong desire for sth: [VN] *She has always craved excitement.* [also V, V to inf] **2** [VN] (*BrE, old use*) to ask for sth seriously: *I must crave your pardon.*

cra·ven /ˈkreɪvn/ *adj.* (*formal, disapproving*) lacking courage SYN COWARDLY ▶ **craven·ly** *adv.*

crav·ing /ˈkreɪvɪŋ/ *noun* ~ (for sth)| ~ (to do sth) a strong desire for sth: *a craving for chocolate* ◇ *a desperate craving to be loved*

craw /krɔː/ *noun* the part of a bird's throat where food is kept IDM see STICK *v.*

craw·fish /ˈkrɔːfɪʃ/ *noun* (*especially AmE*) = CRAYFISH

crawl /krɔːl/ *verb, noun*
■ *verb* [V] [usually +*adv./prep.*] **1** to move forward on your hands and knees, with your body close to the ground: *Our baby is just starting to crawl.* ◇ *A man was crawling away from the burning wreckage.*—picture at KNEEL **2** when an insect **crawls**, it moves forward on its legs: *There's a spider crawling up your leg.* **3** to move forward very slowly: *The traffic was crawling along.* ◇ *The weeks crawled by.* **4** ~ (to sb) (*informal, disapproving*) to be too friendly or helpful to sb in authority, in a way that is not sincere, especially in order to get an advantage from them: *She's always crawling to the boss.* IDM see SKIN *n.*, WOODWORK PHRV be ˈ**crawling with sth** (*informal*) to be full of or completely covered with people, insects or animals, in a way that is unpleasant: *The place was crawling with journalists.* ◇ *Her hair was crawling with lice.*
■ *noun* **1** [sing.] a very slow speed: *The traffic slowed to a crawl.*—see also PUB CRAWL **2** (often **the crawl**) [sing., U] a fast swimming stroke that you do lying on your front moving one arm over your head, and then the other, while kicking with your feet: *a swimmer doing the crawl*—picture at SWIMMING

crawl·er /ˈkrɔːlə(r)/ *noun* (*informal*) **1** (*BrE, disapproving*) a person who tries to get sb's favour by praising them, doing what will please them, etc. **2** a thing or person that crawls, such as a vehicle, an insect or a baby—see also KERB-CRAWLER

cray·fish /ˈkreɪfɪʃ/ (*especially BrE*) (also **craw·fish** *AmE, BrE*) *noun* [C, U] (*pl.* **cray·fish**, **craw·fish**) a shellfish like a small LOBSTER, that lives in rivers and lakes and can be eaten, or one like a large LOBSTER, that lives in the sea and can be eaten

crayon /ˈkreɪən/ *noun* a coloured pencil or stick of soft coloured chalk or WAX, used for drawing ▶ **crayon** *verb* [V, VN]

craze /kreɪz/ *noun* ~ (for sth) an enthusiastic interest in sth that is shared by many people but that usually does not last very long; a thing that people have a craze for:

æ	ɑː	e	ɜː	ə	ɪ	iː	i	ɒ	ɔː	ʌ	ʊ	u	uː
cat	father	ten	bird	about	sit	see	many	got	saw	cup	put	actual	too
								(BrE)					

the latest fitness craze to sweep the country ◊ Pet pigs are the latest craze.

crazed /kreɪzd/ adj. ~ **(with sth)** (written) full of strong feelings and lacking control: crazed with fear/grief/jealousy ◊ a crazed killer roaming the streets

crazy /'kreɪzi/ adj., noun
■ adj. (cra·zier, crazi·est) (informal) **1** (especially AmE) not sensible; stupid: Are you crazy? We could get killed doing that. ◊ She must be crazy to lend him money. ◊ He drove like a madman, passing in the craziest places. ◊ What a crazy idea! ◊ I know it sounds crazy but it just might work. **2** very angry: That noise is **driving me crazy**. ◊ Marie says he **went crazy**, and smashed the room up. **3** ~ **(about sth)** (often in compounds) very enthusiastic or excited about sth: Rick is crazy about football. ◊ He's football-crazy. ◊ I'm not crazy about Chinese food (= I don't like it very much). ◊ The crowd **went crazy** when the band came on stage. ◊ You're so beautiful you're **driving me crazy**. **4**~ **about sb** liking sb very much; in love with sb: I've been crazy about him since the first time I saw him. **5** (especially AmE) mentally ill; INSANE: She's crazy—she ought to be locked up. ▶ **crazi·ly** adv. **cra·zi·ness** noun [U] **like 'crazy**/'mad** (informal) very fast, hard, much, etc: We worked like crazy to get it done on time.
■ noun (pl. **-ies**) (informal, especially AmE) a crazy person

,crazy 'paving noun [U] (BrE) pieces of stone of different shapes and sizes, fitted together on the ground to make a path or PATIO

creak /kriːk/ verb, noun
■ verb to make the sound that a door sometimes makes when you open it or that a wooden floor sometimes makes when you step on it: [V] She heard a floorboard creak upstairs. ◊ a creaking bed/gate/stair ◊ The table creaked and groaned under the weight. ◊ [V-ADJ] The door creaked open. **IDM** ,creak under the 'strain** if a system or service **creaks under the strain**, it cannot deal effectively with all the things it is expected to do or provide
■ noun [C] (also **creak·ing** [U, C]) a sound, for example that sometimes made by a door when it opens or shuts, or by a wooden floor when you step on it: the creak/creaking of the door ◊ Distant creaks and groans echoed eerily along the dark corridors.

creaky /'kriːki/ adj. **1** making creaks: a creaky old chair **2** old and not in good condition: the country's creaky legal machinery

cream /kriːm/ noun, adj., verb
■ noun **1** [U] the thick pale yellowish-white FATTY liquid that rises to the top of milk, used in cooking or as a type of sauce to put on fruit, etc: strawberries and cream ◊ Would you like milk or cream in your coffee? ◊ fresh/whipped cream ◊ (BrE) cream cakes (= containing cream) ◊ (BrE) double/single (= thick/thin cream)—see also CLOTTED CREAM, ICE CREAM, SALAD CREAM, SOUR CREAM, WHIPPING CREAM—picture on page A1 **2** [C] (in compounds) a sweet/candy that has a soft substance like cream inside: a chocolate/peppermint cream **3** [U, C] a soft substance or thick liquid used on your skin to protect it or make it feel soft; a similar substance used for cleaning things: hand/moisturizing cream ◊ antiseptic cream ◊ a cream cleaner—see also COLD CREAM, FACE CREAM, SHAVING CREAM **4** [U] a pale yellowish-white colour: Do you have this blouse in cream? **5 the ~ of sth** the best people or things in a particular group: the cream of New York society ◊ the cream of the crop of this season's movies **IDM** see CAT
■ adj. pale yellowish-white in colour: a cream linen suit
■ verb [VN] **1** to mix things together into a soft smooth mixture: Cream the butter and sugar together. **2** (AmE, informal) to completely defeat sb: We got creamed in the first round. **PHRV** ,cream sb/sth ↔ 'off** to take sth away, usually the best people or things or an amount of money, in order to get an advantage for yourself: The best students were creamed off by the grammar schools.

,cream 'cheese noun [U, C] soft white cheese containing a lot of cream

cream·er /'kriːmə(r)/ noun [U] a liquid or powder that

you can put in coffee, etc. instead of cream or milk: non-dairy creamer

cream·ery /'kriːməri/ noun (pl. **-ies**) a place where milk and cream are made into butter and cheese

,cream 'puff noun (AmE) **1** = PROFITEROLE **2** (slang, disapproving) a person who is not strong or brave **SYN** WIMP,

,cream 'soda noun [U, C] (especially AmE) a FIZZY drink (= one with bubbles) that tastes of VANILLA

,cream 'tea noun (BrE) a special meal eaten in the afternoon, consisting of tea with SCONES, jam and thick cream

creamy /'kriːmi/ adj. (cream·ier, creami·est) **1** thick and smooth like cream; containing a lot of cream: a creamy sauce/soup **2** pale yellowish-white in colour: creamy skin

crease /kriːs/ noun, verb
■ noun **1** an untidy line that is made in fabric or paper when it is pressed or crushed: She smoothed the creases out of her skirt. ◊ a shirt made of crease-resistant material—picture on page A4 **2** a neat line that you make in sth, for example when you fold it: trousers with a sharp crease in the legs **3** a line in the skin, especially on the face: creases around the eyes **4** (in cricket) a white line on the ground near each WICKET that marks the position of the BOWLER and the BATSMAN
■ verb **1** to make lines on fabric or paper by folding or crushing it; to develop lines in this way: [VN] Pack your suit carefully so that you don't crease it. [also V] **2** to make lines in the skin; to develop lines in the skin: [VN] A frown creased her forehead. ◊ [V] Her face creased into a smile. ▶ **creased** adj.: I can't wear this blouse. It's creased. **PHRV** ,crease 'up| ,crease sb 'up** (BrE, informal) to start laughing or make sb start laughing: Ed creased up laughing. ◊ Her jokes really creased me up.

cre·ate /kri'eɪt/ verb **1** [VN] to make sth happen or exist: Scientists disagree about how the universe was created. ◊ The main purpose of industry is to create wealth. ◊ The government plans to create more jobs for young people. ◊ Create a new directory and put all your files into it. ◊ Try this new dish, created by our head chef. **2** [VN] to produce a particular feeling or impression: The company is trying to create a young energetic image. ◊ The announcement only succeeded in creating confusion. ◊ They've painted it red to create a feeling of warmth. **3** to give sb a particular rank or title: [VN] The government has created eight new peers. ◊ [VN-N] He was created a baronet in 1715.

cre·ation /kri'eɪʃn/ noun **1** [U] the act or process of making sth that is new, or of causing sth to exist that did not exist before: the process of database creation ◊ wealth creation ◊ He had been with the company since its creation in 1979.—see also JOB CREATION **2** [C] (often humorous) a thing that sb has made, especially sth artistic or imaginative: a literary creation ◊ The cake was a delicious creation of sponge, cream and fruit. **3** (usually **the Creation**) [sing.] the making of the world, especially by God as described in the Bible **4** (often **Creation**) [U] the world and all the living things in it

cre·ative /kri'eɪtɪv/ adj. **1** [only before noun] involving the use of skill and the imagination to produce sth new or a work of art: a course on **creative writing** (= writing stories, plays and poems) ◊ the creative and performing arts ◊ **creative thinking** (= thinking about problems in a new way or thinking of new ideas) ◊ the company's creative team ◊ the creative process **2** having the skill and ability to produce sth new, especially a work of art; showing this ability: She's very creative—she writes poetry and paints. ◊ Do you have any ideas? You're the creative one. ▶ **cre·ative·ly** adv. **cre·ativ·ity** /,kriːeɪ'tɪvəti/ noun [U]: Creativity and originality are more important than technical skill.

cre,ative ac'counting noun [U] (disapproving) a way of doing or presenting the accounts of a business that might not show what the true situation really is

cre·ator /kri'eɪtə(r)/ noun **1** [C] a person who has made or invented a particular thing: Walt Disney, the creator of Mickey Mouse **2** (**the Creator**) [sing.] God

crea·ture /'kriːtʃə(r)/ noun **1** a living thing, real or

aɪ	aʊ	eɪ	əʊ	oʊ	ɔɪ	ɪə	eə	ʊə	j	w
my	now	say	go (BrE)	go (AmE)	boy	near	hair	pure	yes	wet

imaginary, that can move around, such as an animal: *The dormouse is a shy, nocturnal creature.* ◊ *respect for all living creatures* ◊ *strange creatures from outer space* **2** (especially following an adjective) a person, considered in a particular way: *You pathetic creature!* ◊ *She was an exotic creature with long red hair and brilliant green eyes.* ◊ *He always goes to bed at ten—he's a creature of habit* (= he likes to do the same things at the same time every day). **IDM a/the creature of sb | sb's creature** (*formal*, *disapproving*) a person or thing that is completely dependent on sb else and is controlled by them

creature 'comforts *noun* [pl.] all the things that make life, or a particular place, comfortable, such as good food, comfortable furniture or modern equipment

crèche (also **creche**) /kreʃ/ *noun* **1** (*BrE*) a place where babies and small children are looked after while their parents are working, studying, shopping, etc. **2** (*AmE*) = CRIB (3)—compare DAY NURSERY

cred /kred/ *noun* [U] = STREET CRED

cre·dence /'kriːdns/ *noun* [U] (*formal*) **1** a quality that an idea or a story has that makes you believe it is true: *Historical evidence lends credence to his theory.* **2** belief in sth as true: *They could give no credence to the findings of the survey.* ◊ *Alternative medicine has been gaining credence* (= becoming more widely accepted) *in recent years.*

cre·den·tial /krə'denʃl/ *verb* [VN] (*AmE*) to provide sb with credentials

cre·den·tials /krə'denʃlz/ *noun* [pl.] **1 ~** (**as/for sth**) the qualities, training or experience that make you suitable to do sth: *He has all the credentials for the job.* ◊ *She will first have to establish her leadership credentials.* **2** documents such as letters that prove that you are who you claim to be, and can therefore be trusted: *to examine sb's credentials*

cred·ibil·ity /ˌkredə'brləti/ *noun* [U] the quality that sb/sth has that makes people believe or trust them: *to gain/lack/lose credibility* ◊ *The prosecution did its best to undermine the credibility of the witness.* ◊ *Newspapers were talking of a credibility gap between what he said and what he did.*—see also STREET CRED

cred·ible /'kredəbl/ *adj.* **1** that can be believed or trusted [SYN] CONVINCING: *a credible explanation/witness* ◊ *It is just not credible that she would cheat.* **2** that can be accepted, because it seems possible that it could be successful: *Community service is seen as the only credible alternative to imprisonment.* ▶ **cred·ibly** /-əbli/ *adv.*: *We can credibly describe the band's latest album as their best yet.*

credit /'kredɪt/ *noun, verb*
■ *noun*
BUY NOW—PAY LATER | **1** [U] an arrangement that you make, with a shop/store for example, to pay later for sth you buy: *to get/refuse credit* ◊ *We bought the dishwasher on credit.* ◊ *to give/offer interest-free credit* (= allow sb to pay later, without any extra charge) ◊ *a credit agreement* ◊ *credit facilities/terms* ◊ *Your credit limit is now £2000.* ◊ *He's a bad credit risk* (= he is unlikely to pay the money later).—compare HIRE PURCHASE
MONEY BORROWED | **2** [U, C] money that you borrow from a bank; a LOAN: *The bank refused further credit to the company.* **3** [U] the status of being trusted to pay back money to sb who lends it to you: *Her credit isn't good anywhere now.*
MONEY IN BANK | **4** [U] if you or your bank account are in credit, there is money in the account **5** [C, U] a sum of money paid into a bank account; a record of the payment: *a credit of £50* ◊ *You'll be paid by direct credit into your bank account.*—compare DEBIT
MONEY BACK | **6** [C, U] (*technical*) a payment that sb has a right to for a particular reason: *a tax credit*
PRAISE | **7** [U] **~** (**for sth**) praise or approval because you are responsible for sth good that has happened: *He's a player who rarely seems to get the credit he deserves.* ◊ *I can't take all the credit for the show's success—it was a team effort.* ◊ *We did all the work and she gets all the credit!* ◊ *Credit will be given in the exam for good spelling*

and grammar. ◊ *At least give him credit for trying* (= praise him because he tried, even if he did not succeed) .—compare BLAME, DISCREDIT **8** [sing.] **~ to sb/sth** a person or a thing whose qualities or achievements are praised and who therefore earns respect for sb/sth else: *She is a credit to the school.*
ON MOVIE/TV PROGRAMME | **9** [C, usually pl.] the act of mentioning sb who worked on a project such as a film/movie or a television programme: *She was given a programme credit for her work on the costumes for the play.* ◊ *The credits* (= the list of all the people involved) *seemed to last almost as long as the film!*
UNIT OF STUDY | **10** [C] a unit of study at a college or university (in the US, also at a school); the fact of having successfully completed a unit of study: *My math class is worth three credits.*
IDM do sb credit | do credit to sb/sth if sth does credit to a person or an organization, they deserve to be praised for it: *Your honesty does you great credit.* **have sth to your credit** to have achieved sth: *He's only 30, and he already has four novels to his credit.* **on the 'credit side** used to introduce the good points about sb/sth, especially after the bad points have been mentioned **to sb's credit** making sb deserve praise or respect: *To his credit, Jack never told anyone exactly what had happened.*
■ *verb*
PUT MONEY IN BANK | **1** [VN] **~ A** (**with B**) | **~ B to A** to add an amount of money to sb's bank account: *Your account has been credited with $50000.* ◊ *$50000 has been credited to your account.*
WITH ACHIEVEMENT | **2** [VN] [usually passive] **~ A** (**with B**) | **~ B to A** to believe or say that sb is responsible for doing sth, especially sth good: *The company is credited with inventing the industrial robot.* ◊ *The invention of the industrial robot is credited to the company.* ◊ *All the contributors are credited on the title page.*
WITH QUALITY | **3** [VN] **~ A with B** to believe that sb/sth has a particular good quality or feature: *I credited you with a little more sense.* **4** [VN] [usually passive] **~ sb/sth as sth** to believe that sb/sth is of a particular type or quality: *The cheetah is generally credited as the world's fastest animal.*
BELIEVE | **5** (*BrE*) (used mainly in questions and negative sentences) to believe sth, especially sth surprising or unexpected: [VN] *He's been promoted—would you credit it?* [also∨wh-, ∨that]

cred·it·able /'kredɪtəbl/ *adj.* (*formal*) **1** of a quite good standard and deserving praise or approval: *It was a very creditable result for the team.* **2** morally good: *There was nothing very creditable in what he did.* ▶ **cred·it·ably** /'kredɪtəbli/ *adv.*

'credit account *noun* (*BrE*) = ACCOUNT (3)

'credit card *noun* a small plastic card that you can use to buy goods and services and pay for them later: *All major credit cards are accepted at our hotels.*—see also CHARGE CARD, CHEQUE CARD, DEBIT CARD, STORE CARD—picture at MONEY

'credit note *noun* (*BrE*) a letter that a shop/store gives you when you have returned sth and that allows you to have goods of the same value in exchange

cred·it·or /'kredɪtə(r)/ *noun* a person, company, etc. that sb owes money to: *The property will be sold to pay off their creditors.*

'credit rating *noun* a judgement made by a bank, etc. about how likely sb is to pay back money that they borrow, and how safe it is to lend money to them

'credit transfer *noun* (*BrE*) the process of sending money from one person's bank account to another's

'credit union *noun* an organization that lends money to its members at low rates of interest

credit·worthy /'kredɪtwɜːði; *AmE* -wɜːrði/ *adj.* able to be trusted to pay back money that is owed; safe to lend money to ▶ **credit·worthi·ness** *noun* [U]

credo /'kriːdəʊ; 'kreɪdəʊ; *AmE* -doʊ/ *noun* (*pl.* **credos**) (*formal*) a set of beliefs

cre·du·lity /krɪ'djuːləti; *AmE* -'duː-/ *noun* [U] (*formal*) the

b	d	f	g	h	k	l	m	n	p	r
bad	**d**id	**f**all	**g**et	**h**at	**c**at	**l**eg	**m**an	**n**ow	**p**en	**r**ed

ability or willingness to believe that sth is real or true: *The plot of the novel stretches credulity to the limit* (= it is almost impossible to believe).

credu·lous /ˈkredjələs; *AmE* -dʒə-/ *adj.* (*formal*) too ready to believe things and therefore easy to deceive—compare INCREDULOUS

creed /kriːd/ *noun* **1** a set of principles or religious beliefs: *people of all races, colours and creeds* ◇ *What is his political creed?* **2** (**the Creed**) [sing.] a statement of Christian belief that is spoken as part of some church services

creek /kriːk/ *noun* **1** (*BrE*) a narrow area of water where the sea flows into the land SYN INLET **2** (*AmE, AustralE*) a small river or stream IDM **up the 'creek (without a 'paddle)** (*spoken*) in a difficult or bad situation: *I was really up the creek without my car.*

creel /kriːl/ *noun* a basket for holding fish that have just been caught

creep /kriːp/ *verb, noun*
■ *verb* (**crept, crept** /krept/) [V] [usually +*adv./prep.*] **1** (of people or animals) to move slowly, quietly and carefully, because you do not want to be seen or heard: *I crept up the stairs, trying not to wake my parents.* **2** (*AmE*) to move with your body close to the ground; to move slowly on your hands and knees SYN CRAWL **3** to move or develop very slowly: *A slight feeling of suspicion crept over me.* **4** (of plants) to grow along the ground or up walls using long stems or roots—see also CREEPER **5 ~ (to sb)** (*BrE, informal, disapproving*) to be too friendly or helpful to sb in authority in a way that is not sincere, especially in order to get an advantage from them IDM see FLESH *n.* PHRV **,creep 'in/'into sth** to begin to happen or affect sth: *As the doctors became more tired, errors began to creep into their work.* **,creep 'up** to gradually increase in amount, price, etc: *House prices are creeping up again.* **,creep 'up on sb 1** to move slowly nearer to sb, usually from behind, without being seen or heard: *Don't creep up on me like that!* **2** to begin to affect sb, especially before they realize it: *Tiredness can easily creep up on you while you're driving.*
■ *noun* (*informal*) **1** a person that you dislike very much and find very unpleasant: *He's a nasty little creep!* **2** (*BrE*) a person who is not sincere but tries to win your approval by being nice to you: *He's the sort of creep who would do that kind of thing!* IDM **give sb the 'creeps** (*informal*) to make sb feel nervous and slightly frightened, especially because sb/sth is unpleasant or strange: *This old house gives me the creeps.*

creep·er /ˈkriːpə(r)/ *noun* a plant that grows along the ground, up walls, etc., often winding itself around other plants—see also VIRGINIA CREEPER

creep·ing /ˈkriːpɪŋ/ *adj.* [only before noun] (of sth bad) happening or moving gradually and not easily noticed: *creeping inflation over the past few years*

creepy /ˈkriːpi/ *adj.* (**creep·ier, creepi·est**) (*informal*) **1** causing an unpleasant feeling of fear or slight horror: *a creepy ghost story* ◇ *It's kind of creepy down in the cellar!* **2** strange in a way that makes you feel nervous: *What a creepy coincidence.*

creepy-crawly /ˌkriːpi ˈkrɔːli/ *noun* (*pl.* -**ies**) (*informal*) an insect, a worm, etc. when you think of it as unpleasant

cre·mate /krəˈmeɪt/ *verb* [VN] (*often passive*) to burn a dead body, especially as part of a funeral ceremony

cre·ma·tion /krəˈmeɪʃn/ *noun* **1** [U] the act of cremating sb **2** [C] a funeral at which the dead person is cremated

crema·tor·ium /ˌkreməˈtɔːriəm/ *noun* (*pl.* **crema·toria** /-ˈtɔːriə/ or **crema·tor·iums**) (*AmE* also **crema·tory** /ˈkriːmətɔːri; ˈkrem-/ *pl.* -**ies**) a building in which the bodies of dead people are burned

crème brûlée /ˌkrem bruːˈleɪ/ *noun* [C, U] (*pl.* **crèmes brûlées** /ˌkrem bruːˈleɪ/) (from *French*) a cold DESSERT (= a sweet dish) made from cream, with burnt sugar on top—picture on page A1

crème caramel /ˌkrem ˈkærəmel/ *noun* [C, U] (*pl.* **crèmes caramels** /ˌkrem ˈkærəmel/) (from *French*) a cold DESSERT (= a sweet dish) made from milk, eggs and sugar

crème de la crème /ˌkrem də lɑː ˈkrem/ *noun* [sing.] (from *French, formal* or *humorous*) the best people or things of their kind: *This school takes only the crème de la crème.*

cren·el·lated (*AmE* also **cren·el·ated**) /ˈkrenəleɪtɪd/ *adj.* (*technical*) (of a tower, castle, etc.) having BATTLEMENTS

Cre·ole /ˈkriːəʊl; *AmE* -oʊl/ (also **creole**) *noun* **1** [C] a person of mixed European and African race, especially one who lives in the West Indies **2** [C] a person whose ancestors were among the first Europeans who settled in the West Indies or Spanish America, or one of the French or Spanish people who settled in the southern states of the US: *Creole cookery* **3** [U] a language formed from a mixture of a European language with a local language (especially an African language spoken by SLAVES in the West Indies)—see also PIDGIN

creo·sote /ˈkriːəsəʊt; *AmE* -soʊt/ *noun, verb*
■ *noun* [U] a thick brown liquid that is made from COAL TAR, used to preserve wood
■ *verb* [VN] to paint or preserve sth with creosote

crêpe (also **crepe**) /ˈkreɪp/ *noun* **1** [U] a light thin fabric, made especially from cotton or silk, with a surface that is covered in lines and folds: *a black crêpe dress* ◇ *a crêpe bandage* **2** [U] a type of strong rubber with a rough surface, used for making the soles of shoes: *crêpe-soled shoes* **3** [C] a thin PANCAKE

'crêpe paper *noun* [U] a type of thin brightly coloured paper that stretches and has a surface covered in lines and folds, used especially for making decorations

crept *pt, pp* of CREEP

cres·cendo /krəˈʃendəʊ; *AmE* -doʊ/ *noun* (*pl.* -**os**) [C, U] **1** (*music*) a gradual increase in how loudly a piece of music is played or sung OPP DIMINUENDO **2** a gradual increase in noise; the loudest point of a period of continuous noise SYN SWELL: *Voices rose in a crescendo and drowned him out.* ◇ (*figurative*) *The advertising campaign reached a crescendo just before Christmas.*

cres·cent /ˈkresnt; *BrE* also ˈkreznt/ *noun* **1** [C] a curved shape that is wide in the middle and pointed at each end: *a crescent moon* **2** [C] (often used in street names) a curved street with a row of houses on it: *I live at 7 Park Crescent.* **3** (**the Crescent**) [sing.] the curved shape that is used as a symbol of Islam—see also THE RED CRESCENT

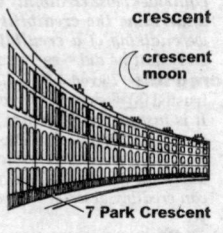

crescent

crescent moon

7 Park Crescent

cress /kres/ *noun* [U] a small plant with thin stems and very small leaves, often eaten in salads and sandwiches—see also WATERCRESS

crest /krest/ *noun, verb*
■ *noun* **1** [usually sing.] **~ (of sth)** the top part of a hill or wave: *surfers riding the crest of the wave* **2** a design used as the symbol of a particular family, organization, etc., especially one that has a long history: *the family/school crest* **3** [C] a group of feathers that stand up on top of a bird's head: *The male is recognizable by its yellow crest.*—picture on page A6 IDM **the crest of a/the 'wave** a situation in which sb is very successful, happy, etc.—more at RIDE *v.*
■ *verb* **1** [VN] (*written*) to reach the top of a hill, mountain or wave: *He slowed the pace as they crested the ridge.* **2** [V] (*AmE*) (of a flood, wave, etc.) to reach its highest level before it falls again: (*figurative*) *The level of debt crested at a massive $290 billion in 1992.*

crest·ed /ˈkrestɪd/ *adj.* **1** marked with a crest: *crested notepaper* **2** used especially in names of birds or animals which have a crest: *crested newts*

crest·fall·en /ˈkrestfɔːlən/ *adj.* sad and disappointed because you have failed and you did not expect to

cre·tin /ˈkretɪn; *AmE* ˈkriːtn/ *noun* (*spoken, offensive*) a very stupid person: *Why did you do that, you cretin?*
▶ **cret·in·ous** /ˈkretɪnəs; *AmE* ˈkriːtnəs/ *adj.*

Creutzfeldt-Jakob disease /ˌkrɔɪtsfelt ˈjækɒb

diːzːz; *AmE* ˈjækɔːb/ *noun* [U] (*abbr.* **CJD**) a brain disease that causes gradual loss of control of the mind and body and, finally, death. It is believed to be caused by PRIONS and is linked to BSE in cows.

cre·vasse /krəˈvæs/ *noun* a deep open crack, especially in ice, for example in a GLACIER—picture at MOUNTAIN

crev·ice /ˈkrevɪs/ *noun* a narrow crack in a rock or wall

crew /kruː/ *noun, verb*

■ *noun* **1** [C+sing./pl. *v.*] all the people working on a ship, plane, etc: *None of the passengers and crew were injured.* ◇ *crew members*—see also AIRCREW, CABIN CREW, FLIGHT CREW **2** [C+sing./pl. *v.*] all the people working on a ship, plane etc. except the officers who are in charge: *the officers and crew* **3** [C+sing./pl. *v.*] a group of people with special technical skills working together: *a film/camera crew* ◇ *an ambulance crew*—see also GROUND CREW **4** [sing.] (*usually disapproving*) a group of people: *The people she invited were a pretty motley crew* (= a strange mix of types of people). **5** [C+sing./pl. *v.*] a team of people who row boats in races: *a member of the Cambridge crew* **6** [U] (*AmE*) the sport of rowing with other people in a boat: *I'm thinking of going out for crew this semester* (= joining the rowing team).

■ *verb* to be part of a crew, especially on a ship: [VN] *Normally the boat is crewed by five people.* ◇ [V] *I crewed for him on his yacht last summer.*

ˈcrew cut *noun* a style of hair for men in which the hair is cut very short—picture at HAIR ▶ **ˈcrew-cut** *adj.*: *crew-cut teenagers*

crew·man /ˈkruːmən/ *noun* (*pl.* **-men** /-mən/) a member of a CREW, usually a man

ˌcrew ˈneck *noun* a round neck on a sweater, etc.

crib /krɪb/ *noun, verb*

■ *noun* **1** (*AmE*) = COT **2** a long open box that horses and cows can eat from SYN MANGER **3** (*BrE*) (*AmE* **crèche**) a model of the scene of Jesus Christ's birth, placed in churches and homes at Christmas **4** (*informal*) written information such as answers to questions, often used dishonestly by students in tests: *a crib sheet* **5** = CRIBBAGE

■ *verb* (**-bb-**) [V, VN] ~ (**sth**) (**from sb**) (*old-fashioned, BrE*) to dishonestly copy work from another student or from a book

crib·bage /ˈkrɪbɪdʒ/ (also **crib**) *noun* [U] a card game in which players score points by collecting different combinations of cards. The score is kept by putting small PEGS in holes in a board.

ˈcrib death *noun* (*AmE*) = COT DEATH

crick /krɪk/ (*AmE also* **kink**) *noun* [usually sing.] a sudden painful stiff feeling in the muscles of your neck or back ▶ **crick** *verb*: [VN] *I suffered a cricked neck during a game of tennis.*

cricket /ˈkrɪkɪt/ *noun* **1** [U] a game played on grass by two teams of 11 players. Players score points (called RUNS) by hitting the ball with a wooden bat and running between two sets of upright wooden sticks, called STUMPS: *a cricket match/team/club/ball*—picture on page 1250 **2** [C] a small brown jumping insect that makes a loud high sound by rubbing its wings together: *the chirping of crickets* IDM **not ˈcricket** (*old-fashioned, BrE, informal*) unfair; not HONOURABLE

crick·et·er /ˈkrɪkɪtə(r)/ *noun* a cricket player

cricket·ing /ˈkrɪkɪtɪŋ/ *adj.* [only before noun] playing cricket; connected with cricket: *cricketing nations* ◇ *a cricketing jersey*

cried *pt, pp* of CRY

crier /ˈkraɪə(r)/ *noun* = TOWN CRIER

cri·key /ˈkraɪki/ *exclamation* (*BrE, old-fashioned, spoken*) used to show that sb is surprised or annoyed: *Crikey, is that the time?*

crime /kraɪm/ *noun* **1** [U] activities that involve breaking the law: *an increase in violent crime* ◇ *the fight against crime* ◇ *Stores spend more and more on crime prevention every year.* ◇ *petty/serious crime* ◇ *the connection between drugs and organized crime* ◇ *He turned to crime when he dropped out of school.* ◇ *The crime rate is rising.* ◇ *crime fiction/novels* (= stories about crime) ◇ *crime fig-*

ures/statistics **2** [C] ~ (**against sb**) an illegal act or activity that can be punished by law: *to commit a crime* (= do sth illegal) ◇ *The massacre was a crime against humanity.*—see also WAR CRIME **3** (**a crime**) [sing.] an act that you think is immoral or is a big mistake: *It's a crime to waste so much money.*

ˈcrime wave *noun* [sing.] a situation in which there is a sudden increase in the number of crimes that are committed

crim·inal /ˈkrɪmɪnl/ *adj., noun*

■ *adj.* **1** [usually before noun] connected with or involving crime: *criminal offences/behaviour* ◇ *criminal damage* (= the crime of damaging sb's property deliberately) ◇ *criminal negligence* (= the illegal act of sb failing to do sth that they should do, with the result that sb else is harmed) **2** [only before noun] connected to the laws that deal with crime: *criminal law* ◇ *the criminal justice system* ◇ *a criminal lawyer* ◇ *to bring criminal charges against sb*—compare CIVIL **3** morally wrong: *This is a criminal waste of resources.*

■ *noun* a person who commits a crime: *Society does not know how to deal with hardened criminals* (= people who regularly commit crimes and are not sorry for what they do). ◇ (*especially AmE*) *a career criminal*

crim·in·al·ity /ˌkrɪmɪˈnæləti/ *noun* [U] the fact of people being involved in crime; criminal acts

crim·in·al·ize (*BrE also* **-ise**) /ˈkrɪmɪnəlaɪz/ *verb* [VN] **1** to make sth illegal by passing a new law: *The use of opium was not criminalized until fairly recently.* **2** to treat sb as a criminal ▶ **crim·in·al·iza·tion, -isa·tion** /ˌkrɪmɪnəlaɪˈzeɪʃn; *AmE* -ləˈz-/ *noun* [U]

crim·in·al·ly /ˈkrɪmɪnəli/ *adv.* according to the laws that deal with crime: *criminally insane*

ˌcriminal ˈrecord *noun* = RECORD (5)

crim·in·ology /ˌkrɪmɪˈnɒlədʒi; *AmE* -ˈnɑː-/ *noun* [U] the scientific study of crime and criminals ▶ **crim·ino·logic·al** /ˌkrɪmɪnəˈlɒdʒɪkl; *AmE* -ˈlɑː-/ *adj.* **crim·in·olo·gist** /-dʒɪst/ *noun*

crimp /krɪmp/ *verb* [VN] **1** to make curls in sb's hair by pressing it with a heated tool: *crimped blonde hair* **2** to press fabric or paper into small folds

crim·son /ˈkrɪmzn/ *adj.* dark red in colour: *She went crimson* (= her face became very red because she was embarrassed). ▶ **crim·son** *noun* [U]

cringe /krɪndʒ/ *verb* [V] **1** to move back and/or away from sb because you are afraid SYN COWER: *a child cringing in terror* **2** to feel very embarrassed and uncomfortable about sth: *I cringe when I think of the poems I wrote then.*

crin·kle /ˈkrɪŋkl/ *verb, noun*

folded   crinkled   crumpled

■ *verb* to become covered with or to form a lot of thin folds or lines, especially in skin, fabric, or paper: [V] *He smiled, his eyes crinkling.* ◇ *Her face crinkled up in a smile.* ◇ *The pages crinkled and curled and turned to ashes in the fire.* [also VN]

■ *noun* a very thin fold or line made on paper, fabric or skin

crin·kly /ˈkrɪŋkli/ *adj.* **1** having a lot of thin folds or lines: *crinkly silver foil* **2** (of hair) having a lot of small curls or waves

crin·ol·ine /ˈkrɪnəlɪn/ *noun* a frame that was worn under a skirt by some women in the past in order to give the skirt a very round full shape

crip·ple /ˈkrɪpl/ *verb, noun*

■ *verb* [VN] [usually passive] **1** to damage sb's body so that they are no longer able to walk or move normally: *He was crippled by polio as a child.* ◇ *to be crippled with arthritis* **2** to seriously damage or harm sb/sth: *The pilot tried to land his crippled plane.* ▶ **crip·pling** *adj.*: *a crippling disease* ◇ *crippling debts*

æ	ɑː	e	ɜː	ə	ɪ	iː	i	ɒ	ɔː	ʌ	ʊ	u	uː
cat	father	ten	bird	about	sit	see	many	got	saw	cup	put	actual	too
								(BrE)					

■ *noun* (*old-fashioned* or *offensive*) a person who is unable to walk or move normally because of a disease or injury: (*figurative*) *He's an emotional cripple* (= he cannot express his feelings). **HELP** People now use **disabled person** instead of 'cripple'.

cri·sis /ˈkraɪsɪs/ *noun* [C, U] (*pl.* **cri·ses** /-siːz/) **1** a time of great danger, difficulty or uncertainty when problems must be solved or important decisions must be made: *a political/financial crisis* ◊ *the government's latest economic crisis* ◊ *The business is still in crisis but it has survived the worst of the recession.* ◊ *The Communist Party was facing an identity crisis.* ◊ *an expert in crisis management* ◊ *We provide help to families in crisis situations.* ◊ *In times of crisis I know which friends I can turn to.* ◊ *The party was suffering a crisis of confidence among its supporters* (= they did not trust it any longer). **2** a time when a problem, a bad situation or an illness is at its worst point: *Their marriage has reached crisis point.* ◊ *The fever has passed its crisis.*—see also CRITICAL

crisp /krɪsp/ *adj., noun, verb*
■ *adj.* (**crisp·er**, **crisp·est**) (usually *approving*) **1** (of food) (also **crispy**) pleasantly hard and dry: *Bake until the pastry is golden and crisp.* **2** (of fruit and vegetables) (also **crispy**) firm and fresh: *a crisp apple/lettuce* **3** (of paper or fabric) fresh and clean; new and slightly stiff without any folds in it: *a crisp new $5 bill* ◊ *a crisp white shirt* **4** (of the air or the weather) pleasantly dry and cold: *a crisp winter morning* ◊ *The air was crisp and clear and the sky was blue.* **5** (of snow, leaves, etc.) firm or dry and making a pleasant noise when crushed: *deep, crisp snow* **6** (of sounds, images, etc.) pleasantly clear and sharp: *The recording sounds very crisp, considering its age.* **7** (sometimes *disapproving*) (of a person's way of speaking) quick and confident in a way that suggests that the person is busy or is not being friendly: *Her answer was crisp, and she gave no details.* ▶ **crisp·ly** *adv.*: *crisply fried potatoes* ◊ *'Take a seat,' she said crisply.* **crisp·ness** *noun* [U]: *The salad had lost its crispness.*
■ *noun* (also **po·tato ˈcrisp**) (both *BrE*) (*AmE* **chip**, **po·tato chip**) a thin round slice of potato that is fried until hard then dried and eaten cold. Crisps are sold in bags and have many different flavours. **IDM** see BURN *v.*
■ *verb* [V, VN] to become or make sth crisp

crisp·bread /ˈkrɪspbred/ *noun* [C, U] a thin crisp biscuit made of wheat or RYE, often eaten with cheese or instead of bread, for example by people who are trying to lose weight

crispy /ˈkrɪspi/ *adj.* (*approving*) = CRISP: *crispy batter*

criss-cross /ˈkrɪs krɒs/ *AmE* /ˈkrɔːs/ *adj., verb*
■ *adj.* [usually before noun] with many straight lines that cross each other: *a criss-cross pattern* ▶ **criss-cross** *noun* [sing.]: *a criss-cross of streets*
■ *verb* to make a pattern on sth with many straight lines that cross each other: [VN] *The city is criss-crossed with canals.* [also V]

cri·ter·ion /kraɪˈtɪəriən; *AmE* -ˈtɪr-/ *noun* (*pl.* **cri·teria** /-riə/) a standard or principle by which sth is judged, or with the help of which a decision is made: *The main criterion is value for money.* ◊ *What criteria are used for assessing a student's ability?*

crit·ic /ˈkrɪtɪk/ *noun* **1** a person who expresses opinions about the good and bad qualities of books, music, etc: *a music/theatre/literary critic* ◊ *The critics loved the movie.* **2** a person who expresses disapproval of sb/sth and talks about their bad qualities, especially publicly: *She is one of the ruling party's most outspoken critics.* ◊ *a critic of private health care*

crit·ic·al /ˈkrɪtɪkl/ *adj.*
EXPRESSING DISAPPROVAL | **1** ~ (of sb/sth) expressing disapproval of sb/sth and saying what you think is bad about them: *a critical comment/report* ◊ *The supervisor is always very critical.* ◊ *Tom's parents were highly critical of the school.*
IMPORTANT | **2** extremely important because a future situation will be affected by it **SYN** CRUCIAL: *a critical factor in the election campaign* ◊ *Reducing levels of carbon dioxide in the atmosphere is of critical importance.* ◊ *Your decision is critical to our future.*
SERIOUS / DANGEROUS | **3** serious, uncertain and possibly dangerous: *The first 24 hours after the operation are the most critical.* ◊ *a critical moment in our country's history* ◊ *One of the victims of the fire remains in a critical condition.*—see also CRISIS
MAKING CAREFUL JUDGEMENTS | **4** involving making fair, careful judgements about the good and bad qualities of sb/sth: *Students are encouraged to develop critical thinking instead of accepting everything they are told without questioning it.*
OF ART / MUSIC / BOOKS, etc. | **5** [only before noun] according to the judgement of critics of art, music, literature, etc: *the film director's greatest critical success* ◊ *In her day she never received the critical acclaim* (= praise from the critics) *she deserved.*
▶ **crit·ic·al·ly** /-kli/ *adv.*: *She spoke critically of her father.* ◊ *He is critically ill in intensive care.* ◊ *I looked at myself critically in the mirror.*

ˌcritical ˈmass *noun* (*physics*) the amount of a substance that is needed for a nuclear CHAIN REACTION to take place

ˌcritical ˈpath *noun* [sing.] (*technical*) the order of work that should be followed to complete a project as fast and as cheaply as possible

criti·cism /ˈkrɪtɪsɪzəm/ *noun* **1** [U, C] ~ (of sb/sth) | ~ (that …) the act of expressing disapproval of sb/sth and opinions about their faults or bad qualities; a statement showing disapproval: *The plan has attracted criticism from consumer groups.* ◊ *There was widespread criticism of the government's handling of the disaster.* ◊ *People in public life must always be open to criticism* (= willing to accept being criticized). ◊ *Ben is very sensitive, he just can't take criticism.* ◊ *to offer sb constructive criticism* (= that is meant to be helpful) ◊ *I didn't mean it as a criticism.* ◊ *criticisms levelled at* (= aimed at/made about) *journalists* ◊ *My only criticism of the house is that it is on a main road.* **2** [U] the work or activity of making fair, careful judgements about the good and bad qualities of sb/sth, especially books, music, etc: *literary criticism*

criti·cize (*BrE* also **-ise**) /ˈkrɪtɪsaɪz/ *verb* **1** ~ sb/sth (for sth) to say that you disapprove of sb/sth; to say what you do not like or think is wrong about sb/sth: [VN] *The decision was criticized by environmental groups.* ◊ *The government has been criticized for not taking the problem seriously.* ◊ [V] *All you ever do is criticize!* **2** [VN] (*BrE*) to judge the good and bad qualities of sth: *We were taught how to criticize poems.*

cri·tique /krɪˈtiːk/ *noun, verb*
■ *noun* a piece of written criticism of a set of ideas, a work of art, etc: *a feminist critique of Freud's theories*
■ *verb* [VN] to write or give your opinion of, or reaction to, a set of ideas, a work of art, etc: *Her job involves critiquing designs by fashion students.*

crit·ter /ˈkrɪtə(r)/ *noun* (*AmE*, *informal*) a living creature: *wild critters*

croak /krəʊk; *AmE* kroʊk/ *verb, noun*
■ *verb* **1** [V] to make a low harsh sound, like the sound a FROG makes **2** to speak or say sth with a low harsh voice: [V] *I had a sore throat and could only croak.* ◊ [VN] *He managed to croak a greeting.* [also V speech] **3** [V] (*slang*) to die
■ *noun* a low harsh sound made in the throat, like the sound made by a FROG

cro·chet /ˈkrəʊʃeɪ; *AmE* kroʊˈʃeɪ/ *noun, verb*
■ *noun* [U] a way of making clothes, etc. from wool or cotton using a special thick needle with a hook at the end to make a pattern of connected threads—picture at SEW
■ *verb* (**cro·chet·ing**, **cro·cheted**) to make sth using crochet: [VN] *a crocheted shawl* [also V]

crock /krɒk; *AmE* kraːk/ *noun* **1** (**crocks**) [pl.] (*old-fashioned*) cups, plates, dishes, etc. **2** [C] (*old use*) a large pot made of baked clay: *a bread crock* **3** [C] (*BrE*, *informal*) an old person **4** [C] (*BrE*, *informal*) an old car in bad condition **IDM** **a ˌcrock of ˈshit** (⚠ *slang*, especially *AmE*) something that is not true—more at GOLD *n.*

aɪ	aʊ	eɪ	əʊ	oʊ	ɔɪ	ɪə	eə	ʊə	j	w
my	now	say	go (BrE)	go (AmE)	boy	near	hair	pure	yes	wet

crocked /krɒkt; *AmE* krɑːkt/ *adj.* [not before noun] (*AmE, slang*) drunk

crock·ery /ˈkrɒkəri; *AmE* ˈkrɑːk-/ *noun* [U] **1** (*especially BrE*) plates, cups, dishes, etc.: *They would like crockery and cutlery as wedding presents.* **2** (*AmE*) dishes, etc. that you use in the oven

croco·dile /ˈkrɒkədaɪl; *AmE* ˈkrɑːk-/ *noun* **1** [C] a large reptile with a long tail, hard skin and very big jaws. Crocodiles live in rivers and lakes in hot countries. **2** [U] crocodile skin made into leather: *crocodile shoes* **3** [C] (*BrE*) a long line of people, especially children, walking in pairs: *a school crocodile* **IDM** ˈcrocodile tears if sb SHEDS (= cries) **crocodile tears**, they pretend to be sad about sth, but they are not really sad at all

cro·cus /ˈkrəʊkəs; *AmE* ˈkroʊ-/ *noun* a small yellow, purple or white flower that appears in early spring

croft /krɒft; *AmE* krɔːft/ *noun* (*BrE*) a small farm or the house on it, especially in Scotland

croft·er /ˈkrɒftə(r); *AmE* ˈkrɔːft-/ *noun* (*BrE*) a person who rents or owns a small family farm, especially in Scotland

crois·sant /ˈkrwæsɒ̃; *AmE* krəˈsɑːnt; krwɑːˈsɑ̃ː/ *noun* (from *French*) a small sweet roll with a curved shape, eaten especially at breakfast—picture on page A1

crone /krəʊn; *AmE* kroʊn/ *noun* (*literary*) an ugly old woman

crony /ˈkrəʊni; *AmE* ˈkroʊni/ *noun* [usually pl.] (*pl.* **-ies**) (often *disapproving*) a person that sb spends a lot of time with: *He was playing cards with his cronies.*

cro·ny·ism /ˈkrəʊnizəm; *AmE* ˈkroʊ-/ *noun* [U] (*disapproving*) the situation in which people in power give jobs to their friends

crook /krʊk/ *noun, verb, adj.*
■ *noun* **1** (*informal*) a dishonest person **SYN** CRIMINAL: *That salesman is a real crook.* **2** ~ **of your arm/elbow** the place where your arm bends at the elbow **3** a long stick with a hook at one end, used especially in the past by SHEPHERDS for catching sheep **IDM** see HOOK *n.*
■ *verb* [VN] to bend your finger or arm
■ *adj.* [not usually before noun] (*AustralE, informal*) ill

crooked /ˈkrʊkɪd/ *adj.* **1** not in a straight line; bent or twisted: *a crooked nose/smile* ◊ *a village of crooked streets and white-walled houses* ◊ *Your glasses are on crooked.* **2** dishonest: *a crooked businessman/deal* ▶ **crook·ed·ly** *adv.*

croon /kruːn/ *verb* to sing sth quietly and gently: [VN] *She gently crooned a lullaby.* [also V]

croon·er /ˈkruːnə(r)/ *noun* (*old-fashioned*) a male singer who sings slow romantic songs

crop /krɒp; *AmE* krɑːp/ *noun, verb*
■ *noun*
PLANTS FOR FOOD | **1** [C] a plant that is grown in large quantities, especially as food: *Sugar has always been an important crop on the island.* ◊ *crop rotation/production/yield* ◊ *The crops are regularly sprayed with pesticides.*—see also CASH CROP **2** [C] the amount of grain, fruit, etc. that is grown in one season: *a fall in this year's coffee crop* ◊ *We are looking forward to a **bumper crop** (= a very large one).*
GROUP OF PEOPLE | **3** [sing.] **a ~ of sth** a group of people who do sth at the same time; a number of things that happen at the same time: *the current crop of graduate trainees* ◊ *She is really **the cream of the crop** (= the best in her group).* ◊ *a crop of disasters/injuries*
WHIP | **4** [C] a short whip used by horse riders: *a riding crop*
HAIR | **5** [C] a very short hairstyle—picture at HAIR **6** [sing.] **a ~ of dark, fair, etc. hair/curls** hair that is short and thick: *He had a thick crop of black curly hair.*
OF BIRD | **7** (*technical*) a part of a bird's throat shaped like a bag where food is stored before it passes into the stomach
■ *verb* (**-pp-**)
HAIR | **1** to cut sb's hair very short: [VN] *closely cropped hair* [also VN-ADJ] —picture at HAIR
PHOTOGRAPH | **2** [VN] (*technical*) to cut off part of a photograph

OF ANIMALS | **3** [VN] to bite off and eat the tops of plants, especially grass: *The horses were quietly cropping the grass.*
PLANTS | **4** [V] (of plants) to produce a crop: *The potatoes cropped well this year.* **5** [VN] to use land to grow crops: *The river valley is intensively cropped.*
PHR V ˌcrop ˈup to appear or happen, especially when it is not expected: *His name just cropped up in conversation.* ◊ *I'll be late—something's cropped up at the office.*

ˈcrop circle (also **ˈcorn circle**) *noun* a circular area in a field of crops that has suddenly become flat. Some people say that crop circles were made by creatures from outer space.

crop·per /ˈkrɒpə(r); *AmE* ˈkrɑːp-/ *noun* **IDM** **come a ˈcropper** (*BrE, informal*) **1** (of a person) to fall over **2** to have a failure or near disaster: *We nearly came a cropper in the second half of the game.*

ˌcrop ˈtop *noun* a woman's informal piece of clothing for the upper body, cut short to leave the stomach bare—picture on page A4

cro·quet /ˈkrəʊkeɪ; *AmE* kroʊˈkeɪ/ *noun* [U] a game played on grass in which players use wooden MALLETS (= hammers with long handles) to knock wooden balls through a series of HOOPS (= curved wires)

cro·quette /krəʊˈket; *AmE* kroʊ-/ *noun* a small amount of MASHED potato, fish, etc., shaped into a ball or tube, covered with BREADCRUMBS and fried

cro·sier (also **croz·ier**) /ˈkrəʊziə(r); *AmE* ˈkroʊʒər/ *noun* a long stick, usually curved at one end, carried by a BISHOP (= a Christian priest of high rank) at religious ceremonies

cross /krɒs; *AmE* krɔːs/ *noun, verb, adj.*
■ *noun*
MARK ON PAPER | **1** [C] a mark or an object formed by two lines crossing each other (X or +); the mark (X) is often used on paper to show sth: *I've put a cross on the map to show where the hotel is.* ◊ *Put a tick if the answer is correct and a cross if it's wrong.* ◊ *Sign your name on the form where I've put a cross.* ◊ *Those who could not write signed with a cross.*—see also NOUGHTS AND CROSSES—compare TICK
FOR PUNISHMENT | **2** [C] a long upright piece of wood with a shorter piece across it near the top. In the past people were hung on crosses and left to die as a punishment.
CHRISTIAN SYMBOL | **3** (**the Cross**) [sing.] the cross that Jesus Christ died on, used as a symbol of Christianity **4** [C] an object, a design, a piece of jewellery, etc. in the shape of a cross, used as a symbol of Christianity: *She wore a small gold cross on a chain around her neck.*
MEDAL | **5** (usually **Cross**) [C] a small decoration in the shape of a cross that is given to sb as an honour for doing sth very brave
MIXTURE | **6** [C, usually sing.] ~ (**between A and B**) a mixture of two different things, breeds of animal, etc: *The play was a cross between a farce and a tragedy.* ◊ *A mule is a cross between a horse and a donkey.*—see also HYBRID
IN SPORT | **7** [C] (in football or hockey) a kick or hit of the ball across the field rather than up or down it—see also THE RED CROSS
IDM **have a (heavy) ˈcross to bear** to have a difficult problem that makes you worried or unhappy but that you have to deal with: *We all have our crosses to bear.*
■ *verb*
GO/PUT ACROSS | **1** ~ (**over**) (**from …**) (**to/into …**) | ~ (**over**) (**sth**) to go across; to pass or stretch from one side to the other: [V] *I waved and she crossed over (= crossed the road towards me).* ◊ *We crossed from Dover to Calais.* ◊ [VN] *to cross a road/the sea/the mountains* ◊ *He crossed over the road and joined me.* ◊ *to cross France by train* ◊ *The bridge crosses the River Dee.* ◊ *A look of annoyance crossed her face.* ◊ *They crossed the finishing line together (= in a race).* **2** [V] to pass across each other: *The roads cross just outside the town.* ◊ *The straps cross over at the back and are tied at the waist.* ◊ *Our letters must have crossed in the mail (= each was sent before the other was received).* ◊ *We seem to have a **crossed line** (= a telephone call that interrupts another call because of a wrong connection).*

b	d	f	g	h	k	l	m	n	p	r
bad	**did**	**fall**	**get**	**hat**	**cat**	**leg**	**man**	**now**	**pen**	**red**

3 [VN] to put or place sth across or over sth else: *to cross your arms / legs* (= place one arm or leg over the other) ◊ *She sat with her legs crossed.* ◊ *a flag with a design of two crossed keys*—picture at CROSS-LEGGED

OPPOSE | **4** [VN] to oppose sb or speak against them or their plans or wishes: *She's really nice until you try to cross her.* ◊ (*literary*) *He had been* **crossed in love** (= was betrayed by the person he loved).

MIX ANIMALS/PLANTS | **5** [VN] **~ A with B | ~ A and B** to make two different types of animal breed together; to mix two types of plant to form a new one: *A mule is the product of a horse crossed with a donkey.* ◊ (*figurative*) *He behaved like an army officer crossed with a professor.*

IN SPORT | **6** [V] (in football, etc.) to kick or pass a ball sideways across the field: *Merson crossed to Joachim.*

DRAW LINE | **7** [VN] to draw a line across sth: *to cross your t's* (= the letters in writing) ◊ (*BrE*) *to cross a cheque* (= to draw two lines across it so that it can only be paid through a bank account)

MAKE CHRISTIAN SYMBOL | **8** [VN] **~ yourself** to make the sign of the CROSS (= the Christian symbol) on your chest

IDM ,**cross your ˈbridges when you ˈcome to them** to worry about a problem when it actually happens and not before **cross your ˈfingers** to hope that your plans will be successful (sometimes putting one finger across another as a sign of hoping for good luck): *I'm crossing my fingers that my proposal will be accepted.* ◊ *Keep your fingers crossed!* **cross my ˈheart (and hope to die)** (*informal*) used to emphasize that you are telling the truth or will do what you promise: *I saw him do it—cross my heart.* **cross your ˈmind** (of thoughts, etc.) to come into your mind: *It never crossed my mind that she might lose* (= I was sure that she would win). ,**cross sb's ˌpalm with ˈsilver** to give sb money so that they will do you a favour, especially tell your FORTUNE ,**cross sb's ˈpath | people's ˌpaths ˈcross** if sb crosses sb's path or their paths cross, they meet by chance: *I hope I never cross her path again.* ◊ *Our paths were to cross again many years later.* **cross ˈswords (with sb)** to fight or argue with sb—more at DOT *v.*, WIRE *n.*

PHR V ,**cross sb/sth↔ˈoff| ,cross sb/sth ˈoff sth** to draw a line through a person's name or an item on a list because they/it is no longer required or involved: *We can cross his name off; he's not coming.* ,**cross sth↔ˈout| ˈthrough** to draw a line through a word, usually because it is wrong ,**cross ˈover (to/into sth)** to move or change from one type of culture, music, political party, etc. to another: *a cult movie that has crossed over to mass appeal*—related noun CROSSOVER

■ *adj.* (**cross·er, cross·est**) **~ (with sb)** (*especially BrE*) annoyed or quite angry: *I was cross with him for being late.* ◊ *Please don't get cross. Let me explain.* ▶ **cross·ly** *adv.*: *'Well what did you expect?' she said crossly.*

cross- /krɒs; AmE krɔːs/ *combining form* (in nouns, verbs, adjectives and adverbs) involving movement or action from one thing to another or between two things: *cross-Channel ferries* ◊ *cross-fertilize* ◊ *crossfire*

cross·bar /ˈkrɒsbɑː(r); AmE ˈkrɔːs-/ *noun* **1** the bar joining the two upright posts of a football goal **2** the bar between the seat and the HANDLEBARS of a man's bicycle—picture at BICYCLE

cross·bones /ˈkrɒsbəʊnz; AmE ˈkrɔːsboʊnz/ *noun* [pl.] ⇨ SKULL AND CROSSBONES

ˈcross-border *adj.* [only before noun] involving activity across a border between two countries: *a cross-border raid by guerrillas*

cross·bow /ˈkrɒsbəʊ; AmE ˈkrɔːsboʊ/ *noun* a weapon which consists of a BOW²(1) that is fixed onto a larger piece of wood, and that shoots short heavy arrows (called BOLTS)

ˈcross-breed *verb, noun*
■ *verb* to make an animal or a plant breed with a different breed; to breed with an animal or a plant of a different breed: [VN] *cross-bred sheep* [also V] ▶ **cross-ˈbreeding** *noun* [U]
■ *noun* an animal or a plant that is a result of cross-breeding—compare HYBRID

,**cross-ˈcheck** *verb* **~ sth (against sth)** to make sure that information, figures etc. are correct by using a different method or system to check them: [VN] *Cross-check your answers with a calculator.* ◊ *Baggage should be cross-checked against the names of individual passengers.* [also V] ▶ **ˈcross-check** *noun*

,**cross-ˈcountry** *adj., noun*
■ *adj.* [usually before noun], *adv.* **1** across fields or open country rather than on roads or a track: *cross-country running/skiing* ◊ *We rode cross-country.*—picture at SKIING **2** from one part of a country to the other, especially not using main roads or routes: *cross-country train journeys*
■ *noun* **1** (**the cross-country**) [sing.] a cross-country running or skiing race **2** [U] the sport of running or skiing across country—compare DOWNHILL *n.*

,**cross-ˈcultural** *adj.* involving or containing ideas from two or more different countries or cultures

ˈcross-current *noun* **1** a current of water in a river or in the sea that flows across the main current **2** [often pl.] (*formal*) a set of beliefs, opinions or ideas that are different from others, especially from those that most people hold

,**cross-curˈricular** *adj.* (*BrE*) affecting or connected with different parts of the school CURRICULUM: *cross-curricular themes*

,**cross-ˈdressing** *noun* [U] the practice of wearing clothes usually worn by a person of the opposite sex, especially for sexual pleasure SYN TRANSVESTISM ▶ ,**cross-ˈdresser** *noun*

,**cross-eˈxamine** *verb* [VN] to question sb carefully and in a lot of detail about answers that they have already given, especially in a court of law: *The witness was cross-examined for over two hours.* ▶ ,**cross-e,xamiˈnation** *noun* [U, C]: *He broke down under cross-examination* (= while he was being cross-examined) *and admitted his part in the assault.*

,**cross-ˈeyed** *adj.* having one or both eyes looking inwards towards the nose

,**cross-ˈfertil·ize** (*BrE also* **-ise**) *verb* [VN] **1** (*biology*) to FERTILIZE a plant using POLLEN from a different type of plant **2** (*written*) to help sth develop in a useful or positive way by mixing ideas from a different area: *The study of psychology has recently been widely cross-fertilized by new discoveries in genetics.* ▶ ,**cross-,fertil·iˈza·tion, -isa·tion** *noun* [U, sing.]

cross·fire /ˈkrɒsfaɪə(r); AmE ˈkrɔːs-/ *noun* [U] the firing of guns from two or more directions at the same time, so that the bullets cross: *The doctor was killed in crossfire as he went to help the wounded.* ◊ (*figurative*) *When two industrial giants clash, small companies can get* **caught in the crossfire** (= become involved and suffer as a result).

ˈcross-hatch *verb* [VN] (*technical*) to mark or colour sth with two sets of parallel lines crossing each other ▶ **ˈcross-hatching** *noun* [U]

cross·ing /ˈkrɒsɪŋ; AmE ˈkrɔːs-/ *noun* **1** a place where you can safely cross a road, a river, etc., or from one country to another: *The child was killed when a car failed to stop at the crossing.* ◊ *The next crossing point is a long way downstream.* ◊ *He was arrested by guards at the border crossing.*—see also LEVEL CROSSING, PEDESTRIAN CROSSING, PELICAN CROSSING, ZEBRA CROSSING **2** a place where two lines, two roads or two tracks cross **3** a journey across a sea or a wide river: *a three-hour ferry crossing* ◊ *a rough crossing from Dover to Calais* ◊ *the first Atlantic crossing* **4** an act of going from one side to another: *attempted crossings of the border*

cross-legged /,krɒs ˈlegd; -ˈlegɪd; AmE ,krɔːs/ *adv.* sitting on the floor with your legs pulled up in front of you and with one leg or foot over the other ▶ **cross-legged** *adj.*: *the cross-legged figure of the Hindu god*

cross·over /ˈkrɒsəʊvə(r); AmE ˈkrɔːsoʊ-/ *noun* the process or result of changing from one area of activity or style of doing sth to another: *The album was an exciting jazz-pop crossover.*

cross·piece /ˈkrɒspiːs; AmE ˈkrɔːs-/ *noun* (*technical*) a

s	t	v	z	ʃ	3	tʃ	dʒ	θ	ð	ŋ
see	tea	van	zoo	shoe	vision	chain	jam	thin	this	sing

cross-legged

with her legs crossed

piece of a structure or a tool that lies or is fixed across another piece

‚cross ˈpurposes *noun* [pl.] if two people are **at cross purposes**, they do not understand each other because they are talking about or aiming at different things, without realizing it: *I think we're talking at cross purposes; that's not what I meant at all.*

‚cross-ˈquestion *verb* to question sb thoroughly and often in a way that seems aggressive: *Two police officers spent the next hour cross-questioning me.*

‚cross-ˈreference *noun, verb*
■ *noun* ~ **(to sth)** a note that tells a reader to look in another part of a book or file for further information
■ *verb* [VN] [usually passive] ~ **sth (to/with sth)** to provide a book with cross-references

cross·roads /ˈkrɒsrəʊdz; *AmE* ˈkrɔːsroʊdz/ *noun* (*pl.* **cross·roads**) a place where two roads meet and cross each other: *At the next crossroads, turn right.* ◇ (*figurative*) *He has reached a career crossroads* (= he must decide which way to go next in his career).—see also INTERSECTION, JUNCTION **IDM** **at a/the ˈcrossroads** at an important point in sb's life or development

ˈcross section *noun* **1** [C, U] what you see when you cut through the middle of sth so that you can see the different layers it is made of; a drawing of this view: *a diagram representing a cross section of the human eye* ◇ *the human eye in cross section* **2** [C, usually sing.] a group of people or things that are typical of a larger group: *a representative cross section of society*

ˈcross stitch *noun* [C, U] a stitch in EMBROIDERY formed by two stitches crossing each other; SEWING in which this stitch is used

ˈcross street *noun* (*AmE*) a street that crosses another street

cross·town /ˌkrɒsˈtaʊn; *AmE* ˌkrɔːs-/ *adj.* (*AmE*) going from one side of a town or city to the other: *a crosstown bus*

cross·walk /ˈkrɒswɔːk; *AmE* ˈkrɔːs-/ *noun* (*AmE*) = PEDESTRIAN CROSSING

cross·wind /ˈkrɒswɪnd; *AmE* ˈkrɔːs-/ *noun* a wind that is blowing across the direction that you are moving in: *Strong crosswinds blew the plane off course.*

cross·wise /ˈkrɒswaɪz; *AmE* ˈkrɔːs-/ *adv.* **1** across, especially from one corner to the opposite one: *Cut the fabric crosswise.* **2** in the form of a cross

cross·word /ˈkrɒswɜːd; *AmE* ˈkrɔːswɜːrd/ (also **ˈcrossword puzzle**) *noun* a game in which you have to fit words across and downwards into spaces with numbers in a square diagram. You find the words by solving CLUES: *to do a/the crossword* ◇ *I've finished the crossword apart from 3 across and 10 down.*

crossword

¹C	R	²E	S	³T	
L		M		H	
⁴U	S	A	G	E	
E		I		R	
⁵S	O	L	V	E	

crotch /krɒtʃ; *AmE* krɑːtʃ/ (also **crutch**) *noun* **1** the part of the body where the legs

join at the top, including the area around the GENITALS **2** the part of a pair of trousers/pants, etc. that covers the crotch: *There's a hole in the crotch.*

crot·chet /ˈkrɒtʃɪt; *AmE* ˈkrɑːtʃ-/ (*BrE*) (*AmE* **quarter note**) *noun* (*music*) a note that lasts half as long as a MINIM/HALF NOTE—picture at MUSIC

crot·chety /ˈkrɒtʃəti; *AmE* ˈkrɑːtʃ-/ *adj.* (*informal*) bad-tempered; easily made angry: *He was tired and crotchety.*

crouch /kraʊtʃ/ *verb, noun*
■ *verb* [V] [usually +*adv./prep.*] to lower your body close to the ground by bending your legs under you: *He crouched down beside her.* ◇ *Doyle crouched behind a hedge.*—picture at KNEEL ▶ **crouched** *adj.*: *She sat crouched in a corner.* **PHRV** **ˈcrouch over sb/sth** to bend over sb/sth so that you are very close to them or it: *He crouched over the papers on his desk.*
■ *noun* [sing.] a crouching position: *She dropped to a crouch.*

croup /kruːp/ *noun* [U] a disease of children that makes them cough a lot and have difficulty breathing

croup·ier /ˈkruːpieɪ; *AmE* also -piər/ *noun* a person whose job is to be in charge of a gambling table and collect and pay out money, give out cards, etc.

crou·ton /ˈkruːtɒn; *AmE* -tɑːn/ *noun* a small piece of cold crisp fried bread served in soup or as part of a salad

crow /krəʊ; *AmE* kroʊ/ *noun, verb*
■ *noun* **1** a large black bird with a harsh cry **2** a sound like that of a COCK/ROOSTER crowing: *She gave a little crow of triumph.* **IDM** **as the ˈcrow flies** in a straight line: *The villages are no more than a mile apart as the crow flies.*—more at EAT, STONE *v.*
■ *verb* **1** [V] (of a COCK/ROOSTER) to make repeated loud high sounds, especially early in the morning **2** ~ **(about/over sth)** (*disapproving*) to talk too proudly about sth you have achieved, especially when sb else has been unsuccessful **SYN** BOAST: [V] *He won't stop crowing about his victory.* ◇ [V speech] *'I've won, I've won!' she crowed.* [also V that] **3** [V] (*BrE*) (of a baby) to make happy sounds

crow·bar /ˈkrəʊbɑː(r); *AmE* ˈkroʊ-/ *noun* a straight iron bar, usually with a curved end, used for forcing open boxes and moving heavy objects

crowd /kraʊd/ *noun, verb*
■ *noun* **1** [C+sing./pl. *v.*] a large number of people gathered together in a public place, for example in the streets or at a sports game: *He pushed his way through the crowd.* ◇ *A small crowd had gathered outside the church.* ◇ *Police had to break up the crowd.* ◇ *Crowds of people poured into the street.* ◇ *I want to get there early to avoid the crowds.* ◇ *The match attracted a capacity crowd of 80000.* ◇ *The crowd cheered the winning hit.* ◇ *crowd control* ◇ *crowd trouble* ◇ *A whole crowd of us are going to the ball* (= a lot of us). ◇ *He left the hotel surrounded by crowds of journalists.* **2** [C+sing./pl. *v.*] (*informal, often disapproving*) a particular group of people: *Bob introduced her to some of the usual crowd* (= people who often meet each other). ◇ *the bright young theatrical crowd* **3** (**the crowd**) [sing.] (sometimes *disapproving*) ordinary people, not special or unusual in any way: *We all like to think we stand out from the crowd* (= are different from and better than other people). ◇ *He prefers to be one of the crowd.* ◇ *She's quite happy to follow the crowd.*
■ *verb* [VN] **1** to fill a place so there is little room to move: *Thousands of people crowded the narrow streets.* **2** to fill your mind so that you can think of nothing else: *Memories crowded his mind.* **3** (*informal*) to stand very close to sb so that they feel uncomfortable or nervous **PHRV** **‚crowd aˈround/ˈround**|**‚crowd aˈround/ˈround sb/sth** to gather in large numbers around sb/sth: *We all crowded around the stove to keep warm.* ◇ *Photographers were crowding around outside.* **‚crowd ˈin (on sb)**|**‚crowd ˈinto sth** (*written*) (of thoughts, questions etc.) to fill your mind so that you can think of nothing else: *Too many uncomfortable thoughts were crowding in on her.* ◇ *Memories came crowding into her mind.* **‚crowd ˈinto/ˈonto sth**|**‚crowd ˈin** to move in large numbers into a small space: *We all crowded into her office to sing 'Happy Birthday'.* **‚crowd sb/sth ˈinto/ˈonto sth**|**‚crowd sb/sth ˈin** to put

C

many people or things into a small space: *Guests were crowded into the few remaining rooms.* **crowd sb/sth 'out** (*BrE*) to fill a place so that other people or things are kept out

crowd·ed /'kraʊdɪd/ *adj.* ~ (**with sth**) **1** having a lot of people or too many people: *crowded streets* ◊ *a crowded bar* ◊ *In the spring the place is crowded with skiers.* ◊ *London was very crowded.*—compare UNCROWDED **2** full of sth: *a room crowded with books* ◊ *We have a very crowded schedule.*

'crowd-pleaser *noun* (*informal*) a person or performance that always pleases an audience

'crowd-puller *noun* (*informal*) a person or thing that always attracts a large audience

crown /kraʊn/ *noun, verb*

■ *noun*

OF KING/QUEEN | **1** [C] a circular ornament, usually made of gold and jewels, that a king or queen wears on his or her head on official occasions—picture at HAT **2** (**the Crown**) [sing.] the government of a country, thought of as being represented by a king or queen: *land owned by the Crown* ◊ *a Minister of the Crown* ◊ *Who's appearing for the Crown* (= bringing a criminal charge against sb on behalf of the state) *in this case?* **3** (**the crown**) [sing.] the position or power of a king or queen: *She refused the crown* (= refused to become queen). ◊ *his claim to the French crown* OF FLOWERS/LEAVES | **4** [C] a circle of flowers, leaves, etc. that is worn on sb's head, sometimes as a sign of victory IN SPORTS COMPETITION | **5** [C, usually sing.] (*informal*) the position of winning a sports competition: *She is determined to retain her Wimbledon crown.* OF HEAD/HAT | **6** (usually **the crown**) [sing.] the top part of the head or a hat HIGHEST PART | **7** (usually **the crown**) [sing.] the highest part of sth: *the crown of a hill* ON TOOTH | **8** [C] an artificial cover for a damaged tooth SHAPE | **9** [C] anything in the shape of a crown, especially an ornament or a BADGE MONEY | **10** [C] a unit of money in several European countries: *Czech crowns* **11** [C] an old British coin worth five SHILLINGS (= now 25p) **IDM** see JEWEL

■ *verb*

KING/QUEEN | **1** to put a crown on the head of a new king or queen as a sign of royal power: [VN] *Queen Elizabeth was crowned in 1953.* ◊ [VN-N] *The prince was soon to be crowned King of England.* COVER TOP | **2** [VN] [usually passive] ~ **sth** (**with sth**) (*written*) to form or cover the top of sth: *His head was crowned with a mop of brown curls.* MAKE COMPLETE | **3** [VN] [often passive] ~ **sth** (**with sth**) to make sth complete or perfect, especially by adding an achievement, a success, etc: *The award of the Nobel Prize has crowned a glorious career in physics.* ◊ *Their efforts were finally crowned with success.* HIT ON HEAD | **4** [VN] (*old-fashioned, slang*) to hit sb on the head TOOTH | **5** [VN] to put an artificial cover on a tooth [SYN] CAP: *I've had one of my teeth crowned.* **IDM** **to crown it 'all** (*BrE*) used to say that sth is the final and worst event in a series of unpleasant or annoying events: *It was cold and raining, and, to crown it all, we had to walk home.*

crown 'colony *noun* a COLONY ruled directly by the British government

Crown 'Court *noun* (in England and Wales) a court of law which deals with criminal cases, with a judge and JURY—compare COUNTY COURT

crown·ing /'kraʊnɪŋ/ *adj.* [only before noun] making sth perfect or complete: *The cathedral is the **crowning glory** of the city.* ◊ *His 'Beethoven' sculpture is seen as the crowning achievement of his career.*

crown 'jewels *noun* [pl.] the CROWN and other royal ornaments worn or carried by a king or queen on formal occasions

Crown 'prince *noun* (in some countries), a prince who will become king when the present king or queen dies: *Crown Prince Wilhelm*

Crown prin'cess *noun* **1** the wife of a Crown prince **2** (in some countries), a princess who will become queen when the present king or queen dies: *Crown Princess Beatrice*

'crow's feet *noun* [pl.] lines in the skin around the outer corner of a person's eye

'crow's-nest *noun* a platform at the top of a ship's MAST (= the post that supports the sails) from which sb can see a long way and watch for land, danger, etc.

croz·ier = CROSIER

cru·cial /'kruːʃl/ *adj.* ~ (**to/ for sth**)| ~ (**that ...**) extremely important, because it will affect other things: *a crucial factor / issue / decision* ◊ *topics of crucial importance for education* ◊ *Winning this contract is crucial to the success of the company.* ◊ *The next few weeks are going to be crucial.* ◊ *It is crucial that we get this right.* ◊ *Parents play a crucial role in preparing their child for school.* ◊ *He wasn't there at the crucial moment* (= when he was needed most). ▶ **cru·cial·ly** /-ʃəli/ *adv.*: *crucially important*

cru·ci·ble /'kruːsɪbl/ *noun* **1** a pot in which substances are heated to high temperatures, metals are melted, etc.—picture at LABORATORY **2** (*formal* or *literary*) a place or situation in which people or ideas are tested severely, often creating sth new or exciting in the process

cru·ci·fix /'kruːsəfɪks/ *noun* a model of a cross with a figure of Jesus Christ on it, as a symbol of the Christian religion

cru·ci·fix·ion /ˌkruːsə'fɪkʃn/ *noun* (sometimes **Crucifixion**) **1** [C, U] the act of killing sb by fastening them to a cross: *the Crucifixion* (= of Jesus) **2** [C] a painting or other work of art representing the crucifixion of Jesus Christ

cru·ci·form /'kruːsɪfɔːm; *AmE* -fɔːrm/ *adj.* (*technical*) (especially of buildings) in the shape of a cross

cru·ci·fy /'kruːsɪfaɪ/ *verb* (**cru·ci·fies, cru·ci·fy·ing, cru·ci·fied, cru·ci·fied**) [VN] **1** to kill sb as a punishment by fastening them to a wooden cross **2** (*informal*) to criticize or punish sb very severely: *The prime minister was crucified in the press for his handling of the affair.*

crud /krʌd/ *noun* [U] (*informal*) any dirty or unpleasant substance

crude /kruːd/ *adj., noun*

■ *adj.* (**cruder, cru·dest**) **1** simple and not very accurate but giving a general idea of sth: *In crude terms, the causes of mental illness seem to be of three main kinds.* **2** (of objects or works of art) simply made, not showing much skill or attention to detail: *a crude drawing of a face* **3** (of people or the way they behave) offensive or rude, especially about sex [SYN] VULGAR: *crude jokes / language* **4** [usually before noun] (of oil and other natural substances) in its natural state, before it has been treated with chemicals: *crude oil / metal* ▶ **crude·ly** *adv.*: *a crudely drawn ship* ◊ *To put it crudely, the poor are going without food so that the rich can drive cars.* **crude·ness** *noun* [U]

■ *noun* (also **crude 'oil**) [U] oil in its natural state, before it has been treated with chemicals: *50000 barrels of crude*

cru·di·tés /'kruːdɪteɪ; *AmE* ˌkruːdɪ'teɪ/ *noun* [pl.] (from French) pieces of raw vegetables that are eaten at the beginning of a meal

cru·dity /'kruːdəti/ *noun* [U, C] (*pl.* **-ies**) (*written*) the fact of being CRUDE; an example of sth CRUDE: *Despite the crudity of their methods and equipment, the experiment was a considerable success.* ◊ *the novel's structural crudities* ◊ *The crudity of her language shocked him.*

cruel /'kruːəl/ *adj.* (**cruel·ler, cruel·lest**) **1** ~ (**to sb/sth**) having a desire to cause pain and suffering: *a cruel dictator* ◊ *I can't stand people who are cruel to animals.* ◊ *Her eyes were cruel and hard.* ◊ *Sometimes you have to be **cruel to be kind** (= make sb suffer because it will be good for them later). **2** causing pain or suffering: *a cruel punishment / joke* ◊ *Her father's death was a **cruel blow**.*

aɪ	aʊ	eɪ	əʊ	oʊ	ɔɪ	ɪə	eə	ʊə	j	w
my	now	say	go (BrE)	go (AmE)	boy	near	hair	pure	yes	wet

▶ **cruel·ly** /ˈkruːəli/ adv.: The dog had been cruelly treated. ◇ I was cruelly deceived.

cruelty /ˈkruːəlti/ noun (pl. -ies) **1** [U] ~ (to sb/sth) behaviour that causes pain or suffering to others, especially deliberately: cruelty to animals ◇ The deliberate cruelty of his words cut her like a knife. **2** [C, usually pl.] a cruel action **3** [C, U] something that happens that seems unfair: the cruelties of life

cruet /ˈkruːɪt/ noun a small container, or set of containers, for salt, pepper, oil, etc. for use on the table at meals

cruise /kruːz/ noun, verb
■ noun a journey by sea, visiting different places, especially as a holiday/vacation: I'd love to go on a round-the-world cruise. ◇ a luxury cruise ship
■ verb **1** to travel in a ship or boat visiting different places, especially as a holiday/vacation: [V, usually +adv./prep.] They cruised down the Nile. ◇ [VN] We spent two weeks cruising the Bahamas. **2** [V] [usually +adv./prep.] (of a car, plane, etc.) to travel at a steady speed: a light aircraft cruising at 4000 feet ◇ a cruising speed of 50 miles an hour **3** (of a car, etc. or its driver) to drive along slowly, especially when you are looking at or for sth: [V, +adv./prep.] She cruised around the block looking for a parking space. ◇ [VN] Taxis cruised the streets, looking for fares. **4** [V+adv./prep.] to win or achieve sth easily: The home team cruised to victory. **5** [V, VN] (slang) to go around in public places looking for a sexual partner

ˈcruise control noun [U] a device in a motor vehicle that allows it to stay at the speed that the driver has chosen

ˌcruise ˈmissile noun a large weapon with a nuclear WARHEAD that flies close to the ground and is guided by its own computer to an exact place

cruiser /ˈkruːzə(r)/ noun **1** a large fast ship used in war **2** (also **ˈcabin cruiser**) a motor boat which you can sleep in, used for pleasure trips—picture at BOAT **3** (AmE) a police car

crumb /krʌm/ noun **1** a very small piece of food, especially of bread or cake, that has fallen off a larger piece: She stood up and brushed the crumbs from her sweater. **2** a small piece or amount: a few crumbs of useful information ◇ The government's only **crumb of comfort** is that their opponents are as confused as they are.

crum·ble /ˈkrʌmbl/ verb, noun
■ verb **1** to break or break sth into very small pieces: [V] Rice flour makes the cake less likely to crumble. ◇ [VN] Crumble the cheese over the salad. **2** [V] if a building or piece of land **is crumbling**, parts of it are breaking off: buildings crumbling into dust ◇ crumbling stonework ◇ The cliff is gradually crumbling away. **3** [V] ~ (into/to sth) | ~ (away) to begin to fail or get weaker or to come to an end: a crumbling business/relationship ◇ All his hopes began to crumble away. ◇ The empire finally crumbled into dust. IDM see WAY n.
■ noun [U, C] (BrE) a DESSERT (= a sweet dish) made from fruit that is covered with a rough mixture of flour, butter and sugar, cooked in the oven and usually served hot: apple crumble and custard

crum·bly /ˈkrʌmbli/ adj. that easily breaks into very small pieces: crumbly soil/cheese

crumbs /krʌmz/ exclamation (old-fashioned, BrE, informal) used to show that you are surprised: Oh crumbs! Is that the time?

crummy /ˈkrʌmi/ adj. (informal) of very bad quality: Most of his songs are pretty crummy.

crum·pet /ˈkrʌmpɪt/ noun (BrE) **1** [C] a small flat round cake with many holes in the top, eaten hot with butter **2** [U] (slang) an offensive way of referring to people who are sexually attractive, usually women

crum·ple /ˈkrʌmpl/ verb **1** ~ (sth) (up) (into sth) to crush sth into folds; to become crushed into folds: [VN] She crumpled the letter up into a ball and threw it on the fire. ◇ [V] This material crumples very easily.—picture at CRINKLE **2** [V] ~ (up) if your face **crumples**, you look sad and disappointed, as if you might cry **3** [V] ~ (up) to fall down in an uncontrolled way because you are injured, unconscious, drunk, etc. SYN COLLAPSE: He crumpled up

in agony. ▶ **crump·led** adj.: crumpled clothes/papers ◇ A crumpled figure lay motionless in the doorway.

crunch /krʌntʃ/ noun, verb, adj.
■ noun **1** [C, usually sing.] a noise like the sound of sth firm being crushed: the crunch of feet on snow ◇ The car drew up with a crunch of gravel. **2** (**the crunch**) [sing.] an important and often unpleasant situation or piece of information: **The crunch came** when she returned from America. ◇ He always says he'll help but **when it comes to the crunch** (= when it is time for action or decision) he does nothing. ◇ The crunch is that we can't afford to go abroad this year. **3** [C, usually sing.] (especially AmE) a situation in which there is suddenly not enough of sth, especially money: a budget/energy/housing crunch
■ verb **1** ~ (on sth) to crush sth noisily between your teeth when you are eating: [VN] She crunched her apple noisily. [also V] **2** to make or cause sth to make a noise like sth hard being crushed SYN SCRUNCH: [V] The snow crunched under our feet. [also VN] **3** [V+adv./prep.] to move over a surface, making a loud crushing noise: I crunched across the gravel to the front door. **4** [VN] (computing) to deal with large amounts of data very quickly—see also NUMBER CRUNCHING PHRV ˌcrunch sth↔ˈup to crush sth completely: He crunched up the empty pack and threw it out of the window.
■ adj. [only before noun] (informal) a **crunch** meeting, sports game, etc. is very important and may be the last chance to succeed: Sunday's crunch game with Leeds

crunchy /ˈkrʌntʃi/ adj. (approving) (especially of food) firm and crisp and making a sharp sound when you bite or crush it: a crunchy salad

cru·sade /kruːˈseɪd/ noun, verb
■ noun **1** ~ (for/against sth) | ~ (to do sth) a long and determined effort to achieve sth that you believe to be right or to stop sth that you believe to be wrong: to lead a crusade against crime ◇ a moral crusade **2** (sometimes **Crusade**) any of the wars fought in Palestine by European Christian countries against the Muslims in the Middle Ages
■ verb [V] to make a long and determined effort to achieve sth that you believe to be right or to stop sth you believe to be wrong SYN CAMPAIGN

cru·sader /kruːˈseɪdə(r)/ noun a person who takes part in a crusade: moral crusaders

crush /krʌʃ/ verb, noun
■ verb **1** to press or squeeze sth so hard that it is damaged or injured, or loses its shape: The car was completely crushed under the truck. ◇ They crush the olives with a heavy wooden press. ◇ Several people were **crushed to death** in the accident. **2** [+adv./prep.] to push or press sb/sth into a small space: Over twenty prisoners were crushed into a small dark cell. **3** to break sth into small pieces or into a powder by pressing hard: Add two cloves of crushed garlic. **4** to become or make sth full of folds or lines **5** to use violent methods to defeat people who are opposing you: The army was sent in to crush the rebellion. **6** to destroy sb's confidence or happiness: She felt completely crushed by the teacher's criticism.
■ noun **1** [C, usually sing.] a crowd of people pressed close together in a small space: a big crush in the theatre bar ◇ I couldn't find a way through the crush. **2** [C] ~ (on sb) a strong feeling of love, that usually does not last very long, that a young person has for sb older: a schoolgirl crush ◇ I had a huge crush on her. **3** [U] a drink made from fruit juice

crush·er /ˈkrʌʃə(r)/ noun (often in compounds) a machine or tool for crushing sth

crush·ing /ˈkrʌʃɪŋ/ adj. [usually before noun] used to emphasize how bad or severe sth is: a **crushing defeat** in the election ◇ The shipyard has been dealt another **crushing blow** with the failure to win this contract. ▶ **crush·ing·ly** adv.

crust /krʌst/ noun **1** [C, U] the hard outer surface of bread: sandwiches with the crusts cut off—picture on page A1 **2** [C, usually sing.] a layer of pastry, especially on top of a pie: Bake until the crust is golden. **3** [C, U] a hard layer or surface, especially above or around sth soft or

C

liquid: *a thin crust of ice* ◊ *the earth's crust*—see also THE UPPER CRUST **IDM** see EARN

crust·acean /krʌˈsteɪʃn/ *noun* (*technical*) any creature with a soft body that is divided into sections, and a hard outer shell. Most crustaceans live in water. CRABS, LOBSTERS and SHRIMPS are all crustaceans.—compare SHELLFISH—picture on page A7

crust·ed /ˈkrʌstɪd/ *adj.* [not usually before noun] ~ (**with sth**) having a hard layer or covering of sth

crusty /ˈkrʌsti/ *adj.* **1** (of food) having a hard outer layer: *fresh crusty bread* **2** (*informal*) (especially of older people) bad-tempered; easily irritated: *a crusty old man*

crutch /krʌtʃ/ *noun* **1** one of two long sticks that you put under your arms to help you walk after you have injured your leg or foot: *After the accident I spent six months on crutches.*—picture on page 598 **2** (usually *disapproving*) a person or thing that gives you help or support but often makes you depend on them too much **3** = CROTCH

crux /krʌks/ *noun* [sing.] **the ~ (of sth)** the most important or difficult part of a problem or an issue: *Now we come to the crux of the matter.*

cry /kraɪ/ *verb, noun*

▪ *verb* (**cries, cry·ing, cried, cried**) **1** ~ (**for sb/sth**)| ~ (**about/over sth**) to produce tears from your eyes because you are unhappy or hurt: [V] *It's all right. Don't cry.* ◊ *The baby was crying for* (= because it wanted) *its mother.* ◊ *There's nothing to cry about.* ◊ *He felt like crying with rage.* ◊ *I just couldn't stop crying.* ◊ [VN] *I found him crying his eyes out* (= crying very much). ◊ *That night she cried herself to sleep.* [also V speech] **2** ~ (**for sth**) to shout loudly: [V] *She ran to the window and cried for help.* ◊ [V speech] *'You're safe!' Tom cried in delight.* ⇨ note at SHOUT **3** [V] (of a bird or an animal) to make a loud harsh noise: *Seagulls followed the boat, crying loudly.* **IDM** ˌcry **ˈfoul** (*informal*) to complain that sb else has done sth wrong or unfair **cry over spilt ˈmilk** (*BrE*) (*AmE* **cry over spilled ˈmilk**) to waste time worrying about sth that has happened that you cannot do anything about **cry ˈwolf** to call for help when you do not need it, with the result that when you do need it people do not believe you **for ˌcrying out ˈloud** (*spoken, informal*) used to show you are angry or surprised: *For crying out loud! Why did you have to do that?*—more at LAUGH *v.*, SHOULDER *n.* **PHRV** ˌcry **ˈoff** (*BrE*) to say that you cannot do sth that you promised to do: *She said she was coming to the party, but cried off at the last moment.* ˌcry **ˈout** to make a loud sound without words because you are hurt, afraid, surprised, etc: *She tried to stop herself from crying out.* ◊ *to cry out in fear/alarm/pain* ˌcry **ˈout**/ˌcry **ˈout sth** to shout sth loudly: *She cried out for help.* ◊ *She cried out his name.* ◊ [+speech] *'Help!' he cried out.* ˌcry **ˈout for sth** (usually in the progressive tenses) to need sth very much: *The company is crying out for fresh new talent.*

▪ *noun* (*pl.* **cries**) **1** [C] a loud sound without words that expresses a strong feeling: *to give a cry of anguish/despair/relief/surprise/terror* **2** [C] a loud shout: *With a cry of 'Stop thief!' he ran after the boy.* ◊ *Her answer was greeted with cries of outrage.* **3** [C] the sound made by a bird or an animal: *the cry of gulls circling overhead* **4** [sing.] an action or a period of crying: *I felt a lot better after a good long cry.* **5** [C] ~ (**for sth**) an urgent demand or request for sth: *Her suicide attempt was really a cry for help.* **6** [C] (especially in compounds) a word or phrase that expresses a group's beliefs and calls people to action: *a battle cry* **IDM in full ˈcry** talking or shouting loudly and in an enthusiastic way: *The Leeds supporters were in full cry.*—more at FAR *adj.*, HUE

cry·baby /ˈkraɪbeɪbi/ *noun* (*pl.* **-ies**) (*informal, disapproving*) a person, especially a child, who cries too often or without good reason: *Don't be such a crybaby.*

cry·ing /ˈkraɪɪŋ/ *adj., noun*

▪ *adj.* [only before noun] **IDM be a crying ˈshame** (*spoken*) used to emphasize that you think sth is extremely bad or shocking: *It's a crying shame to waste all that food.* **a crying ˈneed (for sth)** a great and urgent need for sth

▪ *noun* [U] the sound or act of crying: *the crying of terrified children*

---

cryo·gen·ic /ˌkraɪəˈdʒenɪk/ *adj.* (*technical*) involving the use of very low temperatures: *a cryogenic storage system*

cryo·gen·ics /ˌkraɪəˈdʒenɪks/ *noun* [U] (*physics*) the scientific study of the production and effects of very low temperatures—compare CRYONICS

cry·on·ics /kraɪˈɒnɪks/ *noun* [U] (*medical*) the process of freezing a body at the moment of its death with the hope that it will be brought back to life at some future time—compare CRYOGENICS

crypt /krɪpt/ *noun* a room under the floor of a church, used especially in the past as a place for burying people

cryp·tic /ˈkrɪptɪk/ *adj.* with a meaning that is hidden or not easily understood: *a cryptic message/remark/smile* ◊ *a cryptic crossword clue* ▶ **cryp·tic·al·ly** /-kli/ *adv.*: *'Yes and no,' she replied cryptically.*

crypto- /ˈkrɪptəʊ; *AmE* -toʊ/ *combining form* (in nouns) secret: *a crypto-communist*

crys·tal /ˈkrɪstl/ *noun* **1** [C] a small piece of a substance with many even sides, that is formed naturally when the substance becomes solid: *ice/salt crystals* ◊ *a crystal structure* **2** [U, C] a clear mineral, such as QUARTZ, used in making jewellery and ornaments: *a pair of crystal earrings* **3** [U] glass of very high quality: *a crystal chandelier/vase* **4** [C] (*AmE*) a piece of glass or plastic that covers the face of a watch—see also LIQUID CRYSTAL DISPLAY

ˌcrystal ˈball *noun* a clear glass ball used by people who claim they can predict what will happen in the future by looking into it: *Without a crystal ball, it's impossible to say where we'll be next year.*

ˌcrystal ˈclear *adj.* **1** (of glass, water, etc.) completely clear and bright **2** very easy to understand; completely obvious: *I want to make my meaning crystal clear.*

crys·tal·line /ˈkrɪstəlaɪn/ *adj.* **1** (*technical*) made of or similar to CRYSTALS: *crystalline structure/rocks* **2** (*formal*) very clear **SYN** TRANSPARENT: *water of crystalline purity*

crys·tal·lize (*BrE* also **-ise**) /ˈkrɪstəlaɪz/ *verb* **1** (of thoughts, plans, beliefs, etc.) to become clear and fixed; to make thoughts, beliefs, etc. clear and fixed: [V] *Our ideas began to crystallize into a definite plan.* ◊ [VN] *The final chapter crystallizes all the main issues.* **2** (*technical*) to form or make sth form into CRYSTALS: [V] *The salt crystallizes as the water evaporates.* [also VN] ▶ **crys·tal·liza·tion, -isa·tion** /ˌkrɪstəlaɪˈzeɪʃn; *AmE* -ləˈz-/ *noun* [U, sing.]

crys·tal·lized (*BrE* also **-ised**) /ˈkrɪstəlaɪzd/ *adj.* (especially of fruit) preserved in and covered with sugar

ˈC-section *noun* (*AmE*) = CAESAREAN

CS gas /ˌsiː es ˈɡæs/ *noun* [U] a gas that stings the eyes, producing tears and making it difficult to breathe. CS gas is sometimes used to control crowds.—see also TEAR GAS

CST /ˌsiː es ˈtiː/ *noun* [U] the abbreviation for 'Central Standard Time'

CSYS /ˌsiː es waɪ ˈes/ *abbr.* Certificate of Sixth Year

---

s	t	v	z	ʃ	ʒ	tʃ	dʒ	θ	ð	ŋ
see	tea	van	zoo	shoe	vision	chain	jam	thin	this	sing

Studies (an exam taken by some Scottish school students at the age of 18)

Ct (also **Ct.** especially in *AmE*) *abbr.* (used in written addresses) COURT: *30 Willow Ct*

ct (also **ct.** especially in *AmE*) *abbr.* **1** (in writing) CARAT: *an 18ct gold ring* **2** (in writing) CENT(S): *50 cts*

cu. *abbr.* (in writing) CUBIC: *a volume of 2 cu. m* (= 2 cubic metres)

cub /kʌb/ *noun* **1** [C] a young bear, lion, FOX, etc: *a lioness guarding her cubs* **2** (**the Cubs**) (*BrE*) (*AmE* **the 'Cub Scouts**) [pl.] a branch of the SCOUT ASSOCIATION for boys between the ages of eight and ten or eleven: *to join the Cubs* **3** (Cub) (also '**Cub Scout**) [C] a member of the Cubs—compare BROWNIE

cub·by·hole /ˈkʌbihəʊl; *AmE* -hoʊl/ *noun* a small room or a small enclosed space: *My office is a cubbyhole in the basement.*

cube /kjuːb/ *noun, verb*
■ *noun* **1** a solid or hollow figure with six equal square sides—picture at SOLID **2** a piece of sth, especially food, with six sides: *Cut the meat into cubes.*—see also ICE CUBE, STOCK CUBE, SUGAR CUBE **3** (*mathematics*) the number that you get when you multiply a number by itself twice: *The cube of 5 (5³) is 125 (5×5×5).*
■ *verb* [VN] **1** [usually passive] (*mathematics*) to multiply a number by itself twice: *10 cubed is 1000* **2** to cut food into cubes [SYN] DICE

,**cube 'root** *noun* (*mathematics*) a number which, when multiplied by itself twice, produces a particular number: *The cube root of 64 (∛64) is 4*—compare SQUARE ROOT

cubic /ˈkjuːbɪk/ *adj.* **1** (*abbr.* **cu**) [only before noun] used to show that a measurement is the volume of sth, that is the height multiplied by the length and the width: *cubic centimetres / inches / metres* **2** measured or expressed in cubic units: *The cubic capacity of a car's engine.* **3** having the shape of a cube: *a cubic figure*

cu·bicle /ˈkjuːbɪkl/ *noun* a small room that is made by separating off part of a larger room: *a shower cubicle* ◊ (*BrE*) *a changing cubicle* (= for example at a public swimming pool) ◊ (*especially AmE*) *an office / a library cubicle*

cu·bism (also **Cu·bism**) /ˈkjuːbɪzəm/ *noun* [U] a style and movement in early 20th century art in which objects and people are represented as GEOMETRIC shapes, often shown from many different angles at the same time ▶ **cu·bist** (also **Cu·bist**) *noun*: *The exhibition includes works by the Impressionists and the Cubists.* **cu·bist** (also **Cu·bist**) *adj.* [usually before noun]: *cubist paintings and sculpture*

cu·boid /ˈkjuːbɔɪd/ *noun, adj.*
■ *noun* (*geometry*) a solid object which has six RECTANGULAR sides at RIGHT ANGLES to each other
■ *adj.* shaped approximately like a CUBE

,**cub re'porter** *noun* a young newspaper REPORTER without much experience

cuck·old /ˈkʌkəʊld; *AmE* -oʊld/ *noun, verb*
■ *noun* (*old use, disapproving*) a man whose wife has sex with another man
■ *verb* [VN] **1** (of a man) to make another man a cuckold by having sex with his wife **2** (of a woman) to make her husband a cuckold by having sex with another man

cuckoo /ˈkʊkuː/ *noun, adj.*
■ *noun* (*pl.* **-oos**) a bird with a call that sounds like its name. Cuckoos leave their eggs in the nests of other birds.—see also CLOUD-CUCKOO-LAND
■ *adj.* [not before noun] (*old-fashioned, informal*) crazy

'**cuckoo clock** *noun* a clock that has a small toy bird inside that comes out every hour and marks the hours with a sound like that of a cuckoo

cu·cum·ber /ˈkjuːkʌmbə(r)/ *noun* [C, U] a long vegetable with dark green skin and light green flesh, that is usually eaten raw [IDM] see COOL *adj.*—picture on page A3

cud /kʌd/ *noun* [U] the food that cows and similar animals bring back from the stomach into the mouth to chew again: *cows chewing the cud*

cud·dle /ˈkʌdl/ *verb, noun*
■ *verb* to hold sb/sth close in your arms to show love or affection [SYN] HUG: [V] *A couple of teenagers were kissing and cuddling on the doorstep.* ◊ [VN] *The little boy cuddled the teddy bear close.* [PHRV] **cuddle up (to / against sb/ sth)| cuddle up (together)** to sit or lie very close to sb/sth: *She cuddled up against him.* ◊ *We cuddled up together under the blanket.*
■ *noun* [usually sing.] the action of holding sb close in your arms to show love or affection [SYN] HUG: *to give sb a cuddle*

cud·dly /ˈkʌdli/ *adj.* (*informal*) **1** (*approving*) if a person is **cuddly**, they make you want to cuddle them **2** [only before noun] (of a child's toy) soft and designed to be cuddled: *a cuddly rabbit*

cudgel /ˈkʌdʒl/ *noun, verb*
■ *noun* a short thick stick that is used as a weapon [IDM] **take up (the) cudgels on behalf of sb/sth** (*old-fashioned, written*) to defend or support sb/sth strongly
■ *verb* (*BrE*) (**-ll-**, *AmE* also **-l-**) [VN] to hit sb with a cudgel [IDM] **cudgel your brains** (*old-fashioned, BrE*) to think very hard

cue /kjuː/ *noun, verb*
■ *noun* **1** ~ (**for sth**)|~ (**to do sth**) an action or event that is a signal for sb to do sth: *Jon's arrival was a cue for more champagne.* ◊ *I think that's my cue to explain why I'm here.* **2** a few words or an action in a play that is a signal for another actor to do sth: *She stood in the wings and waited for her cue to go on.* **3** a long wooden stick with a leather tip, used for hitting the ball in the games of BILLIARDS, POOL and SNOOKER—picture on page A8 [IDM] (**right**) **on cue** at exactly the moment you expect or that is appropriate: *'Where is that boy?' As if on cue, Simon appeared in the doorway.* **take your 'cue from sb/sth** to copy what sb else does as an example of how to behave or what to do: *Investors are taking their cue from the big banks and selling sterling.*
■ *verb* (**cue·ing, cued, cued**) [VN] to give sb a signal so they know when to start doing sth: *Can you cue me when you want me to begin speaking?*

cuff /kʌf/ *noun, verb*
■ *noun* **1** [C] the end of a coat or shirt sleeve at the wrist: *a collar and cuffs of white lace*—picture at JEWELLERY—picture on page A4 **2** (**cuffs**) [pl.] (*informal*) = HANDCUFFS **3** [C] (*AmE*) = TURN-UP **4** [C] a light hit with an open hand: *to give sb a friendly cuff* [IDM] ,**off the 'cuff** (of speaking, remarks, etc.) without previous thought or preparation: *I'm just speaking off the cuff here—I haven't seen the results yet.* ◊ *an off-the-cuff remark*
■ *verb* [VN] to hit sb quickly and lightly with your hand, especially in a way that is not serious: *She cuffed him lightly around his head.*

cuff·link /ˈkʌflɪŋk/ *noun* [usually pl.] one of a pair of small decorative objects used for fastening shirt cuffs together: *a pair of gold cufflinks*

cuis·ine /kwɪˈziːn/ *noun* [U, C] (from *French*) **1** a style of cooking: *Italian cuisine* **2** the food served in a restaurant (usually an expensive one): *The hotel restaurant is noted for its excellent cuisine.*—see also HAUTE CUISINE, NOUVELLE CUISINE

cul-de-sac /ˈkʌl də sæk/ *noun* (*pl.* **cul-de-sacs** or **culs-de-sac**) (from *French*) a street that is closed at one end

cu·lin·ary /ˈkʌlɪnəri; *AmE* -neri/ *adj.* [only before noun] (*formal*) connected with cooking or food: *culinary skills / efforts / masterpieces* ◊ *Savour the culinary delights of Mexico.*

cull /kʌl/ *verb, noun*
■ *verb* [VN] to kill a particular number of animals of a group in order to prevent the group from getting too large [PHRV] '**cull sth from sth** to choose or collect sth from a source or several different sources: *an exhibition of paintings culled from regional art galleries*
■ *noun* the act of killing some animals (usually the weakest ones) of a group in order to prevent the group from getting too large: *the annual seal cull*

cul·min·ate /ˈkʌlmɪneɪt/ *verb* [V] ~ (**in/with sth**) (*written*) to end with a particular result, or at a particular

æ	ɑː	e	ɜː	ə	ɪ	iː	i	ɒ	ɔː	ʌ	ʊ	u	uː
cat	father	ten	bird	about	sit	see	many	got	saw	cup	put	actual	too
								(BrE)					

point: *a gun battle which culminated in the death of two police officers* ◇ *Months of hard work culminated in success.* ◇ *Their summer tour will culminate at a spectacular concert in London.*

cul·min·ation /ˌkʌlmɪˈneɪʃn/ *noun* [sing.] (*written*) the highest point or end of sth, usually happening after a long time: *The reforms marked the successful culmination of a long campaign.*

cu·lottes /kjuːˈlɒts; *AmE* kuːˈlɑːts/ *noun* [pl.] women's wide short trousers/pants that are made to look like a skirt: *a pair of culottes*

culp·able /ˈkʌlpəbl/ *adj.* (*formal*) responsible and deserving blame for having done sth wrong: *The accident was the result of a culpable failure to consider the risks involved.* ► **culp·abil·ity** /ˌkʌlpəˈbɪləti/ *noun* [U] **culp·ably** /ˈkʌlpəbli/ *adv.*

cul·prit /ˈkʌlprɪt/ *noun* **1** a person who has done sth wrong or against the law: *The police quickly identified the real culprits.* **2** a person or thing responsible for causing a problem: *The main culprit in the current crisis seems to be modern farming techniques.*

cult /kʌlt/ *noun, adj.* ▪
- *noun* **1** [usually sing.] ~ (**of sth**) a way of life, an attitude, an idea, etc. that has become very popular: *the cult of physical fitness* ◇ *An extraordinary **personality cult** had been created around the leader.* **2** a small group of people who have extreme religious beliefs and who are not part of any established religion: *Their son ran away from home and joined a cult.* **3** (*formal*) a system of religious beliefs and practices: *the Chinese cult of ancestor worship*
- *adj.* [only before noun] very popular with a particular group of people; treating sb/sth as a cult figure, etc.: *a cult movie/book* ◇ *The singer has become a **cult figure** in America.* ◇ *The cartoon has achieved **cult status**.* ◇ *The TV series has a **cult following** among young people.*

cul·ti·vate /ˈkʌltɪveɪt/ *verb* [VN] **1** to prepare and use land for growing plants or crops: *The land around here has never been cultivated.* **2** to grow plants or crops: *The people cultivate mainly rice and beans.* **3** (sometimes *disapproving*) to try to get sb's friendship or support: *He purposely tried to cultivate good relations with the press.* ◇ *It helps if you go out of your way to cultivate the local people.* **4** to develop an attitude, a way of talking or behaving, etc: *She tried to cultivate an air of sophistication.*

cul·ti·vated /ˈkʌltɪveɪtɪd/ *adj.* **1** (of people) having a high level of education and showing good manners: *a cultivated young woman* ◇ *His voice was pleasant and cultivated.* **2** (of land) used to grow crops: *cultivated fields* **3** (of plants that are also wild) grown on a farm, etc. in order to be sold: *cultivated mushrooms*

cul·ti·va·tion /ˌkʌltɪˈveɪʃn/ *noun* [U] **1** the preparation and use of land for growing plants or crops: *fertile land that is **under cultivation** (= being CULTIVATED)* ◇ *rice/ wheat cultivation* **2** the deliberate development of a particular relationship, quality or skill: *the cultivation of a good relationship with local firms*

cul·ti·va·tor /ˈkʌltɪveɪtə(r)/ *noun* **1** a person who CULTIVATES (= grows crops on) the land **2** a machine for breaking up soil and destroying WEEDS (= plants growing where they are not wanted)

cul·tural /ˈkʌltʃərəl/ *adj.* [usually before noun] **1** connected with the culture of a particular society or group, its customs, beliefs, etc: *cultural differences between the two communities* ◇ *economic, social and cultural factors* **2** connected with art, literature, music, etc: *a cultural event* ◇ *Europe's cultural heritage* ◇ *The orchestra is very important for the cultural life of the city.* ► **cul·tur·al·ly** /-rəli/ *adv.*

cul·ture /ˈkʌltʃə(r)/ *noun, verb*
▪ *noun*
WAY OF LIFE | **1** [U] the customs and beliefs, art, way of life and social organization of a particular country or group: *European/Islamic/American culture* ◇ *working-class culture* **2** [C] a country, group, etc. with its own beliefs, etc: *The children are taught to respect different cultures.* ◇ *the effect of technology on traditional cultures*

ART/MUSIC/LITERATURE | **3** [U] art, music, literature, etc., thought of as a group: *Venice is a beautiful city full of culture and history.* ◇ ***popular culture** (= that is enjoyed by a lot of people)* ◇ *the Minister for Culture*

BELIEFS/ATTITUDES | **4** [C, U] the beliefs and attitudes about sth that people in a particular group or organization share: *The political cultures of the United States and the United Kingdom are very different.* ◇ *A culture of failure exists in some schools.* ◇ *company culture* ◇ *We are living in a consumer culture.*

GROWING/BREEDING | **5** [U] (*technical*) the growing of plants or breeding of particular animals in order to get a particular substance or crop from them: *the culture of silkworms (= for silk)*

CELLS/BACTERIA | **6** [C] (*biology, medical*) a group of cells or bacteria, especially one taken from a person or an animal and grown for medical or scientific study; the process of obtaining and growing these cells: *a culture of cells from the tumour* ◇ *Yogurt is made from active cultures.* ◇ *to do/ take a throat culture*
- *verb* [VN] (*biology, medical*) to grow a group of cells or bacteria for medical or scientific study

cul·tured /ˈkʌltʃəd; *AmE* -tʃərd/ *adj.* **1** (of people) well educated and able to understand and enjoy art, literature, etc. **2** (of cells or bacteria) grown for medical or scientific study **3** (of pearls) grown artificially

'culture shock *noun* [C, U] a feeling of confusion and anxiety that sb may feel when they live in or visit another country

cul·vert /ˈkʌlvət; *AmE* -vərt/ *noun* a pipe for water that goes under a road, etc.

cum /kʌm/ *prep.* (used for linking two nouns) and; as well as: *a bedroom-cum-study*

cum·ber·some /ˈkʌmbəsəm; *AmE* -bərs-/ *adj.* **1** large and heavy; difficult to carry: *cumbersome machinery* **2** slow and complicated: *cumbersome legal procedures* **3** (of words or phrases) long or complicated: *The organization changed its cumbersome title to something easier to remember.*

cumin /ˈkʌmɪn/ *noun* [U] the dried seeds of the **cumin** plant, used in cooking as a spice: *cumin seeds*

cum laude /ˌkʊm ˈlɔːdi; ˈlaʊdeɪ/ *adv., adj.* (from *Latin*) (in the US) at the third of the three highest levels of achievement that students can reach when they finish their studies at college: *He graduated cum laude from Georgetown University.*—compare MAGNA CUM LAUDE, SUMMA CUM LAUDE

cum·mer·bund /ˈkʌməbænd; *AmE* -mərb-/ *noun* a wide band of fabric worn around the waist, especially under a DINNER JACKET

cu·mu·la·tive /ˈkjuːmjələtɪv; *AmE* -leɪtɪv/ *adj.* **1** having a result that increases in strength or importance each time more of sth is added: *the **cumulative effect** of human activity on the world environment* **2** including all the amounts that have been added previously: *the monthly sales figures and the cumulative total for the past six months* ► **cu·mu·la·tive·ly** *adv.*

cu·mu·lus /ˈkjuːmjələs/ *noun* [U] (*technical*) a type of thick white cloud

cun·ni·lin·gus /ˌkʌnɪˈlɪŋgəs/ *noun* [U] the act of touching a woman's sex organs with the mouth and tongue in order to give sexual pleasure

cun·ning /ˈkʌnɪŋ/ *adj., noun*
- *adj.* **1** (*disapproving*) able to get what you want in a clever way, especially by tricking or deceiving sb: *a cunning liar* ◇ *He was as cunning as a fox.* **2** clever and skilful: *It was a cunning piece of detective work.* ► **cunning·ly** *adv.*: *The microphone was cunningly concealed in the bookcase.*
- *noun* [U] the ability to achieve sth by tricking or deceiving other people in a clever way: *It took energy and cunning just to survive.* ◇ *She used low cunning (= dishonest behaviour) to get what she wanted.*

cunt /kʌnt/ *noun* (△, *slang*) **1** a woman's VAGINA and outer sexual organs **2** a very offensive word used to insult sb and to show anger or dislike: *You stupid cunt!*

aɪ	aʊ	eɪ	əʊ	oʊ	ɔɪ	ɪə	eə	ʊə	j	w
my	now	say	go (BrE)	go (AmE)	boy	near	hair	pure	yes	wet

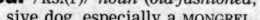

cup

a cup and saucer

plastic cup

egg cup

baby's mug/ beaker

mug

cup

cup /kʌp/ *noun, verb*

■ *noun* **1** [C] a small container shaped like a bowl, usually with a handle, used for drinking tea, coffee, etc: *a teacup* ◇ *a coffee cup* ◇ *a cup and saucer* ◇ *a paper cup* **2** [C] the contents of a cup: *She drank the whole cup.* ◇ *Would you like a cup of tea?* **3** [C] (also **cup·ful**) a unit for measuring quantity used in cooking in the US: *two cups of flour and half a cup of butter* **4** [C] a thing shaped like a cup: *an egg cup* **5** [C] a gold or silver cup on a stem, often with two handles, that is given as a prize in a competition: *She's won several cups for skating.* ◇ *He lifted the cup for the fifth time this year* (= it was the fifth time he had won). **6** [sing.] (usually **Cup**) a sports competition in which a cup is given as a prize: *the World Cup* **7** [C] one of the two parts of a BRA that cover the breast: *a C cup* **8** [C, U] a drink made from wine mixed with, for example, fruit juice **IDM** **not sb's cup of ˈtea** (*informal, spoken*) not what sb likes or is interested in: *An evening at the opera isn't everyone's cup of tea.* ◇ *He's nice enough but not really my cup of tea.*
■ *verb* (-pp-) [VN] **1** ~ **your hand(s) (around/over sth)** to make your hands into the shape of a bowl: *She held the bird gently in cupped hands.* **2** ~ **sth (in your hands)** to hold sth, making your hands into a round shape: *He cupped her face in his hands and kissed her.*

cup·board /ˈkʌbəd; *AmE* -bərd/ *noun* **1** a piece of furniture with doors and shelves used for storing dishes, food, clothes, etc: *kitchen cupboards* **2** (*BrE*) (*AmE* **closet**) a space in a wall with a door that reaches the ground, used for storing things: *built-in cupboards*—see also AIRING CUPBOARD, BROOM CUPBOARD **IDM** **the ˌcupboard is ˈbare** (*BrE*) used to say that there is no money for sth: *They are seeking more funds but the cupboard is bare.* **ˈcupboard love** (*BrE*) affection that sb, especially a child, shows towards sb else in order to get sth—more at SKELETON

cup·cake *noun* /ˈkʌpkeɪk/ *noun* (*especially AmE*) = FAIRY CAKE

ˈcup final (also **ˈCup Final**) *noun* (*especially in* football) the last match in a series of matches in a competition that gives a CUP as a prize to the winners: *cup final tickets* ◇ *the FA Cup Final*

cup·ful /ˈkʌpfʊl/ *noun* the amount that a cup will hold: *3 cupfuls of water*—see also CUP

Cupid /ˈkjuːpɪd/ *noun* **1** the Roman god of love who is shown as a beautiful baby boy with wings, carrying a BOW and arrow **2** (**cupid**) [C] a picture or statue of a baby boy who looks like Cupid **IDM** **play ˈCupid** to try to start a romantic relationship between two people

cu·pid·ity /kjuːˈpɪdəti/ *noun* [U] (*rare, formal, disapproving*) a strong desire for more wealth, possessions, power, etc. than a person needs **SYN** GREED

cu·pola /ˈkjuːpələ/ *noun* a round part on top of a building (like a small DOME)

cuppa /ˈkʌpə/ *noun* (*BrE, informal*) a cup of tea: *Do you fancy a cuppa?*

ˈcup tie *noun* (*BrE*) (especially in football) a match between two teams in a competition that gives a CUP as a prize to the winner

cur /kɜː(r)/ *noun* (*old-fashioned, disapproving*) an aggressive dog, especially a MONGREL

cur·able /ˈkjʊərəbl; *AmE* ˈkjʊr-/ *adj.* (of an illness) that can be cured: *Most skin cancers are curable if treated early.* **OPP** INCURABLE

cur·acy /ˈkjʊərəsi; *AmE* ˈkjʊr-/ *noun* (*pl.* **-ies**) the position of a curate; the time that sb is a curate

cur·ate /ˈkjʊərət; *AmE* ˈkjʊrət/ *noun* (in the Anglican Church) an assistant to a VICAR (= a priest, who is in charge of the church or churches in a particular area) **IDM** **the/a ˌcurate's ˈegg** (*BrE*) something that has some good parts and some bad ones

cura·tive /ˈkjʊərətɪv; *AmE* ˈkjʊr-/ *adj.* (*formal*) able to cure illness **SYN** HEALING: *the curative properties of herbs*—compare PREVENTIVE

cur·ator /kjʊəˈreɪtə(r); *AmE* kjʊˈr-/ *noun* a person whose job is to be in charge of the objects or works of art in a museum or art gallery, etc.

curb /kɜːb; *AmE* kɜːrb/ *verb, noun*
■ *verb* [VN] to control or limit sth, especially sth bad **SYN** CHECK: *He needs to learn to curb his temper.* ◇ *A range of policies have been introduced aimed at curbing inflation.*
■ *noun* **1** ~ **(on sth)** something that controls and puts limits on sth: *curbs on government spending* **2** (*AmE*) = KERB

curb·side (*AmE*) = KERBSIDE

curd /kɜːd; *AmE* kɜːrd/ *noun* [U] (also **curds** [pl.]) a thick soft substance that is formed when milk turns sour

cur·dle /ˈkɜːdl; *AmE* ˈkɜːrdl/ *verb* [V, VN] **1** when a liquid, especially milk, **curdles** or sth **curdles** it, it separates into solid and liquid parts **2** if sth **curdles** your blood or makes your blood **curdle**, it makes you extremely frightened or shocked—see also BLOOD-CURDLING

cure /kjʊə(r); *AmE* kjʊr/ *verb, noun*
■ *verb* [VN] **1** ~ **sb (of sth)** to make a person or an animal healthy again after an illness: *Will you be able to cure him, Doctor?* **2** to make an illness go away: *TB is a serious illness, but it can be cured.* **3** to deal with a problem successfully: *I finally managed to cure the rattling noise in my car.* **4** ~ **sb of sth** to stop sb from behaving in a particular way, especially a way that is bad or annoying **5** to treat food or tobacco with smoke, salt, etc. in order to preserve it **IDM** see KILL *v.*
■ *noun* **1** ~ **(for sth)** a medicine or medical treatment that cures an illness: *the search for a cure for cancer* ◇ *There is no known cure but the illness can be treated.* **2** the act of curing sb of an illness or the process of being cured: *Doctors cannot effect a cure if the disease has spread too far.* ◇ *The cure took six weeks.* **3** ~ **(for sth)** something that will solve a problem, improve a bad situation, etc: *a cure for poverty* **IDM** see PREVENTION

ˈcure-all *noun* something that people believe can cure any problem or any disease **SYN** PANACEA

cur·few /ˈkɜːfjuː; *AmE* ˈkɜːrf-/ *noun* [C, U] **1** a law which says that people must not go outside after a particular time at night until the morning; the time after which nobody must go outside: *The army imposed a dusk-to-dawn curfew.* ◇ *You must get home before curfew.* **2** (*AmE*) a time when children must be home in the evening: *I have a 10 o'clock curfew.*

curio /ˈkjʊəriəʊ; *AmE* ˈkjʊrioʊ/ *noun* (*pl.* **-os**) a small object that is rare or unusual, often sth that people collect

curi·os·ity /ˌkjʊəriˈɒsəti; *AmE* ˌkjʊriˈɑːs-/ *noun* (*pl.* **-ies**) **1** [U, sing.] ~ **(about sth)** | ~ **(to do sth)** a strong desire to know about sth: *Children show curiosity about everything.* ◇ *a certain curiosity to see what would happen next* ◇ *The letter wasn't addressed to me but I opened it out of curiosity.* ◇ *His answer did not satisfy my curiosity at all.* ◇ *Sophie's curiosity was aroused by the mysterious phone call.* ◇ *intellectual curiosity* ◇ *'Why do you ask?' 'Oh, just idle curiosity '* (= no particular reason). **2** [C] an unusual and interesting thing: *The museum is full of historical curiosities.*

curi·ous /ˈkjʊəriəs; *AmE* ˈkjʊr-/ *adj.* **1** ~ **(about sth)** | ~ **(to do sth)** having a strong desire to know about sth:

b	d	f	g	h	k	l	m	n	p	r
bad	did	fall	get	hat	cat	leg	man	now	pen	red

C

They were very curious about the people who lived upstairs. ◊ *I was curious to find out what she had said.* ◊ *Everyone was* **curious as to** *why Mark was leaving.* ◊ *He is such a curious boy, always asking questions.* **2 ~ (that ...)** strange and unusual: *There was a curious mixture of people in the audience.* ◊ *It was a curious feeling, as though we were floating on air.* ◊ *It was curious that she didn't tell anyone.* ▶ **curi·ous·ly** *adv.*: *'Are you really an artist?' Sara asked curiously.* ◊ *His clothes were curiously old-fashioned.* ◊ *Curiously enough, a year later exactly the same thing happened again.*

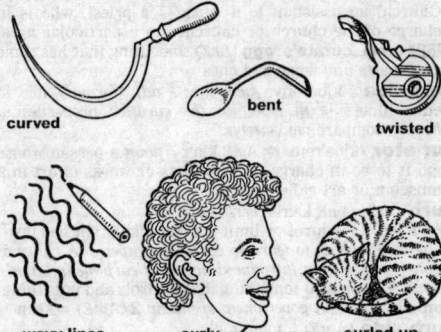

curved   bent   twisted

wavy lines   curly   curled up

curl /kɜːl; *AmE* kɜːrl/ *verb, noun*

■ *verb* **1** to form or make sth form into a curl or curls: [V] *His hair curls naturally.* [also VN] **2** [usually +*adv.* / *prep.*] to form or make sth form into a curved shape: [V] *The cat curled* **into a ball** *and went to sleep.* ◊ [VN] *She curled her legs up under her.* **3** [usually +*adv.* / *prep.*] to move while forming into a twisted or curved shape; to make sth do this: [V] *The smoke curled steadily upwards.* ◊ [VN] *He turned and curled the ball around the goalkeeper.* **4** [V, VN] if you **curl** your lip or your lip **curls**, you move your lip upwards and sideways to show that you think sb/sth is stupid or that you are better than they are **IDM** see TOE *n.* **PHRV** ,**curl 'up** | be ,**curled 'up** to lie or sit with your back curved and your arms and legs bent close to your body: *She curled up and closed her eyes.* ,**curl 'up** | ,**curl sb 'up** (*BrE, informal*) to become or make sb become very embarrassed ,**curl 'up** | ,**curl sth↔'up** to form or make sth form into a tightly curled shape: *The paper started to shrivel and curl up in the heat.*

■ *noun* **1** [C] a small bunch of hair that forms a curved or round shape: *Her hair was a mass of curls.* ◊ *The baby had dark eyes and dark curls.* **2** [C, U] the tendency of hair to form curls: *His hair had a natural curl.* **3** [C] a thing that forms a curved or round shape: *a curl of smoke* ◊ *Decorate the cake with curls of chocolate.* ◊ *a contemptuous curl of the lip* (= an expression showing disapproval)

curl·er /ˈkɜːlə(r); *AmE* ˈkɜːrl-/ *noun* [usually pl.] a small plastic or metal tube which you can wrap wet hair around in order to make it curl **SYN** ROLLER

cur·lew /ˈkɜːljuː; *AmE* ˈkɜːrl-/ *noun* a bird with a long thin beak that curves downwards, that lives near water

curl·ing /ˈkɜːlɪŋ; *AmE* ˈkɜːrlɪŋ/ *noun* [U] a game played on ice, in which players slide heavy flat stones towards a mark

curly /ˈkɜːli; *AmE* ˈkɜːrli/ *adj.* (**curl·ier, curli·est**) having a lot of curls or a curved shape: *short curly hair* ◊ *a dog with a curly tail*—picture at CURL

cur·mudg·eon /kɜːˈmʌdʒən; *AmE* kɜːrˈm-/ *noun* (*old-fashioned*) a bad-tempered person, often an old one ▶ **cur·mudg·eon·ly** *adj.*

cur·rant /ˈkʌrənt; *AmE* ˈkɜːr-/ *noun* **1** a small dried grape, used in cakes, etc: *a currant bun* **2** (usually in compounds) a small black, red or white berry that grows in bunches on bushes: *blackcurrants* ◊ *redcurrants* ◊ *currant bushes*

cur·rency /ˈkʌrənsi; *AmE* ˈkɜːr-/ *noun* (*pl.* **-ies**) **1** [C, U] the system of money that a country uses: *trading in foreign currencies* ◊ *a single European currency* ◊ *You'll*

need some cash in **local currency** but you can also use your credit card.—see also HARD CURRENCY **2** [U] the fact that sth is used or accepted by a lot of people: *The term 'post-industrial' now has* **wide currency**. ◊ *The qualification has* **gained currency** *all over the world.*

cur·rent /ˈkʌrənt; *AmE* ˈkɜːrənt/ *adj., noun*

■ *adj.* **1** [only before noun] happening now; of the present time: *current prices* ◊ *a budget for the current year* ◊ *your current employer* ⇨ note at ACTUAL **2** being used by or accepted by most people: *words that are no longer current*

■ *noun* **1** the movement of water in the sea or a river; the movement of air in a particular direction: *He swam to the shore against a* **strong current**. ◊ *Birds use warm air currents to help their flight.* **2** the flow of electricity through a wire, etc: *a 15 amp electrical current*—see also AC, DC **3** the fact of particular ideas, opinions or feelings being present in a group of people: *Ministers are worried by this current of anti-government feeling.*

ˈ**current account** (*BrE*) (*AmE* ˈ**checking account**) *noun* a type of bank account that you can take money out of at any time, and that provides you with a CHEQUEBOOK and CASH CARD—compare DEPOSIT ACCOUNT

,**current af'fairs** *noun* [pl.] events of political or social importance that are happening now

cur·rent·ly /ˈkʌrəntli; *AmE* ˈkɜːr-/ *adv.* at the present time: *The hourly charge is currently £35.* ◊ *Currently, over 500 students are enrolled on the course.* ◊ *All the options are* **currently available**. ◊ *This matter is currently discussed.*

cur·ricu·lar /kəˈrɪkjələ(r)/ *adj.* connected with the curriculum of a school, etc.—see also EXTRA-CURRICULAR

cur·ricu·lum /kəˈrɪkjələm/ *noun* (*pl.* **cur·ric·ula** /-lə/ or **cur·ricu·lums**) the subjects that are included in a course of study or taught in a school, college, etc: *the school curriculum* ◊ (*BrE*) *Spanish is on the curriculum.* ◊ (*AmE*) *Spanish is in the curriculum.*—compare SYLLABUS

cur·ricu·lum vitae /kəˌrɪkjələm ˈviːtaɪ/ (*abbr.* **CV**) *noun* **1** (*BrE*) (*AmE* **re·sumé**) a written record of your education and employment, that you send when you are applying for a job: *Applications with a full curriculum vitae and two references should reach the Principal by June 12th.* ⇨ Study page B15 **2** (*AmE*) a record of a university/college teacher's education and employment, also including a list of books and articles that they have published and courses that they have taught, used when they are applying for a job

cur·ried /ˈkʌrid; *AmE* ˈkɜːr-/ *adj.* [only before noun] cooked with hot spices: *curried chicken / beef / eggs*

curry /ˈkʌri; *AmE* ˈkɜːri/ *noun, verb*

■ *noun* [C, U] an Indian dish of meat, vegetables, etc. cooked with hot spices, often served with rice: *a chicken curry* ◊ *Would you like some more curry?*

■ *verb* (**cur·ries, curry·ing, cur·ried, cur·ried**) [VN] to make curry out of meat or vegetables **IDM** **curry 'favour (with sb)** (*disapproving*) to try to get sb to like or support you by praising or helping them a lot

ˈ**curry powder** *noun* [U] a powder made from a mixture of spices, used to give a hot flavour to food, especially curry

curse /kɜːs; *AmE* kɜːrs/ *noun, verb*

■ *noun* **1** (also **cuss**) [C] a rude or offensive word or phrase that some people use when they are very angry: *He muttered a curse at the other driver.* **2** [C] a word or phrase that has a magic power to make sth bad happen: *The family thought that they were* **under a curse**.—compare HEX **3** [C] something that causes harm or evil: *the curse of drug addiction* ◊ *Noise is a curse of modern city life.* **4** (**the curse**) [sing.] (*old-fashioned, informal*) MENSTRUATION

■ *verb* **1** [V] to swear: *He hit his head as he stood up and cursed loudly.* **2** [VN] **~ (sb/sth) (for sth)** to say rude things to sb or think rude things about sb/sth: *She cursed her bad luck.* ◊ *He cursed himself for his stupidity.* **3** [VN] to use a magic word or phrase against sb in order to harm them: *Legend has it that the whole village had been cursed by a witch.*—compare HEX **PHRV** be ˈ**cursed with sth** to continuously suffer from or be affected by sth bad: *She seems cursed with bad luck.*

cursed *adj.* **1** /kɜːst; *AmE* kɜːrst/ having a curse (2) on it; suffering from a curse (2): *The necklace was cursed.* ◊ *The whole family seemed cursed.* **2** /ˈkɜːsɪd; *AmE* ˈkɜːrsɪd/ [only before noun] (*old-fashioned*) unpleasant; annoying

cur·sive /ˈkɜːsɪv; *AmE* ˈkɜːrs-/ *adj.* (*technical*) (of HANDWRITING) with the letters joined together

cur·sor /ˈkɜːsə(r); *AmE* ˈkɜːrs-/ *noun* a small mark on a computer screen that can be moved and that shows the position on the screen where, for example, text will be added—picture on page 251

curs·ory /ˈkɜːsəri; *AmE* ˈkɜːrs-/ *adj.* (often *disapproving*) done quickly and without giving enough attention to details: *a cursory glance/examination/inspection* ▸ **cur·sor·ily** /ˈkɜːsərəli; *AmE* ˈkɜːrs-/ *adv.*

curt /kɜːt; *AmE* kɜːrt/ *adj.* (of a person's manner or behaviour) appearing rude because very few words are used, or because sth is done in a very quick way: *a curt reply* ◊ *a curt nod* ◊ *His tone was curt and unfriendly.* ▸ **curt·ly** *adv.* **curt·ness** *noun* [U]

cur·tail /kɜːˈteɪl; *AmE* kɜːrˈt-/ *verb* [VN] (*formal*) to limit sth or make it last for a shorter time: *Spending on books has been severely curtailed.* ◊ *The lecture was curtailed by the fire alarm going off.* ▸ **cur·tail·ment** *noun* [U]: *the curtailment of civil liberties*

cur·tain /ˈkɜːtn; *AmE* ˈkɜːrtn/ *noun, verb*
▪ *noun* **1** [C] a piece of fabric that is hung to cover a window: *to draw/pull/close the curtains* (= to pull them across the window so they cover it) ◊ *to draw/draw back/pull back the curtains* (= to open them, so that the window is no longer covered) ◊ *It was ten in the morning but the curtains were still drawn* (= closed). ◊ *a pair of curtains*—see also DRAPE **2** (*AmE*) = NET CURTAIN **3** [C] a piece of fabric that is hung up as a screen in a room or around a bed, for example: *a shower curtain*—see also THE IRON CURTAIN **4** [sing.] a piece of thick, heavy fabric that hangs in front of the stage in the theatre: *The audience was waiting for the curtain to rise* (= for the play to begin). ◊ *There was tremendous applause when the curtain came down* (= the play ended). ◊ *We left just before the final curtain.* ◊ (*figurative*) *The curtain has fallen on her long and distinguished career* (= her career has ended). ◊ (*figurative*) *It's time to face the final curtain* (= the end; death). **5** [C, usually sing.] a thing that covers, hides or protects sth: *a curtain of rain/smoke* ◊ *She pushed back the curtain of brown hair from her eyes.* **IDM** **be curtains (for sb)** (*informal*) to be a situation without hope or that you cannot escape from: *When I saw he had a gun, I thought it was curtains for me.* **bring down the ˈcurtain on sth** | **bring the ˈcurtain down on sth** to finish or mark the end of sth: *His sudden decision to retire brought down the curtain on a distinguished career.*
▪ *verb* [VN] to provide curtains for a window or a room **PHRV** ˌcurtain sth↔ˈoff to separate an area of a room with a curtain or curtains

ˈcurtain call *noun* the time in the theatre when the actors come to the front of the stage at the end of a play to receive the APPLAUSE of the audience

ˈcurtain-raiser *noun* ~ (to sth) **1** a small event that prepares for a similar, more important one **2** a short performance before the main performance in a theatre, etc.

curtsy (also **curt·sey**) /ˈkɜːtsi; *AmE* ˈkɜːrtsi/ *noun* (*pl.* -ies or -eys) a formal greeting made by a woman or girl in a dance or to an important person, by bending her knees with one foot in front of the other ▸ **curtsy** *verb* (curtsies, curt·sy·ing, curt·sied, curt·sied) (also curt·sey): [V] *She curtsied to the Queen.*

curv·aceous /kɜːˈveɪʃəs; *AmE* kɜːrˈv-/ *adj.* (*informal*) used in newspapers, etc. to describe a woman whose body has attractive curves

curv·ature /ˈkɜːvətʃə(r); *AmE* ˈkɜːrv-/ *noun* [U] (*technical*) the state of being curved; the amount that sth is curved: *the curvature of the earth* ◊ *curvature of the spine*

curve /kɜːv; *AmE* kɜːrv/ *noun, verb*
▪ *noun* **1** a line or surface that bends gradually; a smooth bend: *the delicate curve of her ear* ◊ *a pattern of straight lines and curves* ◊ (especially *AmE*) *a curve in the road* ◊ (especially *AmE*) *The driver lost control on a curve and the vehicle hit a tree.* ◊ *to plot a curve on a graph* ◊ (*technical*) *the unemployment-income curve* (= a line on a GRAPH showing the relationship between the number of unemployed people and national income)—see also LEARNING CURVE **2** (also **ˈcurve ball**) (*AmE*) (in the game of baseball) a ball that moves in a curve when it is thrown to the BATTER: (*figurative*) *One of the journalists threw the senator a curve* (= surprised him by asking a difficult question).
▪ *verb* [usually +adv. / prep.] to move or make sth move in the shape of a curve; to be in the shape of a curve: [V] *The road curved around the bay.* ◊ *The ball curved through the air.* ◊ *His lips curved in a smile.* [also VN]

curved /kɜːvd; *AmE* kɜːrvd/ *adj.* having a round shape: *a curved path/roof/blade*—picture at CURL

curvy /ˈkɜːvi; *AmE* ˈkɜːrvi/ *adj.* (*informal*) having curves: *a curvy body* ◊ *curvy lines*

cush·ion /ˈkʊʃn/ *noun, verb*
▪ *noun* **1** (*AmE* also **pil·low**) a fabric bag filled with soft material or feathers that is used, for example, to make a seat more comfortable: *matching curtains and cushions* ◊ *a floor cushion* (= a large cushion that you put on the floor to sit on) ◊ *a pile of scatter cushions* (= small cushions, often in bright colours, that you put on chairs, etc.) ◊ (*figurative*) *a cushion of moss on a rock* **2** a layer of air between two surfaces that keeps them apart: *A hovercraft rides on a cushion of air.* **3** [usually sing.] ~ (against sth) something that protects you against sth unpleasant that might happen: *His savings were a comfortable cushion against financial problems.* ◊ *The team built up a safe cushion of two goals in the first half.* **4** (in the game of BILLIARDS, etc.) the soft inside edge along each side of the table, that the balls bounce off—picture on page A8
▪ *verb* [VN] **1** to soften the effect of a fall or hit: *My fall was cushioned by the deep snow.* **2** ~ sb/sth (against/from sth) to protect sb/sth from harm or the unpleasant effects of sth: *The south of the country has been cushioned from the worst effects of the recession.* ◊ *He broke the news of my brother's death to me, making no effort to cushion the blow* (= make the news less shocking). **3** [usually passive] to make sth soft with a cushion

cushy /ˈkʊʃi/ *adj.* (**cush·ier**, **cushi·est**) (*informal*, often *disapproving*) very easy and pleasant; needing little or no effort: *a cushy job* **IDM** **a cushy ˈnumber** (*BrE*) an easy job; a pleasant situation that other people would like

cusp /kʌsp/ *noun* **1** (*technical*) a pointed end where two curves meet: *the cusp of a leaf* **2** the time when one sign of the ZODIAC ends and the next begins: *I was born on the cusp between Virgo and Libra.* ◊ (*figurative*) *He was on the cusp between small acting roles and moderate fame.*

cuss /kʌs/ *verb, noun*
▪ *verb* (*old-fashioned*, *informal*) to swear at sb: [V] *My dad used to come home drunk, shouting and cussing.* [also VN]
▪ *noun* (*old-fashioned*, *informal*) **1** used with a negative adjective to describe a person: *He's an awkward cuss.* **2** = CURSE: *cuss words*

cussed /ˈkʌsɪd/ *adj.* (*old-fashioned*, *informal*) (of people) not willing to be helpful **SYN** STUBBORN ▸ **cuss·ed·ly** *adv.* **cuss·ed·ness** *noun* [U]

cus·tard /ˈkʌstəd; *AmE* -tərd/ *noun* **1** [U] (especially *BrE*) (*AmE* usually ˌcustard ˈsauce) a sweet yellow sauce made from milk, sugar, eggs and flour, usually served hot with cooked fruit, PUDDINGS, etc: *apple pie and custard*—picture on page A1 **2** [C, U] a mixture of eggs, milk and sugar baked until it is firm

ˌcustard ˈpie *noun* a flat pie filled with sth soft and wet that looks like custard, that performers throw at each other to make people laugh

cus·to·dial /kʌˈstəʊdiəl; *AmE* -ˈstoʊ-/ *adj.* [usually before noun] (*law*) **1** involving sending sb to prison: *The judge gave him a custodial sentence* (= sent him to prison). **2** connected with the right or duty of looking after sb;

æ	ɑː	e	ɜː	ə	ɪ	iː	i	ɒ	ɔː	ʌ	ʊ	u	uː
cat	father	ten	bird	about	sit	see	many	got	saw	cup	put	actual	too
								(BrE)					

having CUSTODY: *The mother is usually the custodial parent after a divorce.* [OPP] NON-CUSTODIAL

cus·to·dian /kʌˈstəʊdiən; *AmE* -ˈstoʊ-/ *noun* **1** a person who takes responsibility for taking care of or protecting sth: *the museum's custodians* ◇ *a self-appointed custodian of public morals* **2** (*AmE*) = CARETAKER

cus·tody /ˈkʌstədi/ *noun* [U] **1** the legal right or duty to take care of or keep sb/sth; the act of taking care of sth/sb: *Who will have custody of the children?* ◇ *The divorce court awarded custody to the child's mother.* ◇ *The parents were locked in a bitter battle for custody.* ◇ *The bank provides safe custody for valuables.* ◇ *The castle is now in the custody of the state.* **2** the state of being in prison, especially while waiting for trial: *After the riot, 32 people were taken into police custody.* ◇ (*BrE*) *He was remanded in custody, charged with the murder of a policeman.*—see also YOUTH CUSTODY

cus·tom /ˈkʌstəm/ *noun, adj.*
■ *noun*—see also CUSTOMS **1** [C, U] **~ (of doing sth)** an accepted way of behaving or of doing things in a society or a community: *an old/ancient custom* ◇ *the custom of giving presents at Christmas* ◇ *It's a local custom.* ◇ *It is the custom in that country for women to marry young.* **2** [sing.] (*formal* or *literary*) the way a person always behaves; a habit or practice: *It was her custom to rise early.* ◇ *As was his custom, he knocked three times.* **3** [U] (*BrE*, *formal*) (also **business** *AmE*, *BrE*) the fact of a person or people buying goods or services at a shop/store or business: *Thank you for your custom. Please call again.* ◇ *We've lost a lot of custom since prices went up.*
■ *adj.* [only before noun] (*especially AmE*) = CUSTOM-BUILT, CUSTOM-MADE: *a custom motorcycle*

cus·tom·ary /ˈkʌstəməri; *AmE* -meri/ *adj.* **1** if sth is **customary**, it is what people usually do in a particular place or situation: *Is it customary to tip hairdressers in this country?* **2** typical of a person: *She arranged everything with her customary efficiency.* ► **cus·tom·ar·ily** /ˈkʌstəmərəli; *AmE* ˌkʌstəˈmerəli/ *adv.*

ˌcustom-ˈbuilt (also **custom** especially in *AmE*) *adj.* designed and built for a particular person: *a custom-built house*

cus·tom·er /ˈkʌstəmə(r)/ *noun* **1** a person or an organization that buys sth from a shop/store or business: *one of the shop's best/biggest customers* ◇ *They know me—I'm a regular customer.* ◇ *the customer service department* ◇ *The firm has excellent customer relations.* **2** (*old-fashioned, informal*) used after an adjective to describe a particular type of person: *an awkward/tough customer*

WHICH WORD?
customer / client   (?)

A **customer** is someone who buys goods or services from a shop/store or business, or who uses a bank. A **client** pays to use the services or advice of a professional person, such as a lawyer or designer, or an organization.

Customer is increasingly being used now instead of other words such as 'passenger' to suggest that the passenger, etc. has more power or choice than they used to.

---

cus·tom·ize (*BrE* also **-ise**) /ˈkʌstəmaɪz/ *verb* [VN] to make or change sth to suit the needs of the owner: *You can customize the software in several ways.* ► **cus·tom·ized** *adj.*: *a customized car*

ˌcustom-ˈmade (also **cus·tom** especially in *AmE*) *adj.* designed and made for a particular person: *custom-made clothes*—see also BESPOKE

cus·toms /ˈkʌstəmz/ *noun* [pl.] **1** (usually **Customs**) (*BrE* also **Customs and Excise**) (*AmE* also **US Customs Service**) the government department that collects taxes on goods bought and sold and on goods brought into the country, and that checks what is brought in: *The Customs have seized large quantities of smuggled heroin.* ◇ *a customs officer* [HELP] *AmE* uses a singular verb with **customs** in this meaning. **2** the place at a port or an airport where your bags are checked as you come into a

country: *to go through customs and passport control* **3** the taxes that must be paid to the government when goods are brought in from other countries: *to pay customs on sth* ◇ *customs duty/duties*—compare EXCISE

cut /kʌt/ *verb, noun*
■ *verb* (**cut·ting**, **cut**, **cut**)

WOUND/HOLE | **1** to make an opening or a wound in sth, especially with a sharp tool such as a knife or scissors: [VN] *She cut her finger on a piece of glass.* ◇ *He cut himself* (= his face) *shaving.* ◇ *Workmen cut a hole in the pipe.* ◇ *You need a powerful saw to cut through metal.* ◇ (*figurative*) *The canoe cut through the water.* ◇ [VN-ADJ] *She had fallen and cut her head open.*

DIVIDE | **2 ~ sth (from sth)** | **~ sth (in/into sth)** | **~ (sb) sth** | **~ sth (for sb)** to remove sth from sth large, using a knife, etc.; to divide sth into two or more pieces with a knife, etc: [VN] *He cut four thick slices from the loaf.* ◇ *He cut the loaf into thick slices.* ◇ *cut flowers* ◇ *The bus was cut in two by the train.* ◇ *Don't cut the string, untie the knots.* ◇ [VNN, VN] *I cut them all a piece of birthday cake.* ◇ *I cut a piece of birthday cake for them all.*

SHAPE/FORM | **3** [VN] **~ sth (in sth)** to make or form sth by removing material with a knife, etc: *The climbers cut steps in the ice.*

HAIR/NAILS/GRASS, etc. | **4** to make sth shorter by cutting: [VN] *to cut your hair/nails* ◇ *to cut the grass/lawn/hedge* ◇ [VN-ADJ] *He's had his hair cut really short.*

RELEASE | **5 ~ sb (from sth)** to allow sb to escape from somewhere by cutting the rope, object, etc. that is holding them: [VN] *The injured driver had to be cut from the wreckage.* ◇ [VN-ADJ] *Two survivors were cut free after being trapped for twenty minutes.*

CLOTHING | **6** [VN-ADJ] [usually passive] to design and make a piece of clothing in a particular way: *The swimsuit was cut high in the leg.*

ABLE TO CUT/BE CUT | **7** [V] to be capable of cutting: *This knife won't cut.* **8** [V] to be capable of being cut: *Sandstone cuts easily.*

REDUCE | **9** [VN] **~ sth (by ...)** | **~ sth (from ...) (to ...)** to reduce sth by removing a part of it: *to cut prices/taxes/spending/production* ◇ *Buyers will bargain hard to cut the cost of the house they want.* ◇ *His salary has been cut by ten per cent.* ◇ *Could you cut your essay from 5000 to 3000 words?*

REMOVE | **10** [VN] **~ sth (from sth)** to remove sth from sth: *This scene was cut from the final version of the movie.*

COMPUTING | **11** to DELETE (= remove) part of a text on a computer screen in order to place it somewhere else: [V] *You can cut and paste between different programs.* [also VN]

STOP | **12** [VN] (*informal*) used to tell sb to stop doing sth: *Cut the chatter and get on with your work!*

IN MOVIE/TV | **13** [VN] to prepare a film/movie or tape by removing parts of it or putting them in a different order [SYN] EDIT **14** [V] (usually used in orders) to stop filming or recording: *The director shouted 'Cut!'* **15** [V] **~ (from sth) to sth** (in films/movies, radio or television) to move quickly from one scene to another: *The scene cuts from the bedroom to the street.*

MISS CLASS | **16** [VN] (*informal, especially AmE*) to stay away from a class that you should go to: *He's always cutting class.*

UPSET | **17** [VN] (*written*) to hurt sb emotionally: *His cruel remarks cut her deeply.*

IN CARD GAMES | **18** to lift and turn up a pack/deck of playing cards in order to decide who is to play first, etc: [V] *Let's cut for dealer.* [also VN]

GEOMETRY | **19** [VN] (of a line) to cross another line: *The line cuts the circle at two points.*

A TOOTH | **20** [VN] **~ a tooth** to have a new tooth beginning to appear through the GUM: *When did she cut her first tooth?*

A DISC | **21** [VN] **~ a disc** to make a recording of music on a record, CD, etc: *The Beatles cut their first disc in 1962.*

DRUG | **22** [VN] ~ sth (with sth) to mix an illegal drug such as HEROIN with another substance

IDM Most idioms containing **cut** are at the entries for the nouns and adjectives in the idioms, for example **cut your losses** is at **loss**.   **cut and 'run** (*BrE, informal*) to make a quick or sudden escape
PHR V ,cut a'cross sth **1** to affect or be true for different groups that usually remain separate: *Opinion on this issue cuts across traditional political boundaries.* **2** (also ,cut 'through sth) to go across sth in order to make your route shorter: *I usually cut across the park on my way home.*
,cut sth↔'way (from sth) to remove sth from sth by cutting: *They cut away all the dead branches from the tree.*
,cut sth↔'back **1** (also ,cut 'back (on sth)) to reduce sth: *If we don't sell more we'll have to cut back production.* ◊ *to cut back on spending*—related noun CUTBACK **2** to make a bush, etc. smaller by cutting branches off [SYN] PRUNE: *to cut back a rose bush*
,cut sb↔'down (*formal*) to kill sb: *He was cut down by an assassin's bullet.* ,cut sth↔'down to make sth fall down by cutting it at the base: *to cut down a tree* ,cut sth↔'down (to…)| ,cut 'down (on sth) to reduce the size, amount or number of sth: *We need to cut the article down to 1000 words.* ◊ *The doctor told him to cut down on his drinking.* ◊ *I won't have a cigarette, thanks—I'm trying to cut down* (= smoke fewer).
,cut 'in **1** if a motor or an engine **cuts in**, it starts working: *Emergency generators cut in.* **2** (*AmE*) = PUSH IN ,cut 'in (on sb/sth) **1** to interrupt sb when they are speaking: *She kept cutting in on our conversation.* ◊[+speech] *'Forget it!' she cut in.* **2** (of a vehicle or its driver) to move suddenly in front of another vehicle, leaving little space between the two vehicles ,cut sb 'in (on sth) (*informal*) to give sb a share of the profit in a business or an activity
,cut sb↔'off **1** [often passive] to interrupt sb who is speaking on the telephone by breaking the connection: *We were cut off in the middle of our conversation.* **2** (also ,cut sb↔'out (of sth)) to refuse to let sb receive any of your property after you die [SYN] DISINHERIT: *He cut his son off without a penny.* ,cut sb/sth↔'off **1** to interrupt sb and stop them from speaking: *My explanation was cut off by loud protests.* **2** [often passive] to stop the supply of sth to sb: *Our water supply has been cut off.* ◊ *They were cut off for not paying their phone bill.* ,cut sth↔'off **1** (also ,cut sth 'off sth) to remove sth from sth larger by cutting: *He had his finger cut off in an accident at work.* ◊ (*figurative*) *The winner cut ten seconds off* (= ran the distance ten seconds faster than) *the world record.*—see also CUT-OFF **2** to block or get in the way of sth: *They cut off the enemy's retreat.* ◊ *The new factory cuts off our view of the hills.* ,cut sb/sth 'off (from sb/sth) [often passive] to prevent sb/sth from leaving or reaching a place or communicating with people outside a place: *The army was cut off from its base.* ◊ *She feels very cut off living in the country.* ◊ *He cut himself off from all human contact.*
,cut 'out if a motor or an engine **cuts out**, it suddenly stops working—related noun CUT-OUT ,cut sb↔'out (of sth) = CUT SB OFF: *Furious, her mother cut her out of her will.* ,cut sth↔'out **1** to make sth by cutting: *She cut the dress out of some old material.* ◊ (*figurative*) *He's cut out a niche for himself* (= found a suitable job) *in journalism.*—related noun CUT-OUT **2** (*informal*) used to tell sb to stop doing or saying sth annoying: *I'm sick of you two arguing—just cut it out!* **3** to leave sth out of a piece of writing, etc. [SYN] OMIT: *I would cut out the bit about working as a waitress.* **4** to block sth, especially light: *Thick overhanging branches cut out the sunlight.* ,cut sth↔'out (of sth) **1** to remove sth from sth larger by cutting, usually with scissors: *I cut this article out of the newspaper.* **2** to stop doing, using or eating sth: *I've been advised to cut sugar out of my diet.* be ,cut 'out for sth| be ,cut 'out to be sth (*informal*) to have the qualities and abilities needed for sth: *He's not cut out for teaching.* ◊ *He's not cut out to be a teacher.*
,cut 'through sth **1** = CUT ACROSS STH **2** (also ,cut sth 'through sth) to make a path or passage through sth by

cutting: *They used a machete to cut through the bush.* ◊ *The prisoners cut their way through the barbed wire.*
,cut sb↔'up (*informal*) **1** to injure sb badly by cutting or hitting them: *He was badly cut up in the fight.* **2** [usually passive] to upset sb emotionally: *She was pretty cut up about them leaving.* ,cut sth↔'up to divide sth into small pieces with a knife, etc: *He cut up the meat on his plate.*

■ *noun*
WOUND | **1** a wound caused by sth sharp: *cuts and bruises on the face* ◊ *Blood poured from the deep cut on his arm.*
HOLE | **2** a hole or an opening in sth, made with sth sharp: *Using sharp scissors, make a small cut in the material.*
REDUCTION | **3** ~ (in sth) a reduction in amount, size, supply, etc: *price/tax/job cuts* ◊ *They had to take a 20% cut in pay.* ◊ *They announced cuts in public spending.*—see also POWER CUT, SHORT CUT
OF HAIR | **4** [usually sing.] an act of cutting sb's hair; the style in which it is cut: *Your hair could do with a cut* (= it is too long). ◊ *I want to make an appointment for a cut and blow-dry.*
OF CLOTHING | **5** [usually sing.] the shape and style that a piece of clothing has because of the way the fabric is cut: *the elegant cut of her dress*
SHARE OF MONEY | **6** a share in sth, especially money: *They were rewarded with a cut of 5% from the profits.*
OF MOVIE/PLAY, etc. | **7** ~ (in sth) an act of removing part of a film/movie, play, piece of writing, etc: *The director objected to the cuts ordered by the censor.* ◊ *She made some lengthy cuts before handing over the finished novel.*
MEAT | **8** a piece of meat cut from an animal: *a lean cut of pork* ◊ *cheap cuts of stewing lamb*—see also COLD CUTS
IDM a cut above sb/sth better than sb/sth: *His latest novel is a cut above the rest.* the cut and 'thrust (of sth) (*BrE*) the lively or aggressive way that sth is done: *the cut and thrust of political debate*

,cut and 'dried *adj.* [not usually before noun] decided in a way that cannot be changed or argued about: *The inquiry is by no means cut and dried.*

cut·back /ˈkʌtbæk/ *noun* [usually pl.] ~ (in sth) a reduction in sth: *cutbacks in public spending* ◊ *staff cutbacks*

cute /kjuːt/ *adj.* (**cuter, cutest**) **1** pretty and attractive: *a cute little baby* ◊ (*BrE*) *an unbearably cute picture of two kittens* (= it seems sentimental) **2** (*informal*, especially *AmE*) sexually attractive: *Check out those cute guys over there!* **3** (*informal*, especially *AmE*) clever, sometimes in an annoying way because a person is trying to get an advantage for him or herself: *She had a really cute idea.* ◊ *Even as a child, he was always cute enough to get what he wanted.* ◊ *Don't get cute with me!* ▶ **cute·ly** *adv.*: *to smile cutely* **cute·ness** *noun* [U]

cutesy /ˈkjuːtsi/ *adj.* (*informal*) too pretty or attractive in a way that is annoying or not realistic: *She is trying to get away from her cutesy girl-next-door image.*

,cut 'glass *noun* [U] glass with patterns cut in it: *a cut-glass vase*—picture at GLASS

cut·icle /ˈkjuːtɪkl/ *noun* an area of hard skin at the base of the nails on the fingers and toes

cutie /ˈkjuːti/ *noun* (*informal*) a person who is attractive or kind: *He's a real cutie.*

cut·lass /ˈkʌtləs/ *noun* a short SWORD with a curved blade that was used as a weapon by sailors and PIRATES in the past

cut·lery /ˈkʌtləri/ *noun* [U] **1** (*BrE*) (*AmE* **flat·ware, sil·ver·ware**) knives, forks and spoons, used for eating and serving food: *Put the cutlery in the drawer.* ◊ *a stainless steel cutlery set*—picture on page 312 **2** (*AmE*) knives, etc. that are sharp

cut·let /ˈkʌtlət/ *noun* **1** a thick slice of meat, especially LAMB or PORK (= meat from a pig), that is cooked and served with the bone still attached **2** (in compounds) finely chopped pieces of meat, fish, vegetables, etc. that are pressed together into a flat piece, covered with BREADCRUMBS and cooked: *nut cutlets*

'cut-off *noun, adj.*
■ *noun* **1** a point or limit when you stop sth: *The government announced a cut-off in overseas aid.* ◊ *Is there a*

C

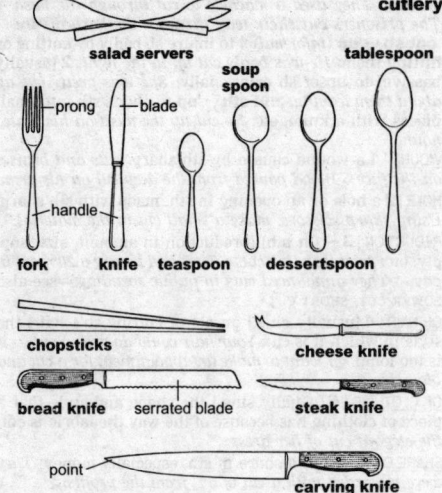

cutlery

salad servers

soup spoon

tablespoon

prong — blade

handle

fork   knife   teaspoon   dessertspoon

chopsticks

cheese knife

bread knife   serrated blade   steak knife

point

carving knife

cut-off point between childhood and adulthood? **2** (**cut-offs**) [pl.] cut-off trousers/pants: *wearing frayed cut-offs*
■ *adj.* [only before noun] (of trousers/pants) made shorter by cutting off part of the legs: *cut-off jeans*

'cut-out *noun* **1** a shape cut out of paper, wood, etc: *a cardboard cut-out* **2** a piece of safety equipment that stops an electric current from flowing through sth

,cut-'price *adj.* [only before noun] (*especially BrE*) (*AmE* usually **,cut-'rate**) **1** sold at a reduced price: *cut-price goods/fares* **2** selling goods at a reduced price: *a cut-price store/supermarket*

cut·ter /'kʌtə(r)/ *noun* **1** (usually in compounds) a person or thing that cuts: *a pastry cutter* **2** (**cutters**) [pl.] (usually in compounds) a tool for cutting: *a pair of wire-cutters* **3** a small fast ship **4** a ship's boat, used for travelling between the ship and the shore

'cut-throat *adj.* [usually before noun] (of an activity) in which people compete with each other in aggressive and unfair ways: *rival companies engaged in cut-throat competition* ◊ *the cut-throat world of politics*

,cut-throat 'razor *noun* a RAZOR (= a tool used for shaving) with a long sharp blade—compare SAFETY RAZOR

cut·ting /'kʌtɪŋ/ *noun, adj.*
■ *noun* **1** (also **'press cutting**) (both *BrE*) (also **clip·ping**, **'press clipping** *AmE, BrE*) an article or a story that you cut from a newspaper or magazine and keep: *newspaper/press cuttings* **2** a piece cut off a plant that will be used to grow a new plant **3** (*BrE*) a narrow open passage that is dug through high ground for a road, railway or canal
■ *adj.* [usually before noun] **1** unkind and likely to hurt sb's feelings: *a cutting remark* **2** (of winds) cold in a sharp and unpleasant way

'cutting board *noun* (*AmE*) = CHOPPING BOARD

,cutting 'edge *noun* [sing.] **1** the ~ (**of sth**) the newest, most advanced stage in the development of sth: *working* **at the cutting edge** *of computer technology* **2** an aspect of sth that gives it an advantage: *We're relying on him to give the team a cutting edge.*

'cutting room *noun* a room in which the different parts of a film/movie are cut and put into order

cuttle·fish /'kʌtlfɪʃ/ *noun* (*pl.* **cuttle·fish**) a sea creature with ten arms and a wide flat shell inside its body, that produces a black substance like ink when it is attacked

cutup /'kʌtʌp/ *noun* (*AmE, informal*) a person who behaves in a silly way in order to attract attention and make people laugh

CV /ˌsiː 'viː/ (*AmE* **resumé**) *noun* a written record of your education and employment that you send when you are applying for a job (abbreviation for 'curriculum vitae'):

Send a full CV with your job application. ⇨ Study page B15

cwt. *abbr.* (*pl.* **cwt.**) (in writing) HUNDREDWEIGHT

-cy (*BrE* also **-acy**) *suffix* (in nouns) **1** the state or quality of: *infancy* ◊ *accuracy* **2** the status or position of: *chaplaincy*

cyan /'saɪən/ *noun* [U] (*technical*) a greenish-blue colour, used in printing

cy·an·ide /'saɪənaɪd/ *noun* [U] a highly poisonous chemical compound

cyber- /'saɪbə(r)/ *combining form* (in nouns and adjectives) connected with electronic communication NETWORKS, especially the Internet: *cybernetics* ◊ *cybercafe*

cy·ber·cafe /'saɪbəkæfeɪ; *AmE* 'saɪbər-/ *noun* a cafe on computers on which customers can use the Internet, send electronic mail, etc.

cy·ber·net·ics /ˌsaɪbə'netɪks; *AmE* -bər'n-/ *noun* [U] the scientific study of communication and control, especially concerned with comparing human and animal brains with machines and electronic devices ► **cy·ber·net·ic** *adj.*

cy·ber·space /'saɪbəspeɪs; *AmE* -bərs-/ *noun* [U] the imaginary place where electronic messages, pictures, etc. exist while they are being sent between computers: *A new electronic link-up that will connect 500 hospitals around the world has checked into cyberspace.*

cy·borg /'saɪbɔːg; *AmE* -bɔːrg/ *noun* (in SCIENCE FICTION stories) a creature that is part human, part machine

cyc·la·men /'sɪkləmən; *AmE* 'saɪk-/ *noun* (*pl.* **cyc·la·men** or **cyc·la·mens**) a plant with pink, purple or white flowers that grow on long stems pointing downwards, often grown indoors

cycle /'saɪkl/ *noun, verb*
■ *noun* **1** a bicycle or motorcycle: *We went for a cycle ride on Sunday.* ◊ *a cycle route/track*—see also BIKE **2** the fact of a series of events being repeated many times, always in the same order: *the cycle of the seasons*—see also LIFE CYCLE **3** a complete set or series, for example of movements in a machine: *eight cycles per second* ◊ *the rinse cycle* (= in a washing machine)
■ *verb* [V] [usually +*adv./prep.*] (*especially BrE*) to ride a bicycle; to travel by bicycle: *I usually cycle home through the park.*—compare BICYCLE, BIKE

'cycle lane (*BrE*) (*AmE* **'bicycle lane**, **'bike lane**) *noun* a part of a road or path that only bicycles are allowed to use

cyc·lic /'saɪklɪk; 'sɪk-/ (also **cyc·lic·al** /'saɪklɪkl; 'sɪk-/) *adj.* [usually before noun] repeated many times and always happening in the same order: *the cyclic processes of nature* ◊ *Economic activity often follows a cyclical pattern.* ► **cyc·lic·al·ly** *adv.*: *events that occur cyclically*

cyc·ling /'saɪklɪŋ/ *noun* [U] the sport or activity of riding a bicycle: *to go cycling* ◊ *Cycling is Europe's second most popular sport.* ◊ *cycling shorts*

cyc·list /'saɪklɪst/ *noun* a person who rides a bicycle—compare BICYCLIST

cyc·lone /'saɪkləʊn; *AmE* -kloʊn/ *noun* a violent tropical storm in which strong winds move in a circle—compare HURRICANE, TYPHOON

cyg·net /'sɪgnət/ *noun* a young SWAN (= a large white bird with a long neck that lives on or near water)

cy·lin·der /'sɪlɪndə(r)/ *noun* **1** a solid or hollow figure with round ends and long straight sides—picture at SOLID **2** an object shaped like a cylinder, especially one used as a container: *a gas/oxygen cylinder* **3** the hollow tube in an engine, shaped like a cylinder, inside which the PISTON moves: *a six-cylinder engine* **IDM** **working/firing on all 'cylinders** (*informal*) using all your energy to do sth; working as well as possible

cy·lin·dric·al /sə'lɪndrɪkl/ *adj.* shaped like a cylinder: *huge cylindrical gas tanks*

cym·bal /'sɪmbl/ *noun* a musical instrument in the form of a round metal plate. It is hit with a stick, or two cymbals are hit against each other: *a clash/crash of cymbals*—picture on page 841

cynic /'sɪnɪk/ *noun* **1** a person who believes that people only do things to help themselves, rather than for good or sincere reasons: *Don't be such a cynic!* **2** a person who does not believe that sth good will happen or that sth is important: *Cynics will say that there is not the slightest chance of success.* ▶ **cyni·cism** /ˈsɪnɪsɪzəm/ *noun* [U]: *In a world full of cynicism she was the one person I felt I could trust.*

cyn·ic·al /ˈsɪnɪkl/ *adj.* **1** believing that people only do things to help themselves rather than for good or honest reasons: *Do you have to be so cynical about everything?* ◇ *a cynical view/smile* **2** not caring that sth might hurt other people, if there is some advantage for you: *a cynical disregard for the safety of others* ◇ *a deliberate and cynical foul* ▶ **cyn·ic·al·ly** /-kli/ *adv.*

cy·pher = CIPHER

cy·press /ˈsaɪprəs/ *noun* a tall straight EVERGREEN tree

cyst /sɪst/ *noun* a GROWTH containing liquid that forms in or on a person's or an animal's body and may need to be removed

cys·tic fi·bro·sis /ˌsɪstɪk faɪˈbrəʊsɪs; *AmE* -ˈbroʊ-/ *noun* [U] a serious medical condition that some people are born with, in which GLANDS in the lungs and other organs do not work correctly. It often leads to infections and can result in early death.

cyst·itis /sɪˈstaɪtɪs/ *noun* [U] an infection of the BLADDER, especially in women, that causes frequent, painful URI-NATION

czar, czar·ina, czar·ism, czar·ist = TSAR, TSARINA, TSARISM, TSARIST

C

æ	ɑː	e	ɜː	ə	ɪ	iː	i	ɒ	ɔː	ʌ	ʊ	u	uː
cat	father	ten	bird	about	sit	see	many	got	saw	cup	put	actual	too

(BrE)

Dd

D /di:/ *noun, abbr., symbol*

■ *noun* (also **d**) [C, U] (*pl.* **D's, d's** /di:z/) **1** the fourth letter of the English alphabet: *'Dog' begins with (a) D/'D'.* **2** (D) (*music*) the second note in the scale of C MAJOR **3** (D) the fourth highest mark/grade that a student can get for a piece of work, showing that it is not very good: *He got (a) D/'D' in/for Geography.*—see also D-DAY

■ *abbr.* (also **D.** especially in *AmE*) (in politics in the US) DEMOCRAT; DEMOCRATIC

■ *symbol* the number 500 in ROMAN NUMERALS

d. *abbr.* **1** (in writing) died: *Emily Clifton, d. 1865* **2** (d) (in the system of money used in the past in Britain) a PENNY

-d *suffix* ⇨ -ED

DA (*BrE*) (*AmE* **D.A.**) *abbr.* DISTRICT ATTORNEY

dab /dæb/ *verb, noun*

■ *verb* (-bb-) **1** ~ (at) sth to touch sth lightly, usually several times: [VN] *She dabbed her eyes and blew her nose.* ◇ [V] *He dabbed at the cut with his handkerchief.* **2** [VN+*adv.*/*prep.*] to put sth on a surface with quick light movements: *She dabbed a little perfume behind her ears.*

■ *noun* **1** a small amount of a liquid, cream or powder that is put on a surface in a quick gentle movement: *She put a dab of perfume behind her ears.* **2** an act of gently touching or pressing sth without rubbing: *He gave the cut a quick dab with the corner of a towel.* **3** a small flat fish

dab·ble /'dæbl/ *verb* **1** ~ (in/with sth) to take part in a sport, an activity, etc. but not very seriously: *She is a talented musician but is content to just dabble.* ◇ *He dabbles in local politics.* **2** [VN] ~ sth (in sth) to move your hands, feet, etc. around in water: *She dabbled her toes in the stream.*

,dab 'hand *noun* (*BrE, informal*) a person who is very good at doing sth or using sth: *He's a dab hand at cooking spaghetti.* ◇ *She's a dab hand with a paintbrush.*

dacha /'dætʃə/ *noun* a Russian country house

dachs·hund /'dæksnd; *AmE* 'dɑ:kshʊnd/ (also *BrE informal* **'sausage dog**) *noun* a small dog with a long body, long ears and very short legs

dad /dæd/ *noun* (*informal*) (often used as a name) father: *That's my dad over there.* ◇ *Do you live with your mum or your dad?* ◇ *Is it OK if I borrow the car, Dad?*

daddy /'dædi/ *noun* used especially by and to young children, and often as a name, to mean 'father': *What does your daddy look like?* ◇ *Daddy, where are you?* ◇ *Come to Daddy.*

,daddy-'long-legs *noun* (*pl.* **daddy-long-legs**) (*informal*) **1** = CRANE FLY **2** (*AmE*) a small creature like a spider with very long legs

dado /'deɪdəʊ; *AmE* -doʊ/ *noun* (*pl.* **-os**, *AmE* **-oes**) the lower part of the wall of a room when it is a different colour or material from the top part

dae·mon /'di:mən/ *noun* a creature in stories from ancient Greece that is half man and half god

daf·fo·dil /'dæfədɪl/ *noun* a tall yellow spring flower shaped like a TRUMPET. It is a national symbol of Wales.

daft /dɑ:ft; *AmE* dæft/ *adj.* (**daft·er, daft·est**) (*BrE, informal*) silly, often in a way that is amusing: *Don't be so daft!* ◇ *She's not as daft as she looks.* ◇ *What a daft thing to say!* ► **daft·ness** *noun* [U] IDM **,daft as a 'brush** (*BrE, spoken*) very silly

dag·ger /'dægə(r)/ *noun* a short pointed knife that is used as a weapon—see also CLOAK-AND-DAGGER IDM **at daggers 'drawn** (*BrE*) if two people are at daggers drawn, they are very angry with each other **look 'daggers at sb** to look at sb in a very angry way

dago /'deɪgəʊ; *AmE* -goʊ/ *noun* (*pl.* **-os** or **-oes**) (△, *slang*)

a very offensive word for a person from Italy, Spain or Portugal

dah·lia /'deɪliə; *AmE* 'dæliə/ *noun* a large brightly coloured garden flower, often shaped like a ball

daily /'deɪli/ *adj., adv., noun*

■ *adj.* [only before noun] **1** happening, done or produced every day: *a daily routine/visit/newspaper* ◇ *events affecting the daily lives of millions of people* ◇ *Invoices are signed on a daily basis.* **2** connected with one day's work: *They charge a daily rate.* IDM **your daily 'bread** the basic things that you need to live, especially food

■ *adv.* every day: *The machines are inspected twice daily.*

■ *noun* (*pl.* **-ies**) **1** a newspaper published every day except Sunday: *The story was in all the dailies.* **2** (also **,daily 'help**) (*old-fashioned, BrE*) a person employed to come to sb's house each day to clean it and do other jobs

dainty /'deɪnti/ *adj.* (**dain·tier, dain·ti·est**) **1** (of people and things) small and delicate in a way that people find attractive: *dainty feet* ◇ *a dainty porcelain cup* **2** (of movements) careful, often in a way that suggests good manners: *She took a dainty little bite of the apple.* ► **dain·tily** *adv.*: *She blew her nose as daintily as possible.* **dain·ti·ness** *noun* [U]

dai·quiri /'daɪkɪri; 'dæk-/ *noun* an alcoholic drink made from RUM mixed with fruit juice, sugar, etc: *a strawberry daiquiri*

dairy /'deəri; *AmE* 'deri/ *noun, adj.*

■ *noun* (*pl.* **-ies**) **1** a place on a farm where milk is kept and where butter and cheese are made **2** a company that sells milk, eggs, cheese and other milk products

■ *adj.* [only before noun] **1** made from milk: *dairy products/produce* **2** connected with the production of milk rather than meat: *the dairy industry* ◇ *dairy cattle/farmers* ◇ *a dairy cow/farm*

dairy·maid /'deərimeɪd; *AmE* 'deri-/ *noun* (*old-fashioned*) a woman who works in a dairy (1)

dairy·man /'deərimən; *AmE* 'deri-/ *noun* (*pl.* **-men** /-mən/) **1** a man who works in a dairy (1) **2** a man who owns or manages a dairy (2) and sells the products

dais /'deɪs/ *noun* a stage, especially at one end of a room, on which people stand to make speeches to an audience

daisy /'deɪzi/ *noun* (*pl.* **-ies**) a small wild flower with white PETALS around a yellow centre; a taller plant with similar but larger flowers—see also MICHAELMAS DAISY IDM see PUSH *v.*

'daisy wheel *noun* a small disc, used in some printers and TYPEWRITERS, that has metal rods around its edge with letters, etc. on them: *a daisy wheel printer*

dale /deɪl/ *noun* (*literary* or *dialect*) a valley, especially in northern England: *the Yorkshire Dales*

dal·li·ance /'dæliəns/ *noun* [U, C] (*old-fashioned* or *humorous*) **1** the behaviour of sb who is dallying with sb/sth: *It turned out to be his last dalliance with the education system.* **2** a sexual relationship that is not serious

dally /'dæli/ *verb* (**dal·lies, dally·ing, dal·lied, dal·lied**) [V] (*old-fashioned*) to do sth too slowly; to take too much time making a decision PHRV **'dally with sb/sth** (*old-fashioned*) to treat sb/sth in a way that is not serious enough—see also DILLY-DALLY

Dal·ma·tian /dæl'meɪʃn/ *noun* a large dog that has short white hair with black spots

dam /dæm/ *noun, verb*

■ *noun* **1** a barrier that is built across a river in order to stop the water from flowing, used especially to make a RESERVOIR (= a lake for storing water) or to produce electricity: *the Narmada dam in India* ◇ *The dam burst.*

aɪ	aʊ	eɪ	əʊ	oʊ	ɔɪ	ɪə	eə	ʊə	j	w
my	now	say	go (BrE)	go (AmE)	boy	near	hair	pure	yes	wet

2 (*technical*) the mother of some animals, especially horses—compare SIRE
- *verb* (-mm-) [VN] ~ **sth (up)** to build a dam across a river, especially in order to make an artificial lake for use as a water supply, etc: *plans to dam Colorado's South Platte river*

dam·age /ˈdæmɪdʒ/ *noun, verb*
- *noun* **1** [U] ~ **(to sth)** physical harm caused to sth which makes it less attractive, useful or valuable: *serious/ severe/extensive/permanent damage ◇ brain/liver damage ◇ smoke/bomb/storm damage ◇ The earthquake caused damage to property estimated at $6 million. ◇ The storm didn't do much damage. ◇ Let's take a look at the damage. ◇ I insist on paying for the damage. ◇ Make sure you insure your camera against loss or damage.* **2** [U] ~ **(to sb/sth)** harmful effects on sb/sth: *emotional damage resulting from divorce ◇ damage to a person's reputation ◇ This could cause serious damage to the country's economy. ◇ I'm going—I've done enough damage here already.* **3** (**damages**) [pl.] an amount of money that is paid to sb by the person, company, etc. that has caused them harm or injury: *He was ordered to pay damages totalling £30 000. ◇ They intend to sue for damages. ◇ Ann was awarded £6000 (in) damages.* **IDM** **what's the 'damage?** (*spoken*) a way of asking how much sth costs
- *verb* [VN] to harm or spoil sth/sb: *The fire badly damaged the town hall. ◇ Several vehicles were damaged in the crash. ◇ Smoking seriously damages your health. ◇ The allegations are likely to damage his political career. ◇ emotionally damaged children*

ˌdamage limiˈtation (also ˌdamage conˈtrol espe- cially in *AmE*) *noun* [U] the process of trying to limit the amount of damage that is caused by sth

dam·aging /ˈdæmɪdʒɪŋ/ *adj.* ~ **(to sb/sth)** causing dam- age; having a bad effect on sb/sth: *damaging conse- quences/effects ◇ Lead is potentially damaging to chil- dren's health.*

dam·ask /ˈdæməsk/ *noun* [U] a thick fabric, usually made from silk or LINEN, with a pattern that is visible on both sides: *a damask tablecloth*

dame /deɪm/ *noun* **1** (**Dame**) (in Britain) a title given to a woman as a special honour because of the work she has done: *Dame Maggie Smith* **2** (*old-fashioned, AmE, infor- mal*) a woman **3** = PANTOMIME DAME

damn /dæm/ *exclamation, adj., verb, adv., noun*
- *exclamation* (also *old-fashioned* **dam·mit** /ˈdæmɪt/ **damn it**) (*informal*) a swear word that people use to show that they are annoyed, disappointed, etc: *Oh damn! I forgot he was coming.*
- *adj.* (also **damned**) [only before noun] (*informal*) **1** a swear word that people use to show that they are annoyed with sb/sth: *Where's that damn book! ◇ The damned thing won't start! ◇ It's none of your damn busi- ness! ◇ He's a damn nuisance!* **2** a swear word that people use to emphasize what they are saying: *What a damn shame!* **IDM** see THING
- *verb* [VN] **1** used when swearing at sb/sth to show that you are angry: *Damn you! I'm not going to let you bully me. ◇ Damn this machine! Why won't it work?* **2** (of God) to decide that sb must suffer in HELL **3** to criticize sb/sth very strongly: *The film was damned by the critics for its mindless violence.* **IDM** **damn the consequences, expense, etc.** (*spoken*) used to say that you are going to do sth even though you know it may be expensive, have bad results, etc: *Let's celebrate and damn the expense!* **damn sb/sth with faint 'praise** to praise sb/sth only a little, in order to show that you do not really like them/it **I'll be damned!** (*old-fashioned, spoken*) used to show that you are very surprised about sth **I'm damned if …** (*spoken*) used to show that you refuse to do sth or do not know sth: *I'm damned if I'll apologize! ◇ I'm damned if I know who he is.*—more at NEAR *adv.*
- *adv.* (also **damned**) (*informal*) **1** a swear word that people use to show that they are annoyed with sb/sth: *Don't be so damn silly! ◇ What a damn stupid question! ◇ You know damn well* (= you know very well) *what I mean! ◇ I'll damn well leave tonight* (= I am determined to). **2** a swear word that people use to emphasize what

they are saying: *damn good/clever/lucky ◇ We got out pretty damned fast!* ◇ *I'm damn sure she had no idea.* **IDM** **damn 'all** (*BrE*) nothing: *I know damn all about com- puters.*
- *noun* **IDM** **not care/give a 'damn (about sb/sth)** (*infor- mal*) to not care at all about sb/sth

dam·nable /ˈdæmnəbl/ *adj.* (*old-fashioned*) bad or annoying ▸ **dam·nably** /ˈdæmnəbli/ *adv.*

dam·na·tion /dæmˈneɪʃn/ *noun* [U] the state of being in HELL; the act of sending sb to HELL: *eternal damnation*

damned /dæmd/ *adj., adv., noun*
- *adj., adv.* = DAMN
- *noun* (**the damned**) [pl.] people who are forced to live in HELL after they die

damned·est ... /ˈdæmdɪst/ *noun, adj.* (*informal*) **IDM** **the damndest ...** (*especially AmE*) the most surprising …: *It's the damnedest thing I ever saw.* **do/ try your 'damnedest (to do sth)** to try as hard as you can (to do sth): *She did her damnedest to get it done on time.*

damn·ing /ˈdæmɪŋ/ *adj.* critical of sb/sth; suggesting that sb is guilty: *damning criticism/evidence ◇ a damning conclusion/report ◇ Her report is expected to deliver a damning indictment of education standards.*

Damo·cles /ˈdæməkliːz/ *noun* **IDM** see SWORD

damp /dæmp/ *adj., noun, verb*
- *adj.* (**damp·er, damp·est**) slightly wet, often in a way that is unpleasant: *The cottage was cold and damp. ◇ It feels damp in here. ◇ damp clothes ◇ Wipe the surface with a damp cloth.* ▸ **damp·ly** *adv.* (*rare*): *The blouse clung damply to her skin.* **IDM** **a damp 'squib** (*BrE, informal*) an event that is disappointing because it is not as excit- ing or impressive as expected
- *noun* [U] (*BrE*) the state of being damp; areas on a wall, etc. that are damp: *The old house smells of damp. ◇ Those marks above the window look like damp to me.*
- *verb* [VN] (*rare*) = DAMPEN: *She damped a towel and wrapped it round his leg.* **PHRV** **ˌdamp 'down sth** to make an emotion or a feeling less strong **ˌdamp sth↔'down** to make a fire burn more slowly or stop burning

'damp course (also **'damp-proof course**) *noun* (both *BrE*) a layer of material near the bottom of a wall that is used to stop damp rising from the ground

damp·en /ˈdæmpən/ *verb* [VN] **1** (also *less frequent* **damp**) to make sth slightly wet: *Perspiration dampened her face and neck. ◇ He dampened his hair to make it lie flat.* **2** to make sth such as a feeling or a reaction less strong: *None of the setbacks could dampen his enthusi- asm for the project. ◇ She wasn't going to let anything dampen her spirits today.*

damp·er /ˈdæmpə(r)/ *noun* **1** a piece of metal that can be moved to allow more or less air into a fire so that the fire burns more or less strongly **2** a device in a piano that is used to reduce the level of the sound produced **IDM** **put a 'damper on sth** (*informal*) to make sth less enjoyable, successful, etc.

damp·ness /ˈdæmpnəs/ *noun* [U] the fact or state of being damp: *To avoid dampness, air the room regularly.*

'damp-proof course *noun* = DAMP COURSE

dam·sel /ˈdæmzl/ *noun* (*old use*) a young woman who is not married **IDM** **a ˌdamsel in diˈstress** (*humorous*) a woman who needs help

dam·son /ˈdæmzn/ *noun* a small purple fruit, like a PLUM: *a damson tree*

dance /dɑːns; *AmE* dæns/ *noun, verb*
- *noun* **1** [C] a series of movements and steps that are usually performed to music; a particular example of these movements and steps: *a dance class/routine ◇ Find a partner and practise these new dance steps. ◇ Do you know any other Latin American dances? ◇ The next dance will be a waltz.* **2** [U] the art of dancing, especially for entertainment: *an evening of drama, music and dance ◇ modern/classical dance ◇ a dance company/troupe* **3** [C] an act of dancing: *Let's have a dance. ◇ He did a little dance of triumph.* **4** [C] a social event at which people dance: *We hold a dance every year to raise money for charity.* **5** [C] a piece of music for dancing to: *The band finished with a few slow dances.* **IDM** see LEAD[1] *v.*, SONG

D

■ *verb* **1** [V] to move your body to the sound and rhythm of music: *Do you want to dance?* ◇ *He asked me to dance.* ◇ *They stayed up all night singing and dancing.* ◇ *They danced to the music of a string quartet.* ◇ *Ruth danced all evening with Richard.* ◇ *Ruth and Richard danced together all evening.* **2** [VN] to do a particular type of dance: *to dance the tango* ◇ *to dance a waltz* **3** [V] to move in a lively way: *The children danced around her.* ◇ *The sun shone on the sea and the waves danced and sparkled.* ◇ *The words danced before her tired eyes.* IDM **¡dance at'tendance on sb** (*BrE, formal*) to be with sb and do things to help and please them **¡dance the 'night away** to dance for the whole evening or night **dance to sb's 'tune** (*BrE*) to do whatever sb tells you to

'dance floor *noun* an area where people can dance in a hotel, restaurant, etc.

'dance hall *noun* a large public room where people pay to go and dance (more common in the past than now) —compare BALLROOM

dan·cer /ˈdɑːnsə(r); *AmE* ˈdæn-/ *noun* a person who dances or whose job is dancing: *She's a fantastic dancer.* ◇ *He's a dancer with the Royal Ballet.*

dan·cing /ˈdɑːnsɪŋ; *AmE* ˈdæn-/ *noun* [U] moving your body to music: *dancing classes/shoes* ◇ *There was music and dancing till two in the morning.* ◇ *disco dancing*

dan·delion /ˈdændɪlaɪən/ *noun* a small wild plant with a bright yellow flower that becomes a soft white ball of seeds called a **dandelion clock**

dan·dle /ˈdændl/ *verb* [VN] (*old-fashioned*) to play with a baby or young child by moving them up and down on your knee

dan·druff /ˈdændrʌf/ *noun* [U] very small pieces of dead skin, seen as a white dust in a person's hair

dandy /ˈdændi/ *noun, adj.*
■ *noun* (*pl.* **-ies**) (*old-fashioned*) a man who cares a lot about his clothes and appearance
■ *adj.* (*old-fashioned, especially AmE*) very good

dang /dæŋ/ *adj., exclamation* (*AmE, informal*) a mild swear word, used instead of DAMN: *It's just dang stupid!*

dan·ger /ˈdeɪndʒə(r)/ *noun* **1** [U] ~ (**of sth**) the possibility of sth happening that will injure, harm or kill sb, or damage or destroy sth: *Danger! Keep Out!* ◇ *Children's lives are in danger every time they cross this road.* ◇ *Doctors said she is now out of danger* (= not likely to die). **2** [C, U] ~ **of sth** | ~ **that** the possibility of sth bad or unpleasant happening: *There is no danger of a bush fire now.* ◇ *The building is in danger of collapsing.* ◇ *How many factory workers are in danger of losing their jobs?* ◇ *There is a danger that the political disorder of the past will return.* ◇ *'Nicky won't find out, will she?' 'Oh, no, there's no danger of that.'* **3** [C] ~ (**to sb/sth**) a person or thing that may cause damage, or harm sb: *Smoking is a serious danger to health.* ◇ *Police said the man was a danger to the public.* ◇ *the hidden dangers in your home*—see also ENDANGER IDM **be on/off the 'danger list** (*BrE*) to be so ill that you may die; to no longer be very ill

'danger money (*BrE*) (*AmE* **'danger pay**) *noun* [U] extra pay for doing work that is dangerous

dan·ger·ous /ˈdeɪndʒərəs/ *adj.* ~ (**for sb**) (**to do sth**) likely to injure or harm sb, or to damage or destroy sth: *a dangerous road/illness/sport* ◇ *The traffic here is very dangerous for children.* ◇ *dangerous levels of carbon monoxide* ◇ *The prisoners who escaped are violent and dangerous.* ◇ *a conviction for dangerous driving* ◇ *The situation is highly dangerous.* ◇ *It would be dangerous for you to stay here.* ▶ **dan·ger·ous·ly** *adv.*: *She was standing dangerously close to the fire.* ◇ *His father is dangerously ill* (= so ill that he might die). ◇ *Mel enjoys living dangerously* (= doing things that involve risk or danger). IDM **dangerous 'ground** a situation or subject that is likely to make sb angry, or that involves risk: *We'd be on dangerous ground if we asked about race or religion.*

dan·gle /ˈdæŋgl/ *verb* **1** [V] [usually+*adv./prep.*] to hang or swing freely: *Gold charms dangled from her bracelet.* ◇ *There was a cigarette dangling from his mouth.* ◇ *A single light bulb dangled from the ceiling.* ◇ *His legs dangled over*

the side of the boat. ◇ *He sat on the edge with his legs dangling over the side.* **2** [VN] to hold sth so that it hangs or swings freely: *She dangled her car keys nervously as she spoke.* PHRV **dangle sth before/in front of sb** to offer sb sth good in order to persuade them to do sth: *He had a company directorship dangled in front of him.*

Danish pastry /ˌdeɪnɪʃ ˈpeɪstri/ (*especially BrE*) (also **Dan·ish** *AmE, BrE*) *noun* a sweet cake made of light pastry, often containing apple, nuts, etc. and/or covered with ICING—picture on page A1

dank /dæŋk/ *adj.* (especially of a place) damp, cold and unpleasant: *a dark dank cave*

dap·per /ˈdæpə(r)/ *adj.* (of a man) small with a neat appearance and nice clothes

dap·pled /ˈdæpld/ *adj.* marked with spots of colour, or shade: *the cool dappled light under the trees*

Darby and Joan /ˌdɑːbi ən ˈdʒəʊn; *AmE* ˌdɑːrbi ən ˈdʒoʊn/ *noun* [pl.] (*BrE*) a way of referring to an old couple who are happily married

dare /deə(r); *AmE* der/ *verb, noun*
■ *verb* **1** (not usually used in the progressive tenses) to be brave enough to do sth: *She said it as loudly as she dared.* ◇ *He didn't dare (to) say what he thought.* ◇ *They daren't ask for any more money.* ◇ (*literary*) *She dared not breathe a word of it to anybody.* ◇ *There was something, dare I say it, a little unusual about him.* **2** to persuade sb to do sth dangerous, difficult or embarrassing so that they can show that they are not afraid: *I'll* (*Go on! Take it! I dare you.* ◇ [VNto inf] *Some of the older boys had dared him to do it.* ⇨ note at MODAL IDM **Don't you dare!** (*spoken*) used to tell sb strongly not to do sth: *'I'll tell her about it.' 'Don't you dare!'* ◇ *Don't you dare say anything to anybody.* **How 'dare you, etc.** used to show that you are angry about sth that sb has done: *How dare you talk to me like that?* ◇ *How dare she imply that I was lying?* **I dare say** (also **I daresay** especially in *BrE*) used when you are saying that sth is probable: *I dare say you know about it already.*
■ *noun* [usually sing.] something dangerous, difficult or embarrassing that you try to persuade sb to do, to see if they will do it: (*BrE*) *He climbed onto the roof for a dare.* ◇ (*AmE*) *She learned to fly on a dare.*

GRAMMAR POINT
dare

Dare (sense 1) usually forms negatives and questions like an ordinary verb and is followed by an infinitive with *to*. It is most common in the negative: *I didn't dare to ask.* ◇ *He won't dare to break his promise.* ◇ *You told him? How did you dare?* ◇ *I hardly dared to hope she'd remember me.* In positive sentences a phrase like **not be afraid** is often used instead: *She wasn't afraid* (= she dared) *to tell him the truth.*

It can also be used like a modal verb especially in present tense negative forms in *BrE*, and is followed by an infinitive without *to*: *I daren't tell her the truth.*

In spoken English, the forms of the ordinary verb are often used with an infinitive without *to*: *Don't you dare tell her what I said!* ◇ *I didn't dare look at him.*

---

dare·devil /ˈdeədevl; *AmE* ˈderd-/ *noun* a person who enjoys doing dangerous things, in a way that other people may think is stupid: *a reckless daredevil* ▶ **dare·devil** *adj.* [only before noun]: *Don't try any daredevil stunts.*

dar·ing /ˈdeərɪŋ; *AmE* ˈder-/ *adj., noun*
■ *adj.* brave; willing to do dangerous or unusual things; involving danger or taking risks: *a daring walk in space* ◇ *There are plenty of activities at the resort for the less daring.* ◇ *The gallery was known for putting on daring exhibitions.* ◇ *a daring strapless dress in black silk* ▶ **dar·ing·ly** *adv.*
■ *noun* [U] courage and the willingness to take risks: *the skill and daring of the mountain climbers*

dark /dɑːk; *AmE* dɑːrk/ *adj., noun*
■ *adj.* (**dark·er, dark·est**)
WITH LITTLE LIGHT | **1** with no or very little light, especially because it is night: *a dark room/street/forest* ◇ *What time*

does it get dark in summer? ◊ *It was dark outside and I couldn't see much.* OPP LIGHT

COLOURS | **2** not light; closer in shade to black than to white: *dark blue/green/red* ◊ *Darker colours are more practical and don't show stains.* OPP LIGHT, PALE **3** having a colour that is close to black: *a dark suit* ◊ *dark-coloured wood* ◊ *The dark clouds in the sky meant that a storm was coming.*

HAIR/SKIN/EYES | **4** brown or black in colour: *Sue has long dark hair.* ◊ *Even if you have dark skin, you still need protection from the sun.* **5** (of a person) having dark hair, eyes, etc: *a dark handsome stranger*

MYSTERIOUS | **6** mysterious; hidden and not known about: *There are no dark secrets in our family.*

EVIL | **7** evil or frightening: *There was a darker side to his nature.* ◊ *the dark forces of the imagination*

WITHOUT HOPE | **8** unpleasant and without any hope that sth good will happen: *the darkest days of Fascism* ◊ *The film is a dark vision of the future.*

IDM **a dark 'horse 1** (*BrE*) a person who does not tell other people much about their life, and who surprises other people by having interesting qualities **2** an unknown competitor in a race, etc. who surprises everyone by winning **keep sth 'dark** (*BrE, informal*) to keep sth secret and not tell people about it

■ *noun*
NO LIGHT | **1** (**the dark**) [sing.] the lack of light in a place, especially because it is night: *All the lights went out and we were left in the dark.* ◊ *Are the children afraid of the dark?* ◊ *animals that can see in the dark*

COLOUR | **2** [U] an amount of sth that is dark in colour: *patterns of light and dark*

IDM **after/before dark** after/before the sun goes down and it is night: *Try to get home before dark.* ◊ *Don't go out àlone after dark.* **in the 'dark (about sth)** knowing nothing about sth: *Workers were kept in the dark about the plans to sell the company.* ◊ *She arrived at the meeting as much in the dark as everyone else.* **a shot/stab in the 'dark** a guess; sth you do without knowing what the result will be: *The figure he came up with was really just a shot in the dark.*—more at LEAP *n.*

the 'dark ages *noun* [pl.] **1** (**the Dark Ages**) the period of European history between the end of the Roman Empire and the 10th century AD **2** (often *humorous*) a period of history or a time when sth was not developed or modern: *Back in the dark ages of computing, in about 1980, they started a software company.*

dark·en /'dɑːkən; *AmE* 'dɑːrk-/ *verb* (*written*) **1** to become dark; to make sth dark: [V] *The sky began to darken as the storm approached.* ◊ [VN] *We walked quickly through the darkened streets.* ◊ *a darkened room* **2** to make sb unhappy or angry; to become unhappy or angry: [VN] *It was a tragedy that darkened his later life.* ◊ [V] *Her mood darkened at the news.* ◊ *Luke's face darkened* (= he looked angry). IDM **never darken my 'door again** (*old-fashioned, humorous*) used to tell sb never to come to your home again

,**dark 'glasses** *noun* [pl.] glasses that have dark-coloured LENSES—see also SUNGLASSES

dark·ly /'dɑːkli; *AmE* 'dɑːrk-/ *adv.* (*written*) **1** in a threatening or unpleasant way: *He hinted darkly that all was not well.* **2** showing a dark colour: *Her eyes burned darkly.*

dark·ness /'dɑːknəs; *AmE* 'dɑːrk-/ *noun* [U] **1** the state of being dark, without any light: *After a few minutes our eyes got used to the darkness.* ◊ *The house was plunged into total darkness when the electricity was cut off.* ◊ *In the west the sun went down and darkness fell* (= it became night). ◊ *There is an extra hour of darkness on winter mornings.* ◊ *Parking is not allowed during the hours of darkness.* ◊ *Her face was in darkness.* ◊ *They managed to escape under cover of darkness.* **2** the quality or state of being dark in colour: *It depends on the darkness of your skin.* **3** (*literary*) evil: *the forces of darkness*

dark·room /'dɑːkruːm; -rʊm; *AmE* 'dɑːrk-/ *noun* a room that can be made completely dark, where you can take film out of a camera and develop photographs

dar·ling /'dɑːlɪŋ; *AmE* 'dɑːrlɪŋ/ *noun, adj.*

■ *noun* **1** (*spoken*) a way of addressing sb that you love: *What's the matter, darling?* **2** a person who is very friendly and kind: *You are a darling, Hugo.* **3** **the ~ of sb/sth** a person who is especially liked and very popular: *She is the darling of the newspapers and can do no wrong.*

■ *adj.* [only before noun] (*informal*) much loved; very attractive, special, etc: *My darling daughter.* ◊ *'Darling Henry,' the letter began.*

darn /dɑːn; *AmE* dɑːrn/ *verb, noun, adj., adv.*

■ *verb* to repair a hole in a piece of clothing by sewing stitches across the hole: [VN] *to darn socks* [alsoV] IDM **'darn it!** (*spoken, especially AmE*) used as a mild swear word to show that you are angry or annoyed about sth, to avoid saying 'damn': *Darn it! I've lost my keys!* **I'll be 'darned!** (*spoken, especially AmE*) used to show that you are surprised about sth

■ *noun* a place on a piece of clothing that has been repaired by darning

■ *adj.* (also **darned**) (*spoken*) used as a mild swear word, to emphasize sth: *Why don't you switch the darn thing off and listen to me!*

■ *adv.* (also **darned**) (*spoken*) used as a mild swear word, instead of saying DAMN, to mean 'extremely' or 'very': *You had a darn good try.* ◊ *It's darn cold tonight.*

darned /dɑːnd; *AmE* dɑːrnd/ *adj., adv.* (*AmE*) a mild swear word that people use to emphasize what they are saying. People say 'darned' to avoid saying 'damn': *That's a darned good idea!* ► **darned·est** *adj.*

dart /dɑːt; *AmE* dɑːrt/ *noun, verb*

■ *noun* **1** [C] a small pointed object, sometimes with feathers to help it fly, that is shot as a weapon or thrown in the game of darts: *a poisoned dart*—picture on page A8 **2** (**darts**) [U] a game in which darts are thrown at a round board marked with numbers for scoring. Darts is often played in British pubs: *a darts match*—picture on page A8 **3** [sing.] a sudden quick movement: *She made a dart for the door.* **4** [sing.] (*written*) a sudden feeling of a strong emotion: *Nina felt a sudden dart of panic.* **5** [C] a pointed fold that is sewn in a piece of clothing to make it fit better

■ *verb* **1** [V+*adv./prep.*] to move suddenly and quickly in a particular direction: *A dog darted across the road in front of me.* ◊ *Her eyes darted around the room, looking for Greg.* **2 ~ a glance/look (at sb)** to look at sb suddenly and quickly: [VN, VNN] *He darted an impatient look at Vicky.* ◊ *He darted Vicky an impatient look.*

dart·board /'dɑːtbɔːd; *AmE* 'dɑːrtbɔːrd/ *noun* a circular board used in the game of darts—picture on page A8

dash /dæʃ/ *noun, verb*

■ *noun*
STH DONE QUICKLY | **1** [sing.] **a ~ (for sth)** an act of going somewhere suddenly and/or quickly: *When the doors opened, there was a mad dash for seats.* ◊ *a 60-mile dash to safety* ◊ *He jumped off the bus and made a dash for the nearest bar.* ◊ *We waited for the police to leave then made a dash for it* (= left quickly in order to escape). **2** [sing.] an act of doing sth quickly because you do not have enough time: *a last-minute dash to buy presents*

SMALL AMOUNT | **3** [C, usually sing.] **~ (of sth)** a small amount of sth that is added to sth else: *Add a dash of lemon juice.* ◊ *The rug adds a dash of colour to the room.*—compare SPLASH

SYMBOL | **4** [C] the mark(—) used to separate parts of a sentence, often instead of a COLON or in pairs instead of BRACKETS—compare HYPHEN ⇨ Appendix 4

RACE | **5** [C, usually sing.] (*especially AmE*) a race in which the competitors run very fast over a short distance SYN SPRINT: *the 100-meter dash*

WAY OF BEHAVING | **6** [U] (*old-fashioned, approving*) a way of behaving that combines style, enthusiasm and confidence

PART OF CAR | **7** [C] (*informal*) = DASHBOARD
—see also PEBBLE-DASH

IDM **cut a 'dash** (*BrE*) to look attractive in a particular set of clothes, especially in a way that makes other people notice you: *He cut quite a dash in his uniform.*

■ *verb*
GO QUICKLY | **1** [V] [usually +*adv./prep.*] to go somewhere

D

æ	ɑː	e	ɜː	ə	ɪ	iː	i	ɒ	ɔː	ʌ	ʊ	u	uː
cat	father	ten	bird	about	sit	see	many	got	saw	cup	put	actual	too

(BrE)

very quickly: *I must dash* (= leave quickly), *I'm late.* ◇ *She dashed off to keep an appointment.* ◇ *He dashed along the platform and jumped on the train.*

THROW/BEAT | **2** [+*adv./prep.*] to throw sth or make sth fall violently onto a hard surface; to beat against a surface: [VN] *The boat was dashed repeatedly against the rocks.* ◇ [V] *The waves were dashing against the harbour wall.*

IDM **dash sb's 'hopes** to destroy sb's hopes by making what they were hoping for impossible **dash (it)! | dash it all!** (*old-fashioned, BrE*) used to show that you are annoyed about sth

PHRV **,dash sth↔'off** to write or draw sth very quickly: *I dashed off a note to my brother.*

dash·board /'dæʃbɔːd; *AmE* -bɔːrd/ (also **fa·scia**) (also **dash** especially in *AmE*) *noun* the part of a car in front of the driver that has instruments and controls in it—picture at CAR

dash·ing /'dæʃɪŋ/ *adj.* (*written*) **1** (usually of a man) attractive, confident and elegant: *a dashing young officer* ◇ *his dashing good looks* **2** (of a thing) attractive and fashionable: *his dashing red waistcoat*

das·tard·ly /'dæstədli; *AmE* -tərd-/ *adj.* (*old-fashioned*) wicked and cruel: *My first part was Captain O'Hagarty, a dastardly villain in a children's play.*

DAT /dæt/ *abbr.* digital audio tape

data /'deɪtə; *BrE* also 'dɑːtə; *AmE* also 'dætə/ *noun* (used as a plural noun in technical English, when the singular is *datum*) **1** [U, pl.] facts or information, especially when examined and used to find out things or to make decisions: *This data was collected from 69 countries.* ◇ *the analysis/interpretation of the data* ◇ *raw data* (= that has not been analysed) ◇ *demographical/historical/personal data* ◇ (*technical*) *These data show that most cancers are detected as a result of clinical follow-up.* **2** [U] information that is stored by a computer: *data capture/retrieval* (= ways of storing or finding information on a computer)

data·bank /'deɪtəbæŋk; *AmE* also 'dætə-/ *noun* a large amount of data on a particular subject that is stored in a computer

data·base /'deɪtəbeɪs; *AmE* also 'dætə-/ *noun* an organized set of data that is stored in a computer and can be looked at and used in various ways

dat·able /'deɪtəbl/ *adj.* that can be DATED to a particular time: *pottery that is datable to the second century*

'data mining *noun* [U] (*computing*) looking at large amounts of information that has been collected on a computer and using it to provide new information

,data 'processing *noun* [U] (*computing*) a series of actions that a computer performs on data to produce an OUTPUT (= information that has been analysed)

,data pro'tection *noun* [U] legal restrictions that keep information stored on computers private and that control who can read it or use it

date /deɪt/ *noun, verb*
■ *noun*
PARTICULAR DAY | **1** [C] a particular day of the month, sometimes in a particular year, given in numbers and words: *'What's the date today?' 'The 10th.'* ◇ *Write today's date at the top of the page.* ◇ *We need to fix a date for the next meeting.* ◇ *They haven't set a date for the wedding yet.* ◇ *I can't come on that date.* ◇ *Please give your name, address and date of birth.* ◇ (*especially AmE*) *name, address and birth date* ◇ *There's no date on this letter.*—see also CLOSING DATE, SELL-BY DATE ⇨ Appendix 3

PAST TIME/FUTURE | **2** [sing., U] a time in the past or future that is not a particular day: *The details can be added at a later date.* ◇ *The work will be carried out at a future date.* ◇ *a building of late Roman date*

ARRANGEMENT TO MEET | **3** [C] (*BrE*) an arrangement to meet sb at a particular time: *Call me next week and we'll try and make a date.*

ROMANTIC MEETING | **4** [C] a meeting that you have arranged with a boyfriend or girlfriend or with sb who might become a boyfriend or girlfriend: *I've got a date with Lucy tomorrow night.* ◇ *Paul's not coming. He's got a hot date* (= an exciting one).—see also BLIND DATE **5** [C] (*especially*

AmE) a boyfriend or girlfriend with whom you have arranged a date: *My date is meeting me at seven.*

FRUIT | **6** [C] a sweet sticky brown fruit that grows on a tree called a **date palm**, common in N Africa and W Asia

IDM **to 'date** until now: *To date, we have received over 200 replies.* ◇ *The exhibition contains some of his best work to date.*—see also OUT OF DATE, UP TO DATE

■ *verb*
WRITE DATE | **1** [VN] to write or print the date on sth: *Thank you for your letter dated 24th March.*

FIND AGE | **2** [VN] to say when sth old existed or was made: *The skeleton has been dated at about 2000 BC.*

OF CLOTHES/WORDS | **3** [V] to become old-fashioned: *She designs classic clothes which do not date.*

PERSON | **4** [VN] if sth dates you, it shows that you are fairly old or older than the people you are with: *I was at the Woodstock festival—that dates me, doesn't it?*

HAVE RELATIONSHIP | **5** (*old-fashioned, AmE*) to have a romantic relationship with sb: [VN] *She's been dating Ron for several months.* [also V]

PHRV **date back (to …) | date from …** to have existed since a particular time in the past or for the length of time mentioned: *The college dates back to medieval times.* ◇ *The custom dates back hundreds of years.* ◇ *a law dating from the 17th century*

date·book /'deɪtbʊk/ *noun* (*AmE*) = DIARY

dated /'deɪtɪd/ *adj.* old-fashioned; belonging to a time in the past—compare UNDATED

'date line *noun* = INTERNATIONAL DATE LINE

'date rape *noun* [U] the crime of RAPING a girl or woman, committed by sb she has gone out with on a DATE

'dating agency (also **'dating service**) *noun* a business or an organization that arranges meetings between single people who want to begin a romantic relationship: *He met his wife through a computer dating agency.*

dat·ive /'deɪtɪv/ *noun* (*grammar*) (in some languages) the form of a noun, a pronoun or an adjective when it is the INDIRECT OBJECT of a verb or is connected with the INDIRECT OBJECT: *In the sentence, 'I sent her a postcard', the word 'her' is in the dative.*—compare ACCUSATIVE, GENITIVE, NOMINATIVE, VOCATIVE ► **dat·ive** *adj.*

datum /'deɪtəm/ *noun* (*pl.* **data**) (*technical*) a fact or piece of information—see also DATA

daub /dɔːb/ *verb, noun*
■ *verb* [VN+*adv./prep.*] ~ **A on, etc. B | ~ B with A** to spread a substance such as paint, mud, etc. thickly and/or carelessly onto sth: *The walls of the building were daubed with red paint.*
■ *noun* **1** [U] a mixture of clay, etc. that was used in the past for making walls: *walls made of wattle and daub* **2** [C] a small amount of a substance such as paint that has been spread carelessly: *a daub of lipstick* **3** [C] a badly painted picture

daugh·ter /'dɔːtə(r)/ *noun* a person's female child—see also GOD-DAUGHTER, GRANDDAUGHTER, STEPDAUGHTER

'daughter-in-law *noun* (*pl.* **daughters-in-law**) the wife of your son—compare SON-IN-LAW

daunt /dɔːnt/ *verb* [VN] [usually passive] to make sb feel nervous and less confident about doing sth: *She was a brave woman but she felt daunted by the task ahead.* ► **daunt·ing** *adj.*: *She has the daunting task of cooking for 20 people every day.* ◇ *Starting a new job can be a daunting prospect.* **daunt·ing·ly** *adv.* **IDM** **nothing 'daunted** (*BrE, formal*) confident about sth difficult you have to do: *Nothing daunted, the people set about rebuilding their homes.*

daunt·less /'dɔːntləs/ *adj.* (*literary*) not easily frightened or stopped from doing sth difficult [SYN] RESOLUTE

daw·dle /'dɔːdl/ *verb* [V] [usually+*adv./prep.*] to take a long time to do sth or go somewhere: *Stop dawdling! We're going to be late!* ◇ *They dawdled along by the river, laughing and talking.*

dawn /dɔːn/ *noun, verb*
■ *noun* **1** [U, C, sing.] the time of day when light first appears [SYN] DAYBREAK, SUNRISE: *They start work at dawn.* ◇ *It's almost dawn.* ◇ *We arrived in Sydney as dawn broke* (= as

aɪ	aʊ	eɪ	əʊ	oʊ	ɔɪ	ɪə	eə	ʊə	j	w
my	now	say	go (BrE)	go (AmE)	boy	near	hair	pure	yes	wet

the first light could be seen). ◊ *I woke up just before dawn.* ◊ *summer's early dawns* ◊ *He works from dawn till dusk* (= from morning till night).—compare DUSK **2** [sing.] **~ (of sth)** the beginning or first signs of sth: *the dawn of civilization/time/history* ◊ *Peace marked a new dawn in the country's history.* IDM see BREAK *n.*, CRACK *n.*
■ *verb* [V] **1** (*written*) (of a day or a period of time) to begin: *The following morning dawned bright and warm.* ◊ *A new technological age had dawned.* **2** to become obvious or easy to understand: *Slowly the awful truth dawned.* IDM see LIGHT *n.* PHRV '**dawn on sb** [no passive] if sth **dawns on you**, you begin to realize it for the first time: [+that] *Suddenly it dawned on me that they couldn't possibly have met before.*

the ˌdawn 'chorus *noun* [sing.] (*BrE*) the sound of birds singing very early in the morning

day /deɪ/ *noun* **1** [C] a period of 24 hours: *I saw Tom three days ago.* ◊ *'What day is it today?' 'Monday.'* ◊ *We're going away in a few days/in a few days' time.* ◊ *They left the day before yesterday* (= two days ago). ◊ *We're meeting the day after tomorrow* (= in two days). ◊ *New Year's Day* ◊ *Take the medicine three times a day.* ◊ *We can't go there today. You can go another day.*—see also FIELD DAY, OFF DAY, RED-LETTER DAY, SPORTS DAY **2** [U] the time between when it becomes light in the morning and when it becomes dark in the evening: *The sun was shining all day.* ◊ *I could sit and watch the river all day long.* ◊ *He works at night and sleeps during the day.* ◊ *Nocturnal animals sleep by day and hunt by night.* **3** [C, usually sing.] the hours of the day when you are awake, working, etc: *a seven-hour working day* ◊ *It's been a long day* (= I've been very busy). ◊ *Did you have a good day?* ◊ *She didn't do a full day's work.* ◊ *I took a half day off yesterday.* ◊ (*AmE*) *Have a nice day!*—see also WORKDAY **4** [C, usually pl.] a particular period of time or history: *in Queen Victoria's day* ◊ *the early days of computers* ◊ *Most women stayed at home in those days.* ◊ (*spoken*) *in the old days* (= in the past)—see also GLORY DAYS, HEYDAY, NOWADAYS, THE PRESENT DAY HELP There are many other compounds ending in **day**. You will find them at their place in the alphabet. IDM **all in a day's 'work** part of your normal working life and not unusual **any day (now)** (*spoken*) very soon: *The letter should arrive any day now.* **carry/win the 'day** (*formal*) to be successful against sb/sth: *Despite strong opposition, the ruling party carried the day.* **day after 'day** each day repeatedly (used especially when sth is boring or annoying): *She hates doing the same work day after day.* **day by 'day** all the time; a little at a time and gradually: *Day by day his condition improved.* **day 'in, day 'out** every day for a long period of time **a day of 'reckoning** the time when sb will have to deal with the result of sth that they have done wrong, or be punished for sth bad that they have done **sb's/sth's days are 'numbered** a person or thing will not continue to live, exist or be successful for much longer: *His days as leader of the party are numbered.* **from day 'one** (*spoken*) from the beginning: *It's never worked from day one.* **from day to 'day 1** with no thoughts or plans for the future: *They live from day to day, looking after their sick daughter.* **2** if a situation changes **from day to day**, it changes often: *A baby's need for food can vary from day to day.* **from one ˌday to the 'next** if a situation changes **from one day to the next**, it is uncertain and not likely to stay the same each day: *I never know what to expect from one day to the next.* **have had your 'day** to no longer be successful, powerful, etc: *She's had her day as a supermodel.* **have seen/known better 'days** (*humorous*) to be in poor condition: *Our car has seen better days!* **if he's, she's, etc. a 'day** (*spoken*) (used when talking about sb's age) at least: *He must be 70 if he's a day!* **in sb's 'day 1** during the part of sb's life when they were most successful, famous, etc: *She was a great dancer in her day.* **2** when sb was young: *In my day, there were plenty of jobs when you left school.* **in 'this day and age** now, in the modern world **it's not sb's 'day** (*spoken*) used when several unfortunate or unpleasant things happen on the same day: *My car broke down and then I locked myself out—it's just not my day!* **make sb's 'day** to make

sb feel very happy on a particular day: *The phone call from Mike really made my day.* **make a day of it** (*spoken*) to make a particular enjoyable activity last for a whole day instead of only part of it **not have all 'day** to not have much time: *Come on! We don't have all day!* **of sb's 'day** during a particular period of time when sb lived: *the best writer/actor/player of his day* ◊ *Bessie Smith was the Madonna of her day.* **of the 'day** that is served on a particular day in a restaurant: *soup of the day* **'one day** at some time in the future, or on a particular day in the past: *One day, I want to leave the city and move to the country.* ◊ *One day, he walked out of the house with a small bag and never came back.* **'one of these days** before a long time has passed: *One of these days you'll come back and ask me to forgive you.* **one of those 'days** (*spoken*) a day when there are a lot of mistakes and a lot of things go wrong: *It's been one of those days!* **'some day** at an unknown time in the future: *Some day I'll be famous.* **take it/things one ˌday at a 'time** (*spoken*) to not think about what will happen in the future: *I don't know if he'll get better. We're just taking it one day at a time.* **'that'll be the day** (*spoken, ironic*) used when you are saying that sth is very unlikely to happen: *Paul? Apologize? That'll be the day!* **'these days** (*spoken*) used to talk about the present, especially when you are comparing it with the past: *These days kids grow up so quickly.* **'those were the days** (*spoken*) used to suggest that a time in the past was happier or better than now **to the 'day** exactly: *It's been three years to the day since we met.* **to this 'day** even now, when a lot of time has passed: *To this day, I still don't understand why he did it.*—more at BORN, BREAK *n.*, CALL *v.*, CLEAR *adj.*, COLD *adj.*, DEED, DOG *n.*, EARLY *adj.*, END *n.*, END *v.*, FORTH, GIVE *v.*, HIGH *adj.*, LATE *adv.*, LIVE¹, NICE, NIGHT, OLD, ORDER *n.*, OTHER *adj.*, PASS *v.*, PLAIN *adj.*, RAINY, ROME, SALAD, SAVE *v.*

'**day boy** *noun* (*BrE*) a boy DAY PUPIL

day·break /'deɪbreɪk/ *noun* [U] the time of day when light first appears SYN DAWN: *We left before daybreak.*

'**day care** *noun* [U] care for small children, or for old or sick people, away from home, during the day: *Day care is provided by the company she works for.* ◊ *a day care centre*

'**day centre** *noun* (*BrE*) a place that provides care for old or sick people during the day

day·dream /'deɪdriːm/ *noun* pleasant thoughts that make you forget about the present: *She stared out of the window, lost in a daydream.* ▶ **day·dream** *verb* [V] **~ (about sb/sth):** *I would spend hours daydreaming about a house of my own.*

'**day girl** *noun* (*BrE*) a girl DAY PUPIL

Day-Glo™ /'deɪ gləʊ; *AmE* gloʊ/ *adj.* having a very bright orange, yellow, green or pink colour: *Day-Glo cycling shorts*

'**day job** *noun* [sing.] the paid work that sb normally does IDM **don't give up the 'day job** (*informal, humorous*) used to tell sb that they should continue doing what they are used to, rather than trying sth new which they are likely to fail at: *So you want to be a writer? Well my advice is, don't give up the day job.*

day·light /'deɪlaɪt/ *noun* [U] the light that comes from the sun during the day: *They emerged from the church into the bright daylight.* ◊ *The street looks very different in daylight.* ◊ *They left before daylight* (= before the sun had risen). IDM **ˌdaylight 'robbery** (*informal*) the fact of sb charging too much money for sth: *You wouldn't believe some of the prices they charge; it's daylight robbery.*—more at BROAD *adj.*

day·lights /'deɪlaɪts/ *noun* [pl.] IDM **beat/knock the (living) 'daylights out of sb** (*informal*) to hit sb very hard several times and hurt them very much **frighten/scare the (living) 'daylights out of sb** (*informal*) to frighten sb very much

'**daylight saving time** (also '**daylight time**) *noun* (*abbr.* DST) [U] (*AmE*) = SUMMER TIME

day·long /'deɪlɒŋ; *AmE* -lɔːŋ/ *adj.* [only before noun] (*especially AmE*) lasting for a whole day: *a daylong conference/meeting*

D

'day nursery (also **nursery**) (both *BrE*) (*AmE* **'day care center**) *noun* a place where small children are cared for while their parents are at work—compare CRÈCHE, NURSERY SCHOOL

,**day 'off** *noun* (*pl.* **days off**) a day on which you do not have to work: *Most weeks, Sunday is my only day off.* ◊ *Why not take a few days off?*

the ,Day of 'Judgement *noun* [sing.] = JUDGEMENT DAY

,**day 'out** *noun* (*pl.* **days out**) a trip or visit somewhere for a day: *We had a day out in the country.*

'day pupil (*BrE*) (also **'day student** *AmE, BrE*) *noun* a school student who lives at home but who goes to a school where other students live in the school

,**day re'lease** *noun* (*BrE*) [U] a system of allowing employees days off work for education: *time off for study on day release* ◊ *a day release course*

,**day re'turn** *noun* (*BrE*) a ticket at a reduced price for a journey to a place and back again on the same day

'day room *noun* a room in a hospital or other institution where people can sit, relax, watch television, etc. during the day

'day school *noun* **1** (*old-fashioned*) a private school with students who live at home and only go to school during the day—compare BOARDING SCHOOL **2** (*BrE*) a course of education lasting one day, at which a particular topic is discussed: *a day school at Leeds University on women in Victorian times*

'day student *noun* (*especially AmE*) = DAY PUPIL

day·time /'deɪtaɪm/ *noun* [U] the period during the day between the time when it gets light and the time when it gets dark: *You don't often see this bird in (the) daytime.* ◊ *The park is open during (the) daytime throughout the summer.* ◊ *Daytime temperatures never fell below 80°F.* ◊ *Please give your name, address and daytime phone number.*

,**day-to-'day** *adj.* [only before noun] **1** planning for only one day at a time: *I have organized the cleaning on a day-to-day basis, until our usual cleaner returns.* **2** involving the usual events or tasks of each day: *She has been looking after the day-to-day running of the school.*

'day trip *noun* a trip or visit completed in one day: *a day trip to France* ► **'day tripper** *noun* (*BrE*)

daze /deɪz/ *noun* **IDM** **in a daze** in a confused state: *I've been in a complete daze since hearing the news.*

dazed /deɪzd/ *adj.* unable to think clearly, especially because of a shock or blow: *Survivors waited for the rescue boats, dazed and frightened.* ◊ *Jimmy was still dazed by the blow to his head.*

daz·zle /'dæzl/ *verb, noun*
■ *verb* [often passive] **1** if a strong light **dazzles** you, it is so bright that you cannot see for a short time: [VN] *He was momentarily dazzled by the strong sunlight.* [also V] **2** [VN] to impress sb a lot with your beauty, skill, knowledge, etc: *He was dazzled by the warmth of her smile.* ► **dazzling** *adj.*: *a dazzling display of oriental dance and music* **daz·zlingly** *adv.*: *She was dazzlingly beautiful.*
■ *noun* [U, sing.] **1** the quality that bright light has that stops you from seeing clearly **2** a thing or quality that impresses you but may prevent you from understanding or thinking clearly: *the dazzle of publicity*

d.b.a. /ˌdiː biː 'eɪ/ *abbr.* (*AmE*) doing business as: *Philip Smith, d.b.a. Phil's Signs*

DC /ˌdiː 'siː/ *abbr.* **1** direct current (an electric current that flows in one direction)—compare AC **2** District of Columbia in the US: *Washington, DC*

'D-Day *noun* [U] a date on which sth important is expected to happen

DDT /ˌdiː diː 'tiː/ *noun* [U] a colourless chemical used, especially in the past, for killing insects that harm crops

de- /diː/ *prefix* (in verbs and related nouns, adjectives and adverbs) **1** the opposite of: *decentralization* **2** removing sth: *to defrost the refrigerator* (= remove layers of ice from it)

dea·con /'diːkən/ *noun* **1** (in the Roman Catholic, Anglican and Orthodox Churches) a religious leader just below the rank of a priest **2** (in some Nonconformist Churches) a person who is not a member of the CLERGY, but who helps a MINISTER with church business affairs

dea·con·ess /ˌdiːkə'nes; *AmE* 'diːkənəs/ *noun* (in some Christian Churches) a woman who has duties that are similar to those of a deacon

dead /ded/ *adj., noun, adv.*
■ *adj.*

NOT ALIVE | **1** no longer alive: *My mother's dead; she died in 1987.* ◊ *a dead person/animal* ◊ *dead leaves/wood/skin* ◊ *He was shot dead by a gunman outside his home.* ◊ *Catherine's dead body lay peacefully on the bed.* ◊ *He dropped dead* (= died suddenly) *last week.* ◊ *The poor child looks more dead than alive.* ◊ (*figurative*) *In ten years he'll be dead and buried as a politician.*

IDEA/BELIEF/PLAN | **2** [not before noun] no longer believed in or aimed for: *Many believe the peace plan is dead.* ◊ *Unfortunately racism is not yet dead.* ◊ *Though the idea may be dead, it is far from being buried* (= people still talk about it, even though there is nothing new to say).

NOT USED | **3** belonging to the past; no longer practised or fashionable: *Is the Western a dead art form?* ◊ *a dead language* (= one that is no longer spoken, for example Latin) ◊ *By the seventies the suit was dead, kept for weddings, funerals and job interviews.*

FINISHED | **4** (*informal*) finished; not able to be used any more: *dead matches* ◊ *There were two dead bottles of wine on the table.*

MACHINE | **5** (of machines or equipment) not working because of a lack of power: *a dead battery/engine* ◊ *The hard disk seems to be dead.* ◊ *Suddenly the phone went dead.*

PLACE | **6** (*informal, disapproving*) very quiet, without activity or interest: *There were no theatres, no cinemas, no coffee bars. It was dead as anything.*

BUSINESS | **7** (*informal, disapproving*) without activity; with nobody buying or selling anything: *'The market is absolutely dead this morning,' said one foreign exchange trader.* ◊ *Winter is traditionally the dead season for the housing market.*

TIRED | **8** [not usually before noun] (*informal*) extremely tired; not well: *half dead with cold and hunger* ◊ *She felt dead on her feet and didn't have the energy to question them further.*

WITHOUT FEELING | **9** [not before noun] (of a part of the body) unable to feel because of cold, etc. **SYN** NUMB: *My left arm had gone dead.* **10** ~ **to sth** unable to feel or understand emotions **SYN** INSENSITIVE: *He was dead to all feelings of pity.* **11** (especially of sb's voice, eyes or face) showing no emotion **SYN** EXPRESSIONLESS: *She said, 'I'm sorry, too,' in a quiet, dead voice.* ◊ *His usually dead grey eyes were sparkling.*

COMPLETE/EXACT | **12** [only before noun] complete or exact: *a dead silence/calm* ◊ *The dead centre of the target* ◊ *The car gave a sudden jerk and came to a dead stop.* ◊ (*BrE*) *This horse is a dead cert for* (= will certainly win) *the race tomorrow.* ◊ *She crumpled to the floor in a dead faint* (= completely unconscious).

NEVER ALIVE | **13** never having been alive: *dead matter* (= for example rock) ◊ *a dead planet* (= one with no life on it)

IN SPORT | **14** outside the playing area

IDM **be a dead 'ringer for sb** (*informal*) to look very like sb: *She's a dead ringer for a girl I used to know.* **(as) ,dead as a/the 'dodo** (*BrE, informal*) completely dead; no longer interesting or valid **(as) ,dead as a 'doornail** (*informal*) completely dead **a ,dead 'duck** (*informal*) a plan, an event, etc. that has failed or is certain to fail and is therefore not worth discussing **be dead and 'gone** (*informal*) to be dead: *You'll be sorry you said that when I'm dead and gone.* **the dead hand of sth** (*written*) an influence that controls or restricts sth: *We need to free business from the dead hand of bureaucracy.* **,dead in the 'water** a person or plan that is **dead in the water** has failed and has little hope of succeeding in the future: *His leadership campaign is dead in the water.* **dead 'meat** (*informal*) in serious trouble: *If anyone finds out, you're dead meat.* **,dead to the 'world** fast asleep **over ,my**

s	t	v	z	ʃ	ʒ	tʃ	dʒ	θ	ð	ŋ
see	tea	van	zoo	shoe	vision	chain	jam	thin	this	sing

dead **'body** (*spoken*) used to show you are strongly opposed to sth: *She moves into our home over my dead body.* **sb wouldn't be seen/caught 'dead ...** (*spoken*) used to say that you would not like to wear particular clothes, or to be in a particular situation: *She wouldn't be seen dead in a hat.* ◊ *He wouldn't be caught dead going to a club with his mother.*—more at FLOG, KNOCK *v.*
- *noun* (**the dead**) **1** [pl.] people who have died: *The dead and wounded in that one attack amounted to 6000.* **2** [sing.] the state of being dead: *Christians believe that God raised Jesus from the dead.* ◊ (*figurative*) *In nine years he has brought his party back from the dead almost to the brink of power.*
  IDM **in the ˌdead of 'night** (*BrE* also **at ˌdead of 'night**) in the quietest part of the night: *I crept out of bed in the dead of night and sneaked downstairs.* **in the ˌdead of 'winter** in the coldest part of winter
- *adv.* (*informal*)
  COMPLETELY | **1** completely; exactly: *You're dead right!* ◊ (*BrE*) *a dead straight road* ◊ (*BrE*) *The train was dead on time.* ◊ *He's dead against the idea.* ◊ *The sight made him stop dead in his tracks* (= stop suddenly). ◊ *She's dead set on getting* (= determined to get) *this new job.*
  VERY | **2** (*BrE, informal*) very; extremely: *The instructions are dead easy to follow.* ◊ *You were dead lucky to get that job.* ◊ *I was dead scared.*
  IDM **cut sb 'dead** (*BrE*) to pretend not to have seen sb; to refuse to greet sb: *She saw me, recognized me and cut me dead.*—more at RIGHT *n.*

ˌdead **'beat** (also *informal* **beat**) *adj.* [not before noun] (*informal*) very tired: *You look dead beat.*

dead·beat /'dedbiːt/ *noun* (*informal*) **1** (*especially AmE*) a lazy person; a person with no job and no money, who is not part of normal society **2** (*AmE*) a person or company that tries to avoid paying their debts

dead·bolt /'dedbəʊlt; *AmE* -boʊlt/ *noun* (*especially AmE*) = DEADLOCK

dead·en /'dedn/ *verb* [VN] to make sth such as a sound, a feeling, etc. less strong SYN DULL: *He was given drugs to deaden the pain.* ▶ **dead·en·ing** *adj.* [only before noun]: *the deadening effect of alcohol on your reactions*

ˌdead **'end** *noun* **1** a road, passage, etc. that is closed at one end: *The first street we tried turned out to be a dead end.* **2** a point at which you can make no further progress in what you are doing: *We had come to a dead end in our research.* ◊ *This line of investigation could prove to be a complete dead end.* ◊ *He's in a dead-end job in the local factory* (= one with low wages and no hope of promotion).

ˌdead **'heat** *noun* **1** (*especially BrE*) a result in a race when two competitors finish at exactly the same time **2** (*AmE*) a situation during a race or competition, etc. when two or more people are at the same level: *The two candidates are in a dead heat in the polls.*

ˌdead **'letter** *noun* **1** [usually sing.] a law or an agreement that still exists but that is ignored **2** (*especially AmE*) a letter that cannot be delivered to an address or to the person who sent it

dead·line /'dedlaɪn/ *noun* ~ (**for sth**) a point in time by which sth must be done: *I prefer to work to a deadline.* ◊ *The deadline for applications is 30 April.* ◊ *the January 15 deadline set by the United Nations*

dead·lock /'dedlɒk; *AmE* -lɑːk/ *noun* **1** [sing., U] a complete failure to reach agreement or settle a dispute: *European agriculture ministers failed to break the deadlock over farm subsidies.* ◊ (*BrE*) *The strike appeared to have reached deadlock.* ◊ (*AmE, BrE*) *The strike has reached a deadlock.* **2** [C] (*BrE*) (also **dead·bolt** *AmE, BrE*) a type of lock on a door that needs a key to open or close it ▶ **dead·locked** *adj.* [not before noun]: *Despite months of discussion the negotiations remained deadlocked.*

ˌdead **'loss** *noun* [usually sing.] (*BrE, informal*) a person or thing that is not helpful or useful: *He may be a very talented designer, but as a manager he's a dead loss.*

dead·ly /'dedli/ *adj., adv.*
- *adj.* (**dead·lier, dead·li·est**) HELP More **deadly** and **deadliest** are the usual forms. You can also use **most deadly**. **1** causing or likely to cause death: *a deadly weapon/*

disease ◊ *deadly poison* ◊ *The cobra is one of the world's deadliest snakes.* ◊ *The terrorists have chosen to play a deadly game with the civilian population.* ◊ *the seven deadly sins* (= for which you could be sent to HELL) **2** [only before noun] extreme; complete: *I'm in deadly earnest.* ◊ *We sat in deadly silence.* ◊ *They are deadly enemies* (= will always remain enemies, and are full of hatred for each other). **3** extremely effective, so that no defence is possible: *His aim is deadly* (= so accurate that he can kill easily). ◊ *It was the deadly striker's 11th goal of the season.* **4** (*BrE, informal*) very boring: *The lecture was absolutely deadly.*
- *adv.* **1** (*informal*) extremely: *deadly serious/dull* **2** (*rare*) = DEATHLY: *deadly pale/cold*

ˌdead·ly **'night·shade** (also **bella·donna**) *noun* [U] a very poisonous plant with purple flowers and black berries

dead·pan /'dedpæn/ *adj.* without any expression or emotion; often pretending to be serious when you are joking: *ˌdeadpan humour*

dead·weight /ˌded'weɪt/ *noun* [usually sing.] **1** a thing that is very heavy and difficult to lift or move **2** a person or thing that makes it difficult for sth to succeed or change

ˌdead **'wood** *noun* [U] people or things that have become useless or unnecessary in an organization

deaf /def/ *adj.* (**deaf·er, deaf·est**) **1** unable to hear anything or unable to hear very well: *to become/go deaf* ◊ *She was born deaf.*—see also STONE DEAF, TONE-DEAF **2** (**the deaf**) *noun* [pl.] people who cannot hear: *television subtitles for the deaf and hard of hearing* **3** [not before noun] ~ **to sth** not willing to listen or pay attention to sth: *He was deaf to my requests for help.* ▶ **deaf·ness** *noun* [U]
IDM **(as) ˌdeaf as a 'post** (*informal*) very deaf **fall on deaf 'ears** to be ignored or not noticed by other people: *Her advice fell on deaf ears.* **turn a deaf 'ear (to sb/sth)** to ignore or refuse to listen to sb/sth: *He turned a deaf ear to the rumours.*

deaf·en /'defn/ *verb* [VN] [usually passive] **1** to make sb unable to hear the sounds around them because there is too much noise: *The noise of the siren was deafening her.* **2** to make sb deaf

deaf·en·ing /'defnɪŋ/ *adj.* very loud: *deafening applause* ◊ *The noise of the machine was deafening.* ◊ *The government's response to the report has been a deafening silence* (= it was very noticeable that nothing was said or done). ▶ **deaf·en·ing·ly** *adv.*

ˌdeaf **'mute** *noun* (sometimes *offensive*) a person who is unable to hear or speak

deal /diːl/ *verb, noun*
- *verb* (**dealt, dealt** /delt/)
  CARDS | **1** ~ (**sth**) (**out**) | ~ (**sth**) (**to sb**) to give cards to each player in a game of cards: [V] *Whose turn is it to deal?* ◊ [VN] *Start by dealing out ten cards to each player.* ◊ [VNN] *He dealt me two aces.*
  DRUGS | **2** to buy and sell illegal drugs: [V] *You can often see people dealing openly on the streets.* [also VN]
  IDM **deal sb/sth a 'blow | deal a 'blow to sb/sth** (*formal*) **1** to be very shocking or harmful to sb/sth: *Her sudden death dealt a blow to the whole country.* **2** to hit sb/sth—more at WHEEL *v.*
  PHRV **'deal in sth 1** to buy and sell a particular product: *The company deals in computer software.* **2** to accept sth as a basis for your decisions, attitudes, or actions: *We don't deal in rumours or guesswork.* **ˌdeal sth↔'out 1** to share sth out among a group of people SYN DISTRIBUTE: *The profits were dealt out among the investors.* **2** to say what punishment sb should have: *Many judges deal out harsher sentences to men than to women.* **'deal with sb** to take appropriate action in a particular situation or according to who you are talking to, managing, etc. SYN HANDLE: *She is used to dealing with all kinds of people in her job.* **'deal with sb/sth** to do business with a person, a company or an organization **'deal with sth 1** to solve a problem, carry out a task, etc: *to deal with enquiries/issues/complaints* ◊ *Have you dealt with these letters yet?* ◊

æ	ɑː	e	ɜː	ə	ɪ	iː	i	ɒ	ɔː	ʌ	ʊ	u	uː
cat	father	ten	bird	about	sit	see	many	got	saw	cup	put	actual	too

(BrE)

D

He's good at dealing with pressure. **2** to be about sth: *Her poems often deal with the subject of death.*

■ *noun*

A LOT | **1** [sing.] **a good/great ~** much; a lot: *They spent a great deal of money.* ◊ *It took a great deal of time.* ◊ *I'm feeling a good deal better.* ◊ *We see them a great deal* (= often).

BUSINESS AGREEMENT | **2** [C] an agreement, especially in business, on particular conditions for buying or doing sth: *to make/sign/conclude/close a deal* (*with sb*) ◊ (*informal*) *Did you cut a deal* (= make one)*?* ◊ *We did a deal with the management on overtime.* ◊ *They were hoping for a better pay deal.* ◊ *A deal was struck after lengthy negotiations.* ◊ *The deal fell through* (= no agreement was reached). ◊ *I got a good deal on the car* (= bought it cheaply). ◊ *It's a deal!* (= I agree to your terms) ◊ *Listen. This is the deal* (= this is what we have agreed and are going to do).—see also PACKAGE

TREATMENT | **3** [C, usually sing.] the way that sb/sth is treated: *If elected, the party has promised a new deal* (= better and fairer treatment) *for teachers.* ◊ *They knew they'd been given a raw/rough deal* (= been treated unfairly). ◊ *We tried to ensure that everyone got a fair deal.* ◊ *It was a square deal for everyone.*

IN CARD GAMES | **4** [C, usually sing.] the action of giving out cards to the players: *It's your deal.*

WOOD | **5** [U] (*especially BrE*) the soft pale wood of FIR or PINE trees, especially when it is cut into boards for making things: *a deal table*

IDM see BIG *adj.*, STRIKE *v.*

deal·er /ˈdiːlə(r)/ *noun* **1 ~** (**in sth**) a person whose business is buying and selling a particular product: *an art/antique dealer* ◊ *He's a dealer in second-hand cars.*—see also WHEELER-DEALER **2** a person who sells illegal drugs **3** the person who gives out the cards in a card game

deal·er·ship /ˈdiːləʃɪp; AmE -lərʃ-/ *noun* a business that buys and sells products, especially cars, for a particular company; the position of being a dealer who can buy and sell sth: *a Ford dealership*

deal·ing /ˈdiːlɪŋ/ *noun* **1** (**dealings**) [pl.] business activities; the relations that you have with sb in business: *Have you had any previous dealings with this company?* ◊ *I knew nothing of his business dealings.* ◊ *She has always been very polite in her dealings with me.* **2** [U] a way of doing business with sb: *a reputation for fair/honest dealing* **3** [U, C] buying and selling: *drug dealing* ◊ *dealings in shares*

dealt *pt, pp* of DEAL

dean /diːn/ *noun* **1** (in the Anglican Church) a priest of high rank who is in charge of the other priests in a CATHEDRAL **2** (also ˌrural ˈdean) (*BrE*) a priest who is in charge of the priests of several churches in an area **3** a person in a university who is in charge of a department of studies: *the dean of the Faculty of Medicine* **4** (in a college or university, especially at Oxford or Cambridge) a person who is responsible for the discipline of students **5** (*AmE*) = DOYEN

dean·ery /ˈdiːnəri/ *noun* (*pl.* **-ies**) **1** a group of PARISHES controlled by a dean (2) **2** the office or house of a dean (1,2)

dear /dɪə(r); AmE dɪr/ *adj., exclamation, noun, adv.*

■ *adj.* (**dear·er, dear·est**) **1 ~** (**to sb**) loved by or important to sb: *He's one of my dearest friends.* ◊ *Her daughter is very dear to her.* **2** (**Dear**) used at the beginning of a letter before the name or title of the person that you are writing to: *Dear Sir or Madam* ◊ *Dear Mrs Jones* **3** [not usually before noun] (*BrE*) expensive; costing a lot of money: *Everything's so dear now, isn't it?* **4** (**dear old/little …**) (*BrE*) used to describe sb in a way that shows affection: *Dear old Sue! I knew she'd help.* ◊ *Their baby's a dear little thing.* IDM **hold sb/sth ˈdear** (*formal*) to care very much for sb/sth; to value sb/sth highly: *He had destroyed everything we held dear.*—more at HEART, LIFE, NEAR *adj.*

■ *exclamation* used in expressions that show that you are surprised, upset, annoyed or worried: *Oh dear! I think I've lost my purse.* ◊ *Oh dear! What a shame.* ◊ *Dear me!*

What a mess! ◊ *Dear oh dear! What are you going to do now?*

■ *noun* **1** (*BrE, spoken*) a kind person: *Isn't he a dear?* ◊ *Be a dear and fetch me my coat.* **2** used when speaking to sb you love: *Would you like a drink, dear?* ◊ *Come here, my dear.* **3** used when speaking to sb in a friendly way, for example by an older person to a young person or a child: *What's your name, dear?*—compare DUCK

■ *adv.* (*BrE*) at a high price: *to buy cheap and sell dear* IDM see COST *v.*

dear·est /ˈdɪərɪst; AmE ˈdɪr-/ *adj., noun*

■ *adj.* (*old-fashioned*) **1** used when writing to sb you love: *'Dearest Nina', the letter began.* **2** [usually before noun] that you feel deeply: *It was her dearest wish to have a family.*

■ *noun* (*old-fashioned*) used when speaking to sb you love: *Come (my) dearest, let's go home.* IDM see NEAR *n.*

dearie /ˈdɪəri; AmE ˈdɪri/ *noun* (*old-fashioned, BrE, spoken*) used to address sb in a friendly way: *Sit down, dearie.*

dear·ly /ˈdɪəli; AmE ˈdɪrli/ *adv.* **1** very much: *She loves him dearly.* ◊ *I would dearly like/love to know what he was thinking.* ◊ *dearly beloved* (= used by a minister at a Christian church service to address people) **2** in a way that causes a lot of suffering or damage, or that costs a lot of money: *Success has cost him dearly.* ◊ *She paid dearly for her mistake.*

dearth /dɜːθ; AmE dɜːrθ/ *noun* [sing.] **~** (**of sth**) a lack of sth; the fact of there not being enough of sth: *There was a dearth of reliable information on the subject.*

death /deθ/ *noun* **1** [C] the fact of sb dying or being killed: *a sudden/violent/peaceful death* ◊ *the anniversary of his wife's death* ◊ *an increase in deaths from cancer* ◊ *He died a slow and painful death.* **2** [U] the end of life; the state of being dead: *Two children were burnt to death in the fire* (= they died as a result of the fire). ◊ *He's drinking himself to death* (= so that it will kill him). ◊ *Police are still trying to establish the cause of death.* ◊ *Do you believe in life after death?* ◊ *a death camp* (= a place where prisoners are killed, usually in a war) ◊ *He was sentenced to death* (= to be executed). **3** [U] **~ of sth** the permanent end or destruction of sth: *the death of all my plans* ◊ *the death of communism* **4** (also **Death**) [U] (*literary*) the power that destroys life, imagined as human in form: *Death is often shown in paintings as a human skeleton.*—see also SUDDEN DEATH IDM **at death's ˈdoor** (*often humorous*) so ill that you may die **be the ˈdeath of sb** to worry or upset sb very much: *Those kids will be the death of me.* ˌ**do sth to ˈdeath** to do or perform sth so often that people become tired of seeing or hearing it: *That joke's been done to death.* **frighten/scare sb to ˈdeath** to frighten sb very much **look/feel like death warmed ˈup** (*BrE*) (*AmE* **like death warmed ˈover**) (*spoken*) to look or feel very ill or tired **put sb to death** to kill sb as a punishment SYN EXECUTE: *The prisoner will be put to death at dawn.* **to death** extremely; very much: *to be bored/frightened/scared/worried to death* ◊ *I'm sick to death of your endless criticism.* **to the death** until sb is dead: *a fight to the death*—more at CATCH *v.*, CHEAT *v.*, DICE *v.*, DIE *v.*, FATE, FIGHT *v.*, FLOG, GRIM, KISS *n.*, LIFE, MATTER *n.*

death·bed /ˈdeθbed/ *noun* [usually sing.] the bed in which sb is dying or dies: *a deathbed confession/conversion/repentance* ◊ *He told me the truth on his deathbed* (= as he lay dying). ◊ *She was on her deathbed* (= going to die very soon). ◊ (*humorous*) *You'd have to be practically on your deathbed before the doctor would come and see you!*

ˈ**death blow** *noun* an event that destroys or puts an end to sth: *They thought the arrival of television would deal a death blow to mass cinema audiences.*

ˈ**death certificate** *noun* an official document, signed by a doctor, that states the cause and time of sb's death

ˈ**death duty** *noun* [usually pl.] (*old-fashioned, BrE*) = INHERITANCE TAX

ˈ**death knell** (also **knell**) *noun* [sing.] an event that means that the end or destruction of sth will come soon

aɪ	aʊ	eɪ	əʊ	oʊ	ɔɪ	ɪə	eə	ʊə	j	w
my	now	say	go (BrE)	go (AmE)	boy	near	hair	pure	yes	wet

death·less /'deθləs/ adj. (written) never dying or forgotten: (ironic) written in his usual deathless prose (= very bad)

death·ly /'deθli/ (also less frequent **dead·ly**) adv. like a dead person; suggesting death: Her face was deathly pale. ◊ The house was deathly still. ▶ **death·ly** adj.: A deathly hush fell over the room as he walked in.

'**death mask** noun a model of the face of a person who has just died, made by pressing a soft substance over their face and removing it when it becomes hard

the 'death penalty noun [sing.] the punishment of being killed that is used in some countries for very serious crimes: the abolition/return of the death penalty

'**death rate** noun **1** the number of deaths every year for every 1000 people in the population of a place: a high/low death rate **2** the number of deaths every year from a particular disease or in a particular group: Death rates from heart disease have risen considerably in recent years.

'**death rattle** noun [sing.] a sound sometimes heard in the throat of a dying person

,**death 'row** noun [U] the cells in a prison for prisoners who are waiting to be killed as punishment for a serious crime: prisoners on death row

'**death sentence** noun the legal punishment of being killed for a serious crime: to be given/to receive the death sentence for murder

'**death's head** noun a human SKULL (= the bone structure of the head) used as a symbol of death

'**death toll** noun the number of people killed in an accident, a war, a disaster, etc.

'**death trap** noun (informal) a building, road, vehicle, etc. that is dangerous and could turn this place into a death cars blocking the exits could turn this place into a death trap.

'**death warrant** noun an official document stating that sb should receive the punishment of being killed for a crime that they have committed: The President signed the death warrant. ◊ If you pay the ransom, you may be signing your son's death warrant. ◊ (figurative) By withdrawing the funding, the government signed the project's death warrant.

,**death-watch 'beetle** noun a small insect that eats into old wood, making sounds like a watch TICKING

'**death wish** noun [sing.] a desire to die, often that sb is not aware of

deb /deb/ noun (informal) = DEBUTANTE

de·bacle /deɪ'bɑːkl/ noun an event or a situation that is a complete failure and causes embarrassment

debar /dɪ'bɑː(r)/ verb (-rr-) [VN] [usually passive] ~ sb (from sth/from doing sth) (formal) to prevent sb from doing sth, joining sth, etc: He was debarred from holding public office.

de·base /dɪ'beɪs/ verb [VN] to make sb/sth less valuable or respected: Sport is being debased by commercial sponsorship. ▶ **de·base·ment** noun [U]

de·bat·able /dɪ'beɪtəbl/ adj. not certain because people can have different ideas and opinions about the thing being discussed: a debatable point ◊ It is highly debatable whether conditions have improved for low-income families.

de·bate /dɪ'beɪt/ noun, verb
■ noun [C, U] ~ (on/about/over sth) **1** a formal discussion of an issue at a public meeting or in a parliament. In a debate two or more speakers express opposing views and then there is often a vote on the issue: a debate on abortion ◊ The minister opened the debate (= was the first to speak). ◊ The motion under debate (= being discussed) was put to a vote. ◊ After a long debate, Congress approved the proposal. **2** an argument or discussion expressing different opinions: a heated/wide-ranging/lively debate ◊ the current debate about tax ◊ There had been much debate on the issue of childcare. ◊ Whether he deserves what has happened to him is open to debate/a matter for debate (= cannot be certain or decided yet). ◊ The theatre's future is a subject of considerable debate.
■ verb **1** to discuss sth, especially formally, before making a decision or finding a solution: [VN] Politicians will be

debating the bill later this week. ◊ The question of the origin of the universe is still hotly debated (= strongly argued about) by scientists. ◊ [V wh-] The committee will debate whether to lower the age of club membership to 16. [also V] **2** ~ (with yourself) to think carefully about sth before making a decision: She debated with herself for a while, and then picked up the phone. ◊ [V wh-] We're debating whether or not to go skiing this winter. [also V -ing]

de·bater /dɪ'beɪtə(r)/ noun a person who is involved in a debate

de·bauched /dɪ'bɔːtʃt/ adj. a debauched person is immoral in their sexual behaviour, drinks a lot of alcohol, takes drugs, etc.

de·bauch·ery /dɪ'bɔːtʃəri/ noun [U] immoral behaviour involving sex, alcohol or drugs

de·ben·ture /dɪ'bentʃə(r)/ noun (BrE, finance) an official document that is given by a company, showing it has borrowed money from a person and stating the interest payments that it will make to them

de·bili·tate /dɪ'bɪlɪteɪt/ verb [VN] (formal) **1** to make sb's body or mind weaker: a debilitating disease ◊ The troops were severely debilitated by hunger and disease. **2** to make a country, an organization, etc. weaker: Prolonged strike action debilitated the industry.

de·bil·ity /dɪ'bɪləti/ noun [U, C] (pl. -ies) (formal) physical weakness, especially as a result of illness: chronic muscle debility

debit /'debɪt/ noun, verb
■ noun **1** a written note in a bank account or other financial record of a sum of money owed or spent: on the debit side of an account ◊ (figurative) On the debit side (= a negative result will be that) the new shopping centre will increase traffic problems. **2** a sum of money taken from a bank account—compare CREDIT n.—see also DIRECT DEBIT
■ verb [VN] when a bank debits an account, it takes money from it: The money will be debited from your account each month.

'**debit card** noun a plastic card that can be used to take money directly from your bank account when you pay for sth—compare CREDIT CARD

de·bon·air /,debə'neə(r); AmE -'ner/ adj. (old-fashioned) (usually of men) fashionable and confident

de·brief /,diː'briːf/ verb [VN] ~ sb (on sth) to ask sb questions officially, in order to get information about the task that they have just completed: He was taken to a US airbase to be debriefed on the mission.—compare BRIEF ▶ **de·brief·ing** noun [U, C]: a debriefing session

deb·ris /'debriː; 'deɪ-; AmE də'briː/ noun [U] **1** pieces of wood, metal, brick, etc. that are left after sth has been destroyed: Emergency teams are still clearing the debris from the plane crash. **2** (written or formal) pieces of material that are not wanted and rubbish/garbage that are left somewhere: Clear away leaves and other garden debris from the pond.

debt /det/ noun **1** [C] a sum of money that sb owes: I need to pay off all my debts before I leave the country. ◊ an outstanding debt of £300 ◊ He had run up credit card debts of thousands of dollars. **2** [U] the situation of owing money, especially when you cannot pay: He died heavily in debt. ◊ The club is £4 million in debt. ◊ We were poor but we never got into debt. ◊ It's hard to stay out of debt when you are a student. ◊ a country's foreign debt burden—see also BAD DEBT **3** [C, usually sing.] the fact that you should feel grateful to sb because they have helped you or been kind to you: to owe a debt of gratitude to sb ◊ I would like to acknowledge my debt to my teachers. **IDM be in sb's 'debt** (formal) to feel grateful to sb for their help, kindness, etc.

debt·or /'detə(r)/ noun a person, a country or an organization that owes money

debug /,diː'bʌg/ verb (-gg-) [VN] (computing) to look for and remove the faults in a computer program

de·bunk /,diː'bʌŋk/ verb [VN] to show that an idea, a belief, etc. is false; to show that sth is not as good as

D

people think it is: *His theories have been debunked by recent research.*

debut (also **début**) /'deɪbjuː; 'debjuː; *AmE* deɪ'bjuː/ *noun* the first public appearance of a performer or sports player: *He will* **make his debut** *for the first team this week.* ◊ *the group's debut album*

debu·tante /'debjutɑːnt/ (also *informal* **deb**) *noun* a young, rich or UPPER-CLASS woman who is going to fashionable social events for the first time

deca- /'dekə/ *combining form* (in nouns) ten; having ten: *decathlon*—compare DECI-

dec·ade /'dekeɪd; dɪ'keɪd/ *noun* a period of ten years, especially a period such as 1910–1919 or 1990–1999

deca·dence /'dekədəns/ *noun* [U] (*disapproving*) behaviour, attitudes, etc. which show a fall in standards, especially moral ones, and an interest in pleasure and enjoyment rather than more serious things: *the decadence of modern Western society*

deca·dent /'dekədənt/ *adj.* (*disapproving*) having or showing low standards, especially moral ones, and an interest only in pleasure and enjoyment rather than serious things: *the decadent rich* ◊ *a decadent lifestyle/society*

de·caf·fein·ated /diː'kæfɪneɪtɪd/ (also *informal* **decaf** *AmE*, *BrE*) (*BrE* also **decaff**) /'diːkæf/ *adj.* (of coffee or tea) with most or all of the CAFFEINE removed ▶ **de·caf·fein·ated** (also *informal* **decaf** *AmE*, *BrE*) (*BrE* also **decaff**) *noun* [U, C]: *Regular coffee or decaf?* ◊ *I'll have a decaf, please.*

decal /'diːkæl/ *noun* (*AmE*) = TRANSFER (5)

de·camp /dɪ'kæmp/ *verb* [V] ~ (**from** …) (**to** …) to leave a place suddenly, often secretly

de·cant /dɪ'kænt/ *verb* [VN] ~ **sth** (**into sth**) to pour liquid, especially wine, from one container into another

de·cant·er /dɪ'kæntə(r)/ *noun* a glass bottle, often decorated, that wine and other alcoholic drinks are poured into from an ordinary bottle before serving

de·capi·tate /dɪ'kæpɪteɪt/ *verb* [VN] to cut off sb's head: *His decapitated body was found floating in a canal.* ▶ **de·capi·ta·tion** /dɪˌkæpɪ'teɪʃn/ *noun* [U, C]

dec·ath·lete /dɪ'kæθliːt/ *noun* a person who competes in a decathlon

dec·ath·lon /dɪ'kæθlən/ *noun* [sing., U] a sporting event in which people compete in ten different sports—compare BIATHLON, HEPTATHLON, PENTATHLON, TRIATHLON

decay /dɪ'keɪ/ *noun, verb*
- *noun* [U] **1** the process or result of being destroyed by natural causes or by not being cared for (= of decaying): *tooth decay* ◊ *The landlord had let the building* **fall into decay.** ◊ *The smell of death and decay hung over the town.* **2** the gradual destruction of a society, an institution, a system, etc: *economic/moral/urban decay* ◊ *the decay of the old industries*
- *verb* **1** to be destroyed gradually by natural processes; to destroy sth in this way SYN ROT: [V] *decaying leaves/teeth/food* [also VN] **2** [V] if a building or an area decays, its condition slowly becomes worse: *decaying inner city areas* **3** [V] to become less powerful and lose influence over people, society, etc: *decaying standards of morality*

de·cease /dɪ'siːs/ *noun* [U] (*law* or *formal*) the death of a person

de·ceased /dɪ'siːst/ *adj.* (*law* or *formal*) **1** dead: *her deceased parents* **2** (**the deceased**) *noun* (*pl.* **the deceased**) a person who has died, especially recently

de·ceit /dɪ'siːt/ *noun* [U, C] dishonest behaviour that is intended to make sb believe sth that is not true; an example of this behaviour: *He was accused of lies and deceit.* ◊ *Everyone was involved in this web of deceit.* ◊ *Their marriage was an illusion and a deceit.*

de·ceit·ful /dɪ'siːtfl/ *adj.* behaving in a dishonest way by telling lies and making people believe things that are not true ▶ **de·ceit·ful·ly** /-fəli/ *adv.* **de·ceit·ful·ness** *noun* [U]

de·ceive /dɪ'siːv/ *verb*
1 [VN] ~ **sb** (**into doing sth**) to make sb believe sth that is not true: *Her husband had been deceiving her for years.* ◊ *She deceived him into handing over all his savings.* **2** ~ **yourself** to refuse to admit to yourself that sth unpleasant is true: [VN] *You're deceiving yourself if you think he'll change his mind.* [also VN that] **3** to make sb have a wrong idea about sb/sth SYN MISLEAD: [VN] *Unless my eyes deceive me, that's the woman he introduced as his wife.* [also V] —see also DECEPTIVE ▶ **de·ceiv·er** *noun*

> **WORD FAMILY**
> deceive *v.*
> deceit *n.*
> deceitful *adj.*
> deception *n.*
> deceptive *adj.*

de·cel·er·ate /diː'seləreɪt/ *verb* (*written*) **1** [V, VN] to reduce the speed at which a vehicle is travelling **2** to become or make sth become slower: [V] *Economic growth decelerated sharply in January.* [also VN] OPP ACCELERATE ▶ **de·cel·er·ation** /diːˌselə'reɪʃn/ *noun* [U]

De·cem·ber /dɪ'sembə(r)/ *noun* [U, C] (*abbr.* **Dec.**) the 12th and last month of the year HELP To see how **December** is used, look at the examples at **April**.

de·cency /'diːsnsi/ *noun* **1** [U] honest, polite behaviour that follows accepted moral standards and shows respect for others: *Her behaviour showed a total lack of* **common decency.** ◊ *Have you no sense of decency?* ◊ *He might have* **had the decency to** *apologize.* **2** (**the decencies**) [pl.] (*formal*) standards of behaviour in society that people think are acceptable: *the basic decencies of civilized society*

de·cent /'diːsnt/ *adj.* **1** (especially *spoken*) of a good enough standard or quality: *a decent meal/job/place to live* ◊ *I need a decent night's sleep.* **2** (of people or behaviour) honest and fair; treating people with respect: *ordinary, decent, hard-working people* ◊ *Everyone said he was a decent sort of guy.* **3** acceptable to people in a particular situation: *a decent burial* ◊ *That dress isn't decent.* ◊ *She ought to have waited for a decent interval before getting married again.* **4** (*informal*) wearing enough clothes to allow sb to see you: *I can't go to the door—I'm not decent.*—compare INDECENT ▶ **de·cent·ly** *adv.* IDM **to do the decent 'thing** to do what people or society expect, especially in a difficult situation: *He did the decent thing and resigned.*

de·cen·tral·ize (*BrE* also **-ise**) /diː'sentrəlaɪz/ *verb* to give some of the power of a central government, organization, etc. to smaller parts or organizations around the country: [VN] *decentralized authority/administration* ◊ *Many European governments were decentralized after the war.* [also V] ▶ **de·cen·tral·iza·tion, -isa·tion** /diːˌsentrəlaɪ'zeɪʃn; *AmE* -lə'z-/ *noun* [U, sing.]

de·cep·tion /dɪ'sepʃn/ *noun* **1** [U] the act of deliberately making sb believe sth that is not true: *a drama full of lies and deception* ◊ *He was accused of obtaining property by deception.* **2** [C] a trick intended to make sb believe sth that is not true: *The whole episode had been a cruel deception.*

de·cep·tive /dɪ'septɪv/ *adj.* likely to make you believe sth that is not true SYN MISLEADING: *a deceptive advertisement* ◊ *Appearances can often be deceptive* (= things are not always what they seem to be). ◊ *the deceptive simplicity of her writing style* (= it seems simple but is not really) ▶ **de·cep·tive·ly** *adv.*: *a deceptively simple idea*

deci- /'desɪ/ *combining form* (in nouns; often used in units of measurement) one TENTH: *decilitre*—compare DECA-

deci·bel /'desɪbel/ *noun* a unit for measuring how loud a sound is: *Noise from the disco reached 110 decibels.*

de·cide /dɪ'saɪd/ *verb* **1** ~ (**between A and B**) | (**against sth**) to think carefully about the different possibilities that are available and choose one of them: [V] *It was difficult to decide between the two candidates.* ◊ *They decided against taking legal action.* ◊ *It's up to you to decide.* ◊ [V wh-] *I can't decide what to wear.* ◊

> **WORD FAMILY**
> decide *v.*
> decision *n.* (≠ indecision)
> decisive *adj.* (≠ indecisive)
> undecided *adj.*

[V**(that)**] *She decided (that) she wanted to live in France.* ◇ [Vto inf] *We've decided not to go away after all.* ◇ [VN] *We might be hiring more people but nothing has been decided yet.* ◇ [VN**(that)**] *It was decided (that) the school should purchase new software.* **2** (*law*) ~ (**for/against sb**) to make an official or legal judgement: [VN] *The case will be decided by a jury.* ◇ [V] *The Appeal Court decided in their favour.* ◇ *It is always possible that the judge may decide against you.* **3** to affect the result of sth: [VN] *A mixture of skill and good luck decided the outcome of the game.* ◇ [V**wh-**] *A number of factors decide whether a movie will be successful or not.* [also V] **4** to be the reason why sb does sth: [VN] *They offered me free accommodation for a year, and that decided me.* [also VN to inf] **PHRV** **de'cide on/ upon sth** to choose sth from a number of possibilities: *We're still trying to decide on a venue.*

de·cid·ed /dɪˈsaɪdɪd/ *adj.* [only before noun] obvious and definite: *His height was a decided advantage in the job.*— compare UNDECIDED

de·cid·ed·ly /dɪˈsaɪdɪdli/ *adv.* **1** (used with an adjective or adverb) definitely and in an obvious way: *Amy was looking decidedly worried.* ◇ *Their relationship is beginning to look decidedly shaky.* **2** (*BrE*) in a way that shows that you are sure and determined about sth: *'I won't go,' she said decidedly.*

de·cid·er /dɪˈsaɪdə(r)/ *noun* [usually sing.] the game, race, etc. that will decide who the winner is in a competition

de·cidu·ous /dɪˈsɪdʒuəs; -dju-/ *adj.* (of a tree, bush etc.) that loses its leaves every year—compare EVERGREEN

deci·litre (*BrE*) (*AmE* **deci·liter**) /ˈdesɪliːtə(r)/ *noun* a unit for measuring liquids. There are 10 decilitres in a litre.

deci·mal /ˈdesɪml/ *adj., noun*
■ *adj.* based on or counted in tens or TENTHS: *the decimal system* ◇ *The figure is accurate to two decimal places* (= shows two figures after the decimal point).
■ *noun* (also ˌdecimal ˈfraction) a FRACTION (= a number less than one) that is shown as a dot or point followed by the number of TENTHS, HUNDREDTHS, etc: *The decimal 0.61 stands for 61 hundredths.*—compare VULGAR FRACTION ⫐ Appendix 3

ˌdecimal ˈpoint *noun* a dot or point used to separate the whole number from the TENTHS, HUNDREDTHS, etc. of a decimal, for example in 0.61

deci·mate /ˈdesɪmeɪt/ *verb* [VN] **1** [usually passive] to kill large numbers of animals, plants or people in a particular area: *The rabbit population was decimated by the disease.* **2** (*informal*) to severely damage sth or make sth weaker. ▶ **deci·ma·tion** /ˌdesɪˈmeɪʃn/ *noun* [U]

deci·metre (*BrE*) (*AmE* **deci·meter**) /ˈdesɪmiːtə(r)/ *noun* a unit for measuring length. There are 10 decimetres in a metre.

de·cipher /dɪˈsaɪfə(r)/ *verb* [VN] to succeed in finding the meaning of sth that is difficult to read or understand: *to decipher a code* ◇ *Can anyone decipher his handwriting?*— see also INDECIPHERABLE

de·ci·sion /dɪˈsɪʒn/ *noun* **1** [C] ~ (**on/about sth**)| ~ (**to do sth**) a choice or judgement that you make after thinking and talking about what is the best thing to do: *to take a decision* (= to decide) ◇ (*BrE*) *to make a decision* (= to decide) ◇ *We need a decision on this by next week.* ◇ *Who took the decision to go ahead with the project?* ◇ *He is really bad at making decisions.* ◇ *We finally reached a decision* (= decided after some difficulty). ◇ *We must come to a decision about what to do next by tomorrow.* ◇ *a big* (= an important) *decision* ◇ *The final decision is yours.* ◇ *It's a difficult decision for any doctor.* ◇ *The editor's decision is final.* ◇ *Mary is the decision-maker in the house.* **2** (also **de·cisive·ness**) [U] the ability to decide sth clearly and quickly: *This is not a job for someone who lacks decision.*—compare INDECISION **3** [U] the process of deciding sth: *The moment of decision had arrived.*

de'cision-making *noun* [U] the process of deciding about sth important, especially in a group of people or in an organization

de·cisive /dɪˈsaɪsɪv/ *adj.* **1** very important for the final result of a particular situation: *a decisive factor/victory/ battle* ◇ *She has played a decisive role in the peace negotiations.* ◇ *a decisive step* (= an important action that will change a situation) *towards a cleaner environment* **2** able to decide sth quickly and with confidence: *decisive management* ◇ *The government must take decisive action on gun control.*—compare INDECISIVE ▶ **de·cisive·ly** *adv.*

de·cisive·ness /dɪˈsaɪsɪvnəs/ *noun* [U] = DECISION (2)

deck /dek/ *noun, verb*
■ *noun* **1** the top outside floor of a ship or boat: *I was the only person on deck at that time of night.* ◇ *As the storm began, everyone disappeared below deck(s).* **2** one of the floors of a ship or a bus: *the upper/lower/main deck of a ship* ◇ *We sat on the top deck of the bus.* ◇ *My cabin is on deck C.*—see also DOUBLE-DECKER, FLIGHT DECK, SINGLE-DECKER **3** (also ˌdeck of ˈcards) (*especially AmE*) = PACK—picture on page A8 **4** (*especially AmE*) a wooden floor that is built outside the back of a house where you can sit and relax—picture at HOUSE **5** a part of a music system that records and/or plays sounds on a disc or tape: *a cassette/tape deck* **IDM** see CLEAR *v.*, HIT *v.*
■ *verb* [VN] **1** [often passive] ~ **sb/sth (out) (in/with sth)** to decorate sb/sth with sth: *The room was decked out in flowers and balloons.* **2** (*slang*) to hit sb very hard so that they fall to the ground

deck·chair /ˈdektʃeə(r); *AmE* -tʃer/ *noun* a folding chair with a long fabric seat on a wooden or metal frame, used for example on a beach or beside a swimming pool— picture at CHAIR

deck·hand /ˈdekhænd/ *noun* a worker on a ship who does work that is not skilled

ˈdeck shoe *noun* a flat shoe made of strong fabric

de·claim /dɪˈkleɪm/ *verb* (*formal*) to say sth loudly; to speak loudly and forcefully about sth you feel strongly about, especially in public: [VN] *She declaimed the famous opening speech of the play.* ◇ [V] *He declaimed against the evils of alcohol.* ◇ [also V **speech**, V **that**]

dec·lam·ation /ˌdekləˈmeɪʃn/ *noun* (*formal*) **1** [U] the act of speaking or of expressing sth to an audience in a formal way **2** [C] a speech or piece of writing that strongly expresses feelings and opinions

de·clama·tory /dɪˈklæmətəri; *AmE* -tɔːri/ *adj.* (*formal*) expressing feelings or opinions in a strong way in a speech or a piece of writing

dec·lar·ation /ˌdekləˈreɪʃn/ *noun* **1** [C, U] an official or formal statement, especially about the plans of a government or an organization; the act of making such a statement: *to issue/sign a declaration* ◇ *the declaration of war* ◇ *the Declaration of Independence* (= of the United States) **2** [C] a written or spoken statement, especially about what people feel or believe: *a declaration of love/faith/ guilt* **3** [C] an official written statement giving information: *a declaration of income* ◇ *customs declarations* (= giving details of goods that have been brought into a country)

de·clare /dɪˈkleə(r); *AmE* dɪˈkler/ *verb* **1** to say sth officially or publicly: [VN] *The government has declared a state of emergency.* ◇ *Germany declared war on France on 1 August 1914.* ◇ *The government has declared war on* (= officially stated its intention to stop) *illiteracy.* ◇ [V **that**] *The court declared that strike action was illegal.* ◇ [VN-N] *The area has been declared a national park.* ◇ [VN to inf] *The painting was declared to be a forgery.* ◇ [VN-ADJ] *The contract was declared void.* ◇ *I declare this bridge open.* **2** to state sth firmly and clearly: [V **speech**] *'I'll do it!'* *Tom declared.* ◇ [V **that**] *He declared that he was in love with her.* ◇ [VN] *Few people dared to declare their opposition to the regime.* ◇ [VN-ADJ] *She declared herself extremely hurt by his lack of support.* [also VN-N] **3** [VN] to tell the tax authorities how much money you have earned: *All income must be declared.* **4** [VN] to tell CUSTOMS officers (= at the border of a country) that you are carrying goods on which you should pay tax: *Do you have anything to declare?* **5** [V] (in cricket) to decide to end your INNINGS (= the period during which your team is BATTING) before all your players have BATTED **PHRV**

æ	ɑː	e	ɜː	ə	ɪ	iː	i	ɒ	ɔː	ʌ	ʊ	u	uː
cat	father	ten	bird	about	sit	see	many	got (BrE)	saw	cup	put	actual	too

D

de·clare a·gainst sb/sth (BrE, formal) to say publicly that you do not support sb/sth de·clare for sb/sth (BrE, formal) to say publicly that you support sb/sth

de·clared /dɪˈkleəd; AmE -ˈklerd/ adj. [only before noun] stated in an open way so that people know about it: *the government's declared intention to reduce crime*

de·clas·sify /ˌdiːˈklæsɪfaɪ/ verb (de·clas·si·fies, de·clas·si·fy·ing, de·clas·si·fied, de·clas·si·fied) [VN] to state officially that secret government information is no longer secret: *declassified information/documents* ▶ de·clas·si·fi·ca·tion /ˌdiːˌklæsɪfɪˈkeɪʃn/ noun [U]

de·cline /dɪˈklaɪn/ noun, verb
■ noun [C usually sing, U] ~ (in sth)| ~ (of sth) a continuous decrease in the number, value, quality, etc. of sth: *a rapid/sharp/gradual decline* ◊ *urban/economic decline* ◊ *The company reported a small decline in its profits.* ◊ *An increase in cars has resulted in the decline of public transport.* ◊ *The town fell into (a) decline* (= started to be less busy, important, etc.) *after the mine closed.* ◊ *Industry in Britain has been in decline since the 1970s.*
■ verb **1** [V] to become smaller, fewer, weaker, etc: *Support for the party continues to decline.* ◊ *The number of tourists to the resort declined by 10% last year.* ◊ *Her health was declining rapidly.* **2** (formal) to refuse politely to accept or to do sth: [V] *I offered to give them a lift but they declined.* ◊ [VN] *to decline an offer/invitation* ◊ [V to inf] *Their spokesman declined to comment on the allegations.* **3** [V, VN] (grammar) if a noun, an adjective or a pronoun **declines**, it has different forms according to whether it is the subject or the object of a verb, whether it is in the singular or plural, etc. When you **decline** a noun, etc., you list these forms.—compare CONJUGATE **IDM** **sb's declining years** (literary) the last years of sb's life

de·code /ˌdiːˈkəʊd; AmE -ˈkoʊd/ verb [VN] **1** to find the meaning of sth, especially sth that has been written in CODE **SYN** DECIPHER: *I was involved in decoding enemy documents.*—compare ENCODE **2** to receive an electronic signal and change it into pictures that can be shown on a television screen: *decoding equipment*

de·coder /ˌdiːˈkəʊdə(r); AmE -ˈkoʊ-/ noun a device that changes an electronic signal into a form that people can understand, such as sound and pictures: *a satellite/video decoder*

dé·col·le·tage /ˌdeɪkɒlˈtɑːʒ; AmE -kɑːləˈt-/ (also **dé·col·leté** /deɪˈkɒlteɪ; AmE ˌdeɪkɑːlˈteɪ/) noun (from French) the top edge of a woman's dress, etc. that is designed to be very low in order to show her shoulders and the top part of her breasts ▶ **dé·col·leté** adj.

de·col·on·iza·tion (BrE also **-isa·tion**) /ˌdiːˌkɒlənaɪˈzeɪʃn; AmE -ˌkɑːlənəˈz-/ noun [U] the process of a COLONY or COLONIES becoming independent

de·com·mis·sion /ˌdiːkəˈmɪʃn/ verb [VN] to officially stop using weapons, a nuclear power station, etc.

de·com·pose /ˌdiːkəmˈpəʊz; AmE -ˈpoʊz/ verb **1** to be destroyed gradually by natural chemical processes **SYN** DECAY, ROT: [V] *a decomposing corpse* ◊ *As the waste materials decompose, they produce methane gas.* ◊ [VN] *a decomposed body* **2** [VN, V] ~ (sth) (into sth) (technical) to divide sth into smaller parts; to divide into smaller parts ▶ **de·com·pos·ition** /ˌdiːkɒmpəˈzɪʃn; AmE -kɑːm-/ noun [U]: *the decomposition of organic waste*

de·com·press /ˌdiːkəmˈpres/ verb **1** [V, VN] to have the air pressure in sth reduced to a normal level or to reduce it to its normal level **2** [VN] (computing) to return files, etc. to their original size after they have been COMPRESSED

de·com·pres·sion /ˌdiːkəmˈpreʃn/ noun [U] **1** a reduction in air pressure; the act of reducing the pressure of the air: *a decompression chamber* (= a piece of equipment that divers sit in so that they can return slowly to normal air pressure after being deep in the sea) ◊ *decompression sickness* (= severe pain and difficulty in breathing experienced by divers who come back to the surface of deep water too quickly)—see also BENDS **2** (technical) the act or process of allowing sth that has been compressed (= made smaller) to fill the space that it originally took up

de·con·gest·ant /ˌdiːkənˈdʒestənt/ noun a medicine

that helps sb with a cold to breathe more easily: *a nasal decongestant*

de·con·struct /ˌdiːkənˈstrʌkt/ verb [VN] (technical) (in literature and philosophy) to analyse a text in order to show that there is no fixed meaning within the text but that the meaning is created each time in the act of reading

de·con·struc·tion /ˌdiːkənˈstrʌkʃn/ noun [U] (technical) (in literature and philosophy) a theory that states that it is impossible for a text to have one fixed meaning, and emphasizes the role of the reader in the production of meaning—compare STRUCTURALISM ▶ **de·con·struc·tion·ist** noun, adj.: *a deconstructionist critic/approach*

de·con·tam·in·ate /ˌdiːkənˈtæmɪneɪt/ verb [VN] to remove harmful substances from a place or thing: *the process of decontaminating areas exposed to radioactivity* ▶ **de·con·tam·in·ation** /ˌdiːkənˌtæmɪˈneɪʃn/ noun [U]

de·con·trol /ˌdiːkənˈtrəʊl; AmE -ˈtroʊl/ verb (-ll-) [VN] (formal, especially AmE) if a government **decontrols** sth, it removes legal controls from it **SYN** DEREGULATE ▶ **de·con·trol** noun [U]

decor /ˈdeɪkɔː(r); AmE deɪˈkɔːr/ noun [U, C, usually sing.] the style in which the inside of a building is decorated: *interior decor* ◊ *the restaurant's elegant new decor*

dec·or·ate /ˈdekəreɪt/ verb **1** [VN] ~ sth (with sth) to make sth look more attractive by putting things on it: *They decorated the room with flowers and balloons.* ◊ *The cake was decorated to look like a car.* **2** (especially BrE) to put paint, WALLPAPER, etc. on the walls and ceilings of a room or house: [V] *I hate decorating.* ◊ *He has his own painting and decorating business.* ◊ [VN] *We need to decorate the sitting room.* ◊ *The sitting room needs decorating.* **3** [VN] to be placed on sth in order to make it look more attractive **SYN** ADORN: *Photographs of actors decorated the walls of the restaurant.* **4** [VN] [usually passive] ~ sb (for sth) to give sb a medal as a sign of respect for sth they have done

dec·or·ation /ˌdekəˈreɪʃn/ noun **1** [C, usually pl.] a thing that makes sth look more attractive on special occasions: *Christmas decorations* ◊ *a table decoration* **2** [U, C] a pattern, etc. that is added to sth and that stops it from being plain: *the elaborate decoration on the carved wooden door* **3** [U] the style in which sth is decorated: *a Chinese theme in the interior decoration* **4** [U] (BrE) the act or process of decorating sth such as the inside of a house by painting it, etc. **5** [C] a medal that is given to sb as an honour

dec·ora·tive /ˈdekərətɪv; AmE ˈdekəreɪtɪv/ adj. (of an object or a building) decorated in a way that makes it attractive; intended to look attractive or pretty: *The mirror is functional yet decorative.* ◊ *purely decorative arches*

dec·or·ator /ˈdekəreɪtə(r)/ noun a person whose job is painting and decorating houses

dec·or·ous /ˈdekərəs/ adj. (formal) polite and appropriate in a particular social situation; not shocking: *a decorous kiss* ▶ **dec·or·ous·ly** adv.

de·corum /dɪˈkɔːrəm/ noun [U] (formal) polite behaviour that is appropriate in a social situation: *a sense of decorum*

de·couple /ˌdiːˈkʌpl/ verb [VN] ~ sth (from sth) (formal) to end the connection or relationship between two things

decoy /ˈdiːkɔɪ/ noun [C] **1** an animal or a bird, or a model of one, that attracts other animals or birds, especially so that they can be shot by people who are hunting them **2** a thing or a person that is used to trick sb into doing what you want them to do; going where you want them to go, etc. ▶ **decoy** /dɪˈkɔɪ/ verb [VN]

de·crease verb, noun
■ verb /dɪˈkriːs/ ~ (from sth) (to sth) to become or make sth become smaller in size, number, etc: [V] *The number of new students decreased from 210 to 160 this year.* ◊ *The price of wheat has decreased by 15%.* ◊ *This species of bird is decreasing in numbers every year.* ◊ *a decreasing population* ◊ [VN] *People should decrease the amount of fat they eat.* **OPP** INCREASE
■ noun /ˈdiːkriːs/ [C, U] ~ (in sth)| ~ (of sth) the process of reducing sth or the amount that sth is reduced by:

aɪ	aʊ	eɪ	əʊ	oʊ	ɔɪ	ɪə	eə	ʊə	j	w
my	now	say	go	go	boy	near	hair	pure	yes	wet
			(BrE)	(AmE)						

There has been some decrease in military spending this year. ◊ *a decrease of nearly 6% in the number of visitors to the museum* OPP INCREASE

de·cree /dɪˈkriː/ *noun, verb*

■ *noun* **1** [C, U] an official order from a ruler or a government that becomes the law: *to issue/sign a decree* ◊ *a leader who rules by decree* (= not in a DEMOCRATIC way) **2** [C] a decision that is made in a court of law

■ *verb* (**de·cree·ing, de·creed, de·creed**) to decide, judge or order sth officially: [VN] *The government decreed a state of emergency.* ◊ [VN that] *It was decreed that the following day would be a holiday.* [also V, V wh-]

de·cree ˈab·so·lute *noun* [sing.] (*BrE, law*) an order from a court of law that finally ends a marriage, making the two people divorced: *The period between the decree nisi and the decree absolute was six weeks.*

decree nisi /dɪˌkriː ˈnaɪsaɪ/ *noun* [sing.] (*BrE, law*) an order from a court of law that a marriage will end after a fixed amount of time unless there is a good reason why it should not

de·crepit /dɪˈkrepɪt/ *adj.* (of a thing or person) very old and not in good condition or health: *a decrepit building/vehicle* ◊ *a decrepit old man*

de·crepi·tude /dɪˈkrepɪtjuːd; *AmE* -tuːd/ *noun* [U] (*formal*) the state of being old and in poor condition or health

de·crim·in·al·ize (*BrE* also **-ise**) /diːˈkrɪmɪnəlaɪz/ *verb* [VN] to change the law so that sth is no longer illegal: *There are moves to decriminalize some soft drugs.* ▶ **de·crim·in·al·iza·tion, -isa·tion** /diːˌkrɪmɪnəlaɪˈzeɪʃn; *AmE* -ləˈz-/ *noun* [U]

decry /dɪˈkraɪ/ *verb* (**de·cries, de·cry·ing, de·cried, de·cried**) [VN] ~ **sb/sth** (**as sth**) (*formal*) to strongly criticize sb/sth, especially publicly SYN CONDEMN: *The measures were decried as useless.* [also VN]

dedi·cate /ˈdedɪkeɪt/ *verb* [VN] **1** ~ **yourself/sth to sth/to doing sth** to give a lot of your time and effort to a particular activity or purpose because you think it is important: *She dedicates herself to her work.* ◊ *He dedicated his life to helping the poor.* **2** ~ **sth to sb** to say at the beginning of a book, a piece of music or a performance that you are doing it for sb, as a way of thanking them or showing respect: *This book is dedicated to my parents.* **3** ~ **sth** (**to sb/sth**) to hold an official ceremony to say that a church or other building, or an object has a special purpose or is special to the memory of a particular person: *The chapel was dedicated in 1880.* ◊ *A memorial stone was dedicated to those who lost their lives in the war.*

dedi·cated /ˈdedɪkeɪtɪd/ *adj.* **1** ~ (**to sth**) working hard at sth because it is very important to you SYN COMMITTED: *a dedicated teacher* ◊ *She is dedicated to her job.* **2** [only before noun] designed to do only one particular type of work; used for one particular purpose only: *a dedicated word processor/server* ◊ *Software is exported through a dedicated satellite link.*

ded·ica·tion /ˌdedɪˈkeɪʃn/ *noun* **1** [U] ~ (**to sth**) (*approving*) the hard work and effort that sb puts into an activity or purpose because they think it is important: *hard work and dedication* **2** [C] a ceremony that is held to show that a church or other building, or an object, has a special purpose or is special to the memory of a particular person **3** [C] the words that are used at the beginning of a book, piece of music, a performance, etc. to offer it to sb as a sign of thanks or respect

de·duce /dɪˈdjuːs; *AmE* dɪˈduːs/ *verb* ~ (**sth**) (**from sth**) (*formal*) to form an opinion about sth based on the information or evidence that is available SYN INFER: [V that] *Can we deduce from your silence that you do not approve?* ◊ [VN] *We can deduce a lot from what people spend their money on.* [also V wh-] —see also DEDUCTION ▶ **de·du·cible** /dɪˈdjuːsəbl; *AmE* -ˈduːs-/ *adj.*

de·duct /dɪˈdʌkt/ *verb* [VN] [often passive] ~ **sth** (**from sth**) to take away money, points, etc. from a total amount: *The cost of your uniform will be deducted from your wages.* ◊ *Ten points will be deducted for a wrong answer.*

de·duct·ible /dɪˈdʌktəbl/ *adj.* that can be taken away

from an amount of money you earn, from tax, etc: *These costs are deductible from profits.* ◊ *tax-deductible expenses* (= that you do not have to pay tax on) ▶ **de·duct·ible** *noun* [C] (*AmE*): *The donation he made was a deductible on his tax form.* ◊ *After a $75 deductible, Medicare pays 80 per cent of doctors' bills.*

de·duc·tion /dɪˈdʌkʃn/ *noun* **1** [U, C] the process of using information you have in order to understand a particular situation or to find the answer to a problem: *He arrived at the solution by a simple process of deduction.* ◊ *If my deductions are correct, I can tell you who the killer was.*—see also DEDUCE—compare INDUCTION (3) **2** [U, C] the process of taking an amount of sth, especially money, away from a total; the amount that is taken away: *deductions from your pay for tax, pension contributions, etc.* ◊ *tax deductions*

de·duct·ive /dɪˈdʌktɪv/ *adj.* [usually before noun] using knowledge about things that are generally true in order to think about and understand particular situations or problems: *deductive logic/reasoning*—compare INDUCTIVE

deed /diːd/ *noun* **1** (*formal, literary*) a thing that sb does that is usually very good or very bad: *a brave/charitable/evil deed* ◊ *a tale of heroic deeds* **2** (often plural in British English) a legal document that you sign, especially one that proves that you own a house or a building: *the deeds of the house*—see also TITLE DEED IDM **your good deed for the** ˈ**day** a helpful, kind thing that you do

deed of ˈ**covenant** *noun* (*BrE*) an agreement to pay a regular amount of money to sb/sth, especially a charity, that means that they also receive the tax that would have to be paid on this money: *Signing a deed of covenant makes £1 worth £1.33.*

ˈ**deed poll** *noun* [U, sing.] (*BrE*) a legal document signed by only one person, especially in order to change their name: *Smith changed his name by deed poll to Jervis-Smith.*

deem /diːm/ *verb* (*formal*) (not usually used in the progressive tenses) to have a particular opinion about sth SYN CONSIDER: [VN-N] *The evening was deemed a great success.* ◊ [VN-ADJ] *She deemed it prudent not to say anything.* ◊ *They would take any action deemed necessary.* [also V (that), VN to inf]

deep /diːp/ *adj., adv., noun*

■ *adj.* (**deep·er, deep·est**)

TOP TO BOTTOM | **1** having a large distance from the top or surface to the bottom: *a deep hole/well/river* ◊ *deep water/snow* OPP SHALLOW

FRONT TO BACK | **2** having a large distance from the front edge to the furthest point inside: *a deep cut/wound* ◊ *a deep space* OPP SHALLOW

MEASUREMENT | **3** used to describe or ask about the depth of sth: *The water is only a few inches deep.* ◊ *How deep is the wound?*

FAR INSIDE | **4** ~ **in sth** far inside or down in sth: *deep in the desert/forest* ◊ *He stood with his hands deep in his pockets.*

-DEEP | **5** (in adjectives) as far up or down as the point mentioned: *The water was only waist-deep so I walked ashore.* **6** (in adjectives) in the number of rows mentioned, one behind the other: *They were standing three-deep at the bar.*

BREATH/SIGH | **7** [usually before noun] taking in or giving out a lot of air: *She took a deep breath.* ◊ *He gave a deep sigh.*

SOUNDS | **8** low: *I heard his deep warm voice filling the room.* ◊ *a deep roar/groan*

COLOURS | **9** strong and dark: *a rich deep red* OPP PALE

SLEEP | **10** a person in a **deep** sleep is difficult to wake: *to be in a deep sleep/trance/coma* OPP LIGHT

SERIOUS | **11** extreme or serious: *He's in deep trouble.* ◊ *a deep economic recession* ◊ *The affair had exposed deep divisions within the party.* ◊ *a place of great power and of deep significance*

EMOTIONS | **12** strongly felt; sincere: *deep concern/regret/affection/respect* ◊ *a deep sense of loss*

KNOWLEDGE | **13** showing great knowledge or understanding: *a deep understanding/insight/analysis*

b	d	f	g	h	k	l	m	n	p	r
bad	did	fall	get	hat	cat	leg	man	now	pen	red

D

DIFFICULT TO UNDERSTAND | **14** difficult to understand SYN PROFOUND: *This discussion's getting too deep for me.* ◊ *He pondered, as if over some deep philosophical point.*

INVOLVED | **15** ~ **in sth** fully involved in an activity or a state: *to be deep in thought/conversation/prayer* ◊ *He is often so deep in his books that he forgets to eat.* ◊ *The firm ended up deep in debt.*

PERSON | **16** if a person is **deep**, they hide their real feelings and opinions: *She's always been a deep one, trusting no one.*

IN SPORT | **17** to or from a position far down or across the field: *a deep ball from Beckham*

—see also DEPTH

IDM **go off the 'deep end** (*informal*) to suddenly become very angry or emotional **in deep 'water(s)** (*informal*) in trouble or difficulty **jump/be thrown in at the 'deep end** (*informal*) to start or be made to start a new and difficult activity that you are not prepared for: *Junior hospital doctors are thrown in at the deep end in their first jobs.*—more at DEVIL, SHIT *n.*

■ *adv.* (**deep·er, deep·est**) ~ (**below, into, under, etc.**) a long way below the surface of sth or a long way inside or into sth: *Dig deeper!* ◊ *The miners were trapped deep underground.* ◊ *whales that feed deep beneath the waves* ◊ *He gazed deep into her eyes.* ◊ *They sat and talked deep into the night* (= until very late).

IDM **deep 'down 1** if you know sth **deep down**, you know your true feelings about sth, although you may not admit them to yourself: *Deep down I still loved him.* **2** if sth is true **deep down**, it is really like that, although it may not be obvious to people: *He seems confident but deep down he's quite insecure.* **go/run 'deep** (of emotions, beliefs, etc.) to be felt in a strong way, especially for a long time: *Dignity and pride run deep in this community.*—more at DIG *v.*, STILL

■ *noun* [sing.] (**the deep**) (*literary*) the sea

WHICH WORD?
deep / deeply

The adverbs **deep** and **deeply** can both mean 'a long way down or into something'. **Deep** can only mean this and is more common than **deeply** in this sense. It is usually followed by a word like *into* or *below*: *We decided to go deeper into the jungle.*

Deeply usually means 'very much': *deeply in love* ◊ *deeply shocked.* You can use **deep down** (but not **deeply**) to talk about a person's real nature: *She can seem stern, but deep down she's a very kind person.* ◊ ~~She can seem stern, but deeply she's a very kind person.~~

---

deep·en /'diːpən/ *verb* **1** if an emotion or a feeling **deepens**, or if sth **deepens** it, it becomes stronger: [V] *Their friendship soon deepened into love.* [also VN] **2** to become worse; to make sth worse: [V] *Warships were sent in as the crisis deepened.* ◊ *a deepening economic recession* [also VN] **3** [V] to become deeper; to make sth deeper: [V] *The water deepened gradually.* ◊ *His frown deepened.* [VN] *There were plans to deepen a stretch of the river.* **4** [VN] to improve your knowledge or understanding of sth: *an opportunity for students to deepen their understanding of different cultures* **5** [V, VN] if colour or light **deepens** or if sth **deepens** it, it becomes darker: *deepening shadows* **6** if a sound or voice **deepens** or if you **deepen** it, it becomes lower or you make it lower: [V] *His voice deepened to a growl.* [also VN] **7** [V] if your breathing **deepens**, you breathe more deeply than usual

deep 'freeze (*BrE*) (*AmE* **Deep·freeze**™) **,deep 'freezer**) *noun* = FREEZER

deep-'frozen *adj.* preserved at an extremely low temperature

deep-'fry *verb* [VN] [usually passive] to cook food in oil that covers it completely: *deep-fried chicken pieces*

deep·ly /'diːpli/ *adv.* **1** very; very much: *She is deeply religious.* ◊ *They were deeply disturbed by the accident.* ◊ *Opinion is deeply divided on this issue.* ◊ *deeply rooted customs/ideas* ◊ *deeply held beliefs/convictions/views* (=

that sb feels very strongly) **2** used with some verbs to show that sth is done in a very complete way: *to breathe/sigh/exhale deeply* (= using all of the air in your lungs) ◊ *sleep deeply* (= in a way that makes it difficult for you to wake up) ◊ *to think deeply* (= about all the aspects of sth) **3** to a depth that is quite a long way from the surface of sth: *to drill deeply into the wood* ⇨ note at DEEP

,deep-'rooted, ,deep-'seated *adj.* [usually before noun] (of feelings and beliefs) very fixed and strong; difficult to change or to destroy: *a deep-rooted desire/fear/problem* ◊ *The country's political divisions are deep-seated.*

'deep-sea (also *less frequent* **'deep-water**) *adj.* [only before noun] of or in the deeper parts of the sea: *a deep-sea diver* ◊ *deep-sea fishing/diving*

,deep-'set *adj.* (*written*) eyes that are **deep-set** seem to be quite far back in a person's face

,deep-'six *verb* [VN] [usually passive] (*AmE, informal*) to decide not to do or use sth that you had planned to do or use: *Plans to build a new mall were deep-sixed after protests from local residents.*

the ,Deep 'South *noun* [sing.] the southern states of the US, especially Georgia, Alabama, Mississippi, Louisiana and South Carolina

deer /dɪə(r); *AmE* dɪr/ *noun* (*pl.* **deer**) an animal with long legs, that eats grass, leaves, etc. and can run fast. Most male deer have ANTLERS (= horns shaped like branches). There are many types of deer: *a herd of red deer* ◊ *a deer park*—see also FALLOW DEER, REINDEER, ROE DEER, DOE, FAWN, STAG

deer·stalk·er /'dɪəstɔːkə(r); *AmE* 'dɪrs-/ *noun* a cap with two PEAKS, one in front and one behind, and two pieces of fabric which are usually tied together on top but can be folded down to cover the ears

de·face /dɪ'feɪs/ *verb* [VN] to damage the appearance of sth especially by drawing or writing on it ► **de·face·ment** *noun* [U]

de facto /,deɪ 'fæktəʊ; *AmE* -toʊ/ *adj.* [usually before noun] (from *Latin, formal*) existing as a fact although it may not be legally accepted as existing: *The general took de facto control of the country.* ► **de facto** *adv.*: *He continued to rule the country de facto.*—compare DE JURE

def·am·a·tion /,defə'meɪʃn/ *noun* [U, C] (*formal*) the act of causing harm to sb by saying or writing bad or false things about them: *The company sued for defamation.*

de·fama·tory /dɪ'fæmətri; *AmE* -tɔːri/ *adj.* (*formal*) (of speech or writing) intended to harm sb by saying or writing bad or false things about them

de·fame /dɪ'feɪm/ *verb* [VN] (*formal*) to harm sb by saying or writing bad or false things about them

de·fault /dɪ'fɔːlt; 'diː-/ *noun, verb*

■ *noun* **1** [U, C] failure to do sth that must be done by law, especially paying a debt: *The company is in default on the loan.* ◊ *Mortgage defaults have risen in the last year.* **2** [U, C, usually sing.] (especially *computing*) what happens or appears if you do not make any other choice or change: *The default option is to save your work every five minutes.* ◊ *On this screen, 256 colours is the default.* IDM **by de'fault 1** a game or competition can be won **by default** if there are no other competitors **2** if sth happens **by default**, it happens because you have not made any other decision or choices which would make things happen differently **in de'fault of sth** (*formal*) because of a lack of sth: *They accepted what he had said in default of any evidence to disprove it.*

■ *verb* [V] **1** ~ (**on sth**) to fail to do sth that you legally have to do, especially by not paying a debt: *to default on a loan/debt* ◊ *defaulting borrowers/tenants* **2** ~ (**to sth**) (especially *computing*) to happen when you do not make any other choice or change ► **de·fault·er** *noun*: *mortgage defaulters*

de·feat /dɪ'fiːt/ *verb, noun*

■ *verb* [VN] **1** to win against sb in a war, competition, sports game, etc. SYN BEAT: *He defeated the champion in three sets.* ◊ *a defeated army* **2** (*formal*) if sth **defeats** you, you cannot understand it: *The instruction manual completely defeated me.* **3** to stop sth from being successful: *The*

---

s	t	v	z	ʃ	ʒ	tʃ	dʒ	θ	ð	ŋ
see	tea	van	zoo	shoe	vision	chain	jam	thin	this	sing

motion was defeated by 19 votes. ◊ *Staying late at the office to discuss shorter working hours rather defeats the object of the exercise!*

■ noun **1** [U, C] failure to win or to be successful: *The party faces defeat in the election.* ◊ *a narrow/heavy defeat* ◊ *The world champion has only had two defeats in 20 fights.* ◊ *They finally had to admit defeat* (= stop trying to be successful). **2** [C, usually sing.] the act of winning a victory over sb/sth: *the defeat of fascism*

de·feat·ist /dɪˈfiːtɪst/ *adj.* expecting not to succeed, and showing it in a particular situation: *a defeatist attitude/view* ▶ **de·feat·ist** *noun: He is a pessimist and a defeatist.* **de·feat·ism** *noun* [U]

defe·cate /ˈdefəkeɪt; ˈdiː-/ *verb* [V] (*formal*) to get rid of solid waste from your body through your bowels ▶ **defe·ca·tion** /ˌdefəˈkeɪʃn; ˌdiː-/ *noun* [U]

de·fect *noun, verb*
■ noun /ˈdiːfekt; dɪˈfekt/ a fault in sth or in the way it has been made which means that it is not perfect: *a speech defect* ◊ *a defect in the glass*
■ verb /dɪˈfekt/ [V] ~ (**from sth**) (**to sth**) to leave a political party, country, etc. to join another that is considered to be an enemy: *A number of writers and musicians defected from the Soviet Union to the West in the 1960s.* ▶ **de·fec·tion** /dɪˈfekʃn/ *noun* [U, C] ~ (**from sth**) (**to sth**): *There have been several defections from the ruling party.* **de·fect·or** *noun*

de·fect·ive /dɪˈfektɪv/ *adj.* having a fault or faults; not perfect or complete [SYN] FAULTY: *defective goods* ◊ *Her hearing was found to be slightly defective.* ▶ **de·fect·ive·ly** *adv.* **de·fect·ive·ness** *noun* [U]

de·fence (*BrE*) (*AmE* **de·fense**) /dɪˈfens/ *noun*
PROTECTION AGAINST ATTACK | **1** [U] the act of protecting sb/sth from attack, criticism, etc: *soldiers who died in defence of their country* ◊ *When her brother was criticized she leapt to his defence.* ◊ *What points can be raised in defence of this argument?* ◊ *I have to say in her defence that she knew nothing about it beforehand.*—see also SELF-DEFENCE **2** [C, U] ~ (**against sth**) something that provides protection against attack from enemies, the weather, illness, etc: *The town walls were built as a defence against enemy attacks.* ◊ *The harbour's sea defences are in poor condition.* ◊ *The body has natural defence mechanisms to protect it from disease.* ◊ *Humour is a more effective defence than violence.* **3** [U] the organization of the people and systems that are used by a government to protect a country from attack: (*BrE*) *the Ministry of Defence* ◊ (*AmE*) *the Department of Defense* ◊ *Further cuts in defence spending are being considered.*
SUPPORT | **4** [C] something that is said or written in order to support sth: *a defence of Marxism*
LAW | **5** [C] what is said in a court of law to prove that a person did not commit a crime; the act of presenting this argument in a court of law: *Her defence was that she was somewhere completely different at the time of the crime.* ◊ *He wanted to conduct his own defence.* **6** (**the defence**) [sing.+ sing./pl. v.] the lawyer or lawyers whose job is to prove in a court of law that a person did not commit a crime—compare PROSECUTION
IN SPORT | **7** [sing., U] the players who must prevent the other team from scoring; the position of these players on the sports field: *Welford cut through the defence to score the winning goal.* ◊ (*BrE*) *She plays in defence.* ◊ (*AmE*) *He plays on defense.*—compare ATTACK, OFFENSE **8** [C] a contest, game, etc. in which the previous winner or winners compete in order to try to win again: *Milan's defence of the European Cup*

de·fence·less /dɪˈfensləs/ *adj.* weak; not able to protect yourself; having no protection: *defenceless animals/children* ◊ *The village is defenceless against attack.*

de·fend /dɪˈfend/ *verb*
PROTECT AGAINST ATTACK | **1** ~ (**sb/yourself/sth**) (**from/against sb/sth**) to protect sb/sth from attack: [VN] *All our officers are trained to defend themselves against knife attacks.* ◊ *Troops have been sent to defend the borders.* ◊ [V] *It is impossible to defend against an all-out attack.*

SUPPORT | **2** [VN] ~ **sb/yourself/sth** (**from/against sb/sth**) to say or write sth in support of sb/sth that has been criticized: *Politicians are skilled at defending themselves against their critics.* ◊ *How can you defend such behaviour?*
IN SPORT | **3** [V, VN] (in football, hockey, etc.) to protect your own goal to stop your opponents from scoring
IN COMPETITIONS | **4** [VN] to take part in a competition that you won the last time and try to win it again: *He is defending champion.* ◊ *She will be defending her title at next month's championships.* ◊ (*politics*) *He intends to defend his seat in the next election.*
LAW | **5** to act as a lawyer for sb who has been charged with a crime: [VN] *He has employed one of the UK's top lawyers to defend him.* [also V]

de·fend·ant /dɪˈfendənt/ *noun* the person in a court of law who is accused of committing a crime, or who is being sued by another person—compare PLAINTIFF, ACCUSED

de·fend·er /dɪˈfendə(r)/ *noun* **1** a player who must stop the other team from scoring in games such as football **2** a person who defends and believes in protecting sth: *a passionate defender of human rights*

de·fense (*AmE*) = DEFENCE

de·fens·ible /dɪˈfensəbl/ *adj.* **1** able to be supported by reasons or arguments that show that it is right or should be allowed: *Is abortion morally defensible?* **2** (of a place) able to be defended from an attack

de·fen·sive /dɪˈfensɪv/ *adj., noun*
■ adj. **1** protecting sb/sth against attack: *a defensive measure* ◊ *Troops are taking up a defensive position around the town.*—compare OFFENSIVE **2** behaving in a way that shows that you feel that people are criticizing you: *Don't ask him about his plans—he just gets defensive.* **3** (*sport*) connected with trying to prevent the other team or player from scoring points or goals: *defensive play*—compare OFFENSIVE ▶ **de·fen·sive·ly** *adv.* **de·fen·sive·ness** *noun* [U]
■ noun [IDM] **on/onto the defensive** acting in a way that shows that you expect to be attacked or criticized; having to defend yourself: *Their questions about the money put her on the defensive.* ◊ *Warnings of an enemy attack forced the troops onto the defensive.*

defer /dɪˈfɜː(r)/ *verb* (**-rr-**) to delay sth until a later time: [VN] *The department deferred the decision for six months.* ◊ *She had applied for deferred admission to college.* [also V-ing] ▶ **de·fer·ment, de·fer·ral** /dɪˈfɜːrəl/ *noun* [U, C]
[PHRV] **deˈfer to sb/sth** (*formal*) to agree to accept what sb has decided or what they think about sb/sth because you respect him or her: *We will defer to whatever the committee decides.*

def·er·ence /ˈdefərəns/ *noun* [U] (*written*) behaviour that shows that you respect sb/sth: *The women wore veils in deference to the customs of the country.* ◊ *The flags were lowered out of deference to the bereaved family.* ▶ **def·er·en·tial** /ˌdefəˈrenʃl/ *adj.* **def·er·en·tial·ly** /-ʃəli/ *adv.*

de·fi·ance /dɪˈfaɪəns/ *noun* [U] open refusal to obey sb/sth: *a look/an act/a gesture of defiance* ◊ *Nuclear testing was resumed in defiance of an international ban.*

de·fi·ant /dɪˈfaɪənt/ *adj.* openly refusing to obey sb/sth, sometimes in an aggressive way: *a defiant teenager* ◊ *The terrorists sent a defiant message to the government.* ▶ **de·fi·ant·ly** *adv.*

de·fib·ril·la·tor /diːˈfɪbrɪleɪtə(r)/ *noun* (*medical*) a piece of equipment used to control the movements of the heart muscles by giving the heart a controlled electric shock

de·fi·ciency /dɪˈfɪʃnsi/ *noun* (pl. **-ies**) ~ (**in/of sth**) **1** [U, C] the state of not having, or not having enough of, sth that is essential: *Vitamin deficiency in the diet can cause illness.* ◊ *a deficiency of Vitamin B* **2** [C] a fault or a weakness in sth/sb that makes it or them less successful: *deficiencies in the computer system*

de·fi·cient /dɪˈfɪʃnt/ *adj.* **1** ~ (**in sth**) not having enough of sth, especially sth that is essential: *a diet that is deficient in vitamin A* **2** (*formal*) not good enough: *Deaf people are sometimes treated as being mentally deficient.*

def·icit /ˈdefɪsɪt/ *noun* **1** (*economics*) the amount by

D

æ	ɑː	e	ɜː	ə	ɪ	iː	i	ɒ	ɔː	ʌ	ʊ	u	uː
cat	father	ten	bird	about	sit	see	many	got	saw	cup	put	actual	too
(BrE)

which money spent or owed is greater than money earned in a particular period of time: *a budget/trade deficit* ◊ *The trade balance has been in deficit for the past five years.*—compare SURPLUS **2** the amount by which sth, especially an amount of money, is too small or smaller than sth else: *There's a deficit of $3 million in the total needed to complete the project.* ◊ *The team has to come back from a 2–0 deficit in the first half.*

de·fied *pt, pp* of DEFY

de·file¹ /dɪˈfaɪl/ *verb* [VN] (*formal* or *literary*) to make sth dirty or no longer pure, especially sth that people consider important or holy: *Many victims of burglary feel their homes have been defiled.* ◊ *The altar had been defiled by vandals.* ▶ **de·file·ment** *noun*

de·file² /dɪˈfaɪl; ˈdiːfaɪl/ *noun* (*formal*) a narrow way through mountains

de·fine /dɪˈfaɪn/ *verb* **1** [VN] ~ sth (**as sth**) to say or explain what the meaning of a word or phrase is: *The term 'mental illness' is difficult to define.* ◊ *Life imprisonment is defined as 60 years under state law.* **2** to describe or show sth accurately: [VN] *We need to define the task ahead very clearly.* ◊ *The difficulty of a problem was defined in terms of how long it took to complete.* ◊ [V wh-] *It is difficult to define what makes him so popular.* **3** [VN] to show clearly a line, shape or edge: *The mountain was sharply defined against the sky.* ▶ **de·fin·able** *adj.*

def·in·ite /ˈdefɪnət/ *adj., noun*
■ *adj.* **1** ~ (**that …**) sure or certain; unlikely to change: *Can you give me a definite answer by tomorrow?* ◊ *Is it definite that he's leaving?* ◊ *I've heard rumours, but nothing definite.* ◊ *a definite offer of a job* ◊ *I'm not sure—I can find out for definite if you like.* ◊ *That's definite then, is it?* ◊ *They have very definite ideas on how to bring up children.* **2** easily or clearly seen or understood; obvious: *The look on her face was a definite sign that sth was wrong.* ◊ *There was a definite feeling that things were getting worse.* **3** [not before noun] ~ (**about sth**) | ~ (**that …**) (of a person) sure that sth is true or that sth is going to happen and stating it to other people: *I'm definite about this.*
■ *noun* [sing.] (*informal*) something that you are certain about or that you know will happen; sb who is sure to do sth: *'We're moving our office to Glasgow.' 'That's a definite, is it?'* ◊ *'Is Sarah coming to the party?' 'Yes, she's a definite.'*

ˌdefinite ˈarticle *noun* (*grammar*) the word *the*—compare INDEFINITE ARTICLE

def·in·ite·ly /ˈdefɪnətli/ *adv.* **1** (especially *spoken*) a way of emphasizing that sth is true and that there is no doubt about it: *I definitely remember sending the letter.* ◊ *'Was it what you expected?' 'Yes, definitely.'* ◊ *'Do you plan to have children?' 'Definitely not!'* ◊ *Some old people want help; others most definitely do not.* **2** in a way that is certain or that shows that you are certain: *The date of the move has not been definitely decided yet* (= it may change). ◊ *Please say definitely whether you will be coming or not.*

def·in·ition /ˌdefɪˈnɪʃn/ *noun* **1** [C, U] an explanation of the meaning of a word or phrase, especially in a dictionary; the act of stating the meanings of words and phrases: *clear simple definitions* ◊ *Neighbours by definition live close by* (= this is what being a neighbour means). **2** [C] what an idea, etc. means: *What's your definition of happiness?* **3** [U] the quality of being clear and easy to see: *The definition of the digital TV pictures is excellent.*

de·fini·tive /dɪˈfɪnətɪv/ *adj.* **1** final; not able to be changed: *a definitive agreement/answer/statement* ◊ *The definitive version of the text is ready to be published.* **2** [usually before noun] considered to be the best of its kind and almost impossible to improve: *the definitive biography of Einstein* ▶ **de·fini·tive·ly** *adv.*

de·flate *verb* **1** /dɪˈfleɪt; diː-/ [VN, V] to let air or gas out of a tyre, BALLOON, etc.; to become smaller because of air or gas coming out **2** /dɪˈfleɪt/ [VN] [often passive] to make sb feel less confident; to make sb/sth feel or seem less important: *All the criticism had left her feeling totally deflated.* **3** /ˌdiːˈfleɪt/ [VN] (*economics*) to reduce the amount of money being used in a country so that prices fall or stay steady—compare INFLATE (3), REFLATE

de·fla·tion /dɪˈfleɪʃn; diː-/ *noun* [U] **1** (*economics*) a reduction in the amount of money in a country's economy so that prices fall or remain the same **2** the action of air being removed from sth OPP INFLATION ▶ **de·fla·tion·ary** /ˌdiːˈfleɪʃənri; AmE -neri/ *adj.*: *deflationary policies*

de·flect /dɪˈflekt/ *verb* **1** to change direction or make sth change direction, especially after hitting sth: [V] *The ball deflected off Reid's body into the goal.* ◊ [VN] *He raised his arm to try to deflect the blow.* **2** [VN] to succeed in preventing sth from being directed towards you: *All attempts to deflect attention from his private life have failed.* ◊ *She sought to deflect criticism by blaming her family.* **3** [VN] ~ sb (**from sth**) to prevent sb from doing sth that they are determined to do: *The government will not be deflected from its commitments.*

de·flec·tion /dɪˈflekʃn/ *noun* [U, C, usually sing.] a sudden change in the direction that sth is moving in, usually after it has hit sth; the act of causing sth to change direction: *the angle of deflection* ◊ *the deflection of the missile away from its target* ◊ *The goal was scored with a deflection off the goalkeeper.*

de·flower /ˌdiːˈflaʊə(r)/ *verb* [VN] (*old-fashioned, literary*) to have sex with a woman who has not had sex before

de·fog /ˌdiːˈfɒg; AmE -ˈfɔːg; -ˈfɑːg/ *verb* [VN, V] (*AmE*) = DEMIST

de·foli·ate /ˌdiːˈfəʊlieɪt; AmE -ˈfoʊ-/ *verb* [VN] (*technical*) to destroy the leaves of trees or plants, especially with chemicals ▶ **de·foli·ation** /ˌdiːˌfəʊliˈeɪʃn; AmE -ˌfoʊ-/ *noun* [U]

de·for·est /ˌdiːˈfɒrɪst; AmE -ˈfɔːr-; -ˈfɑːr-/ (also **dis·af·for·est**) *verb* [VN] [usually passive] to cut down and destroy all the trees in a place: *Two thirds of the region has been deforested in the past decade.*

de·for·est·ation /ˌdiːˌfɒrɪˈsteɪʃn; AmE -ˌfɔːr-; -ˌfɑːr-/ *noun* [U] the act of cutting down or burning the trees in an area: *land erosion caused by widespread deforestation*—compare AFFORESTATION, REFORESTATION

de·form /dɪˈfɔːm; AmE -ˈfɔːrm/ *verb* [VN] to change or spoil the usual or natural shape of sth: *The disease had deformed his spine.*

de·form·ation /ˌdiːfɔːˈmeɪʃn; AmE -fɔːrˈm-/ *noun* **1** [U] the process or result of changing and spoiling the normal shape of sth **2** [C] a change in the normal shape of sth as a result of injury or illness: *a deformation of the spine*

de·formed /dɪˈfɔːmd; AmE -ˈfɔːrmd/ *adj.* (of a person or a part of the body) having a shape that is not normal because it has grown wrongly: *She was born with deformed hands.*

de·form·ity /dɪˈfɔːməti; AmE -ˈfɔːrm-/ *noun* (*pl.* -ies) [C, U] a condition in which a part of the body is not the normal shape because of injury, illness or because it has grown wrongly: *Drugs taken during pregnancy may cause physical deformity in babies.*

de·fraud /dɪˈfrɔːd/ *verb* ~ sb (**of sth**) to get money illegally from a person or an organization by tricking them: [VN] *They were accused of defrauding the company of $14000.* ◊ [V] *All three men were charged with conspiracy to defraud.*

de·fray /dɪˈfreɪ/ *verb* [VN] ~ costs/expenses (*formal*) to give sb back the money that they have spent on sth

de·frock /ˌdiːˈfrɒk; AmE -ˈfrɑːk/ *verb* [VN] [usually passive] to officially remove a priest from his or her job, because he or she has done sth wrong: *a defrocked priest*

de·frost /ˌdiːˈfrɒst; AmE -ˈfrɔːst/ *verb* **1** to become or make sth warmer, especially food, so that it is no longer frozen: [VN] *Make sure you defrost the chicken completely before cooking.* ◊ [V] *It will take about four hours to defrost.* **2** [VN, V] when you **defrost** a refrigerator or FREEZER, or when it **defrosts**, you remove the ice from it—compare DE-ICE, MELT, THAW, UNFREEZE **3** [VN] (*AmE*) to remove ice from the surface of a car's windows ▶ **de·frost·er** *noun*—picture at CAR

deft /deft/ *adj.* (especially *written*) **1** (of a person's movements) skilful and quick: *deft hands/fingers/footwork* ◊ *He finished off the painting with a few deft strokes of the brush.* **2** skilful: *her deft command of the language*

▶ **deft·ly** *adv.*: *I threw her a towel which she deftly caught.* ◊ *They deftly avoided answering my questions.* **deft·ness** *noun* [U]

de·funct /dɪˈfʌŋkt/ *adj.* (*formal*) no longer existing, operating or being used

de·fuse /ˌdiːˈfjuːz/ *verb* [VN] **1** to stop a possibly dangerous or difficult situation from developing, especially by making people less angry or nervous: *Local police are trying to defuse racial tension in the community.* **2** to remove the FUSE from a bomb so that it cannot explode

defy /dɪˈfaɪ/ *verb* (**de·fies, defy·ing, de·fied, de·fied**) [VN] **1** to refuse to obey or show respect for sb in authority, a law, a rule, etc: *I wouldn't have dared to defy my teachers.* ◊ *Hundreds of people today defied the ban on political gatherings.* **2 ~ belief, explanation, description, etc.** to be impossible or almost impossible to believe, explain, describe, etc: *a political move that defies explanation* ◊ *The beauty of the scene defies description.* **3** to successfully resist sb/sth to a very unusual degree: *The baby boy defied all the odds and survived* (= stayed alive when it seemed certain that he would die).

> **WORD FAMILY**
> **defy** *v.*
> **defiance** *n.*
> **defiant** *adj.*

deg. *abbr.* degree(s): *26 deg. C*

de·gen·er·ate *verb, adj., noun*
■ *verb* /dɪˈdʒenəreɪt/ [V] **~ (into sth)** to become worse, for example by becoming lower in quality or weaker: *The march degenerated into a riot.* ◊ *Her health degenerated quickly.*
■ *adj.* /dɪˈdʒenərət/ **1** having moral standards that have fallen to a level that is very low and unacceptable to most people: *a degenerate popular culture* **2** (*technical*) having returned to a simple structure; lacking sth that is usually present ▶ **de·gen·er·acy** /dɪˈdʒenərəsi/ *noun* [U]
■ *noun* /dɪˈdʒenərət/ (*written*) a person whose behaviour shows moral standards that have fallen to a very low level

de·gen·er·ation /dɪˌdʒenəˈreɪʃn/ *noun* [U] the process of becoming worse or less acceptable in quality or condition: *social/moral degeneration* ◊ *Intensive farming in the area has caused severe degeneration of the land.*

de·gen·era·tive /dɪˈdʒenərətɪv/ *adj.* (*technical*) (of an illness) getting or likely to get worse as time passes: *degenerative diseases such as arthritis*

de·grad·able /dɪˈgreɪdəbl/ *adj.* (*especially AmE, technical*) that can be changed to a simpler form—see also BIODEGRADABLE

deg·rad·ation /ˌdegrəˈdeɪʃn/ *noun* [U] **1** a situation in which sb has lost all SELF-RESPECT and the respect of other people: *the degradation of being sent to prison* **2** (*technical*) the process of sth being damaged or made worse: *environmental degradation*

de·grade /dɪˈgreɪd/ *verb* **1** [VN] to show or treat sb in a way that makes them seem not worth any respect or not worth taking seriously: *This poster is offensive and degrades women.* **2** [V, VN] (*technical*) to change or make sth change to a simpler chemical form **3** [VN] (*technical*) to make sth become worse, especially in quality

de·grad·ing /dɪˈgreɪdɪŋ/ *adj.* treating sb as if they have no value, so that they lose their SELF-RESPECT and the respect of other people: *the inhuman and degrading treatment of prisoners*

de·gree /dɪˈgriː/ *noun* **1** [C] a unit for measuring angles: *an angle of ninety degrees* (*90°*) **2** [C] (*abbr.* **deg.**) a unit for measuring temperature: *Water freezes at 32 degrees Fahrenheit* (*32°F*) *or zero/nought degrees Celsius* (*0°C*). **3** [C, U] the amount or level of sth: *Her job demands a high degree of skill.* ◊ *I agree with you* **to a certain degree.** ◊ *To what degree can parents be held responsible for a child's behaviour?* ◊ *Most pop music is influenced, to a greater or lesser degree, by the blues.* **4** [C] the qualification obtained by students who successfully complete a university or college course: *My brother has a master's degree from Harvard.* ◊ *She has a degree in Biochemistry from London University.* ◊ *a four-year degree course* **5** [C]

(*BrE*) a university or college course, normally lasting three years or more: *I'm hoping to do a chemistry degree.* **6** [C] a level in a scale of how serious sth is: *murder in the first degree* (= of the most serious kind) ◊ *first-degree murder* ◊ *third-degree* (= very serious) *burns* IDM **by deˈgrees** slowly and gradually: *By degrees their friendship grew into love.*—more at NTH

> **WHICH WORD?** (?)
> **degree / certificate / diploma**
>
> A **degree** is usually the qualification that you get by completing a course of study at a college or university: *a bachelor's degree* ◊ *I got my degree in 1987.* In *BrE* it can also mean the course itself: *She's doing a physics degree.*
>
> **Diploma** and **certificate** are both words for official documents that show you have done or achieved something. **Diploma** is used for degrees and other courses of study but **certificate** can be more general: *a High School diploma* ◊ *a degree certificate* ◊ *a certificate of attendance* ◊ *a swimming certificate.*
>
> In *BrE* the qualification or course of study can also be called a **diploma** or a **certificate**: *a two-year diploma course* ◊ *I'm studying for the First Certificate in English.*

de·hu·man·ize (*BrE also* **-ise**) /ˌdiːˈhjuːmənaɪz/ *verb* [VN] to make sb lose their human qualities such as kindness, pity, etc: *the dehumanizing effects of poverty and squalor* ▶ **de·hu·man·iza·tion, -isa·tion** /ˌdiːˌhjuːmənaɪˈzeɪʃn; *AmE* -nəˈz-/ *noun* [U]

de·hu·midi·fier /ˌdiːhjuːˈmɪdɪfaɪə(r)/ *noun* an electrical machine for removing water from the air—see also HUMIDIFIER

de·hy·drate /diːˈhaɪdreɪt/ *verb* **1** [VN] [usually passive] to remove the water from sth, especially food, in order to preserve it **2** to lose too much water from your body; to make a person's body lose too much water: [V] *Runners can dehydrate very quickly in this heat.* ◊ [VN] *the dehydrating effects of alcohol* ▶ **de·hy·dra·tion** /ˌdiːhaɪˈdreɪʃn/ *noun* [U]: *to suffer from dehydration*

de·ice /ˌdiː ˈaɪs/ *verb* [VN] to remove the ice from sth—compare DEFROST, MELT, THAW, UNFREEZE

deify /ˈdeɪfaɪ; ˈdiːfaɪ/ *verb* (**dei·fies, dei·fy·ing, dei·fied, dei·fied**) [VN] (*formal*) to treat or worship sb as a god ▶ **dei·fi·ca·tion** /ˌdeɪfɪˈkeɪʃn; ˌdiːfɪˈkeɪʃn/ *noun* [U]: *the deification of medieval kings*

deign /deɪn/ *verb* [V to inf] (*disapproving*) to do sth in a way that shows you that you are too important to do it SYN CONDESCEND: *She just grunted, not deigning to look up from the page.*

deity /ˈdeɪəti; ˈdiːəti/ *noun* (*pl.* **-ies**) **1** [C] a god or GODDESS: *Greek/Roman/Hindu deities* **2** (**the Deity**) [sing.] (*formal*) God

déjà vu /ˌdeɪʒɑː ˈvuː/ *noun* [U] (from *French*) the feeling that you have previously experienced sth which is happening to you now: *I had a strong sense of déjà vu as I entered the room.*

de·ject·ed /dɪˈdʒektɪd/ *adj.* unhappy and disappointed: *She looked so dejected when she lost the game.* ▶ **de·ject·ed·ly** *adv.*

de·jec·tion /dɪˈdʒekʃn/ *noun* [U] a feeling of unhappiness and disappointment

de jure /ˌdeɪ ˈdʒʊəri; *AmE* ˈdʒʊri/ *adj., adv.* (from *Latin, law*) according to the law: *He held power de jure and de facto* (= both according to the law and in reality).—compare DE FACTO

delay /dɪˈleɪ/ *noun, verb*
■ *noun* **1** [C] a period of time when sb/sth has to wait because of a problem that makes sth slow or late: *Commuters will face long delays on the roads today.* ◊ *We apologize for the delay in answering your letter.* ◊ *a delay of two hours/a two-hour delay* **2** [C, U] a situation in which sth does not happen when it should; the act of delaying: *There's no time for delay.* ◊ *Report it to the police* **without delay** (= immediately).

b	d	f	g	h	k	l	m	n	p	r
bad	did	fall	get	hat	cat	leg	man	now	pen	red

■ **verb 1** to not do sth until a later time or to make sth happen at a later time: [VN] *The judge will delay his verdict until he receives medical reports on the offender.* ◊ *She's suffering a delayed reaction* (= a reaction that did not happen immediately) *to the shock.* ◊ [V-ing] *He delayed telling her the news, waiting for the right moment.* ◊ [V] *Don't delay—call us today!* **2** [VN] to make sb late or force them to do sth more slowly: *Thousands of commuters were delayed for over an hour.* ◊ *The government is accused of using delaying tactics* (= deliberately doing sth to delay a process, decision, etc.).

de·lect·able /dɪˈlektəbl/ *adj.* (*written*) **1** (of food and drink) extremely pleasant to taste, smell or look at: *the delectable smell of freshly baked bread* **2** (*humorous*) (of a person) very attractive: *his delectable body*

de·lect·ation /ˌdiːlekˈteɪʃn/ *noun* [U] (*formal* or *humorous*) enjoyment or entertainment

dele·gate *noun, verb*
■ *noun* /ˈdelɪgət/ a person who is chosen or elected to represent the views of a group of people and vote and make decisions for them: *The conference was attended by delegates from 56 countries.*
■ *verb* /ˈdelɪgeɪt/ **1 ~ (sth) (to sb)** to give part of your work, power or authority to sb in a lower position than you: [V] *Some managers find it difficult to delegate.* ◊ [VN] *The job had to be delegated to an assistant.* **2** [VN to inf] [usually passive] to choose sb to do sth: *I've been delegated to organize the Christmas party.*

dele·ga·tion /ˌdelɪˈgeɪʃn/ *noun* **1** [C+sing./ pl. *v.*] a group of people who represent the views of an organization, a country, etc: *the Dutch delegation to the United Nations* ◊ *a delegation of teachers* **2** [U] the process of giving sb work or responsibilities that would usually be yours: *delegation of authority/decision-making*

de·lete /dɪˈliːt/ *verb* [VN] **~ sth (from sth)** to remove sth that has been written or printed, or that has been stored on a computer: *Your name has been deleted from the list.* ◊ *This command deletes files from the directory.* ◊ (*BrE*) *Mr/ Mrs/Ms* (*delete as appropriate*) ▶ **de·le·tion** /dɪˈliːʃn/ *noun* [U, C]: *He made several deletions to the manuscript.*

dele·teri·ous /ˌdeləˈtɪəriəs; *AmE* -ˈtɪr-/ *adj.* (*formal*) harmful and damaging: *the deleterious effect of stress on health*

deli /ˈdeli/ *noun* = DELICATESSEN

de·lib·er·ate *adj., verb*
■ *adj.* /dɪˈlɪbərət/ **1** done on purpose rather than by accident [SYN] PLANNED: *a deliberate act of vandalism* ◊ *The speech was a deliberate attempt to embarrass the government.* **2** (of a movement or an action) done slowly and carefully: *She spoke in a slow and deliberate way.*
■ *verb* /dɪˈlɪbəreɪt/ to think very carefully about sth, usually before making a decision: [V] *The jury deliberated for five days before finding him guilty.* ◊ *They deliberated on whether to continue with the talks.* [also V wh-]

de·lib·er·ate·ly /dɪˈlɪbərətli/ *adv.* **1** done in a way that was planned, not by chance [SYN] INTENTIONALLY, ON PURPOSE: *She's been deliberately ignoring him all day.* **2** slowly and carefully: *He packed up his possessions slowly and deliberately.*

de·lib·er·ation /dɪˌlɪbəˈreɪʃn/ *noun* **1** [U, C, usually pl.] the process of carefully considering or discussing sth: *After ten hours of deliberation, the jury returned a verdict of 'not guilty'.* ◊ *The deliberations of the committee are completely confidential.* **2** [U] the quality of being slow and careful in what you say or do: *She signed her name with great deliberation.*

deli·cacy /ˈdelɪkəsi/ *noun* (*pl.* **-ies**) **1** [U] the quality of being, or appearing to be, easy to damage or break: *the delicacy of the fabric* **2** [U] the quality of being done carefully and gently: *the delicacy of his touch* **3** [U] very careful behaviour in a difficult situation so that nobody is offended: *She handled the situation with great sensitivity and delicacy.* **4** [U] the fact that a situation is difficult and sb may be easily offended: *I need to talk to you about a matter of some delicacy.* **5** [C] a type of food considered to be very special in a particular place: *local delicacies*

deli·cate /ˈdelɪkət/ *adj.* **1** easily damaged or broken

[SYN] FRAGILE: *delicate china teacups* ◊ *The eye is one of the most delicate organs of the body.* ◊ *the delicate ecological balance of the rainforest* ◊ *Babies have very delicate skin.* ◊ *a cool wash cycle for delicate fabrics* **2** (of a person) not strong and easily becoming ill: *a delicate child/constitution* **3** small and having a beautiful shape or appearance: *his delicate hands* ◊ *Women were treated like delicate flowers needing special treatment.* **4** made or formed in a very careful and detailed way: *the delicate mechanisms of a clock* **5** showing or needing skilful, careful or sensitive treatment: *I admired your delicate handling of the situation.* ◊ *a delicate problem* ◊ *The delicate surgical operation took five hours.* **6** (of colours, flavours and smells) light and pleasant; not strong: *a delicate fragrance/flavour* ◊ *a river scene painted in delicate watercolours* ▶ **deli·cate·ly** *adv.*: *He stepped delicately over the broken glass.* ◊ *delicately balanced flavours*

deli·ca·tes·sen /ˌdelɪkəˈtesn/ (also **deli**) *noun* a shop/ store or part of one that sells cooked meats and cheeses, and special or unusual foods that come from other countries

de·li·cious /dɪˈlɪʃəs/ *adj.* **1** having a very pleasant taste or smell: *Who cooked this? It's delicious.* **2** (*literary*) extremely pleasant or enjoyable: *the delicious coolness of the breeze* ▶ **de·li·cious·ly** *adv.*: *deliciously creamy soup*

de·light /dɪˈlaɪt/ *noun, verb*
■ *noun* **1** [U] a feeling of great pleasure: *a feeling of sheer/ pure delight* ◊ *The children squealed with delight when they saw the puppy.* ◊ *She won the game easily, to the delight of all her fans.* ◊ *He takes (great) delight in* (= enjoys) *proving others wrong.* **2** [C] something that gives you great pleasure: *This guitar is a delight to play.* ◊ *the delights of living in the country*
■ *verb* [VN] to give sb a lot of pleasure and enjoyment: *This news will delight his fans all over the world.* [PHRV] **delight in sth/doing sth** [no passive] to enjoy doing sth very much, especially sth that makes other people feel embarrassed, uncomfortable, etc.

de·light·ed /dɪˈlaɪtɪd/ *adj.* **~ (to do sth)| ~ (that...)| ~ (at/with sth)** very pleased: *a delighted smile* ◊ *I'd be absolutely delighted to come.* ◊ *I was delighted that you could stay.* ◊ *She was delighted by/at the news of the wedding.* ◊ *I was delighted with my presents.* ▶ **de·light·ed·ly** *adv.*

de·light·ful /dɪˈlaɪtfl/ *adj.* very pleasant: *a delightful book/restaurant/town* ◊ *a delightful child* ▶ **de·light·ful·ly** /dɪˈlaɪtfəli/ *adv.*

de·limit /diˈlɪmɪt/ *verb* [VN] (*formal*) to decide what the limits of sth are

de·lin·eate /dɪˈlɪnieɪt/ *verb* [VN] (*formal*) to describe, draw or explain sth in detail: *Our objectives need to be precisely delineated.* ◊ *The ship's route is clearly delineated on the map.* ▶ **de·lin·ea·tion** /dɪˌlɪniˈeɪʃn/ *noun* [U, C]

de·lin·quency /dɪˈlɪŋkwənsi/ *noun* [U, C] (*pl.* **-ies**) bad or criminal behaviour, usually of young people: *an increase in juvenile delinquency*

de·lin·quent /dɪˈlɪŋkwənt/ *adj.* **1** (especially of young people or their behaviour) showing a tendency to commit crimes: *delinquent teenagers* **2** (*AmE, finance*) having failed to pay money that is owed: *a delinquent borrower* **3** (*AmE, finance*) (of a sum of money) not having been paid in time: *a delinquent loan* ▶ **de·lin·quent** *noun*—see also JUVENILE DELINQUENT

de·li·ri·ous /dɪˈlɪriəs; *BrE* also -ˈlɪəriəs/ *adj.* **1** in an excited state and not able to think or speak clearly, usually because of fever: *He became delirious and couldn't recognize people.* **2** extremely excited and happy: *The crowds were delirious with joy.* ▶ **de·li·ri·ous·ly** *adv.*

de·lir·ium /dɪˈlɪriəm; *BrE* also -ˈlɪəriəm/ *noun* [U] a mental state where sb becomes delirious, usually because of illness: *fits of delirium*

delirium tremens /dɪˌlɪriəm ˈtriːmenz; *BrE* also -ˌlɪəriəm/ *noun* [U] (*medical*) = DTs

de·liver /dɪˈlɪvə(r)/ *verb*
TAKE GOODS/LETTERS **1 ~ (sth) (to sb/sth)** to take goods, letters, etc. to the person or people they have been sent to; to take sb somewhere: [VN] *Leaflets have been delivered*

to every household. ◊ *Do you have your milk delivered?* ◊ [V] *We promise to deliver within 48 hours.*

GIVE SPEECH | **2** [VN] to give a speech, talk, etc. or other official statement: *She is due to deliver a lecture on genetic engineering.* ◊ *He delivered his lines confidently.* ◊ *The jury finally delivered its verdict.*

KEEP PROMISE | **3 ~ (on sth)** to do what you promised to do or what you are expected to do; to produce or provide what people expect you to: [V] *He has promised to finish the job by June and I am sure he will deliver.* ◊ *She always delivers on her promises.* ◊ [VN] *If you can't deliver improved sales figures, you're fired.* ◊ *The team delivered a stunning victory last night.*

GIVE TO SB'S CONTROL | **4** [VN] **~ sb/sth (up/over) (to sb)** (*formal*) to give sb/sth to sb else so that they are under this person's control: *They delivered their prisoner over to the invading army.*

BABY | **5** [VN] **~ a baby** to help a woman to give birth to a baby: *The baby was delivered by Caesarean section.* **6** [VN] **be delivered of a baby** (*formal*) to give birth to a baby: *She was delivered of a healthy boy.*

THROW | **7** [VN] to throw or aim sth: *He **delivered the** blow* (= hit sb hard) *with all his force.*

RESCUE | **8** [VN] **~ sb (from sth)** (*old use*) to rescue sb from sth bad

IDM see GOODS, SIGN *v.*

de·liver·able /dɪˈlɪvərəbl/ *noun* [usually pl.] a product that a company promises to have ready for a customer: *computer software deliverables*

de·liv·er·ance /dɪˈlɪvərəns/ *noun* [U] **~ (from sth)** (*formal*) the state of being rescued from danger, evil or pain

de·liv·ery /dɪˈlɪvəri/ *noun* (*pl.* **-ies**) **1** [U, C] the act of taking goods, letters, etc. to the people they have been sent to: *a delivery van* ◊ *Please pay for goods **on delivery*** (= when you receive them). ◊ *Allow 28 days **for delivery**.* ◊ *Is there a postal/mail delivery on Saturdays?* ◊ (*formal*) *When can you **take delivery of** (= be available to receive) the car?* ◊ (*figurative*) *the delivery of public services* **2** [C, U] the process of giving birth to a baby: *an easy/difficult delivery* ◊ *a delivery room/ward* (= in a hospital, etc.) **3** [sing.] the way in which sb speaks, sings a song, etc. in public: *The beautiful poetry was ruined by her poor delivery.* **4** [C] a ball that is thrown, especially in cricket or baseball: *a fast delivery* **IDM** see CASH *n.*

dell /del/ *noun* (*literary*) a small valley with trees growing in or around it

del·phin·ium /delˈfɪniəm/ *noun* a tall garden plant with blue or white flowers growing up its stem

delta /ˈdeltə/ *noun* **1** the fourth letter of the Greek alphabet (Δ,δ) **2** an area of land, shaped like a triangle, where a river has split into several smaller rivers before entering the sea: *the Nile Delta*

de·lude /dɪˈluːd/ *verb* **~ sb/yourself (into doing sth)** to make sb believe sth that is not true **SYN** DECEIVE: [VN] *Don't be deluded into thinking that we are out of danger yet.* ◊ *You poor deluded creature.* ◊ *He's deluding himself if he thinks it's going to be easy.* ◊ [VN that] *She had been deluding herself that he loved her.*—see also DELUSION

del·uge /ˈdeljuːdʒ/ *noun, verb*
■ *noun* [usually sing.] **1** a sudden very heavy fall of rain; a flood **2** a large number of things that happen or arrive at the same time: *a deluge of calls/complaints/letters*
■ *verb* [VN] **1 ~ sb/sth (with sth)** [usually passive] to send or give sb/sth a large number of things at the same time **SYN** INUNDATE: *We have been deluged with applications for the job.* **2** [often passive] (*formal*) to flood a place with water: *The campsite was deluged by a flash flood.*

de·lu·sion /dɪˈluːʒn/ *noun* **1** [C] a false belief or opinion about yourself or your situation: *the delusions of the mentally ill* ◊ *Don't go getting **delusions of grandeur*** (= a belief that you are more important than you actually are). **2** [U] the act of believing or making yourself believe sth that is not true

de luxe /də ˈlʌks; ˈlʊks/ *adj.* [usually before noun] of a higher quality and more expensive than usual: *a de luxe hotel*

delve /delv/ *verb* [V+adv./prep.] to search for sth inside a bag, container, etc: *She delved in her handbag for a pen.* **PHRV** **delve into sth** to try hard to find out more information about sth **SYN** PROBE: *She had started to delve into her father's distant past.*

Dem. *abbr.* (in politics in the US) DEMOCRAT; DEMOCRATIC

dema·gogue /ˈdeməɡɒɡ; *AmE* -ɡɑːɡ/ *noun* (*disapproving*) a political leader who tries to win support by using arguments based on emotion rather than reason ► **dema·gog·ic** /ˌdeməˈɡɒɡɪk; *AmE* -ˈɡɑːɡ-/ *adj.* **dema·gogy** /ˈdeməɡɒɡi; *AmE* -ɡɑːɡi/ *noun* [U]

de·mand /dɪˈmɑːnd; *AmE* dɪˈmænd/ *noun, verb*
■ *noun* **1** [C] **~ (for sth/that…)** a very firm request for sth; sth that sb needs: *a demand for higher pay* ◊ *demands that the law on gun ownership should be changed* ◊ *firms attempting to **meet/satisfy** their customers' **demands*** (= to give them what they are asking for) **2** (**demands**) [pl.] **~ (of sth)| ~ (on sb)** things that sb/sth makes you do, especially things that are difficult, make you tired, worried, etc: *the demands of children/work* ◊ *Flying makes enormous **demands** on pilots.* **3** [U, C] **~ (for sth/sb)** the desire or need of customers for goods or services which they want to buy or use: *to meet the demand for a product* ◊ *There's an increased demand for organic produce these days.* ◊ *Demand is exceeding supply.* **IDM** **by popular de'mand** because a lot of people have asked for sth: *By popular demand, the play will run for another week.* **in de'mand** wanted by a lot of people: *Good secretaries are always in demand* **on de'mand** done or happening whenever sb asks: *Feed the baby on demand.*—see also SUPPLY AND DEMAND
■ *verb* **1** to ask for sth very firmly: [VN] *She demanded an immediate explanation.* ◊ [V that] *The UN has demanded that all troops be withdrawn.* ◊ (*BrE* also) *They are demanding that all troops should be withdrawn.* ◊ [V to inf] *I demand to see the manager.* ◊ [V speech] *'Who the hell are you?' he demanded angrily.* **2** [VN] to need sth in order to be done successfully: *This sport demands both speed and strength.*

de·mand·ing /dɪˈmɑːndɪŋ; *AmE* -ˈmæn-/ *adj.* **1** (of a piece of work) needing a lot of skill, patience, effort, etc: *The work is physically demanding.* **2** (of a person) expecting a lot of work or attention from others; not easily satisfied: *a demanding boss/child* **OPP** UNDEMANDING

de·mar·cate /ˈdiːmɑːkeɪt; *AmE* -mɑːrk-/ *verb* [VN] (*formal*) to mark or establish the limits of sth: *Plots of land have been demarcated by barbed wire.*

de·mar·ca·tion /ˌdiːmɑːˈkeɪʃn; *AmE* -mɑːrˈk-/ *noun* [U, C] a border or line that separates two things, such as types of work, groups of people or areas of land: *It was hard to draw clear lines of demarcation between work and leisure.* ◊ *social demarcations*

de·mean /dɪˈmiːn/ *verb* [VN] **1 ~ yourself** to do sth that makes people have less respect for you: *I wouldn't demean myself by asking for charity.* **2** to make people have less respect for sb/sth **SYN** DEGRADE: *Such images demean women.*

de·mean·ing /dɪˈmiːnɪŋ/ *adj.* putting sb in a position that does not give them the respect that they should have: *He found it demeaning to work for his former employee.*

de·mean·our (*BrE*) (*AmE* **de·meanor**) /dɪˈmiːnə(r)/ *noun* [U] (*formal*) the way that sb looks or behaves: *He maintained a professional demeanour throughout.*

de·men·ted /dɪˈmentɪd/ *adj.* **1** (*especially BrE*) behaving in a crazy way because you are extremely upset or worried: *I've been nearly demented with worry about you.* **2** (*old-fashioned* or *medical*) having a mental illness ► **de·men·ted·ly** *adv.*

de·men·tia /dɪˈmenʃə/ *noun* [U] (*medical*) a serious mental disorder caused by brain disease or injury, that affects the ability to think, remember and behave normally—see also SENILE DEMENTIA

dem·er·ara sugar /ˌdeməreərə ˈʃʊɡə(r); *AmE* -rerə/ *noun* [U] (*BrE*) a type of rough brown sugar

de·merit /diːˈmerɪt/ *noun* (*formal*) **1** [usually pl.] a fault in sth or a disadvantage of sth: *the merits and demerits of the scheme* **2** (*AmE*) a mark on sb's school record showing that they have done sth wrong: *You'll get three demerits if you're caught smoking on school grounds.*

demi- /'demi/ *prefix* (in nouns) half; partly: *demigod*

de·mili·tar·ize (*BrE* also **-ise**) /ˌdiːˈmɪlɪtəraɪz/ *verb* [VN] [usually passive] to remove military forces from an area: *a demilitarized zone* OPP MILITARIZE ▶ **de·mili·tar·iza·tion,** **-isa·tion** /ˌdiːˌmɪlɪtəraɪˈzeɪʃn; *AmE* -rəˈz-/ *noun* [U]

de·mise /dɪˈmaɪz/ *noun* [sing.] **1** the end or failure of an institution, an idea, a company, etc. **2** (*formal or humorous*) death: *his imminent/sudden/sad demise*

de·mist /ˌdiːˈmɪst/ (*BrE*) (*AmE* **de·fog**) *verb* [VN] to remove the CONDENSATION from a car's windows so that you can see clearly

demo /'deməʊ; *AmE* -moʊ/ *noun* (*pl.* **-os**) (*informal*) **1** (*especially BrE*) = DEMONSTRATION (1): *They all went on the demo.* **2** = DEMONSTRATION (2): *I'll give you a demo.* **3** a record or tape with an example of sb's music on it: *a demo tape*

demo- *prefix* (in nouns, adjectives and adverbs) connected with people or population: *democracy* ◇ *democratic*

demob /ˌdiːˈmɒb; *AmE* -ˈmaːb/ *verb* (**-bb-**) [VN] [usually passive] (*BrE, informal*) = DEMOBILIZE: *He was demobbed in 1946.* ▶ **demob** *noun* [U] (*BrE*)

de·mo·bil·ize (*BrE* also **-ise**) /diːˈməʊbəlaɪz; *AmE* -ˈmoʊ-/ (*also BrE informal* **demob**) *verb* [VN] to release sb from military service, especially at the end of a war—compare MOBILIZE ▶ **de·mo·bil·iza·tion,** **-isa·tion** /ˌdiːˌməʊbəlaɪˈzeɪʃn; *AmE* -ˌmoʊbələˈz-/ *noun* [U]

dem·oc·racy /dɪˈmɒkrəsi; *AmE* -ˈmaːk-/ *noun* (*pl.* **-ies**) **1** [U] a system of government in which all the people of a country can vote to elect their representatives: *parliamentary democracy* ◇ *the principles of democracy* **2** [C] a country which has this system of government: *Western democracies* ◇ *I thought we were supposed to be living in a democracy.* **3** [U] fair and equal treatment of everyone in an organization, etc., and their right to take part in making decisions: *the fight for justice and democracy*

demo·crat /'deməkræt/ *noun* **1** a person who believes in or supports democracy **2** (**Democrat**) (*abbr.* **D, Dem.**) a member or supporter of the Democratic party of the US—compare REPUBLICAN

demo·crat·ic /ˌdeməˈkrætɪk/ *adj.* **1** (of a country, state, system, etc.) controlled by representatives who are elected by the people of a country; connected with this system: *a democratic country* ◇ *a democratic system/election* ◇ *democratic government/rule/accountability* ◇ *They are aiming to make the institutions of the EU truly democratic.* **2** based on the principle that all members have an equal right to be involved in running an organization, etc: *democratic involvement/participation* ◇ *a democratic decision* **3** based on the principle that all members of society are equal rather than divided by money or social class: *a democratic society/outlook* ◇ *democratic values/reforms* **4** (**Democratic**) (*abbr.* **Dem., D**) connected with the Democratic party in the US: *the Democratic senator from Oregon* ▶ **demo·crat·ic·al·ly** /-kli/ *adv.*: *a democratically elected government/leader* ◇ *democratically accountable/controlled* ◇ *The decision was taken democratically.*

the Demo'cratic Party *noun* [sing.] one of the two main political parties in the US, usually considered to be in favour of social REFORM—compare THE REPUBLICAN PARTY

dem·oc·ra·tize (*BrE* also **-ise**) /dɪˈmɒkrətaɪz; *AmE* -ˈmaːk-/ *verb* [VN] (*formal*) to make a country or an institution more democratic ▶ **dem·oc·ra·tiza·tion,** **-isa·tion** /dɪˌmɒkrətaɪˈzeɪʃn; *AmE* -ˌmaːkrətəˈz-/ *noun* [U]

dem·og·raphy /dɪˈmɒɡrəfi; *AmE* -ˈmaːɡ-/ *noun* [U] the changing number of births, deaths, diseases, etc. in a community over a period of time; the scientific study of these changes: *the social demography of Africa* ▶ **dem·og·raph·er** /dɪˈmɒɡrəfə(r); *AmE* -ˈmaːɡ-/ *noun* **demo·graph·ic** /ˌdeməˈɡræfɪk/ *adj.*: *demographic changes/trends/factors*

de·mol·ish /dɪˈmɒlɪʃ; *AmE* -ˈmaːl-/ *verb* [VN] **1** to pull or knock down a building: *The factory was demolished in 1980.* **2** to show that an idea or theory is completely

wrong: *A recent book has demolished this theory.* **3** to defeat sb easily and completely: *They demolished New Zealand 22–6 in the final.* **4** (*BrE, informal*) to eat sth very quickly: *The children demolished their burgers and chips.* ▶ **demo·li·tion** /ˌdeməˈlɪʃn/ *noun* [U, C]: *The whole row of houses is scheduled for demolition.* ◇ *His speech did a very effective demolition job on the government's proposals.*

demolition 'derby *noun* (*AmE*) = STOCK-CAR RACING

demon /'diːmən/ *noun* **1** an evil spirit: *demons torturing the sinners in Hell* **2** (*informal*) a person who does sth very well or with a lot of energy: *He skis like a demon.* **3** something that causes a person to worry and makes them unhappy: *the demons of jealousy* IDM **the demon 'drink** (*BrE, humorous*) alcoholic drink

de·mon·ic /diːˈmɒnɪk; *AmE* -ˈmaːn-/ *adj.* connected with, or like, a demon (1): *demonic forces/powers* ◇ *a demonic appearance/nature*

dem·on·strable /dɪˈmɒnstrəbl; *AmE* -ˈmaːn- *BrE* also 'demənstrəbl/ *adj.* (*formal*) that can be shown or proved: *a demonstrable need* ▶ **dem·on·strably** /-bli/ *adv.*: *demonstrably unfair*

dem·on·strate /'demənstreɪt/ *verb* **1** ~ sth (**to sb**) to show sth clearly by giving proof or evidence: [V that] *These results demonstrate convincingly that our campaign is working.* ◇ [VN] *Let me demonstrate to you some of the difficulties we are facing.* ◇ [V wh-] *His sudden departure had demonstrated how unreliable he was.* ◇ [VN to inf] *The theories were demonstrated to be false.* ◇ [VN that] *It has been demonstrated that this drug is effective.* **2** [VN] to show by your actions that you have a particular quality, feeling or opinion SYN DISPLAY: *You need to demonstrate more self-control.* ◇ *We want to demonstrate our commitment to human rights.* **3** ~ sth (**to sb**) to show and explain how sth works or how to do sth: [VN] *Her job involves demonstrating new educational software.* [also V wh-] **4** [V] ~ (**against sth**)| ~ **in favour/support of sth**) to take part in a public meeting or march, usually as a protest or to show support for sth SYN PROTEST: *students demonstrating against the war* ◇ *They are demonstrating in favour of free higher education.*

de·mon·stra·tion /ˌdemənˈstreɪʃn/ *noun* **1** (also *informal* **demo** especially in *BrE*) [C] ~ (**against sb/sth**) a public meeting or march at which people show that they are protesting against or supporting sb/sth: *to take part in/go on a demonstration* ◇ *to hold/stage a demonstration* ◇ *mass demonstrations in support of the exiled leader* ◇ *anti-government demonstrations* ◇ *a peaceful/violent demonstration*—compare MARCH **2** (also *informal* **demo**) [C, U] an act of showing or explaining how sth works or is done: *We were given a brief demonstration of the computer's functions.* ◇ *a practical demonstration* ◇ *We provide demonstration of videoconferencing over the Internet.* **3** [C, U] an act of giving proof or evidence for sth: *a demonstration of the connection between the two sets of figures* ◇ *a demonstration of how something that seems simple can turn out to be very complicated* **4** [C] an act of showing a feeling or an opinion: *a public demonstration of affection* ◇ *a demonstration of support for the reforms*

de·mon·stra·tive /dɪˈmɒnstrətɪv; *AmE* -ˈmaːn-/ *adj., noun*
■ *adj.* **1** showing feelings openly, especially feelings of affection: *Some people are more demonstrative than others.* ◇ *a demonstrative greeting/friendship* **2** (*grammar*) used to identify the person or thing that is being referred to: *'This' and 'that' are demonstrative pronouns.*
■ *noun* (*grammar*) a demonstrative pronoun or DETERMINER

dem·on·stra·tor /'demənstreɪtə(r)/ *noun* **1** a person who takes part in a public meeting or march in order to protest against sb/sth or to show support for sb/sth: *pro-democracy demonstrators* **2** a person whose job is to show or explain how sth works or is done

de·mor·al·ize (*BrE* also **-ise**) /dɪˈmɒrəlaɪz; *AmE* -ˈmɔːr-; -ˈmaːr-/ *verb* [VN] [usually passive] to make sb lose confidence or hope SYN DISHEARTEN: *Constant criticism is enough to demoralize anybody.* ▶ **de·mor·al·ized, -ised** *adj.*: *The workers here seem very demoralized.* **de·mor·al-**

iz·ing, -is·ing *adj.*: *the demoralizing effects of unemployment* **de·mor·al·iza·tion, -isa·tion** /dɪˌmɒrəlaɪˈzeɪʃn; AmE -ˌmɔːrələˈz-, -ˌmɑːrələˈz-/ *noun* [U]

de·mote /ˌdiːˈməʊt; AmE -ˈmoʊt/ *verb* [VN] [often passive] **~ sb (from sth) (to sth)** to move sb to a lower position or rank, often as a punishment OPP PROMOTE ▶ **de·mo·tion** /ˌdiːˈməʊʃn; AmE -ˈmoʊ-/ *noun* [C, U]

dem·ot·ic /dɪˈmɒtɪk; AmE -ˈmɑːt-/ *adj.* (*formal*) used by or typical of ordinary people

demur /dɪˈmɜː(r)/ *verb, noun*
- *verb* (**-rr-**) (*formal*) to say that you do not agree with sth or that you refuse to do sth: [V] *At first she demurred, but then finally agreed.* [also Vspeech]
- *noun* IDM **without de·mur** (*formal*) without objecting or hesitating: *They accepted without demur.*

de·mure /dɪˈmjʊə(r); AmE dɪˈmjʊr/ *adj.* **1** (of a woman or a girl) behaving in a way that does not attract attention to herself or her body; quiet and serious: *a demure young lady* ◇ suggesting that a woman or girl is demure: *a demure smile* ◇ *a demure navy blouse with a white collar* ▶ **de·mure·ly** *adv.*

de·mys·tify /ˌdiːˈmɪstɪfaɪ/ *verb* (**de·mys·ti·fies, de·mys·ti·fy·ing, de·mys·ti·fied, de·mys·ti·fied**) [VN] (*written*) to make sth easier to understand and less complicated by explaining it in a clear and simple way ▶ **de·mys·ti·fi·ca·tion** /ˌdiːˌmɪstɪfɪˈkeɪʃn/ *noun* [U]

den /den/ *noun* **1** the hidden home of some types of wild animal: *a bear's/lion's den* **2** (*disapproving*) a place where people meet in secret, especially for some illegal or immoral activity: *a den of thieves* ◇ *a drinking/gambling den* ◇ *He thought of New York as **a den of iniquity**.* **3** (*AmE*) a room in a house where people go to relax, watch television, etc. **4** (*old-fashioned, BrE, informal*) a room in a house where a person can work or study without being disturbed: *He would often retire to his den.* **5** a secret enclosed place where children play: *They made themselves a den in the woods.* IDM see BEARD *v.*, LION

de·nation·al·ize (*BrE* also **-ise**) /ˌdiːˈnæʃnəlaɪz/ *verb* [VN] to sell a company or an industry so that it is no longer owned by the government SYN PRIVATIZE OPP NATIONALIZE ▶ **de·nation·al·iza·tion, -isa·tion** /ˌdiːˌnæʃ-nəlaɪˈzeɪʃn; AmE -ləˈz-/ *noun* [U]

de·nial /dɪˈnaɪəl/ *noun* **1** [C] **~ (of sth/that …)** a statement that says sth is not true or does not exist: *the prisoner's repeated denials of the charges against him* ◇ *The terrorists issued a denial of responsibility for the attack.* ◇ *an official denial that there would be an election before the end of the year* **2** [C, U] **(a) ~ of sth** a refusal to allow sb to have sth they have a right to expect: *the denial of basic human rights* **3** [U] (*psychology*) a refusal to accept that sth unpleasant or painful is true: *The patient is still in denial.*

den·ier /ˈdeniə(r)/ *noun* (*especially BrE*) a unit for measuring how fine threads of NYLON, silk, etc. are: *15 denier stockings*

deni·grate /ˈdenɪɡreɪt/ *verb* [VN] (*formal*) to criticize sb/sth unfairly; to say sb/sth does not have any value or is not important: *I didn't intend to denigrate her achievements.* ▶ **deni·gra·tion** /ˌdenɪˈɡreɪʃn/ *noun* [U]

denim /ˈdenɪm/ *noun* **1** [U] a strong cotton fabric that is usually blue and is used for making clothes, especially JEANS: *a denim jacket*—picture on page A4 ORIGIN From the French *serge de Nîmes*, meaning serge (a type of fabric) from the town of Nimes. **2** (**denims**) [pl.] (*old-fashioned*) trousers/pants made of denim SYN JEANS

deni·zen /ˈdenɪzn/ *noun* (*formal or humorous*) a person, an animal or a plant that lives, grows or is often found in a particular place: *polar bears, denizens of the frozen north* ◇ *the denizens of the local pub*

de·nom·in·ation /dɪˌnɒmɪˈneɪʃn; AmE -ˌnɑːm-/ *noun* (*formal*) **1** a branch of the Christian Church: *Christians of all denominations attended the conference.* **2** a unit of value, especially of money: *coins and banknotes of various denominations*

de·nom·in·ation·al /dɪˌnɒmɪˈneɪʃənl; AmE -ˌnɑːm-/ *adj.* belonging to a particular branch of the Christian Church

de·nom·in·ator /dɪˈnɒmɪneɪtə(r); AmE -ˈnɑːm-/ *noun* (*mathematics*) the number below the line in a FRACTION showing how many parts the whole is divided into, for example 4 in ¾—compare NUMERATOR, COMMON DENOMINATOR

de·note /dɪˈnəʊt; AmE dɪˈnoʊt/ *verb* (*formal*) **1** to be a sign of sth SYN INDICATE: [VN] *A very high temperature often denotes a serious illness.* [also Vthat] **2** to mean sth SYN REPRESENT: [VN] *In this example 'X' denotes the time taken and 'Y' denotes the distance covered.* ◇ *The red triangle denotes danger.* ◇ *Here 'family' denotes mother, father and children.* [also Vwh-] —compare CONNOTE

de·noue·ment (also **dé·noue·ment**) /ˌdeɪˈnuːmɒ̃; AmE ˌdeɪnuːˈmɑː/ *noun* (from *French*) the end of a play, book, etc., in which everything is explained or settled; the end result of a situation: *an exciting/unexpected denouement*

de·nounce /dɪˈnaʊns/ *verb* [VN] **1 ~ sb/sth (as sth)** to strongly criticize sb/sth that you think is wrong, illegal, etc: *She publicly denounced the government's handling of the crisis.* ◇ *The project was denounced as a scandalous waste of public money.* **2 ~ sb (as sth)** to tell the police, the authorities, etc. about sb's illegal political activities: *They were denounced as spies.* ◇ *Many people denounced their friends and neighbours to the secret police.*—see also DENUNCIATION

dense /dens/ *adj.* (**dens·er, dens·est**) **1** containing a lot of people, things, plants, etc. with little space between them: *a dense crowd/forest* ◇ *areas of dense population* **2** difficult to see through: *dense fog/smoke/fumes* **3** (*informal*) stupid: *How can you be so dense?* **4** difficult to understand because it contains a lot of information: *a dense piece of writing* **5** (*technical*) heavy in relation to its size: *Less dense substances move upwards to form a crust.* ▶ **dense·ly** *adv.*: *a densely populated area* ◇ *densely covered/packed*

dens·ity /ˈdensəti/ *noun* (*pl.* **-ities**) **1** [U] the quality of being dense; the degree to which sth is dense: *population density* ◇ *low density forest* **2** [C, U] (*physics*) the thickness of a solid, liquid or gas measured by its MASS (= weight) per unit of volume: *the density of a gas* **3** [U] (*computing*) the amount of space available on a disk for recording data: *a high/double density floppy*

dent /dent/ *verb, noun*
- *verb* [VN] **1** to make a hollow place in a hard surface, usually by hitting it: *The back of the car was badly dented in the collision.* **2** to damage sb's confidence, reputation, etc: *It seemed that nothing could dent his confidence.*
- *noun* a hollow place in a hard surface, usually caused by sth hitting it: *a large dent in the passenger door* IDM **make, etc. a 'dent in sth** to reduce the amount of sth, especially money: *The lawyer's fees will make a dent in our finances.*

dent·al /ˈdentl/ *adj.* [only before noun] **1** connected with the teeth: *dental disease/care/treatment/health* ◇ *a dental appointment* ◇ *dental records* ◇ (*BrE*) *a dental surgery* (= where a dentist sees patients) **2** (*phonetics*) (of a consonant) produced with the tongue against the upper front teeth, for example /ð/, or against the RIDGE of the teeth, for example /n, d, t/

'dental floss (also **floss**) *noun* [U] a type of thread that is used for cleaning between the teeth

'dental hygienist *noun* (*especially AmE*) = HYGIENIST

'dental surgeon *noun* (*formal*) = DENTIST

den·tist /ˈdentɪst/ *noun* **1** (also *formal* **'dental surgeon**) a person whose job is to take care of people's teeth **2** (**dentist's**) a place where a dentist sees patients: *an appointment at the dentist's*

den·tis·try /ˈdentɪstri/ *noun* [U] **1** the medical study of the teeth and mouth **2** the work of a dentist: *preventive dentistry*

den·tures /ˈdentʃəz; AmE -tʃərz/ *noun* [pl.] artificial teeth on a thin piece of plastic (= a PLATE), worn by sb who no longer has all their own teeth ▶ **den·ture** *adj.*: *denture adhesive*—compare FALSE TEETH, PLATE *n.* (14)

de·nude /dɪˈnjuːd; AmE dɪˈnuːd/ *verb* [VN] [usually passive] **~ sth (of sth)** (*formal*) to make sth bare: *hillsides denuded of trees*

de·nun·ci·ation /dɪˌnʌnsiˈeɪʃn/ *noun* [C, U] **~ (of sb/**

	b	d	f	g	h	k	l	m	n	p	r
	bad	did	fall	get	hat	cat	leg	man	now	pen	red

D

sth) an act of criticizing sb/sth strongly in public: *an angry denunciation of the government's policies* ◊ *All parties joined in bitter denunciation of the terrorists.*—see also DENOUNCE

Denver boot /ˈdenvə buːt; *AmE* -vər/ *noun* (*AmE*) = CLAMP (2)

deny /dɪˈnaɪ/ *verb* (**de·nies**, **deny·ing**, **de·nied**, **de·nied**) **1** to say that sth is not true: [VN] *to deny a claim/a charge/an accusation* ◊ *The spokesman refused either to confirm or deny the reports.* ◊ *There's no denying (the fact) that quicker action could have saved them.* ◊ [V-ing] *He denies attempting to murder his wife.* ◊ [V(that)] *She denied (that) there had been any cover-up.* ◊ [VN that] *It can't be denied that we need to devote more resources to this problem.* **2** [VN] to refuse to admit or accept sth: *She denied all knowledge of the incident.* ◊ *The department denies responsibility for what occurred.* **3** ~ sth (to sb)| ~ (sb) (sth) (*formal*) to refuse to allow sb to have sth that they want or ask for: [VNN, VN] *They were denied access to the information.* ◊ *Access to the information was denied to them.* **4** [VN] ~ yourself (sth) (*formal*) to refuse to let yourself have sth that you would like to have, especially for moral or religious reasons

> **WORD FAMILY**
> deny v.
> denial n.
> undeniable adj.

de·odor·ant /diˈəʊdərənt; *AmE* diˈoʊ-/ *noun* [C, U] a substance that people put on their bodies to remove or hide unpleasant smells: (*a*) *roll-on deodorant*—see also ANTI-PERSPIRANT

dep. *abbr.* (in writing) DEPART(S); DEPARTURE—compare ARR.

de·part /dɪˈpaːt; *AmE* dɪˈpaːrt/ *verb* (rather *formal*) **1** ~ (for...) (from...) to leave a place, especially to start a trip: [V] *Flights for Amsterdam depart from Terminal 3.* ◊ *She waited until the last of the guests had departed.* ◊ [VN] (*AmE*) *The train departed Amritsar at 6.15 p.m.* **2** (*AmE*) to leave your job: [V] *the departing president* ◊ [VN] *He departed his job December 16.*—see also DEPARTURE IDM **depart this 'life** to die. People say 'depart this life' to avoid saying 'die'. PHRV **de'part from sth** to behave in a way that is different from usual: *Departing from her usual routine, she took the bus to work.*

de·part·ed /dɪˈpaːtɪd; *AmE* -ˈpaːrt-/ *adj.* [only before noun] (*formal*) **1** dead. People say 'departed' to avoid saying 'dead': *your dear departed brother* **2** (**the departed**) *noun* (*pl.* **the de·part·ed**) the person who has died

de·part·ment /dɪˈpaːtmənt; *AmE* -ˈpaːrt-/ *noun* (*abbr.* Dept) a section of a large organization such as a government, business, university, etc: *the Department of the Environment* ◊ *the Treasury Department* ◊ *a government/university department* ◊ *the marketing/sales department* ◊ *the children's department* (= in a large store) ◊ *the English department*—see also THE STATE DEPARTMENT IDM **be sb's department** (*spoken*) to be sth that sb is responsible for or knows a lot about: *Don't ask me about it—that's her department.*

de·part·ment·al /ˌdiːpaːtˈmentl; *AmE* -paːrt-/ *adj.* [only before noun] connected with a department rather than with the whole organization: *a departmental manager/meeting*

de'partment store *noun* a large shop/store that is divided into several parts, each part selling a different type of goods

de·part·ure /dɪˈpaːtʃə(r); *AmE* -ˈpaːrt-/ *noun* **1** [C, U] ~ (from...) the act of leaving a place; an example of this: *His sudden departure threw the office into chaos.* ◊ *Flights should be confirmed 48 hours before departure.* ◊ *They had received no news of him since his departure from the island.* **2** [C] a plane, train, etc. leaving a place at a particular time: *arrivals and departures* ◊ *All departures are from Manchester.* ◊ *the departure lounge/time/gate* ◊ *the departures board* **3** [C] **a** ~ (from sth) an action that is different from what is usual or expected: *It was a radical departure from tradition.* ◊ *Their latest single represents a new departure for the band.* IDM see POINT *n.*

de·pend /dɪˈpend/ *verb* IDM **that de'pends | it (all) de'pends** used to say that you are not certain about sth because other things have to be considered: *'Is he coming?' 'That depends. He may not have the time.'* ◊ *I don't know if we can help—it all depends.* ◊ *I might not go. It depends how tired I am.* ◊ *'Your job sounds fun.' 'It depends what you mean by 'fun'.'* ◊ *I shouldn't be too late. But it depends if the traffic's bad.* PHRV **de'pend on/upon sb/sth 1** to rely on sb/sth and be able to trust them: *He was the sort of person you could depend on.* ◊ [+to inf] *He knew he could depend upon her to deal with the situation.* **2** to be sure or expect that sth will happen: *Depend upon it* (= you can be sure) *we won't give up.* ◊ [+-ing] *Can we depend on you coming in on Sunday?* ◊ (*formal*) *You can depend on his coming in on Sunday.* [+to inf] (*ironic*) *You can depend on her to be* (= she always is) *late.* **de'pend on/upon sb/sth (for sth)** (not usually used in the progressive tenses) to need money, help, etc. from sb/sth else for a particular purpose: *The community depends on the shipping industry for its survival.* ◊ *I don't want to depend too much on my parents.* **de'pend on/upon sth** (not used in the progressive tenses) to be affected or decided by sth: *Does the quality of teaching depend on class size?* ◊ *It would depend on the circumstances.* ◊ [+wh-] *We might need more food depending on how many people turn up.*

> **GRAMMAR POINT**
> **depend on**
>
> In informal English, it is quite common to say **depend** rather than **depend on** before words like *what*, *how* or *whether*. *It depends what you mean by 'hostile'.* In formal written English, **depend** should always be followed by *on* or *upon*: *It depends on how you define the term 'hostile'. Upon* is more formal and less frequent than *on.*

de·pend·able /dɪˈpendəbl/ *adj.* that can be relied on to do what you want or need: *a dependable person/car* ▶ **de·pend·abil·ity** /dɪˌpendəˈbɪləti/ *noun* [U]

de·pend·ant /dɪˈpendənt/ (*BrE*) (also **de·pend·ent** *AmE, BrE*) *noun* a person, especially a child, who depends on another person for a home, food, money, etc.

de·pend·ence /dɪˈpendəns/ *noun* [U] **1** ~ (on/upon sb/sth) the state of needing the help and support of sb/sth in order to survive or be successful: *his dependence on his parents* ◊ *Our relationship was based on mutual dependence.* ◊ *the dependence of Europe on imported foods* ◊ *financial/economic dependence* OPP INDEPENDENCE **2** (also **de·pend·ency**) the state of being ADDICTED (= unable to stop taking or using it): *drug/alcohol dependence* **3** ~ of A and B (*technical*) the fact of one thing being affected by another: *the close dependence of soil and landforms*

de·pend·ency /dɪˈpendənsi/ *noun* (*pl.* -ies) **1** [U] ~ (on/upon sb/sth) the state of relying on sb/sth for sth, especially when this is not normal or necessary: *financial/economic dependency* ◊ *Their aim is to reduce people's dependency on the welfare state.* ◊ *the dependency culture* (= a way of life on which people are too dependent on money from the government) **2** [C] a country, an area, etc. that is controlled by another country: *The Orkney islands were formerly dependencies of Norway and Denmark.* **3** = DEPENDENCE

de·pend·ent /dɪˈpendənt/ *adj., noun*
■ *adj.* **1** ~ (on/upon sb/sth) (for sth) needing sb/sth in order to survive or be successful: *a woman with several dependent children* ◊ *You can't be dependent on your parents all your life.* ◊ *The festival is heavily dependent on sponsorship for its success.* **2** ~ on/upon sth ADDICTED to sth (= unable to stop taking or using it): *to be dependent on drugs/alcohol* **3** ~ on/upon sth (*formal*) affected or decided by sth: *A child's development is dependent on many factors.* ◊ *The price is dependent on how many extras you choose.*
■ *noun* (*especially AmE*) = DEPENDANT

s	t	v	z	ʃ	ʒ	tʃ	dʒ	θ	ð	ŋ
see	tea	van	zoo	shoe	vision	chain	jam	thin	this	sing

de·pendent 'clause *noun* (*grammar*) = SUBORDINATE CLAUSE

de·per·son·al·ize (*BrE* also **-ise**) /ˌdiːˈpɜːsənəlaɪz; *AmE* -ˈpɜːrs-/ *verb* [VN] [often passive] (*written*) to make sth less personal so that it does not seem as if human beings with feelings and personality are involved

de·pict /dɪˈpɪkt/ *verb* ~ **sb/sth (as sb/sth)** (rather *formal*) **1** to show an image of sb/sth in a picture: [VN] *a painting depicting the Virgin and Child* ◇ [VN-ing] *The artist had depicted her lying naked on a bed.* **2** [VN] to describe sth in words, or give an impression of sth in words or with a picture: *The novel depicts French society in the 1930s.* ◇ *The advertisements depict smoking as glamorous and attractive.* ▶ **de·pic·tion** /dɪˈpɪkʃn/ *noun* [U, C]: *They object to the movie's depiction of gay people.*

de·pila·tory /dɪˈpɪlətri; *AmE* -tɔːri/ *noun* (*pl.* **-ies**) a substance used for removing body hair ▶ **de·pila·tory** *adj.* [only before noun]: *depilatory creams*

de·plane /diːˈpleɪn/ *verb* [V] (*AmE*) to get off a plane SYN DISEMBARK

de·plete /dɪˈpliːt/ *verb* [VN] [usually passive] to reduce sth by a large amount so that there is not enough left: *Food supplies were severely depleted.* ▶ **de·ple·tion** /dɪˈpliːʃn/ *noun* [U]: *ozone depletion* ◇ *the depletion of fish stocks*

de·plor·able /dɪˈplɔːrəbl/ *adj.* (*formal*) very bad and unacceptable, often in a way that shocks people: *a deplorable episode / incident* ◇ *They were living in the most deplorable conditions.* ◇ *The acting was deplorable.* ▶ **de·plor·ably** /-əbli/ *adv.*: *They behaved deplorably.* ◇ *deplorably high / low / bad*

de·plore /dɪˈplɔː(r)/ *verb* [VN] (*formal*) to strongly disapprove of sth and criticize it, especially publicly: *Like everyone else, I deplore and condemn this killing.*

de·ploy /dɪˈplɔɪ/ *verb* [VN] **1** (*technical*) to move soldiers or weapons into a position where they are ready for military action: *US forces deployed in the Gulf* ◇ *At least 5000 missiles were deployed along the border.* **2** (*formal*) to use sth effectively: *to deploy arguments / resources* ▶ **de·ploy·ment** *noun* [U]

de·popu·late /ˌdiːˈpɒpjuleɪt; *AmE* -ˈpɑːp-/ *verb* [VN] [usually passive] to reduce the number of people living in a place: *Whole stretches of land were laid waste and depopulated.* ▶ **de·popu·la·tion** /ˌdiːˌpɒpjuˈleɪʃn; *AmE* -ˌpɑːp-/ *noun* [U]

de·port /dɪˈpɔːt; *AmE* dɪˈpɔːrt/ *verb* [VN] to force sb to leave a country, usually because they have broken the law or because they have no legal right to be there: *He was convicted of drug offences and deported.* ▶ **de·port·ation** /ˌdiːpɔːˈteɪʃn; *AmE* -pɔːrˈt-/ [C, U]: *Several of the asylum seekers now face deportation.* ◇ *a deportation order*

de·port·ment /dɪˈpɔːtmənt; *AmE* -ˈpɔːrt-/ *noun* [U] (*formal*) **1** (*BrE*) the way in which a person stands and moves: *lessons for young ladies in deportment and etiquette* **2** (*old-fashioned, especially AmE*) the way in which a person behaves

de·pose /dɪˈpəʊz; *AmE* dɪˈpoʊz/ *verb* [VN] to remove sb, especially a ruler, from power: *The president was deposed in a military coup.*

de·posit /dɪˈpɒzɪt; *AmE* -ˈpɑːz-/ *noun, verb*
■ *noun*
MONEY | **1** [usually sing.] **a** ~ **(on sth)** a sum of money that is given as the first part of a larger payment: *We've put down a 5% deposit on the house.* ◇ *They normally ask you to pay £100 (as a) deposit.* **2** [usually sing.] a sum of money that is paid by sb when they rent sth and that is returned to them if they do not lose or damage the thing that they are renting: *to pay a deposit* **3** a sum of money that is paid into a bank account: *Deposits can be made at any branch.* **4** (in Britain) the amount of money that a candidate in an election to Parliament has to pay, and that is returned if he/she gets enough votes: *All the other candidates lost their deposits.*
SUBSTANCE | **5** a layer of a substance that has formed naturally underground: *mineral / gold / coal deposits* **6** a layer of a substance that has been left somewhere, especially by a river, flood, etc., or is found at the bottom of a liquid:

The rain left a deposit of mud on the windows. ◇ *Turkish coffee always leaves a thick deposit at the bottom of the cup.* ◇ *fatty deposits in the arteries of the heart*
■ *verb* [VN]
PUT DOWN | **1** [+*adv. / prep.*] to put or lay sb/sth down in a particular place: *She deposited a pile of books on my desk.* ◇ (*informal*) *I was whisked off in a taxi and deposited outside the hotel.*
LEAVE SUBSTANCE | **2** (especially of a river or a liquid) to leave a layer of sth on the surface of sth, especially gradually and over a period of time: *Sand was deposited which hardened into sandstone.*
MONEY | **3** to put money into a bank account: *Millions were deposited in Swiss bank accounts.* **4** to pay a sum of money as the first part of a larger payment; to pay a sum of money that you will get back if you return in good condition sth that you have rented
PUT IN SAFE PLACE | **5** ~ **sth (in sth)** | ~ **sth (with sb/sth)** to put sth valuable or important in a place where it will be safe: *Guests may deposit their valuables in the hotel safe.*

de'posit account *noun* (*BrE*) a type of account at a bank or BUILDING SOCIETY that pays interest on money that is left in it—compare CURRENT ACCOUNT

de·pos·ition /ˌdepəˈzɪʃn/ *noun* **1** [U, C] (*technical*) the natural process of leaving a layer of a substance on rocks or soil; a substance left in this way: *marine / river deposition* **2** [U, C] the act of removing sb, especially a ruler, from power: *the deposition of the King* **3** [C] (*law*) a formal statement, taken from sb and used in a court of law

de·pos·it·or /dɪˈpɒzɪtə(r); *AmE* -ˈpɑːz-/ *noun* a person who puts money in a bank account

de·posi·tory /dɪˈpɒzɪtri; *AmE* dɪˈpɑːzətɔːri/ *noun* (*pl.* **-ies**) a place where things can be stored

depot /ˈdepəʊ; *AmE* ˈdiːpoʊ/ *noun* **1** a place where large amounts of food, goods or equipment are stored: *an arms depot* **2** (*BrE*) a place where vehicles, for example, buses are kept and repaired **3** (*AmE*) a small station where trains or buses stop

de·prave /dɪˈpreɪv/ *verb* [VN] (*formal*) to make sb morally bad SYN CORRUPT: *In my view this book would deprave young children.*

de·praved /dɪˈpreɪvd/ *adj.* (*formal*) morally bad SYN WICKED, EVIL: *This is the work of a depraved mind.*

de·prav·ity /dɪˈprævəti/ *noun* [U] (*formal*) the state of being morally bad: *a life of depravity*

dep·re·cate /ˈdeprəkeɪt/ *verb* [VN] (*formal*) to feel and express strong disapproval of sth ▶ **dep·re·cat·ing** (also *less frequent* **dep·re·ca·tory** /ˌdeprəˈkeɪtəri; *AmE* ˈdeprɪkətɔːri/) *adj.*: *a deprecating comment* **dep·re·cat·ing·ly** *adv.*

de·pre·ci·ate /dɪˈpriːʃieɪt/ *verb* **1** [V] to become less valuable over a period of time: *New cars start to depreciate as soon as they are on the road.* ◇ *Shares continued to depreciate on the stock markets today.* OPP APPRECIATE **2** [VN] (*business*) to reduce the value, as stated in the company's accounts, of a particular ASSET over a particular period of time: *The bank depreciates PCs over a period of five years.* **3** [VN] (*formal*) to make sth seem unimportant or of no value: *I had no intention of depreciating your contribution.* ▶ **de·pre·ci·ation** /dɪˌpriːʃiˈeɪʃn/ *noun* [U]: *currency depreciation* ◇ *the depreciation of fixed assets*

dep·re·da·tion /ˌdeprəˈdeɪʃn/ *noun* [usually pl.] (*formal*) acts that cause harm or damage

de·press /dɪˈpres/ *verb* **1** to make sb sad and without enthusiasm or hope: [VN] *Wet weather always depresses me.* ◇ [VN to inf] *It depresses me to see so many young girls smoking.* **2** [VN] to make trade, business, etc. less active: *The recession has depressed the housing market.* **3** [VN] to lower the value of prices or wages: *to depress wages / prices* **4** [VN] (*formal*) to press or push sth down, especially part of a machine: *to depress the clutch pedal* (= when driving).

de·pressed /dɪˈprest/ *adj.* **1** very sad and without hope: *She felt very depressed about the future.* **2** suffering from the medical condition of DEPRESSION **3** (of a place or an industry) without enough economic activity or employment: *an attempt to bring jobs to depressed areas* **4** having

D

æ	ɑː	e	ɜː	ə	ɪ	iː	i	ɒ	ɔː	ʌ	ʊ	u	uː
cat	father	ten	bird	about	sit	see	many	got	saw	cup	put	actual	too

(BrE)

a lower amount or level than usual: *depressed rates/ prices*

de·press·ing /dɪˈpresɪŋ/ *adj.* making you feel very sad and without enthusiasm: *a depressing sight/thought/ experience* ◊ *Looking for a job these days can be very depressing.* ▶ **de·press·ing·ly** *adv.*: *a depressingly familiar experience*

de·pres·sion /dɪˈpreʃn/ *noun* **1** [U] a medical condition in which a person feels very sad and anxious and often has physical SYMPTOMS such as being unable to sleep, etc: *clinical depression* ◊ *She suffered from severe depression after losing her job.* ◊ *post-natal depression* **2** [U, C] the state of feeling very sad and without hope: *There was a feeling of gloom and depression in the office when the news of the job cuts was announced.* **3** [C, U] a period when there is little economic activity and many people are poor or without jobs: *The country was in the grip of (an) economic depression.* ◊ *the great Depression of the 1930s* **4** [C] (*written*) a part of a surface that is lower than the parts around it [SYN] HOLLOW: *Rainwater collects in shallow depressions on the ground.* **5** [C] (*technical*) a weather condition in which the pressure of the air becomes lower, often causing rain—compare ANTICYCLONE

de·pres·sive /dɪˈpresɪv/ *adj., noun*
■ *adj.* connected with the medical condition of depression: *depressive illness*
■ *noun* a person who is suffering from the medical condition of depression—see also MANIC-DEPRESSIVE

de·pres·sor /dɪˈpresə(r)/ ⊏> TONGUE DEPRESSOR

de·priv·ation /ˌdeprɪˈveɪʃn/ *noun* [U] the fact of not having sth that you need, like enough food, money or a home; the process that causes this: *neglected children suffering from social deprivation* ◊ *sleep deprivation* ◊ *government policies to reduce urban/rural deprivation* ◊ *the deprivation of war* (= the suffering caused by not having enough of some things)

de·prive /dɪˈpraɪv/ *verb* [PHRV] **de'prive sb/sth of sth** to prevent sb from having or doing sth, especially sth important: *They were imprisoned and deprived of their basic rights.* ◊ *Why should you **deprive yourself** of such simple pleasures?*

de·prived /dɪˈpraɪvd/ *adj.* without enough food, education, and all the things that are necessary for people to live a happy and comfortable life: *a deprived childhood/ background/area* ◊ *economically/emotionally/socially deprived*

Dept (also **Dept.** especially in *AmE*) *abbr.* (in writing) department

depth /depθ/ *noun*
MEASUREMENT | **1** [C, U] the distance from the top or surface to the bottom of sth: *What's the depth of the water here?* ◊ *Water was found at a depth of 30 metres.* ◊ *They dug down to a depth of two metres.* ◊ *Many dolphins can dive to depths of 200 metres.* ◊ *The oil well extended several hundreds of feet in depth.* ◊ *the depth of a cut/wound/ crack* **2** [C, U] the distance from the front to the back of sth: *The depth of the shelves is 30 centimetres.*

OF FEELINGS | **3** [U] the strength and power of feelings: *the depth of her love/friendship/anger/fear*

OF KNOWLEDGE | **4** [U] (*approving*) the quality of knowing or understanding a lot of details about sth; the ability to provide and explain these details: *a writer of great wisdom and depth* ◊ *a job that doesn't require any great **depth of knowledge*** ◊ *His ideas lack depth.*

DEEPEST PART | **5** [C, usually pl.] the deepest, most extreme or serious part of sth: *the depths of the ocean* ◊ *to live in the depths of the country* (= a long way from a town) ◊ *in the depths of winter* (= when it is coldest) ◊ *She was in the depths of despair* ◊ *He gazed into the depths of her eyes.* ◊ *Her paintings reveal hidden depths* (= unknown and interesting things about her character).

OF COLOUR | **6** [U] the strength of a colour: *Strong light will affect the depth of colour of your carpets and curtains.*

PICTURE/PHOTOGRAPH | **7** [U] (*technical*) the quality in a

work of art or a photograph which makes it appear not to be flat
—see also DEEP
[IDM] **in 'depth** in a detailed and thorough way: *I haven't looked at the report in depth yet.* ◊ *an in-depth study* **be out of your 'depth 1** (*BrE*) to be in water that is too deep to stand in with your head above water **2** to be unable to understand sth because it is too difficult; to be a situation that you cannot control: *He felt totally out of his depth in his new job.*—more at PLUMB *v.*

'depth charge *noun* a bomb that is set to explode underwater, used to destroy SUBMARINES

depu·ta·tion /ˌdepjuˈteɪʃn/ *noun* [C+sing./pl. *v.*] a small group of people who are asked or allowed to act or speak for others

de·pute /dɪˈpjuːt/ *verb* [VN to inf] [often passive] (*formal*) to give sb else the authority to represent you or do sth for you [SYN] DELEGATE: *He was deputed to put our views to the committee.*

depu·tize (*BrE* also **-ise**) /ˈdepjutaɪz/ *verb* [V] ~ **(for sb)** to do sth that sb in a higher position than you would usually do: *Ms Green has asked me to deputize for her at the meeting.*

dep·uty /ˈdepjuti/ *noun* (*pl.* **-ies**) **1** a person who is the next most important person below a business manager, a head of a school, a political leader, etc. and who does the person's job when he or she is away: *I'm acting as deputy till the manager returns.* ◊ *the deputy head of a school* **2** the name for a member of parliament in some countries **3** (in the US) a police officer who helps the SHERIFF of an area

de·rail /dɪˈreɪl/ *verb* [VN] to make a train leave the track: (*figurative*) *This latest incident could derail the peace process.* ▶ **de·rail·ment** *noun* [C, U]

de·ranged /dɪˈreɪndʒd/ *adj.* unable to behave and think normally, especially because of mental illness: *mentally deranged* ◊ *a deranged attacker/mind/laugh* ▶ **de·range·ment** *noun* [U]: *He seemed to be on the verge of total derangement.*

derby /ˈdɑːbi; *AmE* ˈdɜːrbi/ *noun* (*pl.* **-ies**) **1** (*AmE*) = BOWLER (2) **2** (*BrE*) a sports competition between teams from the same area or town: *a local derby between the two North London sides* ◊ *a derby match* **3** a race or sports competition: *a motorcycle derby*—see also DEMOLITION DERBY **4** (**Derby**) used in the name of several horse races which happen every year: *the Epsom Derby* ◊ *the Kentucky Derby*

de·regu·late /ˌdiːˈregjuleɪt/ *verb* [VN] [often passive] to free a trade, a business activity, etc. from rules and controls [SYN] DECONTROL: *deregulated financial markets* ▶ **de·regu·la·tion** /ˌdiːˌregjuˈleɪʃn/ *noun* [U] **de·regu·la·tory** /ˌdiːˈregjələtəri; *AmE* -tɔːri/ *adj.* [only before noun]: *deregulatory reforms*

dere·lict /ˈderəlɪkt/ *adj., noun*
■ *adj.* (especially of land or buildings) not used or cared for and in bad condition: *derelict land/buildings/sites*
■ *noun* (*formal*) a person without a home, a job or property: *derelicts living on the streets* [SYN] VAGRANT

dere·lic·tion /ˌderəˈlɪkʃn/ *noun* (*written*) **1** [U] the state of being derelict: *industrial/urban dereliction* ◊ *a house in a state of dereliction* **2** [U, sing.] ~ **of duty** (*formal* or *law*) the fact of deliberately not doing what you ought to do, especially when it is part of your job: *The police officers were found guilty of serious **dereliction of duty**.*

de·ride /dɪˈraɪd/ *verb* [VN] [often passive] ~ **sb/sth (as sth)** (*formal*) to treat sb/sth as ridiculous and not worth considering seriously [SYN] MOCK: *His views were derided as old-fashioned.* [also V speech]

de ri·gueur /ˌdə rɪˈɡɜː(r)/ *adj.* [not before noun] (from French) considered necessary if you wish to be accepted socially: *Evening dress is de rigueur at the casino.*

de·ri·sion /dɪˈrɪʒn/ *noun* [U] unkind laughter or remarks that show you think sb/sth is ridiculous and not worth considering seriously: *Her speech was greeted with howls of derision.* ◊ *He became an object of universal derision.*

de·ri·sive /dɪˈraɪsɪv/ (also *less frequent* **de·ri·sory**) *adj.*

unkind and showing that you think sb/sth is ridiculous: *She gave a short, derisive laugh.* ▶ **de·ri·sive·ly** *adv.*

de·ri·sory /dɪˈraɪsəri/ *adj.* (*formal*) **1** too small or of too little value to be considered seriously SYN LAUGHABLE: *They offered us a derisory £10 a week.* **2** (*rare*) = DERISIVE

der·iv·ation /ˌderɪˈveɪʃn/ *noun* [U, C] the origin or development of sth, especially a word: *a word of Greek derivation*

de·riva·tive /dɪˈrɪvətɪv/ *noun, adj.*
- *noun* a word or thing that has been developed or produced from another word or thing: *'Happiness' is a derivative of 'happy'.* ◊ *Crack is a highly potent and addictive derivative of cocaine.*
- *adj.* (usually *disapproving*) copied from sth else; not having new or original ideas: *a derivative design/style* ◊ *I found the novel thin and derivative. I had expected more.*

de·rive /dɪˈraɪv/ *verb* PHRV **de·rive sth from sth 1** (*formal*) to get sth from sth: *He derived great pleasure from painting.* **2** (*technical*) to obtain a substance from sth: *The new drug is derived from fish oil.* **de·rive from sth | be de·rived from sth** to come or develop from sth: *The word 'politics' is derived from a Greek word meaning 'city'.*

derma·titis /ˌdɜːməˈtaɪtɪs; *AmE* ˌdɜːrm-/ *noun* [U] (*medical*) a skin condition in which the skin becomes red, swollen and sore

derma·tolo·gist /ˌdɜːməˈtɒlədʒɪst; *AmE* ˌdɜːrməˈtɑːl-/ *noun* a doctor who studies and treats skin diseases

derma·tol·ogy /ˌdɜːməˈtɒlədʒi; *AmE* ˌdɜːrməˈtɑːl-/ *noun* [U] the scientific study of skin diseases ▶ **derma·to·logi·cal** /ˌdɜːmətəˈlɒdʒɪkl; *AmE* ˌdɜːrmətəˈlɑːdʒ-/ *adj.*

de·roga·tory /dɪˈrɒɡətri; *AmE* dɪˈrɑːɡətɔːri/ *adj.* showing a critical attitude towards sb SYN INSULTING: *derogatory remarks/comments*

der·rick /ˈderɪk/ *noun* **1** a tall machine used for moving or lifting heavy weights, especially on a ship; a type of CRANE **2** a tall structure over an oil WELL for holding the DRILL (= the machine that makes the hole in the ground for getting the oil out)

derring-do /ˌderɪŋ ˈduː/ *noun* [U] (*old-fashioned, humorous*) brave actions, like those in adventure stories

der·vish /ˈdɜːvɪʃ; *AmE* ˈdɜːrvɪʃ/ *noun* a member of a Muslim religious group whose members make a promise to stay poor and live without comforts or pleasures. They perform a fast lively dance as part of their worship: *He threw himself around the stage like a whirling dervish.*

de·sal·in·ation /ˌdiːˌsælɪˈneɪʃn/ *noun* [U] the process of removing salt from sea water: *a desalination plant*

de·scale /ˌdiːˈskeɪl/ *verb* [VN] (*BrE*) to remove the SCALE (= the hard white material left on pipes, etc. by water when it is heated) from sth

des·cant /ˈdeskænt/ *noun* (*music*) a tune that is sung or played at the same time as, and usually higher than, the main tune

des·cend /dɪˈsend/ *verb* **1** (*formal*) to come or go down from a higher to a lower level: [V] *The plane began to descend.* ◊ *The results, ranked in descending order* (= from the highest to the lowest) *are as follows:* ◊ [VN] *She descended the stairs slowly.* OPP ASCEND **2** [V] (*formal*) (of a hill, etc.) to slope downwards: *At this point the path descends steeply.* OPP ASCEND **3** [V] ~ (**on/upon sb/sth**) (*literary*) (of night, darkness, a mood, etc.) to arrive and begin to affect sb/sth SYN FALL: *Night descends quickly in the tropics.* ◊ *Calm descended on the crowd.* PHRV **be des'cended from sb** to be related to sb who lived a long time ago: *He claims to be descended from a Spanish prince.* **des'cend into sth** [no passive] (*formal*) to gradually get into a bad state: *The country was descending into chaos.* **des'cend on/upon sb/sth** to visit sb/sth in large numbers, sometimes unexpectedly: *Hundreds of football fans descended on the city.* **des'cend to sth** [no passive] to do sth that makes people stop respecting you: *They descended to the level of personal insults.*

des·cend·ant /dɪˈsendənt/ *noun* **1** a person's **descendants** are their children, their children's children, and all the people who live after them who are related to them: *He was an O'Conor and a direct descendant of the last*

High King of Ireland. ◊ *Many of them are descendants of the original settlers.* **2** something that has developed from sth similar in the past

des·cent /dɪˈsent/ *noun* **1** [C, usually sing.] an action of coming or going down: *The plane began its descent to Heathrow.* ◊ (*figurative*) *the country's swift descent into anarchy* OPP ASCENT **2** [C] a slope going downwards: *There is a gradual descent to the sea.* OPP ASCENT **3** [U] ~ (**from sb**) a person's family origins SYN ANCESTRY: *to be of Scottish descent* ◊ *He traces his line of descent from the Stuart kings.*

de·scribe /dɪˈskraɪb/ *verb* **1** ~ **sb/sth (to/for sb)** | ~ **sb/sth (as sth)** to say what sb/sth is like: [VN] *Can you describe him to me?* ◊ *The man was described as tall and dark, and aged about 20.* ◊ *Jim was described by his colleagues as 'unusual'.* [V-**wh**-] *Describe how you did it.* ◊ [V-ing] *Several people described seeing strange lights in the sky.* [also VN-ing] **2** [VN] (*formal or technical*) to make a movement which has a particular shape; to form a particular shape: *The shark described a circle around the shoal of fish.* ▶ **de·scrib·able** *adj.*

de·scrip·tion /dɪˈskrɪpʃn/ *noun* **1** [C, U] ~ (**of sb/sth**) a piece of writing or speech that says what sb/sth is like; the act of writing or saying in words what sb/sth is like: *to give a **detailed/full description** of the procedure* ◊ *a **brief/general description** of the software* ◊ *Police have issued a description of the gunman.* ◊ *'Scared stiff' is an apt description of how I felt at that moment.* ◊ *a personal pain that goes beyond description* (= is too great to express in words) ◊ *the novelist's powers of description* **2** [C] of some, all, every, etc. ~ of some, etc. type: *boats of every description/all descriptions* ◊ *Their money came from trade of some description.* ◊ *medals, coins and things of that description* IDM **answer/fit a description (of sb/sth)** to be like a particular person or thing: *A child answering the description of the missing boy was found safe and well in London yesterday.*—more at BEGGAR *v.*

de·scrip·tive /dɪˈskrɪptɪv/ *adj.* **1** saying what sb/sth is like; describing sth: *the descriptive passages in the novel* ◊ *The term I used was meant to be purely descriptive* (= not judging). **2** (*linguistics*) saying how language is actually used, without giving rules for how it should be used OPP PRESCRIPTIVE

dese·crate /ˈdesɪkreɪt/ *verb* [VN] to damage a holy thing or place or treat it without respect: *desecrated graves* ▶ **dese·cra·tion** /ˌdesɪˈkreɪʃn/ *noun* [U]: *the desecration of a cemetery* ◊ (*figurative*) *the desecration of the countryside by new roads*

de·seg·re·gate /ˌdiːˈseɡrɪɡeɪt/ *verb* [VN] to end the policy of SEGREGATION in a place in which people of different races are kept separate in public places, etc: *to desegregate schools* ▶ **de·seg·re·ga·tion** /ˌdiːˌseɡrɪˈɡeɪʃn/ *noun* [U]

de·select /ˌdiːsɪˈlekt/ *verb* [VN] **1** if the local branch of a political party in Britain **deselects** the existing Member of Parliament, it does not choose him or her as a candidate at the next election **2** (*computing*) to remove sth from the list of possible choices on a computer MENU ▶ **de·selec·tion** *noun* [U]

des·ert *noun, verb*
- *noun* /ˈdezət; *AmE* ˈdezərt/—see also DESERTS [C, U] a large area of land that has very little water and very few plants growing on it. Many deserts are covered with sand: *the Sahara Desert* ◊ *Somalia is mostly desert.* ◊ *burning desert sands* ◊ (*figurative*) *a cultural desert* (= a place without any culture)
- *verb* /dɪˈzɜːt; *AmE* dɪˈzɜːrt/ **1** [VN] to leave sb without help or support SYN ABANDON: *She was deserted by her husband.* **2** [VN] [often passive] to go away from a place and leave it empty SYN ABANDON: *The villages had been deserted.* ◊ *The owl seems to have deserted its nest.* **3** to leave the armed forces without permission: [V] *Large numbers of soldiers deserted as defeat became inevitable.* [also VN] **4** [VN] to stop using, buying or supporting sth: *Why did you desert teaching for politics?* **5** [VN] (*written*) if a particular quality **deserts** you, it is not there when you need it: *Her courage seemed to desert her for a moment.*

b	d	f	g	h	k	l	m	n	p	r
bad	**did**	**fall**	**get**	**hat**	**cat**	**leg**	**man**	**now**	**pen**	**red**

▶ **de·ser·tion** /dɪˈzɜːʃn/ *noun* [U, C]: *She felt betrayed by her husband's desertion.* ◊ *The army was badly affected by desertions.* **IDM** see SINK *v.*

'desert boot *noun* a SUEDE boot that just covers the ankle

des·ert·ed /dɪˈzɜːtɪd; *AmE* -ˈzɜːrt-/ *adj.* **1** (of a place) with no people in it: *deserted streets* ◊ *The office was completely deserted.* **2** left by a person or people who do not intend to return **SYN** ABANDONED: *a deserted village* ◊ *deserted wives*

de·sert·er /dɪˈzɜːtə(r); *AmE* -ˈzɜːrt-/ *noun* a person who leaves from the army, navy, etc. without permission (= DESERTS)

desert·ifi·ca·tion /dɪˌzɜːtɪfɪˈkeɪʃn; *AmE* -ˌzɜːrt-/ *noun* [U] (*technical*) the process of becoming or making sth a DESERT

ˌdesert 'island *noun* a tropical island where no people live

des·erts /dɪˈzɜːts; *AmE* dɪˈzɜːrts/ *noun* [pl.] **IDM** **sb's (just) deserts** what sb deserves, especially when it is sth bad: *The family of the victim said that the killer had got his just deserts when he was jailed for life.*

de·serve /dɪˈzɜːv; *AmE* dɪˈzɜːrv/ *verb* (not used in the progressive tenses) if sb/sth **deserves** sth, it is right that they should have it, because of the way they have behaved or because of what they are: [VN] *You deserve a rest after all that hard work.* ◊ *The report deserves careful consideration.* ◊ *One player in particular deserves a mention.* ◊ *What have I done to deserve this?* ◊ [Vtoinf] *They didn't deserve to win.* ◊ *He deserves to be locked up for ever for what he did.* [also V-ing] **IDM** **sb deˌserves a 'medal** (*spoken*) used to say that you admire sb because they have done sth difficult or unpleasant **ˌget what you deˈserve | deˌserve all/everything you 'get** (*informal*) used to say that you think sb has earned the bad things that happen to them—more at TURN *n.*

de·served·ly /dɪˈzɜːvɪdli; *AmE* -ˈzɜːrv-/ *adv.* in the way that is deserved; correctly: *The restaurant is deservedly popular.* ◊ *He has just been chosen for the top job, and deservedly so.*

de·serv·ing /dɪˈzɜːvɪŋ; *AmE* -ˈzɜːrv-/ *adj.* ~ (of sth) (*formal*) that deserves help, praise, a reward, etc: *to give money to a deserving cause* ◊ *This family is one of the most deserving cases.* ◊ *an issue deserving of attention* **OPP** UNDESERVING

des·ic·cated /ˈdesɪkeɪtɪd/ *adj.* **1** (of food) dried in order to preserve it: *desiccated coconut* **2** (*technical*) completely dry: *treeless and desiccated soil*

des·ic·ca·tion /ˌdesɪˈkeɪʃn/ *noun* [U] (*technical*) the process of becoming completely dry

de·sid·er·atum /dɪˌzɪdəˈrɑːtəm; -ˈreɪtəm/ *noun* (*pl.* -ata /-ɑːtə; -eɪtə/) (from *Latin, formal*) a thing that is wanted or needed

de·sign /dɪˈzaɪn/ *noun, verb*
■ *noun*
ARRANGEMENT | **1** [U, C] the general arrangement of the different parts of sth that is made, such as a building, book, machine etc: *The basic design of the car is very similar to that of earlier models.* ◊ *special new design features* ◊ *The machine's unique design prevents it from overheating.* ◊ *The magazine will appear in a new design from next month.*
DRAWING/PLAN/MODEL | **2** [U] the art or process of deciding how sth will look, work, etc. by drawing plans, making models, etc: *a course in art and design* ◊ *a design studio* ◊ *computer-aided design* ◊ *the design and development of new products*—see also INTERIOR DESIGN **3** [C] ~ (for sth) a drawing or plan from which sth may be made: *designs for aircraft* ◊ *new and original designs*
PATTERN | **4** [C] an arrangement of lines and shapes as a decoration: *floral/abstract/geometric designs* ◊ *The tiles come in a huge range of colours and designs.*
INTENTION | **5** [U, C] a plan or an intention: *It happened—whether by accident or design—that the two of them were left alone after all the others had gone.* ◊ *It is all part of his grand design for government.*

IDM **have designs on sb** (*formal* or *humorous*) to want to start a sexual relationship with sb: *He was quite aware of her marital designs on him.* **have designs on sth** to be planning to get sth for yourself, often in a way that other people do not approve of: *Rumours spread that the Duke had designs on the crown* (= wanted to make himself king).
■ *verb*
DRAW PLANS | **1** ~ sth (for sb/sth) to decide how sth will look, work, etc., especially by drawing plans or making models: [VN] *to design a car/a dress/an office* ◊ *a badly designed kitchen* ◊ *They asked me to design a poster for the campaign.* [also VNN]
PLAN STH | **2** [VN] to think of and plan a system, a way of doing sth, etc: *We need to design a new syllabus for the third year.*
FOR SPECIAL PURPOSE | **3** [usually passive] ~ sth (for sth) | ~ sth (as sth) to make, plan or intend sth for a particular purpose or use: [VN] *The method is specifically designed for use in small groups.* ◊ [VNtoinf] *The programme is designed to help people who have been out of work for a long time.*

des·ig·nate *verb, adj.*
■ *verb* /ˈdezɪɡneɪt/ [often passive] **1** ~ sth (as) sth | ~ sth (as being sth) to say officially that sth has a particular character or name; to describe sth in a particular way: [VN-N] *This area has been designated (as) a National Park.* ◊ *This floor has been designated a no-smoking area.* ◊ [VN] *Several pupils were designated as having moderate or severe learning difficulties.* ◊ *a designated nature reserve* ◊ *designated seats for the elderly* **2** ~ sb (as) sth to choose or name sb for a particular job or position: [VN] *The director is allowed to designate his/her successor.* ◊ [VN-N] *Who has she designated (as) her deputy?* ◊ *the man designated to succeed the president* **3** [VN] to show sth using a particular mark or sign: *The different types are designated by the letters A, B and C.*
■ *adj.* /ˈdezɪɡnət; -nət/ [after noun] (*written*) chosen to do a job but not yet having officially started it: *an interview with the director designate*

ˌdesignated 'driver *noun* (*informal*) the person who agrees to drive and not drink alcohol when people go to a party, a bar, etc.

ˌdesignated 'hitter *noun* (in baseball) a player who is named at the start of the game as the person who will hit the ball instead of the PITCHER

des·ig·na·tion /ˌdezɪɡˈneɪʃn/ *noun* (*formal*) **1** [U] ~ (as sth) the action of choosing a person or thing for a particular purpose, or of giving them or it a particular status: *The district is under consideration for designation as a conservation area.* **2** [C] a name, title or description: *Her official designation is Financial Controller.*

de·sign·er /dɪˈzaɪnə(r)/ *noun, adj.*
■ *noun* a person whose job is to decide how things such as clothes, furniture, tools, etc. will look or work by making drawings, plans or patterns: *a fashion/jewellery designer* ◊ *an industrial designer*
■ *adj.* [only before noun] made by a famous designer; expensive and having a famous BRAND name: *designer jeans/jewellery/labels* ◊ *designer beer/water* ◊ *He had a trendy haircut, an earring and designer stubble* (= a short beard, grown for two or three days and thought to look fashionable).

deˌsigner 'drug *noun* a drug produced artificially, usually one that is illegal: *a tablet of the designer drug Ecstasy*

de·sir·able /dɪˈzaɪərəbl/ *adj.* **1** (*formal*) ~ (that) ...| ~ (for sb) (to do sth) that you would like to have or do; worth having or doing: (*BrE*) *It is desirable that interest rates should be reduced.* ◊ (*AmE*) *It is desirable that interest rates be reduced.* ◊ *highly desirable* ◊ *The house has many desirable features.* ◊ *It is no longer desirable for adult children to live with their parents.* ◊ *She chatted for a few minutes about the qualities she considered desirable in a secretary.* ◊ *Such measures are desirable if not essential.* **OPP** UNDESIRABLE **2** (of a person) causing other

D

people to feel sexual desire: *She suddenly saw herself as a desirable young woman.* ▶ **de·sir·abil·ity** /dɪˌzaɪərə'bɪləti/ *noun* [U] (*formal*): *No one questions the desirability of cheaper fares.*

de·sire /dɪ'zaɪə(r)/ *noun, verb*
■ *noun* **1** [C, U] ~ (**for sth**)| ~ (**to do sth**) a strong wish to have or do sth: *a strong desire for power* ◇ *enough money to satisfy all your desires* ◇ *She felt an overwhelming desire to return home.* ◇ (*formal*) *I have no desire* (= I do not want) *to discuss the matter further.* ◇ (*formal*) *He has expressed a desire to see you.* **2** [U, C] ~ (**for sb**) a strong wish to have sex with sb: *She felt a surge of love and desire for him.* **3** [C, usually sing.] a person or thing that is wished for: *When she agreed to marry him he felt he had achieved his heart's desire.*
■ *verb* (not used in the progressive tenses) **1** (*formal*) to want sth; to wish for sth: [VN] *We all desire health and happiness.* ◇ *The house had everything you could desire.* ◇ *The medicine did not achieve the desired effect.* ◇ [V to inf] *Fewer people desire to live in the north of the country.* [also VN to inf] **2** to be sexually attracted to sb: [VN] *He still desired her, and she him.* **IDM** **leave a lot, much, something, etc. to be de'sired** to be bad or unacceptable

de·sir·ous /dɪ'zaɪərəs/ *adj.* [not before noun] ~ (**of sth/ of doing sth**)| ~ (**to do sth**) (*formal*) having a wish for sth; wanting sth: *At that point Franco was desirous of prolonging the war.*

de·sist /dɪ'zɪst; dɪ'sɪst/ *verb* [V] ~ (**from sth/from doing sth**) (*formal*) to stop doing sth: *They agreed to desist from the bombing campaign.*

desk /desk/ *noun* **1** a piece of furniture like a table, usually with drawers in it, that you sit at to read, write, work, etc: *He used to be a pilot but now he has a desk job.* **2** a place where you can get information or be served at an airport, a hotel, etc: *the check-in desk* ◇ *the reception desk*—see also CASH DESK **3** an office at a newspaper, television company, etc. that deals with a particular subject: *the news/sports desk*—see also CITY DESK

'desk clerk *noun* (*AmE*) = CLERK

de·skill /ˌdiː'skɪl/ *verb* [VN] (*technical*) to reduce the amount of skill that is needed to do a particular job ▶ **de·skill·ing** *noun* [U]

desk·top /'desktɒp; *AmE* -tɑːp/ *noun* **1** the top of a desk **2** = DESKTOP COMPUTER

desktop com'puter (also **desk·top**) *noun* a computer with a keyboard, screen and main processing unit, that fits on a desk—compare LAPTOP, NOTEBOOK

desktop 'publishing *noun* [U] (*abbr.* **DTP**) the use of a small computer and a printer to produce a small book, a magazine, or other printed material

deso·late *adj., verb*
■ *adj.* /'desələt/ **1** (of a place) empty and without people, making you feel sad or frightened: *a bleak and desolate landscape* **2** very lonely and unhappy: *The thought that her husband did not want the baby made her feel utterly desolate.*
■ *verb* /'desəleɪt/ [VN] [usually passive] (*literary*) to make sb feel sad and without hope: *She had been desolated by the death of her friend.*

deso·la·tion /ˌdesə'leɪʃn/ *noun* [U] (*written*) **1** the feeling of being very lonely and unhappy: *Her death left him with a terrible sense of desolation.* **2** the state of a place that is ruined or destroyed and offers no joy or hope to people: *a scene of utter desolation*

des·pair /dɪ'speə(r); *AmE* dɪ'sper/ *noun, verb*
■ *noun* [U] the feeling of having lost all hope: *She uttered a wordless cry of despair.* ◇ *A deep sense of despair overwhelmed him.* ◇ *He gave up the struggle in despair.* ◇ *One harsh word would send her into the depths of despair.* ◇ *Eventually, driven to despair, he threw himself under a train.*—see also DESPERATE **IDM** **be the despair of sb** to make sb worried or unhappy, because they cannot help: *My handwriting was the despair of my teachers.*—more at COUNSEL *n.*
■ *verb* [V] ~ (**of sth/sb**)| ~ (**of doing sth**) to stop having any hope that a situation will change or improve: *Don't despair! We'll think of a way out of this.* ◇ *They'd almost*

despaired of ever having children. ◇ *I despair of him; he can't keep a job for more than six months.*

des·pair·ing /dɪ'speərɪŋ; *AmE* -'sper-/ *adj.* showing or feeling the loss of all hope: *a despairing cry/look/sigh* ◇ *With every day that passed he became ever more despairing.* ▶ **des·pair·ing·ly** *adv.*: *She looked despairingly at the mess.*

des·patch (*BrE*) = DISPATCH

des·per·ado /ˌdespə'rɑːdəʊ; *AmE* -doʊ/ *noun* (*pl.* -**oes** or -**os**) (*old-fashioned*) a man who does dangerous and criminal things without caring about himself or other people

des·per·ate /'despərət/ *adj.* **1** feeling or showing that you have little hope and are ready to do anything without worrying about danger to yourself or others: *The prisoners grew increasingly desperate.* ◇ *Stores are getting desperate after two years of poor sales.* ◇ *Somewhere out there was a desperate man, cold, hungry, hunted.* ◇ *I heard sounds of a desperate struggle, just above my room.* **2** [usually before noun] (of an action) giving little hope of success; tried when everything else has failed: *a desperate bid for freedom* ◇ *She clung to the edge in a desperate attempt to save herself.* ◇ *His increasing financial difficulties forced him to take desperate measures.* ◇ *Doctors were fighting a desperate battle to save the little girl's life.* **3** [not usually before noun] ~ (**for sth**)| ~ (**to do sth**) needing or wanting sth very much: *He was so desperate for a job he would have done anything.* ◇ *I was absolutely desperate to see her.* ◇ (*informal*) *I'm desperate for a cigarette.* **4** (of a situation) extremely serious or dangerous: *The children are in desperate need of love and attention.* ◇ *They face a desperate shortage of clean water.* ▶ **des·per·ate·ly** *adv.*: *desperately ill/unhappy/lonely* ◇ *He took a deep breath, desperately trying to keep calm.* ◇ *They desperately wanted a child.* ◇ *She looked desperately around for a weapon.*

des·per·ation /ˌdespə'reɪʃn/ *noun* [U] the state of being desperate: *In desperation, she called Louise and asked for her help.* ◇ *There was a note of desperation in his voice.* ◇ *an act of sheer desperation*

de·spic·able /dɪ'spɪkəbl; *rarely* 'despɪkəbl/ *adj.* (*formal*) very unpleasant or evil: *a despicable act/crime* ◇ *I hate you! You're despicable.*

des·pise /dɪ'spaɪz/ *verb* [VN] (not used in the progressive tenses) to dislike and have no respect for sb/sth: *She despised gossip in any form.* ◇ *He despised himself for being so cowardly.*

des·pite /dɪ'spaɪt/ *prep.* **1** used to show that sth happened or is true in spite of sth: *Her voice was shaking despite all her efforts to control it.* ◇ *Despite applying for hundreds of jobs, he is still out of work.* ◇ *She was good at physics despite the fact that she found it boring.* **2** (**despite yourself**) used to show that sb did not intend to do the thing mentioned: *He had to laugh despite himself.*

de·spoil /dɪ'spɔɪl/ *verb* [VN] ~ **sth** (**of sth**) (*literary*) to steal sth valuable from a place; to make a place less attractive by damaging or destroying it

des·pond·ent /dɪ'spɒndənt; *AmE* -'spɑːn-/ *adj.* ~ (**about sth**)| (*especially AmE*) ~ (**over sth**) sad, without much hope: *She was becoming increasingly despondent about the way things were going.* ▶ **des·pond·ency** /dɪ'spɒndənsi; *AmE* -'spɑːn-/ *noun* [U]: *a mood of despondency* ◇ *Life's not all gloom and despondency.* **des·pond·ent·ly** *adv.*

des·pot /'despɒt; *AmE* 'despət/ *noun* a ruler with great power, especially one who uses it in a cruel way: *an enlightened despot* (= one who tries to use his/her power in a good way) ▶ **des·pot·ic** /dɪ'spɒtɪk; *AmE* -'spɑːt-/ *adj.*: *despotic power/rule*

des·pot·ism /'despətɪzəm/ *noun* [U] the rule of a despot

des·sert /dɪ'zɜːt; *AmE* dɪ'zɜːrt/ *noun* [U, C] sweet food eaten at the end of a meal: *What's for dessert?* ◇ *a rich chocolate dessert* ◇ *a dessert wine* ◇ (*BrE*) *the dessert trolley* (= a table on wheels from which you choose your dessert in a restaurant)—compare AFTERS, PUDDING, SWEET—picture on page A1

des·sert·spoon /dɪ'zɜːtspuːn; *AmE* -'zɜːrt-/ *noun* **1** a spoon of medium size—picture at CUTLERY **2** (also **des-**

D

æ	ɑː	e	ɜː	ə	ɪ	iː	i	ɒ	ɔː	ʌ	ʊ	u	uː
cat	father	ten	bird	about	sit	see	many	got	saw	cup	put	actual	too
								(BrE)					

sert·spoon·ful /-fʊl/) the amount a dessertspoon can hold

de·sta·bil·ize (BrE also **-ise**) /ˌdiːˈsteɪbəlaɪz/ verb [VN] to make a system, country, government, etc. become less firmly established or successful: *Terrorist attacks on senior officials were threatening to destabilize the government.* ◊ *The news had a destabilizing effect on the stock market.*—compare STABILIZE ▸ **de·sta·bil·iza·tion, -isa·tion** /ˌdiːˌsteɪbəlaɪˈzeɪʃn; AmE -ləˈz-/ noun [U]

des·tin·ation /ˌdestɪˈneɪʃn/ noun a place to which sb/ sth is going or being sent: *popular holiday destinations like the Bahamas* ◊ *to arrive at/reach your destination* ◊ *Our luggage was checked all the way through to our final destination.*

des·tined /ˈdestɪnd/ adj. (formal) **1 ~ for sth | ~ to do sth** having a future which has been decided or planned at an earlier time, especially by fate: *He was destined for a military career, like his father before him.* ◊ *We seem destined never to meet.* **2 ~ for** on the way to or intended for a place: *goods destined for Poland*

des·tiny /ˈdestəni/ noun (pl. **-ies**) **1** [C] what happens to sb or what will happen to them in the future, especially things that they cannot change or avoid: *the destinies of nations* ◊ *He wants to be in control of his own destiny.* **2** [U] the power believed to control events [SYN] FATE: *I believe there's some force guiding us—call it God, destiny or fate.* ◊ *She was spurred on by a strong sense of destiny and ambition.*

des·ti·tute /ˈdestɪtjuːt; AmE -tuːt/ adj. **1** without money, food and the other things necessary for life: *When he died, his family was left completely destitute.* **2 (the destitute)** noun [pl.] people who are destitute: *homes and refuges for the destitute* **3 ~ of sth** (formal) lacking sth: *They seem destitute of ordinary human feelings.* ▸ **des·ti·tu·tion** /ˌdestɪˈtjuːʃn; AmE -ˈtuːʃn/ noun [U]: *homelessness and destitution*

des·troy /dɪˈstrɔɪ/ verb [VN] **1** to damage sth so badly that it no longer exists, works, etc: *The building was completely destroyed by fire.* ◊ *They've destroyed all the evidence.* ◊ *Heat gradually destroys vitamin C.* ◊ *You have destroyed my hopes of happiness.* ◊ *Failure was slowly destroying him* (= making him less and less confident and happy). **2** to kill an animal deliberately, usually because it is sick or not wanted: *The injured horse had to be destroyed.*—see also SOUL-DESTROYING

> **WORD FAMILY**
> destroy v.
> destroyer n.
> destruction n.
> destructive adj.
> indestructible adj.

des·troy·er /dɪˈstrɔɪə(r)/ noun **1** a small fast ship used in war, for example to protect larger ships **2** a person or thing that destroys: *Sugar is the destroyer of healthy teeth.*

de·struc·tion /dɪˈstrʌkʃn/ noun [U] the act of destroying sth; the process of being destroyed: *the destruction of the rainforests* ◊ *weapons of mass destruction* ◊ *a tidal wave bringing **death and destruction** in its wake* ◊ *The central argument is that capitalism **sows the seeds of its own destruction** (= creates the forces that destroy it).*

de·struc·tive /dɪˈstrʌktɪv/ adj. causing destruction or damage: *the destructive power of modern weapons* ◊ *the destructive effects of anxiety*—compare CONSTRUCTIVE ▸ **de·struc·tive·ly** adv. **de·struc·tive·ness** noun [U]

des·ul·tory /ˈdesəltri; AmE -tɔːri/ adj. (formal) going from one thing to another, without a definite plan and without enthusiasm: *I wandered about in a desultory fashion.* ◊ *a desultory conversation* ▸ **des·ul·tor·ily** adv.

Det abbr. (BrE) (in writing) DETECTIVE: *Det Insp* (= Inspector) *Cox*

de·tach /dɪˈtætʃ/ verb **1 ~ (sth) (from sth)** to remove sth from sth larger; to become separated from sth: [VN] *Detach the coupon and return it as soon as possible* ◊ *One of the panels had become detached from the main structure.* ◊ [V] *The skis should detach from the boot if you fall.* **2** [VN] **~ yourself (from sb/sth)** (formal) to leave or separate yourself from sb/sth: *She detached herself from his embrace.* ◊ (figurative) *I tried to detach myself from the*

reality of these terrible events.—compare ATTACH **3** [VN] (technical) to send a group of soldiers, etc. away from the main group, especially to do special duties

de·tach·able /dɪˈtætʃəbl/ adj. that can be taken off: *a coat with a detachable hood*

de·tached /dɪˈtætʃt/ adj. **1** (of a house) not joined to another house on either side—compare SEMI-DETACHED **2** showing a lack of feeling [SYN] INDIFFERENT: *She wanted him to stop being so cool, so detached, so cynical.* **3** (approving) not influenced by other people or by your own feelings [SYN] IMPARTIAL: *a detached observer*

de·tach·ment /dɪˈtætʃmənt/ noun **1** [U] the state of not being involved in sth in an emotional or personal way: *He answered with an air of detachment.* ◊ *She felt a sense of detachment from what was going on.* **2** [U] (approving) the state of not being influenced by other people or by your own feelings: *In judging these issues a degree of critical detachment is required.* **3** [C] a group of soldiers, ships, etc. sent away from a larger group, especially to do special duties: *a detachment of artillery* **4** [U] the act of detaching sth; the process of being detached from sth: *to suffer detachment of the retina*

de·tail /ˈdiːteɪl; AmE also dɪˈteɪl/ noun, verb
■ noun
FACTS/INFORMATION | **1** [C] a small individual fact or item; a less important fact or item: *an expedition planned down to the last detail* ◊ *He stood still, absorbing every detail of the street.* ◊ *Tell me the main points now; leave **the details** till later.* **2** [U] the small facts or features of sth, when you consider them all together: *This issue will be discussed **in more detail** in the next chapter.* ◊ *The research has been carried out with scrupulous **attention to detail**.* ◊ *The sketch was from memory but he had an eye for detail* (= noticed and remembered small details). ◊ *The fine detail of the plan has yet to be worked out.* **3** (details) [pl.] information about sth: *Please supply the following details: name, age and sex.* ◊ *Further details and booking forms are available on request.* ◊ *They didn't give any details about the game.* ◊ 'We had a terrible time—' 'Oh, spare me **the details** (= don't tell me any more).'
SMALL PARTS | **4** [C, U] a small part of a picture or painting; the smaller or less important parts of a picture, pattern, etc. when you consider them all together: *This is a detail from the 1844 Turner painting.* ◊ *a huge picture with a lot of detail in it*
SOLDIERS | **5** [C] a group of soldiers given special duties
[IDM] **go into 'detail(s)** to explain sth fully: *I can't go into details now; it would take too long.*
■ verb
GIVE FACTS/INFORMATION | **1** [VN] to give a list of facts or all the available information about sth: *The brochure details all the hotels in the area and their facilities.*
ORDER SOLDIER | **2** [often passive] to give an official order to sb, especially a soldier, to do a particular task: [VN to inf] *Several of the men were detailed to form a search party.* [also VN]
CLEAN CAR | **3** [VN] (AmE) to clean a car extremely thoroughly: *He got work for a while detailing cars.*

de·tailed /ˈdiːteɪld; AmE also dɪˈteɪld/ adj. giving many details and a lot of information; paying great attention to details: *a detailed description/analysis/study* ◊ *detailed instructions*

de·tail·ing /ˈdiːteɪlɪŋ; AmE also dɪˈteɪlɪŋ/ noun [U] small details put on a building, piece of clothing, etc., especially for decoration

de·tain /dɪˈteɪn/ verb [VN] **1** to keep sb in an official place, such as a police station, a prison or a hospital, and prevent them from leaving: *One man has been detained for questioning.* **2** (formal) to delay sb or prevent them from going somewhere: *I'm sorry—he'll be late; he's been detained at a meeting.*—see also DETENTION

de·tain·ee /ˌdiːteɪˈniː/ noun a person who is kept in prison, usually because of his or her political opinions

de·tect /dɪˈtekt/ verb [VN] to discover or notice sth, especially sth that is not easy to see, hear, etc: *The tests are designed to detect the disease early.* ◊ *an instrument that can detect small amounts of radiation* ◊ *Do I detect a note* *of criticism?* ▶ **de·tect·able** *adj.*: *The noise is barely detectable by the human ear.* OPP UNDETECTABLE

de·tec·tion /dɪˈtekʃn/ *noun* [U] the process of detecting sth; the fact of being detected: *crime prevention and detection* ◇ *Last year the detection rate for car theft was just 13%.* ◇ *Many problems, however, escape detection.* ◇ *Early detection of cancers is vitally important.*

de·tect·ive /dɪˈtektɪv/ *noun* (*abbr.* **Det**) **1** a person, especially a police officer, whose job is to examine crimes and catch criminals: *Detective Inspector (Roger) Brown* ◇ *detectives from the anti-terrorist squad* ◇ *a detective story/novel*—see also STORE DETECTIVE **2** a person employed by sb to find out information about sb/sth—see also PRIVATE DETECTIVE

de·tect·or /dɪˈtektə(r)/ *noun* a piece of equipment for discovering the presence of sth, such as metal, smoke, explosives or changes in pressure or temperature: *a smoke detector*

dé·tente (also **de·tente** especially in *AmE*) /ˌdeɪˈtɑːnt/ *noun* [U] (from *French, formal*) an improvement in the relationship between two or more countries which have been unfriendly towards each other in the past: *a new international climate of détente*

de·ten·tion /dɪˈtenʃn/ *noun* **1** [U] the state of being kept in a place, especially a prison, and prevented from leaving: *a sentence of 12 months' detention in a young offender institution* ◇ *police powers of arrest and detention* ◇ *allegations of torture and detention without trial* ◇ *a detention camp* **2** [U, C] the punishment of being kept at school for a time after other students have gone home: *They can't give me (a) detention for this.*—see also DETAIN

de'tention centre (*BrE*) (*AmE* **de'tention center**) *noun* **1** a place where young people who have committed offences are kept in detention **2** a place where people are kept in detention, especially people who have entered a country illegally

deter /dɪˈtɜː(r)/ *verb* (**-rr-**) ~ **sb (from sth/from doing sth)** to make sb decide not to do sth or continue doing sth, especially by making them understand the difficulties and unpleasant results of their actions: [VN] *I told him I wasn't interested, but he wasn't deterred.* ◇ *The high price of the service could deter people from seeking advice.* [also V] —see also DETERRENT

de·ter·gent /dɪˈtɜːdʒənt/ *AmE* -ˈtɜːrdʒ-/ *noun* [U, C] a liquid or powder that helps remove dirt, for example from clothes or dishes

de·teri·or·ate /dɪˈtɪəriəreɪt/ *AmE* -ˈtɪr-/ *verb* [V] ~ **(into sth)** to become worse: *Her health deteriorated rapidly and she died shortly afterwards.* ◇ *deteriorating weather conditions* ◇ *The discussion quickly deteriorated into an angry argument.* ▶ **de·teri·or·ation** /dɪˌtɪəriəˈreɪʃn; *AmE* -ˌtɪr-/ *noun* [U, C]: *a serious deterioration in relations between the two countries*

de·ter·min·able /dɪˈtɜːmɪnəbl/ *AmE* -ˈtɜːrm-/ *adj.* (*formal*) that can be found out or calculated: *During the third month of pregnancy the sex of the child becomes determinable.*

de·ter·min·ant /dɪˈtɜːmɪnənt/ *AmE* -ˈtɜːrm-/ *noun* (*formal*) a thing that decides whether or how sth happens: *Interest rates are a major determinant of currency trends.*

de·ter·min·ate /dɪˈtɜːmɪnət/ *AmE* -ˈtɜːrm-/ *adj.* (*formal*) fixed and definite: *a sentence with a determinate meaning*

de·ter·min·ation /dɪˌtɜːmɪˈneɪʃn/ *AmE* -ˌtɜːrm-/ *noun* **1** [U] ~ **(to do sth)** the quality that makes you continue trying to do sth even when this is difficult: *fierce/grim/dogged determination* ◇ *He fought the illness with courage and determination.* ◇ *I admire her determination to get it right.* ◇ *They had survived by sheer determination.* **2** [U] (*formal*) the process of deciding sth officially: *factors influencing the determination of future policy* **3** [U, C] (*technical*) the act of finding out or calculating sth: *Both methods rely on the accurate determination of the pressure of the gas.*

de·ter·mine /dɪˈtɜːmɪn/ *AmE* -ˈtɜːrm-/ *verb* (*formal*) **1** to discover the facts about sth; to calculate sth exactly: [VN] *An inquiry was set up to determine the cause of the acci-*

dent. ◇ [V wh-] *We set out to determine exactly what happened that night.* [also V that] **2** to make sth happen in a particular way or be of a particular type: [VN] *Age and experience will be determining factors in our choice of candidate.* ◇ *Upbringing plays an important part in determining a person's character.* [also V wh-] **3** to officially decide and/or arrange sth: [VN] *A date for the meeting has yet to be determined.* ◇ [V(that)] *The court determined (that) the defendant should pay the legal costs.* **4** ~ **on sth/to do sth** to decide definitely to do sth: [V to inf] *They determined to start early.* [also V, V(that)]

de·ter·mined /dɪˈtɜːmɪnd; *AmE* -ˈtɜːrm-/ *adj.* **1** [not before noun] ~ **(to do sth)** if you are **determined** to do sth, you have made a firm decision to do it and you will not let anyone prevent you: *I'm determined to succeed.* **2** showing a person's determination to do sth: *a determined effort to stop smoking* ◇ *The proposal had perished in the face of determined opposition.* ▶ **de·ter·mined·ly** *adv.*

de·ter·miner /dɪˈtɜːmɪnə(r); *AmE* -ˈtɜːrm-/ *noun* (*grammar*) (abbreviated as *det.* in this dictionary) a word such as *the, some, my,* etc. that comes before a noun to show how the noun is being used

de·ter·min·ism /dɪˈtɜːmɪnɪzəm; *AmE* -ˈtɜːrm-/ *noun* [U] (*philosophy*) the belief that people are not free to choose what they are like or how they behave, because these things are decided by their background, surroundings and other things over which they have no control ▶ **de·ter·min·is·tic** /dɪˌtɜːmɪˈnɪstɪk; *AmE* -ˌtɜːrm-/ *adj.*

de·ter·rent /dɪˈterənt; *AmE* -ˈtɜːr-/ *noun* ~ **(to sb/sth)** a thing that makes sb less likely to do sth (= that deters them): *Hopefully his punishment will act as a deterrent to others.* ◇ *the country's nuclear deterrents* (= nuclear weapons that are intended to stop an enemy from attacking) ▶ **de·ter·rence** /dɪˈterəns; *AmE* -ˈtɜːr-/ *noun* [U] (*formal*) **de·ter·rent** *adj.*: *a deterrent effect*

de·test /dɪˈtest/ *verb* (not used in the progressive tenses) to hate sb/sth very much: [VN] *They detested each other on sight.* [also V -ing] ▶ **de·test·ation** /ˌdiːteˈsteɪʃn/ *noun* [U]

de·test·able /dɪˈtestəbl/ *adj.* that deserves to be hated: *All terrorist crime is detestable, whoever the victims.* ◇ *'You're detestable!' she said, shaking.*

de·throne /ˌdiːˈθrəʊn; *AmE* -ˈθroʊn/ *verb* [VN] to remove a king or queen from power; to remove sb from a position of authority or power

det·on·ate /ˈdetəneɪt/ *verb* to explode, or to make a bomb or other device explode: [V] *Two other bombs failed to detonate.* [also VN]

det·on·ation /ˌdetəˈneɪʃn/ *noun* [C, U] an explosion; the action of making sth explode

det·on·ator /ˈdetəneɪtə(r)/ *noun* a device for making sth, especially a bomb, explode

de·tour /ˈdiːtʊə(r); *AmE* -tʊr/ *noun, verb*
■ *noun* **1** a longer route that you take in order to avoid a problem or to visit a place: *We had to make a detour around the flooded fields.* ◇ *It's well worth making a detour to see the village.* **2** (*AmE*) = DIVERSION
■ *verb* (*AmE*) ~ **(to …)** to take a longer route in order to avoid a problem or to visit a place; to make sb/sth take a longer route: [V] *The President detoured to Chicago for a special meeting.* [also VN]

de·toxi·fi·ca·tion /ˌdiːˌtɒksɪfɪˈkeɪʃn; *AmE* -ˌtɑːks-/ (also *informal* **detox** /ˈdiːtɒks; *AmE* -tɑːks/) *noun* [U] treatment given to people to help them stop drinking alcohol or taking drugs: *a detoxification unit*

de·tox·ify /ˌdiːˈtɒksɪfaɪ; *AmE* -ˈtɑːks-/ *verb* (**de·toxi·fies, de·toxi·fy·ing, de·toxi·fied, de·toxi·fied**) [VN] **1** to remove harmful substances or poisons from sth **2** to treat sb in order to help them stop drinking too much alcohol or taking drugs

de·tract /dɪˈtrækt/ *verb* PHRV **de'tract from sth| de'tract sth from sth** (not used in the progressive tenses) to make sth seem less good or enjoyable: *He was determined not to let anything detract from his enjoyment of the trip.*

de·tract·or /dɪˈtræktə(r)/ *noun* [usually pl.] (especially *written*) a person who tries to make sb/sth seem less good or valuable by criticizing it

de·train /ˌdiːˈtreɪn/ *verb* [V, VN] (*formal*) to leave a train or make sb leave a train

det·ri·ment /ˈdetrɪmənt/ *noun* [U, C, usually sing.] (*formal*) the act of causing harm or damage; sth that causes harm or damage **IDM** **to the detriment of sb/sth | to sb/sth's detriment** resulting in harm or damage to sb/sth: *He was engrossed in his job to the detriment of his health.* **without detriment (to sb/sth)** not resulting in harm or damage to sb/sth

det·ri·ment·al /ˌdetrɪˈmentl/ *adj.* ~ **(to sb/sth)** harmful: *the sun's **detrimental effect** on skin* ◇ *The policy will be detrimental to the peace process.* ► **det·ri·men·tal·ly** /-təli/ *adv.*

de·tritus /dɪˈtraɪtəs/ *noun* [U] **1** (*technical*) natural waste material that is left after sth has been used or broken up: *organic detritus from fish and plants* **2** (*formal*) any kind of rubbish/garbage that is left after an event or when sth has been used: *the detritus of everyday life*

de trop /ˌdə ˈtrəʊ; *AmE* ˈtroʊ/ *adj.* [not before noun] (from French, *formal*) not wanted, especially in a social situation with other people

deuce /djuːs; *AmE* duːs/ *noun* **1** [U, C] (in tennis) the situation when both players have 40 as a score, after which one player must win two points one after the other in order to win the game **2** [C] (*AmE*) a playing card with two PIPS on it: *the deuce of clubs* **3** (**the deuce**) [sing.] (*old-fashioned, spoken*) used in questions to show that you are annoyed: *What the deuce is he doing?*

deus ex machina /ˌdeɪʊs eks ˈmækɪnə/ *noun* [sing.] (*literary*) an unexpected power or event that saves a situation that seems without hope, especially in a play or novel

Deutsch·mark /ˈdɔɪtʃmɑːk; *AmE* -mɑːrk/ (also **mark**) *noun* (*abbr.* **DM**) **1** [C] the unit of money in Germany (to be replaced by the euro) **2** (**the Deutschmark**) [sing.] (*finance*) the value of the Deutschmark compared with the value of the money of other countries: *The pound slumped to 2.47 against the Deutschmark.*

de·value /ˌdiːˈvæljuː/ *verb* **1** [V, VN] ~ **(sth) (against sth)** (*finance*) to reduce the value of the money of one country when it is exchanged for the money of another country **OPP** REVALUE **2** [VN] to give a lower value to sth, making it seem less important than it really is: *Work in the home is often ignored and devalued.* ► **de·valu·ation** /ˌdiːˌvæljuˈeɪʃn/ *noun* [C, U]: *There has been a further small devaluation against the dollar.*

dev·as·tate /ˈdevəsteɪt/ *verb* [VN] **1** to completely destroy a place or an area: *The bomb devastated much of the old part of the city.* **2** [often passive] to make sb feel very shocked and sad

dev·as·tated /ˈdevəsteɪtɪd/ *adj.* extremely upset and shocked: *His family is absolutely devastated.*

dev·as·tat·ing /ˈdevəsteɪtɪŋ/ *adj.* **1** causing a lot of damage and destruction: *a devastating explosion/fire/cyclone* ◇ *Oil spills are having a **devastating effect** on coral reefs in the ocean.* ◇ *He received devastating injuries in the accident.* ◇ *It will be a **devastating blow** to the local community if the factory closes.* **2** extremely shocking to a person: *the devastating news that her father was dead* **3** impressive and powerful: *his devastating performance in the 100 metres* ◇ *Her smile was devastating.* ◇ *a devastating attack on the President's economic record* ► **dev·as·tat·ing·ly** *adv.*: *a devastatingly handsome man*

dev·as·ta·tion /ˌdevəˈsteɪʃn/ *noun* [U] great destruction or damage, especially over a wide area: *The bomb caused widespread devastation.*

de·velop /dɪˈveləp/ *verb*
GROW BIGGER/STRONGER | **1** ~ **(sth) (from sth) (into sth)** to gradually grow or become bigger, more advanced, stronger, etc.; to make sth do this: [V] *The child is developing normally.* ◇ *The place has rapidly developed from a small fishing community into a thriving tourist resort.* ◇ [VN] *She developed the company from nothing.*
NEW IDEA/PRODUCT | **2** [VN] to think of or produce a new

idea, product, etc. and make it successful: *The company develops and markets new software.*
DISEASE/PROBLEM | **3** to begin to have sth such as a disease or a problem; to start to affect sb/sth: [VN] *Her son developed asthma when he was two.* ◇ *The car developed engine trouble and we had to stop.* [also V]
BECOME SERIOUS/IMPORTANT | **4** [V] to start to happen and then become more serious or important: *A crisis was rapidly developing in the Gulf.*
BECOME BETTER | **5** to start to have a skill, ability, quality, etc. that becomes better and stronger; to become better and stronger: [VN] *He's developed a real flair for management.* ◇ [V] *Their relationship has developed over a number of years.*
BUILD HOUSES | **6** [VN] to build new houses, factories, etc. on an area of land, especially land that was not being used effectively before: *The site is being developed by a French company.*
IDEA/STORY | **7** [VN] to make an idea, a story, etc. clearer by explaining it further: *She develops the theme more fully in her later books.*
PHOTOGRAPHS | **8** [VN] to treat photographic film with chemicals so that the pictures can be seen: *I had the film developed yesterday.*

de·veloped /dɪˈveləpt/ *adj.* **1** (of a country, society, etc.) having many industries and a complicated economic system: *financial aid to less developed countries* ◇ *The average citizen in the developed world uses over 155kg of paper per year.*—compare UNDERDEVELOPED **2** in an advanced state: *children with highly developed problem-solving skills*—see also WELL DEVELOPED

de·vel·op·er /dɪˈveləpə(r)/ *noun* **1** [C] a person or company that buys land or buildings in order to build new houses, shops/stores, etc., or to improve the old ones, and makes a profit from doing this: *property developers* **2** [C] a person or a company that designs and creates new products: *a software developer* **3** [U] a chemical substance that is used for developing photographs from a film

de·vel·op·ing /dɪˈveləpɪŋ/ *adj.* [only before noun] (of a country, society, etc.) poor, and trying to make its industry and economic system more advanced: *developing countries/nations/economies*—compare UNDERDEVELOPED

de·vel·op·ment /dɪˈveləpmənt/ *noun*
GROWTH | **1** [U] the gradual growth of sth so that it becomes more advanced, stronger, etc: *a baby's development in the womb* ◇ *the development of basic skills such as literacy and numeracy* ◇ *career development*
NEW PRODUCT | **2** [U, C] the process of producing or creating sth new or more advanced; a new or advanced product: *the development of vaccines against tropical diseases* ◇ *The government is encouraging the development of small businesses.* ◇ *developments in aviation technology* ◇ *This piece of equipment is an exciting new development.*—see also RESEARCH AND DEVELOPMENT
NEW EVENT | **3** [C] a new event or stage that is likely to affect what happens in a continuing situation: *the latest developments in the war* ◇ *Are there further developments in the investigation?*
NEW BUILDINGS | **4** [C] a piece of land with new buildings on it: *a commercial/business/housing development* **5** [U] the process of using an area of land especially to make a profit by building on it, etc: *He bought the land for development.*

de·vel·op·men·tal /dɪˌveləpˈmentl/ *adj.* **1** in a state of developing or being developed: *The product is still at a developmental stage.* **2** connected with the development of sb/sth: *developmental psychology*

de'velopment area *noun* (*BrE*) an area where new industries are encouraged in order to create jobs

de·vi·ant /ˈdiːviənt/ *adj.* different from what most people consider to be normal and acceptable: *deviant behaviour/sexuality* ► **de·vi·ant** *noun*: *sexual deviants* **de·vi·ance** /-viəns/, **de·vi·ancy** /ˈdiːviənsi/ *noun* [U]: *a study of social deviance and crime*

de·vi·ate /ˈdiːvieɪt/ *verb* [V] ~ **(from sth)** to be different from sth; to do sth differently from what is usual or

s	t	v	z	ʃ	ʒ	tʃ	dʒ	θ	ð	ŋ
see	tea	van	zoo	shoe	vision	chain	jam	thin	this	sing

expected: *The bus had to deviate from its usual route because of a road closure.* ◊ *He never deviated from his original plan.*

de·vi·ation /ˌdiːviˈeɪʃn/ *noun* ~ **(from sth)** **1** [U, C] the act of moving away from what is normal or acceptable; a difference from what is expected or acceptable: *deviation from the previously accepted norms* ◊ *sexual deviation* ◊ *a deviation from the plan* **2** [C] (*technical*) the amount by which a single measurement is different from the average: *a compass deviation of 5°* (= from true north)—see also STANDARD DEVIATION

de·vice /dɪˈvaɪs/ *noun* **1** an object or a piece of equipment that has been designed to do a particular job: *a water-saving device* ◊ *electrical labour-saving devices around the home* **2** a bomb or weapon that will explode: *A powerful device exploded outside the station.* ◊ *the world's first atomic device* **3** a method of doing sth that produces a particular result or effect: *Sending advertising by mail is very successful as a marketing device.* ◊ *The report was a device used to hide rather than reveal problems.* **IDM** **leave sb to their own de'vices** to leave sb alone to do as they wish, and not tell them what to do

devil /ˈdevl/ *noun* **1** (**the Devil**) (in the Christian, Jewish and Muslim religions) the most powerful evil being **SYN** SATAN **2** a wicked evil spirit: *They believed she was possessed by devils.* **3** (*informal*) a person who behaves badly, especially a child: *a naughty little devil* **4** (*informal*) used to talk about sb and to emphasize an opinion that you have of them: *I miss the old devil, now that he's gone.* ◊ *She's off to Greece for a month—lucky devil!* **IDM** **be a 'devil** (*BrE*) people say **Be a devil!** to encourage sb to do sth that they are not sure about doing: *Go on, be a devil, buy both of them.* **better the ˌdevil you 'know (than the ˌdevil you 'don't)** (*saying*) used to say that it is easier and wiser to stay in a bad situation that you know and can deal with rather than change to a new situation which may be much worse **between the ˌdevil and the ˌdeep blue 'sea** in a difficult situation where there are two equally unpleasant or unacceptable choices **the 'devil** (*old-fashioned*) very difficult or unpleasant: *These berries are the devil to pick because they're so small.* **a devil of a job/time** (*old-fashioned*) a very difficult or unpleasant job or time: *I've had a devil of a job finding you.* **go to the 'devil!** (*old-fashioned, spoken*) used, in an unfriendly way, to tell sb to go away **like the 'devil** (*old-fashioned, informal*) very hard, fast, etc: *We ran like the devil.* **speak/talk of the 'devil** (*informal*) people say **speak/talk of the devil** when sb they have been talking about appears unexpectedly: *Well, speak of the devil—here's Alice now!* **what, where, who, why, etc. the 'devil ...** (*old-fashioned*) used in questions to show that you are annoyed or surprised: *What the devil do you think you're doing?*—more at PAY *v.*

devil·ish /ˈdevəlɪʃ/ *adj.* **1** cruel or wicked: *a devilish conspiracy* **2** morally bad, but in a way that people find attractive: *He was handsome, with a devilish charm.*

devil·ish·ly /ˈdevəlɪʃli/ *adv.* (*old-fashioned*) extremely; very: *a devilishly hot day*

ˌdevil-may-'care *adj.* [not usually before noun] cheerful and not worrying about the future: *a devil-may-care attitude to life*

dev·il·ment /ˈdevlmənt/ (also **dev·il·ry** /ˈdevlri/) *noun* (*formal*) wild behaviour that causes trouble **SYN** MISCHIEF

ˌdevil's 'advocate *noun* a person who expresses an opinion that they do not really hold in order to encourage a discussion about a subject: *Often the interviewer will need to play devil's advocate in order to get a discussion going.*

de·vi·ous /ˈdiːviəs/ *adj.* **1** behaving in a dishonest or indirect way, or deceiving people, in order to get sth **SYN** CUNNING: *a devious politician* ◊ *He got rich by devious means.* **2** ~ **route/path** a route or path that is not straight but has many changes in direction; not direct: *a devious route from the airport* ▶ **de·vi·ous·ly** *adv.* **de·vi·ous·ness** *noun* [U]

de·vise /dɪˈvaɪz/ *verb* [VN] to invent sth new or a new way of doing sth **SYN** THINK UP: *A new system has been devised to control traffic in the city.*

de·void /dɪˈvɔɪd/ *adj.* ~ **of sth** (*written*) completely lacking in sth: *The letter was devoid of warmth and feeling.*

de·vo·lu·tion /ˌdiːvəˈluːʃn; *AmE* ˌdev-/ *noun* [U] the act of giving power from a central authority or government to an authority or a government in a local region: *a supporter of devolution for Scotland*

de·volve /dɪˈvɒlv; *AmE* -ˈvɑːlv/ *verb* **PHRV** **de'volve on/ upon sb/sth** (*written*) **1** if property, money, etc. **devolves on/upon** you, you receive it after sb else dies **2** if a duty, responsibility, etc. **devolves on/upon** you, it is given to you by sb at a higher level of authority **devolve sth to/ on/upon sb** to give a duty, responsibility, power, etc. to sb who has less authority than you: *The central government devolved most tax-raising powers to the regional authorities.*

de·volved /dɪˈvɒlvd; *AmE* -ˈvɑːlvd/ *adj.* if power or authority is **devolved**, it has been passed to sb who has less power: *devolved responsibility* ◊ *a system of devolved government*

de·vote /dɪˈvəʊt; *AmE* dɪˈvoʊt/ *verb* **PHRV** **devote yourself to sb/sth** to give most of your time, energy, attention, etc. to sb/sth: *She devoted herself to her career.* **devote sth to sth** to give an amount of time, attention, etc. to sth: *I could only devote two hours a day to work on the project.*

de·voted /dɪˈvəʊtɪd; *AmE* -ˈvoʊt-/ *adj.* ~ **(to sb/sth)** having great love for sb/sth and being loyal to them: *They are devoted to their children.* ◊ *a devoted son/friend/fan* ▶ **de·voted·ly** *adv.*

de·votee /ˌdevəˈtiː/ *noun* ~ **(of sb/sth)** **1** a person who admires and is very enthusiastic about sb/sth: *a devotee of science fiction* **2** a very religious person who belongs to a particular group: *devotees of Krishna*

de·vo·tion /dɪˈvəʊʃn; *AmE* -ˈvoʊ-/ *noun* ~ **(to sb/sth)** **1** [U, sing.] great love, care and support for sb/sth: *His devotion to his wife and family is touching.* **2** [U, sing.] the action of spending a lot of time or energy on sth: *devotion to duty/a cause* ◊ *Her devotion to the job left her with very little free time.* **3** (**devotions**) [pl.] prayers and other religious practices

de·vo·tion·al /dɪˈvəʊʃənl; *AmE* -ˈvoʊ-/ *adj.* (of music, literature, etc.) connected with or used in religious services

de·vour /dɪˈvaʊə(r)/ *verb* [VN] **1** to eat all of sth quickly especially because you are very hungry: *He devoured half of his burger in one bite.* **2** to read or look at sth with great interest and enthusiasm: *She devoured everything she could lay her hands on: books, magazines and newspapers.* **3** (*formal*) to destroy sb/sth: *Flames devoured the house.* **IDM** **be devoured by sth** to be filled with a strong emotion that seems to control you: *She was devoured by envy and hatred.*

de·vout /dɪˈvaʊt/ *adj.* (of a person) believing strongly in a particular religion and obeying its laws and practices: *a devout Christian/Muslim* ▶ **de·vout·ly** *adv.*: *She devoutly* (= very strongly) *hoped he was telling the truth.* ◊ *a devoutly Catholic region*

dew /djuː; *AmE* duː/ *noun* [U] the very small drops of water that form on the ground, etc. during the night: *The grass was wet with early morning dew.*

dew·drop /ˈdjuːdrɒp; *AmE* ˈduːdrɑːp/ *noun* a small drop of dew or other liquid

dewy /ˈdjuːi; *AmE* ˈduːi/ *adj.* wet with DEW

ˌdewy-'eyed *adj.* (*disapproving*) showing emotion about sth, perhaps with a few tears in the eyes **SYN** SENTIMENTAL

dex·ter·ity /dekˈsterəti/ *noun* [U] **1** skill in using your hands: *You need manual dexterity to be good at video games.* **2** the ability to do sth skilfully: *mental/verbal dexterity*

dex·ter·ous (also **dex·trous**) /ˈdekstrəs/ *adj.* (*written*) skilful with your hands; skilfully done: *animals that are naturally dexterous* ▶ **dex·ter·ous·ly** (also **dex·trous·ly**) *adv.*

D

æ	ɑː	e	ɜː	ə	ɪ	iː	i	ɒ	ɔː	ʌ	ʊ	u	uː
cat	father	ten	bird	about	sit	see	many	got	saw	cup	put	actual	too
								(BrE)					

dex·trose /ˈdekstrəʊz; -əʊs; *AmE* -oʊz; -oʊs/ *noun* [U] (*chemistry*) a form of GLUCOSE (= a type of natural sugar)

DfEE /ˌdi: ef i: ˈi:/ *abbr.* Department for Education and Employment (the government department in Britain that is responsible for education and employment policy)

dhow /daʊ/ *noun* an Arab ship with one large sail in the shape of a triangle

di- /daɪ/ *combining form* (*chemistry*) (in nouns that are names of chemical compounds) containing two atoms or groups of the type mentioned: *carbon dioxide*

dia·betes /ˌdaɪəˈbiːtiːz/ *noun* [U] a medical condition, caused by a lack of INSULIN, which makes the patient produce a lot of URINE and feel very thirsty

dia·bet·ic /ˌdaɪəˈbetɪk/ *adj., noun*
■ *adj.* **1** having or connected with diabetes: *She's diabetic.* ◊ *a diabetic patient* ◊ *diabetic complications* **2** suitable for or used by sb who has diabetes: *a diabetic diet*
■ *noun* a person who suffers from DIABETES

dia·bol·ical /ˌdaɪəˈbɒlɪkl; *AmE* -ˈbɑːl-/ *adj.* **1** (*informal, especially BrE*) extremely bad or annoying: *The traffic was diabolical.* **2** (*also less frequent* **dia·bol·ic** /ˌdaɪəˈbɒlɪk; *AmE* -ˈbɑːl-/) evil and wicked; like a devil ▶ **dia·bol·ic·al·ly** /-kli/ *adv.*

dia·crit·ic /ˌdaɪəˈkrɪtɪk/ *noun* (*linguistics*) a mark such as an ACCENT, placed over, under or through a letter in some languages, to show that the letter should be pronounced differently from the same letter without a mark ▶ **dia·crit·ic·al** /-ˈkrɪtɪkl/ *adj.*: *diacritical marks*

dia·dem /ˈdaɪədem/ *noun* a CROWN, worn especially as a sign of royal power

diag·nose /ˈdaɪəgnəʊz; -ˈnəʊz; *AmE* ˌdaɪəgˈnoʊs/ *verb* ~ **sb (as/with) (sth)** | ~ **sth (as sth)** to say exactly what an illness or the cause of a problem is: [VN] *The test is used to diagnose a variety of diseases.* ◊ *The illness was diagnosed as cancer.* ◊ *He has recently been diagnosed with angina.* ◊ [VN-N] *He was diagnosed (as) a diabetic when he was 64.* [also V, VN-ADJ]

diag·no·sis /ˌdaɪəgˈnəʊsɪs; *AmE* -ˈnoʊ-/ *noun* [C, U] (*pl.* **diag·noses** /-siːz/) ~ **(of sth)** the act of discovering or identifying the exact cause of an illness or a problem: *diagnosis of lung cancer* ◊ *They are waiting for the doctor's diagnosis.* ◊ *An accurate diagnosis was made after a series of tests.*

diag·nos·tic /ˌdaɪəgˈnɒstɪk; *AmE* -ˈnɑːs-/ *adj., noun*
■ *adj.* [usually before noun] (*technical*) connected with identifying sth, especially an illness: *to carry out diagnostic assessments/tests* ◊ *specific conditions which are diagnostic of Aids*
■ *noun* (*computing*) **1** (also ˌdiagˈnostic program) a program used for identifying a computer fault **2** a message on a computer screen giving information about a fault

di·ag·onal /daɪˈægənl/ *adj., noun*
■ *adj.* (of a straight line) at an angle; joining two opposite sides of sth at an angle: *diagonal stripes* ▶ **di·ag·onal·ly** /-nəli/ *adv.*: *Walk diagonally across the field to the far corner and then turn left.*
■ *noun* a straight line that joins two opposite sides of sth at an angle; a straight line that is at an angle

dia·gram /ˈdaɪəgræm/ *noun* a simple drawing using lines to explain where sth is, how sth works, etc: *a diagram of the wiring system* ◊ *The results are shown in diagram 2.* ▶ **dia·gram·mat·ic** /ˌdaɪəgrəˈmætɪk/ *adj.* **dia·gram·mat·ic·al·ly** /-kli/ *adv.*

dial /ˈdaɪəl/ *noun, verb*
■ *noun* **1** the face of a clock or watch, or a similar control on a machine, piece of equipment or vehicle that shows a measurement of time, amount, speed, temperature, etc: *an alarm clock with a luminous dial* ◊ *Check the tyre pressure on the dial.*—see also SUNDIAL **2** the round control on a radio, cooker/stove, etc. that you turn in order to adjust sth, for example to choose a particular station or to choose a particular temperature **3** the round part on some older telephones, with holes for the fingers, that you move around to call a particular number

■ *verb* (**-ll-**, *AmE* **-l-**) to use a telephone by turning the dial or pushing buttons to call a number: [VN] *He dialled the number and waited.* ◊ *Dial 0033 for France.* [also V]

dia·lect /ˈdaɪəlekt/ *noun* [C, U] the form of a language that is spoken in one area with grammar, words and pronunciation that may be different from other forms of the same language: *the Yorkshire dialect*—compare ACCENT, IDIOLECT ▶ **dia·lect·al** /ˌdaɪəˈlektl/ *adj.*

dia·lect·ic /ˌdaɪəˈlektɪk/ *noun* [sing.] (also *less frequent* **dia·lect·ics** [U]) **1** (*philosophy*) a method of discovering the truth of ideas by discussion and logical argument and by considering ideas that are opposed to each other **2** (*formal*) the way in which two aspects of a situation affect each other ▶ **dia·lect·ic·al** /-kl/ *adj.*

'**dialling code** (also **code**) *noun* (*BrE*) the numbers that are used for a particular town, area or country, in front of an individual telephone number: *international dialling codes*—compare AREA CODE

'**dialling tone** (*BrE*) (*AmE* '**dial tone**) *noun* the sound that you hear when you pick up a telephone that means you can make a call

dia·logue (*AmE* also **dia·log**) /ˈdaɪəlɒg; *AmE* -lɔːg; -lɑːg/ *noun* [C, U] **1** conversations in a book, play, or film/movie: *The novel has long descriptions and not much dialogue.* ◊ *dialogues for language learners* **2** a formal discussion between two groups or countries, especially when they are trying to solve a problem, end a dispute, etc: *The President told waiting reporters there had been a constructive dialogue.*—compare MONOLOGUE

'**dialogue box** (*BrE*) (also '**dialog box** *AmE, BrE*) *noun* a box that appears on a computer screen asking the user to choose what they want to do next—picture on page 251

dia·ly·sis /ˌdaɪˈæləsɪs/ *noun* [U] (*technical*) a process for separating substances from a liquid, especially for taking waste substances out of the blood of people with damaged KIDNEYS: *kidney/renal dialysis* ◊ *a dialysis machine*

dia·manté /ˌdiːəˈmɒnteɪ; *AmE* ˌdiːəmɑːnˈteɪ/ *adj.* decorated with glass that is cut to look like diamonds: *diamanté earrings*

diam·eter /daɪˈæmɪtə(r)/ *noun* **1** a straight line going from one side of a circle or any other round object to the other side, passing through the centre—compare RADIUS: *the diameter of a tree trunk* ◊ *The dome is 42.3 metres in diameter.*—picture at CIRCLE **2** (*technical*) a measurement of the power of an instrument to MAGNIFY sth: *a lens magnifying 300 diameters* (= making sth look 300 times larger than it really is).

dia·met·ric·al·ly /ˌdaɪəˈmetrɪkli/ *adv.* ~ **opposed/opposite** completely different: *We hold diametrically opposed views.*

dia·mond /ˈdaɪəmənd/ *noun* **1** [U, C] a clear colourless precious stone of pure CARBON, the hardest substance known. Diamonds are used in jewellery and also in industry, especially for cutting glass: *a ring with a diamond in it* ◊ *a diamond ring/necklace* ◊ *She was wearing her diamonds* (= jewellery with diamonds in it). ◊ *The lights shone like diamonds.*—see also ROUGH DIAMOND **2** [C] a shape with four straight sides of equal length and with angles that are not RIGHT ANGLES **3** (**diamonds**) [pl., U] one of the four SUITS (= sets) in a pack/deck of cards. The cards are marked with red diamond shapes: *ten of diamonds*—picture on page A8 **4** [C] a card of this SUIT: *You must play a diamond if you have one.* **5** [C] (in baseball) the space inside the lines that connect the four BASES; also used to mean the whole baseball field

ˌ**dia·mond in the 'rough** *noun* (*AmE*) = ROUGH DIAMOND

ˌ**diamond 'jubilee** *noun* [usually sing.] the 60th anniversary of an important event, especially of sb becoming king/queen; a celebration of this event—compare GOLDEN JUBILEE, SILVER JUBILEE

ˌ**diamond 'wedding** (*BrE*) (*AmE* ˌ**diamond anni'versary**) (also ˌ**diamond 'wedding anniversary** *AmE, BrE*) *noun* the 60th anniversary of a wedding—compare GOLDEN WEDDING, RUBY WEDDING, SILVER WEDDING

di·aper /ˈdaɪəpə(r); *AmE* ˈdaɪpər/ *noun* (*AmE*) = NAPPY: *a diaper rash*

aɪ	aʊ	eɪ	əʊ	oʊ	ɔɪ	ɪə	eə	ʊə	j	w
my	now	say	go (BrE)	go (AmE)	boy	near	hair	pure	yes	wet

di·aph·an·ous /daɪˈæfənəs/ *adj.* (*written*) (of cloth or fabric) so light, delicate and fine that you can almost see through it

dia·phragm /ˈdaɪəfræm/ *noun* **1** (*anatomy*) the layer of muscle between the lungs and the stomach, used especially to control breathing **2** (*BrE also* **cap**) a rubber or plastic device that a woman places inside her VAGINA before having sex to prevent SPERM from entering the WOMB and making her pregnant **3** any thin piece of material used to separate the parts of a machine, etc. **4** (*technical*) a thin disc used to turn electronic signals into sound and sound into electronic signals in telephones, LOUDSPEAKERS, etc.

diar·ist /ˈdaɪərɪst/ *noun* a person who writes a diary, especially one that is later published: *Samuel Pepys, the famous 17th century diarist*

diar·rhoea (*BrE*) (*AmE* **diar·rhea**) /ˌdaɪəˈrɪə; *AmE* -ˈriːə/ (*also informal* **the runs**) *noun* [U] an illness in which waste matter is emptied from the bowels much more frequently than normal, and in liquid form: *Symptoms include diarrhoea and vomiting.*

diary /ˈdaɪəri/ *noun* (*pl.* **-ies**) **1** (*BrE*) (*AmE* **date·book**) a book with spaces for each day of the year in which you can write down things you have to do in the future: *a desk diary* ◇ *I'll make a note of our next meeting in my diary.* **2** a book in which you can write down the experiences you have each day, your private thoughts, etc: *Do you keep a diary* (= write one regularly)? ◇ *The writer's letters and diaries are being published next year.*—compare JOURNAL ⇨ note at AGENDA

dias·pora /daɪˈæspərə/ *noun* [sing.] (*formal*) **1** (**the diaspora**) the movement of the Jewish people away from their own country to live and work in other countries **2** the movement of people from any nation or group away from their own country

dia·ton·ic /ˌdaɪəˈtɒnɪk; *AmE* -ˈtɑːn-/ *adj.* (*music*) using only the notes of the appropriate MAJOR or MINOR scale—compare CHROMATIC

dia·tribe /ˈdaɪətraɪb/ *noun* ~ (**against sb/sth**) (*formal*) a long and angry speech or piece of writing attacking and criticizing sb/sth: *He launched a bitter diatribe against the younger generation.*

dibs /dɪbz/ ᴵᴰᴹ **dibs on …** (*AmE*) = BAGS (I) … at BAG *v.*

dice /daɪs/ *noun, verb*

■ *noun* (*pl.* **dice**) **1** (also **die** especially in *AmE*) [C] a small CUBE of wood, plastic, etc., with a different number of spots on each of its sides, used in games of chance: *a pair of dice* ◇ *to roll / throw / shake the dice* **2** [U] a game played with dice: *We played dice all night.*—picture on page A8 ᴵᴰᴹ **no ˈdice** (*spoken, especially AmE*) used to show that you refuse to do sth or that sth cannot be done: *'Did you get that job?' 'No dice.'*—more at LOAD *v.*

■ *verb* [VN] to cut meat, vegetables, etc. into small square pieces: *diced carrots* ᴵᴰᴹ **dice with death** (*informal*) to risk your life by doing sth that you know is dangerous

dicey /ˈdaɪsi/ *adj.* (*BrE, informal*) uncertain and dangerous SYN RISKY: *The fog made driving pretty dicey.*

di·chot·omy /daɪˈkɒtəmi; *AmE* -ˈkɑːt-/ *noun* [usually sing.] (*pl.* **-ies**) ~ (**between A and B**) (*formal*) the separation that exists between two groups or things that are completely opposite to and different from each other

dick /dɪk/ *noun* (⚠, *slang*) **1** a man's PENIS **2** = DICKHEAD—see also CLEVER DICK

dick·ens /ˈdɪkɪnz/ *noun* (**the dickens**) (*old-fashioned, informal*) **1** used in questions instead of 'devil' to show that you are annoyed or surprised: *Where the dickens did he go?* **2** (*AmE*) used when you are saying how attractive, etc. sb is: *cute as the dickens*

Dick·ens·ian /dɪˈkenziən/ *adj.* connected with or typical of the novels of Charles Dickens, which often describe social problems and bad social conditions: *a Dickensian slum*

dicker /ˈdɪkə(r)/ *verb* [V] ~ (**with sb**) (**over sth**) (*especially AmE*) to argue about or discuss sth with sb, especially in order to agree on a price SYN BARGAIN

dick·head /ˈdɪkhed/ (also **dick**) *noun* (⚠, *slang*) a very

rude way of referring to sb, especially a man, that you think is stupid SYN IDIOT

dicky /ˈdɪki/ *adj.* (*old-fashioned, BrE, informal*) not healthy; not working correctly: *a dicky heart*

ˈdicky bird *noun* (*BrE*) (used by or when speaking to young children) a bird ᴵᴰᴹ **not say, hear, etc. a dicky bird** (*BrE, informal*) to say, hear, etc. nothing: *He won't say a dicky bird but we think he knows who did it.*

Dicta·phone™ /ˈdɪktəfəʊn; *AmE* -foʊn/ *noun* a small machine used to record on tape people speaking, so that their words can be played back later and written down

dic·tate *verb, noun*

■ *verb* /dɪkˈteɪt; *AmE* ˈdɪkteɪt/ **1** ~ (**sth**) (**to sb**) to say words aloud for sb else to write down: [VN] *He dictated a letter to his secretary.* [also V] **2** ~ (**sth**) (**to sb**) to tell sb what to do, especially in an annoying way: [VN] *They are in no position to dictate terms* (= tell other people what to do). ◇ [V wh-] *What right do they have to dictate how we live our lives?* [also V that] **3** to control or influence how sth happens: [VN] *When we take our vacations is very much dictated by Greg's work schedule.* ◇ [V wh-] *It's generally your job that dictates where you live now.* [also V, V that] ᴾᴴᴿⱽ **dicˈtate to sb** [often passive] to give orders to sb, often in a rude or aggressive way: *She refused to be dictated to by anyone.*

■ *noun* /ˈdɪkteɪt/ [usually pl.] (*formal*) an order, a rule or a command that you must obey: *to follow the dictates of fashion*

dic·ta·tion /dɪkˈteɪʃn/ *noun* **1** [U] the act of speaking or reading aloud so that sb can write down the words **2** [C, U] a test in which students write down what is being read aloud to them, especially in language lessons

dic·ta·tor /dɪkˈteɪtə(r); *AmE* ˈdɪkteɪtər/ *noun* (*disapproving*) **1** a ruler who has complete power over a country, especially one who has gained it using military force **2** a person who behaves as if they have complete power over other people, and tells them what to do

dic·ta·tor·ial /ˌdɪktəˈtɔːrial/ *adj.* (*disapproving*) **1** connected with or controlled by a dictator: *a dictatorial ruler* ◇ *a dictatorial regime* **2** using power in an unreasonable way by telling people what to do and not listening to their views or wishes: *dictatorial behaviour* ▶ **dic·ta·tori·al·ly** /-əli/ *adv.*

dic·ta·tor·ship /ˌdɪkˈteɪtəʃɪp; *AmE* -tərʃ-/ *noun* **1** [C, U] government by a dictator **2** [C] a country that is ruled by a dictator

dic·tion /ˈdɪkʃn/ *noun* [U] **1** the way that sb pronounces words: *clear diction* **2** (*technical*) the choice and use of words in literature

dic·tion·ary /ˈdɪkʃənri; *AmE* -neri/ *noun* (*pl.* **-ies**) **1** a book that gives a list of the words of a language in alphabetical order and explains what they mean, or gives a word for them in a foreign language: *a Spanish-English dictionary* **2** a book that explains the words that are used in a particular subject: *a dictionary of mathematics* **3** a list of words in electronic form, for example stored in a computer's SPELLCHECKER

dic·tum /ˈdɪktəm/ *noun* (*pl.* **dicta** /-tə/ or **dic·tums**) (*formal*) a statement that expresses sth that people believe is always true or should be followed

did *pt* of DO

di·dac·tic /daɪˈdæktɪk/ *adj.* (*formal*) **1** designed to teach people sth, especially a moral lesson: *didactic art / poetry* **2** (usually *disapproving*) telling people things rather than letting them find out for themselves ▶ **di·dac·tic·al·ly** /-kli/ *adv.*

did·dle /ˈdɪdl/ *verb* [VN] ~ **sb** (**out of sth**) (*BrE, informal*) to get money or some advantage from sb by cheating them

diddly /ˈdɪdli/ (also **diddly·squat** /ˌdɪdliˈskwɒt; *AmE* -ˈskwɑːt/) *noun* (*AmE, informal*) (used in negative sentences) not anything; nothing: *She doesn't know diddly about it.*

didn't /ˈdɪdnt/ *short form* did not

die /daɪ/ *verb, noun*

■ *verb* (**dies, dying, died, died**) **1** ~ (**of / from sth**) | ~ (**for sth**) to stop living: [V] *to die of / from cancer* ◇ *Her husband*

D

died suddenly last week. ◊ He died for his beliefs. ◊ That plant's died. ◊ I'll never forget it **to my dying day** (= until I die). ◊ (spoken) **I nearly died** when I saw him there (= it was very embarrassing). ◊ [VN] to die a violent/painful/natural death ◊ [V-ADJ] She died young. ◊ At least they died happy. ◊ [V-N] He died a poor man. **2** [V] to stop existing; to disappear: The old customs are dying. ◊ His secret died with him (= he never told anyone). ◊ The words died on my lips (= I stopped speaking). **3** [V] (of a machine) to stop working: The engine spluttered and died. ◊ My car just died on me. **IDM** be **'dying for sth/to do sth** (informal) to want sth or want to do sth very much: I'm dying for a glass of water. ◊ I'm dying to know what happened. **die a/the 'death** (BrE, informal) to fail completely: The play got terrible reviews and quickly died a death. **die in your 'bed** to die of old age or illness **die 'laughing** to find sth extremely funny: I nearly died laughing when she said that. **old ˌhabits, ˌtraditions, etc. die 'hard** used to say that things change very slowly **to 'die for** (informal) if you think sth is **to die for**, you really want it, and would do anything to get it: She was wearing a dress to die for.—more at CROSS v., FLY n., SAY v. **PHR V** ˌdie a'way to become gradually weaker or fainter and finally disappear: The sound of their laughter died away. ˌdie 'back if a plant **dies back**, it loses its leaves but remains alive ˌdie 'down to become gradually less strong, loud, noticeable, etc: The flames finally died down. ◊ When the applause had died down, she began her speech. ˌdie 'off to die one after the other until there are none left ˌdie 'out to stop existing: This species has nearly died out because its habitat is being destroyed.

■ noun **1** a block of metal with a special shape or with a pattern cut into it, that is used for shaping other pieces of metal such as coins, or for making patterns on paper or leather **2** (especially AmE) = DICE **IDM** **the die is cast** (saying) used to say that an event has happened or a decision has been made that cannot be changed

die·hard /'daɪhɑːd; AmE -hɑːrd/ adj. strongly opposing change and new ideas: diehard supporters of the exiled king ▶ **die·hard** noun: A few diehards are trying to stop the reforms.

diesel /'diːzl/ noun **1** (also **'diesel fuel, 'diesel oil**) [U] a type of heavy oil used as a fuel instead of petrol/gas: a diesel engine (= one that burns diesel) ◊ diesel cars/locomotives/trains—compare PETROL **2** [C] a vehicle that uses diesel fuel: Our new car is a diesel.

diet /'daɪət/ noun, verb
■ noun **1** [C, U] the food that you eat and drink regularly: to have a healthy, balanced diet ◊ the Japanese diet of rice, vegetables and fish ◊ to receive advice on diet **2** [C] a limited variety or amount of food that you eat for medical reasons or because you want to lose weight; a time when you only eat this limited variety or amount: a low-fat, salt-free diet ◊ diet drinks (= with fewer calories than normal) ◊ I decided to **go on a diet** (= to lose weight) before my holiday. **3** [sing.] **a ~ of sth** (disapproving) a large amount of a restricted range of activities: Children today are brought up on a diet of television cartoons and soap operas. ▶ **diet·ary** /'daɪətəri; AmE -teri/ adj. [usually before noun]: dietary advice/changes/habits ◊ dietary fibre
■ verb [V] to eat less food or only food of a particular type in order to lose weight: She's always dieting but she never seems to lose any weight.

diet·er /'daɪətə(r)/ noun a person who is trying to lose weight on a DIET

diet·et·ics /ˌdaɪə'tetɪks/ noun [U] the scientific study of DIET and healthy eating ▶ **diet·et·ic** adj.: dietetic advice

diet·ician (also **diet·itian**) /ˌdaɪə'tɪʃn/ noun a person whose job is to advise people on what kind of food they should eat to keep healthy

dif·fer /'dɪfə(r)/ verb [V] **1 A and B ~ (from each other)** | **A ~s from B** to be different from sb/sth: They hold differing views. ◊ French differs from English in this respect. ◊ French and English differ in this respect. ◊ Ideas on child-care may differ considerably between the parents. **2 ~ (with sb) (about/on/over sth)** to disagree with sb: I have

to differ with you on that. ◊ Medical opinion differs as to how to treat the disease. **IDM** see AGREE, BEG

dif·fer·ence /'dɪfrəns/ noun **1** [C, U] **~ (between A and B)** | **~ (in sth)** the way in which two people or things are not like each other; the way in which sb/sth has changed: There are no significant differences between the education systems of the two countries. ◊ He was studying the complex similarities and differences between humans and animals. ◊ There's no difference in the results. ◊ She noticed a marked difference in the children on her second visit. ◊ I can never **tell the difference** (= distinguish) between the twins ◊ There's **a world of difference** between liking someone and loving them. ◊ **What a difference!** You look great with your hair like that. **OPP** SIMILARITY **2** [sing., U] **~ (in sth) (between A and B)** the amount that sth is greater or smaller than sth else: There's not much difference in price between the two computers. ◊ There's an age difference of six years between the boys (= one is six years older than the other). ◊ I'll lend you £500 and you'll have to find the difference (= the rest of the money that you need). ◊ We measured the difference in temperature. **3** [C] a disagreement between people: We have our differences, but she's still my sister. ◊ Why don't you settle your differences and be friends again? ◊ There was **a difference of opinion** over who had won. **IDM** make a, no, some, etc. **difference (to/in sb/sth)** to have an effect/no effect on sb/sth: The rain didn't make much difference to the game. ◊ Your age shouldn't make any difference to whether you get the job or not. ◊ Changing schools made a big difference to my life. ◊ What difference will it make if he knows or not? ◊ I don't think it makes **a lot of difference** what colour it is (= it is not important). ◊ 'Shall we go on Friday or Saturday?' 'It makes no difference (to me).' **make all the 'difference (to sb/sth)** to have an important effect on sb/sth; to make sb feel better: A few kind words at the right time make all the difference. **same 'difference** (spoken) used to say that you think the differences between two things are not important: 'That's not a xylophone, it's a glockenspiel.' 'Same difference.' **with a 'difference** (informal) (after nouns) used to show that sth is interesting or unusual: The traditional backpack with a difference—it's waterproof.—more at BURY, SINK v., SPLIT v., WORLD

dif·fer·ent /'dɪfrənt/ adj. **1 ~ (from/to/than sb/sth)** not the same as sb/sth; not like sb/sth else: American English is significantly different from British English. ◊ (BrE) It's very different to what I'm used to. ◊ (AmE) He saw he was no different than anybody else. ◊ It's different now than it was a year ago. ◊ People often give very different accounts of the same event. ◊ My son's terribly untidy; my daughter's **no different**. **OPP** SIMILAR **2** [only before noun] separate and individual: She offered us five different kinds of cake. ◊ The programme was about customs in different parts of the country. ◊ They are sold in many different colours. ◊ I looked it up in three different dictionaries. **3** [not usually before noun] (informal) unusual; not like other people or things: 'Did you enjoy the play?' 'Well, it was certainly different!' ▶ **dif·fer·ent·ly** adv.: Boys and girls may behave differently. ◊ The male bird has a differently shaped head. **IDM** a **different kettle of fish** (informal) a completely different situation or person from the one previously mentioned—more at COMPLEXION, KNOW v., MATTER n., SING v., TELL

BRITISH / AMERICAN
different from / to / than

Different from is the most common structure in both BrE and AmE. **Different to** is also used in BrE: Paul's very different from/to his brother ◊ This visit is very different from/to last time.

In AmE people also say **different than**: Your trains are different than ours. ◊ You look different than before.

Before a clause you can also use **different from** (and **different than** in AmE): She looked different from what I'd expected. ◊ She looked different than (what) I'd expected.

s	t	v	z	ʃ	ʒ	tʃ	dʒ	θ	ð	ŋ
see	tea	van	zoo	shoe	vision	chain	jam	thin	this	sing

dif·fer·en·tial /ˌdɪfəˈrenʃl/ *noun, adj.*

- *noun* **1** ~ **(between A and B)** a difference in the amount, value or size of sth, especially the difference in rates of pay for people doing different work in the same industry or profession: *wage/pay/income differentials* **2** (also ˌ**differential** ˈ**gear**) a GEAR that makes it possible for a vehicle's back wheels to turn at different speeds when going around corners
- *adj.* [only before noun] (*formal*) showing or depending on a difference; not equal: *the differential treatment of prisoners based on sex and social class* ◊ *differential rates of pay*

dif·fer·en·ti·ate /ˌdɪfəˈrenʃieɪt/ *verb* **1** ~ **(between A and B)** / ~ A **(from B)** to recognize or show that two things are not the same SYN DISTINGUISH: [V] *It's difficult to differentiate between the two varieties.* ◊ [VN] *I can't differentiate one variety from another.* **2** [VN] ~ **sth (from sth)** to be the particular thing that shows that things or people are not the same SYN DISTINGUISH: *The male's yellow beak differentiates it from the female.* **3** [V] ~ **between A and B** to treat people or things in a different way, especially in an unfair way SYN DISCRIMINATE ▶ **dif·fer·en·ti·ation** /ˌdɪfəˌrenʃiˈeɪʃn/ *noun* [U]

dif·fi·cult /ˈdɪfɪkəlt/ *adj.* **1** ~ **(for sb) (to do sth)** not easy; needing effort or skill to do or to understand: *a difficult problem/task/exam* ◊ *It's difficult for them to get here much before seven.* ◊ *It's really difficult to read your writing.* ◊ *Your writing is really difficult to read.* ◊ *She finds it very difficult to get up early.* **2** full of problems; causing a lot of trouble: *to be in a difficult position/situation* ◊ *My boss is making life very difficult for me.* ◊ *13 is a difficult age.* **3** (of people) not easy to please; not helpful: *a difficult child/customer/boss* ◊ *Don't pay any attention to her—she's just being difficult.* IDM see JOB, LIFE

dif·fi·culty /ˈdɪfɪkəlti/ *noun* (*pl.* **-ies**) **1** [C, usually pl., U] a problem; a thing or situation that causes problems: *the difficulties of English syntax* ◊ *children with severe learning difficulties* ◊ *We've run into difficulties/difficulty with the new project.* ◊ *He got into difficulties while swimming and had to be rescued.* ◊ *The bank is in difficulty/difficulties.* ◊ *It was a time fraught with difficulties and frustration.* **2** [U] the state or quality of being hard to do or to understand; the effort that sth involves: *I had considerable difficulty (in) persuading her to leave.* ◊ *I had no difficulty (in) making myself understood. The changes were made with surprisingly little difficulty.* ◊ *He spoke slowly and with great difficulty.* ◊ *We found the house without difficulty.* ◊ *They discussed the difficulty of studying abroad.* ◊ *You cannot say 'have difficulty to do sth': I had difficulty to persuade her to leave.* **3** [U] how hard sth is: *varying levels of difficulty* ◊ *questions of increasing difficulty*

dif·fi·dent /ˈdɪfɪdənt/ *adj.* ~ **(about sth)** not having much confidence in yourself; not wanting to talk about yourself SYN SHY: *a diffident manner/smile* ◊ *He was modest and diffident about his own success.* ▶ **dif·fi·dence** /-dəns/ *noun* [U]: *She overcame her natural diffidence and spoke with great frankness.* **dif·fi·dent·ly** *adv.*

dif·fract /dɪˈfrækt/ *verb* [VN] (*physics*) to break up a beam of light into a series of dark and light bands or into the different colours of the SPECTRUM ▶ **dif·frac·tion** /dɪˈfrækʃn/ *noun* [U]

dif·fuse *adj., verb*

- *adj.* /dɪˈfjuːs/ **1** spread over a wide area: *diffuse light* ◊ *a diffuse community* **2** not clear or easy to understand; using a lot of words: *a diffuse style of writing* ▶ **diffuse·ly** *adv.* **dif·fuse·ness** *noun* [U]
- *verb* /dɪˈfjuːz/ **1** (*formal*) to spread or become spread widely in all directions: [VN] *The problem is how to diffuse power without creating anarchy.* ◊ [V] *Technologies diffuse rapidly.* **2** [V, VN] (*technical*) if a gas or liquid **diffuses** or **is diffused** in a substance, it becomes slowly mixed with that substance **3** [VN] (*formal*) to make light shine less brightly by spreading it in many directions: *The moon was fuller than the night before, but the light was diffused by cloud.* ▶ **dif·fu·sion** /dɪˈfjuːʒn/ *noun* [U]

dig /dɪɡ/ *verb, noun*

- *verb* (**dig·ging, dug, dug** /dʌɡ/) **1** ~ **(for sth)** to make a hole in the ground or to move soil from one place to another using your hands, a tool or a machine: [V] *to dig for coal/gold/Roman remains* ◊ *They dug deeper and deeper but still found nothing.* ◊ *I think I'll do some digging in the garden.* ◊ [VN] *to dig a ditch/grave/hole/tunnel* ◊ (*BrE*) *I've been digging the garden.* **2** [VN] to remove sth from the ground with a tool: *I'll dig some potatoes for lunch.* **3** [V] [usually +adv./prep.] to search in sth in order to find an object in sth: *I dug around in my bag for a pen.* **4** [VN] (*old-fashioned, spoken*) (*slang*) to approve of or like sth very much IDM **dig** ˈ**deep (into sth)** **1** to search thoroughly for information: *You'll need to dig deep into the records to find the figures you want.* **2** to try hard to provide the money, equipment, etc. that is needed: *We're asking you to dig deep for the earthquake victims.* **dig your** ˈ**heels/**ˈ**toes in** to refuse to do sth or to change your mind about sth: *They dug in their heels and would not lower the price.* **dig (deep) in/into your pocket(s), savings, etc.** to spend a lot of your own money on sth **dig sb in the** ˈ**ribs** to push your finger or your elbow into sb's side, especially to attract their attention **dig yourself into a** ˈ**hole** to get yourself into a bad situation that it will be very difficult to get out of **dig your own** ˈ**grave | dig a** ˈ**grave for yourself** to do sth that will have very harmful results for you PHRV ˌ**dig** ˈ**in** (*spoken*) **1** used to tell sb to start to eat: *Help yourselves, everybody! Dig in!* **2** to wait, or deal with a difficult situation, with great patience: *There is nothing we can do except dig in and wait.* ˌ**dig sth** ↔ ˈ**in 1** to mix soil with another substance by digging the two substances together: *The manure should be well dug in.* **2** to push sth into sth else: *He dug his fork into the steak.* ˌ**dig yourself** ˈ**in** (of soldiers) to protect yourself against an attack by making a safe place in the ground ˌ**dig** ˈ**into sth 1** (*informal*) to start to eat food with enthusiasm: *She dug into her bowl of pasta.* **2** to push or rub against your body in a painful or uncomfortable way: *His fingers dug painfully into my arm.* **3** to find out information by searching or asking questions: *Will you dig a little into his past and see what you find?* ˌ**dig sth** ˈ**into sth 1** to mix soil with another substance by digging the two substances together **2** to push or press sth into sth else: *She dug her hands deeper into her pockets.* ˌ**dig sb/sth** ↔ ˈ**out (of sth) 1** to remove sb/sth from somewhere by digging the ground around them or it: *More than a dozen people were dug out of the avalanche alive.* **2** to find sth that has been hidden or forgotten for a long time: *I went to the attic and dug out Grandad's medals.* ˌ**dig sth** ↔ ˈ**over** to prepare ground by digging the soil to remove stones, etc. ˌ**dig sth** ↔ ˈ**up 1** to break the ground into small pieces before planting seeds, building sth, etc: *They are digging up the football field to lay a new surface.* **2** to remove sth from the ground by digging SYN UNEARTH: *An old Roman vase was dug up here last month.* **3** to discover information about sb/sth SYN UNEARTH: *Tabloid newspapers love to dig up scandal.*
- *noun*—see also DIGS **1** a small push with your finger or elbow: *She gave him a dig in the ribs.* **2** ~ **(at sb/sth)** a remark that is intended to annoy or upset sb: *He kept making sly little digs at me.* ◊ *to have a dig at sb/sth* **3** an occasion when an organized group of people dig in the ground to discover old buildings or objects, in order to find out more about their history SYN EXCAVATION: *to go on a dig* ◊ *an archaeological dig*

di·gest *verb, noun*

- *verb* /daɪˈdʒest; dɪ-/ **1** when you **digest** food, or it **digests**, it is changed into substances that your body can use: [VN] *Humans cannot digest plants such as grass.* ◊ [V] *You should allow a little time after a meal for the food to digest.* **2** [VN] to think about sth so that you fully understand it: *He paused, waiting for her to digest the information.*
- *noun* /ˈdaɪdʒest/ a short report containing the most important facts of a longer report or piece of writing; a collection of short reports: *a monthly news digest*

di·gest·ible /daɪˈdʒestəbl; dɪ-/ *adj.* easy to digest; pleasant to eat or easy to understand OPP INDIGESTIBLE

di·ges·tion /daɪˈdʒestʃən; dɪ-/ *noun* **1** [U] the process of digesting food—compare INDIGESTION **2** [C, usually sing.] the ability to digest food: *to have a good/poor digestion*

æ	ɑː	e	ɜː	ə	ɪ	iː	i	ɒ	ɔː	ʌ	ʊ	u	uː
cat	father	ten	bird	about	sit	see	many	got	saw	cup	put	actual	too

(BrE)

di·gest·ive /daɪˈdʒestɪv; dɪ-/ *adj.* [only before noun] connected with the digestion of food: *the digestive system / tract ◊ digestive problems*

di'gestive biscuit (also **digestive**) *noun* (*BrE*) a round sweet biscuit made from WHOLEMEAL flour, sometimes covered with chocolate: *a packet of chocolate digestives*

dig·ger /ˈdɪgə(r)/ *noun* **1** a large machine that is used for digging up the ground **2** a person or an animal that digs—see also GOLD-DIGGER

digit /ˈdɪdʒɪt/ *noun* **1** any of the ten numbers from 0 to 9: *The number 57306 contains five digits.* **2** (*anatomy*) a finger, thumb or toe

digit·al /ˈdɪdʒɪtl/ *adj., noun*
■ *adj.* **1** using a system of receiving and sending information as a series of the numbers one and zero, showing that an electronic signal is there or is not there: *a digital camera ◊ digital terrestrial and digital satellite broadcasting* **2** (of clocks, watches, etc.) showing information by using figures, rather than with HANDS that point to numbers: *a digital clock / watch*—compare ANALOGUE ▸ **digit·al·ly** /-təli/: *digitally remastered tapes*
■ *noun* [U] digital television: *How long have you had digital? ◊ With digital you can choose the camera angle you want.*

ˌdigital reˈcording *noun* [C, U] a recording in which sounds or pictures are represented by a series of numbers showing that an electronic signal is there or is not there; the process of making a recording in this way

ˌdigital ˈtelevision *noun* **1** [U] the system of broadcasting television using digital signals **2** [C] a television set that can receive digital signals

digit·ize (*BrE* also **-ise**) /ˈdɪdʒɪtaɪz/ *verb* [VN] to change data into a DIGITAL form that can be easily read and processed by a computer: *a digitized map*

dig·ni·fied /ˈdɪgnɪfaɪd/ *adj.* calm and serious and deserving respect: *a dignified person / manner / voice ◊ Throughout his trial he maintained a dignified silence.* OPP UNDIGNIFIED

dig·ni·fy /ˈdɪgnɪfaɪ/ *verb* (**dig·ni·fies, dig·ni·fy·ing, dig·ni·fied**) [VN] (*formal*) **1** to make sb/sth seem impressive: *The mayor was there to dignify the celebrations.* **2** to make sth appear important when it is not really: *I'm not going to dignify his comments by reacting to them.*

dig·ni·tary /ˈdɪgnɪtəri; AmE -teri/ *noun* (*pl.* **-ies**) a person who has an important official position

dig·nity /ˈdɪgnəti/ *noun* [U] **1** a calm and serious manner that deserves respect: *She accepted the criticism with quiet dignity.* **2** the fact of being given honour and respect by people: *the dignity of work ◊ The terminally ill should be allowed to die with dignity.* **3** a sense of your own importance and value: *It's difficult to preserve your dignity when you have no job and no home.* IDM **beˌneath your ˈdignity** below what you see as your own importance or worth **ˌstand on your ˈdignity** (*formal*) to demand to be treated with the respect that you think that you deserve

di·gress /daɪˈgres/ *verb* [V] (*formal*) to start to talk about sth that is not connected with the main point of what you are saying ▸ **di·gres·sion** /daɪˈgreʃn/ *noun* [C, U]: *After several digressions, he finally got to the point.*

digs /dɪgz/ *noun* [pl.] (*old-fashioned, BrE, informal*) a room or rooms that you rent to live in SYN LODGINGS

dike *noun* = DYKE

dik·tat /ˈdɪktæt/ *noun* [C, U] (*disapproving*) an order given by a government, for example, that people must obey: *an EU diktat from Brussels ◊ government by diktat*

di·lapi·dated /dɪˈlæpɪdeɪtɪd/ *adj.* (of furniture and buildings) old and in very bad condition ▸ **di·lapi·da·tion** /dɪˌlæpɪˈdeɪʃn/ *noun* [U]: *in a state of dilapidation*

di·late /daɪˈleɪt/ *verb* to become or to make sth larger, wider or more open: [V] *Her eyes dilated with fear. ◊* [VN] *dilated pupils / nostrils ◊ Red wine can help to dilate blood vessels.* ▸ **dila·tion** /daɪˈleɪʃn/ *noun* [U, C]

dila·tory /ˈdɪlətəri; AmE -tɔːri/ *adj.* **~ (in doing sth)** (*formal*) not acting quickly enough; causing delay: *The government has been dilatory in dealing with the problem of unemployment.*

dildo /ˈdɪldəʊ; AmE -doʊ/ *noun* (*pl.* **dildos** or **dildoes**) an object shaped like a PENIS that is used for sexual pleasure

di·lemma /dɪˈlemə; daɪ-/ *noun* a situation which makes problems, often one in which you have to make a very difficult choice between things of equal importance: *to face a dilemma ◊ to be in a dilemma* IDM see HORN

dil·et·tante /ˌdɪləˈtænti/ *noun* (*pl.* **dil·et·tanti** /-tiː/ or **dil·et·tan·tes**) (*disapproving*) a person who does or studies sth but is not serious about it and does not have much knowledge ▸ **di·let·tante** *adj.*: *a dilettante artist*

dili·gence /ˈdɪlɪdʒəns/ *noun* [U] (*formal*) careful and thorough work or effort: *She shows great diligence in her schoolwork. ◊ The captain exercised all reasonable diligence to prevent the ship from sinking.*

dili·gent /ˈdɪlɪdʒənt/ *adj.* (*formal*) showing care and effort in your work or duties: *a diligent student / worker ◊ After a diligent search, the police found the missing child.* ▸ **dili·gent·ly** *adv.*

dill /dɪl/ *noun* [U] a plant with yellow flowers whose leaves and seeds have a strong taste and are used in cooking as a herb. Dill is often added to vegetables kept in VINEGAR: *dill pickles*

dilly-dally /ˈdɪli dæli/ *verb* (**dilly-dallies, dilly-dallying, dilly-dallied, dilly-dallied**) [V] (*old-fashioned, informal*) to take too long to do sth, go somewhere or make a decision

di·lute *verb, adj.* /daɪˈluːt; BrE also -ˈljuːt/
■ *verb* [VN] **1 ~ sth (with sth)** to make a liquid weaker by adding water or another liquid to it SYN WATER DOWN: *The paint can be diluted with water to make a lighter shade.* **2** to make sth weaker or less effective SYN WATER DOWN: *Large classes dilute the quality of education that children receive.* ▸ **di·lu·tion** /daɪˈluːʃn; BrE also -ˈljuːʃn/ *noun* [U]: *the dilution of sewage ◊ This is a serious dilution of their election promises.*
■ *adj.* (also **di·luted**) (of a liquid) made weaker by adding water or another substance: *a dilute acid / solution*

dim /dɪm/ *adj., verb*
■ *adj.* (**dim·mer, dim·mest**)
LIGHT | **1** not bright: *the dim glow of the fire in the grate ◊ This light is too dim to read by.*
PLACE | **2** where you cannot see well because there is not much light: *a dim room / street*
OBJECT | **3** that you cannot see well because there is not much light: *the dim outline of a house in the moonlight ◊ I could see a dim shape in the doorway.*
EYES | **4** not able to see well: *His eyesight is getting dim.*
MEMORIES | **5** that you cannot remember or imagine clearly: *dim memories ◊ She had a dim recollection of a visit to a big house. ◊* (*humorous*) *in the **dim and distant** past*
PERSON | **6** (*informal, especially BrE*) not intelligent: *He's very dim.*
SITUATION | **7** not hopeful or good: *Her future career prospects look dim.*
▸ **dim·ness** *noun* [U]: *It took a while for his eyes to adjust to the dimness.*—see also DIMLY
IDM **take a dim view of sb/sth** to disapprove of sb/sth; to not have a good opinion of sb/sth: *She took a dim view of my suggestion.*
■ *verb* (**-mm-**)
LIGHT | **1** if a light **dims** or if you **dim** it, it becomes or you make it less bright: [V] *The lights in the theatre dimmed as the curtain rose.* [also VN]
FEELING / QUALITY | **2** if a feeling or quality **dims**, or if sth **dims** it, it becomes less strong: [V] *Her passion for dancing never dimmed over the years.* [also VN]

dime /daɪm/ *noun* a coin of the US and Canada worth ten cents IDM **a ˌdime a ˈdozen** (*AmE*) = TWO / TEN A PENNY

di·men·sion /daɪˈmenʃn; dɪ-/ *noun* **1** a measurement in space for example, the height, width or length of sth: *We measured the dimensions of the kitchen. ◊ Computer design tools that work in three dimensions.*—see also THE FOURTH DIMENSION **2** [usually pl.] the size and extent of a situation: *a problem of considerable dimensions* **3** an aspect, or way of looking at or thinking about sth: *Her job added*

aɪ	aʊ	eɪ	əʊ	oʊ	ɔɪ	ɪə	eə	ʊə	j	w
my	now	say	go	go	boy	near	hair	pure	yes	wet
			(BrE)	(AmE)						

a new dimension to her life. ◊ *the social dimension of unemployment* **4** (**-dimensional**) (in adjectives) having the number of dimensions mentioned: *a multi-dimensional model*—see also THREE-DIMENSIONAL, TWO-DIMENSIONAL

'dime store *noun* (*old-fashioned, AmE*) = FIVE-AND-DIME

di·min·ish /dɪˈmɪnɪʃ/ *verb* **1** to become or to make sth become smaller, weaker, etc. [SYN] DECREASE: [V] *The world's resources are rapidly diminishing.* ◊ *His influence has diminished with time.* ◊ *Our efforts were producing diminishing returns* (= we achieved less although we spent more time or money). [also VN] **2** [VN] to make sb/ sth seem less important than they really are: *I don't wish to diminish the importance of their contribution.*

di,minished responsi'bility *noun* [U] (*BrE, law*) a state in which a person who is accused of a crime is not considered to be responsible for their actions, because they are mentally ill: *He was found not guilty of murder on the grounds of diminished responsibility.*

di·minu·endo /dɪˌmɪnjuˈendəʊ; *AmE* -doʊ/ *noun* (*pl.* **-os**) [C, U] (*music*) a gradual decrease in how loudly a piece of music is played or sung [OPP] CRESCENDO

dim·in·ution /ˌdɪmɪˈnjuːʃn; *AmE* -ˈnuːʃn/ *noun* ~ (**of/in sth**) (*formal*) **1** [U] the act of reducing sth or of being reduced: *the diminution of political power* **2** [C, usually sing.] a reduction; an amount reduced: *a diminution in population growth*

di·minu·tive /dɪˈmɪnjətɪv/ *adj., noun*
■ *adj.* (*formal*) very small: *She was a diminutive figure beside her husband.*
■ *noun* **1** a word or an ending of a word that shows that sb/sth is small, for example *piglet* (= a young pig), *kitchenette* (= a small kitchen) **2** a short informal form of a word, especially a name: *'Nicky' is a common diminutive of 'Nicholas'*

dimly /ˈdɪmli/ *adv.* not very brightly or clearly: *a dimly lit room* ◊ *I was dimly aware* (= only just aware) *of the sound of a car in the distance.* ◊ *I did remember, but only dimly.*

'dim·mer switch (also **dim·mer**) *noun* **1** a switch that allows you to make an electric light brighter or less bright **2** (*AmE*) = DIP SWITCH

dimple /ˈdɪmpl/ *verb, noun*
■ *verb* [V] to make a hollow place appear on each of your cheeks, especially by smiling
■ *noun* **1** a small hollow place in the skin, especially in the cheek or chin: *She had a dimple which appeared when she smiled.* **2** any small hollow place in a surface: *a pane of glass with a dimple pattern* ▶ **dimpled** /ˈdɪmpld/: *a dimpled chin*

dimple

dim-'witted *adj.* (*informal*) stupid: *a dim-witted child* ▶ **dim·wit** *noun*

din /dɪn/ *noun* [sing.] a loud, unpleasant noise that lasts for a long time: *The children were making an awful din.*

dinar /ˈdiːnɑː(r)/ *noun* a unit of money in Yugoslavia, Bosnia and various countries in the Middle East and N Africa

dine /daɪn/ *verb* [V] (*formal*) to eat dinner: *We dined with my parents at a restaurant in town.* [PHRV] **'dine on sth** to have a particular type of food for dinner **,dine 'out** to eat dinner in a restaurant or sb else's home **,dine 'out on sth** (*informal*) to tell other people about sth that has happened to you, in order to make them interested in you [IDM] see WINE *v.*

diner /ˈdaɪnə(r)/ *noun* **1** a person eating a meal, especially in a restaurant: *a restaurant capable of seating 100 diners* **2** (*especially AmE*) a small, usually cheap, restaurant: *a roadside diner*

din·ette /daɪˈnet/ *noun* (*especially AmE*) a small room or part of a room for eating meals

ding·bat /ˈdɪŋbæt/ *noun* (*AmE, slang*) a stupid person

ding-dong /ˈdɪŋ dɒŋ; *AmE* dɑːŋ; dɔːŋ/ *noun* **1** [U] used to represent the sound made by a bell: *I rang the doorbell.*

Ding-dong! No answer. **2** (*BrE, informal*) an argument or fight: *The two men were having a real ding-dong on the doorstep.*

dinghy /ˈdɪŋi; ˈdɪŋgi/ *noun* (*pl.* **-ies**) **1** a small open boat that you sail or row: *a sailing dinghy*—picture at BOAT **2** = RUBBER DINGHY—compare YACHT

dingo /ˈdɪŋgəʊ; *AmE* -goʊ/ *noun* (*pl.* **-oes**) a wild Australian dog

dingy /ˈdɪndʒi/ *adj.* (**din·gier, din·gi·est**) dark and dirty: *a dingy room/hotel* ◊ *dingy curtains/clothes* ▶ **din·gi·ness** *noun* [U]

'dining car (*BrE* also **'restaurant car**) *noun* a railway carriage in which meals are served

'dining room *noun* a room used mainly for eating meals in

'dining table *noun* a table for having meals on—compare DINNER TABLE

dinky /ˈdɪŋki/ *adj.* (*informal*) **1** (*BrE, approving*) small and neat in an attractive way: *What a dinky little hat!* **2** (*AmE, disapproving*) too small: *I grew up in a dinky little town that didn't even have a movie theater.*

din·ner /ˈdɪnə(r)/ *noun* **1** [U, C] the main meal of the day, eaten either in the middle of the day or in the evening: *It's time for dinner.* ◊ *Have you had dinner yet?* ◊ *What time do you serve dinner?* ◊ *Let's invite them to dinner tomorrow.* ◊ *What shall we have for dinner tonight?* ◊ *It's your turn to cook dinner.* ◊ *She didn't eat much dinner.* ◊ *I never eat a big dinner.* ◊ *Christmas dinner* ◊ *a three-course dinner* ◊ *I'd like to take you out to dinner tonight.* ◊ (*BrE*) *school dinners* (= meals provided at school in the middle of the day) ⇨ note at MEAL **2** [C] a large formal social gathering at which dinner is eaten: *The club's annual dinner will be held on 3 June.*—see also DINNER PARTY [IDM] see DOG *n.*

'dinner dance *noun* a social event in the evening that includes a formal meal and dancing

'dinner jacket (*BrE*) *noun* a black or white jacket worn with a BOW TIE at formal occasions in the evening—compare TAILS *n.* (6), TUXEDO

'dinner lady *noun* (in Britain) a woman whose job is to serve meals to children in schools

'dinner party *noun* a social event at which a small group of people eat dinner at sb's house

'dinner service *noun* a set of matching plates, dishes, etc. for serving a meal

'dinner suit (*BrE*) (*AmE* **tux·edo**) *noun* a DINNER JACKET and trousers/pants, worn with a BOW TIE at formal occasions in the evening

'dinner table *noun* (often **the dinner table**) [usually sing.] the table at which people are eating dinner; an occasion when people are eating together: *conversation at the dinner table*—compare DINING TABLE

'dinner theater *noun* (*AmE*) a restaurant where you see a play after your meal

'dinner time *noun* the time at which dinner is normally eaten

din·ner·ware /ˈdɪnəweə(r)/; *AmE* ˈdɪnərwer/ *noun* [U] (*AmE*) plates, dishes, etc. used for serving a meal

dino·saur /ˈdaɪnəsɔː(r)/ *noun* **1** an animal that lived millions of years ago but is now EXTINCT (= it no longer exists). There were many types of dinosaur, some of which were very large. **2** (*disapproving*) a person or thing that is old-fashioned and cannot change in the changing conditions of modern life

dint /dɪnt/ *noun* [IDM] **by dint of sth/of doing sth** (*formal*) by means of sth: *He succeeded by dint of hard work.*

dio·cese /ˈdaɪəsɪs/ *noun* (in the Christian Church) a district for which a BISHOP is responsible ▶ **dio·cesan** /daɪˈɒsɪsn; *AmE* -ˈɑːs-/ *adj.*

diode /ˈdaɪəʊd; *AmE* -oʊd/ *noun* (*technical*) an electronic device in which the electric current passes in one direction only, for example a SILICON CHIP

di·ox·ide /daɪˈɒksaɪd; *AmE* -ˈɑːks-/ *noun* [U, C] (*chemistry*) a compound formed by combining two atoms of OXYGEN and one atom of another chemical element—see also CARBON DIOXIDE

b	d	f	g	h	k	l	m	n	p	r
bad	did	fall	get	hat	cat	leg	man	now	pen	red

D

di·oxin /daɪˈɒksɪn; *AmE* -ˈɑːks-/ *noun* a chemical used in industry and farming. Most dioxins are poisonous.

dip /dɪp/ *verb, noun*

■ *verb* (**-pp-**) **1** [VN] ~ **sth (into sth)** | ~ **sth (in)** to put sth quickly into a liquid and take it out again: *He dipped the brush into the thick white paint.* ◊ *Dip your hand in to see how hot the water is.* ◊ *The fruit had been dipped in chocolate.* **2** [usually +*adv. / prep.*] to go downwards or to a lower level; to make sth do this: [V] *The sun dipped below the horizon.* ◊ *Sales for this quarter have dipped from 38.7 million to 33 million.* ◊ *The road dipped suddenly as we approached the town.* ◊ [VN] *The plane dipped its wings.* **3** [VN] (*BrE*) if you dip your HEADLIGHTS when driving a car at night, you make the beam from them point down so that other drivers do not have the light in their eyes **4** [VN] when farmers dip animals, especially sheep, they put them in a bath of a liquid containing chemicals in order to kill insects, etc. **IDM** **dip into your ˈpocket** (*informal*) to spend some of your own money on sth **dip a ˈtoe in/into sth** | **dip a ˈtoe in/into the water** (*informal*) to start doing sth very carefully to see if it will be successful or not **PHRV** **ˌdip ˈinto sth 1** to put your hand into a container to take sth out: *She dipped into her purse and took out some coins.* **2** to read or watch only parts of sth: *I have only had time to dip into the report.* **3** to take an amount from money that you have saved: *We took out a loan for the car because we didn't want to dip into our savings.*

■ *noun* **1** [C] (*informal*) a quick swim: *Let's go for a dip before breakfast.* **2** [C] a decrease in the amount or success of sth, usually for only a short period: *a sharp dip in earnings / profits* **3** [C] a place where a surface suddenly drops to a lower level and then rises again: *a dip in the road* ◊ *Puddles had formed in the dips.* **4** [C, U] a thick mixture into which biscuits and pieces of raw vegetables are dipped before being eaten **5** [U, C] a liquid containing a chemical into which sheep and other animals can be dipped in order to kill insects on them **6** [sing.] ~ **into sth** a quick look at sth: *A brief dip into history serves to confirm this view.* **7** [C, usually sing.] a quick movement of sth down and up: *He gave a dip of his head.*—see also LUCKY DIP

diph·theria /dɪfˈθɪəriə; *AmE* -ˈθɪriə; ˈdɪp-/ *noun* [U] a serious infectious disease of the throat that causes difficulty in breathing

diph·thong /ˈdɪfθɒŋ; *AmE* -θɔːŋ; ˈdɪp-/ *noun* (*phonetics*) a combination of two vowel sounds or vowel letters, for example the sounds /aɪ/ in *pipe* / paɪp/ or the letters *ou* in *doubt*

dip·loma /dɪˈpləʊmə; *AmE* -ˈploʊ-/ *noun* **1** (*BrE*) a course of study at a college or university: *a two-year diploma course* ◊ *She is taking a diploma in management studies.* **2** a document showing that you have completed a course of study or part of your education: *a High School diploma* ⇨ note at DEGREE

dip·lo·macy /dɪˈpləʊməsi; *AmE* -ˈploʊ-/ *noun* [U] **1** the activity of managing relations between different countries; the skill in doing this: *international diplomacy* ◊ *Diplomacy is better than war.* **2** skill in dealing with people in difficult situations without upsetting or offending them [SYN] TACT—see also SHUTTLE DIPLOMACY

dip·lo·mat /ˈdɪpləmæt/ *noun* **1** (also *old-fashioned* **diplomatist**) a person whose job is to represent his or her country in a foreign country, for example, in an EMBASSY **2** a person who is skilled at dealing with other people

dip·lo·mat·ic /ˌdɪpləˈmætɪk/ *adj.* **1** connected with managing relations between countries (= DIPLOMACY): *a diplomatic crisis* ◊ *Attempts are being made to settle the dispute by diplomatic means.* ◊ *to break off / establish / restore diplomatic relations with a country* **2** having or showing skill in dealing with people in difficult situations: *a diplomatic answer / move / smile* ▶ **dip·lo·mat·ic·al·ly** /-kli/ *adv.*: *The country remained diplomatically isolated.* ◊ *'Why don't we take a break for coffee?' she suggested diplomatically.*

ˌdiploˌmatic ˈbag *noun* a container that is used for sending official letters and documents between a govern-

ment and its representatives in another country and that cannot be opened by CUSTOMS officers

ˌdiploˈmatic ˈcorps *noun* (usually **the diplomatic corps**) [C+sing./ pl. *v.*] (*pl.* **diplomatic corps**) all the DIPLOMATS who work in a particular city or country

ˌdiploˌmatic imˈmunity *noun* [U] special rights given to diplomats working in a foreign country which mean they cannot be arrested, taxed, etc. in that country

the Diploˈmatic Service (*especially BrE*) (*AmE* usually **the ˈForeign Service**) *noun* [sing.] the government department concerned with representing a country in foreign countries

dip·lo·ma·tist /dɪˈpləʊmətɪst; *AmE* -ˈploʊ-/ *noun* (*old-fashioned*) = DIPLOMAT

dip·per /ˈdɪpə(r)/ *noun* a bird that lives near rivers—see also BIG DIPPER

dippy /ˈdɪpi/ *adj.* (*informal*) stupid; crazy

dipso·maniac /ˌdɪpsəˈmeɪniæk/ *noun* a person who has a strong desire for alcoholic drink that they cannot control

dip·stick /ˈdɪpstɪk/ *noun* **1** a metal rod used for measuring the amount of liquid in a container, especially the amount of oil in an engine **2** (*informal*) a stupid person

ˈdip switch (*BrE*) (*AmE* **ˈdimmer switch**) *noun* a switch that allows you to make the beam from the front lights on a car point downwards

dire /ˈdaɪə(r)/ *adj.* (**direr, dir·est**) **1** [usually before noun] (*formal*) very serious: *living in dire poverty* ◊ *dire warnings / threats* ◊ *Such action may have dire consequences.* ◊ *We're in dire need of your help.* ◊ *The firm is in dire straits* (= in a very difficult situation) *and may go bankrupt.* **2** (*BrE, informal*) very bad: *The acting was dire.*

dir·ect /dəˈrekt; dɪ-; daɪ-/ *adj., verb, adv.*

■ *adj.*

NOBODY/NOTHING IN BETWEEN | **1** [usually before noun] happening or done without involving other people, actions, etc. in between: *They are in direct contact with the hijackers.* ◊ *His death was a direct result of your action.* ◊ *We are looking for somebody with direct experience of this type of work.* ◊ *This information has a direct bearing on* (= it is closely connected with) *the case.* OPP INDIRECT

JOURNEY/ROUTE | **2** going in the straightest line between two places without stopping or changing direction: *the most direct route / course* ◊ *a direct flight* (= a flight that does not stop) ◊ *There's a direct train to Leeds* (= it may stop at other stations but you do not have to change trains). ◊ *a direct hit* (= a hit that is accurate and does not touch sth else first) OPP INDIRECT

HEAT/LIGHT | **3** [only before noun] with nothing between sth and the source of the heat or light: *Protect your child from direct sunlight by using a sunscreen.*

EXACT | **4** [only before noun] exact: *That's the direct opposite of what you told me yesterday.* ◊ *a direct quote* (= one using a person's exact words)

SAYING WHAT YOU MEAN | **5** saying exactly what you mean in a way that nobody can pretend not to understand: *a direct answer / question* ◊ *You'll have to get used to his direct manner.* OPP INDIRECT

RELATIONSHIP | **6** [only before noun] related through parents and children rather than brothers, sisters, aunts, etc: *a direct descendant of the country's first president* OPP INDIRECT

■ *verb*

AIM | **1** [VN] ~ **sth to/towards sth/sb** | ~ **sth at/against sth/sb** to aim sth in a particular direction or at a particular person: *The machine directs a powerful beam at the affected part of the body.* ◊ *There are three main issues that we need to direct our attention to.* ◊ *Most of his anger was directed against himself.* ◊ *Was that remark directed at me?*

CONTROL | **2** [VN] to control or be in charge of sb/sth: *A new manager has been appointed to direct the project.* ◊ *He was asked to take command and direct operations.*

MOVIE/PLAY/MUSIC | **3** to be in charge of actors in a play, or a film/movie, or musicians in an orchestra, etc: [V] *She prefers to act rather than direct.* ◊ [VN] *The movie was*

s	t	v	z	ʃ	ʒ	tʃ	dʒ	θ	ð	ŋ
see	tea	van	zoo	shoe	vision	chain	jam	thin	this	sing

directed by Steven Spielberg. ◊ She now directs a large choir.

SHOW THE WAY | **4** [VN] **~ sb (to …)** to tell or show sb how to get to somewhere or where to go: Could you direct me to the station? ◊ A police officer was directing the traffic.

GIVE ORDER | **5** (formal) to give an official order: [VN to inf] The police officers had been directed to search the building. ◊ [V that] The judge directed that the mother be given custody of the children. ◊ (BrE also) The judge directed that the mother should be given custody of the children.

LETTER/COMMENT | **6** [VN] **~ sth to …** (formal) to send a letter, etc. to a particular place or to a particular person: Direct any complaints to the Customer Services department.

■ adv.

JOURNEY/ROUTE | **1** without stopping or changing direction: It costs more to fly direct to Hong Kong. ◊ The 10.40 goes direct to Leeds.

NOBODY IN BETWEEN | **2** without involving other people: I prefer to deal with him direct.

di,rect 'access noun [U] (computing) the ability to get data immediately from any part of a computer file

di,rect 'action noun [U, C] the use of strikes, protests, etc. instead of discussion in order to get what you want

di,rect 'current noun [C, U] (abbr. DC) an electric current that flows in one direction only—compare ALTERNATING CURRENT

di,rect 'debit noun [U, C] (in Britain) an instruction to your bank to allow sb else to take an amount of money from your account on a particular date, especially to pay bills: We pay all our bills by direct debit.—compare STANDING ORDER

di,rect de'posit noun [U] (AmE) the system of paying sb's wages straight into their bank account

dir·ec·tion /dəˈrekʃn; dɪ-; daɪ-/ noun

WHERE TO | **1** [C, U] the general position a person or thing moves or points towards: Tom went off in the direction of the post office. ◊ She glanced in his direction. ◊ The aircraft was flying in a northerly direction. ◊ The road was blocked in both directions. ◊ They hit a truck coming in **the opposite direction**. ◊ Has the wind changed direction? ◊ When the police arrived, the crowd scattered in **all directions**. ◊ I lost all **sense of direction** (= I didn't know which way to go).

DEVELOPMENT | **2** [C, U] the general way in which a person or thing develops: The exhibition provides evidence of several new directions in her work. ◊ I am very unhappy with the direction the club is taking. ◊ It's only a small improvement but at least it's **a step in the right direction**.

WHERE FROM | **3** [C] the general position a person or thing comes or develops from: Support came from an unexpected direction. ◊ Let us approach the subject from a different direction.

PURPOSE | **4** [U] a purpose; an aim: We are looking for somebody with a clear **sense of direction**. ◊ Once again her life felt lacking in direction.

INSTRUCTIONS | **5** [C, usually pl.] instructions about how to do sth, where to go, etc: Let's stop and ask for directions. ◊ Simple directions for assembling the model are printed on the box.

CONTROL | **6** [U] the art of managing or guiding sb/sth: All work was produced by the students **under the direction of** John Williams.

FILM/MOVIE | **7** [U] the instructions given by sb directing a film/movie: There is some clever direction and the film is very well shot.

dir·ec·tion·al /dəˈrekʃənl; dɪ-; daɪ-/ adj. (technical) **1** producing or receiving signals, sound, etc. better in one particular direction: a directional microphone / aerial **2** connected with the direction in which sth is moving: directional control / stability

dir·ec·tion·less /dəˈrekʃnləs; dɪ-; daɪ-/ adj. (written) without a direction, purpose or aim

dir·ect·ive /dəˈrektɪv; dɪ-; daɪ-/ noun, adj.

■ noun an official instruction: The EU has issued a new set of directives on pollution.
■ adj. (formal) giving instructions: They are seeking a central, directive role in national energy policy.

dir·ect·ly /dəˈrektli; dɪ-; daɪ-/ adv., conj.

■ adv. **1** in a direct line or manner: He drove her directly to her hotel. ◊ She looked directly at us. ◊ He's directly responsible to the boss. ◊ We have not been directly affected by the latest cuts. OPP INDIRECTLY **2** exactly in a particular position: directly opposite / below / ahead ◊ They remain directly opposed to these new plans. **3** immediately: She left directly after the show. **4** (old-fashioned, BrE) soon: Tell them I'll be there directly.
■ conj. (BrE) as soon as: I went home directly I had finished work.

di,rect 'mail noun [U] advertisements that are sent to people through the post / mail

di,rect 'marketing noun [U] the business of selling products or services directly to customers who order by mail or by telephone instead of going to a shop / store

dir·ect·ness /dəˈrektnəs; dɪ-; daɪ-/ noun [U] the quality of being simple and clear, so that it is impossible not to understand: 'What's that?' she asked with her usual directness.

di,rect 'object noun (grammar) a noun, noun phrase or pronoun that refers to a person or thing that is directly affected by the action of a verb: In 'I met him in town', the word 'him' is the direct object.—compare INDIRECT OBJECT

dir·ect·or /dəˈrektə(r); dɪ-; daɪ-/ noun **1** one of a group of senior managers who run a company: the managing director ◊ an executive / non-executive director ◊ He's on the **board of directors**. **2** a person who is in charge of a particular activity or department in a company, a college, etc: a musical / art director ◊ a regional / technical / finance director ◊ the director of education / finance **3** a person in charge of a film / movie or play who tells the actors and staff what to do—compare PRODUCER

dir·ect·or·ate /dəˈrektərət; dɪ-; daɪ-/ noun **1** a section of a government department in charge of one particular activity: the environmental directorate **2** the group of directors who run a company

di,rector-'general noun (especially BrE) the head of a large organization, especially a public organization: the director-general of the BBC

dir·ect·or·ial /ˌdaɪrekˈtɔːriəl/ adj. [only before noun] connected with the position or work of a DIRECTOR, especially of a director of films / movies: The film marks her directorial debut.

Di,rector of ,Public Prose'cutions noun (abbr. DPP) (in England and Wales) a public official whose job is to decide whether people who are suspected of a crime should be brought to trial

dir·ect·or·ship /dəˈrektəʃɪp; dɪ-; daɪ-; AmE -tərʃ-/ noun the position of a company DIRECTOR; the period during which this is held

dir·ec·tory /dəˈrektəri; dɪ-; daɪ-/ noun (pl. -ies) **1** a book containing lists of information, usually in alphabetical order, for example people's telephone numbers or the names and addresses of businesses in a particular area: a telephone / trade directory ◊ a directory of European Trade Associations **2** a file containing a group of other files or programs in a computer

di,rectory en'quiries (BrE) (AmE **di,rectory as'sistance** or informal **in·for·ma·tion**) noun [U+sing. / pl. v.] a telephone service that you can use to find out a person's telephone number

di,rect 'rule noun [U] government of a region by a central government, when that region has had its own government in the past

di,rect 'speech noun [U] (grammar) a speaker's actual words; the use of these in writing: Only direct speech should go inside inverted commas.—compare INDIRECT SPEECH, REPORTED SPEECH

di,rect 'tax noun (technical) a tax which is collected directly from the person who pays it, for example income tax—compare INDIRECT TAX ▶ **di,rect tax'ation** noun [U]

dirge /dɜːdʒ; AmE dɜːrdʒ/ noun **1** a song sung in the past

æ	ɑː	e	ɜː	ə	ɪ	iː	i	ɒ	ɔː	ʌ	ʊ	u	uː
cat	father	ten	bird	about	sit	see	many	got	saw	cup	put	actual	too

(BrE)

at a funeral or for a dead person **2** (*informal, disapproving*) any song or piece of music that is too slow and sad

dirk /dɜːk; *AmE* dɜːrk/ *noun* a long heavy pointed knife that was used as a weapon in Scotland in the past

dirt /dɜːt; *AmE* dɜːrt/ *noun* [U] **1** any substance that makes sth dirty, for example dust, soil or mud: *His clothes were covered in dirt.* ◊ *First remove any grease or dirt from the surface.* **2** (*especially AmE*) loose earth or soil: *He picked up a handful of dirt and threw it at them.* ◊ *Pack the dirt firmly round the plants.* ◊ *They lived in a shack with a dirt floor.* **3** (*informal*) unpleasant or harmful information about sb that could be used to damage their reputation, career, etc: *Do you have any dirt on the new guy?* **4** (*informal*) = EXCREMENT: *dog dirt* **IDM** see DISH *v.*, TREAT *v.*

dirt ˈcheap *adj., adv.* (*informal*) very cheap: *It was dirt cheap.* ◊ *I got it dirt cheap.*

ˈdirt farmer *noun* (*AmE*) a farmer who has poor land and does not make much money, and who does not pay anyone else to work on the farm

dirt ˈpoor *adj.* (*AmE, informal*) extremely poor

ˈdirt road (*AmE also* **ˈdirt track**) *noun* a rough road in the country that is made from hard earth

ˈdirt track *noun* **1** (*AmE*) = DIRT ROAD **2** a track made of CINDERS, soil etc. used for motorcycle racing: *a dirt-track race/meeting*

dirty /ˈdɜːti; *AmE* ˈdɜːrti/ *adj., verb, adv.*
■ *adj.* (**dirt·ier**, **dirti·est**)
UNDERLINE NOT CLEAN | **1** not clean: *dirty hands/clothes* ◊ *a dirty mark* ◊ *Try not to get too dirty!* ◊ *I always get given the dirty jobs* (= jobs that make you become dirty).
OFFENSIVE | **2** [usually before noun] connected with sex in an offensive way: *a dirty joke/book* ◊ *He's got a dirty mind* (= he often thinks about sex).
UNPLEASANT/DISHONEST | **3** [usually before noun] unpleasant or dishonest: *a dirty lie/liar* ◊ *She's a dirty player.* ◊ *He's a great man for doing the dirty jobs* (= jobs which are unpleasant because they involve being dishonest or mean to people).
COLOURS | **4** [only before noun] dull: *a dirty brown carpet*
DRUGS | **5** (*AmE, slang*) using illegal drugs
IDM **be a dirty ˈword** to be a subject or an idea that people think is bad or immoral: *Profit is not a dirty word around here.* (**do sb's**) **ˈdirty work** (to do) the unpleasant or dishonest jobs that sb else does not want to **do do the ˈdirty on sb** (*BrE, informal*) to cheat or betray sb; to treat sb unfairly: *I'd never do the dirty on my friends.* **give sb a dirty ˈlook** to look at sb in a way that shows you are annoyed with them—more at HAND *n.*, WASH *v.*
■ *verb* (**dirt·ies**, **dirty·ing**, **dirt·ied**, **dirt·ied**) [VN] to make sth dirty
■ *adv.*
IDM **dirty great/big** (*BrE, informal*) used to emphasize how large sth is: *When I turned round he was pointing a dirty great gun at me.* **play ˈdirty** (*informal*) to behave or play a game in an unfair way—more at TALK *v.*

dirty old ˈman *noun* (*informal*) an older man whose interest in sex or in sexually attractive young women is considered to be offensive or not natural for sb of his age

dirty ˈtrick *noun* **1** [usually pl.] dishonest, secret and often illegal activity by a political group or other organization, that is intended to harm the reputation or success of an opponent: *a dirty tricks campaign* **2** an unpleasant and dishonest act: *What a dirty trick to play!*

dirty weekˈend *noun* (*BrE, humorous*) a WEEKEND spent away with a sexual partner, often in secret

dis (*also* **diss**) /dɪs/ *verb* (**-ss-**) [VN] (*slang, especially AmE*) to show a lack of respect for sb, especially by saying insulting things to them: *If he disses me again, I'll hit him.*

dis- /dɪs/ *prefix* (in adjectives, adverbs, nouns and verbs) not; the opposite of: *dishonest* ◊ *disagreeably* ◊ *disadvantage* ◊ *disappear*

dis·abil·ity /ˌdɪsəˈbɪləti/ *noun* (*pl.* **-ies**) **1** [C] a physical or mental condition that means you cannot use a part of your body completely or easily, or that you cannot learn easily: *a physical/mental/permanent disability* ◊ *people*

with severe learning disabilities **2** [U] the state of not being able to use a part of your body completely or easily; the state of not being able to learn easily: *He qualifies for help on the grounds of disability.* ⇨ note at DISABLED

dis·able /dɪsˈeɪbl/ *verb* [VN] **1** to injure or affect sb permanently so that, for example, they cannot walk or cannot use a part of their body: *He was disabled in a car accident.* ◊ *a disabling condition/illness* **2** to prevent sth from working correctly: *The burglars gained entry to the building after disabling the alarm.*

dis·abled /dɪsˈeɪbld/ *adj.* **1** unable to use a part of your body completely or easily because of a physical condition, illness, injury, etc.; unable to learn easily: *physically/mentally disabled* ◊ *severely disabled* ◊ *He was born disabled.* ◊ *facilities for disabled people* **2** (**the disabled**) *noun* [pl.] people who are disabled: *caring for the sick, elderly and disabled*

WHICH WORD?
disabled / handicapped ⃝?

Disabled is the most generally accepted term to refer to people with a permanent illness or injury that makes it difficult for them to use part of their body completely or easily. **Handicapped** is slightly old-fashioned and many people now think it is offensive. People also now prefer to use the word **disability** rather than **handicap**. The expression **disabled people** is often preferred to **the disabled** because it sounds more personal.

Disabled and **disability** can be used with other words to talk about a mental condition: *mentally disabled* ◊ *learning disabilities*.

If somebody's ability to hear, speak or see has been damaged but not destroyed completely, they have **impaired hearing/speech/sight** (or **vision**). They can be described as **visually/hearing impaired** or **partially sighted**: *The museum has special facilities for blind and partially sighted visitors.*

---

dis·able·ment /dɪsˈeɪblmənt/ *noun* [U] (*formal*) the state of being disabled or the process of becoming disabled: *The insurance policy covers sudden death or disablement.*

dis·abuse /ˌdɪsəˈbjuːz/ *verb* [VN] ~ sb (of sth) (*formal*) to tell sb that what they think is true is, in fact, not true

dis·ad·van·tage /ˌdɪsədˈvɑːntɪdʒ; *AmE* -ˈvæn-/ *noun* [C, U] ~ (of sth) | ~ (to sth) something that causes problems and tends to stop sb/sth from succeeding or making progress: *a serious/severe/considerable disadvantage* ◊ *One major disadvantage of the area is the lack of public transport.* ◊ *There are disadvantages to the plan.* ◊ *What's the main disadvantage?* ◊ *I was at a disadvantage compared to the younger members of the team.* ◊ *The fact that he didn't speak a foreign language put him at a distinct disadvantage.* ◊ *I hope my lack of experience won't be to my disadvantage.* ◊ *The advantages of the scheme far outweighed the disadvantages.* ◊ *Many children in the class suffered severe social and economic disadvantage.* ▶ **dis·ad·van·tage** *verb* [VN]

dis·ad·van·taged /ˌdɪsədˈvɑːntɪdʒd; *AmE* -ˈvæn-/ **1** *adj.* not having the things, such as education, and enough money, that people need in order to succeed in life **SYN** DEPRIVED: *disadvantaged groups/children* ◊ *a severely disadvantaged area* **OPP** ADVANTAGED **2** (**the disadvantaged**) *noun* [pl.] people who are disadvantaged

dis·ad·van·ta·geous /ˌdɪsædvænˈteɪdʒəs/ *adj.* ~ (to/for sb) (*formal*) causing sb to be in a worse situation compared to other people: *The deal will not be disadvantageous to your company.* **OPP** ADVANTAGEOUS

dis·af·fect·ed /ˌdɪsəˈfektɪd/ *adj.* not longer satisfied with your situation, organization, belief etc. and therefore not loyal to it: *Some disaffected members left to form a new party.* ▶ **dis·af·fec·tion** /ˌdɪsəˈfekʃn/ *noun* [U]: *There are signs of growing disaffection amongst voters.*

dis·af·for·est /ˌdɪsəˈfɒrɪst; *AmE* -ˈfɔːr-; -ˈfɑːr-/ *verb* [VN] = DEFOREST

---

dis·agree /ˌdɪsəˈgriː/ *verb* **1** [V] ~ **(with sb) (about/on/over sth)** if two people **disagree** or one person **disagrees** with another about sth, they have a different opinion about it: *Even friends disagree sometimes.* ◇ *He disagreed with his parents on most things.* ◇ *Some people disagree with this argument.* ◇ *No, I disagree. I don't think it would be the right thing to do.* [also V that] **2** [V] if statements or reports **disagree**, they give different information OPP AGREE PHRV **disa'gree with sb** if sth, especially food, **disagrees** with you, it has a bad effect on you and makes you feel ill **disa'gree with sth/with doing sth** to believe that sth is bad or wrong; to disapprove of sth: *I disagree with violent protests.*

dis·agree·able /ˌdɪsəˈgriːəbl/ *adj.* (*formal*) **1** not nice or enjoyable SYN UNPLEASANT: *a disagreeable smell/experience/job* **2** (of a person) rude and unfriendly SYN UNPLEASANT: *a disagreeable bad-tempered man* OPP AGREEABLE ▶ **dis·agree·ably** /-əbli/ *adv.*

dis·agree·ment /ˌdɪsəˈgriːmənt/ *noun* [U, C] ~ **(about/on/over/as to sth)** | ~ **(among …)** | ~ **between A and B** a situation where people disagree about sth and often argue: *Disagreement arose about exactly how to plan the show.* ◇ *disagreement on the method to be used* ◇ *There is considerable disagreement over the safety of the treatment.* ◇ *It was a source of disagreement between the two states.* ◇ *There is disagreement among archaeologists as to the age of the sculpture.* ◇ *They have had several disagreements with their neighbours.* OPP AGREEMENT

dis·allow /ˌdɪsəˈlaʊ/ *verb* [VN] (often passive) to officially refuse to accept sth because it is not valid: *to disallow a claim/an appeal* ◇ *The second goal was disallowed.*— compare ALLOW (6)

dis·ap·pear /ˌdɪsəˈpɪə(r); *AmE* -ˈpɪr/ *verb* [V] **1** [often + adv. / prep.] to become impossible to see SYN VANISH: *The plane disappeared behind a cloud.* ◇ *Lisa watched until the train disappeared from view.* **2** to stop existing SYN VANISH: *Her nervousness quickly disappeared once she was on stage.* ◇ *The problem won't just disappear.* ◇ *Our countryside is disappearing at an alarming rate.* **3** to be lost or impossible to find SYN VANISH: *I can never find a pen in this house. They disappear as soon as I buy them.* ◇ *The child disappeared from his home some time after four.* ▶ **dis·ap·pear·ance** /-ˈpɪərəns; *AmE* -ˈpɪr-/ *noun* [U, C]: *the disappearance of many species of plants and animals from our planet* ◇ *Police are investigating the disappearance of a young woman.* IDM see ACT n., FACE n.

dis·ap·point /ˌdɪsəˈpɔɪnt/ *verb* **1** to make sb feel sad because sth that they hope for or expect to happen does not happen or is not as good as they hoped: [VN] *Her decision to cancel the concert is bound to disappoint her fans.* ◇ *I hate to disappoint you, but I'm just not interested.* ◇ *The movie had disappointed her* (= it wasn't as good as she had expected). ◇ [V] *His latest novel does not disappoint.* [also VN that] **2** [VN] to prevent sth that sb hopes for from becoming a reality: *The new government had soon disappointed the hopes of many of its supporters.*

dis·ap·point·ed /ˌdɪsəˈpɔɪntɪd/ *adj.* ~ **(at/by sth)** | ~ **(in/with sb/sth)** | ~ **(to see, hear, etc.)** | ~ **(that …)** | ~ **(not) to be …** upset because sth you hoped for has not happened or been as good, successful, etc. as you expected: *They were bitterly disappointed at the result of the game.* ◇ *I was disappointed by the quality of the wine.* ◇ *I'm disappointed in you—I really thought I could trust you!* ◇ *I was very disappointed with myself.* ◇ *He was disappointed to see she wasn't at the party.* ◇ *I'm disappointed (that) it was sold out.* ◇ *She was disappointed not to be chosen.*

dis·ap·point·ing /ˌdɪsəˈpɔɪntɪŋ/ *adj.* not as good, successful, etc. as you had hoped; making you feel disappointed: *a disappointing result/performance* ◇ *The outcome of the court case was disappointing for the family involved.* ▶ **dis·ap·point·ing·ly** *adv.*: *The room was disappointingly small.*

dis·ap·point·ment /ˌdɪsəˈpɔɪntmənt/ *noun* **1** [U] sadness because sth has not happened or been as good, successful, etc. as you expected or hoped: *Book early for the show to avoid disappointment.* ◇ *To our great disap-*

pointment, it rained every day of the trip. ◇ *He found it difficult to hide his disappointment when she didn't arrive.* **2** [C] ~ **(to sb)** a person or thing that is disappointing: *a bitter/major disappointment* ◇ *That new restaurant was a big disappointment.* ◇ *I always felt I was a disappointment to my father.*

dis·ap·pro·ba·tion /ˌdɪsˌæprəˈbeɪʃn/ *noun* [U] (*formal*) disapproval of sb/sth that you think is morally wrong

dis·ap·proval /ˌdɪsəˈpruːvl/ *noun* [U] ~ **(of sb/sth)** a feeling that you do not like an idea, an action or sb's behaviour because you think it is bad, not suitable or going to have a bad effect on sb else: *disapproval of his methods* ◇ *to show/express disapproval* ◇ *He shook his head in disapproval.* ◇ *She looked at my clothes with disapproval.* OPP APPROVAL

dis·ap·prove /ˌdɪsəˈpruːv/ *verb* [V] ~ **(of sb/sth)** to think that sb/sth is not good or suitable; to not approve of sb/sth: *She wants to be an actress but her parents disapprove.* ◇ *He strongly disapproved of the changes that had been made.* OPP APPROVE

dis·ap·prov·ing /ˌdɪsəˈpruːvɪŋ/ *adj.* showing that you do not approve of sb/sth: *a disapproving glance/tone/look* OPP APPROVING ▶ **dis·ap·prov·ing·ly** *adv.*: *He looked disapprovingly at the row of empty wine bottles.*

dis·arm /dɪsˈɑːm; *AmE* -ˈɑːrm/ *verb* **1** [VN] to take a weapon or weapons away from sb: *Most of the rebels were captured and disarmed.* **2** [V] (of a country or a group of people) to reduce the size of an army or to give up some or all weapons, especially nuclear weapons **3** [VN] (*written*) to make sb feel less angry or critical: *He disarmed her immediately by apologizing profusely.* ◇ *The best way to disarm your critics is to make them laugh.*—compare ARM

dis·arma·ment /dɪsˈɑːməmənt; *AmE* -ˈɑːrm-/ *noun* [U] the fact of a country reducing the size of its armed forces or the number of weapons, especially nuclear weapons, that it has: *nuclear disarmament* ◇ *disarmament talks*—compare ARMAMENT

dis·arm·ing /dɪsˈɑːmɪŋ; *AmE* -ˈɑːrm-/ *adj.* making people feel less angry or suspicious than they were before: *a disarming smile* ▶ **dis·arm·ing·ly** *adv.*: *disarmingly frank*

dis·ar·range /ˌdɪsəˈreɪndʒ/ *verb* [VN] (usually passive) (*formal*) to make sth untidy

dis·array /ˌdɪsəˈreɪ/ *noun* [U] a state of confusion and lack of organization in a situation or a place: *The peace talks broke up in disarray.* ◇ *Our plans were thrown into disarray by her arrival.*

dis·as·so·ci·ate /ˌdɪsəˈsəʊʃieɪt; -ˈsəʊs-; *AmE* -ˈsoʊ-/ *verb* [VN] = DISSOCIATE

dis·as·ter /dɪˈzɑːstə(r); *AmE* -ˈzæs-/ *noun* **1** [C] an unexpected event such as a very bad accident, a flood or a fire that kills a lot of people or causes a lot of damage SYN CATASTROPHE: *an air/a ferry disaster* ◇ *environmental disasters* ◇ *Thousands died in the disaster.* ◇ *a natural disaster* (= one that is caused by nature) **2** [C, U] a very bad situation that causes problems: *Losing your job doesn't have to be such a disaster.* ◇ *Disaster struck when the wheel came off.* ◇ *financial disaster* ◇ *Letting her organize the party is a recipe for disaster* (= something that is likely to go badly wrong). **3** [C, U] (*informal*) a complete failure: *As a teacher, he's a disaster.* ◇ *The play's first night was a total disaster.* IDM see WAIT v.

di'saster area *noun* **1** a place where a disaster has happened and which needs special help **2** (*informal*) a place or situation that has a lot of problems, is a failure, or is badly organized

dis·as·trous /dɪˈzɑːstrəs; *AmE* -ˈzæs-/ *adj.* very bad, harmful or unsuccessful: *a disastrous harvest/fire/result* ◇ *Lowering interest rates could have disastrous consequences for the economy.* ▶ **dis·as·trous·ly** *adv.*: *How could everything go so disastrously wrong?*

dis·avow /ˌdɪsəˈvaʊ/ *verb* [VN] (*formal*) to state publicly that you have no knowledge of sth or that you are not responsible for sth/sb: *They disavowed claims of a split in the party.* ▶ **dis·avowal** /-ˈvaʊəl/ *noun* [C, U]

dis·band /dɪsˈbænd/ *verb* to stop sb/sth from operating as a group; to separate or no longer operate as a group:

D

[VN] *They set about disbanding the terrorist groups.* ◊ [V] *The committee formally disbanded in August.* ▶ **dis·band·ment** *noun* [U]

dis·bar /dɪsˈbɑː(r)/ *verb* (-rr-) [VN] [usually passive] ~ **sb (from sth/from doing sth)** to stop a lawyer from working in the legal profession, especially because he or she has done sth illegal

dis·be·lief /ˌdɪsbɪˈliːf/ *noun* [U] the feeling of not being able to believe sth: *He stared at me* **in disbelief.** ◊ *To enjoy the movie you have to* **suspend your disbelief** (= pretend to believe sth, even if it seems very unlikely).—compare BELIEF (3)—compare UNBELIEF

dis·be·lieve /ˌdɪsbɪˈliːv/ *verb* (not used in the progressive tenses) (*formal*) to not believe that sth is true or that sb is telling the truth: [VN] *Why should I disbelieve her story?* [also V] ▶ **dis·be·liev·ing** *adj.*: *a disbelieving look/ smile/laugh* **dis·be·liev·ing·ly** *adv.* PHRV **disbe'lieve in sth** to not believe that sth exists

dis·burse /dɪsˈbɜːs; AmE -ˈbɜːrs/ *verb* [VN] (*formal*) to pay money to sb from a large amount that has been collected for a purpose ▶ **dis·burse·ment** *noun* [U, C]: *the disbursement of funds* ◊ *aid disbursements*

disc (also **disk** especially in AmE) /dɪsk/ *noun* **1** a thin flat circular object: *He wears an identity disc around his neck.* **2** = CD: *This recording is available on disc or cassette.* **3** (*BrE, rare*) a disk for a computer **4** (*old-fashioned*) = RECORD (2) **5** one of the layers of CARTILAGE between the bones of the back: *He's been off work with a **slipped disc*** (= one that has moved from its correct position, causing pain).

dis·card *verb, noun*
▪ *verb* /dɪsˈkɑːd; AmE -ˈkɑːrd/ **1** [VN] ~ **sth/sb (as sth)** to get rid of sth that you no longer want or need [SYN] CAST ASIDE: *The room was littered with discarded newspapers.* ◊ *He had discarded his jacket because of the heat.* ◊ *10% of the data was discarded as unreliable* ◊ (*figurative*) *She could now discard all thought of promotion.* **2** [VN, V] (in card games) to get rid of a card that you do not want
▪ *noun* /ˈdɪskɑːd; AmE -kɑːrd/ a person or a thing that is not wanted or thrown away, especially a card in a card game

'disc brake *noun* [usually pl.] a BRAKE that works by two surfaces pressing onto a disc in the centre of a wheel

dis·cern /dɪˈsɜːn; AmE -ˈsɜːrn/ *verb* (not used in the progressive tenses) (*formal*) **1** to know, recognize or understand sth, especially sth that is not obvious: [VN] *It is possible to discern a number of different techniques in her work.* ◊ *He discerned a certain coldness in their welcome.* ◊ [V wh-] *It is often difficult to discern how widespread public support is.* [also V that] **2** [VN] to see or hear sth, but not very clearly: *She could just discern the house in the distance.* ▶ **dis·cern·ible** *adj.*: *There is often no discernible difference between rival brands.* ◊ *His face was barely discernible in the gloom.*

dis·cern·ing /dɪˈsɜːnɪŋ; AmE -ˈsɜːrn-/ *adj.* (*approving*) able to show good judgement about the quality of sb/sth

dis·cern·ment /dɪˈsɜːnmənt; AmE -ˈsɜːrn-/ *noun* [U] (*formal, approving*) the ability to show good judgement about the quality of sb/sth: *He shows great discernment in his choice of friends.*

dis·charge *verb, noun*
▪ *verb* /dɪsˈtʃɑːdʒ; AmE -ˈtʃɑːrdʒ/
FROM HOSPITAL/JOB **1** [VN] [usually passive] ~ **sb (from sth)** to give sb official permission to leave a place or job; to make sb leave a job: *Patients were being discharged from the hospital too early.* ◊ *She had discharged herself against medical advice.* ◊ *He was discharged from the army following his injury.* ◊ *She was discharged from the police force for bad conduct.*
FROM PRISON/COURT **2** [VN] [often passive] to allow sb to leave prison or a court of law: *He was **conditionally discharged** after admitting the theft.*
GAS/LIQUID **3** ~ **(sth) (into sth)** when a gas or a liquid **discharges** or is **discharged**, or sb **discharges** it, it flows somewhere: [V] *The river is diverted through the power station before discharging into the sea.* ◊ [VN] *The factory was fined for discharging chemicals into the river.*
FORCE/POWER **4** (*technical*) to release force or power: [VN]

Lightning is caused by clouds discharging electricity. [also V]
DUTY **5** [VN] (*formal*) to do everything that is necessary to perform and complete a particular duty: *to discharge your responsibilities/obligations* ◊ *to discharge a debt* (= to pay it)
GUN **6** [VN] (*formal*) to fire a gun, etc.
▪ *noun* /ˈdɪstʃɑːdʒ; AmE -tʃɑːrdʒ/
OF LIQUID/GAS **1** [U, C] the action of releasing a substance such as a liquid or gas; a substance that comes out from inside somewhere: *a ban on the discharge of toxic waste* ◊ *thunder and lightning caused by electrical discharges* ◊ *nasal/vaginal discharge* (= from the nose/vagina)
FROM HOSPITAL/JOB **2** [U, C] ~ **(from sth)** the act of officially allowing sb, or of telling sb, to leave somewhere, especially sb in a hospital or the army
OF DUTY **3** [U] (*formal*) the act of carrying out a task or a duty or of paying money that is owed: *the discharge of debts/obligations*

dis·ciple /dɪˈsaɪpl/ *noun* **1** a person who believes in and follows the teachings of a religious or political leader: *a disciple of the economist John Maynard Keynes* **2** one of the people who followed Jesus Christ and his teachings when he was living on earth, especially one of the twelve APOSTLES

dis·cip·lin·ar·ian /ˌdɪsəplɪˈneəriən; AmE -ˈner-/ *noun* a person who believes in using rules and punishments for controlling people: *She's a very strict disciplinarian.*

dis·cip·lin·ary /ˈdɪsəplɪnəri; ˌdɪsəˈplɪnəri; AmE ˈdɪsəpləneri/ *adj.* connected with the punishment of people who break rules: *a disciplinary hearing* (= to decide if sb has done sth wrong) ◊ *The company will be taking **disciplinary action** against him.*

dis·cip·line /ˈdɪsəplɪn/ *noun, verb*
▪ *noun* **1** [U] the practice of training people to obey rules and orders and punishing them if they do not; the controlled behaviour or situation that results from this training: *The school has a reputation for high standards of discipline.* ◊ *Strict discipline is imposed on army recruits.* ◊ *She keeps good discipline in class.* **2** [C] a method of training your mind or body or of controlling your behaviour; an area of activity where this is necessary: *Yoga is a good discipline for learning to relax.* **3** [U] the ability to control your behaviour or the way you live, work, etc: *He'll never get anywhere working for himself— he's got no discipline.*—see also SELF-DISCIPLINE **4** [C] an area of knowledge; a subject that people study or are taught, especially in a university
▪ *verb* **1** [VN] ~ **sb (for sth)** to punish sb for sth they have done: *The officers were disciplined for using racist language.* **2** [VN] to train sb, especially a child, to obey particular rules and control the way they behave: *a guide to the best ways of disciplining your child* **3** ~ **yourself** to control the way you behave and make yourself do things that you believe you should do: [VN to inf] *He disciplined himself to exercise at least three times a week.* ◊ [VN] *Dieting is a matter of disciplining yourself.* ▶ **dis·cip·lined** *adj.*: *a disciplined army/team* ◊ *a disciplined approach to work*

'disc jockey *noun* (*abbr.* **DJ**) a person whose job is to introduce and play popular recorded music, on radio or television or at a club

dis·claim /dɪsˈkleɪm/ *verb* [VN] (*formal*) **1** to state publicly that you have no knowledge of sth, or that you are not responsible for sth [SYN] DENY: *She disclaimed any knowledge of her husband's whereabouts.* ◊ *The rebels disclaimed all responsibility for the explosion.* **2** to give up your right to sth, such as property or a title

dis·claim·er /dɪsˈkleɪmə(r)/ *noun* **1** (*formal*) a statement in which sb says that they are not connected with or responsible for sth, or that they do not have any knowledge of it **2** (*law*) a statement in which a person says officially that they do not claim the right to do sth

dis·close /dɪsˈkləʊz; AmE -ˈkloʊz/ *verb* **1** ~ **sth (to sb)** to give sb information about sth, especially sth that was previously secret [SYN] REVEAL: [VN] *The spokesman refused to disclose details of the takeover to the press.* ◊

[v that] *The report discloses that human error was to blame for the accident.* ◊ [VN that] *It was disclosed that two women were being interviewed by the police.* [also v wh-] **2** [VN] (*written*) to allow sth that was hidden to be seen SYN REVEAL: *The door swung open, disclosing a long dark passage.*

dis·clo·sure /dɪsˈkləʊʒə(r); *AmE* -ˈkloʊ-/ *noun* (*formal*) **1** [U] the act of making sth known or public that was previously secret or private SYN REVELATION: *the newspaper's disclosure of defence secrets* **2** [C] information or a fact that is made known or public that was previously secret or private SYN REVELATION: *startling disclosures about his private life*

disco /ˈdɪskəʊ; *AmE* ˈdɪskoʊ/ *noun* **1** (also *old-fashioned* **disco·theque**) a club, a party, etc. where people dance to recorded pop music: *disco music/dancing* ◊ *the youth club disco* **2** the lights and sound equipment for such an event

dis·col·or·ation (*BrE* also **dis·col·our·ation**) /ˌdɪsˌkʌləˈreɪʃn/ *noun* **1** [U] the process of becoming discoloured: *discoloration caused by the sun* **2** [C] a place where sth has become discoloured

dis·col·our (*BrE*) (*AmE* **dis·color**) /dɪsˈkʌlə(r)/ *verb* to change colour, or to make the colour of sth change, in a way that makes it look less attractive: [V] *Plastic tends to discolour with age.* ◊ [VN] *The pipes were beginning to rust, discolouring the water.*

dis·comfit /dɪsˈkʌmfɪt/ *verb* [VN] [often passive] (*literary*) to make sb feel confused or embarrassed ▶ **dis·com·fit·ure** /dɪsˈkʌmfɪtʃə(r)/ *noun* [U]: *He was clearly taking delight in her discomfiture.*

dis·com·fort /dɪsˈkʌmfət; *AmE* -fərt/ *noun, verb*
■ *noun* **1** [U] a feeling of slight pain or of being physically uncomfortable: *You will experience some minor discomfort during the treatment.* ◊ *abdominal discomfort* **2** [U] a feeling of worry or embarrassment: *John's presence caused her considerable discomfort.* **3** [C] (*formal*) something that makes you feel uncomfortable or causes you a slight feeling of pain
■ *verb* [VN] [often passive] (*formal*) to make sb feel anxious or embarrassed

dis·com·pose /ˌdɪskəmˈpəʊz; *AmE* -ˈpoʊz/ *verb* [VN] (*rare, formal*) to disturb sb and make them feel anxious ▶ **dis·com·pos·ure** /ˌdɪskəmˈpəʊʒə(r); *AmE* -ˈpoʊ-/ *noun* [U]

dis·con·cert /ˌdɪskənˈsɜːt; *AmE* -ˈsɜːrt/ *verb* [VN] to make sb feel anxious, confused or embarrassed: *His answer rather disconcerted her.* ▶ **dis·con·cert·ed** *adj.*: *I was very disconcerted to find that everyone else already knew it.* **dis·con·cert·ing** *adj.*: *She had the disconcerting habit of saying exactly what she thought.* **dis·con·cert·ing·ly** *adv.*

dis·con·nect /ˌdɪskəˈnekt/ *verb* [VN] **1** ~ sth (**from sth**) to remove a piece of equipment from a supply of gas, water or electricity: *First, disconnect the boiler from the water mains.* **2** [usually passive] to officially stop the supply of telephone lines, water, electricity or gas to a building: *You may be disconnected if you do not pay the bill.* **3** ~ sth (**from sth**) to separate sth from sth: *The ski had become disconnected from the boot.* **4** [usually passive] to break the contact between two people who are talking on the telephone: *We were suddenly disconnected.* OPP CONNECT ▶ **dis·con·nec·tion** *noun* [U, C]

dis·con·nect·ed /ˌdɪskəˈnektɪd/ *adj.* **1** not related to or connected with the things or people around: *disconnected images/thoughts/ideas* ◊ *I felt disconnected from the world around me.* **2** (of speech or writing) with the parts not connected in a logical order

dis·con·so·late /dɪsˈkɒnsələt; *AmE* -ˈkɑːn-/ *adj.* (*formal*) very unhappy and disappointed SYN DEJECTED: *The disconsolate players left for home without a trophy.* ▶ **dis·con·so·late·ly** *adv.*

dis·con·tent /ˌdɪskənˈtent/ (also **dis·con·tent·ment** /ˌdɪskənˈtentmənt/) *noun* [U, C] ~ (**at/over/with sth**) a feeling of being unhappy because you are not satisfied with a particular situation; sth that makes you have this feeling SYN DISSATISFACTION: *There is widespread discon-*

tent among the staff at the proposed changes to pay and conditions.—compare CONTENTMENT

dis·con·tent·ed /ˌdɪskənˈtentɪd/ *adj.* ~ (**with sth**) unhappy because you are not satisfied with your situation OPP CONTENTED ▶ **dis·con·tent·ed·ly** *adv.*

dis·con·tinue /ˌdɪskənˈtɪnjuː/ *verb* **1** to stop doing, using or providing sth, especially sth that you have been doing, using or providing regularly: [VN] *It was decided to discontinue the treatment after three months.* [also v -ing] **2** [VN] [usually passive] to stop making a product: *a sale of discontinued china*

dis·con·tinu·ity /ˌdɪskɒntɪˈnjuːəti; *AmE* -ˌkɑːntəˈnuː-/ *noun* (*pl.* **-ies**) (*formal*) **1** [U] the state of not being continuous: *discontinuity in the children's education* **2** [C] a break or change in a continuous process: *Changes in government have led to discontinuities in policy.* OPP CONTINUITY

dis·con·tinu·ous /ˌdɪskənˈtɪnjuəs/ *adj.* (*formal*) not continuous; stopping and starting again SYN INTERMITTENT

dis·cord /ˈdɪskɔːd; *AmE* -kɔːrd/ *noun* **1** [U] (*formal*) disagreement; quarrelling: *marital/family discord* ◊ *A note of discord surfaced during the proceedings.* OPP CONCORD—compare HARMONY **2** [C, U] (*music*) a combination of musical notes that sound harsh together

dis·cord·ant /dɪsˈkɔːdənt; *AmE* -ˈkɔːrd-/ *adj.* **1** [usually before noun] (*formal*) not in agreement; combining with other things in a way that is strange or unpleasant: *discordant views* **2** (of sounds) sounding harsh together

disco·theque /ˈdɪskətek/ *noun* (*old-fashioned*) = DISCO

dis·count *noun, verb*
■ *noun* /ˈdɪskaʊnt/ [C, U] an amount of money that is taken off the usual cost of sth SYN REDUCTION: *to get/give/offer a discount* ◊ *discount rates/prices* ◊ *a 10% discount* ◊ *They were selling everything at a discount* (= at reduced prices). ◊ *a discount shop* (= one that regularly sells goods at reduced prices) ◊ *Do you give any discount?*
■ *verb* /dɪsˈkaʊnt; *AmE* also ˈdɪskaʊnt/ [VN] **1** ~ sth (**as sth**) (*formal*) to think or say that sth is not important or not true: *We cannot discount the possibility of further strikes.* ◊ *The news reports were being discounted as propaganda.* **2** to take an amount of money off the usual cost of sth; to sell sth at a discount: *discounted prices/fares*

dis·counter /ˈdɪskaʊntə(r)/ (also **ˈdiscount store**) *noun* a shop/store that sells things very cheaply, often in large quantities or from a limited range of goods

dis·cour·age /dɪsˈkʌrɪdʒ; *AmE* -ˈkɜːr-/ *verb* **1** ~ sth | ~ sb **from doing sth** to try to prevent sth or to prevent sb from doing sth, especially by making it difficult to do or by showing that you do not approve of it: [VN] *a campaign to discourage smoking among teenagers* ◊ *I leave a light on when I'm out to discourage burglars.* ◊ *His parents tried to discourage him from being an actor.* [also v -ing] **2** [VN] ~ sb (**from doing sth**) to make sb feel less confident or enthusiastic about doing sth: *Don't be discouraged by the first failure—try again!* ◊ *The weather discouraged most people from attending.* OPP ENCOURAGE ▶ **dis·cour·aged** *adj.* [not usually before noun]: *Learners can feel very discouraged if an exercise is too difficult.* **dis·cour·aging** *adj.*: *a discouraging experience/response/result* **dis·cour·aging·ly** *adv.*

dis·cour·age·ment /dɪsˈkʌrɪdʒmənt; *AmE* -ˈkɜːr-/ *noun* **1** [U] a feeling that you no longer have the confidence or enthusiasm to do sth: *an atmosphere of discouragement and despair* **2** [U] the action of trying to stop sth: *the government's discouragement of political protest* **3** [C] a thing that discourages sb from doing sth: *Despite all these discouragements, she refused to give up.*

dis·course *noun, verb*
■ *noun* /ˈdɪskɔːs; *AmE* -kɔːrs/ **1** [C, U] (*formal*) a long and serious treatment or discussion of a subject in speech or writing: *a discourse on issues of gender and sexuality* ◊ *He was hoping for some lively political discourse at the meeting.* **2** [U] (*linguistics*) the use of language in speech and writing in order to produce meaning; language that is studied, usually in order to see how the different parts of

æ	ɑː	e	ɜː	ə	ɪ	iː	i	ɒ	ɔː	ʌ	ʊ	u	uː
cat	father	ten	bird	about	sit	see	many	got	saw	cup	put	actual	too

(BrE)

a text are connected: *spoken/written discourse* ◊ *discourse analysis*

■ *verb* /dɪsˈkɔːs; *AmE* -ˈkɔːrs/ **PHRV** **disˈcourse on/upon sth** (*formal*) to talk or give a long speech about sth that you know a lot about

dis·cour·teous /dɪsˈkɜːtiəs; *AmE* -ˈkɜːrt-/ *adj.* (*formal*) having bad manners and not showing respect for other people **SYN** IMPOLITE: *He didn't wish to appear discourteous.* **OPP** COURTEOUS

dis·cour·tesy /dɪsˈkɜːtəsi; *AmE* -ˈkɜːrt-/ *noun* [U, C] (*pl.* **-ies**) (*formal*) behaviour or an action that is not polite

dis·cover /dɪsˈkʌvə(r)/ *verb* **1** [VN] to be the first person to become aware that a particular place or thing exists: *Cook is credited with discovering Hawaii.* ◊ *Scientists around the world are working to discover a cure for Aids.* **2** to find sb/sth that was hidden or that you did not expect to find: [VN] *Police discovered a large stash of drugs while searching the house.* ◊ *We discovered this beach while we were sailing around the island.* ◊ [VN-ing] *He was discovered hiding in a shed.* ◊ [VN-ADJ] *She was discovered dead at her home in Leeds.* **3** to find out about sth; to find some information about sth: [VN] *I've just discovered hang-gliding!* ◊ [V(that)] *It was a shock to discover (that) he couldn't read.* ◊ [Vwh-] *We never did discover why she gave up her job.* ◊ [VNthat] *It was later discovered that the diaries were a fraud.* ◊ [VNtoinf] *He was later discovered to be seriously ill.* **HELP** This pattern is usually used in the passive. **4** [VN] [often passive] to be the first person to realize that sb is very good at singing, acting, etc. and help them to become successful and famous: *The singer was discovered while still at school.* ▶ **dis·cov·er·er** *noun*: *the discoverer of penicillin*

> **WHICH WORD?**
> **discover / invent / find out / learn / know** (?)
>
> If you **invent** something, you make or design something that did not exist before.
>
> If you **discover** something, you find something that already exists or learn about it for the first time, before anyone else does: *Who discovered America?*
>
> You can also **discover** a piece of information that other people knew but you didn't: *When did you discover that she's married?*
>
> If you **learn** something, you come to know it by study or enquiry: *learning new vocabulary.*
>
> If you **find** something **out** either by chance or by study or enquiry: *When did you find out that she's married?*
>
> If you **know** something, you have that knowledge or information in your mind: *I couldn't find out what the word meant as it wasn't in my dictionary, but John told me, so now I know it.*

dis·cov·ery /dɪsˈkʌvəri/ *noun* (*pl.* **-ies**) **1** [C, U] ~ (of sth)|~ (that ...) an act or the process of finding sb/sth, or learning about sth that was not known about before: *the discovery of antibiotics in the 20th century* ◊ *The discovery of a child's body in the river has shocked the community.* ◊ *Researchers in this field have made some important new discoveries.* ◊ *He saw life as a voyage of discovery.* ◊ *She was shocked by the discovery that he had been unfaithful.* ◊ *the discovery of new talent in the art world* **2** [C] a thing, fact or person that is found or learned about for the first time: *The drug is not a new discovery—it's been known about for years.*

dis·credit /dɪsˈkredɪt/ *verb, noun*
■ *verb* [VN] **1** to make people stop respecting sb/sth: *The photos were deliberately taken to discredit the President.* ◊ *a discredited government/policy* **2** to make people stop believing that sth is true; to make sth appear unlikely to be true: *These theories are now largely discredited among linguists.*
■ *noun* [U] (*formal*) damage to sb's reputation; loss of respect: *Violent football fans bring discredit on the teams they support.* ◊ *Britain, to its discredit, did not speak out against these atrocities.*—compare CREDIT *n.* (7)

dis·cred·it·able /dɪsˈkredɪtəbl/ *adj.* (*formal*) bad and unacceptable; causing people to lose respect for sb/sth

dis·creet /dɪsˈkriːt/ *adj.*
careful in what you say or do, in order to keep sth secret or to avoid causing embarrassment or difficulty for sb **SYN** TACTFUL:

> **WORD FAMILY**
> **discreet** *adj.* (≠ indiscreet)
> **discretion** *n.* (≠ indiscretion)

He was always very discreet about his love affairs. ◊ *You ought to make a few discreet enquiries before you sign anything.* ▶ **dis·creet·ly** *adv.*: *She coughed discreetly to announce her presence.*

dis·crep·ancy /dɪsˈkrepənsi/ *noun* (*pl.* **-ies**) [C, U] ~ (in sth)|~ (between A and B) a difference between two or more things that should be the same: *wide discrepancies in prices quoted for the work* ◊ *What are the reasons for the discrepancy between girls' and boys' performance in school?*

dis·crete /dɪsˈkriːt/ *adj.* (*formal* or *technical*) independent of other things of the same type **SYN** SEPARATE: *The organisms can be divided into discrete categories.* ▶ **dis·crete·ly** *adv.* **dis·crete·ness** *noun* [U]

dis·cre·tion /dɪsˈkreʃn/ *noun* [U] **1** the freedom or power to decide what should be done in a particular situation: *I'll leave it up to you to use your discretion.* ◊ *How much to tell terminally ill patients is left to the discretion of the doctor.* **2** care in what you say or do, in order to keep sth secret or to avoid causing embarrassment or difficulty for sb; the quality of being DISCREET: *This is confidential, but I know that I can rely on your discretion.*—compare INDISCRETION **IDM** **at sb's diˈscretion** according to what sb decides or wishes to do: *Bail is granted at the discretion of the court.* ◊ *There is no service charge and tipping is at your discretion.* **diˌscretion is the ˌbetter part of ˈvalour** (*saying*) you should avoid danger and not take unnecessary risks

dis·cre·tion·ary /dɪsˈkreʃənəri; *AmE* -neri/ *adj.* [usually before noun] (*formal*) decided according to the judgement of a person in authority about what is necessary in each particular situation; not decided by rules: *You may be eligible for a discretionary grant for your university course.*

dis·crim·in·ate /dɪsˈkrɪmɪneɪt/ *verb* **1** ~ (between A and B)|~ A from B to recognize that there is a difference between people or things; to show a difference between people or things: [V] *The computer program was unable to discriminate between letters and numbers.* ◊ [VN] *When do babies learn to discriminate voices?* ◊ *A number of features discriminate this species from others.* **2** [V] ~ (against sb)|~ (in favour of sb) to treat one person or group worse/better than another in an unfair way: *practices that discriminate against women and in favour of men* ◊ *It is illegal to discriminate on grounds of race, sex or religion.*

dis·crim·in·at·ing /dɪsˈkrɪmɪneɪtɪŋ/ *adj.* (*approving*) able to judge the good quality of sth: *a discriminating audience/customer*

dis·crim·in·ation /dɪˌskrɪmɪˈneɪʃn/ *noun* **1** [U] ~ (against sb) the practice of treating sb or a particular group in society less fairly than others: *racial/sex/sexual discrimination* (= because of sb's race or sex) ◊ *discrimination against the elderly* ◊ *discrimination in favour of the young* ◊ *discrimination on the grounds of race, gender, or sexual orientation*—see also POSITIVE DISCRIMINATION **2** [U] (*approving*) the ability to judge what is good, true, etc. **SYN** DISCERNMENT: *He showed great discrimination in his choice of friends.* **3** (*formal*) [U, C] the ability to recognize a difference between one thing and another; a difference that is recognized: *to learn discrimination between right and wrong* ◊ *fine discriminations*

dis·crim·in·atory /dɪsˈkrɪmɪnətəri; *AmE* dɪˈskrɪmɪnətɔːri/ *adj.* unfair; treating sb or one group of people worse than others: *discriminatory practices/rules/measures* ◊ *sexually/racially discriminatory laws*

dis·cur·sive /dɪsˈkɜːsɪv; *AmE* -ˈkɜːrs-/ *adj.* (of a style of writing or speaking) moving from one point to another without any strict structure: *the discursive style of the novel*

aɪ	aʊ	eɪ	əʊ	oʊ	ɔɪ	ɪə	eə	ʊə	j	w
my	now	say	go (BrE)	go (AmE)	boy	near	hair	pure	yes	wet

dis·cus /'dɪskəs/ *noun* **1** [C] a heavy flat circular object thrown in a sporting event **2 (the discus)** [sing.] the event or sport of throwing a discus as far as possible—picture on page 1251

dis·cuss /dɪ'skʌs/ *verb* **1 ~ sth (with sb)** to talk about sth with other people, especially in order to decide sth: [VN] *Have you discussed the problem with anyone?* ◇ *I'm not prepared to discuss this on the phone.* ◇ [V wh-] *We need to discuss when we should go.* ◇ [V-ing] *We briefly discussed buying a second car.* [also VN-ing] **HELP** You cannot say 'discuss about sth': ~~I discussed about my problem with my parents.~~ Look also at **discussion**. **2** to write or talk about sth in detail, showing the different ideas and opinions about it: [VN] *This topic will be discussed at greater length in the next chapter.* [also V wh-]

dis·cus·sion /dɪ'skʌʃn/ *noun* **1** [U, C] the process of discussing sb/sth; a conversation about sb/sth: *a topic/ subject for discussion* ◇ *After considerable discussion, they decided to accept our offer.* ◇ *The plans have been under discussion* (= being talked about) *for a year now.* ◇ *Discussions are still taking place between the two leaders.* ◇ *We had a discussion about the differences between Britain and the US.* **2** [C] a speech or a piece of writing that discusses many different aspects of a subject: *Her article is a discussion of the methods used in research.*

dis·dain /dɪs'deɪn/ *noun, verb*
- *noun* [U, sing.] **~ (for sb/sth)** the feeling that sb/sth is not good enough to deserve your respect or attention [SYN] CONTEMPT: *to treat sb with disdain* ◇ *a disdain for the law*
- *verb* (*formal*) **1** [VN] to think that sb/sth is not good enough to deserve your respect: *She disdained his offer of help.* **2** [V to inf] to refuse to do sth because you think that you are too important to do it: *He disdained to turn to his son for advice.*

dis·dain·ful /dɪs'deɪnfl/ *adj.* **~ (of sb/sth)** showing disdain: *She's always been disdainful of people who haven't been to college.* ▸ **dis·dain·ful·ly** /-fəli/ *adv.*

dis·ease /dɪ'ziːz/ *noun* [U, C] **1** an illness affecting humans, animals or plants, often caused by infection: *heart/liver/kidney disease* ◇ *health measures to prevent the spread of disease* ◇ *an infectious/contagious disease* (= one that can be passed to sb very easily) ◇ *It is not known what causes the disease.* ◇ *protection against sexually transmitted diseases* ◇ *He suffers from a rare blood disease.* ⇨ vocabulary notes on page 599 **2** [C] (*formal*) something that is very wrong with people's attitudes, way of life or with society: *Greed is a disease of modern society.*

dis·eased /dɪ'ziːzd/ *adj.* suffering from a disease: *diseased tissue* ◇ *the diseased social system*

dis·em·bark /ˌdɪsɪm'bɑːk; *AmE* -'bɑːrk/ *verb* [V] **~ (from sth)** (*informal*) to leave a vehicle, especially a ship or an aircraft, at the end of a journey [OPP] EMBARK ▸ **dis·em·bark·ation** /ˌdɪsembɑː'keɪʃn/ *noun* [U]

dis·em·bod·ied /ˌdɪsɪm'bɒdid; *AmE* -'bɑːdid/ *adj.* [usually before noun] **1** (of sounds) coming from a person or place that cannot be seen or identified: *a disembodied voice* **2** separated from the body: *disembodied spirits*

dis·em·bowel /ˌdɪsɪm'baʊəl/ *verb* (**-ll-**, *AmE* **-l-**) [VN] to take the stomach, bowels and other organs out of a person or animal

dis·en·chant·ed /ˌdɪsɪn'tʃɑːntɪd; *AmE* -'tʃænt-/ *adj.* **~ (with sb/sth)** no longer feeling enthusiasm for sb/sth; not believing sth is good or worth doing: *He was becoming disenchanted with his job as a lawyer.* ▸ **dis·en·chant·ment** *noun* [U]: *a growing sense/feeling of disenchantment with his job*

dis·en·fran·chise /ˌdɪsɪn'fræntʃaɪz/ *verb* [VN] to take away sb's rights, especially their right to vote: *a disenfranchised group/minority* [OPP] ENFRANCHISE

dis·en·gage /ˌdɪsɪn'ɡeɪdʒ/ *verb* **1 ~ (sth/sb) (from sth/ sb)** | **~ yourself (from sb/sth)** (*formal*) to free sb/sth from the person or thing that is holding them or it; to become free: [VN] *She gently disengaged herself from her sleeping son.* ◇ *to disengage the clutch* (= when driving a car) ◇ (*figurative*) *They wished to disengage themselves from these policies.* ◇ [V] *We saw the booster rockets disengage and fall into the sea.* **2** [V, VN] (*technical*) if an army

disengages or sb disengages it, it stops fighting and moves away—compare ENGAGE ▸ **dis·en·gage·ment** *noun* [U]

dis·en·tan·gle /ˌdɪsɪn'tæŋɡl/ *verb* [VN] **1 ~ sth (from sth)** to separate different arguments, ideas, etc. that have become confused: *It's not easy to disentangle the truth from the official statistics.* **2 ~ sth/sb (from sth)** to free sb/sth from sth that has become wrapped or twisted around it or them: *He tried to disentangle his fingers from her hair.* ◇ (*figurative*) *She has just disentangled herself from a painful relationship.* **3** to get rid of the twists and knots in sth: *He was sitting on the deck disentangling a coil of rope.*

dis·equi·lib·rium /ˌdɪs,iːkwɪ'lɪbriəm; -,ekw-/ *noun* [U] (*formal* or *technical*) a loss or lack of balance in a situation

dis·es·tab·lish /ˌdɪsɪ'stæblɪʃ/ *verb* [VN] (*formal*) to end the official status of a national Church: *a campaign to disestablish the Church of England* ▸ **dis·es·tab·lish·ment** *noun* [U]

dis·favour (*BrE*) (*AmE* **dis·favor**) /dɪs'feɪvə(r)/ *noun* [U] (*formal*) the feeling that you do not like or approve of sb/sth: *They looked upon the birth of a girl with disfavour.*

dis·fig·ure /dɪs'fɪɡə(r); *AmE* -ɡjər/ *verb* [VN] to spoil the appearance of a person, thing or place: *Her face was disfigured by a long red scar.* ▸ **dis·fig·ure·ment** *noun* [U, C]: *He suffered permanent disfigurement in the fire.*

dis·gorge /dɪs'ɡɔːdʒ; *AmE* -'ɡɔːrdʒ/ *verb* [VN] (*written*) **1** to pour sth out in large quantities: *The pipe disgorges sewage into the sea.* **2** if a vehicle or building **disgorges** people, they come out of it in large numbers: *The bus disgorged a crowd of noisy children.*

dis·grace /dɪs'ɡreɪs/ *noun, verb*
- *noun* **1** [U] the loss of other people's respect and approval because of the bad way sb has behaved [SYN] SHAME: *Her behaviour has brought disgrace on her family.* ◇ *The swimmer was sent home from the Olympics in disgrace.* ◇ *There is no disgrace in being poor.* ◇ *Sam was in disgrace with his parents.* **2** [sing.] **a ~ (to sb/sth)** a person or thing that is so bad that people connected with them or it feel or should feel ashamed: *Your homework is an absolute disgrace.* ◇ *That sort of behaviour is a disgrace to the legal profession.* ◇ *The state of our roads is a national disgrace.* ◇ *It's a disgrace that* (= it is very wrong that) *they are paid so little.*
- *verb* [VN] **1** to behave badly in a way that makes you or other people feel ashamed: *I disgraced myself by drinking far too much.* ◇ *He had disgraced the family name.* **2 (be disgraced)** to lose the respect of people, usually so that you lose a position of power: *He was publicly disgraced and sent into exile.* ◇ *a disgraced politician/leader*

dis·grace·ful /dɪs'ɡreɪsfl/ *adj.* very bad or unacceptable; that people should feel ashamed about: *His behaviour was absolutely disgraceful!* ◇ *It's disgraceful that none of the family tried to help her.* ◇ *a disgraceful waste of money* ▸ **dis·grace·ful·ly** /-fəli/ *adv.*

dis·grun·tled /dɪs'ɡrʌntld/ *adj.* **~ (at sb/sth)** annoyed or disappointed because sth has happened to upset you: *I left feeling disgruntled at the way I'd been treated.* ◇ *disgruntled employees*

dis·guise /dɪs'ɡaɪz/ *verb, noun*
- *verb* [VN] **1 ~ sb (as sb/sth)** to change your appearance so that people cannot recognize you: *The hijackers were heavily disguised.* ◇ *She disguised herself as a boy.* ◇ *They got in disguised as security guards.* **2** to hide sth or change it, so that it cannot be recognized: *She made no attempt to disguise her surprise.* ◇ *It was a thinly disguised attack on the President.* ◇ *She couldn't disguise the fact that she felt uncomfortable.*
- *noun* **1** [C, U] a thing that you wear or use to change your appearance so that people do not recognize you: *She wore glasses and a wig as a disguise.* ◇ *The star travelled in disguise* (= wearing a disguise). ◇ (*figurative*) *A vote for the Liberal Democrats is just a Labour vote in disguise.* **2** [U] the art of changing your appearance so that people

D

do not recognize you: *He is a master of disguise.* **IDM** see BLESSING

dis·gust /dɪsˈɡʌst/ *noun, verb*

■ *noun* [U] ~ **(at/with sth)**| ~ **(for sb)** a strong feeling of dislike or disapproval for sb/sth that you feel is unacceptable, or for sth that looks, smells, etc. unpleasant: *She expressed her disgust at the programme by writing a letter to complain.* ◊ *The idea fills me with disgust.* ◊ *I can only feel disgust for these criminals.* ◊ *He walked away in disgust.* ◊ *Much to my disgust, they refused to help.* ◊ *She wrinkled her nose in disgust at the smell of urine.*

■ *verb* [VN] if sth **disgusts** you, it makes you feel shocked and almost ill because it is so unpleasant: *The level of violence in the film really disgusted me.*

dis·gust·ed /dɪsˈɡʌstɪd/ *adj.* ~ **(at/by/with sb/sth/yourself)** feeling or showing disgust: *I was disgusted at/by the thought that he had touched her.* ◊ *He was disgusted to see such awful living conditions.* ◊ *I was disgusted with myself for eating so much.* ▶ **dis·gust·ed·ly** /dɪsˈɡʌstɪdli/ *adv.*: *'This champagne is warm!', he said disgustedly.*

dis·gust·ing /dɪsˈɡʌstɪŋ/ *adj.* **1** extremely unpleasant: *The kitchen was in a disgusting state when she left.* ◊ *What a disgusting smell!* **2** unacceptable and shocking: *I think it's disgusting that they're closing the local hospital.* ◊ *His language is disgusting* (= he uses a lot of obscene words).

dis·gust·ing·ly /dɪsˈɡʌstɪŋli/ *adv.* **1** (sometimes *humorous*) extremely (in a way that other people feel jealous of): *He looked disgustingly healthy when he got back from the Bahamas.* **2** in a disgusting way: *disgustingly dirty*

dish /dɪʃ/ *noun, verb*

■ *noun* **1** [C] a flat shallow container for cooking food in or serving it from: *a glass dish* ◊ *an ovenproof dish* ◊ *a baking/serving dish* ◊ *They helped themselves from a large dish of pasta.* **2 (the dishes)** [pl.] the plates, bowls, cups, etc. that have been used for a meal and need to be washed: *I'll do the dishes* (= wash them). **3** [C] food prepared in a particular way as part of a meal: *a vegetarian/fish dish* ◊ *This makes an excellent hot main dish.* ◊ *I can recommend the chef's dish of the day.*—see also SIDE DISH **4** [C] any object that is shaped like a dish or bowl: *a soap dish*—see also SATELLITE DISH **5** [C] (*informal*) a sexually attractive person: *What a dish!*

■ *verb* **IDM** **dish the ˈdirt (on sb)** (*informal*) to tell people unkind or unpleasant things about sb, especially about their private life **PHRV** **ˌdish it ˈout** (*disapproving*) to criticize other people: *He enjoys dishing it out, but he really can't take it* (= cannot accept criticism from other people). **ˌdish sth↔ˈout 1** (*informal*) to give sth, often to a lot of people or in large amounts: *Students dished out leaflets to passers-by.* ◊ *She's always dishing out advice, even when you don't want it.* **2** to serve food onto plates for a meal: *Can you dish out the potatoes please?* **ˌdish ˈup| ˌdish sth↔ˈup** to serve food onto plates for a meal **ˌdish ˈup sth** to offer sth to sb, especially sth that is not very good

dis·har·mony /dɪsˈhɑːməni; *AmE* -ˈhɑːrm-/ *noun* [U] (*formal*) a lack of agreement about important things, which causes bad feelings between people or groups of people: *marital/racial/social disharmony*

dish·cloth /ˈdɪʃklɒθ; *AmE* -klɔːθ/ (*AmE* usually **dish·rag**) *noun* a cloth for washing dishes

dis·heart·en /dɪsˈhɑːtn; *AmE* -ˈhɑːrtn/ *verb* [VN] (*written*) to make sb lose hope or confidence: *Don't let this defeat dishearten you.* ▶ **dis·heart·ened** *adj.*: *a disheartened team/community* **dis·heart·en·ing** /-ˈhɑːtnɪŋ; *AmE* -ˈhɑːrt-/ *adj.*: *a disheartening experience/failure*

dish·ev·elled /dɪˈʃevld/ (*especially BrE*) (*AmE* usually **dish·ev·eled**) *adj.* (of hair, clothes or sb's general appearance) very untidy: *He looked tired, dishevelled and very pale.*

dis·hon·est /dɪsˈɒnɪst; *AmE* -ˈɑːn-/ *adj.* not honest; intending to deceive people: *Beware of dishonest traders in the tourist areas.* ◊ *I don't like him, and it would be dishonest of me to pretend otherwise.* ▶ **dis·hon·est·ly** *adv.* **dis·hon·esty** *noun* [U]

dis·hon·our (*BrE*) (*AmE* **dis·honor**) /dɪsˈɒnə(r); *AmE* -ˈɑːn-/ *noun, verb*

■ *noun* [U] (*formal*) a loss of honour or respect because you have done sth immoral or unacceptable

■ *verb* [VN] (*formal*) **1** to make sb/sth lose the respect of other people: *You have dishonoured the name of the school.* **2** to refuse to keep an agreement or promise: *He had dishonoured nearly all of his election pledges.* **OPP** HONOUR

dis·hon·our·able (*BrE*) (*AmE* **dis·hon·or·able**) /dɪsˈɒnərəbl; *AmE* -ˈɑːn-/ *adj.* not deserving respect; immoral or unacceptable: *It would have been dishonourable of her not to keep her promise.* ◊ *He was given a* **dishonourable discharge** (= an order to leave the army for unacceptable behaviour). ▶ **dis·hon·our·ably** /-nərəbli/ *adv.*

dish·pan /ˈdɪʃpæn/ *noun* (*AmE*) a bowl for washing plates, etc. in

dish·rag /ˈdɪʃræɡ/ *noun* (*AmE*) = DISHCLOTH

dish·towel /ˈdɪʃtaʊəl/ *noun* (*AmE*) = TEA TOWEL

dish·wash·er /ˈdɪʃwɒʃə(r); *AmE* -wɑːʃ-; -wɔːʃ-/ *noun* **1** a machine for washing plates, cups, etc: *to load/stack the dishwasher* **2** a person whose job is to wash plates, etc., for example in a restaurant

dish·water /ˈdɪʃwɔːtə(r)/ *noun* [U] water that sb has used to wash dirty plates, etc. **IDM** see DULL *adj.*

dishy /ˈdɪʃi/ *adj.* (*old-fashioned informal, especially BrE*) (of a person) physically attractive

dis·il·lu·sion /ˌdɪsɪˈluːʒn/ *verb* [VN] to destroy sb's belief in or good opinion of sb/sth: *I hate to disillusion you, but not everyone is as honest as you.* ▶ **dis·il·lu·sion** *noun* [U] = DISILLUSIONMENT

dis·il·lu·sioned /ˌdɪsɪˈluːʒnd/ *adj.* ~ **(by/with sb/sth)** disappointed because the person you admired or the idea you believed to be good and true now seems without value: *I soon became disillusioned with the job.*

dis·il·lu·sion·ment /ˌdɪsɪˈluːʒnmənt/ (also **dis·il·lu·sion**) *noun* [U, sing.] ~ **(with sth)** the state of being disillusioned: *There is widespread disillusionment with the present government.*

dis·in·cen·tive /ˌdɪsɪnˈsentɪv/ *noun* [C] ~ **(to sth)** a thing that makes sb less willing or less keen to do sth: *A sudden fall in profits provided a further disincentive to new investors.* **OPP** INCENTIVE

dis·in·clin·ation /ˌdɪsˌɪnklɪˈneɪʃn/ *noun* [sing., U] (*formal*) a lack of willingness to do sth; a lack of enthusiasm for sth: *There was a general disinclination to return to the office after lunch.*

dis·in·clined /ˌdɪsɪnˈklaɪnd/ *adj.* [not before noun] ~ **(to do sth)** (*formal*) not willing **SYN** RELUCTANT: *He was strongly disinclined to believe anything that she said.*

dis·in·fect /ˌdɪsɪnˈfekt/ *verb* [VN] **1** to clean sth using a substance that kills bacteria: *to disinfect a surface/room/wound* **2** to run a computer program to get rid of a computer VIRUS

dis·in·fect·ant /ˌdɪsɪnˈfektənt/ *noun* [U, C] a substance that disinfects: *a strong smell of disinfectant*

dis·in·for·ma·tion /ˌdɪsˌɪnfəˈmeɪʃn; *AmE* -fər-/ *noun* [U] false information that is given deliberately, especially by government organizations

dis·in·genu·ous /ˌdɪsɪnˈdʒenjuəs/ *adj.* [not usually before noun] (*formal*) not sincere, especially when you pretend to know less about sth than you really do: *It would be disingenuous of me to claim I had never seen it.*—compare INGENUOUS ▶ **dis·in·genu·ous·ly** *adv.*

dis·in·herit /ˌdɪsɪnˈherɪt/ *verb* [VN] to prevent sb, especially your son or daughter, from receiving your money or property after your death—compare INHERIT (1)

dis·in·te·grate /dɪsˈɪntɪɡreɪt/ *verb* [VN] **1** to break into small parts or pieces and be destroyed: *The plane disintegrated as it fell into the sea.* **2** to become much less strong or united and be gradually destroyed: *The authority of the central government was rapidly disintegrating.* ▶ **dis·in·te·gra·tion** /dɪsˌɪntɪˈɡreɪʃn/ *noun* [U]: *the gradual disintegration of traditional values*

dis·in·ter /ˌdɪsɪnˈtɜː(r)/ *verb* (-rr-) [VN] (*formal*) **1** to dig up

s	t	v	z	ʃ	ʒ	tʃ	dʒ	θ	ð	ŋ
see	tea	van	zoo	shoe	vision	chain	jam	thin	this	sing

sth, especially a dead body, from the ground OPP INTER **2 ~ sth (from sth)** to find sth that has been hidden or lost for a long time

dis·in·ter·est /dɪs'ɪntrəst; -trest/ *noun* [U] **1 ~ (in sth)** lack of interest: *His total disinterest in money puzzled his family.* **2** the fact of not being involved in sth

dis·in·ter·est·ed /dɪs'ɪntrəstɪd; -trestɪd/ *adj.* **1** not influenced by personal feelings, or by the chance of getting some advantage for yourself: *a disinterested onlooker/spectator* ◊ *Her advice appeared to be disinterested.* **2** (*informal*) not interested ⇨ note at INTERESTED ▶ **dis·in·ter·est·ed·ly** *adv.*

dis·in·vest·ment /ˌdɪsɪn'vestmənt/ *noun* [U] (*finance*) the process of selling the shares you have bought in a company

dis·joint·ed /dɪs'dʒɔɪntɪd/ *adj.* not communicated or described in a clear or logical way; not connected: *the disjointed thoughts of a dying man*

dis·junc·tion /dɪs'dʒʌŋkʃn/ (also *less frequent* **dis·junc·ture** /dɪs'dʒʌŋktʃə(r)/) *noun* **~ (between A and B)** (*formal*) a difference between two things that you would expect to be in agreement with each other

disk /dɪsk/ *noun* **1** (*especially AmE*) = DISC **2** (also **mag·netic 'disk**) (*computing*) a device for storing information on a computer, with a MAGNETIC surface that records information received in electronic form—see also FLOPPY DISK, HARD DISK

'disk drive *noun* a device that passes data between a disk and the memory of a computer or from one disk or computer to another: *a floppy/hard disk*

disk·ette /dɪs'ket/ *noun* = FLOPPY DISK

dis·like /dɪs'laɪk/ *verb, noun*
■ *verb* (rather *formal*) to not like sb/sth: [VN] *Why do you dislike him so much?* ◊ *He disliked it when she behaved badly in front of his mother.* ◊ [V-ing] *I dislike being away from my family.* ◊ *Much as she disliked going to funerals* (= although she did not like it at all)*, she knew she had to be there.* ◊ [VN-ing] *He disliked her staying away from home.*
■ *noun* **1** [U, sing.] **~ (of/for sb/sth)** a feeling of not liking sb/sth: *He did not try to hide his dislike of his boss.* ◊ *She took an instant dislike to the house and the neighbourhood.* **2** [C, usually pl.] a thing that you do not like: *I've told you all my likes and dislikes.*

dis·lo·cate /'dɪsləkeɪt; AmE -loʊk-; dɪs'loʊ-/ *verb* [VN] **1** to put a bone out of its normal position in a joint: *He dislocated his shoulder in the accident.* ◊ *a dislocated finger* **2** to stop a system, plan etc. from working or continuing in the normal way SYN DISRUPT ▶ **dis·lo·ca·tion** /ˌdɪslə'keɪʃn; AmE -loʊ-/ *noun* [C, U]: *a dislocation of the shoulder* ◊ *These policies could cause severe economic and social dislocation.*

dis·lodge /dɪs'lɒdʒ; AmE -'lɑːdʒ/ *verb* [VN] **1 ~ sth (from sth)** to force or knock sth out of its position: *The wind dislodged one or two tiles from the roof.* **2 ~ sb (from sth)** to force sb to leave a place, position or job: *The rebels have so far failed to dislodge the President.*

dis·loyal /dɪs'lɔɪəl/ *adj.* **~ (to sb/sth)** not loyal or faithful to your friends, family, country, etc: *He was accused of being disloyal to the government.* ▶ **dis·loy·alty** /-'lɔɪəlti/ *noun* [U]

dis·mal /'dɪzməl/ *adj.* **1** causing or showing sadness SYN MISERABLE, GLOOMY: *dismal conditions/surroundings/weather* ◊ *Christmas will be dismal without the children.* **2** (*informal*) not skilful or successful; of very low quality: *The singer gave a dismal performance of some old songs.* ◊ *Their recent attempt to increase sales has been a dismal failure.* ▶ **dis·mal·ly** /-məli/ *adv.*: *I tried not to laugh but failed dismally* (= was completely unsuccessful).

dis·man·tle /dɪs'mæntl/ *verb* [VN] **1** to take apart a machine or structure so that it is in separate pieces: *I had to dismantle the engine in order to repair it.* ◊ *The steel mill was dismantled piece by piece.* **2** to end an organization or system gradually in an organized way: *The government was in the process of dismantling the state-owned industries.* ▶ **dis·mant·ling** *noun* [U]

dis·may /dɪs'meɪ/ *noun, verb*
■ *noun* [U] a worried, sad feeling after you have received an unpleasant surprise: *She could not hide her dismay at the result.* ◊ *He looked at her in dismay.* ◊ *To her dismay, her name was not on the list.* ◊ *The news has been greeted with dismay by local business leaders.*
■ *verb* [VN] to make sb feel shocked and disappointed: *Their reaction dismayed him.* ▶ **dis·mayed** *adj.* **~ (at/by sth)| ~ to find, hear, see, etc.**: *He was dismayed at the change in his old friend.* ◊ *The suggestion was greeted by a dismayed silence.* ◊ *They were dismayed to find that the ferry had already left.*

dis·mem·ber /dɪs'membə(r)/ *verb* [VN] **1** to cut or tear the dead body of a person or an animal into pieces: *Police say the body had been dismembered.* **2** (*formal*) to divide a country, an organization, etc. into smaller parts ▶ **dis·mem·ber·ment** *noun* [U]

dis·miss /dɪs'mɪs/ *verb* [VN] **1 ~ sb/sth (as sth)** to decide that sb/sth is not important and not worth thinking or talking about SYN WAVE ASIDE: *I think we can safely dismiss their objections.* ◊ *Vegetarians are no longer dismissed as cranks.* ◊ *He dismissed the opinion polls as worthless.* ◊ *The suggestion should not be dismissed out of hand* (= without thinking about it). **2 ~ sth (from sth)** to put thoughts or feelings out of your mind: *Dismissing her fears, she climbed higher.* ◊ *He dismissed her from his mind.* **3 ~ sb (from sth)** to officially remove sb from their job: *She claims she was unfairly dismissed from her post.* **4** to send sb away or allow them to leave: *At 12 o'clock the class was dismissed.* **5** (*law*) to say that a trial or legal case should not continue, usually because there is not enough evidence: *The case was dismissed.* **6** (in cricket) to end the INNINGS of a player or team

dis·missal /dɪs'mɪsl/ *noun* **1** [U, C] the act of dismissing sb from their job; an example of this: *He still hopes to win his claim against unfair dismissal.* ◊ *The dismissals followed the resignation of the chairman.* **2** [U] the failure to consider sth as important: *Her casual dismissal of the threats seemed irresponsible.*

dis·mis·sive /dɪs'mɪsɪv/ *adj.* **~ (of sb/sth)** showing that you do not believe a person or thing to be important or worth considering: *a dismissive gesture/tone* ▶ **dis·mis·sive·ly** *adv.*: *to shrug/wave dismissively*

dis·mount /dɪs'maʊnt/ *verb* [V] **~ (from sth)** to get off a horse, bicycle or motorcycle OPP MOUNT

dis·obedi·ence /ˌdɪsə'biːdiəns/ *noun* [U] failure or refusal to obey—see also CIVIL DISOBEDIENCE OPP OBEDIENCE

dis·obedi·ent /ˌdɪsə'biːdiənt/ *adj.* failing or refusing to obey: *a disobedient child* OPP OBEDIENT

dis·obey /ˌdɪsə'beɪ/ *verb* to refuse to do what a person, law, etc. tells you to do; to refuse to obey: [VN] *He was punished for disobeying orders.* [also V] OPP OBEY

dis·order /dɪs'ɔːdə(r); AmE -'ɔːrd-/ *noun* **1** [U] an untidy state; a lack of order or organization: *His financial affairs were in complete disorder.* ◊ *The room was in a state of disorder.* OPP ORDER **2** [U] violent behaviour of large groups of people: *an outbreak of rioting and public disorder*—compare ORDER (3) **3** [C, U] an illness that causes a part of the body to stop functioning correctly: *a blood/bowel disorder* ◊ *eating disorders* ◊ *He was suffering from some form of psychiatric disorder.*

dis·ordered /dɪs'ɔːdəd; AmE -'ɔːrdərd/ *adj.* **1** showing a lack of order or control: *disordered hair* ◊ *a disordered state* OPP ORDERED **2** (*technical*) suffering from a mental or physical disorder: *emotionally disordered children*

dis·or·der·ly /dɪs'ɔːdəli; AmE -'ɔːrdərli/ *adj.* [usually before noun] (*formal*) **1** (of people or behaviour) showing lack of control; publicly violent or noisy: *disorderly conduct* ◊ *They were arrested for being drunk and disorderly.* **2** untidy: *newspapers in a disorderly pile by the door* OPP ORDERLY

dis·or·gan·ized (*BrE* also **-ised**) /dɪs'ɔːgənaɪzd; AmE -'ɔːrg-/ (also *less frequent* **un·or·gan·ized, -ised**) *adj.* badly planned; not able to plan or organize well: *It was a hectic disorganized weekend.* ◊ *She's so disorganized.—*

æ	ɑː	e	ɜː	ə	ɪ	iː	i	ɒ	ɔː	ʌ	ʊ	u	uː
cat	father	ten	bird	about	sit	see	many	got	saw	cup	put	actual	too
								(BrE)					

compare ORGANIZED ▶ **dis·or·gan·iza·tion, -isa·tion** /dɪsˌɔːɡənaɪˈzeɪʃn; AmE -ˌɔːrɡənəˈz-/ noun [U]

dis·orien·tate /dɪsˈɔːrientett/ (also **dis·orient** /dɪsˈɔːrient/, AmE, BrE) verb [VN] **1** to make sb unable to recognize where they are or where they should go: *The darkness had disorientated him.* **2** to make sb feel confused: *Ex-soldiers can be disorientated by the transition to civilian life.*—compare ORIENT ▶ **dis·orien·tated** (also **dis·orient·ed**) adj.: *She felt shocked and totally disorientated.* **dis·orien·ta·tion** /dɪsˌɔːriənˈteɪʃn/ noun [U]

dis·own /dɪsˈəʊn; AmE -ˈoʊn/ verb [VN] to decide that you no longer want to be connected with or responsible for sb/sth: *Her family disowned her for marrying a foreigner.*

dis·par·age /dɪˈspærɪdʒ/ verb [VN] (formal) to suggest that sb/sth is not important or valuable: *I don't mean to disparage your achievements.* ▶ **dis·par·age·ment** noun [U] **dis·para·ging** adj.: *disparaging remarks* **dis·para·ging·ly** adv.: *He spoke disparagingly of his colleagues.*

dis·par·ate /ˈdɪspərət/ adj. (formal) **1** made up of parts or people that are very different from each other: *a disparate group of individuals* **2** (of two or more things) so different from each other that they cannot be compared or cannot work together

dis·par·ity /dɪˈspærəti/ noun [U, C] (pl. **-ies**) (formal) a difference, especially one connected with unfair treatment: *the wide disparity between rich and poor*

dis·pas·sion·ate /dɪsˈpæʃənət/ adj. (approving) not influenced by emotion SYN IMPARTIAL: *taking a calm, dispassionate view of the situation* ◇ *a dispassionate observer* ▶ **dis·pas·sion·ate·ly** adv.

dis·patch (BrE also **des·patch**) /dɪˈspætʃ/ verb, noun
■ verb [VN] **1** ~ sb/sth (to ...) (formal) to send sb/sth somewhere, especially for a special purpose: *Troops have been dispatched to the area.* ◇ *A courier was dispatched to collect the documents.* **2** ~ sth (to sb/sth) (formal) to send a letter, parcel/package or message somewhere: *Goods are dispatched within 24 hours of your order reaching us.* **3** (formal) to deal or finish with sb/sth quickly and completely: *He dispatched the younger player in straight sets.* **4** (old-fashioned) to kill a person or an animal
■ noun **1** [U] (formal) the act of sending sb/sth somewhere: *More food supplies are ready for immediate dispatch.* **2** [C] a message or report sent quickly from one military officer to another or between government officials **3** [C] a report sent to a newspaper by a journalist who is working in a foreign country: *dispatches from the war zone* IDM **with di'spatch** (formal) quickly and efficiently: *He carries out his duties with efficiency and dispatch.*

di'spatch box (also **de'spatch box**) (both BrE) noun **1** [C] a container for carrying official documents **2** (**the Dispatch Box**) [sing.] a box on a table in the centre of the House of Commons in the British parliament, which ministers stand next to when they speak

dis·patch·er /dɪˈspætʃə(r)/ noun (AmE) a person whose job is to see that trains, buses, planes, etc. leave on time

di'spatch rider (also **de'spatch rider**) noun (both BrE) a person whose job is to carry messages or packages by motorcycle

dis·pel /dɪˈspel/ verb (**-ll-**) [VN] to make sth, especially a feeling or belief, go away or disappear: *His speech dispelled any fears about his health.*

dis·pens·able /dɪˈspensəbl/ adj. [not usually before noun] not necessary; that can be got rid of: *They looked on music and art lessons as dispensable.* OPP INDISPENSABLE, ESSENTIAL

dis·pens·ary /dɪˈspensəri/ noun (pl. **-ies**) **1** a place in a hospital, shop/store, etc. where medicines are prepared for patients **2** (old-fashioned) a place where patients are treated, especially one run by a charity

dis·pen·sa·tion /ˌdɪspenˈseɪʃn/ noun **1** [C, U] special permission, especially from a religious leader, to do sth that is not usually allowed or legal: *She needed a special dispensation to remarry.* ◇ *The sport's ruling body gave him dispensation to compete in national competitions.* **2** [U] (formal) the act or process of providing sth, especially by sb in authority: *the dispensation of justice* **3** [C] (technical) a political or religious system that operates in a country at a particular time

dis·pense /dɪˈspens/ verb [VN] **1** ~ sth (to sb) to give out sth to people: *The machine dispenses a range of drinks and snacks.* **2** ~ sth (to sb) (formal) to provide sth, especially a service, for people: *The organization dispenses free health care to the poor.* ◇ *to dispense justice/advice* **3** to prepare medicine and give it to people, as a job: *to dispense a prescription* ◇ (BrE) *to dispense medicine* ◇ (BrE) *a dispensing chemist* PHRV **di'spense with sb/sth** to get rid of sth or stop using it because you no longer need it: *Debit cards dispense with the need for cash altogether.* ◇ *I think we can dispense with the formalities* (= speak openly and naturally to each other).

dis·pens·er /dɪˈspensə(r)/ noun a machine or container holding money, drinks, paper towels, etc., that you can obtain quickly by pulling a handle or pressing buttons: *a soap dispenser*—see also CASH DISPENSER

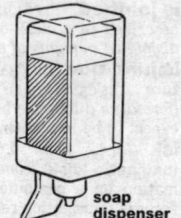
soap dispenser

dis'pensing chemist noun (BrE) = CHEMIST (1)

dis·per·sal /dɪˈspɜːsl; AmE dɪˈspɜːrsl/ noun [U, C] (written) the process of sending sb/sth in different directions; the process of spreading sth over a wide area: *police trained in crowd dispersal* ◇ *the dispersal of seeds*

dis·perse /dɪˈspɜːs; AmE dɪˈspɜːrs/ verb **1** to move apart and go away in different directions; to make sb/sth do this: [V] *The fog began to disperse.* ◇ *The crowd dispersed quickly.* ◇ [VN] *Police dispersed the protesters with tear gas.* **2** to spread or to make sth spread over a wide area: [VN] *The seeds are dispersed by the wind.* [also V]

dis·per·sion /dɪˈspɜːʃn; AmE dɪˈspɜːrʒn/ noun [U] (technical) the process by which people or things are spread over a wide area: *population dispersion* ◇ *the dispersion of light*

dis·pir·ited /dɪˈspɪrɪtɪd/ adj. (written) having no hope or enthusiasm: *She looked tired and dispirited.*—compare SPIRITED

dis·pir·it·ing /dɪˈspɪrɪtɪŋ/ adj. (written) making sb lose their hope or enthusiasm: *a dispiriting experience/failure*

dis·place /dɪsˈpleɪs/ verb [VN] [often passive] **1** to take the place of sb/sth: *Gradually factory workers were displaced by machines.* ◇ (technical) *The ship displaces 58000 tonnes* (= as a way of measuring of its size). **2** to force people to move away from their home to another place: *Around 10000 people have been displaced by the fighting.* **3** to move sth from its usual position: *Check for roof tiles that have been displaced by the wind.* **4** (especially AmE) to remove sb from a job or position: *The nation's displaced workers are not receiving enough help with job-seeking.*

di,splaced 'person noun (pl. **di,splaced 'persons**) (technical) a REFUGEE

dis·place·ment /dɪsˈpleɪsmənt/ noun [U] **1** (formal) the act of displacing sb/sth; the process of being displaced: *the largest displacement of civilian population since World War Two* **2** [C] (physics) the amount of a liquid moved out of place by sth floating or put in it, especially a ship floating in water: *a ship with a displacement of 10000 tonnes*

dis·play /dɪˈspleɪ/ verb, noun
■ verb ~ sth (to sb) **1** [VN] to put sth in a place where people can see it easily; to show sth to people: *The exhibition gives local artists an opportunity to display their work.* ◇ *She displayed her bruises for all to see.* **2** [VN] to show signs of sth, especially a quality or feeling: *I have rarely seen her display any sign of emotion.* ◇ *These statistics display a definite trend.* **3** [VN] (of a computer, etc.) to show information: *The screen will display the user name in the top right-hand corner.* ◇ *This column displays the title of the mail message.* **4** [V] (technical) (of male birds

and animals) to show a special pattern of behaviour that is intended to attract a female bird or animal

■ *noun* **1** an arrangement of things in a public place to inform or entertain people or advertise sth for sale: *a beautiful floral display outside the Town Hall* ◊ *a window display* ◊ *a display cabinet* **2** an act of performing a skill or of showing sth happening, in order to entertain: *a firework display* ◊ *a breathtaking display of aerobatics* **3** an occasion when you show a particular quality, feeling or ability by the way that you behave: *a display of affection / strength / wealth* **4** the words, pictures, etc. shown on a computer screen: *a high resolution colour display*—see also LIQUID CRYSTAL DISPLAY, VDU **IDM** **on di'splay** put in a place where people can look at it: *Designs for the new sports hall are on display in the library.* ◊ *to put sth on temporary / permanent display*

dis·please /dɪsˈpliːz/ *verb* [VN] (*formal*) to make sb feel upset, annoyed or not satisfied: *The tone of the letter displeased her.* **OPP** PLEASE ▶ **dis·pleased** *adj.* ~ **(with sb/sth)**: *Are you displeased with my work?* **dis·pleas·ing** *adj.* ~ **(to sb/sth)**: *His remarks were clearly not displeasing to her.*

dis·pleas·ure /dɪsˈpleʒə(r)/ *noun* [U] ~ **(at/with sb/sth)** (*formal*) the feeling of being upset and annoyed: *She made no attempt to hide her displeasure at the prospect.*—compare PLEASURE

dis·port /dɪsˈpɔːt; *AmE* dɪsˈpɔːrt/ *verb* [VN] ~ **yourself** (*old-fashioned* or *humorous*) to enjoy yourself by doing sth active

dis·pos·able /dɪsˈpəʊzəbl; *AmE* -ˈspoʊ-/ *adj.* [usually before noun] **1** made to be thrown away after use: *disposable gloves / razors* ◊ (*BrE*) *disposable nappies* ◊ (*AmE*) *disposable diapers* **2** (*finance*) available for use: *disposable assets / capital / resources* ◊ *a person's disposable income* (= money they are free to spend after paying taxes, etc.)

dis·pos·ables /dɪsˈpəʊzəblz; *AmE* -ˈspoʊ-/ *noun* [pl.] NAPPIES / DIAPERS that are thrown away after use

dis·posal /dɪsˈpəʊzl; *AmE* -ˈspoʊ-/ *noun* **1** [U] the act of getting rid of sth: *a bomb disposal squad* ◊ *sewage disposal systems* ◊ *the disposal of nuclear waste* **2** [C] (*business*) the sale of part of a business, property, etc. **3** [C] (*AmE*) = WASTE-DISPOSAL UNIT **IDM** **at your/sb's disposal** available for use as you prefer/sb prefers: *He will have a car at his disposal for the whole month.* ◊ *Well, I'm at your disposal* (= I am ready to help you in any way I can).

dis·pose /dɪsˈpəʊz; *AmE* dɪsˈpoʊz/ *verb* (*formal*) **1** [VN+*adv./prep.*] to arrange things or people in a particular way or position **2** ~ **sb to/toward(s) sth** to make sb behave in a particular way: [VN] *a drug that disposes the patient towards sleep* [also VN to inf] **PHR V** **di'spose of sb/sth 1** to get rid of sb/sth that you do not want or cannot keep: *the difficulties of disposing of nuclear waste* ◊ *to dispose of stolen property* **2** to deal with a problem, question or threat successfully: *That seems to have disposed of most of their arguments.* **3** to defeat or kill sb: *It took her a mere 20 minutes to dispose of her opponent.*

dis·posed /dɪsˈpəʊzd; *AmE* dɪsˈpoʊzd/ *adj.* [not before noun] (*formal*) **1** ~ **(to do sth)** willing or prepared to do sth: *I'm not disposed to argue.* ◊ *You're most welcome to join us if you feel so disposed.* **2** (following an adverb) ~ **to/towards sb/sth** having a good/bad opinion of a person or thing: *She seems favourably disposed to the move.*—see also ILL-DISPOSED, WELL DISPOSED

dis·pos·ition /ˌdɪspəˈzɪʃn/ *noun* **1** [C, usually sing.] the natural qualities of a person's character: *to have a cheerful disposition* ◊ *people of a nervous disposition* **2** [C, usually sing.] ~ **to/towards sth** | ~ **to do sth** (*formal*) a tendency to behave in a particular way: *to have / show a disposition towards acts of violence* **3** [C, usually sing.] (*formal*) the way sth is placed or arranged **4** [C, U] (*law*) a formal act of giving property or money to sb

dis·pos·sess /ˌdɪspəˈzes/ *verb* [VN] [usually passive] ~ **sb (of sth)** (*formal*) to take sb's property, land or house away from them ▶ **dis·pos·ses·sion** /ˌdɪspəˈzeʃn/ *noun* [U]

the dis·pos·sessed /ˌdɪspəˈzest/ *noun* [pl.] people who have had property taken away from them

dis·pro·por·tion /ˌdɪsprəˈpɔːʃn; *AmE* -ˈpɔːrʃn/ *noun* [U, C] ~ **(between A and B)** (*written*) the state of two things not being at an equally high or low level; an example of this: *the disproportion between the extra responsibilities and the small salary increase* ◊ *a profession with a high disproportion of male to female employees*

dis·pro·por·tion·ate /ˌdɪsprəˈpɔːʃənət; *AmE* -ˈpɔːrʃ-/ *adj.* ~ **(to sth)** too large or too small when compared with sth else: *The area contains a disproportionate number of young middle-class families.*—compare PROPORTIONATE ▶ **dis·pro·por·tion·ate·ly** *adv.*: *The lower-paid spend a disproportionately large amount of their earnings on food.*

dis·prove /ˌdɪsˈpruːv/ *verb* [VN] to show that sth is wrong or false: *The theory has now been disproved.* **OPP** PROVE

dis·put·able /dɪˈspjuːtəbl/ *adj.* (*formal*) that can or should be questioned or argued about—compare INDISPUTABLE

dis·pu·ta·tion /ˌdɪspjuˈteɪʃn/ *noun* [C, U] (*formal*) a discussion about sth that people cannot agree on

dis·pute *noun, verb*

■ *noun* /dɪˈspjuːt; ˈdɪspjuːt/ [C, U] ~ **(between A and B)** | ~ **(over/about sth)** an argument or a disagreement between two people, groups or countries; discussion about a subject where there is disagreement: *a dispute between the two countries about the border* ◊ *the latest dispute over fishing rights* ◊ *industrial / pay disputes* ◊ *The union is **in dispute with** management over working hours.* ◊ *The cause of the accident was still **in dispute*** (= being argued about). ◊ *The matter was settled **beyond dispute** by the court judgment* (= it could no longer be argued about). ◊ *His theories are **open to dispute*** (= can be disagreed with).

■ *verb* /dɪˈspjuːt/ **1** to question whether sth is true and valid: [VN] *These figures have been disputed.* ◊ *to dispute a decision / claim* ◊ *The family wanted to dispute the will.* ◊ [V that] *No one is disputing that there is a problem.* [also V wh-] **2** to argue or disagree strongly with sb about sth, especially about who owns sth: [VN] *The ownership of this land has been disputed for centuries.* ◊ *disputed territory* ◊ *The issue remains **hotly disputed**.* [also V] **3** [VN] to fight to get control of sth or to win sth: *On the last lap three runners were disputing the lead.*

dis·qual·ify /dɪsˈkwɒlɪfaɪ; *AmE* -ˈkwɑːl-/ *verb* (**dis·quali·fies, dis·quali·fy·ing, dis·quali·fied, dis·quali·fied**) [VN] ~ **sb (from sth/from doing sth)** | ~ **sb (for sth)** to prevent sb from doing sth because they have broken a rule or are not suitable: *He was disqualified from the competition for using drugs.* ◊ (*BrE*) *You could be disqualified from driving for up to three years.* ◊ *A heart condition disqualified him for military service.* ▶ **dis·quali·fi·ca·tion** /dɪsˌkwɒlɪfɪˈkeɪʃn; *AmE* -ˌkwɑːl-/ *noun* [C, U]: *Any form of cheating means automatic disqualification.*

dis·quiet /dɪsˈkwaɪət/ *noun* [U] ~ **(about/over sth)** (*formal*) feelings of worry and unhappiness about sth: *There is considerable public disquiet about the safety of the new trains.*

dis·quiet·ing /dɪsˈkwaɪətɪŋ/ *adj.* (*formal*) causing worry and unhappiness

dis·quisi·tion /ˌdɪskwɪˈzɪʃn/ *noun* (*formal*) a long complicated speech or written report on a particular subject

dis·re·gard /ˌdɪsrɪˈɡɑːd; *AmE* -ˈɡɑːrd/ *verb, noun*

■ *verb* [VN] to not consider sth; to treat sth as unimportant: *The board completely disregarded my recommendations.* ◊ *Safety rules were disregarded.*

■ *noun* [U] ~ **(for/of sb/sth)** the act of treating sb/sth as unimportant and not caring about them/it: *She shows a total disregard for other people's feelings.*

dis·re·pair /ˌdɪsrɪˈpeə(r); *AmE* -ˈper/ *noun* [U] a building, road, etc. that is in a state of **disrepair** has not been looked after and is broken or in bad condition: *The station quickly **fell into disrepair** after it was closed.*

dis·rep·ut·able /dɪsˈrepjətəbl/ *adj.* that people consider to be dishonest and bad **OPP** RESPECTABLE: *She spent the evening with her disreputable brother Stefan.* ◊ *a disreputable area of the city*—compare REPUTABLE

dis·re·pute /ˌdɪsrɪˈpjuːt/ *noun* [U] the fact that sb/sth

D

loses the respect of other people: *The players' behaviour on the field is likely to bring the game into disrepute.*

dis·res·pect /ˌdɪsrɪˈspekt/ *noun* [U, C] ~ (for/to sb/sth) a lack of respect for sb/sth: *disrespect for the law/the dead* ◊ *No disrespect intended sir; it was just a joke.* ▶ **dis·res·pect·ful** /-fl/ *adj.* ~ (to sb/sth) **dis·res·pect·ful·ly** /-fəli/ *adv.*

dis·robe /dɪsˈrəʊb; *AmE* -ˈroʊb/ *verb* (*formal or humorous*) to take off your or sb else's clothes; to take off clothes worn for an official ceremony: [V] *She went behind the screen to disrobe.* [also VN]

dis·rupt /dɪsˈrʌpt/ *verb* [VN] to make it difficult for sth to continue in the normal way: *Demonstrators succeeded in disrupting the meeting.* ◊ *Bus services will be disrupted tomorrow because of the bridge closure.* ▶ **dis·rup·tion** /dɪsˈrʌpʃn/ *noun* [U, C]: *We aim to help you move house with minimum disruption to yourself.* ◊ *disruptions to rail services* ◊ *The strike caused serious disruptions for several days.*

dis·rup·tive /dɪsˈrʌptɪv/ *adj.* causing problems, noise, etc. so that sth cannot continue normally: *She had a disruptive influence on the rest of the class.*

diss = DIS

dis·sat·is·fac·tion /ˌdɪsˌsætɪsˈfækʃn/ *noun* [U] ~ (with/ at sb/sth) a feeling that you are not pleased and satisfied: *Many people have expressed their dissatisfaction with the arrangement.*

dis·sat·is·fied /dɪsˈsætɪsfaɪd; dɪˈsæt-/ *adj.* ~ (with sb/ sth) not happy or satisfied with sth: *dissatisfied customers* ◊ *If you are dissatisfied with our service, please write to the manager.* OPP SATISFIED—compare UNSATISFIED

dis·sect /dɪˈsekt; daɪ-/ *verb* [VN] **1** to cut up a dead person, animal or plant in order to study it **2** to study sth closely and/or discuss it in great detail: *Her latest novel was dissected by the critics.* **3** to divide sth into smaller pieces, areas, etc: *The city is dissected by a network of old canals.* ▶ **dis·sec·tion** /dɪˈsekʃn; daɪ-/ *noun* [U, C]: *anatomical dissection* ◊ *Your enjoyment of a novel can suffer from too much analysis and dissection.*

dis·sem·ble /dɪˈsembl/ *verb* (*formal*) to hide your real feelings or intentions, often by pretending to have different ones: [V] *She was a very honest person who was incapable of dissembling.* [also VN]

dis·sem·in·ate /dɪˈsemɪneɪt/ *verb* [VN] (*formal*) to spread information, knowledge, etc. so that it reaches many people: *Their findings were widely disseminated.* ▶ **dis·sem·in·ation** /dɪˌsemɪˈneɪʃn/ *noun* [U]

dis·sen·sion /dɪˈsenʃn/ *noun* [U] (*formal*) disagreement between people or within a group: *dissension within the government*

dis·sent /dɪˈsent/ *noun, verb*
■ *noun* **1** [U] the fact of having or expressing opinions that are different from those that are officially accepted: *political/religious dissent* **2** [C] (*AmE*) a judge's statement giving reasons why he or she disagrees with a decision made by the other judges in a court case
■ *verb* [V] ~ (from sth) (*formal*) to have or express opinions that are different from those that are officially accepted: *Only two ministers dissented from the official view.* ▶ **dis·sent·ing** *adj.*: *dissenting groups/voices/views/opinion*

dis·sent·er /dɪˈsentə(r)/ *noun* **1** a person who does not agree with opinions that are officially or generally accepted **2** (**Dissenter**) (in Britain in the past) a Protestant who refused to accept the teachings of the Church of England—compare NONCONFORMIST

dis·ser·ta·tion /ˌdɪsəˈteɪʃn; *AmE* -sərˈt-/ *noun* ~ (on sth) a long piece of writing on a particular subject, especially one written for a university degree

dis·ser·vice /dɪsˈsɜːvɪs; dɪˈsɜː-; *AmE* -ˈsɜːrv-/ *noun* [sing.] IDM **do sb a dis'service** to do sth that harms sb and the opinion that other people have of them: *The minister's comments do teachers a great disservice.*

dis·si·dent /ˈdɪsɪdənt/ *noun* a person who strongly disagrees with and criticizes their government, especially in a country where this kind of action is dangerous: *left-wing dissidents* ▶ **dis·si·dence** /ˈdɪsɪdəns/ *noun* [U] **dis·si·dent** *adj.*

dis·si·mi·lar /dɪˈsɪmɪlə(r)/ *adj.* ~ (from/to sb/sth) not the same: *These wines are not dissimilar* (= are similar). OPP SIMILAR ▶ **dis·si·mi·lar·ity** /ˌdɪsɪmɪˈlærəti/ *noun* [C, U]

dis·simu·late /dɪˈsɪmjuleɪt/ *verb* [VN, V] (*formal*) to hide your real feelings or intentions, often by pretending to have different ones SYN DISSEMBLE ▶ **dis·simu·la·tion** /dɪˌsɪmjuˈleɪʃn/ *noun* [U]: *He was capable of great dissimulation and hypocrisy.*

dis·si·pate /ˈdɪsɪpeɪt/ *verb* (*formal*) **1** to gradually become or make sth become weaker until it disappears: [V] *Eventually, his anger dissipated.* ◊ [VN] *Her laughter soon dissipated the tension in the air.* **2** [VN] to waste sth, such as time or money, especially by not planning the best way of using it

dis·si·pated /ˈdɪsɪpeɪtɪd/ *adj.* (*disapproving*) enjoying activities that are harmful such as drinking too much alcohol

dis·si·pa·tion /ˌdɪsɪˈpeɪʃn/ *noun* [U] (*formal*) **1** the process of disappearing or of making sth disappear: *the dissipation of energy in the form of heat* **2** the act of wasting money or spending money until there is none left: *concerns about the dissipation of the country's wealth* **3** (*disapproving*) living a life of harmful but enjoyable activities

dis·so·ci·ate /dɪˈsəʊsieɪt; -ʃeɪt; *AmE* -ˈsoʊ-/ *verb* [VN] **1** (also **dis·as·so·ci·ate**) ~ yourself/sb from sb/sth to say or do sth to show that you are not connected with or do not support sb/sth; to make it clear that sth is not connected with a particular plan, action, etc: *He tried to dissociate himself from the party's more extreme views.* ◊ *They were determined to dissociate the UN from any agreement to impose sanctions.* **2** ~ sb/sth (from sth) (*formal*) to think of two people or things as separate and not connected with each other: *She tried to dissociate the two events in her mind.* OPP ASSOCIATE ▶ **dis·so·ci·ation** /dɪˌsəʊsiˈeɪʃn; -ʃeɪʃn; *AmE* -ˌsoʊ-/ *noun* [U]: *the dissociation of political and moral ideas*

dis·sol·ute /ˈdɪsəluːt/ *adj.* (*formal, disapproving*) enjoying immoral activities and not caring about behaving in a morally acceptable way

dis·sol·ution /ˌdɪsəˈluːʃn/ *noun* [U] ~ (of sth) (*written*) **1** the act of officially ending a marriage, a business agreement, or a parliament **2** the process in which sth gradually disappears: *the dissolution of barriers of class and race* **3** the act of breaking up an organization, etc: *the dissolution of the Soviet Union*

dis·solve /dɪˈzɒlv; *AmE* -ˈzɑːlv/ *verb* **1** [V] ~ (in sth) (of a solid) to mix with a liquid and become part of it: *Salt dissolves in water.* ◊ *Heat gently until the sugar dissolves.* **2** [VN] ~ sth (in sth) to make a solid become part of a liquid: *Dissolve the tablet in water.* **3** [VN] to officially end a marriage, business agreement or parliament: *Their marriage was dissolved in 1989.* ◊ *The election was announced and parliament was dissolved.* **4** (*written*) to disappear; to make sth disappear: [V] *When the ambulance had gone, the crowd dissolved.* ◊ [VN] *His calm response dissolved her anger.* **5** [V] ~ into laughter, tears, etc. to suddenly start laughing, crying, etc: *When the teacher looked up, the children dissolved into giggles.* ◊ *Every time she heard his name, she dissolved into tears.* **6** ~ (sth) (away) to remove or destroy sth, especially by a chemical process; to be destroyed in this way: [VN] *a new detergent that dissolves stains* ◊ [V] *All the original calcium had dissolved away.*

dis·son·ance /ˈdɪsənəns/ *noun* **1** [C, U] (*music*) a combination of musical notes that sound harsh together OPP CONSONANCE **2** [U] (*formal*) lack of agreement ▶ **dis·son·ant** /ˈdɪsənənt/ *adj.*: *dissonant voices/notes*

dis·suade /dɪˈsweɪd/ *verb* [VN] ~ sb (from sth/from doing sth) to persuade sb not to do sth: *I tried to dissuade him from giving up his job.* ◊ *They were going to set off in the fog, but were dissuaded.*

dis·taff /ˈdɪstɑːf; *AmE* ˈdɪstæf/ *noun* a stick that was used in the past for holding wool when it was spun by hand IDM **on the distaff side** (*old-fashioned*) on the woman's side of the family

s	t	v	z	ʃ	ʒ	tʃ	dʒ	θ	ð	ŋ
see	tea	van	zoo	shoe	vision	chain	jam	thin	this	sing

dis·tance /'dɪstəns/ *noun, verb*

■ *noun* **1** [C, U] the amount of space between two places or things: *a short/long distance* ◊ *the distance of the earth from the sun* ◊ *a distance of 200 kilometres* ◊ *What's the distance between New York City and Boston/from New York City to Boston?* ◊ *In the US, distance is measured in miles.* ◊ *The beach is within walking distance of my house* (= you can walk there easily). ◊ *Paul has to drive very long distances as part of his job.* ◊ *Our parents live some distance away* (= quite far away).—see also LONG-DISTANCE, MIDDLE DISTANCE, OUTDISTANCE **2** [U] being far away in space or in time: *Distance is no problem on the Internet.* **3** [sing.] a point that is a particular amount of space away from sth else: *You'll never get the ball in from that distance.* **4** [U, C] a situation in which there is a lack of friendly feelings or of a close relationship between two people or groups of people: *The coldness and distance in her voice took me by surprise.* **IDM** **at/from a 'distance** from a place or time that is not near; from far away: *She had loved him at a distance for years.* **go the (full) 'distance** to continue playing in a competition or sports contest until the end: *Nobody thought he would last 15 rounds but he went the full distance.* **in/into the 'distance** far away but still able to be seen or heard: *We saw lights in the distance.* ◊ *Alice stood staring into the distance.* **keep sb at a 'distance** to refuse to be friendly with sb; to not let sb be friendly towards you **keep your 'distance (from sb/sth) 1** to make sure you are not too near sb/sth **2** to avoid getting too friendly or involved with a person, group, etc: *She was warned to keep her distance from Charles if she didn't want to get hurt.*—more at SHOUTING, SPIT *v.*, STRIKE *v.*

■ *verb* [VN] **~ yourself sb/sth (from sb/sth)** to become less involved or connected with sb/sth: *When he retired, he tried to distance himself from politics.* ◊ *It's not always easy for nurses to distance themselves emotionally.*

dis·tant /'dɪstənt/ *adj.* **1** far away in space or time: *the distant sound of music* ◊ *distant stars/planets* ◊ *The time we spent together is now a distant memory.* ◊ *(formal) The airport was about 20 kilometres distant.* ◊ *a star 30000 light years distant from the Earth* ◊ *(figurative) Peace was just a distant hope* (= not very likely). **2 ~ (from sth)** not like sth else: *Their life seemed utterly distant from his own.* **3** [only before noun] (of a person) related to you but not closely: *a distant cousin/aunt/relative* **4** not friendly; not wanting a close relationship with sb: *Pat sounded very cold and distant on the phone.* **5** not paying attention to sth but thinking about sth completely different: *There was a distant look in her eyes, her mind was obviously on something else.* ▶ **dis·tant·ly** *adv.*: *Somewhere, distantly, he could hear the sound of the sea.* ◊ *We're distantly related.* ◊ *Holly smiled distantly.* **IDM** **the (,dim and) ,distant 'past** a long time ago: *stories from the distant past* **in the not too ,distant 'future** not a long time in the future but fairly soon

dis·taste /dɪs'teɪst/ *noun* [U, sing.] **~ (for sb/sth)** a feeling that sb/sth is unpleasant or offensive: *He looked around the filthy room in distaste.* ◊ *a distaste for politics of any sort*

dis·taste·ful /dɪs'teɪstfl/ *adj.* unpleasant or offensive

dis·tem·per /dɪs'tempə(r)/ *noun* [U] **1** an infectious disease of animals, especially cats and dogs, that causes fever and coughing **2** (*BrE*) a type of paint that is mixed with water and used on walls

dis·tend /dɪ'stend/ *verb* (*formal* or *medical*) to swell or make sth swell because of pressure from inside: [VN] *starving children with huge distended bellies* [alsoV] ▶ **dis·ten·sion** /dɪ'stenʃn/ *noun* [U]: *distension of the stomach*

dis·til (*AmE* also **dis·till**) /dɪ'stɪl/ *verb* (-ll-) [VN] **1 ~ sth (from sth)** to make a liquid pure by heating it until it becomes a gas, then cooling it and collecting the drops of liquid that form: *to distil fresh water from sea water* ◊ *distilled water* **2** to make sth such as a strong alcoholic drink in this way: *The factory distils and bottles whisky.* **3 ~ sth (from/into sth)** (*formal*) to get the essential meaning or ideas from thoughts, information, experiences, etc: *The notes I made on my travels were distilled into a*

book. ▶ **dis·til·la·tion** /ˌdɪstɪ'leɪʃn/ *noun* [C, U]: *the distillation process*

dis·til·ler /dɪ'stɪlə(r)/ *noun* a person or company that produces SPIRITS (= strong alcoholic drinks) such as whisky by distilling them

dis·til·lery /dɪ'stɪləri/ *noun* (*pl.* **-ies**) a factory where strong alcoholic drink is made by the process of distilling

dis·tinct /dɪ'stɪŋkt/ *adj.* **1** easily or clearly heard, seen, felt, etc: *There was a distinct smell of gas.* ◊ *His voice was quiet but every word was distinct.* **2 ~ (from sth)** clearly different or of a different kind: *The results of the survey fell into two distinct groups.* ◊ *Jamaican reggae music is quite distinct from North American jazz or blues.* ◊ *rural areas, as distinct from major cities* **3** [only before noun] used to emphasize that you think an idea or situation definitely exists and is important: *Being tall gave Tony a distinct advantage.* ◊ *I had the distinct impression I was being watched.* ◊ *A strike is now a distinct possibility.* ▶ **dis·tinct·ly** *adv.*: *I distinctly heard someone calling me.* ◊ *a distinctly Australian accent* ◊ *He could remember everything very distinctly.* **dis·tinct·ness** *noun* [U]

dis·tinc·tion /dɪ'stɪŋkʃn/ *noun* **1** [C] **~ (between A and B)** a clear difference or contrast especially between people or things that are similar or related: *distinctions between traditional and modern societies* ◊ *Philosophers did not use to make a distinction between arts and science.* **2** [U] the quality of being excellent or important: *a writer of distinction* **3** [sing.] the quality of being sth that is special: *She had the distinction of being the first woman to fly the Atlantic.* **4** [U] the separation of people or things into different groups: *The new law makes no distinction between adults and children* (= treats them equally). ◊ *All groups are entitled to this money without distinction.* **5** [C, U] a special mark/grade or award that is given to sb, especially a student, for excellent work: *Naomi got a distinction in maths.* ◊ *He graduated with distinction.*

dis·tinct·ive /dɪ'stɪŋktɪv/ *adj.* having a quality or characteristic that makes sth different and easily noticed: *clothes with a distinctive style* ◊ *The male bird has distinctive black and white markings on its head.* ▶ **dis·tinct·ive·ly** *adv.*: *a distinctively nutty flavour*

dis·tin·guish /dɪ'stɪŋgwɪʃ/ *verb* **1 ~ (between) A and B| ~ A from B** to recognize the difference between two people or things: [V] *At what age are children able to distinguish between right and wrong?* ◊ [VN] *It was hard to distinguish one twin from the other.* ◊ *Sometimes reality and fantasy are hard to distinguish.* **2** [VN] (not used in the progressive tenses) **~ A (from B)** to be a characteristic that makes two people, animals or things different: *What was it that distinguished her from her classmates?* ◊ *The male bird is distinguished from the female by its red beak.* ◊ *Does your cat have any distinguishing marks?* **3** [VN] (not used in the progressive tenses) to be able to see or hear sth: *I could not distinguish her words, but she sounded agitated.* **4** [VN] **~ yourself (as sth)** to do sth so well that people notice and admire you: *She has already distinguished herself as an athlete.* ▶ **dis·tin·guish·able** /dɪ'stɪŋgwɪʃəbl/ *adj.* **~ (from sb/sth)**: *The male bird is easily distinguishable from the female.* ◊ *The coast was barely distinguishable in the mist.*

dis·tin·guished /dɪ'stɪŋgwɪʃt/ *adj.* **1** very successful and admired by other people: *a distinguished career in medicine* **2** having an appearance that makes sb look important or that makes people admire or respect them: *I think grey hair makes you look very distinguished.*

dis·tort /dɪ'stɔːt; *AmE* dɪ'stɔːrt/ *verb* [VN] **1** to change the shape, appearance or sound of sth so that it is strange or not clear: *a fairground mirror that distorts your shape* ◊ *The loudspeaker seemed to distort his voice.* **2** to twist or change facts, ideas, etc. so that they are no longer correct or true: *Newspapers are often guilty of distorting the truth.* ◊ *The article gave a distorted picture of his childhood.* ▶ **dis·tort·ion** /dɪ'stɔːʃn; *AmE* dɪ'stɔːrʃn/ [C, U]: *modern alloys that are resistant to wear and distortion* ◊ *a distortion of the facts*

dis·tract /dɪ'strækt/ *verb* [VN] **~ sb/sth (from sth)** to take

D

æ	ɑː	e	ɜː	ə	ɪ	iː	i	ɒ	ɔː	ʌ	ʊ	u	uː
cat	father	ten	bird	about	sit	see	many	got	saw	cup	put	actual	too
								(BrE)					

sb's attention away from what they are trying to do: *You're distracting me from my work.* ◊ *Don't talk to her— she's very easily distracted.* ◊ *It was another attempt to distract attention from the truth.* ▶ **dis·tract·ing** *adj.*: *distracting thoughts* ◊ *a distracting noise*

dis·tract·ed /dɪˈstræktɪd/ *adj.* ~ **(by sb/sth)** unable to pay attention to sb/sth, because you are worried or thinking about sth else ▶ **dis·tract·ed·ly** *adv.*

dis·trac·tion /dɪˈstrækʃn/ *noun* **1** [C, U] a thing that takes your attention away from what you are doing or thinking about: *I find it hard to work at home because there are too many distractions.* ◊ *cinema audiences looking for distraction* **2** [C] an activity that amuses or entertains you **IDM to diˈstraction** so that you become upset, excited, or angry and not able to think clearly: *The children are driving me to distraction today.*

dis·traught /dɪˈstrɔːt/ *adj.* extremely upset and anxious so that you cannot think clearly: *She's still too distraught to speak about the tragedy.*

dis·tress /dɪˈstres/ *noun, verb*
■ *noun* [U] **1** a feeling of great worry or unhappiness; great suffering: *The newspaper article caused the actor considerable distress.* ◊ *She was obviously in distress after the attack.* ◊ *deep emotional distress* **2** suffering and problems caused by not having enough money, food, etc: *economic/financial distress* **3** a situation in which a ship, plane, etc. is in danger or difficulty and needs help: *a distress signal* (= a message asking for help) ◊ *It is a rule of the sea to help another boat in distress.* **IDM** see DAMSEL
■ *verb* [VN] to make sb feel very worried or unhappy: *It was clear that the letter had deeply distressed her.* ◊ *Don't distress yourself* (= don't worry).

dis·tressed /dɪˈstrest/ *adj.* **1** upset and anxious: *He was too distressed and confused to answer their questions.* **2** suffering pain; in a poor physical condition: *When the baby arrived, it was blue and distressed.* **3** (of a piece of clothing or furniture) made to look older and more worn than it really is: *a distressed leather jacket*

dis·tress·ing /dɪˈstresɪŋ/ *adj.* making you feel extremely upset, especially because of sb's suffering ▶ **dis·tress·ing·ly** *adv.*

dis·trib·ute /dɪˈstrɪbjuːt; ˈdɪstrɪbjuːt/ *verb* [VN] **1** ~ **(to/among sb/sth)** to give things to a large number of people; to share sth between a number of people: *The organization distributed food and blankets to the earthquake victims.* ◊ *The newspaper is distributed free.* ◊ *The money was distributed among schools in the area.* **2** to send goods to shops/stores and businesses so that they can be sold: *'Plastika' distributes our products in the UK.* **3** [often passive] to spread sth, or different parts of sth, over an area: *Make sure that your weight is evenly distributed.*

dis·tri·bu·tion /ˌdɪstrɪˈbjuːʃn/ *noun* **1** [U, C] the way that sth is shared or exists over a particular area or among a particular group of people: *the unfair distribution of wealth* ◊ *The map shows the distribution of this species across the world.* ◊ *They studied the geographical distribution of the disease.* **2** [U] the act of giving or delivering sth to a number of people: *the distribution of food and medicines to the flood victims* ◊ *He was arrested on drug distribution charges.* **3** [U] (*business*) the system of transporting and delivering goods: *distribution costs* ◊ *worldwide distribution systems* ◊ *marketing, sales and distribution* ▶ **dis·tri·bu·tion·al** *adj.*

dis·tribu·tive /dɪˈstrɪbjətɪv/ *adj.* [usually before noun] (*business*) connected with distribution

dis·tribu·tor /dɪˈstrɪbjətə(r)/ *noun* **1** a person or company that supplies goods to shops/stores, etc: *Japan's largest software distributor* **2** a device in an engine that sends electric current to the SPARK PLUGS

dis·trict /ˈdɪstrɪkt/ *noun* **1** an area of a country or town, especially one that has particular features: *the City of London's financial district* **2** an area of a country, town or state that has official BOUNDARIES (= borders), for administrative purposes: *a tax/postal district* ◊ *a school district* ◊ *congressional districts* ◊ *district councils*

ˌdistrict aˈttorney *noun* (*abbr.* **DA**) (in the US) a lawyer who is responsible for bringing criminal CHARGES against sb in a particular area or state

ˌdistrict ˈnurse *noun* (in Britain) a nurse who visits patients in their homes

dis·trust /dɪsˈtrʌst/ *noun, verb*
■ *noun* [U, sing.] ~ **(of sb/sth)** a feeling of not being able to trust sb/sth: *They looked at each other with distrust.* ◊ *He has a deep distrust of all modern technology.* ▶ **dis·trust·ful** /-fl/ *adj.*: *distrustful of authority*
■ *verb* [VN] to feel that you cannot trust or believe sb/sth: *She distrusted his motives for wanting to see her again.*—compare MISTRUST

> **WHICH WORD?**
> **distrust / mistrust**
>
> There is very little difference between these two words, but **distrust** is more common and perhaps slightly stronger. If you are sure that someone is acting dishonestly or cannot be relied on, you are more likely to say that you **distrust** them. If you are expressing doubts and suspicions, on the other hand, you would probably use **mistrust**.

dis·turb /dɪˈstɜːb; *AmE* -ˈstɜːrb/ *verb* **1** [VN] to interrupt sb when they are trying to work, sleep, etc: *I'm sorry to disturb you, but can I talk to you for a moment?* ◊ *If you get up early, try not to disturb everyone else.* ◊ *She awoke early after a disturbed night.* **2** [VN] to move sth or change its position: *Don't disturb the papers on my desk.* **3** to make sb worry: [VN] *The letter shocked and disturbed me.* ◊ [VN to inf] *It disturbed her to realize that she was missing him.*

dis·turb·ance /dɪˈstɜːbəns; *AmE* -ˈstɜːrb-/ *noun* **1** [U, C, usually sing.] actions that make you stop what you are doing, or that upset the normal state that sth is in; the act of disturbing sb/sth or the fact of being disturbed: *The building work is creating constant noise, dust and disturbance.* ◊ *a disturbance in the usual pattern of events* ◊ *the disturbance of the local wildlife by tourists* **2** [C] a situation in which people behave violently in a public place: *serious disturbances in the streets* ◊ *He was charged with causing a disturbance after the game.* **3** [U, C] a state in which sb's mind or a function of the body is upset and not working normally: *emotional disturbance*

dis·turbed /dɪˈstɜːbd; *AmE* -ˈstɜːrbd/ *adj.* **1** mentally ill, especially because of very unhappy or shocking experiences: *a special school for emotionally disturbed children* **2** unhappy and full of bad or shocking experiences: *The killer had a disturbed family background.* **3** very anxious and unhappy about sth: *I was deeply disturbed and depressed by the news.*—compare UNDISTURBED

dis·turb·ing /dɪˈstɜːbɪŋ; *AmE* -ˈstɜːrb-/ *adj.* making you feel anxious and upset or shocked: *a disturbing piece of news* ▶ **dis·turb·ing·ly** *adv.*

dis·unite /ˌdɪsjuˈnaɪt/ *verb* [VN] [usually passive] (*formal*) to make a group of people unable to agree with each other or work together: *a disunited political party*

dis·unity /dɪsˈjuːnəti/ *noun* [U] (*formal*) a lack of agreement between people: *disunity within the Conservative party*

dis·use /dɪsˈjuːs/ *noun* [U] a situation in which sth is no longer being used: *The factory fell into disuse twenty years ago.*

dis·used /ˌdɪsˈjuːzd/ *adj.* [usually before noun] no longer used: *a disused station*—compare UNUSED

ditch /dɪtʃ/ *noun, verb*
■ *noun* a long channel dug at the side of a field or road, to hold or take away water
■ *verb* **1** [VN] (*informal*) to get rid of sth/sb because you no longer want or need it/them: *The new road building programme has been ditched.* ◊ *He ditched his girlfriend.* **2** [VN, V] if a pilot ditches an aircraft, or if it ditches, it lands in the sea in an emergency

ditch·water /ˈdɪtʃwɔːtə(r)/ *noun* [U] **IDM** see DULL *adv.*

dither /ˈdɪðə(r)/ *noun, verb*

aɪ	aʊ	eɪ	əʊ	oʊ	ɔɪ	ɪə	eə	ʊə	j	w
my	now	say	go (BrE)	go (AmE)	boy	near	hair	pure	yes	wet

■ *noun* [sing.] (*BrE, informal*) a state of not being able to decide what you should do: *to be in a dither about sth*

■ *verb* [V] ~ (**over sth**) (*especially BrE*) to hesitate about what to do because you are unable to decide: *She was dithering over what to wear.* ◊ *Stop dithering and get on with it.*

ditto /'dɪtəʊ; *AmE* -toʊ/ *noun* **1** (*abbr.* **do.**) (*symb* ") used, especially in a list, underneath a particular word or phrase, to show that it is repeated and to avoid having to write it again **2** (*informal*) used instead of a particular word or phrase, to avoid repeating it: *The waiters were rude and unhelpful, the manager ditto.*

ditty /'dɪti/ *noun* (*pl.* **-ies**) (often *humorous*) a short simple song

di·ur·et·ic /ˌdaɪjuˈretɪk/ *noun* (*medical*) a substance that causes an increase in the flow of URINE ▶ **di·ur·et·ic** *adj.*: *diuretic drugs/effects*

di·ur·nal /daɪ'ɜːnl; *AmE* -'ɜːrnl/ *adj.* **1** (*biology*) (of animals) active during the day OPP NOCTURNAL **2** (*astronomy*) taking one day: *the diurnal rotation of the earth*

Div. *abbr.* (in writing) DIVISION: *League Div. 1* (= in football)

diva /'diːvə/ *noun* a famous woman singer, especially an opera singer

Di·vali = DIWALI

divan /dɪ'væn; *AmE* 'daɪvæn/ *noun* **1** (also **di,van 'bed**) (both *BrE*) a bed with a thick base and a MATTRESS and no HEADBOARD—picture at BED **2** a long low soft seat without a back or arms

dive /daɪv/ *verb, noun*

■ *verb* (**dived, dived,** *AmE* also **dove** /dəʊv; *AmE* doʊv/ **dived**) [V]

JUMP INTO WATER | **1** ~ (**from/off sth**) (**into sth**)| ~ (**in**) to jump into water with your head and arms going in first: *We dived into the river to cool off.*

UNDERWATER | **2** (usually **go diving**) to swim underwater wearing breathing equipment, collecting or looking at things: *to dive for pearls* ◊ *The main purpose of his holiday to Greece was to go diving.*—see also DIVING **3** to go to a deeper level underwater: *The whale dived as the harpoon struck it.*

OF BIRDS/AIRCRAFT | **4** to go steeply down through the air: *The seagulls soared then dived.*—see also NOSEDIVE

OF PRICES | **5** to fall suddenly: *The share price dived from 49p to an all-time low of 40p.*

MOVE/JUMP/FALL | **6** [+*adv./prep.*] ~ (**for sth**) (*informal*) to move or jump quickly in a particular direction, especially to avoid sth, to try to catch a ball, etc: *We heard an explosion and dived for cover* (= got into a place where we would be protected). ◊ *The goalie dived for the ball, but missed it.* ◊ *It started to rain so we dived into the nearest cafe.* **7** (*BrE*) (in football) to fall deliberately when sb TACKLES you, so that the REFEREE awards a FOUL

PHRV **'dive into sth** (*informal*) to put your hand quickly into sth such as a bag or pocket: *She dived into her bag and took out a couple of coins.*

■ *noun*

JUMP INTO WATER | **1** a jump into deep water with your head first and your arms in front of you: *a spectacular high dive* (= from high above the water)

UNDERWATER | **2** an act of going underwater and swimming there with special equipment: *a dive to a depth of 18 metres*

OF BIRDS/AIRCRAFT | **3** an act of suddenly flying downwards

BAR/CLUB | **4** (*informal*) a bar, music club, etc. that is cheap, and perhaps dark or dirty: *The band played in every smoky dive in town.*

IDM **make a 'dive (for sth)** to suddenly move or jump forward to do sth or reach sb/sth: *The goalkeeper made a dive for the ball.* **take a 'dive** (*informal*) to suddenly get worse: *Profits really took a dive last year.*

'dive-bomb *verb* [VN] (of an aircraft or its pilot) to dive steeply through the air and drop bombs on sth

diver /'daɪvə(r)/ *noun* **1** a person who works underwater, usually with special equipment: *a deep-sea diver*—com-

pare FROGMAN **2** a person who jumps into the water with their head first and their arms in front of them

di·verge /daɪ'vɜːdʒ; *AmE* -'vɜːrdʒ/ *verb* [V] (*written*) **1** ~ (**from sth**) to separate and go in different directions: *The parallel lines appear to diverge.* ◊ *The coastal road diverges from the freeway just north of Santa Monica.* ◊ *Many species have diverged from a single ancestor.* ◊ *We went through school and college together, but then our paths diverged.* **2** ~ (**from sth**) (*formal*) (of opinions, views, etc.) to be different: *Opinions diverge greatly on this issue.* **3** ~ **from sth** to be or become different from what is expected, planned, etc: *to diverge from the norm* ◊ *He diverged from established procedure.* OPP CONVERGE ▶ **di·ver·gence** /daɪ'vɜːdʒəns; *AmE* -'vɜːrdʒ-/ *noun* [C, U]: *a wide divergence of opinion* **di·ver·gent** /-dʒənt/ *adj.*: *divergent paths/opinions*

divers /'daɪvəz; *AmE* -vərz/ *adj.* [only before noun] (*old use*) of many different kinds

di·verse /daɪ'vɜːs; *AmE* -'vɜːrs/ *adj.* very different from each other and of various kinds: *people from diverse cultures* ◊ *My interests are very diverse.*

di·ver·sify /daɪ'vɜːsɪfaɪ; *AmE* -'vɜːrs-/ *verb* (**di·ver·si·fies, di·ver·si·fy·ing, di·ver·si·fied, di·ver·si·fied**) **1** ~ (**sth**) (**into sth**) (especially of a business or company) to develop a wider range of products, interests, skills, etc. in order to be more successful or reduce risk: [V] *Farmers are being encouraged to diversify into new crops.* [also VN] **2** to change or to make sth change so that there is greater variety: [V] *Patterns of family life are diversifying and changing.* ◊ [VN] *The culture has been diversified with the arrival of immigrants.* ▶ **di·ver·si·fi·ca·tion** /daɪˌvɜːsɪfɪ'keɪʃn; *AmE* -ˌvɜːrs-/ *noun* [U]

di·ver·sion /daɪ'vɜːʃn; *AmE* -'vɜːrʒn/ *noun* **1** [C, U] the act of changing the direction that sb/sth is following, or what sth is used for: *a river diversion project* ◊ *We made a short diversion to go and look at the castle.* ◊ *the diversion of funds from the public to the private sector of industry* **2** [C] something that takes your attention away from sb/sth while sth else is happening: *For the government, the war was a welcome diversion from the country's economic problems.* ◊ *A smoke bomb created a diversion while the robbery took place.* **3** [C] (*BrE*) (*AmE* **de·tour**) a road or route that is used when the usual one is closed: *Diversions will be signposted.* **4** [C] (*formal*) an activity that is done for pleasure, especially because it takes your attention away from sth else: *The party will make a pleasant diversion.* ◊ *The city is full of diversions.*

di·ver·sion·ary /daɪ'vɜːʃənəri; *AmE* -'vɜːrʒəneri/ *adj.* intended to take sb's attention away from sth

di·ver·sity /daɪ'vɜːsəti; *AmE* -'vɜːrs-/ *noun* **1** [U, C, usually sing.] a range of many people or things that are very different from each other: *the biological diversity of the rainforests* ◊ *a great/wide/rich diversity of opinion* **2** [U] the quality or fact of including a range of many people or things: *There is a need for greater diversity and choice in education.*

di·vert /daɪ'vɜːt; *AmE* -'vɜːrt/ *verb* [VN] ~ **sb/sth (from sth)** (**to sth**) to make sb/sth change direction: *Northbound traffic will have to be diverted onto minor roads.* **2** to use money, materials, etc. for a different purpose from their original purpose **3** to take sb's thoughts or attention away from sth SYN DISTRACT: *The war diverted people's attention away from the economic situation.* **4** (*formal*) to entertain people: *Children are easily diverted.*

di·vert·ing /daɪ'vɜːtɪŋ; *AmE* -'vɜːrt-/ *adj.* (*formal*) entertaining and amusing

di·vest /daɪ'vest/ *verb* [VN] (*formal*) **1** ~ **sb/yourself of sth** to remove clothes: *He divested himself of his jacket.* **2** ~ **yourself of sth** to get rid of sth: *The company is divesting itself of some of its assets.* **3** ~ **sb/sth of sth** to take sth away from sb/sth: *After her illness she was divested of much of her responsibility.*

di·vest·ment /daɪ'vestmənt/ *noun* [U, C] (*finance*) the act of selling the shares you have bought in a company or of taking money away from where you have invested it

D

b	d	f	g	h	k	l	m	n	p	r
bad	did	fall	get	hat	cat	leg	man	now	pen	red

div·ide /dɪˈvaɪd/ *verb, noun*

■ *verb*

> **WORD FAMILY**
> divide *v., n.*
> division *n.*
> divisive *adj.*

SEPARATE | **1 ~** **(sth) (up)** **(into sth)** to separate or make sth separate into parts: [V] *The cells began to divide rapidly.* ◇ [VN] *A sentence can be divided up into meaningful segments.* **2** [VN] **~ sth (up/out)** **(between/ among sb)** to separate sth into parts and give a share to each of a number of different people, etc: *Jack divided up the rest of the cash.* ◇ *We divided the work between us.* **3** [VN] **~ sth (between A and B)** to use different parts of your time, energy, etc. for different activities, etc: *He divides his energies between politics and business.* **4** [VN] **~ A from B** (*formal*) to separate two people or things: *Can it ever be right to divide a mother from her child?* **5** [VN] **~ sth (off)| ~ A from B** to be the real or imaginary line or barrier that separates two people or things: *A fence divides off the western side of the grounds.*

CAUSE DISAGREEMENT | **6** [VN] to make two or more people disagree: *The issue has divided the government.* ◇ *The government is divided on this issue.* ◇ *a divided society*

MATHEMATICS | **7** [VN] **~ sth by sth** to find out how many times one number is contained in another: *30 divided by 6 is 5* (30 ÷ 6 = 5). **8** [VN] **~ into sth** to be able to be multiplied to give another number: *5 divides into 30 6 times.*

IDM **di,vide and ˈrule** to keep control over people by making them disagree with and fight each other, therefore not giving them the chance to unite and oppose you together: *a policy of divide and rule* **divided aˈgainst itself** (of a group which should be united) split by disagreements: *The regime is profoundly divided against itself.*

■ *noun* [usually sing.]

DIFFERENCE | **1 ~** **(between A and B)** a difference between two groups of people that separates them from each other: *the North/South divide* ◇ *the divide between Catholics and Protestants in Northern Ireland*

BETWEEN RIVERS | **2** (*especially AmE*) a line of high land that separates two river systems [SYN] WATERSHED [IDM] see BRIDGE *v.*

di,vided ˈhighway *noun (AmE)* = DUAL CARRIAGEWAY

divi·dend /ˈdɪvɪdend/ *noun* **1** an amount of the profits that a company pays to people who own shares in the company: *dividend payments of 50 cents a share* **2** (*BrE*) a money prize that is given to winners in the FOOTBALL POOLS [IDM] see PAY *v.*

div·ider /dɪˈvaɪdə(r)/ *noun* **1** [C] a thing that divides sth: *a room divider* (= a screen or door that divides a room into two parts) **2** (**dividers**) [pl.] an instrument made of two long thin metal parts joined together at the top, used for measuring lines and angles: *a pair of dividers*

diˈviding line *noun* [usually sing.] **1** something that marks the separation between two things or ideas: *There is no clear dividing line between what is good and what is bad.* **2** a place that separates two areas: *The river was chosen as a dividing line between the two districts.*

div·in·ation /ˌdɪvɪˈneɪʃn/ *noun* [U] the act of finding out and saying what will happen in the future

di·vine /dɪˈvaɪn/ *adj., verb*

■ *adj.* **1** [usually before noun] coming from or connected with God or a god: *divine law/love/will* ◇ *divine intervention* (= help from God to change or improve a situation) **2** (*old-fashioned*) wonderful; beautiful ▶ **div·ine·ly** *adv.*

■ *verb* **1** (*formal*) to find out sth by guessing: [V wh-] *She could divine what he was thinking just by looking at him.* [also VN] **2** [VN, V] to search for underground water using a stick in the shape of a Y, called a **divining rod**

div·ing /ˈdaɪvɪŋ/ *noun* [U] **1** the sport or activity of diving into water with your head and arms first: *a diving competition* **2** the activity of swimming underwater using special breathing equipment: *I'd love to go diving in the Aegean.* ◇ *a diving suit*—see also SKIN DIVING

ˈdiving board *noun* a board at the side of or above a swimming pool from which people can jump or DIVE into the water

div·in·ity /dɪˈvɪnəti/ *noun* (*pl.* **-ies**) **1** [U] the quality of being a god or like God: *the divinity of Christ* **2** [C] a god or GODDESS: *Roman/Greek/Egyptian divinity* **3** [U] the study of the nature of God and religious belief [SYN] THEOLOGY: *a doctor of Divinity*

div·is·ible /dɪˈvɪzəbl/ *adj.* [not before noun] **~ (by sth)** that can be divided, usually with nothing remaining: *8 is divisible by 2 and 4, but not by 3.* [OPP] INDIVISIBLE

div·ision /dɪˈvɪʒn/ *noun*

INTO SEPARATE PARTS | **1** [U, sing.] **~ (of sth between A and B)| (of sth) (into sth)** the process or result of dividing into separate parts; the process or result of dividing sth or sharing it out: *cell division* ◇ *the division of labour between the sexes* ◇ *a fair division of time and resources* ◇ *the division of the population into age groups* ◇ *a distinction which cuts right across the familiar division into arts and sciences*

MATHEMATICS | **2** [U] the process of dividing one number by another: *the division sign* (÷)—compare MULTIPLICATION— see also LONG DIVISION

DISAGREEMENT/ DIFFERENCE | **3** [C, U] **~ (in/within sth)|** **(between A and B)** a disagreement or difference in opinion, way of life, etc., especially between members of a society or an organization: *There are deep divisions in the party over European monetary union.* ◇ *the work of healing the divisions within society* ◇ *divisions between rich and poor* ◇ *social/class divisions*

PART OF ORGANIZATION | **4** [C+sing./ pl. *v.*] (*abbr.* **Div.**) a large and important unit or section of an organization: *the company's sales division*

IN SPORT | **5** [C+sing./ pl. *v.*] (*abbr.* **Div.**) (in Britain) one of the group of teams that a sport competition is divided into, especially in football: *the first division/division one* ◇ *a first-division team*

PART OF ARMY | **6** [C+sing./ pl. *v.*] (*abbr.* **Div.**) a unit of an army, consisting of several BRIGADES or REGIMENTS: *the Guards Armoured Division*

BORDER | **7** [C] a line that divides sth: *A hedge forms the division between their land and ours.*

IN PARLIAMENT | **8** [C] (*technical*) the separation of members of the British parliament into groups to vote for or against sth: *The Bill was read without a division.*

div·ision·al /dɪˈvɪʒənl/ *adj.* [only before noun] belonging to or connected with a division (= a section of the army or department of an organization): *the divisional commander/headquarters*

div·isive /dɪˈvaɪsɪv/ *adj.* (*disapproving*) causing people to be split into groups that disagree with or oppose each other: *He believes that unemployment is socially divisive.*— see also DIVIDE ▶ **div·isive·ly** *adv.* **div·isive·ness** *noun* [U]

di·vorce /dɪˈvɔːs; *AmE* dɪˈvɔːrs/ *noun, verb*

■ *noun* **1** [U, C] the legal ending of a marriage: *The marriage ended in divorce in 1996.* ◇ *an increase in the divorce rate* (= the number of divorces in a year) ◇ *They have agreed to get a divorce.* ◇ *Divorce proceedings* (= the legal process of divorce) *started today.*—compare SEPARATION **2** [C] (*formal*) **~ (between A and B)** a separation; the ending of a relationship between two things: *the divorce between religion and science*

■ *verb* **1** to end your marriage to sb legally: [VN] *They're getting divorced.* ◇ *She's divorcing her husband.* ◇ [V] *I'd heard they're divorcing.* **2** [VN] [often passive] (*formal*) **~ sb/sth from sth** to separate, a person, an idea, a subject, etc. from sth; to keep two things separate: *They believed that art should be divorced from politics.* ◇ *When he was depressed, he felt utterly divorced from reality.*

di·vorcé /dɪˌvɔːˈseɪ; *AmE* dɪˌvɔːrˈseɪ/ *noun (AmE)* a man whose marriage has been legally ended

di·vorced /dɪˈvɔːst; *AmE* -ˈvɔːrst/ *adj.* **1** no longer married: *Many divorced men remarry and have second families.* ◇ *My parents are divorced.* ◇ *Are they going to get divorced?* **2~ from sth** (*formal*) appearing not to be affected by sth; separate from sth: *He seems completely divorced from reality.*

di·vor·cee /dɪˌvɔːˈsiː; *AmE* dɪˌvɔːrˈseɪ/ *noun (BrE)* a person whose marriage has been legally ended, especially a woman

divot /'dɪvət/ *noun* a piece of grass and earth that is dug out by accident, for example by a CLUB when sb is playing golf

di·vulge /daɪ'vʌldʒ/ *verb* ~ **sth** (**to sb**) (*formal*) to give sb information that is supposed to be secret SYN REVEAL: [VN] *Police refused to divulge the identity of the suspect.* [also ∨ wh-]

divvy /'dɪvi/ *verb* (**div·vies, divvy·ing, div·vied, div·vied**) PHRV ,**divvy sth** ↔ '**up** (*informal*) to divide sth, especially money into two or more parts

Di·wali (also **Di·vali**) /dɪ'wɑːli/ *noun* [U] a Hindu festival that is held in the autumn/fall, celebrated by lighting candles and clay lamps, and with FIREWORKS

Dixie·land /'dɪksilænd/ *noun* [U] a type of traditional jazz—see also TRAD

DIY /,di: aɪ 'waɪ/ *noun* [U] (*BrE*) the activity of making, repairing or decorating things in the home yourself, instead of paying sb to do it (abbreviation for 'do it yourself'): *a DIY store*

dizzy /'dɪzi/ *adj.* **1** feeling as if everything is spinning around you and that you are not able to balance: *Climbing so high made me **feel dizzy**.* ◊ *I suffer from **dizzy spells*** (= short periods when I am dizzy). **2** making you feel dizzy; making you feel that a situation is changing very fast: *the dizzy descent from the summit* ◊ *the dizzy pace of life in Hong Kong* **3** (*informal, especially AmE*) silly or stupid: *a dizzy blonde* ▶ **diz·zily** *adv.* **diz·zi·ness** *noun* [U] IDM **the dizzy 'heights (of sth)** (*informal*) an important or impressive position

dizzy·ing /'dɪziɪŋ/ *adj.* making you feel dizzy: *The car drove past with dizzying speed.*

DJ /,di: 'dʒeɪ/ *noun* a person who plays records and talks about music on the radio or in a club (abbreviation for 'disc jockey')

djinn /dʒɪn/ *noun* (in Arabian stories) a spirit with magic powers SYN GENIE

DNA /,di: en 'eɪ/ *noun* [U] (*chemistry*) the chemical in the cells of animals and plants that carries GENETIC information and is a type of NUCLEIC ACID: *DNA fingerprinting*

do¹ /'də; du; strong form du:/ *verb, auxiliary verb, noun*—see also DO² ⇨ Appendix 1
■ *verb* (**does** /dʌz/ **did** /dɪd/ **done** /dʌn/)
ACTION | **1** [VN] used to refer to actions that you do not mention by name or do not know about: *What are you doing this evening?* ◊ *We will do what we can to help.* ◊ *Are you doing anything tomorrow evening?* ◊ *The company ought to do something about the poor service.* ◊ *There's **nothing to do*** (= no means of passing the time in an enjoyable way) *in this place.* ◊ *There's **nothing we can do** about it* (= we can't change the situation). ◊ *What can I do for you* (= how can I help)?
BEHAVE | **2** [V+adv./prep.] ~ (**as ...**) to act or behave in the way mentioned: *Do as you're told!* ◊ *They are free to do as they please.* ◊ *You **would do well to*** (= I advise you to) *consider all the options before buying.*
SUCCEED/PROGRESS | **3** [V+adv./prep.] used to ask or talk about the success or progress of sb/sth: *How is the business doing?* ◊ *She **did well** out of* (= made a big profit from) *the deal.* ◊ *He's **doing very well** at school* (= his work is good). ◊ *Both mother and baby are **doing well*** (= after the birth of the baby). ◊ (*informal*) *How are you **doing*** (= how are you)?
TASK/ACTIVITY | **4** [VN] to work at or perform an activity or a task: *I'm doing some research on the subject.* ◊ *I have a number of things to do today.* ◊ *I do aerobics once a week.* ◊ (*especially AmE*) *Let's **do*** (= meet for) *lunch.* ◊ (*spoken*) *Sorry. I **don't do funny*** (= I can't be funny). **5** [VN] used with nouns to talk about tasks such as cleaning, washing, arranging, mending, etc: *to **do*** (= wash) *the dishes* ◊ *to **do*** (= arrange) *the flowers* ◊ *I like the way you've **done** your hair.* ⇨ note on page 370 **6** [VN] ~ **the ironing, cooking, shopping, etc.** | ~ **some, a little, etc. acting, writing, etc.** to perform the activity or task mentioned: *I like listening to the radio when I'm **doing the ironing**.* ◊ *She **did a lot of acting** when she was at college.*

JOB | **7** [VN] (usually used in questions) to work at sth as a job: *What do you do* (= what is your job)? ◊ *What does she want to do when she leaves school?* ◊ *What did she **do for a living**?* ◊ *What's Tom doing these days?*
STUDY | **8** [VN] to learn or study sth: *I'm doing physics, biology and chemistry.* ◊ *Have you done any* (= studied anything by) *Keats?*
SOLVE | **9** [VN] to find the answer to sth; to solve sth: *I can't do this sum.* ◊ *Are you good at doing crosswords?*
MAKE | **10** ~ **sth (for sb)** | ~ **sth** to produce or make sth: [VN] *to do a drawing/painting/sketch* ◊ *Does this pub do* (= provide) *lunches?* ◊ *Who's doing* (= organizing and preparing) *the food for the wedding reception?* ◊ [VN, VNN] *I'll do a copy for you.* ◊ *I'll do you a copy.*
PERFORM | **11** [VN] to perform or produce a play, an opera, etc: *The local dramatic society is doing 'Hamlet' next month.*
COPY SB | **12** [VN] to copy sb's behaviour or the way sb speaks, sings, etc., especially in order to make people laugh: *He does a great Elvis Presley.* ◊ *Can you do a Welsh accent?*
FINISH | **13** (**have/be done, get sth done**) (*formal*) to finish sth: [V] *Sit there and wait till I've done.* ◊ [V-ing] *I've done talking—let's get started.* ◊ [VN] *Did you get your article done in time?*
TRAVEL | **14** [VN] to travel a particular distance: *How many miles did you do during your tour?* ◊ *My car does 40 miles to the gallon* (= uses one GALLON *of petrol/gas to travel 40 miles*). **15** [VN] to complete a journey/trip: *We did the round trip in two hours.*
SPEED | **16** [VN] to travel at or reach a particular speed: *The car was doing 90 miles an hour.*
VISIT | **17** [VN] (*informal*) to visit a place as a tourist: *We did Tokyo in three days.*
SPEND TIME | **18** [VN] to spend a period of time doing sth: *She did a year at college, but then dropped out.* ◊ *He did six years* (= in prison) *for armed robbery.*
DEAL WITH | **19** [VN] to deal with or attend to sb/sth: *The hairdresser said she could do me* (= cut my hair) *at three.*
BE SUITABLE/ENOUGH | **20** ~ **(for sb/sth)** | ~ **(as sth)** to be suitable or be enough for sb/sth: [V] *These shoes **won't do** for the party.* ◊ *'Can you lend me some money?' 'Sure—will $20 do?'* ◊ *The box will **do fine** as a table.* ◊ [VN] (*especially BrE*) *This room **will do** me nicely, thank you* (= it has everything I need). ⇨ note at ENOUGH
COOK | **21** [VN] to cook sth: *How would you like your steak done?*
CHEAT | **22** [VN] [usually passive] (*BrE, informal*) to cheat sb: *This isn't a genuine antique—you've been done.*
PUNISH | **23** (*BrE*) ~ **sb (for sth)** (*informal*) to punish sb: *They did him for tax evasion.* ◊ *She **got done** for speeding.*
ROB | **24** [VN] (*informal*) to rob a place: *The gang did a warehouse and a supermarket.*
TAKE DRUGS | **25** [VN] (*informal*) to take an illegal drug: *He doesn't smoke, drink or **do drugs**.*
HAVE SEX | **26** [VN] ~ **it** (*slang*) to have sex

IDM Most idioms containing **do** are at the entries for the nouns and adjectives in the idioms, for example **do a bunk** is at **bunk**.   **be/have to do with sb/sth** to be about or connected with sb/sth: *'What do you want to see me about?' 'It's to do with that letter you sent me.'* **have (got) something, nothing, a lot, etc. to do with sb/sth** used to talk about how much sb/sth is connected with sb/sth: *Her job has something to do with computers.* ◊ *'How much do you earn?' 'What's it got to do with you?'* ◊ *Hard work has a lot to do with* (= is an important reason for) *her success.* ◊ *We don't have very much to do with our neighbours* (= we do not speak to them very often). ◊ *I'd have nothing to do with him, if I were you.* **it won't 'do** (*especially BrE*) used to say that a situation is not satisfactory and should be changed or improved: *This is the third time you've been late this week; it simply won't do.* **not 'do anything/a lot/much for sb** (*informal*) used to say that sth does not make sb look attractive: *That hairstyle doesn't do anything for her.* ,**nothing 'doing** (*informal*) used to refuse a request: *'Can you lend me ten*

æ	ɑː	e	ɜː	ə	ɪ	iː	i	ɒ	ɔː	ʌ	ʊ	u	uː
cat	father	ten	bird	about	sit	see	many	got	saw	cup	put	actual	too
								(BrE)					

D

D

dollars?' 'Nothing doing!' **no you** '**don't** (*spoken*) used to show that you intend to stop sb from doing sth that they were going to do: *Sharon went to get into the taxi. 'Oh no you don't,' said Steve.* **that** '**does it** (*informal*) used to show that you will not accept sth any longer: *That does it, I'm off. I'm not having you swear like that at me.* **that's** '**done it** (*informal*) used to say that an accident, a mistake, etc. has spoiled or ruined sth: *That's done it. You've completely broken it this time.* **that will** '**do** used to order sb to stop doing or saying sth: *That'll do, children—you're getting far too noisy.* **what do you do for sth?** used to ask how sb manages to obtain the thing mentioned: *What do you do for entertainment out here?* **what is sb/sth doing …?** used to ask why sb/sth is in the place mentioned: *What are these shoes doing on my desk?* **PHRV** ,**do a**'**way with sb/yourself** (*informal*) to kill sb/yourself ,**do a**'**way with sth** (*informal*) to stop doing or having sth; to make sth end **SYN** ABOLISH: *He thinks it's time we did away with the monarchy.* ,**do sb/sth** '**down** (*BrE, informal*) to criticize sb/sth unfairly '**do for sb/sth** [usually passive] (*informal*) to ruin, destroy or kill sb/sth: *Without that contract, we're done for.* ,**do sb/ yourself** '**in** (*informal*) **1** to kill sb/yourself: *He was so depressed he felt like doing himself in.* **2** [usually passive] to make sb very tired: *Come and sit down—you look done in.* ,**do sth↔**'**in** (*informal*) to injure a part of the body: *He did his back in lifting heavy furniture.* ,**do sb** '**out of sth** (*informal*) to unfairly prevent sb from having what they ought to have: *She was done out of her promotion.* ,**do sb** '**over** (*informal, especially BrE*) to attack and beat sb severely: *He was done over by a gang of thugs.* ,**do sth↔**'**over 1** to clean or decorate sth again: *The paintwork will need doing over soon.* **2** (*AmE*) to do sth again: *She insisted that everything be done over.* ,**do** '**up** to be fastened: *The skirt does up at the back.* ,**do sth↔**'**up 1** to fasten a coat, skirt, etc: *He never bothers to do his jacket up.* **OPP** UNDO **2** to make sth into a package **SYN** WRAP: *She was carrying a package done up in brown paper.* **3** (*BrE*) to repair and decorate a house, etc: *He makes money by buying old houses and doing them up.* ,**do yourself** '**up** (*informal*) to make yourself more attractive by putting on MAKE-UP, attractive clothes, etc. '**do sth with sb/sth** (used in negative sentences and questions with *what*): *I don't know what to do with* (= how to use) *all the food that's left over.* ◊ *What have you done with* (= where have you put) *my umbrella?* ◊ *What have you been doing with yourselves* (= how have you been passing the time)?—see also COULD DO WITH, CAN'T BE DOING WITH ,**do with**'**out**|,**do with**'**out sth** to manage without sb/sth: *She can't do without a secretary.* ◊ *If they can't get it to us in time, we'll just have to do without.* [+ -ing] (*ironic*) *I could have done without being* (= I wish I had not been) *woken up at three in the morning.*

■ *auxiliary verb* (**does** /dʌz/ **did** /dɪd/ **done** /dʌn/) **1** used before a full verb to form negative sentences and questions: *I don't like fish.* ◊ *They didn't go to Paris.* ◊ *Don't forget to write.* ◊ *Does she speak French?* **2** used to make QUESTION TAGS (= short questions at the end of statements): *You live in New York, don't you?* ◊ *She doesn't work here, does she?* **3** used to avoid repeating a full verb: *He plays better than he did a year ago.* ◊ *She works harder than he does.* ◊ *'Who won?' 'I did.'* ◊ *'I love peaches.' 'So do I.'* ◊ *'I don't want to go back.' 'Neither do I.'* **4** used when no other AUXILIARY verb is present, to emphasize what you are saying: *He does look tired.* ◊ *She did at least write to say thank you.* ◊ (*BrE*) *Do shut up!* **5** used to change the order of the subject and verb when an adverb is moved to the front: *Not only does she speak Spanish, she's also good with computers.*

■ *noun* /duː/ (*pl.* **dos** or **do's** /duːz/) (*BrE, informal*) a party; a social event: *Are you having a big do for your birthday?*
IDM **do's and don'ts** (*informal*) rules that you should follow: *Here are some do's and don'ts for exercise during pregnancy.*—more at FAIR *adj.*

do² /dəʊ; *AmE* doʊ/ *noun* = DOH—see also DO¹

do. *abbr.* DITTO

dob /dɒb; *AmE* daːb/ *verb* (*BrE, AustralE, informal*) **PHRV**

To talk about jobs in the home you can use such phrases as **wash the dishes, clean the kitchen floor, set the table**, etc. In conversation the verb **do** is often used instead: *Let me do the dishes.* ◊ *Michael said he would do the kitchen floor.* ◊ *It's your turn to do the table.* **Do** is often used with nouns ending -*ing*: *to do the shopping/cleaning/ironing/vacuuming*.

The verb **make** is used especially in the phrase **make the beds** and when you are talking about preparing or cooking food: *He makes a great lasagne.* ◊ *I'll make breakfast while you're having a shower.* You can also say **get, get ready** and, especially in *AmE*, **fix** for preparing meals: *Can you get dinner while I put the kids to bed?* ◊ *Sit down—I'll fix supper for you.*

,**dob sb** '**in (to sb)** to tell sb about sth that another person has done wrong: *Sue dobbed me in to the teacher.*

Dobermann (pinscher) (also **Doberman (pinscher)** especially in *AmE*) /ˌdəʊbəmən ('pɪnʃə(r)); *AmE* ˌdoʊbərmən/ *noun* a large dog with short dark hair, often used for guarding buildings

doc /dɒk; *AmE* dɑːk/ *noun* (*informal, especially AmE*) a way of addressing or talking about a doctor

do·cile /'dəʊsaɪl; *AmE* 'dɑːsl/ *adj.* quiet and easy to control: *a docile child/horse/temperament* ▶ **do·cile·ly** /-saɪlli; *AmE* -səli/ *adv.* (*rare*) **do·cil·ity** /dəʊ'sɪləti; *AmE* dɑː's-/ *noun* [U]

dock /dɒk; *AmE* dɑːk/ *noun, verb*

■ *noun* **1** [C] a part of a port where ships are repaired or where goods are put onto or taken off them: *dock workers* ◊ *a dock strike* ◊ *The ship was in dock.*—see also DRY DOCK **2** (**docks**) [pl.] a group of docks in a port and the buildings around them that are used for repairing ships, storing goods, etc. **3** [C] (*AmE*) = JETTY **4** [C] (*AmE*) a raised platform for loading vehicles or trains **5** [C] the part of a court of law where the person who has been accused of a crime stands or sits during a trial: *He's been in the dock* (= on trial for a crime) *several times already.* **6** [U] a wild plant of Northern Europe with large thick leaves that can be rubbed on skin that has been stung by NETTLES to make it less painful: *dock leaves*

■ *verb* **1** if a ship **docks** or you **dock** a ship, it sails into a harbour and stays there: [V] *The ferry is expected to dock at 6.* [also VN] **2** if two spacecraft **dock**, or **are docked**, they are joined together in space: [VN] *Next year, a technology module will be docked on the space station.* [also V] **3** [VN] **~ sth (from/off sth)** to take away part of sb's wages, etc: *If you're late, your wages will be docked.* ◊ *They've docked 15% off my pay for this week.* **4** [VN] to cut an animal's tail short

dock·er /'dɒkə(r); *AmE* 'dɑːk-/ *noun* a person whose job is moving goods on and off ships

docket /'dɒkɪt; *AmE* 'dɑːk-/ *noun* **1** (*business*) a document or label that shows what is in a package, which goods have been delivered, which jobs have been done, etc. **2** (*AmE*) a list of cases to be dealt with in a particular court of law

dock·land /'dɒklænd; *AmE* 'dɑːk-/ *noun* [U] (also **docklands** [pl.]) (*BrE*) the district near DOCKS (= the place where ships are loaded and unloaded in a port): *plans to further redevelop Bristol's docklands*

dock·side /'dɒksaɪd; *AmE* 'dɑːk-/ *noun* [sing.] the area around the DOCKS (= the place where ships are loaded and unloaded) in a port

dock·yard /'dɒkjɑːd; *AmE* 'dɑːkjɑːrd/ *noun* an area with DOCKS (= the place where ships are loaded and unloaded in a port) and equipment for building and repairing ships

doc·tor /'dɒktə(r); *AmE* 'dɑːk-/ *noun, verb*

■ *noun* (*abbr.* Dr) **1** a person who has been trained in medical science, whose job is to treat people who are ill or injured: *You'd better see a doctor about that cough.* ◊ *Doctor Staples* (= as a title/form of address) **2** (**doctor's**) a place where a doctor sees patients: *an appointment at the doctor's* **3** a person who has received the highest

---

aɪ	aʊ	eɪ	əʊ	oʊ	ɔɪ	ɪə	eə	ʊə	j	w
my	now	say	go	go	boy	near	hair	pure	yes	wet
			(BrE)	(AmE)						

university degree: *a Doctor of Philosophy/Law* ◊ *Doctor Franks* (= as a title/form of address) **4** (*especially AmE*) used as a title or form of address for a dentist
■ *verb* [VN] **1** to change sth in order to deceive sb [SYN] FALSIFY: *He was accused of doctoring the figures.* **2** to add sth harmful to food or drink: *The wine had been doctored.* **3** (*informal*) to remove part of the sex organs of an animal [SYN] NEUTER

doc·tor·al /ˈdɒktərəl; *AmE* ˈdɑːk-/ *adj.* [only before noun] connected with a doctorate: (*BrE*) *a doctoral thesis* ◊ (*AmE*) *a doctoral dissertation*

doc·tor·ate /ˈdɒktərət; *AmE* ˈdɑːk-/ *noun* the highest university degree: *She's studying for her doctorate.*

doc·trin·aire /ˌdɒktrɪˈneə(r); *AmE* ˌdɑːktrəˈner/ *adj.* (*disapproving*) strictly following a theory in all circumstances, even if there are practical problems or disagreement: *a doctrinaire communist* ◊ *doctrinaire attitudes/beliefs/policies*

doc·tri·nal /dɒkˈtraɪnl; *AmE* ˈdɑːktrənl/ *adj.* (*formal*) relating to a doctrine or doctrines: *the doctrinal position of the English church* ◊ *doctrinal beliefs/disputes* ◊ (*disapproving*) *a rigidly doctrinal approach* ▶ **doc·tri·nal·ly** *adv.*

doc·trine /ˈdɒktrɪn; *AmE* ˈdɑːk-/ *noun* **1** [C, U] a belief or set of beliefs held and taught by a Church, a political party, etc: *the doctrine of parliamentary sovereignty* ◊ *Christian doctrine* **2** (**Doctrine**) [C] (*AmE*) a statement of government policy: *the Monroe Doctrine*

docu·drama /ˈdɒkjudrɑːmə; *AmE* ˈdɑːk-/ *noun* a film/movie, usually made for television, in which real events are shown in the form of a story

docu·ment *noun, verb*
■ *noun* /ˈdɒkjumənt; *AmE* ˈdɑːk-/ **1** an official paper or book that gives information about sth, or that can be used as evidence or proof of sth: *legal documents* ◊ *travel documents* ◊ *Copies of the relevant documents must be filed at court.* ◊ *One of the documents leaked to the press was a memorandum written by the head of the security police.* **2** a computer file that contains text that has a name that identifies it: *Save the document before closing.*—picture on page 251
■ *verb* /ˈdɒkjument; *AmE* ˈdɑːk-/ [VN] **1** to record the details of sth: *Causes of the disease have been well documented.* **2** to prove or support sth with documents: *documented evidence*

docu·men·tary /ˌdɒkjuˈmentri; *AmE* ˌdɑːk-/ *noun, adj.*
■ *noun* (*pl.* **-ies**) a film or a radio or television programme giving facts about sth: *a television documentary about/on the future of nuclear power*
■ *adj.* [only before noun] **1** consisting of documents: *documentary evidence/sources/material* **2** giving a record or report of the facts about sth, especially by using pictures, recordings, etc. of people involved: *a documentary account of the Vietnam war* ◊ *The film was given a documentary style by the director.*

docu·men·ta·tion /ˌdɒkjumenˈteɪʃn; *AmE* ˌdɑːk-/ *noun* [U] **1** the documents that are required for sth, or that give evidence or proof of sth: *I couldn't enter the country because I didn't have all the necessary documentation.* **2** the act of recording sth in a document; the state of being recorded in a document: *the documentation of an agreement*

docu·soap /ˈdɒkju səʊp; *AmE* ˈdɑːkju soʊp/ *noun* (*BrE*) a television programme about the lives of real people, presented as entertainment—see also SOAP OPERA

DOD /ˌdiː əʊ ˈdiː; *AmE* oʊ/ *abbr.* Department of Defense (the government department in the US that is responsible for defence)

dod·der·ing /ˈdɒdərɪŋ; *AmE* ˈdɑːd-/ (*BrE* also **dod·dery** /ˈdɒdəri; *AmE* ˈdɑːd-/) *adj.* (of people) weak, slow and not able to walk in a steady way, especially because of old age: *a doddering old fool*

dod·dle /ˈdɒdl; *AmE* ˈdɑːdl/ *noun* [sing.] (*BrE, informal*) a task or an activity that is very easy: *The first year of the course was an absolute doddle.* ◊ *The machine is a doddle to set up and use.*

dodge /dɒdʒ; *AmE* dɑːdʒ/ *verb, noun*
■ *verb* **1** to move quickly and suddenly to one side in order to avoid sb/sth: [VN] *He ran across the road, dodging the traffic.* ◊ [V] [*usually +adv./prep.*] *The girl dodged behind a tree to hide from the other children.* **2** to avoid doing sth, especially in a dishonest way: [VN] *He dodged his military service.* ◊ [V-ing] *She tried to dodge paying her taxes.*
■ *noun* a clever and dishonest trick, played in order to avoid sth: *a tax dodge* ◊ *When it comes to getting off work, he knows all the dodges.*

dodgem /ˈdɒdʒəm; *AmE* ˈdɑːdʒəm/ *noun* (*BrE*) **1** (**the dodgems**) [pl.] a ride at a FUNFAIR in which people drive small electric cars around an enclosed space, trying to chase and hit the other cars: *The kids wanted to go on the dodgems.* **2** (also **dodgem car**) (also **bumper car** *AmE, BrE*) one of the small electric cars that you drive in the dodgems

dodger /ˈdɒdʒə(r); *AmE* ˈdɑːdʒr/ *noun* (*informal*) a person who dishonestly avoids doing sth: *tax dodgers* ◊ *a crackdown on fare dodgers on trains*—see also DRAFT DODGER

dodgy /ˈdɒdʒi; *AmE* ˈdɑːdʒi/ *adj.* (*informal, BrE*) **1** seeming or likely to be dishonest [SYN] SUSPICIOUS: *He made a lot of money, using some very dodgy methods.* ◊ *I don't want to get involved in anything dodgy.* **2** not working well; not in good condition: *I can't play—I've got a dodgy knee.* ◊ *The marriage had been distinctly dodgy for a long time.* **3** involving risk, danger or difficulty: *If you get into any dodgy situations, call me.*

dodo /ˈdəʊdəʊ; *AmE* ˈdoʊdoʊ/ *noun* (*pl.* **-os**) **1** a large bird that could not fly and that is now EXTINCT (= no longer exists) **2** (*AmE*) a stupid person [IDM] see DEAD *adj.*

doe /dəʊ; *AmE* doʊ/ *noun* a female deer, rabbit or HARE—compare BUCK, HIND, STAG

doer /ˈduːə(r)/ *noun* (*approving*) a person who does things rather than thinking or talking about them: *We need fewer organizers and more doers.*

does /dʌz/ ➪ DO

doesn't /ˈdʌznt/ *short form* does not

doff /dɒf; *AmE* dɑːf; dɔːf/ *verb* [VN] (*old-fashioned*) to take off your hat, especially to show respect for sb/sth

dog /dɒg; *AmE* dɔːg/ *noun, verb*
■ *noun* **1** [C] an animal with four legs and a tail, often kept as a pet or trained for work, for example hunting or guarding buildings. There are many types of dog, some of which are wild: *I took the dog for a walk.* ◊ *I could hear a dog barking.* ◊ *dog food* ◊ *guard dogs* ◊ *a dog and her puppies*—see also GUIDE DOG, GUN DOG, LAPDOG, SHEEPDOG, SNIFFER DOG, TRACKER DOG **2** [C] a male dog, FOX or WOLF—compare BITCH **3** (**the dogs**) [pl.] (*BrE, informal*) GREYHOUND racing **4** [C] (*slang, especially AmE*) a thing of low quality; a failure: *Her last movie was an absolute dog.* **5** [C] (*slang, especially AmE*) an offensive way of describing a woman who is not considered attractive **6** [C] (*informal, disapproving*) used, especially after an adjective, to describe a man who has done sth bad: *You dirty dog!*—see also HOT DOG, SHAGGY-DOG STORY, TOP DOG, WATCHDOG [IDM] **(a case of) ,dog eat ˈdog** a situation in business, politics, etc. where there is a lot of competition and people are willing to harm each other in order to succeed: *I'm afraid in this line of work it's a case of dog eat dog.* ◊ *We're operating in a dog-eat-dog world.* **a ˌdog in the ˈmanger** a person who stops other people from enjoying what he or she cannot use or does not want **a dog's ˈbreakfast/ ˈdinner** (*BrE, informal*) a thing that has been done badly [SYN] MESS: *He's made a real dog's breakfast of these accounts.* **a ˈdog's life** an unhappy life, full of problems or unfair treatment **every dog has his/its ˈday** (*saying*) everyone has good luck or success at some point in their life **go to the ˈdogs** (*AmE* also **go to hell in a ˈhandbasket**) (*informal*) to get into a very bad state: *This firm's gone to the dogs since the new management took over.* **not have a ˈdog's chance** to have no chance at all: *He hasn't a dog's chance of passing the exam.*—more at HAIR, RAIN *v.*, SICK *adj.*, SLEEP *v.*, TAIL *n.*, TEACH
■ *verb* (**-gg-**) [VN] **1** (of a problem or bad luck) to cause you trouble for a long time: *He had been dogged by bad health*

b	d	f	g	h	k	l	m	n	p	r
bad	did	fall	get	hat	cat	leg	man	now	pen	red

all his life. **2** to follow sb closely: *She had the impression that someone was dogging her steps.*

'dog biscuit *noun* a small hard biscuit fed to dogs

'dog collar *noun* **1** a collar for a dog **2** (*informal*) a stiff white collar fastened at the back and worn by some Christian priests

'dog days *noun* [pl.] the hottest period of the year: *the dog days of summer*

'dog-eared *adj.* (of a book) used so much that the corners of many of the pages are turned down—picture at JAGGED

,dog-'end *noun* (*BrE, informal*) the end of a cigarette that has been smoked

dog·fight /'dɒgfaɪt; *AmE* 'dɔːg-/ *noun* **1** a fight between aircraft in which they fly around close to each other **2** a struggle between two people or groups in order to win sth **3** (**dog fight**) a fight between dogs, especially one that is arranged illegally, for entertainment ▶ **dog·fight·ing** *noun* [U]

dog·fish /'dɒgfɪʃ; *AmE* 'dɔːg-/ *noun* (*pl.* **dog·fish**) a small SHARK (= a large fierce sea fish with very sharp teeth)

dog·ged /'dɒgɪd; *AmE* 'dɔːg-/ *adj.* [usually before noun] (*approving*) showing determination; not giving up easily: *dogged determination / persistence* ◊ *their dogged defence of the city* ▶ **dog·ged·ly** *adv.* **dog·ged·ness** *noun* [U]

dog·gerel /'dɒgərəl; *AmE* 'dɔːg-/ *noun* [U] poetry that is badly written or ridiculous, sometimes because the writer has not intended it to be serious

doggo /'dɒgəʊ; *AmE* 'dɔːgoʊ/ *adv.* **lie ~** (*old-fashioned, informal*) to lie still and quiet, so that other people will not notice you

dog·gone /'dɒgɒn; *AmE* 'dɔːgɔːn/ *adj.* [only before noun] (*AmE, informal*) used to show that you are annoyed or surprised: *Where's the doggone key?* ◊ *Don't drive so doggone fast.* ◊ *Well, doggone it!*

doggy /'dɒgi; *AmE* 'dɔːgi/ *noun, adj.*
■ *noun* (also **dog·gie**) (*pl.* **-ies**) (*informal*) a child's word for a dog
■ *adj.* [only before noun] of or like a dog: *a doggy smell*

'doggy bag (also **'doggie bag**) *noun* (*informal*) a bag for taking home any food that is left after a meal in a restaurant

'doggy-paddle *noun* = DOG-PADDLE

'dog handler *noun* a police officer who works with a trained dog

dog·house /'dɒghaʊs; *AmE* 'dɔːg-/ *noun* (*AmE*) = KENNEL
IDM **be in the doghouse** (*informal, AmE, BrE*) if you are in the doghouse, sb is annoyed with you because of sth that you have done

dogie /'dəʊgi; *AmE* 'doʊgi/ *noun* (*AmE*) a young cow that has lost its mother

'dog-leg *noun* a sharp bend, especially in a road or on a golf course

dogma /'dɒgmə; *AmE* 'dɔːgmə/ *noun* [U, C] (*often disapproving*) a belief or set of beliefs held by a group or organization, which others are expected to accept without argument: *political / social / religious / party dogma* ◊ *He has caused a storm by calling into question one of the central dogmas of the Church.*

dog·mat·ic /dɒg'mætɪk; *AmE* dɔːg-/ *adj.* (*disapproving*) being certain that your beliefs are right and that others should accept them, without paying attention to evidence or other opinions: *a dogmatic approach / statement* ◊ *There is a danger of becoming too dogmatic about teaching methods.* ▶ **dog·mat·ic·al·ly** /-kli/ *adv.*

dog·ma·tism /'dɒgmətɪzəm; *AmE* 'dɔːg-/ *noun* [U] (*disapproving*) behaviour and attitudes that are dogmatic

,do-'gooder *noun* (*informal, disapproving*) a person who tries to help other people but who does it in a way that is annoying

'dog-paddle (also **'doggy-paddle**) *noun* [U] a simple swimming stroke, with short quick movements like those of a dog in the water

dogs·body /'dɒgzbɒdi; *AmE* 'dɔːgzbɑːdi/ *noun* (*pl.* **-ies**) (*BrE, informal*) a person who does all the boring jobs that

nobody else wants to do, and who is treated as being less important than other people: *I got myself a job as a typist and general dogsbody on a small magazine.*

dog·sled /'dɒgsled; *AmE* 'dɔːg-/ *noun* (*AmE*) a SLEDGE (= a vehicle that slides over snow) pulled by dogs, used especially in Canada and Alaska

'dog tag *noun* (*AmE, slang*) a small piece of metal that US soldiers wear round their necks with their name and number on it

,dog-'tired *adj.* [not usually before noun] (*informal*) very tired

dog·wood /'dɒgwʊd; *AmE* 'dɔːg-/ *noun* [U, C] a bush or small tree with red or pink berries and red stems, that grows in northern regions; the hard wood of this tree

DoH *abbr.* (in Britain) Department of Health: *the DoH Aids prevention policy*

doh (also **do**) /dəʊ; *AmE* doʊ/ *noun* (*music*) the 1st and 8th note of a MAJOR scale

doily /'dɔɪli/ *noun* (*pl.* **-ies**) **1** (*BrE*) a small circle of paper or fabric with a pattern of very small holes in it, that you put on a plate under a cake or sandwiches **2** (*AmE*) a small decorative MAT that you put on top of a piece of furniture

doing /'duːɪŋ/ *noun* [C, usually pl., U] a thing done or caused by sb: *I've been hearing a lot about your doings recently.* ◊ *I promise you this was none of my doing* (= I didn't do it). **IDM** **take some 'doing | take a lot of 'doing** to be hard work; to be difficult: *Getting it finished by tomorrow will take some doing.*

,do it your'self *noun* [U] (*especially BrE*) = DIY: *The materials you need are available from any good do-it-yourself store.*

Dolby™ /'dɒlbi; 'dəʊlbi; *AmE* 'dɔːlbi; 'doʊlbi/ *noun* [U] a system for reducing background noise in sound recordings

dol·drums /'dɒldrəmz; *AmE* 'doʊl-/ *noun* [pl.] (usually **the doldrums**) **1** the state of feeling sad or depressed: *He's been in the doldrums ever since she left him.* **2** a lack of activity or improvement: *The bond market normally revives after the summer doldrums.* ◊ *Despite these measures, the economy remains in the doldrums.*

dole /dəʊl; *AmE* doʊl/ *noun, verb*
■ *noun* [sing.] (usually **the dole**) (*BrE, informal*) money paid by the state to unemployed people: *He's been on the dole* (= without a job) *for a year.* ◊ *It is feared the government might change the rules for claiming dole.* ◊ *lengthening dole queues* ◊ *We could all be in the dole queue on Monday* (= have lost our jobs).
■ *verb* **PHRV** **,dole sth↔'out (to sb)** to give out an amount of food, money, etc. to a number of people in a group

dole·ful /'dəʊlfl; *AmE* 'doʊlfl/ *adj.* (*written*) very sad: *a doleful expression / face / song* ◊ *a doleful looking man* ▶ **dole·ful·ly** /-fəli/ *adv.*

doll /dɒl; *AmE* dɑːl/ *noun, verb*
■ *noun* **1** a child's toy in the shape of a person, especially a baby or a child: *a rag doll* (= one made out of fabric) **2** (*old-fashioned slang, especially AmE*) a word used to describe a pretty or attractive woman, now often considered offensive: *She's quite a doll.*
■ *verb* **PHRV** **,doll sb / yourself 'up** (*informal*) to make yourself look attractive for a party, etc., with fashionable clothes: *Are you getting dolled up for the party?*

dol·lar /'dɒlə(r); *AmE* 'dɑːl-/ *noun* **1** [C] (*symb* $) the unit of money in the US, Canada, Australia and several other countries: *You will be paid in American dollars.*—compare BUCK **2** [C] a BANKNOTE or coin worth one dollar: *Do you have a dollar?* ◊ *a dollar bill* **3** (**the dollar**) [sing.] (*finance*) the value of the US dollar compared with the value of the money of other countries: *The dollar closed two cents down.* **IDM** see BET *v.*, MILLION

doll·house /'dɒlhaʊs; *AmE* 'dɑːl-/ *noun* (*AmE*) = DOLL'S HOUSE

dol·lop /'dɒləp; *AmE* 'dɑːləp/ *noun* (*informal*) **1** a lump of soft food, often dropped from a spoon: *a dollop of whipped cream* **2** an amount of sth: *A dollop of romance now and then is good for everybody.*

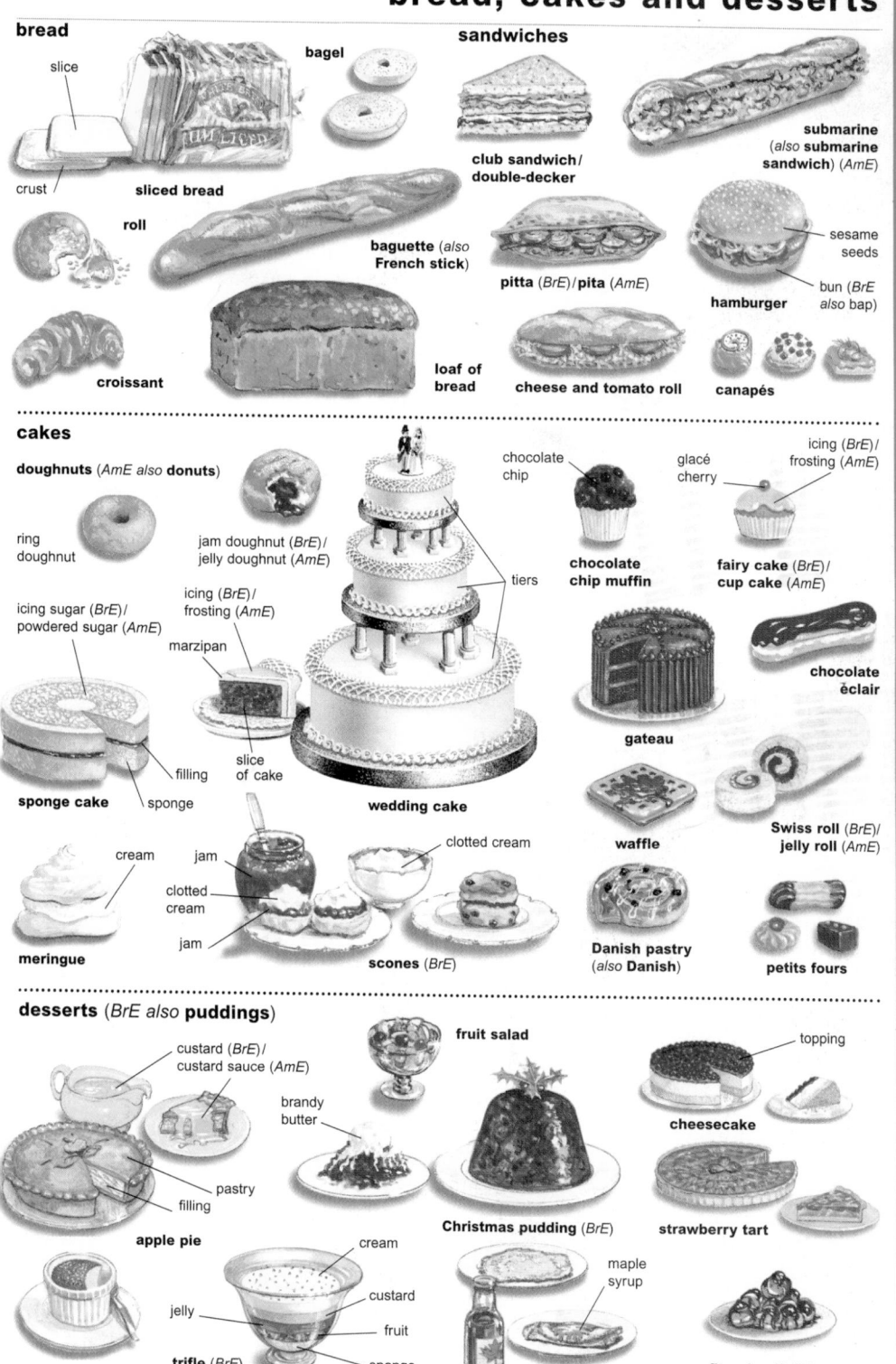

bread

slice

crust

sliced bread

roll

croissant

bagel

baguette (*also* **French stick**)

loaf of bread

sandwiches

club sandwich / double-decker

submarine (*also* **submarine sandwich**) (*AmE*)

pitta (*BrE*) / **pita** (*AmE*)

sesame seeds

bun (*BrE* also bap)

hamburger

cheese and tomato roll

canapés

cakes

doughnuts (*AmE also* **donuts**)

ring doughnut

jam doughnut (*BrE*) / **jelly doughnut** (*AmE*)

icing sugar (*BrE*) / powdered sugar (*AmE*)

icing (*BrE*) / **frosting** (*AmE*)

marzipan

slice of cake

filling

sponge

sponge cake

tiers

wedding cake

chocolate chip

glacé cherry

icing (*BrE*) / frosting (*AmE*)

chocolate chip muffin

fairy cake (*BrE*) / **cup cake** (*AmE*)

chocolate éclair

gateau

waffle

Swiss roll (*BrE*) / **jelly roll** (*AmE*)

cream

jam

clotted cream

jam

meringue

clotted cream

scones (*BrE*)

Danish pastry (*also* **Danish**)

petits fours

desserts (*BrE also* **puddings**)

custard (*BrE*) / custard sauce (*AmE*)

brandy butter

pastry

filling

apple pie

fruit salad

Christmas pudding (*BrE*)

topping

cheesecake

strawberry tart

cream

custard

jelly

fruit

trifle (*BrE*)

sponge

crème brûlée

maple syrup

pancakes

profiteroles (*BrE*) / **cream puffs** (*AmE*)

A2 fruit and vegetables

Some fruit and vegetables are always countable:
- *Do you like bananas?*

Some are always uncountable:
- *Celery is usually eaten raw.*

Some may be countable or uncountable, depending on whether you are thinking of them as plants or as food and on how they are prepared as food. If you are thinking of a fruit or vegetable as a plant you are usually talking about the whole fruit or vegetable, so it will be countable:
- *Plant the cabbages in rows.*

Larger fruit or vegetables, that you do not eat whole, are uncountable as food:
- *duck with spring cabbage*

Others may be eaten whole (countable)...
- *baked apples*
- *baby carrots*

... or prepared in such a way that they are not eaten whole (uncountable in British English but still countable in American English)
- *stewed apple (BrE)/stewed apples (AmE)*
- *grated raw carrot (BrE)/grated raw carrots (AmE)*

cherries

stalk (*BrE*)/ stem (*AmE*)

apple

core

banana

skin (*BrE*)/peel (*AmE*)

pip (*BrE*)/ seed (*AmE*)

peach

stone (*BrE*)/ pit (*AmE*)

flesh

kiwi fruit

fig

watermelon

seeds

avocado

a bunch of grapes

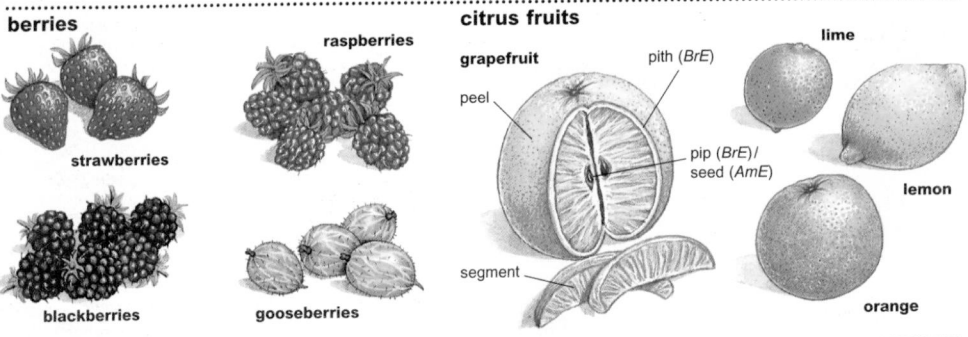

berries

strawberries

raspberries

blackberries

gooseberries

citrus fruits

grapefruit

peel

pith (*BrE*)

pip (*BrE*)/ seed (*AmE*)

segment

lime

lemon

orange

tropical fruits

pineapple

mango

lychee

shell

coconut

flesh

milk

passion fruit

pomegranate

seeds

starfruit

onion

shallots

cabbage

cauliflower

clove

leek

spring onions (*BrE*)/
green onions (*AmE*)

garlic

floret (*BrE*)

Brussels
sprouts

broccoli

mushrooms

aubergine (*BrE*)/
eggplant (*AmE*)

artichoke
(*also* **globe artichoke**)

spear

asparagus

okra

sweet potato

corn on
the cob

celery

potato

fennel

sweetcorn (*BrE*)/**corn** (*AmE*)

yam

squash

marrow (*BrE*)

courgette (*BrE*)/
zucchini (*AmE*)

pumpkin

peas and beans

pod

green
beans

peas

kidney beans

bean
sprouts

root vegetables

carrot

parsnip

swede (*BrE*)/
rutabaga (*AmE*)

turnip

beetroot (*BrE*)/**beet** (*AmE*)

salad vegetables

radishes

lettuce

tomato

peppers (*BrE*)/**bell
peppers** (*AmE*)

cucumber

A4 clothes and fabrics

pinstripe suit

double-breasted jacket

single-breasted jacket

lapel

breast pocket

tweed

cuff

waistcoat (*BrE*)/ **vest** (*AmE*)

trousers (*BrE*)/ **pants** (*AmE*)

lining

bow tie

polka dots

crease

cravat

pinstripe

turn-up (*BrE*)/ cuff (*AmE*)

paisley

striped shirt

button-down collar

patterned/print blouse

collar

sleeve

crop top

tie (*esp BrE*)/ **necktie** (*AmE fml*)

cuff

leggings

braces (*BrE*)/ **suspenders** (*AmE*)

belt

fly (*BrE* also flies)

waistband

corduroy (*also* **cord**)

jeans (*made of* **denim**)

flared trousers (*BrE*)/ **pants** (*AmE*) (*also* **flares**)

trousers (*BrE*)/ **pants** (*AmE*)

check pyjamas (*BrE*)/ **checked pajamas** (*AmE*)

nightdress (*BrE*)/ **nightgown** (*AmE*)

lace

polo neck (*BrE*)/ **turtleneck** (*AmE*)

V-neck

cardigan

sweater (*BrE* also **jumper**)

sweatshirt

round neck

kilt

tartan/ plaid

tracksuit (*BrE*)/**sweats** (*AmE*)

towelling (*BrE*)/ **toweling** (*AmE*)

bathrobe (*BrE* also **dressing gown**)

tracksuit bottoms (*BrE*)/ **sweatpants** (*AmE*)

coats   hood

jacket   **overcoat**   **raincoat**

fleece

anorak (*BrE*)/ **jacket** (*AmE*)

drawstring

fleece

cagoule (*BrE*)/ **jacket** (*AmE*)

belt

buckle

trench coat

A6 the animal kingdom

birds

crest

finch

beak/bill

wing

tail

talons

claw

toe

nest

webbed foot

feather

egg

poultry and game

chicken

duck

turkey

pheasant

birds of prey

golden eagle

vulture

carrion

barn owl

puffin

seabirds

albatross

gull

primates

spider monkey

prehensile tail

chimpanzee (*also* chimp)

bat

mammals

coat

muzzle

whisker

mane

paw

claw

snout

tail

lion

marsupials

koala

eucalyptus tree

joey

pouch

kangaroo

antlers

horns

horns

tusk

trunk

hooves

pachyderms

hide

horn

blowhole

rodents

beaver

rhinoceros (*also* rhino)

red squirrel

hippopotamus (*also* hippo)

sperm whale

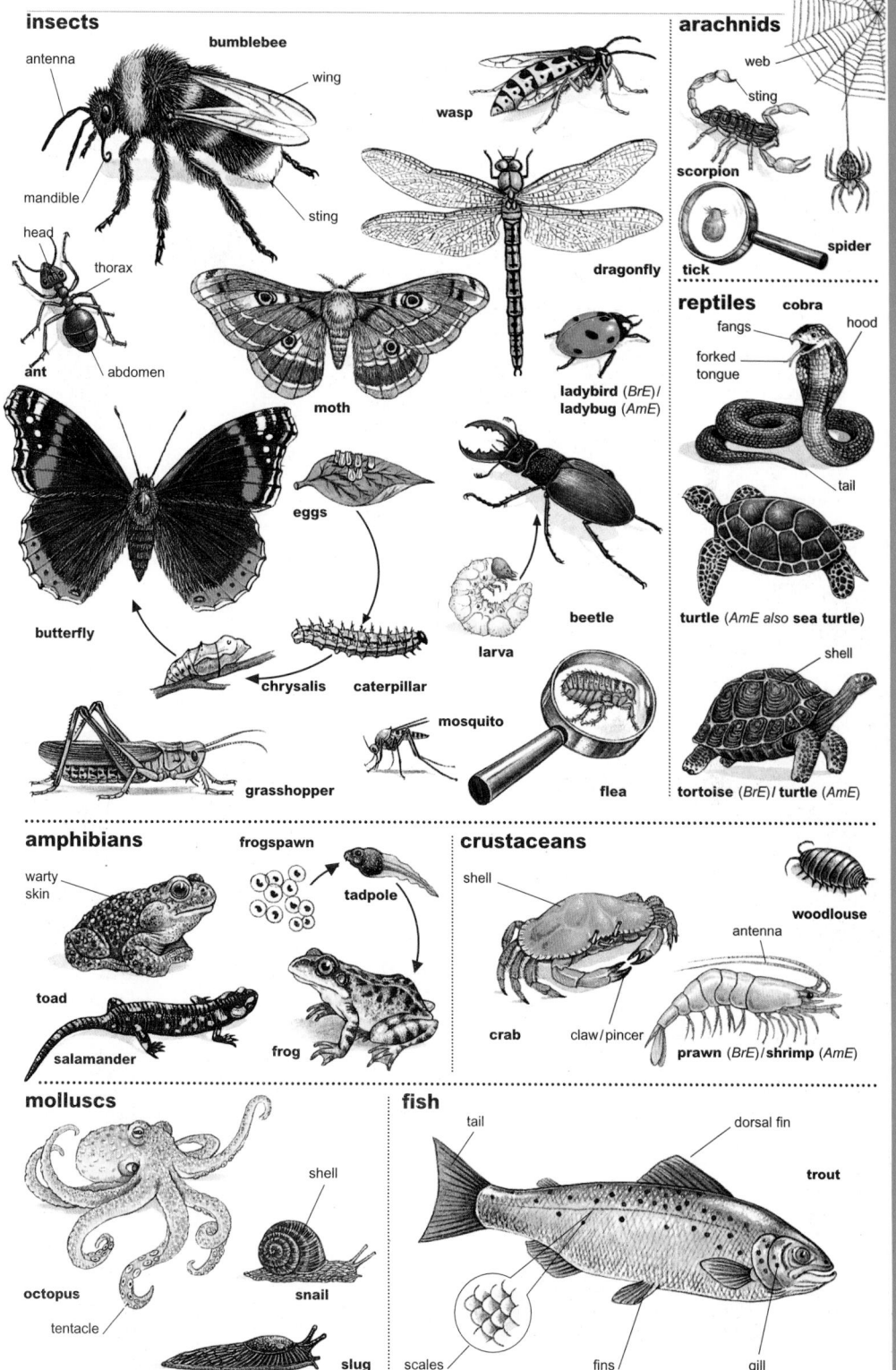

insects

antenna
wing
bumblebee
mandible
sting
head
thorax
ant
abdomen
moth
wasp
dragonfly
ladybird (*BrE*) /
ladybug (*AmE*)
butterfly
eggs
beetle
larva
chrysalis   **caterpillar**
mosquito
grasshopper
flea

arachnids

web
sting
scorpion
spider
tick

reptiles

cobra
fangs
hood
forked
tongue
tail
turtle (*AmE also* **sea turtle**)
shell
tortoise (*BrE*) / **turtle** (*AmE*)

amphibians

frogspawn
warty
skin
tadpole
toad
salamander
frog

crustaceans

shell
woodlouse
antenna
crab
claw/pincer
prawn (*BrE*) / **shrimp** (*AmE*)

molluscs

shell
octopus
tentacle
snail
slug

fish

tail
dorsal fin
trout
scales
fins
gill

A8 games and toys

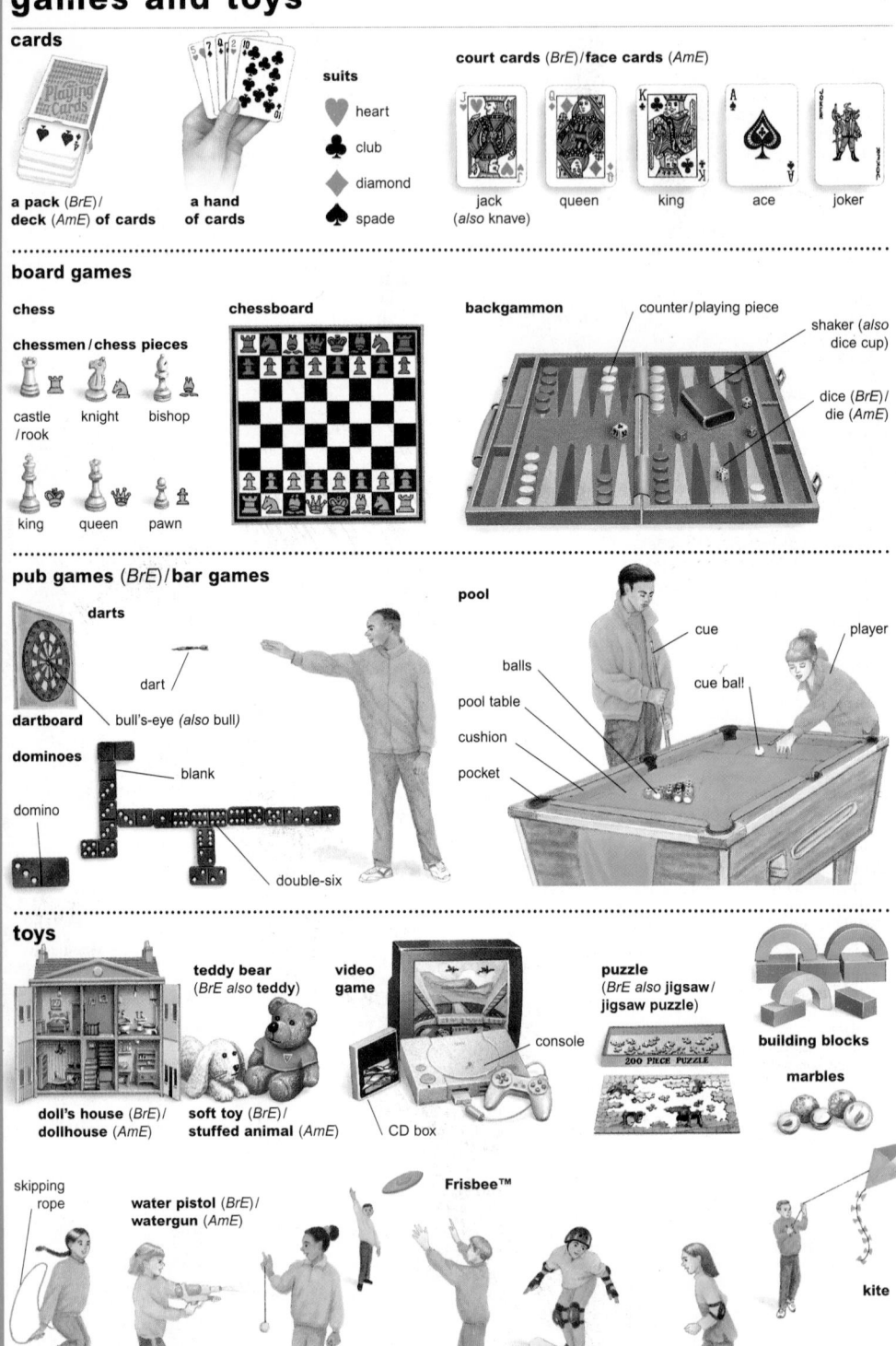

cards

a pack (BrE) /
deck (AmE) of cards

a hand
of cards

suits

♥ heart
♣ club
♦ diamond
♠ spade

court cards (BrE) / **face cards** (AmE)

jack
(also knave)

queen

king

ace

joker

board games

chess

chessmen / chess pieces

castle
/rook

knight

bishop

king

queen

pawn

chessboard

backgammon

counter / playing piece

shaker (also
dice cup)

dice (BrE) /
die (AmE)

pub games (BrE) / bar games

darts

dart

dartboard

bull's-eye (also bull)

dominoes

domino

blank

double-six

pool

cue

player

balls

cue ball

pool table

cushion

pocket

toys

doll's house (BrE) /
dollhouse (AmE)

teddy bear
(BrE also **teddy**)

soft toy (BrE) /
stuffed animal (AmE)

**video
game**

console

CD box

puzzle
(BrE also **jigsaw** /
jigsaw puzzle)

200 PIECE PUZZLE

building blocks

marbles

skipping
rope

water pistol (BrE) /
watergun (AmE)

Frisbee™

kite

skipping

Yo Yo™

skateboard

Rollerblade™
(also **in-line skate**)

'doll's house (*BrE*) (*AmE* **doll·house** *noun* a toy house with small furniture and sometimes DOLLS in it for children to play with—picture on page A8

dolly /'dɒli; *AmE* 'dɑːli; 'dɔːli/ *noun* (*pl.* **-ies**) **1** a child's word for a DOLL **2** (*especially AmE*) a low platform on wheels for moving heavy objects

'dolly-bird *noun* (*old-fashioned, BrE, informal*) a way of referring to a young woman who is considered attractive but not very intelligent

dol·men /'dɒlmen; *AmE* 'doʊl-/ *noun* a pair or group of upright stones with a large flat stone on top, built in ancient times to mark a place where sb was buried

dol·phin /'dɒlfɪn; *AmE* 'dɑːl-/ *noun* a sea animal that looks like a large fish with a pointed mouth. Dolphins are very intelligent and often friendly towards humans. There are several types of dolphin: *a school of dolphins*—compare PORPOISE

dolt /dəʊlt; *AmE* doʊlt/ *noun* (*disapproving*) a stupid person ▶ **dol·tish** *adj.*

-dom *suffix* (in nouns) **1** the condition or state of: *freedom* ◇ *martyrdom* **2** the rank of; an area ruled by: *kingdom* **3** the group of: *officialdom*

do·main /də'meɪn; dəʊ-; *AmE* doʊ-/ *noun* **1** an area of knowledge or activity; especially one that sb is responsible for: *The care of older people is being placed firmly within the domain of the family.* ◇ *Physics used to be very much a male domain.*—see also PUBLIC DOMAIN **2** lands owned or ruled by a particular person, government, etc., especially in the past: *The Spice Islands were within the Spanish domains.*

dome /dəʊm; *AmE* doʊm/ *noun* **1** a round roof with a circular base: *the dome of St Paul's Cathedral* **2** a thing or a building shaped like a dome: *his bald dome of a head* ◇ *the Millennium Dome in London* **3** (*AmE*) (in names) a sports STADIUM whose roof is shaped like a dome: *the Houston Astrodome*

dome

dome

domed /dəʊmd; *AmE* doʊmd/ *adj.* [usually before noun] having or shaped like a dome: *a domed forehead/ceiling*

do·mes·tic /də'mestɪk/ *adj., noun*

■ *adj.* **1** [usually before noun] of or inside a particular country; not foreign or international: *domestic affairs/politics* ◇ *domestic flights* (= to and from places within a country) ◇ *Output consists of both exports and sales on the domestic market.* **2** [only before noun] used in the home; connected with the home or family: *domestic appliances* ◇ *domestic tasks/chores* ◇ *the growing problem of domestic violence* (= violence between members of the same family) ◇ *domestic service* (= the work of a servant in a large house) ◇ *domestic help* (= help with the work in a house; the person or people who do this work) **3** liking home life; enjoying or good at cooking, cleaning the house, etc: *I'm not a very domestic sort of person.* **4** (of animals) kept on farms or as pets; not wild ▶ **do·mes·tic·al·ly** /-kli/ *adv.*: *domestically produced goods*

■ *noun* **1** (also **,domestic 'help, ,domestic 'worker**) a servant who works in sb's house, doing the cleaning and other jobs **2** (*informal*) a fight between two members of the same family: *The police were called to sort out a domestic.*

do·mes·ti·cate /də'mestɪkeɪt/ *verb* [VN] **1** to make a wild animal used to living with or working for humans **2** to grow plants or crops for human use [SYN] CULTIVATE **3** (*often humorous*) to make sb good at cooking, caring for a house, etc.; to make sb enjoy home life: *Some men are very hard to domesticate.* ▶ **do·mes·ti·cated** *adj.*: *domesticated animals* ◇ *They've become a lot more domesticated since they got married.* **do·mes·ti·ca·tion** /də,mestɪ'keɪʃn/ *noun* [U]: *the domestication of cattle*

do·mes·ti·city /,dəʊme'stɪsəti; ,dɒm-; *AmE* ,doʊs-; ,dɑːm-/ *noun* [U] (*written*) home or family life: *an atmosphere of happy domesticity* ◇ *a life of domesticity and motherhood*

do,mestic 'science *noun* (*old-fashioned, BrE*) = HOME ECONOMICS

domi·cile /'dɒmɪsaɪl; *AmE* 'dɑːm-; 'doʊm-/ *noun* (*formal* or *law*) the place where sb lives, especially when it is stated for official or legal purposes

domi·ciled /'dɒmɪsaɪld; *AmE* 'dɑːm-; 'doʊm-/ *adj.* [not before noun] (*formal* or *law*) living in a particular place: *to be domiciled in the United Kingdom*

domi·cil·iary /,dɒmɪ'sɪliəri; *AmE* ,dɑːmə'sɪlieri; ,doʊ-/ *adj.* [only before noun] (*formal*) in sb's home: *a domiciliary visit* (= for example, by a doctor) ◇ *domiciliary care/services/treatment*

dom·in·ant /'dɒmɪnənt; *AmE* 'dɑːm-/ *adj.* **1** more important, powerful or noticeable than other things: *The firm has achieved a dominant position in the world market.* ◇ *The dominant feature of the room was the large open fireplace.* **2** (*biology*) a **dominant** GENE causes a person to have a particular physical characteristic, for example brown eyes, even if only one of their parents has passed on this GENE—compare RECESSIVE ▶ **dom·in·ance** /'dɒmɪnəns; *AmE* 'dɑː-/ *noun* [U]: *to achieve/assert dominance over sb* ◇ *political/economic dominance*

dom·in·ate /'dɒmɪneɪt; *AmE* 'dɑːm-/ *verb* **1** to control or have a lot of influence over sb/sth, especially in an unpleasant way: [VN] *As a child he was dominated by his father.* ◇ [V] *She always says a lot in meetings, but she doesn't dominate.* **2** [VN] to be the most important or noticeable feature of sth: *In recent years, social policy has been dominated by cuts in spending.* **3** [VN] to be the largest, highest or most obvious thing in a place: *The cathedral dominates the city.* ▶ **dom·in·ation** /,dɒmɪ'neɪʃn; *AmE* ,dɑː-/ *noun* [U]: *colonial/economic/political domination* ◇ *companies fighting for domination of the software market*

dom·in·eer·ing /,dɒmɪ'nɪərɪŋ; *AmE* ,dɑːmə'nɪr-/ *adj.* (*disapproving*) trying to control other people without considering their wishes, opinions or feelings: *He was brought up by a cold and domineering father.* ◇ *a domineering manner/personality*

Do·min·ic·an /də'mɪnɪkən/ *noun* a member of a Christian group of MONKS or NUNS following the rules of St Dominic ▶ **Do·min·ic·an** *adj.*

do·min·ion /də'mɪniən/ *noun* **1** [U] ~ (**over sb/sth**) (*literary*) authority to rule; control: *Man has dominion over the natural world.* ◇ *Soon the whole country was under his sole dominion.* **2** [C] (*formal*) an area controlled by one ruler: *the vast dominions of the Chinese Empire* **3** (often **Dominion**) [C] (in the past) any of the countries of the British Commonwealth that had their own government—compare COLONY, PROTECTORATE

dom·ino /'dɒmɪnəʊ; *AmE* 'dɑːmənoʊ/ *noun* (*pl.* **-oes**) **1** [C] a small flat block, often made of wood, marked on one side with two groups of dots representing numbers, used for playing games—picture on page A8 **2** (**dominoes**) [U] a game played with a set of dominoes, in which players take turns to put them onto a table—picture on page A8

'domino effect *noun* [usually sing.] a situation in which one event causes a series of similar events to happen one after the other

don /dɒn; *AmE* dɑːn/ *noun, verb*
■ *noun* **1** (*BrE*) a teacher at a university, especially Oxford or Cambridge—see also DONNISH **2** (*informal*) the leader of a group of criminals involved with the Mafia
■ *verb* (**-nn-**) [VN] (*formal*) to put clothes, etc. on: *He donned his jacket and went out.*

do·nate /dəʊ'neɪt; *AmE* 'doʊneɪt/ *verb* [VN] ~ **sth** (**to sb/sth**) **1** to give money, food, clothes, etc. to sb/sth, especially a charity: *He donated thousands of pounds to charity.* **2** to allow doctors to remove blood or a body organ in order to help sb who needs it: *All donated blood is tested for HIV and other infections.*

do·na·tion /dəʊ'neɪʃn; *AmE* doʊ-/ *noun* [C, U] ~ (**to sb/sth**)| ~ (**of…**) something that is given to a person or an organization such as a charity, in order to help them; the

æ	ɑː	e	ɜː	ə	ɪ	iː	i	ɒ	ɔː	ʌ	ʊ	u	uː
cat	father	ten	bird	about	sit	see	many	got	saw	cup	put	actual	too
								(BrE)					

act of giving sth in this way: *to make a donation to charity* ◊ *a generous/large/small donation* ◊ *a donation of £200/a £200 donation* ◊ *The work of the charity is funded by voluntary donations.* ◊ *organ donation* (= allowing doctors to use an organ from your body after your death in order to save a sick person's life)

done /dʌn/ *adj., exclamation*—see also DO *v.*
- *adj.* [not before noun] **1 ~ (with)** finished; completed: *When you're done, perhaps I can say something.* ◊ *I'll be glad when this job is over and done with.* **2** (of food) cooked enough: *The meat isn't quite done yet.* **3** (*BrE, informal*) socially acceptable, especially among people who have a strict set of social rules: *At school, it simply wasn't done to show that you cared for anything except cricket.* **IDM** **be 'done for** (*informal*) to be in a very bad situation; to be certain to fail: *Unless we start making some sales, we're done for.* ◊ *When he pointed the gun at me, I thought I was done for* (= about to die). **be done 'in** (*informal*) to be extremely tired **be the ˌdone 'thing** (*BrE*) to be socially acceptable behaviour **be/get 'done for sth/for doing sth** (*BrE, informal*) to be caught and punished for doing sth illegal but not too serious: *I got done for speeding on my way back.* **be/have 'done with sth** to have finished dealing with sb, or doing or using sth: *If you've done with that magazine, can I have a look at it?* **have 'done with it** (*BrE*) to do sth unpleasant, as quickly as possible, so that it is finished: *Why not tell her you're quitting and have done with it?*—more at EASY *adv.*, HARD *adv.*, SOON
- *exclamation* used to show that you accept an offer: *'I'll give you £800 for it.' 'Done!'*

Don Juan /ˌdɒn ˈdʒuːən; -ˈ(h)wɑːn; *AmE* ˌdɑːn-/ *noun* (*informal*) a man who has sex with a lot of women

don·key /ˈdɒŋki; *AmE* ˈdɑːŋ-; ˈdɔːŋ-/ *noun* an animal of the horse family, with short legs and long ears. People ride donkeys or use them to carry heavy loads. **IDM** **'donkey's years** (*BrE, informal*) a very long time: *We've known each other for donkey's years.* ◊ *I met him once, but that was donkey's years ago.*—more at TALK *v.*

'donkey jacket *noun* (*BrE*) a thick short coat, usually dark blue, worn especially by people working outside

'donkey work *noun* [U] (*BrE, informal*) the hard boring part of a job or task

don·nish /ˈdɒnɪʃ; *AmE* ˈdɑːn-/ *adj.* (*BrE*) (of a man) serious and concerned with academic rather than practical matters: *He has a somewhat donnish air about him.*

donor /ˈdəʊnə(r); *AmE* ˈdoʊ-/ *noun* **1** a person or an organization that makes a gift of money, clothes, food, etc. to a charity, etc: *international aid donors* (= countries which give money, etc. to help other countries) ◊ *She is one of the charity's main donors.* **2** a person who gives blood or a part of his or her body to be used by doctors to help sick people: *a blood donor* ◊ *The heart transplant will take place as soon as a suitable donor can be found.* ◊ *donor organs* ◊ *a donor card* (= a card that you carry giving permission for doctors to use parts of your body after your death)

don't /dəʊnt/ *short form* do not

donut *noun* (*especially AmE*) = DOUGHNUT

doo·dah /ˈduːdɑː/ (*BrE*) (*AmE* **doo·dad** /ˈduːdæd/) *noun* (*informal*) a small object whose name you have forgotten or do not know

doo·dle /ˈduːdl/ *verb* [V] to draw lines, shapes, etc., especially when you are bored or thinking about sth else: *I often doodle when I'm on the phone.* ► **doo·dle** *noun*

doo·hickey /ˈduːhɪki/ *noun* (*AmE, informal*) a small object whose name you have forgotten or do not know, especially part of a machine

doo·lal·ly /duːˈlæli/ *adj.* [not before noun] (*BrE, informal*) crazy: *The poor chap's gone doolally.*

doom /duːm/ *noun, verb*
- *noun* [U] death or destruction; any terrible event that you cannot avoid: *to meet your doom* ◊ *She had a sense of impending doom* (= felt that sth very bad was going to happen). **IDM** **ˌdoom and 'gloom** | **ˌgloom and 'doom** a general feeling of having lost all hope and of PESSIMISM (=

expecting things to go badly): *Despite the obvious setbacks, it is not all doom and gloom for the England team.* **ˌprophet of 'doom** | **'doom merchant** a person who predicts that things will go very badly: *The prophets of doom who said television would kill off the book were wrong.*
- *verb* [usually passive] **~ sb/sth (to sth)** to make sb/sth certain to fail, suffer, die, etc: *The plan was doomed to failure.* ◊ *The marriage was doomed from the start.* [also VN to inf]

'doom-laden *adj.* [usually before noun] predicting or leading to death or destruction: *doom-laden economic forecasts*

doom·sayer /ˈduːmseɪə(r)/ (*especially AmE*) (*BrE* also **doom·ster** /ˈduːmstə(r)/) *noun* a person who says that sth very bad is going to happen

dooms·day /ˈduːmzdeɪ/ *noun* [sing.] the last day of the world when Christians believe that everyone will be judged by God **IDM** **till 'doomsday** (*informal*) a very long time; for ever: *This job's going to take me till doomsday.*

door /dɔː(r)/ *noun* **1** a piece of wood, glass, etc. that is opened and closed so that people can get in and out of a room, building, car, etc.; a similar thing in a cupboard/closet: *a knock on the door* ◊ *to open/shut/close/slam/lock/bolt the door* ◊ *to answer the door* (= to go and open it because sb has knocked on it or rung the bell) ◊ *the front/back door* (= at the entrance at the front/back of a building) ◊ *the bedroom door* ◊ *the door frame* ◊ *a four-door saloon car* ◊ *the fridge door* ◊ *Shut the door!* ◊ *Close the door behind you, please.* ◊ *The door closed behind him.*—see also BACK-DOOR, FIRE DOOR, FRENCH DOOR, OPEN-DOOR, REVOLVING DOOR, SLIDING DOOR, STAGE DOOR, SWING DOOR, TRAPDOOR **2** the space when a door is open: *Marc appeared through a door at the far end of the room.* ◊ (*spoken*) *She's just arrived—she's just come in the door.* ◊ (*spoken*) *He walked out the door.* **3** the area close to the entrance of a building: *There's somebody at the door* (= at the front door of a house). ◊ *'Can I help you?' asked the man at the door.*—see also DOORWAY **4** a building or home that is a particular number of buildings or homes away from another: *the family that lives three doors up from us* ◊ *Our other branch is just a few doors down the road.*—see also NEXT DOOR **IDM** **be on the door** to work at the entrance to a theatre, club, etc., for example collecting tickets from people as they enter **close/shut the 'door on sth** to make it unlikely that sth will happen: *She was careful not to close the door on the possibility of further talks.* **(from) ˌdoor to 'door** from building to building: *The journey takes about an hour, door to door.* ◊ *a door-to-door salesman* **(open) the 'door to sth** (to provide) the means of getting or reaching sth; (to create) the opportunity for sth: *The agreement will open the door to increased international trade.* ◊ *Our courses are the door to success in English.* **lay sth at sb's 'door** (*formal*) to say that sb is responsible for sth that has gone wrong **leave the door 'open (for sth)** to make sure that there is still the possibility of doing sth **out of 'doors** in the open air **SYN** OUTDOORS: *You should spend more time out of doors in the fresh air.* **shut/slam the door in sb's face 1** to shut a door hard when sb is trying to come in **2** to refuse to talk to sb or meet them, in a rude way—more at BACK *adj.*, BARN, BEAT *v.*, CLOSE[1] *v.*, CLOSED, DARKEN, DEATH, FOOT *n.*, OPEN *v.*, SHOW *v.*, STABLE *n.*, WOLF *n.*

door·bell /ˈdɔːbel; *AmE* ˈdɔːrbel/ *noun* a bell with a button outside a house that you push to let the people inside know that you are there: *to ring the doorbell*—picture at RING

door·keeper /ˈdɔːkiːpə(r); *AmE* ˈdɔːrk-/ *noun* a person who guards the entrance to a large building, especially to check on people going in

door·knob /ˈdɔːnɒb; *AmE* ˈdɔːrnɑːb/ *noun* a type of round handle for a door, that you turn in order to open the door

'door knocker *noun* = KNOCKER

door·man /ˈdɔːmən; *AmE* ˈdɔːrmən/ *noun* (*pl.* **-men** /-mən/) a man, often in uniform, whose job is to stand at the entrance to a large building such as a hotel or a

aɪ	aʊ	eɪ	əʊ	oʊ	ɔɪ	ɪə	eə	ʊə	j	w
my	now	say	go (BrE)	go (AmE)	boy	near	hair	pure	yes	wet

theatre, and open the door for visitors, find them taxis, etc.—compare PORTER (3)

door·mat /'dɔːmæt; AmE 'dɔːrmæt/ noun **1** a small piece of strong material near a door that people can clean their shoes on **2** (informal) a person who allows other people to treat them badly but usually does not complain

door·nail /'dɔːneɪl; AmE 'dɔːrn-/ noun **IDM** see DEAD adj.

door·step /'dɔːstep; AmE 'dɔːrs-/ noun **1** a step outside a door of a building, or the area that is very close to the door: *The police turned up on their doorstep at 3 o'clock this morning.*—picture at HOUSE **2** (BrE, informal) a thick piece of bread, usually one that is made into a sandwich **IDM on the/your 'doorstep** very close to where a person lives: *The nightlife is great with bars and clubs right on the doorstep.*

door·stop /'dɔːstɒp; AmE 'dɔːrstɑːp/ noun a thing that is used to stop a door from closing or to prevent it from hitting and damaging a wall when it is opened

door·way /'dɔːweɪ; AmE 'dɔːrweɪ/ noun an opening into a building or a room, where the door is: *She stood **in the doorway** for a moment before going in.* ◊ *homeless people sleeping in shop doorways*

dope /dəʊp; AmE doʊp/ noun, verb
■ noun **1** [U] (informal) a drug that is taken illegally for pleasure, especially CANNABIS or, in the US, HEROIN: *to peddle/smoke dope* **2** [U] a drug that is taken by a person or given to an animal to affect their performance in a race or sport: *The athlete failed a dope test* (= a medical test showed that he had taken such drugs). **3** [C] (informal) a stupid person **4** [U] the ~ (on sb/sth) (informal) information on sb/sth, especially details that are not generally known: *Give me the dope on the new boss.*
■ verb [VN] **1** to give a drug to a person or an animal in order to affect their performance in a race or sport **2** to give sb a drug, often in their food or drink, in order to make them unconscious: *Thieves doped a guard dog and stole $10000 worth of goods.* ◊ *The wine was doped.* **3** ~ sb **(up)** [usually passive] (informal) if sb is **doped** or **doped up**, they cannot think clearly or act normally because they are under the influence of drugs

dopey /'dəʊpi; AmE 'doʊpi/ adj. (informal) **1** rather stupid: *a dopey grin* **2** not fully awake or thinking clearly, sometimes because you have taken a drug: *I felt dopey and drowsy after the operation.*

dork /dɔːk; AmE dɔːrk/ noun (informal) a stupid or boring person that other people laugh at ▶ **dorky** adj.

dorm /dɔːm; AmE dɔːrm/ noun (informal) = DORMITORY

dor·mant /'dɔːmənt; AmE 'dɔːrm-/ adj. not active or growing now but able to become active or to grow in the future: *a dormant volcano* ◊ *During the winter the seeds lie dormant in the soil.* ▶ **dor·mancy** noun [U]

,dormer 'window (also **dormer**) noun a vertical window in a room that is built into a sloping roof—picture at HOUSE, THATCH

dor·mi·tory /'dɔːmətri; AmE 'dɔːrmətɔːri/ noun (pl. -ies) (also informal **dorm**) **1** a room for several people to sleep in, especially in a school or other institution **2** (AmE) = HALL OF RESIDENCE

'dormitory town (BrE) (AmE **'bedroom community**, **'bedroom suburb**) noun a town that people live in and from where they travel to work in a bigger town or city

dor·mouse /'dɔːmaʊs; AmE 'dɔːrm-/ noun (pl. **dor·mice** /-maɪs/) a small animal like a mouse, with a tail covered in fur

dor·sal /'dɔːsl; AmE 'dɔːrsl/ adj. [only before noun] (technical) on or connected with the back of a fish or an animal: *a shark's dorsal fin*—picture on page A7

dos·age /'dəʊsɪdʒ; AmE 'doʊ-/ noun [usually sing.] an amount of sth, usually a medicine or a drug, that is taken regularly over a particular period of time: *a high/low dosage* ◊ *to increase/reduce the dosage* ◊ *Do not exceed the recommended dosage.*

do's and don'ts ⇨ DO¹ n.

dose /dəʊs; AmE doʊs/ noun, verb
■ noun **1** an amount of a medicine or a drug that is taken once, or regularly over a period of time: *a high/low/*

lethal dose ◊ *Repeat the dose after 12 hours if necessary.* **2** (informal) an amount of sth: *A dose of flu kept me off work for two weeks.* ◊ *Workers at the nuclear plant were exposed to high doses of radiation.* ◊ *I can cope with her **in small doses** (= for short amounts of time).* **IDM like a dose of 'salts** (old-fashioned, BrE, informal) very fast and easily—more at MEDICINE
■ verb [VN] ~ sb/yourself (up) (with sth) to give sb/yourself a medicine or drug: *She dosed herself up with vitamin pills.* ◊ *He was heavily dosed with painkillers.*

dosh /dɒʃ; AmE dɑːʃ/ noun [U] (BrE, slang) money

doss /dɒs; AmE dɑːs/ verb, noun
■ verb [V] (BrE, slang) **1** ~ **(down)** to sleep somewhere, especially somewhere uncomfortable or without a real bed: *You can doss down on my floor.* **2** ~ **(about/around)** to spend your time not doing very much: *We were just dossing about in lessons today.*
■ noun (BrE, slang) something that does not need much effort

doss·er /'dɒsə(r); AmE 'dɑːs-/ noun (BrE) **1** a person who has no permanent home and who lives and sleeps on the streets or in cheap HOSTELS **2** (spoken) a person who is very lazy

doss·house /'dɒshaʊs; AmE 'dɑːs-/ (BrE) (AmE **flophouse**) noun (slang) a cheap place to stay for people who have no home

dos·sier /'dɒsieɪ; AmE 'dɔːs-; 'dɑːs-/ noun ~ (on sb/sth) a collection of documents that contain information about a person, an event or a subject **SYN** FILE: *to assemble/compile a dossier* ◊ *We have a dossier on him.*

dot /dɒt; AmE dɑːt/ noun, verb
■ noun a small round mark, especially one that is printed: *There are dots above the letters i and j.* ◊ *Text and graphics are printed at 300 dots per inch.* ◊ *The helicopters appeared as two black dots on the horizon.* **IDM on the 'dot** (informal) exactly on time or at the exact time mentioned: *The taxi showed up on the dot.* ◊ *Breakfast is served at 8 on the dot.*—more at YEAR
■ verb (-tt-) [VN] **1** to put a dot above or next to a letter or word: *Why do you never dot your i's?* **2** [usually passive] to spread things or people over an area; to be spread over an area: *The countryside was dotted with small villages.* ◊ *Small villages dot the countryside.* ◊ *There are lots of Italian restaurants dotted around London.* **3** ~ **A on/over B/ ~ B with A** to put very small amounts of sth in a number of places on a surface: *Dot the cream all over your face.* ◊ *Dot your face with the cream.* **IDM dot your ,i's and cross your 't's** to pay attention to the small details when you are finishing a task

dot·age /'dəʊtɪdʒ; AmE 'doʊ-/ noun **IDM be in your dotage** to be old and not always able to think clearly

dote /dəʊt; AmE doʊt/ verb **PHRV 'dote on/upon sb** to feel and show great love for sb, ignoring their faults: *He dotes on his children.*

dot·ing /'dəʊtɪŋ; AmE 'doʊtɪŋ/ adj. [only before noun] showing a lot of love for sb, often ignoring their faults: *a doting mother/father*

,dot 'matrix printer noun a machine that prints letters, numbers, etc. formed from very small dots

dot·ted /'dɒtɪd; AmE 'dɑːt-/ adj. **1** covered in dots **2** [only before noun] (music) (of a musical note) followed by a DOT to show that it is one and a half times the length of an ordinary note: (BrE) *a dotted minim* = (AmE) *a dotted half note*

,dot·ted 'line noun a line made of dots: *Country boundaries are shown on this map as dotted lines.* ◊ *A page break is represented as a dotted line on screen.* ◊ *Fold along the dotted line.* ◊ *Write your name on the dotted line.* **IDM** see SIGN v.

dotty /'dɒti; AmE 'dɑːti/ adj. (old-fashioned, BrE, informal) **1** slightly crazy or silly **SYN** ECCENTRIC **2** ~ about sb/sth having romantic feelings for sb; being enthusiastic about sth

double /'dʌbl/ adj., det., adv., noun, verb
■ adj. [usually before noun]
TWICE AS MUCH/MANY | **1** twice as much or as many as usual: *a double helping* ◊ *two double whiskies*

b	d	f	g	h	k	l	m	n	p	r
bad	did	fall	get	hat	cat	leg	man	now	pen	red

WITH TWO PARTS | **2** having or made of two things or parts that are equal or similar: *double doors* ◊ *a double-page advertisement* ◊ *'Otter' is spelt with a double t.* ◊ *My extension is two four double 0 (2400).*

FOR TWO PEOPLE | **3** made for two people or things: *a double bed/room*—compare SINGLE *adj.* (4)

COMBINING TWO THINGS | **4** combining two things or qualities: *a double meaning/purpose/aim* ◊ *It has the double advantage of being both easy and cheap.*

■ *det.*

TWICE AS MUCH/MANY | twice as much or as many as: *His income is double hers.* ◊ *He earns double what she does.* ◊ *We need double the amount we already have.*

■ *adv.*

IN TWO PARTS | in twos or in two parts: *I thought I was seeing double* (= seeing two of sth). ◊ *Fold the blanket double.* ◊ *I had to bend double to get under the table.*

■ *noun*

TWICE AS MUCH/MANY | **1** [U] twice the number or amount: *He gets paid double for doing the same job I do.*

ALCOHOLIC DRINK | **2** [C] a glass of strong alcoholic drink containing twice the usual amount: *Two Scotches, please—and make those doubles, will you?*

PERSON/THING | **3** [C] a person or thing that looks exactly like another: *She's the double of her mother.* **4** [C] an actor who replaces another actor in a film/movie to do dangerous or other special things—see also BODY DOUBLE

BEDROOM | **5** [C] = DOUBLE ROOM: *Is that a single or a double you want?*—compare SINGLE *n.* (3)

IN SPORT | **6** (**doubles**) [pl.] a game, especially of tennis, in which one pair plays another: *mixed doubles* (= in which each pair consists of a man and a woman)—compare SINGLES *n.* (5) **7** (**the double**) [sing.] the fact of winning two important competitions or beating the same player or team twice, in the same season or year

IDM **at the 'double** (*BrE*) (*AmE* **on the 'double**) (*informal*) quickly; hurrying ,**double or 'quits** (*BrE*) (*AmE* ,**double or 'nothing**) (in gambling) a risk in which you could win twice the amount you pay, or you could lose all your money

■ *verb*

BECOME TWICE AS MUCH/MANY | **1** to become, or make sth become, twice as much or as many: [V] *Membership almost doubled in two years.* ◊ [VN] *Double all the quantities in the recipe to make enough for eight people.*

FOLD | **2** [VN] ~ **sth** (**over**) to bend or fold sth so that there are two layers: *She doubled the blanket and put it under his head.*

IN BASEBALL | **3** [V] to hit the ball far enough for you to get to second BASE: *He doubled to left field.*

PHRV **'double as sth**| ,**double 'up as sth** to have another use or function as well as the main one: *The kitchen doubles as a dining room.* ,**double 'back** to turn back and go in the direction you have come from ,**double 'up (on sth/with sb)** (*informal*) to form a pair in order to do sth or to share sth: *We'll have to double up on books; there aren't enough to go around.* ◊ *They only have one room left: you'll have to double up with Peter.* ,**double 'up/ 'over**| ,**double sb 'up/'over** to bend or to make your body bend over quickly, for example because you are in pain: *Jo doubled up with laughter.* ◊ *I was doubled over with pain.*

'**double act** *noun* two people who work together, usually to entertain an audience

,**double 'agent** *noun* a person who is a SPY for a particular country, and also for another country which is an enemy of the first one

,**double-'barrelled** (*BrE*) (*AmE* ,**double-'barreled**) *adj.* [usually before noun] **1** (of a gun) having two BARRELS (= places where the bullets come out) **2** (*BrE*) (of a family name) having two parts, sometimes joined by a HYPHEN, for example 'Day-Lewis' **3** (*AmE*) (of a plan, etc.) having two parts, and therefore likely to be effective

,**double 'bass** (also **bass**) *noun* the largest musical instrument in the violin family, that plays very low notes—picture on page 840

,**double 'bill** (*AmE* also ,**double 'feature**) *noun* two films/movies, television programmes, etc. that are shown one after the other: *a cartoon double bill*

,**double 'bind** *noun* [usually sing.] a situation in which it is difficult to choose what to do because whatever you choose will have negative results

,**double 'bluff** *noun* a way of trying to deceive sb by telling them the truth while hoping that they think you are lying

,**double-'book** *verb* [VN] [often passive] to promise the same room, seat, table, etc. to two different people at the same time—compare OVERBOOK ▶ ,**double-'booking** *noun* [C, U]

,**double-'breasted** *adj.* a double-breasted jacket or coat has two front parts so that one part covers the other when the buttons are done up, and two rows of buttons can be seen—compare SINGLE-BREASTED—picture on page A4

,**double-'check** *verb* to check sth for a second time or with great care: [VN] *I'll double-check the figures.* [also V, V(that)] ▶ ,**double-'check** *noun*

,**double 'chin** *noun* a fold of fat under a person's chin, that looks like another chin

,**double-'cross** *verb* [VN] to cheat or deceive sb who trusts you (usually in connection with sth illegal or dishonest): *He double-crossed the rest of the gang and disappeared with all the money.* ▶ ,**double-'cross** *noun* [usually sing.]

,**double-'dealer** *noun* (*informal*) a dishonest person who deceives other people ▶ ,**double-'dealing** *noun* [U]

,**double-'decker** *noun* **1** a bus with two floors, one on top of the other—compare SINGLE-DECKER—picture at BUS **2** (*AmE*) a sandwich made from three pieces of bread with two layers of food between them—picture on page A1

,**double 'digits** *noun* [pl.] (*AmE*) = DOUBLE FIGURES ▶ ,**double-'digit** *adj.* (*AmE*) = DOUBLE-FIGURE

,**double 'Dutch** *noun* [U] (*BrE, informal*) speech or writing that is impossible to understand, and that seems to be nonsense

,**double-'edged** *adj.* **1** (of a knife, etc.) having two cutting edges **2** (of a remark, comment, etc.) having two possible meanings [SYN] AMBIGUOUS **3** having two different parts or uses, often parts that contrast with each other: *the double-edged quality of life in a small town—security and boredom* IDM **be a double-edged 'sword/ 'weapon** to be sth that has both advantages and disadvantages

double en·ten·dre /ˌduːbl ɒ̃ˈtɒ̃drə; *AmE* ɑ̃ːˈtɑ̃ːdrə/ *noun* (from *French*) a word or phrase that can be understood in two different ways, one of which usually refers to sex

,**double 'feature** *noun* (*AmE*) = DOUBLE BILL

,**double 'figures** (*especially BrE*) (*AmE usually* ,**double 'digits**) *noun* [pl.] used to describe a number that is not less than 10 and not more than 99: *Inflation is in double figures.* ▶ ,double-'figure (*especially BrE*) (*AmE* usually ,double-'digit) *adj.* [only before noun]: *a double-figure pay rise*

,double 'glazing *noun* [U] (*especially BrE*) windows that have two layers of glass with a space between them, designed to make the room warmer and to reduce noise: *We're having double-glazing fitted.* ▶ ,double-'glaze *verb* [VN] ,double-'glazed *adj.*: *double-glazed windows*

,double 'jeopardy *noun* (*AmE, law*) the fact of taking sb to a court of law twice for the same crime, or punishing sb twice for the same reason

,double-'jointed *adj.* having joints in your fingers, arms, etc. that allow you to bend them both backwards and forwards

,double 'life *noun* a life of a person who leads two different lives which are kept separate from each other, usually because one of them involves secret, often illegal or immoral, activities: *to live/lead a double life*

,double-'park *verb* [usually passive] to park a car or other vehicle beside one that is already parked in a street: [VN] *A red sports car stood double-parked almost in the middle of the road.* ◊ *I'll have to rush—I'm double-parked.* [also V]

,double 'quick *adv.* (*BrE, informal*) very quickly ▶ ,double-'quick *adj.* [only before noun]: *The TV was repaired in double-quick time.*

,double 'room (also double) *noun* a bedroom for two people

double-speak /ˈdʌblspiːk/ (also 'double-talk) *noun* [U] language that is intended to deceive people, or that can be understood in two different ways

,double 'standard *noun* a rule or moral principle that is unfair because it is used in one situation, but not in another, or because it treats one group of people differently from another

doub·let /ˈdʌblət/ *noun* a short, tightly fitting jacket worn by men from the 14th to the 17th century: *dressed in doublet and hose*

,double 'take *noun* if you do a double take, you wait for a moment before you react to sth that has happened, because it is very surprising

double-talk /ˈdʌbltɔːk/ *noun* [U] = DOUBLESPEAK

,double 'time *noun* [U] twice sb's normal pay, that they earn for working at times which are not normal working hours

doubly /ˈdʌbli/ *adv.* (used before adjectives) **1** more than usual: *doubly difficult/hard/important* ◊ *I made doubly sure I locked all the doors when I went out.* **2** in two ways; for two reasons: *I was doubly attracted to the house—by its size and its location.*

doubt /daʊt/ *noun, verb*

■ *noun* [U, C] ~ (about sth)| ~ (that ...)| ~ (as to sth) a feeling of being uncertain about sth or not believing sth: *a feeling of doubt and uncertainty* ◊ *There is some doubt about the best way to do it.* ◊ *There is no doubt at all that we did the right thing.* ◊ *New evidence has cast doubt on the guilt of the man jailed for the crime.* ◊ *The article raised doubts about how effective the new drug really was.* ◊ *If you are in any doubt as to whether you should be doing these exercises, consult your doctor.* ◊ *She knew without a shadow of a doubt that he was lying to her.* ◊ *Whether he will continue to be successful in future is open to doubt.* **IDM** beyond (any) 'doubt in a way that shows that sth is completely certain: *The research showed beyond doubt that smoking contributes to heart disease.* ◊ (*law*) *The prosecution was able to establish beyond reasonable doubt that the woman had been lying.* be in 'doubt to be uncertain: *The success of the system is not in doubt.* have your 'doubts (about sth) to have reasons why you are not certain about whether sth is good or whether sth good will happen: *I've had my doubts about his work since he joined the firm.* ◊ *It may be all right. Personally, I have my doubts.* if in 'doubt used to give advice to sb who cannot decide what to do: *If in doubt, wear black.* ,no 'doubt **1** used when you are saying that sth is probable: *No doubt she'll call us when she gets there.*

2 used when you are saying that sth is certainly true: *He's made some great movies. There's no doubt about it.* without/beyond 'doubt used when you are giving your opinion and emphasizing the point that you are making: *This meeting has been, without doubt, one of the most useful we have had so far.*—more at BENEFIT *n.*

■ *verb* **1** to feel uncertain about sth; to feel that sth is not true, will probably not happen, etc: *There seems no reason to doubt her story.* ◊ *'Do you think England will win?'—'I doubt it.'* ◊ [V(that)] *I never doubted (that) she would come.* ◊ [Vwh-] *I doubt whether/if the new one will be any better.* **2** [VN] to not trust sb/sth; to not believe sb: *I had no reason to doubt him.* ▶ doubt·er *noun*

doubt·ful /ˈdaʊtfl/ *adj.* **1** ~ (about sth)| ~ (about doing sth) (of a person) not sure; uncertain and feeling doubt: *Rose was doubtful about the whole idea.* ◊ *He was doubtful about accepting extra work.* **2** ~ (if/that/whether ...) unlikely; not probable: *It's doubtful if this painting is a Picasso.* ◊ *With her injuries it's doubtful that she'll ever walk again.* ◊ *It's doubtful whether the car will last another year.* ◊ *Giggs is injured and is doubtful for the game tomorrow* (= unlikely to play). **3** [not usually before noun] (of a thing) uncertain and likely to get worse: *At the beginning of the war things were looking very doubtful.* **4** [only before noun] of low value; probably not genuine and that you cannot rely on: *This wine is of doubtful quality.* ▶ doubt·ful·ly /-fəli/ *adv.*

doubt·ing Thomas /ˌdaʊtɪŋ ˈtɒməs; *AmE* ˈtɑːm-/ *noun* [sing.] (*old-fashioned*) a person who is unlikely to believe sth until they see proof of it

doubt·less /ˈdaʊtləs/ *adv.* (also less frequent ·doubt·less·ly) (*written*) almost certainly: *He would doubtless disapprove of what Kelly was doing.*

douche /duːʃ/ *noun* a method of washing inside a woman's VAGINA using a stream of water ▶ douche *verb* [V, VN]

dough /dəʊ; *AmE* doʊ/ *noun* **1** [U, sing.] a mixture of flour, water, etc. that is made into bread and pastry: *Knead the dough on a floured surface.* **2** [U] (*old-fashioned, slang*) money

dough·nut (also donut especially in *AmE*) /ˈdəʊnʌt; *AmE* ˈdoʊ-/ *noun* a small cake made of fried dough, usually in the shape of a ring or round and filled with jam/jelly, fruit, cream, etc.—picture on page A1

doughty /ˈdaʊti/ *adj.* [usually before noun] (*old-fashioned*) brave and strong

doula /ˈduːlə/ *noun* (*AmE*) a woman whose role is to provide emotional support to a woman who is giving birth—compare MIDWIFE

dour /ˈdaʊə(r); *BrE also* dʊə(r); *AmE also* dʊr/ *adj.* **1** (of a person) giving the impression of being unfriendly and severe **2** (of a thing, a place, or a situation) not pleasant; with no features that make it lively or interesting: *The city, drab and dour by day, is transformed at night.* ◊ *The game proved to be a dour struggle, with both men determined to win.* ▶ dour·ly *adv.*

douse (also dowse) /daʊs/ *verb* [VN] **1** ~ sth (with sth) to stop a fire from burning by pouring water over it; to put out a light: *He doused the flames with a fire extinguisher.* **2** ~ sb/sth (in/with sth) to pour a lot of liquid over sb/sth; to soak sb/sth in liquid: *The car was doused in petrol and set alight.*

dove[1] /dʌv/ *noun* **1** a bird of the PIGEON family. The white dove is often used as a symbol of peace: *A dove cooed softly.* ◊ *He wore a dove-grey suit.*—see also TURTLE DOVE **2** a person, especially a politician, who prefers peace and discussion to war—compare HAWK

dove[2] /dəʊv; *AmE* doʊv/ (*AmE*) *pt* of DIVE

dove·cote /ˈdʌvkɒt; ˈdʌvkəʊt; *AmE* -kɑːt; -koʊt/ (also dove·cot /ˈdʌvkɒt; *AmE* -kɑːt/) *noun* a small building for DOVES or PIGEONS to live in

dove·tail /ˈdʌvteɪl/ *verb, noun*

■ *verb* (*formal*) ~ (sth) (with/into sth) if two things dovetail or if one thing dovetails with another, they fit together well: [V] *My plans dovetailed nicely with hers.* [also VN]

æ	ɑː	e	ɜː	ə	ɪ	iː	i	ɒ	ɔː	ʌ	ʊ	u	uː
cat	father	ten	bird	about	sit	see	many	got	saw	cup	put	actual	too
								(BrE)					

■ *noun* (also ˌ**dovetail** ˈ**joint**) a joint for fixing two pieces of wood together

dow·ager /ˈdaʊədʒə(r)/ *noun* **1** a woman of high social rank who has a title from her dead husband: *the dowager Duchess of Norfolk* **2** (*informal*) an impressive, usually rich, old woman

dowdy /ˈdaʊdi/ *adj.* **1** (of a woman) not attractive or fashionable: *He had a rather dowdy wife and several children.* **2** (of a thing) dull or boring and not attractive: *a dowdy dress*

down /daʊn/ *adv., prep., verb, adj., noun*
■ *adv.* HELP For the special uses of **down** in phrasal verbs, look at the entries for the verbs. For example **climb down** is in the phrasal verb section at **climb**. **1** to or at a lower place or position: *She jumped down off the chair.* ◊ *He looked down at her.* ◊ *We watched as the sun went down.* ◊ *She bent down to pick up her glove.* ◊ *Mary's not down yet* (= she is still upstairs). ◊ *The baby can't keep any food down* (= in her body). **2** from a standing or upright position to a sitting or horizontal one: *Please sit down.* ◊ *He had to go and lie down for a while.* **3** at a lower level or rate: *Prices have gone down recently.* ◊ *We're already two goals down* (= the other team has two goals more). **4** used to show that the amount or strength of sth is lower, or that there is less activity: *Turn the music down!* ◊ *The class settled down and she began the lesson.* **5** (in a CROSSWORD) reading from top to bottom, not from side to side: *I can't do 3 down.* **6** to or in the south of a country: *They flew down to Texas.* ◊ *Houses are more expensive down south.* **7** on paper; on a list: *Did you get that down?* ◊ *I always write everything down.* ◊ *Have you got me down for the trip?* **8** used to show the limits in a range or an order: *Everyone will be there, from the Principal down.* **9** having lost the amount of money mentioned: *At the end of the day we were £20 down.* **10** if you pay an amount of money **down**, you pay that to start with, and the rest later **11** (*informal*) used to say how far you have got in a list of things you have to do: *Well, I've seen six apartments so far. That's six down and four to go!* IDM **be down to sb** (*informal*) to be the responsibility of sb: *It's down to you to check the door.* **be down to sb/sth** to be caused by a particular person or thing: *She claimed her problems were down to the media.* **be down to sth** to have only a little money left: *I'm down to my last dollar.* **be/go down with sth** to have or catch an illness **down through sth** (*written*) during a long period of time: *Down through the years this town has seen many changes.* **down ˈunder** (*informal*) in Australia **down with sb/sth** used to say that you are opposed to sth, or to a person: *The crowds chanted 'Down with NATO!'*
■ *prep.* **1** from a high or higher point on sth to a lower one: *The stone rolled down the hill.* ◊ *Tears ran down her face.* ◊ *Her hair hung down her back to her waist.* **2** along; towards the direction in which you are facing: *He lives just down the street.* ◊ *Go down the road till you reach the traffic lights.* ◊ *There's a bridge a mile down the river from here.* **3** all through a period of time: *an exhibition of costumes down the ages* (= from all periods of history)
■ *verb* [VN] (*informal*) **1** to finish a drink or eat sth quickly: *We downed our coffees and left.* **2** to force sb/sth down to the ground: *to down a plane* IDM ˌ**down** ˈ**tools** (*BrE*) (of workers) to stop work; to go on strike
■ *adj.* [not before noun] **1** (*informal*) sad or depressed: *I feel a bit down today.* **2** (of a computer or computer system) not working: *The system was down all morning.*—see also DOWN TIME IDM see HIT *v.*, KICK *v.*, LUCK *n.*, MOUTH *n.*
■ *noun* [U]—see also DOWNS **1** the very fine soft feathers of a bird: *duck down* **2** fine soft hair—see also DOWNY IDM **have a** ˈ**down on sb/sth** (*BrE, informal*) to have a bad opinion of sb and not treat them well—**more at** UP *n.*

ˌ**down-and-**ˈ**out** *noun* a person who has no home or money and lives on the street

ˌ**down at** ˈ**heel** *adj.* looking less attractive and fashionable than before, usually because of a lack of money: *The town has become very down at heel.* ◊ *a down-at-heel hotel*

down·beat /ˈdaʊnbiːt/ *adj.* (*informal*) **1** dull or depressing; not hopeful about the future: *The overall mood of the meeting was downbeat.* OPP UPBEAT **2** not showing strong feelings or enthusiasm

down·cast /ˈdaʊnkɑːst/ *adj.* (*written*) **1** (of eyes) looking down: *Eyes downcast, she continued eating and did not speak again.* **2** (of a person or an expression) sad or depressed: *A group of downcast men stood waiting for food.*

down·er /ˈdaʊnə(r)/ *noun* (*informal*) **1** [usually pl.] a drug, especially a BARBITURATE, that relaxes you or makes you want to sleep—compare UPPER **2** an experience that makes you feel sad or depressed: *Not getting the promotion was a real downer.* ◊ *He's really on a downer isn't he?* (= very depressed)

down·fall /ˈdaʊnfɔːl/ *noun* [sing.] the loss of a person's money, power, social position, etc.; the thing that causes this: *The sex scandal finally led to his downfall.* ◊ *Greed was her downfall.*

down·grade /ˌdaʊnˈɡreɪd/ *verb* [VN] **1** ~ **sb/sth (from sth) (to sth)** to move sb/sth down to a lower rank or level: *She's been downgraded from principal to vice-principal.* **2** to make sth/sb seem less important or valuable than it/they really are—compare UPGRADE ▶ **down·grad·ing** *noun* [U, C]: *a downgrading of diplomatic relations*

down·heart·ed /ˌdaʊnˈhɑːtɪd; *AmE* -ˈhɑːrtɪd/ *adj.* [not before noun] feeling depressed or sad: *We're disappointed by these results but we're not downhearted.*

down·hill /ˌdaʊnˈhɪl/ *adv., adj., noun*
■ *adv.* towards the bottom of a hill; in a direction that goes down: *to run/walk/cycle downhill* OPP UPHILL IDM ˌ**go down**ˈ**hill** to get worse in quality, health, etc. SYN DETERIORATE: *Their marriage went downhill after the first child was born.*
■ *adj.* going or sloping towards the bottom of a hill: *a downhill path* OPP UPHILL IDM **be (all) downhill | be** ˌ**downhill all the** ˈ**way** (*informal*) **1** to be easy compared to what came before: *It's all downhill from here. We'll soon be finished.* **2** becoming worse or less successful: *It's been all downhill for his career since then, with four defeats in five games.* ◊ *I started work as a journalist and it was downhill all the way for my health.*
■ *noun* [U] the type of skiing in which you go directly down a mountain; a race in which people ski down a mountain—compare CROSS-COUNTRY—picture at SKIING

ˌ**down-**ˈ**home** *adj.* (*AmE*) used to describe a person or thing that reminds you of a simple way of life, typical of the country, not the town

Down·ing Street /ˈdaʊnɪŋ striːt/ *noun* [sing.] (not used with *the*) a way of referring to the British PRIME MINISTER and government, taken from the name of the street where the PRIME MINISTER lives: *Downing Street issued a statement late last night.*

down·load /ˌdaʊnˈləʊd; *AmE* -ˈloʊd/ *verb* [VN] (*computing*) to move data to a smaller computer system from a larger one—compare LOAD

down·mark·et /ˌdaʊnˈmɑːkɪt; *AmE* -ˈmɑːrkɪt/ (*BrE*) (*AmE* **down·scale**) *adj.* (*disapproving*) cheap and of poor quality: *The company wants to break away from its downmarket image.* OPP UPMARKET ▶ **down·mark·et** *adv.*: *To get more viewers the TV station will have to go downmarket.*

down·play /ˌdaʊnˈpleɪ/ *verb* [VN] to make people think that sth is less important than it really is: *The coach is downplaying the team's poor performance.*

down·pour /ˈdaʊnpɔː(r)/ *noun* [usually sing.] a heavy fall of rain that often starts suddenly

down·right /ˈdaʊnraɪt/ *adj.* [only before noun] used as a way of emphasizing sth negative or unpleasant: *There was suspicion and even downright hatred between them.* ▶ **down·right** *adv.*: *She couldn't think of anything to say that wasn't downright rude.* ◊ *It's not just stupid—it's downright dangerous.*

down·river /ˌdaʊnˈrɪvə(r)/ *adv.* = DOWNSTREAM

downs /daʊnz/ *noun* (**the downs**) [pl.] an area of open land with low hills, especially in southern England: *the South Downs*

down·scale /ˈdaʊnskeɪl/ *adj., adv.* (*AmE*) = DOWNMARKET

down·shift /ˈdaʊnʃɪft/ *verb* [V] **1** (*AmE*) to change to a

aɪ	aʊ	eɪ	əʊ	oʊ	ɔɪ	ɪə	eə	ʊə	j	w
my	now	say	go	go	boy	near	hair	pure	yes	wet
			(BrE)	(AmE)						

lower GEAR in a vehicle **2** to change to a job or style of life where you may earn less but which puts less pressure on you and involves less stress ▶ **down·shift** noun [C, U] **down·shift·er** noun

down·side /'daʊnsaɪd/ noun [sing.] the disadvantages or less positive aspects of sth OPP UPSIDE

down·size /'daʊnsaɪz/ verb [V, VN] (business) to reduce the number of people who work in a company, business, etc. in order to reduce costs

down·spout /'daʊnspaʊt/ noun (AmE) = DRAINPIPE

'Down's syndrome noun [U] an ABNORMAL condition in which a person is born with a wide, flat face, sloping eyes and a mental ability that is below average

down·stairs /,daʊn'steəz; AmE -'sterz/ adv., noun
■ adv. down the stairs; on or to a floor or a house or building lower than the one you are on, especially the one at ground level: *She rushed downstairs and burst into the kitchen.* ◊ *Wait downstairs in the hall.* OPP UPSTAIRS ▶ **down·stairs** adj. [only before noun]: *a downstairs bathroom*
■ noun [sing.] the lower floor of a house or building, especially the one at ground level: *We're painting the downstairs.* OPP UPSTAIRS

down·stream /,daʊn'striːm/ (also less frequent **down·river**) adv. ~ (of/from sth) in the direction in which a river flows: *to drift/float downstream* ◊ *downstream of/from the bridge* OPP UPSTREAM ▶ **down·stream** adj.: *downstream areas*

'down time noun [U] the time during which a machine, especially a computer, is not working

down-to-'earth adj. (approving) sensible and practical, in a way that is helpful and friendly: *She was friendly and down-to-earth and quickly put me at my ease.*

down·town /,daʊn'taʊn/ adv. (especially AmE) in or towards the centre of a city, especially its main business area: *to go/work downtown*—compare MIDTOWN, TOWN CENTRE, UPTOWN ▶ **down·town** adj.: *a downtown store*

down·trend /'daʊntrend/ noun [sing.] (AmE) a situation in which business activity or performance decreases or becomes worse over a period of time OPP UPTREND

down·trod·den /'daʊntrɒdn; AmE -trɑːdn/ adj. **down·trodden** people are treated so badly by the people with authority and power that they no longer have the energy or ability to fight back

down·turn /'daʊntɜːn; AmE -tɜːrn/ noun [usually sing.] ~ (in sth) a fall in the amount of business that is done; a time when the economy becomes weaker: *a downturn in sales/trade/business* ◊ *the economic downturn of the late 1990s* OPP UPTURN

down·ward /'daʊnwəd; AmE -wərd/ adj. [usually before noun] moving or pointing towards a lower level: *the downward slope of a hill* ◊ *A rise in interest rates would reverse the downward trend in inflation.* ◊ *She was trapped in a downward spiral of personal unhappiness.* OPP UPWARD

down·wards /'daʊnwədz; AmE -wərdz/ (also **downward** especially in AmE) adv. towards the ground or towards a lower level: *She was lying face downwards on the grass.* ◊ *The garden sloped gently downwards to the river.* ◊ *It was a policy welcomed by world leaders from the US president downwards.* OPP UPWARDS

down·wind /,daʊn'wɪnd/ adv. ~ (of sth) in the direction in which the wind is blowing: *sailing downwind* ◊ *Warnings were issued to people living downwind of the fire to stay indoors.* OPP UPWIND ▶ **down·wind** adj.

downy /'daʊni/ adj. covered in sth very soft, especially hair or feathers—see also DOWN n.

dowry /'daʊri/ noun (pl. **-ies**) **1** money and/or property that, in some societies, a wife or her family must pay to her husband when they get married **2** money and/or property that, in some societies, a husband must pay to his wife's family when they get married

dowse /daʊz/ verb **1** [V] to look for underground water or minerals by using a special stick or rod that moves when it comes near water, etc. **2** = DOUSE ▶ **dowser** noun

doyen /'dɔɪən/ (feminine **doy·enne** /dɔɪ'en/) (AmE usu-

ally **dean**) noun the most respected or most experienced member of a group or profession: *Clive James, that doyen of television critics ...*

doz. abbr. (in writing) DOZEN: *2 doz. eggs*

doze /dəʊz; AmE doʊz/ verb, noun
■ verb [V] to sleep lightly for a short time: *I dozed fitfully until dawn.* PHRV **,doze 'off** to go to sleep, especially during the day: *She dozed off in front of the fire.*
■ noun [sing.] a short period of sleep, usually during the day: *I had a doze on the train.*

dozen /'dʌzn/ noun, det. (pl. **dozen**) **1** [C] (abbr. **doz.**) a group of twelve of the same thing: *Give me a dozen, please.* ◊ *two dozen eggs* ◊ *three dozen red roses* **2** [C] a group of approximately twelve people or things: *several dozen/a few dozen people* ◊ *The company employs no more than a couple of dozen people.* ◊ *Only about half a dozen people turned up.* ◊ *There was only space for a half-dozen tables.* **3** (**dozens**) [pl.] ~ (of sth) (informal) a lot of people or things: *They arrived in dozens* (= in large numbers). ◊ *I've been there dozens of times.* IDM see BAKER, DIME, NINETEEN, SIX

dozy /'dəʊzi; AmE 'doʊzi/ adj. (informal) **1** not looking or feeling awake **2** (BrE) stupid; not intelligent

DPhil /,diː'fɪl/ noun (BrE) the abbreviation for 'Doctor of Philosophy': *to be/have/do a DPhil* ◊ *James Mendelssohn DPhil*

DPP /,diː piː 'piː/ abbr. (in England and Wales) DIRECTOR OF PUBLIC PROSECUTIONS

Dr (BrE) (also **Dr.** AmE, BrE) abbr. **1** (in writing) Doctor: *Dr (Jane) Walker* **2** (in street names) DRIVE

drab /dræb/ adj. (**drab·ber, drab·best**) without interest or colour; dull and boring: *a cold drab little office* ◊ *drab women, dressed in browns and greys* ▶ **drab·ness** [U]

drabs /dræbz/ noun IDM see DRIBS

drachma /'drækmə/ noun (pl. **drachmas** or **drachmae** /'drækmiː/) the unit of money in Greece

dra·co·nian /drə'kəʊniən; AmE -'koʊ-/ adj. (formal) (of a law, punishment, etc.) extremely harsh and severe: *a call for draconian measures against drug-related crime*

draft /drɑːft; AmE dræft/ noun, adj., verb
■ noun **1** [C] a rough written version of sth that is not yet in its final form: *I've made a rough draft of the letter.* ◊ *This is only the first draft of my speech.* ◊ *the final draft* (= the final version) ◊ *The legislation is still in draft form.* ◊ *a draft constitution/treaty/agreement* **2** [C] (finance) a written order to a bank to pay money to sb: *Payment must be made by bank draft drawn on a UK bank.* **3** (**the draft**) [sing.] (especially AmE) = CONSCRIPTION **4** [sing.] (AmE) a system in which professional teams in some sports choose players each year from among college students **5** [C] (AmE) = DRAUGHT
■ adj. (AmE) = DRAUGHT
■ verb (also **draught** especially in BrE) [VN] **1** to write the first rough version of sth such as a letter, speech, or book: *to draft a constitution/contract/bill* ◊ *I'll draft a letter for you.* **2** [+adv./prep.] to choose people and send them somewhere for a special task: *Extra police are being drafted in to control the crowds.* **3** [usually passive] (AmE) = CONSCRIPT: *He had been drafted to fight in the Vietnam war.* ◊ *They were drafted into the army.*

'draft dodger noun (AmE, disapproving) a person who illegally tries to avoid doing military service—compare CONSCIENTIOUS OBJECTOR

draft·ee /,drɑːf'tiː; AmE ,dræf'tiː/ noun (AmE) = CONSCRIPT

draft·er /'drɑːftə(r)/ noun **1** a person who prepares a rough version of a plan, document, etc. **2** (AmE) = DRAFTSMAN (2)

drafts·man /'drɑːftsmən/, **drafts·woman** /'drɑːftswʊmən/ noun (pl. **-men** /-mən/) (pl. **-women** /-wɪmɪn/) **1** (AmE) = DRAUGHTSMAN, DRAUGHTSWOMAN **2** (AmE also **drafter**) a person who writes official or legal documents: *the draftsmen of the treaty/bill/constitution*

drafts·pers·on /'drɑːftspɜːsn; AmE -pɜːrsn/ noun (AmE) = DRAUGHTSMAN (1)

drafty (AmE) = DRAUGHTY

D

D

drag /dræg/ *verb, noun*

■ *verb* (**-gg-**)

PULL | **1** [VN] [usually+*adv./prep.*] to pull sb/sth along with effort and difficulty: *I dragged the chair over to the window.* ◊ *They dragged her from her bed.*

MOVE SLOWLY | **2** [+*adv./prep.*] to move yourself slowly and with effort: [VN] *I managed to drag myself out of bed.* ◊ [V] *She always drags behind when we walk anywhere.*

PERSUADE SB TO GO | **3** [VN+*adv./prep.*] to persuade sb to come or go somewhere they do not really want to come or go to: *I'm sorry to drag you all this way in the heat.* ◊ *The party was so good I couldn't drag myself away.*

OF TIME | **4** [V] (of time or an event) to pass very slowly: *Time dragged terribly.* ◊ *The meeting really dragged.*—see also DRAG ON

TOUCH GROUND | **5** to move, or make sth move, partly touching the ground: [V] *This dress is too long—it drags on the ground when I walk.* ◊ [VN] *He was dragging his coat in the mud.*

SEARCH RIVER | **6** [VN] ~ **sth (for sb/sth)** to search the bottom of a river, lake, etc. with nets or hooks: *They dragged the canal for the missing children.*

COMPUTING | **7** [VN+*adv./prep.*] to move some text, an ICON, etc. across the screen of a computer using the mouse

IDM **drag your 'feet/'heels** to be deliberately slow in doing sth or in making a decision—more at BOOTSTRAP PHRV **,drag sb↔'down** to make sb feel weak or unhappy **,drag sb/sth↔'down (to sth)** to bring sb/sth to a lower social or economic level, a lower standard of behaviour, etc: *If he fails, he'll drag us all down with him.* **,drag sth/sb 'into sth| ,drag sth/sb↔'in 1** to start to talk about sth/sb that has nothing to do with what is being discussed: *Do you have to drag politics into everything?* **2** to try to get sb involved in a situation who is not connected with it: *Don't drag the children into our argument.* **,drag 'on** (*disapproving*) to go on for too long: *The dispute has dragged on for months.* **,drag sth↔'out** to make sth last longer than necessary SYN PROLONG: *Let's not drag out this discussion; we need to reach a decision.* **,drag sth 'out of sb** to make sb say sth they do not want to say: *We dragged a confession out of him.* **,drag sth↔'up** to mention an unpleasant story, fact, etc. that people do not want to remember or talk about: *Why do you have to keep dragging up my divorce?*

■ *noun*

BORING PERSON/THING | **1** [sing.] (*informal*) a boring person or thing; sth that is annoying: *He's such a drag.* ◊ *Walking's a drag—let's drive there.* ◊ *Having to work late every day is a drag.*

SB/STH STOPPING PROGRESS | **2** [sing.] ~ **on sb/sth** (*informal*) a person or thing that makes progress difficult: *He came to be seen as a drag on his own party's prospects.*

ON CIGARETTE | **3** [C] (*informal*) an act of breathing in smoke from a cigarette, etc: *She took a long drag on her cigarette.*

WOMEN'S CLOTHES | **4** [U] (*informal*) clothes that are usually worn by the opposite sex (usually women's clothes worn by men): *He performed in drag.* ◊ *a drag queen* (= a man dressed in women's clothes usually in order to entertain people)

PHYSICS | **5** [U] the force of the air that acts against the movement of an aircraft or other vehicle—see also MAIN DRAG—compare LIFT

dragon /'drægən/ *noun* **1** (in stories) a large fierce animal with wings and a long tail, that can breathe out fire **2** (*disapproving, especially BrE*) a woman who behaves in a fierce and frightening way

dragon·fly /'drægənflaɪ/ *noun* (*pl.* **-ies**) an insect with a long thin body, often brightly coloured, and two pairs of large transparent wings. Dragonflies are often seen over water.—picture on page A7

drag·oon /drə'guːn/ *noun, verb*
■ *noun* a soldier in the past who rode a horse and carried a gun
■ *verb* PHRV **dra'goon sb into sth/into doing sth** (*written*) to force or persuade sb to do sth that they do not want to do

drain /dreɪn/ *verb, noun*

■ *verb* **1** to make sth empty or dry by removing all the liquid from it; to become empty or dry in this way: [VN] *Drain and rinse the pasta.* ◊ *The marshes have been drained.* ◊ *You will need to drain the central heating system before you replace the radiator.* ◊ [V] *The swimming pool drains very slowly.* ◊ *Leave the dishes to drain.* **2** ~ **(sth) (from/out of sth)| ~ (sth) (away/off)** to make liquid flow away from sth; to flow away: [VN] *We had to drain the oil out of the engine.* ◊ *Drain off the excess fat from the meat.* ◊ [V] *She pulled out the plug and the water drained away.* ◊ *The river drains into a lake.* ◊ *All the colour drained from his face when I told him the news* ◊ (*figurative*) *My anger slowly drained away.* **3** [VN] to empty a cup or glass by drinking everything in it: (*written*) *In one gulp, he drained the glass.* ◊ *She quickly drained the last of her drink.* **4** [VN] ~ **sb/sth (of sth)** to make sb/sth weaker, poorer, etc. by using up their/its strength, money, etc: *My mother's hospital expenses were slowly draining my income.* ◊ *I felt drained of energy.* ◊ *The experience left her* **emotionally drained.** ◊ *an exhausting and draining experience*

■ *noun* **1** [C] a pipe that carries away dirty water or other liquid waste: *We had to call in a plumber to unblock the drain.* ◊ *The drains* (= the system of pipes) *date from the beginning of the century.* **2** [C] (*BrE*) (*AmE* **grate, 'sewer grate**) a frame of metal bars over the opening to a drain in the ground—picture at HOUSE **3** [C] (*AmE*) = PLUGHOLE **4** [sing.] ~ **on sb/sth** a thing that uses a lot of the time, money, etc. that could be used for sth else: *Military spending is a huge drain on the country's resources.*—see also BRAIN DRAIN IDM **(go) down the 'drain** (*BrE* also **(go) down the 'plughole**) (*informal*) (to be) wasted; (to get) very much worse: *It's just money down the drain, you know.* ◊ *Safety standards have gone down the drain.*—more at LAUGH *v.*

drain·age /'dreɪnɪdʒ/ *noun* [U] **1** the process by which water or liquid waste is drained from an area: *a drainage system/channel/ditch* ◊ *The area has good natural drainage.* **2** a system of drains

drained /dreɪnd/ *adj.* [not usually before noun] very tired and without energy: *She suddenly felt totally drained.*

'draining board (*BrE*) (*AmE* **'drain·board**) *noun* the area next to a kitchen SINK where cups, plates, etc. are put for the water to run off, after they have been washed

drain·pipe /'dreɪnpaɪp/ *noun* **1** (*AmE* also **down·spout**) a pipe that carries RAINWATER from the roof of a building to a drain—picture at HOUSE **2** a pipe that carries dirty water or other liquid waste away from a building

drake /dreɪk/ *noun* a male duck

dram /dræm/ *noun* (especially *ScotE*) a small amount of an alcoholic drink, especially whisky

drama /'drɑːmə/ *noun* **1** [C] a play for the theatre, television or radio: *a costume/historical drama* **2** [U] plays considered as a form of literature: *classical/Elizabethan/modern drama* ◊ *a drama critic* ◊ *a drama student* ◊ *I studied English and Drama at college.* **3** [C] an exciting event: *A powerful human drama was unfolding before our eyes.* **4** [U, C] excitement: *You couldn't help being thrilled by the drama of the situation.* IDM **make a drama out of sth** to make a small problem or event seem more important or serious than it really is

dra·mat·ic /drə'mætɪk/ *adj.* **1** (of a change, an event, etc.) sudden, very great and often surprising: *a dramatic increase/fall/change/improvement* ◊ *dramatic results/developments/news* ◊ *The announcement had a dramatic effect on house prices.* **2** exciting and impressive: *a dramatic victory/ending* ◊ *They watched dramatic pictures of the police raid on TV.* **3** [usually before noun] connected with the theatre or plays: *a local dramatic society* **4** exaggerated in order to create a special effect and attract people's attention: *He flung out his arms in a dramatic gesture.* ◊ *Don't be so dramatic!* ▶ **dra·mat·ic·al·ly** /-kli/ *adv.*: *Prices have fallen dramatically.* ◊ *At any point events could have developed in a dramatically different way.* ◊ *'At last!' she cried dramatically.*

s	t	v	z	ʃ	ʒ	tʃ	dʒ	θ	ð	ŋ
see	tea	van	zoo	shoe	vision	chain	jam	thin	this	sing

dra‚matic 'irony *noun* [U] a situation in a play when a character's words carry an extra meaning to the audience because they know more than the character, especially about what is going to happen

dra·mat·ics /drə'mætɪks/ *noun* [pl.] behaviour that does not seem sincere because it is exaggerated or too emotional—see also AMATEUR DRAMATICS

drama·tist /'dræmətɪst/ *noun* a person who writes plays for the theatre, television or radio SYN PLAYWRIGHT: *a TV dramatist*

drama·tize (*BrE* also **-ise**) /'dræmətaɪz/ *verb* **1** [VN] to present a book, an event, etc. as a play or a film/movie: *Jane Austen's 'Emma' was dramatized on television recently.* **2** to make sth seem more exciting or important than it really is: [VN] *Don't worry too much about what she said—she tends to dramatize things.* [also V] ► **drama·tiza·tion, -isa·tion** /ˌdræmətaɪ'zeɪʃn; -tə'z-/ *noun* [U, C]: *a television dramatization of the trial*

drank *pt* of DRINK

drape /dreɪp/ *verb, noun*
▪ *verb* [VN+*adv./prep.*] **1 ~ sth around/over/across, etc. sth** to hang clothes, materials, etc. loosely on sb/sth: *She had a shawl draped around her shoulders.* ◊ *He draped his coat over the back of the chair.* **2 ~ sb/sth in/with sth** to cover or decorate sb/sth with material: *walls draped in ivy* ◊ *She draped some velvety material over the old sofa.* **3 ~ around/round/over, etc. sth** to allow part of your body to rest on sth in a relaxed way: *His arm was draped casually around her shoulders.*
▪ *noun* (*especially AmE*) (*AmE* also **dra·pery**) [usually pl.] a long thick curtain: *blue velvet drapes*

draper /'dreɪpə(r)/ *noun* (*old-fashioned, BrE*) **1** a person who owns or manages a shop that sells fabric, curtains, etc. **2** (**draper's**) (*pl.* **drapers**) a shop/store that sells fabric, curtains, etc.

dra·pery /'dreɪpəri/ *noun* (*pl.* **-ies**) **1** [U] (also **dra·per·ies** [pl.]) fabric or clothing hanging in loose folds: *a cradle swathed in draperies and blue ribbon* **2** [C, usually pl.] (*AmE*) = DRAPE **3** [U] (*old-fashioned*) fabric and materials for sewing sold by a draper: *a drapery shop/business*—compare DRY GOODS

dras·tic /'dræstɪk; *BrE* also 'drɑːs-/ *adj.* extreme in a way that has a sudden, serious or violent effect on sth: *drastic measures/changes* ◊ *The government is threatening to take drastic action.* ◊ *a drastic shortage of food* ◊ *Talk to me before you do anything drastic.* ► **dras·tic·al·ly** /-kli/ *adv.*: *Output has been drastically reduced.* ◊ *Things have started to go drastically wrong.*

drat /dræt/ *exclamation* (*old-fashioned, informal*) used to show that you are annoyed: *Drat! I forgot my key.* ► **drat·ted** *adj.* [only before noun] (*old-fashioned, BrE, informal*): *This dratted pen won't work.*

draught /drɑːft/ (*BrE*) (*AmE* **draft** /dræft/) *noun, adj., verb*
▪ *noun* **1** [C] a flow of cool air in a room or other enclosed space: *There's a draught in here.* ◊ *A cold draught of air blew in from the open window.* ◊ *I was sitting in a draught.* **2** [C] (*formal*) one continuous action of swallowing liquid; the amount swallowed: *He took a deep draught of his beer.* **3** [C] (*old use* or *literary*) medicine in a liquid form: *a sleeping draught* (= one that makes you sleep) **4** (**draughts**) (*BrE*) (*AmE* **check·ers**) [U] a game for two players using 24 round pieces on a board marked with black and white squares **5** [C] (*BrE*) (*AmE* **check·er**) one of the round pieces used in a game of draughts IDM **on 'draught** (*of beer*) taken from a large container (= a BARREL): *This beer is not available on draught* (= it is available only in bottles or cans).
▪ *adj.* **1** [usually before noun] served from a large container (= a BARREL) rather than in a bottle: *draught beer* **2** [only before noun] used for pulling heavy loads: *a draught horse*
▪ *verb* [VN] (*especially BrE*) = DRAFT

draught·board /'drɑːftbɔːd; *AmE* 'dræftbɔːrd/ (*BrE*) (*AmE* **'check·er·board**) *noun* a board with black and white squares, used for playing DRAUGHTS/CHECKERS

'draught excluder (*BrE*) (*AmE* **'weather strip**) *noun* [C, U] a piece of material that helps to prevent cold air coming through a door, window, etc.

draughts·man /'drɑːftsmən/ (*BrE*) (*AmE* **drafts·man** /'dræfts-/) *noun* (*pl.* **-men** /-mən/) **1** a person whose job is to draw detailed plans of machinery, buildings, etc. **2** a person who draws: *He's a poor draughtsman.*—see also DRAUGHTSWOMAN, DRAUGHTSPERSON ► **draughts·man·ship** (*BrE*) (*AmE* **drafts·man·ship**) *noun* [U]

draughts·person /'drɑːftspɜːsn/ (*BrE*) (*AmE* **drafts·person** /'dræftspɜːrsn/) *noun* a draughtsman or a draughtswoman

draughts·woman /'drɑːftswʊmən/ (*BrE*) (*AmE* **drafts·woman** /'dræfts-/) *noun* (*pl.* **-women** /-wɪmɪn/) **1** a woman whose job is to draw detailed plans of machinery, buildings, etc. **2** a woman who draws—see also DRAUGHTS·MAN

draughty /'drɑːfti/ (*BrE*) (*AmE* **drafty** /'dræfti/) *adj.* (**draught·ier, draughti·est**) (of a room, etc.) uncomfortable because cold air is blowing through: *a draughty room/corridor*

draw /drɔː/ *verb, noun*
▪ *verb* (**drew** /druː/ **drawn** /drɔːn/)
MAKE PICTURES | **1** to make pictures, or a picture of sth, with a pencil, pen or chalk (but not paint): [V] *You draw beautifully.* ◊ [VN] *to draw a picture/diagram/graph* ◊ *She drew a house.* ◊ *He drew a circle in the sand with a stick.* ◊ (*figurative*) *The report drew a grim picture of inefficiency and corruption.*

PULL | **2** [VN+*adv./prep.*] to move sth/sb by pulling it or them gently: *He drew the cork out of the bottle.* ◊ *I drew my chair up closer to the fire.* ◊ *She drew me onto the balcony.* ◊ *I tried to draw him aside* (for example where I could talk to him privately). ◊ (*figurative*) *My eyes were drawn to the man in the corner.* **3** [VN] (of horses, etc.) to pull a vehicle such as a carriage: *The Queen's coach was drawn by six horses.* ◊ *a horse-drawn carriage*

CURTAINS | **4** [VN] to open or close curtains, etc: *The blinds were drawn.* ◊ *It was getting dark so I switched on the light and drew the curtains.* ◊ *She drew back the curtains and let the sunlight in.*

MOVE | **5** [V+*adv./prep.*] (*written*) to move in the direction mentioned: *The train drew into the station.* ◊ *The train drew in.* ◊ *The figures in the distance seemed to be drawing closer.* ◊ *Their car drew alongside ours.* ◊ (*figurative*) *Her retirement is drawing near.* ◊ (*figurative*) *The meeting was drawing to a close.*

WEAPON | **6 ~ (sth) (on sb)** to take out a weapon, such as a gun or a SWORD, in order to attack sb: [VN] *She drew a revolver on me.* ◊ *He came towards them with his sword drawn.* [also V]

ATTRACT | **7** [VN] **~ sb (to sth)** to attract or interest sb: *The movie is drawing large audiences.* ◊ *Her screams drew passers-by to the scene.* ◊ *The course draws students from all over the country.* ◊ *She felt drawn to the man standing by the door.*

GET REACTION | **8** [VN] **~ sth (from sb)** to produce a reaction or response: *The announcement drew loud applause from the audience.* ◊ *The plan has drawn a lot of criticism.*

MAKE SB TALK | **9** [VN] **~ sb (about/on sth)** [often passive] (*BrE*) to make sb say more about sth: *Spielberg refused to be drawn on his next movie.*

CONCLUSION | **10** [VN] **~ sth (from sth)** to have a particular idea after you have studied sth or thought about it: *What conclusions did you draw from the report?* ◊ *We can draw some lessons for the future from this accident.*

COMPARISON | **11** [VN] to express a comparison or a contrast: *to draw an analogy/a comparison/a parallel/a distinction between two events*

CHOOSE | **12** to decide sth by picking cards, tickets or numbers by chance: [V] *We drew for partners.* ◊ [VN] *They had to draw lots to decide who would go.* ◊ *He drew the winning ticket.* ◊ *Names were drawn from a hat for the last few places.* ◊ *Italy has been drawn against Spain in the first round.* ◊ [VN to inf] *Italy has been drawn to play Spain.*

GAME | **13 ~ (with/against sb)** to finish a game without either team winning: [V] *England and France drew.* ◊

æ	ɑː	e	ɜː	ə	ɪ	iː	i	ɒ	ɔː	ʌ	ʊ	u	uː
cat	father	ten	bird	about	sit	see	many	got	saw	cup	put	actual	too

(BrE)

D

England drew with/against France. ◇ *England and France drew 3–3.* ◇ [VN] *England drew their game against France.*

MONEY | **14** [VN] ~ sth (from sth)| ~ sth out (of sth)| ~ sth on sth to take money or payments from a bank account or post office: *Can I draw $80 out of my account?* ◇ *I drew out £200.* ◇ *She went to the post office to draw her pension.* ◇ *The cheque was drawn on his personal account.*

LIQUID/GAS | **15** [VN] to take or pull liquid or gas from somewhere: *to draw water from a well* ◇ *The device draws water along the pipe.*

SMOKE/AIR | **16** ~ at/on sth| ~ sth in (written) to breathe in smoke or air: [V] *He drew thoughtfully on his pipe.* ◇ [VN] *She breathed deeply, drawing in the fresh mountain air.*

IDM **draw a 'blank** to get no response or result: *So far, the police investigation has drawn a blank.* **draw 'breath** (*BrE*) (*AmE* **draw a 'breath**) **1** to stop doing sth and rest: *She talks all the time and hardly stops to draw breath.* **2** (*literary*) to live; to be alive: *He was as kind a man as ever drew breath.* **draw sb's 'fire** to make sb direct their anger, criticism, etc. at you, so that others do not have to face it **draw the 'line (at sth/at doing sth)** to refuse to do sth; to set a limit: *I don't mind helping, but I draw the line at doing everything myself.* ◇ *We would have liked to invite all our relatives, but you have to draw the line somewhere.* **draw the 'line (between sth and sth)** to distinguish between two closely related ideas: *Where do you draw the line between genius and madness?* **draw the short 'straw** (*BrE*) (*AmE* **get the short end of the 'stick**) to be the person in a group who is chosen or forced to perform an unpleasant duty or task: *I drew the short straw and had to clean the toilets.* **draw 'straws (for sth)** to decide on sb to do or have sth, by choosing pieces of paper, etc: *We drew straws for who went first.*—more at BATTLE *n.*, DAGGER, HEIGHT, HORN, LOT *n.*, SIDE *n.*

PHRV **draw 'back** to move away from sb/sth: *He came close but she drew back.* **draw 'back (from sth/from doing sth)** to choose not to take action, especially because you feel nervous: *We drew back from taking our neighbours to court.* **draw sth from sb/sth** to take or obtain sth from a particular source: *to draw support/comfort/strength from your family* ◇ *She drew her inspiration from her childhood experiences.* **draw 'in** to become dark earlier in the evening as winter gets nearer: *The nights/days are drawing in.* **draw sb into sth/into doing sth| draw sb ⟷ 'in** to involve or make sb take part in sth, although they may not want to take part at first: *youngsters drawn into a life of crime* ◇ *The book starts slowly, but it gradually draws you in.* **draw sth ⟷ 'off** to remove some liquid from a larger supply: *The doctor drew off some fluid to relieve the pressure.* **draw 'on** (*written*) if a time or a season draws on, it passes: *Night was drawing on.* **draw on/upon sth** to use a supply of sth that is available to you: *I'll have to draw on my savings.* ◇ *The novelist draws heavily on her personal experiences.* **draw 'out** to become lighter in the evening as summer gets nearer: *The days/evenings are drawing out.* **draw sb ⟷ 'out** to encourage sb to talk or express themselves freely **draw sth ⟷ 'out** to make sth last longer than usual or necessary: *She drew the interview out to over an hour.*—see also LONG-DRAWN-OUT **draw 'up** if a vehicle draws up, it arrives and stops: *The cab drew up outside the house.* **draw sth ⟷ 'up** to make or write sth that needs careful thought or planning: *to draw up a contract/list*

■ *noun*
CHOOSING | **1** (*AmE* also **draw·ing**) [usually sing.] ~ (for sth) the act of choosing sth, for example the winner of a prize or the teams who play each other in a competition, usually by taking pieces of paper, etc. out of a container without being able to see what is written on them: *the draw for the second round of the European Cup* ◇ *The draw for the raffle takes place on Saturday.*
SPORTS/GAMES | **2** (*especially BrE*) a game in which both teams or players finish with the same number of points: *The match ended in a two-all draw.* ◇ *He managed to hold Smith to a draw* (= to stop him from winning when he seemed likely to do so).—compare TIE *n.* (5) **3** (*AmE* usu-

ally **draw·ing**) a competition in which the winners are chosen in a draw: *a prize draw*—compare LOTTERY **4** (*BrE*) a sports match for which the teams or players are chosen in a draw: *Liverpool have an away draw against Manchester United.* **5** [usually sing.] a set of matches for which the teams or players are chosen in a draw: *There are only two seeded players left in the top half of the draw.*
ATTRACTION | **6** a person, a thing or an event that attracts a lot of people [SYN] ATTRACTION: *She is currently one of the biggest draws on the Irish music scene.*
SMOKE | **7** an act of breathing in the smoke from a cigarette [SYN] DRAG
IDM **be quick/fast on the 'draw 1** (*informal*) to be quick to understand or react in a new situation: *You can't fool him, he's always quick on the draw.* **2** to be quick at pulling out a gun in order to shoot it—more at LUCK *n.*

draw·back /'drɔːbæk/ *noun* ~ (of/to sth)| ~ (of/to doing sth) a disadvantage or problem that makes sth a less attractive idea: *The main drawback to it is the cost.* ◇ *This is the one major drawback of the new system.*

draw·bridge /'drɔːbrɪdʒ/ *noun* a bridge that can be pulled up, for example to stop people from entering a castle or to allow ships to pass under it: *to raise/lower the drawbridge*

drawer *noun* **1** /drɔː(r)/ a part of a piece of furniture such as a desk, used for keeping things in. It is shaped like a box and has a handle on the front for pulling it out: *in the top/middle/bottom drawer of the desk*—see also CHEST OF DRAWERS, TOP DRAWER **2** /'drɔː(r)ə/ (*formal*) a person who writes a cheque

drawers /drɔːz; *AmE* drɔːrz/ *noun* [pl.] (*old-fashioned*) KNICKERS or UNDERPANTS, especially ones that cover the upper parts of the legs

draw·ing /'drɔːɪŋ/ *noun* **1** [C] a picture made using a pencil or pen rather than paint: *a pencil/charcoal drawing* ◇ *a drawing of a yacht* ◇ *He did/made a drawing of the old farmhouse.* **2** [U] the art or skill of making pictures, plans, etc. using a pen or pencil: *I'm not very good at drawing.* ◇ *technical drawing* = DRAW (1, 3)

'drawing board *noun* a large flat board used for holding a piece of paper while a drawing or plan is being made **IDM** **(go) back to the 'drawing board** to start thinking about a new way of doing sth after a previous plan or idea has failed **on the 'drawing board** being prepared or considered: *It's just one of several projects on the drawing board.*

'drawing pin (*BrE*) (*AmE* **thumb·tack**, **tack**) *noun* a short pin with a large round flat head, used especially for fastening paper to a board or wall—picture at STATIONERY

'drawing power *noun* [U] (*AmE*) = PULLING POWER

'drawing room *noun* (*formal* or *old-fashioned*) a room in a large house in which people relax and guests are entertained—compare LIVING ROOM

drawl /drɔːl/ *verb* to speak or say sth slowly with vowel sounds that are longer than usual: [V speech] *'Hi there!'* *she drawled lazily.* ◇ [V] *He had a smooth drawling voice.* [also VN] ▶ **drawl** *noun* [sing.]: *She spoke in a slow southern drawl.*

drawn /drɔːn/ *adj.* (of a person or their face) looking pale and thin because the person is ill, tired or worried: *She looked very pale and drawn.*—see also DRAW *v.*

draw·string /'drɔːstrɪŋ/ *noun* a piece of string sewn inside the material at the top of a bag, pair of trousers/pants, etc. that can be pulled tighter in order to make the opening smaller: *They fasten with a drawstring.*—picture at FASTENER and on page A5

dray /dreɪ/ *noun* a low flat vehicle, pulled by horses, and used in the past for carrying heavy loads, especially BARRELS of beer

dread /dred/ *verb, noun*
■ *verb* to be very afraid of sth; to fear that sth bad is going to happen: [VN] *This was the moment he had been dreading.* ◇ [V-ing] *I dread being sick.* ◇ [VN-ing] *She dreads her husband finding out.* ◇ [V to inf] *I dread to think what would happen if there really was a fire here.* [also V that]

aɪ	aʊ	eɪ	əʊ	oʊ	ɔɪ	ɪə	eə	ʊə	j	w
my	now	say	go (BrE)	go (AmE)	boy	near	hair	pure	yes	wet

■ *noun* [U, C, usually sing.] a feeling of great fear about sth that might or will happen in the future; a thing that causes this feeling: *The prospect of growing old fills me with dread.* ◇ *She has an irrational dread of hospitals.* ◇ *The committee members live in dread of* (= are always worried about) *anything that may cause a scandal.* ◇ *My greatest dread is that my parents will find out.*

dread·ed /'dredɪd/ (*also formal* **dread**) *adj.* [only before noun] causing fear: *The dreaded moment had finally arrived.* ◇ (*humorous*) *Did I hear the dreaded word 'homework'?*

dread·ful /'dredfl/ *adj.* (*especially BrE*) **1** very bad or unpleasant: *What dreadful weather!* ◇ *What a dreadful thing to say!* ◇ *It's dreadful the way they treat their staff.* ◇ *How dreadful!* ◇ *Jane looked dreadful* (= looked ill or tired). **2** [only before noun] used to emphasize how bad sth is: *He's a dreadful snob.* ◇ *She's making a dreadful mess of things.* ◇ *I'm afraid there's been a dreadful mistake.* **3** [usually before noun] causing fear or suffering: *a dreadful accident/disease/scream* ◇ *They suffered dreadful injuries.*

dread·ful·ly /'dredfəli/ *adv.* (*especially BrE*) **1** extremely; very much: *I'm dreadfully sorry.* ◇ *I miss you dreadfully.* **2** very badly: *They suffered dreadfully during the war.*

dread·locks /'dredlɒks; *AmE* -lɑːks/ (*also informal* **dreads** /dredz/) *noun* [pl.] hair that is twisted into long thick pieces that hang down from the head, worn especially by RASTAFARIANS—picture at HAIR

dream /driːm/ *noun, verb*
■ *noun* **1** [C] a series of images, events and feelings that happen in your mind while you are asleep: *I had a vivid dream about my old school.* ◇ *I thought someone came into the bedroom, but it was just a dream.* ◇ *'Good night. Sweet dreams.'*—compare NIGHTMARE—see also WET DREAM **2** [C] a wish to have or be sth, especially one that seems difficult to achieve: *Her lifelong dream was to be a famous writer.* ◇ *He wanted to be rich but it was an impossible dream.* ◇ *If I win, it will be a **dream come true**.* ◇ *She tried to turn her dream of running her own business into reality.* ◇ *a dream car/house/job* ◇ *If he thinks it's easy to get a job he's **living in a dream world**.* ◇ *I've finally found the man of my dreams.* ◇ *a chance to fulfil a childhood dream* ◇ *It was the end of all my hopes and dreams.*—see also PIPE DREAM **3** [sing.] a state of mind or a situation in which things do not seem real or part of normal life: *She walked around in a dream all day.*—see also DAYDREAM, WET DREAM **4** [sing.] (*informal*) a beautiful or wonderful person or thing: *That meal was an absolute dream.* **IDM** **go/ work like a 'dream 1** to work very well: *My new car goes like a dream.* **2** to happen without problems, in the way that you had planned: *The wedding celebrations went like a dream.* **in your 'dreams** (*spoken*) used to tell sb that sth they are hoping for is not likely to happen: *'I'll be a manager before I'm 30.' 'In your dreams.'* **like a bad 'dream** (of a situation) so unpleasant that you cannot believe it is true: *In broad daylight the events of the night before seemed like a bad dream.*—more at WILD *adj.*
■ *verb* (**dreamt, dreamt** /dremt/) *or* (**dreamed, dreamed**) **1** ~ (*of/about sb/sth*) to experience a series of images, events and feelings in your mind while you are asleep: [V] *Did I talk in my sleep? I must have been dreaming.* ◇ *I dreamt about you last night.* ◇ [VN] *Did it really happen or did I just dream it?* ◇ [V(that)] *I dreamt (that) I got the job.* **2** ~ (*of/about sth*)| ~ (*of/about doing sth*) to imagine and think about sth that you would like to happen: [V] *She dreams of running her own business.* ◇ *It was the kind of trip most of us only dream about.* ◇ (*spoken*) *I wouldn't **dream** of going without you* (= I would never go without you). ◇ [VN] *Who'd have dreamt it? They're getting married.* ◇ [V(that)] *I **never** dreamt (that) I'd actually get the job.* **PHRV** **,dream sth a'way** to waste time just thinking about things you would like to do without actually doing anything **,dream 'on** (*spoken, informal*) you say **dream on** to tell sb that an idea is not practical or likely to happen **,dream sth↔'up** (*informal*) to have an idea, especially a very unusual or silly one: *Trust you to dream up a crazy idea like this!*

dream·er /'driːmə(r)/ *noun* **1** (sometimes *disapproving*) a person who has ideas or plans that are not practical or realistic **2** (usually *disapproving*) a person who does not pay attention to what is happening around them, but thinks about other things instead **3** a person who dreams: *Dreamers do not always remember their dreams.*

dream·land /'driːmlænd/ *noun* [U] (*especially BrE, disapproving*) a pleasant but not very realistic situation that only exists in your mind: *You must be living in dreamland if you think he'll change his mind.*

dream·less /'driːmləs/ *adj.* (of sleep) without dreams; deep and peaceful: *I fell straight into a dreamless sleep.*

dream·like /'driːmlaɪk/ *adj.* as if existing or happening in a dream: *The place had an almost dreamlike quality.*

'dream ticket *noun* [sing.] (used especially in newspapers about candidates for an election) a combination of people who, together, are considered to be the best

dreamy /'driːmi/ *adj.* (**dream·ier, dreami·est**) **1** looking as though you are thinking about other things and not paying attention to what is happening around you: *She had a dreamy look in her eyes.* ◇ *a dreamy expression* **2** (of a person or an idea) imaginative, but not very realistic: *Paul was dreamy and not very practical.* **3** as if you are in a dream or asleep: *He moved in the dreamy way of a man in a state of shock.* **4** (*informal*) pleasant and gentle; that makes you feel relaxed: *a slow, dreamy melody* **5** (*informal*) beautiful; wonderful: *What's he like? I bet he's really dreamy.* ▶ **dream·ily** /-ɪli/ *adv.* **dreami·ness** *noun* [U]

dreary /'drɪəri/ *AmE* /'drɪri/ *adj.* (**drear·ier, dreari·est**) that makes you feel sad; dull and not interesting: *a dreary winter's day* ◇ *a dreary film* ◇ *a long and dreary journey on the train* ▶ **drear·ily** /'drɪərəli/ *AmE* /'drɪr-/ *adv.*: *'I didn't get the job,' he said drearily.* **dreari·ness** *noun* [U]: *She hated the dreariness of her everyday life.*

dredge /dredʒ/ *verb* **1** ~ (*sth*) (*for sth*) to remove mud, stones, etc. from the bottom of a river, canal, etc. using a boat or special machine, to make it deeper or to search for sth: [VN] *They're dredging the harbour so that larger ships can use it.* ◇ *They dredge the bay for gravel.* [also V] **2** ~ *sth* (*up*) (*from sth*) to bring sth up from the bottom of a river, etc. using a boat or special machine: [VN] *waste dredged (up) from the sea bed* **3** [VN] ~ (*in/with*) to cover food lightly with sugar, flour, etc: *Dredge the top of the cake with icing sugar.* **PHRV** **,dredge sth↔'up 1** (usually *disapproving*) to mention sth that has been forgotten, especially sth unpleasant or embarrassing: *The papers keep trying to dredge up details of his past love life.* **2** to manage to remember sth, especially sth that happened a long time ago: *Now she was dredging up memories from the depths of her mind.*

dredger /'dredʒə(r)/ *noun* a boat or machine that is used to clear mud, etc. from the bottom of a river, or to make the river wider

dregs /dregz/ *noun* [pl.] **1** the last drops of a liquid, mixed with little pieces of solid material that are left in the bottom of a container: *She threw the coffee dregs down the sink.* **2** the worst and most useless parts of sth: *the dregs of society/humanity* **3** (*literary*) the last parts of sth: *the last dregs of daylight*

drench /drentʃ/ *verb* [VN] [often passive] ~ *sb/sth* (*in/ with sth*) to make sb/sth completely wet: *We were caught in the storm and got drenched to the skin.* ◇ *His face was drenched with sweat.* ◇ (*figurative*) *She drenched herself in perfume.*

dress /dres/ *noun, verb*
■ *noun*
CLOTHES **1** [C] a piece of women's clothing that is made in one piece and covers the body down to the legs, sometimes reaching to below the knees, or to the ankles: *a long white dress* ◇ *a wedding dress*—see also COCKTAIL DRESS, EVENING DRESS, SUNDRESS **2** [U] clothes for either men or women: *to wear casual/formal dress* ◇ *He has no **dress sense*** (= no idea of how to dress well). ◇ *The company has a strict **dress code**—all male employees are expected to wear suits.*—see also EVENING DRESS, FANCY DRESS, MORNING DRESS, HEADDRESS
■ *verb*
CLOTHES **1** ~ (*sb*) (*in sth*) to put clothes on yourself/sb: [V]

b	d	f	g	h	k	l	m	n	p	r
bad	did	fall	get	hat	cat	leg	man	now	pen	red

I dressed quickly. ◊ [VN] *She dressed herself and the children in their best clothes.* ◊ *Get up and get dressed!* OPP UNDRESS **2** [V] ~ **(sb) (for/in/as sth)** to wear a particular type or style of clothes: *to dress well/badly/fashionably/comfortably* ◊ *You should dress for cold weather today.* ◊ *She always dressed entirely in black.* ◊ *He was dressed as a woman* (= he was wearing women's clothes). **3** [V] to put on formal clothes: *Do they expect us to dress for dinner?* **4** [VN] to provide clothes for sb: *He dresses many of Hollywood's most famous young stars.*

WOUND | **5** [VN] to clean, treat and cover a wound: *The nurse will dress that cut for you.*

FOOD | **6** [VN] to prepare food for cooking or eating: *to dress a salad* (= put oil or vinegar, etc. on it) ◊ *to dress a chicken* (= clean it ready for cooking)

DECORATE | **7** [VN] (*formal*) to decorate or arrange sth: *to dress a shop window* (= arrange a display of clothes or goods in it)

STONE/WOOD/LEATHER | **8** [VN] to prepare a material such as stone, wood, leather, etc. for use

IDM see MUTTON, PART *n*.

PHRV ,dress 'down to wear clothes that are more informal than those you usually wear, for example in an office ,dress sb 'down to criticize or be angry with sb because they have done sth wrong ,dress 'up to wear clothes that are more formal than those you usually wear: *There's no need to dress up—come as you are.* ,dress 'up | ,dress sb 'up to put on special clothes, especially to pretend to be sb/sth different: *Kids love dressing up.* ◊ *The boys were all dressed up as pirates.* ◊ (*BrE*) *dressing-up clothes* ◊ (*AmE*) *dress-up clothes* ,dress sth 'up to present sth in a way that makes it seem better or different: *However much you try to dress it up, office work is not glamorous.*

dress·age /'dresɑːʒ/ *noun* [U] a set of controlled movements that a rider trains a horse to perform; a competition in which these movements are performed

,dress 'circle (*especially BrE*) (*AmE usually* ,first 'bal·cony) *noun* the first level of seats above the ground floor in a theatre

dressed /drest/ *adj.* [not before noun] **1** wearing clothes and not naked or wearing clothes for sleeping: *Hurry up and get dressed.* ◊ *fully dressed* ◊ *I can't go to the door—I'm not dressed yet.* **2** ~ **(in ...)** wearing clothes of a particular type: *smartly dressed* ◊ *The bride was dressed in white.* ◊ *He was casually dressed in jeans and a T-shirt.* **IDM** dressed to 'kill (*informal*) wearing the kind of clothes that will make people notice and admire you dressed (up) to the 'nines (*informal*) wearing very elegant or formal clothes—more at MUTTON

dress·er /'dresə(r)/ *noun* **1** (also ,Welsh 'dresser) (*BrE*) a large piece of wooden furniture with shelves in the top part and cupboards below, used for displaying and storing cups, plates, etc. **2** (*AmE*) = CHEST OF DRAWERS **3** (used with an adjective) a person who dresses in the way mentioned: *a snappy dresser* **4** (in a theatre) a person whose job is to look after an actor's clothes for a play and help him/her to get dressed

dress·ing /'dresɪŋ/ *noun* **1** (also 'salad dressing) [C, U] a thin sauce used to add flavour to salads, usually made from oil, VINEGAR, salt, pepper, etc: *a low-calorie dressing*—see also FRENCH DRESSING **2** [U] (*AmE*) = STUFFING (1) **3** [C] a piece of soft material placed over a wound in order to protect it **4** [U] the act of putting on clothes: *Many of our patients need help with dressing.*—see also CROSS-DRESSING, POWER DRESSING, WINDOW DRESSING

,dressing-'down *noun* [sing.] (*old-fashioned, informal*) an occasion when sb speaks angrily to a person because they have done sth wrong

'dressing gown (*BrE*) (*AmE* bath·robe, robe) *noun* a long loose piece of clothing, usually with a belt, worn indoors over night clothes, for when you first get out of bed ⇨ Picture on page A5

'dressing room *noun* **1** a room for changing your clothes in, especially one for actors or, in British English, for sports players **2** a small room next to a bedroom in some large houses, in which clothes are kept and people get dressed **3** (*AmE*) = FITTING ROOM

'dressing table (*AmE* also van·ity) *noun* a piece of bedroom furniture like a table with drawers and a mirror on top, used by women to sit at while they comb their hair, etc.

dress·maker /'dresmeɪkə(r)/ *noun* a person who makes women's clothes, especially as a job ▶ dress·mak·ing *noun* [U]

,dress re'hearsal *noun* the final practice of a play in the theatre, using the clothes and lights that will be used for the real performance: (*figurative*) *The earlier protests had just been dress rehearsals for full-scale revolution.*

'dress uniform *noun* [U] a uniform that army, navy, etc. officers wear for formal occasions and ceremonies: *wearing full dress uniform*

dressy /'dresi/ *adj.* (dress·ier, dressi·est) **1** (of clothes) elegant and formal **2** (of people) liking to wear elegant or fashionable clothes

drew *pt* of DRAW

drib·ble /'drɪbl/ *verb, noun*
■ *verb* **1** [V, VN] to let SALIVA or another liquid come out of your mouth and run down your chin **SYN** DROOL **2** [V+adv./prep.] to fall in small drops or in a thin stream: *Melted wax dribbled down the side of the candle.* **3** [VN+adv./prep.] ~ **sth (into/over/onto sth)** to pour sth slowly, in drops or a thin stream **SYN** DRIZZLE: *Dribble a little olive oil over the salad.* **4** (in football and some other sports) to move the ball along with several short kicks, hits or bounces: [VN] *She dribbled the ball the length of the field.* ◊ [V] *He dribbled past two defenders and scored a magnificent goal.*—picture on page 1250
■ *noun* **1** [C] a very small amount of liquid, in a thin stream: *a dribble of blood* ◊ *Add just a dribble of oil.* **2** [U] (*especially BrE*) SALIVA (= liquid) from a person's mouth: *There was dribble all down the baby's front.* **3** [C] the act of dribbling in a sport

dribs /drɪbz/ *noun* [pl.] **IDM** in ,dribs and 'drabs (*informal*) in small amounts or numbers over a period of time: *She paid me in dribs and drabs, not all at once*

dried *pt, pp* of DRY

,dried 'fruit *noun* [U, C] fruit (for example, CURRANTS or RAISINS) that has been dried to be used in cooking or eaten on its own

drier = DRYER—see also DRY *adj.*

drift /drɪft/ *noun, verb*
■ *noun*
SLOW MOVEMENT | **1** [sing., U] a slow steady movement from one place to another; a gradual change or development from one situation to another, especially to sth bad: *a population drift away from rural areas* ◊ *attempts to halt the drift towards war*
OF SHIP | **2** [U] the movement of a ship or plane away from its direction because of currents or wind: *Remember to allow for drift.*
OF SEA/AIR | **3** [U, C] the movement of the sea or air **SYN** CURRENT: *the general direction of drift on the east coast* ◊ *He knew the hidden drifts in that part of the river.*
OF SNOW | **4** [C] a large pile of sth, especially snow, made by the wind: *The road was blocked by deep drifts of snow.*—see also SNOWDRIFT
OF FLOWERS | **5** [C] a large mass of sth, especially flowers: *Plant daffodils in informal drifts.*
MEANING | **6** [sing.] the general meaning of what sb says or writes: *Do you catch my drift?* ◊ *My German isn't very good, but I got the drift of what she said.*
—see also CONTINENTAL DRIFT
■ *verb*
MOVE SLOWLY | **1** [V] [usually +adv./prep.] to move along smoothly and slowly in water or air: *Clouds drifted across the sky.* ◊ *The empty boat drifted out to sea.* ◊ *A cool breeze drifted through the open window.* **2** [V+adv./prep.] to move or go somewhere slowly: *The crowd drifted away from the scene of the accident.* ◊ *Her gaze drifted around the room.*
WITHOUT PURPOSE | **3** [V] [usually +adv./prep.] to happen or

change or to do sth without a particular plan or purpose: *I didn't intend to be a teacher—I just drifted into it.* ◊ *He hasn't decided what to do yet—he's just drifting.* ◊ *The conversation drifted onto politics.*

INTO STATE/SITUATION | **4** [V] ~ **in/into sth** to go from one situation or state to another without realizing it: *Finally she drifted into sleep.* ◊ *The injured man tried to speak but soon drifted into unconsciousness.*

OF SNOW/SAND | **5** [V] to be blown into large piles by the wind: *drifting sand* ◊ *Some roads are closed because of drifting.*

FLOAT | **6** [VN] to make sth float somewhere: *The logs are drifted downstream to the mill.*

PHRV ,drift a'**part** to become less friendly or close to sb: *As children we were very close, but as we grew up we just drifted apart.* ,drift '**off (to sleep)** to fall asleep: *I didn't hear the storm, I must have drifted off by then.*

drift·er /'drɪftə(r)/ *noun* (*disapproving*) a person who moves from one job or place to another with no real purpose

'**drift net** *noun* a very large net used by fishing boats. The net is hung in the sea behind the boat and pulled along.

drift·wood /'drɪftwʊd/ *noun* [U] wood that the sea carries up onto the shore, or that floats on the water

drill /drɪl/ *noun, verb*

■ *noun* **1** [C] a tool or machine with a pointed end for making holes: *an electric drill* ◊ *a pneumatic drill* ◊ *a hand drill* ◊ *a dentist's drill* ◊ *a drill bit* (= the pointed part at the end of the drill)—picture at TOOL **2** [C, U] a way of learning sth by means of repeated exercises: *tense drills* **3** [C, U] a practice of what to do in an emergency, for example if there is a fire: *There'll be a fire drill sometime this morning.* **4** [U] military training in marching, the use of weapons, etc: *rifle drill* **5** (**the drill**) [sing.] (*old-fashioned, BrE*) the correct or usual way to do sth: *What's the drill for claiming expenses?* **6** [U] strong cotton fabric **7** [C] a machine for planting seeds in rows

■ *verb* **1** to make a hole in sth, using a drill: [VN] *Drill a series of holes in the frame.* ◊ [V] *They're drilling for oil off the Irish coast.* ◊ *He drilled through the wall by mistake.* **2** ~ **sb** (**in sth**) to teach sb to do sth by making them repeat it a lot of times: [VN to inf] *The children were drilled to leave the classroom quickly when the fire bell rang.* ◊ [VN] *a well-drilled team* **3** [VN] to train soldiers to perform military actions: *The soldiers were being drilled outside the barracks.* **PHRV** '**drill sth into sb** to make sb remember or learn sth by repeating it often: *It was drilled into us at an early age never to drop litter.*

drily (also **dryly**) /'draɪli/ *adv.*—see also DRY **1** if sb speaks **drily**, they are being humorous, but not in an obvious way: *'Well, at least it's not purple,' she commented drily.* **2** in a way that shows no emotion: *He smiled drily and leaned back in his chair.* **3** in a way that shows that there is no liquid present: *She coughed drily.* ◊ *He swallowed drily and nodded.*

drink /drɪŋk/ *noun, verb*

■ *noun* **1** [C, U] a liquid for drinking; an amount of a liquid that you drink: *Can I have a drink?* ◊ *soft drinks* (= cold drinks without alcohol) ◊ *a drink of water* ◊ *food and drink* ◊ *She took a drink from the glass and then put it down.* **2** [C, U] alcohol or an alcoholic drink; sth that you drink on a social occasion: *Let's go for a drink.* ◊ *The drinks are on me* (= I'll pay for them). ◊ *I need a stiff drink* (= a very strong drink). ◊ (*BrE*) *He's got a drink problem.* ◊ (*AmE*) *He has a drinking problem.* ◊ (*humorous*) *The children are enough to drive me to drink.* ◊ (*BrE*) *They came home the worse for drink* (= drunk). ◊ *She took to drink* (= drank too much alcohol) *after her marriage broke up.* **3** (**drinks**) [pl.] (*BrE*) a social occasion where you have alcoholic drinks: *Would you like to come for drinks on Sunday?* ◊ *a drinks party* **IDM** see DEMON, MEAT

■ *verb* (**drank** /dræŋk/, **drunk** /drʌŋk/) **1** to take liquid into your mouth and swallow it: [VN] *What would you like to drink?* ◊ [VN] *In hot weather, you should drink plenty of water.* ◊ *I don't drink coffee.* **2** to drink alcohol, especially when it is done regularly: [V] *He doesn't drink.* ◊ *Don't*

drink and drive (= drive a car after drinking alcohol). ◊ *She's been drinking heavily since she lost her job.* ◊ [VN] *I drank far too much last night.* ◊ [VN-ADJ] *He had drunk himself unconscious on vodka.*—see also DRUNK **IDM** **drink sb's 'health** to wish sb good health as you lift your glass, and then drink from it **drink like a 'fish** to drink a lot of alcohol regularly ,**drink sb under the 'table** (*informal*) to drink more alcohol than sb else without becoming as drunk as they are **PHRV** ,**drink sth↔'in** to look at or listen to sth with great interest and enjoyment: *We just stood there drinking in the scenery.* '**drink to sb/sth** to wish sb good luck, health or success as you lift your glass and then drink from it [SYN] TOAST: *All raise your glasses and drink to Katie and Tom!* ,**drink 'up** | ,**drink (sth)↔'up** to drink all of sth: *Drink up and let's go.* ◊ *Come on, drink up your juice.*

drink·able /'drɪŋkəbl/ *adj.* **1** clean and safe to drink **2** pleasant to drink: *a very drinkable wine*

,**drink-'driver** (*BrE*) (also ,**drunk 'driver** *AmE, BrE*) *noun* a person who drives a vehicle after drinking too much alcohol

,**drink-'driving** (also ,**drunken 'driving**) (both *BrE*) (also '**drunk driving** *AmE, BrE*) *noun* [U] driving a vehicle after drinking too much alcohol

drink·er /'drɪŋkə(r)/ *noun* **1** a person who drinks alcohol regularly, especially sb who drinks too much: *a heavy/moderate drinker* ◊ *I'm not much of a drinker.* **2** (after a noun) a person who regularly drinks the particular drink mentioned: *a coffee/tea/beer drinker*

drink·ing /'drɪŋkɪŋ/ *noun* [U] the act of drinking alcohol: *Drinking is not advised during pregnancy.* ◊ *There are tough penalties for drinking and driving.*

'**drinking chocolate** *noun* [U] (*BrE*) a sweet chocolate powder or a hot drink made from this powder mixed with hot milk and/or water—compare COCOA

'**drinking fountain** (*especially BrE*) (*AmE usually* '**water fountain**) *noun* a device that supplies water for drinking in public places—picture at FOUNTAIN

'**drinking straw** *noun* = STRAW

'**drinking water** *noun* [U] water that is safe for drinking

drip /drɪp/ *verb, noun*

■ *verb* (**-pp-**) **1** [V] [usually +*adv./prep.*] (of liquid) to fall in small drops: *She was hot and sweat dripped into her eyes.* ◊ *Water was dripping down the walls.* **2** to produce drops of liquid: [V] *The tap was dripping.* ◊ *Her hair dripped down her back.* ◊ [VN] *Be careful, you're dripping paint everywhere!* **3** ~ (**with**) **sth** (*written*) to contain or hold a lot of sth: [V] *The trees were dripping with fruit.* ◊ [VN] *His voice dripped sarcasm.*

■ *noun* **1** [sing.] the sound or action of small drops of liquid falling continuously: *The silence was broken only by the steady drip, drip of water from the roof.* **2** [C] a small drop of liquid that falls from sth: *We put a bucket under the hole in the roof to catch the drips.* **3** (*AmE also* **IV**) [C] (*medical*) a piece of equipment that passes liquid food, medicine or blood very slowly through a tube into a patient's VEIN: *She's been put on a drip.* **4** [C] (*informal, becoming old-fashioned*) a boring or stupid person with a weak personality: *Don't be such a drip—come and join in the fun!*

,**drip-'dry** *adj.* made of a fabric that will dry quickly without CREASES when you hang it up wet: *a drip-dry shirt*

'**drip-feed** *verb* (**drip-fed, drip-fed**) [VN] to give sb sth in separate small amounts ► '**drip feed** *noun* [U, C]: *the steady drip feed of leaked documents in the papers*

drip·ping /'drɪpɪŋ/ *adj., noun*

■ *adj.* ~ (**with sth**) very wet: *Her face was dripping with sweat.* ◊ *His clothes were still dripping wet.* ◊ (*figurative*) *His wife came in, dripping with diamonds.*

■ *noun* [U] fat that comes out of meat when it is cooked, often kept for frying other food in

drive /draɪv/ *verb, noun*

■ *verb* (**drove** /drəʊv; *AmE* droʊv/, **driven** /'drɪvn/)
VEHICLE | **1** to operate a vehicle so that it goes in a particular direction: [V] *Can you drive?* ◊ *Don't drive so fast!* ◊ *I drove to work this morning.* ◊ *Shall we drive* (= go there

æ	ɑː	e	ɜː	ə	ɪ	iː	i	ɒ	ɔː	ʌ	ʊ	u	uː
cat	father	ten	bird	about	sit	see	many	got	saw	cup	put	actual	too
								(BrE)					

D

by car) *or go by train?* ◊ [VN] *He drives a taxi* (= that is his job). **2** [VN] [usually +*adv.* / *prep.*] to take sb somewhere in a car, taxi, etc: *Could you drive me home?* **3** [VN] to own or use a particular type of vehicle: *What car do you drive?*

<u>MACHINE</u> | **4** [VN] [usually passive] to provide the power that makes a machine work: *a steam-driven locomotive*

<u>MAKE SB DO STH</u> | **5** [VN] to force sb to act in a particular way: *The urge to survive drove them on.* ◊ *You're driving yourself too hard.* **6** to make sb very angry, crazy, etc. or to make them do sth extreme: [VN-ADJ] *to drive sb crazy/ mad* ◊ [VN to inf] *Hunger drove her to steal.* ◊ [VN] *Those kids are driving me to despair.* ◊ (*humorous*) *It's enough to drive you to drink* (= to make you start drinking too much alcohol)*!*

<u>MAKE SB/STH MOVE</u> | **7** [VN +*adv.* / *prep.*] to force sb/sth to move in a particular direction: *to drive sheep into a field* ◊ *The enemy was driven back.*

<u>HIT/PUSH</u> | **8** [VN +*adv.* / *prep.*] to force sth to go in a particular direction or into a particular position by pushing it, hitting it, etc: *to drive a nail into a piece of wood*

<u>MAKE A HOLE</u> | **9** [VN +*adv.* / *prep.*] to make an opening in or through sth by using force: *They drove a tunnel through the solid rock.*

<u>IN SPORT</u> | **10** to hit a ball with force, sending it forward: [VN] *to drive the ball into the rough* (= in golf) [also V]

<u>WIND/WATER</u> | **11** [VN] [usually +*adv.* / *prep.*] to carry sth along: *Huge waves drove the yacht onto the rocks.* **12** [V] [usually +*adv.* / *prep.*] to fall or move rapidly and with great force: *The waves drove against the shore.* ◊ *driving rain*

IDM **drive a coach and 'horses through sth** to spoil sth, for example a plan **drive sth 'home (to sb)** to make sb understand or accept sth, by saying it often, loudly, angrily, etc: *You will really need to drive your point home.* **drive sb in'sane** to make sb more and more angry or irritated, especially over a long period of time: *This job is driving me insane.* **what sb is 'driving at** the thing sb is trying to say: *I wish I knew what they were really driving at.*—more at GROUND *n.*, HARD *adj.*, SNOW *n.*

PHRV **,drive a'way**| **,drive sb/sth a'way** to leave in a vehicle; to take sb away in a vehicle: *We heard him drive away.* ◊ *Someone drove the car away in the night.* **,drive sb a'way** to make sb not want to stay or not want to go somewhere: *Her constant nagging drove him away.* ◊ *Terrorist threats are driving away tourists.* **,drive 'off 1** (of a driver, car, etc.) to leave: *The robbers drove off in a stolen vehicle.* **2** (in golf) to hit the ball to begin a game **,drive sb/sth↔'off** to force sb/sth to go back or away: *The defenders drove off each attack.* **,drive 'on** to continue driving: *Don't stop—drive on!* **,drive sb/sth↔'out (of sth)** to make sb/sth disappear or stop doing sth: *New fashions drive out old ones.* **,drive sth↔'up/'down** to make sth such as prices rise or fall quickly

■ *noun*

<u>IN/OF VEHICLE</u> | **1** [C] a journey in a car or other vehicle: *Let's go for a drive.* ◊ *a drive through the mountains* ◊ *It's a three-hour drive to London.* **2** [C, U] the equipment in a vehicle that takes power from the engine to the wheels: *the drive shaft* ◊ *a car with four-wheel drive* ◊ *a left-/ right-hand drive car* (= a car where the driver and the controls are on the left / right)

<u>OUTSIDE HOUSE</u> | **3** (also **drive·way**) [C] a wide hard path or a private road that leads from the street to a house: *There were two cars parked in/on the drive.*—picture at HOUSE

<u>EFFORT</u> | **4** [C] ~ **(for sth)**| ~ **(to do sth)** an organized effort by a group of people to achieve sth: *a recruitment / export / economy drive* ◊ *a drive for greater efficiency* ◊ *the government's drive to reduce energy consumption*

<u>DESIRE/ENERGY</u> | **5** [C, U] a strong desire or need in people: *a strong sexual drive* **6** [U] (*approving*) a strong desire to do things and achieve sth; great energy: *He'll do very well—he has tremendous drive.*

<u>IN SPORT</u> | **7** [C] a long hard hit or kick: *She has a strong forehand drive* (= in tennis). ◊ *He scored with a brilliant 25-yard drive* (= for example, in football).

<u>COMPUTING</u> | **8** [C] the part of a computer that reads and

stores information on disks or tapes: *a 224 MB hard drive* ◊ *a CD drive*—see also DISK DRIVE

<u>GAMES</u> | **9** [C] (*BrE*) a social occasion when a lot of people compete in a game such as WHIST or BINGO

<u>ANIMALS/ENEMY</u> | **10** [C] an act of chasing animals or the enemy and making them go into a smaller area, especially in order to kill or capture them

<u>ROAD</u> | **11** (**Drive**) (*abbr.* **Dr**) used in the names of roads: *21 Island Heights Drive*

'drive-by *adj.* (*AmE*) [only before noun] a **drive-by** shooting, etc. is done from a moving car: *a drive-by killing* ▶ **'drive-by** *noun*

'drive-in *noun* a place where you can watch films/movies, eat, etc. without leaving your car: *We stopped at a drive-in for a hamburger.* ◊ *drive-in movies*

drivel /'drɪvl/ *noun, verb*
■ *noun* [U] (*informal, disapproving*) silly nonsense: *How can you watch that drivel on TV?*
■ *verb* (**-ll-**, *AmE* **-l-**) [V] ~ **(on) (about sth)** (usually used in the progressive tenses) to keep talking about silly or unimportant things

driven /'drɪvn/ *adj.* (of a person) determined to succeed, and working very hard to do so—see also DRIVE, DROVE, DRIVEN *v.*

driver /'draɪvə(r)/ *noun* **1** a person who drives a vehicle: *a bus / train / ambulance / taxi driver* ◊ *She climbed into the driver's seat.* ◊ (*BrE*) *a learner driver* (= one who has not yet passed a driving test) ◊ (*AmE*) *a student driver* ◊ *The car comes equipped with a driver's airbag.* **2** (in golf) a CLUB with a wooden head **3** (*computing*) software that controls the sending of data between a computer and a piece of equipment that is attached to it such as a printer **IDM** see BACK SEAT, SEAT *n.*

'driver's license *noun* (*AmE*) = DRIVING LICENCE

'drive-through (also **'drive-thru**) *noun* (*AmE*) a restaurant, bank, etc. where you can be served without having to get out of your car

'drive·way /'draɪvweɪ/ *noun* = DRIVE (3): *There was a car parked in/on the driveway.*—picture at HOUSE

driv·ing /'draɪvɪŋ/ *noun, adj.*
■ *noun* [U] the way that sb drives a vehicle; the act of driving: *dangerous driving* ◊ *driving lessons* **IDM** see SEAT *n.*
■ *adj.* [only before noun] **1** strong and powerful; having a strong influence in making sth happen: *Who was the driving force* (= the person with the strongest influence) *in the band?* **2** (of rain, snow, etc.) falling very fast and at an angle

'driving licence (*BrE*) (*AmE* **'driver's license**) *noun* an official document that shows that you are qualified to drive

'driving school *noun* a business that gives people lessons in how to drive a car

'driving test *noun* a test that must be passed before you are qualified to drive

,driving under the 'influence *noun* [U] (*abbr.* **DUI**) (*AmE*) (in some states in the US) the crime of driving a vehicle after drinking too much alcohol. It is a less serious crime than 'driving while intoxicated'.

,driving while in'toxicated *noun* [U] (*abbr.* **DWI**) (*AmE*) the crime of driving a vehicle after drinking too much alcohol

driz·zle /'drɪzl/ *verb, noun*
■ *verb* **1** [V] when it is drizzling, it is raining lightly **2** [VN] ~ **sth (over sth)** to pour a small amount of liquid over the surface of sth: *Drizzle the lemon juice over the fish.*
■ *noun* [U, sing.] light fine rain: *A light drizzle was falling.* ▶ **driz·zly** /'drɪzli/ *adj.*: *a dull, drizzly morning*

droll /drəʊl; *AmE* droʊl/ *adj.* (*old-fashioned* or *ironic*) amusing, but not in a way that you expect

drom·ed·ary /'drɒmədəri; *AmE* 'drɑːmədəri/ *noun* (*pl.* **-ies**) an animal of the CAMEL family, with only one HUMP, that lives in desert countries

drone /drəʊn; *AmE* droʊn/ *noun, verb*
■ *noun* **1** [usually sing.] a continuous low noise: *the distant drone of traffic* ◊ *He spoke in a low drone.* **2** [usually sing.]

aɪ	aʊ	eɪ	əʊ	oʊ	ɔɪ	ɪə	eə	ʊə	j	w
my	now	say	go	go	boy	near	hair	pure	yes	wet
			(BrE)	(AmE)						

a continuous low sound made by some musical instruments, for example the BAGPIPES, over which other notes are played or sung **3** a male bee that does not work and only lives in order to reproduce—compare QUEEN BEE, WORKER **4** a person who is lazy and gives nothing to society while others work
■ *verb* [V] to make a continuous low noise: *A plane was droning in the distance.* ◊ *a droning voice* PHRV **,drone 'on (about sth)** to talk for a long time in a boring way

drool /druːl/ *verb* **1** [V] to let SALIVA (= liquid) come out of your mouth SYN DRIBBLE: *The dog was drooling at the mouth.* **2 ~ (over sb/sth)** (*disapproving*) to show in a silly or exaggerated way that you want or admire sb/sth very much: *teenagers drooling over photos of movie stars*

droop /druːp/ *verb* [V] **1** to bend, hang or move downwards, especially because of being weak or tired: *She was so tired, her eyelids were beginning to droop.* **2** to become sad or depressed: *Our spirits drooped when we heard the news.* ▶ **droop** *noun* [sing.]: *the slight droop of her mouth* **droopy** *adj.*: *a droopy moustache*

drop /drɒp; *AmE* drɑːp/ *verb, noun*
■ *verb* (**-pp-**)
FALL | **1** to fall or allow sth to fall by accident: [V] *The climber slipped and dropped to his death.* ◊ [VN] *Be careful not to drop that plate.* **2** to fall or make sth fall deliberately: [V, +*adv. / prep.*] *He staggered in and dropped into a chair.* ◊ [VN] *Medical supplies are being dropped into the stricken area.* ◊ (*BrE*) *He dropped his trousers* (= undid them and let them fall). ◊ (*AmE*) *He dropped his pants.* **3** [V] to fall down or be no longer able to stand because you are extremely tired: *I feel ready to drop.* ◊ *She expects everyone to work till they drop.*
BECOME WEAKER/LESS | **4** to become or make sth weaker, lower or less: [V] *The temperature has dropped considerably.* ◊ *At last the wind dropped.* ◊ *His voice dropped to a whisper.* ◊ *The Dutch team have dropped to fifth place.* ◊ *The price of shares dropped by 14p.* ◊ *Shares dropped in price by 14p.* ◊ [VN] *She dropped her voice dramatically.* ◊ *You must drop your speed in built-up areas.*
EYES | **5 ~ your eyes/gaze | your eyes/gaze ~** (*written*) to look down: [V] *Her eyes dropped to her lap.* [also VN]
SLOPE DOWNWARDS | **6** [V] **~ (away) (from sth)** to slope steeply downwards: *In front of them the valley dropped sharply away from the road.*
DELIVER/SEND | **7** [VN] **~ sb/sth (off)** to stop so that sb can get out of a car, etc.; to deliver sth on the way to somewhere else: *Can you drop me near the bank?* ◊ *You left your jacket, but I can drop it off on my way to work tomorrow.* **8** [VNN] **~ sb a line/note** to send a short letter to sb: *Drop me a line when you get there.*
LEAVE OUT | **9** [VN] **~ sb/sth (from sth)** to leave sb/sth out by accident or deliberately: *She's been dropped from the team because of injury.* ◊ *He spoke with a cockney accent and dropped his aitches* (= did not pronounce the letter 'h' at the start of words).
FRIENDS | **10** [VN] to stop seeing sb socially: *She's dropped most of her old friends.*
STOP | **11** [VN] to stop doing or discussing sth; to not continue with sth: *I dropped German* (= stopped studying it) *when I was 14.* ◊ *Drop everything and come at once!* ◊ *Look, can we just drop it* (= stop talking about it)? ◊ *I think we'd better drop the subject.* ◊ *Let's drop the formalities—please call me Mike.* ◊ *The police decided to drop the charges against her.*
HINT | **12** [VN] **~ a hint** to say or do sth in order to show sb, in an indirect way, what you are thinking
IN KNITTING | **13** [VN] **~ a stitch** to let a stitch go off the needle
IDM **drop a 'brick/'clanger** (*BrE, informal*) to say sth that offends or embarrasses sb, although you did not intend to **drop 'dead 1** (*informal*) to die suddenly and unexpectedly **2** (*spoken*) used to tell sb, rudely, to stop annoying you, interfering, etc.—see also DROP-DEAD **drop sb 'in it** (*BrE, informal*) to put sb in an embarrassing situation, especially by telling a secret that you should not have told **drop 'names** to mention famous people you know or have met in order to impress others—related

noun NAME-DROPPING **let sb/sth 'drop 1** to do or say nothing more about sb/sth: *I suggest we let the matter drop.* **2** to mention sb/sth in a conversation, by accident or as if by accident: *He let it drop that the Prime Minister was a close friend of his.*—more at BOTTOM *n.*, FLY *n.*, HEAR, JAW *n.*, LAP *n.*, PENNY
PHRV **,drop 'back/be'hind | ,drop be'hind sb** to move or fall into position behind sb else: *We cannot afford to drop behind our competitors.* **,drop 'by/'in/'round | ,drop 'in on sb | ,drop 'into sth** to pay an informal visit to a person or a place: *Drop by sometime.* ◊ *I thought I'd drop in on you while I was passing.* ◊ *Sorry we're late—we dropped into the pub on the way.* **,drop 'off** (*BrE, informal*) **1** to fall into a light sleep: *I dropped off and missed the end of the film.* **2** to become fewer or less: *Traffic in the town has dropped off since the bypass opened.* **,drop 'out (of sth) 1** to no longer take part in or be part of sth: *He has dropped out of active politics.* ◊ *a word that has dropped out of the language* **2** to leave school, college, etc. without finishing your studies: *She started an engineering degree but dropped out after only a year.*—related noun DROP-OUT (1) **3** (*disapproving*) to reject the ideas and ways of behaving that are accepted by the rest of society—related noun DROPOUT (2)
■ *noun*
OF LIQUID | **1** [C] a very small amount of liquid that forms a round shape: *drops of rain* ◊ *a drop of blood* ◊ *Mix a few drops of milk into the cake mixture.*—see also RAINDROP, TEARDROP **2** [C, usually sing.] (*especially spoken*) a small quantity of a liquid: *Could I have a drop more milk in my coffee, please?* ◊ *I haven't touched a drop* (= drunk any alcohol) *all evening.*
FALL | **3** [C, usually sing.] **~ (in sth)** a fall or reduction in the amount, level or number of sth: *a drop in prices/ temperature* ◊ *a dramatic/sharp drop in profits* ◊ *If you want the job, you must be prepared to take a drop in salary.* ◊ *a five per cent drop*
DISTANCE | **4** [sing.] a distance down from a high point to a lower point: *There was a sheer drop of fifty metres to the rocks below.* ◊ *a twenty-foot drop*
MEDICINE | **5** (**drops**) [pl.] a liquid medicine that you put one drop at a time into your eyes, ears or nose: *eye drops*
DELIVERING | **6** [C] the act of delivering sth/sb in a vehicle or by plane; the act of dropping sth: *Aid agencies are organizing food drops to civilians in the war zone.* ◊ *a parachute drop*
SWEET/CANDY | **7** [C] a small round sweet/candy of the type mentioned: *fruit drops* ◊ *cough drops* (= sweets/candy to help a cough)
IDM **at the ,drop of a 'hat** immediately; without hesitating: *The company can't expect me to move my home and family at the drop of a hat.* **a ,drop in the 'ocean** (*BrE*) (*AmE* **a ,drop in the 'bucket**) an amount of sth that is too small or unimportant to make any real difference to a situation

,drop-'dead *adv.* (*informal*) used before an adjective to emphasize that sb/sth is attractive in a very noticeable way: *a drop-dead gorgeous Hollywood star* ▶ **,drop-'dead** *adj.*

drop·let /'drɒplət; *AmE* 'drɑːp-/ *noun* a small drop of a liquid

drop·out /'drɒpaʊt; *AmE* 'drɑːp-/ *noun* **1** a person who leaves school or college before they have finished their studies: *college dropouts* ◊ *a university with a high drop-out rate* **2** (*disapproving*) a person who rejects the ideas and ways of behaving that are accepted by the rest of society

drop·per /'drɒpə(r); *AmE* 'drɑːp-/ *noun* a short glass tube with a hollow rubber end used for measuring medicine or other liquids in drops—picture at LABORATORY

drop·pings /'drɒpɪŋz; *AmE* 'drɑːp-/ *noun* the solid waste matter of birds and animals (usually small animals)

dross /drɒs; *AmE* drɔːs; drɑːs/ *noun* [U] **1** (*BrE*) something of very low quality; the least valuable part of sth: *mass-produced dross* **2** (*technical*) a waste substance, especially that separated from a metal when it is melted

D

b	d	f	g	h	k	l	m	n	p	r
bad	did	fall	get	hat	cat	leg	man	now	pen	red

drought /draʊt/ *noun* [U, C] a long period of time when there is little or no rain: *two years of severe drought* ◊ *one of the worst droughts on record*

drove /drəʊv; *AmE* droʊv/ *noun* [usually pl.] a large number of people or animals, often moving or doing sth as a group: *droves of tourists* ◊ *People were leaving the countryside in droves to look for work in the cities.*—see also DRIVE *v.*

drover /ˈdrəʊvə(r); *AmE* ˈdroʊv-/ *noun* a person who moves groups of cows or sheep from one place to another, especially to market

drown /draʊn/ *verb* 1 to die because you have been underwater too long and you cannot breathe; to kill sb in this way: [V] *Two children drowned after falling into the river.* ◊ *He had attempted to rescue the drowning man.* ◊ [VN] *She tried to drown herself.* ◊ *He was drowned at sea.* ◊ *They had drowned the unwanted kittens.* 2 [VN] ~ **sth (in sth)** to make sth very wet; to completely cover sth in water or another liquid: *The fruit was drowned in cream.* 3 [VN] ~ **sb/sth (out)** (of a sound) to be louder than other sounds so that you cannot hear them: *She turned up the radio to drown out the noise from next door.* ▶ **drown·ing** *noun* [U, C]: *death by drowning* ◊ *Alcohol plays a part in an estimated 30% of drownings.* [IDM] **drown your 'fears/'loneliness/'sorrows, etc.** (especially *humorous*) to get drunk in order to forget your problems

drowse /draʊz/ *verb* [V] to be in a light sleep or almost asleep: *My mother was sitting on the porch drowsing in the sun.*

drowsy /ˈdraʊzi/ *adj.* (**drows·ier, drowsi·est**) 1 tired and almost asleep [SYN] SLEEPY: *The tablets may make you feel drowsy.* 2 making you feel relaxed and tired: *a drowsy afternoon in the sunshine* ▶ **drows·ily** /-əli/ *adv.* **drow·si·ness** *noun* [U]: *The drugs tend to cause drowsiness.*

drub·bing /ˈdrʌbɪŋ/ *noun* (*informal*) (in a sport) a situation where one team easily beats another: *We gave them a drubbing in the match on Saturday.*

drudge /drʌdʒ/ *noun* a person who has to do long hard boring jobs

drudg·ery /ˈdrʌdʒəri/ *noun* [U] hard boring work: *domestic drudgery*

drug /drʌɡ/ *noun, verb*
■ *noun* 1 an illegal substance that some people smoke, INJECT, etc. to give them pleasant or exciting feelings: *He does not smoke or* **take drugs**. ◊ *teenagers experimenting with drugs* ◊ *I found out Steve was* **on drugs** (= regularly used drugs). ◊ *drug and alcohol abuse* ◊ *a* **hard** (= very harmful) *drug such as heroin* ◊ *a* **soft drug** (= one that is not considered very harmful) ◊ *Drugs have been seized with a street value of two million dollars.* ◊ *She was a* **drug addict** (= could not stop using drugs). ◊ *He was charged with* **pushing drugs** (= selling them). ◊ (*informal*) *I don't* **do drugs** (= use them). ◊ *drug rehabilitation* 2 a substance used as a medicine or used in a medicine: *prescribed drugs* ◊ *The doctor put me on a course of pain-killing drugs.* ◊ *drug companies* ◊ *The drug has some bad side effects.*—see also DESIGNER DRUG
■ *verb* (**-gg-**) [VN] 1 to give a person or an animal a drug, especially to make them unconscious, or to affect their performance in a race or competition: *He was drugged and bundled into the back of the car.* ◊ *It's illegal to drug horses before a race.* 2 to add a drug to sb's food or drink to make them unconscious or sleepy: *Her drink must have been drugged.* [IDM] **drugged up to the 'eyeballs** to have taken or been given a lot of drugs

'drug dealer *noun* a person who sells illegal drugs

drug·gie /ˈdrʌɡi/ *noun* (*informal*) a person who takes illegal drugs regularly

drug·gist /ˈdrʌɡɪst/ *noun* (*AmE*) = CHEMIST (1), PHARMACIST (1)

drug·store /ˈdrʌɡstɔː(r)/ *noun* (*AmE*) a shop/store that sells medicines and also other types of goods, for example COSMETICS—see also CHEMIST (2)—compare PHARMACY

Druid /ˈdruːɪd/ *noun* a priest of an ancient Celtic religion

drum /drʌm/ *noun, verb*
■ *noun* 1 a musical instrument made of a hollow round frame with plastic or skin stretched tightly across one or both ends. You play it by hitting it with sticks or with your hands: *a bass drum* ◊ *Tony Cox on drums* ◊ *to play the drums* ◊ *a regular drum beat*—picture on page 841

drumming her fingers

2 a large container for oil or chemicals, shaped like a CYLINDER: *a 50 gallon drum* ◊ *an oil drum* 3 a thing shaped like a drum, especially part of a machine: *The mixture flows to a revolving drum where the water is filtered out.* [IDM] **beat/bang the 'drum (for sb/sth)** (especially *BrE*) to speak with enthusiasm in support of sb/sth: *She's really banging the drum for the new system.*
■ *verb* (**-mm-**) 1 [V] to play a drum 2 ~ **(sth) on sth** to make a sound by hitting a surface again and again: [VN] *Impatiently, he drummed his fingers on the table.* [also V] [IDM] **'drum sth into sb's head** = DRUM STH INTO SB [PHRV] **'drum sth into sb** to make sb remember sth by repeating it a lot of times: *We had it drummed into us that we should never talk to strangers.* **,drum sb 'out (of sth)** [usually passive] to force sb to leave an organization as a punishment for doing sth wrong **,drum sth↔'up** to try hard to get support or business: *He had flown to the north of the country to drum up support for the campaign.*

drum·beat /ˈdrʌmbiːt/ *noun* the sound that a beat on a drum makes

'drum kit *noun* a set of drums—picture on page 841

,drum 'major *noun* the leader of a marching band of musicians, especially in the army

,drum majo'rette (especially *BrE*) (*AmE* usually **major·ette**) *noun* a girl in special brightly coloured clothes who walks in front of a marching band spinning, throwing and catching a long stick (called a BATON)

drum·mer /ˈdrʌmə(r)/ *noun* a person who plays a drum or drums

drum·ming /ˈdrʌmɪŋ/ *noun* [U, sing.] 1 the act of playing a drum; the sound of a drum being played 2 a continuous sound or feeling like the beats of a drum: *the steady drumming of the rain on the tin roof*

drum·stick /ˈdrʌmstɪk/ *noun* 1 the lower part of the leg of a chicken or other bird that is cooked and eaten as food: *a chicken/turkey drumstick* 2 a stick used for playing a drum—picture on page 841

drunk /drʌŋk/ *adj., noun*—see also DRINK *v.*
■ *adj.* 1 [not usually before noun] having drunk so much alcohol that it is impossible to think or speak clearly: *She was too drunk to remember anything about the party.* ◊ *His only way of dealing with his problems was to go out and get drunk.* ◊ *They got drunk on vodka.* 2 ~ **with sth** (*written*) in a great state of excitement because of a particular emotion or situation: *drunk with optimism/success* [IDM] **(as) drunk as a 'lord** (*BrE*) (*AmE* **as drunk as a 'skunk**) (*informal*) very drunk—more at BLIND *adv.*, ROARING
■ *noun* a person who is drunk or who often gets drunk

drunk·ard /ˈdrʌŋkəd; *AmE* -ərd/ *noun* (*old-fashioned*) a person who gets drunk very often [SYN] ALCOHOLIC

,drunk 'driver *noun* (especially *AmE*) = DRINK-DRIVER

,drunk 'driving *noun* [U] (especially *AmE*) = DRINK-DRIVING

drunk·en /ˈdrʌŋkən/ *adj.* [only before noun] 1 drunk or often getting drunk: *a drunken driver* ◊ *She was often beaten by her drunken husband.* 2 showing the effects of too much alcohol; involving people who are drunk: *He came home to find her in a drunken stupor.* ◊ *a drunken brawl* ▶ **drunk·en·ly** *adv.*: *He staggered drunkenly to his feet.* **drunk·en·ness** *noun* [U]

dry /draɪ/ *adj., verb*
■ *adj.* (**drier, dri·est**)
NOT WET 1 not wet, damp or sticky; without water or MOISTURE: *Is my shirt dry yet?* ◊ *Store onions in a cool dry*

place. ◊ *I'm afraid this cake has turned out very dry and crumbly.* ◊ *Her mouth felt* **as dry as a bone** (= completely dry). ◊ *When the paint is completely dry, apply another coat.* ◊ *It was high summer. The trees were dusty and the rivers were dry* (= had no water in them).—see also BONE DRY

LITTLE RAIN | **2** with very little rain: *weeks of hot dry weather* ◊ *a dry climate* ◊ *the dry season* ◊ *I hope it stays dry for our picnic.* ◊ *Rattlesnakes occur in the warmer, drier parts of North America.*

SKIN/HAIR | **3** without the natural oils that makes it soft and healthy: *a moisturizing shampoo and conditioner for dry hair*

COUGH | **4** that does not produce any PHLEGM (= the thick liquid that forms in the nose and throat): *a dry hacking cough*

BREAD | **5** eaten on its own without any butter, jam, etc: *Breakfast consisted of dry bread and a cup of tea.*

WINE | **6** not sweet: *a crisp dry white wine* ◊ *a dry sherry* ◊ *This wine is too dry for me.*

HUMOUR | **7** (*approving*) very clever and expressed in a quiet way that is not obvious; often using IRONY: *He was a man of few words with a delightful dry sense of humour.*

WITHOUT EMOTION | **8** not showing emotion: *a dry tone/ voice/manner*

BORING | **9** not interesting: *Government reports tend to make dry reading.*

WITHOUT ALCOHOL | **10** without alcohol; where it is illegal to buy, sell or drink alcohol: *We had a dry wedding* (= no alcoholic drinks were served). ◊ *a dry county/state*

THIRSTY | **11** (*informal, especially BrE*) thirsty; that makes you thirsty: *I'm a bit dry.* ◊ *This is dry work.*

▶ **dryly** = DRILY **dry·ness** *noun* [U]

IDM **milk/suck sb/sth 'dry** to get from sb/sth all the money, help, information, etc. they have, usually giving nothing in return **not a dry eye in the 'house** (*humorous*) used to say that everyone was very emotional about sth: *There wasn't a dry eye in the house when they announced their engagement.* **run 'dry** to stop supplying water; to be all used so that none is left: *The wells in most villages in the region have run dry.* ◊ *Vaccine supplies started to run dry as the flu outbreak reached epidemic proportions.*—more at BLEED, HIGH *adj.*, HOME *adv.*, POWDER *n.*, SQUEEZE *v.*

■ *verb* (**dries, dry·ing, dried, dried**) to become dry; to make sth dry:[V] *Be careful. The paint hasn't dried yet.* ◊ *You wash the dishes and I'll dry.* ◊ [VN] *You can use this towel to dry your hands.* ◊ *I'll just finish drying my hair then I'll come down.* ◊ *to dry your eyes/tears*

PHRV **,dry'off | ,dry sb/sth↔'off** to become dry or make sth dry: *We went swimming then lay in the sun to dry off.* ◊ *We dried our boots off by the fire.* **,dry 'out | ,dry sb↔'out** (*informal*) to stop drinking alcohol after you have continuously been drinking too much; to cure sb of drinking too much alcohol: *He went to an expensive clinic to dry out.* **,dry 'out | ,dry sth↔'out** to become or to allow sth to become dry, in a way that is not wanted: *Water the plant regularly, never letting the soil dry out.* ◊ *Hot sun and cold winds can soon dry out your skin.* **,dry 'up 1** (of rivers, lakes, etc.) to become completely dry: *During the drought the river dried up.* **2** if a supply of sth **dries up**, there is gradually less of it until there is none left: *As she got older, offers of modelling work began to dry up.* **3** to suddenly stop talking because you do not know what to say next **,dry 'up | ,dry sth↔'up** (*BrE*) to dry dishes with a towel after you have washed them: *I'll wash and you can dry up.*

dryad /'draɪæd/ *noun* (in stories) a female spirit who lives in a tree

,dry 'cell *noun* the type of cell in a **dry battery** which contains chemicals only in solid form

,dry-'clean (also **clean**) *verb* [VN] to clean clothes using chemicals instead of water: *This garment must be dry-cleaned only.* ▶ **,dry-'cleaning** *noun* [U]

,dry-'cleaner's *noun* = CLEANER

,dry 'dock *noun* [C, U] an enclosed part of a port, from which the water can be removed, for building or repairing ships: *The ship is in dry dock.*

dryer (also **drier**) /'draɪə(r)/ *noun* (especially in compounds) a machine for drying sth: *a hair dryer* ◊ *Don't put that sweater in the dryer.*—see also SPIN DRYER, TUMBLE-DRYER

,dry-'eyed *adj.* [not before noun] not crying: *She remained dry-eyed throughout the trial.*

'dry goods *noun* [pl.] **1** types of food that are solid and dry, such as tea, coffee and flour **2** (*old-fashioned, AmE*) fabric and things that are made out of fabric, such as clothes and sheets: *a dry goods store*—compare DRAPERY

,dry 'ice *noun* [U] solid CARBON DIOXIDE used for keeping food, etc. cold and producing special effects in the theatre

,dry 'land *noun* [U] land, rather than sea: *It was a great relief to be back* **on dry land** *after such a rough crossing.*

dryly = DRILY

,dry 'rot *noun* [U] **1** wood that has decayed and turned to powder **2** any FUNGUS that causes this decay

,dry 'run *noun* [usually sing.] a complete practice of a performance or way of doing sth, before the real one

dry-stone wall /,draɪstəun 'wɔːl; *AmE* -stoun/ *noun* (*BrE*) (*AmE* **'dry wall**) a stone wall built without MORTAR (= a substance usually used to hold bricks or stones together in building) between the stones

'dry wall *noun* [U] (*AmE*) **1** = PLASTERBOARD **2** = DRYSTONE WALL

DSS /,di: es 'es/ *abbr.* (in Britain) Department of Social Security

DST /,di: es 'ti:/ *abbr.* daylight saving time

DTI /,di: ti: 'aɪ/ *abbr.* (in Britain) Department of Trade and Industry

DTP /,di: ti: 'pi:/ *abbr.* DESKTOP PUBLISHING

DTs (*BrE*) (*AmE* **D.T.'s**) /,di: 'ti:z/ *noun* [pl.] a physical condition in which people who drink too much alcohol feel their body shaking and imagine that they are seeing things that are not really there (abbreviation for 'delirium tremens')

dual /'dju:əl; *AmE* 'du:əl/ *adj.* [only before noun] having two parts or aspects: *his dual role as composer and conductor* ◊ *She has* **dual nationality** (= is a citizen of two different countries). ◊ *The piece of furniture serves a dual purpose as a cupboard and as a table.*—see also DUAL-PURPOSE ⇨ note at DOUBLE

,dual 'carriageway (*BrE*) (*AmE* **di,vided 'highway**) *noun* a road with a strip of land in the middle that divides the lines of traffic moving in opposite directions

dual·ism /'dju:əlɪzəm; *AmE* 'du:-/ *noun* [U] **1** (*philosophy*) the theory that there are two opposite principles in everything, for example good and evil **2** (*formal*) the state of having two parts ▶ **dual·ist, dual·ist·ic** *adj.* **dual·ist** *noun*

dual·ity /dju:'æləti; *AmE* du:-/ *noun* [U, C] (*pl.* **-ies**) (*formal*) the state of having two parts or aspects

,dual-'purpose *adj.* that can be used for two different purposes: *a dual-purpose vehicle* (= for carrying passengers or goods)

dub /dʌb/ *verb, noun*

■ *verb* (**-bb-**) **1** [VN-N] to give sb/sth a particular name, often in a humorous or critical way: *The Belgian actor Jean Claude Van Damme has been dubbed 'Muscles from Brussels'.* **2** [VN] **~ sth (into sth)** to replace the original speech in a film/movie or television programme with words in another language: *an American movie dubbed into Italian*—compare SUBTITLE **3** [VN] (*especially BrE*) to make a piece of music by mixing sounds from different recordings

■ *noun* a type of West Indian music or poetry with a strong beat

du·bi·ous /'dju:biəs; *AmE* 'du:-/ *adj.* **1** [not usually before noun] **~ (about sth)/(about doing sth)** (of a person) not certain and slightly suspicious about sth; not knowing whether sth is good or bad SYN DOUBTFUL: *I was rather dubious about the whole idea.* **2** (*disapproving*) probably

æ	ɑː	e	ɜː	ə	ɪ	iː	i	ɒ	ɔː	ʌ	ʊ	u	uː
cat	father	ten	bird	about	sit	see	many	got	saw	cup	put	actual	too
								(BrE)					

not honest: *They indulged in some highly dubious business practices to obtain their current position in the market.* **3** that you cannot be sure about; that is probably not
good: *They consider the plan to be of dubious benefit to
most families.* ◊ *(ironic) She had the dubious honour of
being the last woman to be hanged in England* (= it was
not an honour at all). ▶ **du·bi·ous·ly** *adv.*

ducal /ˈdjuːkl; *AmE* ˈduːkl/ *adj.* [only before noun] of or
belonging to a DUKE: *the ducal palace in Rouen*

duch·ess /ˈdʌtʃəs/ *noun* **1** the wife of a DUKE **2** the Duchess *of York* **2** a woman who has the rank of a DUKE

duchy /ˈdʌtʃi/ (also **duke·dom**) *noun* an area of land that
is owned and controlled by a DUKE or DUCHESS: *the Duchy
of Cornwall*

duck /dʌk/ *noun, verb*
■ *noun* **1** (*pl.* **ducks** or **duck**)
[C] a common bird that
lives on or near water,
with short legs, WEBBED
feet (= feet with thin pieces
of skin between the toes)
and a wide beak. There are
many types of duck, some
of which are kept for their
meat or eggs: *wild ducks* ◊
duck eggs ◊ *Every afternoon
they went to the park to feed*

He ducked.

the ducks.—picture on page A6 **2** [C] a female duck—
compare DRAKE **3** [U] meat from a duck: *roast duck with
orange sauce* **4** (also **duckie, ducks, ducky**) [C, usually
sing.] (*BrE, informal*) a friendly way of addressing sb:
Anything else, duck?—compare DEAR, LOVE **5** (**a duck**)
[sing.] (in cricket) a BATSMAN's score of zero: *He was out
for a duck.*—see also LAME DUCK, SITTING DUCK **IDM** (**take
to sth) like a ˌduck to ˈwater** (to become used to sth)
very easily, without any problems or fears: *She has taken
to teaching like a duck to water.*—more at DEAD *adj.*,
WATER *n.*
■ *verb* **1** ~ (**down**)| ~ (**behind/under sth**) to move your
head or body downwards to avoid being hit or seen: [V]
He had to duck as he came through the door. ◊ *We ducked
down behind the wall so they wouldn't see us.* ◊ *He just
managed to* **duck out of sight.** ◊ [VN] *She ducked her head
and got into the car.* **2** [VN] to avoid sth by moving your
head or body out of the way **SYN** DODGE: *He ducked the
first few blows then started to fight back.* **3** [V+*adv.*/*prep.*]
to move somewhere quickly, especially in order to avoid
being seen: *She ducked into the adjoining room as we
came in.* **4** ~ (**out of**) **sth** to avoid a difficult or unpleasant
duty or responsibility: [V] *It's his turn to cook dinner, but
I bet he'll try to duck out of it.* ◊ [VN] *The government is
ducking the issue.* **5** (*AmE* also **dunk**) [VN] to push sb
underwater and hold them there for a short time: *The
kids were ducking each other in the pool.*

ˌduck-billed ˈplatypus *noun* = PLATYPUS

duck·boards /ˈdʌkbɔːdz; *AmE* -bɔːrdz/ *noun* [pl.] long
narrow wooden boards used to make a path over wet
ground

duck·ling /ˈdʌklɪŋ/ *noun* [C, U] a young duck; the meat
of a young duck—see also UGLY DUCKLING

duck·weed /ˈdʌkwiːd/ *noun* [U] a very small plant that
grows on the surface of still water

duct /dʌkt/ *noun* **1** a pipe or tube carrying liquid, gas,
electric or telephone wires, etc: *a heating/ventilation
duct* **2** a tube in the body or in plants through which
liquid passes: *the bile duct*

duc·tile /ˈdʌktaɪl/ *adj.* (*technical*) (of a metal) that can be
made into a thin wire

duct·ing /ˈdʌktɪŋ/ *noun* [U] **1** a system of ducts **2** material in the form of a duct or ducts: *a short piece of ducting*

dud /dʌd/ *noun, adj.*
■ *noun* **1** [C] (*informal*) a thing that is useless, especially
because it does not work correctly: *Two of the fireworks
in the box were duds.* **2** (**duds**) [pl.] (*slang*) clothes
■ *adj.* [only before noun] useless; that does not work correctly: *a dud battery* ◊ *a dud cheque* (= written by sb who
has not enough money in their bank account)

dude /duːd; djuːd/ *noun* (*slang, especially AmE*) a man:
He's a real cool dude. ◊ *Hey, dude, what's up?*

ˈdude ranch *noun* an American RANCH (= a large farm)
where people can go on holiday/vacation and do the sort
of activities that COWBOYS do

dudgeon /ˈdʌdʒən/ *noun* **IDM** see HIGH *adj.*

due /djuː; *AmE* duː/ *adj., noun, adv.*
■ *adj.*
CAUSED BY | **1** [not before noun] ~ **to sth/sb** caused by
sb/sth; because of sb/sth: *The team's success was largely
due to her efforts.* ◊ *Most of the problems were due to
human error.* ◊ *The project had to be abandoned due to a
lack of government funding.* **HELP** Some people think that
it is more correct to use **owing** to to mean 'because of'
after a verb or at the beginning of a clause, as **due** is an
adjective.
EXPECTED | **2** [not before noun] ~ (**to do sth**)| ~ (**for sth**)
arranged or expected: *When's the baby due?* ◊ *Rose is due
to start school in January.* ◊ *The band's first album is due
for release later this month.* ◊ *The next train is due in five
minutes.* ◊ (*especially AmE*) *My essay's due next Friday* (=
it has to be given to the teacher by then).
OWED | **3** [not usually before noun] when a sum of money
is **due**, it must be paid immediately: *Payment is due on 1
October.* **4** [not before noun] ~ (**to sb**) owed to sb as a
debt, because it is their right or because they have done
sth to deserve it: *Have they been paid the money that is
due to them?* ◊ *Our thanks are due to the whole team.*
5 [not before noun] ~ (**for**) **sth** owed sth; deserving sth:
I'm still due 15 day's leave. ◊ *She's due for promotion soon.*
SUITABLE/RIGHT | **6** [only before noun] (*formal*) that is suit-
able or right in the circumstances: *After due consideration, we have decided to appoint Mr. Davis to the job.* ◊ *to
make due allowance for sth* ◊ (*BrE*) *He was charged with
driving without* **due care and attention.**—compare
UNDUE
IDM **in ˌdue ˈcourse** at the right time and not before:
Your request will be dealt with in due course. **with (all)
due reˈspect** used when you are going to disagree, usually quite strongly, with sb: *With all due respect, the
figures simply do not support you on this.*
■ *noun* **1** (**your/sb's ~**) [U] a thing that should be given to
sb by right: *He received a large reward, which was no
more than his due* (= than what he deserved). ◊ *She's a
slow worker, but to give her her due* (= to be fair to her),
she does try very hard. **2** (**dues**) [pl.] charges, for example
to be a member of a club: *to pay your dues*
■ *adv.* ~ **north/south/east/west** exactly; in a straight line:
to sail due east ◊ *The village lies five miles due north of
York.*

ˌdue ˈdate *noun* [usually sing.] the date on or by which
sth, especially a sum of money, is owed or expected

duel /ˈdjuːəl; *AmE* ˈduːəl/ *noun* **1** a formal fight with
weapons between two people, used in the past to settle a
quarrel, especially over a matter of honour: *to fight/win
a duel* ◊ *to challenge sb to a duel* **2** a competition or
struggle between two people or groups: *a verbal duel*
▶ **duel** *verb* (**-ll-,** *AmE* **-l-**): [V] *The two men duelled to the
death.*

du·el·ling /ˈdjuːəlɪŋ/ (*BrE*) (*AmE* **du·el·ing** /ˈduːəlɪŋ/)
noun [U] the practice of fighting duels

duet /djuˈet; *AmE* duˈet/ (also *less frequent* **duo**) *noun* a
piece of music for two players or singers: *a piano duet*—
compare SOLO, TRIO

duff /dʌf/ *adj., noun, verb*
■ *adj.* (*BrE, informal*) useless; that does not work as it
should: *He sold me a duff radio.*
■ *noun* (*AmE, informal*) a person's bottom
■ *verb* **PHRV** **ˌduff sb↔ˈup** (*BrE, informal*) to hit or kick sb
severely **SYN** BEAT UP

duf·fel bag (also **duf·fle bag**) /ˈdʌfl bæg/ *noun* **1** (*BrE*) a
bag made out of fabric, shaped like a tube and closed by a
string around the top. It is usually carried over the
shoulder. **2** (*AmE*) a similar bag, but closed with a ZIP
along the top and carried in your hand—compare HOLD-
ALL—picture at BAG

duf·fel coat (also **duf·fle coat**) /ˈdʌfl kəʊt; *AmE* koʊt/

aɪ	aʊ	eɪ	əʊ	oʊ	ɔɪ	ɪə	eə	ʊə	j	w
my	now	say	go (BrE)	go (AmE)	boy	near	hair	pure	yes	wet

noun a coat made of heavy woollen fabric, that usually has a HOOD and is fastened with TOGGLES

duf·fer /ˈdʌfə(r)/ *noun* (*old-fashioned*, *BrE*, *informal*) a person who is stupid or unable to do anything well: *I was a bit of a duffer at school.*

dug *pt, pp* of DIG

dug·out /ˈdʌɡaʊt/ *noun* **1** a rough shelter, made by digging a hole in the ground and covering it, used by soldiers **2** a shelter by the side of a football or baseball field where a team's manager, etc. can sit and watch the game **3** (also **ˌdugout caˈnoe**) a CANOE (= a type of light narrow boat) made by cutting out the inside of a tree TRUNK

DUI /ˌdiː juː ˈaɪ/ *abbr.* (*AmE*) = DRIVING UNDER THE INFLUENCE

duke /djuːk; *AmE* duːk/ *noun* **1** a NOBLEMAN of the highest rank: *the Duke of Edinburgh* **2** (in some parts of Europe, especially in the past) a male ruler of a small independent state—see also ARCHDUKE, DUCHESS, DUCHY, GRAND DUKE

duke·dom /ˈdjuːkdəm; *AmE* ˈduːk-/ *noun* **1** the rank or position of a duke **2** = DUCHY

dul·cet /ˈdʌlsɪt/ *adj.* [only before noun] (*humorous* or *ironic*) sounding sweet and pleasant: *I thought I recognized your dulcet tones* (= the sound of your voice)

dul·ci·mer /ˈdʌlsɪmə(r)/ *noun* **1** a musical instrument that you play by hitting the metal strings with two hammers **2** a musical instrument with strings, popular in American traditional music, that you lay on your knee and play with your fingers

dull /dʌl/ *adj., verb*
- *adj.* (**dull·er, dull·est**)
  BORING | **1** not interesting or exciting: *Life in a small town could be deadly dull.* ◊ *The countryside was flat, dull and uninteresting.* ◊ *The first half of the game was pretty dull.* ◊ *There's never a dull moment when John's around.*
  LIGHT/COLOURS | **2** not bright or shiny: *a dull colour/glow* ◊ *dull, lifeless hair* ◊ *Her eyes were dull with dark shadows beneath them.*
  SOUNDS | **3** not clear or loud: *The gates shut behind him with a dull thud.*
  WEATHER | **4** not bright, with a lot of clouds: *It was a dull, grey day.*
  PAIN | **5** not very severe, but continuous: *a dull ache/pain*
  PERSON | **6** slow in understanding [SYN] STUPID: *a dull pupil/class/mind*
  TRADE | **7** (*especially AmE*) not busy; slow: *Don't sell into a dull market.*
  ▶ **dull·ness** *noun* [U] **dully** /ˈdʌli/ *adv.*: *'I suppose so,' she said dully.* ◊ *His leg ached dully.*
  [IDM] **(as) dull as ˈditchwater** (*BrE*) (*AmE* **(as) dull as ˈdishwater**) extremely boring
- *verb*
  PAIN | **1** (of pain or an emotion) to become or be made weaker or less severe: [VN] *The tablets they gave him dulled the pain for a while.* [also V]
  PERSON | **2** [VN] (*written*) to make a person slower or less lively: *He felt dulled and stupid with sleep.*
  COLOURS, SOUNDS | **3** to become or to make sth less bright, clean or sharp: [V] *His eyes dulled and he slumped to the ground.* ◊ [VN] *The endless rain seemed to dull all sound.*

dull·ard /ˈdʌlɑːd; *AmE* -lɑːrd/ *noun* (*old-fashioned*) a stupid person with no imagination

duly /ˈdjuːli; *AmE* ˈduːli/ *adv.* **1** (*formal*) in the correct or expected manner: *The document was duly signed and authorized by the inspector.* **2** at the expected and correct time: *They duly arrived at 9.30 in spite of torrential rain.*—compare UNDULY

dumb /dʌm/ *adj., verb*
- *adj.* (**dumb·er, dumb·est**) **1** (*old-fashioned*, sometimes *offensive*) unable to speak: *She was born deaf and dumb.* [HELP] **Dumb** used in this meaning is old-fashioned and can be offensive. It is better to use **speech-impaired** instead. **2** temporarily not speaking or refusing to speak: *We were all struck dumb with amazement.* ◊ *We all sat there in dumb silence.* **3** (*informal, especially AmE*) stupid: *That was a pretty dumb thing to do.* ◊ *If the police question*

you, act dumb (= pretend you do not know anything). ◊ *In all her early movies she always played a dumb blonde.* ▶ **dumb·ly** *adv.*: *'Are you all right?' Laura nodded dumbly.* **dumb·ness** *noun* [U]
- *verb* [PHRV] **ˌdumb ˈdown|** **ˌdumb sth↔ˈdown** (*disapproving*) to make sth less accurate or EDUCATIONAL, and of worse quality, by trying to make it easier for people to understand: *The BBC denies that its broadcasting has been dumbed down.* ▶ **ˌdumbing ˈdown** *noun* [U]

ˌdumb ˈanimal *noun* [usually pl.] (*BrE*) an animal, especially when seen as deserving pity

ˈdumb-bell *noun* **1** a short bar with a weight at each end, used for strengthening the arm and shoulder muscles **2** (*AmE, informal*) a stupid person

dumb·found·ed /dʌmˈfaʊndɪd/ (also *less frequent* **dumb·struck** /ˈdʌmstrʌk/) *adj.* unable to speak because of surprise: *She was completely dumbfounded by the news.*

dumbo /ˈdʌmbəʊ; *AmE* -boʊ/ *noun* (*pl.* **-oes**) (*informal*) a stupid person

ˌdumb ˈwaiter *noun* a small lift/elevator for carrying food and plates from one floor to another in a restaurant

dum·dum /ˈdʌmdʌm/ (also **ˌdumdum ˈbullet**) *noun* a bullet that spreads out and breaks into many pieces when it hits sb, causing serious injuries

dummy /ˈdʌmi/ *noun, adj.*
- *noun* (*pl.* **-ies**) **1** [C] a model of a person, used especially when making clothes or for showing them in a shop window: *a tailor's dummy* **2** [C] a thing that seems to be real but is only a copy of the real thing **3** [C] (*AmE, informal*) a stupid person: *Don't just stand there you dummy.* **4** [C] (in some sports, such as football) an occasion when you pretend to pass the ball to another player and then do not do so **5** [C] (*BrE*) (*AmE* **paci·fier**) a specially shaped rubber or plastic object for a baby to suck **6** [U] (in card games, especially BRIDGE) the cards which are placed facing upwards on the table and which can be seen by all the players
- *adj.* [only before noun] made to look real, although it is actually a copy which does not work: *a dummy bomb/rifle*

ˌdummy ˈrun *noun* (*BrE*) a practice attack, performance, etc. before the real one

dump /dʌmp/ *verb, noun*
- *verb* [VN]
  GET RID OF | **1** to get rid of sth you do not want, especially in a place which is not suitable: *Too much toxic waste is being dumped at sea.* ◊ *The dead body was just dumped by the roadside.* **2 ~ sth (on sb)** (*informal*) to get rid of sb/sth or leave them for sb else to deal with: *He's got no right to keep dumping his problems on me.* **3** (*business*) to get rid of goods by selling them at a very low price, often in another country
  PUT DOWN | **4** to put sth down in a careless or untidy way: *Just dump your stuff over there—we'll sort it out later.*
  END RELATIONSHIP | **5** (*informal*) to end a romantic relationship with sb: *Did you hear he's dumped his girlfriend?*
  COMPUTING | **6** to copy information and move it somewhere to store it
  [IDM] see LAP *n.*
  [PHRV] **ˈdump on sb** (*AmE*) to criticize sb severely or treat them badly
- *noun*—see also DUMPS
  FOR WASTE | **1** a place where waste or rubbish/garbage is taken and left: *the municipal dump* ◊ *a toxic/nuclear waste dump*
  DIRTY PLACE | **2** (*informal, disapproving*) a dirty or unpleasant place: *How can you live in this dump?*

D

FOR WEAPONS | **3** a temporary store for military supplies: *an ammunition dump*

COMPUTING | **4** an act of copying data stored in a computer; a copy or list of the contents of this data: *a screen dump* (= a copy of what is on a computer screen)

WASTE FROM BODY | **5** [C] (*slang*) an act of passing waste matter from the body through the bowels: *to have a dump*

dump·er /'dʌmpə(r)/ *noun* (*especially AmE*) a person who throws away dangerous or harmful things, especially in the wrong place

'dumper truck (*BrE*) (*AmE* **'dump truck**) *noun* a vehicle for carrying earth, stones, etc. in a container which can be lifted up for the load to fall out—picture at TRUCK

dump·ing /'dʌmpɪŋ/ *noun* [U] the act or practice of DUMPING sth, especially dangerous substances: *a ban on the dumping of radioactive waste at sea*

'dumping ground *noun* [usually sing.] a place where sth that is not wanted is DUMPED

dump·ling /'dʌmplɪŋ/ *noun* **1** a small ball of DOUGH (= a mixture of flour, fat and water) that is cooked and served with meat dishes: *chicken with herb dumplings* **2** a small ball of pastry often with fruit in it, eaten as a DESSERT: *apple dumplings*

dumps /dʌmps/ *noun* [pl.] **IDM** **down in the 'dumps** (*informal*) feeling unhappy **SYN** DEPRESSED

Dump·ster™ /'dʌmpstə(r)/ *noun* (*AmE*) = SKIP

'dump truck *noun* (*AmE*) = DUMPER TRUCK

dumpy /'dʌmpi/ *adj.* (especially of a person) short and fat

dun /dʌn/ *adj.* greyish-brown in colour ▶ **dun** *noun* [U]

dunce /dʌns/ *noun* (*old-fashioned*) a person, especially a child at school, who is stupid or slow to learn

dune /dju:n; *AmE* du:n/ (also **'sand dune**) *noun* a small hill of sand formed by the wind, near the sea or in a desert

'dune buggy *noun* = BEACH BUGGY

dung /dʌŋ/ *noun* [U] solid waste from animals, especially from large ones: *cow dung*

dun·garees /ˌdʌŋgə'ri:z/ *noun* [pl.] **1** (*BrE*) (*AmE* **overalls**, **'bib overalls**) a piece of clothing that consists of trousers/pants with an extra piece of fabric covering the chest, held up by straps over the shoulders: *a pair of dungarees* ◊ *His dungarees were covered in grease.* **2** (*AmE*) heavy cotton trousers/pants for working in

dun·geon /'dʌndʒən/ *noun* a dark underground room used as a prison, especially in a castle: *Throw him into the dungeons!*

dunk /dʌŋk/ *verb* **1** [VN] ~ **sth (in/into sth)** to put food quickly into liquid before eating it: *She sat reading a magazine, dunking cookies in her coffee.* **2** [VN] (*especially AmE*) to push sb underwater for a short time, as a joke; to put sth into water: *The camera survived being dunked in the river.* **3** [V, VN] (in basketball) to jump very high and put the ball through the basket with great force from above—picture on page 1250

dunno /də'nəʊ; *AmE* də'noʊ/ (*non-standard*) a way of writing the informal spoken form of 'I don't know'

duo /'dju:əʊ; *AmE* 'du:oʊ/ *noun* (*pl.* **-os**) **1** two people who perform together or are often seen or thought of together: *the comedy duo Laurel and Hardy*—compare TRIO **2** = DUET

duo·de·num /ˌdju:ə'di:nəm; *AmE* ˌdu:ə-/ *noun* (*pl.* **duo·de·nums** or **duo·dena** /-'di:nə/) (*anatomy*) the first part of the small INTESTINE, next to the stomach—picture at BODY ▶ **duo·denal** /ˌdju:ə'di:nl; *AmE* ˌdu:ə-/ *adj.*: *a duodenal ulcer*

du·op·oly /dju:'ɒpəli; *AmE* du:'ɑ:-/ *noun* (*pl.* **-ies**) (*business*) **1** a right to trade in a particular product or service, held by only two companies or organizations **2** a group of two companies or organizations who hold a duopoly—compare MONOPOLY

dupe /dju:p; *AmE* du:p/ *verb, noun*
■ *verb* [VN] ~ **sb (into doing sth)** to trick or cheat sb: *They soon realized they had been duped.* ◊ *He was duped into giving them his credit card.*

■ *noun* (*formal*) a person who is tricked or cheated

du·plex /'dju:pleks; *AmE* 'du:-/ *noun* (*especially AmE*) **1** a building divided into two separate homes **2** a flat/apartment with rooms on two floors

du·pli·cate *verb, adj., noun*
■ *verb* /'dju:plɪkeɪt; *AmE* 'du:-/ [VN] **1** [often passive] to make an exact copy of sth: *a duplicated form/letter* **2** to do sth again, especially when it is unnecessary: *There's no point in duplicating work already done.* ▶ **du·pli·ca·tion** /ˌdju:plɪ'keɪʃn; *AmE* ˌdu:-/ *noun* [U, C]
■ *adj.* /'dju:plɪkət; *AmE* 'du:-/ [only before noun] exactly like sth else; made as a copy of sth else: *a duplicate invoice*
■ *noun* /'dju:plɪkət; *AmE* 'du:-/ one of two or more things that are the same in every detail **SYN** COPY: *Is this a duplicate or the original?* **IDM** **in duplicate** (of documents, etc.) as two copies that are exactly the same in every detail: *to prepare a contract in duplicate* —compare TRIPLICATE

du·pli·city /dju:'plɪsəti; *AmE* du:-/ *noun* [U] (*formal*) dishonest behaviour that is intended to make sb believe sth which is not true ▶ **du·pli·ci·tous** /dju:'plɪsɪtəs; *AmE* du:-/ *adj.*

dur·able /'djʊərəbl; *AmE* 'dʊr-/ *adj.* likely to last for a long time without breaking or getting weaker: *durable plastics* ◊ *negotiations for a durable peace* ▶ **dur·abil·ity** /ˌdjʊərə'bɪləti; *AmE* ˌdʊr-/ *noun* [U]: *the durability of gold*—see also CONSUMER DURABLES

ˌdurable 'goods *noun* [pl.] (*AmE*) = CONSUMER DURABLES

dur·ation /dju'reɪʃn; *AmE* du-/ *noun* [U] (*formal*) the length of time that sth lasts or continues: *The school was used as a hospital for the duration of the war.* ◊ *a contract of three years' duration* **IDM** **for the duration** (*informal*) until the end of a particular situation

dur·ess /dju'res; *AmE* du-/ *noun* [U] (*formal*) threats or force that are used to make sb do sth: *He signed the confession under duress.*

Durex™ /'djʊəreks; *AmE* 'dʊr-/ *noun* (*pl.* **Durex**) (*BrE*) a CONDOM

durian /'dʊəriən; *AmE* 'dʊr-/ *noun* a large tropical fruit with a strong unpleasant smell but a sweet flavour

dur·ing /'djʊərɪŋ; *AmE* 'dʊr-/ *prep.* **1** all through a period of time: *during the 1990s* ◊ *There are extra flights to Colorado during the winter.* ◊ *Please remain seated during the performance.* **2** at some point in a period of time: *He was taken to the hospital during the night.* ◊ *I only saw her once during my stay in Rome.* **HELP** **During** is used to say when something happens; **for** answers the question 'how long?': *I stayed in London for a week.* ◊ *I stayed in London during a week.*

dusk /dʌsk/ *noun* [U] the time of day when the light has almost gone, but it is not yet dark: *The street lights go on at dusk.*—compare DAWN

dusky /'dʌski/ *adj.* (*literary*) not very bright; dark or soft in colour: *the dusky light inside the cave* ◊ *dusky pink*

dust /dʌst/ *noun, verb*
■ *noun* **1** [U] a fine powder that consists of very small pieces of sand, earth, etc: *A cloud of dust rose as the truck drove off.* ◊ *The workers wear masks to avoid inhaling the dust.* **2** the fine powder of dirt that forms in buildings, on furniture, floors, etc: *The books were all covered with dust.* ◊ *There wasn't a speck of dust anywhere in the room.* ◊ *That guitar's been sitting gathering dust* (= not being used) *for years now.* **3** a fine powder that consists of very small pieces of a particular substance: *coal/gold dust*—see also DUSTY **IDM** **leave sb in the 'dust** (*AmE*) to leave sb far behind **let the dust settle** | **wait for the dust to settle** to wait for a situation to become clear or certain—more at BITE *v.*
■ *verb* **1** to clean furniture, a room, etc. by removing dust from surfaces with a cloth: [V] *I broke the vase while I was dusting.* ◊ [VN] *Could you dust the sitting room?* **2** [VN] [usually +*adv./prep.*] to remove dirt from sb/sth/yourself with your hands or a brush: *She dusted some ash from her sleeve.* **3** [VN] ~ **sth (with sth)** to cover sth with fine powder: *Dust the cake with sugar.* **PHRV** **ˌdust sb/sth ↔ 'down** (*especially BrE*) to remove dust, dirt, etc.

s	t	v	z	ʃ	ʒ	tʃ	dʒ	θ	ð	ŋ
see	tea	van	zoo	shoe	vision	chain	jam	thin	this	sing

from sb/sth: *Mel stood up and dusted herself down.* ,**dust sb/sth**↔'**off** to remove dust, dirt, etc. from sb/sth: *(figurative) For the concert, he dusted off some of his old hits.*

dust·bin /'dʌstbɪn/ (*BrE*) (*AmE* '**garbage can**, '**trash can**) *noun* a large container with a lid, used for putting rubbish/garbage in, usually kept outside the house ⇨ note at RUBBISH

'**dust bowl** *noun* an area of land that has been turned into desert by lack of rain or too much farming

dust·cart /'dʌstkɑːt; *AmE* -kɑːrt/ (*BrE*) (*AmE* '**garbage truck**) *noun* a vehicle for collecting rubbish/garbage from outside houses, etc.

'**dust cover** *noun* **1** = DUST JACKET **2** a hard or soft plastic cover on a piece of equipment, etc. that protects it when it is not being used—picture at COVER

dust·er /'dʌstə(r)/ *noun* **1** a cloth for removing dust from furniture **2** (*old-fashioned, AmE*) a piece of clothing that you wear over your other clothes when you are cleaning the house, etc.

'**dust jacket** (also '**dust cover**) *noun* a paper cover on a book that protects it but that can be removed

dust·man /'dʌstmən/ *noun* (*pl.* -**men** /-mən/) (also *informal* **bin·man**, *formal* '**refuse collector**) (all *BrE*) (*AmE* '**garbage man**) a person whose job is to remove waste from outside houses, etc. ⇨ note at RUBBISH

dust·pan /'dʌstpæn/ *noun* a small flat container with a handle into which dust is brushed from the floor

'**dust sheet** *noun* a large cloth that is used to protect furniture from dust or paint

'**dust storm** *noun* a storm that carries clouds of dust in the wind over a wide area

'**dust-up** *noun* (*BrE, slang*) a quarrel or fight

dusty /'dʌsti/ *adj.* (**dust·ier**, **dusti·est**) **1** full of dust; covered with dust: *a dusty road* ◊ *piles of dusty books* **2** (of a colour) not bright; dull: *dusty pink*

Dutch /dʌtʃ/ *adj.* of or connected with the Netherlands, its people or its language **IDM** **go Dutch (with sb)** to share the cost of sth with sb

,**Dutch** '**barn** *noun* (*BrE*) a farm building without walls that has a roof supported on poles, used for storing HAY (= dried grass), etc.

,**Dutch** '**courage** *noun* [U] (*BrE, informal*) the false courage or confidence that a person gets from drinking alcohol

duti·ful /'djuːtɪfl; *AmE* 'duː-/ *adj.* doing everything that you are expected to do; willing to obey and to show respect: *a dutiful daughter/son/wife* ▶ **duti·ful·ly** /-fəli/ *adv.*

duty /'djuːti; *AmE* 'duːti/ *noun* (*pl.* -**ies**) **1** [C, U] something that you feel you have to do because it is your moral or legal responsibility: *It is my duty to report it to the police.* ◊ *Local councillors have a duty to serve the community.* ◊ *I don't want you to visit me simply out of a sense of duty.* ◊ *your duties as a parent* ◊ *to do your duty for your country* **2** [U] the work that is your job: *Report for duty at 8 a.m.*—see also NIGHT DUTY **3** (**duties**) [pl.] tasks that are part of your job: *I spend a lot of my time on administrative duties.* ◊ *Your duties will include setting up a new computer system.*—see also HEAVY-DUTY **4** [C, U] ~ (**on sth**) a tax that you pay on things that you buy especially those that you bring into a country: *customs/excise/import duties* ◊ *duty on wine and beer*—see also DEATH DUTY, STAMP DUTY **IDM** **on/off duty** (of nurses, police officers, etc.) working/not working at a particular time: *Who's on duty today?* ◊ *What time do you go off duty?*—see also OFF-DUTY—more at BOUNDEN, LINE *n.*

,**duty-'bound** *adj.* [not before noun] (*formal*) having to do sth because it is your duty: *I felt duty-bound to help him.*

,**duty-'free** *adj.* (of goods) that you can bring into a country without paying tax on them: *duty-free cigarettes/alcohol/shopping* ▶ ,**duty-'free** *adv.* ,**duty-'free** *noun* (*BrE, informal*): *We bought a load of duty-frees* (= duty-free goods) *at the airport.*

,**duty-'free shop** (also ,**duty-'free**) *noun* a shop/store in an airport or on a ship, etc. that sells goods such as cigarettes, alcohol, PERFUME, etc. without tax on them

duvet /'duːveɪ/ (also ,**continental** '**quilt**, **quilt**) *noun* (all *BrE*) a large fabric bag that is filled with feathers or other soft material and used as a cover on a bed: *a duvet cover*—picture at BED

DVD /ˌdiː viː 'diː/ *noun* a disk on which large amounts of information, especially photographs and video, can be stored, for use on a computer (an abbreviation for 'digital videodisc' or 'digital versatile disk'): *a DVD-ROM drive*—picture on page 250

dwarf /dwɔːf; *AmE* dwɔːrf/ *noun, adj., verb*
■ *noun* (*pl.* **dwarfs** or **dwarves** /dwɔːvz; *AmE* dwɔːrvz/) **1** (in stories) a creature like a small man, who has magic powers and who is usually described as living and working under the ground, especially working with metal **2** (sometimes *offensive*) an extremely small person, who will never grow to a normal size because of a physical problem; a person suffering from DWARFISM **HELP** There is no other word that is generally considered more acceptable.
■ *adj.* [only before noun] (of a plant or an animal) much smaller than the normal size: *dwarf conifers*
■ *verb* [VN] to make sth seem small or unimportant compared with sth else: *The old houses were dwarfed by the huge new tower blocks.*

dwarf·ism /'dwɔːfɪzəm; *AmE* 'dwɔːrf-/ *noun* the medical condition of being a dwarf. People who suffer from this condition are very short and often have short arms and legs.

dweeb /dwiːb/ *noun* (*AmE, slang, disapproving*) a person, especially a boy or a man, who does not have good social skills and is not fashionable

dwell /dwel/ *verb* (**dwelt, dwelt** or **dwelled, dwelled**) [V+*adv./prep.*] (*formal* or *literary*) to live somewhere: *He dwelt in a ruined cottage on the hillside.* ◊ *For ten years she dwelled among the nomads of North America.* **PHR V** '**dwell on/upon sth 1** to think or talk a lot about sth, especially sth it would be better to forget: *So you made a mistake, but there's no need to dwell on it.* **2** (*written*) to look at sth for a long time

dwell·er /'dwelə(r)/ *noun* (especially in compounds) a person or an animal that lives in the particular place that is mentioned: *apartment dwellers*

dwell·ing /'dwelɪŋ/ *noun* (*formal*) a house, flat/apartment, etc. where a person lives: *The development will consist of 66 dwellings and a number of offices.*

'**dwelling house** *noun* (*BrE, law*) a house that people live in, not one that is used as an office, etc.

'**dwelling place** *noun* (*old-fashioned*) the place where sb lives

DWI /ˌdiː dʌblju: 'aɪ/ *abbr.* (*AmE*) = DRIVING WHILE INTOXICATED

dwin·dle /'dwɪndl/ *verb* [V] ~ (**away**) (**to sth**) to become gradually less or smaller: *dwindling audiences/numbers/popularity* ◊ *Support for the party has dwindled away to nothing.* ◊ *Membership of the club has dwindled from 70 to 20.*

dye /daɪ/ *verb, noun*
■ *verb* (**dyes, dye·ing, dyed, dyed**) to change the colour of sth, especially by using a special liquid or substance: [VN] *to dye wool/fabric/clothes* ◊ [VN-ADJ] *She dyed her hair blonde.*—see also TIE-DYE
■ *noun* [C, U] a substance that is used to change the colour of things such as cloth or hair: *black dye* ◊ *hair dye* ◊ *natural/chemical/vegetable dyes*

,**dyed in the 'wool** *adj.* [usually before noun] (usually *disapproving*) having strong beliefs or opinions that are never going to change: *dyed in the wool traditionalists* **ORIGIN** From the idea that dye produced a more even and lasting colour if the wool was dyed in its raw state.

dying /'daɪɪŋ/ *adj.* **1** [only before noun] connected with or happening at the time of sb's death: *I will remember it to my dying day.* ◊ *her dying wishes/words* **2** (**the dying**) *noun* [pl.] people who are dying: *doctors who care for the dying* **IDM** see BREATH—see also DIE *v.*

dyke (also **dike**) /daɪk/ *noun* **1** a long thick wall that is built to stop water flooding onto a low area of land, especially from the sea **2** (*especially BrE*) a channel that carries water away from the land **3** (△, *slang*) (usually *offensive*) = LESBIAN

dy·nam·ic /daɪˈnæmɪk/ *noun, adj.*

■ *noun* **1** (**dynamics**) [pl.] the way in which people or things behave and react to each other in a particular situation: *the dynamics of political change* ◊ *group dynamics* (= the way in which members of a group react to each other) **2** (**dynamics**) [U] the science of the forces involved in movement: *fluid dynamics*—compare STATICS **3** [sing.] (*formal*) a force that produces change, action or effects **4** (**dynamics**) [pl.] (*music*) changes in volume in music

■ *adj.* **1** (*approving*) (of a person) forceful, and having a lot of energy: *a dynamic personality* **2** (of a process) always changing and making progress OPP STATIC **3** (*physics*) (of a force or power) producing movement OPP STATIC

dyna·mism /ˈdaɪnəmɪzəm/ *noun* [U] energy and enthusiasm to make new things happen or to make things succeed

dyna·mite /ˈdaɪnəmaɪt/ *noun, verb*

■ *noun* [U] **1** a powerful explosive: *a stick of dynamite* **2** a thing that is likely to cause a violent reaction or a lot of trouble: *The abortion issue is political dynamite.* **3** (*informal, approving*) an extremely impressive or exciting person or thing: *Their new album is dynamite.*

■ *verb* [VN] to destroy or damage sth using dynamite

dy·namo /ˈdaɪnəməʊ; *AmE* -moʊ/ *noun* (*pl.* **-os**) **1** a device for turning MECHANICAL energy (= energy from

movement) into electricity; a GENERATOR **2** (*informal*) a person with a lot of energy: *the team's midfield dynamo* ◊ *She's a human dynamo.*

dyn·asty /ˈdɪnəsti; *AmE* ˈdaɪ-/ *noun* (*pl.* **-ies**) **1** a series of rulers of a country who all belong to the same family: *the Nehru-Gandhi dynasty* **2** a period of years during which members of a particular family rule a country ▶ **dyn·as·tic** /dɪˈnæstɪk; *AmE* daɪ-/ *adj.* [usually before noun]: *dynastic history*

dys·en·tery /ˈdɪsəntri; *AmE* -teri/ *noun* [U] an infection of the bowels that causes severe DIARRHOEA with loss of blood

dys·func·tion·al /dɪsˈfʌŋkʃənl/ *adj.* (*technical*) not working in a satisfactory or successful way: *children from dysfunctional families*

dys·lexia /dɪsˈleksiə/ *noun* [U] a slight disorder of the brain that causes difficulty in reading and spelling, for example, but does not affect intelligence ▶ **dys·lex·ic** /dɪsˈleksɪk/ *adj.*: *He's dyslexic.* **dys·lex·ic** *noun*: *Writing courses for dyslexics.*

dys·pep·sia /dɪsˈpepsiə; *AmE* dɪsˈpepʃə/ *noun* [U] (*medical*) pain caused by difficulty in DIGESTING food SYN INDIGESTION

dys·pep·tic /dɪsˈpeptɪk/ *adj.* **1** (*medical*) connected with or suffering from dyspepsia **2** (*formal, rare*) bad-tempered

dys·trophy ⇨ MUSCULAR DYSTROPHY

Ee

E /iː/ *noun, abbr.*
- *noun* (also **e**) [C, U] (*pl.* **E's, e's** /iːz/) **1** the fifth letter in the English alphabet: *'Egg' begins with (an) E/'E'.* **2** (E) (*music*) the third note in the scale of C MAJOR **3** (E) the fifth highest mark/grade that a student can get for a piece of work, showing that it is very bad: *He got an E in/for French.*—see also E-NUMBER
- *abbr.* **1** East; Eastern: *E Asia* **2** (*slang*) the drug ECSTASY

e- /iː/ *combining form* (in nouns and verbs) connected with the use of electronic communication, especially the Internet, for sending information, doing business, etc: *e-commerce* ◊ *e-business*—see also E-FIT, E-MAIL

each /iːtʃ/ *det., pron.* used to refer to every one of two or more people or things, when you are thinking about them separately: *Each answer is worth 20 points.* ◊ *Each of the answers is worth 20 points.* ◊ *The answers are worth 20 points each.* ◊ *'Red or blue?' 'I'll take one of each, please.'* ◊ *We each have our own car.* ◊ *There aren't enough books for everyone to have one each.* ◊ *They lost $40 each.* ◊ *Each day that passed he grew more and more desperate.*

> **GRAMMAR POINT**
> **each / every**
>
> **Each** is used in front of a singular noun and is followed by a singular verb: *Each student has been given his or her own e-mail address.* The use of *his* or *her* sometimes sounds slightly formal and it is becoming more common to use the plural pronoun *their*. *Each student has been given their own e-mail address.*
> When **each** is used after a plural subject, it has a plural verb: *They each have their own e-mail address.*
> **Every** is always followed by a singular verb: *Every student in the class is capable of passing the exam.*
> **Each of, each one of** and **every one of** are followed by a plural noun or pronoun, but the verb is usually singular: *Each (one) of the houses was slightly different.* ◊ *I bought a dozen eggs and every one of them was bad.* A plural verb is more informal.

each 'other *pron.* used as the object of a verb or preposition to show that each member of a group does sth to or for the other members: *Don and Susie really loved each other* (= he loved her and she loved him). ◊ *They looked at each other and laughed.* ◊ *We can wear each other's clothes.*

,each 'way *adv.* (*BrE*) if you bet money **each way** on a race, you win if your horse, etc. comes first, second or third in the race

eager /'iːɡə(r)/ *adj.* ~ **(for sth/to do sth)** very interested and excited by sth that is going to happen or about sth that you want to do [SYN] KEEN: *eager crowds outside the stadium* ◊ *She is eager for* (= wants very much to get) *her parents' approval.* ◊ *Everyone in the class seemed eager to learn.* ◊ *They're eager to please* (= wanting to be helpful). ▶ **eager·ly** *adv.*: *the band's eagerly awaited new CD* **eager·ness** *noun* [U, sing.]: *I couldn't hide my eagerness to get back home.*

,eager 'beaver *noun* (*informal*) an enthusiastic person who works very hard

eagle /'iːɡl/ *noun* **1** a large BIRD OF PREY (= a bird that kills other creatures for food) with a sharp curved beak and very good sight: *eagles soaring overhead*—see also BALD EAGLE, GOLDEN EAGLE **2** (in golf) a score of two strokes less than the standard score for a hole (= two under PAR)—compare BIRDIE, BOGEY

,eagle 'eye *noun* [usually sing.] if sb has an **eagle eye**, they watch things carefully and are good at noticing things: *Nothing escaped our teacher's eagle eye.* ▶ **,eagle-'eyed** *adj.*: *An eagle-eyed tourist found the suspicious package.*

ear /ɪə(r); *AmE* ɪr/ *noun* **1** [C] either of the organs on the sides of the head that you hear with: *an ear infection* ◊ *the inner/outer ear* ◊ *She whispered something in his ear.* ◊ *He put his hands over his ears.* ◊ *She's had her ears pierced.* ◊ *The elephant flapped its ears.* ◊ *He was always there with a sympathetic ear* (= a willingness to listen to people).—see also CAULIFLOWER EAR, GLUE EAR, MIDDLE EAR—picture at BODY **2 (-eared)** (in adjectives) having the type of ears mentioned: *a long-eared owl* **3** [sing.] an ability to recognize and copy sounds well: *She has always had an ear for languages.* ◊ *You need a good ear to master the piano.* **4** [C] the top part of a grain plant, such as wheat, that contains the seeds: *ears of corn*—picture at CEREAL [IDM] **be all 'ears** (*informal*) to be waiting with interest to hear what sb has to say: *'Do you know what he said?' 'Go on—I'm all ears.'* **be out on your 'ear** (*informal*) to be forced to leave (a job, etc.) **be up to your ears in sth** to have a lot of sth to deal with: *We're up to our ears in work.* **sth comes to/reaches sb's 'ears** somebody hears about sth, especially when other people already know about it: *News of his affair eventually reached her ears.* **sb's 'ears are burning** a person thinks that other people are talking about them, especially in an unkind way: *'I bumped into your ex-wife last night.' 'I thought I could feel my ears burning!'* **sb's 'ears are flapping** (*BrE, informal*) a person is trying to listen to sb else's conversation **go in 'one ear and out the 'other** (*informal*) (of information, etc.) to be forgotten quickly: *Everything I tell them just goes in one ear and out the other.* **have sb's ear | have the ear of sb** to be able to give sb advice, influence them, etc. because they trust you: *He had the ear of the monarch.* **keep/have an/your ear to the 'ground** to make sure that you always find out about the most recent developments in a particular situation **play (sth) by 'ear** to play music by remembering how it sounds rather than by reading it **play it by 'ear** (*informal*) to decide how to deal with a situation as it develops rather than by having a plan to follow: *I don't know what they'll want when they arrive—we'll have to play it by ear.* **shut/close your 'ears to sth** to refuse to listen to sth: *She decided to shut her ears to all the rumours.* **smile/grin/beam from ear to 'ear** to be smiling, etc. a lot because you are very pleased about sth **with half an 'ear** without giving your full attention to what is being said, etc.—more at BELIEVE, BEND *v.*, BOX *n.*, BOX *v.*, COCK *v.*, DEAF *adj.*, EASY *adj.*, FEEL *v.*, FLEA, LEND, MUSIC, OPEN *adj.*, PIG *n.*, PRICK *v.*, RING *v.*, SILK, THICK *adj.*, WALL *n.*, WET *adj.*, WORD *n.*

ear·ache /'ɪəreɪk; *AmE* 'ɪr-/ *noun* [U, C] pain inside the ear: *to have (an) earache*

'ear drops *noun* [pl.] liquid medicine that can be put into the ears

ear·drum /'ɪədrʌm; *AmE* 'ɪr-/ *noun* the piece of thin tightly stretched skin inside the ear which is moved by sound waves, making you able to hear: *a perforated eardrum*

ear·ful /'ɪəfʊl; *AmE* 'ɪrfʊl/ *noun* [sing.] (*informal*) if sb gives you an **earful**, they tell you for a long time how angry they are about sth that you have done

earl /ɜːl; *AmE* ɜːrl/ *noun* a NOBLEMAN of high rank: *Earl Spencer* ◊ *the Earl of Northumberland*—see also COUNTESS

earli·est /'ɜːliɪst; *AmE* 'ɜːrl-/ *noun* [sing.] **(the earliest)** the time before which sth cannot happen: *The earliest we* can finish is next Friday. ◊ We can't finish before next Friday **at the earliest**.

'ear lobe (also **lobe**) *noun* the soft part at the bottom of the ear—picture at BODY

early /'ɜːli; *AmE* 'ɜːrli/ *adj., adv.*

■ *adj.* (**earl·ier, earli·est**) **1** near the beginning of a period of time, an event etc: *the early morning* ◊ *my earliest memories* ◊ *The project is still in the early stages.* ◊ *the early 1990s* ◊ *in* **the early days** *of space exploration* (= when it was just beginning) ◊ *The earliest possible date I can make it is the third.* ◊ *He's in his early twenties.* ◊ *Mozart's early works* (= those written at the beginning of his career) ◊ *Early booking is essential, as space is limited.* **2** arriving, or done before the usual, expected or planned time: *You're early! I wasn't expecting you till seven.* ◊ *The bus was ten minutes early.* ◊ *an early breakfast* ◊ *Let's* **make an early start** *tomorrow.* ◊ *She's an* **early riser** (= she gets up early in the morning) ◊ *He learnt to play the piano at an early age.* ◊ *early potatoes* (= that are ready to eat at the beginning of the season) OPP LATE ▶ **earli·ness** *noun* [U] IDM **an 'early bird** (*humorous*) a person who gets up, arrives, etc. very early **at your earliest con'venience** (*written, business*) as soon as possible: *Please telephone at your earliest convenience.* **it's early 'days (yet)** (*BrE*) used to say that it is too soon to be sure how a situation will develop: *It's early days yet. We don't know if the play will be a success.*—more at BRIGHT *adj.*, HOUR, NIGHT

■ *adv.* (**earl·ier, earli·est**) **1** near the beginning of a period of time, an event, a piece of work, etc: *early in the week/year/season/morning* ◊ *The best rooms go to those who book earliest.* ◊ *We arrived early the next day.* ◊ *He started writing music as early as 1989.* OPP LATE ⇨ note at SOON **2** before the usual, expected or planned time: *The bus came five minutes early.* ◊ *I woke up early this morning.* ◊ *The baby arrived earlier than expected.* OPP LATE **3** (**earlier**) before the present time or the time mentioned: *As I mentioned earlier ...* ◊ *a week earlier* ◊ *She had seen him earlier in the day.* OPP LATER IDM **early 'on** at an early stage of a situation, relationship, period of time, etc: *I knew quite early on that I wanted to marry her.*

early 'closing *noun* [U] (*BrE*) the practice of closing shops on a particular afternoon every week (now no longer very common)

early 'warning *noun* [U, sing.] a thing that tells you in advance that sth serious or dangerous is going to happen: *an early warning of heart disease* ◊ *an early warning system* (= of enemy attack)

ear·mark /'ɪəmɑːk; *AmE* 'ɪrmɑːrk/ *verb* [VN] [usually passive] **~ sb/sth (for/as sb/sth)** to decide that sth will be used for a particular purpose, or to state that sth will happen to sb/sth in the future: *The money had been earmarked for spending on new school buildings.* ◊ *The factory has been earmarked for closure.* ◊ *She was earmarked early as a possible champion.*

ear·muff /'ɪəmʌf; *AmE* 'ɪrmʌf/ *noun* [usually pl.] either of a pair of coverings for the ears connected by a band across the top of the head, and worn to protect the ears, especially from cold: *a pair of earmuffs*—picture at HAT

earn /ɜːn; *AmE* ɜːrn/ *verb* **1** to get money for work that you do: [VN] *He earns about £20000 a year.* ◊ *She earned a* **living** *as a part-time secretary.* ◊ *She must* **earn a fortune** (= earn a lot of money). ◊ [VNN] *His victory in the tournament earned him $50000.* ◊ [V] *All the children are earning now.* **2** [VN] to get money as profit or interest on money you lend, have in a bank, etc: *Your money would earn more in a high-interest account.* **3** to get sth that you deserve, usually because of sth good you have done or because of the good qualities you have: [VN] *He earned a reputation as an expert on tax law.* ◊ *As a teacher, she had earned the respect and admiration of her students.* ◊ *I need a rest. Think I've earned it, don't you?* ◊ *She's having a well-earned rest this week.* ◊ [VNN] *His outstanding ability earned him a place on the team.* IDM **earn a/your 'crust** (*BrE, informal*) to earn enough money to live on **earn your 'keep 1** to do useful or helpful things in return for being allowed to live or stay somewhere **2** to be worth the amount of time or money that is being spent: *He felt he no*

longer deserved such a high salary. He just wasn't earning his keep.—more at SPUR *n.*

earn·er /'ɜːnə(r); *AmE* 'ɜːrn-/ *noun* **1** a person who earns money for a job that they do: *high/low earners*—see also WAGE EARNER **2** an activity or a business that makes a profit: *Tourism is the country's biggest foreign currency earner.* ◊ (*BrE, informal*) *Her new business has turned out a* **nice little earner**.

earn·est /'ɜːnɪst; *AmE* 'ɜːrn-/ *adj.* very serious and sincere: *an earnest young man* ◊ *Despite her earnest efforts, she could not find a job.* ▶ **earn·est·ly** *adv.* **earn·est·ness** *noun* [U] IDM **in 'earnest 1** more seriously and with more force or effort than before: *The work on the house will* **begin in earnest** *on Monday.* **2** very serious and sincere about what you are saying and about your intentions; in a way that shows that you are serious: *You may laugh but I'm in* **deadly earnest**. ◊ *I could tell she spoke in earnest.*

earn·ings /'ɜːnɪŋz; *AmE* 'ɜːrn-/ *noun* [pl.] **1** the money that you earn for the work that you do: *a rise in average earnings* ◊ *compensation for loss of earnings caused by the accident* **2** the profit that a company makes: *earnings per share* ◊ *export earnings*

earnings-re'lated *adj.* (*BrE*) (of payments, etc.) connected to and changing according to the amount of money that you earn: *an earnings-related pension scheme*

ear·phones /'ɪəfəʊnz; *AmE* 'ɪrfoʊnz/ *noun* [pl.] = HEADPHONES

ear·piece /'ɪəpiːs; *AmE* 'ɪrpiːs/ *noun* the part of a telephone or piece of electrical equipment that you hold next to or put into your ear so that you can listen

ear·plug /'ɪəplʌg; *AmE* 'ɪrp-/ *noun* [usually pl.] a piece of soft material that you put into your ear to keep out noise, water or air

ear·ring /'ɪərɪŋ; *AmE* 'ɪrɪŋ/ *noun* [often pl.] a piece of jewellery that you fasten in or on your ear: *a pair of earrings*

ear·shot /'ɪəʃɒt; *AmE* 'ɪrʃɑːt/ *noun* IDM **out of 'earshot (of sb/sth)** too far away to hear sb/sth or to be heard: *We waited until Ted was safely out of earshot before discussing it.* **within 'earshot (of sb/sth)** near enough to hear sb/sth or to be heard: *As she came within earshot of the group, she heard her name mentioned.*

'ear-splitting *adj.* extremely loud

earth /ɜːθ; *AmE* ɜːrθ/ *noun, verb*

■ *noun* **1** (also **Earth, the Earth**) [U, sing.] the world; the planet that we live on: *the planet Earth* ◊ *the history of life on earth* ◊ *the earth's ozone layer* ◊ *The earth revolves around the sun.* ◊ *I must be the happiest person on earth!* **2** [U, sing.] land; the hard surface of the world that is not the sea or the sky; the ground: *After a week at sea, it was good to feel the earth beneath our feet again.* ◊ *You could feel the earth shake as the truck came closer.* **3** [U] the substance that plants grow in SYN SOIL: *a clod/lump/mound of earth* ◊ *I cleaned off the earth clinging to my boots.* **4** [C] the hole where an animal, especially a FOX, lives **5** (*BrE*) (*AmE* **ground**) [C, usually sing.] a wire that connects an electric CIRCUIT with the ground and makes it safe IDM **charge, cost, pay, etc. the 'earth** (*BrE, informal*) to charge, etc. a lot of money: *I'd love that dress, but it costs the earth.* **come back/down to 'earth (with a 'bang/'bump)** | **bring sb (back) down to 'earth (with a 'bang/'bump)** (*informal*) to return, or to make sb return, to a normal way of thinking or behaving after a time when they have been very excited, not very practical, etc.—see also DOWN-TO-EARTH **go to 'earth/'ground** (*BrE*) to hide, especially to escape from sb who is chasing you **how, why, where, who, etc. on 'earth** (*informal*) used to emphasize the question you are asking when you are surprised or angry or cannot think of an obvious answer: *What on earth are you doing?* ◊ *How on earth can she afford that?* **be, feel, look, taste, etc. like nothing on 'earth** (*informal*) to be, feel, look, taste, etc. very bad **on 'earth** used after negative nouns or pronouns to emphasize what you are saying: *Nothing on earth would persuade me to go with him.* **run sb/sth to 'earth/'ground** (*BrE*) to find sb/sth after looking hard for a long time—

E

more at END *n*., FACE *n*., MOVE *v*., PROMISE *v*., SALT *n*., WIPE *v*.

■ *verb* (*BrE*) (*AmE* **ground**) [VN] [usually passive] to make electrical equipment safe by connecting it to the ground with a wire

---

WHICH WORD? ❓

earth / floor / ground / soil / land

To talk about our planet, use **the earth**.

For the surface of the earth that is not the sea or the sky, use **earth**, **land** or **ground**: *The parachute floated gently down to earth.* ◊ *We did not see land again until the ship reached Australia.* ◊ *a plane 2 500 feet above the ground.*

For the hard surface you walk on, use **ground** outside and **floor** inside: *He flung his bike to the ground and rushed inside.* ◊ *Her clothes were just lying on the floor.*

Trees and plants grow in **soil**, **earth** (*BrE*), or **dirt** (*AmE*) : *These plants prefer alkaline soil.* ◊ *We filled a few trays with earth/dirt and planted the seeds.* What you buy in bags to put your plants or seeds in is usually called **compost** or **soil**. **Ground** is an area of soil: *fertile/soft ground* ◊ *a piece of ground where the kids play.*

---

earth·bound /'ɜːθbaʊnd; *AmE* 'ɜːrθ-/ *adj.* **1** unable to leave the surface of the earth: *birds and their earthbound predators* **2** (*literary*) not imaginative or spiritual

earth·en /'ɜːθn; *AmE* 'ɜːrθn/ *adj.* [only before noun] **1** (of floors or walls) made of earth **2** (of objects) made of baked clay: *earthen pots*

earth·en·ware /'ɜːθnweə(r); *AmE* 'ɜːrθnwer/ *adj.* made of very hard baked clay: *an earthenware bowl* ▶ **earth·en·ware** *noun* [U]

earth·ling /'ɜːθlɪŋ; *AmE* 'ɜːrθ-/ *noun* a word used in SCIENCE FICTION stories by creatures from other planets to refer to a person living on the earth

earth·ly /'ɜːθli; *AmE* 'ɜːrθ-/ *adj.* [usually before noun] **1** (*written*) connected with life on earth and not with any spiritual life: *earthly desires* ◊ *the sorrows of this earthly life* **2** (often used in questions and negatives for emphasis) possible: *There's no earthly reason why you shouldn't go.* ◊ *What earthly difference is my opinion going to make?* ◊ *He didn't have an earthly chance of getting the job.*

ˈearth mother *noun* **1** (also **Earth Mother**) a GODDESS who represents the earth as the source of life; a GODDESS of FERTILITY **2** (*informal*) a woman who seems very suited to being a mother

earth·quake /'ɜːθkweɪk; *AmE* 'ɜːrθ-/ (also *informal* **quake**) *noun* a sudden, violent shaking of the earth's surface: *damage caused by a powerful earthquake*

ˈearth science *noun* [C, U] a science concerned with studying the earth or part of it. Geography and GEOLOGY are both earth sciences.—compare LIFE SCIENCES, NATURAL SCIENCE

ˈearth-shattering *adj.* having a very great effect and of great importance: *an earth-shattering discovery*

earth·work /'ɜːθwɜːk; *AmE* 'ɜːrθwɜːrk/ *noun* [usually pl.] a large bank of earth that was built long ago in the past and used as a defence

earth·worm /'ɜːθwɜːm; *AmE* 'ɜːrθwɜːrm/ *noun* a common long thin worm that lives in soil

earthy /'ɜːθi; *AmE* 'ɜːrθi/ *adj.* (**earth·ier**, **earthi·est**) **1** concerned with the body, sex, etc. in an open and direct way that some people find rude or embarrassing: *an earthy sense of humour* **2** of or like earth or soil: *earthy colours/ smells* ▶ **earthi·ness** *noun* [U]

ear·wig /'ɪəwɪg; *AmE* 'ɪrwɪg/ *noun* a small brown insect with a long body and two curved pointed parts called PINCERS that stick out at the back end of its body

ease /iːz/ *noun, verb*
■ *noun* [U] **1** lack of difficulty: *He passed the exam with ease.* ◊ *The ease with which she learns languages is astonishing.* ◊ *This computer is popular for its good design and*

---

ease of use. ◊ *All important points are numbered for ease of reference* (= so that you can find them easily). **2** the state of feeling relaxed or comfortable without worries, problems or pain: *In his retirement, he lived a life of ease.* **IDM** **(stand) at ˈease** used as a command to soldiers to tell them to stand with their feet apart and their hands behind their backs—compare ATTENTION *n.* (5) **at (your) ˈease** relaxed and confident and not nervous or embarrassed: *I never feel completely at ease with him.* **put sb at (their) ˈease** to make sb feel relaxed and confident, not nervous or embarrassed: *Try to put the candidate at ease by being friendly and informal.*—more at ILL *adj.*, MIND *n.*

■ *verb* **1** to become or to make sth less unpleasant, painful, severe, etc: [VN] *This should help ease the pain.* ◊ *The plan should ease traffic congestion in the town.* ◊ *It would ease my mind* (= make me less worried) *to know that she was settled.* ◊ [V] *The pain immediately eased.* **2** [+adv. / prep.] to move, or to move sb/sth, slowly and carefully: [V] *He eased slowly forwards.* ◊ [VN] *She eased herself into a chair.* ◊ *He eased off his shoes.* **3** [VN] to make sth easier: *Ramps have been built to ease access for the disabled.* **4** to make sth or to become less tight and more relaxed: [VN] *Ease your grip on the wheel a little.* (also V) **5** to become or make sth lower in price or value [SYN] REDUCE: [V] *Share prices eased back from yesterday's levels.* (also VN) **PHR V** **ˌease ˈinto sth** | **ˌease yourself/sb into sth** to become or help sb to become familiar with sth new, especially a new job **ˌease ˈoff** | **ˌease ˈoff sth** to become or make sth become less strong, unpleasant, etc: *We waited until the traffic had eased off.* ◊ *Ease off the training a few days before the race.* **ˌease sb↔ˈout (of sth)** to force sb to leave a job or position of authority, especially by making it difficult or unpleasant for them over a period of time **ˌease ˈup 1** to reduce the speed at which you are travelling **2** to become less strong, unpleasant, etc.

easel /'iːzl/ *noun* a wooden frame to hold a picture while it is being painted or (in the past) a BLACKBOARD

eas·ily /'iːzəli/ *adv.* **1** without problems or difficulty: *I can easily finish it tonight.* ◊ *The museum is easily accessible by car.* **2** very probably; very likely: *Are you sure you locked the gate? You could easily have forgotten.* ◊ *The situation might all too easily have become a disaster.* **3 ~ the best, nicest, etc.** without doubt; definitely: *It's easily the best play I've seen this year.* **4** quickly; more quickly than is usual: *I get bored easily.* ◊ *He's easily distracted.*

east /iːst/ *noun, adj., adv.*
■ *noun* [U, sing.] (*abbr.* E) **1** (usually **the east**) the direction that you look towards to see the sun rise; one of the four main points of the COMPASS: *Which way is east?* ◊ *A gale was blowing from the east.* ◊ *a town to the east of* (= further east than) *Chicago*—compare NORTH, SOUTH, WEST—picture at COMPASS **2** (also **East**) the eastern part of a country, region or city: *I was born in the East, but now live in San Francisco.* **3** (**the East**) the countries of Asia, especially China, Japan and India **4** (**the East**) (in the past) the Communist countries of Eastern Europe: *East-West relations*

■ *adj.* [only before noun] **1** (also **East**) (*abbr.* E) in or towards the east: *East Africa* ◊ *They live on the east coast.* **2** an **east** wind blows from the east—compare EASTERLY
■ *adv.* towards the east: *The house faces east.*

east·bound /'iːstbaʊnd/ *adj.* travelling or leading towards the east: *eastbound traffic* ◊ *the eastbound carriageway of the motorway*

the ˌEast ˈEnd *noun* an area of East London traditionally connected with working people ▶ **ˌEast ˈEnder** *noun*: *He's a real East Ender.*

Easter /'iːstə(r)/ *noun* **1** [U, C] (also **ˌEaster ˈDay**, **ˌEaster ˈSunday**) (in the Christian religion) a Sunday in March or April when Christians remember the death of Christ and his return to life: *Easter services* **2** (also **Easter·time**) the period that includes Easter Day and the days close to it: *the Easter holidays/vacation*

ˈEaster egg *noun* **1** (*BrE*) an egg made of chocolate that is given as a present and eaten at Easter **2** an egg with a shell that is painted and decorated at Easter

east·er·ly /'iːstəli; *AmE* -ərli/ *adj., noun*

E

■ *adj.* [only before noun] **1** in or towards the east: *travelling in an easterly direction* **2** [usually before noun] (of winds) blowing from the east: *a cold easterly wind*—compare EAST

■ *noun* (*pl.* **-ies**) a wind that blows from the east

east·ern /'i:stən; *AmE* -ərn/ *adj.* **1** (also **Eastern**) [only before noun] (*abbr.* **E**) situated in the east or facing east: *eastern Spain* ◊ *Eastern Europe* ◊ *the eastern slopes of the mountain* **2** (usually **Eastern**) connected with the part of the world that is to the east of Europe: *Eastern cookery*

east·ern·er /'i:stənə(r); *AmE* 'i:stərnər/ *noun* a person who comes from or lives in the eastern part of a country, especially the US

east·ern·most /'i:stənməʊst; *AmE* -ərnmoʊst/ *adj.* furthest east: *the easternmost city in Europe*

the ˌEastern ˌOrthodox ˈChurch *noun* = THE ORTHODOX CHURCH

East·er·time /'i:stətaɪm; *AmE* 'i:stərt-/ *noun* [U, C] = EASTER

east·wards /'i:stwədz; *AmE* -wərdz/ (also **east·ward**) *adv.* towards the east: *to go/look/turn eastwards* ▶ **east·ward** *adj.*: *in an eastward direction*

easy /'i:zi/ *adj., adv.*

■ *adj.* (**eas·ier, easi·est**) **1** not difficult; done or obtained without a lot of effort or problems: *an easy exam/job* ◊ *He didn't make it easy for me to leave.* ◊ *Their house isn't the easiest place to get to.* ◊ *vegetables that are easy to grow* ◊ *Several schools are within easy reach* (= not far away). ◊ *It can't be easy for her, on her own with the children.* ◊ *It's easy for you to tell me to keep calm, but you're not in my position.* OPP HARD **2** comfortable, relaxed and not worried: *I'll agree to anything for an easy life.* ◊ *I don't feel easy about letting the kids go out alone.* OPP UNEASY **3** [only before noun] open to attack; not able to defend yourself: *She's an easy target for their criticisms.* ◊ *The baby fish are easy prey for birds.* **4** [only before noun] pleasant and friendly; not awkward: *He had a very easy manner.* **5** [not usually before noun] (*informal, disapproving*) (of women) willing to have sex with many different people—see also EASILY ▶ **easi·ness** *noun* [U] IDM **as ˌeasy as ˈanything/as ˈpie/as ABˈC/as falling off a ˈlog** (*informal*) very easy or very easily **ˌeasy ˈmoney** money that you get without having to work very hard for it **ˌeasy on the ˈear/ˈeye** (*informal*) pleasant to listen to or look at **have an easy ˈtime (of it)** (*BrE*) to have no difficulties or problems **I'm ˈeasy** (*BrE, informal*) used to say that you do not have a strong opinion when sb has offered you a choice: *'Do you want to watch this or the news?' 'Oh, I'm easy. It's up to you.'* **of easy ˈvirtue** (*old-fashioned*) (of a woman) willing to have sex with anyone **on ˈeasy street** (*AmE*) enjoying a comfortable way of life with plenty of money **take the easy way ˈout** to end a difficult situation by choosing the simplest solution even if it is not the best one—more at FREE *adj.*, OPTION, REACH *n.*, RIDE *n.*, TOUCH *n.*

■ *adv.* (**eas·ier, easi·est**) used to tell sb to be careful when doing sth: *Easy with that chair—one of its legs is loose.* IDM **ˌeasier ˌsaid than ˈdone** much more difficult to do than to talk about: *'Why don't you get yourself a job?' 'That's easier said than done.'* **ˌeasy ˈcome, ˌeasy ˈgo** (*saying*) used to mean that sb does not care very much about money or possessions especially if they spend it or lose sth **ˌeasy ˈdoes it** (*informal*) used to tell sb to do sth, or move sth, slowly and carefully **go ˈeasy on sb** (*informal*) used to tell sb to treat a person in a gentle way and not to be too angry or severe: *Go easy on her—she's having a really hard time at the moment.* **go ˈeasy on/with sth** (*informal*) used to tell sb not to use too much of sth: *Go easy on the sugar.* **ˌstand ˈeasy** used as a command to soldiers who are already standing AT EASE to tell them that they can stand in an even more relaxed way **ˌtake it ˈeasy** (*spoken*) used to tell sb not to be worried or angry: *Take it easy! Don't panic.* **ˌtake it/things ˈeasy** to relax and avoid working too hard or doing too much: *The doctor told me to take it easy for a few weeks.*

ˌeasy ˈchair *noun* a large comfortable chair: *to sit in an easy chair*

ˌeasy-ˈgoing *adj.* relaxed and happy to accept things without worrying or getting angry: *I wish I had such easy-going parents!*

ˌeasy ˈlistening *noun* [U] music that is pleasant and relaxing but that some people think is not very interesting

easy-peasy /ˌi:zi ˈpi:zi/ *adj.* (*BrE, spoken*) (used especially by children) very easy

eat /i:t/ *verb* (**ate** /et; *especially AmE* eɪt/, **eaten** /'i:tn/) **1** to put food in your mouth, chew it and swallow it: [V] *I was too nervous to eat.* ◊ *She doesn't eat sensibly* (= doesn't eat food that is good for her). ◊ [VN] *I don't eat meat.* ◊ *Would you like something to eat?* ◊ *I couldn't eat another thing* (= I have had enough food). **2** [V] to have a meal: *Where shall we eat tonight?* ◊ *We ate at a pizzeria in town.* IDM **ˌeat sb aˈlive** (*informal*) **1** to criticize or punish sb severely because you are extremely angry with them **2** to defeat sb completely in an argument, a competition, etc: *The defence lawyers are going to eat you alive tomorrow.* **3** [usually passive] (of insects, etc.) to bite sb many times: *I was being eaten alive by mosquitoes.* **eat your ˈheart out!** (*spoken*) used to compare two things and say that one of them is better: *Look at him dance! Eat your heart out, John Travolta* (= he dances even better than John Travolta). **eat your ˈheart out (for sb/sth)** (*especially BrE*) to feel very unhappy, especially because you want sb/sth you cannot have **eat humble ˈpie** (*BrE*) (*AmE* eat ˈcrow**) to say and show that you are sorry for a mistake that you made ORIGIN From a pun on the old word *umbles*, meaning 'offal', which was considered inferior food. **eat like a ˈhorse** (*informal*) to eat a lot: *She may be thin, but she eats like a horse.* **eat out of your/sb's ˈhand** to trust sb and be willing to do what they say: *She'll have them eating out of her hand in no time.* **eat sb out of ˌhouse and ˈhome** (*informal, often humorous*) to eat a lot of sb else's food **eat your ˈwords** to admit that what you said was wrong **I could eat a ˈhorse** (*spoken*) used to say that you are very hungry **I'll eat my ˈhat** (*spoken*) used to say that you think sth is very unlikely to happen: *If she's here on time, I'll eat my hat!* **what's eating him, etc.?** (*spoken*) used to ask what sb is annoyed or worried about—more at CAKE *n.*, DOG *n.* PHRV **ˌeat sth↔aˈway** to reduce or destroy sth gradually: *The coastline is being eaten away year by year.* **ˌeat aˈway at sth/sb 1** to reduce or destroy sth gradually: *Woodworm had eaten away at the door frame.* ◊ *His constant criticism ate away at her self-confidence.* **2** to worry sb over a period of time **ˈeat into sth 1** to use up a part of sth, especially sb's money or time: *Those repair bills have really eaten into my savings.* **2** to destroy or damage the surface of sth: *Rust had eaten into the metal.* **ˌeat ˈout** to have a meal in a restaurant, etc. rather than at home: *Do you feel like eating out tonight?* **ˌeat ˈup|ˌeat sth↔ˈup** to eat all of sth: *Eat up! We've got to go out soon.* ◊ *Come on. Eat up your potatoes.* **ˌeat sb ˈup** [usually passive] to fill sb with a particular emotion so that they cannot think of anything else: *She was eaten up by regrets.* **ˌeat sth↔ˈup** to use sth in large quantities: *Legal costs had eaten up all the savings she had.*

eat·able /'i:təbl/ *adj.* (*rare*) good enough to be eaten—see also EDIBLE

eater /'i:tə(r)/ *noun* (usually after an adjective or a noun) a person or an animal that eats a particular thing or in a particular way: *We're not great meat eaters.* ◊ *He's a big eater* (= he eats a lot).

eat·ery /'i:təri/ (*pl.* **-ies**) *noun* (*informal, especially AmE*) a restaurant or other place that serves food

eat·ing /'i:tɪŋ/ *noun* [U] the act of eating sth: *healthy eating* ◊ *eating disorders such as anorexia or bulimia* IDM see PROOF

ˈeating apple *noun* (*BrE*) any type of apple that can be eaten raw—compare COOKING APPLE

eats /i:ts/ *noun* [pl.] (*informal*) food, especially at a party

eau de Cologne /ˌəʊ də kəˈləʊn; *AmE* ˌoʊ də kəˈloʊn/ *noun* [U] = COLOGNE

eaves /i:vz/ *noun* [pl.] the lower edges of a roof that stick

aɪ	aʊ	eɪ	əʊ	oʊ	ɔɪ	ɪə	eə	ʊə	j	w
my	now	say	go	go	boy	near	hair	pure	yes	wet
			(BrE)	(AmE)						

out over the walls: *birds nesting under the eaves*—picture at HOUSE

eaves·drop /'iːvzdrɒp; *AmE* -drɑːp/ *verb* (**-pp-**) [V] **~ (on sb/sth)** to listen secretly to what other people are saying: *We caught him eavesdropping outside the window.* ▶ **eaves·drop·per** *noun*

ebb /eb/ *noun, verb*
■ *noun* (**the ebb**) [usually sing.] the period of time when the sea flows away from the land: *the ebb tide* ▸IDM◂ **the ¦ebb and 'flow (of sth/sb)** the repeated, often regular, movement from one state to another; the repeated change in level, numbers or amount: *the ebb and flow of the tides/ seasons* ◊ *the ebb and flow of money* ◊ *She sat in silence enjoying the ebb and flow of conversation.*—more at LOW *adj.*
■ *verb* [V] **1** (*formal*) (of the TIDE in the sea) to move away from the land ▸SYN◂ GO OUT ▸OPP◂ FLOW **2 ~ (away)** to become gradually weaker or less ▸SYN◂ DECREASE: *The pain was ebbing.* ◊ *As night fell, our enthusiasm began to ebb away.*

ebony /'ebəni/ *noun, adj.*
■ *noun* [U] the hard black wood of various tropical trees: *an ebony carving*
■ *adj.* black in colour: *ebony skin*

ebul·li·ent /ɪ'bʌliənt; -'bʊl-/ *adj.* (*written*) full of confidence, energy and good humour: *The Prime Minister was in ebullient mood.* ▶ **ebul·li·ence** /-əns/ *noun* [U]

ec·cen·tric /ɪk'sentrɪk/ *adj.* considered by other people to be strange or unusual: *eccentric behaviour/clothes* ◊ *an eccentric aunt* ▶ **ec·cen·tric** *noun*: *Most people considered him a harmless eccentric.* **ec·cen·tric·al·ly** /-kli/ *adv.*

ec·cen·tri·city /ˌeksen'trɪsəti/ (*pl.* **-ies**) *noun* **1** [U] behaviour that people think is strange or unusual; the quality of being unusual and different from other people: *As a teacher, she had a reputation for eccentricity.* ◊ *Arthur was noted for the eccentricity of his clothes.* **2** [C, usually pl.] an unusual act or habit: *We all have our little eccentricities.*

ec·cle·si·as·tic /ɪˌkliːzi'æstɪk/ *noun* (*formal*) a priest or MINISTER in the Christian Church

ec·cle·si·as·tic·al /ɪˌkliːzi'æstɪkəl/ *adj.* [usually before noun] connected with the Christian Church: *ecclesiastical history*

ECG /ˌiː siː 'dʒiː/ (*AmE* also **EKG**) *noun* the abbreviation for 'electrocardiogram' (a medical test that measures and records electrical activity of the heart)

ech·elon /'eʃəlɒn; *AmE* -lɑːn/ *noun* **1** [usually pl.] a rank or position of authority in an organization or a society: *the lower/upper/top/higher echelons of the Civil Service* **2** an arrangement of soldiers, planes, etc. in which each one is behind and to the side of the one in front

echo /'ekəʊ; *AmE* 'ekoʊ/ *noun, verb*
■ *noun* (*pl.* **-oes**) **1** the reflecting of sound off a wall or inside an enclosed space so that a noise appears to be repeated; a sound that is reflected back in this way: *There was an echo on the line and I couldn't hear clearly.* ◊ *The hills sent back a faint echo.* ◊ *the echo of footsteps running down the corridor* ◊ *'So you love him, do you?' Magda's voice was a mocking echo of my own.* **2** the fact of an idea, event, etc. being like another and reminding you of it; sth that reminds you of sth else: *Yesterday's crash has grim echoes of previous disasters.* **3** an opinion or attitude that agrees with or repeats one already expressed or thought: *His words were an echo of what she had heard many times before.* ◊ *The speech found an echo in the hearts of many of the audience* (= they agreed with it).
■ *verb* (**echoes, echo·ing, echoed, echoed**) **1** [V] if a sound echoes, it bounces off a wall, the side of a mountain, etc. so that you can hear it again: *Her footsteps echoed in the empty room.* ◊ *The gunshot echoed through the forest.* **2 ~ (to/with sth)| ~ sth (back)** to send back and repeat a sound; to be full of a sound: [V] *The whole house echoed.* ◊ *The street echoed with the cries of children.* ◊ [VN] *The valley echoed back his voice.* **3** [VN] (*written*) to repeat an idea or opinion because you agree with it: *This is a view echoed by many on the right of the party.* **4** (*written*) to repeat what sb else has just said, especially because you

find it surprising: [V**speech**] *'He's gone!' Viv echoed incredulously.* [also VN]

eclair /ɪ'kleə(r); *AmE* ɪ'kler/ *noun* a long thin cake for one person, made of light pastry, filled with cream and usually with chocolate on top: *a chocolate eclair*—picture on page A1

eclec·tic /ɪ'klektɪk/ *adj.* (*formal*) not following one style or set of ideas but choosing from or using a wide variety: *She has very eclectic tastes in literature.* ▶ **eclec·tic·al·ly** /-tɪkli/ *adv.* **eclec·ti·cism** /ɪ'klektɪsɪzəm/ *noun* [U]: *Critics praised the originality and eclecticism of her work.*

eclipse /ɪ'klɪps/ *noun, verb*
■ *noun* **1** [C] an occasion when the moon passes between the earth and the sun so that you cannot see all or part of the sun for a time; an occasion when the earth passes between the moon and the sun so that you cannot see all or part of the moon for a time: *an eclipse of the sun/moon* ◊ *a total/partial eclipse* **2** [sing., U] (*written*) a loss of importance, power, etc. especially because sb/sth else has become more important, powerful, etc: *The election result marked the eclipse of the right wing.* ◊ *Her work was in eclipse for most of the 20th century.*
■ *verb* [VN] **1** [often passive] (of the moon, the earth, etc.) to cause an eclipse **2** (*written*) to make sb/sth seem dull or unimportant by comparison ▸SYN◂ OUTSHINE: *Though a talented player, he was completely eclipsed by his brother.*

eco- /'iːkəʊ; *AmE* 'iːkoʊ/ *combining form* (in nouns, adjectives and adverbs) connected with the environment: *eco-friendly* ◊ *eco-warriors* (= people who protest about damage to the environment)

eco·logic·al /ˌiːkə'lɒdʒɪkl; *AmE* -'lɑːdʒ-/ *adj.* **1** connected with the relation of plants and living creatures to each other and to their environment: *We risk upsetting the ecological balance of the area.* ◊ *an ecological disaster* (= one that alters the whole balance of ecology in an area) **2** interested in and concerned about the ecology of a place: *the ecological movement* ▶ **eco·logic·al·ly** /-kli/: *The system is both practical and ecologically sound.*

ecolo·gist /i'kɒlədʒɪst; *AmE* i'kɑːl-/ *noun* **1** a scientist who studies ecology **2** a person who is interested in ecology and believes the environment should be protected

ecol·ogy /i'kɒlədʒi; *AmE* i'kɑːl-/ *noun* [U] the relation of plants and living creatures to each other and to their environment; the study of this: *plant/animal/human ecology* ◊ *the ecology movement* ◊ *Oil pollution could damage the ecology of the coral reefs.*

eco·nom·ic /ˌiːkə'nɒmɪk; ˌekə-; *AmE* -'nɑːm-/ *adj.* **1** [only before noun] connected with the trade, industry and development of wealth of a country, an area or a society: *social, economic and political issues* ◊ *economic growth/ cooperation/development/reform* ◊ *the government's economic policy* ◊ *economic history* ◊ *the current economic climate* **2** (of a process, a business or an activity) producing enough profit to continue ▸SYN◂ PROFITABLE

WHICH WORD?

economic / economical

Economic means 'connected with the economy of a country or an area, or with the money that a society or an individual has': *the government's economic policy* ◊ *the economic aspects of having children.*
— see also ECONOMY 1

Economical means 'spending money or using something in a careful way that avoids waste': *It is usually economical to buy washing powder in large quantities.*
— see also ECONOMY 3

---

eco·nom·ic·al /ˌiːkə'nɒmɪkl; ˌekə-; *AmE* -'nɑːm-/ *adj.* **1** providing good service or value in relation to the amount of time or money spent: *an economical car to run* (= one that does not use too much petrol/gas) ◊ *It would be more economical to buy the bigger size.* **2** using no more of sth than is necessary: *an economical use of land/space*

◊ *an economical prose style* (= one that uses no unnecessary words) **3** not spending more money than necessary: *He was economical in all areas of his life.* **IDM** **economical with the 'truth** a way of saying that sb has left out some important facts, when you do not want to say that they are lying

eco·nom·ic·al·ly /ˌiːkəˈnɒmɪkli; ˌekə-; *AmE* -ˈnɑːm-/ *adv.* **1** in a way connected with the trade, industry and development of wealth of a country, an area or a society: *The factory is no longer economically viable.* ◊ *Economically, the centre of Spain has lost its dominant role.* ◊ *the economically active/inactive population* (= those who are employed/unemployed) **2** in a way that provides good service or value in relation to the amount of time or money spent: *I'll do the job as economically as possible.* **3** in a way that uses no more of sth than is necessary: *The design is intended to use space as economically as possible.* ◊ *She writes elegantly and economically.*

eco·nom·ics /ˌiːkəˈnɒmɪks; ˌekə-; *AmE* -ˈnɑːm-/ *noun* **1** [U] the study of how a society organizes its money, trade and industry: *He studied politics and economics at Yale.* ◊ *Keynsian/Marxist economics*—see also HOME ECONOMICS **2** [pl., U] the way in which money influences, or is organized within an area of business or society: *The economics of the project are very encouraging.*

econo·mist /ɪˈkɒnəmɪst; *AmE* ɪˈkɑːn-/ *noun* a person who studies or writes about economics

econo·mize (*BrE* also **-ise**) /ɪˈkɒnəmaɪz; *AmE* ɪˈkɑːn-/ *verb* [V] ~ **(on sth)** to use less money, time, etc. than you normally use: *Old people often try to economize on heating, thus endangering their health.*

econ·omy /ɪˈkɒnəmi; *AmE* ɪˈkɑːn-/ *noun* (*pl.* **-ies**) **1** (often **the economy**) [C] the relationship between production, trade and the supply of money in a particular country or region: *The economy is in recession.* ◊ *the world economy* ◊ *a market economy* (= one in which the price is fixed according to both cost and demand) **2** [C] a country, when you are thinking about its economic system: *Ireland was one of the fastest-growing economies in Western Europe in the 1990s.* **3** [C, U] the use of the time, money, etc. that is available in a way that avoids waste: *We need to make substantial economies.* ◊ *It's a false economy to buy cheap clothes* (= it seems cheaper but it is not really since they do not last very long). ◊ *She writes with a great economy of words* (= using only the necessary words). ◊ *(BrE)* We're on an economy drive at home. (= trying to avoid waste and spend as little money as possible) ◊ *Buy the large economy pack!* (= the one that gives you better value for money) ◊ *to fly economy (class)* (= by the cheapest class of air travel) ◊ *an economy fare* (= the cheapest)

eco·sys·tem /ˈiːkəʊsɪstəm; *AmE* ˈiːkoʊ-/ *noun* all the plants and living creatures in a particular area considered in relation to their physical environment

ec·stasy /ˈekstəsi/ *noun* (*pl.* **-ies**) **1** [U, C] a feeling or state of very great happiness **2** (**Ecstasy**) [U] (*abbr.* E) an illegal drug, taken especially by young people at parties, that gives feelings of great energy and pleasure

ec·stat·ic /ɪkˈstætɪk/ *adj.* very happy, excited and enthusiastic; feeling or showing great enthusiasm: *Sally was ecstatic about her new job.* ◊ *ecstatic applause/praise/ reviews* ◊ *He gave an ecstatic sigh of happiness.* ▶ **ec·stat·ic·al·ly** /-kli/ *adv.*: *He sighed ecstatically.*

-ec·tomy *combining form* (in nouns) a medical operation in which part of the body is removed: *appendectomy* (= removal of the APPENDIX)

ecu (also **ECU**) /ˈekjuː; ˈiː-/ *noun* (*pl.* **ecu** or **ecus**) the abbreviation for European Currency Unit, a unit of money of the European Union. In 1999 it was replaced by the euro.

ecu·men·ic·al /ˌiːkjuːˈmenɪkl; ˌekjuː-/ *adj.* involving or uniting members of different branches of the Christian Church: *an ecumenical committee*

ecu·men·ism /ɪˈkjuːmənɪzəm/ *noun* [U] the principle or aim of uniting different branches of the Christian Church

ec·zema /ˈeksɪmə; *AmE* ɪɡˈziːmə/ *noun* [U] a skin condition in which areas of skin become red, rough and sore

-ed, -d *suffix* **1** (in adjectives) having; having the charac-

teristics of: *talented* ◊ *bearded* ◊ *diseased* **2** (makes the past tense and past participle of regular verbs): *hated* ◊ *walked* ◊ *loved*

ed. (also **Ed.**) *abbr.* EDITED (BY), EDITION, EDITOR: *'Eighteenth Century Women Poets', Ed. Lonsdale* ◊ *6th ed.*

Edam /ˈiːdæm/ *noun* [U, C] a type of round yellow Dutch cheese that is covered with red WAX

eddy /ˈedi/ *noun, verb*
■ *noun* (*pl.* **-ies**) a circular movement of air, dust or water
■ *verb* (**ed·dies, eddy·ing, ed·died, ed·died**) [V] (of air, dust, water, etc.) to move around in a circle: *The waves swirled and eddied around the rocks.*

Eden /ˈiːdn/ (also **the ˌGarden of 'Eden**) *noun* [sing.] (in the Bible) the beautiful garden where Adam and Eve, the first human beings, lived before they did sth God had told them not to and were sent away, often seen as a place of happiness and INNOCENCE

edge /edʒ/ *noun, verb*
■ *noun* **1** [C] the outside limit of an object, a surface or an area; the part furthest from the centre: *He stood on the edge of the cliff.* ◊ *a big house on/at the edge of town* ◊ *Don't put that glass so near the edge of the table.* ◊ *I sat down at the water's edge.* ◊ *Stand the coin on its edge.*—see also LEADING EDGE **2** [C] the sharp part of a blade, knife or SWORD that is used for cutting: *Be careful—it has a sharp edge.*—see also KNIFE-EDGE **3** (usually **the edge**) [sing.] the point at which sth, especially sth bad, may begin to happen **SYN** BRINK, VERGE: *They had brought the country to the edge of disaster.*—see also CUTTING EDGE **4** [sing.] ~ **(on/over sb/sth)** a slight advantage over sb/ sth: *The company needs to improve its **competitive edge**.* ◊ *They have the edge on us.* **5** [sing.] a strong, often exciting, quality: *Her show now has a hard political edge to it.* **6** [sing.] a sharp tone of voice, often showing anger: *He did his best to remain calm, but there was a distinct edge to his voice.* **7** (**-edged**) (in adjectives) having the type of edge or edges mentioned: *a lace-edged handkerchief*—see also GILT-EDGED **IDM** **be on 'edge** to be nervous, excited or bad-tempered **on the edge of your 'seat** very excited and giving your full attention to sth: *The game had the crowd on the edge of their seats.* **take the 'edge off sth** to make sth less strong, less bad, etc: *The sandwich took the edge off my appetite.*—more at FRAY *v.*, RAZOR, ROUGH *adj.*, TEETER, TOOTH

the rim of the glass
the edge of the table

■ *verb* **1** [+*adv./prep.*] to move or to move sth slowly and carefully in a particular direction: [V] *She edged a little closer to me.* ◊ *I edged nervously past the dog.* ◊ [VN] *Emily edged her chair forward.* **2** [VN] [usually passive] ~ **sth (with/in sth)** to put sth around the edge of sth: *The handkerchief is edged with lace.* **3** [V+*adv./prep.*] to increase or decrease slightly: *Prices edged up 2% in the year to December.* **PHRV** **ˌedge sb/sth↔'out (of sth)** to move sb from their position or job gradually, especially when they are not fully aware of what is happening: *She was edged out of the company by the new director.*

edge·ways /ˈedʒweɪz/ (*BrE*) (*AmE* **edge·wise** /-waɪz/) *adv.* with the edge upwards or forwards; on one side: *You'll only get the desk through the door if you turn it edgeways.* **IDM** see WORD *n.*

edging /ˈedʒɪŋ/ *noun* [U, C] something that forms the border or edge of sth, usually added to make it more attractive

edgy /ˈedʒi/ *adj.* (*informal*) nervous, especially about what might happen: *She's been very edgy lately.* ◊ *After the recent unrest there is an edgy calm in the capital.* ▶ **edgi·ly** *adv.*: *'I'm not sure I can make it tomorrow,' he said edgily.* **edgi·ness** *noun* [U, sing.]

ed·ible /ˈedəbl/ *adj.* fit or suitable to be eaten; not poisonous: *The food at the hotel was barely edible.* ◊ *edible fungi/ snails/flowers*

s	t	v	z	ʃ	ʒ	tʃ	dʒ	θ	ð	ŋ
see	tea	van	zoo	shoe	vision	chain	jam	thin	this	sing

edict /'iːdɪkt/ *noun* [U, C] (*formal*) an official order or statement given by sb in authority

edi·fi·ca·tion /ˌedɪfɪ'keɪʃn/ *noun* [U] (*formal or humorous*) the improvement of sb's mind or character: *The books were intended for the edification of the masses.*

edi·fice /'edɪfɪs/ *noun* (*formal*) a large impressive building: *an imposing edifice from the 19th century* ◊ (*figurative*) *Their new manifesto hardly threatens to bring the whole edifice of capitalism crashing down.* ◊ (*figurative*) *an edifice of lies*

edify /'edɪfaɪ/ *verb* (**edi·fies**, **edify·ing**, **edi·fied**, **edi·fied**) [V, VN] (*formal*) to improve people's minds or characters by teaching them about sth

edify·ing /'edɪfaɪɪŋ/ *adj.* (*formal or humorous*) likely to improve your mind or your character: *edifying literature* ◊ *Watching soccer fans howling racist remarks was not an edifying sight.*

edit /'edɪt/ *verb* **1** to prepare a piece of writing, a book, etc. to be published by correcting the mistakes, making improvements to it, etc: [VN] *He's editing a book of essays by Isaiah Berlin.* ◊ *This is the edited version of my speech* (= some parts have been taken out). [also V] **2** [VN] when sb **edits** a film/movie, television programme, etc. they take what has been filmed or recorded and decide which parts to include and in which order: *They're showing the edited highlights of last month's game.* **3** to be responsible for planning and publishing a newspaper, magazine, etc. (= to be the EDITOR): *She used to edit a women's magazine.* PHRV ˌedit sth↔'out (of sth) to remove words, phrases or scenes from a book, programme, etc. before it is published or shown: *They edited out references to her father in the interview.*

edi·tion /ɪ'dɪʃn/ *noun* **1** the form in which a book is published: *a paperback/hardback/hardcover edition* ◊ *She collects first editions of Victorian novels.* ◊ *the electronic edition of 'The Guardian'* **2** a particular newspaper or magazine, or radio or television programme, especially one in a regular series: *Tonight's edition of 'Panorama' looks at unemployment.* **3** (*abbr.* **ed.**) the total number of copies of a book, newspaper or magazine, etc. published at one time: *The dictionary is now in its sixth edition.* ◊ *The article appeared in the evening edition of 'The Mercury'.*—see also LIMITED EDITION—compare IMPRESSION (7)

edi·tor /'edɪtə(r)/ *noun* **1** a person who is in charge of a newspaper, magazine, etc., or part of one, and who decides what should be included: *the editor of the Washington Post* ◊ *the sports/financial/fashion editor* **2** a person who prepares a book to be published, for example by checking and correcting the text, making improvements, etc.—see also COPY EDITOR, SUBEDITOR **3** a person who prepares a film/movie, radio or television programme for being shown or broadcast by deciding what to include, and what order it should be in **4** a person who works as a journalist for radio or television reporting on a particular area of news: *our economics editor* **5** a person who chooses texts written by one or by several writers and prepares them to be published in a book: *She's the editor of a new collection of ghost stories.* **6** (*computing*) a program that allows you to change stored text or data ▶ **edit·or·ship** *noun* [U]: *the editorship of 'The Times'*

edi·tor·ial /ˌedɪ'tɔːriəl/ *adj., noun*
■ *adj.* [usually before noun] connected with the task of preparing sth such as a newspaper, a book or a television or radio programme, to be published or broadcast: *the magazine's editorial staff* ◊ *an editorial decision*
■ *noun* (*BrE* also **lead·er**, **ˌleading 'article**) an important article in a newspaper, that expresses the editor's opinion about an item of news or an issue; in the US also a comment on radio or television that expresses the opinion of the STATION or NETWORK

edu·cate /'edʒukeɪt/ *verb* **1** [VN] [often passive] to teach sb over a period of time at a school, college, university, etc: *She was educated in the US.* ◊ *He was educated at his local comprehensive school and then at Oxford.* **2 ~ sb (in/on sth)** to teach sb about sth or how to do sth: [VN] *Children need to be educated on the dangers of drug-taking.* ◊

[VN to inf] *The campaign is intended to educate the public to respect the environment.*

edu·cated /'edʒukeɪtɪd/ *adj.* **1** (**-educated**) having had the kind of education mentioned; having been to the school, college or university mentioned: *privately educated children* ◊ *a British-educated lawyer* ◊ *He's a Princeton-educated Texan.* **2** having had a high standard of education; showing a high standard of education: *an educated and articulate person* ◊ *the educated elite* ◊ *He spoke in an educated voice.* IDM **an ˌeducated 'guess** a guess that is based on some degree of knowledge, and is therefore likely to be correct

edu·ca·tion /ˌedʒu'keɪʃn/ *noun* **1** [U, sing.] a process of teaching, training and learning, especially in schools or colleges, to improve knowledge and develop skills: *primary/elementary education* ◊ *secondary education* ◊ *further/higher/post-secondary education* ◊ *students in full-time education* ◊ *adult education classes* ◊ *a college/university education* ◊ *the state education system* ◊ *a man of little education* ◊ *She completed her formal education in 1995.* **2** [U, sing.] a particular kind of teaching or training: *health education* **3** (also **Education**) [U] the institutions or people involved in teaching and training: *the Education Department* ◊ *the Department of Health, Education and Welfare* ◊ *There should be closer links between education and industry.* **4** (usually **Education**) [U] the subject of study that deals with how to teach: *a College of Education* ◊ *a Bachelor of Education degree* ◊ *She's an education major.* **5** [sing.] (often *humorous*) an interesting experience that teaches you sth: *The rock concert was quite an education for my parents!*

edu·ca·tion·al /ˌedʒu'keɪʃənl/ *adj.* connected with education; providing education: *children with special educational needs* ◊ *an educational psychologist* ◊ *an educational visit* ◊ *educational games/toys* (= that teach you sth as well as amusing you) ◊ *Watching television can be very educational.* ▶ **edu·ca·tion·al·ly** /-ʃənəli/ *adv.*: *Children living in inner-city areas may be educationally disadvantaged.* ◊ (*old-fashioned*) *educationally subnormal*

edu·ca·tion·al·ist /ˌedʒu'keɪʃənəlɪst/ (also **edu·ca·tion·ist** /ˌedʒu'keɪʃənɪst/) *noun* a specialist in theories and methods of teaching

edu·ca·tive /'edʒukətɪv/ *adj.* (*formal*) that teaches sth: *the educative role of the community*

edu·ca·tor /'edʒukeɪtə(r)/ *noun* (*formal*) **1** a person whose job is to teach or educate people: *adult educators* (= who teach adults) **2** (*especially AmE*) a person who is an expert in the theories and methods of education—see also EDUCATIONALIST

edu·tain·ment /ˌedju'teɪnmənt/ *noun* [U] products such as books, television programmes and especially computer SOFTWARE that both educate and entertain

-ee *suffix* (in nouns) **1** a person affected by an action: *employee*—compare -ER, -OR **2** a person described as or concerned with: *absentee* ◊ *refugee*

EEG /ˌiː iː 'dʒiː/ *noun* the abbreviation for 'electroencephalogram' (a medical test that measures and records electrical activity in the brain)

eel /iːl/ *noun* [C, U] a long thin sea or FRESHWATER fish that looks like a snake. There are several types of eel, some of which are are used for food: *jellied eels*

-eer *suffix* **1** (in nouns) a person concerned with: *auctioneer* ◊ *mountaineer* **2** (in verbs) (often *disapproving*) to be concerned with: *profiteer* ◊ *commandeer*

eerie /'ɪəri; *AmE* 'ɪri/ *adj.* strange, mysterious and frightening: *an eerie yellow light* ◊ *I found the silence underwater really eerie.* ▶ **eer·ily** /'ɪərəli; *AmE* 'ɪr-/ *adv.*

eff /ef/ *verb* IDM **eff and 'blind** (*BrE, informal*) to use swear words: *There was a lot of effing and blinding going on.* PHRV ˌeff 'off (△, *BrE*) a rude way of telling sb to go away, used instead of 'fuck off'—see also EFFING

ef·face /ɪ'feɪs/ *verb* [VN] (*formal*) to make sth disappear; to remove sth—see also SELF-EFFACING

ef·fect /ɪ'fekt/ *noun, verb*
■ *noun* **1** [C, U] **~ (on sb/sth)** a change that sb/sth causes in sb/sth else; a result: *the effect of heat on metal* ◊ *dramatic/long-term effects* ◊ *to learn to distinguish between cause*

æ	ɑː	e	ɜː	ə	ɪ	iː	i	ɒ	ɔː	ʌ	ʊ	u	uː
cat	father	ten	bird	about	sit	see	many	got	saw	cup	put	actual	too
								(BrE)					

E

and effect ◊ *the beneficial effects of exercise* ◊ *Modern farming methods can have an adverse effect on the environment.* ◊ *Her criticisms had the effect of discouraging him completely.* ◊ *Despite her ordeal, she seems to have suffered no ill effects.* ◊ *I can certainly feel the effects of too many late nights.* ◊ *'I'm feeling really depressed.' 'The winter here has that effect sometimes.'* ◊ *I tried to persuade him, but with little or no effect.*—see also GREENHOUSE EFFECT, KNOCK-ON, SIDE EFFECT ⇨ note at AFFECT **2** [C, U] a particular look, sound or impression that sb, such as an artist or a writer, wants to create: *The overall effect of the painting is overwhelming.* ◊ *The stage lighting gives the effect of a moonlit scene.* ◊ *Add a scarf for a casual effect.* ◊ *He only behaves like that for effect* (= in order to impress people).—see also SPECIAL EFFECTS, SOUND EFFECT **3 (effects)** [pl.] *(formal, written)* your personal possessions: *The insurance policy covers all baggage and personal effects.* **IDM** **bring/put sth into ef'fect** to cause sth to come into use: *The recommendations will soon be put into effect.* **come into ef'fect** to come into use; to begin to apply: *New controls come into effect next month.* **in ef'fect 1** used when you are stating what the facts of a situation are: *In effect, the two systems are identical.* ◊ *His wife had, in effect, run the government for the past six months.* **2** (of a law or rule) in use: *These laws are in effect in twenty states.* **take ef'fect 1** to start to produce the results that are intended: *The aspirins soon take effect.* **2** to come into use; to begin to apply: *The new law takes effect from tomorrow.* **to the effect that … | to this/that ef'fect** used to show that you are giving the general meaning of what sb has said or written rather than the exact words: *He left a note to the effect that he would not be coming back.* ◊ *She told me to get out—or words to that effect.* **to good, great, dramatic, etc. ef'fect** producing a good, successful, dramatic, etc. result or impression **to no ef'fect** not producing the result you intend or hope for: *We warned them, but to no effect.* **with immediate effect | with effect from …** *(formal)* starting now; starting from …: *The government has cut interest rates with effect from the beginning of next month.*
■ *verb* [VN] *(formal)* to make sth happen: *to effect a cure/change/recovery* ⇨ note at AFFECT

ef·fec·tive /ɪˈfektɪv/ *adj.* **1** producing the result that is wanted or intended; producing a successful result: *Long prison sentences can be a very effective deterrent for offenders.* ◊ *Aspirin is a simple but highly effective treatment.* ◊ *drugs that are effective against cancer* ◊ *I admire the effective use of colour in her paintings.* **OPP** INEFFECTIVE— see also COST-EFFECTIVE **2** [only before noun] in reality, although not officially intended: *the effective, if not the actual, leader of the party* ◊ *He has now taken effective control of the country.* **3** *(formal)* (of laws and rules) coming into use: *The new speed limit on this road becomes effective from 1 June.* ▸ **ef·fec·tive·ness** (also *less frequent* **ef·fect·iv·ity** /ˌɪfekˈtɪvɪti/) *noun* [U]: *to check the effectiveness of the security system*

ef·fect·ive·ly /ɪˈfektɪvli/ *adv.* **1** in a way that produces the intended result or a successful result: *The company must reduce costs to compete effectively.* ◊ *You dealt with the situation very effectively.* **OPP** INEFFECTIVELY **2** used when you are saying what the facts of a situation are: *He was very polite but effectively he was telling me that I had no chance of getting the job.*

ef·fec·tual /ɪˈfektʃuəl/ *adj.* *(formal)* (of things, not of people) producing the result that was intended **SYN** EFFECTIVE: *an effectual remedy*—compare INEFFECTUAL ▸ **ef·fec·tual·ly** *adj.*

ef·fem·in·ate /ɪˈfemɪnət/ *adj.* *(disapproving)* (of a man or a boy) looking, behaving or sounding like a woman or a girl ▸ **ef·fem·in·acy** /ɪˈfemɪnəsi/ *noun* [U]

ef·fer·ves·cent /ˌefəˈvesnt; *AmE* ˌefərˈv-/ *adj.* **1** *(approving)* (of people and their behaviour) excited, enthusiastic and full of energy **SYN** BUBBLY **2** (of a liquid) having or producing small bubbles of gas ▸ **ef·fer·ves·cence** /ˌefəˈvesns; *AmE* ˌefərˈvesns/ *noun* [U]

ef·fete /ɪˈfiːt/ *adj.* *(disapproving)* **1** weak; without the power that it once had: *an effete monarchy* **2** (of a man) without strength; looking or behaving like a woman

ef·fi·ca·cious /ˌefɪˈkeɪʃəs/ *adj.* *(formal)* (of things, not of people) producing the result that was wanted or intended **SYN** EFFECTIVE: *They hope the new drug will prove especially efficacious in the relief of pain.*

ef·fi·cacy /ˈefɪkəsi/ *noun* [U] *(formal)* the ability of sth, especially a drug or a medical treatment, to produce the results that are wanted **SYN** EFFECTIVENESS

ef·fi·ciency /ɪˈfɪʃnsi/ *noun* **1** [U] the quality of doing sth well with no waste of time or money: *improvements in efficiency at the factory* ◊ *I was impressed by the efficiency with which she handled the crisis.* **2 (efficiencies)** [pl.] ways of wasting less time and money or of saving time or money: *We are looking at our business to see where savings and efficiencies can be made.* **3** [U] *(technical)* the relationship between the amount of energy that goes into a machine or an engine, and the amount that it produces

ef·fi·cient /ɪˈfɪʃnt/ *adj.* doing sth well and thoroughly with no waste of time, money, or energy: *an efficient secretary/teacher/manager* ◊ *efficient heating equipment* ◊ *the efficient use of energy* ◊ *As we get older, our bodies become less efficient at burning up calories.* ◊ *fuel-efficient cars* (= that do not use much fuel) **OPP** INEFFICIENT ▸ **ef·fi·cient·ly** /-li/ *adv.*: *a very efficiently organized event*

ef·figy /ˈefɪdʒi/ *noun* (*pl.* **-ies**) **1** a statue of a famous person, a saint or a god: *stone effigies in the church* **2** a model of a person that makes them look ugly: *The demonstrators burned a crude effigy of the president.*

eff·ing /ˈefɪŋ/ *adj.* [only before noun] *(BrE, △, spoken)* a swear word that many people find offensive that is used to emphasize a comment or an angry statement; used instead of saying 'fucking'

ef·flu·ent /ˈefluənt/ *noun* [U, C] *(formal)* liquid waste, especially chemicals produced by factories, or SEWAGE

ef·fort /ˈefət; *AmE* ˈefərt/ *noun* **1** [U, C] the physical or mental energy that you need to do sth; sth that takes a lot of energy: *You should put more effort into your work.* ◊ *A lot of effort has gone into making this event a success.* ◊ *It's a long climb to the top, but well worth the effort.* ◊ *Getting up this morning was quite an effort* (= it was difficult). ◊ *(BrE)* **With (an) effort** (= with difficulty) *she managed to stop herself laughing.* **2** [C] **~ (to do sth)** an attempt to do sth especially when it is difficult to do: *to make a determined/real/special effort to finish on time* ◊ *The company has laid off 150 workers in an effort to save money.* ◊ *I didn't really feel like going out, but I am glad* **I made the effort**. ◊ *The local clubs are* **making every effort** *to interest more young people.* ◊ *We need to make a* **concerted effort** *to finish on time.* ◊ *I spent hours cleaning the house, but there isn't much to show* **for all my efforts**. ◊ *With an effort of will he resisted the temptation.* ◊ *The prospect was a joint/group effort.* **3** [C] (usually after a noun) a particular activity that a group of people organize in order to achieve sth: *the Russian space effort* ◊ *the United Nations' peacekeeping effort* **4** [C] the result of an attempt to do sth: *I'm afraid this essay is a poor effort.* **IDM** see BEND *v.*

ef·fort·less /ˈefətləs; *AmE* ˈefərt-/ *adj.* needing little or no effort, so that it seems easy: *She dances with effortless grace.* ◊ *He made playing the guitar look effortless.* ▸ **ef·fort·less·ly** *adv.*

ef·front·ery /ɪˈfrʌntəri/ *noun* [U] *(formal)* behaviour that is confident and very rude, without any feeling of shame **SYN** NERVE: *He had the effrontery to accuse me of lying!*

ef·fu·sion /ɪˈfjuːʒn/ *noun* [C, U] **1** *(technical)* something, especially a liquid, that flows out of sb/sth; the act of flowing out **2** *(formal)* the expression of feelings in an exaggerated way; feelings that are expressed in this way

ef·fu·sive /ɪˈfjuːsɪv/ *adj.* showing much or too much emotion: *an effusive welcome* ◊ *He was effusive in his praise.* ▸ **ef·fu·sive·ly** *adv.*

e-fit /ˈiːfɪt/ *noun* *(BrE)* a picture of a person who is wanted by the police, made using a computer program that puts together and makes changes to pictures of different features of faces, based on information that is given by sb who has seen the person—compare IDENTIKIT, PHOTO-FIT

EFL /ˌiː ef ˈel/ *abbr.* *(BrE)* English as a foreign language

aɪ	aʊ	eɪ	əʊ	oʊ	ɔɪ	ɪə	eə	ʊə	j	w
my	now	say	go	go	boy	near	hair	pure	yes	wet
			(BrE)	(AmE)						

(refers to the teaching of English to people for whom it is not the first language)

EFTA /'eftə/ *abbr.* European Free Trade Association (an economic association of some European countries)

e.g. /ˌiː 'dʒiː/ *abbr.* for example (from the Latin 'exempli gratia'): *popular pets, e.g. cats and dogs*

egali·tar·ian /iˌɡælɪ'teəriən; *AmE* -'ter-/ *adj.* based on, or holding, the belief that everyone is equal and should have the same rights and opportunities: *an egalitarian society* ▶ **egali·tar·ian** *noun: He described himself as 'an egalitarian'.* **egali·tar·ian·ism** /-ɪzəm/ *noun* [U]

egg /eɡ/ *noun, verb*
■ *noun* **1** [C] a small OVAL object with a thin hard shell produced by a female bird and containing a young bird; a similar object produced by a female fish, insect, etc: *The female sits on the eggs until they hatch.* ◇ *The fish lay thousands of eggs at one time.* ◇ *crocodile eggs*—picture on pages A6, A7 **2** [C, U] a bird's egg, especially one from a chicken, that is eaten as food: *a boiled egg* ◇ *bacon and eggs* ◇ *fried/poached/scrambled eggs* ◇ *Bind the mixture together with a little beaten egg.* ◇ *You've got some egg on your shirt.* ◇ *egg yolks/whites* ◇ *egg noodles/pasta* ◇ *ducks'/quails' eggs* ◇ *a chocolate egg* (= made from chocolate in the shape of an egg)—see also EASTER EGG, SCOTCH EGG **3** [C] (in women and female animals) a cell that combines with a SPERM to create a baby or young animal: *The male sperm fertilizes the female egg.* ◇ *an egg donor*—see also NEST EGG **IDM** **have 'egg on/all over your face** (*informal*) to be made to look stupid: *They were left with egg on their faces when only ten people showed up.* **put all your eggs in one 'basket** to rely on one particular course of action for success rather than giving yourself several different possibilities: *I've applied for several jobs. I don't want to put all my eggs in one basket.* —more at CHICKEN *n.*, CURATE, KILL *v.*, OMELETTE, SURE *adv.*, TEACH
■ *verb* **PHRV** **ˌegg sb↔'on** to encourage sb to do sth, especially sth that they should not do: *He hit the other boy again and again as his friends egged him on.*

'egg cup *noun* a small cup for holding a boiled egg

egg·head /'eɡhed/ *noun* (*informal, disapproving* or *humorous*) a person who is very intelligent and is only interested in studying

egg·plant /'eɡplɑːnt/ *noun* [C, U] (*AmE*) = AUBERGINE—picture on page A3

ˌegg 'roll *noun* (*AmE*) a type of SPRING ROLL in which the pastry is made with eggs

egg·shell /'eɡʃel/ *noun* **1** [C, U] the hard thin outside of an egg **2** [U] (*BrE*) a type of paint that is smooth but not shiny when it dries

'egg timer *noun* a device that you use to measure the time needed to boil an egg

ego /'iːɡəʊ; *AmE* also *AmE* 'iːɡoʊ/ *noun* (*pl.* -os) **1** your sense of your own value and importance: *He has the biggest ego of anyone I've ever met.* ◇ *Winning the prize really boosted her ego.* **2** (*psychology*) the part of the mind that is responsible for your sense of who you are (= your IDENTITY)—see also ALTER EGO—compare SUPEREGO, ID

ego·cen·tric /ˌeɡəʊ'sentrɪk; ˌiːɡ-; *AmE* ˌiːɡoʊ-/ *adj.* thinking only about yourself and not about what other people need or want **SYN** SELFISH

ego·ism /'eɡəʊɪzəm; 'iːɡ-; *AmE* -oʊ-/ (also **egot·ism** /'eɡətɪzəm; 'iːɡ-/) *noun* [U] (*disapproving*) the fact of thinking that you are better or more important than anyone else ▶ **ego·is·tic** /ˌeɡəʊ'ɪstɪk; ˌiːɡ-; *AmE* -oʊ-/ (also **egot·is·tic·al** /ˌeɡə'tɪstɪkl; ˌiːɡə-/) **ego·is·tic** /ˌeɡə-'tɪstɪk; ˌiːɡə-/) *adj.* **ego·is·tic·al·ly** /-kli/ *adv.*

ego·ist /'eɡəʊɪst; 'iːɡ-; *AmE* 'iːɡoʊ-/ (also **egot·ist** /'eɡətɪst; 'iːɡə-/) *noun* (*disapproving*) a person who thinks that they are better than other people and who thinks and talks too much about himself or herself: *You need to be an egotist to succeed in politics.*

'ego trip *noun* (usually *disapproving*) an activity that sb does because it makes them feel good and important

egre·gious /ɪ'ɡriːdʒiəs/ *adj.* (*formal*) extremely bad

egret /'iːɡrət/ *noun* a bird of the HERON family, with long legs and long white tail feathers

eh /eɪ/ *exclamation* (*BrE*) (*AmE* usually **huh**) **1** the sound that people make when they want sb to repeat sth: *'I'm not hungry.' 'Eh?' 'I said I'm not hungry.'* **2** the sound that people make when they want sb to agree or reply: *So what do you think, eh?* **3** the sound people make when they are surprised: *Another new dress, eh!*

Eid (also **Id**) /iːd/ *noun* one of the two main Muslim festivals, either **Eid ul-Fitr** /ˌiːd ʊl 'fɪtrə/ at the end of Ramadan, or **Eid ul-Adha** /ˌiːd ʊl 'ɑːdə/ which celebrates the end of the PILGRIMAGE to Mecca and Abraham's SACRIFICE of a sheep

ei·der·down /'aɪdədaʊn; *AmE* -dərd-/ *noun* (*BrE*) a thick, warm cover for a bed, filled with feathers or other soft material, and usually placed on top of a sheet and BLANKETS

eider duck /'aɪdə dʌk; *AmE* 'aɪdər/ *noun* a large duck with soft feathers, that lives in northern countries

eight /eɪt/ **1** *number* 8 **HELP** There are examples of how to use numbers at the entry for **five**. **2** *noun* a team of eight people who row a long narrow boat in races; the boat they row—see also FIGURE OF EIGHT

eight·een /ˌeɪ'tiːn/ *number* 18 ▶ **eight·eenth** /ˌeɪ'tiːnθ/ *ordinal number*

eighth /eɪtθ/ *ordinal number, noun*
■ *ordinal number* 8th **HELP** There are examples of how to use ordinal numbers at the entry for **fifth**.
■ *noun* each of eight equal parts of sth

'eighth note *noun* (*AmE, music*) = QUAVER

eighty /'eɪti/ *number* **1** 80 **2** (**the eight·ies**) [pl.] numbers, years or temperatures from 80 to 89 ▶ **eight·ieth** /'eɪtiəθ/ *ordinal number* **IDM** **in your eighties** between the ages of 80 and 89

ei·stedd·fod /aɪ'steðvɒd; *AmE* -vɑːd/ *noun* a festival, held in Wales, in which there are singing, music and poetry competitions

ei·ther /'aɪðə(r); 'iːðə(r)/ *det., pron., adv.*
■ *det., pron.* **1** one or the other of two; it does not matter which: *You can park on either side of the street.* ◇ *You can keep one of the photos. Either of them—whichever you like.* ◇ *There are two types of qualification—either is acceptable.* ⇨ note at NEITHER **2** each of two: *The offices on either side were empty.* ◇ *There's a door at either end of the corridor.*
■ *adv.* **1** used after negative phrases to state that a feeling or situation is similar to one already mentioned: *Pete can't go and I can't either.* ◇ (*AmE, informal*) *'I don't like it.' 'Me either.'* (= Neither do I). **2** used to add extra information to a statement: *I know a good Italian restaurant. It's not far from here, either.* **3** (**either...or...**) used to show a choice of two things: *Well, I think she's either Russian or Polish.* ◇ *I'm going to buy either a camera or a CD player with the money.* ◇ *Either he could not come or he did not want to.*—compare OR ⇨ note at NEITHER

ejacu·late /i'dʒækjuleɪt/ *verb* **1** [V, VN] when a man or a male animal **ejaculates**, SEMEN comes out through the PENIS **2** [V speech] (*old-fashioned*) to say or shout sth suddenly

ejacu·la·tion /iˌdʒækju'leɪʃn/ *noun* **1** [C, U] the act of ejaculating; the moment when SPERM comes out of a man's PENIS: *premature ejaculation* **2** [C] (*formal*) a sudden shout or sound that you make when you are angry or surprised

eject /i'dʒekt/ *verb* **1** [VN] ~ **sb (from sth)** (*formal*) to force sb to leave a place: *Police ejected a number of violent protesters from the hall.* **2** [VN] ~ **sth (from sth)** to push sth out suddenly and with a lot of force: *Used cartridges are ejected from the gun after firing.* **3** [V] to escape from an aircraft that is going to crash, sometimes using an EJECTOR SEAT: *The pilot managed to eject moments before the plane crashed.* **4** [VN, V] when you eject a tape, disk, etc., or when it ejects, it comes out of the machine after you have pressed a button ▶ **ejec·tion** /i'dʒekʃn/ *noun* [U, C]

eject·or seat /i'dʒektə siːt; *AmE* -tər/ (*AmE* also **ejection seat**) *noun* a seat that allows a pilot to be thrown out of an aircraft in an emergency

eke /iːk/ *verb* **PHRV** **ˌeke sth↔'out 1** to make a small supply of sth such as food or money last longer by using

b	d	f	g	h	k	l	m	n	p	r
bad	did	fall	get	hat	cat	leg	man	now	pen	red

only small amounts of it: *She managed to eke out her student loan till the end of the year.* **2 ~ a living, etc.** (*written*) to manage to live with very little money

EKG /ˌiː keɪ ˈdʒiː/ *abbr.* (*AmE*) = ECG

elab·or·ate *adj., verb*

■ *adj.* [usually before noun] very complicated and detailed; carefully prepared and organized: *elaborate designs/decorations* ◊ *She had prepared a very elaborate meal.* ◊ *an elaborate computer system* ▶ **elab·or·ate·ly** *adv.: an elaborately decorated room*

■ *verb* /ɪˈlæbəreɪt/ **1 ~ (on/upon sth)** to explain or describe sth in a more detailed way: [V] *He said he was resigning but did not elaborate on his reasons.* ◊ [VN] *She went on to elaborate her argument.* [also V speech] **2** [VN] to develop a plan, an idea, etc. and make it complicated or detailed: *In his plays he takes simple traditional tales and elaborates them.* ▶ **elab·or·ation** /ɪˌlæbəˈreɪʃn/ *noun* [U, C]: *The importance of the plan needs no further elaboration.*

elan /eɪˈlɒ̃; eɪˈlæn; *AmE* eɪˈlɑː/ *noun* [U] (*from French, written*) showing great enthusiasm and energy, style and confidence

elapse /ɪˈlæps/ *verb* [V] (not usually used in the progressive tenses) (*formal*) if a period of time **elapses**, it passes: *Many years elapsed before they met again.*

e·lapsed ˈtime *noun* [U] (*technical*) used to describe the time that passes between the start and end of a project or a computer operation, in contrast to the actual time needed to do a particular task which is part of the project

elas·tic /ɪˈlæstɪk/ *noun, adj.*

■ *noun* [U] material made with rubber, that can stretch and then return to its original size: *This skirt needs some new elastic in the waist.*

■ *adj.* **1** made with elastic: *an elastic headband* **2** able to stretch and return to its original size and shape: *elastic materials* **3** that can change or be changed: *The demand for the product is elastic.* ◊ *Our plans are fairly elastic.*

elas·ti·cated /ɪˈlæstɪkeɪtɪd/ (*BrE*) (*AmE* **elas·ti·cized** /ɪˈlæstɪsaɪzd/) *adj.* (of clothing, or part of a piece of clothing) made using elastic material that can stretch: *a skirt with an elasticated waist*

e·lastic ˈband *noun* (*BrE*) = RUBBER BAND

elas·ti·city /ˌiːlæˈstɪsəti; ˌelæ-; ˌɪˌlæ-/ *noun* [U] the quality that sth has of being able to stretch and return to its original size and shape (= of being elastic)

elated /iˈleɪtɪd/ *adj.* **~ (at/by sth)** very happy and excited because of sth good that has happened, or will happen: *They were elated at the result.* ◊ *I was elated by the prospect of the new job ahead.*

ela·tion /iˈleɪʃn/ *noun* [U] a feeling of great happiness and excitement

elbow /ˈelbəʊ; *AmE* -boʊ/ *noun, verb*

■ *noun* **1** the joint between the upper and lower parts of the arm where it bends in the middle: *She jabbed him with her elbow.* ◊ *He's fractured his elbow.*—picture at BODY **2** the part of a piece of clothing that covers the elbow: *The jacket was worn at the elbows.* **3** a part of a pipe, chimney, etc. where it bends at a sharp angle **IDM get the ˈelbow** (*BrE, informal*) to be told by sb that they no longer want to have a relationship with you; to be told to go away **give sb the ˈelbow** (*BrE, informal*) to tell sb that you no longer want to have a relationship with them; to tell sb to go away—more at KNOW *v.*, POWER *n.*, RUB *v.*

■ *verb* [VN] [usually +*adv./prep.*] to push sb with your elbow, usually in order to get past them: *She elbowed me out of the way to get to the front of the line.* ◊ *He elbowed his way through the crowd.*

ˈelbow grease *noun* [U] (*informal*) the effort used in physical work, especially in cleaning or polishing sth

ˈelbow room *noun* [U] (*informal*) enough space to move or walk in

elder /ˈeldə(r)/ *adj., noun*

■ *adj.* **1** [only before noun] (of people, especially two members of the same family) older: *my elder brother* ◊ *his elder sister* **2** (**the elder**) used without a noun immediately after it to show who is the older of two people: *the elder of their two sons* **3** (**the elder**) (*formal*) used before or after sb's

name to show that they are the older of two people who have the same name: *the elder Pitt* ◊ *Pitt the elder—* compare THE YOUNGER at YOUNG *adj.* (6) ⇨ note at OLD

■ *noun* **1** (**elders**) [pl.] people of greater age, experience and authority: *Children have no respect for their elders nowadays.* ◊ *the village elders* (= the old and respected people of the village) **2** (**my, etc. elder**) [sing.] (*formal*) a person older than me, etc: *He is her elder by several years.* **3** [C] an official in some Christian churches **4** [C] a small tree with white flowers with a sweet smell (**elderflowers**) and bunches of small black berries (**elderberries**) **IDM your ˌelders and ˈbetters** people who are older and wiser than you and whom you should respect

elder·berry /ˈeldəberi; *AmE* -derb-/ *noun* (*pl.* **-ies**) a small black berry that grows in bunches on an elder tree: *elderberry wine*

eld·er·ly /ˈeldəli; *AmE* -ərli/ *adj.* **1** (of people) used as a polite word for 'old': *an elderly couple* ◊ *elderly relatives* **2** (**the elderly**) *noun* [pl.] people who are old

ˌelder ˈstatesman *noun* **1** an old and respected politician or former politician whose advice is still valued because of his or her long experience **2** any experienced and respected person whose advice or work is valued: *an elder statesman of golf*

eld·est /ˈeldɪst/ *adj.* **1** (of people, especially of three or more members of the same family) oldest: *Tom is my eldest son.* **2** (**the eldest**) used without a noun immediately after it to show who is the oldest of three or more people: *the eldest of their three children* ⇨ note at OLD

elect /ɪˈlekt/ *verb, adj.*

■ *verb* **1 ~ sb (to sth) | ~ sb (as) sth** to choose sb to do a particular job by voting for them: [VN] *an elected assembly/leader/representative* ◊ *the newly elected Labour government* ◊ *She became the first black woman to be elected to the Senate.* ◊ [VN-N] *He was elected (as) MP for Oxford East.* **2** [V to inf] (*formal*) to choose to do sth: *Increasing numbers of people elect to work from home nowadays.*

■ *adj.* **1** used after nouns to show that sb has been chosen for a job, but is not yet doing that job: *the president elect* **2** (**the elect**) *noun* [pl.] (*religion*) people who have been chosen to be saved from punishment after death

elec·tion /ɪˈlekʃn/ *noun* **1** [U, C] the process of choosing a person or a group of people for a position, especially a political position, by voting: *election campaigns/results* ◊ *to win/lose an election* ◊ *to vote in an election* ◊ *In America, presidential elections are held every four years.* ◊ (*BrE*) *How many candidates are* **standing for election**? ◊ (*AmE*) *to* **run for election 2** [U] the fact of having been chosen by election: *We welcome his election as president.*—see also BY-ELECTION, GENERAL ELECTION

elec·tion·eer·ing /ɪˌlekʃəˈnɪərɪŋ; *AmE* -ˈnɪr-/ *noun* [U] the activity of making speeches and visiting people to try to persuade them to vote for a particular politician or political party in an election

elect·ive /ɪˈlektɪv/ *adj., noun*

■ *adj.* [usually before noun] (*formal*) **1** using or chosen by election: *an elective democracy* ◊ *an elective assembly* ◊ *an elective member* ◊ *He had never held the elective office* (= a position which is filled by election). **2** having the power to elect: *an elective body* **3** (of medical treatment) that you choose to have; that is not urgent: *elective surgery* **4** (of a course or subject) that a student can choose

■ *noun* (*especially AmE*) a course or subject at a college or school which a student can choose to do

elect·or /ɪˈlektə(r)/ *noun* a person who has the right to vote in an election

elect·oral /ɪˈlektərəl/ *adj.* [only before noun] connected with elections: *electoral systems/reforms* ▶ **elect·or·al·ly** /-rəli/ *adv.: an electorally effective campaign*

e·lectoral ˈcollege *noun* **1** (**the Electoral College**) (in the US) a group of people who come together to elect the President and Vice-President, based on the votes of people in each state **2** (*BrE*) a group of people who are chosen to represent the members of a political party, etc. in the election of a leader

e·lectoral ˈregister (also **e·lectoral ˈroll**) *noun* (in

	s	t	v	z	ʃ	ʒ	tʃ	dʒ	θ	ð	ŋ
	see	tea	van	zoo	shoe	vision	chain	jam	thin	this	sing

Britain) the official list of people who have the right to vote in a particular area

elect·or·ate /ɪˈlektərət/ *noun* [C+sing./pl. *v.*] **1** the people in a country or an area who have the right to vote, thought of as a group: *Only 70% of the electorate voted in the last election.* **2** (*AustralE, NZE*) = CONSTITUENCY (1)

elec·tric /ɪˈlektrɪk/ *adj., noun*
■ *adj.* **1** [usually before noun] connected with electricity; using, produced by or producing electricity: *an electric motor ◇ an electric light/guitar ◇ an electric current/charge ◇ an electric generator ◇ an electric plug/socket/switch* (= that carries electricity)—see also ELECTRIC SHOCK, ELECTRIC STORM **2** full of excitement; making people excited: *The atmosphere was electric. ◇ The news had an electric effect on the waiting crowd.*
■ *noun* [U] (*spoken, informal*) used to refer to the supply of electricity to a building: *The electric will be off tomorrow. ◇ I haven't paid the electric* (= the bill for the supply of electricity) *yet.*

WHICH WORD?
electric / electrical (?)

These adjectives are frequently used with the following nouns:

electric ~	electrical ~
light	equipment
guitar	wiring
drill	signal
chair	engineer
shock	shock

Electric is usually used to describe something that uses or produces electricity. You use **electrical** with more general nouns such as *equipment* and *wiring* and things that are concerned with electricity: *an electrical fault.* However, the distinction is not always so clear now: *an electric/electrical company ◇ an electric/electrical current ◇ an electric/electrical shock.*

---

elec·tric·al /ɪˈlektrɪkl/ *adj.* connected with electricity; using or producing electricity: *an electrical fault in the engine ◇ electrical equipment/appliances ◇ electrical power/energy* ► **elec·tric·al·ly** /-kli/ *adv.*: *a car with electrically operated windows ◇ electrically charged particles*

e·lectrical engiˈneering *noun* [U] the design and building of machines and systems that use or produce electricity; the study of this subject ► **e·lectrical engiˈneer** *noun*

e·lectrical ˈstorm *noun* (*especially AmE*) = ELECTRIC STORM

e·lectric ˈblanket *noun* a BLANKET for a bed that is heated by electricity passing through the wires inside it (usually used under the bottom sheet of the bed)

e·lectric ˈblue *noun* [U] a bright or METALLIC blue colour

e·lectric ˈchair (usually **the electric chair**) (also *informal* **the chair**) *noun* [sing.] (especially in the US) a chair in which criminals are killed by passing a powerful electric current through their bodies; the method of EXECUTION which uses this chair: *He was sent to the electric chair. ◇ They face death by the electric chair.*

e·lectric ˈfence *noun* a wire fence through which an electric current can be passed

elec·tri·cian /ɪˌlekˈtrɪʃn/ *noun* a person whose job is to connect, repair, etc. electrical equipment

elec·tri·city /ɪˌlekˈtrɪsəti/ *noun* **1** [U] a form of energy from charged ELEMENTARY PARTICLES, usually supplied as electric current through cables, wires, etc. for lighting, heating, driving machines, etc: *a waste of electricity ◇ The electricity is off* (= there is no electric power supply to the house). **2** [U, sing.] (*written*) a feeling of great emotion, excitement, etc.

e·lectric ˈrazor *noun* = SHAVER

elec·trics /ɪˈlektrɪks/ *noun* [pl.] (*BrE, informal*) the sys-

tem of electrical wires in a house, car or machine: *There's a problem with the electrics.*

e·lectric ˈshock (also **shock**) *noun* a sudden painful feeling that you get when electricity passes through your body

e·lectric ˈstorm (*BrE*) (also **e·lectrical ˈstorm** *AmE, BrE*) *noun* a violent storm in which electricity is produced in the atmosphere

elec·tri·fi·ca·tion /ɪˌlektrɪfɪˈkeɪʃn/ *noun* [U] the process of changing sth so that it works by electricity: *the electrification of the railway line from Manchester to Preston*

elec·trify /ɪˈlektrɪfaɪ/ *verb* (**elec·tri·fies, elec·tri·fy·ing, elec·tri·fied, elec·tri·fied**) [VN] **1** [usually passive] to make sth work by using electricity; to pass an electrical current through sth: *The railway line was electrified in the 1950s. ◇ He had all the fences around his home electrified.* **2** (*written*) to make sb feel very excited and enthusiastic about sth: *Her performance electrified the audience.*

elec·tri·fy·ing /ɪˈlektrɪfaɪɪŋ/ *adj.* (*written*) very exciting: *The dancers gave an electrifying performance.*

elec·tro- /ɪˈlektrəʊ; AmE -troʊ/ *combining form* (in nouns, adjectives, verbs and adverbs) connected with electricity: *electromagnetism*

elec·tro·car·dio·gram /ɪˌlektrəʊˈkɑːdiəʊɡræm; AmE ɪˌlektroʊˈkɑːrdioʊ-/ *noun* = ECG

elec·tro·con·vul·sive therapy /ɪˌlektrəʊkənˈvʌlsɪv θerəpi; AmE -troʊ-/ (also **eˈlec·tro·shock ther·apy**) *noun* [U] a medical treatment of mental illness that passes electricity through the patient's brain

elec·tro·cute /ɪˈlektrəkjuːt/ *verb* [VN] [usually passive] to injure or kill sb by passing electricity through their body: *The boy was electrocuted when he wandered onto a railway track. ◇ James Roach was electrocuted in South Carolina in 1986* (= punished by being killed in the electric chair). ► **elec·tro·cu·tion** /ɪˌlektrəˈkjuːʃn/ *noun* [U]: *Six people were drowned; five died from electrocution. ◇ He was sentenced to death by electrocution.*

elec·trode /ɪˈlektrəʊd; AmE -troʊd/ *noun* either of two points (or TERMINALS) by which an electric current enters or leaves a battery or other electrical device—see also ANODE, CATHODE

elec·tro·enceph·alo·gram /ɪˌlektrəʊɪnˈsefələɡræm; -ˈkefələ-; AmE -troʊɪnˈsef-/ *noun* = EEG

elec·troly·sis /ɪˌlekˈtrɒləsɪs; AmE -ˈtrɑːl-/ *noun* [U] **1** the destruction of the roots of hairs by means of an electric current, as a beauty treatment **2** (*chemistry*) the separation of a liquid (or electrolyte) into its chemical parts by passing an electric current through it

elec·tro·lyte /ɪˈlektrəlaɪt/ *noun* (*chemistry*) a liquid that an electric current can pass through, especially in an electric cell or battery ► **elec·tro·ly·tic** /ɪˌlektrəˈlɪtɪk/ *adj.*

elec·tro·mag·net·ic /ɪˌlektrəʊmæɡˈnetɪk; AmE -troʊ-/ *adj.* (*physics*) having both electrical and MAGNETIC characteristics (or PROPERTIES): *an electromagnetic wave/field*

elec·tro·mag·net·ism /ɪˌlektrəʊˈmæɡnətɪzəm; AmE -troʊ-/ *noun* [U] (*physics*) the production of a MAGNETIC FIELD by means of an electric current, or of an electric current by means of a MAGNETIC FIELD

elec·tron /ɪˈlektrɒn; AmE -trɑːn/ *noun* (*physics*) a very small piece of MATTER (= a substance) with a negative electric CHARGE, found in all atoms—see also NEUTRON, PROTON

elec·tron·ic /ɪˌlekˈtrɒnɪk; AmE -ˈtrɑːnɪk/ *adj.* [usually before noun] **1** (of a device) having or using many small parts, such as MICROCHIPS, that control and direct a small electric current: *an electronic calculator ◇ electronic music ◇ This dictionary is available in electronic form.* **2** concerned with electronic equipment: *an electronic engineer*

elec·tron·ic·al·ly /ɪˌlekˈtrɒnɪkli/ *adv.* in an electronic way, or using a device that works in an electronic way: *to process data electronically* (= using a computer)

ˌelectronic ˈmail *noun* [U] (*formal*) = E-MAIL

elec·tron·ics /ɪˌlekˈtrɒnɪks; AmE -ˈtrɑːn-/ *noun* **1** [U] the branch of science and technology that studies electronic

E

æ	ɑː	e	ɜː	ə	ɪ	iː	i	ɒ	ɔː	ʌ	ʊ	u	uː
cat	father	ten	bird	about	sit	see	many	got	saw	cup	put	actual	too

(BrE)

currents in electronic equipment **2** [U] the use of electronic technology, especially in developing new equipment: *the electronics industry* **3** (**electronics**) [pl.] the electronic CIRCUITS and COMPONENTS (= parts) used in electronic equipment: *There may be a fault in the electronics.*

elec·tronic 'tagging *noun* [U] the system of attaching an electronic device to a person so that the police, etc. know where the person is

e·lectron 'microscope *noun* a very powerful MICROSCOPE that uses ELECTRONS instead of light rays

elec·tro·plate /ɪˈlektrəpleɪt/ *verb* [VN] [usually passive] to cover sth with a thin layer of metal using ELECTROLYSIS

elec·tro·shock ther·apy /ɪˈlektrəʊʃɒk ˈθerəpi; *AmE* -troʊʃɑːk/ *noun* = ELECTROCONVULSIVE THERAPY

ele·gant /ˈelɪɡənt/ *adj.* **1** (of people or their behaviour) graceful and attractive: *She was tall and elegant.* **2** (of clothes, places and things) attractive and designed well: *an elegant dress ◇ an elegant room/restaurant* **3** (of a plan or an idea) clever but simple: *an elegant solution to the problem* ▶ **ele·gance** /ˈelɪɡəns/ *noun* [U]: *She dresses with casual elegance. ◇ His writing combines elegance and wit.* **ele·gant·ly** *adv.*: *elegantly dressed ◇ elegantly furnished ◇ He leaned elegantly against the door.*

ele·giac /ˌelɪˈdʒaɪək/ *adj.* (*formal* or *literary*) expressing sadness, especially about the past or people who have died: *Her poetry has an elegiac quality.*

elegy /ˈelədʒi/ *noun* (*pl.* **-ies**) a poem or song that expresses sadness, especially for sb who has died

elem·ent /ˈelɪmənt/ *noun*

PART/AMOUNT | **1** [C] ~ (**in/of sth**) a necessary or typical part of sth: *Cost was a key element in our decision. ◇ The story has all the elements of a soap opera. ◇ Customer relations is an important element of the job.* **2** [C, usually sing.] ~ **of surprise, risk, truth, etc.** a small amount of a quality or feeling: *We need to preserve the element of surprise. ◇ There appears to be an element of truth in his story.*

GROUP OF PEOPLE | **3** [C, usually pl.] a group of people who form a part of a larger group or society: *moderate/radical elements within the party ◇ unruly elements in the school*

CHEMISTRY | **4** [C] a simple chemical substance that consists of atoms of only one type and cannot be split by chemical means into a simpler substance. Gold, OXYGEN and CARBON are all elements.—compare COMPOUND

EARTH/AIR/FIRE/WATER | **5** [C] one of the four substances: earth, air, fire and water, which people used to believe everything else was made of

WEATHER | **6** (**the elements**) [pl.] the weather, especially bad weather: *Are we going to brave the elements and go for a walk? ◇ to be exposed to the elements*

BASIC PRINCIPLES | **7** (**elements**) [pl.] the basic principles of a subject that you have to learn first: *He taught me the elements of map-reading.*

ENVIRONMENT | **8** [C, usually sing.] a natural or suitable environment, especially for an animal: *Water is a fish's natural element.*

ELECTRICAL PART | **9** [C] the part of a piece of electrical equipment that gives out heat: *The kettle needs a new element.*

IDM **in your 'element** doing what you are good at and enjoy: *She's really in her element at parties.* **out of your 'element** in a situation that you are not used to and that makes you feel uncomfortable: *I feel out of my element talking about politics.*

elem·en·tal /ˌelɪˈmentl/ *adj.* [usually before noun] (*formal*) **1** wild and powerful; like the forces of nature: *the elemental fury of the storm* **2** basic and important: *an elemental truth*

elem·en·tary /ˌelɪˈmentri/ *adj.* **1** in or connected with the first stages of a course of study: *an elementary English course ◇ a book for elementary students ◇ at an elementary level*—compare PRIMARY, SECONDARY **2** of the most basic kind: *the elementary laws of economics ◇ an elementary mistake* **3** very simple and easy: *elementary questions*

elementary 'particle *noun* (*physics*) any of the different types of very small pieces of MATTER (= a substance) smaller than an atom

ele'mentary school (also *informal* **'grade school**) *noun* (in the US) a school for children between the ages of about 6 and 12

ele·phant /ˈelɪfənt/ *noun* a very large animal with thick grey skin, large ears, two curved outer teeth called TUSKS and a long nose called a TRUNK. There are two types of elephant, the African and the Asian: *herds of elephants/ elephant herds ◇ a baby elephant*—see also WHITE ELEPHANT

ele·phant·ine /ˌelɪˈfæntaɪn; *AmE* -tiːn/ *adj.* (*formal* or *humorous*) very large and CLUMSY; like an elephant

ele·vate /ˈelɪveɪt/ *verb* [VN] **1** ~ **sb/sth** (**to sth**) | ~ **sth** (**into sth**) (*formal*) to give sb/sth a higher position or rank, often more important than they deserve **SYN** RAISE, PROMOTE: *He elevated many of his friends to powerful positions within the government. ◇ It was an attempt to elevate football to a subject worthy of serious study.* **2** (*technical* or *formal*) to lift sth up or put sth in a higher position: *It is important that the injured leg should be elevated.* **3** (*technical*) to make the level of sth increase: *Smoking often elevates blood pressure.* **4** (*formal*) to improve a person's mood, so that they feel happy: *The song never failed to elevate his spirits.*

ele·vated /ˈelɪveɪtɪd/ *adj.* [usually before noun] **1** high in rank: *an elevated status* **2** (*formal*) having a high moral or INTELLECTUAL level: *elevated language/sentiments/ thoughts* **3** higher than the area around; above the level of the ground: *The house is in an elevated position, overlooking the town. ◇ an elevated highway/railway/road* (= one that runs on a bridge above the ground or street) **4** (*technical*) higher than normal: *elevated blood pressure*

ele·va·tion /ˌelɪˈveɪʃn/ *noun* **1** [U] (*formal*) the process of sb getting a higher or more important rank: *his elevation to the presidency* **2** [C, usually sing.] (*technical*) the height of a place, especially its height above sea level: *The city is at an elevation of 2000 metres.* **3** [C] (*formal*) a piece of ground that is higher than the area around **4** [C] (*architecture*) one side of a building, or a drawing of this by an ARCHITECT: *the front/rear/side elevation of a house*—compare PLAN *n.* (4) **5** [U, sing.] (*technical*) an increase in the level or amount of sth: *elevation of blood sugar levels*

ele·va·tor /ˈelɪveɪtə(r)/ *noun* **1** (*AmE*) = LIFT (1) **2** a place for storing large quantities of grain **3** a part in the tail of an aircraft that is moved to make it go up or down—picture at PLANE

eleven /ɪˈlevn/ **1** *number* 11 **2** *noun* a team of eleven players for football, cricket or hockey: *She was chosen for the first eleven.* ▶ **elev·enth** /ɪˈlevnθ/ *ordinal number* **IDM** **at the e‚leventh 'hour** at the last possible moment; just in time

e‚leven-'plus *noun* (usually **the eleven-plus**) [sing.] an exam that all children used to take in Britain at the age of eleven to decide which type of secondary school they should go to. It is still taken in a few areas.

elev·enses /ɪˈlevnzɪz/ *noun* [U] (*old-fashioned, BrE, informal*) a very small meal, for example biscuits with tea or coffee, that people sometimes have at about eleven o'clock in the morning

elf /elf/ *noun* (*pl.* **elves** /elvz/) (in stories) a creature like a small person with pointed ears, who has magic powers

elfin /ˈelfɪn/ *adj.* (*written*) (of a person or their features) small and delicate: *an elfin face*

elicit /iˈlɪsɪt/ *verb* [VN] ~ **sth** (**from sb**) (*written*) to get information or a reaction from sb, often with difficulty: *I could elicit no response from him. ◇ Her tears elicited great sympathy from her audience.*

elide /iˈlaɪd/ *verb* [VN] (*phonetics*) to leave out the sound of part of a word when you are pronouncing it: *The 't' in 'often' may be elided.*—see also ELISION

eli·gible /ˈelɪdʒəbl/ *adj.* **1** ~ (**for sth**) | ~ (**to do sth**) a person who is **eligible** for sth or to do sth, is able to have or do it because they have the right qualifications, are the right age, etc: *Only those over 70 are eligible for the special payment. ◇ When are you eligible to vote in your* *country?* [OPP] INELIGIBLE **2** an eligible young man or woman is thought to be a good choice as a husband/wife, usually because they are rich or attractive ▸ **eli·gi·bil·ity** /ˌelɪdʒəˈbɪləti/ *noun* [U]

elim·in·ate /ɪˈlɪmɪneɪt/ *verb* **1** [VN] ~ sth/sb (from sth) to remove or get rid of sth/sb: *Credit cards eliminate the need to carry a lot of cash.* ◊ *The police have eliminated two suspects from their investigation.* ◊ *This diet claims to eliminate toxins from the body.* **2** [VN] ~ sb (from sth) [usually passive] to defeat a person or a team so that they no longer take part in a competition, etc: *All the English teams were eliminated in the early stages of the competition.* ◊ *She was eliminated from the tournament in the first round.* **3** [VN] (*written*) to kill sb, especially an enemy or opponent: *Most of the enemy's left-wing opponents were eliminated.* ▸ **elim·in·ation** /ɪˌlɪmɪˈneɪʃn/ *noun* [U, C]: *the elimination of disease/poverty/crime* ◊ *There were three eliminations in the first round of the competition.* ◊ *the elimination of toxins from the body*

eli·sion /ɪˈlɪʒn/ *noun* [U, C] (*phonetics*) the act of leaving out the sound of part of a word when you are pronouncing it, as in *we'll*, *don't* and *let's*—see also ELIDE

elite /eɪˈliːt; ɪˈliːt/ *noun* [C+sing./pl. v.] a group of people in a society, etc. who are powerful and have a lot of influence, because they are rich, intelligent, etc: *a member of the ruling/intellectual elite* ◊ *Public opinion is influenced by the small elite who control the media.* ◊ *In these countries, only the elite can afford an education for their children.* ▸ **elite** *adj.* [only before noun]: *an elite group of senior officials* ◊ *an elite military academy*

elit·ism /eɪˈliːtɪzəm; ɪ-/ *noun* [U] (often *disapproving*) **1** a way of organizing a system, society, etc. so that only a few people (= an elite) have power or influence: *Many people believe that private education encourages elitism.* **2** the feeling of being better than other people that being part of an elite encourages ▸ **elit·ist** *adj.*: *an elitist model of society* ◊ *She accused him of being elitist.* **elit·ist** *noun*

elixir /ɪˈlɪksə(r); BrE also -sɪə(r)/ *noun* (*literary*) a magic liquid that is believed to cure illnesses or to make people live for ever: *the elixir of life/youth*

Eliza·bethan /ɪˌlɪzəˈbiːθn/ *adj.* connected with the time when Queen Elizabeth I was queen of England (1558–1603) ▸ **Eliza·bethan** *noun*: *Shakespeare was an Elizabethan.*

elk /elk/ *noun* (*pl.* **elk** or **elks**) **1** (*BrE*) a large deer that lives in northern Europe and Asia. In N America it is called a MOOSE. **2** (*AmE*) = WAPITI

el·lipse /ɪˈlɪps/ *noun* (*technical*) a regular OVAL shape, like a circle that has been pressed inwards from two sides—picture at OVAL

el·lip·sis /ɪˈlɪpsɪs/ *noun* (*pl.* **el·lip·ses** /-siːz/) [C, U] **1** (*grammar*) the act of leaving out a word or words from a sentence deliberately, when the meaning can be understood without them **2** three dots (…) used to show that a word or words have been left out ⇨ Appendix 4

el·lip·tic·al /ɪˈlɪptɪkl/ *adj.* **1** (especially *grammar*) with a word or words left out of a sentence deliberately: *an elliptical remark* (= one that suggests more than is actually said) **2** (also *less frequent* **el·lip·tic** /ɪˈlɪptɪk/) (*geometry*) connected with or in the form of an ELLIPSE ▸ **el·lip·tic·al·ly** /-kli/ *adv.*: *to speak/write elliptically*

elm /elm/ *noun* **1** [C, U] (also **'elm tree**) a tall tree with broad leaves: *a line of stately elms* ◊ *The hedgerows were planted with elm.* **2** [U] the hard wood of the elm tree

elo·cu·tion /ˌeləˈkjuːʃn/ *noun* [U] the ability to speak clearly and correctly, especially in public and pronouncing the words in a way that is considered to be socially acceptable

elong·ate /ˈiːlɒŋgeɪt; AmE ɪˈlɔːŋ-/ *verb* to become longer; to make sth longer: [V] *The seal pup's body elongates as it grows older.* [also VN] ▸ **elonga·tion** /ˌiːlɒŋˈgeɪʃn; AmE ˌiːlɔːŋ-/ *noun* [U]: *the elongation of vowel sounds*

elong·ated /ˈiːlɒŋgeɪtɪd; AmE ɪˈlɔːŋ-/ *adj.* long and thin, often in a way that is not normal: *Modigliani's women have strangely elongated faces.*

elope /ɪˈləʊp; AmE ɪˈloʊp/ *verb* [V] ~ (with sb) to run away with sb in order to marry them secretly ▸ **elope·ment** /ɪˈləʊpmənt; AmE ɪˈloʊp-/ *noun* [C, U]

elo·quent /ˈeləkwənt/ *adj.* **1** able to use language and express your opinions well, especially when you are speaking in public: *an eloquent speech/speaker* **2** (of a look or movement) able to express a feeling: *His eyes were eloquent.* ▸ **elo·quence** /ˈeləkwəns/ *noun* [U]: *a speech of passionate eloquence* ◊ *the eloquence of his smile* **elo·quent·ly** *adv.*: *She spoke eloquently on the subject for about an hour.* ◊ *His face expressed his grief more eloquently than any words.*

else /els/ *adv.* (used in questions or after *nothing*, *nobody*, *something*, *anything*, etc.) **1** in addition to sth already mentioned: *What else did he say?* ◊ *I don't want anything else, thanks.* ◊ *I'm taking a few clothes and some books, not much else.* **2** different: *Ask somebody else to help you.* ◊ *Haven't you got anything else to wear?* ◊ *Why didn't you come? Everybody else was there.* ◊ *Yes I did give it to her. What else could I do?* [IDM] **or else 1** if not; OTHERWISE: *Hurry up or else you'll be late.* ◊ *They can't be coming or else they'd have called.* **2** (*informal*) used to threaten or warn sb: *Just shut up, or else!*

else·where /ˌelsˈweə(r); AmE ˈelswer/ *adv.* in, at or to another place: *The answer to the problem must be sought elsewhere.* ◊ *Our favourite restaurant was closed, so we had to go elsewhere.* ◊ *Elsewhere, the weather today has been fairly sunny.* ◊ *Prices are higher here than elsewhere.*

ELT /ˌiː el ˈtiː/ *abbr.* (*BrE*) English Language Teaching (the teaching of English to people for whom it is not the first language)

elu·ci·date /ɪˈluːsɪdeɪt/ *verb* (*formal*) to make sth clearer by explaining it more fully: [VN] *He elucidated a point of grammar.* ◊ [V wh-] *I will try to elucidate what I think the problems are.* ◊ [V] *Let me elucidate.* ▸ **elu·ci·da·tion** /ɪˌluːsɪˈdeɪʃn/ *noun* [U, C]: *Their objectives and methods require further elucidation.*

elude /ɪˈluːd/ *verb* [VN] **1** to manage to avoid or escape from sb/sth, especially in a clever way: *The two men managed to elude the police for six weeks.* **2** if sth eludes you, you are not able to achieve it, or not able to remember or understand it: *He was extremely tired but sleep eluded him.* ◊ *They're a popular band but chart success has eluded them so far.* ◊ *Finally he remembered the tiny detail that had eluded him the night before.*

elu·sive /ɪˈluːsɪv/ *adj.* difficult to find, define, or achieve: *Eric, as elusive as ever, was nowhere to be found.* ◊ *the elusive concept of 'literature'* ◊ *A solution to the problem of toxic waste is proving elusive in the extreme.* ▸ **elu·sive·ly** *adv.* **elu·sive·ness** *noun* [U]

elves *pl.* of ELF

em- ⇨ EN-

'em /əm/ *pron.* (*informal*) = THEM: *Don't let 'em get away.*

ema·ci·ated /ɪˈmeɪʃieɪtɪd/ *adj.* thin and weak, usually because of illness or lack of food ▸ **ema·ci·ation** /ɪˌmeɪsiˈeɪʃn/ *noun* [U]: *She was very thin, almost to the point of emaciation.*

e-mail (also **email**) /ˈiːmeɪl/ *noun, verb*
■ *noun* **1** (also *formal* **electronic 'mail**) [U] a way of sending messages and data to other people by means of computers connected together in a NETWORK: *to send a message by e-mail*—picture on page 251 **2** [C, U] a message sent by e-mail ⇨ Study page B13
■ *verb* ~ sth (to sb) to send a message to sb by e-mail: [VN] *Patrick e-mailed me yesterday.* ◊ [VN, VNN] *I'll e-mail the documents to her.* ◊ *I'll e-mail her the documents.*

em·an·ate /ˈeməneɪt/ *verb* (*formal*) [VN] to produce or show sth: *He emanates power and confidence.* ▸ **em·an·ation** /ˌeməˈneɪʃn/ *noun* [C, U] [PHRV] **'emanate from sth** to come from sth or somewhere: *The sound of loud music emanated from the building.* ◊ *The proposal originally emanated from the UN.*

eman·ci·pate /ɪˈmænsɪpeɪt/ *verb* [VN] [often passive] ~ sb (from sth) to free sb, especially from legal, political or social restrictions: *Slaves were not emancipated until 1863 in the United States.* ▸ **eman·ci·pated** *adj.*: *Are women now fully emancipated* (= with the same rights and opportunities as men)? ◊ *an emancipated young woman* (= one with modern ideas about women's place in society)

eman·ci·pa·tion /ɪˌmænsɪˈpeɪʃn/ *noun* [U]: *the emancipation of slaves*

emas·cu·late /iˈmæskjuleɪt/ *verb* [VN] [often passive] (*formal*) **1** to make sb/sth less powerful or less effective **2** to make a man feel that he has lost his male role or qualities: *He felt emasculated by her dominance.* ▶ **emas·cu·la·tion** /iˌmæskjuˈleɪʃn/ *noun* [U]

em·balm /ɪmˈbɑːm/ *verb* [VN] to prevent a dead body from decaying by treating it with special substances to preserve it ▶ **em·balm·er** /ɪmˈbɑːmə(r)/ *noun*

em·bank·ment /ɪmˈbæŋkmənt/ *noun* **1** a wall of stone or earth made to keep water back or to carry a road or railway/railroad over low ground **2** a slope made of earth or stone that rises up from either side of a road or railway/railroad

em·bargo /ɪmˈbɑːgəʊ; *AmE* ɪmˈbɑːrgoʊ/ *noun, verb*
■ *noun* (*pl.* **-oes**) ~ **(on sth)** an official order that forbids trade with another country: *an arms embargo* ◊ *an embargo on arms sales to certain countries* ◊ *a trade embargo against/on certain countries* ◊ *to impose/ enforce/lift an embargo*
■ *verb* (**em·bar·goes, em·bargo·ing, em·bar·goed, em·bar·goed**) [VN] to place an embargo on sth: *There have been calls to embargo all arms shipments to the region.*

em·bark /ɪmˈbɑːk; *AmE* ɪmˈbɑːrk/ *verb* to get onto a ship; to put sth onto a ship: [V] *We stood on the pier and watched as they embarked.* ◊ [VN] *They embarked the troops by night.* OPP DISEMBARK ▶ **em·bark·ation** /ˌembɑːˈkeɪʃn/ *noun* [U, C]: *Embarkation will be at 14:20 hours.* PHRV **emˈbark on/upon sth** to start to do sth new or difficult: *She is about to embark on a diplomatic career.*

em·bar·rass /ɪmˈbærəs/ *verb* [VN] **1** to make sb feel shy, awkward or ashamed, especially in a social situation: [VN] *Her questions about my private life embarrassed me.* ◊ *I didn't want to embarrass him by kissing him in front of his friends.* ◊ [VNtoinf] *It embarrassed her to meet strange men in the corridor at night.* **2** to cause problems or difficulties for sb: *The speech was deliberately designed to embarrass the prime minister.*

em·bar·rassed /ɪmˈbærəst/ *adj.* **1** ~ **(about/at sth)** | ~ **(to do sth)** (of a person or their behaviour) shy, awkward or ashamed, especially in a social situation: *She's embarrassed about her height.* ◊ *He felt embarrassed at being the centre of attention.* ◊ *Some women are too embarrassed to consult their doctor about the problem.* ◊ *Her remark was followed by an embarrassed silence.* ◊ *I've never felt so embarrassed in my life!* ⇨ note at ASHAMED **2 financially** ~ (*informal*) not having any money; in a difficult financial situation

em·bar·rass·ing /ɪmˈbærəsɪŋ/ *adj.* **1** making you feel shy, awkward or ashamed: *an embarrassing mistake/ question/situation* ◊ *It can be embarrassing for children to tell complete strangers about such incidents.* ◊ *It was so embarrassing having to sing in public.* **2** causing sb to look stupid, dishonest, etc: *The report is likely to prove highly embarrassing to the government.* ▶ **em·bar·rass·ing·ly** *adv.*: *The play was embarrassingly bad.*

em·bar·rass·ment /ɪmˈbærəsmənt/ *noun* **1** [U] shy, awkward or guilty feelings; a feeling of being embarrassed: *I nearly died of embarrassment when he said that.* ◊ *I'm glad you offered—it saved me the embarrassment of having to ask.* ◊ *Much to her embarrassment she realized that everybody had been listening to her singing.* **2** [C] ~ **(to/for sb)** a situation which causes problems for sb: *Her resignation will be a severe embarrassment to the party.* **3** [C] ~ **(to sb)** a person who causes problems for another person or other people and makes them feel embarrassed IDM **an embarrassment of ˈriches** so many good things that it is difficult to choose just one

em·bassy /ˈembəsi/ *noun* (*pl.* **-ies**) **1** a group of officials led by an AMBASSADOR who represent their government in a foreign country: *the American embassy in London* ◊ *embassy officials* ◊ *to inform the embassy of the situation* **2** the building in which an embassy works: *a demonstration outside the Russian Embassy*—compare CONSULATE, HIGH COMMISSION

em·bat·tled /ɪmˈbætld/ *adj.* (*written*) **1** surrounded by problems and difficulties: *the embattled party leader* **2** (of an army, a city, etc.) involved in war; surrounded by the enemy

embed (also **imbed**) /ɪmˈbed/ *verb* (**-dd-**) [VN] [usually passive] ~ **sth (in sth)** to fix sth firmly into a substance or solid object: *an operation to remove glass that was embedded in his leg* ◊ *The bullet embedded itself in the wall.* ◊ (*figurative*) *These attitudes are deeply embedded in our society* (= felt very strongly and difficult to change).

em·bel·lish /ɪmˈbelɪʃ/ *verb* [VN] (*written*) **1** to make sth more beautiful by adding decorations to it **2** to make a story more interesting by adding details that are not always true SYN EMBROIDER ▶ **em·bel·lish·ment** *noun* [U, C]: *Good pasta needs very little embellishment.* ◊ *a 16th century church with 18th century embellishments*

ember /ˈembə(r)/ *noun* [usually pl.] a piece of wood or coal that is not burning but is still red and hot after a fire has died

em·bez·zle /ɪmˈbezl/ *verb* to steal money that you are responsible for or that belongs to your employer: [VN] *He was found guilty of embezzling $150000 of public funds.* [alsoV] ▶ **em·bezzle·ment** *noun* [U]: *She was found guilty of embezzlement.* **em·bez·zler** /ɪmˈbezlə(r)/ *noun*

em·bit·ter /ɪmˈbɪtə(r)/ *verb* [VN] to make sb feel angry or disappointed about sth over a long period of time: *Years of caring for her ageing parents had embittered her.* ▶ **em·bit·tered** *adj.*: *a sick and embittered old man* ◊ *an embittered laugh*

em·bla·zon /ɪmˈbleɪzn/ (also **blazon**) *verb* [VN+adv./ prep.] [usually passive] ~ **A with B** | ~ **B on, across, etc. A** to decorate sth with a design, a symbol or words so that people will notice it easily: *baseball caps emblazoned with the team's logo* ◊ *The team's logo was emblazoned on the baseball caps.*

em·blem /ˈembləm/ *noun* ~ **(of sth)** **1** a design or picture that represents a country or an organization: *America's national emblem, the bald eagle* ◊ *the club emblem* **2** something that represents a perfect example or a principle: *The dove is an emblem of peace.*

em·blem·at·ic /ˌembləˈmætɪk/ *adj.* (*formal*) ~ **(of sth)** **1** that represents or is a symbol of sth **2** that is considered typical of a situation, an area of work, etc: *The violence is emblematic of what is happening in our inner cities.*

em·bodi·ment /ɪmˈbɒdimənt; *AmE* -ˈbɑːd-/ *noun* [usually sing.] (*formal*) ~ **of sth** a person or thing that represents or is a typical example of an idea or a quality: *He is the embodiment of the young successful businessman.*

em·body /ɪmˈbɒdi; *AmE* ɪmˈbɑːdi/ *verb* (**em·bodies, em·body·ing, em·bodied, em·bodied**) [VN] **1** to express or represent an idea or a quality: *a politician who embodied the hopes of black youth* ◊ *the principles embodied in the Declaration of Human Rights* **2** (*formal*) to include or contain sth: *This model embodies many new features.*

em·bold·en /ɪmˈbəʊldən; *AmE* -ˈboʊl-/ *verb* **1** [usually passive] (*formal*) to make sb feel braver or more confident: *Emboldened by the wine, he went over to introduce himself to her.* ◊ [VNtoinf] *With such a majority, the administration was emboldened to introduce radical new policies.* **2** [VN] (*technical*) to make a piece of text appear in BOLD print

em·boss /ɪmˈbɒs; *AmE* ɪmˈbɔːs/ *verb* [VN] [usually passive] ~ **A with B** | ~ **B on A** to put a raised design or piece of writing on paper, leather, etc: *stationery embossed with the hotel's name* ◊ *The hotel's name was embossed on the stationery.* ▶ **em·bossed** *adj.*: *embossed stationery*

em·brace /ɪmˈbreɪs/ *verb* **1** to put your arms around sb as a sign of love or friendship SYN HUG: [V] *They embraced and wept and promised to keep in touch.* ◊ [VN] *She embraced her son warmly.* **2** [VN] (*formal*) to accept an idea, a proposal, a set of beliefs, etc., especially when it is done with enthusiasm: *to embrace democracy/ feminism/Islam* ◊ *It is unlikely that such countries will embrace capitalist ideas.* **3** [VN] (*formal*) to include sth: *The talks embraced a wide range of issues.* ▶ **em·brace** *noun* [C, U]: *He held her in a warm embrace.* ◊ *There were*

s	t	v	z	ʃ	ʒ	tʃ	dʒ	θ	ð	ŋ
see	tea	van	zoo	shoe	vision	chain	jam	thin	this	sing

tears and embraces as they said goodbye. ◊ the country's eager embrace of foreign influences

em·bro·ca·tion /ˌembrəˈkeɪʃn/ noun [U] a liquid for rubbing on sore muscles to make them less painful, for example after too much exercise

em·broi·der /ɪmˈbrɔɪdə(r)/ verb **1** ~ A (on B)| ~ B (with A) to decorate fabric with a pattern of stitches usually using coloured thread: [VN] an embroidered blouse ◊ She embroidered flowers on the cushion covers. ◊ She embroidered the cushion cover with flowers. [also V] **2** [VN] (written) to make a story more interesting by adding details that are not true SYN EMBELLISH: He is inclined to embroider the facts.

em·broi·dery /ɪmˈbrɔɪdəri/ noun **1** [U, C] patterns that are sewn onto fabric using threads of various colours; fabric that is decorated in this way: a beautiful piece of embroidery ◊ Indian embroideries **2** [U] the skill or activity of decorating fabric in this way—picture at SEW

em·broil /ɪmˈbrɔɪl/ verb [VN] [often passive] ~ sb/yourself (in sth) (written) to involve sb/yourself in an argument or a difficult situation: He became embroiled in a dispute with his neighbours. ◊ I was reluctant to embroil myself in his problems.

em·bryo /ˈembriəʊ; AmE -brioʊ/ noun (pl. -os) a young animal or plant in the very early stages of development before birth, or before coming out of its egg or seed, especially a human egg in the first eight weeks after FERTILIZATION: human embryos ◊ (figurative) the embryo of an idea ◊ an embryo politician (= one who is not yet very experienced) ◊ emigrants to Canada—compare IMMIGRANT IDM **in embryo** existing but not yet fully developed: The idea already existed in embryo in his earlier novels.

em·bry·ology /ˌembriˈɒlədʒi; AmE -ˈɑːl-/ noun [U] the scientific study of the development of embryos ▶ **em·bryo·logic·al** /ˌembriəˈlɒdʒɪkl; AmE -ˈlɑːdʒ-/ adj. **em·bry·olo·gist** /ˌembriˈɒlədʒɪst; AmE -ˈɑːl-/ noun

em·bry·on·ic /ˌembriˈɒnɪk; AmE -ˈɑːnɪk/ adj. [usually before noun] **1** (formal) in an early stage of development: The plan, as yet, only exists in embryonic form. **2** (technical) of an embryo: embryonic cells

emcee /emˈsiː/ noun (AmE, informal) a person who introduces guests or entertainers at a formal occasion SYN MASTER OF CEREMONIES ▶ **emcee** verb [V, VN]

emend /iˈmend/ verb [VN] (formal) to remove the mistakes in a piece of writing, especially before it is printed SYN CORRECT

emend·ation /ˌiːmenˈdeɪʃn/ noun [C, U] (formal) a letter or word that has been changed or corrected in a text; the act of making changes to a text

em·er·ald /ˈemərəld/ noun **1** [C, U] a bright green precious stone: an emerald ring **2** (also ˌemerald ˈgreen) [U] a bright green colour ▶ **em·er·ald** (also ˌemerald ˈgreen) adj.

emerge /iˈmɜːdʒ; AmE iˈmɜːrdʒ/ verb **1** [V] ~ (from sth) to come out of a dark, enclosed or hidden place: The swimmer emerged from the lake. ◊ She finally emerged from her room at noon. ◊ We emerged into bright sunlight. **2** (of facts, ideas, etc.) to become known: [V] No new evidence emerged during the investigation. ◊ [V that] It emerged that the company was going to be sold. **3** [V] ~ (as sth) to start to exist; to appear or become known: After the elections opposition groups began to emerge. ◊ He emerged as a key figure in the campaign ◊ the emerging markets of South Asia **4** [V] ~ (from sth) to survive a difficult situation or experience: She emerged from the scandal with her reputation intact. ▶ **emer·gence** /-dʒəns/ noun [U]: the island's emergence from the sea 3000 years ago ◊ the emergence of new technologies/evidence

emer·gency /iˈmɜːdʒənsi; AmE iˈmɜːrdʒ-/ noun (pl. -ies) [C, U] a sudden serious and dangerous event or situation which needs immediate action to deal with it: The government has declared a **state of emergency** following the earthquake. ◊ This door should only be used in an emergency. ◊ the emergency exit (= to be used in an emergency) ◊ The government had to take emergency action. ◊ The pilot made an emergency landing in a field. ◊ I always have some extra cash with me **for emergencies**. ◊ The govern-

ment has been granted **emergency powers** (= to deal with an emergency).

eˈmergency brake noun (AmE) **1** = HANDBRAKE **2** a BRAKE on a train that can be pulled in an emergency

eˈmergency room noun (abbr. ER) (AmE) = ACCIDENT AND EMERGENCY

eˈmergency services noun [pl.] (BrE) the public organizations that deal with emergencies: the police, fire, AMBULANCE and COASTGUARD services

emer·gent /iˈmɜːdʒənt; AmE iˈmɜːrdʒ-/ adj. [usually before noun] (written) new and still developing: emergent nations/states

emeri·tus /iˈmerɪtəs/ adj. (often **Emeritus**) used with a title to show that a person, usually a university teacher, keeps the title as an honour, although he or she has stopped working: the Emeritus Professor of Biology HELP In AmE the form **Emerita** /iˈmerɪtə/ is used for women: Professor Emerita Mary Judd

emery /ˈeməri/ noun [U] a hard mineral used especially in powder form for polishing things and making them smooth

ˈemery board noun a small strip of wood or cardboard covered in emery, used for shaping the fingernails

emet·ic /iˈmetɪk/ noun (medical) a substance that makes you VOMIT (= bring up food from the stomach) ▶ **emet·ic** adj.

emi·grant /ˈemɪɡrənt/ noun a person who leaves their country to live in another: emigrant families/labour/workers ◊ emigrants to Canada—compare IMMIGRANT

emi·grate /ˈemɪɡreɪt/ verb [V] ~ (from ...) (to ...) to leave your own country to go and live permanently in another country—compare IMMIGRATE ▶ **emi·gra·tion** /ˌemɪˈɡreɪʃn/ noun [U, C]: the mass emigration of Jews from Eastern Europe—compare IMMIGRATION

émi·gré /ˈemɪɡreɪ/ noun (from French) a person who has left their own country, usually for political reasons: the son of Russian émigrés

emi·nence /ˈemɪnəns/ noun **1** [U] (formal) the quality of being famous and respected, especially in a profession: a man of political eminence **2** [C] (**His/Your Eminence**) a title used in speaking to or about a CARDINAL (= a priest of the highest rank in the Roman Catholic Church): Their Eminences will see you now. **3** [C] (old-fashioned or formal) an area of high ground

emi·nent /ˈemɪnənt/ adj. [usually before noun] **1** (of people) famous and respected, especially in a particular profession: an eminent architect **2** (of good qualities) unusual; excellent: a man of eminent good sense

emi·nent·ly /ˈemɪnəntli/ adv. (formal) (used to emphasize a positive quality) very; extremely: She seems eminently suitable for the job.

emir /eˈmɪə(r); ˈeɪmɪə(r); AmE eˈmɪr; eɪˈmɪr/ noun the title given to some Muslim rulers: the Emir of Kuwait

emir·ate /ˈemɪərət; ˈemɪrət; AmE ˈemərət/ noun **1** the position of an emir **2** an area of land that is ruled over by an emir: the United Arab Emirates **3** the period of time that an emir rules

emis·sary /ˈemɪsəri; AmE -seri/ noun (pl. -ies) (formal) a person who is sent to deliver an official message, especially from one country to another, or to perform a special task: the King's special emissary

emis·sion /iˈmɪʃn/ noun **1** [U] (formal) the production or sending out of light, heat, gas, etc: the emission of carbon dioxide into the atmosphere ◊ emission controls **2** [C] gas, etc. that is sent out into the air: The government has pledged to clean up industrial emissions.

emit /iˈmɪt/ verb (-tt-) [VN] (formal) to send out sth such as light, heat, sound, gas, etc: The metal container began to emit a clicking sound. ◊ Sulphur gases were emitted by the volcano.

emol·li·ent /iˈmɒliənt; AmE iˈmɑːl-/ adj., noun
■ adj. (formal) **1** making a person or situation calmer in the hope of keeping relations peaceful: an emollient reply **2** (technical) used for making your skin soft or less painful: an emollient cream

æ	ɑː	e	ɜː	ə	ɪ	iː	i	ɒ	ɔː	ʌ	ʊ	u	uː
cat	father	ten	bird	about	sit	see	many	got	saw	cup	put	actual	too
								(BrE)					

■ *noun* [C, U] (*technical*) a liquid or cream that is used to make the skin soft

emol·u·ment /ɪˈmɒljumənt; *AmE* ɪˈmɑːl-/ *noun* [usually pl.] (*formal*) money paid to sb for work they have done, especially to sb who earns a lot of money

emote /ɪˈməʊt; *AmE* ɪˈmoʊt/ *verb* [V] (*written*) to show emotion in a very obvious way

emo·tion /ɪˈməʊʃn; *AmE* ɪˈmoʊʃn/ *noun* [C, U] a strong feeling such as love, fear or anger; the part of a person's character that consists of feelings: *He lost control of his emotions.* ◊ *They expressed mixed emotions at the news.* ◊ ***Emotions are running high*** (= people are feeling very excited, angry, etc.)*.* ◊ *The decision was based on emotion rather than rational thought.* ◊ *She showed no emotion at the verdict.* ◊ *Mary was overcome with emotion.*

emo·tion·al /ɪˈməʊʃənl; *AmE* ɪˈmoʊ-/ *adj.* **1** [usually before noun] connected with people's feelings (= with the emotions): *emotional problems/needs* ◊ *emotional stress* ◊ *a child's emotional and intellectual development* ◊ *Mothers are often the ones who provide emotional support for the family.* **2** causing people to feel strong emotions: *emotional language* ◊ *abortion and other **emotional issues*** **3** (sometimes *disapproving*) showing strong emotions, sometimes in a way that other people think is unnecessary: *an emotional outburst/response/reaction* ◊ *They made an emotional appeal for help.* ◊ *He tends to get emotional on these occasions.* ▶ **emo·tion·al·ly** /-ʃənəli/ *adv.*: *emotionally disturbed children* ◊ *I try not to become emotionally involved.* ◊ *They have suffered physically and emotionally.* ◊ *an emotionally charged atmosphere*

emo·tion·less /ɪˈməʊʃənləs; *AmE* ɪˈmoʊ-/ *adj.* not showing any emotion: *an emotionless voice*

emo·tive /ɪˈməʊtɪv; *AmE* ɪˈmoʊ-/ *adj.* causing people to feel strong emotions: *emotive language/words* ◊ *Capital punishment is a highly emotive issue.*

em·panel = IMPANEL

em·pa·thize (*BrE* also **-ise**) /ˈempəθaɪz/ *verb* [V] ~ **(with sb/sth)** to understand another person's feelings and experiences, especially because you have been in a similar situation

em·pathy /ˈempəθi/ *noun* [U] ~ **(with sb/sth)** | ~ **(for sb/sth)** | ~ **(between A and B)** the ability to understand another person's feelings, experience, etc: *the writer's imaginative empathy with his subject* ◊ *empathy for other people's situations* ◊ *It is important to develop the empathy between dogs and their handlers.*

em·peror /ˈempərə(r)/ *noun* the ruler of an empire: *the Roman emperors* ◊ *the Emperor Napoleon*—see also EMPRESS

em·phasis /ˈemfəsɪs/ *noun* (*pl.* **em·phases** /-siːz/) [U, C] **1** ~ **(on/upon sth)** special importance that is given to sth: *to put/lay/place emphasis on sth* ◊ *There has been **a shift of emphasis** from manufacturing to service industries.* ◊ *The emphasis is very much on learning the spoken language.* ◊ *The course has a vocational emphasis.* ◊ *We provide all types of information, **with an emphasis on** legal advice.* ◊ *The examples we will look at have quite different emphases.* **2** the extra force given to a word or phrase when spoken, especially in order to show that it is important; a way of writing a word (for example drawing a line underneath it) to show that it is important: *'I can assure you,' she added with emphasis, 'the figures are correct.'*

em·pha·size (*BrE* also **-ise**) /ˈemfəsaɪz/ *verb* **1** to give special importance to sth: [VN] *His speech emphasized the importance of attracting industry to the town.* ◊ [V that] *She emphasized that their plan would mean sacrifices and hard work.* ◊ [V wh-] *He emphasized how little was known about the disease.* ◊ [VN that] *It should be emphasized that this is only one possible explanation.* [also V speech] **2** [VN] to make sth more noticeable: *She swept her hair back from her face to emphasize her high cheekbones.* **3** [VN] to give extra force to a word or phrase when you are speaking, especially to show that it is important SYN STRESS

em·phat·ic /ɪmˈfætɪk/ *adj.* **1** an **emphatic** statement, answer, etc. is given in a strong and forceful way to show

that it is important: *an emphatic denial/rejection* **2** (of a person) making it very clear what you mean by using forceful language: *He was emphatic that he could not work with her.* ◊ *She was equally emphatic about the importance of discipline.* **3** an **emphatic** victory, win, or defeat is one in which one team or player wins by a large amount ▶ **em·phat·ic·al·ly** /-kli/ *adv.*: *'Certainly not,' he replied emphatically.* ◊ *She is emphatically opposed to the proposals.* ◊ *He has always emphatically denied the allegations.* ◊ *The proposal was emphatically defeated.*

em·phy·se·ma /ˌemfɪˈsiːmə/ *noun* [U] (*medical*) a condition that affects the lungs, making it difficult to breathe

em·pire /ˈempaɪə(r)/ *noun* **1** a group of countries or states that are controlled by one ruler or government: *the Roman empire* **2** a group of commercial organizations controlled by one person or company: *a business empire*

ˈempire ˌbuilding *noun* [U] (usually *disapproving*) the process of obtaining extra land, authority, etc. in order to increase your own power or position

em·pir·ic·al /ɪmˈpɪrɪkl/ *adj.* [usually before noun] based on experiments or experience rather than ideas or THEORIES: *empirical evidence/knowledge/research* ◊ *an empirical study* ▶ **em·pir·ic·al·ly** /-kli/ *adv.*: *Such claims need to be tested empirically.*

em·piri·cism /ɪmˈpɪrɪsɪzəm/ *noun* [U] (*philosophy*) the use of experiments or experience as the basis for your ideas; the belief in these methods ▶ **em·piri·cist** /-sɪst/ *adj.*: *an empiricist theory* **em·piri·cist** *noun*: *the English empiricist, John Locke*

em·place·ment /ɪmˈpleɪsmənt/ *noun* (*technical*) a position that has been specially prepared so that a large gun can be fired from it

em·ploy /ɪmˈplɔɪ/ *verb, noun*

■ *verb* **1** ~ **sb (as sth)** to give sb a job to do for payment: [VN] *How many people does the company employ?* ◊ *For the past three years he has been employed as a firefighter.* ◊ [VN to inf] *A number of people have been employed to deal with the backlog of work.*—see also SELF-EMPLOYED, UNEMPLOYED **2** [VN] (*formal*) to use sth such as a skill, method etc. for a particular purpose: *He criticized the repressive methods employed by the country's government.* ◊ *The police had to employ force to enter the building.* **IDM** **be employed in doing sth** (*written*) if a person or their time is **employed in doing sth**, the person spends time doing that thing: *She was employed in making a list of all the jobs to be done.*

■ *noun* [U] **IDM** **in sb's em·ploy** | **in the em·ploy of sb** (*formal*) working for sb; employed by sb

---

WHICH WORD?

employ / take on

If a company **employs** a person, he or she is working on the staff of the company or is paid to do some work for them: *The company employs 1 200 people.* ◊ *He was employed as an electrician at the shipyard.*

In *BrE* you can also say that a company **takes** someone on when the company starts to employ them: *Business has been so good that we've had to take on more staff.* In *AmE* the word **hire** would be used.

---

em·ploy·able /ɪmˈplɔɪəbl/ *adj.* having the skills and qualifications that will make sb want to employ you

em·ploy·ee /ɪmˈplɔɪiː/ *noun* a person who is paid to work for sb: *The firm has over 500 employees.* ◊ *hospital/government employees* ◊ *employee rights/relations*

em·ploy·er /ɪmˈplɔɪə(r)/ *noun* a person or company that pays people to work for them: *They're very good employers* (= they treat the people that work for them well)*.* ◊ *one of the largest employers in the area*

em·ploy·ment /ɪmˈplɔɪmənt/ *noun* **1** [U, C] work, especially when it is done to earn money; the state of being employed: *to be in paid employment* ◊ *full-time/part-time employment* ◊ *conditions/terms of employment* ◊ *Graduates are finding it more and more difficult to find employment.* ◊ *pensions from previous employments* **2** [U] the situation in which people have work: *The government is aiming at **full employment***.* ◊ *Changes in farming methods have*

badly affected employment in the area. OPP UNEMPLOY-
MENT **3** [U] the act of employing sb: *The law prevented the
employment of children under ten in the cotton mills.* **4** [U]
~ **(of sth)** (*formal*) the use of sth: *the employment of
artillery in the capture of the town*

em·ploy·ment agency *noun* a business that helps
people to find work and employers to find workers

em·por·ium /emˈpɔːriəm/ *noun* (*pl.* **em·por·iums** or **em-
poria** /-riə/) **1** (*old-fashioned*) a large shop/store **2** a
shop/store that sells a particular type of goods: *an arts
and crafts emporium*

em·power /ɪmˈpaʊə(r)/ *verb* [often passive] **1** (*formal*) to
give sb the power or authority to do sth SYN AUTHORIZE:
[VN to inf] *The courts were empowered to impose the death
sentence for certain crimes.* [also VN] **2** to give sb more
control over their own life or the situation they are in:
[VN] *The movement actively empowered women and gave
them confidence in themselves.* [also VN to inf] ▸ **em-
power·ment** *noun* [U]: *the empowerment of the individual*

em·press /ˈemprəs/ *noun* **1** a woman who is the ruler of
an empire: *the Empress of Egypt* **2** the wife of an EMPEROR

emp·ties /ˈemptiz/ *noun* [pl.] empty bottles or glasses

emp·ti·ness /ˈemptinəs/ *noun* [U, sing.] **1** a feeling of
being sad and lonely because nothing seems to have any
value: *There was an aching emptiness in her heart.* **2** the
fact that there is nothing or nobody in a place: *The silence
and emptiness of the house did not scare her.* **3** (*formal*) a
place that is empty: *He stared out at the vast emptiness
that was the sea.*

empty /ˈempti/ *adj., verb*
■ *adj.* (**emp·tier**, **emp·ti·est**) **1** ~ **(of sth)** with no people or
things inside: *an empty box/glass* ◊ *empty hands* (= not
holding anything) ◊ *an empty plate* (= with no food on it) ◊
The theatre was half empty. ◊ *an empty house/room/bus* ◊
Is this an empty chair (= not one that another person will
be using)? ◊ *The house had been standing empty* (=
without people living in it) *for some time.* ◊ *It's not good to
drink alcohol on an empty stomach* (= without having
eaten something). ◊ (*formal*) *The room was empty of furniture.* **2** [usually before noun] (of sth that sb says or does)
with no meaning; not meaning what is said: *empty words*
◊ *an empty promise* ◊ *an empty gesture aimed at pleasing
the crowds* **3** (of a person, or a person's life) unhappy
because life does not seem to have a purpose, usually
after sth sad has happened: *Three months after his death,
she still felt empty.* ◊ *My life seems empty without you.* **4** ~
of sth without a quality that you would expect to be
there: *words that were empty of meaning* ▸ **emp·ti·ly**
adv.: *She stood staring emptily into space.* IDM **the empty
ˈnest** the situation that parents are in when their children have left home: *the empty nest syndrome*
■ *verb* (**emp·ties**, **empty·ing**, **emp·tied**, **emp·tied**) **1** [VN] ~
sth (out/out of sth) | ~ **sth (of sth)** to remove everything
that is in a container, etc: *I emptied out my pockets but
could not find my keys.* ◊ *She emptied the water out of the
vase.* ◊ *He emptied his glass and asked for a refill.* ◊ *He
emptied the ashtrays, washed the glasses and went to bed.* ◊
The room had been emptied of all furniture. ◊ (*figurative*)
She emptied her mind of all thoughts of home. **2** [V] ~ **(out)**
to become empty: *The tank empties out in five minutes.* ◊
The streets soon emptied when the rain started. **3** [VN] ~
sth (out) to take out the contents of sth and put them
somewhere else: *She emptied the contents of her bag onto
the table.* ◊ *Many factories emptied their waste into the
river.* **4** [VN] to make sure that everyone leaves a room,
building, etc. SYN EVACUATE: *Police had instructions to
empty the building because of a bomb threat.* **5** [V] ~ **(out)
into/onto sth** to flow or move out from one place to
another: *The Rhine empties into the North Sea.* ◊ *Fans
emptied out onto the streets after the concert.*

empty-ˈhanded *adj.* [not usually before noun] without
getting what you wanted; without taking sth to sb: *The
robbers fled empty-handed.* ◊ *She visited every Sunday and
never arrived empty-handed.*

empty-ˈheaded *adj.* unable to think or behave in an
intelligent way

EMU /ˌiː em ˈjuː/ *abbr.* Economic and Monetary Union (of
the European Union)

emu /ˈiːmjuː/ *noun* a large Australian bird that can run
fast but cannot fly

emu·late /ˈemjuleɪt/ *verb* [VN] **1** (*formal*) to try to do sth
as well as sb else because you admire them: *She hopes to
emulate her sister's sporting achievements.* **2** (*computing*)
(of a computer program, etc.) to work in the same way as
another computer, etc. and perform the same tasks
▸ **emu·la·tion** /ˌemjuˈleɪʃn/ *noun* [U, C]

emu·la·tor /ˈemjuleɪtə(r)/ *noun* (*computing*) a device or
piece of SOFTWARE that makes it possible to use programs,
etc. on one type of computer even though they have been
designed for a different type

emul·sify /ɪˈmʌlsɪfaɪ/ *verb* (**emul·si·fies**, **emul·si·fy·ing**,
emul·si·fied, **emul·si·fied**) [V, VN] (*technical*) if two
liquids of different thicknesses **emulsify** or **are emulsi-
fied**, they combine to form a smooth mixture

emul·sion /ɪˈmʌlʃn/ *noun* [C, U] **1** any mixture of liquids
that do not normally mix together, such as oil and water
2 (also **eˈmulsion paint**) (*BrE*) a type of paint used on
walls and ceilings that dries without leaving a shiny
surface **3** (*technical*) a substance on the surface of PHOTO-
GRAPHIC film that makes it sensitive to light

en- /ɪn/ (also **em-** /ɪm/ before *b, m* or *p*) *prefix* (in verbs)
1 to put into the thing or condition mentioned: *encase* ◊
endanger ◊ *empower* **2** to cause to be: *enlarge* ◊ *embolden*

-en *suffix* **1** (in verbs) to make or become: *blacken* ◊ *sadden*
2 (in adjectives) made of; looking like: *wooden* ◊ *golden*

en·able /ɪˈneɪbl/ *verb* [VN to inf] to make it possible for
sb to do sth: *The software enables you to access the Internet in seconds.* ◊ *a new programme to enable older people
to study at college* **2** to make it possible for sth to happen
or exist by creating the necessary conditions: [VN to inf]
Insulin enables the body to use and store sugar. ◊ [VN] *a
new train line to enable easier access to the stadium*

enact /ɪˈnækt/ *verb* **1** [often passive] (*law*) to pass a law:
[VN] *legislation enacted by parliament* [also VN that] **2** [VN]
[often passive] (*formal*) to perform a play or act a part in
a play: *scenes from history enacted by local residents* **3** [VN]
(**be enacted**) (*formal*) to take place SYN BE PLAYED OUT:
*They seemed unaware of the drama being enacted a few
feet away from them.*

en·act·ment /ɪˈnæktmənt/ *noun* [U, C] (*law*) the process
of a law becoming official; a law which has been made
official: *the enactment of environmental legislation* ◊ *legal
enactments covering food safety*

en·amel /ɪˈnæml/ *noun* **1** [U, C] a substance that is
melted onto metal, pots, etc. and forms a hard shiny
surface to protect or decorate them; an object made from
enamel: *a chipped enamel bowl* ◊ *a handle inlaid with
bone and enamel* ◊ *an exhibition of enamels and jewellery*
2 [U] the hard white outer layer of a tooth **3** (also
eˌnamel ˈpaint) [U, C] a type of paint that dries to leave a
hard shiny surface and is used to protect or decorate
objects

en·am·elled (*BrE*) (*AmE* **en·am·eled**) /ɪˈnæmld/ *adj.*
[usually before noun] covered or decorated with enamel

en·am·oured (*BrE*) (*AmE* **en·amored**) /ɪˈnæməd; *AmE*
-ərd/ *adj.* **1** ~ **of/with sth** (*formal*) (often in negative
sentences) liking sth a lot: *He was less than enamoured of
the music.* ◊ (*humorous*) *I'm not exactly enamoured with
the idea of spending a whole day with them.* **2** ~ **of/with
sb** (*literary*) in love with sb

en bloc /ˌɒ̃ ˈblɒk; *AmE* ˌɑː ˈblɑːk/ *adv.* (from *French*) as a
group rather than separately: *There are reports of teachers resigning en bloc.*

enc. = ENCL.

en·camp /ɪnˈkæmp/ *verb* (*formal*) [V, VN] if a group of
people **encamp** or **are encamped** somewhere, they set up
a camp or have set up a camp there

en·camp·ment /ɪnˈkæmpmənt/ *noun* a group of tents,
huts, etc. where people live together, usually for only a
short period of time: *a military encampment*

en·cap·su·late /ɪnˈkæpsjuleɪt/ *verb* [VN] ~ **sth (in sth)**
(*formal*) to express the most important parts of sth in a

E

few words, a small space or a single object: *The poem encapsulates many of the central themes of her writing.* ▶ **en·cap·su·la·tion** *noun* [U, C]

en·case /ɪnˈkeɪs/ *verb* [VN] [often passive] ~ **sth (in sth)** (*formal*) to surround or cover sth completely, especially to protect it: *The reactor is encased in concrete and steel.* ◇ *His upper body was completely encased in bandages.*

en·cash /ɪnˈkæʃ/ *verb* [VN] (*BrE, formal*) to exchange a cheque, etc. for money [SYN] CASH ▶ **en·cash·ment** *noun* [U, C]

-ence ⇨ -ANCE

en·ceph·al·itis /enˌsefəˈlaɪtɪs; -ˌkefə-/ *noun* [U] (*medical*) a condition in which the brain becomes swollen, caused by an infection or ALLERGIC reaction

en·ceph·al·op·athy /enˌsefəˈlɒpəθi; -ˌkefə-; *AmE* -ˈlɑːp-/ *noun* [U] (*medical*) a disease in which the functioning of the brain is affected by infection, BLOOD POISONING, etc.— see also BSE

en·chant /ɪnˈtʃɑːnt; *AmE* -ˈtʃænt/ *verb* [VN] **1** (*formal*) to attract sb strongly and make them feel very interested, excited, etc: *The happy family scene had enchanted him.* **2** to place sb/sth under a magic SPELL (= magic words that have special powers)

en·chant·ed /ɪnˈtʃɑːntɪd; *AmE* -ˈtʃæntɪd/ *adj.* **1** placed under a SPELL (= magic words that have special powers): *an enchanted forest/kingdom* **2** (*formal*) filled with great pleasure: *He was enchanted to see her again after so long.* ◇ *The children were enchanted with the present.*

en·chant·er /ɪnˈtʃɑːntə(r); *AmE* -ˈtʃæn-/ *noun* (in stories) a man who has magic powers that he uses to control people

en·chant·ing /ɪnˈtʃɑːntɪŋ; *AmE* -ˈtʃæntɪŋ/ *adj.* attractive and pleasing: *an enchanting view* ▶ **en·chant·ing·ly** *adv.*

en·chant·ment /ɪnˈtʃɑːntmənt; *AmE* -ˈtʃænt-/ *noun* **1** [U] (*formal*) a feeling of great pleasure **2** [U] the state of being under a magic SPELL: *It was a place of deep mystery and enchantment.* **3** [C] (*literary*) = SPELL: *They had been turned to stone by an enchantment.*

en·chant·ress /ɪnˈtʃɑːntrəs; *AmE* -ˈtʃæn-/ *noun* **1** (in stories) a woman who has magic powers that she uses to control people **2** (*literary*) a woman that men find very attractive and interesting

en·chil·ada /ˌentʃɪˈlɑːdə/ *noun* (from *Spanish*) a Mexican dish consisting of a TORTILLA filled with meat and covered with a spicy sauce [IDM] see BIG *adj.*

en·cir·cle /ɪnˈsɜːkl; *AmE* ɪnˈsɜːrkl/ *verb* [VN] (*written*) to surround sb/sth completely in a circular shape or movement: *Jack's arms encircled her waist.* ◇ *The island is encircled by a coral reef.* ▶ **en·circle·ment** *noun* [U]

encl. (also **enc.**) *abbr.* (*business*) enclosed (used on business letters to show that another document is being sent in the same envelope)

en·clave /ˈenkleɪv/ *noun* an area of a country or city where the people have a different religion, culture or NATIONALITY from those who live in the country or city that surrounds it

en·close /ɪnˈkləʊz; *AmE* ɪnˈkloʊz/ *verb* [VN] **1** [usually passive] ~ **sth (in/with sth)** to build a wall, fence, etc. around sth: *The yard had been enclosed with iron railings.* ◇ *The land was enclosed in the seventeenth century* (= in Britain, when public land was made private property). ◇ (*figurative*) *All translated words should be enclosed in brackets.* **2** (especially of a wall, fence, etc.) to surround sth: *Low hedges enclosed the flower beds.* ◇ *She felt his arms enclose her.* **3** ~ **sth (with sth)** to put sth in the same envelope, parcel/package, etc. as sth else: *Please return the completed form, enclosing a recent photograph.* ◇ *Please find enclosed a cheque for £100.*

en·closed /ɪnˈkləʊzd; *AmE* ɪnˈkloʊzd/ *adj.* **1** with walls, etc. all around: *Do not use this substance in an enclosed space.* **2** (*abbr.* **encl.**) sent with a letter, etc: *Please complete the enclosed application form.* **3** (of religious communities) having little contact with the outside world: *an enclosed order of monks*

en·clos·ure /ɪnˈkləʊʒə(r); *AmE* -ˈkloʊ-/ *noun* **1** [C] a piece of land that is surrounded by a fence or wall and is used

for a particular purpose: *a wildlife enclosure* **2** [U, C] the act of placing a fence on such land around a piece of land: *the enclosure of common land in the seventeenth century* **3** [C] something that is placed in an envelope with a letter

en·code /ɪnˈkəʊd; *AmE* ɪnˈkoʊd/ *verb* [VN] **1** to change ordinary language into letters, symbols, etc. in order to send secret messages **2** (*computing*) to change information into a form that can be processed by a computer— compare DECODE

en·com·pass /ɪnˈkʌmpəs/ *verb* [VN] (*formal*) **1** to include a large number or range of things: *The job encompasses a wide range of responsibilities.* ◇ *The group encompasses all ages.* **2** to surround or cover sth completely: *The fog soon encompassed the whole valley.*

en·core /ˈɒŋkɔː(r); *AmE* ˈɑːŋ-/ *noun, exclamation*
■ *noun* an extra short performance given at the end of a concert; a request for this made by an audience calling out: *She played a Chopin waltz as an encore.* ◇ *The group got three encores.*
■ *exclamation* an audience calls out **encore!** at the end of a concert to ask the performer to play or sing another piece of music

en·coun·ter /ɪnˈkaʊntə(r)/ *verb, noun*
■ *verb* [VN] **1** to experience sth, especially sth unpleasant or difficult, while you are trying to do sth else: *We encountered a number of difficulties in the first week.* ◇ *I had never encountered such resistance before.* **2** (*formal*) to meet sb, or discover or experience sth, especially sb/sth new, unusual or unexpected [SYN] COME ACROSS: *She was the most remarkable woman he had ever encountered.*
■ *noun* **1** ~ **(with sb/sth)** | ~ **(between A and B)** a meeting, especially one that is sudden, unexpected or violent: *Three of them were killed in the subsequent encounter with the police.* ◇ *The story describes the extraordinary encounter between a man and a dolphin.* ◇ *a chance encounter* ◇ *I've had a number of close encounters* (= situations that could have been dangerous) *with bad drivers.* ◇ *It was his first sexual encounter* (= first experience of sex). ◇ *Flaubert was her first encounter with French literature.* **2** a sports match against a particular player or team: *She has beaten her opponent in all of their previous encounters.*

en·cour·age /ɪnˈkʌrɪdʒ; *AmE* -ˈkɜːr-/ *verb* **1** [VN] ~ **sb (in sth)** to give sb support, courage or hope: *My parents have always encouraged me in my choice of career.* ◇ *We were greatly encouraged by the positive response of the public.* **2** to persuade sb to do sth by making it easier for them and making them believe it is a good thing to do: [VNtoinf] *Banks actively encourage people to borrow money.* [alsoV-ing] **3** ~ **sth (in sb)** to make sth more likely to happen or develop: [VN] *They claim that some computer games encourage violent behaviour in young children.* ◇ [VNtoinf] *Music and lighting are used to encourage shoppers to buy more.* [alsoV-ing] [OPP] DISCOURAGE ▶ **en·cour·aging** *adj.* [not usually before noun]: *This month's unemployment figures are not very encouraging.* ◇ *You could try being a little more encouraging!* **en·cour·aging·ly** *adv.*: *to smile/nod encouragingly* ◇ *The attendance was encouragingly high.*

en·cour·age·ment /ɪnˈkʌrɪdʒmənt; *AmE* -ˈkɜːr-/ *noun* [U, C, usually sing.] ~ **(to sb) (to do sth)** the act of encouraging sb to do sth; something that encourages sb: *a few words of encouragement* ◇ *He needs all the support and encouragement he can get.* ◇ *With a little encouragement from his parents he should do well.* ◇ *She was given every encouragement to try something new.* ◇ *Her words were a great encouragement to them.*

en·croach /ɪnˈkrəʊtʃ; *AmE* ɪnˈkroʊtʃ/ *verb* [V] ~ **(on/ upon sth)** (*formal*) **1** (*disapproving*) to begin to affect or use up too much of sb's time, rights, personal life, etc: *I won't encroach on your time any longer.* ◇ *He never allows work to encroach upon his family life.* **2** to slowly begin to cover more and more of an area: *The growing town soon encroached on the surrounding countryside.* ◇ *the encroaching tide* (= that is coming in) ▶ **en·croach·ment** *noun* [U, C] ~ **(on/upon sth)**: *the regime's many encroachments on human rights*

en·crust·ation /ˌenkrʌˈsteɪʃn/ *noun* = INCRUSTATION

en·crust·ed /ɪnˈkrʌstɪd/ adj. ~ (with/in sth) covered with a thin hard layer of sth; forming a thin hard layer on sth: a crown encrusted with diamonds ◊ encrusted blood

en·crypt /ɪnˈkrɪpt/ verb [VN] (especially computing) to put information into a special CODE, especially in order to prevent people from looking at it without authority ▶ **en·cryp·tion** /ɪnˈkrɪpʃn/ noun [U]

en·cum·ber /ɪnˈkʌmbə(r)/ verb [VN] [usually passive] ~ sb/sth (with sth) (written) **1** to make it difficult for sb to do sth or for sth to happen: The police operation was encumbered by crowds of reporters. ◊ The business is encumbered with debt. **2** to be large and/or heavy and make it difficult for sb to move: The frogmen were encumbered by their diving equipment.

en·cum·brance /ɪnˈkʌmbrəns/ noun (formal) a person or thing that prevents sb from moving easily or from doing what they want: I felt I was being an encumbrance to them.

-ency ⇨ -ANCY

en·cyc·lic·al /ɪnˈsɪklɪkl/ noun an official letter written by the Pope and sent to all Roman Catholic BISHOPS

en·cyc·lo·pe·dia (BrE also **-pae·dia**) /ɪnˌsaɪkləˈpiːdiə/ noun a book or set of books giving information about all areas of knowledge or about different areas of one particular subject, usually arranged in alphabetical order; a similar collection of information on a CD-ROM

en·cyclo·pe·dic (BrE also **-paedic**) /ɪnˌsaɪkləˈpiːdɪk/ adj. **1** connected with encyclopedias or the type of information found in them: encyclopedic information ◊ an encyclopedic dictionary **2** having a lot of information about a wide variety of subjects; containing complete information about a particular subject: She has an encyclopedic knowledge of natural history.

end /end/ noun, verb

■ noun

FINAL PART | **1** the final part of a period of time, an event, an activity or a story: at the end of the week/month/year ◊ We didn't leave until the very end. ◊ They finally get named at the end of the book. ◊ We had to hear about the whole journey from beginning to end. ◊ It's the end of an era.

FURTHEST PART | **2** the part of an object or a place that is the furthest away from its centre: Turn right at the end of the road. ◊ His office is the room at the other end of the corridor. ◊ I joined the end of the queue. ◊ Go to the end of the line! ◊ You've got something on the end of your nose. ◊ Tie the ends of the string together. ◊ That's his wife sitting at the far end of the table. ◊ These two products are from opposite ends of the price range. ◊ We've travelled from one end of Mexico to the other. ◊ They live in the end house.— see also DEAD END, EAST END, SPLIT ENDS, TAIL END

FINISH | **3** a situation in which sth does not exist any more: the end of all his dreams ◊ The meeting came to an end (= finished). ◊ The war was finally at an end. ◊ The coup brought his corrupt regime to an end. ◊ There's no end in sight to the present crisis. ◊ They have called for an end to violence. ◊ That was by no means the end of the matter.

AIM | **4** an aim or a purpose: They are prepared to use violence in pursuit of their ends. ◊ She is exploiting the current situation for her own ends. ◊ With this end in view (= in order to achieve this) they employed 50 new staff. ◊ We are willing to make any concessions necessary to this end (= in order to achieve this).

PART OF ACTIVITY | **5** [usually sing.] a part of an activity with which sb is concerned, especially in business: We need somebody to handle the marketing end of the business. ◊ Are there any problems at your end? ◊ I have kept my end of the bargain.

OF TELEPHONE LINE/JOURNEY | **6** [usually sing.] either of two places connected by a telephone call, journey, etc: I answered the phone but there was no one at the other end. ◊ Jean is going to meet me at the other end.

OF SPORTS FIELD | **7** one of the two halves of a sports field: The teams changed ends at half-time.

PIECE LEFT | **8** (BrE) a small piece that is left after sth has been used: a cigarette end—see also FAG END, LOOSE END, ODDS AND ENDS

DEATH | **9** [usually sing.] a person's death. People say 'end' to avoid saying 'death': She came to an untimely end (= died young). ◊ I was with him at the end (= when he died). ◊ (literary) He met his end (= died) at the Battle of Waterloo.

IDM at the ˌend of the ˈday (BrE, spoken) used to introduce the most important fact after everything has been considered: At the end of the day, he'll still have to make his own decision. a bad/sticky ˈend (BrE) something unpleasant that happens to sb, for example punishment or a violent death, usually because of their own actions: He'll come to a sticky end one of these days if he carries on like that. be at the end of sth to have almost nothing left of sth: I'm at the end of my patience. ◊ They are at the end of their food supply. be at the ˌend of your ˈtether (BrE) (AmE be at the ˌend of your ˈrope) to feel that you cannot deal with a difficult situation any more because you are too tired, worried, etc. be the ˈend (BrE, spoken) when you say that people or situations are the end, you mean that you are annoyed with them an ˌend in itˈself a thing that is itself important and not just a part of sth more important the end justifies the ˈmeans (saying) bad or unfair methods of doing sth are acceptable if the result of that action is good or positive (reach) the end of the ˈline/ˈroad (to reach) the point at which sth can no longer continue in the same way: A defeat in the second round marked the end of the line for last year's champion. end of ˈstory (spoken) used when you are stating that there is nothing more that can be said or done about sth ˌend to ˈend in a line, with the ends touching: They arranged the tables end to end. get/have your ˈend away (BrE, slang) to have sex go to the ˌends of the ˈearth to do everything possible, even if it is difficult, in order to get or achieve sth: I'd go to the ends of the earth to see her again. in the ˈend **1** after a long period of time or series of events: He tried various jobs and in the end became an accountant. **2** after everything has been considered: You can try your best to impress the interviewers but in the end it's often just a question of luck. keep your ˈend up (BrE, informal) to continue to be cheerful in a difficult situation make (both) ends ˈmeet to earn just enough money to be able to buy the things you need: Many families struggle to make ends meet. no ˈend (spoken) very much: It upset me no end to hear they'd split up. no ˈend of sth (spoken) a lot of sth: We had no end of trouble getting them to agree. not the end of the ˈworld (spoken) not the worst thing that could happen to sb: Failing one exam is not the end of the world. on ˈend **1** in an upright position: It'll fit if you stand it on end. **2** for the stated length of time, without stopping: He would disappear for weeks on end. put an ˈend to yourself | put an ˈend to it all to kill yourself—more at BEGINNING, BITTER adj., BURN v., DEEP adj., HAIR, HEAR, LIGHT n., LOOSE END, MEANS, RECEIVE, SHARP adj., SHORT n., THIN adj., WIT, WRONG adj.

■ verb ~ (sth) (with sth) to finish; to make sth finish: [V] The road ends here. ◊ How does the story end? ◊ The speaker ended by suggesting some topics for discussion. ◊ Her note ended with the words: 'See you soon.' ◊ [VN] They decided to end their relationship. ◊ They ended the play with a song. [also V speech]

IDM ˌend your ˈdays/ˈlife (in sth) to spend the last part of your life in a particular state or place: He ended his days in poverty. ˌend in ˈtears (BrE, spoken) if you say that sth will end in tears, you are warning sb that what they are doing will have an unhappy or unpleasant result ˈend it all | ˌend your ˈlife to kill yourself the sth to end all sths used to emphasize that sth is large, important, exciting, etc. you think sth is: The movie has a car chase to end all car chases.

PHRV ˈend in sth [no passive] **1** to have sth as an ending: The word I'm thinking of ends in '-ous'. **2** to have sth as a result: Their long struggle ended in failure. ◊ The debate ended in uproar. ˌend ˈup to find yourself in a place or situation that you did not intend or expect to be in: If you go on like this you'll end up in prison. ◊ [+ -ing] At first they hated each other, but they ended up getting married. ◊ [+ADJ] If he carries on driving like that, he'll end up dead.

E

æ	ɑː	e	ɜː	ə	ɪ	iː	i	ɒ	ɔː	ʌ	ʊ	u	uː
cat	father	ten	bird	about	sit	see	many	got	saw	cup	put	actual	too
								(BrE)					

en·dan·ger /ɪnˈdeɪndʒə(r)/ *verb* [VN] to put sb/sth in a situation in which they could be harmed or damaged: *The health of our children is being endangered by exhaust fumes.* ◊ *That one mistake seriously endangered the future of the company.* ◊ *The sea turtle is an endangered species* (= it may soon no longer exist).

en·dear /ɪnˈdɪə(r); AmE -ˈdɪr/ *verb* [VN] PHRV **en'dear sb/ yourself to sb** to make sb/yourself popular: *Their policies on taxation didn't endear them to voters.* ◊ *She was a talented teacher who endeared herself to all who worked with her.*

en·dear·ing /ɪnˈdɪərɪŋ; AmE -ˈdɪr-/ *adj.* causing people to feel affection: *an endearing remark/smile/habit* ▶ **en·dear·ing·ly** *adv.*: *an endearingly old-fashioned idea*

en·dear·ment /ɪnˈdɪəmənt; AmE -ˈdɪrm-/ *noun* [C, U] a word or an expression that is used to show affection: *They were whispering endearments to each other.* ◊ *'Darling' is a term of endearment.*

en·deav·our (*BrE*) (*AmE* **en·deav·or**) /ɪnˈdevə(r)/ *noun, verb*
■ *noun* [U, C] (*formal*) an attempt to do sth, especially sth new or difficult: *Please make every endeavour to arrive on time.* ◊ *advances in the field of scientific endeavour* ◊ *The manager is expected to use his or her best endeavours to promote the artist's career.*
■ *verb* [Vtoinf] (*formal*) to try very hard to do sth SYN STRIVE: *I will endeavour to do my best for my country.*

en·dem·ic /enˈdemɪk/ *adj.* ~ **(in/to …)** regularly found in a particular place or among a particular group of people and difficult to get rid of: *Malaria is endemic in many hot countries.* ◊ *Corruption is endemic in the system.* ◊ *an attitude endemic among senior members of the profession* ◊ *species endemic to* (= only found in) *Madagascar* ◊ *the endemic problem of racism*—compare PANDEMIC

end·ing /ˈendɪŋ/ *noun* **1** the last part of a story, film/ movie, etc: *His stories usually have a happy ending.* OPP OPENING **2** the act of finishing sth; the last part of sth: *the anniversary of the ending of the Pacific War* ◊ *It was the perfect ending to the perfect day.* **3** the last part of a word, that is added to a main part: *verb endings* ◊ *a masculine/ feminine ending*

en·dive /ˈendaɪv; -dɪv/ *noun* [C, U] **1** (*BrE*) (*AmE* **chicory** [U]) a plant with green curly leaves that are eaten raw as a vegetable **2** (*AmE*) = CHICORY (1)

end·less /ˈendləs/ *adj.* **1** very large in size or amount and seeming to have no end: *endless patience* ◊ *endless opportunities for making money* ◊ *The possibilities are endless.* ◊ *an endless list of things to do* ◊ *We don't have an endless supply of money, you know.* **2** continuing for a long time and seeming to have no end: *an endless round of parties and visits* ◊ *The journey seemed endless.* ◊ *I've had enough of their endless arguing.* **3** (*technical*) (of a loop, etc.) having the ends joined together so it forms one piece: *an endless loop of tape* ▶ **end·less·ly** *adv.*: *She talks endlessly about her problems.* ◊ *an endlessly repeated pattern*

en·dorse /ɪnˈdɔːs; AmE ɪnˈdɔːrs/ *verb* [VN] **1** to say publicly that you support a person, statement or course of action: *I wholeheartedly endorse his remarks.* ◊ *Members of all parties endorsed a ban on land mines.* **2** to say in an advertisement that you use and like a particular product so that other people will want to buy it: *I wonder how many celebrities actually use the products they endorse.* **3** to write your name on the back of a cheque so that it can be paid into a bank account **4** [usually passive] (*BrE*) to write details of a driving offence on sb's DRIVING LICENCE: *You risk being fined and having your licence endorsed.*

en·dorse·ment /ɪnˈdɔːsmənt; AmE -ˈdɔːrs-/ *noun* [C, U] **1** a public statement or action showing that you support sb/sth: *The election victory is a clear endorsement of their policies.* ◊ *a letter of endorsement* **2** a statement made in an advertisement, usually by sb famous or important, saying that they use and like a particular product **3** (*BrE*) details of a driving offence written on sb's DRIVING LICENCE: *How many endorsements can you have before you lose your licence?*

endow /ɪnˈdaʊ/ *verb* [VN] to give a large sum of money to a school, a college or another institution to provide it with an income PHRV **be en'dowed with sth** to naturally have a particular feature, quality, etc: *She was endowed with intelligence and wit.* ◊ *The stones are believed to be endowed with magical powers.*—see also WELL ENDOWED **en'dow sb/sth with sth 1** to believe or imagine that sb/sth has a particular quality: *She had endowed Marcus with the qualities she wanted him to possess.* **2** (*formal*) to give sth to sb/sth: *to endow sb with a responsibility*

en·dow·ment /ɪnˈdaʊmənt/ *noun* **1** [C, U] money that is given to a school, a college or another institution to provide it with an income; the act of giving this money **2** [C, usually pl.] (*formal*) a quality or an ability that you are born with

en'dowment mortgage *noun* (*BrE*) a type of MORT-GAGE (= money borrowed to buy property) in which money is regularly paid into an endowment policy. At the end of a particular period of time this money is then used to pay back the money that was borrowed—compare REPAYMENT MORTGAGE

en'dowment policy *noun* (*BrE*) a type of life insurance in which a person regularly pays money to an insurance company, and receives a sum of money from them at the end of a particular period of time

'end product *noun* something that is produced by a particular activity or process

'end re'sult *noun* [usually sing.] the final result of a particular activity or process: *The end result of using this method is that learners leave the classroom discouraged.*

en·dur·ance /ɪnˈdjʊərəns; AmE -ˈdʊr-/ *noun* [U] the ability to continue doing sth painful or difficult for a long period of time without complaining: *He showed remarkable endurance throughout his illness.* ◊ *They were humiliated beyond endurance.* ◊ *This event tests both physical and mental endurance.* ◊ *powers of endurance* ◊ *The party turned out to be more of an endurance test than a pleasure.*

en·dure /ɪnˈdjʊə(r); AmE -ˈdʊr/ *verb* **1** (*written*) to experience and deal with sth that is painful or unpleasant, especially without complaining SYN BEAR: [VN] *They had to endure a long wait before the case came to trial.* ◊ *She could not endure the thought of parting.* ◊ *The pain was almost too great to endure.* ◊ (*formal*) *a love that endures all things and never fails* ◊ [V-ing, Vtoinf] *He can't endure being defeated.* ◊ *He can't endure to be defeated.* **2** [V] (*formal*) to continue to exist for a long time SYN LAST: *a success that will endure* ▶ **en·dur·able** /ɪnˈdjʊərəbl; AmE -ˈdʊr-/ *adj.*: *I felt that life was no longer endurable.* OPP UNENDURABLE

en·dur·ing /ɪnˈdjʊərɪŋ; AmE -ˈdʊr-/ *adj.* lasting for a long time: *enduring memories* ◊ *an enduring relationship/ influence* ◊ *What is the reason for the game's enduring appeal?* ▶ **en·dur·ing·ly** *adv.*: *an enduringly popular style*

'end-'user *noun* a person who actually uses a product rather than one who makes or sells it, especially a person who uses a product connected with computers

'end zone *noun* the area at the end of an American football field into which the ball must be carried or passed in order to score points

enema /ˈenəmə/ *noun* a liquid that is put into a person's RECTUM (= the opening through which solid waste leaves the body) in order to clean out the bowels, especially before a medical operation; the act of cleaning out the bowels in this way

enemy /ˈenəmi/ *noun* (*pl.* **-ies**) **1** [C] a person who hates sb or who acts or speaks against sb/sth: *He has a lot of enemies in the company.* ◊ *After just one day, she had already made an enemy of her manager.* ◊ *It is rare to find a prominent politician with few political enemies.* ◊ *The state has a duty to protect its citizens against external enemies.* ◊ *Birds are the natural enemies of many insect pests* (= they kill them).—see also ENMITY **2 (the enemy)** [sing.+ sing./pl. v.] a country that you are fighting a war against; the soldiers, etc. of this country: *The enemy was/ were forced to retreat.* ◊ *enemy forces/aircraft/territory* ◊ *behind enemy lines* (= the area controlled by the enemy)

aɪ	aʊ	eɪ	əʊ	oʊ	ɔɪ	ɪə	eə	ʊə	j	w
my	now	say	go	go	boy	near	hair	pure	yes	wet
			(BrE)	(AmE)						

3 [C] ~ (of sth) (*formal*) anything that harms sth or prevents it from being successful: *Poverty and ignorance are the enemies of progress.* **IDM** see WORST *adj.*

en·er·get·ic /ˌenəˈdʒetɪk; *AmE* ˌenərˈdʒ-/ *adj.* having or needing a lot of energy and enthusiasm: *He knew I was energetic and dynamic and would get things done.* ◊ *an energetic member/supporter* ◊ *The heart responds well to energetic exercise.* ◊ *For the more energetic* (= people who prefer physical activities), *we offer windsurfing and diving.* ◊ *I think I'd prefer something a little less energetic.* ▶ **en·er·get·ic·al·ly** /-kli/ *adv.*: *He energetically denied the charge.*

en·er·gize (*BrE* also **-ise**) /ˈenədʒaɪz; *AmE* ˈenərdʒ-/ *verb* [VN] **1** to make sb enthusiastic about sth **2** to give sb more energy, strength, etc: *a refreshing and energizing fruit drink* **3** (*technical*) to supply power or energy to a machine, an atom, etc: *positively energized particles*

en·ergy /ˈenədʒi; *AmE* -ərdʒi/ *noun* **1** [U] the ability to put effort and enthusiasm into an activity, work, etc: *It's a waste of time and energy.* ◊ *She's always full of energy.* ◊ *nervous energy* (= energy produced by feeling nervous) **2** (**energies**) [pl.] the physical and mental effort that you use to do sth: *She put all her energies into her work.* ◊ *creative/destructive energies* **3** [U] a source of power, such as fuel, used for driving machines, providing heat, etc: *solar/nuclear energy* ◊ *It is important to conserve energy.* ◊ *an energy crisis* (= for example when fuel is not freely available) **4** [U] (*physics*) the ability of MATTER or RADIATION to work because of its MASS, movement, electric CHARGE, etc: *kinetic/potential energy*

ener·vate /ˈenəveɪt; *AmE* ˈenərv-/ *verb* [VN] (*formal*) to make sb feel weak and tired: *an enervating disease/climate* ▶ **en·er·va·tion** /ˌenəˈveɪʃn; *AmE* ˌenərˈv-/ *noun* [U]

en·fant ter·rible /ˌɒ̃fɒ̃ teˈriːbl; *AmE* ˌɑ̃ːfɑː/ *noun* (*pl.* **enfants ter·ribles** /ˌɒ̃fɒ̃ teˈriːbl; *AmE* ˌɑ̃ːfɑː/) (from *French*) a person who is young and successful and whose behaviour and ideas may be unusual and may shock or embarrass other people

en·fee·ble /ɪnˈfiːbl/ *verb* [VN] (*formal*) to make sb/sth weak ▶ **en·fee·bled** *adj.*

en·fold /ɪnˈfəʊld; *AmE* ɪnˈfoʊld/ *verb* [VN] ~ sb/sth (in sth) (*literary*) **1** to hold sb in your arms in a way that shows affection: *She lay quietly, enfolded in his arms.* **2** to surround or cover sb/sth completely: *Darkness spread and enfolded him.*

en·force /ɪnˈfɔːs; *AmE* ɪnˈfɔːrs/ *verb* [VN] **1** ~ sth (on/against sb/sth) to make sure that people obey a particular law or rule: *It's the job of the police to enforce the law.* ◊ *The legislation will be difficult to enforce.* ◊ *United Nations troops enforced a ceasefire in the area.* **2** ~ sth (on sb) to make sth happen or force sb to do sth: *You can't enforce cooperation between the players.* ◊ *a period of enforced absence* ▶ **en·force·able** /-əbl/ *adj.*: *A gambling debt is not legally enforceable.* **en·force·ment** *noun* [U]: *strict enforcement of regulations* ◊ *law enforcement agencies/officers/procedures*

en·fran·chise /ɪnˈfræntʃaɪz/ *verb* [VN] [usually passive] (*formal*) to give sb the right to vote in an election **OPP** DISENFRANCHISE ▶ **en·fran·chise·ment** /ɪnˈfræntʃɪzmənt/ *noun* [U]

eng. *abbr.* (*BrE*) (in writing) engineer; engineering

en·gage /ɪnˈɡeɪdʒ/ *verb* **1** [VN] (*formal*) to succeed in attracting and keeping sb's attention and interest: *It is a movie that engages both the mind and the eye.* **2** ~ sb (as sth) (*formal*) to employ sb to do a particular job: [VN] *He is currently engaged as a consultant.* [also VN to inf] **3** [V] ~ (with sth/sb) to become involved with and try to understand sth/sb: *She has the ability to engage with young minds.* **4** (*formal*) to begin fighting with sb: [VN] *to engage the enemy* [also V] **5** ~ (with sth) when a part of a machine **engages**, or when you **engage** it, it fits together with another part of the machine and the machine begins to work: [V] *One cogwheel engages with the next.* ◊ *The cogwheels are not engaging.* ◊ [VN] *Engage the clutch before selecting a gear.* **OPP** DISENGAGE **PHRV** **en'gage in sth| en'gage sb in sth** to take part in sth; to make sb take

part in sth: *Even in prison, he continued to engage in criminal activities.* ◊ *She tried desperately to engage him in conversation.*

en·gaged /ɪnˈɡeɪdʒd/ *adj.* **1** ~ (in/on sth) (*formal*) busy doing sth: *They are engaged in talks with the Irish government.* ◊ *He is now engaged on his second novel.* ◊ *I can't come to dinner on Tuesday—I'm otherwise engaged* (= I have already arranged to do something else). ◊ *They were engaged in conversation.* **2** ~ (to sb) having agreed to marry sb: *She's engaged to Peter.* ◊ *They are engaged to be married* (= to each other). ◊ *When did you get engaged?* ◊ *an engaged couple* **3** (*BrE*) (*AmE* **busy**) (of a telephone line) being used: *I couldn't get through—the line's engaged.* ◊ *I phoned earlier but you were engaged* (= using your phone). ◊ *the engaged tone/signal* **4** (*BrE*) (of a public toilet) being used—compare VACANT

en·gage·ment /ɪnˈɡeɪdʒmənt/ *noun*

<u>BEFORE MARRIAGE</u> | **1** [C] ~ (to sb) an agreement to marry sb; the period during which two people are engaged: *Their engagement was announced in the local paper.* ◊ *She has broken off her engagement to Charles.* ◊ *an engagement party* ◊ *a long/short engagement*

<u>ARRANGEMENT TO DO STH</u> | **2** [C] an arrangement to do sth at a particular time, especially sth official or sth connected with your job: *an engagement book/diary* ◊ *He has a number of social engagements next week.* ◊ *It was her first official engagement.* ◊ *I had to refuse because of a prior engagement.*

<u>FIGHTING</u> | **3** [C, U] (*technical*) fighting between two armies, etc: *The general tried to avoid an engagement with the enemy.*

<u>BEING INVOLVED</u> | **4** [U] ~ (with sb/sth) (*formal*) being involved with sb/sth in an attempt to understand them/it: *Her views are based on years of engagement with the problems of the inner city.*

<u>EMPLOYMENT</u> | **5** [U, C] (*BrE*) an arrangement to employ sb; the process of employing sb: *The terms of engagement are to be agreed in writing.*

en'gagement ring *noun* a ring, usually with precious stones, that a man gives to a woman when they agree to get married

en·gaging /ɪnˈɡeɪdʒɪŋ/ *adj.* (*written*) interesting ‧ or pleasant in a way that attracts your attention: *an engaging smile/manner/person* ▶ **en·ga·ging·ly** *adv.*

en·gen·der /ɪnˈdʒendə(r)/ *verb* [VN] (*formal*) to make a feeling or situation exist: *The issue engendered controversy.*

en·gine /ˈendʒɪn/ *noun* **1** the part of a vehicle that produces power to make the vehicle move: *a diesel/petrol engine* ◊ *My car had to have a new engine.* ◊ *engine trouble/problems* ◊ *Switch the engine on/off.* ◊ *the engine room* (= the part of a ship where the engine is situated)—see also INTERNAL-COMBUSTION ENGINE, JET ENGINE, TRACTION ENGINE **2** (also **loco·mo·tive**) a vehicle that pulls a train **3** (**-engined**) (in adjectives) having the type or number of engines mentioned: *a twin-engined speedboat*—see also FIRE ENGINE

'engine driver (*BrE*, becoming *old-fashioned*) (*AmE* **engin·eer**) *noun* a person whose job is driving a railway/railroad engine

en·gin·eer /ˌendʒɪˈnɪə(r); *AmE* -ˈnɪr/ *noun, verb*
▪ *noun* **1** a person whose job involves designing and building engines, machines, roads, bridges, etc: *an electrical/a mechanical engineer*—see also CHEMICAL ENGINEER, CIVIL ENGINEER, LIGHTING ENGINEER, SOFTWARE ENGINEER, SOUND ENGINEER **2** a person who is trained to repair machines and electrical equipment: *They're sending an engineer to fix the phone.* **3** a person whose job is to control and repair engines, especially on a ship or an aircraft: *a flight engineer* ◊ *the chief engineer on a cruise liner* **4** (*AmE*) = ENGINE DRIVER **5** a soldier trained to design and build military structures
▪ *verb* [VN] **1** (often *disapproving*) to arrange for sth to happen or take place, especially when this is done secretly in order to give yourself an advantage: *She engineered a further meeting with him.* **2** [usually passive] to design and build sth: *The car is beautifully engineered*

E

and a pleasure to drive. **3** to change the GENETIC structure of sth: *genetically engineered crops*

en·gin·eer·ing /ˌendʒɪˈnɪərɪŋ; *AmE* -ˈnɪr-/ *noun* [U] **1** the activity of applying scientific knowledge to the design, building and control of machines, roads, bridges, electrical equipment, etc: *The bridge is a triumph of modern engineering.* **2** (also ˌengineering ˈscience) the study of engineering as a subject: *a degree in engineering*—see also CHEMICAL ENGINEERING, CIVIL ENGINEERING, ELECTRICAL ENGINEERING, GENETIC ENGINEERING, MECHANICAL ENGINEERING, SOCIAL ENGINEERING

Eng·lish /ˈɪŋɡlɪʃ/ *noun, adj.*
■ *noun* **1** [U] the language of Britain, Ireland, N America, Australia and some other countries: *She speaks good English.* ◊ *I need to improve my English.* **2** [U] English language or literature as a subject of study: *a degree in English* ◊ *English is my best subject.* **3** (**the English**) [pl.] the people of England (sometimes wrongly used to mean the British, including the Scots, the Welsh and the Northern Irish) **IDM** the ˌKing's/ˌQueen's ˈEnglish (*old-fashioned*) (in Britain) correct standard English—more at PLAIN *adj.*
■ *adj.* connected with England, its people or its language: *the English countryside* ◊ *an English man/woman* ◊ *typically English attitudes* ◊ *an English dictionary* ⊏> note at BRITISH

ˌEnglish ˈbreakfast *noun* [C, U] a large breakfast, usually consisting of CEREAL (= food made from grain), cooked BACON and eggs, toast and tea or coffee—compare CONTINENTAL BREAKFAST

ˌEnglish ˈhorn *noun* (*especially AmE*) = COR ANGLAIS

Eng·lish·man /ˈɪŋɡlɪʃmən/ *noun* (*pl.* **-men** /-mən/) a man from England **IDM** an ˌEnglishman's ˌhome is his ˈcastle (*BrE*) (*AmE* a ˌman's ˌhome is his ˈcastle) (*saying*) a person's home is a place where they can be private and safe and do as they like

ˌEnglish ˈmuffin *noun* (*AmE*) = MUFFIN (1)

en·grave /ɪnˈɡreɪv/ *verb* [VN] [often passive] **~ A** (**with B**)| **~ B on A** to cut words or designs on wood, stone, metal, etc: *The silver cup was engraved with his name.* ◊ *His name was engraved on the silver cup.* **IDM** be engraved on/in your ˈheart, ˈmemory, ˈmind, etc. to be sth that you will never forget because it affected you so strongly

en·graver /ɪnˈɡreɪvə(r)/ *noun* a person whose job is to cut words or designs on wood, stone, metal, etc.

en·grav·ing /ɪnˈɡreɪvɪŋ/ *noun* **1** [C] a picture made by cutting a design on a piece of metal and then printing the design on paper **2** [U] the art or process of cutting designs on wood, stone, metal, etc.

en·gross /ɪnˈɡrəʊs; *AmE* ɪnˈɡroʊs/ *verb* [VN] if sth engrosses you, it is so interesting that you give it all your attention and time: *As the business grew, it totally engrossed him.* ▶ **en·gross·ing** /ɪnˈɡrəʊsɪŋ; *AmE* -ˈɡroʊs-/: *an engrossing problem*

en·grossed /ɪnˈɡrəʊst; *AmE* ɪnˈɡroʊst/ *adj.* **~ (in/with sth)** so interested or involved in sth that you give it all your attention: *She was engrossed in conversation.*

en·gulf /ɪnˈɡʌlf/ *verb* [VN] (*written*) **1** to surround or to cover sb/sth completely: *He was engulfed by a crowd of reporters.* ◊ *The vehicle was **engulfed in flames**.* **2** to affect sb/sth very strongly: *Fear engulfed her.*

en·hance /ɪnˈhɑːns; *AmE* -ˈhæns/ *verb* [VN] to increase or further improve the good quality, value or status of sb/sth: *This is an opportunity to enhance the reputation of the company.* ◊ *the skilled use of make-up to enhance your best features* ▶ **en·hanced** *adj.*: *enhanced efficiency/ security* **en·hance·ment** *noun* [U,C]: *equipment for the enhancement of sound quality* ◊ *software enhancements*

en·hancer /ɪnˈhɑːnsə(r); *AmE* -ˈhæns-/ *noun* (*technical*) a substance or device that is designed to improve sth: *flavour enhancers*

en·igma /ɪˈnɪɡmə/ *noun* a person, thing or situation that is mysterious and difficult to understand: *Even after years he still remains an enigma to me.*

en·ig·mat·ic /ˌenɪɡˈmætɪk/ *adj.* mysterious and difficult to understand: *an enigmatic smile* ▶ **en·ig·mat·ic·al·ly** /-kli/ *adv.*: *'I might,' he said enigmatically.*

en·jambe·ment (also **en·jamb·ment**) /ɪnˈdʒæmbmənt/ *noun* [U, C] (from *French, technical*) the fact of a sentence continuing beyond the end of a line of poetry—compare CAESURA

en·join /ɪnˈdʒɔɪn/ *verb* **1** [VN, VNtoinf] [often passive] (*formal*) to order or strongly advise sb to do sth; to say that a particular action or quality is necessary **2** [VN] **~ sb from doing sth** (*law*) to legally prevent sb from doing sth, for example with an INJUNCTION

enjoy /ɪnˈdʒɔɪ/ *verb* **1** to get pleasure from sth: [VN] *We thoroughly enjoyed our time in New York.* ◊ *Thanks for a great evening. I really enjoyed it.* ◊ [V-ing] *I enjoy playing tennis and squash.* **2** [VN] **~ yourself** to be happy and get pleasure from what you are doing: *They all enjoyed themselves at the party.* **3** [VN] (*written*) to have sth good that is an advantage to you: *People in this country enjoy a high standard of living.* ◊ *He's always enjoyed good health.* **4** [V] (**enjoy!**) (*spoken*) used to say that you hope sb gets pleasure from sth that you are giving them or recommending to them: *Here's that book I promised you. Enjoy!*

GRAMMAR POINT

enjoy

Note the following patterns:

I enjoyed myself at the party. ~~I enjoyed at the party.~~
Thanks. I really enjoyed it. ~~Thanks. I really enjoyed.~~
I enjoy playing basketball. ~~I enjoy to play basketball.~~
I enjoy reading very much. ~~I enjoy very much reading.~~
I hope you enjoy your trip. ~~I hope you enjoy with your trip.~~

---

en·joy·able /ɪnˈdʒɔɪəbl/ *adj.* giving pleasure: *an enjoyable weekend/experience* ◊ *highly/really/thoroughly/very enjoyable* ▶ **en·joy·ably** /-əbli/ *adv.*: *The evening passed enjoyably.*

en·joy·ment /ɪnˈdʒɔɪmənt/ *noun* **1** [U] the pleasure that you get from sth: *He spoiled my enjoyment of the game by talking all through it.* ◊ *The rules are there to ensure everyone's safety and enjoyment.* ◊ *Children seem to have lost their enjoyment in reading.* ◊ *I get a lot of enjoyment from my grandchildren.* **2** [C] something that gives you pleasure: *Children like to share interests and enjoyments with their parents.* **3** [U] **~ of sth** (*formal*) the fact of having and using sth: *the enjoyment of equal rights*

en·large /ɪnˈlɑːdʒ; *AmE* -ˈlɑːrdʒ/ *verb* **1** to make sth bigger; to become bigger: [VN] *There are plans to enlarge the recreation area.* ◊ *Reading will enlarge your vocabulary.* [also V] **2** [VN] (*usually passive*) to make a bigger copy of a photograph or document: *We're going to have this picture enlarged.* ▶ **en·larged** *adj.*: *an enlarged heart* **PHRV** **en·large on/upon sth** (*formal*) to say or write more about sth that has been mentioned **SYN** ELABORATE

en·large·ment /ɪnˈlɑːdʒmənt; *AmE* -ˈlɑːrdʒ-/ *noun* **1** [U, sing.] **~ (of sth)** the process or result of sth becoming or being made larger: *the enlargement of the company's overseas business activities* **2** [C] something that has been made larger, especially a photograph: *If you like the picture I can send you an enlargement of it.* **OPP** REDUCTION

en·light·en /ɪnˈlaɪtn/ *verb* [VN] (*formal*) to give sb information so that they understand sth better: *She didn't enlighten him about her background.* ▶ **en·light·en·ing** *adj.*: *It was a very enlightening interview.*

en·light·ened /ɪnˈlaɪtnd/ *adj.* [usually before noun] (*approving*) having or showing an understanding of people's needs, a situation, etc. that is not based on old-fashioned attitudes and PREJUDICE: *enlightened opinions/attitudes/ideas* ◊ *an enlightened approach to teaching*

en·light·en·ment /ɪnˈlaɪtnmənt/ *noun* **1** [U] knowledge about and understanding of sth; the process of understanding sth or making sb understand it: *The newspapers provided little enlightenment about the cause of the accident.* ◊ *cultural/spiritual enlightenment* **2** (**the Enlightenment**) [sing.] the period in the 18th century when many

s	t	v	z	ʃ	ʒ	tʃ	dʒ	θ	ð	ŋ
see	tea	van	zoo	shoe	vision	chain	jam	thin	this	sing

writers and scientists began to argue that science and reason were more important than religion and tradition

en·list /ɪnˈlɪst/ *verb* **1** ~ sth/sb (in sth) | ~ sb (as sth) to persuade sb to help you or to join you in doing sth: [VN] *They hoped to **enlist the help** of the public in solving the crime.* ◊ *We were enlisted as helpers.* [also VN to inf] **2** ~ (sb) (in/into/for sth) | ~ (sb) (as sth) to join or to make sb join the armed forces [SYN] JOIN UP: [V] *They both enlisted in 1915.* ◊ *to enlist as a soldier* ◊ [VN] *He was enlisted into the US Navy.* ▶ **en·list·ment** [U]: *the enlistment of expert help* ◊ *his enlistment in the Royal Air Force*

en·list·ed /ɪnˈlɪstɪd/ *adj.* (*especially AmE*) (of a member of the army, etc.) having a rank that is below that of an officer: *enlisted men and women* ◊ *enlisted personnel*

en·liven /ɪnˈlaɪvn/ *verb* [VN] (*formal*) to make sth more interesting or more fun

en masse /ˌɒ̃ ˈmæs; *AmE* ˌɑ̃-/ *adv.* (from *French*) all together, and usually in large numbers: *The young folk were emigrating en masse.*

en·mesh /ɪnˈmeʃ/ *verb* [VN] [usually passive] ~ sb/sth (in sth) (*written*) to involve sb/sth in a bad situation that it is not easy to escape from

en·mity /ˈenmɪti/ *noun* [U, C] (*pl.* **-ies**) ~ (between A and B) feelings of hatred towards sb: *the traditional problem of the enmity between Protestants and Catholics* ◊ *personal enmities and political conflicts* ◊ *Her action earned her the enmity of two or three colleagues.*—see also ENEMY

en·noble /ɪˈnəʊbl; *AmE* ɪˈnoʊbl/ *verb* [VN] (*formal*) **1** [usually passive] to make sb a member of the NOBILITY **2** to give sb/sth a better moral character: *In a strange way she seemed ennobled by her grief.* ▶ **en·noble·ment** *noun* [U]

ennui /ɒnˈwiː; *AmE* ɑːn-/ *noun* [U] (from *French, literary*) feelings of being bored and not satisfied because nothing interesting is happening

enor·mity /ɪˈnɔːməti; *AmE* ɪˈnɔːrm-/ *noun* (*pl.* **-ies**) **1** [U] the ~ of sth (of a problem, etc.) the very great size, effect, etc. of sth; the fact of sth being very serious: *the enormity of a task/problem/decision* ◊ *People are still coming to terms with the enormity of the disaster.* ◊ *The full enormity of the crime has not yet been revealed.* **2** [C, usually pl.] (*formal*) a very serious crime: *the enormities of the Hitler regime*

enor·mous /ɪˈnɔːməs; *AmE* ɪˈnɔːrməs/ *adj.* extremely large [SYN] HUGE, IMMENSE: *an enormous house/dog* ◊ *an enormous amount of time/money/information* ◊ *enormous interest/pressure/responsibility* ◊ *The problems facing the President are enormous.*

enor·mous·ly /ɪˈnɔːməsli; *AmE* ɪˈnɔːrm-/ *adv.* very; very much: *enormously rich/powerful/grateful* ◊ *The price of wine varies enormously depending on where it comes from.* ◊ *She was looking forward to the meeting enormously.*

enough /ɪˈnʌf/ *det., pron., adv.*
■ *det.* used before plural or uncountable nouns to mean 'as many or as much as sb needs or wants' [SYN] SUFFICIENT: *Have you made enough copies?* ◊ *Is there enough room for me?* ◊ *I didn't have enough clothes to last a week.* ◊ *Don't ask me to do it. I've got enough problems as it is.* ◊ (*old-fashioned*) *There was food enough for all.* [HELP] Although **enough** after a noun now sounds old-fashioned, **time enough** is still fairly common: *There'll be time enough to relax when you've finished your work.*
■ *pron.* as many or as much as sb needs or wants: *Six bottles should be enough.* ◊ *Have you had enough* (= to eat)? ◊ *If enough of you are interested, we'll organize a trip to the theatre.* ◊ *There was **nowhere near enough** for everybody.* ◊ *We've nearly run out of paper. Do you think there's enough for today?* [IDM] **e,nough is e'nough** (*saying*) used when you think that sth should not continue any longer **e,nough 'said** used to say that you understand a situation and there is no need to say any more: *'He's a politician, remember.' 'Enough said.'* **have had e'nough (of sth/sb)** used when sth/sb is annoying you and you no longer want to do, have or see it or them: *I've had enough of driving the kids around.*
■ *adv.* (used after verbs, adjectives and adverbs) **1** to the necessary degree: *I hadn't trained enough for the game.* ◊ *This house isn't big enough for us.* ◊ *She's old enough to*

decide for herself. ◊ *We didn't leave early enough.* ◊ *Tell them it's just not good enough.* **2** to a satisfactory degree, but not to a very great degree: *He seemed pleasant enough to me.* **3** to a degree that you do not wish to get any greater: *I hope my job's safe. Life is hard enough as it is.* [IDM] **,curiously, ,funnily, ,oddly, ,strangely, etc. e'nough** used to show that sth is surprising: *Funnily enough, I said the same thing myself only yesterday.*—more at FAR *adv.*, FAIR *adj.*, LIKE *adv.*, MAN *n.*, NEAR *adv.*, RIGHT *adj.*, SURE *adv.*

> **WHICH WORD?**
>
> **enough / adequate / sufficient / satisfactory / acceptable / will do**
>
> **Enough** is the usual word that you use to say that you have as much as you need of something: *Five copies should be enough.* ◊ *Do you have enough money?* ◊ *We haven't got enough time.*
>
> **Adequate** and **sufficient** have the same meaning but are very formal. In informal English you can use **will do**: *Can you lend me some money? Ten pounds will do.*
>
> If you are talking about the quality of something, you can say that it is **good enough**: *Is the light good enough to take photos?* In formal language you can also say that it is **adequate, satisfactory** or **acceptable**. These words on their own may suggest that something is only just good enough and could be better. Compare: *This piece of work is satisfactory* and *This piece of work is very satisfactory.*
>
> In informal English you can use **will do**, but it can also mean 'only just': *Will this do?* ◊ *It isn't very good but it'll do.*

en pas·sant /ˌɒ̃ ˈpæsɒ̃; *AmE* ˌɑ̃ː pæˈsɑ̃ː/ *adv.* (from *French*) while talking about sth else and without giving much information: *He mentioned en passant that he was going away.*

en·quire (also **inquire** *especially in AmE*) /ɪnˈkwaɪə(r)/ *verb* ~ (about sb/sth) (*rather formal*) to ask sb for some information: [V] *I called the station to enquire about train times.* ◊ *She **enquired as to** your whereabouts.* ◊ [V wh-] *Might I enquire why you have not mentioned this until now?* ◊ [VN] *He enquired her name.* [also V speech] [PHRV] **en'quire after sb** (*formal*) to ask for information about sb, especially about their health or about what they are doing **en'quire into sth** to find out more information about sth [SYN] INVESTIGATE: *A committee was appointed to enquire into the allegations.* **en'quire sth of sb** (*formal*) to ask sb sth: [+ speech] *'Will you be staying for lunch?' she enquired of Charles.*

en·quir·er (also **in·quirer** *especially in AmE*) /ɪnˈkwaɪərə(r)/ *noun* (*formal*) a person who asks for information

en·quir·ing (also **in·quir·ing** *especially in AmE*) /ɪnˈkwaɪərɪŋ/ *adj.* [usually before noun] **1** showing an interest in learning new things: *a child with an enquiring mind* **2** asking for information: *an enquiring look* ▶ **en·quir·ing·ly** (also **in·quir·ing·ly** *especially in AmE*) *adv.*

en·quiry (also **in·quiry** *especially in AmE*) /ɪnˈkwaɪəri; *AmE* usually ˈɪnkwəri/ *noun* (*pl.* **-ies**) **1** [C] ~ (into sth) an official process to find out the cause of sth or to find out information about sth: *to hold/order/set up an enquiry into the affair* ◊ *a murder enquiry* ◊ *a public enquiry into the environmental effects of the proposed new road* **2** [C] ~ (from sb) (about sb/sth) a request for information about sb/sth; a question about sb/sth: *a telephone enquiry* ◊ *We received over 300 enquiries about the job.* ◊ *I'll have to **make** a few **enquiries** (= try to find out about it) and get back to you.* ◊ *enquiries from prospective students* ◊ (*BrE*) *Two men have been **helping police with their enquiries** (= are being questioned about a crime, but have not been charged with it).* **3** [U] the act of asking questions or collecting information about sb/sth: *scientific enquiry* ◊ *The police are following several **lines of enquiry**.* ◊ *a committee of enquiry* **4** (**enquiries**) [pl.] (*BrE*) a place where you can get information: *Ask at enquiries to see if*

æ	ɑː	e	ɜː	ə	ɪ	iː	i	ɒ	ɔː	ʌ	ʊ	u	uː
cat	father	ten	bird	about	sit	see	many	got	saw	cup	put	actual	too
	(BrE)												

your bag has been handed in.—see also DIRECTORY ENQUIR-IES

en·rage /ɪnˈreɪdʒ/ *verb* [VN] [usually passive] (*written*) to make sb very angry

en·rap·ture /ɪnˈræptʃə(r)/ *verb* [VN] [usually passive] (*formal*) to give sb great pleasure or joy [SYN] ENCHANT

en·rich /ɪnˈrɪtʃ/ *verb* [VN] **1** ~ sth (with sth) to improve the quality of sth, often by adding sth to it: *The study of science has enriched all our lives.* ◊ *Most breakfast cereals are enriched with vitamins.* **2** to make sb/sth rich or richer: *a nation enriched by oil revenues* ◊ *They were accused of using their position to enrich themselves.* ▶ **en·rich·ment** *noun* [U]

enrol /ɪnˈrəʊl; *AmE* ɪnˈroʊl/ *verb* (**-ll-**) (*especially BrE*) (*AmE* usually **en·roll**) to arrange for yourself or for sb else to officially join a course, school, etc: [V] *You need to enrol before the end of August.* ◊ (*BrE*) *to enrol on a course* ◊ (*AmE*) *to enroll in a course* ◊ [VN] *The centre will soon be ready to enrol candidates for the new-style programme.*

en·rol·lee /ɪnˈrəʊˈliː; *AmE* ɪnˌroʊ-/ *noun* (*AmE*) a person who has officially joined a course, an organization, etc.

en·rol·ment (*BrE*) (*AmE* **en·roll·ment**) /ɪnˈrəʊlmənt; *AmE* -ˈroʊl-/ *noun* [U, C] the act of officially joining a course, school, etc.; the number of people who do this: *Enrolment is the first week of September.* ◊ *School enrolments are currently falling.*

en route /ˌɒ̃ ˈruːt; ˌɒn; *AmE* ˌɑː-; ˌɑːn/ *adv.* ~ (**from** ...) (**to** ...)| (*BrE*) ~ (**for** ...) (*from French*) on the way; while travelling from/to a particular place: *We stopped for a picnic en route.* ◊ *The bus broke down en route from Boston to New York.* ◊ *a plane en route for Heathrow*

en·sconce /ɪnˈskɒns; *AmE* -ˈskɑːns/ *verb* [VN] [usually+adv./prep.] (*formal*) if you **are ensconced** or **ensconce yourself** somewhere, you are made or make yourself comfortable and safe in that place or position

en·sem·ble /ɒnˈsɒmbl; *AmE* ɑːnˈsɑːmbl/ *noun* **1** [C+sing./pl. v.] a small group of musicians, dancers or actors who perform together: *a brass/wind/string ensemble* ◊ *The ensemble is/are based in Lyons.* **2** [C, usually sing.] (*formal*) a number of things considered as a group **3** [C, usually sing.] a set of clothes that are worn together: *A pair of pink shoes completed her striking ensemble.*

en·shrine /ɪnˈʃraɪn/ *verb* [VN] [usually passive] ~ sth (in sth) (*formal*) to make a law, right, etc. respected or official, especially by stating it in an important written document: *These rights are enshrined in the country's constitution.*

en·shroud /ɪnˈʃraʊd/ *verb* [VN] (*literary*) to cover or surround sth completely so that it cannot be seen or understood: *The island was enshrouded in mist.* ◊ *Secrecy enshrouded the Party's central committee.*

en·sign /ˈensən/ *noun* **1** a flag flown on a ship to show which country it belongs to: *the White Ensign* (= the flag of the British Navy) **2** an officer of lower rank in the US navy: *Ensign Marshall*

en·slave /ɪnˈsleɪv/ *verb* [VN] [usually passive] **1** to make sb a slave **2** ~ sb/sth (to sth) (*formal*) to make sb/sth completely dependent on sth so that they cannot manage without it ▶ **en·slave·ment** *noun* [U]

en·snare /ɪnˈsneə(r); *AmE* ɪnˈsner/ *verb* [VN] (*formal*) to make sb/sth unable to escape from a difficult situation or from a person who wants to control them: *young homeless people who become ensnared in a life of crime*

ensue /ɪnˈsjuː; *AmE* -ˈsuː/ *verb* [V] (*written*) to happen after or as a result of another event [SYN] FOLLOW: *An argument ensued.* ▶ **en·su·ing** *adj.: He had become separated from his parents in the ensuing panic.* ◊ *They lost track of each other in the ensuing years.*

en suite /ˌɒ̃ ˈswiːt; *AmE* ˌɑ̃-/ *adj., adv.* (*BrE*, from French) (of a bathroom) joined onto a bedroom and for use only by people in that bedroom: *Each bedroom in the hotel has a bathroom en suite/an en suite bathroom.* ◊ *an en suite bedroom* (= a bedroom with an en suite bathroom) ◊ *en suite facilities*

en·sure (also **in·sure** especially in *AmE*) /ɪnˈʃʊə(r); -ˈʃɔː(r); *AmE* ɪnˈʃʊr/ *verb* to make sure that sth happens or is

definite: [VN] *The book ensured his success.* ◊ [V(**that**)] *Please ensure (that) all lights are switched off.* [alsoVNN]

-ent ⇨ -ANT

en·tail /ɪnˈteɪl/ *verb* to involve sth that cannot be avoided: [VN] *The job entails a lot of hard work.* ◊ *The girls learn exactly what is entailed in caring for a newborn baby.* ◊ [V-ing] *It will entail driving a long distance every day.* [alsoVN-ing]

en·tan·gle /ɪnˈtæŋgl/ *verb* [VN] [usually passive] **1** ~ sb/sth (in/with sth) to make sb/sth become caught or twisted in sth: *The bird had become entangled in the wire netting.* **2** ~ sb in sth/with sb to involve sb in a difficult or complicated situation: *He became entangled in a series of conflicts with the management.* ◊ *She didn't want to get entangled* (= emotionally involved) *with him.*

en·tangle·ment /ɪnˈtæŋglmənt/ *noun* **1** [C] a difficult or complicated relationship with another person or country: *emotional/political entanglements* **2** [U] the act of becoming entangled in sth; the state of being entangled: *Many dolphins die each year from entanglement in fishing nets.* **3** (**en·tangle·ments**) [pl.] (*technical*) barriers made of BARBED WIRE, used to stop an enemy from getting close

en·tente /ɒnˈtɒnt; *AmE* ɑːnˈtɑːnt/ *noun* [U, sing.] (from *French*) a friendly relationship between two countries: *the Franco-Russian entente*

en·tente cor·di·ale /ˌɒntɒnt ˌkɔːdiˈɑːl; *AmE* ˌɑːntɑːnt ˌkɔːrd-/ *noun* [U, sing.] (from *French*) a friendly relationship between two countries, especially between Britain and France

enter /ˈentə(r)/ *verb*

COME/GO IN | **1** (not usually used in the passive) (*formal*) to come or go into sth: [V] *Knock before you enter.* ◊ [VN] *Someone entered the room behind me.* ◊ *Where did the bullet enter the body?* ◊ (*figurative*) *A note of defiance entered her voice.* ◊ (*figurative*) *It never entered my head* (= I never thought) *that she would tell him about me.*

JOIN INSTITUTION/START WORK | **2** [VN] [no passive] to become a member of an institution; to start working in an organization or a profession: *to enter a school/college/university* ◊ *to enter politics/the legal profession* ◊ *to enter Parliament* (= become an MP) ◊ *to enter the Church* (= become a priest)

BEGIN ACTIVITY | **3** [VN] to begin or become involved in an activity, a situation, etc: *to enter a relationship/conflict/war* ◊ *Several new firms have now entered the market.* ◊ *The investigation has entered a new phase.* ◊ *The strike is entering its fourth week.*

EXAM/COMPETITION | **4** ~ (**for sth**)| ~ **sb** (**in/for sth**) to put your name on the list for an exam, a race, a competition, etc.; to do this for sb: [VN] *1000 children entered the competition.* ◊ *Irish trainers have entered several horses in the race.* ◊ *How many students have been entered for the exam?* ◊ [V] *Only four British players have entered for the championship.*

WRITE INFORMATION | **5** [VN] ~ **sth** (**in/into/on sth**) to put names, numbers, details, etc. in a list, book or computer: *Enter your name and occupation in the boxes* (= on a form). ◊ *to enter data into a computer* ◊ *to enter figures on a spreadsheet*

SAY OFFICIALLY | **6** [VN] (*formal*) to say sth officially so that it can be recorded: *to enter a plea of not guilty* (= at the beginning of a court case) ◊ *to enter a protest/an offer* —see also ENTRANCE, ENTRY [IDM] see FORCE *n.*, NAME *n.* [PHRV] '**enter into sth** (*formal*) **1** to begin to discuss or deal with sth: *Let's not enter into details at this stage.* **2** to take an active part in sth: *They entered into the spirit of the occasion* (= began to enjoy and feel part of it). **3** [no passive] to form part of sth or have an influence on sth: *This possibility never entered into our calculations.* ◊ *Your personal feelings shouldn't enter into this at all.* '**enter into sth** (**with sb**) to begin sth or become involved in sth: *to enter into a contract/an agreement* ◊ *to enter into negotiations/correspondence* '**enter on/upon sth** (*formal*) to start to do sth or become involved in it: *to enter on a new career*

en·ter·itis /ˌentəˈraɪtəs/ *noun* [U] (*medical*) a painful

entrance

infection in the INTESTINES that usually causes DIAR-RHOEA—see also GASTRO-ENTERITIS

en·ter·prise /'entəpraɪz; AmE -tərp-/ noun **1** [C] a company or business: *an enterprise with a turnover of $26 billion* ◊ *state-owned/public enterprises* ◊ *small and medium-sized enterprises* **2** [C] a large project, especially one that is difficult SYN VENTURE: *his latest business/commercial enterprise* ◊ *a joint enterprise* **3** [U] the development of businesses by the people of a country rather than by the government: *grants to encourage enterprise in the region* ◊ *an enterprise culture* (= in which people are encouraged to develop small businesses)—see also FREE ENTERPRISE, PRIVATE ENTERPRISE **4** [U] (*approving*) the ability to think of new projects and make them successful: *a job in which enterprise is rewarded* ◊ *a man of enterprise*

en·ter·pris·ing /'entəpraɪzɪŋ; AmE -tərp-/ adj. (*approving*) having or showing the ability to think of new projects or new ways of doing things and make them successful: *One enterprising farmer opened up his field as a car park and charged people £10 to park there.*

en·ter·tain /ˌentə'teɪn; AmE -tər't-/ verb **1** to invite people to eat or drink with you as your guests, especially in your home: [V] *The job involves a lot of entertaining.* ◊ [VN] *Barbecues are a favourite way of entertaining friends.* **2 ~ (sb) (with sth)** to interest and amuse sb in order to please them: [VN] *He entertained us for hours with his stories and jokes.* ◊ [V] *The aim of the series is both to entertain and inform.* **3** [VN] (not used in the progressive tenses) (*formal*) to consider or allow yourself to think about an idea, a hope, a feeling, etc: *He had entertained hopes of a reconciliation.* ◊ *to entertain a doubt/suspicion*

en·ter·tain·er /ˌentə'teɪnə(r); AmE -tər't-/ noun a person whose job is amusing or interesting people, for example, by singing, telling jokes or dancing: *a street entertainer*

en·ter·tain·ing /ˌentə'teɪnɪŋ; AmE -tər't-/ adj. interesting and amusing: *an entertaining speech/evening* ◊ *I found the talk both informative and entertaining.* ◊ *She was always so funny and entertaining.* ► **en·ter·tain·ing·ly** adv.

en·ter·tain·ment /ˌentə'teɪnmənt; AmE -tər't-/ noun **1** [U, C] films/movies, music, etc. used to entertain people; an example of this: *radio, television and other forms of entertainment* ◊ *live/family entertainment* ◊ *The entertainment was provided by a folk band.* ◊ *Local entertainments are listed in the newspaper.* ◊ *The show was good entertainment value.* **2** [U] the act of entertaining sb: *a budget for the entertainment of clients*

en·thral (*BrE*) (*AmE* **en·thrall**) /ɪn'θrɔːl/ verb (**-ll-**) (usually passive) if sth **enthrals** you, it is so interesting, beautiful, etc. that you give it all your attention: [VN] *The child watched, enthralled by the bright moving images.* [also V] ► **en·thral·ling** adj.: *an enthralling performance*

en·throne /ɪn'θrəʊn; AmE ɪn'θroʊn/ verb [VN] [usually passive] when a king, queen or important member of a Church is **enthroned**, they sit on a THRONE (= a special chair) in a ceremony to mark the beginning of their rule ► **en·throne·ment** noun [U, C]

en·thuse /ɪn'θjuːz; AmE -'θuːz/ verb **1 ~ (about/over sth/sb)** to talk in an enthusiastic and excited way about sth: [V] *The article enthused about the benefits that the new system would bring.* ◊ [V speech] *'It's a wonderful idea', he enthused.* [also V that] **2** [VN] [usually passive] **~ sb (with sth)** to make sb feel very interested and excited: *Everyone present was enthused by the idea.*

en·thu·si·asm /ɪn'θjuːziæzəm; AmE -'θuːz-/ noun **1** [U] **~ (for sth/for doing sth)** a strong feeling of excitement and interest in sth and a desire to become involved in it: *I can't say I share your enthusiasm for the idea.* ◊ *She never lost her enthusiasm for teaching.* ◊ *He had a real enthusiasm for the work.* ◊ *The news was greeted with a lack of enthusiasm by those at the meeting.* ◊ *'I don't mind,' she said, without much enthusiasm.* ◊ *full of enthusiasm* **2** [C] (*formal*) something that you are very interested in and spend a lot of time doing

en·thu·si·ast /ɪn'θjuːziæst; AmE -'θuːz-/ noun **~ (for/of sth)** **1** a person who is very interested in sth and spends a

lot of time doing it: *a football enthusiast* ◊ *an enthusiast of jazz* **2** a person who approves of sth and shows enthusiasm for it: *enthusiasts for a united Europe*

en·thu·si·ast·ic /ɪnˌθjuːzi'æstɪk; AmE -ˌθuːz-/ adj. **~ (about sb/sth)** | **~ (about doing sth)** feeling or showing a lot of excitement and interest about sb/sth: *an enthusiastic supporter/crowd* ◊ *an enthusiastic welcome* ◊ *You don't sound very enthusiastic about the idea.* ◊ *She was even less enthusiastic about going to Spain.* ► **en·thu·si·as·tic·al·ly** /-kli/ adv.

en·tice /ɪn'taɪs/ verb [usually+adv./prep.] **~ sb (into doing sth)** to persuade sb/sth to go somewhere or to do sth, usually by offering them sth: [VN] *The bargain prices are expected to entice customers away from other stores.* ◊ *The animal refused to be enticed from its hole.* ◊ [VN to inf] *Try and entice the child to eat by offering small portions of their favourite food.* ► **en·tice·ment** noun [C, U]: *The party is offering low taxation as its main enticement.*

en·ticing /ɪn'taɪsɪŋ/ adj. something that is **enticing** is so attractive and interesting that you want to have it or know more about it: *The offer was too enticing to refuse.* ► **en·ticing·ly** adv.

en·tire /ɪn'taɪə(r)/ adj. [only before noun] (used when you are emphasizing that the whole of sth is involved) including everything, everyone or every part SYN WHOLE: *The entire village was destroyed.* ◊ *I wasted an entire day on it.* ◊ *I have never in my entire life heard such nonsense!* ◊ *The disease threatens to wipe out the entire population.*

en·tire·ly /ɪn'taɪəli; AmE ɪn'taɪərli/ adv. in every way possible; completely: *I entirely agree with you.* ◊ *I'm not entirely happy about the proposal.* ◊ *That's an entirely different matter.* ◊ *The audience was almost entirely female.*

en·tir·ety /ɪn'taɪərəti/ noun [sing.] (*formal*) **the ~ of sth** the whole of sth **IDM in its/their en·tirety** as a whole, rather than in parts: *The poem is too long to quote in its entirety.*

en·title /ɪn'taɪtl/ verb **1** [often passive] **~ sb to sth** to give sb the right to have or to do sth: [VN] *You will be entitled to your pension when you reach 65.* ◊ *Everyone's entitled to their own opinion.* ◊ [VN to inf] *This ticket does not entitle you to travel first class.* **2** [VN-N] [usually passive] to give a title to a book, play, etc: *He read a poem entitled 'Salt'.*

en·title·ment /ɪn'taɪtlmənt/ noun (*formal*) **1** [U] **~ (to sth)** the official right to have or do sth: *This may affect your entitlement to compensation.* **2** [C] something that you have an official right to; the amount that you have the right to receive: *Your contributions will affect your pension entitlements.* **3** [C] (*AmE*) a government system that provides financial support to a particular group of people: *a reform of entitlements* ◊ *Medicard, Medicare and other entitlement programs*

en·tity /'entəti/ noun (*pl.* **-ies**) (*formal*) something that exists separately from other things and has its own identity: *The unit has become part of a larger department and no longer exists as a separate entity.* ◊ *These countries can no longer be viewed as a single entity.*

en·tomb /ɪn'tuːm/ verb [VN] [usually passive] **~ sb/sth (in sth)** (*formal*) **1** to bury or completely cover sb/sth so that they cannot get out, be seen, etc. **2** to put a dead body in a TOMB

en·to·mol·ogy /ˌentə'mɒlədʒi; AmE -'mɑː-/ noun [U] the scientific study of insects ► **en·to·mo·logic·al** /ˌentəmə'lɒdʒɪkl; AmE -'lɑːdʒ-/ adj. **en·to·molo·gist** /ˌentə'mɒlədʒɪst; AmE -'mɑː-/ noun

en·tou·rage /'ɒntʊrɑːʒ; AmE 'ɑːn-/ noun [C+sing./pl. v.] a group of people who travel with an important person: *the President and members of his immediate entourage* ◊ *an entourage of adoring fans*

en·trails /'entreɪlz/ noun [pl.] the organs inside the body of a person or an animal, especially their INTESTINES SYN INNARDS

en·trance¹ /'entrəns/ noun—see also ENTRANCE² DOOR/GATE **1** [C] **~ (to/of sth)** a door, gate, passage, etc. used for entering a room, building or place: *the entrance* to the museum/the museum entrance ◊ the front/back/ side entrance of the house ◊ A lighthouse marks the entrance to the harbour. ◊ an entrance hall/lobby ◊ I'll meet you at the **main entrance**.—compare EXIT n. (1)

GOING IN | **2** [C, usually sing.] ~ **(of sb)** the act of entering a room, building or place, especially in a way that attracts the attention of other people: *His sudden entrance took everyone by surprise.* ◊ *A fanfare signalled the entrance of the king.* ◊ *She made her entrance after all the other guests had arrived.* ◊ *The hero makes his entrance* (= walks onto the stage) *in Scene 2.* **3** [U] ~ **(to sth)** the right or opportunity to enter a building or place: *They were refused entrance to the exhibition.* ◊ *(BrE) an entrance fee* (= money paid to go into a museum, etc.) ◊ *The police were unable to gain entrance to the house.*

BECOMING INVOLVED | **4** [C] ~ **(into sth)** the act of becoming involved in sth: *The company made a dramatic entrance into the export market.*

TO CLUB/INSTITUTION | **5** [U] ~ **(to sth)** permission to become a member of a club, society, university, etc: *a university entrance exam* ◊ *entrance requirements* ◊ *Entrance to the golf club is by sponsorship only.*

—compare ENTRY

WHICH WORD?

entrance / entry / admission

Both **entrance** and **entry** can be used to mean the act of going into a room or building: *She looked up at the sound of my entrance/entry.*

Entrance, **entry** and **admission** all mean the right to enter a place: *We were refused entrance/entry/admission.*

Entrance, **entry** and **admission** are also used for the right to join a club, an institution or a group: *an entrance exam* ◊ *entry requirements* ◊ *selecting students for admission.*

The physical way in to a building is an **entrance** (*AmE* also **entryway**): *I'll meet you at the entrance.*

---

en·trance² /ɪnˈtrɑːns; *AmE* -ˈtræns/ *verb* [VN] [usually passive] (*written*) to make sb feel great pleasure and admiration so that they give sb/sth all their attention: *He listened to her, entranced.*—see also ENTRANCE¹ ▶ **en·tran·cing** *adj.*: *entrancing music*

'entrance hall *noun* (*especially BrE*) a large room inside the entrance of a large or public building

en·trant /ˈentrənt/ *noun* ~ **(to sth) 1** a person who has recently joined a profession, university, etc: *new women entrants to the police force* ◊ *university entrants* **2** a person or an animal that enters a race or a competition; a person that enters an exam

en·trap /ɪnˈtræp/ *verb* (**-pp-**) [VN] [often passive] (*formal*) **1** to put or catch sb/sth in a place or situation from which they cannot escape: *She felt entrapped by her family's expectations.* **2** ~ **sb (into doing sth)** to trick sb, and encourage them to do sth, especially to commit a crime, so that they can be arrested for it

en·trap·ment /ɪnˈtræpmənt/ *noun* [U] (*law*) the illegal act of tricking sb into committing a crime so that they can be arrested for it

en·treat /ɪnˈtriːt/ *verb* (*formal*) to ask sb to do sth in a serious and often emotional way [SYN] BEG, IMPLORE: [VN] *Please help me, I entreat you.* ◊ [VN to inf] *She entreated him not to go.* [also V speech, VN speech]

en·treaty /ɪnˈtriːti/ *noun* (*pl.* **-ies**) [C, U] (*formal*) a serious and often emotional request

en·trée /ˈɒntreɪ; *AmE* ˈɑːn-/ *noun* (from *French*) **1** [C] (in a restaurant or at a formal meal) the main dish of the meal or a dish served before the main course **2** [U, C] ~ **(into/to sth)** (*formal*) the right or ability to enter a social group or place: *Her wealth and reputation gave her an entrée into upper-class circles.*

en·trench (also **in·trench**) /ɪnˈtrentʃ/ *verb* [VN] [usually passive] (sometimes *disapproving*) to establish sth very firmly so that it is very difficult to change: *Sexism is*

deeply *entrenched in our society.* ◊ *entrenched attitudes/ interests/opposition*

en·trench·ment /ɪnˈtrentʃmənt/ *noun* **1** [U] ~ **(of sth)** the fact of sth being firmly established **2** [C, usually pl.] a system of TRENCHES (= long narrow holes dug in the ground by soldiers to provide defence)

entre·pre·neur /ˌɒntrəprəˈnɜː(r); *AmE* ˌɑːn-/ *noun* a person who makes money by starting or running businesses, especially when this involves taking financial risks ▶ **en·tre·pre·neur·ial** /-ˈnɜːriəl/ *adj.*: *entrepreneurial skills/flair* **entre·pre·neur·ship** *noun* [U]

en·trust /ɪnˈtrʌst/ *verb* [VN] ~ **A to (B)| ~ B with A** to make sb responsible for doing sth or taking care of sb: *He entrusted the task to his nephew.* ◊ *He entrusted his nephew with the task.*

entry /ˈentri/ *noun* (*pl.* **-ies**)

GOING IN | **1** [C, U] ~ **(into sth)** an act of going into or getting into a place: *She made her entry to the sound of thunderous applause.* ◊ *The children were surprised by the sudden entry of their teacher.* ◊ *How did the thieves gain entry into the building?* **2** [U] ~ **(to/into sth)** the right or opportunity to enter a place: *No Entry* (= for example, on a sign) ◊ *Entry to the museum is free.* ◊ *to be granted/ refused entry into the country* ⇨ note at ENTRANCE¹

JOINING GROUP | **3** [U] ~ **(into sth)** the right or opportunity to take part in sth or become a member of a group: *countries seeking entry into the European Union* ◊ *the entry of women into the workforce*

IN COMPETITION | **4** [C] something that you do, write or make to take part in a competition, for example answering a set of questions: *There have been some impressive entries in the wildlife photography section* (= impressive photographs). ◊ *The closing date for entries is 31 March.* ◊ *The sender of the first correct entry drawn will win a weekend for two in Venice.* **5** [U] the act of taking part in a competition, race, etc: *Entry is open to anyone over the age of 18.* ◊ *an entry form* **6** [sing.] the total number of people who are taking part in a competition, race, etc: *There's a record entry for this year's marathon.*

WRITTEN INFORMATION | **7** [C] ~ **(in sth)** an item, for example a piece of information, that is written or printed in a dictionary, an account book, a DIARY, etc: *an encyclopedia entry* ◊ *There is no entry in his diary for that day.* **8** [U] the act of recording information in a computer, book, etc: *More keyboarding staff are required for data entry.*

DOOR/GATE | **9** (also **entry·way** /ˈentriweɪ/) (both *AmE*) [C] a door, gate or passage where you enter a building; an entrance hall: *You can leave your umbrella in the entry.* ⇨ note at ENTRANCE¹

Entry·phone™ /ˈentrifəʊn; *AmE* -foʊn/ *noun* (*BrE*) a type of telephone on the wall next to the entrance to a building enabling a person inside the building to speak to a person outside before opening the door

en·twine /ɪnˈtwaɪn/ *verb* [VN] [usually passive] **1** ~ **sth (with/in/around sth)** to twist or wind sth around sth else: *They strolled through the park, with arms entwined.* **2** (**be entwined (with sth)**) to be very closely involved or connected with sth: *Her destiny was entwined with his.*

'E-number *noun* (*BrE*) a number beginning with the letter E that is printed on packets and containers to show what artificial flavours and colours have been added to food and drink; an artificial flavour, colour, etc. added to food and drink: *This sauce is full of E-numbers.*

enu·mer·ate /ɪˈnjuːməreɪt; *AmE* ɪˈnuː-/ *verb* [VN] (*formal*) to name things on a list one by one: *She enumerated the main points.*

enun·ci·ate /ɪˈnʌnsieɪt/ *verb* **1** to say or pronounce words clearly: [VN] *She enunciated each word slowly and carefully.* [also V, V speech] **2** [VN] (*formal*) to express an idea clearly and exactly: *He enunciated his vision of the future.* ▶ **enun·ci·ation** /ɪˌnʌnsiˈeɪʃn/ *noun* [U]

en·velop /ɪnˈveləp/ *verb* [VN] ~ **sb/sth (in sth)** (*formal*) to wrap sb/sth up or cover them or it completely: *She was enveloped in a huge white towel.* ◊ *Clouds enveloped the mountain tops.* ◊ *Darkness fell and enveloped the town.*

en·vel·ope /ˈenvələʊp; ˈɒn-; *AmE* ˈenvəloʊp; ˈɑːn-/ *noun* **1** a flat paper container used for sending letters in: *writ-*

---

s	t	v	z	ʃ	ʒ	tʃ	dʒ	θ	ð	ŋ
see	tea	van	zoo	shoe	vision	chain	jam	thin	this	sing

ing paper and envelopes ◊ *an airmail/padded/prepaid envelope*—see also SAE, SASE **2** a flat container made of plastic for keeping papers in

en·vi·able /'enviəbl/ *adj.* something that is enviable is the sort of thing that is good and that other people want to have too: *He is in the enviable position of having two job offers to choose from.* OPP UNENVIABLE ▶ **en·vi·ably** /-bli/ *adv.*: *an enviably mild climate*

en·vi·ous /'enviəs/ *adj.* ~ (**of sb/sth**) wanting to be in the same situation as sb else; wanting sth that sb else has: *Everyone is so envious of her.* ◊ *They were envious of his success.* ◊ *He saw the envious look in the other boy's eyes.* ▶ **en·vi·ous·ly** *adv.*: *They look enviously at the success of their European counterparts.*—see also ENVY

en·vir·on·ment /ɪn'vaɪrənmənt/ *noun* **1** [C, U] the conditions that affect the behaviour and development of sb/sth; the physical conditions that sb/sth exists in: *a pleasant working/learning environment* ◊ *An unhappy home environment can affect a child's behaviour.* ◊ *They have created an environment in which productivity should flourish.* ◊ *These rocks are common to certain climate environments.* ◊ *the political/financial environment* ◊ *tests carried out in a controlled environment* **2** (**the environment**) [sing.] the natural world in which people, animals and plants live: *the Department of the Environment* ◊ *measures to protect the environment* ◊ *pollution of the environment* ◊ *damage to the environment* **3** [C] (*computing*) the complete structure within which a user, computer or program operates: *a desktop development environment*

en·vir·on·men·tal /ɪn,vaɪrən'mentl/ *adj.* [only before noun] **1** connected with the natural conditions in which people, animals and plants live; connected with the environment: *the environmental impact of pollution* ◊ *environmental issues/problems* ◊ *an environmental group/movement* (= that aims to improve or protect the natural environment) ◊ *environmental damage* **2** connected with the conditions that affect the behaviour and development of sb/sth: *environmental influences* ◊ *an environmental health officer* ▶ **en·vir·on·men·tal·ly** /-təli/ *adv.*: *an environmentally sensitive area* (= one that is easily damaged or that contains rare animals, plants, etc.) ◊ *environmentally damaging*

en·vir·on·men·tal·ist /ɪn,vaɪrən'mentəlɪst/ *noun* a person who is concerned about the natural environment and wants to improve and protect it ▶ **en·vir·on·ment·al·ism** *noun* [U]

en,vironmentally 'friendly (also **en,vironment-'friendly**) *adj.* (of products) not harming the environment: *environmentally friendly packaging*

en·vir·ons /ɪn'vaɪrənz/ *noun* [pl.] (*formal*) the area surrounding a place: *Berlin and its environs* ◊ *people living in the immediate environs of a nuclear plant*

en·vis·age /ɪn'vɪzɪdʒ/ (*especially BrE*) (*AmE* usually **en·vis·ion**) *verb* to imagine what will happen in the future: [VN] *What level of profit do you envisage?* ◊ [V-ing] *I don't envisage working with him again.* ◊ [VN-ing] *I can't envisage her coping with this job.* ◊ [VNthat] *It is envisaged that the talks will take place in the spring.* [also Vthat, Vwh-]

en·vis·ion /ɪn'vɪʒn/ *verb* [VN] **1** to imagine what a situation will be like in the future, especially a situation you intend to work towards: *They envision an equal society, free of poverty and disease.* **2** (*especially AmE*) = ENVISAGE: *They didn't envision any problems with the new building.*

envoy /'envɔɪ/ *noun* a person who represents a government or an organization and is sent as a messenger to talk to other governments and organizations

envy /'envi/ *noun, verb*
■ *noun* [U] ~ (**of sb**)| ~ (**at/of sth**) the feeling of wanting to be in the same situation as sb else; the feeling of wanting sth that sb else has: *He couldn't conceal his envy of me.* ◊ *She felt a pang of envy at the thought of his success.* ◊ *They looked with envy at her latest purchase.* ◊ *Her colleagues were green with envy* (= they had very strong feelings of envy). IDM **be the envy of sb/sth** to be a person or thing that other people admire and that causes feelings of envy:

British television is the envy of the world.—see also ENVIABLE, ENVIOUS
■ *verb* (**en·vies, envy·ing, en·vied, en·vied**) to wish you had the same qualities, possessions, opportunities, etc. as sb else: [VN] *He envied her—she seemed to have everything she could possibly want.* ◊ *She has always envied my success.* ◊ [VNN] *I don't envy Ed that job* (= I am pleased I do not have it). ◊ [VN-ing] *I envy you having such a close family.*

en·zyme /'enzaɪm/ *noun* (*biology*) a substance, usually produced by plants and animals, which helps a chemical change happen or happen more quickly, without being changed itself

eon = AEON

ep·aul·ette (*especially BrE*) (*AmE* usually **ep·aulet**) /'epəlet/ *noun* a decoration on the shoulder of a coat, jacket, etc., especially when part of a military uniform

ephem·era /ɪ'femərə/ *noun* [pl.] things that are important or used for only a short period of time: *a collection of postcards, tickets and other ephemera*

ephem·eral /ɪ'femərəl/ *adj.* (*formal*) lasting or used for only a short period of time: *ephemeral pleasures* ◊ *leaflets, handouts and other ephemeral material*

epic /'epɪk/ *noun, adj.*
■ *noun* **1** [C, U] a long poem about the actions of great men and women or about a nation's history; this style of poetry: *one of the great Hindu epics* ◊ *the creative genius of Greek epic*—compare LYRIC **2** [C] a long film/movie or book that contains a lot of action, usually about a historical subject **3** [C] (sometimes *humorous*) a long and difficult job or activity that you think people should admire: *Their four-hour match on Centre Court was an epic.*
■ *adj.* [usually before noun] **1** having the features of an epic: *an epic poem*—compare LYRIC **2** taking place over a long period of time and involving a lot of difficulties: *an epic journey/struggle* **3** very great and impressive: *a tragedy of epic proportions*

epi·centre (*BrE*) (*AmE* **epi·cen·ter**) /'epɪsentə(r)/ *noun* **1** the point on the earth's surface where the effects of an earthquake are felt most strongly **2** (*formal*) the central point of sth

epi·cure /'epɪkjʊə(r); *AmE* -kjʊr/ *noun* (*formal*) a person who enjoys food and drink of high quality and knows a lot about it

epi·dem·ic /,epɪ'demɪk/ *noun* **1** a large number of cases of a particular disease happening at the same time in a particular community: *the outbreak of a flu epidemic* ◊ *an epidemic of measles* **2** a sudden rapid increase in how often sth bad happens: *an epidemic of crime in the inner cities* ▶ **epi·dem·ic** *adj.*: *Car theft is now reaching epidemic proportions.*—compare PANDEMIC

epi·demi·ology /,epɪ,di:mi'ɒlədʒi; *AmE* -'ɑ:l-/ *noun* [U] the scientific study of the spread and control of diseases ▶ **epi·demi·ologic·al** /,epɪ,di:miə'lɒdʒɪkl; *AmE* -'lɑ:dʒ-/ *adj.* **epi·demi·olo·gist** /,epɪ,di:mi'ɒlədʒɪst; *AmE* -'ɑ:l-/ *noun*

epi·der·mis /,epɪ'dɜːmɪs; *AmE* -'dɜːrm-/ *noun* [sing., U] (*anatomy*) the outer layer of the skin

epi·dural /,epɪ'djʊərəl; *AmE* usually -'dʊr-/ *noun* (*medical*) an ANAESTHETIC that is put into the lower part of the back so that no pain is felt below the waist: *Some mothers choose to have an epidural when giving birth.*

epi·glot·tis /,epɪ'glɒtɪs; *AmE* -'glɑːtɪs/ *noun* (*anatomy*) a thin piece of tissue at the back of the tongue that prevents food or drink from entering the lungs

epi·gram /'epɪɡræm/ *noun* a short poem or phrase that expresses an idea in a clever or amusing way ▶ **epi·gram·mat·ic** /,epɪɡrə'mætɪk/ *adj.*

epi·graph /'epɪɡrɑːf; *AmE* -ɡræf/ *noun* a line of writing, short phrase, etc. on a building or statue, or as an introduction to part of a book

epi·lepsy /'epɪlepsi/ *noun* [U] a disorder of the nervous system that causes a person to become unconscious suddenly, often with violent movements of the body ▶ **epi·lep·tic** /,epɪ'leptɪk/ *adj.*: *an epileptic fit* **epi·lep·tic** *noun*: *Is she an epileptic?*

epi·logue /'epɪlɒɡ; *AmE* -lɔːɡ; -lɑːɡ/ *noun* a speech, etc. at

æ	ɑː	e	ɜː	ə	ɪ	iː	i	ɒ	ɔː	ʌ	ʊ	u	uː
cat	father	ten	bird	about	sit	see	many	got	saw	cup	put	actual	too

(BrE)

E

the end of a play, book, or film/movie that comments on or acts as a CONCLUSION to what has happened—compare PROLOGUE

Epiph·any /ɪˈpɪfəni/ *noun* a Christian festival, held on the 6 January, in memory of the time when the MAGI came to see the baby Jesus at Bethlehem

epis·cop·al /ɪˈpɪskəpl/ *adj.* **1** connected with a BISHOP or BISHOPS: *episcopal power* **2** (usually **Episcopal**) (also **Epis·co·pa·lian**) (of a Christian Church) that is governed by BISHOPS: *the Episcopal Church* (= the Anglican Church in Scotland and the US)

Epis·co·pa·lian /ɪˌpɪskəˈpeɪliən/ *noun* a member of the Episcopal Church

epi·sode /ˈepɪsəʊd; *AmE* -soʊd/ *noun* **1** an event, a situation, or a period of time in sb's life, a novel, etc. that is important or interesting in some way: *I'd like to try and forget the whole episode.* ◇ *One of the funniest episodes in the book occurs in Chapter 6.* **2** one part of a story that is broadcast on television or radio in several parts

epi·sod·ic /ˌepɪˈsɒdɪk; *AmE* -ˈsɑːd-/ *adj.* (*formal*) **1** happening occasionally and not at regular intervals: *her episodic acting career* **2** (of a story, etc.) containing or consisting of many separate and different events: *My memories of childhood are hazy and episodic.*

epis·tle /ɪˈpɪsl/ *noun* **1** (**Epistle**) any of the letters in the New Testament of the Bible, written by the first people who followed Christ: *the Epistles of St Paul* **2** (*formal* or *humorous*) a long, serious letter on an important subject

epis·tol·ary /ɪˈpɪstələri; *AmE* -leri/ *adj.* (*formal*) written or expressed in the form of letters: *an epistolary novel*

epi·taph /ˈepɪtɑːf; *AmE* -tæf/ *noun* **1** words that are written or said about a dead person, especially words on a GRAVESTONE **2 ~ (to sb/sth)** something which is left to remind people of a particular person, a period of time or an event: *These slums are an epitaph to the housing policy of the 1960s.*

epi·thet /ˈepɪθet/ *noun* **1** an adjective or phrase that is used to describe sb/sth's character or most important quality, especially in order to give praise or criticism: *The film is long and dramatic but does not quite earn the epithet 'epic'.* **2** (*especially AmE*) an offensive word or phrase that is used about a person or group of people: *Racial epithets were scrawled on the walls.*

epit·ome /ɪˈpɪtəmi/ *noun* [sing.] **the ~ of sth** a perfect example of sth: *He is the epitome of a modern young man.* ◇ *clothes that are the epitome of good taste*

epit·om·ize (*BrE* also **-ise**) /ɪˈpɪtəmaɪz/ *verb* [VN] to be a perfect example of sth: *The fighting qualities of the team are epitomized by the captain.* ◇ *These movies seem to epitomize the 1950s.*

epoch /ˈiːpɒk; *AmE* ˈepək/ *noun* (*formal* or *literary*) **1** a period of time in history, especially one during which important events or changes happen: *The death of the emperor marked the end of an epoch in the country's history.* **2** (*technical*) a long period of time in the world's history or in the earth's development: *geological epochs*

epoch-making *adj.* (*formal*) having a very important effect on people's lives and on history: *the epoch-making events that ended the Cold War*

epony·mous /ɪˈpɒnɪməs; *AmE* ɪˈpɑːn-/ *adj.* [only before noun] the **eponymous** character of a book, play, film/ movie, etc. is the one mentioned in the title: *Don Quixote, eponymous hero of the great novel by Cervantes*

epoxy /ɪˈpɒksi; *AmE* ɪˈpɑːksi/ *noun* [U, C] (*pl.* **-ies**) (also e₁poxy ˈresin) a type of strong glue

Epsom salts /ˌepsəm ˈsɔːlts/ *noun* [pl.] a white powder that can be mixed with water and used as a medicine or LAXATIVE

equ·able /ˈekwəbl/ *adj.* (*formal*) **1** calm and not easily upset or annoyed: *an equable temperament* **2** (of weather) keeping a steady temperature with no sudden changes: *an equable climate* ▶ **equ·ably** /ˈekwəbli/ *adv.*

equal /ˈiːkwəl/ *adj., noun, verb*
■ *adj.* **1 ~ (to sb/sth)** the same in size, quantity, value, etc. as sth else: *There is an equal number of boys and girls in the class.* ◇ *One unit of alcohol is equal to half a pint of beer.* ◇ *two pieces of wood equal in length/of equal length* **HELP** You can use **exactly**, **precisely**, **approximately**, etc. with **equal** in this meaning. **2** having the same rights or being treated the same as other people, without differences such as race, religion or sex being considered: *equal rights/pay* ◇ *The company has an equal opportunities policy* (= gives the same chances of employment to everyone). ◇ *the desire for a more equal society* (= in which everyone has (he same rights and chances) **HELP** You can use **more** with **equal** in this meaning. **3 ~ to sth** (*formal*) having the necessary strength, courage and ability to deal with sth successfully: *I hope that he proves equal to the challenge.*—see also EQUALLY **IDM on ˌequal ˈterms (with sb)** having the same advantages and disadvantages as sb else: *Can our industry compete on equal terms with its overseas rivals?*—more at THING

■ *noun* a person or thing of the same quality or with the same status, rights, etc. as another: *She treats the people who work for her as her equals.* ◇ *Our cars are the equal of those produced anywhere in the world.* **IDM be without ˈequal | have no ˈequal** (*formal*) to be better than anything else or anyone else of the same type: *He is a player without equal.*—more at FIRST *n.*

■ *verb* (**-ll-**, *AmE* **-l-**) **1** *linking verb* [V-N] to be the same in size, quantity, value, etc. as sth else: *2x plus y equals 7* (2x+y=7) ◇ *A metre equals 39.38 inches.* **2** [VN] to be as good as sth else or do sth to the same standard as sb else: *This achievement is unlikely ever to be equalled.* ◇ *Her hatred of religion is equalled only by her loathing for politicians.* ◇ *With his last jump he equalled the world record.* **3** [VN] to lead to or result in sth: *Cooperation equals success.*

equal·ity /iˈkwɒləti; *AmE* iˈkwɑː-/ *noun* [U] the fact of being equal in rights, status, advantages, etc: *racial/ social/sexual equality* ◇ *equality of opportunity* ◇ *the principle of equality before the law* (= the law treats everyone the same) ◇ *Don't you believe in equality between men and women?* **OPP** INEQUALITY

equal·ize (*BrE* also **-ise**) /ˈiːkwəlaɪz/ *verb* **1** [VN] to make things equal in size, quantity, value, etc. in the whole of a place or group: *a policy to equalize the distribution of resources throughout the country* **2** [V] (*BrE*) (especially in football) to score a goal that makes the score of both teams equal: *Owen equalized early in the second half.* ▶ **equal·iza·tion, -isa·tion** /ˌiːkwəlaɪˈzeɪʃn; *AmE* -ləˈzeɪ-/ *noun* [U]

equal·izer (*BrE* also **-iser**) /ˈiːkwəlaɪzər/ *noun* [usually sing.] (*BrE*) (especially in football) a goal that makes the score of both teams equal: *Owen scored the equalizer for Liverpool.*

equal·ly /ˈiːkwəli/ *adv.* **1** to the same degree; in the same or in a similar way: *Diet and exercise are equally important.* ◇ *This job could be done equally well by a computer.* ◇ *We try to treat every member of staff equally.* **2** in equal parts, amounts, etc: *The money was divided equally among her four children.* ◇ *They share the housework equally.* **3** used to introduce another phrase or idea that adds to and is as important as what you have just said: *I'm trying to do what is best, but equally I've got to consider the cost.*

equa·nim·ity /ˌekwəˈnɪməti/ *noun* [U] (*formal*) a calm state of mind which means that you do not become angry or upset, especially in difficult situations: *She accepted the prospect of her operation with equanimity.*

equate /iˈkweɪt/ *verb* [VN] **~ sth (with sth)** to think that sth is the same as sth else or is as important: *Some parents equate education with exam success.* ◇ *I don't see how you can equate the two things.* **PHRV eˈquate to sth** to be equal to sth else: *A $5000 raise equates to 25%.*

equa·tion /iˈkweɪʒn/ *noun* **1** [C] (*mathematics*) a statement showing that two amounts or values are equal, for example 2x+y=54 **2** [U, sing.] the act of making sth equal or considering sth as equal (= equating them): *The equation of wealth with happiness can be dangerous.* **3** [C, usually sing.] a problem or situation in which several things must be considered and dealt with: *When children enter the equation, further tensions may arise within a marriage.*

equa·tor /ɪˈkweɪtə(r)/ (usually **the equator**) *noun* [sing.] an imaginary line around the earth at an equal distance from the North and South Poles—picture on page A7

equa·tor·ial /ˌekwəˈtɔːriəl/ *adj.* near the equator or typical of a country that is near the equator: *equatorial rainforests* ◊ *an equatorial climate*

equerry /ɪˈkweri; ˈekwəri/ *noun* (*pl.* **-ies**) a male officer who acts as an assistant to a member of a royal family

eques·trian /ɪˈkwestriən/ *adj.* [usually before noun] connected with riding horses, especially as a sport: *equestrian events at the Olympic Games*

equi- /ˈiːkwɪ-; ˈek-/ *combining form* (in nouns, adjectives and adverbs) equal; equally: *equidistant* ◊ *equilibrium*

equi·dis·tant /ˌiːkwɪˈdɪstənt; ˌek-/ *adj.* [not before noun] **~** (**from sth**) (*formal*) equally far from two or more places: *All points on a circle are equidistant from the centre.*

equi·lat·eral /ˌiːkwɪˈlætərəl; ˌek-/ *adj.* (*geometry*) (of a triangle) having all sides the same length—picture at TRIANGLE

equi·lib·rium /ˌiːkwɪˈlɪbriəm; ˌek-/ *noun* [U, sing.] **1** a state of balance, especially between opposing forces or influences: *The point at which the solid and the liquid are in equilibrium is called the freezing point.* ◊ *Any disturbance to the body's state of equilibrium can produce stress.* ◊ *We have achieved an equilibrium in the economy.* **2** a calm state of mind and a balance of emotions: *He sat down to try and recover his equilibrium.*

equine /ˈekwaɪn/ *adj.* (*formal*) connected with horses; like a horse

equi·nox /ˈiːkwɪnɒks; ˈek-; *AmE* -naːks/ *noun* one of the two times in the year (around 20 March and 22 September) when the sun is above the EQUATOR and day and night are of equal length: *the spring/autumn equinox*

equip /ɪˈkwɪp/ *verb* (**-pp-**) **~** **yourself/sb/sth** (**with sth**) (**for sth**) **1** [VN] to provide yourself/sb/sth with the things that are needed for a particular purpose or activity: *to be fully/specially/poorly equipped* ◊ *She got a bank loan to rent and equip a small workshop.* ◊ *He equipped himself with a street plan.* ◊ *The centre is well equipped for canoeing and mountaineering.* **2** to prepare sb for an activity or task, especially by teaching them what they need to know: [VN] *The course is designed to equip students for a career in nursing.* [also VN to inf]

equip·ment /ɪˈkwɪpmənt/ *noun* [U] **1** the things that are needed for a particular purpose or activity: *a useful piece of equipment for the kitchen* ◊ *medical/office equipment* ◊ *new equipment for the sports club* **2** the process of providing a place or person with necessary things: *The equipment of the photographic studio was expensive.*

equit·able /ˈekwɪtəbl/ *adj.* (*formal*) fair and reasonable; treating everyone in an equal way: *an equitable distribution of resources* OPP INEQUITABLE ▶ **equit·ably** /-bli/ *adv.*

equity /ˈekwəti/ *noun* **1** [U] (*finance*) the value of a company's shares; the value of a property after all charges and debts have been paid—see also NEGATIVE EQUITY **2** (**equities**) [pl.] (*finance*) shares in a company which do not pay a fixed amount of interest **3** [U] (*formal*) a situation in which everyone is treated equally SYN FAIRNESS: *a society where justice and equity prevail* **4** [U] (*law*) (especially *BrE*) a system of natural justice allowing a fair judgement in a situation where the existing laws are not satisfactory

equiva·lent /ɪˈkwɪvələnt/ *adj., noun*
■ *adj.* **~** (**to sth**) equal in value, amount, meaning, importance, etc: *Eight kilometres is roughly equivalent to five miles.* ◊ *250 grams or an equivalent amount in ounces* ▶ **equiva·lence** /-ləns/ *noun* [U] (*formal*): *There is no straightforward equivalence between economic progress and social well-being.*
■ *noun* **~** (**of/to sth**) a thing, amount, word, etc. that is equivalent to sth else: *Send £20 or the equivalent in your own currency.* ◊ *Creutzfeldt-Jakob disease, the human equivalent of BSE* ◊ *The 'Gymnasium' is the closest equivalent to the grammar school in England.* ◊ *Breathing such*

polluted air is the equivalent of (= has the same effect as) smoking ten cigarettes a day.

equivo·cal /ɪˈkwɪvəkl/ *adj.* (*formal*) **1** (of words or statements) not having one clear or definite meaning or intention; able to be understood in more than one way SYN AMBIGUOUS: *She gave an equivocal answer, typical of a politician.* **2** (of actions or behaviour) difficult to understand or explain clearly or easily: *The experiments produced equivocal results.*

equivo·cate /ɪˈkwɪvəkeɪt/ *verb* [V speech, V] (*formal*) to talk about sth in a way that is deliberately not clear in order to avoid or hide the truth

equivo·ca·tion /ɪˌkwɪvəˈkeɪʃn/ *noun* [C, U] (*formal*) a way of behaving or speaking that is not clear or definite and is intended to avoid or hide the truth: *These actions must be condemned without equivocation.*

ER /ˌiː ˈɑː(r)/ *abbr.* EMERGENCY ROOM

er /ɜː(r)/ *exclamation* (*BrE*) the sound that people make when they are deciding what to say next: *'Will you do it?' 'Er, yes, I suppose so.'*

-er *suffix* **1** (in nouns) a person or thing that: *lover* ◊ *computer*—compare -EE, -OR **2** (in nouns) a person or thing that has the thing or quality mentioned: *three-wheeler* ◊ *foreigner* **3** (in nouns) a person concerned with: *astronomer* ◊ *philosopher* **4** (in nouns) a person belonging to: *New Yorker* **5** (makes comparative adjectives and adverbs): *wider* ◊ *bigger* ◊ *happier* ◊ *sooner*—compare -EST

era /ˈɪərə; *AmE* ˈɪrə; ˈerə/ *noun* a period of time, usually in history, that is different from other periods because of particular characteristics or events: *the Victorian/modern/post-war era* ◊ *When she left the firm, it was the end of an era* (= things were different after that).

eradi·cate /ɪˈrædɪkeɪt/ *verb* [VN] **~** **sth** (**from sth**) to destroy or get rid of sth completely, especially sth bad: *Polio has been virtually eradicated in Brazil.* ◊ *We are determined to eradicate racism from our sport.* ▶ **eradi·ca·tion** /ɪˌrædɪˈkeɪʃn/ *noun* [U]

erase /ɪˈreɪz; *AmE* ɪˈreɪs/ *verb* [VN] **1 ~** **sth** (**from sth**) to remove sth completely: *She tried to erase the memory of that evening.* ◊ *All doubts were suddenly erased from his mind.* ◊ *You cannot erase injustice from the world.* **2** to make a mark or sth you have written disappear, for example by rubbing it, especially in order to correct it: *He had erased the wrong word.* ◊ *All the phone numbers had been erased.* **3** to remove a recording from a tape or information from a computer's memory: *Parts of the recording have been erased.*

eraser /ɪˈreɪzə(r); *AmE* ɪˈreɪsər/ *noun* (*AmE* or *formal*) = RUBBER

eras·ure /ɪˈreɪʒə(r)/ *noun* [U] (*formal*) the act of removing or destroying sth: *the accidental erasure of important computer disks* (= the removal of information from them)

ere /eə(r); *AmE* er/ *conj., prep.* (*old use* or *literary*) before: *Ere long* (= soon) *they returned.*

erect /ɪˈrekt/ *adj., verb*
■ *adj.* **1** (*formal*) in an upright position SYN STRAIGHT: *Stand with your arms by your side and your head erect.* **2** (of the PENIS or NIPPLES) larger than usual, stiff and upright because of sexual excitement
■ *verb* [VN] (*formal*) **1** to build sth: *The church was erected in 1582.* ◊ *to erect a wall/monument/statue* **2** to put sth in position and make it stand upright SYN PUT STH UP: *Police had to erect barriers to keep crowds back.* ◊ *to erect a tent/sign* **3** to create or establish sth: *to erect trade barriers*

erec·tion /ɪˈrekʃn/ *noun* **1** [C] if a man has an **erection**, his PENIS is hard and upright because he is sexually excited: *to get/have an erection* **2** [U] (*formal*) the act of building sth or putting it in an upright position: *the erection of temporary scaffolding around the building site* **3** [C] (*formal*) a structure or building, especially a large one

ergo /ˈɜːɡəʊ; *AmE* ˈɜːrɡoʊ/ *adv.* (from Latin, *formal* or *humorous*) therefore

er·go·nom·ic /ˌɜːɡəˈnɒmɪk; *AmE* ˌɜːrɡəˈnɑːm-/ *adj.* designed to improve people's working conditions and to help them work more efficiently: *the ergonomic design*

b	d	f	g	h	k	l	m	n	p	r
bad	did	fall	get	hat	cat	leg	man	now	pen	red

and installation of VDUs ▶ **er·go·nom·ic·al·ly** adv.: The layout is hard to fault ergonomically.

er·go·nom·ics /ˌɜːgəˈnɒmɪks; AmE ˌɜːrgəˈnɑːm-/ noun [U] the study of working conditions, especially the design of equipment and furniture, in order to help people work more efficiently

er·mine /ˈɜːmɪn; AmE ˈɜːrmɪn/ noun [U] the white winter fur of the STOAT, used especially to decorate the formal clothes of judges, kings, etc.

erode /ɪˈrəʊd; AmE ɪˈroʊd/ verb [often passive] ~ **(sth) (away) 1** to gradually destroy the surface of sth through the action of wind, rain, etc.; to be gradually destroyed in this way [SYN] WEAR AWAY: [VN] The cliff face has been steadily eroded by the sea. ◇ [V] The rocks have eroded away over time. **2** (written) to gradually destroy sth or make it weaker over a period of time; to be destroyed or made weaker in this way: [VN] Her confidence has been slowly eroded by repeated failures. ◇ Mortgage payments have been eroded (= decreased in value) by inflation. [also V] ▶ **ero·sion** /ɪˈrəʊʒn; AmE ɪˈroʊʒn/ noun [U]: the erosion of the coastline by the sea ◇ soil erosion ◇ the erosion of her confidence

er·ogen·ous zone /ɪˈrɒdʒənəs zəʊn; AmE ɪˈrɑːdʒ- zoʊn/ noun an area of the body that gives sexual pleasure when it is touched

erot·ic /ɪˈrɒtɪk; AmE ɪˈrɑːtɪk/ adj. showing or involving sexual desire and pleasure; intended to make sb feel sexual desire: erotic art / poetry / pictures ◇ an erotic dream / fantasy ▶ **erot·ic·al·ly** /-kli/ adv.

erot·ica /ɪˈrɒtɪkə; AmE ɪˈrɑːt-/ noun [U] books, pictures, etc. that are intended to make sb feel sexual desire

eroti·cism /ɪˈrɒtɪsɪzəm; AmE ɪˈrɑːt-/ noun [U] the fact of expressing or describing sexual feelings and desire, especially in art, literature, etc: the film's blatant eroticism

err /ɜː(r); AmE er/ verb [V] (old-fashioned, formal) to make a mistake: To err is human ... [IDM] **err on the side of sth** to show too much of a good quality: I thought it was better to err on the side of caution (= to be too careful rather than take a risk).

er·rand /ˈerənd/ noun a job that you do for sb that involves going somewhere to take a message, to buy sth, deliver goods, etc: He often **runs errands** for his grandmother. ◇ Her boss sent her on an errand into town.

er·rant /ˈerənt/ adj. [only before noun] (formal or humorous) **1** doing sth that is wrong; not behaving in an acceptable way: errant fathers who refuse to pay maintenance for their children **2** (of a husband or wife) not sexually faithful

er·rat·ic /ɪˈrætɪk/ adj. (often disapproving) not happening at regular times; not following any plan or regular pattern; that you cannot rely on [SYN] UNPREDICTABLE: The electricity supply here is quite erratic. ◇ She had learnt to live with his sudden changes of mood and erratic behaviour. ◇ Mary is a gifted but erratic player (= she does not always play well). ▶ **er·rat·ic·al·ly** /-kli/ adv.: He was obviously upset and was driving erratically.

er·ratum /eˈrɑːtəm/ noun [usually pl.] (pl. **er·rata** /-tə/) (technical) a mistake in a book (shown in a list at the back or front)

er·ro·ne·ous /ɪˈrəʊniəs; AmE ɪˈroʊ-/ adj. (formal) not correct; based on wrong information: erroneous conclusions / assumptions ▶ **er·ro·ne·ous·ly** adv.

error /ˈerə(r)/ noun [C, U] ~ **in sth / in doing sth** a mistake, especially one that causes problems or affects the result of sth: No payments were made last week because of a computer error. ◇ There are too many errors in your work. ◇ I think you have made an error in calculating the total. ◇ A simple **error of judgement** meant that there was not enough food to go around. ◇ an **error message** (= one that tells you sth is wrong in a computer program) on the screen ◇ a **grave error** (= a very serious mistake) ◇ The delay was due to **human error** (= a mistake made by a person rather than by a machine). ◇ The computer system was switched off **in error** (= by mistake). ◇ There is no room for error in this job. [IDM] **see, realize, etc. the ˌerror of your ˈways** (formal or humorous) to realize or

admit that you have done sth wrong and decide to change your behaviour—more at TRIAL n.

er·satz /ˈeəzæts; AmE ˈersɑːts/ adj. artificial and not as good as the real thing or product: ersatz coffee

Erse /ɜːs; AmE ɜːrs/ noun [U] the Scottish or Irish Gaelic language—compare GAELIC, IRISH

erst·while /ˈɜːstwaɪl; AmE ˈɜːrst-/ adj. [only before noun] (formal) former; that until recently was the type of person or thing described but is not any more: an erstwhile opponent / ally / colleague ◇ His erstwhile friends turned against him.

eru·dite /ˈerudaɪt/ adj. (formal) having or showing great knowledge that is gained from academic study

eru·di·tion /ˌeruˈdɪʃn/ noun [U] (formal) great academic knowledge

erupt /ɪˈrʌpt/ verb **1** when a VOLCANO **erupts** or burning rocks, smoke, etc. **erupt** or **are erupted**, the burning rocks are thrown out from the volcano: [V] The volcano could erupt at any time. ◇ Ash began to erupt from the crater. ◇ [VN] An immense volume of rocks and molten lava was erupted. **2** [V] ~ **(into sth)** to start happening, suddenly and violently [SYN] BREAK OUT: Violence erupted outside the embassy gates. ◇ The unrest erupted into revolution. **3** ~ **(in / into sth)** to suddenly express your feelings very strongly, especially by shouting loudly: [V] My father just erupted into fury. ◇ When Davis scored for the third time the crowd erupted. [also V **speech**] **4** [V] (of spots, etc.) to suddenly appear on your skin: A rash had erupted all over his chest and arms. ▶ **erup·tion** /ɪˈrʌpʃn/ noun [C, U]: a major volcanic eruption ◇ an eruption of violent protest ◇ skin rashes and eruptions

-ery, -ry suffix (in nouns) **1** the group or class of: greenery ◇ gadgetry **2** the state or character of: bravery ◇ rivalry **3** the art or practice of: cookery ◇ archery **4** a place where sth is made, grows, lives, etc: bakery ◇ orangery

es·cal·ate /ˈeskəleɪt/ verb ~ **(sth) (into sth)** to become or make sth greater, worse, more serious, etc: [V] The fighting escalated into a full-scale war. ◇ the escalating costs of health care ◇ [VN] We do not want to escalate the war. ▶ **es·cal·ation** /ˌeskəˈleɪʃn/ noun [C, U]: an escalation in food prices ◇ further escalation of the conflict

es·cal·ator /ˈeskəleɪtə(r)/ noun a moving staircase that carries people between different floors of a large building

es·cal·ope /ˈeskəlɒp; eˈskæləp; AmE ɪˈskɑːləp; ɪˈskæ-/ noun a thin slice of meat with no bones in it, often covered with BREADCRUMBS and fried: escalopes of veal

es·cap·ade /ˌeskəˈpeɪd; ˈeskəpeɪd/ noun an exciting adventure (often one that people think is dangerous or stupid): Isabel's latest romantic escapade

es·cape /ɪˈskeɪp/ verb, noun
■ verb **1** [V] ~ **(from sb/sth)** to get away from a place where you have been kept as a prisoner or not allowed to leave: Two prisoners have escaped. ◇ He escaped from prison this morning. **2** ~ **(from sth)** to get away from an unpleasant or dangerous situation: [V] She managed to escape from the burning car. ◇ (figurative) As a child he would often escape into a dream world of his own. ◇ [VN] They were glad to have **escaped the clutches** of winter for another year. **3** [no passive] to avoid sth unpleasant or dangerous: [VN] She was lucky to escape punishment. ◇ The pilot escaped death by seconds. ◇ There was no escaping the fact that he was overweight. ◇ [V-ing] He narrowly escaped being killed. **4** ~ **(with sth)** to suffer no harm or less harm than you would expect: [V] I was lucky to escape with minor injuries. ◇ [V-ADJ] Both drivers escaped unhurt. **5** [VN] [no passive] to be forgotten or not noticed: Her name escapes me (= I can't remember it). ◇ It might have **escaped your notice**, but I'm very busy at the moment. **6** [V] (of gases, liquids, etc.) to get out of a container, especially through a hole or crack: Put a lid on to prevent heat escaping. ◇ toxic waste escaping into the sea **7** (of a sound) to come out from your mouth without you intending to: [VN] A groan escaped her lips. [also V]
■ noun **1** [C, U] ~ **(from sth)** the act or a method of escaping from a place or an unpleasant or dangerous situation: an escape from a prisoner of war camp ◇ I had a **narrow escape** (= I was lucky to have escaped). ◇ There was no

hope of escape from her disastrous marriage. ◇ *He took an elaborate* **escape route** *from South Africa to Britain.* ◇ *As soon as he turned his back, she would* **make her escape.**—see also FIRE ESCAPE **2** [sing., U] a way of forgetting sth unpleasant or difficult for a short time: *For her travel was an escape from the boredom of her everyday life.* **3** [C] the fact of a liquid, gas, etc. coming out of a pipe or container by accident; the amount that comes out: *an escape of gas* **IDM** **make ˌgood your eˈscape** (*written*) to manage to escape completely—more at BARN

es·caped /ɪˈskeɪpt/ *adj.* [only before noun] having escaped from a place: *an escaped prisoner/lion*

es·capee /ɪˌskeɪˈpiː/ *noun* (*formal*) a person or an animal that has escaped from somewhere, especially sb who has escaped from prison

es·cap·ism /ɪˈskeɪpɪzəm/ *noun* [U] an activity, a form of entertainment, etc. that helps you avoid or forget unpleasant or boring things: *the pure escapism of adventure movies* ◇ *For John, books are a* **form of escapism.**
▶ **es·cap·ist** /-pɪst/ *adj.*

es·carp·ment /ɪˈskɑːpmənt; *AmE* ˈskɑːrp-/ *noun* a steep slope that separates an area of high ground from an area of lower ground

es·chew /ɪsˈtʃuː/ *verb* [VN] (*formal*) to deliberately avoid or keep away from sth

es·cort *noun, verb*
■ *noun* /ˈeskɔːt; *AmE* ˈeskɔːrt/ **1** [C, U] a person or group of people or vehicles that travels with sb/sth in order to protect or guard them: *Armed escorts are provided for visiting heads of state.* ◇ *Prisoners are taken to court* **under police escort. 2** [C] (*formal* or *old-fashioned*) a person, especially a man, who takes sb to a particular social event **3** [C] a person, especially a woman, who is paid to go out socially with sb: *an escort service/agency*
■ *verb* /ɪˈskɔːt; *AmE* ɪˈskɔːrt/ [VN] [usually +adv. / prep.] to go with sb to protect or guard them or to show them the way: *The President arrived, escorted by twelve soldiers.*

es·cudo /eˈskuːdəʊ; *AmE* -doʊ/ *noun* (*pl.* **-os**) the unit of money in Portugal (to be replaced by the euro)

-ese *suffix* **1** (in adjectives and nouns) of a country or city; a person who lives in a country or city; the language spoken there: *Chinese* ◇ *Viennese* **2** (in nouns) (often *disapproving*) the style or language of: *journalese* ◇ *officialese*

Es·kimo /ˈeskɪməʊ; *AmE* -moʊ/ *noun* (*pl.* **Es·kimo** or **Es·kimos**) (sometimes *offensive*) a member of a race of people from northern Canada, and parts of Alaska, Greenland and Siberia. Many of these people prefer to use the name Inuit.—compare INUIT

ESL /ˌiː es ˈel/ *abbr.* English as a second language (refers to the teaching of English as a foreign language to people who are living in a country in which English is either the first or second language)

ESOL /ˈiːsɒl; *AmE* -sɑːl/ *abbr.* English for speakers of other languages

esopha·gus (*AmE*) = OESOPHAGUS

eso·ter·ic /ˌesəˈterɪk; ˌiːsə-/ *adj.* (*formal*) likely to be understood or enjoyed by only a few people with a special knowledge or interest: *a programme of music for everyone, even those with the most esoteric taste*

ESP /ˌiː es ˈpiː/ *abbr.* **1** English for specific/special purposes (the teaching of English for scientific, technical, etc. purposes to people whose first language is not English) **2** extrasensory perception (the ability to know things without using the senses of sight, hearing, etc., for example to know what people are thinking or what will happen in the future)

esp. *abbr.* (in writing) especially

es·pa·drille /ˈespədrɪl/ *noun* a light shoe made of strong fabric with a sole made of rope

es·pe·cial /ɪˈspeʃl/ *adj.* [only before noun] (*BrE, formal*) greater or better than usual; special in some way or for a particular group: *a matter of especial importance* ◇ *The lecture will be of especial interest to history students.*—compare SPECIAL *adj.* (5)

es·pe·cial·ly /ɪˈspeʃəli/ *adv.* (*abbr.* **esp.**) **1** more with one person, thing, etc. than with others, or more in

particular circumstances than in others **SYN** PARTICU-LARLY: *The car is quite small, especially if you have children.* ◇ *Teenagers are very fashion conscious, especially girls.* ◇ *I love Rome, especially in the spring.* **2** for a particular purpose, person, etc: *I made it especially for you.* **3** very much; to a particular degree: *I wasn't feeling especially happy that day.* ◇ *'Do you like his novels?' 'Not especially.'*

> **WHICH WORD?**
> **especially / specially**
>
> **Especially** usually means 'particularly': *She loves all sports, especially swimming.* It is not placed first in a sentence: *I especially like sweet things.* ◇ ~~*Especially I like sweet things.*~~
> **Specially** usually means 'for a particular purpose' and is often followed by a past participle, such as *designed, developed* or *made*: *a course specially designed to meet your needs* ◇ *She has her clothes specially made in Paris.*
> In *BrE*, **especially** and **specially** are often used in the same way and it can be hard to hear the difference when people speak. **Specially** is less formal: *I bought this especially/specially for you.* ◇ *It is especially/specially important to remember this.*
> The adjective for both **especially** and **specially** is usually **special**.

Es·per·anto /ˌespəˈræntəʊ; *AmE* -toʊ/ *noun* [U] an artificial language invented in 1887 as a means of international communication, based on the main European languages but with easy grammar and pronunciation

es·pi·on·age /ˈespiənɑːʒ/ *noun* [U] the activity of secretly getting important political or military information about another country or of finding out about another company's secrets by using SPIES: *Some of the commercial activities were a cover for espionage.* ◇ *She may call it research; I call it industrial espionage.*—see also COUNTER-ESPIONAGE

es·plan·ade /ˌespləˈneɪd/ *noun* a level area of open ground in a town for people to walk along, often by the sea or a river

es·pouse /ɪˈspaʊz/ *verb* [VN] (*formal*) to give your support to a belief, policy etc: *They espoused the notion of equal opportunity for all in education.* ▶ **es·pousal** /ɪˈspaʊzl/ *noun* [U, sing.] **~ of sth**: *his recent espousal of populism*

es·presso /eˈspresəʊ; *AmE* -soʊ/ *noun* (*pl.* **-os**) **1** [U] strong black coffee made by forcing steam or boiling water through ground coffee **2** [C] a cup of espresso: *Two espressos, please.*

es·prit de corps /eˌspriː də ˈkɔː(r)/ *noun* [U] (from *French*) feelings of pride, care and support for each other, etc. that are shared by the members of a group

espy /eˈspaɪ/ *verb* (**espies, espy·ing, espied, espied**) [VN] (*literary*) to see sb/sth suddenly

Esq. *abbr.* **1** (becoming *old-fashioned, especially BrE*) Esquire (a polite title written after a man's name, especially on an official letter addressed to him. If Esq. is used, Mr is not then used): *Edward Smith, Esq.* **2** (*AmE*) used as a title after the name of a male or female lawyer

-esque *suffix* (in adjectives) in the style of: *statuesque* ◇ *Kafkaesque*

-ess *suffix* (in nouns) female: *lioness* ◇ *actress*

essay *noun, verb*
■ *noun* /ˈeseɪ/ **1 ~** (**on sth**) a short piece of writing by a student as part of a course of study: *an essay on the causes of the First World War* **2 ~** (**on sth**) a short piece of writing on a particular subject, written in order to be published: *The book contains a number of interesting essays on women in society.* **3 ~** (**in sth**) (*formal*) an attempt to do sth: *His first essay in politics was a complete disaster.*
■ *verb* /eˈseɪ/ [VN] (*literary*) to try to do sth

es·say·ist /ˈeseɪɪst/ *noun* a person who writes essays to be published

æ	ɑː	e	ɜː	ə	ɪ	iː	i	ɒ	ɔː	ʌ	ʊ	u	uː
cat	father	ten	bird	about	sit	see	many	got (BrE)	saw	cup	put	actual	too

es·sence /ˈesns/ *noun* **1** [U] ~ (of sth) the most important quality or feature of sth, that makes it what it is: *His paintings capture the essence of France.* ◇ *In essence* (= when you consider the most important points), *your situation isn't so different from mine.* **2** [U, C] a liquid taken from a plant, etc. that contains its smell and taste in a very strong form: *essence of rosewood* ◇ (*BrE*) *coffee/vanilla/almond essence*—see also EXTRACT **IDM** **of the ˈessence** necessary and very important: *In this situation time is of the essence* (= we must do things as quickly as possible).

es·sen·tial /ɪˈsenʃl/ *adj., noun*
■ *adj.* **1** ~ (to/for sth) | ~ (to do sth) | ~ (that …) completely necessary; extremely important in a particular situation or for a particular activity **SYN** VITAL: *an essential part/ingredient/component of sth* ◇ *Money is not essential to happiness.* ◇ *Experience is essential for this job.* ◇ *essential services such as gas, water and electricity* ◇ *The museum is closed while essential repairs are being carried out.* ◇ *It is essential to keep the two groups separate* ◇ *Even in small companies, computers are an essential tool.*—compare INESSENTIAL, NON-ESSENTIAL **OPP** DISPENSABLE **2** [only before noun] connected with the most important aspect or basic nature of sb/sth **SYN** FUNDAMENTAL: *The essential difference between Sara and me is in our attitude to money.* ◇ *The essential character of the town has been destroyed by the new road.*
■ *noun* [usually pl.] **1** something that is needed in a particular situation or in order to do a particular thing: *I only had time to pack the bare essentials* (= the most necessary things). ◇ *The studio had all the essentials like heating and running water.* **2** an important basic fact or piece of knowledge about a subject: *the essentials of English grammar*

es·sen·tial·ly /ɪˈsenʃəli/ *adv.* when you think about the true, important or basic nature of sb/sth **SYN** BASICALLY, FUNDAMENTALLY: *There are three essentially different ways of tackling the problem.* ◇ *The pattern is essentially the same in all cases.* ◇ *Essentially, what we are suggesting is that the firm needs to change.* ◇ *He was, essentially, a teacher, not a manager.* ◇ *The article was essentially concerned with her relationship with her parents* (= it dealt with other things, but this was the most important).

es,sential ˈoil *noun* an oil taken from a plant, used because of its strong smell for making PERFUME and in AROMATHERAPY

-est *suffix* (makes superlative adjectives and adverbs): *widest* ◇ *biggest* ◇ *happiest* ◇ *soonest*—compare -ER

es·tab·lish /ɪˈstæblɪʃ/ *verb* **1** [VN] to start or create an organization, a system, etc. that is meant to last for a long time **SYN** SET UP: *The committee was established in 1912.* ◇ *The new treaty establishes a free trade zone.* **2** [VN] to start having a relationship, especially a formal one, with another person, group or country: *The school has established a successful relationship with the local community.* **3** [VN] ~ sb/sth/yourself (in sth) (as sth) to hold a position for long enough or succeed in sth well enough to make people accept and respect you: *By then she was established as a star.* ◇ *He has just set up his own business but it will take him a while to get established.* **4** [VN] to make people accept a belief, claim, custom etc: *It was this campaign that established the paper's reputation.* ◇ *Traditions get established over time.* **5** to discover or prove the facts of a situation **SYN** ASCERTAIN: [VN] *Police are still trying to establish the cause of the accident.* ◇ [Vthat] *They have established that his injuries were caused by a fall.* ◇ [VWh-] *We need to establish where she was at the time of the shooting.* ◇ [VNthat] *It has since been established that the horse was drugged.*

es·tab·lished /ɪˈstæblɪʃt/ *adj.* [only before noun] **1** respected or given official status because it has existed or been used for a long time: *They are an established company with a good reputation.* ◇ *This unit is now an established part of the course.*—see also WELL ESTABLISHED **2** (of a person) well known and respected in a job, etc. that they have been doing for a long time: *an established actor* **3** (of a Church or a religion) made official for a country

es·tab·lish·ment /ɪˈstæblɪʃmənt/ *noun* **1** [C] (*formal*) an organization, a large institution or a hotel: *an educational establishment* ◇ *a research establishment* ◇ *The hotel is a comfortable and well-run establishment.* **2** (usually **the Establishment**) [sing.+ sing./pl. v.] (often *disapproving*) the people in a society or a profession who have influence and power and who usually do not support change: *the medical/military/political establishment* ◇ *young people rebelling against the Establishment* **3** [U] the act of starting or creating sth that is meant to last for a long time: *The speaker announced the establishment of a new college.* ◇ *the establishment of diplomatic relations between the countries*

es·tate /ɪˈsteɪt/ *noun* **1** a large area of land, usually in the country, that is owned by one person or family **2** (*BrE*) an area of land with a lot of houses or factories of the same type on it: *She lives in a tower block on an estate in London.*—see also COUNCIL ESTATE, HOUSING ESTATE, INDUSTRIAL ESTATE, TRADING ESTATE **3** (*law*) all the money and property that a person owns, especially everything that is left when they die: *Her estate was left to her daughter.*

esˈtate agent (*BrE*) (*AmE* **Real·tor**™ **ˈreal estate agent**) *noun* a person whose job is to sell houses and land for people

esˈtate car (*BrE*) (*AmE* **ˈstation wagon**) *noun* a car with a lot of space behind the back seats and a door at the back for loading large items—picture at CAR

eˈstate tax *noun* [U] (*AmE*) = INHERITANCE TAX

es·teem /ɪˈstiːm/ *noun, verb*
■ *noun* [U] (*formal*) great respect and admiration; a good opinion of sb: *She is held in high esteem by her colleagues.* ◇ *Please accept this small gift as a token of our esteem.*—see also SELF-ESTEEM
■ *verb* (*formal*) (not used in the progressive tenses) **1** [VN] [usually passive] to respect and admire sb/sth very much: *a highly esteemed scientist* ◇ *Many of these qualities are esteemed by managers.* **2** [VN-N] (*old-fashioned, formal*) to think of sb/sth in a particular way: *She was esteemed the perfect novelist.*

es·thete, es·thet·ic (*AmE*) = AESTHETE, AESTHETIC

es·tim·able /ˈestɪməbl/ *adj.* (*old-fashioned* or *formal*) deserving respect and admiration

es·ti·mate *noun, verb*
■ *noun* /ˈestɪmət/ **1** a judgement that you make without having the exact details or figures about the size, amount, cost, etc. of sth: *I can give you a rough estimate of the amount of wood you will need.* ◇ *a ballpark estimate* (= an approximate estimate) ◇ *official government estimates of traffic growth over the next decade* ◇ *At least 5000 people were killed, and that's a conservative estimate* (= the real figure will be higher). **2** a statement of how much a piece of work will probably cost
■ *verb* /ˈestɪmeɪt/ [often passive] ~ sth (at sth) to form an idea of the cost, size, value etc. of sth, but without calculating it exactly: [VN] *The satellite will cost an estimated £400 million.* ◇ *Police estimate the crowd at 30000.* ◇ [VN to inf] *The deal is estimated to be worth around $1.5 million.* ◇ [V (that)] *We estimated (that) it would cost about £5 000.* ◇ [VN (that)] *It is estimated (that) the project will last four years.* ◇ [VWh-] *It is hard to estimate how many children suffer from dyslexia.*

es·ti·ma·tion /ˌestɪˈmeɪʃn/ *noun* (*formal*) **1** [sing.] a judgement or opinion about the value or quality of sb/sth: *Who is the best candidate in your estimation?* ◇ *Since he left his wife he's certainly gone down in my estimation* (= I have less respect for him). ◇ *She went up in my estimation* (= I have more respect for her) *when I discovered how much charity work she does.* **2** [C] a judgement about the levels or quantity of sth: *Estimations of our total world sales are around 50 million.*

es·tranged /ɪˈstreɪndʒd/ *adj.* (*formal*) **1** [usually before noun] no longer living with your husband or wife: *his estranged wife Emma* **2** ~ (from sb) no longer friendly, loyal or in contact with sb: *He became estranged from his family after the argument.* **3** ~ (from sth) no longer involved in or connected with sth, especially sth that

aɪ	aʊ	eɪ	əʊ	oʊ	ɔɪ	ɪə	eə	ʊə	j	w
my	now	say	go	go	boy	near	hair	pure	yes	wet
			(BrE)	(AmE)						

used to be important to you: *She felt estranged from her former existence.*

es·trange·ment /ɪˈstreɪndʒmənt/ *noun* [U, C] ~ (from sb/sth)| ~ (between A and B) the state of being estranged; a period of being estranged: *a period of estrangement from his wife* ◊ *The misunderstanding had caused a seven-year estrangement between them.*

estrogen (*AmE*) = OESTROGEN

es·tu·ary /ˈestʃuəri; *AmE* -eri/ (*pl.* **-ies**) *noun* the wide part of a river where it flows into the sea: *the Thames estuary*—picture at COAST

Estuary 'English *noun* [U] a way of speaking which combines standard English with the way of speaking that is typical of London, used by many people in the south-east of England

et al. /ˌet ˈæl/ *abbr.* (used especially after names) and other people or things (from Latin 'et alii/alia'): *research by West et al., 1996*

etc. /et ˈsetərə; ˌɪt/ *abbr.* used after a list to show that there are other things that you could have mentioned (the abbreviation for 'et cetera'): *Remember to take some paper, a pen, etc.* ◊ *We talked about the contract, pay, etc.*

et cet·era /ˌet ˈsetərə; ˌɪt/ = ETC.

etch /etʃ/ *verb* ~ A (with B)| ~ B (in/into/on A) **1** to cut lines into a piece of glass, metal etc. in order to make words or a picture: [VN] *a glass tankard with his initials etched on it* ◊ *a glass tankard etched with his initials* [also V] **2** [VN] [usually passive] (*literary*) if a feeling is etched on sb's face, or sb's face is etched with a feeling, that feeling can be seen very clearly: *Tiredness was etched on his face.* ◊ *His face was etched with tiredness.* **3** [VN] [usually passive] to make a strong clear mark or pattern on sth: *a mountain etched* (= having a clear outline) *against the sky* **IDM** **be etched on your 'heart/'memory/'mind** (*written*) if sth is etched on your memory, you remember it because it has made a strong impression on you

etch·ing /ˈetʃɪŋ/ *noun* [C, U] a picture that is printed from an etched piece of metal; the art of making these pictures

eter·nal /ɪˈtɜːnl; *AmE* ɪˈtɜːrnl/ *adj.* **1** without an end; existing or continuing for ever: *the promise of eternal life in heaven* ◊ *She's an eternal optimist* (= she always expects that the best will happen). ◊ *eternal truths* (= ideas that are always true and never change) **2** [only before noun] (*disapproving*) happening often and seeming never to stop: *I'm tired of your eternal arguments.* ▶ **eter·nal·ly** /ɪˈtɜːnəli; *AmE* -ˈtɜːrn-/ *adv.*: *I'll be eternally grateful to you for this.* ◊ *women trying to look eternally young*

e,ternal 'triangle *noun* a situation where two people are in love with or having a sexual relationship with the same person

eter·nity /ɪˈtɜːnəti; *AmE* ɪˈtɜːrn-/ *noun* **1** [U] (*formal*) time without end, especially life continuing without end after death: *There will be rich and poor for all eternity.* ◊ *They believed that their souls would be condemned to burn in hell for eternity.* **2** (**an eternity**) [sing.] (*informal*) a period of time that seems to be very long or to never end: *After what seemed like an eternity the nurse returned with the results of the test.*

etha·nol /ˈeθənɒl; *AmE* -noʊl/ (also **ethyl alcohol**) *noun* [U] (*chemistry*) the type of alcohol in alcoholic drinks, also used as a fuel or SOLVENT

ether /ˈiːθə(r)/ *noun* [U] **1** a colourless liquid made from alcohol, used in industry as a SOLVENT and, in the past, in medicine to make people unconscious before an operation **2** (**the ether**) (*old use* or *literary*) the upper part of the sky: *Her words disappeared into the ether.* **3** (**the ether**) the air, when it is thought of as the air in which radio or electronic communication takes place

ether·eal /iˈθɪəriəl; *AmE* iˈθɪr-/ *adj.* (*formal*) extremely delicate and light; seeming to belong to another, more spiritual, world: *ethereal music* ◊ *her ethereal beauty*

Ether·net /ˈiːθənet; *AmE* ˈiːθərnet/ *noun* [U] (*computing*) a system for connecting a number of computer systems to form a NETWORK

ethic /ˈeθɪk/ *noun* **1** (**ethics**) [pl.] moral principles that

control or influence a person's behaviour: *professional/business/medical ethics* ◊ *to draw up a code of ethics* ◊ *He began to question the ethics of his position.* **2** [sing.] a system of moral principles or rules of behaviour: *a strongly defined work ethic* ◊ *the Protestant ethic* **3** (**ethics**) [U] the branch of philosophy that deals with moral principles

eth·ic·al /ˈeθɪkl/ *adj.* **1** [not before noun] connected with beliefs and principles about what is right and wrong: *ethical issues/standards/questions* ◊ *the ethical problems of human embryo research* **2** morally correct or acceptable: *Is it ethical to promote cigarettes through advertising?* ◊ *ethical investment* (= investing money in businesses that are considered morally acceptable) ▶ **eth·ic·al·ly** /-kli/ *adv.*: *The committee judged that he had not behaved ethically.*

eth·nic /ˈeθnɪk/ *adj.* **1** connected with or belonging to a nation, race or tribe that shares a cultural tradition: *ethnic groups/communities* ◊ *ethnic strife/tensions/violence* (= between people from different races or tribes) ◊ *ethnic Albanians living in Germany* **2** typical of a country or culture that is very different from modern western culture and therefore interesting for people in western countries: *ethnic clothes/jewellery/cooking* ▶ **eth·nic·al·ly** /-kli/ *adv.*: *an ethnically divided region*

,ethnic 'cleansing *noun* [U] (used especially in news reports) the policy of forcing the people of a particular race or religion to leave an area or a country

eth·ni·city /eθˈnɪsəti/ *noun* [U] (*technical*) the fact of belonging to a particular race: *Many factors are important, for example class, gender, age and ethnicity.*

,ethnic mi'nority *noun* a group of people from a particular culture or of a particular race living in a country where the main group is of a different culture or race

ethno·cen·tric /ˌeθnəʊˈsentrɪk; *AmE* ˌeθnoʊ-/ *adj.* based on the ideas and beliefs of one particular culture and using these to judge other cultures: *a white, ethnocentric school curriculum* ▶ **ethno·cen·trism** *noun* [U]

eth·nog·raph·er /eθˈnɒɡrəfə(r); *AmE* -ˈnɑːɡ-/ *noun* a person who studies different races and cultures

eth·nog·raphy /eθˈnɒɡrəfi; *AmE* -ˈnɑːɡ-/ *noun* [U] the scientific description of different races and cultures ▶ **ethno·graph·ic** /ˌeθnəˈɡræfɪk/ *adj.*: *ethnographic research/studies*

eth·no·logy /eθˈnɒlədʒi; *AmE* -ˈnɑːl-/ *noun* [U] the scientific study and comparison of human races ▶ **ethno·logic·al** /ˌeθnəˈlɒdʒɪkl; *AmE* -ˈlɑːdʒ-/ *adj.* **eth·nolo·gist** /eθˈnɒlədʒɪst; *AmE* -ˈnɑːl-/ *noun*

ethos /ˈiːθɒs; *AmE* ˈiːθɑːs/ *noun* [sing.] (*formal*) the moral ideas and attitudes that belong to a particular group or society: *an ethos of public service*

ethyl alcohol /ˌeθɪl ˈælkəhɒl; ˌiːθaɪl; *AmE* -hɔːl; -hɑːl/ *noun* [U] (*chemistry*) = ETHANOL

eti·ology (*AmE*) = AETIOLOGY

eti·quette /ˈetɪket; -kət/ *noun* [U] the formal rules of correct or polite behaviour in society or among members of a particular profession: *advice on etiquette* ◊ *medical/legal/professional etiquette*

-ette *suffix* (in nouns) **1** small: *kitchenette* **2** female: *usherette*

étude /ˈeɪtjuːd; *AmE* also -tuːd/ *noun* (*music*) (*especially AmE*) = STUDY *n.* (8)

ety·mol·ogy /ˌetɪˈmɒlədʒi; *AmE* -ˈmɑːl-/ *noun* (*pl.* **-ies**) **1** [U] the study of the origin and history of words and their meanings **2** [C] the origin and history of a particular word ▶ **etymo·logic·al** /ˌetɪməˈlɒdʒɪkl; *AmE* -ˈlɑːdʒ-/ *adj.*: *an etymological dictionary*

EU /ˌiː ˈjuː/ *abbr.* EUROPEAN UNION

eu·ca·lyp·tus /ˌjuːkəˈlɪptəs/ *noun* [C, U] (*pl.* **eu·ca·lyp·ti** /-taɪ/) (also **euca'lyptus tree**, **'gum tree**) a tall straight tree with leaves that produce an oil with a strong smell, that is used in medicine. There are several types of eucalyptus and they grow especially in Australasia.

eu·char·ist /ˈjuːkərɪst/ *noun* (**the Eucharist**) [sing.] a ceremony in the Christian Church during which people eat bread and drink wine in memory of the last meal that

Christ had with his DISCIPLES; the bread and wine taken at this ceremony—see also COMMUNION, MASS

eu·gen·ics /juːˈdʒenɪks/ *noun* [U] the study of methods to improve the mental and physical characteristics of the human race by choosing who may become parents ▶ **eu·gen·ic** *adj.* **eu·gen·ist** /juːˈdʒiːnɪst/ (also **eu·geni·cist**) /juːˈdʒenɪsɪst/ *noun*

eu·lo·gize (*BrE* also **-ise**) /ˈjuːlədʒaɪz/ *verb* [VN] ~ **sb/sth** (**as sth**) (*formal*) to praise sb/sth very highly: *He was eulogized as a hero.* ▶ **eu·lo·gis·tic** /ˌjuːləˈdʒɪstɪk/ *adj.*

eu·logy /ˈjuːlədʒi/ *noun* [C, U] (*pl.* **-ies**) **1** ~ (**of/to sb/sth**) a speech or piece of writing praising sb/sth very much: *a eulogy to marriage* **2** ~ (**for/to sb**) (*especially AmE*) a speech given at a funeral praising the person who has died

eu·nuch /ˈjuːnək/ *noun* **1** a man who has been CASTRATED, especially one who guarded women in some eastern countries in the past **2** (*formal*) a person without power or influence: *a political eunuch*

eu·phem·ism /ˈjuːfəmɪzəm/ *noun* ~ (**for sth**) an indirect word or phrase that people often use to refer to sth embarrassing or unpleasant, sometimes to make it seem more acceptable than it really is: *'Pass away' is a euphemism for 'die'.* ◊ *'User fees' is just a politician's euphemism for taxes.* ▶ **eu·phem·is·tic** /ˌjuːfəˈmɪstɪk/ *adj.*: *euphemistic language* **eu·phem·is·tic·al·ly** /ˌjuːfəˈmɪstɪkli/ *adv.*: *The prison camps were euphemistically called 'retraining centres'.*

eu·pho·nium /juːˈfəʊniəm; *AmE* -ˈfoʊ-/ *noun* a large BRASS musical instrument like a TUBA

eu·phoria /juːˈfɔːriə/ *noun* [U] an extremely strong feeling of happiness and excitement that usually lasts only a short time: *I was in a state of euphoria all day.* ▶ **eu·phor·ic** /juːˈfɒrɪk; *AmE* -ˈfɔːr-; -ˈfɑːr-/ *adj.*: *My euphoric mood could not last.*

eur·eka /juˈriːkə/ *exclamation* used to show pleasure at having found sth, especially the answer to a problem

Euro /ˈjʊərəʊ; *AmE* ˈjʊroʊ/ *adj.* (*informal*) (used especially in newspapers) connected with Europe, especially the European Union: *Euro rules*

euro /ˈjʊərəʊ; *AmE* ˈjʊroʊ/ *noun* (*symb* €) (*pl.* **-os**) (since 1999) a unit of money of eleven countries of the European Union: *The price is given in dollars or euros.*

Euro- /ˈjʊərəʊ; *AmE* ˈjʊroʊ/ *combining form* (in nouns and adjectives) connected with Europe or the European Union: *a Euro-MP* ◊ *Euro-elections*

Euro·crat /ˈjʊərəkræt; *AmE* ˈjʊr-/ *noun* (sometimes *disapproving*) an official of the European Union, especially a senior one

Eur·ope /ˈjʊərəp; *AmE* ˈjʊrəp/ *noun* [U] **1** the continent next to Asia in the east, the Atlantic Ocean in the west, and the Mediterranean Sea in the south: *western/eastern/central Europe* **2** the European Union: *countries wanting to join Europe* ◊ *He's very pro-Europe.* **3** (*BrE*) all of Europe except for Britain: *British holidaymakers in Europe*

Euro·pean /ˌjʊərəˈpiːən; *AmE* ˌjʊr-/ *adj., noun*

■ *adj.* **1** of or connected with Europe: *European languages* **2** of or connected with the European Union: *European law* ◊ *our European partners*

■ *noun* **1** a person from Europe, or whose ancestors came from Europe **2** (*BrE*) a person who supports the principles and aims of the European Union: *a good European*

the ˌEuropean ˈUnion *noun* [sing.] (*abbr.* EU) an economic and political organization that many European countries belong to

eu·tha·nasia /ˌjuːθəˈneɪziə; *AmE* -ˈneɪʒə/ *noun* [U] the practice (illegal in most countries) of killing without pain a person who is suffering from a disease that cannot be cured: *They argued in favour of legalizing voluntary euthanasia* (= people being able to ask for euthanasia themselves).

evacu·ate /ɪˈvækjueɪt/ *verb* **1** [VN] to move people from a place of danger to a safer place: *Police evacuated nearby buildings.* ◊ *Children were evacuated from London to escape the bombing.* **2** to move out of a place because of

danger, and leave the place empty: [VN] *Employees were urged to evacuate their offices immediately.* ◊ [V] *Locals were told to evacuate.* **3** [VN] (*formal*) to empty your bowels ▶ **evacu·ation** /ɪˌvækjuˈeɪʃn/ *noun* [U, C]: *the emergency evacuation of thousands of people after the earthquake*

evac·uee /ɪˌvækjuˈiː/ *noun* a person who is sent away from a place because it is dangerous, especially during a war

evade /ɪˈveɪd/ *verb* **1** to escape from sb/sth or avoid meeting sb: [VN] *For two weeks they evaded the press.* ◊ *He managed to evade capture.* [also V-ing] **2** to find a way of not doing sth, especially sth that legally or morally you should do: [VN] *to evade payment of taxes* ◊ *She is trying to evade all responsibility for her behaviour.* [also V-ing] **3** to avoid dealing with or talking about sth: [VN] *Come on, don't you think you're evading the issue?* ◊ [V-ing] *to evade answering a question* **4** [VN] (*formal*) to not come or happen to sb SYN ELUDE: *The answer evaded him* (= he could not think of it).—see also EVASION, EVASIVE

evalu·ate /ɪˈvæljueɪt/ *verb* to form an opinion of the amount, value or quality of sth after thinking about it carefully SYN ASSESS: [VN] *Our research attempts to evaluate the effectiveness of the different drugs.* ◊ [VWh-] *We need to evaluate how well the policy is working.* ▶ **evalu·ation** /ɪˌvæljuˈeɪʃn/ *noun* [C, U]: *a preliminary evaluation of the health care system*

evan·es·cent /ˌiːvəˈnesnt; *AmE* usually ˌev-/ *adj.* (*literary*) disappearing quickly from sight or memory

evan·gel·ic·al /ˌiːvænˈdʒelɪkl/ *adj., noun*

■ *adj.* **1** of or belonging to a Christian group that emphasizes the authority of the Bible and the importance of personal SALVATION through faith: *They're evangelical Christians.* **2** wanting very much to persuade people to accept your views and opinions: *He delivered his speech with evangelical fervour.*

■ *noun* a member of the evangelical branch of the Christian Church

evan·gel·ist /ɪˈvændʒəlɪst/ *noun* **1** a person who tries to persuade people to become Christians, especially by travelling around the country holding religious meetings or speaking on radio or television—see also TELEVANGELIST **2** (**Evangelist**) one of the four writers (Matthew, Mark, Luke, John) of the books called the GOSPELS in the Bible ▶ **evan·gel·ism** *noun* [U] **evan·gel·ist·ic** /ɪˌvændʒəˈlɪstɪk/ *adj.*: *an evangelistic meeting/crusade* ◊ *evangelistic zeal*

evan·gel·ize (*BrE* also **-ise**) /ɪˈvændʒəlaɪz/ *verb* [VN] to try to persuade people to become Christians

evap·or·ate /ɪˈvæpəreɪt/ *verb* **1** if a liquid **evaporates** or if sth **evaporates** it, it changes into a gas, especially steam: [V] *Heat until all the water has evaporated.* ◊ [VN] *The sun is constantly evaporating the earth's moisture.* **2** [V] to disappear, especially by gradually becoming less and less: *Her confidence had now completely evaporated.* ▶ **evap·or·ation** /ɪˌvæpəˈreɪʃn/ *noun* [U]

eˌvaporated ˈmilk *noun* [U] thick sweet milk sold in cans, often served with fruit instead of cream

eva·sion /ɪˈveɪʒn/ *noun* [C, U] **1** the act of avoiding sb or of avoiding sth that you are supposed to do: *His behaviour was an evasion of his responsibilities as a father.* ◊ *She's been charged with tax evasion.* **2** a statement that sb makes that avoids dealing with sth or talking about sth honestly and directly: *His speech was full of evasions and half-truths.*—see also EVADE

eva·sive /ɪˈveɪsɪv/ *adj.* not willing to give clear answers to a question: *evasive answers/comments/replies* ◊ *Tessa was evasive about why she had not been at home that night.* ▶ **eva·sive·ly** *adv.*: *'I'm not sure,' she replied evasively.* **eva·sive·ness** *noun* [U] IDM **take evasive action** to act in order to avoid danger or an unpleasant situation

eve /iːv/ *noun* **1** the day or evening before an event, especially a religious festival or holiday: *Christmas Eve* (= 24 December) ◊ *a New Year's Eve party* (= on 31 December) ◊ *on the eve of the election* **2** (*old use* or *literary*) evening

even /ˈiːvn/ *adv., adj., verb*

■ *adv.* **1** used to emphasize sth unexpected or surprising: *He never even opened the letter* (= so he certainly didn't read it). ◇ *It was cold there even in summer* (= so it must have been very cold in winter). ◇ *Even a child can understand it* (= so adults certainly can). ◇ *She didn't even call to say she wasn't coming.* **2** used when you are comparing things, to make the comparison stronger: *You know even less about it than I do.* ◇ *She's even more intelligent than her sister.* **3** used to introduce a more exact description of sb/sth: *It's an unattractive building, ugly even.* ⇨ note at ALTHOUGH
IDM **even as** (*formal*) just at the same time as sb does sth or as sth else happens: *Even as he shouted the warning the car skidded.* **even if/though** in spite of the fact or belief that; no matter whether: *I'll get there, even if I have to walk.* ◇ *I like her, even though she can be annoying at times.* ⇨ note at ALTHOUGH ˌeven ˈnow/ˈthen **1** in spite of what has/had happened: *I've shown him the photographs but even now he won't believe me.* ◇ *Even then she would not admit her mistake.* **2** (*formal*) at this or that exact moment: *The troops are even now preparing to march into the city.* ˌeven ˈso in spite of that: *There are a lot of spelling mistakes; even so, it's quite a good essay.*—more at LESS *adv.*

■ *adj.*
SMOOTH/LEVEL | **1** smooth, level and flat: *You need an even surface to work on.* OPP UNEVEN
NOT CHANGING | **2** not changing very much in amount, speed, etc: *an even temperature all year* ◇ *Children do not learn at an even pace.* OPP UNEVEN
EQUAL | **3** (of an amount of sth) equal or the same for each person, team, place, etc: *Our scores are now even.* ◇ *the even distribution of food* OPP UNEVEN **4** (of two people or teams) equally balanced or of an equal standard: *an even contest* ◇ *The two players were pretty even.* OPP UNEVEN
NUMBERS | **5** that can be divided exactly by two: *4, 6, 8, 10 are all even numbers* OPP ODD
SAME SIZE | **6** equally spaced and the same size: *even features/teeth* OPP UNEVEN
CALM | **7** calm; not changing or becoming upset: *She has a very even temperament.* ◇ *He spoke in a steady, even voice.*
▶ **even·ness** /ˈiːvənnəs/ *noun* [U]
IDM **be ˈeven** (*informal*) to no longer owe sb money or a favour: *If I pay for the meals then we're even.* **be/get ˈeven (with sb)** (*informal*) to cause sb the same amount of trouble or harm as they have caused you: *I'll get even with you for this, just you wait.* **break ˈeven** to complete a piece of business, etc. without either losing money or making a profit: *The company just about broke even last year.* **have an even ˈchance (of doing sth)** to be equally likely to do or not do sth: *She has more than an even chance of winning tomorrow.* **on an even ˈkeel** living, working or happening in a calm way, with no sudden changes, especially after a difficult time—more at HONOUR *n.*

■ *verb*
IDM ˌeven the ˈscore to harm or punish sb who has harmed or cheated you in the past
PHRV ˌeven ˈout to become level or steady, usually after varying a lot: *House prices keep rising and falling but they should eventually even out.* ˌeven sth↔ˈout to spread things evenly over a period of time or among a number of people: *He tried to even out the distribution of work among his employees.* ˌeven sth↔ˈup to make a situation or a competition more equal

ˌeven-ˈhanded *adj.* completely fair, especially when dealing with different groups of people: *He had an even-handed approach to the negotiations.*

even·ing /ˈiːvnɪŋ/ *noun* **1** [C, U] the part of the day between the afternoon and the time you go to bed: *I'll come and see you tomorrow evening.* ◇ *What do you usually do in the evening?* ◇ *She's going to her sister's for the evening.* ◇ *the long winter evenings* ◇ *the evening performance* **2** [C] an event of a particular type happening in the evening: *a musical evening at school* (= when music is performed) ▶ **even·ings** *adv.* (*especially AmE*): *He works*

evenings. **IDM** **Good ˈevening** (also *informal* **Evening**) used as a polite greeting, or reply to a greeting, when people first see each other in the evening: *Good evening, everyone.* ◇ *Evening, Mike.*—more at OTHER *adj.*

ˈ**evening class** *noun* a course of study for adults in the evening: *an evening class in car maintenance* ◇ *to go to/attend evening classes*

ˈ**evening dress** *noun* **1** [U] elegant clothes worn for formal occasions in the evening: *Everyone was in evening dress.* **2** [C] a woman's long formal dress

even·ly /ˈiːvnli/ *adv.* **1** in a smooth, regular or equal way: *Make sure the paint covers the surface evenly.* ◇ *She was fast asleep, breathing evenly.* ◇ *evenly spaced at four cm apart* **2** with equal amounts for each person or in each place: *evenly distributed/divided* ◇ *Incidence of the disease is fairly evenly spread across Europe.* ◇ *The two teams are very evenly matched* (= are equally likely to win). **3** calmly; without showing any emotion: *'I warned you not to phone me,' he said evenly.*

ˌeven ˈmoney *noun* (*BrE* also **evens** [pl.]) (in betting) ODDS that give an equal chance of winning or losing and that mean a person has the chance of winning the same amount of money that he or she has bet

even·song /ˈiːvnsɒŋ; *AmE* -sɔːŋ/ *noun* [U] the service of evening prayer in the Anglican Church—compare MATINS, VESPERS

event /ɪˈvent/ *noun* **1** a thing that happens, especially sth important: *The election was the main event of 1999.* ◇ *In the light of later events the decision was proved right.* ◇ *The decisions we take now may influence the course of events* (= the way things happen) *in the future.* ◇ *Everyone was frightened by the strange sequence of events.* ◇ *In the normal course of events* (= if things had happened as expected) *she would have gone with him.* **2** a planned public or social occasion: *a fund-raising event* ◇ *the social event of the year* **3** one of the races or competitions in a sports programme: *The 800 metres is the fourth event of the afternoon.*—see also FIELD EVENT, TRACK EVENT **IDM** **in ˈany event | at ˈall events** used to emphasize or show that sth is true or will happen in spite of other circumstances: *I think she'll agree to do it but in any event, all she can say is 'no'.* **in the eˈvent** when the situation actually happened: *I got very nervous about the exam, but in the event, I needn't have worried; it was really easy.* **in the event of sth | in the event that sth happens** if sth happens: *In the event of an accident, call this number.* ◇ *Sheila will inherit everything in the event of his death.* **in ˈthat event** if that happens: *In that event, we will have to reconsider our offer.*—more at HAPPY, WISE *adj.*

> **WHICH WORD?**
>
> **event / occurrence / incident / happening**
>
> All these words describe something that happens.
> An **event** is often something important or interesting: *I'll never forget the terrible events of that summer.* It can refer to something such as a concert, festival or sports competition: *The tourist guide lists the major events in the town throughout the year.*
> **Occurrence** is a formal word and is usually used, with words like *common* or *rare*, to talk about how often something happens: *Divorce has become a common occurrence in this country.*
> An **incident** is often something not very important but that you remember because it is unusual or unpleasant: *The movie is based on a real-life incident.* It can also refer to a crime or an accident: *The police reported several thefts and one violent incident.*
> **Happening** is used to describe something unusual or strange: *strange happenings in the town.*

ˌeven-ˈtempered *adj.* not easily made angry or upset

event·ful /ɪˈventfl/ *adj.* full of things that happen, especially exciting, important or dangerous things: *an eventful day/life/journey*

event·ing /ɪˈventɪŋ/ (also ˌthree-day eˈventing) *noun* [U] the sport of taking part in competitions riding horses.

| æ | ɑː | e | ɜː | ə | ɪ | iː | i | ɒ | ɔː | ʌ | ʊ | u | uː |
| cat | father | ten | bird | about | sit | see | many | got | saw | cup | put | actual | too |
(BrE)

E

These are often held over three days and include riding across country, jumping and DRESSAGE.

even·tual /ɪ'ventʃuəl/ *adj.* [only before noun] happening at the end of a period of time or of a process: *the eventual winner of the tournament* ◊ *It is impossible to predict what the eventual outcome of global warming will be.* ◊ *The village school may face eventual closure.*

even·tu·al·ity /ɪˌventʃu'æləti/ *noun* (*pl.* **-ies**) (*formal*) something that may possibly happen, especially sth unpleasant: *We were prepared for every eventuality.* ◊ *The money had been saved for just such an eventuality.*

even·tu·al·ly /ɪ'ventʃuəli/ *adv.* at the end of a period of time or a series of events: *Our flight eventually left five hours late.* ◊ *I'll get round to mending it eventually.* ◊ *She hopes to get a job on the local newspaper and eventually work for 'The Times'.* HELP Use **finally** for the last in a list of things.

ever /'evə(r)/ *adv.* **1** used in negative sentences and questions, or sentences with *if* to mean 'at any time': *Nothing ever happens here.* ◊ *Don't you ever get tired?* ◊ *If you're ever in Miami, come and see us.* ◊ *'Have you ever thought of changing your job?' 'No, never / No I haven't.'* ◊ *'Have you ever been to Rome?' 'Yes, I have, actually. Not long ago.'* ◊ *She hardly ever* (= almost never) *goes out.* ◊ *We see them very seldom, if ever.* ◊ (*informal*) *I'll never ever do that again!* **2** used for emphasis when you are comparing things: *It was raining harder than ever.* ◊ *It's my best ever score.* **3** (*rather formal*) all the time or every time; always: *Paul, ever the optimist, agreed to try again.* ◊ *She married the prince and they lived happily ever after.* ◊ *He said he would love her for ever.* ◊ *Their debts grew ever larger* (= kept increasing). ◊ *the ever-growing problem* ◊ *an ever-present danger* **4** used after *when, why,* etc. to show that you are surprised or shocked: *Why ever did you agree?* IDM **did you 'ever (…)!** (*old-fashioned, informal*) used to show that you are surprised or shocked: *Did you ever hear anything like it?* **ever since (…)** continuously since the time mentioned: *He's had a car ever since he was 18.* ◊ *I was bitten by a dog once and I've been afraid of them ever since.* **'ever so/'ever such a** (*spoken, especially BrE*) very; really: *He looks ever so smart.* ◊ *She's ever such a nice woman.* ◊ *It's ever so easy.* **if ,ever there 'was (one)** (*spoken*) used to emphasize that sth is certainly true: *That was a disaster if ever there was one!* **yours 'ever/ ever 'yours** sometimes used at the end of an informal letter, before you write your name

ever·green /'evəɡriːn; *AmE* 'evərɡr-/ *noun* a tree or bush that has green leaves all through the year—compare CONIFER, DECIDUOUS ▶ **ever·green** *adj.*: *evergreen shrubs* ◊ (*figurative*) *a new production of Rossini's evergreen* (= always popular) *opera*

ever·last·ing /ˌevə'lɑːstɪŋ; *AmE* ˌevər'læstɪŋ/ *adj.* **1** continuing for ever; never changing SYN ETERNAL: *everlasting life / love* ◊ *an everlasting memory of her smile* ◊ *To his everlasting credit, he never told anyone what I'd done.* **2** (*disapproving*) continuing too long; repeated too often SYN INTERMINABLE, NEVER-ENDING: *I'm tired of your everlasting complaints.* ▶ **ever·last·ing·ly** *adv.*

ever·more /ˌevə'mɔː(r); *AmE* ˌevər'm-/ (also **for ever/more**) *adv.* (*literary*) always

every /'evri/ *det.* **1** used with singular nouns to refer to all the members of a group of things or people: *She knows every student in the school.* ◊ *I could hear every word they said.* ◊ *We enjoyed every minute of our stay.* ◊ *Every day seemed the same to him.* ◊ *Every single time he calls, I'm out.* ◊ *They were watching her every movement.* ◊ *Every one of their CDs has been a hit.* ➪ note at EACH **2** all possible: *We wish you every success.* ◊ *He had every reason to be angry.* **3** used to say how often sth happens or is done: *The buses go every 10 minutes.* ◊ *We had to stop every few miles.* ◊ *One in every three marriages ends in divorce.* ◊ *He has every third day off* (= he works for two days then has one day off then works for two days and so on). ◊ *We see each other every now and again.* ◊ *Every now and then he regretted his decision.* IDM **every other** each ALTERNATE one (= the first, third, fifth, etc. one, but not the second, fourth, sixth, etc.): *They visit us every other week.*

every·body /'evribɒdi; *AmE* -baːdi; -bɑdi/ *pron.* = EVERYONE: *Everybody knows Tom.* ◊ *Have you asked everybody? Didn't you like it? Everybody else did.*

every·day /'evrideɪ/ *adj.* [only before noun] used or happening every day or regularly; ordinary: *everyday objects* ◊ *The Internet has become part of everyday life.* ◊ *a small dictionary for everyday use*

every·one /'evriwʌn/ (also **every·body**) *pron.* every person; all people: *Everyone cheered and clapped.* ◊ *The police questioned everyone in the room.* ◊ *The teacher commented on everyone's work.* ◊ *Everyone else was there.*

every·place /'evripleɪs/ *adv.* (*AmE*) = EVERYWHERE

every·thing /'evriθɪŋ/ *pron.* (with a singular verb) **1** all things: *Everything had gone.* ◊ *When we confronted him, he denied everything.* ◊ *Take this bag, and leave everything else to me.* ◊ *She seemed to have everything—looks, money, intelligence.* **2** the situation now; life generally: *Everything in the capital is now quiet.* ◊ *'How's everything with you?' 'Fine, thanks.'* **3** the most important thing: *Money isn't everything.* ◊ *My family means everything to me.* IDM **and everything** (*spoken*) and so on; and other similar things: *Have you got his name and address and everything?* ◊ *She told me about the baby and everything.*

every·where /'evriweə(r); *AmE* -wer/ (*AmE* also **every·place**) *adv.* in, to or at every place: *I've looked everywhere.* ◊ *He follows me everywhere.* ◊ *We'll have to eat here—everywhere else is full.*

evict /ɪ'vɪkt/ *verb* [VN] **~ sb (from sth)** to force sb to leave a house or land, especially when you have the legal right to do so: *A number of tenants have been evicted for not paying the rent.* ◊ *Police had to evict demonstrators from the building.* ▶ **evic·tion** /ɪ'vɪkʃn/ *noun* [U, C]: *to face eviction from your home*

evi·dence /'evɪdəns/ *noun, verb*
- *noun* **1** [U, C] **~ (of/for sth) | ~ (that …) | ~ (to suggest, show, etc.)** the facts, signs or objects that make you believe that sth is true: *There is convincing evidence of a link between exposure to sun and skin cancer.* ◊ *We found further scientific evidence for this theory.* ◊ *There is not a shred of evidence that the meeting actually took place.* ◊ *Have you any evidence to support this allegation?* ◊ *The room bore evidence of a struggle.* ◊ *On the evidence of their recent matches, it is unlikely the Spanish team will win the cup.* **2** [U] the information that is used in a court of law to try to prove sth: *I was asked to give evidence* (= to say what I knew, describe what I had seen, etc.) *at the trial.* ◊ *He was released when the judge ruled there was no evidence against him.*—see also CIRCUMSTANTIAL IDM **(be) in 'evidence** present and clearly seen: *The police were much in evidence at today's demonstration.* **turn King's/ Queen's 'evidence** (*BrE*) (*AmE* **turn State's 'evidence**) to give information against other criminals in order to get a less severe punishment—compare PLEA BARGAINING—more at BALANCE *n.*, STATE *n.*
- *verb* [VN] [usually passive] (*formal*) to prove or show sth; to be evidence of sth SYN TESTIFY TO: *The legal profession is still a largely male world, as evidenced by the small number of women judges.*

evi·dent /'evɪdənt/ *adj.* **~ (to sb) (that …) | ~ (in/from sth)** clear; easily seen; obvious: *It has now become evident to us that a mistake has been made.* ◊ *The growing interest in history is clearly evident in the number of people visiting museums and country houses.* ◊ *The orchestra played with evident enjoyment.*—see also SELF-EVIDENT

evi·dent·ly /'evɪdəntli/ *adv.* **1** clearly; that can be seen or understood easily: *She walked slowly down the road, evidently in pain.* ◊ *'I'm afraid I couldn't finish the work last night.' 'Evidently not.'* **2** according to what people say: *He evidently hated maths at school, so it's amazing he became an accountant!* ◊ *Evidently, she had nothing to do with the whole affair.*

evil /'iːvl; 'iːvɪl/ *adj., noun*
- *adj.* **1** (of people) enjoying harming others; wicked and cruel: *an evil man* ◊ *an evil grin / laugh* **2** having a harmful effect on people; morally bad: *evil deeds* ◊ *the evil effects of racism* **3** connected with the Devil and with what is bad in the world: *evil spirits / beings* **4** extremely

aɪ	aʊ	eɪ	əʊ	oʊ	ɔɪ	ɪə	eə	ʊə	j	w
my	now	say	go	go	boy	near	hair	pure	yes	wet
			(BrE)	(AmE)						

unpleasant: *an evil smell* **IDM** **the evil 'hour/'day/ 'moment** the time when you have to do sth difficult or unpleasant: *I'd better go and see the dentist—I can't put off the evil hour any longer.*—more at BREW *n.*, GENIUS *n.*

■ *noun* (*formal*) **1** [U] a force that causes wicked or bad things to happen; wicked behaviour: *the eternal struggle between good and evil* ◊ *the forces of evil* ◊ *You cannot pretend there's no evil in the world.* **2** [C, usually pl.] a wicked or harmful thing; the bad effect of sth: *the evils of drugs/alcohol* ◊ *social evils* **IDM** see LESSER, NECESSARY

the ˌevil 'eye *noun* [sing.] the magic power to harm sb by looking at them

evil·ly /'i:vəli/ *adv.* in a wicked or very unpleasant way: *to grin evilly* ◊ *to look evilly at sb*

evince /ɪ'vɪns/ *verb* [VN] (*formal*) to show clearly that you have a feeling or quality: *He evinced a strong desire to be reconciled with his family.*

evis·cer·ate /ɪ'vɪsəreɪt/ *verb* [VN] (*formal*) to remove the inner organs of a body

evoca·tive /ɪ'vɒkətɪv/; *AmE* ɪ'vɑːk-/ *adj.* ~ (**of sth**) (*approving*) making you think of or remember a strong image or feeling, in a pleasant way: *evocative smells/ sounds/music* ◊ *Her new book is wonderfully evocative of village life.*

evoke /ɪ'vəʊk/; *AmE* ɪ'voʊk/ *verb* [VN] (*written*) to bring a feeling, a memory or an image into your mind: *The music evoked memories of her youth.* ◊ *His case is unlikely to evoke public sympathy.* ▶ **evo·ca·tion** /ˌiːvəʊ'keɪʃn; *AmE* ˌiːvoʊ-/ *noun* [C, U]: *a brilliant evocation of childhood in the 1940s*

evo·lu·tion /ˌiːvə'luːʃn; ˌev-/ *noun* [U] **1** (*biology*) the gradual development of plants, animals, etc. over many years, from simple to more complicated forms: *The evolution of the human species.* ◊ *Darwin's theory of evolution* **2** the gradual development of sth: *In politics Britain has preferred evolution to revolution* (= gradual development to sudden violent change).

evo·lu·tion·ary /ˌiːvə'luːʃənri; ˌev-; *AmE* -neri/ *adj.* connected with evolution; connected with gradual development and change: *evolutionary theory/biology* ◊ *evolutionary change*

evolve /i'vɒlv; *AmE* i'vɑːlv/ *verb* **1 ~ (sth) (from sth) (into sth)** to develop gradually, especially from a simple to a more complicated form; to develop sth in this way: [V] *The idea evolved from a drawing I discovered in the attic.* ◊ *The company has evolved into a major chemical manufacturer.* ◊ [VN] *Each school must evolve its own way of working.* **2 ~ (from sth)** (*biology*) (of plants, animals, etc.) to develop gradually over many GENERATIONS from a simple form to a more complicated one: [V] *The three species evolved from a single ancestor.* ◊ [VN] *The dolphin has evolved a highly developed jaw.*

ewe /juː/ *noun* a female sheep—compare RAM

ewer /'juːə(r)/ *noun* a large JUG used in the past for carrying water

ex /eks/ *noun, prep.*

■ *noun* (*pl.* **exes**) (*informal*) a person's former wife, husband or other partner: *The children are spending the weekend with my ex and his new wife.*

■ *prep.* (*BrE*) not including sth: *The price is £1500 ex VAT.*

ex- /eks/ *prefix* (in nouns) former: *ex-wife* ◊ *ex-president*

ex·acer·bate /ɪɡ'zæsəbeɪt; *AmE* ɪɡ'zæsərb-/ *verb* [VN] (*written*) to make sth worse, especially a disease or problem **SYN** AGGRAVATE: *His aggressive reaction only exacerbated the situation.* ◊ *The symptoms may be exacerbated by certain drugs.* ▶ **ex·acer·ba·tion** *noun* [U, C]

exact /ɪɡ'zækt/ *adj., verb*

■ *adj.* **1** correct in every detail; accurate: *She gave an exact description of the attacker.* ◊ **an exact copy/replica** *of the painting* ◊ *We need to know the exact time the incident occurred.* ◊ *What were his exact words?* ◊ *She's in her mid-thirties—thirty-six to be exact.* ◊ *The colours were an exact match.* ◊ *He started to phone me at the exact moment I started to phone him* (= at the same time). ◊ *The two men were exact contemporaries at university.* ◊ *Her second husband was **the exact opposite** of her first* (= completely different). **2** (of people) very accurate and careful about

details **SYN** METICULOUS **3** (of a science) using accurate measurements and following set rules: *Assessing insurance risk can never be an exact science.* ▶ **exact·ness** *noun* [U]

■ *verb* [VN] **~ sth (from sb)** (*formal*) **1** to demand and get sth from sb: *She was determined to exact a promise from him.* **2** to make sth bad happen to sb: *Stress can exact a high price from workers* (= can affect them badly). ◊ *He exacted* (= took) *a terrible revenge for their treatment of him.* ▶ **exac·tion** /ɪɡ'zækʃn/ *noun* [C, U] (*formal*)

exact·ing /ɪɡ'zæktɪŋ/ *adj.* needing or demanding a lot of effort and care about details: *exacting work* ◊ *products designed to meet the exacting standards of today's international marketplace* ◊ *He was an exacting man to work for.*

exac·ti·tude /ɪɡ'zæktɪtjuːd; *AmE* -tuːd/ *noun* [U] (*formal*) the quality of being very accurate and exact: *scientific exactitude*

exact·ly /ɪɡ'zæktli/ *adv.* **1** used to emphasize that sth is correct in every way or in every detail **SYN** PRECISELY: *I know exactly how she felt.* ◊ *Do exactly as I tell you.* ◊ *It happened almost exactly a year ago.* ◊ *It's exactly nine o'clock.* ◊ *You haven't changed at all—you still look **exactly the same.*** ◊ *His words had **exactly the opposite** effect.* ◊ *Your answer is exactly right.* ◊ *It was a warm day, if not exactly hot.* **2** (*spoken*) used to ask for more information about sth: *Where exactly did you stay in France?* ◊ (*disapproving*) *Exactly what are you trying to tell me?* **3** used as a reply, agreeing with what sb has just said, or emphasizing that it is correct: *'You mean somebody in this room must be the murderer?' 'Exactly.'* **IDM** **not exactly** (*spoken*) **1** used when you are saying the opposite of what you really mean: *He wasn't exactly pleased to see us—in fact he refused to open the door.* ◊ *It's not exactly beautiful, is it?* (= it's ugly) **2** used when you are correcting sth that sb has said: *'So he told you you'd got the job?' 'Not exactly, but he said they were impressed with me.'*

ex·ag·ger·ate /ɪɡ'zædʒəreɪt/ *verb* to make sth seem longer, better, worse or more important than it really is: [V] *The hotel was really filthy and I'm not exaggerating.* ◊ [VN] *He tends to exaggerate the difficulties.* ◊ *I'm sure he exaggerates his Irish accent* (= tries to sound more Irish than he really is). ◊ *Demand for satellite television has been greatly exaggerated.*

ex·ag·ger·ated /ɪɡ'zædʒəreɪtɪd/ *adj.* **1** made to seem larger, better, worse or more important than it really is or needs to be: *to make greatly/grossly/wildly exaggerated claims* ◊ *She has an exaggerated sense of her own importance.* **2** (of an action) done in a way that makes people notice it: *an exaggerated laugh* ◊ *He looked at me with exaggerated surprise.* ▶ **ex·ag·ger·ated·ly** *adv.*

ex·ag·ger·ation /ɪɡˌzædʒə'reɪʃn/ *noun* [C usually sing, U] a statement or description that makes sth seem larger, better, worse or more important than it really is; the act of making a statement like this: *a slight/gross/ wild exaggeration* ◊ *It would be an exaggeration to say I knew her well—I only met her twice.* ◊ *It's no exaggeration to say that most students have never read a complete Shakespeare play.* ◊ *He told his story simply and without exaggeration.*

exalt /ɪɡ'zɔːlt/ *verb* [VN] (*formal*) **1** to make sb rise to a higher rank or position, sometimes to one that they do not deserve **2** to praise sb/sth very much

exalt·ation /ˌeɡzɔː'leɪʃn/ *noun* [U] (*formal*) **1** a feeling of very great joy or happiness: *a moment of extreme joy and exaltation* **2** an act of raising sth/sb to a high position or rank: *the exaltation of emotion and intuition above logical reasoning*

exalt·ed /ɪɡ'zɔːltɪd/ *adj.* **1** (*formal* or *humorous*) of high rank, position or great importance: *She was the only woman to rise to such an exalted position.* ◊ *You're moving in very exalted circles!* **2** (*formal*) full of great joy and happiness: *I felt exalted and newly alive.*

exam /ɪɡ'zæm/ *noun* (*also formal* **exam·in·ation**) *noun* a formal written, spoken or practical test, especially at school or college, to see how much you know about a subject, or what you can do: *to take an exam* ◊ (*formal*) *to*

b	d	f	g	h	k	l	m	n	p	r
bad	did	fall	get	hat	cat	leg	man	now	pen	red

E

sit an exam ◇ to pass/fail an exam ◇ (BrE) to mark an exam ◇ (AmE) to grade an exam ◇ an exam paper ◇ I got my exam results today. ◇ (BrE) She did well in her exams. ◇ (AmE) She did well on her exams. ◇ A lot of students suffer from exam nerves. ◇ He's practising hard for his piano exam. **HELP** Use take/do/sit an exam not ~~write an exam~~.

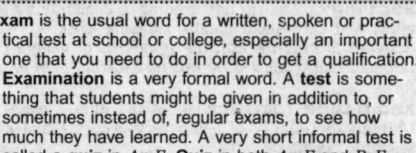

WHICH WORD?

exam / examination / test / quiz

Exam is the usual word for a written, spoken or practical test at school or college, especially an important one that you need to do in order to get a qualification. Examination is a very formal word. A test is something that students might be given in addition to, or sometimes instead of, regular exams, to see how much they have learned. A very short informal test is called a quiz in AmE. Quiz in both AmE and BrE also means a contest in which people try to answer questions: a trivia quiz ◇ a quiz show.

exam·in·a·tion /ɪɡˌzæmɪˈneɪʃn/ noun **1** [C] (formal) = EXAM: to sit an examination in mathematics ◇ successful candidates in GCSE examinations ◇ Applicants are selected for jobs on the results of a competitive examination. **HELP** Use take/do/sit an examination not ~~write an examination~~. **2** [U,C] the act of looking at or considering sth very carefully: Careful examination of the ruins revealed an even earlier temple. ◇ **On closer examination** it was found that the signature was not genuine. ◇ Your proposals are still **under examination**. ◇ The issue needs **further examination**. ◇ The chapter concludes with a brief examination of some of the factors causing family break-up. **3** [C] a close look at sth/sb, especially to see if there is anything wrong or to find the cause of a problem: a medical examination ◇ a post-mortem examination—see also CROSS-EXAMINATION

exam·ine /ɪɡˈzæmɪn/ verb **1** to consider or study an idea, a subject, etc. very carefully: [VN] These ideas will be examined in more detail in Chapter 10. ◇ [V wh-] It is necessary to examine how the proposals can be carried out. **2** [VN] ~ sth/sb (for sth) to look at sth/sb closely, to see if there is anything wrong or to find the cause of a problem: The goods were examined for damage on arrival. ◇ The doctor examined her but could find nothing wrong. **3** [VN] ~ sb (in/on sth) (formal) to give sb a test to see how much they know about a subject or what they can do· The students will be examined in all subjects at the end of term. ◇ You are only being examined on this semester's work. **4** [VN] (law) to ask sb questions formally, especially in a court of law—see also CROSS-EXAMINE **IDM** see NEED v.

exam·in·er /ɪɡˈzæmɪnə(r)/ noun **1** a person who writes the questions for, or marks/grades, a test of knowledge or ability: The papers are sent to external examiners (= ones not connected with the students' school or college). **2** (especially AmE) a person who has the official duty to check that things are being done correctly and according to the rules of an organization; a person who officially examines sth—see also MEDICAL EXAMINER

ex·ample /ɪɡˈzɑːmpl; AmE -ˈzæmpl/ noun **1** ~ (of sth) something such as an object, a fact or a situation that shows, explains or supports what you say: Can you give me an example of what you mean? ◇ It is important to cite examples to support your argument. ◇ This dictionary has many examples of how words are used. ◇ Just to give you an example of his generosity—he gave me his old car and wouldn't take any money for it. **2** ~ (of sth) a thing that is typical of or represents a particular group or set: This is a good example of the artist's early work. ◇ It is a **perfect example** of a medieval castle. ◇ Japan is often quoted as the **prime example** of a modern industrial nation. ◇ It is a **classic example** of how not to design a new city centre. **3** ~ (to sb) a person or their behaviour that is thought to be a good model for others to copy: Her courage is an example to us all. ◇ He **sets an example** to the other students. ◇ She is a **shining example** of what people with disabilities can achieve. ◇ He is a captain who leads by

example. **4** a person's behaviour, either good or bad, that other people copy: It would be a mistake to **follow his example**. **IDM for example** (abbr. **e.g.**) used to emphasize sth that explains or supports what you are saying; used to give an example of what you are saying: There is a similar word in many languages, for example in French and Italian. ◇ The report is incomplete; it does not include sales in France, for example. ◇ It is possible to combine Computer Science with other subjects, for example Physics. **make an example of sb** to punish sb as a warning to others not to do the same thing

ex·as·per·ate /ɪɡˈzæspəreɪt; BrE also -ˈzɑːsp-/ verb [VN] to annoy or irritate sb very much: Her moods exasperated him. ▶ **ex·as·per·ation** /ɪɡˌzæspəˈreɪʃn; BrE also -ˈzɑːsp-/ noun [U]: He shook his head in exasperation. ◇ a groan/look/sigh of exasperation

ex·as·per·ated /ɪɡˈzæspəreɪtɪd; BrE also -ˈzɑːsp-/ adj. extremely annoyed, especially if you cannot do anything to improve the situation: 'Why won't you answer me?' he asked in an exasperated voice. ◇ She was becoming exasperated with all the questions they were asking.

ex·as·per·at·ing /ɪɡˈzæspəreɪtɪŋ; BrE also -ˈzɑːsp-/ adj. extremely annoying: He's the most difficult and exasperating man I know.

ex·cav·ate /ˈekskəveɪt/ verb [VN] **1** to dig in the ground to look for old buildings or objects that have been buried for a long time; to find sth by digging in this way: The site has been excavated by archaeologists. ◇ pottery and weapons excavated from the burial site **2** (formal) to make a hole, etc. in the ground by digging: The body was discovered when builders excavated the area.

ex·cav·ation /ˌekskəˈveɪʃn/ noun **1** [C, U] the activity of digging in the ground to look for old buildings or objects that have been buried for a long time: the recent excavations at Pompeii **2** [C, usually pl.] a place where people are digging to look for old buildings or objects: The excavations are open to the public. **3** [U] the act of digging, especially with a machine

ex·cav·ator /ˈekskəveɪtə(r)/ noun **1** a large machine that is used for digging and moving earth—picture at TRUCK **2** a person who digs in the ground to look for old buildings and objects

ex·ceed /ɪkˈsiːd/ verb [VN] (formal) **1** to be greater than a particular number or amount: The price will not exceed £100. ◇ His achievements have **exceeded expectations**. **2** to do more than the law or an order, etc. allows you to do: She was exceeding the speed limit (= driving faster than is allowed). ◇ The officers had exceeded their authority.—see also EXCESS

ex·ceed·ing·ly /ɪkˈsiːdɪŋli/ adv. (formal, becoming old-fashioned) extremely; very; very much

excel /ɪkˈsel/ verb (-ll-) **1** [V] ~ (in/at sth/at doing sth) to be very good at doing sth: She has always excelled in foreign languages. ◇ The team excels at turning defence into attack. ◇ As a child he excelled at music and art. **2** [VN] ~ yourself (BrE) to do extremely well and even better than you usually do: Rick's cooking was always good but this time he really excelled himself.

ex·cel·lence /ˈeksələns/ noun [U] ~ (in sth) the quality of being extremely good: a reputation for academic excellence ◇ The hospital is recognized as a **centre of excellence** in research and teaching.—see also PAR EXCELLENCE

Ex·cel·lency /ˈeksələnsi/ noun (His/Her/Your Excellency) (pl. -ies) a title used when talking to or about sb who has a very important official position, especially an AMBASSADOR: Good evening, your Excellency. ◇ their Excellencies the French and Spanish Ambassadors

ex·cel·lent /ˈeksələnt/ adj. **1** extremely good: an excellent meal ◇ excellent service ◇ At $300 the bike is excellent **value**. ◇ She speaks excellent French. ◇ (spoken) It was absolutely excellent. **2** used to show that you are very pleased about sth or that you approve of sth: You can all come? Excellent! ▶ **ex·cel·lent·ly** adv.

ex·cept /ɪkˈsept/ prep., conj., verb
■ prep. (also ex'cept for) used before you mention the only thing or person about which a statement is not true **SYN** APART FROM: We work every day except Sunday. ◇ They all

E

came except Matt. ◊ *I had nothing on except for my socks.*
⇨ note at BESIDES

■ *conj.* ~ (that ...) used before you mention sth that makes a statement not completely true SYN APART FROM THE FACT THAT: *I didn't tell him anything except that I needed the money.* ◊ *Our dresses were the same except mine was red.*

■ *verb* [VN] [usually passive] ~ sb/sth (from sth) (*written*) to not include sb/sth: *Children under five are excepted from the survey.* ◊ *The sanctions ban the sale of any products excepting medical supplies and food.* ◊ *Tours are arranged all year round (January excepted).* IDM see PRESENT *adj.*

ex·cep·tion /ɪkˈsepʃn/ *noun* **1** a person or a thing that is not included in a general statement: *Most of the buildings in the town are modern, but the church is an exception.* ◊ *With very few exceptions, private schools get the best exam results.* ◊ *Nobody had much money at the time and I was no exception.* **2** a thing that does not follow a rule: *Good writing is unfortunately the exception rather than the rule* (= it is unusual). ◊ *There are always a lot of exceptions to grammar rules.* IDM **the exception that proves the 'rule** people say that sth is the exception that proves the rule when they are stating sth that seems to be different from the normal situation, but they mean that the normal situation remains true in general: *Most electronics companies have not done well this year, but ours is the exception that proves the rule.* **make an ex'ception** to allow sb not to follow the usual rule on one occasion: *Children are not usually allowed in, but I'm prepared to make an exception in this case.* **take ex'ception to sth** to object strongly to sth; to be angry about sth: *I take great exception to the fact that you told my wife before you told me.* ◊ *No one could possibly take exception to his comments.* **with the ex'ception of** except; not including: *All his novels are set in Italy with the exception of his last.* **without ex'ception** used to emphasize that the statement you are making is always true and everyone or everything is included: *All students without exception must take the English examination.*

ex·cep·tion·al /ɪkˈsepʃənl/ *adj.* **1** unusually good: *At the age of five he showed exceptional talent as a musician.* ◊ *The quality of the recording is quite exceptional.* **2** very unusual: *This deadline will be extended only in exceptional circumstances.* OPP UNEXCEPTIONAL

ex·cep·tion·al·ly /ɪkˈsepʃənəli/ *adv.* **1** used before an adjective or adverb to emphasize how strong or unusual the quality is: *The weather, even for January, was exceptionally cold.* ◊ *I thought Bill played exceptionally well.* **2** only in unusual circumstances: *Exceptionally, students may be accepted without formal qualifications.*

ex·cerpt /ˈeksɜːpt; *AmE* -sɜːrpt/ *noun* ~ (from sth) a short piece of writing, music, film, etc. taken from a longer whole ▶ **ex·cerpt** *verb* [VN] ~ sth (from sth): *The document was excerpted from an unidentified FBI file.*

ex·cess *noun, adj.*

■ *noun* /ɪkˈses/ **1** [sing., U] ~ (of sth) more than is necessary, reasonable or acceptable: *Are you suffering from an excess of stress in your life?* ◊ *In an excess of enthusiasm I agreed to work late.* ◊ *You can throw away any excess.* ◊ *He started drinking to excess after losing his job.* ◊ *The increase will not be in excess of* (= more than) *two per cent.* **2** [C, U] an amount by which sth is larger than sth else: *We cover costs up to £600 and then you pay the excess.* **3** (excesses) [pl.] extreme behaviour that is unacceptable, illegal or immoral: *We need a free press to curb government excesses.*

■ *adj.* /ˈekses/ [only before noun] in addition to an amount that is necessary, usual or legal: *Excess food is stored as fat.* ◊ *Driving with excess alcohol in the blood is a serious offence.*

ˌexcess 'baggage *noun* [U] bags, cases, etc. taken on to a plane that weigh more than the amount each passenger is allowed to carry without paying extra

ex·ces·sive /ɪkˈsesɪv/ *adj.* greater than what seems reasonable or appropriate; extreme: *They complained about the excessive noise coming from the upstairs flat.* ◊ *The amounts she borrowed were not excessive.* ◊ *Excessive*

drinking can lead to stomach disorders. ▶ **ex·ces·sive·ly** *adv.*: *excessively high prices*

ex·change /ɪksˈtʃeɪndʒ/ *noun, verb*

■ *noun*

GIVING AND RECEIVING | **1** [C, U] an act of giving sth to sb or doing sth for sb and receiving sth in return: *The exchange of prisoners took place this morning.* ◊ *We need to promote an open exchange of ideas and information.* ◊ *an exchange of glances/insults* ◊ *an exchange of fire* (= between enemy soldiers) ◊ *I get you out of the country and you keep your mouth shut. Is that a fair exchange?* ◊ *Would you like my old TV in exchange for this camera?* ◊ *I'll type your report if you'll babysit in exchange.*—see also PART EXCHANGE

CONVERSATION/ARGUMENT | **2** [C] a conversation or an argument: *There was only time for a brief exchange.* ◊ *The Prime Minister was involved in a heated exchange with opposition MPs.*

OF MONEY | **3** [U] the process of changing an amount of one CURRENCY (= the money used in one country) for an equal value of another: *currency exchange facilities* ◊ *Where can I find the best exchange rate/rate of exchange?*—see also FOREIGN EXCHANGE

BETWEEN TWO COUNTRIES | **4** [C] an arrangement when two people or groups from different countries visit each other's homes or do each other's jobs for a short time: *Our school does an exchange with a school in France.* ◊ *Nick went on the French exchange.* ◊ *trade and cultural exchanges with China*

BUILDING | **5** (often **Exchange**) [C] (in compounds) a building where business people met in the past to buy and sell a particular type of goods: *the old Corn Exchange*—see also STOCK EXCHANGE

TELEPHONE | **6** [C] = TELEPHONE EXCHANGE

■ *verb* [VN]

GIVE AND RECEIVE | **1** ~ sth (with sb) to give sth to sb and at the same time receive the same type of thing from them: *to exchange ideas/news/information* ◊ *Juliet and David exchanged glances* (= they looked at each other). ◊ *I shook hands and exchanged a few words with the manager.* ◊ *The two men exchanged blows* (= hit each other). ◊ *Everyone in the group exchanged telephone numbers.*

MONEY/GOODS | **2** ~ **A for B** to give or return sth that you have and get sth different or better instead: *You can exchange your currency for dollars in the hotel.* ◊ *If it doesn't fit, take it back and the store will exchange it.*

CONTRACTS | **3** ~ **contracts** (*especially BrE*) to sign a contract with the person that you are buying sth from, especially a house or land

IDM see WORD *n.*

ex·change·able /ɪksˈtʃeɪndʒəbl/ *adj.* that can be exchanged: *These tokens are exchangeable for CDs and cassettes only.*

ex·chequer /ɪksˈtʃekə(r)/ *noun* [sing.] **1** (often **the Exchequer**) (in Britain) the government department that controls public money SYN TREASURY—see also CHANCELLOR OF THE EXCHEQUER **2** the public or national supply of money: *This resulted in a considerable loss to the exchequer.*

ex·cise¹ /ˈeksaɪz/ *noun* [U] a government tax on some goods made, sold or used within a country: *new excise duties on low-alcohol drinks* ◊ *a sharp increase in vehicle excise* ◊ *an excise officer* (= an official whose job is to collect excise)—compare CUSTOMS

ex·cise² /ɪkˈsaɪz/ *verb* [VN] ~ sth (from sth) (*formal*) to remove sth completely: *Certain passages were excised from the book.*

ex·ci·sion /ɪkˈsɪʒn/ *noun* [U, C] (*formal or technical*) the act of removing sth completely from sth; the thing removed

ex·cit·able /ɪkˈsaɪtəbl/ *adj.* (of people or animals) likely to become easily excited: *a class of excitable ten-year-olds* ▶ **ex·cit·abil·ity** /ɪkˌsaɪtəˈbɪləti/ *noun* [U]

ex·cite /ɪkˈsaɪt/ *verb* [VN] **1** to make sb feel very pleased, interested or enthusiastic, especially about sth that is going to happen: *The prospect of a year in India greatly excited her.* **2** to make sb nervous or upset and unable to

æ	ɑː	e	ɜː	ə	ɪ	iː	i	ɒ	ɔː	ʌ	ʊ	u	uː
cat	father	ten	bird	about	sit	see	many	got	saw	cup	put	actual	too

(BrE)

E

relax: *Don't excite yourself* (= keep calm). ◊ *Try not to excite your baby too much before bedtime.* **3 ~ sth (in sb)** to make sb feel a particular emotion or react in a particular way SYN AROUSE: *The European Parliament is not an institution which excites interest in voters.* ◊ *to excite attention/criticism/curiosity* ◊ *The news has certainly excited comment* (= made people talk about it). **4** to make sb feel sexual desire SYN AROUSE **5** (*formal*) to make a part of the body or part of a physical system more active SYN STIMULATE

ex·cit·ed /ɪkˈsaɪtɪd/ *adj.* **1 ~ (about/at/by sth)| ~ (to do sth)** feeling or showing happiness and enthusiasm: *The children were excited about opening their presents.* ◊ *I'm really excited at the prospect of working abroad.* ◊ *Don't get too excited by the sight of your name in print.* ◊ *He was very excited to be asked to play for Wales.* ◊ *The new restaurant is **nothing to get excited about*** (= not particularly good). ◊ *An excited crowd of people gathered around her.* ⇨ note at WORRIED **2** nervous or upset and unable to relax: *Some horses become excited when they're in traffic.* **3** feeling sexual desire ▶ **ex·cit·ed·ly** *adv.*: *She waved excitedly as the car approached.*

ex·cite·ment /ɪkˈsaɪtmənt/ *noun* **1** [U] the state of feeling excited: *The news caused great excitement among her friends.* ◊ *to feel a surge/thrill/shiver of excitement* ◊ *He was flushed **with excitement** at the thought.* ◊ *The dog leapt and wagged its tail **in excitement**.* ◊ *In her excitement she dropped her glass.* **2** [C] (*formal*) something that you find exciting: *The new job was not without its excitements.*

ex·cit·ing /ɪkˈsaɪtɪŋ/ *adj.* causing great interest or excitement: *one of the most exciting developments in biology in recent years* ◊ *They waited and waited for something exciting to happen.* ◊ *an exciting prospect/possibility* ◊ *an exciting story/discovery* ◊ *I still find the job exciting.* ▶ **ex·cit·ing·ly** *adv.*

ex·claim /ɪkˈskleɪm/ *verb* (*written*) to say sth suddenly and loudly, especially because of strong emotion or pain: [V speech] *'It isn't fair!', he exclaimed angrily.* ◊ [V] *She opened her eyes and exclaimed in delight at the scene.* [also V that]

ex·clam·ation /ˌekskləˈmeɪʃn/ *noun* a short sound, word or phrase spoken suddenly to express an emotion. *Oh!, Look out!* and *Ow!* are exclamations: *He gave an exclamation of surprise.*

excla'mation mark (*especially BrE*) (*AmE usually* **excla'mation point**) *noun* the mark (!) that is written after an exclamation ⇨ Appendix 4

ex·clude /ɪkˈskluːd/ *verb* [VN] **1 ~ sth (from sth)** to deliberately not include sth in what you are doing or considering: *The cost of borrowing has been excluded from the inflation figures.* ◊ *Try excluding sugar and fat from your diet.* ◊ *Buses run every hour, Sundays excluded.* OPP INCLUDE **2 ~ sb/sth (from sth)** to prevent sb/sth from entering a place or taking part in sth: *Women are still excluded from some London clubs.* ◊ (*BrE*) *Concern is growing over the number of children excluded from school* (= forbidden to attend because of bad behaviour). ◊ *She felt excluded by the other girls* (= they did not let her join in what they were doing). **3** to decide that sth is not possible: *We should not **exclude the possibility** of negotiation.* ◊ *The police have excluded theft as a motive for the murder.*

ex·clud·ing /ɪkˈskluːdɪŋ/ *prep.* not including: *Lunch costs £10 per person, excluding drinks.*

ex·clu·sion /ɪkˈskluːʒn/ *noun* **1** [U, C] **~ (of sb/sth) (from sth)** the act of excluding sb/sth; an example of this: *Exclusion of air creates a vacuum in the bottle.* ◊ *the exclusion of robbery as a motive* ◊ *Memories of the past filled her mind **to the exclusion** of all else.* ◊ (*BrE*) *the exclusion of disruptive students from school* ◊ (*BrE*) *Two exclusions from one school in the same week is unusual.* **2** [C] a person or thing that is excluded: *Check the list of exclusions in the insurance policy.* OPP INCLUSION

ex·clu·sion·ary /ɪkˈskluːʒənri/ *adj.* (*formal*) designed to prevent a particular person or group of people from taking part in sth or doing sth

ex'clusion zone *noun* an area where people are not allowed to enter because it is dangerous or is used for secret activities

ex·clu·sive /ɪkˈskluːsɪv/ *adj., noun*
■ *adj.* **1** only to be used by one particular person or group; only given to one particular person or group: *The hotel has exclusive access to the beach.* ◊ *exclusive rights to televise the World Cup* ◊ *His mother has told 'The Times' about his death in an exclusive interview* (= not given to any other newspaper). **2** (of a group, society, etc.) not very willing to allow new people to become members, especially if they are from a lower social class: *He belongs to an exclusive club.* **3** of a high quality and expensive and therefore not often bought or used by most people: *an exclusive hotel* ◊ *exclusive designer shops/clothes* **4** not able to exist or be a true statement at the same time as sth else: *The two options are not **mutually exclusive*** (= you can have them both). **5 ~ of sb/sth** not including sb/sth: *The price is for accommodation only, exclusive of meals.* OPP INCLUSIVE ▶ **ex·clu·sive·ly** *adv.*: *a charity that relies almost exclusively on voluntary contributions*
■ *noun* an item of news or a story about famous people that is published in only one newspaper or magazine

ex·clu·siv·ity /ˌekskluːˈsɪvəti/ (also **ex·clu·sive·ness** /ɪkˈskluːsɪvnəs/) *noun* [U] the quality of being exclusive: *The resort still preserves a feeling of exclusivity.* ◊ *a designer whose clothes have not lost their exclusiveness*

ex·com·mu·ni·cate /ˌekskəˈmjuːnɪkeɪt/ *verb* [VN] **~ sb (for sth)** to punish sb by officially stating that they can no longer be a member of a Christian Church, especially the Roman Catholic Church ▶ **ex·com·mu·ni·ca·tion** /ˌekskəˌmjuːnɪˈkeɪʃn/ *noun* [U, C]

ex·cori·ate /ˌeksˈkɔːrieɪt/ *verb* [VN] **1** (*medical*) to irritate a person's skin so that it starts to come off **2** (*rare, formal*) to criticize sb/sth severely ▶ **ex·cori·ation** *noun* [U, C]

ex·cre·ment /ˈekskrɪmənt/ *noun* [U] (*formal*) solid waste matter that is passed from the body through the bowels SYN FAECES: *the pollution of drinking water by untreated human excrement* ▶ **ex·cre·men·tal** *adj.*

ex·cres·cence /ɪkˈskresns/ *noun* (*formal*) an ugly lump that has grown on a part of an animal's body or on a plant: (*figurative*) *The new office block is an excrescence* (= it is very ugly).

ex·creta /ɪkˈskriːtə/ *noun* [U] (*formal*) solid and liquid waste matter passed from the body: *human excreta*

ex·crete /ɪkˈskriːt/ *verb* [V] (*technical*) to pass solid or liquid waste matter from the body ▶ **ex·cre·tion** /ɪkˈskriːʃn/ *noun* [U, C]

ex·cru·ci·at·ing /ɪkˈskruːʃieɪtɪŋ/ *adj.* extremely painful: *The pain in my back was excruciating.* ◊ *She groaned at the memory, suffering all over again the excruciating embarrassment of those moments.* ▶ **ex·cru·ci·at·ing·ly** *adv.*: *excruciatingly uncomfortable* ◊ *excruciatingly painful/boring/embarrassing*

ex·cul·pate /ˈekskʌlpeɪt/ *verb* [VN] (*formal*) to prove or state officially that sb is not guilty of sth ▶ **ex·cul·pa·tion** *noun* [U]

ex·cur·sion /ɪkˈskɜːʃn; *AmE* ɪkˈskɜːrʒn/ *noun* **1** a short journey made for pleasure, especially one that has been organized for a group of people: *They've gone **on an excursion** to York.* **2 ~ into sth** (*formal*) a short period of trying a new or different activity: *After a brief excursion into drama, he concentrated on his main interest, which was poetry.*

ex·cus·able /ɪkˈskjuːzəbl/ *adj.* [not usually before noun] that can be excused: *Doing it once was just about excusable—doing it twice was certainly not.* OPP INEXCUSABLE

ex·cuse *noun, verb*
■ *noun* /ɪkˈskjuːs/ **1 ~ (for sth/for doing sth)** a reason, either true or invented, that you give to explain or defend your behaviour: *Late again! What's your excuse this time?* ◊ *There's **no excuse** for such behaviour.* ◊ *His excuse for forgetting her birthday was that he had lost his diary.* ◊ *You don't have to **make excuses** for her* (= try to think of reasons for her behaviour). ◊ *It's late. I'm afraid I'll have to **make my excuses*** (= say I'm sorry, give my reasons

and leave). ⇨ note at REASON **2 ~ (for sth/for doing sth)|
~ (to do sth)** a good reason that you give for doing sth
that you want to do for other reasons: *It's just an excuse
for a party.* ◊ *It gave me an excuse to take the car.* **3** a very
bad example of sth: *Why get involved with that pathetic
excuse for a human being?* **4** (*AmE*) a note written by a
doctor or parent to explain why a student cannot go to
school

■ *verb* /ɪkˈskjuːz/ **1 ~ sth| ~ sb (for sth/for doing sth)** to
forgive sb for sth that they have done, for example not
being polite or making a small mistake: [VN] *Please excuse
the mess.* ◊ *I hope you'll excuse me for being so late.* ◊ *You
must excuse my father—he's not always that rude.* ◊ (*BrE*)
You might be excused for thinking that Ben is in charge
(= he is not, but it is an easy mistake to make). ◊ [VN-ing]
(*formal*) *Excuse my interrupting you.* **2** [VN] **~ sth| ~ sb/
yourself (for sth/for doing sth)** to make your or sb else's
behaviour seem less offensive by finding reasons for it
[SYN] JUSTIFY: *Nothing can excuse such rudeness.* **3** [VN] **~
sb/yourself (from sth)** to allow sb to leave; to say in a
polite way that you are leaving: *Now if you'll excuse me,
I'm a very busy man.* ◊ *She excused herself and left the
meeting early.* **4 ~ sb (from sth/from doing sth)** [usually
passive] to allow sb to not do sth that they should normally do: [VN] *She was excused from giving evidence
because of her age.* [also VNN] **IDM** **ex'cuse me 1** used to
politely get sb's attention, especially sb you do not know:
Excuse me, is this the way to the station? **2** used to politely
ask sb to move so that you can get past them: *Excuse me,
could you let me through?* **3** used to say that you are sorry
for interrupting sb or behaving in a slightly rude way:
Guy sneezed loudly. 'Excuse me,' he said. **4** used to disagree politely with sb: *Excuse me, but I don't think that's
true.* **5** used to politely tell sb that you are going to leave
or talk to sb else: *'Excuse me for a moment,' she said and
left the room.* **6** (*especially AmE*) used to say sorry for
pushing sb or doing sth wrong: *Oh, excuse me. I didn't see
you there.* **7 (excuse me?)** (*AmE*) used when you did not
hear what sb said and you want them to repeat it

ex-di'rectory *adj.* (*BrE*) (of a person or telephone number) not listed in the public telephone book, at the
request of the owner of the telephone. The telephone
company will not give ex-directory numbers to people
who ask for them: *an ex-directory number* ◊ *She's ex-
directory.*—see also UNLISTED

exec /ɪgˈzek/ *noun* (*informal*) an EXECUTIVE in a business:
The role of the chief exec is to empower the team.

exe-crable /ˈeksɪkrəbl/ *adj.* (*formal*) very bad [SYN] TER-
RIBLE: *execrable poetry*

exe-cute /ˈeksɪkjuːt/ *verb* [VN] **1** [usually passive] **~ sb
(for sth)** to kill sb, especially as a legal punishment: *He
was executed for treason.* ◊ *The prisoners were executed
by firing squad.* **2** (*formal*) to do a piece of work, perform
a duty, put a plan into action, etc: *They drew up and
executed a plan to reduce fuel consumption.* ◊ *The crime
was very cleverly executed.* ◊ *Check that the computer has
executed your commands.* **3** (*formal*) to successfully perform a skilful action or movement: *The pilot executed a
perfect landing.* **4** (*formal*) to make or produce a work of
art: *Picasso also executed several landscapes at Horta de
San Juan.* **5** (*law*) to follow the instructions in a legal
document; to make a document legally valid: *His will was
executed by his lawyers in 1978.*

exe-cu-tion /ˌeksɪˈkjuːʃn/ *noun* **1** [U, C] the act of killing
sb, especially as a legal punishment: *He faced execution by
hanging for murder.* ◊ *Over 200 executions were carried out
last year.* **2** [U] (*formal*) the act of doing a piece of work,
performing a duty, or putting a plan into action: *He had
failed in the execution of his duty.* ◊ *The idea was good, but
the execution was poor.* **3** [U] (*formal*) skill in performing
or making sth, such as a piece of music or work of art:
Her execution of the piano piece was perfect. **4** [U] (*law*) the
act of following the instructions in a legal document,
especially those in sb's WILL: *The solicitors are proceeding
with the execution of her mother's will.* **IDM** see STAY *n.*

exe-cu-tion-er /ˌeksɪˈkjuːʃənə(r)/ *noun* a public official
whose job is to execute criminals

ex-ecu-tive /ɪgˈzekjətɪv/ *noun, adj.*

■ *noun* **1** [C] a person who has an important job as a
manager of a company or an organization: *advertising/
business/sales executives* ◊ *a chief/senior/top executive in
a computer firm* **2** [C+sing./pl. *v.*] a group of people who
run a company or an organization: *The union's executive
has/have yet to reach a decision.* **3 (the executive)** [sing.+
sing./pl. *v.*] the part of a government responsible for
putting laws into effect—compare JUDICIARY, LEGISLATURE

■ *adj.* [only before noun] **1** connected with managing a
business or an organization, and with making plans and
decisions: *She has an executive position in a finance company.* ◊ *executive decisions/duties/jobs/positions* ◊ *the
executive dining room* **2** having the power to put important laws and decisions into effect: *executive authority* ◊ *an
executive board/body/committee/officer* ◊ *Executive power
is held by the president.* **3** expensive; for the use of sb who
is important: *an executive car* ◊ *an executive suite* (= in a
hotel) ◊ *an executive lounge* (= at an airport)

e,xecutive 'privilege *noun* [U] (in the US) the right of
the President and the executive part of the government to
keep official documents secret

ex-ecu-tor /ɪgˈzekjətə(r)/ *noun* (*technical*) a person,
bank, etc. that is chosen by sb who is making their WILL
to carry out the instructions in it

exe-gesis /ˌeksɪˈdʒiːsɪs/ *noun* [U, C] (*pl.* **exe-geses**
/-siːz/) (*formal*) the detailed explanation of a piece of
writing, especially religious writing

ex-em-plar /ɪgˈzemplɑː(r)/ *noun* (*formal*) a person or
thing that is a good or typical example of sth [SYN] MODEL

ex-em-plary /ɪgˈzempləri/ *adj.* **1** providing a good
example for people to copy: *Her behaviour was exemplary.*
◊ *a man of exemplary character* **2** [usually before noun]
(*law* or *formal*) (of punishment) severe; used especially as
a warning to others

ex-em-plify /ɪgˈzemplɪfaɪ/ *verb* (**ex-em-pli-fies, ex-em-
pli-fy-ing, ex-em-pli-fied, ex-em-pli-fied**) [VN] [often pas-
sive] (*formal*) **1** to be a typical example of sth: *Her early
work is exemplified in her book, 'A Study of Children's
Minds'.* ◊ *His food exemplifies Italian cooking at its best.*
2 to give an example in order to make sth clearer: *She
exemplified each of the points she was making with an
amusing anecdote.* ▶ **ex-em-pli-fi-ca-tion** /ɪgˌzem-
plɪfɪˈkeɪʃn/ *noun* [U, C]

ex-empt /ɪgˈzempt/ *adj., verb*

■ *adj.* [not before noun] **~ (from sth)** if sb/sth is exempt
from sth, they are not affected by it, do not have to do it,
pay it, etc: *The interest on the money is exempt from tax.* ◊
Some students are exempt from certain exams. ▶ **-exempt**
(in compounds, forming adjectives): *tax-exempt donations
to charity*

■ *verb* [VN] **~ sb/sth (from sth)** (*formal*) to give or get sb's
official permission not to do sth or not to pay sth they
would normally have to do or pay: *His bad eyesight
exempted him from military service.* ◊ *In 1983, charities
were exempted from paying the tax.*

ex-emp-tion /ɪgˈzempʃn/ *noun* **1** [U, C] **~ (from sth)**
official permission not to do sth or pay sth that you
would normally have to do or pay: *She was given exemp-
tion from the final examination.* **2** [C] a part of your
income that you do not have to pay tax on: *a tax exemp-
tion on money donated to charity*

ex-er-cise /ˈeksəsaɪz; *AmE* -sərs-/ *noun, verb*

■ *noun*

ACTIVITY/MOVEMENTS | **1** [U] physical or mental activity that
you do to stay healthy or become stronger: *Swimming is
good exercise.* ◊ *I don't get much exercise sitting in the
office all day.* ◊ *The mind needs exercise as well as the
body.* ◊ *vigorous/gentle exercise* ◊ (*BrE*) *to take exercise*
2 [C] a set of movements or activities that you do to stay
healthy or develop a skill: *breathing/relaxation/stretch-
ing exercises* ◊ *exercises for the piano* ◊ *Repeat the exercise
ten times on each leg.*

QUESTIONS | **3** [C] a set of questions in a book that tests
your knowledge or practises a skill: *grammar exercises* ◊
Do exercise one for homework.

USE OF POWER/RIGHT/QUALITY | **4** [U] **~ of sth** the use of
power, a skill, a quality or a right to make sth happen:

b	d	f	g	h	k	l	m	n	p	r
bad	did	fall	get	hat	cat	leg	man	now	pen	red

the exercise of power/authority by the government ◇ the exercise of patience/discretion/judgement

FOR PARTICULAR RESULT | **5** [C] ~ (**in sth**) an activity that is designed to achieve a particular result: *an exercise in public relations* ◇ *Staying calm was an exercise in self-control.* ◇ *a communications exercise* ◇ *In the end it proved a pointless exercise.*

FOR SOLDIERS | **6** [C, usually pl.] a set of activities or movements for training soldiers: *military exercises*

CEREMONIES | **7** (**exercises**) [pl.] (*AmE*) ceremonies: *college graduation exercises*

■ *verb*

USE POWER/RIGHT/QUALITY | **1** [VN] (*formal*) to use your power, rights or personal qualities in order to achieve sth: *When she appeared in court she exercised her right to remain silent.* ◇ *He was a man who exercised considerable influence over people.*

DO PHYSICAL ACTIVITY | **2** to do sports or other physical activities in order to stay healthy or become stronger; to make an animal do this: [V] *an hour's class of exercising to music* ◇ *How often do you exercise?* ◇ [VN] *Horses need to be exercised regularly.* **3** [VN] to give a part of the body the movement and activity it needs to keep strong and healthy: *These movements will exercise your arms and shoulders.*

BE ANXIOUS | **4** [VN] [usually passive] ~ **sb/sth** (**about sth**) (*formal*) if sb is **exercised** about sth, they are very anxious about it

'exercise bike *noun* a bicycle that does not move forward but is used for getting exercise indoors

'exercise book *noun* **1** (*BrE*) (*AmE* **note·book**) a small book for students to write their work in **2** (*AmE*) = WORK-BOOK

exert /ɪgˈzɜːt; *AmE* ɪgˈzɜːrt/ *verb* [VN] **1** to use power or influence to affect sb/sth: *He exerted all his authority to make them accept the plan.* ◇ *The moon exerts a force on the earth that causes the tides.* **2** ~ **yourself** to make a big effort: *In order to be successful he would have to exert himself.*

ex·er·tion /ɪgˈzɜːʃn; *AmE* -ˈzɜːrʃ-/ *noun* **1** [U] (also **ex·er·tions** [pl.]) physical or mental effort; the act of making an effort: *She was hot and breathless from the exertion of cycling uphill.* ◇ *He needed to relax after the exertions of a busy day at work.* **2** [sing.] the use of power to make sth happen: *the exertion of force/strength/authority*

exe·unt /ˈeksiʌnt/ *verb* [V] (from *Latin*) used in a play as a written instruction that tells two or more actors to leave the stage: *Exeunt Antony and Cleopatra.*—compare EXIT

ex·foli·ate /eksˈfəʊlieɪt; *AmE* -ˈfoʊ-/ *verb* [V, VN] to remove rough or dead cells from the surface of skin in order to make your skin smoother ▶ **ex·foli·ation** *noun* [U]

ex gra·tia /ˌeks ˈgreɪʃə/ *adj.* (*written*, from *Latin*) given or done as a gift or favour, not because there is a legal duty to do it: *ex gratia payments* ▶ **ex gra·tia** *adv.*: *The sum was paid ex gratia.*

ex·hale /eksˈheɪl/ *verb* to breathe out the air or smoke, etc. in your lungs: [V] *He sat back and exhaled deeply.* ◇ [VN] *She exhaled the smoke through her nose.* OPP INHALE ▶ **ex·hal·ation** /ˌekshəˈleɪʃn/ *noun* [U, C]

ex·haust /ɪgˈzɔːst/ *noun, verb*

■ *noun* **1** [U] waste gases that come out of a vehicle, an engine or a machine: *car exhaust fumes/emissions* **2** (also **ex'haust pipe**) (also **tail·pipe** especially in *AmE*) [C] a pipe through which exhaust gases come out: *My car needs a new exhaust.*—picture at CAR

■ *verb* [VN] **1** to make you feel very tired: *Even a short walk exhausted her.* ◇ *There's no need to exhaust yourself clearing up—we'll do it.* **2** to use all of sth so that there is none left: *Within three days they had exhausted their supply of food.* ◇ *Don't give up until you have exhausted all the possibilities.* **3** to talk about or study a subject until there is nothing else to say about it: *I think we've exhausted that particular topic.*

ex·haust·ed /ɪgˈzɔːstɪd/ *adj.* **1** very tired: *I'm exhausted!* ◇

◇ *to feel completely/utterly exhausted* ◇ *The exhausted climbers were rescued by helicopter.* **2** completely used or finished: *You cannot grow crops on exhausted land.*

ex·haust·ing /ɪgˈzɔːstɪŋ/ *adj.* making you feel very tired: *an exhausting day at work* ◇ *I find her exhausting—she never stops talking.*

ex·haus·tion /ɪgˈzɔːstʃən/ *noun* [U] **1** the state of being very tired: *suffering from physical/mental/nervous exhaustion* ◇ *Her face was grey with exhaustion.* **2** (*formal*) the act of using sth until it is completely finished: *the exhaustion of natural resources*

ex·haust·ive /ɪgˈzɔːstɪv/ *adj.* very thorough; looking at every detail: *exhaustive research/tests* ◇ *an exhaustive study of sth* ▶ **ex·haust·ive·iy** *adv.*: *Every product is exhaustively tested before being sold.*

ex'haust pipe *noun* = EXHAUST

ex·hibit /ɪgˈzɪbɪt/ *verb, noun*

■ *verb* **1** ~ (**sth**) (**at/in …**) to show sth in a public place for people to enjoy or to give them information: [VN] *They will be exhibiting their new designs at the trade fairs this spring.* ◇ [V] *He exhibits regularly in several local art galleries.* **2** [VN] (*written*) to show clearly that you have or feel a particular feeling, quality or ability: *The patient exhibited signs of fatigue and memory loss.*

■ *noun* **1** an object or a work of art put in a public place, for example a museum, so that people can see it **2** a thing that is used in a court of law to prove that sb is guilty or not guilty: *The first exhibit was a knife which the prosecution claimed was the murder weapon.* **3** (*AmE*) = EXHIBITION (1): *The new exhibit will tour a dozen US cities next year.*

ex·hib·ition /ˌeksɪˈbɪʃn/ *noun* **1** (*especially BrE*) (*AmE* usually **ex·hibit**) [C] a collection of things, for example works of art, that are shown to the public: *Have you seen the Picasso exhibition?* ◇ *an exhibition of old photographs* **2** [U] ~ **of sth** the act of showing sth, for example works of art, to the public: *She refused to allow the exhibition of her husband's work.* **3** [sing.] **an** ~ **of sth** the act of showing a skill, a feeling, or a kind of behaviour: *We were treated to an exhibition of the footballer's speed and skill.* ◇ *an appalling exhibition of bad manners* **4** [C] (*BrE*) an amount of money that is given as a prize to a student IDM **make an exhi'bition of yourself** (*disapproving*) to behave in a bad or stupid way in public

ex·hib·ition·ism /ˌeksɪˈbɪʃənɪzəm/ *noun* [U] **1** (*disapproving*) behaviour that is intended to make people notice or admire you **2** (*psychology*) the mental condition that makes sb want to show their sexual organs in public

ex·hib·ition·ist /ˌeksɪˈbɪʃənɪst/ *noun* (usually *disapproving*) a person who likes to make other people notice him or her: *Children are natural exhibitionists.*

ex·hib·it·or /ɪgˈzɪbɪtə(r)/ *noun* a person or a company that shows their work or products to the public

ex·hil·ar·ate /ɪgˈzɪləreɪt/ *verb* [VN] to make sb feel very happy and excited: *Speed had always exhilarated him.* ▶ **ex·hil·ar·ated** *adj.*: *I felt exhilarated after a morning of skiing.* **ex·hil·ar·ation** /ɪgˌzɪləˈreɪʃn/ *noun* [U]: *the exhilaration of performing on stage*

ex·hil·ar·at·ing /ɪgˈzɪləreɪtɪŋ/ *adj.* very exciting and enjoyable: *My first parachute jump was an exhilarating experience.*

ex·hort /ɪgˈzɔːt; *AmE* ɪgˈzɔːrt/ *verb* ~ **sb** (**to sth/to do sth**) (*formal*) to try hard to persuade sb to do sth SYN URGE: [VN to inf] *The party leader exhorted his members to start preparing for government.* ◇ [VN] *They had been exhorted to action.* [also V speech, VN speech] ▶ **ex·hort·ation** /ˌegzɔːˈteɪʃn; *AmE* -zɔːrˈt-/ *noun* [C, U]

ex·hume /eksˈhjuːm; ɪgˈzjuːm; *AmE* ɪgˈzuːm/ *verb* [VN] [usually passive] (*formal*) to remove a dead body from the ground especially in order to examine how the person died: *The body was exhumed on the order of the judge.* ▶ **ex·hum·ation** /ˌekshjuːˈmeɪʃn/ *noun* [U]

exi·gency /ˈeksɪdʒənsi; ɪgˈzɪdʒ-/ *noun* [C, usually pl., U] (*pl.* **-ies**) (*formal*) an urgent need or demand that you must deal with: *the exigencies of war* ◇ *political/financial exigencies*

exile /ˈeksaɪl; ˈegzaɪl/ *noun, verb*

E

■ *noun* **1** [U, sing.] the state of being sent to live in another country that is not your own, especially for political reasons or as a punishment: *to be/live in exile* ◊ *to be forced/sent into exile* ◊ *to go into exile* ◊ *a place of exile* ◊ *He returned after 40 years of exile.* **2** [C] a person who chooses, or is forced to live away from his or her own country: *political exiles* ◊ *a tax exile* (= a rich person who moves to another country where taxes are lower)

■ *verb* [VN] [usually passive] ~ **sb** (**from ...**) to force sb to leave their country, especially for political reasons or as a punishment; to send sb into exile: *the party's exiled leaders* ◊ *an American, exiled from his homeland*

exist /ɪɡˈzɪst/ *verb* [V] **1** (not used in the progressive tenses) to be real; to be present in a place or situation: *Does life exist on other planets?* ◊ *The problem only exists in your head, Jane.* ◊ *Few of these monkeys still exist in the wild.* ◊ *A temple existed here hundreds of years ago.* **2** ~ (**on sth**) to live, especially in a difficult situation or with very little money: *We existed on a diet of rice and very little else.* ◊ *They can't exist on the money he's earning.*

ex·ist·ence /ɪɡˈzɪstəns/ *noun* **1** [U] the state or fact of being real or living: *I was unaware of his existence until today.* ◊ *This is the oldest Hebrew manuscript in existence.* ◊ *Pakistan came into existence as an independent country after the war.* ◊ *a crisis that threatens the industry's continued existence* **2** [C] a way of living especially when this is difficult or boring: *The family endured a miserable existence in a cramped and noisy apartment.* ◊ *We led a poor but happy enough existence as children.* ◊ *They eke out a precarious existence* (= they have hardly enough money to live on). ◊ *The peasants depend on a good harvest for their very existence* (= in order to continue to live).

ex·ist·ent /ɪɡˈzɪstənt/ *adj., noun*
■ *adj.* (*formal*) existing; real: *creatures existent in nature* OPP NON-EXISTENT
■ *noun* (*philosophy*) a thing that is real and exists: *The self is the only knowable existent.*

ex·ist·en·tial /ˌeɡzɪˈstenʃəl/ *adj.* [only before noun] **1** (*formal*) connected with human existence **2** (*philosophy*) connected with the theory of existentialism

ex·ist·en·tial·ism /ˌeɡzɪˈstenʃəlɪzəm/ *noun* [U] (*philosophy*) the theory that human beings are free and responsible for their own actions in a world without meaning ▶ **ex·ist·en·tial·ist** /-ʃəlɪst/ *noun*: *Sartre was an existentialist.* **ex·ist·en·tial·ist** *adj.*: *existentialist theory*

existing /ɪɡˈzɪstɪŋ/ *adj.* [only before noun] found or used now: *New laws will soon replace existing legislation.*

exit /ˈeksɪt; ˈeɡzɪt/ *noun, verb*
■ *noun* **1** a way out of a public building or vehicle: *Where's the exit?* ◊ *There is a fire exit on each floor of the building.* ◊ *The emergency exit is at the back of the bus.*—compare ENTRANCE **2** an act of leaving, especially of an actor from the stage: *The heroine made her exit to great applause.* ◊ *He made a quick exit to avoid meeting her.* ◊ *an exit visa* (= a stamp in a passport giving sb permission to leave a particular country) **3** a place where vehicles can leave a road to join another road: *Leave the roundabout at the second exit.* ◊ *Take the exit for Trento.*
■ *verb* **1** (*formal*) to go out; to leave a building, stage, vehicle, etc: [V] *The bullet entered her back and exited through her chest.* ◊ *We exited via a fire door.* ◊ [VN] *As the actors exited the stage the lights went on.* **2** to finish using a computer program: [V] *To exit from this page, press the return key.* ◊ [VN] *I exited the database and switched off the computer.* **3** [V] (**exit ...**) used in the instructions printed in a play to say that an actor must leave the stage: *Exit Macbeth*—compare EXEUNT

ˈ**exit poll** *noun* in an **exit poll** immediately after an election, people are asked how they voted, in order to predict the result of the election

exo·dus /ˈeksədəs/ *noun* [sing.] ~ (**from ...**) (**to ...**) (*formal* or *humorous*) a situation in which many people leave a place at the same time: *the mass exodus from Paris to the country in the summer*

ex of·fi·cio /ˌeks əˈfɪʃiəʊ; AmE -ˈfɪʃioʊ/ *adj.* (from *Latin, formal*) included or allowed because of your job, position

or rank: *an ex officio member of the committee* ▶ **ex of·fi·cio** *adv.*

ex·on·er·ate /ɪɡˈzɒnəreɪt; AmE -ˈzɑːn-/ *verb* [VN] ~ **sb** (**from sth**) (*formal*) to officially state that sb is not responsible for sth that they have been blamed for: *The police report exonerated Lewis from all charges of corruption.* ▶ **ex·on·er·ation** /ɪɡˌzɒnəˈreɪʃn; AmE -ˌzɑːnə-/ *noun* [U]

ex·or·bi·tant /ɪɡˈzɔːbɪtənt; AmE -ˈzɔːrb-/ *adj.* (*formal*) (of a price) much too high: *exorbitant costs/fares/fees/prices/rents* ▶ **ex·or·bi·tant·ly** *adv.*: *Prices are exorbitantly high in this shop.*

ex·or·cism /ˈeksɔːsɪzəm; AmE -sɔːrs-/ *noun* [U, C] **1** the act of getting rid of an evil spirit from a place or a person's body by prayers or magic; a ceremony where this is done **2** (*written*) the act of making yourself forget a bad experience or memory

ex·or·cist /ˈeksɔːsɪst; AmE -sɔːrs-/ *noun* a person who makes evil spirits leave a place or a person's body by prayers or magic

ex·or·cize (*BrE* also **-ise**) /ˈeksɔːsaɪz; AmE -sɔːrs-/ *verb* [VN] **1** ~ **sth** (**from sb/sth**) to make an evil spirit leave a place or sb's body by special prayers or magic: *The ghost was exorcized from the house.* **2** (*written*) to remove sth that is bad or painful from your mind: *She had managed to exorcize these unhappy memories from her mind.*

exot·ic /ɪɡˈzɒtɪk; AmE -ˈzɑːtɪk/ *adj.* from or in another country, especially a tropical one; seeming exciting and unusual because it is connected with foreign countries: *brightly-coloured exotic flowers/plants/birds* ◊ *She travels to all kinds of exotic locations all over the world.*

exot·ica /ɪɡˈzɒtɪkə; AmE ɪɡˈzɑːt-/ *noun* [U] unusual and exciting things, especially from other countries: *a sale of antiques and exotica*

ex·pand /ɪkˈspænd/ *verb* **1** to become greater in size, number or importance; to make sth greater in size, number or importance: [V] *Metals expand when they are heated.* ◊ *Student numbers are expanding rapidly.* ◊ *A child's vocabulary expands through reading.* ◊ *The waist expands to fit all sizes.* ◊ [VN] *In breathing the chest muscles expand the rib cage and allow air to be sucked into the lungs.* ◊ *The new system expanded the role of family doctors.* ◊ *There are no plans to expand the local airport.* OPP CONTRACT **2** if a business **expands** or is **expanded**, new branches are opened, it makes more money, etc: [VN] *We've expanded the business by opening two more stores.* ◊ [V] *an expanding economy* (= with more businesses starting and growing) **3** [V] to talk more; to add details to what you are saying: *I repeated the question and waited for her to expand.* PHR V **ex'pand on/upon sth** to say more about sth and add some details: *Could you expand on that point, please?*

ex·pand·able /ɪkˈspændəbl/ *adj.* ~ (**to sth**) (especially *technical*) that can be expanded: *an expandable briefcase* ◊ *The system is expandable to 16 processors, with a maximum of 512MB RAM.*

ex·panse /ɪkˈspæns/ *noun* ~ (**of sth**) a wide and open area of sth, especially land or water: *a wide/vast expanse of blue sky* ◊ *I looked out over flat expanses of open farmland.*

ex·pan·sion /ɪkˈspænʃn/ *noun* [U, C] an act of increasing or making sth increase in size, amount or importance: *a period of rapid economic expansion* ◊ *Despite the recession the company is confident of further expansion.* ◊ *The book is an expansion of a series of lectures given last year.*

ex·pan·sion·ary /ɪkˈspænʃənri/ *adj.* (*formal*) encouraging economic expansion: *This budget will have a net expansionary effect on the economy.*

ex·pan·sion·ism /ɪkˈspænʃənɪzəm/ *noun* [U] (sometimes *disapproving*) the belief in and process of increasing the size and importance of sth, especially in a country or a business: *the economic expansionism of Europe and America* ◊ *military/territorial expansionism* ▶ **ex·pan·sion·ist** /-ʃənɪst/ *adj.*: *expansionist policies* ◊ *an expansionist state* **ex·pan·sion·ist** *noun*: *He was a ruthless expansionist.*

ex·pan·sive /ɪkˈspænsɪv/ *adj.* **1** covering a large

æ	ɑː	e	ɜː	ə	ɪ	iː	i	ɒ	ɔː	ʌ	ʊ	u	uː
cat	father	ten	bird	about	sit	see	many	got	saw	cup	put	actual	too
								(BrE)					

amount of space: *She opened her arms wide in an expansive gesture of welcome.* ◊ *landscape with expansive skies* **2** covering a large subject area, rather than trying to be exact and use few words: *We need to look at a more expansive definition of the term.* ◊ *The piece is written in his usual expansive style.* **3** friendly and willing to talk a lot: *She was clearly relaxed and in an expansive mood.* **4** (especially of a period of time) encouraging economic EXPANSION: *In the expansive 1960s bright graduates could advance rapidly.* ► **ex·pan·sive·ly** *adv.*: *He waved his arms expansively.* **ex·pan·sive·ness** *noun* [U]

ex·pati·ate /ɪkˈspeɪʃieɪt/ *verb* PHRV **exˈpatiate on/ upon sth** (*rare, formal*) to write or speak in detail about a subject

ex·patri·ate /ˌeksˈpætriət; *AmE* -ˈpeɪt-/ (also *informal* **expat**) *noun* a person living in a country that is not their own: *American expatriates in Paris* ► **ex·patri·ate** *adj.* [only before noun]: *expatriate Britons in Spain* ◊ *expatriate workers*

ex·pect /ɪkˈspekt/ *verb* **1** to think or believe that sth will happen or that sb will do sth: [VN] *We are expecting a rise in food prices this month.* ◊ *Don't expect sympathy from me!* ◊ *That's not the sort of behaviour I expect of you!* ◊ *Double the expected number of people came to the meeting.* ◊ [V to inf] *You can't expect to learn a foreign language in a few months.* ◊ *I looked back, half expecting to see someone following me.* ◊ [VN to inf] *House prices are expected to rise sharply.* ◊ *I didn't expect him to become a successful writer.* ◊ *Do you really expect me to believe you?* ◊ [V (that)] *Many people were expecting (that) the peace talks would break down.* ◊ [VN that] *It is expected that the report will suggest some major reforms.* **2** (often used in the progressive tenses) to be waiting for sb/sth to arrive, as this has been arranged: [VN] *to expect a visit/call/letter from sb* ◊ *Are you expecting visitors?* ◊ [VN, VN to inf] *We were expecting him yesterday.* ◊ *We were expecting him to arrive yesterday.* **3 ~ sth (of/from sb)** to demand that sb will do sth because it is their duty or responsibility: [VN] *Her parents expected high standards from her.* ◊ *Are you clear what is expected of you?* ◊ *He's still getting over his illness, so don't expect too much from him.* ◊ [VN to inf] *They expected all their children to be high achievers.* ◊ *We are expected to work on Saturdays.* ◊ [V to inf] *I expect to be paid promptly for the work.* [also V that] **4** (*informal, especially BrE*) (not used in the progressive tenses) used when you think sth is probably true: [V] *'Will you be late?' 'I expect so.'* ◊ *'Are you going out tonight?' 'I don't expect so.'* ◊ [V, V (that)] *'Who's eaten all the cake?' 'Tom, I expect/I expect it was Tom.'* HELP 'That' is nearly always left out.—compare UNEXPECTED IDM **be expecting a baby/child** (*informal*) to be pregnant: *Ann's expecting a baby in June.* **be (only) to be exˈpected** to be likely to happen; to be quite normal: *A little tiredness after taking these drugs is to be expected.* **what (else) do you exˈpect?** (*spoken*) used to tell sb not to be surprised by sth: *She swore at you? What do you expect when you treat her like that?*

ex·pect·ancy /ɪkˈspektənsi/ *noun* [U] the state of expecting or hoping that sth, especially sth good or exciting, will happen: *There was an air of expectancy among the waiting crowd.*—see also LIFE EXPECTANCY

ex·pect·ant /ɪkˈspektənt/ *adj.* **1** hoping for sth, especially sth good and exciting: *children with expectant faces waiting for the fireworks to begin* ◊ *A sudden roar came from the expectant crowd.* **2 ~ mother/father/parent** used to describe sb who is going to have a baby soon or become a father ► **ex·pect·ant·ly** *adv.*: *She looked at him expectantly.* ◊ *waiting expectantly*

ex·pect·ation /ˌekspekˈteɪʃn/ *noun* **1** [U, C] **~ (of sth)| ~ (that...)** a belief that sth will happen because it is likely: *We are confident in our expectation of a full recovery.* ◊ *There was a general expectation that he would win.* ◊ *I applied for the post more in hope than expectation.* ◊ *The expectation is that property prices will rise.* ◊ **Contrary to expectations**, *interest rates did not rise.* ◊ **Against all expectations**, *she was enjoying herself.* **2** [C, usually pl., U] a hope that sth good will happen: *She went to college with great expectations.* ◊ *There was an air of expectation and great curiosity.* ◊ *The results exceeded our expect-*

ations. ◊ *The numbers attending fell short of expectations.* ◊ *The event did not live up to expectations.* **3** [C, usually pl.] a strong belief about the way sth should happen or how sb should behave: *Some parents have unrealistic expectations of their children.* ◊ *Unfortunately the new software has failed to meet expectations.*

expectation of ˈlife *noun* [U] = LIFE EXPECTANCY

ex·pec·tor·ant /ɪkˈspektərənt/ *noun* (*medical*) a cough medicine that helps you to get rid of thick liquid (= PHLEGM) from the lungs

ex·pec·tor·ate /ɪkˈspektəreɪt/ *verb* [V] (*formal*) to cough and make PHLEGM come up from your lungs into your mouth so you can SPIT it out ► **ex·pec·tor·ation** /ɪkˌspektəˈreɪʃn/ *noun* [U]

ex·pe·di·ent /ɪkˈspiːdiənt/ *noun, adj.*
■ *noun* an action that is useful or necessary for a particular purpose, but not always fair or right: *The disease was controlled by the simple expedient of not allowing anyone to leave the city.*
■ *adj.* [not usually before noun] (of an action) useful or necessary for a particular purpose, but not always fair or right: *The government has clearly decided that a cut in interest rates would be politically expedient.* ► **ex·pe·di·ency** /-ənsi/ *noun* [U]: *He acted out of expediency, not principle.*

ex·ped·ite /ˈekspədaɪt/ *verb* [VN] (*formal*) to make a process happen more quickly SYN SPEED UP: *We have developed rapid order processing to expedite deliveries to customers.*

ex·ped·ition /ˌekspəˈdɪʃn/ *noun* **1** an organized journey with a particular purpose, especially to find out about a place that is not well known: *to plan/lead/go on an expedition to the North Pole* ◊ *a military/scientific expedition* **2** the people who go on an expedition: *Three members of the Everest expedition were killed.* **3** (sometimes *humorous*) a short trip that you make when you want or need sth: *a shopping/fishing expedition*

ex·ped·ition·ary force /ˌekspəˈdɪʃənri fɔːs; *AmE* -neri fɔːrs/ *noun* a group of soldiers who are sent to another country to fight in a war

ex·ped·itious /ˌekspəˈdɪʃəs/ *adj.* (*formal*) that works well without wasting time, money, etc. SYN EFFICIENT ► **ex·ped·itious·ly** *adv.*: *The work was carried out as expeditiously as possible.*

ex·pel /ɪkˈspel/ *verb* (-ll-) [VN] **~ sb/sth (from sth)** **1** to officially make sb leave a school or an organization: *She was expelled from school at 15.* ◊ *Olympic athletes expelled for drug-taking* **2** to force sb to leave a country: *Foreign journalists are being expelled.* **3** (*technical*) to force air or water out of a part of the body or from a container: *to expel air from the lungs*—see also EXPULSION

ex·pend /ɪkˈspend/ *verb* [VN] **~ sth (in/on sth)| ~ sth (in/**

on/doing sth) (*formal*) to use or spend a lot of time, money, energy, etc: *She expended all her efforts on the care of home and children.* ◊ *Smith had expended large sums in pursuing his claim through the court.*

ex·pend·able /ɪkˈspendəbl/ *adj.* (*formal*) if you consider people or things to be **expendable**, you think that you can get rid of them when they are no longer needed, or think it is acceptable if they are killed or destroyed

ex·pend·iture /ɪkˈspendɪtʃə(r)/ *noun* [U, C] **1** the act of spending or using money; an amount of money spent: *a reduction in public/government/military expenditure* ◊ *plans to increase expenditure on health and education* ◊ *The budget provided for a total expenditure of £27 billion.* **2** the use of energy, time, materials, etc: *the expenditure of emotion* ◊ *This study represents a major expenditure of time and effort.*—compare INCOME

ex·pense /ɪkˈspens/ *noun* **1** [U] the money that you spend on sth: *The garden was transformed at great expense.* ◊ *No expense was spared* (= they spent as much money as was needed) *to make the party a success.* ◊ *He's arranged everything, no expense spared.* ◊ *She always travels first-class regardless of expense.* ◊ *The results are well worth the expense.* **2** [C, usually sing.] something that makes you spend money: *Running a car is a big expense.* **3** (**expenses**) [pl.] money spent in doing a particular job, or for a particular purpose: *living/household/medical/legal expenses* ◊ *Can I give you something towards expenses?* ◊ *financial help to meet the expenses of an emergency* ◊ *The payments he gets barely cover his expenses.* **4** (**expenses**) [pl.] money that you spend while you are working that your employer will pay back to you later: *You can claim back your travelling/travel expenses.* ◊ (*BrE*) *to take a client out for a meal on expenses* ◊ *an all-expenses-paid trip* **IDM** **at sb's expense 1** paid for by sb: *We were taken out for a meal at the company's expense.* **2** if you make a joke **at sb's expense**, you laugh at them and make them feel silly **at the expense of sb/sth** with loss or damage to sb/sth: *He built up the business at the expense of his health.* **go to the expense of sth/of doing sth | go to a lot of, etc. expense** to spend money on sth: *They went to all the expense of redecorating the house and then they moved.* **put sb to the expense of sth/of doing sth | put sb to a lot of, etc. expense** to make sb spend money on sth: *Their visit put us to a lot of expense.*—more at OBJECT *n.*

ex·pense account *noun* an arrangement by which money spent by sb while they are at work is later paid back to them by their employer; a record of money spent in this way: *Put the cost of the train fare on your expense account.*

ex·pen·sive /ɪkˈspensɪv/ *adj.* costing a lot of money: *an expensive car/restaurant/holiday* ◊ *Art books are expensive to produce.* ◊ *I can't afford it, it's too expensive.* ◊ *Making the wrong decision could prove expensive.* OPP INEXPENSIVE ▶ **ex·pen·sive·ly** *adv.*: *expensively dressed/furnished* ◊ *There are other restaurants where you can eat less expensively.*

ex·peri·ence /ɪkˈspɪəriəns; *AmE* -ˈspɪr-/ *noun, verb*
■ *noun* **1** [U] the knowledge and skill that you have gained through doing sth for a period of time; the process of gaining this: *to have over ten years' teaching experience* ◊ *Do you have any previous experience of this type of work?* ◊ *a doctor with experience in dealing with patients suffering from stress* ◊ *My lack of practical experience was a disadvantage.* ◊ *She didn't get paid much but it was all good experience.* ◊ *He gained valuable experience whilst working on the project.* ◊ *We all learn by experience.*—see also WORK EXPERIENCE **2** [U] the things that have happened to you that influence the way you think and behave: *Experience has taught me that life can be very unfair.* ◊ *It is important to try and learn from experience.* ◊ *In my experience, very few people really understand the problem.* ◊ *She knew from past experience that Ann would not give up easily.* ◊ *The book is based on personal experience.* ◊ *direct/first-hand experience of poverty* **3** [C] ~ (of sth) an event or activity that affects you in some way: *an enjoyable/exciting/unusual/unforgettable experience* ◊ *It was her first experience of living alone.* ◊

Living in Africa was very different from home and quite an experience (= unusual for us). ◊ *I had a bad experience with fireworks once.* ◊ *He seems to have had some sort of religious experience.* **4** (**the … experience**) [sing.] events or knowledge shared by all the members of a particular group in society, that influences the way they think and behave: *musical forms like jazz that emerged out of the Black American experience* **IDM** see CHALK *v.*
■ *verb* [VN] **1** to have a particular situation affect you or happen to you: *The country experienced a foreign currency shortage for several months.* ◊ *Everyone experiences these problems at some time in their lives.* **2** to have and be aware of a particular emotion or physical feeling: *to experience pain/pleasure/unhappiness* ◊ *I experienced a moment of panic as I boarded the plane.*

ex·peri·enced /ɪkˈspɪəriənst; *AmE* -ˈspɪr-/ *adj.* **1** ~ (in sth) having knowledge or skill in a particular job or activity: *an experienced teacher* ◊ *He's very experienced in looking after animals.* **2** having knowledge as a result of doing sth for a long time, or having had a lot of different experiences: *She's very young and not very experienced.* ◊ *an experienced traveller* (= sb who has travelled a lot)

ex·peri·en·tial /ɪkˌspɪəriˈenʃl; *AmE* -ˌspɪr-/ *adj.* (*formal or technical*) based on or involving experience: *experiential knowledge* ◊ *experiential learning methods*

ex·peri·ment /ɪkˈsperɪmənt/ *noun, verb*
■ *noun* [C, U] **1** a scientific test that is carried out in order to study what happens and to gain new knowledge: *to do/perform/carry out/conduct an experiment* ◊ *proved/shown by experiment* ◊ *laboratory experiments* ◊ *Many people do not like the idea of experiments on animals.* **2** ~ (in sth) a new activity, idea or method that you try out to see what happens or what effect it has: *the country's brief experiment in democracy* ◊ *I've never cooked this before so it's an experiment.*
■ *verb* [V] ~ (on sb/sth)| ~ (with sth) **1** to carry out a scientific experiment or experiments: *Some people feel that experimenting on animals causes unnecessary suffering.* **2** to try or test new ideas, methods, etc. to find out what effect they have: *He wanted to experiment more with different textures in his paintings.* ◊ *I experimented until I got the recipe just right.* ▶ **ex·peri·ment·er** *noun*

ex·peri·men·tal /ɪkˌsperɪˈmentl/ *adj.* **1** based on new ideas, forms or methods that are used to find out what effect they have: *experimental teaching methods* ◊ *experimental theatre/art/music* ◊ *The equipment is still at the experimental stage.* **2** connected with scientific experiments: *experimental conditions/data/evidence* ▶ **ex·peri·men·tal·ly** /-təli/ *adv.*: *This theory can be confirmed experimentally.* ◊ *The new drug is being used experimentally on some patients.* ◊ *He moved his shoulder experimentally to see if it still hurt.*

ex·peri·men·ta·tion /ɪkˌsperɪmenˈteɪʃn/ *noun* [U] (*formal*) the activity or process of EXPERIMENTING: *experimentation with new teaching methods* ◊ *Many people object to experimentation on embryos.*

ex·pert /ˈekspɜːt; *AmE* -pɜːrt/ *noun, adj.*
■ *noun* ~ (at/in/on sth)| ~ (at/in/on doing sth) a person with special knowledge, skill or training in sth: *a computer/medical expert* ◊ *an expert in child psychology* ◊ *an expert on modern literature* ◊ *He's an expert at getting his own way.* ◊ *Don't ask me—I'm no expert!*
■ *adj.* ~ (at/in sth)| ~ (at/in doing sth) done with, having or involving great knowledge or skill: *to seek expert advice/an expert opinion* ◊ *an expert gardener/driver* ◊ *We need some expert help.* ◊ *She's expert at making cheap, but stylish clothes.* ◊ *They are all expert in this field.*—compare INEXPERT ▶ **ex·pert·ly** *adv.*: *The roads were icy but she stopped the car expertly.* ◊ *The music was expertly performed.*

ex·pert·ise /ˌekspɜːˈtiːz; *AmE* -pɜːrˈt-/ *noun* [U] ~ (in sth/in doing sth) expert knowledge or skill in a particular subject, activity or job: *professional/scientific/technical expertise* ◊ *They have considerable expertise in dealing with oil spills.* ◊ *We have the expertise to help you run your business.*

b	d	f	g	h	k	l	m	n	p	r
bad	did	fall	get	hat	cat	leg	man	now	pen	red

,**expert 'system** noun (computing) a computer system that can provide information and expert advice on a particular subject. The program asks users a series of questions about their problem and gives them advice based on its store of knowledge: *expert systems to aid medical diagnosis*

ex·pi·ate /'ekspieɪt/ verb [VN] (formal) to accept punishment for sth that you have done wrong in order to show that you are sorry: *He had a chance to confess and expiate his guilt.* ▶ **ex·pi·ation** /ˌekspiˈeɪʃn/ noun [U, sing.]

ex·pir·ation /ˌekspəˈreɪʃn/ noun [U] (AmE, formal) = EXPIRY

expi'ration date noun (AmE) **1** = EXPIRY DATE: *Check the expiration date on your passport.* **2** the date by which an item of food should be eaten: *The expiration date on this yogurt was November 20.*

ex·pire /ɪkˈspaɪə(r)/ verb [V] **1** (of a document, an agreement, etc.) to be no longer valid because the period of time for which it could be used has ended SYN RUN OUT: *When does your driving licence expire?* **2** (of a period of time, especially one during which sb holds a position of authority) to end: *His term of office expires at the end of June.* **3** (literary) to die—see also UNEXPIRED

ex·piry /ɪkˈspaɪəri/ (especially BrE) (AmE usually **ex·pir·ation**) noun [U] an ending of the period of time when an official document can be used, or when an agreement is valid: *the expiry of a fixed-term contract* ◇ *The licence can be renewed on expiry.*

ex'piry date (BrE) (AmE **expi'ration date**) noun the date after which an official document, agreement, etc. is no longer valid

ex·plain /ɪkˈspleɪn/ verb
1 ~ sth (to sb) to tell sb about sth in a way that makes it easy to understand: [VN] *First, I'll explain the rules of the game.* ◇ *It was difficult to explain the problem to beginners.* ◇ [V] *'Let me explain!' he added helpfully.* ◇ *She explained to them what to do in an emergency.* ◇ [Vthat] *I explained that an ambulance would be coming soon.* ◇ [Vwh-] *He explained who each person in the photo was.* ◇ *Can you explain how the e-mail system works?* ◇ [Vspeech] *'It works like this,' she explained.* [also Vthat] **2** ~ sth (to sb) to give a reason, or be a reason, for sth: [V] *She tried to explain but he wouldn't listen.* ◇ [Vthat] *Alex explained that his car had broken down.* ◇ [Vwh-] *Well, that doesn't explain why you didn't phone.* ◇ [VN] *Scientific findings that help explain the origins of the universe.* ◇ *The government now has to explain its decision to the public.* ◇ (spoken) *Oh well then, that explains it* (= I understand now why sth happened.' HELP You cannot say 'explain me, him, her, etc.': *Can you explain the situation to me?* ◇ *~~Can you explain me the situation?~~* ◇ *I'll explain to you why I like it.* ◇ *~~I'll explain you why I like it.~~* IDM **ex'plain yourself 1** to give sb reasons for your behaviour, especially when they are angry or upset because of it: *I really don't see why I should have to explain myself to you.* **2** to say what you mean in a clear way: *Could you explain yourself a little more—I didn't understand.* PHRV **ex'plain sth↔a'way** to give reasons why sth is not your fault or why sth is not important

WORD FAMILY
explain v.
explanation n.
explanatory adj.
explicable adj. (≠ inexplicable)

ex·plan·ation /ˌekspləˈneɪʃn/ noun **1** [C, U] ~ (for sth/ for doing sth) a statement, fact, or situation that tells you why sth happened; a reason given for sth: *The most likely explanation is that his plane was delayed.* ◇ *to offer/ provide an explanation* ◇ *I can't think of any possible explanation for his absence.* ◇ *She left the room abruptly without explanation.* ◇ *'I had to see you,' he said, by way of explanation.* ◇ *She didn't give a very adequate explanation for being late.* ◇ *The book opens with **an explanation** of why some drugs are banned.* ◇ **an explanation as to why** he had left early ⇨ note at REASON **2** [C] a statement or piece of writing that tells you how sth works or makes sth easier to understand: *For a full explanation*

of how the machine works, turn to page 5. ◇ *The teacher gave the children a detailed explanation of the story.*

ex·plana·tory /ɪkˈsplænətri; AmE -tɔːri/ adj. [usually before noun] giving the reasons for sth; intended to describe how sth works or to make sth easier to understand: *There are explanatory notes at the back of the book.*—see also SELF-EXPLANATORY

ex·ple·tive /ɪkˈspliːtɪv; AmE ˈeksplətɪv/ noun (formal) a word, especially a rude word, that you use when you are angry, or in pain SYN SWEAR WORD

ex·plic·able /ɪkˈsplɪkəbl; ˈeksplɪkəbl/ adj. [not usually before noun] (formal) that can be explained or understood: *His behaviour is only explicable in terms of* (= because of) *his recent illness.* OPP INEXPLICABLE

ex·pli·cate /'eksplɪkeɪt/ verb [VN] (formal) to explain an idea or a work of literature in a lot of detail: *How can we best explicate 'King Lear' and understand it?* ▶ **ex·pli·ca·tion** /ˌeksplɪˈkeɪʃn/ noun [C, U]

ex·pli·cit /ɪkˈsplɪsɪt/ adj. **1** (of a statement or piece of writing) clear and easy to understand: *He gave me very explicit directions on how to get there.* **2** (of a person) saying sth clearly, exactly and openly: *She was quite explicit about why she had left.* **3** said, done or shown in an open or direct way, so that you do not doubt what is happening: *The reasons for the decision should be made explicit.* ◇ *She made some very explicit references to my personal life.* ◇ *a sexually explicit film*—compare IMPLICIT ▶ **ex·pli·cit·ly** adv.: *The report states explicitly that the system was to blame.*—compare IMPLICITLY **ex·pli·cit·ness** noun [U]: *He didn't like the degree of sexual explicitness in the film.*

ex·plode /ɪkˈspləʊd; AmE ɪkˈsploʊd/ verb
BURST VIOLENTLY | **1** to burst or make sth burst loudly and violently, causing damage SYN BLOW UP: [V] *Bombs were exploding all around the city.* ◇ [VN] *There was a huge bang as if someone had exploded a rocket outside.* ◇ *Bomb disposal experts exploded the device under controlled conditions.*—compare IMPLODE

WORD FAMILY
explode v.
explosion n.
explosive adj., n.
unexploded adj.

GET ANGRY/DANGEROUS | **2** ~ (into/with sth) (of a person or situation) to suddenly become very angry or dangerous: [V] *Suddenly Charles exploded with rage.* ◇ *The protest exploded into a riot.* ◇ [Vspeech] *'Of course there's something wrong!' Jem exploded.*

EXPRESS EMOTION | **3** [V] ~ (into/with sth) to suddenly express an emotion: *We all exploded into wild laughter.*

MOVE SUDDENLY | **4** [V] ~ (into sth) to suddenly and quickly do sth; to move suddenly with a lot of force: *After ten minutes the game exploded into life.*

MAKE LOUD NOISE | **5** [V] to make a sudden very loud noise: *Thunder exploded overhead.*

INCREASE QUICKLY | **6** [V] to increase suddenly and very quickly in number: *the exploding world population*

SHOW STH IS NOT TRUE | **7** [VN] to show that sth is not true, especially sth that people believe: *At last, a women's magazine to explode the myth that thin equals beautiful.*

ex·ploded /ɪkˈspləʊdɪd; AmE ɪkˈsploʊ-/ adj. (technical) (of a drawing or diagram) showing the parts of sth separately but also showing how they are connected to each other—compare UNEXPLODED

ex·ploit verb, noun
■ verb /ɪkˈsplɔɪt/ [VN] **1** (disapproving) to treat a person or situation as an opportunity to gain an advantage for yourself: *He exploited his father's name to get himself a job.* ◇ *She realized that her youth and inexperience were being exploited.* **2** (disapproving) to treat sb unfairly by making them work and not giving them much in return: *What is being done to stop employers from exploiting young people?* **3** to use sth well in order to gain as much from it as possible: *She fully exploits the humour of her role in the play.* **4** ~ sth (for sth) to develop or use sth for business or industry: *countries exploiting the rainforests for hardwood* ◇ *No minerals have yet been exploited in Antarctica.* ▶ **ex·ploit·er** noun [C]

s	t	v	z	ʃ	ʒ	tʃ	dʒ	θ	ð	ŋ
see	tea	van	zoo	shoe	vision	chain	jam	thin	this	sing

E

■ *noun* /ˈeksplɔɪt/ [usually pl.] a brave, exciting or interesting act: *the daring exploits of Roman heroes*

ex·ploit·ation /ˌeksplɔɪˈteɪʃn/ *noun* [U] **1** (*disapproving*) a situation in which sb treats sb else in an unfair way, especially in order to make money from their work: *the exploitation of children* **2** the use of land, oil, minerals, etc: *commercial exploitation of the mineral resources in Antarctica* **3** (*disapproving*) the fact of using a situation in order to get an advantage for yourself: *exploitation of the situation for his own purposes*

ex·ploit·ative /ɪkˈsplɔɪtətɪv/ (*AmE* also **ex·ploit·ive** /ɪkˈsplɔɪtɪv/) *adj.* treating sb unfairly in order to gain an advantage or to make money: *an exploitative economic system*

ex·plor·ation /ˌekspləˈreɪʃn/ *noun* [C, U] **1** the act of travelling through a place in order to find out about it or look for sth in it: *the exploration of space* ◊ *oil exploration* (= searching for oil in the ground) **2** an examination of sth in order to find out about it: *the book's explorations of the human mind*

ex·plora·tory /ɪkˈsplɒrətri; *AmE* ɪkˈsplɔːrətɔːri/ *adj.* done with the intention of examining sth in order to find out more about it: *exploratory surgery* ◊ *exploratory drilling for oil*

ex·plore /ɪkˈsplɔː(r)/ *verb* **1** ~ (**sth**) (**for sth**) to travel to or around an area or a country in order to learn about it: [VN] *The city is best explored on foot.* ◊ *They explored the land to the south of the Murray river.* ◊ [V] *As soon as we arrived on the island we were eager to explore.* ◊ *companies exploring for* (= searching for) *oil* **2** [VN] to examine sth completely or carefully in order to find out more about it: *These ideas will be explored in more detail in chapter 7.* **3** [VN] to feel sth with your hands or another part of the body: *She explored the sand with her toes.*—see also UNEXPLORED

ex·plorer /ɪkˈsplɔːrə(r)/ *noun* a person who travels to unknown places in order to find out more about them

ex·plo·sion /ɪkˈspləʊʒn; *AmE* -ˈsploʊ-/ *noun* **1** [C, U] the sudden violent bursting and loud noise of sth such as a bomb exploding; the act of deliberately causing sth to explode: *a bomb/nuclear/gas explosion* ◊ *There were two loud explosions and then the building burst into flames.* ◊ *Bomb Squad officers carried out a controlled explosion of the device.* ◊ *300 people were injured in the explosion.* **2** [C] a large, sudden or rapid increase in the amount or number of sth: *a population explosion* ◊ *an explosion of interest in learning Japanese* **3** [C] (*formal*) a sudden, violent expression of emotion, especially anger [SYN] OUTBURST

ex·plo·sive /ɪkˈspləʊsɪv; -zɪv; *AmE* -ˈsploʊ-/ *adj.*, *noun*
■ *adj.* **1** easily able or likely to explode: *an explosive device* (= a bomb) ◊ *an explosive mixture of chemicals* **2** likely to cause violence or strong feelings of anger or hatred: *a potentially explosive situation* **3** often having sudden violent or angry feelings: *an explosive temper* **4** increasing suddenly and rapidly: *the explosive growth of the export market* **5** (of a sound) sudden and loud ▶ **ex·plo·sive·ly** *adv.*
■ *noun* [C, U] a substance that is able or likely to cause an explosion: *nuclear/plastic explosives* ◊ *The bomb was packed with several pounds of high explosive.*

ex·po·nent /ɪkˈspəʊnənt; *AmE* -ˈspoʊ-/ *noun* **1** a person who supports an idea, theory, etc. and persuades others that it is good: *She was a leading exponent of free trade during her political career* **2** a person who is able to perform a particular activity with skill: *the most famous exponent of the art of mime* **3** (*mathematics*) a raised figure or symbol that shows how many times a quantity must be multiplied by itself, for example the figure 4 in a^4

ex·po·nen·tial /ˌekspəˈnenʃl/ *adj.* **1** (*mathematics*) of or shown by an exponent: 2^4 *is an exponential expression.* ◊ *an exponential curve/function* **2** (*written*) (of a rate of increase) becoming faster and faster: *exponential growth/increase* ▶ **ex·po·nen·ti·al·ly** /-ʃəli/ *adv.*: *to increase exponentially*

ex·port *verb*, *noun*
■ *verb* /ɪkˈspɔːt; *AmE* ɪkˈspɔːrt/ **1** ~ (**sth**) (**to sb**) to sell and send goods to another country: [VN] *The islands export sugar and fruit.* ◊ *90% of the engines are exported to Europe.* [also V] **2** [VN] to introduce an idea or activity to another country or area: *American pop music has been exported around the world.* [OPP] IMPORT
■ *noun* /ˈekspɔːt; *AmE* ˈekspɔːrt/ **1** [U] the selling and transporting of goods to another country: *a ban on the export of live cattle* ◊ *This is where the fruit is packaged for export.* ◊ *export earnings/markets/industries* ◊ *an export licence* **2** [C, usually pl.] a product that is sold to another country: *the country's major exports* ◊ *a fall in the value of exports* [OPP] IMPORT

ex·port·ation /ˌekspɔːˈteɪʃn; *AmE* ˌekspɔːrˈt-/ *noun* [U] the process of transporting goods to another country for sale

ex·port·er /ekˈspɔːtə(r); *AmE* ekˈspɔːrt-/ *noun* a person, company or country that sells goods to another country: *the world's largest/major/leading exporter of cars* ◊ *The country is now a net exporter of fuel* (= it exports more than it imports).—compare IMPORTER

ex·pose /ɪkˈspəʊz; *AmE* ɪkˈspoʊz/ *verb* [VN]
SHOW STH HIDDEN | **1** to show sth that is usually hidden: *He smiled suddenly, exposing a set of amazingly white teeth.* ◊ *Miles of sand are exposed at low tide.* ◊ *My job as a journalist is to expose the truth.* ◊ *He did not want to expose his fears and insecurity to anyone.*
SHOW TRUTH | **2** to tell the true facts about a person or a situation, and show them/it to be immoral, illegal, etc: *She was exposed as a liar and a fraud.* ◊ *He threatened to expose the racism that existed within the police force.*
TO STH HARMFUL | **3** ~ **sb/sth/yourself** (**to sth**) to put sb/sth in a place or situation where they are not protected from sth harmful or unpleasant: *to expose yourself to criticism/ridicule* ◊ *Do not expose babies to strong sunlight.*
GIVE EXPERIENCE | **4** ~ **sb to sth** to let sb find out about sth by giving them experience of it or showing them what it is like: *We want to expose the kids to as much art and culture as possible.*
FILM IN CAMERA | **5** to allow light onto the film inside a camera when taking a photograph
YOURSELF | **6** ~ **yourself** a man who **exposes** himself shows his sexual organs in public in a way that is offensive to other people
—see also EXPOSURE

ex·posé /ekˈspəʊzeɪ; *AmE* ˌekspoʊˈzeɪ/ *noun* an account of the facts of a situation, especially when these are shocking or have deliberately been kept secret

ex·posed /ɪkˈspəʊzd; *AmE* ɪkˈspoʊzd/ *adj.* **1** (of a place) not protected from the weather by trees, buildings or high ground **2** (of a person) not protected from attack or criticism: *She was left feeling exposed and vulnerable.* **3** (*finance*) likely to experience financial losses

ex·pos·ition /ˌekspəˈzɪʃn/ *noun* (*formal*) **1** [C, U] a full explanation of a theory, plan, etc: *a clear and detailed exposition of their legal position* **2** [C] (*rare*) an event at which people, businesses, etc. show and sell their goods; a TRADE FAIR

ex·pos·tu·late /ɪkˈspɒstʃuleɪt; *AmE* ɪkˈspɑːs-/ *verb* [V, V speech] (*formal*) to argue, disagree or protest about sth ▶ **ex·pos·tu·la·tion** /ɪkˌspɒstʃuˈleɪʃn; *AmE* ɪkˌspɑːs-/ *noun* [U, C]

ex·pos·ure /ɪkˈspəʊʒə(r); *AmE* -ˈspoʊ-/ *noun*
TO STH HARMFUL | **1** [U] ~ (**to sth**) the state of being in a place or situation where there is no protection from sth harmful or unpleasant: *prolonged exposure to harmful radiation* ◊ (*finance*) *the company's exposure on the foreign exchange markets* (= to the risk of making financial losses)
SHOWING TRUTH | **2** [U] the state of having the true facts about sb/sth told after they have been hidden because they are bad, immoral or illegal: *exposure as a liar and a fraud* ◊ *the exposure of illegal currency deals*
ON TV/IN NEWSPAPERS, etc. | **3** [U] the fact of being discussed or mentioned on television, in newspapers, etc. [SYN] PUBLICITY: *Her new movie has had a lot of exposure in the media.*
MEDICAL CONDITION | **4** [U] a medical condition caused by being out in very cold weather for too long without

æ	ɑː	e	ɜː	ə	ɪ	iː	i	ɒ	ɔː	ʌ	ʊ	u	uː
cat	father	ten	bird	about	sit	see	many	got	saw	cup	put	actual	too
								(BrE)					

E

protection: *Two climbers were brought in suffering from exposure.*

<u>FILM IN CAMERA</u> | **5** [C] a length of film in a camera that is used to take a photograph: *There are three exposures left on this roll of film.* **6** [C] the length of time for which light is allowed to reach the film when taking a photograph: *I used a long exposure for this one.*

<u>SHOWING STH HIDDEN</u> | **7** [U] the act of showing sth that is usually hidden—see also INDECENT EXPOSURE

ex·pound /ɪk'spaʊnd/ *verb* ~ **sth (to sb)**| ~ **on sth** (*formal*) to explain sth by talking about it in detail: [VN] *He expounded his views on the subject to me at great length.* ◊ [V] *We listened as she expounded on the government's new policies.*

ex·press /ɪk'spres/ *verb, adj., adv., noun*
■ *verb* **1** to show or make known a feeling, an opinion, etc. by words, looks or actions: [VN] *Teachers have expressed concern about the emphasis on testing.* ◊ *His views have been expressed in numerous speeches.* ◊ *to express fears/doubts/reservations* ◊ *to express interest/regret/surprise* ◊ [V wh-] *Words cannot express how pleased I am.* **2** ~ **yourself** to speak, write or communicate in some other way what you think or feel: [VN] *Teenagers often have difficulty expressing themselves.* ◊ *Perhaps I have not expressed myself very well.* ◊ *She expresses herself most fully in her paintings.* ◊ (*formal*) [VN-ADJ] *They expressed themselves delighted.* **3** [VN] ~ **itself** (*formal*) (of a feeling) to become obvious in a particular way: *Their pleasure expressed itself in a burst of applause.* **4** [VN] ~ **sth as/in sth** (especially *mathematics*) to represent sth in a particular way, for example by symbols: *The figures are expressed as percentages.* ◊ *Educational expenditure is often expressed in terms of the amount spent per student.*—see also UNEXPRESSED
■ *adj.* [only before noun] **1** travelling very fast; sent or done very quickly: *an express bus/coach/train* ◊ *express delivery services* **2** (*formal*) (of a wish or an aim) clearly and openly stated [SYN] DEFINITE: *It was his express wish that you should have his gold watch after he died.* ◊ *I came here with the express purpose of speaking with the manager.*
■ *adv.* (especially *BrE*) using a special fast service: *I'd like to send this parcel express, please.*
■ *noun* **1** (also **ex'press train**) [C] a fast train that does not stop at many places: *the 8.27 express to Edinburgh* ◊ *the Trans-Siberian Express* **2** (also **ˌspecial de'livery**) [U] (*BrE*) a service for sending or transporting things quickly

ex·pres·sion /ɪk'spreʃn/ *noun*
<u>SHOWING FEELINGS/IDEAS</u> | **1** [U, C] things that people say, write or do in order to show their feelings, opinions and ideas: *an expression of support* ◊ *Expressions of sympathy flooded in from all over the country.* ◊ **Freedom of expression** (= freedom to say what you think) *is a basic human right.* ◊ (*formal*) *The poet's anger finds expression in* (= is shown in) *the last verse of the poem.* ◊ *Only in his dreams does he give expression to his fears.*
<u>ON FACE</u> | **2** [C] a look on a person's face that shows their thoughts or feelings: *There was a worried expression on her face.* ◊ *an expression of amazement/disbelief/horror* ◊ *His expression changed from surprise to one of amusement.* ◊ *The expression in her eyes told me something was wrong.* ◊ *facial expressions*
<u>WORDS</u> | **3** [C] a word or phrase: *a polite/slang/old-fashioned expression* ◊ (*spoken*) *He's a pain in the butt, if you'll pardon the expression.*
<u>IN MUSIC/ACTING</u> | **4** [U] a strong show of feeling when you are playing music, speaking, acting, etc: *Try to put a little more expression into it!*
<u>MATHEMATICS</u> | **5** [C] a group of signs that represent an idea or a quantity

ex·pres·sion·ism (also **Ex·pres·sion·ism**) /ɪk'spreʃənɪzəm/ *noun* [U] a style and movement in early 20th century art, theatre, cinema and music that tries to express people's feelings and emotions rather than showing events or objects in a realistic way ▶ **ex·pres·sion·ist** (also **Ex·pres·sion·ist**) /-ʃənɪst/ *noun*: *the younger*

Expressionists **ex·pres·sion·ist** (also **Ex·pres·sion·ist**) *adj.*: *expressionist art/cinema*

ex·pres·sion·less /ɪk'spreʃənləs/ *adj.* not showing feelings, thoughts, etc: *an expressionless face/tone/voice*—compare EXPRESSIVE

ex·pres·sive /ɪk'spresɪv/ *adj.* **1** showing or able to show your thoughts and feelings: *She has wonderfully expressive eyes.* ◊ *the expressive power of his music*—compare EXPRESSIONLESS **2** [not before noun] ~ **of sth** (*formal*) showing sth; existing as an expression of sth: *Every word and gesture is expressive of the artist's sincerity.* ▶ **ex·pres·sive·ly** *adv.* **ex·pres·sive·ness** *noun* [U]

ex·press·ly /ɪk'spresli/ *adv.* (*formal*) **1** clearly; definitely: *She was expressly forbidden to touch my papers.* **2** for a special and deliberate purpose [SYN] ESPECIALLY: *The rule was introduced expressly for this purpose.*

ex·press·way /ɪk'spreswei/ *noun* = FREEWAY

ex·pro·pri·ate /eks'prəʊprieɪt; *AmE* -'proʊ-/ *verb* [VN] **1** (*formal* or *law*) (of a government or an authority) to officially take away private property from its owner for public use **2** (*formal*) to take sb's property and use it without permission ▶ **ex·pro·pri·ation** /ˌeksprəʊˈprieɪʃn; *AmE* -ˌproʊ-/ *noun* [U]

ex·pul·sion /ɪk'spʌlʃn/ *noun* ~ **(from ...)** **1** [U, C] the act of forcing sb to leave a place; the act of EXPELLING sb: *These events led to the expulsion of senior diplomats from the country.* **2** [U, C] the act of sending sb away from a school or an organization, so that they can no longer belong to it; the act of EXPELLING sb: *The headteacher threatened the three girls with expulsion.* ◊ *The club faces expulsion from the football league.* **3** [U] (*formal*) the act of sending or driving a substance out of your body or a container

ex·punge /ɪk'spʌndʒ/ *verb* [VN] ~ **sth (from sth)** (*formal*) to remove or get rid of sth, such as a name, piece of information or a memory, from a book or list, or from your mind: *Details of his criminal activities were expunged from the file.* ◊ *What happened just before the accident was expunged from his memory.*

ex·pur·gate /'ekspəgeɪt; *AmE* -pərg-/ *verb* [VN] [usually passive] (*formal*) to remove or leave out parts of a piece of writing or a conversation when printing or reporting it, because you think those parts could offend people: *She gave an expurgated account of what had happened.*

ex·quis·ite /ɪk'skwɪzɪt; 'ekskwɪzɪt/ *adj.* **1** extremely beautiful or carefully made: *exquisite craftsmanship* ◊ *Her wedding dress was absolutely exquisite.* **2** (*formal*) (of a feeling) strongly felt [SYN] ACUTE: *exquisite pain/pleasure* **3** (*formal*) delicate and sensitive: *The room was decorated in exquisite taste.* ◊ *an exquisite sense of timing* ▶ **ex·quis·ite·ly** *adv.*

ˌex·'serviceman, **ˌex-'service woman** *noun* (*pl.* **-men** /-mən/ **-women** /-wɪmɪn/) (*BrE*) a person who used to be in the armed forces

ext. *abbr.* (used as part of a telephone number) extension: *Ext. 4299*

ex·tant /ek'stænt; 'ekstənt/ *adj.* (*formal*) (of sth very old) still in existence: *extant remains of the ancient wall*

ex·tem·pore /ek'stempəri/ *adj.* (*formal*) spoken or done without any previous thought or preparation: *an extempore speech* ▶ **ex·tem·pore** *adv.*

ex·tem·por·ize (*BrE* also **-ise**) /ɪk'stempəraɪz/ *verb* [V] (*formal*) to speak or perform without preparing or practising [SYN] IMPROVISE ▶ **ex·tem·por·iza·tion**, **-isa·tion** /ɪk,stempəraɪ'zeɪʃn; *AmE* -rə'z-/ *noun* [U]

ex·tend /ɪk'stend/ *verb*
<u>MAKE LONGER/LARGER/WIDER</u> | **1** [VN] to make sth longer or larger: *to extend a fence/road/house* ◊ *There are plans to extend the no-smoking area.* **2** [VN] to make sth last longer: *to extend a deadline/visa* ◊ *The show has been extended for another six weeks.* ◊ *Careful maintenance can extend the life of your car by several years.* **3** [VN] to make a business, an idea, an influence, etc. cover more areas or operate in more places: *The company plans to extend its operations into Europe.* ◊ *The school is extending the range of subjects taught.*
<u>INCLUDE</u> | **4** [V+adv./prep.] to relate to or include sb/sth:

aɪ	aʊ	eɪ	əʊ	oʊ	ɔɪ	ɪə	eə	ʊə	j	w
my	now	say	go (BrE)	go (AmE)	boy	near	hair	pure	yes	wet

extravagance. **3** [C, U] something that is impressive or noticeable because it is unusual or extreme: *the extravagance of Strauss's music*

ex·trava·gant /ɪkˈstrævəgənt/ *adj.* **1** spending a lot more money or using a lot more of sth than you can afford or than is necessary: *I felt very extravagant spending £100 on a dress.* ◊ *She's got very extravagant tastes.* ◊ *Residents were warned not to be* **extravagant with** *water, in view of the low rainfall this year.* **2** costing a lot more money than you can afford or is necessary: *an extravagant present* **3** (of ideas, speech or behaviour) very extreme or impressive but not reasonable or practical SYN EXAGGERATED: *the extravagant claims/promises of politicians* ◊ *I was embarrassed by all the extravagant praise I was getting.* ▶ **ex·trava·gant·ly** *adv.*: *extravagantly expensive* ◊ *extravagantly high hopes*

ex·trava·ganza /ɪkˌstrævəˈɡænzə/ *noun* a large, expensive and impressive entertainment: *a musical extravaganza*

ex·tra·vert *(rare)* = EXTROVERT

ex·treme /ɪkˈstriːm/ *adj., noun*
■ *adj.* **1** [usually before noun] very great in degree: *We are working under extreme pressure at the moment.* ◊ *thousands of people living in extreme poverty* ◊ *The heat in the desert was extreme.* **2** not ordinary or usual; serious or severe: *Children will be removed from their parents only* **in extreme circumstances.** ◊ *Don't go doing anything extreme like leaving the country.* ◊ *It was the most extreme example of cruelty to animals I had ever seen.* ◊ *extreme weather conditions* ◊ *extreme sports* (= dangerous sports, for example SNOWBOARDING and BUNGEE JUMPING) **3** (of people, political organizations, opinions, etc.) far from what most people consider to be normal, reasonable or acceptable: *extreme left-wing/right-wing views* **4** [only before noun] as far as possible from the centre, the beginning or in the direction mentioned: *Kerry is in the extreme west of Ireland.* ◊ *She sat on the extreme edge of her seat.*
■ *noun* **1** a feeling, situation, way of behaving, etc. that is as different as possible from another or is opposite to it: *extremes of love and hate* ◊ *He used to be very shy, but now he's gone to* **the opposite extreme** (= changed from one extreme kind of behaviour to another). **2** the greatest or highest degree of sth: *extremes of cold, wind or rain* IDM **go, etc. to ex·tremes | take sth to ex·tremes** to act or be forced to act in a way that is far from normal or reasonable: *It's embarrassing the extremes he'll go to in order to impress his boss.* ◊ *Taken to extremes, this kind of behaviour can be dangerous.* **in the ex·treme** *(formal)* to a great degree: *The journey would be dangerous in the extreme.*

ex·treme·ly /ɪkˈstriːmli/ *adv.* (usually with adjectives and adverbs) to a very high degree: *extremely important/useful/complicated* ◊ *She found it extremely difficult to get a job.*

ex·tre·mis ⇨ IN EXTREMIS

ex·trem·ism /ɪkˈstriːmɪzəm/ *noun* [U] political, religious, etc. ideas or actions that are extreme and not normal, reasonable or acceptable to most people: *political extremism*

ex·trem·ist /ɪkˈstriːmɪst/ *noun* (usually *disapproving*) a person whose opinions, especially about religion or politics, are extreme, and who may do things that are violent, illegal, etc. for what they believe: *left-wing/right-wing/political/religious extremists* ▶ **ex·trem·ist** *adj.* [usually before noun]: *extremist attacks/groups/policies*

ex·trem·ity /ɪkˈstreməti/ *noun* (*pl.* **-ies**) **1** [C] the furthest point, end or limit of sth: *The lake is situated at the eastern extremity of the mountain range.* **2** [C, U] the degree to which a situation, a feeling, an action, etc. is extreme, difficult or unusual: *the extremities/extremity of pain* **3** (**extremities**) [pl.] *(formal)* the parts of your body that are furthest from the centre, especially your hands and feet

ex·tri·cate /ˈekstrɪkeɪt/ *verb* [VN] ~ **sb/sth/yourself** **(from sth)** *(written)* **1** to escape or enable sb to escape from a difficult situation: *He had managed to extricate himself from most of his official duties.* **2** to free sb/sth or yourself from a place where they/it or you are trapped: *They managed to extricate the pilot from the tangled control panel.*

ex·trin·sic /eksˈtrɪnsɪk; -zɪk/ *adj.* *(formal)* not belonging naturally to sb/sth; coming from or existing outside sb/sth rather than within them: *extrinsic factors*—compare INTRINSIC

ex·tro·vert (also *less frequent* **ex·tra·vert**) /ˈekstrəvɜːt; *AmE* -vɜːrt/ *noun* a lively and confident person who enjoys being with other people OPP INTROVERT ▶ **ex·tro·vert** *(BrE)* (also **ex·tro·vert·ed** *AmE, BrE*) *adj.*

ex·trude /ɪkˈstruːd/ *verb* **1** *(formal)* to force or push sth out of sth; to be forced or pushed in this way: [VN] *Lava is extruded from the volcano.* [also V] **2** [VN] *(technical)* to shape metal or plastic by forcing it through a hole ▶ **ex·tru·sion** /ɪkˈstruːʒn/ *noun* [U]

ex·uber·ant /ɪɡˈzjuːbərənt; *AmE* -ˈzuː-/ *adj.* **1** full of energy, excitement and happiness: *She gave an exuberant performance.* ◊ *an exuberant personality/imagination* ◊ *a picture painted in exuberant reds and yellows* **2** (of plants, etc.) strong and healthy; growing quickly and well ▶ **ex·uber·ance** /-rəns/ *noun* [U]: *We can excuse his behaviour as youthful exuberance.* **ex·uber·ant·ly** *adv.*

exude /ɪɡˈzjuːd; *AmE* -ˈzuːd/ *verb* **1** if you **exude** a particular feeling or quality, or it **exudes** from you, people can easily see that you have it: [VN] *She exuded confidence.* [also V] **2** if sth **exudes** a liquid or smell, or a liquid or smell **exudes** from somewhere, the liquid, etc. comes out slowly: [VN] *The plant exudes a sticky fluid.* ◊ [V] *An awful smell exuded from the creature's body.*

exult /ɪɡˈzʌlt/ *verb* ~ **(at/in sth)** *(formal)* to feel and show that you are very excited and happy because of sth that has happened: [V] *He leaned back, exulting at the success of his plan.* ◊ [V speech] *'We won!' she exulted.* [also V that]

ex·ult·ant /ɪɡˈzʌltənt/ *adj.* ~ **(at sth)** *(formal)* feeling or showing great pride or happiness especially because of sth exciting that has happened SYN TRIUMPHANT: *The fans were exultant at their team's victory.* ▶ **ex·ult·ant·ly** *adv.*

ex·ult·ation /ˌeɡzʌlˈteɪʃn/ *noun* [U] *(formal)* great pride or happiness, especially because of sth exciting that has happened

-ey ⇨ -Y

eye /aɪ/ *noun, verb*
■ *noun*
PART OF BODY | **1** [C] either of the two organs on the face that you see with: *The suspect has dark hair and green eyes.* ◊ *to close/open your eyes* ◊ *to drop/lower your eyes* (= to look down) ◊ *There were tears in his eyes.* ◊ *I have something in my eye.* ◊ *to make/avoid eye contact with sb* (= to look/avoid looking at them at the same time as they look at you) ◊ *All eyes were on him* (= everyone was looking at him) *as he walked on to the stage.*—see also BLACK EYE, SHUT-EYE—picture at BODY **2** (**-eyed**) (in adjectives) having the type or number of eyes mentioned: *a blue-eyed blonde* ◊ *a one-eyed monster*

ABILITY TO SEE | **3** [sing.] the ability to see: *A surgeon needs a good eye and a steady hand.*—see also EAGLE EYE

WAY OF SEEING | **4** [C, usually sing.] a particular way of seeing sth: *He looked at the design* **with the eye of** *an engineer.* ◊ *She viewed the findings with a critical eye.* ◊ **To my eye,** *the windows seem out of proportion.* ◊ *She can do no wrong* **in his eyes.**

OF NEEDLE | **5** [C] the hole in the end of a needle that you put the thread through—picture at SEW

ON CLOTHES | **6** [C] a small thin piece of metal curved round, that a small hook fits into, used for fastening clothes: *It fastens with a* **hook and eye.**—picture at FASTENER

OF STORM | **7** [sing.] **a/the ~ of a/the** storm, tornado, hurricane, etc. a calm area at the centre of a storm, TORNADO, etc.

æ	ɑː	e	ɜː	ə	ɪ	iː	i	ɒ	ɔː	ʌ	ʊ	u	uː
cat	father	ten	bird	about	sit	see	many	got	saw	cup	put	actual	too
							(BrE)						

ON POTATO | **8** [C] a dark mark on a potato from which another plant will grow

—see also CATSEYE, BULLSEYE, THE EVIL EYE, FISHEYE LENS, RED-EYE

IDM **be all 'eyes** to be watching sb/sth carefully and with a lot of interest **before/in front of sb's (very) eyes** in sb's presence; in front of sb: *He had seen his life's work destroyed before his very eyes.* **be up to your eyes in sth** to have a lot of sth to deal with: *We're up to our eyes in work.* **cast/run an eye/your eyes over sth** to look at or examine sth quickly: *Could you just run your eyes over this report?* **clap/lay/set eyes on sb/sth** (*spoken*) (usually used in negative sentences) to see sb/sth: *I haven't clapped eyes on them for weeks.* ◊ *I hope I never set eyes on this place again!* **an ,eye for an 'eye (and a ,tooth for a 'tooth)** (*saying*) used to say that you should punish sb by doing to them what they have done to you or to sb else **sb's eyes are bigger than their 'stomach** used to say that sb has been GREEDY by taking more food than they can eat **for sb's eyes 'only** to be seen only by a particular person: *I'll lend you the letters but they're for your eyes only.* **get/keep your 'eye in** (*BrE*) (in ball games) to practise so that you are able to judge more clearly how fast and where the ball is going **have an eye for sth** to be able to judge if things look attractive, valuable, etc: *I've never had much of an eye for fashion.* ◊ *She has an eye for a bargain.* **have eyes in the back of your 'head** to be aware of everything that is happening around you, even things that seem difficult or impossible to see **have one eye/half an eye on sth** to look at or watch sth while doing sth else, especially in a secret way so that other people do not notice: *During his talk, most of the delegates had one eye on the clock.* **have your 'eye on sb 1** to be watching sb carefully, especially to check that they do not do anything wrong **2** to be thinking about asking sb out, offering sb a job, etc. because you think they are attractive, good at their job, etc: *He's got his eye on the new girl in your class.* **have your 'eye on sth** to be thinking about buying sth **in the eyes of the 'law, 'world, etc.** according to the law, most people in the world, etc. **keep an eye on sb/sth** to take care of sb/sth and make sure that they are not harmed, damaged, etc: *We've asked the neighbours to keep an eye on the house for us while we are away.* **keep an eye open/out (for sb/sth)** to look for sb/sth while you are doing other things: *Police have asked residents to keep an eye out for anything suspicious.* **keep your 'eyes peeled/skinned (for sb/sth)** to look carefully for sb/sth: *We kept our eyes peeled for any signs of life.* **look sb in the 'eye(s)/'face** (usually used in negative sentences and questions) to look straight at sb without feeling embarrassed or ashamed: *Can you look me in the eye and tell me you're not lying?* ◊ *I'll never be able to look her in the face again!* **make 'eyes at sb | give sb the 'eye** to look at sb in a way that shows that you find them sexually attractive: *He's definitely giving you the eye!* **,my 'eye!** (*BrE, spoken*) used to show that you do not believe sb/sth: *'It's an antique.' 'An antique, my eye!'* **not see eye to 'eye with sb (on sth)** to not share the same views as sb about sth **not (be able to) take your 'eyes off sb/sth** to find sb/sth so interesting, attractive, etc. that you watch them all the time **one in the eye (for sb/sth)** (*informal*) a result, action, etc. that represents a defeat or disappointment for sb/sth: *The appointment of a woman was one in the eye for male domination.* **only have eyes for/have eyes only for sb** to be in love with only one particular person: *He's only ever had eyes for his wife.* **see, look at, etc. sth through sb's eyes** to think about or see sth from another person's point of view: *Try looking at it through her eyes for a change.* **shut/close your eyes to sth** to pretend that you have not noticed sth so that you do not have to deal with it **under the (watchful) eye of sb** being watched carefully by sb: *The children played under the watchful eye of their father.* **with an eye for/on/to the main chance** (*BrE, usually disapproving*) with the hope of using a particular situation in order to gain some advantage for yourself **with an eye to sth/to doing sth** with the intention of doing sth: *He bought the*

warehouse with an eye to converting it into a hotel. **with your 'eyes open** fully aware of the possible problems or results of a particular course of action: *I went into this with my eyes open so I guess I only have myself to blame.* **with your 'eyes shut/closed** having enough experience to be able to do sth easily: *I've made this trip so often, I could do it with my eyes shut.*—more at APPLE, BAT *v.*, BEAUTY, BELIEVE, BIRD, BLIND *adj.*, BLINK *n.*, BLUE *adj.*, CATCH *v.*, CLOSE² *adj.*, COCK *v.*, CORNER *n.*, DRY *n.*, EASY *adj.*, FAR *adv.*, FEAST *v.*, HIT *v.*, MEET *v.*, MIND *n.*, NAKED, OPEN *adj.*, OPEN *v.*, PLEASE *v.*, PUBLIC *adj.*, PULL *v.*, ROVING, SIGHT *n.*, TWINKLING, WEATHER *n.*

■ *verb* (**eye·ing** or **eying, eyed, eyed**) [VN] to look at sb/sth carefully, especially because you want sth or you are suspicious of sth: *to eye sb curiously/doubtfully/suspiciously/thoughtfully* ◊ *He couldn't help eyeing the cakes hungrily.* ◊ *They eyed us with alarm.*
PHRV **,eye sb↔'up** (*informal*) to look at sb in a way that shows you have a special interest in them, especially a sexual interest

eye·ball /'aɪbɔːl/ *noun, verb*
■ *noun* the whole of the eye, including the part inside the head that cannot be seen—picture at BODY **IDM** **,eyeball to 'eyeball (with sb)** very close to sb and looking at them, especially during an angry conversation, meeting, etc: *The protesters and police stood eyeball to eyeball.* ◊ *an eyeball-to-eyeball confrontation* **be up to your eyeballs in sth** to have a lot of sth to deal with: *They're up to their eyeballs in work.*—more at DRUG *v.*
■ *verb* [VN] (*informal*) to look at sb/sth in a way that is very direct and not always polite or friendly: *They eyeballed each other across the room.*

eye·brow /'aɪbraʊ/ (also **brow**) *noun* [usually pl.] the line of hair above the eye—picture at BODY **IDM** **be up to your eyebrows in sth** to have a lot of sth to deal with: *He's in it (= trouble) up to his eyebrows.*—more at RAISE *v.*

'eye-catching *adj.* (of a thing) immediately noticeable because it is particularly interesting, bright or attractive: *an eye-catching advertisement*

eye·ful /'aɪfʊl/ *noun* **1** an amount of sth such as liquid or dust that has been thrown, or blown into your eye: *an eyeful of sand* **2** (*informal*) a person or thing that is beautiful or interesting to look at **IDM** **have/get an eyeful (of sth)** (*BrE, spoken*) to look carefully at sth that is interesting or unusual

eye·glass /'aɪɡlɑːs; *AmE* -ɡlæs/ *noun* **1** a LENS for one eye used to help you see more clearly with that eye **2** (**eyeglasses**) (*AmE*) = GLASSES

eye·lash /'aɪlæʃ/ (also **lash**) *noun* [usually pl.] one of the hairs growing on the edge of the EYELIDS: *false eyelashes* ◊ *She just flutters her eyelashes and the men come running!*—picture at BODY

eye·let /'aɪlət/ *noun* a hole with a metal ring around it in a piece of cloth or leather normally used for passing a rope or string through

'eye level *noun* [U] the height of a person's eyes: *Computer screens should be at eye level.* ◊ *an eye-level grill/oven/monitor*

eye·lid /'aɪlɪd/ (also **lid**) *noun* either of the pieces of skin above and below the eye that cover it when you BLINK or close the eye—picture at BODY **IDM** see BAT *v.*

eye·liner /'aɪlaɪnə(r)/ (also **liner**) *noun* [U] a type of MAKE-UP, usually black, that is put around the edge of the eyes to make them more noticeable and attractive

'eye-opener *noun* [usually sing.] an event, experience, etc. that is surprising and shows you sth that you did not already know: *Travelling around India was a real eye-opener for me.*

eye·patch /'aɪpætʃ/ *noun* a piece of fabric worn over one eye, usually because the eye is damaged

eye·piece /'aɪpiːs/ *noun* the piece of glass (= a LENS) at the end of a TELESCOPE or MICROSCOPE that you look through—picture at LABORATORY

eye·shadow /'aɪʃædəʊ; *AmE* -doʊ/ *noun* [C, U] a type of coloured MAKE-UP that is put on the skin above the eyes (= the EYELIDS) to make them look more attractive

aɪ	aʊ	eɪ	əʊ	oʊ	ɔɪ	ɪə	eə	ʊə	j	w
my	now	say	go (BrE)	go (AmE)	boy	near	hair	pure	yes	wet

eye·sight /ˈaɪsaɪt/ *noun* [U] the ability to see: *to have good/bad/poor eyesight* ◇ *an eyesight test* ⇨ note at SIGHT

eye·sore /ˈaɪsɔː(r)/ *noun* a building, an object, etc. that is unpleasant to look at: *That old factory is a real eyesore!*

ˈeye teeth *noun* [pl.] **IDM** **give your eye teeth for sth/ to do sth** (*informal*) used when you are saying that you want sth very much: *I'd give my eye teeth to own a car like that.*

eye·wit·ness /ˈaɪwɪtnəs/ *noun* a person who has seen a crime, accident, etc. and can describe it afterwards: *an eyewitness account of the suffering of the refugees*—see also WITNESS

eyrie (*especially BrE*) (*AmE* usually **aerie**) /ˈɪəri; ˈeəri; ˈaɪəri; *AmE* ˈɪri; ˈeri/ *noun* **1** a nest that is built high up among rocks by a BIRD OF PREY (= a bird that kills other creatures for food) such as an EAGLE **2** a room or building in a high place that is often difficult to reach and from which sb can see what is happening below

E

Ff

F *noun, abbr.*

■ *noun* (also **f**) /ef/ [C, U] (*pl.* **F's, f's** /efs/) **1** the 6th letter of the English alphabet: *'Fox' begins with (an) F/'F'.* **2** (F) (*music*) the fourth note in the scale of C MAJOR **3** the 6th highest mark/grade that a student can get for a piece of work, showing that it is very bad and the student has failed: *He got (an) F/'F' in/for Chemistry.*—see also F-WORD

■ *abbr.* **1** FAHRENHEIT: *Water freezes at 32°F.* **2** (*BrE*) (in academic titles) FELLOW of: *FRCM (= Fellow of the Royal College of Music)*

f (*BrE*) (also **f.** *AmE, BrE*) *abbr.* **1** female **2** (*grammar*) feminine **3** (*music*) loudly (from Italian 'forte')

fa = FAH

fab /fæb/ *adj.* (*old-fashioned, BrE, informal*) extremely good

fable /'feɪbl/ *noun* **1** [C, U] a traditional short story that teaches a moral lesson, especially one with animals as characters; these stories considered as a group: *Aesop's Fables ◊ a land rich in fable* **2** [U, C] a statement, or an account of sth, that is not true

fabled /'feɪbld/ *adj.* (*literary* or *humorous*) famous and often talked about, but rarely seen: *a fabled monster ◊ For the first week he never actually saw the fabled Jack.*—compare LEGENDARY

fab·ric /'fæbrɪk/ *noun* **1** [U, C] material made by weaving wool, cotton, silk, etc., used for making clothes, curtains, etc. and for covering furniture: *cotton/knitted fabric ◊ furnishing fabrics*—picture at SEW—picture on page A4 **2** [sing.] **the ~ (of sth)** (*written*) the basic structure of a society, an organization, etc. that enables it to function successfully: *a trend which threatens the very fabric of society* **3** [sing.] **the ~ (of sth)** the basic structure of a building, such as the walls, floor and roof

fab·ri·cate /'fæbrɪkeɪt/ *verb* [VN] [often passive] **1** to invent false information in order to deceive people: *The evidence was totally fabricated.* **2** (*technical*) to make or produce goods, equipment, etc. from various different materials **SYN** MANUFACTURE ▶ **fab·ri·ca·tion** /ˌfæbrɪ-'keɪʃn/ *noun* [C, U]: *Her story was a complete fabrication from start to finish.*

fabu·lous /'fæbjələs/ *adj.* **1** (*informal*) extremely good: *a fabulous performance/view ◊ Jane is a fabulous cook. ◊ The food looks fabulous.* **2** (*written*) very great: *fabulous wealth/riches/beauty*

fabu·lous·ly /'fæbjələsli/ *adv.* (*written*) extremely: *fabulously wealthy/rich*

fa·çade /fə'sɑːd/ *noun* **1** the front of a building: *a classical façade* **2** [usually sing.] the way that sb/sth appears to be, which is different from the way sb/sth really is: *She managed to maintain a façade of indifference. ◊ Squalor and poverty lay behind the city's glittering façade.*

face /feɪs/ *noun, verb*

■ *noun*

FRONT OF HEAD | **1** the front part of the head between the forehead and the chin: *a pretty/round/freckled face ◊ He buried his face in his hands. ◊ You should have seen the look on her face when I told her! ◊ The expression on his face never changed.*—picture at BODY

EXPRESSION | **2** an expression that is shown on sb's face: *a sad/happy/smiling face ◊ Her face lit up (= showed happiness) when she spoke of the past. ◊ His face fell (= showed disappointment, sadness, etc.) when he read the headlines. ◊ Sue's face was a picture (= she looked very surprised, angry, etc.) as she listened to her husband's speech.*

-FACED | **3** (in adjectives) having the type of face or expression mentioned: *pale-faced ◊ grim-faced*

PERSON | **4** (in compounds) used to refer to a person of the type mentioned: *She looked around for a familiar face. ◊ a well-known face on our television screens ◊ It's nice to see some new faces here this evening. ◊ I'm fed up of seeing the same old faces every time we go out!*

SIDE/SURFACE | **5** a side or surface of sth: *the north face of the mountain ◊ The birds build their nests in the rock face. ◊ How many faces does a cube have?*—see also COALFACE

FRONT OF CLOCK | **6** the front part of a clock or watch

CHARACTER/ASPECT | **7** ~ **of sth** (*written*) the particular character of sth: *the changing face of Britain* **8** ~ **of sth** a particular aspect of sth: *the unacceptable face of capitalism*
—see also IN-YOUR-FACE, TYPEFACE, VOLTE-FACE

IDM **disappear/vanish off the face of the 'earth** to disappear completely: *Keep looking—they can't just have vanished off the face of the earth.* **sb's face doesn't fit** used to say that sb will not get a particular job or position because they do not have the appearance, personality, etc. that the employer wants, even when this should not be important: *It doesn't matter how qualified you are, if your face doesn't fit, you don't stand a chance.* **sb's face is like 'thunder** | **sb has a face like 'thunder** sb looks very angry **,face to 'face (with sb)** close to and looking at sb: *The two have never met face to face before.* **,face to 'face with sth** in a situation where you have to accept that sth is true and deal with it: *She was at an early age brought face to face with the horrors of war.* **,face 'up/'down 1** (of a person) with your face and stomach facing upwards/downwards: *She lay face down on the bed.* **2** (of a playing card) with the number or picture facing upwards/downwards: *Place the card face up on the pile.* **have the 'face to do sth** (*BrE, informal*) to do sth that other people think is rude or shows a lack of respect without feeling embarrassed or ashamed **in the face of 'sth 1** in spite of problems, difficulties, etc: *She showed great courage in the face of danger.* **2** as a result of sth: *He was unable to deny the charges in the face of new evidence.* **lose 'face** to be less respected or look stupid because of sth you have done **on the 'face of it** (*informal*) used to say that sth seems to be good, true, etc. but that this opinion may need to be changed when you know more about it: *On the face of it, it seems like a great deal.* **pull/ make 'faces/a 'face (at sb)** to produce an expression on your face to show that you do not like sb/sth or in order to make sb laugh: *What are you pulling a face at now?* **put your 'face on** (*informal*) to put on MAKE-UP **set your face against sb/sth** (*written, especially BrE*) to be determined to oppose sb/sth: *Her father had set his face against the marriage.* **to sb's 'face** if you say sth to sb's face, you say it to them directly rather than to other people—compare BEHIND SB'S BACK **'what's his/her face** (*spoken*) used to refer to a person whose name you cannot remember: *Are you still working for what's her face?*—more at BLOW *v.*, BLUE *adj.*, BRAVE *adj.*, DOOR *n.*, FEED *v.*, EGG *n.*, EYE *n.*, FLAT *adv.*, FLY *v.*, LAUGH *v.*, LONG *adj.*, NOSE *n.*, PLAIN *adj.*, PRETTY *adj.*, SAVE *v.*, SHOW *v.*, SHUT *v.*, SLAP *n.*, STARE *v.*, STRAIGHT *n.*, WIPE *v.*, WRITE

■ *verb*

BE OPPOSITE | **1** to be opposite sb/sth; to have your face or front pointing towards sb/sth or in a particular direction: [VN] *She turned and faced him. ◊ Most of the rooms face the sea.* ◊ [V+adv./prep.] *The terrace faces south. ◊ a north-facing wall ◊ Stand with your feet apart and your hands facing upwards. ◊ Which direction are you facing?*—picture at FRONT *n.*

s	t	v	z	ʃ	ʒ	tʃ	dʒ	θ	ð	ŋ
see	tea	van	zoo	shoe	vision	chain	jam	thin	this	sing

SB/STH DIFFICULT | **2** [VN] if you **face** a particular situation, or it **faces** you, you have to deal with it: *the problems faced by one-parent families* ◊ *The company is facing a financial crisis.* ◊ *She's faced with a difficult decision.* **3** [VN] to accept that a difficult situation exists, although you would prefer not to: *It's not always easy to face the truth.* ◊ *She had to face the fact that her life had changed forever.* ◊ *Face facts—she isn't coming back.* ◊ *Let's face it, we're not going to win.* **4** if you **can't face** sth unpleasant, you feel unable or unwilling to deal with it: [VN] *I just can't face work today.* ◊ [V-ing] *I can't face seeing them.* **5** [VN] to talk to or deal with sb, even though this is difficult or unpleasant: *How can I face Tom? He'll be so disappointed.*

COVER SURFACE | **6** [VN] to cover a surface with another material: *a brick building faced with stone*

IDM **face the 'music** (*informal*) to accept and deal with criticism or punishment for sth you have done: *The others all ran off, leaving me to face the music.*
PHR V **,face sb↔'down** to oppose or beat sb by dealing with them directly and confidently **,face 'off** (*especially AmE*) **1** to start a game such as ice hockey: *Both teams are ready to face off.* **2** to get ready to argue, fight or compete with sb: *The candidates are preparing to face off on TV tonight.*—related noun FACE-OFF **,face 'up to sth** to accept and deal with sth that is difficult or unpleasant: *She had to face up to the fact that she would never walk again.*

> **VOCABULARY BUILDING**
> expressions on your **face**
>
> To **beam** is to have a big happy smile on your face.
> To **frown** is to make a serious, angry or worried expression by bringing your eyebrows closer together so that lines appear on your forehead.
> To **glare** or **glower** is to look in an angry, aggressive way.
> To **grimace** is to make an ugly expression with your face to show pain, disgust, etc.
> To **scowl** is to look at someone in an angry or annoyed way.
> To **smirk** is to smile in a silly or unpleasant way that shows that you are pleased with yourself, know something that other people do not know, etc.
> To **sneer** is to show that you have no respect for someone by turning your upper lip upwards.
>
> These words can also be used as nouns: *She looked up with a puzzled frown.* ◊ *He gave me an icy glare.* ◊ *a grimace of pain.*

'face card *noun* (*especially AmE*) = COURT CARD
face·cloth /'feɪsklɒθ; *AmE* -klɔːθ/ *noun* (*BrE*) = FLANNEL
'face cream *noun* [U, C] a thick cream that you put on your face to clean the skin or keep it soft
face·less /'feɪsləs/ *adj.* [usually before noun] (*disapproving*) having no noticeable characteristics or identity: *faceless high-rise apartment blocks*
face·lift /'feɪslɪft/ *noun* [usually sing.] **1** a medical operation in which the skin on a person's face is tightened in order to make them look younger: *to have a facelift* **2** changes made to a building, room or place to make it look more attractive: *The town has recently been given a facelift.*
'face-off *noun* **1** (*informal, especially AmE*) an argument or a fight: *a face-off between the presidential candidates* ◊ *There were minor face-offs between demonstrators and police.* **2** the way of starting play in a game of ice hockey
'face pack *noun* (*BrE*) a substance that you put on your face and take off after a short period of time, used to clean and improve the quality of your skin
'face powder *noun* powder that you put on your face to make it look less shiny
'face-saving *adj.* [only before noun] intended to protect sb's reputation and to avoid embarrassment: *a face-saving compromise*
facet /'fæsɪt/ *noun* **1** ~ (**of sth**) a particular part or aspect

of sth: *Now let's look at another facet of the problem.* **2** one of the flat sides of a cut stone or jewel
fa·cetious /fə'siːʃəs/ *adj.* trying to appear amusing and intelligent at a time when other people do not think it is appropriate, and when it would be better to be serious: *a facetious comment/remark* ◊ *Stop being facetious; this is serious.* ► **fa·cetious·ly** *adv.* **fa·cetious·ness** *noun* [U]
,face 'value *noun* [U, sing.] the value of a stamp, coin, ticket, etc. that is shown on the front of it: *Tickets were changing hands at three times their face value.* IDM **take sth at face 'value** to believe that sth is what it appears to be, without questioning it: *Taken at face value, the figures look very encouraging.* ◊ *You shouldn't take anything she says at face value.*
fa·cia = FASCIA
fa·cial /'feɪʃl/ *adj., noun*
■ *adj.* [usually before noun] connected with a person's face; on a person's face: *a facial expression/injury* ◊ *facial hair* ► **fa·cial·ly** /'feɪʃəli/ *adv.*: *Facially the two men were very different.*
■ *noun* a beauty treatment in which a person's face is cleaned using creams, steam, etc. in order to improve the quality of the skin
fa·cile /'fæsaɪl; *AmE* 'fæsl/ *adj.* (*disapproving*) **1** produced without effort or careful thought: *a facile remark/generalization* **2** [only before noun] (*formal*) obtained too easily and having little value: *a facile victory*
fa·cili·tate /fə'sɪlɪteɪt/ *verb* [VN] (*formal*) to make an action or a process possible or easier: *The new trade agreement should facilitate more rapid economic growth.* ◊ *Structured teaching facilitates learning.* ► **fa·cili·ta·tion** /fə,sɪlɪ'teɪʃn/ *noun* [U, sing.]
fa·cili·ta·tor /fə'sɪlɪteɪtə(r)/ *noun* **1** a person who helps sb do sth more easily by discussing problems, giving advice, etc. rather than telling them what to do: *The teacher acts as a facilitator of learning.* **2** (*formal*) a thing that helps a process take place
fa·cil·ity /fə'sɪləti/ *noun* **1** (**facilities**) [pl.] buildings, services, equipment, etc. that are provided for a particular purpose: *sports/leisure facilities* ◊ *conference/storage facilities* ◊ *shopping/banking/cooking facilities* ◊ *The hotel has special facilities for welcoming disabled people.* ◊ *All rooms have private facilities* (= a private bathroom). **2** [C] a special feature of a machine, service, etc. that makes it possible to do sth extra: *a bank account with an overdraft facility* ◊ *a facility for checking spelling* **3** [C] a place, usually including buildings, used for a particular purpose or activity: *the world's largest nuclear waste facility* ◊ *a new health care facility* **4** [sing., U] ~ (**for sth**) a natural ability to learn or do sth easily: *She has a great facility for languages.* ◊ *He plays the piano with surprising facility.*
fa·cing /'feɪsɪŋ/ *noun* **1** [C, U] a layer of brick, stone, etc. that covers the surface of a wall to make it look more attractive **2** [C, U] a layer of stiff material sewn around the inside of the neck, ARMHOLES, etc. of a piece of clothing to strengthen them **3** (**facings**) [pl.] the collar, cuffs, etc. of a piece of clothing that are made in a different colour or material
fac·sim·ile /fæk'sɪməli/ *noun* **1** [C] an exact copy of sth: *a facsimile edition* ◊ *a manuscript reproduced in facsimile* **2** [C, U] (*formal*) = FAX: *a facsimile machine*
fact /fækt/ *noun* **1** [sing.] ~ (**that…**) used to refer to a particular situation that exists: *I could no longer ignore the fact that he was deeply unhappy.* ◊ *Despite the fact that she was wearing a seat belt, she was thrown sharply forward.* ◊ *Due to the fact that they did not read English, the prisoners were unaware of what they were signing.* ◊ *She was happy apart from the fact that she could not return home.* ◊ *Voluntary work was particularly important in view of the fact that women were often forced to give up paid work on marriage.* ◊ *How do you account for the fact that unemployment is still rising?* ◊ *The fact remains that we are still two teachers short.* ◊ *The mere fact of being poor makes such children criminals in the eyes of the police.* **2** [C] a thing that is known to be true, especially when it can be proved: *Isn't it a fact that the firm is losing*

F

æ	ɑː	e	ɜː	ə	ɪ	iː	i	ɒ	ɔː	ʌ	ʊ	u	uː
cat	father	ten	bird	about	sit	see	many	got	saw	cup	put	actual	too
								(BrE)					

money? ◊ (*informal*) *I haven't spoken to anyone in English for days and that's a fact.* ◊ *I know for a fact* (= I am certain) *that she's involved in something illegal.* ◊ *The judge instructed both lawyers to* **stick to the facts** *of the case.* ◊ *First, some basic facts about healthy eating!* ◊ *The report is based on* **hard facts** (= information that can be proved to be true). ◊ *If you're going to make accusations, you'd better* **get your facts right** (= make sure your information is correct). ◊ *It's about time you learnt to* **face (the) facts** (= accepted the truth about the situation). **3** [U] things that are true rather than things that have been invented: *The story is based on fact.* ◊ *It's important to* **distinguish fact from fiction.** **IDM** **,after the 'fact** after sth has happened or been done when it is too late to prevent it or change it: *On some vital decisions employees were only informed after the fact.* **the fact (of the matter) is (that) …** used to emphasize a statement, especially one that is the opposite of what has just been mentioned: *A new car would be wonderful but the fact of the matter is that we can't afford one.* **a ,fact of 'life** a situation that cannot be changed, especially one that is unpleasant **,facts and 'figures** accurate and detailed information: *I've asked to see all the facts and figures before I make a decision.* **the ,facts of 'life** the details about sex and about how babies are born, especially as told to children **the facts speak for them'selves** it is not necessary to give any further explanation about sth because the information that is available already proves that it is true **in (actual) fact 1** used to give extra details about sth that has just been mentioned: *I used to live in France; in fact, not far from where you're going.* **2** used to emphasize a statement, especially one that is the opposite of what has just been mentioned: *I thought the work would be difficult. In actual fact, it's very easy.* **Is that a 'fact?** (*spoken*) used to reply to a statement that you find interesting or surprising, or that you do not believe: *'She says I'm one of the best students she's ever taught.' 'Is that a fact?'*—more at MATTER *n.*, POINT *n.*

'fact-finding *adj.* [only before noun] that aims to find out information about a country, an organization, a situation, etc: *a fact-finding mission/visit*

fac·tion /ˈfækʃn/ *noun* **1** [C] a small group of people within a larger one whose members have some different aims and beliefs to those of the larger group: *rival factions within the administration* **2** [U] opposition, disagreement, etc. that exists between small groups of people within an organization or political party: *a party divided by faction and intrigue* **3** [U] films/movies, books, etc. that combine fact with FICTION (= imaginary events)

fac·tion·al /ˈfækʃnəl/ *adj.* [only before noun] connected with the factions of an organization or political party: *factional conflict/infighting* ▶ **fac·tion·al·ism** *noun* [U]

fac·ti·tious /fækˈtɪʃəs/ *adj.* (*rare, formal*) not genuine but created deliberately and made to appear to be true

fac·tor /ˈfæktə(r)/ *noun, verb*

■ *noun* **1** [C] one of several things that cause or influence sth: *environmental/economic factors* ◊ *The closure of the mine was the single most important factor in the town's decline.* ◊ *the* **key/crucial/deciding factor 2** [C] (*mathematics*) a number that divides into another number exactly: *2, 3, 4 and 6 are factors of 12.* **3** [C] the amount by which sth increases or decreases: *The real wage of the average worker has increased by a factor of over ten in the last 70 years.* **4** [C] a particular level on a scale of measurement: *a suntan lotion with a protection factor of 10* ◊ *The wind-chill factor will make it seem colder.* **5** [U] (*medical*) a substance in the blood that helps the CLOTTING process. There are several types of this substance: *Haemophiliacs have no factor 8 in their blood* **IDM** see FEEL-GOOD

■ *verb* **PHRV** **,factor sth↔'in| factor sth↔'into sth** (*technical*) to include a particular fact or situation when you are thinking about or planning sth: *Remember to factor in staffing costs when you are planning the project.*

fac·tor·ial /fækˈtɔːriəl/ *noun* (*mathematics*) the result when you multiply a whole number by all the numbers below it: *factorial 5 (represented as 5!)* $= 5 \times 4 \times 3 \times 2 \times 1$

fac·tory /ˈfæktri; -təri/ *noun* (*pl.* **-ies**) a building or group

of buildings where goods are made: *a car factory* ◊ *factory workers*

'factory farm *noun* (*BrE*) a type of farm in which animals are kept inside in small spaces and are fed special food so that a large amount of meat, milk, etc. is produced as quickly and cheaply as possible—compare BATTERY FARM ▶ **'factory farming** *noun* [U]

,factory 'floor *noun* (often **the factory floor**) [sing.] the part of a factory where the goods are actually produced: *Jobs are at risk, not just* **on the factory floor** (= among the workers, rather than the managers) *but throughout the business.*

'factory ship *noun* a large ship used for catching fish, that has equipment for cleaning and freezing the fish on board

fac·to·tum /fækˈtəʊtəm; *AmE* -ˈtoʊ-/ *noun* (*formal* or *humorous*) a person employed to do a wide variety of jobs for sb

'fact sheet *noun* a piece of paper giving information about a subject, especially (in Britain) one discussed on a radio or television programme

fac·tual /ˈfæktʃuəl/ *adj.* based on or containing facts: *a factual account of events* ◊ *factual information/knowledge* ◊ *The essay contains a number of factual errors.* ▶ **factual·ly** /-tʃuəli/ *adv.*: *factually correct/accurate*

fac·ulty /ˈfæklti/ *noun* (*pl.* **-ies**) **1** [C, usually pl.] any of the physical or mental abilities that a person is born with: *the faculty of sight* ◊ *She retained her mental faculties* (= the ability to think and understand) *until the day she died.* ◊ *to be* **in full possession of your faculties** (= be able to speak, hear, see, understand, etc.) **2** [sing.] **~ of (doing) sth** (*formal*) a particular ability for doing sth: *the faculty of understanding complex issues* ◊ *a faculty for seeing his own mistakes* **3** [C] a department or group of related departments in a college or university: *the Faculty of Law* ◊ *the Arts Faculty* **4** [C+sing./pl. *v.*] all the teachers in a faculty of a college or university: *the Law School faculty* ◊ *a faculty meeting* ◊ *faculty members* **5** [C, U] (often **the faculty**) (*AmE*) all the teachers of a particular university or college: *faculty members*

fad /fæd/ *noun* something that people are interested in for only a short period of time: *the latest/current fad* ◊ *a fad for physical fitness* ◊ *Rap music proved to be more than just a* **passing fad.**

faddy /ˈfædi/ *adj.* (*BrE, informal, disapproving*) liking some things and not others, especially food, in a way that other people think is unreasonable: *a faddy eater* ▶ **faddi·ness** *noun* [U]

fade /feɪd/ *verb* **1** to become or to make sth become paler or less bright: [V] *All colour had faded from the sky.* ◊ *The curtains had faded in the sun.* ◊ [VN] *The sun had faded the curtains.* ◊ *He was wearing faded blue jeans.* **2** [V] **~ (away)** to disappear gradually: *Her smile faded.* ◊ *Hopes of reaching an agreement seem to be fading away.* ◊ *His voice faded to a whisper* (= gradually became quieter). ◊ *The laughter faded away.* ◊ *All other issues* **fade into insignificance** compared with the struggle for survival. **3** if a sports player, team, actor, etc. **fades**, they stop playing or performing as well as they did before: *Black faded on the final bend.* **IDM** see WOODWORK **PHRV** **,fade a'way** (of a person) to become very weak or ill/sick and die: *In the last weeks of her life she simply faded away.* **,fade 'in/'out** to become clearer or louder / less clear or quieter: *George saw the monitor black out and then a few words faded in.* **,fade sth 'in/'out** to make a picture or a sound clearer or louder / less clear or quieter: *Fade out the music at the end of the scene.*

'fade-out *noun* [U, C] (in cinema or broadcasting) the process of making sound or a picture gradually less loud or clear

fae·ces (*BrE*) (*AmE* **feces**) /ˈfiːsiːz/ *noun* [pl.] (*formal*) solid waste material that leaves the body through the ANUS ▶ **fae·cal** (*BrE*) (*AmE* **fecal**) /ˈfiːkl/ *adj.* [only before noun]

faff /fæf/ *verb* **PHRV** **,faff a'bout/a'round** (*BrE, spoken*) to spend time doing things in a way that is not well

F

organized and that does not achieve much: *Stop faffing about and get on with it!*

fag /fæg/ *noun* **1** [C] (*BrE, informal*) = CIGARETTE **2** [C] (*AmE, △, slang*) an offensive word for a male HOMOSEXUAL **3** [sing.] (*BrE, informal*) something that is boring and tiring to do: *It's too much of a fag to go out.* **4** [C] (*BrE*) (especially in the past) a boy at a PUBLIC SCHOOL who has to do jobs for an older boy

fag 'end *noun* (*BrE, informal*) **1** [C] the last part of a cigarette that is left after it has been smoked **2** [sing.] **the ~ of sth** the last part of sth, especially when it is less important or interesting: *I only caught the fag end of their conversation.*

fagged /fægd/ (*also* **fagged 'out**) *adj.* [not before noun] (*BrE, spoken*) very tired [IDM] **I can't be 'fagged (to do sth)** used to say that you are too tired or bored to do sth

fag·got /ˈfægət/ *noun* **1** (*BrE*) a ball of finely chopped meat mixed with bread, baked or fried and eaten hot **2** (*also* **fag**) (*AmE, informal, △*) an offensive word for a HOMOSEXUAL man **3** a bunch of sticks tied together, used for burning on a fire

fah (*also* **fa**) /fɑː/ *noun* (*music*) the fourth note of a MAJOR scale

Fahr·en·heit /ˈfærənhaɪt/ *adj.* (*abbr.* F) of or using a scale of temperature in which water freezes at 32° and boils at 212°: *fifty degrees Fahrenheit* ⇨ Appendix 3 ▶ **Fahr·en·heit** *noun* [U]: *to give the temperature in Fahrenheit*

fail /feɪl/ *verb, noun*
■ *verb*
NOT SUCCEED | **1 ~ (in sth)** to not be successful in achieving sth: [V] *I failed in my attempt to persuade her.* ◊ *Many diets fail because they are boring.* ◊ *a failing school* ◊ [Vtoinf] *She failed to get into art college.* ◊ *The song can't fail to be a hit* (= definitely will be a hit).
NOT DO STH | **2** to not do sth: [Vtoinf] *He failed to keep the appointment.* ◊ *She never fails to e-mail every week.* ◊ *I fail to see* (= I don't understand) *why you won't even give it a try.* ◊ [V] *He felt he would be failing in his duty if he did not report it.*
TEST/EXAM | **3** to not pass a test or an exam; to decide that sb/sth has not passed a test or an exam: [VN] *He failed his driving test.* ◊ *The examiners failed over half the candidates.* ◊ *She was disqualified after failing a drugs test.* ◊ [V] *What will you do if you fail?* [OPP] PASS
OF MACHINES/PARTS OF BODY | **4** [V] to stop working: *The brakes on my bike failed half way down the hill.*
OF HEALTH/SIGHT | **5** [V] (especially in the progressive tenses) to become weak: *Her eyesight is failing.* ◊ *His last months in office were marred by failing health.*
DISAPPOINT SB | **6** [VN] to DISAPPOINT sb; to be unable to help when needed: *When he lost his job, he felt he had failed his family.* ◊ *She tried to be brave, but her courage failed her.* ◊ (*figurative*) *Words fail me* (= I cannot express how I feel).
NOT BE ENOUGH | **7** [V] to not be enough when needed or expected: *The crops failed again last summer.* ◊ *The rains had failed and the rivers were dry.*
OF COMPANY/BUSINESS | **8** [V] to be unable to continue: *Several banks failed during the recession.*
■ *noun* the result of an exam in which a person is not successful: *I got three passes and one fail.* [IDM] **without 'fail 1** when you tell sb to do sth **without fail**, you are telling them that they must do it: *I want you here by two o'clock without fail.* **2** always: *He writes every week without fail.*

failed /feɪld/ *adj.* [only before noun] not successful: *a failed writer* ◊ *a failed coup*

fail·ing /ˈfeɪlɪŋ/ *noun, prep.*
■ *noun* [usually pl.] a weakness or fault in sb/sth: *She is aware of her own failings.* ◊ *The inquiry acknowledges failings in the judicial system.*
■ *prep.* used to introduce a suggestion that could be considered if the one just mentioned is not possible: *Ask a friend to recommend a doctor or, **failing that**, ask for a list in your local library.*

'fail-safe *adj.* [usually before noun] (of machinery or equipment) designed to stop working if anything goes wrong: *a fail-safe device/mechanism/system*

fail·ure /ˈfeɪljə(r)/ *noun*
NOT SUCCESSFUL | **1** [U] lack of success in doing or achieving sth: *The success or failure of the plan depends on you.* ◊ *The attempt was **doomed to failure**.* ◊ *All my efforts ended in failure.* ◊ *the problems of economic failure and increasing unemployment* ◊ *She is still coming to terms with the failure of her marriage.* [OPP] SUCCESS **2** [C] somebody or something that is not successful: *The whole thing was a complete failure.* ◊ *He was a failure as a teacher.* [OPP] SUCCESS
NOT DOING STH | **3** [U, C] **~ to do sth** an act of not doing sth, especially sth that you are expected to do: *the failure of the United Nations to maintain food supplies* ◊ *Failure to comply with the regulations will result in prosecution.*
OF MACHINE/PART OF BODY | **4** [U, C] the state of not working correctly or as expected; an occasion when this happens: *patients suffering from heart/kidney failure* ◊ *A power failure plunged everything into darkness.* ◊ *The cause of the crash was given as engine failure.*
OF BUSINESS | **5** [C, U] **business ~** a situation in which a business has to close because it is not successful
OF CROP/HARVEST | **6** [U, C] **crop/harvest ~** a situation in which crops do not grow correctly and do not produce food

faint /feɪnt/ *adj., verb, noun*
■ *adj.* (**faint·er, faint·est**) **1** that cannot be clearly seen, heard or smelt: *a faint glow/glimmer/light* ◊ *a faint smell of perfume* ◊ *We could hear their voices growing fainter as they walked down the road.* ◊ *His breathing became faint.* **2** very small; possible but unlikely: *There is still a faint hope that she may be cured.* ◊ *They don't have the faintest chance of winning.* **3** not enthusiastic: *a faint show of resistance* ◊ *a faint smile* **4** [not before noun] feeling weak and tired and likely to lose consciousness: *She suddenly felt faint.* ◊ *The walkers were faint from hunger.* ▶ **faint·ly** *adv.*: *She smiled faintly.* ◊ *He looked faintly embarrassed.* [IDM] **not have the 'faintest (idea)** (*informal*) to not know anything at all about sth: *I didn't have the faintest idea what you meant.*—more at DAMN *v.*
■ *verb* [V] to become unconscious when not enough blood is going to your brain, usually because of the heat, a shock, etc: *to faint from hunger* ◊ *Suddenly the woman in front of me fainted.* ◊ (*informal*) *I almost fainted* (= I was very surprised) *when she told me.*
■ *noun* [sing.] the state of losing consciousness: *He fell to the ground in a dead faint.*

faint-'hearted *adj.* lacking confidence and not brave; afraid of failing [SYN] COWARDLY: *He tried not to appear faint-hearted.* ▶ **the ,faint-'hearted** *noun* [pl.]: *The climb is not for the faint-hearted* (= people who are not brave).

faint·ness /ˈfeɪntnəs/ *noun* [U] the state of feeling weak and tired and likely to lose consciousness: *The side effects include nausea and faintness.*

fair /feə(r); *AmE* fer/ *adj., adv., noun*
■ *adj.* (**fair·er, fair·est**)
ACCEPTABLE/APPROPRIATE | **1 ~ (to/on sb)** acceptable and appropriate in a particular situation: *a fair deal/wage/price/question* ◊ *The punishment was very fair.* ◊ *Was it really fair to him to ask him to do all the work?* ◊ *It's not fair on the students to keep changing the timetable.* ◊ *It's only fair to add that they were not told about the problem until the last minute.* ◊ *It seems only fair that they should give us something in return.* ◊ *I think it is fair to say that they are pleased with this latest offer.* ◊ *To be fair, she behaved better than we expected.* ◊ (*especially BrE*) 'You should really have asked me first.' 'Right, okay, **fair comment**.' [OPP] UNFAIR
TREATING PEOPLE EQUALLY | **2 ~ (to sb)** treating everyone equally and according to the rules or law: *She has always been scrupulously fair.* ◊ *demands for a fairer distribution of wealth* ◊ *We have to be fair to both players.* ◊ *to receive a fair trial* ◊ *free and fair elections* ◊ *It's not fair! He always gets more than me.* ◊ *The new tax is fairer than the old system.* [OPP] UNFAIR

b	d	f	g	h	k	l	m	n	p	r
bad	did	fall	get	hat	cat	leg	man	now	pen	red

F

QUITE LARGE | **3** [only before noun] quite large in number, size or amount: *A fair number of people came along.* ◇ *a fair-sized town* ◇ *We've still got a fair bit/amount* (= quite a lot) *to do.*

QUITE GOOD | **4** (*especially BrE*) quite good: *There's a fair chance that we might win this time.* ◇ *It's a fair bet that they won't turn up.* ◇ *I have a fair idea of what happened.* ◇ *His knowledge of French is only fair.*

HAIR/SKIN | **5** pale in colour: *a fair complexion* ◇ *She has long fair hair.* ◇ *All her children are fair* (= they all have fair hair).

WEATHER | **6** bright and not raining: *a fair and breezy day* **7** (*literary*) (of winds) not too strong and blowing in the right direction: *They set sail with the first fair wind.*

BEAUTIFUL | **8** (*literary* or *old use*) beautiful: *a fair maiden*

IDM **all's fair in love and 'war** (*saying*) in some situations any type of behaviour is acceptable to get what you want **be 'fair!** (*spoken*) used to tell sb to be reasonable in their judgement of sb/sth: *Be fair! She didn't know you were coming.* **by fair means or 'foul** using dishonest methods if honest ones do not work **a fair crack of the 'whip** (*BrE, informal*) a reasonable opportunity to show that you can do sth: *I felt we weren't given a fair crack of the whip.* **fair e'nough** (*spoken, especially BrE*) used to say that an idea or suggestion seems reasonable: *'We'll meet at 8.' 'Fair enough.'* ◇ *If you don't want to come, fair enough, but let Bill know.* **(give sb) a fair 'hearing** (to allow sb) the opportunity to give their point of view about sth before deciding if they have done sth wrong, often in a court of law: *I'll see that you get a fair hearing.* **fair's 'fair** (*spoken*) (*BrE also* **fair 'dos/'do's**) used, especially as an exclamation, to say that you think that an action, decision, etc. is acceptable and appropriate because it means that everyone will be treated fairly: *Fair's fair—you can't expect them to cancel everything just because you can't make it.* **(give sb/get) a fair 'shake** (*AmE, informal*) (to give sb/get) fair treatment that gives you the same chance as sb else **(more than) your fair share of sth** (more than) an amount of sth that is considered to be reasonable or acceptable: *He has more than his fair share of problems.* ◇ *I've had my fair share of success in the past.* **it's a fair 'cop** (*BrE, spoken, humorous*) used by sb who is caught doing sth wrong, to say that they admit that they are wrong

■ *adv.* according to the rules; in a way that is considered to be acceptable and appropriate: *Come on, you two, fight fair!* ◇ *They'll respect you as long as you play fair* (= behave honestly).

IDM **fair and 'square** (also **fairly and 'squarely**) **1** honestly and according to the rules: *We won the election fair and square.* **2** (*BrE*) in a direct way that is easy to understand: *I told him fair and square to pack his bags.* **3** (*BrE*) exactly in the place you were aiming for: *I hit the target fair and square.* **set fair (to do sth/for sth)** (*BrE*) having the necessary qualities or conditions to succeed: *She seems set fair to win the championship.* ◇ *Conditions were set fair for stable economic development.*—more at SAY *v.*

■ *noun*

ENTERTAINMENT | **1** (*BrE also* **fun-fair**) (*AmE also* **car·ni·val**) a type of entertainment in a field or park at which people can ride on large machines and play games to win prizes: *Let's take the kids to the fair.* ◇ *all the fun of the fair* **2** (*AmE*) a type of entertainment in a field or park at which farm animals and products are shown and take part in competitions: *the county/state fair* **3** (*BrE*) = FÊTE

BUSINESS | **4** an event at which people, businesses, etc. show and sell their goods: *a world trade fair* ◇ *a craft/a book/an antique fair*

ANIMAL MARKET | **5** (*BrE*) (in the past) a market at which animals were sold: *a horse fair*

JOBS | **6** **job/careers ~** an event at which people who are looking for jobs can get information about companies who might employ them

ˌfair 'copy *noun* (*BrE*) a neat version of a piece of writing

ˌfair 'game *noun* [U] if a person or thing is said to be **fair game**, it is considered acceptable to play jokes on them,

criticize them, etc: *The younger teachers were considered fair game by most of the kids.*

fair·ground /ˈfeəɡraʊnd; *AmE* ˈferɡ-/ *noun* **1** an outdoor area where a FAIR with entertainments is held **2** [usually pl.] (*AmE*) a place where a FAIR showing farm animals, farm products, etc. is held: *the Ohio State Fairgrounds* **3** [usually pl.] (*AmE*) a place where companies and businesses hold a FAIR to show their products: *the Milan trade fairgrounds*

ˌfair-'haired *adj.* with light or BLONDE hair

fair·ly /ˈfeəli; *AmE* ˈferli/ *adv.* **1** (before adjectives and adverbs) to some extent but not very: *a fairly easy book* ◇ *a fairly typical reaction* ◇ *I know him fairly well, but I wouldn't say we were really close friends.* ◇ *I go jogging fairly regularly.* ◇ *We'll have to leave fairly soon* (= before very long). ◇ *I'm fairly certain I can do the job.* ◇ *The report was fairly incomprehensible.* ◇ *I think you'll find it fairly difficult* (= you do not want to say that it is very difficult). ⇨ note at QUITE **2** in a fair and reasonable way; honestly: *He has always treated me very fairly.* ◇ *Her attitude could fairly be described as hostile.* **3** (*old-fashioned*) used to emphasize sth that you are saying: *I fairly jumped for joy.* ◇ *The time fairly raced by.* **IDM** **fairly and squarely** = FAIR AND SQUARE

ˌfair-'minded *adj.* (of people) looking at and judging things in a fair and open way

fair·ness /ˈfeənəs; *AmE* ˈfernəs/ *noun* [U] **1** the quality of treating people equally or in a way that is reasonable: *the fairness of the judicial system* **2** (of skin or hair) a pale colour: *A tan emphasized the fairness of her hair.* **IDM** **in (all) fairness (to sb)** used to introduce a statement that defends sb who has just been criticized, or that explains another statement that may seem unreasonable: *In all fairness to him, he did try to stop her leaving.*

ˌfair 'play *noun* [U] the fact of playing a game or acting honestly, fairly and according to the rules: *a player admired for his sense of fair play* ◇ *The task of the organization is to ensure fair play when food is distributed to the refugees.*

the ˌfair 'sex (also **the ˌfairer 'sex**) *noun* [sing.+ sing./pl. v.] (*old-fashioned*) women

fair·way /ˈfeəweɪ; *AmE* ˈferweɪ/ *noun* (in golf) the long strip of short grass that you must hit the ball along before you get to the GREEN and the hole—compare THE ROUGH—picture at GOLF

ˈfair-weather *adj.* [only before noun] (*disapproving*) (of people) behaving in a particular way or doing a particular activity only when it is pleasant for them: *a fair-weather friend* (= sb who stops being a friend when you are in trouble)

fairy /ˈfeəri; *AmE* ˈferi/ *noun* (*pl.* **-ies**) **1** (in stories) a creature like a small person, who has magic powers: *a good/wicked fairy* **2** (*disapproving, slang*) an offensive word for a HOMOSEXUAL man

ˈfairy cake (*BrE*) (also **cup·cake** *AmE, BrE*) *noun* a small cake, baked in a paper container shaped like a cup and often with ICING on top—picture on page A1

ˌfairy 'godmother *noun* a person who rescues you when you most need help

fairy·land /ˈfeərilænd; *AmE* ˈferi-/ *noun* **1** [U] the home of FAIRIES **2** [sing.] a beautiful, special or unusual place: *The toyshop is a fairyland for young children.*

ˈfairy lights *noun* [pl.] (*BrE*) small coloured electric lights used for decoration, especially on a tree at Christmas

ˈfairy tale (also ˈfairy story) *noun* **1** a story about magic or FAIRIES, usually for children: *the prince in a fairy tale* **2** a story that sb tells that is not true; a lie: *Now tell me the truth: I don't want any more of your fairy stories.*

ˈfairy-tale *adj.* typical of sth in a fairy tale: *a fairy-tale castle on an island* ◇ *a fairy-tale wedding in the cathedral*

fait ac·com·pli /ˌfeɪt əˈkɒmpli:; *AmE* əˈkɑ:m-/ *noun* [usually sing.] (*pl.* **faits ac·com·plis** /ˌfeɪz əˈkɒmpli:; *AmE* əˈkɑ:m-/) (from French) something that has already happened or been done and that you cannot change: *We got married secretly and then presented our parents with a fait accompli.*

s	t	v	z	ʃ	ʒ	tʃ	dʒ	θ	ð	ŋ
see	tea	van	zoo	shoe	vision	chain	jam	thin	this	sing

faith /feɪθ/ *noun* **1** [U] ~ (**in sb/sth**) trust in sb's ability or knowledge; trust that sb/sth will do what has been promised: *I have great faith in you—I know you'll do well.* ◇ *We've lost faith in the government's promises.* ◇ *Her friend's kindness has restored her faith in human nature.* **2** [U, sing.] strong religious belief: *blind/unquestioning faith* ◇ *to lose your faith* ◇ *Faith is stronger than reason.* **3** [C] a particular religion: *the Christian faith* ◇ *The children are learning to understand people of different faiths.* **4** (**good ~**) [U] the intention to do sth right: *They handed over the weapons as a gesture of good faith.* **IDM** **break/keep faith with sb** to break/keep a promise that you have made to sb; to stop/continue being loyal to sb **in bad 'faith** knowing that what you are doing is wrong **in good 'faith** believing that what you are doing is right; believing that sth is correct: *We printed the report in good faith but have now learnt that it was incorrect.* ◇ *He bought the painting in good faith (= he did not know that it had been stolen).*—more at PIN *v.*

faith·ful /ˈfeɪθfl/ *adj.* **1** ~ (**to sb/sth**) staying with or supporting a particular person, organization or belief **SYN** LOYAL: *a faithful servant/friend/dog* ◇ *He remained faithful to the ideals of the party until his death.* ◇ *She was rewarded for her 40 years' faithful service with the company.* ◇ *I have been a faithful reader of your newspaper for many years.* **2** (**the faithful**) *noun* [pl.] people who believe in a religion; the loyal supporters of a political party: *The president will keep the support of the party faithful.* **3** (of a wife, husband or partner) ~ (**to sb**) not having a sexual relationship with anyone else **4** ~ (**to sth**) true and accurate; not changing anything: *a faithful copy/account/description/representation* ◇ *His translation manages to be faithful to the spirit of the original.* **5** [only before noun] able to be trusted; that you can rely on: *a faithful worker/correspondent* ◇ *my faithful old car* ▶ **faith·ful·ness** *noun* [U]: *faithfulness to tradition* ◇ *She had doubts about his faithfulness.*

faith·ful·ly /ˈfeɪθfəli/ *adv.* **1** accurately; carefully: *to follow instructions faithfully* ◇ *The events were faithfully recorded in her diary.* **2** in a loyal way; in a way that you can rely on: *He had supported the local team faithfully for 30 years.* ◇ *She promised faithfully not to tell anyone my secret.* **IDM** **Yours faithfully** (*BrE*) used at the end of a formal letter before you sign your name, when you have addressed sb as 'Dear Sir/Dear Madam, etc.' and not by their name ⇨ Study page B14

'faith healing *noun* [U] a method of treating a sick person through the power of belief and prayer ▶ **'faith healer** *noun*

faith·less /ˈfeɪθləs/ *adj.* (*formal*) not loyal; that you cannot rely on or trust: *a faithless friend/wife/ally*

fake /feɪk/ *adj., noun, verb*
■ *adj.* **1** (*disapproving*) not genuine; appearing to be sth it is not: *fake designer clothing* ◇ *a fake American accent* **2** made to look like sth else: *a Jean Paul Gaultier jacket in fake fur* ◇ *Don't go out in the sun—get a fake tan from a bottle.*
■ *noun* **1** an object such as a work of art, a coin or a piece of jewellery that is not genuine but has been made to look as if it is: *All the paintings proved to be fakes.* **2** a person who pretends to be what they are not in order to deceive people
■ *verb* **1** [VN] to make sth false appear to be genuine, especially in order to deceive sb: *She faked her mother's signature on the document.* ◇ *He arranged the accident in order to fake his own death.* **2** to pretend to have a particular feeling, illness, etc: [VN] *She's not really sick—she's just faking it.* ◇ *He faked a yawn.* [also V] ▶ **faker** *noun*

fakir /ˈfeɪkɪə(r); *AmE* fəˈkɪr/ *noun* a Muslim holy man without possessions who lives by asking other people for money or food (= by BEGGING)

fal·con /ˈfɔːlkən; *AmE* ˈfælkən/ *noun* a BIRD OF PREY (= a bird that kills other creatures for food) with long pointed wings

fal·con·er /ˈfɔːlkənə(r); *AmE* ˈfælkənər/ *noun* a person who keeps and trains falcons, often using them for hunting

fal·con·ry /ˈfɔːlkənri; *AmE* ˈfæl-/ *noun* [U] the art or sport of breeding falcons and training them to hunt and kill other birds or animals

fall /fɔːl/ *verb, noun*
■ *verb* (**fell** /fel/ **fall·en** /ˈfɔːlən/)
DROP DOWN | **1** [V] [usually +*adv./prep.*] to drop down from a higher level to a lower level: *Several of the books had fallen onto the floor.* ◇ *One of the kids fell into the river.* ◇ *The handle had fallen off the drawer.* ◇ *September had come and the leaves were starting to fall.* ◇ *He fell 20 metres onto the rocks below.* ◇ *The rain was falling steadily.* ◇ *They were injured by falling rocks.*
STOP STANDING | **2** [V] [usually +*adv./prep.*] to suddenly stop standing: *She slipped on the ice and fell.* ◇ *I fell over and cut my knee.* ◇ *The house looked as if it was about to fall down.*—see also FALLEN
OF HAIR/MATERIAL | **3** [V+*adv./prep.*] to hang down: *Her hair fell over her shoulders in a mass of curls.*
SLOPE DOWNWARDS | **4** [V] ~ (**away/off**) to slope downwards: *Beyond the hill, the land falls away sharply towards the river.*
DECREASE | **5** to decrease in amount, number or strength: [V] *Their profits have fallen by 30 per cent.* ◇ *Prices continued to fall on the stock market today.* ◇ *The temperature fell sharply in the night.* ◇ *falling birth rates* ◇ (*written*) *Her voice fell to a whisper.* ◇ [VN] *Share prices fell 30p.*
BE DEFEATED | **6** [V] to be defeated or captured: *The coup failed but the government fell shortly afterwards.* ◇ *Troy finally fell to the Greeks.*
DIE IN BATTLE | **7** [V] (*literary*) to die in battle; to be shot: *a memorial to those who fell in the two world wars*
BECOME | **8** to pass into a particular state; to begin to be sth: [V-ADJ] *He had fallen asleep on the sofa.* ◇ *The book fell open at a page of illustrations.* ◇ (*written*) *The room had fallen silent.* ◇ *She fell ill soon after and did not recover.* ◇ [V] *I had fallen into conversation with a man on the train.* ◇ *The house had fallen into disrepair.* ◇ [V-N] *She knew she must not fall prey to his charm.*
HAPPEN/OCCUR | **9** [V] ~ (**on sb/sth**) (*literary*) to come quickly and suddenly **SYN** DESCEND: *A sudden silence fell.* ◇ *Darkness falls quickly in the tropics.* ◇ *An expectant hush fell on the guests.* **10** [V+*adv./prep.*] to happen or take place: *My birthday falls on a Monday this year.* **11** [V+*adv./prep.*] to move in a particular direction or come in a particular position: *My eye fell on (= I suddenly saw) a curious object.* ◇ *Which syllable does the stress fall on?* ◇ *A shadow fell across her face.*
BELONG TO GROUP | **12** [V+*adv./prep.*] to belong to a particular class, group or area of responsibility: *Out of over 400 staff there are just 7 that fall into this category.* ◇ *This case falls outside my jurisdiction.* ◇ *This falls under the heading of scientific research.*
IDM Idioms containing **fall** are at the entries for the nouns and adjectives in the idioms, for example **fall by the wayside** is at **wayside**.
PHRV **fall a'bout** (*BrE, informal*) to laugh a lot: [+-ing] *We all fell about laughing.*
fall a'part 1 to be in very bad condition so that parts are breaking off: *My car is falling apart.* **2** to have so many problems that it is no longer possible to exist or function: *Their marriage finally fell apart.* ◇ *The deal fell apart when we failed to agree on a price.*
fall a'way to become gradually fewer or smaller; to disappear: *His supporters fell away as his popularity declined.* ◇ *The market for their products fell away to almost nothing.* ◇ *All our doubts fell away.* ◇ *The houses fell away as we left the city.*
fall 'back 1 to move or turn back **SYN** RETREAT: *The enemy fell back as our troops advanced.* **2** to decrease in value or amount **fall 'back on sb/sth** [no passive] to go to sb for support; to have sth to use when you are in difficulty: *I have a little money in the bank to fall back on.* ◇ *She fell back on her usual excuse of having no time.*—related noun FALLBACK
fall be'hind | **fall be'hind sb/sth** to fail to keep level with sb/sth: *She soon fell behind the leaders.* **fall be'hind with sth** to not pay or do sth at the right time: *They had*

fallen behind with their mortgage repayments. ◊ *He's fallen behind with his school work again.*

,fall ˈdown to be shown to be not true or not good enough: *And that's where the theory falls down.*—see also FALL *v.* (2)

ˈfall for sb [no passive] (*informal*) to be strongly attracted to sb; to fall in love with sb: *They fell for each other instantly.* ˈfall for sth [no passive] (*informal*) to be tricked into believing sth that is not true: *I'm surprised you fell for that trick.*

,fall ˈin if soldiers fall in, they form lines: *The sergeant ordered his men to fall in.* ,fall ˈin with sb/sth [no passive] (*BrE*) to agree to sth: *She fell in with my idea at once.* ˈfall into sth to be able to be divided into sth: *My talk falls naturally into three parts.*

,fall ˈoff to decrease in quantity or quality: *Attendance at my lectures has fallen off considerably.*

ˈfall on/upon sb/sth [no passive] (*especially BrE*) **1** to attack or take hold of sb/sth with a lot of energy and enthusiasm: *They fell on him with sticks.* ◊ *The children fell on the food and ate it greedily.* **2** to be the responsibility of sb: *The full cost of the wedding fell on us.*

,fall ˈout **1** to become loose and drop: *His hair is falling out.* ◊ *My tooth fell out.* **2** if soldiers fall out, they leave their lines and move away ,fall ˈout (with sb) (*BrE*) to quarrel with sb so that you are no longer friendly with them

,fall ˈover sb/sth [no passive] to hit your foot against sth when you are walking and fall, or almost fall: *I rushed for the door and fell over the cat in the hallway.*—see also FALL *v.* (2) ,fall ˈover yourself to do sth (*informal*) to try very hard or want very much to do sth: *He was falling over himself to be nice to me.*

,fall ˈthrough to not be completed, or not happen: *Our plans fell through because of lack of money.*

ˈfall to sth (*literary*) to begin to do sth: [+ -ing] *She fell to brooding about what had happened to her.* ˈfall to sb to become the duty or responsibility of sb: *With his partner away, all the work now fell to him.* ◊ [+ to inf] *It fell to me to inform her of her son's death.*

■ *noun*

ACT OF FALLING | **1** [C] an act of falling: *I had a bad fall and broke my arm.* ◊ *She was killed in a fall from a horse.*

OF SNOW/ROCKS | **2** [C] ~ (of sth) an amount of snow, rocks, etc. that falls or has fallen: *a heavy fall of snow* ◊ *a rock fall*

WAY STH FALLS/HAPPENS | **3** [sing.] ~ of sth the way in which sth falls or happens: *the fall of the cards/dice* ◊ *the dark fall of her hair* (= the way her hair hangs down)

OF WATER | **4** (falls) [pl.] (especially in names) a large amount of water falling down from a height SYN WATER-FALL: *The falls upstream are full of salmon.* ◊ *Niagara Falls*

AUTUMN | **5** [C] (*AmE*) = AUTUMN: *in the fall of 1990* ◊ *last fall*

DECREASE | **6** [C] ~ (in sth) a decrease in size, number, rate or level: *a steep fall in prices/profits* ◊ *a big fall in unemployment*

DEFEAT | **7** [sing.] ~ (of sth) a loss of political, economic, etc. power or success; the loss or defeat of a city, country, etc. in war: *the fall of the Roman Empire* ◊ *the rise and fall of British industry* ◊ *the fall of Berlin*

LOSS OF RESPECT | **8** [sing.] a situation in which a person, an organization, etc. loses the respect of other people because they have done sth wrong: *the TV preacher's spectacular fall from grace*

IN BIBLE | **9** (the Fall) [sing.] the occasion when Adam and Eve did not obey God and had to leave the Garden of Eden

IDM see PRIDE *n.*, RIDE *v.*

fal·la·cious /fəˈleɪʃəs/ *adj.* (*formal*) wrong; based on a false idea: *a fallacious argument*

fal·lacy /ˈfæləsi/ *noun* (*pl.* -ies) **1** [C] a false idea that many people believe is true: *It is a fallacy to say that the camera never lies.* **2** [U, C] a false way of thinking about sth: *He detected the fallacy of her argument.*—see also PATHETIC FALLACY

fall·back /ˈfɔːlbæk/ *noun* a plan or course of action that

is ready to be used in an emergency if other things fail: *What's your fallback if they don't come up with the money?* ◊ *We need a fallback position if they won't do the job.*

fall·en /ˈfɔːlən/ *adj.* [only before noun] **1** lying on the ground, after falling: *The road was blocked by a fallen tree.* **2** (*formal*) (of a soldier) killed in a war—see also FALL *v.*

,fallen ˈwoman *noun* (*old-fashioned*) a way of describing a woman in the past who had a sexual relationship with sb who was not her husband

ˈfall guy *noun* (*especially AmE*) a person who is blamed or punished for sth wrong that sb else has done SYN SCAPE-GOAT

fall·ible /ˈfæləbl/ *adj.* able to make mistakes or be wrong: *Memory is selective and fallible.* ◊ *All human beings are fallible.* OPP INFALLIBLE ▶ fal·li·bil·ity /ˌfæləˈbɪləti/ *noun* [U]: *human fallibility*

ˈfalling-off *noun* [sing.] (*BrE*) = FALL-OFF

,falling ˈstar *noun* = SHOOTING STAR

ˈfall-off (*BrE* also *less frequent* ˈfalling-off) *noun* [sing.] ~ (in sth) a reduction in the number, amount or quality of sth: *a recent fall-off in sales*

Fal·lo·pian tubes /fəˌləʊpiən ˈtjuːbz; *AmE* fəˈloʊpiən tuːbz/ *noun* [pl.] (*anatomy*) the two tubes in the body of a woman or female animal along which eggs pass from the OVARIES to the UTERUS

fall·out /ˈfɔːlaʊt/ *noun* [U] **1** dangerous RADIOACTIVE dust that is in the air after a nuclear explosion **2** the bad results of a situation or an action: *the political fallout of the current crisis*

fal·low /ˈfæləʊ; *AmE* -loʊ/ *adj.* **1** (of farm land) not used for growing crops, especially so that the quality of the land will improve: *Farmers are now paid to let their land lie fallow.* **2** (of a period of time) when nothing is created or produced; not successful: *Contemporary dance is coming onto the arts scene again after a long fallow period.*

ˈfallow deer *noun* a small European deer with white spots on its back

false /fɔːls/ *adj.*

NOT TRUE | **1** wrong; not correct or true: *A whale is a fish. True or false?* ◊ *Predictions of an early improvement in the housing market proved false.* ◊ *She gave false information to the insurance company.* ◊ *He used a false name to get the job.*

NOT NATURAL | **2** not natural; artificial: *false teeth/eyelashes* ◊ *a false beard*

NOT GENUINE | **3** not genuine, but made to look real to deceive people: *a false passport* ◊ *a suitcase with a false bottom*

NOT SINCERE | **4** (of people's behaviour) not real or sincere: *false modesty* ◊ *She flashed him a false smile of congratulation.*

WRONG/MISTAKEN | **5** [usually before noun] wrong or MIS-TAKEN, because it is based on sth that is not true or correct: *a false argument/assumption/belief* ◊ *to give a false impression of wealth* ◊ *to lull sb into a false sense of security* (= make sb feel safe when they are really in danger) ◊ *They didn't want to raise any false hopes, but they believed her husband had escaped capture.* ◊ *Buying a cheap computer is a false economy* (= will not actually save you money).

NOT FAITHFUL | **6** (*literary*) (of people) not faithful: *a false lover*

▶ false·ly *adv.*: *to be falsely accused of sth* ◊ *She smiled falsely at his joke.*

IDM by/under/on false preˈtences by pretending to be sth that you are not, in order to gain some advantage for yourself: *She was accused of obtaining money under false pretences.*—more at RING² *v.*

,false aˈlarm *noun* a warning about a danger that does not happen; a belief that sth bad is going to happen, when it is not: *The fire service was called out but it was a false alarm.*

,false ˈdawn *noun* [usually sing.] (*formal*) a situation in which you think that sth good is going to happen but it does not: *a false dawn for the economy*

aɪ	aʊ	eɪ	əʊ	oʊ	ɔɪ	ɪə	eə	ʊə	j	w
my	now	say	go	go	boy	near	hair	pure	yes	wet
			(BrE)	(AmE)						

,false **'friend** noun **1** a person who seems to be your friend, but who is not loyal and cannot be trusted **2** a word in a foreign language that looks similar to a word in your own language, but has a different meaning: *The English word 'sensible' and the French word 'sensible' are false friends.*

false·hood /'fɔːlshʊd/ noun (*formal*) **1** [U] the state of not being true; the act of telling a lie: *to test the truth or falsehood of her claims* **2** [C] a statement that is not true; a lie

,false im'prisonment noun [U] (*law*) the crime of illegally keeping sb as a prisoner somewhere

,false **'move** noun [usually sing.] an action that is not allowed or not recommended and that may cause a bad result: *One false move and the bomb might blow up.*

,false **'start** noun **1** an attempt to begin sth that is not successful: *After a number of false starts, she finally found a job she liked.* **2** (*sport*) a situation when a competitor in a race starts before the official signal has been given

,false **'teeth** noun [pl.] a set of artificial teeth used by sb who has lost their natural teeth—compare DENTURES

fal·setto /fɔːlˈsetəʊ; AmE -toʊ/ noun (pl. **-os**) an unusually high voice, especially the voice that men use to sing very high notes

fals·ify /'fɔːlsɪfaɪ/ verb (**fal·si·fies, fal·si·fy·ing, fal·si·fied, fal·si·fied**) [VN] to change a written record or information so that it is no longer true: *to falsify data/records/accounts* ▶ **fal·si·fi·ca·tion** /ˌfɔːlsɪfɪˈkeɪʃn/ noun [U, C]: *the deliberate falsification of the company's records*

fal·sity /'fɔːlsəti/ noun [U] the state of not being true or genuine OPP TRUTH

fal·ter /'fɔːltə(r)/ verb **1** [V] to become weaker or less effective: *The economy shows no signs of faltering.* ◇ *Her courage never faltered.* **2** to speak in a way that shows that you are not confident: [V] *His voice faltered as he began his speech.* [also V speech] **3** [V] to walk or behave in a way that shows that you are not confident: *She walked up to the platform without faltering.* ◇ *He never faltered in his commitment to the party.* ▶ **fal·ter·ing** /'fɔːltərɪŋ/ adj.: *the faltering peace talks* ◇ *the baby's first faltering steps*

fame /feɪm/ noun [U] the state of being known and talked about by many people: *to achieve/win instant fame* ◇ *to rise/shoot to fame overnight* ◇ *Andrew Lloyd Webber of 'Evita' fame* (= famous for 'Evita') ◇ *The town's only claim to fame is that there was once a riot there.* ◇ *She went to Hollywood in search of fame and fortune.*—see also FAMOUS IDM see CLAIM n.

famed /feɪmd/ adj. ~ (**for sth**) (*written*) very well known SYN RENOWNED: *Las Vegas, famed for its casinos* ◇ *a famed poet and musician*—see also FAMOUS

fa·mil·ial /fəˈmɪliəl/ adj. [only before noun] (*formal*) **1** related to or typical of a family: *familial obligations* **2** (*medical*) (of diseases, conditions, etc.) affecting several members of a family: *familial left-handedness*

fa·mil·iar /fəˈmɪliə(r)/ adj. **1** ~ (**to sb**) well known to you; often seen or heard and therefore easy to recognize: *to look/sound/taste familiar* ◇ *He's a familiar figure in the neighbourhood.* ◇ *The smell is very familiar to everyone who lives near a bakery.* ◇ *Something about her voice was vaguely familiar.* ◇ *Violent attacks are becoming all too familiar* (= sadly familiar). OPP UNFAMILIAR **2** ~ **with sth** knowing sth very well: *an area with which I had been familiar since childhood* ◇ *Are you familiar with the computer software they use?* OPP UNFAMILIAR **3** ~ (**with sb**) (of a person's behaviour) very informal, sometimes in a way that is unpleasant: *You seem to be on very familiar terms with your tutor.* ◇ *After a few drinks her boss started getting too familiar for her liking.*

fa·mil·iar·ity /fəˌmɪliˈærəti/ noun [U] **1** ~ (**with sth**) | ~ (**to sb**) the state of knowing sb/sth well; the state of recognizing sb/sth: *His familiarity with the language helped him enjoy his stay.* ◇ *When she saw the house, she had a feeling of familiarity.* **2** a friendly informal manner: *She addressed me with an easy familiarity that made me feel at home.* IDM **familiarity breeds con'tempt** (*saying*)

knowing sb/sth very well may cause you to lose admiration and respect for them/it

fa·mil·iar·ize (BrE also **-ise**) /fəˈmɪliəraɪz/ verb [VN] ~ **yourself/sb** (**with sth**) to learn about sth or teach sb about sth, so that you/they start to understand it: *You'll need time to familiarize yourself with our office procedures.* ▶ **fa·mil·iar·iza·tion, -isa·tion** /fəˌmɪliəraɪˈzeɪʃn; AmE -rəˈz-/ noun [U]

fa·mil·iar·ly /fəˈmɪliəli; AmE -ərli/ adv. **1** in a friendly and informal manner, sometimes in a way that is too informal to be pleasant: *John Hunt, familiarly known to his friends as Jack* ◇ *He touched her cheek familiarly.* **2** in the way that is well known to people: *The elephant's nose or, more familiarly, trunk is the most versatile organ in the animal kingdom.*

fam·ily /'fæməli/ noun, adj.
■ noun (pl. **-ies**) **1** [C+sing./pl. v.] a group consisting of one or two parents and their children: *the other members of my family* ◇ *Almost every family in the country owns a television.* ◇ *All my family enjoy skiing.* ◇ *one-parent/single-parent families* ◇ *a family of four* ◇ *families with young children*—see also NUCLEAR FAMILY **2** [C+sing./pl. v., U] a group consisting of one or two parents, their children and close relations: *All our family came to Grandad's eightieth birthday party.* ◇ *The support of family and friends is vital.* ◇ *We've only told the immediate family* (= the closest relations). ◇ *the Royal Family* (= the children and close relations of the king or queen) ◇ *I always think of you as one of the family.* ◇ (*informal*) *She's family* (= she is a relation).—see also EXTENDED FAMILY **3** [C+sing./pl. v.] all the people who are related to each other, including those who are now dead: *Some families have farmed in this area for hundreds of years.* ◇ *This painting has been in our family for generations.* **4** [C+sing./pl. v., U] a couple's or a person's children, especially young children: *They have a large family.* ◇ *I addressed it to Mr and Mrs Jones and family.* ◇ *Do they plan to start a family* (= have children)? ◇ *to bring up/raise a family* **5** [C] a group of related animals and plants; a group of related things, especially languages: *Lions belong to the cat family.* ◇ *the Germanic family of languages* IDM (**be/get**) **in the 'family way** (*old-fashioned, informal*) (to be/become) pregnant **run in the 'family** to be a common feature in a particular family: *Heart disease runs in the family.*
■ adj. [only before noun] **1** connected with the family or a particular family: *family life* ◇ *your family background* **2** owned by a family: *a family business* **3** suitable for all members of a family, both adults and children: *a family show*

,family **'doctor** noun (*informal, especially BrE*) = GENERAL PRACTITIONER

'**family man** noun a man who has a wife or partner and children; a man who enjoys being at home with his wife or partner and children: *I see he's become a family man.* ◇ *a devoted family man*

'**family name** noun the part of your name that shows which family you belong to—compare SURNAME

,family **'planning** noun [U] the process of controlling the number of children you have by using CONTRACEPTION

,family **'practitioner** noun (*especially BrE*) = GENERAL PRACTITIONER

'**family room** noun **1** (AmE) a room in a house where the family can relax, watch television, etc. **2** a room in a hotel for three or four people to sleep in, especially parents and children **3** (in Britain) a room in a pub where children are allowed to sit

,family **'tree** noun a diagram that shows the relationship between members of a family over a long period of time: *How far back can you trace your family tree?*

fam·ine /'fæmɪn/ noun [C, U] a lack of food during a long period of time in a region: *a severe famine* ◇ *disasters such as floods and famine* ◇ *the threat of widespread famine in Africa* ◇ *to raise money for famine relief*

fam·ished /'fæmɪʃt/ adj. [not usually before noun] (*informal, becoming old-fashioned*) very hungry SYN STARVING: *When's lunch? I'm famished!*

F

	b	d	f	g	h	k	l	m	n	p	r
	bad	did	fall	get	hat	cat	leg	man	now	pen	red

fam·ous /ˈfeɪməs/ adj. ~ (for sth)| ~ (as sth) known about by many people: *a famous artist/hotel* ◊ *the most famous lake in Scotland* ◊ *He became internationally famous for his novels and poetry.* ◊ *One day, I'll be **rich and famous**.* ◊ *She was more famous as a writer than as a singer.*—see also FAME, INFAMOUS, NOTORIOUS, WORLD-FAMOUS

fam·ous·ly /ˈfeɪməsli/ adv. in a way that is famous: *Some newspapers, most famously the New York Times, refuse to print the word Ms.* **IDM** **get on/along ˈfamously** (*informal*, becoming *old-fashioned*) to have a very good relationship: *My mother and my mother-in-law are getting on famously.*

fan /fæn/ noun, verb
■ noun **1 a** a person who admires sb/sth or enjoys watching or listening to sb/sth very much: *movie fans* ◊ *crowds of football fans* ◊ *a big fan of Pavarotti* ◊ *fan mail* (= letters from fans to the person they admire) **2** a machine with blades that go round to create a current of air: *to switch on the electric fan* ◊ *a fan heater*—see also EXTRACTOR **3 a** thing that you hold in your hand and wave to create a current of cool air **IDM** see SHIT *n.*

fan

■ verb (**-nn-**) [VN] **1** to make air blow onto sb/sth by waving a fan, your hand, etc: *He fanned himself with a newspaper to cool down.* **2** to make a fire burn more strongly by blowing on it: *Fanned by a westerly wind, the fire spread rapidly through the city.* **3** (*written*) to make a feeling, an attitude, etc. stronger **SYN** FUEL: *His reluctance to answer her questions simply fanned her curiosity.* **IDM** **fan the ˈflames (of sth)** to make a feeling such as anger, hatred, etc. worse: *His writings fanned the flames of racism.* **PHRV** **ˌfan ˈout**| **ˌfan sth↔ˈout** to spread out or spread sth out over an area: *The police fanned out to surround the house.* ◊ *The bird fanned out its tail feathers.*

fan·at·ic /fəˈnætɪk/ noun **1** (*informal*) a person who is extremely enthusiastic about sth **SYN** ENTHUSIAST: *a fitness/crossword fanatic* **2** (*disapproving*) a person who holds extreme or dangerous opinions **SYN** EXTREMIST: *religious fanatics* ▶ **fan·at·ic·al** /-kl/ adj.: *a fanatical supporter* ◊ *fanatical anti-royalists* ◊ *a fanatical interest in football* ◊ *She's fanatical about healthy eating.* **fan·at·ic·al·ly** /-kli/ adv.: *fanatically fit*

fan·ati·cism /fəˈnætɪsɪzəm/ noun [U] (*disapproving*) extreme beliefs or behaviour, especially in connection with religion or politics

ˈfan belt noun a belt that operates the machinery that cools a car engine

fan·ci·able /ˈfænsiəbl/ adj. (*BrE, informal*) sexually attractive

fan·cier /ˈfænsiə(r)/ noun (usually in compounds) (*especially BrE*) a person who has a special interest in sth, especially sb who keeps or breeds birds, animals or plants: *a pigeon fancier*

fan·ci·ful /ˈfænsɪfl/ adj. (*written*) **1** (*disapproving*) based on imagination and not facts or reason **2** (of things) decorated in an unusual and imaginative style: *a fanciful gold border* ▶ **fan·ci·ful·ly** /-fəli/ adv.

ˈfan club noun an organization that a person's FANS belong to and that sends them information, etc. about that person

fancy /ˈfænsi/ verb, noun, adj.
■ verb (**fan·cies, fancy·ing, fan·cied, fan·cied**) **1** (*BrE, informal*) to want sth or want to do sth: [VN] *Fancy a drink?* ◊ *She didn't fancy* (= did not like) *the idea of going home in the dark.* ◊ [V-ing] *Do you fancy going out this evening?* **2** [VN] (*BrE, informal*) to be sexually attracted to sb: *I think she fancies me.* **3** [VN] ~ **yourself** (*BrE, informal, disapproving*) to think that you are very popular, attractive or intelligent: *He started to chat to me and I could tell that he really fancied himself.* **4** [VN-N] ~ **yourself (as) sth** (*BrE*) to like the idea of being sth or to believe, often wrongly, that you are sth: *She fancies her-*

self (as) a serious actress. **5** (**Fancy!**) (*BrE, spoken, becoming old-fashioned*) used to show that you are surprised or shocked by sth: [V] *Fancy! She's never been in a plane before.* ◊ [V-ing] *Fancy meeting you here!* ◊ [VN] *'She remembered my name after all those years.' ' Fancy that! '* **6** (*BrE*) [VN] to think that sb will win or be successful at sth, especially in a race: *Which horse do you fancy in the next race?* ◊ *He's hoping to get the job but I don't fancy his chances.* **7** [V (that)] (*literary*) to believe or imagine sth: *She fancied (that) she heard footsteps behind her.*
■ noun (*pl.* **-ies**) **1** [C, U] something that you imagine; your imagination **SYN** FANTASY: *teenage/girlish fancies* ◊ *night-time fancies that disappear in the morning* ◊ *a child's wild flights of fancy* **2** [sing.] a feeling that you would like to have or to do sth **SYN** WHIM: *She said she wanted a dog but it was only a passing fancy.* **3** [C, usually pl.] (*BrE*) a small decorated cake **IDM** **as/whenever etc. the fancy ˈtakes you** as/whenever, etc. you feel like doing sth: *We bought a camper van so we could go away whenever the fancy took us.* **catch/take sb's ˈfancy** to attract or please sb: *She looked through the hotel advertisements until one of them caught her fancy.* **take a ˈfancy to sb/sth** (*especially BrE*) to start liking sb/sth, often without an obvious reason—more at TICKLE *v.*
■ adj. (**fan·cier, fan·ci·est**) **1** unusually complicated, often in an unnecessary way: *a kitchen full of fancy gadgets* ◊ *They applied a lot of fancy footwork to the dance.* **OPP** SIMPLE **2** [only before noun] (especially of small things) with a lot of decorations or bright colours: *fancy goods* (= things sold as ornaments or gifts)—compare PLAIN **3** (sometimes *disapproving*) expensive or connected with an expensive way of life: *fancy restaurants with fancy prices* ◊ *Don't come back with any fancy ideas.*

ˌfancy ˈdress noun [U] (*BrE*) clothes that you wear, especially at parties, to make you appear to be a different character: *guests **in fancy dress**—*see also COSTUME, MASQUERADE

ˌfancy-ˈfree adj. free to do what you like because you are not emotionally involved with anyone: *I was still footloose and fancy-free* (= free to enjoy myself) *in those days.*

fan·fare /ˈfænfeə(r); AmE -fer/ noun **1** [C] a short loud piece of music that is played to celebrate sb/sth important arriving **2** [U, C] a large amount of activity and discussion on television, in newspapers, etc. to celebrate sb/sth: *The new century will begin amid much fanfare worldwide.*

fang /fæŋ/ noun [usually pl.] either of two long sharp teeth at the front of the mouths of some animals, such as a snake or dog—picture on page A7

fan·light /ˈfænlaɪt/ (*BrE*) (*AmE* **tran·som**) noun a small window above a door or another window

Fanny /ˈfæni/ noun **IDM** see SWEET *adj.*

fanny /ˈfæni/ noun (*pl.* **-ies**) **1** (*BrE, ⚠, slang*) the female sex organs **2** (*slang, especially AmE*) a person's bottom

ˈfanny pack noun (*AmE*) = BUMBAG

fan·ta·sia /fænˈteɪziə/ noun a piece of music that does not have a regular form or style, including one based on several well-known tunes

fan·ta·size (*BrE* also **-ise**) /ˈfæntəsaɪz/ verb ~ (**about sth**) to imagine that you are doing sth that you would like to do, or that sth that you would like to happen is happening, even though this is very unlikely: [V] *He sometimes fantasized about winning the gold medal.* [also V that] ▶ **fan·ta·sist** /ˈfæntəsɪst/ noun

fan·tas·tic /fænˈtæstɪk/ adj. **1** (*informal*) extremely good; excellent **SYN** GREAT, BRILLIANT: *a fantastic beach in Australia* ◊ *a fantastic achievement* ◊ *The weather was absolutely fantastic.* ◊ *You've got the job? Fantastic!* **2** (*informal*) very large; larger than you expected **SYN** ENORMOUS, AMAZING: *The response to our appeal was fantastic.* ◊ *The car costs a fantastic amount of money.* **3** (also less frequent **fan·tas·tic·al**) [usually before noun] strange and imaginative **SYN** WEIRD: *fantastic dreams of forests and jungles* **4** impossible to put into practice: *a fantastic scheme/project* ▶ **fan·tas·tic·al·ly** /fænˈtæstɪkli/ adv.:

s	t	v	z	ʃ	ʒ	tʃ	dʒ	θ	ð	ŋ
see	tea	van	zoo	shoe	vision	chain	jam	thin	this	sing

F

fantastically expensive/successful ◇ *a fantastically shaped piece of stone*

fan·ta·sy /ˈfæntəsi/ *noun* (*pl.* **-ies**) **1** [C] a pleasant situation that you imagine but that is unlikely to happen: *his childhood fantasies about becoming a famous football player* **2** [C] a product of your imagination: *Her books are usually escapist fantasies.* **3** [U] the act of imagining things; a person's imagination: *a work of fantasy* ◇ *Stop living in a fantasy world.*

fan·zine /ˈfænziːn/ *noun* a magazine that is written and read by FANS of a musician, sports team, etc.

FAQ *abbr.* used in writing to mean 'frequently asked questions'

far /fɑː(r)/ *adv., adj.*

■ *adv.* (**far·ther, far·thest** or **fur·ther, fur·thest**)
DISTANCE | **1** ~ (**from, away, below,** etc.) a long distance away: *We didn't go far.* ◇ *Have you come far?* ◇ *It's not far to the beach.* ◇ *There's not far to go now.* ◇ *The restaurant is not far from here.* ◇ *countries as far apart as Japan and Brazil* ◇ *He looked down at the traffic far below.* ◇ *Far away in the distance, a train whistled.* ◇ *The farther north they went, the colder it became.* **HELP** In positive sentences it is more usual to use **a long way**: *We went a long way.* ◇ *We went far.* ◇ *The restaurant is a long way from here.* **2** used when you are asking or talking about the distance between two places or the distance that has been travelled or is to be travelled: *How far is it to your house from here?* ◇ *How much further is it?* ◇ *We'll go by train as far as London, and then take a bus.* ◇ *We didn't go as far as the others.* ◇ *I'm not sure I can walk so far.*
TIME | **3** ~ (**back/ahead**)| ~ (**into sth**) a long time from the present; for a large part of a particular period of time: *The band made their first record as far back as 1980.* ◇ *Let's try to plan further ahead.* ◇ *We worked far into the night.*
DEGREE | **4** very much; to a great degree: *That's a far better idea.* ◇ *There are far more opportunities for young people than there used to be.* ◇ *It had been a success far beyond their expectations.* ◇ *He's fallen far behind in his work.* ◇ *She always gives us far too much homework.* **5** used when you are asking or talking about the degree to which sth is true or possible: *How far can we trust him?* ◇ *His parents supported him as far as they could.* ◇ *Plan your route in advance, using main roads as far as possible.*
PROGRESS | **6** used to talk about how much progress has been made in doing or achieving sth: *How far have you got with that report?* ◇ *I read as far as the third chapter.*
⇨ note at FARTHER
IDM as far as the eye can/could 'see to the HORIZON (= where the sky meets the land or sea): *The bleak moorland stretched on all sides as far as the eye could see.* **as far as I 'know | as far as I can re'member, 'see, 'tell,** etc. used to say that you think you know, remember, understand, etc. sth but you cannot be completely sure, especially because you do not know all the facts: *As far as we knew, there was no cause for concern.* ◇ *As far as I can see, you've done nothing wrong.* ◇ *She lived in Chicago, as far as I can remember.* **as/so far as 'I am concerned** used to give your personal opinion on sth: *As far as I am concerned, you can do what you like.* **as/so far as sb/sth is concerned** used to give facts or an opinion about a particular aspect of sth **as/so far as it 'goes** to a limited degree, usually less than is satisfactory: *It's a good plan as far as it goes, but there are a lot of things they haven't thought of.* **by 'far** (used with comparative or superlative adjectives or adverbs) by a great amount: *The last of these reasons is by far the most important.* ◇ *Amy is the smartest by far.* **carry/take sth too,** etc. **'far** to continue doing sth beyond reasonable limits **far and a'way** (followed by comparative or superlative adjectives) by a very great amount: *She's far and away the best player.* **far and 'wide** over a large area: *They searched far and wide for the missing child.* **far be it from me to do sth (but ...)** (*informal*) used when you are just about to disagree with sb or to criticize them and you would like them to think that you do not really want to do this: *Far be it from me to interfere in your affairs but I would like to give you just one piece of advice.* **far from sth/from doing sth** almost

the opposite of sth or of what is expected: *It is far from clear* (= it is not clear) *what he intends to do.* ◇ *Computers, far from destroying jobs, can create employment.* **far 'from it** (*informal*) used to say that the opposite of what sb says is true: *'You're not angry then?' 'Far from it. I've never laughed so much in my life.'* **go 'far** (of people) to be very successful in the future: *She is very talented and should go far.* **go far enough** (used in questions and negative sentences) to achieve all that is wanted: *The new legislation is welcome but does not go far enough.* ◇ *Do these measures go far enough?* ◇ (*disapproving*) *Stop it now. This joke has gone far enough* (= it has continued too long). **go so/as far as to ...** to be willing to go to extreme or surprising limits in dealing with sth: *I wouldn't go as far as to say that he's a liar* (= but I think he may be slightly dishonest). **go too 'far | go 'this/'that far** to behave in an extreme way that is not acceptable: *He's always been quite crude, but this time he's gone too far.* ◇ *I never thought she'd go this far.* **in so/as 'far as** to the degree that: *That's the truth, in so far as I know it.* **not far 'off/'out/ 'wrong** (*informal*) almost correct: *Your guess wasn't far out at all.* **not go 'far 1** (of money) to not be enough to buy a lot of things: *Five pounds doesn't go very far these days.* **2** (of a supply of sth) to not be enough for what is needed: *Four bottles of wine won't go far among twenty people.* **'so far | 'thus far** until now; up to this point: *What do you think of the show so far?* **,so far at a loss** to explain the reason for his death. **,so far** (*informal*) only to a limited degree: *I trust him only so far.* **,so far, so 'good** (*saying*) used to say that things have been successful until now and you hope they will continue to do so, but you know the task, etc. is not finished yet—more at AFIELD, FEW *adj.*, NEAR *adv.*

■ *adj.* (**far·ther, far·thest** or **fur·ther, fur·thest**) [only before noun]
DISTANT | **1** at a greater distance away from you: *I saw her on the far side of the road.* ◇ *at the far end of the room* ◇ *They made for an empty table in the far corner.* **2** at the furthest point in a particular direction: *the far north of Scotland* ◇ *Who is that on the far left of the photograph?* ◇ *She is on the far right of the party* (= holds extreme RIGHT-WING political views). **3** (*old-fashioned* or *literary*) a long distance away: *a far country*
IDM a far cry from sth a very different experience from sth

far·away /ˈfɑːrəweɪ/ *adj.* [only before noun] **1** a long distance away: *a war in a faraway country* **2** a ~ **look/ expression** an expression on your face that shows that your thoughts are far away from your present surroundings: *There was a faraway look in her eyes.*

farce /fɑːs; *AmE* fɑːrs/ *noun* **1** [C, U] a funny play for the theatre based on ridiculous and unlikely situations and events; this type of writing or performance: *a bedroom farce* (= a funny play about sex) **2** [C] a situation or an event that is so unfair or badly organized that it becomes ridiculous: *The trial was a complete farce.*

far·ci·cal /ˈfɑːsɪkl; *AmE* ˈfɑːrs-/ *adj.* ridiculous and not worth taking seriously: *It was a farcical trial.* ◇ *a situation verging on the farcical*

fare /feə(r); *AmE* fer/ *noun, verb*
■ *noun* **1** [C, U] the money that you pay to travel by bus, plane, taxi, etc: *air/bus/taxi fares* ◇ *train/rail fares* ◇ *Children travel (at) half fare.* ◇ *When do they start paying full fare?*—see also RETURN FARE **2** [C] a passenger in a taxi: *The taxi driver picked up a fare at the station.* **3** [U] (*old-fashioned* or *formal*) food that is offered as a meal: *The restaurant provides good traditional fare.*
■ *verb* [V] ~ **well, badly, better,** etc. to be successful/ unsuccessful in a particular situation [SYN] GET ON: *The party fared very badly in the last election.*

the ,Far 'East *noun* China, Japan and other countries of E and SE Asia—compare THE MIDDLE EAST ▶ ,Far 'East·ern *adj.*

fare·well /ˌfeəˈwel; *AmE* ˌferˈwel/ *noun, exclamation*
■ *noun* [C, U] the act of saying goodbye to sb: *She said her farewells and left.* ◇ *a farewell party/drink*

F

æ	ɑː	e	ɜː	ə	ɪ	iː	i	ɒ	ɔː	ʌ	ʊ	u	uː
cat	father	ten	bird	about	sit	see	many	got	saw	cup	put	actual	too
								(BrE)					

■ *exclamation* (*old use* or *formal*) goodbye

far-'fetched *adj.* very difficult to believe: *The whole story sounds very far-fetched.*

far-'flung *adj.* [usually before noun] (*written*) **1** a long distance away: *expeditions to the far-flung corners of the world* **2** spread over a wide area: *a newsletter that helps to keep all our far-flung graduates in touch*

far 'gone *adj.* [not before noun] (*informal*) very ill/sick, crazy or drunk: *She was too far gone to understand anything we said to her.*

farm /fɑːm; *AmE* fɑːrm/ *noun, verb*
■ *noun* **1** an area of land, and the buildings on it, used for growing crops and/or keeping animals: *a 200-acre farm* ◇ *a farm worker/labourer* ◇ *farm buildings/machinery* ◇ *to live/work on a farm* **2** the main house on a farm, where the farmer lives **3** (especially in compounds) a place where particular fish or animals are bred: *a trout/mink/pig farm*—see also BATTERY FARM, COLLECTIVE FARM, DAIRY, FACTORY FARM, HEALTH FARM, TRUCK FARM, WIND FARM
■ *verb* to use land for growing crops and/or keeping animals: [V] *The family has farmed in Kent for over two hundred years.* ◇ [VN] *They farm dairy cattle.* ◇ *He farmed 200 acres of prime arable land.* ◇ *organically farmed pro-* duce **PHRV** **,farm sb↔'out (to sb)** (*BrE, disapproving*) to arrange for sb to be cared for by other people **,farm sb/sth↔'out to sb** to send out work for other people to do: *The company farms out a lot of work to freelancers.*

'farm belt *noun* (*AmE*) an area where there are a lot of farms

farm·er /ˈfɑːmə(r); *AmE* ˈfɑːrm-/ *noun* a person who owns or manages a farm

farm·hand /ˈfɑːmhænd; *AmE* ˈfɑːrm-/ *noun* a person who works for a farmer

farm·house /ˈfɑːmhaʊs; *AmE* ˈfɑːrm-/ *noun* the main house on a farm, where the farmer lives

farm·ing /ˈfɑːmɪŋ; *AmE* ˈfɑːrmɪŋ/ *noun* [U] the business of managing or working on a farm: *to take up farming* ◇ *sheep/fish/organic farming* ◇ *modern farming methods* ◇ *a farming community*

farm·land /ˈfɑːmlænd; *AmE* ˈfɑːrm-/ *noun* [U, pl.] land that is used for farming: *250 acres of farmland* ◇ *the prosperous farmlands of Picardy*

farm·stead /ˈfɑːmsted; *AmE* ˈfɑːrm-/ *noun* (*AmE or formal*) a FARMHOUSE and the buildings near it: *a few scattered farmsteads*

farm·yard /ˈfɑːmjɑːd; *AmE* ˈfɑːrmjɑːrd/ *noun* an area that is surrounded by farm buildings

'far-off *adj.* [only before noun] **1** a long distance away: *a far-off land* **2** a long time ago: *memories of those far-off days*

far·rago /fəˈrɑːɡəʊ; *AmE* -ɡoʊ/ *noun* [usually sing.] (*pl.* **-oes** or **-os**) (*formal, disapproving*) a confused mixture of different things

,far-'reaching *adj.* likely to have a lot of influence or many effects: *far-reaching consequences/implications* ◇ *far-reaching changes/reforms*

far·rier /ˈfæriə(r)/ *noun* a person whose job is making and fitting HORSESHOES for horses' feet

Farsi /ˈfɑːsiː; *AmE* ˈfɑːrsi/ *noun* [U] = PERSIAN

,far-'sighted *adj.* **1** having or showing an understanding of the effects in the future of actions that you take now, and being able to plan for them: *the most far-sighted of politicians* ◇ *a far-sighted decision* **2** (*especially AmE*) = LONG-SIGHTED ▶ **,far-'sighted·ness** *noun* [U]

fart /fɑːt; *AmE* fɑːrt/ *verb, noun*
■ *verb* (⚠, *slang*) [V] to let air from the bowels come out through the ANUS, especially when it happens loudly **HELP** A more polite way of expressing this is 'to break wind'. **PHRV** **,fart a'round** (*BrE also* **,fart a'bout**) (⚠, *slang*) to waste time by behaving in a silly way: *Stop farting around and give me a hand with this!*
■ *noun* (⚠, *slang*) **1** an act of letting air from the bowels come out through the ANUS, especially when it happens

loudly **2** an unpleasant, boring or stupid person: *He's just a boring old fart.*

far·ther /ˈfɑːðə(r); *AmE* ˈfɑːrð-/ *adv., adj.*
■ *adv.* (comparative of *far*) at or to a greater distance in space or time: *farther north/south* ◇ **farther along** *the road* ◇ *I can't go any farther.* ◇ *As a family we grew* **farther and farther** *apart.* ◇ *We watched their ship moving gradually* **farther away**. ◇ *How much farther is it?* ◇ *They hadn't got any farther with the work* (= they had made no progress) **IDM** see AFIELD
■ *adj.* (comparative of *far*) at a greater distance in space, direction or time: *the farther shore of the lake*

>
>
> **WHICH WORD?**
> ## farther / further / farthest / furthest
>
> These are the comparative and superlative forms of **far**.
> To talk about distance, use either **farther, farthest** or **further, furthest**. In *BrE*, **further, furthest** are the most common forms and in *AmE*, **further** and **farthest**: *I have to travel further/farther to work now.*
> To talk about the degree or extent of something, **further/furthest** are usually preferred: *Let's consider this point further.*
> **Further**, but not **farther**, can also mean 'more' or 'additional': *Are there any further questions?* This sounds very formal in *AmE*.

far·thest /ˈfɑːðɪst; *AmE* ˈfɑːrð-/ (also **fur·thest**) *adv., adj.*
■ *adv.* (superlative of *far*) at or to the greatest distance in space or time: *the house* **farthest away** *from the road* ◇ *a competition to see who could throw (the) farthest*
■ *adj.* (also **fur·thest**) (superlative of *far*) most distant in space, direction or time: *the farthest point of the journey* ◇ *the part of the garden farthest from the house* ⇨ note at FARTHER

far·thing /ˈfɑːðɪŋ; *AmE* ˈfɑːrðɪŋ/ *noun* an old British coin worth one quarter of an old PENNY

fa·scia /ˈfeɪʃə/ *noun* (*BrE*) **1** (also **facia**) = DASHBOARD **2** (also **'fascia board**) a board on the roof of a house, at the end of the RAFTERS **3** (also **facia**) a board above the entrance of a shop, with the name of the shop on it

fas·cin·ate /ˈfæsɪneɪt/ *verb* to attract or interest sb very much: [VN] *China has always fascinated me.* ◇ *It was a question that had fascinated him since he was a boy.* ◇ [V] *It seems that the private lives of movie stars never fail to fascinate.*

fas·cin·ated /ˈfæsɪneɪtɪd/ *adj.* ~ **(by sth)**| ~ **to see, learn, etc.** very interested: *The children watched, fascinated, as the picture began to appear.* ◇ *I've always been fascinated by his ideas.* ◇ *They were fascinated to see that it was similar to one they had at home.*

fas·cin·at·ing /ˈfæsɪneɪtɪŋ/ *adj.* extremely interesting and attractive: *a fascinating story/subject* ◇ *The results of the survey made fascinating reading.* ◇ *It's fascinating to see how different people approach the problem.* ◇ *I fail to see what women find so fascinating about him.* ▶ **fas·cin·at·ing·ly** *adv.*

fas·cin·ation /ˌfæsɪˈneɪʃn/ *noun* **1** [C, usually sing.] a very strong attraction, that makes sth very interesting: *Water holds a fascination for most children.* ◇ *The fascination of the game lies in trying to guess what your opponent is thinking.* **2** [U, sing.] ~ **(for/with sb/sth)** the state of being very attracted to and interested in sb/sth: *the public's enduring fascination with the Royal Family* ◇ *The girls listened* **in fascination** *as the story unfolded.* ◇ *They stared in horrified fascination as the snake approached.*

fas·cism /ˈfæʃɪzəm/ (also **Fascism**) *noun* [U] an extreme RIGHT-WING political system or attitude which is in favour of strong central government and which does not allow any opposition

fas·cist /ˈfæʃɪst/ (also **Fascist**) *noun* **1** a person who supports fascism **2** a way of referring to sb that you disapprove of because they have RIGHT-WING attitudes ▶ **fas·cist** *adj.*: *a fascist state* ◇ *fascist sympathies*

aɪ	aʊ	eɪ	əʊ	oʊ	ɔɪ	ɪə	eə	ʊə	j	w
my	now	say	go	go	boy	near	hair	pure	yes	wet
			(BrE)	(AmE)						

fash·ion /ˈfæʃn/ *noun, verb*

■ *noun* **1** [U, C] a popular style of clothes, hair, etc. at a particular time or place; the state of being popular: *dressed in the latest fashion* ◇ *the new season's fashions* ◇ *Long skirts have* **come into fashion** *again.* ◇ *Jeans are still* **in fashion**. ◇ *Some styles never* **go out of fashion**. **2** [C] a popular way of behaving, doing an activity, etc: *The fashion at the time was for teaching mainly the written language.* ◇ *Fashions in art and literature come and go.* **3** [U] the business of making or selling clothes in new and different styles: *a fashion designer/magazine/show* ◇ *the world of fashion* ◇ *the fashion industry* [IDM] **after a ˈfashion** to some extent, but not very well: *I can play the piano,* **after a fashion.** **after the fashion of sb/sth** (*formal*) in the style of sb/sth: *The new library is very much after the fashion of Nash.* **in (a) ...ˈfashion** (*formal*) in a particular way: *How could they behave in such a fashion?* ◇ *She was proved right,* **in** *dramatic* **fashion**, *when the whole department resigned.* **like it's going out of ˈfashion** (*spoken*) used to emphasize that sb is doing sth or using sth a lot: *She's been spending money like it's going out of fashion.*—see also PARROT-FASHION

■ *verb* [VN] **~ A (from/out of B)** | **~ B (into A)** to make or shape sth, especially with your hands: *She fashioned a pot from the clay.* ◇ *She fashioned the clay into a pot.*

fash·ion·able /ˈfæʃnəbl/ *adj.* **1** following a style that is popular at a particular time: *fashionable clothes/furniture/ideas* ◇ *It's becoming fashionable to have long hair again.* ◇ *Such thinking is fashionable among right-wing politicians at the moment.* **2** used or visited by people following a current fashion, especially by rich people: *a fashionable address/resort/restaurant* ◇ *She lives in a very fashionable part of London.* [OPP] UNFASHIONABLE—compare OLD-FASHIONED ▶ **fash·ion·ably** /-əbli/ *adv.*: *fashionably dressed* ◇ *His wife was blonde and fashionably thin.*

ˈfashion-conscious *adj.* aware of the latest fashions and wanting to follow them: *fashion-conscious teenagers/shoppers*

fast /fɑːst; *AmE* fæst/ *adj., adv., verb, noun*

■ *adj.* (**fast·er, fast·est**)

‣ QUICK | **1** moving or able to move quickly: *a fast car/horse* ◇ *the world's fastest runner* **2** happening in a short time or without delay: *the fastest rate of increase for several years* ◇ *a fast response time* **3** able to do sth quickly: *a fast learner/reader*

‣ SURFACE | **4** producing or allowing quick movement: *a fast road/pitch*—see also FAST LANE

‣ WATCH/CLOCK | **5** [not before noun] showing a time later than the true time: *I'm early—my watch must be fast.* ◇ *That clock's ten minutes fast.*

‣ PHOTOGRAPHIC FILM | **6** (*technical*) very sensitive to light, and therefore useful when taking photographs in poor light or of sth that is moving very quickly

‣ FIRMLY FIXED | **7** (of a boat, etc.) firmly fixed and safe: *He made the boat fast.*

‣ COLOURS IN CLOTHES | **8** not likely to change or to come out when washed

[HELP] There is no noun related to **fast**. Use **speed** in connection with vehicles, actions, etc.; **quickness** is used about thinking.

[IDM] **fast and ˈfurious** (of films/movies, shows, etc.) full of rapid action and sudden changes: *In his latest movie, the action is fast and furious.* **a fast ˈtalker** a person who can talk very quickly and easily, but who cannot always be trusted **a fast ˈworker** (*informal*) a person who knows how to get what they want quickly, especially when beginning a sexual relationship with sb—more at BUCK *n.*, HARD *adj.*, PULL *v.*

■ *adv.* (**fast·er, fast·est**)

‣ QUICKLY | **1** quickly: *Don't drive so fast!* ◇ *How fast were you going?* ◇ *I can't go any faster.* ◇ *The water was rising fast.* ◇ *Her heart beat faster.* ◇ (*formal*) *Night was fast approaching.* ◇ *a fast-flowing stream* ⇨ note at QUICK **2** in a short time; without delay: *Children grow up so fast these days.* ◇ *Britain is* **fast** *becoming a nation of fatties.* ◇ *The police said that they had reacted as fast as they could.*

‣ FIRMLY | **3** firmly; completely: *Within a few minutes she was*

fast asleep (= sleeping deeply). ◇ *The boat was stuck fast* (= unable to move) *in the mud.*

[HELP] There is no noun related to **fast**. Use **speed** in connection with vehicles, actions, etc.; **quickness** is used about thinking.

[IDM] **as fast as your legs can carry you** as quickly as you can **hold ˈfast to sth** (*formal*) to continue to believe in an idea, etc. in spite of difficulties **play fast and ˈloose (with sb/sth)** (*old-fashioned*) to treat sb/sth in a way that shows that you feel no responsibility or respect for them **stand ˈfast/ˈfirm** to refuse to move back; to refuse to change your opinions—more at THICK *adv.*

■ *verb* [V] to eat little or no food for a period of time, especially for religious reasons: *Muslims fast during Ramadan.*

■ *noun* a period during which you do not eat food, especially for religious or health reasons: *to go on a fast* ◇ *to break* (= end) *your fast*

WHICH WORD?
fast / quick / rapid

These adjectives are frequently used with the following nouns:

fast ~	quick ~	rapid ~
car	glance	change
train	look	growth
bowler	reply	increase
grower	decision	decline
pace	method	progress
lane	way	development

Fast is used especially to describe a person or thing that moves or is able to move at great speed.

Quick is more often used to describe something that is done in a short time or without delay.

Rapid, swift and **speedy** are more formal words.

Rapid is most commonly used to describe the speed at which something changes. It is not used to describe the speed at which something moves or is done: ~~*a rapid train*~~ ◇ ~~*We had a rapid coffee.*~~

Swift usually describes something that happens or is done quickly and immediately: *a swift decision* ◇ *The government took swift action.*

Speedy has a similar meaning: *a speedy recovery.* It is used less often to talk about the speed at which something moves: ~~*a speedy car.*~~

For the use of **fast** and **quick** as adverbs, see the usage note at **quick**.

---

fas·ten /ˈfɑːsn; *AmE* ˈfæsn/ *verb* **1** **~ (sth) (up)** to close or join together the two parts of sth; to become closed or joined together [SYN] DO UP: [VN] *Fasten your seatbelts, please.* ◇ *He fastened up his coat and hurried out.* ◇ [V] *The dress fastens at the back.* [OPP] UNFASTEN **2** to close sth firmly so that it will not open; to be closed in this way: [VN] *Fasten the gates securely so that they do not blow open.* ◇ [V] *The window wouldn't fasten.* [OPP] UNFASTEN **3** [VN + *adv./prep.*] to fix or place sth in a particular position, so that it will not move: *He fastened back the shutters.* **4** [VN] **~ A to B** | **~ A and B (together)** to attach or tie one thing to another thing: *He fastened the papers together with a paper clip.* **5** if you **fasten** your arms around sb, your teeth into sb, etc., or if your arms, teeth, etc. **fasten** around, into, etc. sb/sth, you hold the person/thing firmly with your arms, etc: [VN] *The dog fastened its teeth in his leg.* ◇ [V] *His hand fastened on her arm.* **6** if you **fasten** your eyes on sb/sth or your eyes **fasten** on sb/sth, you look at them for a long time: [VN] *He fastened his gaze on her face.* [also V] [PHRV] **ˈfasten on(to) sb/sth** to choose or follow sb/sth in a determined way [SYN] LATCH ON TO SB/STH

fas·ten·er /ˈfɑːsnə(r); *AmE* ˈfæs-/ (also **fas·ten·ing**) *noun* a device, such as a button or a zip/zipper, used to close a piece of clothing; a device used to close a window, suitcase, etc. tightly

fas·ten·ing /ˈfɑːsnɪŋ; *AmE* ˈfæs-/ *noun* **1** = FASTENER

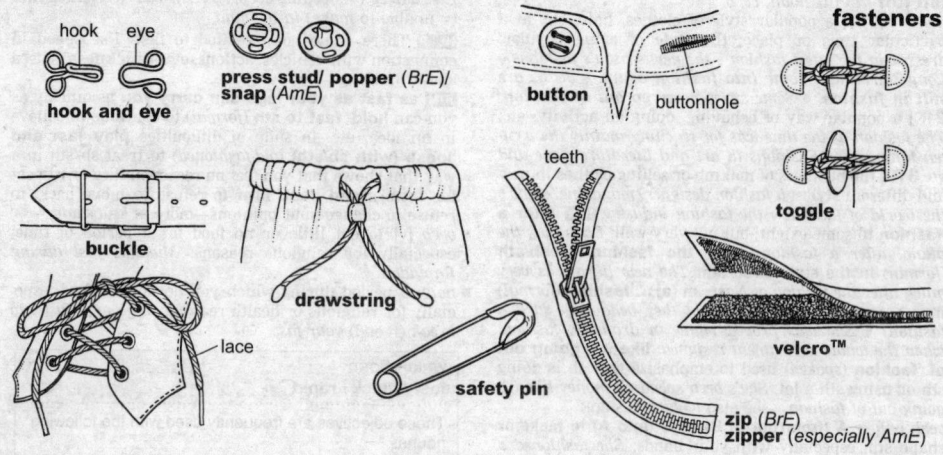

fasteners

hook · eye
hook and eye

press stud/ popper (BrE)/
snap (AmE)

button · buttonhole

teeth

toggle

buckle

drawstring

lace

safety pin

velcro™

zip (BrE)
zipper (especially AmE)

---

2 the place where sth, especially a piece of clothing, fastens; the way sth fastens: *The trousers have a fly fastening.*

,fast 'food *noun* [U] hot food that is served very quickly in special restaurants, and often taken away to be eaten in the street

,fast 'forward *verb* [VN, V] to wind a tape or video forward without playing it ▶ **,fast 'forward** *noun* [U]: *Press fast forward to advance the tape.* ◇ *the fast-forward button*

fas·tidi·ous /fæ'stɪdiəs/ *adj.* **1** being careful that every detail of sth is correct SYN METICULOUS: *Everything was planned in fastidious detail.* ◇ *He was fastidious in his preparation for the big day.* **2** (sometimes *disapproving*) not liking things to be dirty or untidy: *She wasn't very fastidious about personal hygiene.* ▶ **fas·tidi·ous·ly** *adv.* **fas·tidi·ous·ness** *noun* [U]

'fast lane *noun* [sing.] the part of a main road such as a motorway where vehicles drive fastest IDM **in the 'fast lane** where things are most exciting and where a lot is happening: *He had a good job, plenty of money and he was enjoying* **life in the fast lane.**

fast·ness /'fɑːstnəs; *AmE* 'fæs-/ *noun* (*literary*) a place that is thought to be safe because it is difficult to get to or easy to defend SYN STRONGHOLD

'fast track *noun* [sing.] a quick way to achieve sth, for example a high position in a job ▶ **fast-track** *adj.*: *the fast-track route to promotion* ◇ *fast-track graduates*

fat /fæt/ *adj., noun*

■ *adj.* (**fat·ter, fat·test**) **1** (of a person's or an animal's body) having too much flesh on it and weighing too much: *a big fat man/ woman* ◇ *You'll get fat if you eat so much chocolate.* ◇ *He grew fatter and fatter.* ◇ *fat flabby legs* **2** thick or wide: *a fat volume on American history* **3** [only before noun] (*informal*) large in quantity; worth a lot of money: *a fat sum/profit* ◇ *He gave me a nice fat cheque.* ▶ **fat·ness** *noun* [U]: *Fatness tends to run in families.* IDM **(a) fat 'chance (of sth/doing sth)** (*spoken*) used for saying that you do not believe sth is likely to happen: *'They might let us in without tickets.' 'Fat chance of that!'* **a fat lot of good, use, etc.** (*spoken*) not at all good or useful: *Paul can't drive so he was a fat lot of use when I broke my arm.*

■ *noun* **1** [U] a white or yellow substance in the bodies of animals and humans, stored under the skin: *excess body fat* ◇ *This ham has too much fat on it.* **2** [C, U] a solid or liquid substance from animals or plants, treated so that it becomes pure for use in cooking: *Cook the meat in shallow fat.* **3** [C, U] animal and vegetable fats, when you are

> **WORD FAMILY**
> fat *adj.*
> fatty *adj.*
> fatten *v.*
> fattening *adj.*

thinking of them as part of what a person eats: *You should cut down on fats and carbohydrates.* ◇ *foods which are low in fat* ◇ *fat free yoghurts* ◇ *reduced fat margarines* IDM see CHEW *v.*, LIVE¹

> **VOCABULARY BUILDING**
> saying that someone is **fat**
>
> **Fat** is the most common and direct word, but it is not polite to say to someone that they are fat: *Does this dress make me look fat?* ◇ ~~You're looking fat now.~~
>
> **Overweight** is a more neutral word: *I'm a bit overweight.* It can also mean too fat, especially so that you are not fit.
>
> **Large** or **heavy** is less offensive than **fat**: *She's a rather large woman.* **Big** describes someone who is tall as well as fat: *Her sister is a big girl, isn't she?*
>
> **Plump** means slightly fat in an attractive way, often used to describe women.
>
> **Chubby** is used mainly to describe babies and children who are fat in a pleasant, healthy-looking way: *the baby's chubby cheeks.*
>
> **Tubby** (*informal*) is used in a friendly way to describe people who are short and round, especially around the stomach.
>
> **Stocky** is a neutral word and means fairly short, broad and strong.
>
> **Stout** is often used to describe older people who have a round and heavy appearance: *a short stout man with a bald head.*
>
> **Flabby** describes flesh that is fat and loose and it can sound offensive: *exercises to firm up flabby thighs.*
>
> **Obese** is used by doctors to describe people who are so fat that they are unhealthy. It is also used in a general way to mean 'really fat'.
>
> Note that although people talk a lot about their own size or weight, it is generally not considered polite to refer to a person's large size or their weight when you talk to them.
>
> ⇨ note at THIN

fatal /'feɪtl/ *adj.* **1** causing or ending in death: *a fatal accident/blow/illness* ◇ *a **potentially fatal** form of cancer* ◇ *If she gets ill again it could **prove fatal.***—compare MORTAL **2** causing disaster or failure: *a fatal error/mistake* ◇ *Any delay would be fatal.* ◇ *There was a **fatal flaw** in the plan.* ◇ *It'd be fatal to try and stop them now.* ▶ **fa·tal·ly** /-təli/ *adv.*: *fatally injured/wounded* ◇ *The plan was fatally flawed from the start.*

fa·tal·ism /'feɪtəlɪzəm/ *noun* [U] the belief that events are decided by fate and that you cannot control them; the fact of accepting that you cannot prevent sth from happening: *There is a mood of profound fatalism amongst party members.* ▶ **fa·tal·ist** *noun*: *I'm a fatalist.*

fa·tal·is·tic /ˌfeɪtəˈlɪstɪk/ *adj.* showing a belief in fate and feeling that you cannot control events or stop them from happening: *a fatalistic attitude/outlook* ▶ **fa·tal·is·tic·al·ly** /ˌfeɪtəˈlɪstɪkəli/ *adv.*

fa·tal·ity /fəˈtæləti/ *noun* (*pl.* **-ies**) **1** [C] a death that is caused in an accident or a war or by some other act of violence: *Several people were injured, but there were no fatalities.* **2** [U] the fact that a particular disease will result in death: *to reduce the fatality of certain types of cancer* ◊ *Different forms of cancer have different fatality rates.* **3** [U] the belief or feeling that we have no control over what happens to us: *A sense of fatality gripped her.*

ˌfat ˈcat *noun* (*informal, disapproving*) a person who earns, or who has, a lot of money (especially when compared to people who do not earn so much)

fate /feɪt/ *noun* **1** [C] the things, especially bad things, that will happen or have happened to sb/sth: *The fate of the three men is unknown.* ◊ *She sat outside, waiting to find out her fate.* ◊ *The court will decide our fate/fates.* ◊ *Each of the managers suffered the same fate.* ◊ *The government had abandoned the refugees to their fate.* ◊ *From that moment our fate was sealed* (= our future was decided). **2** [U] the power that is believed to control everything that happens and that cannot be stopped or changed: *Fate was kind to me that day.* ◊ *By a strange twist of fate, Andy and I were on the same plane.* **IDM** **a fate worse than ˈdeath** (*often humorous*) a terrible thing that could happen—more at **TEMPT**

fated /ˈfeɪtɪd/ *adj.* **1** ~ (**to do sth**) unable to escape a particular fate; certain to happen because everything is controlled by fate: *We were fated never to meet again.* ◊ *He believes that everything in life is fated.* **2** = **ILL-FATED**

fate·ful /ˈfeɪtfl/ *adj.* [usually before noun] having an important, often very bad, effect on future events: *She looked back now to that fateful day in December.* ◊ *his final fateful journey to Moscow*

father /ˈfɑːðə(r)/ *noun, verb*
■ *noun* **1** a male parent of a child or an animal; a person who is acting as the father to a child: *Ben's a wonderful father.* ◊ *You've been like a father to me.* ◊ *Our new boss is a father of three* (= he has three children). ◊ *He was a wonderful father to both his natural and adopted children.* ◊ (*old-fashioned*) *Father, I cannot lie to you.*—see also GODFATHER, GRANDFATHER, STEPFATHER **2** (**fathers**) [pl.] (*literary*) a person's ANCESTORS (= people who are related to you who lived in the past): *the land of our fathers*—see also FOREFATHERS **3** ~ (**of sth**) the first man to introduce a new way of thinking about sth or of doing sth: *Henry Moore is considered to be the father of modern British sculpture.*—see also FOUNDING FATHER **4** (**Father**) used by Christians to refer to God: *Father, forgive us.* ◊ *God the Father* **5** (**Father**) (*abbr.* **Fr**) the title of a priest, especially in the Roman Catholic Church and the Orthodox Church: *Father Dominic*—see also HOLY FATHER **IDM** **from ˌfather to ˈson** from one GENERATION of a family to the next **like ˌfather, like ˈson** used to say that a son's character or behaviour is similar to that of his father—more at **OLD**
■ *verb* [VN] **1** to become the father of a child by making its mother pregnant: *He claims to have fathered over 20 children.* **2** (*written*) to create new ideas or a new way of doing sth

ˌFather ˈChristmas (*BrE*) (also **ˈSanta Claus** *AmE, BrE*) *noun* an imaginary old man with red clothes and a long white BEARD. Parents tell small children that he brings them presents at Christmas.

ˈfather figure *noun* an older man that sb respects because he will advise and help them like a father

father·hood /ˈfɑːðəhʊd; *AmE* -ðərhʊd/ *noun* [U] the state of being a father

ˈfather-in-law *noun* (*pl.* **fathers-in-law**) the father of your husband or wife—compare MOTHER-IN-LAW

ˈfather·land /ˈfɑːðəlænd; *AmE* -ðərlænd/ *noun* [usually sing.] (*old-fashioned*) (used especially about Germany) the country where a person, or their family, was born, especially when they feel very loyal towards it

father·less /ˈfɑːðələs; *AmE* -ðərləs/ *adj.* [usually before noun] without a father, either because he has died or because he does not live with his children: *fatherless children/families*

father·ly /ˈfɑːðəli; *AmE* -ðərli/ *adj.* typical of a good father: *fatherly advice* ◊ *He keeps a fatherly eye on his players.*

ˈFather's Day *noun* a day when fathers receive cards and gifts from their children, usually the third Sunday in June

fathom /ˈfæðəm/ *verb, noun*
■ *verb* ~ **sb/sth** (**out**) to understand or find an explanation for sth: [VN] *It is hard to fathom the pain felt at the death of a child.* ◊ [V wh-] *He couldn't fathom out what the man could possibly mean.*
■ *noun* a unit for measuring the depth of water, equal to 6 feet or 1.8 metres: *The ship sank in 20 fathoms.* ◊ (*figurative*) *She kept her feelings hidden fathoms deep.*

fa·tigue /fəˈtiːɡ/ *noun* **1** [U] a feeling of being extremely tired, usually because of hard work or exercise: *physical and mental fatigue* ◊ *Driver fatigue was to blame for the accident.* ◊ *I was dropping with fatigue and could not keep my eyes open.* **2** [U] (usually after another noun) a feeling of not wanting to do a particular activity any longer because you have done too much of it: *battle fatigue* **3** [U] weakness in metal or wood caused by repeated bending or stretching: *The wing of the plane showed signs of metal fatigue.* **4** (**fatigues**) [pl.] loose clothes worn by soldiers **5** (**fatigues**) [pl.] (*especially AmE*) duties, such as cleaning and cooking, that soldiers have to do, especially as a punishment

fa·tigued /fəˈtiːɡd/ *adj.* [not usually before noun] (*formal*) very tired, both physically and mentally

fa·tiguing /fəˈtiːɡɪŋ/ *adj.* (*formal*) very tiring, both physically and mentally

fatso /ˈfætsəʊ; *AmE* -soʊ/ *noun* (*pl.* **-oes**) = FATTY

fat·ten /ˈfætn/ *verb* ~ (**sb/sth**) **up** to make sb/sth fatter, especially an animal before killing it for food; to become fatter: [VN] *The piglets are taken from the sow to be fattened for market.* ◊ *She's very thin after her illness—but we'll soon fatten her up.* [also V]

fat·ten·ing /ˈfætnɪŋ/ *adj.* (of food) likely to make you fat: *fattening cakes*

fatty /ˈfæti/ *adj., noun*
■ *adj.* (**fat·tier, fat·ti·est**) containing a lot of fat; consisting of fat: *fatty foods* ◊ *fatty tissue*
■ *noun* (*pl.* **-ies**) (also **fatso**) (*informal, disapproving*) a fat person: *Britain is fast becoming a nation of fatties.*

fatu·ous /ˈfætʃuəs/ *adj.* (*formal*) very silly and showing a lack of intelligence: *a fatuous comment/grin* ▶ **fatu·ous·ly** *adv.*

fau·cet /ˈfɔːsɪt/ *noun* (*AmE*) (*BrE* **tap**) a device that controls the flow of water from a pipe: *the hot/cold faucet* ◊ *to turn a faucet on/off*—picture at PLUG

fault /fɔːlt/ *noun, verb*
■ *noun*
RESPONSIBILITY **1** [U] ~ (**that...**) | ~ (**for doing sth**) the responsibility for sth wrong that has happened or been done: *It was his fault that we were late.* ◊ *Why should I say sorry when it's not my fault?* ◊ *It's nobody's fault.* ◊ *It's your own fault for being careless.* ◊ *Many people live in poverty through no fault of their own.* ◊ *I think the owners are at fault* (= responsible) *for not warning us.*

IN SB'S CHARACTER **2** [C] a bad or weak aspect of sb's character: *He's proud of his children and blind to their faults.* ◊ *I love her for all her faults* (= in spite of them).

STH WRONG **3** [C] something that is wrong or not perfect with sth; something that is wrong with a machine or system that stops it from working correctly: *The book's virtues far outweigh its faults.* ◊ *The system, for all its faults, is the best available at the moment.* ◊ *a major fault in the design* ◊ *a structural/an electrical fault*

IN TENNIS **4** [C] a mistake made when SERVING: *He has served a number of double faults in this set.*

GEOLOGY **5** [C] a place where there is a break that is

F

æ	ɑː	e	ɜː	ə	ɪ	iː	i	ɒ	ɔː	ʌ	ʊ	u	uː
cat	father	ten	bird	about	sit	see	many	got	saw	cup	put	actual	too
	(BrE)												

F

longer than usual in the layers of rock in the earth's CRUST: *the San Andreas fault* ◇ *a fault line*

IDM **to a 'fault** (*written*) used to say that sb has a lot, or even too much, of a particular good quality: *She is generous to a fault.*—more at FIND *v.*

■ *verb* [VN] (often used in negative sentences with *can* and *could*) to find a mistake or a weakness in sb/sth **SYN** CRITICIZE: *Her colleagues could not fault her dedication to the job.* ◇ *He had always been polite—she couldn't fault him on that.*

'fault-finding *noun* [U] the act of looking for faults in sb/sth

fault·less /'fɔːltləs/ *adj.* perfect; having no mistakes: *faultless English* ▶ **fault·less·ly** *adv.*

faulty /'fɔːlti/ *adj.* **1** not perfect; not working or made correctly: *Ask for a refund if the goods are faulty.* ◇ *faulty workmanship* ◇ *an accident caused by a faulty signal* **2** (of a way of thinking) wrong or containing mistakes, often resulting in bad decisions: *faulty reasoning*

faun /fɔːn/ *noun* (in ancient Roman stories) a god of the woods, with a man's face and body and a goat's legs and horns

fauna /'fɔːnə/ *noun* [U, C] all the animals living in an area or in a particular period of history: *the local flora and fauna* (= plants and animals) ◇ (*technical*) *land and marine faunas*

faux pas /ˌfəʊ 'pɑː; *AmE* ˌfoʊ/ *noun* (*pl.* **faux pas** /ˌfəʊ 'pɑːz; *AmE* ˌfoʊ/) (from *French*) an action or a remark that causes embarrassment because it is not socially correct

fave /feɪv/ *noun* (*informal*) a favourite person or thing: *That song is one of my faves.* ▶ **fave** *adj.*: *her fave TV show*

fa·vour (*BrE*) (*AmE* **favor**) /'feɪvə(r)/ *noun, verb*
■ *noun*

HELP | **1** [C] a thing that you do to help sb: *Could you do me a favour and pick up Sam from school today?* ◇ *Can I ask a favour?* ◇ *I would never ask for any favours from her.* ◇ *I'm going as a favour to Ann, not because I want to.* ◇ *I'll ask Steve to take it. He owes me a favour.* ◇ *Thanks for helping me out. I'll return the favour* (= help you because you have helped me) *some time.* ◇ *Do yourself a favour* (= help yourself) *and wear a helmet on the bike.*

APPROVAL | **2** [U] approval or support for sb/sth: *The suggestion to close the road has found favour with* (= been supported by) *local people.* ◇ *The programme has lost favour with viewers recently.* ◇ *an athlete who fell from favour after a drugs scandal* ◇ (*formal*) *The government looks with favour upon* (= approves of) *the report's recommendations.* ◇ *She's not in favour with* (= supported or liked by) *the media just now.* ◇ *It seems Tim is back in favour with the boss* (= the boss likes him again).

BETTER TREATMENT | **3** [U] treatment that is generous to one person or group in a way that seems unfair to others: *As an examiner, she showed no favour to any candidate.*

PARTY GIFT | **4** (favors) [pl.] (*AmE*) = PARTY FAVORS

SEX | **5** (favours) [pl.] (*old-fashioned*) agreement to have sex with sb: *demands for sexual favours*

IDM **do sb no 'favours** to do sth that is not helpful to sb or that gives a bad impression of them: *You're not doing yourself any favours, working for nothing.* ◇ *The orchestra did Beethoven no favours.* **Do me a 'favour!** (*spoken*) used in reply to a question that you think is silly: '*Do you think they'll win?' 'Do me a favour! They haven't got a single decent player.'* **in favour (of sb/sth) 1** if you are in favour of sb/sth, you support and agree with them/it: *He argued in favour of a strike.* ◇ *There were 247 votes in favour (of the motion) and 152 against.* ◇ *I'm all in favour of* (= completely support) *equal pay for equal work.* ◇ *Most of the 'don't knows' in the opinion polls came down in favour of* (= eventually chose to support) *the Democrats.* **2** if you replace one thing **in favour** of another, you think the second thing is better or you want it more: *He abandoned teaching in favour of a career as a musician.* **in sb's favour 1** if sth is **in sb's favour**, it gives them an advantage or helps them: *The exchange rate is in our favour at the moment.* ◇ *She was willing to bend the rules in Mary's favour.* **2** a decision or judgement that is in

sb's favour benefits that person or says that they were right—more at CURRY *v.*, FEAR *n.*, STACKED

■ *verb*

PREFER | **1** to prefer one system, plan, way of doing sth, etc. to another: [VN] *Many countries favour a presidential system of government.* [also V-*ing*, VN-*ing*]

TREAT BETTER | **2** [VN] to treat sb better than you treat other people, especially in an unfair way: *The treaty seems to favour the US.*

HELP | **3** [VN] to provide suitable conditions for a particular person, group, etc.: *The warm climate favours many types of tropical plants.*

LOOK LIKE PARENT | **4** [VN] (*old-fashioned* or *AmE*) to look like one of your parents or older relations: *She definitely favours her father.*

fa·vour·able (*BrE*) (*AmE* **fa·vor·able**) /'feɪvərəbl/ *adj.* **1** making people have a good opinion of sb/sth: *She made a favourable impression on his parents.* ◇ *The biography shows him in a favourable light.* **2** positive and showing your good opinion of sb/sth: *favourable comments* **3** ~ **(to/for sb/sth)** good for sth and making it likely to be successful or have an advantage: *The terms of the agreement are favourable to both sides.* ◇ *favourable economic conditions* **4** fairly good and not too expensive: *They offered me a loan on very favourable terms.* **OPP** UNFAVOURABLE ▶ **fa·vour·ably** (*BrE*) (*AmE* **fa·vor·ably**) /-əbli/ *adv.*: *He speaks very favourably of your work.* ◇ *These figures compare favourably with last year's.* ◇ *I was very favourably impressed with her work.*

fa·voured (*BrE*) (*AmE* **favored**) /'feɪvəd; *AmE* -vərd/ *adj.* **1** treated in a special way or receiving special help or advantages in a way that may seem unfair: *a member of the President's favoured circle of advisers* **2** preferred by most people: *the favoured candidate* **3** (*formal*) particularly pleasant and worth having: *Their house is in a very favoured position near the park.*

fa·vour·ite (*BrE*) (*AmE* **fa·vor·ite**) /'feɪvərɪt/ *adj., noun*
■ *adj.* liked more than others of the same kind: *It's one of my favourite movies.* ◇ *Who is your favourite writer?* **IDM** **sb's favourite 'son** a performer, politician, sports player, etc., who is popular where they were born
■ *noun* **1** a person or thing that you like more than the others of the same type: *These biscuits are great favourites with the children.* ◇ *This song is a particular favourite of mine.* ◇ *Which one's your favourite?* ◇ *The programme has become a firm favourite with young people.* **2** a person who is liked better by sb and receives better treatment than others: *She loved all her grandchildren but Ann was her favourite.* **3** ~ **(for sth)**| ~ **(to do sth)** the horse, competitor, team, etc. that is expected to win: *The favourite came third.* ◇ *Her horse is the hot favourite for the race.* ◇ *AC Milan, the hot favourites to win the European Cup* **4** ~ **(for sth)**| ~ **(to do sth)** the person who is expected by most people to get a particular job or position: *She's the favourite for the job.* ◇ *She's the favourite to succeed Blair as leader.*

fa·vour·it·ism /'feɪvərɪtɪzəm/ (*BrE*) (*AmE* **fa·vor·it·ism**) *noun* [U] (*disapproving*) the act of unfairly treating one person better than others because you like them better: *The students accused the teacher of favouritism.*

fawn /fɔːn/ *adj., noun, verb*
■ *adj.* light yellowish-brown in colour: *a fawn coat*
■ *noun* **1** [C] a deer less than one year old **2** [U] a light yellowish-brown colour
■ *verb* [V] ~ **(on/over sb)** (*disapproving*) to try to please sb by praising them or paying them too much attention: *He seemed unaware of the girl's fawning admiration.*

fax /fæks/ *noun, verb*
■ *noun* (also *formal* **fac·sim·ile**) **1** (also **'fax machine**) [C] a machine that sends and receives documents in an electronic form along telephone wires and then prints them: *Do you have a fax?* **2** [U] a system for sending documents using a fax machine: *Can you send it to me by fax?* ◇ *What is your fax number?* **3** [C] a letter or message sent by fax: *Did you get my fax?* ◇ *You can send faxes by e-mail from your computer.* ⇨ Study page B13

■ *verb* ~ **sth (to sb)**| ~ **sb (sth)** to send sb a document, message, etc. by fax: [VNN, VN] *Could you fax me the latest version?* ◊ *Could you fax it to me?* ◊ [VN] *I faxed the list of hotels through to them.*

faze /feɪz/ *verb* [VN] [often passive] (*informal*) to make you feel confused or shocked, so that you do not know what to do: *She wasn't fazed by his comments.* ◊ *He looked as if nothing could faze him.*

FBI /ˌef biː ˈaɪ/ *abbr.* Federal Bureau of Investigation. The FBI is the police department in the US that is controlled by the national government and that is responsible for dealing with crimes that affect more than one state.

FC /ˌef ˈsiː/ *abbr.* (*BrE*) football club: *Tottenham FC*

FCO /ˌef siː ˈəʊ; *AmE* ˈoʊ/ *abbr.* FOREIGN AND COMMONWEALTH OFFICE

FE /ˌef ˈiː/ *abbr.* (in Britain) FURTHER EDUCATION

fear /fɪə(r); *AmE* fɪr/ *noun, verb*

■ *noun* [C, U] ~ **(of sb/sth)**| ~ **(for sb/sth)**| ~ **(that ...)** the bad feeling that you have when you are in danger, when sth bad might happen, or when a particular thing frightens you: (*a*) *fear of the dark/spiders/flying* ◊ *Her eyes showed no fear.* ◊ *The child was shaking with fear.* ◊ *We lived in constant fear of losing our jobs.* ◊ *her fears for her son's safety* ◊ *the fear that he had cancer* ◊ *The doctor's report confirmed our worst fears.* ◊ *Alan spoke of his fears for the future.* **IDM** **for fear of sth/of doing sth | for fear (that) ...** to avoid the danger of sth happening: *We spoke quietly for fear of waking the guards.* ◊ *I had to run away for fear (that) he might one day kill me.* **in ˌfear of your ˈlife** feeling frightened that you might be killed **ˌno ˈfear** (*BrE, spoken*) used to say that you definitely do not want to do sth: *'Are you coming climbing?' 'No fear!'* **put the fear of ˈGod into sb** to make sb very frightened, especially in order to make them do sth **without fear or ˈfavour** (*formal*) in a fair way—more at STRIKE *v.*

■ *verb* **1** to be frightened of sb/sth or frightened of doing sth: [VN] *All his employees fear him.* ◊ *to fear death/persecution/the unknown* ◊ *Don't worry, you have nothing to fear from us.* ◊ [V to inf] (*formal*) *She feared to tell him the truth.* [also V -ing] **2** to feel that sth bad might have happened or might happen in the future: [VN] *She has been missing for three days now and police are beginning to fear the worst* (= think that she is dead). ◊ [VN-ADJ] *Hundreds of people are feared dead.* ◊ [VN to inf] *Women and children are feared to be among the victims.* **HELP** This pattern is only used in the passive. ◊ [VN (that)] *It is feared (that) he may have been kidnapped.* ◊ [V] *Never fear/Fear not* (= Don't worry), *I shall return.* [also V (that)] **3** (**I fear**) [V] (*formal*) used to tell sb that you think that sth bad has happened or is true: *They are unlikely to get here on time, I fear.* ◊ *'He must be dead then?' 'I fear so.'* ◊ *'She's not coming back?' 'I fear not.'* **PHRV** **ˈfear for sb/sth** to be worried about sb/sth: *We fear for his safety.* ◊ *He feared for his mother, left alone on the farm.*

fear·ful /ˈfɪəfl; *AmE* ˈfɪrfl/ *adj.* **1** ~ **(for sb)**| ~ **(of sth/of doing sth)**| ~ **(that)** ... (*formal*) nervous and afraid: *Parents are ever fearful for their children.* ◊ *fearful of an attack* ◊ *She was fearful that she would fail.* **2** [only before noun] (*formal*) terrible and frightening **3** (*old-fashioned, informal*) extremely bad: *We made a fearful mess of the room.* ▸ **fear·ful·ly** /-fəli/ *adv.*: *We watched fearfully.* ◊ *fearfully* (= extremely) *expensive* **fear·ful·ness** *noun* [U]

fear·less /ˈfɪələs; *AmE* ˈfɪrləs/ *adj.* (*approving*) not afraid, in a way that people admire: *a fearless mountaineer* ▸ **fear·less·ly** *adv.* **fear·less·ness** *noun* [U]

fear·some /ˈfɪəsəm; *AmE* ˈfɪrsəm/ *adj.* (*formal*) making people feel very frightened: *a fearsome dinosaur* ◊ *He has a fearsome reputation as a fighter.*

feas·ible /ˈfiːzəbl/ *adj.* that is possible and likely to be achieved **SYN** PRACTICABLE: *a feasible plan/suggestion/idea* ◊ *It's just not feasible to manage the business on a part-time basis.* **OPP** UNFEASIBLE ▸ **feasi·bil·ity** /ˌfiːzə-ˈbɪləti/ *noun* [U]: *a feasibility study on the proposed new airport* ◊ *I doubt the feasibility of the plan.*

feast /fiːst/ *noun, verb*

■ *noun* (*formal*) **1** a large or special meal, especially for a lot of people and to celebrate sth: *a wedding feast* **2** a day or period of time when there is a religious festival: *the feast of Christmas* ◊ *a feast day* **3** [usually sing.] a thing or an event that brings great pleasure: *a feast of colours* ◊ *The evening was a real feast for music lovers.*

■ *verb* [V] ~ **(on sth)** to eat a large amount of food, with great enjoyment **IDM** **feast your ˈeyes (on sb/sth)** to look at sb/sth and get great pleasure

feat /fiːt/ *noun* (*approving*) an action or piece of work that needs skill, strength or courage: *The tunnel is a brilliant feat of engineering.* ◊ *to perform/attempt/achieve astonishing feats* ◊ *That was **no mean feat** (= it was difficult to do).

fea·ther /ˈfeðə(r)/ *noun, verb*

■ *noun* one of the many soft light parts covering a bird's body: *a peacock feather* ◊ *a feather pillow* (= one containing feathers)—picture on page A6 **IDM** **a ˈfeather in your cap** an action that you can be proud of—more at BIRD, KNOCK *v.*, RUFFLE *v.*, SMOOTH *v.*

■ *verb* **IDM** **feather your (own) ˈnest** to make yourself richer, especially by spending money on yourself that should be spent on sth else—more at TAR *v.*

ˌfeather-ˈbed *verb* (**-dd-**) [VN] (*BrE*) to make things easy for sb, especially by giving them money or good conditions of work

ˌfeather ˈboa (also **boa**) *noun* a long thin piece of clothing like a SCARF, made of feathers and worn over the shoulders by women, especially in the past

ˌfeather ˈduster *noun* a stick with feathers on the end of it that is used for cleaning

fea·thered /ˈfeðəd; *AmE* -ðərd/ *adj.* covered with feathers or having feathers

fea·ther·weight /ˈfeðəweɪt; *AmE* ˈfeðərw-/ *noun* a boxer weighing between 53.5 and 57 kilograms, heavier than a BANTAMWEIGHT: *a featherweight champion*

fea·thery /ˈfeðəri/ *adj.* light and soft; like a feather: *feathery leaves/snowflakes*

fea·ture /ˈfiːtʃə(r)/ *noun, verb*

■ *noun* [C] **1** something important, interesting or typical of a place or thing: *An interesting feature of the city is the old market.* ◊ *Teamwork is a **key feature** of the training programme.* ◊ *Which features do you look for when choosing a car?* ◊ *The software has no particular **distinguishing features**.* ◊ *geographical features* **2** [usually pl.] a part of sb's face such as their nose, mouth and eyes: *his strong handsome features* ◊ *Her eyes are her most **striking feature**.* **3** ~ **(on sb/sth)** (in newspapers, on television, etc.) a special article or programme about sb/sth: *a special feature on education* **4** (*old-fashioned*) the main film/movie in a cinema programme

■ *verb* **1** [VN] ~ **sb/sth (as sb/sth)** to include a particular person or thing as a special feature: *The film features Anthony Hopkins as Picasso.* ◊ *The latest model features alloy wheels and an electronic alarm.* ◊ *Many of the hotels featured in the brochure offer special deals for weekend breaks.* **2** [V] ~ **(in sth)** to have an important part in sth: *Olive oil and garlic feature prominently in his recipes.*

ˈfeature film *noun* a main film/movie with a story, rather than a DOCUMENTARY, etc.

fea·ture·less /ˈfiːtʃələs; *AmE* -tʃərl-/ *adj.* without any qualities or noticeable characteristics: *The countryside is flat and featureless.*

fe·brile /ˈfiːbraɪl; *AmE* also ˈfeb-/ *adj.* **1** (*formal*) nervous, excited and very active: *a product of her febrile imagination* **2** (*medical*) (of an illness) caused by fever

Feb·ru·ary /ˈfebruəri; *AmE* -ueri/ *noun* [U, C] (*abbr.* Feb.) the 2nd month of the year, between January and March **HELP** To see how **February** is used, look at the examples at **April**.

fecal, feces (*AmE*) = FAECAL, FAECES

feck·less /ˈfekləs/ *adj.* having a weak character; not behaving in a responsible way: *Her husband was a charming, but lazy and feckless man.* ▸ **feck·less·ness** *noun* [U]

fec·und /ˈfiːkənd; ˈfek-/ *adj.* (*formal*) **1** able to produce a lot of children, crops, etc. **SYN** FERTILE **2** producing new and useful things, especially ideas ▶ **fe·cund·ity** /fɪ-ˈkʌndəti/ *noun* [U]

Fed /fed/ *noun* (*AmE, informal*) an officer of the FBI or another federal organization

fed *pt, pp* of FEED

fed·eral /ˈfedərəl/ *adj.* **1** having a system of government in which the individual states of a country have control over their own affairs, but are controlled by a central government for national decisions, etc: *a federal republic* **2** (within a federal system, especially the US) connected with national government rather than the local government of an individual state: *a federal law* ◇ *state and federal income taxes* ▶ **fed·er·al·ly** *adv.*: *federally funded health care*

the ˌFederal ˌBureau of Investiˈgation = FBI

fed·er·al·ist /ˈfedərəlɪst/ *noun* a supporter of a FEDERAL system of government ▶ **fed·er·al·ist** *adj.*: *a federalist future in Europe* **fed·er·al·ism** /ˈfedərəlɪzəm/ *noun* [U]: *European federalism*

fed·er·ate /ˈfedəreɪt/ *verb* [V] (*technical*) (of states, organizations, etc.) to unite under a central government or organization while keeping some local control

fed·er·ation /ˌfedəˈreɪʃn/ *noun* **1** [C] a country consisting of a group of individual states that have control over their own affairs but are controlled by a central government for national decisions, etc: *the Russian Federation* **2** [C] a group of clubs, trade unions, etc. that have joined together to form an organization: *the International Tennis Federation* **3** [U] the act of forming a federation: *Many MPs are against federation in Europe.*

fe·dora /fɪˈdɔːrə/ *noun* a low soft hat with a curled BRIM

ˌfed ˈup *adj.* [not before noun] ~ (**with sb/sth**) (especially *spoken*) bored or unhappy, especially with a situation that has continued for too long: *You look fed up. What's the matter?* ◇ *I'm fed up with waiting for her.* ◇ *People are fed up with all these traffic jams.* ◇ *In the end, I just got* **fed up with** *his constant complaining.* ◇ *I wish he'd get a job. I'm* **fed up with it** (= with the situation). **HELP** Some people say 'fed up of sth' in BrE, but this is not considered correct in standard English.

fee /fiː/ *noun* **1** an amount of money that you pay for professional advice or services: *legal fees* ◇ *Does the bank* **charge a fee** *for setting up the account?* ◇ *fee-paying schools* (= that you have to pay to go to) **2** an amount of money that you pay to join an organization, or to do sth: *membership fees* ◇ *There is no* **entrance fee** *to the gallery.*

fee·ble /ˈfiːbl/ *adj.* (**fee·bler** /ˈfiːblə(r)/, **feeb·lest** /ˈfiːblɪst/) **1** very weak: *a feeble old man* ◇ *The heartbeat was feeble and irregular.* **2** not effective; not showing determination or energy: *a feeble argument/excuse/joke* ◇ *a feeble attempt to explain* ◇ *Don't be so feeble! Tell her you don't want to go.* ▶ **feeble·ness** *noun* [U] **feebly** /ˈfiːbli/ *adv.*

ˌfeeble-ˈminded *adj.* **1** (*old use, offensive*) having less than usual intelligence **2** weak and unable to make decisions

feed /fiːd/ *verb, noun*
■ *verb* (**fed, fed** /fed/)

GIVE/EAT FOOD | **1** ~ **sb/sth (on) sth** | ~ **sth to sb/sth** to give food to a person or an animal: [VN] *Have you fed the cat yet?* ◇ *The baby can't feed itself yet* (= can't put food into its own mouth). ◇ *The cattle are fed on barley.* ◇ [VNN, VN] *The cattle are fed barley.* ◇ *The barley is fed to the cattle.* **2** [V] (of a baby or an animal) to eat food: *Slugs and snails feed at night.*—see also FEED ON/OFF STH **3** [VN] to provide food for a family or group of people: *They have a large family to feed.* ◇ *There's enough here to feed an army.*

PLANT | **4** [VN] to give a plant a special substance to make it grow: *Feed the plants once a week.*

GIVE ADVICE/INFORMATION | **5** ~ **sb sth** | ~ **sth to sb** to give advice, information, etc. to sb/sth: [VNN, VN] *We are constantly fed gossip and speculation by the media.* ◇ *Gossip and speculation are constantly fed to us by the media.*

SUPPLY | **6** [VN] ~ **A (with B)** | ~ **B into A** to supply sth to sb/sth: *The electricity line is fed with power through an underground cable.* ◇ *Power is fed into the electricity line through an underground cable.*

PUT INTO MACHINE | **7** [VN] ~ **A (with B)** | ~ **B into A** | ~ **sth (into/through sth)** to put or push sth into or through a machine: *He fed coins into the meter.* ◇ *He fed the meter with coins.* ◇ *The fabric is fed through the machine.*

SATISFY NEED | **8** [VN] to satisfy a need, desire, etc. and keep it strong: *For drug addicts, the need to feed the addiction takes priority over everything else.*

IDM **feed your ˈface** (*informal, usually disapproving*) to eat a lot of food or too much food **a ˈfeeding frenzy** (*especially AmE*) a period of time during which sb/sth eats, spends, etc. a lot in a way that does not seem to be controlled—more at BITE *v.*

PHRV **ˈfeed on/off sth 1** (of an animal) to eat sth: *Butterflies feed on the flowers of garden plants.* **2** (often *disapproving*) to become stronger because of sth else: *Racism feeds on fear.* ◇ *He feeds off the work and reputation of others.* **ˌfeed ˈthrough (to sb/sth)** to reach sb/sth after going through a process or system: *It will take time for the higher rates to feed through to investors.* **ˌfeed sb↔ˈup** (*BrE*) to give a lot of food to sb to make them fatter or stronger

■ *noun*
MEAL FOR BABY/ANIMAL | **1** [C] a meal of milk for a young baby; a meal for an animal: *her morning feed*

FOR ANIMALS/PLANTS | **2** [U, C] food for animals or plants: *winter feed for the horses*

FOR MACHINE | **3** [U] material supplied to a machine **4** [C] a pipe, device, etc. which supplies a machine with sth: *the cold feed to the water cylinder* ◇ *The printer has an automatic paper feed.*

LARGE MEAL | **5** [C] (*informal*) a large meal: *They needed a bath and a good feed.*

TELEVISION PROGRAMMES | **6** [U] (*AmE*) television programmes that are sent from a central station to other stations in a NETWORK; the system of sending out these programmes: *network feed*

feed·back /ˈfiːdbæk/ *noun* [U] **1** advice, criticism or information about how good or useful sth or sb's work is: *I'd appreciate some feedback on my work.* ◇ *The teacher will give you feedback on the test.* ◇ *We need both positive and negative feedback from our customers.* **2** the unpleasant noise produced by electrical equipment such as an AMPLIFIER when some of the power returns to the system

feed·bag /ˈfiːdbæg/ *noun* (*AmE*) = NOSEBAG

feed·er /ˈfiːdə(r)/ *noun, adj.*
■ *noun* **1** (used with an adjective or a noun) an animal or plant that eats a particular thing or eats in a particular way: *plankton feeders* **2** a mechanism that supplies sth to a machine **3** a container filled with food for birds or animals
■ *adj.* [only before noun] **1** (of roads, rivers, etc.) leading to a bigger road, etc: *a feeder road to the motorway/freeway* **2** supplying goods, services, etc. to a large organization **3** (*AmE*) (of animals on a farm) kept to be killed and used for meat

ˈfeeder school *noun* (*BrE*) a school from which most of the children go to a particular SECONDARY SCHOOL or college in the same area

feed·ing /ˈfiːdɪŋ/ *noun* [U] the act of giving food to a person, an animal or a plant: *breast/bottle feeding*

ˈfeeding bottle *noun* (*BrE*) a plastic bottle with a rubber top which a baby or young animal can suck milk through

feel /fiːl/ *verb, noun*
■ *verb* (**felt, felt** /felt/)

WELL/SICK/HAPPY/SAD, etc. | **1** *linking verb* to experience a particular feeling or emotion: [V-ADJ] *The heat made him feel faint.* ◇ *She sounded more confident than she felt.* ◇ *I was feeling guilty.* ◇ *You'll feel better after a good night's sleep.* ◇ *She felt betrayed.* ◇ *I feel sorry for him.* ◇ [V+adv./prep.] *How are you feeling today?* ◇ *I know exactly how you feel* (= I feel sympathy for you). ◇ *Luckily I was feeling in a good mood.* ◇ [VN] *He seemed to feel no remorse at all.* ◇ [V-N] *Standing there on stage I felt a complete idiot.* ◇ [V] *I felt like a complete idiot.*

BE/BECOME AWARE | **2** (not usually used in the progressive tenses) to notice or be aware of sth because it is touching you or having a physical effect on you $\boxed{\text{SYN}}$ SENSE: [VN] *I could feel the warm sun on my back.* ◇ *She could not feel her legs.* ◇ *He felt a hand on his shoulder.* ◇ [VN-**ing**] *He felt a hand touching his shoulder.* ◇ *She could feel herself blushing.* ◇ [VNinf] *I felt something crawl up my arm.* ◇ *We felt the ground give way under our feet.* **3** [VN] (not usually used in the progressive tenses) to become aware of sth even though you cannot see it, hear it, etc. $\boxed{\text{SYN}}$ SENSE: *Can you feel the tension in this room?*

HAVE IMPRESSION | **4** linking verb (not used in the progressive tenses) to give you a particular feeling or impression: [V-ADJ] *It felt strange to be back in my old school.* ◇ *My mouth felt completely dry.* ◇ [V] *The interview only took ten minutes, but it felt like hours.* ◇ *It feels like rain* (= seems likely to rain). ◇ *Her head felt as if it would burst.* ◇ *It felt as though he had run a marathon.* ◇ *How does it feel to be alone all day?* $\boxed{\text{HELP}}$ In spoken English people often use **like** instead of **as if** or **as though** in this meaning, especially in *AmE: He felt like he'd run a marathon.* This is considered incorrect in written *BrE.*

TOUCH | **5** linking verb (not used in the progressive tenses) to have a particular physical quality which you become aware of by touching: [V-ADJ] *The water feels warm.* ◇ *Its skin feels really smooth.* ◇ [V] *This wallet feels like leather.* **6** to deliberately move your fingers over sth in order to find out what it is like: [VN] *Can you feel the bump on my head?* ◇ *Try to tell what this is just by feeling it.* ◇ [Vwh-] *Feel how rough this is.*

THINK/BELIEVE | **7** (not usually used in the progressive tenses) to think or believe that sth is the case; to have a particular opinion or attitude $\boxed{\text{SYN}}$ THINK: [V(**that**)] *We all felt (that) we were unlucky to lose.* ◇ *I felt (that) I had to apologize.* ◇ [VNtoinf] *She felt it to be her duty to tell the police.* ◇ [VN-N] *She felt it her duty to tell the police.* ◇ [VN-ADJ] *I felt it advisable to do nothing.* ◇ [V] *This decision is, I feel, a huge mistake.* ◇ *This is something I feel strongly about.*

BE STRONGLY AFFECTED | **8** [VN] to experience the effects or results of sth, often strongly: *He feels the cold a lot.* ◇ *Cathy was really feeling the heat.* ◇ *She felt her mother's death very deeply.* ◇ *The effects of the recession are being felt everywhere.* ◇ *We all felt the force of her arguments.*

SEARCH WITH HANDS | **9** [V] ~ (**about**/**around**) (**for sth**) to search for sth with your hands, feet, etc: *He felt in his pockets for some money.* ◇ *I had to feel about in the dark for the light switch.*

$\boxed{\text{IDM}}$ ˌfeel your ˈage to realize that you are getting old, especially compared with people you are with who are younger than you **feel your ˈears burning** to think or imagine that other people are talking about you **feel ˈfree (to do sth)** (*informal*) used to tell sb that they are allowed to do sth: *Feel free to ask questions if you don't understand.* ◇ *'Can I use your phone?' 'Feel free.'* **feel ˈgood** to feel happy, confident, etc: *It makes me feel good to know my work is appreciated.* **feel (it) in your ˈbones (that ...)** to be certain about sth even though you do not have any direct proof and cannot explain why you are certain: *I know I'm going to fail this exam—I can feel it in my bones.* **feel like sth/like doing sth** to want to have or do sth: *I feel like a drink.* ◇ *We all felt like celebrating.* ◇ *We'll go for a walk if you feel like it.* **feel the ˈpinch** (*informal*) to not have enough money: *Lots of people who have lost their jobs are starting to feel the pinch.* **feel ˈsick** (*especially BrE*) (*AmE usually* **feel ˌsick to your ˈstomach**) to feel as though you will VOMIT soon: *Mum! I feel sick.* **feel your ˈway 1** to move along carefully, for example when it is dark, by touching walls, objects, etc. **2** to be careful about how you do things, usually because you are in a situation that you are not familiar with: *She was new in the job, still feeling her way.* **not feel yourˈself** to not feel healthy and well: *I'm not quite feeling myself today.*—more at DEATH, FLATTER, HARD *adv.*, HONOUR *n.*, HONOUR *v.*, JELLY, MARK *n.*, MILLION, PRESENCE, SMALL *adj.*

$\boxed{\text{PHRV}}$ ˈfeel for sb to have sympathy for sb: *I really felt for her when her husband died.* ◇ *I do feel for you, honestly.* ˌfeel sb‹·›ˈup (*informal*) to touch sb sexually, especially when they do not want you to ˌfeel ˈup to sth to have the

strength and energy to do or deal with sth: *Do we have to go to the party? I really don't feel up to it.* ◇ [+-**ing**] *After the accident she didn't feel up to driving.*

■ *noun* [sing.]

TOUCH | **1** (**the feel**) the feeling you get when you touch sth or are touched: *You can tell it's silk by the feel.* ◇ *She loved the feel of the sun on her skin.* **2** an act of feeling or touching: *I had a feel of the material.* ◇ *rough/smooth to the feel*

IMPRESSION | **3** the impression that is created by a place, situation, etc.; atmosphere: *It's a big city but it has the feel of a small town.* ◇ *The room has a comfortable feel to it.*

$\boxed{\text{IDM}}$ **get the feel of sth/of doing sth** to become familiar with sth or with doing sth: *I haven't got the feel of the brakes in this car yet.* **have a feel for sth** to have an understanding of sth or be naturally good at doing it: *She has a real feel for languages.*

feel·er /ˈfiːlə(r)/ *noun* [usually pl.] either of the two long thin parts on the heads of some insects and of some animals that live in shells that they use to feel and touch things with $\boxed{\text{SYN}}$ ANTENNA $\boxed{\text{IDM}}$ **put out ˈfeelers** (*informal*) to try to find out what people think about a particular course of action before you do it

ˈfeel-good *adj.* making you feel happy and pleased about life: *a feel-good movie* $\boxed{\text{IDM}}$ **the ˈfeel-good factor** (*BrE*) (used especially in newspapers, etc.) the hopeful feeling about the future that is shared by many people

feel·ing /ˈfiːlɪŋ/ *noun*

STH THAT YOU FEEL | **1** [C] ~ (**of sth**) something that you feel through the mind or through the senses: *a feeling of hunger/excitement/sadness* ◇ *guilty feelings* ◇ *I've got a tight feeling in my stomach.* ◇ (*spoken*) *'I really resent the way he treated me.' 'I know the feeling.'* (= I know how you feel) ◇ *'I'm going to miss you.' 'The feeling's mutual* (= I feel exactly the same).*'*

IDEA/BELIEF | **2** [sing.] ~ (**of sth**)| ~ (**that ...**) the idea or belief that a particular thing is true or a particular situation is likely to happen: *He suddenly had the feeling of being followed.* ◇ *I got the feeling that he didn't like me much.* ◇ *I had a nasty feeling that we were lost.*

ATTITUDE/OPINION | **3** [U, C] ~ (**about/on sth**) an attitude or opinion about sth: *The general feeling of the meeting was against the decision.* ◇ *I don't have any strong feelings about it one way or the other.* ◇ *My own feeling is that we should buy the cheaper one.* ◇ *She had mixed feelings about giving up her job.* ◇ *Public feeling is being ignored by the government.*

EMOTIONS | **4** (**feelings**) [pl.] a person's emotions rather than their thoughts or ideas: *He hates talking about his feelings.* ◇ *I didn't mean to hurt your feelings* (= offend you). **5** [U, C] strong emotion: *She spoke with feeling about the plight of the homeless.* ◇ *Feelings are running high* (= people are very angry or excited).

UNDERSTANDING | **6** [U] ~ (**for sb/sth**) the ability to understand sb/sth or to do sth in a sensitive way: *She has a wonderful feeling for colour.* ◇ *He played the piano with great feeling.*

SYMPATHY/LOVE | **7** [U] ~ (**for sb/sth**) sympathy or love for sb/sth: *You have no feeling for the sufferings of others.* ◇ *She still had a lot of feeling for David.*

PHYSICAL | **8** [U] the ability to feel physically: *I've lost all feeling in my legs.*

ATMOSPHERE | **9** [sing.] the atmosphere of a place, situation, etc: *They have managed to recreate the feeling of the original theatre.*

$\boxed{\text{IDM}}$ **bad/ill ˈfeeling** (also **bad/ill ˈfeelings** especially in *AmE*) anger between people, especially after an argument or disagreement: *There was a lot of bad feeling between the two groups of students.*—more at HARD *adj.*, SINK *v.*, SPARE

feel·ing·ly /ˈfiːlɪŋli/ *adv.* with strong emotion $\boxed{\text{SYN}}$ EMOTIONALLY: *He spoke feelingly about his dead father.*

feet *pl.* of FOOT

feign /feɪn/ *verb* (*written*) to pretend that you have a particular feeling or that you are ill, tired, etc: [VN] *He survived the massacre by feigning death.* ◇ *'Who cares?' said Alex, feigning indifference.* [also Vtoinf]

æ	ɑː	e	ɜː	ə	ɪ	iː	i	ɒ	ɔː	ʌ	ʊ	u	uː
cat	father	ten	bird	about	sit	see	many	got	saw	cup	put	actual	too

(BrE)

F

feint /feɪnt/ noun, verb
- noun (especially in sport) a movement that is intended to make your opponent think you are going to do one thing when you are really going to do sth else
- verb [V] (especially in sport) to confuse your opponent by making them think you are going to do one thing when you are really going to do sth else

feisty /ˈfaɪsti/ adj. (feist·ier, feisti·est) (informal, approving) (of people) strong, determined and not afraid of arguing with people

fe·lici·tous /fəˈlɪsɪtəs/ adj. (formal or literary) (especially of words) chosen well; very suitable; giving a good result: a felicitous turn of phrase ▶ fe·lici·tous·ly adv.

fe·li·city /fəˈlɪsəti/ noun (pl. -ies) (formal or literary) 1 [U] great happiness 2 [U] the quality of being well chosen or suitable: The story is told with great felicity of style. 3 (felicities) [pl.] well-chosen or successful features, especially in a speech or piece of writing

fe·line /ˈfiːlaɪn/ adj., noun
- adj. like a cat; connected with an animal of the cat family: She walks with feline grace.
- noun (formal) a cat; an animal of the cat family

fell /fel/ noun, verb, adj.—see also FALL, FELL, FALLEN v.
- noun a hill or an area of hills in northern England
- verb [VN] 1 to cut down a tree 2 (written) to make sb fall to the ground: He felled his opponent with a single blow.
- adj. IDM at/in one fell swoop all at the same time; in a single action, especially a sudden or violent one

fella (also **fell·er**) /ˈfelə(r)/ noun (spoken) 1 an informal way of referring to a man 2 an informal way of referring to sb's boyfriend: Have you met her new fella?

fel·la·tio /fəˈleɪʃiəʊ; AmE -ʃioʊ/ noun [U] (formal) the practice of touching a man's PENIS with the tongue and lips to give sexual pleasure

fel·low /ˈfeləʊ; AmE ˈfeloʊ/ noun, adj.
- noun 1 (informal, becoming old-fashioned) a way of referring to a man or boy: He's a nice old fellow.—see also FELLA 2 [usually pl.] a person that you work with or that is like you; a thing that is similar to the one mentioned: She has a very good reputation among her fellows. ◇ Many caged birds live longer than their fellows in the wild. 3 (BrE) a senior member of some colleges or universities: a fellow of New College, Oxford 4 a member of an academic or professional organization: a fellow of the Royal College of Surgeons 5 (especially AmE) a GRADUATE student who holds a FELLOWSHIP: a graduate fellow ◇ a teaching fellow
- adj. [only before noun] used to describe sb who is the same as you in some way, or in the same situation: fellow members/citizens/workers ◇ my fellow passengers on the train

fellow ˈfeeling noun [U, C] a feeling of sympathy for sb because you have shared similar experiences

fel·low·ship /ˈfeləʊʃɪp; AmE -loʊ-/ noun 1 [U] a feeling of friendship between people who do things together or share an interest: They offer students counselling and fellowship. 2 [C] an organized group of people who share an interest, aim or belief 3 [C] (especially BrE) the position of being a senior member of a college or university 4 [C] an award of money to a GRADUATE student to allow them to continue their studies or to do research 5 [C, U] the state of being a member of an academic or professional organization: to be elected to fellowship of the British Academy

felon /ˈfelən/ noun (law) a person who has committed a felony

fel·ony /ˈfeləni/ noun [C, U] (pl. -ies) (AmE or old-fashioned, law) the act of committing a serious crime such as murder or RAPE; a crime of this type: a charge of felony—compare MISDEMEANOUR

felt /felt/ noun [U] a soft thick fabric made from wool or hair that has been pressed tightly together: a felt hat—see also FEEL, FELT, FELT v.

felt-tip ˈpen (also **ˌfelt tip, ˌfelt-tipped ˈpen**) noun a pen that has a point made of felt

fe·male /ˈfiːmeɪl/ adj., noun

- adj. 1 being a woman or a girl: a female student/employee/artist ◇ Two of the candidates must be female. 2 of the sex that can lay eggs or give birth to babies: a female cat 3 of women; typical of women; affecting women: female characteristics ◇ the female role—compare FEMININE 4 (of plants and flowers) that can produce fruit 5 (technical) (of electrical equipment) having a hole that another part fits into: a female plug
- noun 1 an animal that can lay eggs or give birth to babies; a plant that can produce fruit 2 a woman or a girl: More females than males are employed in the factory.

femi·nine /ˈfemənɪn/ adj., noun
- adj. 1 having the qualities or appearance considered to be typical of women; connected with women: That dress makes you look very feminine. ◇ He had delicate, almost feminine, features. ◇ How far do you think the traditional feminine role has changed?—compare FEMALE, MASCULINE 2 (grammar) belonging to a class of words that refer to female people or animals and often have a special form: Some people prefer not to use the feminine form 'actress' and use the word 'actor' for both sexes. 3 (grammar) (in some languages) belonging to a class of nouns, pronouns or adjectives that have feminine GENDER not MASCULINE or NEUTER: The French word for 'table' is feminine.
- noun (grammar) 1 (the feminine) [sing.] the feminine GENDER (= form of nouns, adjectives and pronouns) 2 [C] a feminine word or word form—compare MASCULINE, NEUTER

femi·nin·ity /ˌfeməˈnɪnəti/ noun [U] the fact of being a woman; the qualities that are considered to be typical of women

femi·nism /ˈfemənɪzəm/ noun [U] the belief and aim that women should have the same rights and opportunities as men; the struggle to achieve this aim

femi·nist /ˈfemənɪst/ noun a person who supports the belief that women should have the same rights and opportunities as men ▶ femi·nist adj. [usually before noun]: feminist demands/ideas/theories ◇ the feminist movement

femme fa·tale /ˌfæm fəˈtɑːl/ noun (pl. femmes fa·tales /ˌfæm fəˈtɑːl/) (from French) a very beautiful woman that men find sexually attractive but who brings them trouble or unhappiness

femur /ˈfiːmə(r)/ noun (pl. fe·murs or fem·ora /ˈfemərə/) (anatomy) the THIGH BONE—picture at BODY ▶ fem·oral /ˈfemərəl/ adj. [only before noun]

fen /fen/ noun an area of low flat wet land, especially in the east of England

fence /fens/ noun, verb
- noun 1 a structure made of wood or wire supported with posts that is put between two areas of land as a BOUNDARY, or around a garden/yard, field, etc. to keep animals in, or to keep people and animals out 2 a structure that horses must jump over in a race or a competition 3 (slang) a criminal who buys and sells stolen goods IDM see GRASS n., MEND v., SIDE n., SIT
- verb 1 [VN] to surround or divide an area with a fence: His property is fenced with barbed wire.—see also UNFENCED 2 [V] to take part in the sport of FENCING 3 [V] ~ (with sb) to speak to sb in a clever way in order to gain an advantage in the conversation PHRV ˌfence sb/sth↔ˈin [often passive] 1 to surround sb/sth with a fence 2 to restrict sb's freedom SYN HEM SB IN: She felt fenced in by domestic routine. ˌfence sth↔ˈoff [often passive] to divide one area from another with a fence

fen·cer /ˈfensə(r)/ noun a person who takes part in the sport of FENCING

fen·cing /ˈfensɪŋ/ noun [U] 1 the sport of fighting with long thin SWORDS 2 fences; wood, wire, or other material used for making fences: The factory is surrounded by electric fencing.

fend /fend/ verb PHRV ˌfend for yourˈself to look after yourself without help from anyone else: His parents agreed to pay the rent for his apartment but otherwise left him to fend for himself. ˌfend sth/sb↔ˈoff 1 to defend or protect yourself from sb/sth that is attacking you: The police officer fended off the blows with his riot shield. 2 to

aɪ	aʊ	eɪ	əʊ	oʊ	ɔɪ	ɪə	eə	ʊə	j	w
my	now	say	go	go	boy	near	hair	pure	yes	wet
			(BrE)	(AmE)						

protect yourself from difficult questions, criticisms, etc., especially by avoiding them: *She managed to fend off questions about new tax increases.*

fend·er /'fendə(r)/ *noun* **1** (*AmE*) = WING (4) **2** (*AmE*) = MUDGUARD **3** a frame around a FIREPLACE to prevent burning coal or wood from falling out **4** a soft solid object such as an old tyre or a piece of rope that is hung over the side of a boat so the boat is not damaged if it touches another boat or a harbour wall

'fender bender *noun* (*AmE, informal*) a car accident in which there is not a lot of damage

feng shui /ˌfeŋ 'ʃuːi; ˌfʊŋ 'ʃweɪ/ *noun* [U] a Chinese system for deciding the right position for a building and for placing objects inside a building in order to make people feel comfortable and happy

fen·land /'fenlænd; -lənd/ *noun* [U, C] an area of low flat wet land in the east of England

fen·nel /'fenl/ *noun* [U] a vegetable that has a thick round stem with a strong taste. The seeds and leaves are also used in cooking.—picture on page A3

feral /'ferəl/ *adj.* (of animals) living wild, especially after escaping from life as a pet or on a farm: *feral cats*

fer·mata /fɜː'mɑːtə; *AmE* fɜːr'm-/ *noun* (*music*) (*especially AmE*) = PAUSE

fer·ment *verb, noun*

■ *verb* /fə'ment; *AmE* fər'm-/ to experience a chemical change because of the action of YEAST or bacteria, often changing sugar to alcohol; to make sth change in this way: [V] *Fruit juices ferment if they are kept for too long.* ◊ (*figurative*) *A blend of emotions fermented inside her.* ◊ [VN] *Red wine is fermented at a higher temperature than white.* ▶ **fer·men·ta·tion** /ˌfɜːmen'teɪʃn; *AmE* ˌfɜːrm-/ *noun* [U]

■ *noun* /'fɜːment; *AmE* 'fɜːrm-/ [U, sing.] (*formal*) a state of political or social excitement and confusion: *a period of intense political ferment* ◊ *The country is in ferment.*

fern /fɜːn; *AmE* fɜːrn/ *noun* [C, U] a plant with large delicate leaves and no flowers that grows in wet areas or is grown in a pot. There are many types of fern.—see also MAIDENHAIR FERN ▶ **ferny** *adj.*

fer·ocious /fə'rəʊʃəs; *AmE* -'rəʊ-/ *adj.* very fierce, violent or aggressive; very strong: *a ferocious beast/war/attack/storm* ◊ *a man driven by ferocious determination* ◊ *ferocious opposition to the plan* ▶ **fer·ocious·ly** *adv.*

fer·ocity /fə'rɒsəti; *AmE* fə'rɑːs-/ *noun* [U] violence; fierce or aggressive behaviour: *The police were shocked by the ferocity of the attack.*

fer·ret /'ferɪt/ *noun, verb*

■ *noun* a small fierce animal with a long thin body, kept for chasing rabbits from their holes, killing rats, etc.

■ *verb* **1** [V+*adv./prep.*] ~ (**about/around**) (**for sth**) (*informal*) to search for sth that is lost or hidden among a lot of things: *She opened the drawer and ferreted around for her keys.* **2** [V] to hunt rabbits, rats, etc. using ferrets PHRV **ferret sb/sth↔'out** (*informal*) to discover information or to find sb/sth by searching thoroughly, asking a lot of questions, etc.

Fer·ris wheel /'ferɪs wiːl/ *noun* (*especially AmE*) = BIG WHEEL

fer·rous /'ferəs/ *adj.* [only before noun] (*technical*) containing iron; connected with iron: *ferrous and non-ferrous metals*

fer·rule /'feruːl; *AmE* 'ferəl/ *noun* a piece of metal or rubber that covers the end of an umbrella or a stick to protect it

ferry /'feri/ *noun, verb*

■ *noun* (*pl.* -**ies**) a boat that carries people, vehicles and goods across a river or across a narrow part of the sea: *the cross-channel ferry service* ◊ *We caught the ferry at Ostend.* ◊ *the Dover-Calais ferry crossing* ◊ *the Staten Island ferry*—picture at BOAT

■ *verb* (**fer·ries, ferry·ing, fer·ried, fer·ried**) [usually+*adv./prep.*] to carry people or goods in a boat or other vehicle from one place to another, often for a short distance and as a regular service: [VN] *He offered to ferry us across the river in his boat.* ◊ *The children need to be ferried to and from school.* [also V]

'ferry boat *noun* a boat that is used as a ferry

ferry·man /'ferimən/ *noun* (*pl.* -**men** /-mən/) a person in charge of a ferry across a river

fer·tile /'fɜːtaɪl; *AmE* 'fɜːrtl/ *adj.* **1** (of land or soil) that plants grow well in: *a fertile valley/region* **2** (of people, animals or plants) that can produce babies, young animals, fruit or new plants: *The treatment has been tested on healthy fertile women under the age of 35.* **3** [usually before noun] that produces good results; that encourages activity: *a fertile partnership* ◊ *The region at the time was fertile ground for revolutionary movements* (= there were the necessary conditions for them to develop easily). **4** [usually before noun] (of a person's mind or imagination) that produces a lot of new ideas: *the product of a fertile imagination* OPP INFERTILE—compare STERILE

fer·til·ity /fə'tɪləti; *AmE* fər't-/ *noun* [U] the state of being fertile: *the fertility of the soil/land* ◊ *a god of fertility* ◊ *fertility treatment* (= medical help given to a person to help them have a baby)

fer·til·ize (*BrE* also **-ise**) /'fɜːtəlaɪz; *AmE* 'fɜːrt-/ *verb* [VN] **1** to put POLLEN into a plant so that a seed develops; to join SPERM with an egg so that a baby or young animal develops: *Flowers are often fertilized by bees as they gather nectar.* ◊ *a fertilized egg* **2** to add a substance to soil to make plants grow more successfully ▶ **fer·til·ization, -isa·tion** /ˌfɜːtəlaɪ'zeɪʃn; *AmE* ˌfɜːrtələ'z-/ *noun* [U]: *Immediately after fertilization, the cells of the egg divide.* ◊ *the fertilization of soil with artificial chemicals*

fer·til·izer (*BrE* also **-iser**) /'fɜːtəlaɪzə(r); *AmE* 'fɜːrt-/ *noun* [C, U] a substance added to soil to make plants grow more successfully: *artificial/chemical fertilizers* ◊ *liquid fertilizer*

fer·vent /'fɜːvənt; *AmE* 'fɜːrv-/ *adj.* [usually before noun] having or showing very strong and sincere feelings about sth SYN ARDENT: *a fervent admirer/believer/supporter* ◊ *a fervent belief/hope/desire* ▶ **fer·vent·ly** *adv.*

fer·vid /'fɜːvɪd; *AmE* 'fɜːrvɪd/ *adj.* (*rare, formal*) feeling sth too strongly; showing feelings that are too strong ▶ **fer·vid·ly** *adv.*

fer·vour (*BrE*) (*AmE* **fer·vor**) /'fɜːvə(r); *AmE* 'fɜːrv-/ *noun* [U] very strong feelings about sth SYN ENTHUSIASM: *She kissed him with unusual fervour.* ◊ *religious/patriotic fervour*

fess /fes/ *verb* PHRV **fess 'up** (*AmE, informal*) to admit that you have done sth wrong

-fest /fest/ *combining form* (in nouns) a festival or large meeting involving a particular activity or with a particular atmosphere: *a jazzfest* ◊ *a talkfest* ◊ *a lovefest*

fes·ter /'festə(r)/ *verb* [V] **1** (of a wound or cut) to become badly infected: *festering sores/wounds* **2** (of bad feelings or thoughts) to become much worse because you do not deal with them successfully

fes·ti·val /'festɪvl/ *noun* **1** a series of performances of music, plays, films/movies, etc., usually organized in the same place once a year; a series of public events connected with a particular activity or idea: *the Edinburgh festival* ◊ *the Cannes film festival* ◊ *a beer festival* ◊ *a rock festival* (= where bands perform, often outdoors and over a period of several days) **2** a day or period of the year when people stop working to celebrate a special event, often a religious one: *Christmas and Easter are the main Christian festivals.*—see also HARVEST FESTIVAL

fes·tive /'festɪv/ *adj.* **1** typical of a special event or celebration: *a festive atmosphere/occasion* ◊ *The whole town is in festive mood.* **2** (*BrE*) connected with the period when people celebrate Christmas: *the festive season/period* ◊ *festive decorations/food*

fes·tiv·ity /fe'stɪvəti/ *noun* **1** (**festivities**) [pl.] the activities that are organized to celebrate a special event **2** [U] the happiness and enjoyment that exist when people celebrate sth: *The wedding was an occasion of great festivity.* ◊ *an air of festivity*

fes·toon /fe'stuːn/ *verb, noun*

■ *verb* [VN] [usually passive] ~ **sb/sth** (**with sth**) to decorate sb/sth with flowers, coloured paper, etc., often as part of a celebration

■ *noun* a chain of lights, coloured paper, flowers, etc., used to decorate sth

	b		d		f		g		h		k		l		m		n		p		r
	bad		did		fall		get		hat		cat		leg		man		now		pen		red

Fest·schrift /ˈfestʃrɪft/ noun (pl. **Fest·schrift·en** or **Fest·schrifts**) (from German) a collection of articles published in honour of a SCHOLAR

feta cheese /ˌfetə ˈtʃiːz/ (also **feta**) noun [U] a type of Greek cheese made from sheep's milk

fetal (especially AmE) = FOETAL

fetch /fetʃ/ verb **1** (especially BrE) to go to where sb/sth is and bring them/it back: [VN] to fetch help / a doctor ◇ The inhabitants have to walk a mile to fetch water. ◇ She's gone to fetch the kids from school. ◇ [VNN] Could you fetch me my bag? **2** [VN] to be sold for a particular price: The painting is expected to fetch £10000 at auction. **IDM** **fetch and ˈcarry (for sb)** to do a lot of little jobs for sb as if you were their servant **PHRV** **ˌfetch ˈup** (informal, especially BrE) to arrive somewhere without planning to: And then, a few years after leaving college, he somehow fetched up in Rome.

fetch·ing /ˈfetʃɪŋ/ adj. (informal) (especially of a person or their clothes) attractive: She looked very fetching in a little red hat. ◇ a fetching blue sweater ◇ a fetching smile ▶ **fetch·ing·ly** adv.

fête /feɪt/ noun, verb
■ noun (also **fete**, **fair**) (all BrE) (AmE **car·ni·val**) an outdoor entertainment at which people can play games to win prizes, buy food and drink, etc., usually arranged to make money for a special purpose: the school / village / church fête
■ verb (also **fete** especially in AmE) [VN] [usually passive] (written) to welcome, praise or entertain sb publicly

fetid (also less frequent **foe·tid** /ˈfetɪd; ˈfiːtɪd/) adj. [usually before noun] (formal) smelling very unpleasant: fetid air

fet·ish /ˈfetɪʃ/ noun **1** (usually disapproving) the fact that a person spends too much time doing or thinking about a particular thing: She has a fetish about cleanliness. ◇ He makes a fetish of his work. **2** the fact of getting sexual pleasure from a particular object: to have a leather fetish **3** an object that some people worship because they believe that it has magic powers ▶ **fet·ish·ism** noun [U]: a magazine specializing in rubber fetishism ◇ the importance of animal fetishism in the history of Egypt **fet·ish·ist** noun: a leather fetishist **fet·ish·is·tic** /ˌfetɪˈʃɪstɪk/ adj.

fet·lock /ˈfetlɒk; AmE -lɑːk/ noun the part at the back of a horse's leg, just above its HOOF, where long hair grows

fet·ter /ˈfetə(r)/ verb, noun
■ verb [VN] [usually passive] **1** (literary) to restrict sb's freedom to do what they want **2** to put chains around a prisoner's feet
■ noun **1** [usually pl.] (literary) something that stops sb from doing what they want: They were at last freed from the fetters of ignorance. **2** (fetters) [pl.] chains that are put around a prisoner's feet

fet·tle /ˈfetl/ noun **IDM** **in fine / good ˈfettle** (old-fashioned, informal) healthy; in good condition

fetus (especially AmE) = FOETUS

feud /fjuːd/ noun, verb
■ noun ~ (between A and B) | ~ (with sb) | ~ (over sb/sth) an angry and bitter argument between two people or groups of people that continues over a long period of time: a long-running feud between the two artists ◇ a feud with the neighbours ◇ a family feud (= within a family or between two families) ◇ a feud over money
■ verb [V] ~ (with sb) to have an angry and bitter argument with sb over a long period of time: He has been feuding with his brother for years. ◇ feuding families / gangs ▶ **feud·ing** noun [U]: stories of bitter feuding between rival drug dealers

feu·dal /ˈfjuːdl/ adj. [usually before noun] connected with or similar to feudalism: the feudal system

feu·dal·ism /ˈfjuːdəlɪzəm/ noun [U] the social system that existed during the Middle Ages in Europe in which people were given land and protection by a NOBLEMAN, and had to work and fight for him in return ▶ **feu·dal·ist·ic** /ˌfjuːdəˈlɪstɪk/ adj.

fever /ˈfiːvə(r)/ noun **1** [C, U] a medical condition in which a person has a temperature that is higher than normal: He has a high fever. ◇ Aspirin should help reduce the fever.—compare TEMPERATURE **2** [C, U] (old-fashioned) (used mainly in compounds) a particular type of disease in which sb has a high temperature: She caught a fever on her travels in Africa, and died.—see also GLANDULAR FEVER, HAY FEVER, RHEUMATIC FEVER, SCARLET FEVER, YELLOW FEVER **3** [sing.] ~ (of sth) a state of nervous excitement: He waited for her arrival in a fever of impatience. **4** [U] (especially in compounds) great interest or excitement about sth: election fever

fe·vered /ˈfiːvəd; AmE -vərd/ adj. [only before noun] (written) **1** showing great excitement or worry: fevered excitement / speculation ◇ a fevered imagination / mind (= that imagines strange things) **2** suffering from a fever: She mopped his fevered brow.

fe·ver·ish /ˈfiːvərɪʃ/ adj. **1** [usually before noun] showing strong feelings of excitement or worry, often with a lot of activity or quick movements: The whole place was a scene of feverish activity. ◇ a state of feverish excitement ◇ feverish with desire / longing **2** suffering from a fever; caused by a fever: She was aching and feverish. ◇ a feverish cold / dream / sleep ▶ **fe·ver·ish·ly** adv.: The team worked feverishly to the November deadline. ◇ Her mind raced feverishly.

ˈfever pitch noun [U, C] a very high level of excitement or activity: Speculation about his future had reached fever pitch. ◇ Excitement has been at fever pitch for days.

few /fjuː/ det., adj., pron.
■ det., adj. (**fewer**, **few·est**) **1** used with plural nouns and a plural verb to mean 'not many': Few people understand the difference. ◇ There seem to be fewer tourists around this year. ◇ Very few students learn Latin now. **2** (usually **a few**) used with plural nouns and a plural verb to mean 'a small number', 'some': We've had a few replies. ◇ I need a few things from the store. ◇ Quite a few people are going to arrive early. ◇ I try to visit my parents every few weeks. **IDM** **ˌfew and ˌfar beˈtween** not frequent; not happening often
■ pron. **1** not many people, things or places: Very few of his books are worth reading. ◇ You can pass with as few as 25 points. ◇ (formal) Few will argue with this conclusion. **2** (**a few**) a small number of people, things or places; some: I recognized a few of the other people. ◇ I've seen most of his movies. Only a few are as good as his first one. ◇ Could you give me a few more details? **3** (**fewer**) not as many as: Fewer than 20 students passed all the exams. ◇ There are no fewer than 100 different species in the area. **4** (**the few**) used with a plural verb to mean 'a small group of people': Real power belongs to the few. ◇ She was one of the chosen few (= the small group with special privileges). **IDM** **quite a ˈfew** (BrE also **a good ˈfew**) a fairly large number: I've been there quite a few times. **have ˈhad a few** (informal) to have had enough alcohol to make you drunk

fey /feɪ/ adj. (literary, sometimes disapproving) (usually of a person) sensitive and rather mysterious or strange; not acting in a very practical way: One of the guests was a slightly fey romantic novelist.

fez /fez/ noun (pl. **fezzes**) a round red hat with a flat top and a TASSEL but no BRIM, worn by men in some Muslim countries

ff abbr. (music) very loudly (from Italian 'fortissimo')

ff. abbr. written after the number of a page or line to mean 'and the following pages or lines': See pp. 96 ff.

fi·ancé /fiˈɒnseɪ; -ˈɑːns-; AmE ˌfiːɑːnˈseɪ/ noun the man that a woman is ENGAGED to (= has officially agreed to marry): Linda and her fiancé were there.

fi·an·cée /fiˈɒnseɪ; AmE ˌfiːɑːnˈseɪ/ noun the woman that a man is ENGAGED to (= has officially agreed to marry): Paul and his fiancée were there.

fi·asco /fiˈæskəʊ; AmE fiˈæskoʊ/ noun (pl. **-os**, AmE also **-oes**) something that does not succeed, often in a way that causes embarrassment: The party was a complete fiasco. ◇ What a fiasco!

fiat /ˈfiːæt; ˈfaɪæt/ noun [C, U] (formal) an official order given by sb in authority

fib /fɪb/ noun, verb
■ noun (informal) a statement that is not true; a lie about sth that is not important: Stop telling fibs.

s	t	v	z	ʃ	ʒ	tʃ	dʒ	θ	ð	ŋ
see	tea	van	zoo	shoe	vision	chain	jam	thin	this	sing

F

■ *verb* (**-bb-**) [V] (*informal*) to tell a lie, usually about sth that is not important: *Come on, don't fib! Where were you really last night?* ► **fib·ber** *noun*: *You fibber!*

fibre (*BrE*) (*AmE* **fiber**) /ˈfaɪbə(r)/ *noun* **1** [U] the part of food that helps to keep a person healthy by keeping the bowels working and moving other food quickly through the body $\overline{\text{SYN}}$ ROUGHAGE: *dietary fibre* ◊ *Dried fruits are especially high in fibre.* ◊ *a high/low fibre diet* **2** [C, U] a material such as fabric or rope that is made from a mass of natural or artificial threads: *nylon and other man-made fibres* **3** [C] one of the many thin threads that form body tissue, such as muscle, and natural materials, such as wood and cotton: *cotton/wood/nerve/muscle fibres* ◊ (*literary*) *She loved him with every fibre of her being.*—see also MORAL FIBRE, OPTICAL FIBRE

fibre·glass (*BrE*) (*AmE* **fiber-**) /ˈfaɪbəɡlɑːs; *AmE* ˈfaɪbərɡlæs/ (*BrE* also ˌglass ˈfibre) (*AmE* also ˌglass ˈfiber) *noun* [U] a strong light material made from glass fibres and plastic, used for making boats, parts of cars, etc: *a fibreglass racing yacht*

fibre ˈoptics (*BrE*) (*AmE* ˌfiber ˈoptics) *noun* [U] the use of thin fibres of glass, etc. for sending information in the form of light signals ► **fibre-ˈoptic** *adj.*: *fibre-optic cables*

fi·brous /ˈfaɪbrəs/ *adj.* [usually before noun] (*technical*) made of many fibres; looking like fibres: *fibrous tissue* ◊ *fibrous roots*

fib·ula /ˈfɪbjələ/ *noun* (*pl.* **fibu·lae** or **fibu·las**) (*anatomy*) the outer bone of the two bones in the lower part of the leg between the knee and the ankle—see also TIBIA—picture at BODY

fickle /ˈfɪkl/ *adj.* (*disapproving*) **1** changing often and suddenly: *The weather here is notoriously fickle.* ◊ *the fickle world of fashion* **2** (of a person) often changing their mind in an unreasonable way so that you cannot rely on them: *a fickle friend* ◊ *another example of his fickle behaviour* ► **fickle·ness** *noun* [U]: *the fickleness of the English climate*

fic·tion /ˈfɪkʃn/ *noun* **1** [U] a type of literature that describes imaginary people and events, not real ones: *a work of popular fiction* ◊ *historical/romantic fiction* $\overline{\text{OPP}}$ NON-FICTION—see also SCIENCE FICTION **2** [C] a thing that is invented or imagined and is not true: *For years he managed to keep up the fiction that he was not married.* $\boxed{\text{IDM}}$ see TRUTH

fic·tion·al /ˈfɪkʃənl/ *adj.* not real or true; existing only in stories; connected with fiction: *fictional characters* ◊ *a fictional account of life on a desert island* ◊ *fictional techniques* $\overline{\text{OPP}}$ REAL-LIFE

fic·tion·al·ize (*BrE* also **-ise**) /ˈfɪkʃənəlaɪz/ *verb* [VN] [usually passive] to write a book or make a film/movie about a true story, but changing some of the details, characters, etc: *a fictionalized account of his childhood*

fic·ti·tious /fɪkˈtɪʃəs/ *adj.* invented by sb rather than true: *All the places and characters in my novel are fictitious* (= they do not exist in real life).

fid·dle /ˈfɪdl/ *verb, noun*
■ *verb* **1** [V] ~ (**with sth**) to keep touching or moving sth with your hands, especially because you are bored or nervous: *He was fiddling with his keys while he talked to me.* **2** [VN] (*informal*) to change the details or figures of sth in order to try to get money dishonestly, or gain an advantage: *to fiddle the accounts* ◊ *She fiddled the books* (= changed a company's financial records) *while working as an accountant.* **3** [V] (*informal*) to play music on the violin $\boxed{\text{PHRV}}$ ˌfiddle aˈbout/aˈround to spend your time doing things that are not important ˌfiddle aˈbout/aˈround with sth|ˈfiddle with sth **1** to keep touching and changing sth because you are not satisfied with it: *I've been fiddling about with this design for ages, but I'm still not happy with it.* **2** to touch or move the parts of sth to try to change it or repair it: *He likes to fiddle around with old cars.* ◊ *Who's been fiddling with the TV again?*
■ *noun* (*informal*) **1** [C] = VIOLIN **2** [C] (*BrE*) something that is done dishonestly to get money: *an insurance/tax fiddle* **3** [sing.] (*BrE*) an act of moving sth or adjusting sth in order to make it work **4** [sing.] (*BrE*) something that is

difficult to do $\boxed{\text{IDM}}$ be on the ˈfiddle (*BrE*) to be doing sth dishonest to get money **play second ˈfiddle (to sb/sth)** to be treated as less important than sb/sth; to have a less important position than sb/sth else—more at FIT *adj.*

fid·dler /ˈfɪdlə(r)/ *noun* a person who plays the violin, especially to play FOLK MUSIC

fiddle·sticks /ˈfɪdlstɪks/ *exclamation* (*old-fashioned, informal*) used to say that you disagree with sb

fid·dly /ˈfɪdli/ *adj.* (*BrE, informal*) difficult to do or use because small objects are involved: *Changing a fuse is one of those fiddly jobs I hate.*

fi·del·ity /fɪˈdeləti/ *noun* [U] **1** ~ (**to sth**) (*formal*) the quality of being loyal and not betraying sb/sth; *fidelity to your principles/religion* **2** ~ (**to sb**) the quality of being faithful to your husband, wife or partner by not having a sexual relationship with anyone else: *marital/sexual fidelity* $\overline{\text{OPP}}$ INFIDELITY **3** ~ (**of sth**) (**to sth**) (*formal*) the quality of being accurate: *the fidelity of the translation to the original text*—see also HIGH FIDELITY

fidget /ˈfɪdʒɪt/ *verb, noun*
■ *verb* [V] ~ (**with sth**) to keep moving your body, your hands or your feet because you are nervous, bored, excited, etc: *Sit still and stop fidgeting!*
■ *noun* a person who is always fidgeting

fidgety /ˈfɪdʒɪti/ *adj.* (of a person) unable to remain still or quiet, usually because of being bored or nervous: *The children get fidgety if they have nothing to do.*

field /fiːld/ *noun, verb*
■ *noun*
AREA OF LAND | **1** [C] an area of land in the country used for growing crops or keeping animals in, usually surrounded by a fence, etc: *People were working in the fields.* ◊ *a ploughed field* ◊ *a field of wheat* ◊ *We camped in a field near the village.* **2** [C] (usually in compounds) an area of land used for the purpose mentioned: *a landing field* ◊ *a medal for bravery in the field* (*of battle*)—see also AIRFIELD, BATTLEFIELD, MINEFIELD **3** [C] (usually in compounds) a large area of land covered with the thing mentioned; an area from which the thing mentioned is obtained: *ice fields in the mountains* ◊ *gas fields*—see also COALFIELD, GOLDFIELD, OILFIELD, SNOWFIELD

SUBJECT/ACTIVITY | **4** [C] a particular subject or activity that sb works in or is interested in: *famous in the field of politics/science/music* ◊ *All of them are experts in their chosen field.* ◊ *This discovery has opened up a whole new field of research.*

PRACTICAL WORK | **5** [C] (usually used as an adjective) the fact of people doing practical work or study, rather than working in a classroom or LABORATORY: *a field study/investigation* ◊ *field research/methods* ◊ *essential reading for those working in the field*—see also FIELD TRIP, FIELDWORK

IN SPORT | **6** (*BrE* also **pitch**) [C] (usually in compounds) an area of land used for playing a sport on: *a baseball/rugby/football field* ◊ *a sports field* ◊ *Today they take the field* (= go on to the field to play a game) *against county champions Essex.*—see also PLAYING FIELD **7** (in cricket and baseball) [sing.+ sing./pl. *v.*] the team that is trying to catch the ball rather than hit it **8** [sing.+ sing./pl. *v.*] all the people or animals competing in a particular sports event: *The field includes three world record holders.*

IN BUSINESS | **9** [sing.+ sing./pl. *v.*] all the people or products competing in a particular area of business: *They lead the field in home entertainment systems.*

PHYSICS | **10** [C] (usually in compounds) an area within which the force mentioned has an effect: *the earth's gravitational field* ◊ *an electro-magnetic field*

COMPUTING | **11** [C] part of a record that is a separate item of data: *You will need to create separate fields for first name, surname and address.*

$\boxed{\text{IDM}}$ leave the field ˈclear for sb | leave sb in possession of the ˈfield to enable sb to be successful in a particular area of activity because other people or groups have given up competing with them **play the ˈfield** (*informal*) to have sexual relationships with a lot of different people

æ	ɑː	e	ɜː	ə	ɪ	iː	i	ɒ	ɔː	ʌ	ʊ	u	uː
cat	father	ten	bird	about	sit	see	many	got	saw	cup	put	actual	too
								(BrE)					

■ *verb*

CANDIDATE/TEAM | **1** [VN] to provide a candidate, speaker, team, etc. to represent you in an election, a competition, etc: *Each of the main parties fielded more than 300 candidates.* ◊ *England will field a young side in the World Cup.*

IN CRICKET/BASEBALL | **2** [V] to be the person or the team that catches the ball and throws it back after sb has hit it: *Hussain won the toss and chose to field first.* **3** [VN] to catch the ball and throw it back: *He fielded the ball expertly.*

QUESTIONS | **4** [VN] to receive and deal with questions or comments: *The BBC had to field more than 300 phone calls after last night's programme.*

'field corn *noun* [U] (*AmE*) MAIZE (= a type of corn) grown as food for animals rather than people

'field day *noun* (*AmE*) = SPORTS DAY **IDM** **have a 'field day** (*AmE, BrE*) to be given the opportunity to do sth that you enjoy, especially sth that other people do not approve of: *The tabloid press had a field day with the latest government scandal.*

field·er /'fiːldə(r)/ *noun* (*BrE* also **fields·man**) (in cricket and baseball) a member of the team that is trying to catch the ball rather than hit it

'field event *noun* [usually pl.] a sport done by ATHLETES that is not a race, for example jumping or throwing the JAVELIN—compare TRACK EVENT—picture on page 1251

'field glasses *noun* [pl.] = BINOCULARS

'field goal *noun* **1** (in American football or rugby) a goal scored by kicking the ball over the bar of the goal **2** (in basketball) a goal scored by throwing the ball through the net during normal play

'field hockey *noun* [U] (*AmE*) = HOCKEY

'field hospital *noun* a temporary hospital near a BATTLE-FIELD

,field 'marshal *noun* (*abbr.* **FM**) an officer of the highest rank in the British army: *Field Marshal Montgomery*

'field officer *noun* **1** a person in a company or other organization whose job involves practical work in a particular area or region **2** an officer of high rank in the army (= a MAJOR, LIEUTENANT COLONEL or COLONEL)

,field of 'fire *noun* (*pl.* **fields of fire**) the area that you can hit when shooting from a particular position

,field of 'vision (also **,field of 'view** or *technical* **,visual 'field**) *noun* (*pl.* **fields of vision/view, visual fields**) the total amount of space that you can see from a particular point without moving your head

fields·man /'fiːldzmən/ *noun* (*pl.* **-men** /-mən/) (*BrE*) = FIELDER

'field sports *noun* [pl.] (*BrE*) outdoor sports such as hunting, fishing and shooting

'field test *verb* [VN] to test sth, such as a piece of equipment, in the place where it will be used ▶ **'field test** *noun*: *Laboratory and field tests have been conducted.*

'field trip *noun* a journey made by a group of people, often students, to study sth in its natural environment: *We went on a geology field trip.*

field·work /'fiːldwɜːk; *AmE* -wɜːrk/ *noun* [U] research or study that is done in the real world rather than in a classroom or LABORATORY ▶ **field·worker** *noun*

fiend /fiːnd/ *noun* **1** a very cruel or unpleasant person **2** (*informal*) (used after another noun) a person who is very interested in the thing mentioned [SYN] FANATIC: *a crossword/health fiend* **3** an evil spirit

fiend·ish /'fiːndɪʃ/ *adj.* [usually before noun] **1** cruel and unpleasant: *a fiendish act/grin* ◊ *shrieks of fiendish laughter* **2** (*informal*) extremely clever and complicated, often in an unpleasant way: *a puzzle of fiendish complexity* ◊ *a fiendish plan* **3** (*informal*) extremely difficult: *a fiendish problem*

fiend·ish·ly /'fiːndɪʃli/ *adv.* (*informal*) very; extremely: *fiendishly clever/complicated*

fierce /fɪəs; *AmE* fɪrs/ *adj.* (**fier·cer**, **fier·cest**) **1** (especially of people or animals) angry and aggressive in a way that is frightening: *a fierce dog* ◊ *Who was that fierce old lady?* ◊ *Two fierce eyes glared at them.* ◊ *He suddenly looked fierce.* ◊ *She spoke in a fierce whisper.* **2** (especially

of actions or emotions) showing strong feelings or a lot of activity, often in a way that is violent: *fierce loyalty/hatred* ◊ *the scene of fierce fighting* ◊ *He launched a fierce attack on the Democrats.* ◊ *Competition from abroad became fiercer in the 1990s.* **3** (of weather conditions or temperatures) very strong in a way that could cause damage: *protection against the fierce wind coming in off the sea* ◊ *the fierce heat of the flames* ▶ **fierce·ly** *adv.*: *'Let go of me,' she said fiercely.* ◊ *fiercely competitive/independent/proud* ◊ *The aircraft was burning fiercely.* **fierce·ness** *noun* [U] **IDM** **something 'fierce** (*AmE, spoken*) very much; more than usual: *I sure do miss you something fierce!*

fiery /'faɪəri/ *adj.* [usually before noun] **1** looking like fire; consisting of fire: *fiery red hair* ◊ *The sun was now sinking, a fiery ball of light in the west.* **2** quickly or easily becoming angry: *a fiery temper/character* ◊ *a fiery young man* **3** showing strong emotions, especially anger: *a fiery look* **4** (of food or drink) causing a part of your body to feel as if it is burning: *a fiery Mexican dish*

fi·esta /fi'estə/ *noun* (from *Spanish*) a public event when people celebrate and are entertained with music and dancing, usually connected with a religious festival in countries where the people speak Spanish

fife /faɪf/ *noun* a musical instrument like a small FLUTE that plays high notes and is used with drums in military music

fif·teen /ˌfɪf'tiːn/ **1** *number* 15 **2** *noun* a team of Rugby Union players: *He's in the first fifteen.* ▶ **fif·teenth** /ˌfɪf'tiːnθ/ *ordinal number*

fifth /fɪfθ/ *ordinal number, noun*

■ *ordinal number* 5th: *Today is the fifth (of May).* ◊ *the fifth century BC* ◊ *It's her fifth birthday.* ◊ *My office is on the fifth floor.* ◊ *It's the fifth time that I've been to America.* ◊ *Her mother had just given birth to another child, her fifth.* ◊ *the world's fifth-largest oil exporter* ◊ *He finished fifth in the race.* ◊ *Edward V* (= Edward the fifth)

■ *noun* each of five equal parts of sth: *She cut the cake into fifths.* ◊ *He gave her a fifth of the total amount.*

,fifth 'column *noun* a group of people working secretly to help the enemy of the country or organization they are in ▶ **,fifth 'columnist** *noun*

fifth·ly /'fɪfθli/ *adv.* used to introduce the fifth of a list of points you want to make in a speech or piece of writing: *Fifthly, we need to consider the effect on the local population.*

fifty /'fɪfti/ **1** *number* 50 **2** (**the fifties**) *noun* [pl.] numbers, years or temperatures from 50 to 59: *She was born in the fifties.* ▶ **fif·ti·eth** /'fɪftiəθ/ *ordinal number* **IDM** **in your 'fifties** between the ages of 50 and 59

fifty-'fifty *adj., adv.* (*informal*) divided equally between two people, groups or possibilities: *Costs are to be shared on a fifty-fifty basis between the government and local businesses.* ◊ *She has a fifty-fifty chance of winning* (= an equal chance of winning or losing). ◊ *Let's split this fifty-fifty.*

,fifty 'pence (also **,fifty pence 'piece, 50p** /ˌfɪfti 'piː/) *noun* a British coin worth 50 pence: *Put a fifty pence in the machine.* ◊ *Have you got a 50p?*

fig /fɪg/ *noun* a soft sweet fruit that is full of small seeds and often eaten dried: *a fig tree*—picture on page A2 **IDM** **not care/give a 'fig (for sb/sth)** (*old-fashioned, BrE, informal*) not to care at all about sth; to think that sth is not important

fig. *abbr.* **1** (in writing) FIGURE: *See fig. 3.* **2** (in writing) FIGURATIVE(LY)

fight /faɪt/ *verb, noun*

■ *verb* (**fought, fought** /fɔːt/)

IN WAR/BATTLE | **1** ~ (**against sb**) to take part in a war or battle against an enemy: [V] *soldiers trained to fight* ◊ *He fought in Vietnam.* ◊ *My grandfather fought against the Fascists in Spain.* ◊ [VN] *to fight a war/battle* ◊ *They gathered soldiers to fight the invading army.*

STRUGGLE/HIT | **2** to struggle physically with sb: [V] *My little brothers are always fighting.* ◊ *She'll fight like a tiger to protect her children.* [also VN]

IN CONTEST | **3** ~ **sb/sth (for sth)** to take part in a contest

aɪ	aʊ	eɪ	əʊ	oʊ	ɔɪ	ɪə	eə	ʊə	j	w
my	now	say	go	go	boy	near	hair	pure	yes	wet
			(BrE)	(AmE)						

against sb: [VN] *to fight an election/a campaign* ◇ [V] *She's fighting for a place in the national team.*

OPPOSE | **4** to try hard to stop, deal with or oppose sth bad: [VN] *to fight racism/corruption/poverty* ◇ *Workers are fighting the decision to close the factory.* ◇ [V] *We will fight for as long as it takes.*

TRY TO GET/DO STH | **5** ~ **(for sth)** to try very hard to get sth or to achieve sth: [V] *He's still fighting for compensation after the accident.* ◇ [VN] *She gradually* **fought her way to** *the top of the company.* ◇ [V to inf] *Doctors fought for more than six hours to save his life.*

ARGUE | **6** [V] ~ **(with sb) (about/over sth)** to have an argument with sb about sth: *It's a trivial matter and not worth fighting about.*

IN BOXING | **7** to take part in a boxing match: [V] *Doctors fear he may never fight again following his injury.* [also VN]

LAW | **8** [VN] ~ **sb (for sth)** to try to get what you want in a court of law: *He fought his wife for custody of the children.* ◇ *I'm determined to fight the case.*

▶ **fight·ing** noun [U]: *Fighting broke out in three districts of the city last night.* ◇ *outbreaks of street fighting*

IDM **fight fire with fire** to use similar methods in a fight or an argument to those your opponent is using **fight for (your) life** to make a great effort to stay alive, especially when you are badly injured or seriously ill: *A young cyclist is fighting for his life after the accident.* **a fighting chance** a small chance of being successful if a great effort is made **fighting fit** extremely fit or healthy **fighting spirit** a feeling that you are ready to fight very hard for sth or to try sth difficult **fighting talk** comments or remarks that show that you are ready to fight very hard for sth: *What we want from the management is fighting talk.* **fight a losing battle** to try to do sth that you will probably never succeed in doing **fight shy of sth/of doing sth** to be unwilling to accept sth or do sth, and to try to avoid it: *Successive governments have fought shy of such measures.* **fight to the death/finish** to fight until one of the two people or groups is dead, or until one person or group defeats the other **fight tooth and nail** to fight in a very determined way for what you want: *The residents are fighting tooth and nail to stop the new development.* **fight your own battles** to be able to win an argument or get what you want without anyone's help: *I wouldn't get involved—he's old enough to fight his own battles.*—more at LIVE[1]

PHRV **fight back (against sb/sth)** to resist strongly or attack sb who has attacked you: *Don't let them bully you. Fight back!* ◇ *It is time to fight back against street crime.* **fight sth ↔ back/down** to try hard not to do or show sth, especially not to show your feelings: *She fought back the urge to run.* ◇ *He fought down his disgust.* **fight sb/sth ↔ off** to resist sb/sth by fighting against them/it: *The jeweller was stabbed as he tried to fight the robbers off.* **fight out sth, fight it out** to fight or argue until an argument has been settled: *The conflict is still being fought out.* ◇ *They still hadn't reached any agreement so we left them to fight it out.*

■ *noun*

STRUGGLE | **1** [C] ~ **(with sb/sth)** | ~ **(between A and B)** a struggle against sb/sth using physical force: *He* **got into a fight** *with a man in the bar.* ◇ *a street/gang fight* ◇ *A fight broke out between rival groups of fans.* ◇ *a world title fight* (= fighting as a sport)

TRYING TO GET/DO STH | **2** [sing.] ~ **(against/for sth)** | ~ **(to do sth)** the work of trying to destroy, prevent or achieve sth: *the fight against crime* ◇ *a fight for survival*

COMPETITION | **3** [sing.] a competition or an act of competing, especially in a sport: *The team* **put up a good fight** (= they played well) *but were finally beaten.* ◇ *She now* **has a fight on her hands** (= will have to play very well) *to make it through to the next round.*

ARGUMENT | **4** [C] ~ **(with sb)** | ~ **(over/about sth)** (*especially AmE*) an argument about sth: *Did you have a fight with him?* ◇ *We had a fight over money.*

BATTLE/WAR | **5** [C] a battle, especially for a particular

place or position: *In the fight for Lemburg, the Austrians lost.*

DESIRE TO FIGHT | **6** [U] the desire or ability to keep fighting for sth: *In spite of many defeats, they still had plenty of fight left in them.*

IDM **a fight to the finish** a sports competition, election, etc. between sides that are so equal in ability that they continue fighting very hard until the end—more at PICK *v.*, SPOIL *v.*

fight·back /'faɪtbæk/ noun [usually sing.] (*BrE*) an effort by a person, group or team to get back to a strong position that they have lost

fight·er /'faɪtə(r)/ noun **1** a fast military plane designed to attack other aircraft: *a jet fighter* ◇ *a fighter pilot* ◇ *fighter planes/bases* **2** a person who fights—see also FIRE-FIGHTER, FREEDOM FIGHTER, PRIZEFIGHTER **3** (*approving*) a person who does not give up hope or admit that they are defeated

fig leaf noun **1** a leaf of a FIG tree, traditionally used for covering the sex organs of naked bodies in paintings and on statues **2** a thing that is used to hide an embarrassing fact or situation

fig·ment /'fɪgmənt/ noun **IDM** **a figment of sb's imagi'nation** something that sb has imagined and that does not really exist

fig·ura·tive /'fɪgərətɪv; *AmE* also 'fɪgjə-/ *adj.* [usually before noun] **1** (of language, words, phrases, etc.) used in a way that is different from the usual meaning, in order to create a particular mental image. For example, 'He exploded with rage' shows a figurative use of the verb 'explode'.—compare LITERAL, METAPHORICAL **2** (of paintings, art, etc.) showing people, animals and objects as they really look: *a figurative artist/painter*—compare ABSTRACT ▶ **fig·ura·tive·ly** *adv.*: *She is, figuratively speaking, holding a gun to his head.*

fig·ure /'fɪgə(r); *AmE* 'fɪgjər/ *noun, verb*
■ *noun*

NUMBERS | **1** [C, often pl.] a number representing a particular amount, especially one given in official information: *the latest trade/sales/unemployment figures* ◇ *By 1998, this figure had risen to 14 million.* ◇ *Experts put the real figure at closer to 75%.* **2** [C] a symbol rather than a word representing one of the numbers between 0 and 9: *Write the figure '7' on the board.* ◇ *a six-figure salary* (= over 100000 pounds or dollars) ◇ *His salary is now in six figures.*—see also DOUBLE FIGURES, SINGLE FIGURES **3** (*figures*) [pl.] (*informal*) the area of mathematics that deals with adding, multiplying, etc. numbers: *Are you any good at figures?* ◇ *I'm afraid I don't* **have a head for figures** (= I am not good at adding, etc.).

PERSON | **4** [C] a person of the type mentioned: *a leading figure in the music industry* ◇ *a cult/public/political figure* ◇ *a figure of authority* ◇ *When she last saw him, he was a sad figure—old and tired.*—see also FATHER FIGURE, MOTHER FIGURE **5** [C] the shape of a person seen from a distance or not clearly: *a tall figure in black*

SHAPE OF BODY | **6** [C] the shape of the human body, especially a woman's body that is attractive: *She's always had a good figure.* ◇ *I'm watching my figure* (= trying not to get fat).

IN PAINTING/STORY | **7** [C] a person or an animal in a drawing, painting, etc., or in a story: *The central figure in the painting is the artist's daughter.*

STATUE | **8** [C] a statue of a person or an animal: *a bronze figure of a horse*

PICTURE/DIAGRAM | **9** [C] (*abbr.* **fig.**) a picture, diagram, etc. in a book, that is referred to by a number: *The results are illustrated in figure 3 opposite.*

GEOMETRY | **10** [C] a particular shape formed by lines or surfaces: *a five-sided figure* ◇ *a solid figure*

MOVEMENT ON ICE | **11** [C] a pattern or series of movements performed on ice

IDM **be/become a figure of 'fun** to be/become sb that other people laugh at **cut a … 'figure** (of a person) to have a particular appearance: *He cut a striking figure in his white dinner jacket.* **put a figure on sth** to say the exact price or number of sth—more at FACT

F

F

■ *verb*

BE IMPORTANT | **1** [V] ~ **(as sth)** **(in/among sth)** to be part of a process, situation, etc. especially an important part: *The question of the peace settlement is likely to figure prominently in the talks.* ◊ *My feelings about the matter didn't seem to figure at all.* ◊ *It did not figure high on her list of priorities.* ◊ *Do I still figure in your plans?*

THINK/DECIDE | **2** to think or decide that sth will happen or is true: [V(**that**)] *I figured (that) if I took the night train, I could be in Scotland by morning.* ◊ *We figured the sensible thing to do was to wait.* ◊ [VN] *That's what I figured.* [also V wh-]

CALCULATE | **3** [VN] (*AmE*) to calculate an amount or the cost of sth: *We figured the attendance at 150000.*

IDM **it/that figures** used to say that sth was expected or seems logical: *'John called in sick.' 'That figures, he wasn't feeling well yesterday.'* ◊ (*disapproving*) *'She was late again.' 'Yes, that figures.'*

PHRV **'figure on sth** | **'figure on (sb/sth) doing sth** to plan sth or to do sth; to expect sth (to happen): *I hadn't figured on getting home so late.* ,**figure sb/sth** ↔ **'out 1** to think about sb/sth until you understand them/it: *We've never been able to figure her out.* ◊ [+wh-] *I can't figure out how to do this.* **2** to calculate an amount or the cost of sth: [+wh-] *Have you figured out how much the trip will cost?*

fig·ured /ˈfɪɡəd; *AmE* ˈfɪɡjərd/ *adj.* [only before noun] (*technical*) decorated with a small pattern: *figured pottery*

fig·ure·head /ˈfɪɡəhed; *AmE* -ɡjərh-/ *noun* **1** a person who is in a high position in a country or an organization but who has no real power or authority **2** a large wooden statue, usually representing a woman, that used to be fixed to the front end of a ship

,**figure of 'eight** (*BrE*) (*AmE* ,**figure 'eight**) *noun* (*pl.* **figures of eight, figure eights**) a pattern or movement that looks like the shape of the number 8

,**figure of 'speech** *noun* (*pl.* **figures of speech**) a word or phrase used in a different way from its usual meaning in order to create a particular mental image or effect

'**figure-skating** *noun* [U] a type of ICE SKATING in which you cut patterns in the ice and do jumps and SPINS—compare SPEED SKATING

fig·ur·ine /ˈfɪɡəriːn; *AmE* ˌfɪɡjəˈriːn/ *noun* a small statue of a person or an animal used as an ornament

fila·ment /ˈfɪləmənt/ *noun* **1** a thin wire in a LIGHT BULB that produces light when electricity is passed through it **2** (especially *technical*) a long thin piece of sth that looks like a thread: *glass/metal filaments*

fil·bert /ˈfɪlbət; *AmE* -bərt/ *noun* (especially *AmE*) = HAZELNUT

filch /fɪltʃ/ *verb* [VN] (*informal*) to steal sth, especially sth small or not very valuable

file /faɪl/ *noun, verb*

■ *noun* **1** a box or folded piece of card, often with a wire or metal rod, for keeping loose papers together and in order: *a box file* ◊ *A stack of files awaited me on my desk.*—picture at STATIONERY **2** a collection of information stored together in a computer, under a particular name: *to access/copy/create/delete/save a file* ◊ *Every file on the same disk must have a different name.* **3** ~ (**on sb**) a file and the information it contains, for example about a particular person or subject: *secret police files* ◊ *to have/open/keep a confidential file on sb* ◊ *Your application will be kept on file* (= in a file, to be used later). ◊ *Police have reopened the file* (= have started collecting information again) *on the missing girl.* **4** a metal tool with a rough surface for cutting or shaping hard substances or for making them smooth—see also NAIL FILE—picture at TOOL **5** a line of people or things, one behind the other: *They set off* **in file** *behind the teacher.* IDM **(in) Indian/single 'file** (in) one line, one behind the other: *They made their way in single file along the cliff path.*

■ *verb* **1** [VN] ~ **sth (away)** to put and keep documents, etc. in a particular place and in a particular order so that you can find them easily; to put a document into a file: *The forms should be filed alphabetically.* ◊ *I filed the letters away in a drawer.* ◊ *Please file it in my 'Research' file.* **2** ~ **(for sth)** (*law*) to present sth so that it can be officially recorded and dealt with: [V] *to file for divorce/bankruptcy* ◊ [VN] *to file a claim/a complaint/a petition/a lawsuit* [also V to inf] **3** [VN] (of a journalist) to send a report or a story to your employer **4** [V + adv./prep.] to walk in a line of people, one after the other, in a particular direction: *The doors of the museum opened and the visitors began to file in.* **5** [VN] ~ **sth (away/down, etc.)** to cut or shape sth or make sth smooth using a file: *to file your nails*

'**file cabinet** *noun* (*AmE*) = FILING CABINET

'**file clerk** *noun* (*AmE*) = FILING CLERK

filet *noun* (*AmE*) = FILLET

fil·ial /ˈfɪliəl/ *adj.* [usually before noun] (*formal*) connected with the way children behave towards their parents: *filial affection/duty*

fili·bus·ter /ˈfɪlɪbʌstə(r)/ *noun* (especially *AmE*) a long speech made in a parliament in order to delay a vote ▶ **fili·bus·ter** *verb* [V]

fili·gree /ˈfɪlɪɡriː/ *noun* [U] delicate decoration made from gold, silver or COPPER wire

fil·ing /ˈfaɪlɪŋ/ *noun* **1** [U] the act of putting documents, letters, etc. into a file **2** [C] (especially *AmE*) something that is placed in an official record: *a bankruptcy filing* **3** (**filings**) [pl.] very small pieces of metal, made when a larger piece of metal is FILED: *copper/iron filings*

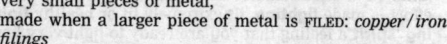

filigree

filigree earring

'**filing cabinet** (*BrE*) (*AmE* '**file cabinet**) *noun* a piece of office furniture with deep drawers for storing files

'**filing clerk** (*BrE*) (*AmE* '**file clerk**) *noun* a person whose job is to file letters, etc. and do general office tasks

Fi·li·pino /ˌfɪlɪˈpiːnəʊ; *AmE* -noʊ/ *noun, adj.*

■ *noun* **1** [C] a person from the Philippines **2** [U] the language of the Philippines

■ *adj.* connected with the Philippines, its people or their language

fill /fɪl/ *verb, noun*

■ *verb*

MAKE FULL | **1** ~ **(sth)** **(with sth)** to make sth full of sth; to become full of sth: [VN] *to fill a hole with earth/a bucket with water* ◊ *to fill a vacuum/void* ◊ *Please fill this glass for me.* ◊ *The school is* **filled to capacity**. ◊ *Smoke filled the room.* ◊ *The wind filled the sails.* ◊ *A Disney film can always fill cinemas* (= attract a lot of people to see it). ◊ [VN-ADJ] *Fill a pan half full of water.* ◊ [V] *The room was filling quickly.* ◊ *Her eyes suddenly filled with tears.* ◊ *The sails filled with wind.*

BLOCK HOLE | **2** [VN] to block a hole with a substance: *The crack in the wall had been filled with plaster.* ◊ *I need to have two teeth filled* (= to have FILLINGS put in them). ◊ (*figurative*) *The product has filled a gap in the market.*

WITH FEELING | **3** [VN] ~ **sb (with sth)** to make sb have a strong feeling: *We were all filled with admiration for his achievements.*

WITH SMELL/SOUND/LIGHT | **4** [VN] ~ **sth (with sth)** if a smell, sound or light fills a place, it is very strong, loud or bright and easy to notice

-FILLED | **5** (in adjectives) full of the thing mentioned: *a smoke-filled room* ◊ *a fun-filled day*

A NEED | **6** [VN] to stop people from continuing to want or need sth: *More nurseries will be built to fill the need for high-quality child care.*

JOB | **7** [VN] to do a job, have a role or position, etc: *He fills the post satisfactorily* (= performs his duties well). ◊ *The team needs someone to fill the role of manager very soon.* **8** [VN] to appoint sb to a job: *The vacancy has already been filled.*

TIME | **9** [VN] ~ **sth (up)** to use up a particular period of time doing sth: *How do you fill your day now that you've retired?*

WITH FOOD | **10** [VN] ~ **sb/yourself (up)** **(with sth)** (*informal*) to make sb/yourself feel unable to eat any more: *The* *kids filled themselves with snacks and now they don't want any lunch.*

AN ORDER | **11** [VN] if sb **fills** an order or a PRESCRIPTION, they give the customer what they have asked for

—see also UNFILLED

IDM **fill sb's shoes/boots** to do sb's job in a satisfactory way when they are not there—more at BILL *n.*

PHRV ,fill 'in (for sb) to do sb's job for a short time while they are not there, **fill sth↔'in 1** (also ,fill sth↔'up especially in *AmE*) to complete a form, etc. by writing information on it: *to fill in an application form ◊ To order, fill in the coupon on p 54.* **2** to fill sth completely: *The hole has been filled in.* **3** to spend time doing sth while waiting for sth more important: *He filled in the rest of the day watching television.* **4** to complete a drawing, etc. by covering the space inside the outline with colour ,fill sb 'in (on sth) to tell sb about sth that has happened ,fill 'out to become larger, rounder or fatter ,fill sth↔'out = FILL STH IN (1) ,fill 'up (with sth)| ,fill sth↔'up (with sth) to become completely full; to make sth completely full: *The ditches had filled up with mud and debris.* ◊ *to fill up the tank with oil*

■ *noun* [sing.] **1** your ~ (of sth/sb) as much of sth/sb as you are willing to accept: *I've had my fill of entertaining for one week.* **2** your ~ (of food/drink) as much as you can eat/drink

fill·er /'fɪlə(r)/ *noun* [U, C] **1** a substance used to fill holes or cracks, especially in walls before painting them **2** (*informal*) something that is not important but is used to complete sth else because nothing better is available: *The song was originally a filler on their first album.*—see also STOCKING FILLER

'**filler cap** *noun* a lid for covering the end of the pipe through which petrol/gas is put into a motor vehicle—picture at CAR

fil·let /'fɪlɪt; *AmE* fɪ'leɪ/ *noun, verb*
■ *noun* (*AmE* also **filet**) [C, U] a piece of meat or fish that has no bones in it: *plaice fillets ◊ a fillet of cod ◊ fillet steak*
■ *verb* [VN] to remove the bones from a piece of fish or meat; to cut fish or meat into fillets

fill·ing /'fɪlɪŋ/ *noun, adj.*
■ *noun* **1** [C] a small amount of metal or other material used to fill a hole in a tooth: *I had to have two fillings at the dentist's today.* **2** [C, U] food put inside a sandwich, cake, pie, etc: *a sponge cake with cream and jam filling ◊ a wide range of sandwich fillings*—picture on page A1 **3** [C, U] soft material used to fill cushions, PILLOWS, etc: *synthetic fillings*
■ *adj.* (of food) making your stomach feel full: *This cake is very filling.*

'**filling station** *noun* = PETROL STATION

fil·lip /'fɪlɪp/ *noun* [sing.] a ~ (to/for sth) (*formal*) a thing or person that causes sth to improve suddenly [SYN] BOOST: *A drop in interest rates gave a welcome fillip to the housing market.*

filly /'fɪli/ *noun* (*pl.* **-ies**) a young female horse—compare COLT, MARE

film /fɪlm/ *noun, verb*
■ *noun*
MOVING PICTURES | **1** [C] (*especially BrE*) (*AmE* usually **movie**) a series of moving pictures recorded with sound that tells a story, shown on television or at the cinema/ movie theater: *Let's go to the cinema—there's a good film on this week. ◊ Let's stay in and watch a film. ◊ a horror/ documentary/feature film ◊ a silent film (= one recorded without sound) ◊ an international film festival ◊ a film crew/critic/director/producer ◊ the film version of the novel* **2** [U] (*especially BrE*) (*AmE* usually **the movies** [pl.]) (*BrE* also **the cin·ema**) the art or business of making films/movies: *to study film and photography ◊ the film industry*—compare CINEMA **3** [U] moving pictures of real events, shown for example on television [SYN] FOOT-AGE: *television news film of the riots*

IN CAMERAS | **4** [U, C] thin plastic that is sensitive to light, used for taking photographs and making films/movies; a roll of this plastic, used in cameras: *a roll of film ◊ 35mm/*

colour film ◊ She put a new film in her camera. ◊ to have a film developed

THIN LAYER | **5** [C, usually sing.] ~ (of sth) a thin layer of sth, usually on the surface of sth else: *Everything was covered in a film of dust.*

—see also CLING FILM

■ *verb* to make a film/movie of a story or a real event:[V] *They are filming in Moscow right now.* ◊ [VN] *It took them six weeks to film the documentary.* ◊ *The show was filmed on location in New York.* ◊ [VN-ing] *Two young boys were filmed stealing CDs on the security video.* ▶ **film·ing** *noun* [U]: *Filming was delayed because of bad weather.*

'**film-goer** (*especially BrE*) (*AmE* usually **movie·goer**) (*BrE* also **cinema-goer**) *noun* a person who goes to the cinema/movies, especially when they do it regularly

'**film-maker** *noun* a person who makes films/movies

'**film star** (*especially BrE*) (*AmE* usually '**movie star**) *noun* a male or female actor who is famous for being in films/movies

filmy /'fɪlmi/ *adj.* [usually before noun] thin and almost transparent: *a filmy cotton blouse*

Filo·fax™ /'faɪləʊfæks; *AmE* -loʊ-/ *noun* a small book with pages that can be added or removed easily, used for writing notes, addresses, etc. in—see also PERSONAL ORGANIZER

filo pastry /'fiːləʊ ˌpeɪstri; *AmE* 'fiːloʊ/ (also **filo**) *noun* [U] a type of pastry with a lot of very thin layers

fil·ter /'fɪltə(r)/ *noun, verb*

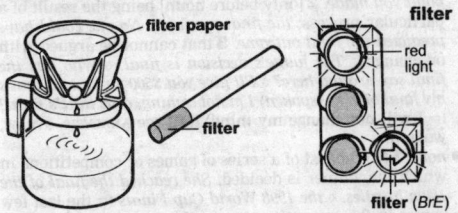

filter paper

filter

filter

red light

filter (*BrE*)

■ *noun* **1** a device containing paper, sand, chemicals, etc. that a liquid or gas is passed through in order to remove any materials that are not wanted: *an air/oil filter ◊ a coffee/water filter ◊ filter paper for the coffee machine ◊ He smokes cigarettes without filters.*—picture at CAFETIERE **2** a device that allows only particular types of light or sound to pass through it **3** (*BrE*) a light on a set of TRAFFIC LIGHTS showing that traffic can turn left or right while traffic that wants to go straight ahead must wait: *a filter lane*
■ *verb* **1** [VN] to pass liquid, light, etc. through a special device, especially to remove sth that is not wanted: *All drinking water must be filtered. ◊ filtered air/coffee ◊ Use a sun block that filters UVA effectively. ◊ (figurative) My secretary is very good at filtering my calls (= making sure that calls that I do not want do not get through).*—see also FILTRATION **2** [V+adv./prep.] (of people) to move slowly in a particular direction: *The doors opened and people started filtering through.* **3** [V+adv./prep.] (of information, news, etc.) to slowly become known: *More details about the crash are filtering through.* **4** [V+adv./prep.] (of light or sound) to come into a place slowly or in small amounts: *Sunlight filtered in through the curtains.* **5** [V] (*BrE*) (of traffic at traffic lights) to turn left at traffic lights while other vehicles wanting to go straight ahead or turn right must wait **PHRV** ,filter sth↔'out to remove sth that you do not want from a liquid, light, etc. by using a special device or substance: *to filter out dust particles/ light/impurities ◊ (figurative) The test is used to filter out candidates who may be unsuitable.*

'**filter tip** *noun* a filter at the end of a cigarette that removes some of the harmful substances from the smoke; a cigarette that has this filter

filth /fɪlθ/ *noun* [U] **1** any very dirty and unpleasant substance: *The floor was covered in grease and filth.* **2** words, magazines, etc. that are connected with sex and are considered very rude and offensive: *How can you read* such *filth?* **3 (the filth)** [U] (*BrE, slang*) an offensive word for the police

filthy /ˈfɪlθi/ *adj., adv.*

■ *adj.* (**filth·ier, filthi·est**) **1** very dirty and unpleasant: *filthy rags/streets* ◇ *It's filthy in here!* **2** very rude and offensive and usually connected with sex: *filthy language/words* ◇ *He's got a filthy mind* (= is always thinking about sex). **3** (*informal*) showing anger: *He was in a filthy mood.* ◇ *She has a filthy temper.* ◇ *Ann gave him a filthy look.* **4** (*BrE, informal*) (of the weather) cold and wet: *Isn't it a filthy day?* ▶ **filth·ily** *adv.* **filthi·ness** *noun* [U]

■ *adv.* (*informal*) **1** ~ **dirty** extremely dirty **2** ~ **rich** so rich that you think the person is too rich and you find it offensive

fil·tra·tion /fɪlˈtreɪʃn/ *noun* [U] the process of FILTERING a liquid or gas

fin /fɪn/ *noun* **1** a thin flat part that sticks out from the body of a fish, used for swimming and keeping balance—picture on page A7 **2** a thin flat part that sticks out from the body of a vehicle, aircraft, etc., used for improving its balance and movement: *tail fins*—picture at PLANE

fin·agle /fɪˈneɪgl/ *verb* (*informal, especially AmE*) to behave dishonestly or to obtain sth dishonestly: [VN] *He finagled some tickets for tonight's big game.* [also V]

final /ˈfaɪnl/ *adj., noun*

■ *adj.* **1** [only before noun] being or happening at the end of a series of events, actions, statements, etc: *his final act as party leader* ◇ *The referee blew the final whistle.* ◇ *The project is in its final stages.* ◇ *I'd like to return to the final point you made.* **2** [only before noun] being the result of a particular process: *the final product* ◇ *No one could have predicted the final outcome.* **3** that cannot be argued with or changed: *The judge's decision is final.* ◇ *Who has the final say around here?* ◇ *I'll give you $500 for it, and that's my final offer!* ◇ (*spoken*) *I'm not coming, and that's final!* (= I will not change my mind) **IDM** see ANALYSIS, STRAW, WORD *n.*

■ *noun* **1** [C] the last of a series of games or competitions in which the winner is decided: *She reached the final of the 100m hurdles.* ◇ *the 1998 World Cup Finals* (= the last few games in the competition)—see also QUARTER-FINAL, SEMI-FINAL **2** (**finals**) [pl.] (*BrE*) the last exams taken by university students at the end of their final year: *to sit/take your finals* **3** [C] (*AmE*) an exam taken by school, university or college students at the end of a SEMESTER or QUARTER, usually in a topic that they will not study again

fi·nale /fɪˈnɑːli; *AmE* fɪˈnæli/ *noun* **1** the last part of a show or a piece of music: *the rousing finale of Beethoven's Ninth Symphony* **2** ~ (**to sth**) (after an adjective) an ending to sth of the type mentioned: *a fitting/superb/dramatic finale to the day's events*

fi·nal·ist /ˈfaɪnəlɪst/ *noun* a person who takes part in the FINAL of a game or competition: *an Olympic finalist*

fi·nal·ity /faɪˈnæləti/ *noun* [U] the quality of being final and impossible to change: *the finality of death* ◇ *There was a note of finality in his voice.*

fi·nal·ize (*BrE* also **-ise**) /ˈfaɪnəlaɪz/ *verb* [VN] to complete the last part of a plan, trip, project, etc: *to finalize your plans/arrangements* ◇ *They met to finalize the terms of the treaty.* ▶ **fi·nal·iza·tion, -isa·tion** *noun* [U]

fi·nal·ly /ˈfaɪnəli/ *adv.* **1** after a long time, especially when there has been some difficulty or delay: *The performance finally started half an hour late.* ◇ *I finally managed to get her attention.* ◇ *When they finally arrived it was well past midnight.* **2** used to introduce the last in a list of things: *And finally, I would like to thank you all for coming here today.* **3** in a way that ends all discussion about sth: *The matter was not finally settled until much later.*

fi·nance /ˈfaɪnæns; faɪˈnæns; fəˈnæns/ *noun, verb*

■ *noun* **1** [U] ~ (**for sth**) money used to run a business, an activity or a project: *Finance for education comes from taxpayers.* **2** [U] the activity of managing money, especially by a government or commercial organization: *the Minister of Finance* ◇ *the finance director/department* ◇ *a diploma in banking and finance* ◇ *the world of high finance* (= finance involving large companies or coun-

tries) **3** (**finances**) [pl.] the money available to a person, an organization or a country; the way this money is managed: *government/public/personal finances* ◇ *It's about time you sorted out your finances.* ◇ *Moving house put a severe strain on our finances.*

■ *verb* [VN] to provide money for a project **SYN** FUND: *The building project will be financed by the government and by public donations.* ◇ *He took a job to finance his stay in Germany.*

'finance company (*BrE* also **'finance house**) *noun* a company that lends money to people or businesses

fi·nan·cial /faɪˈnænʃl; fəˈnæ-/ *adj.* [usually before noun] connected with money and FINANCE: *financial services/institutions* ◇ *to give financial advice/assistance/support* ◇ *to be in financial difficulties* ◇ *an independent financial adviser* ◇ *Tokyo and New York are major financial centres.* ▶ **fi·nan·cial·ly** /-ʃəli/ *adv.*: *She is still financially dependent on her parents.* ◇ *Financially, I'm much better off than before.* ◇ *Such projects are not financially viable without government funding.*

fi,nancial 'aid *noun* [U] (*AmE*) money that is given or lent to students at a university or college who cannot pay the full cost of their education: *to apply for financial aid*

fi,nancial 'year (*BrE*) (*AmE* ,fiscal 'year) *noun* [usually sing.] a period of twelve months over which the accounts and taxes of a company or a person are calculated: *the current financial year*

fi·nan·cier /faɪˈnænsiə(r); fə-; *AmE* ˌfɪnənˈsɪr/ *noun* a person who lends large amounts of money to businesses: *a leading/corporate financier*

finch /fɪntʃ/ *noun* (often in compounds) a small bird with a short beak. There are several types of finch.—see also BULLFINCH, CHAFFINCH, GOLDFINCH—picture on page A6

find /faɪnd/ *verb, noun*

■ *verb* (**found, found** /faʊnd/)

BY CHANCE **1** to discover sb/sth unexpectedly or by chance: [VN] *Look what I've found!* ◇ *We've found a great new restaurant near the office.* ◇ [VN-ADJ] *A whale was found washed up on the shore.* ◇ *I didn't expect to come home and find him gone.*

BY SEARCHING **2** ~ **sth (for sb)** | ~ **(sb) sth** to get back sth/sb that was lost after searching for it/them: [VN, VNN] *Can you find my bag for me?* ◇ *Can you find me my bag?* ◇ [VN] *I wanted to talk to him but he was nowhere to be found.* ◇ [VN-ADJ] *The child was eventually found safe and well.*

BY STUDYING/THINKING **3** to discover sth/sb by searching, studying or thinking carefully: [VN] *scientists trying to find a cure for cancer* ◇ *I managed to find a solution to the problem.* ◇ *I'm having trouble finding anything new to say on this subject.* ◇ *Have they found anyone to replace her yet?* ◇ [VN, VNN] *Can you find a hotel for me?* ◇ *Can you find me a hotel?*

BY EXPERIENCE/TESTING **4** to discover that sth is true after you have tried it, tested it or experienced it: [V (that)] *I find (that) it pays to be honest.* ◇ *The report found that 30% of the firms studied had failed within a year.* ◇ [VN-ADJ] *We found the beds very comfortable.* ◇ [VN to inf, VN that] *Her blood was found to contain poison.* ◇ *It was found that her blood contained poison.* ◇ [VN to inf] *They found him to be charming.* [also VN-N]

HAVE OPINION/FEELING **5** to have a particular feeling or opinion about sth: [VN-ADJ] *You may find your illness hard to accept.* ◇ *You may find it hard to accept your illness.* ◇ *I find it amazing that they're still together.* ◇ [VN-N] *She finds it a strain to meet new people.*

HAVE/MAKE AVAILABLE **6** [VN] to have sth available so that you can use it: *I keep meaning to write, but never seem to find (the) time.* ◇ *Where are we going to find £5000 for a new car?*

IN UNEXPECTED SITUATIONS **7** to discover sb/sth/yourself doing sth or in a particular situation, especially when this is unexpected: [VN] *She woke up and found herself in a hospital bed.* ◇ [VN-ADJ] *We came home and found him asleep on the sofa.* ◇ [VN-ing] *I suddenly found myself running down the street.* ◇ [V (that)] *I was disappointed to find that they had left already.*

REACH | **8** [VN] (of things) to arrive at sth naturally; to reach sth: *Water will always find its own level.* ◊ *Most of the money finds its way to the people who need it.* ◊ *The criticism found its mark* (= had the effect intended).

EXIST/GROW | **9** [VN] used to say that sth exists, grows, etc. somewhere: *These flowers are found only in Africa.* ◊ *You'll find this style of architecture all over the town.*

IN COURT OF LAW | **10** (*formal*) to make a particular decision in a court of law: [VN] *How do you find the accused?* ◊ [VN-ADJ] *The jury found him guilty of manslaughter.* ◊ [V] *The court found in her favour.*

IDM all 'found (*old-fashioned, BrE*) with free food and accommodation in addition to your wages **find fault (with sb/sth)** to look for and discover mistakes in sb/sth; to complain about sb/sth **find your 'feet** to become able to act independently and with confidence: *I only recently joined the firm so I'm still finding my feet.* **find it in your heart/yourself to do sth** (*literary*) to be able or willing to do sth: *Can you find it in your heart to forgive her?* ◊ *He couldn't find it in himself to trust anyone again.* **find your 'voice/'tongue** to be able to speak or express your opinion **find your way (to ...)** to discover the right route (to a place): *I hope you can find your way home.* **find your/ its 'way (to/into ...)** to come to a place or a situation by chance or without intending to: *He eventually found his way into acting.* **take sb as you 'find them** to accept sb as they are without expecting them to behave in a special way or have special qualities—more at BEARING, MATCH *n.*, NOWHERE

PHR V 'find for/against sb [no passive] (*law*) to make a decision in favour of/against sb in a court of law: *The jury found for the defendant.* ˌfind 'out (about sth/sb)| find out sth (about sth/sb) to get some information about sth/sb by asking, reading, etc: *She'd been seeing the boy for a while, but didn't want her parents to find out.* ◊ *I haven't found anything out about him yet.* ◊ [+wh-] *Can you find out what time the meeting starts?* ◊ [+that] *We found out later that we had been at the same school.* ⇨ note at DISCOVER ˌfind sb 'out to discover that sb has done sth wrong: *He had been cheating the taxman but it was years before he was found out.*

■ *noun* a thing or person that has been found, especially one that is interesting, valuable or useful: *an important archaeological find* ◊ *Our new babysitter is a real find.*

find·er /ˈfaɪndə(r)/ *noun* a person who finds sth—see also VIEWFINDER

fin de siècle /ˌfæ̃ də ˈsjekl/ *adj.* (from *French*) typical of the end of the 19th century, especially of its art, literature and attitudes

find·ing /ˈfaɪndɪŋ/ *noun* **1** [often pl.] information that is discovered as the result of research into sth: *The findings of the commission will be published today.* **2** (*law*) a decision made by the judge or JURY in a court of law

fine /faɪn/ *adj., adv., noun, verb*
■ *adj.* (**fin·er, fin·est**)
VERY GOOD | **1** [usually before noun] of high quality; good: *a very fine performance* ◊ *fine clothes/wines/workmanship* ◊ *a particularly fine example of Saxon architecture* ◊ *Jim has made a fine job of the garden.* ◊ *people who enjoy the finer things in life* (= for example art, good food, etc.). ◊ *He tried to appeal to their finer feelings* (= feelings of duty, love, etc.). ◊ *It was his finest hour* (= most successful period) *as manager of the England team.*

VERY WELL | **2** (of a person) in good health: '*How are you?*' '*Fine, thanks.*' ◊ *I was feeling fine when I got up this morning.*

ACCEPTABLE/SATISFACTORY | **3** (*spoken*) (also used as an exclamation) used to tell sb that an action, a suggestion or a decision is acceptable: '*I'll leave this here, OK?*' '*Fine.*' ◊ '*Bob wants to know if he can come too.*' '*That's fine by me.*' **4** (*spoken*) used to say you are satisfied with sth: *Don't worry. Your speech was fine.* ◊ *You go on without me. I'll be fine.* ◊ '*Can I get you another drink?*' '*No, thanks. I'm fine.*' ◊ (*ironic*) *This is a fine* (= terrible) *mess we're in!* ◊ (*ironic*) *You're a fine one to talk!* (= you are not in a position to criticize, give advice, etc.)

ATTRACTIVE | **5** [usually before noun] pleasing to look at: *a fine view* ◊ *a fine-looking woman* ◊ *a fine figure of a man*

DELICATE | **6** [usually before noun] attractive and delicate: *fine bone china* ◊ *She has inherited her mother's fine features* (= a small nose, mouth, etc.).

WEATHER | **7** (*especially BrE*) bright and not raining: *a fine day/evening* ◊ *I hope it stays fine for the picnic.*

VERY THIN | **8** very thin or narrow: *fine blond hair* ◊ *a fine thread* ◊ *a brush with a fine tip*

DETAIL/DISTINCTIONS | **9** [usually before noun] difficult to see or describe: *You really need a magnifying glass to appreciate all the fine detail.* ◊ *There's no need to make such fine distinctions.* ◊ *There's a fine line between love and hate* (= it is easy for one to become the other).

WITH SMALL GRAINS | **10** made of very small grains: *fine sand/flour* ◊ *Use a finer piece of sandpaper to finish.*

PERSON | **11** [only before noun] that you have a lot of respect for: *He was a fine man and a fine soldier* (= respected both as a man and as a soldier).

WORDS/SPEECHES | **12** sounding important and impressive but unlikely to have any effect: *His speech was full of fine words which meant nothing.*

METALS | **13** (*technical*) containing only a particular metal and no other substances that reduce the quality: *fine gold*

IDM get sth down to a fine 'art (*informal*) to learn to do sth well and efficiently: *I spend so much time travelling that I've got packing down to a fine art.* **not to put too fine a 'point on it** used to emphasize sth that is expressed clearly and directly, especially a criticism: *Not to put too fine a point on it, I think you are lying.*—more at CHANCE *n.*, FETTLE, LINE *n.*, TALK *v.*

■ *adv.* (*informal*) in a way that is satisfactory or acceptable: *Keep going like that—you're doing fine.* ◊ *Things were going fine until you showed up.* ◊ *That arrangement suits me fine.* ◊ (*BrE*) *An omelette will do me fine* (= will be enough for me).

IDM cut it/things 'fine (*informal*) to leave yourself just enough time to do sth: *If we don't leave till after lunch we'll be cutting it very fine.*

■ *noun* a sum of money that must be paid as punishment for breaking a law or rule: *a parking fine* ◊ *Offenders will be liable to a heavy fine* (= one that costs a lot of money). ◊ *She has already paid over $2000 in fines.*

■ *verb* [often passive] **~ sb (sth) (for sth/for doing sth)** to make sb pay money as an official punishment: [VN] *She was fined for speeding.* ◊ [VNN] *The company was fined £20000 for breaching safety regulations.*

fine 'art *noun* [U] (also **fine 'arts** [pl.]) forms of art, especially painting, drawing and SCULPTURE, that are created to be beautiful rather than useful: *the Slade School of Fine Art*

fine·ly /ˈfaɪnli/ *adv.* **1** into very small grains or pieces: *finely chopped herbs* **2** in a beautiful or impressive way: *a finely furnished room* ◊ *finely dressed servants* **3** in a very delicate or exact way: *a finely tuned engine* ◊ *The match was finely balanced throughout.*

fine·ness /ˈfaɪnnəs/ *noun* [U] **1** the quality of being made of thin threads or lines very close together: *fineness of detail* **2** (*technical*) the quality of sth: *the fineness of the gold*

the ˌfine 'print *noun* [U] (*AmE*) = THE SMALL PRINT

fin·ery /ˈfaɪnəri/ *noun* [U] (*written*) colourful and elegant clothes and jewellery, especially those that are worn for a special occasion: *The mayor was dressed in all his finery.*

fi·nesse /fɪˈnes/ *noun, verb*
■ *noun* [U] great skill in dealing with people or situations, especially in a delicate way
■ *verb* [VN] (*especially AmE*) **1** to deal with sth in a way that is clever but slightly dishonest: *to finesse a deal* **2** to do sth with a lot of skill or style

ˌfine-tooth 'comb (also **ˌfine-toothed 'comb**) *noun* a comb in which the pointed parts are thin and very close together **IDM** go over/through sth with a fine-tooth/fine-toothed comb to examine or search sth very carefully

fine-'tune *verb* [VN] to make very small changes to sth so that it is as good as it can possibly be ▶ **fine-'tuning**

b	d	f	g	h	k	l	m	n	p	r
bad	did	fall	get	hat	cat	leg	man	now	pen	red

F

noun [U]: *The system is set up but it needs some fine-tuning.*

fin·ger /ˈfɪŋgə(r)/ *noun, verb*

■ *noun* **1** one of the four long thin parts that stick out from the hand (or five, if the thumb is included): *She ran her fingers through her hair.* ◊ *Hold the material between finger and thumb.* ◊ *He was about to speak but she raised a finger to her lips.*—see also BUTTER-FINGERS, FOREFINGER, GREEN FINGERS, INDEX FINGER, LITTLE FINGER, MIDDLE FINGER, RING FINGER **2** (-fingered) (in adjectives) having the type of fingers mentioned; having or using the number of fingers mentioned: *long-fingered* ◊ *nimble-fingered* ◊ *a four-fingered chord*—see also LIGHT-FINGERED **3** the part of a glove that covers the finger **4** ~ (of sth) a long narrow piece of bread, cake, land, etc: *a finger of toast* ◊ *chocolate fingers*—see also FISH FINGER **5** ~ (of sth) an amount of alcohol that fills a glass to the same depth as the width of a person's finger IDM the ˌfinger of susˈpicion *if the finger of suspicion points or is pointed at sb, they are suspected of having committed a crime, being responsible for sth, etc.* **get, pull, etc. your ˈfinger out** (*BrE, informal*) used to tell sb to start doing some work or making an effort: *You're going to have to pull your finger out if you want to pass this exam.* **give sb the ˈfinger** (*AmE, informal*) to raise your middle finger in the air with the back part of your hand facing sb, done to be rude to sb or to show them that you are angry **have a finger in every ˈpie** (*informal*) to be involved in a lot of different activities and have influence over them, especially when other people think that this is annoying **have, etc. your ˈfingers in the till** (*BrE, informal*) to be stealing money from the place where you work **have/keep your finger on the ˈpulse (of sth)** to always be aware of the most recent developments in a particular situation **lay a ˈfinger on sb** (usually used in negative sentences) to touch sb with the intention of hurting them physically: *I never laid a finger on her.* **not put your finger on sth** to not be able to identify what is wrong or different about a particular situation: *There was something odd about him but I couldn't put my finger on it.* **put/stick two ˈfingers up at sb** (*BrE, informal*) to form the shape of a V with the two fingers nearest your thumb and raise your hand in the air with the back part of it facing sb, done to be rude to them or to show them that you are angry—see also V-SIGN **work your fingers to the ˈbone** to work very hard—more at BURN *v.*, COUNT *v.*, CROSS *v.*, LIFT *v.*, POINT *v.*, SLIP *v.*, SNAP *v.*, STICKY, THUMB *n.*

■ *verb* [VN] **1** to touch or feel sth with your fingers: *Gary sat fingering his beard, saying nothing.* **2** ~ sb (for sth) | ~ sb (as sth) (*informal, especially AmE*) to accuse sb of doing sth illegal and tell the police about it: *Who fingered him for the burglaries?*

fin·ger·ing /ˈfɪŋgərɪŋ/ *noun* [U, C] the positions in which you put your fingers when playing a musical instrument; the order you use your fingers: *a guitar piece with tricky fingering*

fin·ger·mark /ˈfɪŋgəmɑːk; *AmE* ˈfɪŋgərmɑːrk/ *noun* [usually pl.] (*especially BrE*) a mark made by a finger, for example on a clean surface

fin·ger·nail /ˈfɪŋgəneɪl; *AmE* -gərn-/ *noun* the thin hard layer that covers the outer tip of each finger

fin·ger·print /ˈfɪŋgəprɪnt; *AmE* -gərp-/ *noun* (*especially BrE*) a mark made by the pattern of lines on the tip of a person's finger, often used by the police to identify criminals: *His fingerprints were all over the gun.* ◊ *to take a suspect's fingerprints*—see also GENETIC FINGERPRINT ▶ **fin·ger·print** *verb* [VN]

fin·ger·print·ing /ˈfɪŋgəprɪntɪŋ; *AmE* -gərp-/ *noun* [U] the practice of recording sb's fingerprints, often used by the police to identify criminals—see also GENETIC FINGER-PRINTING

fin·ger·tip /ˈfɪŋgətɪp; *AmE* -gərt-/ *noun* [usually pl.] the end of the finger that is furthest from the hand: *Apply the cream gently using your fingertips.* IDM **have sth at your ˈfingertips** to have the information, knowledge, etc. that is needed in a particular situation and be able to find it easily and use it quickly **to your ˈfingertips** (*BrE*) in every way: *She's a perfectionist to her fingertips.*

fin·icky /ˈfɪnɪki/ *adj.* **1** (*disapproving*) too worried about what you eat, wear, etc.; disliking many things SYN FUSSY: *a finicky eater* **2** needing great care and attention to detail: *It's a very finicky job.*

fin·ish /ˈfɪnɪʃ/ *verb, noun*

■ *verb* **1** to stop doing sth or making sth because it is complete: [VN] *Haven't you finished your homework yet?* ◊ *She finished law school last year.* ◊ *I'll just finish the chapter then I'll come.* ◊ *a beautifully finished piece of furniture* ◊ *He put the finishing touches to his painting* (= did the things that made it complete). ◊ [V-ing] *Be quiet! He hasn't finished speaking.* ◊ [V] *I thought you'd never finish!* [also V speech] **2** to come to an end; to bring sth to an end: [V] *The play finished at 10.30.* ◊ *The symphony finishes with a flourish.* ◊ [VN] *A cup of coffee finished the meal perfectly.* **3** [VN] ~ sth (off/up) to eat, drink or use what remains of sth: *He finished off his drink with one large gulp.* ◊ *We might as well finish up the cake—there isn't much left.* **4** to end in a particular state or position at the end of a race or a competition: [V-ADJ] *She was delighted to finish second.* ◊ *The dollar finished the day slightly down.* ◊ *He finished 12 seconds outside the world record.* **5** [VN] ~ sb (off) (*informal*) to make sb so tired or impatient that they cannot do any more: *Climbing that hill really finished me off.* ◊ *A lecture from my parents now would just finish me.* PHRV ˌfinish sb/sth↔ˈoff (*informal*) to destroy sb/sth, especially sb/sth that is badly injured or damaged: *The hunter moved in to finish the animal off.* ˌfinish sth↔ˈoff to do the last part of sth; to make sth end by doing one last thing: *I need about an hour to finish off this report.* ◊ *They finished off the show with one of their most famous songs.* ˌfinish ˈup … (*BrE*) to be in a particular state or at a particular place after a series of events: [+ADJ] *If you're not careful, you could finish up seriously ill.* ˈfinish with sb **1** (*BrE*) to end a relationship with sb: *She finished with her boyfriend last week.* **2** to stop dealing with a person: *He'll regret he ever said it once I've finished with him.* ˈfinish with sth **1** to no longer need to use sth: *When you've finished with the book, can I see it?* **2** (*BrE, informal*) to stop doing sth: *I've finished with gambling.* **finish (up) with sth** to have sth at the end: *We had a five-course lunch and finished up with coffee and mints.* ◊ *To finish with, we'll listen to a few songs.*

■ *noun* **1** [C, usually sing.] the last part or the end of sth: *a dramatic finish to the race* ◊ *It was a close finish, as they had predicted.* ◊ *They won in the end but it was a tight finish.* ◊ *The story was a lie from start to finish.* ◊ *I want to see the job through to the finish.*—see also PHOTO FINISH **2** [C, U] the last covering of paint, polish, etc. that is put onto the surface of sth; the condition of the surface: *to apply extra coats of finish* ◊ *a gloss/matt finish* ◊ *furniture available in a range of finishes* **3** [C, U] the final details that are added to sth to make it complete: *The bows will give a feminine finish to the curtains.* IDM see FIGHT *v.*

fin·ished /ˈfɪnɪʃt/ *adj.* **1** [not before noun] ~ (with sb/sth) no longer doing sth or dealing with sb/sth: *I won't be finished for another hour.* ◊ *I'm not finished with you yet.* **2** [not before noun] no longer powerful, effective or able to continue: *If the newspapers find out, he's finished in politics.* ◊ *Their marriage was finished.* **3** [usually before noun] fully completed, especially in a particular way: *the finished product/article* ◊ *a beautifully finished suit*

fin·ish·er /ˈfɪnɪʃə(r)/ *noun* a person or an animal that finishes a race, etc.

ˈfin·ish·ing line (*BrE*) (*AmE* **ˈfinish line**) *noun* the line across a sports track, etc. that marks the end of a race: *The two horses crossed the finishing line together.*

ˈfin·ish·ing school *noun* a private school where young women from rich families are taught how to behave in fashionable society

fi·nite /ˈfaɪnaɪt/ *adj.* **1** having a definite limit or fixed size: *a finite number of possibilities* ◊ *The world's resources are finite.* OPP INFINITE **2** (*grammar*) a finite verb form or CLAUSE shows a particular tense, PERSON and NUMBER: *'Am', 'is', 'are', 'was' and 'were' are the finite forms of 'be'; 'being', and 'been' are the non-finite forms.* OPP NON-FINITE

fink /fɪŋk/ noun (informal, especially AmE) an unpleasant person

fiord = FJORD

fir /fɜː(r)/ (also **'fir tree**) noun an EVERGREEN forest tree with leaves like needles, that grows in cool northern countries

'fir cone (BrE) (also **cone** AmE, BrE) noun the hard fruit of the FIR tree—picture at CONE

fire /ˈfaɪə(r)/ noun, verb
■ noun
  STH BURNING ‖ **1** [U] the flames, light and heat, and often smoke, that are produced when sth burns: *Most animals are afraid of fire.* **2** [U, C] flames that are out of control and destroy buildings, trees, etc: *The car was now on fire.* ◇ *The warehouse has been badly damaged by fire.* ◇ *fire-fighting equipment* ◇ *Several youths had set fire to the police car* (= had made it start burning). ◇ *A candle had set the curtains on fire.* ◇ *These thatched roofs frequently catch fire* (= start to burn). ◇ *forest fires* ◇ *Five people died in a house fire last night.* ◇ *A small fire had started in the kitchen.* ◇ *Fires are breaking out everywhere.* ◇ *It took two hours to put out the fire* (= stop it burning).
  FOR HEATING/COOKING ‖ **3** [C] a pile of burning fuel, such as wood or coal, used for cooking food or heating a room: *to make/build a fire* ◇ *a log/coal fire* ◇ *Sam had lit a fire to welcome us home.* ◇ *Come and get warm by the fire.* ◇ *We sat in front of a roaring fire.*—see also BONFIRE, CAMP-FIRE—picture at ·MANTELPIECE **4** [C] (especially BrE) a piece of equipment for heating a room: *a gas/electric fire* ◇ *Shall I put the fire on?*—see also HEATER
  FROM GUNS ‖ **5** [U] shots from guns: *a burst of machine-gun fire* ◇ *to return fire* (= to fire back at sb who is shooting at you) ◇ *The gunmen opened fire on* (= started shooting at) *the police.* ◇ *Their vehicle came under fire* (= was being shot at). ◇ *He ordered his men to hold their fire* (= not to shoot). ◇ *A young girl was in the line of fire* (= between the person shooting and what he/she was shooting at).
  ANGER/ENTHUSIASM ‖ **6** [U] very strong emotion, especially anger or enthusiasm: *Her eyes were full of fire.* ◇ *The fire seemed to die in him when his wife left.*
  IDM **be/come under 'fire** to be criticized severely for sth you have done: *The health minister has come under fire from all sides.* **hang/hold 'fire** to delay or be delayed in taking action: *The project had hung fire for several years for lack of funds.* **on 'fire** giving you a painful burning feeling: *He couldn't breathe. His chest was on fire.* **play with 'fire** to act in a way that is not sensible and take dangerous risks—more at ADD v., BAPTISM, DRAW v., FIGHT v., FRYING PAN, HOUSE n., IRON n., SMOKE n., WORLD
■ verb
  SHOOT ‖ **1** ~ (sth) (at sb/sth)| ~ (sth) (into sth)| ~ (on sb/sth) to shoot bullets from a gun: [V] *The officer ordered his men to fire.* ◇ *Soldiers fired on the crowd, killing several people.* ◇ [VN] *He fired the gun into the air.* ◇ *They ran away as soon as the first shot was fired.* ◇ *Missiles were fired at the enemy.* **2** (of a gun) to shoot bullets out: [V] *We heard the sound of guns firing.* ◇ [VN] *A starter's pistol fires only blanks.* **3** [VN] to shoot an arrow: *She fired an arrow at the target.*
  FROM JOB ‖ **4** [VN] to force sb to leave their job SYN SACK: *We had to fire him for dishonesty.* ◇ *She got fired from her first job.* ◇ *He was responsible for hiring and firing staff.*
  MAKE SB ENTHUSIASTIC ‖ **5** [VN] ~ sb (with sth) to make sb feel very excited about sth or interested in sth: *The talk had fired her with enthusiasm for the project.* ◇ *His imagination had been fired by the film.*
  OF ENGINE ‖ **6** [V] when an engine fires, an electrical SPARK is produced that makes the fuel burn and the engine start to work
  -FIRED ‖ **7** (in adjectives) using the fuel mentioned in order to operate: *gas-fired central heating*
  CLAY OBJECTS ‖ **8** [VN] to heat a clay object to make it hard and strong: *to fire pottery* ◇ *to fire bricks in a kiln*
  IDM **fire 'questions, 'insults, etc. at sb** to ask sb a lot of questions one after another or make a lot of comments

very quickly: *The room was full of journalists, all firing questions at them.*—more at CYLINDER
  PHRV **fire a'way** (informal) used to tell sb to begin to speak or ask a question: *'I've got a few questions.' 'OK then, fire away.'* **,fire sth↔'off 1** to shoot a bullet from a gun: *They fired off a volley of shots.* **2** to write or say sth to sb very quickly, often when you are angry: *He fired off a letter of complaint.* **,fire sb/sth↔'up** to make sb excited or interested in sth: *She's all fired up about her new job.*

'fire alarm noun a bell or other device that gives people warning of a fire in a building: *Who set off the fire alarm?*

fire·arm /ˈfaɪərɑːm; AmE -ɑːrm/ noun [usually pl.] (formal) a gun that can be carried: *The police were issued with firearms.*

fire·ball /ˈfaɪəbɔːl; AmE ˈfaɪərb-/ noun a bright ball of fire, especially one at the centre of an explosion

fire·bomb /ˈfaɪəbɒm; AmE ˈfaɪərbɑːm/ noun a bomb that makes a fire start burning after it explodes ▶ **fire·bomb** verb [VN]

fire·brand /ˈfaɪəbrænd; AmE ˈfaɪərb-/ noun a person who is always encouraging other people to take strong political action, often causing trouble

fire·break /ˈfaɪəbreɪk; AmE ˈfaɪərb-/ noun a thing that stops a fire from spreading, for example a special door or a strip of land in a forest that has been cleared of trees—see also FIRE LINE

'fire brigade (also **'fire service**) (both BrE) (AmE **'fire department**) noun [C+sing./pl. v.] an organization of people who are trained and employed to put out fires and to rescue people from fires; the people who belong to this organization: *to call out the fire brigade* ◇ *The fire brigade were superb and quickly got everyone out.*

fire·crack·er /ˈfaɪəkrækə(r); AmE ˈfaɪərk-/ noun a small FIREWORK that explodes with a loud noise

'fire de·part·ment noun [usually sing.] (AmE) = FIRE BRIGADE

'fire door noun a heavy door that is used to prevent a fire from spreading in a building

'fire drill (BrE also **'fire practice**) noun [C, U] a practice of what people must do in order to escape safely from a fire in a building

'fire engine (AmE also **'fire truck**) noun a special vehicle that carries equipment for fighting large fires

'fire es·cape noun a metal staircase or ladder on the outside of a building, which people can use to escape from a fire

'fire extinguisher (also **ex·tin·guish·er**) noun a metal container with water or chemicals inside for putting out small fires

fire·fight /ˈfaɪəfaɪt; AmE ˈfaɪərf-/ noun (technical) a battle where guns are used, involving soldiers or the police

fire·fight·er /ˈfaɪəfaɪtə(r); AmE ˈfaɪərf-/ noun a person whose job is to put out fires—see also FIREMAN ▶ **fire·fight·ing** noun [U]: *firefighting equipment/vehicles*

fire·fly /ˈfaɪəflaɪ; AmE ˈfaɪərf-/ noun (pl. **-ies**) a flying insect with a tail that shines in the dark

fire·guard /ˈfaɪəgɑːd; AmE ˈfaɪərgɑːrd/ (AmE also **'fire screen**) noun a metal frame that is put in front of a fire in a room to prevent people from burning themselves

'fire hose noun a long tube that is used for directing water onto fires

fire·house /ˈfaɪəhaʊs; AmE ˈfaɪərh-/ noun (AmE) a FIRE STATION in a small town

'fire hydrant (also **hy·drant**) noun a pipe in the street that water can be pumped from in order to put out fires or to clean the streets

fire·light /ˈfaɪəlaɪt; AmE ˈfaɪərl-/ noun [U] the light that comes from a fire in a room

fire·light·er /ˈfaɪəlaɪtə(r); AmE ˈfaɪərl-/ noun [C, U] (BrE) a block of material that burns easily and is used to help start a coal or wood fire

'fire line noun (AmE) a strip of land that has been cleared in order to stop a fire from spreading—see also FIREBREAK

fire·man /ˈfaɪəmən; AmE ˈfaɪərmən/ noun (pl. **-men** /-mən/) a person, usually a man, whose job is to put out fires—see also FIREFIGHTER ⇨ note at GENDER

æ	ɑː	e	ɜː	ə	ɪ	iː	i	ɒ	ɔː	ʌ	ʊ	u	uː
cat	father	ten	bird	about	sit	see	many	got	saw	cup	put	actual	too
								(BrE)					

F

fire·place /'faɪəpleɪs; *AmE* 'faɪərp-/ *noun* an open space for a fire in the wall of a room—picture at MANTELPIECE

fire·power /'faɪəpaʊə(r); *AmE* 'faɪərp-/ *noun* [U] the number and size of guns that an army, a ship, etc. has available: (*figurative*) *The company has enormous financial firepower.*

'fire prac·tice *noun* [C, U] (*BrE*) = FIRE DRILL

fire·proof /'faɪəpruːf; *AmE* 'faɪərp-/ *adj.* able to resist great heat without burning or being badly damaged: *a fireproof door* ◇ *a fireproof dish* (= that can be heated in an oven)

fire-retardant /'faɪə rɪˌtɑːdənt; *AmE* 'faɪər rɪˌtɑːrd-/ (also **'flame-retardant**) *adj.* [usually before noun] that makes a fire burn more slowly: *The chair had fire-retardant covers.*

'fire sale *noun* a sale of goods at a cheap price because they have been damaged by a fire or because they cannot be stored after a fire

'fire screen *noun* **1** (*AmE*) = FIREGUARD **2** a screen, often decorative, that is put in front of an open fire in a room to protect people from the heat or from SPARKS, or to hide it when it is not lit

'fire ser·vice *noun* [usually sing.] (*BrE*) = FIRE BRIGADE

fire·side /'faɪəsaɪd; *AmE* 'faɪərs-/ *noun* [usually sing.] the part of a room beside the fire: *sitting by the fireside*

'fire station *noun* a building for a FIRE BRIGADE or FIRE DEPARTMENT and its equipment

fire·storm /'faɪəstɔːm; *AmE* 'faɪərstɔːrm/ *noun* a very large fire, usually started by bombs, that is not under control and is made worse by the winds that it causes

'fire trap *noun* a building that would be very dangerous if a fire started there, especially because it would be difficult for people to escape

'fire truck *noun* (*AmE*) = FIRE ENGINE

fire·wall /'faɪəwɔːl; *AmE* 'faɪərw-/ *noun* (*computing*) a part of a computer system that is designed to prevent people from getting at information without authority but still allows them to receive information that is sent to them

fire·wood /'faɪəwʊd; *AmE* 'faɪərwʊd/ *noun* [U] wood that has been cut into pieces to be used for burning in fires: *to collect/chop firewood*

fire·work /'faɪəwɜːk; *AmE* 'faɪərwɜːrk/ *noun* **1** [C] a small device containing powder that burns or explodes and produces bright coloured lights and loud noises, used especially at celebrations: (*BrE*) *to let off a few fireworks* ◇ (*AmE*) *to set off a few fireworks* ◇ *a firework(s) display* **2** (**fireworks**) [pl.] a display of fireworks: *When do the fireworks start?* **3** (**fireworks**) [pl.] (*informal*) strong or angry words; exciting actions: *There'll be fireworks when he finds out!*

fir·ing /'faɪərɪŋ/ *noun* **1** [U] the action of firing guns: *There was continuous firing throughout the night.* **2** [U, C] (*especially AmE*) the action of forcing sb to leave their job: *teachers protesting against the firing of a colleague* ◇ *She's responsible for the hirings and firings.*

'firing line *noun* **IDM** **be in the 'firing line** (*BrE*) (*AmE* **be on the 'firing line**) **1** to be in a position where you can be shot at **2** to be in a position where people can criticize or blame you: *The employment secretary found himself in the firing line over recent job cuts.*

'firing squad *noun* [C+sing./pl. *v.*, U] a group of soldiers who are ordered to shoot and kill sb who is found guilty of a crime: *He was executed by (a) firing squad.*

firm /fɜːm; *AmE* fɜːrm/ *noun, adj., adv., verb*
■ *noun* a business or company: *an engineering firm* ◇ *a firm of accountants*
■ *adj.* (**firm·er, firm·est**) **1** fairly hard; not easy to press into a different shape: *a firm bed/mattress* ◇ *These peaches are still firm.* ◇ *Bake the cakes until they are firm to the touch.* **2** not likely to change: *a firm believer in socialism* ◇ *a firm agreement/date/decision/offer/promise* ◇ *firm beliefs/conclusions/convictions/views* ◇ *She is a firm favourite with the children.* ◇ *We have no firm evidence to support the case.* ◇ *They remained firm friends.* **3** strongly fixed in place **SYN** SECURE: *Stand the fish tank on a firm base.* ◇ *No*

building can stand without firm foundations, and neither can a marriage. **4** (of sb's voice or hand movements) strong and steady: *'No,' she repeated, her voice firmer this time.* ◇ *With a firm grip on my hand, he pulled me away.* ◇ *Her handshake was cool and firm.* **5** (of sb's behaviour, position or understanding of sth) strong and in control: *to exercise firm control/discipline/leadership* ◇ *Parents must be firm with their children.* ◇ *The company now has a firm footing in the marketplace.* ◇ *This book will give your students a firm grasp of English grammar.* ◇ *We need to keep a firm grip on the situation.* **6** [usually before noun] **~ (against sth)** (of a country's money, etc.) not lower than another: *The pound remained firm against the dollar, but fell against the yen.*—see also FIRMLY ▶ **firm·ness** *noun* [U] **IDM** **be on firm 'ground** to be in a strong position in an argument, etc. because you know the facts: *Everyone agreed with me, so I knew I was on firm ground.* **a firm 'hand** strong control or discipline: *Those children need a firm hand to make them behave.* **take a firm 'line/ 'stand (on/against sth)** to make your beliefs known and to try to make others follow them: *We need to take a firm line on tobacco advertising.* ◇ *They took a firm stand against drugs in the school.*
■ *adv.* **IDM** **hold 'firm (to sth)** (*formal*) to believe sth strongly and not change your mind: *She held firm to her principles.* **stand 'fast/'firm** to refuse to move back; to refuse to change your opinions
■ *verb* **1** [VN] to make sth become stronger or harder: *Firm the soil around the plant.* ◇ *This product claims to firm your body in six weeks.* **2** [V] **~ (to/at...)** (*finance*) (of shares, prices, etc.) to become steady or rise steadily: *Rank's shares firmed 3p to 696p.* **PHRV** **,firm 'up** to become harder or more solid: *Put the mixture somewhere cool to firm up.* **,firm 'up sth 1** to make arrangements more final and fixed: *The company has not yet firmed up its plans for expansion.* ◇ *The precise details still have to be firmed up.* **2** to make sth harder or more solid: *A few weeks of aerobics will firm up that flabby stomach.*

firma·ment /'fɜːməmənt; *AmE* 'fɜːrm-/ *noun* (**the firmament**) [sing.] (*old use* or *literary*) the sky: (*figurative*) *a rising star in the literary firmament*

firm·ly /'fɜːmli; *AmE* 'fɜːrm-/ *adv.* in a strong or definite way: *'I can manage,' she said firmly.* ◇ *It is now firmly established as one of the leading brands in the country.* ◇ *Keep your eyes firmly fixed on the road ahead.*

firm·ware /'fɜːmweə(r); *AmE* 'fɜːrmwer/ *noun* [U] (*computing*) a type of computer SOFTWARE that is stored in such a way that it cannot be changed or lost

first /fɜːst; *AmE* fɜːrst/ *det., ordinal number, adv., noun*
■ *det., ordinal number* **1** happening or coming before all other similar things or people; 1st: *his first wife* ◇ *It was the first time they had ever met.* ◇ *I didn't take the first bus.* ◇ *students in their first year at college* ◇ *your first impressions* ◇ *She resolved to do it at the first* (= earliest) *opportunity.* ◇ *King Edward I* (= said as 'King Edward the First') **2** the most important or best: *Your first duty is to your family.* ◇ *She won first prize in the competition.* ◇ *an issue of the first importance* **IDM** see ORDER *n.*
■ *adv.* **1** before anyone or anything else; at the beginning: *'Do you want a drink?' 'I'll finish my work first.'* ◇ *First I had to decide what to wear.* ◇ *Who came first in the race* (= who won)*?* ◇ *It plunged nose first into the river.* **2** for the first time: *When did you first meet him?* **3** used to introduce the first of a list of points you want to make in a speech or piece of writing **SYN** FIRSTLY: *This method has two advantages: first it is cheaper and secondly it is quicker.* **4** used to emphasize that you are determined not to do sth: *She swore that she wouldn't apologize—she'd die first!* **IDM** **at 'first** at or in the beginning: *I didn't like the job much at first.* ◇ *At first I thought he was shy, but then he was just not interested in other people.* ◇ (*saying*) *If at first you don't succeed, try, try again.* ⇨ note at FIRSTLY **come 'first** to be considered more important than anything else: *In any decision she makes, her family always comes first.* **,first and 'foremost** more than anything else: *He does a little teaching, but first and foremost he's a writer.* **,first and 'last** in every way that is important; completely: *She regarded herself, first and last, as a*

aɪ	aʊ	eɪ	əʊ	oʊ	ɔɪ	ɪə	eə	ʊə	j	w
my	now	say	go (BrE)	go (AmE)	boy	near	hair	pure	yes	wet

musician. ,first 'come, ,first 'served (*saying*) people will be dealt with, seen, etc. strictly in the order in which they arrive: *Tickets are available on a first come, first served basis.* ,first of 'all **1** before doing anything else; at the beginning: *First of all, let me ask you something.* **2** as the most important thing: *The content of any article needs, first of all, to be relevant to the reader.* ⇨ note at FIRSTLY ,first 'off (*informal, especially BrE*) before anything else: *First off, let's see how much it'll cost.* ,first 'up (*BrE, informal*) to start with; before anything else ,put sb/sth 'first to consider sb/sth to be more important than anyone/anything else: *She always puts her children first.*—more at HEAD *n.*, SAFETY

■ *noun* **1** (the first) [C] (*pl.* the first) the first person or thing mentioned; the first person or thing to do a particular thing: *I was the first in my family to go to college.* ◊ *Sheila and Jim were the first to arrive.* ◊ *I'd be the first to admit* (= I will most willingly admit) *I might be wrong.* ◊ *The first I heard about the wedding* (= the first time I became aware of it) *was when I saw it in the local paper.* **2** [C, usually sing.] an achievement, event, etc., never done or experienced before: *We went on a cruise, a first for both of us.* **3** (also ,first 'gear) [U] the lowest GEAR on a car, bicycle, etc. that you use when you are moving slowly: *He stuck the car in first and revved.* **4** [C] ~ (in sth) the highest level of university degree at British universities: *She got a first in maths at Exeter.*—compare SECOND, THIRD **IDM** ,first among 'equals the person or thing with the highest status in a group from the (very) 'first from the beginning: *They were attracted to each other from the first.* from ,first to 'last from beginning to end; during the whole time: *It's a fine performance that commands attention from first to last.*

,first 'aid *noun* [U] simple medical treatment that is given to sb before a doctor comes or they can be taken to a hospital: *to give first aid* ◊ *a first-aid course/kit/manual*

,first 'aider *noun* (*BrE*) a person who is trained to give first aid

,first 'balcony *noun* (*AmE*) = DRESS CIRCLE

,first 'base *noun* (in baseball) the first of the BASES that players must touch: *He didn't make it past first base.*—picture on page 1250 **IDM** not get to first 'base (with sth/sb) (*informal, especially AmE*) to fail to make a successful start in a project, relationship, etc.; to fail to get through the first stage

first-born /'fɜːstbɔːn; *AmE* 'fɜːrstbɔːrn/ *noun* (*old-fashioned*) a person's first child ▶ first-born *adj.* [only before noun]: *their firstborn son*

,first 'class *noun, adv.*
■ *noun* [U] **1** the best and most expensive seats or accommodation on a train, ship, etc: *There was more room in first class.* **2** (in Britain) the class of mail that is delivered most quickly: *First class costs more.* **3** (in the US) the class of mail that is used for letters and POSTCARDS **4** the highest standard of degree given by a British university
■ *adv.* **1** using the best and most expensive seats or accommodation in a train, ship, etc: *to travel first class* **2** by the quickest form of mail: *I sent the package first class on Monday.*

,first-'class *adj.* **1** [usually before noun] in the best group; of the highest standard **SYN** EXCELLENT: *a first-class novel* ◊ *a first-class writer* ◊ *The car was in first-class condition.* ◊ *I know a place where the food is first-class.* **2** [only before noun] connected with the best and most expensive way of travelling on a train, ship, etc: *first-class rail travel* ◊ *a first-class cabin/seat/ticket* **3** [only before noun] (in Britain) connected with letters, parcels/packages, etc. that are delivered most quickly, or that cost more to send: *first-class mail/post/postage/stamps* **4** [only before noun] used to describe a university degree of the highest class from a British university: *She was awarded a first-class degree in English.*

,first 'cousin *noun* = COUSIN (1)

'first degree *noun* (*especially BrE*) an academic qualification given by a university or college, for example a BA or BSc, that is given to sb who does not already have a

degree in that subject: *What was your first degree in?* ◊ *to study geography at first-degree level*

,first-de'gree *adj.* [only before noun] **1** (*especially AmE*) ~ murder, assault, robbery, etc. murder, etc. of the most serious kind **2** ~ burns burns of the least serious of three kinds, affecting only the surface of the skin—compare SECOND-DEGREE, THIRD-DEGREE

,first e'dition *noun* one of the copies of a book that was produced the first time the book was printed

,first-'ever *adj.* [only before noun] never having happened or been experienced before: *his first-ever visit to London* ◊ *the first-ever woman vice-president*

the ,first 'family *noun* [sing.] the family of the President of the United States

'first finger *noun* = INDEX FINGER

,first 'floor *noun* [sing.] **1** (*BrE*) the level of a building above the ground level: *Menswear is on the first floor.* **2** (*AmE*) = GROUND FLOOR ▶ ,first-'floor *adj.* [only before noun]: *a first-floor flat/apartment* ⇨ note at FLOOR

,first-'foot *verb* [VN] to be the first person to enter sb's house in the New Year. **First-footing** is a Scottish custom. ▶ ,first-'footer *noun*

'first fruit *noun* [usually pl.] the first result of sb's work or effort

,first gene'ration *noun* [sing.] **1** people who have left their country to go and live in a new country; the children of these people **2** the first type of a machine to be developed: *the first generation of personal computers* ▶ ,first-gene'ration *adj.*: *first-generation Caribbeans in the UK*

,first-'hand *adj.* [only before noun] obtained or experienced yourself: *to have first-hand experience of poverty*—compare SECOND-HAND ▶ ,first-'hand *adv.*: *to experience poverty first-hand*

,first 'lady *noun* [usually sing.] **1** (the First Lady) (in the US) the wife of the President **2** (*AmE*) the wife of the leader of a state **3** the woman who is thought to be the best in a particular profession, sport, etc: *the first lady of country music*

,first 'language *noun* the language that you learn to speak first as a child; the language that you speak best: *His first language is Welsh.*—compare SECOND LANGUAGE

,first lieu'tenant *noun* **1** an officer in the navy with responsibility for managing a ship, etc. **2** an officer in the US army and air force just below the rank of a captain **3** (*informal*) a person who is the next most important to sb

,first 'light *noun* [U] the time when light first appears in the morning **SYN** DAWN, DAYBREAK: *We left at first light.*

first-ly /'fɜːstli; *AmE* 'fɜːrst-/ *adv.* used to introduce the first of a list of points you want to make in a speech or piece of writing: *There are two reasons for this decision: firstly …*

> **WHICH WORD?** ⑦
> **firstly / first of all / at first**
>
> **Firstly** and **first (of all)** are used to introduce a series of facts, reasons, opinions, etc.: *The brochure is divided into two sections, dealing firstly with basic courses and secondly with advanced ones.* **Firstly** is more common in *BrE* than in *AmE*.
>
> **At first** is used to talk about the situation at the beginning of a period of time, especially when you are comparing it with a different situation at a later period: *Maggie had seen him nearly every day at first. Now she saw him much less.*

,first 'mate (also ,first 'officer) *noun* the officer on a commercial ship just below the rank of captain or MASTER

'first name (also 'given name especially in *AmE*) *noun* the name or names that were given to you when you were born, that come before your family name: *His first name is Tom and his surname is Green.* ◊ *Please give all your first names.* ◊ (*BrE*) *to be on first-name terms with sb* (= to call them by their first name as a sign of a

F

friendly informal relationship) ◊ (*AmE*) *to be on a first-name basis*

,first '**night** *noun* the first public performance of a play, film/movie, etc: *I got tickets for the first night of 'Romeo and Juliet'.*

,first of'**fender** *noun* a person who has been found guilty of a crime for the first time

,first '**officer** *noun* = FIRST MATE

,first-,past-the-'**post** *adj.* [only before noun] (of a system of elections) in which only the person who gets the most votes is elected—compare PROPORTIONAL REPRESENTATION

the ,first '**person** *noun* [sing.] **1** (*grammar*) a set of pronouns and verb forms used by a speaker to refer to himself or herself, or to a group including himself or herself: *'I am' is the first person singular of the present tense of the verb 'to be'.* ◊ *'I', 'me', 'we' and 'us' are first-person pronouns.* **2** a way of writing a novel, etc. as if one of the characters is telling the story using the word *I: a novel written in the first person*—compare THE SECOND PERSON, THE THIRD PERSON

,first-'**rate** *adj.* excellent; of the highest quality: *a first-rate swimmer* ◊ *The food here is absolutely first-rate.*

,first re'**fusal** *noun* [U] (*BrE*) the right to decide whether to accept or refuse sth before it is offered to others: *Will you give me first refusal on the car, if you decide to sell it?*

'**first school** *noun* (in Britain) a school for children between the ages of 5 and 8 or 9

,first '**strike** *noun* an attack on an enemy made before they attack you

'**first-time** *adj.* [only before noun] doing or experiencing sth for the first time: *houses for first-time buyers* ◊ *a computer program designed for first-time users*

,first-'**timer** *noun* a person who does sth for the first time: *conference first-timers*

,First '**World** *noun* [sing.] the rich industrial countries of the world—compare THE THIRD WORLD

the ,First World '**War** (also ,World War 'I) *noun* [sing.] the first large international war that was fought mainly in Europe between 1914 and 1918

firth /fɜːθ; *AmE* fɜːrθ/ *noun* (especially in Scottish place names) a narrow strip of the sea that runs a long way into the land, or a part of a river where it flows into the sea: *the Moray Firth* ◊ *the Firth of Clyde*

fis·cal /'fɪskl/ *adj.* connected with government or public money, especially taxes: *fiscal policies/reforms* ▶ **fis·cal·ly** *adv.* —see also PROCURATOR FISCAL

,fiscal '**year** *noun* (*AmE*) = FINANCIAL YEAR

fish /fɪʃ/ *noun, verb*

■ *noun* (*pl.* **fish** or **fishes**) HELP Fish is the usual plural form. The older form, **fishes**, can be used to refer to different kinds of fish. **1** [C] a creature that lives in water, breathes through GILLS, and uses FINS and a tail for swimming: *They caught several fish.* ◊ *tropical/marine/freshwater fish* ◊ *shoals* (= groups) *of fish* ◊ *a fish tank/pond* ◊ *There are about 30000 species of fish in the world.* ◊ *The list of endangered species includes nearly 600 fishes.* ◊ *Fish stocks in the Baltic are in decline.*—see also COARSE FISH, FLATFISH, SEA FISH, SHELLFISH—picture on page A7 **2** [U] the flesh of fish eaten as food: *frozen/smoked/fresh fish* ◊ *fish pie* IDM **a ,fish out of 'water** a person who feels uncomfortable or awkward because he or she is in surroundings that are not familiar **have bigger/other fish to 'fry** to have more important or more interesting things to do **neither ,fish nor 'fowl** neither one thing nor another **an odd/a queer '<b>fish** (*old-fashioned*, *BrE*) a person who is slightly strange or crazy **there are plenty more fish in the 'sea** there are many other people or things that are as good as the one sb has failed to get—more at BIG *adj.*, COLD *adj.*, DIFFERENT, DRINK *v.*

■ *verb* **1** [V] ~ **(for sth)** to try to catch fish with a hook, nets, etc: *You can fish for trout in this stream.* ◊ *The trawler was fishing off the coast of Iceland.* **2** (**go fishing**) to spend time fishing for pleasure: *Let's go fishing this weekend.* **3** [VN] to try to catch fish in the area of water mentioned: *They fished the loch for salmon.* **4** [V+*adv.*/*prep.*] to

search for sth, using your hands: *She fished around in her bag for her keys.* PHRV '**fish for sth** to try to get sth, or to find out sth, although you are pretending not to: *to fish for compliments/information* ,**fish sth/sb↔'out (of sth)** to take or pull sth/sb out of a place: *She fished a piece of paper out of the pile on her desk.* ◊ *They fished a dead body out of the river.*

,fish and '**chips** *noun* [U] a dish of fish that has been fried in BATTER served with CHIPS/FRIES, and usually bought in the place where it has been cooked and eaten at home, etc., especially in Britain: *Three portions of fish and chips, please.* ◊ *a fish and chip shop*

'**fish cake** *noun* (*especially BrE*) pieces of fish mixed with MASHED potato made into a flat round shape, covered with BREADCRUMBS and fried

fish·er·man /'fɪʃəmən; *AmE* 'fɪʃərmən/ *noun* (*pl.* **-men** /-mən/) a person who catches fish, either as a job or as a sport—compare ANGLER

fish·ery /'fɪʃəri/ *noun* (*pl.* **-ies**) **1** a part of the sea or a river where fish are caught in large quantities: *a herring/tuna fishery* ◊ *coastal/freshwater fisheries* **2** = FISH FARM: *a trout fishery* **3** the business or industry of catching fish: *the Ministry of Agriculture, Fisheries and Food*

'**fish-eye lens** /,fɪʃaɪ 'lenz/ *noun* a camera LENS with a wide angle that gives the view a curved shape

'**fish farm** (also **fish·ery**) *noun* a place where fish are bred as a business

,fish '**finger** *noun* a long narrow piece of fish covered with BREADCRUMBS or BATTER, usually frozen and sold in packets

'**fish-hook** *noun* a sharp metal hook for catching fish, that has a point which curves backwards to make it difficult to pull out—picture at HOOK

fish·ing /'fɪʃɪŋ/ *noun* [U] the sport or business of catching fish: *They often go fishing.* ◊ *deep-sea fishing* ◊ *a fishing boat* ◊ *fishing grounds* ◊ *We enjoyed a day's fishing by the river.*

'**fishing line** *noun* a long thread with a sharp hook attached, that is used for catching fish

'**fishing rod** (also **rod**) (*AmE* also '**fishing pole**) *noun* a long wooden or plastic stick with a fishing line and hook attached, that is used for catching fish—picture at REEL

'**fishing tackle** *noun* [U] equipment used for catching fish

'**fish knife** *noun* a knife with a broad blade and without a sharp edge, used for eating fish

fish·mon·ger /'fɪʃmʌŋgə(r)/ *noun* (*especially BrE*) **1** a person whose job is to sell fish in a shop (**fish·mon·ger's**) (*pl.* **fish·mon·gers**) a shop that sells fish

fish·net /'fɪʃnet/ *noun* [U] a fabric made of threads that produce a pattern of small holes like a net: *fishnet stockings*

'**fish slice** *noun* (*BrE*) (*AmE* **spat·ula**) a kitchen UTENSIL that has a broad flat blade with narrow holes in it, attached to a long handle, used for turning and lifting food when cooking—picture at KITCHEN

'**fish·wife** /'fɪʃwaɪf/ *noun* (*pl.* **-wives** /-waɪvz/) (*disapproving*) a woman with a loud voice and bad manners

fishy /'fɪʃi/ *adj.* (**fish·ier**, **fishi·est**) **1** (*informal*) that makes you suspicious because it seems dishonest: *There's something fishy going on here.* **2** smelling or tasting like a fish: *What's that fishy smell?*

fis·sile /'fɪsaɪl; *AmE* 'fɪsl/ *adj.* (*physics*) capable of nuclear FISSION: *fissile material*

fis·sion /'fɪʃn/ *noun* [U] **1** (also ,**nuclear 'fission**) (*physics*) the act or process of splitting the NUCLEUS (= central part) of an atom, when a large amount of energy is released—compare FUSION **2** (*biology*) the division of cells into new cells as a method of reproducing cells

fis·sure /'fɪʃə(r)/ *noun* (*technical*) a long deep crack in sth, especially in rock or in the earth ▶ **fis·sured** *adj.*: *fissured soil/terrain*

fist /fɪst/ *noun* a hand when it is tightly closed with the fingers bent into the PALM: *He punched me with his fist.* ◊ *She clenched her fists to stop herself trembling.* ◊ *He got into a fist fight in the bar.*—see also HAM-FISTED, TIGHT-

s	t	v	z	ʃ	ʒ	tʃ	dʒ	θ	ð	ŋ
see	tea	van	zoo	shoe	vision	chain	jam	thin	this	sing

F

FISTED **IDM** **make a better, good, poor, etc. fist of sth**
(*BrE, informal*) to make a good, bad, etc. attempt to do
sth—more at IRON *adj., MONEY*

fist·ful /'fɪstfʊl/ *noun* a number or an amount of sth that
can be held in a fist: *a fistful of coins*

fisti·cuffs /'fɪstɪkʌfs/ *noun* [pl.] (*old-fashioned* or *humorous*) a fight in which people hit each other with their
FISTS

fit /fɪt/ *verb, adj., noun*

■ *verb* (**fit·ting, fit·ted, fit·ted**) (*AmE* usually **fit·ting, fit, fit**
except in the passive)

RIGHT SIZE/TYPE | **1** (not used in the progressive tenses) to
be the right shape and size for sb/sth: [V] *I tried the dress
on but it didn't fit.* ◇ *That jacket fits well.* ◇ *a close-fitting
dress* ◇ [VN] *I can't find clothes to fit me.* ◇ *The key doesn't
fit the lock.* **2** [V] [usually +adv./prep.] to be of the right
size, type or number to go somewhere: *I'd like to have a
desk in the room but it won't fit.* ◇ *All the kids will fit in the
back of the car.* **3** [VN] **~ sb (for sth)** [often passive] to put
clothes on sb and make them the right size and shape: *I'm
going to be fitted for my wedding dress today.*

PUT STH SOMEWHERE | **4** [VN] to put or fix sth somewhere:
They fitted a smoke alarm to the ceiling. ◇ *The rooms were
all fitted with smoke alarms.* **5** [+adv./prep.] to put or join
sth in the right place: [V] *The glass fits on top of the jug to
form a lid.* ◇ [VN] *We fitted together the pieces of the
puzzle.*

AGREE/MATCH | **6** (not used in the progressive tenses) to
agree with, match or be suitable for sth; to make sth do
this: [V] *Something doesn't quite fit here.* ◇ *His pictures
don't fit into any category.* ◇ [VN] *The facts certainly fit
your theory.* ◇ *The punishment ought to fit the crime.* ◇ *We
should fit the punishment to the crime.*

MAKE SUITABLE | **7 ~ sb/sth (for sth)** (*especially BrE*) to
make sb/sth suitable for a particular job: [VN, VN to inf]
His experience fitted him perfectly for the job. ◇ *His experience fitted him to do the job.*

—see also FITTED

IDM **fit (sb) like a 'glove** to be the perfect size or shape
for sb: *The dress fits me like a glove.*—more at BILL *n.*, CAP
n., DESCRIPTION, FACE *n.*

PHR V ˌfit sb/sth↔'in | ˌfit sb/sth 'in/'into sth **1** to find
time to see sb or to do sth: *I'll try and fit you in after
lunch.* ◇ *I had to fit ten appointments into one morning.*
2 to find or have enough space for sb/sth in a place: *We
can't fit in any more chairs.* ˌfit 'in (with sb/sth) to live,
work, etc. in an easy and natural way with sb/sth: *He's
never done this type of work before; I'm not sure how he'll
fit in with the other people.* ◇ *Where do I fit in?* ◇ *Do these
plans fit in with your arrangements?* ˌfit sb/sth↔'out/'up
(**with sth**) to supply sb/sth with all the equipment,
clothes, food, etc. they need: *to fit out a ship before a long
voyage* ◇ *The room has been fitted out with a stove and a
sink.* ˌfit sb↔'up (for sth) (*BrE, informal*) to make it look
as if sb is guilty of a crime they have not committed **SYN**
FRAME: *I didn't do it—I've been fitted up!*

■ *adj.* (**fit·ter, fit·test**)

HEALTHY | **1 ~ (for sth) | ~ (to do sth)** healthy and strong,
especially because you do regular physical exercise: *Top
athletes have to be very fit.* ◇ (*BrE*) *He won't be fit to play in
the match on Saturday.* ◇ *She tries to keep fit by jogging
every day.* ◇ (*BrE*) *He's been ill and isn't fit enough for
work yet.* ◇ *I feel really fighting fit* (= very healthy and
full of energy). ◇ *The government aims to make British
industry leaner and fitter* (=employing fewer people and
with lower costs). **OPP** UNFIT ➪ vocabulary notes on page
598

SUITABLE | **2 ~ for sb/sth | ~ to do sth** suitable; of the right
quality; with the right qualities or skills: *The food was
not fit for human consumption.* ◇ *It was a meal fit for a
king* (= of very good quality). ◇ *Your car isn't fit to be on
the road!* ◇ *The children seem to think I'm only fit for
cooking and washing!* ◇ *He's so angry he's in no fit state
to see anyone.* ◇ (*formal*) *This is not a fit place for you to
live.* **OPP** UNFIT

READY | **3 ~ to do sth** (*BrE, informal*) ready or likely to do
sth extreme: *They worked until they were fit to drop* (= so

tired that they were likely to fall). ◇ *I've eaten so much I'm
fit to burst.* ◇ *She was laughing fit to burst* (= very much).

ATTRACTIVE | **4** (*BrE, informal*) sexually attractive

IDM **(as) ˌfit as a 'fiddle** (*spoken*) in very good physical
condition see/think ¹**fit (to do sth)** (*formal*) to consider
it right or acceptable to do sth; to decide or choose to do
sth: *You must do as you think fit* (= but I don't agree with
your decision). ◇ *The newspaper did not see fit to publish
my letter* (= and I criticize it for that).—more at SURVIVAL

■ *noun*

ILLNESS | **1** [C] a sudden attack of an illness, such as EPI-
LEPSY, in which sb becomes unconscious and their body
may make violent movements: *to have an epileptic fit* ◇
Her fits are now controlled by drugs.

OF COUGHING/LAUGHTER | **2** [C] a sudden short period of
coughing or of laughter, that you cannot control: *a fit of
coughing* ◇ *He had us all in fits (of laughter) with his
jokes.*

OF STRONG FEELING | **3** [C] a short period of very strong
feeling: *to act in a fit of anger/rage/temper/pique*

OF CLOTHING | **4** [C, U] (often with an adjective) the way
that sth, especially a piece of clothing, fits: *a good/bad/
close/perfect fit*

MATCH | **5** [C] **~ (between A and B)** the way that two things
match each other or are suitable for each other: *We need
to work out the best fit between the staff required and the
staff available.*

IDM **by/in ˌfits and 'starts** frequently starting and stopping again; not continuously: *Because of other commitments I can only write my book in fits and starts.* **have/
throw a ¹fit** (*informal*) to be very shocked, upset or
angry: *Your mother would have a fit if she knew you'd
been drinking!*

fit·ful /'fɪtfʊl/ *adj.* (*written*) happening only for short
periods; not continuous or regular: *a fitful night's sleep* ◇
a fitful burst of energy ▶ **fit·ful·ly** /'fɪtfʊli/ *adv.*: *to sleep
fitfully*

fit·ment /'fɪtmənt/ *noun* [usually pl.] (*BrE, technical*) a
piece of furniture or equipment, especially one that is
made for and fixed in a particular place: *kitchen fitments* ◇
a shower fitment

fit·ness /'fɪtnəs/ *noun* [U] **1** the state of being physically
healthy and strong: *a magazine on health and fitness* ◇ *a
fitness instructor/class/test* ◇ *a high level of physical fitness* **2 ~ for sth/to do sth** the state of being suitable or
good enough for sth: *He convinced us of his fitness for the
task.* ◇ *There were doubts about her fitness to hold office.*

fit·ted /'fɪtɪd/ *adj.* **1** [only before noun] (*especially BrE*) (of
furniture) built to be fixed into a particular space **SYN**
BUILT-IN: *fitted wardrobes/cupboards* **2** [only before noun]
(*especially BrE*) (of a room) with matching cupboards and
other furniture built for the space and fixed in place: *a
fitted kitchen/bedroom* **3** [only before noun] (of clothes)
made to follow the shape of the body; not loose: *a fitted
jacket* **4 ~ for/to sth | ~ to do sth** (*especially BrE*) suit-
able; with the right qualities and skills: *She was well
fitted to the role of tragic heroine.* **5 ~ with sth** having sth
as equipment: *Insurance costs will be reduced for houses
fitted with window locks.*

ˌfitted 'carpet *noun* (*BrE*) a carpet that is cut and fixed
to cover the floor of a room completely—see also WALL-TO-
WALL CARPET

fit·ter /'fɪtə(r)/ *noun* **1** a person whose job is to put
together, or repair equipment: *a gas fitter* **2** a person
whose job is to cut and fit clothes or carpets, etc.

fit·ting /'fɪtɪŋ/ *adj., noun*

■ *adj.* **1** (*formal*) suitable or right for the occasion **SYN**
APPROPRIATE: *The award was a fitting tribute to her years
of devoted work.* ◇ *A fitting end to the meal would be a
glass of port.* ◇ *It is fitting that the new centre for European studies should be in a university that teaches every
European language.* **2** (**-fitting**) (in adjectives) having a
particular FIT: *a tight-fitting dress*

■ *noun* **1** [usually pl.] a small part on a piece of equipment
or furniture: *light fittings* ◇ *a pine cupboard with brass
fittings* **2** [usually pl.] (*BrE*) items in a house such as a
cooker, lights or shelves that are usually fixed but that

æ	ɑː	e	ɜː	ə	ɪ	iː	i	ɒ	ɔː	ʌ	ʊ	u	uː
cat	father	ten	bird	about	sit	see	many	got	saw	cup	put	actual	too

(BrE)

you can take with you when you move to a new house—compare FIXTURE **3** an occasion when you try on a piece of clothing that is being made for you to see if it fits: *to have a fitting for a wedding dress*

'fitting room (*AmE* also **'dressing room**) *noun* a room or CUBICLE in a shop/store where you can put on clothes to see how they look

five /faɪv/ *number* 5: *There are only five cookies left.* ◊ *five of Sweden's top financial experts* ◊ *Ten people were invited but only five turned up.* ◊ *Do you have change for five dollars?* ◊ *a five-month contract* ◊ *Look at page five.* ◊ *Five and four is nine.* ◊ *Three fives are fifteen.* ◊ *I can't read your writing—is this meant to be a five?* ◊ *The bulbs are planted in threes or fives* (= groups of three or five). ◊ *We moved to America when I was five* (= five years old). ◊ *Shall we meet at five* (= at five o'clock), *then?*—see also HIGH FIVE **IDM** **,give sb 'five** (*informal*) to hit the inside of sb's hand with your hand as a greeting or to celebrate a victory: *Give me five!*—more at NINE

,five-and-'dime (also **'dime store**) *noun* (*old-fashioned, AmE*) a shop/store that sells a range of cheap goods

,five-a-'side *noun* [U] (*BrE*) a game of football played indoors with five players on each team: *a five-a-side tournament*

five·fold /'faɪvfəʊld; *AmE* -foʊld/ *adj., adv.* ⇨ -FOLD

,five o'clock 'shadow *noun* [sing.] (*informal*) the dark colour that appears on a man's chin and face when the hair has grown a little during the day

,five 'pence (also **,five pence 'piece, 5p**) *noun* a British coin worth five pence: *Have you got a five pence?*

fiver /'faɪvə(r)/ *noun* (*BrE, informal*) £5 or a five-pound note: *Can you lend me a fiver?*

fix /fɪks/ *verb, noun*
■ *verb*
ATTACH | **1** [VN] (*especially BrE*) to put sth firmly in a place so that it will not move: *to fix a shelf to the wall* ◊ *to fix a post in the ground* ◊ (*figurative*) *He noted every detail so as to fix the scene in his mind.*
ARRANGE | **2** [VN] to decide on a date, time, amount, etc. for sth [SYN] SET: *Has the date of the next meeting been fixed?* ◊ *They fixed the rent at £100 a week.* ◊ *Their prices are fixed until the end of the year* (= will not change before then). **3** ~ **sth (up) (for sb)** to arrange or organize sth: [VN] *I'll fix a meeting.* ◊ *You have to fix visits up in advance with the museum.* ◊ *How are you fixed* (= do you have any plans) *for Thursday?* ◊ (*informal*) *Don't worry, I'll fix it with Sarah.* ◊ [Vtoinf] *I've fixed up (for us) to go to the theatre next week.*
POSITION/TIME | **4** [VN] to discover or say the exact position, time, etc. of sth: *We can fix the ship's exact position at the time the fire broke out.*
FOOD/DRINK | **5** ~ **sth (for sb)** | ~ **sb sth** (*especially AmE*) to provide or prepare sth, especially food: [VNN] *Can I fix you a drink?* ◊ *Can I fix a drink for you?* ◊ [VN] *I'll fix supper.*
REPAIR | **6** [VN] to repair or correct sth: *The car won't start—can you fix it?* ◊ *I've fixed the problem.*
HAIR/FACE | **7** [VN] (*especially AmE*) to make sth such as your hair or face neat and attractive: *I'll fix my hair and then I'll be ready.*
RESULT | **8** [VN] (*informal*) [often passive] to arrange the result of sth in a way that is not honest or fair: *I'm sure the race was fixed.*
PUNISH | **9** [VN] (*informal*) to punish sb who has harmed you and stop them doing you any more harm: *Don't worry—I'll fix him.*
IN PHOTOGRAPHY | **10** [VN] (*technical*) to treat photographic film, etc. with a chemical so that the colours do not change or become less bright
ANIMAL | **11** [VN] (*AmE, informal*) to make an animal unable to have young by means of an operation—see also NEUTER **IDM** **fix sb with a 'look, 'stare, 'gaze, etc.** to look directly at sb for a long time: *He fixed her with an angry stare.* **PHRV** **'fix on sb/sth** to choose sb/sth: *They've fixed on Paris for their honeymoon.* ◊ *Have you fixed on a date for the meeting?* **'fix sth on sb/sth** [often passive] if your

eyes or your mind are **fixed on** sth, you are looking at or thinking about sth with great attention **,fix sth↔'up** to repair, decorate or make sth ready: *They fixed up the house before they moved in.* **,fix sb 'up (with sb)** (*informal*) to arrange for sb to have a meeting with sb who might become a boyfriend or girlfriend **,fix sb 'up (with sth)** (*informal*) to arrange for sb to have sth; to provide sb with sth: *I'll fix you up with a place to stay.*
■ *noun*
SOLUTION | **1** [C] (*informal*) a solution to a problem, especially an easy or temporary one: *There is no quick fix for the steel industry.*
DRUG | **2** [sing.] (*informal*) an amount of sth that you need and want frequently, especially an illegal drug such as HEROIN: *to get yourself a fix* ◊ *I need a fix of coffee before I can face the day.*
DIFFICULT SITUATION | **3** [sing.] a difficult situation [SYN] MESS: *We've got ourselves in a fix about this.*
ON POSITION | **4** [sing.] the act of finding the position of a ship or an aircraft: *They managed to get a fix on the yacht's position.*
UNDERSTANDING | **5** [sing.] (*informal*) an act of understanding sth: *He tried to get a fix on the young man's motives, but he just couldn't understand him.*
DISHONEST RESULT | **6** [sing.] (*informal*) a thing that is dishonestly arranged; a trick: *Her promotion was a fix, I'm sure!*

fix·ated /fɪk'seɪtɪd/ *adj.* [not before noun] ~ **(on sb/sth)** always thinking and talking about sb/sth in a way that is not normal: *He is fixated on things that remind him of his childhood.*

fix·ation /fɪk'seɪʃn/ *noun* **1** [C] ~ **(with/on sb/sth)** a very strong interest in sb/sth, that is not normal or natural: *a mother fixation* ◊ *He's got this fixation with cleanliness.* **2** [U] (*technical*) the process of a gas becoming solid: *nitrogen fixation*

fixa·tive /'fɪksətɪv/ *noun* [C, U] **1** a substance that is used to prevent colours or smells from changing or becoming weaker, for example in photography, art or the making of PERFUME **2** a substance that is used to stick things together or keep things in position, for example false teeth

fixed /fɪkst/ *adj.* **1** staying the same; not changing or able to be changed: *fixed prices* ◊ *a fixed rate of interest* ◊ *people living on fixed incomes* ◊ *The money has been invested for a fixed period.*—see also ABODE **2** (often *disapproving*) (of ideas and wishes) held very firmly; not easily changed: *My parents had fixed ideas about what I should become.* **3** [only before noun] (of expressions on sb's face) not changing and not sincere: *He greeted all his guests with a fixed smile on his face.* **IDM** **how are you, etc. 'fixed (for sth)?** (*spoken*) used to ask how much of sth a person has, or to ask about arrangements: *How are you fixed for cash?* ◊ *How are we fixed for Saturday* (= have we arranged to do anything)?

fixed 'assets *noun* [pl.] (*business*) land, buildings and equipment that are owned and used by a company

fixed 'costs *noun* [pl.] (*business*) the costs that a business must pay that do not change even if the amount of work produced changes

fix·ed·ly /'fɪksɪdli/ *adv.* (*written*) continuously, without looking away, but often with no real interest: *to stare/gaze fixedly at sb/sth*

'fixed-term *adj.* [only before noun] a **fixed-term** contract, etc. is one that only lasts for the agreed period of time

fixer /'fɪksə(r)/ *noun* **1** (*informal*) a person who arranges things for other people, sometimes dishonestly: *a great political fixer* ◊ *an unscrupulous loan fixer* **2** a chemical substance used in photography to prevent a photograph from changing and becoming too dark

fix·ings /'fɪksɪŋz/ *noun* [pl.] (*AmE*) = TRIMMINGS: *a hamburger with all the fixings*

fix·ity /'fɪksəti/ *noun* [U] (*formal*) the quality of being firm and not changing

fix·ture /'fɪkstʃə(r)/ *noun* **1** (*BrE*) a sports event that has been arranged to take place on a particular date and at a

aɪ	aʊ	eɪ	əʊ	oʊ	ɔɪ	ɪə	eə	ʊə	j	w
my	now	say	go	go	boy	near	hair	pure	yes	wet
			(BrE)	(AmE)						

particular place: *an annual fixture* ◇ *Saturday's fixture against Liverpool* ◇ *the season's fixture list* **2** (especially *BrE*) a thing such as a bath or a toilet that is fixed in a house and that you do not take with you when you move house: *plumbing fixtures* ◇ *The price of the house includes* **fixtures and fittings.** ◇ (*figurative*) *He has stayed with us so long he seems to have become* **a permanent fixture.**—compare FITTING

fizz /fɪz/ *verb, noun*

■ *verb* [V] when a liquid **fizzes**, it produces a lot of bubbles and makes a long sound like an 's': *Champagne was fizzing in the glass.* ◇ (*figurative*) *He started to fizz with enthusiasm.* ◇ (*figurative*) *Share prices are fizzing.*

■ *noun* **1** [U, sing.] the small bubbles of gas in a liquid: (*figurative*) *There is plenty of fizz and sparkle in the show.* ◇ (*figurative*) *The fizz has gone out of the market.* **2** [U, sing.] the sound that is made by bubbles of gas in a liquid, or a sound similar to this: *the fizz of a firework* **3** [U] (*BrE*, *informal*) a drink that has a lot of bubbles of gas, especially CHAMPAGNE

fiz·zle /ˈfɪzl/ *verb* [V] when sth, especially sth that is burning, **fizzles**, it makes a sound like a long 's' SYN HISS PHRV **,fizzle 'out** (*informal*) to gradually become less successful and end in a disappointing way

fizzy /ˈfɪzi/ *adj.* (*BrE*) (of a drink) having bubbles of gas in it: *fizzy drinks* ◇ *The wine was pink and slightly fizzy.* ◇ *'A bottle of mineral water, please.' 'Fizzy or still?'*

fjord (also **fiord**) /ˈfjɔːd; *AmE* ˈfjɔːrd/ *noun* a long narrow strip of sea between high cliffs, especially in Norway

flab /flæb/ *noun* [U] (*informal*, *disapproving*) soft, loose flesh on a person's body: *Fight the flab with exercise!*

flab·ber·gast·ed /ˈflæbəgɑːstɪd; *AmE* ˈflæbərgæstɪd/ *adj.* [not usually before noun] (*informal*) extremely surprised and/or shocked

flabby /ˈflæbi/ *adj.* (*informal*, *disapproving*) **1** having soft, loose flesh; fat: *flabby thighs* ◇ *He's got soft and flabby since he gave up running.* **2** weak; with no strength or force: *a flabby grip* ◇ *a flabby argument/personality*

flac·cid /ˈflæsɪd; ˈflæk-/ *adj.* (*formal*) soft and weak; not firm and hard: *flaccid breasts*

flack /flæk/ *noun* **1** [U] = FLAK **2** [C] (*AmE*, *informal*) = PRESS AGENT

flag /flæg/ *noun, verb*

■ *noun* **1** a piece of fabric with a special coloured design on it that may be the symbol of a particular country or organization, or may have a particular meaning. A flag can be attached to a pole or held in the hand: *the Italian flag* ◇ *the flag of Italy* ◇ *The hotel flies the American flag when it has guests from the US.* ◇ *The American flag was flying.* ◇ *All the flags were at half mast* (= in honour of a famous person who has died). ◇ *The black and white flag went down, and the race began.* **2** used to refer to a particular country or organization and its beliefs and values: *to swear allegiance to the flag* ◇ *He was working under the flag of the United Nations.* **3** a piece of fabric that is attached to a pole and used as a signal or MARKER in various sports—picture at GOLF **4** a flower that is a type of IRIS and that grows near water: *yellow flags* **5** = FLAGSTONE IDM **fly/show/wave the 'flag** to show your support for your country, an organization or an idea to encourage or persuade others to do the same **keep the 'flag flying** to represent your country or organization: *Our exporters keep the flag flying at international trade exhibitions.*

■ *verb* (**-gg-**) **1** [VN] to put a special mark next to information that you think is important: *I've flagged the paragraphs that we need to look at in more detail.* **2** [V] to become tired, weaker or less enthusiastic: *It had been a long day and the children were beginning to flag.* ◇ *Her confidence never flagged.* ◇ *flagging support/enthusiasm* PHRV **,flag sb/sth↔'down** to signal to the driver of a vehicle to stop by waving at them

'flag day *noun* **1** (*BrE*) a day when money is collected in public places for a charity, and people who give money receive a small paper STICKER **2** (**Flag Day**) 14 June, the anniversary of the day in 1777 when the Stars and Stripes became the national flag of the United States

fla·gel·late /ˈflædʒəleɪt/ *verb* [VN] (*formal*) to whip yourself or sb else, especially as a religious punishment or as a way of experiencing sexual pleasure ▶ **fla·gel·la·tion** /ˌflædʒəˈleɪʃn/ *noun* [U]

,flag 'football *noun* [U] (*AmE*) a type of American football played without the usual form of TACKLING. A tackle is made, instead, by pulling a piece of fabric from an opponent's WAISTBAND.—compare TOUCH FOOTBALL

flagged /flægd/ *adj.* covered with large flat stones (called FLAGSTONES): *a flagged floor*

,flag of con'venience *noun* a flag of a foreign country that is used by a ship from another country for legal or financial reasons

flagon /ˈflægən/ *noun* a large bottle or similar container, often with a handle, in which wine, CIDER, etc. is sold or served

flag·pole /ˈflægpəʊl; *AmE* -poʊl/ (also **flag·staff**) *noun* a tall pole on which a flag is hung

fla·grant /ˈfleɪɡrənt/ *adj.* (of an action) shocking because it is done in a very obvious way and shows no respect for people, laws, etc: *a flagrant abuse of human rights* ◇ *a flagrant breach of copyright* ◇ *He showed a flagrant disregard for anyone else's feelings.* ▶ **fla·grant·ly** *adv.*

fla·grante /fləˈɡrænti/ *adv.* IDM **in fla'grante** (*literary* or *humorous*) if sb is found or caught **in flagrante**, they are discovered doing sth that they should not be doing, especially having sex

flag·ship /ˈflægʃɪp/ *noun* **1** the main ship in a FLEET of ships in the navy **2** [usually sing.] the most important product, service, building, etc. that an organization owns or produces: *The company is opening a new flagship store in London.*

flag·staff /ˈflægstɑːf; *AmE* -stæf/ *noun* = FLAGPOLE

flag·stone /ˈflægstəʊn; *AmE* -stoʊn/ (also **flag**) *noun* a large flat square piece of stone that is used for floors, paths, etc.

'flag-waving *noun* [U] the expression of strong national feelings, especially in a way that people disapprove of

flail /fleɪl/ *verb, noun*

■ *verb* (*written*) **1** ~ (sth) (**about/around**) to move around without control; to move your arms and legs around without control: [V] *The boys flailed around on the floor.* ◇ *He was running along, his arms flailing wildly.* [also VN] **2** [VN] to hit sb/sth very hard, especially with a stick

■ *noun* a tool that has a long handle with a stick swinging from it, used especially in the past to separate grains of wheat from their dry outer covering, by beating the wheat

flair /fleə(r); *AmE* fler/ *noun* **1** [sing., U] ~ **for sth** a natural ability to do sth well: *He has a flair for languages.* **2** [U] a quality showing the ability to do things in an interesting and imaginative way: *artistic flair* ◇ *She dresses with real flair.*

flak (also **flack**) /flæk/ *noun* [U] **1** guns on the ground that are shooting at enemy aircraft; bullets from these guns **2** (*informal*) severe criticism: *He's taken a lot of flak for his left-wing views.* ◇ *She came in for a lot of flak from the press.*

flake /fleɪk/ *noun, verb*

■ *noun* **1** a small, very thin layer or piece of sth, especially one that has broken off from sth larger: *flakes of snow/ paint* ◇ *dried onion flakes*—see also CORNFLAKES, SNOWFLAKE, SOAP FLAKES **2** (*AmE*, *informal*) a person who is strange or unusual or who forgets things easily

■ *verb* **1** [V] ~ (**off**) to fall off in small thin pieces: *You could see bare wood where the paint had flaked off.* ◇ *His skin was dry and flaking.* **2** to break sth, especially fish or other food into small thin pieces; to fall into small thin pieces: [VN] *Flake the tuna and add to the sauce.* ◇ *flaked almonds* [also V] PHRV **,flake 'out 1** (*informal*) to lie down or fall asleep because you are extremely tired: *When I got home he'd already flaked out on the bed.* **2** (*AmE*, *informal*) to begin to behave in a strange way

'flak jacket *noun* a heavy jacket without sleeves that is strengthened with metal and is worn by soldiers and police officers to protect them from bullets

flaky /ˈfleɪki/ *adj.* **1** tending to break into small, thin pieces: *flaky pastry* ◊ *dry flaky skin* **2** (*AmE, informal*) (of a person) behaving in a strange or unusual way; tending to forget things: *He plays a flaky tourist visiting Europe.* ▶ **flaki·ness** *noun* [U]

flam·bé /ˈflɒmbeɪ; *AmE* flɑːmˈbeɪ/ *adj.* [after noun] (from French) (of food) covered with alcohol, especially BRANDY and allowed to burn for a short time ▶ **flambé** *verb* [VN] —picture on page 275

flam·boy·ant /flæmˈbɔɪənt/ *adj.* **1** (of people or their behaviour) different, confident and exciting in a way that attracts attention: *a flamboyant gesture/style/personality* ◊ *He was flamboyant and temperamental on and off the stage.* **2** bright, colourful and noticeable: *flamboyant clothes/designs* ▶ **flam·boy·ance** /-ˈbɔɪəns/ *noun* [U] **flam·boy·ant·ly** *adv.*

flame /fleɪm/ *noun, verb*
■ *noun* **1** [C, U] a hot bright stream of burning gas that comes from sth that is on fire: *the tiny yellow flame of a match* ◊ *The flames were growing higher and higher.* ◊ *The building was in flames* (= was burning). ◊ *The plane burst into flame(s)* (= suddenly began burning strongly). ◊ *Everything went up in flames* (= was destroyed by fire).—picture at LABORATORY **2** [U] a bright red or orange colour: *a flame-red car* **3** [C] (*literary*) a very strong feeling: *a flame of passion*—see also OLD FLAME **IDM** see ADD *v.*, FAN *v.*
■ *verb* **1** (*literary*) to burn with a bright flame: [V] *The logs flamed on the hearth.* ◊ (*figurative*) *Hope flamed in her.* [also V-ADJ] **2** (*literary*) (of a person's face) to become red as a result of a strong emotion; to make sth become red: [V] *Her cheeks flamed with rage.* [also V-ADJ, VN] **3** [VN] (*informal*) to send sb an angry or insulting message on the Internet

fla·menco /fləˈmeŋkəʊ; *AmE* -koʊ/ *noun* (*pl.* -os) **1** [U, C] a fast exciting Spanish dance that is usually danced to music played on a guitar: *flamenco dancing* ◊ *to dance the flamenco* **2** [U] the guitar music that is played for this dance: *to play some flamenco*

flame·proof /ˈfleɪmpruːf/ *adj.* made of or covered with a special material that will not burn easily

flame-retard·ant /ˈfleɪm rɪˌtɑːdənt; *AmE* -ˌtɑːrd-/ *adj.* = FIRE-RETARDANT

flame-thrower *noun* a weapon like a gun that shoots out burning liquid or flames and is often used for clearing plants from land

flam·ing /ˈfleɪmɪŋ/ *adj.* [only before noun] **1** full of anger: *a flaming argument/temper* **2** burning and covered in flames: *Flaming fragments were still falling from the sky.* **3** (*BrE, informal*) used to emphasize that you are annoyed: *You flaming idiot!* **4** bright red or orange in colour: *flaming (red) hair* ◊ *a flaming sunset*

fla·mingo /fləˈmɪŋgəʊ; *AmE* -goʊ/ *noun* (*pl.* -oes *or* -os) a large pink bird with long thin legs and a long neck, that lives near water in warm countries

flam·mable /ˈflæməbl/ (also **in·flam·mable** especially in *BrE*) *adj.* that can catch fire and burn easily: *highly flammable liquids/materials* **OPP** NON-FLAMMABLE

flan /flæn/ *noun* [C, U] (*especially BrE*) an open pie made of pastry or cake filled with eggs and cheese, fruit, etc: *a mushroom/strawberry flan* ◊ *Have some more flan.*—compare QUICHE, TART

flange /flændʒ/ *noun* an edge that sticks out from an object and strengthens it or (as in a railway/railroad wheel) keeps it in the correct position

flank /flæŋk/ *noun, verb*
■ *noun* **1** the side of sth such as a building or mountain **2** the left or right of an army during a battle, or a sports team during a game **3** the side of an animal between the RIBS and the hip: *She patted the horse's flank.*
■ *verb* [VN] **1** (be flanked by sb/sth) to have sb/sth on one or both sides: *She left the courtroom flanked by armed guards.* **2** to be placed on one or both sides of sth: *They drove through the flat cotton fields that flanked Highway 17.*

flank·er /ˈflæŋkə(r)/ *noun* an attacking player in rugby or American football

flan·nel /ˈflænl/ *noun* **1** [U] a soft light fabric, containing cotton or wool, used for making clothes: *a flannel shirt/coat* ◊ *a grey flannel suit* **2** (also **face-cloth**) (both *BrE*) (*AmE* **wash-cloth**) [C] a small piece of cloth used for washing yourself: *a face flannel* **3** (flannels) [pl.] trousers/pants made of flannel: *cricket flannels* **4** [U] (*BrE, informal*) words that do not have much meaning and that avoid telling sb what they want to know

flan·nel·ette /ˌflænəˈlet/ *noun* [U] a soft cotton fabric, used especially for making sheets and NIGHTCLOTHES

flap /flæp/ *noun, verb*
■ *noun*
FLAT PIECE OF PAPER, etc. ▸ **1** [C] a flat piece of paper, fabric, metal, etc. that is attached to sth along one side and that hangs down or covers an opening: *the flap of an envelope* ◊ *I zipped the tent flaps shut.*—see also CAT FLAP
MOVEMENT ▸ **2** [C, usually sing.] a quick often noisy movement of sth up and down or from side to side: *With a flap of its wings, the bird was gone.* ◊ *the flap of the sails*
WORRY/EXCITEMENT ▸ **3** [sing.] (*informal, especially BrE*) a state of worry, confusion and excitement: *She gets in a flap over the slightest thing.*
PUBLIC DISAGREEMENT ▸ **4** [sing.] (*AmE*) public disagreement, anger or criticism caused by sth a public figure has said or done: *the flap about the President's business affairs*
PART OF AIRCRAFT ▸ **5** [C] a part of the wing of an aircraft that can be raised or lowered to control upward or downward movement—picture at PLANE
■ *verb* (-pp-)
MOVE QUICKLY ▸ **1** if a bird **flaps** its wings, or if its wings **flap**, they move quickly up and down: [VN] *The bird flapped its wings and flew away.* ◊ [V] *The gulls flew off, wings flapping.* **2** to move or to make sth move up and down or from side to side, often making a noise: [V] *The sails flapped in the breeze.* ◊ *Two large birds flapped* (= flew) *slowly across the water.* ◊ [VN] *She walked up and down, flapping her arms to keep warm.* ◊ *A gust of wind flapped the tents.*
BE WORRIED/EXCITED ▸ **3** [V] (*BrE, informal*) to behave in an anxious or excited way: *There's no need to flap—I've got everything firmly under control.*
IDM see EAR

flap·jack /ˈflæpdʒæk/ *noun* **1** [U, C] (*BrE*) a thick soft biscuit made from OATS, butter, sugar and SYRUP **2** [C] (*AmE*) a thick PANCAKE

flap·per /ˈflæpə(r)/ *noun* a young woman in the 1920s who wore fashionable clothes, had short hair and was interested in modern music and new ideas

flare /fleə(r); *AmE* fler/ *verb, noun*
■ *verb* **1** [V] to burn brightly, but usually for only a short time or not steadily: *The match flared and went out.* ◊ *The fire flared into life.* ◊ (*figurative*) *Colour flared in her cheeks.* **2** [V] ~ (up) (especially of anger and violence) to suddenly start or become much stronger **SYN** ERUPT: *Violence flared when the police moved in.* ◊ *Tempers flared towards the end of the meeting.*—related noun FLARE-UP (1) **3** to say sth in an angry and aggressive way: [V speech] *'You should have told me!' she flared at him.* [also V] **4** [V] (of clothes) to become wider towards the bottom: *The sleeves are tight to the elbow, then flare out.* **5** if a person or animal **flares** their NOSTRILS (= the openings at the end of the nose), or if their nostrils **flare**, they become wider, especially as a sign of anger: [V] *The horse backed away, its nostrils flaring with fear.* [also VN]
PHRV ˌflare ˈup **1** (of flames, a fire, etc.) to suddenly start burning more brightly—related noun FLARE-UP (3) **2** (of a person) to suddenly become angry—related noun FLARE-UP (1) **3** (of an illness, injury, etc.) to suddenly start again or become worse—related noun FLARE-UP (2)
■ *noun* **1** [usually sing.] a bright but unsteady light or flame that does not last long: *The flare of the match lit up his face.* **2** a device that produces a bright flame, used especially as a signal; a flame produced in this way: *The ship sent up distress flares to attract the attention of the coastguard.* **3** a shape that becomes gradually wider: *a skirt with a slight flare* **4** (flares) (*BrE* also ˌflared ˈtrousers) [pl.] (*informal*) trousers/pants that become very wide at the bottom of the legs: *a pair of flares*

s	t	v	z	ʃ	ʒ	tʃ	dʒ	θ	ð	ŋ
see	tea	van	zoo	shoe	vision	chain	jam	thin	this	sing

flared /fleəd; AmE flerd/ adj. (of clothes) wider at the bottom edge than at the top: *flared trousers*—picture on page A4

'flare-up noun [usually sing.] **1** a sudden expression of angry or violent feeling: *a flare-up of tension between the two sides* **2** (of an illness) a sudden painful attack, especially after a period without any problems or pain **3** the fact of a fire suddenly starting to burn again more strongly than before: *a flare-up of the bushfires*

flash /flæʃ/ verb, noun, adj.
■ verb
SHINE BRIGHTLY | **1** to shine very brightly for a short time; to make sth shine in this way: [V] *Lightning flashed in the distance.* ◊ *A neon sign flashed on and off above the door.* ◊ *the flashing blue lights of a police car* ◊ [VN] *The guide flashed a light into the cave.*
GIVE SIGNAL | **2** ~ (sth) (at sb) | ~ sb (sth) to use a light to give sb a signal: [VN, VNN] *Red lights flashed a warning at them.* ◊ *Red lights flashed them a warning.* ◊ [VN] *Why is that driver flashing his lights at us?*
SHOW QUICKLY | **3** [VN] to show sth to sb quickly: *He flashed his pass at the security officer.*
MOVE QUICKLY | **4** [V+adv./prep.] to move or pass very quickly: *The countryside flashed past the train windows.* ◊ *A look of terror flashed across his face.*
OF THOUGHTS/MEMORIES | **5** [V+adv./prep.] to come into your mind suddenly: *A terrible thought flashed through my mind.*
ON SCREEN | **6** [+adv./prep.] ~ (sth) (up) to appear on a television screen, computer screen, etc. for a short time; to make sth do this: [V] *A message was flashing on his pager.* ◊ [VN] *His name was flashed up on the screen.*
SEND NEWS | **7** [VN+adv./prep.] to send information quickly by radio, computer, etc: *News of their triumph was flashed around the world.*
SHOW EMOTION | **8** [V] (literary) to show a strong emotion suddenly and quickly: *Her eyes flashed with anger.*
OF A MAN | **9** [V] (informal) if a man **flashes**, he shows his sexual organs in public
IDM flash sb a 'smile, 'look, etc. to smile, look, etc. at sb suddenly and quickly
PHRV ,flash sth a'round (disapproving) to show sth to other people in order to impress them: *He's always flashing his money around.* **,flash 'back (to sth) 1** if your mind **flashes back** to sth, you remember sth that happened in the past: *Her thoughts flashed back to their wedding day.*—related noun FLASHBACK(2) **2** if a film/movie **flashes back** to sth, it shows things that happened at an earlier time, for example in an earlier part of sb's life—related noun FLASHBACK (1) **3** (written) to reply very quickly and/or angrily **,flash 'by/'past** (of time) to go very quickly: *The morning has just flashed by.*
■ noun
LIGHT | **1** [C] a sudden bright light that shines for a moment and then disappears: *a flash of lightning* ◊ *Flashes of light were followed by an explosion.* ◊ *There was a blinding flash and the whole building shuddered.*
SIGNAL | **2** [C] the act of shining a light on sth, especially as a signal
SUDDEN IDEA/EMOTION | **3** [C] ~ of sth a particular feeling or idea that suddenly comes into your mind or shows in your face: *a flash of anger/inspiration*
OF BRIGHT COLOUR | **4** [C] ~ of sth the sudden appearance for a short time of sth bright or colourful: *a flash of white teeth* ◊ *On the horizon, she saw a flash of silver—the sea!*
IN PHOTOGRAPHY | **5** [C, U] a piece of equipment that produces a bright light for a very short time, used for taking photographs indoors, when it is dark, etc; the use of this when taking a photograph: *a camera with a built-in flash* ◊ *I'll need flash for this shot.* ◊ *flash photography*
NEWS | **6** [C] = NEWSFLASH
ON UNIFORM | **7** [C] (BrE) a band or small piece of fabric worn on a military uniform to show a person's rank
ON BOOK/PACKET | **8** [C] a band of colour or writing across a book, packet, etc.
IDM a ,flash in the 'pan a sudden success that lasts only a short time and is not likely to be repeated **in/like a**

'flash very quickly and suddenly: *The weekend seemed to be over in a flash.*—more at QUICK adv.
■ adj. (BrE, informal, disapproving) attracting attention by being large or expensive, or by having expensive clothes, etc.: *a flash car* ◊ *He's very flash, isn't he?*

flash-back /'flæʃbæk/ noun **1** [C, U] a part of a film/movie, play, etc. that shows a scene that happened earlier in time than the main story: *The events that led up to the murder were shown in a series of flashbacks.* ◊ *The reader is told the story in flashback.* **2** [C] a sudden, very clear, strong memory of sth that happened in the past that is so real you feel that you are living through the experience again: *war veterans suffering from nightmares and flashbacks*

flash-bulb /'flæʃbʌlb/ noun a small electric BULB that can be attached to a camera to take photographs indoors or when it is dark

flash-card /'flæʃkɑːd; AmE -kɑːrd/ noun a card with a word or picture on it, that teachers use during lessons

flash-er /'flæʃə(r)/ noun **1** (informal) a man who shows his sexual organs in public, especially in order to shock or frighten women **2** a device that turns a light on and off quickly

'flash flood noun a sudden flood of water caused by heavy rain

flash-gun /'flæʃɡʌn/ noun a piece of equipment that holds and operates a bright light that is used to take photographs indoors or when it is dark

flash-ing /'flæʃɪŋ/ noun [U, pl.] a strip of metal put on a roof where it joins a wall to prevent water getting through

flash-light /'flæʃlaɪt/ noun (especially AmE) = TORCH

flash-point /'flæʃpɔɪnt/ noun [C, U] a situation or place in which violence or anger starts and cannot be controlled: *Tension in the city is rapidly reaching flashpoint.* ◊ *potential flashpoints in the south of the country*

flashy /'flæʃi/ adj. (flash-ier, flashi-est) (informal, usually disapproving) **1** (of things) attracting attention by being bright, expensive, large, etc: *a flashy hotel* ◊ *I just want a good reliable car, nothing flashy.* **2** (of people) attracting attention by wearing expensive clothes, etc. **3** intended to impress by looking very skilful: *He specializes in flashy technique, without much depth.* ▶ **flash-ily** adv.: *flashily dressed*

flask /flɑːsk; AmE flæsk/ noun **1** a bottle with a narrow top, used in scientific work for mixing or storing chemicals—picture at LABORATORY **2** (BrE) = VACUUM FLASK: *a flask of tea/coffee*—compare THERMOS **3** (especially AmE) = HIP FLASK

flat /flæt/ adj., noun, adv.
■ adj. (flat-ter, flat-test)
LEVEL | **1** having a level surface, not curved or sloping: *low buildings with flat roofs* ◊ *People used to think the earth was flat.* ◊ *Exercise is the only way to get a flat stomach after having a baby.* ◊ *The sails hung limply in the flat calm* (= conditions at sea when there is no wind and the water is completely level). **2** (of land) without any slopes or hills: *The road stretched ahead across the flat landscape.* **3** (of surfaces) smooth and even; without lumps or holes: *I need a flat surface to write on.* ◊ *We found a large flat rock to sit on.*
NOT HIGH | **4** broad but not very high: *Chapatis are a kind of flat Indian bread.* ◊ *flat shoes* (= with no heels or very low ones)
DULL | **5** dull; lacking interest or enthusiasm: *He felt very flat after his friends had gone home.*
VOICE | **6** not showing much emotion; not changing much in tone: *Her voice was flat and expressionless.*
COLOURS/PICTURES | **7** very smooth, with no contrast between light and dark, and giving no impression of depth: *Acrylic paints can be used to create large, flat blocks of colour.*
BUSINESS | **8** not very successful because very little is being sold: *The housing market has been flat for months.*
REFUSAL/DENIAL | **9** [only before noun] not allowing discussion or argument; definite: *Her request was met with a flat refusal.* ◊ *He gave a flat 'No!' to one reporter's question.*

F

æ	ɑː	e	ɜː	ə	ɪ	iː	i	ɒ	ɔː	ʌ	ʊ	u	uː
cat	father	ten	bird	about	sit	see	many	got	saw	cup	put	actual	too
								(BrE)					

IN MUSIC | **10** used after the name of a note to mean a note a SEMITONE/HALF-TONE lower: *That note should be B flat, not B.* OPP SHARP—compare NATURAL—picture at MUSIC **11** below the correct PITCH (= how high or low a note sounds): *The high notes were slightly flat.* OPP SHARP

DRINK | **12** no longer having bubbles in it; not fresh: *The soda was warm and had gone flat.*

BATTERY | **13** (*BrE*) unable to supply any more electricity

TYRE | **14** not containing enough air, usually because of a hole

FEET | **15** completely flat with no natural raised curves underneath—see also FLAT-FOOTED

IDM **and ,that's 'flat!** (*BrE, spoken*) that is my final decision and I will not change my mind: *You can't go and that's flat!* **as ,flat as a 'pancake** completely flat—more at BACK *n.*, SPIN *n.*

■ *noun*

ROOMS | **1** [C] (*BrE*) a set of rooms for living in, including a kitchen, usually on one floor of a building: *Do you live in a flat or a house?* ◊ *They're renting a furnished flat on the third floor.* ◊ *a ground-floor flat* ◊ *a new block of flats* ◊ *Many large old houses have been converted into flats.* ◊ *Children from the flats* (= the block of flats) *across the street were playing outside.*—compare APARTMENT

LEVEL PART | **2** [sing.] **the ~ of sth** the flat level part of sth: *He beat on the door with the flat of his hand.* ◊ *the flat of a sword/blade*

LAND | **3** [C, usually pl.] an area of low flat land, especially near water: *salt flats*—see also MUDFLAT

HORSE RACING | **4** (**the flat, the Flat**) [sing.] (*BrE*) the season for racing horses on flat ground with no jumps

IN MUSIC | **5** [C] a note played a SEMITONE/HALF TONE lower than the note that is named. The written symbol is (♭): *There are no sharps or flats in the key of C major.* OPP SHARP—compare NATURAL

TYRE | **6** [C] (*especially AmE*) a tyre that has lost air usually because of a hole: *We got a flat on the way home.* ◊ *We had to stop to fix a flat.*

IN THEATRE | **7** [C] (*technical*) an upright section of scenery used on a theatre stage

SHOES | **8** (**flats**) [pl.] = FLATTIES

IDM **on the 'flat** (*BrE*) on level ground, without hills or jumps (= for example in horse racing)

■ *adv.* (*comparative* **flat·ter**, no *superlative*)

LEVEL | **1** spread out in a level, straight position, especially against another surface: *Lie flat and breathe deeply.* ◊ *They pressed themselves flat against the tunnel wall as the train approached.*

REFUSING/DENYING | **2** (*BrE*) (*AmE* ,flat 'out) (*informal*) in a definite and direct way: *She told me flat she would not speak to me again.* ◊ *I made them a reasonable offer but they turned it down flat.*

IN MUSIC | **3** lower than the correct PITCH (= how high or low a note sounds): *He sings flat all the time.* OPP SHARP

IDM **fall 'flat** if a joke, a story, or an event **falls flat**, it completely fails to amuse people or to have the effect that was intended **fall flat on your 'face 1** to fall so that you are lying on your front **2** to fail completely, usually causing embarrassment: *His next television venture fell flat on its face.* **flat 'broke** (*BrE also* **stony 'broke**) (*informal*) completely broke **flat 'out** (*informal*) **1** as fast or as hard as possible: *Workers are working flat out to meet the rise in demand for new cars.* **2** (*especially AmE*) in a definite and direct way; completely: *I told him flat out 'No'.* ◊ *It's a 30-year mortgage we just flat out can't handle.* **in ...'flat** (*informal*) used with an expression of time to say that sth happened or was done very quickly, in no more than the time stated: *They changed the wheel in three minutes flat* (= in exactly three minutes).

flat·bed /'flætbed/ (also ,flatbed 'truck, ,flatbed 'trailer) *noun* (*especially AmE*) an open truck or TRAILER without high sides, used for carrying large objects—picture at TRUCK

,**flat 'cap** *noun* (*BrE*) = CLOTH CAP

flat·car /'flætkɑː(r)/ *noun* (*AmE*) a railway carriage without a roof or sides, used for carrying goods

,**flat-'chested** *adj.* (*disapproving*) (of a woman) having small breasts

flat·fish /'flætfɪʃ/ *noun* (*pl.* **flat·fish**) any sea fish with a flat body, for example a PLAICE

,**flat-'footed** *adj.* **1** without naturally raised curves (= ARCHES) under the feet **2** (*especially AmE*) not prepared for what is going to happen: *They were **caught flat-footed** by the attack.*

flat·let /'flætlət/ *noun* (*BrE*) a very small flat/apartment

flat·ly /'flætli/ *adv.* **1** in a way that is very definite and will not be changed SYN ABSOLUTELY: *to flatly deny/reject/oppose sth* ◊ *I flatly refused to spend any more time helping him.* ◊ *Our request was flatly rejected.* **2** in a dull way with very little interest or emotion: *'Oh, it's you,' she said flatly.*

flat·mate /'flætmeɪt/ (*BrE*) (*AmE* '**room-mate**) *noun* a person who shares a flat/apartment with one or more others

'**flat-pack** *noun* (*BrE*) a piece of furniture that is sold in pieces in a flat box and that you have to build yourself

'**flat racing** *noun* [U] the sport of horse racing over flat ground with no jumps—compare STEEPLECHASE

flat·ten /'flætn/ *verb* **1** to become or make sth become flat or flatter: [V] *The cookies will flatten slightly while cooking.* ◊ [VN] *These exercises will help to flatten your stomach.* ◊ *He flattened his hair down with gel.* **2** [VN] to destroy or knock down a building, tree, etc: *Most of the factory was flattened by the explosion.* **3** [VN] (*informal*) to defeat sb easily in a competition, argument, etc: *Our team was flattened this evening!* **4** [VN] (*informal*) to hit sb very hard so that they fall down: *He flattened the intruder with a single punch.* ◊ *I'll flatten you if you do that again!* PHRV **flatten sth/yourself against/on sb/sth** to press sth/your body against sb/sth: *She flattened her nose against the window and looked in.* ◊ *Greg flattened himself against the wall to let me pass.* ,**flatten 'out 1** to gradually become completely flat: *The hills first rose steeply then flattened out towards the sea.* **2** to stop growing or going up: *Export growth has started to flatten out.* ,**flatten sth↔'out** to make sth completely flat

flat·ter /'flætə(r)/ *verb* **1** [VN] to say nice things about sb, often in a way that is not sincere, because you want them to do sth for you or you want to please them: *Are you trying to flatter me?* **2 ~ yourself** to choose to believe sth good about yourself and your abilities, especially when other people do not share this opinion: [VN] *'How will you manage without me?' 'Don't flatter yourself.'* [also VN (that)] **3** [VN] to make sb seem more attractive or better than they really are: *That colour doesn't flatter many people.* ◊ *The scoreline flattered England* (= they did not deserve to get such a high score). ▶ **flat·ter·er** /'flætərə(r)/ *noun* IDM **be/feel 'flattered** to be pleased because sb has made you feel important or special: *He was flattered by her attention.* ◊ *I felt flattered at being asked to give a lecture.*

flat·ter·ing /'flætərɪŋ/ *adj.* **1** making sb look more attractive: *a flattering dress* ◊ *The photo is not very flattering.* **2** saying nice things about sb: *flattering remarks* **3** making sb feel pleased and special: *I found it flattering that he still recognized me after all these years.*

flat·tery /'flætəri/ *noun* [U] praise that is not sincere, especially in order to obtain sth from sb: *You're too intelligent to fall for his flattery.* IDM **flattery will get you 'everywhere/'nowhere** (*spoken, humorous*) praise that is not sincere will/will not get you what you want

flat·ties /'flætiz/ (also **flats**) *noun* [pl.] (*informal*) shoes with a very low heel: *a pair of flatties*

'**flat-top** *noun* a type of hair style in which the hair is cut short and flat across the top—picture at HAIR

flatu·lence /'flætjʊləns; *AmE* -tʃə-/ *noun* [U] an uncomfortable feeling caused by having too much gas in the stomach

flatu·lent /'flætjʊlənt; *AmE* -tʃə-/ *adj.* **1** (*disapproving*) sounding important and impressive in a way that exaggerates the truth or facts **2** suffering from too much gas in the stomach

aɪ	aʊ	eɪ	əʊ	oʊ	ɔɪ	ɪə	eə	ʊə	j	w
my	now	say	go (BrE)	go (AmE)	boy	near	hair	pure	yes	wet

flat·ware /ˈflætweə(r)/; *AmE* -wer/ *noun* [U] (*AmE*) = CUT-LERY

flaunt /flɔːnt/ *verb* [VN] (*disapproving*) **1** to show sth you are proud of to other people, in order to impress them: *He did not believe in flaunting his wealth.* ◊ *She openly flaunted her affair with the senator.* **2 ~ yourself** to behave in a confident and sexual way to attract attention **IDM if you've ˌgot it, ˈflaunt it** (*humorous, saying*) used to tell sb that they should not be afraid of allowing other people to see their qualities and abilities

flaut·ist /ˈflɔːtɪst/ (*BrE*) (*AmE* **flut·ist**) *noun* a person who plays the FLUTE

fla·vour (*AmE* **fla·vor**) /ˈfleɪvə(r)/ *noun, verb*
- *noun* **1** [U] how food or drink tastes: *The tomatoes give extra flavour to the sauce.* ◊ *It is stronger in flavour than other traditional Dutch cheeses.* **2** [C] a particular type of taste: *This yogurt comes in ten different flavours.* ◊ *a wine with a delicate fruit flavour* **3** [sing.] a particular quality or atmosphere: *the distinctive flavour of South Florida* ◊ *Foreign visitors help to give a truly international flavour to the occasion.* **4** [sing.] **a/the ~ of sth** an idea of what sth is like: *I have tried to convey something of the flavour of the argument.* **5** (*computing*) a particular type of sth, especially computer SOFTWARE **IDM flavour of the ˈmonth** (*especially BrE*) somebody or something that is very popular at a particular time
- *verb* [VN] **~ sth (with sth)** to add sth to food or drink to give it more flavour or a particular flavour

fla·voured (*BrE*) (*AmE* **fla·vored**) /ˈfleɪvəd; *AmE* -vərd/ *adj.* **1** (-flavoured) having the type of flavour mentioned: *lemon-flavoured sweets/candy* **2** having had flavour added to it: *flavoured yogurt*

fla·vour·ing (*BrE*) (*AmE* **fla·vor·ing**) /ˈfleɪvərɪŋ/ *noun* [U, C] a substance added to food or drink to give it a particular flavour: *orange/vanilla flavouring* ◊ *This food contains no artificial flavourings.*

fla·vour·less (*BrE*) (*AmE* **fla·vor·less**) /ˈfleɪvələs; *AmE* -ərləs/ *adj.* having no flavour: *The meat was tough and flavourless.*

fla·vour·some /ˈfleɪvəsəm; *AmE* -vərs-/ (*BrE*) (*AmE* **fla·vor·ful** /ˈfleɪvəfʊl; *AmE* -vərf-/) *adj.* having a lot of FLA-VOUR

flaw /flɔː/ *noun* **1 ~ (in sth)** a mistake in sth that means that it is not correct or does not work correctly: *The argument is full of fundamental flaws.* ◊ *The report reveals fatal flaws in security at the airport.* **2 ~ (in sth)** a crack or fault in sth that makes it less attractive or valuable: *The vase is in excellent condition except for a few small flaws in its base.* **3 ~ (in sb/sth)** a weakness in sb's character: *There is always a flaw in the character of a tragic hero.*

flawed /flɔːd/ *adj.* having a flaw; damaged or spoiled: *seriously/fundamentally/fatally flawed* ◊ *a flawed argument* ◊ *the book's flawed heroine*

flaw·less /ˈflɔːləs/ *adj.* without FLAWS and therefore perfect: *a flawless complexion/performance* ◊ *Her English is almost flawless.* ▶ **flaw·less·ly** *adv.*

flax /flæks/ *noun* [U] **1** a plant with blue flowers, grown for its stem that is used to make thread and its seeds that are used to make LINSEED OIL **2** threads from the stem of the flax plant, used to make LINEN

flax·en /ˈflæksn/ *adj.* (*written*) (of hair) pale yellow in colour

flay /fleɪ/ *verb* [VN] **1** to remove the skin from an animal or person, usually when they are dead **2** to hit or whip sb very hard so that some of their skin comes off **3** (*formal*) to criticize sb/yourself severely: *He flayed himself for his lack of tact.*

flea /fliː/ *noun* a very small jumping insect without wings, that bites animals and humans and sucks their blood: *The dog has fleas.* **IDM with a ˈflea in your ear** if sb sends a person away **with a flea in their ear**, they tell them angrily to go away—picture on page A7

ˈflea market *noun* an outdoor market that sells SECOND-HAND (= old or used) goods at low prices

flea·pit /ˈfliːpɪt/ *noun* (*old-fashioned, BrE, informal*) an old and dirty cinema or theatre

fleck /flek/ *noun, verb*
- *noun* [usually pl.] **~ (of sth) 1** a very small area of a particular colour: *His hair was dark, with flecks of grey.* **2** a very small piece of sth: *flecks of dust/foam/dandruff*
- *verb* [VN] [usually passive] **~ sth (with sth)** to cover or mark sth with small areas of a particular colour or with small pieces of sth: *The fabric was red, flecked with gold.* ◊ *His hair was flecked with paint.*

fled *pt, pp* of FLEE

fledged /fledʒd/ *adj.* (of birds) able to fly—see also FULLY-FLEDGED

fledg·ling (*BrE* also **fledge·ling**) /ˈfledʒlɪŋ/ *noun* **1** a young bird that has just learnt to fly **2** (usually before another noun) a person, an organization or a system that is new and without experience: *fledgling democracies*

flee /fliː/ *verb* (**fled, fled** /fled/) [no passive] **~ (from) sb/sth| ~ (to …/into …)** (*written*) to leave a person or place very quickly, especially because you are afraid of possible danger: *a camp for refugees fleeing from the war* ◊ *He fled to London after an argument with his family.* ◊ *She burst into tears and fled.* ◊ [VN] *He was caught trying to flee the country.*—compare FLY *v.* (12)

fleece /fliːs/ *noun, verb*
- *noun* **1** [C] the wool coat of a sheep; this coat when it has been removed from a sheep (by SHEARING) **2** [U, C] a soft warm fabric that feels like sheep's wool; a jacket or a SWEATSHIRT that is made from this fabric: *a fleece lining* ◊ *a bright red fleece*—picture on page A5
- *verb* [VN] (*informal*) to take a lot of money from sb by charging them too much: *Some local shops have been fleecing tourists.*

fleecy /ˈfliːsi/ *adj.* [usually before noun] made of soft material, like the wool coat of a sheep; looking like this: *a fleecy sweatshirt* ◊ *a blue sky dappled with fleecy clouds*

fleet /fliːt/ *noun, adj.*
- *noun* **1** [C] a group of military ships commanded by the same person **2** [C] a group of ships fishing together: *a fishing/whaling fleet* **3** (**the fleet**) [sing.] all the military ships of a particular country: *a reduction in the size of the British fleet* **4** [C] **~ (of sth)** a group of planes, buses, taxis, etc. travelling together or owned by the same organization: *the company's new fleet of vans*
- *adj.* (*literary*) able to run fast: *fleet of foot* ◊ *fleet-footed*

ˌFleet ˈAdmiral *noun* (*AmE*) = ADMIRAL OF THE FLEET: *Fleet Admiral William Hunter*

fleet·ing /ˈfliːtɪŋ/ *adj.* [usually before noun] lasting only a short time: *a fleeting glimpse/smile* ◊ *a fleeting moment of happiness* ◊ *We paid a fleeting visit to Paris.* ▶ **fleet·ing·ly** *adv.*

ˈFleet Street *noun* [U] a street in central London where many national newspapers used to have their offices (now used to mean British newspapers and journalists in general)

Flem·ish /ˈflemɪʃ/ *noun* [U] the Dutch language as spoken in northern Belgium, one of the two official languages of Belgium

flesh /fleʃ/ *noun, verb*
- *noun* **1** [U] the soft substance between the skin and bones of animal or human bodies: *The trap had cut deeply into the rabbit's flesh.* ◊ *Tigers are flesh-eating animals.* ◊ *the smell of rotting flesh* **2** [U] the skin of the human body: *His fingers closed around the soft flesh of her arm.* ◊ *flesh-coloured* (= the colour of white people's skin) **3** [U] the soft part of fruit and vegetables, especially when it is eaten—picture on page A2 **4** (**the flesh**) [sing.] (*literary*) the human body when considering its physical and sexual needs, rather than the mind or soul: *the pleasures/sins of the flesh* **IDM ˌflesh and ˈblood** when you say that sb is **flesh and blood**, you mean that they are a normal human being with needs, emotions and weaknesses: *Listening to the cries was more than flesh and blood could stand.* **your (ˌown) ˌflesh and ˈblood** a person that you are related to **in the ˈflesh** if you see sb **in the flesh**, you are in the same place as them and actually see them rather than just seeing a picture of them **make your ˈflesh creep** to make you feel afraid or full of disgust **put flesh on (the bones of) sth** to develop a basic idea, etc.

b	d	f	g	h	k	l	m	n	p	r
bad	did	fall	get	hat	cat	leg	man	now	pen	red

by giving more details to make it more complete: *The strength of the book is that it puts flesh on the bare bones of this argument.*—more at POUND *n.*, PRESS *v.*, SPIRIT *n.*, THORN, WAY *n.*

■ *verb* PHRV ,**flesh sth**↔'**out** to add more information or details to a plan, argument, etc: *These points were fleshed out in the later parts of the speech.*

flesh·pots /'fleʃpɒts; *AmE* -pɑːts/ *noun* [pl.] (*humorous*) places supplying food, drink and sexual entertainment: *the fleshpots of the capital*

'**flesh wound** *noun* an injury in which the skin is cut but the bones and organs inside the body are not damaged

fleshy /'fleʃi/ *adj.* **1** (of parts of the body or people) having a lot of flesh: *fleshy arms/lips* ◊ *a large fleshy man* **2** (of plants or fruit) thick and soft: *fleshy fruit/leaves*

fleur-de-lis (also **fleur-de-lys**) /ˌflɜː də 'liː; -'liːs; *AmE* ˌflɜːr/ *noun* (pl. **fleurs-de-lis** /ˌflɜː də 'liː; -'liːs; *AmE* ˌflɜːr/) (from *French*) a design representing a flower with three PETALS joined together at the bottom, often used in COATS OF ARMS

flew *pt* of FLY

flex /fleks/ *verb, noun*
■ *verb* to bend, move or stretch an arm or leg, or tighten a muscle, especially in order to prepare for a physical activity: [VN] *to flex your fingers/feet/legs* ◊ *He stood on the side of the pool flexing his muscles.* [also V] IDM **flex your 'muscles** to show sb how powerful you are, especially as a warning or a threat
■ *noun* (*BrE*) (also **cord** *AmE, BrE*) [C, U] a piece of wire that is covered with plastic, used for carrying electricity to a piece of equipment: *an electric flex* ◊ *a length of flex*—picture at ROPE

flex·ible /'fleksəbl/ *adj.* **1** (*approving*) able to change to suit new conditions or situations: *a more flexible design/approach* ◊ *flexible working hours* ◊ *Our plans need to be flexible enough to cater for the needs of everyone.* ◊ *You need to be more flexible and imaginative in your approach.* **2** able to bend easily without breaking: *flexible plastic tubing* OPP INFLEXIBLE ▶ **flexi·bil·ity** /ˌfleksə'bɪləti/ *noun* [U]: *Computers offer a much greater degree of flexibility in the way work is organized.* ◊ *exercises to develop the flexibility of dancers' bodies* **flex·ibly** *adv.*

flexi·time /'fleksitaɪm/ (*especially BrE*) (*AmE* usually **flex·time** /'flekstaɪm/) *noun* [U] a system in which employees work a particular number of hours each week or month but can choose when they start and finish work each day: *She works flexitime.*

flick /flɪk/ *verb, noun*
■ *verb* **1** [VN+*adv./prep.*] to hit sth with a sudden quick movement, especially using your finger and thumb together, or your hand: *She flicked the dust off her collar.* ◊ *The horse was flicking flies away with its tail.* ◊ *James flicked a peanut at her.* ◊ *Please don't flick ash on the carpet!* **2** to move or make sth move with sudden quick movements: [V, +*adv./prep.*] *The snake's tongue flicked out.* ◊ *Her eyes flicked from face to face.* ◊ [VN] (*usually+adv./prep.*) *He lifted his head, flicking his hair off his face.* ◊ *The horse moved off, flicking its tail.* **3** ~ a smile/look, etc. at sb | ~ sb a smile/look, etc. to smile or look at sb suddenly and quickly: [VN] *She flicked a nervous glance at him.* ◊ *She flicked him a nervous glance.* **4** [VN] ~ sth (on/off) to press a button or switch quickly in order to turn a machine, etc. on or off: *He flicked a switch and all the lights went out.* ◊ *She flicked the TV on.* **5** [VN] ~ A (with B) | ~ B (at A) to move sth up and down with a sudden movement so that the end of it hits sth: *He flicked me with a wet towel.* ◊ *He flicked a wet towel at me.* ◊ *to flick a whip* PHRV ,**flick 'through sth** to turn the pages of a book, etc. quickly and look at them without reading everything
■ *noun* **1** [C, usually sing.] a small sudden, quick movement or hit, for example with a whip or part of the body: *Bell's flick into the penalty area helped to create the goal.* ◊ *All this information is available at the flick of a switch* (= by simply turning on a machine). ◊ *He threw the ball back with a quick flick of the wrist.* **2** [sing.] a ~ through sth a

quick look through the pages of a book, magazine, etc: *I had a flick through the catalogue while I was waiting.* **3** [C] (*old-fashioned, informal*) a film/movie **4** (**the flicks**) [pl.] (*old-fashioned, BrE, informal*) a cinema

flicker /'flɪkə(r)/ *verb, noun*
■ *verb* **1** [V] (of a light or a flame) to keep going on and off as it shines or burns: *The lights flickered and went out.* ◊ *the flickering screen of the television* **2** [V+*adv./prep.*] (of an emotion, a thought, etc.) to be expressed or appear somewhere for a short time: *Anger flickered in his eyes.* ◊ *A smile flickered across her face.* **3** [V] to move with small quick movements: *Her eyelids flickered as she slept.*
■ *noun* [usually sing.] ~ (of sth) **1** a light that shines in an unsteady way: *the flicker of a television/candle* **2** a small, sudden movement with part of the body: *the flicker of an eyelid* **3** a feeling or an emotion that lasts for only a very short time: *a flicker of hope/doubt/interest* ◊ *A flicker of a smile crossed her face.*

'**flick knife** (*BrE*) (also **switch·blade** *AmE, BrE*) *noun* a knife with a blade inside the handle that jumps out quickly when a button is pressed

flier *noun* = FLYER

flies /flaɪz/ *noun* [pl.] **1** *pl.* of FLY **2** (*BrE*) = FLY *n.* (3) **3** (**the flies**) the space above the stage in a theatre, used for lights and for storing scenery

flight /flaɪt/ *noun, verb*
■ *noun*

JOURNEY BY AIR ▸ **1** [C] a journey made by air, especially in a plane: *a smooth/comfortable/bumpy flight* ◊ *a domestic/an international flight* ◊ *a hot-air balloon flight* ◊ *We met on a flight from London to Paris.*—see also IN-FLIGHT

PLANE ▸ **2** [C] a plane making a particular journey: *We're booked on the same flight.* ◊ *Flight BA 4793 is now boarding at Gate 17.* ◊ *If we leave now, I can catch the earlier flight.* ◊ *mercy/relief flights* (= planes taking help to countries where there is a war)

FLYING ▸ **3** [U] the act of flying: *the age of supersonic flight* ◊ *flight safety* ◊ *The bird is easily recognized in flight* (= when it is flying) *by the black band at the end of its tail.*

MOVEMENT OF OBJECT ▸ **4** [U] the movement or direction of an object as it travels through the air: *the flight of a ball/dart/missile*

OF STEPS ▸ **5** [C] a series of steps between two floors or levels: *She fell down a flight of stairs/steps and hurt her back.*

RUNNING AWAY ▸ **6** [U, sing.] the act of running away from a dangerous or difficult situation: *the flight of refugees from the advancing forces* ◊ *The main character is a journalist in flight from a failed marriage.*

OF FANCY/IMAGINATION ▸ **7** [C] ~ of fancy/imagination an idea or a statement that is very imaginative but not practical or sensible: *This idea was one of my wilder flights of fancy.*

GROUP OF BIRDS/AIRCRAFT ▸ **8** [C] a group of birds or aircraft flying together: *a flight of geese* ◊ *an aircraft of the Queen's flight*

—see also TOP-FLIGHT

IDM **in the first/top 'flight** among the best of a particular group **put sb to 'flight** (*old-fashioned*) to force sb to run away **take 'flight** to run away: *The gang took flight when they heard the police car.*
■ *verb* [VN] [usually passive] (*BrE, sport*) to kick, hit or throw a ball through the air in a skilful way: *He equalized with a beautifully flighted shot.*

'**flight attendant** *noun* (especially *AmE*) a person whose job is to serve and take care of passengers on an aircraft

'**flight crew** *noun* [C+sing./pl. *v.*] the people who work on a plane during a flight

'**flight deck** *noun* **1** an area at the front of a large plane where the pilot sits to use the controls and fly the plane—picture at PLANE **2** a long flat surface on top of a ship that carries aircraft (= an AIRCRAFT CARRIER) where they take off and land

flight·less /'flaɪtləs/ *adj.* [usually before noun] (of birds or insects) unable to fly

ˌflight lieuˈtenant noun (abbr. **Flt. Lt.**) an officer of fairly high rank in the British air force: *Flight Lieutenant Richard Clarkson*

ˈflight path noun the route taken by an aircraft through the air: *The pilot was instructed to change his flight path.*

ˈflight recorder noun = BLACK BOX

ˈflight sergeant noun a member of the British air force, just below the rank of an officer: *Flight Sergeant Bob Andrews*

ˈflight simulator noun a device that reproduces the conditions that exist when flying an aircraft, used for training pilots

flighty /ˈflaɪti/ adj. (informal) a **flighty** woman is one who cannot be relied on because she is always changing activities, ideas and partners without treating them seriously

flimsy /ˈflɪmzi/ adj. (flim·sier, flim·si·est) **1** badly made and not strong enough for the purpose for which it is used: *a flimsy bridge/table* **2** (of material) thin and easily torn: *a flimsy piece of paper/fabric/plastic* **3** difficult to believe: *a flimsy excuse/explanation* ◊ *The evidence against him is pretty flimsy.* ▶ **flim·sily** adv. **flim·si·ness** noun [U]

flinch /flɪntʃ/ verb [V] **~ (at sth)| ~ (away)** to make a sudden movement with your face or body as a result of pain, fear, surprise, etc: *He flinched at the sight of the blood.* ◊ *She flinched away from the dog.* ◊ *He met my gaze without flinching.*—see also UNFLINCHING **PHRV** **ˈflinch from sth| ˈflinch from doing sth** (often used in negative sentences) to avoid thinking about or doing sth unpleasant: *He never flinched from facing up to trouble.*

fling /flɪŋ/ verb, noun
■ verb (flung, flung /flʌŋ/) **1** [VN+adv./prep.] to throw sb/sth somewhere with force, especially because you are angry: *Someone had flung a brick through the window.* ◊ *He flung her to the ground.* ◊ *She flung the letter down on the table.* ◊ *The door was suddenly flung open.* ◊ *He had his enemies flung into prison.* **2** [VN+adv./prep.] to move yourself or part of your body suddenly and with a lot of force: *She flung herself onto the bed.* ◊ *He flung out an arm to stop her from falling.* **3 ~ sth (at sb)** to say sth to sb in an aggressive way: [VN] *They were flinging insults at each other.* [also V speech] —see also FAR-FLUNG **PHRV** **ˈfling yourself at sb** (informal, disapproving) to make it too obvious to sb that you want to have a sexual relationship with them **ˈfling yourself into sth** to start to do sth with a lot of energy and enthusiasm: *They flung themselves into the preparations for the party.* **ˌfling sth↔ˈoff/ˈon** (informal) to take off or put on clothing in a quick and careless way: *He flung off his coat and collapsed on the sofa.* **ˌfling sb↔ˈout** (BrE, informal) to make sb leave a place suddenly **ˌfling sth↔ˈout** (BrE, informal) to get rid of sth that you do not want any longer
■ noun [usually sing.] (informal) **1** a short period of enjoyment when you do not allow yourself to worry or think seriously about anything: *He was determined to have one last fling before retiring.* **2 ~ (with sb)** a short sexual relationship with sb: *We had a brief fling, but it's over now.*—see also HIGHLAND FLING

flint /flɪnt/ noun **1** [U, C] a type of very hard grey stone that can produce a SPARK when it is hit against steel: *prehistoric flint implements* ◊ *His eyes were as hard as flint.* **2** [C] a piece of flint or hard metal that is used to produce a SPARK

flinty /ˈflɪnti/ adj. **1** (written) showing no emotion: *a flinty look/gaze/stare* **2** containing flint: *flinty pebbles/soils*

flip /flɪp/ verb, noun, adj.
■ verb (-pp-) **1** to turn over into a different position with a sudden quick movement; to make sth do this: [V] *The plane flipped and crashed.* ◊ (figurative) *She felt her heart flip* (= with excitement, etc.). ◊ [VN] *He flipped the lid open and looked inside the case.*—see also FLIP OVER **2** [VN] **~ sth (on/off)** to press a button or switch in order to turn a machine, etc. on or off **SYN** FLICK: *to flip a switch* ◊ *She reached over and flipped off the light.* **3** [VN+adv./prep.] to throw sth somewhere using your thumb and/or fingers: *They flipped a coin to decide who would get the ticket.* ◊ *He*

flipped the keys onto the desk. **4** [V] **~ (out)** (informal) to become very angry, excited or unable to think clearly: *She finally flipped under the pressure.* ◊ *He completely flipped when he saw the mess in the kitchen.* **IDM** **ˌflip your ˈlid** (informal) to become very angry and lose control of what you are saying or doing: *She'll flip her lid when she finds out.* **PHRV** **ˌflip ˈover** to turn onto the other side or upside down: *The car hit a tree and flipped over.* ◊ *He flipped over and sat up.* **ˌflip sth↔ˈover** to turn sth onto the other side or upside down: *The wind flipped over several cars.* **ˈflip through sth** to turn the pages of a book, etc. quickly and look at them without reading everything: *She flipped through the magazine looking for the letters page.*
■ noun **1** [C] a small quick hit with a part of the body that causes sth to turn over: *The whole thing was decided on the flip of a coin.* **2** [C] a movement in which the body turns over in the air: *The handstand was followed by a back flip.* ◊ (figurative) *Her heart did a flip.* **3** [sing.] **~ through sth** a quick look through the pages of a book, magazine, etc: *I had a quick flip through the report while I was waiting.*
■ adj. (informal) = FLIPPANT: *a flip answer/comment* ◊ *Don't be flip with me.*

ˈflip chart noun large sheets of paper fixed at the top to a stand so that they can be turned over, used for presenting information at a talk or meeting

ˈflip-flop noun, verb
■ noun (AmE also **thong**) a type of SANDAL (= open shoe) that has a strap that goes between the big toe and the toe next to it: *a pair of flip-flops*—picture at SHOE
■ verb (-pp-) [V] **~ (on sth)** (informal, especially AmE) to change your opinion about sth, especially when you then hold the opposite opinion: *The vice-president was accused of flip-flopping on several major issues.*

flip·pant /ˈflɪpənt/ (also informal **flip**) adj. showing that you do not take sth as seriously as other people think you should: *a flippant answer/attitude* ◊ *Sorry, I didn't mean to sound flippant.* ▶ **flip·pancy** /-ənsi/ noun [U] **flip·pant·ly** adv.

flip·per /ˈflɪpə(r)/ noun [usually pl.] **1** a flat limb that is part of the body of some sea animals such as SEALS and TURTLES, used for swimming **2** a long flat piece of rubber or plastic that you wear on your foot to help you swim more quickly, especially below the surface of the water—picture at SNORKELLING

flip·ping /ˈflɪpɪŋ/ adj., adv. (BrE, spoken) used as a mild swear word by some people to emphasize sth or to show that they are annoyed: *I hate this flipping hotel!* ◊ *Flipping kids!* ◊ *It's flipping cold today!*

ˈflip side noun [usually sing.] **~ (of/to sth)** **1** different and less welcome aspects of an idea, argument or action **2** (old-fashioned) the side of a record that does not have the main song or piece of music on it

flirt /flɜːt; AmE flɜːrt/ verb, noun
■ verb [V] **~ (with sb)** to behave towards sb as if you find them sexually attractive, without seriously wanting to have a relationship with them: *He flirts outrageously with his female clients.* **PHRV** **ˈflirt with sth** (written) **1** to think about or be interested in sth for a short time but not very seriously: *She flirted with the idea of becoming an actress when she was younger.* **2** to take risks or not worry about a dangerous situation that may happen: *to flirt with danger/death/disaster*
■ noun [usually sing.] a person who flirts with a lot of people: *She's a real flirt.*

flir·ta·tion /flɜːˈteɪʃn; AmE flɜːrˈt-/ noun **1** [C, U] **~ with sth** a short period of time during which sb is involved or interested in sth, often not seriously: *a brief and unsuccessful flirtation with the property market* **2** [U] behaviour that shows you find sb sexually attractive but are not serious about them: *Frank's efforts at flirtation had become tiresome to her.* **3** [C] **~ (with sb)** a short sexual relationship with sb that is not taken seriously: *She had a mild flirtation with him when they first met.*

flir·ta·tious /flɜːˈteɪʃəs; AmE flɜːrˈt-/ (also informal **flirty**) adj. behaving in a way that shows a sexual attraction to

F

æ	ɑː	e	ɜː	ə	ɪ	iː	i	ɒ	ɔː	ʌ	ʊ	u	uː
cat	father	ten	bird	about	sit	see	many	got	saw	cup	put	actual	too

(BrE)

sb that is not serious: *a flirtatious young woman* ◊ *a flirtatious giggle/smile* ▶ **flir·ta·tious·ly** *adv.* **flir·ta·tious·ness** *noun* [U]

flit /flɪt/ *verb, noun*

■ *verb* (**-tt-**) [V] [usually +adv./prep.] ~ (**from A to B**)| ~ (**between A and B**) to move lightly and quickly from one place or thing to another: *Butterflies flitted from flower to flower.* ◊ *He flits from one job to another.* ◊ *A smile flitted across his face.* ◊ (*figurative*) *A thought flitted through my mind.*

■ *noun* **IDM** **do a moonlight/midnight 'flit** (*BrE, informal*) to leave a place suddenly and secretly at night, usually in order to avoid paying money that you owe to sb

float /fləʊt; *AmE* floʊt/ *verb, noun*

■ *verb*
ON WATER/IN AIR | **1** [V +adv./prep.] to move slowly on water or in the air [SYN] DRIFT: *A group of swans floated by.* ◊ *The smell of new bread floated up from the kitchen.* ◊ *Beautiful music came floating out of the window.* ◊ (*figurative*) *An idea suddenly floated into my mind.* ◊ (*figurative*) *People seem to float in and out of my life.* **2** [V] ~ (**in/on sth**) to stay on or near the surface of a liquid and not sink: *Wood floats.* ◊ *A plastic bag was floating in the water.* ◊ *Can you float on your back?* **3** [VN] to make sth move on or near the surface of a liquid: *There wasn't enough water to float the ship.* ◊ *They float the logs down the river to the towns.*
WALK LIGHTLY | **4** [V +adv./prep.] (*literary*) to walk or move in an easy, graceful way: *She floated down the steps to greet us.*
SUGGEST IDEA | **5** [VN] to suggest an idea or a plan for other people to consider: *They floated the idea of increased taxes on alcohol.*
BUSINESS/ECONOMICS | **6** [VN] (*business*) to sell shares in a company or business to the public for the first time: *The company was floated on the stock market in 1995.* ◊ *Shares were floated at 585p.* **7** [VN, V] (*economics*) if a government **floats** its country's money or allows it to **float**, it allows its value to change freely according to the value of the money of other countries
IDM see AIR *n.*
PHRV **,float a'bout/a'round** (usually used in the progressive tenses) if an idea, etc. is **floating around**, it is talked about by a number of people or passed from one person to another

■ *noun*
VEHICLE | **1** a large vehicle on which people dressed in special COSTUMES are carried in a festival: *a carnival float*
IN FISHING | **2** a small light object attached to a FISHING LINE that stays on the surface of the water and moves when a fish has been caught
FOR SWIMMING | **3** a light object that floats in the water and is held by a person who is learning to swim to stop them from sinking
DRINK | **4** (*AmE*) a drink with ice cream floating in it: *a Coke float*
MONEY | **5** (*especially BrE*) a sum of money consisting of coins and notes of low value that is given to sb before they start selling things so that they can give customers CHANGE
BUSINESS | **6** = FLOTATION

float·ing /'fləʊtɪŋ; *AmE* 'floʊt-/ *adj.* [usually before noun] not fixed permanently in one particular position or place: *floating exchange rates* ◊ *a floating population* (= one in which people frequently move from one place to another)

,floating 'voter *noun* (*BrE*) a person who does not always vote for the same political party and who has not decided which party to vote for in an election

flock /flɒk; *AmE* flɑːk/ *noun, verb*

■ *noun* **1** [C+sing./pl. *v.*] ~ (**of sth**) a group of sheep, goats or birds of the same type—compare HERD **2** [C+sing./pl. *v.*] ~ (**of sb**) a large group of people, especially of the same type: *a flock of children/reporters* ◊ *They came in flocks to see the procession.* **3** [C+sing./pl. *v.*] (*literary*) the group of people who regularly attend the church of a particular priest, etc. **4** [U] small pieces of soft fabric used for filling cushions, chairs, etc: *a flock mattress* **5** [U]

small pieces of soft material on the surface of a fabric or paper that produce a raised pattern: *flock wallpaper*

■ *verb* to go or gather together somewhere in large numbers: [V +adv./prep.] *Thousands of people flocked to the beach this weekend.* ◊ *Huge numbers of birds had flocked together by the lake.* ◊ [V to inf] *People flocked to hear him speak.* **IDM** see BIRD

floe /fləʊ; *AmE* floʊ/ *noun* = ICE FLOE

flog /flɒg; *AmE* flɑːg; flɔːg/ *verb* (**-gg-**) **1** [VN] [often passive] to punish sb by hitting them many times with a whip or stick: *He was publicly flogged for breaking the country's alcohol laws.* **2** ~ **sth** (**to sb**)| ~ **sth** (**off**) (*BrE, informal*) to sell sth to sb: [VN] *She flogged her guitar to another student.* ◊ *We buy them cheaply and then flog them off at a profit.* ◊ [VNN] *I had a letter from a company trying to flog me insurance.* **IDM** **,flog a dead 'horse** (*BrE, informal*) to waste your effort by trying to do sth that is no longer possible **,flog sth to 'death** (*BrE, informal*) to use an idea, a story, etc. so often that it is no longer interesting: *The story has been flogged to death in the press.*

flog·ging /'flɒgɪŋ; *AmE* 'flɑːg-; 'flɔːg-/ *noun* [C, U] a punishment in which sb is hit many times with a whip or stick: *a public flogging*

flood /flʌd/ *noun, verb*

■ *noun*
WATER | **1** [C, U] a large amount of water covering an area that is usually dry: *The heavy rain has caused floods in many parts of the country.* ◊ *flood water/damage* ◊ *The river is in flood* (= has more water in it than normal and has caused a flood).—see also FLASH FLOOD
LARGE NUMBER | **2** [C] ~ (**of sth**) a very large number of things or people that appear at the same time: *a flood of complaints* ◊ *a flood of refugees* ◊ *The child was in floods of tears* (= crying a lot).

■ *verb*
FILL WITH WATER | **1** if a place **floods** or sth **floods** it, it becomes filled or covered with water: [V] *The cellar floods whenever it rains heavily.* ◊ [VN] *If the pipe bursts it could flood the whole house.*
OF RIVER | **2** to become so full that it spreads out onto the land around it: [V] *When the Ganges floods, it causes considerable damage.* ◊ [VN] *The river flooded the valley.*
LARGE NUMBERS | **3** ~ **in/into/out of sth** to arrive or go somewhere in large numbers: *Refugees continue to flood into neighbouring countries.* ◊ *Telephone calls came flooding in from all over the country.* **4** [VN] [usually passive] ~ **sb/sth with sth** to send sth somewhere in large numbers: *The office was flooded with applications for the job.* **5** [VN] ~ **sth** (**with sth**) to become or make sth become available in a place in large numbers: *Cheap imported goods are flooding the market.* ◊ *A man who planned to flood Britain with cocaine was jailed for 15 years.*
OF FEELING/ THOUGHT | **6** to affect sb suddenly and strongly: [V, +adv./prep.] *A great sense of relief flooded over him.* ◊ *Memories of her childhood came flooding back.* ◊ [VN] *The words flooded him with self-pity.*
OF LIGHT/COLOUR | **7** to spread suddenly into sth; to cover sth: [V, +adv./prep.] *She drew the curtains and the sunlight flooded in.* ◊ [VN] *She looked away as the colour flooded her cheeks.* ◊ *The room was flooded with evening light.*
ENGINE | **8** [V, VN] if an engine **floods** or if you **flood** it, it becomes so full of petrol/gas that it will not start
▶ **flood·ed** *adj.*: *flooded fields* **flood·ing** *noun* [U]: *There will be heavy rain with flooding in some areas.*
PHRV **,flood sb↔'out** [usually passive] to force sb to leave their home because of a flood

flood·gate /'flʌdgeɪt/ *noun* [usually pl.] a gate that can be opened or closed to control the flow of water on a river: (*figurative*) *If the case is successful, it may open the floodgates to more damages claims against the industry* (= start sth that will be difficult to stop).

flood·light /'flʌdlaɪt/ *noun, verb*

■ *noun* [usually pl.] a large powerful lamp, used for lighting sports grounds, theatre stages and the outside of build-

aɪ	aʊ	eɪ	əʊ	oʊ	ɔɪ	ɪə	eə	ʊə	j	w
my	now	say	go (BrE)	go (AmE)	boy	near	hair	pure	yes	wet

ings: *a match played under floodlights* ▶ **flood·light·ing** *noun* [U]: *The floodlighting had been turned off.*
■ *verb* (**flood-lit**, **flood-lit** /-lɪt/) [VN] [usually passive] to light a place or a building using floodlights: *The swimming pool is floodlit in the evenings.* ◇ *floodlit tennis courts*

'**flood plain** *noun* an area of flat land beside a river that regularly becomes flooded when there is too much water in the river

'**flood tide** *noun* a very high rise in the level of the sea that happens at particular times of the year—compare HIGH TIDE

floor /flɔː(r)/ *noun, verb*
■ *noun*
OF ROOM | **1** [C, usually sing.] the surface of a room that you walk on: *a wooden/concrete/marble floor* ◇ *ceramic floor tiles* ◇ *The body was lying on the kitchen floor.* ◇ *The alterations should give us extra floor space.* ⇨ note at EARTH
OF VEHICLE | **2** (*AmE* also **floor·board**) [C, usually sing.] the bottom surface of a vehicle: *The floor of the car was covered in cigarette ends.*
LEVEL OF BUILDING | **3** [C] all the rooms that are on the same level of a building: *Her office is on the second floor.* ◇ *the Irish guy who lives two floors above* ◇ *There is a lift to all floors.* ◇ *Their house is on three floors* (= it has three floors).—see also GROUND FLOOR ⇨ note at STOREY
OF THE SEA/FORESTS | **4** [C, usually sing.] the ground at the bottom of the sea, a forest, etc: *the ocean/valley/cave/forest floor*
IN PARLIAMENT | **5** (**the floor**) [sing.] the part of a building where discussions or debates are held, especially in a parliament; the people who attend a discussion or debate: *Opposition politicians registered their protest on the floor of the House.* ◇ *We will now take any questions from the floor.*
AREA FOR WORK | **6** [C, usually sing.] an area in a building that is used for a particular activity: *on the floor of the Stock Exchange* (= where trading takes place)—see also DANCE FLOOR, FACTORY FLOOR, SHOP FLOOR
FOR WAGES/PRICES | **7** [C, usually sing.] the lowest level allowed for wages or prices: *Prices have gone through the floor* (= fallen to a very low level).—compare CEILING (2)
IDM **get/be given/have the 'floor** to get/be given/have the right to speak during a discussion or debate ,**hold the 'floor** to speak during a discussion or debate, especially for a long time so that nobody else is able to say anything ,**take (to) the 'floor** to start dancing on a DANCE FLOOR: *Couples took the floor for the last dance of the evening.*—more at GROUND FLOOR, WIPE *v.*
■ *verb* [VN]
SURPRISE/CONFUSE | **1** to surprise or confuse sb so that they are not sure what to say or do: *His reply completely floored me.*
HIT | **2** [usually passive] to make sb fall down by hitting them, especially in a sport: *He was floored by the first punch.*
BUILDING/ROOM | **3** [usually passive] to provide a building or room with a floor

---

BRITISH / AMERICAN
floor

In *BrE* the floor of a building at street level is the **ground floor**, the one above it is the **first floor** and the one below it is the **basement**, or **lower ground floor** in a public building.

In *AmE* the floor at street level is usually called the **first floor**, the one above it is the **second floor** and the one below it is the **basement**. In public buildings the floor at street level can also be called the **ground floor**.
⇨ note at STOREY

---

floor·board /'flɔːbɔːd; *AmE* 'flɔːrbɔːrd/ *noun* **1** a long flat piece of wood in a wooden floor: *bare/polished floorboards*– picture at JOIST **2** [usually sing.] (*AmE*) =

FLOOR (2): *a car floorboard* ◇ *He had his foot to the floorboard* (= was going very fast).

floor·ing /'flɔːrɪŋ/ *noun* [U] material used to make the floor of a room: *vinyl/wooden flooring* ◇ *kitchen/bathroom flooring*

'**floor lamp** *noun* (*AmE*) = STANDARD LAMP

'**floor plan** *noun* (*technical*) a drawing of the shape of a room or building, as seen from above, showing the position of the furniture, etc.

'**floor show** *noun* a series of performances by singers, dancers, etc. at a restaurant or club

floo·zie (also **floozy**) /'fluːzi/ *noun* (*pl.* -**ies**) (*old-fashioned, informal, disapproving*) a woman who has sexual relationships with many different men

flop /flɒp; *AmE* flɑːp/ *verb, noun*
■ *verb* (-**pp**-) [V] **1** ~ **into/on sth** | ~ (**down/back**) to sit or lie down in a heavy and sudden way because you are very tired: *Exhausted, he flopped down into a chair.* **2** [+*adv./prep.*] to fall, move or hang in a heavy or awkward way, without control: *Her hair flopped over her eyes.* ◇ *The young man flopped back, unconscious.* ◇ *The fish were flopping around in the bottom of the boat.* **3** (*informal*) to be a complete failure: *The play flopped on Broadway.*
■ *noun* a film/movie, play, party, etc. that is not successful—see also BELLYFLOP

flop·house /'flɒphaʊs; *AmE* 'flɑːp-/ *noun* (*AmE*) = DOSS-HOUSE

floppy /'flɒpi; *AmE* 'flɑːpi/ *adj.* (**flop·pier**, **flop·piest**) hanging or falling loosely; not hard and stiff: *a floppy hat* ◇ *Hugh Grant and his floppy fringe*

,**floppy 'disk** (also **floppy** *pl.* -**ies**) (also **disk·ette**) *noun* a flat disk inside a plastic cover, that is used to store data in the form that a computer can read, and that can be removed from the computer—compare HARD DISK—picture on page 250

flora /'flɔːrə/ *noun* [U] (*technical*) the plants of a particular area, type of environment or period of time: *alpine flora* ◇ *rare species of flora and fauna* (= plants and animals)

floral /'flɔːrəl/ *adj.* [usually before noun] **1** consisting of pictures of flowers; decorated with pictures of flowers: *wallpaper with a floral design/pattern* ◇ *a floral dress* **2** made of flowers: *a floral arrangement/display* ◇ *Floral tributes were sent to the church.*

floret /'flɒrət; *AmE* 'flɔː-; 'flɑː-/ *noun* (*BrE*) a flower part of some vegetables, for example BROCCOLI and CAULIFLOWER. Each vegetable has several florets coming from one main stem.—picture on page A3

florid /'flɒrɪd; *AmE* 'flɔː-; 'flɑː-/ *adj.* (*written*) **1** (of a person's face) red: *a florid complexion* **2** (usually *disapproving*) having too much decoration or detail: *florid language* ▶ **florid·ly** *adv.*

florin /'flɒrɪn; *AmE* 'flɔː-; 'flɑː-/ *noun* an old British coin worth two SHILLINGS (= now 10p)

flor·ist /'flɒrɪst; *AmE* 'flɔː-; 'flɑː-/ *noun* **1** a person who owns or works in a shop/store that sells flowers and plants **2** (**flor·ist's**) (*pl.* **flor·ists**) a shop/store that sells flowers and plants: *I've ordered some flowers from the florist's.*

floss /flɒs; *AmE* flɔːs; flɑːs/ *noun, verb*
■ *noun* [U] **1** = DENTAL FLOSS **2** thin silk thread—see also CANDYFLOSS
■ *verb* [V, VN] to clean between your teeth with DENTAL FLOSS

flo·ta·tion /fləʊ'teɪʃn; *AmE* floʊ-/ *noun* **1** (also **float**) [C, U] (*business*) the process of selling shares in a company to the public for the first time in order to raise money: *plans for (a) flotation on the stock exchange* ◇ *a stock-market flotation* **2** [U] the act of floating on or in water: *a flotation tank* (= where people float in the dark as a way of relaxing)

flo·tilla /flə'tɪlə; *AmE* floʊ't-/ *noun* a group of boats or small ships sailing together

flot·sam /'flɒtsəm; *AmE* 'flɑːt-/ *noun* [U] **1** parts of boats, pieces of wood or rubbish/garbage, etc. that are found

F

floating on the sea or along the shore; any kind of rubbish/garbage: *The beaches are wide and filled with interesting flotsam and jetsam.*—compare JETSAM **2** people who have no home or job and who move from place to place, often rejected by society: *the human flotsam of inner cities*

flounce /flaʊns/ *verb, noun*
- *verb* [V] [usually +adv. / prep.] (*written*) to move somewhere in a way that draws attention to yourself, for example because you are angry or upset: *She flounced out of the room.*
- *noun* **1** a strip of fabric that is sewn around the edge of a skirt, dress, curtain, etc. **2** (*written*) a quick and exaggerated movement that you make when you are angry or want people to notice you: *She left the room with a flounce.* ▶ **flounced** *adj.*: *a flounced skirt*

floun·der /ˈflaʊndə(r)/ *verb, noun*
- *verb* **1** to struggle to know what to say or do or how to continue with sth: [V] *His abrupt change of subject left her floundering helplessly.* [also V **speech**] **2** [V] to have a lot of problems and to be in danger of failing completely: *At that time the industry was floundering.* **3** [V] [usually +adv. /prep.] to struggle to move or get somewhere in water, mud, etc: *She was floundering around in the deep end of the swimming pool.*
- *noun* (*pl.* **floun·der** or **floun·ders**) a small flat sea fish that is used for food

flour /ˈflaʊə(r)/ *noun, verb*
- *noun* [U] a fine white or brown powder made from grain, especially wheat, and used in cooking for making bread, cakes, etc.—see also PLAIN FLOUR, SELF-RAISING FLOUR
- *verb* [VN] [usually passive] to cover sth with a layer of flour: *Roll the dough on a lightly floured surface.*

flour·ish /ˈflʌrɪʃ; *AmE* ˈflɜːrɪʃ/ *verb, noun*
- *verb* **1** [V] to develop quickly and be successful or common [SYN] THRIVE: *Few businesses are flourishing in the present economic climate.* **2** [V] to grow well; to be healthy and happy [SYN] THRIVE: *These plants flourish in a damp climate.* ◇ (*especially BrE*) *I'm glad to hear you're all flourishing.* **3** [VN] (*written*) to wave sth around in a way that makes people look at it
- *noun* **1** [usually sing.] an exaggerated movement that you make when you want sb to notice you: *He opened the door for her with a flourish.* **2** [usually sing.] an impressive act or way of doing sth: *The season ended with a flourish for Owen, when he scored in the final minute of the match.* **3** details and decoration that are used in speech or writing: *a speech full of rhetorical flourishes* **4** a curved line, that is used as decoration, especially in writing **5** [usually sing.] a loud short piece of music, that is usually played to announce an important person or event: *a flourish of trumpets*

floury /ˈflaʊəri/ *adj.* **1** covered with flour: *floury hands* **2** like flour; tasting of flour: *a floury texture* **3** (of potatoes) soft and light when they are cooked

flout /flaʊt/ *verb* [VN] to show that you have no respect for a law, etc. by openly not obeying it [SYN] DEFY: *Motorists regularly flout the law.* ◇ *to flout authority / convention*

flow /fləʊ; *AmE* floʊ/ *noun, verb*
- *noun* [C usually sing, U]
  CONTINUOUS MOVEMENT | **1** ~ (**of sth/sb**) the steady and continuous movement of sth in one direction: *She tried to stop the flow of blood from the wound.* ◇ *an endless flow of refugees into the country* ◇ *to improve traffic flow* (= make it move faster) ◇ *to control the direction of flow*

  PRODUCTION/SUPPLY | **2** ~ (**of sth**) the continuous production or supply of sth: *the flow of goods and services to remote areas* ◇ *to encourage the free flow of information* ◇ *data flow*—see also CASH FLOW

  OF SPEECH/WRITING | **3** continuous talk by sb: *You've interrupted my flow—I can't remember what I was saying.* ◇ *As usual, Tom was in full flow.* **4** ~ **of sth** the way that words and ideas are linked together in speech or writing: *Too many examples can interrupt the smooth flow of the text.*

  OF THE SEA | **5** the movement of the sea towards the land: *the ebb and flow of the tide*
  [IDM] **go with the ˈflow** (*informal*) to be relaxed and not worry about what you should do—more at EBB *n.*
- *verb* [V]
  MOVE CONTINUOUSLY | **1** ~ (**back/ down, etc.**)| ~ (**into, through, etc. sth**) (of liquid, gas or electricity) to move steadily and continuously in one direction: *It's here that the river flows down into the ocean.* ◇ *Blood flowed from a cut on her head.* ◇ *This can prevent air from flowing freely to the lungs.* ◇ *She lost control and the tears began to flow.* **2** [V] [usually +adv. / prep.] (of people or things) to move or pass continuously from one place or person to another, especially in large numbers or amounts: *constant streams of traffic flowed past.* ◇ *Election results flowed in throughout the night.*

  OF IDEAS/CONVERSATION | **3** to develop or be produced in an easy and natural way: *Conversation flowed freely throughout the meal.*

  BE AVAILABLE EASILY | **4** to be available easily and in large amounts: *It was obvious that money flowed freely in their family.* ◇ *The party got better as the drink began to flow.*

  OF FEELING | **5** [+adv. / prep.] to be felt strongly by sb: *Fear and excitement suddenly flowed over me.*

  OF CLOTHES/HAIR | **6** ~ (**down/over sth**) to hang loosely and freely: *Her hair flowed down over her shoulders.* ◇ *long flowing skirts*

  OF THE SEA | **7** (of the TIDE in the sea / ocean) to come in towards the land [OPP] EBB *v.*
  [PHRV] **ˈflow from sth** (*formal*) to come or result from sth

ˈflow chart (also **ˈflow diagram**) *noun* a diagram that shows the connections between the different stages of a process or parts of a system—picture at CHART

flower /ˈflaʊə(r)/ *noun, verb*
- *noun* **1** the coloured part of a plant from which the seed or fruit develops. Flowers usually grow at the end of a stem and last only a short time: *The plant has a beautiful bright red flower.* ◇ *The roses are in flower early this year.* ◇ *The crocuses are late coming into flower.*—picture at PLANT **2** a plant grown for the beauty of its flowers: *a garden full of flowers* ◇ *a flower garden / show* **3** a flower with its stem that has been picked as a decoration: *I picked some flowers.* ◇ *a bunch of flowers* ◇ *a flower arrangement*—see also BOUQUET [IDM] **the flower of sth** (*literary*) the finest or best part of sth
- *verb* [V] **1** (of a plant or tree) to produce flowers [SYN] BLOOM: *This particular variety flowers in July.* ◇ *early-flowering spring bulbs* **2** (*literary*) to develop and become successful [SYN] BLOSSOM

ˈflower arranging *noun* [U] the art of arranging cut flowers in an attractive way

ˈflower bed *noun* a piece of ground in a garden / yard or park where flowers are grown

flowered /ˈflaʊəd; *AmE* ˈflaʊərd/ *adj.* [usually before noun] decorated with patterns of flowers

flower·ing /ˈflaʊərɪŋ/ *noun* **1** [U] the time when a plant has flowers **2** [C, usually sing.] ~ **of sth** the time when sth, especially a period of new ideas in art, music, science, etc., reaches its most complete and successful stage of development

flower·pot /ˈflaʊəpɒt; *AmE* ˈflaʊərpɑːt/ *noun* a container made of plastic or clay for growing plants in—picture at POT

flowery /ˈflaʊəri/ *adj.* [usually before noun] **1** covered with flowers or decorated with pictures of flowers **2** smelling or tasting of flowers **3** (usually *disapproving*) (of speech or writing) too complicated; not expressed in a clear and simple way

flown *pp* of FLY

fl oz *abbr.* (*pl.* **fl oz**) (in writing) FLUID OUNCE: *Add 8 fl oz water.*

flu /fluː/ (often **the flu**) (also *formal* **in·flu·enza**) *noun* [U] an infectious disease like a very bad cold, that causes fever, pains and weakness: *The whole family has the flu.* ◇ (*BrE*) *She's got flu.*

flub /flʌb/ *verb* (**-bb-**) (*AmE*) to do sth badly or make a

F

mistake [SYN] FLUFF, BUNGLE: [VN] *She flubbed the first line of the song.* [also V] ▶ **flub** *noun*

fluc·tu·ate /ˈflʌktʃueɪt/ *verb* [V] **~ (between A and B)** to change frequently in size, amount, quality, etc., especially from one extreme to another: *fluctuating prices* ◇ *During the crisis, oil prices fluctuated between $20 and $40 a barrel.* ◇ *Temperatures can fluctuate by as much as 10 degrees.* ◇ *My weight fluctuated wildly depending on how much I ate.* ◇ *My mood seems to fluctuate from day to day.* ▶ **fluc·tu·ation** /ˌflʌktʃuˈeɪʃn/ *noun* [C, U] **~ (in/of sth)**: *wild fluctuations in interest rates*

flue /fluː/ *noun* a pipe or tube that takes smoke, gas or hot air away from a fire, a HEATER or an oven

flu·ency /ˈfluːənsi/ *noun* [U, sing.] the quality of being able to speak or write a language, especially a foreign language, easily and well: *Fluency in French and Spanish is required for this job.* ◇ *to achieve / acquire / develop greater fluency*

flu·ent /ˈfluːənt/ *adj.* **1 ~ (in sth)** able to speak, read or write a language, especially a foreign language, easily and well: *She's fluent in Polish.* ◇ *a fluent speaker / reader* **2** (of a language, especially a foreign language) expressed easily and well: *He speaks fluent Italian.* **3** (of an action) done in a smooth and skilful way: *fluent handwriting* ◇ *fluent movements* ▶ **flu·ent·ly** *adv.*

fluff /flʌf/ *noun, verb*
■ *noun* **1** [U] **1** (*BrE*) (also **lint** *AmE, BrE*) small pieces of wool, cotton, etc. that gather on clothes and other surfaces **2** soft animal fur or bird feathers, that is found especially on young animals or birds **3** (*informal, especially AmE*) entertainment that is not serious and is not considered to have great value
■ *verb* [VN] **1** (*informal*) to do sth badly or to fail at sth [SYN] BUNGLE: *He completely fluffed an easy shot* (= in sport). ◇ *Most actors fluff their lines occasionally.* **2 ~ sth (out/up)** to shake or brush sth so that it looks larger and/or softer: *The female sat on the eggs, fluffing out her feathers.* ◇ *Let me fluff up your pillows for you.*

fluffy /ˈflʌfi/ *adj.* (**fluf·fier, fluf·fiest**) **1** like fluff; covered in fluff: *a little fluffy kitten* **2** (of food) soft, light and containing air: *Beat the butter and sugar until soft and fluffy.* **3** looking as if it is soft and light: *fluffy white clouds*

fluid /ˈfluːɪd/ *noun, adj.*
■ *noun* [C, U] a liquid; a substance that can flow: *body fluids* (= for example, blood) ◇ *The doctor told him to drink plenty of fluids.* ◇ *cleaning fluid*
■ *adj.* **1** (*formal*) (of movements, designs, music, etc.) smooth, graceful and flowing: *a loose, fluid style of dancing* ◇ *fluid guitar playing* ◇ *the fluid lines of the drawing* **2** (*formal*) (of a situation) likely to change; not fixed: *a fluid political situation* **3** (*technical*) that can flow freely, as gases and liquids do: *a fluid consistency*

flu·id·ity /fluˈɪdəti/ *noun* [U] **1** (*formal*) the quality of being smooth and graceful: *She danced with great fluidity of movement.* **2** (*formal*) the quality of being likely to change: *the fluidity of human behaviour* ◇ *social fluidity* **3** (*technical*) the quality of being able to flow freely, as gases and liquids do

ˌfluid ˈounce *noun* (*abbr.* **fl oz**) a unit for measuring liquids. There are 20 fluid ounces in a British PINT and 16 in an American pint.

fluke /fluːk/ *noun* [usually sing.] (*informal*) a lucky or unusual thing that happens by accident, not because of planning or skill: *They are determined to show that their last win was no fluke.* ◇ *a fluke goal* ▶ **fluky** (also **flukey**) /ˈfluːki/ *adj.*

flume /fluːm/ *noun* **1** a narrow channel made to carry water for use in industry **2** a water CHUTE (= a tube for sliding down) at an amusement park or a swimming pool

flum·mox /ˈflʌməks/ *verb* [VN] [usually passive] (not used in the progressive tenses) (*informal*) to confuse sb so that they do not know what to say or do: *I was flummoxed by her question.* ▶ **flum·moxed** *adj.*

flung *pt, pp* of FLING

flunk /flʌŋk/ *verb* (*informal, especially AmE*) **1** to fail an exam, a test or a course: [VN] *I flunked math in second grade.* [also V] **2** [VN] to make sb fail an exam, a test, or a

course by giving them a low mark / grade: *She's flunked 13 of the 18 students.* [PHRV] **ˌflunk ˈout (of sth)** (*AmE, informal*) to have to leave a school or a college because your marks / grades are not good enough

flun·key (also **flunky**) /ˈflʌŋki/ *noun* (*pl.* **-eys** or **-ies**) **1** (*disapproving*) a person who tries to please sb who is important and powerful by doing small jobs for them **2** (*old-fashioned*) a servant in uniform

fluor·es·cent /ˌflɔːˈresnt; ˌfluəˈr-; *AmE* also ˌfluˈr-/ *adj.* **1** (of substances) producing bright light by using some forms of RADIATION: *a fluorescent lamp* (= one that uses such a substance) ◇ *fluorescent lighting* **2** (of a colour, material, etc.) appearing very bright when light shines on it; that can be seen in the dark: *fluorescent armbands worn by cyclists*—compare PHOSPHORESCENT ▶ **fluor·es·cence** *noun* [U]

fluorid·ation /ˌflɔːrɪˈdeɪʃn; *BrE* also ˌfluər-; *AmE* also ˌflur-/ *noun* [U] the practice of adding fluoride to drinking water to prevent tooth decay

fluor·ide /ˈflɔːraɪd; *BrE* also ˈfluər-; *AmE* also ˈflur-/ *noun* [U] a chemical compound of fluorine that protects teeth from decay and is often added to TOOTHPASTE and sometimes to drinking water

fluor·ine /ˈflɔːriːn; *BrE* also ˈfluər-; *AmE* also ˈflur-/ *noun* [U] (*symb* F) a chemical element. Fluorine is a poisonous pale yellow gas.

flur·ried /ˈflʌrid; *AmE* ˈflɜːrid/ *adj.* nervous and confused; especially because there is too much to do

flurry /ˈflʌri; *AmE* ˈflɜːri/ *noun* (*pl.* **-ies**) **1** [usually sing.] an occasion when there is a lot of activity, interest, excitement, etc. within a short period of time: *a sudden flurry of activity* ◇ *Her arrival caused a flurry of excitement.* ◇ *A flurry of shots rang out in the darkness.* **2** a small amount of snow, rain, etc. that falls for a short time and then stops: *snow flurries* ◇ *flurries of snow* **3** a sudden short movement of paper or fabric, especially clothes: *The ladies departed in a flurry of silks and satins.*

flush /flʌʃ/ *verb, noun, adj.*
■ *verb* **1** (of a person or their face) to become red, especially because you are embarrassed, excited or hot: [V] *She flushed with anger.* ◇ [V-ADJ] *Sam felt her cheeks flush red.* [also VN] **2** [V, VN] when a toilet **flushes** or you **flush** it, water passes through it to clean it, after a handle, etc. has been pressed **3** [VN] **~ sth out (with sth)** | **~ sth through sth** to clean sth by causing water to pass through it: *Flush the pipe out with clean water.* ◇ *Flush clean water through the pipe.* **4** [VN + *adv. / prep.*] to get rid of sth with a sudden flow of water: *They flushed the drugs down the toilet.* ◇ *Drinking lots of water will help to flush toxins out of the body.* [PHRV] **ˌflush sb/sth ˈout (of sth)** | **ˌflush sb/sth↔ˈout** to force a person or an animal to leave the place where they are hiding
■ *noun* **1** [C, usually sing.] a red colour that appears on your face or body because you are embarrassed, excited or hot: *A pink flush spread over his cheeks.*—see also HOT FLUSH **2** [C, usually sing.] a sudden strong feeling; the hot feeling on your face or body caused by this: *a flush of anger / embarrassment / enthusiasm / guilt* **3** [sing.] the act of cleaning a toilet with a sudden flow of water: *Give the toilet a flush.* **4** [C] (in card games) a set of cards that a player has that are all of the same SUIT [IDM] **(in) the first flush of sth** (*written*) (at) a time when sth is new, exciting and strong: *in the first flush of youth / enthusiasm / romance*
■ *adj.* [not before noun] **1** (*informal*) having a lot of money, usually for a short time: *I'm flush this week—I'll pay.* **2 ~ with sth** (of two surfaces) completely level with each other: *Make sure the paving stones are flush with the lawn.*

flushed /flʌʃt/ *adj.* (of a person) red; with a red face: *flushed cheeks* ◇ *Her face was flushed with anger.* ◇ (*figurative*) *He was flushed with success* (= very excited and pleased) *after his first novel was published.*

flus·ter /ˈflʌstə(r)/ *verb, noun*
■ *verb* [VN] [often passive] to make sb nervous and/or confused, especially by giving them a lot to do or by making

them hurry ▶ **flus·tered** *adj.*: *She arrived late, looking hot and flustered.*
■ *noun* [sing.] (*BrE*) a state of being nervous and confused

flute /fluːt/ *noun* **1** a musical instrument of the WOODWIND group, shaped like a thin pipe. The player holds it sideways and blows across a hole at one end.—picture on page 840 **2 champagne ~** a tall narrow glass used for drinking CHAMPAGNE—picture at GLASS

fluted /ˈfluːtɪd/ *adj.* (especially of a round object) with a pattern of curves cut around the outside: *fluted columns* ▶ **flut·ing** *noun* [U]

flut·ist /ˈfluːtɪst/ *noun* (*AmE*) = FLAUTIST

flut·ter /ˈflʌtə(r)/ *verb, noun*
■ *verb* **1** to move lightly and quickly; to make sth move in this way: [V] *Flags fluttered in the breeze.* ◇ *Her eyelids fluttered but did not open.* ◇ [VN] *He fluttered his hands around wildly.* ◇ *She **fluttered her eyelashes** at him (= tried to attract him in order to persuade him to do sth).* **2** [V, VN] when a bird or an insect **flutters** its wings, or its wings **flutter**, the wings move lightly and quickly up and down **3** [V+*adv./prep.*] (of a bird or an insect) to fly somewhere moving the wings quickly and lightly: *The butterfly fluttered from flower to flower.* **4** [V] (of your heart, etc.) to beat very quickly and not regularly: *I could feel a fluttering pulse.* ◇ (*figurative*) *The sound of his voice in the hall made her heart flutter.*
■ *noun* **1** [C, usually sing.] a quick, light movement: *the flutter of wings* ◇ *with a flutter of her long, dark eyelashes* ◇ (*figurative*) *to feel a flutter of panic in your stomach* **2** [C, usually sing.] **~ (on sth)** (*BrE, informal*) a small bet: *to have a flutter on the horses* **3** [sing.] a state of nervous or confused excitement: *Her sudden arrival caused quite a flutter.* **4** [C] a very fast, unsteady HEARTBEAT: *Her heart gave a flutter when she saw him.*

flu·vial /ˈfluːviəl/ *adj.* (*technical*) connected with rivers: *fluvial erosion/deposits*

flux /flʌks/ *noun* **1** [U] continuous movement and change: *Our society is **in a state of flux**.* **2** [C usually sing, U] (*technical*) a flow; an act of flowing: *a flux of neutrons* ◇ *magnetic flux*

fly /flaɪ/ *verb, noun*
■ *verb* (**flies, fly·ing, flew** /fluː/ **flown** /fləʊn/; *AmE* floʊn/)
HELP In sense 15 **flied** is used for the past tense and past participle.
OF BIRD/INSECT | **1** [V] to move through the air, using wings: *A stork flew slowly past.* ◇ *A wasp had flown in through the window.*
AIRCRAFT/SPACECRAFT | **2** [V] (of an aircraft or a spacecraft) to move through air or space: *They were on a plane flying from London to New York.* ◇ *to fly at the speed of sound* ◇ *Lufthansa fly to La Paz from Frankfurt.* **3** [V] to travel in an aircraft or a spacecraft: *I'm flying to Hong Kong tomorrow.* ◇ *Is this the first time that you've flown?* ◇ *I always fly business class.* ◇ *We're flying KLM.* **4** to control an aircraft, etc. in the air: [VN] *a pilot trained to fly large passenger planes* ◇ *children flying kites* ◇ [V] *He's learning to fly.* **5** [VN+*adv./prep.*] to transport goods or passengers in a plane: *The stranded tourists were finally flown home.* ◇ *He had flowers specially flown in for the ceremony.* **6** [VN] to travel over an ocean or area of land in an aircraft: *to fly the Atlantic*
MOVE QUICKLY/SUDDENLY | **7** [V] (often +*adv./prep.*] to go or move quickly: *The train was flying along.* ◇ *She gasped and her hand flew to her mouth.* ◇ *It's late—I must fly.* **8** [usually +*adv./prep.*] to move suddenly and with force: [V] *A large stone came flying in through the window.* ◇ *Several people were hit by flying glass.* ◇ [V-ADJ] *David gave the door a kick and it flew open.*
OF TIME | **9** [V] **~ (by/past)** to seem to pass very quickly: *Doesn't time fly?* ◇ *Summer has just flown by.*
FLAG | **10** if a flag **flies**, or if you **fly** it, it is displayed, for example on a long pole: [VN] *to fly the Union Jack/Stars and Stripes* ◇ [V] *Flags were flying at half mast on all public buildings.*
MOVE FREELY | **11** [V] to move around freely: *hair flying in the wind*
OF STORIES/RUMOURS | **12** [V] to be talked about by many people
ESCAPE | **13** (*written*) to escape from sb/sth: [VN] *Both suspects have flown the country.* [also V] —compare FLEE
OF PLAN | **14** [V] (*AmE*) to be successful: *It remains to be seen whether his project will fly.*
IN BASEBALL | **15** (**flies, flying, flied, flied**) [VN] to hit a ball high into the air
IDM **fly the ˈcoop** (*informal, especially AmE*) to escape from a place **fly ˈhigh** to be successful **fly in the face of ˈsth** (*written*) to oppose or be the opposite of sth that is usual or expected: *Such a proposal is flying in the face of common sense.* **fly into a ˈrage, ˈtemper, etc.** to become suddenly very angry **(go) fly a/your ˈkite** (*AmE, informal*) used to tell sb to go away and stop annoying you or interfering **ˌfly the ˈnest 1** (of a young bird) to become able to fly and leave its nest **2** (*informal*) (of sb's child) to leave home and live somewhere else **fly off the ˈhandle** (*informal*) to suddenly become very angry **go ˈflying** (*BrE, informal*) to fall, especially as a result of not seeing sth under your feet: *Someone's going to go flying if you don't pick up these toys.* **let ˈfly (at sb/sth) (with sth)** to attack sb by hitting them or speaking angrily to them: *He let fly at me with his fist.* ◇ *She let fly with a stream of abuse.*—more at BIRD, CROW *n.*, FLAG *n.*, PIG *n.*, SEAT *n.*, TANGENT, WINDOW
PHR V **ˈfly at sb** (of a person or an animal) to attack sb suddenly
■ *noun* (*pl.* **flies**)
INSECT | **1** [C] a small flying insect with two wings. There are many different types of fly: *A fly was buzzing against the window.* ◇ *Flies rose in thick black swarms.*
IN FISHING | **2** [C] a fly or sth made to look like a fly, that is put on a hook and used as BAIT to catch fish: *fly fishing*
ON TROUSERS/PANTS | **3** [sing.] (*BrE* also **flies** [pl.]) an opening down the front of a pair of trousers/pants that fastens with a ZIP or buttons and is usually covered over by a strip of material: *Your fly is undone!* ◇ *Your flies are undone!*—picture on page A4
ON TENT | **4** [C] a piece of fabric that covers the entrance to a tent
—see also FLIES
IDM **die/fall/drop like ˈflies** to die or fall down in very large numbers: *People were dropping like flies in the intense heat.* **a/the fly in the ˈointment** a person or thing that spoils a situation or an occasion that is satisfactory in all other ways **a fly on the ˈwall** a person who watches others without being noticed: *I'd love to be a fly on the wall when he tells her the news.* ◇ *fly-on-the-wall documentaries (= in which people are filmed going about their normal lives as if the camera were not there)* **(there are) no flies on ˈsb** (*informal*) the person mentioned is clever and not easily tricked **not harm/hurt a ˈfly** to be kind and gentle and unwilling to cause unhappiness **on the ˈfly** (*informal*) if you do sth on the fly, you do it quickly while sth else is happening, and without thinking about it very much

fly·away /ˈflaɪəweɪ/ *adj.* (especially of hair) soft and fine; difficult to keep tidy

fly·blown /ˈflaɪbləʊn; *AmE* -bloʊn/ *adj.* (*BrE*) dirty and in bad condition; not fit to eat

ˈfly-by *noun* (*pl.* **fly-bys**) **1** the flight of a spacecraft near a planet to record data **2** (*AmE*) = FLY-PAST

ˈfly-by-night *adj.* [only before noun] (of a person or business) dishonest and only interested in making money quickly ▶ **ˈfly-by-night** *noun*

flyer (also **flier**) /ˈflaɪə(r)/ *noun* **1** (*informal*) a person who flies an aircraft (usually a small one, not a passenger plane) **2** a person who travels in a plane as a passenger: *frequent flyers* **3** a person who operates sth such as a model aircraft or a KITE from the ground **4** a thing, especially a bird or an insect, that flies in a particular way: *Butterflies can be strong flyers.* **5** a small sheet of paper that advertises a product or an event and is given to a large number of people **6** (*informal*) a person, an animal or a vehicle that moves very quickly: *Ford's flashy new flyer* **7** = FLYING START—see also HIGH-FLYER

fly-fishing *noun* [U] the sport of fishing in a river or lake using an artificial fly to attract and catch the fish

fly·ing /'flaɪŋ/ *adj., noun*
- *adj.* [only before noun] able to fly: *flying insects* **IDM** **with ˌflying 'colours** very well; with a very high mark/grade: *She passed the exam with flying colours.*
- *noun* [U] travelling in an aircraft: *I'm terrified of flying.*

ˌflying 'buttress *noun* (*architecture*) a half arch of brick or stone that supports the outside wall of a large building such as a church

ˌflying 'doctor *noun* (especially in Australia) a doctor who travels in an aircraft to visit patients who live far from a town

ˌflying 'fish *noun* a tropical sea fish that can rise and move forwards above the surface of the water, using its FINS (= flat parts that stick out from its body) as wings

ˌflying 'fox *noun* a large BAT (= an animal like a mouse with wings) that lives in hot countries and eats fruit

ˌflying 'officer *noun* an officer of lower rank in the British air force: *Flying Officer Ian Wall*

ˌflying 'saucer *noun* a round spacecraft that some people claim to have seen and that some people believe comes from another planet—compare UFO

ˌflying 'squad *noun* (usually **the Flying Squad**) a group of police officers in Britain who are ready to travel very quickly to the scene of a serious crime

ˌflying 'start (also *less frequent* **flyer**) *noun* [sing.] a very fast start to a race, competition, etc. **IDM** **get off to a ˌflying 'start | get off to a 'flyer** to make a very good start; to begin sth well: *She's got off to a flying start in her new career.*

ˌflying 'visit *noun* (*BrE*) a very short visit

fly·leaf /'flaɪliːf/ *noun* (*pl.* **fly·leaves**) an empty page at the beginning or end of a book

fly·over /'flaɪəʊvə(r); *AmE* -oʊvər/ *noun* **1** (*BrE*) (*AmE* **over·pass**) a bridge that carries one road over another one **2** (*AmE*) = FLY-PAST

fly·past (*BrE*) (*AmE* **'fly-by, 'flyover**) *noun* a special flight by a group of aircraft, for people to watch at an important ceremony

fly·sheet /'flaɪʃiːt/ (*BrE*) *noun* an extra sheet of fabric on the outside of a tent that keeps the rain out

fly·weight /'flaɪweɪt/ *noun* a boxer, WRESTLER, etc. of the lightest class, usually weighing between 48 and 51 kilograms: *a flyweight champion*

fly·wheel /'flaɪwiːl/ *noun* a heavy wheel in a machine or an engine that helps to keep it working smoothly and at a steady speed

FM *abbr.* **1** /ˌef 'em/ frequency modulation (a method of broadcasting high-quality sound by radio): *Radio 1 FM* **2** (in writing) Field Marshall

foal /fəʊl; *AmE* foʊl/ *noun, verb*
- *noun* a very young horse or DONKEY **IDM** **in foal** (of a female horse) pregnant
- *verb* [V] to give birth to a foal

foam /fəʊm; *AmE* foʊm/ *noun, verb*
- *noun* **1** (also ˌfoam 'rubber) [U] a soft light rubber material, full of small holes, that is used for seats, MATTRESSES, etc: *a foam mattress* ◊ *foam packaging* **2** [U] a mass of very small air bubbles on the surface of a liquid: *a glass of beer with a good head of foam* ◊ *The breaking waves left the beach covered with foam.* **3** [U, C] a chemical substance that forms or produces a soft mass of very small bubbles, used for washing, shaving, or putting out fires, for example: *shaving foam*
- *verb* [V] (of a liquid) to have or produce a mass of small bubbles **SYN** FROTH: *She looked down at the foaming white water.* ◊ *The toothpaste foamed in his mouth.* **IDM** **foam at the 'mouth 1** (especially of an animal) to have a mass of small bubbles in and around its mouth, especially because it is ill or angry **2** (*informal*) (of a person) to be very angry

foamy /'fəʊmi; *AmE* 'foʊmi/ *adj.* consisting of or produc-

cing a mass of small bubbles; like foam: *foamy beer/ shampoo* ◊ *foamy clouds*

fob /fɒb; *AmE* fɑːb/ *verb, noun*
- *verb* (**-bb-**) **PHRV** ˌfob sb↔'off (with sth) **1** to try to stop sb asking questions or complaining by telling them sth that is not true: *Don't let him fob you off with any more excuses.* ◊ *She wouldn't be fobbed off this time.* **2** to give sb sth that they want or is of worse quality than they want: *He was unaware that he was being fobbed off with out-of-date stock.*
- *noun* **1** a short chain that is attached to a watch that is carried in a pocket **2** (also **'fob watch**) a watch that is attached to a fob **3** a small ornament that is attached to a KEY RING, etc.

focal /'fəʊkl; *AmE* 'foʊkl/ *adj.* [only before noun] central; very important; connected with or providing a focus

ˌfocal 'length *noun* (*physics*) the distance between the centre of a mirror or a LENS and its FOCUS

'focal point *noun* **1** a thing or a person that is the centre of interest or activity: *In rural areas, the school is often the focal point for the local community.* ◊ *He quickly became the focal point for those who disagreed with government policy.* **2** (*technical*) = FOCUS

focus /'fəʊkəs; *AmE* 'foʊ-/ *verb, noun*
- *verb* (**-s-** or **-ss-**) **1** ~ (**on/upon sb/sth**) to give attention, effort, etc. to one particular subject, situation or person rather than another: [V] *The discussion focused on three main problems.* ◊ *Each exercise focuses on a different grammar point.* ◊ [VN] *The visit helped to focus world attention on the plight of the refugees.* **2** ~ (**sth**) (**on sb/sth**) (of your eyes, a camera, etc.) to adapt or be adjusted so that things can be seen clearly; to adjust sth so that you can see things clearly: [V] *Let your eyes focus on objects that are further away from you.* ◊ *It took a few moments for her eyes to focus in the dark.* ◊ *In this scene, the camera focuses on the actor's face.* ◊ [VN] *He focused his blue eyes on her.* ◊ *I quickly focused the camera on the children.* **3** [VN] ~ **sth** (**on sth**) (*technical*) to aim rays of light onto a particular point using a LENS
- *noun* (*pl.* **fo·cuses** or **foci** /'fəʊsaɪ; *AmE* 'foʊ-/) **1** [U, C, usually sing.] ~ (**for/on sth**) the thing or person that people are most interested in; the act of paying special attention to sth and making people interested in it: *It was the main focus of attention at the meeting.* ◊ *His comments provided a focus for debate.* ◊ *In today's lecture the focus will be on tax structures within the European Union.* ◊ *The incident brought the problem of violence in schools into sharp focus.* ◊ *We shall maintain our focus on the needs of the customer.* ◊ *What we need now is a change of focus* (= to look at things in a different way). **2** (also **'focal point**) a point or distance at which the outline of an object is clearly seen by the eye or through a LENS: *The children's faces are badly out of focus* (= not clearly shown) *in the photograph.* ◊ *The binoculars were not in focus* (= were not showing things clearly). **3** (also **'focal point**) [C] (*physics*) a point at which rays or waves of light, sound, etc. meet after REFLECTION or REFRACTION; the point from which rays or waves of light, sound, etc. seem to come **4** [C] (*geology*) the point at which an earthquake starts to happen

fo·cused (also **fo·cussed**) /'fəʊkəst; *AmE* 'foʊ-/ *adj.* with your attention directed to what you want to do; with very clear aims

'focus group *noun* a small group of people, specially chosen to represent different social classes, etc., who are asked to discuss and give their opinions about a particular subject. The information obtained is used by people doing MARKET RESEARCH, for example about new products or for a political party.

fod·der /'fɒdə(r); *AmE* 'fɑːd-/ *noun* [U] **1** food for horses and farm animals **2** (*disapproving*) (often after a noun) people or things that are considered to have only one use: *Without education, these children will end up as factory fodder* (= only able to work in a factory). ◊ *This story will be more fodder for the gossip columnists.*—see also CANNON FODDER

F

b	d	f	g	h	k	l	m	n	p	r
bad	did	fall	get	hat	cat	leg	man	now	pen	red

foe /fəʊ; AmE foʊ/ noun (old-fashioned or formal) an enemy

foe·tal (BrE) (also **fetal** AmE, BrE) /ˈfiːtl/ adj. [only before noun] connected with a foetus; typical of a foetus: *foetal abnormalities/heartbeats* ◇ *She lay curled up in a foetal position.*

foe·tid = FETID

foetus (BrE) (also **fetus** AmE, BrE) /ˈfiːtəs/ noun a young human or animal before it is born, especially a human more than eight weeks after FERTILIZATION

fog /fɒg; AmE fɔːg; fɑːg/ noun, verb
- noun [U, C] **1** a thick cloud of very small drops of water in the air close to the land or sea, that is very difficult to see through: *Dense/thick fog is affecting roads in the north and visibility is poor.* ◇ *freezing fog* ◇ *Patches of fog will clear by mid-morning.* ◇ *We get heavy fogs on this coast in winter.* ◇ *The town was covered in a thick blanket of fog.*—compare MIST **2** a state of confusion, in which things are not clear: *He went through the day with his mind in a fog.*
- verb (**-gg-**) **1** [V, VN] ~ (sth) (up) if a glass surface **fogs** or **is fogged** up, it becomes covered in steam or small drops of water so that you cannot see through **2** [VN] to make sb/sth confused or less clear: *I tried to clear the confusion that was fogging my brain.* ◇ *The government was trying to fog the real issues before the election.*

fog·bound /ˈfɒgbaʊnd; AmE ˈfɔːg-; ˈfɑːg-/ adj. unable to operate because of fog; unable to travel or to leave a place because of fog: *a fogbound airport* ◇ *fogbound passengers* ◇ *She spent hours fogbound in Brussels.*

fogey (also **fogy**) /ˈfəʊgi; AmE ˈfoʊgi/ noun (pl. **fogeys** or **fo·gies**) a person with old-fashioned ideas that he or she is unwilling to change: *He sounds like such an old fogey!*

foggy /ˈfɒgi; AmE ˈfɔːgi; ˈfɑːgi/ adj. (**fog·gier**, **fog·gi·est**) not clear because of FOG: *foggy conditions* ◇ *a foggy road* **IDM** **not have the ˈfoggiest (idea)** (informal) to not know anything at all about sth: *'Do you know where she is?' 'Sorry, I haven't the foggiest.'*

fog·horn /ˈfɒghɔːn; AmE ˈfɔːghɔːrn; ˈfɑːg-/ noun an instrument that makes a loud noise to warn ships of danger in FOG: *He's got a voice like a foghorn* (= a loud unpleasant voice).

ˈfog lamp (BrE) (also **ˈfog light** AmE, BrE) noun a very bright light on the front or back of a car to help the driver to see or be seen in FOG—picture at CAR

foi·ble /ˈfɔɪbl/ noun a silly habit or a strange or weak aspect of a person's character, that is considered harmless by other people: *We have to tolerate each other's little foibles.*

ˌfoie ˈgras noun [U] = PÂTÉ DE FOIE GRAS

foil /fɔɪl/ noun, verb
- noun (BrE also ˌsilver ˈfoil) **1** [U] metal made into very thin sheets that is used for covering or wrapping things, especially food: (BrE) *aluminium foil* ◇ (AmE) *aluminum foil*—see also TINFOIL **2** [U] paper that is covered in very thin sheets of metal: *The chocolates are individually wrapped in gold and silver foil.* **3** [C] ~ (for sb/sth) a person or thing that contrasts with, and therefore emphasizes, the qualities of another person or thing: *The pale walls provide a perfect foil for the brightly coloured furniture.* **4** [C] a long thin light SWORD used in the sport of FENCING
- verb [VN] [often passive] (written) to stop sth from happening, especially sth illegal; to prevent sb from doing sth **SYN** THWART: *to foil a plan/crime/plot* ◇ *Customs officials foiled an attempt to smuggle priceless paintings out of the country.* ◇ *They were foiled in their attempt to smuggle priceless paintings.*

foist /fɔɪst/ verb **PHRV** **ˈfoist sb/sth on/upon sb** to force sb to accept sb/sth that they do not want: *The title for her novel was foisted on her by the publishers.*

fold /fəʊld; AmE foʊld/ verb, noun
- verb **1** [VN] ~ sth (up) | ~ sth (back, down, over, etc.) to bend sth, especially paper or fabric, so that one part lies on top of another part: *He folded the map up and put it in his pocket.* ◇ *First, fold the paper in half/in two.* ◇ *The blankets had been folded down.* ◇ *a pile of neatly folded*

clothes ◇ *The bird folded its wings.* **OPP** UNFOLD—see also FOLD-UP—picture at CRINKLE **2** ~ (sth)(away/down) to bend sth so that it becomes smaller or flatter and can be stored or carried more easily; to be able to bend or be able to bend in this way: [VN] *The bed can be folded away during the day.* ◇ [V] *The table folds up when not in use.* ◇ (figurative) *When she heard the news, her legs just folded under her* (= she fell). ◇ [V-ADJ] *The ironing board folds flat for easy storage.* **3** [VN] ~ A in B | ~ B round/over A to wrap sth around sb/sth: *She gently folded the baby in a blanket.* ◇ *She folded a blanket around the baby.* **4** [V] (of a company, a play, etc.) to close because it is not successful **IDM** **fold sb in your ˈarms** (literary) to put your arms around sb and hold them against your body **fold your ˈarms** to put one of your arms over the other one and hold them against your body **fold your ˈhands** to bring or hold your hands together: *She kept her hands folded in her lap.* **PHRV** **ˌfold sth↔ˈin** | **ˌfold sth ˈinto sth** (in cooking) to add one substance to another and gently mix them together: *Fold in the beaten egg whites.*
- noun **1** [C] a part of sth, especially fabric, that is folded or hangs as if it had been folded: *the folds of her dress* ◇ *loose folds of skin* **2** [C] a mark or line made by folding sth, or showing where sth should be folded **3** [C] an area in a field surrounded by a fence or wall where sheep are kept for safety **4** (**the fold**) [sing.] a group of people with whom you feel you belong or who share the same ideas or beliefs: *He called on former Republican voters to return to the fold.* **5** [C] (geology) a curve or bend in the line of the layers of rock in the earth's CRUST **6** [C] (BrE) a hollow place among hills or mountains

-fold suffix (in adjectives and adverbs) multiplied by; having the number of parts mentioned: *to increase tenfold*

fold·away /ˈfəʊldəweɪ; AmE ˈfoʊld-/ adj. = FOLDING

fold·er /ˈfəʊldə(r); AmE ˈfoʊld-/ noun **1** a cardboard or plastic cover for holding loose papers, etc.—picture at STATIONERY **2** (in some computer systems) a way of organizing and storing computer files

fold·ing /ˈfəʊldɪŋ; AmE ˈfoʊ-/ (also less frequent **fold-away**) adj. [only before noun] (of a piece of furniture, a bicycle, etc.) that can be folded, so that it can be carried or stored in a small space: *a folding chair* ◇ *a foldaway bed*

ˈfold-up adj. [only before noun] (of an object) that can be made smaller by closing or folding so that it takes up less space

fo·li·age /ˈfəʊliɪdʒ; AmE ˈfoʊ-/ noun [U] the leaves of a tree or plant; leaves and branches together: *dense green foliage*

folic acid /ˌfɒlɪk ˈæsɪd; ˌfəʊ-; AmE ˌfoʊ-/ noun [U] a VITAMIN found in green vegetables, LIVER and KIDNEY, needed by the body for the production of red blood cells

folio /ˈfəʊliəʊ; AmE ˈfoʊlioʊ/ noun (pl. **-os**) **1** a book made with large sheets of paper, especially as used in early printing **2** (technical) a single sheet of paper from a book

folk /fəʊk; AmE foʊk/ noun, adj.
- noun **1** (also **folks** especially in AmE) [pl.] (informal) people in general: *ordinary working-class folk* ◇ *I'd like a job working with old folk or kids.* ◇ *the folks back home* (= from the place where you come from) **2** (**folks**) [pl.] (informal) a friendly way of addressing more than one person: *Well, folks, what are we going to do today?* **3** (**folks**) [pl.] (informal, especially AmE) the members of your family, especially your parents: *How are your folks?* **4** [pl.] people from a particular country or region, or who have a particular way of life: *country folk* ◇ *townsfolk* ◇ *farming folk* **5** (also **ˈfolk music**) [U] music in the traditional style of a country or community: *a folk festival/concert*
- adj. [only before noun] **1** (of art, culture, etc.) traditional and typical of the ordinary people of a country or community: *folk art* ◇ *a folk museum* **2** based on the beliefs of ordinary people: *folk wisdom* ◇ *Garlic is widely used in Chinese folk medicine.*

ˈfolk dance noun [C, U] a traditional dance of a particular area or country; a piece of music for such a dance

ˈfolk hero noun a person that people in a particular place admire because of sth special they have done

s	t	v	z	ʃ	ʒ	tʃ	dʒ	θ	ð	ŋ
see	tea	van	zoo	shoe	vision	chain	jam	thin	this	sing

folk·lore /ˈfəʊklɔː(r); AmE ˈfoʊk-/ noun [U] the traditions and stories of a country or community: *Irish/Indian folklore* ◊ *The story rapidly became part of family folklore.*

folk ˈmemory noun [C, U] a memory of sth in the past that the people of a country or community never forget

folk music noun [U] = FOLK

folk singer noun a person who sings folk songs

folk song noun **1** a song in the traditional style of a country or community **2** a type of song that became popular in the US in the 1960s, played on a guitar and often about political topics

folksy /ˈfəʊksi; AmE ˈfoʊksi/ adj. **1** (especially AmE) simple, friendly and informal: *They wanted the store to have a folksy small-town image.* **2** (sometimes disapproving) done or made in a traditional style that is typical of simple customs in the past: *a folksy ballad*

folk tale noun a very old traditional story from a particular place that was originally passed on to people in a spoken form

fol·licle /ˈfɒlɪkl; AmE ˈfɑːl-/ noun one of the very small holes in the skin which hair grows from

fol·low /ˈfɒləʊ; AmE ˈfɑːloʊ/ verb

GO AFTER **1** to come or go after or behind sb/sth: [VN] *He followed her into the house.* ◊ *Follow me please. I'll show you the way.* ◊ *I think we're being followed.* ◊ (figurative) *She followed her mother into the medical profession.* ◊ [V] *Wherever she led, they followed.* ◊ *Sam walked in, with the rest of the boys following closely behind.*

HAPPEN/DO AFTER **2** to come after sth/sb else in time or order; to happen as a result of sth else: [VN] *The first two classes are followed by a break of ten minutes.* ◊ *I remember little of the days that followed the accident.* ◊ *A period of unrest followed the president's resignation.* ◊ [V] *A detailed news report will follow shortly.* ◊ *There followed a short silence.* ◊ *The opening hours are as follows …* ◊ *A new proposal followed on from the discussions.* [VN] ~ **sth (up) with sth** to do sth after sth else: *Follow your treatment with plenty of rest.* ◊ *They follow up their March show with four UK dates next month.*

BE RESULT **4** ~ **(from sth)** (not usually used in the progressive tenses) to be the logical result of sth: [V] *I don't see how that follows from what you've just said.* ◊ [V that] *If a = b and b = c it follows that a = c.*

OF PART OF MEAL **5** to come or be eaten after another part: [VN] *The main course was followed by fresh fruit.* HELP This pattern is usually used in the passive. [V] (spoken) *I'll have soup and fish to follow.*

ROAD/PATH **6** [VN] to go along a road, path, etc: *Follow this road until you get to the school, then turn left.* **7** [VN] (of a road, path, etc.) to go in the same direction as sth or parallel to sth: *The lane follows the edge of a wood for about a mile.*

ADVICE/INSTRUCTIONS **8** [VN] to accept advice, instructions, etc. and do what you have been told or shown to do: *to follow a diet/recipe* ◊ *He has trouble following simple instructions.* ◊ *Why didn't you follow my advice?*

COPY **9** [VN] to accept sb/sth as a guide, a leader or an example; to copy sb/sth: *They followed the teachings of Buddha.* ◊ *He always followed the latest fashions (= dressed in fashionable clothes).* ◊ *I don't want you to follow my example and rush into marriage.* ◊ *The movie follows the book faithfully.*

UNDERSTAND **10** to understand an explanation or the meaning of sth: [V, VN] *Sorry, I don't follow.* ◊ *Sorry, I don't follow you.* ◊ [VN] *The plot is almost impossible to follow.*

WATCH/LISTEN **11** [VN] to watch or listen to sb/sth very carefully: *The children were following every word of the story intently.* ◊ *Her eyes followed him everywhere (= she was looking at him all the time).*

BE INTERESTED IN **12** [VN] to take an active interest in sth and be aware of what is happening: *Have you been following the basketball championships?* ◊ *Millions of people followed the trial on TV.*

OF BOOK/MOVIE **13** [VN] to be concerned with the life or development of sb/sth: *The novel follows the fortunes of a village community in Scotland.*

PATTERN/COURSE **14** [VN] to develop or happen in a particular way: *The day followed the usual pattern.*

IDM **follow in sb's ˈfootsteps** to do the same job, have the same style of life, etc. as sb else, especially sb in your family: *She works in television, following in her father's footsteps.* **follow your ˈnose 1** to be guided by your sense of smell **2** to go straight forward: *The garage is a mile ahead up the hill—just follow your nose.* **3** to act according to what seems right or reasonable, rather than following any particular rules **follow ˈsuit 1** (in card games) to play a card of the same SUIT that has just been played **2** to act or behave in the way that sb else has just done PHRV **follow sb aˈround/aˈbout** to keep going with sb wherever they go: *Will you stop following me around!* **follow ˈon** to go somewhere after sb else has gone there: *You go to the beach with the kids and I'll follow on when I've finished work.* **follow ˈthrough** (in tennis, golf, etc.) to complete a stroke by continuing to move the club, RACKET, etc. after hitting the ball—related noun FOLLOW-THROUGH (1) **follow ˈthrough (with sth)| follow sth↔ˈthrough** to finish sth that you have started—related noun FOLLOW-THROUGH (2) **follow sth↔ˈup 1** to add to sth that you have just done by doing sth else: *You should follow up your phone call with an e-mail or a letter.* **2** to find out more about sth that has told you or suggested to you SYN INVESTIGATE: *The police are following up several leads after their TV appeal for information.*—related noun FOLLOW-UP

fol·low·er /ˈfɒləʊə(r); AmE ˈfɑːloʊ-/ noun **1** a person who supports and admires a particular person or set of ideas: *the followers of Mahatma Gandhi* **2** a person who is very interested in a particular activity and follows all the recent news about it: *keen followers of football* ◊ *a follower of fashion* **3** a person who does things after sb else has done them first: *She is a leader, not a follower.*

fol·low·ing /ˈfɒləʊɪŋ; AmE ˈfɑːloʊɪŋ/ adj., noun, prep.
- adj. (**the following …**) **1** next in time: *the following afternoon/month/year/week* ◊ *They arrived on Monday evening and we got there the following day.* **2** that are going to be mentioned next: *Answer the following questions.* IDM **a ˌfollowing ˈwind** a wind blowing in the same direction as a ship or other vehicle that helps it move faster
- noun **1** [usually sing.] a group of supporters: *The band has a huge following in Spain and Italy.* **2** (**the following**) (used with either a singular or a plural verb, depending on whether you are talking about one thing or person or several things or people) the thing or things that you will mention next; the person or people that you will mention next: *The following is a brief summary of events.* ◊ *The following have been chosen to take part: Watts, Hodges and Lennox.*
- prep. after or as a result of a particular event: *He took charge of the family business following his father's death.*

follow-ˈthrough noun **1** (in tennis, golf, etc.) the final part of a stroke after the ball has been hit **2** the actions that sb takes in order to complete a plan: *The project could fail if there is inadequate follow-through.*

follow-up noun [C, U] an action or a thing that continues sth that has already started or comes after sth similar that was done earlier: *The book is a follow-up to her excellent television series.* ▶ **follow-up** adj. [only before noun]: *a follow-up study*

folly /ˈfɒli; AmE ˈfɑːli/ noun (pl. -ies) **1** [U, C] ~ **(to do sth)** a lack of good judgement; the fact of doing sth stupid; an activity or idea that shows a lack of judgement: *an act of sheer folly* ◊ *the follies of youth* ◊ *Giving up a secure job seems to be the height of folly.* ◊ *It would be folly to turn the offer down.* **2** [C] (BrE) a building that has no practical purpose but was built in the past as an ornament, often in the garden of a large country house

fo·ment /fəʊˈment; AmE foʊ-/ verb [VN] (formal) to create trouble or violence or make it worse SYN INCITE: *They accused him of fomenting political unrest.*

fond /fɒnd; AmE fɑːnd/ adj. (**fond·er, fond·est**) **1** ~ **of sb** feeling affection for sb, especially sb you have known for a long time: *Over the years, I have grown quite fond of her.* **2** ~ **of (doing) sth** finding sth pleasant or enjoyable,

F

especially sth you have liked or enjoyed for a long time: *fond of music/cooking/going to parties* ◊ *We had grown fond of the house and didn't want to leave.* **3 ~ of (doing) sth** liking to do sth which other people find annoying or unpleasant, and doing it often: *Sheila's very fond of telling other people what to do.* ◊ *He's rather too fond of the sound of his own voice* (= he talks too much). **4** [only before noun] kind and loving SYN AFFECTIONATE: *a fond look/embrace/farewell* ◊ *I have very fond memories of my time in Spain* (= I remember it with affection and pleasure). **5** [only before noun] (**~ hope**) a hope about sth that is not likely to happen: *I waited all day in the fond hope that she would change her mind.* ▶ **fond·ness** *noun* [U, sing.] **~ (for sb/sth)**: *He will be remembered by the staff with great fondness.* ◊ *a fondness for animals*

fon·dant /'fɒndənt; *AmE* 'fɑːn-/ *noun* **1** [U] a thick sweet soft mixture made from sugar and water, used especially to cover cakes: *fondant icing* **2** [C] a soft sweet/candy that melts in the mouth, made of fondant

fon·dle /'fɒndl; *AmE* 'fɑːndl/ *verb* [VN] to touch and move your hand gently over sb/sth, especially in a sexual way, or in order to show love SYN CARESS

fond·ly /'fɒndli; *AmE* 'fɑːndli/ *adv.* **1** in a way that shows great affection: *He looked at her fondly.* ◊ *I fondly remember my first job as a reporter.* **2** in a hopeful way that is silly or unreasonable: *I fondly imagined that you cared for me.*

fon·due /'fɒndjuː; *AmE* fɑːn'duː/ *noun* [C, U] **1** a Swiss dish of melted cheese and wine into which pieces of bread are DIPPED **2** a dish of hot oil into which small pieces of meat, vegetables, etc. are DIPPED

font /fɒnt; *AmE* fɑːnt/ *noun* **1** a large stone bowl in a church that holds water for the ceremony of BAPTISM **2** (*technical*) the particular size and style of a set of letters that are used in printing, etc.

food /fuːd/ *noun* **1** [U] things that people or animals eat: *a shortage of food/food shortages* ◊ *food and drink* ◊ *the food industry* **2** [C, U] a particular type of food: *Do you like Italian food?* ◊ *frozen foods* ◊ *a can of dog food* (= for a dog to eat) ◊ *He's off his food* (= he does not want to eat anything).—see also CONVENIENCE FOOD, FAST FOOD, HEALTH FOOD, JUNK FOOD, SEAFOOD, SOUL FOOD, WHOLEFOOD **IDM** **food for 'thought** an idea that makes you think seriously and carefully

'food bank *noun* (in the US) a place where poor people can go to get free food

'food chain *noun* (usually **the food chain**) a series of living creatures in which each type of creature feeds on the one below it in the series: *Insects are fairly low down (on) the food chain.*

foodie /'fuːdi/ *noun* (*informal*) a person who is very interested in cooking and eating different kinds of food

'food poisoning *noun* [U] an illness of the stomach caused by eating food that contains harmful bacteria

'food processor *noun* a piece of equipment that is used to mix or cut up food—picture at MIXER

'food stamp *noun* (*AmE*) a piece of paper that is given by the government to poor people, for them to buy food with

food·stuff /'fuːdstʌf/ *noun* [usually pl.] (especially *technical*) any substance that is used as food: *basic foodstuffs*

fool /fuːl/ *noun, verb, adj.*
■ *noun* **1** [C] a person who you think behaves or speaks in a way that lacks intelligence or good judgement SYN IDIOT: *Don't be such a fool!* ◊ *I felt a fool when I realized my mistake.* ◊ *He told me he was an actor and I was fool enough to believe him.* **2** [C] (in the past) a man employed by a king or queen to entertain people by telling jokes, singing songs, etc. SYN JESTER **3** [U, C] (*BrE*) (usually in compounds) a cold light DESSERT (= a sweet dish) made from fruit that is cooked and crushed and mixed with cream or CUSTARD: *rhubarb fool* **IDM** **act/play the 'fool** to behave in a stupid way in order to make people laugh, especially in a way that may also annoy them: *Quit playing the fool and get some work done!* **any fool can/could ...** (*spoken*) used to say that sth is very easy to do: *Any fool could tell she was lying.* **be ,no/,nobody's 'fool**

to be too intelligent or know too much about sth to be tricked by other people: *She's nobody's fool when it comes to dealing with difficult patients.* **make a 'fool of sb** to say or do sth deliberately so that people will think that sb is stupid: *Can't you see she's making a fool of you?* **make a 'fool of yourself** to do sth stupid which makes other people think that you are a fool: *I made a complete fool of myself in front of everyone!* **,more fool 'sb (for doing sth)** (*spoken*) used to say that you think that sb was stupid to do sth, especially when it causes them problems: *'He's not an easy person to live with.' 'More fool her for marrying him!'*—more at SUFFER
■ *verb* **1** [VN] **~ sb (into doing sth)** to trick sb into believing sth that is not true: *She certainly had me fooled—I really believed her!* ◊ *You don't fool me!* ◊ *You're fooling yourself if you think none of this will affect you.* ◊ *Don't be fooled into thinking they're going to change anything.* **2** [V] **~ (about/around) (with sth)** to say or do stupid or silly things, often in order to make people laugh: *Stop fooling around and sit down!* ◊ *If you fool about with matches, you'll end up getting burned.* **IDM** **you could have fooled 'me** (*spoken*) used to say that you do not believe sth that sb has just told you: *'I'm trying as hard as I can!' 'You could have fooled me!'* **PHRV** **,fool a'round 1** (*BrE* also **,fool a'bout**) to waste time instead of doing sth that you should be doing **2 ~ (with sb)** to have a sexual relationship with another person's partner; to have a sexual relationship with sb who is not your partner: *She's been fooling around with a married man.*
■ *adj.* [only before noun] (*informal*) stupid; FOOLISH: *That was a damn fool thing to do!*

fool·hardy /'fuːlhɑːdi; *AmE* -hɑːrdi/ *adj.* (*disapproving*) taking unnecessary risks: *It would be foolhardy to sail in weather like this.* ▶ **fool·hardi·ness** *noun* [U]

fool·ish /'fuːlɪʃ/ *adj.* **1** (of actions or behaviour) not showing good sense or judgement SYN SILLY: *She's just a vain, foolish woman.* ◊ *I was foolish enough to believe what Jeff told me.* ◊ *The accident was my fault—it would be foolish to pretend otherwise.* ◊ *How could she have been so foolish as to fall in love with him?* ◊ *a foolish idea/dream/mistake* ◊ *It was a very foolish thing to do.* **2** [not usually before noun] made to feel or look silly and embarrassed: *I felt foolish and a failure.* ◊ *He's afraid of looking foolish in front of his friends.* ▶ **fool·ish·ly** *adv.*: *We foolishly thought that everyone would speak English.* ◊ *Foolishly, I allowed myself to be persuaded to enter the contest.* **fool·ish·ness** *noun* [U]: *Jenny had to laugh at her own foolishness.*

fool·proof /'fuːlpruːf/ *adj.* (of a plan, machine, method, etc.) very well designed and easy to use so that it cannot fail and you cannot use it wrongly: *This recipe is foolproof—it's perfect every time.*

fools·cap /'fuːlskæp/ *noun* (*BrE*) [U] a large size of paper for writing on

,fool's 'paradise *noun* [usually sing.] a state of happiness that is based on sth that is false or cannot last although the happy person does not realize it

foot /fʊt/ *noun, verb*
■ *noun* (*pl.* **feet** /fiːt/)
PART OF BODY | **1** [C] the lowest part of the leg, below the ankle, on which a person or an animal stands: *My feet are aching.* ◊ *to get/rise to your feet* (= stand up) ◊ *I've been on my feet* (= standing or walking around) *all day.* ◊ *We came on foot* (= we walked). ◊ *walking around the house in bare feet* (= not wearing shoes or socks) ◊ *a foot brake/pump* (= operated using your foot, not your hand) ◊ *a foot passenger* (= one who travels on a ferry without a car) ◊ *a foot soldier* (= one without a vehicle or horse)—see also ATHLETE'S FOOT, BAREFOOT, CLUB FOOT, UNDERFOOT—picture at BODY

-FOOTED | **2** (in adjectives and adverbs) having or using the type or number of foot/feet mentioned: *bare-footed* ◊ *four-footed* ◊ *a left-footed shot into the corner*—see also FLAT-FOOTED, SURE-FOOTED

PART OF SOCK | **3** [C, usually sing.] the part of a sock, STOCKING, etc. that covers the foot

aɪ	aʊ	eɪ	əʊ	oʊ	ɔɪ	ɪə	eə	ʊə	j	w
my	now	say	go	go	boy	near	hair	pure	yes	wet
			(BrE)	(AmE)						

BASE/BOTTOM | **4** [sing.] **the ~ of sth** the lowest part of sth; the base or bottom of sth: *the foot of the stairs / page / mountain* ◊ *The nurse hung a chart at the foot of the bed* (= the part of the bed where your feet normally are when you are lying in it).

MEASUREMENT | **5** (*pl.* **feet** or **foot**) (*abbr.* **ft**) a unit for measuring length equal to 12 INCHES or 30.48 CENTIMETRES: *a 6-foot high wall* ◊ *We're flying at 35000 feet.* ◊ *'How tall are you?' 'Five foot nine'* (= five feet and nine inches).

-FOOTER | **6** (in compound nouns) a person or thing that is a particular number of feet tall or long: *His boat is an eighteen-footer.*

IN POETRY | **7** [sing.] (*technical*) a unit of rhythm in a line of poetry containing one stressed syllable and one or more syllables without stress. Each of the four divisions in the following line is a foot: *For 'men / may 'come / and 'men / may 'go.*

IDM be rushed / run off your 'feet to be extremely busy; to have too many things to do **fall / land on your 'feet** to be lucky in finding yourself in a good situation, or in getting out of a difficult situation **get / have a / your ˌfoot in the 'door** to manage to enter an organization, a field of business, etc. that could bring you success: *I always wanted to work in TV but it took me two years to get a foot in the door.* **get / start off on the right / wrong 'foot (with sb)** (*informal*) to start a relationship well / badly: *I seem to have got off on the wrong foot with the new boss.* **have feet of 'clay** to have a fault or weakness in your character **have / keep your 'feet on the ground** to have a sensible and realistic attitude to life **have / keep a foot in both 'camps** to be involved in or connected with two different or opposing groups **have ˌone foot in the 'grave** (*informal*) to be so old or ill that you are not likely to live much longer **...my 'foot!** (*informal, humorous*) a strong way of saying that you disagree completely with what has just been said: *'Ian can't come because he's tired.' 'Tired my foot! Lazy more like!'* **on your 'feet** completely well or in a normal state again after an illness or a time of trouble: *Sue's back on her feet again after her operation.* ◊ *The new chairman hopes to get the company back on its feet within six months.* **put your best foot 'forward** to make a great effort to do sth, especially if it is difficult or you are feeling tired **put your 'feet up** to sit down and relax, especially with your feet raised and supported: *After a hard day's work, it's nice to get home and put your feet up.* **put your 'foot down 1** to be very strict in opposing what sb wishes to do: *You've got to put your foot down and make him stop seeing her.* **2** (*BrE*) to drive faster: *She put her foot down and roared past them.* **put your 'foot in it** (*BrE*) (also **put your foot in your 'mouth** *AmE, BrE*) to say or do sth that upsets, offends or embarrasses sb: *I really put my foot in it with Ella—I didn't know she'd split up with Tom.* **put a foot 'wrong** (usually used in negative sentences) to make a mistake: *In the last two games he has hardly put a foot wrong.* **set 'foot in / on sth** to enter or visit a place: *the first man to set foot on the moon* ◊ *I vowed never to set foot in the place again.* **set sb / sth on their / its 'feet** to make sb / sth independent or successful: *His business sense helped set the club on its feet again.* **stand on your own (two) 'feet** to be independent and able to take care of yourself: *When his parents died he had to learn to stand on his own two feet.* **under your 'feet** in the way; stopping you from working, etc: *I don't want you kids under my feet while I'm cooking.*—more at BOOT *n.*, COLD *adj.*, DRAG *v.*, FIND *v.*, GRASS *n.*, GROUND *n.*, HAND *n.*, HEAD *n.*, ITCHY, LEFT *adj.*, PATTER *n.*, PULL *v.*, SHOE *n.*, SHOOT *v.*, SIT, STOCKING, SWEEP *v.*, THINK *v.*, VOTE *v.*, WAIT *v.*, WALK *v.*, WEIGHT *n.*, WORLD
■ *verb*
IDM foot the 'bill (*informal*) to be responsible for paying the cost of sth: *Once again it will be the taxpayer who has to foot the bill.*

foot·age /ˈfʊtɪdʒ/ *noun* [U] part of a film showing a particular event: *old film footage of the moon landing*

ˌfoot-and-'mouth disˌease *noun* [U] a disease that cows, sheep, etc. can die from, which causes sore places on the mouth and feet

foot·ball /ˈfʊtbɔːl/ *noun* **1** [U] (also *formal* Asˌsociation 'Football) (both *BrE*) (also **socˈcer** *AmE, BrE*) (also *BrE* informal **footy, footie**) [U] a game played by two teams of 11 players, using a round ball which players kick up and down the playing field (= the PITCH). Teams try to kick the ball into the other team's goal: *to play football* ◊ *a football match / team / stadium*—picture on page 1250 **2** [U] (*AmE*) = AMERICAN FOOTBALL **3** [C] a large round or OVAL ball made of leather or plastic and filled with air **4** [C] (always used with an adjective) an issue or problem that frequently causes argument and disagreement: *Health care should not become a political football.*

'football boot *noun* (*BrE*) a leather shoe with pieces of rubber on the bottom to stop it slipping, worn for playing football—compare CLEATS—picture at SHOE

foot·baller /ˈfʊtbɔːlə(r)/ *noun* (*BrE*) a person who plays football, especially as a profession

foot·ball·ing /ˈfʊtbɔːlɪŋ/ *adj.* [only before noun] (*BrE*) connected with the game of football: *footballing skills*

'football pools (also **the pools**) *noun* [pl.] a form of gambling in Britain in which people try to win money by saying what the results of football matches will be: *They've had a big win on the football pools.*

foot·bridge /ˈfʊtbrɪdʒ/ *noun* a narrow bridge used only by people who are walking

foot·er /ˈfʊtə(r)/ *noun* a line or block of text that is automatically added to the bottom of every page that is printed from a computer—compare HEADER

foot·fall /ˈfʊtfɔːl/ *noun* (*literary*) the sound of the steps made by sb walking

'foot fault *noun* (in tennis) a mistake that is made by not keeping behind the line when SERVING

foot·hill /ˈfʊthɪl/ *noun* [usually pl.] a hill or low mountain at the base of a higher mountain or range of mountains: *the foothills of the Himalayas*

foot·hold /ˈfʊthəʊld; *AmE* -hoʊld/ *noun* **1** a crack, hole or branch where your foot can be safely supported when climbing **2** [usually sing.] a strong position in a business, profession, etc. from which sb can make progress and achieve success: *The company is eager to gain a foothold in Europe.*

footie /ˈfʊti/ *noun* [U] (*BrE, informal*) = FOOTBALL (1)

foot·ing /ˈfʊtɪŋ/ *noun* [sing.] **1** the position of your feet when they are safely on the ground or some other surface: *She lost her footing* (= she slipped or lost her balance) *and fell backwards into the water.* ◊ *I slipped and struggled to regain my footing.* **2** the basis on which sth is established or organized: *The company is now on a sound financial footing.* ◊ *The country has been on a war footing* (= prepared for war) *since March.* **3** the position or status of sb / sth in relation to others; the relationship between two or more people or groups: *The two groups must meet on an equal footing.* ◊ *They were demanding to be treated on the same footing as the rest of the teachers.*

foot·lights /ˈfʊtlaɪts/ *noun* [pl.] a row of lights along the front of the stage in a theatre

foot·loose /ˈfʊtluːs/ *adj.* free to go where you like or do what you want because you have no responsibilities: *Bert was a footloose, unemployed actor.* ◊ *Ah, I was still footloose and fancy-free* (= free to enjoy myself) *in those days.*

foot·man /ˈfʊtmən/ *noun* (*pl.* **-men** /-mən/) a male servant in a house in the past, who opened the door to visitors, served food at table, etc.

foot·note /ˈfʊtnəʊt; *AmE* -noʊt/ *noun* **1** an extra piece of information that is printed at the bottom of a page in a book **2** (of an event or a person) that may be remembered but only as sth that is not important

foot·path /ˈfʊtpɑːθ; *AmE* -pæθ/ *noun* a path that is made for people to walk along, especially in the country: *a public footpath*

foot·plate /ˈfʊtpleɪt/ *noun* (*BrE*) the part of a steam train's engine where the driver stands

foot·print /ˈfʊtprɪnt/ *noun* [usually pl.] a mark left on a surface by a person's foot or shoe or by an animal's foot:

F

footprints in the sand ◇ *muddy footprints on the kitchen floor*

foot·rest /ˈfʊtrest/ *noun* a support for your foot or feet, for example on a motorcycle or when you are sitting down

foot·sie /ˈfʊtsi/ *noun* (*informal*) **IDM** **play ˈfootsie with sb** to touch sb's feet lightly with your own feet, especially under a table, as an expression of affection or sexual interest

foot·sore /ˈfʊtsɔː(r)/ *adj.* (*formal*) having sore or tired feet, especially after walking a long way: *They limped in weary and footsore.*

foot·step /ˈfʊtstep/ *noun* [usually pl.] the sound or mark made each time your foot touches the ground when you are walking or running: *the sound of footsteps on the stairs* ◇ *footsteps in the snow* **IDM** see FOLLOW

foot·stool /ˈfʊtstuːl/ *noun* a low piece of furniture used for resting your feet on when you are sitting—picture at CHAIR

foot·wear /ˈfʊtweə(r); *AmE* -wer/ *noun* [U] anything that people wear on their feet, for example shoes and boots: *Be sure to wear the correct footwear to prevent injuries to your feet.*

foot·work /ˈfʊtwɜːk; *AmE* -wɜːrk/ *noun* [U] **1** the way in which a person moves their feet when playing a sport or dancing **2** the ability to react quickly and skilfully to a difficult situation: *It was going to take some deft political footwork to save the situation.*

footy /ˈfʊti/ *noun* [U] (*BrE, informal*) = FOOTBALL (1)

fop /fɒp; *AmE* fɑːp/ *noun* (*old-fashioned*) a man who is too interested in his clothes and the way he looks ▶ **fop·pish** *adj.*

for /fə(r); *strong form* fɔː(r)/ *prep., conj.*

■ *prep.* **HELP** For the special uses of **for** in phrasal verbs, look at the entries for the verbs. For example **fall for sb** is in the phrasal verb section at **fall**. **1** used to show who is intended to have or use sth or where sth is intended to be put: *There's a letter for you.* ◇ *It's a book for children.* ◇ *We got a new table for the dining room.* ◇ *This is the place for me* (= I like it very much). **2** in order to help sb/sth: *What can I do for you* (= how can I help you)? ◇ *Can you translate this letter for me?* ◇ *I took her classes for her while she was sick.* ◇ *soldiers fighting for their country* **3** concerning sb/sth: *They are anxious for her safety.* ◇ *Fortunately for us, the weather changed.* **4** as a representative of: *I am speaking for everyone in this department.* **5** employed by: *She's working for IBM.* **6** meaning: *Shaking your head for 'No' is not universal.* **7** in support of sb/sth: *Are you for or against the proposal?* ◇ *They voted for independence in a referendum.* ◇ *There's a strong case for postponing the exam.* ◇ *I'm all for people having fun.*—compare AGAINST(2) **8** used to show purpose or function: *a machine for slicing bread* ◇ *Let's go for a walk.* ◇ *Are you learning English for pleasure or for your work?* ◇ *What did you do that for* (= Why did you do that)? **9** used to show a reason or cause: *The town is famous for its cathedral.* ◇ *She gave me a watch for my birthday.* ◇ *He got an award for bravery.* ◇ *I couldn't speak for laughing.* **10** in order to obtain sth: *He came to me for advice.* ◇ *For more information, call this number.* ◇ *There were over fifty applicants for the job.* **11** in exchange for sth: *Copies are available for two dollars each.* ◇ *I'll swap these two bottles for that one.* **12** considering what can be expected from sb/sth: *The weather was warm for the time of year.* ◇ *She's tall for her age.* ◇ *That's too much responsibility for a child.* **13** better, happier, etc. ~ sth better, happier, etc. following sth: *You'll feel better for a good night's sleep.* ◇ *This room would look more cheerful for a spot of paint.* **14** used to show where sb/sth is going: *Is this the bus for Chicago?* ◇ *She knew she was destined for a great future.* **15** used to show a length of time: *I'm going away for a few days.* ◇ *That's all the news there is for now.* **16** used to show that sth is arranged or intended to happen at a particular time: *an appointment for May 12* ◇ *We're invited for 7.30.* **17** used to show the occasion when sth happens: *I'm warning you for the last time—stop talking!* **18** used to show a distance: *The road went on for miles and miles.* **19** used to say how difficult, necessary, pleasant, etc. sth

is that sb might do or has done: *It's useless for us to continue.* ◇ *There's no need for you to go.* ◇ *For her to have survived such an ordeal was remarkable.* ◇ *The box is too heavy for me to lift.* ◇ *Is it clear enough for you to read?* **20** used to show who can or should do sth: *It's not for me to say why he left.* ◇ *How to spend the money is for you to decide.* **IDM** **be ˈin for it** (*BrE* also **be ˈfor it**) (*informal*) to be going to get into trouble or -be punished: *We'd better hurry or we'll be in for it.* **for ˈall 1** in spite of: *For all its clarity of style, the book is not easy reading.* **2** used to say that sth is not important or of no interest or value to you/sb: *For all I know she's still living in Boston.* ◇ *You can do what you like, for all I care.* ◇ *For all the good it's done we might as well not have bothered.* **there's/ that's …for you** (*often ironic*) used to say that sth is a typical example of its kind: *She might at least have called to explain. There's gratitude for you.*

■ *conj.* (*old-fashioned* or *literary*) used to introduce the reason for sth mentioned in the previous statement: *We listened eagerly, for he brought news of our families.* ◇ *I believed her—for surely she would not lie to us.*

for·age /ˈfɒrɪdʒ; *AmE* ˈfɔː-; ˈfɑː-/ *verb, noun*

■ *verb* [V] ~ (**for sth**) (*written*) **1** (especially of an animal) to search for food **2** (of a person) to search for sth, especially using the hands

■ *noun* [U] food for horses and cows: *forage crops / grass*

foray /ˈfɒreɪ; *AmE* ˈfɔː-; ˈfɑː-/ *noun* **1** ~ (**into sth**) an attempt to become involved in a different activity or profession: *the company's first foray into the computer market* **2** ~ (**into sth**) a short sudden attack made by a group of soldiers: *Those on the front line make regular forays into occupied territory.* **3** ~ (**to/into …**) a short journey to find a particular thing or to visit a new place: *weekend shopping forays to France*

for·bade *pt* of FORBID

for·bear *verb, noun*

■ *verb* /fɔːˈbeə(r); *AmE* fɔːrˈber/ (**for·bore** /fɔːˈbɔː(r); *AmE* fɔːrˈbɔːr/, **for·borne** /fɔːˈbɔːn; *AmE* fɔːrˈbɔːrn/) ~ (**from sth/ from doing sth**) (*formal*) to stop yourself from saying or doing sth that you could or would like to say or do: [V] *He wanted to answer back, but he forbore from doing so.* ◇ [Vto inf] *She forbore to ask any further questions.*

■ *noun* = FOREBEAR

for·bear·ance /fɔːˈbeərəns; *AmE* fɔːrˈber-/ *noun* [U] (*formal*) the quality of being patient and sympathetic towards other people, especially when they have done sth wrong

for·bear·ing /fɔːˈbeərɪŋ; *AmE* fɔːrˈber-/ *adj.* (*formal*) showing forbearance: *Thank you for being so forbearing.*

for·bid /fəˈbɪd; *AmE* fərˈb-/ *verb* (**for·bade** /fəˈbæd; fəˈbeɪd; *AmE* fərˈb-/ **for·bid·den** /fəˈbɪdn; *AmE* fərˈb-/) **1** ~ **sb** (**from doing sth**) to order sb not to do sth; to order that sth must not be done: [VN] *He forbade them from mentioning the subject again.* ◇ *Her father forbade the marriage.* ◇ [VN to inf] *You are all forbidden to leave.* ◇ [VNN] *My doctor has forbidden me sugar.* [also VN -ing, V -ing] **2** (*formal*) to make it difficult or impossible to do sth: [VN] *Lack of space forbids further treatment of the topic here.* [also VN to inf] **IDM** **God/ Heaven for'bid (that …)** (*spoken*) used to say that you hope that sth will not happen: *'Maybe you'll end up as a lawyer, like me.' 'God forbid!'* **HELP** Some people find this use offensive.

for·bid·den /fəˈbɪdn; *AmE* fərˈb-/ *adj.* not allowed: *Photography is strictly forbidden in the museum.* ◇ *The conversation was in danger of wandering into forbidden territory* (= topics that they were not allowed to talk about). **IDM** **for,bidden ˈfruit** a thing that is not allowed and that therefore seems very attractive

for·bid·ding /fəˈbɪdɪŋ; *AmE* fərˈb-/ *adj.* seeming unfriendly and frightening and likely to cause harm or danger: *a forbidding appearance / look / manner* ◇ *The house looked dark and forbidding.* ▶ **for·bid·ding·ly** *adv.*

for·bore *pt* of FORBEAR

for·borne *pp* of FORBEAR

s	t	v	z	ʃ	ʒ	tʃ	dʒ	θ	ð	ŋ
see	tea	van	zoo	shoe	vision	chain	jam	thin	this	sing

force /fɔːs; *AmE* fɔːrs/
noun, verb

WORD FAMILY
force *n., v.*
forceful *adj.*
forced *adj.* (≠ unforced)
forcible *adj.*
enforce *v.*

■ *noun*

VIOLENT ACTION | **1** [U] violent physical action used to obtain or achieve sth: *The release of the hostages could not be achieved without the use of force.* ◊ *The rioters were taken away by force.* ◊ *The ultimatum contained the threat of military force.* ◊ *We will achieve much more by persuasion than by brute force.*

PHYSICAL STRENGTH | **2** [U] the physical strength of sth that is shown as it hits sth else: *the force of the blow/explosion/collision* ◊ *The shopping centre took the full force of the blast.* ⇨ note at STRENGTH

STRONG EFFECT | **3** [U] the strong effect or influence of sth: *They realized the force of her argument.* ◊ *He controlled himself by sheer force of will.* ◊ *She spoke with force and deliberation.*

SB/STH WITH POWER | **4** [C] a person or thing that has a lot of power or influence: *economic/market forces* ◊ *the forces of good/evil* ◊ *Ron is the driving force* (= the person who has the most influence) *behind the project.* ◊ *She's a force to be reckoned with* (= a person who has a lot of power and influence and should therefore be treated seriously). ◊ *The expansion of higher education should be a powerful force for change.*

AUTHORITY | **5** [U] the authority of sth: *These guidelines do not have the force of law.* ◊ *The court ruled that these standards have force in British law.*

GROUP OF PEOPLE | **6** [C+sing./pl. *v.*] a group of people who have been organized for a particular purpose: *a member of the sales force* ◊ *A large proportion of the labour force* (= all the people who work in a particular company, area, etc.) *is unskilled.*—see also WORKFORCE

MILITARY | **7** [C+sing./pl. *v.*] a group of people who have been trained to protect other people, usually by using weapons: *a member of the security forces* ◊ *rebel/government forces* ◊ *a peace-keeping force*—see also AIR FORCE, POLICE FORCE, TASK FORCE **8** (the forces) [pl.] (*BrE*) the army, navy and air force: *allied/defence forces*—see also THE ARMED FORCES **9** (forces) [pl.] the weapons and soldiers that an army, etc. has, considered as things that may be used: *strategic nuclear forces.*

POLICE | **10** (the force) [sing.] (*BrE*) the police force: *He joined the force twenty years ago.*

PHYSICS | **11** [C, U] an effect that causes things to move in a particular way: *The moon exerts a force on the earth.* ◊ *the force of gravity* ◊ *magnetic/centrifugal force*

OF WIND | **12** [C, usually sing.] a unit for measuring the strength of the wind: *a force 9 gale* ◊ *a gale force wind*—see also TOUR DE FORCE

IDM **bring sth into 'force** to cause a law, rule, etc. to start being used: *They are hoping to bring the new legislation into force before the end of the year.* **come/enter into 'force** (of a law, rule, etc.) to start being used: *When do the new regulations come into force?* **force of 'habit** if you do sth from or out of **force of habit**, you do it automatically and in a particular way because you have always done it that way in the past **the forces of 'nature** the power of the wind, rain, etc., especially when it causes damage or harm **in 'force 1** (of people) in large numbers: *Protesters turned out in force.* **2** (of a law, rule, etc.) being used: *The new regulations are now in force.* **join/combine 'forces (with sb)** to work together in order to achieve a shared aim: *The two firms joined forces to win the contract.*—more at SPENT

■ *verb*

MAKE SB DO STH | **1** [often passive] ~ sb (into sth/into doing sth) to make sb do sth that they do not want to do SYN COMPEL [VN, VN to inf] *The President was forced into resigning.* ◊ *The President was forced to resign.* ◊ [VN to inf] *I was forced to take a taxi because the last bus had left.* ◊ *She forced herself to be polite to them.* ◊ [VN] *He didn't force me—I wanted to go.* ◊ *Ill health forced him into early retirement.* ◊ (*spoken, humorous*) *'I shouldn't really have any more.' 'Go on—force yourself!'*

USE PHYSICAL STRENGTH | **2** to use physical strength to move sb/sth into a particular position: [VN] *to force a lock/window/door* (= to break it open using force) ◊ *He tried to force a copy of his book into my hand.* ◊ *to force an entry* (= to enter a building using force) ◊ *She forced her way through the crowd of reporters.* ◊ [VN-ADJ] *The door had been forced open.*

MAKE STH HAPPEN | **3** [VN] to make sth happen, especially before other people are ready: *He was in a position where he had to force a decision.* ◊ *Building a new road here will force house prices down.*

A SMILE/LAUGH | **4** [VN] to make yourself smile, laugh, etc. rather than doing it naturally

FRUIT/PLANTS | **5** [VN] to make fruit, plants, etc. grow or develop faster than normal by keeping them in special conditions: *forced rhubarb* ◊ (*figurative*) *It is unwise to force a child's talent.*

IDM **force sb's 'hand** to make sb do sth that they do not want to do or make them do it sooner than they had intended **force the issue** to do sth to make people take action on sth quickly **force the 'pace** (*especially BrE*) **1** to run very fast in a race in order to make the other competitors run faster **2** to make sb do sth faster than they want to: *The demonstrations have succeeded in forcing the pace of change.*—more at THROAT PHR V **force sth ↔ 'back** to make yourself hide an emotion: *She swallowed hard and forced back her tears.* **force sth ↔ 'down 1** to make yourself eat or drink sth that you do not really want **2** to make a plane, etc. land, especially by threatening to attack it **force sb/sth on/upon sb** to make sb accept sth that they do not want: *to force your attentions/opinions/company on sb* **force sth 'out of sb** to make sb tell you sth, especially by threatening them: *I managed to force the truth out of him.*

forced /fɔːst; *AmE* fɔːrst/ *adj.* **1** happening or done against sb's WILL (= without the person concerned wanting it): *forced relocation to a job in another city* ◊ *a forced sale of his property* **2** not sincere; not the result of genuine emotions: *She said she was enjoying herself but her smile was forced.*—see also UNFORCED

forced 'entry *noun* [U, C] an occasion when sb enters a building illegally, using force

forced 'labour (*BrE*) (*AmE* **forced 'labor**) *noun* [U] **1** hard physical work that sb, often a prisoner or slave, is forced to do **2** prisoners or slaves who are forced to work: *The mines were manned by forced labour from conquered countries.*

forced 'landing *noun* an act of having to land an aircraft unexpectedly in order to avoid a crash: *to make a forced landing*

forced 'march *noun* a long march, usually made by soldiers in difficult conditions

force-'feed *verb* [VN] to use force to make sb, especially a prisoner, eat or drink, by putting food or drink down their throat

force·ful /'fɔːsfl; *AmE* 'fɔːrsfl/ *adj.* **1** (of people) expressing opinions firmly and clearly in a way that persuades other people to believe them SYN ASSERTIVE: *a forceful woman/speaker* ◊ *a forceful character/personality* **2** (of opinions, etc.) expressed firmly and clearly so that other people believe them: *a forceful argument/speech* **3** using force: *the forceful suppression of minorities* ▶ **force·ful·ly** /-fəli/ *adv.*: *He argued his case forcefully.* **force·ful·ness** *noun* [U]

force ma·jeure /ˌfɔːs mæˈʒɜː(r); *AmE* ˌfɔːrs/ *noun* [U] (from *French, law*) unexpected circumstances, such as war, that can be used as an excuse when they prevent sb from doing sth that is written in a contract

for·ceps /'fɔːseps; *AmE* 'fɔːrs-/ *noun* [pl.] an instrument used by doctors, with two long thin parts for picking up and holding things: *a pair of forceps* ◊ *a forceps delivery* (= a birth in which the baby is delivered with the help of forceps)

for·cible /'fɔːsəbl; *AmE* 'fɔːrs-/ *adj.* [only before noun] involving the use of physical force: *forcible repatriation* ◊ *The police checked all windows and doors for signs of forcible entry.*

æ	ɑː	e	ɜː	ə	ɪ	iː	i	ɒ	ɔː	ʌ	ʊ	u	uː
cat	father	ten	bird	about	sit	see	many	got	saw	cup	put	actual	too

(BrE)

for·cibly /ˈfɔːsəbli; AmE ˈfɔːrs-/ adv. **1** in a way that involves the use of physical force: *Supporters were forcibly removed from the court.* **2** in a way that makes sth very clear: *It struck me forcibly how honest he'd been.*

ford /fɔːd; AmE fɔːrd/ noun, verb
- noun a shallow place in a river where it is possible to drive or walk across
- verb [VN] to walk or drive across a river or stream

fore /fɔː(r)/ noun, adj., adv.
- noun IDM **be/come to the ˈfore** (BrE) (AmE **be at the ˈfore**) to be/become important and noticed by people; to play an important part: *She has always been to the fore at moments of crisis.* ◇ *The problem has come to the fore again in recent months.* **bring sth to the ˈfore** to make sth become noticed by people
- adj. [only before noun] (technical) situated at the front of a ship, an aircraft or an animal—compare AFT, HIND
- adv. at or towards the front of a ship or an aircraft—compare AFT

fore- /fɔː(r)/ combining form (in nouns and verbs) **1** before; in advance: *foreword* ◇ *foretell* **2** in the front of: *the foreground of the picture*

fore·arm¹ /ˈfɔːrɑːm; AmE -ɑːrm/ noun the part of the arm between the elbow and the wrist—picture at BODY

fore·arm² /ˌfɔːrˈɑːm; AmE -ˈɑːrm/ verb IDM see FOREWARN

fore·bear (also **for·bear**) /ˈfɔːbeə(r); AmE ˈfɔːrber/ noun [usually pl.] (formal or literary) a person who you are descended from, especially one who lived a long time ago SYN ANCESTOR

fore·bod·ing /fɔːˈbəʊdɪŋ; AmE fɔːrˈboʊ-/ noun [U, C] a strong feeling that sth unpleasant or dangerous is going to happen: *She had a sense of foreboding that the news would be bad.* ◇ *The letter filled him with foreboding.* ◇ *He knew from her face that his forebodings had been justified.* ► **fore·bod·ing** adj.: *a foreboding feeling that something was wrong*

fore·cast /ˈfɔːkɑːst; AmE ˈfɔːrkæst/ noun, verb
- noun a statement about what will happen in the future, based on information that is available now: *sales forecasts* ◇ *The forecast said there would be sunny intervals and showers.*—see also WEATHER FORECAST
- verb (fore·cast, fore·cast) or (fore·cast·ed, fore·cast·ed) to say what you think will happen in the future based on information that you have now SYN PREDICT: [VN] *Experts are forecasting a recovery in the economy.* ◇ *Snow is forecast for tomorrow.* ◇ *Temperatures were forecast to reach 40°C.* ◇ [V that] *The report forecasts that prices will rise by 3% next month.* [also V wh-]

fore·cast·er /ˈfɔːkɑːstə(r); AmE ˈfɔːrkæstər/ noun a person who says what is expected to happen, especially sb whose job is to forecast the weather: *a weather forecaster* ◇ *an economic forecaster*

fore·close /fɔːˈkləʊz; AmE fɔːrˈkloʊz/ verb **1** [V, VN] ~ (on sb/sth) (finance) (especially of a bank) to take control of sb's property because they have not paid back money that they borrowed to buy it **2** [VN] (formal) to reject sth as a possibility SYN EXCLUDE

fore·clos·ure /fɔːˈkləʊʒə(r); AmE fɔːrˈkloʊ-/ noun [U, C] (finance) the act of foreclosing on money that has been borrowed; an example of this

fore·court /ˈfɔːkɔːt; AmE ˈfɔːrkɔːrt/ noun (BrE) a large open space in front of a building, for example a PETROL/GAS STATION or hotel, often used for parking cars on

fore·father /ˈfɔːfɑːðə(r); AmE ˈfɔːrf-/ noun [usually pl.] (formal or literary) a person (especially a man) who you are descended from, especially one who lived a long time ago

fore·fin·ger /ˈfɔːfɪŋɡə(r); AmE ˈfɔːrf-/ noun the finger next to the thumb SYN INDEX FINGER

fore·foot /ˈfɔːfʊt; AmE ˈfɔːrfʊt/ noun (pl. -feet /-fiːt/) either of the two front feet of an animal that has four feet

fore·front /ˈfɔːfrʌnt; AmE ˈfɔːrf-/ noun [sing.] IDM **at/in/ to the ˈforefront (of sth)** in or into an important or leading position in a particular group or activity: *Women have always been at the forefront of the Green movement.* ◇ *The new product took the company to the forefront of the computer software field.* ◇ *The court case was constantly in*

the forefront of my mind (= I thought about it all the time).

fore·gather (also **for·gather**) /ˌfɔːˈɡæðə(r); AmE ˌfɔːrˈɡ-/ verb [V] (formal) to meet together in a group

forego = FORGO

fore·going /ˈfɔːɡəʊɪŋ; AmE ˈfɔːrɡoʊɪŋ/ adj. [only before noun] (written) **1** used to refer to sth that has just been mentioned: *the foregoing analysis/discussion/example* **2 (the foregoing)** noun [sing.+ sing./pl. v.] what has just been mentioned: *The foregoing is a description of the proposed plan.*

fore·gone /ˈfɔːɡɒn; AmE ˈfɔːrɡɔːn; -ɡɑːn/ adj. IDM **a ˌfore·gone conˈclusion** if you say that sth is a **foregone conclusion**, you mean that it is a result that is certain to happen

fore·ground /ˈfɔːɡraʊnd; AmE ˈfɔːrɡ-/ noun, verb
- noun **(the foreground) 1** [C, usually sing.] the part of a view, picture, etc. that is nearest to you when you look at it: *The figure in the foreground is the artist's mother.* **2** [sing.] an important position that is noticed by people: *Inflation and interest rates will be very much in the foreground of their election campaign.*—compare BACK-GROUND
- verb [VN] (written) to give particular importance to sth: *The play foregrounds the relationship between father and daughter.*

fore·hand /ˈfɔːhænd; AmE ˈfɔːrh-/ noun [usually sing.] (in tennis, etc.) a way of hitting a ball in which the inner part of the hand (PALM) faces the ball as it is hit: *She has a strong forehand.* ◇ *a forehand volley* ◇ *He served to his opponent's forehand.*—compare BACKHAND

fore·head /ˈfɔːhed; AmE ˈfɒrɪd; ˈfɔːrhed; ˈfɔːred; ˈfɑːr-/ noun the part of the face above the eyes and below the hair SYN BROW—picture at BODY

for·eign /ˈfɒrən; AmE ˈfɔːrən; ˈfɑːrən/ adj. **1** in or from a country that is not your own: *a foreign accent/language/ student* ◇ *a foreign-owned company* ◇ *foreign holidays* ◇ *You could tell she was foreign by the way she dressed.* **2** [only before noun] dealing with or involving other countries: *foreign affairs/news/policy/trade* ◇ *foreign aid* ◇ *a foreign correspondent* (= one who reports on foreign countries in newspapers or on television) OPP HOME **3 ~ to sb/sth** (formal) not typical of sb/sth; not known to sb/sth and therefore seeming strange: *Dishonesty is foreign to his nature.* **4 ~ object/body** (formal) an object that has entered sth by accident and should not be there: *Tears help to protect the eye from potentially harmful foreign bodies.*

the ˌForeign and ˈCommonwealth Office noun [sing.+ sing./pl. v.] (abbr. **FCO**) the British government department that deals with relations with other countries. It used to be called **the Foreign Office** and it is still sometimes referred to as this.

for·eign·er /ˈfɒrənə(r); AmE ˈfɔːr-; ˈfɑːr-/ noun (sometimes offensive) **1** a person who comes from a different country: *The fact that I was a foreigner was a big disadvantage.* **2** a person who does not belong in a particular place: *I have always been regarded as a foreigner by the local folk.*

ˌforeign exˈchange noun **1** [U, C] the system of exchanging the money of one country for that of another country; the place where money is exchanged: *The pound fell on the foreign exchanges yesterday.* **2** [U] money that is obtained using this system: *our largest source of foreign exchange*

the ˈForeign Office noun [sing.] = THE FOREIGN AND COMMONWEALTH OFFICE

the ˌForeign ˈSecretary noun the British government minister in charge of THE FOREIGN AND COMMON-WEALTH OFFICE

ˈForeign Service noun (AmE) = DIPLOMATIC SERVICE

fore·know·ledge /fɔːˈnɒlɪdʒ; AmE fɔːrˈnɑːl-/ noun [U] (formal) knowledge of sth before it happens

fore·leg /ˈfɔːleg; AmE ˈfɔːrleg/ noun either of the two front legs of an animal that has four legs

fore·lock /ˈfɔːlɒk; AmE ˈfɔːrlɑːk/ noun **1** a piece of hair that grows at the front of the head and hangs down over the forehead **2** a part of a horse's MANE that grows forwards between its ears **IDM** **touch/tug your ˈforelock (to sb)** (*BrE, disapproving*) to show too much respect for sb, especially because you are anxious about what they think of you

fore·man /ˈfɔːmən; *AmE* ˈfɔːrmən/, **fore·woman** /ˈfɔːwʊmən; *AmE* ˈfɔːrw-/ *noun* (*pl.* **-men** /-mən/ **-women** /-wɪmɪn/) **1** a worker who is in charge of a group of other factory or building workers **2** a person who acts as the leader of a JURY in a court of law

fore·most /ˈfɔːməʊst; *AmE* ˈfɔːrmoʊst/ *adj., adv.*

■ *adj.* the most important or famous; in a position at the front: *the world's foremost authority on the subject* ◊ *The Prime Minister was foremost among those who condemned the violence.* ◊ *This question has been foremost in our minds recently.*

■ *adv.* **IDM** see FIRST *adv.*

fore·name /ˈfɔːneɪm; *AmE* ˈfɔːrn-/ *noun* (*formal*) a person's first name rather than the name that they share with the other members of their family (their SURNAME): *Please check that your surname and forenames have been correctly entered.*

fo·ren·sic /fəˈrensɪk; -ˈrenzɪk/ *adj.* [only before noun] **1** connected with the scientific tests used by the police when trying to solve a crime: *forensic evidence/medicine/science/tests* ◊ *the forensic laboratory* ◊ *a forensic pathologist* **2** connected with or used in a court of law: *a forensic psychiatrist* (= one who examines people who have been accused of a crime)

fore·play /ˈfɔːpleɪ; *AmE* ˈfɔːrp-/ *noun* [U] sexual activity, such as touching the sexual organs and kissing, that takes place before people have sex

fore·run·ner /ˈfɔːrʌnə(r)/ *noun* ~ **(of sb/sth)** a person or thing that came before and influenced sb/sth else that is similar; a sign of what is going to happen: *Country music was undoubtedly one of the forerunners of rock and roll.*

fore·see /fɔːˈsiː; *AmE* fɔːrˈsiː-/ *verb* (**fore·saw** /fɔːˈsɔː; *AmE* fɔːrˈsɔː/, **fore·seen** /fɔːˈsiːn; *AmE* fɔːrˈsiːn/) to think sth is going to happen in the future; to know about sth before it happens **SYN** PREDICT: [VN] *We do not foresee any problems.* ◊ [V(that)] *No one could have foreseen (that) things would turn out this way.* ◊ [V wh-] *It is impossible to foresee how life will work out.* [also VN-ing] —compare UNFORESEEN

fore·see·able /fɔːˈsiːəbl; *AmE* fɔːrˈs-/ *adj.* that you can predict will happen; that can be foreseen: *foreseeable risks/consequences* **OPP** UNFORESEEABLE **IDM** **for/in the foreseeable ˈfuture** for/in the period of time when you can predict what is going to happen, based on the present circumstances: *The statue will remain in the museum for the foreseeable future.* ◊ *It's unlikely that the hospital will be closed in the foreseeable future* (= soon).

fore·shadow /fɔːˈʃædəʊ; *AmE* fɔːrˈʃædoʊ/ *verb* [VN] (*written*) to be a sign of sth that will happen in the future

fore·shore /ˈfɔːʃɔː(r)/ *noun* [C usually sing, U] **1** (on a beach or by a river) the part of the shore between the highest and lowest levels reached by the water **2** the part of the shore between the highest level reached by the water and the area of land that has buildings, plants, etc. on it

fore·short·en /fɔːˈʃɔːtn; *AmE* fɔːrˈʃɔːrtn/ *verb* [VN] **1** (*technical*) to draw, photograph, etc. objects or people so that they look smaller or closer together than they really are **2** (*written*) to end sth before it would normally finish **SYN** CURTAIL: *a foreshortened education*

fore·sight /ˈfɔːsaɪt; *AmE* ˈfɔːrs-/ *noun* [U] (*approving*) the ability to predict what is likely to happen and to use this to prepare for the future: *She had had the foresight to prepare herself financially in case of an accident.*—compare HINDSIGHT

fore·skin /ˈfɔːskɪn; *AmE* ˈfɔːrs-/ *noun* the loose piece of skin that covers the end of a man's PENIS

for·est /ˈfɒrɪst; *AmE* ˈfɔːr-; ˈfɑːr-/ *noun* **1** [C, U] a large area of land that is thickly covered with trees: *a tropical forest* ◊ *a forest fire* ◊ *Thousands of hectares of forest are des-*

troyed each year.—see also RAINFOREST **2** [C] ~ **(of sth)** a mass of tall narrow objects that are close together: *a forest of television aerials* **IDM** **not see the ˌforest for the ˈtrees** (*AmE*) = NOT SEE THE WOOD FOR THE TREES at WOOD

fore·stall /fɔːˈstɔːl; *AmE* fɔːrˈs-/ *verb* [VN] (*written*) to prevent sth from happening or sb from doing sth by doing sth first: *Try to anticipate what your child will do and forestall problems.*

for·est·ed /ˈfɒrɪstɪd; *AmE* ˈfɔːr-; ˈfɑːr-/ *adj.* covered in forest: *thickly forested hills* ◊ *The province is heavily forested and sparsely populated.*

for·est·er /ˈfɒrɪstə(r); *AmE* ˈfɔːr-; ˈfɑːr-/ *noun* a person who works in a forest, taking care of the trees, planting new ones, etc.

for·est·ry /ˈfɒrɪstri; *AmE* ˈfɔːr-; ˈfɑːr-/ *noun* [U] the science or practice of planting and taking care of trees and forests

fore·taste /ˈfɔːteɪst; *AmE* ˈfɔːrt-/ *noun* [sing.] **a** ~ **(of sth)** a small amount of a particular experience or situation that shows you what it will be like when the same thing happens on a larger scale in the future: *They were unaware that the street violence was just a foretaste of what was to come.*

fore·tell /fɔːˈtel; *AmE* fɔːrˈtel/ *verb* (**fore·told, fore·told** /fɔːˈtəʊld; *AmE* fɔːrˈtoʊld/) (*literary*) to know or say what will happen in the future, especially by using magic powers **SYN** PREDICT: [VN] *to foretell the future* ◊ [V that] *The witch foretold that she would marry a prince.* ◊ [V wh-] *None of us can foretell what lies ahead.*

fore·thought /ˈfɔːθɔːt; *AmE* ˈfɔːrθ-/ *noun* [U] careful thought to make sure that things are successful in the future: *Some forethought and preparation is necessary before you embark on the project.* **IDM** see MALICE

fore·told *pt, pp* of FORETELL

for·ever /fərˈevə(r)/ *adv.* **1** (*BrE* also **for ever**) used to say that a particular situation or state will always exist: *I'll love you forever!* ◊ *After her death, their lives changed forever.* ◊ *Just keep telling yourself that it won't last forever.* **2** (*BrE* also **for ever**) (*informal*) a very long time: *It takes her forever to get dressed.* **3** (*spoken*) used with verbs in the progressive tenses to say that sb does sth very often and in a way that is annoying to other people: *She's forever going on about how poor they are.*

fore·warn /fɔːˈwɔːn; *AmE* fɔːrˈwɔːrn/ *verb* [often passive] ~ **sb (of sth)** (*written*) to warn sb about sth bad or unpleasant before it happens: [VN] *The commander had been forewarned of the attack.* [also VN that] ▶ **fore·warn·ing** *noun* [U, C] **IDM** **foreˌwarned is foreˈarmed** (*saying*) if you know about problems, dangers, etc. before they happen, you can be better prepared for them

fore·word /ˈfɔːwɜːd; *AmE* ˈfɔːrwɜːrd/ *noun* a short introduction at the beginning of a book—compare PREFACE

for·feit /ˈfɔːfɪt; *AmE* ˈfɔːrfət/ *verb, noun, adj.*

■ *verb* [VN] to lose sth or have sth taken away from you because you have done sth wrong: *If you cancel your flight, you will forfeit your deposit.* ◊ *He has forfeited his right to be taken seriously.*

■ *noun* something that a person has to pay, or sth that is taken from them, because they have done sth wrong

■ *adj.* [not before noun] (*formal*) taken away from sb as a punishment

for·feit·ure /ˈfɔːfɪtʃə(r); *AmE* ˈfɔːrfətʃər/ *noun* [U] (*law*) the act of forfeiting sth: *the forfeiture of property*

for·gather *verb* [V] = FOREGATHER

for·gave *pt* of FORGIVE

forge /fɔːdʒ; *AmE* fɔːrdʒ/ *verb, noun*

■ *verb* **1** [VN] to put a lot of effort into making sth successful or strong so that it will last: *a move to forge new links between management and workers* ◊ *Strategic alliances are being forged with major European companies.* ◊ *She forged a new career in the music business.* **2** [VN] to make an illegal copy of sth in order to deceive people: *to forge a passport/banknote/cheque* ◊ *He's getting good at forging his mother's signature.*—compare COUNTERFEIT **3** [VN] to shape metal by heating it in a fire and hitting it with a hammer; to make an object in this way: *swords forged from steel* **4** [V+adv./prep.] (*written*) to move forward in a

F

b	d	f	g	h	k	l	m	n	p	r
bad	did	fall	get	hat	cat	leg	man	now	pen	red

steady but powerful way: *He forged through the crowds to the front of the stage.* ◊ *She forged into the lead* (= in a competition, race, etc.). PHRV ¦forge a'head (with sth) to move forward quickly; to make a lot of progress quickly: *The company is forging ahead with its plans for expansion.* ◊ *Quick learners should be allowed to forge ahead.*

■ noun **1** a place where objects are made by heating and shaping pieces of metal, especially one where a BLACKSMITH works **2** a large piece of equipment used for heating metals in; a building or part of a factory where this is found

for·ger /'fɔːdʒə(r); AmE 'fɔːrdʒ-/ noun a person who makes illegal copies of money, documents, etc. in order to deceive people—compare COUNTERFEITER

for·gery /'fɔːdʒəri; AmE 'fɔːrdʒ-/ noun **1** [U] the crime of copying money, documents, etc. in order to deceive people **2** [C] something, for example a document, piece of paper money, etc., that has been copied in order to deceive people: *Experts are dismissing claims that the painting is a forgery.*—compare COUNTERFEIT

for·get /fə'get; AmE fər'g-/ verb (**for·got** /fə'gɒt; AmE fər'gɑːt/ **for·got·ten** /fə'gɒtn; AmE fər'gɑːtn/)

EVENTS/FACTS **1** ~ (about) sth (not usually used in the progressive tenses) to be unable to remember sth that has happened in the past or information that you knew in the past: [V] *I'd completely forgotten about the money he owed me.* ◊ *Before I forget, there was a call from Italy for you.* ◊ [VN] *I never forget a face.* ◊ *Who could forget his speech at last year's party?* ◊ [V(that)] *She keeps forgetting (that) I'm not a child any more.* ◊ *I was forgetting* (= I had forgotten) *(that) you've been here before.* ◊ [Vwh-] *I've forgotten where they live exactly.* ◊ *I forget how much they paid for it.* ◊ [V-ing] *I'll never forget hearing this piece of music for the first time.* ◊ [VNthat] *It should not be forgotten that people used to get much more exercise.* [alsoVN-ing]

TO DO STH **2** ~ (about) sth to not remember to do sth that you ought to do, or to bring or buy sth that you ought to bring or buy: [V] *'Why weren't you at the meeting?' 'Sorry—I forgot.'* ◊ [Vtoinf] *Take care, and don't forget to write.* ◊ *I forgot to ask him for his address.* ◊ [VN] *I forgot my purse* (= I did not remember to bring it). ◊ *'Hey, don't forget me* (= don't leave without me)*!'* ◊ *Aren't you forgetting something?* (= I think you have forgotten to do sth) HELP You cannot use **forget** if you want to mention the place where you have left something: *I've left my book at home.* ◊ *I've forgotten my book at home.*

STOP THINKING ABOUT STH **3** ~ (about) sb/sth to deliberately stop thinking about sb/sth: [V] *Try to forget about what happened.* ◊ *Could you possibly forget about work for five minutes?* ◊ [VN] *Forget him! Let's forget our differences and be friends.* ◊ [V(that)] *Forget (that) I said anything!* **4** ~ (about) sth to stop thinking that sth is a possibility: [V] *If I lose this job, we can forget about buying a new car.* ◊ [VN] *'I was hoping you might be able to lend me the money.' 'You can forget that!'*

YOURSELF **5** [VN] ~ yourself to behave in a way that is not socially acceptable: *I'm forgetting myself. I haven't offered you a drink yet!*

IDM **for'get it** (*spoken*) **1** used to tell sb that sth is not important and that they should not worry about it: *'I still owe you for lunch yesterday.' 'Forget it.'* **2** used to tell sb that you are not going to repeat what you said: *'Now, what were you saying about John?' 'Forget it, it doesn't matter.'* **3** used to emphasize that you are saying 'no' to sth: *'Any chance of you helping out here?' 'Forget it, I've got too much to do.'* **4** used to tell sb to stop talking about sth because they are annoying you: *Just forget it, will you!* **not forgetting …** (*BrE*) used to include sth in the list of things that you have just mentioned: *I share the house with Jim, Ian and Sam, not forgetting Spike, the dog.*—more at FORGIVE

for·get·ful /fə'getfl; AmE fər'g-/ adj. **1** often forgetting things: *She has become very forgetful in recent years.* **2** ~ of sb/sth (*formal*) not thinking about sb/sth that you should be thinking about ▶ **for·get·ful·ly** /-fəli/ adv. **for·get·ful·ness** noun [U]

for'get-me-not noun a small wild plant with light blue flowers

for·get·table /fə'getəbl; AmE fər'g-/ adj. not interesting or special and therefore easily forgotten: *an instantly forgettable tune* OPP UNFORGETTABLE

for·giv·able /fə'gɪvəbl; AmE fər'g-/ adj. that you can understand and forgive: *His rudeness was forgivable in the circumstances.* OPP UNFORGIVABLE

for·give /fə'gɪv; AmE fər'gɪv/ verb (**for·gave** /fə'geɪv; AmE fər'g-/, **for·given** /fə'gɪvn; AmE fər'g-/) **1** ~ sb/yourself (for sth/for doing sth) to stop feeling angry with sb who has done sth to harm, annoy or upset you; to stop feeling angry with yourself: [VN] *I'll never forgive her for what she did.* ◊ *I can't forgive that type of behaviour.* ◊ *I'd never forgive myself if she heard the truth from someone else.* ◊ [VNN] *She'd forgive him anything.* [alsoV] **2** ~ me (for doing sth) used to say in a polite way that you are sorry if what you are doing or saying seems rude or silly: [VN] *Forgive my ignorance, but what exactly does the company do?* ◊ *Forgive me, but I don't see that any of this concerns me.* ◊ *Forgive me for interrupting, but I really don't agree with that.* ◊ [VN-ing] *Forgive my interrupting but I really don't agree with that.* **3** (*formal*) (of a bank, country, etc.) to say that sb does not need to pay back money that they have borrowed: [VN] *The government has agreed to forgive a large part of the debt.* [alsoVNN] IDM **sb could/might be forgiven for doing sth** used to say that it is easy to understand why sb does or thinks sth, although they are wrong: *Looking at the crowds out shopping, you could be forgiven for thinking that everyone has plenty of money.* **for,give and for'get** to stop feeling angry with sb for sth they have done to you and to behave as if it had not happened

for·give·ness /fə'gɪvnəs; AmE fər'g-/ noun [U] the act of forgiving sb; willingness to forgive sb: *to pray for God's forgiveness* ◊ *the forgiveness of sins* ◊ *He begged forgiveness for what he had done.*

for·giv·ing /fə'gɪvɪŋ; AmE fər'g-/ adj. ~ (of sth) willing to forgive: *She had not inherited her mother's forgiving nature.* ◊ *The public was more forgiving of the president's difficulties than the press and fellow politicians.*

forgo (also **forego**) /fɔː'gəʊ; AmE fɔːr'goʊ/ verb (**for·went** /fɔː'went; AmE fɔːr'went/, **for·gone** /fɔː'gɒn; AmE fɔːr'gɔːn; -'gɑːn/) [VN] (*formal*) to decide not to have or do sth that you would like to have or do: *No one was prepared to forgo their lunch hour to attend the meeting.*

for·got pt of FORGET

for·got·ten pp of FORGET

fork /fɔːk; AmE fɔːrk/ noun, verb

■ noun **1** a tool with a handle and three or four sharp points, (called PRONGS), used for picking up and eating food: *to eat with a knife and fork*—picture at CUTLERY **2** a garden tool with a long or short handle and three or four sharp metal points, used for digging—see also PITCHFORK—picture at GARDEN **3** a place where a road, river, etc. divides into two parts; either of these two parts: *Shortly before dusk they reached a fork and took the left-hand track.* ◊ *Take the right fork.* **4** a thing shaped like a fork, with two or more long parts: *a jagged fork of lightning*—see also TUNING FORK **5** either of two metal supporting pieces into which a wheel on a bicycle or motorcycle is fitted—picture at BICYCLE

■ verb **1** [V] [often+adv. /prep.] (not used in the progressive tenses) (of a road, river, etc.) to divide into two parts that lead in different directions: *The path forks at the bottom of the hill.* ◊ *The road forks right after the bridge.* **2** [V+adv. /prep.] (not used in the progressive tenses) (of a person) to turn left or right where a road, river, etc. divides into two: *Fork right after the bridge.* **3** [VN] [often+adv./prep.] to move, carry or dig sth using a fork: *Clear the soil of weeds and fork in plenty of compost.* PHRV ¦fork 'out (for sth)¦ ¦fork 'out sth (for/on sth) (*informal*) to spend a lot of money on sth, especially unwillingly: *Why fork out for a taxi when there's a perfectly good bus service?* ◊ *We've forked out a small fortune on home improvements over the years.*

forked /fɔːkt; AmE fɔːrkt/ adj. with one end divided into

s	t	v	z	ʃ	ʒ	tʃ	dʒ	θ	ð	ŋ
see	tea	van	zoo	shoe	vision	chain	jam	thin	this	sing

two parts, like the shape of the letter 'Y': *a bird with a black and white forked tail* ◊ *the long forked tongue of a snake*—picture on page A7

,forked 'lightning *noun* [U] the type of LIGHTNING that is like a line that divides into smaller lines near the ground—compare SHEET LIGHTNING

fork·ful /'fɔːkfʊl; *AmE* 'fɔːrk-/ *noun* the amount that a fork holds

,fork-lift 'truck (also **'fork-lift**) *noun* a vehicle with special equipment on the front for moving and lifting heavy objects—picture at TRUCK

for·lorn /fə'lɔːn; *AmE* fər'lɔːrn/ *adj.* **1** (of a person) appearing lonely and unhappy: *She looked so forlorn, standing there in the pouring rain.* **2** (of a place) not cared for and with no people in it: *Empty houses quickly take on a forlorn look.* **3** unlikely to succeed, come true, etc: *She waited in the forlorn hope that he would one day come back to her.* ◊ *His father smiled weakly in a forlorn attempt to reassure him that everything was all right.* ► **for·lorn·ly** *adv.*

form /fɔːm; *AmE* fɔːrm/ *noun, verb*
■ *noun*
TYPE | **1** [C] a type or variety of sth: *forms of transport/ government/energy* ◊ *one of the most common forms of cancer* ◊ *Music is not like most other art forms.* ◊ *all the millions of different life forms on the planet today*
WAY STH IS/LOOKS | **2** [C, U] the particular way sth is, seems, looks or is presented: *The disease can take several different forms.* ◊ *Help in the form of money will be very welcome.* ◊ *Help arrived in the form of two police officers.* ◊ *The training programme takes the form of a series of workshops.* ◊ *Most political questions involve morality in some form or other.* ◊ *We need to come to some form of agreement.* ◊ *I'm opposed to censorship in any shape or form.* ◊ *This dictionary is also available in electronic form.*
DOCUMENT | **3** [C] an official document containing questions and spaces for answers: *an application/entry/order form* ◊ (*especially BrE*) *to fill in a form* ◊ (*especially AmE*) *to fill out a form* ◊ *to complete a form* ◊ (*BrE*) *a booking form* ◊ (*AmE*) *a reservation form*
SHAPE | **4** [C] the shape of sb/sth; a person or thing of which only the shape can be seen: *her slender form* ◊ *The human form has changed little over the last 30000 years.* ◊ *They made out a shadowy form in front of them.*
ARRANGEMENT OF PARTS | **5** [U] the arrangement of parts in a whole, especially in a work of art or piece of writing: *Shape and form are of greater importance to me than colour.* ◊ *In a novel form and content are equally important.*
BEING FIT/HEALTHY | **6** [U] (*BrE*) how fit and healthy sb is; the state of being fit and healthy: *After six months' training the whole team is in superb form.* ◊ *I really need to get back in form.* ◊ *The horse was clearly out of form.*
PERFORMANCE | **7** [U] how well sb/sth is performing; the fact that sb/sth is performing well: *Midfielder Elliott has shown disappointing form recently.* ◊ *On current/present form the party is heading for another election victory.* ◊ *Hingis signalled her return to form with a convincing victory.* ◊ *He's right on form* (= performing well) *as a crazy science teacher in his latest movie.* ◊ *The whole team was on good form and deserved the win.* ◊ *She was in great form* (= happy and cheerful and full of energy) *at the wedding party.*
WAY OF DOING THINGS | **8** [U, C] (*especially BrE*) the usual way of doing sth: *What's the form when you apply for a research grant?* ◊ *conventional social forms* ◊ *True to form* (= as he usually does) *he arrived an hour late.* ◊ *Partners of employees are invited as a matter of form.* **9** [U] (*good/ bad* ~) (*old-fashioned, BrE*) the way of doing things that is socially acceptable/not socially acceptable
IN SCHOOL | **10** (*BrE, old-fashioned*) a class in a school: *Who's your form teacher?*—see also SIXTH FORM **11** (- *former*) (in compounds) (*BrE, old-fashioned*) a student in the form mentioned at school: *a third-former*—see also SIXTH-FORMER
OF WORD | **12** [C] a way of writing or saying a word that

shows, for example, if it is plural or in a particular tense: *the infinitive form of the verb*
IDM **take 'form** (*formal*) to gradually form into a particular shape; to gradually develop: *In her body a new life was taking form.*—more at SHAPE *n.*, TRUE *adj.*
■ *verb*
START TO EXIST | **1** (especially of natural things) to begin to exist and gradually develop into a particular shape; to make sth begin to exist in a particular shape: [V] *Flowers appeared, but fruits failed to form.* ◊ *Storm clouds are forming on the horizon.* ◊ [VN] *These hills were formed by glaciation.* **2** to start to exist and develop; to make sth start to exist and develop: [V] *A plan formed in my head.* ◊ [VN] *I formed many close friendships at college.* ◊ *I didn't see enough of the play to form an opinion about it.*
MAKE SHAPE/FORM | **3** [VN] (often passive) ~ **sth (into sth)** | ~ **sth (from/of sth)** to produce sth in a particular way or make it have a particular shape: *Form the dough into balls with your hands.* ◊ *Bend the wire so that it forms a 'V'.* ◊ *Rearrange the letters to form a new word.* ◊ *Games can help children learn to form letters.* ◊ *Do you know how to form the past tense? The chain is formed from 136 links.* **4** ~ **(sb/sth) (up) (into sth)** to move or arrange objects or people so that they are in a group with a particular shape; to become arranged in a group like this: [VN] *to form a line/queue/circle* ◊ *First get students to form groups of three or four.* ◊ [V] *Queues were already forming outside the theatre.* ◊ *The teams formed up into lines.*
HAVE FUNCTION/ROLE | **5** [VN] to have a particular function or pattern: *The trees form a natural protection from the sun's rays.* **6** linking verb [V-N] to be sth: *The castle forms the focal point of the city.* ◊ *The survey formed part of a larger programme of research.* ◊ *These drawings will form the basis of the exhibition.*
ORGANIZATION | **7** to start a group of people, such as an organization, a committee, etc.; to come together in a group of this kind: [VN] *They hope to form the new government.* ◊ *He formed a band with some friends from school.* ◊ *a newly-formed political party* ◊ [V] *The band formed in 1998.*
HAVE INFLUENCE ON | **8** [VN] to have an influence on the way that sth develops: *Positive and negative experiences form a child's character.*

for·mal /'fɔːml; *AmE* 'fɔːrml/ *adj.* **1** (of a style of dress, speech, writing, behaviour, etc.) very correct and suitable for official or important occasions: *formal evening dress* ◊ *The dinner was a formal affair.* ◊ *He kept the tone of the letter formal and businesslike.* ◊ *She has a very formal manner, which can seem unfriendly.*—compare INFORMAL **2** official; following an agreed or official way of doing things: *formal legal processes* ◊ *to make a formal apology/complaint/request* ◊ *Formal diplomatic relations between the two countries were re-established in December.* ◊ *It is time to put these arrangements on a slightly more formal basis.* **3** (of education or training) received in a school, college or university, with lessons, exams, etc., rather than gained just through practical experience: *He has no formal teaching qualifications.* ◊ *Young children are beginning their formal education sometimes as early as four years old.* **4** concerned with the way sth is done rather than what is done: *Getting approval for the plan is a purely formal matter; nobody will seriously oppose it.* ◊ *Critics have concentrated too much on the formal elements of her poetry, without really looking at what it is saying.* **5** (of a garden, room or building) arranged in a regular manner, according to a clear, exact plan: *delightful formal gardens, with terraced lawns and an avenue of trees* ► **for·mal·ly** /-məli/ *adv.*: *'How do you do?' she said formally.* ◊ *The accounts were formally approved by the board.* ◊ *Although not formally trained as an art historian, he is widely respected for his knowledge of the period.*

for·mal·de·hyde /fɔː'mældɪhaɪd; *AmE* fɔːr'm-/ *noun* [U] **1** (*symb* **CH₂O**) a colourless gas with a strong smell **2** (also *technical* **for·mal·in** /'fɔːməlɪn; *AmE* 'fɔːrm-/) a liquid made by mixing formaldehyde and water, used for preserving BIOLOGICAL SPECIMENS, making plastics and as a DISINFECTANT

æ	ɑː	e	ɜː	ə	ɪ	iː	i	ɒ	ɔː	ʌ	ʊ	u	uː
cat	father	ten	bird	about	sit	see	many	got (BrE)	saw	cup	put	actual	too

for·mal·ism /'fɔːməlɪzəm; *AmE* 'fɔːrm-/ *noun* [U] a style or method in art, music, literature, science, etc. that pays more attention to the rules and the correct arrangement and appearance of things than to inner meaning and feelings ▶ **for·mal·ist** /'fɔːməlɪst; *AmE* 'fɔːrm-/ *noun* **for·mal·ist** *adj.* [usually before noun]: *formalist theory*

for·mal·ity /fɔː'mæləti; *AmE* fɔːr'm-/ *noun* (*pl.* -ies) **1** [C, usually pl.] a thing that you must do as a formal or official part of a legal process, a social situation, etc: *to go through all the formalities necessary in order to get a gun licence* ◊ *Let's skip the formalities and get down to business.* **2** [C, usually sing.] a thing that you must do as part of an official process, but which has little meaning and will not affect what happens: *He already knows he has the job so the interview is a mere formality.* **3** [U] correct and formal behaviour: *Different levels of formality are appropriate in different situations.* ◊ *She greeted him with stiff formality.*

for·mal·ize (*BrE* also **-ise**) /'fɔːməlaɪz; *AmE* 'fɔːrm-/ *verb* [VN] (*written*) **1** to make an arrangement, a plan or a relationship official: *They decided to formalize their relationship by getting married.* **2** to give sth a fixed structure or form by introducing rules: *The college has a highly formalized system of assessment.* ▶ **for·mal·iza·tion, -isa·tion** /ˌfɔːməlaɪ'zeɪʃn; *AmE* ˌfɔːrmələ'z-/ *noun* [U]

for·mat /'fɔːmæt; *AmE* 'fɔːrmæt/ *noun, verb*
■ *noun* **1** the general arrangement, plan, design, etc. of sth: *The format of the new quiz show has proved popular.* **2** the shape and size of a book, magazine, etc: *They've brought out the magazine in a new format.* **3** (*computing*) the way in which data is stored or held for PROCESSING by a computer
■ *verb* (**-tt-**) [VN] **1** to prepare a computer disk so that data can be recorded on it **2** (*technical*) to arrange text in a particular way on a page or a screen

for·ma·tion /fɔː'meɪʃn; *AmE* fɔːr'm-/ *noun* **1** [U] the action of forming sth; the process of being formed: *An agreement on the formation of a new government was reached on June 6.* ◊ *evidence of recent star formation in the galaxy* **2** [C] a thing that has been formed, especially in a particular place or in a particular way: *massive rock formations* **3** [U, C] a particular arrangement or pattern: *aircraft flying in formation* ◊ *formation flying/dancing* ◊ *Flying low across the river was a formation of swans—five of them at least.*

for·ma·tive /'fɔːmətɪv; *AmE* 'fɔːrm-/ *adj.* [only before noun] having an important and lasting influence on the development of sth or of sb's character: *the formative years of childhood* ◊ *formative influences in the development of the labour movement*

for·mer /'fɔːmə(r); *AmE* 'fɔːrm-/ *adj.* [only before noun] **1** that used to exist in earlier times: *in former times* ◊ *the countries of the former Soviet Union* ◊ *This beautiful old building has been restored to its former glory.* **2** that used to have a particular position or status in the past: *the former world champion* ◊ *my former boss/colleague/wife* **3** (**the former ...**) used to refer to the first of two things or people mentioned: *The former option would be much more sensible.*—compare LATTER **4** (**the former**) *pron.* the first of two things or people mentioned: *He had to choose between giving up his job and giving up his principles. He chose the former.*—compare LATTER **IDM** **be a shadow/ghost of your former 'self** to not have the strength, influence, etc. that you used to have

for·mer·ly /'fɔːməli; *AmE* 'fɔːrmərli/ *adv.* in earlier times **SYN** PREVIOUSLY: *Namibia, formerly known as South West Africa* ◊ *I learnt that the house had formerly been an inn.* ◊ *John Marsh, formerly of London Road, Leicester, now living in France*

For·mica™ /fɔː'maɪkə; *AmE* fɔːr'm-/ *noun* [U] a hard plastic that can resist heat, used for covering work surfaces, etc.

for·mid·able /'fɔːmɪdəbl; fə'mɪd-; *AmE* 'fɔːrm-; fər'm-/ *adj.* if people, things or situations are **formidable**, you feel fear and/or respect for them, because they are impressive or powerful, or because they seem very difficult: *In debate he was a formidable opponent.* ◊ *She has a formidable list of qualifications.* ◊ *The two players together make a formidable combination.* ◊ *The task was a formidable one.* ◊ *They had to overcome formidable obstacles.* ▶ **for·mid·ably** /-əbli/ *adv.*: *He now has the chance to prove himself in a formidably difficult role.* ◊ *She's formidably intelligent.*

form·less /'fɔːmləs; *AmE* 'fɔːrm-/ *adj.* (*written*) without a clear or definite shape or structure: *formless dreams* ◊ *a formless landscape, thickly blanketed with snow* ▶ **form·less·ness** *noun* [U]

for·mula /'fɔːmjələ/ *noun* (*pl.* **for·mu·las** or, especially in scientific use, **for·mu·lae** /-liː/) **1** [C] (*mathematics*) a series of letters, numbers or symbols that represent a rule or law: *The formula πr^2 is used to calculate the area of a circle.* **2** [C] (*chemistry*) letters and symbols that show the parts of a chemical compound, etc: *CO is the formula for carbon monoxide.* **3** [C] **~ (for sth/for doing sth)** a particular method of doing or achieving sth: *They're trying to work out a **peace formula** acceptable to both sides in the dispute.* ◊ *There's no **magic formula** for a perfect marriage.* **4** [C] a list of the things that sth is made from, giving the amount of each substance to use: *the secret formula for the blending of the whisky* **5** (also **'formula milk**) [U, C] (*especially AmE*) a type of liquid food for babies, given instead of breast milk **6** (**Formula One, Two, Three etc.**) [U] a class of racing car, based on engine size, etc: *Formula One racing* **7** [C] a fixed form of words used in a particular situation: *legal formulae* ◊ *The minister keeps coming out with the same tired formulas.*

for·mu·la·ic /ˌfɔːmju'leɪɪk; *AmE* ˌfɔːrm-/ *adj.* (*formal*) made up of fixed patterns of words or ideas: *Traditional stories make use of formulaic expressions like 'Once upon a time ...'.*

for·mu·late /'fɔːmjuleɪt; *AmE* 'fɔːrm-/ *verb* **1** to create or prepare sth carefully, giving particular attention to the details: [VN] *to formulate a policy/theory/plan/proposal* ◊ *The compost is specially formulated for pot plants.* ◊ [VN to inf] *This new kitchen cleaner is formulated to cut through grease and dirt.* **2** [VN] to express your ideas in carefully chosen words: *She has lots of good ideas, but she has difficulty formulating them.* ◊ *He struggled to formulate an answer.* ▶ **for·mu·la·tion** /ˌfɔːmju'leɪʃn; *AmE* ˌfɔːrm-/ *noun* [U, C]: *the formulation of new policies*

for·ni·cate /'fɔːnɪkeɪt; *AmE* 'fɔːrn-/ *verb* [V] (*formal, disapproving*) to have sex with sb that you are not married to ▶ **for·ni·ca·tion** /ˌfɔːnɪ'keɪʃn; *AmE* ˌfɔːrn-/ *noun* [U] **for·ni·ca·tor** *noun*

for·sake /fə'seɪk; *AmE* fər's-/ *verb* (**for·sook** /fə'sʊk; *AmE* fər's-/, **for·saken** /fə'seɪkən; *AmE* fər's-/) [VN] **~ sb/sth (for sb/sth)** (*literary*) **1** to leave sb/sth, especially when you have a responsibility to stay: *He had made it clear to his wife that he would never forsake her.* **2** to stop doing sth, or leave sth, especially sth that you enjoy: *She forsook the glamour of the city and went to live in the wilds of Scotland.*—see also GODFORSAKEN

for·swear /fɔː'sweə(r); *AmE* fɔːr'swer/ *verb* (**for·swore** /fɔː'swɔː(r); *AmE* fɔːr's-/, **for·sworn** /fɔː'swɔːn; *AmE* fɔːr'swɔːrn/) [VN] (*formal* or *literary*) to stop doing or using sth; to make a promise that you will stop doing or using sth: *The group forswears all worldly possessions.* ◊ *The country has not forsworn the use of chemical weapons.*

for·sythia /fɔː'saɪθiə; *AmE* fər'sɪθiə/ *noun* [U, C] a bush that has small bright yellow flowers in the early spring

fort /fɔːt; *AmE* fɔːrt/ *noun* a building or buildings built in order to defend an area against attack: *the remains of a Roman fort* **IDM** **hold the 'fort** (*BrE*) (*AmE* **hold down the 'fort**) (*spoken*) to have the responsibility for sth or care of sb while other people are away or out: *Why not have a day off? I'll hold the fort for you.*

forte /'fɔːteɪ; *AmE* fɔːrt/ *noun, adv.*
■ *noun* [sing.] a thing that sb does particularly well: *Languages were never my forte.*
■ *adv.* (*abbr.* **f**) (*music*) played or sung loudly **OPP** PIANO ▶ **forte** *adj.*

forth /fɔːθ; *AmE* fɔːrθ/ *adv.* (*literary* except in particular idioms and phrasal verbs) **1** away from a place; out: *They set forth at dawn.* ◊ *Huge chimneys belched forth smoke*

aɪ	aʊ	eɪ	əʊ	oʊ	ɔɪ	ɪə	eə	ʊə	j	w
my	now	say	go (BrE)	go (AmE)	boy	near	hair	pure	yes	wet

and grime. **2** towards a place; forwards: *Water gushed forth from a hole in the rock.*—see also BRING FORTH **IDM** **from that day/time** **'forth** (*literary*) beginning on that day; from that time—more at BACK *adv.*, SO *adv.*

forth·com·ing /ˌfɔːθˈkʌmɪŋ; *AmE* ˌfɔːrθ-/ *adj.* **1** [only before noun] going to happen, be published, etc. very soon: *the forthcoming elections ◊ a list of forthcoming books ◊ the band's forthcoming UK tour* **2** [not before noun] ready or made available when needed: *Financial support was not forthcoming.* **3** [not before noun] willing to give information about sth: *She's never very forthcoming about her plans.* **OPP** UNFORTHCOMING

forth·right /ˈfɔːθraɪt; *AmE* ˈfɔːrθ-/ *adj.* direct and honest in manner and speech: *a woman of forthright views ◊ He spoke in a forthright manner but without anger.* ▶ **forth·right·ly** *adv.* **forth·right·ness** *noun* [U]

forth·with /ˌfɔːθˈwɪθ; -ˈwɪð; *AmE* ˌfɔːrθ-/ *adv.* (*formal*) immediately; at once: *The agreement between us is terminated forthwith.*

for·ti·eth ⇨ FORTY

for·ti·fi·ca·tion /ˌfɔːtɪfɪˈkeɪʃn; *AmE* ˌfɔːrt-/ *noun* **1** [C, usually pl.] a tower, wall, gun position, etc. built to defend a place against attack: *the ramparts and fortifications of the Old Town* **2** [U] the act of fortifying or strengthening sth: *plans for the fortification of the city*

for·tify /ˈfɔːtɪfaɪ; *AmE* ˈfɔːrt-/ *verb* (**for·ti·fies**, **for·ti·fy·ing**, **for·ti·fied**, **for·ti·fied**) [VN] **1 ~ sth (against sb/sth)** to strengthen a place against attack, especially by building high walls: *a fortified town ◊ They fortified the area against attack.* **2 ~ sb/yourself (against sb/sth)** to make sb/yourself feel stronger, braver, etc: *He fortified himself against the cold with a stiff brandy.* **3** to make a feeling or an attitude stronger: *The news merely fortified their determination.* **4 ~ sth (with sth)** to increase the strength or quality of food or drink by adding sth to it: *Sherry is fortified wine* (= wine with extra alcohol added). *◊ cereal fortified with extra vitamins*

for·tis·simo /fɔːˈtɪsɪməʊ; *AmE* fɔːrˈtɪsɪmoʊ/ *adv.* (*abbr.* ff) (*music*) played or sung very loudly **OPP** PIANISSIMO ▶ **for·tis·simo** *adj.*

for·ti·tude /ˈfɔːtɪtjuːd; *AmE* ˈfɔːrtətuːd/ *noun* [U] (*formal*) courage shown by sb who is suffering great pain or facing great difficulties: *She endured her illness with great fortitude.*

fort·night /ˈfɔːtnaɪt; *AmE* ˈfɔːrt-/ *noun* [usually sing.] (*BrE*) two weeks: *a fortnight's holiday ◊ a fortnight ago ◊ in a fortnight's time ◊ He's had three accidents in the past fortnight.*

fort·night·ly /ˈfɔːtnaɪtli; *AmE* ˈfɔːrt-/ *adj.* (*BrE*) happening once a fortnight: *Meetings take place at fortnightly intervals.* ▶ **fort·night·ly** *adv.*: *The committee meets fortnightly.*

fort·ress /ˈfɔːtrəs; *AmE* ˈfɔːrt-/ *noun* a building or a place that has been strengthened and protected against attack: *a fortress town enclosed by four miles of ramparts ◊ Fear of terrorist attack has turned the conference centre into a fortress.*

for·tuit·ous /fɔːˈtjuːɪtəs; *AmE* fɔːrˈtuː-/ *adj.* (*formal*) happening by chance, especially a lucky chance that brings a good result: *a fortuitous meeting ◊ His success depended on a fortuitous combination of circumstances.* ▶ **for·tuit·ous·ly** *adv.*

for·tu·nate /ˈfɔːtʃənət; *AmE* ˈfɔːrtʃ-/ *adj.* ~ **(to do sth)** | ~ **(in having ...)** | ~ **(for sb)(that ...)** having or bringing an advantage, an opportunity, a piece of good luck, etc. **SYN** LUCKY: *I have been fortunate enough to visit many parts of the world as a lecturer. ◊ I was fortunate in having a good teacher. ◊ Remember those less fortunate than yourselves. ◊ It was very fortunate for him that I arrived on time.* **OPP** UNFORTUNATE

for·tu·nate·ly /ˈfɔːtʃənətli; *AmE* ˈfɔːrtʃ-/ *adv.* by good luck **SYN** LUCKILY: *I was late, but fortunately the meeting hadn't started. ◊ Fortunately for him, he was very soon offered another job.* **OPP** UNFORTUNATELY

for·tune /ˈfɔːtʃuːn; *AmE* ˈfɔːrtʃ-/ *noun* **1** [U] chance or luck, especially in the way it affects people's lives: *I have had the good fortune to work with some brilliant direct-*

ors. *◊ By a stroke of fortune he found work almost immediately. ◊ Fortune smiled on me* (= I had good luck). **2** [C] a large amount of money: *He made a fortune in real estate. ◊ She inherited a share of the family fortune. ◊ A car like that costs a small fortune. ◊ You don't have to spend a fortune to give your family tasty, healthy meals. ◊ She is hoping her US debut will be the first step on the road to* ***fame and fortune***. *◊ That ring must be* ***worth a fortune***. **3** [C, usually pl., U] the good and bad things that happen to a person, family, country, etc: *the changing fortunes of the film industry ◊ the fortunes of war ◊ a reversal of fortune(s)* **4** [C] a person's fate or future: *She can* ***tell*** *your* ***fortune*** *by looking at the lines on your hand.* **IDM** see HOSTAGE, SEEK—see also SOLDIER OF FORTUNE

'fortune cookie *noun* a thin hollow biscuit/cookie, served in Chinese restaurants, containing a short message that predicts what will happen to you in the future

'fortune teller *noun* a person who claims to have magic powers and who tells people what will happen to them in the future

forty /ˈfɔːti; *AmE* ˈfɔːrti/ **1** *number* 40 **2** *noun* (**the for·ties**) [pl.] numbers, years or temperatures from 40 to 49 ▶ **for·tieth** /ˈfɔːtiəθ; *AmE* ˈfɔːrt-/ *ordinal number* **IDM** **in your forties** between the ages of 40 and 49

forty 'winks *noun* [pl.] (*informal*) a short sleep, especially during the day: *I'll feel much better when I've had forty winks.*

forum /ˈfɔːrəm/ *noun* **1 ~ (for sth)** a place where people can exchange opinions and ideas on a particular issue; a meeting organized for this purpose: *Television is now an important forum for political debate. ◊ to hold an international forum on drug abuse* **2** (in ancient Rome) a public place where meetings were held

for·ward /ˈfɔːwəd; *AmE* ˈfɔːrwərd/ *adv., adj., verb, noun*
■ *adv.* **1** (also **for·wards** especially in *BrE*) towards a place or position that is in front: *She leaned forward and kissed him on the cheek. ◊ He took two steps forward. ◊ They ran forward to welcome her.* **OPP** BACK, BACKWARDS **2** towards a good result: *We consider this agreement to be an important step forward. ◊ Cutting our costs is the only way forward. ◊ We are not getting any further forward with the discussion. ◊ The project will go forward* (= continue) *as planned.* **OPP** BACKWARDS **3** towards the future; ahead in time: *Looking forward, we hope to expand our operations in several of our overseas branches. ◊ The next scene takes the story forward five years. ◊* (*old use*) *from this day forward* **4** earlier; sooner: *It was decided to bring the meeting forward two weeks.* **5** (*technical*) in or towards the front part of a ship or plane: *The main cabin is situated forward of* (= in front of) *the mast.*—see also LOOK FORWARD, PUT FORWARD **IDM** see BACKWARDS, CLOCK *n.*, FOOT *n.*
■ *adj.* **1** [only before noun] directed or moving towards the front: *The door opened, blocking his forward movement. ◊ a forward pass* (for example in football) **2** [only before noun] (*technical*) situated in front, especially on a ship, plane or other vehicle: *the forward cabins ◊ A bolt may have fallen off the plane's forward door.* **3** relating to the future: *the forward movement of history ◊ A little* ***forward planning*** *at the outset can save you a lot of expense. ◊ The plans are still* ***no further forward*** *than they were last month.* **4** behaving towards sb in a manner which is too confident or too informal: *I hope you don't think I'm being too forward.*—compare BACKWARD
■ *verb* **1 ~ sth (to sb)** | ~ **(sb) sth** (*formal*) to send or pass goods or information to sb: [VN, VNN] *We will be forwarding our new catalogue to you next week. ◊ We will be forwarding you our new catalogue next week.* **2** [VN] to **forward** *a request/complaint/proposal* **2** [VN] ~ **sth (to sb)** to send a letter, etc. received at the address a person used to live at to their new address: *Could you forward any mail to us in New York? ◊ I put 'please forward' on the envelope.* **3** [VN] (*formal*) to help to improve or develop sth **SYN** FURTHER: *He saw the assignment as a way to forward his career. ◊ She uses various devices to forward the plot.*—see also FAST FORWARD
■ *noun* an attacking player whose position is near the front of a team in football, hockey, etc.—compare BACK

b	d	f	g	h	k	l	m	n	p	r
bad	did	fall	get	hat	cat	leg	man	now	pen	red

'forwarding address *noun* a new address to which letters should be sent on from an old address that sb has moved away from

'forward-looking *adj.* (*approving*) planning for the future; willing to consider modern ideas and methods: *a forward-looking company* ◊ *We need someone dynamic and forward-looking.*

for·ward·ness /'fɔːwədnəs; *AmE* 'fɔːrwərd-/ *noun* [U] behaviour that is too confident or too informal

for·went *pt* of FORGO

fos·sil /'fɒsl; *AmE* 'fɑːsl/ *noun* **1** the remains of an animal or a plant which have become hard and turned into rock: *superbly preserved fossils over two million years old* **2** (*informal, disapproving*) an old person, especially one who is unable to accept new ideas or adapt to changes

'fossil fuel *noun* [C, U] fuel such as coal or oil, that was formed over millions of years from the remains of animals or plants: *Carbon dioxide is produced in huge amounts when fossil fuels are burned.*

fos·sil·ize (*BrE* also **-ise**) /'fɒsəlaɪz; *AmE* 'fɑːs-/ *verb* **1** [usually passive] to become or make sth become a fossil: [VN] *fossilized bones* [also V] **2** [V, VN] (*disapproving*) to become, or make sb/sth become, fixed and unable to change or develop ▶ **fos·sil·iza·tion, -isa·tion** /ˌfɒsəlaɪˈzeɪʃn; *AmE* ˌfɑːsələˈz-/ *noun* [U]

fos·ter /'fɒstə(r); *AmE* 'fɔːs-; 'fɑːs-/ *verb, adj.*

■ *verb* **1** [VN] (*written*) to encourage sth to develop: *The club's aim is to foster better relations within the community.* **2** (*especially BrE*) to take another person's child into your home for a period of time, without becoming his or her legal parents: [VN] *They have fostered over 60 children during the past ten years.* ◊ [V] *We couldn't adopt a child, so we decided to foster.*—compare ADOPT

■ *adj.* [only before noun] used with some nouns in connection with the fostering of a child: *a foster mother / father / family* ◊ *foster parents* ◊ *a foster child* ◊ *a foster home* ◊ *foster care*

fought *pt, pp* of FIGHT

foul /faʊl/ *adj., verb, noun*

■ *adj.* (**foul·er, foul·est**) **1** dirty and smelling bad: *foul air / breath* ◊ *a foul-smelling prison* ◊ *Foul drinking water was blamed for the epidemic.* **2** (*especially BrE*) very unpleasant; very bad: *She's in a foul mood.* ◊ *His boss has a foul temper.* ◊ *This tastes foul.* **3** (of language) including rude words and swearing SYN OFFENSIVE: *foul language* ◊ *He called her the foulest names imaginable.* ◊ *I'm sick of her foul mouth* (= habit of swearing). **4** (of weather) very bad, with strong winds and rain: *a foul night* **5** (*literary*) very evil or wicked: *a foul crime / murder* ▶ **foul·ly** /'faʊlli/ *adv.*: *He swore foully.* ◊ *She had been foully murdered during the night.* **foul·ness** *noun* [U]: *The air was heavy with the stink of damp and foulness.* IDM **fall foul of 'sb/ 'sth** to get into trouble with a person or an organization because of doing sth wrong or illegal: *to fall foul of the law*—more at FAIR *adj.*, CRY *v.*

■ *verb* **1** [VN] (in sport) to do sth to another player that is against the rules of the game: *He was fouled inside the penalty area.* **2** [V, VN] (in baseball) to hit the ball outside the playing area **3** [VN] to make sth dirty, usually with waste material: *Do not permit your dog to foul the grass.* **4** ~ (**sth**) (**up**) to become caught or twisted in sth and stop it working or moving: [VN] *The rope fouled the propeller.* ◊ [V] *A rope fouled up* (= became twisted) *as we pulled the sail down.* PHRV **foul 'up** (*informal*) to make a lot of mistakes; to do sth badly: *I've fouled up badly again, haven't I?*—related noun FOUL-UP **foul sth↔'up** (*informal*) to spoil sth, especially by doing sth wrong—related noun FOUL-UP

■ *noun* (in sport) an action that is against the rules of the game: *It was a clear foul by Ford on the goalkeeper.* ◊ (*AmE*) *to hit a foul* (= in baseball, a ball that is too far left or right, outside the lines that mark the side of the field)—see also PROFESSIONAL FOUL

ˌfoul·'mouthed *adj.* using rude, offensive language: *a foul-mouthed racist*

ˌfoul 'play *noun* [U] **1** criminal or violent activity that causes sb's death: *Police immediately began an investiga-*

tion, but did not suspect foul play (= did not suspect that the person had been murdered). **2** (*BrE*) dishonest or unfair behaviour, especially during a sports game

'foul-up *noun* (*informal*) a problem caused by bad organization or a stupid mistake: *There was a computer foul-up at the bank and customers were sent the wrong statements.*

found /faʊnd/ *verb* [VN] **1** to start sth, such as an organization or an institution, especially by providing money: *to found a club / company* ◊ *Her family founded the college in 1895.* **2** to be the first to start building and living in a town or country: *The town was founded by English settlers in 1790.* **3** [usually passive] ~ **sth** (**on sth**) to base sth on sth: *Their marriage was founded on love and mutual respect.*—see also ILL-FOUNDED, WELL FOUNDED, UNFOUNDED **4** (*technical*) to melt metal and pour it into a MOULD; to make objects using this process—see also FIND *v.*

foun·da·tion /faʊnˈdeɪʃn/ *noun* **1** [C, usually pl.] a layer of bricks, CONCRETE, etc. that forms the solid underground base of a building: *The builders are now beginning to lay the foundations of the new school.* ◊ *The explosion shook the foundations of the houses nearby.* **2** [C, U] a principle, an idea or a fact that sth is based on and that it grows from: *Respect and friendship provide a solid foundation for marriage.* ◊ *The rumour is totally without foundation* (= not based on any facts). ◊ *These stories have no foundation* (= are not based on any facts). **3** [C] an organization that is established to provide money for a particular purpose, for example for scientific research or charity: *The money will go to the San Francisco AIDS Foundation.* **4** [U] the act of starting a new institution or organization: *The organization has grown enormously since its foundation in 1955.* **5** [U] a skin-coloured cream that is put on the face underneath other MAKE-UP IDM **shake / rock the 'foundations of sth | shake / rock sth to its 'foundations** to cause people to question their basic beliefs about sth: *This issue has shaken the foundations of French politics.*

foun'dation course *noun* (*BrE*) a general course at a college that prepares students for longer or more difficult courses

foun'dation stone *noun* a large block of stone that is put at the base of an important new public building in a special ceremony: *to lay the foundation stone of the new museum*

foun·der /'faʊndə(r)/ *noun, verb*

■ *noun* a person who starts an organization, institution, etc. or causes sth to be built: *the founder and president of the company*

■ *verb* [V] ~ (**on sth**) (*written*) **1** (of a plan, etc.) to fail because of a particular problem or difficulty: *The project foundered after problems with funding.* ◊ *The peace talks foundered on a basic lack of trust.* **2** (of a ship) to fill with water and sink: *Our boat foundered on a reef.*

ˌfounder 'member (*BrE*) (*AmE* ˌcharter 'member) *noun* one of the first members of a society, an organization, etc., especially one who helped start it

ˌfounding 'father *noun* **1** (*formal*) a person who starts or develops a new movement, institution or idea: *one of the founding fathers of modern psychology* **2** (**Founding Father**) a member of the group of people who wrote the Constitution of the US in 1787

found·ling /'faʊndlɪŋ/ *noun* (*old-fashioned*) a baby who has been left by its parents and who is found and looked after by sb else

foun·dry /'faʊndri/ *noun* (*pl.* **-ies**) a factory where metal or glass is melted and made into different shapes or objects: *an iron foundry* ◊ *foundry workers*

fount /faʊnt/ *noun* ~ (**of sth**) (*literary or humorous*) the place where sth important comes from SYN SOURCE: *She treats him as if he were the fount of all knowledge.*

foun·tain /'faʊntən; *AmE* 'faʊntn/ *noun* **1** a structure from which water is pumped up into the air, found as an ornament in parks and gardens / yards—see also DRINKING FOUNTAIN **2** a strong flow of liquid or of another substance that is forced into the air: *The amplifier exploded in a fountain of sparks.* **3** a rich source or supply of sth: *Tourism is a fountain of wealth for the city.*

s	t	v	z	ʃ	ʒ	tʃ	dʒ	θ	ð	ŋ
see	tea	van	zoo	shoe	vision	chain	jam	thin	this	sing

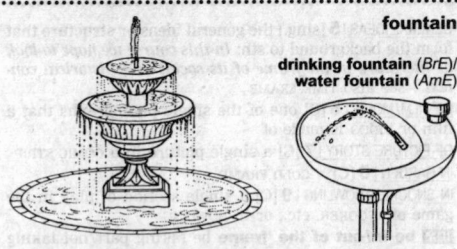

fountain

drinking fountain (BrE)/
water fountain (AmE)

'fountain pen *noun* a pen with a container that you fill with ink that flows to a NIB—picture at STATIONERY

four /fɔː(r)/ **1** *number* 4 HELP There are examples of how to use numbers at the entry for **five**. **2** *noun* a group of four people or things: *to make up a four at tennis* ◇ *a coach and four* (= four horses) **3** *noun* (in cricket) a shot that scores four RUNS **4** *noun* a team of four people who row a long narrow boat in races; the boat that they row IDM **on all 'fours** (of a person) bent over with hands and knees on the ground: *We were crawling around on all fours.* **these four 'walls** used when you are talking about keeping sth secret: *Don't let this go further than these four walls* (= Don't tell anyone else who is not in the room now).

four-by-'four (also **4x4**) *noun* (*AmE*) a vehicle with FOUR-WHEEL DRIVE (= a system in which power is given to all four wheels)

four-fold /'fɔːfəʊld; *AmE* 'fɔːrfoʊld/ *adj., adv.* ⇨ -FOLD

four-letter 'word *noun* a short word that is considered rude or offensive, especially because it refers to sex or other functions of the body: *The play is full of four-letter words.*

four-poster 'bed (also **four-'poster**) *noun* a large bed with a tall post at each of the four corners, a cover over the top and curtains around the sides—picture at BED

four-some /'fɔːsəm; *AmE* 'fɔːrsəm/ *noun* a group of four people taking part in a social activity or sport together: *Can you make up a foursome for tennis tomorrow?*

four-'square *adj.* **1** (of a building) square in shape, solid and strong **2** (of a person) firm, steady and determined ▶ **four-'square** *adv.*: *I stand four-square with the President on this issue.*

four-teen /ˌfɔːˈtiːn; *AmE* ˌfɔːrˈt-/ *number* 14 ▶ **four-teenth** /ˌfɔːˈtiːnθ; *AmE* ˌfɔːrˈt-/ *ordinal number*

fourth /fɔːθ; *AmE* fɔːrθ/ *ordinal number, noun*
  ■ *ordinal number* 4th HELP There are examples of how to use ordinal numbers at the entry for **fifth**.
  ■ *noun* (especially *AmE*) = QUARTER

the ˌfourth diˈmension *noun* [sing.] **1** (used by scientists and writers of SCIENCE FICTION) time **2** an experience that is outside normal human experience

the ˌfourth eˈstate *noun* [sing.] newspapers and journalists in general and the political influence that they have SYN THE PRESS

fourth-ly /'fɔːθli; *AmE* 'fɔːrθ-/ *adv.* used to introduce the fourth of a list of points you want to make in a speech or a piece of writing: *Fourthly, I should like to mention ...*

the ˌFourth of Juˈly *noun* [sing.] a national holiday in the US when people celebrate the anniversary of the Declaration of Independence in 1776—see also INDEPENDENCE DAY

four-wheel 'drive *noun* a system in which power is applied to all four wheels of a vehicle, making it easier to control; a vehicle with this system: *a car with four-wheel drive* ◇ *We rented a four-wheel drive to get around the island.*—see also ATV, FOUR-BY-FOUR—picture at CAR

four-'wheeler *noun* a vehicle with four-wheel drive—see also ATV

fowl /faʊl/ *noun* **1** [C, U] (*pl.* **fowl** or **fowls**) a bird that is kept for its meat and eggs, for example a chicken: *a variety of domestic fowl* **2** [C] (*old use*) any bird—see also GUINEAFOWL, WATERFOWL, WILDFOWL IDM See FISH *n.*

fox /fɒks; *AmE* fɑːks/ *noun, verb*

  ■ *noun* **1** [C] a wild animal of the dog family, with reddish-brown fur, a pointed face and a thick heavy tail—see also FLYING FOX, VIXEN **2** [U] the skin and fur of the fox, used to make coats, etc. **3** [C] (often *disapproving*) a person who is clever and able to get what they want by influencing or tricking other people: *He's a wily old fox.*
  ■ *verb* [VN] (*informal, especially BrE*) to be too difficult for sb to understand or solve; to trick or confuse sb: *The last question foxed even our panel of experts.*

fox-glove /'fɒksɡlʌv; *AmE* 'fɑːks-/ *noun* [C, U] a tall plant with purple or white flowers shaped like bells growing up its stem

fox-hole /'fɒkshəʊl; *AmE* 'fɑːkshoʊl/ *noun* a hole in the ground that soldiers use as a shelter against the enemy or as a place to fire back from—compare HOLE

fox-hound /'fɒkshaʊnd; *AmE* 'fɑːks-/ *noun* a dog with a very good sense of smell, that is trained to hunt FOXES

fox-hunting (*BrE* also **hunt-ing**) *noun* [U] a sport in which FOXES are hunted by specially trained dogs and by people on horses: *to go fox-hunting*

fox-trot /'fɒkstrɒt; *AmE* 'fɑːkstrɑːt/ *noun* a formal dance for two people together, with both small fast steps and longer slow ones; a piece of music for this dance

foxy /'fɒksi; *AmE* 'fɑːksi/ *adj.* **1** like a FOX in appearance **2** (*informal, especially AmE*) (of a woman) sexually attractive **3** clever at tricking others SYN CUNNING

foyer /'fɔɪeɪ; *AmE* 'fɔɪər/ *noun* **1** a large open space inside the entrance of a theatre or hotel where people can meet or wait SYN LOBBY: *I'll meet you in the foyer at 7 o'clock.* **2** (*AmE*) an entrance hall in a private house or flat/apartment

Fr (also **Fr.** especially in *AmE*) *abbr.* Father (used in front of the name of some Christian priests): *Fr (Paul) O'Connor*

fra-cas /'frækɑː; *AmE* 'freɪkəs/ *noun* (*pl.* **fra-cas** /-kɑːz/, *AmE* **fra-cases**) [usually sing.] a noisy argument or fight, usually involving several people: *a fracas between the supporters of the two teams*

frac-tion /'frækʃn/ *noun* **1** a small part or amount of sth: *Only a small fraction of a bank's total deposits will be withdrawn at any one time.* ◇ *She hesitated for the merest fraction of a second.* HELP If **fraction** is used with a plural noun, the verb is usually plural: *Only a fraction of cars in the UK use leaded petrol.* If it is used with a singular noun that represents a group of people, the verb can be singular or plural in *BrE*, but is usually singular in *AmE*: *A tiny fraction of the population never vote/votes.* **2** a division of a number, for example ⅝—see also VULGAR FRACTION—compare INTEGER ⇨ Appendix 3

frac-tion-al /'frækʃənl/ *adj.* **1** (*written*) very small; not important: *a fractional decline in earnings* **2** (*mathematics*) of or in fractions: *a fractional equation*

frac-tion-al-ly /'frækʃənəli/ *adv.* to a very small degree: *He was just fractionally ahead at the finishing line.*

frac-tious /'frækʃəs/ *adj.* (*especially BrE*) **1** bad-tempered or easily upset, especially by small things: *Children often get fractious and tearful when tired.* **2** (*written*) making trouble and complaining: *The six fractious republics are demanding autonomy.*

frac-ture /'fræktʃə(r)/ *noun, verb*
  ■ *noun* **1** a break in a bone or other hard material: *a fracture of the leg/skull* ◇ *a compound/simple fracture* (= one in which the broken bone comes/does not come through the skin) **2** [U] the fact of sth breaking, especially a bone: *Old people's bones are more prone to fracture.*
  ■ *verb* **1** to break or crack; to make sth break or crack: [V] *His leg fractured in two places.* ◇ [VN] *She fell and fractured her skull.* ◇ *a fractured pipeline* **2** (*formal*) (of a society, organization, etc.) to split into several parts so that it no longer functions or exists; to split a society or organization, etc. in this way: [V] *Many people predicted that the party would fracture and split.* ◇ [VN] *The company was fractured into several smaller groups.* ▶ **frac-tured** *adj.* [usually before noun]: *He suffered a badly fractured arm.* ◇ (*figurative*) *They spoke a sort of fractured German.*

F

fra·gile /ˈfrædʒaɪl; *AmE* -dʒl/ *adj.* **1** easily broken or damaged: *fragile china/glass/bones* **2** weak and uncertain; easily destroyed or spoilt: *a fragile alliance/ceasefire/relationship* ◇ *The economy remains extremely fragile.* **3** delicate and often beautiful: *fragile beauty* ◇ *The woman's fragile face broke into a smile.* **4** not strong and likely to become ill: *Her father is now 86 and in fragile health.* ◇ (*BrE, spoken*) *I'm feeling a bit fragile after last night* (= not well, perhaps because of drinking too much alcohol). ▶ **fra·gil·ity** /frəˈdʒɪləti/ *noun* [U]: *the fragility of the human body*

frag·ment *noun, verb*
■ *noun* /ˈfrægmənt/ a small part of sth that has broken off or comes from sth larger: *Police found fragments of glass near the scene.* ◇ *The shattered vase lay in fragments on the floor.* ◇ *I overheard a fragment of their conversation.*
■ *verb* /frægˈment/ [V, VN] (*written*) to break or make sth break into small pieces or parts ▶ **frag·men·ta·tion** /ˌfrægmenˈteɪʃn/ *noun* [U]: *the fragmentation of the country into small independent states* **frag·ment·ed** *adj.*: *a fragmented society*

frag·men·tary /ˈfrægməntri; *AmE* -teri/ *adj.* made of small parts that are not connected or complete: *There is only fragmentary evidence to support this theory.*

fra·grance /ˈfreɪgrəns/ *noun* **1** [C, U] a pleasant smell: *The bath oil comes in various fragrances.* **2** [C] a liquid that you put on your skin in order to make yourself smell nice [SYN] PERFUME: *an exciting new fragrance from Dior*

fra·grant /ˈfreɪgrənt/ *adj.* having a pleasant smell: *fragrant herbs/flowers/oils* ◇ *The air was fragrant with scents from the sea and the hills.* ▶ **fra·grant·ly** *adv.*

frail /freɪl/ *adj.* (**frail·er**, **frail·est**) **1** (especially of an old person) physically weak and thin: *Mother was becoming too frail to live alone.* ◇ *his frail hands* **2** weak; easily damaged or broken: *the frail stems of the flowers* ◇ *Human nature is frail.*

frailty /ˈfreɪlti/ *noun* (*pl.* -**ies**) **1** [U] weakness and poor health: *Increasing frailty meant that she was more and more confined to bed.* **2** [U, C] weakness in a person's character or morals: *human frailty* ◇ *the frailties of human nature*

frame /freɪm/ *noun, verb*

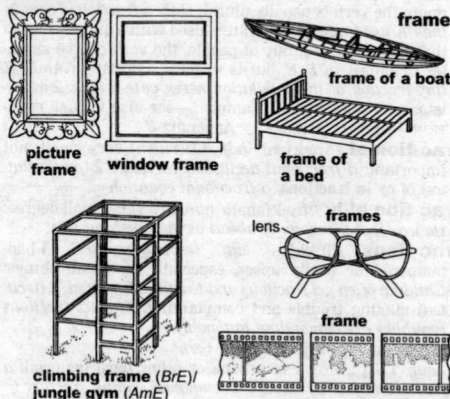

frame

frame of a boat

picture frame

window frame

frame of a bed

climbing frame (*BrE*)/ **jungle gym** (*AmE*)

lens

frames

frame

■ *noun*
BORDER | **1** [C] a strong border or structure of wood, metal, etc. that holds a picture, door, piece of glass, etc. in position: *a picture frame* ◇ *aluminium window frames*
STRUCTURE | **2** [C] the supporting structure of a piece of furniture, a building, a vehicle, etc. that gives it its shape: *the frame of an aircraft/a car/a bicycle*—see also CLIMBING FRAME—picture at BICYCLE
OF GLASSES | **3** [C, usually pl.] a structure of plastic or metal that holds the LENSES in a pair of glasses: *gold-rimmed frames*—picture at GLASS
PERSON/ANIMAL'S BODY | **4** [C, usually sing.] the form or structure of a person or animal's body: *to have a small/slender/large frame*

GENERAL IDEAS | **5** [sing.] the general ideas or structure that form the background to sth: *In this course we hope to look at literature in the frame of its social and historical context.*—see also TIME FRAME
OF FILM/MOVIE | **6** [C] one of the single photographs that a film or VIDEO is made of
OF PICTURE STORY | **7** [C] a single picture in a COMIC STRIP
IN GARDEN | **8** [C] = COLD FRAME
IN SNOOKER/BOWLING | **9** [C] a single section of play in the game of SNOOKER, etc., or in BOWLING
[IDM] **be in/out of the 'frame** be taking part/not taking part in sth: *We won our match, so we're still in the frame for the championship.*
■ *verb* [VN]
MAKE BORDER | **1** [usually passive] to put or make a frame or border around sth: *The photograph had been framed and hung on the wall.* ◇ *Her thick blonde hair framed her face.* ◇ *He stood there, head back, framed against the blue sky.*
PRODUCE FALSE EVIDENCE | **2** [usually passive] ~ **sb** (**for sth**) to produce false evidence against an innocent person so that people think he or she is guilty [SYN] FIT UP: *He says he was framed.*
DEVELOP PLAN/SYSTEM | **3** (*formal*) to create and develop sth such as a plan, a system or a set of rules
EXPRESS STH | **4** to express sth in a particular way: *You'll have to be careful how you frame the question.*
▶ **framed** *adj.* (often in compounds): *a framed photograph* ◇ *a gilt-framed mirror* ◇ *a timber-framed house* (= with a supporting structure of wood)

,frame of 'mind *noun* [sing.] the way you feel or think about sth at a particular time: *We'll discuss this when you're in a better frame of mind.*

,frame of 'reference *noun* (*pl.* **frames of reference**) a particular set of beliefs, ideas or experiences that affects how a person understands or judges sth: *It is easy to choose our own frame of reference and attack any ideas that do not fit it.*

'frame-up *noun* (*informal*) a situation in which false evidence is produced in order to make people think that an innocent person is guilty of a crime

frame·work /ˈfreɪmwɜːk; *AmE* -wɜːrk/ *noun* **1** the parts of a building or an object that support its weight and give it shape: *built on a wooden/metal framework* **2** ~ (**of/for sth**) a set of beliefs, ideas or rules that is used as the basis for making judgements, decisions, etc: *The report provides a framework for further research.* **3** the structure of a particular system: *We need to establish a legal framework for the protection of the environment.* ◇ *the basic framework of society*

franc /fræŋk/ *noun* **1** [C] the unit of money in France, Belgium, Switzerland and several other countries (to be replaced in France, Belgium and Luxembourg by the euro) **2** (**the franc**) [sing.] (*finance*) the value of the franc compared with the value of the money of other countries: *the movement of sterling against the franc*

fran·chise /ˈfræntʃaɪz/ *noun, verb*
■ *noun* **1** [C, U] formal permission given by a company to sb who wants to sell its goods or services in a particular area; formal permission given by a government to sb who wants to operate a public service as a business: *a franchise agreement/company* ◇ *a catering/rail franchise* ◇ *In the reorganization, Southern Television lost their franchise.* ◇ *to operate a business under franchise* **2** [C] a business or service run under franchise: *They operate franchises in London and Paris.* ◇ *a burger franchise* **3** [U] (*formal*) the right to vote in a country's elections: *universal adult franchise*—see also ENFRANCHISE
■ *verb* [VN] [usually passive] to give or sell a franchise (1) to sb: *Catering has been franchised* (*out*) *to a private company.* ◇ *franchised restaurants* ▶ **fran·chis·ing** *noun* [U]

fran·chisee /ˌfræntʃaɪˈziː/ *noun* a person or company that has been given a franchise

fran·chiser /ˈfræntʃaɪzə(r)/ *noun* a company or an organization that gives sb a franchise

franco·phone /ˈfræŋkəfəʊn; *AmE* -foʊn/ *adj.* [only

before noun] speaking French as the main language: *the francophone countries of West Africa* ▶ **franco·phone** *noun*: *the special needs of francophones living in Canada*

frank /fræŋk/ *adj., verb*
■ *adj.* (**frank·er, frank·est** HELP more frank is also common) honest and direct in what you say, sometimes in a way that other people might not like: *a full and frank discussion ◊ a frank admission of guilt ◊ He was very frank about his relationship with the actress.* ◊ **To be frank with you,** *I think your son has little chance of passing the exam.* ▶ **frank·ness** *noun* [U]: *They outlined their aims with disarming frankness.*
■ *verb* [VN] [often passive] to stamp a mark on an envelope, etc. to show that the cost of posting it has been paid or does not need to be paid: *a franking machine*

frank·furt·er /'fræŋkfɜːtə(r); *AmE* -fɜːrt-/ (*AmE* also **wiener,** *informal* **wee·nie**) *noun* a long thin smoked sausage with a reddish-brown skin, often eaten in a long bread roll as a HOT DOG

frank·in·cense /'fræŋkɪnsens/ *noun* [U] a substance that is burnt to give a pleasant smell, especially during religious ceremonies

frank·ly /'fræŋkli/ *adv.* **1** in an honest and direct way that people might not like: *He spoke frankly about the ordeal.* ◊ *They frankly admitted their responsibility.* **2** used to show that you are being honest about sth, even though people might not like what you are saying: *Frankly, I couldn't care less what happens to him.* ◊ *Quite frankly, I'm not surprised you failed.*

fran·tic /'fræntɪk/ *adj.* **1** done quickly and with a lot of activity, but in a way that is not very well organized: *a frantic dash/search/struggle ◊ They made frantic attempts to revive him.* ◊ *Things are frantic in the office right now.* **2** unable to control your emotions because you are extremely frightened or worried about sth: *frantic with worry ◊ Let's go back. Your parents must be getting frantic by now.* ◊ *The children are driving me frantic* (= making me very annoyed). ▶ **fran·tic·al·ly** /-kli/ *adv.*: *They worked frantically to finish on time.*

frat /fræt/ *noun* (*AmE, informal*) = FRATERNITY (2): *a frat boy* (= a member of a fraternity)

fra·ter·nal /frə'tɜːnl; *AmE* -'tɜːrnl/ *adj.* [usually before noun] **1** connected with the relationship that exists between people or groups that share the same ideas or interests: *a fraternal organization/society* **2** connected with the relationship that exists between brothers: *fraternal feelings/rivalry* ▶ **fra·ter·nal·ly** *adv.*

fra,ternal 'twin *noun* either of two children or animals born from the same mother at the same time but not from the same egg—compare IDENTICAL TWIN

fra·ter·nity /frə'tɜːnəti; *AmE* -'tɜːrn-/ *noun* (*pl.* **-ies**) **1** [C+sing./pl. *v.*] a group of people sharing the same profession, interests or beliefs: *members of the medical/banking/racing fraternity* **2** (also *AmE informal* **frat**) [C] a club for a group of male students at an American college or university—compare SORORITY **3** [U] (*formal*) a feeling of friendship and support that exists between the members of a group: *the ideals of liberty, equality and fraternity*

frat·er·nize (*BrE* also **-ise**) /'frætənaɪz; *AmE* -tərn-/ *verb* [V] **~** (**with sb**) to behave in a friendly manner, especially towards sb that you are not supposed to be friendly with: *She was accused of fraternizing with the enemy.* ▶ **frat·er·niza·tion, -isa·tion** /ˌfrætənaɪ'zeɪʃn; *AmE* -tərnə'z-/ *noun* [U]

frat·ri·cide /'frætrɪsaɪd/ *noun* [U] **1** (*formal*) the crime of killing your brother or sister; a person who is guilty of this crime—compare MATRICIDE, PARRICIDE, PATRICIDE **2** the crime of killing people of your own country or group; a person who is guilty of this crime ▶ **frat·ri·cidal** /ˌfrætrɪ'saɪdl/ *adj.*: *to be engaged in a fratricidal struggle*

fraud /frɔːd/ *noun* **1** [U, C] the crime of deceiving sb in order to get money or goods illegally: *She was charged with credit card fraud.* ◊ *property that has been obtained by fraud ◊ a $100 million fraud* **2** [C] a person who pretends to have qualities, abilities, etc. that they do not really have in order to deceive other people: *He's nothing but a liar and a fraud.* ◊ *She felt a fraud accepting their sympathy* (= because she was not really sad). **3** [C] something that is not as good, useful, etc. as people claim it is

fraud·ster /'frɔːdstə(r)/ *noun* (*BrE*) a person who commits fraud

fraudu·lent /'frɔːdjələnt; *AmE* -dʒə-/ *adj.* intended to deceive sb, usually in order to make money illegally: *fraudulent advertising ◊ fraudulent insurance claims* ▶ **fraudu·lence** /'frɔːdjələns; *AmE* -dʒə-/ *noun* [U] **fraudu·lent·ly** /'frɔːdjələntli; *AmE* -dʒə-/ *adv.*

fraught /frɔːt/ *adj.* **1 ~ with sth** filled with sth unpleasant: *a situation fraught with danger/difficulty/problems* **2** (*especially BrE*) causing or feeling worry and anxiety: *She looked/sounded fraught.* ◊ *There was a fraught silence.* ◊ *Things are as fraught as ever in the office.*

fray /freɪ/ *verb, noun*
■ *verb* **1** if fabric **frays** or sth **frays** it, the threads in it start to come apart: [V] *The cuffs of his shirt were fraying.* ◊ *This material frays easily.* ◊ [VN] *It was fashionable to fray the bottoms of your jeans.*—picture at JAGGED **2** if sb's nerves or temper **frays** or sth **frays,** the person starts to get irritated or annoyed: [V] *As the debate went on, tempers began to fray.* [also VN] ▶ **frayed** *adj.*: *frayed denim shorts ◊ Tempers were getting very frayed.* IDM **fray at/around the 'edges/'seams** to start to come apart or to fail: *Support for the leader was fraying at the edges.*
■ *noun* (**the fray**) [sing.] a fight, competition or argument, especially one that is exciting or seen as a test of your ability: *ready/eager for the fray ◊ to enter/join the fray ◊ At 71, he has now retired from the political fray.*

fraz·zle /'fræzl/ *noun* IDM **be burnt, worn, etc. to a 'frazzle** (*informal*) to be completely burnt/extremely tired

fraz·zled /'fræzld/ *adj.* (*informal*) tired and easily annoyed: *They finally arrived home, hot and frazzled.*

freak /friːk/ *noun, adj., verb*
■ *noun* **1** (*informal*) a person with a very strong interest in a particular subject: *a health/fitness/jazz freak*—see also CONTROL FREAK **2** (*disapproving*) a person who is considered to be unusual because of the way they behave, look or think: *She was treated like a freak because she didn't want children.* ◊ *He's going out with a real freak.* **3** (also **,freak of 'nature**) (sometimes *offensive*) a person, an animal, a plant or a thing that is not physically normal **4** a very unusual and unexpected event: *By some freak of fate they all escaped without injury.*
■ *adj.* [only before noun] (of an event or the weather) very unusual and unexpected: *a freak accident/storm/occurrence ◊ freak weather conditions*
■ *verb* **~** (**sb**) (**out**) (*informal*) if sb **freaks** or if sth **freaks** them, they react very strongly to sth that makes them suddenly feel shocked, surprised, frightened, etc: [V] *My parents really freaked when they saw my hair.* ◊ [VN] *Snakes really freak me out.*

freak·ish /'friːkɪʃ/ *adj.* very strange, unusual or unexpected: *freakish weather/behaviour* ▶ **freak·ish·ly** *adv.*

freaky /'friːki/ (*informal*) *adj.* very strange or unusual

freckle /'frekl/ *noun* [usually pl.] a small, pale brown spot on a person's skin, especially on their face, caused by the sun—compare MOLE ▶ **freckled** /'frekld/ *adj.*: *a freckled face/schoolgirl*

free /friː/ *adj., verb, adv.*
■ *adj.* (**freer** /'friːə(r)/ **freest** /'friːɪst/)
NOT CONTROLLED **1 ~** (**to do sth**) not under the control or in the power of sb else; able to do what you want: *I have no ambitions other than to have a happy life and be free.* ◊ *Students have a free choice of courses in their final year.* ◊ *You are free to come and go as you please.* ◊ (*spoken*) *'Can I use the phone?' 'Please, feel free* (= of course you can use it).*'* **2** not restricted or controlled by anyone else; able to do or say what you want: *A true democracy complete with free speech and a free press was called for. ◊ the country's first free election ◊ They gave me free access to all the files.*
NOT PRISONER **3** (of a person) not a prisoner or slave: *He walked out of jail a free man.*
ANIMAL/BIRD **4** not tied up or in a cage: *The researchers set the birds free.*

b	d	f	g	h	k	l	m	n	p	r
bad	did	fall	get	hat	cat	leg	man	now	pen	red

NO PAYMENT | 5 costing nothing: *Admission is free.* ◊ *free samples/tickets/advice* ◊ *We're offering a fabulous free gift with each copy you buy.* ◊ *You can't expect people to work for free* (= without payment).

NOT BLOCKED | 6 clear; not blocked: *Ensure there is a free flow of air around the machine.*

WITHOUT STH | 7 ~ from/of sth not containing or affected by sth harmful or unpleasant: *free from difficulty/doubt/fear* ◊ *free from artificial colours and flavourings* ◊ *It was several weeks before he was completely free of pain.* **8 (-free)** (in adjectives) without the thing mentioned: *virtually fat-free yoghurt* ◊ *tax-free earnings* ◊ *a trouble-free life*

NOT ATTACHED/TRAPPED | 9 ~ (of sth) not attached to sth or trapped by sth: *Pull gently on the free end of the rope.* ◊ *They had to be cut free from their car after the accident.* ◊ *She finally managed to pull herself free.*

NOT BEING USED | 10 not being used: *He held out his free hand and I took it.* ◊ *Is this seat free?*

NOT BUSY | 11 ~ (for sth) (of a person or time) without particular plans or arrangements; not busy: *If Sarah is free for lunch I'll take her out.* ◊ *Keep Friday night free for my party.* ◊ *What do you like to do in your free time* (= when you are not working)?

READY TO GIVE | 12 ~ with sth (often *disapproving*) ready to give sth, especially when it is not wanted: *He's too free with his opinions.*

TRANSLATION | 13 a free TRANSLATION is not exact but gives the general meaning—compare LITERAL

IDM **free and 'easy** informal; relaxed: *Life was never going to be so free and easy again.* **get, have, etc. a free 'hand** to get, have, etc. the opportunity to do what you want to do and to make your own decisions: *I was given a free hand in designing the syllabus.* **get, take, etc. a free 'ride** to get or take sth without paying because sb else is paying for it **it's a free 'country** (*spoken*) used as a reply when sb suggests that you should not do sth: *It's a free country; I'll say what I like!* **there's no such ,thing as a free 'lunch** (*spoken*) used to say that it is not possible to get sth for nothing—more at HOME *adv.*, REIN *n.*

■ *verb*

PRISONER | 1 [VN] **~ sb (from sth)** to allow sb to leave prison or somewhere they have been kept against their WILL (= where they did not want to be kept): *By the end of May nearly 100 of an estimated 2000 political prisoners had been freed.* ◊ *The hijackers agreed to free a further ten hostages.*

SB/STH TRAPPED | 2 [VN] **~ sb/sth/yourself (from sth)** to move sb/sth that is caught or fixed on sth: *Three people were freed from the wreckage.* ◊ *She struggled to free herself.*

REMOVE STH | 3 [VN] **~ sb/sth of/from sb/sth** to remove sth that is unpleasant or not wanted from sb/sth **SYN** RID: *These exercises help free the body of tension.* ◊ *The police are determined to free the town of violent crime.* ◊ *The centre aims to free young people from dependency on drugs.*

MAKE AVAILABLE | 4 [VN] **~ sb/sth (up)** to make sb/sth available for a particular purpose: *We freed time each week for a project meeting.* ◊ *The government has promised to free up more resources for education.* **5** [VN to inf] to give sb the extra time to do sth that they want to do: *Winning the prize freed him to paint full-time.*

■ *adv.*

WITHOUT PAYMENT | 1 (also **,free of 'charge**) without payment: *Children under five travel free.*

NOT TRAPPED | 2 away from or out of a position in which sb/sth is stuck or trapped: *The wagon broke free from the train.*—see also SCOT-FREE

IDM **make free with 'sth** (*disapproving*) to use sth a lot, even though it does not belong to you **run 'free** (of an animal) to be allowed to go where it likes; not tied to anything or kept in a cage—more at WALK *v.*

,free 'agent *noun* a person who can do whatever they want because they are not responsible to or for anyone else

free·base /'fri:beɪs/ *noun* [U] (*slang*) a specially prepared form of the powerful illegal drug COCAINE

free·bas·ing /'fri:beɪsɪŋ/ *noun* [U] (*slang*) the activity of smoking freebase

free·bie /'fri:bi/ *noun* (*informal*) something that is given to sb without payment, usually by a company: *He took all the freebies that were on offer.* ◊ *a freebie holiday*

free·boot·er /'fri:bu:tə(r)/ *noun* a person who takes part in a war in order to steal goods and money ▶ **free·boot·ing** *adj.*, *noun* [U]

free·born /'fri:bɔːn; *AmE* -bɔːrn/ *adj.* [only before noun] (*formal*) not born as a slave

,Free 'Church *noun* a Christian Church that does not belong to the established Church in a particular country

free·dom /'fri:dəm/ *noun* **1** [U, C] **~ (of sth)** the right to do or say what you want without anyone stopping you: *freedom of speech/thought/expression/worship* ◊ *a threat to press/academic freedom* ◊ *rights and freedoms guaranteed by the constitution* ◊ **freedom of information** (= the right to see secret information that a government has about people and organizations) **2** [U, sing.] **~ (of sth) | ~ (to do sth)** the state of being able to do what you want, without anything stopping you: *freedom of action/choice* ◊ *complete freedom to do as you wish* ◊ *Thanks to the automobile, Americans soon had a freedom of movement previously unknown.* **3** [U] the state of not being a prisoner or slave: *He finally won his freedom after twenty years in jail.* **4** [U] **~ from sth** the state of not being affected by the thing mentioned: *freedom from fear/pain/hunger* **IDM** **the freedom of the 'city** (in Britain) an honour that is given to sb by a city as a reward for work they have done—see also FREEMAN **IDM** see MANOEUVRE *n.*

'freedom fighter *noun* a name used to describe a person who uses violence to try to remove a government from power, by people who support this—compare GUERRILLA, TERRORIST

,free 'enterprise *noun* [U] an economic system in which private businesses compete with each other without much government control—compare PRIVATE ENTERPRISE

,free 'fall *noun* [U] **1** the movement of an object or a person falling through the air without engine power or a PARACHUTE: *a free fall display* **2** a sudden drop in the value of sth that cannot be stopped: *Share prices have gone into free fall.*

,free-'floating *adj.* not attached to or controlled by anything: *a free-floating currency/exchange rate*

Free·fone™ *noun* [U] = FREEPHONE

'free-for-all *noun* [sing.] **1** a situation in which there are no rules or controls and everyone acts for their own advantage: *The lowering of trade barriers has led to a free-for-all among exporters.* **2** a noisy fight or argument in which a lot of people take part

'free-form *adj.* [only before noun] (of art or music) not created according to standard forms or structures: *a free-form jazz improvisation*

free·hand /'fri:hænd/ *adj.* [only before noun] drawn without using a ruler or other instruments: *a freehand drawing* ▶ **free·hand** *adv.*: *to draw freehand*

free·hold /'fri:həʊld; *AmE* -hoʊld/ *noun* [C, U] (*law*) (especially *BrE*) the fact of owning a building or piece of land for a period of time that is not limited ▶ **free·hold** *adj.*: *a freehold property* **free·hold** *adv.*: *to buy a house freehold*—compare LEASEHOLD

free·hold·er /'fri:həʊldə(r); *AmE* -hoʊld-/ *noun* (*law*) (especially *BrE*) a person who owns the freehold of a building or piece of land—compare LEASEHOLDER

,free 'house *noun* (in Britain) a pub that can sell different types of beer because it is not owned and controlled by one particular BREWERY (= a company producing beer)—compare TIED HOUSE

,free 'kick *noun* (in football) an opportunity to kick the ball without any opposition, that is given to one team when the other team does sth wrong: *to take a free kick*

free·lance /'fri:lɑːns; *AmE* -læns/ *adj.*, *verb*

■ *adj.* earning money by selling your work or services to several different organizations rather than being employed by one particular organization: *a freelance jour-*

s	t	v	z	ʃ	ʒ	tʃ	dʒ	θ	ð	ŋ
see	tea	van	zoo	shoe	vision	chain	jam	thin	this	sing

nalist ◊ *freelance work* ▶ **free·lance** *adv.*: *I work freelance from home.*

■ *verb* [V] to earn money by selling your work to several different organizations

free·lancer /ˈfriːlɑːnsə(r); *AmE* -lænsər/ (also **free·lance**) *noun* a person who works freelance

free·load·er /ˈfriːləʊdə(r); *AmE* -loʊd-/ *noun* (*informal, disapproving*) a person who is always accepting free food and accommodation from other people without giving them anything in exchange ▶ **free·load** *verb* [V] **free·load·ing** *adj., noun* [U]

ˌfree ˈlove *noun* [U] (*old-fashioned*) the practice of having sex without being married or having several sexual relationships at the same time

free·ly /ˈfriːli/ *adv.* **1** without anyone trying to prevent or control sth: *the country's first freely elected president* ◊ *EU citizens can now travel freely between member states.* **2** without anything stopping the movement or flow of sth: *When the gate is raised, the water can flow freely.* ◊ *Traffic is now moving more freely following an earlier accident.* ◊ *The book is now freely available in the shops* (= it is not difficult to get a copy). ◊ (*figurative*) *The wine flowed freely* (= there was a lot of it to drink). **3** without trying to avoid the truth even though it might be unpleasant or embarrassing: *I freely admit that I made a mistake.* **4** in an honest way without worrying about what people will say or do: *For the first time he was able to speak freely without the fear of reprisals against his family.* **5** in a willing and generous way: *Millions of people gave freely in response to the appeal for the victims of the earthquake.* **6** a piece of writing that is translated **freely** is not translated exactly but the general meaning is given

free·man /ˈfriːmən/ *noun* (*pl.* **free·men** /-mən/) **1** (*BrE*) a person who has been given the FREEDOM of a particular city as a reward for the work that they have done **2** a person who is not a slave

ˌfree ˈmarket *noun* an economic system in which the price of goods and services is affected by supply and demand rather than controlled by a government: *to compete in a free market*

ˌfree marke'teer *noun* a person who believes that prices should be allowed to rise and fall according to supply and demand and not be controlled by the government

Free·mason /ˈfriːmeɪsn/ (also **Mason**) *noun* a man belonging to a secret society whose members help each other and communicate using secret signs

Free·mason·ry /ˈfriːmeɪsnri/ *noun* [U] **1** the system and practices of Freemasons **2** (**freemasonry**) the friendship that exists between people who have the same profession or interests: *the freemasonry of actors*

ˌfree ˈpardon *noun* (*BrE, law*) = PARDON

ˌfree ˈperiod *noun* (*BrE*) a period of time in a school day when a student or teacher does not have a class

Free·phone (also **Free·fone**™) /ˈfriːfəʊn; *AmE* -foʊn/ *noun* [U] (in Britain) a system in which the cost of a telephone call is paid for by the organization being called, rather than by the person making the call—compare TOLL-FREE

ˌfree ˈport *noun* a port at which tax is not paid on goods that have been brought there temporarily before being sent to a different country

Free·post /ˈfriːpəʊst; *AmE* -poʊst/ *noun* [U] (in Britain) a system in which the cost of sending a letter is paid for by the organization receiving it, rather than by the person sending it

ˌfree-ˈrange *adj.* [usually before noun] connected with a system of farming in which animals are kept in natural conditions and can move around freely: *free-range chickens* ◊ *free-range eggs*—compare BATTERY (4), BATTERY FARM

free·sia /ˈfriːʒə; ˈfriːziə/ *noun* a plant with yellow, pink, white or purple flowers with a sweet smell, which are also called **freesias**

ˌfree ˈspirit *noun* a person who is independent and does what they want instead of doing what other people do

ˌfree-ˈstanding *adj.* **1** not supported by or attached to anything: *a free-standing sculpture* **2** not a part of sth else: *a free-standing adult education service*

free·style /ˈfriːstaɪl/ *noun* [U] **1** a swimming race in which competitors can use any stroke they want (usually CRAWL): *the men's 400 m freestyle* **2** (often used as an adjective) a sports competition in which competitors can use any style that they want: *freestyle skiing / wrestling*

free·think·er /ˌfriːˈθɪŋkə(r)/ *noun* a person who forms their own ideas and opinions rather than accepting those of other people, especially in religious teaching ▶ **free·think·ing** *adj.* [only before noun]

ˌfree ˈtrade *noun* [U] a system of international trade in which there are no restrictions or taxes on imports and exports

ˌfree ˈverse *noun* [U] (*technical*) poetry without a regular rhythm or RHYME—compare BLANK VERSE

ˌfree ˈvote *noun* (in Britain) a vote by members of parliament in which they can vote according to their own beliefs rather than following the policy of their political party

free·ware /ˈfriːweə(r); *AmE* -wer/ *noun* [U] (*computing*) computer SOFTWARE that is offered free of charge for anyone to use—compare SHAREWARE

free·way /ˈfriːweɪ/ (also **ex·press·way**) *noun* (in the US) a wide road, with at least two LANES in each direction, where traffic can travel fast for long distances between large towns. You can only enter and leave freeways at special RAMPS: *a freeway exit* ◊ *an accident on the freeway* ◊ *to get onto / to exit the freeway*—compare MOTORWAY

free·wheel /ˌfriːˈwiːl/ *verb* [V] [usually +*adv. / prep.*] to ride a bicycle without using the PEDALS: *I freewheeled down the hill to the village.*

free·wheel·ing /ˌfriːˈwiːlɪŋ/ *adj.* [only before noun] (*informal*) not concerned about rules or the possible results of what you do: *a freewheeling lifestyle*

ˌfree ˈwill *noun* [U] the power to make your own decisions without being controlled by God or fate **IDM of your own free ˈwill** because you want to do sth rather than because sb has told or forced you to do it: *She left of her own free will.*

freeze /friːz/ *verb, noun*

■ *verb* (**froze** /frəʊz; *AmE* froʊz/ **fro·zen** /ˈfrəʊzn; *AmE* ˈfroʊzn/)

BECOME ICE **1** to become hard, and often turn to ice, as a result of extreme cold; to make sth do this: [V] *Water freezes at 0°C.* ◊ *It's so cold that even the river has frozen.* ◊ [VN] *The cold weather had frozen the ground.* ◊ [V-ADJ] *The clothes froze solid on the washing-line.* OPP THAW

OF PIPE / LOCK / MACHINE **2** ~ (**sth**) (**up**) if a pipe, lock or machine **freezes**, or sth **freezes** it, it becomes blocked with frozen liquid and therefore cannot be used: [V] *The pipes have frozen, so we've got no water.* ◊ [VN] *Ten degrees of frost had frozen the locks on the car.*

OF WEATHER **3** [V] when it **freezes**, the weather is at or below 0° Celsius: *It may freeze tonight, so bring those plants inside.*

BE VERY COLD **4** to be very cold; to be so cold that you die: [V] *Every time she opens the window we all freeze.* ◊ [V, VN] *Two men froze to death on the mountain.* ◊ *Two men were frozen to death on the mountain.*

FOOD **5** [VN] to keep food at a very low temperature in order to preserve it: *Can you freeze this cake?* ◊ *These meals are ideal for home freezing.* **6** [V] to be able to be kept at a very low temperature: *Some fruits freeze better than others.*

STOP MOVING **7** [V] to stop moving suddenly because of fear, etc.: *I froze with terror as the door slowly opened.* ◊ (*figurative*) *The smile froze on her lips.* ◊ *The police officer shouted 'Freeze!' and the man dropped the gun.*

FILM / MOVIE **8** [VN] to stop a film / movie or video in order to look at a particular picture: *Freeze the action there!*— see also FREEZE-FRAME

WAGES / PRICES **9** [VN] to hold wages, prices, etc. at a fixed level for a period of time: *Salaries have been frozen for the current year.*

MONEY / BANK ACCOUNT **10** [VN] to prevent money, a bank

æ ɑː e ɜː ə ɪ iː i ɒ ɔː ʌ ʊ u uː
cat father ten bird about sit see many got saw cup put actual too
(BrE)

account, etc. from being used by getting a court order which forbids it: *The company's assets have been frozen.*

IDM **freeze your 'blood | make your 'blood freeze** to make you extremely frightened or shocked—more at TRACK *n.*

PHR V ,freeze sb↔'out (of sth) (*informal*) to be deliberately unfriendly to sb, creating difficulties, etc. in order to stop or DISCOURAGE them from doing sth or taking part in sth ,freeze 'over to become completely covered by ice: *The lake freezes over in winter.*

■ *noun*

OF WAGES/PRICES **1** the act of keeping wages, prices, etc. at a particular level for a period of time: *a wage/price freeze*

STOPPING STH **2** [usually sing.] ~ (on sth) the act of stopping sth: *a freeze on imports*

COLD WEATHER **3** [usually sing.] (*BrE*) an unusually cold period of weather during which temperatures stay below 0° Celsius: *Farmers are still talking about the big freeze of '94.* **4** (*AmE*) a short period of time, especially at night, when the temperature is below 0° Celsius: *A freeze warning was posted for Thursday night.*

'freeze-dry *verb* [VN] [usually passive] to preserve food or drink by freezing and drying it very quickly

'freeze-frame *noun* [U] the act of stopping a moving film at one particular FRAME (= picture)

freezer /'friːzə(r)/ (*BrE also* ,deep 'freeze) (*AmE also* Deepfreeze™ ,deep 'freezer) *noun* a large piece of electrical equipment in which you can store food for a long time at a low temperature so that it stays frozen—see also FRIDGE-FREEZER

freez·ing /'friːzɪŋ/ *adj.* **1** extremely cold: *It's freezing in here!* ◊ *I'm freezing!* **2** [only before noun] having temperatures that are below 0° Celsius: *freezing fog* ◊ *freezing temperatures* ▶ **freez·ing** *adv.* (*informal*): *It's freezing cold outside.*

'freezing point *noun* **1** (also freez·ing) [U] 0° Celsius, the temperature at which water freezes: *Tonight temperatures will fall well below freezing (point).* **2** [C, usually sing.] the temperature at which a particular liquid freezes: *the freezing point of polar sea water*

freight /freɪt/ *noun, verb*

■ *noun* [U] goods that are transported by ships, planes, trains or lorries/trucks; the system of transporting goods in this way: *to send goods by air freight* ◊ *a freight business* ◊ *passenger and freight transportation services*

■ *verb* [VN] **1** to send or carry goods by air, sea or train **2** [usually passive] (*literary*) to fill sth with a particular mood or tone: *Each word was freighted with anger.*

'freight car *noun* (*AmE*) = WAGON

freight·er /'freɪtə(r)/ *noun* a large ship or plane that carries goods

'freight train (*BrE also* 'goods train) *noun* a train that carries only goods

French /frentʃ/ *adj.* of or connected with France, its people or its language **IDM** **take French 'leave** (*BrE*) to leave work without asking permission first

,**French 'bean** *noun* (*BrE*) = GREEN BEAN

,**French 'bread** *noun* [U] white bread in the shape of a long thick stick

,**French 'door** *noun* (*especially AmE*) = FRENCH WINDOW—picture at HOUSE

,**French 'dressing** *noun* [U, C] a mixture of oil, VINEGAR, etc. used to add flavour to a salad SYN VINAIGRETTE

,**French 'fry** *noun* [usually pl.] (*especially AmE*) = CHIP

,**French 'horn** (also **horn** especially in *BrE*) *noun* a BRASS musical instrument that consists of a long tube curled around in a circle with a wide opening at the end—picture on page 840

,**French 'kiss** *noun* a kiss during which people's mouths are open and their tongues touch

,**French 'letter** *noun* (*old-fashioned, BrE, informal*) = CONDOM

,**French 'loaf** *noun* = BAGUETTE

,**French 'plait** (*BrE*) (*AmE* ,French 'braid) *noun* a woman's hairstyle in which all the hair is gathered into one large PLAIT/BRAID down the back of the head, starting from the forehead—picture at HAIR

,**French 'polish** *noun* [U] (*BrE*) a type of transparent liquid (= VARNISH) that is painted onto wooden furniture to give it a hard shiny surface ▶ ,French 'polish *verb* [VN]

,**French 'stick** *noun* = BAGUETTE

,**French 'window** (*BrE*) (also ,French 'door *AmE, BrE*) *noun* [usually pl.] a glass door, usually one of a pair, that leads to a garden/yard or BALCONY—picture at HOUSE

fre·net·ic /frə'netɪk/ *adj.* involving a lot of energy and activity in a way that is not organized: *a scene of frenetic activity* ▶ **fre·net·ic·al·ly** /-kli/ *adv.*

fren·zied /'frenzid/ *adj.* [usually before noun] involving a lot of activity and strong emotions in a way that is often violent or frightening and not under control: *a frenzied attack* ◊ *frenzied activity* ▶ **fren·zied·ly** *adv.*

frenzy /'frenzi/ *noun* [C usually sing, U] (*pl.* **-ies**) ~ (of sth) a state of great activity and strong emotion that is often violent or frightening and not under control: *in a frenzy of activity/excitement/violence* ◊ *The speaker worked the crowd up into a frenzy.* ◊ *an outbreak of patriotic frenzy* ◊ *a killing frenzy* **IDM** see FEED *v.*

fre·quency /'friːkwənsi/ *noun* (*pl.* **-ies**) **1** [U, C] the rate at which sth happens or is repeated: *Fatal road accidents have decreased in frequency over recent years.* ◊ *a society with a high/low frequency* (= happening often/not very often) *of stable marriages* **2** [U] the fact of sth happening often: *the alarming frequency of computer errors* ◊ *Objects like this turn up at sales with surprising frequency.* **3** [C, U] (*technical*) the rate at which a sound wave VIBRATES (= moves up and down): *a high/low frequency* **4** [C, U] (*technical*) the number of radio waves for every second of a radio signal: *a frequency band* ◊ *There are only a limited number of broadcasting frequencies.*

fre·quent *adj., verb*

■ *adj.* /'friːkwənt/ happening often: *He is a frequent visitor to this country.* ◊ *Her calls became less frequent.* ◊ *There is a frequent bus service into the centre of town.* OPP INFREQUENT

■ *verb* /fri'kwent/ [VN] (*formal*) to visit a particular place often: *We met in a local bar much frequented by students.*

fre·quent·ly /'friːkwəntli/ *adv.* often: *Buses run frequently between the city and the airport.* ◊ *some of the most frequently asked questions about the Internet* OPP INFREQUENTLY

fresco /'freskəʊ; *AmE* -koʊ/ *noun* (*pl.* **-oes** or **-os**) [C, U] a picture that is painted on a wall while the PLASTER is still wet; the method of painting in this way: *The church is famous for its frescoes.*—see also ALFRESCO

fresh /freʃ/ *adj., adv.*

■ *adj.* (**fresh·er, fresh·est**)

FOOD **1** (usually of food) recently produced or picked and not frozen, dried or preserved in tins or cans: *Is this milk fresh?* ◊ *fresh bread/flowers* ◊ *Eat plenty of fresh fruit and vegetables.* ◊ *vegetables fresh from the garden* ◊ *Our chefs use only the freshest produce available.*

NEW **2** made or experienced recently: *fresh tracks in the snow* ◊ *Let me write it down while it's still fresh in my mind.* **3** [usually before noun] new or different in a way that adds to or replaces sth: *fresh evidence* ◊ *I think it's time we tried a fresh approach.* ◊ *a fresh coat of paint* ◊ *Could we order some fresh coffee?* ◊ *This is the opportunity he needs to make a fresh start* (= to try sth new after not being successful at sth else).

CLEAN/COOL **4** [usually before noun] pleasantly clean, pure or cool: *a toothpaste that leaves a nice fresh taste in your mouth* ◊ *Let's go and get some fresh air* (= go outside where the air is cooler).

WATER **5** [usually before noun] containing no salt: *There is a shortage of fresh water on the island.*—see also FRESHWATER

WEATHER **6** (*BrE*) quite cold with some wind: *It's fresh this morning, isn't it?* **7** (of the wind) quite strong and cold: *a fresh breeze*

CLEAR/BRIGHT **8** looking clear, bright and attractive: *He*

aɪ	aʊ	eɪ	əʊ	oʊ	ɔɪ	ɪə	eə	ʊə	j	w
my	now	say	go	go	boy	near	hair	pure	yes	wet
			(BrE)	(AmE)						

looked fresh and neat in a clean white shirt. ◊ a collection of summer dresses in fresh colours ◊ a fresh complexion
FULL OF ENERGY | **9** [not usually before noun] full of energy: Regular exercise will help you feel fresher and fitter. ◊ I managed to sleep on the plane and arrived feeling **as fresh as a daisy**.
JUST FINISHED | **10 ~ from sth** having just come from a particular place; having just had a particular experience: students fresh from college ◊ fresh from her success at the Olympic Games
RUDE/CONFIDENT | **11** [not before noun] **~ (with sb)** (informal) rude and too confident in a way that shows a lack of respect for sb or a sexual interest in sb: Don't get fresh with me!

▶ **fresh·ness** noun [U]: We guarantee the freshness of all our produce. ◊ the cool freshness of the water ◊ I like the freshness of his approach to the problem. **IDM** see BLOOD, BREATH, HEART
■ adv.
IDM fresh out of sth (informal, especially AmE) having recently finished a supply of sth: Sorry, we're fresh out of milk.

fresh·en /ˈfreʃn/ verb **1** [VN] **~ sth (up)** to make sth cleaner, cooler, newer or more pleasant: The walls need freshening up with a bit of white paint. ◊ The rain had freshened the air. ◊ Using a mouthwash regularly freshens the breath. **2** [VN] **~ sth (up)** (especially AmE) to add more liquid to a drink, especially an alcoholic one—see also TOP UP **3** [V] (of the wind) to become stronger and colder: The wind will freshen tonight. **PHRV** ,freshen 'up, ,freshen yourself 'up to wash and make yourself look clean and tidy: I'll just go and freshen up before supper.

fresh·ener /ˈfreʃnə(r)/ noun [U, C] (often in compounds) a thing that makes sth cleaner, purer or more pleasant: air freshener

fresh·er /ˈfreʃə(r)/ noun (BrE, informal) a student who has just started his or her first term at a university or college

ˈfresh-faced adj. having a young, healthy-looking face: fresh-faced kids

fresh·ly /ˈfreʃli/ adv. usually followed by a past participle showing that sth has been made, prepared, etc. recently: freshly brewed coffee

fresh·man /ˈfreʃmən/ noun (pl. **-men** /-mən/) (especially AmE) a student who is in his or her first year at a university, college or high school: high school/college freshmen ◊ during my freshman year—compare SOPHOMORE

fresh·water /ˈfreʃwɔːtə(r)/ adj. [only before noun] **1** living in water that is not the sea and is not salty: freshwater fish **2** having water that is not salty: freshwater lakes/pools—compare SALT WATER

fret /fret/ verb, noun
■ verb (-tt-) (especially BrE) **~ (about/over sth)** to be worried or unhappy and not able to relax: [V] Fretting about it won't help. ◊ Her baby starts to fret as soon as she goes out of the room. [also VN, V that]
■ noun one of the bars on the long thin part of a guitar, etc. Frets show you where to press the strings with your fingers to produce particular sounds.—picture on page 841

fret·ful /ˈfretfl/ adj. behaving in a way that shows you are unhappy or uncomfortable ▶ **fret·ful·ly** adv.

fret·work /ˈfretwɜːk; AmE -wɜːrk/ noun [U] patterns cut into wood, metal, etc. to decorate it; the process of making these patterns

Freud·ian /ˈfrɔɪdiən/ adj. **1** connected with the ideas of Sigmund Freud about the way the human mind works, especially his theories of SUBCONSCIOUS sexual feelings **2** (of sb's speech or behaviour) showing your secret thoughts or feelings, especially those connected with sex

Freudian 'slip noun something you say by mistake but which is believed to show your true thoughts

fri·able /ˈfraɪəbl/ adj. (technical) easily broken up into small pieces: friable soil

friar /ˈfraɪə(r)/ noun a member of one of several Roman Catholic religious communities of men who in the past travelled around teaching people about Christianity and lived by asking other people for food (= by BEGGING)—compare MONK

fri·ary /ˈfraɪəri/ noun (pl. **-ies**) a building in which friars live

frica·tive /ˈfrɪkətɪv/ noun (phonetics) a speech sound, such as /f/ /θ/ /ʃ/ or /z/, made by forcing breath out through a narrow space in the mouth with the lips, teeth or tongue in a particular position ▶ **frica·tive** adj. —compare PLOSIVE

fric·tion /ˈfrɪkʃn/ noun **1** [U] the action of one object or surface moving against another: Friction between moving parts had caused the engine to overheat. **2** [U] (physics) the RESISTANCE (= the force that stops sth moving) of one surface to another surface or substance moving over or through it: The force of friction slows the spacecraft down as it re-enters the earth's atmosphere. **3** [U, C] **~ (between A and B)** disagreement or a lack of friendship among people who have different opinions about sth: conflicts and frictions that have still to be resolved

Fri·day /ˈfraɪdeɪ; -di/ noun [C, U] (abbr. **Fri.**) the day of the week after Thursday and before Saturday **HELP** To see how **Friday** is used, look at the examples at **Monday**. **ORIGIN** Originally translated from the Latin for 'day of the planet Venus ' Veneris dies and named after the Germanic goddess Frigga.

fridge /frɪdʒ/ (BrE) (AmE or formal **re·friger·ator**) noun a piece of electrical equipment in which food is kept cold so that it stays fresh

,fridge-'freezer noun (BrE) a piece of kitchen equipment that consists of a fridge and a FREEZER together

fried pt, pp of FRY

friend /frend/ noun
PERSON YOU LIKE | **1** a person you know well and like, and who is not usually a member of your family: This is my friend Tom. ◊ Is he **a friend of yours**? ◊ She's an **old friend** (= I have known her a long time). ◊ He's one of my **best friends**. ◊ a close/good friend ◊ a childhood/family/lifelong friend ◊ I heard about it through a friend of a friend. ◊ She has a wide **circle of friends**.—see also BOYFRIEND, FAIR-WEATHER FRIEND, FALSE FRIEND, GIRLFRIEND, PENFRIEND, SCHOOL FRIEND, BEFRIEND
SUPPORTER | **2** a person who supports an organization, a charity, etc., especially by giving or raising money; a person who supports a particular idea, etc: the Friends of St Martin's Hospital ◊ a friend of democracy
NOT ENEMY | **3** a person who has the same interests and opinions as yourself, and will help and support you: You're among friends here—you can speak freely. ◊ His eyes were moving from face to face: friend or foe?
SILLY/ANNOYING PERSON | **4** (ironic) used to talk about sb you do not know who has done sth silly or annoying: I wish our friend at the next table would shut up.
IN PARLIAMENT/COURT | **5** (in Britain) used by a member of parliament to refer to another member of parliament or by a lawyer to refer to another lawyer in a court of law: my honourable friend, the member for Henley (= in the House of Commons) ◊ my noble friend (= in the House of Lords) ◊ my learned friend (= in a court of law)
IN RELIGION | **6** (**Friend**) a member of the Society of Friends **SYN** QUAKER
IDM be/make 'friends (with sb) to be/become a friend of sb: They had a quarrel, but they're friends again now. ◊ Simon finds it hard to make friends with other children. **be (just) good 'friends** used to say that two friends are not having a romantic relationship with each other **a ,friend in 'need (is a ,friend in'deed)** (saying) a friend who gives you help when you need it (is a true friend) **have ,friends in high 'places** to know important people who can help you—more at MAN n.

friend·less /ˈfrendləs/ adj. (written) without any friends

friend·ly /ˈfrendli/ adj., noun
■ adj. (friend·lier, friend·li·est) **1 ~ to/toward(s) sb** behaving in a kind and pleasant way because you like sb or want to help them: a warm and friendly person ◊ Everyone

F

was very friendly towards me. **2** showing kindness; making you feel relaxed and as though you are among friends: *a friendly smile/welcome* ◊ *a small hotel with a friendly atmosphere* **3** ~ **(with sb)** treating sb as a friend: *We soon became friendly with the couple next door.* ◊ *She was on friendly terms with most of the hospital staff.* **4** (especially of the relationship between countries) not treating sb/sth as an enemy: *to establish/maintain friendly relations with all countries* **5** (often in compound adjectives) that is helpful and easy to use; that helps sb/sth or does not harm it: *This software is much friendlier than the previous version.* ◊ *environmentally-friendly farming methods* ◊ *ozone-friendly cleaning materials*—see also USER-FRIENDLY **6** in which the people, teams, etc. taking part are not seriously competing against each other: *a friendly argument* ◊ *friendly rivalry* ◊ (*BrE*) *It was only a friendly match.* ▶ **friend·li·ness** *noun* [U]
■ *noun* (*pl.* **-ies**) (also **'friendly match**) (both *BrE*) a game of football, etc. that is not part of an important competition

,friendly 'fire *noun* [U] in a war, if people are killed or injured by **friendly fire**, they are hit by a bomb or weapon that is fired by their own side

friend·ship /ˈfrendʃɪp/ *noun* **1** [C] ~ **(with sb)**| ~ **(between A and B)** a relationship between friends: *a close/lasting/lifelong friendship* ◊ *friendships formed while she was at college* ◊ *He seemed to have already struck up* (= begun) *a friendship with Jo.* **2** [U] the feeling or relationship that friends have; the state of being friends: *Your friendship is very important to me.* ◊ *a conference to promote international friendship*

frier = FRYER

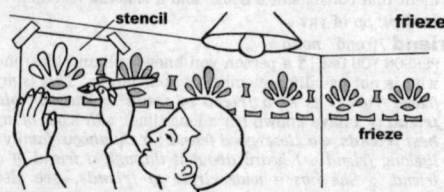

stencil · frieze · frieze

frieze /friːz/ *noun* **1** a border that goes around the top of a room or building with pictures or CARVINGS on it **2** a long narrow picture, usually put up in a school, that children have made or that teaches them sth

frig·ate /ˈfrɪgət/ *noun* a small fast ship in the navy that travels with other ships in order to protect them

frig·ging /ˈfrɪgɪŋ/ *adv., adj.* [only before noun] (△, *slang*) a swear word that many people find offensive, used to emphasize a comment or an angry statement to avoid saying 'fucking': *It's frigging cold outside.* ◊ *Mind your own frigging business!*

fright /fraɪt/ *noun* **1** [U] a feeling of fear: *to cry out in fright* ◊ *He was shaking with fright.*—see also STAGE FRIGHT **2** [C] an experience that makes you feel fear: *You gave me a fright jumping out at me like that.* ◊ *I got the fright of my life.* **IDM** **look a 'fright** (*old-fashioned, BrE*) to look ugly or ridiculous **take 'fright (at sth)** (*written*) to be frightened by sth: *The birds took fright and flew off.*

fright·en /ˈfraɪtn/ *verb* to make sb suddenly feel afraid: [VN] *Sorry, I didn't mean to frighten you.* ◊ *She's not easily frightened.* ◊ [V] *She doesn't frighten easily* (= it is not easy to make her afraid). [also VN to inf] **IDM** see DAYLIGHTS, DEATH, LIFE **PHRV** ,frighten sb/sth ↔ a'way/'off| ,frighten sb/sth a'way from sth **1** to make a person or an animal go away by making them feel afraid: *He threatened the intruders with a gun and frightened them off.* **2** to make sb afraid or nervous so that they no longer want to do sth: *The high prices have frightened off many customers.* **'frighten sb into sth/into doing sth** to make sb do sth by making them afraid

fright·ened /ˈfraɪtnd/ *adj.* ~ **(of sth/of doing sth)**| ~ **(to do sth)**| ~ **(that ...)** afraid; feeling fear: *a frightened child* ◊ *Don't be frightened.* ◊ *What are you frightened of?* ◊ *I'm frightened of walking home alone in the dark.* ◊ *He sounded frightened.* ◊ *I'm too frightened to ask him now.* ◊

She was frightened that the plane would crash. ◊ *I'm frightened for him* (= that he will be hurt, etc.). ◊ (*spoken*) *I'd never do that. I'd be frightened to death.* ▷ note at AFRAID **IDM** see SHADOW *n.*, WIT

fright·en·ers /ˈfraɪtnəz; *AmE* -nərz/ *noun* **IDM** **put the 'frighteners on sb** (*BrE, slang*) to threaten sb in order to make them do what you want

fright·en·ing /ˈfraɪtnɪŋ/ *adj.* making you feel afraid: *a frightening experience/prospect/thought* ◊ *It's frightening to think it could happen again.* ▶ **fright·en·ing·ly** *adv.*

fright·ful /ˈfraɪtfl/ *adj.* (*especially BrE*) **1** (*old-fashioned, informal*) used to emphasize how bad sth is: *It was absolutely frightful!* ◊ *This room's in a frightful mess.* **2** (*old-fashioned*) very serious or unpleasant: *a frightful accident*

fright·ful·ly /ˈfraɪtfəli/ *adv.* (*old-fashioned, especially BrE*) very; extremely: *I'm frightfully sorry.*

fri·gid /ˈfrɪdʒɪd/ *adj.* **1** (of a woman) not able to enjoy sex **2** very cold: *frigid air* **3** not showing any feelings of friendship or kindness: *a frigid voice* ◊ *There was a frigid atmosphere in the room.* ▶ **fri·gid·ly** *adv.*

fri·gid·ity /frɪˈdʒɪdəti/ *noun* [U] (in a woman) the lack of the ability to enjoy sex

frill /frɪl/ *noun* **1** (*BrE*) [C] a narrow strip of fabric with a lot of folds that is attached to the edge of a dress, CUSHION, etc. to decorate it: *a white blouse with frills at the cuffs* **SYN** RUFFLE **2** [pl.] things that are not necessary but are added to make sth more attractive or interesting: *a simple meal with no frills*

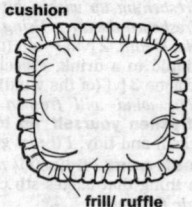

cushion

frill/ ruffle

frilled /frɪld/ *adj.* (*BrE*) decorated with frills **SYN** RUFFLED

frilly /ˈfrɪli/ *adj.* having a lot of frills: *a frilly blouse*

fringe /frɪndʒ/ *noun, verb*
■ *noun* **1** [C, usually sing.] (*BrE*) (*AmE* **bangs** [pl.]) the front part of sb's hair that is cut so that it hangs over their forehead—picture at HAIR **2** [C] a strip of hanging threads attached to the edge of sth to decorate it **3** [C] a narrow strip of trees, buildings, etc. along the edge of sth: *a fringe of woodland* ◊ *Along the coast, an industrial fringe had already developed.* **4** [C] (*BrE*) the outer edge of an area or a group: *on the northern fringe of the city* ◊ *the urban/rural fringe* ◊ *the fringes of society* ◊ *Nina remained on the fringe of the crowd.* **5** [sing.] (usually **the fringe**) groups of people, events and activities that are not part of the main group or activity: *Street musicians have been gathering as part of the festival fringe.* ◊ *fringe meetings at the party conference* **IDM** see LUNATIC *adj.*
■ *verb* [VN] [usually passive] to form a border around sth: *The beach was fringed by coconut palms.* ▶ **fringed (with sth)** *adj.*: *a carpet with a fringed edge*

'fringe benefit *noun* [usually pl.] extra things that an employer gives you as well as your wages: *The fringe benefits include free health insurance.*

,fringe 'theatre *noun* [U, C] (*BrE*) plays, often by new writers, that are unusual and question the way people think; a theatre where such plays are performed—compare OFF-BROADWAY

frip·pery /ˈfrɪpəri/ *noun* [C, usually pl., U] (*pl.* **-ies**) (*disapproving, especially BrE*) objects, decorations and other items that are considered unnecessary and expensive

Fris·bee™ /ˈfrɪzbi/ *noun* a light plastic object, shaped like a plate, that is thrown from one player to another in a game—picture on page A8

frisk /frɪsk/ *verb* **1** [VN] to pass your hands over sb's body to search them for hidden weapons, drugs, etc. **2** [V] ~ **(around)** (of animals) to run and jump in a lively and happy way: *Lambs frisked in the fields.*

frisky /ˈfrɪski/ *adj.* **1** (of people or animals) full of energy; wanting to play: *a frisky puppy* **2** (*informal*) wanting to enjoy yourself in a sexual way

fris·son /ˈfriːsɒ̃; *AmE* friːˈsoʊn/ *noun* [usually sing.] (from

French) a sudden strong feeling, especially of excitement or fear

frit·ter /ˈfrɪtə(r)/ *verb, noun*

■ *verb* PHR V ˌfritter sth↔aˈway (on sth) to waste time or money on things that are not important: *He frittered away the millions his father had left him.*

■ *noun* (usually in compounds) a piece of fruit, meat or vegetable that is covered with BATTER and fried

fritz /frɪts/ *noun* IDM **on the ˈfritz** (*AmE, informal*) not working: *The TV is on the fritz again.*

fri·vol·ity /frɪˈvɒləti; *AmE* -ˈvɑːl-/ *noun* (*pl.* **-ies**) (often *disapproving*) [U, C] behaviour that is silly or amusing, especially when this is not suitable: *It was just a piece of harmless frivolity.* ◇ *I can't waste time on such frivolities.*

frivo·lous /ˈfrɪvələs/ *adj.* (*disapproving*) **1** (of people or their behaviour) silly or amusing, especially when such behaviour is not suitable: *frivolous comments/suggestions* ◇ *Sorry, I was being frivolous.* **2** having no useful or serious purpose: *frivolous pastimes/pleasures* ▶ **frivo·lous·ly** *adv.*

frizz /frɪz/ *verb, noun*

■ *verb* [V, VN] (*informal*) (of hair) to curl very tightly; to make hair do this ▶ **frizzy** *adj.*: *frizzy hair*

■ *noun* [U] (*disapproving*) hair that is very tightly curled

fro /frəʊ; *AmE* froʊ/ *adv.* IDM see TO *adv.*

frock /frɒk; *AmE* frɑːk/ *noun* (*old-fashioned, especially BrE*) a dress: *a party frock*

ˈfrock coat *noun* a long coat worn in the past by men, now worn only for special ceremonies

frog /frɒg; *AmE* frɔːg; frɑːg/ *noun* **1** a small animal with smooth skin, that lives both on land and in water (= is an AMPHIBIAN). Frogs have very long back legs for jumping, and no tail: *the croaking of frogs*—picture on page A7 **2** (**Frog**) (*informal*) an offensive word for a French person IDM **have, etc. a ˈfrog in your throat** to lose your voice or be unable to speak clearly for a short time

frog·man /ˈfrɒgmən; *AmE* ˈfrɔːg-; ˈfrɑːg-/ *noun* (*pl.* **-men** /-mən/) a person who works underwater, wearing a rubber suit, FLIPPERS, and special equipment to help them breathe: *Police frogmen searched the lake for the murder weapon.*—compare DIVER

frog·march /ˈfrɒgmɑːtʃ; *AmE* ˈfrɔːgmɑːrtʃ; ˈfrɑːg-/ *verb* [VN+*adv.*/*prep.*] (*BrE*) to force sb to go somewhere by holding their arms tightly so they have to walk along with you: *He was grabbed by two men and frogmarched out of the hall.*

frog·spawn /ˈfrɒgspɔːn; *AmE* ˈfrɔːg-; ˈfrɑːg-/ *noun* [U] an almost transparent substance that looks like jelly and contains the eggs of a FROG—picture on page A7

fro·ing /ˈfrəʊɪŋ; *AmE* ˈfroʊɪŋ/ *noun* IDM see TOING

frolic /ˈfrɒlɪk; *AmE* ˈfrɑːl-/ *verb, noun*

■ *verb* (**-ck-**) [V] to play and move around in a lively, happy way: *children frolicking on the beach*

■ *noun* [C, U] (*old-fashioned*) a lively and enjoyable activity during which people forget their problems and responsibilities: *It was just a harmless frolic.*

from /frəm; *strong form* frɒm; *AmE* frʌm; frɑːm/ *prep.* HELP For the special uses of **from** in phrasal verbs, look at the entries for the verbs. For example **keep sth from sb** is in the phrasal verb section at **keep**. **1** used to show where sb/sth starts: *She began to walk away from him.* ◇ *Has the train from Bristol arrived?* **2** used to show when sth starts: *We're open from 8 to 7 every day.* ◇ *He was blind from birth.* **3** used to show who sent or gave sth/sb: *a letter from my brother* ◇ *information from witnesses* ◇ *the man from* (= representing) *the insurance company* **4** used to show what the origin of sb/sth is: *I'm from Italy.* ◇ *documents from the sixteenth century* ◇ *quotations from Shakespeare* ◇ *heat from the sun* **5** used to show the material that sth is made of: *Steel is made from iron.* **6** used to show how far apart two places are: *100 metres from the scene of the accident* **7** used to show sb's position or point of view: *You can see the island from here.* ◇ *From a financial point of view the project was a disaster.* **8 ~ sth (to sth)** used to show the range of sth: *The temperature varies from 30 degrees to minus 20.* ◇ *The store sells everything from shoelaces to computers.* ◇ *Conditions vary*

from school to school. **9 ~ sth (to sth)** used to show the state or form of sth/sb before a change: *Things have gone from bad to worse.* ◇ *translating from English to Spanish* ◇ *You need a break from routine.* **10** used to show that sb/sth is separated or removed: *The party was ousted from power after eighteen years.* **11** used to show that sth is prevented: *She saved him from drowning.* **12** used to show the reason for sth: *She felt sick from tiredness.* **13** used to show the reason for making a judgement: *You can tell a lot about a person from their handwriting.* ◇ *From what I heard the company's in deep trouble.* **14** used when distinguishing between two people or things: *Is Portuguese very different from Spanish?* ◇ *I can't tell one twin from the other.* IDM **from ... on** starting at the time mentioned and continuously after that: *From now on you can work on your own.* ◇ *She never spoke to him again from that day on.*

from·age frais /ˌfrɒmɑːˈʒ ˈfreɪ; *AmE* frəˈmɑːʒ/ *noun* [U] (from *French*) a type of very soft cheese, similar to YOGURT

frond /frɒnd; *AmE* frɑːnd/ *noun* **1** a long leaf, often divided into parts along the edge, of some plants or trees, especially PALMS or FERNS **2** a long piece of SEAWEED that looks like one of these leaves

front /frʌnt/ *noun, adj., verb*

They're sitting opposite/ facing each other.

She's sitting in front of him.

■ *noun*

FORWARD PART/POSITION | **1** [C, usually sing.] (usually **the front**) the part or side of sth that faces forward; the side of sth that you look at first: *The front of the building was covered with ivy.* ◇ *The book has a picture of Rome on the front.* ◇ *The front of the car was badly damaged.*—see also SHOPFRONT, Y-FRONTS **2** (**the front**) [sing.] the position that is in the direction that sb/sth is facing: *Keep your eyes to the front and walk straight ahead.* ◇ *There's a garden at the front of the house.* **3** (**the front**) [sing.] the part of sth that is furthest forward: *I prefer to travel in the front of the car* (= next to the driver). ◇ *The teacher made me move my seat to the front of the classroom.* ◇ *Write your name in the front of the book* (= the first few pages).

CHEST | **4** (sb's front) [sing.] the part of sb's body that faces forwards; sb's chest: *She was lying on her front.* ◇ *I spilled coffee down my front.*

SIDE OF BUILDING | **5** [C] **the west, north, south, east, etc. ~** the side of a large building, especially a church, that faces west, north, etc: *the west front of the cathedral*

EDGE OF SEA/LAKE | **6** (**the front**) [sing.] (*BrE*) the road or area of land along the edge of the sea, a lake or a river: *Couples walked hand in hand along the front.*—see also SEA FRONT

IN WAR | **7** [C, usually sing.] an area where fighting takes place during a war: *More British troops have been sent to the front.* ◇ *to serve at the front* ◇ *fighting a war on two fronts*

AREA OF ACTIVITY | **8** [C] a particular area of activity: *Things are looking unsettled on the economic front.* ◇ *Progress has been made on all fronts.*

HIDING TRUE FEELINGS | **9** [sing.] behaviour that is not genuine, done in order to hide your true feelings or opinions: *Rudeness is just a front for her shyness.* ◇ *It's not always easy putting on a brave front for the family.* ◇ *The prime minister stressed the need to present a united front* (= show people that all members of the group have the same opinion about things).

æ	ɑː	e	ɜː	ə	ɪ	iː	i	ɒ	ɔː	ʌ	ʊ	u	uː
cat	father	ten	bird	about	sit	see	many	got (BrE)	saw	cup	put	actual	too

F

HIDING STH ILLEGAL | **10** [C, usually sing.] ~ (for sth) a person or an organization that is used to hide an illegal or secret activity: *The travel company is just a front for drug trafficking.*

POLITICAL ORGANIZATION | **11** (Front) [sing.] used in the names of some political organizations: *the Animal Liberation Front*

WEATHER | **12** [C] the line where a mass of cold air meets a mass of warm air: *a cold/warm front*

IDM ¦front and ¦center (AmE) in or into the most important position **in** ¦front adv. **1** in a position that is further forward than sb/sth but not very far away: *Their house is the one with the big garden in front.* **2** in first place in a race or competition: *The blue team is currently in front with a lead of six points.* **in** ¦front of prep. **1** in a position that is further forward than sb/sth but not very far away: *The car in front of me stopped suddenly and I had to brake.* ◊ *The bus stops right in front of our house.* ◊ *He was standing in front of me in the line.* ◊ *She spends all day sitting in front of* (= working at) *her computer.* **2** if you do sth **in front of** sb, you do it when they are there: *Please don't talk about it in front of the children.* **3** ~ sb (of time) still to come; not yet passed: *Don't give up. You still have your whole life in front of you.* **out** ¦front **1** in the part of a theatre, restaurant, etc. where the public sits: *There's only a small audience out front tonight.* **2** (also BrE informal **out the** ¦front) in the area near to the entrance to a building: *I'll wait for you out (the) front.* **up** ¦front (informal) **1** as payment in advance: *We'll pay you half up front and the other half when you've finished the job.* **2** (in football) in a forward position: *to play up front*—see also UPFRONT—more at BACK *n.*, CASH *n.*, LEAD *v.*

■ *adj.* [only before noun] on or at the front of sth: *the front page of the newspaper* ◊ *front teeth* ◊ *the front wheels of the car* ◊ *We had seats in the front row.* ◊ *an animal's front legs* ◊ *Let's go through to the front room* (= the main room in a house where people sit and entertain guests). ◊ *a front-seat passenger*—compare BACK, HIND *adj.*

IDM on the ¦front burner (informal, especially AmE) (of an issue, a plan, etc.) being given a lot of attention because it is considered important: *Anything that keeps education on the front burner is good.*—compare ON THE BACK BURNER at BACK *adj.*

■ *verb*

FACE STH | **1** ~ (onto sth) to face sth or be in front of sth; to have the front pointing towards sth: [VN] *The cathedral fronts the city's main square.* ◊ [V] *The line of houses fronted straight onto the road.*

COVER FRONT | **2** [VN] [usually passive] to have the front covered with sth: *a glass-fronted bookcase*

LEAD GROUP | **3** [VN] to lead or represent an organization, a group, etc: *He fronts a multinational company.* ◊ *A former art student fronted the band* (= was the main singer).

PRESENT TV PROGRAMME | **4** [VN] (BrE) to present a television programme, a show, etc.

PHRV ¦front for sb/sth to represent a group or an organization and try to hide its secret or illegal activities: *He fronted for them in several illegal property deals.*

WHICH WORD?
in front of / in the front of ❓

In front of can mean the same as **outside** but not **opposite**: *I'll meet you in front of/outside your hotel.* ◊ *There's a bus stop in front of the house* (= on the same side of the road). ◊ *There's a bus stop opposite the house* (= on the other side of the road). — picture on page 517

In/at the front (of sth) means 'in the most forward part of something': *The driver sits at the front of the bus.* ◊ *Put the shortest flowers in the front (of the bunch).*

front·age /ˈfrʌntɪdʒ/ noun **1** [C, U] the front of a building, especially when this faces a road or river: *the baroque frontage of Milan Cathedral* ◊ *a restaurant with good river frontage* **2** [U] (especially AmE) land that is next to a building, street or area of water: *They bought two miles of river frontage along the Colorado.*

frontage road noun (AmE) = SERVICE ROAD

front·al /ˈfrʌntl/ adj. [only before noun] **1** connected with the front of sth: *Air bags are designed to protect the driver in the event of a severe frontal impact.* ◊ *full-frontal nudity* (= showing the whole of the front of a person's body) **2** (frontal attack/assault) an attack or criticism that is very strong and direct: *They launched a frontal attack on company directors.* **3** connected with a weather FRONT: *a cold frontal system* **4** (medical) connected with the front part of the head: *the frontal lobes of the brain* ▶ **front·al·ly** /-təli/ adv.

the ¦front ¦bench noun [C+sing./pl. v.] the most important members of the government and the OPPOSITION in the British parliament, who sit in the front rows of seats: *an Opposition front-bench spokesman on defence*—compare BACK BENCH

front·bench·er /ˌfrʌntˈbentʃə(r)/ noun an important member of the government or the OPPOSITION in the British parliament, who sits in the front rows of seats—compare BACK-BENCHER

¦front ¦door noun the main entrance to a house, usually at the front: *There's someone at the front door.*—picture at HOUSE

¦front-¦end ¦loader noun (especially AmE) a large vehicle with machinery for digging worked by a system of HYDRAULICS

fron·tier /ˈfrʌntɪə(r); AmE frʌnˈtɪr/ noun **1** (BrE) [C] ~ (between A and B) | ~ (with sth) a line that separates two countries, etc.; the land near this line: *the frontier between the land of the Saxons and that of the Danes* ◊ *border guards on the frontier with Kuwait* ◊ *a frontier town/zone/post* **2** (the frontier) [sing.] the edge of land where people live and have built towns, beyond which the country is wild and unknown, especially in the Western US in the 19th century: *a remote frontier settlement* **3** [C, usually pl.] ~ (of sth) the limit of sth, especially the limit of what is known about a particular subject or activity: *to push back the frontiers of science* (= to increase knowledge of science) ◊ *to roll back the frontiers of government* (= to limit the powers of the government)

fron·tiers·man /ˈfrʌntɪəzmən; AmE frʌnˈtɪrz-/ noun (pl. -men /-mən/) a man living on the frontier, especially one who lived in the western US during the 19th century

fron·tis·piece /ˈfrʌntɪspiːs/ noun [usually sing.] a picture at the beginning of a book, on the page opposite the page with the title on it

the ¦front ¦line noun [sing.] an area where the enemies are facing each other during a war and where fighting takes place: *Tanks have been deployed all along the front line.* ◊ *front-line troops* **IDM** in the front line (of sth) doing work that will have an important effect on sth: *a life spent in the front line of research*

front·man /ˈfrʌntmæn/ noun (pl. -men /-men/) **1** a person who represents an organization and tries to make its activities seem acceptable to the public, although in fact they may be illegal: *He acted as a frontman for a drugs cartel.* **2** the leader of a group of musicians **3** (BrE) a person who presents a television programme

¦front ¦office noun [sing.] (especially AmE) the part of a business concerned with managing things or dealing with the public

¦front-of-¦house noun [U] (BrE) **1** the parts of a theatre that are used by the audience **2** (often used as an adjective) the business of dealing with an audience at a theatre, for example selling tickets and programmes

¦front-¦page adj. [only before noun] important or interesting enough to be printed on the front page of a newspaper: *The divorce made front-page news.*

¦front ¦runner noun a person, an animal or an organization that seems most likely to win a race or competition: *He is one of the front runners in the presidential election.*

frost /frɒst; AmE frɔːst/ noun, verb

■ *noun* **1** [U, C] a weather condition in which the temperature drops below 0°C (= FREEZING POINT) so that a thin

white layer of ice forms on the ground and other surfaces, especially at night: *It will be a clear night with some* **ground frost**. ◊ *a sharp/hard/severe frost* ◊ *There were ten degrees of frost* (= the temperature dropped to -10°C) *last night.* ◊ *frost damage* **2** [U] the thin white layer of ice that forms when the temperature drops below 0°C: *The car windows were covered with frost.*—see also HOAR FROST
- *verb* **1** ~ **(sth) (over/up)** to cover sth or to become covered with a thin white layer of ice: [VN] *The mirror was frosted up.* ◊ [V] *The windows had frosted over.* **2** [VN] *(especially AmE)* to cover a cake with ICING/FROSTING

frost·bite /ˈfrɒstbaɪt; AmE ˈfrɔːst-/ *noun* [U] a medical condition in which parts of the body, especially the fingers and toes, become damaged as a result of extremely cold temperatures ▶ **frost·bit·ten** /ˈfrɒstbɪtn; AmE ˈfrɔːst-/ *adj.*

frost·ed /ˈfrɒstɪd; AmE ˈfrɔːstɪd/ *adj.* **1** [only before noun] (of glass) that has been given a rough surface, so that it is difficult to see through: *frosted windows* **2** *(especially AmE)* (of cakes, etc.) covered with ICING/FROSTING **3** covered with FROST: *the frosted garden/ground*

frost·ing /ˈfrɒstɪŋ; AmE ˈfrɔːst-/ *noun* [U] *(AmE)* = ICING

frosty /ˈfrɒsti; AmE ˈfrɔːsti/ *adj.* **1** (of the weather) extremely cold; cold with FROST: *a frosty morning* ◊ *He breathed in the frosty air.* **2** covered with FROST: *frosty fields* **3** unfriendly, in a way that suggests that sb does not approve of sth: *a frosty look/reply* ◊ *The latest proposals were given a frosty reception.* ▶ **frost·ily** /-ɪli/ *adv.*: *'No, thank you,' she said frostily.*

froth /frɒθ; AmE frɔːθ/ *noun, verb*
- *noun* **1** [U] a mass of small bubbles, especially on the surface of a liquid SYN FOAM: *a glass of beer with thick froth on top* **2** [U] ideas, activities, etc. that seem attractive and enjoyable but have no real value **3** [sing.] ~ **of sth** something that looks like a mass of small bubbles on liquid: *a froth of black lace*
- *verb* **1** if a liquid **froths**, or if sb/sth **froths** it, a mass of small bubbles appears on the surface: [V] *a cup of frothing coffee* ◊ *The water gushed and frothed.* [also VN] **2** [V] to produce a lot of SALIVA (= liquid in your mouth): *The dog was frothing at the mouth.* ◊ *(figurative) He frothed at the mouth* (= was very angry) *when I asked for more money.*

froth

frothy /ˈfrɒθi; AmE ˈfrɔːθi/ *adj.* **1** (of liquids) having a mass of small bubbles on the surface: *frothy coffee* **2** seeming attractive and enjoyable but having no real value: *frothy romantic novels* **3** (of clothes or fabric) light and delicate: *a frothy pink dress*

frown /fraʊn/ *verb, noun*
- *verb* ~ **(at sb/sth)** to make a serious, angry or worried expression by bringing your EYEBROWS closer together so that lines appear on your forehead: [V] *What are you frowning at me for?* ◊ *She frowned with concentration.* [also V speech] PHRV **ˈfrown on/upon sb/sth** to disapprove of sb/sth: *In her family, any expression of feeling was frowned upon.*
- *noun* [usually sing.] a serious, angry or worried expression on a person's face that causes lines on their forehead: *She looked up with a puzzled frown on her face.* ◊ *a slight frown of disapproval/concentration*

frow·sty /ˈfraʊsti/ *adj.* *(BrE)* smelling bad because there is no fresh air: *a small frowsty office/room*

froze *pt* of FREEZE

fro·zen /ˈfrəʊzn; AmE ˈfroʊzn/ *adj.* **1** [usually before noun] (of food) kept at a very low temperature in order to preserve it: *frozen peas* **2** [not usually before noun] (of people or parts of the body) extremely cold: *I'm absolutely frozen!* ◊ *You look frozen stiff.* **3** (of rivers, lakes, etc.) with a layer of ice on the surface **4** (especially of ground) so cold that it has become very hard: *The ground was frozen solid.* **5** ~ **with/in sth** unable to move because of a strong emotion such as fear or horror: *She stared at him, frozen with shock.*—see also FREEZE *v.*

fruc·tose /ˈfrʌktəʊs; -təʊz; AmE -toʊs, -toʊz/ *noun* [U] *(chemistry)* a type of sugar found in fruit juice and HONEY

fru·gal /ˈfruːɡl/ *adj.* **1** using only as much money or food as is necessary: *a frugal existence/life* ◊ *He has always been hard-working and frugal.* **2** (of meals) small, plain and not costing very much: *a frugal lunch of bread and cheese* ▶ **fru·gal·ity** /fruˈɡæləti/ *noun* [U] **fru·gal·ly** /-ɡəli/ *adv.*: *to live/eat frugally*

fruit /fruːt/ *noun, verb*
- *noun* **1** [C, U] the part of a plant that consists of a stone/pit or seeds and flesh, can be eaten as food and usually tastes sweet: *tropical fruits, such as bananas and pineapples* ◊ *Eat plenty of fresh fruit and vegetables.* ◊ *fruit juice* ◊ *fruit trees*—see also DRIED FRUIT, FIRST FRUIT, SOFT FRUIT—compare VEGETABLE—picture on page A2 **2** [C] *(technical)* a part of a plant or tree that is formed after the flowers have died and in which seeds develop **3** [C, usually pl.] *(literary)* all the natural things that the earth produces IDM **the fruit/fruits of sth** the good results of an activity or a situation: *to enjoy the fruits of your labours* (= the rewards for your hard work) ◊ *The book is the fruit of years of research.*—more at BEAR *v.*, FORBIDDEN
- *verb* [V] *(technical)* (of a tree or plant) to produce fruit

ˈfruit bat *noun* a BAT (= an animal like a mouse with wings) that lives in hot countries and eats fruit

ˈfruit cake *noun* **1** [C, U] a cake containing dried fruit **2** **(fruitcake)** [C] *(informal)* a person who behaves in a strange or crazy way: *She's nutty as a fruitcake.*

fruit·er·er /ˈfruːtərə(r)/ *noun* *(old-fashioned, especially BrE)* a person who owns or manages a shop/store selling fruit—compare GREENGROCER

ˈfruit fly *noun* a small fly that eats plants that are decaying, especially fruit

fruit·ful /ˈfruːtfl/ *adj.* **1** producing many useful results: *a fruitful collaboration/discussion* OPP FRUITLESS **2** *(literary)* (of land or trees) producing a lot of crops ▶ **fruit·ful·ly** /ˈfruːtfəli/ *adv.* **fruit·ful·ness** /ˈfruːtfəlnəs/ *noun* [U]

fru·ition /fruˈɪʃn/ *noun* [U] *(formal)* the successful result of a plan, a process or an activity: *After months of hard work, our plans finally came to fruition.* ◊ *His extravagant ideas were never brought to fruition.*

fruit·less /ˈfruːtləs/ *adj.* producing no useful results: *a fruitless attempt/search* ◊ *Our efforts to persuade her proved fruitless.* OPP FRUITFUL ▶ **fruit·less·ly** *adv.*

ˈfruit machine *(BrE)* (also **ˌone-armed ˈbandit**, **ˈslot machine** *AmE, BrE*) *noun* a gambling machine that you put coins into and that gives money back if particular pictures appear together on the screen

ˌfruit ˈsalad *noun* [U, C] a cold DESSERT (= a sweet dish) consisting of small pieces of different types of fruit—picture on page A1

fruity /ˈfruːti/ *adj.* (**fruit·ier**, **fruiti·est**) **1** smelling or tasting strongly of fruit: *The wine from this region is rich and fruity.* **2** (of a voice or laugh) deep and pleasant in quality **3** *(AmE, informal)* (of people) slightly crazy

frump /frʌmp/ *noun* *(disapproving)* a woman who wears clothes that are not fashionable ▶ **frumpy** (also *less frequent* **frump·ish**) *adj.*: *frumpy clothes/shoes* ◊ *a frumpy housewife*

frus·trate /frʌˈstreɪt; AmE ˈfrʌstreɪt/ *verb* [VN] **1** to make sb feel annoyed or impatient because they cannot do or achieve what they want: *What frustrates him is that there's too little money to spend on the project.* **2** *(written)* to prevent sb from doing sth; to prevent sth from happening or succeeding: *The rescue attempt was frustrated by bad weather.*

frus·trated /frʌˈstreɪtɪd; AmE ˈfrʌstreɪtɪd/ *adj.* **1** [not before noun] ~ **(at/with sth)** feeling annoyed and impatient because you cannot do or achieve what you want: *It's very easy to get frustrated in this job.* ◊ *They felt frustrated at the lack of progress.* **2** (of an emotion) having no effect; not being satisfied: *He stamped his foot in frustrated rage.* ◊ *frustrated desires/passions* **3** [only before noun] unable to be successful in a particular career: *a frustrated artist* **4** not satisfied sexually

frus·trat·ing /frʌˈstreɪtɪŋ; AmE ˈfrʌstreɪtɪŋ/ *adj.* causing you to feel annoyed and impatient because you cannot do

b	d	f	g	h	k	l	m	n	p	r
bad	did	fall	get	hat	cat	leg	man	now	pen	red

F

or achieve what you want: *It's frustrating to have to wait so long.* ▶ **frus·trat·ing·ly** *adv.*: *Progress was frustratingly slow.*

frus·tra·tion /frʌˈstreɪʃn/ *noun* **1** [U] the feeling of being frustrated: *Dave thumped the table **in frustration**.* ◊ *She couldn't stand the frustration of not being able to help.* **2** [C, usually pl.] something that causes you to feel frustrated: *Every job has its difficulties and frustrations.* ◊ *Inevitably she took out her frustrations on the children.* **3** [U] **~ of sth** (*formal*) the fact that sth is preventing sth/sb from succeeding: *the frustration of all his ambitions*

fry /fraɪ/ *verb, noun*
■ *verb* (**fries, fry·ing, fried, fried**) to cook sth in hot fat or oil; to be cooked in hot fat or oil: [VN] *fried fish* ◊ [V] *the smell of bacon frying*—related noun FRY-UP ⇨ vocabulary notes on page 274—see also STIR-FRY **IDM** see FISH *n.*
■ *noun* **1** [pl.] very small young fish—see also SMALL FRY **2** [C] (usually **fries**) [pl.] (*especially AmE*) = CHIP

fryer (also **frier**) /ˈfraɪə(r)/ *noun* **1** a large deep pan used for frying food in: *a deep-fat fryer* **2** (*AmE*) a young chicken that is suitable for frying

ˈfrying pan (*AmE* also **fry·pan, skil·let**) *noun* a large shallow pan with a long handle, used for frying food in—picture at PAN **IDM** **out of the ˈfrying pan into the ˈfire** from a bad situation to one that is worse

ˈfry-up *noun* (*BrE, informal*) a meal of fried food, such as BACON and eggs

FT (also **F/T**) *abbr.* (in writing) FULL-TIME: *The course is 1 year FT, 2 years PT.*—compare PT

ft (*BrE*) (also **ft.** *AmE, BrE*) *abbr.* (in writing measurements) feet; foot: *The room is 12ft x 9ft.*

fuch·sia /ˈfjuːʃə/ *noun* [C, U] a small bush with flowers in two colours of red, purple or white, that hang down

fuck /fʌk/ *verb, noun*
■ *verb* (⚠, *slang*) **1** [V, VN] to have sex with sb **2** a swear word that many people find offensive that is used to express anger, disgust or surprise: [V] *Oh, fuck! I've lost my keys.* ◊ [VN] *Fuck it! We've missed the train.* ◊ *Fuck you—I'm leaving.* **IDM** **fuck ˈme** used to express surprise: *Fuck me! Have you seen how much this costs?* **PHRV** **ˌfuck aˈround** (*BrE* also **ˌfuck aˈbout**) to waste time by behaving in a silly way: *Stop fucking around and come and help.* **HELP** A more polite, informal way of saying this is **mess about** (*BrE*) or **mess around** (*AmE,BrE*). **ˌfuck sb aˈround** (*BrE* also **ˌfuck sb aˈbout**) to treat sb in a way that is deliberately not helpful to them or wastes their time: *This damn company keeps fucking me around.* **HELP** A more polite, informal way of saying this is **mess sb about/around** (*BrE*). **ˌfuck ˈoff** (usually used in orders) to go away: *Why don't you just fuck off?* **ˌfuck ˈup** to do sth badly or make a bad mistake: *You've really fucked up this time!* **HELP** A more polite way to express this is **mess up.** **ˌfuck sb↔ˈup** to upset or confuse sb so much that they are not able to deal with problems in their life: *My parents' divorce really fucked me up.* **HELP** A more polite way to express this is **mess sb up.** **ˌfuck sth↔ˈup** to do sth badly or spoil sth: *I completely fucked up my exams.* **HELP** A more polite, informal way of saying this is **foul sth up, cock sth up** (slang), **mess sth up** or **bungle sth.** **ˈfuck with sb** to treat sb badly in a way that makes them annoyed: *Don't fuck with him.* **HELP** A more polite way to express this is **mess with sb.**
■ *noun* (⚠, *slang*) **1** [C, usually sing.] an act of sex **2** (**the fuck**) [sing.] used for emphasis, or to show that you are angry, annoyed or surprised: *What the fuck are you doing?* ◊ *Let's get the fuck out of here!* **IDM** **not give a ˈfuck (about sb/sth)** to not care at all about sb/sth: *He doesn't give a fuck about anyone else.*—see also F-WORD

ˌfuck ˈall *noun* [U] (*BrE*, ⚠, *slang*) a phrase that many people find offensive, used to mean 'none at all' or 'nothing at all': *You've done fuck all today.* ◊ *These instructions make fuck all sense to me.*

fuck·er /ˈfʌkə(r)/ *noun* (⚠, *slang*) a very offensive word used to insult sb

fuck·ing /ˈfʌkɪŋ/ *adj., adv.* (⚠, *spoken*) a swear word that many people find offensive that is used to emphasize a

comment or an angry statement: *I'm fucking sick of this fucking rain!* ◊ *He's a fucking good player.* **IDM** **ˈfucking well** (*especially BrE*) used to emphasize an angry statement or an order: *You're fucking well coming whether you want to or not.*

fud·dled /ˈfʌdld/ *adj.* unable to think clearly, usually as a result of old age or drinking alcohol

fuddy-duddy /ˈfʌdi dʌdi/ *noun* (*pl.* **fuddy-duddies**) (*informal*) a person who has old-fashioned ideas or habits: *You're such an old fuddy-duddy!* ▶ **fuddy-duddy** *adj.*: *fuddy-duddy ideas*

fudge /fʌdʒ/ *noun, verb*
■ *noun* **1** [U] a type of soft brown sweet/candy made from sugar, butter and milk **2** (**a fudge**) [sing.] (*especially BrE*) a way of dealing with a situation that does not really solve the problems but is intended to appear to do so: *This solution is a fudge rushed in to win cheers at the party conference.*
■ *verb* **~ (on) sth** to avoid giving clear and accurate information, or a clear answer: [VN] *I asked how long he was staying, but he fudged the answer.* ◊ *Politicians are often very clever at **fudging the issue**.* [also V]

fuel /ˈfjuːəl/ *noun, verb*
■ *noun* [U, C] any material that produces heat or power, usually when it is burnt: *solid fuel* (= wood, coal, etc.) ◊ *nuclear fuels* ◊ *a car with high fuel consumption*—see also FOSSIL FUEL **IDM** see ADD *v.*
■ *verb* (**-ll-,** *AmE* **-l-**) **1** [VN] to supply sth with material that can be burnt to produce heat or power: *Uranium is used to fuel nuclear plants.* ◊ *oil-fuelled power stations* **2** **~ (sth) (up)** to put petrol/gas into a vehicle: [VN] *The helicopter was already fuelled (up) and ready to go.* [also V] **3** [VN] (*written*) to increase sth; to make sth stronger: *to fuel speculation/rumours/fears* ◊ *Higher salaries helped to fuel inflation.*

ˈfuel injection *noun* [U] a system of putting fuel into the engine of a car under pressure as a way of improving its performance

fug /fʌg/ *noun* [sing.] (*BrE, informal*) air in a room that is hot and smells unpleasant because there are too many people in the room or because people are smoking

fu·gi·tive /ˈfjuːdʒətɪv/ *noun, adj.*
■ *noun* **~ (from sb/sth)** a person who has escaped or is running away from somewhere and is trying to avoid being caught: *a fugitive from justice*
■ *adj.* [only before noun] **1** trying to avoid being caught: *a fugitive criminal* **2** (*literary*) lasting only for a very short time: *a fugitive idea/thought*

fugue /fjuːg/ *noun* a piece of music in which one or more tunes are introduced and then repeated in a complicated pattern

-ful *suffix* **1** (in adjectives) full of; having the qualities of; tending to: *sorrowful* ◊ *masterful* ◊ *forgetful* **2** (in nouns) an amount that fills sth: *handful* ◊ *spoonful*

ful·crum /ˈfʊlkrəm; ˈfʌlk-/ *noun* (*pl.* **ful·crums** or **ful·cra** /ˈfʊlkrə; ˈfʌlk-/) **1** (*physics*) the point on which a LEVER turns or is supported **2** [usually sing.] (*written*) the most important part of an activity, or a situation

ful·fil (*BrE*) (*AmE* **ful·fill**) /fʊlˈfɪl/ *verb* (**ful·fill·ing, ful·filled, ful·filled**) [VN] **1** to do or achieve what was hoped for or expected: *to fulfil your dream/ambition/potential* **2** to do or have what is required or necessary: *to fulfil a duty/obligation/promise* ◊ *to fulfil the terms/conditions of an agreement* ◊ *No candidate fulfils all the criteria for this position.* **3** to have a particular role or purpose: *Nursery schools should fulfil the function of preparing children for school.* **4** **~ sb/yourself** to make sb feel happy and satisfied with what they are doing or have done: *I need a job that really fulfils me.* ◊ *He was able to fulfil himself through his painting.* ▶ **ful·fil·ment** (*BrE*) (*AmE* **ful·fill·ment**) *noun* [U]: *the fulfilment of dreams/desires/hopes* ◊ *to find emotional/personal fulfilment*

ful·filled /fʊlˈfɪld/ *adj.* feeling happy and satisfied that you are doing sth useful with your life: *He doesn't feel fulfilled in his present job.* **OPP** UNFULFILLED

ful·fil·ling /fʊlˈfɪlɪŋ/ *adj.* causing sb to feel satisfied and useful: *a fulfilling experience*

full /fʊl/ *adj., adv.*
■ *adj.* (**full·er, fullest**)
WITH NO EMPTY SPACE | **1 ~ (of sth)** containing or holding as much or as many as possible; having no empty space: *a full bottle of wine* ◊ *She could only nod, because her mouth was full.* ◊ *My suitcase was full of books.* ◊ *There were cardboard boxes stuffed full of clothes.* ◊ (*BrE*) *Sorry, the hotel is full up tonight.*

HAVING A LOT | **2 ~ of sth** having or containing a large number or amount of sth: *The sky was full of brightly coloured fireworks.* ◊ *Life is full of coincidences.* ◊ *Our new brochure is crammed full of inspirational ideas.* ◊ *animals pumped full of antibiotics* ◊ *She was full of admiration for the care she had received.* ◊ *He smiled, his eyes full of laughter.*

TALKING A LOT | **3** (of a person) **~ of sth** thinking or talking a lot about a particular thing: *He was full of his new job and everything he'd been doing.*

WITH FOOD | **4** (*BrE* also **full up**) having had enough to eat: *No more for me, thanks—I'm full up.* ◊ *The kids still weren't full, so I gave them an ice cream each.* ◊ *You can't run on a full stomach.*

COMPLETE | **5** [usually before noun] complete; with nothing missing: *Full details are available on request.* ◊ *I still don't think we've heard the full story.* ◊ *a full English breakfast* ◊ *A full refund will be given if the item is faulty.* ◊ *Fill in your full name and address.* ◊ *The address must be printed in full.* ◊ *The country applied for full membership of the European Union.*

AS MUCH AS POSSIBLE | **6** [usually before noun] to the highest level or greatest amount possible: *Many people don't use their computers to their full potential.* ◊ *measures to achieve full employment* ◊ *Students should take full advantage of the university's facilities.* ◊ *I've always believed in living life to the full.* ◊ *She came round the corner at full speed.*

FOR EMPHASIS | **7** [only before noun] used to emphasize an amount or a quantity: *She is a full four inches shorter than her sister.*

BUSY | **8** busy; involving a lot of activities: *He'd had a very full life.* ◊ *Her life was too full to find time for hobbies.*

MOON | **9** appearing as a complete circle: *The moon was full, the sky clear.*—see also FULL MOON

FAT | **10** (of a person or part of the body) large and round. 'Full' is sometimes used to avoid saying 'fat': *He kissed her full sensual lips.* ◊ *They specialize in clothes for women with a fuller figure.*

CLOTHES | **11** made with plenty of fabric; fitting loosely: *a full skirt*

TONE/VOICE/FLAVOUR | **12** deep, strong and rich: *He draws a unique full sound from the instrument.* ◊ *the full fruity flavour of the wine*

IDM Most idioms containing **full** are at the entries for the nouns and verbs in the idioms, for example **full of the joys of spring** is at joy. **full of yourself** (*disapproving*) very proud; thinking only of yourself
■ *adv.* **~ in/on sth** directly: *She looked him full in the face.*

full·back /ˈfʊlbæk/ *noun* **1** [C] one of the defending players in football/soccer, hockey or rugby whose position is near the goal they are defending **2** [C] the attacking player in American football whose position is behind the QUARTERBACK and beside the HALFBACKS **3** [U] the position a fullback plays at: *Hunter is at fullback.*

full-'blooded *adj.* [only before noun] **1** involving very strong feelings or actions; done in an enthusiastic way: *a full-blooded attack* **2** having parents, grandparents, etc. from only one race: *a full-blooded Scotsman*

full-'blown *adj.* [only before noun] having all the characteristics of sb/sth; fully developed: *full-blown Aids* ◊ *The border dispute turned into a full-blown crisis.*

full 'board *noun* [U] a type of accommodation in a hotel, etc. that includes all meals: *Do you require full or half board?*—compare BED AND BREAKFAST, HALF BOARD

full-'bodied *adj.* having a pleasantly strong taste or sound: *a full-bodied red wine* ◊ *a full-bodied string section*

full-'colour (*BrE*) (*AmE* **full-'color**) *adj.* [only before noun] printed using colours rather than just black and white

full-court 'press *noun* [sing.] (*AmE*) **1** (in basketball) a way of attacking in which the members of a team stay close to their opponents over the whole area of play **2** (*informal*) a strong effort to influence sb or a group of people by putting pressure on them

full·er's earth /ˌfʊləz ˈɜːθ; *AmE* ˌfʊlərz ˈɜːrθ/ *noun* [U] a type of clay used for cleaning cloth and making it thicker

full-'face *adj., adv.* showing the whole of sb's face; not in PROFILE: *a full-face view/portrait*

full-'fat *adj.* [usually before noun] (*especially BrE*) (of milk, cheese, etc.) without any of the fat removed

full-'fledged *adj.* (*especially AmE*) = FULLY-FLEDGED

full-'grown *adj.* (of people, animals or plants) having reached the greatest size to which they can grow and stopped growing

full 'house *noun* **1** an occasion in a theatre, cinema/movie theater, etc. when there are no empty seats: *They played to a full house.* **2** (in the card game of POKER) three cards of one kind and two of another kind

full-'length *adj., adv.*
■ *adj.* [only before noun] **1** (of a mirror or picture) showing the whole of a person's body: *a full-length portrait* **2** (of a book, play, etc.) not made shorter; of the usual length: *a full-length novel* **3** (of curtains or a window) reaching the ground **4** (of clothing) reaching a person's ankles: *a full-length skirt/coat*
■ *adv.* a person who is lying **full-length** is lying flat with their legs straight: *He was sprawled full-length across the bed.*

full 'marks *noun* [pl.] (*BrE*) the highest mark/grade in a test, etc. (when you get nothing wrong): *She got full marks in the exam.* ◊ (*figurative*) *Full marks to Bill for an excellent idea!* (= he deserves praise)

full 'moon *noun* [C usually sing, U] the moon when it appears as a full circle; a time when this happens—compare HALF-MOON, NEW MOON

full·ness /ˈfʊlnəs/ *noun* [U, sing.] **1** (of the body or part of the body) the quality of being large and round: *the fullness of her lips* **2** (of colours, sounds and flavours) the quality of being deep and rich **3** the quality of being complete and satisfying: *the fullness of life* **IDM** **in the fullness of 'time** when the time is appropriate, usually after a long period

full-'page *adj.* [only before noun] filling a complete page of a newspaper or magazine: *a full-page ad*

full professor *noun* (*AmE*) = PROFESSOR (1)

full-'scale *adj.* [only before noun] **1** that is as complete and thorough as possible: *a full-scale attack* ◊ *The police made a full-scale search of the area.* **2** that is the same size as sth that is being copied: *a full-scale model*

full-size (also **full-sized**) *adj.* [only before noun] not made smaller; of the usual size: *a full-size model* ◊ *a full-size snooker table*

full 'stop *noun, adv.*
■ *noun* (also less frequent **stop**) (both *BrE*) (*AmE* **period**) the mark (.) used at the end of a sentence and in some abbreviations, for example *e.g.* ⇨ Appendix 4 **IDM** **come to a full 'stop** to stop completely
■ *adv.* (*BrE*) (also **period** *AmE, BrE*) (*spoken*) used at the end of a sentence to emphasize that there is nothing more to say about a subject: *I've already told you—we can't afford it, full stop!*

full-'term *adj.* (*technical*) **1** (of a pregnancy) lasting the normal length of time **2** (of a baby) born after a pregnancy lasting the normal length of time

full 'time *noun* [U] (*BrE*) (in a game of football, rugby, etc: *The referee blew his whistle for full time.* ◊ *The full-time score was 1-1.*—compare HALF-TIME

full-'time *adj., adv.* (*abbr.* **FT**) for all the hours of a week during which people normally work or study, rather than just for a part of it: *students in full-time education* ◊ *a full-time employee* ◊ *a full-time job* ◊ *Looking after a child is a full-time job* (= hard work that takes a lot of time). ◊

F

æ	ɑː	e	ɜː	ə	ɪ	iː	i	ɒ	ɔː	ʌ	ʊ	u	uː
cat	father	ten	bird	about	sit	see	many	got	saw	cup	put	actual	too
								(BrE)					

She works full-time and still manages to run a home.—
compare PART-TIME

full·timer *noun* a person who works full-time

fully /ˈfʊli/ *adv.* **1** completely: *fully recovered/developed/
equipped* ◊ *We are fully aware of the dangers.* ◊ *I fully
understand your motives.* **2** (*formal*) (used to emphasize
an amount) the whole of; as much as: *The disease affects
fully 30 per cent of the population.*

fully-ˈfledged (*BrE*) (also **full-ˈfledged** *AmE, BrE*) *adj.*
[usually before noun] completely developed; with all the
qualifications necessary for sth: *the emergence of a fully-
fledged market economy* ◊ *She was now a fully-fledged
member of the teaching profession.*

ful·min·ate /ˈfʊlmɪneɪt; ˈfʌl-/ *verb* [V] **~ against (sb/sth)**
(*formal*) to criticize sb/sth angrily ▶ **ful·min·ation**
/ˌfʊlmɪˈneɪʃn; ˌfʌl-/ *noun* [C, U]

ful·some /ˈfʊlsəm/ *adj.* (*disapproving*) too generous in
praising or thanking sb, or in saying sorry, so that you
do not sound sincere: *a fulsome apology/tribute* ◊ *He was
fulsome in his praise of the Prime Minister.* ▶ **ful·some·ly**
adv.

fum·ble /ˈfʌmbl/ *verb, noun*
■ *verb* **1 ~ (at/with/in sth) (for sth)|~ (around)** to use your
hands in an awkward way when you are doing sth or
looking for sth: [V] *She fumbled in her pocket for a handkerchief.* ◊ *He fumbled with the buttons on his shirt.* ◊ *She
was fumbling around in the dark looking for the light
switch.* ◊ [VN] *He fumbled the key into the ignition.*
[also V to inf] **2** to have difficulty speaking clearly or finding the right words to say: [V] *During the interview, she
fumbled helplessly for words.* ◊ [VN] *to fumble an
announcement* **3** [VN] (especially in sport) to drop a ball or
to fail to stop or kick it
■ *noun* **1** [sing.] (also **fum·bling** [C, usually pl.]) an awkward action using the hands **2** [C] (*AmE*) the action of
dropping the ball while it is in play in American football:
After a Pittsburgh fumble, Miami scored a touchdown.

fum·bling /ˈfʌmblɪŋ/ *adj.* awkward, uncertain or hesitating: *a fumbling schoolboy*

fume /fjuːm/ *verb* **1 ~ (at/over/about sb/sth)** to be very
angry about sth: [V] *She sat in the car, silently fuming at
the traffic jam.* ◊ *He was fuming with indignation.*
[also V speech] **2** [V] to produce smoke or fumes

fumes /fjuːmz/ *noun* [pl.] (also *less frequent* **fume** [U])
smoke, gas, or sth similar that smells strongly or is
dangerous to breathe in: *diesel/petrol/exhaust fumes* ◊ *to
be overcome by smoke and fumes* ◊ *Clouds of toxic fumes
escaped in a huge chemical factory blaze.* ◊ *The body of a
man was found in a fume filled car yesterday.*

fu·mi·gate /ˈfjuːmɪgeɪt/ *verb* [VN] to use special chemicals, smoke or gas to destroy the harmful insects or
bacteria in a place: *to fumigate a room* ▶ **fu·mi·ga·tion**
/ˌfjuːmɪˈgeɪʃn/ *noun* [U, C]

fun /fʌn/ *noun, adj.*
■ *noun* [U] **1** enjoyment; pleasure; a thing that gives enjoyment or pleasure and makes you feel happy: *We had a lot
of fun at Sarah's party.* ◊ *Sailing is good fun.* ◊ *Have fun*
(= Enjoy yourself)! ◊ *I decided to learn Spanish, just for
fun.* ◊ *I didn't do all that work just for the fun of it.* ◊ *It's
not much fun going to a party on your own.* ◊ *'What fun!'*
she said with a laugh. ◊ *Walking three miles in the pouring rain is not my idea of fun.* ◊ *'What do you say to a
weekend in New York?' 'Sounds like fun.'* **2** behaviour or
activities that are not serious but come from a sense of
enjoyment: *She's very lively and full of fun.* ◊ *We didn't
mean to hurt him. It was just a bit of fun.* ◊ *It wasn't
serious - it was all done in fun.* IDM **fun and ˈgames**
(*informal*) activities that are not serious and that other
people may disapprove of **make ˈfun of sb/sth** to laugh
at sb/sth or make other people laugh at them, usually in
an unkind way: *It's cruel to make fun of people who
stammer.*—more at FIGURE *n.*, POKE *v.*
■ *adj.* amusing or enjoyable: *She's really fun to be with.* ◊
This game looks fun! ◊ *There are lots of fun things for
young people to do here.*

func·tion /ˈfʌŋkʃn/ *noun, verb*

■ *noun* **1** [C, U] a special activity or purpose of a person or
thing: *to fulfil/perform a useful function* ◊ *bodily functions*
(= for example eating, sex, using the toilet) ◊ *The function
of the heart is to pump blood through the body.* ◊ *This
design aims for harmony of form and function.* **2** [C] a
social event or official ceremony: *The hall provided a
venue for weddings and other functions.* **3** [C] (*mathematics*) a quantity whose value depends on the varying values of others. In the statement 2x=y, y is a function of x:
(*figurative*) *Salary is a function of age and experience.*
4 [C] (*computing*) a part of a program, etc. that carries
out a basic operation
■ *verb* [often +*adv./prep.*] to work in the correct way SYN
OPERATE: *Despite the power cuts, the hospital continued to
function normally.* ◊ *We now have a functioning shower.* ◊
Many children can't function effectively in large classes.
PHRV **ˈfunction as sb/sth** to perform the action or the
job of the thing or person mentioned: *The sofa also functions as a bed.* ◊ *I need money to be able to function as an
artist.*

func·tion·al /ˈfʌŋkʃənl/ *adj.* **1** practical and useful; with
little or no decoration: *Bathrooms don't have to be purely
functional.* ◊ *The office was large and functional rather
than welcoming.* **2** having a special purpose; making it
possible for sb to do sth or for sth to happen: *a functional
disorder* (= an illness caused when an organ of the body
fails to perform its function) ◊ *a functional approach to
language learning* ◊ *These units played a key functional
role in the military operation.* **3** (especially of a machine,
an organization or a system) working; able to work: *a
fully functional hospital* ▶ **func·tion·al·ly** /-ʃənəli/ *adv.*

func·tion·al·ism /ˈfʌŋkʃənəlɪzəm/ *noun* [U] the idea or
belief that the most important thing about the style or
design of a building or object is how it is going to be used,
not how it will look ▶ **func·tion·al·ist** /-ʃənəlɪst/ *noun*
func·tion·al·ist *adj.* [usually before noun]

func·tion·al·ity /ˌfʌŋkʃəˈnæləti/ *noun* **1** [U] the quality
in sth of being very suitable for the purpose it was
designed for SYN PRACTICALITY **2** [U] the purpose that sth
is designed for or expected to perform: *Manufacturing
processes may be affected by the functionality of the product.* **3** [U, C] (*computing*) the range of functions that a
computer or other electronic system can perform: *new
software with additional functionality*

func·tion·ary /ˈfʌŋkʃənəri; *AmE* -neri/ *noun* (*pl.* **-ies**)
(*disapproving*) a person with official duties: *party/state/
government functionaries*

ˈfunction key *noun* (*computing*) one of several keys on a
computer keyboard, each marked with 'F' and a number,
that can be used to do sth, such as save a file or get to the
'help' function in a program

fund /fʌnd/ *noun, verb*
■ *noun* **1** [C] an amount of money that has been saved or
has been made available for a particular purpose: *a
disaster relief fund* ◊ *the company's pension fund* ◊ *the
International Monetary Fund* **2** (**funds**) [pl.] money that is
available to be spent: *government funds* ◊ *The hospital is
trying to raise funds for a new kidney machine.* ◊ *The
project has been cancelled because of lack of funds* ◊ *I'm
short of funds at the moment—can I pay you back next
week?* **3** [sing.] **~ of sth** an amount or a supply of sth: *a
fund of knowledge*
■ *verb* [VN] to provide money for sth, usually sth official: *a
dance festival funded by the Arts Council* ◊ *The museum is
privately funded.* ◊ *a government-funded programme*

fun·da·men·tal /ˌfʌndəˈmentl/ *adj., noun*
■ *adj.* **1** serious and very important; affecting the most
central and important parts of sth: *There is a fundamental difference between the two points of view.* ◊ *A fundamental change in the organization of health services was
required.* ◊ *a question of fundamental importance* **2 ~ (to
sth)** central; forming the necessary basis of sth: *Hard
work is fundamental to success.* **3** [only before noun]
(*physics*) forming the source or base from which everything else is made; not able to be divided any further: *a
fundamental particle*

aɪ	aʊ	eɪ	əʊ	oʊ	ɔɪ	ɪə	eə	ʊə	j	w
my	now	say	go	go	boy	near	hair	pure	yes	wet
			(BrE)	(AmE)						

■ *noun* [usually pl.] a basic rule or principle; an essential part: *the fundamentals of modern physics* ◊ *He taught me the fundamentals of the job.*

fun·da·men·tal·ism /ˌfʌndəˈmentəlɪzəm/ *noun* [U] **1** the practice of following very strictly the basic rules and teachings of any religion **2** (in Christianity) the belief that everything that is written in the Bible is completely true ▶ **fun·da·men·tal·ist** /-ɪst/ *noun: Muslim fundamentalists* **fun·da·men·tal·ist** /-ɪst/ *adj.*

fun·da·men·tal·ly /ˌfʌndəˈmentəli/ *adv.* **1** in every way that is important; completely: *The two approaches are fundamentally different.* ◊ *By the 1960s the situation had changed fundamentally.* ◊ *They remained fundamentally opposed to the plan.* **2** used when you are introducing a topic and stating sth important about it SYN BASICALLY: *Fundamentally, there are two different approaches to the problem.* **3** used when you are saying what is the most important thing about sb/sth SYN BASICALLY: *She is fundamentally a nice person, but she finds it difficult to communicate.*

fun·der /ˈfʌndə(r)/ *noun* a person or an organization that provides money for a particular purpose

fund·ing /ˈfʌndɪŋ/ *noun* [U] money for a particular purpose; the act of providing money for such a purpose: *There have been large cuts in government funding for scientific research.*

ˈfund-raiser *noun* **1** a person who collects money for a charity or an organization **2** a social event or entertainment held in order to collect money for a charity or an organization ▶ **ˈfund-raising** *noun* [U]

fu·neral /ˈfjuːnərəl/ *noun* a ceremony, usually a religious one, for burying or CREMATING (= burning) a dead person: *Hundreds of people attended the funeral.* ◊ *a funeral procession* ◊ *a funeral march* (= a sad piece of music suitable for funerals) IDM **it's ˈyour funeral** (*informal*) used to tell sb that they, and nobody else, will have to deal with the unpleasant results of their own actions

ˈfuneral director *noun* (*formal*) = UNDERTAKER

ˈfuneral parlour (*BrE*) (*AmE* **ˈfuneral parlor**) (also **ˈfuneral home** *AmE, BrE*) (*AmE* also **mor·tu·ary**) *noun* a place where dead people are prepared for being buried or CREMATED (= burned) and where visitors can see the body

fu·ner·ary /ˈfjuːnərəri; *AmE* -reri/ *adj.* [only before noun] (*formal*) of or used at a funeral: *funerary monuments/rites*

fu·ner·eal /fjuˈnɪəriəl; *AmE* -ˈnɪr-/ *adj.* (*formal*) suitable for a funeral; sad: *a funereal atmosphere*

fun·fair /ˈfʌnfeə(r); *AmE* -fer/ *noun* (*BrE*) = FAIR

fung·al /ˈfʌŋgl/ *adj.* of or caused by FUNGUS: *a fungal infection*

fun·gi·cide /ˈfʌŋgɪsaɪd; *AmE* ˈfʌndʒɪ-/ *noun* [C, U] a substance that kills fungus

fun·gus /ˈfʌŋgəs/ *noun* (*pl.* **fungi** /ˈfʌŋgiː; -gaɪ; ˈfʌndʒaɪ/) **1** [C, often pl.] any plant without leaves, flowers or green colouring, usually growing on other plants or on decaying matter. MUSHROOMS and MILDEW are both fungi. **2** [U, C] a covering of MOULD or a similar fungus, for example on a plant or wall: *fungus infections*

fu·nicu·lar /fjuːˈnɪkjələ(r)/ (also **fu,nicular ˈrailway**) *noun* a railway on a steep slope, with the carriages being pulled up and down by a moving cable

funk /fʌŋk/ *noun, verb*
■ *noun* **1** [U] a type of modern dance music with a strong rhythm **2** (also ,blue ˈfunk) [sing.] (*old-fashioned, informal*) a state of fear or anxiety
■ *verb* [VN] (*BrE, informal*) to avoid doing sth because you are afraid to or find it difficult

funky /ˈfʌŋki/ *adj.* (**funk·ier, funki·est**) (*informal*) **1** (of pop music) with a strong rhythm that is easy to dance to: *a funky disco beat* **2** (*approving, especially AmE*) fashionable and unusual: *She wears really funky clothes.*

ˈfun-loving *adj.* (of people) liking to enjoy themselves

fun·nel /ˈfʌnl/ *noun, verb*
■ *noun* **1** a device that is wide at the top and narrow at the bottom, used for pouring liquids or powders into a small opening—picture at LABORATORY **2** (*BrE*) (also **smoke-**

stack *AmE, BrE*) a metal chimney, for example on a ship or an engine, through which smoke comes out—picture at BOAT
■ *verb* (**-ll-,** *AmE* **-l-**) to move or make sth move through a narrow space, or as if through a funnel: [V] *Wind was funnelling through the gorge.* ◊ [VN] *Huge pipes funnel the water down the mountainside.* ◊ *Barricades funnelled the crowds towards the square.* ◊ (*figurative*) *Some $10 million in aid was funnelled into the country through government agencies.*

fun·nies /ˈfʌniz/ *noun* (**the funnies**) [pl.] (*AmE, informal*) the part of a newspaper where there are several COMIC STRIPS (= series of drawings that tell a funny story)

fun·nily /ˈfʌnəli/ *adv.* in a strange way IDM **funnily eˈnough** used to show that you expect people to find a particular fact surprising: *Funnily enough, I met her only yesterday.*

funny /ˈfʌni/ *adj.* (**fun·nier, fun·ni·est**)

AMUSING | **1** making you laugh; amusing: *a funny story* ◊ *That's the funniest thing I've ever heard.* ◊ *It's not funny! Someone could have been hurt.* ◊ *I was really embarrassed, but then I saw the funny side of it.* ◊ (*ironic*) *Oh very funny! You expect me to believe that?* ◊ *'What's so funny?'* *she demanded.* HELP Note that **funny** does not mean 'enjoyable': *The party was great fun.* ◊ ~~The party was very funny.~~

STRANGE | **2** (especially *spoken*) difficult to explain or understand: *A funny thing happened to me today.* ◊ *It's funny how things never happen the way you expect them to.* ◊ *That's funny—he was here a moment ago and now he's gone.* ◊ *The funny thing is it never happened again after that.* ◊ *The engine's making a very funny noise.* ◊ *I'm pleased I didn't get that job, in a funny sort of way.*

SUSPICIOUS/ILLEGAL | **3** (*informal*) suspicious and probably illegal or dishonest: *I suspect there may be something funny going on.* ◊ *If there has been any funny business, we'll soon find out.*

WITHOUT RESPECT | **4** (*BrE*, especially *spoken*) humorous in a way that shows a lack of respect for sb SYN CHEEKY: *Don't you get funny with me!*

ILL/SICK | **5** (*informal*) slightly ill/sick: *I feel a bit funny today—I don't think I'll go to work.*

CRAZY | **6** (*BrE, informal*) slightly crazy; not like other people: *That Dave's a funny chap, isn't he?* ◊ *She went a bit funny after her husband died.*

MACHINE | **7** (*informal*) not working as it should: *My computer keeps going funny.*

ˈfunny bone *noun* [usually sing.] (*informal*) the part of the elbow containing a very sensitive nerve that is painful if you hit it against sth

ˈfun run *noun* (*especially BrE*) an event in which people run a long distance, for fun, and to collect money for charity

fur /fɜː(r)/ *noun* **1** [U] the soft thick mass of hair that grows on the body of some animals **2** [U] the skin of an animal with the fur still on it, used especially for making clothes: *a fur coat* ◊ *the fur trade* ◊ *a fur farm* (= where animals are bred and killed for their fur) ◊ *The animal is hunted for its fur.* ◊ *fur-lined gloves* **3** [U] an artificial fabric that looks and feels like fur **4** [C] a piece of clothing, especially a coat or jacket, made of real or artificial fur: *elegant ladies in furs* **5** (*BrE*) = SCALE *n.* (9) **6** [U] a greyish-white layer that forms on a person's tongue, especially when they are ill—see also FURRED

furi·ous /ˈfjʊəriəs; *AmE* ˈfjʊr-/ *adj.* **1** ~ (**with sb**) | ~ (**at sth/sb**) very angry: *She was absolutely furious at having been deceived.* ◊ *He was furious with himself for letting things get so out of control.* **2** with great energy, speed or anger: *a furious argument/debate* ◊ *She drove off at a furious pace.*—see also FURY ▶ **furi·ous·ly** *adv.: furiously angry* ◊ *'Damn!' he said furiously.* ◊ *They worked furiously all weekend, trying to get it finished on time.* IDM see FAST *adj.*

furl /fɜːl; *AmE* fɜːrl/ *verb* [VN] to roll and fasten sth such as a sail, a flag or an umbrella

fur·long /ˈfɜːlɒŋ; *AmE* ˈfɜːrlɔːŋ/ *noun* (especially in horse

F

racing) a unit for measuring distance, equal to 220 YARDS or 201 metres; one EIGHTH of a mile

fur·lough /ˈfɜːləʊ; *AmE* ˈfɜːrloʊ/ *noun* [U, C] **1** permission to leave your duties for a period of time, especially for soldiers working in a foreign country: *to go home on furlough* ◊ *a six-week furlough* **2** (*AmE*) permission for a prisoner to leave prison for a period of time **3** (*AmE*) a period of time during which workers are told not to come to work, usually because there is not enough money to pay them ▶ **fur·lough** *verb* [VN]

fur·nace /ˈfɜːnɪs; *AmE* ˈfɜːrnɪs/ *noun* **1** an enclosed space or room for heating metal or glass to very high temperatures: *It's like a furnace* (= very hot) *in here!*—see also BLAST FURNACE **2** (*especially AmE*) = BOILER

fur·nish /ˈfɜːnɪʃ; *AmE* ˈfɜːrnɪʃ/ *verb* [VN] **1** to put furniture in a house, room, etc: *The house was simply furnished.* ◊ *The room was furnished with antiques.* ◊ *furnished accommodation* (= to rent complete with furniture) **2** ~ **sb/sth with sth** | ~ **sth** (*formal*) to supply or provide sb/sth with sth; to supply sth to sb: *She furnished him with the facts surrounding the case.*

fur·nish·ings /ˈfɜːnɪʃɪŋz; *AmE* ˈfɜːrn-/ *noun* [pl.] the furniture, carpets, curtains, etc. in a room or house: *soft furnishings* ◊ *The wallpaper should match the furnishings.*

fur·ni·ture /ˈfɜːnɪtʃə(r); *AmE* ˈfɜːrn-/ *noun* [U] objects that can be moved, such as tables, chairs and beds, that are put into a house or an office to make it suitable for living or working in: *a piece of furniture* ◊ *garden/office furniture* ◊ *We need to buy some new furniture.*—see also STREET FURNITURE **IDM** see PART *n.*

ˈfurniture van *noun* (*BrE*) = REMOVAL VAN

fur·ore /fjuˈrɔːri; ˈfjʊərɔː(r); *AmE* ˈfjɔr-/ (also **furor** /ˈfjʊərɔː(r); *AmE* ˈfjɔr-/ especially in *AmE*) *noun* [sing.] ~ (**about/over sth**) great anger or excitement shown by a number of people, usually caused by a public event: *His novel about Jesus caused a furore among Christians.* ◊ *the recent furore over the tax increases*

fur·red /fɜːd; *AmE* fɜːrd/ *adj.* covered with fur or with sth that looks like fur: *a furred tongue*

fur·rier /ˈfʌrɪə(r)/ *noun* a person who prepares or sells clothes made from fur

fur·row /ˈfʌrəʊ; *AmE* ˈfɜːroʊ/ *noun, verb*
■ *noun* **1** a long narrow cut in the ground, especially one made by a PLOUGH for planting seeds in: *dark ploughed earth, with white chalk in the furrows* ◊ *Truck wheels had dug furrows in the track.* **2** a deep line in the skin of the face: *Suddenly he looked tired and there were deep furrows in his brow.* **IDM** see PLOUGH *v.*
■ *verb* **1** [VN] to make a furrow in the earth: *furrowed fields* **2** [V, VN] (*written*) if your BROWS or EYEBROWS **furrow** or **are furrowed**, you pull them together, usually because you are worried, and so produce lines on your face

furry /ˈfɜːri/ *adj.* **1** covered with fur: *small furry animals* **2** like fur: *The moss was soft and furry to the touch.*

fur·ther /ˈfɜːðə(r); *AmE* ˈfɜːrð-/ *adv., adj., verb*
■ *adv.* **1** (comparative of *far*) (*especially BrE*) at or to a greater distance **SYN** FARTHER: *We had walked further than I had realized.* ◊ *Two miles further on we came to a small town.* ◊ *The hospital is further down the road.* ◊ *Can you stand a bit further away?* **2** a longer way in the past or the future: *Think further back into your childhood.* ◊ *How will the company be doing ten years further on?* **3** to a greater degree or extent: *The police decided to investigate further.* ◊ *My life is further complicated by having to work such long hours.* ◊ *Nothing could be further from the truth.* **4** (*formal*) in addition to what has just been said **SYN** FURTHERMORE: *Further, it is important to consider the cost of repairs.* ⇨ note at FARTHER **IDM** **further along/down the ˈroad** at some time in the future: *There are certain to be more job losses further down the road.* **go ˈfurther 1** to say more about sth, or make a more extreme point about it: *I would go even further and suggest that the entire government is corrupt.* **2** to last longer; to serve more people: *They watered down the soup to make it go further.* **go no ˈfurther | not go any ˈfurther** if you tell sb that a secret will **go no further**, you promise not to tell it to anyone else **take sth ˈfurther** to take more serious

action about sth or speak to sb at a higher level about it: *I am not satisfied with your explanation and intend to take the matter further.*—more at AFIELD
■ *adj.* (comparative of *far*) more; ADDITIONAL: *Cook for a further 2 minutes.* ◊ *Have you any further questions?* ◊ *For further details call this number.* ◊ *We have decided to take no further action.* ◊ *The museum is closed **until further notice** (= until we say that it is open again).
■ *verb* [VN] to help sth to develop or be successful: *They hoped the new venture would further the cause of cultural cooperation in Europe.* ◊ *She took the new job to further her career.*

fur·ther·ance /ˈfɜːðərəns; *AmE* ˈfɜːrð-/ *noun* [U] (*formal*) the process of helping sth to develop or to be successful **SYN** ADVANCEMENT: *He took these actions purely in (the) furtherance of his own career.*

ˌfurther eduˈcation *noun* [U] (*abbr.* FE) (*BrE*) education that is provided for people after leaving school, but not at a university—compare HIGHER EDUCATION

fur·ther·more /ˌfɜːðəˈmɔː(r); *AmE* ˌfɜːrðərˈmɔːr/ *adv.* (*formal*) in addition to what has just been stated. Furthermore is used especially to add a point to an argument. **SYN** MOREOVER: *He said he had not discussed the matter with her. Furthermore, he had not even contacted her.*

fur·ther·most /ˈfɜːðəməʊst; *AmE* ˈfɜːrðərmoʊst/ *adj.* (*formal*) situated at the greatest distance from sth: *at the furthermost end of the street*

fur·thest /ˈfɜːðɪst; *AmE* ˈfɜːrð-/ *adj., adv.* = FARTHEST

fur·tive /ˈfɜːtɪv; *AmE* ˈfɜːrtɪv/ *adj.* (*disapproving*) behaving in a way that shows that you want to keep sth secret and do not want to be noticed: *She cast a furtive glance over her shoulder.* ◊ *He looked sly and furtive.* ▶ **fur·tive·ly** *adv.* **fur·tive·ness** *noun* [U]

fury /ˈfjʊəri; *AmE* ˈfjʊri/ *noun* **1** [U] (*written*) extreme anger that often includes violent behaviour: *Her eyes blazed with fury.* ◊ *Fury over tax increases* (= as a newspaper HEADLINE). ◊ (*figurative*) *There was no shelter from the fury of the storm.* **2** [sing.] a state of being extremely angry about sth: *He flew into a fury when I refused.* **3** (**the Furies**) [pl.] (in ancient Greek stories) three GODDESSES who punish people for their crimes—see also FURIOUS **IDM** **like fury** (*informal*) with great effort, power, speed, etc.—more at HELL

furze /fɜːz; *AmE* fɜːrz/ *noun* [U] (*BrE*) = GORSE

fuse /fjuːz/ *noun, verb*
■ *noun* **1** a small wire or device inside a piece of electrical equipment that breaks and stops the current if the flow of electricity is too strong: *to change a fuse* ◊ *Check whether a fuse has blown.* **2** a long piece of string or paper which is lit to make a bomb or a FIREWORK explode **3** (*AmE* also **fuze**) a device that makes a bomb explode when it hits sth or at a particular time: *He set the fuse to three minutes.* ◊ *The bombs inside were on a one-hour fuse.* **IDM** see BLOW *v.*, SHORT *n.*
■ *verb* **1** when one thing **fuses** with another, or two things **fuse** or **are fused**, they are joined together to form a single thing: [V] *As they heal, the bones will fuse together.* ◊ *Our different ideas fused into a plan.* ◊ *The sperm fuses with the egg to begin the process of fertilization.* ◊ [VN] *The two companies have been fused into a single organization.* ◊ *Atoms of hydrogen are fused to make helium.* **2** [V, VN] (*technical*) when a substance, especially metal, **fuses**, or you **fuse** it, it is heated until it melts **3** (*BrE*) to stop working or to make sth stop working because a fuse melts: [V] *The lights have fused.* ◊ [VN] *I've fused the lights.* **4** [VN] [usually passive] to put a fuse in a CIRCUIT or in a piece of equipment: *Is this plug fused?*

ˈfuse box *noun* a small box or cupboard that contains the fuses of the electrical system of a building

fu·sel·age /ˈfjuːzəlɑːʒ; *AmE* ˈfjuːs-/ *noun* the main part of an aircraft in which passengers and goods are carried—picture at PLANE

fu·sil·lade /ˌfjuːzəˈleɪd; *AmE* -sə-/ *noun* a rapid series of shots fired from one or more guns; a rapid series of objects that are thrown: *a fusillade of bullets/stones* ◊ (*figurative*) *He faced a fusillade of questions from the waiting journalists.*

fu·sion /ˈfjuːʒn/ *noun* **1** [U, sing.] the process or result of joining two or more things together to form one: *the fusion of copper and zinc to produce brass* ◊ *The movie displayed a perfect fusion of image and sound.* **2** (also **,nuclear ˈfusion**) [U] (*physics*) the act or process of combining the NUCLEI (= central parts) of atoms to form a heavier NUCLEUS, with energy being released—compare FISSION

fuss /fʌs/ *noun, verb*
■ *noun* **1** [U, sing.] unnecessary excitement, worry or activity: *He does what he's told without any fuss.* ◊ *All that fuss over a few pounds!* ◊ *It's a very ordinary movie—I don't know what all the fuss is about* (= why other people think it is so good). ◊ *It was all a fuss about nothing.* ◊ *We'd like a quiet wedding without any fuss.* **2** [sing.] anger or complaints about sth, especially sth that is not important: *I'm sorry for making such a fuss about the noise.* ◊ *Steve kicks up a fuss every time I even suggest seeing you.* IDM **make a fuss of/over sb** to pay a lot of attention to sb, usually to show how much you like them: *They made a great fuss of the new baby.* ◊ *The dog loves being made a fuss of.*
■ *verb* [V] **1 ~ (around)|~ (with/over sth)** to do things, or pay too much attention to things, that are not important or necessary: *Stop fussing around and find something useful to do!* ◊ *Don't fuss with your hair!* **2 ~ (about sth)** to worry about things that are not very important: *Don't fuss, Mum, everything is all right.* IDM **not be fussed (about sb/sth)** (*BrE, informal*) to not mind about sth; to not have feelings about sth: *It'd be good to be there, but I'm not that fussed.* PHR V **ˈfuss over sb** to pay a lot of attention to sb

fuss·pot /ˈfʌspɒt; *AmE* -pɑːt/ (*BrE*) (*AmE* **fuss·budget** /ˈfʌsbʌdʒɪt/*) noun* (*informal*) a person who is often worried about unimportant things and is difficult to please

fussy /ˈfʌsi/ *adj.* (**fuss·ier**, **fussi·est**) **1 ~ (about sth)** too concerned or worried about details or standards, especially unimportant ones: *fussy parents* ◊ *Our teacher is very fussy about punctuation.* ◊ *She's such a fussy eater.* ◊ *'Where do you want to go for lunch?' 'I'm not fussy* (= I don't care).*'* **2** doing sth with small, quick, nervous movements: *a fussy manner* ◊ *the quick, fussy movements of her small hands* **3** having too much detail or decoration: *a dress covered in fussy bows* ◊ *You should avoid patterned wallpaper and fussy ornaments.* ▶ **fuss·ily** *adv.* **fussi·ness** *noun* [U]

fusty /ˈfʌsti/ *adj.* (*disapproving*) **1** smelling old, damp or not fresh SYN MUSTY: *a dark fusty room* **2** old-fashioned: *fusty ideas* ◊ *a fusty old professor*

fu·tile /ˈfjuːtaɪl; *AmE* -tl/ *adj.* having no purpose because there is no chance of success SYN POINTLESS: *a futile attempt/exercise/gesture* ◊ *Their efforts to revive him were futile.* ◊ *It would be futile to protest.* ◊ *My appeal proved futile.* ▶ **fu·til·ity** /fjuːˈtɪləti/ *noun* [U]: *a sense of futility* ◊ *the futility of war*

fu·ton /ˈfuːtɒn; *AmE* -tɑːn/ *noun* a Japanese MATTRESS, often on a wooden frame, that can be used for sitting on or rolled out to make a bed—picture at BED

fu·ture /ˈfjuːtʃə(r)/ *noun, adj.*
■ *noun* **1** (**the future**) [sing.] the time that will come after the present or the events that will happen then: *We need to plan for the future.* ◊ *What will the cities of the future look like?* ◊ *The movie is set in the future.* ◊ *The exchange rate is likely to fall **in the near future*** (= soon). ◊ *She will not be well enough to work **in the foreseeable future*** (= during the period of time when you know what is going to happen). ◊ *What does the future hold?* **2** [C] what will happen to sb/sth at a later time: *Her future is uncertain.* ◊ *This deal could safeguard the futures of the 2000 employees.* **3** [sing., U] the possibility of being successful or surviving at a later time: *She has **a great future** ahead of her.* ◊ *I can't see any future in this relationship.* **4** (**futures**) [pl.] (*finance*) goods or SHARES that are bought at agreed prices but that will be delivered and paid for at a later time: *oil futures* ◊ *the futures market* **5** (**the future**) [sing.] (*grammar*) (also **the ,future ˈtense**) the form of a verb that expresses what will happen after the present IDM **in future** (*BrE*) (*AmE* **in the future**) from now on: *Please be more careful in future.* ◊ *In future, make sure the door is never left unlocked.*—more at DISTANT, FORESEEABLE
■ *adj.* [only before noun] taking place or existing at a time after the present: *future generations* ◊ *at a future date* ◊ *future developments in computer software* ◊ *He met his future wife at law school.*

fu·tur·ism /ˈfjuːtʃərɪzəm/ *noun* [U] a movement in art and literature in the 1920s and 30s that did not try to show realistic figures and scenes but aimed to express confidence in the modern world, particularly in modern machines ▶ **fu·tur·ist** *noun* **fu·tur·ist** *adj.*: *futurist poets*

fu·tur·is·tic /ˌfjuːtʃəˈrɪstɪk/ *adj.* **1** extremely modern and unusual in appearance, as if belonging to a future time: *futuristic design/furniture* **2** imagining what the future will be like: *a futuristic movie/novel*

fu·tur·ity /fjuːˈtjʊərəti; *AmE* -ˈtʊr-/ *noun* [U] (*rare, formal*) the time that will come after the present and what will happen then: *a vision of futurity*

fuze (*AmE*) = FUSE *n.* (3)

fuzz /fʌz/ *noun* **1** [U] short soft fine hair or fur that covers sth, especially a person's face or arms SYN DOWN **2** [sing.] a mass of hair in tight curls: *a fuzz of blonde hair* **3** (**the fuzz**) [sing.+ sing./pl. *v.*] (*old-fashioned, slang*) the police **4** [U] something that you cannot see clearly SYN BLUR: *I saw it as a dim fuzz through the binoculars.*

fuzzy /ˈfʌzi/ *adj.* **1** covered with short soft fine hair or fur SYN DOWNY **2** (of hair) in a mass of tight curls **3** not clear in shape or sound SYN BLURRED: *a fuzzy image* ◊ *The soundtrack is fuzzy in places.* **4** confused and not expressed clearly: *fuzzy ideas/thinking* ◊ *a somewhat fuzzy definition of 'in the national interest'* ▶ **fuzz·ily** *adv.* **fuzzi·ness** *noun* [U]

,fuzzy ˈlogic *noun* [U] (*computing*) a type of LOGIC that is used to try to make computers behave like the human brain

ˈF-word *noun* (*informal*) used to refer to the offensive swear word 'fuck', to avoid having to say it: *He was shocked at how often she used the F-word.*

FX /ˌef ˈeks/ *abbr.* a short way of writing SPECIAL EFFECTS

-fy ⇨ -IFY

FYI *abbr.* used in writing to mean 'for your information'

æ	ɑː	e	ɜː	ə	ɪ	iː	i	ɒ	ɔː	ʌ	ʊ	u	uː
cat	father	ten	bird	about	sit	see	many	got	saw	cup	put	actual	too
	(BrE)												

Gg

G /dʒiː/ *noun, abbr.*

■ *noun* (also **g**) [C, U] (*pl.* **G's, g's** /dʒiːz/) **1** the 7th letter of the English alphabet: *'Gold' begins with (a) G/'G'.* **2** (**G**) (*music*) the fifth note in the scale of C MAJOR—see also G AND T, G-STRING

■ *abbr.* (*AmE*) general audience (a label for a film/movie that is suitable for anyone, including children)

g *abbr.* **1** gram(s): *400g flour* **2** /dʒiː/ (*technical*) GRAVITY or a measurement of the force with which sth moves faster through space because of GRAVITY: *Spacecraft re-entering the earth's atmosphere are affected by g forces.*

gab /gæb/ *noun* **IDM** see GIFT *n.*

gab·ar·dine (also **gab·er·dine**) /ˌgæbəˈdiːn; ˈgæbədiːn; *AmE* -bərd-/ *noun* **1** [U] a strong fabric used especially for making RAINCOATS **2** [C] a coat, especially a RAINCOAT, made of gabardine

gab·ble /ˈgæbl/ *verb, noun*

■ *verb* ~ (**on/away**) (*informal*) to talk quickly so that people cannot hear you clearly or understand you: [V] *They were gabbling on about the past.* ◊ *She was nervous and started to gabble.* ◊ [VN] *He was gabbling nonsense.* [also V speech]

■ *noun* [sing.] fast speech that is difficult to understand, especially when a lot of people are talking at the same time

gab·fest /ˈgæbfest/ *noun* (*AmE, informal*) an informal meeting to talk and exchange news; a long conversation: *Three old friends stopped by and we had a real gabfest.*

gable /ˈgeɪbl/ *noun* the upper part of the end wall of a building, between the two sloping sides of the roof, that is shaped like a triangle—picture at HOUSE

gabled /ˈgeɪbld/ *adj.* having one or more gables: *a gabled house/roof*

gad /gæd/ *verb* (**-dd-**) **PHRV** **,gad a'bout/a'round** (*informal, especially BrE*) to visit different places and have fun, especially when you should be doing sth else

gad·fly /ˈgædflaɪ/ *noun* (*pl.* **-ies**) (usually *disapproving*) a person who annoys or criticizes other people in order to make them do sth

gadget /ˈgædʒɪt/ *noun* a small tool or device that does sth useful

gadget·ry /ˈgædʒɪtri/ *noun* [U] (sometimes *disapproving*) a collection of modern tools and devices: *His desk is covered with electronic gadgetry.*

Gael·ic *noun* **1** /ˈgeɪlɪk; ˈgælɪk/ the Celtic language of Scotland—compare SCOTS **2** /ˈgeɪlɪk/ (also **,Irish 'Gaelic**) the Celtic language of Ireland—compare ERSE, IRISH ▶ **Gael·ic** *adj.*

gaff /gæf/ *noun* **1** a pole with a hook on the end used to pull large fish out of the water **2** (*BrE, slang*) the house, flat/apartment, etc. where sb lives **IDM** see BLOW *v.*

gaffe /gæf/ *noun* a mistake that a person makes in public or in a social situation, especially sth embarrassing **SYN** FAUX PAS: *a social gaffe* ◊ *He made some real gaffes early in his career.*

gaf·fer /ˈgæfə(r)/ *noun* **1** (*BrE, informal*) a person who is in charge of a group of people, for example, workers in a factory, a football team, etc. **SYN** BOSS: *The gaffer told us we're a good team.* **2** the person who is in charge of the electrical work and the lights when a film/movie or television programme is being made

gag /gæg/ *noun, verb*

■ *noun* **1** a piece of cloth that is put over or in sb's mouth to stop them speaking **2** an order that prevents sth from being publicly reported or discussed: *a press gag* ◊ *a gag rule/order* (= one made by a court of law) **3** (*informal*) a joke or a funny story, especially one told by a professional COMEDIAN: *to tell/crack a gag* ◊ *a running gag* (=

one that is regularly repeated during a performance) **4** (*especially AmE*) a trick you play on sb: *It was just a gag—we didn't mean to upset anyone.*

■ *verb* (**-gg-**) **1** [VN] to put a piece of cloth in or over sb's mouth to prevent them from speaking or shouting: *The hostages were bound and gagged.* **2** [VN] to prevent sb from speaking freely or expressing their opinion: *The new laws are seen as an attempt to gag the press.* **3** [V] ~ (**on sth**) to have the unpleasant feeling in your mouth and stomach as if you are going to VOMIT **SYN** RETCH: *She gagged on the blood that filled her mouth.*

gaga /ˈgɑːgɑː/ *adj.* [not usually before noun] (*informal*) **1** (*offensive*) confused and not able to think clearly, especially because of old age: *He has gone completely gaga.* **2** slightly crazy because you are very excited about sb/sth, or very much in love: *The fans went totally gaga over the band.*

gage (*AmE*) = GAUGE

gag·gle /ˈgægl/ *noun* **1** a group of noisy people: *a gaggle of tourists/schoolchildren* **2** a group of GEESE

gai·ety /ˈgeɪəti/ *noun* [U] (*old-fashioned*) the state of being cheerful and full of fun: *The colourful flags added to the gaiety of the occasion.*—see also GAILY, GAY—compare GAYNESS

gaily /ˈgeɪli/ *adv.* **1** in a bright and attractive way: *a gaily decorated room* **2** in a cheerful way: *gaily laughing children* ◊ *She waved gaily to the little crowd.* **3** without thinking or caring about the effect of your actions on other people: *She gaily announced that she was leaving the next day.*—see also GAIETY, GAY

gain /geɪn/ *verb, noun*

■ *verb*

OBTAIN/WIN | **1** to obtain or win sth, especially sth that you need or want: [VN] *to gain entrance/entry/access to sth* ◊ *The country gained its independence ten years ago.* ◊ *The party gained over 50% of the vote.* ◊ [VNN] *Her unusual talent gained her worldwide recognition.* **2** ~ (**sth**) (**by/ from sth**) to obtain an advantage or benefit from sth or from doing sth: [VN] *There is nothing to be gained from delaying the decision.* ◊ [V] *Who stands to gain from this decision?*

GET MORE | **3** [VN] to gradually get more of sth: *to gain confidence/strength/experience* ◊ *I've gained weight recently.*

OF WATCH/CLOCK | **4** to go too fast: [VN] *My watch gains two minutes every 24 hours.* [also V] **OPP** LOSE

OF CURRENCIES/SHARES | **5** ~ **against sth** to increase in value: [VN] *The shares gained 14p to 262p.* ◊ [V] *The pound gained against the dollar again today.*

REACH PLACE | **6** [VN] (*formal*) to reach a place, usually after a lot of effort: *At last she gained the shelter of the forest.*

IDM **gain 'ground** to become more powerful or successful: *Sterling continues to gain ground against the dollar.* **gain 'time** to delay sth so that you can have more time to make a decision, deal with a problem, etc.—more at VENTURE *v.* **PHRV** **'gain in sth** to get more of a particular quality: *to gain in confidence* ◊ *Wine bars have gained in popularity in recent years.* **'gain on sb/sth** to get closer to sb/sth that you are chasing

■ *noun*

INCREASE | **1** [C, U] an increase in the amount of sth, especially in wealth or weight: *a £3000 gain from our investment* ◊ *Regular exercise is the best way of preventing weight gain.*

ADVANTAGE | **2** [C] an advantage or improvement: *efficiency*

aɪ	aʊ	eɪ	əʊ	oʊ	ɔɪ	ɪə	eə	ʊə	j	w
my	now	say	go	go	boy	near	hair	pure	yes	wet
			(BrE)	(AmE)						

gains ◇ *These policies have resulted in great gains in public health.* ◇ *Our loss is their gain.*

PROFIT **3** [U] (often *disapproving*) financial profit: *He only seems to be interested in personal gain.* ◇ *It's amazing what some people will do for gain.*

gain·ful /'geɪnfl/ *adj.* (*formal*) used to describe useful work that you are paid for: *gainful employment* ▶ **gain·ful·ly** /-fəli/ *adv.*: *gainfully employed*

gain·say /,geɪn'seɪ/ *verb* (**gain·says** /-'sez/, **gain·said**, **gain·said** /-'sed/) [VN] (*formal*) (often used in negative sentences) to say that sth is not true; to disagree with or deny sth: *Nobody can gainsay his claims.*

gait /geɪt/ *noun* [sing.] (*written*) a way of walking: *He walked with a rolling gait.*

gai·ter /'geɪtə(r)/ *noun* [usually pl.] a fabric or leather covering for the leg between the knee and the ankle. Gaiters were worn by men in the past and are now mainly worn by people who go walking or climbing: *a pair of gaiters*

gal /gæl/ *noun* (*old-fashioned informal, especially AmE*) a girl or woman

gal. *abbr.* (in writing) GALLON(S)

gala /'gɑːlə; *AmE* 'geɪlə/ *noun* **1** a special public celebration or entertainment: *a charity gala* ◇ *a gala dinner/ night* **2** (*BrE*) a sports competition, especially in swimming: *a swimming gala*

ga·lac·tic /gə'læktɪk/ *adj.* relating to a galaxy

gal·axy /'gæləksi/ *noun* (*pl.* -ies) **1** [C] any of the large systems of stars, etc. in outer space **2** (**the Galaxy**) (also **the ,Milky 'Way**) [sing.] the system of stars that contains our sun and its planets, seen as a bright band in the night sky **3** [C] (*informal*) a group of famous people, or people with a particular skill: *a galaxy of Hollywood stars*

gale /geɪl/ *noun* **1** an extremely strong wind: *The gale blew down hundreds of trees.* ◇ **gale-force winds** ◇ (*BrE*) *It's blowing a gale outside* (= a strong wind is blowing). **2** (**gale(s) of laughter**) the sound of very loud laughter: *His speech was greeted with gales of laughter.*

gall /gɔːl/ *noun, verb*
▪ *noun* **1** rude behaviour showing a lack of respect that is surprising because the person doing it is not embarrassed: *Then they had the gall to complain!* **2** (*formal*) a bitter feeling full of hatred SYN RESENTMENT **3** a swelling on plants and trees caused by insects, disease, etc. **4** (*old-fashioned*) = BILE
▪ *verb* to make sb feel upset and angry, especially because sth is unfair: [VN to inf] *It galls me to have to apologize to her.* [also VN, VN that] —see also GALLING

gal·lant *adj., noun*
▪ *adj.* /'gælənt/ **1** (*old-fashioned* or *literary*) brave, especially in a very difficult situation: *gallant soldiers/heroes* ◇ *She made a gallant attempt to hide her tears.* **2** (of a man) giving polite attention to women ▶ **gal·lant·ly** *adv.*: *She gallantly battled on alone.* ◇ *He bowed and gallantly kissed my hand.*
▪ *noun* /gə'lænt; 'gælənt/ (*old-fashioned*) a fashionable young man, especially one who gives polite attention to women

gal·lant·ry /'gæləntri/ *noun* [U] (*formal*) **1** courage, especially in a battle: *a medal for gallantry* **2** polite attention given by men to women

'gall bladder *noun* an organ attached to the LIVER in which BILE is stored

gal·leon /'gæliən/ *noun* a large Spanish sailing ship, used between the 15th and the 17th centuries

gal·lery /'gæləri/ *noun* (*pl.* -ies) **1** a room or building for showing works of art, especially to the public: *an art/a picture gallery* ◇ *the National Gallery*—see also ART GALLERY **2** a small private shop/store where you can see and buy works of art **3** an upstairs area at the back or sides of a large hall where people can sit: *Relatives of the victim watched from the public gallery as the murder charge was read out in court.*—see also PRESS GALLERY **4** the highest level in a theatre where the cheapest seats are **5** a long narrow room, especially one used for a particular purpose—see also SHOOTING GALLERY **6** a level passage under the ground in a mine or CAVE IDM **play to the 'gallery** to behave in an exaggerated way to attract people's attention

gal·ley /'gæli/ *noun* **1** a long flat ship with sails, usually rowed by slaves or criminals, especially one used by the ancient Greeks or Romans in war **2** the kitchen on a ship or plane

Gal·lic /'gælɪk/ *adj.* connected with or considered typical of France or its people: *Gallic charm*

gall·ing /'gɔːlɪŋ/ *adj.* [not usually before noun] (of a situation or fact) making you angry because it is unfair: *It was galling to have to apologize to a man she hated.*

gal·li·vant /'gælɪvænt/ *verb* [V] (usually used in the progressive tenses) ~ (**about/ around**) (*old-fashioned, informal*) to go from place to place enjoying yourself: *You're too old to go gallivanting around Europe.*

gal·lon /'gælən/ *noun* (*abbr.* **gal.**) a unit for measuring liquid. In the UK it is equal to about 4.5 litres; in the US it is equal to about 3.8 litres. There are four QUARTS in a gallon.

gal·lop /'gæləp/ *verb, noun*
▪ *verb* [usually +*adv./prep.*] **1** [V] when a horse or similar animal **gallops**, it moves very fast and each STRIDE includes a stage when all four feet are off the ground together—compare CANTER **2** to ride a horse very fast, usually at a gallop: [V] *Jo galloped across the field towards him.* ◇ [VN] *He galloped his horse home.*—compare CANTER **3** [V] (*informal*) (of a person) to run very quickly: *She came galloping down the street.*
▪ *noun* **1** [sing.] the fastest speed at which a horse can run, with a stage in which all four feet are off the ground together: *He rode off at a gallop.* ◇ *My horse suddenly broke into a gallop.* **2** [C] a ride on a horse at its fastest speed: *to go for a gallop* **3** [sing.] an unusually fast speed

gal·lop·ing /'gæləpɪŋ/ *adj.* [only before noun] increasing or spreading rapidly: *Galloping inflation is pushing up prices.*

gal·lows /'gæləʊz; *AmE* -loʊz/ *noun* (*pl.* **gal·lows**) a structure on which people, for example criminals, are killed by hanging: *to send a man to the gallows* (= to send him to his death by hanging)

,gallows 'humour (*BrE*) (*AmE* ,gallows 'humor) *noun* [U] jokes about unpleasant things like death

gall·stone /'gɔːlstəʊn; *AmE* -stoʊn/ *noun* a hard painful mass that can form in the GALL BLADDER

gal·ore /gə'lɔː(r)/ *adv.* [after noun] (*informal*) in large quantities: *There will be games and prizes galore.*

gal·oshes /gə'lɒʃɪz; *AmE* -'lɑːʃ-/ *noun* [pl.] rubber shoes (no longer very common) that are worn over normal shoes in wet weather: *a pair of galoshes*

gal·van·ic /gæl'vænɪk/ *adj.* **1** (*technical*) producing an electric current by the action of a chemical on metal **2** (*formal*) making people react in a sudden and dramatic way

gal·van·ize (*BrE* also **-ise**) /'gælvənaɪz/ *verb* [VN] **1** ~ **sb** (**into sth/into doing sth**) (*written*) to make sb take action by shocking them or by making them excited: *The urgency of his voice galvanized them into action.* **2** (*technical*) to cover metal with ZINC in order to protect it from RUST: *a galvanized bucket* ◇ *galvanized steel*

gam·bit /'gæmbɪt/ *noun* **1** a thing that sb does, or sth that sb says, at the beginning of a situation or conversation, that is intended to give them some advantage: *an opening gambit* (= the first thing you say) ◇ *The opposition have dismissed promises of tax cuts as a pre-election gambit.* **2** a move or moves made at the beginning of a game of CHESS in order to gain an advantage later

gam·ble /'gæmbl/ *verb, noun*
▪ *verb* **1** ~ (**sth**) (**on sth**) to risk money on a card game, horse race, etc: [V] *to gamble at cards/on the horses* ◇ [VN] *I gambled all my winnings on the last race.* **2** ~ (**sth**) (**on sth**) to risk losing sth in the hope of being successful: [VN] *He's gambling his reputation on this deal.* ◇ [V] *It was wrong to gamble with our children's future.* ▶ **gam·bler** /'gæmblə(r)/ *noun*: *He was a compulsive gambler* (= found it difficult to stop). PHR V **,gamble sth↔a'way** to lose sth such as money, possessions, etc. by gambling:

G

b	d	f	g	h	k	l	m	n	p	r
bad	**did**	**fall**	**get**	**hat**	**cat**	**leg**	**man**	**now**	**pen**	**red**

Every weekend he drinks and gambles away his earnings.
'gamble on sth/on doing sth to take a risk with sth,
hoping that you will be successful: *He gambled on being
able to buy a ticket at the last minute.*

■ *noun* [sing.] an action that you take when you know there
is a risk but when you hope that the result will be a
success: *She knew she was **taking a gamble** but decided it
was worth it.* ◊ *They invested money in the company right
at the start and **the gamble paid off** (= brought them
success).*

gam·bling /ˈɡæmblɪŋ/ *noun* [U] the activity of playing
games of chance for money and of betting on horses, etc:
heavy gambling debts

gam·bol /ˈɡæmbl/ *verb* (-ll-, *AmE* also -l-) [V] [usu-
ally +*adv.* / *prep.*] to jump or run about in a lively way:
lambs gambolling in the meadow

game /ɡeɪm/ *noun, adj.*

■ *noun*

ACTIVITY/SPORT | **1** [C] an activity or a sport with rules in
which people or teams compete against each other: *card
games* ◊ *board games* ◊ *a game of chance/skill* ◊ *ball
games, such as soccer or tennis* ◊ *(AmE) We're going to the
ball game* (= baseball match).—picture on page A8 **2** [C]
an occasion of playing a game: *to play a game of football/
chess* ◊ *Saturday's League game against Swansea* ◊ *Let's
have a game of table tennis.* ◊ *They're in training for the
big game.* **3** [sing.] *sb's* ~ the way in which sb plays a
game: *Hendry raised his game to collect the £40000 first
prize.* ◊ *Stretching exercises can help you avoid injury and
improve your game.*
SPORTS | **4** (**games**) [pl.] (*old-fashioned, BrE*) sport as a
lesson or an activity at school: *I always hated games at
school.* **5** (**games**) [pl.] a large organized sports event: *the
Olympic Games*
PART OF SPORTS MATCH | **6** [C] a section of some games, such
as tennis, which forms a unit in scoring: *two games all* (=
both players have won two games)
CHILDREN'S ACTIVITY | **7** [C] a children's activity when they
play with toys, pretend to be sb else, etc: *a game of cops
and robbers*
FUN | **8** [C] an activity that you do to have fun: *He was
playing games with the dog.*
BUSINESS | **9** [C] a type of activity or business: *How long
have you been in this game?* ◊ *the game of politics/life* ◊ *I'm
new to this game myself.* ◊ *Getting dirty was **all part of
the game** to the kids.*—see also WAITING GAME
SECRET PLAN | **10** [C] (*informal*) a secret and clever plan; a
trick: *So that's his little game* (= now I know what he has
been planning).
WILD ANIMALS/BIRDS | **11** [U] wild animals or birds that
people hunt for sport or food—picture on page A6—see
also BIG GAME, FAIR GAME

IDM **be on the 'game** (*BrE, slang*) to be a prostitute **the
game is 'up** (*BrE, informal*) said to sb who has done sth
wrong, when they are caught and the crime or trick has
been discovered **give the 'game away** to tell a secret,
especially by accident; to show sth that should be kept
hidden **play the 'game** to behave in a fair and honest
way **play sb's 'game** to do sth which helps sb else's
plans, especially by accident, when you did not intend to
help them **play (silly) 'games (with sb)** not to treat a
situation seriously, especially in order to cheat or
deceive sb: *Don't play silly games with me; I know you did
it.* **'two can play at 'that game** used to tell sb who has
played a trick on you that you can do the same thing to
them **what's sb's/your 'game?** (*BrE, spoken*) used to
ask why sb is behaving as they are—more at BEAT *v.*, CAT,
FUN *n.*, MUG *n.*, NAME *n.*, NUMBER *n.*, RULE *n.*, WORTH *adj.*

■ *adj.* ~ (**for sth/to do sth**) ready and willing to do sth new,
difficult or dangerous: *She's game for anything.* ◊ *We need
a volunteer for this exercise. Who's game to try?*

'game bird *noun* a bird that people hunt for sport or food
game·keep·er /ˈɡeɪmkiːpə(r)/ *noun* a person whose job
is to take care of and breed wild animals and birds that
are kept on private land in order to be hunted **IDM** see
POACHER

game·ly /ˈɡeɪmli/ *adv.* in a way that seems brave,

although a lot of effort is involved: *She tried gamely to
finish the race.*

'game plan *noun* a plan for success in the future, especially in sport, politics or business

'game reserve (also **'game park**) (both *BrE*) (*AmE*
'game preserve) *noun* a large area of land where wild
animals can live in safety

'game show *noun* a television programme in which
people play games or answer questions to win prizes

games·man·ship /ˈɡeɪmzmənʃɪp/ *noun* [U] the ability
to win games by making your opponent less confident
and using rules to your advantage

'game warden *noun* a person whose job is to manage
and take care of the wild animals in a GAME RESERVE

gam·ine /ˈɡæmiːn/ *adj.* (*written*) (of a young woman)
thin and attractive; looking like a boy ▸ **gam·ine** *noun*

gam·ing /ˈɡeɪmɪŋ/ *noun* [U] (*old-fashioned or law*) =
GAMBLING: *He spent all night at the gaming tables.*

gamma /ˈɡæmə/ *noun* the third letter of the Greek alphabet (Γ, γ)

gamma radi'ation *noun* [U] (also **'gamma rays** [pl.])
rays of very short WAVELENGTH sent out by some RADIO-
ACTIVE substances

gam·mon /ˈɡæmən/ *noun* [U] (*BrE*) meat from the back
leg or side of a pig that has been CURED (= preserved
using salt or smoke), usually served in thick slices: *gammon steaks*—compare BACON, HAM, PORK

gammy /ˈɡæmi/ *adj.* [usually before noun] (*old-fashioned, BrE, informal*) (of a leg or knee) injured

gamut /ˈɡæmət/ *noun* (**the gamut**) [sing.] the complete
range of a particular kind of thing: *The network will
provide the gamut of computer services to your home.* ◊ *She
felt she had **run the** (**whole**) **gamut** of human emotions
from joy to despair in one day.*

gan·der /ˈɡændə(r)/ *noun* a male GOOSE (= a bird like a
large duck) **IDM** **have/take a 'gander (at sth)** (*informal*)
to look at sth—more at SAUCE

G and T /ˌdʒiː ənd ˈtiː/ *noun* a drink consisting of GIN
mixed with TONIC WATER

gang /ɡæŋ/ *noun, verb*

■ *noun* **1** an organized group of criminals: *criminal gang
members and drug dealers* ◊ *a gang of pickpockets* ◊ *A
four-man gang carried out the robbery.* **2** a group of young
people who spend a lot of time together and often cause
trouble or fight against other groups: *a gang of youths* ◊ *a
street gang* **3** (*informal*) a group of friends who meet
regularly: *The whole gang will be there.* **4** an organized
group of workers or prisoners doing work together—see
also CHAIN GANG

■ *verb* **PHRV** **gang to'gether** (*informal*) to join together in
a group in order to have more power or strength **gang
'up (on/against sb)** (*informal*) to join together in a
group to hurt, frighten or oppose sb: *At school the older
boys ganged up on him and called him names.*

'gang bang *noun* (*slang*) **1** an occasion when a number
of people have sex with each other in a group **2** the RAPE
of a person by a number of people one after the other
▸ **'gang-bang** *verb* [VN]

gang·bust·ers /ˈɡæŋbʌstəz; *AmE* -ərz/ *noun* **IDM** **like
'gangbusters** (*AmE, informal*) with a lot of energy and
enthusiasm

gang·land /ˈɡæŋlænd/ *noun* [sing.] the world of organized and violent crime: *gangland killings*

gan·gling /ˈɡæŋɡlɪŋ/ (also **gan·gly** /ˈɡæŋɡli/) *adj.* (of a
person) tall thin and awkward in their movements: *a
gangling youth/adolescent*

gan·glion /ˈɡæŋɡliən/ *noun* (*pl.* **gan·glia** /-liə/) (*medical*)
1 a mass of nerve cells **2** a swelling in a TENDON, often at
the back of the hand

gang·plank /ˈɡæŋplæŋk/ *noun* a board for people to
walk on between the side of a boat and the shore

'gang rape *noun* the RAPE of a person by a number of
people one after the other ▸ **'gang-rape** *verb* [VN]

gan·grene /ˈɡæŋɡriːn/ *noun* [U] the decay that takes
place in a part of the body when the blood supply to it has

G

been stopped because of an illness or injury: *Gangrene set in and he had to have his leg amputated.* ► **gan·gren·ous** /ˈɡæŋɡrɪnəs/ *adj.*

gang·sta /ˈɡæŋstə/ *noun* **1** [C] (*AmE, slang*) a member of a street GANG **2** (also ˌ**gangsta** ˈ**rap**) [U] a type of modern music in which the words of a song are spoken to a steady rhythm. The words are usually aggressive and may be critical of women.

gang·ster /ˈɡæŋstə(r)/ *noun* a member of a group of violent criminals: *Chicago gangsters*

gang·way /ˈɡæŋweɪ/ *noun* **1** (*BrE*) a passage between rows of seats in a theatre, an aircraft, etc.—compare AISLE **2** a bridge placed between the side of a ship and the shore so people can get on and off

ganja /ˈɡændʒə; ˈɡɑːn-/ *noun* [U] (*slang*) = MARIJUANA

gan·net /ˈɡænɪt/ *noun* a large seabird that catches fish by DIVING (= going head first into the sea)

gan·try /ˈɡæntri/ *noun* (*pl.* **-ies**) a tall metal frame that is used to support a CRANE, road signs, a spacecraft while it is still on the ground, etc.

gaol, gaoler (*BrE*) = JAIL, JAILER

gap /ɡæp/ *noun* ~ (**in/between sth**) **1** a space between two things or in the middle of sth, especially because there is a part missing: *a gap in a hedge/fence/wall* ◊ *Leave a gap between your car and the next.* **2** a period of time when sth stops, or between two events: *a gap in the conversation* ◊ *They met again after a gap of twenty years.* ◊ (*BrE*) *a **gap year** (= a year between school and university when some students earn money, travel, etc.) **3** a difference that separates people, or their opinions, situation, etc: *the gap between rich and poor* ◊ *the gap between theory and practice*—see also CREDIBILITY, GENERATION GAP **4** a space where sth is missing: *His death left an enormous gap in my life.* ◊ *There were several gaps in my education.* ◊ *We think we've identified **a gap in the market** (= a business opportunity to make or sell sth that is not yet available).* **IDM** see BRIDGE *v.*

gape /ɡeɪp/ *verb* [V] **1** ~ (**at sb/sth**) to stare at sb/sth with your mouth open because you are shocked or surprised: *Isabel gaped at him, horrified.* **2** ~ (**open**) to be or become wide open: *a gaping hole/mouth/wound* ◊ *He stood yawning, his pyjama jacket gaping open.* ◊ *A huge chasm gaped before them.* ► **gape** *noun*

ˌ**gap-ˈtoothed** *adj.* [usually before noun] having wide spaces between your teeth

gar·age /ˈɡærɑːʒ; -rɑːdʒ; -rɪdʒ; *AmE* ɡəˈrɑːʒ; -ˈrɑːdʒ/ *noun, verb*
■ *noun* **1** a building for keeping one or more cars or other vehicles in: (*BrE*) *a house with a built-in garage* ◊ (*AmE*) *a house with an attached garage* ◊ *a double garage* (= one for two cars) ◊ *a bus garage* ◊ *an underground garage* (= for example under an office building)—picture at HOUSE **2** a place where vehicles are repaired and where you can buy a car or buy petrol/gas and oil: *a garage mechanic*—see also PETROL STATION
■ *verb* [VN] to put or keep a vehicle in a garage

ˈ**garage sale** *noun* a sale of used clothes, furniture, etc., held in the garage of sb's house

garb /ɡɑːb; *AmE* ɡɑːrb/ *noun* (*formal* or *humorous*) clothes, especially unusual clothes or those worn by a particular type of person: *military/prison garb*

gar·bage /ˈɡɑːbɪdʒ; *AmE* ˈɡɑːrb-/ *noun* [U] **1** (*especially AmE*) waste food, paper, etc. that you throw away: *garbage collection* ◊ *Don't forget to take out the garbage.* **2** (*especially AmE*) a place or container where waste food, paper, etc. can be placed: *Throw it in the garbage.* **3** (*informal*) something stupid or not true [SYN] RUBBISH: *'You mean you believe all that garbage?' he said.* ➪ note at RUBBISH

ˈ**garbage can** *noun* (*AmE*) = DUSTBIN

ˈ**garbage man** (also *formal* ˈ**garbage collector**) *noun* (both *AmE*) = DUSTMAN

ˈ**garbage truck** *noun* (*AmE*) = DUSTCART

gar·banzo /ɡɑːˈbænzəʊ; *AmE* ɡɑːrˈbɑːnzoʊ; -ˈbæn-/ (also **garˈbanzo ˌbean**) (both *AmE*) *noun* = CHICKPEA

garbed /ɡɑːbd; *AmE* ɡɑːrbd/ *adj.* [not before noun] (*formal*) ~ (**in sth**) dressed in a particular way: *brightly garbed*

gar·bled /ˈɡɑːbld; *AmE* ˈɡɑːrbld/ *adj.* (of a message or story) told in a way that confuses the person listening, usually by sb who is shocked or in a hurry: *He gave a garbled account of what had happened.* ◊ *There was a garbled message from her on my answering machine.*

Garda /ˈɡɑːdə; *AmE* ˈɡɑːrdə/ *noun* **1** (**the Garda**) [U] the police force of the Republic of Ireland **2** (also **garda**) (*pl.* **gardai** /ˈɡɑːdiː; *AmE* ˈɡɑːrdiː/) a police officer of the Republic of Ireland

gar·den /ˈɡɑːdn; *AmE* ˈɡɑːrdn/ *noun, verb*

garden equipment

trowel
hand fork
rake
hoe
fork shovel spade
reel
rose
watering can
wheelbarrow hose
nozzle

G

■ *noun* **1** [C] (*BrE*) (*AmE* **yard**) a piece of land next to or around your house where you can grow flowers, fruit, vegetables, etc., usually with an area of grass, (called a LAWN): *a front/back garden* ◊ *children playing in the garden* ◊ *garden flowers/plants* ◊ *out in the garden* ◊ *a rose garden* (= where only roses are grown)—see also KITCHEN GARDEN, MARKET GARDEN, ROCK GARDEN, ROOF GARDEN—picture at HOUSE **2** [C] (*AmE*) an area in a yard where you grow flowers or plants **3** [C] (usually **gardens**) a public park: *the botanical gardens in Edinburgh* ◊ (*AmE*) *The garden closes at 6 p.m.*—see also ZOOLOGICAL GARDEN **4** (**gardens**) [pl.] (*abbr.* **Gdns**) (*BrE*) used in the name of streets: *39 Belvoir Gardens* **IDM** **everything in the garden is ˈrosy** (*BrE, saying*) everything is satisfactory—more at COMMON *adj.*, LEAD[1] *v.*
■ *verb* [V] to work in a garden ► **gar·den·er** /ˈɡɑːdnə(r); *AmE* ˈɡɑːrd-/ *noun*: *My wife's a keen gardener.* ◊ *We employ a gardener two days a week.* **gar·den·ing** /ˈɡɑːdnɪŋ; *AmE* ˈɡɑːrd-/ *noun* [U]: *organic gardening* ◊ *gardening gloves* ◊ *a gardening programme on TV*

ˈ**garden centre** *noun* (*BrE*) a place that sells plants, seeds, garden equipment, etc.

ˌ**garden ˈcity**, ˌ**garden ˈsuburb** *nouns* (*BrE*) a city or part of a city that has been specially designed to have a lot of open spaces, parks and trees

gar·denia /ɡɑːˈdiːniə; *AmE* ɡɑːrˈd-/ *noun* a bush with shiny leaves and large white or yellow flowers with a sweet smell, also called **gardenias**

the ˌGarden of ˈEden *noun* [sing.] = EDEN

ˈ**garden party** *noun* a formal social event that takes place in the afternoon in a large garden

ˈ**garden-variety** *adj.* [only before noun] (*AmE*) = COMMON OR GARDEN at COMMON *adj.*: *He is not one of your garden-variety criminals.*

gar·gan·tuan /ɡɑːˈɡæntʃuən; *AmE* ɡɑːrˈɡ-/ *adj.* [usually before noun] extremely large: *a gargantuan appetite/meal*

gar·gle /ˈɡɑːɡl; *AmE* ˈɡɑːrɡl/ *verb, noun*

■ *verb* [V] ~ **(with sth)** to wash inside your mouth and throat by moving a liquid around at the back of your throat and then SPITTING it out
■ *noun* **1** [C, U] a liquid used for gargling: *an antiseptic gargle* **2** [sing.] an act of gargling or a sound like that made when gargling: *to have a gargle with salt water*

gar·goyle /'gɑːgɔɪl; *AmE* 'gɑːrg-/ *noun* an ugly figure of a person or an animal that is made of stone and through which water is carried away from the roof of a building, especially a church

gar·ish /'geərɪʃ; *AmE* 'gerɪʃ/ *adj.* very brightly coloured in an unpleasant way: *garish clothes/colours/lights* ▶ **gar·ish·ly** *adv.*: *garishly decorated/lit/painted*

gar·land /'gɑːlənd; *AmE* 'gɑːrl-/ *noun, verb*
■ *noun* a circle of flowers and leaves that is worn on the head or around the neck or is hung in a room as decoration
■ *verb* [VN] [usually passive] (*literary*) to decorate sb/sth with a garland or garlands

gar·lic /'gɑːlɪk; *AmE* 'gɑːrlɪk/ *noun* [U] a vegetable of the onion family with a very strong taste and smell, used in cooking to give flavour to food: *a clove of garlic* (= one section of it) ▶ **gar·licky** *adj.*: *garlicky breath/food*—picture on page A3

gar·ment /'gɑːmənt; *AmE* 'gɑːrm-/ *noun* (*formal*) a piece of clothing: *a strange shapeless garment that had once been a jacket* ◊ *woollen/winter/outer garments*—see also UNDERGARMENT

gar·ner /'gɑːnə(r); *AmE* 'gɑːrn-/ *verb* [VN] (*formal*) to obtain or collect sth such as information, support, etc. **SYN** GATHER, ACQUIRE

gar·net /'gɑːnɪt; *AmE* 'gɑːrn-/ *noun* a clear dark red precious stone that is fairly valuable

gar·nish /'gɑːnɪʃ; *AmE* 'gɑːrnɪʃ/ *verb, noun*
■ *verb* [VN] ~ **sth (with sth)** to decorate a dish of food with a small amount of another food
■ *noun* [C, U] a small amount of food that is used to decorate a larger dish of food

gar·otte (*BrE*) = GARROTTE

gar·ret /'gærət/ *noun* a room, often a small dark unpleasant one, at the top of a house, especially in the roof—compare ATTIC—see also LOFT

gar·rison /'gærɪsn/ *noun, verb*
■ *noun* [C+sing./pl. *v.*] a group of soldiers living in a town or FORT to defend it; the buildings these soldiers live in: *a garrison of 5000 troops* ◊ *a garrison town* ◊ *Half the garrison is/are on duty.*
■ *verb* [VN] to put soldiers in a place in order to defend it from attack: *Two regiments were sent to garrison the town.* ◊ *100 soldiers were garrisoned in the town.*

gar·rotte (*BrE* also **gar·otte**) (*AmE* also **gar·rote**) /gə'rɒt; *AmE* gə'rɑːt/ *verb, noun*
■ *verb* [VN] to kill sb by putting a piece of wire, etc. around their neck and pulling it tight
■ *noun* a piece of wire, etc. used for garrotting sb

gar·rul·ous /'gærələs; *BrE* also -rjʊl-/ *adj.* talking a lot, especially about unimportant things **SYN** TALKATIVE: *He became positively garrulous after a few glasses of wine.* ▶ **gar·rul·ous·ly** *adv.*

gar·ter /'gɑːtə(r); *AmE* 'gɑːrt-/ *noun* **1** a band, usually made of elastic, that is worn around the leg to keep up a sock or STOCKING **2** (*AmE*) = SUSPENDER **IDM** see GUT *n.*

'garter belt *noun* (*AmE*) = SUSPENDER BELT

'garter snake *noun* a harmless American snake with coloured lines along its back

gas /gæs/ *noun, verb*
■ *noun* (*pl.* **gases** or *less frequent* **gas·ses**)
NOT SOLID/LIQUID | **1** [C, U] any substance like air that is neither a solid nor a liquid, for example HYDROGEN and OXYGEN are both gases: *Air is a mixture of gases.* ◊ *CFC gases* ◊ *a gas bottle/cylinder* (= for storing gas)—see also GREENHOUSE GAS **2** [U] a particular type of gas or mixture of gases used as fuel for heating and cooking: *a gas cooker/fire/furnace/oven/ring/stove* ◊ *a gas explosion/leak* ◊ *gas central heating* ◊ (*BrE*) *Preheat the oven to gas mark 5* (= a particular temperature of a gas oven)—see

also CALOR GAS, COAL GAS, NATURAL GAS **3** [U] a particular type of gas used during a medical operation, to make the patient sleep or to make the pain less: *an anaesthetic gas* ◊ *During the birth she was given gas and air.*—see also LAUGHING GAS **4** [U] a particular type of gas used in war to kill or injure people, or used by the police to control people: *a gas attack*—see also CS GAS, NERVE GAS, TEAR GAS
IN VEHICLE | **5** [U] (*AmE*) = PETROL: *a gas station* **6** (**the gas**) [sing.] (*especially AmE*) = GAS PEDAL: *Step on the gas, we're late.*
FUN | **7** [sing.] (*especially AmE*) a person or an event that is fun: *The party was a real gas.*
IN STOMACH | **8** [U] (*AmE*) = WIND¹ (2)
IDM see COOK *v.*
■ *verb* (**-ss-**)
KILL/HARM WITH GAS | **1** [VN] to kill or harm sb by making them breathe poisonous gas
TALK | **2** [V] (usually used in the progressive tenses) (*old-fashioned, informal*) to talk for a long time about things that are not important **SYN** CHAT

'gas chamber *noun* a room that can be filled with poisonous gas for killing animals or people

'gas-cooled *adj.* [only before noun] using gas to keep the temperature cool: *gas-cooled nuclear reactors*

gas·eous /'gæsiəs; 'geɪsiəs/ *adj.* [usually before noun] like or containing gas: *a gaseous mixture/emission* ◊ *in gaseous form*

gas-'fired *adj.* [usually before noun] (*BrE*) using gas as a fuel: *gas-fired central heating*

'gas-guzzler (also **guz·zler**) *noun* (*informal, especially AmE*) a car that needs a lot of petrol/gas ▶ **'gas-guzzling** *adj.* [only before noun]

gash /gæʃ/ *noun, verb*
■ *noun* ~ **(in/on sth)** a long deep cut in the surface of sth, especially a person's skin
■ *verb* [VN] to make a long deep cut in sth, especially a person's skin: *He gashed his hand on a sharp piece of rock.*

gas·hold·er /'gæshəʊldə(r); *AmE* -hoʊl-/ *noun* = GASOMETER

gas·ket /'gæskɪt/ *noun* a flat piece of rubber, etc. placed between two metal surfaces in a pipe or an engine to prevent steam, gas or oil from escaping: *The engine had blown a gasket* (= had allowed steam, etc. to escape). ◊ (*figurative, informal*) *He blew a gasket at the news* (= became very angry).

'gas lamp (also **gas·light**) *noun* a lamp in the street or in a house, that produces light from burning gas

gas·light /'gæslaɪt/ *noun* **1** [U] light produced from burning gas: *In the gaslight she looked paler than ever.* **2** [C] = GAS LAMP

gas·man /'gæsmæn/ *noun* (*pl.* **-men** /-men/) (*informal*) a man whose job is to visit people's houses to see how much gas they have used, or to fit and check gas equipment

'gas mantle *noun* = MANTLE

'gas mask *noun* a piece of equipment worn over the face as protection against poisonous gas

gaso·hol /'gæsəhɒl; *AmE* -hɔːl; -hɑːl/ *noun* [U] (*AmE*) a mixture of petrol/gas and alcohol which can be used in cars

gas·oline (also **gas·olene**) /'gæsəliːn/ *noun* [U] (*AmE*) = PETROL

gas·om·eter /gæ'sɒmɪtə(r); *AmE* -'sɑːm-/ (also **gas·hold·er**) *noun* a very large round container or building in which gas is stored and from which it is sent through pipes to other buildings

gasp /gɑːsp; *AmE* gæsp/ *verb, noun*
■ *verb* **1** ~ **(at sth)** to take a quick deep breath with your mouth open, especially because you are surprised or in pain: [V] *She gasped at the wonderful view.* ◊ *They gasped in astonishment at the news.* ◊ [V speech] *'What was that noise?' he gasped.* **2** ~ **(sth) (out)** to have difficulty breathing or speaking: [V] *He came to the surface of the water gasping for air.* ◊ [VN] *She managed to gasp out her name.* [also V speech] **3** **be gasping (for sth)** [V] (*BrE, spoken*) to

aɪ	aʊ	eɪ	əʊ	oʊ	ɔɪ	ɪə	eə	ʊə	j	w
my	now	say	go (BrE)	go (AmE)	boy	near	hair	pure	yes	wet

want or need sth very badly, especially a drink or a cigarette
- *noun* a quick deep breath, usually caused by a strong emotion: *to give a gasp of horror/surprise/relief* ◊ *His breath came in short gasps.* **IDM** see LAST *det.*

'gas pedal *noun* (*especially AmE*) = ACCELERATOR

'gas station *noun* (*AmE*) = PETROL STATION

gassy /'gæsi/ *adj.* **1** (*BrE*) (of drinks) containing too much gas in the form of bubbles **2** (*AmE*) (of people) having a lot of gas in your stomach, etc.

gas·tric /'gæstrɪk/ *adj.* [only before noun] (*medical*) connected with the stomach: *a gastric ulcer* ◊ *gastric flu* ◊ *gastric juices* (= the acids in your stomach that help you to digest food)

gas·tri·tis /gæ'straɪtɪs/ *noun* [U] (*medical*) an illness in which the inside of the stomach becomes swollen and painful

gastro-enteritis /ˌgæstrəʊˌentə'raɪtɪs; *AmE* ˌgæstroʊ/ *noun* [U] (*medical*) an illness of the stomach and other food passages that causes DIARRHOEA and VOMITING

gas·tro·nom·ic /ˌgæstrə'nɒmɪk; *AmE* -'nɑːm-/ *adj.* [only before noun] connected with cooking and eating good food: *a gastronomic delight* ▶ **gas·tro·nom·ic·al·ly** /-kli/ *adv.*

gas·tron·omy /gæ'strɒnəmi; *AmE* -'strɑːn-/ *noun* [U] (*formal*) the art and practice of cooking and eating good food

gas·works /'gæswɜːks; *AmE* -wɜːrks/ *noun* (*pl.* **gasworks**) [C+sing./pl. *v.*] a factory where gas for lighting and heating is made from coal

gate /geɪt/ *noun* **1** [C] a barrier like a door that is used to close an opening in a fence or a wall outside a building: *an iron gate* ◊ *He pushed open the garden gate.* ◊ *A crowd gathered at the factory gates.* ◊ *the gates of the city*—see also STARTING GATE **2** [C] an opening that can be closed by a gate or gates: *We drove through the palace gates.* **3** [C] a barrier that is used to control the flow of water on a river or canal: *a lock/sluice gate* **4** [C] a way out of an airport through which passengers go to get on their plane: *BA flight 726 to Paris is now boarding at gate 16.* **5** [C] the number of people who attend a sports event: *Tonight's game has attracted the largest gate of the season.* **6** (also **'gate money**) [U] the amount of money made by selling tickets for a sports event: *Today's gate will be given to charity.* **7** (-**gate**) (forming nouns from the names of people or places; used especially in newspapers) a political SCANDAL connected with the person or place mentioned: *Whitewatergate* **ORIGIN** From **Watergate**, the scandal in the United States that brought about the resignation of President Nixon in 1974.

gat·eau /'gætəʊ; *AmE* gæ'toʊ/ *noun* [C, U] (*pl.* **gat·eaux** /'gætəʊ; *AmE* gæ'toʊ/) a large cake filled with cream and usually decorated with fruit, nuts, etc: *a strawberry gateau* ◊ *Is there any gateau left?*—picture on page A1

gate·crash /'geɪtkræʃ/ (also *informal* **crash**) *verb* [VN, V] to go to a party or social event without being invited ▶ **gate·crash·er** *noun*

gated /'geɪtɪd/ *adj.* [usually before noun] (of a road) having gates that need to be opened and closed by drivers

ˌgated com'munity *noun* a group of houses enclosed by a wall or fence, with an entrance that is guarded

gate·house /'geɪthaʊs/ *noun* a house built at or over a gate, for example at the entrance to a park or castle

gate·keep·er /'geɪtkiːpə(r)/ *noun* a person whose job is to check and control who is allowed to go through a gate

'gate money *noun* [U] = GATE (6)

gate·post /'geɪtpəʊst; *AmE* -poʊst/ *noun* a post to which a gate is attached or against which it is closed **IDM** **between you, me and the 'gatepost** (*BrE*, *informal*) used to show that what you are going to say next is a secret

gate·way /'geɪtweɪ/ *noun* **1** an opening in a wall or fence that can be closed by a gate: *They turned through the gateway on the left.* **2** [usually sing.] **~ to/into …** a place through which you can go to reach another larger place: *Perth, the gateway to Western Australia* **3** [usually sing.]

~ to sth a means of getting or achieving sth: *A good education is the gateway to success.* **4** (*computing*) a device that connects two computer NETWORKS (= systems of linked computers) that cannot be connected in any other way

gather /'gæðə(r)/ *verb*
COME/BRING TOGETHER | **1** to come together, or bring people together, in one place to form a group: [V] *A crowd soon gathered.* ◊ *Can you all gather round? I've got something to tell you.* ◊ *The whole family gathered together at Ray's home.* ◊ *His supporters gathered in the main square.* ◊ [VN] *They were all gathered round the TV.* ◊ *A large crowd was gathered outside the studio.* ◊ *The kids were gathered together in one room.* **2** [VN] **~ sth (together/up)** to bring things together that have been spread around: *People slowly gathered their belongings and left the hall.* ◊ *I waited while he gathered up his papers.*
COLLECT | **3** [VN] to collect information from different sources: *Detectives have spent months gathering evidence.* **4** [VN] to collect plants, fruit, etc. from a wide area: *to gather wild flowers*
CROPS/HARVEST | **5** [VN] **~ sth (in)** to pick or cut and collect crops to be stored: *It was late August and the harvest had been safely gathered in.*
BELIEVE/UNDERSTAND | **6** (not used in the progressive tenses) to believe or understand that sth is true because of information or evidence you have: [V(that)] *I gather (that) you wanted to see me.* ◊ *I gather from your letter that you're not enjoying your job.* ◊ [VN] *'There's been a delay.' 'I gathered that.'* ◊ [V] *'She won't be coming.' ' So I gather.'* ◊ *You're self-employed, I gather.* ◊ *As far as I can gather, he got involved in a fight.* ◊ *From what I can gather, there's been some kind of problem.*
INCREASE | **7** [VN] to increase in speed, force, etc: *The truck gathered speed.* ◊ *During the 1980s the green movement gathered momentum.* ◊ *Thousands of these machines are gathering dust* (= not being used) *in stockrooms.*
OF CLOUDS/DARKNESS | **8** [V] to gradually increase in number or amount: *The storm clouds were gathering.* ◊ *the gathering gloom of a winter's afternoon*
CLOTHING | **9** [VN] **~ sth around you/sth | ~ sth up** to pull a piece of clothing tighter to your body: *He gathered his cloak around him.* ◊ *She gathered up her skirts and ran.* **10** [VN] **~ sth (in)** to pull parts of a piece of clothing together in folds and sew them in place: *She wore a skirt gathered (in) at the waist.*
HOLD SB | **11** [VN+*adv./prep.*] (*written*) to pull sb towards you and put your arms around them: *She gathered the child in her arms and held him close.* ◊ *He gathered her to him.*
PREPARE YOURSELF | **12** [VN] to prepare yourself to do sth that requires effort: *I sat down for a moment to gather my strength.* ◊ *She was still trying to gather her thoughts together when the door opened.* ◊ *Fortunately the short delay gave him time to gather himself.*

gath·er·er /'gæðərə(r)/ *noun* a person who collects sth: *prehistoric hunters and gatherers*

gath·er·ing /'gæðərɪŋ/ *noun* **1** [C] a meeting of people for a particular purpose: *a social/family gathering* ◊ *a gathering of religious leaders* **2** [U] the process of collecting sth: *methods of information gathering*

gathers /'gæðəz; *AmE* 'gæðərz/ *noun* [pl.] small folds that are sewn into a piece of clothing

gauche /gəʊʃ; *AmE* goʊʃ/ *adj.* awkward when dealing with people and often saying or doing the wrong thing: *a gauche schoolgirl/manner* ▶ **gauche·ness** (also **gauch·erie** /'gəʊʃəri; *AmE* ˌgoʊʃə'riː/) *noun* [U]: *the gaucheness of youth*

gau·cho /'gaʊtʃəʊ; *AmE* -tʃoʊ/ *noun* (*pl.* **-os**) a S American cowboy

gaudy /'gɔːdi/ *adj.* (**gaud·ier**, **gaudi·est**) (*disapproving*) too brightly coloured in a way that lacks taste: *gaudy clothes/colours* ▶ **gaud·ily** /'gɔːdɪli/ *adv.*: *gaudily dressed/painted* **gaudi·ness** /'gɔːdinəs/ *noun* [U]

gauge (*AmE* also **gage**) /geɪdʒ/ *noun*, *verb*
- *noun* **1** (often in compounds) an instrument for measuring the amount or level of sth: *a fuel/petrol/temperature*

G

gauge **2** a measurement of the width or thickness of sth: *What gauge of wire do we need?* **3** (also **bore** especially in *BrE*) a measurement of the width of the BARREL of a gun: *a 12-gauge shotgun* **4** the distance between the rails of a railway/railroad track or the wheels of a train: *standard gauge* (= 56½ inches in Britain) ◊ *a narrow gauge* (= narrower than standard) *railway/train* **5** [usually sing.] **~ (of sth)** (*written*) a fact or an event that can be used to estimate or judge sth: *Tomorrow's game against Arsenal will be a good gauge of their promotion chances.*
■ *verb* **1** to make a judgement about sth, especially people's feelings or attitudes: [VN] *They interviewed employees to gauge their reaction to the changes.* ◊ *He tried to gauge her mood.* ◊ [V wh-] *It was difficult to gauge whether she was angry or not.* **2** [VN] to measure sth accurately using a special instrument: *precision instruments that can gauge the diameter to a fraction of a millimetre* **3** to calculate sth approximately: [VN] *We were able to gauge the strength of the wind from the movement of the trees.* [also V wh-]

gaunt /gɔːnt/ *adj.* **1** (of a person) very thin, usually because of illness, hunger or worry: *a gaunt face* **2** (of a building) not attractive and without any decoration: *the gaunt ruin of Pendragon Castle* ▶ **gaunt·ness** *noun* [U]

gaunt·let /ˈgɔːntlət/ *noun* **1** a metal glove worn as part of a suit of ARMOUR by soldiers in the Middle Ages **2** a strong glove with a wide covering for the wrist, used for example when driving: *motorcyclists with leather gauntlets* IDM **run the ˈgauntlet** to be criticized or attacked by a lot of people, especially a group of people that you have to walk through: *Some of the witnesses had to run the gauntlet of television cameras and reporters.* **take up the ˈgauntlet** to accept sb's invitation to fight or compete **throw down the ˈgauntlet** to invite sb to fight or compete with you

gauze /gɔːz/ *noun* **1** [U] a light transparent fabric, usually made of cotton or silk **2** [U] a thin cotton fabric used for covering and protecting wounds: *a gauze dressing* **3** [U, C] material made of a NETWORK of wire; a piece of this: *a wire gauze*—picture at LABORATORY ▶ **gauzy** *adj.* [usually before noun]: *a gauzy material*

gave ,pt of GIVE

gavel /ˈgævl/ *noun* a small hammer used by a person in charge of a meeting or an AUCTION, or by a judge in a court of law, in order to get people's attention

ga·votte /gəˈvɒt; *AmE* gəˈvɑːt/ *noun* a French dance that was popular in the past; a piece of music for this dance

Gawd /gɔːd/ *noun, exclamation* (*informal*) used in written English to show that the word 'God' is being pronounced in a particular way to express surprise, anger or fear: *For Gawd's sake hurry up!*

gawk /gɔːk/ *verb* [V] **~ (at sb/sth)** (*informal*) to stare at sb/sth in a rude or stupid way

gawky /ˈgɔːki/ *adj.* (especially of a tall young person) awkward in the way they move or behave: *a shy gawky teenager* ▶ **gawk·ily** /ˈgɔːkɪli/ *adv.* **gawki·ness** /ˈgɔːkinəs/ *noun* [U]

gawp /gɔːp/ *verb* [V] **~ (at sb/sth)** (*BrE, informal*) to stare at sb/sth in a rude or stupid way

gay /geɪ/ *adj., noun*
■ *adj.* **1** (of people, especially men) sexually attracted to people of the same sex SYN HOMOSEXUAL: *gay men* ◊ *I didn't know he was gay.* ◊ *Is she gay?* OPP STRAIGHT **2** [only before noun] connected with people who are gay: *a gay club/bar* ◊ *the lesbian and gay community* **3** (gayer, gayest) (*old-fashioned*) happy and full of fun: *gay laughter* ◊ *She felt lighthearted and gay.* **4** (*old-fashioned*) brightly coloured: *The garden was gay with red geraniums.*—see also GAIETY, GAILY IDM **with ˈgay abandon** without thinking about the results or effects of a particular action
■ *noun* a person who is HOMOSEXUAL, especially a man

gay·ness /ˈgeɪnəs/ *noun* [U] the state of being HOMOSEXUAL—compare GAIETY

gaze /geɪz/ *verb, noun*
■ *verb* [V +adv./prep.] (especially *written*) to look steadily at sb/sth for a long time, either because you are very interested or surprised, or because you are thinking of sth

else: *She gazed at him in amazement.* ◊ *He sat for hours just gazing into space.*
■ *noun* [usually sing.] a long steady look at sb/sth: *He met her gaze* (= looked at her while she looked at him). ◊ *She dropped her gaze* (= stopped looking).

gaz·ebo /gəˈziːbəʊ; *AmE* -boʊ/ *noun* (*pl.* **-os**) a small building with open sides in a garden/yard, especially one with a view

gaz·elle /gəˈzel/ *noun* (*pl.* **gaz·elle** or **gaz·elles**) a small graceful ANTELOPE (= an African animal like a deer)

gaz·ette /gəˈzet/ *noun* **1** an official newspaper published by a particular organization containing important information about decisions that have been made and people who have been employed **2** (**Gazette**) used in the titles of some newspapers: *the Evening Gazette*

gaz·et·teer /ˌgæzəˈtɪə(r); *AmE* -ˈtɪr/ *noun* a list of place names published as a book or at the end of a book

gaz·ump /gəˈzʌmp/ *verb* [VN] [usually passive] (*BrE*) when sb who has made an offer to pay a particular price for a house and who has had this offer accepted is **gaz·umped**, their offer is no longer accepted by the person selling the house, because sb else has made a higher offer ▶ **gaz·ump·ing** /gəˈzʌmpɪŋ/ *noun* [U]

GB /ˌdʒiː ˈbiː/ *abbr.* Great Britain

GBH /ˌdʒiː biː ˈeɪtʃ/ *abbr.* (*BrE, law*) GRIEVOUS BODILY HARM

GCE /ˌdʒiː siː ˈiː/ *noun* [C, U] a British exam taken by students in England and Wales and some other countries in any of a range of subjects. GCE O levels were replaced in 1988 by GCSE exams. (abbreviation for 'General Certificate of Education')—compare O LEVEL, A LEVEL

GCSE /ˌdʒiː siː es ˈiː/ *noun* [C, U] a British exam taken by students in England and Wales and some other countries, usually around the age of 16. GCSE can be taken in any of a range of subjects (abbreviation for 'General Certificate of Secondary Education'): *She's got 10 GCSEs.* ◊ *He's doing German at GCSE.*—compare A LEVEL

Gdns *abbr.* (*BrE*) (used in written addresses) Gardens: *7 Windsor Gdns*

GDP /ˌdʒiː diː ˈpiː/ *noun* the abbreviation for 'gross domestic product' (the total value of all the goods and services produced by a country in one year)—compare GNP

GDR /ˌdʒiː diː ˈɑː(r)/ *abbr.* German Democratic Republic (the former East Germany)

gear /gɪə(r); *AmE* gɪr/ *noun, verb*
■ *noun*
IN VEHICLE **1** [C, usually pl.] machinery in a vehicle that turns engine power (or power on a bicycle) into movement forwards or backwards: *Careless use of the clutch may damage the gears.*—picture at BICYCLE **2** [U, C] a particular position of the gears in a vehicle that gives a particular range of speed and power: *first/second, etc. gear* ◊ *reverse gear* ◊ *low/high gear* ◊ (*BrE*) *bottom/top gear* ◊ (*BrE*) *to change gear* ◊ (*AmE*) *to shift gear* ◊ *When parking on a hill, leave the car in gear.* ◊ *What gear are you in?* ◊ *He drove wildly, crashing through the gears like a maniac.*
EQUIPMENT/CLOTHES **3** [U] the equipment or clothing needed for a particular activity: *climbing/fishing/sports gear*—see also HEADGEAR, RIOT GEAR **4** [U] (*informal*) clothes: *wearing the latest gear*
POSSESSIONS **5** [U] (*informal*) the things that a person owns: *I've left all my gear at Dave's house.*
MACHINERY **6** [U] (often in compounds) a piece of machinery used for a particular purpose: *lifting/towing/winding gear*—see also LANDING GEAR
SPEED/EFFORT **7** [U, C] the speed or effort involved in doing sth: (*BrE*) *The party organization is moving into top gear as the election approaches.* ◊ (*AmE*) *to move into high gear* ◊ *Coming out of the final bend, the runner stepped up a gear to overtake the rest of the pack.*
DRUGS **8** [U] (*slang*) illegal drugs
IDM **get into ˈgear** | **get sth into ˈgear** to start working, or to start sth working, in an efficient way (**slip/be thrown**) **out of ˈgear** (of emotions or situations) (to

s	t	v	z	ʃ	ʒ	tʃ	dʒ	θ	ð	ŋ
see	tea	van	zoo	shoe	vision	chain	jam	thin	this	sing

become) out of control: *She said nothing in case her temper slipped out of gear.* **IDM** see ASS

■ *verb*

PHR V 'gear sth to/towards sth [usually passive] to make, change or prepare sth so that it is suitable for a particular purpose: *The course had been geared towards the specific needs of its members.* ˌgear 'up (for/to sth)| ˌgear sb/sth↔'up (for/to sth) to prepare yourself/sb/sth to do sth: *Cycle organizations are gearing up for National Bike Week.*—see also GEARED

gear·box /'ɡɪəbɒks; *AmE* 'ɡɪrbɑːks/ *noun* the part containing the GEARS of a vehicle

geared /ɡɪəd; *AmE* ɡɪrd/ *adj.* [not before noun] **1** ~ to/towards sth| ~ to do sth designed or organized to achieve a particular purpose, or to be suitable for a particular group of people: *The programme is geared to preparing students for the world of work.* ◇ *The resort is geared towards children.* **2** ~ up (for sth)| ~ up (to do sth) prepared and ready for sth: *We have people on board geared up to help with any problems.*

gear·ing /'ɡɪərɪŋ; *AmE* 'ɡɪrɪŋ/ *noun* [U] **1** (*BrE*) (*AmE* **lever·age**) (*finance*) the relationship between the amount of money that a company owes and the value of its shares **2** a particular set or arrangement of GEARS in a machine or vehicle

'**gear lever** (also '**gear·stick**) (both *BrE*) (*AmE* '**gear shift**, '**stick shift**) *noun* a handle used to change the GEARS of a vehicle—picture at CAR, STICK

gecko /'ɡekəʊ; *AmE* 'ɡekoʊ/ *noun* (*pl.* **-os** *or* **-oes**) a small LIZARD (= a type of reptile) that lives in warm countries

ged·dit? /'ɡedɪt/ *abbr.* (*informal, spoken*) Do you get it? (= Do you understand the joke?)

gee /dʒiː/ *exclamation, verb*

■ *exclamation* (*especially AmE*) a word that some people use to show that they are surprised, impressed or annoyed: *Gee, what a great idea!*

■ *verb* (*BrE*) **PHR V** ˌgee sb↔'up| ˌgee sb↔'on to encourage sb to work harder, perform better, etc. ˌgee 'up used to tell a horse to start moving or to go faster

'**gee-gee** *noun* (*BrE, informal*) (used especially by and to young children) a horse

geek /ɡiːk/ *noun* (*slang, especially AmE*) a person who is boring, who wears clothes that are not fashionable, etc. ▶ **geeky** *adj.*

geese *pl.* of GOOSE

gee whiz /ˌdʒiː 'wɪz/ *exclamation* (*old-fashioned, especially AmE*) = GEE

gee·zer /'ɡiːzə(r)/ *noun* (*informal*) **1** (*BrE*) a man: *Some geezer called Danny did it.* **2** (*AmE*) an old man, especially one who is rather strange

Gei·ger count·er /'ɡaɪɡə kaʊntə(r); *AmE* 'ɡaɪɡər/ *noun* a device used for finding and measuring RADIOACTIVITY

gei·sha /'ɡeɪʃə/ (also '**geisha girl**) *noun* a Japanese woman who is trained to entertain men with conversation, dancing and singing

gel /dʒel/ *noun, verb*

■ *noun* [U, C] a thick substance like jelly, especially one used in products for the hair or skin: *hair/shower gel*

■ *verb* (-ll-) **1** [V] (*BrE*) (also **jell** *AmE, BrE*) (of two or more people) to work well together; to form a successful group: *We just didn't gel as a group.* **2** [V] (*BrE*) (also **jell** *AmE, BrE*) (of an idea, a thought, a plan, etc.) to become clearer and more definite; to work well: *Ideas were beginning to gel in my mind.* ◇ *That day, everything gelled.* **3** [V] (also **jell** especially in *AmE*) (*technical*) (of a liquid) to become thicker and more solid; to form a gel **4** [VN] [usually passive] to put gel on your hair

gel·atin /'dʒelətɪn/ (also **gel·atine** /'dʒelətiːn/) *noun* [U] a clear substance without any taste that is made from boiling animal bones and is used to make jelly, photographic film, etc.

gel·at·in·ous /dʒə'lætɪnəs/ *adj.* thick and sticky, like a jelly: *a gelatinous mixture/substance*

geld /ɡeld/ *verb* [VN] (*technical*) to remove the TESTICLES of a male animal, especially a horse **SYN** CASTRATE

geld·ing /'ɡeldɪŋ/ *noun* a horse that has been CASTRATED—compare STALLION

gel·ig·nite /'dʒelɪɡnaɪt/ *noun* [U] a powerful explosive

gem /dʒem/ *noun* **1** (also *less frequent* **gem·stone** /'dʒemstəʊn; *AmE* -stoʊn/) a precious stone that has been cut and polished and is used in jewellery: *a crown studded with gems* **2** a person, place or thing that is especially good: *This picture is the gem* (= the best) *of the collection.* ◇ *a gem of a place* ◇ *She's a real gem!*—compare JEWEL

Gem·ini /'dʒemɪnaɪ; -ni/ *noun* **1** [U] the third sign of the ZODIAC, the TWINS **2** [C] a person born under the influence of this sign, that is between 22 May and 21 June

Gen. *abbr.* (in writing) General: *Gen. (Stanley) Armstrong*

gen /dʒen/ *noun, verb*

■ *noun* [U] ~ (on sth) (*old-fashioned, BrE, informal*) information

■ *verb* (-nn-) **PHR V** ˌgen 'up (on sth)| ˌgen sb/yourself 'up (on sth) (*old-fashioned, BrE, informal*) to find out or give sb information about sth

gen·darme /'ʒɒndɑːm; *AmE* 'ʒɑːndɑːrm/ *noun* (from French) a member of the French police force

gen·der /'dʒendə(r)/ *noun* [C, U] the fact of being male or female: *issues of class, race and gender* ◇ *gender differences/relations/roles* **2** [C] (*grammar*) (in some languages) each of the classes (MASCULINE, FEMININE and sometimes NEUTER) into which nouns, pronouns and adjectives are divided. Different genders may have different endings, etc. **3** [U] (*grammar*) (in some languages) the division of nouns, pronouns and adjectives into different genders: *In French the adjective must agree with the noun in number and gender.* ⇨ note on page 534

'**gender-specific** *adj.* connected with women only or with men only: *The report was redrafted to remove gender-specific language.*

gene /dʒiːn/ *noun* (*biology*) a unit inside a cell which controls a particular quality in a living thing that has been passed on from its parents: *a dominant/recessive gene* ◇ *genes that code for the colour of the eyes*—see also GENETIC

ge·neal·ogist /ˌdʒiːni'ælədʒɪst/ *noun* a person who studies family history

ge·neal·ogy /ˌdʒiːni'ælədʒi/ *noun* (*pl.* **-ies**) **1** [U] the study of family history, including the study of who the ancestors of a particular person were **2** [C] a particular person's line of ancestors; a diagram that shows this ▶ **ge·nea·logic·al** /ˌdʒiːniə'lɒdʒɪkl; *AmE* -'lɑːdʒ-/ *adj.* [only before noun]: *a genealogical chart/table/tree* (= a chart with branches that shows a person's ancestors)

'**gene pool** *noun* (*biology*) all of the GENES available to a particular SPECIES of animal or plant

gen·era *pl.* of GENUS

gen·eral /'dʒenrəl/ *adj., noun*

■ *adj.*

AFFECTING ALL | **1** affecting all or most people, places or things: *The general opinion is that the conference was a success.* ◇ *the general belief/consensus* ◇ *a general strike* ◇ *books of general interest* (= of interest to most people) ◇ *The bad weather has been fairly general* (= has affected most areas).

USUAL | **2** [usually before noun] normal; usual: *There is one exception to this general principle.* ◇ *As a general rule* (= usually) *he did what he could to be helpful.* ◇ *This opinion is common among the general population* (= ordinary people).

NOT DETAILED | **3** including the most important aspects of sth; not exact or detailed **SYN** OVERALL: *I check the bookings to get a general idea of what activities to plan.* ◇ *I know how it works in general terms.* ◇ *They gave a general description of the man.*

DIRECTION/AREA | **4** the ~ direction/area approximately, but not exactly, the direction/area mentioned: *They fired in the general direction of the enemy.*

NOT LIMITED | **5** not limited to a particular subject, use or activity: *a general hospital* ◇ *general education* ◇ *We shall at this stage keep the discussion fairly general.* **6** not limited to one part or aspect of a person or thing: *a general anaesthetic* ◇ *The building was in a general state of disrepair.*

æ	ɑː	e	ɜː	ə	ɪ	iː	i	ɒ	ɔː	ʌ	ʊ	u	uː
cat	father	ten	bird	about	sit	see	many	got	saw	cup	put	actual	too

(BrE)

G

MORE ABOUT
gender

Ways of talking about men and women

When you are writing or speaking English it is important to use language that includes both men and women equally. Some people may be very offended if you do not.

The human race

Man and **mankind** have traditionally been used to mean 'all men and women'. Many people now prefer to use **humanity, the human race, human beings** or **people.**

Jobs

The suffix **-ess** in names of occupations such as **actress, hostess** and **waitress** shows that the person doing the job is a woman. Many people now avoid these. Instead you can use **actor** or **host**, (although **actress** and **hostess** are still very common) or a neutral word, such as **server** for *waiter* and *waitress.*

Neutral words like **assistant, worker, person** or **officer** are now often used instead of *-man* or *-woman* in the names of jobs. For example, you can use **police officer** instead of *policeman* or *police-woman,* and **spokesperson** instead of *spokesman* or *spokeswoman.* Neutral words are very common in newspapers, on television and radio and in official writing, in both *BrE* and *AmE.*

When talking about jobs that are traditionally done by the other sex, some people say: *a* **male secretary /nurse/model** (NOT **man**) or a **woman/female doctor/barrister/driver.** However this is now not usually used unless you need to emphasize which sex the person is, or it is still unusual for the job to be done by a man/woman: *My daughter prefers to see a woman doctor.* ◊ *They have a male nanny for their kids.* ◊ *a female racing driver.*

Pronouns

He used to be considered to cover both men and women: *Everyone needs to feel he is loved,* but this is not now acceptable. Instead, after **everybody, everyone, anybody, anyone, somebody, some-one,** etc. one of the plural pronouns **they, them, and their** is often used: *Does everybody know what they want?* ◊ *Somebody's left their coat here.* ◊ *I hope nobody's forgotten to bring their passport with them.* ▪

Some people prefer to use **he or she, his or her,** or **him or her** in speech and writing: *Everyone knows what's best for him or herself.* **He/she** or **(s)he** can also be used in writing: *If in doubt, ask your doctor. He/she can give you more information.* (You may find that some writers just use 'she'.) These uses can seem awkward when they are used a lot. It is better to try to change the sentence, using a plural noun. Instead of saying: *A baby cries when he or she is tired* you can say *Babies cry when they are tired.*

HIGHEST IN RANK | **7** [only before noun] (also **General** [after noun]) highest in rank; CHIEF: *the general manager* ◊ *the Inspector General of Police*—see also ATTORNEY-GENERAL, DIRECTOR-GENERAL, GOVERNOR GENERAL, SECRETARY GEN-ERAL, SOLICITOR GENERAL, SURGEON GENERAL

IDM **in** ˌ**general 1** usually; mainly: *In general, Japanese cars are very reliable and breakdowns are rare.* **2** as a whole: *This is a crucial year for your relationships in general and your love life in particular.*

▪ *noun* (*abbr.* **Gen.**) an officer of very high rank in the army and the US air force; the officer with the highest rank in the Marines: *a four-star general* ◊ *General Tom Parker*—see also BRIGADIER GENERAL, MAJOR GENERAL

ˌ**General Cerˌtificate of Eduˈcation** *noun* = GCE

ˌ**General Cerˌtificate of ˌSecondary Eduˈca-tion** *noun* = GCSE

ˌ**general ˈcounsel** *noun* (in the US) the main lawyer who gives legal advice to a company

ˌ**general deˈlivery** *noun* [U] (*AmE*) = POSTE RESTANTE

ˌ**general eˈlection** *noun* an election in which all the people of a country vote to choose a government—com-pare BY-ELECTION

ˌ**general headˈquarters** *noun* [U+sing./pl. *v.*] = GHQ

gen·er·al·ist /ˈdʒenrəlɪst/ *noun* a person who has know-ledge of several different subjects or activities—compare SPECIALIST

gen·er·al·ity /ˌdʒenəˈræləti/ *noun* (*pl.* **-ies**) **1** [C, usually pl.] a statement that discusses general principles or issues rather than details or particular examples: *to speak in broad generalities* ◊ *As usual, he confined his comments to generalities.* **2** (**the generality**) [pl.] (*formal*) most of a group of people or things: *This view is held by the generality of leading scholars.* **3** [U] (*formal*) the qual-ity of being general rather than detailed or exact: *An account of such generality is of little value.*

gen·er·al·iza·tion (*BrE* also **-isa·tion**) /ˌdʒenrəl-aɪˈzeɪʃn; *AmE* -ləˈz-/ *noun* [C, U] a general statement that is based on only a few facts or examples; the act of making such statements: *a speech full of broad/sweeping generalizations* ◊ *to* **make generalizations about** *sth* ◊ *Try to avoid generalization.*

gen·er·al·ize (*BrE* also **-ise**) /ˈdʒenrəlaɪz/ *verb* **1** [V] **~ (from sth)** to use a particular set of facts or ideas in order to form an opinion that is considered valid for a different situation: *It would be foolish to generalize from a single example.* **2** [V] **~ (about sth)** to make a general statement about sth and not look at the details: *It is dangerous to generalize about the poor.* **3** [VN] [often passive] **~ sth (to sth)** (*formal*) to apply a theory, idea, etc. to a wider group or situation than the original one: *These conclusions can-not be generalized to the whole country.*

gen·er·al·ized (*BrE* also **-ised**) /ˈdʒenrəlaɪzd/ *adj.* [usually before noun] not detailed; not limited to one particular area: *a generalized discussion/statement/view* ◊ *a generalized disease/rash* (= affecting the whole body)

ˌ**general ˈknowledge** *noun* [U] knowledge of facts about a lot of different subjects: *a general knowledge quiz*

gen·er·al·ly /ˈdʒenrəli/ *adv.* **1** by or to most people: *The plan was generally welcomed.* ◊ *It is now generally accepted that ...* ◊ *The new drug will be generally available from January.* ◊ *He was a generally unpopular choice for captain.* **2** in most cases **SYN** USUALLY: *I generally get up at six.* ◊ *The male is generally larger with a shorter beak.* **3** without discussing the details of sth: *Let's talk just about investment generally.*

ˌ**general ˈpractice** *noun* [U, C] (*BrE*) the work of a doctor who treats people in the community rather than at a hospital and who is not a specialist in one particular area of medicine; a place where a doctor like this works: *to be in general practice* ◊ *She runs a general practice in Hull.*

ˌ**general pracˈtitioner** (also ˌ**family pracˈtitioner**) (*abbr.* **GP**) (also *informal* ˌ**family ˈdoctor**) *noun* (*espe-cially BrE*) a doctor who is trained in general medicine and who treats patients in a local community rather than at a hospital

the ˌ**general ˈpublic** *noun* [sing.+ sing./pl. *v.*] ordin-ary people who are not members of a particular group or organization: *At that time, the general public was/were not aware of the health risks.* ◊ *The exhibition is not open to the general public.*

ˌ**general ˈpurpose** *adj.* [only before noun] having a wide range of different uses: *a general purpose farm vehicle*

ˌ**general ˈstaff** (often **the general staff**) *noun* [sing.+ sing./pl. *v.*] officers who advise a military leader and help to plan a military operation

ˌ**general ˈstore** (*BrE* also ˌ**general ˈstores** [pl.]) a shop/store that sells a wide variety of goods, especially one in a small town or village: *She runs the post office and general store.*

gen·er·ate /ˈdʒenəreɪt/ *verb* [VN] to produce or create

---

sth: *to generate electricity / heat / power* ◊ *to generate income / profit* ◊ *We need someone to generate new ideas.* ◊ *The proposal has generated a lot of interest.*

gen·er·ation /ˌdʒenəˈreɪʃn/ *noun* **1** [C+sing./ pl. *v.*] all the people who were born at about the same time: *the younger / older generation* ◊ *My generation have grown up without the experience of a world war.* ◊ *I often wonder what future generations will make of our efforts.* **2** [C] the average time in which children grow up, become adults and have children of their own, (usually considered to be about 30 years): *a generation ago* ◊ *My family have lived in this house for generations.* **3** [C, U] a single stage in the history of a family: *stories passed down from generation to generation* ◊ *a first- / second- generation American* (= a person whose family has lived in America for one / two generations) **4** [C, usually sing.] a group of people of similar age involved in a particular activity: *She has inspired a whole generation of fashion school graduates.* **5** [C, usually sing.] a stage in the development of a product, usually a technical one: *fifth-generation computing* ◊ *a new generation of vehicle* **6** [U] the production of sth, especially electricity, heat, etc: *the generation of electricity* ◊ *methods of income generation* **7** [U] (*biology*) the development of animals, plants, etc: *spontaneous generation*

gen·er·ation·al /ˌdʒenəˈreɪʃənl/ *adj.* [usually before noun] connected with a particular generation or with the relationship between different generations: *generational conflict*

the gene'ration gap *noun* [sing.] the difference in attitude or behaviour between young and older people that causes a lack of understanding: *a movie that is sure to bridge the generation gap*

Gene,ration 'X *noun* [U] the group of people who were born between the early 1960s and the middle of the 1970s, who seem to lack a sense of direction in life and to feel that they have no part to play in society

gen·era·tive /ˈdʒenərətɪv/ *adj.* (*formal*) that can produce sth: *generative processes*

gen·er·ator /ˈdʒenəreɪtə(r)/ *noun* **1** a machine for producing electricity: *The factory's emergency generators were used during the power cut.* ◊ *a wind generator* (= a machine that uses the power of the wind to produce electricity) **2** a machine for producing a particular substance: *The museum uses smells and smoke generators to create atmosphere.* ◊ (*figurative*) *The company is a major generator of jobs.* **3** (*BrE*) a company that produces electricity to sell to the public: *the UK's major electricity generator*

gen·er·ic /dʒəˈnerɪk/ *adj.* **1** shared by, including or typical of a whole group of things; not SPECIFIC: *'Vine fruit' is the generic term for currants and raisins.* **2** (of a product, especially a drug) not using the name of the company that made it: *generic brands* ◊ *The doctor offered me a choice of a branded or a generic drug.* ▶ **gen·er·ic·al·ly** /dʒəˈnerɪkli/ *adv.*

gen·er·os·ity /ˌdʒenəˈrɒsəti; *AmE* -ˈrɑːs-/ *noun* [U, sing.] ~ **(to/towards sb)** the fact of being generous (= willing to give sb money, gifts, time or kindness freely): *He treated them with generosity and thoughtfulness.*

gen·er·ous /ˈdʒenərəs/ *adj.* (*approving*) **1** ~ **(with sth)** giving or willing to give freely; given freely: *a generous benefactor* ◊ *to be generous with your time / money* ◊ *to be generous in giving help* ◊ *a generous gift / offer* ◊ *It was generous of him to offer to pay for us both.* **OPP** MEAN **2** more than is necessary; large: *a generous helping of meat* ◊ *a generous increase in salary* ◊ *The car has a generous amount of space.* **3** kind in the way you treat people; willing to see what is good about sb/sth: *a generous mind / spirit* ◊ *He wrote a very generous assessment of my work.* ▶ **gen·er·ous·ly** *adv.*: *Please give generously.* ◊ *a dress that is generously cut* (= uses plenty of fabric)

gen·esis /ˈdʒenəsɪs/ *noun* [sing.] (*formal*) the beginning or origin of sth

gen·et·ic /dʒəˈnetɪk/ *adj.* connected with GENES (= the units in the cells of a living thing that control its physical characteristics) or GENETICS (= the study of genes): *genetic*

and environmental factors ◊ *genetic abnormalities* ▶ **gen·et·ic·al·ly** /-kli/ *adv.*: *genetically engineered / determined / modified / transmitted*

ge,netic 'code *noun* the arrangement of GENES that controls how each living thing will develop

ge,netic ,engi'neering *noun* [U] the science of changing how a living creature or plant develops by changing the information in its GENES

ge,netic 'fingerprinting *noun* [U] the method of finding the particular pattern of GENES in an individual person, particularly to identify sb or find out if sb has committed a crime ▶ **ge,netic 'fingerprint** *noun* [C]

gen·eti·cist /dʒəˈnetɪsɪst/ *noun* a scientist who studies genetics

gen·et·ics /dʒəˈnetɪks/ *noun* [U] the scientific study of the ways in which different characteristics are passed from each GENERATION of living things to the next

gen·ial /ˈdʒiːniəl/ *adj.* friendly and cheerful: *a genial person* ◊ *a genial smile / tone* ▶ **geni·al·ity** /ˌdʒiːniˈæləti/ *noun* [U]: *an atmosphere of warmth and geniality* **geni·al·ly** /ˈdʒiːniəli/ *adv.*: *to smile genially*

genie /ˈdʒiːni/ *noun* (*pl.* **gen·ies** or **genii** /ˈdʒiːniaɪ/) (in Arabian stories) a spirit with magic powers, especially one that lives in a bottle or a lamp **SYN** DJINN

geni·tal /ˈdʒenɪtl/ *adj.* [only before noun] connected with the outer sexual organs of a person or an animal: *the genital area* ◊ *genital infections*

geni·tals /ˈdʒenɪtlz/ (also **geni·talia** /ˌdʒenɪˈteɪliə/) *noun* [pl.] (*anatomy*) a person's sex organs that are outside their body

geni·tive /ˈdʒenətɪv/ *noun* (*grammar*) (in some languages) the special form of a noun, a pronoun or an adjective that is used to show possession or close connection between two things—compare ACCUSATIVE, DATIVE, NOMINATIVE, POSSESSIVE, VOCATIVE ▶ **geni·tive** *adj.*

ge·nius /ˈdʒiːniəs/ *noun* (*pl.* **ge·niuses**) **1** [U] unusually great intelligence, skill or artistic ability: *the genius of Shakespeare* ◊ *a statesman of genius* ◊ *Her idea was a stroke of genius.* **2** [C] a person who is unusually intelligent or artistic, or who has a very high level of skill, especially in one area: *a mathematical / comic genius* ◊ *He's a genius at organizing people.* ◊ *You don't have to be a genius to see that they are in love!* **3** [sing.] ~ **for sth / for doing sth** a special skill or ability: *He had a genius for making people feel at home.* **IDM** **sb's good / evil 'genius** (*especially BrE*) a person or spirit who is thought to have a good / bad influence over you

geno·cide /ˈdʒenəsaɪd/ *noun* [U] the murder of a whole race or group of people ▶ **geno·cidal** *adj.*

gen·ome /ˈdʒiːnəʊm; *AmE* -oʊm/ *noun* (*biology*) the complete set of GENES in a cell or living thing: *the human genome*

genre /ˈʒɑːnrə/ *noun* (*formal*) a particular type or style of literature, art, film or music that you can recognize because of its special features

gent /dʒent/ *noun* (*BrE*) **1** (*old-fashioned* or *humorous*) a man; a GENTLEMAN: *a gent's hairdresser* ◊ *This way please, ladies and gents!* **2** (**a/the gents, a/the Gents**) [sing.] (*informal*) a public toilet for men: *Is there a gents near here?* ◊ *Where's the gents?*

gen·teel /dʒenˈtiːl/ *adj.* (sometimes *disapproving*) **1** of people and their way of life) quiet and polite, often in an exaggerated way; from, or pretending to be from, a high social class: *a genteel manner / upbringing* ◊ *Her genteel accent irritated me.* ◊ *He lived in genteel poverty* (= trying to keep the style of a high social class, but with little money). **2** (of places) quiet and old-fashioned and perhaps slightly boring ▶ **gen·teel·ly** /dʒenˈtiːlli/ *adv.*

gen·tian /ˈdʒenʃn/ *noun* [C, U] a small plant with bright blue flowers that grows in mountain areas

gen·tile /ˈdʒentaɪl/ (also **Gen·tile**) *noun* a person who is not Jewish ▶ **gen·tile** (also **Gen·tile**) *adj.* [only before noun]

gen·til·ity /dʒenˈtɪləti/ *noun* [U] (*formal*) **1** very good manners and behaviour; the fact of belonging to a high social class: *He took her hand with discreet gentility.* ◊ *She* *thinks expensive clothes are a mark of gentility.* **2** the fact of being quiet and old-fashioned: *the faded gentility of the town*

gen·tle /ˈdʒentl/ *adj.* (**gent·ler** /ˈdʒentlə(r)/ **gent·lest** /ˈdʒentlɪst/) **1** calm and kind; doing things in a quiet and careful way: *a quiet and gentle man* ◊ *a gentle voice/ laugh/touch* ◊ *She was the gentlest of nurses.* ◊ *He lived in a gentler age than ours.* ◊ *Be gentle with her!* ◊ *She agreed to come, after a little gentle persuasion.* ◊ *He looks scary but he's really a **gentle giant**.* **2** (of weather, temperature, etc.) not strong or extreme: *a gentle breeze* ◊ *the gentle swell of the sea* ◊ *Cook over a gentle heat.* **3** having only a small effect; not strong or violent: *We went for a gentle stroll.* ◊ *a little gentle work/exercise* ◊ *This soap is very gentle on the hands.* **4** not steep or sharp: *a gentle slope/ curve/angle*—see also GENTLY ▶ **gentle·ness** /ˈdʒentl- nəs/ *noun* [U]

gentle·man /ˈdʒentlmən/ *noun* (*pl.* **-men** /-mən/) **1** [C] a man who is polite and well educated, who has excellent manners and always behaves well: *Thank you—you're a real gentleman.* ◊ *He's no gentleman!*—compare LADY **2** [C, often pl.] (*formal*) used to address or refer to a man, especially sb you do not know: *Ladies and gentlemen! Can I have your attention, please?* ◊ *Gentlemen of the jury!* ◊ *Can I help you, gentlemen?* ◊ *There's a gentleman to see you.* HELP In more informal speech, you could say: *Can I help you?* ◊ *There's someone to see you.* **3** (*old-fashioned*) a man from a high social class, especially one who does not need to work: *a country gentleman* ◊ *a gentleman farmer* (= one who owns a farm, but does no physical work)

gentle·man·ly /ˈdʒentlmənli/ *adj.* (*approving*) behaving very well and showing very good manners; like a gentleman: *gentlemanly behaviour* ◊ *So far, the election campaign has been a very gentlemanly affair.*

gentleman's aˈgreement (also **gentlemen's aˈgreement**) *noun* an agreement made between people who trust each other, which is not written down and which has no legal force

gentle·woman /ˈdʒentlwʊmən/ *noun* (*pl.* **-women** /-wɪmɪn/) (*old use*) a woman who belongs to a high social class; a woman who is well educated and has excellent manners

gen·tly /ˈdʒentli/ *adv.* **1** in a gentle way: *She held the baby gently.* ◊ *'You miss them, don't you?' he asked gently.* ◊ *Simmer the soup gently for 30 minutes.* ◊ *Massage the area gently but firmly.* ◊ *leaves moving gently in the breeze* ◊ *The path ran gently down to the sea.* **2** (*Gently!*) (*BrE, spoken*) used to tell sb to be careful: *Gently! You'll hurt the poor thing!* ◊ *Don't go too fast—gently does it!*

gen·tri·fy /ˈdʒentrɪfaɪ/ *verb* (**gen·tri·fies, gen·tri·fy·ing, gen·tri·fied, gen·tri·fied**) [VN] [usually passive] to change an area, a person, etc. so that they are suitable for, or can mix with, people of a higher social class than before: *Old working class areas of the city are being gentrified.* ▶ **gen·tri·fi·ca·tion** *noun* [U]

gen·try /ˈdʒentri/ *noun* [pl.] (usually **the gentry**) (*old-fashioned*) people belonging to a high social class: *the local gentry* ◊ *the landed gentry* (= those who own a lot of land)

genu·flect /ˈdʒenjuflekt/ *verb* [V] (*formal*) **1** to lower your body by bending one or both knees, as a sign of respect during worship in a church **2 ~ (to sth)** (*disapproving*) to show too much respect to sb/sth ▶ **genu·flec·tion** (*BrE* also **genu·flex·ion**) /ˌdʒenjuˈflekʃn/ *noun* [C, U]

genu·ine /ˈdʒenjuɪn/ *adj.* **1** real; exactly what it appears to be; not artificial: *Is the painting a genuine Picasso?* ◊ *Fake designer watches are sold at a fraction of the price of **the genuine article**.* ◊ *Only genuine refugees can apply for asylum.* **2** sincere and honest; that can be trusted: *He made a genuine attempt to improve conditions.* ◊ *genuine concern for others* ◊ *a very genuine person* ▶ **genu·ine·ly** *adv.*: *genuinely sorry* **genu·ine·ness** *noun* [U]

genus /ˈdʒiːnəs/ *noun* (*pl.* **gen·era** /ˈdʒenərə/) (*biology*) a group into which animals, plants, etc. that have similar characteristics are divided, smaller than a family and larger than a SPECIES—compare CLASS, KINGDOM, ORDER, PHYLUM—see also GENERIC

geo- *combining form* (in nouns, adjectives and adverbs) of the earth: *geochemical* ◊ *geoscience*

geog·raph·er /dʒiˈɒɡrəfə(r)/; *AmE* -ˈɑːɡ-/ *noun* a person who studies geography; an expert in geography

geog·raphy /dʒiˈɒɡrəfi/; *AmE* -ˈɑːɡ-/ *noun* **1** [U] the scientific study of the earth's surface, physical features, divisions, products, population, etc: *human/physical/ economic/social geography* ◊ *a geography lesson/depart- ment/teacher/textbook* ◊ *a degree in geography* **2** [sing.] the way in which the physical features of a place are arranged: *the geography of New York City* ◊ *Kim knew the geography of the building and strode along the corridor.* **3** [sing.] the way in which a particular aspect of life or society is influenced by geography or varies according to geography: *The geography of poverty and the geography of voting are connected.* ▶ **geo·graph·ic·al** /ˌdʒiːəˈɡræfɪkl/ *adj.*: *The survey covers a wide geographical area.* ◊ *The importance of the town is due to its geographical location.* **geo·graph·ic·al·ly** /ˌdʒiːəˈɡræfɪkli/ *adv.*: *geographically remote areas*

geolo·gist /dʒiˈɒlədʒɪst; *AmE* -ˈɑːl-/ *noun* a scientist who studies geology

geol·ogy /dʒiˈɒlədʒi; *AmE* -ˈɑːl-/ *noun* **1** [U] the scientific study of the earth, including the origin and history of the rocks and soil of which the earth is made **2** [sing.] the origin and history of the rocks and soil of a particular area: *the geology of the British Isles* ▶ **geo·logic·al** /ˌdʒiːəˈlɒdʒɪkl/; *AmE* -ˈlɑːdʒ-/ *adj.*: *a geological survey/map* **geo·logic·al·ly** /ˌdʒiːəˈlɒdʒɪkli/; *AmE* -ˈlɑːdʒ-/ *adv.*

geo·met·ric /ˌdʒiːəˈmetrɪk/ (also *less frequent* **geo·met·ric·al** /-ɪkl/) *adj.* of GEOMETRY; of or like the lines, shapes, etc. used in GEOMETRY, especially because of having regular shapes or lines: *a geometric design* ▶ **geo·met·ric·al·ly** /ˌdʒiːəˈmetrɪkli/ *adv.*

geoˌmetric ˈmean *noun* = MEAN

geoˌmetric proˈgression *noun* a series of numbers in which each is multiplied or divided by a fixed number to produce the next, for example 1, 3, 9, 27, 81—compare ARITHMETIC PROGRESSION

geom·etry /dʒiˈɒmətri; *AmE* -ˈɑːm-/ *noun* **1** [U] the branch of mathematics that deals with the measurements and relationships of lines, angles, surfaces and solids **2** [sing.] the measurements and relationships of lines, angles, etc. in a particular object or shape: *the geometry of a spider's web*

geo·phys·ics /ˌdʒiːəʊˈfɪzɪks; *AmE* ˌdʒiːoʊ-/ *noun* [U] the scientific study of the earth's atmosphere, oceans and climate ▶ **geo·phys·ic·al** /-ˈfɪzɪkl/ *adj.*: *geophysical data/surveys* **geo·physi·cist** /-ˈfɪzɪsɪst/ *noun*

geo·pol·it·ics /ˌdʒiːəʊˈpɒlətɪks; *AmE* ˌdʒiːoʊˈpɑːl-/ *noun* [U+sing./pl. *v.*] the political relations between countries and groups of countries in the world; the study of these relations ▶ **geo·pol·it·ical** /ˌdʒiːəʊpəˈlɪtɪkl/; *AmE* ˌdʒiːoʊ-/ *adj.*

Geor·die /ˈdʒɔːdi/; *AmE* ˈdʒɔːrdi/ *noun* (*BrE, informal*) **1** [C] a person from Tyneside in NE England **2** [U] a way of speaking typical of people from Tyneside in NE England ▶ **Geor·die** *adj.*: *a Geordie accent*

Geor·gian /ˈdʒɔːdʒən/; *AmE* ˈdʒɔːrdʒən/ *adj.* (especially of architecture and furniture) from the time of the British kings George I–IV (1714–1830): *a fine Georgian house*

ge·ra·nium /dʒəˈreɪniəm/ *noun* a garden plant with a mass of red, pink or white flowers on the end of each stem

ger·bil /ˈdʒɜːbɪl; *AmE* ˈdʒɜːrbɪl/ *noun* a small desert animal like a mouse, that is often kept as a pet

geri·at·ric /ˌdʒeriˈætrɪk/ *noun* **1** (**geriatrics**) [U] the branch of medicine concerned with the diseases and care of old people **2** [C] (*informal, offensive*) an old person, especially one with poor physical or mental health: *I'm not a geriatric yet, you know!* ▶ **geri·at·ric** *adj.*: *the geriatric ward* (= in a hospital) ◊ *a geriatric vehicle* (= old and in bad condition)

geria·tri·cian /ˌdʒeriəˈtrɪʃn/ *noun* a doctor who studies and treats the diseases of old people

G

s	t	v	z	ʃ	ʒ	tʃ	dʒ	θ	ð	ŋ
see	tea	van	zoo	shoe	vision	chain	jam	thin	this	sing

germ /dʒɜːm; *AmE* dʒɜːrm/ *noun* **1** [C, usually pl.] a very small living thing that can cause infection and disease: *Disinfectant kills germs.* ◇ *Dirty hands can be a breeding ground for germs.* **2** [sing.] ~ **of sth** an early stage of the development of sth: *Here was the germ of a brilliant idea.* **3** [C] (*biology*) the part of a plant or an animal that can develop into a new one—see also WHEATGERM

ger·mane /dʒɜːˈmeɪn; *AmE* dʒɜːrˈm-/ *adj.* [not usually before noun] ~ **(to sth)** (*formal*) (of ideas, remarks, etc.) connected with sth in an important or appropriate way: *remarks that are germane to the discussion*

Ger·man·ic /dʒɜːˈmænɪk; *AmE* dʒɜːrˈm-/ *adj.* **1** connected with or considered typical of Germany or its people: *She had an almost Germanic regard for order.* **2** connected with the language family that includes German, English, Dutch and Swedish among others

German measles /ˌdʒɜːmən ˈmiːzlz; *AmE* ˌdʒɜːrmən-/ (also **ru·bella**) *noun* [U] a mild infectious disease that causes a sore throat and red spots all over the body. It can seriously affect babies born to women who catch it soon after they become pregnant.

German 'shepherd *noun* (*especially AmE*) = ALSATIAN

ger·min·ate /ˈdʒɜːmɪneɪt; *AmE* ˈdʒɜːrm-/ *verb* when the seed of a plant **germinates** or **is germinated**, it starts to grow: [V] (*figurative*) *An idea for a novel began to germinate in her mind.* [also VN] ▶ **ger·min·ation** /ˌdʒɜːmɪˈneɪʃn; *AmE* ˌdʒɜːrm-/ *noun* [U]

germ 'warfare *noun* [U] = BIOLOGICAL WARFARE

ger·ont·olo·gist /ˌdʒerɒnˈtɒlədʒɪst; *AmE* -rənˈtɑːl-/ *noun* (*especially AmE*) a person who studies the process of people growing old

ge·ron·tol·ogy /ˌdʒerɒnˈtɒlədʒi; *AmE* -rənˈtɑːl-/ *noun* [U] the scientific study of old age and the process of growing old

ger·ry·man·der /ˈdʒerimændə(r)/ *verb* [VN] (*disapproving*) to change the size and borders of an area for voting in order to give an unfair advantage to one party in an election ▶ **ger·ry·man·der·ing** *noun* [U]

ger·und /ˈdʒerənd/ *noun* (*grammar*) a noun in the form of the present PARTICIPLE of a verb (that is, ending in *-ing*) for example *travelling* in the sentence *I preferred travelling alone.*

ges·ta·tion /dʒeˈsteɪʃn/ *noun* **1** [U, sing.] the time that the young of a person or an animal develops inside its mother's body until it is born; the process of developing inside the mother's body: *a baby born at 38 weeks' gestation* ◇ *The gestation period of a horse is about eleven months.* ◇ *Gestation lasts about nine months.* **2** [U] (*formal*) the process by which an idea or a plan develops: *His book was nearly twenty years in gestation.*

ges·ticu·late /dʒeˈstɪkjuleɪt/ *verb* [V] (usually *written*) to move your hands and arms about in order to attract attention or make sb understand what you are saying: *He gesticulated wildly at the clock.* ▶ **ges·ticu·la·tion** /dʒeˌstɪkjuˈleɪʃn/ *noun* [C, U]: *wild/frantic gesticulations*

ges·ture /ˈdʒestʃə(r)/ *noun*, *verb*

■ *noun* **1** [C, U] a movement that you make with your hands, your head or your face to show a particular meaning: *He made a rude gesture at the driver of the other car.* ◇ *She finished what she had to say with a gesture of despair.* ◇ *They communicated entirely by gesture.* **2** [C] something that you do or say to show a particular feeling or intention: *They sent some flowers as a gesture of sympathy to the parents of the child.* ◇ *It was a nice gesture* (= it was kind) *to invite his wife too.* ◇ *We do not accept responsibility but we will refund the money as a gesture of goodwill.* ◇ *The government has made a gesture towards public opinion* (= has tried to do sth that the public will like).

■ *verb* ~ **(for/to sb) (to do sth)** to move your hands, head, face, etc. as a way of expressing what you mean or want: [V] [usually +*adv./prep.*] *'I see you read a lot,' he said, gesturing at the wall of books.* ◇ *She gestured for them to come in.* ◇ [Vthat] *He gestured (to me) that it was time to go.* ◇ *They gestured that I should follow.* [also VN]

ge·sund·heit /ɡəˈzʊndhaɪt/ *exclamation* (*AmE*, from *German*) used when sb has SNEEZED to wish them good health

get /ɡet/ *verb* (**getting**, **got**, **got** /ɡɒt; *AmE* ɡɑːt/) **HELP** In spoken *AmE* the past participle **got·ten** /ˈɡɒtn; *AmE* ˈɡɑːtn/ is almost always used.

RECEIVE/OBTAIN | **1** [VN] [no passive] to receive sth: *I got a letter from Dave this morning.* ◇ *What* (= What presents) *did you get for your birthday?* ◇ *He gets* (= earns) *about $40000 a year.* ◇ *This room gets very little sunshine.* ◇ *I got a shock when I saw the bill.* ◇ *I get the impression that he is bored with his job.* **2** [no passive] ~ **sth (for yourself/sb)** | ~ **(yourself/sb) sth** to obtain sth: [VN] *Where did you get* (= buy) *that skirt?* ◇ *Did you manage to get tickets for the concert?* ◇ *She opened the door wider to get a better look.* ◇ *Try to get some sleep.* ◇ *He has just got a new job.* ◇ [VNN] *Why don't you get yourself a car?* ◇ [VN, VNN] *Did you get a present for your mother?* ◇ *Did you get your mother a present?* **3** [VN] [no passive] ~ **sth (for sth)** to obtain or receive an amount of money by selling sth: *How much did you get for your car?* ◇ *We got £120000 for the house.*

BRING | **4** to go to a place and bring sb/sth back [SYN] FETCH: *Quick—go and get a cloth!* ◇ *Somebody get a doctor!* ◇ *I have to go and get my mother from the airport* (= pick her up). ◇ [VN, VNN] *Get a drink for John.* ◇ *Get John a drink.*

PUNISHMENT | **5** [VN] [no passive] to receive sth as a punishment: *He got ten years* (= was sent to prison for ten years) *for armed robbery.*

BROADCASTS | **6** [VN] [no passive] to receive broadcasts from a particular television or radio station: *We can't get Channel 5 in our area.*

BUY | **7** [VN] [no passive] to buy sth, for example a newspaper or magazine, regularly [SYN] TAKE: *Which newspaper do you get?*

MARK/GRADE | **8** [VN] [no passive] to achieve or be given a particular mark/grade in an exam: *He got a 'C' in Chemistry and a 'B' in English.*

ILLNESS | **9** [VN] [no passive] to become infected with an illness; to suffer from a pain, etc: *I got this cold off* (= from) *you!* ◇ *She gets* (= often suffers from) *really bad headaches.*

CONTACT | **10** [VN] [no passive] to be connected with sb by telephone: *I wanted to speak to the manager but I got his secretary instead.*

STATE/CONDITION | **11** to reach a particular state or condition; to make sb/sth/yourself reach a particular state or condition: [V-ADJ] *to get angry/bored/hungry/fat* ◇ *You'll soon get used to the climate here.* ◇ *We ought to go; it's getting late.* ◇ *to get dressed/undressed* (= to put your clothes on/take your clothes off) ◇ *They plan to get married in the summer.* ◇ *She's upstairs getting ready.* ◇ *I wouldn't go there alone; you might get* (= be) *mugged.* ◇ *My car got* (= was) *stolen at the weekend.* ◇ [VN-ADJ] *Don't get your dress dirty!* ◇ *He got his fingers caught in the door.* ◇ *She soon got the children ready for school.* ⇨ note at BECOME **12** [Vtoinf] to reach the point at which you feel, know, are, etc. sth: *After a time you get to realize that these things don't matter.* ◇ *You'll like her once you get to know her.* ◇ *His drinking is getting to be a problem.* ◇ *She's getting to be an old lady now.*

MAKE/PERSUADE | **13** to make, persuade, etc. sb/sth to do sth: [VNtoinf] *I couldn't get the car to start this morning.* ◇ *He got his sister to help him with his homework.* ◇ *You'll never get him to understand.* ◇ [VN-ing] *Can you really get that old car going again?* ◇ *It's not hard to get him talking—the problem is stopping him!*

GET STH DONE | **14** [VN-ADJ] ~ **sth done** to cause sth to happen or be done: *I must get my hair cut.* ◇ *I'll never get all this work finished.*

START | **15** [V-ing] to start doing sth: *I got talking to her.* ◇ *We need to get going soon.*

OPPORTUNITY | **16** (*informal*) [Vtoinf] to have the opportunity to do sth: *He got to try out all the new software.* ◇ *It's not fair—I never get to go first.*

ARRIVE | **17** [V+*adv./prep.*] to arrive at or reach a place or point: *We got to San Diego at 7 o'clock.* ◇ *You got in very*

G

late last night. ◇ *What time did you get here?* ◇ *I haven't got very far with the book I'm reading.*

MOVE/TRAVEL | **18** [+*adv./prep.*] to move to or from a particular place or in a particular direction, sometimes with difficulty; to make sb/sth do this: [V] *The bridge was destroyed so we couldn't get across the river.* ◇ *She got into bed.* ◇ *He got down from the ladder.* ◇ *We didn't get* (= go) **to bed** *until 3 a.m.* ◇ *I'm **getting off*** (= leaving the train) *at the next station.* ◇ *Where have they got to* (= where are they)*?* ◇ *We must be **getting home**; it's past midnight.* ◇ [VN] *The general had to get his troops across the river.* ◇ *We couldn't get the piano through the door.* ◇ *We'd better call a taxi and get you home.* ◇ *I can't get the lid off.* **19** [VN] [no passive] to use a bus, taxi, plane, etc: *We're going to be late—let's get a taxi.* ◇ *I usually get the bus to work.*

MEAL | **20 ~ sth (for yourself/sb)** | **~ (yourself/sb) sth** (*especially BrE*) to prepare a meal: [VN] *Who's getting the lunch?* ◇ [VN, VNN] *I must go home and get tea for the kids.* ◇ *I must go home and get the kids their tea.*

TELEPHONE/DOOR | **21** [VN] (*spoken*) to answer the telephone or a door when sb calls, knocks, etc: *Will you get the phone?*

CATCH/HIT | **22** [VN] to catch or take hold of sb, especially in order to harm or punish them: *He was on the run for a week before the police got him.* ◇ *to get sb by the arm/wrist/throat* ◇ *She fell overboard and the sharks got her.* ◇ *He thinks everybody is **out to get him*** (= trying to harm him). ◇ (*informal*) *I'll get you for that!* **23** [VN +*adv./prep.*] to hit or wound sb: *The bullet got him in the neck.*

UNDERSTAND | **24** [VN] [no passive] (*informal*) to understand sb/sth: *I don't get you.* ◇ *She didn't get the joke.* ◇ *I don't get it—why would she do a thing like that?* ◇ *I get the message—you don't want me to come.*

HAPPEN/EXIST | **25** [VN] [no passive] (*informal*) used to say that sth happens or exists: *You get* (= There are) *all these kids hanging around in the street.* ◇ *They still get cases of typhoid there.*

CONFUSE/ANNOY | **26** [VN] [no passive] (*spoken*) to make sb feel confused because they do not understand sth [SYN] PUZZLE: *'What's the capital of Bulgaria?' 'You've got me there!'* (= I don't know). **27** [VN] [no passive] (*spoken*) to annoy sb: *What gets me is having to do the same thing all day long.*

[HELP] Get is one of the most common words in English, but some people try to avoid it in formal writing.

[IDM] Most idioms containing **get** are at the entries for the nouns and adjectives in the idioms, for example **get sb's goat** is at **goat**. **be getting 'on** (*informal*) **1** (of a person) to be becoming old **2** (of time) to be becoming late: *The time's getting on—we ought to be going.* **be getting on for ...** (*especially BrE*) to be nearly a particular time, age or number: *It must be getting on for midnight.* ◇ *He's getting on for eighty.* **can't get 'over sth** (*spoken*) used to say that you are shocked, surprised, amused, etc. by sth: *I can't get over how rude she was.* **get a'way from it all** (*informal*) to have a short holiday/vacation in a place where you can relax **get (sb) anywhere/somewhere/nowhere** to achieve or cause sb to achieve something/nothing; to make or cause sb to make progress/no progress: *After six months' work on the project, at last I feel I'm getting somewhere.* ◇ *This line of investigation is getting us nowhere.* **get it 'on (with sb)** (*slang, especially AmE*) to have sex with sb **'get it** (*AmE*) = CATCH IT **get it 'up** (*slang*) (of a man) to have an ERECTION **'get there** to achieve your aim or complete a task: *I'm sure you'll get there in the end.* ◇ *It's not perfect but we're getting there* (= making progress). **how selfish, stupid, ungrateful, etc. can you 'get?** (*spoken*) used to express surprise or disapproval that sb has been so selfish, etc. **there's no getting a'way from sth | you can't get a'way from sth** you have to admit that sth unpleasant is true **what are you, was he, etc. 'getting at?** (*spoken*) used to ask, especially in an angry way, what sb is/was suggesting: *I'm partly to blame? What exactly are you getting at?* **what has got into sb?** (*spoken*) used to say that sb has suddenly started to

behave in a strange or different way: *What's got into Alex? He never used to worry like that.*

[PHR V] ,**get a'bout** (*BrE*) = GET AROUND

,**get a'bove yourself** (*especially BrE*) to have too high an opinion of yourself

,**get a'cross (to sb)** | ,**get sth↔a'cross (to sb)** to be communicated or understood; to succeed in communicating sth: *Your meaning didn't really get across.* ◇ *He's not very good at getting his ideas across.*

,**get a'head (of sb)** to make progress (further than others have done): *She wants to get ahead in her career.* ◇ *He soon got ahead of the others in his class.*

,**get a'long 1** (usually used in the progressive tenses) to leave a place: *It's time we were getting along.* **2** = GET ON ,**get a'round 1** (*BrE* also ,**get a'bout**) to move from place to place or from person to person: *She gets around with the help of a stick.* ◇ *News soon got around that he had resigned.* **2** (*especially AmE*) = GET ROUND

'**get at sb** (usually used in the progressive tenses) to keep criticizing sb: *He's always getting at me.* ◇ *She feels she's being got at.* '**get at sb/sth** to reach sb/sth; to gain ACCESS to sb/sth: *The files are locked up and I can't get at them.* '**get at sth** to learn or find out sth: *The truth is sometimes difficult to get at.*

,**get a'way** to have a holiday/vacation: *We're hoping to get away for a few days at Easter.*—related noun GETAWAY ,**get a'way (from ...)** to succeed in leaving a place: *I won't be able to get away from the office before 7.* ,**get a'way (from/...)** to escape from sb or a place ,**get a'way with sth 1** to steal sth and escape with it: *Thieves got away with computer equipment worth $30 000.*—related noun GETAWAY **2** to receive a relatively light punishment: *He was lucky to get away with only a fine.* **3** to do sth wrong and not be punished for it: *Don't be tempted to cheat—you'll never get away with it.* ◇ [+-ing] *Nobody gets away with insulting me like that.*

,**get 'back** to return, especially to your home: *What time did you get back last night?* ,**get sth↔'back** to obtain sth again after having lost it: *She's got her old job back.* ◇ *I never lend books—you never get them back.* ,**get 'back (in)** (of a political party) to win an election after having lost the previous one ,**get 'back at sb** (*informal*) to do sth bad to sb who has done sth bad to you; to get REVENGE on sb: *I'll find a way of getting back at him!* ,**get 'back to sb** to speak or write to sb again later, especially in order to give a reply: *I'll find out and get back to you.* ,**get 'back to sth** to return to sth: *Could we get back to the question of funding?*

,**get be'hind (with sth)** to fail to make enough progress or to produce sth at the right time: *I'm getting behind with my work.* ◇ *He got behind with the payments for his car.*

,**get 'by (on/in/with sth)** to manage to live or do a particular thing using the money, knowledge, equipment, etc. that you have: *How does she get by on such a small salary?* ◇ *I can just about get by in German* (= I can speak basic German).

,**get 'down** (of children) (*BrE*) to leave the table after a meal ,**get sb 'down** (*informal*) to make sb feel sad or depressed ,**get sth↔'down 1** to swallow sth, usually with difficulty **2** to make a note of sth [SYN] WRITE DOWN: *Did you get his number down?* ,**get 'down to sth** to begin to do sth; to give serious attention to sth: *Let's get down to business.* ◇ *I like to get down to work by 9.* ◇ [+-ing] *It's time I got down to thinking about that essay.*

,**get 'in** | ,**get 'into sth 1** to arrive at a place: *The train got in late.* ◇ *What time do you get into Heathrow?* **2** to win an election: *The Republican candidate stands a good chance of getting in.* ◇ *She first got into Parliament* (= became an MP) *in 1997.* **3** to be admitted to a school, university, etc: *She's got into Durham to study law.* ,**get sb↔'in** to call sb to your house to do a job ,**get sth↔'in 1** to collect or gather sth: *to get the crops/harvest in* **2** to buy a supply of sth: *Remember to get in some beers for this evening.* **3** to manage to do or say sth: *I got in an hour's work while the baby was asleep.* ◇ *She talks so much it's impossible to get a word in.* ,**get 'in on sth** to take part in an activity: *He's hoping to get in on any discussions about the new project.*

aɪ	aʊ	eɪ	əʊ	oʊ	ɔɪ	ɪə	eə	ʊə	j	w
my	now	say	go (BrE)	go (AmE)	boy	near	hair	pure	yes	wet

,get 'in with sb (*informal*) to become friendly with sb, especially in order to gain an advantage

,get 'into sth **1** to put on a piece of clothing, especially with difficulty: *I can't get into these shoes—they're too small.* **2** to start a career in a particular profession: *What's the best way to get into journalism?* **3** to become involved in sth; to start sth: *I got into conversation with an Italian student.* ◊ *to get into a fight/an argument* **4** to develop a particular habit: *Don't let yourself get into bad habits.* ◊ *You should get into the routine of saving the document you are working on every ten minutes.* ◊ *How did she get into (= start taking) drugs?* **5** (*informal*) to become interested in sth: *I'm really getting into jazz these days.* **6** to become familiar with sth; to learn sth: *I haven't really got into my new job yet.* ,get 'into sth| ,get yourself/sb 'into sth to reach a particular state or condition; to make sb reach a particular state or condition: *He got into trouble with the police while he was still at school.* ◊ *Three people were rescued from a yacht which got into difficulties.* ◊ *She got herself into a real state (= became very anxious) before the interview.*

,get 'off| ,get 'off sb used especially to tell sb to stop touching you or another person: *Get off me, that hurts!* ,get 'off| ,get sb 'off **1** to leave a place or start a journey; to help sb do this: *We got off straight after breakfast.* ◊ *He got the children off to school.* **2** (*BrE*) to fall asleep; to make sb do this: *I had great difficulty getting off to sleep.* ◊ *They couldn't get the baby off till midnight.* ,get 'off| ,get 'off sth to leave work with permission: *Could you get off (work) early tomorrow?* ,get 'off sth| ,get sb 'off sth to stop discussing a particular subject; to make sb do this: *Please can we get off the subject of dieting?* ◊ *I couldn't get him off politics once he had started.* ,get sth 'off to send sth by post/mail: *I must get these letters off first thing tomorrow.* ,get 'off on sth (*informal*) to be excited by sth, especially in a sexual way ,get 'off (with sth) to have no or almost no injuries in an accident: *She was lucky to get off with just a few bruises.* ,get 'off (with sth)| ,get sb 'off (with sth) to receive no or almost no punishment; to help sb do this: *He was lucky to get off with a small fine.* ◊ *A good lawyer might be able to get you off.* ,get 'off with sb (*informal, especially BrE*) to have a sexual or romantic experience with sb; to start a sexual relationship with sb: *Steve got off with Tracey at the party.*

,get 'on **1** (also ,get a'long) used to talk or ask about how well sb is doing in a particular situation: *He's getting on very well at school.* **2** to be successful in your career: *Parents are always anxious for their children to get on.* **3** (also ,get a'long) to manage or survive: *We can get on perfectly well without her.* ◊ *I just can't get along without a secretary.* ,get 'on to sb **1** to contact sb by telephone or letter: *The heating isn't working; I'll get on to the landlord about it.* **2** to become aware of sb's activities, especially when they have been doing sth bad or illegal: *He had been stealing money from the company for years before they got on to him.* ,get 'on to sth to begin to talk about a new subject: *It's time we got on to the question of costs.* ,get 'on/a'long with sb| ,get 'on/a'long (together) to have a friendly relationship with sb: *She's never really got on with her sister.* ◊ *She and her sister have never really got on.* ◊ *We get along just fine together.* ,get 'on with sth **1** (also ,get a'long with sth) used to talk or ask about how well sb is doing a task: *I'm not getting on very fast with this job.* **2** to continue doing sth, especially after an interruption: *Be quiet and get on with your work.* ◊ *(spoken) Get on with it! We haven't got all day.*

,get 'out to become known: *If this gets out there'll be trouble.* ,get sth↔'out **1** to produce or publish sth: *Will we get the book out by the end of the year?* **2** to say sth with difficulty: *She managed to get out a few words of thanks.* ,get 'out (of sth) to leave a place, especially in order to visit other places, meet people, etc: *You ought to get out of the house more.* ,get 'out of sth **1** to avoid a responsibility or duty: *We promised we'd go—we can't get out of it now.* ◊[+ -ing] *I wish I could get out of going to that meeting.* **2** to stop having a particular habit: *I can't get out of the habit of waking at six in the morning.* ,get sth 'out of sb to persuade sb to tell or give you sth,

especially by force: *The police finally got a confession out of her.* ,get sth 'out of sb/sth to gain or obtain sth good from sb/sth: *She seems to get a lot out of life.* ◊ *He always gets the best out of people.*

,get 'over sth to deal with or gain control of sth [SYN] OVERCOME: *She can't get over her shyness.* ◊ *I think the problem can be got over without too much difficulty.* ,get 'over sth/sb to return to your usual state of health, happiness, etc. after an illness, a shock, the end of a relationship, etc: *He was disappointed at not getting the job, but he'll get over it.* ,get sth↔'over (to sb) to make sth clear to sb: *He didn't really get his meaning over to the audience.* ,get sth 'over (with) (*informal*) to complete sth unpleasant but necessary: *I'll be glad to get the exam over and done with.*

,get 'round/a'round sb to persuade sb to agree or to do what you want, usually by doing nice things for them: *She knows how to get round her dad.* ,get 'round/a'round sth to deal with a problem successfully [SYN] OVERCOME: *A clever lawyer might find a way of getting round that clause.* ,get 'round/a'round to sth to find the time to do sth: *I meant to do the ironing but I didn't get round to it.* ◊[+ -ing] *I hope to get around to answering your letter next week.*

'get through sth **1** to use up a large amount of sth: *We got through a fortune while we were in New York!* **2** to manage to do or complete sth: *Let's start—there's a lot to get through.* ,get 'through (sth) (*BrE*) to be successful in an exam, etc. ,get sb 'through sth to help sb to be successful in an exam: *She got all her students through the exam.* ,get 'through (sth)| ,get sth 'through (sth) to be officially accepted; to make sth be officially accepted: *They got the bill through Congress.* ,get 'through (to sb) **1** to reach sb: *Thousands of refugees will die if these supplies don't get through to them.* **2** to make contact with sb by telephone: *I tried calling you several times but I couldn't get through.* ,get 'through (to sth) (of a player or team) to reach the next stage of a competition: *Moya has got through to the final.* ,get 'through to sb to make sb understand or accept what you say, especially when you are trying to help them: *I find it impossible to get through to her.* ,get 'through with sth to finish or complete a task 'get to sb (*informal*) to annoy or affect sb: *The pressure of work is beginning to get to him.*

,get sb/sth to'gether to collect people or things in one place: *I'm trying to get a team together for Saturday.* ,get to'gether (with sb) to meet with sb socially or in order to discuss sth: *We must get together for a drink sometime.* ◊ *Management should get together with the union.*—related noun GET-TOGETHER

,get 'up **1** to stand up after sitting, kneeling, etc. [SYN] RISE: *The class got up when the teacher came in.* **2** if the sea or wind gets up, it increases in strength and becomes violent ,get 'up| ,get sb 'up to get out of bed; to make sb get out of bed: *He always gets up early.* ◊ *Could you get me up at 6.30 tomorrow?* ,get yourself/sb 'up as sth [often passive] (*BrE*) to dress yourself/sb as sb/sth else: *She was got up as an Indian princess.*—related noun GET-UP ,get sth↔'up to arrange or organize sth: *We're getting up a party for her birthday.* ,get 'up to sth **1** to reach a particular point: *We got up to page 72 last lesson.* **2** to be busy with sth, especially sth surprising or unpleasant: *What on earth will he get up to next?* ◊ *She's been getting up to her old tricks again!*

get·away /'getəweɪ/ *noun* [usually sing.] **1** an escape from a difficult situation, especially after committing a crime: *to make a quick getaway* ◊ *a getaway car* **2** a short holiday/vacation; a place that is suitable for a holiday/vacation: *a romantic weekend getaway in New York* ◊ *the popular island getaway of Penang*

get·ting /'getɪŋ/ *noun* [sing.] [IDM] **while the ,getting is 'good** (*AmE*) = WHILE THE GOING IS GOOD

'get-together *noun* (*informal*) an informal meeting; a party: *a family get-together at Christmas*

'get-up *noun* (*old-fashioned, informal*) a set of clothes, especially strange or unusual ones

,get-up-and-'go *noun* [U] (*informal*) energy and determination to get things done

b	d	f	g	h	k	l	m	n	p	r
bad	**did**	**fall**	**get**	**hat**	**cat**	**leg**	**man**	**now**	**pen**	**red**

G

gey·ser /ˈɡiːzə(r); *AmE* ˈɡaɪzər/ *noun* **1** a natural SPRING that sometimes sends hot water or steam up into the air—picture at VOLCANO **2** (*BrE*) a piece of equipment in a kitchen or bathroom that heats water, usually by gas

ghastly /ˈɡɑːstli; *AmE* ˈɡæstli/ *adj.* (**ghast·lier, ghast·li·est**) **1** (of an event) very frightening and unpleasant, because it involves pain, death, etc: *a ghastly crime/murder* ◊ *She woke up in the middle of a ghastly nightmare.* **2** (*informal*) (of an experience or a situation) very bad; unpleasant: *The weather was ghastly.* ◊ *It's all been a ghastly mistake.* **3** (*informal*) (of a person or thing) that you find unpleasant and dislike very much: *her ghastly husband* ◊ *This lipstick is a ghastly colour.* **4** [not usually before noun] ill/sick or upset: *I felt ghastly the next day.* **5** (*literary*) very pale in appearance, like a dead person: *His face was ghastly white.*

ghee /ɡiː/ *noun* [U] a type of butter used in Indian cooking

gher·kin /ˈɡɜːkɪn; *AmE* ˈɡɜːrkɪn/ *noun* **1** (*BrE*) (*AmE* **pickle**) a small CUCUMBER that has been preserved in VINEGAR before being eaten **2** (*AmE*) a small CUCUMBER

ghetto /ˈɡetəʊ; *AmE* ˈɡetoʊ/ *noun* (*pl.* **-os** or **-oes**) **1** an area of a city where many people of the same race or background live, separately from the rest of the population. Ghettos are often crowded, with bad living conditions: *a poor kid growing up in the ghetto* ◊ *The south coast of Spain has become something of a tourist ghetto.* **2** the area of a town where Jews were forced to live in the past: *the Warsaw ghetto*

ghetto blaster (also **boom box** especially in *AmE*) *noun* (*informal*) a large radio and cassette player that can be carried around, especially to play loud music in public

ghil·lie *noun* = GILLIE

ghost /ɡəʊst; *AmE* ɡoʊst/ *noun, verb*
■ *noun* **1** [C] the spirit of a dead person that a living person believes they can see or hear: *Do you believe in ghosts* (= believe that they exist)? ◊ *the ghost of her father that had come back to haunt her* ◊ *He looked as if he had seen a ghost* (= looked very frightened). **2** [C] the memory of sth, especially sth bad: *The ghost of anti-Semitism still haunts Europe.* **3** [sing.] ~ **of sth** a very slight amount of sth that is left behind or that you are not sure really exists: *There was a ghost of a smile on his face.* ◊ *You don't have a ghost of a chance* (= you have no chance). **4** [sing.] a second image on a television screen that is not as clear as the first, caused by a fault **IDM** **give up the ghost 1** to die **2** (*humorous*) (of a machine) to stop working: *My car finally gave up the ghost.*—more at FORMER
■ *verb* **1** = GHOSTWRITE **2** [V+adv./prep.] (*literary*) to move without making a sound: *They ghosted up the smooth waters of the river.*

ghost·ly /ˈɡəʊstli; *AmE* ˈɡoʊstli/ *adj.* looking or sounding like a ghost; full of ghosts: *a ghostly figure* ◊ *ghostly footsteps* ◊ *the ghostly churchyard*

ghost story *noun* a story about ghosts that is intended to frighten you

ghost town *noun* a town that used to be busy and have a lot of people living in it, but is now empty

ghost train *noun* (*BrE*) a small train at a FUNFAIR that goes through a dark tunnel full of frightening things

ghost·write /ˈɡəʊstraɪt; *AmE* ˈɡoʊst-/ (also **ghost**) *verb* to write a book, an article, etc. for another person who publishes it as their own work: [VN] [often passive] *Her memoirs were ghostwritten.* [also V]

ghost·writer /ˈɡəʊstraɪtə(r); *AmE* ˈɡoʊst-/ *noun* a person who writes a book, etc. for another person, under whose name it is then published

ghoul /ɡuːl/ *noun* **1** (in stories) an evil spirit that opens graves and eats the dead bodies in them **2** (*disapproving*) a person who is too interested in unpleasant things such as death and disaster ▶ **ghoul·ish** /ˈɡuːlɪʃ/ *adj.*: *ghoulish laughter*

GHQ /ˌdʒiː eɪtʃ ˈkjuː/ *noun* [U] the abbreviation for 'general headquarters' (the main centre of a military organization): *He was posted to GHQ Cairo.*

GI /ˌdʒiː ˈaɪ/ *noun* (*pl.* **GIs**) a soldier in the US armed forces

giant /ˈdʒaɪənt/ *noun, adj.*
■ *noun* **1** (in stories) a very large strong person who is often cruel and stupid—see also GIANTESS **2** an unusually large person, animal or plant: *He's a giant of a man.* **3** a very large and powerful organization: *the multinational oil giants* **4** a person who is very good at sth: *literary giants*
■ *adj.* [only before noun] very large; much larger or more important than similar things usually are: *a giant crab* ◊ *a giant-size box of tissues* ◊ *a giant step towards achieving independence*

giant·ess /ˌdʒaɪənˈtes/ *noun* (in stories) a female giant

giant-killer *noun* (*BrE*) (especially in sports) a person or team that defeats another much stronger opponent

giant 'panda *noun* = PANDA (1)

gib·ber /ˈdʒɪbə(r)/ *verb* to speak quickly in a way that is difficult to understand, often because of fear: [V] *He cowered in the corner, gibbering with terror.* ◊ *By this time I was a gibbering wreck.* [also V speech]

gib·ber·ish /ˈdʒɪbərɪʃ/ *noun* [U] (*informal*) words that have no meaning or are impossible to understand **SYN** NONSENSE: *You were talking gibberish in your sleep.*

gib·bet /ˈdʒɪbɪt/ *noun* (*old-fashioned*) an upright wooden structure on which criminals used to be hanged **SYN** GALLOWS

gib·bon /ˈɡɪbən/ *noun* a small APE (= an animal like a large monkey without a tail) with long arms, that lives in SE Asia

gibe = JIBE

gib·lets /ˈdʒɪbləts/ *noun* [pl.] the inside parts of a chicken or other bird, including the heart and LIVER, that are usually removed before it is cooked

giddy /ˈɡɪdi/ *adj.* (**gid·dier, gid·di·est**) **1** [not usually before noun] feeling that everything is moving and that you are going to fall **SYN** DIZZY: *When I looked down from the top floor, I felt giddy.* **2** [not usually before noun] ~ (**with sth**) so happy and excited that you cannot behave normally: *She was giddy with happiness.* **3** [usually before noun] making you feel as if you were about to fall: *The kids were pushing the roundabout at a giddy speed.* ◊ (*figurative*) *the giddy heights of success* **4** (*old-fashioned*) (of people) not serious **SYN** SILLY: *Isabel's giddy young sister* ▶ **gid·di·ly** /ˈɡɪdɪli/ *adv.*: *She swayed giddily across the dance floor.* **gid·di·ness** /ˈɡɪdinəs/ *noun* [U]: *Symptoms include nausea and giddiness.*

gift /ɡɪft/ *noun, verb*
■ *noun* **1** a thing that you give to sb, especially on a special occasion or to say thank you **SYN** PRESENT: *The watch was a gift from my mother.* ◊ *Thank you for your generous gift.* ◊ *a free gift for every reader* ◊ *the gift of life/love* ◊ (*formal*) *The family made a gift of his paintings to the gallery.* ◊ *gifts of toys for the children* **2** ~ (**for sth/for doing sth**) a natural ability **SYN** TALENT: *She has a great gift for music.* ◊ *He has the gift of making friends easily.* ◊ *She can pick up a tune instantly on the piano, it's a gift.* **3** [usually sing.] (*informal*) a thing that is very easy to do or cheap to buy: *Their second goal was an absolute gift.* ◊ *At £500 it's a gift.* **IDM** **the gift of the 'gab** (*BrE*) (*AmE* **a gift for/of 'gab**) (*informal*, sometimes *disapproving*) the ability to speak easily and to persuade other people with your words **look a gift horse in the 'mouth** (usually with negatives) (*informal*) to refuse or criticize sth that is given to you for nothing—more at GOD
■ *verb* (*BrE*, *written*) (used especially in journalism) to give sth to sb without their having to make any effort to get it: [VNN] *They gifted their opponents a goal.* ◊ [VN] *They gifted a goal to their opponents.*

gift certificate (*AmE*) *noun* = GIFT TOKEN

gift·ed /ˈɡɪftɪd/ *adj.* **1** having a lot of natural ability or intelligence: *a gifted musician/player* ◊ *gifted children* **2** ~ **with sth** having sth pleasant: *He was gifted with a charming smile.*

gift shop *noun* a shop/store that sells goods that are suitable for giving as presents

gift token (also **gift voucher**) (both *BrE*) (*AmE* **gift certificate**) *noun* a piece of paper that is worth a particular amount of money and that can be exchanged for goods in a shop/store

s	t	v	z	ʃ	ʒ	tʃ	dʒ	θ	ð	ŋ
see	tea	van	zoo	shoe	vision	chain	jam	thin	this	sing

gift-wrap verb (-pp-) [VN] [often passive] to wrap sth as a present for sb, especially in a shop/store: *Would you like the chocolates gift-wrapped?* ◊ *The store offers a gift-wrapping service.*

gig /gɪg/ noun **1** a performance by musicians playing pop music or jazz in front of an audience: *to do a gig* ◊ *a Verve gig in Leeds* **2** a small light carriage with two wheels, pulled by one horse

gi·gan·tic /dʒaɪˈgæntɪk/ adj. extremely large: *a gigantic house*

gig·gle /ˈgɪgl/ verb, noun
■ verb ~ (at/about sb/sth) to laugh in a silly way because you are amused, embarrassed or nervous: [V] *The girls giggled at the joke.* ◊ *They giggled nervously as they waited for their turn.* [also V speech]
■ noun **1** [C] a slight silly repeated laugh: *She gave a nervous giggle.* ◊ *Matt collapsed into giggles and hung up the phone.* **2** [sing.] (*BrE, informal*) a thing that you think is amusing: *We only did it for a giggle.* **3** (the giggles) [pl.] (*informal*) continuous giggling that you cannot control or stop: *I get the giggles when I'm nervous.* ◊ *She had a fit of the giggles and had to leave the room.*

gig·gly /ˈgɪgli/ adj. laughing a lot in a silly, nervous way

gig·olo /ˈʒɪgələʊ; ˈdʒɪ-; AmE -loʊ/ noun (pl. -os) a man who is paid to be the lover of an older woman, usually one who is rich

gild /gɪld/ verb [VN] (*literary*) to make sth look bright, as if covered with gold: *The golden light gilded the sea.* IDM **gild the 'lily** to spoil sth that is already good or beautiful by trying to improve it

gild·ed /ˈgɪldɪd/ adj. [only before noun] **1** covered with a thin layer of gold or gold paint **2** (*literary*) rich and belonging to the upper classes: *the gilded youth* (= rich, upper-class young people) *of the Edwardian era*

gild·ing /ˈgɪldɪŋ/ noun [U] a layer of gold or gold paint; the surface that this makes

gill¹ /gɪl/ noun [usually pl.] one of the openings on the side of a fish's head that it breathes through—picture on page A7 IDM **to the 'gills** (*informal*) completely full: *I was stuffed to the gills with chocolate cake.*

gill² /dʒɪl/ noun a unit for measuring liquids. There are four gills in a PINT.

gil·lie (also **ghil·lie**) /ˈgɪli/ noun (*ScotE*) a man or boy who helps sb who is shooting or fishing for sport in Scotland

gilt /gɪlt/ noun **1** [U] a thin layer of gold, or sth like gold that is used on a surface for decoration: *gilt buttons/ lettering* **2** (gilts) [pl.] (*BrE, finance*) gilt-edged INVESTMENTS **3** [C] (*especially AmE*) a young female pig IDM **take the gilt off the 'gingerbread** (*BrE*) to do or be sth that makes a situation or ACHIEVEMENT less attractive or impressive

gilt-'edged adj. (*finance*) very safe: *gilt-edged securities/ shares/stocks* (= INVESTMENTS that are considered safe because they have been sold by the government)

gim·crack /ˈdʒɪmkræk/ adj. [only before noun] (*rare*) badly made and of little value

gim·let /ˈgɪmlət/ noun a small tool for making holes in wood to put screws in: (*figurative*) *eyes like gimlets* (= looking very hard at things and noticing every detail)

gimme /ˈgɪmi/ (*informal*) a way of writing the way that the words 'give me' are sometimes spoken: *Gimme back my bike!*

gim·mick /ˈgɪmɪk/ noun (often *disapproving*) an unusual trick or unnecessary device that is intended to attract attention or to persuade people to buy sth: *a promotional/publicity/sales gimmick* ◊ *We don't use gimmicks to sell our products.* ▶ **gim·micky** /ˈgɪmɪki/ adj.: *a gimmicky idea/fashion*

gim·mick·ry /ˈgɪmɪkri/ noun [U] (*disapproving*) the use of gimmicks in selling, etc.

gin /dʒɪn/ noun **1** [U] an alcoholic drink made from grain and flavoured with JUNIPER berries. Gin is usually drunk mixed with TONIC WATER or fruit juice: *Do you like gin?*—see also PINK GIN **2** [C] a glass of gin: *I'll have a gin and tonic, please.*

gin·ger /ˈdʒɪndʒə(r)/ noun, adj., verb

■ noun [U] **1** the root of the **ginger** plant used in cooking as a spice: *a teaspoon of ground ginger* ◊ (*BrE*) *ginger biscuits* **2** a light brownish-orange colour
■ adj. (*BrE*) light brownish-orange in colour: *ginger hair* ◊ *a ginger cat*
■ verb PHRV ˌginger sth/sb↔'up (*BrE*) to make sth/sb more active or exciting

ˌginger 'ale noun **1** [U] a clear FIZZY drink (= with bubbles) that does not contain alcohol, flavoured with ginger, and often mixed with alcoholic drinks **2** [C] a bottle or glass of ginger ale

ˌginger 'beer noun **1** [U] a FIZZY drink (= with bubbles) with a very small amount of alcohol in, flavoured with ginger **2** [C] a bottle or glass of ginger beer

gin·ger·bread /ˈdʒɪndʒəbred; AmE -dʒɑrb-/ noun [U] a sweet cake or soft biscuit/cookie flavoured with GINGER: *a gingerbread man* (= a gingerbread biscuit/cookie in the shape of a person) IDM see GILT

'ginger group noun (*BrE*) a group of people within a political party or an organization, who work to persuade other members to accept their policies or ideas

gin·ger·ly /ˈdʒɪndʒəli; AmE -dʒərli/ adv. in a careful way, because you are afraid of being hurt, of making a noise, etc: *He opened the box gingerly and looked inside.*

'ginger nut (*BrE*) (also **'ginger snap** *AmE, BrE*) noun a hard sweet biscuit/cookie flavoured with GINGER

gin·gery /ˈdʒɪndʒəri/ adj. like GINGER in colour or flavour

ging·ham /ˈgɪŋəm/ noun [U] a cotton fabric with a pattern of white and coloured checks: *a blue and white gingham dress*

gin·gi·vitis /ˌdʒɪndʒɪˈvaɪtəs/ noun [U] (*medical*) a condition in which the GUMS around the teeth become painful, red and swollen

gi·nor·mous /dʒaɪˈnɔːməs; AmE -ˈnɔːrm-/ adj. (*BrE, spoken*) extremely large

gin·seng /ˈdʒɪnseŋ/ noun [U] a medicine obtained from a plant root that some people believe helps you stay young and healthy

gipsy = GYPSY

gir·affe /dʒəˈrɑːf; AmE -ˈræf/ noun (pl. **gir·affe** or **gir·affes**) a tall African animal with a very long neck, long legs, and dark marks on its coat

gird /gɜːd; AmE gɜːrd/ verb IDM **gird (up) your 'loins** (*literary or humorous*) to get ready to do sth difficult: *The company is girding its loins for a plunge into the overseas market.* PHRV **gird yourself/sb/sth (up) for sth** (*literary*) to prepare for sth difficult, especially a fight, contest, etc.

gird·er /ˈgɜːdə(r); AmE ˈgɜːrd-/ noun a long strong iron or steel beam used for building bridges and the FRAMEWORK of large buildings

gir·dle /ˈgɜːdl; AmE ˈgɜːrdl/ noun, verb
■ noun **1** a piece of women's underwear that fits closely around the body from the waist to the THIGH, designed to make a woman look thinner **2** (*literary*) a thing that surrounds sth else: *carefully tended lawns set in a girdle of trees* **3** (*old-fashioned*) a belt or thick string fastened around the waist to keep clothes in position
■ verb [VN] (*literary*) to surround sth: *A chain of volcanoes girdles the Pacific.*

girl /gɜːl; AmE gɜːrl/ noun **1** [C] a female child: *a baby girl* ◊ *a little girl of six* ◊ *Hello, girls and boys!* **2** [C] a daughter: *Our youngest girl is at college.* **3** [C] (sometimes *offensive*) a young woman: *Alex is not interested in girls yet.* ◊ *He married the girl next door.* **4** [C] (usually in compounds) (*old-fashioned, offensive*) a female worker: *an office girl/a shop girl* **5** [C] (*old-fashioned*) a man's girlfriend **6** (girls) [pl.] (used especially as a form of address by women) a woman's female friends: *I'm having a night out with the girls.* ◊ *Good morning, girls!* **7** [sing.] (*old girl*) (often *offensive*) an old woman, especially sb's wife or mother: *How is the old girl these days?*

ˌgirl 'Friday noun a girl or a woman who is employed in an office to do several different jobs, helping other people

girl·friend /ˈgɜːlfrend; AmE ˈgɜːrl-/ noun **1** a girl or a

G

æ	ɑː	e	ɜː	ə	ɪ	iː	i	ɒ	ɔː	ʌ	ʊ	u	uː
cat	father	ten	bird	about	sit	see	many	got	saw	cup	put	actual	too
								(BrE)					

woman that sb is having a romantic relationship with **2** (*especially AmE*) a woman's female friend: *I had lunch with a girlfriend.*

Girl 'Guide *noun* (*old-fashioned*, *BrE*) = GUIDE

girl·hood /ˈgɜːlhʊd; *AmE* ˈgɜːrl-/ *noun* [U] (*old-fashioned*) the time when sb is a girl; the fact of being a girl

girl·ie /ˈgɜːli; *AmE* ˈgɜːrli/ *adj.* [only before noun] (*informal*) **1** containing photographs of naked or nearly naked women, that are intended to make men sexually excited: *girlie magazines* (*disapproving*) *suitable for or like girls, not boys: girlie games*

girl·ish /ˈgɜːlɪʃ; *AmE* ˈgɜːrlɪʃ/ *adj.* like a girl; of a girl: *a girlish giggle/figure/face*

Girl 'Scout *noun* (*AmE*) = GUIDE

giro /ˈdʒaɪrəʊ; *AmE* -roʊ/ *noun* (*pl.* **-os**) (*BrE*) **1** [U] (*finance*) a system in which money can be moved from one bank or post office account to another by a central computer: *to pay by giro* ◊ *a giro credit/payment/transfer* **2** (also **'giro cheque**) [C] a cheque that the government pays through the giro system to people who are unemployed or sick, or who have a very small income: *It is easy for families to run out of money before the weekly giro arrives.*

girth /gɜːθ; *AmE* gɜːrθ/ *noun* **1** [U, C] the measurement around sth, especially a person's waist: *a man of enormous girth* ◊ *a tree one metre in girth/with a girth of one metre* **2** [C] a leather or cloth strap that is fastened around the middle of a horse to keep the seat, (called a SADDLE), or a load in place

gismo = GIZMO

gist /dʒɪst/ *noun* (usually **the gist**) [sing.] **~ (of sth)** the main or general meaning of a piece of writing, a speech or a conversation: *to get* (= understand) *the gist of an argument* ◊ *I missed the beginning of the lecture—can you give me the gist of what he said?* ◊ *I'm afraid I don't quite follow your gist* (= what you really mean).

git /gɪt/ *noun* (*BrE*, *slang*) a stupid or unpleasant man

give /gɪv/ *verb*, *noun*

■ *verb* (**gave** /geɪv/ **given** /ˈgɪvn/)

HAND/PROVIDE | **1 ~ sth to sb | ~ sb sth** to hand sth to sb so that they can look at it, use it or keep it for a time: [VN, VNN] *Give the letter to your mother when you've read it.* ◊ *Give your mother the letter.* ◊ [VNN] *They were all given a box to carry.* ◊ [VN] *She gave her ticket to the woman at the check-in desk.* **2 ~ sth to sb | ~ sb sth** to hand sth to sb as a present; to allow sb to have sth as a present: [VNN] *What are you giving your father for his birthday?* ◊ *She was given a huge bunch of flowers.* ◊ *Did you give the waiter a tip?* ◊ [VN] *We don't usually give presents to people at work.* ◊ [V] *They say it's better to give than to receive.* **3 ~ sth to sb | ~ sb sth** to provide sb with sth: [VNN] *They were all thirsty so I gave them a drink.* ◊ *Give me your name and address.* ◊ *We've been given a 2% pay increase.* ◊ *I was hoping you would give me a job.* ◊ *He was given a new heart in a five-hour operation.* ◊ *She wants a job that gives her more responsibility.* ◊ *Can I give you a ride to the station?* ◊ *They couldn't give me any more information.* ◊ *I'll give you* (= allow you to have) *ten minutes to prepare your answer.* ◊ *Don't give me any of that backchat* (= don't be rude). ◊ [VN] *He gives Italian lessons to his colleagues.* ◊ *The reforms should give a better chance to the less able children.*

MONEY | **4 ~ (sth) to sth** to pay money to a charity, etc., to help people: [V] *We need your help—please give generously.* ◊ *They both gave regularly to charity.* ◊ [VN] *I gave a small donation.* **5 ~ (sb) sth for sth** to pay in order to have or do sth: [VNN] *How much will you give me for the car?* ◊ *I'd give anything to see him again.* ◊ [VN] *I gave £50 for the lot.*

TREAT AS IMPORTANT | **6 ~ sth to sb/sth** to use time, energy, etc. for sb/sth: [VNN, VN] *I gave the matter a lot of thought.* ◊ *I gave a lot of thought to the matter.* ◊ [VN] *The government has given top priority to reforming the tax system.*

PUNISHMENT | **7 ~ sth to sb | ~ sb sth** to make sb suffer a particular punishment: [VNN] *The judge gave him a nine-month suspended sentence.* ◊ [VN] *We discussed what punishment should be given to the boys.*

ILLNESS | **8 ~ sth to sb | ~ sb sth** to infect sb with an illness: [VNN] *You've given me your cold.* ◊ [VN] *She'd given the bug to all her colleagues.*

PARTY/EVENT | **9** [VN] if you **give** a party, you organize it and invite people **10** [VN] to perform sth in public: *She gave a reading from her latest volume of poetry.* ◊ *The President will be giving a press conference this afternoon.*

DO/PRODUCE STH | **11** used with a noun to describe a particular action, giving the same meaning as the related verb: [VN] *She gave a shrug of her shoulders* (= she shrugged). ◊ *He turned to us and gave a big smile* (= smiled broadly). ◊ *She looked up from her work and gave a yawn* (= yawned). ◊ *He gave a loud cry* (= cried out loudly) *and fell to the floor.* ◊ *to give a groan/laugh/sigh* ◊ *Her work has given pleasure to* (= pleased) *millions of readers.* ◊ [VNN] *He gave her a kiss* (= kissed her). ◊ *I have to admit that the news gave us a shock* (= shocked us). ◊ *We'll give you all the help we can* (= help you in every way we can). **HELP** For other similar expressions, look up the nouns in each. For example, you will find **give your approval** at **approval**. **12** [VNN] to produce a particular feeling in sb: *All that driving has given me a headache.* ◊ *Go for a walk. It'll give you an appetite.*

TELEPHONE CALL | **13** [VNN] to make a telephone call to sb: *Give me a call tomorrow.* ◊ (*BrE*) *I'll give you a ring.*

MARK/GRADE | **14** to judge sb/sth to be of a particular standard: [VNN] *She had given the assignment an A.* ◊ *I give it ten out of ten for originality.* [also VN]

PREDICT HOW LONG | **15** [VNN] to predict that sth will last a particular length of time: *That marriage won't last. I'll give them two years, at the outside.*

IN SPORT | **16** [VN-ADJ] to say that a player or the ball is in a particular position: *The umpire gave the ball out.*

BEND | **17** [V] to bend or stretch under pressure: *The branch began to give under his weight.* ◊ (*figurative*) *We can't go on like this—something's got to give.*

IDM Most idioms containing **give** are at the entries for the nouns and adjectives in the idioms, for example, **give rise to sth** is at **rise** *n*. **don't give me 'that** (*spoken*, *informal*) used to tell sb that you do not accept what they say: *'I didn't have time to do it.' 'Oh, don't give me that!'* **give and 'take** to be willing, in a relationship, to accept what sb else wants and to give up some of what you want: *You're going to have to learn to give and take.* **give as good as you 'get** to react with equal force when sb attacks or criticizes you: *She can give as good as she gets.* **give me sth/sb (any day/time)** (*spoken*) used to say that you prefer a particular thing or person to the one that has just been mentioned: *We don't go out much. Give me a quiet night in front of the TV any day!* **give or 'take (sth)** if sth is correct **give or take** a particular amount, it is approximately correct: *It'll take about three weeks, give or take a day or so.* **give sb to believe/understand (that) …** [often passive] (*formal*) to make sb believe/understand sth: *I was given to understand that she had resigned.* **I give you …** (*spoken*, *formal*) used to ask people to drink a TOAST to sb: *Ladies and gentlemen, I give you Geoff Ogilby!* **I/I'll give you 'that** (*spoken*) used when you are admitting that sth is true **what 'gives?** (*spoken*, *informal*) what is happening?; what is the news?

PHRV **give sb a'way** (in a marriage ceremony) to lead the BRIDE to the BRIDEGROOM and formally allow her to marry him: *The bride was given away by her father.* **give sth↔a'way 1** to give sth as a gift: *He gave away most of his money to charity.* ◊ (*informal*) *Check out the prices of our pizzas—we're virtually giving them away!*—related noun GIVEAWAY **2** to present sth: *The mayor gave away the prizes at the school sports day.* **3** to carelessly allow sb to have an advantage: *They've given away two goals already.* **give sb/sb↔a'way** to make known sth that sb wants to keep secret **SYN** BETRAY: *She gave away state secrets to the enemy.* ◊ *It was supposed to be a surprise but the children gave the game away.* ◊ *His voice gave him away* (= showed who he really was).—related noun GIVE-AWAY

give sb 'back sth | give sth↔'back (to sb) 1 to return sth to its owner: *Could you give me back my pen?* ◊ *Could you give me my pen back?* ◊ *I picked it up and gave it back* to him. ◊ (*spoken, informal*) Give it me back! **2** to allow sb to have sth again: *The operation gave him back the use of his legs.*

,give 'in (to sb/sth) 1 to admit that you have been defeated by sb/sth: *The rebels were forced to give in.* **2** to agree to do sth that you do not want to do: *The authorities have shown no signs of giving in to the kidnappers' demands.* **,give sth 'in (to sb)** to hand over sth to sb in authority: *Please give your work in before Monday.*

,give 'off sth to produce sth such as a smell, heat, light, etc: *The flowers gave off a fragrant perfume.*

'give on to/onto sth [no passive] (*BrE*) to have a view of sth; to lead directly to sth: *The bedroom windows give on to the street.* ◊ *This door gives onto the hall.*

,give 'out 1 to come to an end; to be completely used up: *After a month their food supplies gave out.* ◊ *Her patience finally gave out.* **2** to stop working: *One of the plane's engines gave out in mid-Atlantic.* ◊ *Her legs gave out and she collapsed.* **,give sth↔'out** to give sth to a lot of people: *The teacher gave out the exam papers.* **,give 'out sth 1** to produce sth such as heat, light, etc: *The radiator gives out a lot of heat.* **2** [often passive] (*especially BrE*) to tell people about sth or broadcast sth

,give 'over (*BrE, spoken, informal*) used to tell sb to stop doing sth: *Give over, Chris! You're hurting me.* ◊[+-ing] *Give over complaining!* **,give yourself 'over to sth** (also **,give yourself 'up to sth**) to spend all your time doing sth or thinking about sth; to allow sth to completely control your life **,give sth↔'over to sth** [usually passive] to use sth for one particular purpose: *The gallery is given over to British art.*

,give 'up to stop trying to do sth: *They gave up without a fight.* ◊ *She doesn't give up easily.* ◊ *I give up—tell me the answer.* **,give sb 'up 1** (also **,give 'up on sb** especially in *AmE*) to believe that sb is never going to arrive, get better, be found, etc: *There you are at last! We'd given you up.* ◊ *We hadn't heard from him for so long, we'd given him up for dead.* **2** to stop having a relationship with sb: *Why don't you give him up?* **,give sth↔'up 1** [no passive] to stop doing or having sth: *She didn't give up work when she had the baby.* ◊ *We'd given up hope of ever having children.* ◊[+-ing] *You ought to give up smoking.* **2** to spend time on a task that you would normally spend on sth else: *I gave up my weekend to help him paint his apartment.* **,give sth↔'up (to sb)** to hand sth over to sb else: *We had to give our passports up to the authorities.* ◊ *He gave up his seat to a pregnant woman* (= stood up to allow her to sit down). **,give yourself/sb 'up (to sb)** to offer yourself/sb to be captured: *After a week on the run he gave himself up to the police.* **,give yourself 'up to sth** = GIVE YOURSELF OVER TO STH **,give 'up on sb 1** to stop hoping or believing that sb will change, get better, etc: *His teachers seem to have given up on him.* **2** (*especially AmE*) = GIVE SB UP

■ *noun* [U] the ability of sth to bend or stretch under pressure: *The shoes may seem tight at first, but the leather has plenty of give in it.*

IDM **,give and 'take 1** willingness in a relationship to accept what sb else wants and give up some of what you want **2** an exchange of words or ideas: *to encourage a lively give and take*

give·away /'gɪvəweɪ/ *noun, adj.*
■ *noun* (*informal*) **1** something that a company gives free, usually with sth else that is for sale **2** something that makes you guess the real truth about sth/sb: *She pretended she wasn't excited but the expression on her face was a **dead giveaway**.*
■ *adj.* [only before noun] (*informal*) (of prices) very low

given /'gɪvn/ *adj., prep., noun*
■ *adj.* [usually before noun] **1** already arranged: *They were to meet at a given time and place.* **2** that you have stated and are discussing; particular: *We can find out how much money is spent on food in any given period.* **IDM** **be given to sth/to doing sth** (*formal*) to do sth often or regularly: *She's much given to outbursts of temper.* ◊ *He's given to going for long walks on his own.*
■ *prep.* when you consider sth: *Given his age,* (= considering how old he is) *he's remarkably active.* ◊ *Given her*

interest in children, teaching seems the right job for her.
▶ **given that** *conj.*: *It was surprising the government was re-elected, given that they had raised taxes so much.*
■ *noun* something that is accepted as true, for example when you are discussing sth, or planning sth

'given name *noun* (*especially AmE*) = FIRST NAME

giver /'gɪvə(r)/ *noun* (often in compounds) a person or an organization that gives: *They are very generous givers to charity.*

gizmo (also **gismo**) /'gɪzməʊ; *AmE* -moʊ/ *noun* (*informal*) (*pl.* **-os**) a general word for a small piece of equipment, often one that does sth in a new and clever way

giz·zard /'gɪzəd; *AmE* -zərd/ *noun* the part of a bird's stomach in which food is broken up into smaller pieces before being DIGESTED

glacé /'glæseɪ; *AmE* glæ'seɪ/ *adj.* [only before noun] (of fruit) preserved in sugar: *glacé fruits* ◊ *glacé cherries* —picture on page A1

gla·cial /'gleɪʃl; 'gleɪsiəl/ *adj.* **1** [usually before noun] (*geology*) connected with the Ice Age: *the glacial period* (= the time when much of the northern half of the world was covered by ice) **2** (*technical*) caused or made by glaciers; connected with glaciers: *a glacial landscape* ◊ *glacial deposits/erosion* ◊ *glacial processes* **3** (*written*) very cold; like ice: *glacial winds/temperatures* ◊ *the glacial waters of the Arctic* **4** (*written*) (used about people) cold and unfriendly; not showing feelings: *Her expression was glacial.* ◊ *Relations between the two countries had always been glacial.*

gla·cier /'glæsiə(r); *AmE* 'gleɪʃər/ *noun* a large mass of ice, formed by snow on mountains, that moves very slowly down a valley—picture at MOUNTAIN

glad /glæd/ *adj.* **1** [not before noun] ~ (about sth)| ~ (to do sth)| ~ (to know, hear, see …)| ~ (that …) pleased; happy: *'I passed the test!' 'I'm so glad (for you).'* ◊ *'He doesn't need the pills any more.' 'I'm glad about that.'* ◊ *I'm glad to hear you're feeling better.* ◊ *I'm glad (that) you're feeling better.* ◊ *I'm glad to meet you. I've heard a lot about you.* ◊ *He was glad he'd come.* ◊ *I've never been so glad to see anyone in my life!* ◊ *I'm so glad (that) you're safe!* ◊ *She was glad when the meeting was over.* **2** ~ **of sth| ~ if …** grateful for sth: *She was very glad of her warm coat in the biting wind.* ◊ *I'd be glad of your help.* ◊ *I'd be glad if you could help me.* **3** ~ **to do sth** very willing to do sth: *I'd be glad to lend you the money.* ◊ *If you'd like me to help you, I'd **be only too glad** to.* **4** [only before noun] (*old-fashioned*) bringing joy; full of joy: *glad news/tidings* ◊ *They greeted each other with glad cries.* **IDM** **I'm glad to say (that …)** (*spoken*) used when you are commenting on a situation and saying that you are happy about it: *Most teachers, I'm glad to say, take their jobs very seriously.*

glad·den /'glædn/ *verb* (*old-fashioned*) to make sb feel pleased or happy: [VN] *The sight of the flowers **gladdened her heart**.* ◊ [VN to inf] *It **gladdened** him to see them all enjoying themselves.*

glade /gleɪd/ *noun* (*literary*) a small open area of grass in a wood or a forest

gladi·ator /'glædieɪtə(r)/ *noun* (in ancient Rome) a man trained to fight other men or animals in order to entertain the public ▶ **gladia·tor·ial** /ˌglædiə'tɔːriəl/ *adj.*: *gladiatorial combat*

gladi·olus /ˌglædi'əʊləs; *AmE* -'oʊləs/ *noun* (*pl.* **gladi·oli** /-laɪ/) a tall garden plant with long thin leaves and brightly coloured flowers growing up the stem

glad·ly /'glædli/ *adv.* **1** willingly: *I would gladly pay extra for a good seat.* **2** happily; with thanks: *When I offered her my seat, she accepted it gladly.* **IDM** see SUFFER

glad·ness /'glædnəs/ *noun* [U] (*literary*) joy; happiness

'glad rags *noun* [pl.] (*old-fashioned, informal*) a person's best clothes, worn on a special occasion

glam·or·ize (*BrE* also **-ise**) /'glæməraɪz/ *verb* [VN] (usually *disapproving*) to make sth bad appear attractive or exciting: *Television tends to glamorize violence.*

glam·or·ous /'glæmərəs/ (also *informal* **glam**) *adj.* especially attractive and exciting, and different from ordinary things or people: *glamorous movie stars* ◊ *a glamorous*

G

job [OPP] UNGLAMOROUS ▶ **glam·or·ous·ly** *adv.*: *glamorously dressed*

glam·our (*BrE*) (*AmE* **glamor**) /ˈɡlæmə(r)/ *noun* [U]
1 the attractive and exciting quality that makes a person, a job or a place seem special, often because of wealth or status: *hopeful young actors and actresses dazzled by the glamour of Hollywood* ◊ *Now that she's a stewardess, foreign travel has lost its glamour for her.* **2** physical beauty that also suggests wealth or success: *Add a cashmere scarf under your jacket for a touch of glamour.*

glance /ɡlɑːns; *AmE* ɡlæns/ *verb, noun*
■ *verb* [V+adv./prep.] **1** to look quickly at sth/sb: *She glanced in at her watch.* ◊ *He glanced around the room.* ◊ *I glanced up quickly to see who had come in.* **2** ~ **at/down/over/through sth** to read sth quickly and not thoroughly: *I only had time to glance at the newspapers.* ◊ *He glanced briefly down the list of names.* ◊ *She glanced through the report.* [PHRV] **glance on/off sth** (of light) to flash on a surface or be reflected off it **glance 'off (sth)** to hit sth at an angle and move off it in a different direction: *The ball glanced off the post into the net.*
■ *noun* ~ **(at sb/sth)** a quick look: *to take/have a glance at the newspaper headlines* ◊ *a cursory/brief/casual/furtive glance* ◊ *The sisters **exchanged glances** (= looked at each other).* ◊ *She shot him a **sideways glance**.* ◊ *He walked away **without a backward glance**.* ◊ *She **stole a glance** (= looked secretly) at her watch.* [IDM] **at a (single) 'glance** immediately; with only a quick look: *He could tell at a glance what was wrong.* **at first 'glance** when you first look at or think about sth, often rather quickly: *At first glance the problem seemed easy.*

glan·cing /ˈɡlɑːnsɪŋ; *AmE* ˈɡlænsɪŋ/ *adj.* [only before noun] hitting sth/sb at an angle, not with full force: *to strike sb/sth a **glancing blow***

gland /ɡlænd/ *noun* an organ in a person's or an animal's body that produces a chemical substance for the body to use. There are many different glands in the body: *a snake's poison glands* ◊ *Her glands are swollen.*—see also PITUITARY ▶ **glan·du·lar** /ˈɡlændjələ(r); *AmE* -dʒə-/ *adj.* [usually before noun]: *glandular tissue*

glandular 'fever (*BrE*) (*AmE* or *medical* **mono·nucle·osis**) (also *AmE informal* **mono**) *noun* [U] an infectious disease that causes swelling of the LYMPH GLANDS and makes the person feel very weak for a long time

glare /ɡleə(r); *AmE* ɡler/ *verb, noun*

■ *verb* [V] **1** ~ **(at sb/sth)** to look at sb/sth in an angry way: *He didn't shout, he just glared at me silently.* ◊ *I looked at her and she glared furiously back.* **2** to shine with a very bright unpleasant light
■ *noun* **1** [U, sing.] a very bright, unpleasant light: *the glare of the sun* ◊ *The rabbit was caught in the glare of the car's headlights.* ◊ *These sunglasses are designed to reduce glare.* ◊ *(figurative) The divorce was conducted **in the full glare of publicity** (= with continuous attention from newspapers and television).* **2** [C] a long, angry look: *to give sb a hostile glare*

glar·ing /ˈɡleərɪŋ; *AmE* ˈɡler-/ *adj.* **1** [usually before noun] (of sth bad) very easily seen [SYN] BLATANT: *a glaring omission/inconsistency/injustice* ◊ *the most glaring example of this problem* **2** (of a light) very bright and unpleasant: *a glaring white light* **3** angry; fierce: *glaring eyes* ▶ **glar·ing·ly** *adv.*: *glaringly obvious*

glass /ɡlɑːs; *AmE* ɡlæs/ *noun, verb*
■ *noun*

TRANSPARENT SUBSTANCE | **1** [U] a hard, usually transparent, substance used, for example, for making windows and bottles: *a sheet/pane of glass* ◊ *frosted/toughened glass* ◊ *a glass bottle/dish/roof* ◊ *I cut myself on a piece of broken glass.* ◊ *The vegetables are grown **under glass** (= in a glasshouse).*—see also CUT GLASS, PLATE GLASS, STAINED GLASS, GLAZIER

FOR DRINKING | **2** [C] (often in compounds) a container made of glass, used for drinking out of: *a sherry glass* ◊ *a wine glass* **3** [C] the contents of a glass: *a glass of sherry/wine/water* ◊ *He drank three whole glasses.*

GLASS OBJECTS | **4** [U] objects made of glass: *We keep all our glass and china in this cupboard.* ◊ *She has a fine collection of Bohemian glass.*

ON WATCH/PICTURE | **5** [sing.] a protecting cover made of glass on a watch, picture or photograph frame, FIRE ALARM, etc: *In case of emergency, break the glass and press the button.*

FOR EYES | **6** (**glasses**) (*AmE also* **eye·glasses**) (also *old-fashioned* or *formal* **spec·tacles**, *informal* **specs** especially in *BrE*) [pl.] two LENSES in a frame that rests on the nose and ears. People wear glasses in order to be able to see better or to protect their eyes from bright sunlight: *a pair of glasses* ◊ *dark glasses* ◊ *I wear glasses for driving.*—see also FIELD GLASSES, MAGNIFYING GLASS, SUNGLASSES

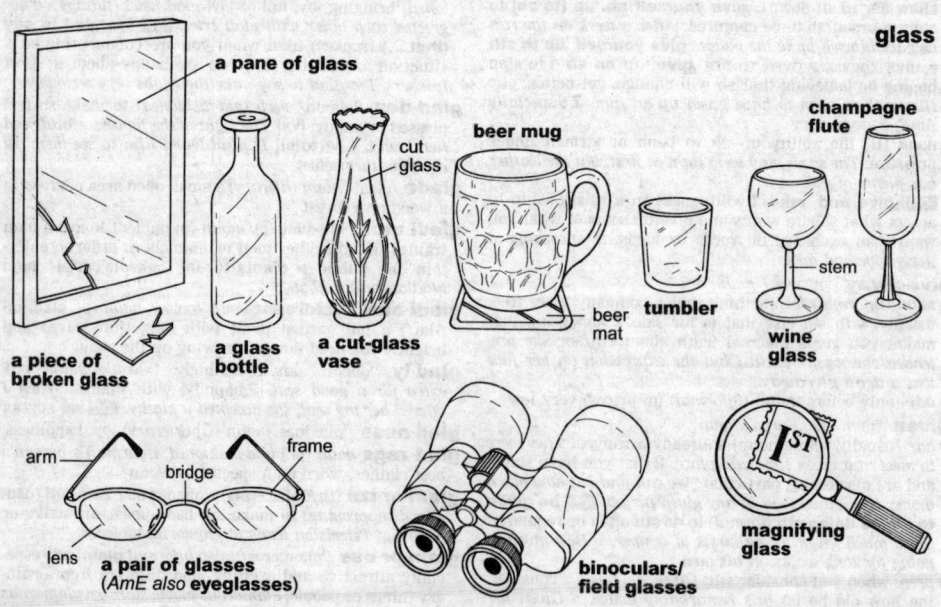

glass

a pane of glass

cut glass

beer mug

champagne flute

a piece of broken glass

a glass bottle

a cut-glass vase

beer mat

tumbler

stem

wine glass

arm

frame

bridge

lens

a pair of glasses
(*AmE also* **eyeglasses**)

binoculars/
field glasses

magnifying glass

	s	t	v	z	ʃ	ʒ	tʃ	dʒ	θ	ð	ŋ
	see	tea	van	zoo	shoe	vision	chain	jam	thin	this	sing

G

MIRROR | **7** [C, usually sing.] (*old-fashioned*) a mirror—see also LOOKING GLASS

BAROMETER | **8** (**the glass**) [sing.] a BAROMETER

IDM see PEOPLE *n.*, RAISE *v.*

■ *verb* [VN] (*BrE, informal*) to hit sb in the face with a glass **PHR V** ,**glass sth 'in/'over** [usually passive] to cover sth with a roof or wall made of glass: *a glassed-in pool*—compare GLAZE

,**glass 'ceiling** *noun* [usually sing.] the imaginary barrier that stops women, or other groups, from getting the best jobs in a company, etc. although there are no official rules to prevent them from getting these jobs

,**glass 'fibre** (*BrE*) (*AmE* ,**glass 'fiber**) *noun* [U] = FIBRE-GLASS

glass·ful /'glɑːsfʊl; *AmE* 'glæs-/ *noun* the amount that a drinking glass will hold

glass·house /'glɑːshaʊs; *AmE* 'glæs-/ *noun* (*BrE*) **1** a building with glass sides and a glass roof, for growing plants in; a type of large GREENHOUSE **2** (*slang*) a military prison

glass·ware /'glɑːsweə(r); *AmE* 'glæswer/ *noun* [U] objects made of glass, especially drinking glasses, dishes, and containers for water or flowers

glassy /'glɑːsi; *AmE* 'glæsi/ *adj.* **1** like glass; smooth and shiny: *a glassy lake ◇ a glassy material* **2** showing no feeling or emotion: *glassy eyes ◇ a glassy look/stare ◇ He looked flushed and glassy-eyed.*

Glas·we·gian /glæz'wiːdʒən/ *noun* a person from Glasgow in Scotland ▶ **Glas·we·gian** *adj.*

glau·coma /glɔː'kəʊmə; *AmE* glaʊ'koʊmə; glɔː-/ *noun* [U] an eye disease that causes gradual loss of sight

glaze /gleɪz/ *verb, noun*
■ *verb* **1** [V] ~ (**over**) if a person's eyes **glaze** or **glaze over**, the person begins to look bored or tired: *A lot of people's eyes glaze over if you say you are a feminist. ◇ 'I'm feeling rather tired,' he said, his eyes glazing.* **2** [VN] to fit sheets of glass into sth: *to glaze a window/house ◇ a glazed door*—see also DOUBLE GLAZING—compare GLASS **3** [VN] ~ **sth** (**with sth**) to cover sth with a glaze to give it a shiny surface: *Glaze the pie with beaten egg. ◇ glazed pottery/tiles ◇* (*AmE*) *a glazed doughnut*
■ *noun* [C, U] **1** a thin clear liquid put on clay objects such as cups and plates before they are finished, to give them a hard shiny surface **2** a thin liquid, made of egg, milk or sugar, for example, that is put on cake, bread, etc. to make it look shiny

glazed /gleɪzd/ *adj.* (especially of the eyes) showing no feeling or emotion; dull: *eyes glazed with boredom*

glaz·ier /'gleɪziə(r); *AmE* -ʒər/ *noun* a person whose job is to fit glass into the frames of windows, etc.

gleam /gliːm/ *verb, noun*
■ *verb* **1** [V] to shine with a pale clear light: *The moonlight gleamed on the water. ◇ Her eyes gleamed in the dark.* **2** ~ (**with sth**) to look very clean or bright: [V] *The house was gleaming with fresh white paint. ◇* [V-ADJ] *Her teeth gleamed white against the tanned skin of her face.* **3** [V] ~ (**with/in sth**) if a person's eyes **gleam** with a particular emotion, or an emotion **gleams** in a person's eyes, the person shows that emotion: *His eyes gleamed with amusement. ◇ Amusement gleamed in his eyes.*
■ *noun* [usually sing.] **1** a pale clear light, often reflected from sth: *the gleam of moonlight on the water ◇ a gleam of light from a lamp ◇ A few gleams of sunshine lit up the gloomy afternoon. ◇ I saw the gleam of the knife as it flashed through the air.* **2** a small amount of sth: *a faint gleam of hope ◇ a serious book with an occasional gleam of humour* **3** an expression of a particular feeling or emotion that shows in sb's eyes: *a gleam of triumph in her eyes ◇ a mischievous gleam in his eye ◇ The gleam in his eye made her uncomfortable* (= as if he was planning sth secret or unpleasant).

glean /gliːn/ *verb* [VN] ~ **sth** (**from sb/sth**) to obtain information, knowledge etc., sometimes with difficulty and often from various different places: *These figures have been gleaned from a number of studies.*

glee /gliː/ *noun* [U] a feeling of happiness, usually because sth good has happened to you, or sth bad has

happened to sb else: *He rubbed his hands in glee as he thought of all the money he would make. ◇ She couldn't disguise her glee at their embarrassment.*

glee·ful /'gliːfl/ *adj.* happy because of sth good you have done or sth bad that has happened to sb else: *a gleeful laugh* ▶ **glee·ful·ly** /-fəli/ *adv.*

glen /glen/ *noun* a deep narrow valley, especially in Scotland or Ireland

glib /glɪb/ *adj.* (*disapproving*) (of speakers and speech) using words that are clever, but are not sincere, and do not show much thought: *a glib talker/salesman ◇ glib answers/explanations* ▶ **glib·ly** *adv.*

glide /glaɪd/ *verb, noun*
■ *verb* [V] [usually +*adv./prep.*] **1** to move smoothly and quietly, especially as though it takes no effort: *Swans went gliding past. ◇ The skaters were gliding over the ice.* **2** (of birds or aircraft) to fly using air currents, without the birds moving their wings or the aircraft using the engine: *An eagle was gliding high overhead. ◇ The plane managed to glide down to the runway.*
■ *noun* **1** [sing.] a continuous smooth movement: *the graceful glide of a skater* **2** [C] (*phonetics*) a speech sound made while moving the tongue from one position to another

glider /'glaɪdə(r)/ *noun* a light aircraft that flies without an engine

glid·ing /'glaɪdɪŋ/ *noun* [U] the sport of flying in a glider

glim·mer /'glɪmə(r)/ *noun, verb*
■ *noun* **1** a faint unsteady light: *We could see a glimmer of light on the far shore.* **2** (also **glim·mer·ing**) a small sign of sth: *a glimmer of hope/amusement/recognition ◇ I caught the glimmer of a smile in his eyes. ◇ the glimmering of an idea*
■ *verb* [V] to shine with a faint unsteady light: *The candles glimmered in the corner. ◇* (*figurative*) *Amusement glimmered in his eyes.*

glimpse /glɪmps/ *noun, verb*
■ *noun* [usually sing.] **1** ~ (**at sb/sth**) | ~ (**of sb/sth**) a look at sb/sth for a very short time, when you do not see the person or thing completely: *He caught a glimpse of her in the crowd. ◇ I came up on deck to get my first glimpse of the island.* **2** ~ (**into sth**) | ~ (**of sth**) a short experience of sth that helps you to understand it: *a fascinating glimpse into life in the ocean ◇ The programme gives us a rare glimpse of a great artist at work.*
■ *verb* [VN] **1** to see sb/sth for a moment, but not very clearly: *He'd glimpsed her through the window as he passed.* **2** to start to understand sth: *Suddenly she glimpsed the truth about her sister.*

glint /glɪnt/ *verb, noun*
■ *verb* [V] **1** to produce small bright flashes of light: *The sea glinted in the moonlight. ◇ The sun glinted on the windows.* **2** if a person's eyes **glint** with a particular emotion, or an emotion **glints** in a person's eyes, the person shows that emotion, which is usually a strong one: *Her eyes glinted angrily. ◇ Hostility glinted in his eyes.*
■ *noun* **1** a sudden flash of light or colour shining from a bright surface: *the glint of the sun on the water ◇ golden glints in her red hair ◇ She saw a glint of silver in the grass.* **2** an expression in sb's eyes showing a particular emotion, often a negative one: *He had a wicked glint in his eye. ◇ a glint of anger/mockery*

glis·ten /'glɪsn/ *verb* (of sth wet) to shine: [V] *Her eyes were glistening with tears. ◇ Sweat glistened on his forehead. ◇* [V-ADJ] *The road glistened wet after the rain.*

glitch /glɪtʃ/ *noun* (*informal*) a small problem or fault that stops sth working successfully

glit·ter /'glɪtə(r)/ *verb, noun*
■ *verb* [V] **1** to shine brightly with little flashes of light, like a diamond **SYN** SPARKLE: *The ceiling of the cathedral glittered with gold. ◇ The water glittered in the sunlight.* **2** ~ (**with sth**) (*written*) (of the eyes) to shine brightly with a particular emotion, usually a strong one: *His eyes glittered with greed.*
■ *noun* **1** [U] bright light consisting of many little flashes: *the glitter of diamonds* **2** [sing.] a bright expression in sb's eyes showing a particular emotion **SYN** GLINT: *There was a triumphant glitter in his eyes.* **3** [U] the attractive,

G

æ	ɑː	e	ɜː	ə	ɪ	iː	i	ɒ	ɔː	ʌ	ʊ	u	uː
cat	father	ten	bird	about	sit	see	many	got	saw	cup	put	actual	too
								(BrE)					

exciting qualities that sb/sth, especially a rich and famous person or place, seems to have $\overline{\text{SYN}}$ GLAMOUR: *the superficial glitter of show business* **4** [U] very small shiny pieces of thin metal or paper that are stuck to things as a decoration: *gold/silver glitter*

glit·ter·ati /ˌglɪtəˈrɑːti/ *noun* [pl.] (used in newspapers) fashionable, rich and famous people

glit·ter·ing /ˈglɪtərɪŋ/ *adj.* [usually before noun] **1** very impressive and successful: *He has a glittering career ahead of him.* **2** very impressive and involving rich and successful people: *a glittering occasion/ceremony* ◊ *a glittering array of stars* **3** shining brightly with many small flashes of light: *glittering jewels*

glit·tery /ˈglɪtəri/ *adj.* shining brightly with many little flashes of light: *a glittery suit*

glitz /glɪts/ *noun* [U] (sometimes *disapproving*) the quality of appearing very attractive, exciting and impressive, in a way that is not always genuine: *the glitz and glamour of the music scene* ▶ **glitzy** *adj.*: *a glitzy, Hollywood-style occasion*

gloam·ing /ˈgləʊmɪŋ; *AmE* ˈgloʊ-/ *noun* (**the gloaming**) [sing.] (*ScotE* or *literary*) the faint light after the sun sets $\overline{\text{SYN}}$ TWILIGHT, DUSK

gloat /gləʊt; *AmE* gloʊt/ *verb* [V] ~ (**about/at/over sth**) to show that you are happy about your own success or sb else's failure, in an unpleasant way: *She was still gloating over her rival's disappointment.* ▶ **gloat·ing** *adj.*: *a gloating look/remark*

glob /glɒb; *AmE* glɑːb/ *noun* (*informal*) a small amount of a liquid or substance in a round shape: *thick globs of paint on the floor*

global /ˈgləʊbl; *AmE* ˈgloʊbl/ *adj.* [usually before noun] **1** covering or affecting the whole world: *global issues* ◊ *The commission is calling for a global ban on whaling.* ◊ *the company's domestic and global markets* **2** considering or including all parts of sth: *We need to take a more global approach to the problem.* ◊ *global searches on the database* ◊ *They sent a global e-mail to all staff.* ▶ **glob·al·ly** /-bəli/ *adv.*: *We need to start thinking globally.*

glob·al·ize (*BrE* also **-ise**) /ˈgləʊbəlaɪz; *AmE* ˈgloʊ-/ *verb* [V, VN] (*economics*) if sth, for example a business company, **globalizes** or is **globalized**, it operates all around the world ▶ **glob·al·iza·tion, -isa·tion** /ˌgləʊbəlaɪˈzeɪʃn; *AmE* ˌgloʊbələˈz-/ *noun* [U]: *the globalization of world trade*

ˌglobal ˈvillage *noun* [sing.] the whole world, looked at as a single community that is connected by electronic communication systems

ˌglobal ˈwarming *noun* [U] the increase in temperature of the earth's atmosphere, that is caused by the increase of particular gases, especially CARBON DIOXIDE—see also GREENHOUSE EFFECT

globe /gləʊb; *AmE* gloʊb/ *noun* **1** [C] an object shaped like a ball with a map of the world on its surface, usually on a STAND so that it can be turned **2** (**the globe**) [sing.] the world (used especially to emphasize its size): *tourists from every corner of the globe* **3** [C] a thing shaped like a ball

ˌglobe ˈartichoke *noun* = ARTICHOKE (1)

globe·trot·ting /ˈgləʊbtrɒtɪŋ; *AmE* ˈgloʊbtrɑːtɪŋ/ *adj.* (*informal*) travelling in many countries all over the world: *a globetrotting journalist* ▶ **globe·trot·ter** *noun* **globe·trot·ting** *noun* [U]

globu·lar /ˈglɒbjələ(r); *AmE* ˈglɑːb-/ *adj.* shaped like a ball, GLOBE or globule; consisting of globules

glob·ule /ˈglɒbjuːl; *AmE* ˈglɑːb-/ *noun* a very small drop or ball of a liquid or of a solid that has been melted: *a globule of fat*

glock·en·spiel /ˈglɒkənʃpiːl; *AmE* ˈglɑːk-/ *noun* a musical instrument made up of a row of metal bars of different lengths, that you hit with two small hammers—compare XYLOPHONE

gloom /gluːm/ *noun* **1** [U, sing.] a feeling of being sad and without hope: *The gloom deepened as the election results came in.* **2** [U] (*literary*) almost total darkness: *We watched the boats come back in the gathering gloom.* $\overline{\text{IDM}}$ see DOOM *n.*, PILE *v.*

gloomy /ˈgluːmi/ *adj.* (**gloom·ier**, **gloomi·est**) **1** nearly dark, or badly lit in a way that makes you feel sad: *a gloomy room/atmosphere* ◊ *It was a wet and gloomy day.* **2** sad and without hope: *a gloomy expression* ◊ *We sat in gloomy silence.* **3** without much hope of success or happiness in the future: *a gloomy picture of the country's economic future* ◊ *Suddenly, the future didn't look so gloomy after all.* ▶ **gloom·ily** /-ɪli/ *adv.*: *He stared gloomily at the phone.*

glop /glɒp; *AmE* glɑːp/ *noun* [U] (*informal, especially AmE*) a thick wet substance that looks, tastes or feels unpleasant

glori·fied /ˈglɔːrɪfaɪd/ *adj.* [only before noun] making sb/sth seem more important or better than they are: *The restaurant was no more than a glorified fast-food cafe.*

glor·ify /ˈglɔːrɪfaɪ/ *verb* (**glori·fies**, **glori·fy·ing**, **glori·fied**, **glori·fied**) [VN] **1** (often *disapproving*) to make sth seem better or more important than it really is: *He denies that the movie glorifies violence.* **2** (*formal*) to praise and worship God ▶ **glori·fi·ca·tion** /ˌglɔːrɪfɪˈkeɪʃn/ *noun* [U]: *the glorification of war*

glori·ous /ˈglɔːriəs/ *adj.* **1** (*formal*) deserving or bringing great fame and success: *a glorious deed/victory* ◊ *a glorious chapter in our country's history*—compare INGLORIOUS **2** (*formal*) very beautiful and impressive: *a glorious sunset/view* **3** extremely enjoyable: *a glorious trip to Rome* **4** (of weather) hot, with the sun shining: *They had three weeks of glorious sunshine.* ▶ **glori·ous·ly** *adv.*

glory /ˈglɔːri/ *noun, verb*

■ *noun* **1** [U] fame, praise or honour that is given to sb because they have achieved sth important: *Olympic glory in the 100 metres* ◊ *I do all the work and he gets all the glory.* ◊ *She wanted to enjoy her moment of glory.* ◊ *He came home a rich man, **covered in glory**.* **2** [U] praise and worship of God: *'Glory to God in the highest'* **3** [U] great beauty: *The city was spread out beneath us **in all its glory**.* ◊ *The house has now been restored to its **former glory**.* **4** [C] a special cause for pride, respect or pleasure: *The temple is one of the glories of ancient Greece.* ◊ *Her long black hair is her **crowning glory** (= most impressive feature).*—see also REFLECTED GLORY

■ *verb* (**glor·ies**, **glory·ing**, **glor·ied**, **glor·ied**) $\overline{\text{PHRV}}$ **ˈglory in sth** (*written*) to get great pleasure or enjoyment from sth $\overline{\text{SYN}}$ REVEL: *She gloried in her new-found independence.*

ˈglory days *noun* [pl.] a time in the past which people look back on as being better than the present

gloss /glɒs; *AmE* glɔːs; glɑːs/ *noun, verb*

■ *noun* **1** [U, sing.] a shine on a smooth surface: *paper with a high gloss on one side* ◊ *The gel gives your hair a gloss.* ◊ *You can have the photos with either a gloss or a matt finish.* **2** [U] (often in compounds) a substance designed to make sth shiny: *lip gloss* **3** (also **ˌgloss ˈpaint**) [U] paint which, when dry, has a hard shiny surface: *two coats of gloss* **4** [U, sing.] an attractive appearance that is only on the surface and hides what is not so attractive: *Beneath the gloss of success was a tragic private life.* ◊ *This scandal has taken the gloss off the occasion.* **5** [C] ~ (**on sth**) a way of explaining sth to make it seem more attractive or acceptable: *The director puts a Hollywood gloss on the civil war.* **6** [C] ~ (**on sth**) a note or comment added to a piece of writing to explain a difficult word or phrase

■ *verb* [VN] ~ **sth** (**as sth**) to add a note or comment to a piece of writing to explain a difficult word, phrase or idea $\overline{\text{PHRV}}$ **ˌgloss ˈover sth** to avoid talking about sth unpleasant or embarrassing by not dealing with it in detail: *to gloss over a problem/difficulty/situation* ◊ *He glossed over any splits in the party.*

gloss·ary /ˈglɒsəri; *AmE* ˈglɔːs-; ˈglɑːs-/ *noun* (*pl.* **-ies**) a list of technical or special words, especially those in a particular text, explaining their meanings: *a glossary of financial terms*

glossy /ˈglɒsi; *AmE* ˈglɔːsi; ˈglɑːsi/ *adj., noun*

■ *adj.* **1** smooth and shiny: *glossy hair* ◊ *a glossy brochure/magazine* (= printed on shiny paper) **2** giving an appearance of being important and expensive: *the glossy world of fashion*

aɪ	aʊ	eɪ	əʊ	oʊ	ɔɪ	ɪə	eə	ʊə	j	w
my	now	say	go	go	boy	near	hair	pure	yes	wet
			(BrE)	(AmE)						

■ *noun* (*pl.* **-ies**) (*BrE, informal*) an expensive magazine printed on glossy paper, with a lot of colour photographs, etc.

glot·tal stop /ˌglɒtl ˈstɒp; *AmE* ˌglɑːtl ˈstɑːp/ *noun* (*phonetics*) a speech sound made by closing and opening the glottis, which in English sometimes takes the place of a /t/, in *butter*, for example

glot·tis /ˈglɒtɪs; *AmE* ˈglɑːt-/ *noun* (*anatomy*) the part of the throat that contains the VOCAL CORDS and the narrow opening between them

glove /glʌv/ *noun* a covering for the hand, made of wool, leather, etc. with separate parts for each finger and the thumb: *a pair of gloves* ◊ *rubber gloves* ◊ *gardening gloves*—compare MITTEN—see also BOXING, OVEN GLOVE [IDM] **the gloves are off** used to say that sb is ready for a fight or an argument—more at FIT *v.*, HAND *n.*, IRON *adj.*, KID *n.*

glove compartment (also **glove box**) *noun* a small enclosed space or shelf facing the front seats of a car, used for keeping small things in—picture at CAR

gloved /glʌvd/ *adj.* [usually before noun] (of a hand) wearing a glove

glove puppet (*BrE*) (*AmE* **hand puppet**) *noun* a type of PUPPET that you put over your hand and move using your fingers

glow /gləʊ; *AmE* gloʊ/ *verb, noun*

■ *verb* **1** (especially of sth hot or warm) to produce a dull, steady light: [V] *The embers still glowed in the hearth.* ◊ *The strap has a fluorescent coating that glows in the dark.* ◊ [V-ADJ] *A cigarette end glowed red in the darkness.* **2** [V] ~ (**with sth**) (of a person's body or face) to look or feel warm or pink, especially after exercise or because of excitement, embarrassment, etc: *Her cheeks were glowing.* ◊ *His face glowed with embarrassment.* **3** [V] ~ (**with sth**) to look very pleased or satisfied: *She was positively glowing with pride.* ◊ *He gave her a warm glowing smile.* **4** ~ (**with sth**) to appear a strong, warm colour: [V] *The countryside glowed with autumn colours.* ◊ [V-ADJ] *The brick walls glowed red in the late afternoon sun.*

■ *noun* [sing.] **1** a dull steady light, especially from a fire that has stopped producing flames: *The city was just a red glow on the horizon.* ◊ *There was no light except for the occasional glow of a cigarette.* **2** the pink colour in your face when you have been doing exercise or feel happy and excited: *The fresh air had brought a healthy glow to her cheeks.* **3** a gold or red colour: *the glow of autumn leaves* **4** a feeling of pleasure and satisfaction: *When she looked at her children, she felt a glow of pride.*

glow·er /ˈglaʊə(r)/ *verb* [V] ~ (**at sb/sth**) to look in an angry, aggressive way [SYN] GLARE ▶ **glow·er** *noun*

glow·ing /ˈgləʊɪŋ; *AmE* ˈgloʊɪŋ/ *adj.* giving enthusiastic praise: *a glowing account/report/review* ◊ *He spoke of her performance in the film* **in glowing terms** (= praising her highly). ▶ **glow·ing·ly** *adv.*

glow-worm *noun* a type of insect. The female has no wings and produces a green light at the end of the tail.

glu·cose /ˈgluːkəʊs; -kəʊz; *AmE* -koʊs; -koʊz/ *noun* [U] a type of sugar that is found in fruit and is easily changed into energy by the human body

glue /gluː/ *noun, verb*

■ *noun* [U, C] a sticky substance that is used for joining things together: *a tube of glue* ◊ *He sticks to her like glue* (= never leaves her).

■ *verb* [VN] ~ **A** (**to/onto B**) | ~ **A and B** (**together**) to join two things together using glue: *She glued the label onto the box.* ◊ *Glue the two pieces of cardboard together.* ◊ *Make sure the edges are glued down.* [IDM] **be glued to sth** (*informal*) to give all your attention to sth; to stay very close to sth: *He spends every evening glued to the TV.* ◊ *Her eyes were glued to the screen* (= she did not stop watching it). **glued to the spot** not able to move, for example because you are frightened or surprised

glue ear *noun* [U] (*BrE*) a medical condition in which the tubes going from the nose to the ear are blocked with MUCUS

glue-sniffing *noun* [U] the habit of breathing in the gases from some kinds of glue in order to produce a state of excitement; a type of SOLVENT ABUSE

glum /glʌm/ *adj.* sad, quiet and unhappy: *The players sat there with glum looks on their faces.* ▶ **glum·ly** *adv.*: *The three of us sat glumly looking out to sea.*

glut /glʌt/ *noun, verb*

■ *noun* [usually sing.] ~ (**of sth**) a situation in which there is more of sth than is needed or can be used: *a glut of cheap videos on the market*

■ *verb* (**-tt-**) [VN] [usually passive] to supply or provide sth with too much of sth: *The market has been glutted with foreign cars.*

glu·ten /ˈgluːtn/ *noun* [U] a sticky substance that is a mixture of two PROTEINS and is left when STARCH is removed from flour, especially wheat flour

glu·tin·ous /ˈgluːtənəs/ *adj.* sticky: *glutinous rice*

glut·ton /ˈglʌtn/ *noun* **1** (*disapproving*) a person who eats too much **2** ~ **for punishment/work** a person who enjoys doing difficult or unpleasant tasks ▶ **glut·ton·ous** /ˈglʌtənəs/ *adj.*

glut·tony /ˈglʌtəni/ *noun* [U] the habit of eating and drinking too much

gly·cer·ine /ˈglɪsəriːn; -rɪn; *AmE* -rən/ (*AmE* usually **gly·cerin** /-rɪn; *AmE* -rən/) *noun* [U] a thick sweet colourless liquid made from fats and oils and used in medicines, beauty products and explosives

GM /ˌdʒiː ˈem/ *abbr.* **1** (*BrE*) genetically modified: *GM foods or 'Frankenstein foods' as they are popularly called* **2** grant-maintained (used in Britain to describe schools that receive money from central, not local government)

gm (*BrE*) (also **gm.** *AmE, BrE*) *abbr.* (*pl.* **gm** or **gms**) gram(s)

GMT /ˌdʒiː em ˈtiː/ *noun* [U] the abbreviation for 'Greenwich Mean Time' (the time at Greenwich in England on the line of 0° LONGITUDE, used for calculating time everywhere in the world)

gnarled /nɑːld; *AmE* nɑːrld/ *adj.* **1** (of trees) twisted and rough; covered with hard lumps: *a gnarled oak/branch/trunk* **2** (of a person or part of the body) bent and twisted because of age or illness: *gnarled hands*

gnarly /ˈnɑːli; *AmE* ˈnɑːrli/ *adj.* (*AmE, slang*) **1** very good; excellent: *Wow, man! That's totally gnarly!* **2** not very good

gnash /næʃ/ *verb* [IDM] **gnash your teeth** to feel very angry and upset about sth, especially because you cannot get what you want: *He'll be gnashing his teeth when he hears that we lost the contract.*

gnat /næt/ *noun* a small fly with two wings, that bites

gnaw /nɔː/ *verb* ~ (**away**) (**at/on sth**) to keep biting sth or chewing it hard, so that it gradually disappears: [VN] *The dog was gnawing a bone.* ◊ [V] *Rats had gnawed through the cable* ◊ *She gnawed at her fingernails.* ◊ (*figurative*) *Self-doubt began to gnaw away at her confidence.* [PHRV] **gnaw at sb** to make sb feel anxious, frightened or uncomfortable over a long period of time: *The problem had been gnawing at him for months.*

gnaw·ing /ˈnɔːɪŋ/ *adj.* [only before noun] making you feel worried over a period of time: *gnawing doubts*

gnome /nəʊm; *AmE* noʊm/ *noun* **1** (in stories) a creature like a small man with white hair and a pointed hat who lives under the ground and guards gold and precious things: (*informal*) *the gnomes of Zurich* (= Swiss bankers who control foreign money) **2** a plastic or stone figure of a gnome, used as a garden ornament

gno·mic /ˈnəʊmɪk; *AmE* ˈnoʊ-/ *adj.* (*formal*) (of a person or a remark) clever and wise but sometimes difficult to understand

GNP /ˌdʒiː en ˈpiː/ *noun* the abbreviation for 'gross national product' (the total value of all the goods and services produced by a country in one year, including the total income from foreign countries)—compare GDP

gnu /nuː; njuː/ *noun* (*pl.* **gnu** or **gnus**) = WILDEBEEST

GNVQ /ˌdʒiː en viː ˈkjuː/ *noun* a course of study taken in British schools by students aged 15-18 to prepare them for university or employment (the abbreviation for 'General

G

	b	d	f	g	h	k	l	m	n	p	r
	bad	did	fall	get	hat	cat	leg	man	now	pen	red

National Vocational Qualification'): *She's doing GNVQ Business Studies at college.*—compare A LEVEL

go /gəʊ; *AmE* goʊ/ *verb, noun*

■ *verb* (**goes** /gəʊz; *AmE* goʊz/ **went** /went/ **gone** /gɒn; *AmE* gɔːn; gɑːn/) **HELP** **Been** is used as the past participle of **go** when sb has gone somewhere and come back.

MOVE/TRAVEL | **1** to move or travel from one place to another: [V, +*adv./prep.*] *She went into her room and shut the door behind her.* ◊ *He goes to work by bus.* ◊ *I have to go to Rome on business.* ◊ *She has gone to China* (= is now in China or is on her way there). ◊ *She has been to China* (= she went to China and has now returned). ◊ *I think you should go to the doctor's.* ◊ *Are you going home for Christmas?* ◊ [V to inf] *She has gone to see her sister this weekend.* **HELP** In spoken English **go** can be used with **and** plus another verb to show purpose or to tell sb what to do: *I'll go and answer the door.* ◊ *Go and get me a drink!* The **and** is sometimes left out, especially in *AmE*: *Go ask your mom!* **2** [V] **~ (to sth) (with sb)** to move or travel, especially with sb else, to a particular place or in order to be present at an event: *Are you going to Dave's party?* ◊ *Who else is going?* ◊ *His dog goes everywhere with him.* **3** [+*adv./prep.*] to move or travel in a particular way or over a particular distance: [V] *He's going too fast.* ◊ [VN] *We had gone about fifty miles when the car broke down.* **4** [V-ing, usually +*adv./prep.*] **~ flying, singing, etc.** to move in a particular way or while doing sth else: *The car went skidding off the road into a ditch.* ◊ *She went sobbing up the stairs.* ◊ *She crashed into a waiter and his tray of drinks went flying.*

LEAVE | **5** [V] to leave one place in order to reach another [SYN] DEPART: *I must be going now.* ◊ *They came at six and went at nine.* ◊ *Has she gone yet?* ◊ *He's been gone an hour* (= he left an hour ago). ◊ *When does the train go?* **6** [V] **~ on sth** to leave a place and do sth different: *to go on a journey/a tour/a trip/a cruise* ◊ *Richard has gone on leave for two weeks.*

VISIT/ATTEND | **7** [V] **~ to sth** to visit or attend a place for a particular purpose: (*BrE*) *I have to go to hospital for an operation.* ◊ (*AmE*) *I have to go to the hospital.* ◊ *to go to prison* (= to be sent there as punishment for a crime) ◊ *Do you go to church* (= regularly attend church services)?

SWIMMING/FISHING/JOGGING, etc. | **8** **~ for sth** to leave a place or travel to a place in order to take part in an activity or a sport: *to go for a walk/drive/swim/run* ◊ *Shall we go for a drink* (= at a pub or bar) *after work?* ◊ *I have to go shopping this afternoon.* ◊ *We're going sailing on Saturday.*

BE SENT | **9** [V] [usually +*adv./prep.*] to be sent or passed somewhere: *I want this memo to go to all managers.*

LEAD | **10** [V+*adv./prep.*] **~ (from...) to...** to lead or EXTEND from one place to another: *I want a rope that will go from the top window to the ground.* ◊ *Where does this road go?*

PLACE/SPACE | **11** [V+*adv./prep.*] to have as a usual or correct position; to be placed: *This dictionary goes on the top shelf.* ◊ *Where do you want the piano to go* (= be put)? **12** [V] **will/would not ~ (in/into sth)** used to say that sth does/did not fit into a particular place or space: *My clothes won't all go in that one suitcase.* ◊ *He tried to push his hand through the gap but it wouldn't go.*

NUMBERS | **13** **~ (into sth)** if a number will **go into** another number, it is contained in that number an exact number of times: [V-N] *3 into 12 goes 4.* ◊ [V] *7 into 15 won't go.* ◊ (*AmE*) *7 into 15 doesn't go.* ◊ *7 won't go into 15.*

PROGRESS | **14** [V+*adv./prep.*] used to talk about how well or badly sth makes progress or succeeds: *'How did your interview go?' 'It went very well, thank you.'* ◊ *Did everything go smoothly?* ◊ *How's it going* (= is your life enjoyable, successful, etc. at the moment)? ◊ *The way things are going the company will be bankrupt by the end of the year.*

STATE/CONDITION | **15** [V] **~ to/into sth** | **~ out of sth** used in many expressions to show that sb/sth has reached a particular state/is no longer in a particular state: *She went to sleep.* ◊ *That colour has gone out of fashion.* **16** *linking verb* [V-ADJ] to become different in a particular way, especially a bad way: *to go bald/blind/mad/bank-*

rupt ◊ *Her hair is going grey.* ◊ *This milk has gone sour.* ◊ *The children went wild with excitement.* ⇨ note at BECOME **17** [V-ADJ] to live or move around in a particular state: *to go naked/barefoot* ◊ *She cannot bear the thought of children going hungry.* **18** [V-ADJ] **~ unnoticed, unreported, etc.** to not be noticed, reported, etc: *Police are worried that many crimes go unreported.*

SONG/STORY | **19** used to talk about what tune or words a song or poem has or what happens in a story: [V,+*adv./prep.*] *How does that song go?* ◊ *I forget how the next line goes.* ◊ [V that] *The story goes that she's been married five times.*

SOUND/MOVEMENT | **20** to make a particular sound or movement: [V-N] *The gun went 'bang'.* ◊ [V+*adv./prep.*] *She went like this with her hand.* **21** [V] to be sounded as a signal or warning: *The whistle went for the end of the game.*

SAY | **22** [V speech] (*informal*) (used when telling a story) to say: *I asked 'How much?' and he goes, 'Fifty.' and I go, 'Fifty? You must be joking!'*

START | **23** [V] to start an activity: *I'll say 'One, two, three, go!' as a signal for you to start.* ◊ *As soon as he gets here we're ready to go.*

MACHINE | **24** [V] if a machine **goes**, it works: *This clock doesn't go.*

DISAPPEAR | **25** [V] to stop existing; to be lost or stolen [SYN] DISAPPEAR: *Has your headache gone yet?* ◊ *I left my bike outside the library and when I came out again it had gone.*

BE THROWN OUT | **26** [V] **sb/sth must/has to/can ~** used to talk about wanting to get rid of sb/sth: *The old sofa will have to go.* ◊ *He's useless—he'll have to go.*

NOT WORK | **27** [V] to get worse; to become damaged or stop working correctly: *Her sight is beginning to go.* ◊ *His mind is going* (= he is losing his mental powers). ◊ *I was driving home when my brakes went.*

DIE | **28** [V] to die. People say 'go' to avoid saying 'die': *You can't take your money with you when you go.*

MONEY | **29** [V] **~ (on sth)** when money **goes**, it is spent or used for sth: *I don't know where the money goes!* ◊ *Most of my salary goes on the rent.* ◊ *The money will go to finance a new community centre.* **30** [V] **~ (to sb) (for sth)** to be sold: *We won't let the house go for less than $200000.* ◊ *There was usually some bread going cheap* (= being sold cheaply) *at the end of the day.* **31** [V+*adv./prep.*] to be willing to pay a particular amount of money for sth: *He's offered £3000 for the car and I don't think he'll go any higher.* ◊ *I'll go to $1000 but that's my limit.*

HELP | **32** [V to inf] to help; to play a part in doing sth: *This all goes to prove my theory.* ◊ *It* (= what has just happened) *just goes to show you can't always tell how people are going to react.*

BE AVAILABLE | **33** (**be going**) [V] (*informal*) to be available: *There just aren't any jobs going in this area.*

TIME | **34** [V+*adv./prep.*] used to talk about how quickly or slowly time seems to pass: *Hasn't the time gone quickly?*

USE TOILET | **35** [V] (*informal*) to use a toilet: *Do you need to go, Billy?*

IDM Most idioms containing **go** are at the entries for the nouns and adjectives in the idioms, for example **go it alone** is at **alone**. **anything goes** (*informal*) anything that sb says or does is accepted or allowed, however shocking or unusual it may be: *Almost anything goes these days.* **as people, things, etc. go** in comparison with the average person, thing, etc: *As teachers go, he's not bad.* **be going on (for) sth** (*BrE*) to be nearly a particular age, time or number: *It was going on (for) midnight.* **be going to do sth 1** used to show what sb intends to do in the future: *We're going to buy a house when we've saved enough money.* **2** used to show that sth is likely to happen very soon or in the future: *I think I'm going to faint.* ◊ *If the drought continues there's going to be a famine.* **don't go doing sth** (*spoken*) used to tell or warn sb not to do sth: *Don't go getting yourself into trouble.* **enough/something to be going on with** (*BrE*) something that is enough for a short time: *£50 should be enough to be going on with.* **go all 'out for sth | go all out to 'do sth** to make a very great effort to get sth or do

s	t	v	z	ʃ	ʒ	tʃ	dʒ	θ	ð	ŋ
see	tea	van	zoo	shoe	vision	chain	jam	thin	this	sing

sth **go and do sth** used to show that you are angry or annoyed that sb has done sth stupid: *Trust him to go and mess things up!* ◊ *Why did you have to go and upset your mother like that?* ◊ *You've really gone and done it* (= done sth very stupid) *now!* **go down well, badly, etc. (with sb)** | **go off well** used to talk about whether people like sth such as a speech, performance, etc: *Her speech went down well with the audience.* **go 'on (with you)** (*old-fashioned*) used to express the fact that you do not believe sth, or that you disapprove of sth: *Go on with you—you're never forty. You don't look a day over thirty.* **(have) a lot, nothing, etc. 'going for you** (to have) many/not many advantages: *You're young, intelligent, attractive—you have a lot going for you!* ,**no 'go** (*informal*) not possible or allowed: *If the bank won't lend us the money it's no go, I'm afraid.*—see also NO-GO AREA **to 'go 1** remaining; still left: *I only have one exam to go.* **2** (*AmE, informal*) if you buy cooked food **to go** in a restaurant or shop/store, you buy it to take away and eat somewhere else: *Two pizzas to go.* ,**where does sb ,go from 'here?** used to ask what action sb should take, especially in order to improve the difficult situation that they are in ,**who goes 'there?** used by a soldier who is guarding a place to order sb to say who they are: *Halt, who goes there?*

PHR V ,**go a'bout** (*BrE*) = GO AROUND **'go about sth** to continue to do sth; to keep busy with sth: *Despite the threat of war, people went about their business as usual.* ,**go a'bout sth** to start working on sth **SYN** TACKLE: *You're not going about the job in the right way.* ◊[+-ing] *How should I go about finding a job?*

,**go 'after sb** to chase or follow sb: *He went after the burglars.* ◊ *She left the room in tears so I went after her.* ,**go 'after sb/sth** to try to get sb/sth: *We're both going after the same job.*

,**go a'gainst sb** to not be in sb's favour or not to their advantage: *The jury's verdict went against him.* ,**go a'gainst sb/sth** to resist or oppose sb/sth: *He would not go against his parents' wishes.* ,**go a'gainst sth** to be opposed to sth; to not fit or agree with sth: *Paying for hospital treatment goes against her principles.* ◊ *His thinking goes against all logic.*

,**go a'head 1** to travel in front of other people in your group and arrive before them: *I'll go ahead and tell them you're on the way.* **2** to happen; to be done **SYN** PROCEED: *The building of the new bridge will go ahead as planned.*—related noun GO-AHEAD ,**go a'head (with sth)** to begin to do sth, especially when sb has given permission or has expressed doubts or opposition: *'May I start now?' 'Yes, go ahead.'* ◊ *The government intends to go ahead with its tax cutting plans*—related noun GO-AHEAD ,**go a'long 1** to continue with an activity: *He made up the story as he went along.* **2** to make progress; to develop: *Things are going along nicely.* ,**go a'long with sb/sth** to agree with sb/sth: *I don't go along with her views on abortion.*

,**go a'round/'round 1** to spin or turn: *to go round in a circle* **2** to be enough for everyone to have one or some: *There aren't enough chairs to go around.* **3** (*BrE also* ,**go a'bout**) to often be in a particular state or behave in a particular way: *She often goes around barefoot.* ◊[+-ing] *It's unprofessional to go round criticizing your colleagues.* **4** to spread from person to person: *There's a rumour going around that they're having an affair.* ,**go a'round/ 'round (to ...)** to visit sb or a place that is near: *I went round to the post office.* ◊ *I'm going around to my sister's* (= her house) *later.*

'**go at sb** to attack sb: *They went at each other furiously.* '**go at sth** to make great efforts to do sth; to work hard at sth: *They went at the job as if their lives depended on it.* ,**go a'way 1** to leave a person or place: *Just go away!* ◊ *Go away and think about it, then let me know.* **2** to leave home for a period of time, especially for a holiday/ vacation: *They've gone away for a few days.* ◊ *I'm going away on business.* **3** to disappear: *The smell still hasn't gone away.*

,**go 'back** if two people **go back** a period of time (usually a long time), they have known each other for that time:

Dave and I go back twenty years. ,**go 'back (to ...)** to return to a place: *She doesn't want to go back to her husband* (= to live with him again). ◊ *This toaster will have to go back* (= be taken back to the shop/store where it was bought)—*it's faulty.* ◊ *Of course we want to go back some day—it's our country, our real home.* ,**go 'back (to sth) 1** to consider sth that happened or was said at an earlier time: *Can I go back to what you said at the beginning of the meeting?* ◊ *Once you have made this decision, there will be no going back* (= you will not be able to change your mind). **2** to have existed since a particular time or for a particular period: *Their family goes back to the time of the Pilgrim Fathers.* ,**go 'back on sth** to fail to keep a promise; to change your mind about sth: *He never goes back on his word* (= never fails to do what he has said he will do). ,**go 'back to sth** to start doing sth again that you had stopped doing: *The kids go back to school next week.* ◊[+-ing] *She's decided to go back to teaching.*

,**go be'fore** (*written*) to exist or happen in an earlier time: *The present crisis is worse than any that have gone before.* '**go before sb/sth** to be presented to sb/sth for discussion, decision or judgement: *My application goes before the planning committee next week.*

,**go be'yond sth** to be more than sth **SYN** EXCEED: *This year's sales figures go beyond all our expectations* (= are much better than we thought they would be).

,**go 'by** (of time) to pass: *Things will get easier as time goes by.* ◊ *The weeks went slowly by.* '**go by sth** to be guided by sth; to form an opinion from sth: *That's a good rule to go by.* ◊ *If past experience is anything to go by, they'll be late.*

,**go 'down 1** to fall to the ground: *She tripped and went down with a bump.* **2** if a ship, etc. **goes down**, it disappears below the water **SYN** SINK **3** when the sun or moon **goes down**, it disappears below the HORIZON **SYN** SET **4** if food or drink will/will not **go down**, it is difficult/easy to swallow: *A glass of wine would go down very nicely* (= I would very much like one). **5** if the price of sth, the temperature, etc. **goes down**, it becomes lower **SYN** FALL: *The price of oil is going down.* ◊ *Oil is going down in price.* **OPP** GO UP **6** (*informal*) to get worse in quality: *The neighbourhood has gone down a lot recently.* **7** (*computing*) to stop working temporarily: *The system is going down in ten minutes.* ,**go 'down (from ...)** (*BrE, formal*) to leave a university, especially Oxford or Cambridge, at the end of a TERM or after finishing your studies: *She went down (from Cambridge) in 1989.* **OPP** GO UP (TO ...) ,**go 'down (in sth)** to be written in sth; to be recorded or remembered in sth: *It all goes down* (= she writes it all) *in her notebook.* ◊ *He will go down in history as a great statesman.* ,**go 'down on sb** (*slang*) to perform ORAL sex on sb (= to use the mouth to stimulate sb's sex organs) ,**go 'down (to sb)** to be defeated by sb, especially in a game or competition: *Italy went down to Brazil by three goals to one.* ,**go 'down (to ...) (from ...)** to go from one place to another, especially further south or from a city or large town to a smaller place: *They've gone down to Brighton for a couple of days.* **OPP** GO UP ,**go 'down with sth** (*especially BrE*) to become ill/sick with sth **SYN** CATCH: *Our youngest boy has gone down with chickenpox.* '**go for sb** to attack sb: *She went for him with a knife.* '**go for sb/sth 1** what I said about Peter goes for you, too. ◊ *They have a high level of unemployment—but the same goes for many other countries.* **2** to go to a place and bring sb/sth back: *She's gone for some milk.* **3** to be attracted by sb/sth; to like or prefer sb/sth: *She goes for tall slim men.* ◊ *I don't really go for modern art.* '**go for sth 1** to choose sth: *I think I'll go for the fruit salad.* **2** to put a lot of effort into sth, so that you get or achieve sth: *Go for it, John! You know you can beat him.* ◊ *It sounds a great idea. Go for it!*

,**go 'in 1** to enter a room, house, etc: *Let's go in, it's getting cold.* **2** if the sun or moon **goes in**, it disappears behind a cloud ,**go 'in for sth 1** (*BrE*) to take an exam or enter a competition: *She's going in for the Cambridge First Certificate.* **2** to have sth as an interest or a hobby: *She doesn't go in for team games.* ,**go 'in with sb** to join sb

G

æ	ɑː	e	ɜː	ə	ɪ	iː	i	ɒ	ɔː	ʌ	ʊ	u	uː
cat	father	ten	bird	about	sit	see	many	got	saw	cup	put	actual	too

(BrE)

in starting a business: *My brothers are opening a garage and they want me to go in with them.*

,go **'into sth 1** (of a vehicle) to hit sth violently: *The car skidded and went into a tree.* **2** (of a vehicle or driver) to start moving in a particular way: *The plane went into a nosedive.* **3** to join an organization, especially in order to have a career in it: *to go into the Army/the Church/Parliament* ◊ *to go into teaching* **4** to begin to do sth or behave in a particular way: *He went into a long explanation of the affair.* **5** to examine sth carefully: *We need to go into the question of costs.* **6** (of money, time, effort, etc.) to be spent on sth or used to do sth: *More government money needs to go into the project.* ◊[+-ing] *Years of work went into researching the book.*

,go **'off 1** to leave a place, especially in order to do sth: *She went off to get a drink.* **2** to be fired; to explode: *The gun went off by accident.* ◊ *The bomb went off in a crowded street.* **3** if an ALARM, etc. **goes off**, it makes a sudden loud noise **4** if a light, the electricity, etc. **goes off**, it stops working: *Suddenly the lights went off.* ◊ *The heating goes off at night.* OPP GO ON **5** (*BrE, informal*) to fall asleep: *Hasn't the baby gone off yet?* **6** (*BrE*) if food or drink **goes off**, it becomes bad and not fit to eat or drink **7** (*BrE*) to get*worse in quality: *Her books have gone off in recent years.* ,go **'off sb/sth** (*BrE, informal*) to stop liking sb/sth or lose interest in them: *Jane seems to be going off Paul.* ◊ *I've gone off beer.* ,go **'off with sb** to leave your husband, wife, partner, etc. in order to have a relationship with sb else: *He went off with his best friend's wife.* ,go **'off with sth** to take away from a place sth that does not belong to you: *He went off with $10000 of the company's money.*

,go **'on 1** when a performer **goes on**, they begin their performance: *She doesn't go on until Act 2.* **2** (in sport) to join a team as a SUBSTITUTE during a game: *Cole went on in place of Beckham just before half-time.* **3** when a light, the electricity, etc. **goes on**, it starts to work: *Suddenly all the lights went on.* OPP GO OFF **4** (of time) to pass: *She became more and more talkative as the evening went on.* **5** (usually **be going on**) to happen: *What's going on here?* **6** if a situation **goes on**, it continues without changing: *This cannot be allowed to go on.* ◊ *How much longer will this hot weather go on for?* ◊ *We can't go on like this—we seem to be always arguing.* **7** to continue speaking, after a short pause: *She hesitated for a moment and then went on.* ◊[+speech] *'You know,' he went on, 'I think my brother could help you.'* **8** used to encourage sb to do sth: *Go on! Have another drink!* ◊ *Go on—jump!* ,go **'on (ahead)** to travel in front of sb else: *You go on ahead—I'll catch you up in a few minutes.* **'go on sth** (used in negative sentences and questions) to base an opinion or a judgement on sth: *The police don't have much to go on.* ,go **'on (about sb/sth)** to talk about sb/sth for a long time, especially in a boring or complaining way: *He went on and on about how poor he was.* ◊ *She does go on sometimes!* ,go **'on (at sb)** (*especially BrE*) to complain to sb about their behaviour, work, etc. SYN CRITICIZE: *She goes on at him continually.* ,go **'on (with sth)** to continue an activity, especially after a pause or break: *That's enough for now—let's go on with it tomorrow.* **go on doing sth** to continue an activity without stopping: *He said nothing but just went on working.* ,go **'on to sth** to pass from one item to the next: *Let's go on to the next item on the agenda.* **go on to do sth** to do sth after completing sth else: *The book goes on to describe his experiences in the army.* ◊ *After her early teaching career she went on to become a doctor.*

,go **'out 1** to leave your house to go to a social event: *She goes out a lot.* ◊[+-ing] *He goes out drinking most evenings.* **2** when the TIDE **goes out**, it moves away from the land SYN EBB OPP COME IN **3** to be sent: *Have the invitations gone out yet?* **4** (*BrE*) when a radio or television programme **goes out**, it is broadcast **5** when news or information **goes out**, it is announced or published: [+that] *Word went out that the director had resigned* **6** if a fire or light **goes out**, it stops burning or shining ,go **'out (of sth) 1** to fail to reach the next stage of a competition, etc: *She went out of the tournament in the first round.* **2** to be no longer fashionable or generally used: *Those skirts*

went out years ago. ,go **'out of sb/sth** (of a quality or a feeling) to be no longer present in sb/sth; to disappear from sb/sth: *All the fight seemed to go out of him.* ◊ *The heat has gone out of the argument.* ,go **'out with sb** ,go **'out (together)** (especially of young people) to spend time with sb and have a romantic or sexual relationship with them: *Tom has been going out with Kate for six weeks.* ◊ *How long have Tom and Kate been going out together?*

,go **'over sth 1** to examine or check sth carefully: *Go over your work before you hand it in.* **2** to study sth carefully, especially by repeating it: *He went over the events of the day in his mind* (= thought about them carefully). ,go **'over (to …)** to move from one place to another, especially when this means crossing sth such as a room, town or city: *He went over and shook hands with his guests.* ◊ *Many Irish people went over to America during the famine.* ,go **'over to sb/sth** (in broadcasting) to change to a different person or place for the next part of a broadcast: *We are now going over to the news desk for an important announcement.* ,go **'over to sth** to change from one side, opinion, habit, etc. to another: *Two Conservative MPs have gone over to the Liberal Democrats.*

,go **'round** = GO AROUND ,go **'round (to …)** = GO AROUND (TO …)

,go **'through** if a law, contract, etc. **goes through**, it is officially accepted or completed: *The deal did not go through.* **go through sth 1** to look at or examine sth carefully, especially in order to find sth: *I always start the day by going through my mail.* ◊ *She went through the company's accounts, looking for evidence of fraud.* **2** to study or consider sth in detail, especially by repeating it: *Let's go through the arguments again.* ◊ *Could we go through* (= practise) *Act 2 once more?* **3** to perform a series of actions; to follow a method or PROCEDURE: *Certain formalities have to be gone through before you can emigrate.* **4** to experience or suffer sth: *She's been going through a bad patch recently.* ◊ *He's amazingly cheerful considering all he's had to go through.* **5** to use up or finish sth completely: *The boys went through two whole loaves of bread.* ,go **'through with sth** to do what is necessary to complete a course of action, especially one that is difficult or unpleasant: *She decided not to go through with* (= not to have) *the operation.*

'go to sb/sth to be given to sb/sth: *Proceeds from the concert will go to charity.* ◊ *All her property went to her eldest son* (= when she died).

,go **to'gether** = GO WITH STH

'go towards sth to be used as part of the payment for sth: *The money will go towards a new car.* ◊[+-ing] *Part of my pay cheque went towards buying a CD player.*

,go **'under 1** (of sth that floats) to sink below the surface **2** (*informal*) to become BANKRUPT (= be unable to pay what you owe): *The firm will go under unless business improves.*

,go **'up 1** to be built: *New offices buildings are going up everywhere.* **2** when the curtain across the stage in a theatre **goes up**, it is raised or opened **3** to be destroyed by fire or an explosion: *The whole building went up in flames.* **4** if the price of sth, the temperature, etc. **goes up**, it becomes higher SYN RISE: *The price of cigarettes is going up.* ◊ *Cigarettes are going up in price.* OPP GO DOWN ,go **'up (to …)** (*BrE, formal*) to arrive at a university, especially Oxford or Cambridge, at the beginning of a TERM or in order to begin your studies: *She went up to Oxford in 1989.* OPP GO DOWN (FROM …) ,go **'up (to …) (from …)** to go from one place to another, especially further north or to a city or large town from a smaller place: *When are you next going up to Scotland?* ◊ *We went up to London last weekend.* OPP GO DOWN

'go with sb (*old-fashioned, informal*) to have a sexual or romantic relationship with sb **'go with sth 1** to be included with or as part of sth: *A car goes with the job.* **2** to agree to accept sth, for example a plan or an offer: *You're offering £500? I think we can go with that.* **3** (also **'go (together)**) to combine well with sth SYN MATCH: *Does this jacket go with this skirt?* ◊ *Those colours don't really go (together).* **4** (also ,go **to'gether**) to exist at the same time or in the same place as sth; to be found together: *Disease often goes with poverty.* ◊ *Disease and poverty often go together.*

go wi'thout (sth) to manage without sth that you usually have or need: *There wasn't time for breakfast, so I had to go without.* ◊ *How long can a human being go (= survive) without sleep?* ◊[+ -ing] *She went without eating for three days.*

■ *noun (pl.* **goes** /gəʊz/) **1** [C] (*BrE*) (also **turn** *AmE, BrE*) a person's turn to move or play in a game or an activity: *Whose go is it?* ◊ *It's your go.* ◊ *'How much is it to play?' 'It's 50p a go.'* ◊ *Can I have a go on your new bike?* **2** [C] (*BrE*) (also **try** *AmE, BrE*) an attempt at doing sth: *It took three goes to get it right.* ◊ *I doubt if he'll listen to advice from me, but I'll give it a go (= I'll try but I don't think I will succeed).* **3** [U] (*BrE*) energy and enthusiasm: *Mary's always got plenty of go.*—see also GET-UP-AND-GO

IDM **at one 'go** (*BrE*) in one single attempt or try: *She blew out the candles at one go.* **be all 'go** (*BrE, informal*) to be very busy or full of activity: *It was all go in the office today.* **be on the 'go** (also **be on the 'move**) (*informal*) to be very active and busy: *I've been on the go all day.* ◊ *Having four children keeps her on the go.* **first, second, etc. 'go** (*BrE*) at the first, second, etc. attempt: *I passed my driving test first go.* **have a 'go (at sth/at doing sth)** to make an attempt to do sth: *'I can't start the engine.' 'Let me have a go.'* ◊ *I'll have a go at fixing it tonight.* **have a 'go** (*spoken, especially BrE*) to attack sb physically: *There were about seven of them standing round him, all waiting to have a go.* **have a 'go at sb** (*informal*) to criticize sb or complain about sb: *The boss had a go at me for being late for work.* **in one 'go** (*especially spoken*) all together on one occasion: *I'd rather do the journey in one go, and not stop on the way.* ◊ *They ate the packet of biscuits all in one go.* **make a 'go of sth** (*informal*) to be successful in sth: *We've had a few problems in our marriage, but we're both determined to make a go of it.*—more at LEAVE *v.,* LET *v.*

goad /gəʊd; *AmE* goʊd/ *verb, noun*
■ *verb* [VN] ~ **sb/sth (into sth/into doing sth)** to keep irritating or annoying sb/sth until they react: *Goaded beyond endurance, she turned on him and hit out.* ◊ *He finally goaded her into answering his question.* **PHRV** **goad sb↔'on** to drive or encourage sb to do sth: *The boxers were goaded on by the shrieking crowd.*
■ *noun* **1** a pointed stick used for making cows, etc. move forwards **2** something that makes sb do sth, usually by annoying them

'go-ahead *noun, adj.*
■ *noun* (**the go-ahead**) [sing.] permission for sb to start doing sth: *The council has given the go-ahead to start building.*
■ *adj.* [usually before noun] willing to try new ideas, methods, etc. and therefore likely to succeed: *a go-ahead company/school/manager*

goal /gəʊl; *AmE* goʊl/ *noun* **1** (in football, hockey, etc.) a wooden frame with a net into which players must kick or hit the ball in order to score a point: *He headed the ball into an open goal (= one that had nobody defending it).* ◊ *Who is in goal (= is the goalkeeper) for Arsenal?*—picture on page 1250 **2** the act of kicking or hitting the ball into the goal; a point that is scored for this: *The winning goal was scored by Hill.* ◊ *Liverpool won by three goals to one.* ◊ *a penalty goal*—see also OWN GOAL **3** something that you hope to achieve: *to pursue/achieve a goal* ◊ *The company has set itself some long-term organizational goals.*

goal·keep·er /'gəʊlkiːpə(r); *AmE* 'goʊl-/ (also *informal* **goalie** /'gəʊli; *AmE* 'goʊli/; *AmE* also **goal·tend·er**) (also *BrE informal* **keeper**) *noun* (in football, hockey, etc.) a player whose job is to stop the ball from going into his or her own team's goal—picture on page 1250

'goal kick *noun* (in football) a kick taken by one team after the ball has been kicked over their GOAL LINE by the other team without a goal being scored

goal·less /'gəʊlləs; *AmE* 'goʊl-/ *adj.* [usually before noun] without either team scoring a goal: (*BrE*) *The match ended in a goalless draw.*

'goal line *noun* (in football, hockey, etc.) the line at either end of a sports field on which the goal stands

goal·mouth /'gəʊlmaʊθ; *AmE* 'goʊl-/ *noun* the area directly in front of a goal

goal·post /'gəʊlpəʊst; *AmE* 'goʊlpoʊst/ (also **post**) *noun* one of the two vertical posts that form part of a goal—picture on page 1250 **IDM** **move, etc. the 'goalposts** (*BrE, informal, disapproving*) to change the rules for sth, or conditions under which it is done, so that the situation becomes more difficult for sb

goal·scorer /'gəʊlskɔːrə(r); *AmE* 'goʊl-/ *noun* a player in football, etc. who scores a goal

goal·tend·er /'gəʊltendə(r); *AmE* 'goʊl-/ *noun* (*AmE*) = GOALKEEPER

goat /gəʊt; *AmE* goʊt/ *noun* **1** an animal with horns and a hairy coat, that lives wild in mountain areas or is kept on farms for its milk or meat: *a mountain goat* ◊ *goat's milk/cheese*—see also BILLY GOAT, NANNY GOAT **2** **old ~** (*informal*) an unpleasant old man who is annoying in a sexual way **IDM** **get sb's 'goat** (*informal*) to annoy sb very much—more at SHEEP

goatee /gəʊ'tiː; *AmE* goʊ-/ *noun* a small pointed BEARD (= hair growing on a man's face) that is grown only on the chin—picture at HAIR

goat·herd /'gəʊthɜːd; *AmE* 'goʊthɜːrd/ *noun* a person whose job is to take care of a group of goats

gob /gɒb; *AmE* gɑːb/ *noun, verb*
■ *noun* (*informal*) **1** (*BrE*) a rude way of referring to a person's mouth: *Shut your gob! (= a rude way of telling sb to be quiet)* **2** a small amount of a thick wet substance: *Gobs of spittle ran down his chin.* **3** [usually pl.] (*AmE*) a large amount of sth: *great gobs of cash*
■ *verb* (**-bb-**) [V] (*BrE, slang*) to blow SALIVA out of your mouth **SYN** SPIT

gob·bet /'gɒbɪt; *AmE* 'gɑːb-/ *noun* ~ **(of sth)** a small amount of sth: *gobbets of blood/food*

gob·ble /'gɒbl; *AmE* 'gɑːbl/ *verb* **1** ~ **sth (up/down)** to eat sth very fast, in a way that people consider rude or GREEDY: [VN] *Don't gobble your food like that!* ◊ *They gobbled down all the sandwiches.* [also V] **2** [V] when a TURKEY **gobbles** it makes a noise in its throat **PHRV** **gobble sth↔'up** (*informal*) **1** to use sth very quickly: *Hotel costs gobbled up most of their holiday budget.* **2** if a business company, etc. **gobbles up** a smaller one, it takes control of it

gobble·de·gook (also **gobble·dy·gook**) /'gɒbldiguːk; *AmE* 'gɑːbl-/ *noun* [U] (*informal*) complicated language that is difficult to understand, especially when used in official documents: *It's all gobbledegook to me.*

'go-between *noun* [C, U] a person who takes messages between one person or group and another: *to act as (a) go-between*

gob·let /'gɒblət; *AmE* 'gɑːb-/ *noun* a cup for wine, usually made of glass or metal, with a stem and base but no handle

gob·lin /'gɒblɪn; *AmE* 'gɑːb-/ *noun* (in stories) a small ugly creature that likes to trick people or cause trouble

gob·smacked /'gɒbsmækt; *AmE* 'gɑːb-/ *adj.* (*BrE, informal*) so surprised that you do not know what to say: *I was gobsmacked when she told me the news.*

'go-cart *noun* (*AmE*) = GO-KART

god /gɒd; *AmE* gɑːd/ *noun* **1** (**God**) [sing.] (not used with *the*) (in Christianity, Judaism and Islam) the being or spirit that is worshipped and is believed to have created the universe: *Do you believe in God?* ◊ *Good luck and God bless you.* ◊ *the Son of God (= Christ)* **2** [C] (in some religions) a being or spirit who is believed to have power over a particular part of nature or who is believed to represent a particular quality: *Mars was the Roman god of war.* ◊ *the rain/sky god* ◊ *Hindu gods*—see also GODDESS **3** [C] a person who is loved or admired very much by other people: *To her fans she's a god.*—see also GODDESS **4** [C] something to which too much importance or attention is given: *Money is his god.* **5** (**the gods**) [pl.] (*BrE, informal*) the seats that are high up at the back of a theatre **IDM** **by 'God!** (*spoken, old-fashioned*) used to emphasize a feeling of determination or surprise **HELP** Some people find this use offensive. **God | God al'mighty | God in 'heaven | good 'God | my 'God | oh 'God**

(*spoken*) used to emphasize what you are saying when you are surprised, shocked or annoyed: *God, what a stupid thing to do!* **HELP** Some people find this use offensive. **God 'bless** used when you are leaving sb, to say that you hope they will be safe, etc: *Good night, God bless.* **God 'rest his/her soul | God 'rest him/her** (*spoken, old-fashioned*) used to show respect when you are talking about sb who is dead **God's gift (to sb/sth)** (*ironic*) a person who thinks that they are particularly good at sth or who thinks that sb will find them particularly attractive: *He seems to think he's God's gift to women.* **God 'willing** (*spoken*) used to say that you hope that things will happen as you have planned and that there will be no problems: *I'll be back next week, God willing.* **play 'God** to behave as if you control events or other people's lives: *It is unfair to ask doctors to play God and end someone's life.* **to 'God/'goodness/'Heaven** used after a verb to emphasize a particular frame, wish, etc: *I wish to God you'd learn to pay attention!* **HELP** Some people find this use offensive. **ye 'gods!** (*spoken*) used to show surprise, lack of belief, etc.—more at ACT *n.*, FEAR *n.*, FORBID, GRACE *n.*, HELP *v.*, HONEST, KNOW *v.*, LAP *n.*, LOVE *n.*, MAN *n.*, NAME *n.*, PLEASE *v.*, THANK

God-awful *adj.* [usually before noun] (*informal*) extremely bad: *He made a God-awful mess of it!* **HELP** Some people find this use offensive.

god·child /ˈgɒdtʃaɪld; *AmE* ˈɡɑːd-/ *noun* (*pl.* **god·chil·dren** /ˈgɒdtʃɪldrən; *AmE* ˈɡɑːd-/) a child that a GODPARENT at a Christian BAPTISM ceremony promises to be responsible for and to teach about the Christian religion

god·dam (also **god·damn**) /ˈgɒddæm; *AmE* ˈɡɑːd-/ (also **god·damned** /ˈgɒddæmd; *AmE* ˈɡɑːd-/) *adj., adv.* (⚠, *slang*) a swear word that many people find offensive, used to show that you are angry or annoyed: *There's no need to be so goddam rude!* ◇ *Where's that goddamned pen?*

god·daughter *noun* a female GODCHILD

god·dess /ˈgɒdes; -əs; *AmE* ˈɡɑːdəs/ *noun* **1** a female god: *Diana, the goddess of hunting* **2** a woman who is loved or admired very much by other people: *a screen goddess* (= a female film/movie star)

god·father /ˈgɒdfɑːðə(r); *AmE* ˈɡɑːd-/ *noun* **1** a male GODPARENT **2** (often **Godfather**) a very powerful man in a criminal organization, especially the Mafia **3 ~ of sth** a person who began or developed sth: *He's the godfather of punk.*

God-fearing *adj.* [usually before noun] (*old-fashioned*) living a moral life based on religious principles

god·for·saken /ˈgɒdfəseɪkən; *AmE* ˈɡɑːdfər-/ *adj.* [only before noun] (of places) boring, depressing and ugly: *I can't stand living in this godforsaken hole.*

God-given *adj.* [usually before noun] given or created by God: *a God-given duty/talent* ◇ *What gives you a God-given right to know all my business?*

god·head /ˈgɒdhed; *AmE* ˈɡɑːd-/ *noun* (**the Godhead**) [sing.] (*formal*) used in the Christian religion to mean God, including the Father, Son and HOLY SPIRIT

god·less /ˈgɒdləs; *AmE* ˈɡɑːd-/ *adj.* [usually before noun] not believing in or respecting God; wicked: *a godless generation/world* ▶ **god·less·ness** *noun* [U]

god·like /ˈgɒdlaɪk; *AmE* ˈɡɑːd-/ *adj.* like God or a god in some quality: *his godlike beauty/status*

godly /ˈgɒdli; *AmE* ˈɡɑːdli/ *adj.* [usually before noun] (*old-fashioned*) living a moral life based on religious principles: *a godly man/society* ▶ **god·li·ness** *noun* [U]

god·mother /ˈgɒdmʌðə(r); *AmE* ˈɡɑːd-/ *noun* a female GODPARENT—see also FAIRY GODMOTHER

god·par·ent /ˈgɒdpeərənt; *AmE* ˈɡɑːdperənt/ *noun* a person who promises at a Christian BAPTISM ceremony to be responsible for a child (= his or her GODCHILD) and to teach them about the Christian religion

god·send /ˈgɒdsend; *AmE* ˈɡɑːd-/ *noun* [sing.] **~ (for sb/ sth) | ~ (to sb/sth)** something good that happens unexpectedly and helps sb/sth when they need help: *This new benefit has come as a godsend for low-income families.*

god·son /ˈgɒdsʌn; *AmE* ˈɡɑːd-/ *noun* a male GODCHILD

goer /ˈɡəʊə(r); *AmE* ˈɡoʊər/ *noun* **1** (**-goer**) (in compounds)

a person who regularly goes to the place or event mentioned: *a cinema-goer* ◇ *a moviegoer* **2** (*BrE, informal*) a woman who enjoys having sex frequently, especially with different men

gofer /ˈɡəʊfə(r); *AmE* ˈɡoʊ-/ *noun* (*informal*) a person whose job is to do small boring tasks for other people in a company **SYN** DOGSBODY: *They call me the gofer—go for this, go for that ...*

go-getter *noun* (*informal*) a person who is determined to succeed, especially in business

gog·gle /ˈgɒgl; *AmE* ˈɡɑːgl/ *verb* [V] **~ (at sb/sth)** (*old-fashioned, informal*) to look at sb/sth with your eyes wide open, especially because you are surprised or shocked

goggle-'eyed *adj.* with your eyes wide open, staring at sth, especially because you are surprised

gog·gles /ˈgɒglz; *AmE* ˈɡɑːglz/ *noun* [pl.] a pair of glasses that fit closely to the face to protect the eyes from wind, dust, water, etc: *a pair of swimming/ski/safety goggles*—picture at SKIING

go-go *adj.* **1** connected with a style of dancing to pop music in which girls dance wearing very few clothes: *a go-go dancer/club* **2** (*AmE, informal*) of a period of time when businesses are growing and people are making money fast: *the go-go years of the 1980s*

going /ˈɡəʊɪŋ; *AmE* ˈɡoʊɪŋ/ *noun, adj.*

▪ *noun* **1** [sing.] (*formal*) an act of leaving a place: *We were all sad at her going.* **2** [U] (used with an adjective) the speed with which sb does sth; how difficult it is to do sth: *Walking four miles in an hour is pretty good going for me.* ◇ *She had her own company by 25—not bad going!* ◇ *It was hard going getting up at five every morning.* **3** [U] the condition of the ground, especially in horse racing: *The going is good to firm.*—see also OUTGOINGS **IDM when the going gets 'tough (the ,tough get 'going)** (*saying*) when conditions or progress become difficult (strong and determined people work even harder to succeed) **while the ,going is 'good** (*BrE*) (*AmE* **while the ,getting is 'good**) before a situation changes and it is no longer possible to do sth: *Don't you think we should quit while the going is good?*—more at COMING, HEAVY

▪ *adj.* (**-going**) (in compounds) going regularly to the place or event mentioned: *the theatre-going public*—see also OCEAN-GOING, ONGOING, OUTGOING **IDM a ,going con'cern** a business or an activity that is making a profit and is expected to continue to do well: *He sold the cafe as a going concern.* **the ,going 'rate (for sth)** the usual amount of money paid for goods or services at a particular time: *They pay slightly more than the going rate for freelance work.*

going-'over *noun* [sing.] (*informal*) **1** a thorough examination of sb/sth: *The garage gave the car a thorough going-over.* **2** a serious physical attack on sb: *The gang gave him a real going-over.*

goings-'on *noun* [pl.] (*informal*) activities or events that are strange, surprising or dishonest: *There were some strange goings-on next door last night.*

goitre (*BrE*) (*AmE* **goi·ter**) /ˈɡɔɪtə(r)/ *noun* [U, C] a swelling of the throat caused by a disease of the THYROID GLAND

go-kart (*BrE*) (also **go-cart** *AmE, BrE*) /ˈɡəʊ kɑːt; *AmE* ˈɡoʊ kɑːrt/ *noun* a vehicle like a small low car with no roof or doors, used for racing

gold /ɡəʊld; *AmE* ɡoʊld/ *noun, adj.*

▪ *noun* **1** [U] (*symb* Au) a chemical element. Gold is a yellow precious metal used for making coins, jewellery, ornaments, etc: *a gold bracelet/ring/watch* ◇ *18-carat gold* ◇ *the country's gold reserves* ◇ *made of solid/pure gold* **2** [U] money, jewellery, etc. that is made of gold: *His wife was dripping with* (= wearing a lot of) *gold.* **3** [U, C] the colour of gold: *I love the reds and golds of autumn.* **4** [U, C] = GOLD MEDAL: *The team took its first Olympic gold.* ◇ *He won three golds and a bronze.* **IDM a crock/pot of 'gold** a large prize or reward that sb hopes for but is unlikely to get **(as) good as 'gold** (*informal*) behaving in a way that other people approve of: *The kids have been as good as gold all day.*—more at HEART, STREET, STRIKE *v.*, WORTH *adj.*

s	t	v	z	ʃ	ʒ	tʃ	dʒ	θ	ð	ŋ
see	tea	van	zoo	shoe	vision	chain	jam	thin	this	sing

■ *adj.* [only before noun] bright yellow in colour, like gold: *The company name was spelled out in gold letters.*

'gold card *noun* a type of CREDIT CARD that enables a person to buy more goods and services than a normal card does

'gold-digger *noun* (*informal, disapproving*) a woman who uses the fact that she is attractive to get money from men

'gold dust *noun* [U] gold in the form of powder IDM **like 'gold dust** (*BrE*) difficult to find or obtain: *Tickets for the final are like gold dust.*

gold·en /'gəʊldən; *AmE* 'goʊldən/ *adj.* **1** (especially *literary*) made of gold: *a golden crown* **2** bright yellow in colour like gold: *golden hair* ◇ *miles of golden beaches* **3** special; wonderful: *golden memories* ◇ *Businesses have a golden opportunity to expand into new markets.* ◇ *Hollywood's golden boy* IDM see KILL *v.*, MEAN *n.*, SILENCE *n.*

,golden 'age *noun* [usually sing.] ~ (of sth) a period during which sth is very successful, especially in the past: *the golden age of cinema*

,golden anni'versary *noun* (*AmE*) = GOLDEN JUBILEE, GOLDEN WEDDING

,golden 'eagle *noun* a large BIRD OF PREY (= a bird that kills other creatures for food) of the EAGLE family, with brownish feathers, that lives in northern parts of the world—picture on page A6

,golden 'handshake *noun* a large sum of money that is given to sb when they leave their job, or to persuade them to leave their job

,golden 'jubilee (*BrE*) (*AmE* **,golden anni'versary**) *noun* the 50th anniversary of an important event: *Queen Victoria's Golden Jubilee celebrations* ◇ *a party to mark the company's golden jubilee*—compare DIAMOND JUBILEE, SILVER JUBILEE

,golden 'oldie *noun* (*informal*) **1** a song or film/movie that is quite old but still well known and popular **2** a person who is no longer young but still successful in their particular career, sport, etc.

,golden 'parachute *noun* (*informal*) part of an employment contract in which a business person is promised a large amount of money if they have to leave their job

,golden 'raisin *noun* (*AmE*) = SULTANA

,golden re'triever *noun* a large dog with thick yellow hair

,golden 'rule *noun* [usually sing.] an important principle that should be followed when doing sth in order to be successful: *The golden rule in tennis is to keep your eye on the ball.*

,golden 'syrup (also **trea·cle**) (both *BrE*) *noun* [U] a very sweet thick yellow liquid made from sugar

,golden 'wedding (*BrE*) (*AmE* **,golden anni'versary**) (also **,golden 'wedding anniversary** *AmE, BrE*) *noun* the 50th anniversary of a wedding: *The couple celebrated their golden wedding in January.*—compare DIAMOND WEDDING, RUBY WEDDING, SILVER WEDDING

gold·field /'gəʊldfiːld; *AmE* 'goʊld-/ *noun* an area where gold is found in the ground

gold·finch /'gəʊldfɪntʃ; *AmE* 'goʊld-/ *noun* a small brightly coloured European bird of the FINCH family, with yellow feathers on its wings

gold·fish /'gəʊldfɪʃ; *AmE* 'goʊld-/ *noun* (*pl.* **gold·fish**) a small orange or red fish. Goldfish are kept as pets in bowls or PONDS.

'goldfish bowl *noun* **1** a glass bowl for keeping fish in as pets **2** a situation in which people can see everything that happens and nothing is private: *Living in this goldfish bowl of publicity would crack the strongest marriage.*

,gold 'leaf (also **,gold 'foil**) *noun* [U] gold that has been made into a very thin sheet and is used for decoration

,gold 'medal *noun* (also **gold** [U,C]) a medal made of gold that is given to the winner of a race or competition: *an Olympic gold medal winner*—compare BRONZE MEDAL, SILVER MEDAL ▶ **,gold 'medallist** (*BrE*) (*AmE* **,gold 'medalist**) *noun*: *an Olympic gold medallist*

'gold mine *noun* **1** a place where gold is dug out of the ground **2** a business or an activity that makes a large profit: *This restaurant is a potential gold mine.*

,gold 'plate *noun* [U] **1** dishes, etc. made of gold **2** a thin layer of gold used to cover another metal; objects made in this way

,gold-'plated *adj.* covered with a thin layer of gold: *gold-plated earrings*

'gold rush *noun* a situation in which a lot of people suddenly go to a place where gold has recently been discovered

gold·smith /'gəʊldsmɪθ; *AmE* 'goʊld-/ *noun* a person who makes, repairs or sells articles made of gold

'gold standard *noun* (usually **the gold standard**) [sing.] an economic system in which the value of money is based on the value of gold: *the ending of the gold standard in 1931*

golf /gɒlf; *AmE* gɑːlf; gɔːlf/ *noun* [U] a game played over a large area of ground using specially shaped sticks to hit a small hard ball into a series of 9 or 18 holes, using as few strokes as possible: *He enjoyed a round of golf on a Sunday morning.* ▶ **golf·ing** *noun* [U]: *a golfing holiday*

'golf club *noun* **1** (also **club**) a long metal stick with a piece of metal or wood at one end, used for hitting the ball in golf: *a set of golf clubs*—picture at GOLF **2** an organization whose members play golf; the place where these people meet and play golf: *Pine Ridge Golf Club* ◇ *We're going for lunch at the golf club.*

'golf course (also **course**) *noun* a large area of land that is designed for playing golf on—picture at GOLF

golf·er /'gɒlfə(r); *AmE* 'gɑːl-; 'gɔːl-/ *noun* a person who plays golf

'golf links (also **links**) *noun* (*pl.* **golf links**) a golf course, especially one by the sea

gol·li·wog /'gɒliwɒg; *AmE* 'gɑːliwɑːg/ (also *informal* **golly** /'gɒli; *AmE* 'gɑːli/ *pl.* **-ies**) *noun* a DOLL (= a model of a person for a child to play with) made of cloth with a black face and short black hair

golly /'gɒli; *AmE* 'gɑːli/ *exclamation* (*old-fashioned, informal*) used to express surprise: *Golly, you're early!*

gonad /'gəʊnæd; *AmE* 'goʊ-/ *noun* (*anatomy*) a male sex organ that produces SPERM; a female sex organ that produces eggs

gon·dola /'gɒndələ; *AmE* 'gɑːn-; gɑːn'doʊlə/ *noun* **1** a long boat with a flat bottom and high parts at each end, used on canals in Venice **2** the part on a CABLE CAR or SKI LIFT where the passengers sit **3** (*especially AmE*) the part of a hot air BALLOON or AIRSHIP where the passengers sit

gon·do·lier /ˌgɒndə'lɪə(r); *AmE* ˌgɑːndə'lɪr/ *noun* a person whose job is to move and steer a gondola in Venice

gone /gɒn; *AmE* gɔːn; gɑːn/ *adj., prep.*—see also GO, GOES, WENT, GONE *v.*

G

æ	ɑː	e	ɜː	ə	ɪ	iː	i	ɒ	ɔː	ʌ	ʊ	u	uː
cat	father	ten	bird	about	sit	see	many	got	saw	cup	put	actual	too
								(BrE)					

- *adj.* [not before noun] **1** (of a thing) used up: *'Where's the coffee?' 'It's all gone.'* **2** (of a person) having left a place; away from a place: *'Is Tom here?' 'No, he was gone before I arrived'.* **3** (*formal*) used to say that a particular situation no longer exists: *The days are gone when you could leave your door unlocked at night.* **4** (*BrE, informal*) having been pregnant for the length of time mentioned: *She's seven months gone.* ◊ *How far gone are you?* **IDM** ,going, ,going, 'gone (*BrE*) (also going 'once, going 'twice, 'sold *AmE, BrE*) said by an AUCTIONEER to show that an item has been sold—more at DEAD *adj.*
- *prep.* (*BrE, informal*) later than the time mentioned: *It's gone six o'clock already.*

goner /'ɡɒnə(r); *AmE* 'ɡɔ:n-; 'ɡɑ:n-/ *noun* (*informal*) a person who is going to die soon or who cannot be saved from a dangerous situation

gong /ɡɒŋ; *AmE* ɡɔ:ŋ; ɡɑ:ŋ/ *noun* **1** a round piece of metal that hangs in a frame and makes a loud deep sound when it is hit with a stick. Gongs are used as musical instruments or to give signals, for example that a meal is ready. **2** (*BrE, informal*) an award or medal given to sb for the work they have done

gonna /'ɡənə; 'ɡɒnə; *AmE* 'ɡɔ:nə/ (*informal, non-standard*) a way of saying or writing 'going to' in informal speech, when it refers to the future: *What's she gonna do now?* **HELP** You should not write this form unless you are copying somebody's speech.

go·nor·rhoea (*BrE*) (*AmE* **go·nor·rhea**) /,ɡɒnə'rɪə; *AmE* ,ɡɑ:nə'ri:ə/ *noun* [U] a disease of the sexual organs, caught by having sex with an infected person—see also VENEREAL DISEASE

gonzo journalism /'ɡɒnzəʊ dʒɜ:nəlɪzəm; *AmE* 'ɡɑ:nzoʊ dʒɜ:rn-/ *noun* [U] (*AmE, informal*) reporting in newspapers that tries to shock or excite readers rather than to give true information

goo /ɡu:/ *noun* [U] (*informal*) any unpleasant sticky wet substance—see also GOOEY

VOCABULARY BUILDING
good and **very good**

Instead of saying that something is **good** or **very good**, try to use more precise and interesting adjectives to describe things:
  delicious/tasty food
  an **exciting/entertaining/absorbing** movie
  an **absorbing/a fascinating/an informative** book
  a **pleasant/an enjoyable/a fun** (*informal*) trip
  a **skilful/talented/fine** player
  impressive/high-quality acting
  useful/helpful advice

In conversation you can use words like **great**, **super**, **wonderful**, **lovely** and **excellent** (especially in *BrE*): *That's a super idea!*

⇨ note at NICE

---

good /ɡʊd/ *adj., noun, adv.*

- *adj.* (**bet·ter** /'betə(r)/ **best** /best/)

HIGH QUALITY **1** of high quality or an acceptable standard: *a good book* ◊ *good food* ◊ *The piano was in good condition.* ◊ *Your work is just not good enough.* ◊ *The results were pretty good.* ◊ *Sorry, my English is not very good.* ◊ *This is as good a place as any to spend the night.* ◊ *You'll never marry her—she's much too good for you.*

PLEASANT **2** pleasant; that you enjoy or want: *Did you have a good time in London?* ◊ *It's good to see you again.* ◊ *This is very good news.* ◊ *Let's hope we have good weather tomorrow.* ◊ *We are still friends, though, which is good.* ◊ *It's a good thing* (= it's lucky) *you're not a vegetarian.*

SENSIBLE/STRONG **3** sensible, logical or strongly supporting what is being discussed: *Thank you, good question.* ◊ *Yes, that's a good point.* ◊ *I have good reason to be suspicious.* ◊ *What a good idea!*

FAVOURABLE **4** showing or getting approval or respect: *The play had good reviews.* ◊ *The hotel has a good reputation.*

SKILFUL **5** ~ (**at sth/at doing sth**) able to do sth well: *to be a good actor/cook* ◊ *to be good at languages/your job* ◊ *Nick has always been good at finding cheap flights.* **6** ~ **with sth/sb** able to use sth or deal with people well: *She's good with her hands* (= able to make things, etc.). ◊ *He's very good with children.*

MORALLY RIGHT **7** morally right; behaving in a way that is morally right: *She has tried to lead a good life.* ◊ *a good deed* ◊ *Giving her that money was a good thing to do.* ◊ *He is a very good man.*

FOLLOWING RULES **8** following strictly a set of rules or principles: *It is good practice to supply a written report to the buyer.* ◊ *She was a good Catholic girl.*

KIND **9** ~ (**to sb**)| ~ (**of sb**) (**to do sth**) willing to help; showing kindness to other people: *He was very good to me when I was ill.* ◊ *It was very good of you to come.* ◊ *I had to take a week off work but my colleagues were very good about it.*

CHILD **10** behaving well or politely: *You can stay up late if you're good.* ◊ *Get dressed now, there's a good girl.*

HEALTHY **11** healthy or strong: *Can you speak into my good ear?* ◊ *I don't feel too good today.*

USEFUL/HELPFUL **12** ~ (**for sb/sth**) having a useful or helpful effect on sb/sth: *Too much sun isn't good for you.* ◊ *It's probably good for you to get some criticism now and then.* ◊ (*spoken*) *Shut your mouth, if you know what's good for you* (= used as a threat). **13** **no ~ doing sth**| **no ~ to sb** not having a useful or helpful effect: *It's no good complaining—they never listen.* ◊ *This book is no good to me: I need the new edition.*

SUITABLE **14** ~ (**for sth/to do sth**)| ~ (**for sb**) suitable or appropriate: *Now is a good time to buy a house.* ◊ *She would be good for the job.* ◊ *Can we change our meeting—Monday isn't good* (= convenient) *for me.*

SHOWING APPROVAL **15** (*spoken*) used to show that you approve of or are pleased about sth that has been said or done, or to show that you want to move on to a new topic of conversation: *'Dinner's ready.' 'Good—I'm starving.'* ◊ *'I got the job.' 'Oh, good.'* ◊ *Good, I think we've come to a decision.* **16** [only before noun] (*spoken*) used as a form of praise: *Good old Jack!* ◊ *'I've ordered some drinks.' 'Good man!'*

IN EXCLAMATIONS **17** (*spoken*) used in exclamations: *Good heavens!* ◊ *Good God!*

LARGE **18** [only before noun] great in number, amount or degree: *a good many people* ◊ *The kitchen is a good size.* ◊ *We spent a good while* (= quite a long time) *looking for the house.* ◊ *He devoted a good deal of* (= a lot of) *attention to the problem.* ◊ *There's a good chance* (= it is likely) *that I won't be here next year.*

AT LEAST **19** not less than; rather more than: *We waited for a good hour.* ◊ *It's a good three miles to the station.*

THOROUGH **20** [only before noun] thorough; complete: *We had a good laugh about it afterwards.* ◊ *You'll feel better after a good sleep.*

AMUSING **21** [usually before noun] amusing: *a good story/joke* ◊ (*spoken*) *That's a good one!*

FOR PARTICULAR TIME/DISTANCE **22** ~ **for sth** having enough energy, health, strength, etc. to last for a particular length of time or distance: *You're good for* (= you will live) *a few years yet.* **23** ~ **for sth** valid for sth: *The ticket is good for three months.*

LIKELY TO PROVIDE **24** ~ **for sth** likely to provide sth: *He's always good for a laugh.* ◊ *Bobby should be good for a few drinks.*

IDM Most idioms containing **good** are at the entries for the nouns and verbs in the idioms, for example **(as) good as gold** is at **gold**. **as 'good as** very nearly: *The matter is as good as settled.* ◊ *He as good as called me a coward* (= suggested that I was a coward without actually using the word 'coward'). **as ,good as it 'gets** used when you are saying that a situation is not going to get any better **good and ...** (*informal*) completely: *I won't go until I'm good and ready.* **a good 'few** several: *There are still a good few empty seats.* **,good for 'you, 'sb, 'them, etc.** (especially *AustralE*) **good 'on you, etc.**) (*informal*) used to praise sb for doing sth well: *'I passed first time.' 'Good for you!'*

---

aɪ	aʊ	eɪ	əʊ	oʊ	ɔɪ	ɪə	eə	ʊə	j	w
my	now	say	go (BrE)	go (AmE)	boy	near	hair	pure	yes	wet

■ *noun*—see also GOODS

MORALLY RIGHT | **1** [U] behaviour that is morally right or acceptable: *the difference between good and evil* ◊ *Is religion always a force for good?* **2** (**the good**) [pl.] people who live a moral life; people who are admired for the work they do to help other people: *a gathering of the great and the good*

STH HELPFUL | **3** [U] something that helps sb/sth: *Cuts have been made for the good of the company.* ◊ *I'm only telling you this for your own good.* ◊ *What's the good of* (= how does it help you) *earning all that money if you don't have time to enjoy it?* ◊ *What good is it redecorating if you're thinking of moving?*—see also DO-GOODER

IDM **all to the 'good** used to say that if sth happens, it will be good, even if it is not exactly what you were expecting: *If these measures also reduce unemployment, that is all to the good.* **be no 'good | not be any/much 'good 1** to not be useful; to have no useful effect: *This gadget isn't much good.* ◊ *It's no good trying to talk me out of leaving.* ◊ *Was his advice ever any good?* **2** to not be interesting or enjoyable: *His latest film isn't much good.* **do 'good | do sb 'good** to have a useful effect; to help sb: *Do you think these latest changes will do any good?* ◊ *Don't you think talking to her would do some good?* ◊ *I'm sure a few days off would do you a power of good* (= improve your health). **for 'good** (*BrE*) also **for ˌgood and 'all**) permanently: *This time she's leaving for good* (= she will never return). **to the 'good** used to say that sb now has a particular amount of money that they did not have before: *We are £500 to the good.* **up to no 'good** (*informal*) doing sth wrong or dishonest: *Those kids are always up to no good.*—more at ILL *adj.*, POWER *n.*, WORLD

■ *adv.* (*especially AmE, informal*) well: *'How's it going?' 'Pretty good.'* ◊ (*non-standard*) *Now, you listen to me good!*

> **WHICH WORD?**
> **good / goodness**
>
> The noun **good** means actions and behaviour that are morally right. You can talk about a person doing **good**: *The charity does a lot of good.* ◊ *the difference between good and evil.*
>
> **Goodness** is the quality of being good. You can talk about a person's **goodness**: *Her goodness shone through.*

good-bye /ˌgʊd'baɪ/ *exclamation, noun* used when you are leaving sb or when sb else is leaving: *She didn't even say goodbye to her mother.* ◊ *We waved them goodbye.* ◊ *We've already said our goodbyes.* ◊ *Kiss me goodbye!* ◊ (*figurative*) *Take out our service contract and say goodbye to costly repair bills.* IDM see KISS *v.*

good 'faith *noun* [U] the intention to be honest and helpful: *a gesture of good faith* ◊ *He acted in good faith.*

'good-for-nothing *noun* (*informal*) a person who is lazy and has no skills: *an idle good-for-nothing* ▶ **'good-for-nothing** *adj.* [usually before noun]: *Where's that good-for-nothing son of yours?*

ˌGood 'Friday *noun* [U, C] the Friday before Easter, the day when Christians remember the Crucifixion of Christ

ˌgood-'hearted *adj.* kind; willing to help other people

ˌgood 'humour (*BrE*) (*AmE* **ˌgood 'humor**) *noun* [U, sing.] a cheerful mood: *Everyone admired her patience and unfailing good humour.* OPP ILL HUMOUR ▶ **ˌgood-'humoured** (*BrE*) (*AmE* **ˌgood-'humored**) *adj.*: *a good-humoured atmosphere* **ˌgood-'humoured·ly** (*BrE*) (*AmE* **ˌgood-'humored·ly**) *adv.*: *to reply good-humouredly*

goodie = GOODY

ˌgood-'looking *adj.* (especially of people) physically attractive: *a good-looking man/couple/face* ◊ *She's strikingly good-looking.*

ˌgood 'looks *noun* [pl.] the physical beauty of a person: *an actor famous for his rugged good looks*

good·ly /'gʊdli/ *adj.* [only before noun] **1** (*old-fashioned, formal*) quite large in size or amount: *a goodly number* **2** (*old use*) physically attractive; of good quality

ˌgood 'name *noun* [sing.] the good opinion that people have of sb/sth: *He told the police he didn't know her, to protect her good name.* ◊ *My election chances are not as important as the good name of the party.*

ˌgood 'nature *noun* [U] the quality of being kind, friendly and patient when dealing with people: *People are always taking advantage of her good nature.*

ˌgood-'natured *adj.* kind, friendly and patient when dealing with people: *a good-natured person/discussion* ▶ **ˌgood-'natured·ly** *adv.*: *to smile good-naturedly*

ˌgood-'neighbourliness *noun* [U] (*BrE*) good relations that exist between people who live in the same area or between countries that are near each other

good·ness /'gʊdnəs/ *noun* [U] **1** (*spoken*) used to express surprise: *Goodness, what a big balloon!* ◊ *My goodness!* ◊ *Goodness me, no!* ◊ *Goodness gracious!* **2** the quality of being good: *the essential goodness of human nature* ◊ *evidence of God's goodness* ◊ (*formal*) *At least have the goodness* (= good manners) *to look at me when I'm talking to you.* ▷ note at GOOD **3** the part of sth that has a useful effect on sb/sth, especially sb's health: *These vegetables have had all the goodness boiled out of them.* IDM **out of the goodness of your 'heart** from feelings of kindness, without thinking about what advantage there will be for you: *You're not telling me he offered to lend you the money out of the goodness of his heart?*—more at GOD, HONEST, KNOW *v.*, THANK

Goodnight = GOOD NIGHT at NIGHT

goods /gʊdz/ *noun* [pl.] **1** things that are produced to be sold: *cheap/expensive goods* ◊ *leather/cotton/paper goods* ◊ *electrical/sports goods* ◊ *perishable/durable goods* ◊ *increased tax on goods and services*—see also CONSUMER GOODS **2** possessions that can be moved: *stolen goods* ◊ *The plastic bag contained all his worldly goods* (= everything he owned). **3** (*BrE*) things (not people) that are transported by rail or road: *a goods train* ◊ *a heavy goods vehicle*—compare FREIGHT IDM **be the 'goods** (*BrE, spoken*) to be very good or impressive **deliver the 'goods | come up with the 'goods** (*informal*) to do what you have promised to do or what people expect or want you to do: *We expected great things of the England team, but on the day they simply failed to deliver the goods.*

ˌgoods and 'chattels *noun* [pl.] (*BrE, especially law*) personal possessions that are not land or buildings

ˌgood 'sense *noun* [U] **~ (to do sth)** the ability to make the right decision about sth; good judgement: *a man of honour and good sense* ◊ *Keeping to a low-fat diet makes very good sense* (= is a sensible thing to do).

'goods train *noun* (*BrE*) = FREIGHT TRAIN

ˌgood-'tempered *adj.* cheerful and not easily made angry

good·will /ˌgʊd'wɪl/ *noun* [U] **1** friendly or helpful feelings towards other people or countries: *a spirit of goodwill in international relations* ◊ *a goodwill gesture/a gesture of goodwill* ◊ *Given goodwill on both sides, I am sure we can reach an agreement.* **2** the good relationship between a business and its customers that is calculated as part of its value when it is sold

goody /'gʊdi/ *noun, exclamation*

■ *noun* (also **goodie**) [usually pl.] (*pl.* **-ies**) (*informal*) **1** a thing that is very nice to eat: *a basket of goodies for the children* **2** anything that is attractive and that people want to have: *Our magazine is giving away lots of free goodies—T-shirts, hats and videos!* **3** a good person, especially in a book or a film/movie: *It's sometimes difficult to tell who are the goodies and who are the baddies.*

■ *exclamation* (becoming *old-fashioned*) a word children use when they are excited or pleased about sth

'goody-goody *noun* (*pl.* **goody-goodies**) (*informal, disapproving*) (used especially by and about children) a person who behaves very well to please people in authority such as parents or teachers

gooey /'guːi/ *adj.* (*informal*) soft and sticky: *a gooey mess* ◊ *gooey cakes*

goof /guːf/ *verb, noun*

G

■ *verb* [V] (*informal, especially AmE*) to make a stupid mistake: *Sorry, guys. I goofed.* **PHRV** ˌgoof aˈround (*informal, especially AmE*) to spend your time doing silly or stupid things **SYN** MESS AROUND ˌgoof ˈoff (*AmE, informal*) to spend your time doing nothing, especially when you should be working

■ *noun* (*informal, especially AmE*) **1** a stupid mistake **2** a silly or stupid person

goofy /ˈguːfi/ *adj.* (*informal, especially AmE*) silly; stupid: *a goofy grin*

googly /ˈguːgli/ *noun* (*pl.* **-ies**) (in cricket) a ball that is BOWLED so that it looks as if it will turn in one direction, but that actually turns the opposite way: (*figurative*) *He bowled the prime minister a googly* (= asked him a difficult question).

goolie (also **gooly**) /ˈguːli/ *noun* [usually pl.] (*pl.* **-ies**) (*BrE, slang*) a rude word for a man's TESTICLE

goon /guːn/ *noun* (*informal*) **1** (*especially AmE*) a criminal who is paid to frighten or injure people **2** (*old-fashioned, especially BrE*) a stupid or silly person

goose /guːs/ *noun, verb*

■ *noun* (*pl.* **geese** /giːs/) **1** [C] a bird like a large duck with a long neck. Geese either live wild or are kept on farms. **2** [U] meat from a goose: *roast goose* **3** [C] a female goose—compare GANDER **4** [C] (*old-fashioned, informal*) a silly person—see also WILD GOOSE CHASE **IDM** see COOK *v.*, KILL *v.*, SAUCE

■ *verb* [VN] (*informal*) **1** to touch or squeeze sb's bottom: *Jack goosed her as she reached for a file.* **2** ~ **sth** (**along/up**) (*AmE*) to make sth move or work faster

goose·berry /ˈguzbəri; *AmE* ˈguːsberi/ *noun* (*pl.* **-ies**) a small green fruit that grows on a prickly bush. Gooseberries taste sour and are usually cooked to make jam, pies, etc: *a gooseberry bush*—picture on page A2 **IDM** **play ˈgooseberry** (*BrE*) to be a third person with two people who have a romantic relationship and want to be alone together

ˈgoose pimples *noun* [pl.] (also *less frequent* **gooseflesh** [U]) (*especially BrE*) (also **ˈgoose bumps**) (*AmE, BrE*) a condition in which there are raised spots on your skin because you feel cold, frightened or excited: *It gave me goose pimples just to think about it.*

ˈgoose-step *noun* [sing.] (often *disapproving*) a way of marching, used by soldiers in some countries, in which the legs are raised high and straight ▶ **ˈgoose-step** *verb* (**-pp-**) [V]

GOP /ˌdʒiː əʊ ˈpiː; *AmE* oʊ/ *abbr.* Grand Old Party (the Republican political party in the US)

go·pher /ˈgəʊfə(r); *AmE* ˈgoʊ-/ (also **ˈground squirrel**) *noun* a N American animal like a rat, that lives in holes in the ground

Gor·dian knot /ˌgɔːdiən ˈnɒt; *AmE* ˌgɔːrdiən ˈnɑːt/ *noun* a very difficult or impossible task or problem: *to cut/untie the Gordian knot* (= to solve a problem with forceful action) **ORIGIN** From the legend in which King Gordius tied a very complicated knot and said that whoever untied it would become the ruler of Asia. Alexander the Great cut through the knot with his sword.

gore /gɔː(r)/ *verb, noun*

■ *verb* [VN] (of an animal) to wound a person or another animal with a horn or TUSK: *He was gored by a bull.*

■ *noun* [U] thick blood that has flowed from a wound, especially in a violent situation: *The movie is not just blood and gore* (= scenes of violence); *it has a thrilling story.*—see also GORY

gorge /gɔːdʒ; *AmE* gɔːrdʒ/ *noun, verb*

■ *noun* [C] a deep narrow valley with steep sides: *the Rhine Gorge*—picture at MOUNTAIN

■ *verb* [VN, V] ~ (**yourself**) (**on sth**) (sometimes *disapproving*) to eat a lot of sth, until you are too full to eat any more

gor·geous /ˈgɔːdʒəs; *AmE* ˈgɔːrdʒəs/ *adj.* **1** (*informal*) very beautiful and attractive; giving pleasure and enjoyment: *a gorgeous girl/man* ◇ *a gorgeous view* ◇ *gorgeous weather* (= warm and with a lot of sun) ◇ *You look gorgeous!* **2** [usually before noun] (of colours, clothes, etc.) with very deep colours; impressive: *exotic birds with feathers of gorgeous colours* ▶ **gor·geous·ly** *adv.*: *gorgeously dressed/decorated*

gor·gon /ˈgɔːgən; *AmE* ˈgɔːrgən/ *noun* **1** (in ancient Greek stories) one of three sisters with snakes on their heads instead of hair, who can change anyone that looks at them into stone **2** an ugly woman who behaves in a fierce and frightening way

gor·illa /gəˈrɪlə/ *noun* a very large powerful African APE (= an animal like a large monkey without a tail) with a black or brown hairy coat

gorm·less /ˈgɔːmləs; *AmE* ˈgɔːrm-/ *adj.* (*BrE, informal*) stupid: *a gormless boy/face* ◇ *Don't just stand there looking gormless—do something!*

gorp /gɔːp; *AmE* gɔːrp/ *noun* [U] (*AmE*) a mixture of nuts, dried fruit, etc. eaten between meals to provide extra energy, especially by people on camping trips, etc.

gorse /gɔːs; *AmE* gɔːrs/ (*BrE* also **furze**) *noun* [U] a bush with thin prickly leaves and small yellow flowers. Gorse often grows on land that is not used or cared for.

gory /ˈgɔːri/ *adj.* **1** (*informal*) involving a lot of blood or violence; showing or describing blood and violence: *a gory accident/operation* ◇ *the gory task of the pathologist* ◇ *a gory movie/book* ◇ (*humorous*) *He insisted on telling us all the gory details about their divorce* (= the unpleasant facts). **2** (*literary*) covered with blood: *a gory figure*

gosh /ɡɒʃ; *AmE* ɡɑːʃ/ *exclamation* (*old-fashioned, informal*) people say '**Gosh!**' when they are surprised or shocked: *Gosh, is that the time?*

gos·ling /ˈgɒzlɪŋ; *AmE* ˈgɑːz-/ *noun* a young GOOSE (= a bird like a large duck)

ˌgo-ˈslow (*BrE*) (*AmE* **slow·down**) *noun* a protest that workers make by doing their work more slowly than usual—compare WORK-TO-RULE

gos·pel /ˈgɒspl; *AmE* ˈgɑːspl/ *noun* **1** [C] (also **Gospel**) one of the four books in the Bible about the life and teaching of Jesus: *the Gospel according to St John* ◇ *St Mark's Gospel* **2** [sing.] (also **the Gospel**) the life and teaching of Jesus as explained in the Bible: *preaching/spreading the gospel* **3** [C, usually sing.] a set of ideas that sb believes in and tries to persuade others to accept: *He preached a gospel of military strength.* **4** (also ˌgospel ˈtruth**) [U] (*informal*) the complete truth: *Is that gospel?* ◇ *Don't take his word as gospel.* **5** (also **ˈgospel music**) [U] a style of religious singing popular among African Americans and other black people: *a gospel choir*

gos·samer /ˈgɒsəmə(r); *AmE* ˈgɑːs-/ *noun* [U] **1** the very fine thread made by spiders **2** (*literary*) any very light delicate material: *a gown of gossamer silk* ◇ *the gossamer wings of a dragonfly*

gos·sip /ˈgɒsɪp; *AmE* ˈgɑːsɪp/ *noun, verb*

■ *noun* **1** [U] (*disapproving*) informal talk or stories about other people's private lives, that may be unkind or not true: *Don't believe all the gossip you hear.* ◇ *Tell me all the latest gossip!* ◇ *The gossip was that he had lost a fortune on the stock exchange.* ◇ *It was common gossip* (= everyone said so) *that they were having an affair.* ◇ *She's a great one for idle gossip* (= she enjoys spreading stories about other people that are probably not true). **2** [C, usually sing.] a conversation about other people and their private lives: *I love a good gossip.* **3** [C] (*disapproving*) a person who enjoys talking about other people's private lives ▶ **gos·sipy** /ˈgɒsɪpi; *AmE* ˈgɑːs-/ *adj.*: *a gossipy letter/neighbour*

■ *verb* [V] to talk about other people's private lives, often in an unkind way: *I can't stand here gossiping all day.* ◇ *She's been gossiping about you.*

ˈgossip column *noun* a piece of writing in a newspaper about social events and the private and personal lives of famous people ▶ **ˈgossip columnist** *noun*: *No photographers or gossip columnists were allowed in.*

got *pt, pp* of GET

gotcha /ˈgɒtʃə; *AmE* ˈgɑːtʃə/ *exclamation* (*non-standard*) the written form of the way some people pronounce 'I've got you', which is not considered to be correct: '*Gotcha!*' *I yelled as I grabbed him by the arm.* (= used when you have caught sb, or have beaten them at sth). ◇ '*Don't let go.*' '*Yeah, gotcha.*' (= Yes, I understand.) **HELP** You

G

should not write this form unless you are copying somebody's speech.

goth /gɒθ; *AmE* gɑːθ/ *noun* **1** [U] a style of rock music, popular in the 1980s, that developed from PUNK music. The words often expressed ideas about the end of the world, death or the devil. **2** [C] a member of a group of people who listen to goth music and wear black clothes and black and white MAKE-UP ▶ **goth** (also **gothic**) *adj.*

Goth·ic /'gɒθɪk; *AmE* 'gɑːθ-/ *adj., noun*
■ *adj.* **1** connected with the Goths (= a Germanic people who fought against the Roman Empire) **2** (*architecture*) built in the style that was popular in Western Europe from the 12th to the 16th centuries, and which has pointed arches and windows and tall thin PILLARS: *a Gothic church* **3** (of a novel, etc.) written in the style popular in the 18th and 19th centuries, which described romantic adventures in mysterious or frightening surroundings **4** (of type and printing) having pointed letters with thick lines and sharp angles. German books used to be printed in this style. **5** connected with goths
■ *noun* [U] **1** the Gothic style of architecture **2** Gothic printing type or printed letters

gotta /'gɒtə; *AmE* 'gɑːtə/ (*informal, non-standard*) the written form of the word some people use to mean 'have got to' or 'have got a', which is not considered to be correct: *He's gotta go.* ◇ *Gotta cigarette?* **HELP** You should not write this form unless you are copying somebody's speech.

got·ten (*AmE*) *pp of* GET

gou·ache /ɡuˈɑːʃ; gwɑːʃ/ *noun* **1** [U] a method of painting using colours that are mixed with water and made thick with a type of glue; the paints used in this method **2** [C] a picture painted using this method

gouge /gaʊdʒ/ *verb, noun*
■ *verb* [VN] **1** ~ **sth (in sth)** to make a hole or cut in sth with a sharp object in a rough or violent way: *The lion's claws had gouged a wound in the horse's side.* ◇ *He had gouged her cheek with a screwdriver.* **2** (*AmE*) to force sb to pay an unfairly high price for sth; to raise prices unfairly: *Price gouging is widespread.* **PHR V** ,**gouge sth↔'out (of sth)** to remove or form sth by digging into a surface: *The man's eyes had been gouged out.* ◇ *Glaciers gouged out valleys from the hills.*
■ *noun* **1** a sharp tool for making hollow areas in wood **2** a deep, narrow hole or cut in a surface

gou·lash /'ɡuːlæʃ/ *noun* [C, U] a hot spicy Hungarian dish of meat that is cooked slowly in liquid with PAPRIKA

gourd /ɡʊəd; ɡɔːd; *AmE* ɡʊrd; ɡɔːrd/ *noun* a type of large fruit, not normally eaten, with hard skin and soft flesh. Gourds are often dried and used as containers.

gour·mand /'ɡʊəmənd; *AmE* 'ɡʊrmɑːnd/ *noun* (often *disapproving*) a person who enjoys eating and eats large amounts of food

gour·met /'ɡʊəmeɪ; *AmE* 'ɡʊrm-/ *noun* a person who knows a lot about good food and wines and who enjoys choosing, eating and drinking them ▶ **gour·met** *adj.* [only before noun]: *gourmet food* (= of high quality and often expensive)

gout /ɡaʊt/ *noun* **1** [U] a disease that causes painful swelling in the joints, especially of the toes, knees and fingers **2** [C] (*literary*) a drop or mass of thick liquid, flame, etc: *gouts of blood*

gov·ern /'ɡʌvn; *AmE* 'ɡʌvərn/ *verb* **1** to legally control a country or its people and be responsible for introducing new laws, organizing public services, etc: [VN] *The country is governed by elected representatives of the people.* ◇ [V] *He accused the opposition party of being unfit to govern.* **2** [VN] [often passive] to control or influence sb/sth or how sth happens, functions, etc: *Prices are very much governed by market demand.* ◇ *All his decisions have been entirely governed by self-interest.* ◇ *We need changes in the law governing school attendance.* **3** [VN] (*grammar*) if a word **governs** another word or phrase, it affects how that word or phrase is formed or used

gov·ern·ance /'ɡʌvənəns; *AmE* -vərn-/ *noun* [U] (*technical*) the activity of governing a country or controlling a company or an organization; the way in which a country is governed or a company or institution is controlled

gov·ern·ess /'ɡʌvənəs; *AmE* -vərn-/ *noun* (especially in the past), a woman employed to teach the children of a rich family in their home and to live with them

gov·ern·ing /'ɡʌvənɪŋ; *AmE* -vərn-/ *adj.* [only before noun] having the right and the authority to control sth such as a country or an institution: *The Conservatives were then the governing party.* ◇ *The school's governing body* (= the group of people who control the organization of the school) *took responsibility for the decision.*

gov·ern·ment /'ɡʌvənmənt; *AmE* -vərn-/ *noun* **1** [C+sing./pl. *v.*] (often **the Government**) (*abbr.* **govt**) the group of people who are responsible for controlling a country or a state: *to lead/form a government* ◇ *the last Conservative government* ◇ *the government of the day* ◇ *Foreign governments have been consulted about this decision.* ◇ *She has resigned from the Government.* ◇ *The Government has/have been considering further tax cuts.* ◇ *government policies/officials/ministers* ◇ *a government department/agency/grant* ◇ *government expenditure/intervention* ◇ *government-controlled industries* **2** [U] a particular system or method of controlling a country: *coalition/communist/totalitarian government* ◇ *Democratic government has now replaced military rule.* ◇ *central/federal government* **3** [U] the activity or the manner of controlling a country: *corrupt/strong government* ◇ *The Democrats are now in government in the US.*

gov·ern·men·tal /,ɡʌvn'mentl; *AmE* ,ɡʌvərn-/ *adj.* connected with government; of a government: *governmental agencies* ◇ *governmental actions*

gov·ern·or /'ɡʌvənə(r); *AmE* -vərn-/ *noun* **1** (also **Governor**) a person who is the official head of a country or region that is politically controlled by another country: *the former governor of the colony* ◇ *a provincial governor* **2** (also **Governor**) a person who is chosen to be in charge of the government of a state in the US: *the governor of Arizona* ◇ *the Arizona governor* ◇ *Governor Tom Kean* **3** (*especially BrE*) a member of a group of people who are responsible for controlling an institution such as a school, a college or a hospital: *a school governor* ◇ *the board of governors of the college* **4** (*BrE*) a person who is in charge of an institution: *a prison governor* ◇ *the governor of the Bank of England* ◇ (*spoken*) *I can't decide. I'll have to ask the governor* (= the man in charge, who employs sb).—see also GUV'NOR

,**Governor-'General** *noun* (*pl.* **Governors-General** or **Governor-Generals**) the official representative in a country of the country that has or had political control over it, especially the representative of the British King or Queen in a Commonwealth country

govt (also **govt.** especially in *AmE*) *abbr.* (in writing) government

gown /ɡaʊn/ *noun* **1** a woman's dress, especially a long one for special occasions: *an evening/wedding gown* **2** a long loose piece of clothing that is worn over other clothes by judges and (in Britain) by other lawyers, and by members of universities (at special ceremonies): *a graduation gown* **3** a piece of clothing that is worn over other clothes to protect them, especially in a hospital: *a surgeon's gown*—see also DRESSING GOWN

gowned /ɡaʊnd/ *adj.* wearing a gown

GP /,dʒiː 'piː/ *noun* (*BrE*) a doctor who is trained in general medicine and who works in the local community, not in a hospital. (abbreviation for 'general practitioner'): *Go and see your GP as soon as possible.* ◇ *There are four GPs in our local practice.*

GPA /,dʒiː piː 'eɪ/ *noun* (*AmE*) the abbreviation for GRADE POINT AVERAGE: *He graduated with a GPA of 3·8.*

Gp Capt *abbr.* GROUP CAPTAIN

grab /ɡræb/ *verb, noun*
■ *verb* (-bb-) **1** ~ **sth (from sb/sth)** to take or hold sb/sth with your hand suddenly, firmly or roughly SEIZE: [VN] *She grabbed the child's hand and ran.* ◇ *He grabbed hold of me and wouldn't let go.* ◇ *Jim grabbed a cake from the plate.* ◇ [V] *Don't grab—there's plenty for everyone.* **2** [V] ~ **at/for sth** to try to take hold of sth: *She grabbed at the*

G

æ	ɑː	e	ɜː	ə	ɪ	iː	i	ɒ	ɔː	ʌ	ʊ	u	uː
cat	father	ten	bird	about	sit	see	many	got	saw	cup	put	actual	too
								(BrE)					

branch, missed and fell. ◊ Kate grabbed for the robber's gun. **3 ~ (at sth)** to take advantage of an opportunity to do or have sth SYN SEIZE: [VN] This was my big chance and I grabbed it with both hands. ◊ [V] He'll grab at any excuse to avoid doing the dishes. **4** [VN] to have or take sth quickly, especially because you are in a hurry: Let's grab a sandwich before we go. ◊ I managed to grab a couple of hours' sleep on the plane. ◊ Grab a seat, I won't keep you a moment. **5** [VN] to take sth for yourself, especially in a selfish or GREEDY way: By the time we arrived, someone had grabbed all the good seats. ◊ She's always trying to grab the limelight. **6** [VN] to get sb's attention: I'll see if I can grab the waitress and get the bill. ◊ Glasgow's drugs problem has **grabbed the headlines tonight** (= been published as an important story in the newspapers). IDM **how does … grab you?** (spoken) used to ask sb whether they are interested in sth or in doing sth: How does the idea of a trip to Rome grab you?
■ noun [usually sing.] **~ (at/for sb/sth)** a sudden attempt to take or hold sb/sth: He made a grab for her bag.—see also SMASH-AND-GRAB IDM **up for 'grabs** (informal) available for anyone who is interested: There are £25000 worth of prizes up for grabs in our competition!

'grab bag noun (AmE) **1** = LUCKY DIP **2** (informal) a mixed collection of things: He offered a grab bag of reasons for his decision.

grace /greɪs/ noun, verb
■ noun
OF MOVEMENT | **1** [U] an attractive quality of movement that is smooth, elegant and controlled: She moves with the natural grace of a ballerina.
BEHAVIOUR | **2** [U] a quality of behaviour that is polite and pleasant and deserves respect: He conducted himself with grace and dignity throughout the trial. **3 (graces)** [pl.] (especially BrE) ways of behaving that people think are polite and acceptable: He was not particularly well versed in the social graces.
EXTRA TIME | **4** [U] extra time that is given to sb to enable them to pay a bill, finish a piece of work, etc: They've given me a month's grace to get the money.
OF GOD | **5** [U] the kindness that God shows towards the human race: the power of divine grace ◊ It was only by the grace of God that they survived.
PRAYER | **6** [U, C] a short prayer that is usually said before a meal to thank God for the food: Let's say grace.
TITLE | **7 (His/Her/Your Grace)** [C] used as a title of respect when talking to or about an ARCHBISHOP, a DUKE or a DUCHESS: Good Morning, Your Grace. ◊ Their Graces the Duke and Duchess of Kent.
—see also COUP DE GRÂCE, SAVING GRACE
IDM **be in sb's good 'graces** (formal) to have sb's approval and be liked by them ,**fall from 'grace** to lose the trust or respect that people have for you, especially by doing sth wrong or immoral **sb's ,fall from 'grace** a situation in which sb loses the trust or respect that people have for them, especially because of sth wrong or immoral that they have done **have the (good) grace to do sth** to be polite enough to do sth, especially when you have done sth wrong: He didn't even have the grace to look embarrassed. ,**there but for the grace of 'God (go 'I)** (saying) used to say that you could easily have been in the same difficult or unpleasant situation that sb else is in **with (a) bad 'grace** in an unwilling and/or rude way: He handed over the money with typical bad grace. **with (a) good 'grace** in a willing and pleasant way: You must learn to accept defeat with good grace.—more at AIR n., STATE n., YEAR
■ verb [VN] (formal) **1** to make sth more attractive; to decorate sth: The table had once graced a duke's drawing room. **2 ~ sb/sth (with sth)** (usually ironic) to bring honour to sb/sth; to be kind enough to attend or take part in sth: She is one of the finest players ever to have graced the game. ◊ Will you be gracing us with your presence tonight?

grace·ful /'greɪsfl/ adj. **1** moving in a controlled, attractive way or having a smooth, attractive form: The dancers were all tall and graceful. ◊ He gave a graceful bow to the

audience. ◊ the graceful curves of the hills **2** polite and kind in your behaviour, especially in a difficult situation: His father had always taught him to be graceful in defeat. ▶ **grace·ful·ly** /-fəli/ adv.: The cathedral's white towers climb gracefully into the sky. ◊ I think we should just **give in gracefully**.

grace·less /'greɪsləs/ adj. **1** not knowing how to be polite and pleasant to other people: a graceless, angry young man **2** not pleasing or attractive to look at: the graceless architecture of the 1960s **3** moving in an awkward way: She swam with a graceless stroke. ▶ **grace·ly** adv.

gra·cious /'greɪʃəs/ adj. **1** (of people or behaviour) kind, polite and generous, especially to sb of a lower social position: a gracious lady/hostess ◊ a gracious smile ◊ Lady Caroline was gracious enough to accept our invitation. ◊ He has not yet learned how to be gracious in defeat. **2** [usually before noun] showing the comfort and easy way of life that wealth can bring: gracious living **3** [only before noun] (BrE, formal) used as a very polite word for royal people or their actions: her gracious Majesty the Queen **4 ~ (to sb)** (of God) showing kindness and MERCY: a gracious act of God **5** (becoming old-fashioned) used for expressing surprise: Goodness gracious! ◊ 'I hope you didn't mind my phoning you.' 'Good gracious, no, of course not.' ▶ **gra·cious·ly** adv.: She graciously accepted our invitation. **gra·cious·ness** noun [U]

grad /græd/ noun (especially AmE) = GRADUATE

grad·ation /grə'deɪʃn/ noun **1** [C, U] (formal) any of the small changes or levels which sth is divided into; the process or result of sth changing gradually: gradations of colour ◊ gradation in size **2** (also **gradu·ation**) [C] a mark showing a division on a scale: the gradations on a thermometer

grade /greɪd/ noun, verb
■ noun **1** the quality of a particular product or material: All the materials used were of the highest grade. **2** a level of ability or rank that sb has in an organization: salary grades (= levels of pay) ◊ She's still only on a secretarial grade. **3** a mark given in an exam or for a piece of school work: (BrE) She got good grades in her exams. ◊ (AmE) She got good grades on her exams. ◊ 70% of pupils got Grade C or above. **4** (in the US school system) one of the levels in a school with children of similar age: Sam is in (the) second grade. **5** (technical) how serious an illness is: low/high grade fever **6** (especially AmE) = GRADIENT **7** (BrE) a level of exam in musical skill IDM **make the 'grade** (informal) to reach the necessary standard; to succeed: About 10% of trainees fail to make the grade.
■ verb **1 ~ sth/sb (by/according to sth)| ~ sth (as sth)** [often passive] to arrange people or things in groups according to their ability, quality, size, etc: [VN] The containers are graded according to size. ◊ Eggs are graded from small to extra large ◊ Ten beaches were graded as acceptable. ◊ Responses were graded from 1 (very satisfied) to 5 (not at all satisfied). [also VN-ADJ] **2** (especially AmE) to give a mark/grade to a student or to a piece of their written work: [VN] I spent all weekend grading papers. ◊ [VN-N] The best students are graded A.—compare MARK

'grade point average noun [usually sing.] (abbr. GPA) the average of a student's marks/grades over a period of time in the American education system

grader /'greɪdə(r)/ noun (AmE) **1** first, second, etc. **~ a** student who is in the grade mentioned: The play is open to all seventh and eighth graders. **2** = MARKER (4)

'grade school noun (informal) = ELEMENTARY SCHOOL

gra·di·ent /'greɪdiənt/ noun **1** (also **grade** especially in AmE) the degree to which the ground slopes, especially on a road or railway: a steep gradient ◊ a hill with a gradient of 1 in 4 (or 25%) **2** (technical) the rate at which temperature, pressure, etc. changes, or increases and decreases, between one region and another

grad·ing /'greɪdɪŋ/ noun [U] (AmE) = MARKING (3)

grad·ual /'grædʒuəl/ adj. **1** happening slowly over a long period; not sudden: a gradual change in the climate ◊ Recovery from the disease is very gradual. **2** (of a slope) not steep

aɪ	aʊ	eɪ	əʊ	oʊ	ɔɪ	ɪə	eə	ʊə	j	w
my	now	say	go	go	boy	near	hair	pure	yes	wet
			(BrE)	(AmE)						

G

grad·ual·ism /ˈɡrædʒuəlɪzəm/ *noun* [U] a policy of gradual change in society rather than sudden change or revolution ▶ **grad·ual·ist** *noun*

grad·ual·ly /ˈɡrædʒuəli/ *adv.* slowly, over a long period of time: *The weather gradually improved.* ◊ *Gradually, the children began to understand.*

gradu·ate *noun, verb*
▪ *noun* /ˈɡrædʒuət/ (also *informal* **grad** especially in *AmE*) **1** ~ (**in sth**) a person who has a university degree: *a graduate in history* ◊ *a science graduate* ◊ *a graduate of Yale/a Yale graduate* ◊ *a graduate student/course* **2** (*AmE*) a person who has completed their school studies: *a high-school graduate* ⇨ note at STUDENT
▪ *verb* /ˈɡrædʒueɪt/ **1** [V] ~ (**in sth**)| ~ (**from…**) to get a degree, especially your first degree, from a university or college: *Only thirty students graduated in Chinese last year.* ◊ *She graduated from Harvard this year.* ◊ *He graduated from York with a degree in Psychology.* **2** [V] ~ (**from…**) (*AmE*) to complete a course in education, especially at HIGH SCHOOL: *Martha graduated from high school two years ago.* **3** [VN] ~ **sb** (**from sth**) (*AmE*) to give a degree, DIPLOMA, etc. to sb: *The college graduated 50 students last year.* **4** [V] ~ (**from sth**) **to sth** to start doing sth more difficult or important than what you were doing before: *She recently graduated from being a dancer to having a small role in a movie.*

gradu·ated /ˈɡrædʒueɪtɪd/ *adj.* **1** divided into groups or levels on a scale: *graduated lessons/tests* **2** (of a container or measure) marked with lines to show measurements: *a graduated jar*

ˈgraduate school (also *informal* **ˈgrad school**) (both *AmE*) *noun* a part of a college or university where you can study for a second or further degree

gradu·ation /ˌɡrædʒuˈeɪʃn/ *noun* **1** [U] the act of successfully completing a university degree, or studies at an American HIGH SCHOOL: *It was my first job after graduation.* **2** [U,C] a ceremony at which degrees, etc. are officially given out: *graduation day* ◊ *My whole family came to my graduation.* **3** [C] = GRADATION: *The graduations are marked on the side of the flask.*

graf·fiti /ɡrəˈfiːti/ *noun* [U, pl.] drawings or writing on a wall, etc. in a public place. They are usually rude, humorous or political: *The subway was covered in graffiti.*

graft /ɡrɑːft; *AmE* ɡræft/ *noun, verb*
▪ *noun* **1** [C] a piece cut from a living plant and fixed in a cut made in another plant, so that it grows there; the process or result of doing this **2** [C] a piece of skin, bone, etc. removed from a living body and placed in another part of the body which has been damaged; the process or result of doing this: *a skin graft* **3** [U] (*BrE, informal*) hard work: *Their success was the result of years of hard graft.* **4** (*especially AmE*) the use of illegal or unfair methods, especially BRIBERY, to gain advantage in business, politics, etc.; money obtained in this way
▪ *verb* **1** [VN] ~ **sth** (**onto/to/into sth**)| ~ **sth** (**on**) (**from sth**) to take a piece of skin, bone, etc. from one part of the body and attach it to a damaged part: *newly grafted tissue* ◊ *New skin had to be grafted on from his back.* **2** [VN] ~ **sth** (**onto sth**) to cut a piece from a living plant and attach it to another plant **3** [VN] ~ **sth** (**onto sth**) to make one idea, system, etc. become part of another one: *Old values are being grafted onto a new social class.* **4** [V] (*BrE, informal*) to work hard: *She's been grafting all day.*

grail /ɡreɪl/ (also **the ˌHoly ˈGrail**) *noun* **1** [sing.] the cup or bowl believed to have been used by Jesus Christ before he died, that became a holy thing that people wanted to find **2** [C] a thing that you try very hard to find or achieve, but never will

grain /ɡreɪn/ *noun* **1** [U,C] the small hard seeds of food plants such as wheat, rice, etc.; a single seed of such a plant: *America's grain exports* ◊ *a few grains of rice*—see also WHOLEGRAIN—picture at CEREAL **2** [C] a small hard piece of particular substances: *a grain of salt/sand/sugar* **3** [C] (used especially in negative sentences) a very small amount: *There isn't a grain of truth in those rumours.* **4** [C] the smallest unit of weight, equal to 0.00143 of a pound or 0.0648 of a GRAM, used for example

for weighing medicines **5** [U] the natural direction of lines in wood, fabric, etc. or of layers of rock; the pattern of lines that you can see: *to cut a piece of wood along/across the grain* **6** [U,C] how rough or smooth a surface feels: *wood of coarse/fine grain* **IDM** **be/go against the ˈgrain** to be or do sth different from what is normal or natural: *It really goes against the grain to have to work on a Sunday.*

grained /ɡreɪnd/ *adj.* (of wood, stone, etc.) **1** having noticeable lines or a pattern on the surface **2** (**-grained**) having a TEXTURE of the type mentioned: *fine-grained stone* ◊ (*figurative*) *coarse-grained information* (= lacking detail)

grainy /ˈɡreɪni/ *adj.* **1** (especially of photographs) not having completely clear images because they look as if they are made of a lot of small dots and marks: *The film is shot in grainy black and white.* **2** having a rough surface or containing small bits, seeds, etc: *grainy texture*

gram /ɡræm/ *noun* **1** (*BrE* also **gramme**) (*abbr.* **g, gm**) a unit for measuring weight. There are 1000 grams in one kilogram. **2** (**-gram**) a thing that is written or drawn: *telegram* ◊ *hologram*

gram·mar /ˈɡræmə(r)/ *noun* **1** [U] the rules in a language for changing the form of words and joining them into sentences: *the basic rules of grammar* ◊ *English grammar* **2** [U] a person's knowledge and use of a language: *His grammar is appalling.* ◊ *bad grammar* **3** [C] a book containing a description of the rules of a language: *a French grammar* **4** [C] (*linguistics*) a particular theory that is intended to explain the rules of a language or of language in general: *a generative grammar*

gram·mar·ian /ɡrəˈmeəriən; *AmE* -ˈmer-/ *noun* a person who is an expert in the study of grammar

ˈgrammar school *noun* **1** (in Britain, especially in the past) a school for young people between the ages of 11 and 18 who are good at academic subjects **2** (*old-fashioned*) = ELEMENTARY SCHOOL

gram·mat·ical /ɡrəˈmætɪkl/ *adj.* **1** connected with the rules of grammar: *a grammatical error* **2** correctly following the rules of grammar: *That sentence is not grammatical.* ▶ **gram·mat·ical·ly** /-kli/ *adv.*: *a grammatically correct sentence*

gramme (*BrE*) = GRAM

gramo·phone /ˈɡræməfəʊn; *AmE* -foʊn/ *noun* (*old-fashioned*) = RECORD PLAYER

gran /ɡræn/ *noun* (*BrE, informal*) grandmother: *Do you want to go to your gran's?* ◊ *Gran, can I have some more toast?*

Gran·ary™ /ˈɡrænəri/ *adj.* [only before noun] (*BrE*) (of bread) containing whole grains of wheat

gran·ary /ˈɡrænəri/ *noun* (*pl.* **-ies**) a building where grain is stored

grand /ɡrænd/ *adj., noun*
▪ *adj.* (**grand·er, grand·est**) **1** impressive and large or important: *It's not a very grand house.* ◊ *The wedding was a very grand occasion.* **2** (**Grand**) [only before noun] used in the names of impressive or very large buildings, etc: *the Grand Canyon* ◊ *We stayed at the Grand Hotel.* **3** needing a lot of effort, money or time to succeed but intended to achieve impressive results: *a grand design/plan/strategy* ◊ *New Yorkers built their city on a grand scale.* **4** (of people) behaving in a proud way because they are rich or from a high social class **5** (*dialect* or *informal*) very good or enjoyable; excellent: *I had a grand day out at the seaside.* ◊ *Thanks. That'll be grand!* ◊ *Fred did a grand job of painting the house.* **6** (**Grand**) used in the titles of people of very high social rank: *the Grand Duchess Elena*—see also GRANDEUR ▶ **grand·ly** *adv.*: *He described himself grandly as a 'landscape architect'.* **grand·ness** *noun* [U] **IDM** **a/the ˌgrand old ˈage** a great age: *She finally learned to drive at the grand old age of 70.* **a/the ˌgrand old ˈman (of sth)** a man who is respected in a particular profession that he has been involved in for a long time
▪ *noun* **1** (*pl.* **grand**) (*informal*) $1000; £1000: *It'll cost you five grand!* **2** = GRAND PIANO

G

gran·dad (also **grand·dad** especially in *AmE*) /ˈgræn-dæd/ *noun* (*informal*) grandfather

grand·child /ˈgræntʃaɪld/ *noun* (*pl.* **grand·chil·dren**) a child of your son or daughter

grand·daddy (also **gran·daddy**) /ˈgrændædi/ *noun* (*AmE, informal*) **1** = GRANDFATHER **2** (**the granddaddy**) the first or greatest example of sth

grand·daugh·ter /ˈgrændɔːtə(r)/ *noun* a daughter of your son or daughter—compare GRANDSON

,**grand 'duchess** *noun* **1** the wife of a grand duke **2** (in some parts of Europe, especially in the past), a female ruler of a small independent state **3** (in Russia in the past) a daughter of the TSAR

,**grand 'duke** *noun* **1** (in some parts of Europe, especially in the past), a male ruler of a small independent state: *The Grand Duke of Tuscany* **2** (in Russia in the past), a son of the TSAR—compare ARCHDUKE

gran·dee /grænˈdiː/ *noun* **1** (in the past) a Spanish or Portuguese NOBLEMAN of high rank **2** a person of high social rank and importance

grand·eur /ˈgrændʒə(r); -djə(r)/ *noun* [U] **1** the quality of being great and impressive in appearance: *the grandeur and simplicity of Roman architecture* ◊ *The hotel had an air of faded grandeur.* **2** the importance or social status sb has or thinks they have: *He has a sense of grandeur about him.* ◊ *She is clearly suffering from delusions of grandeur* (= thinks she is more important than she really is).—see also GRAND

grand·father /ˈgrænfɑːðə(r)/ *noun* the father of your father or mother—see also GRANDAD, GRANDDADDY, GRANDPA—compare GRANDMOTHER

,**grandfather 'clock** *noun* an old-fashioned type of clock in a tall wooden case that stands on the floor

grandfather clock
weights
pendulum
case

grand·ilo·quent /grænˈdɪləkwənt/ *adj.* (*formal, disapproving*) using long or complicated words in order to impress people [SYN] POMPOUS: *a grandiloquent speaker/speech* ▶ **grand·ilo·quence** /-əns/ *noun* [U]

gran·di·ose /ˈgrændiəʊs; *AmE* -oʊs/ *adj.* (*disapproving*) seeming very impressive but too large, complicated, expensive, etc. to be practical or possible: *The grandiose scheme for a journey across the desert came to nothing.* ◊ *a grandiose opera house*

,**grand 'jury** *noun* (*law*) (in the US) a JURY which has to decide whether there is enough evidence against an accused person for a trial in a court of law

grand·ma /ˈgrænmɑː/ *noun* (*informal*) grandmother

,**grand 'master** *noun* a CHESS player of the highest standard

grand·mother /ˈgrænmʌðə(r)/ *noun* the mother of your father or mother—see also GRAN, GRANDMA, GRANNY—compare GRANDFATHER [IDM] see TEACH

,**grand 'opera** *noun* [U, C] opera in which everything is sung and there are no spoken parts

grand·pa /ˈgrænpɑː/ *noun* (*informal*) grandfather—see also GRANDAD

grand·par·ent /ˈgrænpeərənt; *AmE* -perənt/ *noun* [usually pl.] the father or mother of your father or mother: *The children are staying with their grandparents.*

,**grand 'piano** *noun* a large piano in which the strings are horizontal—compare UPRIGHT PIANO—picture at PIANO

Grand Prix /ˌgrɑː ˈpriː/ *noun* (*pl.* **Grands Prix** /ˌgrɑːˈpriː/) one of a series of important international races for racing cars or motorcycles

,**grand 'slam** *noun* **1** (also **Grand Slam**) a very important sports event, contest, etc: *a Grand Slam tournament/cup/title* **2** the winning of every part of a sports contest or all the main contests in a year for a particular sport: *Will France win the grand slam this year?* (= in rugby) **3** (also **grand ,slam home 'run**) (in baseball) a HOME RUN that is worth four points **4** (in card games, especially BRIDGE) the winning of all the TRICKS in a single game

grand·son /ˈgrænsʌn/ *noun* a son of your son or daughter—compare GRANDDAUGHTER

grand·stand /ˈgrænstænd/ *noun* a large covered structure with rows of seats for people to watch sports events

grand·stand·ing /ˈgrænstændɪŋ/ *noun* [U] (*AmE*) (especially in business, politics, etc.) the fact of behaving or speaking in a way that is intended to make people impressed in order to gain some advantage for yourself

,**grand 'total** *noun* the final total when a number of other totals have been added together: *That makes a grand total of 220 dollars.*

,**grand 'tour** *noun* **1** (often *humorous*) a visit around a building or house in order to show it to sb: *Steve took us on a grand tour of the house and gardens.* **2** (also ,**Grand 'Tour**) a visit to the main cities of Europe made by rich young British or American people as part of their education in the past

grange /greɪndʒ/ *noun* (*BrE*) (often as part of a name) a country house with farm buildings: *Thrushcross Grange*

gran·ite /ˈgrænɪt/ *noun* [U] a type of hard grey stone, often used in building

granny (also *less frequent* **gran·nie**) /ˈgræni/ *noun* (*pl.* -**ies**) (*informal*) grandmother—see also GRANDMA ▶ **granny** (also *less frequent* **gran·nie**) *adj.*: *a pair of granny glasses*

,**granny flat** *noun* (*BrE, informal*) a set of rooms for an old person, especially in a relative's house

gran·ola /grəˈnəʊlə; *AmE* -ˈnoʊ-/ *noun* [U] (*especially AmE*) a type of breakfast CEREAL made of grains, nuts, etc. that have been TOASTED

grant /grɑːnt; *AmE* grænt/ *verb, noun*
■ *verb* **1** [often passive] ~ sth (to sb/sth)| ~ (sb) sth to agree to give sb what they ask for, especially formal or legal permission to do sth: [VN, VNN] *The bank finally granted a £500 loan to me.* ◊ *The bank finally granted me a £500 loan.* ◊ [VN] *My request was granted.* ◊ [VNN] *I was granted permission to visit the palace.* ◊ *She was granted a divorce.* **2** to admit that sth is true, although you may not like or agree with it: [VN] *She's a smart woman, I grant you, but she's no genius.* ◊ [VN (that)] *I grant you (that) it looks good, but it's not exactly practical.* [also V that] [IDM] **take it for 'granted (that…)** to believe sth is true without first making sure that it is: *I just took it for granted that he'd always be around.* **take sb/sth for 'granted** to be so used to sb/sth that you do not recognize their true value any more and do not show that you are grateful: *Her husband was always there and she just took him for granted.* ◊ *We take having an endless supply of clean water for granted.*
■ *noun* ~ (to do sth) a sum of money that is given by the government or by another organization to be used for a particular purpose: *student grants* (= to pay for their education) ◊ *He has been awarded a research grant.*

grant·ed /ˈgrɑːntɪd; *AmE* ˈgræn-/ **1** *adv.* used to show that you accept that sth is true, often before you make another statement about it: *'You could have done more to help.' 'Granted.'* ◊ *Granted, it's not the most pleasant of jobs but it has to be done.* **2** ~ (that…) *conj.* because of the fact that: *Granted that it is a simple test to perform, it should be easy to get results quickly.*

,**grant-main'tained** *adj.* (*abbr.* **GM**) (of a school in Britain) receiving financial support from central government rather than local government

granu·lar /ˈgrænjələ(r)/ *adj.* consisting of small GRANULES; looking or feeling like a collection of granules

granu·lated sugar /ˌgrænjuleɪtɪd ˈʃʊgə(r)/ *noun* [U] white sugar in the form of small grains

gran·ule /ˈgrænjuːl/ *noun* [usually pl.] a small, hard piece of sth; a small grain: *instant coffee granules*

grape /greɪp/ *noun* a small green or purple fruit that

grows in bunches on a climbing plant (called a VINE). Wine is made from grapes: *a bunch of grapes* ◊ *black/ white grapes* (= grapes that are actually purple/green in colour)—picture on page A2 **IDM** see SOUR *adj.*

grape·fruit /'greɪpfruːt/ *noun* (*pl.* **grapefruit** or **grape-fruits**) [C, U] a large round yellow CITRUS fruit with a lot of slightly sour juice—picture on page A2

grape·vine /'greɪpvaɪn/ *noun* **IDM** **on/through the 'grapevine** by talking in an informal way to other people: *I heard on the grapevine that you're leaving.*

graph /ɡræf; *BrE also* ɡrɑːf/ *noun* a planned drawing, consisting of a line or lines, showing how two or more sets of numbers are related to each other: *Plot a graph of height against age.* ◊ *The graph shows how house prices have risen since the 1980s.*

graph·ic /'ɡræfɪk/ *adj.* **1** [only before noun] connected with drawings and design, especially in the production of books, magazines, etc: *graphic design* ◊ *a graphic artist/ designer* **2** (of descriptions, etc.) very clear and full of details, especially about sth unpleasant: *a graphic account/description of a battle* ◊ *He kept telling us about his operation, in the most graphic detail.*

graph·ic·al·ly /'ɡræfɪkli/ *adv.* **1** in the form of drawings or diagrams: *This data is shown graphically on the opposite page.* **2** very clearly and in great detail: *The murders are graphically described in the article.*

graph·ics /'ɡræfɪks/ *noun* [pl.] designs, drawings or pictures, that are used especially in the production of books, magazines, etc: *computer graphics* ◊ *Text and graphics are prepared separately and then combined.*

graph·ite /'ɡræfaɪt/ *noun* [U] a soft black mineral that is a form of CARBON. Graphite is used to make pencils, to LUBRICATE machinery, and in nuclear REACTORS.

'graph paper *noun* [U] paper with small squares of equal size printed on it, used for drawing GRAPHS and other diagrams

-graphy *combining form* (in nouns) **1** a type of art or science: *choreography* ◊ *geography* **2** a method of producing images: *radiography* **3** a form of writing or drawing: *calligraphy* ◊ *biography*

grap·ple /'ɡræpl/ *verb* **1** ~ (with sb/sth) to take a firm hold of sb/sth and struggle with them: [V] *Passers-by grappled with the man after the attack.* ◊ [VN] *They managed to grapple him to the ground.* **2** ~ (with sth) to try hard to find a solution to a problem: [V] *The new government has yet to grapple with the problem of air pollution.* ◊ [Vtoinf] *I was grappling to find an answer to his question.*

'grappling iron (also **'grappling hook**) *noun* a tool with several hooks attached to a long rope, used for dragging sth along or holding a boat still

grasp /ɡrɑːsp; *AmE* ɡræsp/ *verb, noun*
■ *verb* **1** [VN] to take a firm hold of sb/sth: *He grasped my hand and shook it warmly.* ◊ *Kay grasped him by the wrist.* **2** to understand sth completely: [VN] *They failed to grasp the importance of his words.* ◊ [Vwh-] *She was unable to grasp how to do it.* ◊ [Vthat] *It took him some time to grasp that he was now a public figure.* **3** [VN] ~ a chance/an opportunity to take an opportunity without hesitating and use it: *I grasped the opportunity to work abroad.* **IDM** **grasp the 'nettle** (*BrE*) to deal with a difficult situation firmly and without hesitating—more at STRAW **PHRV** **'grasp at sth 1** to try to take hold of sth in your hands: *She grasped at his coat as he rushed past her.* **2** to try to take an opportunity
■ *noun* [usually sing.] **1** a firm hold of sb/sth or control over sb/sth: *I grabbed him, but he slipped from my grasp.* ◊ *She felt a firm grasp on her arm.* ◊ *Don't let the situation escape from your grasp.* **2** a person's understanding of a subject or of difficult facts: *He has a good grasp of German grammar.* ◊ *These complex formulae are beyond the grasp of the average pupil.* **3** the ability to get or achieve sth: *Success was within her grasp.*

grasp·ing /'ɡrɑːspɪŋ; *AmE* 'ɡræs-/ *adj.* (*disapproving*) always trying to get money, possessions, power, etc. for yourself [SYN] GREEDY: *a grasping landlord*

grass /ɡrɑːs; *AmE* ɡræs/ *noun, verb*
■ *noun* **1** [U] a common wild plant with narrow green leaves and stems that are eaten by cows, horses, sheep, etc: *a blade of grass* ◊ *The dry grass caught fire.* **2** [C] any type of grass: *ornamental grasses* **3** [sing., U] (usually **the grass**) an area of ground covered with grass: *to cut/mow the grass* ◊ *Don't walk on the grass.* **4** [U] (*slang*) MARI-JUANA **5** [C] (*BrE, slang*, usually *disapproving*) a person, usually a criminal, who tells the police about sb's criminal activities and plans—compare SUPERGRASS **IDM** **the grass is (always) greener on the other side (of the fence)** (*saying*) said about people who never seem happy with what they have and always think that other people have a better situation than they have **not let the grass grow under your feet** to not delay in getting things done **put sb out to 'grass** (*informal*) to force sb to stop doing their job, especially because they are old—more at SNAKE *n.*
■ *verb* [V] ~ (on sb) (also **grass sb 'up**) (both *BrE, informal*) to tell the police about sb's criminal activities **PHRV** **grass sth↔'over** to cover an area with grass

grass 'court *noun* a TENNIS COURT with a grass surface

grassed /ɡrɑːst; *AmE* ɡræst/ *adj.* covered with grass: *grassed areas*

grass·hop·per /'ɡrɑːshɒpə(r); *AmE* 'ɡræshɑːp-/ *noun* an insect with long back legs, that can jump very high and that makes a sound with its legs—picture on page A7 **IDM** see KNEE-HIGH

grass·land /'ɡrɑːslænd; *AmE* 'ɡræs-/ *noun* [U] (also **grass·lands** [pl.] a large area of open land covered with wild grass: *turning grassland into farm land*

grass 'roots (*BrE*) *noun* [pl.] (often **the grass roots**) ordinary people in society or in an organization, rather than the leaders or people who make decisions: *the grass roots of the party* ▶ **grass-'roots** *adj.* [only before noun]: *We need to win support at grass-roots level.*

'grass snake *noun* a small harmless snake

grassy /'ɡrɑːsi; *AmE* 'ɡræsi/ *adj.* covered with grass: *a grassy bank/slope/hillside*

grate /ɡreɪt/ *noun, verb*
■ *noun* **1** a metal frame for holding the wood or coal in a FIREPLACE **2** (*AmE*) = DRAIN
■ *verb* **1** [VN] to rub food against a GRATER in order to cut it into small pieces: *grated apple/carrot/cheese* ◊ *Grate the cheese and sprinkle it over the tomatoes.* **2** [V] ~ (on/with sb) to irritate or annoy sb: *Her voice really grates on me.* ◊ *It grated with him when people implied he wasn't really British.* **3** when two hard surfaces **grate** as they rub together, they make a sharp unpleasant sound; sb can also make one thing **grate** against another: [V] *The rusty hinges grated as the gate swung back.* ◊ [VN] *He grated his knife across the plate.*

grate·ful /'ɡreɪtfl/ *adj.* **1** ~ (to sb) (for sth)| ~ (to do sth)| ~ (that...) feeling or showing thanks because sb has done sth kind for you or has done as you asked: *I am extremely grateful to all the teachers for their help.* ◊ *We would be grateful for any information you can give us.* ◊ *She seems to think I should be grateful to have a job at all.* ◊ *He was grateful that she didn't tell his parents about the incident.* ◊ *Grateful thanks are due to the following people for their help ...* ◊ *Kate gave him a grateful smile.* **2** used to make a request, especially in a letter or in a formal situation: *I would be grateful if you could send the completed form back as soon as possible.* ▶ **grate-ful·ly** /-fəli/ *adv.: He nodded gratefully.* ◊ *All donations will be gratefully received.* ◊ *I gratefully acknowledge the help of many people here today.* **IDM** see SMALL *adj.*

> **WORD FAMILY**
> **grateful** *adj.* (≠ ungrateful)
> **gratitude** *n.* (≠ ingratitude)

grater /'ɡreɪtə(r)/ *noun* a kitchen UTENSIL (= a tool) with a rough surface, used for GRATING food: *a cheese/nutmeg grater*—picture at KITCHEN

grat·ifi·ca·tion /ˌɡrætɪfɪ'keɪʃn/ *noun* [U, C] (*formal*) the state of feeling pleasure when sth goes well for you or when your desires are satisfied; sth that gives you pleasure: *sexual gratification* ◊ *A feed will usually provide instant gratification to a crying baby.*

G

æ	ɑː	e	ɜː	ə	ɪ	iː	i	ɒ	ɔː	ʌ	ʊ	u	uː
cat	father	ten	bird	about	sit	see	many	got	saw	cup	put	actual	too
								(BrE)					

grat·ify /ˈgrætɪfaɪ/ *verb* (**grati·fies**, **grati·fy·ing**, **grati·fied**, **grati·fied**) **1** (*written*) to please or satisfy sb: [VN to inf] *It gratified him to think that it was all his work.* ◊ [VN] *I was gratified by their invitation.* **2** [VN] (*formal*) to satisfy a wish, need, etc: *He only gave his consent in order to gratify her wishes.* ▶ **grati·fied** *adj.* [not usually before noun] ~ (**at sth**)| ~ (**to find, hear, see, etc.**): *She was gratified to find that they had followed her advice.*

grati·fy·ing /ˈgrætɪfaɪɪŋ/ *adj.* (*formal*) pleasing and giving satisfaction: *It is gratifying to see such good results.* ◊ *He felt a gratifying sense of being respected and appreciated.* ▶ **grati·fy·ing·ly** *adv.*

grat·ing /ˈgreɪtɪŋ/ *noun, adj.*
■ *noun* a flat frame with metal bars across it, used to cover a window, a hole in the ground, etc.—see also GRATE (2)
■ *adj.* (of a sound or sb's voice) unpleasant and harsh to listen to

gra·tis /ˈgrætɪs; ˈgreɪtɪs/ *adv.* done or given without having to be paid for [SYN] FREE OF CHARGE ▶ **gra·tis** *adj.*: *I knew his help wouldn't be given gratis.* ◊ *a gratis copy of a book*

grati·tude /ˈgrætɪtjuːd; *AmE* -tuːd/ *noun* [U] ~ (**to sb**) (**for sth**) the feeling of being grateful and wanting to express your thanks: *He smiled at them with gratitude.* ◊ *I would like to express my gratitude to everyone for their hard work.* ◊ *She was presented with the gift in gratitude for her long service.* ◊ *a deep sense of gratitude* ◊ *I owe you a great debt of gratitude* (= feel extremely grateful). [OPP] INGRATITUDE

gra·tuit·ous /grəˈtjuːɪtəs; *AmE* -ˈtuː-/ *adj.* (*disapproving*) done without any good reason or purpose and often having harmful effects [SYN] UNNECESSARY: *gratuitous violence on television* ▶ **gra·tuit·ous·ly** *adv.*

gra·tu·ity /grəˈtjuːəti; *AmE* -ˈtuː-/ *noun* (*pl.* **-ies**) **1** (*formal*) money that you give to sb who has provided a service for you [SYN] TIP **2** (*BrE*) money that is given to employees when they leave their job

grave¹ /greɪv/ *noun, adj.*—see also GRAVE²
■ *noun* **1** a place in the ground where a dead person is buried: *We visited Grandma's grave.* ◊ *There were flowers on the grave.* **2** [sing.] (often **the grave**) (usually *literary*) death; a person's death: *Is there life beyond the grave* (= life after death)? ◊ *He followed her to the grave* (= died soon after her). ◊ *She smoked herself into an early grave* (= died young as a result of smoking). [IDM] **turn in his/her grave** (*BrE*) (*AmE* **roll in his/her grave**) (of a person who is dead) likely to be very shocked or angry: *My father would turn in his grave if he knew.*—more at CRADLE *n.*, DIG *v.*, FOOT *n.*
■ *adj.* (**graver**, **grav·est**) (*formal*) **1** (of situations, feelings, etc.) very serious and important; giving you a reason to feel worried: *The police have expressed grave concern about the missing child's safety.* ◊ *The consequences will be very grave if nothing is done.* ◊ *We were in grave danger.* **2** (of people) serious in manner, as if sth sad, important or worrying has just happened: *He looked very grave as he entered the room.*—see also GRAVITY ▶ **grave·ly** *adv.*: *She is gravely ill.* ◊ *Local people are gravely concerned.* ◊ *He nodded gravely as I poured out my troubles.*

grave² /grɑːv/ (*also* ˌgrave ˈaccent) *noun* a mark placed over a vowel in some languages to show how it should be pronounced, as over the *e* in the French word *pere*—compare ACUTE ACCENT, CIRCUMFLEX, TILDE, UMLAUT—see also GRAVE¹

grave·dig·ger /ˈgreɪvdɪgə(r)/ *noun* a person whose job is to dig graves

gravel /ˈgrævl/ *noun* [U] small stones, often used to make the surface of paths and roads: *a gravel path* ◊ *a gravel pit* (= a place where gravel is taken from the ground)

grav·elled (*BrE*) (*AmE* **grav·eled**) /ˈgrævld/ *adj.* (of a road, etc.) covered with gravel

grav·el·ly /ˈgrævəli/ *adj.* **1** full of or containing many small stones: *a dry gravelly soil* **2** (of a voice) deep and with a rough sound

grave·stone /ˈgreɪvstəʊn; *AmE* -stoʊn/ *noun* a stone that is put upright on a grave, showing the name, etc. of

the person buried there [SYN] HEADSTONE—compare TOMBSTONE

grave·yard /ˈgreɪvjɑːd; *AmE* -jɑːrd/ *noun* **1** an area of land, often near a church, where people are buried—compare CEMETERY, CHURCHYARD **2** a place where things or people that are not wanted are sent or left: *a graveyard for cars*

ˈgraveyard shift *noun* (especially *AmE*) a period of time working at night or in the very early morning

gravi·tate /ˈgrævɪteɪt/ *verb* (*written*) [PHRV] **ˈgravitate to/toward(s) sb/sth** to move towards sb/sth that you are attracted to: *Many young people gravitate to the cities in search of work.*

gravi·ta·tion /ˌgrævɪˈteɪʃn/ *noun* [U] (*physics*) a force of attraction that causes objects to move towards each other

gravi·ta·tion·al /ˌgrævɪˈteɪʃənl/ *adj.* connected with or caused by the force of gravity: *a gravitational field* ◊ *the gravitational pull of the moon*

grav·ity /ˈgrævəti/ *noun* [U] **1** (*abbr.* **g**) the force that attracts objects in space towards each other, and that on the earth pulls them towards the centre of the planet, so that things fall to the ground when they are dropped: *Newton's law of gravity*—see also CENTRE OF GRAVITY **2** (*formal*) extreme importance and a cause for worry [SYN] SERIOUSNESS: *I don't think you realise the gravity of the situation.* ◊ *Punishment varies according to the gravity of the offence.* **3** (*formal*) serious behaviour, speech or appearance: *They were asked to behave with the gravity that was appropriate in a court of law.*—see also GRAVE¹

gravy /ˈgreɪvi/ *noun* [U] **1** a brown sauce made by adding flour to the juices that come out of meat while it is cooking **2** (*AmE, informal*) something, especially money, that is obtained when you do not expect it: *Anything on top of eight percent profit is just gravy for the industry.*

ˈgravy boat *noun* a long low JUG used for serving and pouring gravy at a meal

ˈgravy train *noun* (*informal, especially AmE*) a situation where people seem to be making a lot of money without much effort

gray /greɪ/ (especially *AmE*) = GREY

gray·ish /ˈgreɪɪʃ/ *adj.* (especially *AmE*) = GREYISH

graze /greɪz/ *verb, noun*
■ *verb* **1** (of cows, sheep, etc.) to eat grass that is growing in a field: [V] *There were cows grazing beside the river.* ◊ *Parents have been warned against allowing children to graze on sweets and snacks* (= to keep eating them, instead of real meals). ◊ [VN] *The field had been grazed by sheep.* **2** [VN] to put cows, sheep, etc. in a field so that they can eat the grass there: *The land is used by local people to graze their animals.* **3** [VN] to break the surface of your skin by rubbing it against sth rough: *I fell and grazed my knee.* **4** [VN] to touch sth lightly while passing it: *The bullet grazed his cheek.*
■ *noun* a small injury where the surface of the skin has been slightly broken by rubbing against sth: *Adam walked away from the crash with just cuts and grazes.*

graz·ing /ˈgreɪzɪŋ/ *noun* [U] land with grass that cows, sheep, etc. can eat: *There is poor grazing in the hills.*

grease /griːs/ *noun, verb*
■ *noun* [U] **1** any thick OILY substance, especially one that is used to make machines run smoothly: *Grease marks can be removed with liquid detergent.* ◊ *Her hands were covered with oil and grease.* ◊ *the grease in his hair*—see also ELBOW GREASE **2** animal fat that has been softened by cooking or heating: *plates covered with grease*
■ *verb* [VN] to rub grease or fat on sth: *to grease a cake tin/pan* [IDM] **grease sb's ˈpalm** (*old-fashioned, informal*) to give sb money in order to persuade them to do sth dishonest [SYN] BRIBE **grease the ˈwheels** (*AmE*) = OIL THE WHEELS

grease·paint /ˈgriːspeɪnt/ *noun* [U] a thick substance used by actors as MAKE-UP

grease·proof paper /ˌgriːspruːf ˈpeɪpə(r)/ (*BrE*) (*AmE* ˈwax paper) *noun* [U] paper that does not let GREASE, oil, etc. pass through it, used in cooking and for wrapping food in

greasy /ˈgriːsi; ˈgriːzi/ *adj.* (**greas·ier**, **greasi·est**)

1 covered in a lot of GREASE or oil: *greasy fingers/marks/overalls* **2** (*disapproving*) (of food) cooked with too much oil: *greasy chips* **3** (*disapproving*) (of hair or skin) producing too much natural oil: *long greasy hair* **4** (*informal, disapproving*) (of people or their behaviour) friendly in a way that does not seem sincere [SYN] SMARMY: *a greasy smile*

greasy 'spoon *noun* (*informal, often disapproving*) a small cheap restaurant, usually one that is not very clean or attractive

great /ɡreɪt/ *adj., noun, adv.*
■ *adj.* (**great·er, great·est**)

LARGE | **1** [usually before noun] very large; much bigger than average in size or quantity: *A great crowd had gathered.* ◇ *People were arriving in great numbers.* ◇ *The great majority of* (= most) *people seem to agree with this view.* ◇ *He must have fallen from a great height.* ◇ *She lived to a great age.* **2** [only before noun] (*informal*) used to emphasize an adjective of size or quality: *There was a great big pile of books on the table.* ◇ *He cut himself a great thick slice of cake.* **3** much more than average in degree or quantity: *a matter of great importance* ◇ *The concert had been a great success.* ◇ *Her death was a great shock to us all.* ◇ *It gives me great pleasure to welcome you here today.* ◇ *Take great care of it.* ◇ *You've been a great help.* ◇ *We are all to a great extent the products of our culture.* ⇨ note at BIG

ADMIRED | **4** extremely good in ability or quality and therefore admired by many people: *He has been described as the world's greatest violinist.* ◇ *Sherlock Holmes, the great detective* ◇ *Great art has the power to change lives.*

PLEASANT | **5** (*informal*) very good or pleasant: *He's a great bloke.* ◇ *It's great to see you again.* ◇ *What a great goal!* ◇ *We had a great time in Madrid.* ◇ *'I'll pick you up at seven.' 'That'll be great, thanks.'* ◇ (*ironic*) *Oh great, they left without us.* ◇ *You've been a great help, I must say* (= no help at all).

IMPORTANT/IMPRESSIVE | **6** [only before noun] important and impressive: *The wedding was a great occasion.* ◇ *As the great day approached, she grew more and more nervous.* ◇ *The great thing is to get it done quickly.* ◇ *One great advantage of this metal is that it doesn't rust.*

WITH INFLUENCE | **7** having high status or a lot of influence: *the great powers* (= important and powerful countries) ◇ *We can make this country great again.* ◇ *Alexander the Great*

IN GOOD HEALTH | **8** in a very good state of physical or mental health: *She seemed in great spirits* (= very cheerful). ◇ *I feel great today.* ◇ *Everyone's in great form.*

SKILLED | **9** [not usually before noun] ~ **at (doing) sth** (*informal*) able to do sth well: *She's great at chess.*

USEFUL | **10** ~ **for (doing) sth** (*informal*) very suitable or useful for sth: *This gadget's great for opening jars.* ◇ *Try this cream—it's great for spots.*

FOR EMPHASIS | **11** [only before noun] used when you are emphasizing a particular description of sb/sth: *We are great friends.* ◇ *I've never been a great reader* (= I do not read much). ◇ *She's a great talker, isn't she?*

FAMILY | **12** added to words for family members to show a further stage in relationship: *my great-aunt* (= my father's or mother's aunt) ◇ *her great-grandson* (= the grandson of her son or daughter)

LARGER ANIMALS/PLANTS | **13** [only before noun] used in the names of animals or plants which are larger than similar kinds: *the great tit*

CITY NAME | **14** (**Greater**) used with the name of a city to describe an area that includes the centre of the city and a large area all round it: *Greater London*

▶ **great·ness** *noun* [U]

IDM **be going great 'guns** (*informal*) to be doing sth quickly and successfully: *Work is going great guns now.* **be a 'great one for (doing) sth** to do sth a lot; to enjoy sth: *I've never been a great one for writing letters.* ◇ *You're a great one for quizzes, aren't you?* **be no great 'shakes** (*informal*) to be not very good, efficient, suitable, etc. **great and 'small** of all sizes or types: *all creatures great and small* **the great sth in the 'sky** (*humorous*) used to

refer to where a particular person or thing is imagined to go when they die or are no longer working, similar to the place they were connected with on earth: *Their pet rabbit had gone to the great rabbit hutch in the sky.*—more at PAINS, SUM *n.*

■ *noun* [usually pl.] (*informal*) a very well-known and successful person or thing: *He was one of boxing's all-time greats.*

■ *adv.* (*informal, non-standard*) very well: *Well done. You did great.*

great·coat /'ɡreɪtkəʊt; *AmE* -koʊt/ *noun* a long heavy coat, especially one worn by soldiers

Great Dane /ˌɡreɪt 'deɪn/ *noun* a very large dog with short hair

great·ly /'ɡreɪtli/ *adv.* (*formal*) (usually before a verb or participle) very much: *People's reaction to the film has varied greatly.* ◇ *a greatly increased risk* ◇ *Your help would be greatly appreciated.*

the ˌGreat 'War *noun* [sing.] (*old-fashioned*) = THE FIRST WORLD WAR

Gre·cian /'ɡriːʃn/ *adj.* from Ancient Greece or like the styles of Ancient Greece: *Grecian architecture*

greed /ɡriːd/ *noun* [U] ~ (**for sth**) (*disapproving*) **1** a strong desire for more wealth, possessions, power, etc. than a person needs: *His actions were motivated by greed.* ◇ *Nothing would satisfy her greed for power.* **2** a strong desire for more food or drink when you are no longer hungry or thirsty: *I had another helping of ice cream out of pure greed.*

greedy /'ɡriːdi/ *adj.* (**greed·ier, greedi·est**) ~ (**for sth**) wanting more money, power, food, etc. than you really need: *You greedy pig! You've already had two helpings!* ◇ *The shareholders are greedy for profit.* ◇ *He stared at the diamonds with greedy eyes.* ▶ **greed·ily** *adv.*: *He ate noisily and greedily.*

Greek /ɡriːk/ *noun* **1** [C] a person from modern or ancient Greece **2** [U] the language of modern or ancient Greece **3** [C] (*AmE*) a member of a FRATERNITY or a SORORITY at a college or university IDM **it's all 'Greek to me** (*informal, saying*) I cannot understand it: *She tried to explain how the system works, but I'm afraid it's all Greek to me.*

green /ɡriːn/ *adj., noun, verb*
■ *adj.* (**green·er, green·est**)

COLOUR | **1** having the colour of grass or the leaves of most plants and trees: *green beans* ◇ *Wait for the light to turn green* (= on traffic lights).

COVERED WITH GRASS | **2** covered with grass or other plants: *green fields/hills* ◇ *After the rains, the land was green with new growth.*

FRUIT | **3** not yet ripe: *green tomatoes*

PERSON | **4** (*informal*) (of a person) young and lacking experience: *The new trainees are still very green.* **5** (of a person or their skin) being a pale colour, as if the person is going to VOMIT: *It was a rough crossing and most of the passengers looked distinctly green.*

POLITICS | **6** concerned with the protection of the environment; supporting the protection of the environment as a political principle: *green politics/tourism* ◇ *Try to adopt a greener lifestyle.* ◇ *the Green Party*

▶ **green·ness** *noun* [U]: *the greenness of the countryside* ◇ *Supermarkets have started proclaiming the greenness of their products.*

IDM **ˌgreen with 'envy** very jealous—more at GRASS *n.*
■ *noun*

COLOUR | **1** [U, C] the colour of grass and the leaves of most plants and trees: *the green of the countryside in spring* ◇ *The room was decorated in a combination of greens and blues.* ◇ *She was dressed all in green.*

VEGETABLES | **2** (**greens**) [pl.] (*especially BrE*) green vegetables: *Eat up your greens.*

AREA OF GRASS | **3** [C] (*BrE*) an area of grass, especially in the middle of a town or village: *Children were playing on the village green.* **4** [C] (in golf) an area of grass cut short around a hole in a golf course: *the 18th green* ◇ *Did the ball land on the green?*—see also BOWLING GREEN, PUTTING GREEN—picture at GOLF

G

POLITICS | **5 (the Greens)** [pl.] the Green Party (= the party whose main aim is the protection of the environment)

■ *verb* [VN]

CREATE PARKS | **1** to create parks and other areas with trees and plants in a city: *projects for greening the inner cities*

POLITICS | **2** to make sb more aware of issues connected with the environment: *an attempt to green industry bosses* ▶ **green·ing** *noun* [U]: *the greening of British politics*

green·back /'gri:nbæk/ *noun* (*AmE, informal*) an American BANKNOTE

green 'bean (*BrE also* ,**French 'bean**) (*AmE also* ,**string 'bean**) *noun* a type of bean which is a long thin green POD, cooked and eaten whole as a vegetable—picture on page A3

green 'belt *noun* [U, C, usually sing.] (*BrE*) an area of open land around a city where building is strictly controlled: *New roads are cutting into the green belt.*

green 'card *noun* **1** a document that legally allows sb from another country to live and work in the US **2** (*BrE*) an insurance document that you need when you drive your car in another country

green·ery /'gri:nəri/ *noun* [U] attractive green leaves and plants: *The room was decorated with flowers and greenery.*

green·field /'gri:nfi:ld/ *adj.* [only before noun] (*BrE*) used to describe an area of land that has not yet had buildings on it, but for which building development may be planned: *a greenfield site*

green 'fingers *noun* [pl.] (*BrE*) (*AmE* ,**green 'thumb** [sing.]) if you have **green fingers**, you are good at making plants grow ▶ ,**green-'fingered** *adj.* (*BrE*)

green·fly /'gri:nflaɪ/ *noun* [U, C] (*pl.* **green·flies** *or* **green·fly**) a small flying insect that is harmful to plants: *The roses have got greenfly.*

green·gage /'gri:ngeɪdʒ/ *noun* a small soft green fruit that is a type of PLUM: *a greengage tree*

green·gro·cer /'gri:ngrəʊsə(r); *AmE* -groʊ-/ *noun* (*especially BrE*) **1** a person who owns, manages or works in a shop/store selling fruit and vegetables—compare FRUITERER **2** (**green·gro·cer's**) (*pl.* **green·gro·cers**) a shop/store that sells fruit and vegetables

green·house /'gri:nhaʊs/ *noun* a building with glass sides and a glass roof for growing plants in

the 'greenhouse effect *noun* [sing.] the problem of the gradual rise in temperature of the earth's atmosphere, caused by an increase of gases such as CARBON DIOXIDE in the air surrounding the earth, which trap the heat of the sun: *The destruction of forests is contributing to the greenhouse effect.*—see also GLOBAL WARMING

greenhouse 'gas *noun* any of the gases that are thought to cause the greenhouse effect, especially CARBON DIOXIDE

green·ish /'gri:nɪʃ/ *adj.* fairly green in colour

green·keep·er /'gri:nki:pə(r)/ (*AmE also* **greens·keep·er**) *noun* a person whose job is to take care of a GOLF COURSE

green 'light *noun* [sing.] permission for a project, etc. to start or continue: *The government has decided to give the green light to the plan.*

green 'onion *noun* (*AmE*) = SPRING ONION

Green 'Paper *noun* (in Britain) a document containing government proposals on a particular subject, intended for general discussion—compare WHITE PAPER

green 'pepper *noun* a hollow green fruit that is eaten, raw or cooked, as a vegetable

'green room *noun* a room in a theatre, television STUDIO, etc. where the performers can relax when they are not performing

green 'salad *noun* [C, U] (*BrE*) a salad that is made with raw green vegetables, especially LETTUCE: *Serve with a green salad.*

greens·keep·er /'gri:nzki:pə(r)/ *noun* (*AmE*) = GREEN-KEEPER

green 'tea *noun* [U] a pale tea made from leaves that have been dried but not FERMENTED

green 'thumb *noun* (*AmE*) = GREEN FINGERS

green 'vegetable *noun* [C, usually pl.] (*BrE also* **greens**) [pl.] a vegetable with dark green leaves, for example CABBAGE or SPINACH

Green·wich Mean Time /ˌɡrenɪtʃ 'mi:n taɪm; -nɪdʒ/ = GMT

greet /gri:t/ *verb* [VN] **1** ~ **sb** (**with sth**) to say hello to sb or to welcome them: *He greeted all the guests warmly as they arrived.* ◊ *She greeted us with a smile.* **2** [usually passive] ~ **sb/sth** (**with/as sth**) to react to sth in a particular way: *The changes were greeted with suspicion.* ◊ *The team's win was greeted as a major triumph.* ◊ *Loud cheers greeted the news.* **3** [usually passive] (*of sights, sounds or smells*) to be the first thing that you see, hear or smell at a particular time: *When she opened the door she was greeted by a scene of utter confusion.*

greet·ing /'gri:tɪŋ/ *noun* **1** [C, U] something that you say or do to greet sb: *She waved a friendly greeting.* ◊ *They exchanged greetings and sat down to lunch.* ◊ *He raised his hand in greeting.* **2** (**greetings**) [pl.] a message of good wishes for sb's health, happiness, etc: *Christmas/birthday greetings* ◊ *My mother sends her greetings to you all.* IDM see SEASON *n.*

'greetings card (*BrE*) (*AmE* **'greeting card**) *noun* a card with a picture on the front and a message inside that you send to sb on a particular occasion such as their birthday

gre·gari·ous /grɪ'geəriəs; *AmE* -'ger-/ *adj.* **1** liking to be with other people SYN SOCIABLE: *She's very outgoing and gregarious.* **2** (*biology*) (of animals or birds) living in groups ▶ **gre·gari·ous·ly** *adv.* **gre·gari·ous·ness** *noun* [U]

Gre·gor·ian calendar /grɪˌɡɔ:riən 'kælɪndə(r)/ *noun* [sing.] the system used since 1582 in Western countries of arranging the months in the year and the days in the months and of counting the years from the birth of Christ

Gre·gorian 'chant *noun* [U, C] a type of church music for voices alone, used since the Middle Ages

grem·lin /'gremlɪn/ *noun* an imaginary creature that people blame when a machine suddenly stops working

gren·ade /grə'neɪd/ *noun* a small bomb that can be thrown by hand or fired from a gun—see also HAND GRENADE

grena·dier /ˌgrenə'dɪə(r); *AmE* -'dɪr/ *noun* a soldier in the part of the British army known as the **Grenadiers** or **Grenadier Guards**

grew *pt* of GROW

grey (*especially BrE*) (*AmE usually* **gray**) /greɪ/ *adj., noun, verb*

■ *adj.* **1** having the colour of ashes or smoke: *grey eyes/hair* ◊ *wisps of grey smoke* ◊ *a grey suit* **2** [not usually before noun] having grey hair: *He's gone very grey.* **3** (of a person's skin colour) pale and dull, because they are ill/sick, tired or sad: *The next morning she looked very grey and hollow-eyed.* **4** (of the sky or weather) dull; full of clouds: *grey skies* ◊ *I hate these grey days.* **5** without interest or variety; making you feel sad: *Life seems grey and pointless without him.* **6** (*disapproving*) not interesting or attractive: *The company was full of faceless grey men who all looked the same.* ▶ **grey·ness** (*especially BrE*) (*AmE usually* **gray·ness**) *noun* [U, sing.]

■ *noun* **1** [U, C] the colour of ashes or smoke: *the dull grey of the sky* ◊ *dressed in grey* **2** [C] a grey or white horse: *She's riding the grey.*

■ *verb* [V] (of hair) to become grey: *His hair was greying at the sides.* ◊ *a tall woman with greying hair*

grey 'area (*especially BrE*) (*AmE usually* ,**gray 'area**) *noun* an area of a subject or situation that is not clear or does not fit into a particular group and is therefore difficult to define or deal with: *Exactly what can be called an offensive weapon is still a grey area.*

grey-'haired (*especially BrE*) (*AmE usually* ,**gray-'haired**) *adj.* with grey hair

grey·hound /'greɪhaʊnd/ *noun* a large thin dog with smooth hair and long thin legs, that can run very fast and is used in the sport of **greyhound racing**

s	t	v	z	ʃ	ʒ	tʃ	dʒ	θ	ð	ŋ
see	tea	van	zoo	shoe	vision	chain	jam	thin	this	sing

grey·ish (*especially BrE*) (*AmE* usually **gray·ish**) /'greɪɪʃ/ *adj.* fairly grey in colour: *greyish hair*

'grey matter (*especially BrE*) (*AmE* usually **'gray mat·ter**) *noun* [U] (*informal*) a person's intelligence

grid /grɪd/ *noun* **1** a pattern of straight lines, usually crossing each other to form squares: *New York's grid of streets* **2** a frame of metal or wooden bars that are parallel or cross each other—see also CATTLE GRID **3** a pattern of squares on a map that are marked with letters or numbers to help you find the exact position of a place: *The grid reference is C8.* **4** (*especially BrE*) a system of electric wires or pipes carrying gas, for sending power over a large area: *the national grid* (= the electricity supply in a country) **5** (in motor racing) a pattern of lines marking the starting positions for the racing cars

grid·dle /'grɪdl/ *noun* a circular iron plate that is heated on a stove or over a fire and used for cooking

grid·iron /'grɪdaɪən; *AmE* -aɪərn/ *noun* **1** a frame made of metal bars that is used for cooking meat or fish on, over an open fire **2** (*AmE*) a field used for American football marked with a pattern of parallel lines

grid·lock /'grɪdlɒk; *AmE* -lɑːk/ *noun* [U] **1** a situation in which there are so many cars in the streets of a town that the traffic cannot move at all **2** (usually in politics) a situation in which people with different opinions are not able to agree with each other and so no action can be taken: *Congress is in gridlock.* ▶ **grid·locked** *adj.*

grief /griːf/ *noun* **1** [U, C] ~ (**over/at sth**) a feeling of great sadness, especially when sb dies: *She was overcome with grief when her husband died.* ◊ *They were able to share their common joys and griefs.* **2** [C, usually sing.] something that causes great sadness: *It was a grief to them that they had no children.* **3** [U] (*informal*) problems and worry: *He caused his parents a lot of grief.* **IDM come to 'grief** (*informal*) **1** to end in total failure: *All his schemes for making money seem to come to grief.* **2** to be harmed in an accident: *Several pedestrians came to grief on the icy pavement.* **give sb 'grief (about/over sth)** (*informal*) to be annoyed with sb and criticize their behaviour **good 'grief!** (*informal*) used to express surprise or shock: *Good grief! What a mess!*

'grief-stricken *adj.* feeling extremely sad because of sth that has happened, especially the death of sb

griev·ance /'griːvəns/ *noun* ~ (**against sb**) something that you think is unfair and that you complain or protest about: *Parents were invited to air their grievances* (= express them) *at the meeting.* ◊ *He had been nursing a grievance against his boss for months.* ◊ *Does the company have a formal grievance procedure* (= a way of telling sb your complaints at work)?

grieve /griːv/ *verb* **1** ~ (**for/over sb/sth**) to feel very sad, especially because sb has died: [V] *They are still grieving for their dead child.* ◊ *grieving relatives* ◊ [VN] *She grieved the death of her husband.* **2** (*formal*) to make you feel very sad: [VN that] *It grieved him that he could do nothing to help her.* ◊ [VN] *Their lack of interest grieved her.* ◊ [VN to inf] *It grieved her to leave.*

griev·ous /'griːvəs/ *adj.* (*formal*) very serious and often causing great pain or suffering: *He had been the victim of a grievous injustice.* ▶ **griev·ous·ly** *adv.*: *grievously hurt/wounded*

grievous ˌbodily 'harm *noun* [U] (*abbr.* GBH) (*law*) the crime of causing sb serious physical injury

grif·fin /'grɪfɪn/ (also **grif·fon, gry·phon** /'grɪfən/) *noun* (in stories) a creature with a lion's body and an EAGLE'S wings and head

grill /grɪl/ *noun, verb*
■ *noun* **1** (*BrE*) the part of a cooker that directs heat downwards to cook food that is placed underneath it: *Put it under a hot grill to brown for two minutes.*—compare BROILER—picture on page 275 **2** a flat metal frame that you put food on to cook over a fire—see also BARBECUE **3** a dish of grilled food, especially meat—see also MIXED GRILL **4** (*especially* in names) a restaurant serving grilled food: *Harry's Bar and Grill* **5** = GRILLE
■ *verb* [VN] **1** (*BrE*) to cook food under or over a very strong heat: *Grill the sausages for ten minutes.* ◊ *grilled bacon*—

compare BROIL—picture on page 275 **2** (*AmE*) to cook food over a fire, especially outdoors: *grilled meat and shrimp* **3** ~ **sb (about sth)** to ask sb a lot of questions about their ideas, actions, etc., often in an unpleasant way: *They grilled her about where she had been all night.* ◊ *He was grilled by detectives for several hours.*—see also GRILLING

grille (also **grill**) /grɪl/ *noun* a screen made of metal bars or wire that is placed in front of a window, door or piece of machinery in order to protect it: *a radiator grille* (= at the front of a car) ◊ *a security grille*

grill·ing /'grɪlɪŋ/ *noun* [usually sing.] a period of being questioned closely about your ideas, actions, etc: *The minister faced a tough grilling at today's press conference.*

grim /grɪm/ *adj.* (**grim·mer, grim·mest**) **1** looking or sounding very serious: *a grim face/look/smile* ◊ *She looked grim.* ◊ *with a look of grim determination on his face* ◊ *grim-faced policemen* **2** unpleasant and depressing: *grim news* ◊ *We face the grim prospect of still higher unemployment.* ◊ *The outlook is pretty grim.* ◊ *a grim struggle for survival* ◊ *Things are looking grim for workers in the building industry.* **3** (of a place or building) not attractive; depressing: *The house looked grim and dreary in the rain.* ◊ *the grim walls of the prison* **4** [not before noun] (*BrE, informal*) ill: *I feel pretty grim this morning.* **5** [not usually before noun] (*BrE, informal*) of very low quality: *Their performance was fairly grim, I'm afraid!* ▶ **grim·ly** *adv.*: *a face covered with grime determined* **grim·ness** *noun* [U] **IDM hang/hold on for/like grim 'death** (*BrE*) (also **hang/hold on for dear 'life** *AmE, BrE*) (*informal*) to hold sb/sth very tightly because you are afraid

grim·ace /grɪ'meɪs; 'grɪməs/ *verb, noun*
■ *verb* [V] ~ (**at sb/sth**) to make an ugly expression with your face to show pain, disgust, etc: *He grimaced at the bitter taste.* ◊ *She grimaced as the needle went in.*
■ *noun* an ugly expression made by twisting your face, used to show pain, disgust, etc. or to make sb laugh: *to make/give a grimace of pain* ◊ *'What's that?' she asked with a grimace.*

grime /graɪm/ *noun* [U] dirt that forms a layer on the surface of sth: *a face covered with grime and sweat*

the ˌGrim 'Reaper *noun* an imaginary figure who represents death. It looks like a SKELETON, wears a long CLOAK and carries a SCYTHE.

grimy /'graɪmi/ *adj.* (**grimi·er, grimi·est**) covered with GRIME: *grimy hands/windows*

grin /grɪn/ *verb, noun*
■ *verb* (**-nn-**) ~ (**at sb**) to smile widely: [V] *She grinned amiably at us.* ◊ *They grinned with delight when they heard our news.* ◊ *He was grinning from ear to ear.* ◊ [VN] *He grinned a welcome.* **IDM grin and 'bear it** (only used as an infinitive and in orders) to accept pain, disappointment or a difficult situation without complaining: *There's nothing we can do about it. We'll just have to grin and bear it.*
■ *noun* a wide smile: *She gave a broad grin.* ◊ *a wry/ sheepish grin* ◊ *'No,' he said with a grin.* ◊ *Take that grin off your face!*

grind /graɪnd/ *verb, noun*
■ *verb* (**ground, ground** /graʊnd/)
FOOD/FLOUR/COFFEE | **1** [VN] ~ **sth (down/up)** | ~ **sth (to/ into sth)** to break or crush sth into very small pieces between two hard surfaces or using a special machine: *to grind coffee/corn* ◊ *The animal has teeth that grind its food into a pulp.*—see also GROUND (4) **2** [VN] to produce sth such as flour by crushing: *The flour is ground using traditional methods.*

MAKE SHARP/SMOOTH | **3** [VN] to make sth sharp or smooth by rubbing it against a hard surface: *a special stone for grinding knives*

PRESS INTO SURFACE | **4** [VN] ~ **sth into sth** | ~ **sth in** to press or rub sth into a surface: *He ground his cigarette into the ashtray.* ◊ *The dirt on her hands was ground in.*

RUB TOGETHER | **5** to rub together, or to make hard objects rub together, often producing an unpleasant noise: [V] *Parts of the machine were grinding together noisily.* ◊ [VN]

æ	ɑː	e	ɜː	ə	ɪ	iː	i	ɒ	ɔː	ʌ	ʊ	u	uː
cat	father	ten	bird	about	sit	see	many	got	saw	cup	put	actual	too

(BrE)

G

*She **grinds her teeth** when she is asleep.* ◊ *He ground the gears on the car.*

MACHINE | **6** [VN] to turn the handle of a machine that grinds sth: *to grind a pepper mill*

IDM **bring sth to a grinding halt** to make sth slow down gradually until it stops completely **grind to a 'halt | come to a grinding 'halt** to slow down gradually and then stop completely: *Production ground to a halt during the strike.*—more at AXE *n.*

PHRV ,**grind sb** ↔ '**down** to treat sb in a cruel or harsh way over a long period of time, so that they become very unhappy: *Don't let them grind you down.* ◊ *Years of oppression had ground the people down.* ,**grind 'on** to continue for a long time, when this is unpleasant: *The argument ground on for almost two years.* ,**grind sth** ↔ '**out** to produce sth in large quantities, often sth that is not good or interesting: *She grinds out romantic novels at the rate of five a year.*

■ *noun*

BORING ACTIVITY | **1** [sing.] (*informal*) an activity that is tiring or boring and takes a lot of time: *the **daily grind** of family life* ◊ *It's a long grind to the top of that particular profession.*

OF MACHINES | **2** [sing.] the harsh noise made by machines

SWOT | **3** [C] (*AmE, informal*) = SWOT

grind·er /'graɪndə(r)/ *noun* **1** a machine or tool for grinding a solid substance into a powder: *a coffee grinder* **2** a person whose job is to make knives sharper; a machine which does this—see also ORGAN-GRINDER

grind·ing /'graɪndɪŋ/ *adj.* [only before noun] (of a difficult situation) that never ends or improves: *grinding poverty*

grind·stone /'graɪndstəʊn; *AmE* -stoʊn/ *noun* a round stone that is turned like a wheel and is used to make knives and other tools sharp **IDM** see NOSE *n.*

gringo /'grɪŋgəʊ; *AmE* -goʊ/ *noun* (*pl.* **-os**) (*informal, disapproving*) used in Latin American countries to refer to a person from the US

grip /grɪp/ *noun, verb*

■ *noun*

HOLDING TIGHTLY | **1** [C, usually sing.] ~ **(on sb/sth)** an act of holding sb/sth tightly; a particular way of doing this: *Keep a tight grip on the rope.* ◊ *to loosen/release/relax your grip* ◊ *She tried to **get a grip on** the icy rock.* ◊ *The climber slipped and lost her grip.* ◊ *She struggled from his grip.* ◊ *Try adjusting your grip on the racket.*

CONTROL/POWER | **2** [sing.] ~ **(on sb/sth)** control or power over sb/sth: *The home team took a firm grip on the game in the second half.* ◊ *Our main objective now is to tighten the grip we have on the market.*

UNDERSTANDING | **3** [sing.] ~ **(on sth)** an understanding of sth: *I couldn't get a grip on what was going on.* ◊ *You need to keep a good grip on reality in this job.*

MOVING WITHOUT SLIPPING | **4** [U] the ability of sth to move over a surface without slipping: *These tyres give the bus better grip in slippery conditions.*

STOPS HANDS SLIPPING | **5** [C] a part of sth that has a special surface so that it can be held without the hands slipping: *the grip on a golf club* ◊ *a rubber/plastic grip*

FOR HAIR | **6** [C] (*BrE*) = HAIRGRIP

JOB IN THE MOVIES | **7** [C] a person who prepares and moves the cameras, and sometimes the lighting equipment, when a film/movie is being made

BAG | **8** [C] (*old-fashioned*) a large soft bag, used when travelling

IDM **come/get to 'grips with sth** to begin to understand and deal with sth difficult: *I'm slowly getting to grips with the language* **get/take a 'grip (on yourself)** to improve your behaviour or control your emotions after being afraid, upset or angry: *I have to take a grip on myself, he told himself firmly.* ◊ (*informal*) *Get a grip* (= make an effort to control your emotions)! **in the 'grip of sth** experiencing sth unpleasant that cannot be stopped: *a country in the grip of recession* **lose your 'grip (on sth)** to become unable to understand or control a situation: *Sometimes I feel I'm losing my grip.*

■ *verb* (**-pp-**)

HOLD TIGHTLY | **1** to hold sth tightly: [VN] *'Please don't go,' he said, gripping her arm.* ◊ [V] *She gripped on to the railing with both hands.*

INTEREST/EXCITE | **2** [VN] to interest or excite sb; to hold sb's attention: *The book grips you from start to finish.* ◊ *I was totally gripped by the story.*—see also GRIPPING

HAVE POWERFUL EFFECT | **3** [VN] (of an emotion or a situation) to have a powerful effect on sb/sth: *I was gripped by a feeling of panic.* ◊ *Terrorism has gripped the country for the past two years.*

MOVE/HOLD WITHOUT SLIPPING | **4** to hold onto or to move over a surface without slipping: [VN] *tyres that grip the road* [also V]

gripe /graɪp/ *noun, verb*

■ *noun* (*informal*) a complaint about sth: *My only gripe about the hotel was the food.*

■ *verb* [V] ~ **(about sb/sth)** (*informal*) to complain about sb/sth in an annoying way: *He's always griping about the people at work.*

'Gripe Water™ *noun* [U] (*BrE*) medicine that is given to babies when they have stomach pains

grip·ing /'graɪpɪŋ/ *adj.* [only before noun] a **griping** pain is a sudden strong pain in your stomach

grip·ping /'grɪpɪŋ/ *adj.* exciting or interesting in a way that keeps your attention: *a gripping drama/story* ◊ *His books are always so gripping.*

grisly /'grɪzli/ *adj.* [usually before noun] extremely unpleasant and frightening and usually connected with death and violence: *a grisly crime*

grist /grɪst/ *noun* **IDM** **(all) grist to the/sb's 'mill** (*BrE*) (*AmE* **(all) grist for the/sb's 'mill**) something that is useful to sb for a particular purpose: *Political sex scandals are all grist to the mill of the tabloid newspapers.*

gris·tle /'grɪsl/ *noun* [U] a hard substance in meat that is unpleasant to eat: *a lump of gristle*

grit /grɪt/ *noun, verb*

■ *noun* [U] **1** very small pieces of stone or sand: *I had a piece of grit in my eye.* ◊ *They were spreading grit and salt on the icy roads.* **2** the courage and determination that makes it possible for sb to continue doing sth difficult or unpleasant

■ *verb* (**-tt-**) [VN] to spread grit, salt or sand on a road that is covered with ice **IDM** **grit your 'teeth 1** to bite your teeth tightly together: *She gritted her teeth against the pain.* ◊ *'Stop it!' he said through gritted teeth.* **2** to be determined to continue to do sth in a difficult or unpleasant situation: *It started to rain harder, but we gritted our teeth and carried on.*

grits /grɪts/ *noun* [pl.] corn that is partly crushed before cooking, often eaten for breakfast or as part of a meal in the southern US

grit·ter /'grɪtə(r)/ (*BrE*) (*AmE* **'salt truck**) *noun* a large vehicle used for putting salt, sand, or GRIT on the roads in winter when there is ice on them

gritty /'grɪti/ *adj.* **1** containing or like GRIT: *a layer of gritty dust* **2** showing the courage and determination to continue to do sth difficult or unpleasant: *gritty determination* ◊ *a gritty performance from the British player* **3** showing sth unpleasant as it really is: *a gritty description of urban violence* ◊ *gritty realism*—see also NITTY-GRITTY ▶ **grit·tily** *adv.* **grit·ti·ness** *noun* [U]

griz·zle /'grɪzl/ *verb* [V] (*BrE, informal*) (especially of a baby or child) to cry or complain continuously in a way that is annoying

griz·zled /'grɪzld/ *adj.* (*literary*) having hair that is grey or partly grey: *He looked old and grizzled.* ◊ *a grizzled beard*

griz·zly bear /,grɪzli 'beə(r); *AmE* -'ber/ (also **'griz·zly**) *noun* a large fierce brown bear that lives in N America and parts of Russia

groan /grəʊn; *AmE* groʊn/ *verb, noun*

■ *verb* **1** ~ **(at/with sth)** to make a long deep sound because you are annoyed, upset or in pain, or with pleasure: [V] *to groan with pain/pleasure* ◊ *He lay on the floor groaning.* ◊ *We all groaned at his terrible jokes.* ◊ *They were all*

aɪ	aʊ	eɪ	əʊ	oʊ	ɔɪ	ɪə	eə	ʊə	j	w
my	now	say	go	go	boy	near	hair	pure	yes	wet
			(BrE)	(AmE)						

moaning and groaning (= complaining) *about the amount of work they had.* ◇ '[V**speech**] *'It's a complete mess!' she groaned.* ◇ '*Don't move me,' he groaned.* **2** [V] to make a sound like a person groaning: *The trees creaked and groaned in the wind.* **IDM** **groan under the weight of sth** (*written*) used to say that there is too much of sth **PHRV** **'groan with sth** (*written*) to be full of sth: *tables groaning with food*
■ *noun* a long deep sound made when sb/sth groans: *She let out a groan of dismay.* ◇ *He fell to the floor with a groan.* ◇ *The house was filled with the cello's dismal squeaks and groans.*

gro·cer /ˈɡrəʊsə(r); *AmE* ˈɡroʊ-/ *noun* **1** a person who owns, manages or works in a shop/store selling food and other things used in the home **2** (**gro·cer's**) (*pl.* **gro·cers**) a shop/store that sells these things

gro·cery /ˈɡrəʊsəri; *AmE* ˈɡroʊ-/ *noun* (*pl.* **-ies**) **1** (*especially BrE*) (*AmE* usually **'grocery store**) [C] a shop/store that sells food and other things used in the home. In American English 'grocery store' is often used to mean 'supermarket'. **2** (**groceries**) [pl.] food and other goods sold by a grocer or at a supermarket ▶ **gro·cery** *adj.* [only before noun]: *a grocery bag* ◇ *the grocery bill/business*

grog /ɡrɒɡ; *AmE* ɡrɑːɡ/ *noun* [U] **1** a strong alcoholic drink, originally RUM, mixed with water **2** (*informal, especially AustralE*) any alcoholic drink, especially beer

groggy /ˈɡrɒɡi; *AmE* ˈɡrɑːɡi/ *adj.* [not usually before noun] (*informal*) weak and unable to think or move well because you are ill/sick or very tired: *The sleeping pills left her feeling very groggy.*

groin /ɡrɔɪn/ *noun* **1** the part of the body where the legs join at the top including the area around the GENITALS (= sex organs): *She kicked her attacker in the groin.* ◇ *He's been off all season with a groin injury.*—picture at BODY **2** (*especially AmE*) = GROYNE

grom·met /ˈɡrɒmɪt; *AmE* ˈɡrɑːm-/ *noun* **1** a small metal ring placed around a hole in fabric or leather, to make it stronger **2** (*BrE*) (*AmE* **tube**) a small tube placed in a child's ear in order to DRAIN liquid from it

groom /ɡruːm/ *verb, noun*
■ *verb* **1** [VN] to clean or brush an animal: *to groom a horse/dog/cat* ◇ *The horses are all well fed and groomed.* **2** [VN] (of an animal) to clean the fur or skin of another animal or itself: *a female ape grooming her mate* **3** ~ **sb** (**for/as sth**) to prepare or train sb for an important job or position: [VN] *Our junior employees are being groomed for more senior roles.* ◇ [VN**to** inf] *The eldest son is being groomed to take over when his father dies.*
■ *noun* **1** a person whose job is to feed and take care of horses, especially by brushing and cleaning them **2** = BRIDEGROOM

groomed /ɡruːmd/ *adj.* (usually following an adverb) used to describe the way in which a person cares for their clothes and hair: *She is always perfectly groomed.*—see also WELL-GROOMED

groom·ing /ˈɡruːmɪŋ/ *noun* [U] the things that you do to keep your clothes and hair clean and neat, or to keep an animal's fur or hair clean: *You should always pay attention to personal grooming.* ◇ *Grooming is a vital part of caring for your dog.*

grooms·man /ˈɡruːmzmən/ *noun* (*pl.* **-men** /-mən/) (*AmE*) a friend of the BRIDEGROOM at a wedding, who has special duties

groove /ɡruːv/ *noun* **1** a long narrow cut in the surface of sth hard: *Cut a groove 3 cm from the top of the piece of wood.* **2** (*informal*) a particular type of musical rhythm: *a jazz/Latin groove* **IDM** **be (stuck) in a 'groove** (*BrE*) to be unable to change sth that you have been doing the same way for a long time and that has become boring

grooved /ɡruːvd/ *adj.* having a groove or grooves

groovy /ˈɡruːvi/ *adj.* (*old-fashioned, informal*) fashionable, attractive and interesting

grope /ɡrəʊp; *AmE* ɡroʊp/ *verb, noun*
■ *verb* **1** [V] ~ **(around/for sth)** to try and find sth that you cannot see, by feeling with your hands: *I groped for the light switch.* ◇ *He groped around in the dark for his other*

sock. ◇ (*figurative*) '*It's so …, so …' I was groping for the right word to describe it.* **2** [+*adv./prep.*] to try and reach a place by feeling with your hands because you cannot see clearly: [VN] *He groped his way up the staircase in the dark.* ◇ [V] *She groped through the darkness towards the doors.* **3** [VN] (*informal*) to touch sb sexually, especially when they do not want you to
■ *noun* (*informal*) an act of groping sb (= touching them sexually)

gross /ɡrəʊs; *AmE* ɡroʊs/ *adj., adv., verb, noun*
■ *adj.* (**gross·er, gross·est**) **1** [only before noun] being the total amount of sth before anything is taken away: *gross weight* (= including the container or wrapping) ◇ *gross income/wage* (= before taxes, etc. are taken away) ◇ *Investments showed a gross profit of 26%.*—compare NET **2** [only before noun] (*formal or law*) (of a crime, etc.) very obvious and unacceptable: *gross indecency/negligence/misconduct* ◇ *a gross violation of human rights* **3** (*spoken*) very unpleasant: *'He ate it with mustard.' 'Oh, gross!'* **4** very rude: *gross behaviour/language/manners* **5** very fat and ugly: *She's not just fat, she's positively gross!* ▶ **gross·ness** *noun* [U]
■ *adv.* in total, before anything is taken away: *She earns £25 000 a year gross.*—compare NET *adj.*
■ *verb* [VN] to earn a particular amount of money before tax has been taken off it: *It is one of the biggest grossing movies of all time.* **PHRV** **,gross sb 'out** (*AmE, informal*) to be very unpleasant and make sb feel disgusted: *His bad breath really grossed me out.*
■ *noun* **1** (*pl.* **gross**) a group of 144 things: *two gross of apples* ◇ *to sell sth by the gross* **2** (*pl.* **grosses**) (*especially AmE*) a total amount of money earned by sth, especially a film/movie, before any costs are taken away

gross do,mestic 'product *noun* [sing., U] = GDP

gross·ly /ˈɡrəʊsli; *AmE* ˈɡroʊsli/ *adv.* (*disapproving*) (used to describe unpleasant qualities) extremely: *grossly overweight/unfair/inadequate* ◇ *Press reports have been grossly exaggerated.*

gross ,national 'product *noun* [sing., U] = GNP

gro·tesque /ɡrəʊˈtesk; *AmE* ɡroʊ-/ *adj., noun*
■ *adj.* **1** strange in a way that is unpleasant or offensive: *a grotesque distortion of the truth* ◇ *The story was too grotesque to believe.* ◇ *It's grotesque to expect a person of her experience to work for so little money.* **2** extremely ugly in a strange way, often causing fear or laughter: *a grotesque building/figure* ◇ *tribal dancers wearing grotesque masks* ▶ **gro·tesque·ly** *adv.*
■ *noun* **1** [C] a person who is extremely ugly in a strange way, especially in a book or painting **2** (**the grotesque**) [sing.] a style of art using grotesque figures and designs

grotto /ˈɡrɒtəʊ; *AmE* ˈɡrɑːtoʊ/ *noun* (*pl.* **-oes** or **-os**) a small CAVE especially one that has been made artificially, for example in a garden

grotty /ˈɡrɒti; *AmE* ˈɡrɑːti/ *adj.* (*BrE, informal*) unpleasant or of poor quality: *a grotty little hotel* ◇ *I'm feeling pretty grotty* (= ill).

grouch *noun* /ɡraʊtʃ/ (*informal*) **1** a person who complains a lot **2** a complaint about sth unimportant ▶ **grouch** *verb* [V]

grouchy /ˈɡraʊtʃi/ *adj.* (*informal*) bad-tempered and often complaining

ground /ɡraʊnd/ *noun, verb, adj.*—see also GRIND *v.*
■ *noun*

SURFACE OF EARTH ▏ **1** (often **the ground**) [U] the solid surface of the earth: *I found her lying on the ground.* ◇ *He lost his balance and fell to the ground.* ◇ *2 metres above/below ground* ◇ *Most of the monkeys' food is found at ground level.* ◇ *ground forces* (= soldiers that fight on land, not in the air or at sea) ⇨ note at EARTH

SOIL ▏ **2** [U] soil on the surface of the earth: *fertile ground for planting crops*

AREA OF LAND ▏ **3** [U] an area of open land: *The kids were playing on waste ground behind the school.* **4** [C] (often in compounds) (*BrE*) an area of land that is used for a particular purpose, activity or sport: *a football/recreation/sports ground* ◇ *ancient burial grounds*—see also BREEDING GROUND, DUMPING GROUND, PARADE GROUND,

G

STAMPING GROUND, TESTING GROUND **5 (grounds)** [pl.] a large area of land or sea that is used for a particular purpose: *fishing/hunting grounds* ◊ *feeding grounds for birds*

GARDENS | **6 (grounds)** [pl.] the land or gardens around a large building: *the school/hospital grounds*

AREA OF KNOWLEDGE/IDEAS | **7** [U] an area of interest, knowledge or ideas: *He managed to* **cover a lot of ground** *in a short talk.* ◊ *We had to* **go over the same ground** (= talk about the same things again) *in class the next day.* ◊ *You're* **on dangerous ground** (= talking about ideas that are likely to offend sb or make people angry) *if you criticize his family.* ◊ *I thought I was* **on safe ground** (= talking about a suitable subject) *discussing music with her.* ◊ *He was back* **on familiar ground**, *dealing with the customers.* ◊ *They are fighting the Conservatives* **on their own ground**.—see also COMMON GROUND, MIDDLE GROUND

GOOD REASON | **8** [C, usually pl.] **~ for sth/for doing sth** a good or true reason for saying, doing or believing sth: *You have no* **grounds** *for complaint.* ◊ *What were his grounds for wanting a divorce?* ◊ *The case was dismissed* **on the grounds that** *there was not enough evidence.* ◊ *He retired from the job* **on health grounds**. ◊ *Employers cannot discriminate* **on grounds of** *age.* ⇨ note at REASON

IN LIQUID | **9 (grounds)** [pl.] the small pieces of solid matter in a liquid that have fallen to the bottom: *coffee grounds*

ELECTRICAL WIRE | **10** [C, usually sing.] *(AmE)* = EARTH (5)

BACKGROUND | **11** [C] a background that a design is painted or printed on: *pink roses on a white ground*

IDM **cut the ground from under sb's 'feet** to suddenly spoil sb's idea or plan by doing sth to stop them from continuing with it **gain/make up 'ground (on sb/sth)** to gradually get closer to sb/sth that is moving or making progress in an activity: *The police car was gaining ground on the suspects.* ◊ *They needed to make up ground on their competitors.* **get (sth) off the 'ground** to start happening successfully; to make sth start happening successfully: *Without more money, the movie is unlikely to get off the ground.* ◊ *to get a new company off the ground* **give/lose 'ground (to sb/sth)** to allow sb to have an advantage; to lose an advantage for yourself: *They are not prepared to give ground on tax cuts.* ◊ *The Conservatives lost a lot of ground to the Liberal Democrats at the election.* **go to 'ground** *(BrE)* to hide, especially to escape sb who is chasing you **hold/stand your 'ground 1** to continue with your opinions or intentions when sb is opposing you and wants you to change: *Don't let him persuade you—stand your ground.* **2** to face a situation and refuse to run away: *It is not easy to hold your ground in front of someone with a gun.* **on the 'ground** in the place where sth is happening and among the people who are in the situation, especially in a war: *On the ground, there are hopes that the fighting will soon stop.* ◊ *There's a lot of support for the policy on the ground.* **run/drive/work yourself into the 'ground** to work so hard that you become extremely tired **run sb/sth into the 'ground** to use sth so much that it is broken; to make sb work so hard that they are no longer able to work **thick/thin on the 'ground** *(BrE)* if people or things are thick/thin on the ground, there are a lot/not many of them in a place: *Customers are thin on the ground at this time of year.*—more at EAR, FIRM *adj.*, FOOT *n.*, GAIN *v.*, HIT *v.*, MORAL *adj.*, NEUTRAL *adv.*, NEW, PREPARE, RIVET *v.*, SHIFT *v.*, STONY, SUIT *v.*

■ *verb*

BOAT | **1** when a boat **grounds** or sth **grounds** it, it touches the bottom of the sea and is unable to move: [VN] *The fishing boat had been grounded on rocks off the coast of Cornwall.* [also V]

AIRCRAFT | **2** [VN] [often passive] to prevent an aircraft from taking off: *The balloon was grounded by strong winds.* ◊ *All planes out of Heathrow have been grounded by the strikes.*

CHILD | **3** [VN] [usually passive] to punish a child by not allowing them to go out with their friends for a period of time: *You're grounded for a week!*

ELECTRICITY | **4** [VN] *(AmE)* = EARTH

IDM **(be) 'grounded in/on sth** (to be) based on sth: *His views are grounded on the assumption that all people are equal.*—see also GROUNDING

■ *adj.* [only before noun] (of food) cut or crushed into very small pieces or powder: *ground coffee*

'ground ball *noun* = GROUNDER

'ground 'beef *noun* [U] *(AmE)* = MINCE

'ground-breaking *adj.* [only before noun] making new discoveries; using new methods: *a ground-breaking report/style*

'ground cloth *noun (AmE)* = GROUNDSHEET

'ground control *noun* [U] the people and equipment on the ground that make sure that planes or spacecraft take off and land safely

'ground crew (also **'ground staff**) *noun* [C+sing./pl. *v.*] the people at an airport whose job is to look after aircraft while they are on the ground

ground·er /ˈɡraʊndə(r)/ (also **'ground ball**) *noun* (in baseball) a ball that runs along the ground after it has been hit

'ground 'floor *(BrE)* *(AmE* **first 'floor**) *noun* the floor of a building that is at the same level as the ground outside: *a ground-floor flat/window* ◊ *I live on the ground floor.* ⇨ note at FLOOR **IDM** **be/get in on the ground 'floor** to become involved in a plan, project, etc. at the beginning

ground·hog /ˈɡraʊndhɒɡ; *AmE* -hɔːɡ; -hɑːɡ/ *noun* = WOODCHUCK

ground·ing /ˈɡraʊndɪŋ/ *noun* **1** [sing.] **~ (in sth)** the teaching of the basic parts of a subject: *a good grounding in grammar* **2** [U, C] the act of keeping a plane on the ground or a ship in a port, especially because it is not in a good enough condition to travel

ground·less /ˈɡraʊndləs/ *adj.* not based on reason or evidence: *groundless allegations* ◊ *Our fears proved groundless.*

ground·nut /ˈɡraʊndnʌt/ *noun (BrE)* = PEANUT

'ground plan *noun* **1** a plan of the ground floor of a building—compare PLAN *n.* (4) **2** a plan for future action

'ground rent *noun* [U, C] (in Britain) rent paid by the owner of a building to the owner of the land on which it is built

'ground rule *noun* **1** (**ground rules**) [pl.] the basic rules on which sth is based: *The new code of conduct lays down the ground rules for management-union relations.* **2** [C] *(AmE, sport)* a rule for the playing of a game on a particular field, etc.

ground·sheet /ˈɡraʊndʃiːt/ *(BrE)* *(AmE* **'ground cloth**) *noun* a large piece of material that does not let water through that is placed on the ground inside a tent

grounds·man /ˈɡraʊndzmən/ *noun* (pl. **-men** /-men/) *(especially BrE)* a man whose job is to take care of a sports ground or large garden

'ground squirrel *noun* = GOPHER

'ground staff *noun* [C+sing./pl. *v.*] **1** *(BrE)* the people at a sports ground whose job it is to look after the grass, equipment, etc. **2** = GROUND CREW

ground·swell /ˈɡraʊndswel/ *noun* [sing.] **~ (of sth)** *(written)* the sudden increase of a particular feeling among a group of people: *a groundswell of support* ◊ *There was a groundswell of opinion that he should resign.*

ground·water /ˈɡraʊndwɔːtə(r)/ *noun* [U] water that is found under the ground in soil, rocks, etc.

ground·work /ˈɡraʊndwɜːk; *AmE* -wɜːrk/ *noun* [U] **~ (for sth)** work that is done as preparation for other work that will be done later: *Officials are laying the groundwork for a summit conference of world leaders.*

group /ɡruːp/ *noun, verb*

■ *noun* [C+sing./pl. *v.*] **1** a number of people or things that are together in the same place or that are connected in some way: *a group of girls/trees/houses* ◊ *A group of us are going to the theatre this evening.* ◊ *Students stood around in groups waiting for their results.* ◊ *a discussion/study/support group* ◊ *the Germanic group of languages* ◊ *The proportion of single parent families varies between*

different income groups. ◊ a group activity (= done by a number of people working together)—see also SUBGROUP **HELP** There are many other compounds ending in **group**. You will find them at their place in the alphabet. **2** (*business*) a number of companies that are owned by the same person or organization: *a newspaper group* ◊ *the Burton group* ◊ *the group sales director* **3** (rather *old-fashioned*) a number of musicians who perform together, especially to play pop music: *She sings in a rock group.*
■ *verb* **1** ~ (**sb/sth**) (**round/ around sb/sth**)| ~ (**sb/sth**) (**together**) to gather into a group; to make sb/sth form a group: [VN] *The children grouped themselves around their teacher.* ◊ [V] *We all grouped around the tree for a photograph.* ◊ *The colleges grouped together to offer a wider range of courses.* **2** [VN] to divide people or things into groups of people or things that are similar in some way: *The books are grouped together by subject.* ◊ *Contestants were grouped according to age and ability.*

,group ˈcaptain *noun* (*abbr.* **Gp Capt**) an officer of high rank in the British air force: *Group Captain (Jonathan) Sutton*

groupie /ˈgruːpi/ *noun* a person, especially a young woman, who follows pop musicians around and tries to meet them

group·ing /ˈgruːpɪŋ/ *noun* **1** [C] a number of people or organizations that have the same interests, aims or characteristics and are often part of a larger group: *These small nations constitute an important grouping within the EU.* **2** [U] the act of forming sth into a group

,group ˈpractice *noun* a group of several doctors or other medical workers who work together in the community and use the same building to see patients

,group ˈtherapy *noun* [U] a type of PSYCHIATRIC treatment in which people with similar personal problems meet together to discuss them

grouse /graʊs/ *noun, verb*
■ *noun* **1** [C, U] (*pl.* **grouse**) a bird with a fat body and feathers on its legs, which people shoot for sport and food; the meat of this bird: *grouse shooting* ◊ *grouse moors* ◊ *roast grouse* **2** [C] (*informal*) a complaint
■ *verb* [V, Vspeech] ~ (**about sb/sth**) (*informal*) to complain about sth in a way that other people find annoying [SYN] GRUMBLE

grout /graʊt/ (also **grout·ing**) *noun* [U] a substance that is used between the TILES on the walls of kitchens, bathrooms, etc. ▶ grout *verb* [VN]

grove /grəʊv; *AmE* groʊv/ *noun* **1** (*literary*) a small group of trees: *a grove of birch trees* **2** a small area of land with fruit trees of particular types on it: *an olive grove* **3** used in the names of streets: *Elm Grove*

grovel /ˈgrɒvl; *AmE* ˈgrɑːvl/ *verb* (**-ll-,** *AmE* **-l-**) [V] **1** ~ (**to sb**) (**for sth**) (*disapproving*) to behave in a very HUMBLE way towards sb who is more important than you or who can give you sth you want [SYN] CRAWL **2** [+*adv. / prep.*] to move along the ground on your hands and knees, especially because you are looking for sth ▶ grov·el·ling (*BrE*) (*AmE* **grov·el·ing**) *adj.* [only before noun]: *a grovelling letter of apology*

grow /grəʊ; *AmE* groʊ/ *verb* (**grew** /gruː/ **grown** /grəʊn; *AmE* groʊn/)
INCREASE **1** ~ (**in sth**) to increase in size, number, strength or quality: [V] *The company profits grew by 5% last year.* ◊ *The family has grown in size recently.* ◊ *She is growing in confidence all the time.* ◊ *A growing number of people are going vegetarian.* ◊ [V-ADJ] *The company is growing bigger all the time.*
OF PERSON/ ANIMAL **2** to become bigger or taller and develop into an adult: [V] *You've grown since the last time I saw you!* ◊ *Nick's grown almost an inch in the last month.* ◊ [V-ADJ] *to grow bigger/taller*
OF PLANT **3** to exist and develop in a particular place; to make plants grow: [V] *The region is too dry for plants to grow.* ◊ *Tomatoes grow best in direct sunlight.* ◊ [VN] *I didn't know they grew rice in France.*—see also HOME-GROWN
OF HAIR/NAILS **4** to become longer; to allow sth to become longer by not cutting it: [V] *I've decided to let my hair

grow.* ◊ [VN] *I've decided to grow my hair.* ◊ *I didn't recognize him—he's grown a beard.*
BECOME/BEGIN **5** *linking verb* [V-ADJ] to begin to have a particular quality or feeling over a period of time: *to grow old / bored / calm* ◊ *As time went on he grew more and more impatient.* ◊ *The skies grew dark and it began to rain.* **6** [Vtoinf] to gradually begin to do sth: *I'm sure you'll grow to like her in time.*
DEVELOP SKILLS **7** [V] ~ (**as sth**) (of a person) to develop and improve particular qualities or skills: *She continues to grow as an artist.*
BUSINESS **8** [VN] to increase the size, quality or number of sth: *We are trying to grow the business.*
IDM **it/money doesn't grow on ˈtrees** (*spoken*) used to tell sb not to use sth or spend money carelessly because you do not have a lot of it—more at GRASS *n.*
PHRV ,grow aˈpart (**from sb**) to stop having a close relationship with sb over a period of time ,grow aˈway from sb [no passive] to become less close to sb; to depend on sb or care for sb less: *When she left school she grew away from her mother.* ,grow ˈback to begin growing again after being cut off or damaged ,grow ˈinto sth [no passive] **1** to gradually develop into a particular type of person over a period of time **2** (of a child) to grow big enough to fit into a piece of clothing that used to be too big: *The dress is too long for her now but she'll grow into it.* **3** to become more confident in a new job, etc. and learn to do it better: *She's still growing into her new role as a mother.* ˈgrow on sb [no passive] if sb/sth grows on you, you start to like them or it more and more ,grow ˈout (of a hairstyle, etc.) to disappear as your hair grows: *I had a perm a year ago and it still hasn't grown out.* ,grow sth↔ˈout to allow your hair to grow in order to change the style: *I've decided to grow my layers out.* ,grow ˈout of sth [no passive] **1** (of a child) to become too big to fit into a piece of clothing [SYN] OUTGROW: *He's already grown out of his school uniform.* **2** to stop doing sth as you become older [SYN] OUTGROW: *Most children suck their thumbs but they grow out of it.* **3** to develop from sth: *The idea for the book grew out of a visit to India.* ,grow ˈup **1** (of a person) to develop into an adult: *She grew up (= spent her childhood) in Boston.* ◊ *Their children have all grown up and left home now.*—related noun GROWN-UP **2** used to tell sb to stop behaving in a silly way: *Why don't you grow up?* ◊ *It's time you grew up.* **3** to develop gradually: *A closeness grew up between the two girls.*

grow·er /ˈgrəʊə(r); *AmE* ˈgroʊ-/ *noun* **1** a person or company that grows plants, fruit or vegetables to sell: *a tobacco grower* ◊ *All our vegetables are supplied by local growers.* **2** a plant that grows in the way mentioned: *a fast/slow grower*

grow·ing /ˈgrəʊɪŋ; *AmE* ˈgroʊɪŋ/ *adj.* [only before noun] increasing in size, amount or degree: *A growing number of people are returning to full-time education.* ◊ *one of the country's fastest growing industries* ◊ *There is growing concern over the safety of the missing teenager.*

ˈgrowing pains *noun* [pl.] **1** pains that some children feel in their arms and legs when they are growing **2** emotional anxieties felt by young people as they grow up **3** problems or difficulties that are experienced by a company when it begins operating but that are not likely to last: *Every business experiences its share of growing pains.*

ˈgrowing season *noun* [usually sing.] the period of the year during which the weather conditions are right for plants to grow: *a part of the world with a long growing season*

growl /graʊl/ *verb, noun*
■ *verb* **1** [V] ~ (**at sb/sth**) (of animals, especially dogs) to make a low sound in the throat, usually as a sign of anger **2** ~ (**at sb**) to say sth in a low angry voice: [Vspeech] *'Who are you?' he growled at the stranger.* ◊ [VN] *She growled a sarcastic reply.*
■ *noun* a deep angry sound made when sb/sth growls

grown /grəʊn; *AmE* groʊn/ *adj.* [only before noun] (of a person) mentally and physically an adult: *It's pathetic that grown men have to resort to violence like this.*—see also FULL-GROWN, HOME-GROWN, GROW *v.*

æ	ɑː	e	ɜː	ə	ɪ	iː	i	ɒ	ɔː	ʌ	ʊ	u	uː
cat	father	ten	bird	about	sit	see	many	got	saw	cup	put	actual	too
								(BrE)					

G

grown-up *adj.* **1** (of a person) mentally and physically an adult: *What do you want to be when you're grown-up?* ◊ *She has a grown-up son.* **2** suitable for or typical of an adult: *The child was clearly puzzled at being addressed in such a grown-up way.*

grown-up *noun* (used especially by and to children) an adult person: *If you're good you can eat with the grown-ups.*

growth /grəʊθ; *AmE* groʊθ/ *noun* **1** [U] (of people, animals or plants) the process of growing physically, mentally or emotionally: *Lack of water will stunt the plant's growth.* ◊ *Remove dead leaves to encourage new growth.* ◊ *a concern with personal* (= mental and emotional) *growth and development* ◊ *growth hormones* (= designed to make sb/sth grow faster) **2** [U] ~ (in/of sth) an increase in the size, amount or degree of sth: *population growth* ◊ *the rapid growth in violent crime* **3** [U] an increase in economic activity: *a disappointing year of little growth in Britain and America* ◊ *policies aimed at sustaining economic growth* ◊ *an annual growth rate of 10%* ◊ *a growth area/industry* **4** [C] a lump caused by a disease that forms on or inside a person, an animal or a plant: *a malignant/cancerous growth* **5** [U, C] something that has grown: *The forest's dense growth provides nesting places for a wide variety of birds.* ◊ *several days' growth of beard*

groyne (*BrE*) (also **groin** *AmE, BrE*) /grɔɪn/ *noun* a low wall built out into the sea to prevent it from washing away sand and stones from the beach

grub /grʌb/ *noun, verb*
- *noun* **1** [C] the young form of an insect, that looks like a small fat worm **2** [U] (*informal*) food: *Grub's up* (= the meal is ready)! ◊ *They serve good pub grub there.*
- *verb* (**-bb-**) [V] ~ (**around/about**) (**for sth**) to look for sth, especially by digging or by looking through or under other things: *birds grubbing for worms* **PHRV** **grub sth··'up/'out** to dig sth out of the ground: *The trees were grubbed up to make way for a new road.*

grubby /ˈgrʌbi/ *adj.* (**grub·bier**, **grub·bi·est**) **1** rather dirty, usually because it has not been washed or cleaned: *grubby hands/clothes* **2** unpleasant because it involves activities that are dishonest or immoral **SYN** SORDID: *a grubby affair/scandal* ▸ **grubbi·ness** *noun* [U]

grudge /grʌdʒ/ *noun, verb*
- *noun* ~ (**against sb**) a feeling of anger or dislike towards sb because of sth bad they have done to you in the past: *I bear him no grudge.* ◊ *He has a grudge against the world.* ◊ *I don't hold any grudges now.* ◊ *He's a man with a grudge.* ◊ *England beat New Zealand in a grudge match* (= a match where there is strong dislike between the teams).
- *verb* **1** to do or give sth unwillingly **SYN** BEGRUDGE: [V-ing] *I grudge having to pay so much tax.* ◊ [VN] *He grudges the time that he spends travelling to work.* **2** [VNN] to think that sb does not deserve to have sth **SYN** BEGRUDGE: *You surely don't grudge her her success?*

grudg·ing /ˈgrʌdʒɪŋ/ *adj.* [usually before noun] given or done unwillingly **SYN** RELUCTANT: *He could not help feeling a grudging admiration for the old lady.* ▸ **grudg·ing·ly** (also *less frequent* **be·grudg·ing·ly**) *adv.*: *She grudgingly admitted that I was right.*

gruel /ˈɡruːəl/ *noun* [U] a simple dish made by boiling OATS in milk or water, eaten especially in the past by poor people

gruel·ling (*especially BrE*) (*AmE usually* **gruel·ing**) /ˈɡruːəlɪŋ/ *adj.* very difficult and tiring, needing great effort for a long time: *a gruelling journey/schedule* ◊ *I've had a gruelling day.*

grue·some /ˈɡruːsəm/ *adj.* very unpleasant and filling you with horror, usually because it is connected with death or injury: *a gruesome murder* ◊ *gruesome pictures of dead bodies* ◊ (*humorous*) *We spent a week in a gruesome apartment in Miami.* ▸ **grue·some·ly** *adv.*

gruff /grʌf/ *adj.* **1** (of a voice) deep and harsh, and often sounding unfriendly **2** (of a person's behaviour) unfriendly and impatient: *Beneath his gruff exterior, he's really very kind-hearted.* ▸ **gruff·ly** *adv.*

grum·ble /ˈgrʌmbl/ *verb, noun*
- *verb* **1** ~ (**at/to sb**) (**about/at sb/sth**) to complain about sb/sth in a bad-tempered way: [V] *She's always grumbling to me about how badly she's treated at work.* ◊ [V speech] *'I'll just have to do it myself,' he grumbled.* ◊ [V that] *They kept grumbling that they were cold.* **2** [V] to make a deep continuous sound **SYN** RUMBLE: *Thunder grumbled in the distance.* ▸ **grum·bler** /ˈgrʌmblə(r)/ *noun*
- *noun* **1** ~ (**about sth**) | ~ (**that…**) something that you complain about because you are not satisfied: *My main grumble is about the lack of privacy.* **2** a long low sound **SYN** RUMBLE: *a distant grumble of thunder*

grum·bling /ˈgrʌmblɪŋ/ *noun* **1** [U] the act of complaining about sth: *We didn't hear any grumbling about the food.* **2** (**grumblings**) [pl.] protests about sth that come from a number of people but that are not expressed very clearly

grump /grʌmp/ *noun* (*informal*) a bad-tempered person

grumpy /ˈɡrʌmpi/ *adj.* (**grump·ier**, **grump·iest**) (*informal*) bad-tempered ▸ **grump·ily** /ˈɡrʌmpɪli/ *adv.*

grunge /grʌndʒ/ *noun* [U] **1** (*informal*) dirt of any kind **SYN** GRIME **2** (also **'grunge rock**) a type of loud rock music, which was popular in the early 1990s **3** a style of fashion worn by people who like grunge music, usually involving clothes that look untidy

grungy /ˈgrʌndʒi/ *adj.* (*especially AmE*) dirty in an unpleasant way

grunt /grʌnt/ *verb, noun*
- *verb* **1** [V] (of animals, especially pigs) to make a short low sound in the throat **2** (of people) to make a short low sound in your throat, especially to show that you are in pain, annoyed or not interested; to say sth using this sound: [V] *He pulled harder on the rope, grunting with the effort.* ◊ *When I told her what had happened she just grunted and turned back to her book.* ◊ [VN] *He grunted something about being late and rushed out.* [also V speech]
- *noun* **1** a short, low sound made by a person or an animal (especially a pig): *to give a grunt of effort/pain* **2** (*AmE, slang*) a worker who does boring tasks for low pay **3** (*AmE, slang*) a soldier of low rank

gryphon /ˈgrɪfən/ *noun* = GRIFFIN

GSOH *abbr.* good sense of humour (used in personal advertisements)

'G-string *noun* a narrow piece of fabric that covers the sexual organs and is held up by a string around the waist

Gt (also **Gt.** especially in *AmE*) *abbr.* (in names of places) Great: *Gt Britain* ◊ *Gt Yarmouth*

guano /ˈɡwɑːnəʊ; *AmE* -noʊ/ *noun* [U] the waste substance passed from the bodies of seabirds, that is used to make plants and crops grow well

guar·an·tee /ˌgærənˈtiː/ *noun, verb*
- *noun* **1** a firm promise that you will do sth or that sth will happen: *to give a guarantee of good behaviour* ◊ *He gave me a guarantee that it would never happen again.* ◊ *They are demanding certain guarantees before they sign the treaty.* **2** a written promise given by a company that sth you buy will be replaced or repaired without payment if it goes wrong within a particular period: *We provide a 5-year guarantee against rust.* ◊ *The watch is still under guarantee.* ◊ *The television comes with a year's guarantee.* ◊ *a money-back guarantee* **3** ~ (**of sth**) | ~ (**that…**) something that makes sth else certain to happen: *Career success is no guarantee of happiness.* ◊ *There's no guarantee that she'll come* (= she may not come). **4** money or sth valuable that you give or promise to a bank, for example, to make sure that you will do what you have promised: *We had to offer our house as a guarantee when getting the loan.*
- *verb* **1** to promise to do sth; to promise sth will happen: [VN] *Basic human rights, including freedom of speech, are now guaranteed.* ◊ [V (that)] *We cannot guarantee (that) our flights will never be delayed.* ◊ [VNN] *The ticket will guarantee you free entry.* ◊ [V to inf] *We guarantee to deliver your goods within a week.* **2** [VN] ~ **sth** (**against sth**) to give a written promise to replace or repair a product free of charge if it goes wrong: *This iron is guaranteed for a*

aɪ	aʊ	eɪ	əʊ	oʊ	ɔɪ	ɪə	eə	ʊə	j	w
my	now	say	go (BrE)	go (AmE)	boy	near	hair	pure	yes	wet

year against faulty workmanship. **3** to make sth certain to happen: [VN] *Tonight's victory guarantees the team's place in the final.* ◊ [VNN] *These days getting a degree doesn't guarantee you a job.* **4** [v(that)] to be certain that sth will happen: *You can guarantee (that) the children will start being naughty as soon as they have to go to bed.* **5** to agree to be legally responsible for sth or for doing sth: [VN] *to guarantee a bank loan* ◊ [Vto inf] *to guarantee to pay sb's debts* ◊ [Vthat] *I guarantee that he will appear in court.* **IDM** **be guaran'teed to do sth** to be certain to have a particular result: *If we try to keep it a secret, she's guaranteed to find out.* ◊ *That kind of behaviour is guaranteed to make him angry.*

guar·an·tor /ˌgærənˈtɔː(r)/ *noun* (*formal or law*) a person who agrees to be responsible for sb or for making sure that sth happens or is done: *The United Nations will act as guarantor of the peace settlement.*

guard /gɑːd; *AmE* gɑːrd/ *noun, verb*
■ *noun*
PEOPLE WHO PROTECT **1** [C] a person, such as a soldier, a police officer or a prison officer, who protects a place or people, or prevents prisoners from escaping: *a security guard* ◊ *border guards* ◊ *The prisoner slipped past the guards on the gate and escaped.* ◊ *A guard was posted outside the building.*—compare WARDER—see also BODYGUARD, COASTGUARD, LIFEGUARD **2** [C+sing./pl. v.] a group of people, such as soldiers or police officers, who protect sb/sth: *the captain of the guard* ◊ *the changing of the guard* (= when one group replaces another) ◊ *The guard is/are being inspected today.* ◊ *Fellow airmen provided a guard of honour at his wedding.* ◊ *The President always travels with an armed guard.*—see also NATIONAL GUARD, OLD GUARD, REARGUARD **3** [U] the act or duty of protecting property, places or people from attack or danger; the act or duty of preventing prisoners from escaping: *a sentry on guard* (= at his or her post, on duty) ◊ *to do guard duty* ◊ *The escaped prisoner was brought back under armed guard.* ◊ *The terrorist was kept under police guard.* ◊ *One of the men kept guard, while the other broke into the house.*
SOLDIERS **4** (**the Guards**) [pl.] (in Britain and some other countries) special REGIMENTS of soldiers whose original duty was to protect the king or queen: *the Scots Guards* ◊ *a Guards officer*
AGAINST INJURY **5** [C] (often in compounds) something that covers a part of a person's body or a dangerous part of a machine to prevent injury: *a mouth guard* ◊ *Ensure the guard is in place before operating the machine.*—see also FIREGUARD, MUDGUARD, SAFEGUARD, SHIN GUARD
ON TRAIN **6** [C] (*BrE*, becoming *old-fashioned*) = CONDUCTOR (2)
IN BOXING/FENCING **7** [U] a position you take to defend yourself, especially in a sport such as boxing or FENCING: *to drop/keep up your guard* ◊ (*figurative*) *In spite of the awkward questions the minister never let his guard fall for a moment.*
IDM **be on your 'guard** to be very careful and prepared for sth difficult or dangerous **mount/stand/keep 'guard (over sb/sth)** to watch or protect sb/sth: *Four soldiers stood guard over the coffin.* **off (your) 'guard** not careful or prepared for sth difficult or dangerous: *The lawyer's apparently innocent question was designed to* **catch the witness off (**his**) guard.**
■ *verb* [VN] **1** to protect property, places or people from attack or danger: *The dog was guarding its owner's luggage.* ◊ *political leaders guarded by the police* ◊ *You can't get in; the whole place is guarded.* ◊ (*figurative*) *a closely guarded secret* **2** to prevent prisoners from escaping: *The prisoners were guarded by soldiers.*
PHRV **'guard against sth** to take care to prevent sth or to protect yourself from sth: *to guard against accidents/ error/loss/disease*

'guard dog *noun* a dog that is kept to guard a building

guard·ed /ˈgɑːdɪd; *AmE* ˈgɑːrdɪd/ *adj.* (of a person or a remark they make) careful; not showing feelings or giving much information: *a guarded reply* ◊ *You should be more guarded in what you say to reporters.* ◊ *They gave the*

news a guarded welcome (= did not show great enthusiasm about it). **OPP** UNGUARDED ▶ **guard·ed·ly** *adv.*

guard·house /ˈgɑːdhaʊs; *AmE* ˈgɑːrd-/ *noun* a building for soldiers who are guarding the entrance to a military camp or for keeping military prisoners in

guard·ian /ˈgɑːdiən; *AmE* ˈgɑːrd-/ *noun* **1** a person who protects sth: *Farmers should be guardians of the countryside.* ◊ *The police are guardians of law and order.* **2** a person who is legally responsible for the care of another person, especially a child whose parents have died

ˌguardian 'angel *noun* a spirit that some people believe protects and guides them, especially when they are in danger: (*figurative*) *A delightful guide was my guardian angel for the first week of the tour.*

guard·ian·ship /ˈgɑːdiənʃɪp; *AmE* ˈgɑːrd-/ *noun* [U] (*formal or law*) the state or position of being responsible for sb/sth: *to grant sb guardianship of the children* ◊ *The land is under the guardianship of the people who use it.*

'guard rail *noun* **1** a rail placed on the edge of a path, a cliff or a boat to protect people and prevent them falling over the edge **2** (*AmE*) = CRASH BARRIER

guard·room /ˈgɑːdruːm; -rʊm; *AmE* ˈgɑːrd-/ *noun* a room for soldiers who are guarding the entrance to a building or for keeping military prisoners in

guards·man /ˈgɑːdzmən; *AmE* ˈgɑːrd-/ *noun* (*pl.* **-men** /-mən/) a soldier in THE GUARDS or in THE NATIONAL GUARD in the US

'guard's van *noun* (*BrE*) the part of a train where the person who is in charge of the train rides

guava /ˈgwɑːvə/ *noun* the fruit of a tropical American tree, with yellow skin and pink flesh

gu·ber·na·tor·ial /ˌguːbənəˈtɔːriəl; *AmE* -bərnə-/ *adj.* (*formal*) connected with the job of state GOVERNOR in the US: *a gubernatorial candidate* ◊ *gubernatorial duties*

guer·rilla (also **guer·illa**) /gəˈrɪlə/ *noun* a member of a small group of soldiers who are not part of an official army and who fight against official soldiers, usually to try to change the government: *urban guerrillas* (= those who fight in towns) ◊ *guerrilla war/warfare* (= fought by guerrillas on one or both sides) ◊ *a guerrilla group/ movement/leader*—compare FREEDOM FIGHTER

guess /ges/ *verb, noun*
■ *verb* **1** ~ **(at sth)** to try and give an answer or make a judgement about sth without being sure of all the facts: [V] *I don't really know. I'm just guessing.* ◊ *We can only guess at her reasons for leaving.* ◊ *He* **guessed right/ wrong.** ◊ [V(that)] *I'd guess that she's about 30.* ◊ [Vwh-] *Can you guess where I've been?* ◊ [VN] *Can you guess his age?* **2** to find the right answer to a question or the truth without knowing all the facts: [VN] *She guessed the answer straight away.* ◊ [Vwh-] *You'll never guess what she told me.* ◊ [V(that)] *You would never guess (that) she had problems. She's always so cheerful.*—see also SECOND-GUESS **3** (**I guess**) (*informal, especially AmE*) to suppose that sth is true or likely: [V(that)] *I guess (that) you'll be looking for a new job now.* ◊ *'He didn't see me, I guess.'* **4** (**guess …!**) used to show that you are going to say sth surprising or exciting: [VN] *Guess what! He's asked me out!* ◊ [Vwh-] *Guess who I've just seen!* **IDM** **keep sb 'guessing** (*informal*) to not tell sb about your plans or what is going to happen next: *It's the kind of book that keeps you guessing right to the end.*
■ *noun* ~ **(about sth)**|~ **(at sth)**|~ **(that …)** an attempt to give an answer or an opinion when you cannot be certain if you are right: (*BrE*) *to have/make a guess (at sth)* ◊ (*AmE*) *to take a guess* ◊ *Go on! Have a guess!* ◊ *The article is based on guesses about what might happen in the future.* ◊ *They might be here by 3—but that's just a* **rough guess** (= not exact). ◊ **My guess is that** *we won't hear from him again.* ◊ **At a guess,** *there were forty people at the party.* ◊ *If I might* **hazard a guess,** *I'd say she was about thirty.* ◊ *Who do you think I saw yesterday? I'll give you three guesses.* **IDM** **'anybody's/'anyone's guess** (*informal*) something that nobody can be certain about: *What will happen next is anybody's guess.* **your ˌguess is as good as 'mine** (*informal*) used to tell sb that you do not know any more about a subject than the person that you are

G

talking to does: *'Who's going to win?' 'Your guess is as good as mine.'*—more at EDUCATED

guess·ti·mate /ˈgestɪmət/ *noun* (*informal*) an attempt to calculate sth that is based more on guessing than on information

guess·work /ˈgeswɜːk; *AmE* -wɜːrk/ *noun* [U] the process of trying to find an answer by guessing when you do not have enough information to be sure: *It was pure guesswork on our part.*

guest /gest/ *noun, verb*

■ *noun* **1** a person that you have invited to your house or to a particular event that you are paying for: *We have guests staying this weekend.* ◊ *more than 100 wedding guests* ◊ *I went to the theatre club as Helen's guest.* ◊ *He was the guest of honour* (= the most important person invited to an event). ◊ *Liz was not on the guest list.* **2** a person who is staying at a hotel, etc: *We have accommodation for 500 guests.* ◊ *a paying guest* (= a person who is living in a private house, but paying as if they were in a hotel) ◊ *Guests should vacate their rooms by 10.30 a.m.* **3** a famous person or performer who takes part in a television show or concert: *a guest artist/star/singer* ◊ *Our special guest tonight is ...* ◊ *He made a guest appearance on the show.* **4** a person who is invited to a particular place or organization, or to speak at a meeting: *The scientists are here as guests of our government.* ◊ *a guest speaker* IDM **be my guest** (*informal*) used to give sb permission to do sth that they have asked to do: *'Do you mind if I use the phone?' 'Be my guest.'*

■ *verb* [V] ~ (**on sth**) to take part in a television or radio show, a concert, a game, etc. as a visiting or temporary performer or player: *She guested on several chat shows while visiting Britain.*

ˈguest house *noun* **1** (*BrE*) a small hotel **2** (*AmE*) a small house built near a large house, for guests to stay in

ˈguest room *noun* a bedroom that is kept for guests to use

ˈguest worker *noun* a person, usually from a poor country, who comes to another richer country in order to work there

guff /gʌf/ *noun* [U] (*informal*) ideas or talk that you think are stupid

guf·faw /gəˈfɔː/ *verb* to laugh noisily: [V] *They all guffawed at his jokes.* [also V speech] ▶ **guf·faw** *noun*: *She let out a loud guffaw.*

guid·ance /ˈgaɪdns/ *noun* [U] **1** ~ (**on sth**) help or advice that is given to sb, especially by sb older or with more experience: *guidance for teachers on how to use video in the classroom* ◊ *Activities all take place under the guidance of an experienced tutor.* ◊ (*AmE*) *a guidance counselor* (= sb who advises students)—see also MARRIAGE GUIDANCE **2** the process of controlling the direction of a rocket, etc., using electronic equipment: *a missile guidance system*

guide /gaɪd/ *noun, verb*

■ *noun*

BOOK/MAGAZINE | **1** ~ (**to sth**) a book, magazine, etc. that gives you information, help or instructions about sth: *a Guide to Family Health* ◊ *Let's have a look at the TV guide and see what's on.* **2** (also **guide·book**) ~ (**to sth**) a book that gives information about a place for travellers or tourists: *a guide to Italy* ◊ *travel guides*

PERSON | **3** a person who shows other people the way to a place, especially sb employed to show tourists around interesting places: *a tour guide* ◊ *We hired a local guide to get us across the mountains.* **4** a person who advises you on how to live and behave: *a spiritual guide*

STH THAT HELPS YOU DECIDE | **5** something that gives you enough information to be able to make a decision about sth or form an opinion: *As a rough guide, allow half a cup of rice per person.* ◊ *I let my feelings be my guide.*

GIRL | **6** (**Guide**) (also *old-fashioned* ˌGirl ˈGuide) (both *BrE*) (*AmE* ˌGirl ˈScout) a member of an organization (called **the Guides** or **the Girl Scouts**) which is similar to THE SCOUTS and which trains girls in practical skills and does a lot of activities with them, for example camping —compare BROWNIE

■ *verb* [VN]

SHOW THE WAY | **1** ~ **sb** (**to/through/around sth**) to show sb the way to a place, often by going with them; to show sb a place that you know well: *She guided us through the busy streets to the cathedral.* ◊ *We were guided around the museums.*

INFLUENCE BEHAVIOUR | **2** to direct or influence sb's behaviour: *He was always guided by his religious beliefs.*

EXPLAIN | **3** ~ **sb** (**through sth**) to explain to sb how to do sth, especially sth complicated or difficult: *The health and safety officer will guide you through the safety procedures.*

HELP SB MOVE | **4** to help sb to move in a particular direction; to move sth in a particular direction: *She took her arm and guided her across the busy road.* ◊ *He guided her hand to his face.*—see also GUIDING

guide·book /ˈgaɪdbʊk/ *noun* = GUIDE

guided /ˈgaɪdɪd/ *adj.* [usually before noun] that is led by sb who works as a guide: *a guided tour/walk*

ˌguided ˈmissile *noun* a MISSILE that can be controlled while in the air by electronic equipment

ˈguide dog (*AmE* also ˌSeeing ˈEye dog™) *noun* a dog trained to guide a blind person

guide·line /ˈgaɪdlaɪn/ *noun* **1** (**guidelines**) [pl.] rules or instructions that are given by an official organization telling you how to do sth, especially sth difficult: *The government has drawn up guidelines on the treatment of the mentally ill.* **2** [C] something that can be used to help you make a decision or form an opinion: *The figures are a useful guideline when buying a house.*

guid·ing /ˈgaɪdɪŋ/ *adj.* [only before noun] giving advice and help; having a strong influence on people: *She was inexperienced and needed a guiding hand.* ◊ *a guiding force*

guild /gɪld/ *noun* [C+sing./pl. v.] **1** an organization of people who do the same job or who have the same interests or aims: *the Screen Actors' Guild* **2** an association of skilled workers in the Middle Ages

guil·der /ˈgɪldə(r)/ *noun* the unit of money in the Netherlands (to be replaced by the euro)

guild·hall /ˈgɪldhɔːl/ *noun* (*BrE*) a building in which the members of a GUILD used to meet, now often used for meetings and performances

guile /gaɪl/ *noun* [U] (*formal*) the use of clever but dishonest behaviour in order to deceive people

guile·less /ˈgaɪlləs/ *adj.* (*formal*) behaving in a very honest way; not knowing how to deceive people ▶ **guile·less·ly** *adv.*

guil·le·mot /ˈgɪlɪmɒt; *AmE* -maːt/ *noun* a black and white seabird with a long narrow beak

guil·lo·tine /ˈgɪlətiːn/ *noun, verb*

■ *noun* **1** [sing.] a machine, originally from France, for cutting people's heads off. It has a heavy blade that slides down a wooden frame. **2** (*BrE*) (*AmE* ˈpaper cutter) [C] a device with a long blade for cutting paper **3** [sing.] (*BrE, politics*) the setting of a time limit on a debate in Parliament

■ *verb* [VN] **1** to kill sb by cutting off their head with a guillotine **2** (*BrE*) to cut paper using a guillotine **3** (*BrE, politics*) to limit the amount of time spent discussing a new law in Parliament: *to guillotine a bill/motion*

guilt /gɪlt/ *noun* [U] **1** ~ (**about sth**) the unhappy feelings caused by knowing or thinking that you have done sth wrong: *She had feelings of guilt about leaving her children and going to work.* ◊ *Many survivors were left with a sense of guilt.* ◊ *a guilt complex* (= an exaggerated sense of guilt) **2** the fact that sb has done sth illegal: *His guilt was proved beyond all doubt by the prosecution.* ◊ *an admission of guilt* OPP INNOCENCE **3** blame or responsibility for doing sth wrong or for sth bad that has happened: *The investigation will try to find out where the guilt for the disaster really lies.* ▶ **guilt·less** *adj.* IDM **a ˈguilt trip** (*informal*) things you say to sb in order to make them feel guilty about sth: *Don't lay a guilt trip on your child about schoolwork.*

guilty /ˈgɪlti/ *adj.* (**guilt·ier, guilti·est**) HELP **more guilty**

s	t	v	z	ʃ	ʒ	tʃ	dʒ	θ	ð	ŋ
see	tea	van	zoo	shoe	vision	chain	jam	thin	this	sing

and **most guilty** are more common **1 ~ (about sth)** feeling ashamed because you have done sth that you know is wrong or have not done sth that you should have done: *I felt guilty about not visiting my parents more often.* ◊ *John had a guilty look on his face.* ◊ *I had a **guilty conscience** and could not sleep.* **2 ~ (of sth)** having done sth illegal; being responsible for sth bad that has happened: *The jury found the defendant **not guilty** of the offence.* ◊ *He **pleaded guilty** to murder.* ◊ *the **guilty party** (= the person responsible for sth bad happening)* ◊ *We've all been guilty of selfishness at some time in our lives.* OPP INNOCENT ▶ **guilt·i·ly** /-ɪli/ *adv.*

guinea /ˈgɪni/ *noun* an old British gold coin or unit of money worth 21 SHILLINGS (= now £1.05). Prices are sometimes still given in guineas, for example when buying or selling horses.

guinea·fowl /ˈgɪnifaʊl/ *noun* [C, U] (*pl.* **guinea·fowl**) a bird of the PHEASANT family, that has dark grey feathers with white spots, and is often used for food; the meat of this bird: *roast guineafowl*

'guinea pig *noun* **1** a small animal with short ears and no tail, often kept as a pet **2** a person used in medical or other experiments: *Students in fifty schools are to act as guinea pigs for these new teaching methods.*

guise /gaɪz/ *noun* a way in which sb/sth appears, often in a way that is different from usual or that hides the truth about them/it: *His speech presented racist ideas **under the guise of** nationalism.* ◊ *The story appears in different guises in different cultures.*

gui·tar /gɪˈtɑː(r)/ *noun* a musical instrument that usually has six strings, that you play with your fingers or with a PLECTRUM/PICK: *an acoustic/an electric/a classical guitar* ◊ *a guitar player* ◊ *As he sang, he strummed his guitar.*—see also BASS—picture on page 841

gui·tar·ist /gɪˈtɑːrɪst/ *noun* a person who plays the guitar

Gu·ja·rati (also **Gu·je·rati**) /ˌguːdʒəˈrɑːti/ *noun* **1** [C] a person from the state of Gujarat in western India **2** [U] the language of Gujarat ▶ **Gu·ja·rati** (also **Gu·je·rati**) *adj.*

gulch /ɡʌltʃ/ *noun* (*especially AmE*) a narrow valley with steep sides, that was formed by a fast stream flowing through it

gulf /ɡʌlf/ *noun* **1** [C] a large area of sea that is partly surrounded by land: *the Gulf of Mexico* **2 (the Gulf)** [sing.] the Persian Gulf, the area of sea between the Arabian PENINSULA and Iran: *the Gulf States* (= the countries with coasts on the Gulf) **3** [C, usually sing.] **~ (between A and B)** a large difference between two people or groups in the way that they think, live or feel: *The gulf between rich and poor is enormous.* **4** [C] a wide deep crack in the ground IDM see BRIDGE *v.*

the 'Gulf Stream *noun* [sing.] a warm current of water flowing across the Atlantic Ocean from the Gulf of Mexico towards Europe

gull /ɡʌl/ (also **sea·gull**) *noun* a seabird with long wings and usually with white and grey or black feathers. There are several types of gull: *a black-headed gull* ◊ *Hundreds of gulls were circling overhead.*—see also HERRING GULL—picture on page A6

gul·let /ˈɡʌlɪt/ *noun* the tube through which food passes from the mouth to the stomach SYN OESOPHAGUS—picture at BODY

gul·lible /ˈɡʌləbl/ *adj.* too willing to believe or accept what other people tell you and therefore easily tricked: *The advertisement is aimed at gullible young women worried about their weight.* ▶ **gul·li·bil·ity** /ˌɡʌləˈbɪləti/ *noun* [U]

gully (also **gul·ley**) /ˈɡʌli/ *noun* (*pl.* **gul·lies**, **gul·leys**) **1** a small, narrow channel, usually formed by a stream or by rain **2** a deep DITCH

gulp /ɡʌlp/ *verb, noun*

■ *verb* **1 ~ sth (down)** to swallow large amounts of food or drink quickly: *He gulped down the rest of his tea and went out.* [also V] **2** to swallow, but without eating or drinking anything, especially because of a strong emotion such as fear or surprise: *She gulped nervously before*

trying to answer. [also V] **speech** **3 ~ (for sth)| ~ sth (in)** to breathe quickly and deeply, because you need more air: [V] *She came up **gulping for air**.* ◊ [VN] *He leant against the car, gulping in the cold air.* PHRV **ˌgulp sth↔'back** to stop yourself showing your emotions by swallowing hard: *She gulped back her tears and forced a smile.*

■ *noun* **1 ~ (of sth)** an amount of sth that you swallow or drink quickly: *He took a gulp of coffee.* ◊ *gulps of sea air* **2** an act of breathing in or of swallowing sth: *'Can you start on Monday?' Amy gave a gulp. 'Of course,' she said.* ◊ *He drank the glass of whisky **in one gulp**.*

gum /ɡʌm/ *noun, verb*

■ *noun* **1** [C, usually pl.] either of the firm areas of flesh in the mouth to which the teeth are attached: *gum disease*—picture at BODY **2** [U] a sticky substance produced by some types of tree **3** [U] a type of glue used for sticking light things together, such as paper **4** [U] = CHEWING GUM **5** [C] a firm transparent fruit-flavoured sweet/candy that you chew: *fruit gums* IDM **by gum!** (*old-fashioned, BrE, spoken*) used to show surprise

■ *verb* (**-mm-**) [usually +*adv. / prep.*] **~ A to B| ~ sth (down)** (rather *old-fashioned*) to spread glue on the surface of sth; to stick two things together with glue: *A large address label was gummed to the package.* ◊ *gummed labels* (= with glue on one side) PHRV **ˌgum sth↔'up** [usually passive] (*BrE, informal*) to cover or fill sth with a sticky substance so that it stops moving or working as it should

gum·ball /ˈɡʌmbɔːl/ *noun* (*AmE*) a small ball of CHEWING GUM that looks like a sweet/candy

gumbo /ˈɡʌmbəʊ; *AmE* -boʊ/ *noun* [U] a thick chicken or SEAFOOD soup, usually made with the vegetable OKRA

gum·boot /ˈɡʌmbuːt/ *noun* (*old-fashioned, BrE*) = WELLINGTON

gummed /ɡʌmd/ *adj.* [usually before noun] (of stamps, paper, etc.) covered with a type of glue that will become sticky when water is put on it

gummy /ˈɡʌmi/ *adj.* (*informal*) **1** sticky or covered in gum (2) **2** a **gummy** smile shows your teeth and gums

gump·tion /ˈɡʌmpʃn/ *noun* [U] (*old-fashioned, informal*) **1** the intelligence needed to know what to do in a particular situation: *He didn't have the gumption to keep his mouth shut.* **2** courage and determination: *She won't tell him because she hasn't got the gumption.*

gum·shoe /ˈɡʌmʃuː/ *noun* (*old-fashioned, AmE, informal*) = DETECTIVE (1)

'gum tree *noun* a EUCALYPTUS tree IDM **be up a 'gum tree** (*BrE, informal*) to be in a very difficult situation

gun /ɡʌn/ *noun, verb*

■ *noun* **1** [C] a weapon that is used for firing bullets or SHELLS: *to fire a gun at sb* ◊ *a toy gun* ◊ *anti-aircraft guns* ◊ *Look out, he's got a gun!* ◊ *a gun battle between rival gangs*—see also AIR GUN, HANDGUN, MACHINE GUN, SHOTGUN, STUN GUN, SUB-MACHINE GUN, TOMMY GUN **2** [C] a tool that uses pressure to send out a substance or an object: *a staple gun*—see also SPRAY GUN **3 (the gun)** [sing.] the signal to begin a race, that is made by firing a special gun, called a **starting pistol**, into the air **4** [C] (*informal, especially AmE*) a person who is paid to shoot sb: *a hired gun*—see also FLASHGUN, SON OF A GUN IDM **hold/put a gun to sb's 'head** to force sb to do sth that they do not want to do, by making threats—more at GREAT *adj.*, JUMP *v.*, SPIKE *v.*, STICK *v.*

■ *verb* (**-nn-**) PHRV **be 'gunning for sb** (*informal*) to be looking for an opportunity to blame or attack sb **be 'gunning for sth** to be competing for or trying hard to get sth: *She's gunning for the top job.* **ˌgun sb↔'down** [usually passive] to shoot sb, especially killing or seriously injuring them: *The policeman was gunned down while on duty.*

gun·boat /ˈɡʌnbəʊt; *AmE* -boʊt/ *noun* a small ship that is fitted with large guns

ˌgunboat di'plomacy *noun* [U] a way of making another country accept your demands by using the threat of force

'gun control *noun* [U] (*especially AmE*) laws that restrict the sale and use of guns

æ	ɑː	e	ɜː	ə	ɪ	iː	i	ɒ	ɔː	ʌ	ʊ	u	uː
cat	father	ten	bird	about	sit	see	many	got	saw	cup	put	actual	too

(BrE)

'gun dog *noun* a dog trained to help in the sport of shooting, for example by finding birds that have been shot

gun·fight /'gʌnfaɪt/ *noun* a fight between people using guns ▶ **gun·fight·er** *noun*

gun·fire /'gʌnfaɪə(r)/ *noun* [U] the repeated firing of guns; the sound of guns firing: *an exchange of gunfire with the police* ◊ *I could hear gunfire.*

gunge /gʌndʒ/ (*BrE*) (also **gunk** *AmE, BrE*) *noun* [U] (*informal*) any unpleasant, sticky or dirty substance ▶ **gungy** *adj.*

gung-ho /ˌgʌŋ ˈhəʊ; *AmE* ˈhoʊ/ *adj.* (*informal, disapproving*) too enthusiastic about sth, without thinking seriously about it, especially about fighting and war

gunk /gʌŋk/ *noun* [U] (*especially AmE*) = GUNGE

gun·man /'gʌnmən/ *noun* (*pl.* **-men** /-mən/) a man who uses a gun to rob or kill people

gun·metal /'gʌnmetl/ *noun* **1** a metal that is a mixture of COPPER, tin or ZINC **2** a dull blue-grey colour

gun·nel = GUNWALE

gun·ner /'gʌnə(r)/ *noun* **1** a member of the armed forces who is trained to use large guns **2** a soldier in the British ARTILLERY (= the part of the army that uses large guns)

gun·nery /'gʌnəri/ *noun* [U] (*technical*) the operation of large military guns

gun·ny·sack /'gʌnisæk/ *noun* (*AmE*) a large bag made from rough material and used to store flour, potatoes, etc.

gun·point /'gʌnpɔɪnt/ *noun* IDM **at 'gunpoint** while threatening sb or being threatened with a gun: *The driver was robbed at gunpoint.*

gun·pow·der /'gʌnpaʊdə(r)/ (also **pow·der**) *noun* [U] explosive powder used especially in bombs or FIREWORKS

gun·run·ner /'gʌnrʌnə(r)/ *noun* a person who secretly and illegally brings guns into a country ▶ **gun·run·ning** *noun* [U]

gun·ship /'gʌnʃɪp/ *noun* an armed military HELICOPTER or other aircraft

gun·shot /'gʌnʃɒt; *AmE* -ʃɑːt/ *noun* **1** [U] the bullets that are fired from a gun: *gunshot wounds* **2** [C] the firing of a gun; the sound of it being fired: *I heard the sound of gunshots out in the street.* **3** [U] the distance that a bullet from a gun can travel: *He was out of/within gunshot.*

gun·sling·er /'gʌnslɪŋə(r)/ *noun* (*AmE*) a person who is paid to kill people, especially in films/movies about the American Wild West

gun·smith /'gʌnsmɪθ/ *noun* a person who makes and repairs guns

gun·wale (also **gun·nel**) /'gʌnl/ *noun* the upper edge of the side of a boat or small ship

gur·gle /'gɜːgl; *AmE* 'gɜːrgl/ *verb, noun*
■ *verb* [V] **1** to make a sound like water flowing quickly through a narrow space: *Water gurgled through the pipes.* ◊ *a gurgling stream* **2** if a baby **gurgles**, it makes a noise in its throat when it is happy
■ *noun* **1** a sound like water flowing quickly through a narrow space **2** the sound that babies make in the throat, especially when they are happy

gur·ney /'gɜːni; *AmE* 'gɜːrni/ *noun* (*AmE*) a type of TROLLEY which is used for moving patients in a hospital

guru /'guːruː/ *noun* **1** a Hindu or Sikh religious teacher or leader **2** (*informal*) a person who is an expert on a particular subject or who is very good at doing sth: *a management/health/fashion guru*

gush /gʌʃ/ *verb, noun*
■ *verb* **1** [V] [usually +adv./prep.] **~ out of/from/into sth | ~ out/in** to flow or pour suddenly and quickly out of a hole in large amounts: *blood gushing from a wound* ◊ *Water gushed out of the pipe.* **2** [VN] (of a container/vehicle etc.) to suddenly let out large amounts of a liquid: *The tanker was gushing oil.* ◊ (*figurative*) *She absolutely gushed enthusiasm.* **3** (*disapproving*) to express so much praise or emotion about sb/sth that it does not seem sincere: [V speech] *'You are clever,' she gushed.* [also V]
■ *noun* [usually sing.] **1 ~ (of sth)** a large amount of liquid suddenly and quickly flowing or pouring out of sth: *a*

gush of blood 2 ~ (of sth) a sudden strong expression of feeling: *a gush of emotion*

gush·er /'gʌʃə(r)/ *noun* **1** (*AmE*) an OIL WELL where the oil comes out quickly and in large quantities **2** a person who gushes (3)

gush·ing /'gʌʃɪŋ/ *adj.* (*disapproving*) expressing so much enthusiasm, praise or emotion that it does not seem sincere ▶ **gush·ing·ly** *adv.*

gus·set /'gʌsɪt/ *noun* an extra piece of fabric sewn into a piece of clothing to make it wider, stronger or more comfortable

gussy /'gʌsi/ *verb* (**gus·sies**, **gussy·ing**, **gus·sied**, **gussied**) PHRV **gussy 'up** (*AmE, informal*) to dress yourself in an attractive way SYN DRESS UP: *Even the stars are tired of gussying up for the awards.*

gust /gʌst/ *noun, verb*
■ *noun* a sudden strong increase in the amount and speed of wind that is blowing: *A gust of wind blew his hat off.* ◊ *The wind was blowing in gusts.* **2** a sudden strong expression of emotion: *a gust of laughter/despair*
■ *verb* [V] (of the wind) to suddenly blow very hard: *winds gusting up to 60 mph*

gusto /'gʌstəʊ; *AmE* -toʊ/ *noun* [U] enthusiasm and energy in doing sth: *They sang with gusto.*

gusty /'gʌsti/ *adj.* [usually before noun] with the wind blowing in GUSTS: *a gusty morning* ◊ *gusty winds*

gut /gʌt/ *noun, verb, adj.*
■ *noun* **1** [C] the tube in the body through which food passes when it leaves the stomach SYN INTESTINE **2** (**guts**) [pl.] the organs in and around the stomach, especially in an animal: *I'll only cook fish if the guts have been removed.* **3** [C] (*informal*) a person's stomach, especially when it is large SYN BELLY: *Have you seen the gut on him!* ◊ *a beer gut* (= caused by drinking beer) **4** (**guts**) [pl.] (*informal*) the courage and determination that it takes to do sth difficult or unpleasant: *He doesn't have the guts to walk away from a well-paid job.* **5** [C, usually pl.] the place where your natural feelings that make you react in a particular way are thought to be: *I had a feeling in my guts that something was wrong.* **6** (**guts**) [pl.] the most important part of sth: *the guts of the problem/argument* **7** [U] = CATGUT IDM **have sb's ˌguts for 'garters** (*BrE, informal*) to be very angry with sb and punish them severely for sth they have done **slog/sweat/work your 'guts out** (*informal*) to work very hard to achieve sth: *I slogged my guts out for those exams.*—more at BUST *v.*, HATE *v.*, SPILL *v.*
■ *verb* (**-tt-**) [VN] **1** [usually passive] to destroy the inside or contents of a building or room: *a factory gutted by fire* ◊ *The house was completely gutted.* **2** to remove the organs from inside a fish or an animal to prepare it for cooking
■ *adj.* [only before noun] based on feelings and emotions rather than thought and reason: *a gut feeling/reaction*

gut·less /'gʌtləs/ *adj.* lacking courage or determination: *her gutless brother* ◊ *a gutless performance*

gutsy /'gʌtsi/ *adj.* (*informal*) **1** showing courage and determination: *a gutsy fighter/win* **2** having strong and unusual qualities: *a gutsy red wine* ◊ *a gutsy song*

gut·ted /'gʌtɪd/ *adj.* [not before noun] (*BrE, informal*) extremely sad or disappointed: *Disappointed? I was gutted!*

gut·ter /'gʌtə(r)/ *noun, verb*
■ *noun* **1** [C] a long curved channel made of metal or plastic that is fixed under the edge of a roof to carry away the water when it rains: *a blocked/leaking gutter*—picture at HOUSE **2** [C] a channel at the edge of a road where water collects and is carried away to DRAINS **3** (**the gutter**) [sing.] the bad social conditions or lack of morals sometimes connected with the lowest level of society: *She rose from the gutter to become a great star.* ◊ *the language of the gutter* (= used when swearing)
■ *verb* [V] (*literary*) (of a flame or candle) to burn in an unsteady way

gut·ter·ing /'gʌtərɪŋ/ *noun* [U] the system of gutters on a building; the material used to make gutters: *a length/piece of guttering*

the ˌgutter 'press *noun* [sing.] (*disapproving*) news-

G

papers that print a lot of shocking stories about people's private lives rather than serious news

gut·tur·al /ˈɡʌtərəl/ *adj.* (of a sound) made or seeming to be made at the back of the throat: *guttural consonants* ◇ *a low guttural growl*

guv /ɡʌv/ (*BrE, informal, spoken*) used by a man to address another man who is a customer, etc., meaning 'sir'

guv'nor /ˈɡʌvnə(r)/ *noun* (*BrE, informal, spoken*) (often used as a way of addressing sb) a man who is in a position of authority, for example your employer: *Do you want me to ask the guv'nor about it?*—see also GOVERNOR

guy /ɡaɪ/ *noun* **1** [C] (*informal*) a man: *a big/nice/tough guy* ◇ *a Dutch guy* ◇ *At the end of the film the bad guy gets shot.*—see also FALL GUY, WISE GUY **2** (guys) [pl.] (*spoken, especially AmE*) a group of people of either sex: *Come on, you guys, let's get going!* **3** [C] (in Britain) a model of a man dressed in old clothes that is burned on a BONFIRE on 5 November during the celebrations for BONFIRE NIGHT **4** (also **ˈguy rope**) [C] a rope used to keep a pole or tent in an upright position

Guy Fawkes night /ˌɡaɪ ˈfɔːks naɪt/ *noun* [U, C] = BONFIRE NIGHT

guz·zle /ˈɡʌzl/ *verb* (*informal*, usually *disapproving*) to drink sth quickly and in large amounts. In British English it also means to eat food quickly and in large amounts: [VN] *The kids seem to be guzzling soft drinks all day.* ◇ (*figurative*) *My car guzzles fuel.* [also V]

guz·zler /ˈɡʌzlə(r)/ *noun* (*informal, especially AmE*) = GAS-GUZZLER

gybe (*especially BrE*) (*AmE* usually **jibe**) /dʒaɪb/ *verb, noun*
■ *verb* [V] to change direction when sailing with the wind behind you, by swinging the sail from one side of the boat to the other
■ *noun* an act of gybing

gym /dʒɪm/ *noun* (*informal*) **1** (also *formal* **gym·na·sium**) [C] a room or hall with equipment for doing physical exercise, for example in a school: *to play basketball in the gym* ◇ *The school has recently built a new gym.* **2** [U] physical exercises done in a gym, especially at school: *I don't enjoy gym.* ◇ *gym shoes* **3** [C] (*especially AmE*) = HEALTH CLUB: *I just joined a gym.* ◇ *I work out at the gym most days.*

gym·khana /dʒɪmˈkɑːnə/ *noun* (*BrE*) an event in which people riding horses take part in various competitions

gym·na·sium /dʒɪmˈneɪziəm/ *noun* (*pl.* **gym·na·siums** or **gym·na·sia** /-ziə/) (*formal*) = GYM

gym·nast /ˈdʒɪmnæst/ *noun* a person who performs gymnastics, especially in a competition

gym·nas·tics /dʒɪmˈnæstɪks/ *noun* [U] physical exercises that develop and show the body's strength and ability to move and bend easily, often done as a sport in competitions: *a gymnastics competition* ◇ (*figurative*) *mental/verbal gymnastics* (= quick or clever thinking or use of words) ▶ **gym·nas·tic** *adj.* [only before noun]

ˈgym shoe *noun* (*BrE*) = PLIMSOLL

gym·slip /ˈdʒɪmslɪp/ *noun* (*BrE*) a dress without sleeves worn over a shirt as a school uniform for girls, especially in the past

gy·nae·colo·gist (*BrE*) (*AmE* **gyne·colo·gist**) /ˌɡaɪnə-ˈkɒlədʒɪst; *AmE* -ˈkɑːl-/ *noun* a doctor who studies and treats the medical conditions and diseases of women

gy·nae·col·ogy (*BrE*) (*AmE* **gyne·cology**) /ˌɡaɪnə-ˈkɒlədʒi; *AmE* -ˈkɑːl-/ *noun* [U] the scientific study and treatment of the medical conditions and diseases of women, especially those connected with sexual REPRODUC-TION ▶ **gy·nae·co·logic·al** (*BrE*) (*AmE* **gyne-**) /ˌɡaɪnə-kəˈlɒdʒɪkl; *AmE* -ˈlɑːdʒ-/ *adj.*: *a gynaecological examination*

gyp /dʒɪp/ *noun, verb*
■ *noun* [sing.] (*AmE, informal*) an act of charging too much money for sth: *That meal was a real gyp.* **IDM** **give sb ˈgyp** (*BrE, informal*) to cause sb a lot of pain: *My back's been giving me gyp lately.*
■ *verb* (**-pp-**) [VN] (*especially AmE*) to cheat or trick sb, especially by taking their money

gyp·sum /ˈdʒɪpsəm/ *noun* [U] a soft white mineral like chalk that is found naturally and is used in making PLASTER OF PARIS

gypsy (also **gipsy**) /ˈdʒɪpsi/ *noun* (*pl.* **-ies**) (sometimes *offensive*) a member of a race of people, originally from Asia, who travel around and traditionally live in CARA-VANS. Many people prefer to use the name Romany.—see also ROMANY—compare TRAVELLER

gyr·ate /dʒaɪˈreɪt; *AmE* ˈdʒaɪreɪt/ *verb* to move around in circles; to make sth, especially a part of your body, move around: [V] *They began gyrating to the music.* ◇ *The leaves gyrated slowly to the ground.* ◇ [VN] *As the lead singer gyrated his hips, the crowd screamed wildly.* ▶ **gyr·ation** /dʒaɪˈreɪʃn/ *noun* [C, usually pl., U]

gyro·scope /ˈdʒaɪrəskəʊp; *AmE* -skoʊp/ (also *informal* **gyro** /ˈdʒaɪrəʊ; *AmE* -roʊ/) *noun* a device consisting of a wheel that spins rapidly inside a frame and does not change position when the frame is moved. Gyroscopes are often used to keep ships and aircraft steady. ▶ **gyro·scop·ic** /ˌdʒaɪrəˈskɒpɪk; *AmE* -ˈskɑːpɪk/ *adj.*

G

Hh

H (also **h**) /eɪtʃ/ *noun* [C, U] (*pl.* **H's**, **h's** /ˈeɪtʃɪz/) the 8th letter of the English alphabet: *'Hat' begins with (an) H/ 'H'.*—compare AITCH—see also H-BOMB

ha¹ /hɑː/ *exclamation* **1** (also **hah**) the sound that people make when they are surprised or pleased or when they have discovered sth: *Ha! It serves you right!* ◊ *Ha! I knew he was hiding something.* **2** (also **ha! ha!**) (*written*) the word for the sound that people make when they laugh **3** (also **ha! ha!**) (*spoken, ironic*) used to show that you do not think that sth is funny: *Ha! Ha! Very funny! Now give me back my shoes.*

ha² *abbr.* (in writing) HECTARE

hab·eas cor·pus /ˌheɪbiəs ˈkɔːpəs; *AmE* ˈkɔːrpəs/ *noun* [U] (from *Latin, law*) a law that states that a person who has been arrested should not be kept in prison longer than a particular period of time unless a judge in a court of law has decided that it is right: *to apply for a writ of habeas corpus*

hab·er·dash·er /ˈhæbədæʃə(r); *AmE* ˈhæbərd-/ *noun* **1** (*old-fashioned, BrE*) a person who owns or works in a shop/store selling small articles for sewing, for example, needles, pins, cotton and buttons **2** (**hab·er·dash·er's**) (*pl.* **hab·er·dash·ers**) a shop/store that sells these things **3** (*AmE*) a person who owns, manages or works in a shop/store that makes and sells men's clothes

hab·er·dash·ery /ˌhæbəˈdæʃəri; *AmE* ˈhæbərd-/ *noun* (*pl.* **-ies**) **1** (*old-fashioned, BrE*) small articles for sewing, for example needles, pins, cotton and buttons **2** [U] (*old-fashioned, AmE*) men's clothes **3** [C] a shop/store or part of a shop/store where haberdashery is sold

habit /ˈhæbɪt/ *noun* **1** [C] a thing that you do often and almost without thinking, especially sth that is hard to stop doing: *You need to change your eating habits.* ◊ *good/ bad habits* ◊ *He has the irritating habit of biting his nails.* ◊ *It's all right to borrow money occasionally, but don't let it become a habit.* ◊ *I'd prefer you not to make a habit of it.* ◊ *I'm not in the habit of letting strangers into my apartment.* ◊ *I've got into the habit of turning on the TV as soon as I get home.* ◊ *I'm trying to break the habit of staying up too late.* **2** [U] usual behaviour: *I only do it out of habit.* ◊ *I'm a creature of habit* (= I have a fixed and regular way of doing things). **3** [C] (*informal*) a strong need to keep using drugs, alcohol or cigarettes regularly: *He began to finance his habit through burglary.* ◊ *She's tried to give up smoking but just can't kick the habit.* ◊ *a 50-a-day habit* **4** [C] a long piece of clothing worn by a MONK or NUN IDM see FORCE *n.*

hab·it·able /ˈhæbɪtəbl/ *adj.* suitable for people to live in: *The house should be habitable by the new year.* OPP UNINHABITABLE

habi·tat /ˈhæbɪtæt/ *noun* [C, U] the place where a particular type of animal or plant is normally found: *The panda's natural habitat is the bamboo forest.* ◊ *the destruction of wildlife habitat*

habi·ta·tion /ˌhæbɪˈteɪʃn/ *noun* **1** [U] the act of living in a place: *They looked around for any signs of habitation.* ◊ *The houses were unfit for human habitation* (= not clean or safe enough for people to live in). **2** [C] (*formal*) a place where people live: *The road serves the scattered habitations along the coast.*

habit-forming *adj.* a **habit-forming** activity or drug is one that makes you want to continue doing it or taking it

ha·bit·ual /həˈbɪtʃuəl/ *adj.* **1** [only before noun] usual or typical of sb/sth: *They waited for his habitual response.* ◊ (*formal*) *a person's place of habitual residence* **2** (of an action) done, often in a way that is annoying or difficult to stop: *habitual complaining/interruptions* ◊ *the habitual*

use of heroin **3** [only before noun] (of a person) doing sth that has become a habit and is therefore difficult to stop: *a habitual criminal/drinker/liar* HELP Some people use *an* instead of *a* before **habitual** and then usually do not pronounce the 'h'. This now sounds old-fashioned. ▶ **ha·bit·ual·ly** /-tʃuəli/ *adv.*: *the dark glasses he habitually wore*

ha·bitu·ated /həˈbɪtʃueɪtɪd/ *adj.* **~** (**to sth**) (*formal*) familiar with sth because you have done it or experienced it often

ha·bi·tué /(h)æˈbɪtʃueɪ/ *noun* (from *French, formal*) a person who goes regularly to a particular place or event: *a(n) habitué of upmarket clubs*

ha·ci·enda /ˌhæsiˈendə/ *noun* a large farm in a Spanish-speaking country

hack /hæk/ *verb, noun*

■ *verb* **1** [+*adv./prep.*] to cut sb/sth with rough, heavy blows: [VN] *I hacked the dead branches off.* ◊ *They were hacked to death as they tried to escape.* ◊ *We had to hack our way through the jungle.* ◊ [V] *We hacked away at the bushes.* **2** [VN+*adv./prep.*] to kick sb/sth roughly or without control: *He hacked the ball away.* **3** (*computing*) **~** (**into**) (**sth**) to secretly find a way of looking at and/or changing information on sb else's computer system without permission: [V] *He hacked into the bank's computer.* ◊ [VN] *They had hacked secret data.* **4** [VN] **can/can't ~ it** (*informal*) to be able/not able to manage in a particular situation: *Lots of people leave this job because they can't hack it.* **5** [V] (usually **go hacking**) (*especially BrE*) to ride a horse for pleasure **6** [V] (*AmE, informal*) to drive a taxi

■ *noun* **1** (*disapproving*) a writer, especially of newspaper articles, who does a lot of low quality work and does not get paid much **2** (*disapproving*) a person who does the hard and often boring work for an organization, especially a politician: *a party hack* **3** a horse for ordinary riding or one that can be hired **4** (*AmE, informal*) a taxi **5** an act of hitting sth, especially with a cutting tool

hacked 'off *adj.* [not before noun] (*BrE, informal*) extremely annoyed: *I'm really hacked off.*

hack·er /ˈhækə(r)/ *noun* a person who spends a lot of time using computers for a hobby, especially to look at data without permission

hacking 'cough *noun* [sing.] a dry painful cough that is repeated often

hackles /ˈhæklz/ *noun* [pl.] the hairs on the back of the neck of a dog, cat, etc. that rise when the animal is afraid or angry IDM **make sb's 'hackles rise | raise sb's 'hackles** to make sb angry: *Her controversial article is bound to raise hackles.* **sb's 'hackles rise** to become angry: *Ben felt his hackles rise as the speaker continued.*

hack·ney car·riage /ˈhækni kærɪdʒ/ (also **'hack·ney cab**) *noun* (*BrE*) a word used in official language for a taxi. In the past hackney carriages were carriages pulled by horses that were used as taxis.

hack·neyed /ˈhæknid/ *adj.* used too often and therefore boring: *a hackneyed phrase/subject*

hack·saw /ˈhæksɔː/ *noun* a tool with a narrow blade in a frame, used for cutting metal

had /həd; əd; *strong form* hæd/ *pt, pp* of HAVE

had·dock /ˈhædək/ *noun* (*pl.* **had·dock**) [C, U] a sea fish like a COD but smaller, with white flesh that is used for food: *smoked haddock*

Hades /ˈheɪdiːz/ *noun* [U] (in ancient Greek stories) the land of the dead; HELL

hadn't /ˈhædnt/ *short form* had not

haema·tol·ogy (*BrE*) (*AmE* **hema·tol·ogy**) /ˌhiːməˈtɒlədʒi; *AmE* -ˈtɑːl-/ *noun* [U] the scientific study

---

s	t	v	z	ʃ	ʒ	tʃ	dʒ	θ	ð	ŋ
see	tea	van	zoo	shoe	vision	chain	jam	thin	this	sing

of the blood and its diseases ▶ **haem·ato·logic·al** (*BrE*) (*AmE* **hem-**) /ˌhiːmətəˈlɒdʒɪkl; *AmE* -ˈlɑːdʒ-/ *adj.* **haema·tolo·gist** (*BrE*) (*AmE* **hem-**) /ˌhiːməˈtɒlədʒɪst; *AmE* -ˈtɑːl-/ *noun*

haemo- (*BrE*) (*AmE* **hemo-**) /ˈhiːməʊ; *AmE* -moʊ/ *combining form* (in nouns and adjectives) connected with blood: *haemophilia*

haemo·globin (*BrE*) (*AmE* **hemo·globin**) /ˌhiːməˈgləʊbɪn; *AmE* -ˈgloʊ-/ *noun* [U] a red substance in the blood that carries OXYGEN and contains iron

haemo·philia (*BrE*) (*AmE* **hemo·philia**) /ˌhiːməˈfɪliə/ *noun* [U] a medical condition that causes severe bleeding from even a slight injury because the blood fails to CLOT normally. It usually affects only men although it can be passed on by women.

haemo·phil·iac (*BrE*) (*AmE* **hemo·phil·iac**) /ˌhiːməˈfɪliæk/ *noun* a person who suffers from haemophilia

haem·or·rhage (*BrE*) (*AmE* **hem·or·rhage**) /ˈhemərɪdʒ/ *noun, verb*
■ *noun* **1** [C, U] a medical condition in which there is severe bleeding inside a person's body: *a massive brain/cerebral haemorrhage* ◊ *The injured were checked for any signs of haemorrhage or shock.* **2** [C, usually sing.] **~ (of sb/sth)** a serious loss of people, money, etc. from a country, a group or an organization: *Poor working conditions have led to a steady haemorrhage of qualified teachers from our schools.*
■ *verb* [V] to bleed heavily, especially from the inside of the body; to have a haemorrhage

haem·or·rhoids (*BrE*) (*AmE* **hem·or·rhoids**) /ˈheməˌrɔɪdz/ *noun* [pl.] (*medical*) painful swollen VEINS at or near the ANUS SYN PILES

hag /hæg/ *noun* (*offensive*) an ugly and/or unpleasant old woman

hag·gard /ˈhægəd; *AmE* -gərd/ *adj.* looking very tired because of illness, worry or lack of sleep: *He looked pale and haggard.* ◊ *a haggard face*

hag·gis /ˈhægɪs/ *noun* [C, U] a Scottish dish that looks like a large round sausage made from the heart, lungs and LIVER of a sheep that are finely chopped, mixed with OATS, herbs, etc. and boiled in a bag that is usually made from part of a sheep's stomach

hag·gle /ˈhægl/ *verb* [V] **~ (with sb) (over sth)** to argue with sb in order to reach an agreement, especially about the price of sth: *I left him in the market haggling over the price of a shirt.*

hagi·og·raphy /ˌhægiˈɒgrəfi; *AmE* -ˈɑːg-/ *noun* (*pl.* **-ies**) [C, U] (*formal*) a book about the life of a person that praises them too much; this style of writing

hah = HA

haiku /ˈhaɪkuː/ *noun* (*pl.* **haiku** or **haikus**) (from *Japanese*) a Japanese poem with three lines and usually 17 syllables

hail /heɪl/ *verb, noun*
■ *verb* **1** [usually passive] **~ sb/sth (as) sth** to describe sb/sth as being very good or special, especially in newspapers, etc: [VN] *The conference was hailed as a great success.* ◊ [VN-N] *Teenager Matt Brown is being hailed as a hero for saving a young child from drowning.* **2** [VN] to signal to a taxi or a bus, in order to get the driver to stop: *to hail a taxi/cab* **3** [VN] (*literary*) to call to sb in order to greet them or attract their attention: *A voice hailed us from the other side of the street.*—see also LOUDHAILER **4** [V] when **it hails**, small balls of ice fall like rain from the sky: *It's hailing!* PHRV **'hail from ...** (*formal*) to come from or have been born in a particular place: *His father hailed from Italy.*
■ *noun* **1** [U] small balls of ice that fall like rain: *We drove through hail and snow.* **2** [sing.] **a ~ of sth** a large number or amount of sth that is aimed at sb in order to harm them: *a hail of arrows/bullets* ◊ *a hail of abuse*

Hail Mary *noun* /ˌheɪl ˈmeəri; *AmE* ˈmeri/ (*pl.* **Hail Marys**) a Roman Catholic prayer to Mary, the mother of Jesus

hail·stone /ˈheɪlstəʊn; *AmE* -stoʊn/ *noun* [usually pl.] a small ball of ice that falls like rain

hail·storm /ˈheɪlstɔːm; *AmE* -stɔːrm/ *noun* a storm during which hail falls from the sky

hair /heə(r); *AmE* her/ *noun* **1** [U, C] the substance that looks like a mass of fine threads growing especially on

H

bald head   shaved head   long hair   crew cut   **hair**

moustache   beard   **ponytail**   stubble   goatee   sideboards/sideburns   **dreadlocks**

parting (*BrE*)/part (*AmE*)

flat-top   **undercut**   **cropped hair**   **layered hair**   **bob**   **permed hair**

pigtails (*BrE*)/**braids** (*AmE*)   fringe (*BrE*)/bangs (*AmE*)   **bun**

French plait (*BrE*)/**French braid** (*AmE*)   **plait** (*BrE*)/**braid** (*AmE*)   **cornrows**   **bunches**

æ	ɑː	e	ɜː	ə	ɪ	iː	i	ɒ	ɔː	ʌ	ʊ	u	uː
cat	father	ten	bird	about	sit	see	many	got	saw	cup	put	actual	too
								(BrE)					

the head; one of these threads growing on the body of people and some animals: *fair/dark hair* ◊ *straight/curly/wavy hair* ◊ *to comb/brush your hair* ◊ *(spoken) I'll be down in a minute. I'm doing* (= brushing, arranging, etc.) *my hair.* ◊ *I'm having my hair cut this afternoon.* ◊ *body/facial/pubic hair* ◊ *There's a hair in my soup.* ◊ *The rug was covered with cat hairs.*—see also CAMEL HAIR, HORSEHAIR—picture at BODY **2** (**-haired**) (in adjectives) having the type of hair mentioned: *dark-haired* ◊ *long-haired* **3** [C] a thing that looks like a fine thread growing on the leaves and stems of some plants **IDM** **get in sb's 'hair** (*informal*) to annoy sb by always being near them, asking them questions, etc. **the hair of the 'dog (that 'bit you)** (*informal*) alcohol that you drink in order to make you feel better when you have drunk too much alcohol the night before **keep your 'hair on** (*BrE*, *spoken*) used to tell sb to stop shouting and become calm when they are angry **let your 'hair down** (*informal*) to relax and enjoy yourself, especially in a lively way: *It's about time you let your hair down and had some fun!* **make sb's 'hair stand on end** to shock or frighten sb: *a chilling tale that will make your hair stand on end* **not harm/touch a hair of sb's 'head** to not hurt sb physically in any way **not have a 'hair out of place** (of a person) to look extremely clean and neat **not turn a 'hair** to show no emotion when sth surprising, shocking, etc. happens—more at HANG *v.*, HIDE *n.*, SPLIT *v.*, TEAR¹ *v.*

hair·band /'heəbænd; *AmE* 'herb-/ *noun* a strip of fabric or curved plastic worn by women in their hair, that fits closely over the top of the head and behind the ears

hair·brush /'heəbrʌʃ; *AmE* 'herb-/ *noun* a brush for making the hair tidy or smooth

hair·cut /'heəkʌt; *AmE* 'herkʌt/ *noun* **1** the act of sb cutting your hair: *You need a haircut.* ◊ *I see you've had a haircut.* **2** the style in which sb's hair is cut: *What do you think of my new haircut?* ◊ *a short/trendy haircut*

hair·do /'heədu:; *AmE* 'herdu/ *noun* (*pl.* **-os**) (*old-fashioned, informal*) the style in which a woman's hair is arranged

hair·dress·er /'heədresə(r); *AmE* 'herd-/ *noun* **1** a person whose job is to cut, wash and shape hair **2** (**hair·dresser's**) (*pl.* **hair·dress·ers**) a place where you can get your hair cut, washed and shaped—compare BARBER ▶ **hair·dress·ing** *noun* [U]

hair·dryer (also **hair·drier**) /'heədraɪə(r); *AmE* 'herd-/ *noun* a small machine used for drying your hair by blowing hot air over it

hair·grip /'heəgrɪp; *AmE* 'herg-/ (also **grip**) (both *BrE*) (*AmE* **bobby pin**) *noun* a small thin piece of metal or plastic folded in the middle, used by women for holding their hair in place—compare HAIRPIN

hair·less /'heələs; *AmE* 'herləs/ *adj.* without hair

hair·line /'heəlaɪn; *AmE* 'herl-/ *noun* **1** the place on a person's forehead where their hair starts growing: *a receding hairline* **2** (often used as an adjective) a very thin crack or line: *a hairline crack/fracture*

hair·net /'heənet; *AmE* 'hernet/ *noun* a net worn over the hair to keep it in place

hair·piece /'heəpi:s; *AmE* 'herp-/ *noun* a piece of false hair worn to make your own hair look longer or thicker

hair·pin /'heəpɪn; *AmE* 'herpɪn/ *noun* **1** a small thin piece of wire that is folded in the middle, used by women for holding their hair in place—compare HAIRGRIP **2** = HAIRPIN BEND

hairpin 'bend (*BrE*) (*AmE* **hairpin 'curve**, **hairpin 'turn**) (also **hair·pin** *BrE*, *AmE*) *noun* a very sharp bend in a road, especially a mountain road

hair-raising *adj.* extremely frightening but often exciting: *a hair-raising adventure/story*

hair's breadth *noun* [sing.] a very small amount or distance: *We won by a hair's breadth.* ◊ *They were within a hair's breadth of being killed.*

hair 'shirt *noun* a shirt made of rough fabric containing hair, worn in the past by people who wished to punish themselves for religious reasons

hair·slide /'heəslaɪd; *AmE* 'hers-/ (also **slide**) (both *BrE*)

(*AmE* **bar·rette**) *noun* a small decorative piece of metal or plastic used by women for holding their hair in place

hair-splitting *noun* [U] (*disapproving*) the act of giving too much importance to small and unimportant differences in an argument **IDM** see SPLIT *v.*

hair·spray /'heəspreɪ; *AmE* 'hers-/ *noun* [U, C] a substance sprayed onto the hair to hold it in a particular style

hair·style /'heəstaɪl; *AmE* 'hers-/ *noun* the style in which sb's hair is cut or arranged

hairy /'heəri; *AmE* 'heri/ *adj.* (**hair·ier**, **hairi·est**) **1** covered with a lot of hair: *a hairy chest/monster* ◊ *plants with hairy stems* **2** (*informal*) dangerous or frightening but often exciting: *Driving on icy roads can be pretty hairy.* ◊ *a hairy experience* ▶ **hairi·ness** *noun* [U]

hajj (also **haj**) /hædʒ/ *noun* (usually **the Hajj**) [sing.] the religious journey to Mecca that all Muslims try to make at least once in their lives

hake /heɪk/ *noun* [C, U] (*pl.* **hake**) a large sea fish that is used for food

halal /'hælæl/ *adj.* [only before noun] (of meat) from an animal that has been killed according to Muslim law: *halal meat/food* ◊ *a halal butcher* (= one who sells halal meat)

hal·cyon /'hælsɪən/ *adj.* [usually before noun] (*literary*) peaceful and happy: *the halcyon days of her youth*

hale /heɪl/ *adj.* **IDM** **hale and 'hearty** (especially of an old person) strong and healthy

half /hɑːf; *AmE* hæf/ *noun, det., pron., adv.*
■ *noun* (*pl.* **halves** /hɑːvz; *AmE* hævz/) **1** either of two equal parts into which sth is or can be divided: *two and a half kilos* (2½) ◊ *One and a half hours is/are allowed for the exam.* ◊ *An hour and a half is allowed for the exam.* ◊ *The second half of the book is more exciting.* ◊ *I've divided the money in half.* ◊ *We'll need to reduce the weight by half.*—see also HALVE **2** either of two periods of time into which a sports game, concert, etc. is divided: *No goals were scored in the first half.* **3** = HALFBACK—see also CENTRE HALF, SCRUM HALF **4** (*BrE, informal*) half a PINT of beer or a similar drink: *Two halves of bitter, please.* **IDM** **and a 'half** (*informal*) bigger, better, more important, etc. than usual: *That was a game and a half!* **do nothing/not do anything by 'halves** to do whatever you do completely and thoroughly: *You're expecting twins? Well, you never did do anything by halves.* **go half and 'half | go 'halves (with sb)** to share the cost of sth equally with sb: *We go halves on all the bills.* **the 'half of it** used in negative sentences to say that a situation is worse or more complicated than sb thinks: *'It sounds very difficult.' ' You don't know the half of it.'* **how the other half 'lives** the way of life of a different social group, especially one much richer than you **too clever, etc. by 'half** (*BrE, informal, disapproving*) clever, etc. in a way that annoys you or makes you suspicious—more at MIND *n.*, SIX, TIME *n.*
■ *det., pron.* **1** an amount equal to half of sth/sb: *half an hour* ◊ *Half (of) the fruit was bad.* ◊ *Half of the money was mine.* ◊ *He has a half share in the company.* ◊ *Out of 36 candidates, half passed.* **2** ~ the time, fun, trouble, etc. the largest part of sth: *Half the fun of gardening is never knowing exactly what's going to come up.* ◊ *Half the time you don't even listen to what I say.* **IDM** **half a 'minute, 'second, etc.** (*informal*) a short time: *Hang on. I'll be ready in half a minute.* **half past 'one, 'two, etc.** (*AmE* also **half after 'one, 'two, etc.**) (also *BrE informal* **half 'one, 'two, etc.**) 30 minutes after any hour on the clock
■ *adv.* **1** to the extent of half: *The glass was half full.* **2** partly: *The chicken was only half cooked.* ◊ *half-closed eyes* ◊ *I'm half inclined to agree.* **IDM** **half as many, much, etc. a'gain** (*AmE* **half a'gain as much**) an increase of 50% of the existing number or amount: *Spending on health is half as much again as it was in 1998.* **not half** (*BrE, informal*) used to emphasize a statement or an opinion: *It wasn't half good* (= it was very good). ◊ *'Was she annoyed?' 'Not half!'* (= she was extremely annoyed). **not 'half as | not 'half such a** not nearly: *He is not half*

such a fool as they think. **not half 'bad** (*informal*) (used to show surprise) not bad at all; good: *It really isn't half bad, is it?*

GRAMMAR POINT
half / whole / quarter

Quarter, **half** and **whole** can all be nouns: *Cut the apple into quarters.* ◇ *Two halves make a whole.*

Whole is also an adjective: *I've been waiting here for a whole hour.*

Half is also a determiner: *Half (of) the work is already finished.* ◇ *They spent half the time looking for a parking space.* ◇ *Her house is half a mile down the road.* Note that you do not put *a* or *the* in front of **half** when it is used in this way: *I waited for half an hour.* ◇ *I waited for a half an hour.*

Half can also be used as an adverb: *This meal is only half cooked.*

,**half-and-'half** *adj., adv., noun*
■ *adj.* being half one thing and half another: *I was in that half-and-half land where you are not completely asleep nor completely awake.* ▶ ,**half-and-'half** *adv.*
■ *noun* [U] (*AmE*) a mixture of milk and cream that is used in tea and coffee

'**half-assed** *adj.* (*AmE, slang*) **1** done without care or effort; not well planned **2** stupid ▶ '**half-assed** *adv.*

half·back /'hɑːfbæk; *AmE* 'hæf-/ (also **half**) *noun* **1** [C] one of the defending players in football/soccer, hockey or rugby whose position is between those who play at the front of a team and those who play at the back **2** [C] one of the two attacking players in American football whose position is behind the QUARTERBACK and beside the FULL-BACKS **3** [U] the position a halfback plays at: *Sammer is at halfback.*

,**half-'baked** *adj.* [usually before noun] (*informal*) not well planned or considered: *a half-baked idea*

'**half-bath** *noun* (*AmE*) a small room in a house, containing a WASHBASIN and a toilet SYN POWDER ROOM

,**half 'board** *noun* [U] (*BrE*) a type of accommodation at a hotel, etc. that includes breakfast and an evening meal—compare BED AND BREAKFAST, FULL BOARD

'**half-breed** *noun* (⚠, *offensive*) a person whose parents are from different races, especially when one is white and the other is a Native American ▶ '**half-breed** *adj.* (⚠, *offensive*) HELP It is more acceptable to talk about 'a person **of mixed race**'.

'**half-brother** *noun* a person's **half-brother** is a boy or man with either the same mother or the same father as they have—compare STEPBROTHER

'**half-caste** *noun* (⚠, *offensive*) a person whose parents are from different races ▶ '**half-caste** *adj.* (⚠, *offensive*) HELP It is more acceptable to talk about 'a person **of mixed race**'.

,**half-'cock** *noun* IDM **go off at ,half-'cock** (*BrE, informal*) to start before preparations are complete, so that the effect or result is not satisfactory

,**half-'crown** (also ,**half a 'crown**) *noun* an old British coin worth 2½ SHILLINGS (= now 12½ pence)

,**half 'day** *noun* a day on which people work only in the morning or in the afternoon: *Tuesday is her half day.*

,**half 'dollar** *noun* a US coin worth 50 cents

,**half-'hearted** *adj.* done without enthusiasm or effort: *He made a half-hearted attempt to justify himself.* ◇ *a half-hearted protest/suggestion* ▶ ,**half-'heartedly** *adv.*

,**half-'hour** (also ,**half an 'hour**) *noun* a period of 30 minutes: *He should arrive within the next half-hour.* ◇ *a half-hour drive*

,**half-'hourly** *adj.* happening every 30 minutes: *a half-hourly bus service* ▶ ,**half-'hourly** *adv.*: *The buses run half-hourly.*

'**half-life** *noun* [C] (*physics*) the time taken for the RADIO-ACTIVITY of a substance to fall to half its original value

'**half-light** *noun* [sing., U] a dull light in which it is difficult to see things: *in the grey half-light of dawn*

,**half 'mast** *noun* IDM **at ,half 'mast** (of a flag) flown at the middle of the MAST as a sign of respect for a person who has just died: *Flags were flown at half mast on the day of his funeral.*

,**half 'measures** *noun* [pl.] (*disapproving*) a policy or plan of action that is weak and does not do enough: *There are no half measures with this company.*

,**half-'moon** *noun* **1** the moon when only half of it can be seen from the earth; the time when this happens—compare FULL MOON, NEW MOON **2** a thing that is shaped like a half-moon

'**half note** *noun* (*AmE, music*) = MINIM

half·penny /'heɪpni/ *noun* (*pl.* -**ies**) a British coin in use until 1984, worth half a PENNY

,**half-'price** *adj.* costing half the usual price: *a half-price ticket/offer/sale* ▶ ,**half-'price** *adv.*: *Children aged under four go half-price.* ,**half 'price** *noun* [U]: *We have many items at half price or less.*

'**half-sister** *noun* a person's **half-sister** is a girl or woman who has either the same mother or the same father as them—compare STEPSISTER

'**half step** *noun* (*AmE, music*) = SEMITONE

,**half-'term** *noun* (in British schools) a short holiday/ vacation in the middle of each TERM: *the half-term break/ holiday* ◇ *What are you doing at half term?*

,**half-'timbered** *adj.* [usually before noun] (of a building) having walls that are made from a wooden frame filled with brick, stone, etc. so that the FRAMEWORK can still be seen

,**half-'time** *noun* [U] a short period between the two halves of a game of football, hockey, etc. during which the players rest: *The score at half-time was two all.* ◇ *the half-time score*—compare FULL TIME

'**half-tone** *noun* **1** (*technical*) a print of a black and white photograph in which the different shades of grey are produced from small and large black dots **2** (*AmE, music*) = SEMITONE

'**half-truth** *noun* (*disapproving*) a statement that gives only part of the truth, especially when it is intended to deceive sb: *The newspaper reports are a mixture of gossip, lies and half-truths.*

half·way /,hɑːf'weɪ; *AmE* ,hæf-/ *adv.* **1** at an equal distance between two points; in the middle of a period of time: *It's about halfway between London and Bristol.* ◇ *He left halfway through the ceremony.* ◇ *I'm afraid we're not even halfway there yet.* **2** ~ **to/towards sth| ~ to/ towards doing sth** part of the way towards doing or achieving sth: *This only goes halfway to explaining what really happened.* **3** ~ **decent** (*informal*) fairly, but not very, good: *Any halfway decent map will give you that information.* ▶ **half·way** *adj.*: *The halfway point/stage.* IDM see MEET *v.*

,**halfway 'house** *noun* **1** [sing.] (*BrE*) something that combines the features of two very different things **2** [C] a place where prisoners, mental patients, etc. can stay for a short time after leaving a prison or hospital, before they start to live on their own again

half-wit /'hɑːfwɪt; *AmE* 'hæf-/ *noun* (*informal*) a stupid person ▶ ,**half-'witted** *adj.*

,**half-'yearly** *adj.* [only before noun] happening every six months; happening after the first six months of the year: *a half-yearly meeting* ◇ *the half-yearly sales figures* ▶ ,**half-'yearly** *adv.*: *Interest will be paid half-yearly in June and December.*

hali·but /'hælɪbət/ *noun* [C, U] (*pl.* **hali·but**) a large flat sea fish that is used for food

hali·tosis /,hælɪ'təʊsɪs; *AmE* -'toʊ-/ *noun* [U] (*medical*) a condition in which the breath smells unpleasant

hall /hɔːl/ *noun* **1** (also **hall·way**) (*AmE* also **entry**) a space or passage inside the entrance or front door of a building: *She ran into the hall and up the stairs.*—see also ENTRANCE HALL **2** (*AmE* also **hall·way**) a passage in a building with rooms down either side SYN CORRIDOR: *I headed for Scott's office down the hall.* **3** a building or large room for public meetings, meals, concerts, etc: *a concert/banqueting/sports/exhibition hall* ◇ *There are*

H

three dining halls on campus. ◊ The Royal Albert Hall ◊ (BrE) A jumble sale will be held in the village hall on Saturday.—see also CITY HALL, DANCE HALL, GUILDHALL, MUSIC HALL, TOWN HALL **4** = HALL OF RESIDENCE: She's living **in hall**. **5** (BrE) (often as part of a name) a large country house: Haddon Hall

hal·le·lu·jah /ˌhælɪˈluːjə/ (also **al·le·luia**) noun a song or shout of praise to God ▶ **hal·le·lu·jah** exclamation

hall·mark /ˈhɔːlmɑːk; AmE -mɑːrk/ noun, verb
■ noun **1** a feature or quality that is typical of sb/sth: Police said the explosion **bore all the hallmarks** of a terrorist attack. **2** a mark put on gold, silver and PLATINUM objects that shows the quality of the metal and gives information about when and where the object was made
■ verb to put a hallmark on metal goods

hallo (BrE) = HELLO

Hall of 'Fame noun (pl. ˌHalls of 'Fame) (especially AmE) [C] **1** a place for people to visit, like a museum, with things connected with famous people from a particular sport or activity: the Country Music Hall of Fame **2** [sing.] the group of people who have done a particular activity or sport particularly well

hall of 'residence (also **hall**) noun (pl. halls of residence, halls) (both BrE) (AmE dor·mi·tory) a building for university or college students to live in

hal·lowed /ˈhæləʊd; AmE -loʊd/ adj. [only before noun] **1** (especially of old things) respected and important: one of the theatre's most hallowed traditions **2** that has been made holy: to be buried in hallowed ground

Hal·low·een (also **Hal·low·e'en**) /ˌhæləʊˈiːn; AmE -loʊ-/ noun [C, U] the night of 31st October when it was believed in the past that dead people appeared from their graves, and which is now celebrated in the US, Canada and Britain by children who dress as GHOSTS, WITCHES, etc.—see also TRICK OR TREAT

hal·lu·cin·ate /həˈluːsɪneɪt/ verb to see or hear things that are not really there because of illness or drugs: [V] Some of these drugs can make you hallucinate. [also VN, V that]

hal·lu·cin·ation /həˌluːsɪˈneɪʃn/ noun **1** [C, U] the fact of seeming to see or hear sb/sth that is not really there, especially because of illness or drugs: to suffer from / have hallucinations ◊ High temperatures can cause hallucination. **2** [C] something that is seen or heard when it is not really there: Was the figure real or just a hallucination? **HELP** Some people use an instead of a before hallucination and then usually do not pronounce the 'h'. This now sounds old-fashioned.

hal·lu·cin·atory /həˈluːsɪnətri; həˌluːsɪˈneɪtəri; AmE həˈluːsənətɔːri/ adj. [only before noun] connected with or causing hallucinations: a hallucinatory experience ◊ hallucinatory drugs

hal·lu·cino·gen /ˌhæˈluːsɪnədʒən/ noun a drug, such as LSD, that affects people's minds and makes them see and hear things that are not really there ▶ **hal·lu·cino·gen·ic** /həˌluːsɪnəˈdʒenɪk/ adj.: hallucinogenic drugs/ effects **HELP** Some people use an instead of a before these words, and then usually do not pronounce the 'h'. This now sounds old-fashioned.

hall·way /ˈhɔːlweɪ/ noun **1** (especially BrE) = HALL (1) **2** (AmE) = HALL (2)

halo /ˈheɪləʊ; AmE -loʊ/ noun (pl. -oes or -os) **1** (in paintings, etc.) a circle of light shown around or above the head of a holy person: She played the part of an angel, complete with wings and a halo. ◊ (figurative) a halo of white frizzy hair **2** (informal) = CORONA

halo·gen /ˈhælədʒən/ noun (chemistry) any of a set of five chemical elements, including FLUORINE, CHLORINE and IODINE, that react with HYDROGEN to form strong acids from which simple salts can be made. Halogens, in the form of gas, are used in lamps and cookers/stoves.

halon /ˈheɪlɒn; AmE -lɑːn/ noun (chemistry) a gas that is a compound of CARBON and one or more halogens, used especially to stop fires

halt /hɔːlt; BrE also hɒlt/ verb, noun
■ verb to stop; to make sb/sth stop: [V] She walked towards him and then halted. ◊ 'Halt!' the Major ordered (= used as

a command to soldiers). ◊ [VN] The police were halting traffic on the parade route. ◊ The trial was halted after the first week. **IDM** see TRACK n.
■ noun **1** [sing.] an act of stopping the movement or progress of sb/sth: Work **came to a halt** when the machine broke down. ◊ The thought **brought her to an** abrupt **halt**. ◊ The car skidded to a halt. ◊ Strikes have led to **a halt in** production. ◊ They decided it was time to **call a halt to** the project (= stop it officially). **2** [C] (BrE) a small railway station in the country that has a platform but no buildings **IDM** see GRIND v.

hal·ter /ˈhɔːltə(r); BrE also ˈhɒlt-/ noun **1** a rope or leather strap put around the head of a horse for leading it with **2** (usually used as an adjective) a strap around the neck that holds a woman's dress or shirt in position, leaving the back and shoulders bare: She was dressed in a halter top and shorts.

halt·ing /ˈhɔːltɪŋ; BrE also ˈhɒlt-/ adj. [usually before noun] (especially of speech or movement) stopping and starting often, especially because you are not certain or are not very confident: a halting conversation ◊ a toddler's first few halting steps ▶ **halt·ing·ly** adv.: 'Well ...' she began haltingly.

halve /hɑːv; AmE hæv/ verb **1** to reduce by a half; to make sth reduce by a half: [V] The shares have **halved in value**. ◊ The company is halving its prices. **2** [VN] to divide sth into two equal parts

halves pl. of HALF

hal·yard /ˈhæljəd; AmE -jərd/ noun (technical) a rope used for raising or lowering a sail or flag

ham /hæm/ noun, verb
■ noun **1** [C, U] the top part of a pig's leg that has been CURED (= preserved using salt or smoke) and is eaten as food; the meat from this: The hams were cooked whole. ◊ a slice of ham ◊ a ham sandwich—compare BACON, GAMMON, PORK **2** [C] a person who sends and receives radio messages as a hobby rather than as a job: a radio ham **3** [C] (informal) (often used as an adjective) an actor who performs badly, especially by exaggerating emotions: a ham actor / performance **4** [C, usually pl.] (informal) the back part of a person's leg above the knee—see also HAMSTRING
■ verb (-mm-) **IDM** ˌham it 'up (informal) (especially of actors) when people **ham it up**, they deliberately exaggerate their emotions or movements

ham·burg·er /ˈhæmbɜːɡə(r); AmE -bɜːrg-/ (also **burg·er**) noun **1** (BrE also **beef·burg·er**) finely chopped beef made into a flat round shape that is then fried, often served in a bread roll—picture on page A1 **2** (also ˈhamburger meat) (both AmE) = MINCE

ˌham-'fisted (BrE) (AmE ˌham-'handed) adj. (informal) lacking skill when using your hands or when dealing with people: his ham-fisted efforts to assist her

ham·let /ˈhæmlət/ noun a very small village

ham·mer /ˈhæmə(r)/ noun, verb
■ noun
TOOL | **1** [C] a tool with a handle and a heavy metal head, used for breaking things or hitting nails: (figurative) The decision is a hammer blow for the steel industry.—see also SLEDGEHAMMER—picture at TOOL **2** [C] a tool with a handle and a wooden head, used by a person in charge of an AUCTION (= a sale at which things are sold to the person who offers the most money) in order to get people's attention: to come / go **under the hammer** (= to be sold at auction)
IN PIANO | **3** [C] a small wooden part inside a piano, that hits the strings to produce a sound
IN GUN | **4** [C] a part inside a gun that makes the gun fire
SPORT | **5** [C] a metal ball attached to a wire, thrown as a sport **6** (the hammer) [sing.] the event or sport of throwing the hammer—picture on page 1251
IDM ˌhammer and 'tongs if two people are **at it hammer and tongs** or **go at it hammer and tongs**, they argue or fight with a lot of energy and noise
■ verb
HIT WITH TOOL | **1** ~ sth (in/into/onto sth) to hit sth with a hammer: [V] I could hear somebody hammering next door.

s	t	v	z	ʃ	ʒ	tʃ	dʒ	θ	ð	ŋ
see	tea	van	zoo	shoe	vision	chain	jam	thin	this	sing

◊ [VN] *She hammered the nail into the wall.* ◊ [VN-ADJ] *He was hammering the sheet of copper flat.*

HIT MANY TIMES | **2** to hit sth hard many times, especially so that it makes a loud noise: [V] *Someone was hammering at the door.* ◊ *Hail was hammering down onto the roof.* ◊ (*figurative*) *I was so scared my heart was hammering* (= beating very fast) *in my chest.* ◊ [VN] *He hammered the door with his fists.*

KICK/HIT BALL | **3** [VN] [usually +adv. / prep.] (*informal*) to kick or hit a ball very hard: *He hammered the ball into the net.*

DEFEAT EASILY | **4** [VN] (*informal*) to defeat sb very easily: *Our team was hammered 5-1.*

PHRV ,hammer a'way at sth to work hard in order to finish or achieve sth; to keep repeating sth in order to get the result that you want ,hammer sth↔'home **1** to emphasize a point, an idea, etc. so that people fully understand it **2** to kick a ball hard and score a goal ,hammer sth 'into sb to make sb learn or remember sth by repeating it many times ,hammer 'out sth **1** to discuss a plan, an idea, etc. until everyone agrees or a decision is made: *to hammer out a compromise / deal* **2** to play a tune, especially on a piano, loudly and not very well

,hammer and 'sickle *noun* [sing.] tools representing the people who work in industry and farming, used on the flag of the former Soviet Union and as a symbol of Communism

ham·mer·ing /'hæmərɪŋ/ *noun* **1** [U, sing.] the sound of sb hitting sth with a hammer or with their FISTS: *the sound of hammering from the next room* **2** [C, usually sing.] (*BrE, informal*) an act of defeating or criticizing sb severely: *Our team took a real hammering in the first half.*

ham·mock /'hæmək/ *noun* a type of bed made from a net or from a piece of strong fabric, with ropes at each end that are used to hang it between two trees, posts, etc.

hammy /'hæmi/ *adj.* (ham·mier, ham·mi·est) (*informal*) (of a style of acting) artificial or exaggerated

ham·per /'hæmpə(r)/ *verb, noun*

▪ *verb* [VN] [often passive] (*written*) to prevent sb from easily doing or achieving sth SYN HINDER

▪ *noun* **1** a large basket with a lid, especially one used to carry food in: *a picnic hamper* **2** (*especially BrE*) a box or parcel containing food, sent as a gift: *a Christmas hamper* **3** (*AmE*) a large basket that you keep your dirty clothes in until they are washed

ham·ster /'hæmstə(r)/ *noun* an animal like a large mouse, with large cheeks for storing food. Hamsters are often kept as pets.

ham·string /'hæmstrɪŋ/ *noun, verb*

▪ *noun* **1** one of the five TENDONS behind the knee that connect the muscles of the upper leg to the bones of the lower leg: *a hamstring injury* ◊ *She's pulled a hamstring.* **2** a TENDON behind the middle joint (= HOCK) of the back leg of a horse and some other animals

▪ *verb* (ham·strung, ham·strung /'hæmstrʌŋ/) [VN] [often passive] (*written*) to prevent sb/sth from working or taking action in the way that is needed

hand /hænd/ *noun, verb*

▪ *noun*

PART OF BODY | **1** [C] the part of the body at the end of the arm, including the fingers and thumb: *Ian placed a hand on her shoulder.* ◊ *Put your hand up if you know the answer.* ◊ *Keep both hands on the steering wheel at all times.* ◊ *She was on (her) hands and knees* (= crawling on the floor) *looking for an earring.* ◊ *Couples strolled past holding hands.* ◊ *Give me your hand* (= hold my hand) *while we cross the road.* ◊ *The crowd threw up their hands* (= lifted them into the air) *in dismay.* ◊ *He killed the snake with his bare hands* (= using only his hands). ◊ *a hand towel* (= a small towel for drying your hands on) ◊ *a hand drill* (= one that is used by turning a handle rather than powered by electricity)—see also LEFT-HAND, RIGHT-HAND—picture at BODY

-HANDED | **2** (in adjectives) using the hand or number of hands mentioned: *a one-handed catch* ◊ *left-handed scissors* (= intended to be held in your left hand)

HELP | **3** (a hand) [sing.] (*informal*) help in doing sth: *Let me give you a hand with those bags* (= help you to carry them). ◊ *Do you need a hand with those invoices?* ◊ *The neighbours are always willing to lend a hand.*

ROLE IN SITUATION | **4** [sing.] ~ in sth the part or role that sb/sth plays in a particular situation; sb's influence in a situation: *Early reports suggest the hand of rebel forces in the bombings.* ◊ *Several of his colleagues had a hand in his downfall.* ◊ *This appointment was an attempt to strengthen her hand in policy discussions.*

ON CLOCK/WATCH | **5** [C] (usually in compounds) a part of a clock or watch that points to the numbers—see also HOUR HAND, MINUTE HAND, SECOND HAND

WORKER | **6** [C] a person who does physical work on a farm or in a factory—see also CHARGEHAND, FARMHAND, HIRED HAND, STAGEHAND

SAILOR | **7** [C] a sailor on a ship: *All hands on deck!*—see also DECKHAND

HAND- | **8** (in compounds) by a person rather than a machine: *hand-painted pottery* ◊ *hand-knitted*—see also HANDMADE

IN CARD GAMES | **9** [C] a set of playing cards given to one player in a game: *to be dealt a good / bad hand*—picture on page A8 **10** [C] one stage of a game of cards: *I'll have to leave after this hand.*

WRITING | **11** [sing.] (*old use*) a particular style of writing—see also FREEHAND

MEASUREMENT FOR HORSE | **12** [C] a unit for measuring the height of a horse, equal to 4 INCHES or 10.16 CENTIMETRES—see also DAB HAND, OLD HAND, SECOND-HAND, UNDERHAND

IDM (close/near) at 'hand close to you in time or distance: *Help was at hand.* ◊ *The property is ideally located with all local amenities close at hand.* **at the hands of sb | at sb's hands** (*written*) if you experience sth at the hands of sb, they are the cause of it **be good with your 'hands** to be skilful at making or doing things with your hands **bind/tie sb hand and 'foot 1** to tie sb's hands and feet together so that they cannot move or escape **2** to prevent sb from doing what they want by creating rules, restrictions, etc. **by 'hand 1** by a person rather than a machine: *The fabric was painted by hand.* **2** if a letter is delivered **by hand**, it is delivered by a messenger or by the person who wrote it, rather than by post/mail **fall into sb's 'hands/the 'hands of sb** (*written*) to become controlled by sb: *The town fell into enemy hands.* ◊ *We don't want this document falling into the wrong hands.* **(at) first 'hand** by experiencing, seeing, etc. sth yourself rather than being told about it by sb else: *The President visited the area to see the devastation at first hand.* **get your 'hands dirty** to do physical work: *He's not frightened of getting his hands dirty.* **sb's 'hand (in marriage)** (*old-fashioned*) permission to marry sb, especially a woman: *He asked the general for his daughter's hand in marriage.* **,hand in 'glove (with sb)** working closely with sb, especially in a secret and/or illegal way **,hand in 'hand 1** if two people are **hand in hand**, they are holding each other's hand **2** if two things **go hand in hand**, they are closely connected and one thing causes the other: *Poverty and poor health often go hand in hand.* **(get/take your) ,hands 'off (sth/sb)** (*spoken*) used to tell sb not to touch sth/sb: *Get your hands off my wife! Hey, hands off! That's my drink!* **,hands 'up! 1** (*spoken*) **1** used to tell a group of people to raise one hand in the air if they know the answer to a question, etc: *Hands up all those who want to go swimming.* **2** used by sb who is threatening people with a gun to tell them to raise both hands in the air **have your 'hands full** to be very busy or too busy to do sth else: *She certainly has her hands full with four kids in the house.* **have your 'hands tied** to be unable to do what you want to do because of rules, promises, etc: *I really wish I could help but my hands are tied.* **hold sb's 'hand** to give sb support in a difficult situation: *Do you want me to come along and hold your hand?* **in sb's capable, safe, etc. 'hands** being taken care of or dealt with by sb that you think you can rely on: *Can I leave these queries in your capable hands?* **in 'hand 1** if you have time or money **in hand**, it is left and available to be

æ	ɑː	e	ɜː	ə	ɪ	iː	i	ɒ	ɔː	ʌ	ʊ	u	uː
cat	father	ten	bird	about	sit	see	many	got	saw	cup	put	actual	too

(BrE)

H

used **2** if you have a particular situation **in hand**, you are in control of it **3** the job, question, etc. **in hand** is the one that you are dealing with **4** if sb works a week, month, etc. **in hand**, they are paid for the work a week, etc. after they have completed it **in the hands of sb** | **in sb's ˈhands** being looked after or controlled by sb: *The matter is now in the hands of my lawyer.* ◊ *At that time, the castle was in enemy hands.* **keep your ˈhand in** to occasionally do sth that you used to do a lot so that you do not lose your skill at it: *She retired last year but still teaches the odd class to keep her hand in.* **lay/get your ˈhands on sb** to catch sb that you are annoyed with: *Wait till I get my hands on him!* **lay/get your ˈhands on sth** to find or get sth: *I know their address is here somewhere, but I can't lay my hands on it right now.* **many hands make light ˈwork** (*saying*) used to say that a job is made easier if a lot of people help **not do a hand's ˈturn** (*old-fashioned*) to do no work: *She hasn't done a hand's turn all week.* **off your ˈhands** no longer your responsibility **on either/ every ˈhand** (*literary*) on both/all sides; in both/all directions **on ˈhand** available, especially to help: *The emergency services were on hand with medical advice.* **on your ˈhands** if you have sb/sth **on your hands**, you are responsible for them or it: *Let me take care of the invitations—you've enough on your hands with the caterers.* **on the ˈone hand ... on the ˈother (hand) ...** used to introduce different points of view, ideas, etc., especially when they are opposites: *On the one hand they'd love to have kids, but on the other, they don't want to give up their freedom.* **out of ˈhand 1** difficult or impossible to control: *Unemployment is getting out of hand.* **2** if you reject sth **out of hand**, you do so immediately without thinking about it fully or listening to other people's arguments: *All our suggestions were dismissed out of hand.* **ˌout of your ˈhands** no longer your responsibility: *I'm afraid the matter is now out of my hands.* **ˌplay into sb's ˈhands** to do exactly what an enemy, opponent, etc. wants so that they gain the advantage in a particular situation: *If we get the police involved, we'll be playing right into the protesters' hands.* **put your ˌhand in your ˈpocket** (*BrE*) to spend money or give it to sb: *I've heard he doesn't like putting his hand in his pocket.* **(at) second, third, etc. ˈhand** by being told about sth by sb else who has seen it or heard about it, not by experiencing, seeing, etc. it yourself: *I'm fed up of hearing about these decisions third hand!* **ˌtake sb in ˈhand** to deal with sb in a strict way in order to improve their behaviour **take sth into your own ˈhands** to deal with a particular situation yourself because you are not happy with the way that others are dealing with it **throw your ˈhand in** (*informal*) to stop doing sth or taking part in sth, especially because you are not successful **to ˈhand** that you can reach or get easily: *I'm afraid I don't have the latest figures to hand.* **turn your ˈhand to sth** to start doing sth or be able to do sth, especially when you do it well: *Jim can turn his hand to most jobs around the house.*—more at BIG *adj.*, BIRD, BITE *v.*, BLOOD *n.*, CAP *n.*, CASH *n.*, CHANGE *v.*, CLOSE² *adv.*, COURAGE, DEAD *adj.*, EAT, FIRM *adj.*, FOLD *v.*, FORCE *v.*, FREE *adj.*, HAT, HEAVY, HELP *v.*, IRON *adj.*, JOIN *v.*, KNOW *v.*, LAW, LIFE, LIFT *v.*, LIVE¹, MONEY, OFFER *v.*, OVERPLAY, PAIR *n.*, PALM *n.*, PUTTY, RAISE *v.*, SAFE *adj.*, SHOW *n.*, SHOW *v.*, SLEIGHT, TIME *n.*, TRY *v.*, UPPER *adj.*, WAIT *v.*, WASH *v.*, WHIP *n.*, WIN *v.*, WRING

■ *verb* ~ **sth to sb** | ~ **sb sth** to pass or give sth to sb: [VN, VNN] *She handed the letter to me.* ◊ *She handed me the letter.*

IDM **hand sth to sb on a ˈplate** (*informal*) to give sth to sb without the person concerned making any effort: *Nobody's going to hand you success on a plate.* **have (got) to ˈhand it to sb** (*informal*) used to say that sb deserves praise for sth: *You've got to hand it to her—she's a great cook.*

PHRV **ˌhand sth↔aˈround/ˈround** to offer or pass sth, especially food or drinks, to all the people in a group **ˌhand sth ˈback (to sb)** to give or return sth to the person who owns it or to where it belongs **ˌhand sth↔ˈdown (to sb) 1** [usually passive] to give or leave sth to sb who is younger than you **SYN** PASS DOWN: *These skills used to be handed down from father to son.*—related

noun HAND-ME-DOWN **2** (*especially AmE*) to officially give a decision/statement, etc. **SYN** ANNOUNCE: *The judge has handed down his verdict.* **ˌhand sth↔ˈin (to sb)** to give sth to a person in authority, especially a piece of work or sth that is lost **SYN** GIVE IN: *You must all hand in your projects by the end of next week.* ◊ *I handed the watch in to the police.* ◊ *to* **hand in your notice/resignation** (= formally tell your employer that you want to stop working for them) **ˌhand sth↔ˈon (to sb)** to give or leave sth for another person to use or deal with **SYN** PASS ON, **ˌhand sth↔ˈout (to sb) 1** to give a number of things to the members of a group **SYN** DISTRIBUTE: *Could you hand these books out, please?*—related noun HANDOUT **2** to give advice, a punishment, etc: *He's always handing out advice to people.* **ˌhand sth↔ˈover (to sb)** | **ˌhand ˈover (to sb)** | **ˌhand sth ˈover (to sb)** to give sb else your position of power or the responsibility for sth: *She resigned and handed over to one of her younger colleagues.* ◊ *He finally handed over his responsibility for the company last year.*—related noun HANDOVER **ˌhand sb ˈover to sb** to let sb listen or speak to another person, especially on the telephone or in a news broadcast: *I'll hand you over to my boss.* **ˌhand sb/sth↔ˈover (to sb)** to give sth/sb officially or formally to another person: *He handed over a cheque for $200000.* ◊ *They handed the weapons over to the police.*—related noun HANDOVER

VOCABULARY BUILDING
using your **hands**

touch
These verbs describe different ways of touching things:

feel	*I felt the bag to see what was in it.*
finger	*She fingered the silk delicately.*
handle	*Handle the fruit with care.*
rub	*She rubbed her eyes wearily.*
stroke	*The cat loves being stroked.*
pat	*He patted my arm and told me not to worry.*
tap	*Someone was tapping lightly at the door.*
squeeze	*I took his hand and squeezed it.*

hold
You can use these verbs to describe taking something quickly:

grab	*I grabbed his arm to stop myself from falling.*
snatch	*She snatched the letter out of my hand.*

These verbs describe holding things tightly:

clasp	*Her hands were clasped behind her head.*
clutch	*The child was clutching a doll in her hand.*
grasp	*Grasp the rope with both hands and pull.*
grip	*He gripped his bag tightly and wouldn't let go.*

---

hand·bag /ˈhændbæg/ (*AmE also* **purse**) *noun* a small bag for money, keys, etc., carried especially by women ⇨ note at PURSE—picture at BAG, MONEY

ˈhand baggage *noun* [U] (*especially AmE*) = HAND LUGGAGE

hand·ball /ˈhændbɔːl/ *noun* **1** [U] (*AmE also* **ˈteam handball**) a team game for two teams of seven players, usually played indoors, in which players try to score goals by throwing a ball with their hand **2** [U] (*AmE*) a game in which players hit a small ball against a wall with their hand **3** [C, U] (in football) the offence of touching the ball with your hands: *a penalty for handball*

hand·basin /ˈhændbeɪsn/ *noun* (*BrE*) a small bowl that has taps/faucets and is fixed to the wall, used for washing your hands in

hand·bas·ket /ˈhændbɑːskɪt; *AmE* -bæs-/ *noun* **IDM** **go to hell in a ˈhandbasket** (*AmE*) = GO TO THE DOGS at DOG *n.*

hand·bill /ˈhændbɪl/ *noun* a small printed advertisement that is given to people by hand

hand·book /ˈhændbʊk/ *noun* a book giving instructions

on how to use sth or information about a particular subject—compare MANUAL

hand·brake /ˈhændbreɪk/ (*especially BrE*) (*AmE* usually ˈemergency brake, ˈparking brake) *noun* a BRAKE in a motor vehicle that is operated by hand, used especially when the vehicle is not moving: *to put the handbrake on* ◊ *to take the handbrake off* ◊ *Is the handbrake on?*—picture at CAR

hand·cart /ˈhændkɑːt; *AmE* -kɑːrt/ *noun* = CART

hand·craft /ˈhændkrɑːft; *AmE* -kræft/ *noun* (*AmE*) = HANDICRAFT

hand·craf·ted /ˈhændkrɑːftɪd; *AmE* -kræft-/ *adj.* skilfully made by hand, not by machine: *a handcrafted chair*

hand·cuff /ˈhændkʌf/ *verb* [VN] (*usually passive*) to put handcuffs on sb or to fasten sb to sth/sb with handcuffs: *Her hands were handcuffed behind her back.*

hand·cuffs /ˈhændkʌfs/ (also *informal* **cuffs**) *noun* [pl.] a pair of metal rings joined by a chain, used for holding the wrists of a prisoner together: *a pair of handcuffs* ◊ *She was led away **in handcuffs**.*

hand·ful /ˈhændfʊl/ *noun* **1** [C] ~ (of sth) the amount of sth that can be held in one hand: *a handful of rice* **2** [sing.] ~ (of sb/sth) a small number of people or things: *Only a handful of people came.* **3 a** ~ [sing.] (*informal*) a person or an animal that is difficult to control: *Her children can be a real handful.*

ˈhand grenade *noun* a small bomb that is thrown by hand

hand·gun /ˈhændɡʌn/ *noun* a small gun that you can hold and fire with one hand

ˌhand-ˈheld *adj.* [usually before noun] small enough to be held in the hand while being used: *a hand-held camera/ computer* ▶ ˈhand-held *noun*

hand·hold /ˈhændhəʊld; *AmE* -hoʊld/ *noun* something on the surface of a steep slope, wall, etc. that a person can hold when climbing up it

handi·cap /ˈhændikæp/ *noun, verb*
■ *noun* **1** [C, U] (becoming *old-fashioned*, sometimes *offensive*) a permanent physical or mental condition that makes it difficult or impossible to use a particular part of your body or mind: *Despite her handicap, Jane is able to hold down a full-time job.* ◊ *mental/physical/visual handicap* ⇨ note at DISABLED **2** [C] something that makes it difficult for sb to do sth: *Not speaking the language proved to be a bigger handicap than I'd imagined.* **3** [C] (*sport*) a race or competition in which the most skilful competitors must run further, carry extra weight, etc. in order to give all the competitors an equal chance of winning; the disadvantage that is given to a competitor in such a race or competition **4** [C] (in golf) an advantage given to a weaker player so that competition is more equal when they play against a stronger player. It is expressed as a number related to the number of times a player hits the ball and gets lower as he/she improves.
■ *verb* (-pp-) [VN] (*usually passive*) to make sth more difficult for sb to do: *British exports have been handicapped by the strong pound.*

handi·capped /ˈhændikæpt/ *adj.* (becoming *old-fashioned*, sometimes *offensive*) **1** suffering from a mental or physical handicap: *a mentally/visually handicapped child* ◊ *The accident left him physically handicapped.* **2 (the handicapped)** *noun* [pl.] people who are handicapped: *a school for the physically handicapped* ⇨ note at DISABLED

han·di·craft /ˈhændikrɑːft; *AmE* -kræft/ (*AmE* also **hand·craft**) *noun* [C, usually pl., U] **1** activities such as sewing and weaving that use skill with your hands and artistic ability to make things: *to teach handicrafts* ◊ *Her hobbies are music, reading and handicraft.* **2** things made in this way: *traditional handicrafts bought by tourists*

hand·ily /ˈhændɪli/ *adv.* **1** in a way that is HANDY (= convenient): *We're handily placed for the train station.* **2** (*especially AmE*) easily: *He handily defeated his challengers.*

han·di·work /ˈhændiwɜːk; *AmE* -wɜːrk/ *noun* [U] **1** work that you do, or sth that you have made, especially using your artistic skill: *We admired her exquisite handiwork.*

2 a thing done by a particular person or group, especially sth bad: *This looks like the handiwork of an arsonist.*

hand·ker·chief /ˈhæŋkətʃɪf; -tʃiːf; *AmE* -kərtʃ-/ *noun* (*pl.* **hand·ker·chiefs** or **hand·ker·chieves** /-tʃiːvz/) (also *informal* **hanky**, **han·kie**) a small piece of material or paper that you use for blowing your nose, etc.

han·dle /ˈhændl/ *verb, noun*
■ *verb*
DEAL WITH | **1** [VN] to deal with or control a situation, a person, an area of work or a strong emotion: *A new man was appointed to handle the crisis.* ◊ *She's very good at handling her patients.* ◊ *The sale was handled by Adams Commercial.* ◊ *We can handle up to 500 calls an hour at our new offices.* ◊ *We all have to learn to handle stress.* ◊ *This matter has been handled very badly.* ◊ (*informal*) *You have to know how to **handle yourself** in this business* (= know the right way to behave). ◊ (*informal*) *'Any problems?' 'Nothing I can't handle.'* ◊ (*informal*) *I've got to go. I can't **handle it** any more* (= deal with a difficult situation).
TOUCH WITH HANDS | **2** [VN] to touch, hold or move sth with your hands: *Our cat hates being handled.* ◊ *The label on the box said: 'Fragile. Handle with care.'*
CONTROL | **3** [VN] to control a vehicle, an animal, a tool, etc: *I wasn't sure if I could handle such a powerful car.* ◊ *She's a difficult horse to handle.*
OF VEHICLE | **4** [V] ~ **well/badly** to be easy/difficult to drive or control: *The car handles well in any weather.*
BUY/SELL | **5** [VN] to buy or sell sth SYN DEAL IN: *They were arrested for **handling stolen goods**.*
■ *noun*
OF DOOR/DRAWER/WINDOW | **1** the part of a door, drawer, window, etc. that you use to open it: *She turned the handle and opened the door.*
OF CUP/BAG/TOOL | **2** the part of an object, such as a cup, a bag, or a tool that you use to hold it, or carry it: *the handle of a knife* ◊ *a broom handle*—picture at BAG, CUTLERY
-HANDLED | **3** (in adjectives) having the number or type of handle mentioned: *a long-handled spoon*
IDM **get/have a ˈhandle on sb/sth** (*informal*) to understand or know about sb/sth, especially so that you can deal with it or them later: *I can't get a handle on these sales figures.* **give sb a ˈhandle (on sth)** (*informal*) to give sb enough facts or knowledge for them to be able to deal with sth—more at FLY *v.*

handle·bar /ˈhændlbɑː(r)/ *noun* [C] (also **handle·bars** [pl.]) a metal bar, with a handle at each end, that you use for steering a bicycle or motorcycle: *to hold onto the handlebars*—picture at BICYCLE

ˌhandlebar mousˈtache *noun* a MOUSTACHE that is curved upwards at each end

hand·ler /ˈhændlə(r)/ *noun* (*especially in compounds*) **1** a person who trains and controls animals, especially dogs **2** a person who carries or touches sth as part of their job: *airport baggage handlers* ◊ *food handlers* **3** (*especially AmE*) sb who organizes sth or advises sb: *the President's campaign handlers*

hand·ling /ˈhændlɪŋ/ *noun* [U] **1** the way that sb deals with or treats a situation, a person, an animal, etc: *I was impressed by his handling of the affair.* ◊ *This horse needs firm handling.* **2** the action of organizing or controlling sth: *data handling on computer* **3** the action of touching, feeling or holding sth with your hands: *toys that can stand up to rough handling* **4** the cost of dealing with an order, delivering goods, booking tickets, etc: *a small handling charge* **5** the way in which a motor vehicle can be controlled by the driver: *a car designed for easy and stable handling* **6** = CARRIAGE

ˈhand luggage (*especially BrE*) (also ˈhand baggage, ˈcarry-on baggage especially in *AmE*) *noun* [U] small bags that you can keep with you on an aircraft

hand·made /ˌhændˈmeɪd/ *adj.* made by a person using their hands rather than by machines: *handmade furniture*—compare MACHINE-MADE

hand·maiden /ˈhændmeɪdn/ (also **hand·maid**

/ˈhændmeɪd/) *noun* **1** (*old-fashioned*) a female servant **2** (*formal*) something that supports and helps sth else: *Mathematics was once dubbed the handmaiden of the sciences.*

ˈhand-me-down *noun* [usually pl.] (*especially AmE*) = CAST-OFF: *She hated having to wear her sister's hand-me-downs.* ▶ **ˈhand-me-down** *adj.* (*especially AmE*) = CAST-OFF

hand·out /ˈhændaʊt/ *noun* **1** (sometimes *disapproving*) food, money or clothes that are given to a person who is poor: *to be dependent on handouts* **2** (often *disapproving*) money that is given to a person or an organization by the government, etc., for example to encourage commercial activity **3** a free document that gives information about an event or a matter of public interest, or that states the views of a political party, etc.—see also PRESS RELEASE **4** a document that is given to students in class and that contains a summary of the lesson, a set of exercises, etc.

hand·over /ˈhændəʊvə(r)/ *AmE* -oʊvar/ *noun* [C, U] **1** the act of moving power or responsibility from one person or group to another; the period during which this is done: *the smooth handover of power from a military to a civilian government* **2** the act of giving a person or thing to sb in authority: *the handover of the hostages*

ˌhand-ˈpicked *adj.* carefully chosen for a special purpose

ˈhand puppet *noun* (*AmE*) = GLOVE PUPPET

hand·rail /ˈhændreɪl/ *noun* a long narrow bar that you can hold onto for support, for example when you are going up or down stairs

hand·saw /ˈhændsɔː/ *noun* a SAW (= a tool with a long blade with sharp teeth along one edge) that is used with one hand only—picture at TOOL

hand·set /ˈhændset/ *noun* **1** the part of a telephone that you hold close to your mouth and ear to speak into and listen—compare RECEIVER **2** a device that you hold in your hand to operate a television, etc.—see also REMOTE CONTROL

hand·shake /ˈhændʃeɪk/ *noun* an act of shaking sb's hand with your own, used especially as a greeting or when you have made an agreement—see also GOLDEN HANDSHAKE

ˌhands-ˈoff *adj.* [usually before noun] dealing with people or a situation by not becoming involved and by allowing people to do what they want to: *a hands-off approach to staff management*—compare HANDS-ON

hand·some /ˈhænsəm/ *adj.* (**hand·somer**, **hand·somest**) **HELP** more **handsome** and **most handsome** are more common **1** (of men) attractive **SYN** GOOD-LOOKING: *a handsome face* ◊ *He's the most handsome man I've ever met.* ◊ *He was aptly described as 'tall, dark, and handsome'.* **2** (of women) attractive, with large strong features rather than small delicate ones: *a tall, handsome woman* **3** beautiful to look at: *a handsome horse/house/ city* ◊ *The two of them made a handsome couple.* **4** large in amount or quantity: *a handsome profit* ◊ *He was elected by a handsome majority* (= a lot of people voted for him). **5** generous: *She paid him a handsome compliment.* ▶ **hand·some·ly** *adv.*: *a handsomely dressed man* ◊ *a handsomely produced book* ◊ *to be paid/rewarded handsomely* **hand·some·ness** *noun* [U]

ˌhands-ˈon *adj.* [usually before noun] doing sth rather than just talking about it: *hands-on computer training* ◊ *to gain hands-on experience of industry* ◊ *a hands-on style of management*—compare HANDS-OFF

hand·stand /ˈhændstænd/ *noun* a movement in which you balance on your hands and put your legs straight up in the air

ˌhand-to-ˈhand *adj.* **hand-to-hand** fighting involves physical contact with your opponent

ˌhand-to-ˈmouth *adj.* [usually before noun] if you have a **hand-to-mouth** life, you spend all the money you earn on basic needs such as food and do not have anything left **IDM** see LIVE¹

hand·writ·ing /ˈhændraɪtɪŋ/ *noun* [U] **1** writing that is done with a pen or pencil, not printed or typed **2** a person's particular style of writing in this way: *I can't*

read his handwriting. **IDM** **the ˌhandwriting on the ˈwall** (*AmE*) = THE WRITING ON THE WALL.

hand·writ·ten /ˌhændˈrɪtn/ *adj.* written by hand, not printed or typed: *a handwritten note/statement*

handy /ˈhændi/ *adj.* (**hand·ier, handi·est**) (*informal*) **1** useful; easy to use or to do: *a handy little tool* ◊ *handy hints/tips for removing carpet stains* **2** [not before noun] ~ (**for sth/for doing sth**) situated near to sb/sth; situated or stored in a convenient place: *Always keep a first-aid kit handy.* ◊ *Have you got a pen handy?* ◊ (*BrE*) *Our house is very handy for the station.* **3** [usually before noun] skilful in using your hands or tools to make or repair things: *to be handy around the house*—see also HANDILY **IDM** **ˌcome in ˈhandy** (*informal*) to be useful: *The extra money came in very handy.* ◊ *Don't throw that away—it might come in handy.*

handy·man /ˈhændimæn/ *noun* (*pl.* **-men** /-men/) a man who is good at doing practical jobs inside and outside the house, either as a hobby or as a job

hang /hæŋ/ *verb, noun*

▪ *verb* (**hung, hung** /hʌŋ/ **HELP** In sense 4, **hanged** is used for the past tense and past participle.)

He hung his head in shame.

ATTACH FROM TOP | **1** ~ (**sth**) (**up**) [+*adv./prep.*] to attach sth, or to be attached, at the top so that the lower part is free or loose: [VN] *Hang your coat up on the hook.* ◊ *Where are we supposed to hang our washing up to dry?* ◊ [V] *There were several expensive suits hanging in the wardrobe.*

FALL LOOSELY | **2** [V+*adv./prep.*] when sth **hangs** in a particular way, it falls in that way: *Her hair hung down to her waist.* ◊ *He had lost weight and the suit hung loosely on him.*

BEND DOWNWARDS | **3** to bend or let sth bend downwards: [V] *The dog's tongue was hanging out.* ◊ *Children hung* (= were leaning) *over the gate.* ◊ *A cigarette hung from her lips.* ◊ [VN] *She hung her head in shame.*

KILL SB | **4** (**hanged, hanged**) to kill sb, usually as a punishment, by tying a rope around their neck and allowing them to drop; to be killed in this way: [VN] *He was the last man to be hanged for murder in this country.* ◊ *She had committed suicide by hanging herself from a beam.* ◊ [V] *At that time you could hang for stealing.*

PICTURES | **5** to attach sth, especially a picture, to a hook on a wall; to be attached in this way: [VN] *We hung her portrait above the fireplace.* ◊ *Several of his paintings hang in the Tate Gallery.* **6** [VN] [usually passive] ~ **sth with sth** to decorate a place by placing paintings, etc. on a wall: *The rooms were hung with tapestries.*

WALLPAPER | **7** [VN] to stick WALLPAPER to a wall

DOOR/GATE | **8** [VN] to attach a door or gate to a post so that it moves freely

STAY IN THE AIR | **9** [V+*adv./prep.*] to stay in the air: *Smoke hung in the air above the city.*

IDM **ˈhang sth** (*BrE, spoken*) used to say that you are not going to worry about sth: *Oh, let's get two and hang the expense!* **hang a ˈleft/ˈright** (*AmE*) to take a left/right turn **hang by a ˈhair/ˈthread** (of a person's life) to be in great danger **hang (on) ˈin there** (*informal*) to remain determined to succeed even when a situation is difficult **hang on sb's ˈwords/on sb's every ˈword** to listen with great attention to sb you admire **hang ˈtough** (*AmE*) to be determined and refuse to change your attitude or ideas **let it all hang ˈout** (*informal*) to express your feelings freely—more at BALANCE *n.*, FIRE *n.*, GRIM, HEAVY *adv.*, LOOSE *adj.*, PEG *n.* **PHRV** **ˌhang aˈbout** (*BrE, informal*) **1** to wait or stay near a place, not doing very much: *kids hanging about in the streets* **2** to be very slow doing sth: *I can't hang about—the boss wants to see me.* **3** (*spoken*) used to tell sb to stop what they are doing or saying for a short time: *Hang about! There's something not quite right here.* **ˌhang**

a'bout with sb (*informal*) to spend a lot of time with sb ,**hang a'round (...)** (*informal*) to wait or stay near a place, not doing very much: *You hang around here in case he comes, and I'll go on ahead.* ,**hang a'round with sb** (*informal*) to spend a lot of time with sb ,**hang 'back** to remain in a place after all the other people have left ,**hang 'back (from sth)** to hesitate because you are nervous about doing or saying sth: *I was sure she knew the answer but for some reason she hung back.* ,**hang 'on 1** to hold sth tightly: *Hang on tight—we're off!* **2** (*spoken*) used to ask sb to wait for a short time or to stop what they are doing: *Hang on—I'm not quite ready.* ◊ *Now hang on a minute—you can't really believe what you just said!* **3** to wait for sth to happen: *I haven't heard if I've got the job yet—they've kept me hanging on for days.* **4** (*spoken*) used on the telephone to ask sb who is calling to wait until they can talk to the person they want: *Hang on—I'll just see if he's here.* **5** to continue doing sth in difficult circumstances: *The team hung on for victory.* '**hang on sth** to depend on sth: *A lot hangs on this decision.* ,**hang 'on to sth 1** to hold sth tightly: *Hang on to that rope and don't let go.* **2** (*informal*) to keep sth, not sell it or give it away: *Let's hang on to those old photographs—they may be valuable.* ,**hang 'out** (*informal*) to spend a lot of time in a place: *The local kids hang out at the mall.*—related noun HANG-OUT ,**hang 'over sb** if sth bad or unpleasant is **hanging over** you, you think about it and worry about it a lot because it is happening or might happen: *The possibility of a court case is still hanging over her.* ,**hang to'gether 1** to fit together well; to be the same as or CONSISTENT with each other: *Their accounts of what happened don't hang together.* **2** (of people) to support or help one another ,**hang 'up** to end a telephone conversation by putting the telephone RECEIVER down or switching the telephone off: *After I hung up I remembered what I'd wanted to say.* ,**hang sth ↔ 'up** (*informal*) to finish using sth for the last time: *Ruth has hung up her dancing shoes.* ,**hang 'up on sb** (*informal*) to end a telephone call by suddenly and unexpectedly putting the telephone down: *Don't hang up on me—we must talk!*—see also HUNG UP
■ *noun* [sing.] the way in which a dress, piece of fabric, etc. falls or moves
IDM **get the 'hang of sth** (*informal*) to learn how to do or to use sth; to understand sth: *It's not difficult once you get the hang of it.*

hangar /ˈhæŋə(r); ˈhæŋɡə(r)/ *noun* a large building in which aircraft are kept

hang·dog /ˈhæŋdɒɡ; *AmE* -dɔːɡ/ *adj.* [only before noun] if a person has a **hangdog** look, they look sad or ashamed

hanger /ˈhæŋə(r)/ (also '**coat hanger**, '**clothes hanger**) *noun* a curved piece of wood, plastic or wire, with a hook at the top, that you use to hang clothes up on

,**hanger-'on** *noun* (*pl.* ,**hangers-'on**) (often *disapproving*) a person who tries to be friendly with a famous person or who goes to important events, in order to get some advantage

'**hang-glider** *noun* **1** the frame used in hang-gliding **2** a person who goes hang-gliding

'**hang-gliding** *noun* [U] a sport in which you fly while hanging from a frame like a large KITE which you control with your body movements: *to go hang-gliding*

hang·ing /ˈhæŋɪŋ/ *noun* **1** [U, C] the practice of killing sb as a punishment by putting a rope around their neck and hanging them from a high place; an occasion when this happens: *to sentence sb to death by hanging* ◊ *public hangings* **2** [C, usually pl.] a large piece of material that is hung on a wall for decoration: *wall hangings*

,**hanging 'basket** *noun* a basket or similar container with flowers growing in it, that is hung from a building by a short chain or rope—picture at HOUSE

hang·man /ˈhæŋmən/ *noun* (*pl.* -**men** /-mən/) a man whose job is to hang criminals

'**hang-out** *noun* (*informal*) a place where sb lives or likes to go often **SYN** HAUNT

hang·over /ˈhæŋəʊvə(r); *AmE* -oʊvər/ *noun* **1** the HEAD-ACHE and sick feeling that you have the day after drinking too much alcohol: *She woke up with a terrible*

hangover. **2** [usually sing.] ~ (**from sth**) a feeling, custom, habit, etc. that remains from the past, although it is no longer practical or suitable: *the insecure feeling that was a hangover from her childhood* ◊ *hangover laws from the previous administration*—see also HOLDOVER

'**hang-up** *noun* ~ (**about sth**) (*informal*) an emotional problem about sth that makes you embarrassed or worried: *He's got a real hang-up about his height.*

hank /hæŋk/ *noun* a long piece of wool, thread, rope, etc. that is wound into a large loose ball

han·ker /ˈhæŋkə(r)/ *verb* ~ **after/for sth** to have a strong desire for sth: [V] *He had hankered after fame all his life.* ◊ [Vto inf] *She hankered to go back to Australia.*

han·ker·ing /ˈhæŋkərɪŋ/ *noun* [usually sing.] ~ (**for/after sth**) | ~ (**to do sth**) a strong desire: *a hankering for a wealthy lifestyle*

hanky (also **han·kie**) /ˈhæŋki/ *noun* (*pl.* -**ies**) (*informal*) = HANDKERCHIEF

hanky-panky /ˌhæŋki ˈpæŋki/ *noun* [U] (*old-fashioned*, *informal*) **1** sexual activity that is not considered acceptable: *There was all sorts of hanky-panky going on at the party.* **2** dishonest behaviour

han·som /ˈhænsəm/ (also '**hansom cab**) *noun* a carriage with two wheels, pulled by one horse, used in the past to carry two passengers

Ha·nuk·kah (also **Cha·nuk·kah**, **Cha·nuk·ah**) /ˈhænʊkə/ *noun* an eight-day Jewish festival and holiday in November or December when Jews remember the occasion when the TEMPLE in Jerusalem was DEDICATED again in 165 BC

hap·haz·ard /hæpˈhæzəd; *AmE* -zərd/ *adj.* (*disapproving*) with no particular order or plan; not organized well: *The books had been piled on the shelves in a haphazard fashion.* ◊ *The government's approach to the problem was haphazard.* ▶ **hap·haz·ard·ly** *adv.*

hap·less /ˈhæpləs/ *adj.* [only before noun] (*formal*) not lucky; unfortunate: *the hapless victims of exploitation*

H

WHICH WORD? ?
happen / occur / take place

Happen is the usual word that you use to refer to events that are not planned or expected: *You look terrible – what's happened?* The word is also used to talk about one event resulting from another: *What happened when you told him the news?*

Occur meaning 'happen' is used only in formal situations: *Police report that the accident occurred at about 9.30 p.m.*

Take place is also quite formal and is usually used to talk about an event that has been planned or arranged or when people take an active part in sth: *The festival takes place in July every year.* ◊ *Filming took place in Ireland.* In informal language you would probably say: *The festival is in July every year.* ◊ *The movie was filmed in Ireland.*

hap·pen /ˈhæpən/ *verb* **1** [V] to take place, especially without being planned: *You'll never guess what's happened!* ◊ *Accidents like this happen all the time.* ◊ *Let's see what happens next week.* ◊ *I'll be there whatever happens.* ◊ *I don't know how this happened.* **2** [V] to take place as the result of sth: *She pressed the button but nothing happened.* ◊ *What happens if nobody comes to the party?* ◊ *Just plug it in and see what happens.* **3** to do or be sth by chance: [Vto inf] *She happened to be out when we called.* ◊ *You don't happen to know his name, do you?* ◊ [Vthat] *It happened that she was out when we called.* **4** [Vto inf] used to tell sb sth, especially when you are disagreeing with them or annoyed by what they have said: *That happens to be my mother you're talking about!* **IDM** **anything can/might 'happen** used to say that it is not possible to know what the result of sth will be **as it happens/happened** used when you say sth that is surprising, or sth connected with what sb else has just said: *I agree with you, as it happens.* ◊ *As it happens, I have a spare set of keys in my office.* **it (just) so happens that ...** by chance: *It just so happened they'd been invited too.*

æ	ɑː	e	ɜː	ə	ɪ	iː	i	ɒ	ɔː	ʌ	ʊ	u	uː
cat	father	ten	bird	about	sit	see	many	got	saw	cup	put	actual	too
								(BrE)					

H

,these things 'happen used to tell sb not to worry about sth they have done: *'Sorry—I've spilt some wine.' 'Never mind. These things happen.'*—more at ACCIDENT, EVENT, WAIT v. **PHRV** **'happen on sth** (*old-fashioned*) to find sth by chance **'happen to sb/sth** to have an effect on sb/sth: *I hope nothing* (= nothing unpleasant) *has happened to them.* ◊ *It's the best thing that has ever happened to me.* ◊ *What's happened to your car?* ◊ *Do you know what happened to Gill Lovecy* (= have you any news about her)?

hap·pen·ing /ˈhæpənɪŋ/ *noun, adj.*
■ *noun* **1** [usually pl.] an event; something that happens, often sth unusual: *There have been strange happenings here lately.* ◊ *The momentous happenings of the past few weeks had left her feeling exhausted.* ⇨ note at EVENT **2** an artistic performance or event that is not planned
■ *adj.* [only before noun] (*informal*) where there is a lot of exciting activity; fashionable: *a happening place*

hap·pen·stance /ˈhæpənstæns; *BrE* also -staːns/ *noun* [U, C] (*literary*) chance, especially when it results in sth good

hap·pily /ˈhæpɪli/ *adv.* **1** in a cheerful way; with feelings of pleasure or satisfaction: *to chat/laugh happily* ◊ *children playing happily on the beach* ◊ *to be happily married* ◊ *I think we can manage quite happily on our own.* ◊ *And they all lived happily ever after* (= used as the end of a fairy story). **2** by good luck **SYN** FORTUNATELY: *Happily, the damage was only slight.* **3** willingly: *I'll happily help, if I can.* **4** (*formal*) in a way that is suitable or appropriate: *This suggestion did not fit very happily with our existing plans.*

happy /ˈhæpi/ *adj.* (**hap·pier, hap·pi·est**)
FEELING/GIVING PLEASURE | **1** ~ **(to do sth)** | ~ **(for sb)** | ~ **(that ...)** feeling or showing pleasure; pleased: *a happy smile/face* ◊ *You don't look very happy today.* ◊ *We are happy to announce the engagement of our daughter.* ◊ *I'm very happy for you.* **2** giving or causing pleasure: *a happy marriage/memory/childhood* ◊ *The story has a happy ending.* ◊ *Those were the happiest days of my life.*
AT CELEBRATION | **3** if you wish sb a **Happy Birthday**, **Happy New Year**, etc. you mean that you hope they have a pleasant celebration
SATISFIED | **4** ~ **(with/about sb/sth)** satisfied that sth is good or right; not anxious: *Are you happy with that arrangement?* ◊ *If there's anything you're not happy about, come and ask.* ◊ *I'm not happy with his work this term.* ◊ *She was happy enough with her performance.* ◊ *I'm not too happy about her living alone.* ◊ *I said I'd go just to keep him happy.*
WILLING | **5** ~ **to do sth** (*formal*) willing or pleased to do sth: *I'm happy to leave it till tomorrow.* ◊ *He will be more than happy to come with us.*
LUCKY | **6** lucky; successful: *By a happy coincidence, we arrived at exactly the same time.* ◊ *He is in the happy position of never having to worry about money.*
SUITABLE | **7** (*formal*) (of words, ideas or behaviour) suitable and appropriate for a particular situation: *That wasn't the happiest choice of words.*
▶ **hap·pi·ness** *noun* [U]: *to find/achieve true happiness* ◊ *Her eyes shone with happiness.*
IDM **a ,happy e'vent** the birth of a baby **a/the happy 'medium** something that is in the middle between two choices or two ways of doing sth: *She tried to strike a happy medium between making the questions too hard and making them too easy.* **many happy re'turns (of the 'day)** used to wish sb a happy and pleasant birthday—more at MEAN *n.*

,happy-go-'lucky *adj.* not caring or worrying about the future: *a happy-go-lucky attitude/person*

'happy hour *noun* [usually sing.] (*informal*) a time, usually in the early evening, when a pub or a bar sells alcoholic drinks at lower prices than usual

hara-kiri /ˌhærə ˈkɪri/ *noun* [U] (from *Japanese*) an act of killing yourself by cutting open your stomach with a SWORD, performed especially by the SAMURAI in Japan in the past, to avoid losing honour

har·angue /həˈræŋ/ *verb, noun*
■ *verb* [VN] to speak loudly and angrily in a way that criticizes sb/sth or tries to persuade people to do sth: *He walked to the front of the stage and began to harangue the audience.*
■ *noun* a long loud angry speech that criticizes sb/sth or tries to persuade sb/sth

har·ass /ˈhærəs; həˈræs/ *verb* [VN] **1** [often passive] to annoy or worry sb by putting pressure on them or saying or doing unpleasant things to them: *He has complained of being harassed by the police.* ◊ *She claims she has been sexually harassed at work.* **2** to make repeated attacks on an enemy **SYN** HARRY: *Our convoys were being continually harassed by enemy submarines.* ▶ **har·ass·ment** *noun* [U]: *racial/sexual/police harassment*

har·assed /ˈhærəst; həˈræst/ *adj.* tired and anxious because you have too much to do: *a harassed-looking waiter* ◊ *harassed mothers with their children*

har·bin·ger /ˈhaːbɪndʒə(r); *AmE* ˈhaːrb-/ *noun* ~ **(of sth)** (*formal* or *literary*) a sign that shows that sth is going to happen soon, often sth bad

har·bour (*BrE*) (*AmE* **har·bor**) /ˈhaːbə(r); *AmE* ˈhaːrb-/ *noun, verb*
■ *noun* [C, U] an area of water on the coast, protected from the open sea by strong walls, where ships can shelter: *Several boats lay at anchor in the harbour.* ◊ *to enter/leave harbour*
■ *verb* [VN] **1** to hide and protect sb who is hiding from the police: *Police believe someone must be harbouring the killer.* **2** (*written*) to keep feelings or thoughts, especially negative ones, in your mind for a long time: *The arsonist may harbour a grudge against the company.* ◊ *She began to harbour doubts about the decision.* **3** (*written*) to contain sth and allow it to develop: *Your dishcloth can harbour many germs.* ◊ *These woodlands once harboured a colony of red deer.*

'harbour master (*BrE*) (*AmE* **har·bor·mas·ter**) *noun* an official in charge of a harbour

hard /haːd; *AmE* haːrd/ *adj., adv.*
■ *adj.* (**hard·er, hard·est**)
SOLID/STIFF | **1** solid, firm or stiff and difficult to bend or break: *Wait for the concrete to go hard.* ◊ *a hard mattress* ◊ *Diamonds are the hardest known mineral.* **OPP** SOFT
DIFFICULT | **2** ~ **(for sb) (to do sth)** difficult to do, understand or answer: *a hard choice/question* ◊ *It is hard to believe that she's only nine.* ◊ *It's hard to see how they can lose.* ◊ *'When will the job be finished?' 'It's hard to say.'* (= it is difficult to be certain) ◊ *I find his attitude very hard to take* (= difficult to accept). ◊ *It's hard for old people to change their ways.* ◊ *It must be hard for her, bringing up four children on her own.* ◊ *We're finding reliable staff hard to come by* (= difficult to get). **OPP** EASY **3** full of difficulty and problems, especially because of a lack of money **SYN** TOUGH: *Times were hard at the end of the war.* ◊ *She's had a hard life.* **OPP** EASY
NEEDING/USING EFFORT | **4** needing or using a lot of physical strength or mental effort: *I've had a hard day shovelling snow.* ◊ *I've had a very hard day.* **5** (of people) putting a lot of effort or energy into an activity: *She's a very hard worker.* ◊ *He's hard at work on a new novel.* ◊ *When I left they were all still hard at it* (= working hard). **6** done with a lot of strength or force: *He gave the door a good hard kick.* ◊ *a hard punch.*
WITHOUT SYMPATHY | **7** showing no sympathy or affection: *My father was a hard man.* ◊ *She gave me a hard stare.* ◊ *He said some very hard things to me.*
NOT AFRAID | **8** (*informal*) (of people) ready to fight and showing no signs of fear or weakness: *Come and get me if you think you're hard enough.* ◊ *You think you're really hard, don't you?*
FACTS/EVIDENCE | **9** [only before noun] definitely true and based on information that can be proved: *Is there any hard evidence either way?* ◊ *The newspaper story is based on hard facts.*
WEATHER | **10** very cold and severe: *It had been a hard winter.* ◊ *There was a hard frost that night.*—compare MILD

DRINK | **11** [only before noun] strongly alcoholic: *hard liquor* ◇ (*informal*) *a drop of the hard stuff* (= a strong alcoholic drink)—compare SOFT DRINK

WATER | **12** containing CALCIUM and other mineral salts that make mixing with soap difficult: *a hard water area* ◇ *Our water is very hard.* OPP SOFT

CONSONANTS | **13** (*phonetics*) used to describe a letter *c* or *g* when pronounced as in 'cat' or 'go', rather than as in 'city' or 'giant' OPP SOFT

▶ **hard·ness** *noun* [U]: *water hardness* ◇ *hardness of heart*

IDM **be 'hard on sb/sth 1** to treat or criticize sb in a very severe or strict way: *Don't be too hard on him—he's very young.* **2** to be difficult or unfair to sb/sth: *It's hard on people who don't have a car.* **3** to be likely to hurt or damage sth: *Looking at a computer screen all day can be very hard on the eyes.* **drive/strike a hard 'bargain** to argue in an aggressive way and force sb to agree on the best possible price or arrangement **give sb a hard 'time** to deliberately make a situation difficult and unpleasant for sb: *They really gave me a hard time at the interview.* **,hard and 'fast** (especially after a negative) that cannot be changed in any circumstances: *There are no hard and fast rules about this.* **(as) ,hard as 'nails** showing no sympathy, kindness or fear **,hard 'cheese** (*BrE, informal*) used as a way of saying that you are sorry about sth, usually in an IRONIC way (= you really mean the opposite) **,hard 'going** difficult to understand or needing a lot of effort: *I'm finding his latest novel very hard going.* **,hard 'luck/'lines** (*BrE*) used to tell sb that you feel sorry for them: *'Failed again, I'm afraid.' 'Oh, hard luck.'* **the 'hard way** by having an unpleasant experience or by making mistakes: *She won't listen to my advice so she'll just have to learn the hard way.* **make hard 'work of sth** to use more time or energy on a task than is necessary **no hard 'feelings** used to tell sb that you no longer feel any anger towards them: *Someone's got to lose. No hard feelings, Dave, eh?* **play hard to 'get** (*informal*) to make yourself seem more attractive or interesting by not immediately accepting an invitation to do sth **too much like hard 'work** needing too much effort: *I can't be bothered making a hot meal—it's too much like hard work.*—more at JOB, NUT *n.*, ROCK *n.*

■ *adv.* (**hard·er**, **hard·est**)

WITH EFFORT | **1** with great effort; with difficulty: *to work hard* ◇ *to fight/struggle hard* ◇ *You must try harder.* ◇ *She tried her hardest not to show how disappointed she was.* ◇ *Don't hit it so hard!* ◇ *He was still breathing hard after his run.* ◇ *Our victory was hard won* (= won with great difficulty).

WITH FORCE | **2** with great force: (*figurative*) *Small businesses have been hit hard/hard hit by the recession.*

CAREFULLY | **3** very carefully and thoroughly: *to think/look/listen hard* ◇ *We thought long and hard before deciding to move house.*

A LOT | **4** heavily; a lot or for a long time: *It was raining hard when we set off.* ◇ *to laugh/cry hard*

LEFT/RIGHT | **5** at a sharp angle to the left/right: *Turn hard right at the next junction.*

WHICH WORD?
hard / hardly (?)

The adverb from the adjective **hard** is **hard**: *I have to work hard today.* ◇ *She has thought very hard about her future plans.* ◇ *It was raining hard outside.*

Hardly is an adverb meaning 'almost not': *I hardly ever go to concerts.* ◇ *I can hardly wait for my birthday.* It cannot be used instead of **hard**: ~~I've been working hardly today.~~ ◇ ~~She has thought very hardly about her future plans.~~ ◇ ~~It was raining hardly outside.~~

⇨ note at HARDLY

IDM **be/feel hard 'done by** (*informal*) to be or feel unfairly treated: *She was every right to feel hard done by—her parents have given her nothing.* **be ,hard 'pressed/'pushed to do sth | be hard 'put (to it) to do sth** to find it very difficult to do sth: *He was hard put to it*

to explain her disappearance. **be hard 'up for sth** to have too few or too little of sth: *We're hard up for ideas.*—see also HARD UP **'hard on sth** (*written*) very soon after: *His death followed hard on hers.* **take sth 'hard** to be very upset by sth: *He took his wife's death very hard.*—more at DIE *v.*, HEEL *n.*

hard·back /'hɑːdbæk; *AmE* 'hɑːrd-/ (also **hard·cover** especially in *AmE*) *noun* [C, U] a book that has a stiff cover: *What's the price of the hardback?* ◇ *It was published in hardback last year.* ◇ *hardback books/editions*—compare PAPERBACK

hard·ball /'hɑːdbɔːl; *AmE* 'hɑːrd-/ *noun* (*AmE*) **1** the game of baseball **2** used to refer to a way of behaving, especially in politics, that shows that a person is determined to get what they want: *I want us to play hardball on this issue.* ◇ *hardball politics*

hard·bit·ten /,hɑːd'bɪtn; *AmE* ,hɑːrd-/ *adj.* not easily shocked and not showing emotion, because you have experienced many unpleasant things: *a hardbitten war journalist*

hard·board /'hɑːdbɔːd; *AmE* 'hɑːrdbɔːrd/ *noun* [U] a type of stiff board made by crushing very small pieces of wood together into thin sheets

,hard-'boiled *adj.* **1** (of an egg) boiled until the inside is hard—compare SOFT-BOILED **2** (of people) not showing much emotion

,hard 'by *prep.* (*old-fashioned*) very near: *a house hard by the river* ▶ **,hard 'by** *adv.*

,hard 'candy *noun* [U] (*AmE*) = BOILED SWEET

,hard 'cash (*BrE*) (*AmE* ,**cold 'cash**) *noun* [U] money, especially in the form of coins and notes, that you can spend

'hard cider *noun* (*AmE*) = CIDER

,hard 'copy *noun* [U] (*computing*) information from a computer that has been printed on paper—picture on page 251

,hard 'core *noun* (*BrE*) **1** [sing.+ sing./pl. *v.*] the small central group in an organization, or in a particular group of people, who are the most active or who will not change their beliefs or behaviour: *It's really only the hard core that bother(s) to go to meetings.* ◇ *A hard core of drivers ignore the law.* **2** [U] (usually **'hardcore**) small pieces of stone, brick, etc. used as a base for building roads on

,hard-'core *adj.* [only before noun] **1** having a belief or a way of behaving that will not change: *hard-core party members* **2** showing or describing sexual activity in a detailed or violent way: *They sell hard-core pornography.*

,hard 'court *noun* an area with a hard surface for playing tennis on, not grass

hard·cover /'hɑːdkʌvə(r); *AmE* 'hɑːrd-/ *noun* (*especially AmE*) = HARDBACK

,hard 'currency *noun* [U, C] money that is easy to exchange for money from another country, because it is not likely to lose its value: *The hotel insisted that we pay in hard currency.*

,hard 'disk *noun* a disk inside a computer that stores data and programs—compare FLOPPY DISK—picture on page 250

'hard-drinking *adj.* drinking a lot of alcohol

,hard 'drug *noun* [usually pl.] a powerful illegal drug, such as HEROIN, that some people take for pleasure and can become ADDICTED to—compare SOFT DRUG

,hard-'earned *adj.* that you get only after a lot of work and effort: *hard-earned cash* ◇ *We finally managed a hard-earned draw.*

,hard-'edged *adj.* powerful, true to life and not affected by emotion: *the movie's hard-edged realism*

hard·en /'hɑːdn; *AmE* 'hɑːrdn/ *verb* **1** to become or make sth become firm, stiff or solid: [V] *The varnish takes a few hours to harden.* ◇ (*figurative*) *Their suspicions hardened into certainty.* ◇ [VN] *a method for hardening and preserving wood* **2** if your voice, face, etc. **hardens**, or you **harden** it, it becomes more serious or severe: [V] *Her face hardened into an expression of hatred.* ◇ [VN] *He hardened*

H

his voice when he saw she wasn't listening. **3** if sb's feelings or attitudes **harden** or sb/sth **hardens** them, they become more fixed and determined: [V] *Public attitudes to the strike have hardened.* ◊ *Opinion seems to be hardening against the invasion.* ◊ [VN] *The incident hardened her resolve to leave the company.* **4** [VN] [usually passive] to make sb less kind or less affected by extreme situations: *Joe sounded different, hardened by the war.* ◊ *They were* **hardened criminals** (= they showed no regret for their crimes). ◊ *In this job you have to* **harden your heart** *to pain and suffering.* ▶ **hard·en·ing** *noun* [U, sing.]: *hardening of the arteries* ◊ *a hardening of attitudes towards one-parent families*

,**hard-'faced** *adj.* (*disapproving*) (of a person) showing no feeling or sympathy for other people

,**hard-'fought** *adj.* that involves fighting very hard: *a hard-fought battle/win/victory*

,**hard 'hat** *noun* a protective hat worn by building workers, etc.—picture at HAT

,**hard-'headed** *adj.* determined and not allowing your emotions to affect your decisions: *a hard-headed businessman*

,**hard-'hearted** *adj.* giving no importance to the feelings or problems of other people—compare SOFT-HEARTED

,**hard-'hitting** *adj.* not afraid to talk about or criticize sb/sth in an honest and very direct way: *a hard-hitting campaign/report/speech*

,**hard 'labour** (*BrE*) (*AmE* ,**hard 'labor**) *noun* [U] punishment in prison that involves a lot of very hard physical work

,**hard 'left** *noun* [sing.+ sing./pl. v.] (*especially BrE*) the members of a LEFT-WING political party who have the most extreme opinions: *hard-left policies*

,**hard 'line** *noun* [sing.] a strict policy or attitude: *the judge's hard line against drug dealers* ◊ *The government took a hard line on the strike.*

,**hard-'line** *adj.* [usually before noun] **1** (of a person) having very fixed beliefs and being unlikely or unwilling to change them: *a hard-line Communist* **2** (of ideas) very fixed and unlikely to change: *a hard-line attitude* ▶ **hard-liner** *noun*: *a Republican hardliner*

,**hard-'luck story** *noun* a story about yourself that you tell sb in order to get their sympathy or help

hard·ly /'hɑːdli; *AmE* 'hɑːrd-/ *adv.* **1** almost no; almost not; almost none: *There's* **hardly any** *tea left.* ◊ *Hardly anyone has bothered to reply.* ◊ *She* **hardly ever** *calls me* (= almost never). ◊ *We hardly know each other.* ◊ **Hardly a day goes by without** *my thinking of her* (= I think of her almost every day). **2** used especially after 'can' or 'could' and before the main verb, to emphasize that it is difficult to do sth: *I* **can hardly keep** *my eyes open* (= I'm almost falling asleep). ◊ *I* **could hardly believe** *it when I read the letter.* **3** used to say that sth has just begun, happened, etc: *We can't stop for coffee now, we've hardly started.* ◊ *We had hardly sat down to supper when the phone rang.* ◊ (*written*) *Hardly had she spoken than she regretted it bitterly.* **4** used to suggest that sth is unlikely or unreasonable or that sb is silly for saying or doing sth: *He is hardly likely to admit he was wrong.* ◊ *It's hardly surprising she was fired; she never did any work.* ◊ *It's* **hardly the time** *to discuss it now.* ◊ *You* **can hardly** *expect her to do it for free.* ◊ '*Couldn't you have just said no?*' '*Well, hardly,* (= of course not) *she's my wife's sister.*' ⇨ note at HARD

,**hard-'nosed** *adj.* not affected by feelings when trying to get what you want: *a hard-nosed journalist*

,**hard of 'hearing** *adj.* [not before noun] **1** unable to hear very well **2** (**the hard of hearing**) *noun* [pl.] people who are unable to hear very well: *subtitles for the deaf and the hard of hearing*

'**hard-on** *noun* (△, *slang*) an ERECTION (1)

,**hard 'porn** *noun* [U] (*informal*) films/movies, pictures, books, etc. that show sexual activity in a very detailed and sometimes violent way—compare SOFT PORN

,**hard-'pressed** *adj.* **1** having a lot of problems, especially too much work, and too little time or money: *Hard-pressed junior doctors want shorter working hours.*

2 ~ **to do sth** finding sth very difficult to do: *You would be hard-pressed to find a better secretary.*

,**hard 'right** *noun* [sing.+ sing./pl. v.] (*especially BrE*) the members of a RIGHT-WING political party who have the most extreme opinions: *hard-right opinions*

,**hard 'rock** *noun* [U] a type of loud modern music with a very strong beat, played on electric guitars

hard·scrab·ble /,hɑːd'skræbl; *AmE* ,hɑːrd-/ *adj.* (*AmE*) not having enough of the basic things you need to live: *a hardscrabble life/upbringing*

,**hard 'sell** *noun* [sing., U] a method of selling sth that puts a lot of pressure on the customer to buy it—compare SOFT SELL

hard·ship /'hɑːdʃɪp; *AmE* 'hɑːrd-/ *noun* [U, C] a situation that is difficult and unpleasant because you do not have enough money, food, clothes, etc: *economic/financial hardship* ◊ *People suffered many hardships during that long winter.* ◊ *It was* **no hardship** *to walk home on such a lovely evening.*

,**hard 'shoulder** (*BrE*) (*AmE* '**breakdown lane**) *noun* [sing.] a strip of ground with a hard surface beside a motorway/freeway where vehicles can stop in an emergency: *to pull over onto the hard shoulder/into the breakdown lane*

hard-top /'hɑːdtɒp; *AmE* 'hɑːrdtɑːp/ *noun* a car with a metal roof

,**hard 'up** *adj.* (*informal*) **1** having very little money, especially for a short period of time: *hard up students* **2** ~ (**for sth**) lacking in sth interesting to do, talk about, etc: '*You could always go out with Steve.*' '*I'm not that hard up!*'

hard·ware /'hɑːdweə(r); *AmE* 'hɑːrdwer/ *noun* [U] **1** (*computing*) the machinery and electronic parts of a computer system—compare SOFTWARE **2** (*BrE* also **iron-mon·gery**) tools and equipment that are used in the house and garden/yard: *a hardware shop*

'**hardware dealer** *noun* (*AmE*) = IRONMONGER

,**hard-'wearing** *adj.* (*BrE*) that lasts a long time and remains in good condition: *a hard-wearing carpet*

,**hard-'wired** *adj.* (*technical*) (of computer functions) built into the permanent system and not provided by SOFTWARE

,**hard-'won** *adj.* [usually before noun] that you only get after fighting or working hard for it: *She was not going to give up her hard-won freedom so easily.*

H

hard·wood /'hɑːdwʊd; AmE 'hɑːrd-/ noun [U,C] hard heavy wood from a DECIDUOUS tree (= one that loses its leaves in winter): *hardwood doors/floors*—compare SOFT-WOOD

hard-'working adj. putting a lot of effort into a job and doing it well: *hard-working nurses*

hardy /'hɑːdi; AmE 'hɑːrdi/ adj. (har·dier, har·di·est) **1** strong and able to survive difficult conditions and bad weather: *a hardy breed of sheep* **2** (of a plant) that can live outside through the winter ▶ **hardi·ness** noun [U]

hare /heə(r); AmE her/ noun, verb
■ noun an animal like a large rabbit with very strong back legs, that can run very fast—compare RABBIT **IDM** see MAD
■ verb [V+adv./prep.] (BrE) to run or go somewhere very fast

hare·bell /'heəbel; AmE 'herbel/ (ScotE **blue·bell**) noun a wild plant with delicate blue flowers shaped like bells

'hare-brained adj. (informal) crazy and unlikely to succeed: *a hare-brained scheme/idea/theory*

hare·lip /'heəlɪp; AmE 'herlɪp/ noun an old-fashioned and now offensive word for CLEFT LIP

harem /'hɑːriːm; -rəm; AmE 'hærəm/ noun **1** the women or wives belonging to a rich man, especially in some Muslim societies **2** the separate part of a traditional Muslim house where the women live **3** (technical) a group of female animals that share the same male for MATING

hari·cot /'hærɪkəʊ; AmE -koʊ/ (also **,haricot 'bean**) (both BrE) (AmE **'navy bean**) noun a type of small white bean that is usually dried before it is sold and then soaked before cooking

hark /hɑːk; AmE hɑːrk/ verb [V] (old use) used only as an order to tell sb to listen: *Hark! I hear a step on the stair!* **PHRV** **'hark at sb** (BrE, spoken) used only as an order to draw attention to sb who has just said sth stupid or who is showing too much pride: *Just hark at him! Who does he think he is?* **,hark 'back (to sth)** **1** to remember or talk about sth that happened in the past: *She's always harking back to how things used to be.* **2** to remind you of, or to be like, sth in the past: *The newest styles hark back to the clothes of the Seventies.*

har·ken = HEARKEN

har·le·quin /'hɑːləkwɪn; AmE 'hɑːrl-/ noun an amusing character in some traditional plays, who wears special brightly coloured clothes with a diamond pattern

har·lot /'hɑːlət; AmE 'hɑːrlət/ noun (old use, disapproving) a prostitute, or a woman who looks and behaves like one

harm /hɑːm; AmE hɑːrm/ noun, verb
■ noun [U] damage or injury that is caused by a person or an event: *He would never frighten anyone or* **cause** *them* **any harm.** ◊ *He may look fierce, but he* **means no harm.** ◊ *The court case will* **do serious harm** *to my business.* ◊ *The accident could have been much worse; luckily* **no harm** *was done.* ◊ *Don't worry, we'll see that the children* **come** *to* **no harm.** ◊ *I can't say I like Mark very much, but I don't* **wish him any harm.** ◊ *Hard work* **never did any-** *one* **any harm.** ◊ *Look, we're just going out for a few drinks,* **where's the harm in that?** ◊ *The treatment they gave him did him* **more harm than good.** **IDM** **,no 'harm done** (spoken) used to tell sb not to worry because they have caused no serious damage or injury: *Forget it, Dave, no harm done.* **out of harm's 'way** in a safe place where sb/sth cannot be hurt or injured or do any damage to sb/sth **there is no harm in (sb's) doing sth | it does no harm (for sb) to do sth** used to tell sb that sth is a good idea and will not cause any problems: *He may say no, but there's no harm in asking.* ◊ *It does no harm to ask.*
■ verb [VN] to hurt or injure sb or to damage sth: *He would never harm anyone.* ◊ *Pollution can harm marine life.* ◊ *These revelations will harm her chances of winning the election.* **IDM** see FLY n., HAIR

harm·ful /'hɑːmfl; AmE 'hɑːrmfl/ adj. ~ **(to sb/sth)** causing damage or injury to sb/sth, especially to a person's health or to the environment: *the harmful effects of alcohol* ◊ *Fruit juices can be harmful to children's teeth.* ◊ *the sun's harmful ultra-violet rays* ◊ *Many household products are potentially harmful.*

harm·less /'hɑːmləs; AmE 'hɑːrm-/ adj. **1** ~ **(to sb/sth)** unable or unlikely to cause damage or harm: *The bacteria is harmless to humans.* **2** unlikely to upset or offend anyone: *It's just a bit of harmless fun.* ▶ **harm·less·ly** adv.: *The missile fell harmlessly into the sea.* **harm·less·ness** noun [U]

har·mon·ic /hɑː'mɒnɪk; AmE hɑːr'mɑːn-/ adj., noun
■ adj. [usually before noun] (music) relating to the way notes are played or sung together to make a pleasing sound: *the harmonic and rhythmic interest of the music*
■ noun [usually pl.] (music) a note that can be played on some musical instruments, that is higher and quieter than the main note being played

har·mon·ica /hɑː'mɒnɪkə; AmE hɑːr'mɑːn-/ (BrE also **'mouth organ**) noun a small musical instrument that you hold near your mouth and play by blowing or sucking air through it

har·mo·ni·ous /hɑː'məʊniəs; AmE hɑːr'moʊ-/ adj. **1** (of relationships, etc.) friendly, peaceful and without any disagreement **2** arranged together in a pleasing way so that each part goes well with the others: *a harmonious combination of colours* **3** (of sounds) very pleasant when played or sung together ▶ **har·mo·ni·ous·ly** adv.: *They worked very harmoniously together.*

har·mo·nium /hɑː'məʊniəm; AmE hɑːr'moʊ-/ noun a musical instrument like a small ORGAN. Air is pumped through metal pipes to produce the sound and the different notes are played on the keyboard.

har·mon·ize (BrE also **-ise**) /'hɑːmənaɪz; AmE 'hɑːrm-/ verb **1** [V] ~ **(with sth)** (written) if two or more things **harmonize** with each other or one thing **harmonizes** with the other, the things go well together and produce an attractive result: *The new building does not harmonize with its surroundings.* **2** [VN] (written) to make systems or rules similar in different countries or organizations: *the need to harmonize tax levels across the European Union* **3** [V] ~ **(with sb/sth)** to play or sing music that combines with the main tune to make a pleasing sound: *Sally sang the melody while I harmonized.* ▶ **har·mon·iza·tion, -isa·tion** /,hɑːmənaɪ'zeɪʃn; AmE ,hɑːrmənə'z-/ noun [U,C]

har·mony /'hɑːməni; AmE 'hɑːrm-/ noun (pl. -ies) **1** [U] a state of peaceful existence and agreement: *the need to be* **in harmony with** *our environment* ◊ *to live together in perfect harmony* ◊ *social/racial harmony*—compare DISCORD **2** [U,C] (music) the way in which different notes that are played or sung together combine to make a pleasing sound: *to sing in harmony* ◊ *to study four-part harmony* ◊ *passionate lyrics and stunning vocal harmonies*—compare DISCORD **3** [C,U] a pleasing combination of related things: *the harmony of colour in nature*

har·ness /'hɑːnɪs; AmE 'hɑːrnɪs/ noun, verb
■ noun **1** a set of leather straps and metal pieces that is put around a horse's head and body so that the horse can be controlled and fastened to a carriage, etc. **2** a set of straps for fastening sth to a person's body or to keep them from moving off or falling: *a safety harness*—picture at CHAIR **IDM** **in 'harness** (BrE) doing your normal work, especially after a rest or a holiday **in harness (with sb)** (BrE) working closely with sb in order to achieve sth
■ verb [VN] **1** ~ **sth (to sth)** to put a harness on a horse or other animal; to attach a horse or other animal to sth with a harness: *to harness a horse* ◊ *We harnessed two ponies to the cart.* ◊ (figurative) *In some areas, the poor feel harnessed to their jobs.* **2** to control and use the force or strength of sth to produce power or to achieve sth: *attempts to harness the sun's rays as a source of energy* ◊ *We must harness the skill and creativity of our workforce.*

harp /hɑːp; AmE hɑːrp/ noun, verb
■ noun a large musical instrument with strings stretched on an upright frame, played with the fingers—picture on page 840
■ verb **PHRV** **,harp 'on (about sth)| 'harp on sth** to keep talking about sth in a boring or annoying way

harp·ist /'hɑːpɪst; AmE 'hɑːrp-/ noun a person who plays the harp

har·poon /hɑː'puːn; AmE hɑːr'p-/ noun, verb

H

æ	ɑː	e	ɜː	ə	ɪ	iː	i	ɒ	ɔː	ʌ	ʊ	u	uː
cat	father	ten	bird	about	sit	see	many	got	saw	cup	put	actual	too
								(BrE)					

■ *noun* a weapon like a SPEAR that you can throw or fire from a gun and is used for catching large fish, WHALES, etc.

■ *verb* [VN] to hit sth with a harpoon

harp·si·chord /ˈhɑːpsɪkɔːd; *AmE* ˈhɑːrpsɪkɔːrd/ *noun* an early type of musical instrument similar to a piano, but with strings that are PLUCKED (= pulled), not hit

harp·si·chord·ist /ˈhɑːpsɪkɔːdɪst; *AmE* ˈhɑːrpsɪkɔːrd-/ *noun* a person who plays the harpsichord

harpy /ˈhɑːpi; *AmE* ˈhɑːrpi/ *noun* (*pl.* -ies) **1** (in ancient Greek and Roman stories) a cruel creature with a woman's head and body and a bird's wings and feet **2** a cruel woman

har·ri·dan /ˈhærɪdən/ *noun* (*old-fashioned* or *literary*) a bad-tempered unpleasant woman

har·rier /ˈhæriə(r)/ *noun* a BIRD OF PREY (= a bird that kills other creatures for food) of the HAWK family

har·row /ˈhærəʊ; *AmE* -roʊ/ *noun* a piece of farming equipment that is pulled over land that has been PLOUGHED to break up the earth before planting ▶ **har·row** *verb* [VN]

har·row·ing /ˈhærəʊɪŋ; *AmE* -roʊ-/ *adj.* very shocking or frightening and making you feel very upset: *a harrowing experience/film*

harry /ˈhæri/ *verb* (**har·ries, harry·ing, har·ried, har·ried**) [VN] (*written*) **1** to annoy or upset sb by continuously asking them questions or for sth: *She has been harried by the press all week.* **2** to make repeated attacks on an enemy SYN HARASS: *They harried the retreating army.*

harsh /hɑːʃ; *AmE* hɑːrʃ/ *adj.* (**harsh·er, harsh·est**) **1** cruel, severe and unkind: *The punishment was harsh and unfair.* ◇ *The minister received some harsh criticism.* ◇ *the harsh treatment of slaves* ◇ *He regretted his harsh words.* ◇ *We had to face up to the harsh realities of life sooner or later.* **2** (of weather or living conditions) very difficult and unpleasant to live in: *a harsh winter/wind/climate* ◇ *the harsh conditions of poverty which existed for most people at that time* **3** too strong and bright; ugly or unpleasant to look at: *harsh colours* ◇ *She was caught in the harsh glare of the headlights.* ◇ *the harsh lines of concrete buildings* **4** unpleasant to listen to: *a harsh voice* **5** too strong and rough and likely to damage sth: *harsh detergents* ▶ **harsh·ly** *adv.*: *She was treated very harshly.* **harsh·ness** *noun* [U]

hart /hɑːt/ *noun* a male deer, especially a red deer; a STAG—compare BUCK, HIND

har·vest /ˈhɑːvɪst; *AmE* ˈhɑːrv-/ *noun, verb*

■ *noun* **1** [C, U] the time of year when the crops are gathered in on a farm, etc.; the act of cutting and gathering crops: *harvest time* ◇ *Farmers are extremely busy during the harvest.* **2** [C] the crops, or the amount of crops, cut and gathered: *the grain harvest* ◇ *a good/bad harvest* (= a lot of crops or few crops) IDM see REAP

■ *verb* [V, VN] to cut and gather a crop; to catch a number of animals or fish to eat

har·vest·er /ˈhɑːvɪstə(r); *AmE* ˈhɑːrv-/ *noun* **1** a machine that cuts and gathers grain—see also COMBINE HARVESTER **2** (*old-fashioned*) a person who helps to gather in the crops

harvest ˈfestival *noun* a service held in Christian churches when people thank God for the crops that have been gathered—compare THANKSGIVING

has /həz; əz; *strong form* hæz/ ⇨ HAVE

has-been /ˈhæz biːn/ *noun* (*informal, disapproving*) a person who is no longer as famous, successful or important as they used to be

hash /hæʃ/ *noun* **1** [U, C] a hot dish of cooked meat and potatoes that are cut into small pieces and mixed together: *corned beef hash* **2** [U] (*informal*) = HASHISH **3** (also ˈhash sign) (both *BrE*) (*AmE* ˈpound sign) [C] the symbol (#), especially one on a telephone IDM **make a ˈhash of sth** (*informal*) to do sth badly: *I made a real hash of the interview.*

hash ˈbrowns *noun* [pl.] (*AmE*) a dish of chopped potatoes and onions, fried until they are brown

hash·ish /ˈhæʃiːʃ; hæˈʃiːʃ/ (also *informal* **hash**) *noun* [U]

a drug made from the RESIN of the HEMP plant, which gives a feeling of being relaxed when it is smoked or chewed. Use of the drug is illegal in many countries. SYN CANNABIS

hasn't /ˈhæznt/ *short form* has not

hasp /hɑːsp; *AmE* hæsp/ *noun* a flat piece of metal with a long narrow hole in it, used with a PADLOCK to fasten doors, boxes, etc.

has·sle /ˈhæsl/ *noun, verb*

■ *noun* [C, U] (*informal*) **1** a situation that is annoying because it involves doing sth difficult or complicated that needs a lot of effort: *It's a hassle having to travel with so many bags.* ◇ *Send them a fax—it's a lot less hassle than phoning.* ◇ *legal hassles* **2** a situation in which people disagree, argue or annoy you: *Do as you're told and don't give me any hassle!* ◇ *Try not to get into a hassle with this guy.*

■ *verb* (*informal*) [VN] to annoy sb or cause them trouble, especially by asking them to do sth many times: *Don't keep hassling me! I'll do it later.*

has·sock /ˈhæsək/ *noun* **1** a thick firm cushion used for kneeling on in a church **2** (*AmE*) = POUFFE

hast /hæst/ (**thou hast**) (*old use*) a way of saying 'you have'

haste /heɪst/ *noun* [U] speed in doing sth, especially because you do not have enough time: *In her haste to complete the work on time, she made a number of mistakes.* ◇ *The letter had clearly been written in haste.* ◇ *After his first wife died, he married again with almost indecent haste.* ◇ (*old-fashioned*) *She made haste to open the door.* IDM ˌmore ˈhaste, ˌless ˈspeed (*BrE, saying*) you will finish doing sth sooner if you do not try to do it too quickly because you will make fewer mistakes

has·ten /ˈheɪsn/ *verb* **1** [Vtoinf] to say or do sth without delay: *She saw his frown and hastened to explain.* ◇ *He has been described as a 'charmless bore'—not by me, I hasten to add.* **2** [VN] (*written*) to make sth happen sooner or more quickly: *The treatment she received may, in fact, have hastened her death.* ◇ *News of the scandal certainly hastened his departure from office.* **3** [V+adv./prep.] (*literary*) to go or move somewhere quickly SYN HURRY: *We hastened back to Rome.*

hasty /ˈheɪsti/ *adj.* (**hasti·er, hasti·est**) **1** said, made or done very quickly, especially when this has bad results: *a hasty departure/meal/farewell* ◇ *The army beat a hasty retreat.* ◇ *Let's not make any hasty decisions.* **2 ~ in doing sth** (of a person) acting or deciding too quickly, without enough thought: *Perhaps I was too hasty in rejecting his offer.* IDM see BEAT *v.* ▶ **hasti·ly** /-ɪli/ *adv.*: *Perhaps I spoke too hastily.* ◇ *She hastily changed the subject.*

hat /hæt/ *noun* **1** a covering made to fit the head, often with a BRIM, (= a flat edge that sticks out) and worn out of doors: *a straw/woolly hat* ◇ *to put on/take off a hat* **2** (*informal*) a position or role, especially an official or professional role, when you have more than one such role: *I'm wearing two hats tonight—parent and teacher.* ◇ *I'm telling you this with my lawyer's hat on, you understand.*—see also OLD HAT IDM **go hat in ˈhand (to sb)** (*AmE*) = GO CAP IN HAND **keep sth under your ˈhat** (*informal*) to keep sth secret and not tell anyone else ˌmy ˈhat (*old-fashioned, BrE*) used to express surprise **out of a/the ˈhat** if sth such as a name is picked out of a/the hat, it is picked at RANDOM from a container into which all the names are put, so that each name has an equal chance of being picked, in a competition, etc. **I take my ˈhat off to sb | hats off to sb** (both *especially BrE*) (*AmE* usually **I tip my ˈhat to sb**) (*informal*) used to say that you admire sb very much for sth they have done **throw your ˈhat into the ring** to announce officially that you are going to compete in an election, a competition, etc.—more at DROP *n.*, EAT, KNOCK *v.*, PASS *v.*, PULL *v.*, TALK *v.*

hat·band /ˈhætbænd/ *noun* a band of fabric placed around a hat as decoration

hatch /hætʃ/ *verb, noun*

■ *verb* **1** [V] **~ (out)** (of a young bird, fish, insect, etc.) to come out of an egg: *Ten chicks hatched (out) this morning.* **2** [V] **~ (out)** (of an egg) to break open so that a young

band

cap   badge

top hat

panama   boater

visor

cowboy hat

bobble (BrE)/ pompom

crash helmet

brim

baseball cap

bowler (BrE)/ derby (AmE)

hard hat

bobble hat

crown

peak (BrE)/ bill (AmE)

sunhats

earmuffs

hood

beret

beanie

cloth cap / flat cap (both BrE)

trilby

bird, fish, insect, etc. can come out: *The eggs are about to hatch.* **3** [VN] to make a young bird, fish, insect, etc. come out of an egg: *The female must find a warm place to hatch her eggs.* **4** [VN] ~ **sth** (**up**) to create a plan or idea, especially in secret: *Have you been hatching up a deal with her?* IDM see COUNT *v*.

■ *noun* **1** (also **hatch·way**) an opening or a door in the DECK of a ship or the bottom of an aircraft, through which goods are to be carried are lowered **2** an opening in a wall between two rooms, especially a kitchen and a DINING ROOM, through which food can be passed: *a serving hatch* **3** a door in an aircraft or a spacecraft: *an escape hatch* **4** an opening or a door in a floor or ceiling: *a hatch to the attic* IDM ,**down the 'hatch** (*informal, saying*) used before drinking sth, especially to express good wishes before drinking alcohol—more at BATTEN

hatch·back /'hætʃbæk/ *noun* a car with a sloping door at the back that opens upwards—picture at CAR

hatch·ery /'hætʃəri/ *noun* (*pl.* **-ies**) a place for HATCHING eggs: *a trout hatchery*

hatchet /'hætʃɪt/ *noun* a small AXE (= a tool with a heavy blade for chopping things) with a short handle—picture at AXE IDM see BURY

'**hatchet-faced** *adj.* (*disapproving*) (of a person) having a long thin face and sharp features

'**hatchet job** *noun* [usually sing.] ~ (**on sb/sth**) (*informal*) strong criticism that is often unfair and is intended to harm sb/sth: *The press did a very effective hatchet job on her last movie.*

'**hatchet man** *noun* (*informal*) a person employed by an organization to make changes that are not popular with the other people who work there

hatch·way /'hætʃweɪ/ *noun* = HATCH

hate /heɪt/ *verb, noun*

■ *verb* (not used in the progressive tenses) **1** to dislike sth very much: [VN] *I hate spinach.* ◇ *I hate Monday mornings.* ◇ *I hate it when people cry.* ◇ *He hated it in France* (= did not like the life there). ◇ *I* **hate the way** *she always criticizes me.* ◇ [V-ing] *She hates making mistakes.* ◇ [V to inf] *He hated to be away from his family.* ◇ *She's a person who hates to make mistakes.* ◇ *I hate to think what would have happened if you hadn't been there.* ◇ [VN-ing] *He hates anyone parking in his space.* ◇ [VN to inf] *She would have hated him to see how her hands shook.* ◇ *I'd hate anything to happen to him.* **2** [VN] ~ **sb** (**for sth**) to dislike sb very much: *The two boys hated each other.* ◇ *I hated myself for feeling jealous.* ◇ *He was her most hated*

enemy. **3** [no passive] [V to inf] used when saying sth that you would prefer not to have to say, or when politely asking to do sth: *I hate to say it, but I don't think their marriage will last.* ◇ *I hate to trouble you, but could I use your phone?* ▶ **hater** *noun*: *I'm not a woman hater, I just don't like Joan.* IDM **hate sb's 'guts** (*informal*) to dislike sb very much

■ *noun* **1** [U] a very strong feeling of dislike for sb SYN HATRED: *She spoke of her hate for the killers.* ◇ *a look of hate* ◇ *a hate campaign* (= cruel comments made about sb over a period of time in order to damage their reputation) ◇ *hate mail* (= letters containing cruel comments) **2** [C] (*informal*) a person or thing that you hate: *Plastic flowers have always been a particular hate of mine.* IDM see PET *adj.*

WHICH WORD?

hate / hatred

These two words have a similar meaning. **Hatred** is more often used to describe a very strong feeling of dislike for a particular person or thing: *Her deep hatred of her sister was obvious.* ◇ *a cat's hatred of water.* **Hate** is more often used when you are talking about this feeling in a general way: *a look of pure hate* ◇ *people filled with hate.*

hate·ful /'heɪtfl/ *adj.* ~ (**to sb**) very unkind or unpleasant: *a hateful person/place/face* ◇ *The idea of fighting against men of their own race was hateful to them.*

hath /hæθ/ (*old use*) has

hat·red /'heɪtrɪd/ *noun* [U, C] ~ (**for/ of sb/sth**)| ~ (**towards sb**) a very strong feeling of dislike for sb/sth: *He looked at me with intense hatred.* ◇ *There was fear and hatred in his voice.* ◇ *She felt nothing but hatred for her attacker.* ◇ *a profound hatred of war* ◇ *racial hatred* (= between people from different races) ◇ *The debate simply revived old hatreds.*

hat·ter /'hætə(r)/ *noun* (*old-fashioned*) a person who makes and sells hats IDM see MAD

'**hat-trick** *noun* three points, goals, etc. scored by the same player in a particular match or game; three successes achieved by one person: *to score a hat-trick* ◇ *a hat-trick of wins*

haughty /'hɔːti/ *adj.* behaving in an unfriendly way towards other people because you think that you are better than them: *a haughty face/look/manner* ◇ *He*

replied with haughty disdain. ▶ **haught·ily** /-ɪli/ adv.
haughti·ness noun [U]

haul /hɔːl/ verb, noun
■ verb **1** [VN] to pull sth/sb with a lot of effort: *The wagons were hauled by horses.* ◊ *He reached down and hauled Liz up onto the wall.* **2** [VN+adv./prep.] ~ **yourself up/out of** etc. to move yourself somewhere slowly and with a lot of effort: *She hauled herself out of bed.* **3** [VN+adv./prep.] to force sb to go somewhere they do not want to go: *A number of suspects have been hauled in for questioning.* **4** [VN] [usually passive] ~ **sb** (**up**) **before sb/sth** to make sb appear in a court of law in order to be judged: *He was hauled up before the local magistrates for dangerous driving.* **IDM** **haul sb over the 'coals** (*BrE*) **rake sb over the 'coals** (*AmE*) to criticize sb severely because they have done sth wrong
■ noun **1** a large amount of sth that has been stolen or that is illegal: *a haul of jewellery/weapons* ◊ *a drugs haul* **2** (especially in sport) a large number of points, goals, etc: *His haul of 40 goals in a season is a record.* **3** [usually sing.] the distance covered in a particular journey: *They began the long slow haul to the summit.* ◊ *Our camp is only a short haul from here.* ◊ *Take the coast road—it'll be less of a haul* (= an easier journey). ◊ (*figurative*) *It's going to be a long haul till you're fit again.* (= it will take a long time).—see also LONG-HAUL, SHORT-HAUL **4** a quantity of fish caught at one time

haul·age /'hɔːlɪdʒ/ noun [U] (*BrE*) the business of transporting goods by road or railway; money charged for this: *the road haulage industry* ◊ *a haulage firm/contractor* ◊ *How much is haulage?*

haul·ier /'hɔːliə(r)/ (*BrE*) (*AmE* **haul·er** /'hɔːlə(r)/) noun a person or company whose business is transporting goods by road or railway/railroad

haunch /hɔːntʃ/ noun **1** (**haunches**) [pl.] the tops of the legs and BUTTOCKS; the similar parts at the back of the body of an animal that has four legs: *to crouch/squat on your haunches* **2** [C] a back leg and LOIN of an animal that has four legs, eaten as food: *a haunch of venison*

haunt /hɔːnt/ verb, noun
■ verb [VN] **1** if the ghost of a dead person **haunts** a place, people say that they have seen it there: *A headless rider haunts the country lanes.* **2** if sth unpleasant **haunts** you, it keeps coming to your mind so that you cannot forget it: *The memory of that day still haunts me.* ◊ *For years she was haunted by guilt.* **3** to continue to cause problems for sb for a long time: *That decision came back to haunt him in later life.*
■ noun a place that sb visits often or where they spend a lot of time: *Is this one of your usual haunts?* ◊ *The pub is a favourite haunt of artists.*

haunt·ed /'hɔːntɪd/ adj. **1** (of a building) believed to be visited by ghosts: *a haunted house* **2** (of an expression on sb's face) showing that sb is very worried: *There was a haunted look in his eyes.*

haunt·ing /'hɔːntɪŋ/ adj. beautiful, sad or frightening in a way that cannot be forgotten: *a haunting melody/experience/image* ▶ **haunt·ing·ly** adv.: *a hauntingly beautiful landscape*

haute cou·ture /ˌəʊt kuˈtjʊə(r); *AmE* ˌoʊt kuˈtʊr/ noun [U] (from *French*) the business of making fashionable and expensive clothes for women; the clothes made in this business

haute cuis·ine /ˌəʊt kwɪˈziːn; *AmE* ˌoʊt/ noun [U] (from *French*) cooking of a very high standard

haut·eur /əʊˈtɜː(r); *AmE* hɔːˈtɜːr; oʊˈt-/ noun [U] (*formal*) an unfriendly way of behaving towards other people suggesting that you think that you are better than they are

have /həv; əv; hæv/ verb, auxiliary verb ⇨ Appendix 1
■ verb (**has, hav·ing, had, had**) (In some senses **have got** is also used, especially in British English.)
OWN/HOLD | **1** (also **have got**) [VN] (not used in the progressive tenses) to own, hold or POSSESS sth: *He had a new car and a boat.* ◊ *Have you got a job yet?* ◊ *I don't have that much money on me.* ◊ *She's got a BA in English.*
CONSIST OF | **2** (also **have got**) [VN] (not used in the pro-

gressive tenses) be made up of: *In 1999 the party had 10000 members.*
QUALITY/FEATURE | **3** (also **have got**) (not used in the progressive tenses) to show a quality or feature: [VN] *The ham had a smoky flavour.* ◊ *The house has gas-fired central heating.* ◊ *They have a lot of courage.* ◊ [VN-ADJ] *He's got a front tooth missing.* **4** (also **have got**) [VN to inf] (not used in the progressive tenses) to show a particular quality by your actions: *Surely she didn't have the nerve to say that to him?*
RELATIONSHIP | **5** (also **have got**) [VN] (not used in the progressive tenses) used to show a particular relationship: *He's got three children.* ◊ *Do you have a client named Peters?*
STH AVAILABLE | **6** (also **have got**) [VN] (not used in the progressive tenses) to be able to make use of sth because it is available: *Have you got time to call him?* ◊ *We have no choice in the matter.*
SHOULD/MUST | **7** (also **have got**) [VN] (not used in the progressive tenses) to be in a position where you ought to do sth: *We have a duty to care for the refugees.* **8** (also **have got**) (not used in the progressive tenses) to be in a position of needing to do sth: [VN] *I've got a lot of homework tonight.* ◊ [VN to inf] *I must go—I have a bus to catch.*
HOLD | **9** (also **have got**) [VN+adv./prep.] (not used in the progressive tenses) to hold sb/sth in the way mentioned: *She'd got him by the collar.* ◊ *He had his head in his hands.*
PUT/KEEP IN A POSITION | **10** (also **have got**) [VN+adv./prep.] (not used in the progressive tenses) to place or keep sth in a particular position: *Mary had her back to me.* ◊ *I soon had the fish in a net.*
FEELING/THOUGHT | **11** (also **have got**) [VN] (not used in the progressive tenses) to let a feeling or thought come into your mind: *He had the strong impression that someone was watching him.* ◊ *We've got a few ideas for the title.* ◊ (*spoken*) *I've got it! We'll call it 'Word Magic'.*
ILLNESS | **12** (also **have got**) [VN] (not used in the progressive tenses) to suffer from an illness or a disease: *I've got a headache.*
EXPERIENCE | **13** [VN] to experience sth: *I went to a few parties and had a good time.* ◊ *I was having difficulty in staying awake.* ◊ *She'll have an accident one day.*
EVENT | **14** [VN] to organize or hold an event: *Let's have a party.*
EAT/DRINK/SMOKE | **15** [VN] to eat, drink or smoke sth: *to have breakfast/lunch/dinner* ◊ *I'll have the salmon* (for example, in a restaurant). ◊ *I had a cigarette while I was waiting.*
DO STH | **16** [VN] to perform a particular action: *I had a swim to cool down.* ◊ (*BrE*) *to have a wash/shower/bath*
GIVE BIRTH | **17** [VN] to give birth to sb/sth: *She's going to have a baby.*
EFFECT | **18** [VN] to produce a particular effect: *His paintings had a strong influence on me as a student.* ◊ *The colour green has a restful effect.*
RECEIVE | **19** [VN] (not usually used in the progressive tenses) to receive sth from sb: *I had a letter from my brother this morning.* ◊ *Can I have the bill, please?* **20** [VN] to be given sth; to have sth done to you: *I'm having treatment for my back problem.* ◊ *How many driving lessons have you had so far?* **21** (also **have got**) [VN-ing] (not used in the progressive tenses) to experience the effects of sb's actions: *We have orders coming in from all over the world.*
HAVE STH DONE | **22** [VN] (used with a past participle) ~ **sth done** to suffer the effects of what sb else does to you: *She had her bag stolen.* **23** [VN] (used with a past participle) ~ **sth done** to cause sth to be done for you by sb else: *You've had your hair cut!* ◊ *We're having our car repaired.* **24** to tell or arrange for sb to do sth for you: [VN inf] *He had the bouncers throw them out of the club.* ◊ (*informal*) *I'll have you know* (= I'm telling you) *I'm a black belt in judo.* ◊ [VN+adv./prep.] *She's always having the builders in to do something or other.*
ALLOW | **25** (used in negative sentences, especially after

will not, cannot, etc.) to allow sth; to accept sth without complaining: [VN] *I'm sick of your rudeness—I won't have it any longer!* ◇ [VN-ing] *We can't have people arriving late all the time.*

<u>PUT SB/STH IN A CONDITION</u> **26** to cause sb/sth to be in a particular state; to make sb react in a particular way: [VN-ADJ] *I want to have everything ready in good time.* ◇ [VN-ing] *He had his audience listening attentively.*

<u>IN ARGUMENT</u> **27** (also **have got**) [VN] (*informal*) (not used in the progressive tenses) to put sb at a disadvantage in an argument: *You've got me there. I hadn't thought of that.*

<u>SEX</u> **28** [VN] (*slang*) to have sex with sb: *He had her in his office.*

<u>TRICK</u> **29** [VN] [usually passive] (*informal*) to trick or deceive sb: *I'm afraid you've been had.*

<u>GUESTS</u> **30** [VN] [no passive] to take care of sb/sth in your home, especially for a limited period: *We're having the kids for the weekend.* **31** [VN+*adv./prep.*] [no passive] to entertain sb in your home: *We had some friends to dinner last night.*

<u>BE WITH</u> **32** (also **have got**) [VN] **~ sb with you** (not used in the progressive tenses) to be with sb: *She had some friends with her.*

<u>FOR A JOB</u> **33** [VN] [no passive] **~ sb as sth** to take or accept sb for a particular role: *Who can we have as treasurer?*

IDM Most idioms containing **have** are at the entries for the nouns and adjectives in the idioms, for example **have your eye on sb** is at **eye** *n.* **have 'done with sth** (*especially BrE*) to finish sth unpleasant so that it does not continue: *Let's have done with this silly argument.* **have 'had it** (*informal*) **1** to be in a very bad condition; to be unable to be repaired: *The car had had it.* **2** to be extremely tired: *I've had it! I'm going to bed.* **3** to have lost all chance of surviving sth: *When the truck smashed into me, I thought I'd had it.* **4** to be going to experience sth unpleasant: *Dad saw you scratch the car—you've had it now!* **5** to be unable to accept a situation any longer: *I've had it (up to here) with him—he's done it once too often.* **have it 'off/a'way (with sb)** (*BrE, slang*) to have sex with sb **have it 'that (that…)** to claim that it is a fact that …: *Rumour has it that we'll have a new manager soon.* **have (got) it/that 'coming (to you)** to be likely to suffer the unpleasant effects of your actions and to deserve to do so: *It was no surprise when she left him— everyone knew he had it coming to him.* **have it 'in for sb** (*informal*) to not like sb and be unpleasant to them **have it 'in you (to do sth)** (*informal*) to be capable of doing sth: *Everyone thinks he has it in him to produce a literary classic.* ◇ *You were great. I didn't know you had it in you.* **have (got) 'nothing on sb/sth** (*informal*) to be not nearly as good as sb/sth—see also HAVE STH ON SB **not 'having any** (*informal*) not willing to listen to or believe sth: *I tried to persuade her to wait but she wasn't having any.* **what 'have you** other things, people, etc. of the same kind: *There's room in the cellar to store old furniture and what have you.*

PHRV **,have (got) sth a'gainst sb/sth** (not used in the progressive tenses) to dislike sb/sth for a particular reason: *What have you got against Ruth? She's always been good to you.* **,have sb↔'back** to allow a husband, wife or partner that you are separated from to return **,have sth 'back** to receive sth that sb has borrowed or taken from you: *You can have your files back after we've checked them.* **,have (got) sth 'in** (not used in the progressive tenses) to have a supply of sth in your home, etc: *Have we got enough food in?* **,have sb 'on** (*informal*) to try to make sb believe sth that is not true, usually as a joke: *You didn't really, did you? You're not having me on, are you?* **,have (got) sth 'on** (not used in the progressive tenses) **1** to be wearing sth: *She had a red jacket on.* ◇ *He had nothing (= no clothes) on.* ⇨ note at WEAR **2** to leave a piece of equipment working: *She has her TV on all day.* **3** to have arranged to do sth: *I can't see you this week—I've got a lot on.* **,have (got) sth 'on sb** [no passive] (*informal*) (not used in the progressive tenses) to know sth bad about sb,

especially sth that connects them with a crime: *I'm not worried—they've got nothing on me.* **,have sth 'out** to cause sth, especially a part of your body, to be removed: *I had to have my appendix out.* **,have sth 'out (with sb)** to try to settle a dispute by discussing or arguing about it openly: *I need to have it out with her once and for all.* **,have sb 'up (for sth)** (*BrE, informal*) [usually passive] to cause sb to be accused of sth in a court of law: *He was had up for manslaughter.*

■ *auxiliary verb* used with the past participle to form perfect tenses: *I've finished my work.* ◇ *He's gone home, hasn't he?* ◇ '*Have you seen it?* ' '*Yes, I have/No, I haven't.*' ◇ *She'll have had the results by now.* ◇ *Had they left before you got there?* ◇ *If I hadn't seen it with my own eyes I wouldn't have believed it.* ◇ (*formal*) *Had I known that* (= if I had known that) *I would never have come.*

BRITISH / AMERICAN
have you got / do you have

Have got is the usual verb in *BrE* to show possession, etc. in positive statements in the present tense, in negative statements and in questions: *They've got a wonderful house.* ◇ *We haven't got a television.* ◇ *Have you got a meeting today?* Questions and negative statements formed with **do** are also common: *Do you have any brothers and sisters?* ◇ *We don't have a car.*

Have is also used but is more formal: *I have no objection to your request.* ◇ *Have you an appointment?* Some expressions with **have** are common even in informal language: *I'm sorry, I haven't a clue.*

In the past tense **had** is used in positive statements. In negatives and questions, forms with **did have** are usually used: *They had a wonderful house.* ◇ *We didn't have much time.* ◇ *Did she have her husband with her?*

In *AmE* **have** and forms with **do/does/did** are the usual way to show possession, etc. in positive statements, negatives and questions: *They have a wonderful house.* ◇ *We don't have a television.* ◇ *Do you have a meeting today?* **Have got** is not used in questions, but is used in positive statements, especially to emphasize that somebody has one thing rather than another: '*Does your brother have brown hair?' 'No, he's got blond hair.'*

In both *BrE* and *AmE* **have** and forms with **do/does** and **did** are used when you are referring to a habit or routine: *In my country people usually have large families.* ◇ *We don't often have time to talk.* ◇ *Do you ever have headaches?*

---

haven /ˈheɪvn/ *noun* a place that is safe and peaceful where people go to rest or to be protected from sth: *The hotel is a haven of peace and tranquility.* ◇ *The river banks are a haven for wildlife.*—see also SAFE HAVEN, TAX HAVEN

the ,have-'nots *noun* [pl.] people who do not have money and possessions—compare THE HAVES

haven't /ˈhævnt/ *short form* have not

hav·er·sack /ˈhævəsæk; *AmE* -vərs-/ *noun* (*old-fashioned, BrE*) a bag that is carried on the back or over the shoulder, especially when walking in the country

the 'haves *noun* [pl.] people who have enough money and possessions: *the division between the haves and the have-nots*—compare THE HAVE-NOTS

have to /ˈhæv tə; ˈhæf/ *modal verb* (**has to** /ˈhæz tə; ˈhæs/ **had to, had to** /ˈhæd tə; ˈhæt/) **1** (also **have got to** especially in *BrE*) used to show that you must do sth: *Sorry, I've got to go.* ◇ *Did she have to pay a fine?* ◇ *You don't have to knock—just walk in.* ◇ *I haven't got to leave till seven.* ◇ *First, you have to think logically about your fears.* ◇ (*spoken*) *I have to admit, the idea of marriage scares me.* ◇ *Do you have to go?* ◇ (*especially BrE*) *Have you got to go?* **2** (also **have got to** especially in *BrE*) used to give advice or recommend sth: *You simply have to get a new job.* ◇ *You've got to try this recipe—it's delicious.* **3** (also **have got to** especially in *BrE*) used to say that sth must be true or must happen:

æ	ɑː	e	ɜː	ə	ɪ	iː	i	ɒ	ɔː	ʌ	ʊ	u	uː
cat	father	ten	bird	about	sit	see	many	got	saw	cup	put	actual	too
								(BrE)					

H

There has to be a reason for his strange behaviour. ◊ *This war has got to end soon.* **4** (*spoken*) used to suggest that an annoying event happens in order to annoy you, or that sb does sth in order to annoy you: *Of course, it had to start raining as soon as we got to the beach.* ◊ **Do you have to hum so loudly?** (= it is annoying) ⇨ note at MODAL, MUST

havoc /ˈhævək/ *noun* [U] a situation in which there is a lot of damage, destruction or disorder: *The floods caused havoc throughout the area.* ◊ *Continuing strikes are beginning to* **play havoc with** *the national economy.* ◊ *These insects can* **wreak havoc on** *crops.*

haw /hɔː/ *verb* **IDM** see HUM *v.*

hawk /hɔːk/ *noun, verb*
■ *noun* **1** a strong fast BIRD OF PREY (= a bird that kills other creatures for food): *He waited,* **watching her like a hawk** (= watching her very closely).—see also SPARROWHAWK **2** a person, especially a politician, who supports the use of military force to solve problems—compare DOVE
■ *verb* **1** [VN] to try to sell things by going from place to place asking people to buy them **SYN** PEDDLE: *He made a living hawking cleaning products from door to door.* **2** [V, VN] to get PHLEGM in your mouth when you cough

hawk·er /ˈhɔːkə(r)/ *noun* a person who makes money by hawking goods

hawk-ʼeyed *adj.* (of a person) watching closely and carefully and noticing small details

hawk·ish /ˈhɔːkɪʃ/ *adj.* (*politics*) preferring to use military action rather than peaceful discussion in order to solve a problem

haw·ser /ˈhɔːzə(r)/ *noun* (*technical*) a thick rope or steel cable used on a ship

haw·thorn /ˈhɔːθɔːn; *AmE* -θɔːrn/ *noun* [U, C] a prickly bush or small tree with white or pink flowers and small dark red berries called **haws**: *a hawthorn hedge*

hay /heɪ/ *noun* [U] **1** grass that has been cut and dried and is used as food for animals: *a bale of hay*—compare STRAW **2** (*AmE, informal*) a small amount of money: *I get $50 for each of these and that's not hay!* **IDM make hay while the ʼsun shines** (*saying*) to make good use of opportunities, good conditions, etc. while they last—more at HIT *v.*, ROLL *n.*

ʼhay fever *noun* an illness that affects the nose, eyes and throat and is caused by POLLEN from plants that is breathed in from the air

hay·mak·ing /ˈheɪmeɪkɪŋ/ *noun* [U] the process of cutting and drying grass to make HAY

hay·ride /ˈheɪraɪd/ *noun* (*AmE*) a ride for pleasure on a CART filled with HAY, pulled by a horse or TRACTOR

hay·stack /ˈheɪstæk/ (also *less frequent* **hay·rick** /ˈheɪrɪk/) *noun* a large pile of HAY, used as a way of storing it until it is needed **IDM** see NEEDLE *n.*

hay·wire /ˈheɪwaɪə(r)/ *adj.* **IDM go ʼhaywire** (*informal*) to stop working correctly or become out of control: *After that, things started to go haywire.*

haz·ard /ˈhæzəd; *AmE* -ərd/ *noun, verb*
■ *noun* **~ (to sb/sth)** | **~ (of sth/of doing sth)** a thing that can be dangerous or cause damage: *a fire/safety hazard* ◊ *Growing levels of pollution represent a serious health hazard to the local population.* ◊ *Everybody is aware of the hazards of smoking.* ◊ **hazard lights** (= flashing lights on a car that warn other drivers of possible danger)
■ *verb* **1** to make a suggestion or guess which you know may be wrong: [VN] *Would you like to* **hazard a guess?** ◊ [V speech] *'Is it Tom you're going with?' she hazarded.* [also V that] **2** [VN] (*formal*) to risk sth or put it in danger **SYN** ENDANGER: *Careless drivers hazard other people's lives as well as their own.*

haz·ard·ous /ˈhæzədəs; *AmE* -ərdəs/ *adj.* involving risk or danger, especially to sb's health or safety: *hazardous waste/chemicals* ◊ *a hazardous journey* ◊ *It would be hazardous to invest so much.* ◊ *a list of products that are potentially hazardous to health*

haze /heɪz/ *noun, verb*
■ *noun* **1** [C, U] air that is difficult to see through because it contains very small drops of water, especially caused by hot weather: *a heat haze* **2** [sing.] air containing sth that

makes it difficult to see through it: *a haze of smoke/dust/steam* **3** [sing.] a mental state in which your thoughts, feelings, etc. are not clear: *an alcoholic haze* ◊ *a haze of pain*
■ *verb* **1** [VN, V] to become covered or to cover sth in a HAZE **2** [VN] (*AmE*) to play tricks on sb, especially a new student, or to give them very unpleasant things to do, sometimes as a condition for entering a FRATERNITY or SORORITY: *Several students were hospitalized for injuries caused by hazing.*

hazel /ˈheɪzl/ *noun, adj.*
■ *noun* [C, U] a small tree that produces small nuts (called **hazelnuts**) that can be eaten
■ *adj.* (of eyes) greenish-brown or reddish-brown in colour

hazel·nut /ˈheɪzlnʌt/ (also **fil·bert** especially in *AmE*) *noun* the small brown nut of the HAZEL tree—picture at NUT

hazy /ˈheɪzi/ *adj.* (**hazi·er, hazi·est**) **1** not clear because of HAZE: *a hazy afternoon/sky* ◊ *hazy light/sunshine* ◊ *The mountains were hazy in the distance.* **2** not clear because of a lack of memory, understanding or detail: *a hazy memory/idea* ◊ *What happened next is all very hazy.* **3** (of a person) uncertain or confused about sth: *I'm a little hazy about what to do next.* ▶ **haz·ily** *adv.*: *'Why now?' she wondered hazily.*

ʼH-bomb *noun* = HYDROGEN BOMB

HE (*BrE*) (also **H.E.** *AmE, BrE*) *abbr.* **1** Her/His EXCELLENCY: *HE the Australian Ambassador* **2** HIGHER EDUCATION

he /hi; i:; i; *strong form* hi:/ *pron., noun*
■ *pron.* (used as the subject of a verb) **1** a male person or animal that has already been mentioned or is easily identified: *Everyone liked my father—he was the perfect gentleman.* ◊ *He* (= the man we are watching) *went through that door.* **2** (*becoming old-fashioned*) a person, male or female, whose sex is not stated or known, especially when referring to sb mentioned earlier or to a group in general: *Every child needs to know that he is loved.* ◊ (*saying*) *He who* (= anyone who) *hesitates is lost.*—compare HIM
■ *noun* /hi:/ **1** [sing.] (*informal*) a male: *What a nice dog—is it a he or a she?* **2** (**he-**) (in compound nouns) a male animal: *a he-goat*

head /hed/ *noun, verb*
■ *noun*
PART OF BODY | **1** [C] the part of the body on top of the neck containing the eyes, nose, mouth and brain: *She nodded her head in agreement.* ◊ *He shook his head in disbelief.* ◊ *The boys hung their heads in shame.* ◊ *The driver suffered head injuries.* ◊ *She always has her head in a book* (= is always reading). ◊ *He still has a good head of hair* (= a lot of hair).—see also DEATH'S HEAD—picture at BODY and on page A7
MIND | **2** [C] the mind or brain: *I sometimes wonder what goes on in that head of yours.* ◊ *I wish you'd use your head* (= think carefully before doing or saying sth). ◊ *The thought never entered my head.* ◊ *I can't work it out in my head—I need a calculator.* ◊ *I can't get that tune out of my head.* ◊ *When will you get it into your head* (= understand) *that I don't want to discuss this any more!* ◊ *For some reason, she's got it into her head* (= believes) *that the others don't like her.* ◊ *Who's been putting such weird ideas into your head* (= making you believe that)? ◊ *Try to put the exams out of your head* (= stop thinking about them) *for tonight.*—see also HOTHEAD
MEASUREMENT | **3** (**a head**) [sing.] the size of a person's or animal's head, used as a measurement of distance or height: *She's a good head taller than her sister.* ◊ *The favourite won by a short head* (= a distance slightly less than the length of a horse's head).
PAIN | **4** [C, usually sing.] (*informal*) a continuous pain in your head **SYN** HEADACHE: *I woke up with a really bad head this morning.*
SIDE OF COIN | **5** (**heads**) [U] the side of a coin that has a picture of the head of a person on it, used as one choice when a coin is TOSSED to decide sth—compare TAILS *n.* (7)
END OF OBJECT | **6** [C, usually sing.] **~ (of sth)** the end of a

aɪ	aʊ	eɪ	əʊ	oʊ	ɔɪ	ɪə	eə	ʊə	j	w
my	now	say	go	go	boy	near	hair	pure	yes	wet
			(BrE)	(AmE)						

long narrow object that is larger or wider than the rest of it: *the head of a nail*—see also BEDHEAD

TOP | **7** [sing.] **~ of sth** the top or highest part of sth: *at the head of the page/stairs* ◇ *They finished the season at the head of their league.*

OF RIVER | **8** [sing.] **the ~ of the river** the place where a river begins SYN SOURCE

OF TABLE | **9** [sing.] **the ~ of the table** the most important seat at a table: *The President sat at the head of the table.*

OF LINE OF PEOPLE | **10** [sing.] **the ~ of sth** the position at the front of a line of people: *The prince rode at the head of his regiment.*

OF PLANT | **11** [C] **~ (of sth)** the mass of leaves or flowers at the end of a stem: *Remove the dead heads to encourage new growth.*

OF GROUP/ORGANIZATION | **12** [C, U] the person in charge of a group of people or an organization: *the heads of government/state* ◇ *She resigned as head of department.* ◇ *the crowned heads* (= the kings and queens) *of Europe* ◇ *the head gardener/waiter* ◇ (*BrE*) *the head boy/girl* (= a student who is chosen to represent the school)

OF SCHOOL/COLLEGE | **13** [C] (often **Head**) (*BrE*) the person in charge of a school or college SYN HEADMASTER, HEADMISTRESS, HEAD TEACHER: *I've been called in to see the Head.* ◇ *the deputy head*

ON BEER | **14** [sing.] the mass of small bubbles on the top of a glass of beer

OF SPOT | **15** [C] the part of a spot on your skin that contains a thick yellowish liquid (= PUS)—see also BLACKHEAD

IN TAPE/VIDEO RECORDER | **16** [C] the part of a TAPE RECORDER or VIDEO RECORDER that touches the tape and changes the electrical signals into sounds and/or pictures

NUMBER OF ANIMALS | **17 ~ of sth** [pl.] used to say how many animals of a particular type are on a farm, in a HERD, etc: *200 head of sheep*

OF STEAM | **18 a ~ of steam** [sing.] the pressure produced by steam in an enclosed space

SEX | **19** [U] (⚠, *slang*) ORAL sex (= using the mouth to stimulate sb's sex organs): *to give head*

IDM **a/per 'head** for each person: *The meal worked out at $20 a head.* **bang/knock your/their 'heads together** (*informal*) to force people to stop arguing and behave in a sensible way **be banging, etc. your head against a brick 'wall** (*informal*) to keep trying to do sth that will never be successful: *Trying to reason with them was like banging my head against a brick wall.* **be/stand head and 'shoulders above sb/sth** to be much better than other people or things **bite/snap sb's 'head off** (*informal*) to shout at sb in an angry way, especially without reason **bring sth to a 'head | come to a 'head** if you **bring** a situation **to a head** or if a situation **comes to a head**, you are forced to deal with it quickly because it suddenly becomes very bad **bury/hide your head in the 'sand** to refuse to admit that a problem exists or refuse to deal with it **can't get your 'head round sth** (*BrE*, *informal*) to be unable to understand sth: *She's dead. I can't get my head round it yet.* **can't make head nor 'tail of sth** to be unable to understand sth: *I couldn't make head nor tail of what he was saying.* **do sb's 'head in** (*BrE*, *informal*) to make you feel confused, upset and/or annoyed: *Shut up! You're doing my head in.* **do sth standing on your 'head** (*informal*) to be able to do sth very easily and without having to think too much **from ,head to 'foot/'toe** covering your whole body: *We were covered from head to foot in mud.* **get your 'head down** (*informal*) **1** (*BrE*) to sleep: *I managed to get my head down for an hour.* **2** = KEEP/get your head down **give sb their 'head** to allow sb to do what they want without trying to stop them **go head to 'head (with sb)** to deal with sb in a very direct and determined way **go to your 'head 1** (of alcohol) to make you feel drunk: *That glass of wine has gone straight to my head.* **2** (of success, praise, etc.) to make you feel too proud of yourself in a way that other people find annoying **have a good 'head on your shoulders** to be a sensible person **have your head in**

the **'clouds 1** to be thinking about sth that is not connected with what you are doing **2** to have ideas, plans, etc. that are not realistic **have a head for sth 1** to be good at sth: *to have a head for figures/business* **2** if sb does not **have a head for heights**, they feel nervous and think they are going to fall when they look down from a high place **have your 'head screwed on (the right way)** (*informal*) to be a sensible person **,head 'first 1** moving forwards or downwards with your head in front of the rest of your body: *He fell head first down the stairs.* **2** without thinking carefully about sth before acting: *She got divorced and rushed head first into another marriage.* **head over heels in 'love** loving sb very much: *He's fallen head over heels in love with his boss.* **heads or 'tails?** (*spoken*) used to ask sb which side of a coin they think will be facing upwards when it is TOSSED in order to decide sth by chance **'heads will roll (for sth)** (*spoken*, usually *humorous*) used to say that some people will be punished because of sth that has happened **hold your 'head high | hold up your 'head** to be proud of or not feel ashamed about sth that you have done: *She managed to hold her head high and ignore what people were saying.* **in over your 'head** involved in sth that is too difficult for you to deal with: *After a week in the new job, I soon realized that I was in over my head.* **keep/get your 'head down** to avoid attracting attention to yourself **keep your 'head | keep a clear/cool 'head** to remain calm in a difficult situation **keep your 'head above water** to deal with a difficult situation, especially one in which you have financial problems, and just manage to survive **laugh, scream, etc. your 'head off** (*informal*) to laugh, etc. a lot and very loudly **lose your 'head** to become unable to act in a calm or sensible way **on your (own) head 'be it** used to tell sb that they will have to accept any unpleasant results of sth that they decide to do: *Tell him the truth if you want to, but on your own head be it!* **out of/off your 'head** (*BrE*, *informal*) **1** crazy **2** not knowing what you are saying or doing because of the effects of alcohol or drugs **over sb's 'head 1** too difficult or complicated for sb to understand: *A lot of the jokes went (= were) right over my head.* **2** to a higher position of authority than sb: *I couldn't help feeling jealous when she was promoted over my head.* **put our/your/their 'heads together** to think about or discuss sth as a group **stand/turn sth on its 'head** to make people think about sth in a completely different way **take it into your head to do sth** to suddenly decide to do sth, especially sth that other people think is stupid **take it into your head that …** to suddenly start thinking sth, especially sth that other people think is stupid **turn sb's 'head** (of success, praise, etc.) to make a person feel too proud in a way that other people find annoying **two heads are better than 'one** (*saying*) used to say that two people can achieve more than one person working alone—more at BEAR *n.*, BLOCK *n.*, BOTHER *v.*, DRUM *v.*, EYE *n.*, GUN *n.*, HAIR, HEART, HIT *v.*, IDEA, KNOCK *v.*, LAUGH *v.*, NEED *v.*, OLD, PRICE *n.*, REAR *v.*, RING *v.*, ROOF *n.*, SCRATCH *v.*, THICK *adj.*, TOP *n.*

■ *verb*

MOVE TOWARDS | **1** [V+*adv.*/*prep.*] to move in a particular direction: *Where are we heading?* ◇ *Let's head back home.* ◇ *She headed for the door.* ◇ (*figurative*) *Can you forecast where the economy is heading?*

GROUP/ORGANIZATION | **2** [VN] (also **,head sth ‹ ›'up**) to lead or be in charge of sth: *She has been appointed to head the research team.*

LIST/LINE OF PEOPLE | **3** [VN] to be at the top of a list of names or at the front of a line of people: *Italy heads the table after two games.* ◇ *to head a march/procession*

BE AT TOP | **4** [VN] [usually passive] to put a word or words at the top of a page or section of a book as a title: *The chapter was headed 'My Early Life'.*

FOOTBALL | **5** [VN] to hit a football with your head: *Walsh headed the ball into an empty goal.*

PHRV **be 'heading for sth** (also **be 'headed for sth** especially in *AmE*) **1** to be going in a particular direction or to a particular place: *Where are you two headed?* **2** to be likely to experience sth bad: *They look as though they're heading for divorce.* **,head sb ‹ ›'off** to get in front of sb in order to make them turn back or change direction $\boxed{\text{SYN}}$ INTERCEPT: *We'll head them off at the bridge!* ˌhead sth↔ˈoff to take action in order to prevent sth from happening: *He headed off efforts to replace him as leader.* ˌhead sth↔ˈup to lead or be in charge of a department, part of an organization, etc.—see also HEAD *v.* (2)

head·ache /ˈhedeɪk/ *noun* **1** a continuous pain in the head: *to suffer from headaches* ◊ *Red wine gives me a headache.* ◊ *I have a splitting headache* (= a very bad one). **2** a person or thing that causes worry or trouble: *The real headache will be getting the bank to lend you the money.*

head·band /ˈhedbænd/ *noun* a strip of fabric worn around the head, especially to keep hair or sweat out of your eyes when playing sports

head·bang·er /ˈhedbæŋə(r)/ *noun* (*informal*) **1** a person who likes to shake their head violently up and down while listening to rock music **2** a stupid or crazy person ▶ **head·banging** *noun* [U]

head·board /ˈhedbɔːd; *AmE* -bɔːrd/ *noun* the upright board at the end of a bed where you put your head

ˌhead ˈboy *noun* (in some British schools) the boy who is chosen each year to represent his school

head·butt /ˈhedbʌt/ *verb* [VN] (*especially BrE*) to deliberately hit sb hard with your head ▶ **head·butt** *noun*

ˈhead case *noun* (*BrE, informal*) a person who behaves in a strange way and who seems to be mentally ill

head·cheese /ˈhedtʃiːz/ *noun* [U] (*AmE*) = BRAWN

head·count /ˈhedkaʊnt/ *noun* an act of counting the number of people who are at an event, employed by an organization, etc.; the number of people that have been counted in this way: *to do a headcount* ◊ *What's the latest headcount?*

head·dress /ˈheddres/ *noun* a covering worn on the head on special occasions

head·ed /ˈhedɪd/ *adj.* **1** (of writing paper) having the name and address of a person, an organization, etc. printed at the top: *headed notepaper* **2** (-headed) (in adjectives) having the type of head or number of heads mentioned: *a bald-headed man* ◊ *a three-headed monster*—see also BIG-HEADED, CLEAR-HEADED, COOL-HEADED, EMPTY-HEADED, HARD-HEADED, LEVEL-HEADED, LIGHT-HEADED, PIG-HEADED, WRONG-HEADED

head·er /ˈhedə(r)/ *noun* **1** (in football) an act of hitting the ball with your head **2** a line or block of text that is automatically added to the top of every page that is printed from a computer—compare FOOTER

head·gear /ˈhedɡɪə(r); *AmE* -ɡɪr/ *noun* [U] anything worn on the head, for example a hat: *protective headgear*

ˌhead ˈgirl *noun* (in some British schools) the girl who is chosen each year to represent her school

head·hunt /ˈhedhʌnt/ *verb* [VN] to find sb who is suitable for a senior job and persuade them to leave their present job: *I was headhunted by a marketing agency.* ▶ **head·hunt·ing** *noun* [U]

head·hunt·er /ˈhedhʌntə(r)/ *noun* **1** a person whose job is to find people with the necessary skills to work for a particular company and to persuade them to join this company **2** a member of a tribe that collects the heads of the people they kill

head·ing /ˈhedɪŋ/ *noun* **1** a title printed at the top of a page or at the beginning of a section of a book: *chapter headings* **2** the subject of each section of a speech or piece of writing: *The company's aims can be grouped under three main headings.*

head·lamp /ˈhedlæmp/ *noun* (*especially BrE*) = HEAD-LIGHT

head·land /ˈhedlənd; -lænd/ *noun* a narrow piece of high land that sticks out from the coast into the sea $\boxed{\text{SYN}}$ PROMONTORY—picture at COAST

head·less /ˈhedləs/ *adj.* [usually before noun] without a head: *a headless body/corpse* $\boxed{\text{IDM}}$ **run around like a ˌheadless ˈchicken** to be very busy and active trying to do sth, but not very organized, with the result that you do not succeed

head·light /ˈhedlaɪt/ *noun* (also **head·lamp** especially

in *BrE*) a large light, usually one of two, at the front of a motor vehicle; the beam from this light: *He dipped his headlights* (= lowered the beam of light) *for the oncoming traffic.*—picture at CAR

head·line /ˈhedlaɪn/ *noun, verb*
■ *noun* **1** [C] the title of a newspaper article printed in large letters, especially at the top of the front page: *They ran the story under the headline 'Home at last!'.* ◊ *The scandal was in the headlines for several days.* ◊ *headline news*—see also BANNER HEADLINE **2** (the headlines) [pl.] a short summary of the most important items of news, read at the beginning of a news programme on the radio or television $\boxed{\text{IDM}}$ **grab/hit/make the ˈheadlines** to be an important item of news in newspapers or on the radio or television
■ *verb* **1** [VN-N] [usually passive] to give a story or article a particular headline: *The story was headlined 'Back to the future.'* **2** (*especially AmE*) to be the main performer in a concert or show: [VN] *The concert is to be headlined by Elton John.* [also V]

head·lock /ˈhedlɒk; *AmE* -lɑːk/ *noun* (in WRESTLING) a way of holding an opponent's head so that they cannot move: *He had him in a headlock.*

head·long /ˈhedlɒŋ; *AmE* -lɔːŋ/ *adv.* **1** with the head first and the rest of the body following: *She fell headlong into the icy pool.* **2** without thinking carefully before doing sth: *The government is taking care not to rush headlong into another controversy.* **3** quickly and without looking where you are going: *He ran headlong into a police car.* ▶ **head·long** *adj.* [only before noun]: *a headlong dive/rush*

head·man /ˈhedmæn; -mən/ *noun* (*pl.* **-men** /-mən; -men/) the leader of a tribe: *the village headman*

head·mas·ter /ˌhedˈmɑːstə(r); *AmE* -ˈmæs-/, **head·mis·tress** /ˌhedˈmɪstrəs/ *noun* (becoming *old-fashioned*) a teacher who is in charge of a school, especially a private school

ˌhead ˈoffice *noun* [C, U+sing./pl. *v.*] the main office of a company; the managers who work there: *Their head office is in New York.* ◊ *I don't know what head office will think about this proposal.*

ˌhead of ˈstate *noun* (*pl.* **heads of state**) the official leader of a country who is sometimes also the leader of the government

ˌhead-ˈon *adj.* [only before noun] **1** in which the front part of one vehicle hits the front part of another vehicle: *a head-on crash/collision* **2** in which people express strong views and deal with sth in a direct way: *There was a head-on confrontation between management and unions.* ▶ ˌhead-ˈon *adv.*: *The cars crashed head-on.* ◊ *We hit the tree head-on.* ◊ *to tackle a problem head-on* (= without trying to avoid it)

head·phones /ˈhedfəʊnz; *AmE* -foʊnz/ (also **ear·phones**) *noun* [pl.] a piece of equipment worn over the ears that makes it possible to listen to music, the radio, etc. without other people hearing it: *a pair/set of headphones*

head·quar·tered /ˌhedˈkwɔːtəd; *AmE* ˈhedkwɔːrtərd/ *adj.* [not before noun] having headquarters in a particular place: *News Corporation is headquartered in Sydney.*

head·quar·ters /ˌhedˈkwɔːtəz; *AmE* ˈhedkwɔːrtərz/ *noun* [U+sing./pl. *v.*, C] (*pl.* **head·quar·ters**) (*abbr.* **HQ**) a place from which an organization or a military operation is controlled; the people who work there: *The firm's headquarters is/are in London.* ◊ *Several companies have their headquarters in the area.* ◊ *I'm now based at headquarters.* ◊ *police headquarters* ◊ *Headquarters in Dublin has/have agreed.*

head·rest /ˈhedrest/ *noun* the part of a seat or chair that supports a person's head, especially on the front seat of a car—picture at CAR

head·room /ˈhedruːm; -rʊm/ *noun* [U] **1** the amount of space between the top of a vehicle and an object it drives under **2** the amount of space between the top of your head and the roof of a vehicle: *There's a lot of headroom for such a small car.*

head·scarf /ˈhedskɑːf; *AmE* -skɑːrf/ *noun* (*pl.* **head-**

scarves) a square piece of fabric tied around the head, usually with a knot under the chin, worn by women instead of a hat

head·set /ˈhedset/ *noun* a pair of HEADPHONES, especially one with a MICROPHONE attached to it

head·ship /ˈhedʃɪp/ *noun* ~ **(of sth) 1** the position of being in charge of an organization: *the headship of the department* **2** (*BrE*) the position of being in charge of a school

ˌhead ˈstart *noun* [sing.] ~ **(on/over sb)** an advantage that sb already has before they start doing sth: *Being able to speak French gave her a head start over the other candidates.*

head·stone /ˈhedstəʊn; *AmE* -stoʊn/ *noun* a piece of stone placed at one end of a grave, showing the name, etc. of the person buried there ▭SYN▭ GRAVESTONE—compare TOMBSTONE

head·strong /ˈhedstrɒŋ; *AmE* -strɔːŋ/ *adj.* (*disapproving*) a **headstrong** person is determined to do things their own way and refuses to listen to advice

ˌhead ˈtable *noun* (*AmE*) = TOP TABLE

ˌhead ˈteacher *noun* (*especially BrE*) (*AmE* usually **principal**) a teacher who is in charge of a school

ˌhead-to-ˈhead *adj.* [only before noun] in which two people or groups face each other directly in order to decide the result of a dispute or competition: *a head-to-head battle/clash/contest* ▶ **ˌhead-to-ˈhead** *adv.*: *They are set to meet head-to-head in next week's final.*

head·waters /ˈhedwɔːtəz; *AmE* -tərz/ *noun* [pl.] streams forming the source of a river

head·way /ˈhedweɪ/ *noun* [U] ▭IDM▭ **make ˈheadway** to make progress, especially when this is slow or difficult: *We are making little headway with the negotiations.* ◊ *The boat was unable to make much headway against the tide.*

head·wind /ˈhedwɪnd/ *noun* a wind that is blowing towards a person or vehicle, so that it is blowing from the direction in which the person or vehicle is moving—compare TAILWIND

head·word /ˈhedwɜːd; *AmE* -wɜːrd/ *noun* (*technical*) a word that forms a HEADING in a dictionary, under which its meaning is explained

heady /ˈhedi/ *adj.* (**head·ier**, **headi·est**) **1** [usually before noun] having a strong effect on your senses; making you feel excited and hopeful: *the heady days of youth* ◊ *the heady scent of hot spices* ◊ *a heady mixture of desire and fear* ◊ *House-buying is like drinking wine—it can be heady stuff.* **2** [not before noun] (of a person) excited in a way that makes you do things without worrying about the possible results: *She felt heady with success.*

heal /hiːl/ *verb* **1** ~ **(up)** to become healthy again; to make sth healthy again: [V] *It took a long time for the wounds to heal.* ◊ *The cut healed up without leaving a scar.* ◊ [VN] *This will help to heal your cuts and scratches.* ◊ (*figurative*) *It was a chance to* **heal the wounds** *in the party* (= to repair the damage that had been done). **2** [VN] ~ **sb** (**of sth**) (*old use* or *formal*) to cure sb who is ill; to make sb feel happy again: *the story of Jesus healing ten lepers of their disease* ◊ *I felt healed by his love.* **3** to put an end to sth or make sth easier to bear; to end or become easier to bear: [VN] *She was never able to heal the rift between herself and her father.* ◊ [V] *The breach between them never really healed.*

heal·er /ˈhiːlə(r)/ *noun* **1** a person who cures people of illnesses and disease using natural powers rather than medicine: *a faith/spiritual healer* **2** something that makes a bad situation easier to deal with: *Time is a great healer.*

heal·ing /ˈhiːlɪŋ/ *noun* [U] the process of becoming or making sb/sth healthy again; the process of getting better after an emotional shock: *the healing process* ◊ *emotional healing*—see also FAITH HEALING

health /helθ/ *noun* [U] **1** the condition of a person's body or mind: *Exhaust fumes are bad for your health.* ◊ *to be in poor/good/excellent/the best of health* ◊ *mental health* ◊ *She was forced to resign because of ill health.* ▭⇨▭ vocabulary notes on page 598 **2** the state of being physically and mentally healthy: *He was nursed back to health by his wife.* ◊ *She was glowing with health and clearly enjoying life.* ◊ *As long as you have your health, nothing else matters.* **3** the work of providing medical services: *All parties are promising to increase spending on health.* ◊ *the Health Minister* ◊ *the Department of Health* ◊ *health insurance* ◊ *health and safety regulations* (= laws that protect the health of people at work) **4** how successful sth is: *the health of your marriage/finances* ▭IDM▭ see CLEAN *adj.*, DRINK *v.*, PROPOSE, RUDE

ˈhealth care *noun* [U] the service of providing medical care: *the costs of health care for the elderly* ◊ *health care workers/professionals*

ˈhealth centre *noun* (*BrE*) a building where a group of doctors see their patients and where some local medical services have their offices

ˈhealth club *noun* (also **gym** especially in *AmE*) a private club where people go to do physical exercises in order to stay or become healthy and fit

ˈhealth farm *noun* (*BrE*) (*AmE* **ˈhealth spa**) *noun* a place where people can stay for short periods of time in order to try to improve their health by eating special food, doing physical exercises, etc.

ˈhealth food *noun* [U, C, usually pl.] food that does not contain any artificial substances and is therefore thought to be good for your health

health·ful /ˈhelθfl/ *adj.* [usually before noun] (*formal*) good for your health

ˈhealth service *noun* a public service providing medical care—see also NATIONAL HEALTH SERVICE

ˈhealth spa *noun* (*AmE*) = HEALTH FARM

ˈhealth visitor *noun* (in Britain) a trained nurse whose job is to visit people in their homes, for example new mothers, and give them advice on some areas of medical care

healthy /ˈhelθi/ *adj.* (**health·ier**, **healthi·est**) **1** having good health and not likely to become ill: *a healthy child/animal/tree* ◊ *Keep healthy by eating well and exercising regularly.* ▭OPP▭ UNHEALTHY **2** [usually before noun] good for your health: *a healthy diet/climate/lifestyle* ▭OPP▭ UNHEALTHY **3** [usually before noun] showing that you are in good health: *to have a healthy appetite* ◊ *a shampoo that keeps hair looking healthy* **4** normal and sensible: *The child showed a healthy curiosity.* ◊ *She has a healthy respect for her rival's talents.* ◊ *It's not healthy the way she clings to the past.* ▭OPP▭ UNHEALTHY **5** successful and working well: *a healthy economy* ◊ *Your car doesn't sound very healthy.* **6** [usually before noun] large and showing success: *a healthy bank balance* ◊ *a healthy profit* ▶ **health·ily** *adv.*: *to eat healthily* **healthi·ness** *noun* [U]

> **WHICH WORD?**
>
> **healthy / well**
>
> **Healthy** describes a person who is rarely ill or things that are good for your health: *a healthy child / diet / lifestyle.*
>
> **Well** describes your health on a particular occasion: *I'm sorry to hear you were not well yesterday.* ◊ *You're looking well.* ◊ *I hope you'll feel* **better** *soon.*

heap /hiːp/ *noun, verb*
■ *noun* **1** ~ **(of sth)** an untidy pile of sth: *The building was reduced to a heap of rubble.* ◊ *a compost heap* ◊ *His clothes lay in a heap on the floor.* ◊ *Worn-out car tyres were stacked in heaps.*—see also SCRAP HEAP, SLAG HEAP **2** [usually pl.] (*informal*) a lot of sth: *There's heaps of time before the plane leaves.* ◊ *I've got heaps to tell you.* **3** (*informal, humorous*) a car that is old and in bad condition ▭IDM▭ **at the top/bottom of the ˈheap** high up/low down in the structure of an organization or a society: *These workers are at the bottom of the economic heap.* **collapse, fall, etc. in a ˈheap** to fall down heavily and not move: *He collapsed in a heap on the floor.* **heaps ˈbetter, ˈmore, ˈolder, etc.** (*BrE, informal*) a lot better, etc: *Help yourself—there's heaps more.* ◊ *He looks heaps better than when I last saw him.*

æ	ɑː	e	ɜː	ə	ɪ	iː	i	ɒ	ɔː	ʌ	ʊ	u	uː
cat	father	ten	bird	about	sit	see	many	got	saw	cup	put	actual	too
								(BrE)					

H

Health

Staying healthy

If you are **fit** (*BrE*), **physically fit**, or **in shape** (especially *AmE*), you are healthy and strong, especially as a result of diet and exercise:

- *Top athletes have to be very fit.* (*BrE*)
- *People who are physically fit have a lower risk of heart disease.*
- *After my heart attack, the doctor advised me to get in shape and stay that way.*

*The doctor said I should **get** more **exercise** (*BrE* also … **take** more exercise).*

- *No cream for me – I'm **on a diet**.*
- *I need to **go on a diet**.*
- *She cycles up to 90 miles a day to **keep fit**.* (*BrE*)
- *She rides her bike up to 90 miles a day to **stay in shape**.* (especially *AmE*)

Accidents and injuries

Injury [U] or **an injury** [C] is something that happens when your body is hurt, for example in an accident.

- *A local man suffered serious injuries when his car went off the road and ran into a tree.*
- *Two drivers escaped injury when their vehicles collided.*

A **wound** is the place on the body where the injury happened and can often be seen.

- *The nurse changed the bandage on the wound every day.*

Cuts and scratches

An injury is usually something fairly serious. Other words are used for less serious things.

- *The knife slipped and cut my finger, but it's only a **scratch**.*
- *I fell on the ice, but only got a small **bruise** (= a place where the skin turns dark).*
- *She fell over and **grazed** her knees.*

Aches and pains

You have **a pain in** a part of your body:

- *She felt a sharp pain in her stomach.*

or you or a part of your body **aches**:

- *He ached all over.*
- *My head was aching dully.*

There are special words for aches or pain in some parts of the body. Some of these aches are countable and some are uncountable. There are also differences between British and American English:

- **headache** [C]
  She told us she had a headache.
- **stomach ache** [C] (*BrE* also [U])
  He went to bed early with a stomach ache.
  He went to bed early with stomach ache.
- **backache**, **earache** and **toothache** [U] (*BrE*), [C] (especially *AmE*)
  He's in excellent health except for occasional backache. (*BrE*)
  I've got earache / toothache. (*BrE*)
  He's in excellent health except for an occasional backache. (*AmE*)
  I have an earache / a toothache. (*AmE*)

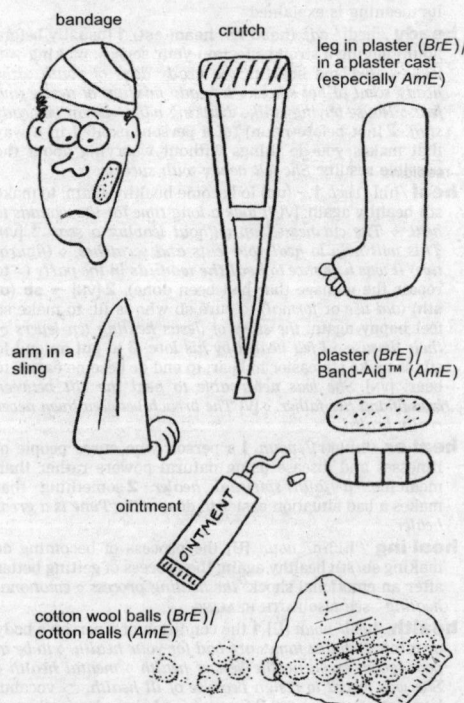

bandage

crutch

leg in plaster (*BrE*) / in a plaster cast (especially *AmE*)

arm in a sling

plaster (*BrE*) / Band-Aid™ (*AmE*)

ointment

cotton wool balls (*BrE*) / cotton balls (*AmE*)

Diseases and illnesses

Illness is a general word for a period of not being in good health:

- *He died unexpectedly after a short illness.*
- *The doctor asked whether she had a history of any serious illness.*

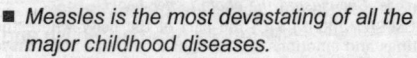

A **disease** is a particular illness with a name, or an illness that affects a particular part of the body:

- *Measles is the most devastating of all the major childhood diseases.*
- *A healthy diet and regular exercise can help prevent heart disease.*

A **condition** is a permanent health problem that affects a particular part of the body:

- *Asthma can be a very frightening condition, especially in a child.*
- *She suffers from a heart condition.*

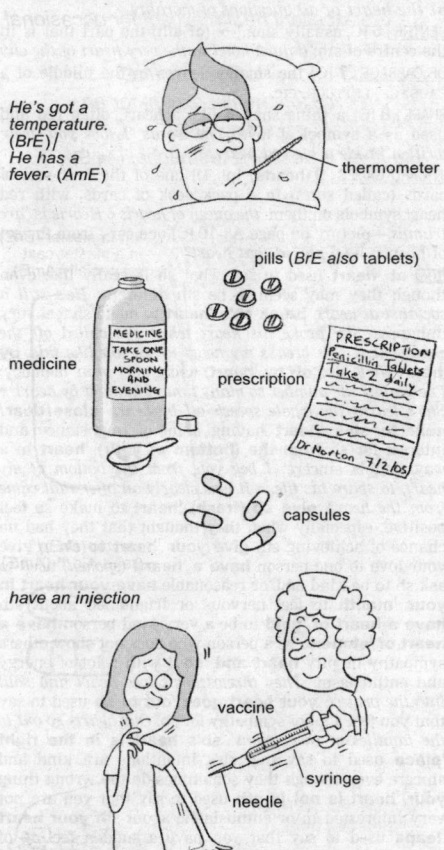

He's got a temperature. (*BrE*)/ He has a fever. (*AmE*)

thermometer

pills (*BrE* also tablets)

medicine

prescription

capsules

have an injection

vaccine

syringe

needle

Having a disease

People usually talk about **having** a disease or an illness:

- *I'm warning you – I have a bad cold.*
- *Have the kids had chickenpox yet?*

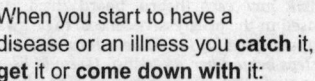

sneeze

When you start to have a disease or an illness you **catch** it, **get** it or **come down with** it:

- *I must have caught this cold from you.*
- *He gets really bad hay fever every summer.*
- *I've been sneezing and coughing all day – I must be coming down with something.*

In more formal contexts and with more serious diseases you can talk about people **suffering from** and **contracting** diseases:

- *This medicine is often recommended by doctors for their patients who suffer from arthritis.*
- *people who contract Aids*

Being ill

There are different ways of talking about being or becoming ill in British and American English:

- *I've never **been** so **ill** in my life.*
- *What's wrong? Are you **feeling unwell**?* (both *BrE*)
- *He's not in the office today – he's **sick**. (AmE)*
- *She **was taken ill** (= became ill suddenly) with severe pains in the stomach. (BrE)*
- *I just can't afford to **get sick**. (AmE)*

cough

To **feel sick** means different things in British and American English. In American English it means that you feel ill:

- *He began feeling sick Friday afternoon and was diagnosed as having suffered a minor heart attack.*

In British English it means that you feel that you want to VOMIT (= bring food up from your stomach):

- *The smell of stale cigarettes always makes me feel sick.*

To express this idea in American English, you can use **sick to your stomach**:

- *The smell of stale cigarettes always makes me sick to my stomach.*

■ *verb* [VN] **1** ~ sth (up) to put things in an untidy pile: *Rocks were heaped up on the side of the road.* **2** ~ A on B | ~ B with A to put a lot of sth in a pile on sth: *She heaped food on my plate.* ◊ *She heaped my plate with food.* **3** ~ A on B | ~ B with A to give a lot of sth such as praise or criticism to sb: *He heaped praise on his team.* ◊ *He heaped his team with praise.* **IDM** see SCORN *n.*

heap·ed /hiːpt/ (*especially BrE*) (*AmE* usually **heap·ing**) *adj.* used to describe a spoon, etc. that has as much in it or on it as it can hold: *a heaped teaspoon of sugar* ◊ *heaping plates of scrambled eggs*—compare LEVEL *adj.* (1)

hear /hɪə(r); *AmE* hɪr/ *verb* (**heard, heard** /hɜːd; *AmE* hɜːrd/) **1** (not used in the progressive tenses) to be aware of sounds with your ears: [V] *I can't hear very well.* ◊ [VN] *She heard footsteps behind her.* ◊ [VN-ing] *He could hear a dog barking.* ◊ [VNinf] *Did you hear him go out?* ◊ [V wh-] *Didn't you hear what I said?* ◊ [VN to inf] *She has been heard to make threats to her former lover.* **HELP** This pattern is only used in the passive. **2** (not used in the progressive tenses) to listen or pay attention to sb/sth: [VN] *Did you hear that play on the radio last night?* ◊ [VNinf] *Be quiet—I can't hear myself think!* (= it is so noisy that I can't think clearly) ◊ [V wh-] *We'd better hear what they have to say.* ◊ *I hear what you're saying* (= I have listened to your opinion), *but you're wrong.* **3** (not usually used in the progressive tenses) ~ (about sb/sth) to be told about sth: [V] *Haven't you heard? She resigned.* ◊ *'I'm getting married.' 'So I've heard.'* ◊ *I was sorry to hear about your accident.* ◊ [VN] *We had heard nothing for weeks.* ◊ [V (that)] *I was surprised to hear (that) he was married.* ◊ [VN (that)] *I've heard it said (that) they met in Italy.* [also V wh-] **4** [VN] to listen to and judge a case in a court of law: *The appeal was heard in private.* ◊ *Today the jury began to hear the evidence.* **IDM** **Have you heard the one about …?** used to ask sb if they have heard a particular joke before ˌhear! ˈhear! used to show that you agree with or approve of what sb has just said, especially during a speech **hear ˈtell (of sth)** (*old-fashioned* or *formal*) to hear people talking about sth: *I've often heard tell of such things.* **not/never hear the ˈend of it** to keep being reminded of sth because sb is always talking to you about it: *If we don't get her a dog we'll never hear the end of it.* **you could hear a ˈpin drop** it was extremely quiet: *The audience was so quiet you could have heard a pin drop.* **(Do) you ˈhear me?** (*spoken*) used to tell sb in an angry way to pay attention and obey you: *You can't go—do you hear me?*—more at LAST *n.*, THING, VOICE *n.* **PHRV** ˈhear from sb | ˈhear sth from sb to receive a letter, telephone call, etc. from sb: (*written*) *I look forward to hearing from you.* ◊ *I haven't heard anything from her for months.* ˈhear of sb/sth | ˈhear sth of sb/sth to know about sb/sth because you have been told about them: *I've never heard of the place.* ◊ *She disappeared and was never heard of again.* ◊ *The last I heard of him he was living in Glasgow.* ◊ *This is the first I've heard of it!* **not ˈhear of sth** to refuse to let sb do sth, especially because you want to help them: *She wanted to walk home but I wouldn't hear of it.* ◊ [+ -ing] *He wouldn't hear of my walking home alone*—see also UNHEARD-OF, **hear sb ˈout** to listen until sb has finished saying what they want to say

hear·er /ˈhɪərə(r); *AmE* ˈhɪr-/ *noun* a person who hears sth or who is listening to sb

hear·ing /ˈhɪərɪŋ; *AmE* ˈhɪr-/ *noun* **1** [U] the ability to hear: *Her hearing is poor.* ◊ *He's hearing-impaired* (= not able to hear well).—see also HARD OF HEARING **2** [C] an official meeting at which the facts about a crime, complaint, etc. are presented to the person or group of people who will have to decide what action to take: *a court/disciplinary hearing* **3** [sing.] an opportunity to explain your actions, ideas or opinions: *to get/give sb a fair hearing* ◊ *His views may be unfashionable but he deserves a hearing.* **IDM** **in/within (sb's) hearing** near enough to sb so that they can hear what is said: *She shouldn't have said such things in your hearing.*—more at FAIR *adj.*

ˈhearing aid *noun* a small device that fits inside the ear and makes sounds louder, used by people who cannot hear well: *to have/wear a hearing aid*

heark·en (also **hark·en**) /ˈhɑːkən; *AmE* ˈhɑːrkən/ *verb* [V] ~ (to sb/sth) (*old use*) to listen to sb/sth

hear·say /ˈhɪəseɪ; *AmE* ˈhɪrseɪ/ *noun* [U] things that you have heard from another person but do not (definitely) know to be true **SYN** RUMOUR: *We can't make a decision based on hearsay and guesswork.* ◊ *hearsay evidence*

hearse /hɜːs; *AmE* hɜːrs/ *noun* a long vehicle used for carrying the coffin (= the box for the dead body) at a funeral

heart /hɑːt; *AmE* hɑːrt/ *noun*

PART OF BODY | **1** [C] the organ in the left side of the chest that pumps blood around the body: *heart trouble/failure* ◊ *to have a weak heart* ◊ *The patient's heart stopped beating for a few seconds.* ◊ *I could feel my heart pounding in my chest* (= because of excitement etc.).—see also CORONARY HEART DISEASE, OPEN-HEART SURGERY—picture at BODY **2** [C] (*literary*) the outside part of the chest where the heart is: *She clasped the photo to her heart.*

FEELINGS/EMOTIONS | **3** [C] the part of the body where the feelings and emotions are thought to be, especially those connected with love: *She has a kind heart.* ◊ *Have you no heart?* ◊ *He returned with a heavy heart* (= sad). ◊ *Her novels tend to deal with affairs of the heart.* ◊ *The story captured the hearts and minds of a generation.*—see also BROKEN HEART

-HEARTED | **4** (in adjectives) having the type of character or personality mentioned: *cold-hearted* ◊ *kind-hearted*

IMPORTANT PART | **5** [sing.] ~ (of sth) the most important part of sth: *the heart of the matter/problem* ◊ *The committee's report went to the heart of the government's dilemma.* ◊ *The distinction between right and wrong lies at the heart of all questions of morality.*

CENTRE | **6** [C, usually sing.] ~ (of sth) the part that is in the centre of sth: *a quiet hotel in the very heart of the city*

OF CABBAGE | **7** [C] the smaller leaves in the middle of a CABBAGE, LETTUCE, etc.

SHAPE | **8** [C] a thing shaped like a heart, often red and used as a symbol of love: *The words 'I love you' were written inside a big red heart.*

IN CARD GAMES | **9** (**hearts**) [pl., U] one of the four sets of cards (called SUITS) in a pack/deck of cards, with red heart symbols on them: *the queen of hearts* ◊ *Hearts is/are trumps.*—picture on page A8 **10** [C] one card from the set of hearts: *Who played that heart?*

IDM **at ˈheart** used to say what sb is really like even though they may seem to be sth different: *He's still a socialist at heart.* **break sb's ˈheart** to make sb feel very unhappy: *She broke his heart when she called off the engagement.* ◊ *It breaks my heart to see you like this.* **by ˈheart** (*BrE* also **off by ˈheart**) using only your memory: *I've dialled the number so many times I know it by heart.* ◊ *She's learnt the whole speech off by heart.* **close/dear/near to sb's ˈheart** having a lot of importance and interest for sb **from the (bottom of your) ˈheart** in a way that is sincere: *I beg you, from the bottom of my heart, to spare his life.* ◊ *It was clearly an offer that came from the heart.* **give sb (fresh) ˈheart** to make sb feel positive, especially when they thought that they had no chance of achieving sth **give your ˈheart to sb** to give your love to one person **have a ˈheart!** (*spoken*) used to ask sb to be kind and/or reasonable **have your heart in your ˈmouth** to feel nervous or frightened about sth **have a heart of ˈgold** to be a very kind person **have a heart of ˈstone** to be a person who does not show others sympathy or pity **heart and ˈsoul** with a lot of energy and enthusiasm: *They threw themselves heart and soul into the project.* **your heart goes ˈout to sb** used to say that you feel a lot of sympathy for sb: *Our hearts go out to the families of the victims.* **sb's heart is in the right ˈplace** used to say that sb's intentions are kind and sincere even though they sometimes do the wrong thing **your ˈheart is not in sth** used to say that you are not very interested in or enthusiastic about sth **your heart ˈleaps** used to say that you have a sudden feeling of happiness or excitement **your heart misses a beat** used to say that you have a sudden feeling of fear, excitement, etc. **your heart ˈsinks** used to say that you suddenly feel

H

sad or depressed about sth: *My heart sank when I saw how much work there was left.* ◇ *She watched him go with a sinking heart.* **in good 'heart** (*BrE*) happy and cheerful **in your 'heart (of 'hearts)** if you know sth **in your heart**, you have a strong feeling that it is true: *She knew in her heart of hearts that she was making the wrong decision.* **it does your 'heart good (to do sth)** it makes you feel happy when you see or hear sth: *It does my heart good to see the old place being taken care of so well.* **let your ,heart rule your 'head** to act according to what you feel rather than to what you think is sensible **lose 'heart** to stop hoping for sth or trying to do sth because you no longer feel confident **lose your 'heart (to sb/sth)** (*written*) to fall in love with sb/sth **a man/woman after your own 'heart** a man/woman who likes the same things or has the same opinions as you **my heart 'bleeds (for sb)** (*ironic*) used to say that you do not feel sympathy or pity for sb: *'I have to go to Brazil on business.' 'My heart bleeds for you!'* **not have the 'heart (to do sth)** to be unable to do sth because you know that it will make sb sad or upset **pour out/open your 'heart to sb** to tell sb all your problems, feelings, etc. **set your 'heart on sth | have your heart 'set on sth** to want sth very much **take 'heart (from sth)** to feel more positive about sth, especially when you thought that you had no chance of achieving sth: *The government can take heart from the latest opinion polls.* **take sth to 'heart** to be very upset by sth that sb says or does **,tear/,rip the 'heart out of sth** to destroy the most important part or aspect of sth **to your heart's con'tent** as much as you want: *a supervised play area where children can run around to their heart's content* **with all your 'heart/your whole 'heart** completely: *I hope with all my heart that things work out for you.*—more at CHANGE *n.*, CROSS *v.*, EAT, ETCH, FIND *v.*, GOODNESS, INTEREST *n.*, SICK *adj.*, SOB *v.*, STEAL *v.*, STRIKE *v.*, TEAR[1] *v.*, WARM *v.*, WAY *n.*, WEAR *v.*, WIN *v.*, YOUNG *adj.*

heart-ache /ˈhɑːteɪk; *AmE* ˈhɑːrt-/ *noun* [U, C] a strong feeling of sadness or worry: *The relationship caused her a great deal of heartache.* ◇ *the heartaches of being a parent*

ˈheart attack *noun* a sudden serious medical condition in which the heart stops working normally, sometimes causing death—compare CORONARY THROMBOSIS

heart-beat /ˈhɑːbiːt; *AmE* ˈhɑːrt-/ *noun* **1** [C, U] the movement or sound of the heart as it pumps blood around the body: *a rapid/regular heartbeat* **2** [sing.] the **~ of sth** (*AmE*) an important feature of sth, that is responsible for making it what it is: *The candidate said that he understood the heartbeat of the Hispanic community in California.*

heart-break /ˈhɑːbreɪk; *AmE* ˈhɑːrt-/ *noun* [U, C] a strong feeling of sadness: *They suffered the heartbreak of losing a child through cancer.* ▶ **ˈheart-break-ing** *adj.*: *a heartbreaking story* ◇ *It's heartbreaking to see him wasting his life like this.*

heart-broken /ˈhɑːbrəʊkən; *AmE* ˈhɑːrtbroʊkən/ *adj.* extremely sad because of sth that has happened: *He was heartbroken when she left him.*—compare BROKEN-HEARTED

heart-burn /ˈhɑːbɜːn; *AmE* ˈhɑːrtbɜːrn/ *noun* [U] a pain that feels like sth burning in your chest caused by INDIGESTION

heart-en /ˈhɑːtn; *AmE* ˈhɑːrtn/ *verb* [VN] [usually passive] to make sb feel encouraged and more hopeful ▶ **heart-en-ing** *adj.*: *It is heartening to see the determination of these young people.*

ˈheart failure *noun* [U] a serious medical condition in which the heart does not work correctly

heart-felt /ˈhɑːtfelt; *AmE* ˈhɑːrt-/ *adj.* [usually before noun] showing strong feelings that are sincere: *a heartfelt apology/plea/sigh* ◇ *heartfelt sympathy/thanks*

hearth /hɑːθ; *AmE* hɑːrθ/ *noun* **1** the floor at the bottom of a FIREPLACE (= the space for a fire in the wall of a room); the area in front of this: *A log fire roared in the open hearth.* ◇ *The cat dozed in its favourite spot on the hearth.*—picture at MANTELPIECE **2** (*literary*) home and family life: *a longing for hearth and home*

hearth-rug /ˈhɑːθrʌɡ; *AmE* ˈhɑːrθ-/ *noun* a RUG (= a small carpet) placed on the floor in front of a FIREPLACE

heart-ily /ˈhɑːtɪli; *AmE* ˈhɑːrt-/ *adv.* **1** with obvious enjoyment and enthusiasm: *to laugh/sing/eat heartily* **2** in a way that shows that you feel strongly about sth: *I heartily agree with her on this.* ◇ *His latest book is heartily recommended to all those who enjoy historical mysteries.* **3** (*written*) extremely: *heartily glad/relieved*

heart-land /ˈhɑːtlænd; *AmE* ˈhɑːrt-/ *noun* (also **heart-lands** [pl.]) **1** the central part of a country or an area: *the great Russian heartlands* **2** an area that is important for a particular activity or political party: *the industrial heartland of Germany* ◇ *the traditional Tory heartland of Britain's boardrooms*

heart-less /ˈhɑːtləs; *AmE* ˈhɑːrt-/ *adj.* feeling no pity for other people: *The decision does seem a little heartless.* ◇ *What a heartless thing to say!* ▶ **heart-less-ly** *adv.* **heart-less-ness** *noun* [U]

ˈheart-rending *adj.* [usually before noun] causing feelings of great sadness: *a heart-rending story*

ˈheart-searching *noun* [U] the process of examining carefully your feelings or reasons for doing sth

ˈheart-stopping *adj.* [usually before noun] causing feelings of great excitement or worry: *For one heart-stopping moment she thought they were too late.*

heart-strings /ˈhɑːtstrɪŋz; *AmE* ˈhɑːrt-/ *noun* [pl.] strong feelings of love or pity: *to tug/pull at sb's heartstrings* (= to cause such feelings in sb)

ˈheart-throb *noun* a famous man, usually an actor or a singer, that a lot of women find attractive: *a Hollywood heart-throb*

,heart-to-'heart *noun* [usually sing.] a conversation in which two people talk honestly about their feelings and personal problems: *to have a heart-to-heart with sb* ▶ **,heart-to-'heart** *adj.*: *a heart-to-heart talk*

ˈheart-warming *adj.* causing feelings of happiness and pleasure: *a heart-warming experience/story*

hearty /ˈhɑːti; *AmE* ˈhɑːrti/ *adj., noun*
■ *adj.* (**heart-ier, hearti-est**) **1** [usually before noun] showing friendly feelings for sb: *a hearty greeting/reception/welcome* **2** (sometimes *disapproving*) loud, cheerful and full of energy: *a hearty and boisterous fellow* ◇ *a hearty voice/handshake* **3** [only before noun] (of a meal or sb's APPETITE) large; making you feel full: *a hearty breakfast* ◇ *to have a hearty appetite* **4** [usually before noun] showing that you feel strongly about sth: *He nodded his head in hearty agreement.* ◇ *Hearty congratulations to everyone involved.* ◇ *a hearty dislike of sth* IDM see HALE ▶ **hearti-ness** *noun* [U]
■ *noun* (*pl.* **-ies**) (*BrE*, sometimes *disapproving*) a person who is loud, cheerful and full of energy, especially one who plays a lot of sport

heat /hiːt/ *noun, verb*
■ *noun*
BEING HOT/TEMPERATURE | **1** [U, sing.] the quality of being hot: *He could feel the heat of the sun on his back.* ◇ *Heat rises.* ◇ *The fire gave out a fierce heat.*—see also WHITE HEAT **2** [U, C, usually sing.] the level of temperature: *to increase/reduce the heat* ◇ *Test the heat of the water before getting in.* ◇ *Set the oven to a low/high/moderate heat.*—see also BLOOD HEAT **3** [U] hot weather; the hot conditions in a building/vehicle, etc: *You should not go out in **the heat of the day** (= at the hottest time).* ◇ *to suffer from the heat* ◇ *the afternoon/midday heat* ◇ *The heat in the factory was unbearable.*
FOR COOKING | **4** [U] a source of heat, especially one that you cook food on: *Return the pan to the heat and stir.*
IN BUILDING/ROOM | **5** [U] (*especially AmE*) = HEATING: *The heat wasn't on and the house was freezing.*
STRONG FEELINGS | **6** [U] strong feelings, especially of anger or excitement: *'No, I won't,' he said with heat in his voice.* ◇ *The chairman tried to take the heat out of the situation* (= to make people calmer). ◇ *In the heat of the moment she forgot what she wanted to say* (= because she was so angry or excited). ◇ *In the heat of the argument he said a lot of things he regretted later.*
PRESSURE | **7** [U] pressure on sb to do or achieve sth: *The*

æ	ɑː	e	ɜː	ə	ɪ	iː	i	ɒ	ɔː	ʌ	ʊ	u	uː
cat	father	ten	bird	about	sit	see	many	got	saw	cup	put	actual	too
								(BrE)					

heat is on now that the election is only a week away. ◊ Leeds United turned up the heat on their opponents with a second goal. ◊ Can she **take the heat** of this level of competition?

RACE | **8** [C] one of a series of races or competitions, the winners of which then compete against each other in the next part of the competition: *a qualifying heat* ◊ *She won her heat.* ◊ *He did well in the heats; hopefully he'll do as well in the final.*—see also DEAD HEAT

IDM **if you can't stand the 'heat (get out of the 'kitchen)** (*informal*) used to tell sb to stop trying to do sth if they find it too difficult, especially in order to suggest that they are less able than other people **be on 'heat** (*BrE*) (*AmE* **be in 'heat**) (of a female mammal) to be in a sexual condition ready for MATING

■ *verb* to make sth hot or warm; to become hot or warm: [VN] *Heat the oil and add the onions.* ◊ *The system produced enough energy to heat several thousand homes.* [also V]

PHRV ,**heat 'up 1** to become hot or warm: *The oven takes a while to heat up.* **2** (*especially AmE*) = HOT UP: *The election contest is heating up.* ,**heat sth ↔ 'up** to make sth hot or warm: *Just heat up the food in the microwave.*

heat·ed /ˈhiːtɪd/ *adj.* **1** (of a person or discussion) full of anger and excitement: *a heated argument/debate* ◊ *She became very heated.* **2** (of a room, building, etc.) made warmer using a heater: *a heated swimming pool* OPP UNHEATED ▶ **heat·ed·ly** *adv.*: *'You had no right!' she said heatedly.*

heat·er /ˈhiːtə(r)/ *noun* a machine used for making air or water warmer: *a gas heater* ◊ *a water heater*—see also IMMERSION HEATER, STORAGE HEATER

heath /hiːθ/ *noun* a large area of open land that is not used for farming and is covered with rough grass and other small wild plants

hea·then /ˈhiːðn/ *noun, adj.*
■ *noun* (*old-fashioned, offensive*) **1** used by people who have a strong religious belief as a way of referring to a person who has no religion or who believes in a religion that is not one of the world's main religions **2** used to refer to a person who shows lack of education
■ *adj.* (*old-fashioned, offensive*) connected with heathens: *heathen gods* ◊ *He set out to convert the heathen* (= people who are heathens).

hea·ther /ˈheðə(r)/ *noun* [U] a low wild plant with small purple, pink or white flowers, that grows on hills and areas of wild open land (= MOORLAND)

Heath Rob·in·son /ˌhiːθ ˈrɒbɪnsən; *AmE* ˈrɑːb-/ (*BrE*) (*AmE* ,**Rube 'Gold·berg**) *adj.* [only before noun] (*humorous*) (of machines and devices) having a very complicated design, especially when used to perform a very simple task; not practical: *a Heath Robinson contraption*

heat·ing /ˈhiːtɪŋ/ *noun* [U] (*especially BrE*) (also **heat** especially in *AmE*) the process of supplying heat to a room or building; a system used to do this: *Who turned the heating off?* ◊ *What type of heating do you have?* ◊ *a gas heating system* ◊ *heating bills*—see also CENTRAL HEATING

heat·proof /ˈhiːtpruːf/ *adj.* that cannot be damaged by heat: *a heatproof dish*

'**heat-resistant** *adj.* not easily damaged by heat: *heat-resistant clothing*

'**heat-seeking** *adj.* [only before noun] (of a weapon) that moves towards the heat coming from the aircraft, etc. that it is intended to hit and destroy: *heat-seeking missiles*

heat·stroke /ˈhiːtstrəʊk; *AmE* -stroʊk/ *noun* [U] an illness with fever and often loss of consciousness, caused by being in too great a heat for too long

heat·wave /ˈhiːtweɪv/ *noun* a period of unusually hot weather

heave /hiːv/ *verb, noun*
■ *verb* **1** [+*adv./prep.*] to lift, pull or throw sb/sth very heavy with one great effort: [VN] *I managed to heave the trunk down the stairs.* ◊ *They heaved the body overboard.* ◊ [V] *We all heaved on the rope.* **2** [V] ~ (**with sth**) to rise up and down with strong, regular movements: *The boat heaved beneath them.* ◊ *Her shoulders heaved with laughter.* **3** [VN] ~ **a sigh, etc.** to make a sound slowly and often

with effort: *We all heaved a sigh of relief.* **4** [V] to experience the tight feeling in your stomach that you get before you VOMIT: *The thought of it makes me heave.* IDM ,**heave into 'sight/'view** HELP Hove is usually used for the past tense and past participle in this idiom. (*written*) (especially of ships) to appear, especially when moving gradually closer from a long way off: *A ship hove into sight.* PHRV ,**heave 'to** HELP Hove is usually used for the past tense and past participle in this phrasal verb. (*technical*) if a ship or its CREW (= the people sailing it) **heave to**, the ship stops moving
■ *noun* [C, U] **1** an act of lifting, pulling or throwing: *With a mighty heave he lifted the sack onto the truck.* **2** (especially *literary*) a rising and falling movement: *the steady heave of the sea*

heave-ho /ˌhiːv ˈhəʊ; *AmE* ˈhoʊ/ *noun* [sing.] IDM **give sb the (old) heave-'ho** (*informal*) to dismiss sb from their job; to end a relationship with sb

heaven /ˈhevn/ *noun* **1** (also **Heaven**) [U] (in some religions) the place believed to be the home of God where good people go when they die: *the kingdom of heaven* ◊ *I feel like I've died and gone to heaven.* **2** [U, C] (*informal*) a place or situation in which you are very happy: *This isn't exactly my idea of heaven!* ◊ *It was heaven being away from the phone for a week.* ◊ *The island is truly a heaven on earth.* **3** (**Heaven**) [U] (*formal*) God: *It was the will of Heaven.* **4** (**the heavens**) [pl.] (*literary*) the sky: *Four tall trees stretched up to the heavens.* IDM (**Good**) '**Heavens!** | ,**Heavens a'bove!** (*spoken*) used to show that you are surprised or annoyed: *Good heavens, what are you doing?* **the heavens 'opened** it began to rain heavily—more at FORBID, GOD, HELP *v.*, HIGH *adj.*, KNOW *v.*, MOVE *v.*, NAME *n.*, SEVENTH, THANK

heav·en·ly /ˈhevnli/ *adj.* **1** [only before noun] connected with heaven: *our heavenly Father* (= God) ◊ *the heavenly kingdom* **2** [only before noun] connected with the sky: *heavenly bodies* (= the sun, moon, stars and planets) **3** (*informal*) very pleasant: *a heavenly morning/feeling* ◊ *This place is heavenly.*

,**heaven-'sent** *adj.* [usually before noun] happening unexpectedly and at exactly the right time: *a heaven-sent opportunity*

heav·en·ward /ˈhevnwəd; *AmE* -wərd/ (also **heav·en·wards**) *adv.* (*literary*) towards heaven or the sky: *to cast/raise your eyes heavenward* (= to show you are annoyed or impatient)

heav·ing /ˈhiːvɪŋ/ *adj.* [not before noun] ~ (**with sb/sth**) full of sth: *The place was heaving with journalists.*

heavy /ˈhevi/ *adj., noun, adv.*
■ *adj.* (**heav·ier, heavi·est**)
WEIGHING A LOT | **1** weighing a lot; difficult to lift or move: *She was struggling with a heavy suitcase.* ◊ *My brother is much heavier than me.* ◊ *He tried to push the heavy door open.* ◊ *How heavy is it* (= how much does it weigh)? ◊ (*figurative*) *Her father carried a heavy burden of responsibility.* OPP LIGHT

WORSE THAN USUAL | **2** more or worse than usual in amount, degree, etc: *the noise of heavy traffic* ◊ *heavy frost/rain/snow* ◊ *the effects of heavy drinking* ◊ *There was heavy fighting in the capital last night.* ◊ *The penalty for speeding can be a heavy fine.* ◊ *She spoke with heavy irony.* OPP LIGHT

NOT DELICATE | **3** (of sb/sth's appearance or structure) large and solid; not delicate: *big, dark rooms full of heavy furniture* ◊ *He was tall and strong, with heavy features.* OPP LIGHT

MATERIAL | **4** (of the material or substance that sth is made of) thick: *heavy curtains* ◊ *a heavy coat* OPP LIGHT

FULL OF STH | **5** ~ **with sth** (*literary*) full of or loaded with sth: *trees heavy with apples* ◊ *The air was heavy with the scent of flowers.* ◊ *His voice was heavy with sarcasm.*

MACHINES | **6** [usually before noun] (of machines, vehicles or weapons) large and powerful: *a wide range of engines and heavy machinery* ◊ *heavy lorries/trucks* ◊ *heavy goods vehicles*

BUSY | **7** [usually before noun] involving a lot of work or activity; very busy: *a heavy schedule* ◊ *She'd had a heavy day.*

WORK | **8** hard, especially because it requires a lot of physical strength: *heavy digging/lifting*

FALL/HIT | **9** falling or hitting sth with a lot of force: *a heavy fall/blow*

MEAL/FOOD | **10** large in amount or very solid: *a heavy lunch/dinner* ◊ *a heavy cake* OPP LIGHT

USING A LOT | **11** ~ on sth (*informal*) using a lot of sth: *Older cars are heavy on gas.* ◊ *Don't go so heavy on the garlic.*

DRINKER/SMOKER/SLEEPER | **12** [only before noun] (of a person) doing the thing mentioned more, or more deeply, than usual: *a heavy drinker/eater/smoker* ◊ *a heavy breather/sleeper*

SOUND | **13** (of a sound that sb makes) loud and deep: *heavy breathing/snoring* ◊ *a heavy groan/sigh*

SERIOUS/DIFFICULT | **14** (usually *disapproving*) (of a book, programme, style, etc.) serious; difficult to understand or enjoy: *We found the play very heavy.* ◊ *The discussion got a little heavy.*

SEA/OCEAN | **15** dangerous because of big waves, etc: *strong winds and heavy seas*

AIR/WEATHER | **16** hot and lacking fresh air, in a way that is unpleasant: *It's very heavy—I think there'll be a storm.*

SOIL | **17** wet, sticky and difficult to dig or to move over

STRICT | **18** (of a person) very strict and harsh: *Don't be so heavy on her—it wasn't her fault.*

▶ **heav·i·ly** *adv.*: *a heavily loaded van* ◊ *to drink heavily* ◊ *to be heavily taxed* ◊ *to rely heavily on sb/sth* ◊ *He fell heavily.* ◊ *It was raining heavily.* **heavi·ness** *noun* [U] IDM **get 'heavy** (*informal*) to become very serious, because strong feelings are involved: *They started shouting at me. It got very heavy.* ,**heavy 'going** used to describe sb/sth that is difficult to deal with or understand: *She's a bit heavy going.* ◊ *I found the course rather heavy going.* **heavy 'hand** a way of doing sth or of treating people that is much stronger and less sensitive than it needs to be: *the heavy hand of management* **a heavy 'heart** a feeling of great sadness: *She left her children behind with a heavy heart.* **the 'heavy mob/ brigade** (*BrE, informal*) a group of strong, often violent people employed to do sth such as protect sb **a heavy 'silence/'atmosphere** a situation when people do not say anything, but feel embarrassed or uncomfortable **make heavy 'weather of sth** to seem to find sth more difficult or complicated than it needs to be—more at CROSS *n.*, TOLL *n.*

■ *noun* (*pl.* **-ies**) **1** [C] (*informal*) a large strong man whose job is to protect a person or place, often using violence **2** [U] (*ScotE*) strong beer, especially BITTER: *a pint of heavy*

■ *adv.*

IDM **hang/lie 'heavy 1** ~ (on/in sth) (of a feeling or sth in the air) to be very noticeable in a particular place in a way that is unpleasant: *Smoke lay heavy on the far side of the water.* ◊ *Despair hangs heavy in the stifling air.* **2** ~ on sb/sth to cause sb/sth to feel uncomfortable or anxious: *The crime lay heavy on her conscience.*

,**heavy 'breather** *noun* a person who gets sexual pleasure from calling sb on the telephone and not speaking to them ▶ ,**heavy 'breathing** *noun* [U]

,**heavy-'duty** *adj.* [only before noun] not easily damaged and therefore suitable for hard physical work or to be used all the time: *a heavy-duty carpet/tyre* ◊ *heavy-duty plastic*

,**heavy 'goods vehicle** *noun* (*BrE*) = HGV

,**heavy-'handed** *adj.* **1** not showing a sympathetic understanding of the feelings of other people: *a heavy-handed approach/manner* **2** using unnecessary force: *heavy-handed police methods* **3** (of a person) using too much of sth in a way that can cause damage: *Don't be too heavy-handed with the salt.*

,**heavy 'hitter** *noun* (*informal, especially AmE*) a person with a lot of power, especially in business or politics

,**heavy 'industry** *noun* [U, C] industry that uses large machinery to produce metal, coal, vehicles, etc.—compare LIGHT INDUSTRY

,**heavy 'metal** *noun* **1** [U] a type of ROCK MUSIC (= loud modern music) with a very strong beat played very loud on electric guitars and often with words that are shouted loudly **2** [C] (*technical*) a metal that has a very high DENSITY (= the relation of its weight to its volume), such as gold or LEAD

,**heavy 'petting** *noun* [U] sexual activity that does not involve full SEXUAL INTERCOURSE

,**heavy-'set** *adj.* having a broad heavy body SYN THICK-SET

heavy·weight /'heviweɪt/ *noun* **1** a boxer of the heaviest class, weighing 79.5 kilograms or more: *a heavyweight champion* ◊ *a person or thing that weighs more than is usual* **3** a very important person, organization or thing that influences others: *a political heavyweight* ◊ *a heavyweight journal*

Heb·raic /hi'breɪk/ *adj.* of or connected with the Hebrew language or people: *Hebraic poetry*

Heb·rew /'hi:bru:/ *noun* **1** a member of an ancient race of people living in what is now Israel and Palestine. Their writings and traditions form the basis of the Jewish religion. **2** the language traditionally used by the Hebrew people **3** a modern form of the Hebrew language which is the official language of modern Israel—compare YIDDISH ▶ **Heb·rew** *adj.*

heck /hek/ *exclamation, noun* (*informal*) used to show that you are slightly annoyed or surprised: *Oh heck, I'm going to be late!* ◊ *We had to wait a heck of a long time!* ◊ *Who the heck are you?* IDM **for the 'heck of it** (*informal*) just for pleasure rather than for a reason **what the 'heck!** (*informal*) used to say that you are going to do sth that you know you should not do: *It means I'll be late for work but what the heck!*

heckle /'hekl/ *verb* to interrupt a speaker at a public meeting by shouting out questions or rude remarks SYN BARRACK: [VN] *He was booed and heckled throughout his speech.* [also V] ▶ **heck·ler** /'heklə(r)/ *noun* **heck·ling** *noun* [U]

hec·tare /'hekteə(r); *AmE* -ter *BrE* also 'hekta:(r)/ *noun* (*abbr.* **ha**) a unit for measuring an area of land; 10000 square metres or about 2.5 ACRES

hec·tic /'hektɪk/ *adj.* very busy; full of activity: *to lead a hectic life* ◊ *a hectic schedule*

hec·tor /'hektə(r)/ *verb* [VN, V speech] (*written*) to try to make sb do sth by talking or behaving in an aggressive way SYN BULLY ▶ **hec·tor·ing** *adj.*: *a hectoring tone of voice*

he'd /hi:d/ *short form* **1** he had **2** he would

hedge /hedʒ/ *noun, verb*

■ *noun* **1** a row of bushes or small trees planted close together, usually along the edge of a field, garden/yard or road: *a privet hedge* **2** ~ against sth a way of protecting yourself against the loss of sth, especially money: *to buy gold as a hedge against inflation*

■ *verb* **1** [V] to avoid giving a direct answer to a question or promising to support a particular idea, etc: *Just answer 'yes' or 'no'—and stop hedging.* **2** [VN] to put a hedge around a field, etc. **3** [VN] [usually passive] ~ sb/sth (about/around) (with sth) (*formal*) to surround or limit sb/sth: *His religious belief was always hedged with doubt.* ◊ *Their offer was hedged around with all sorts of conditions.* IDM ,**hedge your 'bets** to reduce the risk of losing or making a mistake by supporting more than one side in a competition, an argument, etc., or by having several choices available to you PHRV **'hedge against sth** to do sth to protect yourself against problems, especially against losing money: *a way of hedging against currency risks* ,**hedge sb/sth** ↔ **'in** to surround sb/sth with sth SYN HEM SB/STH IN: *The cathedral is now hedged in by other buildings.* ◊ (*figurative*) *Married life made him feel hedged in and restless.*

hedge·hog /'hedʒhɒg; *AmE* -hɔːg; -hɑːg/ *noun* a small brown European animal with stiff parts like needles, (called SPINES), covering its back. Hedgehogs are NOCTUR-NAL (= active mostly at night) and can roll into a ball to defend themselves when they are attacked.

hedge·row /'hedʒrəʊ; AmE -roʊ/ noun (especially in Britain) a line of bushes planted along the edge of a field or road

he·don·ism /'hiːdənɪzəm/ noun [U] the belief that pleasure is the most important thing in life ▶ **he·don·is·tic** /ˌhiːdə'nɪstɪk/ adj.

he·don·ist /'hiːdənɪst/ noun a person who believes that pleasure is the most important thing in life

heed /hiːd/ verb, noun
■ verb [VN] to pay careful attention to sb's advice or warning
☐ noun [U] **IDM** **give/pay 'heed (to sb/sth)** | **take 'heed (of sb/sth)** (formal) to pay careful attention to sb/sth: They gave little heed to the rumours. ◊ I paid no heed at the time but later I had cause to remember what he'd said.

heed·less /'hiːdləs/ adj. [not usually before noun] ~ (of sb/sth) (formal) not paying careful attention to sb/sth ▶ **heed·less·ly** adv.

heel /hiːl/ noun, verb
■ noun
PART OF FOOT | **1** [C] the back part of the foot below the ankle—picture at BODY
PART OF SOCK/SHOE | **2** [C] the part of a sock, etc. that covers the heel **3** [C] the raised part on the bottom of a shoe, boot, etc. that makes the shoe, etc. higher at the back: shoes with a low/high heel ◊ a stiletto heel ◊ The sergeant clicked his heels and walked out.—compare SOLE n. (2)—picture at SHOE
-HEELED | **4** (in adjectives) having the type of heel mentioned: high-heeled shoes—see also WELL HEELED
SHOES | **5** (heels) [pl.] a pair of women's shoes that have high heels: She doesn't often wear heels.
PART OF HAND | **6** [C] ~ of your hand/palm the raised part of the inside of the hand where it joins the wrist
UNPLEASANT MAN | **7** [C] (old-fashioned, informal) a man who is unpleasant to other people and cannot be trusted
—see also ACHILLES' HEEL, DOWN AT HEEL
IDM **at/on sb's 'heels** following closely behind sb: He fled from the stadium with the police at his heels. **bring sb/sth to 'heel** **1** to force sb to obey you and accept discipline **2** to make a dog come close to you **come to 'heel 1** (of a person) to agree to obey sb and accept their discipline **2** (of a dog) to come close to the person who has called it **(hard/hot) on sb's/sth's 'heels** very close behind sb/sth; very soon after sth: News of rising unemployment followed hard on the heels of falling export figures. **ˌtake to your 'heels** to run away from sb/sth **ˌturn/ˌspin on your 'heel** to turn around suddenly so that you are facing in the opposite direction **under the 'heel of sb** (literary) completely controlled by sb—more at COOL v., DIG v., DRAG v., HEAD n., KICK v., TREAD v.
■ verb
REPAIR SHOE | **1** [VN] to repair the heel of a shoe, etc.
OF BOAT | **2** [V] ~ (over) to lean over to one side: The boat heeled over in the strong wind.

hefty /'hefti/ adj. (heft·ier, hefti·est) **1** (of a person or an object) big and heavy: Her brothers were both hefty men in their forties. **2** (of an amount of money) large; larger than usual or expected: They sold it easily and made a hefty profit. ◊ Interest rates have gone up to a hefty 12%. **3** using a lot of force: He gave the door a hefty kick. ▶ **heft·ily** adv.

he·gem·ony /hɪ'dʒeməni; -'ge-; 'hedʒɪməni; AmE -moʊni/ noun [U, C] (pl. -ies) (formal) control by one country, organization, etc. over other countries, etc. within a particular group: the country's continuing desire for political and military hegemony ▶ **hege·mon·ic** /ˌhedʒɪ'mɒnɪk; ˌhegɪ-; AmE -'mɑːnɪk/ adj.: hegemonic power/control

heifer /'hefə(r)/ noun a young female cow, especially one that has not yet had a CALF

height /haɪt/ noun
MEASUREMENT | **1** [U, C] the measurement of how tall a person or thing is: Height: 210 mm. Width: 57 mm. Length: 170 mm. ◊ Please state your height and weight. ◊ It is

almost 2 metres in height. ◊ She is the same height as her sister. ◊ to be of medium/average height ◊ You can adjust the height of the chair. ◊ The table is available in several different heights.
BEING TALL | **2** [U] the quality of being tall or high: She worries about her height (= that she is too tall). ◊ The height of the mountain did not discourage them.
DISTANCE ABOVE GROUND | **3** [C, U] a particular distance above the ground: The plane flew at a height of 3000 metres. ◊ The aircraft was gaining height. ◊ to be at shoulder/chest/waist height ◊ The stone was dropped from a great height.
HIGH PLACE | **4** [C, usually pl.] (often used in names) a high place or position: Brooklyn Heights ◊ He doesn't have a head for heights (= is afraid of high places). ◊ a fear of heights ◊ We looked out over the city from the heights of Edinburgh Castle. ◊ The pattern of the ancient fields is clearly visible from a height.
STRONGEST POINT/LEVEL | **5** [sing.] the point when sth is at its best or strongest: He is at the height of his career. ◊ She is still at the height of her powers. ◊ I wouldn't go there in the height of summer. ◊ The fire reached its height around 2 a.m. ◊ The housing market was at its height in the eighties. **6** (heights) [pl.] a better or greater level of sth; a situation where sth is very good: Their success had reached new heights. ◊ She dreamed of reaching the dizzy heights of stardom. ◊ He didn't know it was possible to reach such heights of happiness.
EXTREME EXAMPLE | **7** [sing.] ~ of sth an extreme example of a particular quality: It would be the height of folly (= very stupid) to change course now. ◊ She was dressed in the height of fashion.
IDM **draw yourself up/rise to your full 'height** to stand straight and tall in order to show your determination or high status—more at DIZZY

height·en /'haɪtn/ verb if a feeling or an effect heightens, or sth heightens it, it becomes stronger or increases SYN INTENSIFY: [V] Tension has heightened after the recent bomb attack. ◊ [VN] The campaign is intended to heighten public awareness of the disease.

hein·ous /'heɪnəs/ adj. [usually before noun] (formal) morally very bad: a heinous crime ▶ **hein·ous·ness** noun [U]

heir /eə(r); AmE er/ noun ~ (to sth) | ~ (of sb) **1** a person who has the legal right to receive sb's property, money or title when that person dies: to be heir to a large fortune ◊ the heir to the throne (= the person who will be the next king or queen) ◊ the son and heir of the Earl of Lancaster **2** a person who is thought to continue the work or a tradition started by sb else: the president's political heirs **HELP** Use an, not a, before heir.

ˌheir ap'parent noun (pl. heirs apparent) ~ (to sth) **1** an HEIR whose legal right to receive sb's property, money or title cannot be taken away because it is impossible for sb with a stronger claim to be born **2** a person who is expected to take the job of sb when that person leaves

heir·ess /'eəres; -rəs; AmE 'er-/ noun ~ (to sth) a female heir, especially one who has received or will receive a large amount of money **HELP** Use an, not a, before heir-ess.

heir·loom /'eəluːm; AmE 'erl-/ noun a valuable object that has belonged to the same family for many years: a family heirloom **HELP** Use an, not a, before heirloom.

ˌheir pre'sumptive noun (pl. heirs presumptive) an HEIR who may lose his or her legal right to receive sb's property, money or title if sb with a stronger claim is born

heist /haɪst/ noun, verb
■ noun (informal, especially AmE) an act of stealing sth valuable from a shop/store or bank: a bank heist
■ verb [VN] (especially AmE) to steal sth valuable from a shop/store or bank

held pt, pp of HOLD

hel·ic·al /'helɪkl; 'hiːl-/ adj. (technical) like a HELIX

heli·cop·ter /'helɪkɒptə(r); AmE -kɑːp-/ (also informal cop·ter, chop·per) noun an aircraft without wings that

H

has large blades on top that go round. It can fly straight up from the ground and can also stay in one position in the air: *He was rushed to the hospital by helicopter.* ◊ *a police helicopter* ◊ *a helicopter pilot*

he·lio·trope /ˈhiːlɪətrəʊp; *AmE* -troʊp/ *noun* **1** [C, U] a garden plant with pale purple flowers with a sweet smell **2** [U] a pale purple colour

heli·pad /ˈhelɪpæd/ (also **ˈhelicopter pad**) *noun* a small area where HELICOPTERS can take off and land

heli·port /ˈhelɪpɔːt; *AmE* -pɔːrt/ *noun* a place where HELI-COPTERS take off and land

he·lium /ˈhiːliəm/ *noun* [U] (*symb* **He**) a chemical element. Helium is a very light colourless gas that does not burn, often used to fill BALLOONS and to freeze food.

helix /ˈhiːlɪks/ *noun* (*pl.* **heli·ces** /ˈhiːlɪsiːz/) a shape like a SPIRAL or a line curved around a CYLIN-DER or CONE

helix

hell /hel/ *noun* **1** [sing.] (usually **Hell**) (used without *a* or *the*) in some religions, the place believed to be the home of devils and where bad people go after death **2** [U, sing.] a very unpleasant experience or situation in which people suffer very much: *The last three months have been hell.* ◊ *He went through hell during the trial.* ◊ *Her parents made her life hell.* ◊ *Being totally alone is my idea of hell on earth.* **3** a swear word that some people use when they are annoyed or surprised or to emphasize sth. Its use is offensive to some people: *Oh hell, I've burned the pan.* ◊ *What the hell do you think you are doing?* ◊ *I can't really afford it, but, what the hell* (= it doesn't matter), *I'll get it anyway.* ◊ *He's as guilty as hell.* ◊ (*AmE*) *'Do you understand?' 'Hell, no. I don't.'* **IDM** **all ˈhell broke loose** (*informal*) suddenly there was a lot of noise, arguing, fighting or confusion: *There was a loud bang and then all hell broke loose.* **beat/kick (the) ˈhell out of sb/sth | knock ˈhell out of sth** (*informal*) to hit sb/sth very hard: *He was a dirty player and loved to kick hell out of the opposition.* **(just) for the ˈhell of it** (*informal*) just for fun; for no real reason: *They stole the car just for the hell of it.* **from ˈhell** (*informal*) used to describe a very unpleasant person or thing; the worst that you can imagine: *They are the neighbours from hell.* **get the hell ˈout (of …)** (*spoken*) to leave a place very quickly: *Let's get the hell out of here.* **give sb ˈhell** (*informal*) **1** to make life unpleasant for sb: *He used to give his mother hell when he was a teenager.* ◊ *My new shoes are giving me hell* (= are hurting me). **2** to shout at or speak angrily to sb: *Dad will give us hell when he sees that mess.* **go to hell in a ˈhandbasket** (*AmE, informal*) → GO TO THE DOGS at DOG *n.* **hell for ˈleather** (*old-fashioned, BrE, informal*) as quickly as possible: *to ride hell for leather* **hell hath no ˈfury (like a woman ˈscorned)** (*BrE*) used to refer to sb, usually a woman, who has reacted very angrily to sth, especially the fact that her husband or lover has been UNFAITHFUL **(come) hell or high ˈwater** (*informal*) in spite of any difficulties: *I was determined to go, come hell or high water.* **Hell's ˈteeth** (*old-fashioned, BrE, spoken*) used to express anger or surprise **like ˈhell 1** (*informal*) used for emphasis: *She worked like hell for her exams.* ◊ *My broken finger hurt like hell.* **2** (*spoken*) used when you are refusing permission or saying that sth is not true: *'I'm coming with you.' 'Like hell you are'* (= you certainly are not). **a/ one hell of a … | a/one helluva** /ˈheləvə/ (*spoken, slang*) used to give emphasis to what a person is saying: *The firm was in a hell of a mess when he took over.* ◊ *This holiday is going to cost a hell of a lot of money.* ◊ *It must have been one hell of a party.* ◊ *It's taken him a hell of a long time to get here.* ◊ *That's one helluva big house you've got.* **play (merry) ˈhell with sth/sb** (*BrE, informal*) to affect sth badly **scare, annoy, etc. the ˈhell out of sb** (*informal*) to scare, annoy, etc. sb very much **to ˈhell and back** (*informal*) used to say that sb has been through a difficult situation: *We'd been to hell and back together and we were still good friends.* **to ˈhell with sb/sth** (*spoken*) used to express anger or dislike and to say that you no

longer care about sb/sth and will take no notice of them: *'To hell with him,' she thought, 'I'm leaving.'* — more at BAT *n.*, CAT, CATCH *v.*, HOPE *n.*, PAY *v.*, RAISE *v.*, SNOWBALL *n.* **HELP** Some people find the use of the spoken idioms offensive.

he'll /hiːl/ *short form* he will

hell-ˈbent *adj.* **~ on sth/on doing sth** determined to do sth even though the results may be bad: *He seems hell-bent on drinking himself to death.*

Hel·ene /ˈheliːn/ *noun* a person from Greece, especially ancient Greece

Hel·len·ic /heˈlenɪk; -ˈliːn-/ *adj.* of or connected with ancient or modern Greece

hell·hole /ˈhelhəʊl; *AmE* -hoʊl/ *noun* a very unpleasant place

hell·ion /ˈheliən/ *noun* (*AmE*) a badly behaved child who annoys other people

hell·ish /ˈhelɪʃ/ *adj.* (*informal, especially BrE*) extremely unpleasant: *His school days were hellish.* ◊ *We've had a hellish time lately.*

hello (also **hullo** especially in *BrE*) (*BrE* also **hallo**) /həˈləʊ; *AmE* həˈloʊ/ *exclamation, noun* **1** used as a greeting when you meet sb, when you answer the telephone or when you want to attract sb's attention: *Hello John, how are you?* ◊ *Hello, is there anybody there?* ◊ *Say hello to Liz for me.* ◊ *They exchanged hellos* (= said hello to each other) *and forced smiles.* **2** (*BrE*) used to show that you are surprised by sth: *Hello, hello, what's going on here?*

MORE ABOUT
greetings

Hello is the most usual word and is used in all situations, including answering the telephone.

Hi is more informal and is now very common.

How are you? or **How are you doing?** (very informal) often follow **Hello** and **Hi**: *'Hello, Mark.' 'Oh, hi, Kathy! How are you?'*

Good morning is often used by members of a family or people who work together when they see each other for the first time in the day. It can also be used in formal situations and on the telephone. In informal speech, people may just say **Morning**.

Good afternoon and **Good evening** are much less common. **Good night** is not used to greet somebody, but only to say goodbye late in the evening or when you are going to bed.

If you are meeting someone for the first time, you can say **Pleased to meet you** or **Nice to meet you** (less formal). Some people use **How do you do?** in formal situations. The correct reply to this is **How do you do?**

---

hel·luva → HELL

helm /helm/ *noun* a handle or wheel used for steering a boat or ship—compare TILLER **IDM** **at the ˈhelm 1** in charge of an organization, project, etc. **2** steering a boat or ship **take the ˈhelm 1** to take charge of an organization, project, etc. **2** to begin steering a boat or ship

hel·met /ˈhelmɪt/ *noun* a type of hard hat that protects the head, worn, for example, by a police officer, a soldier or a person playing some sports—see also CRASH HEL-MET—picture at HOCKEY, BICYCLE

hel·met·ed /ˈhelmɪtɪd/ *adj.* [only before noun] wearing a helmet

helms·man /ˈhelmzmən/ *noun* (*pl.* **-men** /-mən/) a person who steers a boat or ship

help /help/ *verb, noun*
■ *verb*
MAKE EASIER/BETTER **1** ~ (**sb**) (**with sth**) | ~ (**sb**) (**in doing sth**) to make it easier or possible for sb to do sth by doing sth for them or by giving them sth that they need: [V] *Help, I'm stuck!* ◊ *He always helps with the housework.* ◊ *I need contacts that could help in finding a job.* ◊ [VN] *We must all try and help each other.* ◊ *Jo will help us with some of the organization.* ◊ [VN to inf] *The college's aim is to help students (to) achieve their aspirations.* ◊ *This charity*

æ	ɑː	e	ɜː	ə	ɪ	iː	i	ɒ	ɔː	ʌ	ʊ	u	uː
cat	father	ten	bird	about	sit	see	many	got	saw	cup	put	actual	too
								(BrE)					

aims to help people (to) help themselves. ◊ [VNinf] *Come and help me lift this box.* ◊ [Vtoinf] *She helped (to) organize the party.* **HELP** In verb patterns with a **to** infinitive, the 'to' is often left out, especially in informal or spoken English. **2** to improve a situation; to make it easier for sth to happen: [V] *It helped being able to talk about it.* ◊ [VN] *It doesn't really help matters knowing that everyone is talking about us.* ◊ [Vtoinf] *This should help (to) reduce the pain.*

SB TO MOVE | **3** [VN+*adv.* / *prep.*] to help sb move by letting them lean on you, guiding them, etc: *She helped him to his feet.* ◊ *We were helped ashore by local people.*

GIVE FOOD/DRINK | **4** [VN] ~ **yourself/sb (to sth)** to give yourself/sb food, drinks, etc: *If you want another drink, just help yourself.* ◊ *Can I help you to some more salad?*

STEAL | **5** [VN] ~ **yourself to sth** (*informal, disapproving*) to take sth without permission SYN STEAL: *He'd been helping himself to the money in the cash register.*

IDM **sb can (not) help (doing) sth** | **sb can not help but do sth** used to say that it is impossible to prevent or avoid sth: *I can't help thinking he knows more than he has told us.* ◊ *She couldn't help but wonder what he was thinking.* ◊ *It couldn't be helped* (= there was no way of avoiding it and we must accept it). ◊ *I always end up having an argument with her, I don't know why, I just can't help it.* ◊ *I couldn't help it if the bus was late* (= it wasn't my fault). ◊ *She burst out laughing—she couldn't help herself* (= couldn't stop herself). **give/lend a ,helping 'hand** to help sb **God/Heaven 'help sb** (*spoken*) used to say that you are afraid sb will be in danger or that sth bad will happen to them: *God help us if this doesn't work.* **HELP** Some people find this use offensive. **so 'help me (God)** used to swear that what you are saying is true, especially in a court of law

PHRV **,help sb 'off/'on with sth** to help sb put on/take off a piece of clothing: *Let me help you off with your coat.* **,help 'out** | **,help sb↔'out** to help sb, especially in a difficult situation: *He's always willing to help out.* ◊ *When I bought the house, my sister helped me out with a loan.*

■ *noun*

MAKING EASIER/BETTER | **1** [U] ~ **(with sth)** the act of helping sb to do sth: *Thank you for all your help.* ◊ *Do you need any help with that?* ◊ *Can I be of any help to you?* ◊ *None of this would have been possible without their help.* ◊ *She stopped smoking with the help of her family and friends.*

ADVICE/MONEY | **2** [U] ~ **(with sth)** advice, money, etc. that is given to sb in order to solve their problems: *to seek financial/legal/medical help* ◊ *The organization offers practical help in dealing with paperwork.* ◊ *You should qualify for help with the costs of running a car.* ◊ *a help key/screen* (= a function on a computer that provides information on how to use the computer)

BEING USEFUL | **3** [U] the fact of being useful: *The map wasn't much help.* ◊ *With the help of a ladder, neighbours were able to rescue the children from the blaze.* ◊ *Just shouting at him isn't going to be a lot of help.*

FOR SB IN DANGER | **4** [U] the act of helping sb who is in danger: *Quick, get help!* ◊ *She screamed for help.*

PERSON/THING | **5** [sing.] **a** ~ **(to sb)** a person or thing that helps sb: *She was more of a hindrance than a help.* ◊ *Your advice was a big help.* ◊ (*ironic*) *You're a great help, I must say!*

CLEANER | **6** [C] (*old-fashioned*) a person who is employed by sb to clean their house, etc: *The help hasn't come this morning.*—see also HOME HELP

IDM **there is no 'help for it** (*especially BrE*) it is not possible to avoid doing sth that may harm sb in some way: *There's no help for it. We shall have to call the police.*

'help desk *noun* a service, usually in a business company, that gives people information and help, especially if they are having problems with a computer

help·er /ˈhelpə(r)/ *noun* a person who helps sb to do sth: *a willing helper*

help·ful /ˈhelpfl/ *adj.* **1** ~ **(for sb) (to do sth)** | ~ **(in doing sth)** | ~ **(to sb)** useful and able to improve a particular situation: *helpful advice/information/suggestions* ◊ *Sorry I can't be more helpful.* ◊ *It would be helpful for me to see*

the damage for myself. ◊ *Role-play is helpful in developing communication skills.* ◊ *The booklet should be very helpful to parents of disabled children.* **2** (*of a person*) willing to help sb: *I called the police but they weren't very helpful.* ◊ *The staff couldn't have been more helpful.* OPP UNHELPFUL ▶ **help·ful·ly** /-fəli/ *adv.*: *She helpfully suggested that I try the local library.* **help·ful·ness** *noun* [U]

help·ing /ˈhelpɪŋ/ *noun* ~ **(of sth)** an amount of food given to sb at a meal: *a small/generous helping* ◊ *We all had a second helping of pie.*

help·less /ˈhelpləs/ *adj.* **1** unable to take care of yourself or do things without the help of other people: *the helpless victims of war* ◊ *a helpless gesture/look* ◊ *He lay helpless on the floor.* ◊ *It's natural to feel helpless against such abuse.* ◊ *The worst part is being helpless to change anything.* **2** ~ **(with sth)** unable to control a strong feeling: *helpless panic/rage* ◊ *The audience was helpless with laughter.* ▶ **help·less·ly** *adv.*: *They watched helplessly as their home went up in flames.* **help·less·ness** *noun* [U]: *a feeling/sense of helplessness*

help·line /ˈhelplaɪn/ *noun* (*BrE*) a telephone service that provides advice and information about particular problems

help·mate /ˈhelpmeɪt/ (also **help·meet** /ˈhelpmiːt/) *noun* (*formal* or *literary*) a helpful partner, especially a wife

helter-skelter /ˌheltə ˈskeltə(r); *AmE* ˌheltər/ *noun, adj.*
■ *noun* (*BrE*) a tall tower at a FAIRGROUND that has a path twisting around the outside of it from the top to the bottom for people to slide down
■ *adj.* [only before noun] done in a hurry and in a way that lacks organization: *a helter-skelter dash to meet the deadline* ▶ **helter-skelter** *adv.*

hem /hem/ *noun, verb*
■ *noun* the edge of a piece of fabric that has been folded over and sewn, especially on a piece of clothing: *to take up the hem of a dress* (= to make the dress shorter)—picture at SEW

■ *verb* (-mm-) [VN] to make a hem on sth: *to hem a skirt* IDM **,hem and 'haw** (*AmE*) = HUM AND HAW PHR V **,hem sb/sth↔'in** to surround sb/sth so that they cannot move or grow easily SYN HEDGE SB/STH IN: *The village is hemmed in on all sides by mountains.* ◊ (*figurative*) *She felt hemmed in by all their petty rules and regulations.*

'he-man *noun* (*pl.* **-men** /-men/) (often *humorous*) a strong man with big muscles, especially one who likes to show other people how strong he is

hema·tol·ogy (*AmE*) = HAEMATOLOGY

hemi·sphere /'hemɪsfɪə(r); *AmE* -sfɪr/ *noun* **1** one half of the earth, especially the half above or below the EQUATOR: *the northern/southern hemisphere* **2** (*anatomy*) either half of the brain: *the left/right cerebral hemisphere* **3** one half of a SPHERE (= a round solid object)

hemi·spher·ic·al /,hemɪ'sferɪkl/ *adj.* shaped like a hemisphere

hem·line /'hemlaɪn/ *noun* the bottom edge of a dress or skirt; the length of a dress or skirt: *Shorter hemlines are back in this season.*

hem·lock /'hemlɒk; *AmE* -lɑːk/ *noun* **1** [U, C] a poisonous plant with a mass of small white flowers growing at the end of a stem that is covered in spots **2** [U] poison made from hemlock

hemo- ⇨ HAEMO-

hemp /hemp/ *noun* [U] a plant which is used for making rope and fabric, and also to make the drug CANNABIS

hen /hen/ *noun* **1** a female chicken, often kept for its eggs or meat: *a small flock of laying hens* ◊ *battery hens* **2** (especially in compounds) any female bird: *a hen pheasant*—compare COCK—see also MOORHEN

hence /hens/ *adv.* (*formal*) for this reason: *We suspect they are trying to hide something, hence the need for an independent inquiry.* IDM **six days, weeks, etc. 'hence** (*formal*) six days, etc. from now: *The true consequences will only be known several years hence.*

hence·forth /,hens'fɔːθ; *AmE* -'fɔːrθ/ (also **hence·for·ward** /,hens'fɔːwəd; *AmE* -'fɔːrwərd/) *adv.* (*formal*) starting from a particular time and at all times in the future: *Friday 31 July 1925 henceforth became known as 'Red Friday'.*

hench·man /'hentʃmən/ *noun* (*pl.* **-men** /-mən/) a faithful supporter of a powerful person, for example a political leader or criminal, who is prepared to use violence or become involved in illegal activities to help that person: *his ruthless henchmen*

henna /'henə/ *noun* [U] a reddish-brown DYE (= a substance used to change the colour of sth), used especially on the hair and skin

'hen party (also **'hen night**) *noun* (*BrE, informal*) a party for women only, especially one held for a woman who will soon get married—compare STAG NIGHT

hen·pecked /'henpekt/ *adj.* (*informal*) a man who people say is henpecked has a wife who is always telling him what to do, and is too weak to disagree with her

hepa·titis /,hepə'taɪtɪs/ *noun* [U] a serious disease of the LIVER. There are three main forms: **hepatitis A** (the least serious, caused by infected food), **hepatitis B** and **hepatitis C** (both very serious and caused by infected blood).

hepta·gon /'heptəgən; *AmE* -gɑːn/ *noun* (*geometry*) a flat shape with seven straight sides and seven angles ▶ **hept·agon·al** /hep'tægənl/ *adj.*

hept·ath·lon /hep'tæθlən/ *noun* [sing., U] a sporting event, especially one for women, in which people compete in seven different sports—compare BIATHLON, DECATHLON, PENTATHLON, TRIATHLON

her /hə(r); ɜː(r); ə(r); *strong form* hɜː(r)/ *pron.*, *det.*

■ *pron.* used as the object of a verb or after a preposition to refer to a woman or girl who has already been mentioned or is easily identified: *We're going to call her Sophie.* ◊ *Please give her my regards.* ◊ *The manager will be free soon—you can wait for her here.* ◊ *That must be her now.*—compare SHE

■ *det.* (the possessive form of *she*) of or belonging to a woman or girl who has already been mentioned or is easily identified: *Meg loves her job.* ◊ *She broke her leg skiing.*—see also HERS

her·ald /'herəld/ *verb*, *noun*

■ *verb* [VN] (*written*) **1** to be a sign that sth is going to happen: *These talks could herald a new era of peace* **2** ~ **sb/sth (as sth)** [often passive] to say in public that sb/sth is good or important: *The report is being heralded as a blueprint for the future of transport.*

■ *noun* **1** something that shows that sth else is going to happen soon: *The government claims that the fall in unemployment is the herald of economic recovery.* **2** (in the past) a person who carried messages from a ruler

her·ald·ry /'herəldri/ *noun* [U] the study of the COATS OF ARMS and the history of old families ▶ **her·al·dic** /he'rældɪk/ *adj.*

herb /hɜːb; *AmE* hɜːrb/ *noun* **1** a plant whose leaves, flowers or seeds are used to flavour food, in medicines or for their pleasant smell. PARSLEY, MINT and OREGANO are all herbs: *a herb garden* ◊ (*AmE*) *an herb garden* **2** (*technical*) a plant with a soft stem that dies down after flowering ▶ **herb·al** /'hɜːbl; *AmE* 'ɜːrbl; 'hɜːrbl/ *adj.*: *herbal medicine/remedies* ◊ *herbal tea*

herb·aceous /hɜː'beɪʃəs; *AmE* ɜːr'b-; hɜːr'b-/ *adj.* (*technical*) connected with plants that have soft stems: *a herbaceous plant*

her,baceous 'border *noun* a piece of ground in a garden/yard containing plants that produce flowers every year without being replaced

herb·age /'hɜːbɪdʒ; *AmE* 'ɜːrb-; 'hɜːrb-/ *noun* [U] (*technical*) plants in general, especially grass that is grown for cows, etc. to eat

herb·al /'hɜːbl; *AmE* 'ɜːrbl; 'hɜːrbl/ *noun* a book about HERBS, especially those used in medicines

herb·al·ist /'hɜːbəlɪst; *AmE* 'ɜːrb-; 'hɜːrb-/ *noun* a person who grows, sells or uses HERBS for medical purposes

herbi·cide /'hɜːbɪsaɪd; *AmE* 'ɜːrb-; 'hɜːrb-/ *noun* a chemical that is poisonous to plants, used to kill plants that are growing where they are not wanted—see also INSECTICIDE, PESTICIDE

herbi·vore /'hɜːbɪvɔː(r); *AmE* 'ɜːrb-; 'hɜːrb-/ *noun* any animal that eats only plants—compare CARNIVORE, INSECTIVORE, OMNIVORE, VEGETARIAN ▶ **herb·iv·or·ous** /hɜː'bɪvərəs; *AmE* ɜːr'b-; hɜːr'b-/ *adj.*: *herbivorous dinosaurs*

Her·cu·lean /,hɜːkju'liːən; *AmE* ,hɜːrk-/ *adj.* [usually before noun] needing a lot of strength, determination or effort: *a Herculean task* ORIGIN From the Greek myth in which **Hercules** proved his courage and strength by completing twelve very difficult tasks ('the Labours of Hercules').

herd /hɜːd; *AmE* hɜːrd/ *noun*, *verb*

■ *noun* **1** a group of animals of the same type that live and feed together: *a herd of cows/deer/elephants* ◊ *a beef/dairy herd*—compare FLOCK **2** (usually *disapproving*) a large group of people of the same type: *She pushed her way through a herd of lunchtime drinkers.* ◊ *the* **common herd** (= ordinary people) ◊ *If you feel so strongly, why* **follow the herd** (= do and think the same as everyone else)? IDM see RIDE *v.*

■ *verb* **1** [+adv. / prep.] to move or make sb/sth move in a particular direction: [V] *We all herded on to the bus.* ◊ [VN] *They were herded together into trucks and driven away.* **2** [VN] to make animals move together as a group: *a shepherd herding his flock*

'herd instinct *noun* [sing.] the natural tendency in people or animals to behave or think like other people or animals

herds·man /'hɜːdzmən; *AmE* 'hɜːrd-/ *noun* (*pl.* **-men** /-mən/) a man whose job is to take care of a group of animals, such as cows

here /hɪə(r); *AmE* hɪr/ *adv.*, *exclamation*

■ *adv.* **1** used after a verb or preposition to mean 'in, at or to this position or place': *I live here.* ◊ *Put the box here.* ◊ *Let's get out of here.* ◊ *Come over here.* **2** now; at this point: *The countdown to Christmas starts here.* ◊ *Here the speaker paused to have a drink.* **3** (especially *spoken*) used when you are giving or showing sth to sb: *Here's the*

b	d	f	g	h	k	l	m	n	p	r
bad	did	fall	get	hat	cat	leg	man	now	pen	red

H

money I promised you. ◊ *Here's a dish that is simple and quick to make.* ◊ *Here is your opportunity.* ◊ **Here comes the bus.** ◊ *I can't find my keys. Oh,* **here they are.** ◊ *Here* **we are** (= we've arrived). **4 ~ to do sth** used to show your role in a situation: *I'm here to help you.* **5** (used after a noun, for emphasis): *My friend here saw it happen.* **IDM** **here and 'there** in various places: *Papers were scattered here and there on the floor.* **here 'goes** (*spoken*) used when you are telling people that you are just going to do sth exciting, dangerous, etc. **here's to sb/sth** used to wish sb health or success, as you lift a glass and drink a TOAST: *Here's to your future happiness!* **here, there and 'everywhere** in many different places; all around **here we 'go** (*spoken*) said when sth is starting to happen: *'Here we go,' thought Fred, 'she's sure to say something.'* **here we go a'gain** (*spoken*) said when sth is starting to happen again, especially sth bad **here you 'are** (*spoken*) used when you are giving sth to sb: *Here you are. This is what you were asking for.* **here you 'go** (*spoken*) used when you are giving sth to sb: *Here you go. Four copies, is that right?* **neither 'here nor 'there** not important **SYN** IRRELEVANT: *What might have happened is neither here nor there.*
■ *exclamation* **1** (*BrE*) used to attract sb's attention: *Here, where are you going with that ladder?* **2** used when offering sth to sb: *Here, let me carry that for you.*

here·abouts /ˌhɪərəˈbaʊts; *AmE* ˌhɪr-/ (*AmE* also **here·about**) *adv.* near this place: *There aren't many houses hereabouts.*

here·after /ˌhɪərˈɑːftə(r); *AmE* ˌhɪrˈæf-/ *adv.* **1** (also **here·in·after**) (in legal documents, etc.) in the rest of this document **2** (*formal*) from this time; in future—compare THEREAFTER **3** (*formal*) after death: *Do you believe in a life hereafter?*

the here·after /ˌhɪərˈɑːftə(r); *AmE* ˌhɪrˈæf-/ *noun* [sing.] a life believed to begin after death

here·by /ˌhɪəˈbaɪ; *AmE* ˌhɪrˈbaɪ/ *adv.* (in legal documents, etc.) as a result of this statement, and in a way that makes sth legal

her·edi·tary /həˈredɪtri; *AmE* -teri/ *adj.* **1** (especially of illnesses) given to a child by its parents before it is born: *a hereditary disease/condition/problem* ◊ *Epilepsy is hereditary in her family.* **2** that is legally given to sb's child, when that person dies: *a hereditary title/monarchy* **3** holding a rank or title that is hereditary: *hereditary peers/rulers*

her·ed·ity /həˈredəti/ *noun* [U] the process by which mental and physical characteristics are passed by parents to their children; these characteristics in a particular person: *the debate over the effects of heredity and environment*

here·in /ˌhɪərˈɪn; *AmE* ˌhɪrˈɪn/ *adv.* (*formal* or *law*) in this place, document, statement or fact: *Neither party is willing to compromise and herein lies the problem.*

here·in·after /ˌhɪərɪnˈɑːftə(r); *AmE* ˌhɪrɪnˈæf-/ *adv.* (*law*) = HEREAFTER

here·of /ˌhɪərˈɒv; *AmE* ˌhɪrˈʌv; -ˈɑːv/ *adv.* (*law*) of this: *a period of 12 months from the date hereof* (= the date of this document)

her·esy /ˈherəsi/ *noun* [U, C] (*pl.* **-ies**) **1** a belief or an opinion that is against the principles of a particular religion; the fact of holding such beliefs: *He was burned at the stake for heresy.* ◊ *the heresies of the early Protestants* **2** a belief or an opinion that disagrees strongly with what most people believe: *The idea is heresy to most employees of the firm.*

her·et·ic /ˈherətɪk/ *noun* a person who is guilty of heresy ▶ **her·et·ical** /həˈretɪkl/ *adj.*: *heretical beliefs*

here·to /ˌhɪəˈtuː; *AmE* ˌhɪrˈtuː/ *adv.* (*law*) to this

here·to·fore /ˌhɪətuˈfɔː(r); *AmE* ˌhɪrt-/ *adv.* (*formal*) before this time

here·with /ˌhɪəˈwɪð; -ˈwɪθ; *AmE* ˌhɪrˈw-/ *adv.* (*written*) with this letter, book or document: *I enclose herewith a copy of the policy.*

heri·tage /ˈherɪtɪdʒ/ *noun* [usually sing.] the history, traditions and qualities that a country or society has had for many years and that are considered an important

part of its character: *Spain's rich cultural heritage* ◊ *The building is part of our national heritage.*

herm·aph·ro·dite /hɜːˈmæfrədaɪt; *AmE* hɜːrˈm-/ *noun* a person, an animal or a flower that has both male and female sexual organs or characteristics ▶ **herm·aph·ro·dite** *adj.*

her·met·ic /hɜːˈmetɪk; *AmE* hɜːrˈm-/ *adj.* **1** (*technical*) tightly closed so that no air can escape or enter **SYN** AIRTIGHT **2** (*formal, disapproving*) closed and difficult to become a part of: *the strange, hermetic world of the theatre* ▶ **her·met·ic·al·ly** /-kli/ *adv.*: *a hermetically sealed container*

her·mit /ˈhɜːmɪt; *AmE* ˈhɜːrmɪt/ *noun* a person who, usually for religious reasons, lives a very simple life alone and does not meet or talk to other people.

her·mit·age /ˈhɜːmɪtɪdʒ; *AmE* ˈhɜːrm-/ *noun* a place where a hermit lives or lived

'hermit crab *noun* a CRAB (= a sea creature with eight legs and, usually, a hard shell) that has no shell of its own and has to use the empty shells of other sea creatures

her·nia /ˈhɜːniə; *AmE* ˈhɜːrniə/ *noun* [C, U] a medical condition in which part of an organ is pushed through a weak part of the body wall

hero /ˈhɪərəʊ; *AmE* ˈhɪroʊ; ˈhiː-/ *noun* (*pl.* **-oes**) **1** a person, especially a man, who is admired by many people for doing sth brave or good: *a war hero* (= sb who was very brave during a war) ◊ *The Olympic team were given a hero's welcome on their return home.* ◊ *one of the country's national heroes* **2** the main male character in a story, novel, film/movie etc.: *The hero of the novel is a ten-year old boy.* **3** a person, especially a man, that you admire because of a particular quality or skill that they have: *my childhood hero* **4** (*AmE*) = SUBMARINE (2)—see also HEROINE

hero·ic /həˈrəʊɪk; *AmE* -ˈroʊ-/ *adj.* **1** showing extreme courage and admired by many people: *a heroic figure* ◊ *Rescuers made heroic efforts to save the crew.* **2** showing great determination to succeed or to achieve sth, especially sth difficult: *We watched our team's heroic struggle to win back the cup.* **3** that is about or involves a hero: *a heroic story/poem* ◊ *heroic deeds/myths* **4** very large or great: *This was foolishness on a heroic scale.* ▶ **hero·ic·al·ly** /-kli/ *adv.*

hero·ics /həˈrəʊɪks; *AmE* -ˈroʊ-/ *noun* [pl.] **1** (*disapproving*) talk or behaviour that is too brave or dramatic for a particular situation: *Remember, no heroics, we just go in there and do our job.* **2** actions that are brave and determined: *Thanks to Bateman's heroics in the second half, the team won 2–0.*

her·oin /ˈherəʊɪn; *AmE* -roʊ-/ *noun* [U] a powerful illegal drug made from MORPHINE, that some people take for pleasure and can become ADDICTED to: *a heroin addict*

hero·ine /ˈherəʊɪn; *AmE* -roʊ-/ *noun* **1** a girl or woman who is admired by many for doing sth brave or good: *the heroines of the revolution* **2** the main female character in a story, novel, film/movie, etc: *The heroine is played by Demi Moore.* **3** a woman that you admire because of a particular quality or skill that she has: *Madonna was her teenage heroine.*

hero·ism /ˈherəʊɪzəm; *AmE* -roʊ-/ *noun* [U] very great courage

heron /ˈherən/ *noun* a large bird with a long neck and long legs, that lives near water

'hero worship *noun* [U] great admiration for sb because you think they are extremely beautiful, intelligent, etc.

'hero-worship *verb* (**-pp-**) [VN] to admire sb very much because you think they are extremely beautiful, intelligent, etc.

her·pes /ˈhɜːpiːz; *AmE* ˈhɜːrp-/ *noun* [U] an infectious disease that causes painful spots on the skin, especially on the face and sexual organs

her·ring /ˈherɪŋ/ *noun* (*pl.* **her·ring** or **her·rings**) [U, C] a N Atlantic fish that swims in very large groups and is used for food: *shoals of herring* ◊ *fresh herring fillets* ◊ *pickled herrings*—see also RED HERRING

s	t	v	z	ʃ	ʒ	tʃ	dʒ	θ	ð	ŋ
see	tea	van	zoo	shoe	vision	chain	jam	thin	this	sing

her·ring·bone /ˈherɪŋbəʊn; *AmE* -boʊn/ *noun* [U] a pattern used, for example, in fabric consisting of lines of V shapes that are parallel to each other

'**herring gull** *noun* a large N Atlantic bird of the GULL family, with black tips to its wings

hers /hɜːz; *AmE* hɜːrz/ *pron.* of or belonging to her: *His eyes met hers.* ◇ *The choice was hers.* ◇ *a friend of hers*

her·self /hɜːˈself; *weak form* həˈself; *AmE* hɜːrˈs-; hərˈs-/ *pron.* **1** (the reflexive form of *she*) used when the woman or girl who performs an action is also affected by it: *She hurt herself.* ◇ *She must be very proud of herself.* **2** used to emphasize the female subject or object of a sentence: *She told me the news herself.* ◇ *Jane herself was at the meeting.* **IDM** **be, seem, etc. her'self** (of a woman or girl) to be in a normal state of health or happiness; not influenced by other people: *She didn't seem quite herself this morning.* ◇ *She needed space to be herself.* **(all) by her'self 1** alone; with anyone else: *She lives by herself.* **2** without help: *She runs the business by herself.* **(all) to her'self** for only her to have or use: *She wants a room all to herself.*

hertz /hɜːts; *AmE* hɜːrts/ *noun* (*pl.* **hertz**) (*abbr.* **Hz**) a unit for measuring the FREQUENCY of sound waves

he's *short form* **1** /hiːz; hiz; ɪz/ he is **2** /hiːz/ he has

hesi·tancy /ˈhezɪtənsi/ *noun* [U] the state or quality of being slow or uncertain in doing or saying sth: *I noticed a certain hesitancy in his voice.*

hesi·tant /ˈhezɪtənt/ *adj.* slow to speak or act because you feel uncertain, embarrassed or unwilling: *a hesitant smile / reply* ◇ *She's hesitant about signing the contract.* ◇ *the baby's first few hesitant steps* ◇ *Doctors are hesitant to comment on the new treatment.* ▶ **hesi·tant·ly** *adv.*

hesi·tate /ˈhezɪteɪt/ *verb* **1** ~ **(about/over sth)** to be slow to speak or act because you feel uncertain or nervous: [V] *She hesitated before replying.* ◇ *I didn't hesitate for a moment about taking the job.* [also V speech] **2** [V to inf] to be worried about doing sth, especially because you are not sure that it is right or appropriate: *Please do not hesitate to contact me if you have any queries.* ▶ **hesi·ta·tion** /ˌhezɪˈteɪʃn/ *noun* [U, C]: *She agreed without the slightest hesitation.* ◇ *We were trained to speak fluently and without unnecessary hesitations.*

hes·sian /ˈhesiən; *AmE* ˈheʃn/ (*especially BrE*) (*AmE* usually **bur·lap**) *noun* [U] a strong rough brown fabric, used especially for making SACKS

hetero- /ˈhetərəʊ; *AmE* -roʊ/ *combining form* (in nouns, adjectives and adverbs) other; different: *heterogeneous* ◇ *heterosexual*—compare HOMO-

het·ero·dox /ˈhetərədɒks; *AmE* -dɑːks/ *adj.* (*formal*) not following the usual or accepted beliefs and opinions— compare ORTHODOX, UNORTHODOX ▶ **het·ero·doxy** *noun* [U, C] (*pl.* **-ies**)

het·ero·ge·neous /ˌhetərəˈdʒiːniəs/ *adj.* (*formal*) consisting of many different kinds of people or things: *the heterogeneous population of the United States* **OPP** HOMOGENEOUS ▶ **het·ero·gen·eity** /-dʒəˈniːəti/ *noun* [U]

het·ero·sex·ual /ˌhetərəˈsekʃuəl/ *noun* a person who is sexually attracted to people of the opposite sex—compare BISEXUAL, HOMOSEXUAL ▶ **het·ero·sex·ual** *adj.*: *a heterosexual relationship* **het·ero·sexu·al·ity** /ˌhetərəˌsekʃuˈæləti/ *noun* [U]

het up /ˌhet ˈʌp/ *adj.* [not before noun] ~ **(about/over sth)** (*BrE, informal*) anxious, excited or slightly angry: *What are you getting so het up about?*

heur·is·tic /hjuˈrɪstɪk/ *adj.* (*formal*) heuristic teaching or education encourages you to learn by discovering things for yourself

heur·is·tics /hjuˈrɪstɪks/ *noun* [U] (*formal*) a method of solving problems by finding practical ways of dealing with them, learning from past experience

hew /hjuː/ *verb* (**hewed, hewed** or **hewn** /hjuːn/) [VN] **1** (*old-fashioned*) to cut sth large with a tool: *to hew wood / rocks* **2** (*written*) to make or shape sth large by cutting: *roughly hewn timber frames* ◇ *The statues were hewn out of solid rock.*

hex /heks/ *verb* [VN] (*AmE*) to use magic powers in order to harm sb ▶ **hex** *noun*: *to put a hex on sb*—compare CURSE

hexa- /ˈheksə/ (also **hex-**) *combining form* (in nouns, adjectives and adverbs) six; having six: *hexagon* ◇ *hexameter*

hexa·gon /ˈheksəgən; *AmE* -gɑːn/ *noun* (*geometry*) a flat shape with six straight sides and six angles ▶ **hex·agon·al** /heksˈægənl/ *adj.*

hex·am·eter /hekˈsæmɪtə(r)/ *noun* (*technical*) a line of poetry with six stressed syllables

hey /heɪ/ *exclamation* (*informal*) **1** used to attract sb's attention or to express interest, surprise or anger: *Hey, can I just ask you something?* ◇ *Hey, leave my things alone!* **2** used to show that you do not really care about sth or that you think it is not important: *That's the third time I've been late this week - but hey! - who's counting?* **IDM** **hey 'presto** (*BrE*) (*AmE* **presto**) people sometimes say **hey presto** when they have just done sth so quickly and easily that it seems to have been done by magic: *You just press the button and, hey presto, a perfect cup of coffee!*

hey·day /ˈheɪdeɪ/ *noun* [usually sing.] the time when sb/sth had most power or success, or was most popular: *In its heyday, the company ran trains every fifteen minutes.* ◇ *a fine example from the heyday of Italian cinema* ◇ *a picture of Brigitte Bardot in her heyday*

HGV /ˌeɪtʃ dʒiː ˈviː/ *abbr.* (*BrE*) heavy goods vehicle (a large vehicle such as a lorry / truck): *You need an HGV licence for this job.*

hi /haɪ/ *exclamation* (*informal*) used as a greeting: *Hi guys!* ◇ *Hi, there! How're you doing?*

hia·tus /haɪˈeɪtəs/ *noun* [sing.] (*formal*) **1** a pause in activity when nothing happens: *After a five-month hiatus, the talks resumed.* **2** a space, especially in a piece of writing or in a speech, where sth is missing

hi·ber·nate /ˈhaɪbəneɪt; *AmE* -bərn-/ *verb* [V] (of animals) to spend the winter in a state like deep sleep ▶ **hi·ber·na·tion** /ˌhaɪbəˈneɪʃn; *AmE* -bərˈn-/ *noun* [U]

hi·bis·cus /hɪˈbɪskəs; haɪ-/ *noun* [U, C] (*pl.* **hi·bis·cus**) a tropical plant or bush with large brightly coloured flowers

hic·cup (also **hic·cough**) /ˈhɪkʌp/ *noun, verb*

■ *noun* **1** [C] a sharp, usually repeated, sound made in the throat, that is caused by a sudden movement of the DIAPHRAGM and that you cannot control: *She gave a loud hiccup.* **2** (**the**) **hiccups** [pl.] a series of hiccups: *I ate too quickly and got hiccups.* ◇ *He had the hiccups.* **3** (*informal*) a small problem or temporary delay: *There was a slight hiccup in the timetable.*

■ *verb* [V] to have hiccups or a single hiccup

hick /hɪk/ *noun* (*informal, disapproving, especially AmE*) a person from the country who is considered to be stupid and to have little experience of life: *I was just a hick from Texas then.* ▶ **hick** *adj.*: *a hick town*

hickey /ˈhɪki/ *noun* (*AmE*) = LOVE BITE

hick·ory /ˈhɪkəri/ *noun* [U] the hard wood of the N American **hickory tree**

'**hidden a'genda** *noun* (*disapproving*) the secret intention behind what sb says or does: *There are fears of a hidden agenda behind this new proposal.*

hide /haɪd/ *verb, noun*

■ *verb* (**hid** /hɪd/ **hid·den** /ˈhɪdn/) **1** [VN] to put or keep sb/sth in a place where they / it cannot be seen or found: *He hid the letter in a drawer.* ◇ *I keep my private papers hidden.* ◇ *They hid me from the police in their attic.* **2** to go somewhere where you hope you will not be seen or found: [V] *Quick, hide!* ◇ *I hid under the bed.* ◇ (*figurative*) *He hid behind a false identity.* ◇ [VN] *She hides herself away in her office all day.* **3** [VN] to cover sth so that it cannot be seen: *He hid his face in his hands.* ◇ *The house was hidden by trees.* ◇ *No amount of make-up could hide her age.* **4** [VN] to keep sth secret, especially your feelings: *She struggled to hide her disappointment.* ◇ *I have never tried to hide the truth about my past.* ◇ *They claim that they have nothing to hide* (= there was nothing wrong or illegal about what they did)*.* ◇ *She felt sure the letter had some hidden meaning.* **IDM** **hide your light under a 'bushel** (*BrE*) to not let people know that you are good at sth—more at MULTITUDE, HEAD *n.*

æ	ɑː	e	ɜː	ə	ɪ	iː	i	ɒ	ɔː	ʌ	ʊ	u	uː
cat	father	ten	bird	about	sit	see	many	got	saw	cup	put	actual	too
								(BrE)					

H

H

■ *noun* **1** [C] (*BrE*) a place from which people can watch wild animals or birds, without being seen by them **2** [C, U] an animal's skin, especially when it is bought or sold or used for leather: *boots made from buffalo hide* **3** (*informal, especially AmE*) used to refer to sb's life or safety when they are in a difficult situation: *All he's worried about is his own hide* (= himself). ◊ *She'd do anything to save her own hide.* [IDM] **have/tan sb's 'hide** (*old-fashioned, informal* or *humorous*) to punish sb severely **not see hide nor 'hair of sb/sth** (*spoken*) not to see sb/sth for some time: *I haven't seen hide nor hair of her for a month.*

hide-and-seek /ˌhaɪd n 'siːk/ *noun* [U] a children's game in which one player covers his or her eyes while the other players hide, and then tries to find them

hide·away /'haɪdəweɪ/ *noun* a place where you can go to hide or to be alone

hide·bound /'haɪdbaʊnd/ *adj.* (*disapproving*) having old-fashioned ideas, rather than accepting new ways of thinking [SYN] NARROW-MINDED

hid·eous /'hɪdiəs/ *adj.* very ugly or unpleasant: *a hideous face/building/dress* ◊ *Their new colour scheme is hideous!* ◊ *a hideous crime* ◊ *The whole experience had been like some hideous nightmare.* ► **hid·eous·ly** *adv.*: *His face was hideously deformed.*

hide·out /'haɪdaʊt/ *noun* a place where sb goes when they do not want anyone to find them

hid·ing /'haɪdɪŋ/ *noun* **1** [U] the state of being hidden: *After the trial, she had to go into hiding for several weeks.* ◊ *He only came out of hiding ten years after the war was over.* ◊ *We spent months in hiding.* **2** [sing.] (*informal, especially BrE*) a physical punishment, usually involving being hit hard many times [SYN] BEATING: *to give sb/get a (good) hiding* ◊ (*figurative*) *The team got a hiding in their last game.* [IDM] **on a ˌhiding to 'nothing** (*BrE, informal*) having no chance of success

'hiding place *noun* a place where sb/sth can be hidden

hier·arch·ic·al /ˌhaɪə'rɑːkɪkl; *AmE* -'rɑːrk-/ *adj.* arranged in a hierarchy: *a hierarchical society/structure/organization*

hier·archy /'haɪərɑːki; *AmE* -rɑːrki/ *noun* (*pl.* **-ies**) **1** [C, U] a system, especially in a society or an organization, in which people are organized into different levels of importance from highest to lowest: *the social/political hierarchy* ◊ *She's high up in the management hierarchy.* **2** [C+sing./pl. *v.*] the group of people in control of a large organization or institution **3** [C] (*formal*) a system that ideas or beliefs can be arranged into: *a hierarchy of needs*

hiero·glyph /'haɪərəglɪf/ *noun* a picture or symbol of an object, representing a word, syllable or sound, especially as used in ancient Egyptian and other writing systems ► **hiero·glyph·ic** /ˌhaɪərə'glɪfɪk/ *adj.*

hiero·glyph·ics /ˌhaɪərə'glɪfɪks/ *noun* [pl.] writing that uses hieroglyphs

hi-fi /'haɪ faɪ/ *noun* [C, U] equipment for playing recorded music that produces high quality STEREO sound ► **hi-fi** *adj.* [usually before noun]: *a hi-fi system*

higgledy-piggledy /ˌhɪgldi 'pɪgldi/ *adv.* (*informal*) in an untidy way that lacks any order: *Files were strewn higgledy-piggledy over the floor.* ► **higgledy-piggledy** *adj.*: *a higgledy-piggledy collection of houses*

high /haɪ/ *adj., noun, adv.*
■ *adj.* (**high·er, high·est**)
FROM BOTTOM TO TOP | **1** measuring a long distance from the bottom to the top: *What's the highest mountain in the US?* ◊ *The house has a high wall all the way round it.* ◊ *shoes with high heels* ◊ *He has a round face with a high forehead.* [OPP] LOW **2** used to talk about the distance that sth measures from the bottom to the top: *How high is Everest?* ◊ *It's only a low wall—about a metre high.* ◊ *The grass was waist-high.*
FAR ABOVE GROUND | **3** at a level which is a long way above the ground or above the level of the sea: *a high branch/shelf/window* ◊ *The rooms had high ceilings.* ◊ *They were flying at high altitude.* ◊ *the grasslands of the high prairies* [OPP] LOW
GREATER THAN NORMAL | **4** greater than normal in quantity,

size or degree: *a high temperature/speed/price* ◊ *a high rate of inflation* ◊ *Demand is high at this time of year.* ◊ *a high level of pollution* ◊ *a high standard of craftsmanship* ◊ *A high degree of accuracy is needed.* ◊ *We had high hopes for the business* (= we believed it would be successful). ◊ *The cost in terms of human life was high.* ◊ *high* (= strong) *winds*—compare LOW (4)
CONTAINING A LOT | **5** ~ (**in sth**) containing a lot of a particular substance: *foods which are high in fat* ◊ *a high potassium content* [OPP] LOW
RANK/STATUS | **6** (usually before noun) near the top in rank or status: *She has held high office under three prime ministers.* ◊ *The case was referred to a higher court.* ◊ *He has friends in high places* (= among people of power and influence). [OPP] LOW
VALUABLE | **7** of great value: *to play for high stakes* ◊ *My highest card is ten.*
IDEALS/PRINCIPLES | **8** (usually before noun) morally good: *a man of high ideals/principles*
APPROVING | **9** (usually before noun) showing a lot of approval or respect for sb: *She is held in very high regard by her colleagues.* ◊ *You seem to have a high opinion of yourself!* [OPP] LOW
SOUND | **10** at or near the top of a musical scale; not deep or low: *She has a high voice.* ◊ *That note is definitely too high for me.* [OPP] LOW
OF PERIOD OF TIME | **11** [only before noun] used to describe the middle or the most attractive part of a period of time: *high noon* ◊ *high summer*
FOOD | **12** (of meat, cheese, etc.) beginning to go bad and having a strong smell
ON ALCOHOL/DRUGS | **13** [not before noun] ~ (**on sth**) (*informal*) behaving in an excited way because of the effects of alcohol or drugs
—see also HEIGHT
[IDM] **be/get on your high 'horse** (*informal*) to behave in a way that shows you think you are better than other people **have a 'high old time** (*old-fashioned, informal*) to enjoy yourself very much **high and 'dry 1** (of a boat, etc.) in a position out of the water: *Their yacht was left high and dry on a sandbank.* **2** in a difficult situation, without help or money **high and 'mighty** (*informal*) behaving as though you think you are more important than other people **high as a 'kite** (*informal*) behaving in a very excited way because of being strongly affected by alcohol or drugs **high days and 'holidays** festivals and special occasions **in high 'dudgeon** (*old-fashioned, written*) in an angry or offended mood, and showing other people that you are angry: *He stomped out of the room in high dudgeon.* **smell, stink, etc. to high 'heaven** (*informal*) **1** to have a strong unpleasant smell **2** to seem to be very dishonest or morally unacceptable—more at HELL, MORAL *adj.*, ORDER *n.*, PROFILE *n.*, TIME *n.*
■ *noun*
LEVEL/NUMBER | **1** the highest level or number: *Profits reached an all-time high last year.*
WEATHER | **2** an area of high air pressure; an ANTICYCLONE: *A high over southern Europe is bringing fine, sunny weather to all parts.* **3** the highest temperature reached during a particular day, week, etc: *Highs today will be in the region of 25°C.*
FROM DRUGS | **4** (*informal*) the feeling of extreme pleasure and excitement that sb gets after taking some types of drugs: *The high lasted all night.*
FROM SUCCESS/ENJOYMENT | **5** (*informal*) the feeling of extreme pleasure and excitement that sb gets from doing sth enjoyable or being successful at sth: *He was on a real high after winning the competition.* ◊ *the highs and lows of her acting career*
SCHOOL | **6** used in the name of a high school: *He graduated from Little Rock High in 1982.*
[IDM] **on 'high 1** (*formal*) in a high place: *We gazed down into the valley from on high.* **2** (*humorous*) the people in senior positions in an organization: *An order came down from on high that lunchbreaks were to be half an hour and no longer.* **3** in heaven: *The disaster was seen as a judgement from on high.*

aɪ	aʊ	eɪ	əʊ	oʊ	ɔɪ	ɪə	eə	ʊə	j	w
my	**now**	**say**	**go** (BrE)	**go** (AmE)	**boy**	**near**	**hair**	**pure**	**yes**	**wet**

■ *adv.* (**high·er**, **high·est**)

FAR FROM GROUND/BOTTOM | **1** at or to a position or level that is a long way up from the ground or from the bottom: *An eagle circled high overhead.* ◊ *I can't jump any higher.* ◊ *She never got very high in the company.* ◊ *His desk was* **piled high** *with papers.* ◊ *She's* **aiming high** (= hoping to be very successful) *in her exams.*

VALUE/AMOUNT | **2** at or to a large cost, value or amount: *Prices are expected to rise even higher this year.*

SOUND | **3** at a high PITCH: *I can't sing that high.*

IDM **,high and 'low** everywhere: *I've searched high and low for my purse.* **run 'high** (especially of feelings) to be strong and angry or excited: *Feelings ran high as the election approached.*—more at FLY *v.*, HEAD *n.*, RIDE *v.*

> **WHICH WORD?** (?)
> **high / tall**
>
> **High** is used to talk about the measurement from the bottom to the top of something: *The fence is over five metres high.* ◊ *He has climbed some of the world's highest mountains.* You also use **high** to describe the distance of something from the ground: *How high was the plane when the engine failed?*
>
> **Tall** is used instead of **high** to talk about people: *My brother's much taller than me.* **Tall** is also used for things that are high and narrow such as trees: *She ordered cold beer in a tall glass.* ◊ *tall factory chimneys.* Buildings can be **high** or **tall**.

high·ball /'haɪbɔːl/ *noun* (*AmE*) a strong alcoholic drink, such as whisky or GIN, mixed with FIZZY water (= with bubbles) or GINGER ALE, etc. and served with ice

'high beams *noun* [pl.] (*AmE*) the lights on a car when they are pointing a long way ahead, not down at the road: *Turn on your high beams.*

,high-'born *adj.* (*old-fashioned* or *formal*) having parents who are members of the highest social class SYN ARISTOCRATIC

high·boy /'haɪbɔɪ/ *noun* (*AmE*) = TALLBOY

high·brow /'haɪbraʊ/ *adj.* (sometimes *disapproving*) concerned with or interested in serious artistic or cultural ideas SYN INTELLECTUAL: *highbrow newspapers/television programmes* ◊ *highbrow readers* OPP LOWBROW—compare MIDDLEBROW

'high chair *noun* a special chair with long legs and a little seat and table, for a small child to sit in when eating—picture at CHAIR

High 'Church *adj.* connected with the part of the Anglican Church that is most similar to the Roman Catholic Church in its beliefs and practices

,high-'class *adj.* **1** excellent; of good quality: *a high-class restaurant* ◊ *to stay in high-class accommodation* **2** connected with a high social class: *to come from a high-class background* OPP LOW-CLASS

,high com'mand *noun* [usually sing.] the senior leaders of the armed forces of a country

,high com'mission *noun* **1** the office and the staff of an EMBASSY that represents the interests of one Commonwealth country in another **2** a group of people who are working for a government or an international organization on an important project

High Com'missioner *noun* **1** a person who is sent by one Commonwealth country to live in another, to protect the interests of their own country **2** a person who is head of an important international project: *the United Nations High Commissioner for Refugees*

,High 'Court (also **,High Court of 'Justice**) *noun* **1** a court of law in England and Wales that deals with the most serious CIVIL cases but not criminal ones **2** = THE SUPREME COURT

,high-defi'nition *adj.* [only before noun] (*technical*) using or produced by a system that gives very clear detailed images: *high-definition television* ◊ *high-definition displays*

,high-'end *adj.* (*AmE*) expensive and of high quality

,higher 'animals, **,higher 'plants** *noun* [pl.] animals and plants that have reached an advanced stage of development

,higher edu'cation *noun* [U] (*abbr.* **HE**) education and training at college and university, especially to degree level—compare FURTHER EDUCATION

,high ex'plosive *noun* [C, U] a very powerful substance that is used in bombs and can damage a very large area

high·fa·lu·tin /ˌhaɪfə'luːtɪn/ *adj.* (*informal, disapproving*) trying to seem serious or important, but in a way that often appears silly and unnecessary SYN PRETENTIOUS: *highfalutin language/ideas*

,high fi'delity *noun* [U] (*old-fashioned*) = HI-FI

,high 'five *noun* (especially *AmE*) an action to celebrate victory or to express happiness in which two people raise one arm each and hit their open hands together: *Way to go! High five!*

,high-'flown *adj.* (usually *disapproving*) (of language and ideas) very grand and complicated: *His high-flown style just sounds absurd today.*

,high-'flyer (also **,high-'flier**) *noun* a person who has the desire and the ability to be very successful in their job or their studies: *academic high-flyers*

,high-'flying *adj.* [only before noun] **1** very successful: *a high-flying career woman* **2** that flies very high in the air: *high-flying aircraft*

,high-'grade *adj.* [usually before noun] of very good quality: *high-grade petrol*

'high ground *noun* (usually **the high ground**) [sing.] the advantage in a discussion or an argument, etc.: *The government is claiming the high ground in the education debate.* IDM see MORAL

,high-'handed *adj.* (of people or their behaviour) using authority in an unreasonable way, without considering the opinions of other people: *a high-handed attitude/manner*

,high 'heels *noun* [pl.] shoes that have very high heels, usually worn by women ▶ **,high-'heeled** *adj.* [only before noun]: *high-heeled shoes/boots*

,high 'jinks (*AmE* also **hi-jinks**) *noun* [pl.] (*old-fashioned, informal*) lively and excited behaviour SYN FUN

the 'high jump *noun* [sing.] a sporting event in which people try to jump over a high bar that is gradually raised higher and higher: *She won a silver medal in the high jump.*—picture on page 1251 IDM **be for the 'high jump** (*BrE, informal*) to be going to be severely punished

high·land /'haɪlənd/ *adj., noun*
■ *adj.* [only before noun] **1** connected with an area of land that has hills or mountains: *highland regions* ◊ *highland roads* **2** (**Highland**) connected with the Highlands of Scotland: *Highland cattle* ◊ *Highland dress*—compare LOWLAND
■ *noun* **1** [C, usually pl.] an area of land with hills or mountains **2** (**the Highlands**) [pl.] the high mountain region of Scotland—compare LOWLAND

high·land·er /'haɪləndə(r)/ *noun* **1** a person who comes from an area where there are a lot of mountains **2** (**Highland·er**) a person who comes from the Scottish Highlands—compare LOWLANDER

,Highland 'fling *noun* a fast Scottish dance that is danced by one person

,high-'level *adj.* [usually before noun] **1** involving senior people: *high-level talks/negotiations* ◊ *high-level staff* **2** in a high position or place: *a high-level walk in the hills* **3** advanced: *a high-level course* **4** (*computing*) (of a computer language) similar to an existing language such as English, making it fairly simple to use OPP LOW-LEVEL

'high life *noun* (also **the high life**) [sing., U] (also **,high 'living** [U]) (sometimes *disapproving*) a way of life that involves going to parties and spending a lot of money on food, clothes, etc.

high·light /'haɪlaɪt/ *verb, noun*
■ *verb* [VN] **1** to emphasize sth, especially so that people give it more attention: *The report highlights the major problems facing society today.* **2** to mark part of a text with a special coloured pen, or to mark an area on a

H

b	d	f	g	h	k	l	m	n	p	r
bad	did	fall	get	hat	cat	leg	man	now	pen	red

computer screen, to emphasize it or make it easier to see: *I've highlighted the important passages in yellow.* **3** to make some parts of your hair a lighter colour than the rest by using a chemical substance on them

■ *noun* **1** the best, most interesting or most exciting part of sth: *One of the highlights of the trip was seeing the Taj Mahal.* ◊ *The highlights of the match will be shown later this evening.* **2** (**highlights**) [pl.] areas of hair that are lighter than the rest, usually because a chemical substance has been put on them **3** (**highlights**) [pl.] (*technical*) the light or bright part of a picture or photograph

high·light·er /ˈhaɪlaɪtə(r)/ *noun* **1** (also **ˈhighlighter pen**) a special pen used for marking words in a text in bright colours—picture at STATIONERY **2** a coloured substance that you put above your eyes or on your cheeks to make yourself more attractive

high·ly /ˈhaɪli/ *adv.* **1** very: *highly successful/skilled/intelligent* ◊ *highly competitive/critical/sensitive* ◊ *It is highly unlikely that she'll be late.* **2** at or to a high standard, level or amount: *highly trained/educated* ◊ *a highly developed economy* ◊ *a highly paid job* **3** with admiration or praise: *His teachers think very highly of him* (= have a very good opinion of him). ◊ *She speaks highly of you.* ◊ *Her novels are very highly regarded.*

highly ˈstrung (*BrE*) (*AmE* **high-ˈstrung**) *adj.* (of a person or an animal) nervous and easily upset: *a sensitive and highly-strung child* ◊ *Their new horse is very highly strung.*

high-ˈminded *adj.* (of people or ideas) having strong moral principles ▶ **high-ˈminded·ness** *noun* [U]

High·ness /ˈhaɪnəs/ *noun* (**His/Her/Your Highness**) a title of respect used when talking to or about a member of the royal family: *Yes, Your Highness.*—see also ROYAL HIGHNESS

high ˈnoon *noun* **1** exactly twelve o'clock in the middle of the day **2** (*written*) the most important stage of sth, when sth that will decide the future happens

high-ˈoctane *adj.* [only before noun] **1** (of fuel used in engines) of very good quality and very efficient **2** (*slang*) full of energy; powerful: *a high-octane actor/athlete*

high perˈformance *adj.* [only before noun] that can go very fast or do complicated things: *a high performance car/computer*

high-ˈpitched *adj.* (of sounds) very high: *a high-pitched voice/whistle* OPP LOW-PITCHED

high point *noun* the most interesting, enjoyable or best part of sth: *It was the high point of the evening.* OPP LOW POINT

high-ˈpowered *adj.* **1** (of people) having a lot of power and influence; full of energy: *high-powered executives* **2** (of activities) important; with a lot of responsibility: *a high-powered job* **3** (also **high-ˈpower**) (of machines) very powerful: *a high-powered car/computer*

high ˈpressure *noun* [U] **1** the condition of air, gas, or liquid that is kept in a small space by force: *Water is forced through the pipes at high pressure.* **2** a condition of the air which affects the weather, when the pressure is higher than average: *The rain will be followed by warmer, drier weather as areas of high pressure move in.*—compare LOW PRESSURE

high-ˈpressure *adj.* [only before noun] **1** that involves aggressive ways of persuading sb to do sth or to buy sth: *high-pressure sales techniques* **2** that involves a lot of worry and anxiety SYN STRESSFUL: *a high-pressure job* **3** using or containing a great force of a gas or a liquid: *a high-pressure water-jet* .

high-ˈpriced *adj.* [usually before noun] expensive: *high-priced housing/cars*

high ˈpriest *noun* **1** the most important priest in the Jewish religion in the past **2** (*feminine* **high ˈpriestess**) an important priest in some other non-Christian religions: (*figurative*) *Janis Joplin was known as the High Priestess of Rock.*

high-ˈprofile *adj.* [only before noun] receiving or involving a lot of attention and discussion on television, in newspapers, etc: *a high-profile performer/campaign*—see also PROFILE

high-ˈranking *adj.* senior; important: *a high-ranking officer/official* ◊ *a high-ranking post*

high-ˈrise *adj.* [only before noun] (of a building) very tall and having a lot of floors: *high-rise housing* ▶ **ˈhigh-rise** *noun*: *to live in a high-rise*—compare LOW-RISE

high-ˈrisk *adj.* [usually before noun] involving a lot of danger and the risk of injury, death, damage, etc: *a high-risk sport* ◊ *high-risk patients* (= who are very likely to get a particular illness)—compare LOW-RISK

high road *noun* [usually sing.] **1** (*old-fashioned*, *BrE*) a main or important road—compare HIGHWAY **2 ~ (to sth)** the most direct way: *This is the high road to democracy.* IDM **take the ˈhigh road (in sth)** (*AmE*) to take the most positive course of action: *He took the high road in his campaign.*

high ˈroller *noun* (*AmE*, *informal*) a person who spends a lot of money, especially on gambling

high school *noun* [C, U] **1** (in the US and some other countries) a school for young people between the ages of 14 and 18 **2** often used in Britain in the names of schools for young people between the ages of 11 and 18: *Oxford High School*—compare SECONDARY SCHOOL

the ˌhigh ˈseas *noun* [pl.] (*formal* or *literary*) the areas of sea that are not under the legal control of any one country: *international laws to regulate fishing on the high seas*

high ˈseason *noun* [U, sing.] (*especially BrE*) the time of year when a hotel or tourist area receives most visitors—compare LOW SEASON

high-seˈcurity *adj.* [only before noun] **1** (of buildings and places) very carefully locked and guarded: *a high-security prison* **2** (of prisoners) kept in a prison that is very carefully locked and guarded

high-ˈsounding *adj.* (*especially BrE*, often *disapproving*) (of language or ideas) complicated and intended to sound important SYN PRETENTIOUS

high-ˈspeed *adj.* [only before noun] that travels, works or happens very fast: *a high-speed train/computer* ◊ *high-speed car chase*

high-ˈspirited *adj.* **1** (of people) very lively and active: *a high-spirited child* ◊ *high-spirited behaviour* **2** (of animals, especially horses) lively and difficult to control OPP PLACID—see also SPIRIT

high spot *noun* the most enjoyable or important part of sth: *Lunch in an expensive restaurant was the high spot of the day.*

high street (*BrE*) (*AmE* **main street**) *noun* (especially in names) the main street of a town, where most shops/stores, banks, etc. are: *Peckham High Street* ◊ *106 High Street, Peckham* ◊ *high-street banks/shops*

high-ˈstrung *adj.* (*AmE*) = HIGHLY STRUNG

high ˈtable *noun* [C, U] (*BrE*) a table on a raised platform, where the most important people at a formal dinner sit to eat

high·tail /ˈhaɪteɪl/ *verb* IDM **ˈhightail it** (*informal*, *especially AmE*) to leave somewhere very quickly

high ˈtea *noun* (*BrE*) a meal consisting of cooked food, bread and butter and cakes, usually with tea to drink, eaten in the late afternoon or early evening instead of dinner

high-ˈtech (also **hi-ˈtech**) *adj.* (*informal*) **1** using the most modern methods and machines, especially electronic ones: *high-tech industries* ◊ *These new computers are all very high-tech.* **2** (of designs, objects, etc.) very modern in appearance; using modern materials: *a high-tech table made of glass and steel*—compare LOW-TECH

high techˈnology *noun* [U] the most modern methods and machines, especially electronic ones; the use of these in industry, etc.

high-ˈtension *adj.* [only before noun] carrying a very powerful electric current: *high-tension wires/cables*

high ˈtide *noun* [U, C] the time when the sea has risen to its highest level; the sea at this time: *You can't walk along this beach at high tide.*—compare FLOOD TIDE, HIGH WATER OPP LOW TIDE

'high-tops noun [pl.] (*especially AmE*) sports shoes that cover the ankle, worn especially for playing basketball

high 'treason noun [U] = TREASON

'high-up noun (*BrE, informal*) an important person with a high rank

high 'water noun [U] the time when the sea or the water in a river has risen to its highest level: *Fishing is good at high water.*—compare HIGH TIDE **IDM** see HELL

high-'water mark noun a line or mark showing the highest point that the sea or flood water has reached: (*figurative*) *the high-water mark of Parisian fashion* (= the most successful time)—compare LOW-WATER MARK

high·way /ˈhaɪweɪ/ noun **1** (*especially AmE*) a main road, usually connecting large towns: *an interstate highway* ◊ *Highway patrol officers closed the road.* **2** (*BrE, formal*) a public road: *A parked car was obstructing the highway.*—compare HIGH ROAD

the ˌHighway 'Code noun [sing.] (in Britain) the official rules for drivers and other users of public roads; the book that contains these rules

high·way·man /ˈhaɪweɪmən/ noun (*pl.* **-men** /-mən/) a man, usually on a horse and carrying a gun, who robbed travellers on public roads in the past

high 'wire noun [usually sing.] a rope or wire that is stretched high above the ground, and used by CIRCUS performers

hi·jack /ˈhaɪdʒæk/ verb [VN] **1** to use violence or threats to take control of a vehicle, especially a plane, in order to force it to travel to a different place or to demand sth from a government: *The plane was hijacked by two armed men on a flight from London to Cairo.* **2** (*disapproving*) to use or take control of sth, especially a meeting, in order to advertise your own aims and interests ▶ **hi·jack·ing** (also **hi·jack**) noun [C, U]: *There have been a series of hijackings recently in the area.* ◊ *an unsuccessful hijack*—compare CARJACKING

hi·jack·er /ˈhaɪdʒækə(r)/ noun a person who hijacks a plane or other vehicle

hi-jinks (*AmE*) = HIGH JINKS

hike /haɪk/ noun, verb
■ *noun* **1** a long walk in the country: *They went on a ten-mile hike through the forest.* ◊ *We could go into town but it's a real hike* (= a long way) *from here.* **2** ~ (**in sth**) (*informal, especially AmE*) a large or sudden increase in prices, costs, etc: *a tax/price hike* ◊ *the latest hike in interest rates* **IDM** **take a 'hike** (*AmE, informal*) a rude way of telling sb to go away
■ *verb* **1** to go for a long walk in the country, especially for pleasure: *strong boots for hiking over rough country* ◊ [VN] (*AmE*) *to hike the Rockies* **2** [V] (**go hiking**) to spend time hiking for pleasure: *If the weather's fine, we'll go hiking this weekend.* **3** [VN] ~ **sth** (**up**) to increase prices, taxes, etc. suddenly by large amounts: *The government hiked up the price of milk by over 40%.* **PHR V** **ˌhike sth↔'up** (*informal*) to pull or lift sth up, especially your clothing **SYN** HITCH: *She hiked up her skirt and waded into the river.*

hiker /ˈhaɪkə(r)/ noun a person who goes for long walks in the country for pleasure: see also HITCH-HIKER

hik·ing /ˈhaɪkɪŋ/ noun [U] the activity of going for long walks in the country for pleasure: *to go hiking* ◊ *hiking boots*

hil·ari·ous /hɪˈleəriəs; *AmE* -ˈler-/ adj. extremely funny: *a hilarious joke/story* ◊ *Lynn found the whole situation hilarious.* ◊ *Do you know Pete? He's hilarious.* ▶ **hil·ari·ous·ly** adv.: *hilariously funny*

hil·ar·ity /hɪˈlærəti/ noun [U] a state of great amusement causing loud laughter: *The announcement was greeted with great hilarity.*

hill /hɪl/ noun **1** an area of land that is higher than the land around it, but not as high as a mountain: *a region of gently rolling hills* ◊ *a hill farm/town/fort* ◊ *The house is built on the side of a hill overlooking the river.* ◊ *I love walking in the hills* (= in the area where there are hills) .—see also ANTHILL, FOOTHILL, MOLEHILL **2** a slope on a road: *Always take care when driving down steep hills.* ◊ *a*

hill start (= the act of starting a vehicle on a slope)—see also DOWNHILL, UPHILL **IDM** **a ˌhill of 'beans** (*old-fashioned, AmE, informal*) something that is not worth much **ˌover the 'hill** (*informal*) (of a person) old and therefore no longer useful or attractive: *Youngsters seem to think you're over the hill at 40!*—more at OLD

hill·billy /ˈhɪlbɪli/ noun (*pl.* **-ies**) **1** [C] (*AmE, disapproving*) a person who lives in the mountains and is thought to be stupid by people who live in the towns **2** [U] = COUNTRY AND WESTERN

hil·lock /ˈhɪlək/ noun a small hill

hill·side /ˈhɪlsaɪd/ noun the side of a hill: *The crops will not grow on exposed hillsides.* ◊ *Our hotel was on the hillside overlooking the lake.*

'hill station noun a small town in the hills, especially in India, where people go to find cooler weather in summer

hill·top /ˈhɪltɒp; *AmE* -tɑːp/ noun the top of a hill: *the hilltop town of Urbino*

hilly /ˈhɪli/ adj. (**hill·ier**, **hilli·est**) having a lot of hills: *a hilly area/region*

hilt /hɪlt/ noun the handle of a SWORD, knife, etc. **IDM** (**up**) **to the 'hilt** as much as possible: *We're mortgaged up to the hilt.* ◊ *They have promised to back us to the hilt.*

him /hɪm/ pron. used as the object of a verb or after a preposition to refer to a male person or animal that has already been mentioned or is easily identified: *When did you see him?* ◊ *He took the children with him.* ◊ *I'm taller than him.*—compare HE

him·self /hɪmˈself/ pron. **1** (the reflexive form of *he*) used when the man or boy who performs an action is also affected by it: *He introduced himself.* ◊ *Peter ought to be ashamed of himself.* **2** used to emphasize the male subject or object of a sentence: *The doctor said so himself.* ◊ *Did you see the manager himself?* **IDM** **be, seem, etc. him'self** (of a man or boy) to be in a normal state of health or happiness; not influenced by other people: *He didn't seem quite himself this morning.* ◊ *He needed space to be himself.* (**all**) **by him'self 1** alone; without anyone else: *He lives all by himself.* **2** without help: *He managed to repair the car by himself.* (**all**) **to him'self** for only him to have or use: *He has the house to himself during the week.*

hind /haɪnd/ adj., noun
■ *adj.* [only before noun] the **hind** legs or feet of an animal with four legs are those situated at the back: *The horse reared up on its hind legs.* **OPP** FORE, FRONT **IDM** see TALK v.
■ *noun* a female deer, especially a red deer; a DOE—compare HART

hin·der /ˈhɪndə(r)/ verb [VN] ~ **sb/sth** (**from sth/from doing sth**) to make it difficult for sb to do sth or sth to happen: *a political situation that hinders economic growth* ◊ *Some teachers felt hindered by a lack of resources.* ◊ *A former injury was hindering him from playing his best.*—see also HINDRANCE

Hindi /ˈhɪndi/ noun [U] one of the official languages of India, spoken especially in N India ▶ **Hindi** adj.

hind·quar·ters /ˌhaɪndˈkwɔːtəz; *AmE* -ˈkwɔːrtərz/ noun [pl.] the back part of an animal that has four legs, including its two back legs

hin·drance /ˈhɪndrəns/ noun **1** [C, usually sing.] ~ (**to sth/sb**) a person or thing that makes it more difficult for sb to do sth or for sth to happen: *To be honest, she was more of a hindrance than a help.* ◊ *The high price is a major hindrance to potential buyers.* **2** [U] (*formal*) the act of making it more difficult for sb to do sth or for sth to happen: *They were able to complete their journey without further hindrance.*—see also HINDER **IDM** see LET n.

hind·sight /ˈhaɪndsaɪt/ noun [U] the understanding that you have of a situation only after it has happened and that means you would have done things differently: *With hindsight it is easy to say they should not have released him.* ◊ *What looks obvious in hindsight was not at all obvious at the time.* ◊ *It's easy to criticise with the benefit of hindsight.*—compare FORESIGHT

Hindu /ˈhɪnduː; ˌhɪnˈduː/ noun a person whose religion is Hinduism ▶ **Hindu** adj.: *a Hindu temple*

H

æ	ɑː	e	ɜː	ə	ɪ	iː	i	ɒ	ɔː	ʌ	ʊ	u	uː
cat	father	ten	bird	about	sit	see	many	got	saw	cup	put	actual	too
								(BrE)					

Hin·du·ism /'hɪnduːɪzəm/ *noun* [U] the main religion of India which includes the worship of several gods and belief in REINCARNATION

hinge /hɪndʒ/ *noun, verb*
- *noun* a piece of metal, plastic, etc. on which a door, lid or gate moves freely as it opens or closes: *The door had been pulled off its hinges.*

hinge

- *verb* [VN] [usually passive] to attach sth with a hinge
▶ **hinged** *adj.*: *a hinged door/lid* **PHRV** '**hinge on/upon sth** (of an action, a result, etc.) to depend on sth completely: *Everything hinges on the outcome of these talks.* ◊ [+wh-] *His success hinges on how well he does at the interview.*

hint /hɪnt/ *noun, verb*
- *noun* **1** something that you say or do in an indirect way in order to show sb what you are thinking: *He gave a* **broad hint** (= one that was obvious) *that he was thinking of retiring.* ◊ *Should I* **drop a hint** (= give a hint) *to Matt?* **2** something that suggests what will happen in the future: *At the first hint of trouble, they left.* **3** [usually sing.] ~ **(of sth)** a small amount of sth [SYN] TRACE: *a hint of a smile* ◊ *There was more than a hint of sadness in his voice.* ◊ *The walls were painted white with a hint of peach.* **4** [usually pl.] ~ **(on sth)** a small piece of practical information or advice [SYN] TIP: *handy hints on saving money* **IDM** **take a/the** '**hint** to understand what sb wants you to do even though they tell you in an indirect way: *I thought they'd never go—some people just can't take a hint.* ◊ *Sarah hoped he'd take the hint and leave her alone.*
- *verb* ~ **(at sth)** to suggest sth in an indirect way: [V] *What are you hinting at?* ◊ [V(that)] *They hinted (that) there might be more job losses.* [also V speech]

hin·ter·land /'hɪntəlænd; AmE -tərl-/ *noun* [usually sing.] the areas of a country that are away from the coast, from the banks of a large river or from the main cities: *the rural/agricultural hinterland*

hip /hɪp/ *noun, adj., exclamation*
- *noun* **1** the area at either side of the body between the top of the leg and the waist; the joint at the top of the leg: *She stood with her hands on her hips.* ◊ *These jeans are too tight around the hips.* ◊ *a hip replacement operation* ◊ *the hip bone* ◊ *She broke her hip in the fall.*—picture at BODY **2** (-hipped) (in adjectives) having hips of the size or shape mentioned: *large-hipped* ◊ *slim-hipped* **3** (also '**rose hip**) the red fruit that grows on some types of wild rose bush **IDM** see SHOOT *v.*
- *adj.* (**hip·per, hip·pest**) (*informal*) following or knowing what is fashionable in clothes, music, etc.
- *exclamation* **IDM** **hip, hip, hoo'ray!** (also *less frequent* **hip, hip, hur'rah/hur'ray!**) used by a group of people to show their approval of sb. One person in the group says 'hip, hip' and the others then shout 'hooray' or 'hurrah': '*Three cheers for the bride and groom: Hip, hip … 'Hooray!*'

'**hip flask** (*BrE*) (also **flask** *AmE, BrE*) *noun* a small flat bottle made of metal or glass and often covered with leather, used for carrying alcohol

'**hip hop** *noun* [U] **1** a type of modern dance music with spoken words and a steady beat played on electronic instruments, originally played by young African Americans **2** the culture of the young African Americans and others who enjoy this type of music, including special styles of art, dancing, dress, etc.

'**hip-huggers** *noun* (*AmE*) = HIPSTERS

hip·pie (also **hippy**) /'hɪpi/ *noun* (*pl.* **-ies**) a person who rejects the way that most people live in western society, often having long hair, wearing brightly-coloured clothes and taking illegal drugs. The hippie movement was most popular in the 1960s.

hippo /'hɪpəʊ; AmE 'hɪpoʊ/ *noun* (*pl.* **-os**) (*informal*) = HIPPOPOTAMUS—picture on page A6

the Hippo·crat·ic oath /ˌhɪpəkrætɪk 'əʊθ; AmE 'oʊθ/ *noun* [sing.] the promise that doctors make to keep to the principles of the medical profession

hippo·pot·amus /ˌhɪpə'pɒtəməs; AmE -'pɑːtə-/ (also *informal* **hippo**) *noun* (*pl.* **hippo·pot·amuses** /-məsɪz/ or **hip·po·pot·ami** /-maɪ/) a large heavy African animal with thick dark skin and short legs, that lives in rivers and lakes—picture on page A6

hippy = HIPPIE

hip·sters /'hɪpstəz; AmE -stərz/ (*BrE*) (*AmE* '**hip-huggers**) *noun* [pl.] trousers/pants that cover the hips but not the waist: *a pair of hipsters*

hire /'haɪə(r)/ *noun, verb*
- *verb* **1** [VN] (*especially BrE*) to pay money to borrow sth for a short time: *to hire a car/room/video* ⇨ note at RENT **2** (*especially AmE*) to give sb a job: [VN] *She was hired three years ago.* ◊ [V] *He does the hiring and firing in our company.* **3** [VN] to employ sb for a short time to do a particular job: *to hire a lawyer* ◊ *They hired a firm of consultants to design the new system.* **PHRV** **hire sth ↔ out** to let sb use sth for a short time, in return for payment **hire yourself** '**out (to sb)** to arrange to work for sb: *He hired himself out to whoever needed his services.*
- *noun* [U] (*especially BrE*) the act of paying to use sth for a short time: *bicycles for hire, £2 an hour* ◊ *a hire car* ◊ *a car hire firm* ◊ *The price includes the hire of the hall.* ◊ *The costumes are on hire from the local theatre.* ⇨ note at RENT **IDM** see PLY *v.*

,**hired** '**hand** *noun* (*AmE*) a person who is paid to work on a farm

hire·ling /'haɪəlɪŋ; AmE 'haɪərlɪŋ/ *noun* (*disapproving*) a person who is willing to do anything or work for anyone as long as they are paid

,**hire** '**purchase** *noun* [U] (*BrE*) (*abbr.* **hp**) (*AmE* **in'stallment plan** [U, C]) a method of buying an article by making regular payments for it over several months or years. The article only belongs to the person who is buying it when all the payments have been made: *a hire purchase agreement* ◊ *We're buying a new cooker on hire purchase.*—compare CREDIT

hir·sute /'hɜːsjuːt; AmE 'hɜːrsuːt/ *adj.* (*literary* or *humorous*) (especially of a man) having a lot of hair on the face or body

his /hɪz/ *det., pron.*
- *det.* (the possessive form of *he*) of or belonging to a man or boy who has already been mentioned or is easily identified: *James has sold his car.* ◊ *He broke his leg skiing.*
- *pron.* of or belonging to him: *He took my hand in his.* ◊ *The choice was his.* ◊ *a friend of his*

His·pan·ic /hɪ'spænɪk/ *adj., noun*
- *adj.* of or connected with Spain or Spanish-speaking countries, especially those of Latin America
- *noun* a person whose first language is Spanish, especially one from a Latin American country living in the US

hiss /hɪs/ *verb, noun*
- *verb* **1** [V] ~ **(at sb/sth)** to make a sound like a long 's': *The steam escaped with a loud hissing noise.* ◊ *The snake lifted its head and hissed.* **2** to make a sound like a long 's' to show disapproval of sb/sth, especially an actor or a speaker: [VN] *He was booed and hissed off the stage.* [also V] **3** ~ **(at sb)** to say sth in a quiet angry voice: [V] *He hissed at them to be quiet.* ◊ [V speech] '*Leave me alone!' she hissed.*
- *noun* a sound like a long 's'; this sound used to show disapproval of sb: *the hiss of the air brakes* ◊ *the snake's hiss* ◊ *The performance was met with boos and hisses.*

his·ta·mine /'hɪstəmiːn/ *noun* [U] (*medical*) a chemical substance that is given out by the body in response to an injury or an ALLERGY—see ANTIHISTAMINE

histo·gram /'hɪstəgræm/ *noun* (*technical*) = BAR CHART

his·tor·ian /hɪ'stɔːriən/ *noun* a person who studies or writes about history; an expert in history **HELP** Some speakers do not pronounce the 'h' at the beginning of **historian** and use *an* instead of *a* before it. This now sounds old-fashioned.

his·tor·ic /hɪ'stɒrɪk; AmE -'stɔːr-; -'stɑːr-/ *adj.* [usually before noun] **1** important in history; likely to be thought of as important at some time in the future: *a historic building/monument* ◊ *The area is of special historic inter-*

aɪ	aʊ	eɪ	əʊ	oʊ	ɔɪ	ɪə	eə	ʊə	j	w
my	now	say	go	go	boy	near	hair	pure	yes	wet
			(BrE)	(AmE)						

est. ◇ *a(n) historic occasion / decision / day / visit / victory* **2** of a period during which history was recorded: *in historic times*—compare PREHISTORIC **HELP** Some speakers do not pronounce the 'h' at the beginning of **historic** and use *an* instead of *a* before it. This now sounds old-fashioned.

WHICH WORD?

historic / historical

Historic is usually used to describe something that is so important that it is likely to be remembered: *Today is a historic occasion for our country.* **Historical** usually describes something that is connected with the past or with the study of history, or something that really happened in the past: *I have been doing some historical research.* ◇ *Was Robin Hood a historical figure?*

---

his·tor·ic·al /hɪˈstɒrɪkl; *AmE* -ˈstɔːr-; -ˈstɑːr-/ *adj.* [usually before noun] **1** connected with the past: *the historical background to the war* ◇ *You must place these events in their historical context.* **2** connected with the study of history: *historical documents / records / research* ◇ *The building is of historical importance.* **3** (of a book, film / movie, etc.) about people and events in the past: *a historical novel / setting* **HELP** Some speakers do not pronounce the 'h' at the beginning of **historical** and use *an* instead of *a* before it. This now sounds old-fashioned. ▶ **his·tor·ic·al·ly** /-kli/ *adv.*: *The book is historically inaccurate.* ◇ *Historically, there has always been a great deal of rivalry between the two families.*

the his·toric 'present *noun* [sing.] (*grammar*) the simple present tense used to describe events in the past in order to make the description more powerful

his·tor·iog·raphy /ˌhɪstɔriˈɒɡrəfi; *AmE* -ˌstɔːriˈɑːɡ-; -ˌstɑːr-/ *noun* [U] the study of writing about history ▶ **his·tor·iog·raph·ical** /ˌhɪstɔriˈɡræfɪkl; *AmE* -ˌstɔːr-; -ˌstɑːr-/ *adj.*

his·tory /ˈhɪstri/ *noun* (*pl.* **-ies**) **1** [U] all the events that happened in the past: *a turning point in human history* ◇ *one of the worst disasters in recent history* ◇ *a people with no sense of history* ◇ *Many people throughout history have dreamt of a world without war.* ◇ *The area was inhabited long before the dawn of recorded history* (= before people wrote about events). ◇ *These events changed the course of history.* **2** [sing., U] the past events concerned in the development of a particular place, subject, etc: *the history of Ireland / democracy / popular music* ◇ *The local history of the area is fascinating.* ◇ *The school traces its history back to 1865.* **3** [U] the study of past events as a subject at school or university: *a history teacher* ◇ *a degree in History* ◇ *social / economic / political history* ◇ *ancient / medieval / modern history* ◇ *She's studying art history.*—see also NATURAL HISTORY **4** [C] a written or spoken account of past events: *She's writing a new history of Europe.* ◇ *She went on to catalogue a long history of disasters.* **5** [sing.] a record of sth happening frequently in the past life of a person, family or place; the set of facts that are known about sb's past life: *He has a history of violent crime.* ◇ *There is a history of heart disease in my family.* ◇ *a patient's medical history*—see also CASE HISTORY, LIFE HISTORY **6** [U] (*informal*) something that happened in the past that is no longer important: *We won't talk about that—that's history.* ◇ *They had an affair once but that's past history now.* **IDM** **the 'history books** the record of great achievements in history: *She has earned her place in the history books.* **history re'peats itself** used to say that things often happen later in the same way as before **make 'history | go down in 'history** to be or do sth so important that it will be recorded in history—more at REST *n.*

his·tri·on·ic /ˌhɪstriˈɒnɪk; *AmE* -ˈɑːnɪk/ *adj.* [usually before noun] (*formal, disapproving*) **histrionic** behaviour is very emotional and is intended to attract attention in a way that does not seem sincere: *histrionic gestures* ▶ **his·tri·on·ic·al·ly** /-kli/ *adv.*

his·tri·on·ics /ˌhɪstriˈɒnɪks; *AmE* -ˈɑːnɪks/ *noun* [pl.]

(*formal, disapproving*) behaviour that is very emotional and is intended to attract attention in a way that does not seem sincere: *She was used to her mother's histrionics.*

hit /hɪt/ *verb, noun*
■ *verb* (**hit·ting, hit, hit**)
▸ TOUCH SB / STH WITH FORCE | **1** [VN] **~ sb / sth (with sth)** to bring your hand, or an object you are holding, against sb / sth quickly and with force: *My parents never used to hit me.* ◇ *He hit the nail squarely on the head with the hammer.* ◇ *She hit him on the head with her umbrella.* **2** [VN] to come against sth / sb with force, especially causing damage or injury: *The bus hit the bridge.* ◇ *I was hit by a falling stone.* **3** [VN] **~ sth (on / against sth)** to knock a part of your body against sth: *He hit his head on the low ceiling.* **4** [VN] [often passive] (of a bullet, bomb, etc. or a person using them) to reach and touch a person or thing suddenly and with force: *The town was hit by bombs again last night.* ◇ *He was hit by a sniper.*
▸ BALL | **5** [VN] to bring a bat, etc. against a ball and push it away with force: *She hit the ball too hard and it went out of the court.* ◇ *We've hit our ball over the fence.* **6** [VN] (*sport*) to score points by hitting a ball: *to hit a home run*
▸ HAVE BAD EFFECT | **7** to have a bad effect on sb / sth: [VN] *The tax increases will certainly hit the poor.* ◇ *His death didn't really hit me at first.* ◇ *Rural areas have been worst hit by the strike.* ◇ *Spain was one of the **hardest hit** countries.* ◇ [V] *A tornado hit on Tuesday night.*
▸ ATTACK | **8** to attack sb / sth: [VN] *We hit the enemy when they least expected it.* [also V]
▸ REACH | **9** [VN] to reach a place: *Follow this footpath and you'll eventually hit the road.* ◇ *The President **hits town** tomorrow.* **10** [VN] to reach a particular level: *Temperatures hit 40° yesterday.* ◇ *The euro hit a record low in trading today.*
▸ PROBLEM / DIFFICULTY | **11** [VN] (*informal*) to experience sth difficult or unpleasant: *We seem to have hit a problem.* ◇ *Everything was going well but then we hit trouble.*
▸ SUDDENLY REALIZE | **12** [VN] (*informal*) to come suddenly into your mind: *I couldn't remember where I'd seen him before, and then it suddenly hit me.*
▸ PRESS BUTTON | **13** [VN] (*informal*) to press sth such as a button to operate a machine, etc: *Hit the brakes!*
IDM **hit (it) 'big** (*informal*) to be very successful: *The band has hit big in the US.* **hit the 'ceiling / 'roof** (*informal*) to suddenly become very angry **hit the 'buffers** (*informal*) if a plan, sb's career, etc. **hits the buffers**, it suddenly stops being successful **hit the 'deck** (*informal*) to fall to the ground **hit the ground 'running** (*informal*) to start doing sth and continue very quickly and successfully **hit the 'hay / 'sack** (*informal*) to go to bed **hit sb (straight / right) in the 'eye** to be very obvious to sb '**hit it** (*spoken*) used to tell sb to start doing sth, such as playing music: *Hit it, Louis!* **hit it 'off (with sb)** (*informal*) to have a good friendly relationship with sb: *We hit it off straight away.* **hit the 'jackpot** to make or win a lot of money quickly and unexpectedly **hit the nail on the 'head** to say sth that is exactly right **hit the 'road / 'trail** (*informal*) to start a journey / trip **hit the 'roof** = GO THROUGH THE ROOF at ROOF **hit the 'spot** (*informal*) if sth **hits the spot** it does exactly what it should do **hit the 'streets | hit the 'shops / 'stores** (*informal*) to become widely available for sale: *The new magazine hits the streets tomorrow.* **hit sb when they're 'down** to continue to hurt sb when they are already defeated **hit sb where it 'hurts** to affect sb where they will feel it most—more at HEADLINE, HOME *adv.*, KNOW *v.*, MARK *n.*, NERVE *n.*, NOTE *n.*, PAY DIRT, SHIT *n.*, SIX, STRIDE *n.*
PHRV ,**hit 'back (at sb / sth)** to reply to attacks or criticism: *In a TV interview she hit back at her critics.* '**hit on sb** (*AmE, slang*) to start talking to sb to show them that you are sexually attracted to them '**hit on / upon sth** [no passive] to think of a good idea suddenly or by chance: *She hit upon the perfect title for her new novel.* ,**hit 'out (at sb / sth)** to attack sb / sth violently by fighting them or criticizing them: *I just hit out blindly in all directions.* ◇ *In a rousing speech the minister hit out at racism in the armed forces.* **hit sb (up) for sth** (*AmE, slang*) to ask sb

---

for money: *Does he always hit you for cash when he wants new clothes?* '**hit sb with sth** (*informal*) to tell sb sth, especially sth that surprises or shocks them: *How much is it going to cost, then? Come on, hit me with it!*

■ *noun*

ACT OF HITTING | **1** an act of hitting sb/sth with your hand or with an object held in your hand: *Give it a good hit.* ◊ *He made the winning hit.* **2** an occasion when sth that has been thrown, fired, etc. at an object reaches that object: *The bomber scored a direct hit on the bridge.* ◊ *We finished the first round with a score of two hits and six misses.*

STH POPULAR | **3** a person or thing that is very popular: *The duo were a real hit in last year's show.* ◊ *a hit record / single / musical* ◊ *Her new series is a smash hit.*

OF DRUG | **4** (*slang*) an amount of an illegal drug that is taken at one time

MURDER | **5** (*slang, especially AmE*) a violent crime or murder—see also HIT MAN

COMPUTING | **6** a result of a search on a computer, especially on the Internet

IDM **be / make a 'hit (with sb)** to be liked very much by sb when they first meet you: *You've made a big hit with Bill.*

,**hit-and-'miss** (also ,**hit-or-'miss**) *adj.* not done in a careful or planned way and therefore not likely to be successful: *The procedure is far too clumsy and hit-and-miss.*

,**hit-and-'run** *adj.* [only before noun] **1** (of a road accident) caused by a driver who does not stop to help: *a hit-and-run accident / death* ◊ *a hit-and-run driver* (= one who causes an accident but drives away without helping) **2** (of a military attack) happening suddenly and unexpectedly so that the people attacking can leave quickly without being hurt: *hit-and-run raids* ▶ ,**hit-and-'run** *noun*: *A boy was killed this morning in a hit-and-run outside his school.*

hitch /hɪtʃ/ *verb, noun*

■ *verb* **1** to get a free ride in a person's car; to travel around in this way, by standing at the side of the road and trying to get passing cars to stop: [VN] *They hitched a ride in a truck.* ◊ (*BrE also*) *They hitched a lift.* ◊ [V] *We spent the summer hitching around Europe.*—see also HITCH-HIKE **2** [VN] ~ **sth (up)** to pull up a piece of your clothing SYN HIKE: *She hitched up her skirt and waded into the river.* **3** [VN+*adv. / prep.*] ~ **yourself (up, etc.)** to lift yourself into a higher position, or the position mentioned: *She hitched herself up.* ◊ *He hitched himself onto the bar stool.* **4** [VN] ~ **sth (to sth)** to fix sth to sth else with a rope, a hook, etc: *She hitched the pony to the gate.* **IDM** **get 'hitched** (*informal*) to get married

■ *noun* **1** a problem or difficulty that causes a short delay: *The ceremony went off without a hitch.* ◊ *a legal / last-minute / technical hitch* **2** a type of knot: *a clove hitch*

'**hitch-hike** *verb* [V] to travel by asking for free rides in other people's cars, by standing at the side of the road and trying to get passing cars to stop: *They hitch-hiked around Europe.*—see also HITCH ▶ '**hitch-hik·er** *noun*

,**hi-'tech** = HIGH-TECH

hither /'hɪðə(r)/ *adv.* (*old use*) to this place **IDM** ,**hither and 'thither** | ,**hither and 'yon** (especially *literary*) in many different directions

hith·er·to /,hɪðə'tuː; *AmE* ,hɪðər'tuː/ *adv.* (*formal*) until now; until the particular time you are talking about: *a hitherto unknown species of moth*

'**hit list** *noun* (*informal*) a list of people, organizations, etc. against whom some unpleasant action is being planned: *Which services are on the government's hit list?* ◊ *She was at the top of the terrorists' hit list for over two years.*

'**hit man** *noun* (*informal*) a criminal who is paid to kill sb

,**hit-or-'miss** *adj.* = HIT-AND-MISS

the 'hit parade *noun* (*old-fashioned*) a list published every week that shows which pop records have sold the most copies

'**hit squad** *noun* a group of criminals who are paid to kill a person

hit·ter /'hɪtə(r)/ *noun* (often in compounds) **1** (in sports) a person who hits the ball in the way mentioned: *a big / long / hard hitter* **2** (in politics or business) a person who is powerful: *the heavy hitters of Japanese industry*

HIV /,eɪtʃ aɪ 'viː/ *noun* [U] the VIRUS (= simple living thing that causes infections / illnesses) that can cause AIDS (abbreviation for 'human immunodeficiency virus'): *to be infected with HIV* ◊ *to be HIV positive*

hive /haɪv/ *noun, verb*

■ *noun* **1** (also **bee·hive**) [C] a structure made for bees to live in **2** [C] the bees living in a hive **3** [C, usually sing.] **a ~ of activity / industry** a place full of people who are busy **4** (**hives**) [U] a skin disease that causes the skin to become red and painful

■ *verb* **PHRV** **hive sth↔'off (to / into sth)** [often passive] (*especially BrE*) to separate one part of a group from the rest; to sell part of a business: *The IT department is being hived off into a new company.*

hiya /'haɪjə/ *exclamation* used to greet sb, meaning hello

HM (*BrE*) (also **H.M.** *AmE, BrE*) *abbr.* Her/His MAJESTY('s): *HM the Queen* ◊ *HM Customs*

HMG *abbr.* (*BrE*) Her Majesty's Government

hmm (also **hm, h'm**) /m; hm/ *exclamation* used in writing to show the sound that you make to express doubt or when you are hesitating

HMS /,eɪtʃ em 'es/ *abbr.* Her/His Majesty's Ship (used before the name of a ship in the British navy): *HMS Apollo*

HNC /,eɪtʃ en 'siː/ *noun* the abbreviation for 'Higher National Certificate' (a British university or college qualification, especially in a technical or scientific subject): *to do an HNC in electrical engineering*

HND /,eɪtʃ en 'diː/ *noun* the abbreviation for 'Higher National Diploma' (a British university or college qualification, especially in a technical or scientific subject): *to do an HND in fashion design*

hoard /hɔːd; *AmE* hɔːrd/ *noun, verb*

■ *noun* ~ (**of sth**) a collection of money, food, valuable objects, etc., especially one that sb keeps in a secret place so that other people will not find or steal it: *They dug up a hoard of Roman coins.*

■ *verb* [V, VN] to collect and keep large amounts of food, money, etc., especially secretly ▶ **hoard·er** *noun*

hoard·ing /'hɔːdɪŋ; *AmE* 'hɔːrd-/ *noun* **1** (*BrE*) (also **bill·board** *AmE, BrE*) [C] a large board on the outside of a building or at the side of the road, used for putting advertisements on: *advertising hoardings* **2** [C] (*BrE*) a temporary fence made of boards that is placed around an area of land until a building has been built **3** [U] the act of hoarding things

hoar frost /'hɔː frɒst; *AmE* 'hɔːr frɔːst/ *noun* [U] a layer of small pieces of ice that look like white needles and that form on surfaces outside when temperatures are very low

hoarse /hɔːs; *AmE* hɔːrs/ *adj.* (of a person or voice) sounding harsh, especially because of a sore throat: *He shouted himself hoarse.* ◊ *a hoarse cough / cry / scream* ▶ **hoarse·ly** *adv.* **hoarse·ness** *noun* [U]

hoary /'hɔːri/ *adj.* [usually before noun] **1** (*old-fashioned*) very old and well known and therefore no longer interesting: *a hoary old joke* **2** (*literary*) (especially of hair) grey or white because a person is old

hoax /həʊks; *AmE* hoʊks/ *noun, verb*

■ *noun* an act intended to make sb believe sth that is not true, especially sth unpleasant: *a bomb hoax* ◊ *hoax calls*

■ *verb* [VN] to trick sb by making them believe sth that is not true, especially sth unpleasant ▶ **hoax·er** *noun*

hob /hɒb; *AmE* hɑːb/ *noun* **1** (*BrE*) the top part of a cooker where food is cooked in pans; a similar surface that is built into a kitchen unit and is separate from the oven: *an electric / a gas hob* **2** a metal shelf at the side of a fire, used in the past for heating pans, etc. on

hob·ble /'hɒbl; *AmE* 'hɑːbl/ *verb* **1** [V] [usually+*adv. / prep.*] to walk with difficulty, especially because your feet or legs hurt: *The old man hobbled across the road.* **2** [VN] to tie together two legs of a horse or other animal in order to stop it from running away **3** [VN] to make it more difficult for sb to do sth or sth to happen

s	t	v	z	ʃ	ʒ	tʃ	dʒ	θ	ð	ŋ
see	tea	van	zoo	shoe	vision	chain	jam	thin	this	sing

hob·by /ˈhɒbi; *AmE* ˈhɑːbi/ *noun* (*pl.* **-ies**) an activity that you do for pleasure when you are not working: *Her hobbies include swimming and gardening.* ◊ *I only play jazz as a hobby.*

ˈ**hobby horse** *noun* **1** (sometimes *disapproving*) a subject that sb feels strongly about and likes to talk about: *to get on/ride your hobby horse* (= talk about your favourite subject) **2** a toy made from a long stick that has a horse's head at one end and on which children pretend to ride

hob·by·ist /ˈhɒbiːɪst; *AmE* ˈhɑːb-/ *noun* (*formal*) a person who is very interested in a particular hobby

hob·gob·lin /hɒbˈgɒblɪn; ˈhɒbgɒblɪn; *AmE* ˈhɑːbgɑːb-/ *noun* (in stories) a small ugly creature that likes to trick people or cause trouble

hob·nail boot /ˌhɒbneɪl ˈbuːt; *AmE* ˌhɑːb-/ (also ˌ**hob-nailed ˈboot** /-neɪld/) *noun* [usually pl.] a heavy shoe whose sole is attached to the upper part with short heavy nails

hob·nob /ˈhɒbnɒb; *AmE* ˈhɑːbnɑːb/ *verb* (**-bb-**) [V] ~ **(with sb)** (*informal*) to spend a lot of time with sb, especially sb who is rich and/or famous

hobo /ˈhəʊbəʊ; *AmE* ˈhoʊboʊ/ *noun* (*pl.* **-os**) (*old-fashioned, especially AmE*) **1** a person who travels from place to place looking for work, especially on farms **2** = TRAMP

Hob·son's choice /ˌhɒbsnz ˈtʃɔɪs; *AmE* ˌhɑːb-/ *noun* [U] a situation in which sb has no choice because if they do not accept what is offered, they will get nothing

hock /hɒk; *AmE* hɑːk/ *noun, verb*
▪ *noun* **1** [C] the middle joint of an animal's back leg **2** [U, C] (*BrE*) a German white wine **3** [U, C] (*especially AmE*) = KNUCKLE (2) **4** (*informal*) if sth that you own is in **hock**, you have exchanged it for money but hope to buy it back later **IDM** **be in ˈhock (to sb)** to owe sb sth: *I'm in hock to the bank for £6000.*
▪ *verb* [VN] (*informal*) to leave a valuable object with sb in exchange for money that you borrow **SYN** PAWN

hockey /ˈhɒki; *AmE* ˈhɑːki/ *noun* [U] **1** (*BrE*) (*AmE* ˈ**field hockey**) a game played on a field by two teams of 11 players, with curved sticks and a small hard ball. Teams try to hit the ball into the other team's goal: *to play hockey* ◊ *a hockey stick/player/team* **2** (*AmE*) = ICE HOCKEY

hocus-pocus /ˌhəʊkəs ˈpəʊkəs; *AmE* ˌhoʊkəs ˈpoʊkəs/ *noun* [U] language or behaviour that is nonsense and is intended to hide the truth from people: *I still think that horoscopes are a load of hocus-pocus.*

hod /hɒd; *AmE* hɑːd/ *noun* an open box attached to a pole, used by building workers for carrying bricks on the shoulder

hodge·podge /ˈhɒdʒpɒdʒ; *AmE* ˈhɑːdʒpɑːdʒ/ *noun* [sing.] (*AmE*) = HOTCHPOTCH

hoe /həʊ; *AmE* hoʊ/ *noun, verb*
▪ *noun* a garden tool with a long handle and a blade, used for breaking up soil and removing WEEDS (= plants growing where they are not wanted)—picture at GARDEN
▪ *verb* (**hoe·ing, hoed, hoed**) to break up soil, remove plants, etc. with a hoe: [VN] *to hoe the flowerbeds* [also V]

hog /hɒg; *AmE* hɔːg; hɑːg/ *noun, verb*
▪ *noun* **1** (*especially AmE*) a pig, especially one that is kept and made fat for eating **2** (*BrE*) a male pig that has been CASTRATED (= had part of its sex organs removed) and is kept for its meat—compare BOAR, SOW—see also ROAD HOG, WARTHOG **IDM** **go the whole ˈhog** to do sth thoroughly or completely: *We painted the kitchen and then decided to go the whole hog do the other rooms as well.*
▪ *verb* (**-gg-**) [VN] to use or keep most of sth yourself and stop others from using or having it: *to hog the road* (= drive so that other vehicles cannot pass) ◊ *to hog the bathroom* (= to spend a long time in it so that others cannot use it)

Hog·ma·nay /ˈhɒgməneɪ; *AmE* ˌhɑːgməˈneɪ/ *noun* [U] (in Scotland) New Year's Eve (31 December) and the celebrations that happen on that day

hog·wash /ˈhɒgwɒʃ; *AmE* ˈhɔːgwɑːʃ; ˈhɑːg-; -wɔːʃ/ *noun* [U] (*informal, especially AmE*) an idea, argument, etc. that you think is stupid

ho ho /ˌhəʊ ˈhəʊ; *AmE* ˌhoʊ ˈhoʊ/ *exclamation* **1** used to

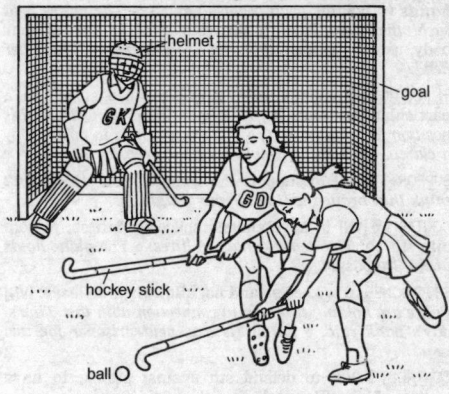

hockey (*BrE*)/ field hockey (*AmE*)

helmet
goal
hockey stick
ball

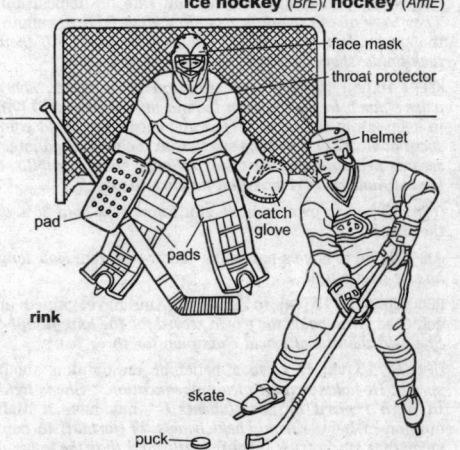

ice hockey (*BrE*)/ hockey (*AmE*)

face mask
throat protector
helmet
pad
catch glove
pads
rink
skate
puck

show the sound of a deep laugh **2** used to show surprise: *Ho, ho! What have we here?*

ho-hum /ˌhəʊ ˈhʌm; *AmE* ˌhoʊ/ *exclamation* used to show that you are bored

hoick /hɔɪk/ *verb* [VN] (*BrE, informal*) to lift or pull sth in a particular direction, especially with a quick sudden movement

the hoi pol·loi /ˌhɔɪ pəˈlɔɪ/ *noun* [pl.] (*disapproving or humorous*) an insulting word for ordinary people

hoist /hɔɪst/ *verb, noun*
▪ *verb* [VN] [usually +*adv. / prep.*] to raise or pull sth up to a higher position, often using ropes or special equipment: *He hoisted himself onto a high stool.* ◊ *The cargo was hoisted aboard by crane.* ◊ *to hoist a flag/sail* **IDM** **be hoist/hoisted by/with your own peˈtard** (*BrE*) be hurt or have problems as a result of your own plans to hurt or trick others
▪ *noun* a piece of equipment used for lifting heavy things, or for lifting people who cannot stand or walk

hokey /ˈhəʊki; *AmE* ˈhoʊki/ *adj.* (*AmE, informal*) expressing emotions in a way that seems exaggerated or silly

hokum /ˈhəʊkəm; *AmE* ˈhoʊ-/ *noun* [U] (*informal, especially AmE*) **1** a film/movie, play, etc. that is not realistic and has no artistic qualities **2** an idea, argument, etc. that you think is stupid: *What a bunch of hokum!*

hold /həʊld; *AmE* hoʊld/ *verb, noun*
▪ *verb* (**held, held** /held/)
IN HAND/ARMS / **1** [VN] to carry sth; to have sb/sth in your hand, arms, etc: *She was holding a large box.* ◊ *I held the mouse by its tail.* ◊ *The girl held her father's hand tightly.* ◊ *He was holding the baby in his arms.* ◊ *The winning*

æ	ɑː	e	ɜː	ə	ɪ	iː	i	ɒ	ɔː	ʌ	ʊ	u	uː
cat	father	ten	bird	about	sit	see	many	got	saw	cup	put	actual	too
								(BrE)					

H

captain held the trophy in the air. ◊ *We were* **holding hands** (= holding each other's hands). ◊ *The lovers held each other close.* **2** [VN] to put your hand on part of your body, usually because it hurts: *She groaned and held her head.*

IN POSITION | **3** [usually +*adv.* / *prep.*] to keep sb/sth in a particular position: [VN] *Hold your head up.* ◊ *Hold this position for a count of 10.* ◊ *The wood is held in position by a clamp.* ◊ [VN-ADJ] *I'll hold the door open for you.*

SUPPORT | **4** [VN] to support the weight of sb/sth: *I don't think that branch will hold your weight.*

CONTAIN | **5** [VN] to have enough space for sth/sb; to contain sth/sb: *This barrel holds 25 litres.* ◊ *The plane holds about 300 passengers.*

SB PRISONER | **6** to keep sb and not allow them to leave: [VN] *Police are holding two men in connection with last Thursday's bank raid.* ◊ [VN-N] *He was held prisoner for two years.*

CONTROL | **7** [VN] to defend sth against attack; to have control of sth: *The rebels held the radio station.*

REMAIN | **8** [V] to remain strong and safe or in position: *They were afraid the dam wouldn't hold.* **9** [V] to remain the same: *How long will the fine weather hold?* ◊ *If their luck holds, they could still win the championship.*

KEEP | **10** [VN] to keep sb's attention or interest: *There wasn't much in the museum to hold my attention.* **11** [VN] to keep sth at the same level, rate, speed, etc: *Hold your speed at 70.* **12** [VN] to keep sth so that it can be used later: *records held on computer* ◊ *Our solicitor holds our wills.* ◊ *We can hold your reservation for three days.*

OWN | **13** [VN] to own or have sth: *Employees hold 30% of the shares.*

JOB | **14** [VN] to have a particular job or position: *How long has he held office?*

RECORD/ TITLE | **15** [VN] to have sth you have gained or achieved: *Who holds the world record for the long jump?* ◊ *She held the title of world champion for three years.*

OPINION | **16** [VN] to have a belief or an opinion about sb/sth: *He holds strange views on education.* ◊ *She is held in high regard by her students* (= they have a high opinion of her). ◊ *firmly-held beliefs* **17** (*formal*) to consider that sth is true: [VthAT] *I still hold that the government's economic policies are mistaken.* ◊ [VN-ADJ] *Parents will be held responsible for their children's behaviour.* ◊ [VNto inf] *These vases are held to be the finest examples of Greek art.* **HELP** This pattern is usually used in the passive.

MEETING | **18** [VN] [usually passive] to organize and have a meeting, competition, conversation, etc: *The meeting will be held in the community centre.* ◊ *It's impossible to hold a conversation with all this noise.*

ROAD/ COURSE | **19** [VN] if a vehicle **holds the road**, it is in close contact with the road and easy to control, especially when driven fast **20** [VN] if a ship or an aircraft **holds a course**, it continues to move in a particular direction

IN MUSIC | **21** [VN] to make a note continue for a particular time

ON TELEPHONE | **22** to wait until you can speak to the person you have telephoned: [V] *That extension is busy right now. Can you hold?* ◊ [VN] *She asked me to hold the line.*

STOP | **23** [VN] used to tell sb to stop doing sth or not to do sth: *Hold your fire!* (= don't shoot) ◊ *Hold the front page!* (= don't print it until a particular piece of news is available) ◊ (*AmE, informal*) *Give me a hot dog, but hold the* (= don't give me any) *mustard.*

IDM Most idioms containing **hold** are at the entries for the nouns and adjectives in the idioms, for example **hold the fort** is at **fort**. **hold ˈgood** to be true: *The same argument does not hold good in every case.* **ˈhold it** (*spoken*) used to ask sb to wait, or not to move: *Hold it a second—I don't think everyone's arrived yet.* **there is no ˈholding sb** a person cannot be prevented from doing sth:

Once she gets onto the subject of politics there's no holding her.

PHRV ˌhold sth aˈgainst sb to allow sth that sb has done to make you have a lower opinion of them: *I admit I made a mistake—but don't hold it against me.*

ˌhold sb/sth↔ˈback **1** to prevent sb/sth from moving forward or crossing sth: *The police were unable to hold back the crowd.* **2** to prevent the progress or development of sb/sth: *Do you think that mixed ability classes hold back the better students?* ˌhold sth↔ˈback **1** to not tell sb sth they want or need to know: *to hold back information* **2** to stop yourself from expressing how you really feel: *She just managed to hold back her anger.* ◊ *He bravely held back his tears.* ˌhold ˈback (from doing sth)| ˌhold sb ˈback (from doing sth) to hesitate or to make sb hesitate to act or speak: *She held back, not knowing how to break the terrible news.* ◊ *I wanted to tell him the truth, but something held me back.*

ˌhold sb↔ˈdown **1** to prevent sb from moving, using force: *It took three men to hold him down.* **2** to prevent sb from having their freedom or rights: *The people are held down by a repressive regime.* ˌhold sth↔ˈdown **1** to keep sth at a low level: *The rate of inflation must be held down.* **2** [no passive] to keep a job for some time: *He was unable to hold down a job after his breakdown.* **3** [no passive] (*AmE, informal*) to limit sth, especially a noise: *Hold it down, will you? I'm trying to sleep!*

ˌhold ˈforth to speak for a long time about sth in a way that other people might find boring

ˌhold sth↔ˈin to not express how you really feel: *to hold in your feelings/ anger* **OPP** LET STH OUT

ˌhold ˈoff **1** (of rain or a storm) to not start: *The rain held off just long enough for us to have our picnic.* **2** to not do sth immediately: *We could get a new computer now or hold off until prices are lower.* ◊ [+-ing] *Could you hold off making your decision for a few days?* ˌhold sb/sth↔ˈoff to stop sb/sth defeating you: *She held off all the last-minute challengers and won the race in a new record time.*

ˌhold ˈon **1** (*spoken*) used to tell sb to wait or stop: *Hold on a minute while I get my breath back.* ◊ *Hold on! This isn't the right road.* **2** to survive in a difficult or dangerous situation: *They managed to hold on until help arrived.* **3** (*spoken*) used on the telephone to ask sb to wait until they can talk to the person they want: *Can you hold on? I'll see if he's here.* ˌhold sth↔ˈon to keep sth in position: *These nuts and bolts hold the wheels on.* ◊ *The knob is only held on by sticky tape.* ˌhold ˈon (to sth/sb)| ˌhold ˈonto sth/sb [no passive] to keep holding sth/sb: *Hold on and don't let go until I say so.* ◊ *He held onto the back of the chair to stop himself from falling.* ˌhold ˈon to sth| ˌhold ˈonto sth **1** to keep sth that is an advantage for you; to not give or sell sth to sb else: *You should hold on to your oil shares.* ◊ *She took an early lead in the race and held onto it for nine laps.* **2** to keep sth for sb else or for longer than usual: *I'll hold onto your mail for you until you get back.*

ˌhold ˈout **1** to last, especially in a difficult situation: *We can stay here for as long as our supplies hold out.* **2** to resist or survive in a dangerous or difficult situation: *The rebels held out in the mountains for several years.* ˌhold ˈout to offer a chance, hope or possibility of sth: *Doctors hold out little hope of her recovering.* ˌhold sth↔ˈout to put your hand or arms, or sth in your hand, towards sb, especially to give or offer sth: *I held out my hand to steady her.* ◊ *He held out the keys and I took them.* ˌhold ˈout for sth [no passive] to cause a delay in reaching an agreement because you hope you will gain sth: *The union negotiators are holding out for a more generous pay settlement.* ˌhold ˈout on sb (*informal*) to refuse to tell or give sb sth

ˌhold sth↔ˈover [usually passive] **1** to not deal with sth immediately; to leave sth to be dealt with later: *The matter was held over until the next meeting.* **2** to show a film/movie, play, etc. for longer than planned: *The movie proved so popular it was held over for another week.* ˌhold sth ˈover sb to use knowledge that you have about sb to threaten them or make them do what you want

ˌhold sb to sth **1** to make sb keep a promise **2** to stop an

aɪ	aʊ	eɪ	əʊ	oʊ	ɔɪ	ɪə	eə	ʊə	j	w
my	now	say	go	go	boy	near	hair	pure	yes	wet
			(BrE)	(AmE)						

opposing team scoring more points than you: *The league leaders were held to a 0–0 draw.*

hold to'gether| **hold sth↔to'gether 1** to remain, or to keep sth, united: *A political party should hold together.* ◊ *It's the mother who usually holds the family together.* **2** (of an argument, a theory or a story) to be logical or CONSISTENT: *Their case doesn't hold together when you look at the evidence.*—compare HANG TOGETHER at HANG **3** if a machine or an object **holds together** or sth **holds it together**, the different parts stay together so that it does not break

hold 'up to remain strong and working effectively: *She's holding up well under the pressure.* **hold sb/sth↔'up** [often passive] **1** to support sb/sth and stop them from falling **2** to delay or block the movement or progress of sb/sth: *An accident is holding up traffic.* ◊ *My application was held up by the postal strike.*—related noun HOLD-UP **3** to use or present sb/sth as an example: *She's always holding up her children as models of good behaviour.* ◊ *His ideas were held up to ridicule.* **hold up 'sth** to rob a bank, shop/store, etc. using a gun—related noun HOLD-UP

hold with sth [no passive] (used in negative sentences or in questions) to agree with or approve of sth: *I don't hold with the use of force.* ◊ [+-ing] *They don't hold with letting children watch as much TV as they want.*

■ *noun*

WITH HAND | **1** (sing., U) the action of holding sb/sth; the way you are holding sb/sth SYN GRIP: *His hold on her arm tightened.* ◊ *She tried to keep hold of the child's hand as they walked along.* ◊ *Make sure you've got a steady hold on the camera.*

IN SPORT | **2** [C] a particular way of holding sb, especially in a sport such as WRESTLING or in a fight: *The wrestler put his opponent into a head hold.* ◊ *The exercise called for the recruits to get out of various holds.*

POWER/CONTROL | **3** [sing.] **~ (on/over sb/sth)** influence, power or control over sb/sth: *What she knew about his past gave her a hold over him.* ◊ *He struggled to get a hold of his anger.*—see also STRANGLEHOLD

IN CLIMBING | **4** [C] a place where you can put your hands or feet when climbing—see also FOOTHOLD, HANDHOLD, TOE-HOLD

ON SHIP/PLANE | **5** [C] the part of a ship or plane where the goods being carried are stored—picture at PLANE

IDM catch/get/grab/take, etc. (a) 'hold of sb/sth to have or take sb/sth in your hands: *He caught hold of her wrists so she couldn't get away.* ◊ *Lee got hold of the dog by its collar.* ◊ *Quick, grab a hold of that rope.* ◊ *Gently, she took hold of the door handle and turned it.* **get 'hold of sb** to contact or find sb: *Where have you been? I've been trying to get hold of you all day.* **get 'hold of sth 1** to find sth that you want or need: *I need to get hold of Tom's address.* ◊ *It's almost impossible to get hold of tickets for the final.* ◊ *It's almost impossible to get hold of tickets for the final.* ◊ *It's almost impossible to understand what sb is allowed to do: There will be no holds barred in his interview with the president this evening.* **on 'hold 1** delayed until a later time or date: *She put her career on hold to have a baby.* ◊ *The project is on hold until more money is available.* **2** if a person on the telephone is put **on hold**, they have to wait until the person that they want to talk to is free **take (a) 'hold** to begin to have complete control over sb/sth; to become very strong: *Panic took hold of him and he couldn't move.* ◊ *They managed to get out of the house just before the flames took hold.* ◊ *It is best to treat the disease early before it takes a hold.*—more at WRONG *adj.*

hold·all /'həʊldɔːl; *AmE* 'hoʊ-/ *noun* (*BrE*) a large bag made of strong fabric or soft leather, used when you are travelling for carrying clothes, etc.—compare DUFFEL BAG—picture at BAG

hold·er /'həʊldə(r); *AmE* 'hoʊ-/ *noun* (often in compounds) **1** a person who has or owns the thing mentioned: *a licence holder* ◊ *a season ticket holder* ◊ *the current holder of the world record* ◊ *holders of high office* ◊ *the holder of a French passport*—see also RECORD HOLDER, TITLE-HOLDER **2** a thing that holds the object mentioned: *a pen holder*—see also CIGARETTE HOLDER

hold·ing /'həʊldɪŋ; *AmE* 'hoʊ-/ *noun* **1 ~ (in sth)** a number of shares that sb has in a company: *She has a 40% holding in the company.*—see also FUNDHOLDING **2** [often pl.] an amount of property that is owned by a person, museum, library, etc: *one of the most important private holdings of Indian art* **3** a piece of land that is rented by sb and used for farming—see also SMALLHOLDING

holding company *noun* a company that is formed to buy shares in other companies which it then controls

holding operation *noun* a course of action that is taken so that a particular situation stays the same or does not become any worse

holding pattern *noun* the route a plane travels in while it is flying above the landing place, waiting for permission to land

hold·over /'həʊldəʊvə(r); *AmE* 'hoʊldoʊvər/ *noun* (*AmE*) a person who keeps a position of power, for example sb who had a particular position in one ADMINISTRATION and who still has it in the next

hold-up *noun* **1** a situation in which sth is prevented from happening for a short time: *What's the hold-up?* ◊ *We should finish by tonight, barring hold-ups.* ◊ (*BrE*) *Sorry I'm late. There was a hold-up on the motorway.* **2** an act of robbing a bank, etc. using a gun: *a hold-up at the local supermarket*

hole /həʊl; *AmE* hoʊl/ *noun, verb*

■ *noun*

HOLLOW SPACE | **1** [C] a hollow space in sth solid or in the surface of sth: *He dug a deep hole in the garden.* ◊ *The bomb blew a huge hole in the ground.* ◊ *Water had collected in the holes in the road.*

OPENING | **2** [C] a space or opening that goes all the way through sth SYN GAP: *to drill/bore/punch/kick a hole in sth* ◊ *There were holes in the knees of his trousers.* ◊ *The children climbed through a hole in the fence.* ◊ *a bullet hole* ◊ *the hole in the ozone layer*—see also OZONE HOLE

ANIMAL'S HOME | **3** [C] the home of a small animal: *a rabbit/mouse hole*—see also BOLT-HOLE—compare FOXHOLE, PIGEON-HOLE

UNPLEASANT PLACE | **4** [C, usually sing.] (*informal, disapproving*) an unpleasant place to live or be in: *I am not going to bring up my child in this hole.*—see also HELL-HOLE

IN GOLF | **5** [C] a hollow in the ground that you must get the ball into; one of the sections of a GOLF COURSE with the TEE at the beginning and the hole at the end: *The ball rolled into the hole and she had won.* ◊ *an eighteen-hole golf course* ◊ *He liked to play a few holes after work.* ◊ *She won the first hole.*—picture at GOLF

FAULT/WEAKNESS | **6** [C, usually pl.] a fault or weakness in sth such as a plan, law or story: *He was found not guilty because of holes in the prosecution case.* ◊ *I don't believe what she says—her story is full of holes.*—see also LOOP-HOLE

EMPTY PLACE/POSITION | **7** [sing.] a place or position that needs to be filled because sb/sth is no longer there: *After his wife left, there was a gaping hole in his life.* ◊ *Buying the new equipment left a big hole in the company's finances.*

HELP There are many other compounds ending in **hole**. You will find them at their place in the alphabet.

IDM in a 'hole (*informal*) in a difficult situation: *He had got himself into a hole and it was going to be difficult to get out of it.* **in the 'hole** (*AmE, informal*) in debt; owing money: *We start the current fiscal year $30 million in the hole.* **make a 'hole in sth** to use up a large amount of sth that you have, especially money: *School fees can make a big hole in your savings.*—more at ACE *n.*, BURN *v.*, DIG *v.*, PICK *v.*

■ *verb*

MAKE A HOLE | **1** [VN] [usually passive] to make a hole or holes in sth, especially a boat or ship

IN GOLF | **2 ~ (out)** to hit a golf ball into the hole: [VN] *She holed a 25 foot putt.* ◊ [V] *She holed out from 25 feet.*

PHRV hole 'up| be ,holed 'up (*informal*) to hide in a place: *He'll hole up now and move again tomorrow, after dark.* ◊ *We believe the gang are holed up in the mountains.*

H

hole-in-'one *noun* (*pl.* **holes-in-one**) an occasion in golf when a player hits the ball from the TEE into the hole using only one shot: *to get a hole-in-one*

,hole-in-the-'wall *noun* [sing.] (*informal*) **1** (*BrE*) = CASH MACHINE **2** (*AmE*) a small dark shop/store or restaurant ▶ **,hole-in-the-'wall** *adj.* [only before noun]: *hole-in-the-wall cash machines/restaurants*

holey /ˈhəʊli; *AmE* ˈhoʊ-/ *adj.* a **holey** piece of clothing or material has a lot of holes in it

holi·day /ˈhɒlədeɪ; *AmE* ˈhɑːl- *BrE also* -di/ *noun, verb*
■ *noun* **1** [U] (also **holi·days** [pl.]) (both *BrE*) (*AmE* **vacation**) a period of time when you are not at work or school: *the school/summer/Christmas holidays* ◇ *I'm afraid Mr Walsh is away on holiday this week.* ◇ *The package includes 20 days' paid holiday a year.* ◇ *holiday pay* ◇ *a holiday job* (= done by students during the school holidays) **2** [C] (*BrE*) (*AmE* **vac·ation**) a period of time spent travelling or resting away from home: *a camping/skiing/walking holiday* ◇ *a family/foreign holiday.* ◇ *a holiday cottage/home/resort* ◇ *the holiday industry* ◇ *Where are you going for your holidays this year?* ◇ *They met while on holiday in Greece.*—see also BUSMAN'S HOLIDAY, PACKAGE TOUR **3** [C] a day when most people do not go to work or school, especially because of a religious or national celebration: *a national holiday* ◇ *Today is a holiday in Wales.*—see also BANK HOLIDAY, PUBLIC HOLIDAY **4** (**holidays**) [pl.] (*AmE*) the time in December and early January that includes Christmas, Hanukkah and New Year: *Happy Holidays!* IDM see HIGH *adj.*
■ *verb* (*BrE*) (*AmE* **vac·ation**) [V] to spend a holiday somewhere: *She was holidaying with her family in Ireland.*

'holiday camp *noun* (*BrE*) a place that provides accommodation and entertainment for large numbers of people who are on holiday/vacation

holi·day·maker /ˈhɒlədeɪmeɪkə(r); *AmE* ˈhɑːl- *BrE also* -dimer-/ *noun* (*BrE*) (*AmE* **vac·ation·er**) a person who is visiting a place on holiday/vacation: *The plane was packed with Dutch holidaymakers.*

holier-than-thou /ˌhəʊliə ðən ˈðaʊ; *AmE* ˌhoʊliər/ *adj.* (*disapproving*) showing that you think that you are morally better than other people: *I can't stand his holier-than-thou attitude.*

holi·ness /ˈhəʊlinəs; *AmE* ˈhoʊ-/ *noun* **1** [U] the quality of being holy **2** (**His/Your Holiness**) [C] a title of respect used when talking to or about the Pope and some other religious leaders: *His Holiness Pope John Paul II*

hol·is·tic /həʊˈlɪstɪk; hɒˈl-; *AmE* hoʊ-; hɑːˈl-/ *adj.* **1** (*informal*) considering a whole thing or being to be more than a collection of parts: *a holistic approach to life* **2** (*medical*) treating the whole person rather than just the SYMPTOMS (= effects) of a disease: *holistic medicine* ▶ **hol·is·tic·al·ly** /-kli/ *adv.*

hol·ler /ˈhɒlə(r); *AmE* ˈhɑːl-/ *verb* (*informal, especially AmE*) to shout loudly SYN YELL: [V] *Don't holler at me!* ◇ [V speech] *'Look out!' I hollered.* [also VN]

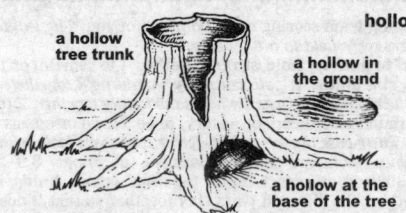

hollow
a hollow tree trunk
a hollow in the ground
a hollow at the base of the tree

hol·low /ˈhɒləʊ; *AmE* ˈhɑːloʊ/ *adj., noun, verb*
■ *adj.* **1** having a hole or empty space inside: *a hollow ball/centre/tube* ◇ *The tree trunk was hollow inside.* ◇ *Her stomach felt hollow with fear.* **2** (of parts of the face) sinking deeply into the face: *hollow eyes/cheeks* ◇ *hollow-eyed from lack of sleep* **3** [usually before noun] (of sounds) making a low sound like that made by an empty object when it is hit: *a hollow groan/echo* **4** [usually before noun] not sincere: *hollow promises/threats* ◇ *a hollow laugh/voice* ◇ *Their appeals for an end to the violence had a hollow ring.* **5** [usually before noun] without real value: *to win a hollow victory* ◇ *The statistics show that it was no hollow warning.* ▶ **hol·low·ly** *adv.*: *to laugh/echo hollowly* **hol·low·ness** *noun* [U]: *the hollowness of success/victory* IDM see RING[2] *v.*
■ *noun* **1** an area that is lower than the surface around it, especially on the ground: *muddy hollows* ◇ *The village lay secluded in a hollow of the hills* (= a small valley). ◇ *She noticed the slight hollows under his cheekbones.* **2** a hole or an enclosed space in sth: *The squirrel disappeared into a hollow at the base of the tree.*
■ *verb* [VN] [usually passive] to make a flat surface curve inwards IDM PHR V **hollow sth ↔ out 1** to make a hole in sth by removing part of it: *Hollow out the cake and fill it with cream.* **2** to form sth by making a hole in sth else: *The cave has been hollowed out of the mountainside.*

holly /ˈhɒli; *AmE* ˈhɑːli/ *noun* (*pl.* **-ies**) [U, C] a bush or small tree with hard shiny prickly leaves and bright red berries in winter, often used as a decoration at Christmas: *a sprig of holly*

hol·ly·hock /ˈhɒlihɒk; *AmE* ˈhɑːlihɑːk/ *noun* a tall garden plant with white, yellow, red or purple flowers growing up its stem

holo·caust /ˈhɒləkɔːst; *AmE* ˈhɑːlə-; ˈhoʊlə-/ *noun* **1** [C] a situation in which many things are destroyed and many people killed, especially because of a war or a fire: *a nuclear holocaust* **2** (**the Holocaust**) [sing.] the killing of millions of Jews by the Nazis in the 1930s and 1940s

holo·gram /ˈhɒləgræm; *AmE* ˈhɑːl-; ˈhoʊl-/ *noun* a special type of picture in which the objects seem to be THREE-DIMENSIONAL (= solid rather than flat)

holo·graph·ic /ˌhɒləˈgræfɪk; *AmE* ˌhɑːl-; ˌhoʊl-/ *adj.* [usually before noun] connected with holograms: *a holographic picture/illusion*

hols /hɒlz; *AmE* hɑːlz/ *noun* [pl.] (*old-fashioned, BrE, informal*) holidays

hol·ster /ˈhəʊlstə(r); *AmE* ˈhoʊ-/ *noun* a leather case worn on a belt or on a strap under the arm, used for carrying a small gun

holy /ˈhəʊli; *AmE* ˈhoʊli/ *adj.* (**holi·er, holi·est**) **1** [usually before noun] connected with God or a particular religion: *the Holy Bible/Scriptures* ◇ *holy ground* ◇ *a holy war* (= one fought to defend the beliefs of a particular religion) ◇ *the holy city of Mecca* ◇ *Islam's holiest shrine* OPP UNHOLY—see also HOLY ORDERS **2** good in a moral and religious way: *a holy life/man* OPP UNHOLY **3** [only before noun] (*informal*) used to emphasize that you are surprised, afraid, etc: *Holy cow! What was that?*—see also HOLIER-THAN-THOU, HOLINESS

,Holy Com'munion *noun* [U] = COMMUNION

the ,Holy 'Father *noun* [sing.] the POPE

the ,Holy 'Ghost *noun* [sing.] = THE HOLY SPIRIT

the ,Holy 'Grail *noun* [sing.] = GRAIL

the ,holy of 'holies *noun* [sing.] **1** the most holy part of a religious building **2** (*humorous*) a special room or building that can only be visited by important people

s	t	v	z	ʃ	ʒ	tʃ	dʒ	θ	ð	ŋ
see	tea	van	zoo	shoe	vision	chain	jam	thin	this	sing

‚holy 'orders *noun* [pl.] the official position of being a priest, BISHOP, etc: *to take holy orders* (= to become a priest)

the ‚Holy 'Spirit (also the ‚Holy 'Ghost) *noun* [sing.] (in Christianity) God in the form of a spirit

'Holy Week *noun* in the Christian Church, the week before Easter Sunday

hom·age /'hɒmɪdʒ; *AmE* 'hɑːm-/ *noun* [U, C, usually sing.] ~ (to sb/sth) (*formal*) something that is said or done to show respect for sb: *The kings of France paid homage to no one.* ◊ *He describes his book as 'a homage to my father'.* ◊ *They stood in silent homage around the grave.*

hom·burg /'hɒmbɜːɡ; *AmE* 'hɑːmbɜːrɡ/ *noun* a man's soft hat with a narrow, curled BRIM

home /həʊm; *AmE* hoʊm/ *noun, adj., adv., verb*

■ *noun*

HOUSE, etc. | 1 [C, U] the house or flat/apartment that you live in, especially with your family: *We are not far from my home now.* ◊ *Old people prefer to stay in their own homes.* ◊ *She leaves home at 7 every day.* ◊ *the family home* ◊ *While travelling she missed the comforts of home.* ◊ *He left home* (= left his parents and began an independent life) *at sixteen.* ◊ *Nowadays a lot of people work from home.* ◊ *I'll call you from home later.* ◊ (*figurative*) *We haven't found a home for all my father's books yet* (= a place where they can be kept). ◊ *stray dogs needing new homes*—see also STAY-AT-HOME 2 [C] a house or flat/apartment, etc., when you think of it as property that can be bought and sold: *a holiday/summer home* ◊ *A lot of new homes are being built on the edge of town.* ◊ *Private home ownership is increasing faster than ever.* ◊ *They applied for a home improvement loan.*—see also MOBILE HOME, SECOND HOME, STATELY HOME

TOWN/COUNTRY | 3 [C, U] the town, district, country, etc. that you come from, or where you are living and that you feel you belong to: *I often think about my friends back home.* ◊ *Jane left England and made Greece her home.* ◊ *Jamaica is home to over two million people.*

FAMILY | 4 [C] used to refer to a family living together, and the way it behaves: *She came from a violent home.* ◊ *He had always wanted a real home with a wife and children.*—see also BROKEN HOME

FOR OLD PEOPLE/CHILDREN | 5 [C] a place where people who cannot care for themselves live and are cared for by others: *a children's home* ◊ *an old people's home* ◊ *a retirement home* ◊ *a home for the mentally ill* ◊ *She has lived in a home since she was six.*—see also NURSING HOME, REST HOME

FOR PETS | 6 [C] a place where pets with no owner are looked after: *a dogs'/cats' home*

OF PLANT/ANIMAL | 7 [sing., U] the place where a plant or animal usually lives; the place where sb/sth can be found: *This region is the home of many species of wild flower.* ◊ *The tiger's home is in the jungle.* ◊ *The Rockies are home to bears and mountain lions.*

WHERE STH FIRST DONE | 8 [sing.] the ~ of sth the place where sth was first discovered, made or invented: *New Orleans, the home of jazz* ◊ *Greece, the home of democracy*

IDM at 'home 1 in a person's own house, flat/apartment, etc: *I phoned you last night, but you weren't at home.* ◊ *Oh no, I left my purse at home.* ◊ *He lived at home* (= with his parents) *until he was thirty.* 2 comfortable and relaxed: *Sit down and make yourself at home.* ◊ *Simon feels very at home on a horse.* 3 (used especially in journalism) in sb's own country, not in a foreign country: *The president is not as popular at home as he is abroad.* 4 if a sports team plays at home, it plays in the town, etc. that it comes from: *Leeds are playing at home this weekend.* ◊ *Is the match on Saturday at home or away?* away from 'home 1 away from a person's own house, flat/apartment, etc: *He works away from home during the week.* ◊ *I don't want to be away from home for too long.* 2 (*BrE*) if a sports team plays away from home, it plays in the town, etc. that its opponent comes from a ‚home from 'home (*BrE*) (*AmE* a ‚home away from 'home) a place where you feel relaxed and comfortable as if you were in your own home **home sweet 'home** (often *ironic*) used to say how pleasant your home is (especially when you really mean that it is not pleasant at all) **set up 'home** (*BrE*) (used especially about a couple) to start living in a new place: *They got married and set up home together in Hull.* **when he's, it's, etc. at 'home** (*BrE, humorous*) used to emphasize a question about sb/sth: *Who's she when she's at home?* (= I don't know her)—more at CHARITY, CLOSE² *adj.*, EAT, ENGLISHMAN, SPIRITUAL

■ *adj.* [only before noun]

WHERE YOU LIVE | 1 connected with the place where you live: *home life* (= with your family) ◊ *a person's home address/town* ◊ *We offer customers a free home delivery service.*

MADE/USED AT HOME | 2 made or used at home: *home movies* ◊ *home cooking* ◊ *a home computer* ◊ *home brew* (= beer that is made at home)

OWN COUNTRY | 3 (*especially BrE*) connected with your own country rather than foreign countries SYN DOMESTIC: *products for the home market* ◊ *home news/affairs* OPP FOREIGN, OVERSEAS

IN SPORT | 4 connected with a team's own sports ground: *a home match/win* ◊ *the home team* ◊ *Rangers were playing in front of their home crowd.*—compare AWAY

■ *adv.*

WHERE YOU LIVE | 1 to or at the place where you live: *Come on, it's time to go home.* ◊ *What time did you get home last night?* ◊ *The trip has been exhausting and I'll be glad to be home.* ◊ *After a month, they went back home to America.* ◊ *It was a lovely day so I walked home.* ◊ *Anna will drive me home after work.* ◊ *Hopefully the doctors will allow her home tomorrow.* ◊ (*AmE*) *I like to stay home in the evenings.*

INTO CORRECT POSITION | 2 into the correct position: *She leaned on the door and pushed the bolt home.* ◊ *He drove the ball home* (= scored a goal) *from 15 metres.* ◊ *The torpedo struck home on the hull of the ship.*

IDM be home and 'dry (*BrE*) (*AmE* be home 'free) to have done sth successfully, especially when it was difficult: *I could see the finish line and thought I was home and dry.* bring home the 'bacon (*informal*) to be successful at sth; to earn money for your family to live on bring sth 'home to sb to make sb realize how important, difficult or serious sth is: *The sight of his pale face brought home to me how ill he really was.* ◊ *The television pictures brought home to us all the full horror of the attack.* come 'home to sb to become completely clear to sb, often in a way that is painful: *It suddenly came home to him that he was never going to see Julie again.* sth comes home to 'roost (also the chickens come home to 'roost) used to say that if sb says or does sth bad or wrong, it will affect them badly in the future hit/strike 'home if a remark, etc. hits/strikes home, it has a strong effect on sb, in a way that makes them realize what the true facts of a situation are: *Her face went pale as his words hit home.*—more at COW *n.*, DRIVE *v.*, PRESS *v.*, RAM *v.*, ROMP *n.*, WRITE

■ *verb*

PHRV 'home 'in on sth 1 to aim at sth and move straight towards it: *The missile homed in on the target.* 2 to direct your thoughts or attention towards sth: *I began to feel I was really homing in on the answer.*

‚home 'base *noun* [sing., U] 1 = HOME PLATE 2 the place where sb/sth usually lives, works or operates from: *The submarine returned to its home base in Vancouver.*

home·body /'həʊmbɒdi; *AmE* 'hoʊmbɑːdi/ *noun* (*pl.* -ies) (*informal, especially AmE*) a person who enjoys spending time at home

home·boy /'həʊmbɔɪ; *AmE* 'hoʊm-/ *noun* (*AmE, slang*) a male friend from the same town as you; a member of your GANG (= a group of young people who go around together)

home·buy·er /'həʊmbaɪə(r); *AmE* 'hoʊm-/ *noun* a person who buys a house, flat/apartment, etc.

home·com·ing /'həʊmkʌmɪŋ; *AmE* 'hoʊm-/ *noun* 1 [C, U] the act of returning to your home after being away for a long time: *She spent the day preparing for his homecoming.* 2 [C] (*AmE*) a social event that takes place

H

æ	ɑː	e	ɜː	ə	ɪ	iː	i	ɒ	ɔː	ʌ	ʊ	u	uː
cat	father	ten	bird	about	sit	see	many	got	saw	cup	put	actual	too

(BrE)

every year at a high school, college or university for people who used to be students there

the ˌHome 'Counties *noun* [pl.] the counties around London

ˌhome eco'nomics *noun* [U] cooking and other skills needed at home, taught as a subject in school

ˌhome 'front *noun* [sing.] the people who do not go to fight in a war but who stay in a country to work **IDM** **on the 'home front** happening at home, or in your own country, rather than in a foreign country

ˌhome 'ground *noun* [sing., U] **1** (*BrE*) a sports ground that a team regularly plays on in their own area or town **2** a place where sb lives or works and where they feel confident, rather than a place that is not familiar to them: *I'd rather meet him here on my own home ground.*

ˌhome-'grown *adj.* **1** (of plants, fruit and vegetables) grown in a person's garden: *home-grown tomatoes* **2** made, trained or educated in your own country, town, etc: *The team has a wealth of home-grown talent.*

ˌhome 'help *noun* (*BrE*) a person whose job is to help old or sick people with cooking, cleaning, etc.

home-land /'həʊmlænd; *AmE* 'hoʊm-/ *noun* **1** [usually sing.] the country where a person was born: *Many refugees have been forced to flee their homeland.* **2** [usually pl.] (in the Republic of S Africa under the APARTHEID system in the past) one of the areas with some SELF-GOVERNMENT that were intended for a group of black African people to live in: *the Transkei homeland*

home-less /'həʊmləs; *AmE* 'hoʊm-/ *adj.* **1** having no home: *The scheme has been set up to help homeless people.* **2** (the homeless) *noun* [pl.] people who have no home: *helping the homeless* ▶ **home·less·ness** *noun* [U]

ˌhome 'loan *noun* (*informal*) = MORTGAGE

home·ly /'həʊmli; *AmE* 'hoʊm-/ *adj.* (**home·lier, home·li·est**) **1** (*BrE, approving*) (of a place) making you feel comfortable, as if you were in your own home: *The hotel has a lovely homely feel to it.* **2** (*approving, especially BrE*) simple and good: *homely cooking/food* **3** (*BrE, approving*) (of a woman) warm and friendly and enjoying the pleasures of home and family: *His landlady was a kind, homely woman.* **4** (*AmE, disapproving*) (of a person's appearance) not attractive: *a homely child*

ˌhome-'made *adj.* made at home, rather than produced in a factory and bought in a shop/store: *home-made jam*

home-maker /'həʊmmeɪkə(r); *AmE* 'hoʊm-/ *noun* (*especially AmE*) a person, especially a woman, who works at home and takes care of the house and family ▶ **home-making** *noun* [U]

the 'Home Office *noun* [sing.+ sing./pl. v.] the British government department that deals with the law, the police and prisons, and with decisions about who can enter the country

homeo·path (*BrE* also **hom·oeo-**) /'həʊmiəpæθ; *AmE* 'hoʊ-/ *noun* a person who treats illness using homeopathic methods

hom·eop·athy (*BrE* also **hom·oeo-**) /ˌhəʊmi'ɒpəθi; ˌhɒmi-; *AmE* ˌhoʊmi'ɑːp-; ˌhɑːm-/ *noun* [U] a system of treating diseases or conditions using very small amounts of the substance that causes the disease or condition ▶ **homeo·path·ic** (*BrE* also **hom·oeo-**) /ˌhəʊmiə'pæθɪk; ˌhɒm-; *AmE* ˌhoʊm-/ *adj.*: *homeopathic medicines/remedies/treatments*

home-own·er /'həʊməʊnə(r); *AmE* 'hoʊmoʊ-/ *noun* a person who owns their house or flat/apartment

'home page *noun* (*computing*) the main page created by a company, an organization, institution, etc. on the WORLD WIDE WEB from which connections to other pages can be made—picture on page 251

'home plate (also **ˌhome 'base**) (*AmE* also **plate**) *noun* (in baseball) the place where the person hitting the ball stands and where they must return to after running around all the bases—picture on page 1250

homer /'həʊmə(r); *AmE* 'hoʊm-/ *noun* (*AmE, informal*) = HOME RUN: *He hit a homer.*

home·room /'həʊmruːm; -rʊm; *AmE* 'hoʊm-/ *noun* [C, U] (*AmE*) a classroom where students go at the beginning of

each school day, so that teachers can check who is in school; the time spent in this room: *Homeroom lasts for ten minutes.*

ˌhome 'rule *noun* [U] the right of a country or region to govern itself, especially after another country or region has governed it

ˌhome 'run (also *AmE informal* **homer**) *noun* (in baseball) a hit that allows the person hitting the ball to run around all the bases without stopping

Home 'Secretary *noun* the British government minister in charge of the Home Office

home·sick /'həʊmsɪk; *AmE* 'hoʊm-/ *adj.* sad because you are away from home and you miss your family and friends: *I felt homesick for Scotland.* ▶ **home·sick·ness** *noun* [U]

home·spun /'həʊmspʌn; *AmE* 'hoʊm-/ *adj.* **1** (especially of ideas) simple and ordinary; not coming from an expert: *homespun philosophy* **2** (of fabric) woven at home

home·stead /'həʊmsted; *AmE* 'hoʊm-/ *noun, verb*
■ *noun* **1** a house with the land and buildings around it, especially a farm **2** (in the US in the past) a piece of land given to sb by the government on condition that they lived on it and grew crops on it
■ *verb* [V] (*old-fashioned, AmE*) to live and work on a homestead (2) ▶ **home·stead·er** *noun*

the ˌhome 'straight (*especially BrE*) (also **the ˌhome 'stretch** *especially in AmE*) *noun* [sing.] **1** the last part of a race **2** the last part of an activity, etc. when it is nearly completed

ˌhome 'town *noun* the place where you were born or lived as a child

ˌhome 'truth *noun* [usually pl.] a true but unpleasant fact about a person, usually told to them by sb else: *It's time you told him a few home truths.*

home·ward /'həʊmwəd; *AmE* 'hoʊmwərd/ *adj.* going towards home: *the homeward journey* ▶ **home·ward** (also **home·wards** *especially BrE*) *adv.*: *Commuters were heading homeward at the end of the day.* ◇ *We drove homewards in silence.* ◇ *We were homeward bound at last.*

home·work /'həʊmwɜːk; *AmE* 'hoʊmwɜːrk/ *noun* [U] **1** work that is given by teachers for students to do at home: *I still haven't done my geography homework.* ◇ *How much homework do you get?* ◇ *I have to write up the notes for homework.* **2** (*informal*) work that sb does to prepare for sth: *You could tell that he had really done his homework* (= found out all he needed to know).

home·work·er /'həʊmwɜːkə(r); *AmE* 'hoʊmwɜːrk-/ *noun* a person who works at home, often doing jobs that are not well paid such as making clothes for shops/stores ▶ **home·work·ing** *noun* [U]

homey (also **homy**) /'həʊmi; *AmE* 'hoʊmi/ *adj.* (especially *AmE*) pleasant and comfortable, like home: *The hotel had a nice, homey atmosphere.*

homi·cidal /ˌhɒmɪ'saɪdl; *AmE* ˌhɑːm-/ *adj.* likely to kill another person; making sb likely to kill another person: *a homicidal maniac* ◇ *He had clear homicidal tendencies.*

homi·cide /'hɒmɪsaɪd; *AmE* 'hɑːm-/ *noun* [C, U] (*especially AmE, law*) the crime of killing sb deliberately **SYN** MURDER—compare MANSLAUGHTER

hom·ily /'hɒməli; *AmE* 'hɑːm-/ *noun* (*pl.* **-ies**) (*formal, often disapproving*) a speech or piece of writing giving advice on the correct way to behave, etc: *She delivered a homily on the virtues of family life.*

hom·ing /'həʊmɪŋ; *AmE* 'hoʊm-/ *adj.* [only before noun] **1** (of a bird or an animal) trained, or having a natural ability, to find the way home from a long distance away: *Many birds have a remarkable homing instinct.* **2** (of a missile, etc.) fitted with an electronic device that enables it to find and hit the place or object it is aimed at: *a homing device*

'homing pigeon *noun* a PIGEON (= a type of bird) that has been trained to find its way home from a long distance away, and that people race against other pigeons for sport

hom·iny /'hɒmɪni; *AmE* 'hɑːm-/ *noun* [U] dried MAIZE,

H

boiled in water or milk, eaten especially in the southern states of the US

homo- /'hɒməʊ-; 'həʊm-; *AmE* 'hoʊmoʊ-/ *combining form* (in nouns, adjectives and adverbs) the same: *homogeneous* ◇ *homosexual*—compare HETERO-

hom·oe·op·athy (*BrE*) = HOMEOPATHY

homo·gen·eity /ˌhɒmədʒə'niːəti; *AmE* ˌhɑːm-/ *noun* [U] (*formal*) the quality of being homogeneous

homo·ge·neous /ˌhɒmə'dʒiːniəs; *AmE* ˌhoʊm-/ *adj.* (*formal*) consisting of things or people that are all the same or all of the same type: *a homogeneous group/ mixture/population* OPP HETEROGENEOUS

hom·ogen·ized (*BrE* also **-ised**) /hə'mɒdʒənaɪzd; *AmE* hə'mɑːdʒ-/ *adj.* (of milk) treated so that the cream is mixed in with the rest

homo·graph /'hɒməɡrɑːf; *AmE* 'hɑːməɡræf/ *noun* (*grammar*) a word that is spelt like another word but has a different meaning from it, and may have a different pronunciation, for example *bow* /baʊ/, *bow* /bəʊ/; *AmE* boʊ/

homo·nym /'hɒmənɪm; *AmE* 'hɑːm-; 'hoʊm-/ *noun* (*grammar*) a word that is spelt like another word (and may be pronounced like it) but which has a different meaning, for example *can* meaning 'be able' and *can* meaning 'put sth in a container'

homo·pho·bia /ˌhɒmə'fəʊbiə; ˌhəʊm-; *AmE* ˌhoʊmə'foʊ-/ *noun* [U] a strong dislike and fear of HOMOSEXUAL people ▶ **homo·pho·bic** *adj.*

homo·phone /'hɒməfəʊn; *AmE* 'hɑːməfoʊn/ *noun* (*grammar*) a word that is pronounced like another word but has a different spelling or meaning, for example *some, sum* /sʌm/

Homo sa·pi·ens /ˌhəʊməʊ 'sæpienz; *AmE* ˌhoʊmoʊ 'seɪp-; 'sæp-/ *noun* [U] (from *Latin, technical*) the kind or SPECIES of human being that exists now

homo·sex·ual /ˌhəʊmə'sekʃuəl; ˌhɒm-; *AmE* ˌhoʊm-/ *noun* a person, usually a man, who is sexually attracted to people of the same sex: *a practising homosexual*—compare BISEXUAL, GAY, HETEROSEXUAL, LESBIAN ▶ **homo·sex·ual** *adj.*: *a homosexual act/relationship* **homo·sexu·al·ity** /ˌhəʊməˌsekʃu'æləti; ˌhɒm-; *AmE* ˌhoʊm-/ *noun* [U]

homy = HOMEY

Hon (also **Hon.** especially in *AmE*) /ɒn; *AmE* ɑːn/ *abbr.* **1** (*BrE*) HONORARY (used in official titles of jobs): *Hon Treasurer: D Shrimpton* **2** HONOURABLE: *the Hon Member for Bolsover*

hon·cho /'hɒntʃəʊ; *AmE* 'hɑːntʃoʊ/ *noun* (*informal, especially AmE*) the person who is in charge SYN BOSS: *Claude is the studio's head honcho.*

hone /həʊn; *AmE* hoʊn/ *verb* [VN] ~ **sth (to sth)** **1** to develop and improve sth, especially a skill, over a period of time: *His body was honed to perfection.* ◇ *She honed her debating skills at college.* ◇ *It was a finely honed piece of writing.* **2** to make a blade sharp or sharper SYN SHARPEN

hon·est /'ɒnɪst; *AmE* 'ɑːn-/ *adj.* **1** always telling the truth, and never stealing or cheating: *an honest man/woman* **2** ~ **(about sth)| ~ (with sb)** not hiding the truth about sth: *an honest answer* ◇ *Are you being completely honest about your feelings?* ◇ *Thank you for being so honest with me.* ◇ *Give me your honest opinion.* ◇ (*spoken*) *To be honest* (= what I really think is), *it was one of the worst books I've ever read.* ◇ *Let's be honest, she's only interested in Mike because of his money.* **3** showing an honest mind or attitude: *She's got an honest face.* **4** (of work or wages) earned or resulting from hard work: *He hasn't done an honest day's work in his life.* ◇ *It's quite a struggle to make an honest living.* HELP Use *an*, not *a*, before honest. IDM **honest!** (*spoken*) used to emphasize that you are not lying: *I didn't mean it, honest!* **honest to 'God/'goodness** used to emphasize that what you are saying is true: *Honest to God, Mary, I'm not joking.* HELP Some people find this use offensive. **make an honest 'woman of sb** (*old-fashioned, humorous*) to marry a woman after having had a sexual relationship with her

ˌhonest 'broker *noun* a person or country that tries to get other people or countries to reach an agreement or to

solve a problem, without getting involved with either side

hon·est·ly /'ɒnɪstli; *AmE* 'ɑːn-/ *adv.* **1** in an honest way: *I can't believe he got that money honestly.* **2** used to emphasize that what you are saying is true, however surprising it may seem: *I didn't tell anyone, honestly!* ◇ *I honestly can't remember a thing about last night.* ◇ *You can't honestly expect me to believe that!* **3** used to show that you disapprove of sth and are irritated by it: *Honestly! Whatever will they think of next?*

ˌhonest-to-'goodness *adj.* [only before noun] (*approving*) simple and good: *honest-to-goodness country food*

hon·esty /'ɒnəsti; *AmE* 'ɑːn-/ *noun* [U] the quality of being honest: *She answered all my questions with her usual honesty.* ◇ *His honesty is not in question.* IDM **in all 'honesty** used to state a fact or an opinion which, though true, may seem disappointing: *The book isn't, in all honesty, as good as I expected.*

honey /'hʌni/ *noun* **1** [U] a sweet sticky yellow substance made by bees that is spread on bread, etc. like jam and used in cooking **2** [C] (*spoken*) a way of addressing sb that you like or love: *Have you seen my keys, honey?* **3** [C] (*spoken*) a person that you like or love and think is very kind: *He can be a real honey when he wants to be.* IDM see LAND *n.*

honey·comb /'hʌnikəʊm; *AmE* -koʊm/ (also **comb**) *noun* [C, U] a structure of cells with six sides, made by bees for holding their honey and their eggs

honey·combed /'hʌnikəʊmd; *AmE* -koʊmd/ *adj.* ~ **(with sth)** filled with holes, tunnels, etc.

honey·dew melon /ˌhʌnidjuː 'melən; *AmE* -duː/ *noun* a type of MELON with a pale skin and green flesh

hon·eyed /'hʌnid/ *adj.* (*literary*) **1** (of words) soft and intended to please, but often not sincere: *She spoke in honeyed tones.* **2** (*literary*) tasting or smelling like honey, or having the gold colour of honey

honey·moon /'hʌnimuːn/ *noun, verb*
■ *noun* [usually sing.] **1** a holiday/vacation taken by a couple who have just got married: *We went to Venice for our honeymoon.* ◇ *They're on their honeymoon.* **2** the period of time at the start of a new activity when nobody is criticized and people feel enthusiastic: *The honeymoon period for the government is now over.*
■ *verb* [V+adv./prep.] to spend your honeymoon somewhere ▶ **honey·moon·er** *noun*

honey·pot /'hʌnipɒt; *AmE* -pɑːt/ *noun* [usually sing.] (*BrE*) a place, thing or person that a lot of people are attracted to: *The toy section of the store is a honeypot for children.*

honey·suckle /'hʌnisʌkl/ *noun* [U, C] a climbing plant with white, yellow or pink flowers with a sweet smell

honk /hɒŋk; *AmE* hɑːŋk; hɔːŋk/ *noun, verb*
■ *noun* **1** the noise made by a GOOSE **2** the noise made by a car horn
■ *verb* **1** if a car horn **honks** or you **honk** or **honk the horn**, the horn makes a loud noise SYN HOOT: [V] *honking taxis* ◇ *Why did he honk at me?* ◇ [VN] *People honked their horns as they drove past.* **2** [V] when a GOOSE **honks**, it makes a loud noise

honky /'hɒŋki; *AmE* 'hɑːŋ-; 'hɔːŋ-/ *noun* (*pl.* **-ies**) (*AmE, slang*) an offensive word for a white person, used by black people

honky-tonk /'hɒŋki tɒŋk; *AmE* 'hɑːŋki tɑːŋk; 'hɔːŋki tɔːŋk/ *noun* **1** [C] (*AmE*) a cheap, noisy bar or dance hall **2** [U] a type of lively jazz played on a piano: *a honky-tonk piano/singer*

honor, hon·or·able (*AmE*) = HONOUR, HONOURABLE

hon·or·arium /ˌɒnə'reəriəm; *AmE* ˌɑːnə'rer-/ *noun* (*pl.* **hon·or·aria** /-riə/) (*formal*) a payment made for sb's professional services HELP Use *an*, not *a*, before honorarium.

hon·or·ary /'ɒnərəri; *AmE* 'ɑːnəreri/ *adj.* (*abbr.* Hon) **1** (of a university degree, a rank, etc.) given as an honour, without the person having to have the usual qualifications: *an honorary doctorate/degree* **2** (of a position in an organization) not paid: *the honorary president* ◇ *The* *post of treasurer is a purely honorary position.* **3** treated like a member of group without actually belonging to it: *She was treated as an honorary man.* **HELP** Use **an**, not **a**, before **honorary**.

hon·or·if·ic /ˌɒnəˈrɪfɪk; *AmE* ˌɑːnə-/ *adj.* (*formal*) showing respect for the person you are speaking to: *an honorific title* **HELP** Use **an**, not **a**, before **honorific**.

'honor roll *noun* (*AmE*) **1** = ROLL OF HONOUR **2** a list of the best students in a college or high school

'honor system *noun* [sing.] (*AmE*) an agreement in which people are trusted to obey rules

hon·our (*BrE*) (*AmE* **honor**) /ˈɒnə(r); *AmE* ˈɑːnər/ *noun, verb*

HELP Use **an**, not **a**, before **honour**.

■ *noun*

RESPECT | **1** [U] great respect and admiration for sb: *the guest of honour* (= the most important one) ◊ *the seat/place of honour* (= given to the most important guest) ◊ *They stood in silence as a mark of honour to her.*—see also MAID OF HONOUR, MATRON OF HONOUR

PRIVILEGE | **2** [sing.] (*formal*) something that you are very pleased or proud to do because people are showing you great respect: *It was a great honour to be invited here today.*

MORAL BEHAVIOUR | **3** [U] the quality of knowing and doing what is morally right: *a man of honour* ◊ *Proving his innocence has become a matter of honour.*

REPUTATION | **4** [U] a good reputation; respect from other people: *upholding the honour of your country* ◊ *The family honour is at stake.*

SB/STH CAUSING RESPECT | **5** [sing.] **~ to sth/sb** a person or thing that causes others to respect and admire sth/sb: *She is an honour to the profession.*

AWARD | **6** [C] an award, official title, etc. given to sb as a reward for sth that they have done: *the New Year's Honours list* (= in Britain, a list of awards and titles given on January 1 each year) ◊ *to win the highest honour* ◊ *He was buried with full military honours* (= with a special military service as a sign of respect).—see also ROLL OF HONOUR

AT UNIVERSITY/SCHOOL | **7** (**honours, honors**) [pl.] (*abbr.* **Hons**) (often used as an adjective) a university course that is of a higher level than a basic course (in the US also used to describe a class in school which is at a higher level than other classes): *an honours degree/course* ◊ *a First Class Honours degree* ◊ (*AmE*) *I took an honors class in English.* **8** (**honours, honors**) [pl.] if you pass an exam or GRADUATE from a university or school **with honours**, you receive a special mark/grade for having achieved a very high standard

JUDGE/MAYOR | **9** (**His/Her/Your Honour**) [C] a title of respect used when talking to or about a judge or a US MAYOR: *No more questions, Your Honour.*

IN CARD GAMES | **10** [C, usually pl.] the cards that have the highest value

IDM **do sb an 'honour | do sb the 'honour (of doing sth)** (*formal*) to do sth to make sb feel very proud and pleased: *Would you do me the honour of dining with me?* **do the 'honours** to perform a social duty or ceremony, such as pouring drinks, making a speech, etc: *Would you do the honours and draw the winning ticket?* **have the 'honour of sth/of doing sth** (*formal*) to be given the opportunity to do sth that makes you feel proud and happy: *May I have the honour of the next dance?* **(there is) honour among 'thieves** (*saying*) used to say that even criminals have standards of behaviour that they respect **(feel) honour 'bound to do sth** (*formal*) to feel that you must do sth because of your sense of moral duty: *She felt honour bound to attend as she had promised to.* **the honours are 'even** no particular person, team, etc. is doing better than the others in a competition, an argument, etc. **in 'honour of sb/sth | in sb's/sth's 'honour** in order to show respect and admiration for sb/sth: *a ceremony in honour of those killed in the explosion* ◊ *A banquet was held in her honour.* **on your 'honour** (*old-fashioned*) **1** used to promise very seriously that you will do sth or that sth is true: *I swear on my honour that I*

knew nothing about this. **2** to be trusted to do sth: *You're on your honour not to go into my room.*—more at POINT *n.*

■ *verb* [VN]

SHOW RESPECT | **1 ~ sb (with sth)** to do sth that shows great respect for sb/sth: *The President honoured us with a personal visit.* ◊ *our honoured guests* ◊ (*ironic*) *I'm glad to see that you've decided to honour us with your presence!*

GIVE AWARD | **2 ~ sb/sth (with sth) (for sth)** to give public praise, an award or a title to sb for sth they have done: *He has been honoured with a knighthood for his scientific work.* **OPP** DISHONOUR

KEEP PROMISE | **3** to do what you have agreed or promised to do: *I have every intention of honouring our contract.* ◊ *to honour a cheque* (= to keep an agreement to pay it) **OPP** DISHONOUR

IDM **be/feel honoured (to do sth)** to feel proud and happy: *I was honoured to have been mentioned in his speech.*

hon·our·able (*BrE*) (*AmE* **hon·or·able**) /ˈɒnərəbl; *AmE* ˈɑːnə-/ *adj.* **1** deserving respect and admiration: *a long and honourable career in government* ◊ *They managed an honourable 2-2 draw.* ◊ *With a few honourable exceptions, the staff were found to be incompetent.* **2** showing high moral standards: *an honourable man* **3** allowing sb to keep their good name and the respect of others: *an honourable compromise* ◊ *They urged her to do the honourable thing and resign.* ◊ *He received an honourable discharge from the army.* **4** (**the Honourable**) (*abbr.* **Hon**) [only before noun] (in Britain) a title used by a child of some ranks of the NOBILITY **5** (**the/my Honourable ...**) (*abbr.* **Hon**) [only before noun] (in Britain), a title used by Members of Parliament when talking about or to another Member during a debate: *If my Honourable Friend would give me a chance to answer, ...* **6** (*abbr.* **Hon**) a title of respect used by an official of high rank: *the Honorable Alan Simpson, US senator*—compare RIGHT HONOURABLE **HELP** Use **an**, not **a**, before **honourable**. ▶ **hon·our·ably** (*BrE*) (*AmE* **hon·or·ably**) /-əbli/ *adv.*: *to behave honourably*

Hons /ɒnz; *AmE* ɑːnz/ *abbr.* (*BrE*) HONOURS (used after the name of a university degree): *Tim Smith BA (Hons)*

hooch /huːtʃ/ *noun* [U] (*informal, especially AmE*) strong alcoholic drink, especially sth that has been made illegally: *a bottle of hooch*

hood /hʊd/ *noun* **1** a part of a coat, etc. that you can pull up to cover the back and top of your head: *a jacket with a detachable hood*—picture at HAT and on page A5 **2** a piece of fabric put over sb's face and head so that they cannot be recognized or so that they cannot see **3** a piece of coloured silk or fur worn over an academic GOWN to show the kind of degree held by the person wearing it **4** (*especially BrE*) a folding cover over a car, etc: *We drove all the way with the hood down.*—picture at PUSHCHAIR **5** (*AmE*) = BONNET (2) **6** a cover placed over a device or machine, for example, to protect it: *a lens hood* ◊ *an extractor hood* (= one that removes cooking smells from a kitchen) **7** (*slang, especially AmE*) = HOODLUM (1)

-hood *suffix* (in nouns) **1** the state or quality of: *childhood* ◊ *falsehood* **2** a group of people of the type mentioned: *the priesthood*

hood·ed /ˈhʊdɪd/ *adj.* **1** having or wearing a hood: *a hooded jacket* ◊ *A hooded figure waited in the doorway.* **2** (of eyes) having large EYELIDS that always look as if they are partly closed

hood·lum /ˈhuːdləm/ *noun* (*informal*) **1** (also *slang* **hood** especially in *AmE*) a violent criminal, especially one who is part of a GANG **2** a violent and noisy young man

hood·wink /ˈhʊdwɪŋk/ *verb* [VN] **~ sb (into doing sth)** to trick sb: *She had been hoodwinked into buying a worthless necklace.*

hooey /ˈhuːi/ *noun* [U] (*informal, especially AmE*) nonsense; stupid talk

hoof /huːf/ *noun, verb*

■ *noun* (pl. **hoofs** or **hooves** /huːvz/) the hard part of the foot of some animals, for example horses **IDM** **on the 'hoof 1** meat that is sold, transported, etc. **on the hoof** is sold, etc. while the cow or sheep is still alive **2** (*BrE*,

s	t	v	z	ʃ	ʒ	tʃ	dʒ	θ	ð	ŋ
see	tea	van	zoo	shoe	vision	chain	jam	thin	this	sing

informal) if you do sth **on the hoof**, you do it quickly and without giving it your full attention because you are doing sth else at the same time

■ *verb* [VN] (*informal*) to kick a ball very hard or a long way **IDM** **'hoof it** to go somewhere on foot; to walk somewhere: *We hoofed it all the way to 42nd Street.*

hoo-ha /'huː haː/ *noun* [U, sing.] (*BrE, informal*) noisy excitement, especially about sth unimportant **SYN** FUSS

hook /hʊk/ *noun, verb*

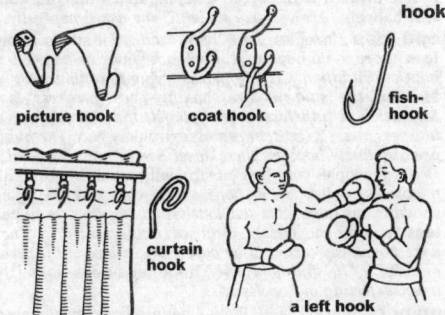

picture hook   coat hook   **hook**   **fish-hook**

curtain hook

a left hook

■ *noun* **1** a curved piece of metal, plastic or wire for hanging things on, catching fish with, etc.: *a picture/curtain/coat hook ◊ a fish-hook ◊ Hang your towel on that hook.—*see also BOATHOOK **2** (in boxing) a short hard blow that is made with the elbow bent: *a left hook to the jaw* **3** (in cricket and golf) a way of hitting the ball so that it curves sideways instead of going straight ahead **IDM** **by ,hook or by 'crook** using any method you can, even a dishonest one **get (sb) off the 'hook | let sb off the 'hook** to free yourself or sb else from a difficult situation or a punishment **hook, line and 'sinker** completely: *What I said was not true, but he fell for it* (= believed it) *hook, line and sinker.* **off the 'hook** if you leave or take the telephone **off the 'hook**, you take the RECEIVER (= the part that you pick up) off the place where it usually rests, so that nobody can call you—more at RING² *v.*, SLING *v.*

■ *verb* **1** [+*adv./prep.*] to fasten or hang sth on sth else using a hook; to be fastened or hanging in this way: [VN] *We hooked the trailer to the back of the car.* ◊ [V] *a dress that hooks at the back* [+*adv./prep.*] to put sth, especially your leg, arm or finger, around sth else so that you can hold onto it or move it; to go around sth else in this way: [VN] *He hooked his foot under the stool and dragged it over.* ◊ *Her thumbs were hooked into the pockets of her jeans.* ◊ [V] *Suddenly an arm hooked around my neck.* **3** [VN] to catch a fish with a hook: *It was the biggest pike I ever hooked.* ◊ (*figurative*) *She had managed to hook a wealthy husband.* **4** [VN] (*especially in golf, cricket or football*) to hit or kick a ball so that it goes to one side instead of straight ahead **PHR V** **,hook** **'up (to sth)** | **,hook sb/sth** **'up (to sth)** to connect sb/sth to a piece of electronic equipment or to a power supply: *She was then hooked up to an IV drip.* ◊ *Check that the computer is hooked up to the printer.*—related noun HOOK-UP **,hook 'up with sb** (*informal*) **1** to meet sb and spend time with them **2** to start working with sb

hoo-kah /'hʊkə/ *noun* a long pipe for smoking, used in some eastern countries, that passes smoke through a container of water to cool it

,hook and 'eye *noun* (*pl.* **hooks and eyes**) a device for fastening clothes, consisting of a small thin piece of metal curved round, and a hook that fits into it—picture at FASTENER

hooked /hʊkt/ *adj.* **1** curved; shaped like a hook: *a hooked nose/beak/finger* **2** [not before noun] ~ **(on sth)** (*informal*) dependent on sth bad, especially a drug **3** [not before noun] ~ **(on sth)** (*informal*) enjoying sth very much, so that you want to do it, see it, etc. as much as possible **4** having one or more hooks

hook·er /'hʊkə(r)/ *noun* **1** the player in a rugby team, whose job is to pull the ball out of the SCRUM with his foot

2 (*informal*) a prostitute (= a woman who has sex with men for money)

hookey = HOOKY

'hook-up *noun* a connection between two pieces of equipment, especially electronic equipment used in broadcasting, or computers: *a satellite hook-up between the major European networks*

hook·worm /'hʊkwɜːm; *AmE* -wɜːrm/ *noun* **1** [C] a worm that lives in the INTESTINES of humans and animals **2** [U] a disease caused by hookworms

hooky (also **hookey**) /'hʊki/ (*especially AmE*) **IDM** **play 'hooky** (*old-fashioned, informal*) = PLAY TRUANT at TRUANT

hooli·gan /'huːlɪɡən/ *noun* a young person who behaves in an extremely noisy and violent way in public, usually in a group: *English football hooligans* ► **hooli·gan·ism** /-ɪzəm/ *noun* [U]

hoop /huːp/ *noun* **1** a large ring of plastic, wood or iron: *a barrel bound with iron hoops* ◊ *hoop earrings* (= in the shape of a hoop) **2** the ring that the players throw the ball through in the game of basketball in order to score points: *Let's shoot some hoops.* **3** a large ring that was used as a children's toy in the past, or for animals or riders to jump through at a CIRCUS **4** a small arch made of metal or plastic, put into the ground: *croquet hoops* ◊ *Grow lettuces under plastic stretched over wire hoops.* **IDM** see JUMP *v.*

hooped /huːpt/ *adj.* shaped like a hoop: *hooped earrings*

hoopla /'huːplaː/ *noun* **1** [U, sing.] (*informal, especially AmE*) excitement about sth which gets a lot of public attention **2** [U] (*BrE*) (*AmE* **ring·toss**) a game in which players try to throw rings over objects in order to win them as prizes

hoo·ray /hu'reɪ/ (also **hur·rah, hur·ray**) *exclamation* used to show that you are happy or that you approve of sth **IDM** see HIP *exclam.*

hoot /huːt/ *verb, noun*
■ *verb* **1** [V] to make a loud noise: *He had the audience hooting with laughter.* ◊ *Some people hooted in disgust.* **2** (*BrE*) if a car horn **hoots** or you **hoot** or **hoot the horn**, the horn makes a loud noise **SYN** HONK: [V] *hooting cars* ◊ *Why did he hoot at me?* ◊ [VN] *Passing motorists hooted their horns.* ◊ *The train hooted a warning* (= the driver sounded the horn to warn people). **3** [V] when an OWL **hoots**, it makes a long calling sound
■ *noun* **1** [C] (*especially BrE*) a short loud laugh or shout: *The suggestion was greeted by **hoots of laughter**.* **2** [sing.] (*spoken*) a situation or a person that you find very funny: *The play was a real hoot!* ◊ *You ought to meet her—she's a hoot!* **3** the loud sound made by the horn of a vehicle **4** the cry of an OWL **IDM** **not care/give a 'hoot | not care/give two 'hoots** (*informal*) not to care at all: *I don't care two hoots about having money, as long as I'm happy.*

hoot·er /'huːtə(r)/ *noun* **1** (*rather old-fashioned*) the device in a vehicle, or a factory, that makes a loud noise as a signal **2** (*BrE, slang*) a person's nose, especially a large one [usually pl.] (*AmE, slang*) a woman's breast

hoo·ver /'huːvə(r)/ *verb* (*BrE*) to clean a carpet, floor, etc. with a Hoover **SYN** VACUUM: [VN] *to hoover the carpet/floor/bedroom* [also V] ► **hoo·ver·ing** *noun* [U]: *It's your turn to do the hoovering.*

Hoo·ver™ /'huːvə(r)/ *noun* (*BrE*) = VACUUM CLEANER

hooves *pl.* of HOOF—picture on page A6

hop /hɒp; *AmE* hɑːp/ *verb, noun*
■ *verb* (**-pp-**) **1** [V] [usually +*adv./prep.*] (*of a person*) to move by jumping on one foot: *I couldn't put my weight on my ankle and had to hop everywhere.* ◊ *kids hopping over puddles* **2** [V+*adv./prep.*] (*of an animal or a bird*) to move by jumping with all or both feet together: *A robin was hopping around on the path.* **3** [V+*adv./prep.*] (*informal*) to go or move somewhere quickly and suddenly: *Hop in, I'll drive you home.* ◊ *to hop into/out of bed* ◊ *We hopped over to Paris for the weekend.* **4** [VN] (*AmE*) ~ **a plane, bus, train, etc.** to get on a plane, bus, etc. **5** [V] ~ **(from sth to sth)** to change from one activity or subject to another: *I like to hop from channel to channel when I watch TV.* **IDM** **'hop it** (*BrE, old-fashioned, informal*)

æ	ɑː	e	ɜː	ə	ɪ	iː	i	ɒ	ɔː	ʌ	ʊ	u	uː
cat	father	ten	bird	about	sit	see	many	got	saw	cup	put	actual	too
								(BrE)					

usually used in orders to tell sb to go away: *Go on, hop it!* ¦hopping 'mad (*informal*) very angry **hop 'to it** (*AmE*) = JUMP TO IT

■ *noun* **1** [C] a short jump by a person on one foot: *He crossed the hall with a hop, skip and a jump.* **2** [C] a short jump by an animal or a bird with both feet together **3** [C] a short journey, especially by plane **4** [C] a tall plant that grows up walls, pots, etc. with green female flowers that are shaped like CONES **5** (**hops**) [pl.] the green female flowers of the hop plant that have been dried, used for making beer **6** [C] (*old-fashioned, informal*) a social event at which people dance in an informal way—see also HIP HOP **IDM** see CATCH *v.*

hope /həʊp; *AmE* hoʊp/ *verb, noun*

■ *verb* ~ (**for sth**) to want sth to happen and think that it is possible: [V] *We are hoping for good weather on Sunday.* ◊ *All we can do now is wait and hope.* ◊ *'Do you think it will rain?' ' I hope not.'* ◊ *'Will you be back before dark?' ' I hope so, yes.'* ◊ [V(**that**)] *I hope (that) you're okay.* ◊ *Let's hope we can find a parking space.* ◊ [VN(**that**)] *It is hoped that over £10000 will be raised.* ◊ [Vto inf] *She is hoping to win the gold medal.* ◊ *We hope to arrive around two.* ⇨ note at EXPECT **HELP** Hope can be used in the passive in the form **it is hoped that....** For must always be used with **hope** in other passive sentences: *The improvement that had been hoped for never came.* ◊ *The hoped-for improvement never came.* **IDM** ¦hope against 'hope (**that...**) to continue to hope for sth although it is very unlikely to happen ¦hope for the 'best to hope that sth will happen successfully, especially where it seems likely that it will not **I should hope so/not | So I should hope** (*spoken*) used to say that you feel very strongly that sth should/should not happen: *'Nobody blames you.' 'I should hope not!'*

■ *noun* **1** [U, C] ~ (**of/for sth**) | ~ (**of doing sth**) | ~ (**that...**) a belief that sth you want will happen: *There is now hope of a cure.* ◊ *Hopes for the missing men are fading.* ◊ *There is little hope that they will be found alive.* ◊ *They have given up hope of finding any more survivors.* ◊ *The future is not without hope.* ◊ *Don't raise your hopes too high, or you may be disappointed.* ◊ *I'll do what I can, but don't get your hopes up.* ◊ *He pinned all his hopes on getting that job.* ◊ *There is still a glimmer of hope.* ◊ *She has high hopes of winning* (= is very confident about it). ◊ *The situation is not good but we live in hope that it will improve.* **2** [C] ~ (**of/for sth**) | ~ (**for sb**) | ~ (**that...**) | ~ (**of doing sth**) something that you wish for: *She told me all her hopes, dreams and fears.* ◊ *They have high hopes for their children.* **3** [C, usually sing.] ~ (**of sth**) | ~ (**for sb**) a person, a thing or a situation that will help you get what you want: *He turned to her in despair and said, 'You're my last hope.'* ◊ *The operation was Kelly's only hope of survival.* **IDM** be beyond 'hope (**of sth**) to be in a situation where no improvement is possible **hold out little, etc. 'hope (of sth/that...) | not hold out any, much, etc. 'hope (of sth/that...)** to offer little, etc. reason for believing that sth will happen: *The doctors did not hold out much hope for her recovery.* **in the hope of sth | in the hope that...** because you want sth to happen: *I called early in the hope of catching her before she went to work.* ◊ *He asked her again in the vain hope that he could persuade her to come* (= it was impossible). **not have a 'hope (in 'hell) (of doing sth)** (*informal*) to have no chance at all: *She doesn't have a hope of winning.* ¦some 'hope! (*BrE, spoken*) used to say that there is no chance at all that sth will happen—more at DASH *v.*, PIN *v.*

'**hoped-for** *adj.* [only before noun] (*written*) wanted and thought possible: *The new policy did not bring the hoped-for economic recovery.*

hope·ful /'həʊpfl; *AmE* 'hoʊp-/ *adj., noun*

■ *adj.* **1** [not usually before noun] ~ (**that...**) | ~ (**about sth**) (of a person) believing that sth you want will happen: *I feel hopeful that we'll find a suitable house very soon.* ◊ *He is not very hopeful about the outcome of the interview.* ◊ (*BrE*) *She is hopeful of returning to work soon.* **2** [only before noun] (of a person's behaviour) showing hope: *a hopeful smile* **3** (of a thing) making you believe that sth you want will happen; bringing hope: *The latest trade figures are a hopeful sign.* ◊ *The future did not seem very hopeful.* ▶ **hope·ful·ness** *noun* [U]

■ *noun* a person who wants to succeed at sth and is likely to: *50 young hopefuls are trying for a place in the England team.*

hope·ful·ly /'həʊpfəli; *AmE* 'hoʊp-/ *adv.* **1** used to express what you hope will happen: *Hopefully, we'll arrive before dark.* **HELP** Although this is the most common use of **hopefully**, it is a fairly new use and some people think it is incorrect. **2** hoping that what you want will happen: *'Are you free tonight?' she asked hopefully.*

hope·less /'həʊpləs; *AmE* 'hoʊp-/ *adj.* **1** if sth is **hopeless**, there is no hope that it will get better or succeed· *a hopeless situation* ◊ *It's hopeless trying to convince her.* ◊ *Most of the students are making good progress, but Michael is a hopeless case.* ◊ *He felt that his life was a hopeless mess.* **2** (*BrE, informal*) extremely bad: *The buses are absolutely hopeless these days!* **3** ~ (**at sth**) (*especially BrE*) (of people) very bad (at sth); with no ability or skill: *a hopeless driver* ◊ *I'm hopeless at science.* **4** feeling or showing no hope: *She felt lonely and hopeless.* ▶ **hope·less·ly** *adv.*: *hopelessly confused/outnumbered* ◊ *They were hopelessly lost.* ◊ *to be hopelessly in love* ◊ *'I'll never manage it,' he said hopelessly.* **hope·less·ness** *noun* [U]: *a sense/feeling of hopelessness*

hop·per /'hɒpə(r); *AmE* 'hɑːp-/ *noun* a container shaped like a V, that holds grain, coal, or food for animals, and lets it out through the bottom

hop·scotch /'hɒpskɒtʃ; *AmE* 'hɑːpskɑːtʃ/ *noun* [U] a children's game played on a pattern of squares marked on the ground. Each child throws a stone into a square then HOPS (= jumps on one leg) and jumps along the empty squares to pick up the stone again.

horde /hɔːd; *AmE* hɔːrd/ *noun* (sometimes *disapproving*) a large crowd of people: *There are always hordes of tourists here in the summer.* ◊ *The car attracted the interest of a horde of children.* ◊ *Football fans turned up in hordes.*

hori·zon /həˈraɪzn/ *noun* **1** (**the horizon**) [sing.] the furthest that you can see, where the sky seems to meet the land or the sea: *The sun sank below the horizon.* ◊ *A ship appeared on the horizon.* **2** [C, usually pl.] the limit of your desires, knowledge or interests: *She wanted to travel to broaden her horizons.* ◊ *The company needs new horizons now.* **IDM** on the ho'rizon likely to happen soon: *There's trouble looming on the horizon.*

hori·zon·tal /ˌhɒrɪˈzɒntl; *AmE* ˌhɔːrəˈzɑːntl; ˌhɑːr-/ *adj., noun*

■ *adj.* flat and level; going across and parallel to the ground rather than going up and down: *horizontal and vertical lines*—compare VERTICAL ▶ **hori·zon·tal·ly** /-təli/ *adv.*: *Cut the cake in half horizontally and spread jam on one half.*

■ *noun* **1** (**the hori·zon·tal**) [U] a horizontal position: *He shifted his position from the horizontal.* **2** [C] a horizontal line or surface

hor·mone /'hɔːməʊn; *AmE* 'hɔːrmoʊn/ *noun* a chemical substance produced in the body or in a plant that encourages growth or influences how the cells and tissues function; an artificial substance that has similar effects: *growth hormones* ◊ *a hormone imbalance* ◊ *Oestrogen is a female sex hormone.* ▶ **hor·mo·nal** /hɔːˈməʊnl; *AmE* hɔːrˈmoʊnl/ *adj.* [usually before noun]: *the hormonal changes occurring during pregnancy*

¦**hormone re'placement therapy** *noun* [U] = HRT

horn /hɔːn; *AmE* hɔːrn/ *noun* **1** [C] a hard pointed part that grows, usually in pairs, on the heads of some animals, such as sheep and cows. Horns are often curved.—picture on page A6 **2** [U] the hard substance of which animal horns are made: *rhino horn* **3** [C] a simple musical instrument that consists of a curved metal tube that you blow into: *a hunting horn* **4** [C] (*especially BrE*) = FRENCH HORN: *a horn concerto* **5** [C] a device in a vehicle for making a loud sound as a warning or signal: *to honk your car horn* ◊ (*BrE*) *to sound/toot your horn*—see also FOGHORN—picture at CAR **IDM** blow/toot your own 'horn (*AmE, informal*) = BLOW YOUR OWN TRUMPET at BLOW *v.*

aɪ	aʊ	eɪ	əʊ	oʊ	ɔɪ	ɪə	eə	ʊə	j	w
my	now	say	go (BrE)	go (AmE)	boy	near	hair	pure	yes	wet

draw/pull your 'horns in to start being more careful in your behaviour, especially by spending less money than before **on the horns of a di'lemma** in a situation in which you have to make a choice between things that are equally unpleasant—more at BULL, LOCK *v.*

horn·beam /'hɔːnbiːm; *AmE* 'hɔːrn-/ *noun* [C, U] a tree with smooth grey bark and hard wood

horned /hɔːnd; *AmE* hɔːrnd/ *adj.* having horns or having sth that looks like horns

hor·net /'hɔːnɪt; *AmE* 'hɔːrnɪt/ *noun* a large WASP (= a black and yellow flying insect) that has a very powerful sting **IDM** **a 'hornet's nest** a difficult situation in which a lot of people get very angry: *His letter to the papers stirred up a real hornet's nest.*

horn of 'plenty *noun* = CORNUCOPIA

horn·pipe /'hɔːnpaɪp; *AmE* 'hɔːrn-/ *noun* a fast dance for one person, traditionally performed by sailors; the music for the dance

horn-rimmed *adj.* (of a pair of glasses) with frames made of material that looks like horn

horny /'hɔːni; *AmE* 'hɔːrni/ *adj.* **1** (*informal*) sexually excited: *to feel horny* **2** (*informal*) sexually attractive: *to look horny* **3** made of a hard substance like horn: *the bird's horny beak* **4** (of skin, etc.) hard and rough: *horny hands*

horo·scope /'hɒrəskəʊp; *AmE* 'hɔːrəskoʊp; 'hɑːr-/ *noun* a description of what is going to happen to sb in the future, based on the position of the stars and the planets when the person was born

hor·ren·dous /hɒ'rendəs; *AmE* hɔː'r-; hɑː'r-/ *adj.* **1** extremely shocking; terrible: *horrendous injuries* **2** extremely unpleasant and unacceptable: *horrendous traffic* **HELP** Some people use *an* instead of *a* before the 'h'. This word and then usually do not pronounce the 'h'. This now sounds old-fashioned. ► **hor·ren·dous·ly** *adv.*: *horrendously expensive*

hor·rible /'hɒrəbl; *AmE* 'hɔːr-; 'hɑːr-/ *adj.* **1** (especially *spoken*) very bad or unpleasant; used to describe sth that you do not like: *horrible weather/children/shoes* ◊ *The coffee tasted horrible.* ◊ *I've got a horrible feeling she lied to us.* **2** making you feel very shocked and frightened: *a horrible crime/nightmare* **3** (especially *spoken*) (of people or their behaviour) unfriendly, unpleasant or unkind: *a horrible man* ◊ *My sister was being horrible to me all day.* ◊ *What a horrible thing to say!* ► **hor·ribly** /-əbli/ *adv.*: *It was horribly painful.* ◊ *The experiment went horribly wrong.*

hor·rid /'hɒrɪd; *AmE* 'hɔːr-; 'hɑːr-/ *adj.* (*old-fashioned* or *informal, especially BrE*) very unpleasant or unkind [SYN] HORRIBLE: *a horrid child* ◊ *a horrid smell* ◊ *Don't be so horrid to your brother.*

hor·rif·ic /hə'rɪfɪk/ *adj.* **1** extremely bad and shocking or frightening [SYN] HORRIFYING: *a horrific murder/accident/attack* ◊ *Her injuries were horrific.* **2** (*informal*) very bad or unpleasant [SYN] HORRENDOUS: *We had a horrific trip.* **HELP** Some people use *an* instead of *a* before this word and then usually do not pronounce the 'h'. This now sounds old-fashioned. ► **hor·rif·ic·al·ly** /-kli/ *adv.*

hor·rify /'hɒrɪfaɪ; *AmE* 'hɔːr-; 'hɑːr-/ *verb* (**hor·ri·fies, hor·ri·fy·ing, hor·ri·fied, hor·ri·fied**) to make sb feel extremely shocked, disgusted or frightened [SYN] APPAL: [VN] *The whole country was horrified by the killings.* ◊ [VN to inf] *It horrified her to think that he had killed someone.* [also VN that] ► **hor·ri·fied** *adj.*: *He was horrified when he discovered the conditions in which they lived.* ◊ *She gazed at him in horrified disbelief.*

hor·ri·fy·ing /'hɒrɪfaɪɪŋ; *AmE* 'hɔːr-; 'hɑːr-/ *adj.* making you feel extremely shocked, disgusted or frightened: *a horrifying sight/experience/story* ◊ *It's horrifying to see such poverty.* ► **hor·ri·fy·ing·ly** *adv.*

hor·ror /'hɒrə(r); *AmE* 'hɔːr-; 'hɑːr-/ *noun* **1** [U] a feeling of great shock, fear or disgust: *People watched **in horror** as the small plane crashed to the ground.* ◊ *With a look of horror, he asked if the doctor thought he had cancer.* ◊ *The thought of being left alone filled her with horror.* ◊ ***To her horror**, the man produced a gun.* ◊ *She recoiled in horror at the sight of an enormous spider.* ◊ ***To his horror**, he*

could feel himself starting to cry (= it upset him very much). ◊ *Her eyes were wide with horror.* **2** [sing.] **~ of sth/of doing sth** a great fear or hatred of sth: *a horror of deep water* ◊ *Most people have a horror of speaking in public.* **3** [U] **the ~ of sth** the very unpleasant nature of sth, especially when it is shocking or frightening: *The full horror of the accident was beginning to become clear.* ◊ *In his dreams he relives the horror of the attack.* **4** [C, usually pl.] a very unpleasant or frightening experience: *the horrors of war* ◊ *You wouldn't believe the horrors they have suffered due to famine and disease.* **5** [U] a type of book, film/movie, etc. that is designed to frighten people: *In this section you'll find horror and science fiction.* ◊ *a horror film/movie*—see also HORROR STORY **6** [C] (*BrE, informal*) a child who behaves badly: *Her son is a little horror.* **IDM** **,horror of 'horrors** (*BrE, humorous* or *ironic*) used to emphasize how bad a situation is: *I stood up to speak and—horror of horrors—realized I had left my notes behind.*—more at SHOCK *n.*

'horror story *noun* **1** a story about strange and frightening things that is designed to entertain people **2** (*informal*) a report that describes a an experience of a situation as very unpleasant: *horror stories about visits to the dentist*

'horror-struck (also **'horror-stricken**) *adj.* suddenly feeling very shocked, frightened or disgusted

hors d'oeuvre /ˌɔː 'dɜːv; *AmE* ˌɔːr 'dɜːrv/ *noun* [C, U] (*pl.* **hors d'oeuvres** /ˌɔː 'dɜːv; *AmE* ˌɔːr 'dɜːrv/) (from *French*) a small amount of food, usually cold, served before the main part of a meal—compare STARTER

horse /hɔːs; *AmE* hɔːrs/ *noun, verb*
■ *noun* **1** a large animal with four legs, a MANE (= long thick hair on its neck) and a tail. Horses are used for riding on, pulling carriages, etc: *He mounted his horse and rode off.* ◊ *a horse and cart*—see also COLT, FILLY, FOAL, GELDING, MARE, STALLION **2** = VAULTING HORSE—see also CLOTHES HORSE, HOBBY HORSE, ROCKING HORSE, SEA HORSE, STALKING HORSE, TROJAN HORSE, WHITE HORSES **IDM** **(straight) from the horse's 'mouth** (*informal*) (of information) given by sb who is directly involved and therefore likely to be accurate **hold your 'horses** (*informal*) used to tell sb that they should wait a moment and not be so excited that they take action without thinking about it first **,horses for 'courses** (*BrE*) the act of matching people with suitable jobs or tasks **a one, two, three, etc. horse 'race** a competition or an election in which there are only one, two, etc. teams or candidates with a chance of winning—more at BACK *v.*, BARN *n.*, CART *n.*, CHANGE *v.*, DARK *adj.*, DRIVE *v.*, EAT, FLOG, GIFT *n.*, HIGH *adj.*, STABLE *n.*, WILD *adj.*
■ *verb* **PHR V** **,horse a'bout/a'round** (*informal*) to play in a way that is noisy and not very careful so that you could hurt sb or damage sth

horse·back /'hɔːsbæk; *AmE* 'hɔːrs-/ *noun, adj.*
■ *noun* **IDM** **on 'horseback** sitting on a horse; using horses: *a soldier on horseback*
■ *adj.* [only before noun] sitting on a horse: *a horseback tour* ► **horse·back** *adv.*: *to ride horseback*

'horseback riding *noun* [U] (*AmE*) = RIDING

horse·box /'hɔːsbɒks; *AmE* 'hɔːrsbɑːks/ *noun* (*BrE*) a vehicle for transporting horses in, sometimes pulled behind another vehicle—see also HORSE TRAILER

,horse 'chestnut *noun* **1** a large tall tree with spreading branches, white or pink flowers and nuts that grow inside prickly cases—see also CHESTNUT **2** the smooth brown nut of the horse chestnut tree—compare CONKER

'horse-drawn *adj.* [only before noun] (of a vehicle) pulled by a horse or horses

horse·flesh /'hɔːsfleʃ; *AmE* 'hɔːrs-/ *noun* [U] horses, especially when being bought or sold

horse·hair /'hɔːsheə(r); *AmE* 'hɔːrsher/ *noun* [U] hair from the MANE or tail of a horse, used, in the past, for filling MATTRESSES, chairs, etc.

horse·man /'hɔːsmən; *AmE* 'hɔːrs-/ *noun* (*pl.* **-men** /-mən/) a rider on a horse; a person who can ride horses: *a good horseman*—see also HORSEWOMAN

b	d	f	g	h	k	l	m	n	p	r
bad	did	fall	get	hat	cat	leg	man	now	pen	red

horse·man·ship /ˈhɔːsmənʃɪp; AmE ˈhɔːrs-/ noun [U] skill in riding horses

horse·play /ˈhɔːspleɪ; AmE ˈhɔːrs-/ noun [U] rough noisy play in which people push or hit each other for fun

horse·power /ˈhɔːspaʊə(r); AmE ˈhɔːrs-/ noun [C, U] (pl. **horse·power**) (abbr. **h.p.**) a unit for measuring the power of an engine: *a powerful car with a 170 horsepower engine* ◇ (informal) *I'll need a bit more horsepower to get up this hill!*

horse race noun a race between horses with riders

horse racing noun [U] a sport in which horses with riders race against each other

horse·rad·ish /ˈhɔːsrædɪʃ; AmE ˈhɔːrs-/ noun [U] **1** a hard white root vegetable that has a taste like pepper **2** (BrE also **horseradish 'sauce**) a sauce made from horseradish, that is eaten with meat: *roast beef and horseradish*

horse riding noun [U] (BrE) = RIDING

horse·shoe /ˈhɔːsʃuː; ˈhɔːʃʃuː; AmE ˈhɔːrʃ-; ˈhɔːrs-/ noun (also **shoe**) **1** a piece of curved iron that is attached with nails to the bottom of a horse's foot. A horseshoe is often used as a symbol of good luck. **2** anything shaped like a horseshoe: *a horseshoe bend in the river*

horse-trading noun [U] the activity of discussing business with sb using clever or secret methods in order to reach an agreement that suits you

horse trailer noun (AmE) a vehicle for transporting horses in, pulled by another vehicle—see also HORSEBOX

horse·woman /ˈhɔːswʊmən; AmE ˈhɔːrs-/ noun (pl. -women /-wɪmɪn/) a woman rider on a horse; a woman who can ride horses: *a good horsewoman*

horsey (also **horsy**) /ˈhɔːsi; AmE ˈhɔːrsi/ adj. **1** interested in and involved with horses or horse racing **2** connected with horses; like a horse: *She had a long, horsey face.*

horti·cul·ture /ˈhɔːtɪkʌltʃə(r); AmE ˈhɔːrt-/ noun [U] the study or practice of growing flowers, fruit and vegetables: *a college of agriculture and horticulture* ▶ **horti·cul·tural** /ˌhɔːtɪˈkʌltʃərəl; AmE ˌhɔːrt-/ adj.: *a horticultural show/society* **horti·cul·tur·al·ist**, **horti·cul·tur·ist** noun

hose /həʊz; AmE hoʊz/ noun, verb
■ noun **1** (also **hose·pipe** /ˈhəʊzpaɪp; AmE ˈhoʊz-/) (BrE) a long tube made of rubber, plastic, etc., used for putting water onto fires, gardens, etc: *a garden hose* ◇ *a length of hose*—see also FIRE HOSE—picture at GARDEN **2** [pl.] = HOSIERY **3** [pl.] trousers/pants that fit tightly over the legs, worn by men in the past: *doublet and hose*
■ verb [VN] to wash or pour water on sth using a hose: *Firemen hosed the burning car.* **PHRV** ,**hose sth↔'down** to wash sth using a hose: *I'll just hose down the car.*

ho·siery /ˈhəʊziəri; AmE ˈhoʊʒəri/ (also **hose**) noun [U] used especially in shops/stores as a word for TIGHTS, STOCKINGS and socks: *the hosiery department*

hos·pice /ˈhɒspɪs; AmE ˈhɑːs-/ noun a hospital for people who are dying: *an Aids hospice*

hos·pit·able /hɒˈspɪtəbl; ˈhɒspɪtəbl; AmE hɑːˈs-; ˈhɑːs-/ adj. **1** ~ (to/towards sb) (of a person) pleased to welcome guests; generous and friendly to visitors: *The local people are very hospitable to strangers.* **2** (especially written) having good conditions that allow things to grow; having a pleasant environment: *a hospitable climate* ◇ *The countryside in the north is less hospitable.* **OPP** INHOSPITABLE ▶ **hos·pit·ably** /-əbli/ adv.

hos·pital /ˈhɒspɪtl; AmE ˈhɑːs-/ noun a large building where people who are ill/sick or injured are given medical treatment and care: (BrE) *He had to go to hospital for treatment.* ◇ (AmE) *He had to go to the hospital for treatment.* ◇ *to be admitted to (the) hospital* ◇ *to be discharged from (the) hospital* ◇ *The injured were rushed to (the) hospital in an ambulance.* ◇ *He died in (the) hospital.* ◇ *I'm going to the hospital to visit my brother.* ◇ *a psychiatric/mental hospital* ◇ *hospital doctors/nurses/staff* ◇ *There is an urgent need for more day care centres and more hospital beds.*—see also COTTAGE HOSPITAL

hos·pi·tal·ity /ˌhɒspɪˈtæləti; AmE ˌhɑːs-/ noun [U] **1** friendly and generous behaviour towards guests: *Thank you for your kind hospitality.* **2** food, drink or services that are provided by an organization for guests, customers, etc: *We were entertained in the company's hospitality suite.* ◇ *the hospitality industry* (= hotels, restaurants, etc.)

hos·pi·tal·ize (BrE also **-ise**) /ˈhɒspɪtəlaɪz; AmE ˈhɑːs-/ verb [VN] [usually passive] to send sb to a hospital for treatment ▶ **hos·pi·tal·iza·tion**, **-isa·tion** /ˌhɒspɪtəlaɪˈzeɪʃn; AmE ˌhɑːspɪtələˈz-/ noun [U]: *a long period of hospitalization*

host /həʊst; AmE hoʊst/ noun, verb
■ noun **1** [C] a person who invites guests to a meal, a party, etc. or who has people staying at their house: *Ian, our host, introduced us to the other guests.* **2** [C] a country, a city or an organization that holds and arranges a special event: *The college is playing host to a group of visiting Russian scientists.* **3** [C] a person who introduces and talks to guests on a television or radio show: *a TV game show host* **4** [C] (technical) an animal or a plant on which another animal or plant lives and feeds **5** [C] ~ of sb/sth a large number of people or things: *A host of musicians will perform at the festival.* ◇ *a host of possibilities* **6** (the Host) [sing.] the bread that is used in the Christian service of COMMUNION, after it has been BLESSED—see also HOSTESS
■ verb [VN] **1** to organize an event to which others are invited and make all the arrangements for them: *Germany is bidding to host the World Cup finals.* **2** to introduce a television or radio programme, a show, etc: *The awards ceremony will be hosted by Sir David Frost.* **3** to organize a party that you have invited guests to: *to host a dinner*

hos·tage /ˈhɒstɪdʒ; AmE ˈhɑːs-/ noun a person who is captured and held prisoner by a person or group, and who may be injured or killed if people do not do what the person or group is asking: *Three children were taken hostage during the bank robbery.* ◇ *He was held hostage for almost a year.* ◇ *The government is negotiating the release of the hostages.* **IDM** a ,**hostage to 'fortune** something that you have, or have promised to do, that could cause trouble or worry in the future

hos·tel /ˈhɒstl; AmE ˈhɑːstl/ noun **1** a building that provides cheap accommodation and meals to students, workers or travellers—see also YOUTH HOSTEL **2** (BrE) (also **shel·ter**) (AmE, BrE) a building, usually run by a charity, where people who have no home can stay for a short time: *a hostel for the homeless*

hos·tel·ry /ˈhɒstəlri; AmE ˈhɑːs-/ (pl. -ies) noun (old use or humorous) a pub or hotel

host·ess /ˈhəʊstəs; -es; AmE ˈhoʊstəs/ noun **1** a woman who invites guests to a meal, a party, etc.; a woman who has people staying at her home: *Mary was always the perfect hostess.* **2** a woman who is employed to welcome and entertain men at a NIGHTCLUB **3** a woman who introduces and talks to guests on a television or radio show **4** (AmE) a woman who greets the customers in a restaurant—see also HOST

hos·tile /ˈhɒstaɪl; AmE ˈhɑːstl; -taɪl/ adj. **1** ~ (to/towards sb/sth) very unfriendly or aggressive and ready to argue or fight: *The speaker got a very hostile reception from the audience.* ◇ *She was openly hostile towards her parents.* **2** ~ (to sth) strongly rejecting or opposed to sth: *hostile to the idea of change* **3** making it difficult for sth to happen or to be achieved: *hostile conditions for plants to grow in* **4** belonging to a military enemy: *hostile territory/aircraft* **5** (business) (of an offer to buy a company, etc.) not wanted by the company that is to be bought: *a hostile takeover bid*

hos·til·ity /hɒˈstɪləti; *AmE* hɑːˈs-/ *noun* **1** [U] ~ **(to/ towards sb/sth)** unfriendly or aggressive feelings or behaviour: *feelings of hostility towards people from other backgrounds* ◊ *There was* **open hostility** *between the two schools.* **2** [U] ~ **(to/towards sth)** strong and angry opposition towards an idea, a plan or a situation: *public hostility to nuclear power* **3 (hostilities)** [pl.] (*formal*) acts of fighting in a war: *the start/outbreak of hostilities between the two sides* ◊ *a cessation of hostilities* (= an end to fighting)

host·ler /ˈhɒslə(r); *AmE* ˈhɑːs-/ *noun* (*AmE*) = OSTLER

hot /hɒt; *AmE* hɑːt/ *adj., verb*

■ *adj.* (**hot·ter, hot·test**)

TEMPERATURE | **1** having a high temperature; producing heat: *Do you like this hot weather?* ◊ *It's hot today, isn't it?* ◊ *It was hot and getting hotter.* ◊ *It was the hottest July on record.* ◊ *a hot dry summer* ◊ *Be careful—the plates are hot.* ◊ *All rooms have hot and cold water.* ◊ *a hot bath* ◊ *a hot meal* (= one that has been cooked) ◊ *I couldn't live in a hot country* (= one which has high average temperatures). ◊ *Cook in a very hot oven.* ◊ *Eat it while it's hot.* ◊ *I touched his forehead. He felt hot and feverish.*—see also BAKING HOT, BOILING HOT, PIPING HOT, RED-HOT, WHITE-HOT **2** (of a person) feeling heat in an unpleasant or uncomfortable way: *Is anyone too hot?* ◊ *I feel hot.* ◊ *Her cheeks were hot with embarrassment.* **3** making you feel hot: *London was hot and dusty.* ◊ *a long hot journey*

FOOD | **4** containing pepper and spices and producing a burning feeling in your mouth: *hot spicy food* ◊ *You can make a curry hotter simply by adding chillies.* ◊ *hot mustard* OPP MILD

CAUSING STRONG FEELINGS | **5** involving a lot of activity, argument or strong feelings: *Today we enter the hottest phase of the election campaign.* ◊ *The environment has become a very hot issue.* ◊ *Competition is getting hotter day by day.*

DIFFICULT/DANGEROUS | **6** difficult or dangerous to deal with and making you feel worried or uncomfortable: *When things got too hot most journalists left the area.* ◊ *They're making life hot for her.*

POPULAR | **7** (*informal*) new, exciting and very popular: *This is one of the hottest clubs in town.* ◊ *They are one of this year's hot new bands on the rock scene.* ◊ *The couple are Hollywood's* **hottest property.**

NEWS | **8** fresh, very recent and usually exciting: *I've got some hot gossip for you!* ◊ *a story that is* **hot off the press** (= has just appeared in the newspapers)

TIP/FAVOURITE | **9** [only before noun] likely to be successful: *She seems to be the* **hot favourite** *for the job.* ◊ *Do you have any* **hot tips** *for today's race?*

GOOD AT STH/KNOWING A LOT | **10** [not before noun] ~ **at/on sth** (*informal*) very good at doing sth; knowing a lot about sth: *Don't ask me—I'm* **not too hot** *on British history.*

ANGER | **11** if sb has a **hot temper** they become angry very easily

SEXUAL EXCITEMENT | **12** feeling or causing sexual excitement: *You were as hot for me as I was for you.* ◊ *I've got a* **hot date** *tonight.*

SHOCKING/CRITICAL | **13** containing scenes, statements, etc. that are too shocking or too critical and are likely to cause anger or disapproval: *Some of the nude scenes were regarded as too hot for Broadway.* ◊ *The report was highly critical of senior members of the Cabinet and was considered too hot to publish.*—see also HOT STUFF

STRICT | **14** [not before noun] ~ **on sth** thinking that sth is very important and making sure that it always happens or is done: *They're very hot on punctuality at work.*

MUSIC | **15** (of music, especially jazz) having a strong and exciting rhythm

GOODS | **16** stolen and difficult to get rid of because they can easily be recognized: *I'd never have touched those CDs if I'd known they were hot.*

IN CHILDREN'S GAMES | **17** [not before noun] used in children's games to say that the person playing is very close

to finding a person or thing, or to guessing the correct answer: *You're getting hot!*

IDM **be in/get into hot 'water** (*informal*) to be in or get into trouble **go hot and 'cold** to experience a sudden feeling of fear or anxiety: *When the phone rang I just went hot and cold.* **go/sell like hot 'cakes** to sell quickly or in great numbers **(all) hot and 'bothered** (*informal*) in a state of anxiety or confusion because you are under too much pressure, have a problem, are trying to hurry, etc. **hot on sb's/sth's 'heels** following sb/sth very closely: *He turned and fled with Peter hot on his heels.* ◊ *Further successes came hot on the heels of her first best-selling novel.* **hot on sb's/sth's 'tracks/'trail** (*informal*) close to catching or finding the person or thing that you have been chasing or searching for **hot under the 'collar** (*informal*) angry or embarrassed: *He got very hot under the collar when I asked him where he'd been all day.* **in hot pur'suit (of sb)** following sb closely and determined to catch them: *She sped away in her car with journalists in hot pursuit.* **not so/too 'hot 1** not very good in quality: *Her spelling isn't too hot.* **2** not feeling well: *'How are you today?' 'Not so hot, I'm afraid.'*—more at BLOW *v.*, CAT, HEEL *n.*, STRIKE *v.*

■ *verb* (**-tt-**)

PHRV **hot 'up** (*BrE*) (also **heat 'up** *AmE, BrE*) (*informal*) to become more exciting or to show an increase in activity: *Things are really hotting up in the election campaign.*

hot 'air *noun* [U] (*informal*) claims, promises or statements that sound impressive but have no real meaning or truth

hot-'air balloon *noun* = BALLOON

hot·bed /ˈhɒtbed; *AmE* ˈhɑːt-/ *noun* [usually sing.] ~ **of sth** a place where a lot of a particular activity, especially sth bad or violent, is happening: *The area was a hotbed of crime.*

hot-'blooded *adj.* (of a person) having strong emotions and easily becoming very excited or angry SYN PASSIONATE: *a hot-blooded lover*—compare WARM-BLOODED

hot 'chocolate (*BrE* also **choc·olate**) *noun* [U, C] a drink made by mixing chocolate powder with hot water or milk; a cup of this drink: *Two coffees and a hot chocolate, please.*

hotch·potch /ˈhɒtʃpɒtʃ; *AmE* ˈhɑːtʃpɑːtʃ/ (*especially BrE*) (*AmE* usually **hodge·podge** /ˈhɒdʒpɒdʒ; *AmE* ˈhɑːdʒpɑːdʒ/) *noun* [sing.] (*informal*) a number of things mixed together without any particular order or reason: *a hotchpotch of ideas*

hot cross 'bun *noun* a small sweet bread roll that contains CURRANTS and has a pattern of a cross on top, traditionally eaten in Britain around Easter

hot-'desking *noun* [U] the practice in an office of giving desks to workers when they are required, rather than giving each worker their own desk

hot dog (*BrE* also **hot 'dog**) *noun* **1** a hot sausage served in a long bread roll **2** (*AmE*) a person who performs clever or dangerous tricks while skiing or SURFING: *He's a real hot dog.*

hot-dog *verb* [V] (*AmE, informal*) to perform clever or dangerous tricks while skiing or SURFING

hotel /həʊˈtel; *AmE* hoʊ-/ *noun* a building where people stay, usually for a short time, paying for their rooms and meals: *We stayed at/in a hotel.* ◊ *hotel rooms/guests* ◊ *a luxury/five-star hotel* ◊ *a friendly, family-run hotel* HELP Some speakers do not pronounce the 'h' at the beginning of *hotel* and use *an* instead of *a* before it. This now sounds old-fashioned.

ho·tel·ier /həʊˈtelɪə(r); -lieɪ; *AmE* hoʊˈteljər; ˌoʊtelˈjeɪ/ *noun* a person who owns or manages a hotel

hot 'flush (*BrE*) (*AmE* **hot 'flash**) *noun* a sudden hot and uncomfortable feeling in the skin, especially experienced by women during the MENOPAUSE

hot·foot /ˈhɒtfʊt; *AmE* ˈhɑːt-/ *adv., verb*

■ *adv.* (*written*) moving quickly and in a hurry: *He had just arrived hotfoot from London.*

■ *verb* IDM **'hotfoot it** (*informal*) to walk or run somewhere quickly: *Once the police arrived, we hotfooted it out of there.*

æ	ɑː	e	ɜː	ə	ɪ	iː	i	ɒ	ɔː	ʌ	ʊ	u	uː
cat	father	ten	bird	about	sit	see	many	got	saw	cup	put	actual	too
								(BrE)					

H

hot·head /ˈhɒthed; AmE ˈhɑːt-/ noun a person who often acts too quickly, without thinking of what might happen ▶ **hot-headed** /ˌhɒtˈhedɪd/ adj.

hot·house /ˈhɒthaʊs; AmE ˈhɑːt-/ noun **1** a heated building, usually made of glass, used for growing delicate plants in: *hothouse flowers* **2** a place or situation that encourages the rapid development of sb/sth, especially ideas and emotions

hot·line /ˈhɒtlaɪn; AmE ˈhɑːt-/ noun **1** a special telephone line that people can use in order to get information or to talk about sth: *a 24-hour confidential hotline* **2** a direct telephone line between the heads of government in different countries

hot·ly /ˈhɒtli; AmE ˈhɑːtli/ adv. **1** done in an angry or excited way or with a lot of strong feeling: *a hotly debated topic* ◊ *Recent reports in the press have been hotly denied.* ◊ *'Nonsense!' he said hotly.* ◊ *The results were hotly disputed.* **2** done with a lot of energy and determination SYN CLOSELY: *hotly contested elections* ◊ *She ran out of the shop, hotly pursued by the store detective.*

ˈhot pants noun [pl.] very short, tight women's SHORTS

hot·plate /ˈhɒtpleɪt; AmE ˈhɑːt-/ noun a flat, heated metal surface, for example on a cooker/stove, that is used for cooking food or for keeping it hot

hot·pot /ˈhɒtpɒt; AmE ˈhɑːtpɑːt/ noun **1** [C, U] (*BrE*) a hot dish of meat, potato, onion, etc. cooked slowly in liquid in the oven **2** [C] (*AmE*) a small electric pot that you can use to heat water or food

ˌhot poˈtato noun [usually sing.] (*informal*) a problem, situation, etc. that is difficult and unpleasant to deal with

hots /hɒts; AmE hɑːts/ noun [pl.] IDM **get/have the ˈhots for sb** (*informal*) to be sexually attracted to sb

the ˈhot seat noun [sing.] (*informal*) if sb is in the hot seat, they have to take responsibility for important or difficult decisions and actions

hot·shot /ˈhɒtʃɒt; AmE ˈhɑːtʃɑːt/ noun (*informal*) a person who is extremely successful in their career or at a particular sport ▶ **hot·shot** adj. [only before noun]: *a hotshot lawyer*

ˈhot spot noun (*informal*) **1** a place where fighting is common, especially for political reasons **2** a place where there is a lot of activity or entertainment **3** (*AmE*) a place that is very hot and dry, where a fire has been burning or is likely to start **4** (*computing*) an area on a computer screen that you can CLICK on to start an operation such as loading a file

ˌhot ˈstuff noun [U] (*informal, especially BrE*) **1** a person who is sexually attractive: *She's pretty hot stuff.* **2** a film/movie, book, etc. which is exciting in a sexual way: *His latest novel is hot stuff.* **3** ~ (at sth) a person who is very skilful at sth: *She's really hot stuff at tennis.* **4** something that is likely to cause anger or disagreement: *These new proposals are proving to be hot stuff.*

ˌhot-ˈtempered adj. (*especially BrE*) tending to become very angry easily

ˌhot ˈtub noun a heated bath that several people can sit in together

ˌhot-ˈwater bottle noun a rubber container that is filled with hot water and put in a bed to make it warm

ˈhot-wire verb [VN] (*informal*) to start the engine of a vehicle by using a piece of wire instead of a key

hou·mus = HUMMUS

hound /haʊnd/ noun, verb
■ noun a dog that can run fast and has a good sense of smell, used for hunting: *The hounds picked up the scent of the fox.*—see also AFGHAN HOUND, BLOODHOUND, FOXHOUND, GREYHOUND, WOLFHOUND
■ verb [VN] to keep following sb and not leave them alone, especially in order to get sth from them or ask them questions SYN HARASS: *They were hounded day and night by the press.* PHRV ˌhound sb ˈout (of sth)|ˈhound sb from sth [usually passive] to force sb to leave a job or a place, especially by making their life difficult and unpleasant: *They were hounded out of the country.*

hour /ˈaʊə(r)/ noun HELP Use an, not a, before hour. **1** [C] (*abbr.* hr) 60 minutes; one of the 24 parts that a day is divided into: *It will take about an hour to get there.*

◊ *The interview lasted half an hour.* ◊ *It was a three-hour exam.* ◊ *I waited for an hour and then I left.* ◊ *He'll be back in an hour.* ◊ *We're paid by the hour.* ◊ *The minimum wage was set at £3.20 an hour.* ◊ *Top speed is 120 miles per hour.* ◊ *York was within an hour's drive.* ◊ *Chicago is two hours away* (= it takes two hours to get there). ◊ *We're four hours ahead of New York* (= referring to the time difference). ◊ *We hope to be there within the hour* (= in less than an hour). **2** [C, usually sing.] a period of about an hour, used for a particular purpose: *I use the Internet at work, during my lunch hour.*—see also HAPPY HOUR, RUSH HOUR **3** (hours) [pl.] a fixed period of time during which people work, an office is open, etc: *Opening hours are from 10 to 6 each day.* ◊ *Most people in this kind of job tend to work long hours.* ◊ *What are your office hours?* ◊ *a hospital's visiting hours* ◊ *Britain's licensing hours* (= when pubs are allowed to open) *used to be very restricted.* ◊ *This is the only place to get a drink after hours* (= after the normal closing time for pubs). ◊ *Clients can now contact us electronically out of hours* (= when the office is closed). **4** [sing.] a particular point in time: *You can't turn him away at this hour of the night.* **5** (hours) [pl.] a long time: *It took hours getting there.* ◊ *I've been waiting for hours.* ◊ *'How long did it last?' 'Oh, hours and hours.'* **6** [C, usually sing.] the time when sth important happens: *This was often thought of as the country's finest hour.* ◊ *She thought her last hour had come.* ◊ *Don't desert me in my hour of need.* **7** (the hour) [sing.] the time when it is exactly 1 o'clock, 2 o'clock, etc: *There's a bus every hour on the hour.* ◊ *The clock in the living room struck the hour.* **8** (hours) [pl.] used when giving the time according to the 24-hour clock, usually in military or other official language: *The first missile was launched at 2300* (= said 23 hundred) *hours* (= at 11 p.m.). IDM **ˈall hours** any time, especially a time which is not usual or suitable: *He's started staying out till all hours* (= until very late at night). ◊ *She thinks she can call me at all hours of the day and night.* **keep ... ˈhours** if you keep regular, strange, etc. hours, the times at which you do things (especially getting up or going to bed) are regular, strange, etc. **the ˌsmall/ˌearly hours** (also **the wee small ˈhours** ScotE, AmE also **the wee ˈhours**) the period of time very early in the morning, soon after midnight: *We worked well into the small hours.* ◊ *The fighting began in the early hours of Saturday morning.*—more at ELEVENTH, EVIL, KILL v., UNEARTHLY, UNGODLY

hour·glass /ˈaʊəɡlɑːs; AmE ˈaʊərɡlæs/ noun a glass container holding sand that takes exactly an hour to pass through a small opening between the top and bottom sections—compare EGG TIMER

ˈhour hand noun the small hand on a clock or watch that points to the hour

hour·ly /ˈaʊəli; AmE ˈaʊərli/ adj., adv. HELP Use an, not a, before hourly.
■ adj. [only before noun] **1** done or happening every hour: *an hourly bus service* ◊ *Trains leave at hourly intervals.* **2** an hourly wage, fee, rate, etc. is the amount that you earn every hour or pay for a service every hour: *an hourly rate of $30 an hour.*
■ adv. every hour: *Reapply sunscreen hourly and after swimming.* ◊ *Dressings are changed four hourly* (= every four hours) *to help prevent infection.*

house noun, verb
■ noun /haʊs/ (*pl.* **houses** /ˈhaʊzɪz/)
BUILDING | **1** [C] a building for people to live in, usually for one family: *He went into the house.* ◊ *a two-bedroom house* ◊ *Let's have the party at my house.* ◊ *House prices in London are still falling.* ◊ *What time do you leave the house in the morning* (= to go to work)?—see also PENTHOUSE, SAFE HOUSE, SHOW HOUSE **2** [sing.] all the people living in a house SYN HOUSEHOLD: *Be quiet or you'll wake the whole house!* **3** [C] (in compounds) a building used for a particular purpose, for example for holding meetings in or keeping animals or goods in: *an opera house* ◊ *a hen house*—see also DOGHOUSE, DOSSHOUSE, HALFWAY HOUSE, HOTHOUSE, LIGHTHOUSE, MADHOUSE, OUTHOUSE, STOREHOUSE, WAREHOUSE **4** (House) [sing.] (*BrE*) used in the names of

house

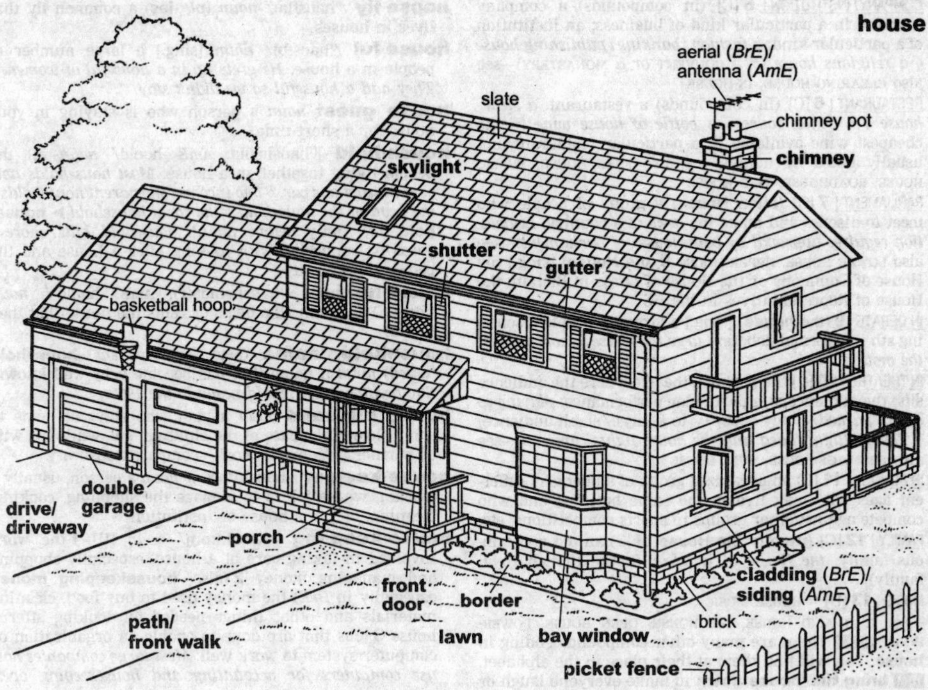

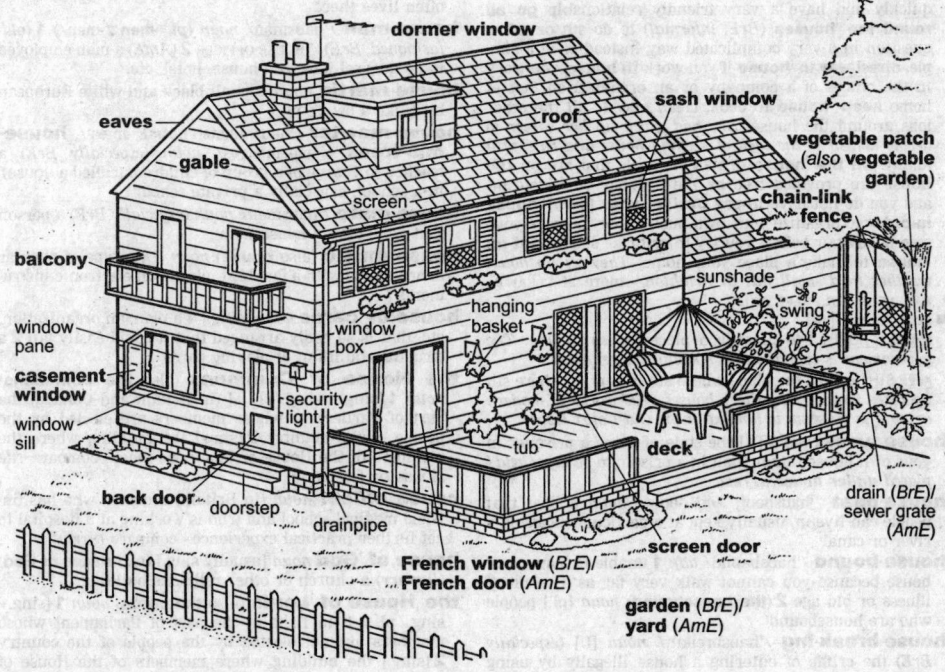

aerial (*BrE*)/
antenna (*AmE*)

chimney pot

chimney

slate

skylight

basketball hoop

shutter

gutter

**double
garage**

**drive/
driveway**

porch

**front
door** **border**

**path/
front walk**

lawn

cladding (*BrE*)/
siding (*AmE*)

brick

bay window

picket fence

dormer window

sash window

eaves

roof

gable

screen

vegetable patch
(*also* **vegetable
garden**)

**chain-link
fence**

balcony

window
pane

**casement
window**

window
sill

window
box

**hanging
basket**

security
light

sunshade

swing

back door

doorstep

drainpipe

tub

deck

drain (*BrE*)/
sewer grate
(*AmE*)

screen door

French window (*BrE*)/
French door (*AmE*)

garden (*BrE*)/
yard (*AmE*)

H

office buildings: *Their offices are on the second floor of Chester House.*

COMPANY/INSTITUTION | **5** [C] (in compounds) a company involved in a particular kind of business; an institution of a particular kind: *a fashion/banking/publishing house* ◊ *a religious house* (= a CONVENT *or a* MONASTERY)—see also CLEARING HOUSE, IN-HOUSE

RESTAURANT | **6** [C] (in compounds) a restaurant: *a steak-house* ◊ *a coffee house* ◊ *a bottle of house wine* (= the cheapest wine available in a particular restaurant, not usually listed by name)—see also FREE HOUSE, PUBLIC HOUSE, ROADHOUSE, TIED HOUSE

PARLIAMENT | **7** [C] (often **House**) a group of people who meet to discuss and make the laws of a country: *Legislation requires approval by both houses of parliament.*—see also LOWER HOUSE, UPPER HOUSE **8** (**the House**) [sing.] the House of Commons or the House of Lords in Britain; the House of Representatives in the US

IN DEBATE | **9** (**the house**) [sing.] a group of people discussing sth in a formal debate: *I urge the house to vote against the motion.*

IN THEATRE | **10** [C] the part of a theatre where the audience sits; the audience at a particular performance: *playing to a full/packed/empty house* (= to a large/small audience) ◊ *The spotlight faded and the house lights came up.*—see also FRONT-OF-HOUSE, FULL HOUSE

IN SCHOOL | **11** [C] an organized group of students of different ages who may live in the same building and who compete against other groups in sports competitions, etc.

FAMILY | **12** [C] (usually **the House of ...**) an old and famous family: *the House of Windsor* (= the British royal family)

MUSIC | **13** [U] = HOUSE MUSIC

—see also ACID HOUSE, ART-HOUSE, OPEN HOUSE, POWER-HOUSE **HELP** There are many other compounds ending in **house**. You will find them at their place in the alphabet. **IDM bring the ˈhouse down** to make everyone laugh or CHEER, especially at a performance in the theatre **get on like a ˈhouse on fire** (*BrE*) (*AmE* **get along like a ˈhouse on fire**) (*informal*) (of people) to become friends quickly and have a very friendly relationship **go all round the ˈhouses** (*BrE, informal*) to do sth or ask a question in a very complicated way instead of in a simple, direct way **in ˈhouse** if you work **in house**, you work in the offices of a company or an organization, not at home **keep ˈhouse** to cook, clean and do all the other jobs around the house: *She had given up her career to devote herself to the task of keeping house and raising a family.* **on the ˈhouse** drinks or meals that are **on the house** are provided free by the pub/bar or restaurant and you do not have to pay **put/set your (own) ˈhouse in order** to organize your own business or improve your own behaviour before you try to criticize sb else **set up ˈhouse** to make a place your home: *They set up house together in a small flat in Brighton.*—more at CLEAN *v.*, EAT, PEOPLE *n.*, SAFE *adj.*

■ *verb* /haʊz/ [VN]
PROVIDE HOME | **1** to provide a place for sb to live: *The government is committed to housing the refugees.*
KEEP STH | **2** to be the place where sth is kept or where sth operates from: *The gallery houses 2000 works of modern art.* ◊ *The museum is housed in the Old Court House.*

ˈhouse arrest *noun* [U] the state of being a prisoner in your own house rather than in a prison: *to be kept/held/placed under house arrest*

house·boat /ˈhaʊsbəʊt; *AmE* -boʊt/ *noun* a boat that people can live in, usually kept at a particular place on a river or canal

house·bound /ˈhaʊsbaʊnd/ *adj.* **1** unable to leave your house because you cannot walk very far as a result of illness or old age **2** (**the housebound**) *noun* [pl.] people who are housebound

house·break·ing /ˈhaʊsbreɪkɪŋ/ *noun* [U] (*especially BrE*) the crime of entering a house illegally by using force, in order to steal things from it **SYN** BURGLARY
▶ house·break·er /ˈhaʊsbreɪkə(r)/ *noun*

ˈhouse-broken *adj.* (*AmE*) = HOUSE-TRAINED

house·coat /ˈhaʊskəʊt; *AmE* -koʊt/ *noun* a long loose piece of clothing, worn in the house by women

house·fly /ˈhaʊsflaɪ/ *noun* (*pl.* -**ies**) a common fly that lives in houses

house·ful /ˈhaʊsfʊl/ *noun* [sing.] a large number of people in a house: *He grew up in a houseful of women.* ◊ *They had a houseful so we didn't stay.*

ˈhouse guest *noun* a person who is staying in your house for a short time

house·hold /ˈhaʊshəʊld; *AmE* -hoʊld/ *noun* all the people living together in a house: *Most households now own at least one car.* ◊ *low-income/one-parent households* ◊ *the head of the household* ◊ *the royal household* ▶ house·hold *adj.* [only before noun]: *household bills/chores/goods* (= connected with looking after a house and the people living in it)

house·hold·er /ˈhaʊshəʊldə(r); *AmE* -hoʊld-/ *noun* (*formal*) a person who owns or rents the house that they live in

ˌhousehold ˈname (also *less frequent* ˌhousehold ˈword) *noun* a name that has become very well known: *She became a household name in the 1960s.*

ˈhouse husband *noun* a man who stays at home to cook, clean, take care of the children, etc. while his wife or partner goes out to work—compare HOUSEWIFE

house·keep·er /ˈhaʊskiːpə(r)/ *noun* a person, usually a woman, whose job is to manage the shopping, cooking, cleaning, etc. in a house or institution

house·keep·ing /ˈhaʊskiːpɪŋ/ *noun* [U] **1** the work involved in taking care of a house, especially shopping and managing money **2** (also ˈhousekeeping money especially in *BrE*) the money used to buy food, cleaning materials and other things needed for looking after a house **3** jobs that are done to enable an organization or computer system to work well: *Most large companies now use computers for accounting and housekeeping operations.*

house·maid /ˈhaʊsmeɪd/ *noun* (*old-fashioned*) a female servant in a large house who cleans the rooms, etc. and often lives there

house·man /ˈhaʊsmən/ *noun* (*pl.* -**men** /-mən/) **1** (*old-fashioned, BrE*) = HOUSE OFFICER **2** (*AmE*) a man employed to do general jobs in a house, hotel, etc.

ˈhouse martin *noun* a small black and white European bird like a SWALLOW

house·mas·ter /ˈhaʊsmɑːstə(r); *AmE* -mæs-/, house·mis·tress /ˈhaʊsmɪstrəs/ *noun* (*especially BrE*) a teacher in charge of a group of children, (called a HOUSE), in a school, especially a private school

house·mate /ˈhaʊsmeɪt/ *noun* (*especially BrE*) a person that you share a house with

ˈhouse music (also **house**) *noun* [U] a type of popular dance music with a fast beat, played on electronic instruments

ˌhouse of ˈcards *noun* [sing.] **1** a plan, an organization, etc. that is so badly arranged that it could easily fail **2** a structure built out of playing cards

the ˌHouse of ˈCommons (also **the Com·mons**) *noun* **1** [sing.+ sing./pl. *v.*] (in Britain and Canada) the part of Parliament whose members are elected by the people of the country **2** [sing.] the building where the members of the House of Commons meet—compare THE HOUSE OF LORDS

ˈhouse officer *noun* (in Britain) a doctor who has finished medical school and who is working at a hospital to get further practical experience—compare INTERN

ˌhouse of ˈGod *noun* [usually sing.] (*pl.* **houses of God**) (*literary*) a church or other religious building

the ˌHouse of ˈLords (also **the Lords**) *noun* **1** [sing.+ sing./pl. *v.*] (in Britain) the part of Parliament whose members are not elected by the people of the country **2** [sing.] the building where members of the House of Lords meet—compare THE HOUSE OF COMMONS

the ˌHouse of Repreˈsentatives *noun* [sing.] the largest part of Congress in the US, or of the Parliament in

s	t	v	z	ʃ	ʒ	tʃ	dʒ	θ	ð	ŋ
see	tea	van	zoo	shoe	vision	chain	jam	thin	this	sing

Australia and New Zealand, whose members are elected by the people of the country—compare SENATE(1)

'house party *noun* a party held at a large house in the country where guests stay for a few days; the guests at this party

'house plant (*BrE* also **'pot plant**) *noun* a plant that you grow in a pot and keep indoors

'house-proud *adj.* spending a lot of time making your house look clean and attractive, and thinking that this is important

house·room /'haʊsruːm, -rʊm/ *noun* [U] space in a house for sb/sth **IDM not give sth 'houseroom** (*BrE*) to not like sth and not want it in your house

'house-sit *verb* [V] (**-tt-**) to live in sb's house while they are away in order to take care of it for them

the ˌHouses of 'Parliament *noun* [pl.] (in Britain) the Parliament that consists of both THE HOUSE OF COMMONS and THE HOUSE OF LORDS; the buildings in London where the British Parliament meets

ˌhouse-to-'house *adj.* [only before noun] visiting every house in a particular area: *a house-to-house collection/search* ◊ *The police are making house-to-house inquiries.*

'house-trained (*BrE*) (*AmE* **'house-broken**) *adj.* (of pet cats or dogs) trained to DEFECATE and URINATE outside the house or in a special box

house·wares /'haʊsweəz; *AmE* -werz/ *noun* [pl.] (*AmE*) (in shops/stores) small items used in the house, especially kitchen equipment

'house-warming *noun* a party given by sb who has just moved into a new house

house·wife /'haʊswaɪf/ *noun* (*pl.* **-wives** /-waɪvz/) a woman who stays at home to cook, clean, take care of the children, etc. while her husband or partner goes out to work—compare HOUSE HUSBAND ▶ **house·wife·ly** *adj.*

house·work /'haʊswɜːk; *AmE* -wɜːrk/ *noun* [U] the work involved in taking care of a home and family, for example cleaning and cooking: *to do the housework*

hous·ing /'haʊzɪŋ/ *noun* **1** [U] houses, flats/apartments, etc. that people live in, especially when referring to their type, price or condition: *public/private housing* ◊ *poor housing conditions* ◊ *the housing shortage* ◊ *the housing market* (= the activity of buying and selling houses, etc.) **2** [U] the job of providing houses, flats/apartments, etc. for people to live in: *a housing committee/department/officer* ◊ *the council's housing policy* **3** [C] a hard cover that protects part of a machine: *a car's rear axle housing*

'housing association *noun* (in Britain) an organization that owns houses, flats/apartments, etc. and helps people to rent or buy them at a low price

'housing benefit *noun* [U, C] (in Britain) money given by the government to people who do not earn much, to help them pay for a place to live in

'housing estate (*BrE*) (also **'housing development** *AmE*, *BrE*) *noun* an area in which a large number of houses or flats/apartments are planned and built together at the same time: *They live on a housing estate.*

'housing project (also **pro·ject**) (both *AmE*) *noun* a group of houses or flats/apartments built for poor families, usually with government money

hove *pt*, *pp* of HEAVE

hovel /'hɒvl; *AmE* 'hʌvl/ *noun* (*disapproving*) a house or room that is not fit to live in because it is dirty or in very bad condition

hover /'hɒvə(r); *AmE* 'hʌvər/ *verb* [V, usually +*adv./prep.*] **1** (of birds, HELICOPTERS, etc.) to stay in the air in one place: *A hawk hovered over the hill.* **2** (of a person) to wait somewhere, especially near sb, in a shy or uncertain manner: *He hovered nervously in the doorway.* **3** [+*adv./prep.*] to stay close to sth, or to stay in an uncertain state: *Temperatures hovered around freezing.* ◊ *He hovered on the edge of consciousness.* ◊ *A smile hovered on her lips.*

hov·er·craft /'hɒvəkrɑːft; *AmE* 'hʌvərkræft/ *noun* a vehicle that travels just above the surface of water or land, driven by engines that make a cushion of air for it to travel on—compare HYDROFOIL—picture at BOAT

how /haʊ/ *adv.* **1** in what way or manner: *How does it*

work? ◊ *He did not know how he ought to behave.* ◊ *I'll show you how to load the software.* ◊ *'Her behaviour was very odd.' 'How so?'* ◊ *It's funny how* (= that) *people always remember him.* ◊ *Do you remember how* (= that) *the kids always loved going there?* ◊ *How ever did you get here so quickly?*—compare HOWEVER **2** used to ask about sb's health: *How are you?* ◊ *How are you feeling now?* **3** used to ask whether sth is successful or enjoyable: *How was your trip?* ◊ *How did they play?* **4** used before an adjective or adverb to ask about the amount, degree, etc. of sth, or about sb's age: *How often do you go swimming?* ◊ *I didn't know how much to bring.* ◊ *How much are those earrings* (= What do they cost)? ◊ *How many people were there?* ◊ *How old is she?* **5** used to express surprise, pleasure, etc: *How kind of you to help!* ◊ *How he wished he had been there!* **6** in any way in which SYN HOWEVER: *I'll dress how I like in my own house!* **IDM how 'can I/'could you!** (*spoken*) used to show that you strongly disapprove of sb's behaviour or are very surprised by it: *Ben! How could you? After all they've done for us!* ◊ *Ugh! How can you eat that stuff?* **how 'come?** (*spoken*) used to ask the reason for sth: *'I think you owe me some money.' 'How come?'* **ˌhow do you 'do** (becoming *old-fashioned*) used as a formal greeting when you meet sb for the first time. The usual reply is also *How do you do?* **ˌhow's 'that?** (*spoken*) **1** used to ask the reason for sth: *'I left work early today.' 'How's that* (= Why)?' **2** used when asking sb's opinion of sth: *I'll tuck your sheets in for you. How's that? Comfortable?* ◊ *Two o'clock on the dot! How's that for punctuality!*

howdy /'haʊdi/ *exclamation* (*AmE*, *informal*, often *humorous*) used to say hello: *Howdy, partner.*

how·ever /haʊ'evə(r)/ *adv.* **1** used with an adjective or adverb to mean 'to whatever degree': *He wanted to take no risks, however small.* ◊ *She has the window open, however cold it is outside.* ◊ *However carefully I explained, she still didn't understand.* **HELP** When **ever** is used to emphasize **how**, meaning 'in what way or manner', it is written as a separate word: *How ever did you get here so quickly?* **2** in whatever way: *However you look at it, it's going to cost a lot.* **3** used to introduce a statement that contrasts with sth that has just been said: *He was feeling bad. He went to work, however, and tried to concentrate.* ◊ *We thought the figures were correct. However, we have now discovered some errors.* ⇨ note at ALTHOUGH

how·itz·er /'haʊɪtsə(r)/ *noun* a heavy gun that fires SHELLS high into the air for a short distance

howl /haʊl/ *verb*, *noun*
■ *verb* **1** [V] (of a dog, WOLF, etc.) to make a long, loud cry **2** [V] to make a loud cry when you are in pain, angry, amused, etc: *to howl in pain/despair/protest* ◊ *We howled with laughter.* ◊ *The baby was howling* (= crying loudly) *all the time I was there.* **3** [V] (of the wind) to blow hard and make a long loud noise: *The wind was howling around the house.* **4** to say sth loudly and angrily: [VN] *The crowd howled its displeasure.* [also V speech] **PHRV** **ˌhowl sb↔'down** to prevent a speaker from being heard by shouting angrily SYN SHOUT SB DOWN
■ *noun* **1** a long loud sad cry made by a dog, WOLF, etc. **2** a loud cry showing pain, anger, amusement, etc: *to let out a howl of fright/frustration/anguish* ◊ *The suggestion was greeted with howls of laughter.* **3** a long loud sound made when the wind is blowing strongly: *They listened to the howl of the wind through the trees.*

howl·er /'haʊlə(r)/ *noun* (*informal*, especially *BrE*) a stupid mistake, especially in what sb says or writes: *The report is full of howlers.*

howl·ing /'haʊlɪŋ/ *adj.* [only before noun] **1** (of a storm, etc.) very fierce, with strong winds: *a howling gale/storm/wind* **2** (*informal*) very great or extreme: *a howling success* ◊ *She flew into a howling rage.*

h.p. /ˌeɪtʃ 'piː/ (also **HP**) *abbr.* **1** HORSEPOWER **2** (*BrE*) HIRE PURCHASE

HQ /ˌeɪtʃ 'kjuː/ *abbr.* HEADQUARTERS: *See you back at HQ.* ◊ *police HQ*

hr (also **hr.** especially in *AmE*) *abbr.* (*pl.* **hrs** or **hr**) (in writing) hour: *Cover and chill for 1 hr.*

æ	ɑː	e	ɜː	ə	ɪ	iː	i	ɒ	ɔː	ʌ	ʊ	u	uː
cat	father	ten	bird	about	sit	see	many	got	saw	cup	put	actual	too
								(BrE)					

HRH /ˌeɪtʃ ɑːr ˈeɪtʃ/ *abbr.* His/Her ROYAL HIGHNESS: *HRH Prince Harry*

HRT /ˌeɪtʃ ɑː ˈtiː;; *AmE* ɑːr/ *noun* [U] medical treatment for women going through the MENOPAUSE in which HORMONES are added to the body (abbreviation for 'hormone replacement therapy')

hua·rache /wæˈrɑːtʃi; wəˈr-/ *noun* a type of SANDAL (= open shoe) made of many narrow strips of leather woven together

hub /hʌb/ *noun* **1** [usually sing.] ~ **(of sth)** the central and most important part of a particular place or activity: *the commercial hub of the city* ◊ *to be at the hub of things* (= where things happen and important decisions are made) ◊ *a hub airport* (= a large important one where people often change from one plane to another) **2** the central part of a wheel—picture at BICYCLE

hub·bub /ˈhʌbʌb/ *noun* [sing., U] **1** the loud sound made by a lot of people talking at the same time: *It was difficult to hear what he was saying over the hubbub.* **2** a situation in which there is a lot of noise, excitement and activity: *the hubbub of city life*

hubby /ˈhʌbi/ *noun* [usually sing.] (*pl.* **-ies**) (*informal*) = HUSBAND

hub·cap /ˈhʌbkæp/ *noun* a round metal cover that fits over the HUB of a vehicle's wheel—picture at CAR

hu·bris /ˈhjuːbrɪs/ *noun* [U] (*literary*) the fact of sb being too proud. In literature, a character with this pride ignores warnings and laws and this usually results in their DOWNFALL and death.

huck·ster /ˈhʌkstə(r)/ *noun* (*old-fashioned, AmE*) **1** (*disapproving*) a person who uses aggressive or annoying methods to sell sth **2** a person who sells things in the street or by visiting people's houses

hud·dle /ˈhʌdl/ *verb, noun*
■ *verb* [V] [usually +*adv. / prep.*] ~ **(up)** **1** (of people or animals) to gather closely together, usually because of cold or fear: *We huddled together for warmth.* ◊ *They all huddled around the fire.* ◊ *People huddled up close to each other.* **2** to hold your arms and legs close to your body, usually because you are cold or frightened: *I huddled under a blanket on the floor.* ▶ **hud·dled** *adj.*: *People were huddled together around the fire.* ◊ *huddled figures in shop doorways* ◊ *We found him huddled on the floor.*
■ *noun* **1** a small group of people, objects or buildings that are close together, especially when they are not in any particular order: *People stood around in huddles.* ◊ *The track led them to a huddle of barns and outbuildings.* **2** (in American football) a time when the players gather round to hear the plan for the next part of the game **IDM** **get/go into a ˈhuddle (with sb)** to move close to sb so that you can talk about sth without other people hearing

hue /hjuː/ *noun* **1** (*literary* or *technical*) a colour; a particular shade of a colour: *His face took on an unhealthy whitish hue.* ◊ *Her paintings capture the subtle hues of the countryside in autumn.* **2** (*formal*) a type of belief or opinion: *supporters of every political hue* **IDM** ,hue and ˈcry strong public protest about sth: *Further cuts in welfare have raised a hue and cry among the American public.*

huff /hʌf/ *verb, noun*
■ *verb* ■ to say sth or make a noise in a way that shows you are offended or annoyed: [V speech] *'Well, nobody asked you,' she huffed irritably.* [also V] **IDM** ,huff and ˈpuff (*informal*) **1** to breathe in a noisy way because you are very tired: *Jack was huffing and puffing to keep up with her.* **2** to make it obvious that you are annoyed about sth without doing anything to change the situation: *After much huffing and puffing, she finally agreed to help.*
■ *noun* **IDM** in a ˈhuff (*informal*) in a bad mood, especially because sb has annoyed or upset you: *She went off in a huff.*

huffy /ˈhʌfi/ *adj.* (*informal*) in a bad mood, especially because sb has annoyed or upset you ▶ **huff·ily** *adv.*

hug /hʌg/ *verb, noun*
■ *verb* (**-gg-**) **1** to put your arms around sb and hold them tightly, especially to show that you like or love them **SYN** EMBRACE: [VN] *They hugged each other.* ◊ *She hugged*

him tightly. ◊ [V] *They put their arms around each other and hugged.* **2** [VN] to put your arms around sth and hold it close to your body: *She sat in the chair, hugging her knees.* ◊ *He hugged the hot-water bottle to his chest.* **3** [VN] (of a path, vehicle, etc.) to keep close to sth for a distance: *The track hugs the coast for a mile.* **4** [VN] to fit tightly around sth, especially a person's body: *figure-hugging jeans*
■ *noun* an act of putting your arms around sb and holding them tightly, especially to show that you like or love them: *She gave her mother a big hug.* ◊ *He stopped to receive hugs and kisses from the fans.*—see also BEAR HUG

huge /hjuːdʒ/ *adj.* extremely large in size or amount; great in degree: *a huge crowd* ◊ *He gazed up at her with huge brown eyes.* ◊ *huge debts / losses / profits* ◊ *huge amounts of data* ◊ *The sums of money involved are potentially huge.* ◊ *The party was a huge success.* ◊ *This is going to be a huge problem for us.*

huge·ly /ˈhjuːdʒli/ *adv.* (*written*) **1** extremely: *hugely entertaining / important / popular / successful* **2** very much: *They intended to invest hugely in new technology.* ◊ *He turned around, grinning hugely.*

huh /hʌ/ *exclamation* **1** people use **Huh?** at the end of questions, suggestions, etc., especially when they want sb to agree with them: *So you won't be coming tonight, huh?* ◊ *Let's get out of here, huh?* **2** people say **Huh!** to show anger, surprise, disagreement, etc. or to show that they are not impressed by sth: *Huh! Is that all you've done?* **3** people say **Huh?** to show that they have not heard what sb has just said: *'Are you feeling OK?' 'Huh?'*

hula hoop /ˈhuːlə huːp/ *noun* a large plastic ring that you swing around your waist by moving your hips

hulk /hʌlk/ *noun* **1** the main part of an old vehicle, especially a ship, that is no longer used: *the hulk of a wrecked ship* **2** a very large person, especially one who is not very graceful: *a great hulk of a man* **3** a very large object, especially one that causes you to feel nervous or afraid

hulk·ing /ˈhʌlkɪŋ/ *adj.* [only before noun] very large or heavy, often in a way that causes you to feel nervous or afraid: *a hulking figure crouching in the darkness* ◊ *I don't want that hulking great computer in my office.*

hull /hʌl/ *noun, verb*
■ *noun* the main, bottom part of a ship, that goes in the water: *a wooden / steel hull* ◊ *They climbed onto the upturned hull and waited to be rescued.*—picture at BOAT
■ *verb* [VN] to remove the outer covering of peas, beans, etc. or the ring of leaves attached to STRAWBERRIES

hul·la·ba·loo /ˌhʌləbəˈluː/ *noun* [sing.] a lot of loud noise, especially made by people who are annoyed or excited about sth: *They looked outside to find out what all the hullabaloo was about.*

hullo (*especially BrE*) = HELLO

hum /hʌm/ *verb, noun*
■ *verb* (**-mm-**) **1** to sing a tune with your lips closed: [V] *She was humming softly to herself.* ◊ [VN] *What's that tune you're humming?* **2** [V] to make a low continuous sound: *The computers were humming away.* **3** [V] (*informal*) to be full of activity: *The streets were beginning to hum with life.* **IDM** ,hum and ˈhaw (*BrE*) (*AmE* ,hem and ˈhaw) (*informal*) to take a long time to make a decision or before you say sth
■ *noun* [sing.] ~ **(of sth)** a low continuous sound: *the hum of bees / traffic / voices* ◊ *The room filled with the hum of conversation.*

human /ˈhjuːmən/ *adj., noun*
■ *adj.* **1** [only before noun] of or connected with people rather than animals, machines or gods: *the human body / brain* ◊ *human anatomy / activity / behaviour / experience* ◊ *a terrible loss of human life* ◊ *Contact with other people is a basic human need.* ◊ *This food is not fit for human consumption.* ◊ *human geography* (= the study of the way different people live around the world) ◊ *The hostages were used as a human shield* (= a person or group of people that is forced to stay in a particular place where they would be hurt or killed if their country attacked it). ◊ *Firefighters formed a human chain* (= a line of people) *to carry the children to safety.*—picture at CHAIN **2** show-

H

ing the weaknesses that are typical of people, which means that other people should not criticize the person too much: *human weaknesses/failings* ◊ *We must allow for **human error**.* ◊ *It's only **human** to want the best for your children.* **3** having the same feelings and emotions as most ordinary people: *He's really very human when you get to know him.* ◊ *The public is always attracted to politicians who have **the human touch** (= the ability to make ordinary people feel relaxed when they meet them).* —compare INHUMAN, NON-HUMAN **IDM** see MILK *n.*
■ *noun* (also **human 'being**) a person rather than an animal or a machine: *Dogs can hear much better than humans.* ◊ *That is no way to treat another human being.*

hu·mane /hjuːˈmeɪn/ *adj.* showing kindness towards people and animals by making sure that they do not suffer more than is necessary: *a caring and humane society* ◊ *These regulations ensure the humane treatment of all refugees.* ◊ *the humane killing of animals* **OPP** INHUMANE ▶ **hu·mane·ly** *adv.*: *to treat sb humanely* ◊ *meat that has been humanely produced* ◊ *The dog was humanely destroyed.*

human 'interest *noun* [U] the part of a story in a newspaper, etc. that people find interesting because it describes the experiences, feelings, etc. of the people involved

hu·man·ism /ˈhjuːmənɪzəm/ *noun* [U] a system of thought that considers that solving human problems with the help of reason is more important than religious beliefs. It emphasizes the fact that the basic nature of human beings is good. ▶ **hu·man·is·tic** /ˌhjuːməˈnɪstɪk/ *adj.*: *humanistic ideals*

hu·man·ist /ˈhjuːmənɪst/ *noun* a person who believes in humanism

hu·mani·tar·ian /hjuːˌmænɪˈteəriən; *AmE* -ˈter-/ *adj.* [usually before noun] concerned with reducing suffering and improving the conditions that people live in: *to provide **humanitarian** aid to the war zone* ◊ *humanitarian concerns/issues/needs* ◊ *a humanitarian organization* ◊ *They are calling for the release of the hostages on **humanitarian grounds**.* ◊ *The expulsion of hundreds of thousands of people represents a humanitarian catastrophe of enormous proportions.* ▶ **hu·mani·tar·ian** *noun* **hu·mani·tar·ian·ism** /-ɪzəm/ *noun* [U]

hu·man·ity /hjuːˈmænəti/ *noun* **1** [U] people in general: *crimes against humanity* **2** [U] the state of being a person rather than a god, an animal or a machine: *The story was used to emphasize the humanity of Jesus.* ◊ *united by a sense of common humanity* **3** [U] the quality of being kind to people and animals by making sure that they do not suffer more than is necessary; the quality of being HUMANE: *The judge was praised for his courage and humanity.* **OPP** INHUMANITY **4 (the) humanities** [pl.] the subjects of study that are concerned with the way people think and behave, for example literature, language, history and philosophy—compare SCIENCE

hu·man·ize (*BrE* also **-ise**) /ˈhjuːmənaɪz/ *verb* [VN] (*written*) to make sth more pleasant or suitable for people; to make sth more HUMANE: *These measures are intended to humanize the prison system.*

hu·man·kind /ˌhjuːmənˈkaɪnd/ *noun* [U] people in general—see also MANKIND

hu·man·ly /ˈhjuːmənli/ *adv.* within human ability; in a way that is typical of human behaviour, thoughts and feelings: *The doctors did all that was **humanly possible**.* ◊ *He couldn't humanly refuse to help her.*

human 'nature *noun* [U] the ways of behaving, thinking and feeling that are shared by most people and are considered to be normal: *Her kindness has restored my faith in human nature (= the belief that people are good).* ◊ *It's only human nature to be worried about change.*

hu·man·oid /ˈhjuːmənɔɪd/ *noun* a machine or creature that looks and behaves like a human being ▶ **hu·man·oid** *adj.*

the human 'race *noun* [sing.] all people, considered together as a group

human re'sources *noun* **1** [pl.] people's skills and abilities, seen as sth a company, an organization, etc. can

make use of **2** [U+sing./pl. *v.*] the department in a company that deals with employing and training people **SYN** PERSONNEL: *the human resources director*

human 'right *noun* [usually pl.] one of the basic rights that everyone has to be treated fairly and not in a cruel way, especially by their government: *The country has a poor record on human rights.* ◊ *to campaign for human rights* ◊ *human rights abuses/violations*

hum·ble /ˈhʌmbl/ *adj., verb*
■ *adj.* (**hum·bler** /ˈhʌmblə(r)/ **hum·blest** /ˈhʌmblɪst/) **1** showing you do not think that you are as important as other people: *Be humble enough to learn from your mistakes.* ◊ *my humble tribute to this great man*—see also HUMILITY **2** (*ironic* or *humorous*) used to suggest that you are not as important as other people, but in a way that is not sincere or not very serious: *In my humble opinion, you were in the wrong.* ◊ *My humble apologies. I did not understand.* **3** having a low rank or social position: *a man of humble birth/origins* ◊ *a humble occupation* ◊ *the daughter of a humble shopkeeper* **4** (of a thing) not large or special in any way: *a humble farmhouse* ◊ *The company has worked its way up from humble beginnings to become the market leader.* ▶ **hum·bly** /ˈhʌmbli/ *adv.*: *I would humbly suggest that there is something wrong here.* ◊ *'Sorry,' she said humbly.* **IDM** see EAT
■ *verb* [VN] **1** to make sb feel that they are not as good or important as they thought they were: *He was humbled by her generosity.* ◊ *a humbling experience* **2** [usually passive] to easily defeat an opponent, especially a strong or powerful one: *The world champion was humbled last night in three rounds.* **3 ~ yourself** to show that you are not too proud to ask for sth, admit that you have been wrong, etc.—see also HUMILITY

hum·bug /ˈhʌmbʌɡ/ *noun* **1** [U] (*written*) dishonest language or behaviour that is intended to deceive people: *political humbug* **2** [C] (*old-fashioned*) a person who is not sincere or honest **3** [C] (*BrE*) a hard sweet/candy made from boiled sugar, especially one that tastes of PEPPERMINT

hum·ding·er /ˌhʌmˈdɪŋə(r)/ *noun* [sing.] (*informal*) something that is very exciting or impressive: *It turned into a real humdinger of a game.*

hum·drum /ˈhʌmdrʌm/ *adj.* boring and always the same: *a humdrum existence/job/life*

hu·merus /ˈhjuːmərəs/ *noun* (*pl.* **hu·meri** /ˈhjuːməraɪ/) (*anatomy*) the large bone in the top part of the arm between the shoulder and the elbow—picture at BODY

humid /ˈhjuːmɪd/ *adj.* (of the air or climate) warm and damp: *These ferns will grow best in a humid atmosphere.* ◊ *The island is hot and humid in the summer.*

hu·midi·fier /hjuːˈmɪdɪfaɪə(r)/ *noun* a machine used for making the air in a room less dry—see also DEHUMIDIFIER

hu·mid·ity /hjuːˈmɪdəti/ *noun* [U] **1** the amount of water in the air: *Instruments constantly monitor temperature and humidity.* ◊ *high/low humidity* ◊ *70% humidity* **2** conditions in which the air is very warm and damp: *These plants need heat and humidity to grow well.* ◊ *The humidity was becoming unbearable.*

hu·mili·ate /hjuːˈmɪlieɪt/ *verb* [VN] to make sb feel ashamed or stupid and lose the respect of other people: *I didn't want to humiliate her in front of her colleagues.* ◊ *I've never felt so humiliated.* ◊ *The party was humiliated in the recent elections.* ▶ **hu·mili·at·ing** *adj.*: *a humiliating defeat* ◊ *It was the most humiliating night of his life.* **hu·mili·ation** /hjuːˌmɪliˈeɪʃn/ *noun* [U, C]: *She suffered the humiliation of being criticized in public.*

hu·mil·ity /hjuːˈmɪləti/ *noun* [U] the quality of not thinking that you are better than other people; the quality of being humble: *Her first defeat was an early lesson in humility.* ◊ *an act of genuine humility*

hum·ming·bird /ˈhʌmɪŋbɜːd; *AmE* -bɜːrd/ *noun* a small brightly coloured bird that lives in warm countries and that can stay in one place in the air by beating its wings very fast, making a continuous low sound (= a HUMMING sound)

hum·mock /ˈhʌmək/ *noun* (*BrE*) a small hill or pile of earth

b	d	f	g	h	k	l	m	n	p	r
bad	did	fall	get	hat	cat	leg	man	now	pen	red

hum·mus (also **hou·mus**) /ˈhuməs; ˈhuːməs/ *noun* [U] a type of Greek food that is a soft mixture of CHICKPEAS, oil and GARLIC

hu·mon·gous /hjuːˈmʌŋgəs/ *adj.* (*informal, especially AmE*) very big

humor, humor·less (*AmE*) = HUMOUR, HUMOURLESS

hu·mor·ist /ˈhjuːmərɪst/ *noun* a person who is famous for writing or telling amusing stories

hu·mor·ous /ˈhjuːmərəs/ *adj.* funny and entertaining; showing a sense of humour: *He gave a humorous account of their trip to Spain.* ◊ *She had not intended to be humorous.* ◊ *He had a wide mouth and humorous grey eyes.* ▶ **hu·mor·ous·ly** *adv.*: *The poem humorously describes local characters and traditions.*

hu·mour (*BrE*) (*AmE* **hu·mor**) /ˈhjuːmə(r)/ *noun, verb*
■ *noun* **1** [U] the quality in sth that makes it funny or amusing; the ability to laugh at things that are amusing: *a story full of gentle humour* ◊ *She ignored his feeble attempt at humour.* ◊ *They failed to see the humour of the situation.* ◊ *He has a good **sense of humour**.* ◊ *I can't stand people with no **sense of humour**.* ◊ *She smiled with a rare flash of humour.* ◊ *She has her very own brand of humour.* ◊ *The film is only funny if you appreciate French humour* (= things that cause French people to laugh). **2** [C, U] (*formal*) the state of your feelings or mind at a particular time: *to be in the best/worst of humours* ◊ *The meeting dissolved in ill humour.* ◊ *to be out of humour* (= in a bad mood)—see also GOOD HUMOUR, GOOD-HUMOURED, ILL-HUMOURED **3** [C] (*old use*) one of the four liquids that were thought in the past to be in a person's body and to influence health and character
■ *verb* [VN] to agree with sb's wishes, even if they seem unreasonable, in order to keep the person happy: *She thought it best to humour him rather than get into an argument.*

hu·mour·less (*BrE*) (*AmE* **hu·mor·less**) /ˈhjuːmələs; *AmE* -ərləs/ *adj.* not having or showing the ability to laugh at things that other people think are amusing: *a humourless person/smile*

hump /hʌmp/ *noun, verb*
■ *noun* **1** a large lump that sticks out above the surface of sth, especially the ground: *the dark hump of the mountain in the distance* ◊ (*BrE*) *a road/speed/traffic hump* (= a hump on a road that forces traffic to drive more slowly) **2** a large lump on the back of some animals, especially CAMELS **3** a large lump on the back of a person, caused by an unusual curve in the SPINE (= the row of bones in the middle of the back) IDM **get/take the 'hump** (*BrE, informal*) to become annoyed or upset about sth: *Fans get the hump when the team loses.* **be over the 'hump** to have done the most difficult part of sth
■ *verb* [VN] **1** (*BrE*) to carry sth heavy: *I've been humping furniture around all day.* **2** (△, *slang*) to have sex with sb

hump·back /ˈhʌmpbæk/ *noun* **1** = HUMPBACK WHALE **2** = HUNCHBACK

humpback 'bridge *noun* (*BrE*) a small bridge that slopes steeply on both sides

humpback 'whale (also **hump·back**) *noun* a large WHALE (= a very large sea animal) with a back shaped like a HUMP

humped /hʌmpt/ *adj.* having a HUMP or HUMPS; shaped like a HUMP: *a humped back* ◊ *He was tall and broad with humped shoulders.*

humph *exclamation* the way of writing the sound /həmf/ that people use to show they do not believe sth or do not approve of it

humus /ˈhjuːməs/ *noun* [U] a substance made from dead leaves and plants, added to soil to help plants grow

Hun /hʌn/ *noun* (*pl.* **Huns** or **the Hun**) (*informal*) an offensive word for a German person, used especially during the First and Second World Wars

hunch /hʌntʃ/ *verb, noun*
■ *verb* [+adv./prep.] to bend the top part of your body forward and raise your shoulders and back: [V] *She leaned forward, hunching over the desk.* ◊ [VN] *He hunched his shoulders and thrust his hands deep into*

his pockets. ▶ **hunched** *adj.*: *a hunched figure* ◊ *He sat hunched over his breakfast.*
■ *noun* a feeling that sth is true even though you do not have any evidence to prove it: *It seemed that the doctor's hunch had been right.* ◊ *My hunch is that the burglars are still in the area.* ◊ *I had a hunch (that) you'd be back.* ◊ *to follow/back your hunches*

hunch·back /ˈhʌntʃbæk/ (also **hump·back**) *noun* (*offensive*) a person who has a HUMP on their back

hun·dred /ˈhʌndrəd/ *number* (*plural verb*) **1** 100 HELP You say **a, one, two, several**, etc. **hundred** without a final 's' on 'hundred'. **Hundreds (of ...)** can be used if there is no number or quantity before it. Always use a plural verb with **hundred** or **hundreds**.: *One hundred (of the children) have already been placed with foster families.* ◊ *There were just a hundred of them there.* **5** *This vase is worth several hundred dollars.* ◊ *She must be over a hundred* (= a hundred years old). ◊ *Hundreds of thousands of people are at risk.* ◊ *a hundred-year lease* **2** **a hundred** or **hundreds (of ...)** (*usually informal*) a large amount: *hundreds of miles away* ◊ *for hundreds of years* ◊ *If I've said it once, I've said it a hundred times.* ◊ *I have a **hundred and one** things to do.* ◊ (*formal*) *Men died in their hundreds.* **3** (**the hundreds**) [pl.] the numbers from 100 to 999: *We're talking about a figure in the low hundreds.* **4** (**the ...hundreds**) [pl.] (*spoken*) the years of a particular century: *the early nineteen hundreds* (= written 'early 1900s') **5** **one, two, three**, etc. **~ hours** (*spoken*) used to express whole hours in the 24-hour system: *twelve hundred hours* (= 12.00, midday) ⇨ Appendix 3 IDM see NINETY

hun·dredth /ˈhʌndrədθ; -ətθ/ *ordinal number, noun*
■ *ordinal number* 100th: *her hundredth birthday*
■ *noun* each of one hundred equal parts of sth: *a/one hundredth of a second*

hun·dred·weight /ˈhʌndrədweɪt/ *noun* (*pl.* **hun·dred·weight**) (*abbr.* **cwt.**) a unit for measuring weight equal to 112 pounds in the UK and 100 pounds in the US. There are 20 hundredweight in a TON.

hung /hʌŋ/ *adj.* [only before noun] **1** (of a parliament or council) (*BrE*) in which no political party has more elected members than all the other parties added together **2** (of a JURY) unable to agree about whether sb is guilty of a crime—see also HANG, *v.*

hun·ger /ˈhʌŋgə(r)/ *noun, verb*
■ *noun* **1** [U] the state of not having enough food to eat, especially when this causes illness or death SYN STARVATION: *Around fifty people die of hunger every day in the camp.* ◊ *The organization works to alleviate world hunger and disease.* **2** [U] the feeling caused by a need to eat: *hunger pangs* ◊ *I felt faint with hunger.* **3** [sing.] **~ (for sth)** (*formal*) a strong desire for sth: *a hunger for knowledge/information/success* ◊ *Nothing seemed to satisfy their hunger for truth.*
■ *verb* PHRV **'hunger for/after sth/sb** (*literary*) to have a strong desire or need for sth/sb

'hunger strike *noun* [C, U] the act of refusing to eat for a long period of time in order to protest about sth: *to be/go on hunger strike* ▶ **'hunger striker** *noun*

hung·over *adj.* [not usually before noun] a person who is **hung-over** is feeling ill/sick because they drank too much alcohol the night before—see also HANGOVER

hun·gry /ˈhʌŋgri/ *adj.* (**hun·grier, hun·gri·est**) **1** feeling that you want to eat sth: *I'm really hungry.* ◊ *Is anyone getting hungry?* ◊ *All this talk of food is making me hungry.* ◊ *I have a hungry family to feed.* **2** not having enough food to eat: *The charity is now targeting hungry people in Africa.* ◊ *Thousands are **going hungry** because of the failure of this year's harvest.* **3** (**the hungry**) *noun* [pl.] people who do not have enough food to eat **4** [only before noun] causing you to feel that you want to eat sth: *All this gardening is hungry work.* **5** **~ (for sth)** having or showing a strong desire for sth: *Both parties are hungry for power.* ◊ *power-hungry* ◊ *The child is simply hungry for affection.* ◊ *His eyes had a wild hungry look in them.*
▶ **hun·grily** /ˈhʌŋgrəli/ *adv.*: *They gazed hungrily at the display of food.* ◊ *He kissed her hungrily.*

s	t	v	z	·ʃ	ʒ	tʃ	dʒ	θ	ð	ŋ
see	tea	van	zoo	shoe	vision	chain	jam	thin	this	sing

‚hung 'up adj. [not before noun] **~ (on/about sth/sb)** (informal, disapproving) very worried about sth/sb; thinking about sth/sb too much: You're not still hung up on that girl? ◊ He's too hung up about fitness.

hunk /hʌŋk/ noun **1** a large piece of sth, especially food, that has been cut or broken from a larger piece: a hunk of bread/cheese/meat **2** (informal) a man who is big, strong and sexually attractive: He's a real hunk.

hun·ker /'hʌŋkə(r)/ verb **PHRV** ‚hunker 'down **1** (especially AmE) to sit on your heels with your knees bent up in front of you **SYN** SQUAT: He hunkered down beside her. **2** to prepare yourself to stay somewhere, keep an opinion, etc. for a long time **3** to refuse to change an opinion, way of behaving, etc.

hun·kers /'hʌŋkəz; AmE -kərz/ noun **IDM** on your 'hunkers sitting on your heels with your knees bent up in front of you

hunky /'hʌŋki/ adj. (hunk·ier, hunk·iest) (of a man) big, strong and sexually attractive: Who is that hunky guy?

hunky-dory /ˌhʌŋki 'dɔːri/ adj. [not before noun] (informal) if you say that **everything is hunky-dory**, you mean that there are no problems and that everyone is happy

hunt /hʌnt/ verb, noun
■ verb **1** to chase wild animals or birds in order to catch or kill them for food, sport or to make money: [V] Lions sometimes hunt alone. ◊ [VN] Whales are still being hunted and killed in the Arctic. **2** [V] **~ (for sth)** to look for sth that is difficult to find **SYN** SEARCH: I've hunted everywhere but I can't find it. ◊ She is still hunting for a new job. **3 ~ (for) sb** to look for sb in order to catch them or harm them: [VN] Police are hunting an escaped criminal. ◊ [V] Detectives are hunting for thieves who broke into a warehouse yesterday. **4** [V, VN] (in Britain) to chase and kill FOXES as a sport, riding horses and using dogs **PHRV** ‚hunt sb↔'down to search for sb until you catch or find them, especially in order to punish or harm them ‚hunt sth↔'down/'out to search for sth until you find it
■ noun **1** [C, usually sing.] **~ (for sb/sth)** an act of looking for sb/sth that is difficult to find: The hunt is on for a suitable candidate. ◊ Hundreds have joined a police hunt for the missing teenager. ◊ a murder hunt (= to find the person who has killed sb)—see also TREASURE HUNT, WITCH-HUNT **2** [C] (often in compounds) an act of chasing wild animals to kill or capture them: a tiger/seal hunt **3** [C] (in Britain) an event at which people ride horses and hunt FOXES as a sport: There will be a hunt on Boxing Day. ◊ a hunt meeting **4** [C+sing./pl. v.] (in Britain) a group of people who regularly hunt FOXES as a sport: There are several different hunts in the area.

hunt·er /'hʌntə(r)/ noun **1** a person who hunts wild animals for food or sport; an animal that hunts its food **2** (usually in compounds) a person who looks for and collects a particular kind of thing: a bargain hunter—see also HEADHUNTER **3** (BrE) a fast strong horse used in hunting FOXES **4** (AmE) a dog used in hunting

hunt·ing /'hʌntɪŋ/ noun [U] **1** chasing and killing wild animals and birds as a sport or for food: to go hunting ◊ Since 1977 otter hunting has been illegal. **2** [U] (BrE) = FOX-HUNTING **3** job/house **~** the process of trying to get a job or find a house to buy or rent: How's the job hunting going?

'hunting ground noun **1** a place where people with a particular interest can easily find what they want: Crowded markets are a happy hunting ground for pickpockets. **2** a place where wild animals are hunted

hunt·ress /'hʌntrəs/ noun (literary) a woman who hunts wild animals

hunts·man /'hʌntsmən/ noun (pl. -men /-mən/) a man who hunts animals

hur·dle /'hɜːdl; AmE 'hɜːrdl/ noun, verb
■ noun **1** each of a series of upright frames that a person or horse jumps over in a race: His horse fell at the final hurdle. ◊ to clear a hurdle (= jump over it successfully) **2** (hurdles) [pl.] a race in which runners or horses have to jump over hurdles: the 300 m hurdles—picture on page 1251 **3** a problem or difficulty that must be solved or dealt with before you can achieve sth: The next hurdle will be getting her parents' agreement. ◊ Well we've cleared the first hurdle; let's see what happens next.
■ verb **1 ~ (over) sth** to jump over sth while you are running: [VN] He hurdled two barriers to avoid reporters. ◊ [V] to hurdle over a fence **2** [V] to run in a hurdles race

hurd·ler /'hɜːdlə(r)/ /'hɜːrd-/ noun a person or horse that runs in races over hurdles

hurd·ling /'hɜːdlɪŋ; AmE 'hɜːrd-/ noun [U] the sport of racing over HURDLES

hurdy-gurdy /'hɜːdi gɜːdi; AmE 'hɜːrdi gɜːrdi/ noun (pl. -ies) a small musical instrument that is played by turning a handle

hurl /hɜːl; AmE hɜːrl/ verb **1** [VN+adv./prep.] to throw sth/sb violently in a particular direction: He hurled a brick through the window. **2** [VN] **~ abuse, accusations, insults, etc. (at sb)** to shout insults, etc. at sb: Rival fans hurled abuse at each other.

hurl·ing /'hɜːlɪŋ; AmE 'hɜːrlɪŋ/ noun [U] an Irish ball game similar to hockey, played by two teams of 15 people

hurly-burly /'hɜːli bɜːli; AmE 'hɜːrli bɜːrli/ noun [U] a very noisy and busy activity or situation: He enjoys the hurly-burly of political debate.

hur·rah /hə'rɑː/ (BrE **hur·ray** /hə'reɪ/) exclamation = HOORAY

hur·ri·cane /'hʌrɪkən; AmE 'hɜːrəkən; -keɪn/ noun a violent storm with very strong winds, especially in the western Atlantic Ocean: hurricane-force winds ◊ Hurricane Betty is now approaching the coast of Florida.—compare CYCLONE, TYPHOON

'hurricane lamp noun a type of lamp with glass sides to protect the flame inside from the wind

hur·ried /'hʌrid; AmE 'hɜːr-/ adj. [usually before noun] done too quickly because you do not have enough time: I ate a hurried breakfast and left. **OPP** UNHURRIED ▶ **hur·ried·ly** adv.: I hurriedly got up and dressed.

hurry /'hʌri; AmE 'hɜːri/ verb, noun
■ verb (hur·ries, hurry·ing, hur·ried, hur·ried) **1** to do sth more quickly than usual because there is not much time **SYN** RUSH: [V] You'll have to hurry if you want to catch that train. ◊ The kids hurried to open their presents. **HELP** In spoken English **hurry** can be used with and plus another verb, instead of with to and the infinitive, especially to tell somebody to do something quickly: Hurry and open your present—I want to see what it is! **2** [V+adv./prep.] to move quickly in a particular direction: He picked up his bags and hurried across the courtyard. ◊ She hurried away without saying goodbye. **3** [VN] **~ sb (into doing sth)** to make sb do sth more quickly **SYN** RUSH: I don't want to hurry you but we are close in twenty minutes. ◊ She was hurried into making an unwise choice. **4** [VN+adv./prep.] to deal with sth quickly **SYN** RUSH: Her application was hurried through. **5** [VN] [usually passive] to do sth too quickly **SYN** RUSH: A good meal should never be hurried. **PHRV** ‚hurry 'on to continue speaking without giving anyone else time to say anything ‚hurry 'up (with sth) to do sth more quickly because there is not much time: I wish the bus would hurry up and come. ◊ Hurry up! We're going to be late. ◊ Hurry up with the scissors. I need them. ‚hurry sb/sth↔'up to make sb do sth more quickly; to make sth happen more quickly: Can you do anything to hurry my order up?
■ noun the need or wish to get sth done quickly: Take your time—there's no hurry. ◊ In my hurry to leave, I forgot my passport. ◊ What's the hurry? The train doesn't leave for an hour. **IDM** in a 'hurry **1** very quickly or more quickly than usual: He had to leave in a hurry. **2** not having enough time to do sth: Sorry, I haven't got time to do it now—I'm in a hurry. ◊ Alice was in a tearing hurry as usual. **in a 'hurry to do sth** impatient to do sth: My daughter is in such a hurry to grow up. ◊ Why are you in such a hurry to sell? **in no 'hurry (to do sth) | not in a/any 'hurry (to do sth) 1** having plenty of time: I don't mind waiting—I'm not in any particular hurry. ◊ Serve this lady first—I'm in no hurry. **2** not wanting or not willing to do sth: We were in no hurry to get back to work after the holiday. **sb will not do sth again in a 'hurry**

(*spoken*) used to say that sb does not want to do sth again because it was not enjoyable: *I won't be going there again in a hurry—the food was terrible.*

hurt /hɜːt; *AmE* hɜːrt/ *verb, adj., noun*

- *verb* (**hurt, hurt**) **1** to cause physical pain to sb/yourself; to injure sb/yourself: [VN] *He hurt his back playing squash.* ◊ *Did you* **hurt** *yourself?* ◊ *Stop it. You're hurting me.* ◊ *My back is really hurting me today.* ◊ [V] *My shoes hurt—they're too tight.* **2** [V] to feel painful: *My feet hurt. Ouch! That hurt!* ◊ *It* **hurts** *when I bend my knee.* **3** to make sb unhappy or upset: [V] *What really hurt was that he never answered my letter.* ◊ [VN] *I'm sorry, I didn't mean to hurt you.* ◊ *I didn't want to* **hurt his feelings.** ◊ [VNto inf] *It* **hurt** *me to think that he would lie to me.* [also V to inf] **4** [V] (**be hurting**) (*informal*) to feel unhappy or upset: *I know you're hurting and I want to help you.* **5** [VN] to have a bad effect on sb/sth: *Many people on low incomes will be hurt by the government's plans.* **6** [V] (**be hurting**) (**for sth**) (*AmE*) to be in a difficult situation because you need sth, especially money: *His campaign is already hurting for money.* **IDM it won't/wouldn't 'hurt (sb/sth) (to do sth)** used to say that sb should do a particular thing: *It wouldn't hurt you to help with the housework occasionally.*—more at FLY *n.*, HIT *v.*
- *adj.* **1** injured physically: *None of the passengers were badly hurt.* **OPP** UNHURT **2** upset and offended by sth that sb has said or done: *a hurt look/expression* ◊ *She was* **deeply hurt** *that she had not been invited.* ◊ *Martha's hurt pride showed in her eyes.*
- *noun* [U, sing.] a feeling of unhappiness because sb has been unkind or unfair to you: *There was hurt and real anger in her voice.* ◊ *It was a hurt that would take a long time to heal.*

hurt·ful /ˈhɜːtfl; *AmE* ˈhɜːrtfl/ *adj.* ~ (**to sb**) (of comments) unkind and making you feel upset and offended: *I cannot forget the hurtful things he said.* ◊ *The bad reviews of her new book were very hurtful to her.* ▶ **hurt·ful·ly** /-fəli/ *adv.*: *He said, rather hurtfully, that he had better things to do than come and see me.*

hur·tle /ˈhɜːtl; *AmE* ˈhɜːrtl/ *verb* [V+adv./prep.] to move or make sb/sth move very fast in a particular direction: *A runaway car came hurtling towards us.*

hus·band /ˈhʌzbənd/ *noun, verb*

- *noun* (also *informal* **hubby**) the man that a woman is married to; a married man: *This is my husband, Steve.* **IDM ,husband and 'wife** a man and woman who are married to each other: *They lived together as husband and wife* (= as if they were married) *for years.* ◊ *a husband-and-wife team*
- *verb* [VN] (*formal*) to use sth very carefully and make sure that you do not waste it

hus·band·ry /ˈhʌzbəndri/ *noun* **1** farming, especially when done carefully and well: *animal/crop husbandry* **2** (*old-fashioned*) the careful use of food, money and supplies

hush /hʌʃ/ *verb, noun*

- *verb* **1** [V] (used especially in orders) to be quiet; to stop talking or crying: *Hush now and try to sleep.* **2** [VN] (*written*) to make sb/sth become quieter; to make sb stop talking, crying, etc. **PHRV ,hush sth↔'up** to hide information about a situation because you do not want people to know about it: *He claimed that the whole affair had been hushed up by the council.*
- *noun* [sing., U] a period of silence, especially following a lot of noise, or when people are expecting sth to happen: *There was a deathly hush in the theatre.* ◊ *A hush descended over the waiting crowd.* ◊ (*BrE, spoken*) *Can we have a bit of hush?* (= please be quiet)

hushed /hʌʃt/ *adj.* **1** (of a place) quiet because nobody is talking; much quieter than usual: *A hushed courtroom listened as the boy gave evidence.* **2** [usually before noun] (of voices) speaking very quietly: *a hushed tone/voice/ whisper*

hush-'hush *adj.* (*informal*) secret and not known about by many people: *Their wedding was very hush-hush.*

'hush money *noun* [U] money that is paid to sb to prevent them from giving other people information that could be embarrassing or damaging

'hush puppy *noun* a small fried cake made of CORNMEAL, eaten especially in the southern US

husk /hʌsk/ *noun, verb*

- *noun* the dry outer covering of nuts, fruits and seeds, especially of grain
- *verb* [VN] to remove the husks from grain, seeds, nuts, etc.

husky /ˈhʌski/ *adj., noun*

- *adj.* (**husk·ier, husk·iest**) (of a person or their voice) sounding deep, quiet and rough, sometimes in an attractive way: *She spoke in a husky whisper.* ▶ **husk·ily** *adv.* **huski·ness** *noun* [U]
- *noun* (*AmE* also **huskie**) (*pl.* **-ies**) a large strong dog with thick hair, used for pulling SLEDGES across snow

hus·sar /həˈzɑː(r)/ *noun* (in the past) a CAVALRY soldier who carried light weapons

hussy /ˈhʌsi/ *noun* (*pl.* **-ies**) (*old-fashioned, disapproving*) a girl or woman who behaves in a way that is considered shocking or morally wrong

hust·ings /ˈhʌstɪŋz/ *noun* (**the hustings**) [pl.] (*especially BrE*) the political meetings, speeches, etc. that take place in the period before an election: *Most politicians will be out on the hustings this week.*

hus·tle /ˈhʌsl/ *verb, noun*

- *verb* **1** [VN+adv./prep.] to make sb move quickly by pushing them in a rough aggressive way: *He grabbed her arm and hustled her out of the room.* ◊ *I was hustled into a waiting car.* **2** [VN] ~ **sb** (**into sth**) to force sb to make a decision before they are ready or sure **3** (*informal, especially AmE*) to sell or obtain sth, often illegally: [VN] *to hustle dope* ◊ [V] *They survive by hustling on the streets.* **4** [V] (*AmE, informal*) to act in an aggressive way or with a lot of energy **5** [V] (*AmE, slang*) to work as a prostitute
- *noun* [U] busy noisy activity of a lot of people in one place: *We escaped from the hustle and bustle of the city for the weekend.*

hus·tler /ˈhʌslə(r)/ *noun* **1** (*informal, especially AmE*) a person who tries to trick sb into giving them money **2** (*AmE, slang*) a prostitute

hut /hʌt/ *noun* a small, simply built house or shelter: *a beach hut* ◊ *a wooden hut*

hutch /hʌtʃ/ *noun* a wooden box with a front made of wire, used for keeping rabbits or other small animals in

hya·cinth /ˈhaɪəsɪnθ/ *noun* a plant with a mass of small blue, white or pink flowers with a sweet smell that grow closely together around a thick stem

hy·aena = HYENA

hy·brid /ˈhaɪbrɪd/ *noun* **1** an animal or plant that has parents of different SPECIES or varieties: *A mule is a hybrid of a male donkey and a female horse.*—compare CROSS-BREED **2** ~ (**between/of A and B**) something that is the product of mixing two or more different things: *The music was a hybrid of western pop and traditional folk song.* ▶ **hy·brid** *adj.*: *hybrid flowers* ◊ *a hybrid language/ system*

hy·brid·ize (*BrE* also **-ise**) /ˈhaɪbrɪdaɪz/ *verb* [V, VN] (*technical*) if an animal or a plant **hybridizes** or **is hybridized** with an animal or a plant of another SPECIES, they join together to produce a hybrid ▶ **hy·brid·iza·tion, -isa·tion** /ˌhaɪbrɪdaɪˈzeɪʃn; *AmE* -dəˈzeɪ-/ *noun* [U]

hy·dran·gea /haɪˈdreɪndʒə/ *noun* a bush with white, pink or blue flowers that grow closely together in the shape of a large ball

hy·drant /ˈhaɪdrənt/ *noun* = FIRE HYDRANT

hy·drate /ˈhaɪdreɪt; haɪˈdreɪt/ *verb* [VN] (*technical*) to make sth absorb water ▶ **hy·dra·tion** /haɪˈdreɪʃn/ *noun* [U]—compare DEHYDRATE

hy·draul·ic /haɪˈdrɔːlɪk; *BrE* also -ˈdrɒl-/ *adj.* [usually before noun] **1** (of water, oil, etc.) moved through pipes, etc. under pressure: *hydraulic fluid* **2** (of a mechanism) operated by liquid moving under pressure: *hydraulic brakes* **3** connected with hydraulic systems: *hydraulic engineering* ▶ **hy·draul·ic·al·ly** /-kli/ *adv.*: *hydraulically operated doors*

hy·draul·ics /haɪˈdrɔːlɪks; *BrE* also -ˈdrɒl-/ *noun* **1** [pl.] machinery that works by the use of liquid moving under pressure **2** [U] the science of the use of liquids moving under pressure

hydr(o)- /'haɪdr(əʊ); *AmE* -dr(oʊ)/ *combining form* (in nouns, adjectives and adverbs) **1** connected with water: *hydroelectricity* **2** (*chemistry*) combined with HYDROGEN: *hydrochloric acid*

hydro·car·bon /ˌhaɪdrəˈkɑːbən; *AmE* -ˈkɑːrb-/ *noun* (*chemistry*) a compound of HYDROGEN and CARBON. There are many different hydrocarbons found in petrol/gas, coal and natural gas: *a cut in hydrocarbon emissions from motor vehicles*

hydro·chlor·ic acid /ˌhaɪdrəˌklɒrɪk ˈæsɪd; *AmE* -ˌklɔːr-/ *noun* [U] (*chemistry*) (*symb* **HCl**) an acid containing HYDROGEN and CHLORINE

hydro·elec·tric /ˌhaɪdrəʊɪˈlektrɪk; *AmE* ˌhaɪdroʊ-/ *adj.* using the power of water to produce electricity; produced by the power of water: *a hydroelectric plant/dam/turbine* ◊ *hydroelectric power* ▶ **hydro·elec·tri·city** /-ˌɪˌlekˈtrɪsəti/ *noun* [U]

hydro·foil /'haɪdrəfɔɪl/ *noun* a boat which rises above the surface of the water when it is travelling fast—compare HOVERCRAFT—picture at BOAT

hydro·gen /'haɪdrədʒən/ *noun* [U] (*symb* **H**) a chemical element. Hydrogen is a colourless gas that is the lightest of all the elements. It combines with OXYGEN to form water.

hydrogen bomb (also **'H-bomb**) *noun* a very powerful nuclear bomb

hydrogen pe'roxide *noun* [U] (*chemistry*) = PEROXIDE

hydro·plane /'haɪdrəpleɪn/ *noun, verb*
■ *noun* **1** a light boat with an engine and a flat bottom, designed to travel fast over the surface of water **2** (*AmE*) = SEAPLANE
■ *verb* [V] (*AmE*) = AQUAPLANE

hydro·pon·ics /ˌhaɪdrəˈpɒnɪks; *AmE* -ˈpɑːn-/ *noun* [U] the process of growing plants in water or sand, rather than in soil

hydro·ther·apy /ˌhaɪdrəʊˈθerəpi; *AmE* ˌhaɪdroʊ-/ *noun* [U] the treatment of disease or injury by doing physical exercises in water

hyena (also **hy·aena**) /haɪˈiːnə/ *noun* a wild animal like a dog, that eats the meat of animals that are already dead and has a cry like a human laugh. Hyenas live in Africa and Asia.

hy·giene /'haɪdʒiːn/ *noun* [U] the practice of keeping yourself and your living and working areas clean in order to prevent illness and disease: *food hygiene* ◊ *personal hygiene* ◊ *In the interests of hygiene, please wash your hands.*

hy·gien·ic /haɪˈdʒiːnɪk; *AmE* also ˌhaɪdʒiˈenɪk; haɪˈdʒenɪk/ *adj.* clean and free of bacteria and therefore unlikely to spread disease: *Food must be prepared in hygienic conditions.* ◊ *The kitchen didn't look very hygienic.* ▶ **hy·gien·ic·al·ly** /-kli/ *adv.*: *Medical supplies are disposed of hygienically.*

hy·gien·ist /haɪˈdʒiːnɪst/ (also **'dental hygienist** especially in *AmE*) *noun* a person who works with a dentist and whose job is to clean people's teeth and give them advice about keeping them clean

hymen /'haɪmən/ *noun* (*anatomy*) a piece of skin that partly covers the opening of the VAGINA in women who have never had sex

hymn /hɪm/ *noun* **1** a song of praise, especially one praising God and sung by Christians **2** [usually sing.] if a film/movie, book, etc. is a **hymn to sth**, it praises it very strongly

hymn book (also *old-fashioned* **hym·nal** /'hɪmnəl/) *noun* a book of hymns

hype /haɪp/ *noun, verb*
■ *noun* [U] (*informal, disapproving*) advertisements and discussion on television, radio, etc. telling the public about a product and about how good or important it is: *marketing/media hype* ◊ *Don't believe all the hype—the book isn't that good.*
■ *verb* [VN] ~ **sth** (**up**) (*informal, disapproving*) to advertise sth a lot and exaggerate its good qualities, in order to get

a lot of public attention for it: *This week his much-hyped new movie opens in London.* ◊ *The meeting was hyped up in the media as an important event.*

hyped 'up *adj.* (*informal*) (of a person) very worried or excited about sth that is going to happen: *She gets really hyped up about job interviews.*

hyper /'haɪpə(r)/ *adj.* (*informal*) excited and nervous; having too much nervous energy

hyper- /'haɪpə(r)/ *prefix* (in adjectives and nouns) more than normal; too much: *hypercritical* ◊ *hypertension*—compare HYPO-

hyper·active /ˌhaɪpərˈæktɪv/ *adj.* (especially of children and their behaviour) too active and only able to keep quiet and still for short periods ▶ **hyper·activ·ity** /ˌhaɪpərækˈtɪvəti/ *noun* [U]

hyper·bole /haɪˈpɜːbəli; *AmE* -ˈpɜːrb-/ *noun* [U, C, usually sing.] a way of speaking or writing that makes sth sound better, more exciting, dangerous, etc. than it really is [SYN] EXAGGERATION: *The film is being promoted with all the usual hyperbole.*

hyper·link /'haɪpəlɪŋk; *AmE* -pərl-/ *noun* a place in an electronic document on a computer that is linked to another electronic document: *Click on the hyperlink.*

hyper·mar·ket /'haɪpəmɑːkɪt; *AmE* -pərmɑːrk-/ *noun* (*BrE*) a very large shop situated outside a town, that sells a wide range of goods

hyper·sen·si·tive /ˌhaɪpəˈsensətɪv; *AmE* -pərˈs-/ *adj.* ~ (to sth) **1** very easily offended: *He's hypersensitive to any kind of criticism.* **2** extremely physically sensitive to particular substances, medicines, light, etc: *Her skin is hypersensitive.* ▶ **hyper·sen·si·tiv·ity** /ˌhaɪpəˌsensəˈtɪvəti; *AmE* -pərˌs-/ *noun* [U]

hyper·ten·sion /ˌhaɪpəˈtenʃn; *AmE* -pərˈt-/ *noun* [U] (*medical*) blood pressure that is higher than is normal

hyper·text /'haɪpətekst; *AmE* -pərt-/ *noun* [U] text stored in a computer system that contains links that allow the user to move from one piece of text or document to another: *a hypertext link on the Internet*

hyper·ven·ti·late /ˌhaɪpəˈventɪleɪt; *AmE* -pərˈv-/ *verb* [V] (*technical*) to breathe too quickly because you are very frightened or excited ▶ **hyper·ven·ti·la·tion** /ˌhaɪpəˌventɪˈleɪʃn; *AmE* -pərˌven-/ *noun* [U]

hy·phen /'haɪfn/ *noun* the mark (-) used to join two words together to make a new one, as in *back-up*, or to show that a word has been divided between the end of one line and the beginning of the next: *Is there a hyphen in post-mortem?*—compare DASH ⇨ Appendix 4

hy·phen·ate /'haɪfəneɪt/ *verb* [VN] to join two words together using a hyphen; to divide a word between two lines of text using a hyphen: *Is your name hyphenated?* ▶ **hy·phen·ation** /ˌhaɪfəˈneɪʃn/ *noun* [U]: *hyphenation rules*

hyp·no·sis /hɪpˈnəʊsɪs; *AmE* -ˈnoʊ-/ *noun* [U] **1** an unconscious state in which sb can still see and hear and can be influenced to follow commands or answer questions: *She only remembered details of the accident under hypnosis.* **2** = HYPNOTISM: *He uses hypnosis as part of the treatment.* ◊ *Hypnosis helped me give up smoking.*

hypno·ther·apy /ˌhɪpnəʊˈθerəpi; *AmE* ˌhɪpnoʊ-/ *noun* [U] a kind of treatment that uses HYPNOSIS to help with physical or emotional problems

hyp·not·ic /hɪpˈnɒtɪk; *AmE* -ˈnɑːt-/ *adj., noun*
■ *adj.* **1** making you feel as if you are going to fall asleep, especially because of a regular, repeated noise or movement: *hypnotic music* ◊ *His voice had an almost hypnotic effect.* **2** [only before noun] connected with or produced by hypnosis: *a hypnotic trance/state* **3** (of a drug) making you sleep
■ *noun* (*technical*) a drug that makes you sleep; a SLEEPING PILL

hyp·no·tism /'hɪpnətɪzəm/ (also **hyp·no·sis**) *noun* [U] the practice of HYPNOTIZING a person (= putting them into an unconscious state)

hyp·no·tist /'hɪpnətɪst/ *noun* a person who HYPNOTIZES

H

people: *She went to a hypnotist hoping he could help her to give up smoking.*

hyp·no·tize (*BrE* also **-ise**) /ˈhɪpnətaɪz/ *verb* [VN] **1** to produce a state of HYPNOSIS in sb **2** [usually passive] (*written*) to interest sb so much that they can think of nothing else [SYN] MESMERIZE: *He was hypnotized by her beauty.*

hypo- /ˈhaɪpəʊ; *AmE* -poʊ/ (also **hyp-**) *prefix* (in adjectives and nouns) under; below normal: *hypodermic ◊ hypothermia*—compare HYPER-

hypo·chon·dria /ˌhaɪpəˈkɒndriə; *AmE* -ˈkɑːn-/ *noun* [U] a state in which sb worries all the time about their health and believes that they are ill when there is nothing wrong with them

hypo·chon·driac /ˌhaɪpəˈkɒndriæk; *AmE* -ˈkɑːn-/ *noun* a person who suffers from hypochondria: *Don't be such a hypochondriac!—there's nothing wrong with you.* ▶ **hypo·chon·driac** (also **hypo·chon·driacal** /ˌhaɪpəˌkɒnˈdraɪəkl; *AmE* /ˌkɑːnˈd-/) *adj.*

hypoc·risy /hɪˈpɒkrəsi; *AmE* hɪˈpɑːk-/ *noun* (*pl.* **-ies**) [U, C] (*disapproving*) behaviour in which sb pretends to have moral standards or opinions that they do not actually have: *He condemned the hypocrisy of those politicians who do one thing and say another. ◊ It's hypocrisy for them to pretend that they were shocked at the news.*

hypo·crite /ˈhɪpəkrɪt/ *noun* (*disapproving*) a person who pretends to have moral standards or opinions that they do not actually have: *Charles was a liar and a hypocrite who married her for money.* ▶ **hypo·crit·ical** /ˌhɪpəˈkrɪtɪkl/ *adj.*: *It would be hypocritical of me to have a church wedding when I don't believe in God.* **hypo·crit·ic·al·ly** /-kli/ *adv.*

hypo·der·mic /ˌhaɪpəˈdɜːmɪk; *AmE* -ˈdɜːrm-/ (also **hypo·dermic ˈneedle**, **hypodermic ˈsyringe**) *noun* a medical instrument with a long thin needle that is used to give sb an INJECTION under their skin = SYRINGE ▶ **hypo·der·mic** *adj.*: *a hypodermic injection* (= one under the skin)

hypot·en·use /haɪˈpɒtənjuːz; *AmE* -ˈpɑːtənuːs; -njuːz/ *noun* (*geometry*) the side opposite the RIGHT-ANGLE of a RIGHT-ANGLED triangle—picture at TRIANGLE

hypo·ther·mia /ˌhaɪpəˈθɜːmiə; *AmE* -ˈθɜːrm-/ *noun* [U] a medical condition in which the body temperature is much lower than normal

hy·poth·esis /haɪˈpɒθəsɪs; *AmE* -ˈpɑːθ-/ *noun* (*pl.* **hy·poth·eses** /-siːz/) **1** [C] an idea or explanation of sth that is based on a few known facts but that has not yet been proved to be true or correct: *to formulate/confirm a hypothesis ◊ a hypothesis about the function of dreams* **2** [U] guesses and ideas that are not based on certain knowledge [SYN] SPECULATION: *It would be pointless to engage in hypothesis before we have the facts.*

hy·poth·esize (*BrE* also **-ise**) /haɪˈpɒθəsaɪz; *AmE* -ˈpɑːθ-/ *verb* (VN, Vthat, V) (*formal*) to suggest a way of explaining sth when you do not definitely know about it; to form a hypothesis

hypo·thet·ic·al /ˌhaɪpəˈθetɪkl/ *adj.* based on situations or ideas which are possible and imagined rather than real and true: *a hypothetical question/situation/example ◊ Let us take the hypothetical case of Sheila, a mother of two … ◊ I wasn't asking about anybody in particular—it was a **purely hypothetical** question.* ▶ **hypo·thet·ic·al·ly** /-kli/ *adv.*

hys·ter·ec·tomy /ˌhɪstəˈrektəmi/ *noun* (*pl.* **-ies**) [C, U] a medical operation to remove a woman's WOMB

hys·teria /hɪˈstɪəriə; *AmE* -ˈstɪr-/ *noun* [U] **1** a state of extreme excitement, fear or anger in which a person, or a group of people, loses control of their emotions and starts to cry, laugh, etc: *There was mass hysteria when the band came on stage. ◊ A note of hysteria crept into her voice.* **2** (*disapproving*) an extremely excited and exaggerated way of behaving or reacting to an event: *the usual media hysteria that surrounds royal visits ◊ public hysteria about Aids* **3** (*medical*) a condition in which sb experiences violent or extreme emotions that they cannot control, especially as a result of shock

hys·ter·ic·al /hɪˈsterɪkl/ *adj.* **1** in a state of extreme excitement, and crying, laughing, etc. in an uncontrolled way: *hysterical screams/laughter ◊ a hysterical giggle ◊ He became almost hysterical when I told him. ◊ Let's not get hysterical. ◊ (disapproving) He thought I was being a hysterical female.* **2** (*informal*) extremely funny: *She seemed to find my situation absolutely hysterical.* [HELP] Some people use *an* instead of *a* before this word, and then usually do not pronounce the 'h'. This now sounds old-fashioned. ▶ **hys·ter·ic·al·ly** /-kli/ *adv.*: *to laugh/cry/scream/sob hysterically ◊ hysterically funny*

hys·ter·ics /hɪˈsterɪks/ *noun* [pl.] **1** an expression of extreme fear, excitement or anger that makes sb lose control of their emotions and cry, laugh, etc: *He went into hysterics when he heard the news.* **2** (*informal*) wild laughter: *She had the audience in hysterics.* [IDM] **have hysterics** (*spoken*) to be extremely upset and angry: *My mum'll have hysterics when she sees the colour of my hair.*

Hz *abbr.* (in writing) HERTZ

s	t	v	z	ʃ	ʒ	tʃ	dʒ	θ	ð	ŋ
see	tea	van	zoo	shoe	vision	chain	jam	thin	this	sing

I i

I /aɪ/ *noun, pron., symbol, abbr.*

- *noun* (also **i**) [C, U] (*pl.* **I's, i's** /aɪz/) the 9th letter of the English alphabet: *'Island' begins with (an) I/'I'*. **IDM** see DOT *v.*
- *pron.* used as the subject of a verb when the speaker or writer is referring to himself/herself: *I think I'd better go now.* ◇ *He and I are old friends.* ◇ *When they asked me if I wanted the job, I said yes.* ◇ *I'm not going to fall, am I?* ◇ *I'm taller than her, aren't I?*—see also ME
- *symbol* (also **i**) the number 1 in ROMAN NUMERALS
- *abbr.* (also **I.**) (especially on maps) Island(s); ISLE(s)

-ial *suffix* (in adjectives) typical of: *dictatorial* ▶ **-ially** (in adverbs): *officially*

iam·bic /aɪˈæmbɪk/ *adj.* (*technical*) (of rhythm in poetry) in which one short or weak syllable is followed by one long or strong syllable: *a poem written in iambic pentameters* (= in lines of ten syllables, five short and five long)

-ian, -an *suffix* **1** (in nouns and adjectives) from; typical of: *Bostonian* ◇ *Brazilian* ◇ *Shakespearian* ◇ *Libran* **2** (in nouns) a specialist in: *mathematician*

-iana, -ana *suffix* (in nouns) a collection of objects, facts, stories, etc. connected with the person, place, period, etc. mentioned: *Mozartiana* ◇ *Americana* ◇ *Victoriana*

ibex /ˈaɪbeks/ *noun* (*pl.* **ibex**) a mountain goat with long curved horns

ibid. (also **ib.**) *abbr.* in the same book or piece of writing as the one that has just been mentioned (from Latin 'ibidem')

-ibility ⇨ -ABLE

ibis /ˈaɪbɪs/ *noun* (*pl.* **ibises**) a bird with a long neck, long legs and a long beak that curves downwards, that lives near water

-ible, ibly ⇨ -ABLE, -ABLY

ibu·profen /ˌaɪbjuˈprəʊfen; *AmE* -ˈproʊ-/ *noun* [U] a drug used to reduce pain and INFLAMMATION

-ic *suffix* **1** (in adjectives and nouns) connected with: *scenic* ◇ *economic* ◇ *Arabic* **2** (in adjectives) that performs the action mentioned: *horrific* ◇ *specific* ▶ **-ical** (in adjectives): *comical* **-ically** (in adverbs): *physically*

ice /aɪs/ *noun, verb*

- *noun* **1** [U] water that has frozen and become solid: *There was ice on the windows.* ◇ *The lake was covered with a sheet of ice.* ◇ *My hands are as cold as ice.*—see also ICY, BLACK ICE, DRY ICE **2** [sing.] (usually **the ice**) a frozen surface that people SKATE on: *The dancers came out onto the ice.* ◇ *Both teams are on the ice, waiting for the whistle.* **3** [U] a piece of ice used to keep food and drinks cold: *I'll have lemonade please—no ice.* **4** [C] (*old-fashioned, especially BrE*) an ice cream—see also CHOC ICE **5** [U] (*AmE*) a type of sweet food that consists of ice that has been crushed and flavoured **IDM** **break the 'ice** to say or do sth that makes people feel more relaxed, especially at the beginning of a meeting, party, etc.—see also ICE-BREAKER (2) **cut no 'ice (with sb)** to have no influence or effect on sb: *His excuses cut no ice with me.* **on 'ice 1** (of wine, etc.) kept cold by being surrounded by ice **2** (of a plan, etc.) not being dealt with now; waiting to be dealt with at a later time: *We've had to put our plans on ice for the time being.* **3** (of entertainment, etc.) performed by SKATERS on an ICE RINK: *Cinderella on ice*—more at THIN *adj.*
- *verb* [VN] to cover a cake with ICING **PHRV** **ˌice 'over/'up**, **ˌice sth↔'over/'up** to cover sth with ice; to become covered with ice: *It was a memorable flight because the wings iced up.*

ˈice age (often **the Ice Age**) *noun* one of the long periods of time, thousands of years ago, when much of the earth's surface was covered in ice

ˈice axe (*BrE*) (*AmE* **ˈice-ax**) *noun* a tool used by people climbing mountains for cutting steps into ice—picture at AXE

ice·berg /ˈaɪsbɜːɡ; *AmE* -bɜːrɡ/ *noun* an extremely large mass of ice floating in the sea **IDM** see TIP *n.*

ˌiceberg 'lettuce *noun* a type of LETTUCE (= a salad vegetable) with crisp pale green leaves

ˌice-'blue *adj.* (especially of eyes) very pale blue in colour

ˈice-bound *adj.* surrounded by or covered in ice

ice-box /ˈaɪsbɒks; *AmE* -bɑːks/ *noun* (*old-fashioned, especially AmE*) = FRIDGE

ˈice-breaker *noun* **1** a strong ship designed to break a way through ice, for example in the Arctic or Antarctic **2** a thing that you do or say, like a game or a joke, to make people feel less nervous when they first meet

ˈice bucket *noun* a container filled with ice and used for keeping bottles of wine, etc. cold

ˈice cap *noun* a layer of ice permanently covering parts of the earth, especially around the North and South Poles

ˌice-'cold *adj.* **1** as cold as ice; very cold: *ice-cold beer* ◇ *My hands were ice-cold.* **2** not having or showing any emotion: *His eyes had grown ice-cold.*

ˌice 'cream (also **ˈice cream** especially in *AmE*) *noun* [U, C] a type of sweet frozen food made from milk fat, flavoured with fruit, chocolate, etc. and often eaten as a DESSERT; a small amount of this food intended for one person, often served in a container made of biscuit that is shaped like a CONE: *Desserts are served with cream or ice cream.* ◇ *Who wants an ice cream?*

ˈice cube *noun* a small, usually square, piece of ice used for making drinks cold

iced /aɪst/ *adj.* **1** (of drinks) made very cold; containing ice: *iced coffee/tea* **2** (of a cake, etc.) covered with ICING: *an iced cake*

ˌiced 'water (*BrE*) (*AmE* **ˈice water**) *noun* water with ice in it for drinking

ˈice floe (also **floe**) *noun* a large area of ice, floating in the sea

ˈice hockey (*BrE*) (*AmE* **hockey**) *noun* [U] a game played on ice, in which players use long sticks to hit a hard rubber disc (= called a PUCK) into the other team's goal—picture at HOCKEY

ˌice 'lolly (also *informal* **lolly**) (both *BrE*) (*AmE* **Popsicle**™) *noun* a piece of ice flavoured with fruit, served on a stick

ˈice pack *noun* a plastic container filled with ice that is used to cool parts of the body that are injured, etc.

ˈice pick *noun* a tool with a very sharp point for breaking ice

ˈice rink (also **ˈskating rink**, **rink**) *noun* a specially prepared flat surface of ice, where you can ice-skate; a building where there is an ice rink

ˈice skate (also **skate**) *noun* a boot with a thin metal blade on the bottom, that is used for SKATING on ice

ˈice-skate *verb* [V] to SKATE on ice ▶ **ˈice skater** *noun*

ˈice skating *noun* [U] = SKATING: *to go ice skating*

ˈice water *noun* (*AmE*) = ICED WATER

icicle /ˈaɪsɪkl/ *noun* a pointed piece of ice that is formed when water freezes as it falls down from sth such as a roof

icily /ˈaɪsɪli/ *adv.* said or done in a very unfriendly way: *'I have nothing to say to you,' she said icily.*

icing /'aɪsɪŋ/ (*especially BrE*) (*AmE* usually **frost·ing**) *noun* [U] a sweet mixture of sugar and water, milk, butter or egg white that is used to cover and decorate cakes—picture on page A1 **IDM** **the icing on the 'cake** something extra and not essential that is added to an already good situation or experience and that makes it even better

'icing sugar (*BrE*) (*AmE* **con'fectioners' sugar**, **'powdered sugar**) *noun* [U] fine white powder made from sugar, that is mixed with water to make icing—picture on page A1

icon /'aɪkɒn; *AmE* -kɑːn/ *noun* **1** (*computing*) a small symbol on a computer screen that represents a program or a file: *Click on the printer icon with the mouse.*—picture on page 251 **2** a famous person or thing that people admire and see as a symbol of a particular idea, way of life, etc: *Madonna and other pop icons of the 1980s* ◊ *a feminist/gay icon* (= sb that feminists, gay people admire) **3** (also **ikon**) (in the Orthodox Church) a painting or statue of a holy person that is also thought of as a holy object

icon·ic /aɪ'kɒnɪk; *AmE* -'kɑːnɪk/ *adj.* (*formal*) acting as a sign or symbol of sth

icono·clast /aɪ'kɒnəklæst; *AmE* -'kɑːnə-/ *noun* (*formal*) a person who criticizes popular beliefs or established customs and ideas

icono·clas·tic /aɪˌkɒnə'klæstɪk; *AmE* ˌkɑːnə-/ *adj.* (*formal*) criticizing popular beliefs or established customs and ideas ► **icono·clasm** /aɪ'kɒnəklæzəm; *AmE* -'kɑːnə-/ *noun* [U]: *the iconoclasm of the early Christians*

-ics *suffix* (in nouns) the science, art or activity of: *physics* ◊ *dramatics* ◊ *athletics*

ICU /ˌaɪ siː 'juː/ *abbr.* intensive care unit (= in a hospital)

icy /'aɪsi/ *adj.* **1** very cold: *icy winds/water* ◊ *My feet were icy cold.* **2** covered with ice: *icy roads* **3** (of a person's voice, manner, etc.) not friendly or kind; showing feelings of dislike or anger: *My eyes met his icy gaze.*—see also ICILY ► **ici·ness** *noun* [U]

ID /ˌaɪ 'diː/ *noun, verb*
▪ *noun* **1** [U, C] an official way of showing who you are, for example a document with your name, date of birth and often a photograph on it (abbreviation for 'identity' or 'identification'): *You must carry ID at all times.* ◊ *The police checked IDs at the gate.* ◊ *an ID card* **2** [C] IDENTIFICATION: *The police need a witness to make a positive ID.*
▪ *verb* (**ID's**, **ID'ing**, **ID'd**, **ID'd**) [VN] (*informal*) = IDENTIFY

Id = EID

id /ɪd/ *noun* (*psychology*) the part of the unconscious mind where many of a person's basic needs, feelings and desires are supposed to exist—compare EGO, SUPEREGO

I'd /aɪd/ *short form* **1** I had **2** I would

-ide *suffix* (*chemistry*) (in nouns) a compound of: *chloride*

idea /aɪ'dɪə; *AmE* -'diːə/ *noun*

PLAN/THOUGHT | **1** [C] ~ **(for sth)** | ~ **(of sth)** | ~ **(of doing sth)** a plan, thought or suggestion, especially about what to do in a particular situation: *It would be **a good idea** to call before we leave.* ◊ *I like the idea of living on a boat.* ◊ *He already had an idea for his next novel.* ◊ *Her family expected her to go to college, but she had **other ideas**. ◊ *The surprise party was Jane's idea.* ◊ (*spoken*) *It might be **an idea** (= it would be sensible) to try again later.* ◊ *We've been toying with the idea of (= thinking about) getting a dog.* ◊ *It seemed like a good idea at the time, and then it all went horribly wrong.* ◊ *The latest **big idea** is to make women more interested in sport.*

IMPRESSION | **2** [U, sing.] ~ **(of sth)** a picture or an impression in your mind of what sb/sth is like: *The brochure should give you **a good idea** of the hotel.* ◊ *I had some **idea** of what the job would be like.* ◊ *She doesn't seem to have any idea of what I'm talking about.* ◊ *I don't want anyone **getting the wrong idea** (= getting the wrong impression about sth).* ◊ *An evening at home watching TV is not my idea of a good time.*

OPINION | **3** [C] ~ **(about sth)** an opinion or a belief about sth: *He has some very strange ideas about education.*

FEELING | **4** [sing.] ~ **(that ...)** a feeling that sth is possible: *What gave you the idea that he'd be here?* ◊ *I have a pretty good idea where I left it—I hope I'm right.*

AIM | **5** (**the idea**) [sing.] ~ **of sth/of doing sth** the aim or purpose of sth: *You'll soon get the idea* (= understand). ◊ *What's the idea of the game?* ◊ *What's the idea of all this?* **IDM** **give sb i'deas** | **put i'deas into sb's head** to give sb hopes about sth that may not be possible or likely; to make sb act or think in an unreasonable way: *Who's been putting ideas into his head?* **have no i'dea** | **not have the faintest, first, etc. idea** (*spoken*) used to emphasize that you do not know sth: *'What's she talking about?' 'I've no idea.'* ◊ *He hasn't the faintest idea how to manage people.* **have the right i'dea** to have found a very good or successful way of living, doing sth, etc: *He's certainly got the right idea—retiring at 55.* **'That's an idea!** (*spoken*) used to reply in a positive way to a suggestion that sb has made: *Hey, that's an idea! And we could get a band, as well.* **'That's the idea!** (*spoken*) used to encourage people and to tell them that they are doing sth right: *That's the idea! You're doing fine.* **You have no i'dea ...** (*spoken*) used to show that sth is hard for sb else to imagine: *You've no idea how much traffic there was tonight.*—more at BUCK *v.*

ideal /aɪ'diːəl/ *adj., noun*
▪ *adj.* **1** ~ **(for sth)** perfect; most suitable: *This beach is ideal for children.* ◊ *She's the ideal candidate for the job.* ◊ *The trip to Paris will be an **ideal opportunity** to practise my French.* **2** [only before noun] existing only in your imagination or as an idea; not likely to be real: *the search for ideal love* ◊ *In an **ideal world** there would be no poverty and disease.* ► **ideal·ly** /aɪ'diːəli/ *adv.*: *She's ideally suited for this job.* ◊ *Ideally, I'd like to live in New York, but that's not possible.*
▪ *noun* **1** [C] an idea or standard that seems perfect, and worth trying to achieve or obtain: *political ideals* ◊ *She found it hard to live up to his high ideals.* **2** [C, usually sing.] ~ **(of sth)** a person or thing that you think is perfect: *It's my ideal of what a family home should be.*

ideal·ism /aɪ'diːəlɪzəm/ *noun* [U] **1** the belief that a perfect life, situation, etc. can be achieved, even when this is not very likely: *He was full of youthful idealism.* ◊ *Idealism has no place in modern politics.* **2** (*philosophy*) the belief that our ideas are the only things that are real and that we can know about—compare MATERIALISM, REALISM ► **ideal·ist** *noun*: *He's too much of an idealist for this government.*

ideal·is·tic /ˌaɪdɪə'lɪstɪk/ *adj.* having a strong belief in perfect standards and trying to achieve them, even when this is not realistic: *She's still young and idealistic.* ► **ideal·is·tic·al·ly** /ˌaɪdɪə'lɪstɪkli/ *adv.*

ideal·ize (*BrE* also **-ise**) /aɪ'diːəlaɪz/ *verb* [VN] to consider or represent sb/sth as being perfect or better than they really are: *It is tempting to idealize the past.* ◊ *an idealized view of married life* ► **ideal·iza·tion, -isa·tion** /aɪˌdiːəlaɪ'zeɪʃn; *AmE* -lə'z-/ *noun* [U, C]

idem /'ɪdem/ *adv.* (from *Latin, written*) from the same book, article, author, etc. as the one that has just been mentioned

iden·ti·cal /aɪ'dentɪkl/ *adj.* **1** ~ **(to/with sb/sth)** similar in every detail: *a row of identical houses* ◊ *Her dress is almost identical to mine.* ◊ *The number on the card should be identical with the one on the cheque book.* ◊ *The two pictures are similar, although not identical.* **2** (**the identical**) [only before noun] the same: *This is the identical room we stayed in last year.* ► **iden·ti·cal·ly** /-kli/ *adv.*: *The children were dressed identically.*

i,dentical 'twin *noun* one of two children or animals who are born at the same time and who have developed from a single egg. Identical twins are of the same sex and look very similar.—compare FRATERNAL TWIN

iden·ti·fi·able /aɪˌdentɪ'faɪəbl/ *adj.* that can be recognized: *identifiable groups/characteristics* ◊ *The house is easily identifiable by the large tree outside.* **OPP** UNIDENTIFIABLE

iden·ti·fi·ca·tion /aɪˌdentɪfɪ'keɪʃn/ *noun* **1** [U, C] (*abbr.* **ID**) the process of showing, proving or recognizing who or what sb/sth is: *The identification of the crash victims was a long and difficult task.* ◊ *Each product has a number for easy identification.* ◊ *an identification number* ◊ *Only one*

aɪ	aʊ	eɪ	əʊ	oʊ	ɔɪ	ɪə	eə	ʊə	j	w
my	now	say	go (BrE)	go (AmE)	boy	near	hair	pure	yes	wet

witness could make a positive identification. **2** [U] the process of recognizing that sth exists, or is important: *The early identification of children with special educational needs is very important.* **3** (*abbr.* ID) [U] official papers or a document that can prove who you are: *Can I see some identification, please?* **4** [U, C] ~ (**with sb/sth**) a strong feeling of sympathy, understanding or support for sb/sth: *her emotional identification with the play's heroine* ◊ *their increasing identification with the struggle for independence* **5** [U, C] ~ (**of sb**) (**with sb/sth**) the process of making a close connection between one person or thing and another: *the voters' identification of the Democrats with high taxes*

i‚dentifi‚cation parade *noun* (also *informal* i'dentity parade) (both *BrE*) (also 'line-up *AmE, BrE*) a row of people, including one person who is suspected of a crime, who are shown to a WITNESS to see if he or she can recognize the criminal

iden·ti·fy /aɪˈdentɪfaɪ/ *verb* (iden·ti·fies, iden·ti·fy·ing, iden·ti·fied, iden·ti·fied) **1** (also *informal* ID) [VN] ~ sb/sth (as sb/sth) to recognize sb/sth and be able to say who or what they are: *The bodies were identified as those of two suspected drug dealers.* ◊ *She was able to identify her attacker.* ◊ *Passengers were asked to identify their own suitcases before they were put on the plane.* ◊ *Many of those arrested refused to identify themselves* (= would not say who they were). ◊ *First of all we must identify the problem areas.* **2** to find or discover sb/sth: [VN] *Scientists have identified a link between diet and cancer.* ◊ *As yet they have not identified a buyer for the company.* ◊ [V wh-] *They are trying to identify what is wrong with the present system.* **3** [VN] ~ sb/sth (as sb/sth) to make it possible to recognize who or what sb/sth is: *In many cases, the clothes people wear identify them as belonging to a particular social class.* **PHRV** i'dentify with sb to feel that you can understand and share the feelings of sb else: *I didn't enjoy the book because I couldn't identify with any of the main characters.* identify sb with sth to consider sb to be sth: *He was not the 'tough guy' the public identified him with.* identify sth with sth to consider sth to be the same as sth else [SYN] EQUATE: *You should not identify wealth with happiness.* be identified with sb/sth | identify yourself with sb/sth to support sb/sth; to be closely connected with sb/sth: *The Church became increasingly identified with opposition to the regime.*

Iden·ti·kit™ /aɪˈdentɪkɪt/ (*BrE*) (*AmE* com·pos·ite, com'posite sketch) *noun* a set of drawings of different features that can be put together to form the face of a person, especially sb wanted by the police, using descriptions given by people who saw the person; a picture made in this way—compare E-FIT, PHOTO-FIT

iden·tity /aɪˈdentəti/ *noun* (*pl.* -ies) **1** [C, U] (*abbr.* ID) who or what sb/sth is: *The police are trying to discover the identity of the killer.* ◊ *Their identities were kept secret.* ◊ *She is innocent; it was a case of mistaken identity.* ◊ *Do you have any proof of identity?* ◊ *The thief used a false identity.* ◊ *She went through an identity crisis in her teens* (= was not sure of who she was or of her place in society). **2** [C, U] the characteristics, feelings or beliefs that distinguish people from others: *a sense of national/cultural/personal/group identity* ◊ *a plan to strengthen the corporate identity of the company* **3** [U] ~ (**with sb/sth**) | ~ (**between A and B**) the state or feeling of being very similar to and able to understand sb/sth: *an identity of interests* ◊ *There's a close identity between fans and their team.*

i'dentity card (also ID card) *noun* a card with a person's name, date of birth, photograph, etc. on it that proves who they are

i'dentity parade *noun* (*informal*) = IDENTIFICATION PARADE

ideo·gram /ˈɪdiəɡræm/ (also ideo·graph /ˈɪdiəɡrɑːf; *AmE* -ɡræf/) *noun* **1** a symbol that is used in a writing system, for example Chinese, to represent the idea of a thing, rather than the sounds of a word **2** (*technical*) a sign or a symbol for sth

ideo·logue /ˈaɪdiəlɒɡ; ˈɪd-; *AmE* -lɔːɡ; -lɑːɡ/ (also ideolo-

gist /ˌaɪdiˈɒlədʒɪst; *AmE* -ˈɑːl-/) *noun* (*formal*, sometimes *disapproving*) a person whose actions are influenced by belief in a set of principles (= by an ideology)

ideol·ogy /ˌaɪdiˈɒlədʒi; *AmE* -ˈɑːl-/ *noun* [C, U] (*pl.* -ies) (sometimes *disapproving*) **1** a set of ideas that an economic or political system is based on: *Marxist/capitalist ideology* **2** a set of beliefs, especially one held by a particular group, that influences the way people behave: *the ideology of gender roles* ◊ *alternative ideologies* ▶ ideo·logic·al /ˌaɪdiəˈlɒdʒɪkl; *AmE* -ˈlɑːdʒ-/ *adj.*: *ideological differences* ideo·logic·al·ly /-kli/ *adv.*: *ideologically correct*

idi·ocy /ˈɪdiəsi/ *noun* (*pl.* -ies) (*formal*) **1** [U] very stupid behaviour; the state of being very stupid [SYN] STUPIDITY: *It is sheer idiocy to go climbing in this weather.* **2** [C] a very stupid act, remark, etc: *the idiocies of bureaucracy*

idio·lect /ˈɪdiəlekt/ *noun* [C, U] (*linguistics*) the way that a particular person uses language—compare DIALECT

idiom /ˈɪdiəm/ *noun* **1** [C] a group of words whose meaning is different from the meanings of the individual words: *'Let the cat out of the bag' is an idiom meaning to tell a secret by mistake.* ⇨ Study page B12 **2** [U, C] (*formal*) the kind of language and grammar used by particular people at a particular time or place **3** [U, C] (*formal*) the style of writing, music, art, etc. that is typical of a particular person, group, period or place: *the classical/contemporary/popular idiom*

idiom·at·ic /ˌɪdiəˈmætɪk/ *adj.* **1** containing expressions that are natural to a native speaker of a language: *She speaks fluent and idiomatic English.* **2** containing an idiom: *an idiomatic expression* ▶ idiom·at·ic·al·ly /-kli/ *adv.*

idio·syn·crasy /ˌɪdiəˈsɪŋkrəsi/ *noun* [C, U] (*pl.* -ies) a person's particular way of behaving, thinking, etc., especially when it is unusual; an unusual feature [SYN] ECCENTRICITY: *Wearing a raincoat, even on a hot day, is one of her idiosyncrasies.* ◊ *The car has its little idiosyncrasies.* ▶ idio·syn·crat·ic /ˌɪdiəsɪŋˈkrætɪk/ *adj.*: *His teaching methods are idiosyncratic but successful.*

idiot /ˈɪdiət/ *noun* **1** (*informal*) a very stupid person [SYN] FOOL: *When I lost my passport, I felt such an idiot.* ◊ *Not that switch, you idiot!* **2** (*old-fashioned, offensive*) a person with very low intelligence who cannot think or behave normally

idi·ot·ic /ˌɪdiˈɒtɪk; *AmE* -ˈɑːtɪk/ *adj.* very stupid: *an idiotic question* ◊ *Don't be so idiotic!* ▶ idi·ot·ic·al·ly /-kli/ *adv.*

idle /ˈaɪdl/ *adj., verb*
■ *adj.* **1** (of people) lazy; not working hard: *an idle student* **2** (of machines, factories, etc.) not in use: *to lie/stand/remain idle* **3** (of people) without work; unemployed: *Over ten per cent of the workforce is now idle.* **4** [usually before noun] with no particular purpose or effect; useless: *idle chatter/curiosity* ◊ *It was just an idle threat* (= not serious). ◊ *It is idle to pretend that their marriage is a success.* **5** [usually before noun] (of time) not spent doing work or sth particular: *In idle moments, he carved wooden figures.* ▶ idle·ness *noun* [U]: *After a period of enforced idleness, she found a new job.*
■ *verb* **1** [usually +*adv.*/*prep.*] (*written*) to spend time doing nothing important: [VN] *They idled the days away, talking and watching television.* ◊ [V] *She idled along by the river* (= walked slowly and with no particular purpose). **2** [V] (of an engine) to run slowly while the vehicle is not moving [SYN] TICK OVER: *She left the car idling at the roadside.* **3** [VN] (*AmE*) to close a factory, etc. or stop providing work for the workers, especially temporarily: *The strikes have idled nearly 4000 workers.*

idler /ˈaɪdlə(r)/ *noun* a person who is lazy and does not work [SYN] LOAFER

idly /ˈaɪdli/ *adv.* without any particular reason, purpose or effect; doing nothing: *She sat in the sun, idly sipping a cool drink.* ◊ *He wondered idly what would happen.* ◊ *We can't stand idly by* (= do nothing) *and let people starve.*

idol /ˈaɪdl/ *noun* **1** a person or thing that is loved and admired very much: *a pop/football/teen idol* ◊ *the idol of countless teenagers* ◊ *a fallen idol* (= sb who is no longer popular) **2** a statue that is worshipped as a god

idol·atry /aɪˈdɒlətri; *AmE* -ˈdɑːl-/ *noun* [U] **1** the practice of worshipping statues as gods **2** (*formal*) too much love or admiration for sb/sth: *football fans whose support for their team borders on idolatry* ▶ **idol·atrous** /aɪˈdɒlətrəs; *AmE* -ˈdɑːl-/ *adj.*

idolize (*BrE* also **-ise**) /ˈaɪdəlaɪz/ *verb* [VN] to admire or love sb very much: *a pop star idolized by millions of fans* ◇ *They idolize their kids.*

idyll /ˈɪdɪl; *AmE* ˈaɪdl/ *noun* **1** (*written*) a happy and peaceful place, event or experience, especially one connected with the countryside **2** (*literature*) a short poem or other piece of writing that describes a peaceful and happy scene

idyl·lic /ɪˈdɪlɪk; *AmE* aɪˈd-/ *adj.* peaceful and beautiful; perfect, without problems: *a house set in idyllic surroundings* ◇ *to lead an idyllic existence* ◇ *The cottage sounds idyllic.* ▶ **idyl·lic·al·ly** /-kli/ *adv.*: *a house idyllically set in wooded grounds*

i.e. /ˌaɪ ˈiː/ *abbr.* used to explain exactly what the previous thing that you have mentioned means (from Latin 'id est'): *the basic essentials of life, i.e. housing, food and water*

-ie ⇨ -Y

if /ɪf/ *conj., noun*

■ *conj.* **1** used to say that one thing can, will or might happen or be true, depending on another thing happening or being true: *If you see him, give him this note.* ◇ *I'll only stay if you offer me more money.* ◇ *If necessary I can come at once.* ◇ *You can stay for the weekend if you like.* ◇ *If anyone calls, tell them I'm not at home.* ◇ *If he improved his IT skills, he'd (= he would) easily get a job.* ◇ *You would know what was going on if you'd (= you had) listened.* ◇ *They would have been here by now if they'd caught the early train.* ◇ *If I was in charge, I'd do things differently.* ◇ (*rather formal*) *If I were in charge ...* ◇ *Even if (= although) you did see someone, you can't be sure it was him.* **2** when; whenever; every time: *If metal gets hot it expands.* ◇ *She glares at me if I go near her desk.* **3** (*formal*) used with *will* or *would* to ask sb politely to do sth: *If you will sit down for a few moments, I'll tell the manager you're here.* ◇ *If you would care to leave your name, we'll contact you as soon as possible.* **4** used after *ask, know, find out, wonder*, etc. to introduce one of two or more possibilities SYN WHETHER: *Do you know if he's married?* ◇ *I wonder if I should wear a coat or not.* ◇ *He couldn't tell if she was laughing or crying.* ◇ *Listen to the tune and see if you can remember the words.* **5** used after verbs or adjectives expressing feelings: *I am sorry if I disturbed you.* ◇ *I'd be grateful if you would keep it a secret.* ◇ *Do you mind if I turn the TV off?* **6** used to admit that sth is possible, but to say that it is not very important: *If she has any weakness, it is her Italian.* ◇ *So what if he was late. Who cares?* **7** used before an adjective to introduce a contrast: *He's a good driver, if a little over-confident.* ◇ *We'll only do it once—if at all.* **8** used to ask sb to listen to your opinion: *If you ask me, she's too scared to do it.* ◇ *If you think about it, those children must be at school by now.* ◇ *If you remember, Mary was always fond of animals.* **9** used before *could, may* or *might* to suggest sth or to interrupt sb politely: *If I may make a suggestion, perhaps we could begin a little earlier next week.* IDM **if and when** used to say sth about an event that may or may not happen: *If and when we ever meet again I hope he remembers what I did for him.* **if anything** used to express an opinion about sth, or after a negative statement to suggest that the opposite is true: *I'd say he was more like his father, if anything.* ◇ *She's not thin—if anything she's on the plump side.* **if I were you** used to give sb advice: *If I were you I'd start looking for another job.* **if not 1** used to introduce a different suggestion, after a sentence with *if*: *I'll go if you're going. If not (= if you are not) I'd rather stay at home.* **2** used after a *yes/no* question to say what will or should happen if the answer is 'no': *Are you ready? If not, I'm going without you.* ◇ *Do you want that cake? If not, I'll have it.* **3** used to suggest that sth may be even larger, more important, etc. than was first stated: *They cost thousands if not millions of pounds to build.* **if only** used to say that you wish sth was true or that sth had happened: *If only I were rich.* ◇ *If only*

I knew her name. ◇ *If only he'd remembered to send that letter.* ◇ *If only I had gone by taxi.* **it's not as if** (*spoken*) used to say that sth that is happening is surprising: *I'm surprised they've invited me to their wedding—it's not as if I know them well.* **only if** (*rather formal*) used to state the only situation in which sth can happen: *Only if a teacher has given permission is a student allowed to leave the room.* ◇ *Only if the red light comes on is there any danger to employees.*

■ *noun* (*informal*) a situation that is not certain: *If he wins—and it's a big if—he'll be the first Englishman to win for fifty years.* ◇ *There are still a lot of ifs and buts before everything's settled.*

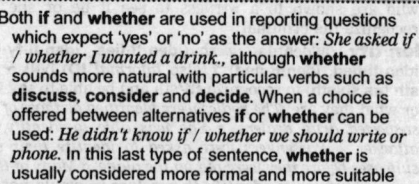

GRAMMAR POINT

if / whether

Both **if** and **whether** are used in reporting questions which expect 'yes' or 'no' as the answer: *She asked if / whether I wanted a drink.*, although **whether** sounds more natural with particular verbs such as **discuss, consider** and **decide**. When a choice is offered between alternatives **if** or **whether** can be used: *He didn't know if / whether we should write or phone.* In this last type of sentence, **whether** is usually considered more formal and more suitable for written English.

iffy /ˈɪfi/ *adj.* (*informal*) **1** (*especially BrE*) not in perfect condition; bad in some way: *That meat smells a bit iffy to me.* **2** not certain: *The weather looks slightly iffy.*

-ify, -fy *suffix* (in verbs) to make or become: *purify* ◇ *solidify*

igloo /ˈɪɡluː/ *noun* (*pl.* **igloos**) a small round house or shelter built from blocks of hard snow by the Inuit people of northern N America

ig·ne·ous /ˈɪɡniəs/ *adj.* (*geology*) (of rocks) formed when MAGMA (= melted or liquid material lying below the earth's surface) becomes solid, especially after it has poured out of a VOLCANO

ig·nite /ɪɡˈnaɪt/ *verb* (*written*) to start to burn; to make sth start to burn: [V] *Gas ignites very easily.* ◇ (*figurative*) *Tempers ignited when the whole family spent Christmas together.* ◇ [VN] *Flames melted a lead pipe and ignited leaking gas.* ◇ (*figurative*) *His words ignited their anger.*

ig·ni·tion /ɪɡˈnɪʃn/ *noun* **1** [C, usually sing.] the electrical system of a vehicle that makes the fuel begin to burn to start the engine; the place in a vehicle where you start this system: *to turn the ignition on/off* ◇ *to put the key in the ignition*—picture at CAR **2** [U] (*technical*) the action of starting to burn or of making sth burn: *The flames spread to all parts of the house within minutes of ignition.*

ig·noble /ɪɡˈnəʊbl; *AmE* -ˈnoʊ-/ *adj.* (*formal*) not good or honest; that should make you feel shame: *ignoble thoughts* ◇ *an ignoble person* OPP NOBLE

ig·no·mini·ous /ˌɪɡnəˈmɪniəs/ *adj.* (*formal*) that makes, or should make, you feel ashamed SYN DISGRACEFUL, HUMILIATING: *an ignominious defeat* ◇ *He made one mistake and his career came to an ignominious end.* ▶ **ig·no·mini·ous·ly** *adv.*

ig·no·miny /ˈɪɡnəmɪni/ *noun* [U] (*formal*) public shame and loss of honour SYN DISGRACE: *They suffered the ignominy of defeat.*

ig·nor·amus /ˌɪɡnəˈreɪməs/ *noun* (*usually humorous*) a person who does not have much knowledge: *When it comes to music, I'm a complete ignoramus.*

ig·nor·ance /ˈɪɡnərəns/ *noun* [U] ~ (**of/about sth**) a lack of knowledge or information about sth: *widespread ignorance of/about the disease* ◇ *They fought a long battle against prejudice and ignorance.* ◇ *She was kept in ignorance of her husband's activities.* ◇ *Children often behave badly out of/through ignorance.* IDM **ignorance is bliss** (*saying*) if you do not know about sth, you cannot worry about it: *Some doctors believe ignorance is bliss and don't give their patients all the facts.*

ig·nor·ant /ˈɪɡnərənt/ *adj.* **1** ~ (**of/about sth**) lacking knowledge or information about sth; not educated: *an ignorant person/question* ◇ *He's completely ignorant about* modern technology. ◊ At that time I was ignorant of events going on elsewhere. ◊ Never make your students feel stupid or ignorant. **2** (informal) with very bad manners: a rude, ignorant person ▶ **ig·nor·ant·ly** adv.

ig·nore /ɪgˈnɔː(r)/ verb [VN] **1** to pay no attention to sth [SYN] DISREGARD: He ignored all the 'No Smoking' signs and lit up a cigarette. ◊ I made a suggestion but they chose to ignore it. ◊ We cannot afford to ignore their advice. **2** to pretend that you have not seen sb or that sb is not there: She ignored him and carried on with her work.

igu·ana /ɪˈgwɑːnə/ noun a large tropical American LIZ-ARD (= a type of reptile)

ikon noun = ICON

il- suffix ⇨ IN-

ilk /ɪlk/ noun [usually sing.] (informal, sometimes disapproving) type; kind: the world of media people and their ilk ◊ I can't stand him, or any others of that ilk.

ill /ɪl/ adj., adv., noun
■ adj. **1** (especially BrE) (AmE usually **sick**) [not usually before noun] suffering from an illness or disease; not feeling well: Her father is seriously ill in St Luke's hospital. ◊ She was taken ill suddenly. ◊ We both started to feel ill shortly after the meal. ◊ Uncle Harry is terminally ill with cancer (= he will die from his illness). ◊ the mentally ill (= people with a mental illness) ◊ (written) He fell ill and died soon after. ⇨ vocabulary notes on page 599—see also ILLNESS **2** [usually before noun] bad or harmful: He resigned because of ill health (= he was often ill). ◊ She suffered no ill effects from the experience. ◊ a woman of ill repute (= considered to be immoral) **3** (formal) that brings, or is thought to bring, bad luck: a bird of ill omen [IDM] **ill at 'ease** feeling uncomfortable and embarrassed: I felt ill at ease in such formal clothes. **it's an ,ill 'wind (that blows nobody any good)** (saying) no problem is so bad that it does not bring some advantage to sb—more at FEELING
■ adv. **1** (especially in compounds) badly or in an unpleasant way: The animals had been grossly ill-treated. **2** (formal) badly; not in a satisfactory way: They live in an area ill served by public transport. **3** (formal) only with difficulty: We're wasting valuable time, time we can ill afford. [IDM] **speak/think 'ill of sb** (formal) to say or think bad things about sb: Don't speak ill of the dead.
■ noun **1** [usually pl.] (formal) a problem or harmful thing; an illness: social/economic ills ◊ the ills of the modern world **2** [U] (literary) harm; bad luck: I may not like him, but I wish him no ill.

I'll /aɪl/ short form **1** I shall **2** I will

ill-ad'vised adj. not sensible; likely to cause difficulties in the future: Her remarks were ill-advised, to say the least. ◊ You would be ill-advised to travel on your own.—compare WELL ADVISED ▶ **ill-ad'visedly** adv.

ill-as'sorted adj. (of a group of people or things) not seeming suited to each other: They seem an ill-assorted couple.

ill-'bred adj. rude or badly behaved, especially because you have not been taught how to behave well [OPP] WELL BRED

ill-con'cealed adj. (formal) (of feelings or expressions of feeling) not hidden well from other people

ill-con'ceived adj. badly planned or designed

ill-con'sidered adj. not carefully thought about or planned

ill-de'fined adj. **1** not clearly described: an ill-defined role/policy **2** not clearly marked or easy to see: an ill-defined path/track [OPP] WELL DEFINED

ill-dis'posed adj. ~ (towards sb) (formal) not feeling friendly towards sb [OPP] WELL DISPOSED

il·legal /ɪˈliːgl/ adj., noun
■ adj. not allowed by the law;: illegal immigrants/aliens ◊ It's illegal to drive through a red light. [OPP] LEGAL ▶ **il·legal·ly** /-gəli/ adv.: an illegally parked car ◊ He entered the country illegally.
■ noun (AmE) a person who lives or works in a country illegally

il·legal·ity /ˌɪliːˈgæləti/ noun (pl. -ies) **1** [U] the state of

being illegal: No illegality is suspected. **2** [C] an illegal act—compare LEGALITY

il·legible /ɪˈledʒəbl/ (also **un·read·able**) adj. difficult or impossible to read: an illegible signature [OPP] LEGIBLE

il·legit·im·ate /ˌɪləˈdʒɪtəmət/ adj. **1** born to parents who are not married to each other **2** not allowed by a particular set of rules or by law: illegitimate use of company property [OPP] LEGITIMATE ▶ **il·legit·im·acy** /ˌɪləˈdʒɪt-əmasi/ noun [U] **il·legit·im·ate·ly** adv.

ill-e'quipped adj. ~ (for sth)| ~ (to do sth) not having the necessary equipment or qualifications: At 18, he was ill-equipped for such a responsible job. ◊ The department is ill-equipped to deal with such a large number of enquiries.

ill-'fated (also **fated**) adj. (written) not lucky and ending sadly, especially in death or failure: an ill-fated expedition

ill-'fitting adj. not the right size or shape: ill-fitting clothes

ill-'founded adj. (formal) not based on fact or truth: All our fears proved ill-founded. [OPP] WELL FOUNDED

ill-'gotten adj. (old-fashioned or humorous) obtained dishonestly or unfairly: ill-gotten gains (= money that was not obtained fairly)

ill 'humour (BrE) (AmE ,ill 'humor) noun [U, C] (literary) a bad mood [OPP] GOOD HUMOUR ▶ **ill-'humoured** (BrE) (AmE ,ill-'humored) adj.

il·lib·eral /ɪˈlɪbərəl/ adj. (formal) not allowing much freedom of opinion or action [SYN] INTOLERANT: illiberal policies/reforms

il·licit /ɪˈlɪsɪt/ adj. **1** not allowed by the law [SYN] ILLEGAL: illicit drugs **2** not approved of by the normal rules of society: an illicit love affair ▶ **illicit·ly** adv.

ill-in'formed adj. having or showing little knowledge of sth [OPP] WELL INFORMED: The public is ill-informed about their legal rights.

il·lit·er·ate /ɪˈlɪtərət/ adj., noun
■ adj. **1** (of a person) not knowing how to read or write [OPP] LITERATE **2** (of a document or letter) badly written, as if by sb without much education **3** (usually after a noun or adverb) not knowing very much about a particular subject area: computer illiterate ◊ musically illiterate ▶ **il·lit·er·acy** /ɪˈlɪtərəsi/ noun [U]
■ noun a person who is illiterate

ill-'judged adj. (formal) that has not been carefully thought about; not appropriate in a particular situation

ill-'mannered adj. (formal) not behaving well or politely in social situations [SYN] RUDE [OPP] WELL MANNERED

ill·ness /ˈɪlnəs/ noun **1** [U] the state of being physically or mentally ill: mental illness ◊ I missed a lot of school through illness last year. **2** [C] a type or period of illness: minor/serious illnesses ◊ childhood illnesses ◊ He died after a long illness. ⇨ vocabulary notes on page 599

il·logic·al /ɪˈlɒdʒɪkl; AmE -ˈlɑːdʒ-/ adj. not sensible or thought out in a logical way: illogical behaviour/arguments ◊ She has an illogical fear of insects. [OPP] LOGICAL ▶ **il·logic·al·ity** /ɪˌlɒdʒɪˈkæləti; AmE -ˌlɑːdʒ-/ noun [U, C] **il·logic·al·ly** /-kli/ adv.

ill-pre'pared adj. **1** ~ (for sth) not ready, especially because you were not expecting sth to happen: The team was ill-prepared for a disaster on that scale. **2** badly planned or organized: an ill-prepared speech

ill-'starred adj. (formal) not lucky and likely to bring unhappiness or to end in failure: an ill-starred marriage

ill-'tempered adj. (formal) angry and rude or irritated, especially when this seems unreasonable

ill-'timed adj. done or happening at the wrong time: an ill-timed visit [OPP] WELL TIMED

ill-'treat verb [VN] to treat sb in a cruel or unkind way: to ill-treat children/animals ▶ **ill-'treatment** noun [U]: the ill-treatment of prisoners

il·lu·min·ate /ɪˈluːmɪneɪt/ (also less frequent **il·lu·mine**) verb [VN] **1** to shine light on sth: Floodlights illuminated the stadium. ◊ The earth is illuminated by the sun. **2** (formal) to make sth clearer or easier to understand [SYN] CLARIFY: This text illuminates the philosopher's early thinking. **3** to decorate a street, building, etc. with bright

æ	ɑː	e	ɜː	ə	ɪ	iː	i	ɒ	ɔː	ʌ	ʊ	u	uː
cat	father	ten	bird	about	sit	see	many	got	saw	cup	put	actual	too
								(BrE)					

lights for a special occasion **4** (*literary*) to make a person's face, etc. seem bright and excited SYN LIGHT UP: *Her smile illuminated her entire being.*

il·lu·min·ated /ɪˈluːmɪneɪtɪd/ *adj.* [usually before noun] **1** lit with bright lights: *the illuminated city at night* **2** (of books, etc.) decorated with gold, silver and bright colours in a way that was done in the past, by hand: *illuminated manuscripts*

il·lu·min·at·ing /ɪˈluːmɪneɪtɪŋ/ *adj.* helping to make sth clear or easier to understand: *We didn't find the examples he used particularly illuminating.*

il·lu·min·ation /ɪˌluːmɪˈneɪʃn/ *noun* **1** [U, C] light or a place that light comes from: *The only illumination in the room came from the fire.* **2** (**illuminations**) [pl.] (*BrE*) bright colourful lights used to decorate a town or building for a special event: *Christmas illuminations* **3** [C, usually pl.] a coloured decoration, usually painted by hand, in an old book **4** [U] (*formal*) understanding or explanation of sth: *spiritual illumination*

il·lu·mine /ɪˈluːmɪn/ *verb* [VN] (*rare*) = ILLUMINATE

ill-'used *adj.* (*old-fashioned* or *formal*) badly treated

il·lu·sion /ɪˈluːʒn/ *noun* **1** [C, U] a false idea or belief, especially about sb or about a situation: *I have no illusions about her feelings for me* (= I know the truth is that she does not love me). ◊ *She's under the illusion that* (= believes wrongly that) *she'll get the job.* ◊ *He could no longer distinguish between illusion and reality.* **2** [C] something that seems to exist but in fact does not, or seems to be sth that it is not: *Mirrors in a room often give an illusion of space.* ◊ *The idea of absolute personal freedom is an illusion.*—see also OPTICAL ILLUSION

il·lu·sion·ist /ɪˈluːʒənɪst/ *noun* an entertainer who performs tricks that seem strange or impossible to believe

il·lu·sory /ɪˈluːsəri/ *adj.* (*formal*) not real, although seeming to be: *an illusory sense of freedom*

il·lus·trate /ˈɪləstreɪt/ *verb* **1** [VN] [usually passive] ~ **sth (with sth)** to use pictures, photographs, diagrams, etc. in a book, etc.: *an illustrated textbook* ◊ *His lecture was illustrated with slides taken during the expedition.* **2** to make the meaning of sth clearer by using examples, pictures, etc.: [VN] *To illustrate my point, let me tell you a little story.* ◊ *Last year's sales figures are illustrated in Figure 2.* [also V wh-] **3** to show that sth is true or that a situation exists SYN DEMONSTRATE: [VN] *The incident illustrates the need for better security measures.* [also V wh-, V that]

il·lus·tra·tion /ˌɪləˈstreɪʃn/ *noun* **1** [C] a drawing or picture in a book, magazine, etc. especially one that explains sth: *50 full-colour illustrations* **2** [U] the process of illustrating sth: *the art of book illustration* **3** [C, U] a story, an event or an example that clearly shows the truth about sth: *The statistics are a clear illustration of the point I am trying to make* ◊ *Let me, by way of illustration, quote from one of her poems.*

il·lus·tra·tive /ˈɪləstrətɪv; *AmE* ɪˈlʌs-/ *adj.* (*formal*) helping to explain sth or show it more clearly: *an illustrative example*

il·lus·tra·tor /ˈɪləstreɪtə(r)/ *noun* a person who draws or paints pictures for books, etc.

il·lus·tri·ous /ɪˈlʌstriəs/ *adj.* (*formal*) very famous and much admired, especially because of what you have achieved: *The composer was one of many illustrious visitors to the town.* ◊ *a long and illustrious career*

ill 'will *noun* [U] bad and unkind feelings towards sb: *I bear Sue no ill will.*

ILO /ˌaɪ el ˈəʊ; *AmE* ˈoʊ/ *abbr.* International Labour Organization (an organization within the United Nations concerned with employment and working conditions)

I'm /aɪm/ *short form* I am

im- ⇨ IN-

image /ˈɪmɪdʒ/ *noun* **1** [C, U] the impression that a person, an organization or a product, etc. gives to the public: *His public image is very different from the real person.* ◊ *The advertisements are intended to improve the company's image.* ◊ *Image is very important in the music world.* ◊ *stereotyped images of women in children's books* **2** [C] a

mental picture that you have of what sb/sth is like or looks like: *images of the past* ◊ *I always had an image of her standing by that particular window.* **3** [C] (*formal*) a copy of sb/sth in the form of a picture or statue: *Images of deer and hunters decorate the cave walls.* ◊ *a wooden image of the Hindu god Ganesh* **4** [C] a picture of sb/sth seen in a mirror, through a camera, or on a television or computer: *He stared at his own image reflected in the water.* ◊ *Slowly, an image began to appear on the screen.*—see also MIRROR IMAGE **5** [C] a word or phrase that describes sth in an imaginative way: *poetic images of the countryside* IDM **be the image of sb** | **be the very/ living/spitting image of sb** to be very similar to, or almost exactly like sb/sth else: *He's the spitting image of his father.*

im·agery /ˈɪmɪdʒəri/ *noun* [U] **1** language that produces pictures in the minds of people reading or listening: *poetic imagery*—see also METAPHOR **2** (*formal*) pictures, photographs, etc: *satellite imagery* (for example, photographs of the earth taken from space)

im·agin·able /ɪˈmædʒɪnəbl/ *adj.* **1** used with superlatives, and with *all* and *every*, to emphasize that sth is the best, worst, etc. that you can imagine, or includes every possible example: *The house has the most spectacular views imaginable.* ◊ *They stock every imaginable type of pasta.* **2** possible to imagine: *These technological developments were hardly imaginable 30 years ago.*

im·agin·ary /ɪˈmædʒɪnəri; *AmE* -neri/ *adj.* existing only in your mind or imagination: *imaginary fears/threats* ◊ *The equator is an imaginary line around the middle of the earth.* ◊ *The story is wholly imaginary.*

im·agin·ation /ɪˌmædʒɪˈneɪʃn/ *noun* **1** [U, C] the ability to create pictures in your mind; the part of your mind that does this: *a vivid/fertile imagination* ◊ *He's got no imagination.* ◊ *It doesn't take much imagination to guess what she meant.* ◊ *Don't let your imagination run away with you* (= don't use too much imagination). ◊ *The new policies appear to have caught the imagination of the public* (= they find them interesting and exciting). ◊ *Nobody hates you—it's all in your imagination.* ◊ (*informal*) *Use your imagination!* (= used to tell sb that they will have to guess the answer to the question they have asked you, usually because it is obvious or embarrassing) **2** [U] something that you have imagined rather than sth that exists: *She was no longer able to distinguish between imagination and reality.* ◊ *Is it my imagination or have you lost a lot of weight?* **3** [U] the ability to have new and exciting ideas: *His writing lacks imagination.* ◊ *With just a little imagination, you could turn this place into a palace.* IDM see FIGMENT, STRETCH *n.*

im·agina·tive /ɪˈmædʒɪnətɪv/ *adj.* having or showing new and exciting ideas SYN INVENTIVE: *an imaginative approach/idea/child* OPP UNIMAGINATIVE ▶ **im·agina·tive·ly** *adv.*: *The stables have been imaginatively converted into offices.*

im·agine /ɪˈmædʒɪn/ *verb* **1** to form a picture in your mind of what sth might be like: [VN] *The house was just as she had imagined it.* ◊ *I can't imagine life without the children now.* ◊ [V (that)] *Close your eyes and imagine (that) you are in a forest.* ◊ [V wh-] *Can you imagine what it must be like to lose your job after 20 years?* ◊ [V -ing] *She imagined walking into the office and handing in her resignation.* ◊ [VN-ing] *I can just imagine him saying that!* ◊ [VN to inf] *I had imagined her to be older than that.* ◊ [V] (*spoken*) *'He was furious.' ' I can imagine.'* [also VN-ADJ, VN-N] **2** to believe sth that is not true: [V (that)] *He's always imagining (that) we're talking about him behind his back.* ◊ [VN] *There's nobody there. You're imagining things.* **3** to think that sth is probably true SYN SUPPOSE, ASSUME: [V (that)] *I don't imagine (that) they'll refuse.* ◊ [V] *'Can we still buy tickets for the concert?' 'I imagine so.'* [also VN that]

im·aging /ˈɪmɪdʒɪŋ/ *noun* (*computing*) the process of capturing, storing and showing an image on a computer screen: *imaging software/techniques*

im·agin·ings /ɪˈmædʒɪnɪŋz/ *noun* [pl.] things that you imagine, that exist only in your mind

aɪ	aʊ	eɪ	əʊ	oʊ	ɔɪ	ɪə	eə	ʊə	j	w
my	now	say	go (BrE)	go (AmE)	boy	near	hair	pure	yes	wet

imam /ɪˈmɑːm/ *noun* (in Islam) **1** a religious man who leads the prayers in a MOSQUE **2** (**Imam**) the title of a religious leader

im·bal·ance /ɪmˈbæləns/ *noun* [C, U] **~ (between A and B)** | **~ (in/of sth)** a situation in which two or more things are not the same size or are treated differently, in a way that is unfair or causes problems: *a global imbalance of/ in power* ◊ *Attempts are being made to redress* (= put right) *the imbalance between our import and export figures.* ◊ *Postnatal depression is usually due to hormonal imbalance.*

im·be·cile /ˈɪmbəsiːl; *AmE* -sl/ *noun* **1** a rude way to describe a person that you think is very stupid [SYN] IDIOT: *They behaved like imbeciles.* **2** (*old-fashioned, offensive*) a person who has a very low intelligence ▶ **im·be·cile** (also **im·be·cil·ic**) *adj.* [usually before noun]: *imbecile remarks* **im·be·cil·ity** /ˌɪmbəˈsɪləti/ *noun* [U, C]

imbed = EMBED

im·bibe /ɪmˈbaɪb/ *verb* **1** [V, VN] (*formal or humorous*) to drink sth, especially alcohol **2** [VN] (*formal*) to absorb sth, especially information

im·bro·glio /ɪmˈbrəʊliəʊ; *AmE* ɪmˈbroʊlioʊ/ *noun* (*pl.* **-os**) (*formal*) a complicated situation that causes confusion or embarrassment, especially one that is political

imbue /ɪmˈbjuː/ *verb* [VN] [often passive] **~ sb/sth (with sth)** (*formal*) to fill sb/sth with strong feelings, opinions or values [SYN] INFUSE: *Her voice was imbued with an unusual seriousness.* ◊ *He was imbued with a desire for social justice.*

IMF /ˌaɪ em ˈef/ *abbr.* International Monetary Fund. The IMF is an organization within the United Nations which is concerned with trade and economic development.

imi·tate /ˈɪmɪteɪt/ *verb* [VN] **1** to copy sb/sth: *Her style of painting has been imitated by other artists.* ◊ *Art imitates Nature.* ◊ *Teachers provide a model for children to imitate.* ◊ *No computer can imitate the complex functions of the human brain.* **2** to copy the way a person speaks or behaves, in order to amuse people [SYN] MIMIC: *She knew that the girls used to imitate her and laugh at her behind her back.*

imi·ta·tion /ˌɪmɪˈteɪʃn/ *noun* **1** [C] a copy of sth, especially sth expensive: *a poor/cheap imitation of the real thing* ◊ *This latest production is a **pale imitation** of the original* (= it is not nearly as good). ◊ *imitation leather/ pearls* **2** [U] the act of copying sb/sth: *A child learns to talk by imitation.* ◊ *Many corporate methods have been adopted by American managers **in imitation of** Japanese practice.* **3** [C] an act of copying the way sb talks and behaves, especially to make people laugh [SYN] IMPERSONATION, IMPRESSION: *He **does a** hilarious **imitation** of Tony Blair.*

imi·ta·tive /ˈɪmɪtətɪv; *AmE* -teɪtɪv/ *adj.* (*formal*, sometimes *disapproving*) that copies sb/sth: *movies that encourage imitative crime* ◊ *His work has been criticized for being imitative and shallow.*

imi·ta·tor /ˈɪmɪteɪtə(r)/ *noun* a person or thing that copies sb/sth else: *The band's success has inspired hundreds of would-be imitators.*

im·macu·late /ɪˈmækjələt/ *adj.* **1** extremely clean and tidy [SYN] SPOTLESS: *She always looks immaculate.* ◊ *an immaculate uniform/room* **2** containing no mistakes [SYN] PERFECT: *an immaculate performance* ▶ **im·macu·late·ly** *adv.*: *immaculately dressed*

im·man·ent /ˈɪmənənt/ *adj.* (*formal*) present as a natural part of sth; present everywhere

im·ma·ter·ial /ˌɪməˈtɪəriəl; *AmE* -ˈtɪr-/ *adj.* **1** [not usually before noun] **~ (to sb/sth)** not important in a particular situation [SYN] IRRELEVANT: *The cost is immaterial.* ◊ *It is immaterial to me whether he stays or goes.* **2** (*formal*) not having a physical form: *an immaterial God* [OPP] MATERIAL

im·ma·ture /ˌɪməˈtjʊə(r); *AmE* -ˈtʃʊr; -ˈtʊr/ *adj.* **1** behaving in a way that is not sensible and is typical of people who are much younger: *immature behaviour* ◊ *He's very immature for his age.* **2** not fully developed or grown: *immature plants* [OPP] MATURE ▶ **im·ma·tur·ity** /ˌɪmə-ˈtjʊərəti; *AmE* -ˈtʃʊr-; -ˈtʊr-/ *noun* [U]

im·meas·ur·able /ɪˈmeʒərəbl/ *adj.* (*formal*) too large,

great etc. to be measured: *to cause immeasurable harm* ◊ *Her contribution was of immeasurable importance.* ▶ **im·meas·ur·ably** /-bli/ *adv.*: *Housing standards improved immeasurably after the war.* ◊ *Stress has an immeasurably more serious effect on our lives than we realize.*

im·me·di·acy /ɪˈmiːdiəsi/ *noun* [U] (*written*) **1** the quality in sth that makes it seem as if it is happening now, close to you and is therefore important, urgent, etc: *the immediacy of the problem/threat* ◊ *Newspapers lack the immediacy of television.* **2** lack of delay; speed: *Our aim is immediacy of response to emergency calls.*

im·me·di·ate /ɪˈmiːdiət/ *adj.* **1** happening or done without delay [SYN] INSTANT: *an immediate reaction/response* ◊ *to take immediate action* **2** [usually before noun] existing now and needing urgent attention: *Our immediate concern is to help the families of those who died.* ◊ *The effects of global warming, while not immediate, are potentially catastrophic.* **3** [only before noun] next to or very close to a particular place or time: *in the immediate vicinity* ◊ *The prospects for the immediate future are good.* ◊ *The director is standing on her immediate right.* ◊ *my immediate predecessor in the job* (= the person who had the job just before me) **4** [only before noun] having a direct effect: *The immediate cause of death is unknown.* [IDM] see EFFECT *n.*

im·me·di·ate·ly /ɪˈmiːdiətli/ *adv., conj.*
▪ *adv.* **1** without delay; at once: *She answered almost immediately.* ◊ *The point of my question may not be immediately apparent.* **2** (usually with prepositions) next to or very close to a particular place or time: *Turn right immediately after the church.* ◊ *the years immediately before the war* **3** (usually with past participles) closely and directly: *Counselling is being given to those most immediately affected by the tragedy.*
▪ *conj.* (*especially BrE*) as soon as: *Immediately she'd gone, I remembered her name.*

im·me·mor·ial /ˌɪməˈmɔːriəl/ *adj.* (*formal or literary*) that has existed for longer than people can remember: *an immemorial tradition* ◊ *My family has lived in this area **from time immemorial*** (= for hundreds of years).

im·mense /ɪˈmens/ *adj.* extremely large or great [SYN] ENORMOUS: *There is still an immense amount of work to be done.* ◊ *The benefits are immense.* ◊ *a project of immense importance*

im·mense·ly /ɪˈmensli/ *adv.* extremely; very much [SYN] ENORMOUSLY: *immensely popular/difficult/grateful* ◊ *We enjoyed ourselves immensely.*

im·mens·ity /ɪˈmensəti/ *noun* [U] the large size of sth: *the immensity of the universe* ◊ *We were overwhelmed by the sheer immensity of the task.*

im·merse /ɪˈmɜːs; *AmE* ɪˈmɜːrs/ *verb* [VN] **1 ~ sb/sth (in sth)** to put sb/sth into a liquid so that they or it are completely covered **2 ~ yourself/sb in sth** to become or make sb completely involved in sth: *She immersed herself in her work.* ◊ *Clare and Phil were immersed in conversation in the corner.*

im·mer·sion /ɪˈmɜːʃn; *AmE* ɪˈmɜːrʒn; -ʃn/ *noun* [U] **1 ~ (in sth)** the act of putting sb/sth into a liquid so that they or it are completely covered; the state of being completely covered by a liquid: *Immersion in cold water resulted in rapid loss of heat.* ◊ *baptism by total immersion* (= putting the whole body underwater) **2 ~ (in sth)** the state of being completely involved in sth: *his long immersion in politics* ◊ *a two-week immersion course in French* (= in which the student will hear and use only French)

imˈmersion heater *noun* (*BrE*) a device that provides hot water for a house by heating water in a TANK (= a large container)

im·mi·grant /ˈɪmɪɡrənt/ *noun* a person who has come to live permanently in a country that is not their own: *illegal immigrants* ◊ *immigrant communities/families/ workers*—compare EMIGRANT, MIGRANT

im·mi·grate /ˈɪmɪɡreɪt/ *verb* [V] **~ (to ...) (from ...)** (*especially AmE*) to come and live permanently in a country after leaving your own country: *About 6.6 million people immigrated to the United States in the 1970s.*—compare EMIGRATE

im·mi·gra·tion /ˌɪmɪˈɡreɪʃn/ *noun* [U] **1** the process of

---

b	d	f	g	h	k	l	m	n	p	r
bad	did	fall	get	hat	cat	leg	man	now	pen	red

coming to live permanently in a country that is not your own; the number of people who do this: *laws restricting immigration into the US* ◊ *a rise/fall in immigration* ◊ *immigration officers*—compare EMIGRATION **2** (also **immi'gration control**) the place at a port, an airport, etc. where the PASSPORTS and other documents of people coming into a country are checked: *to go through immigration*

im·mi·nent /'ɪmɪnənt/ *adj.* (especially of sth unpleasant) likely to happen very soon: *the imminent threat of invasion* ◊ *The system is in imminent danger of collapse.* ◊ *An announcement about his resignation is imminent.* ► **im·mi·nence** /-əns/ *noun* [U]: *the imminence of death* **im·mi·nent·ly** *adv.*

im·mo·bile /ɪ'məʊbaɪl; *AmE* ɪ'moʊbl/ *adj.* **1** not moving SYN MOTIONLESS: *She stood immobile by the window.* **2** unable to move: *His illness has left him completely immobile.* OPP MOBILE ► **im·mo·bil·ity** /ˌɪmə'bɪləti/ *noun* [U]

im·mo·bil·ize (*BrE* also **-ise**) /ɪ'məʊbəlaɪz; *AmE* ɪ'moʊ-/ *verb* [VN] to prevent sth from moving or from working normally: *a device to immobilize the car engine in case of theft* ◊ *Always immobilize a broken leg immediately.* ► **im·mo·bil·iza·tion, -isa·tion** *noun* [U]

im·mo·bil·izer (*BrE* also **-iser**) (*AmE* **im·mo·bil·iser**™) /ɪ'məʊbəlaɪzə(r); *AmE* ɪ'moʊ-/ *noun* a device that is fitted to a car to stop it moving if sb tries to steal it

im·mod·er·ate /ɪ'mɒdərət; *AmE* ɪ'mɑːd-/ *adj.* [usually before noun] (*formal, disapproving*) extreme; not reasonable SYN EXCESSIVE: *immoderate drinking* OPP MODERATE ► **im·mod·er·ate·ly** *adv.*

im·mod·est /ɪ'mɒdɪst; *AmE* ɪ'mɑːd-/ *adj.* **1** (*disapproving*) having or showing a very high opinion of yourself and your abilities SYN CONCEITED: *I am immodest enough to think that I played an important part in her decision.* **2** not considered to be socially acceptable by most people, especially concerning sexual behaviour: *an immodest dress* OPP MODEST

im·mol·ate /'ɪməleɪt/ *verb* [VN] (*formal*) to kill sb by burning them ► **im·mol·ation** /ˌɪmə'leɪʃn/ *noun* [U]

im·moral /ɪ'mɒrəl; *AmE* ɪ'mɔːr-; ɪ'mɑːr-/ *adj.* **1** (of people and their behaviour) not considered to be good or honest by most people: *It's immoral to steal.* ◊ *There's nothing immoral about wanting to earn more money.* **2** not following accepted standards of sexual behaviour: *an immoral act/life/person* ◊ *They were charged with living off immoral earnings* (= money earned by working as a prostitute).—compare AMORAL, MORAL ► **im·mor·al·ity** /ˌɪmə'ræləti/ *noun* [U, C] (*pl.* **-ies**): *the immorality of war* ◊ *a life of immorality* **im·mor·al·ly** /ɪ'mɒrəli; *AmE* ɪ'mɔːr-; ɪ'mɑːr-/ *adv.*

im·mor·tal /ɪ'mɔːtl; *AmE* ɪ'mɔːrtl/ *adj., noun*
▪ *adj.* **1** that lives or lasts for ever: *The soul is immortal.* OPP MORTAL **2** famous and likely to be remembered for ever: *the immortal Goethe* ◊ *In the immortal words of Henry Ford, 'If it ain't broke, don't fix it.'*
▪ *noun* **1** a person who is so famous that they will be remembered for ever: *She is one of the Hollywood immortals.* **2** a god or other being who is believed to live for ever

im·mor·tal·ity /ˌɪmɔː'tæləti; *AmE* ˌɪmɔːr't-/ *noun* [U] the state of being immortal: *belief in the immortality of the soul* ◊ *He is well on his way to showbusiness immortality.*

im·mor·tal·ize (*BrE* also **-ise**) /ɪ'mɔːtəlaɪz; *AmE* ɪ'mɔːrt-/ *verb* [VN] ~ **sb/sth** (**in sth**) to prevent sb/sth from being forgotten in the future, especially by mentioning them in literature, making films/movies about them, painting them, etc: *The poet fell in love with her and immortalized her in his verse.*

im·mov·able /ɪ'muːvəbl/ *adj.* **1** [usually before noun] that cannot be moved: *an immovable object* **2** (of a person or an opinion, etc.) impossible to change or persuade: *On this issue he is completely immovable.*

im·mune /ɪ'mjuːn/ *adj.* [not usually before noun] **1** ~ (**to sth**) that cannot catch or be affected by a particular disease or illness: *Adults are often immune to German measles.* **2** ~ (**to sth**) not affected by sth: *You'll eventually*

become immune to criticism. **3** ~ (**from sth**) protected from sth and therefore able to avoid it SYN EXEMPT: *No one should be immune from prosecution.* ◊ *Not even the President's wife was immune from criticism by the press.*

im,mune res'ponse *noun* (*biology*) the reaction of the body to the presence of an ANTIGEN (= a substance that can cause disease)

im'mune system *noun* the system in your body that produces substances to help it fight against infection and disease

im·mun·ity /ɪ'mjuːnəti/ *noun* [U, C] (*pl.* **-ies**) **1** ~ (**to sth**) | ~ (**against sth**) the body's ability to avoid or not be affected by infection and disease: *immunity to infection* ◊ *The vaccine provides longer immunity against flu.* **2** ~ (**from sth**) the state of being protected from sth: *The spies were all granted immunity from prosecution.* ◊ *parliamentary/congressional immunity* (= protection against particular laws that is given to politicians) ◊ *Officials of all member states receive certain privileges and immunities.*—see also DIPLOMATIC IMMUNITY

im·mun·ize (*BrE* also **-ise**) /'ɪmjunaɪz/ *verb* [VN] ~ **sb/sth** (**against sth**) to protect a person or an animal from a disease, especially by giving them an INJECTION of a VACCINE—compare INOCULATE, VACCINATE ► **im·mun·ization, -isa·tion** /ˌɪmjunaɪ'zeɪʃn; *AmE* -nə'z-/ *noun* [U, C]: *an immunization programme to prevent epidemics*

im·mun·ology /ˌɪmju'nɒlədʒi; *AmE* -'nɑːl-/ *noun* [U] the scientific study of protection against disease

im·mure /ɪ'mjʊə(r); *AmE* ɪ'mjʊr/ *verb* [VN] ~ **sb** (**from/in sth**) (*literary*) to shut sb in a place so that they cannot get out

im·mut·able /ɪ'mjuːtəbl/ *adj.* (*formal*) that cannot be changed; that will never change SYN UNCHANGEABLE: *an immutable fact/law* ► **im·mut·abil·ity** /ɪˌmjuːtə'bɪləti/ *noun* [U]

imp /ɪmp/ *noun* **1** (in stories) a small creature like a little man, that has magic powers and behaves badly **2** a child who behaves badly, but not in a serious way

im·pact *noun, verb*
▪ *noun* /'ɪmpækt/ [C usually sing, U] **1** ~ (**of sth**) (**on sb/sth**) the powerful effect that sth has on sb/sth: *the environmental impact of tourism* ◊ *The report assesses the impact of Aids on the gay community.* ◊ *Her speech made a profound impact on everyone.* ◊ *Businesses are beginning to feel the full impact of the recession.* **2** the act of one object hitting another; the force with which this happens: *craters made by meteorite impacts* ◊ *The impact of the blow knocked Jack off balance.* ◊ *The bomb explodes on impact* (= when it hits something). ◊ *The car is fitted with side impact bars* (= to protect it from a blow from the side).
▪ *verb* /ɪm'pækt/ **1** ~ (**on/upon**) **sth** to have an effect on sth SYN AFFECT: [V] *Her father's death impacted greatly on her childhood years.* ◊ [VN] (*business*) *The company's performance was impacted by the high value of the pound.* **2** [V, VN] ~ (**on/upon/with**) **sth** (*formal*) to hit sth with great force

im·pair /ɪm'peə(r); *AmE* ɪm'per/ *verb* [VN] (*written*) to damage sth or make sth worse: *His age impaired his chances of finding a new job.*

im·paired /ɪm'peəd; *AmE* ɪm'perd/ **1** damaged or not functioning normally: *impaired vision/memory* **2** (**-impaired**) (in adjectives and nouns) having the type of physical or mental problem mentioned: *hearing-impaired children* ◊ *Nowadays we say someone is 'speech-impaired', not dumb.* ⇨ note at DISABLED

im·pair·ment /ɪm'peəmənt; *AmE* -'perm-/ *noun* [U, C] (*technical*) the state of having a physical or mental condition which means that part of your body or brain does not work correctly; a particular condition of this sort: *impairment of the functions of the kidney* ◊ *visual impairments*

im·pale /ɪm'peɪl/ *verb* [VN] **1** to push a sharp pointed object through sth: *She impaled a lump of meat on her fork.* **2** if you **impale** yourself on sth, or **are impaled** on it, you have a sharp pointed object pushed into you and you may be caught somewhere by it: *He had fallen and been impaled on some iron railings.*

s	t	v	z	ʃ	ʒ	tʃ	dʒ	θ	ð	ŋ
see	tea	van	zoo	shoe	vision	chain	jam	thin	this	sing

im·panel (also **em·panel**) /ɪmˈpænl/ verb (-ll-, AmE -l-) [VN] (especially AmE) to choose the members of a JURY in a court of law; to choose sb as a member of a JURY

im·part /ɪmˈpɑːt; AmE ɪmˈpɑːrt/ verb [VN] (formal) **1** ~ sth (to sb) to pass information, knowledge, etc. to other people SYN CONVEY: to impart facts/news/skills **2** ~ sth (to sth) to give a particular quality to sth SYN LEND: The spice imparts an Eastern flavour to the dish.

im·par·tial /ɪmˈpɑːʃl; AmE ɪmˈpɑːrʃl/ adj. not supporting one person or group more than another SYN NEUTRAL, UNBIASED: an impartial inquiry/observer ◊ to give impartial advice ◊ As chairman, I must remain impartial. OPP PARTIAL ▶ **im·par·ti·al·ity** /ˌɪmˌpɑːʃiˈæləti; AmE -ˌpɑːrʃi-/ noun [U] **im·par·tial·ly** /-ʃəli/ adv.

im·pass·able /ɪmˈpɑːsəbl; AmE -ˈpæs-/ adj. (of a road, an area etc.) impossible to travel on or through, especially because it is in bad condition or it has been blocked by sth: The mountain roads are totally impassable to cars in winter. ◊ The river formed an impassable barrier for migrating animals. OPP PASSABLE

im·passe /ˈæmpɑːs; AmE ˈɪmpæs/ noun [usually sing.] a difficult situation in which no progress can be made because the people involved cannot agree what to do SYN DEADLOCK: to break/end the impasse ◊ Negotiations have reached an impasse.

im·pas·sioned /ɪmˈpæʃnd/ adj. [usually before noun] (usually of speech) showing strong feelings about sth SYN FERVENT: an impassioned plea/speech/defence

im·pas·sive /ɪmˈpæsɪv/ adj. not showing any feeling or emotion SYN EMOTIONLESS: her impassive expression/face ▶ **im·pas·sive·ly** adv.: The accused listened impassively as the judge sentenced him.

im·pa·tient /ɪmˈpeɪʃnt/ adj. **1** ~ (with sb/sth)| ~ (at sth) annoyed or irritated by sb/sth, especially because you have to wait for a long time: I'd been waiting for twenty minutes and I was getting impatient. ◊ Try not to be too impatient with her. ◊ Sarah was becoming increasingly impatient at their lack of interest. ◊ He waved them away with an impatient gesture. **2** ~ to do sth| ~ for sth wanting to do sth soon; wanting sth to happen soon: She was clearly impatient to leave. ◊ impatient for change/success **3** ~ of sb/sth (formal) unable or unwilling to accept sth unpleasant: impatient of criticism/delay ▶ **im·pa·tience** /ɪmˈpeɪʃns/ noun [U]: She was bursting with impatience to tell me the news. **im·pa·tient·ly** adv.: We sat waiting impatiently for the movie to start.

im·peach /ɪmˈpiːtʃ/ verb [VN] **1** ~ sb (for sth) (of a court or other official body, especially in the US) to charge an important public figure with a serious crime **2** (formal) to raise doubts about sth SYN QUESTION: to impeach sb's motives ▶ **im·peach·ment** noun [U, C]

im·peach·able /ɪmˈpiːtʃəbl/ adj. (especially AmE) (of a crime) for which a politician or a person who works for the government can be impeached: an impeachable offense

im·pec·cable /ɪmˈpekəbl/ adj. without mistakes or faults; perfect: impeccable manners/taste/credentials ◊ Her written English is impeccable. ◊ He was dressed in a suit and an impeccable white shirt. ▶ **im·pec·cably** /-bli/ adv.: to behave impeccably ◊ impeccably dressed

im·pe·cu·ni·ous /ˌɪmpɪˈkjuːniəs/ adj. (formal or humorous) having little or no money SYN POOR, PENNILESS: an impecunious student

im·ped·ance /ɪmˈpiːdns/ noun [U] (technical) a measurement of the total RESISTANCE of a piece of electrical equipment, etc. to the flow of an ALTERNATING CURRENT

im·pede /ɪmˈpiːd/ verb [VN] [often passive] (formal) to delay or stop the progress of sth SYN HINDER, HAMPER: Work on the building was impeded by severe weather.

im·pedi·ment /ɪmˈpedɪmənt/ noun **1** ~ (to sth) something that delays or stops the progress of sth SYN OBSTACLE: The level of inflation is a serious impediment to economic recovery. **2** a physical problem that makes it difficult to speak normally: a speech impediment

im·pedi·menta /ɪmˌpedɪˈmentə/ noun [pl.] (formal or humorous) the bags and other equipment that you take

with you, especially when travelling, and that are difficult to carry

impel /ɪmˈpel/ verb (-ll-) ~ sb (to sth) if an idea or feeling impels you to do sth, you feel as if you are forced to do it: [VN to inf] He felt impelled to investigate further. ◊ [VN] There are various reasons that impel me to that conclusion.

im·pend·ing /ɪmˈpendɪŋ/ adj. [only before noun] (usually of an unpleasant event) that is going to happen very soon: his impending death/retirement ◊ warnings of impending danger/disaster

im·pene·trable /ɪmˈpenɪtrəbl/ adj. **1** that cannot be entered, passed through or seen through: an impenetrable jungle/fortress ◊ impenetrable darkness OPP PENETRABLE **2** ~ (to sb) impossible to understand: an impenetrable mystery ◊ Their jargon is impenetrable to an outsider. ◊ Her expression was impenetrable. ▶ **im·pene·tra·bil·ity** /ɪmˌpenɪtrəˈbɪləti/ noun [U] **im·pene·trably** /-bli/ adv.

im·pera·tive /ɪmˈperətɪv/ adj., noun
■ adj. **1** [not usually before noun] ~ (that …)| ~ (to do sth) (formal) very important and needing immediate attention or action SYN VITAL: It is absolutely imperative that we finish by next week. ◊ It is imperative for your recovery to continue the treatment for at least two months. **2** (formal) expressing authority: an imperative tone **3** [only before noun] (grammar) expressing an order: an imperative sentence
■ noun **1** (formal) a thing that is very important and needs immediate attention or action: the economic imperative of quality education for all **2** (grammar) the form of a verb that expresses an order; a verb in this form: In 'Go away!' the verb is **in the imperative**. ◊ 'Go away!' is an imperative.

im·per·cept·ible /ˌɪmpəˈseptəbl; AmE -pər's-/ adj. very small and therefore unable to be seen or felt; OPP PERCEPTIBLE: imperceptible changes in temperature ▶ **im·per·cept·ibly** /-əbli/ adv.

im·per·fect /ɪmˈpɜːfɪkt; AmE -ˈpɜːrf-/ adj., noun
■ adj. containing faults or mistakes; not complete or perfect: an imperfect world ◊ an imperfect understanding of English ◊ All our sale items are slightly imperfect. ▶ **im·per·fect·ly** adv.
■ noun (**the imperfect**) (also **the im·perfect 'tense**) [sing.] (grammar) the verb tense that expresses action in the past that is not complete. It is often called the **past progressive** or **past continuous**: In 'while I was washing my hair', the verb is **in the imperfect**.

im·per·fec·tion /ˌɪmpəˈfekʃn; AmE -pər'f-/ noun [C, U] a fault or weakness in sb/sth: They learned to live with each other's imperfections.

im·per·ial /ɪmˈpɪəriəl; AmE -ˈpɪr-/ adj. [only before noun] **1** connected with an empire: the imperial family/palace/army ◊ imperial power/expansion **2** connected with the system for measuring length, weight and volume using pounds, GALLONS, etc.—compare METRIC

im·peri·al·ism /ɪmˈpɪəriəlɪzəm; AmE -ˈpɪr-/ noun [U] (usually disapproving) **1** a system in which one country controls other countries, often after defeating them in a war: Roman imperialism **2** the fact of a powerful country increasing its influence over other countries through business, culture, etc: cultural/economic imperialism ▶ **im·peri·al·is·t** (also **im·peri·al·is·tic** /ɪmˌpɪəriəˈlɪstɪk; AmE -ˌpɪr-/) adj.: an imperialist power ◊ imperialist ambitions

im·peri·al·ist /ɪmˈpɪəriəlɪst; AmE -ˈpɪr-/ noun (usually disapproving) a person, such as a politician, who supports imperialism

im·peril /ɪmˈperəl/ verb (-ll-, AmE -l-) [VN] (formal) to put sth/sb in danger SYN ENDANGER

im·peri·ous /ɪmˈpɪəriəs; AmE -ˈpɪr-/ adj. (formal) expecting people to obey you and treating them as if they are not as important as you: an imperious gesture/voice/command ▶ **im·peri·ous·ly** adv.: 'Get it now,' she demanded imperiously.

im·per·ish·able /ɪmˈperɪʃəbl/ adj. (formal or literary) that will last for a long time or forever SYN ENDURING

im·per·man·ent /ɪmˈpɜːmənənt; AmE -ˈpɜːrm-/ adj.

æ	ɑː	e	ɜː	ə	ɪ	iː	i	ɒ	ɔː	ʌ	ʊ	u	uː
cat	father	ten	bird	about	sit	see	many	got	saw	cup	put	actual	too
							(BrE)						

(*formal*) that will not last or stay the same forever OPP PERMANENT ► **im·per·man·ence** /-əns/ *noun* [U]

im·per·me·able /ɪmˈpɜːmiəbl; *AmE* -ˈpɜːrm-/ *adj.* ~ (**to sth**) (*technical*) not allowing a liquid or gas to pass through: *impermeable rock* OPP PERMEABLE

im·per·mis·sible /ˌɪmpəˈmɪsəbl; *AmE* -pɜːrˈm-/ *adj.* that cannot be allowed: *an impermissible invasion of privacy* OPP PERMISSIBLE

im·per·son·al /ɪmˈpɜːsənl; *AmE* -ˈpɜːrs-/ *adj.* **1** (usually *disapproving*) lacking friendly human feelings or atmosphere; making you feel unimportant: *a vast impersonal organization* ◇ *an impersonal hotel room* ◇ *Business letters need not be formal and impersonal.* ◇ *a cold impersonal stare* **2** not referring to any particular person: *Let's keep the criticism general and impersonal.* **3** (*grammar*) an impersonal verb or sentence has 'it' or 'there' as the subject ► **im·per·son·al·ity** /ɪmˌpɜːsəˈnæləti; *AmE* -ˌpɜːrs-/ *noun* [U]: *the cold impersonality of some modern cities* **im·per·son·ally** /ɪmˈpɜːsənəli; *AmE* -ˈpɜːrs-/ *adv.*

im·per·son·ate /ɪmˈpɜːsəneɪt; *AmE* -ˈpɜːrs-/ *verb* [VN] to pretend to be sb in order to deceive people or to entertain them: *He was caught trying to impersonate a security guard.* ◇ *They do a pretty good job of impersonating Laurel and Hardy.* ► **im·per·son·ation** /ɪmˌpɜːsəˈneɪʃn; *AmE* -ˌpɜːrs-/ *noun* [C, U]: *He did an extremely convincing impersonation of the singer.*

im·per·son·ator /ɪmˈpɜːsəneɪtə(r); *AmE* -ˈpɜːrs-/ *noun* a person who copies the way another person talks or behaves in order to entertain people: *The show included a female impersonator* (= a man dressed as a woman).

im·per·tin·ent /ɪmˈpɜːtɪnənt; *AmE* -ˈpɜːrtn-/ *adj.* rude and not showing respect for sb who is older or more important: *an impertinent question/child* ◇ *Would it be impertinent to ask why you're leaving?* ► **im·per·tin·ence** /-əns/ *noun* [U, C, usually sing.]: *She had the impertinence to ask my age!* **im·per·tin·ent·ly** *adv.*

im·per·turb·able /ˌɪmpəˈtɜːbəbl; *AmE* -pərˈtɜːrb-/ *adj.* (*formal*) not easily upset or worried by a difficult situation; calm ► **im·per·turb·ability** /ˌɪmpəˌtɜːbəˈbɪləti; *AmE* -pərˌtɜːrb-/ *noun* [U] **im·per·turb·ably** /-əbli/ *adv.*

im·per·vi·ous /ɪmˈpɜːviəs; *AmE* -ˈpɜːrv-/ *adj.* **1** ~ **to sth** not affected or influenced by sth: *impervious to criticism/pain* **2** ~ (**to sth**) (*technical*) not allowing a liquid or gas to pass through: *an impervious rock/layer* ◇ *impervious to moisture*

im·petu·ous /ɪmˈpetʃuəs/ *adj.* acting or done quickly and without thinking carefully about the results SYN RASH, IMPULSIVE: *an impetuous young woman* ◇ *an impetuous decision* ► **im·petu·os·ity** /ɪmˌpetʃuˈɒsəti; *AmE* -ˈɑːsəti/ *noun* [U] **im·petu·ous·ly** *adv.*

im·petus /ˈɪmpɪtəs/ *noun* **1** [U, sing.] ~ (**for sth**)| ~ (**to sth/to do sth**) something that encourages a process or activity to develop more quickly SYN STIMULUS: *to give* (*a*) *new/fresh impetus to sth* ◇ *The debate seems to have lost much of its initial impetus.* ◇ *His articles provided the main impetus for change.* **2** [U] (*technical*) the force or energy with which sth moves

im·pinge /ɪmˈpɪndʒ/ *verb* [V] ~ (**on/upon sth/sb**) (*formal*) to have a noticeable effect on sth/sb, especially a bad one SYN ENCROACH: *He never allowed his work to impinge on his private life.*

im·pious /ˈɪmpiəs; ɪmˈpaɪəs/ *adj.* (*formal*) showing a lack of respect for God and religion; OPP PIOUS ► **im·pi·ety** /ɪmˈpaɪəti/ *noun* [U]

imp·ish /ˈɪmpɪʃ/ *adj.* showing a lack of respect for sb/sth in a way that is amusing rather than serious: *an impish grin/look*—see also IMP ► **imp·ish·ly** *adv.*: *to grin/smile impishly*

im·plac·able /ɪmˈplækəbl/ *adj.* **1** (of strong negative opinions or feelings) that cannot be changed: *implacable hatred/opposition* **2** (of a person) unwilling to stop opposing sb/sth: *an implacable enemy* ► **im·plac·ably** /ɪmˈplækəbli/ *adv.*: *to be implacably opposed to the plan*

im·plant *verb, noun*
▪ *verb* /ɪmˈplɑːnt; *AmE* -ˈplænt/ ~ (**sth**) (**in/into sth**) **1** [VN] (*written*) to fix an idea, attitude, etc. firmly in sb's mind: *Prejudices can easily become implanted in the mind.* **2** [VN]

to put sth (usually sth artificial) into a part of the body for medical purposes, usually by means of an operation: *an electrode implanted into the brain*—compare TRANSPLANT **3** [V] (of an egg or an EMBRYO) to become fixed inside the body of a person or an animal so that it can start to develop ► **im·plant·ation** /ˌɪmplɑːnˈteɪʃn; *AmE* -plæn-/ *noun* [U]
▪ *noun* /ˈɪmplɑːnt; *AmE* -plænt/ something that is put into a person's body in a medical operation: *silicone breast implants*—compare TRANSPLANT

im·plaus·ible /ɪmˈplɔːzəbl/ *adj.* not seeming reasonable or likely to be true: *a highly implausible claim/idea/theory* ◇ *Her explanation is not implausible.* OPP PLAUSIBLE ► **im·plaus·ibly** *adv.*

im·ple·ment *verb, noun*
▪ *verb* /ˈɪmplɪment/ [VN] to make sth that has been officially decided start to happen or be used SYN CARRY OUT: *to implement changes/decisions/policies/reforms* ► **im·ple·men·ta·tion** /ˌɪmplɪmenˈteɪʃn/ *noun* [U]: *the implementation of the new system*
▪ *noun* /ˈɪmplɪmənt/ a tool or an instrument, often one that is quite simple and that is used outdoors: *agricultural implements*

im·pli·cate /ˈɪmplɪkeɪt/ *verb* [VN] **1** ~ **sb** (**in sth**) to show or suggest that sb is involved in sth bad or criminal: *He tried to avoid saying anything that would implicate him further.* **2** ~ **sth** (**in/as sth**) to show or suggest that sth is the cause of sth bad: *The results implicate poor hygiene as one cause of the outbreak.* IDM **be implicated in sth** to be involved in a crime; to be responsible for sth bad: *Senior officials were implicated in the scandal.*

im·pli·ca·tion /ˌɪmplɪˈkeɪʃn/ *noun* **1** [C, usually pl.] ~ (**for/of sth**) a possible effect or result of an action or a decision: *The development of the site will have implications for the surrounding countryside.* ◇ *They failed to consider the wider implications of their actions.* **2** [C, U] something that is suggested or indirectly stated (= sth that is IMPLIED): *The implication in his article is that being a housewife is greatly inferior to every other occupation.* ◇ *He criticized the Director and, by implication, the whole of the organization.* **3** [U] ~ (**of sb**) (**in sth**) the fact of being involved, or of involving sb, in sth, especially a crime: *He resigned after his implication in a sex scandal.*

im·pli·cit /ɪmˈplɪsɪt/ *adj.* **1** ~ (**in sth**) suggested without being directly expressed: *Implicit in his speech was the assumption that they were guilty.* ◇ *implicit criticism* **2** ~ (**in sth**) forming part of sth (although perhaps not directly expressed): *The ability to listen is implicit in the teacher's role.* **3** ~ (**in sth**) complete and not doubted: *She had the implicit trust of her staff.*—compare EXPLICIT ► **im·pli·cit·ly** *adv.*: *It reinforces, implicitly or explicitly, the idea that money is all-important.* ◇ *I trust John implicitly.*

im·plode /ɪmˈpləʊd; *AmE* ɪmˈploʊd/ *verb* [V] **1** to burst or explode inwards—compare EXPLODE **2** (of an organization, a system, etc.) to fail suddenly and completely ► **im·plo·sion** /ɪmˈpləʊʒn; *AmE* -ˈploʊ-/ *noun* [C, U]

im·plore /ɪmˈplɔː(r)/ *verb* (*formal* or *literary*) to ask sb to do sth in an anxious way because you want or need it very much SYN BESEECH, BEG: [VN to inf] *She implored him to stay.* ◇ [V speech] *'Help me,' he implored.* ◇ [VN] *Tell me it's true. I implore you.* [also VN speech] ► **im·plor·ing** *adj.*: *She gave him an imploring look.*

imply /ɪmˈplaɪ/ *verb* (**im·plies, im·ply·ing, im·plied, im·plied**) **1** to suggest that sth is true or that you feel or think sth, without saying so directly: [V (that)] *Are you implying (that) I am wrong?* ◇ [VN] *I disliked the implied criticism in his voice.* [also VN that] ⇨ note at INFER **2** to make it seem likely that sth is true or exists: [V (that)] *The survey implies (that) more people are moving house than was thought.* ◇ [VN] *The fact that she was here implies a degree of interest.* [also VN that] **3** [VN] (of an idea, action, etc.) to make sth necessary in order to be successful: *The project implies an enormous investment in training.*—see also IMPLICATION

im·pol·ite /ˌɪmpəˈlaɪt/ *adj.* not polite SYN RUDE: *Some people think it is impolite to ask someone's age.*

aɪ	aʊ	eɪ	əʊ	oʊ	ɔɪ	ɪə	eə	ʊə	j	w
my	now	say	go (BrE)	go (AmE)	boy	near	hair	pure	yes	wet

im·pol·it·ic /ɪmˈpɒlətɪk; AmE -ˈpɑːl-/ adj. (formal) not wise: *It would have been impolitic to refuse his offer.*

im·pon·der·able /ɪmˈpɒndərəbl; AmE -ˈpɑːn-/ noun [usually pl.] (formal) something that is difficult to measure or estimate: *We can't predict the outcome. There are too many imponderables.* ▶ **im·pon·der·able** adj.

im·port noun, verb
■ noun /ˈɪmpɔːt; AmE ˈɪmpɔːrt/ **1** [C, usually pl.] a product or service that is brought into one country from another: *food imports from abroad* OPP EXPORT **2** [U, pl.] the act of bringing a product or service into one country from another: *The report calls for a ban on the import of hazardous waste.* ◊ *import controls* ◊ *an import licence* ◊ *imports of oil* OPP EXPORT **3** [U] (formal) importance: *matters of great import* **4** the ~ (of sth) [sing.] (formal) the meaning of sth, especially when it is not immediately clear: *It is difficult to understand the full import of this statement.*
■ verb /ɪmˈpɔːt; AmE ɪmˈpɔːrt/ [VN] ~ sth (from …)| ~ sth (into …) to bring a product, a service, an idea, etc. into one country from another: *The country has to import most of its raw materials.* ◊ *goods imported from Japan into the US* ◊ *customs imported from the West* OPP EXPORT ▶ **im·port·ation** /ˌɪmpɔːˈteɪʃn; AmE -pɔːrˈt-/ noun [U, C]: *a ban on the importation of ivory*

im·port·ance /ɪmˈpɔːtns; AmE -ˈpɔːrt-/ noun [U] the quality of being important: *She stressed the importance of careful preparation.* ◊ *It's a matter of the greatest importance to me.* ◊ *They attach great importance to the project* ◊ *the relative importance of the two ideas* ◊ *State your reasons in order of importance.* ◊ *He was very aware of his own importance* (= of his status).

im·port·ant /ɪmˈpɔːtnt; AmE -ˈpɔːrt-/ adj. **1** ~ (to sb) having a great effect on people or things; of great value: *an important decision/factor* ◊ *I have an important announcement to make.* ◊ *Money played an important role in his life.* ◊ *Listening is an important part of the job.* ◊ *one of the most important collections of American art* ◊ *It is important to follow the manufacturer's instructions.* ◊ *It is important that he attend every day.* ◊ *(BrE) It is important that he should attend every day.* ◊ *It is important for him to attend every day.* ◊ *It's very important to me that you should be there.* ◊ *The important thing is to keep trying.* **2** (of a person) having great influence or authority: *an important member of the team* ◊ *He likes to feel important.* ▶ **im·port·ant·ly** adv.: *More importantly, can he be trusted?* ◊ *She was sitting importantly behind a big desk.*

im·port·er /ɪmˈpɔːtə(r); AmE -ˈpɔːrt-/ noun a person, company, etc. that buys goods from another country to sell them in their own country: *a London-based importer of Italian goods*—compare EXPORTER

im·por·tun·ate /ɪmˈpɔːtʃənət; AmE -ˈpɔːrt-/ adj. (formal) asking for things many times in a way that is annoying: *importunate demands/pleas*

im·por·tune /ˌɪmpɔːˈtjuːn; AmE -pɔːrˈtuːn/ verb [VN, VN to inf] ~ (sb) (for sth) (formal) to ask sb for sth many times and in a way that is annoying SYN PESTER

im·pose /ɪmˈpəʊz; AmE ɪmˈpoʊz/ verb **1** [VN] ~ sth (on/upon sth/sb) to introduce a new law, rule, tax, etc.; to order that a rule, punishment, etc. be used: *A new tax was imposed on fuel.* **2** [VN] ~ sth (on/upon sb/sth) to force sb/sth to have to deal with sth that is difficult or unpleasant: *to impose limitations/restrictions/constraints on sth* ◊ *This system imposes additional financial burdens on many people.* **3** [VN] ~ sth (on/upon sb) to make sb accept the same opinions, wishes etc. as your own: *She didn't want to impose her values on her family.* ◊ *It was noticeable how a few people managed to impose their will on the others.* **4** [V] ~ (on/upon sb/sth) to expect sb to do sth for you or to spend time with you, when it may not be convenient for them: *'You must stay for lunch.' 'Well, thanks, but I don't want to impose …'* ◊ *Everyone imposes on Dave's good nature.* **5** [VN] ~ yourself (on/upon sb/sth) to make sb/sth accept or be aware of your presence or ideas: *European civilization was the first to impose itself across the whole world.*

im·pos·ing /ɪmˈpəʊzɪŋ; AmE -ˈpoʊz-/ adj. impressive to look at; making a strong impression: *a grand and imposing building* ◊ *a tall imposing woman*

im·pos·ition /ˌɪmpəˈzɪʃn/ noun **1** [U] the act of introducing sth such as a new law or rule, or a new tax: *the imposition of martial law* ◊ *the imposition of tax on domestic fuel* **2** [C] an unfair or unreasonable thing that sb expects or asks you to do: *I'd like to stay if it's not too much of an imposition.*

im·pos·sible /ɪmˈpɒsəbl; AmE -ˈpɑːs-/ adj. **1** that cannot exist or be done; not possible: *almost/virtually impossible* ◊ *It's impossible for me to be there before eight.* ◊ *It's impossible to prove.* ◊ *I find it impossible to lie to her.* ◊ *an impossible dream/goal* OPP POSSIBLE **2** very difficult to deal with: *I've been placed in an impossible position.* ◊ *Honestly, you're impossible at times!* **3** (the impossible) noun [sing.] a thing that is or seems impossible: *to attempt the impossible* ▶ **im·pos·si·bil·ity** /ɪmˌpɒsəˈbɪləti; AmE -ˌpɑːsə-/ noun [U, C, usually sing.]: *the sheer impossibility of providing enough food for everyone* ◊ *a virtual impossibility* **im·pos·sibly** /ɪmˈpɒsəbli; AmE -ˈpɑːs-/ adv.: *an impossibly difficult problem* (= impossible to solve) ◊ *He was impossibly handsome* (= it was difficult to believe that he could be so handsome).

im·pos·tor (BrE also **im·pos·ter**) /ɪmˈpɒstə(r); AmE -ˈpɑːs-/ noun a person who pretends to be sb else in order to deceive people

im·pos·ture /ɪmˈpɒstʃə(r); AmE -ˈpɑːs-/ noun [U, C] (formal) an act of deceiving people deliberately by pretending to be sb else

im·po·tent /ˈɪmpətənt/ adj. **1** having no power to change things or to influence a situation: *Without the chairman's support, the committee is impotent.* ◊ *She blazed with impotent rage.* **2** (of a man) unable to achieve an ERECTION and therefore unable to have full sex ▶ **im·po·tence** /ˈɪmpətəns/ noun [U]: *a feeling of impotence in the face of an apparently insoluble problem* ◊ *male impotence* **im·po·tent·ly** adv.

im·pound /ɪmˈpaʊnd/ verb [VN] (law) **1** (of the police, courts of law, etc.) to take sth away from sb, so that they cannot use it SYN CONFISCATE: *The car was impounded by the police after the accident.* **2** to shut up dogs, cats, etc. found on the streets in a POUND, until their owners collect them

im·pov·er·ish /ɪmˈpɒvərɪʃ; AmE -ˈpɑːv-/ verb [VN] (written) **1** to make sb poor: *These changes are likely to impoverish single parent families even further.* **2** to make sth worse in quality: *Intensive cultivation has impoverished the soil.* ▶ **im·pov·er·ish·ment** noun [U]

im·pov·er·ished /ɪmˈpɒvərɪʃt; AmE -ˈpɑːv-/ adj. **1** very poor; without money: *impoverished peasants* ◊ *the impoverished areas of the city* **2** poor in quality, because sth is missing

im·prac·tic·able /ɪmˈpræktɪkəbl/ adj. impossible or very difficult to do; not PRACTICAL in a particular situation: *It would be impracticable for each member to be consulted on every occasion.*—compare IMPRACTICAL OPP PRACTICABLE ▶ **im·prac·tic·abil·ity** /ɪmˌpræktɪkəˈbɪləti/ noun [U]

im·prac·ti·cal /ɪmˈpræktɪkl/ adj. **1** not sensible or realistic: *It was totally impractical to think that we could finish the job in two months.* **2** (of people) not good at doing things that involve using the hands; not good at planning or organizing things OPP PRACTICAL—compare IMPRACTICABLE ▶ **im·prac·ti·cal·ity** /ɪmˌpræktɪˈkæləti/ [U]

im·pre·ca·tion /ˌɪmprɪˈkeɪʃn/ noun (formal) a CURSE (= an offensive word that is used to express extreme anger)

im·pre·cise /ˌɪmprɪˈsaɪs/ adj. not accurate; not giving exact details or making sth clear: *an imprecise definition* ◊ *imprecise information* ◊ *The witness's descriptions were too imprecise to be of any real value.* OPP PRECISE ▶ **im·pre·cise·ly** adv.: *These terms are often used imprecisely and interchangeably.* **im·pre·ci·sion** /ˌɪmprɪˈsɪʒn/ noun [U]: *There is considerable imprecision in the terminology used.*

im·preg·nable /ɪmˈpregnəbl/ adj. **1** an impregnable building is so strongly built that it cannot be entered by

b	d	f	g	h	k	l	m	n	p	r
bad	did	fall	get	hat	cat	leg	man	now	pen	red

force: *an impregnable fortress* **2** strong and impossible to defeat or change: *The team built up an impregnable 5-1 lead.*

im·preg·nate /ˈɪmpregneɪt; *AmE* ɪmˈpreg-/ *verb* [VN] **1** [usually passive] **~ sth (with sth)** to make a substance spread through an area so that the area is full of the substance: *The pad is impregnated with insecticide.* **2** (*formal*) to make a woman or female animal pregnant ▸ **im·preg·na·tion** /ˌɪmpregˈneɪʃn/ *noun* [U]

im·pres·ario /ˌɪmprəˈsɑːriəʊ; *AmE* -riəʊ/ *noun* (*pl.* **-os**) a person who arranges plays in the theatre, etc., especially a person who manages a theatre, opera or ballet company

im·press /ɪmˈpres/ *verb* **1 ~ sb (with sth/sb)** if a person or thing **impresses** you, you feel admiration for them or it: [VN] *We interviewed a number of candidates but none of them impressed us.* ◊ *She was* **suitably impressed** (= as impressed as sb had hoped) *with the painting.* ◊ *He impressed her with his sincerity.* ◊ *His sincerity impressed her.* ◊ [V] *The Grand Canyon never fails to impress.* ◊ [VN that] *It impressed me that she remembered my name.*—see also IMPRESSIVE **2** [VN] **~ sth on/upon sb** (*formal*) to make sb understand how important, serious etc. sth is by emphasizing it: *He impressed on us the need for immediate action.* **3** [VN] **~ sth/itself on/upon sth** (*formal*) to have a great effect on sth, especially sb's mind, imagination, etc: *Her words impressed themselves on my memory.*—see also UNIMPRESSED

im·pres·sion /ɪmˈpreʃn/ *noun*

IDEA/OPINION **1 ~ (of sb/sth)** | **~ (that …)** an idea, a feeling or an opinion that you get about sb/sth, or that sb/sth gives you: *a general/an overall impression* ◊ *to get a good/bad impression of sb/sth* ◊ *an initial/a lasting impression* ◊ *My first impression of him was favourable.* ◊ *I did not get the impression that they were unhappy about the situation.* ◊ *My impression is that there are still a lot of problems.* ◊ *She gives the impression of being very busy.*

EFFECT **2 ~ (on sb)** the effect that an experience or a person has on sb/sth: *a big/deep/strong impression* ◊ *His trip to India made a strong impression on him.* ◊ *You'll have to play better than that if you really want to make an impression* (= to make people admire you). ◊ *My words made no impression on her.*

DRAWING **3** a drawing showing what a person looks like or what a place or a building will look like in the future: *This is an artist's impression of the new stadium.*

AMUSING COPY OF SB **4 ~ (of sb)** an amusing copy of the way a person acts or speaks: *He did his impression of Tom Hanks.*

FALSE APPEARANCE **5** an appearance that may be false: *Clever lighting creates an impression of space in a room.*

MARK **6** a mark that is left when an object is pressed hard into a surface

BOOK **7** all the copies of a book that are printed at one time, with few or no changes to the contents since the last time the book was printed—compare EDITION

IDM **(be) under the im·pression that …** believing, usually wrongly, that sth is true or is happening: *I was under the impression that the work had already been completed.*

im·pres·sion·able /ɪmˈpreʃənəbl/ *adj.* (of a person, especially a young one) easily influenced or affected by sb/sth: *children at an impressionable age*

Im·pres·sion·ism /ɪmˈpreʃənɪzəm/ *noun* [U] a style in painting developed in France in the late 19th century that uses colour to show the effects of light on things and to suggest atmosphere rather than showing exact details ▸ **Im·pres·sion·ist** *adj.* [usually before noun]: *Impressionist landscapes*

im·pres·sion·ist /ɪmˈpreʃənɪst/ *noun* **1** (usually **Impressionist**) an artist who paints in the style of Impressionism: *Impressionists such as Monet and Pissarro* **2** a person who entertains people by copying the way a famous person speaks or behaves

im·pres·sion·is·tic /ɪmˌpreʃəˈnɪstɪk/ *adj.* (*written*) giving a general idea rather than particular facts or details

im·pres·sive /ɪmˈpresɪv/ *adj.* (of things or people) making you feel admiration, because they are very large,

good, skilful, etc: *an impressive building with a huge tower* ◊ *an impressive performance* ◊ *one of the most impressive novels of recent years* ◊ *She was very impressive in the interview.* **OPP** UNIMPRESSIVE ▸ **im·pres·sive·ly** *adv.*: *impressively high* ◊ *impressively organized*

im·pri·ma·tur /ˌɪmprɪˈmɑːtə(r)/ *noun* [sing.] (*formal*) official approval of sth, given by a person in a position of authority

im·print *verb, noun*
▪ *verb* /ɪmˈprɪnt/ [VN] **~ A in/on B** | **~ B with A 1** to have a great effect on sth so that it cannot be forgotten, changed, etc: *The terrible scenes were indelibly imprinted on his mind.* **2** to print or press a mark or design onto a surface: *clothes imprinted with the logos of sports teams*
▪ *noun* /ˈɪmprɪnt/ **1 ~ (of sth) (in/on sth)** a mark made by pressing or stamping sth onto a surface: *the imprint of a foot in the sand* **2** [usually sing.] **~ (of sth) (on sb/sth)** (*formal*) the lasting effect that a person or an experience has on a place or a situation **3** (*technical*) the name of the PUBLISHER of a book, usually printed below the title on the first page

im·prison /ɪmˈprɪzn/ *verb* [VN] [often passive] to put sb in a prison or another place from which they cannot escape: *They were imprisoned for possession of drugs.* ◊ (*figurative*) *Some young mothers feel imprisoned in their own homes.* ▸ **im·pris·on·ment** /-mənt/ *noun* [U]: *to be sentenced to* **life imprisonment** *for murder*

im·prob·able /ɪmˈprɒbəbl; *AmE* -ˈprɑːb-/ *adj.* **1 ~ (that …)** not likely to be true or to happen: *an improbable story/plot* ◊ *It seems improbable that the current situation will continue.* ◊ *It all sounded* **highly improbable.** **OPP** PROBABLE **2** seeming strange because it is not what you would expect: *Her hair was an improbable shade of yellow.* ▸ **im·prob·abil·ity** /ɪmˌprɒbəˈbɪləti; *AmE* -ˌprɑːbə-/ *noun* [U, C]: *the improbability of finding them alive* ◊ *statistical improbability* **im·prob·ably** /-əbli/ *adv.*: *He claimed, improbably, that he had never been there.* ◊ *an improbably happy end*

im·promptu /ɪmˈprɒmptjuː; *AmE* -ˈprɑːmptuː/ *adj.* done without preparation or planning: *an impromptu speech*

im·proper /ɪmˈprɒpə(r); *AmE* -ˈprɑːp-/ *adj.* **1** dishonest, or morally wrong: *improper business practices* ◊ *improper conduct* ◊ *There was nothing improper about our relationship* (= it did not involve sex). **OPP** PROPER **2** (*formal*) not suited or appropriate to the situation: *It would be improper to comment at this stage.* **OPP** PROPER **3** wrong; not correct: *improper use of the drug* ▸ **im·prop·er·ly** *adv.*: *to behave improperly* ◊ *He was improperly dressed for the occasion.* ◊ *improperly cooked meat*

im·pro·pri·ety /ˌɪmprəˈpraɪəti/ *noun* [U, C] (*pl.* **-ies**) (*formal*) behaviour or actions that are dishonest, morally wrong or not appropriate for a person in a position of responsibility: *There was no evidence of impropriety.* **OPP** PROPRIETY

im·prove /ɪmˈpruːv/ *verb* to become better than before; to make sth/sb better than before: [V] *His quality of life has improved dramatically since the operation.* ◊ *The doctor says she should continue to improve* (= after an illness). ◊ [VN] *to improve efficiency/standards/conditions* ◊ *The company needs to improve performance in all these areas.* ◊ *I need to improve my French.* **PHRV** **im·prove on/upon sth** to achieve or produce sth that is of a better quality than sth else: *We've certainly improved on last year's figures.*

im·prove·ment /ɪmˈpruːvmənt/ *noun* **1** [U] **~ (in/on/to sth)** the act of making sth better; the process of sth becoming better: *Sales figures continue to show signs of improvement.* ◊ *There is still* **room for improvement** *in your work.* ◊ *We expect to see* **further improvement** *over the coming year.* **2** [C] **~ (in/on sth)** a change in sth that makes it better; sth that is better than it was before: *a significant/substantial/dramatic improvement* ◊ *a slight/steady improvement* ◊ *an improvement in Anglo-German relations* ◊ *This is a great improvement on your previous work.* ◊ *improvements to the bus service* ◊ *home improvements* (= changes that are made to a house, that increase its value) **HELP** *Home improvement* is [U] in *AmE*.

s	t	v	z	ʃ	ʒ	tʃ	dʒ	θ	ð	ŋ
see	tea	van	zoo	shoe	vision	chain	jam	thin	this	sing

im·pro·vi·dent /ɪmˈprɒvɪdənt; AmE -ˈprɑːv-/ adj. (formal) not thinking about or planning for the future; spending money in a careless way OPP PROVIDENT ▶ **im·provi·dence** /-əns/ noun [U]

im·pro·vise /ˈɪmprəvaɪz/ verb **1** to make or do sth using whatever is available, usually because you do not have what you really need: [V] *There isn't much equipment. We're going to have to improvise.* ◇ [VN] *We improvised some shelves out of planks of wood and bricks.* **2** ~ (**on sth**) to invent music, the words in a play, a statement, etc. while you are playing or speaking, instead of planning it in advance: [V] *'It'll be ready some time next week, I expect,' she said, improvising.* ◇ *He improvised on the melody.* ◇ [VN] *an improvised response/speech* ▶ **im·pro·visa·tion** /ˌɪmprəvaɪˈzeɪʃn; AmE ɪmˌprɑːvəˈzeɪʃn/ noun [U, C]

im·pru·dent /ɪmˈpruːdnt/ adj. (formal) not wise or sensible SYN UNWISE: *It would be imprudent to invest all your money in one company.* OPP PRUDENT ▶ **im·pru·dence** /-ns/ noun [U] **im·pru·dent·ly** adv.

im·pu·dent /ˈɪmpjədənt/ adj. (formal) rude; not showing respect for other people: *an impudent young fellow* ◇ *an impudent remark* ▶ **im·pu·dence** /-əns/ noun [U]

im·pugn /ɪmˈpjuːn/ verb [VN] (formal) to express doubts about whether sth is right, honest, etc.

im·pulse /ˈɪmpʌls/ noun **1** [C usually sing, U] ~ (**to do sth**) a sudden strong wish or need to do sth, without stopping to think about the results: *He had a sudden impulse to stand up and sing.* ◇ *I resisted the impulse to laugh.* ◇ *Her first impulse was to run away.* ◇ *The door was open and on* (**an**) **impulse** *she went inside.* ◇ *He tends to act on impulse.* **2** [C] (technical) a force or movement of energy that causes sth else to react: *nerve/electrical impulses* **3** [C usually sing, U] (formal) something that causes sb/sth to do sth or to develop and make progress: *to give an impulse to the struggling car industry*

ˈimpulse buying noun [U] buying goods without planning to do so in advance, and without thinking about it carefully

im·pul·sive /ɪmˈpʌlsɪv/ adj. (of people or their behaviour) acting suddenly without thinking carefully about what might happen because of what you are doing: *an impulsive act/decision/gesture/reaction* ◇ *She has an impulsive nature.* ▶ **im·pul·sive·ly** adv.: *Impulsively he reached out and took her hand.* **im·pul·sive·ness** noun [U]

im·pun·ity /ɪmˈpjuːnəti/ noun [U] (formal, disapproving) if a person does sth bad **with impunity**, they do not get punished for what they have done

im·pure /ɪmˈpjuə(r); AmE ɪmˈpjʊr/ adj. **1** not pure or clean; not consisting of only one substance but mixed with one or more substances often of poorer quality: *impure gold* **2** (old-fashioned or written) (of thoughts or feelings) morally bad, especially because they are connected with sex: *impure thoughts/motives* OPP PURE

im·pur·ity /ɪmˈpjʊərəti; AmE -ˈpjʊr-/ noun (pl. **-ies**) **1** [C] a substance that is present in small amounts in another substance, making it dirty or of poor quality: *A filter will remove most impurities found in water.* **2** [U] the state of being dirty or not pure OPP PURITY

im·pute /ɪmˈpjuːt/ PHRV **im'pute sth to sb/sth** (formal) to say, often unfairly, that sb is responsible for sth or has a particular quality SYN ATTRIBUTE: *I denied the motives that my employer was imputing to me.* ▶ **im·put·ation** /ˌɪmpjuˈteɪʃn/ noun [U, C]

in /ɪn/ prep., adv., adj., noun

■ prep. HELP For the special uses of **in** in phrasal verbs, look at the entries for the verbs. For example **deal in sth** is in the phrasal verb section at **deal**. **1** at a point within an area or a space: *a country in Africa* ◇ *The kids were playing in the street.* ◇ *It's in that drawer.* ◇ *I read about it in the paper.* **2** within the shape of sth; surrounded by sth: *She was lying in bed.* ◇ *sitting in an armchair* ◇ *Leave the key in the lock.* ◇ *Soak it in cold water.* **3** into sth: *He dipped his brush in the paint.* ◇ *She got in her car and drove off.* **4** forming the whole or part of sth/sb; contained within sth/sb: *There are 31 days in May.* ◇ *all the* paintings in the collection ◇ *I recognize his father in him* (= his character is similar to his father's). **5** during a period of time: *in 2005* ◇ *in the 18th century* ◇ *in spring/summer/ autumn/winter* ◇ *in the fall* ◇ *in March* ◇ *in the morning/ afternoon/evening* ◇ *I'm getting forgetful in my old age.* **6** after a particular length of time: *to return in a few minutes/hours/days/months.* ◇ *It will be ready in a week's time* (= one week from now). ◇ *She learnt to drive in three weeks* (= after three weeks she could drive). **7** (used in negative sentences or after *first, last,* etc.) for a particular period of time: *I haven't seen him in years.* ◇ *It's the first letter I've had in ten days.* **8** wearing sth: *dressed in their best clothes* ◇ *the man in the hat* ◇ *to be in uniform/disguise* ◇ *She was all in black.* **9** used to describe physical surroundings: *We went out in the rain.* ◇ *He was sitting alone in the darkness.* **10** used to show a state or condition: *I'm in love!* ◇ *The house is in good repair.* ◇ *I must put my affairs in order.* ◇ *a man in his thirties* ◇ *The daffodils were in full bloom.* **11** involved in sth; taking part in sth: *to act in a play* **12** used to show sb's job or profession: *He is in the army.* ◇ *She's in computers.* ◇ *in business/politics* **13** used to show the form, shape, arrangement or quantity of sth: *a novel in three parts* ◇ *Roll it up in a ball.* ◇ *They sat in rows.* ◇ *People flocked in their thousands to see her.* **14** used to show the language, material, etc. used: *Say it in English.* ◇ *She wrote in pencil.* ◇ *Put it in writing.* ◇ *I paid in cash.* ◇ *He spoke in a loud voice.* **15** concerning sth: *She was not lacking in courage.* ◇ *a country rich in minerals* ◇ *three metres in length* **16** while doing sth; while sth is happening: *In attempting to save the child from drowning, she nearly lost her own life.* ◇ *In all the commotion I forgot to tell him the news.* **17** used to introduce the name of a person who has a particular quality: *We're losing a first-rate editor in Kathy.* **18** used to show a rate or relative amount: *a gradient of one in five* ◇ *a tax rate of 22 pence in the pound* IDM **in that** /ɪn ðæt/ (written) for the reason that; because: *She was fortunate in that she had friends to help her.*

■ adv. HELP For the special uses of **in** in phrasal verbs, look at the entries for the verbs. For example **fill in (for sb)** is in the phrasal verb section at **fill**. **1** contained within an object, an area or a substance: *We were locked in.* ◇ *I can't drink coffee with milk in.* **2** into an object, an area or a substance: *She opened the door and went in.* ◇ *The kids were playing by the river and one of them fell in.* **3** (of people) at home or at a place of work: *Nobody was in when we called.* OPP OUT **4** (of trains, buses, etc.) at the place where people can get on or off, for example the station: *The bus is due in* (= it should arrive) *at six.* **5** (of letters, etc.) received: *Applications must be in by April 30.* **6** (of the TIDE) at or towards its highest point on land: *Is the tide coming in or going out?* **7** elected: *Several new Labour councillors got in at the last election.* **8** (in cricket, baseball, etc.) if a team or team member is **in**, they are BATTING: *England were in first.* **9** (in tennis, etc.) if the ball is in, it has landed inside the line: *Her serve was just in.* IDM **be in at sth** to be present when sth happens: *They were in at the start.* **be 'in for sth** (informal) to be going to experience sth soon, especially sth unpleasant: *He's in for a shock!* ◇ *I'm afraid we're in for a storm.* **be/ get 'in on sth** (informal) to be/become involved in sth; to share or know about sth: *I'd like to be in on the plan.* ◇ *Is she in on the secret?* **be (well) 'in with sb** (informal) to be (very) friendly with sb, and likely to get an advantage from the friendship **,in and 'out (of sth)** going regularly to a place: *He was in and out of jail for most of his life.*

■ adj. [usually before noun] (informal) popular and fashionable: *Purple is the in colour this spring.* ◇ *Exotic pets are the in thing right now.* ◇ *Short skirts are in again.*—see also IN-JOKE

■ noun IDM **the ,ins and 'outs (of sth)** all the details, especially the complicated or difficult ones: *the ins and outs of the problem* ◇ *He quickly learned the ins and outs of the job.*

in. abbr. (pl. **in.** or **ins.**) INCH: *Height: 6ft 2in.*

in- prefix /ɪn/ **1** (also **il-** /ɪl/ **im-** /ɪm/ **ir-** /ɪr/) (in adjectives, adverbs and nouns) not; the opposite of: *infinite* ◇

æ	ɑː	e	ɜː	ə	ɪ	iː	i	ɒ	ɔː	ʌ	ʊ	u	uː
cat	father	ten	bird	about	sit	see	many	got	saw	cup	put	actual	too
								(BrE)					

illogical ◇ *immorally* ◇ *irrelevance* **2** (also **im-** /ɪm/) (in verbs) to put into the condition mentioned: *inflame* ◇ *imperil*

-in *combining form* (in nouns) an activity in which many people take part: *a sit-in* ◇ *a teach-in*

in·abil·ity /ˌɪnəˈbɪləti/ *noun* [U, sing.] **~ (to do sth)** the fact of not being able to do sth: *the government's inability to provide basic services* ◇ *Some families go without medical treatment because of their inability to pay.* OPP ABILITY

in ab·sen·tia /ˌɪn æbˈsenʃiə/ *adv.* (from *Latin*) while not present at the event being referred to: *Two foreign suspects will be tried in absentia.*

in·access·ible /ˌɪnækˈsesəbl/ *adj.* **~ (to sb/sth)** difficult or impossible to reach or to get: *They live in a remote area, inaccessible except by car.* ◇ *Dirt can collect in inaccessible places.* ◇ *The temple is now inaccessible to the public.* ◇ (*figurative*) *The language of teenagers is often completely inaccessible to* (= not understood by) *adults.* OPP ACCESSIBLE ▶ **in·access·ibil·ity** /ˌɪnækˌsesəˈbɪləti/ *noun* [U]

in·accur·ate /ɪnˈækjərət/ *adj.* not exact or accurate; with mistakes: *an inaccurate statement/measurement/ description* ◇ *inaccurate information* ◇ *All the maps we had were wildly inaccurate.* OPP ACCURATE ▶ **in·accur·acy** /ɪnˈækjərəsi/ *noun* [C, U] (*pl.* **-ies**): *The article is full of inaccuracies.* ◇ *The writer is guilty of bias and inaccuracy.* **in·accur·ate·ly** *adv.*

in·action /ɪnˈækʃn/ *noun* [U] (usually *disapproving*) lack of action; the state of doing nothing about a situation or a problem: *The police were accused of inaction in the face of a possible attack.*

in·active /ɪnˈæktɪv/ *adj.* **1** not doing anything; not active: *Some animals are inactive during the daytime.* ◇ *The area has a large, but politically inactive population.* ◇ *The volcano has been inactive for 50 years.* **2** not in use; not working: *an inactive oil well* **3** having no effect: *an inactive drug/disease* OPP ACTIVE ▶ **in·activ·ity** /ˌɪnækˈtɪvəti/ *noun* [U]: *periods of enforced inactivity and boredom* ◇ *The inactivity of the government was deplorable.*

in·ad·equacy /ɪnˈædɪkwəsi/ *noun* (*pl.* **-ies**) **1** [U] **~ (of sth)** the state of not being enough or good enough: *the inadequacy of our resources* OPP ADEQUACY **2** [U] a state of not being able or confident to deal with a situation: *a feeling/sense of inadequacy* **3** [C, usually pl.] **~ (of/in sth)** a weakness; a lack of sth: *gross inadequacies in the data* ◇ *He had to face up to his own inadequacies as a father.*

in·ad·equate /ɪnˈædɪkwət/ *adj.* **1 ~ (for sth)|~ (to do sth)** not enough; not good enough: *inadequate supplies/ resources/preparation* ◇ *The system is inadequate for the tasks it has to perform.* ◇ *The food supplies are inadequate to meet the needs of the hungry.* OPP ADEQUATE **2** (of people) not able, or not confident enough, to deal with a situation: *I felt totally inadequate as a parent.* ▶ **in·ad·equate·ly** *adv.*: *to be inadequately prepared/insured/ funded*

in·ad·mis·sible /ˌɪnədˈmɪsəbl/ *adj.* (*formal*) that cannot be allowed or accepted, especially in a court of law: *inadmissible evidence* OPP ADMISSIBLE

in·ad·vert·ent·ly /ˌɪnədˈvɜːtəntli; *AmE* -ˈvɜːrt-/ *adv.* by accident; without intending to: *We had inadvertently left without paying the bill.* ▶ **in·ad·vert·ent** *adj.*: *an inadvertent omission* **in·ad·ver·tence** *noun* [U]

in·ad·vis·able /ˌɪnədˈvaɪzəbl/ *adj.* [not usually before noun] **~ (for sb) (to do sth)** (*formal*) not sensible or wise; that you would advise against: *It is inadvisable to bring children on this trip.* OPP ADVISABLE

in·ali·en·able /ɪnˈeɪliənəbl/ *adj.* [usually before noun] (*formal*) that cannot be taken away from you: *the inalienable right to decide your own future*

inane /ɪˈneɪn/ *adj.* stupid or silly; with no meaning: *an inane remark* ▶ **in·ane·ly** *adv.*: *to grin inanely* **in·an·ity** /ɪˈnænəti/ *noun* [U, C, usually pl.] (*pl.* **-ies**)

in·ani·mate /ɪnˈænɪmət/ *adj.* not alive in the way that people, animals and plants are: *A rock is an inanimate object.* OPP ANIMATE

in·applic·able /ˌɪnəˈplɪkəbl; ɪnˈæplɪkəbl/ *adj.* [not before noun] **~ (to sb/sth)** that cannot be used, or that does not apply, in a particular situation: *These regulations are inapplicable to international students.* OPP APPLICABLE

in·appro·pri·ate /ˌɪnəˈprəʊpriət; *AmE* -ˈproʊ-/ *adj.* **~ (for sb/sth) (to do sth)|~ (to/for sth)** not suitable or appropriate in a particular situation: *inappropriate behaviour/language* ◇ *It would be inappropriate for me to comment on what your tutor said.* ◇ *clothes inappropriate to the occasion* OPP APPROPRIATE ▶ **in·appro·pri·ate·ly** *adv.*: *She was inappropriately dressed for a funeral.* **in·appro·pri·ate·ness** *noun* [U]

in·articu·late /ˌɪnɑːˈtɪkjələt; *AmE* -ɑːrˈtɪk-/ *adj.* **1** (of people) not able to express ideas or feelings clearly or easily **2** (of speech) not using clear words; not expressed clearly: *an inarticulate reply/speech* OPP ARTICULATE ▶ **in·articu·late·ly** *adv.*

in·as·much as /ˌɪnəzˈmʌtʃ əz/ *conj.* (*formal, written*) used to add a comment on sth that you have just said and to say in what way it is true: *He was a very unusual musician inasmuch as he was totally deaf.*

in·atten·tion /ˌɪnəˈtenʃn/ *noun* [U] **~ (to sth/sb)** (usually *disapproving*) lack of attention: *They complained about his inattention to his patients.* ◇ *The accident was the result of a moment's inattention.*

in·atten·tive /ˌɪnəˈtentɪv/ *adj.* **~ (to sth/sb)** (*disapproving*) not paying attention to sth/sb: *an inattentive pupil* ◇ *inattentive to the needs of others* OPP ATTENTIVE ▶ **in·atten·tive·ly** *adv.*

in·aud·ible /ɪnˈɔːdəbl/ *adj.* **~ (to sb)** that you cannot hear: *She spoke in an almost inaudible whisper.* ◇ *The whistle was inaudible to the human ear.* OPP AUDIBLE ▶ **in·audi·bil·ity** /ɪnˌɔːdəˈbɪləti/ *noun* [U] **in·aud·ibly** /ɪnˈɔːdəbli/ *adv.*

in·aug·ural /ɪˈnɔːgjərəl/ *adj.* [only before noun] (of an official speech, meeting, etc.) first, and marking the beginning of sth important, for example the time when a new leader or parliament starts work, when a new organization is formed or when sth is used for the first time: *the President's inaugural address* ◇ *the professor's inaugural lecture* ◇ *the inaugural meeting of the geographical society* ◇ *the inaugural flight of the space shuttle* ▶ **in·aug·ural** *noun* [C, usually sing.] (*especially AmE*): *the presidential inaugural in January*

in·aug·ur·ate /ɪˈnɔːgjəreɪt/ *verb* **1 ~ sb (as sth)** to introduce a new public official or leader at a special ceremony: [VN-N] *He will be inaugurated (as) President in January.* [also VN] **2** [VN] to officially open a building or start an organization with a special ceremony: *The new theatre was inaugurated by the mayor.* **3** [VN] (*formal*) to introduce a new development or an important change: *The moon landing inaugurated a new era in space exploration.* ▶ **in·aug·ur·ation** /ɪˌnɔːgjəˈreɪʃn/ *noun* [U, C]: *the President's inauguration* ◇ *an inauguration speech*

in·aus·pi·cious /ˌɪnɔːˈspɪʃəs/ *adj.* (*formal*) showing signs that the future will not be good or successful: *an inauspicious start* OPP AUSPICIOUS ▶ **in·aus·pi·cious·ly** *adv.*

in·authen·tic /ˌɪnɔːˈθentɪk/ *adj.* not genuine; that you cannot believe or rely on OPP AUTHENTIC ▶ **in·authen·ti·city** /ˌɪnɔːθenˈtɪsəti/ *noun* [U]

in·born /ˌɪnˈbɔːn; *AmE* -ˈbɔːrn/ (also *less frequent* **in·bred**) *adj.* an **inborn** quality is one that you are born with SYN INNATE: *Some people have an inborn tendency to put on weight.*

in·bound /ˈɪnbaʊnd/ *adj.* (*formal*) travelling towards a place rather than leaving it: *inbound flights/passengers* OPP OUTBOUND

'in box *noun* (*AmE*) = IN TRAY

in·bred /ˌɪnˈbred/ *adj.* **1** produced by breeding among closely related members of a group of animals, people or plants: *an inbred racehorse* **2** (*rare*) = INBORN

in·breed·ing /ˈɪnbriːdɪŋ/ *noun* [U] breeding between closely related people or animals

in·built /ˈɪnbɪlt/ *adj.* [only before noun] an **inbuilt** quality exists as an essential part of sth/sb: *His height gives*

aɪ	aʊ	eɪ	əʊ	oʊ	ɔɪ	ɪə	eə	ʊə	j	w
my	now	say	go (BrE)	go (AmE)	boy	near	hair	pure	yes	wet

him an inbuilt advantage over his opponent.—compare
BUILT-IN

in·built /'ɪn'bɪlt/ adj. (rare) = BUILT-IN

Inc. (also **inc**) /ɪŋk/ abbr. Incorporated (used after the
name of a company in the US): *Texaco Inc.*

inc. abbr. (BrE) = INCL.

in·cal·cul·able /ɪn'kælkjələbl/ adj. (formal) very large
or very great; too great to calculate: *The oil spill has
caused incalculable damage to the environment.* ◇ *The
treasures are of incalculable value.*—compare CALCULABLE
▸ **in·cal·cul·ably** /-əbli/ adv.

in·can·des·cent /ˌɪnkæn'desnt/ adj. **1** (technical) giving out light when heated: *incandescent lamps* **2** (formal)
very bright: *incandescent white* **3** (formal) full of strong
emotion: *an incandescent musical performance* ◇ *She was
incandescent with rage.* ▸ **in·can·des·cence** /-sns/ noun
[U]

in·can·ta·tion /ˌɪnkæn'teɪʃn/ noun [C, U] special words
that are spoken or sung to have a magic effect; the act of
speaking or singing these words

in·cap·able /ɪn'keɪpəbl/ adj. **1 ~ of sth/of doing sth** not
able to do sth: *incapable of speech/movement* ◇ *The children seem to be totally incapable of working by themselves.*
2 not able to control yourself or your affairs; not able to
do anything well: *He was found lying in the road, drunk
and incapable.* ◇ *If people keep telling you you're incapable, you begin to lose confidence in yourself.* OPP CAPABLE

in·cap·aci·tate /ˌɪnkə'pæsɪteɪt/ verb [VN] [usually pas-
sive] (formal) to make sb unable to live or work normally: *He was incapacitated by old age and sickness.*

in·cap·acity /ˌɪnkə'pæsəti/ noun [U] (written) **1 ~** (of
sb/sth) (to do sth) lack of ability or skill SYN INABILITY:
their incapacity to govern effectively **2** the state of being
too ill to do your work or look after yourself: *She returned
to work after a long period of incapacity.*

in·car·cer·ate /ɪn'kɑːsəreɪt/ AmE -'kɑːrs-/ verb [VN] [usu-
ally passive] **~ sb (in sth)** (formal) to put sb in prison or
in another place from which they cannot escape SYN
IMPRISON: *Thousands were incarcerated in labour camps.*
▸ **in·car·cer·ation** /ɪnˌkɑːsə'reɪʃn/ AmE -ˌkɑːrs-/ noun
[U]

in·car·nate adj., verb
■ adj. /ɪn'kɑːnət/ AmE -'kɑːrn-/ (usually after nouns)
(formal) in human form: *The leader seemed the devil
incarnate.* ◇ *My aunt is generosity incarnate.*
■ verb /'ɪnkɑːneɪt/ AmE -kɑːrn-/ [VN] (formal) to give a definite or human form to a particular idea or quality

in·car·na·tion /ˌɪnkɑː'neɪʃn/ AmE -kɑːr'n-/ noun **1** [C] a
period of life in a particular form: *one of the incarnations
of Vishnu* ◇ *He believed he had been a prince in a previous
incarnation.* ◇ (figurative) *I worked for her in her earlier
incarnation* (= her previous job) *as a lawyer.* **2** [C] a
person who represents a particular quality, for example,
in human form: *the incarnation of evil* **3** [sing., U] (also
the Incarnation) (in Christianity) the act of God coming
to earth in human form as Jesus

in·cau·tious /ɪn'kɔːʃəs/ adj. (formal) done without
thinking carefully about the results; not thinking about
what might happen ▸ **in·cau·tious·ly** adv.

in·cen·di·ary /ɪn'sendiəri/ AmE -dieri/ adj., noun
■ adj. [only before noun] **1** designed to cause fires: *an
incendiary device/bomb/attack* **2** (formal) causing strong
feelings or violence: *incendiary remarks*
■ noun (pl. **-ies**) a bomb that is designed to make a fire start
burning when it explodes SYN FIREBOMB

in·cense noun, verb
■ noun /'ɪnsens/ [U] a substance that produces a pleasant
smell when you burn it, used particularly in religious
ceremonies
■ verb /ɪn'sens/ [VN] [usually passive] to make sb very
angry: *The decision incensed the workforce.* ◇ *The workforce was incensed by the decision.* ◇ *She was incensed at
the idea.*

in·cen·tive /ɪn'sentɪv/ noun [C, U] **~ (for/to sb/sth) (to
do sth)** something that encourages you to do sth: *tax
incentives to encourage savings* ◇ *There is no incentive for
people to save fuel.* OPP DISINCENTIVE

in·cep·tion /ɪn'sepʃn/ noun [sing.] (formal) the start of
an institution, an organization, etc: *The club has grown
rapidly since its inception in 1990.*

in·ces·sant /ɪn'sesnt/ adj. (usually disapproving) never
stopping: *incessant noise/rain/chatter* ◇ *incessant meetings* ▸ **in·ces·sant·ly** adv.: *to talk incessantly*

in·cest /'ɪnsest/ noun [U] sexual activity between two
people who are very closely related in a family, for
example, a brother and sister, or a father and daughter

in·ces·tu·ous /ɪn'sestjuəs; AmE -tʃuəs/ adj. **1** involving
sex between two people in a family who are very closely
related: *an incestuous relationship* **2** (disapproving)
involving a group of people who have a close relationship
and do not want to include anyone outside the group: *The
music industry is an incestuous business.* ▸ **in·ces·tu-
ous·ly** adv.

inch /ɪntʃ/ noun, verb
■ noun **1** (abbr. **in.**) a unit for measuring length, equal to
2.54 CENTIMETRES. There are twelve inches in a FOOT: *1.14
inches of rain fell last night.* ◇ *She's a few inches taller
than me.* **2** a small amount or distance: *He escaped death
by an inch.* ◇ *The car missed us by inches.* ◇ *Ronaldo was
just inches away from scoring.* IDM **every inch 1** the
whole of sth: *The doctor examined every inch of his body.* ◇
(figurative) *If they try to fire me I'll fight them every inch
of the way.* **2** completely: *In his first game the young
player already looked every inch a winner.* **give sb an
'inch (and they'll take a 'mile/'yard)** (saying) used to
say that if you allow some people a small amount of
freedom or power they will see you as weak and try to
take a lot more **,inch by 'inch** very slowly and with great
care or difficulty: *She crawled forward inch by inch.* **not
budge/give/move an 'inch** to refuse to change your
position, decision, etc. even a little: *We tried to negotiate a
lower price but they wouldn't budge an inch.* **within an
'inch of sth/of doing sth** very close to sth/doing sth:
She was within an inch of being killed. ◇ *They beat him
within an inch of his life* (= very severely).—more at
TRUST v.
■ verb [+adv./prep.] to move or make sth move slowly and
carefully in a particular direction: [V] *She moved forward,
inching towards the rope.* ◇ [VN] *I inched the car forward.* ◇
He inched his way through the narrow passage.

in·cho·ate /ɪn'kəʊət; 'ɪnkəʊeɪt; AmE -'koʊ-/ adj. (rare,
formal) just begun and therefore not clear or developed:
inchoate ideas

in·ci·dence /'ɪnsɪdəns/ noun **1** [C, usually sing.] **~ of
sth** (written) the extent to which sth happens or has an
effect: *an area with a high incidence of crime/disease/
unemployment* **2** [U] (technical) the way in which a ray of
light meets a surface: *the angle of incidence*

in·ci·dent /'ɪnsɪdənt/ noun **1** [C] something that happens, especially sth unusual or unpleasant: *His bad behaviour was just an isolated incident.* ◇ *One particular
incident sticks in my mind.* **2** [C, U] a serious or violent
event, such as a crime, an accident or an attack: *There
was a shooting incident near here last night.* ◇ (BrE) *The
police are setting up an* **incident room** (= where they can collect evidence, etc.). ◇ *The
demonstration passed off* **without incident.** **3** [C] a dis-
agreement between two countries, often involving military forces: *a border/diplomatic incident* ⇨ note at EVENT

in·ci·den·tal /ˌɪnsɪ'dentl/ adj., noun
■ adj. **1 ~ (to sth)** happening in connection with sth else,
but not as important as it, or not intended: *The discovery
was incidental to their main research.* ◇ **incidental music**
(= music used with a play or a film/movie to give
atmosphere) ◇ *You may be able to get help with* **incidental
expenses** (= small costs that you get in connection with
sth). **2 ~ to sth** (technical) happening as a natural result
of sth: *These risks are incidental to the work of a fire-
fighter.*
■ noun [usually pl.] something that happens in connection
with sth else, but is less important: *You'll need money for
incidentals such as tips and taxis.*

in·ci·den·tal·ly /ˌɪnsɪ'dentli/ adv. **1** used to introduce a
new topic, or some extra information, or a question that

you have just thought of [SYN] BY THE WAY: *Incidentally, have you heard the news about Sue?* **2** in a way that was not planned but that is connected with sth else: *The information was only discovered incidentally.*

in·cin·er·ate /ɪnˈsɪnəreɪt/ *verb* [VN] [often passive] to burn sth until it is completely destroyed: *Most of the waste is incinerated.* ▶ **in·cin·er·ation** /ɪnˌsɪnəˈreɪʃn/ *noun* [U]: *high-temperature incineration plants*

in·cin·er·ator /ɪnˈsɪnəreɪtə(r)/ *noun* an enclosed container for burning waste at high temperatures

in·cipi·ent /ɪnˈsɪpiənt/ *adj.* [usually before noun] (*formal*) just beginning: *signs of incipient unrest*

in·cise /ɪnˈsaɪz/ *verb* [VN] ~ sth (in/on/onto sth) (*formal*) to cut words, designs, etc. into a surface—compare ENGRAVE

in·ci·sion /ɪnˈsɪʒn/ *noun* [C, U] a sharp cut made in sth, particularly during a medical operation; the act of making a cut in sth: *Make a small incision below the ribs.*

in·ci·sive /ɪnˈsaɪsɪv/ *adj.* (*approving*) **1** showing clear thought and good understanding of what is important, and the ability to express this: *incisive comments / criticism / analysis* ◊ *an incisive mind* **2** showing sb's ability to take decisions and act forcefully: *an incisive performance* ▶ **in·ci·sive·ly** *adv.* **in·ci·sive·ness** *noun* [U]

in·ci·sor /ɪnˈsaɪzə(r)/ *noun* one of the eight sharp teeth at the front of the mouth that are used for biting—compare CANINE, MOLAR

in·cite /ɪnˈsaɪt/ *verb* ~ sb (to sth) | ~ sth to encourage sb to do sth violent, illegal or unpleasant, especially by making them angry or excited: [VN] *to incite crime / racial hatred / violence* ◊ *They were accused of inciting the crowd to violence.* ◊ [VN to inf] *He incited the workforce to come out on strike.*

in·cite·ment /ɪnˈsaɪtmənt/ *noun* [U, C] ~ (to sth) the act of encouraging sb to do sth violent, illegal or unpleasant: *incitement to racial hatred*

in·civil·ity /ˌɪnsəˈvɪləti/ *noun* [U, C] (*pl.* **-ies**) (*formal*) rude behaviour; rude remarks—see also UNCIVIL

incl. (*BrE* also **inc.**) *abbr.* **1** (in advertisements) including; included: *transport not incl.* ◊ *£29.53 inc. tax* **2** INCLUSIVE: *Open 1 April to 31 October incl.*

in·clem·ent /ɪnˈklemənt/ *adj.* (*formal*) (of the weather) not pleasant; cold, wet, etc. [OPP] CLEMENT ▶ **in·clem·ency** /-ənsi/ *noun* [U]

in·clin·ation /ˌɪnklɪˈneɪʃn/ *noun* **1** [U, C] ~ (to do sth) | ~ (towards / for sth) a feeling that makes you want to do sth: *He did not show the slightest inclination to leave.* ◊ *My natural inclination is to find a compromise.* ◊ *She lacked any inclination for housework.* ◊ *He was a loner by nature and by inclination.* ◊ *She had neither the time nor the inclination to help them.* ◊ *You must follow your own inclinations when choosing a career.* **2** [C] ~ to do sth a tendency to do sth: *There is an inclination to treat geography as a less important subject.* **3** [C usually sing, U] (*technical*) a degree of sloping: *an inclination of 45°* ◊ *the angle of inclination* **4** [C] a small downward movement, usually of the head

in·cline *verb, noun*
■ *verb* /ɪnˈklaɪn/ (*formal*) **1** ~ (sb) to/towards sth to tend to think or behave in a particular way; to make sb do this: [V] *I incline to the view that we should take no action at this stage.* ◊ [V to inf] *The government is more effective than we incline to think.* ◊ [VN] *Lack of money inclines many young people towards crime.* ◊ [VN to inf] *His obvious sincerity inclined me to trust him.* **2** [VN] ~ your head to bend your head forward, especially as a sign of agreement, greeting, etc. **3** ~ (sth) (to/towards sth) to lean or slope in a particular direction; to make sth lean or slope: [V] *The land inclined gently towards the shore.* [also VN]
■ *noun* /ˈɪnklaɪn/ (*formal*) a steep / slight incline

in·clined /ɪnˈklaɪnd/ *adj.* **1** [not before noun] ~ (to do sth) wanting to do sth: *She was inclined to trust him.* ◊ *He writes only when he feels inclined to.* ◊ *There'll be time for a swim if you feel so inclined.* **2** ~ to do sth tending to do sth; likely to do sth: *He's inclined to be lazy.* ◊ *They'll be more inclined to listen if you don't shout.* **3** ~ to agree, believe, think, etc. used when you are expressing an

opinion but do not want to express it very strongly: *I'm inclined to agree with you.* **4** (used with particular adverbs) having a natural ability for sth; preferring to do sth: *musically / academically inclined children* **5** sloping; at an angle

in·clude /ɪnˈkluːd/ *verb* **1** (not used in the progressive tenses) if one thing **includes** another, it has the second thing as one of its parts: [VN] *The tour included a visit to the Science Museum.* ◊ *Does the price include tax?* ◊ [V-ing] *Your duties include typing letters and answering the telephone.* ⇨ note at COMPRISE **2** [VN] ~ sb/sth (as/in/on sth) to make sb/sth part of sth: *You should include some examples in your essay.* ◊ *We all went, me included.* ◊ *Representatives from the country were included as observers at the conference.* [OPP] EXCLUDE

in·clud·ing /ɪnˈkluːdɪŋ/ *prep.* (*abbr.* **incl.**) having sth as part of a group or set: *I've got three days' holiday including New Year's Day.* ◊ *Six people were killed in the riot, including a policeman.* ◊ *It's £7·50, including tax.* [OPP] EXCLUDING

in·clu·sion /ɪnˈkluːʒn/ *noun* **1** [U] the fact of including sb/sth; the fact of being included: *His inclusion in the team is in doubt.* **2** [C] a person or thing that is included: *There were some surprising inclusions in the list.* [OPP] EXCLUSION

in·clu·sive /ɪnˈkluːsɪv/ *adj.* **1** ~ (of sth) having the total cost, or the cost of sth that is mentioned, contained in the price: *The fully inclusive fare for the trip is £52.* ◊ *The rent is inclusive of water and heating.* [OPP] EXCLUSIVE **2** from … to … inclusive including all the days, months, numbers, etc. mentioned: *We are offering free holidays for children aged two to eleven inclusive.* ◊ *The castle is open daily from May to October inclusive.* **3** including a wide range of people, things, ideas, etc: *The party must adopt more inclusive strategies and a broader vision.* [OPP] EXCLUSIVE ▶ **in·clu·sive·ly** *adv.*: *The word 'men' can be understood inclusively* (= including men and women). **in·clu·sive·ness** *noun* [U]

BRITISH / AMERICAN
inclusive / through

In *BrE* **inclusive** is used to emphasize that you are including the days, months, numbers, etc. mentioned, especially in formal or official situations: *Answer questions 8 to 12 inclusive.* ◊ *The amusement park is open daily from May to October inclusive.*

In *AmE* **through** is used: *Answer questions 8 through 12.* ◊ *The amusement park is open (from) May through October.*

To can also be used with this meaning in *BrE* and *AmE*: *The park is open from 1 May to 31 October.*

in·cog·nito /ˌɪnkɒgˈniːtəʊ; *AmE* ˌɪnkɑːgˈniːtoʊ/ *adv.* in a way that prevents other people from finding out who you are: *Movie stars often prefer to travel incognito.* ▶ **in·cog·nito** *adj.*: *an incognito visit*

in·co·her·ent /ˌɪnkəʊˈhɪərənt; *AmE* ˌɪnkoʊˈhɪr-/ *adj.* **1** (of people) unable to express yourself clearly, often because of emotion: *She broke off, incoherent with anger.* [OPP] COHERENT **2** (of sounds) not clear and hard to understand [SYN] UNINTELLIGIBLE: *Rachel whispered something incoherent.* **3** not logical or well organized: *an incoherent text / policy* [OPP] COHERENT ▶ **in·co·her·ence** /-əns/ *noun* [U] **in·co·her·ent·ly** *adv.*

in·come /ˈɪnkʌm; -kəm/ *noun* [C, U] the money that a person, a region, a country, etc. earns from work, from investing money from business, etc: *people on high / low incomes* ◊ *a weekly disposable income* (= the money that you have left to spend after tax, etc.) *of £200* ◊ *a rise in national income* ◊ *They receive a proportion of their income from the sale of goods and services.* ◊ *Tourism is a major source of income for the area.* ◊ *higher / middle / lower income groups*—compare EXPENDITURE

in·comer /ˈɪnkʌmə(r)/ *noun* (*BrE*) a person who comes to live in a particular place

s	t	v	z	ʃ	ʒ	tʃ	dʒ	θ	ð	ŋ
see	tea	van	zoo	shoe	vision	chain	jam	thin	this	sing

'income support *noun* [U] (in Britain) the money that the government pays to people who have no income or a very low income

'income tax *noun* [U, C] the amount of money that you pay to the government according to how much you earn: *The standard rate of income tax was cut to 23p in the pound.*

in·com·ing /ˈɪnkʌmɪŋ/ *adj.* [only before noun] **1** recently elected or chosen: *the incoming government/ president/administration* OPP OUTGOING (2) **2** arriving somewhere, or being received: *incoming flights* ◊ *the incoming tide* ◊ *incoming calls/mail/information* OPP OUTGOING (3)

in·com·men·sur·able /ˌɪnkəˈmenʃərəbl/ *adj.* **~ (with sth)** (*rare, formal*) if two things are **incommensurable**, they are so completely different from each other that they cannot be compared

in·com·mu·ni·cado /ˌɪnkəˌmjuːnɪˈkɑːdəʊ; *AmE* -ˈkɑːdoʊ/ *adj.* without communicating with other people, because you are not allowed to or because you do not want to: *The prisoner has been* **held incommunicado** *for more than a week.* ◊ *She spent her fortieth birthday incommunicado, in Scotland.*

in·com·par·able /ɪnˈkɒmprəbl; *AmE* -ˈkɑːm-/ *adj.* so good or impressive that nothing can be compared to it: *the incomparable beauty of Lake Garda* ◊ *the incomparable Frank Sinatra* ▶ **in·com·par·abil·ity** /ɪnˌkɒmpərəˈbɪləti; *AmE* -ˌkɑːm-/ *noun* [U] **in·com·par·ably** /ɪnˈkɒmprəbli; *AmE* -ˈkɑːm-/ *adv.*: *Her latest book is incomparably better than her earlier ones.*

in·com·pat·ible /ˌɪnkəmˈpætəbl/ *adj.* **1 ~ (with sth)** two actions, ideas, etc. that are **incompatible** are not acceptable or possible together because of basic differences: *The hours of the job are incompatible with family life.* ◊ *These two objectives are* **mutually incompatible.** **2** two people who are **incompatible** are very different from each other and so are not able to live or work happily together: *She and her husband soon proved to be totally incompatible.* **3 ~ (with sth)** two things that are **incompatible** are of different types so that they cannot be used or mixed together: *New computer software is often incompatible with older computers.* ◊ *Those two blood groups are incompatible.* OPP COMPATIBLE ▶ **in·com·pati·bil·ity** /ˌɪnkəmˌpætəˈbɪləti/ *noun* [U, C] (*pl.* **-ies**)

in·com·pe·tence /ɪnˈkɒmpɪtəns; *AmE* -ˈkɑːm-/ *noun* [U] the lack of skill or ability to do your job or a task as it should be done: *professional/managerial incompetence* ◊ *government/police incompetence* ◊ *He was dismissed for incompetence.*

in·com·pe·tent /ɪnˈkɒmpɪtənt; *AmE* -ˈkɑːm-/ *adj., noun*
■ *adj.* not having the skill or ability to do your job or a task as it should be done: *an incompetent teacher/manager* ◊ *his incompetent handling of the affair* ◊ *The Prime Minister was attacked as incompetent to lead.* OPP COMPETENT ▶ **in·com·pe·tent·ly** *adv.*
■ *noun* a person who does not have the skill or ability to do their job or a task as it should be done

in·com·plete /ˌɪnkəmˈpliːt/ *adj., noun*
■ *adj.* not having everything that it should have; not finished or complete: *an incomplete set of figures* ◊ *Spoken language contains many incomplete sentences.* OPP COMPLETE ▶ **in·com·plete·ly** *adv.*: *The causes of the phenomenon are still incompletely understood.* **in·com·plete·ness** *noun* [U]
■ *noun* (*AmE*) the grade that a student gets for a course of education when they have not completed all the work for that course

in·com·pre·hen·sible /ˌɪnˌkɒmprɪˈhensəbl; *AmE* -ˌkɑːm-/ *adj.* **~ (to sb)** impossible to understand SYN UNINTELLIGIBLE: *Some application forms can be incomprehensible to ordinary people.* ◊ *He found his son's actions totally incomprehensible.* OPP COMPREHENSIBLE ▶ **in·com·pre·hen·si·bil·ity** /ɪnˌkɒmprɪˌhensəˈbɪləti; *AmE* -ˌkɑːm-/ *noun* **in·com·pre·hen·sibly** /-səbli/ *adv.*

in·com·pre·hen·sion /ˌɪnˌkɒmprɪˈhenʃn; *AmE* -ˌkɑːm-/ *noun* [U] the state of not being able to understand sb/sth: *Anna read the letter with incomprehension.*

in·con·ceiv·able /ˌɪnkənˈsiːvəbl/ *adj.* impossible to imagine or believe SYN UNTHINKABLE: *It is inconceivable that the minister was not aware of the problem.* OPP CONCEIVABLE ▶ **in·con·ceiv·ably** *adv.*: *She was inconceivably wealthy.*

in·con·clu·sive /ˌɪnkənˈkluːsɪv/ *adj.* not leading to a definite decision or result: *inconclusive evidence/results/ tests* ◊ *inconclusive talks/discussions* OPP CONCLUSIVE ▶ **in·con·clu·sive·ly** *adv.*: *The last meeting had ended inconclusively.*

in·con·gru·ous /ɪnˈkɒŋgruəs; *AmE* -ˈkɑːŋ-/ *adj.* strange, and not suitable in a particular situation: *Such traditional methods seem incongruous in our technical age.* ▶ **in·con·gru·ity** /ˌɪnkɒnˈgruːəti; *AmE* ˌɪnkɑːn-/ *noun* [U, C] (*pl.* **-ies**): *She was struck by the incongruity of the situation.* **in·con·gru·ous·ly** *adv.*: *incongruously dressed*

in·con·se·quen·tial /ɪnˌkɒnsɪˈkwenʃl; *AmE* -ˌkɑːn-/ *adj.* not important or worth considering SYN TRIVIAL: *inconsequential details* ◊ *inconsequential chatter* OPP CONSEQUENTIAL ▶ **in·con·se·quen·tial·ly** /-ʃəli/ *adv.*

in·con·sid·er·able /ˌɪnkənˈsɪdrəbl/ *adj.* IDM **not inconsiderable** (*formal*) large; large enough to be considered important: *We have spent a not inconsiderable amount of money on the project already.*

in·con·sid·er·ate /ˌɪnkənˈsɪdərət/ *adj.* (*disapproving*) not giving enough thought to other people's feelings or needs SYN THOUGHTLESS: *inconsiderate behaviour/ remarks* ◊ *It was inconsiderate of you not to call.* OPP CONSIDERATE ▶ **in·con·sid·er·ate·ly** *adv.*

in·con·sis·tent /ˌɪnkənˈsɪstənt/ *adj.* **1** [not usually before noun] **~ (with sth)** if two statements, etc. are **inconsistent**, or one is **inconsistent with** the other, they cannot both be true because they give the facts in a different way: *The report is inconsistent with the financial statements.* ◊ *The witnesses' statements were inconsistent.* **2 ~ with sth** not matching a set of standards, ideas, etc: *Her behaviour was clearly inconsistent with her beliefs.* **3** (*disapproving*) tending to change too often; not staying the same: *inconsistent results* ◊ *Children find it difficult if a parent is inconsistent.* OPP CONSISTENT ▶ **in·con·sis·tency** /-ənsi/ *noun* [U, C] (*pl.* **-ies**): *There is some inconsistency between the witnesses' evidence and their earlier statements.* ◊ *I noticed a few minor inconsistencies in her argument.* **in·con·sis·tent·ly** *adv.*

in·con·sol·able /ˌɪnkənˈsəʊləbl; *AmE* -ˈsoʊl-/ *adj.* very sad and unable to accept help or comfort: *They were inconsolable when their only child died.* ▶ **in·con·sol·ably** /-əbli/ *adv.*: *to weep inconsolably*

in·con·spicu·ous /ˌɪnkənˈspɪkjuəs/ *adj.* not attracting attention; not easy to notice: *She tried to look as inconspicuous as possible.* OPP CONSPICUOUS ▶ **in·con·spicu·ous·ly** *adv.*

in·con·stant /ɪnˈkɒnstənt; *AmE* -ˈkɑːn-/ *adj.* (*formal*) not faithful in love or friendship SYN FICKLE OPP CONSTANT ▶ **in·con·stancy** /-ənsi/ *noun* [U]

in·con·test·able /ˌɪnkənˈtestəbl/ *adj.* (*formal*) that is true and cannot be disagreed with or DENIED: *an incontestable right/fact* ▶ **in·con·test·ably** /-əbli/ *adv.*

in·con·tin·ence /ɪnˈkɒntɪnəns; *AmE* -ˈkɑːn-/ *noun* [U] the lack of ability to control the BLADDER and bowels OPP CONTINENCE ▶ **in·con·tin·ent** /-ənt/ *adj.*: *Many of our patients are incontinent.*

in·con·tro·vert·ible /ˌɪnkɒntrəˈvɜːtəbl; *AmE* ˌɪnkɑːn-trəˈvɜːrt-/ *adj.* (*formal*) that is true and cannot be disagreed with or DENIED: *incontrovertible evidence/proof* ▶ **in·con·tro·vert·ibly** /ˌɪnkɒntrəˈvɜːtəbli; *AmE* ˌɪnkɑːn-trəˈvɜːrt-/ *adv.*

in·con·veni·ence /ˌɪnkənˈviːniəns/ *noun, verb*
■ *noun* **1** [U] trouble or problems, especially concerning what you need or would like yourself: *We apologize for the delay and regret any inconvenience it may have caused.* ◊ *I have already been put to considerable inconvenience.* **2** [C] a person or thing that causes problems or difficulties: *I can put up with minor inconveniences.*
■ *verb* [VN] to cause trouble or difficulty for sb: *I hope that we haven't inconvenienced you.*

in·con·veni·ent /ˌɪnkənˈviːniənt/ *adj.* causing trouble

æ	ɑː	e	ɜː	ə	ɪ	iː	i	ɒ	ɔː	ʌ	ʊ	u	uː
cat	father	ten	bird	about	sit	see	many	got	saw	cup	put	actual	too
								(BrE)					

or problems, especially concerning what you need or would like yourself: *an inconvenient time/place* ◊ *That's most inconvenient for me. I'm working that weekend.* OPP CONVENIENT ▶ **in·con·veni·ent·ly** *adv.*

in·cor·por·ate /ɪn'kɔːpəreɪt; AmE -'kɔːrp-/ *verb* [VN] ~ **sth (in/into/within sth)** to include sth so that it forms a part of sth: *Many of your suggestions have been incorporated in the plan.* ◊ *The new car design incorporates all the latest safety features.* ◊ *We have incorporated all the latest safety features into the design.* ▶ **in·corp·or·ation** /ɪnˌkɔːpə'reɪʃn; AmE -ˌkɔːrp-/ *noun* [U]: *the incorporation of foreign words into the language*

in·corp·or·ated /ɪn'kɔːpəreɪtɪd; AmE -'kɔːrp-/ *adj.* (*abbr.* **Inc.**) (*business*) formed into a business company with legal status

in·cor·por·eal /ˌɪnkɔː'pɔːriəl; AmE -kɔːr'p-/ *adj.* (*formal*) without a body or form: *material bodies and incorporeal minds*

in·cor·rect /ˌɪnkə'rekt/ *adj.* **1** not accurate or true: *incorrect information/spelling* ◊ *His version of what happened is incorrect.* **2** speaking or behaving in a way that does not follow the accepted standards or rules—see also POLITICALLY CORRECT OPP CORRECT ▶ **in·cor·rect·ly** *adv.*: *an incorrectly addressed letter* **in·cor·rect·ness** *noun* [U]

in·cor·ri·gible /ɪn'kɒrɪdʒəbl; AmE -'kɔːr-/ *adj.* (*disapproving* or *humorous*) having bad habits which cannot be changed or improved: *Her husband is an incorrigible flirt.* ◊ *You're incorrigible!* ▶ **in·cor·ri·gibly** /ɪn'kɒrɪdʒəbli; AmE -'kɔːr-/ *adv.*

in·cor·rupt·ible /ˌɪnkə'rʌptəbl/ *adj.* **1** (of people) not able to be persuaded to do sth wrong or dishonest, even if sb offers them money: *Bribery won't work with him. He's incorruptible.* **2** that cannot decay or be destroyed OPP CORRUPTIBLE ▶ **in·cor·rupt·ibil·ity** /ˌɪnkəˌrʌptə'bɪləti/ *noun* [U]

in·crease *verb*, *noun*
■ *verb* /ɪn'kriːs/ ~ **(sth) (from A) (to B)** | ~ **(sth) (by sth)** to become or to make sth greater in amount, number, value, etc: [V] *The population has increased from 1.2 million to 1.8 million.* ◊ *The rate of inflation increased by 2%.* ◊ *The price of oil increased.* ◊ *Oil increased in price.* ◊ *Disability increases with age* (= the older sb is, the more likely they are to have a disability). ◊ [VN] *We need to increase productivity.* ◊ *They've increased the price by 50%.* OPP DECREASE ▶ **in·creased** *adj.* [only before noun]: *increased demand/pressure/spending*
■ *noun* /'ɪnkriːs/ [C, U] ~ **(in sth)** a rise in the amount, number or value of sth: *an increase in spending/population* ◊ *an increase of 2p in the pound on income tax* ◊ *an increase of nearly 20%* ◊ *a significant/substantial increase in sales* ◊ *price/tax/wage increases* ◊ *Homelessness is* **on the increase** (= increasing). OPP DECREASE

in·creas·ing·ly /ɪn'kriːsɪŋli/ *adv.* more and more all the time: *increasingly difficult/important/popular* ◊ *It is becoming increasingly clear that this problem will not be easily solved.* ◊ *Increasingly, training is taking place in the office rather than outside it.*

in·cred·ible /ɪn'kredəbl/ *adj.* **1** impossible or very difficult to believe: *an incredible story* ◊ *It seemed incredible that she had been there a week already.* **2** (*informal*) extremely good or extremely large: *The hotel was incredible.* ◊ *an incredible amount of work*

in·cred·ibly /ɪn'kredəbli/ *adv.* **1** extremely: *incredibly lucky/stupid/difficult/beautiful* **2** in a way that is very difficult to believe: *Incredibly, it was six months before I realized what was going on.*

in·credu·lous /ɪn'kredjələs; AmE -dʒəl-/ *adj.* not willing or not able to believe sth; showing an inability to believe sth: '*Here?*' *said Kate, incredulous.* ◊ *an incredulous look/face*—compare CREDULOUS ▶ **in·credu·lity** /ˌɪnkrə'djuːləti; AmE -'duː-/ *noun* [U]: *a look of surprise and incredulity* **in·credu·lous·ly** *adv.*: *He laughed incredulously.*

in·cre·ment /'ɪŋkrəmənt/ *noun* **1** a regular increase in the amount of money that sb is paid for their job: *a salary of £25 K with annual increments* **2** (*formal*) an increase in a number or an amount ▶ **in·cre·men·tal** /ˌɪŋkrə'mentl/ *adj.*: *incremental costs* **in·cre·men·tal·ly** /-təli/ *adv.*

in·crim·in·ate /ɪn'krɪmɪneɪt/ *verb* [VN] to make it seem as if sb has done sth wrong or illegal: *They were afraid of answering the questions and incriminating themselves.* ▶ **in·crim·in·at·ing** *adj.* [usually before noun]: *incriminating evidence* **in·crim·in·ation** /ɪnˌkrɪmɪ'neɪʃn/ *noun* [U]

in·crust·ation (also **en·crust·ation**) /ˌɪnkrʌ'steɪʃn/ *noun* [U, C] the process of forming a hard outer covering or layer; the covering or layer that is formed

in·cu·bate /'ɪŋkjubeɪt/ *verb* **1** [VN] (of a bird) to sit on its eggs in order to keep them warm until they HATCH **2** [VN] (*biology*) to keep cells, bacteria, etc. at a suitable temperature so that they develop **3** [VN] (**be incubating sth**) (*medical*) to have an infectious disease developing inside you before SYMPTOMS (= signs of illness) appear **4** [V] (*medical*) (of a disease) to develop slowly without showing any signs: *The BSE bug incubates for three years.*

in·cu·ba·tion /ˌɪŋkju'beɪʃn/ *noun* **1** [U] the HATCHING of eggs **2** [C] (also **incu'bation period**) (*medical* or *biology*) the time between sb being infected with a disease and the appearance of the first SYMPTOMS (= signs) **3** [U] (*biology*) the development and growth of bacteria, etc.

in·cu·ba·tor /'ɪŋkjubeɪtə(r)/ *noun* **1** a piece of equipment in a hospital which new babies are placed in when they are weak or born too early, in order to help them survive **2** a machine like a box where eggs are kept warm until the young birds are born

in·cu·bus /'ɪŋkjubəs/ *noun* (*pl.* **in·cu·buses** or **in·cubi** /-baɪ/) **1** (*literary*) a problem that makes you worry a lot **2** a male evil spirit, supposed in the past to have sex with a sleeping woman—compare SUCCUBUS

in·cul·cate /'ɪnkʌlkeɪt; AmE ɪn'kʌl-/ *verb* [VN] ~ **sth (in/into sb)** | ~ **sb with sth** (*formal*) to cause sb to learn and remember ideas, moral principles, etc., especially by repeating them often: *to inculcate a sense of responsibility in sb* ◊ *to inculcate sb with a sense of responsibility* ▶ **in·cul·ca·tion** /ˌɪnkʌl'keɪʃn/ *noun* [U]

in·cum·bency /ɪn'kʌmbənsi/ *noun* (*pl.* **-ies**) (*formal*) the official position of sb or the time during which they have it

in·cum·bent /ɪn'kʌmbənt/ *noun*, *adj.*
■ *noun* a person who has an official position: *the present incumbent of the White House/10 Downing Street*
■ *adj.* **1** [only before noun] having an official position: *the incumbent president* **2** ~ **upon/on sb** (*formal*) necessary as part of sb's duties: *It was incumbent on them to attend.*

incur /ɪn'kɜː(r)/ *verb* (**-rr-**) [VN] (*formal*) **1** if you **incur** sth unpleasant, you are in a situation in which you have to deal with it: *She had incurred the wrath of her father by marrying without his consent* **2** if you **incur** costs, you have to pay them: *You risk incurring bank charges if you exceed your overdraft limit.*

in·cur·able /ɪn'kjʊərəbl; AmE -'kjʊr-/ *adj.* **1** that cannot be cured: *an incurable disease/illness* OPP CURABLE **2** that cannot be changed: *She's an incurable optimist.* ▶ **in·cur·ably** /-əbli/ *adv.*: *incurably ill/romantic*

in·cur·sion /ɪn'kɜːʃn; AmE ɪn'kɜːrʒn/ *noun* ~ **(into sth)** (*formal*) **1** a sudden attack on a place by foreign armies, etc. **2** the sudden appearance of sth in a particular area of activity that is either not expected or not wanted: *the incursion of English soccer into European competitions*

Ind. *abbr.* (*BrE, politics*) INDEPENDENT: *G Green (Ind.)*

in·debt·ed /ɪn'detɪd/ *adj.* **1** ~ **(to sb) (for sth)** (*formal*) grateful to sb for helping you: *I am deeply indebted to my family for all their help.* **2** (of countries, governments, etc.) owing money to other countries or organizations: *a list of the fifteen most heavily indebted nations* ▶ **in·debt·ed·ness** *noun* [U]

in·decency /ɪn'diːsnsi/ *noun* **1** [U] behaviour that is thought to be morally or sexually offensive: *an act of gross indecency* (= a sexual act that is a criminal offence) **2** [C, usually sing.] an indecent act, expression, etc.

in·decent /ɪn'diːsnt/ *adj.* **1** (of behaviour, talk, etc.) thought to be morally offensive, especially because it involves sex or being naked: *indecent conduct/photos/language*—compare DECENT **2** (of clothes) showing parts of the body that are usually covered: *That skirt of hers is*

aɪ	aʊ	eɪ	əʊ	oʊ	ɔɪ	ɪə	eə	ʊə	j	w
my	now	say	go (BrE)	go (AmE)	boy	near	hair	pure	yes	wet

positively indecent. **3** not done in the appropriate or usual amount of time: *They left the funeral with almost indecent haste* (= too quickly). ▶ **in·decent·ly** *adv.*: *He was charged with indecently assaulting five women.*

in,decent as'sault *noun* [C, U] (*law*) a sexual attack on sb but one that does not include RAPE

in,decent ex'posure *noun* [U] (*law*) the crime of showing your sexual organs to other people in a public place

in·de·cipher·able /ˌɪndɪˈsaɪfrəbl/ *adj.* (of writing or speech) impossible to read or understand: *His signature is indecipherable.*

in·deci·sion /ˌɪndɪˈsɪʒn/ (also *less frequent* **in·deci·sive·ness**) *noun* [U] the state of being unable to decide: *After a moment's indecision, he said yes.*—compare DECISION

in·deci·sive /ˌɪndɪˈsaɪsɪv/ *adj.* **1** (of a person) unable to make decisions: *a weak and indecisive man* **2** not providing a clear and definite answer or result: *an indecisive battle* OPP DECISIVE ▶ **in·deci·sive·ly** *adv.* **in·deci·sive·ness** *noun* [U] = INDECISION

in·deed /ɪnˈdiːd/ *adv.* **1** used to emphasize a positive statement or answer: *'Was he very angry?' 'Indeed he was.' ◇ 'Do you agree?' 'Indeed I do/Yes, indeed.' ◇ 'You said you'd help?' 'I did indeed—yes.' ◇ It is indeed a remarkable achievement.* **2** (*especially BrE*) used after *very* and an adjective or adverb to emphasize a statement, description, etc: *Thank you very much indeed! ◇ I was very sad indeed to hear of your father's death.* **3** (*formal, especially BrE*) used to add information to a statement: *I don't mind at all. Indeed, I would be delighted to help.* **4** (*spoken, especially BrE*) used to show that you are surprised at sth or that you find sth ridiculous: *A ghost indeed! I've never heard anything so silly.* **5** (*spoken*) used when you are repeating a question that sb has just asked and showing that you do not know the answer: *'Why did he do it?' 'Why indeed?'* IDM see FRIEND

in·defat·ig·able /ˌɪndɪˈfætɪɡəbl/ *adj.* (*formal, approving*) never giving up or getting tired of doing sth: *an indefatigable defender of human rights* ▶ **in·defat·ig·ably** /ˌɪndɪˈfætɪɡəbli/ *adv.*

in·defens·ible /ˌɪndɪˈfensəbl/ *adj.* **1** that cannot be defended or excused because it is morally unacceptable: *indefensible behaviour ◇ The minister was accused of defending the indefensible.* **2** (of a place or building) impossible to defend from military attack

in·defin·able /ˌɪndɪˈfaɪnəbl/ *adj.* difficult or impossible to define or explain: *She has that indefinable something that makes an actress a star.* ▶ **in·defin·ably** /-əbli/ *adv.*

in·def·in·ite /ɪnˈdefɪnət/ *adj.* **1** lasting for a period of time that has no fixed end: *She will be away for the indefinite future. ◇ The workers have been on indefinite strike since July.* **2** not clearly defined: *an indefinite science*

in,definite 'article *noun* (*grammar*) the word *a* or *an*—compare DEFINITE ARTICLE

in·def·in·ite·ly /ɪnˈdefɪnətli/ *adv.* for a period of time with no fixed limit: *The trial was postponed indefinitely.*

in·del·ible /ɪnˈdeləbl/ *adj.* **1** impossible to forget or remove: *The experience made an indelible impression on me. ◇ Her unhappy childhood left an indelible mark.* **2** (of ink, pens, etc.) leaving a mark that cannot be removed: *an indelible marker/stain* ▶ **in·del·ibly** /-əbli/ *adv.*: *That day is stamped indelibly on my memory.*

in·deli·cate /ɪnˈdelɪkət/ *adj.* (*formal*) likely to be thought rude or embarrassing: *indelicate questions/comments* ▶ **in·deli·cacy** /-kəsi/ *noun* [U]

in·dem·nify /ɪnˈdemnɪfaɪ/ *verb* (**in·dem·ni·fies**, **in·dem·ni·fy·ing**, **in·dem·ni·fied**, **in·dem·ni·fied**) [VN] (*law*) **1** ~ **sb** (**against sth**) to promise to pay sb an amount of money if they suffer any damage or loss **2** ~ **sb** (**for sth**) to pay sb an amount of money because of the damage or loss that they have suffered ▶ **in·dem·ni·fi·ca·tion** /ɪnˌdemnɪfɪˈkeɪʃn/ *noun* [U]

in·dem·nity /ɪnˈdemnəti/ *noun* (*pl.* **-ies**) (*formal* or *law*) **1** [U] ~ (**against sth**) protection against damage or loss, especially in the form of a promise to pay for any that happens: *an indemnity clause/fund/policy ◇ indemnity*

insurance 2 [C] a sum of money that is given as payment for damage or loss

in·dent *verb, noun*
- *verb* /ɪnˈdent/ [VN] to start a line of print or writing further away from the edge of the page than the other lines: *The first line of each paragraph should be indented.*
- *noun* /ˈɪndent/ **1** ~ (**for sth**) (*business*) (*especially BrE*) an official order for goods or equipment **2** = INDENTATION

in·den·ta·tion /ˌɪndenˈteɪʃn/ *noun* **1** [C] a cut or mark on the edge or surface of sth: *The horse's hooves left deep indentations in the mud.* **2** (also **in·dent**) [C] a space left at the beginning of a line of print or writing **3** [U] the action of indenting sth or the process of being indented

in·dented /ɪnˈdentɪd/ *adj.* (of an edge or a surface) an indented edge is not even, because parts of it are missing or have been cut away: *an indented coastline*

in·den·ture /ɪnˈdentʃə(r)/ *noun* a type of contract in the past that forced a servant or APPRENTICE to work for their employer for a particular period of time ▶ **in·den·tured** *adj.*

in·de·pend·ence /ˌɪndɪˈpendəns/ *noun* [U] **1** ~ (**from sb/sth**) (of a country) freedom from political control by other countries: *Cuba gained independence from Spain in 1898.* **2** the time when a country became politically independent: *independence celebrations ◇ the first elections since independence* **3** the freedom to organize your own life, make your own decisions, etc. without needing help from other people: *He values his independence. ◇ a woman's financial independence* OPP DEPENDENCE

Inde'pendence Day *noun* [U, C] 4 July, celebrated in the US as the anniversary of the day in 1776 when the Americans DECLARED themselves independent of Britain—see also THE FOURTH OF JULY

in·de·pend·ent /ˌɪndɪˈpendənt/ *adj., noun*
- *adj.*

COUNTRY | **1** ~ (**from/of sth**) (of countries) having their own government: *Mozambique became independent in 1975.*

SEPARATE | **2** done or given by sb who is not involved in a situation and is able to judge it fairly: *an independent inquiry/witness ◇ She went to a lawyer for some independent advice.* **3** ~ (**of sb/sth**) not connected with or influenced by sth; not connected with each other: *The police force should be independent of direct government control. ◇ Two independent research bodies reached the same conclusions.*

ORGANIZATION | **4** supported by private money rather than government money: *independent television/schools ◇ the independent sector*

PERSON | **5** ~ (**of sb/sth**) confident and free to do things without needing help from other people: *Going away to college has made me much more independent. ◇ She's a very independent-minded young woman. ◇ Students should aim to become more independent of their teachers.* **6** ~ (**of sb/sth**) having or earning enough money so that you do not have to rely on sb else for help: *It was important to me to be financially independent of my parents. ◇ a man of independent means* (= with a private income)

POLITICIAN | **7** not representing or belonging to a particular political party: *an independent candidate*

▶ **in·de·pend·ent·ly** *adv.* ~ (**of sb/sth**): *The two departments work independently of each other. ◇ It was the first time that she had lived independently.*
- *noun* (*abbr.* **Ind.**) a member of parliament, candidate, etc. who does not belong to a particular political party

inde,pendent 'school *noun* = PRIVATE SCHOOL

,in-'depth *adj.* [usually before noun] very thorough and detailed: *an in-depth discussion/study ◇ We will be providing in-depth coverage of the election as the results come in.*—see also DEPTH

in·des·crib·able /ˌɪndɪˈskraɪbəbl/ *adj.* so extreme or unusual it is almost impossible to describe: *The pain was indescribable. ◇ I felt a sense of indescribable relief.* ▶ **in·des·crib·ably** /-əbli/ *adv.*: *indescribably beautiful/boring*

in·des·truct·ible /ˌɪndɪˈstrʌktəbl/ *adj.* that is very strong and cannot easily be destroyed: *plastic containers* *that are virtually indestructible ◊ an indestructible bond of friendship*

in·de·ter·min·ate /ˌɪndɪˈtɜːmɪnət; *AmE* -ˈtɜːrm-/ *adj.* that cannot be identified easily or exactly: *Her eyes were an indeterminate colour. ◊ She was a tall woman of indeterminate age.* ▶ **in·de·ter·min·acy** /-nəsi/ *noun* [U]

index /ˈɪndeks/ *noun, verb*

■ *noun* **1** (*pl.* **in·dexes**) a list of names or topics that are referred to in a book, etc., usually arranged at the end of a book in alphabetical order or listed in a separate file or book: *Look it up in the index. ◊ Author and subject indexes are available on a library database.* **2** (*BrE*) = CARD INDEX **3** (*pl.* **in·dexes** or **in·dices**) a system that shows the level of prices and wages, etc. so that they can be compared with those of a previous date: *the cost-of-living index ◊ The Dow Jones index fell 15 points this morning. ◊ stockmarket indices ◊ house price indexes* **4** (*pl.* **in·dices**) a sign or MEASURE that sth else can be judged by: *The number of new houses being built is a good index of a country's prosperity.* **5** (usually **indices** [pl.]) (*mathematics*) the small number written above a larger number to show how many times that number must be multiplied by itself. In the EQUATION $4^2 = 16$, the number 2 is an index.

■ *verb* [VN] **1** to make an index of documents, the contents of a book, etc.; to add sth to a list of this type: *All publications are indexed by subject and title.* **2** [usually passive] **~ sth (to sth)** to link wages, etc. to the level of prices of food, clothing, etc. so that they both increase at the same rate

in·dex·ation /ˌɪndekˈseɪʃn/ *noun* [U] the linking of increases in wages, etc. to increases in prices

ˈindex card *noun* a small card that you can write information on and keep with other cards in a box or file—see also CARD INDEX—picture at STATIONERY

ˈindex finger (also **ˈfirst finger**) *noun* the finger next to the thumb SYN FOREFINGER—picture at BODY

ˌindex-ˈlinked *adj.* (*BrE*) (of wages, etc.) rising in value according to increases in the cost of living ▶ **ˌindex-ˈlinking** *noun* [U]

In·dian /ˈɪndiən/ *noun* **1** a person from India **2** (*old-fashioned, offensive*) = NATIVE AMERICAN ▶ **In·dian** *adj.* IDM see CHIEF *n.*, FILE *n.*

ˌIndian ˈcorn *noun* [U] (*especially AmE*) a type of MAIZE with large brown and yellow grains, not usually eaten but sometimes used to make decorations, for example at Thanksgiving

ˌIndian ˈsummer *noun* **1** a period of dry warm weather in the autumn/fall **2** a pleasant period of success or improvement, especially later in sb's life: *As a player, he's experiencing something of an Indian summer.*

in·di·cate /ˈɪndɪkeɪt/ *verb*

SHOW | **1** to show that sth is true or exists: [VN] *Record profits in the retail market indicate a boom in the economy.* ◊ [Vthat] *Research indicates that eating habits are changing fast.* ◊ [V] *Kingston-upon-Thames, as the name indicates, is situated on the banks of the Thames.* [alsoVwh-]

SUGGEST | **2** to be a sign of sth; to show that sth is possible or likely: [VN] *A red sky at night often indicates fine weather the next day.* ◊ [Vthat] *Early results indicate that the government will be returned to power.*

MENTION | **3 ~ sth (to sb)** to mention sth, especially in an indirect way: [V(that)] *In a key speech, the Queen indicated (that) she was willing to pay tax.* ◊ [VN] *During our meeting, he indicated his willingness to cooperate.* [alsoVwh-]

POINT TO | **4 ~ sb/sth (to sb)** to make sb notice sb/sth, especially by pointing or moving your head: [VN] *She took out a map and indicated the quickest route to us.* ◊ [Vwh-] *He indicated where the furniture was to go.* [alsoVthat]

GIVE INFORMATION | **5** [VN] to represent information without using words: *The results are indicated in Table 2.* **6** to give information in writing: [VN] *You are allowed 20kgs of baggage unless indicated otherwise on your ticket.* ◊ [Vwh-] *Please indicate clearly which colour you require.*

SHOW MEASUREMENT | **7** (of an instrument for measuring things) to show a particular measurement: [VN] *When the*

temperature gauge indicates 90°F or more, turn off the engine. [alsoVwh-]

IN VEHICLE | **8** (*BrE*) to show that your vehicle is going to change direction, by using lights or your arm: [V] *Always indicate before moving into another lane.* ◊ [VN] *He indicated left and then turned right.* [alsoV(that)]

BE RECOMMENDED | **9** [VN] [usually passive] (*formal*) to be necessary or recommended: *A course of chemotherapy was indicated.*

in·di·ca·tion /ˌɪndɪˈkeɪʃn/ *noun* [C, U] **~ (of sth/of doing sth)| ~ (that …)** a remark or sign that shows that sth is happening or what sb is thinking or feeling: *They gave no indication of how the work should be done. ◊ There are clear indications that the economy is improving. ◊ All the indications are that the deal will go ahead as planned. ◊ He shows every indication* (= clear signs) *of wanting to accept the post.*

in·di·ca·tive /ɪnˈdɪkətɪv/ *adj., noun*

■ *adj.* **1** [not usually before noun] **~ (of sth)** (*formal*) showing or suggesting sth: *Their failure to act is indicative of their lack of interest.* **2** [only before noun] (*grammar*) stating a fact

■ *noun* (**the indicative**) [sing.] (*grammar*) the form of a verb that states a fact: *In 'Ben likes school', the verb 'like' is in the indicative.*

in·di·ca·tor /ˈɪndɪkeɪtə(r)/ *noun* **1** a sign that shows you what sth is like or how a situation is changing: *The economic indicators for the end of the year are better than expected.* **2** a device on a machine that shows speed, pressure, etc: *a depth indicator* **3** (*BrE*) (*AmE* **ˈturn signal**) (also *informal* **blink·er** *AmE, BrE*) a light on a vehicle that flashes to show that the vehicle is going to turn left or right—picture at CAR

in·dices *pl.* of INDEX

in·dict /ɪnˈdaɪt/ *verb* [VN] [usually passive] **~ sb (for sth)** (*especially AmE, law*) to officially charge sb with a crime: *The senator was indicted for murder.*

in·dict·able /ɪnˈdaɪtəbl/ *adj.* (*especially AmE, law*) **1** (of a crime) for which you can be indicted: *an indictable offense* **2** (of a person) able to be indicted

in·dict·ment /ɪnˈdaɪtmənt/ *noun* **1** [C, usually sing.] **~ (of/on sth)** a sign that a system, society, etc. is very bad or very wrong: *The poverty in our cities is a damning indictment of modern society.* **2** [C] (*especially AmE*) a written statement accusing sb of a crime **3** [U] (*especially AmE*) the act of officially accusing sb of a crime: *This led to his indictment on allegations of conspiracy.*

indie /ˈɪndi/ *adj.* used to describe popular music played by bands that are new and not well known, that is produced by small independent companies: *an indie band/label*

in·dif·fer·ence /ɪnˈdɪfrəns/ *noun* [U, sing.] **~ (to sb/sth)** a lack of interest, feeling or reaction towards sb/sth: *his total indifference to what people thought of him ◊ What she said is a matter of complete indifference to me. ◊ Their father treated them with indifference. ◊ an indifference to the needs of others*

in·dif·fer·ent /ɪnˈdɪfrənt/ *adj.* **1** [not usually before noun] **~ (to sb/sth)** having or showing no interest in sb/sth: *The government cannot afford to be indifferent to public opinion.* **2** not very good SYN MEDIOCRE: *an indifferent meal/performance ◊ The festival has the usual mixture of films—good, bad and indifferent.* ▶ **in·dif·fer·ent·ly** *adv.*: *He shrugged indifferently.*

in·di·gen·ous /ɪnˈdɪdʒənəs/ *adj.* **~ (to …)** (*formal*) belonging to a particular place rather than coming to it from somewhere else SYN NATIVE: *the indigenous peoples/languages of the area ◊ The kangaroo is indigenous to Australia.*

in·di·gent /ˈɪndɪdʒənt/ *adj.* [usually before noun] (*rare, formal*) very poor

in·di·gest·ible /ˌɪndɪˈdʒestəbl/ *adj.* **1** (of food) that cannot easily be DIGESTED in the stomach: *an indigestible meal* **2** (of facts, information, etc.) difficult to understand, and presented in a complicated way: *an indigestible amount of data* OPP DIGESTIBLE

s	t	v	z	ʃ	ʒ	tʃ	dʒ	θ	ð	ŋ
see	tea	van	zoo	shoe	vision	chain	jam	thin	this	sing

in·di·ges·tion /ˌɪndɪˈdʒestʃən/ noun [U] pain caused by difficulty in DIGESTING food SYN DYSPEPSIA

in·dig·nant /ɪnˈdɪɡnənt/ adj. ~ (at/about sth)| ~ (that …) feeling or showing anger and surprise because you think that you have been treated unfairly: an indignant letter/look ◇ She was very indignant at the way she had been treated. ◇ They were indignant that they hadn't been invited. ▶ **in·dig·nant·ly** adv.: 'I'm certainly not asking him!' she retorted indignantly.

in·dig·na·tion /ˌɪndɪɡˈneɪʃn/ noun [U] ~ (at/about sth)| ~ (that …) a feeling of anger and surprise caused by sth that you think is unfair or unreasonable: a storm/chorus of public indignation at the rise in train fares ◇ to arouse sb's indignation ◇ Some benefits apply only to men, much to the indignation of working women. ◇ to be full of righteous indignation (= the belief that you are right to be angry even though other people do not agree)

in·dig·nity /ɪnˈdɪɡnəti/ noun [U, C] (pl. -ies) ~ (of sth/of doing sth) a situation that makes you feel embarrassed or ashamed because you are not treated with respect; an act that causes these feelings SYN HUMILIATION: The chairman suffered the indignity of being refused admission to the meeting. ◇ the daily indignities of imprisonment

in·digo /ˈɪndɪɡəʊ; AmE -ɡoʊ/ adj. very dark blue in colour: an indigo sky ▶ **in·digo** noun [U]

in·dir·ect /ˌɪndəˈrekt; -daɪˈr-/ adj. [usually before noun] **1** happening not as the main aim, cause or result of a particular action, but in addition to it: the indirect effects of the war ◇ to find something out by indirect methods ◇ The building collapsed as an indirect result of the heavy rain and storms. ◇ There would be some benefit, however indirect, to the state. **2** avoiding saying sth in a clear and obvious way: an indirect attack/comment **3** not going in a straight line: an indirect route OPP DIRECT ▶ **in·dir·ect·ly** adv.: The new law will affect us all, directly or indirectly.

indirect 'object noun (grammar) a noun, noun phrase or pronoun in a sentence, used after some verbs, that refers to the person or thing that an action is done to or for: In 'Give him the money', 'him' is the indirect object and 'money' is the direct object.

indirect 'question (also re‚ported 'question) noun (grammar) a question in REPORTED SPEECH, for example She asked where I was going. HELP Do not put a question mark after an indirect question.

indirect 'speech noun [U] (grammar) = REPORTED SPEECH—compare DIRECT SPEECH

indirect 'tax noun [C, U] a tax that is paid as an amount added to the price of goods and services and not paid directly to the government—compare DIRECT TAX ▶ ‚indir·ect ta'xation noun [U]

in·dis·cern·ible /ˌɪndɪˈsɜːnəbl; AmE -ˈsɜːrn-/ adj. that cannot be seen, heard or understood: The differences are almost indiscernible.

in·dis·cip·line /ɪnˈdɪsɪplɪn/ noun [U] (formal) a lack of control in the behaviour of a group of people: The report identifies the causes of violence and indiscipline in schools.

in·dis·creet /ˌɪndɪˈskriːt/ adj. not careful about what you say or do, especially when this embarrasses or offends sb: an indiscreet comment ◇ It was indiscreet of him to disclose that information. OPP DISCREET ▶ **in·dis·creet·ly** adv.

in·dis·cre·tion /ˌɪndɪˈskreʃn/ noun **1** [C] an act or remark that is indiscreet, especially one that is not morally acceptable: political/youthful indiscretions **2** [U] the act of saying or doing sth without thinking about the effect it may have, especially when this embarrasses or offends sb: He talked to the press in a moment of indiscretion.—compare DISCRETION

in·dis·crim·in·ate /ˌɪndɪˈskrɪmɪnət/ adj. **1** an indiscriminate action is done without thought about what the result may be, especially when it causes people to be harmed: indiscriminate attacks on motorists by youths throwing stones ◇ Doctors have been criticized for their indiscriminate use of antibiotics. **2** acting without careful judgement: She's always been indiscriminate in her choice of friends. ▶ **in·dis·crim·in·ate·ly** adv.: The soldiers fired indiscriminately into the crowd.

in·dis·pens·able /ˌɪndɪˈspensəbl/ adj. ~ (to sb/sth)| ~ (for sth/for doing sth) essential; too important to be without: Cars have become an indispensable part of our lives. ◇ She made herself indispensable to the department. ◇ A good dictionary is indispensable for learning a foreign language. OPP DISPENSABLE

in·dis·posed /ˌɪndɪˈspəʊzd; AmE -ˈspoʊzd/ adj. (formal) **1** [not usually before noun] unable to do sth because you are ill, or for a reason you do not want to give SYN UNWELL: She cannot perform tonight as she is indisposed. **2** [not before noun] ~ to do sth not willing to do sth

in·dis·pos·ition /ˌɪndɪspəˈzɪʃn/ noun [C, U] (formal) a slight illness that makes you unable to do sth

in·dis·put·able /ˌɪndɪˈspjuːtəbl/ adj. that is true and cannot be disagreed with or DENIED SYN UNDENIABLE: indisputable evidence ◇ an indisputable fact ◇ It is indisputable that the crime rate has been rising.—compare DISPUTABLE ▶ **in·dis·put·ably** adv.: This painting is indisputably one of his finest works.

in·dis·sol·uble /ˌɪndɪˈsɒljəbl; AmE -ˈsɑːl-/ adj. (formal) (of a relationship) that cannot be ended: an indissoluble friendship ▶ **in·dis·sol·ubly** /ˌɪndɪˈsɒljəbli; AmE -ˈsɑːl-/ adv.: indissolubly linked

in·dis·tinct /ˌɪndɪˈstɪŋkt/ adj. that cannot be seen, heard or remembered clearly SYN VAGUE, HAZY: an indistinct figure in the distance ◇ His memory of the incident was somewhat indistinct. ▶ **in·dis·tinct·ly** adv.

in·dis·tin·guish·able /ˌɪndɪˈstɪŋɡwɪʃəbl/ adj. **1** ~ (from sth) if two things are **indistinguishable**, or one is **indistinguishable from** the other, it is impossible to see any differences between them: The male of the species is almost indistinguishable from the female. **2** not clear; not able to be clearly identified: His words were indistinguishable.

in·di·vid·ual /ˌɪndɪˈvɪdʒuəl/ adj., noun
■ adj. **1** [only before noun] (often used after each) considered separately rather than as part of a group: We interviewed each individual member of the community. ◇ The minister refused to comment on individual cases. **2** [only before noun] connected with one person; designed for one person: respect for individual freedom ◇ an individual pizza **3** (usually approving) typical of one particular person or thing in a way that is different from others SYN ORIGINAL: a highly individual style of dress
■ noun **1** a person considered separately rather than as part of a group: The competition is open to both teams and individuals. ◇ Treatment depends on the individual involved. ◇ donations from private individuals (= ordinary people rather than companies, the government, etc.) **2** a person who is original and very different from others: She's grown into quite an individual. **3** (informal, usually disapproving) a person of a particular type, especially a strange one: an odd-looking individual ◇ So this individual came up and demanded money.

in·di·vidu·al·ism /ˌɪndɪˈvɪdʒuəlɪzəm/ noun [U] **1** the quality of being different from other people and doing things in your own way: She owes her success to her individualism and flair. **2** the belief that individual people in society should have the right to make their own decisions, etc., rather than be controlled by the government: Capitalism stresses innovation, competition and individualism. ▶ **in·di·vidu·al·ist** /-əlɪst/ noun: She's a complete individualist in her art. **in·di·vidu·al·is·tic** /ˌɪndɪˌvɪdʒuəˈlɪstɪk/ (also **in·di·vidu·al·ist**) adj.: an individualistic culture ◇ His music is highly individualistic and may not appeal to everyone.

in·di·vidu·al·ity /ˌɪndɪˌvɪdʒuˈæləti/ noun [U] the qualities that make sb/sth different from other people or things: She expresses her individuality through her clothes.

in·di·vidu·al·ize (BrE also **-ise**) /ˌɪndɪˈvɪdʒuəlaɪz/ verb [VN] (written) to make sth different to suit the needs of a particular person, place, etc: to individualize children's learning

in·di·vidu·al·ized (BrE also **-ised**) /ˌɪndɪˈvɪdʒuəlaɪzd/ adj. designed for a particular person or thing; connected

æ	ɑː	e	ɜː	ə	ɪ	iː	i	ɒ	ɔː	ʌ	ʊ	u	uː
cat	father	ten	bird	about	sit	see	many	got (BrE)	saw	cup	put	actual	too

with a particular person or thing: *individualized teaching* ◊ *a highly individualized approach to management*

in·di·vidu·al·ly /ˌɪndɪˈvɪdʒuəli/ *adv.* separately, rather than as a group: *individually wrapped chocolates* ◊ *The manager spoke to them all individually.* ◊ *The hotel has 100 individually designed bedrooms.*

in·di·vis·ible /ˌɪndɪˈvɪzəbl/ *adj.* that cannot be divided into separate parts OPP DIVISIBLE ► **in·di·vis·ibil·ity** /ˌɪndɪˌvɪzəˈbɪləti/ *noun* [U] **in·di·vis·ibly** /ˌɪndɪˈvɪzəbli/ *adv.*

Indo- /ˈɪndəʊ; *AmE* ˈɪndoʊ/ *combining form* (in nouns and adjectives) Indian: *the Indo-Pakistan border*

in·doc·trin·ate /ɪnˈdɒktrɪneɪt; *AmE* ɪnˈdɑːk-/ *verb* (*disapproving*) to force sb to accept a particular belief or set of beliefs and not allow them to consider any others: [VN] *They had been indoctrinated from an early age with their parents' beliefs.* [also VN to inf] ► **in·doc·trin·ation** /ɪnˌdɒktrɪˈneɪʃn; *AmE* -ˌdɑːk-/ *noun* [U]: *political/religious indoctrination*

Indo-Euro·pean *adj.* of or connected with the family of languages spoken in most of Europe and parts of western Asia (including English, French, Latin, Greek, Swedish, Russian and Hindi)

in·do·lent /ˈɪndələnt/ *adj.* (*formal*) lazy; not wanting to work ► **in·do·lence** /-əns/ *noun* [U]

in·dom·it·able /ɪnˈdɒmɪtəbl; *AmE* ɪnˈdɑːm-/ *adj.* (*formal, approving*) not willing to accept defeat, even in a difficult situation; very brave and determined: *an indomitable spirit* ◊ *an indomitable campaigner for human rights*

in·door /ˈɪndɔː(r)/ *adj.* [only before noun] situated, done or used inside a building: *an indoor swimming pool* ◊ *indoor games* ◊ *the world indoor 200 metres champion* OPP OUTDOOR

in·doors /ˌɪnˈdɔːz; *AmE* ˌɪnˈdɔːrz/ *adv.* inside or into a building: *to go/stay indoors* ◊ *Many herbs can be grown indoors.* OPP OUTDOORS

in·drawn /ˌɪnˈdrɔːn/ *adj.* (*literary*) **indrawn breath** is air that sb breathes in suddenly and quickly, expressing surprise or shock

in·dub·it·ably /ɪnˈdjuːbɪtəbli; *AmE* -ˈduː-/ *adv.* (*formal*) in a way that cannot be doubted; without question SYN UNDOUBTEDLY: *He was, indubitably, the most suitable candidate.* ► **in·dub·it·able** *adj.*: *indubitable proof*

in·duce /ɪnˈdjuːs; *AmE* -duːs/ *verb* **1** [VN to inf] (*formal*) to persuade or influence sb to do sth: *Nothing would induce me to take the job.* **2** [VN] (*formal*) to cause sth: *drugs which induce sleep* ◊ *a drug-induced coma* **3** [VN] (*medical*) to make a woman start giving birth to her baby by giving her special drugs: *an induced labour* ◊ *We'll have to induce her.*

in·duce·ment /ɪnˈdjuːsmənt; *AmE* ɪnˈduːsmənt/ *noun* [C, U] ~ (to sb) (to do sth) something that is given to sb to persuade them to do sth SYN INCENTIVE: *financial inducements to mothers to stay at home* ◊ *There is little inducement for them to work harder.* ◊ *Government officials have been accused of accepting inducements (= BRIBES) from local businessmen.*

in·duct /ɪnˈdʌkt/ *verb* [VN] [often passive] ~ sb (into sth) (as sth) (*formal*) **1** to formally give sb a job or position of authority, especially as part of a ceremony **2** to officially introduce sb into a group or an organization, especially the army **3** to introduce sb to a particular area of knowledge: *They were inducted into the skills of magic.*

in·duct·ee /ˌɪndʌkˈtiː/ *noun* (*especially AmE*) a person who is being, or who has just been, introduced into a special group of people, especially sb who has just joined the army

in·duc·tion /ɪnˈdʌkʃn/ *noun* **1** [U, C] ~ (into sth) the process of introducing sb to a new job, skill, organization, etc.; a ceremony at which this takes place: *induction into the local business community* ◊ *The induction of new students will take place in the main hall.* **2** [U, C] the act of making a pregnant woman start to give birth, using artificial means such as a special drug **3** [U] (*technical*) a method of discovering general rules and principles from particular facts and examples—compare DEDUCTION **4** [U]

(*technical*) the process by which electricity or MAGNETISM passes from one object to another without them touching

in'duction course *noun* (*BrE*) a training course for new employees, students, etc. that is designed to give them a general introduction to the business, school, etc.

in'duction loop *noun* a system in theatres, etc., which helps people who cannot hear well. A ring of wire around the room produces a signal that can be received directly by HEARING AIDS.

in·duct·ive /ɪnˈdʌktɪv/ *adj.* (*technical*) **1** using particular facts and examples to form general rules and principles: *an inductive argument* ◊ *inductive reasoning* —compare DEDUCTIVE **2** connected with the INDUCTION of electricity ► **in·duct·ive·ly** *adv.*: *a theory derived inductively from the data*

in·dulge /ɪnˈdʌldʒ/ *verb* **1** ~ in sth | ~ yourself (with sth) to allow yourself to have or do sth that you like, especially sth that is considered bad for you: [V] *They went into town to indulge in some serious shopping.* ◊ [VN] *I indulged myself with a long hot bath.* **2** [VN] to satisfy a particular desire, interest, etc: *The inheritance enabled him to indulge his passion for art.* **3** [VN] ~ sb (with sth) | ~ sth to be too generous in allowing sb to have or do whatever they like: *She did not believe in indulging the children with presents.* ◊ *Her father had always indulged her every whim.* **4** [V] ~ in sth to take part in an activity, especially one that is illegal

in·dul·gence /ɪnˈdʌldʒəns/ *noun* **1** [U] (usually *disapproving*) the state or act of having or doing whatever you want; the state of allowing sb to have or do whatever they want: *to lead a life of indulgence* ◊ *Avoid excessive indulgence in sweets and canned drinks.* ◊ *There is no limit to the indulgence he shows to his grandchildren.* **2** [C] something that you allow yourself to have even though it is not essential: *The holiday was an extravagant indulgence.*—see also SELF-INDULGENCE **3** [U] (*formal*) willingness to ignore the weaknesses in sb/sth SYN PATIENCE: *They begged the audience's indulgence.*

in·dul·gent /ɪnˈdʌldʒənt/ *adj.* **1** (usually *disapproving*) tending to allow sb to have or do whatever they want: *indulgent parents* ◊ *an indulgent smile* ◊ *Mothers tend to be less indulgent towards daughters.*—see also SELF-INDULGENT **2** willing or too willing to ignore the weaknesses in sb/sth SYN PATIENT: *to take an indulgent view of sth* ► **in·dul·gent·ly** *adv.*: *to laugh indulgently*

in·dus·trial /ɪnˈdʌstriəl/ *adj.* [usually before noun] **1** connected with industry: *industrial conflict/disputes/unrest* ◊ *industrial development/production/output* ◊ *an industrial accident* **2** used by industries: *industrial chemicals* ◊ *industrial-strength cleaning fluid* **3** having many industries: *an industrial area/town* ◊ *an industrial society/economy* ◊ *the world's leading industrial nations* ► **in·dus·tri·al·ly** /-əli/ *adv.*: *industrially advanced countries*

in,dustrial 'action *noun* [U] (*especially BrE*) action that workers take, especially stopping work, to protest to their employers about sth

in,dustrial archae'ology *noun* [U] the study of machines, factories, bridges, etc. used in the past in industry

in,dustrial 'arts (also **shop**, **'shop class**) *noun* [U] (*AmE*) a school subject in which students learn to make things from wood and metal using tools and machines

in,dustrial e'state (*BrE*) (*AmE* **in,dustrial 'park**) an area especially for factories, on the edge of a town—compare TRADING ESTATE

in·dus·tri·al·ism /ɪnˈdʌstriəlɪzəm/ *noun* [U] (*technical*) an economic and social system based on industry

in·dus·tri·al·ist /ɪnˈdʌstriəlɪst/ *noun* a person who owns or runs a large factory or industrial company

in·dus·tri·al·ize (*BrE* also **-ise**) /ɪnˈdʌstriəlaɪz/ *verb* if a country or an area **is industrialized** or if it **industrializes**, industries are developed there: [V] *The southern part of the country was slow to industrialize.* [also VN] ► **in·dus·tri·al·iza·tion**, **-isa·tion** /ɪnˌdʌstriəlaɪˈzeɪʃn; *AmE* -ləˈz-/ *noun* [U]: *the rapid industrialization of Japan* **in·dus·tri·al·ized**, **-ised** *adj.*: *an industrialized country*

in,dustrial re'lations *noun* [pl.] relations between employers and employees

the In,dustrial Revo'lution *noun* [sing.] the period in the 18th and 19th centuries in Europe and the US when machines began to be used to do work, and industry grew rapidly

in,dustrial tri'bunal *noun* (*BrE*) a type of court that can decide on disputes between employees and employers

in·dus·tri·ous /ɪnˈdʌstriəs/ *adj.* (*approving*) working hard; busy SYN HARD-WORKING: *an industrious student* ▶ **in·dus·tri·ous·ly** *adv.*

in·dus·try /ˈɪndəstri/ *noun* (*pl.* **-ies**) **1** [U] the production of goods from raw materials, especially in factories: *heavy/light industry* ◇ *the needs of British industry* ◇ *She got a job in industry.* **2** [C] the people and activities involved in producing a particular thing, or in providing a particular service: *the steel industry* ◇ *the catering/tourist industry* ◇ *We need to develop local industries.* ◇ (*figurative, disapproving*) *the Madonna industry* (= the large number of people involved in making Madonna successful)—see also CAPTAIN OF INDUSTRY, COTTAGE INDUSTRY, HEAVY INDUSTRY **3** [U] (*formal*) the quality of working hard: *We were impressed by their industry.*

in·ebri·ated /ɪˈniːbrieɪtɪd/ *adj.* (*formal* or *humorous*) drunk

in·ed·ible /ɪnˈedəbl/ *adj.* that you cannot eat because it is of poor quality, or poisonous; not edible: *The waiters were rude, the food inedible.*

in·effable /ɪnˈefəbl/ *adj.* (*rare, formal*) too great or beautiful to describe in words: *ineffable joy*

in·ef·fect·ive /ˌɪnɪˈfektɪv/ *adj.* ~ (**in doing sth**) not achieving what you want to achieve; not having any effect: *The new drug was ineffective.* ◇ *ineffective management* ◇ *The law proved ineffective in dealing with the problem.* OPP EFFECTIVE ▶ **in·ef·fect·ive·ness** *noun* [U]: *the ineffectiveness of western medicine in treating this illness* **in·ef·fect·ive·ly** *adv.*

in·ef·fec·tual /ˌɪnɪˈfektʃuəl/ *adj.* (*written*) without the ability to achieve much; weak; not achieving what you want to: *an ineffectual teacher* ◇ *an ineffectual attempt to reform the law* ▶ **in·ef·fec·tu·al·ly** /-tʃuəli/ *adv.*

in·ef·fi·cient /ˌɪnɪˈfɪʃnt/ *adj.* not doing a job well and not making the best use of time, money, energy, etc: *an inefficient heating system* ◇ *inefficient government* ◇ *an extremely inefficient secretary* ◇ *inefficient use of time and energy* OPP EFFICIENT ▶ **in·ef·fi·ciency** /-ənsi/ *noun* [U, C] (*pl.* **-ies**): *waste and inefficiency in government* ◇ *inefficiencies in the system* **in·ef·fi·cient·ly** *adv.*

in·ele·gant /ɪnˈelɪgənt/ *adj.* not attractive or graceful: *an inelegant fall* ◇ *an inelegant phrase* ▶ **in·ele·gant·ly** *adv.*

in·eli·gible /ɪnˈelɪdʒəbl/ *adj.* ~ (**for sth/to do sth**) not having the necessary qualifications to have or to do sth: *ineligible for financial assistance* ◇ *ineligible to vote* OPP ELIGIBLE

in·eluct·able /ˌɪnɪˈlʌktəbl/ *adj.* (*rare, formal*) that you cannot avoid: *the ineluctable signs of ageing* ▶ **in·eluct·ably** /-əbli/ *adv.*

inept /ɪˈnept/ *adj.* acting or done with no skill: *She was left feeling inept and inadequate.* ◇ *an inept remark* ▶ **in·ept·ly** *adv.*

in·epti·tude /ɪˈneptɪtjuːd; *AmE* -tuːd/ *noun* [U] lack of skill: *the ineptitude of the police in handling the situation*

in·equal·ity /ˌɪnɪˈkwɒləti; *AmE* -ˈkwɑːl-/ *noun* [U, C] (*pl.* **-ies**) the unfair difference between groups of people in society, when some have more wealth, status or opportunities than others: *inequality of opportunity* ◇ *economic inequalities between different areas* ◇ *racial inequality* OPP EQUALITY

in·equit·able /ɪnˈekwɪtəbl/ *adj.* (*formal*) not fair; not the same for everyone: *inequitable distribution of wealth* OPP EQUITABLE

in·equity /ɪnˈekwəti/ *noun* [C, U] (*pl.* **-ies**) (*formal*) something that is unfair; the state of being unfair: *a victim of the inequities of/in the legal system*

in·erad·ic·able /ˌɪnɪˈrædɪkəbl/ *adj.* (*formal*) (of a qual-

ity or situation) that cannot be removed or changed: *The slave trade had an ineradicable effect on world history.*

inert /ɪˈnɜːt; *AmE* ɪˈnɜːrt/ *adj.* **1** (*formal*) without power to move or act: *He lay inert with half-closed eyes.* ◇ *The president has to operate within an inert political system.* **2** (*technical*) without active chemical or other PROPERTIES (= characteristics): *inert gases*

in·er·tia /ɪˈnɜːʃə; *AmE* ɪˈnɜːrʃə/ *noun* [U] **1** (usually *disapproving*) lack of energy; lack of desire or ability to move or change: *I can't seem to throw off this feeling of inertia.* ◇ *the forces of institutional inertia in the school system* **2** (*physics*) a PROPERTY (= characteristic) of MATTER (= a substance) by which it stays still or, if moving, continues moving in a straight line unless it is acted on by a force outside itself

in·er·tial /ɪˈnɜːʃl; *AmE* ɪˈnɜːrʃl/ *adj.* (*technical*) connected with or caused by inertia

in·escap·able /ˌɪnɪˈskeɪpəbl/ *adj.* (of a fact or a situation) that you cannot avoid or ignore: *an inescapable fact* ◇ *This leads to the inescapable conclusion that the two things are connected.* ▶ **in·escap·ably** /-əbli/ *adv.*

in·es·sen·tial /ˌɪnɪˈsenʃl/ *adj.* not necessary: *inessential luxuries* ▶ **in·es·sen·tial** *noun*: *Few people had spare cash for inessentials.*—compare ESSENTIAL, NON-ESSENTIAL

in·estim·able /ɪnˈestɪməbl/ *adj.* (*formal*) too great to calculate: *The information he provided was of inestimable value.*

in·ev·it·able /ɪnˈevɪtəbl/ *adj.* **1** that you cannot avoid or prevent: *It was an inevitable consequence of the decision.* ◇ *It was inevitable that there would be job losses.* ◇ *A rise in the interest rates seems inevitable.* **2** [only before noun] (often *humorous*) so frequent that you always expect it: *the English and their inevitable cups of tea* **3** (**the inevit·able**) *noun* [sing.] something that is certain to happen: *You have to accept the inevitable.* ◇ *The inevitable happened—I forgot my passport.* ▶ **in·ev·it·abil·ity** /ɪnˌevɪtəˈbɪləti/ *noun* [U, sing.]: *the inevitability of death* ◇ *There was an inevitability about their defeat.*

in·ev·it·ably /ɪnˈevɪtəbli/ *adv.* **1** as is certain to happen: *Inevitably, the press exaggerated the story.* **2** (often *humorous*) as you would expect: *Inevitably, it rained on the day of the wedding.*

in·exact /ˌɪnɪɡˈzækt/ *adj.* not accurate or exact: *an inexact description* ◇ *Economics is an inexact science.*

in·ex·cus·able /ˌɪnɪkˈskjuːzəbl/ *adj.* too bad to accept or forgive: *inexcusable rudeness* OPP EXCUSABLE ▶ **in·ex·cus·ably** /-əbli/ *adv.*

in·ex·haust·ible /ˌɪnɪɡˈzɔːstəbl/ *adj.* that cannot be EXHAUSTED (= finished); very great: *an inexhaustible supply of good jokes* ◇ *Her energy is inexhaustible.*

in·ex·or·able /ɪnˈeksərəbl/ *adj.* (*formal*) (of a process) that cannot be stopped or changed: *the inexorable rise of crime* ▶ **in·ex·or·ably** /ɪnˈeksərəbli/ *adv.*: *events leading inexorably towards a crisis*

in·ex·pen·sive /ˌɪnɪkˈspensɪv/ *adj.* not costing a lot of money: *a relatively inexpensive hotel* OPP EXPENSIVE ▶ **in·ex·pen·sive·ly** *adv.*

in·ex·peri·ence /ˌɪnɪkˈspɪəriəns; *AmE* -ˈspɪr-/ *noun* [U] lack of knowledge and experience: *His mistake was due to youth and inexperience.*

in·ex·peri·enced /ˌɪnɪkˈspɪəriənst; *AmE* -ˈspɪr-/ *adj.* having little knowledge or experience of sth: *inexperienced drivers/staff* ◇ *inexperienced in modern methods* ◇ *a child too young and inexperienced to recognize danger*

in·ex·pert /ɪnˈekspɜːt; *AmE* -pɜːrt/ *adj.* without much skill—compare EXPERT: *an inexpert dancer* ▶ **in·ex·pert·ly** *adv.*

in·ex·plic·able /ˌɪnɪkˈsplɪkəbl/ *adj.* that cannot be understood or explained SYN INCOMPREHENSIBLE: *inexplicable behaviour* ◇ *For some inexplicable reason he gave up a fantastic job.* OPP EXPLICABLE ▶ **in·ex·plic·ably** *adv.*: *inexplicably delayed/absent* ◇ *She inexplicably withdrew the offer.*

in·ex·press·ible /ˌɪnɪkˈspresəbl/ *adj.* (of feelings) too strong to be put into words: *inexpressible relief/joy*

in ex·tre·mis /ˌɪn ɪkˈstriːmɪs/ *adv.* (from *Latin, formal*)

b	d	f	g	h	k	l	m	n	p	r
bad	did	fall	get	hat	cat	leg	man	now	pen	red

1 in a very difficult situation when very strong action is needed **2** at the moment of death

in·ex·tric·able /ˌɪnɪkˈstrɪkəbl; ɪnˈekstrɪkəbl/ *adj.* (*formal*) too closely linked to be separated: *Knowledge and economic power have become inextricable.* ◊ *an inextricable connection between the past and the present*

in·ex·tric·ably /ˌɪnɪkˈstrɪkəbli; ɪnˈekstrɪkəbli/ *adv.* if two things are **inextricably linked**, etc., it is impossible to separate them: *Europe's foreign policy is inextricably linked with that of the US.* ◊ *She had become inextricably involved in the campaign.*

in·fal·lible /ɪnˈfæləbl/ *adj.* **1** never wrong; never making mistakes: *infallible advice* ◊ *Doctors are not infallible.* [OPP] FALLIBLE **2** that never fails; always doing what it is supposed to do: *an infallible method of memorizing things* ▶ **in·fal·li·bil·ity** /ɪnˌfæləˈbɪləti/ *noun* [U]: *his belief in the infallibility of dreams as a guide to the future* ◊ *papal infallibility* **in·fal·libly** /-əbli/ *adv.*

in·fam·ous /ˈɪnfəməs/ *adj.* (*formal*) well known for being bad or evil [SYN] NOTORIOUS: *a general who was infamous for his brutality* ◊ *the most infamous concentration camp* ◊ (*humorous*) *the infamous British sandwich*—compare FAMOUS

in·famy /ˈɪnfəmi/ *noun* (*pl.* **-ies**) (*formal*) **1** [U] the state of being well known for sth bad or evil: *a day that will live in infamy* **2** [U, C] evil behaviour; an evil act: *scenes of horror and infamy*

in·fancy /ˈɪnfənsi/ *noun* [U] **1** the time when a child is a baby or very young: *to die in infancy* **2** the early development of sth: *a time when the cinema was still in its infancy*

in·fant /ˈɪnfənt/ *noun, adj.*
■ *noun* **1** (*formal or technical*) a baby or very young child: *a nursery for infants under two* ◊ *their infant son* ◊ *She was seriously ill as an infant.* ◊ *the infant mortality rate* ◊ *Mozart was an infant prodigy* (= a child with unusual ability). [HELP] *In AmE* **infant** *is only used for a baby, especially a very young one.* **2** (in British and Australian education) a child at school between the ages of four and seven: *an infant school* ◊ *infant teachers* ◊ *I've known her since we were in the infants* (= at infant school).
■ *adj.* [only before noun] **1** designed to be used by infants: *infant formula* (= milk for babies) **2** new and not yet developed: *infant industries*

in·fanti·cide /ɪnˈfæntɪsaɪd/ *noun* (*formal*) **1** [U, C] the crime of killing a baby; a person who is guilty of this crime **2** [U] (in some cultures) the practice of killing babies that are not wanted, for example because they are girls and not boys

in·fant·ile /ˈɪnfəntaɪl/ *adj.* **1** (*disapproving*) typical of a small child (and therefore not suitable for adults or older children) [SYN] CHILDISH: *infantile jokes* **2** [only before noun] (*formal or technical*) connected with babies or very young children

in·fan·try /ˈɪnfəntri/ *noun* [U+sing./pl. *v.*] soldiers who fight on foot: *infantry units* ◊ *The infantry was/were guarding the bridge.*

in·fan·try·man /ˈɪnfəntrimən/ *noun* (*pl.* **-men** /-mən/) a soldier who fights on foot

in·fatu·ated /ɪnˈfætʃueɪtɪd/ *adj.* **~** (with sb/sth) having a very strong feeling of love or attraction for sb/sth so that you cannot think clearly and in a sensible way: *She was completely infatuated with him.*

in·fatu·ation /ɪnˌfætʃuˈeɪʃn/ *noun* [C, U] **~** (with/for sb/sth) very strong feelings of love or attraction for sb/sth, especially when these are unreasonable and do not last long: *It isn't love, it's just a passing infatuation.*

in·fect /ɪnˈfekt/ *verb* [VN] **~** sb/sth (with sth) **1** to make a disease or an illness spread to a person, an animal or a plant: *It is not possible to infect another person through kissing.* ◊ *people infected with HIV* **2** (usually passive) to make a substance contain harmful bacteria that can spread disease [SYN] CONTAMINATE: *eggs infected with salmonella* **3** to make sb share a particular feeling: *She infected the children with her enthusiasm for music.*

in·fected /ɪnˈfektɪd/ *adj.* containing harmful bacteria:

The wound from the dog bite had become infected. ◊ *an infected water supply*

in·fec·tion /ɪnˈfekʃn/ *noun* **1** [U] the act or process of causing or getting a disease: *to be exposed to infection* ◊ *to increase the risk of infection* **2** [C] an illness that is caused by bacteria or a VIRUS and that affects one part of the body: *an ear/throat infection* ◊ *to pass on/spread an infection*—compare CONTAGION

in·fec·tious /ɪnˈfekʃəs/ *adj.* **1** an **infectious** disease can be passed easily from one person to another, especially through the air they breathe: *Flu is highly infectious.* ◊ (*figurative*) *infectious laughter* **2** [not usually before noun] if a person or an animal is **infectious**, they have a disease that can be spread to others: *I'm still infectious.*—compare CONTAGIOUS ▶ **in·fec·tious·ly** *adv.*: *to laugh infectiously*

infer /ɪnˈfɜː(r)/ *verb* (**-rr-**) **1** **~** sth (from sth) to reach an opinion or decide that sth is true on the basis of information that is available [SYN] DEDUCE: [VN] *Much of the meaning must be inferred from the context.* ◊ [V that] *It is reasonable to infer that the government knew about these deals.* **2** (*non-standard*) to suggest indirectly that sth is true: [V (that)] *Are you inferring (that) I'm not capable of doing the job?* [also VN]

WHICH WORD?
infer / imply

Infer and **imply** have opposite meanings. The two words can describe the same event, but from different points of view. If a speaker or writer **implies** something, they suggest it without saying it directly: *The article implied that the pilot was responsible for the accident.* If you **infer** something from what a speaker or writer says, you come to the conclusion that this is what he or she means: *I inferred from the article that the pilot was responsible for the accident.*

Infer is now often used with the same meaning as **imply**. However, many people consider that a sentence such as *Are you inferring that I'm a liar?* is incorrect, although it is fairly common in speech.

---

in·fer·ence /ˈɪnfərəns/ *noun* **1** [C] something that you can find out indirectly from what you already know: *to draw/make inferences from the data* ◊ *The clear inference is that the universe is expanding.* **2** [U] the act or process of forming an opinion, based on what you already know: *If he is guilty then, by inference, so is his wife* (= it is logical to think so, from the same evidence).

in·fer·ior /ɪnˈfɪəriə(r); AmE -ˈfɪr-/ *adj., noun*
■ *adj.* **1** **~** (to sb/sth) not as good as sb/sth else: *of inferior quality* ◊ *inferior goods/workmanship* ◊ *to make sb feel inferior* ◊ *Modern music is often considered inferior to that of the past.* **2** [usually before noun] (*formal*) of lower rank; lower: *an inferior officer/court* [OPP] SUPERIOR
■ *noun* a person who is not as good as sb else; a person who is lower in rank or status

in·fer·ior·ity /ɪnˌfɪəriˈɒrəti; AmE -ˌfɪriˈɔːr-; -ˈɑːr-/ *noun* [U] the state of not being as good as sb/sth else: *a sense of inferiority* ◊ *social inferiority*

inferi'ority complex *noun* a feeling that you are not as good, as important or as intelligent as other people: *She has always had an inferiority complex about her looks.*

in·fer·nal /ɪnˈfɜːnl; AmE ɪnˈfɜːrnl/ *adj.* **1** [only before noun] (*old-fashioned*) extremely annoying: *Stop that infernal noise!* **2** connected with HELL; terrible: *the infernal regions*

in·ferno /ɪnˈfɜːnəʊ; AmE ɪnˈfɜːrnoʊ/ *noun* [usually sing.] (*pl.* **-os**) a very large dangerous fire that is out of control: *a blazing/raging inferno*

in·fer·tile /ɪnˈfɜːtaɪl; AmE ɪnˈfɜːrtl/ *adj.* **1** (of people, animals and plants) not able to have babies or produce young: *an infertile couple* **2** (of land) not able to produce good crops [OPP] FERTILE ▶ **in·fer·til·ity** /ˌɪnfəˈtɪləti; AmE -fɜːrˈt-/ *noun* [U]: *an infertility clinic* ◊ *infertility treatment for couples*

---

s	t	v	z	ʃ	ʒ	tʃ	dʒ	θ	ð	ŋ
see	tea	van	zoo	shoe	vision	chain	jam	thin	this	sing

in·fest /ɪnˈfest/ *verb* [VN] [usually passive] (especially of insects or animals such as rats) to exist in large numbers in a particular place, often causing damage or disease: *shark-infested waters ◊ The kitchen was infested with ants.* ▶ **in·fes·ta·tion** /ˌɪnfeˈsteɪʃn/ *noun* [C, U]: *an infestation of lice*

in·fi·del /ˈɪnfɪdəl/ *noun* (*old use*) an offensive way of referring to sb who does not believe in what the speaker considers to be the true religion

in·fi·del·ity /ˌɪnfɪˈdeləti/ *noun* [U, C] (*pl.* **-ies**) the act of not being faithful to your wife, husband or partner, by having sex with sb else: *marital infidelity ◊ She could not forgive his infidelities.* **OPP** FIDELITY

in·fight·ing /ˈɪnfaɪtɪŋ/ *noun* [U] arguments and disagreements between people in the same group who are competing for power: *political infighting within the party*

in·fill /ˈɪnfɪl/ *noun* [U] **1** the filling in of a space with sth, especially the building of new houses in spaces between existing ones: *infill development* **2** the material used to fill in a space or a hole: *gravel infill* ▶ **in·fill** *verb* [V, VN]

in·fil·trate /ˈɪnfɪltreɪt/ *verb* **1** ~ (sb) (into sth) to enter or make sb enter a place or an organization secretly, especially in order to get information that can be used against it: [VN] *The headquarters had been infiltrated by enemy spies. ◊ Rebel forces were infiltrated into the country.* ◊ [V] *The CIA agents successfully infiltrated into the terrorist organizations.* **2** ~ (into) sth (*technical*) (especially of liquids or gases) to pass slowly into sth: [V] *Only a small amount of the rainwater actually infiltrates into the soil.* [also VN] ▶ **in·fil·tra·tion** /ˌɪnfɪlˈtreɪʃn/ *noun* [U]: *communist infiltration of the army ◊ the infiltration of rain into the soil*

in·fil·tra·tor /ˈɪnfɪltreɪtə(r)/ *noun* a person who secretly becomes a member of a group or goes to a place, to get information or to influence the group

in·fin·ite /ˈɪnfɪnət/ *adj., noun*
■ *adj.* **1** very great; impossible to measure: *an infinite variety of plants ◊ a teacher with infinite patience ◊* (*ironic*) *The company in its infinite wisdom decided to close the staff restaurant* (= they thought it was a good thing to do, but nobody else agreed). **2** without limits; without end: *an infinite universe* **OPP** FINITE
■ *noun* [sing.] **1** (the infinite) something that has no end **2** (the Infinite) God

in·fin·ite·ly /ˈɪnfɪnətli/ *adv.* **1** (used especially in comparisons) very much: *Your English is infinitely better than my German.* **2** extremely; with no limit: *Human beings are infinitely adaptable.*

in·fini·tesi·mal /ˌɪnfɪnɪˈtesɪml/ *adj.* (*formal*) extremely small: *infinitesimal traces of poison ◊ an infinitesimal risk* ▶ **in·fini·tesi·mal·ly** /-məli/ *adv.*

in·fini·tive /ɪnˈfɪnətɪv/ *noun* (*grammar*) the basic form of a verb such as *be* or *run*. In English, an infinitive is used by itself, as is *swim* in *She can swim*, or with *to* as in *She likes to swim.* **IDM** see SPLIT *v.*

in·fin·ity /ɪnˈfɪnəti/ *noun* (*pl.* **-ies**) **1** [U] (also **in·fin·it·ies** [pl.]) the state of having no end or limit: *the infinity/ infinities of space* **2** [U] a point far away that can never be reached: *The landscape seemed to stretch into infinity.* **3** (*symb* ∞) [U, C] (*mathematics*) a number larger than any other **4** [sing.] a large amount that is impossible to count: *an infinity of stars*

in·firm /ɪnˈfɜːm; *AmE* ɪnˈfɜːrm/ *adj.* **1** ill/sick and weak, especially over a long period or because of old age: *to grow old and infirm* **2** (the infirm) *noun* [pl.] people who are weak and ill/sick for a long period: *care for the elderly and infirm*

in·firm·ary /ɪnˈfɜːməri; *AmE* -ˈfɜːrm-/ *noun* (*pl.* **-ies**) **1** (often used in names) a hospital **2** a special room in a school, prison, etc. for people who are ill/sick: *the college infirmary*

in·firm·ity /ɪnˈfɜːməti; *AmE* -ˈfɜːrm-/ *noun* [U, C] (*pl.* **-ies**) weakness or illness over a long period: *We all fear disability or infirmity. ◊ the infirmities of old age*

in·flame /ɪnˈfleɪm/ *verb* [VN] (*written*) **1** to cause very strong feelings, especially anger or excitement, in a person or in a group of people: *His comments have inflamed teachers all over the country. ◊ Her defiance inflamed his jealousy yet further.* **2** to make a situation worse or more difficult to deal with: *The situation was further inflamed by the arrival of the security forces.*

in·flamed /ɪnˈfleɪmd/ *adj.* **1** (of a part of the body) red, sore and hot because of infection or injury: *an inflamed and swollen finger* **2** (of people, feelings, etc.) very angry or excited: *an inflamed crowd ◊ a man inflamed with jealousy*

in·flam·mable /ɪnˈflæməbl/ *adj.* **1** (*especially BrE*) = FLAMMABLE: *inflammable material* **2** full of strong emotions or violence

in·flam·ma·tion /ˌɪnfləˈmeɪʃn/ *noun* [U, C] a condition in which a part of the body becomes red, sore and swollen because of infection or injury: *inflammation of the ear ◊ a cream to reduce the inflammation*

in·flam·ma·tory /ɪnˈflæmətri; *AmE* -tɔːri/ *adj.* **1** (*disapproving*) intended to cause very strong feelings of anger: *inflammatory remarks* **2** (*medical*) causing or involving inflammation

in·flat·able /ɪnˈfleɪtəbl/ *adj., noun*
■ *adj.* needing to be filled with air or gas before you use it: *an inflatable dinghy/mattress*
■ *noun* **1** an inflatable boat **2** a large object made of plastic or rubber and filled with air or gas, used for children to play on, or as an advertisement for sth

in·flate /ɪnˈfleɪt/ *verb* **1** to fill sth or become filled with gas or air: [VN] *Inflate your life jacket by pulling sharply on the cord.* ◊ [V] *The life jacket failed to inflate.* **2** [VN] (*written*) to make sth appear to be more important or impressive than it really is: *The media have grossly inflated the significance of this meeting.* **3** (*written*) to increase in price; to increase the price of sth: [VN] *The principal effect of the demand for new houses was to inflate prices.* ◊ [V] *Food prices are no longer inflating at the same rate as last year.*—compare DEFLATE, REFLATE

in·flated /ɪnˈfleɪtɪd/ *adj.* **1** (especially of prices) higher than is acceptable or reasonable: *inflated salaries/bills* **2** (of ideas, claims, etc.) believing or claiming that sb/sth is more important or impressive than they really are: *He has an inflated sense of his own importance.*

in·fla·tion /ɪnˈfleɪʃn/ *noun* [U] **1** a general rise in the prices of services and goods in a particular country, resulting in a fall in the value of money; the rate at which this happens: *the fight against rising inflation ◊ to control/curb inflation ◊ to reduce/bring down inflation ◊ a high/low rate of inflation ◊ an inflation rate of 3% ◊ Wage increases must be in line with inflation. ◊ Inflation is currently running at 3%.* **2** the act or process of filling sth with air or gas: *life jackets with an automatic inflation device* **OPP** DEFLATION

in·fla·tion·ary /ɪnˈfleɪʃənri; *AmE* -neri/ *adj.* [usually before noun] causing or connected with a general rise in the prices of services and goods: *the inflationary effects of price rises ◊ Our economy is in an inflationary spiral of wage and price increases* (= a continuing situation in which an increase in one causes an increase in the other).

in·flect /ɪnˈflekt/ *verb* [V] (*grammar*) if a word **inflects**, its ending or spelling changes according to its GRAMMATICAL function in a sentence; if a language **inflects**, it has words that do this ▶ **in·flect·ed** *adj.* [usually before noun]: *an inflected language/form/verb*

in·flec·tion (also **in·flex·ion** especially in *BrE*) /ɪnˈflekʃn/ *noun* [C, U] **1** a change in the form of a word, especially the ending, according to its GRAMMATICAL function in a sentence **2** a change in how high or low your voice is as you are speaking: *She spoke slowly and without inflection.*

in·flex·ible /ɪnˈfleksəbl/ *adj.* **1** (*disapproving*) that cannot be changed or made more suitable for a particular situation **SYN** RIGID: *an inflexible attitude/routine/system ◊ The rules are too inflexible to allow for human error.* **2** (*disapproving*) (of people or organizations) unwilling to change their opinions, decisions, etc., or the way they do things: *He's completely inflexible on the subject.* **3** (of a material) difficult or impossible to bend **SYN** STIFF **OPP**

FLEXIBLE ▶ **in·flex·ibil·ity** /ɪnˌfleksə'bɪləti/ *noun* [U]
in·flex·ibly /-əbli/ *adv.*

in·flict /ɪn'flɪkt/ *verb* [VN] ~ **sth (on/upon sb/sth)** to make sb/sth suffer sth unpleasant: *They in'flicted a humiliating defeat on the home team.* ◇ *They surveyed the damage inflicted by the storm.* ◇ *Heavy casualties were inflicted on the enemy.* ◇ (*humorous*) *Do you have to inflict that music on us?* ▶ **in·flic·tion** /ɪn'flɪkʃn/ *noun* [U]: *the infliction of pain/harm/injury* PHRV **in'flict yourself/sb on sb** (often *humorous*) to force sb to spend time with you/sb when they do not want to: *Sorry to inflict myself on you again like this!*

'**in-flight** *adj.* [only before noun] provided or happening during a journey on a plane: *an in-flight meal/movie* ◇ *in-flight refuelling*

in·flow /'ɪnfləʊ; *AmE* -floʊ/ *noun* **1** [C, U] the movement of a lot of money, people or things into a place from somewhere else SYN INFLUX: *inflows of capital from abroad* ◇ *a steady inflow of refugees* **2** [sing., U] the movement of a liquid or of air into a place from somewhere else: *an inflow pipe* OPP OUTFLOW

in·flu·ence /'ɪnfluəns/ *noun, verb*
■ *noun* **1** [U, C] ~ **(on/upon sb/sth)** the effect that sb/sth has on the way a person thinks or behaves or on the way that sth works or develops: *to have/exert a strong influence on sb* ◇ *the influence of the climate on agricultural production* ◇ *What exactly is the influence of television on children?* **2** [U] ~ **(over sb/sth)** the power that sb/sth has to make sb/sth behave in a particular way: *Her parents no longer have any real influence over her.* ◇ *She could probably exert her influence with the manager and get you a job.* ◇ *He committed the crime* **under the influence of** *drugs.* **3** [C] ~ **(on sb/sth)** somebody or something that affects the way a person behaves and thinks: *cultural/environmental influences* ◇ *Those friends are a bad influence on her.* ◇ *His first music teacher was a major influence in his life.* IDM **under the 'influence** having had too much alcohol to drink: *She was charged with driving under the influence.*
■ *verb* **1** to have an effect on the way that sb behaves or thinks, especially by giving them an example to follow: [VN] *His writings have influenced the lives of millions.* ◇ *to be strongly/greatly/deeply influenced by sth* ◇ *Don't let me influence you either way.* ◇ [V wh-] *The wording of questions can influence how people answer.* [also VN to inf] **2** to have an effect on a particular situation and the way that it develops: [VN] *A number of social factors influence life expectancy.* [also V wh-]

in·flu·en·tial /ˌɪnflu'enʃl/ *adj.* ~ **(in sth/in doing sth)** having a lot of influence on sb/sth: *a highly influential book* ◇ *She is one of the most influential figures in local politics.* ◇ *The committee was influential in formulating government policy on employment.*

in·flu·enza /ˌɪnflu'enzə/ *noun* [U] (*formal*) = FLU

in·flux /'ɪnflʌks/ *noun* [usually sing.] ~ **(of sb/sth) (into ...)** the fact of a lot of people, money or things arriving somewhere: *a massive/sudden influx of visitors* ◇ *the influx of wealth into the region*

info /'ɪnfəʊ; *AmE* 'ɪnfoʊ/ *noun* **1** [U] (*informal*) information: *Have you had any more info about the job yet?* **2** (info-) (in nouns) connected with information: *an infosheet* ◇ *We send all potential clients an infopack.*

info·mer·cial /ˌɪnfəʊ'mɜːʃl; *AmE* ˌɪnfoʊ'mɜːrʃl/ *noun* (*especially AmE*) a long advertisement on television that tries to give a lot of information about a subject, so that it does not appear to be an advertisement

in·form /ɪn'fɔːm; *AmE* ɪn'fɔːrm/ *verb* **1** ~ **sb (of/about sth)** to tell sb about sth, especially in an official way: [VN] *Please inform us of any changes of address.* ◇ [VN that] *I have been reliably informed* (= somebody I trust has told me) *that the couple will marry next year.* ◇ [VN speech] *'He's already left,' she informed us.* [also VN wh-] **2** [VN] ~ **yourself (of/about sth)** to find out information about sth: *We need time to inform ourselves thoroughly of the problem.* **3** [VN] (*formal*) to have an influence on sth: *Religion informs every aspect of their lives.* PHRV **in'form on sb** to give information to the police or sb in authority about

the illegal activities of sb: *He informed on his own brother.*

in·for·mal /ɪn'fɔːml; *AmE* ɪn'fɔːrml/ *adj.* **1** relaxed and friendly; not following strict rules of how to behave or do sth: *an informal atmosphere* ◇ *an informal arrangement/meeting/visit* ◇ *Discussions are on an informal basis within the department.* **2** (of clothes) suitable for wearing at home or when relaxing rather than for a special or an official occasion SYN CASUAL **3** (of language) suitable for normal conversation and writing to friends rather than for serious speech and letters: *an informal expression/style*—compare FORMAL, SLANG ▶ **in·for·mal·ity** /ˌɪnfɔː'mæləti; *AmE* -fɔːr'm-/ *noun* [U] **in·for·mal·ly** /ɪn'fɔːməli; *AmE* -'fɔːrm-/ *adv.*: *They told me informally* (= not officially) *that I had got the job.* ◇ *to dress informally*

in·form·ant /ɪn'fɔːmənt; *AmE* -'fɔːrm-/ *noun* **1** a person who gives secret information about sb/sth to the police or a newspaper: *a police/paid informant* ◇ *The journalist refused to reveal the identity of his informant.* **2** (*technical*) a person who gives sb information about sth, for example to help them with their research: *His informants were middle-class professional women.*

in·for·ma·tion /ˌɪnfə'meɪʃn; *AmE* ˌɪnfər'm-/ (also *informal* **info**) *noun* [U] **1** ~ **(on/about sb/sth)** facts or details about sb/sth: *a piece of information* ◇ *a source of information* ◇ *to provide/give/pass on information* ◇ *to collect/gather/receive/obtain information* ◇ *For further information on the diet, write to us at this address.* ◇ *Our information is that the police will shortly make an arrest.* ◇ *This leaflet is produced* **for the information of** (= to inform) *our customers.* ◇ *an information desk/office* **2** (*AmE, informal*) = DIRECTORY ENQUIRIES ▶ **in·for·ma·tion·al** *adj.* [only before noun]: *the informational content of a book* ◇ *the informational role of the media* IDM **for information 'only** (*written*) written on documents that are sent to sb who needs to know the information in them but does not need to deal with them **for your infor'mation 1** (*abbr.* **FYI**) = FOR INFORMATION ONLY **2** (*informal*) used to tell sb that they are wrong about sth: *For your information, I don't even have a car.*—more at MINE *n.*

infor,mation super'highway (also **super·high·way**) *noun* (*computing*) a large electronic NETWORK such as the Internet, used for sending information such as sound, pictures and video quickly in DIGITAL form

infor,mation tech'nology *noun* [U] (*abbr.* **IT**) the study or use of electronic equipment, especially computers, for storing, analysing and sending out information

in·forma·tive /ɪn'fɔːmətɪv; *AmE* -'fɔːrm-/ *adj.* giving useful information: *The talk was both informative and entertaining.* OPP UNINFORMATIVE

in·formed /ɪn'fɔːmd; *AmE* ɪn'fɔːrmd/ *adj.* having or showing a lot of knowledge about a particular subject or situation: *an informed critic* ◇ *an informed choice/decision/guess/opinion* ◇ *They are not* **fully informed** *about the changes.* ◇ **Keep me informed** *of any developments.* OPP UNINFORMED—see also ILL-INFORMED, WELL INFORMED

in·form·er /ɪn'fɔːmə(r); *AmE* -'fɔːrm-/ *noun* a criminal who gives information to the police about other criminals

info·tain·ment /ˌɪnfəʊ'teɪnmənt; *AmE* ˌɪnfoʊ-/ *noun* [U] television programmes, etc. that present news and serious subjects in an entertaining way

infra- *prefix* (in adjectives) below or beyond a particular limit: *infrared*—compare ULTRA-

in·frac·tion /ɪn'frækʃn/ *noun* [C, U] (*formal*) an act of breaking a rule or law: *minor infractions of EU regulations*

infra dig /ˌɪnfrə 'dɪg/ *adj.* [not before noun] (*old-fashioned, BrE, informal*) considered to be below the standard of behaviour appropriate in a particular situation or to sb's social position

in·fra·red /ˌɪnfrə'red/ *adj.* (*physics*) having or using ELECTROMAGNETIC waves which are longer than those of red light in the SPECTRUM, and which cannot be seen: *infrared radiation* ◇ *an infrared lamp*—compare ULTRAVIOLET

in·fra·struc·ture /'ɪnfrəstrʌktʃə(r)/ *noun* [C, U] the

aɪ	aʊ	eɪ	əʊ	oʊ	ɔɪ	ɪə	eə	ʊə	j	w
my	now	say	go (BrE)	go (AmE)	boy	near	hair	pure	yes	wet

basic systems and services that are necessary for a country or an organization, for example buildings, transport, water and power supplies and administrative systems: *economic / social / transport infrastructure* ▶ **in·fra·struc·tural** /ˌɪnfrəˈstrʌktʃərəl/ *adj.* [usually before noun]: *infrastructural development*

in·fre·quent /ɪnˈfriːkwənt/ *adj.* not happening often SYN RARE: *her infrequent visits home* ◊ *Muggings are relatively infrequent in this area.* OPP FREQUENT ▶ **in·frequent·ly** *adv.*: *This happens not infrequently* (= often).

in·fringe /ɪnˈfrɪndʒ/ *verb* **1** [VN] (of an action, a plan, etc.) to break a law or rule: *The material can be copied without infringing copyright.* **2** ~ **(on/upon) sth** to limit sb's legal rights: [VN] *They said that compulsory identity cards would infringe civil liberties.* ◊ [V] *She refused to answer questions that infringed on her private affairs.* ▶ **in·fringe·ment** /-mənt/ *noun* [U, C]: *copyright infringement* ◊ *an infringement of liberty / rights*

in·furi·ate /ɪnˈfjʊərieɪt; AmE -ˈfjʊr-/ *verb* to make sb extremely angry SYN ENRAGE: [VN] *Her silence infuriated him even more.* ◊ [VN that] *It infuriates me that she was not found guilty.* [also VN to inf]

in·furi·at·ing /ɪnˈfjʊərieɪtɪŋ; AmE -ˈfjʊr-/ *adj.* making you extremely angry: *an infuriating child / delay* ◊ *It is infuriating to talk to someone who just looks out of the window.* ▶ **in·furi·at·ing·ly** *adv.*: *to smile infuriatingly* ◊ *Infuriatingly, the shop had just closed.*

in·fuse /ɪnˈfjuːz/ *verb* **1** [VN] ~ **A into B** | ~ **B with A** (*formal*) to make sb/sth have a particular quality: *Her novels are infused with sadness.* **2** [VN] (*formal*) to have an effect on all parts of sth: *Politics infuses all aspects of our lives.* **3** [V, VN] if you **infuse** herbs, etc. or they **infuse**, you put them in hot water until the flavour has passed into the water

in·fu·sion /ɪnˈfjuːʒn/ *noun* [C, U] **1** ~ **of sth (into sth)** (*formal*) the act of adding sth to sth else in order to make it stronger or more successful: *a cash / capital infusion* ◊ *an infusion of new talent into science education* ◊ *The company needs an infusion of new blood* (= new employees with new ideas). **2** a drink or medicine made by soaking herbs, etc. in hot water

-ing *suffix* used to make the present participle of regular verbs: *hating* ◊ *walking* ◊ *loving*

in·geni·ous /ɪnˈdʒiːniəs/ *adj.* **1** (of an object, a plan, an idea, etc.) very suitable for a particular purpose and resulting from clever new ideas: *an ingenious device / invention / experiment* ◊ *ingenious ways of saving energy* **2** (of a person) having a lot of clever new ideas and good at inventing things: *an ingenious cook* ◊ *She's very ingenious when it comes to finding excuses.* ▶ **in·geni·ous·ly** *adv.*: *ingeniously designed*

in·génue /ˈænzeɪnjuː; AmE ˈændʒənuː/ *noun* (from *French*) an innocent young woman, especially in a film / movie or play

in·genu·ity /ˌɪndʒəˈnjuːəti; AmE -ˈnuː-/ *noun* [U] the ability to invent things or solve problems in clever new ways: *The problem tested the ingenuity of even the most imaginative students.*

in·genu·ous /ɪnˈdʒenjuəs/ *adj.* (*formal, sometimes disapproving*) honest, innocent and willing to trust people SYN NAIVE: *You're too ingenuous.* ◊ *an ingenuous smile* ◊ *It is ingenuous to suppose that money did not play a part in his decision.*—compare DISINGENUOUS ▶ **in·genu·ous·ly** *adv.*

in·gest /ɪnˈdʒest/ *verb* [VN] (*technical*) to take food, drugs, etc. into your body, usually by swallowing ▶ **in·gest·ion** *noun* [U]

ingle·nook /ˈɪŋɡlnʊk/ *noun* a space at either side of a large FIREPLACE where you can sit

in·glori·ous /ɪnˈɡlɔːriəs/ *adj.* [usually before noun] (*literary*) causing feelings of shame: *an inglorious chapter in the nation's history*—compare GLORIOUS ▶ **in·glori·ous·ly** *adv.*

ingot /ˈɪŋɡət/ *noun* a solid piece of metal, especially gold or silver, usually shaped like a brick

in·grained /ɪnˈɡreɪnd/ *adj.* **1** ~ **(in sb/sth)** (of a habit, an attitude, etc.) that has existed for a long time and is

therefore difficult to change: *ingrained prejudices* ◊ *The belief that we should do our duty is deeply ingrained in most of us.* **2** (of dirt) under the surface of sth and therefore difficult to get rid of

in·grati·ate /ɪnˈɡreɪʃieɪt/ *verb* [VN] [no passive] ~ **yourself (with sb)** (*disapproving*) to do things in order to make sb like you, especially sb who will be useful to you: *The first part of his plan was to ingratiate himself with the members of the committee.*

in·grati·at·ing /ɪnˈɡreɪʃieɪtɪŋ/ *adj.* (*disapproving*) trying too hard to please sb: *an ingratiating smile* ▶ **in·grati·at·ing·ly** *adv.*

in·grati·tude /ɪnˈɡrætɪtjuːd; AmE -tuːd/ *noun* [U] the state of not feeling or showing that you are grateful for sth: *Her help was met with ingratitude and unkindness.* OPP GRATITUDE

in·gre·di·ent /ɪnˈɡriːdiənt/ *noun* ~ **(of/in/for sth)** **1** one of the things from which sth is made, especially one of the foods that are used together to make a particular dish: *Coconut is a basic ingredient for many curries.* ◊ *Our skin cream contains only natural ingredients.* **2** one of the things or qualities that are necessary to make sth successful: *the essential ingredients for success* ◊ *It has all the ingredients of a good mystery story.*

in·gress /ˈɪnɡres/ *noun* [U] (*formal*) the act of entering a place; the right to enter a place

'in-group *noun* (usually *disapproving*) a small group of people in an organization or a society whose members share the same interests, language, etc. and try to keep other people out SYN CLIQUE

in·grow·ing /ˈɪnɡrəʊɪŋ; AmE -ɡroʊ-/ (*BrE*) (also **ingrown** *AmE, BrE*) *adj.* [only before noun] (of the nail of a toe) growing inwards into the skin

in·habit /ɪnˈhæbɪt/ *verb* [VN] to live in a particular place: *some of the rare species that inhabit the area* ◊ *The island used to be inhabited* (= have people living here).

WORD FAMILY	
inhabit *v.*	
habitable *adj.*	(≠ uninhabitable)
uninhabited *adj.*	
inhabitant *n.*	
habitation *n.*	

in·hab·it·ant /ɪnˈhæbɪtənt/ *noun* a person or an animal that lives in a particular place: *the oldest inhabitant of the village* ◊ *a town of 11 000 inhabitants*

in·hal·ant /ɪnˈheɪlənt/ *noun* a drug or medicine that you breathe in

in·hale /ɪnˈheɪl/ *verb* to take air, smoke, gas, etc. into your lungs as you breathe SYN BREATHE IN: [V] *She closed her eyes and inhaled deeply.* ◊ *He inhaled deeply on another cigarette.* ◊ [VN] *Local residents needed hospital treatment after inhaling fumes from the fire.* OPP EXHALE ▶ **in·hal·ation** /ˌɪnhəˈleɪʃn/ *noun* [U]: *Hundreds of children were treated for smoke inhalation.*

in·haler /ɪnˈheɪlə(r)/ (also *informal* **puff·er**) *noun* a small device containing medicine that you breathe in through your mouth, used by people who have problems with breathing

in·here /ɪnˈhɪə(r); AmE ɪnˈhɪr/ *verb* PHRV **in'here in sth** (*rare, formal*) to be a natural part of sth: *the meaning which inheres in words*

in·her·ent /ɪnˈhɪərənt; AmE -ˈhɪr-/ *adj.* ~ **(in sb/sth)** that is a basic or permanent part of sb/sth and that cannot be removed SYN INTRINSIC: *the difficulties inherent in a study of this type* ◊ *Violence is inherent in our society.* ◊ *an inherent weakness in the design of the machine* ▶ **in·her·ent·ly** *adv.*: *an inherently unworkable system*

in·herit /ɪnˈherɪt/ *verb* ~ **(sth) (from sb)** **1** to receive money, property, etc. from sb when they die: [VN] *She inherited a fortune from her father.* [also V]—compare DISINHERIT **2** [VN] to have qualities, physical features, etc. that are similar to those of your parents, grandparents, etc: *He has inherited his mother's patience.* ◊ *an inherited disease* **3** [VN] if you **inherit** a particular situation from sb, you are now responsible for dealing with it, especially because you have replaced that person in their job: *policies inherited from the previous administration*

b	d	f	g	h	k	l	m	n	p	r
bad	did	fall	get	hat	cat	leg	man	now	pen	red

in·her·it·ance /ɪnˈherɪtəns/ *noun* **1** [C usually sing, U] the money, property, etc. that you receive from sb when they die; the fact of receiving sth when sb dies: *She spent all her inheritance in a year.* ◊ *The title passes by inheritance to the eldest son.* **2** [U, C] something from the past or from your family that affects the way you behave, look, etc: *our artistic/cultural inheritance* ◊ *Physical characteristics are determined by genetic inheritance.*

in'heritance tax (*AmE* also **e'state tax**) *noun* [U] tax that you must pay on the money or property that you receive from sb when they die

in·her·i·tor /ɪnˈherɪtə(r)/ *noun* **1** [usually pl.] **~ of sth** a person who is affected by the work, ideas, etc. of people who lived before them [SYN] HEIR: *We are the inheritors of a great cultural tradition.* **2** a person who receives money, property, etc. from sb when they die [SYN] HEIR

in·hibit /ɪnˈhɪbɪt/ *verb* [VN] **1** to prevent sth from happening or make it happen more slowly or less frequently than normal: *A lack of oxygen may inhibit brain development in the unborn child.* **2 ~ sb (from sth/from doing sth)** to make sb nervous or embarrassed so that they are unable to do sth: *The managing director's presence inhibited them from airing their problems.*

in·hibit·ed /ɪnˈhɪbɪtɪd/ *adj.* unable to relax or express your feelings in a natural way: *Boys are often more inhibited than girls about discussing their problems.*

in·hib·ition /ˌɪnhɪˈbɪʃn; ˌɪnɪˈb-/ *noun* **1** [C, U] a shy or nervous feeling that stops you from expressing your real thoughts or feelings: *The children were shy at first, but soon lost their inhibitions.* ◊ *She had no inhibitions about making her opinions known.* **2** [U] (*formal*) the act of restricting or preventing a process or an action: *the inhibition of growth*

in·hos·pit·able /ˌɪnhɒˈspɪtəbl; *AmE* ˌɪnhɑːˈs-/ *adj.* **1** (of a place) difficult to stay or live in, especially because there is no shelter from the weather: *inhospitable terrain* ◊ *an inhospitable climate* **2** (of people) not giving a friendly or polite welcome to guests [OPP] HOSPITABLE

'in-house *adj.* [only before noun] existing or happening within a company or an organization: *an in-house magazine* ◊ *in-house language training* ▶ **in-'house** *adv.*: *The software was developed in-house.*

in·human /ɪnˈhjuːmən/ *adj.* **1** lacking the qualities of kindness and pity; very cruel: *inhuman and degrading treatment/conditions* **2** not human; not seeming to be produced by a human being and therefore frightening: *There was a strange inhuman sound.*—compare HUMAN, NON-HUMAN, SUBHUMAN

in·hu·mane /ˌɪnhjuːˈmeɪn/ *adj.* not caring about the suffering of other people; very cruel: *inhumane treatment of animals/prisoners/the mentally ill* [OPP] HUMANE ▶ **in·hu·mane·ly** *adv.*

in·human·ity /ˌɪnhjuːˈmænəti/ *noun* [U] cruel behaviour or treatment; the fact of not having the usual human qualities of kindness and pity: *man's inhumanity to man* ◊ *the inhumanity of the system* [OPP] HUMANITY

in·imi·cal /ɪˈnɪmɪkl/ *adj.* (*formal*) **1 ~ to sth** harmful to sth; not helping sth: *These policies are inimical to the interests of society.* **2** unfriendly: *an inimical stare/look*

in·im·it·able /ɪˈnɪmɪtəbl/ *adj.* too good or individual for anyone else to copy with the same effect: *John related in his own **inimitable way** the story of his trip to Tibet.*

ini·qui·tous /ɪˈnɪkwɪtəs/ *adj.* (*formal*) very unfair or wrong [SYN] WICKED: *an iniquitous system/practice*

ini·quity /ɪˈnɪkwəti/ *noun* [U, C] (*pl.* **-ies**) (*formal*) the fact of being very unfair or wrong; sth that is very unfair or wrong: *the iniquity of racial prejudice* ◊ *the iniquities of the criminal justice system*

ini·tial /ɪˈnɪʃl/ *adj., noun, verb*
■ *adj.* [only before noun] happening at the beginning; first: *an initial payment of £60 and ten instalments of £25* ◊ *in the initial stages* (= at the beginning) *of the campaign* ◊ *My initial reaction was to decline the offer.*
■ *noun* **1** [C] the first letter of a person's first name: *'What initial is it, Mrs Owen?' 'It's J, J for Jane.'* **2** (**initials**) [pl.] the first letters of all of a person's names: *John Fitzgerald Kennedy was often known by his initials JFK.* ◊ *Just write your initials.*
■ *verb* (**-ll-**, *AmE* usually **-l-**) [VN] to mark or sign sth with your initials: *Please initial each page and sign in the space provided.*

ini·tial·ly /ɪˈnɪʃəli/ *adv.* at the beginning: *Initially, the system worked well.* ◊ *The death toll was initially reported at around 250, but was later revised to 300.*

ini·ti·ate *verb, noun*
■ *verb* /ɪˈnɪʃieɪt/ [VN] **1** (*formal*) to make sth begin: *to initiate legal action/proceedings against sb* ◊ *The government has initiated a programme of economic reform.* **2 ~ sb (into sth)** to explain sth to sb and/or make them experience it for the first time: *Many of them had been initiated into drug use at an early age.* **3 ~ sb (into sth)** to make sb a member of a particular group, especially as part of a secret ceremony: *Hundreds are initiated into the sect each year.*
■ *noun* /ɪˈnɪʃiət/ a person who has been allowed to join a particular group, organization, or religion and is learning its rules and secrets

ini·ti·ation /ɪˌnɪʃiˈeɪʃn/ *noun* [U] **1 ~ (into sth)** the act of sb becoming a member of a group, often with a special ceremony; the act of introducing sb to an activity or skill: *an initiation ceremony* ◊ *her initiation into the world of marketing* **2** (*formal*) the act of starting sth: *the initiation of criminal proceedings*

ini·tia·tive /ɪˈnɪʃətɪv/ *noun* **1** [C] a new plan for dealing with a particular problem or for achieving a particular purpose: *a United Nations peace initiative* ◊ *a government initiative to combat unemployment* **2** [U] the ability to decide and act on your own without waiting for sb to tell you what to do: *You won't get much help. You'll have to use your initiative.* ◊ *She did it on her own initiative* (= without anyone telling her to do it). **3** (**the initiative**) [sing.] the power or opportunity to act and gain an advantage before other people do: *to seize/lose the initiative* ◊ *It was up to the US to take the initiative in repairing relations.*

ini·ti·ator /ɪˈnɪʃieɪtə(r)/ *noun* (*formal*) the person who starts sth

in·ject /ɪnˈdʒekt/ *verb* [VN] **1 ~ sth (into yourself/sb/sth)** | **~ yourself/sb/sth (with sth)** to put a drug or other substance into a person's or an animal's body using a SYRINGE: *Adrenalin was injected into the muscle.* ◊ *She has been injecting herself with insulin since the age of 16.* **2 ~ A (into B)** | **~ B (with A)** to put a liquid into sth using a SYRINGE or similar instrument: *Chemicals are injected into the fruit to reduce decay.* ◊ *The fruit is injected with chemicals to reduce decay.* **3 ~ sth (into sth)** to add a particular quality to sth: *His comments injected a note of humour into the proceedings.* **4 ~ sth (into sth)** to give money to an organization, a project, etc. so that it can function: *They are refusing to inject any more capital into the industry.*

in·jec·tion /ɪnˈdʒekʃn/ *noun* **1** [C, U] an act of injecting sb with a drug or other substance: *to give sb an injection* ◊ *He was treated with penicillin injections.* ◊ *An anaesthetic was administered by injection.* ◊ *daily injections of insulin*—picture on page 599 **2** [C] a large sum of money that is spent to help improve a situation, business, etc: *The theatre faces closure unless it gets an urgent cash injection.* **3** [U, C] an act of forcing liquid into sth: *a fuel injection system*

'in-joke *noun* a joke that is only understood by a particular group of people

in·ju·di·cious /ˌɪndʒuˈdɪʃəs/ *adj.* (*formal*) not sensible or wise; not appropriate in a particular situation: *an injudicious act/remark* [OPP] JUDICIOUS ▶ **in·ju·di·cious·ly** *adv.*

in·junc·tion /ɪnˈdʒʌŋkʃn/ *noun* **1 ~ (against sb)** an official order given by a court of law which demands that sth must or must not be done: *to seek/obtain an injunction* ◊ *The court granted an injunction against the defendants.*—compare RESTRAINING ORDER **2** (*formal*) a warning or an order from sb in authority

in·jure /ˈɪndʒə(r)/ *verb* [VN] **1** to harm yourself or sb else physically, especially in an accident: *He injured his knee* *playing hockey.* ◊ *Three people were killed and five injured in the crash.* **2** to damage sb's reputation, pride, etc: *This could seriously injure the company's reputation.*

in·jured /ˈɪndʒəd; *AmE* -dʒərd/ *adj.* **1** physically hurt; having an injury: *an injured leg* ◊ *Luckily, she isn't injured.* ◊ *Carter is playing in place of the injured O'Reilly.* OPP UNINJURED **2** (**the injured**) *noun* [pl.] the people injured in an accident, a battle, etc: *Ambulances took the injured to a nearby hospital.* **3** (of a person or their feelings) upset or offended because sth unfair has been done: *an injured look / tone* ◊ *injured pride*

the ˌinjured ˈparty *noun* [sing.] (especially *law*) the person who has been treated unfairly, or the person who claims in a court of law to have been treated unfairly

in·juri·ous /ɪnˈdʒʊəriəs; *AmE* -ˈdʒʊr-/ *adj.* ~ (**to sb/sth**) (*formal*) causing or likely to cause harm or damage

in·jury /ˈɪndʒəri/ *noun* (*pl.* **-ies**) ~ (**to sb/sth**) **1** [C, U] harm done to a person's or an animal's body, for example in an accident: *serious injury / injuries* ◊ *minor injuries* ◊ *to sustain injuries / an injury* ◊ *to escape injury* ◊ *injury to the head* ◊ *a head injury* ◊ *Two players are out of the team because of injury.* ◊ *There were* **no injuries** *in the crash* (= no people injured). ◊ (*BrE, spoken*) *Don't do that. You'll* **do yourself an injury** (= hurt yourself). ⇨ vocabulary notes on page 598 **2** [U] (especially *law*) damage to a person's feelings: *Damages may be awarded for emotional injury.* IDM see ADD

ˈinjury time *noun* [U] (*BrE*) time added at the end of a game of football, hockey, etc. because the game has been interrupted by injured players needing treatment

in·just·ice /ɪnˈdʒʌstɪs/ *noun* [U, C] the fact of a situation being unfair and of people not being treated equally; an unfair act or an example of unfair treatment: *fighting against poverty and injustice* ◊ *a burning sense of injustice* ◊ *racial / social injustice* ◊ *She was enraged at the injustice of the remark.* ◊ *The report exposes the injustices of the system.* OPP JUSTICE IDM **do yourself/sb an inˈjustice** to judge yourself/sb unfairly: *We may have been doing him an injustice. This work is good.*

ink /ɪŋk/ *noun, verb*
■ *noun* [U, C] coloured liquid for writing, drawing and printing: *written* **in ink** ◊ *a pen and ink drawing* ◊ *different coloured inks*—see also INKY
■ *verb* [VN] **1** to cover sth with ink so that it can be used for printing **2** (*AmE, informal*) to sign a document, especially a contract: *The group has just inked a $10 million deal.* PHRV **ˌink sth ↔ ˈin** to write or draw in ink over sth that has already been drawn or drawn in pencil: (*figurative*) *The date for the presentation should have been inked in* (= made definite) *by now.*

ink-jet printer /ˈɪŋkdʒet prɪntə(r)/ *noun* a printer that uses very small JETS to blow ink onto paper in order to form letters, numbers, etc.

ink·ling /ˈɪŋklɪŋ/ *noun* [usually sing.] ~ (**of sth**) | ~ (**that …**) a slight knowledge of sth that is happening or about to happen SYN SUSPICION: *He had no inkling of what was going on.* ◊ *The first inkling I had that something was wrong was when I found the front door wide open.*

ˈink-pad *noun* a a thick piece of soft material soaked with ink, used with a rubber stamp

ink·well /ˈɪŋkwel/ *noun* a pot for holding ink that fits into a hole in a desk (used in the past)

inky /ˈɪŋki/ *adj.* **1** black like ink: *the inky blackness of the cellar* **2** made dirty with ink: *inky fingers*

in·laid /ˌɪnˈleɪd/ *adj.* ~ (**with sth**) (of furniture, floors, etc.) decorated with designs of wood, metal, etc. that are set into the surface: *an inlaid wooden box* ◊ *a box inlaid with gold*

in·land *adv., adj.*
■ *adv.* /ˌɪnˈlænd/ in a direction towards the middle of a country; away from the coast: *The town lies a few kilometres inland.* ◊ *We travelled further inland the next day.*
■ *adj.* /ˈɪnlænd/ [usually before noun] situated in or near the middle of a country, not near the edge or on the coast: *inland areas / towns / waterways* ◊ *inland seas / lakes*—compare COASTAL

the ˌInland ˈRevenue *noun* [sing.] the government department in Britain that is responsible for collecting taxes—compare THE INTERNAL REVENUE SERVICE

ˈin-laws *noun* [pl.] (*informal*) your relatives by marriage, especially the parents of your husband or wife: *We're visiting my in-laws on Sunday.*

inlay *verb, noun*
■ *verb* /ɪnˈleɪ/ (**in·lay·ing, in·laid, in·laid** /ˌɪnˈleɪd/) [VN] [often passive] ~ **A** (**with B**) | ~ **B** (**in/into A**) to decorate the surface of sth by putting pieces of wood or metal into it in such a way that the surface remains smooth: *The lid of the box had been inlaid with silver.*
■ *noun* /ˈɪnleɪ/ [C, U] a design or pattern on a surface made by setting wood or metal into it; the material that this design is made of: *The table was decorated with gold inlay.*

inlet /ˈɪnlet/ *noun* **1** a narrow strip of water that stretches into the land from the sea or a lake, or between islands **2** (*technical*) an opening through which liquid, air or gas can enter a machine: *a fuel inlet* OPP OUTLET

ˌin-line ˈskate *noun* = ROLLERBLADE™ ▶ **ˌin-line ˈskating** *noun* [U]

in loco par·en·tis /ɪn ˌləʊkəʊ pəˈrentɪs; *AmE* ˌloʊkoʊ/ *adv.* (from *Latin, formal*) having the same responsibility for a child as a parent has

in·mate /ˈɪnmeɪt/ *noun* one of the people living in an institution such as a prison or a mental hospital

in me·mor·iam /ˌɪn məˈmɔːriəm/ *prep.* (from *Latin*) used to mean 'in memory of', for example on the stone over a grave

in·most /ˈɪnməʊst; *AmE* ˈɪnmoʊst/ *adj.* [only before noun] = INNERMOST

inn /ɪn/ *noun* **1** (*old-fashioned, BrE*) a pub, usually in the country and often one where people can stay the night **2** (*AmE*) a small hotel, usually in the country **3** (**Inn**) used in the names of many pubs, hotels and restaurants: *Holiday Inn*

in·nards /ˈɪnədz; *AmE* ˈɪnərdz/ *noun* [pl.] (*informal*) **1** the organs inside the body of a person or an animal, especially the stomach: *turkey innards* **2** the parts inside a machine

in·nate /ɪˈneɪt/ *adj.* (of a quality, feeling, etc.) that you have when you are born: *the innate ability to learn* ▶ **in·nate·ly** *adv.*: *He believes that humans are innately violent.*

inner /ˈɪnə(r)/ *adj.* [only before noun] **1** inside; towards or close to the centre of a place: *an inner room / courtyard* ◊ *inner London* ◊ *the inner ear* OPP OUTER **2** (of feelings, etc.) private and secret; not expressed or shown to other people: *She doesn't reveal much of her inner self.*

ˌinner ˈcircle *noun* the small group of people who have a lot of power in an organization, or who control it

ˌinner ˈcity *noun* the part near the centre of a large city, which often has social problems: *There are huge problems in our inner cities.* ◊ *an inner-city area / school*

in·ner·most /ˈɪnəməʊst; *AmE* ˈɪnərmoʊst/ *adj.* [only before noun] **1** (also *less frequent* **in·most**) most private, personal and secret: *I could not express my innermost feelings to anyone.* **2** nearest to the centre or inside of sth: *the innermost shrine of the temple* OPP OUTERMOST

ˈinner tube *noun* a rubber tube filled with air inside a tyre

in·ning /ˈɪnɪŋ/ *noun* (in baseball) one of the nine periods of a game in which each team has a turn at BATTING

in·nings /ˈɪnɪŋz/ *noun* (*pl.* **in·nings**) (in cricket) a period of time in a game during which a team or a single player is BATTING IDM **sb had a good ˈinnings** (*BrE, informal*) used about sb who has died to say that they had a long life

innit /ˈɪnɪt/ *exclamation* (*BrE, non-standard*) a way of saying 'isn't it': *Cold, innit?*

inn·keep·er /ˈɪnkiːpə(r)/ *noun* (*old-fashioned*) a person who owns or manages an INN

in·no·cence /ˈɪnəsns/ *noun* [U] **1** the fact of not being guilty of a crime, etc: *She protested her innocence* (= said repeatedly that she was innocent). ◊ *This new evidence will prove their innocence.* ◊ *I asked if she was*

æ	ɑː	e	ɜː	ə	ɪ	iː	i	ɒ	ɔː	ʌ	ʊ	u	uː
cat	father	ten	bird	about	sit	see	many	got	saw	cup	put	actual	too
								(BrE)					

married **in all innocence** (= without knowing it was likely to offend or upset her). OPP GUILT **2** lack of knowledge and experience of the world, especially of evil or unpleasant things: *Children lose their innocence as they grow older.*

in·no·cent /ˈɪnəsnt/ *adj., noun*
■ *adj.* **1** ~ **(of sth)** not guilty of a crime, etc.; not having done sth wrong: *They have imprisoned an innocent man.* ◊ *She was found innocent of any crime.* ◊ *He was the innocent party* (= person) *in the breakdown of the marriage.* OPP GUILTY **2** [only before noun] suffering harm or being killed because of a crime, war, etc. although not directly involved in it: *an innocent bystander* ◊ *innocent victims of a bomb blast* **3** not intended to cause harm or upset sb SYN HARMLESS: *It was all innocent fun.* ◊ *It was a perfectly innocent remark.* **4** having little experience of the world, especially of sexual matters, or of evil or unpleasant things: *an innocent young child* ▶ **in·no·cent·ly** *adv.*: *'Oh, Sue went too, did she?' I asked innocently* (= pretending I did not know that this was important).
■ *noun* an innocent person, especially a young child

in·noc·u·ous /ɪˈnɒkjuəs; *AmE* ɪˈnɑːk-/ *adj.* (*formal*) **1** not intended to offend or upset anyone: *It seemed a perfectly innocuous remark.* **2** not harmful or dangerous: *an innocuous substance*

in·nov·ate /ˈɪnəveɪt/ *verb* to introduce new things, ideas, or ways of doing sth: [V] *We must constantly adapt and innovate to ensure success in a growing market.* ◊ [VN] *to innovate new ideas/products* ▶ **in·nov·ator** /ˈɪnəveɪtə(r)/ *noun*

in·nov·ation /ˌɪnəˈveɪʃn/ *noun* ~ **(in sth)** **1** [U] the introduction of new things, ideas or ways of doing sth: *an age of technological innovation* **2** [C] a new idea, way of doing sth, etc. that has been introduced or discovered: *recent innovations in steel-making technology*

in·nova·tive /ˈɪnəveɪtɪv; *BrE* also ˈɪnəvətɪv/ (also *less frequent* **in·nov·atory** /ˌɪnəˈveɪtəri; *AmE* also ˈɪnəvətɔːri/) *adj.* (*approving*) introducing or using new ideas, ways of doing sth, etc: *There will be a prize for the most innovative design.*

in·nu·endo /ˌɪnjuˈendəʊ; *AmE* -doʊ/ *noun* [C, U] (*pl.* **-oes** or **-os**) (*disapproving*) an indirect remark about sb/sth, usually suggesting sth bad or rude; the use of remarks like this: *innuendoes about her private life* ◊ *The song is full of sexual innuendo.*

in·nu·mer·able /ɪˈnjuːmərəbl; *AmE* ɪˈnuː-/ *adj.* too many to be counted; very many: *Innumerable books have been written on the subject.*

in·nu·mer·ate /ɪˈnjuːmərət; *AmE* ɪˈnuː-/ *adj.* unable to count or do simple mathematics OPP NUMERATE

in·ocu·late /ɪˈnɒkjuleɪt; *AmE* ɪˈnɑːk-/ *verb* [VN] ~ **sb (against sth)** to protect a person or an animal from catching a particular disease by INJECTING them with a mild form of the disease—compare IMMUNIZE, VACCINATE ▶ **in·ocu·la·tion** /ɪˌnɒkjuˈleɪʃn; *AmE* ɪˌnɑːk-/ *noun* [C, U]

in·offen·sive /ˌɪnəˈfensɪv/ *adj.* not likely to offend or upset anyone: *a shy, inoffensive young man* OPP OFFENSIVE

in·op·er·able /ɪnˈɒpərəbl; *AmE* ɪnˈɑːp-/ *adj.* **1** (of an illness, especially CANCER) not able to be cured by a medical operation: *an inoperable brain tumour* **2** (*formal*) that cannot be used or made to work; not practical: *The policy was thought to be inoperable.* OPP OPERABLE

in·op·era·tive /ɪnˈɒpərətɪv; *AmE* ɪnˈɑːp-/ *adj.* (*formal*) **1** (of a rule, system, etc.) not valid or able to be used **2** (of a machine) not working; not functioning correctly OPP OPERATIVE

in·op·por·tune /ɪnˈɒpətjuːn; *AmE* ɪnˌɑːpərˈtuːn/ *adj.* (*formal*) not appropriate or convenient; happening at a bad time: *They arrived at an inopportune moment.* OPP OPPORTUNE

in·or·din·ate /ɪnˈɔːdɪnət; *AmE* -ˈɔːrd-/ *adj.* (*formal*) far more than is usual or expected SYN EXCESSIVE: *They spent an inordinate amount of time and money on the production.* ▶ **in·or·din·ate·ly** *adv.*: *inordinately high prices*

in·or·gan·ic /ˌɪnɔːˈgænɪk; *AmE* ˌɪnɔːrˈg-/ *adj.* not consist-

ing of or coming from any living substances: *inorganic fertilizers* OPP ORGANIC

inor·ganic ˈchemistry *noun* [U] the branch of chemistry that deals with substances that do not contain CARBON—compare ORGANIC CHEMISTRY

in·pa·tient /ˈɪnpeɪʃnt/ *noun* a person who stays in a hospital while receiving treatment—compare OUTPATIENT

input /ˈɪnpʊt/ *noun, verb*
■ *noun* **1** [C, U] ~ **(into/to sth)** | ~ **(of sth)** time, knowledge, ideas, etc. that you put into work, a project, etc. in order to make it succeed; the act of putting sth in: *Her specialist input to the discussions has been very useful.* ◊ *I'd appreciate your input on this.* ◊ *There has been a big input of resources into the project from industry.* ◊ *Barley is one of the main inputs to the process of distillation.* **2** [U] (*computing*) the act of putting information into a computer; the information that you put in: *data input* ◊ *This program accepts input from most word processors.* **3** [C] (*technical*) a place or means for electricity, data, etc. to enter a machine or system—compare OUTPUT
■ *verb* (**in·put·ting**, **input**, **input**) or (**in·put·ting**, **in·put·ted**, **in·put·ted**) [VN] to put information into a computer: *to input text/data/figures*—compare OUTPUT

in·quest /ˈɪnkwest/ *noun* ~ **(on/into sth)** **1** an official investigation to find out the cause of sb's death, especially when it has not happened naturally: *An inquest was held to discover the cause of death.* ◊ *a coroner's inquest into his death* **2** a discussion about sth that has failed: *An inquest was held on the team's poor performance.*

in·quire, in·quirer, in·quir·ing, in·quiry (*especially AmE*) = ENQUIRE, ENQUIRER, ENQUIRING, ENQUIRY

in·qui·si·tion /ˌɪnkwɪˈzɪʃn/ *noun* **1 (the Inquisition)** [sing.] the organization set up by the Roman Catholic Church to punish people who opposed its beliefs, especially from the 15th to the 17th century **2** [C] (*formal* or *humorous*) a series of questions that sb asks you, especially when they ask them in an unpleasant way

in·quisi·tive /ɪnˈkwɪzətɪv/ *adj.* **1** (*disapproving*) asking too many questions and trying to find out about what other people are doing, etc: *Don't be so inquisitive. It's none of your business!* **2** very interested in learning about many different things: *an inquisitive nature/mind* ▶ **in·quisi·tive·ly** *adv.* **in·quisi·tive·ness** *noun* [U]

in·quisi·tor /ɪnˈkwɪzɪtə(r)/ *noun* **1** a person who asks a lot of difficult questions, especially in a way that makes you feel threatened **2** an officer of the Inquisition of the Roman Catholic Church ▶ **in·quisi·tor·ial** /ɪnˌkwɪzəˈtɔːriəl/ *adj.*: *He questioned her in a cold inquisitorial voice.* **in·quisi·tor·ial·ly** *adv.*

in·road /ˈɪnrəʊd; *AmE* -roʊd/ *noun* ~ **(into sth)** something that is achieved, especially by reducing the power or success of sth else: *This deal is their first major inroad into the American market.* IDM **make inroads into/on sth** if one thing **makes inroads into** another, it has a noticeable effect on the second thing, especially by reducing it, or influencing it: *Tax rises have made some inroads into the country's national debt.*

in·rush /ˈɪnrʌʃ/ *noun* [usually sing.] a sudden flow towards the inside: *an inrush of air/water*

in·sane /ɪnˈseɪn/ *adj.* **1** seriously mentally ill and unable to live in normal society: *Doctors certified him as insane.* ◊ *The prisoners were slowly going insane.* OPP SANE **2** (**the insane**) *noun* [pl.] people who are insane: *a hospital for the insane* **3** (*informal*) very stupid, crazy or dangerous: *I must have been insane to agree to the idea.*—see also INSANITY ▶ **in·sane·ly** *adv.*: *He is insanely jealous.* IDM SEE DRIVE *v.*

in·sani·tary /ɪnˈsænətri; *AmE* -teri/ (also **un·sani·tary** especially in *AmE*) *adj.* dirty and likely to spread disease OPP SANITARY

in·san·ity /ɪnˈsænəti/ *noun* [U] **1** the state of being INSANE: *He was found not guilty, by reason of insanity.* OPP SANITY **2** actions that are very stupid and possibly dangerous: *It would be sheer insanity to attempt the trip in such bad weather.*

in·sati·able /ɪnˈseɪʃəbl/ *adj.* always wanting more of

sth; not able to be satisfied: *an insatiable appetite/curiosity/thirst* ◊ *There seems to be an insatiable demand for more powerful computers.* ▶ **in·sati·ably** /-ʃəbli/ *adv.*

in·scribe /ɪnˈskraɪb/ *verb* [VN] ~ **A (on/in B)** | ~ **B (with A)** to write or cut words, your name, etc. onto sth: *His name was inscribed on the trophy.* ◊ *The trophy was inscribed with his name.* ◊ *She signed the book and inscribed the words 'with grateful thanks' on it.*

in·scrip·tion /ɪnˈskrɪpʃn/ *noun* words written in the front of a book or cut in stone or metal: *There was an inscription carved over the doorway.*

in·scrut·able /ɪnˈskruːtəbl/ *adj.* if a person or their expression is **inscrutable**, it is hard to know what they are thinking or feeling, because they do not show any emotion ▶ **in·scrut·abil·ity** /ɪnˌskruːtəˈbɪləti/ *noun* [U] **in·scrut·ably** /ɪnˈskruːtəbli/ *adv.*

in·sect /ˈɪnsekt/ *noun* any small creature with six legs and a body divided into three parts. Insects usually also have wings. ANTS, bees and flies are all insects: *insect pests/larvae/species* ◊ *insect repellent* (= a chemical that keeps insects away) ◊ *an insect bite*—picture on page A7—see also STICK INSECT ┃**HELP**┃ Insect is often used to refer to other small crawling creatures, for example spiders, although this is not correct scientific language.

in·secti·cide /ɪnˈsektɪsaɪd/ *noun* [C, U] a chemical used for killing insects: *crops sprayed with insecticides*—see also HERBICIDE, PESTICIDE ▶ **in·secti·cidal** /ɪnˌsektɪˈsaɪdl/ *adj.*

in·sect·ivore /ɪnˈsektɪvɔː(r)/ *noun* any animal that eats insects—compare CARNIVORE, HERBIVORE, OMNIVORE ▶ **in·sect·iv·or·ous** /ˌɪnsekˈtɪvərəs/ *adj.*

in·se·cure /ˌɪnsɪˈkjʊə(r); *AmE* -ˈkjʊr/ *adj.* **1** not confident about yourself or your relationships with other people: *He's very insecure about his appearance.* ◊ *She felt nervous and insecure.* **2** not safe or protected: *Jobs nowadays are much more insecure than they were ten years ago.* ◊ *As an artist he was always financially insecure.* ◊ *Insecure doors and windows* (= for example, without good locks) *make life easy for burglars.* ┃OPP┃ SECURE ▶ **in·se·cure·ly** *adv.* **in·secur·ity** /ˌɪnsɪˈkjʊərəti; *AmE* -ˈkjʊr-/ *noun* [U, C] (*pl.* **-ies**): *feelings of insecurity* ◊ *job insecurity* ◊ *We all have our fears and insecurities.*

in·sem·in·ate /ɪnˈsemɪneɪt/ *verb* [VN] (*technical*) to put SPERM into a woman or female animal in order to make her pregnant: *The cows are **artificially** inseminated.* ▶ **in·sem·in·ation** /ɪnˌsemɪˈneɪʃn/ *noun* [U]:—see also ARTIFICIAL INSEMINATION

in·sens·ibil·ity /ɪnˌsensəˈbɪləti/ *noun* [U] **1** (*formal*) the state of being unconscious **2** the fact of not being able to react to particular things: *insensibility to pain/beauty*

in·sens·ible /ɪnˈsensəbl/ *adj.* (*formal*) **1** [not before noun] ~ **(to sth)** unable to feel sth or react to it: *insensible to pain/cold* **2** [not before noun] ~ **(of sth)** not aware of a situation or of sth that might happen: *They were not insensible of the risks.* ┃OPP┃ SENSIBLE **3** unconscious as the result of injury, illness, etc: *He drank himself insensible.* ▶ **in·sens·ibly** /-əbli/ *adv.*

in·sensi·tive /ɪnˈsensətɪv/ *adj.* ~ **(to sth) 1** not realizing or caring how other people feel, and therefore likely to hurt or offend them: *an insensitive person/remark* ◊ *She's completely insensitive to my feelings.* **2** not aware of changing situations, and therefore of the need to react to them: *The government seems totally insensitive to the mood of the country.* **3** not able to feel or react to sth: *insensitive to pain/cold* ◊ *He seems completely insensitive to criticism.* ┃OPP┃ SENSITIVE ▶ **in·sensi·tive·ly** *adv.* **in·sensi·tiv·ity** /ɪnˌsensəˈtɪvəti/ *noun* [U]

in·sep·ar·able /ɪnˈseprəbl/ *adj.* **1** ~ **(from sth)** not able to be separated: *Our economic fortunes are inseparable from those of Europe.* **2** if people are **inseparable**, they spend most of their time together and are very good friends ▶ **in·sep·ar·ab·il·ity** /ɪnˌseprəˈbɪləti/ *noun* [U] **in·sep·ar·ably** /ɪnˈseprəbli/ *adv.*: *Our lives were inseparably linked.*

in·sert *verb, noun*
■ *verb* /ɪnˈsɜːt; *AmE* ɪnˈsɜːrt/ [VN] **1** ~ **sth (in/into/between sth)** to put sth into sth else or between two things: *Insert*

coins into the slot and press for a ticket. ◊ *They inserted a tube in his mouth to help him breathe.* **2** ~ **sth (into sth)** to add sth to a piece of writing: *Position the cursor where you want to insert a word.* ◊ *Later, he inserted another paragraph into his will.*
■ *noun* /ˈɪnsɜːt; *AmE* ˈɪnsɜːrt/ ~ **(in sth) 1** an extra section added to a book, newspaper or magazine, especially to advertise sth: *an 8-page insert on the new car models* **2** something that is put inside sth else, or added to sth else: *These inserts fit inside any style of shoe.*

in·ser·tion /ɪnˈsɜːʃn; *AmE* ɪnˈsɜːrʃn/ *noun* **1** [U, C] ~ **(in/into sth)** the act of putting sth inside sth else; a thing that is put inside sth else: *An examination is carried out before the insertion of the tube.* **2** [C, U] a thing that is added to a book, piece of writing, etc.; the act of adding sth: *the insertion of an extra paragraph*

'in-service *adj.* [only before noun] (of training, courses of study, etc.) done while sb is working in a job, in order to learn new skills: *in-service training*

inset /ˈɪnset/ *noun, verb*
■ *noun* **1** a small picture, map, etc. inside a larger one: *For the Shetland Islands, see inset.* **2** something that is added on to sth else, or put inside sth else: *The windows have beautiful stained glass insets.*
■ *verb* (**in·set·ting, inset, inset**) [VN] **1** [usually passive] ~ **A (with B)** | ~ **B (into A)** to fix sth into the surface of sth else, especially as a decoration: *The tables were inset with ceramic tiles.* ◊ *Ceramic tiles were inset into the tables.* **2** ~ **sth (into sth)** to put a small picture, map, etc. inside the borders of a bigger one

in·shore /ˈɪnʃɔː(r)/ *adj.* [usually before noun] in the sea but close to the shore: *an inshore breeze* ◊ *an inshore lifeboat* (= that stays close to the land) ▶ **,in'shore** *adv.*: *The boat came inshore* (= towards the land).—compare OFFSHORE

in·side /ˌɪnˈsaɪd/ *prep., adv., noun, adj.*
■ *prep.* (also **in·side of** especially in *AmE*) **1** on or to the inner part of sth/sb; within sth/sb: *Go inside the house.* ◊ *Inside the box was a gold watch.* ◊ *For years we had little knowledge of what life was like inside China.* ◊ *You'll feel better with a good meal inside you.* ◊ (*figurative*) *Inside most of us is a small child screaming for attention.* ┃OPP┃ OUTSIDE **2** in less than the amount of time mentioned: *The job is unlikely to be finished inside (of) a year*
■ *adv.* **1** on or to the inside: *She shook it to make sure there was nothing inside.* ◊ *We had to move inside* (= indoors) *when it started to rain.* ◊ (*figurative*) *I pretended not to care but I was screaming inside.* ┃OPP┃ OUTSIDE **2** (*informal*) in prison: *He was sentenced to three years inside.*

inside out   back to front

■ *noun* **1** [C, usually sing.] (usually **the inside**) the inner part, side or surface of sth: *The inside of the box was blue.* ◊ *The door was locked from the inside.* ◊ *The shell is smooth on the inside.* ◊ *the insides of the windows* ┃OPP┃ THE OUTSIDE **2** (**the inside**) [sing.] the part of a road nearest the edge, that is used by slower vehicles: *He tried to overtake on the inside.* ┃OPP┃ THE OUTSIDE **3** (**the inside**) [sing.] the part of a curved road or track nearest to the middle or shortest side of the curve: *The French runner is coming up fast on the inside.* ┃OPP┃ THE OUTSIDE **4** (**insides**) [pl.] (*informal*) a person's stomach and bowels: *She was so nervous, her insides were like jelly.* ┃IDM┃ **,inside 'out** with the part that is usually inside facing out: *You've got your sweater on inside out.* ◊ *Turn the bag inside out and* *let it dry.*—compare BACK TO FRONT at BACK *n.* **on the in'side** belonging to a group or an organization and therefore able to get information that is not available to other people: *The thieves must have had someone on the inside helping them.* **turn sth inside out 1** to make a place very untidy when you are searching for sth: *The burglars had turned the house inside out.* **2** to cause large changes: *The new manager turned the old systems inside out.*—more at KNOW *v.*

■ *adj.* [only before noun] **1** forming the inner part of sth; not on the outside: *the inside pages of a newspaper* ◊ *an inside pocket* **2** known or done by sb in a group or an organization: *inside information* ◊ *Any newspaper would pay big money to get the inside story on her marriage.* ◊ *The robbery appeared to have been an inside job.*

in·sider /ɪnˈsaɪdə(r)/ *noun* a person who knows a lot about a group or an organization, because they are part of it: *The situation was described by one insider as 'absolute chaos'.*

in,sider 'dealing (also **in,sider 'trading**) *noun* [U] the crime of buying or selling SHARES in a company with the help of information known only by those connected with the business

,inside 'track *noun* [sing.] (*especially AmE*) a position in which you have an advantage over sb else

in·sidi·ous /ɪnˈsɪdiəs/ *adj.* (*formal, disapproving*) spreading gradually or without being noticed, but causing serious harm: *the insidious effects of polluted water supplies* ▶ **in·sidi·ous·ly** *adv.*

in·sight /ˈɪnsaɪt/ *noun* **1** [U] (*approving*) the ability to see and understand the truth about people or situations: *a writer of great insight* ◊ *With a flash of insight I realized what the dream meant.* **2** [C, U] ~ **(into sth)** an understanding of what sth is like: *The book gives us fascinating insights into life in Mexico.* ◊ *I hope you have gained some insight into the difficulties we face.*

in·sight·ful /ˈɪnsaɪtfʊl/ *adj.* (*approving*) showing a clear understanding of a person or situation: *an insightful historian*

in·sig·nia /ɪnˈsɪɡniə/ *noun* [U+sing./pl. *v.*] the symbol, BADGE or sign that shows sb's rank or that they are a member of a group or an organization: *the royal insignia* ◊ *His uniform bore the insignia of a captain.*

in·sig·nifi·cant /ˌɪnsɪɡˈnɪfɪkənt/ *adj.* not big or valuable enough to be considered important: *an insignificant difference* ◊ *The levels of chemicals in the river are not insignificant.* ◊ *He made her feel insignificant and stupid.* **OPP** SIGNIFICANT ▶ **in·sig·nifi·cance** /-kəns/ [U]: *Her own problems paled into insignificance beside this terrible news.* **in·sig·nifi·cant·ly** *adv.*

in·sin·cere /ˌɪnsɪnˈsɪə(r); *AmE* -ˈsɪr/ *adj.* (*disapproving*) saying or doing sth that you do not really mean or believe: *an insincere smile* **OPP** SINCERE ▶ **in·sin·cere·ly** *adv.* **in·sin·cer·ity** /ˌɪnsɪnˈserəti/ *noun* [U]: *She accused him of insincerity.*

in·sinu·ate /ɪnˈsɪnjueɪt/ *verb* **1** to suggest indirectly that sth unpleasant is true: [V that] *The article insinuated that he was having an affair with his friend's wife.* ◊ [VN] *What are you trying to insinuate?* ◊ *an insinuating smile/ glance/tone* **2** [VN] ~ **yourself into sth** (*formal, disapproving*) to succeed in gaining sb's respect, affection, etc. so that you can use the situation to your own advantage: *In the first act, the villain insinuates himself into the household of the man he intends to kill.* **3** [VN+adv./prep.] (*formal*) to slowly move yourself or a part of your body into a particular position or place: *She insinuated her right hand under his arm.*

in·sinu·ation /ɪnˌsɪnjuˈeɪʃn/ *noun* **1** [C] something that sb insinuates: *She resented the insinuation that she was too old for the job.* **2** [U] the act of insinuating sth

in·sip·id /ɪnˈsɪpɪd/ *adj.* (*disapproving*) **1** having almost no taste or flavour: *a cup of insipid coffee* **2** not interesting or exciting: *After an hour of insipid conversation, I left.*

in·sist /ɪnˈsɪst/ *verb* ~ **(on sth) 1** to demand that sth happens or that sb agrees to do sth: [V] *I didn't really want to go but he insisted.* ◊ *'Please come with us' 'Very well then, if you insist.'* ◊ (*formal*) *She insisted on his/him*

wearing a suit. ◊ [V that] *He insists that she come.* ◊ (*BrE* also) *He insists that she should come.* **2** to say firmly that sth is true, especially when other people do not believe you: [V] *He insisted on his innocence.* ◊ [V (that)] *He insisted (that) he was innocent.* [also V speech] **PHRV in'sist on/ upon sth** to demand sth and refuse to be persuaded to accept anything else: *We insisted on a refund of the full amount.* ◊ [+ -ing] *They insisted upon being given every detail of the case.* **in'sist on doing sth** to continue doing sth even though other people think it is annoying: *They insist on playing their music late at night.*

in·sist·ence /ɪnˈsɪstəns/ *noun* [U] ~ **(on sth/on doing sth)|** ~ **(that …)** an act of demanding or saying sth firmly and refusing to accept any opposition or excuses: *their insistence on strict standards of behaviour* ◊ *At her insistence, the matter was dropped.*

in·sist·ent /ɪnˈsɪstənt/ *adj.* **1** ~ **(on sth/on doing sth)|** ~ **(that …)** demanding sth firmly and refusing to accept any opposition or excuses: *They were insistent on having a contract for the work.* ◊ *Why are you so insistent that we leave tonight?* ◊ *She didn't want to go but her brother was insistent.* **2** continuing for a long period of time in a way that cannot be ignored: *insistent demands* ◊ *the insistent ringing of the telephone* ▶ **in·sist·ent·ly** *adv.*

in situ /ˌɪn ˈsɪtjuː; *AmE* also ˈsaɪtuː/ *adv.* (from *Latin*) in the original or correct place

in·so·far as /ˌɪnsəˈfɑːr əz/ = IN SO FAR AS at FAR

in·sole /ˈɪnsəʊl; *AmE* ˈɪnsoʊl/ *noun* a piece of material shaped like your foot that is placed inside a shoe to make it more comfortable

in·so·lent /ˈɪnsələnt/ *adj.* extremely rude and showing a lack of respect: *an insolent child/smile* ▶ **in·so·lence** /-əns/ *noun* [U]: *Her insolence cost her her job.* **in·so·lent·ly** *adv.*

in·sol·uble /ɪnˈsɒljəbl; *AmE* -ˈsɑːl-/ *adj.* **1** (*especially BrE*) (*AmE* usually **in·sol·vable** /ɪnˈsɒlvəbl; *AmE* -ˈsɑːl-/) (of a problem, MYSTERY, etc.) that cannot be solved or explained **2** ~ **(in sth)** (of a substance) that does not dissolve in a liquid **OPP** SOLUBLE

in·solv·ent /ɪnˈsɒlvənt; *AmE* -ˈsɑːl-/ *adj.* not having enough money to pay what you owe **SYN** BANKRUPT: *The company has been declared insolvent.* **OPP** SOLVENT ▶ **in·solv·ency** /-ənsi/ *noun* [U, C] (*pl.* **-ies**)

in·som·nia /ɪnˈsɒmniə; *AmE* -ˈsɑːm-/ *noun* [U] the condition of being unable to sleep: *to suffer from insomnia*—see also SLEEPLESSNESS

in·som·niac /ɪnˈsɒmniæk; *AmE* -ˈsɑːm-/ *noun* a person who finds it difficult to sleep

in·sou·ci·ance /ɪnˈsuːsiəns/ *noun* [U] (*formal*) the state of not being worried about anything **SYN** NONCHALANCE: *She hid her worries behind an air of insouciance.* ▶ **in·sou·ci·ant** /-siənt/ *adj.*

Insp *abbr.* INSPECTOR (especially in the British police force): *Chief Insp (Paul) King*

in·spect /ɪnˈspekt/ *verb* [VN] **1** ~ **sth/sb (for sth)** to look closely at sth/sb, especially to check that everything is satisfactory **SYN** EXAMINE: *The teacher walked around inspecting their work.* ◊ *The plants are regularly inspected for disease.* ◊ *Make sure you inspect the goods before signing for them.* **2** to officially visit a school, factory, etc. in order to check that rules are being obeyed and that standards are acceptable: *Public health officials were called in to inspect the premises.* ▶ **in·spec·tion** /ɪnˈspekʃn/ *noun* [U, C]: *to carry out an inspection of sth* ◊ *On closer inspection, the notes proved to be forgeries.* ◊ *The head went on a tour of inspection of all the classrooms.*

in·spect·or /ɪnˈspektə(r)/ *noun* **1** a person whose job is to visit schools, factories, etc. to check that rules are being obeyed and that standards are acceptable: *a school/ health/safety inspector*—see also TAX INSPECTOR **2** (*abbr.* **Insp**) an officer of middle rank in the POLICE FORCE: *Inspector Maggie Forbes*—see also CHIEF INSPECTOR **3** (in Britain) a person whose job is to check tickets on a bus or train to make sure that they are valid

in·spect·or·ate /ɪnˈspektərət/ *noun* [C+sing./pl. *v.*] (*especially BrE*) an official group of inspectors who work together on the same subject or at the same kind of

s	t	v	z	ʃ	ʒ	tʃ	dʒ	θ	ð	ŋ
see	tea	van	zoo	shoe	vision	chain	jam	thin	this	sing

institution: *The schools inspectorate has/have published a report on science teaching.*

in·spector of 'taxes (also **'tax inspector**) *noun* (in Britain) a person who is responsible for collecting the tax that people must pay on the money they earn—see also TAX COLLECTOR, TAXMAN

in·spir·ation /ˌɪnspəˈreɪʃn/ *noun* **1** [U] ~ **(to do sth)**| ~ **(for sth)** the process that takes place when sb sees or hears sth that causes them to have exciting new ideas or makes them want to create sth, especially in art, music or literature: *She had the time and the inspiration to develop her talent.* ◊ *Dreams can be a rich source of inspiration for an artist.* ◊ *Both poets* **drew their inspiration** *from the countryside.* ◊ *Looking for inspiration for a new dessert? Try this recipe.* **2** [C, usually sing.] ~ **(for sth)** somebody or something that is the reason why sb creates or does sth: *He says my sister was the inspiration for his heroine.* ◊ *Clark was the inspiration behind Saturday's victory.* **3** [C, usually sing.] ~ **(to/for sb)** somebody or something that makes you want to be better, more successful, etc: *Her charity work is an inspiration to us all.* **4** [C usually sing, U] a sudden good idea: *He had an inspiration: he'd give her a dog for her birthday.* ◊ *It came to me in a flash of inspiration.*

in·spir·ation·al /ˌɪnspəˈreɪʃənl/ *adj.* providing inspiration: *an inspirational leader*

in·spire /ɪnˈspaɪə(r)/ *verb* **1** ~ **sb (to sth)** to give sb the desire, confidence or enthusiasm to do sth well: [VN] *The actors inspired the kids with their enthusiasm.* ◊ *The actors' enthusiasm inspired the kids.* ◊ *His superb play inspired the team to a thrilling 5–0 win.* ◊ [VN to inf] *By visiting schools, the actors hope to inspire children to put on their own productions.* **2** [VN] [usually passive] to give sb the idea for sth, especially sth artistic or imaginative: *The choice of decor was inspired by a trip to India.* ◊ *His paintings were clearly inspired by Monet's work.* **3** [VN] ~ **sb (with sth)**| ~ **sth (in sb)** to make sb have a particular feeling or emotion: *Her work didn't exactly* **inspire me with confidence.** ◊ *As a general, he inspired great loyalty in his troops.*

in·spired /ɪnˈspaɪəd; *AmE* ɪnˈspaɪərd/ *adj.* **1** having excellent qualities or abilities; produced with the help of INSPIRATION: *an inspired performance/poet* ◊ *an inspired choice/guess* (= one that is right but based on feelings rather than knowledge) OPP UNINSPIRED **2** (-**inspired**) used with nouns, adjectives and adverbs to form adjectives that show how sth has been influenced: *politically-inspired killings*

in·spir·ing /ɪnˈspaɪərɪŋ/ *adj.* exciting and encouraging you to do or feel sth: *an inspiring teacher* ◊ *(informal) The book is less than inspiring.* OPP UNINSPIRING—see also AWE-INSPIRING

in·stabil·ity /ˌɪnstəˈbɪləti/ *noun* [U, C, usually pl.] (*pl.* -**ies**) **1** the quality of a situation in which things are likely to change or fail suddenly: *political and economic instability* **2** a mental condition in which sb's behaviour is likely to change suddenly: *mental/emotional instability* OPP STABILITY—see also UNSTABLE

in·stall /ɪnˈstɔːl/ *verb* [VN] **1** to fix equipment or furniture into position so that it can be used: *He's getting a phone installed tomorrow.* ◊ *The hotel chain has recently installed a new booking system.* ◊ *I'll need some help installing the software.* **2** ~ **sb (as sth)** to put sb in a new position of authority, often with an official ceremony: *He was installed as President last May.* **3** to make sb/yourself comfortable in a particular place or position: *We installed ourselves in the front row.*

in·stal·la·tion /ˌɪnstəˈleɪʃn/ *noun* **1** [U, C] the act of fixing equipment or furniture in position so that it can be used: *installation costs* ◊ *Installation of the new system will take several days.* **2** [C] a piece of equipment or machinery that has been fixed in position so that it can be used: *a heating installation* **3** [C] a place where specialist equipment is kept and used: *a military/nuclear installation* **4** [U] the act of placing sb in a new position of authority, often with a ceremony: *the installation of the new vice-chancellor* **5** [C] (*art*) a piece of modern SCULP-

TURE that is made using sound, light, etc. as well as objects

in'stallment plan *noun* [U, C] (*AmE*) = HIRE PURCHASE

in·stal·ment (*especially BrE*) (*AmE* usually **in·stall·ment**) /ɪnˈstɔːlmənt/ *noun* **1** one of a number of payments that are made regularly over a period of time until sth has been paid for: *We paid for the car by/in instalments.* ◊ *The final instalment on the loan is due next week.* ◊ *They were unable to keep up* (= continue to pay regularly) *the instalments.* **2** one of the parts of a story that appears regularly over a period of time in a newspaper, on television, etc. SYN EPISODE

in·stance /ˈɪnstəns/ *noun, verb*
■ *noun* a particular example or case of sth: *The report highlights a number of instances of injustice.* ◊ *In most instances, there will be no need for further treatment.* ◊ *I would normally suggest taking time off work, but* **in this instance** *I'm not sure that would do any good.* IDM **for 'instance** for example: *What would you do, for instance, if you found a member of staff stealing?* **in the 'first instance** (*formal*) as the first part of a series of actions: *In the first instance, notify the police and then contact your insurance company.*
■ *verb* [VN] (*formal*) to give sth as an example

in·stant /ˈɪnstənt/ *adj., noun*
■ *adj.* **1** [usually before noun] happening immediately: *She took an instant dislike to me.* ◊ *This account gives you instant access to your money.* ◊ *The show was an instant success.* **2** [only before noun] (of food) that can be made quickly and easily, usually by adding hot water: *instant coffee*
■ *noun* [usually sing.] **1** a very short period of time; a moment: *I'll be back in an instant.* ◊ *Just for an instant I thought he was going to refuse.* **2** a particular point in time: *At that (very) instant, the door opened.* ◊ *I recognized her* **the instant** (*that*) (= as soon as) *I saw her.* ◊ *Come here* **this instant** (= immediately)!

in·stant·an·eous /ˌɪnstənˈteɪniəs/ *adj.* happening immediately: *an instantaneous response* ◊ *Death was almost instantaneous.* ▸ **in·stant·an·eous·ly** *adv.*

in·stant·ly /ˈɪnstəntli/ *adv.* immediately: *Her voice is instantly recognizable.* ◊ *The driver of the car was killed instantly.*

ˌinstant 'replay *noun* (*AmE*) = ACTION REPLAY

in·stead /ɪnˈsted/ *adv.* in the place of sb/sth: *Lee was ill so I went instead.* ◊ *He didn't reply. Instead, he turned on his heel and left the room.* ◊ *(written) She said nothing, preferring instead to save her comments till later.*

in'stead of *prep.* in the place of sb/sth: *We just had soup instead of a full meal.* ◊ *Now I can walk to work instead of going by car.*

in·step /ˈɪnstep/ *noun* **1** the top part of the foot that forms an arch between the ankle and toes **2** the part of a shoe that covers the instep

in·sti·gate /ˈɪnstɪɡeɪt/ *verb* [VN] **1** (*especially BrE*) to make sth start or happen, usually with official SYN BRING STH ABOUT: *The government has instigated a programme of economic reform.* **2** to cause sth bad to happen: *They were accused of instigating racial violence.*

in·sti·ga·tion /ˌɪnstɪˈɡeɪʃn/ *noun* [U] the act of causing sth to begin or happen: *An appeal fund was launched at the instigation of the President.* ◊ *It was done at his instigation.*

in·sti·ga·tor /ˈɪnstɪɡeɪtə(r)/ *noun* ~ **(of sth)** a person who causes sth to happen, especially sth bad: *the instigators of the riots*

in·stil (*BrE*) (*AmE* **in·still**) /ɪnˈstɪl/ *verb* (-**ll**-) [VN] ~ **sth (in/into sb)** to gradually make sb feel, think or behave in a particular way over a period of time: *to instil confidence/discipline/fear into sb*

in·stinct /ˈɪnstɪŋkt/ *noun* [U, C] **1** ~ **(for sth/for doing sth)**| ~ **(to do sth)** a natural tendency for people and animals to behave in a particular way using the knowledge and abilities that they were born with rather than thought or training: *maternal instincts* ◊ *Children do not know by instinct the difference between right and wrong.* ◊ *His first instinct was to run away.* ◊ *Horses have a well-*

æ	ɑː	e	ɜː	ə	ɪ	iː	i	ɒ	ɔː	ʌ	ʊ	u	uː
cat	father	ten	bird	about	sit	see	many	got	saw	cup	put	actual	too
								(BrE)					

developed instinct for fear. ◊ Even at school, he showed he **had an instinct for** (= was naturally good at) business. **2** ~ **(that ...)** a feeling that makes you do sth or believe that sth is true, even though it is not based on facts or reason SYN INTUITION: Her instincts had been right.

in·stinct·ive /ɪnˈstɪŋktɪv/ adj. based on instinct, not thought or training: instinctive knowledge ◊ She's an instinctive player. ◊ My instinctive reaction was to deny everything. ▶ **in·stinct·ive·ly** adv.: He knew instinctively that something was wrong.

in·stinct·ual /ɪnˈstɪŋktʃuəl/ adj. (psychology) based on natural instinct; not learned

in·sti·tute /ˈɪnstɪtjuːt; AmE -tuːt/ noun, verb
■ noun an organization that has a particular purpose, especially one that is connected with education or a particular profession; the building used by this organization: a research institute ◊ the Institute of Chartered Accountants ◊ institutes of higher education
■ verb [VN] (formal) to introduce a system, policy, etc. or start a process: to institute criminal proceedings against sb ◊ The new management intends to institute a number of changes.

in·sti·tu·tion /ˌɪnstɪˈtjuːʃn; AmE -ˈtuːʃn/ noun **1** [C] a large important organization that has a particular purpose, for example, a university or bank: an educational/financial institution ◊ the Smithsonian Institution **2** [C] (usually disapproving) a building where people with special needs are taken care of, for example because they are old or mentally ill: a mental/penal institution ◊ We want this to be like a home, not an institution. **3** [C] a custom or system that has existed for a long time among a particular group of people: the institution of marriage ◊ Fish and chips have become a British institution. **4** [U] the act of starting or introducing sth such as a system or a law: the institution of new safety procedures **5** [C] (informal, humorous) a person who is well known because they have been in a particular place or job for a long time: You must know him—he's an institution around here!

in·sti·tu·tion·al /ˌɪnstɪˈtjuːʃənl; AmE -ˈtuː-/ adj. [usually before noun] connected with an institution: institutional investors ◊ institutional care/food ▶ **in·sti·tu·tion·ally** /-ʃənəli/ adv.

in·sti·tu·tion·al·ize (BrE also **-ise**) /ˌɪnstɪˈtjuːʃənəlaɪz; AmE -ˈtuː-/ verb [VN] **1** to send sb who is not capable of living independently to live in a special house (= an institution) especially when it is for a long period of time **2** to make sth become part of an organized system, society or culture, so that it is considered normal ▶ **in·sti·tu·tion·al·iza·tion, -isa·tion** /ˌɪnstɪˌtjuːʃənəlaɪˈzeɪʃn; AmE -ˌtuːʃ ənələˈ-/ noun [U]

in·sti·tu·tion·al·ized (BrE also **-ised**) /ˌɪnstɪˈtjuːʃənəlaɪzd; AmE -ˈtuː-/ adj. **1** (usually disapproving) that has happened or been done for so long that it is considered normal: institutionalized racism **2** (of people) lacking the ability to live and think independently because they have spent so long in an institution: institutionalized patients

ˌin-ˈstore adj. [only before noun] within a large shop/store: an in-store bakery

in·struct /ɪnˈstrʌkt/ verb **1** (formal) to tell sb to do sth, especially in a formal or official way: [VN to inf] The letter instructed him to report to headquarters immediately. ◊ [VN wh-] You will be instructed where to go as soon as the plane is ready. ◊ [VN] She arrived at 10 o'clock as instructed. ◊ [VN] He instructed that a wall be built around the city. ◊ (BrE also) He instructed that a wall should be built around the city. [also V speech, VN speech] ⇨ note at ORDER **2** [VN] ~ **sb (in sth)** (formal) to teach sb sth, especially a practical skill: All our staff have been instructed in sign language. **3** [VN that] [usually passive] (formal) to give sb information about sth: We have been instructed that a decision will not be made before the end of the week. **4** [VN, VN to inf] (law) to employ sb to represent you in a legal situation, especially as a lawyer

in·struc·tion /ɪnˈstrʌkʃn/ noun, adj.
■ noun **1** (**instructions**) [pl.] detailed information on how to do or use sth SYN DIRECTIONS: Follow the instructions on the packet carefully. **2** [C, usually pl.] ~ **(to do sth)** | ~ **(that ...)** something that sb tells you to do SYN ORDER: to ignore/carry out sb's instructions ◊ I'm under instructions to keep my speech short. **3** [C] a piece of information that tells a computer to perform a particular operation. **4** [U] ~ **(in sth)** (formal) the act of teaching sth to sb: religious instruction
■ adj. [only before noun] giving detailed information on how to do or use sth (= giving instructions): an instruction book/manual

in·struc·tion·al /ɪnˈstrʌkʃənl/ adj. [usually before noun] that teaches people sth: instructional materials/videos

in·struct·ive /ɪnˈstrʌktɪv/ adj. giving a lot of useful information: a most instructive experience ◊ It is instructive to see how other countries are tackling the problem.

in·struct·or /ɪnˈstrʌktə(r)/ noun **1** a person whose job is to teach sb a practical skill or sport: a driving instructor **2** (AmE) a teacher below the rank of ASSISTANT PROFESSOR at a college or university

in·stru·ment /ˈɪnstrəmənt/ noun **1** a tool or device used for a particular task, especially for delicate or scientific work: surgical/optical/precision instruments ◊ instruments of torture **2** = MUSICAL INSTRUMENT: Is he learning an instrument? **3** a device used for measuring speed, distance, temperature, etc. in a vehicle or on a piece of machinery: the flight instruments ◊ the instrument panel **4** ~ **of/for sth** (formal) something that is used by sb in order to achieve sth; a person or thing that makes sth happen: The law is not the best instrument for dealing with family matters. ◊ an instrument of change/oppression **5** ~ **of sb/sth** (formal) a person who is used and controlled by sb/sth that is more powerful: an instrument of God/fate

in·stru·men·tal /ˌɪnstrəˈmentl/ adj., noun
■ adj. **1** ~ **(in sth/in doing sth)** important in making sth happen: He was instrumental in bringing about an end to the conflict. **2** made by or for musical instruments: instrumental music ▶ **in·stru·men·tal·ly** adv.
■ noun a piece of music (usually popular music) in which only musical instruments are used with no singing

in·stru·men·tal·ist /ˌɪnstrəˈmentəlɪst/ noun a person who plays a musical instrument—compare VOCALIST

in·stru·men·ta·tion /ˌɪnstrəmenˈteɪʃn/ noun [U] **1** a set of INSTRUMENTS used in operating a vehicle or a piece of machinery: the aircraft's instrumentation **2** the way in which a piece of music is written for a particular group of instruments

in·sub·or·din·ation /ˌɪnsəˌbɔːdɪˈneɪʃn; AmE -ˌbɔːrd-/ noun [U] (formal) the refusal to obey orders or show respect for sb who has a higher rank SYN DISOBEDIENCE: Two officers were reported for insubordination. ▶ **in·sub·or·din·ate** /ˌɪnsəˈbɔːdɪnət; AmE -ˈbɔːrd-/ adj.

in·sub·stan·tial /ˌɪnsəbˈstænʃl/ adj. **1** not very large, strong or important: an insubstantial construction of wood and glue ◊ an insubstantial argument **2** (literary) not real or solid: as insubstantial as a shadow

in·suf·fer·able /ɪnˈsʌfrəbl/ adj. extremely annoying, unpleasant and difficult to bear SYN UNBEARABLE: insufferable pride ◊ He's insufferable! ▶ **in·suf·fer·ably** /-əbli/ adv.: insufferably hot

in·suf·fi·cient /ˌɪnsəˈfɪʃnt/ adj. ~ **(to do sth)** | ~ **(for sth)** not large, strong or important enough for a particular purpose SYN INADEQUATE: insufficient evidence/time ◊ His salary is insufficient to meet his needs. OPP SUFFICIENT ▶ **in·suf·fi·cient·ly** adv. **in·suf·fi·ciency** /-ˈfənsi/ noun [U, sing.] (usually technical): cardiac insufficiency

in·su·lar /ˈɪnsjələ(r); AmE ˈɪnsələr/ adj. (disapproving) only interested in your own country, ideas, etc. and not in those from outside: The British are often accused of being insular. ▶ **in·su·lar·ity** /ˌɪnsjuˈlærəti; AmE -səˈl-/ noun [U]

in·su·late /ˈɪnsjuleɪt; AmE -səl-/ verb [VN] **1** ~ **sth (from/against sth)** to protect sth with a material that prevents heat, sound, electricity, etc. from passing through: Home

aɪ	aʊ	eɪ	əʊ	oʊ	ɔɪ	ɪə	eə	ʊə	j	w
my	now	say	go (BrE)	go (AmE)	boy	near	hair	pure	yes	wet

owners are being encouraged to insulate their homes to save energy. **2 ~ sb/sth from/against sth** (*written*) to protect sb/sth from unpleasant experiences or influences [SYN] SHIELD: *Until now the industry has been insulated from economic realities.*

in·su·lated /ˈɪnsjuleɪtɪd; *AmE* -səl-/ *adj.* protected with a material that prevents heat, sound, electricity, etc. from passing through: *insulated wires ◊ a well-insulated house*

in·su·lat·ing /ˈɪnsjuleɪtɪŋ; *AmE* ˈɪnsəleɪtɪŋ/ *adj.* [only before noun] preventing heat, sound, electricity, etc. from passing through: *insulating materials/properties*

ˈinsulating tape *noun* [U] a strip of sticky material used for covering bare electrical wires to prevent the possibility of an electric shock

in·su·la·tion /ˌɪnsjuˈleɪʃn; *AmE* -səl-/ *noun* [U] the act of protecting sth with a material that prevents heat, sound, electricity, etc. from passing through; the materials used for this: *Better insulation of your home will help to reduce heating bills. ◊ foam insulation*

in·su·la·tor /ˈɪnsjuleɪtə(r); *AmE* -səl-/ *noun* a material or device used to prevent heat, electricity, or sound from escaping from sth

in·su·lin /ˈɪnsjəlɪn; *AmE* -səl-/ *noun* [U] a chemical substance produced in the body that controls the amount of sugar absorbed by the blood; a similar artificial substance given to people whose bodies do not produce enough naturally: *insulin-dependent diabetes*

in·sult *verb, noun*
■ *verb* /ɪnˈsʌlt/ [VN] to say or do sth that offends sb: *I have never been so insulted in my life! ◊ She felt insulted by the low offer.*
■ *noun* /ˈɪnsʌlt/ **~ (to sb/sth)** a remark or an action that is said or done in order to offend sb: *The crowd were shouting insults at the police. ◊ His comments were seen as an insult to the president. ◊ The questions were an insult to our intelligence* (= too easy). [IDM] see ADD

in·sult·ing /ɪnˈsʌltɪŋ/ *adj.* **~ (to sb/sth)** causing or intending to cause sb to feel offended: *insulting behaviour/remarks ◊ She was really insulting to me.*

in·su·per·able /ɪnˈsuːpərəbl; *BrE* also -ˈsjuː-/ *adj.* (*formal*) (of difficulties, problems, etc.) that cannot be dealt with successfully [SYN] INSURMOUNTABLE

in·sup·port·able /ˌɪnsəˈpɔːtəbl; *AmE* -ˈpɔːrt-/ *adj.* so bad or difficult that you cannot accept it or deal with it [SYN] INTOLERABLE: *Their debt had become an insupportable burden.*

in·sur·ance /ɪnˈʃʊərəns; -ˈʃɔːr-; *AmE* -ˈʃʊr-/ *noun* **1** [U, C] **~ (against sth)** an arrangement with a company in which you pay them regular amounts of money and they agree to pay the costs, for example, if you die or are ill, or if you lose or damage sth: *life/car/travel/household insurance ◊ to have adequate insurance cover ◊ to take out insurance against fire and theft ◊ insurance premiums* (= the regular payments made for insurance) *◊ Can you claim for the loss on your insurance?*—see also NATIONAL INSURANCE **2** [U] the business of providing people with insurance: *an insurance broker/company ◊ He works in insurance.* **3** [U] money paid by or to an insurance company: *to pay insurance on your house ◊ When her husband died, she received £50000 in insurance.* **4** [U, C] **~ (against sth)** something you do to protect yourself against sth bad happening in the future: *At that time people had large families as an insurance against some children dying.*

inˈsurance adjuster *noun* (*AmE*) = LOSS ADJUSTER

inˈsurance policy *noun* a written contract between a person and an insurance company: *a travel insurance policy ◊* (*figurative*) *Always make a back-up disk as an insurance policy.*

in·sure /ɪnˈʃʊə(r); -ˈʃɔː(r); *AmE* -ˈʃʊr/ *verb* **1 ~ (yourself/sth) (against/for sth)** to buy insurance so that you will receive money if your property, car, health, etc. gets damaged, stolen, etc: [VN] *The painting is insured for $1 million. ◊ Luckily he had insured himself against long-term illness. ◊* (*figurative*) *Having a lot of children is a way of insuring themselves against loneliness in old age. ◊* [V] *We strongly recommend insuring against sickness or injury.* **2** [VN] to sell insurance to sb for sth: *The company*

can refuse to insure a property that does not have window locks. **3** (*especially AmE*) = ENSURE

in·sured /ɪnˈʃʊəd; -ˈʃɔːd; *AmE* -ˈʃʊrd/ *adj.* **1 ~ (to do sth)| ~ (against sth)** having insurance: *Was the vehicle insured? ◊ You're not insured to drive our car. ◊ It isn't insured against theft.* **2 (the insured)** *noun* (*pl.* **the insured**) (*law*) the person who has made an agreement with an insurance company and who receives money if, for example, they are ill or if they lose or damage sth

in·surer /ɪnˈʃʊərə(r); -ˈʃɔːr-; *AmE* -ˈʃʊr-/ *noun* a person or company that provides people with insurance

in·sur·gency /ɪnˈsɜːdʒənsi; *AmE* -ˈsɜːrdʒ-/ *noun* [U, C] (*pl.* **-ies**) an attempt to take control of a country by force [SYN] REBELLION—see also COUNTER-INSURGENCY

in·sur·gent /ɪnˈsɜːdʒənt; *AmE* -ˈsɜːrdʒ-/ *noun* [usually pl.] (*formal*) a person fighting against the government or armed forces of their own country [SYN] REBEL: *an attack by armed insurgents ◊ insurgent groups* ▶ **in·sur·gent** *adj.*

in·sur·mount·able /ˌɪnsəˈmaʊntəbl; *AmE* -sərˈm-/ *adj.* (*formal*) (of difficulties, problems, etc.) that cannot be dealt with successfully [SYN] INSUPERABLE

in·sur·rec·tion /ˌɪnsəˈrekʃn/ *noun* [C, U] a situation in which a large group of people try to take political control of their own country with violence [SYN] UPRISING: *an armed insurrection against the regime* ▶ **in·sur·rec·tion·ary** /ˌɪnsəˈrekʃənəri; *AmE* -neri/ *adj.*

in·tact /ɪnˈtækt/ *adj.* [not usually before noun] complete and not damaged: *Most of the house remains intact even after two hundred years. ◊ He emerged from the trial with his reputation intact.*

in·take /ˈɪnteɪk/ *noun* **1** [U, C] the amount of food, drink, etc. that you take into your body: *high fluid intake ◊ to reduce your daily intake of salt* **2** [C, U] the number of people who are allowed to enter a school, college, profession, etc. during a particular period: *the annual student intake ◊ Intake in universities is down by 10%.* **3** [C] a place where liquid, air, etc. enters a machine: *the air/fuel intake* **4** [C, usually sing.] an act of taking sth in, especially breath: *a sharp intake of breath*

in·tan·gible /ɪnˈtændʒəbl/ *adj.* **1** that exists but that is difficult to describe, understand or measure: *The old building had an intangible air of sadness about it. ◊ The benefits are intangible.* **2** (*business*) that does not exist as a physical thing but is still valuable to a company: *intangible assets/property* [OPP] TANGIBLE ▶ **in·tan·gible** *noun* [usually pl.]: *intangibles such as staff morale and goodwill*

in·te·ger /ˈɪntɪdʒə(r)/ *noun* (*mathematics*) a whole number, such as 3 or 4 but not 3.5—compare FRACTION

in·te·gral /ˈɪntɪɡrəl/ *adj.* **1 ~ (to sth)** being an essential part of sth: *Music is an integral part of the school's curriculum. ◊ Practical experience is integral to the course.* **2** [usually before noun] included as part of sth, rather than supplied separately: *All models have an integral CD player.* **3** [usually before noun] having all the parts that are necessary for sth to be complete: *an integral system* ▶ **in·te·gral·ly** /ˈɪntɪɡrəli/ *adv.*

in·te·grate /ˈɪntɪɡreɪt/ *verb* **1 ~ (A) (into/with B)| ~ A and B** to combine two or more things so that they work together; to combine with sth else in this way: [V] *These programs will integrate with your existing software. ◊* [VN] *These programs can be integrated with your existing software.* **2 ~ (sb) (into/with sth)** to become or make sb become accepted as a member of a social group, especially when they come from a different culture: [V] *They have not made any effort to integrate with the local community.* [also VN] [OPP] SEGREGATE

in·te·grated /ˈɪntɪɡreɪtɪd/ *adj.* [usually before noun] in which many different parts are closely connected and work successfully together: *an integrated transport system* (= including buses, trains, taxis, etc.) *◊ an integrated school* (= attended by students of all races and religions)

ˌintegrated ˈcircuit *noun* (*physics*) a small MICROCHIP that contains a large number of electrical connections and performs the same function as a larger CIRCUIT made from separate parts

in·te·gra·tion /ˌɪntɪˈɡreɪʃn/ *noun* **1** the act or process of

b	d	f	g	h	k	l	m	n	p	r
bad	**did**	**fall**	**get**	**hat**	**cat**	**leg**	**man**	**now**	**pen**	**red**

combining two or more things so that they work together (= of integrating them): *The aim is to promote closer economic integration.* **2** the act or process of mixing people who have previously been separated, usually because of colour, race, religion, etc: *racial integration in schools*

in·teg·rity /ɪnˈtegrəti/ *noun* [U] **1** the quality of being honest and having strong moral principles: *personal/ professional/artistic integrity ◊ to behave with integrity* **2** (*formal*) the state of being whole and not divided: *to respect the territorial integrity of the nation*

in·tel·lect /ˈɪntəlekt/ *noun* **1** [U, C] the ability to think in a logical way and understand things, especially at an advanced level; your mind: *a man of considerable intellect* **2** [C] a very intelligent person: *She was one of the most formidable intellects of her time.*

in·tel·lec·tual /ˌɪntəˈlektʃuəl/ *adj., noun*
- *adj.* **1** [usually before noun] connected with or using a person's ability to think in a logical way and understand things [SYN] MENTAL: *intellectual development/curiosity ◊ an intellectual novel* **2** (of a person) well educated and enjoying activities in which you have to think seriously about things: *She's very intellectual.* ▶ **in·tel·lec·tu·al·ly** *adv.*: *intellectually challenging/gifted* **in·tel·lec·tual·ism** /ˌɪntəˈlektʃuəlɪzəm/ *noun* [U] (usually *disapproving*)
- *noun* a person who is well educated and enjoys activities in which they have to think seriously about things

ˌintel·lectual ˈproperty *noun* [U] (*law*) an idea, a design, etc. that sb has created and that the law prevents other people from copying: *intellectual property rights*

in·tel·li·gence /ɪnˈtelɪdʒəns/ *noun* [U] **1** the ability to learn, understand and think in a logical way about things; the ability to do this well: *a person of high/ average/low intelligence ◊ He didn't even have the intelligence to call for an ambulance.*—see also ARTIFICIAL INTELLIGENCE **2** secret information that is collected about a foreign country, especially one that is an enemy; the people that collect this information: *intelligence reports/ operations ◊ the US Central Intelligence Agency*

in'telligence quotient *noun* = IQ

in'telligence test *noun* a test to measure how well a person is able to understand and think in a logical way about things

in·tel·li·gent /ɪnˈtelɪdʒənt/ *adj.* **1** good at learning, understanding and thinking in a logical way about things; showing this ability: *a highly intelligent child ◊ to ask an intelligent question* [OPP] UNINTELLIGENT **2** (of an animal, a being, etc.) able to understand and learn things: *a search for intelligent life on other planets* **3** (*computing*) (of a computer, program, etc.) able to store information and use it in new situations: *intelligent software/systems* ▶ **in·tel·li·gent·ly** *adv.*

in·tel·li·gent·sia /ɪnˌtelɪˈdʒentsiə/ (usually **the intelligentsia**) *noun* [sing.+ sing./pl. *v.*] the people in a country or society who are well educated and are interested in culture, politics, literature, etc.

in·tel·li·gible /ɪnˈtelɪdʒəbl/ *adj.* ~ (to sb) that can be easily understood: *His lecture was readily intelligible to all the students.* [OPP] UNINTELLIGIBLE ▶ **in·tel·li·gi·bil·ity** /ɪnˌtelɪdʒəˈbɪləti/ *noun* [U] **in·tel·li·gibly** *adv.*

in·tem·per·ate /ɪnˈtempərət/ *adj.* (*formal*) **1** showing a lack of control over yourself: *intemperate language* [OPP] TEMPERATE **2** (*especially AmE*) regularly drinking too much alcohol ▶ **in·tem·per·ance** /-pərəns/ *noun* [U]

in·tend /ɪnˈtend/ *verb* **1** to have a plan, result or purpose in your mind when you do sth: [V] *We finished later than intended.* ◊ [V to inf] *I fully intended* (= definitely intended) *to pay for the damage.* *The writer clearly intends his readers to identify with the main character.* ◊ [V-ing] (*BrE*) *I don't intend staying long.* ◊ [VN] *The company intends a slow-down in expansion.* ◊ [VNN] *He intended her no harm* (= it was not his plan to harm her). ◊ [VN that] *It*

> **WORD FAMILY**
> intend *v.*
> intended *adj.* (≠ unintended)
> intention *n.*
> intentional *adj.* (≠ unintentional)

is intended that production will start at the end of the month. [also V that] **2** [VN] ~ sth (by sth)|~ sth (as sth) to plan that sth should have a particular meaning [SYN] MEAN: *What exactly did you intend by that remark? ◊ He intended it as a joke.*

in·tend·ed /ɪnˈtendɪd/ *adj.* [only before noun] **1** that you are trying to achieve or reach: *the intended purpose ◊ his intended victims/audience* **2** ~ for sb/sth|~ as sth|~ to be/do sth planned or designed for sb/sth: *The book is intended for children. ◊ The notes are intended as an introduction to the course.*—see also UNINTENDED

in·tense /ɪnˈtens/ *adj.* **1** very great; very strong; extreme: *intense heat/cold/pain ◊ The President is under intense pressure to resign. ◊ the intense blue of her eyes ◊ intense interest/pleasure/desire/anger* **2** serious and often involving a lot of action in a short period of time: *intense competition/activity/speculation* **3** (of a person) having or showing very strong feelings, opinions or thoughts about sb/sth: *an intense gaze/look ◊ He's very intense about everything.*—compare INTENSIVE ▶ **in·tense·ly** *adv.*: *She disliked him intensely.*

in·ten·si·fier /ɪnˈtensɪfaɪə(r)/ *noun* (*grammar*) a word, especially an adjective or an adverb, for example *so* or *very*, that strengthens the meaning of another word

in·ten·sify /ɪnˈtensɪfaɪ/ *verb* (**in·ten·si·fies, in·ten·si·fy·ing, in·ten·si·fied, in·ten·si·fied**) to increase in degree or strength; to make sth increase in degree or strength [SYN] HEIGHTEN: [V] *Violence intensified during the night. ◊* [VN] *The opposition leader has intensified his attacks on the government.* ▶ **in·tensi·fi·ca·tion** /ɪnˌtensɪfɪˈkeɪʃn/ *noun* [U, sing.]

in·ten·sity /ɪnˈtensəti/ *noun* (*pl.* **-ies**) **1** [U, sing.] the state or quality of being intense: *intensity of light/sound/ colour ◊ intensity of feeling/concentration/relief ◊ He was watching her with an intensity that was unnerving. ◊ The storm resumed with even greater intensity.* **2** [U, C] (usually *technical*) The strength of sth, for example light, that can be measured: *continuously varying intensities of natural light*

in·ten·sive /ɪnˈtensɪv/ *adj.* **1** involving a lot of work or activity done in a short time: *an intensive language course ◊ two weeks of intensive training ◊ intensive diplomatic negotiations* **2** extremely thorough; done with a lot of care: *His disappearance has been the subject of intensive investigation.* **3** (of methods of farming) aimed at producing as much food as possible using as little land or as little money as possible: *Traditionally reared animals grow more slowly than those reared under intensive farming conditions. ◊ intensive agriculture*—see also CAPITALINTENSIVE, LABOUR-INTENSIVE ▶ **in·ten·sive·ly** *adv.*: *This case has been intensively studied. ◊ intensively farmed land*

in,tensive 'care *noun* [U] **1** continuous care and attention, often using special equipment, for people in hospital who are very seriously ill or injured: *She needed intensive care for several days. ◊ intensive care patients/beds* **2** (also **in,tensive 'care unit** [C]) (*abbr.* ICU) the part of a hospital that provides intensive care: *The baby was in intensive care for 48 hours.*

in·tent /ɪnˈtent/ *adj., noun*
- *adj.* **1** showing strong interest and attention: *an intent gaze/look ◊ His eyes were suddenly intent.* **2** ~ on/upon sth|~ on/upon doing sth (*formal*) determined to do sth, especially sth that will harm other people: *They were intent on murder. ◊ Are you intent upon destroying my reputation?* **3** ~ on/upon sth giving all your attention to sth: *I was so intent on my work that I didn't notice the time.* ▶ **in·tent·ly** *adv.*: *She looked at him intently.*
- *noun* [U] ~ (to do sth) (*formal* or *law*) what you intend to do [SYN] INTENTION: *She denies possessing the drug with intent to supply. ◊ a letter/statement of intent ◊ His intent is clearly not to placate his critics.* [IDM] **to all intents and 'purposes** (*BrE*) (*AmE* **for all intents and 'purposes**) in the effects that sth has, if not in reality; almost completely: *By 1981 the docks had, to all intents and purposes, closed. ◊ The two items are, to all intents and purposes, identical.*

in·ten·tion /ɪnˈtenʃn/ *noun* [C, U] ~ (of doing sth)|~ (to

s	t	v	z	ʃ	ʒ	tʃ	dʒ	θ	ð	ŋ
see	tea	van	zoo	shoe	vision	chain	jam	thin	this	sing

do sth)| ~ (that ...) what you intend or plan to do; your aim: *I have no intention of going to the wedding.* ◊ *He has announced his intention to retire.* ◊ *It was not my intention that she should suffer.* ◊ *He left England with the intention of travelling in Africa.* ◊ *I have every intention of paying her back what I owe her.* ◊ *The original intention was to devote three months to the project.* ◊ *She's full of good intentions but they rarely work out.* ◊ *I did it with the best (of) intentions* (= meaning to help), *but I only succeeded in annoying them.*—see also WELL INTENTIONED

in·ten·tion·al /ɪnˈtenʃənl/ *adj.* done deliberately; intended: *I'm sorry I left you off the list—it wasn't intentional.* [OPP] UNINTENTIONAL ▶ **in·ten·tion·al·ly** /-ʃənəli/ *adv.*: *She would never intentionally hurt anyone.* ◊ *I kept my statement intentionally vague.*

inter /ɪnˈtɜː(r)/ *verb* **(-rr-)** [VN] [usually passive] (*formal*) to bury a dead person [OPP] DISINTER—see also INTERMENT

inter- /ˈɪntə(r)/ *prefix* (in verbs, nouns, adjectives and adverbs) between; from one to another: *interface* ◊ *interaction* ◊ *international*—compare INTRA-

inter·act /ˌɪntərˈækt/ *verb* [V] **~ (with sb)** **1** to communicate with sb, especially while you work, play or spend time with them: *Teachers have a limited amount of time to interact with each child.* **2** if one thing **interacts** with another, or if two things **interact**, the two things have an effect on each other: *Perfume interacts with the skin's natural chemicals.* ▶ **inter·action** /-ˈækʃn/ *noun* [U, C] **~ (between sb/sth)| ~ (with sb/sth)**: *the interaction between performers and their audience* ◊ *the interaction of bacteria with the body's natural chemistry*

inter·active /ˌɪntərˈæktɪv/ *adj.* **1** that involves people working together and having an influence on each other: *The school believes in interactive teaching methods.* **2** (*computing*) that allows information to be passed continuously and in both directions between a computer and the person who uses it: *interactive systems/video* ▶ **inter·active·ly** *adv.* **inter·activ·ity** /ˌɪntərækˈtɪvəti/ *noun* [U]

inter alia /ˌɪntər ˈeɪliə/ *adv.* (from *Latin, formal*) among other things

inter·breed /ˌɪntəˈbriːd; *AmE* -tərˈb-/ *verb* [V, VN] if animals from different SPECIES **interbreed**, or sb **interbreeds** them, they produce young together

inter·cede /ˌɪntəˈsiːd; *AmE* -tərˈs-/ *verb* [V] **~ (with sb) (for/on behalf of sb)** (*formal*) to speak to sb in order to persuade them to show pity on sb else or to help settle an argument: *They interceded with the authorities on behalf of the detainees.* ▶ **inter·ces·sion** /ˌɪntəˈseʃn; *AmE* -tərˈs-/ *noun* [U]: *the intercession of a priest*

inter·cept /ˌɪntəˈsept; *AmE* -tərˈs-/ *verb* [VN] to stop sb/ sth that is going from one place to another from arriving: *Reporters intercepted him as he tried to leave the hotel.* ◊ *The letter was intercepted.* ▶ **inter·cep·tion** /ˌɪntəˈsepʃn; *AmE* -tərˈs-/ *noun* [U, C]: *the interception of enemy radio signals*

inter·cept·or /ˌɪntəˈseptə(r); *AmE* -tərˈs-/ *noun* a fast military plane that attacks enemy planes that are carrying bombs

inter·change *noun, verb*
■ *noun* /ˈɪntətʃeɪndʒ; *AmE* -tərtʃ-/ **1** [C, U] the act of sharing or exchanging sth, especially ideas or information: *a continuous interchange of ideas* ◊ *electronic data interchange* **2** [C] a place where a main road joins a motorway/freeway, designed so that vehicles leaving or joining the road do not have to cross other lines of traffic
■ *verb* /ˌɪntəˈtʃeɪndʒ; *AmE* -tərˈtʃ-/ **1** [VN] to share or exchange ideas, information, etc. **2** **~ (A) (with B)| ~ A and B** to put each of two things or people in the other's place; to move or be moved from one place to another in this way: [VN] *to interchange the front and rear tyres of a car* ◊ *to interchange the front tyres with the rear ones* ◊ [V] *The front and rear tyres interchange* (= can be exchanged).

inter·change·able /ˌɪntəˈtʃeɪndʒəbl; *AmE* -tərˈtʃ-/ *adj.* **~ (with sth)** that can be exchanged, especially without affecting the way in which sth works: *The two words are virtually interchangeable* (= have almost the same meaning). ◊ *The V8 engines are all interchangeable with each*

other. ▶ **inter·change·abil·ity** /ˌɪntətʃeɪndʒəˈbɪləti; *AmE* -tərtʃ-/ *noun* [U] **inter·change·ably** *adv.*: *These terms are used interchangeably.*

inter·city /ˌɪntəˈsɪti; *AmE* -tərˈs-/ *adj.* [usually before noun] (of transport) travelling between cities, usually with not many stops on the way: *an intercity rail service* ◊ *intercity travel*

inter·col·le·gi·ate /ˌɪntəkəˈliːdʒiət; *AmE* ˌɪntərkə-/ *adj.* (*especially AmE*) involving competition between colleges: *intercollegiate football/athletics*

inter·com /ˈɪntəkɒm; *AmE* ˈɪntərkɑːm/ *noun* a system of communication by telephone or radio inside an office, plane, etc.; the device you press or switch on to start using this system: *to announce sth over the intercom* ◊ *They called him on the intercom.*

inter·com·mu·ni·ca·tion /ˌɪntəkəˌmjuːnɪˈkeɪʃn; *AmE* -tərkə-/ *noun* [U] the process of communicating between people or groups

inter·con·nect /ˌɪntəkəˈnekt; *AmE* -tərkə-/ *verb* **~ (A) (with B)| ~ A and B** (*written*) to connect similar things; to be connected to or with similar things: [VN] *Bad housing is interconnected with debt and poverty.* ◊ *Bad housing, debt and poverty are interconnected.* ◊ [V] *separate bedrooms that interconnect* ▶ **inter·con·nec·tion** /-ˈnekʃn/ *noun* [C, U]: *interconnections from one part of the brain to another* ◊ *interconnections between different parts of the brain*

inter·con·tin·en·tal /ˌɪntəˌkɒntɪˈnentl; *AmE* ˌɪntərˌkɑːn-/ *adj.* [usually before noun] between continents: *intercontinental flights/missiles/travel/trade*

inter·course /ˈɪntəkɔːs; *AmE* ˈɪntərkɔːrs/ *noun* [U] **1** = SEXUAL INTERCOURSE: *The prosecution stated that intercourse had occurred on several occasions.* ◊ *anal intercourse* **2** (*old-fashioned*) communication and exchange between people, countries, etc: *the importance of social intercourse between different age groups*

inter·de·nom·in·ation·al /ˌɪntədɪˌnɒmɪˈneɪʃənl; *AmE* ˌɪntərdɪˌnɑːm-/ *adj.* shared by different religious groups (= different DENOMINATIONS): *an interdenominational school*

inter·de·part·men·tal /ˌɪntəˌdiːpɑːˈmentl; *AmE* ˌɪntərˌdiːpɑːrt-/ *adj.* between departments; involving more than one department: *interdepartmental committees/meetings/rivalry*

inter·de·pend·ent /ˌɪntədɪˈpendənt; *AmE* -tərdɪ-/ *adj.* that depend on each other; consisting of parts that depend on each other: *interdependent economies/organizations/relationships* ◊ *The world is becoming increasingly interdependent.* ▶ **inter·de·pend·ence** /-əns/ (*also* less frequent **inter·de·pend·ency** *pl.* **-ies**) *noun* [U, C]

inter·dict /ˈɪntədɪkt; *AmE* ˈɪntərd-/ *noun* **1** (*law*) an official order from a court of law that orders you not to do sth **2** (*technical*) (in the Roman Catholic Church) an order forbidding sb to take part in church services, etc.

inter·dic·tion /ˌɪntəˈdɪkʃn; *AmE* -tərˈd-/ *noun* [U] (*formal, especially AmE*) the act of stopping sth that is being transported from one place from reaching another place, especially by using force: *the Customs Service's drug interdiction programs*

inter·dis·cip·lin·ary /ˌɪntəˈdɪsəplɪnəri; *AmE* ˌɪntər-ˈdɪsəplɪneri/ *adj.* involving different areas of knowledge or study: *interdisciplinary research* ◊ *an interdisciplinary approach*

inter·est /ˈɪntrəst; -trest/ *noun, verb*
■ *noun*
WANTING TO KNOW MORE | **1** [sing., U] **~ (in sb/sth)** the feeling that you have when you want to know or learn more about sb/sth: *to feel/have/show/express (an) interest in sth* ◊ *Do your parents take an interest in your friends?* ◊ *By that time I had lost (all) interest in the idea.* ◊ *I watched with interest.* ◊ *As a matter of interest,* (= I'd like to know) *what time did the party finish?* ◊ *Just out of interest,* how much did it cost?—compare DISINTEREST
ATTRACTION | **2** [U] the quality that sth has when it attracts sb's attention or makes them want to know more about it: *There are many places of interest around Oxford.* ◊ *The subject is of no interest to me at all.* ◊ *These plants will add*

æ	ɑː	e	ɜː	ə	ɪ	iː	i	ɒ	ɔː	ʌ	ʊ	u	uː
cat	father	ten	bird	about	sit	see	many	got	saw	cup	put	actual	too
								(BrE)					

interest to your garden in winter.—see also HUMAN INTER-EST

HOBBY | 3 [C] an activity or a subject that you enjoy and that you spend your free time doing or studying: *Her main interests are music and tennis.* ◊ *He was a man of wide interests outside his work.*—compare HOBBY

MONEY | 4 [U] ~ **(on sth)** (*finance*) the extra money that you pay back when you borrow money or that you receive when you invest money: *to pay interest on a loan* ◊ *The money was repaid* **with interest.** ◊ *interest charges/payments* ◊ **Interest rates** *have risen by 1%.* ◊ **high rates of interest**—see also COMPOUND INTEREST, SIMPLE INTEREST

ADVANTAGE | 5 [C, usually pl., U] a good result or an advantage for sb/sth: *to promote/protect/safeguard sb's interests* ◊ *She was acting entirely* **in her own interests.** ◊ *These reforms were* **in the best interests** *of local government.* ◊ *It is* **in the public interest** *that these facts are made known.*—see also SELF-INTEREST

SHARE IN BUSINESS | 6 [C, usually pl., U] ~ **(in sth)** a share in a business or company and its profits: *She has business interests in France.* ◊ *American interests in Europe* (= money invested in European countries)—see also CON-TROLLING INTEREST

CONNECTION | 7 [C, U] ~ **(in sth)** a connection with sth which affects your attitude to it, especially because you may benefit from it in some way: *I should, at this point,* **declare my interest.** ◊ *Organizations* **have an interest in** *ensuring that employee motivation is high.*—compare DIS-INTEREST—see also VESTED INTEREST

GROUP OF PEOPLE | 8 [C, usually pl.] a group of people who are in the same business or who share the same aims which they want to protect: *powerful farming interests* ◊ *relationships between local government and business inter-ests* ◊ *the activities of special* **interest** *groups*

IDM **have sb's interests at 'heart** to want sb to be happy and successful even though your actions may not show this **in the interest(s) of sth** in order to help or achieve sth: *In the interest(s) of safety, smoking is forbid-den.* **to do sth (back) with interest** to do the same thing to sb as they have done to you, but with more force, enthusiasm, etc.—more at CONFLICT *n.*

■ *verb* ~ **sb/yourself (in sth)** to attract your attention and make you feel interested; to make yourself give your attention to sth: [VN] *Politics doesn't interest me.* ◊ *She has always interested herself in charity work.* ◊ [VN to inf] *It may interest you to know that Andy didn't accept the job.* **PHRV** **'interest sb in sth** to persuade sb to buy, do or eat sth: *Could I interest you in this model, Sir?*

inter·est·ed /ˈɪntrəstɪd; -trest-/ *adj.* **1** ~ **(in sth/sb)|** ~ **(in doing sth)|** ~ **(to do sth)** giving your attention to sth because you enjoy finding out about it or doing it; show-ing interest in sth and finding it exciting: *I'm very inter-ested in history.* ◊ *Anyone interested in joining the club should contact us at the address below.* ◊ *We would be interested to hear your views on this subject.* ◊ *an interested audience/reader* ◊ *There's a talk on Italian art—are you interested* (= would you like to go)? ◊ *He sounded genu-inely interested.* **2** in a position to gain from a situation or be affected by it: *As an* **interested party,** *I was not allowed to vote.* ◊ *Interested groups will be given three months to give their views on the new development.*

inter·est-free *adj.* with no interest charged on money borrowed: *an interest-free loan* ◊ *interest-free credit*

'interest group *noun* a group of people who work together to achieve sth that they are particularly inter-ested in, especially by putting pressure on the govern-ment, etc.

inter·est·ing /ˈɪntrəstɪŋ; -trest-/ *adj.* ~ **(to do sth)|** ~ **(that ...)** attracting your attention because it is special, exciting or unusual: *an interesting question/point/example* ◊ *interesting people/places/work* ◊ *It would be interesting to know what he really believed.* ◊ *I find it interesting that she claims not to know him.* ◊ *Can't we do something more interesting?* ◊ *Her account makes interest-ing reading.* ◊ *It is particularly interesting to compare the two versions.* ▶ **inter·est·ing·ly** *adv.*: *Interestingly, there are very few recorded cases of such attacks.*

inter·face /ˈɪntəfeɪs; *AmE* -tərf-/ *noun, verb*
■ *noun* **1** (*computing*) the way a computer program pre-sents information to a user or receives information from a user, in particular the LAYOUT of the screen and the MENUS: *the user interface* **2** (*computing*) an electrical CIR-CUIT, connection or program that joins one device or system to another: *the interface between computer and printer* **3** ~ **(between A and B)** (*written*) the point where two subjects, systems, etc. meet and affect each other: *the interface between manufacturing and sales*
■ *verb* ~ **(sth) (with sth)|** ~ **A and B** (*computing*) to be connected with sth using an interface; to connect sth in this way: [V] *The new system interfaces with existing tele-phone equipment.* [also VN]

inter·fere /ˌɪntəˈfɪə(r); *AmE* ˌɪntərˈfɪr/ *verb* [VN] ~ **(in sth)** to get involved in and try to influence a situation that does not concern you, in a way that annoys other people: *I wish my mother would stop interfering and let me make my own decisions.* ◊ *The police are very unwilling to interfere in family problems.* **PHRV** **inter'fere with sb** (*BrE*) to touch a child in a sexual way **inter'fere with sth** **1** to prevent sth from succeeding or from being done or happening as planned: *She never allows her personal feelings to interfere with her work.* **2** to touch, use or change sth, especially a piece of equipment, so that it is damaged or no longer works correctly: *I'd get fired if he found out I'd been interfering with his records.*

inter·fer·ence /ˌɪntəˈfɪərəns; *AmE* -tərˈfɪr-/ *noun* [U] **1** ~ **(in sth)** the act of interfering: *They resent foreign interfer-ence in the internal affairs of their country.* **2** interruption of a radio signal by another signal on a similar WAVE-LENGTH, causing extra noise that is not wanted

inter·fer·ing /ˌɪntəˈfɪərɪŋ; *AmE* -tərˈfɪr-/ *adj.* [usually before noun] (*disapproving*) involving yourself in an annoying way in other people's private lives: *She's an interfering busybody!*

inter·feron /ˌɪntəˈfɪərɒn; *AmE* ˌɪntərˈfɪrɑːn/ *noun* [U] (*biology*) a substance produced by the body to prevent harmful VIRUSES from causing disease

inter·gal·act·ic /ˌɪntəɡəˈlæktɪk; *AmE* -tərɡə-/ *adj.* [only before noun] existing or happening between GALAXIES of stars: *intergalactic space/travel*

inter·gov·ern·men·tal /ˌɪntəɡʌvənˈmentl; *AmE* ˌɪntərˌɡʌvərn-/ *adj.* [only before noun] concerning the governments of two or more countries: *an intergovern-mental conference*

in·terim /ˈɪntərɪm/ *adj., noun*
■ *adj.* [only before noun] **1** intended to last for only a short time until sb/sth more permanent is found: *an interim government/measure/report* ◊ *The vice-president took power* **in the interim period** *before the election.* **2** (*finance*) calculated before the final results of sth are known **SYN** PROVISIONAL: *interim figures/profits/results*
■ *noun* **IDM** **in the interim** during the period of time between two events; until a particular event happens: *Despite everything that had happened in the interim, they had remained good friends.* ◊ *Her new job does not start until May and she will continue in the old job in the interim.*

in·ter·ior /ɪnˈtɪəriə(r); *AmE* -ˈtɪr-/ *noun, adj.*

■ **noun 1** [C, usually sing.] the inside part of sth: *the interior of a building/a car* OPP EXTERIOR **2 (the interior)** [sing.] the central part of a country or continent that is a long way from the coast: *an expedition into the interior of Australia* **3 (the Interior)** [sing.] a country's own affairs rather than those that involve other countries: *the Department/Minister of the Interior*

■ **adj.** [only before noun] connected with the inside part of sth: *interior walls/doors* OPP EXTERIOR

in·terior de'corator *noun* a person whose job is to design and/or decorate a room or the inside of a house, etc. with paint, paper, fabrics and carpets ▶ **in·terior deco'ration** *noun* [U]: *an interior decoration scheme*

in·terior de'sign *noun* [U] the art or job of choosing the paint, carpets, furniture, etc. to decorate the inside of a house ▶ **in·terior de'signer** *noun*

inter·ject /ˌɪntə'dʒekt; *AmE* -tər'dʒ-/ *verb* (*written*) to interrupt what sb is saying with your opinion or a remark: [Vspeech] *'You're wrong,'* interjected Susan. [alsoVN, V]

inter·jec·tion /ˌɪntə'dʒekʃn; *AmE* -tər'dʒ-/ *noun* (*grammar*) a short sound, word or phrase spoken suddenly to express an emotion. *Oh!, Look out!* and *Ow!* are interjections. SYN EXCLAMATION

inter·lace /ˌɪntə'leɪs; *AmE* -tər'l-/ *verb* ~ (sth) (with sth) (*written*) to weave things together by twisting them over and under each other; to be woven together in this way: [V] *interlacing branches* ◇ [VN] *Her hair was interlaced with ribbons and flowers.*

inter·leave /ˌɪntə'liːv; *AmE* -tər'l-/ *verb* [VN] ~ sth (with sth) to put sth, especially thin layers of sth, between things

inter·link /ˌɪntə'lɪŋk; *AmE* -tər'l-/ *verb* ~ (sth) (with sth) to connect things; to be connected with other things:[VN] [usually passive] *The two processes are interlinked.* ◇ [V] *a series of short interlinking stories*

inter·lock /ˌɪntə'lɒk; *AmE* ˌɪntər'lɑːk/ *verb* ~ (sth) (with sth) to fit or be fastened firmly together: [V] *interlocking shapes/systems/pieces* ◇ *The US space shuttle will interlock with the Russian space station later today.* [alsoVN]

inter·locu·tor /ˌɪntə'lɒkjətə(r); *AmE* ˌɪntər'lɑːk-/ *noun* (*formal*) **1** a person taking part in a conversation with you **2** a person or an organization that talks to another person or organization on behalf of sb else

inter·loper /'ɪntələʊpə(r); *AmE* 'ɪntərloʊpər/ *noun* a person who is present in a place or a situation where they do not belong SYN INTRUDER: *She felt like an interloper in her own family.*

inter·lude /'ɪntəluːd; *AmE* -tərl-/ *noun* **1** a period of time between two events during which sth different happens: *a romantic interlude* (= a short romantic relationship) ◇ *Apart from a brief interlude of peace, the war lasted nine years.* **2** a short period of time between the parts of a play, film/movie, etc: *There will now be a short interlude.* **3** a short piece of music or a talk, etc. that fills this period of time: *a musical interlude* ⇨ note at BREAK

inter·marry /ˌɪntə'mæri; *AmE* -tər'm-/ *verb* (**inter·mar·ries, inter·marry·ing, inter·mar·ried, inter·mar·ried**) [V] **1** to marry sb of a different race or from a different country or a different religious group: *Blacks and whites often intermarried* (= married each other). ◇ *They were not forbidden to intermarry with the local people.* **2** to marry sb within your own family or group: *cousins who intermarry* ▶ **inter·mar·riage** /ˌɪntə'mærɪdʒ/ *noun* [U, C]: *intermarriage between blacks and whites*

inter·medi·ary /ˌɪntə'miːdiəri; *AmE* ˌɪntər'miːdieri/ *noun* (*pl.* -ies) ~ (between A and B) a person or an organization that helps other people or organizations to make an agreement by being a means of communication between them SYN MEDIATOR, GO-BETWEEN: *Financial institutions act as intermediaries between lenders and borrowers.* ◇ *All talks have so far been conducted through an intermediary.* ▶ **inter·medi·ary** *adj.* [only before noun]: *to play an intermediary role in the dispute*

inter·medi·ate /ˌɪntə'miːdiət; *AmE* -tər'm-/ *adj., noun*

■ **adj. 1** [usually before noun] ~ (between A and B) situated between two places, things, states, etc: *an intermediate stage/step in a process* ◇ *Liquid crystals are considered*

to be intermediate between liquid and solid. **2** having more than a basic knowledge of sth but not yet advanced; suitable for sb who is at this level: *an intermediate skier/student* ◇ *an intermediate coursebook* ◇ *pre-/upper-intermediate classes*

■ **noun** a person who is learning sth and who has more than a basic knowledge of it but is not yet advanced

,intermediate tech'nology *noun* [U] technology that is suitable for use in developing countries as it is cheap and simple and can use local materials

in·ter·ment /ɪn'tɜːmənt; *AmE* -'tɜːrm-/ *noun* [C, U] (*formal*) the act of burying a dead person—see also INTER *v.*

in·ter·min·able /ɪn'tɜːmɪnəbl; *AmE* -'tɜːrm-/ *adj.* lasting a very long time and therefore boring or annoying SYN ENDLESS: *an interminable speech/wait/discussion* ◇ *The drive seemed interminable.* ▶ **in·ter·min·ably** /-əbli/ *adv.*: *The meeting dragged on interminably.*

inter·min·gle /ˌɪntə'mɪŋgl; *AmE* -tər'm-/ *verb* ~ (A) (with B)|~ A and B (*written*) to mix people, ideas, colours, etc. together; to be mixed in this way: [VN] *The book intermingles fact with fiction.* ◇ *The book intermingles fact and fiction.* ◇ [V] *tourists and local people intermingling in the market square*

inter·mis·sion /ˌɪntə'mɪʃn; *AmE* -tər'm-/ *noun* [C, U] **1** (*especially AmE*) a short period of time between the parts of a play, film/movie, etc: *Wine was served during the intermission.* ◇ (*AmE*) *After intermission, the second band played.* HELP This meaning is only [U] in *AmE*. ⇨ note at BREAK **2** a period of time during which sth stops before continuing again: *This state of affairs lasted without intermission for a hundred years.*

inter·mit·tent /ˌɪntə'mɪtənt; *AmE* -tər'm-/ *adj.* stopping and starting often over a period of time, but not regularly SYN SPORADIC: *intermittent bursts of applause* ◇ *intermittent rain/showers* ▶ **inter·mit·tent·ly** *adv.*: *Protests continued intermittently throughout November.*

in·tern *verb, noun*

■ **verb** /ɪn'tɜːn; *AmE* ɪn'tɜːrn/ [VN] [often passive] ~ sb (in sth) to put sb in prison during a war or for political reasons, although they have not been charged with a crime—see also INTERNEE ▶ **in·tern·ment** /ɪn'tɜːnmənt; *AmE* -'tɜːrn-/ *noun* [U]: *the internment of suspected terrorists* ◇ *internment camps*

■ **noun** (also **interne**) /'ɪntɜːn; *AmE* 'ɪntɜːrn/ (*AmE*) **1** an advanced student of medicine, whose training is nearly finished and who is working in a hospital to get further practical experience: *Interns and residents at the hospital are working 12-hour shifts.*—compare HOUSE OFFICER **2** a student or new GRADUATE who is getting practical experience in a job, for example during the summer holiday/vacation: *a summer intern at a law firm* ▶ **in·tern·ship** *noun*: *an internship at a television station*—compare WORK EXPERIENCE

in·tern·al /ɪn'tɜːnl; *AmE* ɪn'tɜːrnl/ *adj.* **1** [only before noun] connected with the inside of sth: *the internal structure of a building* ◇ *internal doors/fittings* OPP EXTERNAL **2** [only before noun] connected with the inside of your body: *internal organs/injuries* ◇ *The medicine is not for internal use.* OPP EXTERNAL **3** [usually before noun] involving or concerning only the people who are part of a particular organization rather than people from outside it: *an internal audit/inquiry* ◇ *the internal workings of government* ◇ *internal divisions within the company* OPP EXTERNAL **4** [only before noun] connected with a country's own affairs rather than those that involve other countries SYN DOMESTIC: *internal affairs/trade/markets* ◇ *an internal flight* (= within a country) OPP EXTERNAL **5** coming from within a thing itself rather than from outside it: *a theory which lacks internal consistency* (= whose parts are not consistent) ◇ *Some photos contain internal evidence* (= fashions, transport, etc.) *that may help to date them.* **6** happening or existing in your mind SYN INNER: *internal rage* ▶ **in·tern·al·ly** /-nəli/ *adv.*: *internally connected rooms* ◇ *The new posts were only advertised internally.*

in,ternal-com'bustion engine *noun* a type of

engine used in most cars that produces power by burning petrol/gas inside

in·tern·al·ize (*BrE* also **-ise**) /ɪnˈtɜːnəlaɪz; *AmE* -ˈtɜːrn-/ *verb* [VN] (*technical*) to make a feeling, an attitude, or a belief part of the way you think and behave: *Minority groups tend to internalize the values of the dominant society.*—compare EXTERNALIZE ▶ **in·tern·al·iza·tion, -isa·tion** /ɪnˌtɜːnəlaɪˈzeɪʃn; *AmE* -ˌtɜːrnələˈz-/ *noun* [U]

the In,ternal 'Revenue Service *noun* [sing.] (*abbr.* IRS) (in the US) the government department that is responsible for collecting most national taxes, for example income tax—compare THE INLAND REVENUE

inter·nation·al /ˌɪntəˈnæʃnəl; *AmE* -tərˈn-/ *adj., noun*
■ *adj.* [usually before noun] connected with or involving two or more countries: *international trade / law / sport* ◇ *an international airport / school / company* ◇ *international relations* ◇ *a pianist with an international reputation* ▶ **inter·nation·al·ly** /-nəli/ *adv.*: *internationally famous*
■ *noun* (*BrE*) **1** a sports competition involving teams from two countries: *the France-Scotland rugby international* **2** a player who takes part in a sports competition against another country: *a former swimming international*

the Inter,national 'Date Line (also **'date line**) *noun* [sing.] the imaginary line that goes from north to south through the Pacific Ocean. The date on the west side is one day earlier than that on the east side.

inter·nation·al·ism /ˌɪntəˈnæʃnəlɪzəm; *AmE* -tərˈn-/ *noun* [U] the belief that countries should work together in a friendly way ▶ **inter·nation·al·ist** /-ʃnəlɪst/ *noun, adj.*

inter·nation·al·ize (*BrE* also **-ise**) /ˌɪntəˈnæʃnəlaɪz; *AmE* -tərˈn-/ *verb* [VN] to bring sth under the control or protection of many nations; to make sth international ▶ **inter·nation·al·iza·tion, -isa·tion** /ˌɪntəˌnæʃnəlaɪˈzeɪʃn; *AmE* -tərˌnæʃnələˈz-/ *noun* [U]

interne *noun* = INTERN

inter·necine /ˌɪntəˈniːsaɪn; *AmE* -tərˈn-/ *adj.* [only before noun] (*formal*) happening between members of the same group, country or organization: *internecine struggles / warfare / feuds*

in·tern·ee /ˌɪntɜːˈniː; *AmE* ˌɪntɜːrˈniː/ *noun* a person who is put in prison for political reasons, usually without a trial (= who is INTERNED)

Inter·net /ˈɪntənet; *AmE* -tərn-/ *noun* (usually **the Internet**) (also *informal* **the Net**) [sing.] an international computer NETWORK connecting other NETWORKS and computers from companies, universities, etc: *I got the information from the Internet.* ◇ *Internet service providers* ⇨ vocabulary notes on page 250 —see also INTRANET, WWW

in·tern·ist /ɪnˈtɜːnɪst; *AmE* -ˈtɜːrn-/ *noun* (*AmE*) a doctor who is a specialist in the treatment of diseases of the organs inside the body and who does not usually do medical operations

inter·pene·trate /ˌɪntəˈpenɪtreɪt; *AmE* -tərˈp-/ *verb* [V, VN] (*formal*) to spread completely through sth or from one thing to another in each direction ▶ **inter·pene·tra·tion** /ˌɪntəˌpenɪˈtreɪʃn; *AmE* -tərˌp-/ *noun* [U, C]

inter·per·son·al /ˌɪntəˈpɜːsənl; *AmE* -tərˈpɜːrs-/ *adj.* [only before noun] connected with relationships between people: *interpersonal skills*

inter·plan·et·ary /ˌɪntəˈplænɪtri; *AmE* ˌɪntərˈplænəteri/ *adj.* [only before noun] between planets: *interplanetary space / travel*

inter·play /ˈɪntəpleɪ; *AmE* -tərp-/ *noun* [U, sing.] ~ (of/ between A and B) (*formal*) the way in which two or more things or people affect each other [SYN] INTERACTION: *the interplay between politics and the environment* ◇ *the subtle interplay of colours*

Inter·pol /ˈɪntəpɒl; *AmE* ˈɪntərpoʊl/ *noun* [sing.+ sing./ pl. v.] an international organization that enables the police forces of different countries to help each other to solve crimes

in·ter·pol·ate /ɪnˈtɜːpəleɪt; *AmE* -ˈtɜːrp-/ *verb* (*formal*) **1** to make a remark that interrupts a conversation: [V speech] *'But why?' he interpolated.* [also VN] **2** [VN] ~ sth (into sth) to add sth to a piece of writing: *The lines*

were interpolated into the manuscript at a later date. ▶ **in·ter·pol·ation** /ɪnˌtɜːpəˈleɪʃn; *AmE* -ˌtɜːrp-/ *noun* [U, C]

inter·pose /ˌɪntəˈpəʊz; *AmE* ˌɪntərˈpoʊz/ *verb* (*formal*) **1** to add a question or remark into a conversation: [V speech] *'Just a minute,' Charles interposed. 'How do you know?'* [also VN] **2** [VN] ~ sb/sth (between A and B) to place sth between two people or things: *He quickly interposed himself between Mel and the doorway.*

in·ter·pret /ɪnˈtɜːprɪt; *AmE* -ˈtɜːrp-/ *verb* **1** [VN] to explain the meaning of sth: *The students were asked to interpret the poem.* **2** [VN] ~ sth (as sth) to decide that sth has a particular meaning and to understand it in this way: *I didn't know whether to interpret her silence as acceptance or refusal.* ◇ *The data can be interpreted in many different ways.*—compare MISINTERPRET **3** [V] ~ (for sb) to translate one language into another as you hear it: *She couldn't speak much English so her children had to interpret for her.* **4** [VN] to perform a piece of music, a role in a play, etc. in a way that shows your feelings about its meaning: *He interpreted the role with a lot of humour.* ▶ **in·ter·pret·able** /ɪnˈtɜːprɪtəbl; *AmE* -ˈtɜːrp-/ *adj.*: *interpretable data*

in·ter·pret·ation /ɪnˌtɜːprɪˈteɪʃn; *AmE* -ˌtɜːrp-/ *noun* [C, U] **1** the particular way in which sth is understood or explained: *Her evidence suggests a different interpretation of the events leading to his death.* ◇ *It is not possible for everyone to put their own interpretation on the law.* ◇ *Dreams are open to interpretation* (= they can be explained in different ways). **2** the particular way in which sb chooses to perform a piece of music, a role in a play, etc: *a modern interpretation of 'King Lear'*

in·ter·pret·ative /ɪnˈtɜːprɪtətɪv; *AmE* ɪnˈtɜːrprətətɪv/ (also **in·ter·pret·ive** /ɪnˈtɜːprɪtɪv; *AmE* -ˈtɜːrp-/ especially in *AmE*) *adj.* [usually before noun] connected with the particular way in which sth is understood, explained or performed; providing an interpretation: *an interpretative problem* ◇ *an interpretative exhibition*

in·ter·pret·er /ɪnˈtɜːprɪtə(r); *AmE* -ˈtɜːrp-/ *noun* **1** a person whose job is to translate what sb is saying into another language: *Speaking through an interpreter, the President said that the talks were going well.* ◇ *a sign language interpreter* (= a person who translates what sb is saying into sign language for deaf people)—compare TRANSLATOR **2** a person who performs a piece of music or a role in a play in a way that clearly shows their ideas about its meaning: *She was considered one of the finest interpreters of Debussy's music.* **3** (*computing*) a computer program that changes the instructions of another program into a form that the computer can understand and use

inter·racial /ˌɪntəˈreɪʃl; *AmE* -tərˈr-/ *adj.* [only before noun] involving people of different races: *interracial marriage*

inter·reg·num /ˌɪntəˈregnəm; *AmE* -tərˈr-/ *noun* [usually sing.] (*pl.* **inter·reg·nums**) (*formal*) a period of time during which a country, an organization, etc. does not have a leader and is waiting for a new one

inter·relate /ˌɪntərɪˈleɪt/ *verb* (*written*) if two or more things **interrelate**, or if they are **interrelated**, they are closely connected and they affect each other: [V] *a discussion of how the mind and body interrelate* ◇ *a discussion of how the mind interrelates with the body* [also VN] ▶ **inter·related** *adj.*: *a number of interrelated problems* ◇ *the belief that the mind is closely interrelated with the body*

inter·rela·tion·ship /ˌɪntərɪˈleɪʃnʃɪp/ (also **inter·rela·tion** /ˌɪntərɪˈleɪʃn/) *noun* [C, U] ~ (of/between A and B) the way in which two or more things or people are connected and affect each other

in·ter·ro·gate /ɪnˈterəgeɪt/ *verb* [VN] **1** to ask sb a lot of questions over a long period of time, especially in an aggressive way: *He was interrogated by the police for over 12 hours.* **2** (*technical*) to obtain information from a computer or other machine ▶ **in·ter·ro·ga·tion** /ɪnˌterəˈgeɪʃn/ *noun* [U, C]: *He confessed after four days under interrogation.* ◇ *She hated her parents' endless interrogations about where she'd been.* **in·ter·ro·ga·tor** *noun*

inter·roga·tive /ˌɪntəˈrɒgətɪv; *AmE* -ˈrɑːg-/ *adj., noun*

■ *adj.* **1** (*formal*) asking a question; in the form of a question: *an interrogative gesture/remark/sentence* **2** (*grammar*) used in questions: *interrogative pronouns/determiners/adverbs* (for example, *who, which and why*) ▶ **inter·rog·a·tive·ly** *adv.*

■ *noun* (*grammar*) a question word, especially a pronoun or a DETERMINER such as *who* or *which*

inter·rupt /ˌɪntəˈrʌpt/ *verb* **1** ~ (**sb/sth**) (**with sth**) to say or do sth that makes sb stop what they are saying or doing: [V] *Sorry to interrupt, but there's someone to see you.* ◇ *Would you mind not interrupting all the time?* ◇ [VN] *I hope I'm not interrupting you.* ◇ *They were interrupted by a knock at the door.* [also V speech, VN speech] **2** [VN] to stop the continuous progress of sth for a short time: *The game was interrupted several times by rain.* ◇ *We interrupt this programme to bring you an important news bulletin.* **3** [VN] to stop a line, surface, view, etc. from being even or continuous

inter·rup·tion /ˌɪntəˈrʌpʃn/ *noun* [C, U] **1** something that temporarily stops an activity or a situation; a time when an activity is stopped: *The birth of her son was a minor interruption to her career.* ◇ *an interruption to the power supply* ◇ *I managed to work for two hours without interruption.* **2** the act of interrupting sb/sth and of stopping them from speaking: *He ignored her interruptions.* ◇ *She spoke for 20 minutes without interruption.*

inter·sect /ˌɪntəˈsekt; *AmE* -tərˈs-/ *verb* **1** (of lines, roads, etc.) to meet or cross each other: [V] *a pattern of intersecting streets* ◇ *The lines intersect at right angles.* ◇ *The path intersected with a busy road.* [also VN] **2** [VN] [usually passive] ~ **sth** (**with sth**) to divide an area by crossing it: *The landscape is intersected with spectacular gorges.*

inter·sec·tion /ˌɪntəˈsekʃn; *AmE* -tərˈs-/ *noun* **1** [C] a place where two or more roads, lines, etc. meet or cross each other: *Traffic lights have been placed at all major intersections.* **2** [U] the act of intersecting sth

inter·sperse /ˌɪntəˈspɜːs; *AmE* -tərˈspɜːrs/ *verb* [VN] (*written*) to put sth in sth else or among or between other things: *Lectures will be interspersed with practical demonstrations.*

inter·state /ˈɪntəsteɪt; *AmE* -tərs-/ *adj., noun*

■ *adj.* [only before noun] between states, especially in the US: *interstate commerce*

■ *noun* (also ˌinterstate ˈhighway) (in the US) a large road between states: *Get on the interstate leading toward Miami.*

inter·stel·lar /ˌɪntəˈstelə(r); *AmE* -tərˈst-/ *adj.* [only before noun] between the stars in the sky: *interstellar space/matter*—compare STELLAR

in·ter·stice /ɪnˈtɜːstɪs; *AmE* -ˈtɜːrs-/ *noun* [usually pl.] (*rare, formal*) a small crack or space in sth

inter·twine /ˌɪntəˈtwaɪn; *AmE* -tərˈtw-/ *verb* [usually passive] **1** if two or more things intertwine or are intertwined, they are twisted together so that they are very difficult to separate: [VN] *a necklace of rubies intertwined with pearls* ◇ [V] *intertwining branches* **2** to be or become very closely connected with sth/sb else: [VN] [usually passive] *Their political careers had become closely intertwined.* [also V]

inter·val /ˈɪntəvl; *AmE* ˈɪntərvl/ *noun* **1** a period of time between two events: *The interval between major earthquakes might be 200 years.* **2** (*BrE*) (also **inter·mis·sion** *AmE, BrE*) a short period of time separating parts of a play, film/movie or concert: *There will be an interval of 20 minutes after the second act.* ⇨ note at BREAK **3** [usually pl.] a short period during which sth different happens from what is happening the rest of the time: *She's delirious, but has lucid intervals.* ◇ (*BrE*) *The day should be mainly dry with sunny intervals.* **4** (*music*) a difference in PITCH (= how high or low a note sounds) between two notes: *an interval of one octave* **IDM at (...) intervals 1** with time between: *Buses to the city leave at regular intervals.* ◇ *The runners started at 5-minute intervals.* **2** with spaces between: *Flaming torches were positioned at intervals along the terrace.*

inter·vene /ˌɪntəˈviːn; *AmE* -tərˈv-/ *verb* **1** [V] ~ (**in sth**) to become involved in a situation in order to improve or

help it: *The President intervened personally in the crisis.* ◇ *She might have been killed if the neighbours hadn't intervened.* **2** to interrupt sb when they are speaking in order to say sth: [V speech] *'But,' she intervened, 'what about the others?'* [also V] **3** [V] to happen in a way that delays sth or prevents it from happening: *They were planning to get married and then the war intervened.* **4** [V] (*formal*) to exist between two events or places: *I saw nothing of her during the years that intervened.* ▶ **inter·ven·tion** /ˌɪntəˈvenʃn; *AmE* -tərˈv-/ *noun* [U, C] ~ (**in sth**): *calls for government intervention to save the steel industry* ◇ *armed/military intervention*

inter·ven·tion·ism /ˌɪntəˈvenʃənɪzəm; *AmE* -tərˈv-/ *noun* [U] the policy or practice of a government influencing the economy of its own country, or of becoming involved in the affairs of other countries ▶ **inter·ven·tion·ist** /-ʃənɪst/ *adj., noun: interventionist policies*

inter·view /ˈɪntəvjuː; *AmE* -tərv-/ *noun, verb*

■ *noun* **1** ~ (**for a job, etc.**) a formal meeting at which sb is asked questions to see if they are suitable for a particular job, or for a course of study at a college, university, etc: *a job interview* ◇ *to be called for (an) interview* ◇ *He has an interview next week for the manager's job.* **2** ~ (**with sb**) a meeting (often a public one) at which a journalist asks sb questions in order to find out their opinions: *a television/radio/newspaper interview* ◇ *an interview with the new Governor* ◇ *to give an interview* (= to agree to answer questions) ◇ *Yesterday, in an interview on German television, the minister denied the reports.* ◇ *The interview was published in all the papers.* **3** ~ (**with sb**) a private meeting between people when questions are asked and answered: *an interview with the careers adviser*

■ *verb* **1** ~ **sb** (**for a job, etc.**) to talk to sb and ask them questions at a formal meeting to find out if they are suitable for a job, course of study, etc: [VN] *Which post are you being interviewed for?* ◇ *We interviewed ten people for the job.* [also V] **2** [VN] ~ **sb** (**about sth**) to ask sb questions about their life, opinions, etc., especially on the radio or television or for a newspaper or magazine: *Next week, I will be interviewing Spielberg about his latest movie.* ◇ *The Prime Minister declined to be interviewed.* **3** [VN] ~ **sb** (**about sth**) to ask sb questions at a private meeting: *The police are waiting to interview the injured man.* ▶ **inter·view·ing** *noun* [U]: *The research involves in-depth interviewing.* ◇ *interviewing skills/techniques*

inter·view·ee /ˌɪntəvjuːˈiː; *AmE* -tərv-/ *noun* the person who answers the questions in an interview

inter·view·er /ˈɪntəvjuːə(r); *AmE* -tərv-/ *noun* the person who asks the questions in an interview

inter·war /ˌɪntəˈwɔː(r); *AmE* -tərˈw-/ *adj.* [only before noun] happening or existing between the First and the Second World Wars: *the interwar years/period*

inter·weave /ˌɪntəˈwiːv; *AmE* -tərˈw-/ *verb* (**inter·wove** /-ˈwəʊv; *AmE* -ˈwoʊv/, **inter·woven** /-ˈwəʊvn; *AmE* -ˈwoʊvn/) [usually passive] to weave together two or more pieces of thread, wool, etc: [VN] *The blue fabric was interwoven with red and gold thread.* ◇ (*figurative*) *The problems are inextricably interwoven* (= very closely connected). [also V]

in·tes·tate /ɪnˈtesteɪt/ *adj.* (*law*) not having made a WILL (= a legal document that says what is to happen to a person's property when they die) ▶ **in·tes·tacy** /ɪnˈtestəsi/ *noun* [U]

in·tes·tine /ɪnˈtestɪn/ *noun* [often pl.] a long tube in the body between the stomach and the ANUS. Food passes from the stomach to the **small intestine** and from there to the **large intestine.**—picture at BODY ▶ **in·tes·tinal** /ɪnˈtestɪnl; ˌɪnteˈstaɪnl/ *adj.* [usually before noun]

in·tim·acy /ˈɪntɪməsi/ *noun* (*pl.* **-ies**) **1** [U] the state of having a close personal relationship with sb **2** [C, usually pl.] a thing that a person says or does to sb that they know very well **3** [U] (*formal or law*) sexual activity, especially an act of SEXUAL INTERCOURSE

in·tim·ate *adj., verb, noun*

■ *adj.* /ˈɪntɪmət/ **1** (of people) having a close and friendly relationship: *intimate friends* ◇ *We're not on intimate terms with our neighbours.* **2** private and personal, often

æ	ɑː	e	ɜː	ə	ɪ	iː	i	ɒ	ɔː	ʌ	ʊ	u	uː
cat	father	ten	bird	about	sit	see	many	got	saw	cup	put	actual	too

(BrE)

in a sexual way: *The article revealed intimate details about his family life.* ◇ *the most intimate parts of her body* **3** (of a place or situation) encouraging close, friendly relationships, sometimes of a sexual nature: *an intimate restaurant/dinner/conversation* ◇ *He knew an intimate little bar where they would not be disturbed.* **4** (of knowledge) very detailed and thorough: *an intimate knowledge of the English countryside* **5** (of a link between things) very close: *an intimate connection between class and educational success* **6** ~ **(with sb)** (*formal* or *law*) having a sexual relationship with sb ▶ **in·tim·ate·ly** *adv.*: *intimately connected/linked/related* ◇ *an area of the country that he knew intimately* ◇ *She was intimately involved in the project.* ◇ *They touched each other intimately* (= in a sexual way).

■ *verb* /ˈɪntɪmeɪt/ ~ **sth (to sb)** (*formal*) to let sb know what you think or mean in an indirect way: [VN] *He has already intimated to us his intention to retire.* ◇ [V(that)] *He has already intimated (that) he intends to retire.*

■ *noun* /ˈɪntɪmət/ (*formal*) a close personal friend

in·tim·ation /ˌɪntɪˈmeɪʃn/ *noun* [C, U] (*formal*) the act of stating sth or making it known, especially in an indirect way: *There was no intimation from his doctor that his condition was serious.*

in·timi·date /ɪnˈtɪmɪdeɪt/ *verb* [VN] ~ **sb (into sth/into doing sth)** to frighten or threaten sb so that they will do what you want: *They were accused of intimidating people into voting for them.* ◇ *She refused to be intimidated by their threats.* ▶ **in·timi·da·tion** /ɪnˌtɪmɪˈdeɪʃn/ *noun* [U]: *the intimidation of witnesses*

in·timi·dated /ɪnˈtɪmɪdeɪtɪd/ *adj.* [not usually before noun] feeling frightened and not confident in a particular situation: *We try to make sure children don't feel intimidated on their first day at school.*

in·timi·dat·ing /ɪnˈtɪmɪdeɪtɪŋ/ *adj.* ~ **(for/to sb)** frightening in a way which makes a person feel less confident: *an intimidating manner* ◇ *This kind of questioning can be very intimidating to children.*

in·timi·da·tory /ɪnˌtɪmɪˈdeɪtəri/ *adj.* (*formal*) intended to frighten or threaten sb

into /ˈɪntə; *before vowels strong form* ˈɪntu; *strong form* ˈɪntu/ *prep.* **HELP** For the special uses of **into** in phrasal verbs, look at the entries for the verbs. For example **lay into sb/sth** is in the phrasal verb section at **lay**. **1** to a position in or inside sth: *Come into the house.* ◇ *She dived into the water.* ◇ *He threw the letter into the fire.* ◇ (*figurative*) *She turned and walked off into the night.* **2** in the direction of sth: *Speak clearly into the microphone.* ◇ *Driving into the sun, we had to shade our eyes.* **3** to a point at which you hit sb/sth: *The truck crashed into a parked car.* **4** to a point during a period of time: *She carried on working late into the night.* ◇ *He didn't get married until he was well into his forties.* **5** used to show a change in state: *The fruit can be made into jam.* ◇ *Can you translate this passage into German?* ◇ *They came into power in 1997.* ◇ *She was sliding into depression.* **6** used to show the result of an action: *He was shocked into a confession of guilt.* **7** about or concerning sth: *an inquiry into safety procedures* **8** used when you are dividing numbers: *3 into 24 is 8.* **IDM** be **'into sth** (*informal*) to be interested in sth in an active way: *He's into surfing in a big way.*

in·toler·able /ɪnˈtɒlərəbl; *AmE* -ˈtɑːl-/ *adj.* so bad or difficult that you cannot TOLERATE it; completely unacceptable [SYN] UNBEARABLE: *an intolerable burden/situation* ◇ *The heat was intolerable.* ▶ **in·toler·ably** /-əbli/ *adv.*: *intolerably hot*

in·toler·ant /ɪnˈtɒlərənt; *AmE* -ˈtɑːl-/ *adj.* **1** ~ **(of sb/sth)** (*disapproving*) not willing to accept ideas or ways of behaving that are different from your own [OPP] TOLERANT **2** ~ **(of sth)** (*technical*) not able to eat particular foods, use particular medicines, etc. ▶ **in·toler·ance** /-əns/ *noun* [U]: *religious intolerance* ◇ *food allergy and intolerance*

in·ton·ation /ˌɪntəˈneɪʃn/ *noun* **1** [U, C] (*phonetics*) the rise and fall of the voice in speaking, especially as this affects the meaning of what is being said: *intonation patterns* ◇ *In English, some questions have a rising inton-*

ation.—compare STRESS **2** [U] (*music*) the quality of playing or singing exactly in tune: *The violin's intonation was poor.*

in·tone /ɪnˈtəʊn; *AmE* ɪnˈtoʊn/ *verb* (*formal*) to say sth in a slow and serious voice without much expression: [VN] *The priest intoned the final prayer.* [also **V speech**]

in toto /ɪn ˈtəʊtəʊ; *AmE* ˈtoʊtoʊ/ *adv.* (from *Latin, formal*) completely; including all parts

in·toxi·cant /ɪnˈtɒksɪkənt; *AmE* -ˈtɑːk-/ *noun* (*technical*) a substance such as alcohol that produces false feelings of pleasure and a lack of control

in·toxi·cated /ɪnˈtɒksɪkeɪtɪd; *AmE* -ˈtɑːk-/ *adj.* (*formal*) **1** under the influence of alcohol or drugs: (*AmE*) *He was arrested for DWI* (= driving while intoxicated). **2** ~ **(by/with sth)** very excited by sth, so that you cannot think clearly: *intoxicated with power/success* ▶ **in·toxi·cate** *verb* [VN]

in·toxi·cat·ing /ɪnˈtɒksɪkeɪtɪŋ; *AmE* -ˈtɑːk-/ *adj.* **1** (of drink) containing alcohol **2** making you feel excited so that you cannot think clearly: *Power can be intoxicating.* ▶ **in·toxi·ca·tion** /ɪnˌtɒksɪˈkeɪʃn; *AmE* -ˌtɑːk-/ *noun* [U]

intra- *prefix* (in adjectives and adverbs) inside; within: *intravenous* ◇ *intra-departmental* (= within a department)—compare INTER-

in·tract·able /ɪnˈtræktəbl/ *adj.* (*formal*) (of a problem or a person) very difficult to deal with: *Unemployment was proving to be an intractable problem.* [OPP] TRACTABLE ▶ **in·tract·abil·ity** /ɪnˌtræktəˈbɪləti/ *noun* [U]

intra·mural /ˌɪntrəˈmjʊərəl; *AmE* -ˈmjʊrəl/ *adj.* taking place within a single institution, especially a school or college: *Jeff played intramural basketball in high school.*

Intra·net /ˈɪntrənet/ *noun* (*computing*) a computer NETWORK that is private to a company, university, etc. but is connected to and uses the same SOFTWARE as the Internet

in·transi·gent /ɪnˈtrænsɪdʒənt; *AmE* -ˈtrænz-/ *adj.* (*formal, disapproving*) (of people) unwilling to change their opinions or behaviour in a way that would be helpful to others [SYN] STUBBORN: *an intransigent attitude* ▶ **in·transi·gence** /-əns/ *noun* [U]

in·transi·tive /ɪnˈtrænsətɪv/ *adj.* (*grammar*) (of verbs) used without a DIRECT OBJECT; not TRANSITIVE: *The verb 'die' as in 'He died suddenly', is intransitive.* ▶ **in·transi·tive·ly** *adv.*: *The verb is being used intransitively.*

intra·uter·ine /ˌɪntrəˈjuːtəraɪn/ *adj.* (*medical*) within the UTERUS

intrauterine de'vice *noun* = IUD

intra·ven·ous /ˌɪntrəˈviːnəs/ *adj.* (*abbr.* IV) (*medical*) (of drugs or food) going into a VEIN: *intravenous fluids* ◇ *an intravenous injection* ◇ *an intravenous drug user* ▶ **intra·ven·ous·ly** *adv.*

'in tray (*AmE* also **'in box**) *noun* (in an office) a container on your desk for letters that are waiting to be read or answered—compare OUT TRAY

in·trench = ENTRENCH

in·trepid /ɪnˈtrepɪd/ *adj.* (*formal, often humorous*) very brave; not afraid of danger or difficulties: *an intrepid explorer*

in·tri·cacy /ˈɪntrɪkəsi/ *noun* **1** (**in·tri·ca·cies**) [pl.] the ~ **of sth** the complicated parts or details of sth: *the intricacies of economic policy* **2** [U] the fact of having complicated parts, details or patterns: *the intricacy of the design*

in·tri·cate /ˈɪntrɪkət/ *adj.* having a lot of different parts and small details that fit together: *intricate patterns/designs/structures* ◇ *an intricate network of loyalties and relationships* ▶ **in·tri·cate·ly** /-kətli/ *adv.*: *intricately carved/decorated/patterned*

in·trigue *verb, noun*

■ *verb* /ɪnˈtriːg/ **1** [often passive] to make sb very interested and want to know more about sth: [VN] *The idea intrigued me.* ◇ *You've really intrigued me—tell me more!* [also VN that] **2** [V] ~ **(with sb) (against sb)** (*formal*) to secretly plan with other people to harm sb

■ *noun* /ˈɪntriːg; ɪnˈtriːg/ **1** [U] the activity of making secret plans in order to achieve an aim, often by deceiving people: *political intrigue* ◇ *The young heroine steps into a web of intrigue in the academic world.* **2** [C] a secret plan

aɪ	aʊ	eɪ	əʊ	oʊ	ɔɪ	ɪə	eə	ʊə	j	w
my	now	say	go (BrE)	go (AmE)	boy	near	hair	pure	yes	wet

or relationship, especially one which involves sb else being deceived: *I soon learnt about all the intrigues and scandals that went on in the little town.* **3** [U] the atmosphere of interest and excitement that surrounds sth secret or important

intrigued /ɪnˈtriːɡd/ *adj.* [not usually before noun] **~ (to do sth)** very interested in sth/sb and wanting to know more about it/them: *He was intrigued by her story.* ◊ *I'm intrigued to know what you thought of the movie.*

in·tri·guing /ɪnˈtriːɡɪŋ/ *adj.* very interesting because of being unusual or not having an obvious answer: *These discoveries raise intriguing questions.* ◊ *an intriguing story/possibility* ◊ *He found her intriguing.* ▶ **in·tri·guing·ly** *adv.*

in·trin·sic /ɪnˈtrɪnsɪk; -zɪk/ *adj.* **~ (to sth)** belonging to or part of the real nature of sth/sb: *the intrinsic value of education* ◊ *These tasks were repetitive, lengthy and lacking any intrinsic interest.* ◊ *Small local shops are intrinsic to the town's character.*—compare EXTRINSIC ▶ **in·trin·sic·al·ly** /-kli/ *adv.*: *There is nothing intrinsically wrong with the idea* (= it is good in itself but there may be outside circumstances which mean it is not suitable).

intro /ˈɪntrəʊ; *AmE* ˈɪntroʊ/ *noun* (*pl.* **-os**) (*informal*) an introduction to sth, especially to a piece of music or writing

intro·duce /ˌɪntrəˈdjuːs; *AmE* -ˈduːs/ *verb* [VN]
PEOPLE | **1 ~ A (to B) | ~ A and B | ~ yourself (to sb)** to tell two or more people who have not met before what each others' names are; to tell sb what your name is: *Can I introduce my wife?* ◊ *He introduced me to a Greek girl at the party.* ◊ *We've already been introduced.* ◊ *Can I introduce myself? I'm Helen Robins.* ◊ *'Kay, this is Steve.' 'Yes, I know—we've already introduced ourselves.'*
TV/RADIO SHOW | **2** to be the main speaker in a television or radio show, who gives details about the show and who presents the people who are in it; to tell the audience the name of the person who is going to speak or perform: *The next programme will be introduced by Mary David.* ◊ *May I introduce my first guest on the show tonight …*
NEW EXPERIENCE | **3 ~ sb to sth | ~ sth (to sb)** to make sb learn about sth or do sth for the first time: *The first lecture introduces students to the main topics of the course.* ◊ *It was she who first introduced the pleasures of sailing to me.*
NEW PRODUCT/LAW | **4 ~ sth (into/to sth)** to make sth available for use, discussion, etc. for the first time SYN BRING IN: *The company is introducing a new range of products this year.* ◊ *The new law was introduced in 1991.* ◊ *We want to introduce the latest technology into schools.*
PLANT/ANIMAL/DISEASE | **5 ~ sth (to/into sth)** to bring a plant, an animal or a disease to a place for the first time: *Vegetation patterns changed when goats were introduced to the island.*
START | **6** to be the start of sth new: *Bands like 'James' introduced the craze for indie music.* ◊ *A slow theme introduces the first movement.*
IN PARLIAMENT | **7** to formally present a new law so that it can be discussed: *to introduce a bill* (*before Parliament*)
ADD | **8 ~ sth (into sth)** (*formal*) to put sth into sth: *Particles of glass had been introduced into the baby food.*

intro·duc·tion /ˌɪntrəˈdʌkʃn/ *noun*
BRINGING INTO USE/TO A PLACE | **1** [U] the act of bringing sth into use or existence for the first time, or of bringing sth to a place for the first time: *the introduction of new manufacturing methods* ◊ *the introduction of compulsory military service* ◊ *the 1000th anniversary of the introduction of Christianity to Russia* **2** [C] a thing that is brought into use or introduced to a place for the first time: *The book lists plants suitable for the British flower garden, among them many new introductions.*
OF PEOPLE | **3** [C] **~ (to sb)** the act of making one person formally known to another, in which you tell each the other's name: *Introductions were made and the conversation started to flow.* ◊ *Our speaker today needs no introduction* (= is already well known). ◊ *a letter of introduction* (= a letter which tells sb who you are, writ-

ten by sb who knows both you and the person reading the letter)
FIRST EXPERIENCE | **4** [sing.] **~ (to sth)** a person's first experience of sth: *This album was my first introduction to modern jazz.*
OF BOOK/SPEECH | **5** [C, U] **~ (to sth)** the first part of a book or speech that gives a general idea of what is to follow: *a brief/general introduction* ◊ *a book with an excellent introduction and notes* ◊ *By way of introduction, let me give you the background to the story.*—compare PREFACE
TO SUBJECT | **6** [C] **~ (to sth)** a book or course for people beginning to study a subject: *'An Introduction to Astronomy'* ◊ *It's a useful introduction to an extremely complex subject.*
IN MUSIC | **7** [C] (*music*) a short section at the beginning of a piece of music: *an eight-bar introduction*

intro·duc·tory /ˌɪntrəˈdʌktəri/ *adj.* **1** written or said at the beginning of sth as an introduction to what follows: *introductory chapters/paragraphs/remarks* **2** intended as an introduction to a subject or an activity for people who have never done it before: *introductory courses/lectures* **3** offered for a short time only, when a product is first on sale: *a special introductory price of just £1·99*

intro·spec·tion /ˌɪntrəˈspekʃn/ *noun* [U] the careful examination of your own thoughts, feelings and reasons for behaving in a particular way: *These situations are best resolved with the minimum of introspection or self-analysis.*

intro·spect·ive /ˌɪntrəˈspektɪv/ *adj.* tending to think a lot about your own thoughts, feelings, etc: *There were a lot of family problems and Jim became increasingly introspective.*

intro·vert /ˈɪntrəvɜːt; *AmE* -vɜːrt/ *noun* a quiet person who is more interested in their own thoughts and feelings than in spending time with other people OPP EXTROVERT ▶ **intro·ver·sion** /ˌɪntrəˈvɜːʃn; *AmE* -ˈvɜːrʒn/ *noun* [U]

intro·vert·ed /ˈɪntrəvɜːtɪd; *AmE* -vɜːrt-/ (also **intro·vert**) *adj.* more interested in your own thoughts and feelings than in spending time with other people: *His teachers perceived him as shy and introverted.* OPP EXTROVERT

in·trude /ɪnˈtruːd/ *verb* [V] **1 ~** to go or be somewhere where you are not wanted or are not supposed to be: *I'm sorry to intrude, but I need to talk to someone.* ◊ *legislation to stop newspapers from intruding on people's private lives* **2 ~ (on/into/upon sth)** to disturb sth or have an unpleasant effect on it: *The sound of the telephone intruded into his dreams.*

in·truder /ɪnˈtruːdə(r)/ *noun* **1** a person who enters a building or an area illegally **2** a person who is somewhere where they are not wanted: *The people in the room seemed to regard her as an unwelcome intruder.*

in·tru·sion /ɪnˈtruːʒn/ *noun* [U, C] **~ (into/on/upon sth) 1** something that affects a situation or people's lives in a way that they do not want: *They claim the noise from the new airport is an intrusion on their lives.* ◊ *This was another example of press intrusion into the affairs of the royals.* **2** the act of entering a place which is private or where you may not be wanted: *She apologized for the intrusion but said she had an urgent message.*

in·tru·sive /ɪnˈtruːsɪv/ *adj.* too noticeable, direct, etc. in a way that is disturbing or annoying: *intrusive questions/sales methods* ◊ *When Alison was at home she was an intrusive presence.*

in·tuit /ɪnˈtjuːɪt; *AmE* -ˈtuː-/ *verb* (*formal*) to know that sth is true based on your feelings rather than on facts, what sb tells you, etc: [V that] *She intuited that something was badly wrong.* [also VN, V wh-]

in·tu·ition /ˌɪntjuˈɪʃn; *AmE* -tu-/ *noun* **1** [U] the ability to know sth by using your feelings rather than by considering the facts: *Intuition told her that he had spoken the truth.* **2** [C] **~ (that …)** an idea or a strong feeling that sth is true although you cannot explain why: *I had an intuition that something awful was about to happen.*

in·tui·tive /ɪnˈtjuːɪtɪv; *AmE* -ˈtuː-/ *adj.* **1** (of ideas) obtained by using your feelings rather than by considering the facts: *an intuitive judgement* ◊ *He had an intuitive* sense of what the reader wanted. **2** (of people) able to understand sth by using feelings rather than by considering the facts: *Is the feminine nature generally more intuitive?* ▶ **in·tui·tive·ly** *adv.*: *Intuitively, she knew that he was lying.*

Inuit /ˈɪnjuɪt; ˈɪnuɪt/ *noun* (*pl.* **In·uits** or **Inuit**) a member of a race of people from northern Canada and parts of Greenland and Alaska. The name is sometimes also used to refer to people from Siberia.—compare ESKIMO

in·un·date /ˈɪnʌndeɪt/ *verb* [VN] [usually passive] **1** ~ **sb** **(with sth)** to give or send sb so many things that they cannot deal with them all SYN OVERWHELM, SWAMP: *We have been inundated with offers of help.* **2** (*formal*) to cover an area of land with a large amount of water SYN FLOOD: *Flood waters inundate the river plain each spring.* ▶ **in·un·da·tion** /ˌɪnʌnˈdeɪʃn/ *noun* [U, C]

inure /ɪˈnjʊə(r); *AmE* ɪˈnjʊr/ *verb* PHR V **i'nure sb/yourself to sth** (*formal*) to make sb/sth get used to sth unpleasant so that they are no longer strongly affected by it: *The prisoners quickly became inured to the harsh conditions.*

in·vade /ɪnˈveɪd/ *verb* **1** to enter a country, town, etc. using military force in order to take control of it: [V] *Troops invaded on August 9th that year.* ◇ [VN] *When did the Romans invade Britain?* **2** [VN] to enter a place in large numbers, especially in a way that causes damage or confusion: *Demonstrators invaded the government buildings.* ◇ *As the final whistle blew, fans began invading the field.* ◇ *The cancer cells may invade other parts of the body.* **3** [VN] to affect sth in an unpleasant or annoying way: *Do the press have the right to invade her privacy in this way?*—see also INVASION, INVASIVE

in·vader /ɪnˈveɪdə(r)/ *noun* an army or a country that enters another country by force in order to take control of it; a soldier fighting in such an army: *a foreign invader* ◇ *They prepared to repel the invaders.* ◇ (*figurative*) *The white blood cells attack cells infected with an invader.*

in·valid *adj., noun, verb*
■ *adj.* /ɪnˈvælɪd/ **1** not legally or officially acceptable: *The treaty was declared invalid because it had not been ratified.* ◇ *People with invalid papers are deported to another country.* **2** not based on all the facts, and therefore not correct: *an invalid argument* **3** (*computing*) of a type that the computer cannot recognize: *An error code will be displayed if any invalid information has been entered.* ◇ *invalid characters* OPP VALID
■ *noun* /ˈɪnvəlɪd; *BrE* also ˈɪnvəliːd/ a person who needs other people to take care of them, because of illness that they have had for a long time: *She had been a delicate child and her parents had treated her as an invalid.* ◇ *his invalid wife*
■ *verb* /ˈɪnvəlɪd; ˈɪnvəliːd/ [VN] ~ **sb (out)** | ~ **sb (out of sth)** (*BrE*) to force sb to leave the armed forces because of an illness or injury: *He was invalided out of the army in 1943.*

in·vali·date /ɪnˈvælɪdeɪt/ *verb* [VN] **1** to prove that an idea, a story, an argument, etc. is wrong: *This new piece of evidence invalidates his version of events.* **2** if you invalidate a document, contract, election, etc., you make it no longer legally or officially valid or acceptable OPP VALIDATE ▶ **in·vali·da·tion** /ɪnˌvælɪˈdeɪʃn/ *noun* [U]

in·val·id·ity /ˌɪnvəˈlɪdəti/ *noun* [U] **1** (*BrE, technical*) the state of being unable to look after yourself because of illness or injury **2** (*formal*) the state of not being legally or officially acceptable—compare VALIDITY

in·valu·able /ɪnˈvæljuəbl/ *adj.* ~ **(to/for sb/sth)** | ~ **(in sth)** extremely useful: *invaluable help/information/support* ◇ *The book will be invaluable for students in higher education.* ◇ *The research should prove invaluable in the study of children's language.* ◇ *an invaluable asset/tool*— compare VALUABLE HELP **Invaluable** = 'very valuable or useful'. The opposite of **valuable** is **valueless** or **worthless**.

in·vari·able /ɪnˈveəriəbl; *AmE* -ˈver-/ *adj.* always the same; never changing: *Her routine was invariable.* ◇ *his invariable courtesy and charm* ◇ *an invariable law/principle/practice*—compare VARIABLE

in·vari·ably /ɪnˈveəriəbli; *AmE* -ˈver-/ *adv.* always: *This*

acute infection of the brain is almost invariably fatal. ◇ *This is not invariably the case.* ◇ *Invariably the reply came back, 'Not now!'*

in·vari·ant /ɪnˈveəriənt; *AmE* -ˈver-/ *adj.* (*technical*) always the same; never changing SYN INVARIABLE

in·va·sion /ɪnˈveɪʒn/ *noun* [C, U] **1** the act of an army entering another country by force in order to take control of it: *the Russian invasion of Czechoslovakia in 1968* ◇ *the threat of invasion* ◇ *an invasion force/fleet* **2** the fact of a large number of people or things arriving somewhere, especially people or things that are disturbing or unpleasant: *the annual tourist invasion* ◇ *Farmers are struggling to cope with an invasion of slugs.* **3** an act or a process that affects sb/sth in a way that is not welcome: *The actress described the photographs of her as an invasion of privacy.*—see also INVADE

in·va·sive /ɪnˈveɪsɪv/ *adj.* (*formal*) **1** (especially of diseases within the body) spreading very quickly and difficult to stop: *invasive cancer* **2** (of medical treatment) involving cutting into the body: *invasive surgery*—see also INVADE

in·vec·tive /ɪnˈvektɪv/ *noun* [U] (*formal*) rude language and unpleasant remarks that sb shouts when they are very angry: *The gesture infuriated him and he let out a stream of invective.*

in·veigh /ɪnˈveɪ/ *verb* PHR V **in'veigh against sb/sth** (*formal*) to criticize sb/sth strongly

in·vei·gle /ɪnˈveɪɡl/ *verb* [VN] ~ **sb/yourself (into sth/ into doing sth)** (*formal*) to achieve control over sb in a clever and dishonest way, especially so that they will do what you want: *He inveigled himself into her affections* (= dishonestly made her love him).

in·vent /ɪnˈvent/ *verb* [VN] **1** to produce or design sth that has not existed before: *Who invented the steam engine?* ⇨ note at DISCOVER **2** to say or describe sth that is not true, especially in order to deceive people: *What excuse did he invent this time?* ◇ *Many children invent an imaginary friend.*

in·ven·tion /ɪnˈvenʃn/ *noun* **1** [C] a thing or an idea that has been invented: *Fax machines were a wonderful invention at the time.* ◇ *This combination of cheese and apples is not an invention of the north of England.* **2** [U] the act of inventing sth: *Such changes have not been seen since the invention of the printing press.* **3** [C, U] the act of inventing a story or an idea and pretending that it is true; a story invented in this way: *This story is apparently a complete invention.* **4** [U] the ability to have new and interesting ideas: *John was full of invention—always making up new dance steps and sequences.*

in·vent·ive /ɪnˈventɪv/ *adj.* **1** (especially of people) able to think of new and interesting ideas: *She has a highly inventive mind.* **2** (of ideas) new and interesting: *This is a courageous and inventive piece of film-making.* ▶ **in·vent·ive·ly** *adv.* **in·vent·ive·ness** *noun* [U]

in·vent·or /ɪnˈventə(r)/ *noun* a person who has invented sth or whose job is inventing things

in·ven·tory /ˈɪnvəntri; *AmE* -tɔːri/ *noun* (*pl.* **-ies**) **1** [C] a written list of all the objects, furniture, etc. in a particular building: *an inventory of the museum's contents* **2** [U] (*AmE*) all the goods in a shop SYN STOCK: *The inventory will be disposed of over the next twelve weeks.* ◇ *inventory records/control*—compare STOCKTAKING

in·verse /ˌɪnˈvɜːs; ˌɪnˈvɜːrs/ *adj.* **1** [only before noun] opposite in amount or position to sth else: *A person's wealth is often in inverse proportion to their happiness* (= the more money they have, the less happy they are). ◇ *There is often an inverse relationship between the power of the tool and how easy it is to use.* **2** (**the 'inverse**) *noun* [sing.] (*technical*) the exact opposite of sth ▶ **in·verse·ly** /ˌɪnˈvɜːsli; *AmE* -ˈvɜːrs-/ *adv.*: *We regard health as inversely related to social class.*

in·ver·sion /ɪnˈvɜːʃn; *AmE* ɪnˈvɜːrʃn; -ʒn/ *noun* [U, C] (*technical*) the act of changing the position or order of sth to its opposite, or of turning sth upside down: *the inversion of normal word order* ◇ *an inversion of the truth*

in·vert /ɪnˈvɜːt; *AmE* ɪnˈvɜːrt/ *verb* [VN] (*formal*) to change the normal position of sth, especially by turning it upside down or by arranging it in the opposite order: *Place a plate over the cake tin and invert it.* ◇ *In questions, the subject and verb are often inverted.*

in·ver·te·brate /ɪnˈvɜːtɪbrət; *AmE* -ˈvɜːrt-/ *noun* (*technical*) any animal with no BACKBONE, for example a worm—compare VERTEBRATE

in,verted 'commas *noun* [pl.] (*BrE*) = QUOTATION MARKS **IDM in inverted commas** (*spoken*) used to show that you think a particular word, description, etc. is not true or appropriate: *The manager showed us to our 'luxury apartment', in inverted commas.*

in,verted 'snobbery *noun* [U] (*BrE, disapproving*) the attitude that disapproves of everything connected with high social status and that is proud of low social status

in·vest /ɪnˈvest/ *verb* **1** ~ (sth) (in sth) to buy property, shares in a ompany, etc. in the hope of making a profit: [V] *Now is a good time to invest in the property market.* ◇ [VN] *He invested his life savings in his daughter's business.* **2** ~ (sth) (in/on sth) (of an organization or government, etc.) to spend money on sth in order to make it better or more successful: [V] *The government has invested heavily in public transport.* ◇ [VN] *The college has invested $2 million on a new conference hall.* [also VN to inf] **3** ~ sth (in sth/in doing sth) to spend time, energy, effort, etc. on sth that you think is good or useful: [VN] *She had invested all her adult life in the relationship.* [also VN -ing] **4** [VN] ~ sb (with sth)| ~ sb (as sth) (*formal*) to give sb power or authority, especially as part of their job: *The new position invested her with a good deal of responsibility.* ◇ *The interview was broadcast on the same day he was invested as President.*—see also INVESTITURE **PHR V in'vest in sth** (*informal, often humorous*) to buy sth that is expensive but useful: *Don't you think it's about time you invested in a new coat?* **in'vest sb/sth with sth** (*formal*) to make sb/sth seem to have a particular quality: *Being a model invests her with a certain glamour.*

in·ves·ti·gate /ɪnˈvestɪɡeɪt/ *verb* **1** to carefully examine the facts of a situation, an event, a crime, etc. to find out the truth about it or how it happened: [V] *The FBI has been called in to investigate.* ◇ (*informal*) *'What was that noise?' 'I'll go and investigate.'* ◇ [VN] *Police are investigating possible links between the murders.* [also V wh-] **2** [VN] ~ sb (for sth) to try to find out information about sb's character, activities, etc: *This is not the first time he has been investigated by the police for fraud.* **3** to find out information and facts about a subject or problem by study or research: [VN] *Scientists are investigating the effects of diet on fighting cancer.* ◇ [V wh-] *The research investigates how foreign speakers gain fluency.* [also V]

in·ves·ti·ga·tion /ɪnˌvestɪˈɡeɪʃn/ *noun* [C, U] ~ (into sth) **1** an official examination of the facts about a situation, crime, etc: *a criminal/murder/police investigation* ◇ *The police have completed their investigations into the accident.* ◇ *She is still under investigation.* **2** a scientific or academic examination of the facts of a subject or problem: *an investigation into the spending habits of teenagers*

in·ves·ti·ga·tive /ɪnˈvestɪɡətɪv; *AmE* -ɡeɪtɪv/ (also *less frequent* **in·ves·ti·ga·tory** /ɪnˈvestɪɡətəri; *AmE* -ɡətɔːri/) *adj.* [usually before noun] involving examining an event or a situation to find out the truth: *The article was an excellent piece of investigative journalism.* ◇ *The police have full investigatory powers.*

in·ves·ti·ga·tor /ɪnˈvestɪɡeɪtə(r)/ *noun* a person who examines a situation such as an accident or a crime to find out the truth: *air safety investigators* ◇ *a private investigator* (= a DETECTIVE)

in·ves·ti·ture /ɪnˈvestɪtʃə(r)/ *noun* [U, C] a ceremony at which sb formally receives an official title or special powers

in·vest·ment /ɪnˈvestmənt/ *noun* **1** [U] ~ (in sth) the act of investing money in sth: *to encourage foreign/private investment* ◇ *investment income* ◇ *This country needs investment in education.* **2** [C] the money that you invest, or the thing that you invest in: *a minimum investment of $10000* ◇ *a high return on my investments* ◇ *Our investments are not doing well.* ◇ *We bought the house as an*

investment (= to make money). **3** [C] a thing that is worth buying because it will be useful or helpful: *A microwave is a good investment.* **4** [U, C] the act of giving time or effort to a particular task in order to make it successful: *The project has demanded considerable investment of time and effort.*

in·vest·or /ɪnˈvestə(r)/ *noun* a person or an organization that invests money in sth: *small investors* (= private people) ◇ *institutional investors*

in·vet·er·ate /ɪnˈvetərət/ *adj.* [usually before noun] (*formal, often disapproving*) **1** (of a person) always doing sth or enjoying sth, and unlikely to stop: *an inveterate liar/traveller* **2** (of a bad feeling or habit) done or felt for a long time and unlikely to change: *inveterate hostility*

in·vidi·ous /ɪnˈvɪdiəs/ *adj.* (*formal*) unpleasant and unfair; likely to offend sb or make them jealous: *We were in the invidious position of having to choose whether to break the law or risk lives.* ◇ *It would be invidious to single out any one person to thank.*

in·vigi·late /ɪnˈvɪdʒɪleɪt/ *verb* (*BrE*) (*AmE* **proc·tor**) to watch people while they are taking an exam to make sure that they have everything they need, that they keep to the rules, etc: [VN] *to invigilate an exam* [also V] ▶ **in·vigi·la·tion** /ɪnˌvɪdʒɪˈleɪʃn/ *noun* [U] **in·vigi·la·tor** /ɪnˈvɪdʒɪleɪtə(r)/ (*BrE*) (*AmE* **proc·tor**) *noun*: *If you have a problem, ask the invigilator.*

in·vig·or·ate /ɪnˈvɪɡəreɪt/ *verb* [VN] **1** [often passive] to make sb feel healthy and full of energy: *The cold water invigorated him.* ◇ *They felt refreshed and invigorated after the walk.* **2** to make a situation, an organization, etc. efficient and successful: *They are looking into ways of invigorating the department.* ▶ **in·vig·or·at·ing** *adj.*: *invigorating walk/shower/massage*

in·vin·cible /ɪnˈvɪnsəbl/ *adj.* too strong to be defeated or changed: *The team seemed invincible.* ◇ *an invincible belief in his own ability* ▶ **in·vin·ci·bil·ity** /ɪnˌvɪnsəˈbɪləti/ *noun* [U]

in·viol·able /ɪnˈvaɪələbl/ *adj.* (*formal*) that must be respected and not attacked or destroyed: *the inviolable right to life* ◇ *inviolable territory* ◇ *an inviolable rule* ▶ **in·viol·abil·ity** /ɪnˌvaɪələˈbɪləti/ *noun* [U]

in·viol·ate /ɪnˈvaɪələt/ *adj.* (*formal*) that has been, or must be, respected and cannot be attacked or destroyed: *Their privacy remained inviolate.*

in·vis·ible /ɪnˈvɪzəbl/ *adj.* **1** ~ (to sb/sth) that cannot be seen: *stars invisible to the naked eye* ◇ *a wizard who could make himself invisible* ◇ *She felt invisible in the crowd.* **OPP** VISIBLE **2** (*economics*) connected with a service that a country provides, such as BANKING or TOURISM, rather than goods: *invisible earnings/exports* ▶ **in·vis·ibil·ity** /ɪnˌvɪzəˈbɪləti/ *noun* [U]: *The ink had faded to invisibility.* **in·vis·ibly** /ɪnˈvɪzəbli/ *adv.*: *He moved away invisibly into the background.*

in·vi·ta·tion /ˌɪnvɪˈteɪʃn/ *noun* **1** [C] ~ (to sth/to do sth) a spoken or written request to sb to do sth or to go somewhere: *to issue/extend an invitation* ◇ *to accept/turn down/decline an invitation* ◇ *an invitation to the party* ◇ *I have an open invitation* (= not restricted to a particular date) *to visit my friend in Japan.* **2** [U] the act of inviting sb or of being invited: *A concert was held at the invitation of the mayor.* ◇ *Admission is by invitation only.* **3** [C] a card or piece of paper that you use to invite sb to sth: *Have you ordered the wedding invitations yet?* **4** [sing.] ~ to sb (to do sth)| ~ to sth something that encourages sb to do sth, usually sth bad: *Leaving the doors unlocked is an open invitation to burglars.*

in·vi·ta·tion·al /ˌɪnvɪˈteɪʃənl/ *noun* (*especially AmE*) (often used in names) a sports event that you can take part in only if you are invited ▶ **in·vi·ta·tion·al** *adj.*

in·vite *verb, noun*

■ *verb* /ɪnˈvaɪt/ **1** ~ sb (to sth) to ask sb to come to a social event: [VN] *Have you been invited to their party?* ◇ *I'd have liked to have gone but I wasn't invited.* ◇ [VN to inf] *They have invited me to go to Paris with them.* **2** ~ sb (to/for sth)| ~ sth (from sb) (*formal*) to ask sb formally to go somewhere or do sth: [VN] *Successful candidates will be invited for interview next week.* ◇ *He invited questions from*

æ	ɑː	e	ɜː	ə	ɪ	iː	i	ɒ	ɔː	ʌ	ʊ	u	uː
cat	father	ten	bird	about	sit	see	many	got	saw	cup	put	actual	too

(BrE)

the audience. ◊ [VN to inf] *Readers are invited to write in with their comments.* **3** to make sth, especially sth bad or unpleasant, likely to happen SYN ASK FOR: [VN] *Such comments are just inviting trouble.* [also VN to inf] —see also UNINVITED PHRV **in,vite sb a'long** to ask sb to go somewhere with you and other people: *I got myself invited along.* **in,vite sb 'back 1** to ask sb to come to your home after you have been somewhere together: *After the movie, she invited me back for a drink.* **2** to ask sb to come to your home a second time, or to ask sb to come to your house after you have been to theirs **in,vite sb 'in/'up** to ask sb to come into your home, especially after you have been somewhere together **in,vite sb 'over/'round/ a'round** to ask sb to come to your home
- *noun* /'ɪnvaɪt/ (*informal*) an invitation: *Thanks for your invite.*

in·vit·ing /ɪn'vaɪtɪŋ/ *adj.* making you want to do, try, taste, etc. sth; attractive: *an inviting smell/view* ◊ *The water looks really inviting.* ▶ **in·vit·ing·ly** *adv.*

in vitro /ɪn 'viːtrəʊ; *AmE* 'viːtroʊ/ *adj.* (from *Latin, biology*) (of processes) taking place outside a living body, in scientific APPARATUS: *in vitro experiments* ◊ *the development of in vitro fertilization*—see also IVF ▶ **in vitro** *adv.*: *an egg fertilized in vitro*

in vivo /ɪn 'viːvəʊ; *AmE* 'viːvoʊ/ *adj.* (from *Latin, biology*) (of processes) taking place in a living body ▶ **in vivo** *adv.*

in·vo·ca·tion /,ɪnvə'keɪʃn/ *noun* [U, C] **1** (*formal*) the act of asking for help, from a god or from a person in authority; the act of referring to sth or of calling for sth to appear **2** (*computing*) the act of making a particular function start

in·voice /'ɪnvɔɪs/ *noun, verb*
- *noun* a list of goods that have been sold, work that has been done etc., showing what you must pay BILL: *to send/issue/settle an invoice for the goods* ◊ *an invoice for £250*
- *verb* [VN] **~ sb (for sth)| ~ sth (to sb/sth)** (*business*) to write or send sb a bill for work you have done or goods you have provided: *You will be invoiced for these items at the end of the month.* ◊ *Invoice the goods to my account.*

in·voke /ɪn'vəʊk; *AmE* ɪn'voʊk/ *verb* [VN] (*formal*) **1 ~ sth (against sb)** to mention or use a law, rule, etc. as a reason for doing sth: *It is unlikely that libel laws will be invoked.* **2** to mention a person, a theory, an example, etc. to support your opinions or ideas, or as a reason for sth: *She invoked several eminent scholars to back up her argument.* **3** to mention sb's name to make people feel a particular thing or act in a particular way: *His name was invoked as a symbol of the revolution.* **4** to make a request (for help) to sb, especially a god **5** to make sb have a particular feeling or imagine a particular scene SYN EVOKE: *The opening paragraph invokes a vision of England in the early Middle Ages.* HELP Some people think this use is not correct. **6** to use or apply sth: *He frequently invokes animal metaphors in his poetry.* **7** (*computing*) to begin to run a program, etc: *This command will invoke the HELP system.* **8** to make evil appear by using magic

in·vol·un·tary /ɪn'vɒləntri; *AmE* ɪn'vɑːlənteri/ *adj.* **1** an involuntary movement, etc. is made suddenly, without you intending it or being able to control it: *an involuntary cry of pain* OPP VOLUNTARY **2** happening without you wanting it to: *the involuntary repatriation of immigrants* ◊ *involuntary childlessness* ▶ **in·vol·un·tar·ily** /ɪn'vɒləntrəli; *AmE* ɪn,vɑːlən'terəli/ *adv.*

in·volve /ɪn'vɒlv; *AmE* ɪn'vɑːlv/ *verb* **1** if a situation, an event or an activity **involves** sth, that thing is an important or necessary part of it SYN ENTAIL: [VN] *Any investment involves an element of risk.* ◊ *Many of the crimes involved drugs.* ◊ [V-ing] *The test will involve answering questions about a photograph.* ◊ [VN-ing] *The job involves me travelling all over the country.* ◊ (*formal*) *The job involves my travelling all over the country.* **2** [VN] if a situation, an event or an activity **involves** sb, they take part in it or are affected by it: *There was a serious incident involving a group of youths.* ◊ *How many vehicles were involved in the crash?* **3** [VN] **~ sb (in sth/in doing**

sth) to make sb take part in sth: *We want to involve as many people as possible in the celebrations.* ◊ *Parents should involve themselves in their child's education.* **4** [VN] **~ sb (in sth)** to say or do sth to show that sb took part in sth, especially a crime SYN IMPLICATE: *His confession involved a number of other politicians in the affair.* PHRV **in'volve sb in sth** to make sb experience sth, especially sth unpleasant: *You have involved me in a great deal of extra work.*

in·volved /ɪn'vɒlvd; *AmE* ɪn'vɑːlvd/ *adj.* **1** [not before noun] **~ (in sth)** taking part in sth; being part of sth or connected with sth: *to be/become/get involved in politics* ◊ *We need to examine all the costs involved in the project first.* ◊ *We'll make our decision and contact the people involved.* HELP In this meaning, **involved** is often used after a noun. **2** [not usually before noun] **~ (in/with sth/sb)** giving a lot of time or attention to sb/sth: *She was deeply involved with the local hospital.* ◊ *I was so involved in my book I didn't hear you knock.* ◊ *He's a very involved father* (= he spends a lot of time with his children). **3** [not usually before noun] **~ (with sb/sth)** having a close personal relationship with sb: *They're not romantically involved.* ◊ *You're too emotionally involved with the situation.* **4** complicated and difficult to understand SYN COMPLEX: *an involved sentence/plot*

in·volve·ment /ɪn'vɒlvmənt; *AmE* -'vɑːlv-/ *noun* **1** [U] **~ (in/with sth)** the act of taking part in sth: *US involvement in European wars* **2** [U, C] **~ (in/with sth)** the act of giving a lot of time and attention to sth you care about: *her growing involvement with contemporary music* **3** [C, U] **~ (with sb)** a romantic or sexual relationship with sb that you are not married to: *He spoke openly about his involvement with the actress.*

in·vul·ner·able /ɪn'vʌlnərəbl/ *adj.* **~ (to sth)** that cannot be harmed or defeated; safe: *to be in an invulnerable position* ◊ *The submarine is invulnerable to attack while at sea.* OPP VULNERABLE ▶ **in·vul·ner·abil·ity** /ɪn,vʌl-nərə'bɪləti/ *noun* [U]

in·ward /'ɪnwəd; *AmE* -wərd/ *adj., adv.*
- *adj.* **1** [only before noun] inside your mind and not shown to other people: *an inward smile* ◊ *Her calm expression hid her inward panic.* **2** towards the inside or centre of sth: *an inward flow* ◊ *an inward curve* OPP OUTWARD
- *adv.* (also **in·wards** especially in *BrE*) **1** towards the inside or centre: *The door opens inwards.* **2** towards yourself and your interests: *Her thoughts turned inwards.* ◊ (*disapproving*) *an inward-looking person* (= one who is not interested in other people) OPP OUTWARDS

,inward in'vestment *noun* [U, C] (*business*) money that is invested within a particular country

in·ward·ly /'ɪnwədli; *AmE* -wərd-/ *adv.* in your mind; secretly: *She groaned inwardly.* ◊ *I was inwardly furious.* OPP OUTWARDLY

in·ward·ness /'ɪnwədnəs; *AmE* -wərd-/ *noun* [U] (*formal or literary*) interest in feelings and emotions rather than in the world around

'in-your-face *adj.* (*informal*) used to describe an attitude, a performance, etc. that is aggressive in style and deliberately designed to make people react strongly for or against it: *in-your-face action thrillers*

iod·ine /'aɪədiːn; *AmE* -daɪn/ *noun* [U] (*symb* I) a chemical element. Iodine is a blue-black substance found in sea water. A liquid containing iodine is sometimes used as an ANTISEPTIC (= a substance used on wounds to prevent infection).

ion /'aɪən; *BrE* also 'aɪɒn; *AmE* also 'aɪɑːn/ *noun* (*physics* or *chemistry*) an atom or a MOLECULE with a positive or negative electric CHARGE caused by its losing or gaining one or more ELECTRONS

-ion (also **-ation, -ition, -sion, -tion, -xion**) *suffix* (in nouns) the action or state of: *hesitation* ◊ *competition* ◊ *confession*

ion·ize (*BrE* also **-ise**) /'aɪənaɪz/ *verb* [VN, V] (*technical*) to change sth or be changed into ions ▶ **ion·iza·tion, -isa·tion** /,aɪənaɪ'zeɪʃn; *AmE* -nə'z-/ *noun* [U]

ion·izer (*BrE* also **-iser**) /'aɪənaɪzə(r)/ *noun* a device that is used to make air in a room fresh and healthy by producing negative IONS

iono·sphere /aɪˈɒnəsfɪə(r); *AmE* aɪˈɑːnəsfɪr/ *noun* (**the ionosphere**) [sing.] a layer of the earth's atmosphere between about 80 and 1000 kilometres above the surface of the earth, that reflects radio waves around the earth—compare STRATOSPHERE

iota /aɪˈəʊtə; *AmE* aɪˈoʊtə/ *noun* [sing.] (usually used in negative sentences) an extremely small amount: *There is not one iota of truth* (= no truth at all) *in the story.* ◊ *I don't think that would help one iota.*

IOU /ˌaɪ əʊ ˈjuː; *AmE* -oʊ-/ *noun* (*informal*) a written promise that you will pay sb the money you owe them (a way of writing 'I owe you'): *an IOU for £20*

IPA /ˌaɪ piː ˈeɪ/ *abbr.* International Phonetic Alphabet (an alphabet that is used to show the pronunciation of words in any language)

ipso facto /ˌɪpsəʊ ˈfæktəʊ; *AmE* ˌɪpsoʊ ˈfæktoʊ/ *adv.* (from *Latin, formal*) because of the fact that has been mentioned: *You cannot assume that a speaker of English is ipso facto qualified to teach English.*

IQ /ˌaɪ ˈkjuː/ *noun* a measurement of a person's intelligence that is calculated from the results of special tests (abbreviation for 'intelligence quotient'): *an IQ of 120* ◊ *to have a high/low IQ* ◊ *IQ tests*

ir- ⇨ IN-

IRA /ˌaɪ ɑːr ˈeɪ/ *noun* [sing.] the abbreviation for 'Irish Republican Army'. The IRA is an illegal organization which has fought for Northern Ireland to be united with the Republic of Ireland.

iras·cible /ɪˈræsəbl/ *adj.* (*formal*) becoming angry very easily ▶ **iras·ci·bil·ity** /ɪˌræsəˈbɪləti/ *noun* [U]

irate /aɪˈreɪt/ *adj.* very angry: *irate customers* ◊ *an irate phone call*

ire /ˈaɪə(r)/ *noun* [U] (*formal or literary*) anger SYN WRATH: *to arouse/raise/provoke the ire of local residents* ◊ (*AmE*) *to draw the ire of local residents*

iri·des·cent /ˌɪrɪˈdesnt/ *adj.* (*formal*) showing many bright colours that seem to change in different lights: *a bird with iridescent blue feathers* ▶ **iri·des·cence** /-ˈdesns/ *noun* [U]

irid·ium /ɪˈrɪdiəm/ *noun* [U] (*symb* Ir) a chemical element. Iridium is a very hard yellow-white metal, used especially in making ALLOYS.

iris /ˈaɪrɪs/ *noun* **1** the round coloured part that surrounds the PUPIL of your eye—picture at BODY **2** a tall plant with long pointed leaves and large purple or bright yellow flowers

Irish /ˈaɪrɪʃ/ *noun, adj.*
■ *noun* **1** (also **Irish ˈGaelic, Gaelic**) the Celtic language of Ireland—compare ERSE **2** (**the Irish**) [pl.] the people of Ireland
■ *adj.* of or connected with Ireland, its people or its language

Irish ˈcoffee *noun* **1** [U] hot coffee mixed with whisky and sugar, with thick cream on top **2** [C] a cup or glass of Irish coffee

irk /ɜːk; *AmE* ɜːrk/ *verb* (*formal or literary*) to annoy or irritate sb: [VN] *Her flippant tone irked him.* [also VN that, VN to inf]

irk·some /ˈɜːksəm; *AmE* ˈɜːrk-/ *adj.* (*formal*) annoying or irritating: *I found the restrictions irksome.*

iron /ˈaɪən; *AmE* ˈaɪərn/ *noun, verb, adj.*
■ *noun*
METAL **1** [U] (*symb* Fe) a chemical element. Iron is a hard strong metal that is used to make steel and is also found in small quantities in blood and food: *cast/wrought/corrugated iron* ◊ *iron gates/bars/railings* ◊ *an iron and steel works* ◊ *iron ore* (= rock containing iron) ◊ *patients with iron deficiency* (= not enough iron in their blood) ◊ *iron tablets* (= containing iron prepared as a medicine) ◊ (*figurative*) *She had a will of iron* (= it was very strong).
TOOL **2** [C] a tool with a flat metal base that can be heated and used to make clothes smooth: *a steam iron* **3** [C] (usually in compounds) a tool made of iron—see also BRANDING IRON, SOLDERING IRON, TIRE IRON

FOR PRISONERS **4** (**irons**) [pl.] chains or other heavy objects made of iron, attached to the arms and legs of prisoners, especially in the past: *leg irons* ◊ (*old-fashioned*) *to clap somebody in irons*

IN GOLF **5** [C] one of the set of CLUBS (= sticks for hitting the ball with) that have a metal head: *He hit a magnificent shot with a nine iron.*—compare WOOD

IDM **have several, etc. irons in the ˈfire** to be involved in several activities or areas of business at the same time, hoping that at least one will be successful—more at PUMP *v.*, RULE *v.*, STRIKE *v.*
■ *verb* to make clothes, etc. smooth by using an iron: [VN] *I'll need to iron that dress before I can wear it.* ◊ [V] *He was ironing when I arrived.*—see also IRONING
PHRV **ˌiron sth ↔ ˈout** to remove the CREASES (= folds that you do not want) from clothes, etc. by using an iron ◊ **ˌiron ˈout sth** to get rid of any problems or difficulties that are affecting sth: *There are still a few details that need ironing out.*
■ *adj.* [only before noun] very strong and determined: *She was known as the 'Iron Lady'.* ◊ *a man of iron will*
IDM **an iron ˈfist/ˈhand (in a velvet ˈglove)** if you use the words **an iron fist/hand** when describing the way that sb behaves, you mean that they treat people harshly. The harsh treatment may be hidden behind a kind appearance (the **velvet glove**).

the ˈIron Age *noun* [sing.] the historical period about 3000 years ago when people first used iron tools

the ˌIron ˈCurtain *noun* [sing.] the name that people used for the border that used to exist between Western Europe and the COMMUNIST countries of Eastern Europe

ˌiron-ˈgrey (*especially BrE*) (also **ˌiron-ˈgray** especially in *AmE*) *adj.* dark grey in colour: *iron-grey hair*

iron·ic /aɪˈrɒnɪk; *AmE* -ˈrɑːn-/ (also *less frequent* **iron·ic·al** /aɪˈrɒnɪkl; *AmE* -ˈrɑːn-/) *adj.* **1** showing that you really mean the opposite of what you are saying; expressing IRONY: *an ironic comment/smile* **2** (of a situation) strange or amusing because it is very different from what you expect: *It's ironic that she became a teacher—she used to hate school.*—see also IRONY ▶ **iron·ic·al·ly** /aɪˈrɒnɪkli; *AmE* -ˈrɑːn-/ *adv.*: *Ironically, the book she felt was her worst sold more copies than any of her others.* ◊ *He smiled ironically.*

iron·ing /ˈaɪənɪŋ; *AmE* ˈaɪərnɪŋ/ *noun* [U] **1** the task of pressing clothes, etc. with an IRON to make them smooth: *to do the ironing* **2** the clothes, etc. that you have just IRONED or that need to be done: *a pile of ironing*

ˈironing board *noun* a long narrow board covered with cloth, and usually with folding legs, that you IRON clothes on

iron·mon·ger /ˈaɪənmʌŋɡə(r); *AmE* ˈaɪərn-/ (*BrE*, becoming *old-fashioned*) (*AmE* **ˈhardware dealer**) *noun* **1** a person who owns or works in a shop/store selling tools and equipment for the house and garden/yard **2** (**ironmonger's**) (*pl.* **iron·mon·gers**) a shop that sells tools and equipment for the house and garden/yard ▶ **iron·mon·gery** /-mʌŋɡəri/ *noun* [U] (*BrE*) = HARDWARE

ˌiron ˈrations *noun* [pl.] (*often humorous*) a small amount of food that soldiers and people walking or climbing carry to use in an emergency

iron·stone /ˈaɪənstəʊn; *AmE* ˈaɪərnstoʊn/ *noun* [U] a type of rock that contains iron

iron·work /ˈaɪənwɜːk; *AmE* ˈaɪərnwɜːrk/ *noun* [U] things made of iron, such as gates, parts of buildings, etc.

iron·works /ˈaɪənwɜːks; *AmE* ˈaɪərnwɜːrks/ *noun* (*pl.* **iron·works**) [C+sing./pl. *v.*] a factory where iron is obtained from ORE (= rock containing metal), or where heavy iron goods are made

irony /ˈaɪrəni/ *noun* (*pl.* **-ies**) **1** [U, C] the amusing or strange aspect of a situation that is very different from what you expect; a situation like this: *The irony is that when he finally got the job, he discovered he didn't like it.* ◊ *It was one of life's little ironies.* **2** [U] the use of words that say the opposite of what you really mean, often as a joke and with a tone of voice that shows this: *'England is famous for its food,' she said with heavy irony.* ◊ *There was a note of irony in his voice.* ◊ *a hint/trace of irony*

ir·radi·ate /ɪˈreɪdieɪt/ *verb* [VN] **1** (*technical*) to treat food with RADIOACTIVE rays in order to preserve it **2** ~ **sth (with sth)** (*literary*) to make sth look brighter and happier: *faces irradiated with joy* ▶ **ir·radi·ation** /ɪˌreɪdiˈeɪʃn/ *noun* [U]

ir·ration·al /ɪˈræʃənl/ *adj.* not based on, or not using, clear logical thought: *an irrational fear* ◇ *You're being irrational.* OPP RATIONAL ▶ **ir·ration·al·ity** /ɪˌræʃəˈnæləti/ *noun* [U, C, usually sing.] **ir·ration·al·ly** /ɪˈræʃnəli/ *adv.*: *to behave irrationally*

ir·re·con·cil·able /ɪˈrekənsaɪləbl; ɪˌrekənˈsaɪləbl/ *adj.* **1** if differences or disagreements are **irreconcilable**, they are so great that it is not possible to settle them: *irreconcilable differences/conflicts* **2** if an idea or opinion is **irreconcilable** with another, it is impossible for sb to have both of them together: *This view is irreconcilable with common sense.* **3** people who are **irreconcilable** cannot be made to agree: *irreconcilable enemies*

ir·cov·er·able /ɪˈkʌvərəbl/ *adj.* (*formal*) that you cannot get back; lost: *irrecoverable costs* ◇ *irrecoverable loss of sight* OPP RECOVERABLE ▶ **ir·re·cov·er·ably** /-əbli/ *adv.*

ir·re·deem·able /ɪˈriːdiːməbl/ *adj.* (*formal*) too bad to be corrected, improved or saved ▶ **ir·re·deem·ably** /-əbli/ *adv.*: *irredeemably spoilt*

ir·re·du·cible /ɪˈriːˈdjuːsəbl; AmE -ˈduːs-/ *adj.* (*formal*) that cannot be made smaller or simpler: *to cut staff to an irreducible minimum* ◇ *an irreducible fact* ▶ **ir·re·du·cibly** /-əbli/ *adv.*

ir·re·fut·able /ɪˈfjuːtəbl; ɪˈrefjətəbl/ *adj.* (*formal*) that cannot be proved wrong and that must therefore be accepted: *irrefutable evidence* ▶ **ir·re·fut·ably** /-əbli/ *adv.*

ir·regu·lar /ɪˈreɡjələ(r)/ *adj., noun*
▪ *adj.* **1** not arranged in an even way; not having an even, smooth pattern or shape: *irregular teeth* ◇ *an irregular outline* **2** not happening at times that are at an equal distance from each other; not happening regularly: *irregular meals* ◇ *an irregular heartbeat* ◇ *irregular attendance at school* ◇ *He visited his parents at irregular intervals.* **3** not normal; not according to the usual rules: *an irregular practice* ◇ *His behaviour is highly irregular.* **4** (*grammar*) not formed in the normal way: *an irregular verb* **5** (of a soldier etc.) not part of a country's official army OPP REGULAR ▶ **ir·regu·lar·ly** *adv.*
▪ *noun* a soldier who is not a member of a country's official army

ir·regu·lar·ity /ɪˌreɡjəˈlærəti/ *noun* (*pl.* **-ies**) **1** [C, U] an activity or a practice which is not according to the usual rules, or not normal: *alleged irregularities in the election campaign* ◇ *suspicion of financial irregularity* **2** [C, U] something that does not happen at regular intervals: *a slight irregularity in his heartbeat* **3** [U, C] something that is not smooth or regular in shape or arrangement: *The paint will cover any irregularity in the surface of the walls.*—compare REGULARITY

ir·rele·vance /ɪˈreləvəns/ (*also less frequent* **ir·rele·vancy** /-ənsi/ *pl.* **-ies**) *noun* **1** [U] lack of importance to or connection with a situation: *the irrelevance of the curriculum to children's daily life* OPP RELEVANCE **2** [C, usually sing.] something that is not important to or connected with a situation: *His idea was rejected as an irrelevance.*

ir·rele·vant /ɪˈreləvənt/ *adj.* ~ **(to sth/sb)** not important to or connected with a situation: *totally/completely/largely irrelevant* ◇ *irrelevant remarks* ◇ *That evidence is irrelevant to the case.* ◇ *Many people consider politics is irrelevant to their lives.* ◇ *Whether I believe you or not is irrelevant now.* OPP RELEVANT ▶ **ir·rele·vant·ly** *adv.*

ir·re·li·gious /ɪˈlɪdʒəs/ *adj.* (*rare, formal*) without any religious belief; showing no respect for religion

ir·re·me·di·able /ɪˈriːˈmiːdiəbl/ *adj.* (*rare, formal*) too bad to be corrected or cured: *an irremediable situation* OPP REMEDIABLE ▶ **ir·re·me·di·ably** *adv.*

ir·rep·ar·able /ɪˈrepərəbl/ *adj.* (of a loss, injury, etc.) too bad or too serious to repair or put right: *to cause irreparable damage/harm to your health* ◇ *Her death is an irreparable loss.* OPP REPAIRABLE ▶ **ir·rep·ar·ably** /-əbli/ *adv.*: *irreparably damaged*

ir·re·place·able /ɪˈpleɪsəbl/ *adj.* too valuable or special to be replaced: *These pictures are irreplaceable.* OPP REPLACEABLE

ir·re·press·ible /ɪˈpresəbl/ *adj.* **1** (of a person) lively, happy and full of energy: *The irrepressible Fowler scored two goals.* **2** (of feelings, etc.) very strong; impossible to control or stop: *irrepressible confidence* ▶ **ir·re·press·ibly** /-əbli/ *adv.*

ir·re·proach·able /ɪˈprəʊtʃəbl; AmE -ˈprəʊ-/ *adj.* (of a person or their behaviour) free from fault and impossible to criticize

ir·re·sist·ible /ɪˈzɪstəbl/ *adj.* **1** so strong that it cannot be stopped or resisted: *I felt an irresistible urge to laugh.* ◇ *His arguments were irresistible.* OPP RESISTIBLE **2** ~ **(to sb)** so attractive that you feel you must have it: *an irresistible bargain* ◇ *The bright colours were irresistible to the baby.* ◇ *On such a hot day, the water was irresistible* (= it made you want to swim in it). ▶ **ir·re·sist·ibly** /-əbli/ *adv.*: *They were irresistibly drawn to each other.*

ir·reso·lute /ɪˈrezəluːt/ *adj.* (*formal*) not able to decide what to do OPP RESOLUTE ▶ **ir·reso·lute·ly** *adv.* **ir·reso·lu·tion** /ɪˌrezəˈluːʃn/ *noun* [U]

ir·re·spect·ive of /ɪˈspektɪv əv/ *prep.* (*written*) without considering sth or being influenced by it: *Everyone is treated equally, irrespective of race.* ◇ *The weekly rent is the same irrespective of whether there are three or four occupants.*

ir·re·spon·sible /ɪˈspɒnsəbl; AmE -ˈspɑːn-/ *adj.* (*disapproving*) (of a person) not thinking enough about the effects of what they do; not showing a feeling of responsibility: *an irresponsible teenager* ◇ *an irresponsible attitude* ◇ *It would be irresponsible to ignore the situation.* OPP RESPONSIBLE ▶ **ir·re·spon·si·bil·ity** /ɪˌspɒnsəˈbɪləti; AmE -ˌspɑːnsə-/ *noun* [U] **ir·re·spon·sibly** /-əbli/ *adv.*

ir·re·triev·able /ɪˈtriːvəbl/ *adj.* (*formal*) that you can never make right or get back: *an irretrievable situation* ◇ *the irretrievable breakdown of the marriage* ◇ *The money already paid is irretrievable.* OPP RETRIEVABLE ▶ **ir·re·triev·ably** /-əbli/ *adv.*: *Some of our old traditions are irretrievably lost.*

ir·rev·er·ent /ɪˈrevərənt/ *adj.* (usually *approving*) not showing respect to sb/sth that other people usually respect: *irreverent wit* ◇ *an irreverent attitude to tradition* ▶ **ir·rev·er·ence** /-əns/ *noun* [U] **ir·rev·er·ent·ly** *adv.*

ir·re·vers·ible /ɪˈvɜːsəbl; AmE -ˈvɜːrs-/ *adj.* that cannot be changed back to what it was before: *an irreversible change/decline/decision* ◇ *irreversible brain damage* OPP REVERSIBLE ▶ **ir·re·vers·ibly** /-əbli/ *adv.*

ir·rev·oc·able /ɪˈrevəkəbl/ *adj.* (*formal*) that cannot be changed; final: *an irrevocable decision/step* ▶ **ir·rev·oc·ably** /-əbli/ *adv.*: *irrevocably committed*

ir·ri·gate /ˈɪrɪɡeɪt/ *verb* [VN] **1** to supply water to an area of land through pipes or channels so that crops will grow: *irrigated land/crops* **2** (*medical*) to wash out a wound or part of the body with a flow of water or liquid ▶ **ir·ri·ga·tion** /ɪrɪˈɡeɪʃn/ *noun* [U]: *irrigation channels*

ir·rit·able /ˈɪrɪtəbl/ *adj.* getting annoyed easily; showing your anger: *to be tired and irritable* ◇ *an irritable gesture* ▶ **ir·rit·abil·ity** /ɪrɪtəˈbɪləti/ *noun* [U] **ir·rit·ably** /-əbli/ *adv.*

irritable ˈbowel syndrome *noun* [U] a condition of the bowels that causes pain and DIARRHOEA or CONSTIPATION, often caused by stress or anxiety

ir·ri·tant /ˈɪrɪtənt/ *noun* **1** (*technical*) a substance that makes part of your body sore: *chemical irritants* **2** (*written*) something that makes you annoyed or causes trouble: *The presence of the army has been a constant irritant.* ▶ **ir·ri·tant** *adj.* [usually before noun]: *irritant substances*

ir·ri·tate /ˈɪrɪteɪt/ *verb* [VN] **1** to annoy sb, especially by sth you continuously do or by sth that continuously happens: *The way she puts on that accent really irritates me.* **2** to make your skin or a part of your body sore or painful: *Some painkilling drugs can irritate the lining of the stomach.* ▶ **ir·ri·tat·ing** *adj.*: *I found her extremely irritating* ◇ *an irritating habit* ◇ *an irritating cough/rash* **ir·ri·tat·ing·ly** *adv.* **ir·ri·ta·tion** /ɪrɪˈteɪʃn/ *noun* [U, C]:

s	t	v	z	ʃ	ʒ	tʃ	dʒ	θ	ð	ŋ
see	tea	van	zoo	shoe	vision	chain	jam	thin	this	sing

He noted, with some irritation, that the letter had not been sent. ◊ *a skin irritation*

ir·ri·tated /ˈɪrɪteɪtɪd/ *adj.* ~ **(at/by/with sth)** annoyed or angry: *She was getting more and more irritated at his comments.*

ir·rup·tion /ɪˈrʌpʃn/ *noun* ~ **(of sth) (into sth)** (*formal*) the sudden and violent entry of sb/sth

IRS /ˌaɪ ɑːr ˈes/ *abbr.* Internal Revenue Service

Is. *abbr.* (especially on maps) Island(s); ISLE(s): *Windward Is.*

is /ɪz/ ⇨ BE

ISBN /ˌaɪ es biː ˈen/ *noun* the abbreviation for 'International Standard Book Number' (a number that identifies an individual book and its PUBLISHER): *Can you give me the ISBN, please?*

-ise ⇨ -IZE

ish /ɪʃ/ *adv.* (*spoken*) used after a statement to make it less definite: *I've finished preparing the food. Ish. I just need to make the sauce.*

-ish *suffix* (in adjectives) **1** from the country mentioned: *Turkish* ◊ *Irish* **2** (sometimes *disapproving*) having the nature of; like: *childish* **3** fairly; approximately: *reddish* ◊ *thirtyish* ▶ **-ishly** (in adverbs): *foolishly*

Islam /ˈɪzlɑːm; ɪzˈlɑːm/ *noun* [U] **1** the Muslim religion, based on belief in one God and REVEALED through Muhammad as the Prophet of Allah **2** all Muslims and Muslim countries in the world ▶ **Is·lam·ic** /ɪzˈlæmɪk; -ˈlɑːm-/ *adj.*: *Islamic law*

is·land /ˈaɪlənd/ *noun* **1** (*abbr.* I, I., Is.) a piece of land that is completely surrounded by water: *We spent a week on the Greek island of Kos.* ◊ *a remote island off the coast of Scotland*—see also DESERT ISLAND **2** (*BrE*) = TRAFFIC ISLAND

is·land·er /ˈaɪləndə(r)/ *noun* a person who lives on an island, especially a small one

isle /aɪl/ *noun* (*abbr.* I, I., Is.) used especially in poetry and names to mean 'island': *the Isle of Skye* ◊ *the British Isles*

islet /ˈaɪlət/ *noun* (*rare*) a very small island

ism /ˈɪzəm/ *noun* (usually *disapproving*) used to refer to a set of ideas or system of beliefs or behaviour: *You're always talking in isms—sexism, ageism, racism.*

-ism *suffix* (in nouns) **1** the action or result of: *criticism* **2** the state or quality of: *heroism* **3** the teaching, system or MOVEMENT of: *Buddhism* **4** unfair treatment or hatred for the reason mentioned: *racism* **5** a feature of language of the type mentioned: *Americanism* ◊ *colloquialism* **6** a medical condition or disease: *alcoholism*

isn't /ˈɪznt/ *short form* is not

iso- /ˈaɪsəʊ; *AmE* ˈaɪsoʊ/ *combining form* (in nouns, adjectives and adverbs) equal: *isotope* ◊ *isometric*

iso·bar /ˈaɪsəbɑː(r)/ *noun* (*technical*) a line on a weather map that joins places that have the same air pressure at a particular time

isol·ate /ˈaɪsəleɪt/ *verb* [VN] **1** ~ **sb/yourself/sth (from sb/sth)** to separate sb/sth physically or socially from other people or things: *Patients with the disease should be isolated.* ◊ *He was immediately isolated from the other prisoners.* **2** ~ **sth (from sth)** to separate a part of a situation, problem, idea, etc. so that you can see what it is and deal with it separately: *It is possible to isolate a number of factors that contributed to her downfall.* **3** ~ **sth (from sth)** (*technical*) to separate a single substance, cell, etc. from others so that you can study it: *Researchers are still trying to isolate the gene that causes this abnormality.*

isol·ated /ˈaɪsəleɪtɪd/ *adj.* **1** (of buildings and places) far away from any others: *isolated rural areas* **2** (of people) without much contact with other people [SYN] LONELY: *I felt very isolated in my new job.* ◊ *Elderly people easily become socially isolated.* **3** single; happening once: *The police said the attack was an isolated incident.*

isol·ation /ˌaɪsəˈleɪʃn/ *noun* [U] ~ **(from sb/sth) 1** the act of separating sb/sth; the state of being separate: *geographical isolation* ◊ *an isolation hospital/ward* (= for people with infectious diseases) ◊ *The country was threatened with complete isolation from the international*

community unless the atrocities stop.* ◊ *He lives in **splendid isolation** (= far from, or in a superior position to, everyone else).* **2** the state of being alone or lonely: *Many unemployed people experience feelings of isolation and depression.* [IDM] **in isolation (from sb/sth)** separately; alone: *To make sense, these figures should not be looked at in isolation.*

isol·ation·ism /ˌaɪsəˈleɪʃənɪzəm/ *noun* [U] the policy of not becoming involved in the affairs of other countries or groups ▶ **isol·ation·ist** /-ʃənɪst/ *adj., noun*: *an isolationist foreign policy*

iso·met·ric /ˌaɪsəˈmetrɪk/ *adj.* **1** (*technical*) connected with a type of physical exercise in which muscles are made to work without the whole body moving **2** (*geometry*) connected with a style of drawing in three DIMENSIONS without PERSPECTIVE

isos·celes /aɪˈsɒsəliːz; *AmE* -ˈsɑːs-/ *adj.* (*geometry*) (of a triangle) having two of its three sides the same length—picture at TRIANGLE

iso·therm /ˈaɪsəθɜːm; *AmE* -θɜːrm/ *noun* (*technical*) a line on a weather map that joins places that have the same temperature at a particular time

iso·tope /ˈaɪsətəʊp; *AmE* -toʊp/ *noun* (*physics* or *chemistry*) one of two or more forms of a chemical element with different physical PROPERTIES (= characteristics) but the same chemical ones: *radioactive isotopes* ◊ *the many isotopes of carbon*

issue /ˈɪʃuː; *BrE also* ˈɪsjuː/ *noun, verb*

■ *noun*

<u>TOPIC OF DISCUSSION</u> | **1** [C] an important topic that people are discussing or arguing about: *a key/sensitive/controversial issue* ◊ *This is a big issue; we need more time to think about it.* ◊ *She usually writes about environmental issues.* ◊ *The union plans to **raise the issue** of overtime.* ◊ *The party was divided on this issue.* ◊ *You're just **avoiding the issue**.* ◊ *Don't **confuse the issue**.*

<u>PROBLEM/WORRY</u> | **2** [C] (*informal*) a problem or worry that sb has with sth: *Money is not an issue.* ◊ *I don't think my private life is the issue here.* ◊ *I'm not bothered about the cost—you're the one who's **making an issue** of it.* ◊ *Because I grew up in a dysfunctional family, anger is a big issue for me.* ◊ (*AmE*) *She's always on a diet—she **has issues about** food.*

<u>MAGAZINE/NEWSPAPER</u> | **3** [C] one of a regular series of magazines or newspapers: *the July issue of 'What Car?'* ◊ *The article appeared in issue 25.*

<u>OF STAMPS/COINS/SHARES</u> | **4** [C] a number or set of things that are supplied and made available at the same time: *The company is planning a new share issue.* ◊ *a special issue of stamps*

<u>MAKING AVAILABLE/KNOWN</u> | **5** [U] the act of supplying or making available things for people to buy or use: *I bought a set of the new stamps on the date of issue.* ◊ *the issue of blankets to the refugees* ◊ *the issue of a joint statement by the French and German foreign ministers*

<u>CHILDREN</u> | **6** [U] (*law*) children of your own: *He died without issue.*

[IDM] **be at ˈissue** to be the most important part of the subject that is being discussed: *What is at issue is whether she was responsible for her actions.* **take ˈissue with sb (about/on/over sth)** (*formal*) to start disagreeing or arguing with sb about sth: *I must take issue with you on that point.*—more at FORCE *v.*

■ *verb* [VN]

<u>MAKE KNOWN</u> | **1** ~ **sth (to sb)** to make sth known formally: *They issued a joint statement denying the charges.* ◊ *The police have issued an appeal for witnesses.*

<u>GIVE</u> | **2** [often passive] ~ **sth (to sb)** | ~ **sb with sth** to give sth to sb, especially officially: *to issue passports/visas/tickets* ◊ *New members will be issued with a temporary identity card.* ◊ *Work permits were issued to only 5% of those who applied for them.*

<u>LAW</u> | **3** to start a legal process against sb, especially by means of an official document: *to issue a writ against sb* ◊ *A warrant has been issued for his arrest.*

<u>MAGAZINE</u> | **4** to produce sth such as a magazine, article, etc: *We issue a monthly newsletter.*

æ	ɑː	e	ɜː	ə	ɪ	iː	i	ɒ	ɔː	ʌ	ʊ	u	uː
cat	father	ten	bird	about	sit	see	many	got	saw	cup	put	actual	too
								(BrE)					

STAMPS/COINS/SHARES **5** to produce new stamps, coins, shares, etc. for sale to the public: *The Royal Mail issued a special set of stamps to mark the occasion.*

PHR V **'issue from sth** (*formal*) to come out of sth: *A weak trembling sound issued from his lips.*

-ist *suffix* (in nouns and some related adjectives) **1** a person who believes or practises: *atheist* **2** a member of a profession or business activity: *dentist* **3** a person who uses a thing: *violinist* **4** a person who does sth: *plagiarist*

isth·mus /'ɪsməs/ *noun* a narrow strip of land, with water on each side, that joins two larger pieces of land

IT /ˌaɪ 'tiː/ *noun* [U] the study and use of electronic processes and equipment to store and send information of all kinds, including words, pictures and numbers (abbreviation for 'information technology')

it /ɪt/ *pron.* (used as the subject or object of a verb or after a preposition) **1** used to refer to an animal or a thing that has already been mentioned or that is being talked about now: *'Where's your car?' 'It's in the garage.'* ◇ *Did you see it?* ◇ *Start a new file and put this letter in it.* ◇ *Look! It's going up that tree.* ◇ *We have $500. Will it be enough for a deposit?* **2** used to refer to a baby, especially one whose sex is not known: *Her baby's due next month. She hopes it will be a boy.* **3** used to refer to a fact or situation that is already known or happening: *When the factory closes, it will mean 500 people losing their jobs.* ◇ *Yes, I was at home on Sunday. What about it?* (= Why do you ask?) ◇ *Stop it, you're hurting me!* **4** used to identify a person: *It's your mother on the phone.* ◇ *Hello, Peter, it's Mike here.* ◇ *Hi, it's me!* ◇ *Was it you who put these books on my desk?* **5** used in the position of the subject or object of a verb when the real subject or object is at the end of the sentence: *Does it matter what colour it is?* ◇ *It's impossible to get there in time.* ◇ *It's no use shouting.* ◇ *She finds it boring at home.* ◇ *It appears that the two leaders are holding secret talks.* ◇ *I find it strange that she doesn't want to go.* **6** used in the position of the subject of a verb when you are talking about time, the date, distance, the weather, etc: *It's ten past twelve.* ◇ *It's our anniversary.* ◇ *It's two miles to the beach.* ◇ *It's a long time since they left.* ◇ *It was raining this morning.* ◇ *It's quite warm at the moment.* **7** used when you are talking about a situation: *If it's convenient I can come tomorrow.* ◇ *It's good to talk.* ◇ *I like it here.* **8** used to emphasize any part of a sentence: *It's Jim who's the clever one.* ◇ *It's Spain that they're going to, not Portugal.* ◇ *It was three weeks later that he heard the news.* **9** exactly what is needed: *In this business, either you've got it or you haven't.*—see also ITS IDM **that is 'it 1** this/that is the important point, reason, etc: *That's just it—I can't work when you're making so much noise.* **2** this/that is the end: *I'm afraid that's it—we've lost.* **this is 'it 1** the expected event is just going to happen: *Well, this is it! Wish me luck.* **2** this is the main point: *'You're doing too much.' 'Well, this is it. I can't cope with any more work.'*

Ital·ian·ate /ɪ'tæljəneɪt/ *adj.* in an Italian style: *an Italianate villa*

ital·ic /ɪ'tælɪk/ *adj.* (of printed or written letters) leaning to the right: *The example sentences in this dictionary are printed in italic type.* ◇ *Use an italic font.*—compare ROMAN

itali·cize (*BrE* also **-ise**) /ɪ'tælɪsaɪz/ *verb* [VN] [often passive] to write or print sth in italics

ital·ics /ɪ'tælɪks/ *noun* [pl.] (also **ital·ic** [sing.]) printed letters that lean to the right: *Examples in this dictionary are in italics.* ◇ *Use italics for the names of books or plays.*—compare ROMAN ⇨ Appendix 4

ITC /ˌaɪ tiː 'siː/ *abbr.* Independent Television Commission (an organization that controls what is allowed to be shown on some television channels in Britain that are not part of the BBC)

itch /ɪtʃ/ *verb, noun*
■ *verb* **1** [V] to have an uncomfortable feeling on your skin that makes you want to scratch; to make your skin feel like this: *I itch all over.* ◇ *Does the rash itch?* ◇ *This sweater really itches.* **2** ~ **for sth/to do sth** (*informal*) (often used in the progressive tenses) to want to do sth very much: [V] *The crowd was itching for a fight.* ◇ [V to inf] *He's itching to get back to work.*

■ *noun* **1** [C, usually sing.] an uncomfortable feeling on your skin that makes you want to scratch yourself: *to get/have an itch* **2** [sing.] ~ **(to do sth)** (*informal*) a strong desire to do sth: *She has an itch to travel.* ◇ *the creative itch*

itchy /'ɪtʃi/ *adj.* having or producing an itch on the skin: *an itchy nose/rash* ◇ *I feel itchy all over.* ▶ **itchi·ness** *noun* [U] IDM **(get/have) itchy 'feet** (*informal*) to want to travel or move to a different place; to want to do sth different

it'd /'ɪtəd/ *short form* **1** it had **2** it would

-ite *suffix* (in nouns) (often *disapproving*) a person who follows or supports: *Blairite* ◇ *Trotskyite*

item /'aɪtəm/ *noun* **1** one thing on a list of things to buy, do, talk about, etc: *What's the next item on the agenda?* **2** a single article or object: *Can I pay for each item separately?* ◇ *The computer was my largest single item of expenditure.* ◇ *This clock is a collector's item* (= because it is rare and valuable). **3** a single piece of news in a newspaper, on television, etc: *an item of news/a news item* IDM **be an item** (*informal*) to be involved in a romantic or sexual relationship: *Are they an item?*

item·ize (*BrE* also **-ise**) /'aɪtəmaɪz/ *verb* [VN] to produce a detailed list of things: *The report itemizes 23 different faults.* ◇ *an itemized phone bill* (= each call is shown separately)

it·in·er·ant /aɪ'tɪnərənt/ *adj.* [usually before noun] (*formal*) travelling from place to place, especially to find work: *itinerant workers/musicians* ◇ *to lead an itinerant life* ▶ **it·in·er·ant** *noun*: *homeless itinerants*

it·in·er·ary /aɪ'tɪnərəri; *AmE* aɪ'tɪnəreri/ *noun* (*pl.* **-ies**) a plan of a journey, including the route and the places that you visit: *a detailed itinerary* ◇ *Visits to four different countries are included in your itinerary.* ⇨ note at AGENDA

-ition ⇨ -ION

-itis *suffix* (in nouns) **1** (*medical*) a disease of: *tonsillitis* **2** (*informal*, especially *humorous*) too much of; too much interest in: *World Cup-itis*

it'll /'ɪtl/ *short form* it will

its /ɪts/ *det.* belonging to or connected with a thing, an animal or a baby: *Turn the box on its side.* ◇ *Have you any idea of its value?* ◇ *The dog had hurt its paw.* ◇ *The baby threw its food on the floor.*

it's /ɪts/ *short form* **1** it is **2** it has

it·self /ɪt'self/ *pron.* **1** (the reflexive form of *it*) used when the animal or thing that does an action is also affected by it: *The cat was washing itself.* ◇ *Does the VCR turn itself off?* ◇ *The company has got itself into difficulties.* ◇ *There's no need for the team to feel proud of itself.* **2** (used to emphasize an animal, a thing, etc.): *The village itself is pretty, but the surrounding countryside is rather dull.* IDM **be ,patience, ,honesty, sim,plicity, etc. it'self** to be an example of complete patience, etc: *The manager of the hotel was courtesy itself.* **(all) by it'self 1** automatically, without anyone doing anything: *The machine will start by itself in a few seconds.* **2** alone: *The house stands by itself in an acre of land.* **in it'self** considered separately from other things, in its true nature: *In itself, it's not a difficult problem to solve.* **to it'self** not shared with others: *It doesn't have the market to itself.*

itty-bitty /ˌɪti 'bɪti/ (also **itsy-bitsy** /ˌɪtsi 'bɪtsi/) *adj.* [only before noun] (*informal*, especially *AmE*) very small

ITV /ˌaɪ tiː 'viː/ *abbr.* Independent Television (a group of British companies that produce programmes that are paid for by advertising)

-ity *suffix* (in nouns) the quality or state of: *purity* ◇ *oddity*

IUD /ˌaɪ juː 'diː/ (also **coil**) *noun* a small plastic or metal object placed inside a woman's UTERUS (= where a baby grows before it is born) to stop her becoming pregnant. IUD is an abbreviation for 'intrauterine device'.

IV /ˌaɪ 'viː/ *abbr., noun*
■ *abbr.* INTRAVENOUS, INTRAVENOUSLY
■ *noun* (*AmE*) = DRIP (3)

I've /aɪv/ *short form* I have

-ive *suffix* (in nouns and adjectives) tending to; having the nature of: *explosive* ◇ *descriptive*

aɪ	aʊ	eɪ	əʊ	oʊ	ɔɪ	ɪə	eə	ʊə	j	w
my	now	say	go	go	boy	near	hair	pure	yes	wet
			(BrE)	(AmE)						

IVF /ˌaɪ vi: ˈef/ *noun* [U] (*technical*) the abbreviation for 'in vitro fertilization' (a process which FERTILIZES an egg from a woman outside her body. The egg is then put inside her UTERUS to develop.)—see also TEST-TUBE BABY

ivory /ˈaɪvəri/ (*pl.* -ies) *noun* **1** [U] a hard yellowish-white substance like bone that forms the TUSKS (= long teeth) of elephants and some other animals: *a ban on the ivory trade* ◊ *an ivory chess set* **2** [C] an object made of ivory: *a priceless collection of ivories* **3** [U] a yellowish-white colour

ivory 'tower *noun* (*disapproving*) a place or situation where you are separated from the problems and practical aspects of normal life and therefore do not have to worry about or understand them: *academics living in ivory towers*

ivy /ˈaɪvi/ *noun* [U, C] (*pl.* -ies) a climbing plant, especially one with dark green shiny leaves with five points: *stone walls covered in ivy*—see also POISON IVY

the ˌIvy 'League *noun* [sing.] a group of eight traditional universities in the eastern US with high academic standards and a high social status—compare OXBRIDGE ▶ ˌIvy 'League *adj.*: *Ivy League colleges*

-ize, -ise *suffix* (in verbs) **1** to become, make or make like: *privatize* ◊ *fossilize* ◊ *Americanize* **2** to speak, think, act, treat, etc. in the way mentioned: *criticize* ◊ *theorize* ◊ *deputize* ◊ *pasteurize* **3** to place in: *hospitalize* ▶ **-ization, -isation** (in nouns): *immunization* **-izationally, -isationally** (in adverbs): *organizationally*

Jj

J (also **j**) /dʒeɪ/ *noun* [C, U] (*pl.* **J's, j's** /dʒeɪz/) the 10th letter of the English alphabet: *'Jelly' begins with (a) J/'J'.*

jab /dʒæb/ *verb, noun*
- *verb* (-bb-) ~ (sth) (in sb/sth)| ~ (at sth)| ~ sb/sth (with sth) to push a pointed object into sb/sth, or in the direction of sb/sth, with a sudden strong movement: [VN] *She jabbed him in the ribs with her finger.* ◊ *She jabbed her finger in his ribs.* ◊ [V] *He jabbed at the picture with his finger.* ◊ *The boxer jabbed at his opponent.*
- *noun* **1** a sudden strong hit with sth pointed or with a FIST (= a tightly closed hand): *She gave him a jab in the stomach with her elbow.* ◊ *a boxer's left jab* **2** (*BrE, informal*) an INJECTION to help prevent you from catching a disease: *a flu jab*

jab·ber /'dʒæbə(r)/ *verb* (*disapproving*) to talk quickly and in an excited way so that it is difficult to understand what you are saying: [V] *What is he jabbering about now?* [also V speech] ▶ **jab·ber** *noun* [U]

jack /dʒæk/ *noun, verb*
- *noun* **1** [C] a device for raising heavy objects off the ground, especially motor vehicles so that a wheel can be changed **2** [C] an electronic connection between two pieces of electrical equipment **3** [C] (in a pack/deck of cards) a card with a picture of a young man on it, worth more than a ten and less than a queen: *the jack of clubs*—picture on page A8 **4** [C] (in the game of BOWLS) a small white ball towards which players roll larger balls **5** (**jacks**) [pl.] a children's game in which players bounce a small ball and pick up small metal objects, also called **jacks** including the ball—see also BLACKJACK, FLAP-JACK, UNION JACK **IDM** **a jack of 'all trades** a person who can do many different types of work, but who perhaps does not do them very well—more at ALL RIGHT *adj.*
- *verb* **PHRV** ˌjack sth↔'in (*BrE, informal*) to decide to stop doing sth, especially your job: *After five years, he decided to jack it all in.* ˌjack 'off (⚠, *slang*) (of a man) to MASTURBATE ˌjack sth↔'up **1** to lift sth, especially a vehicle, off the ground using a jack **2** (*informal*) to increase sth, especially prices, by a large amount

jackal /'dʒækl; -kɔːl/ *noun* a wild animal like a dog, that eats the meat of animals that are already dead and lives in Africa and Asia

jack·ass /'dʒækæs/ *noun* (*informal, especially AmE*) a stupid person: *Careful, you jackass!*

jack·boot /'dʒækbuːt/ *noun* **1** [C] a tall boot that reaches up to the knee, worn by soldiers, especially in the past **2** (**the jackboot**) [sing.] used to refer to cruel military rule: *to be under the jackboot of a dictatorial regime*

'Jack cheese *noun* [U] (*AmE*) = MONTEREY JACK

jack·daw /'dʒækdɔː/ *noun* a black and grey bird of the CROW family

jacket /'dʒækɪt/ *noun* **1** a piece of clothing worn on the top half of the body over a shirt, etc. that has sleeves and fastens down the front; a short, light coat: *a denim/tweed jacket* ◊ *I have to wear a jacket and tie to work.*—see also BOMBER JACKET, DINNER JACKET, DONKEY JACKET, FLAK JACKET, LIFE JACKET, SMOKING JACKET, SPORTS JACKET, STRAITJACKET—picture on page A5 **2** (also **'dust jacket**) a loose paper cover for a book, usually with a design or picture on it **3** an outer cover around a hot water pipe, etc., for example to reduce loss of heat **4** (*BrE*) the skin of a baked potato: *jacket potatoes* (= baked potatoes) ◊ *potatoes baked in their jackets* **5** (*especially AmE*) = SLEEVE (3)

jack·ham·mer /'dʒækhæmə(r)/ *noun* (*AmE*) = PNEU-MATIC DRILL

'jack-in-the-box *noun* a toy in the shape of a box with a figure inside on a spring that jumps up when you open the lid

jack·knife /'dʒæknaɪf/ *noun, verb*
- *noun* (*pl.* **jack·knives**) /-naɪvz/ a large knife with a folding blade
- *verb* [V] to form a V-shape. For example if a lorry/truck that is in two parts **jackknifes**, the driver loses control and the back part moves towards the front part.

jack·pot /'dʒækpɒt; *AmE* -pɑːt/ *noun* a large amount of money that is the most valuable prize in a game of chance: *to win the jackpot* ◊ *jackpot winners* ◊ (*figurative*) *United hit the jackpot* (= were successful) *with a 5-0 win over Liverpool.*

jack·rab·bit /'dʒækræbɪt/ *noun* a large N American HARE (= an animal like a large rabbit) with very long ears

Jack 'Robinson /ˌdʒæk 'rɒbɪnsn; *AmE* 'rɑːb-/ *noun* **IDM** **before you can say Jack 'Robinson** (*old-fashioned*) very quickly; very soon

Jack Russell /ˌdʒæk 'rʌsl/ (also ˌJack ˌRussell 'terrier) *noun* a small active dog with short legs

ˌJack the 'Lad *noun* [sing.] (*BrE, slang*) a young man who is very confident in a rude and noisy way, and enjoys going out with male friends, drinking alcohol and trying to attract women

Jaco·bean /ˌdʒækə'biːən/ *adj.* connected with the time when James I (1603–25) was King of England: *Jacobean houses/drama*

Ja·cuzzi ™ /dʒə'kuːzi/ (also **spa** especially in *AmE*) *noun* a large bath with a pump that moves the water around, giving a pleasant feeling to your body

jade /dʒeɪd/ *noun* [U] **1** a hard stone that is usually green and is used in making ornaments and jewellery: *a jade necklace* **2** ornaments made of jade: *a collection of Chinese jade* **3** (also ˌjade 'green) a bright green colour

jaded /'dʒeɪdɪd/ *adj.* tired and bored, usually because you have had too much of sth: *I felt terribly jaded after working all weekend.* ◊ *It was a meal to tempt even the most jaded palate.*

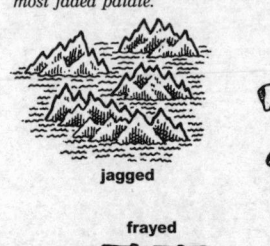
jagged

ragged

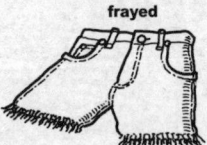
frayed

dog-eared

jagged /'dʒægɪd/ *adj.* with rough, pointed, often sharp edges: *jagged rocks/peaks/edges*

jag·uar /'dʒægjuə(r)/ *noun* a large animal of the cat family, that has yellowish-brown fur with black rings and spots. Jaguars live in parts of central America.

jail (*BrE* also **gaol**) /dʒeɪl/ *noun, verb*
- *noun* [U, C] a prison: *She spent a year in jail.* ◊ *He has been released from jail.* ◊ *a ten-year jail sentence* ◊ *Britain's overcrowded jails* ⇨ note at SCHOOL

s	t	v	z	ʃ	ʒ	tʃ	dʒ	θ	ð	ŋ
see	tea	van	zoo	shoe	vision	chain	jam	thin	this	sing

■ *verb* [VN] [usually passive] ~ **sb (for sth)** to put sb in prison: *He was jailed for life for murder.*

jail·bird /'dʒeɪlbɜːd; *AmE* -bɜːrd/ *noun* (*old-fashioned, informal*) a person who has spent a lot of time in prison

jail·break /'dʒeɪlbreɪk/ *noun* (*especially AmE*) an escape from prison, usually by several people

jail·er /'dʒeɪlə(r)/ (*BrE* also **gaol·er**) *noun* (*old-fashioned*) a person in charge of a prison and the prisoners in it

jail·house /'dʒeɪlhaʊs/ *noun* (*AmE*) a prison

jala·peño /ˌhæləˈpeɪnjəʊ; *AmE* ˌhɑːləˈpeɪnjoʊ/ (also ˌjalaˌpeño **'pepper**) *noun* (from *Spanish*) the small green fruit of a type of pepper plant, that has a very hot taste and is used in Mexican cooking

jam /dʒæm/ *noun, verb*
■ *noun*
SWEET FOOD | **1** [U, C] a thick sweet substance made by boiling fruit with sugar, often sold in JARS and spread on bread: *strawberry jam* ◊ *recipes for jams and preserves* ◊ (*BrE*) *a jam doughnut*—compare JELLY, MARMALADE—picture on page A1

MANY PEOPLE/VEHICLES | **2** [C] a situation in which it is difficult or impossible to move because there are so many people or vehicles in one particular place: *The bus was delayed in a five-mile jam.* ◊ *As fans rushed to leave, jams formed at all the exits.*—see also TRAFFIC JAM

IDM **be in a 'jam** (*informal*) to be in a difficult situation **jam to'morrow** (*BrE, informal*) good things that are promised for the future but never happen: *They refused to settle for a promise of jam tomorrow.*—more at MONEY

■ *verb* (-mm-)
PUSH WITH FORCE | **1** [VN+*adv. / prep.*] to push sth somewhere with a lot of force: *He jammed his fingers in his ears.* ◊ *A stool had been jammed against the door.*

STOP MOVING/WORKING | **2** ~ **(sth) (up)** to become unable to move or work; to make sth do this: [V] *The photocopier keeps jamming up.* ◊ [VN] *There's a loose part that keeps jamming the mechanism.* ◊ [V-ADJ] *The valve has jammed shut.* ◊ [VN-ADJ] *He jammed the door open with a piece of wood.*

PUT INTO SMALL SPACE | **3** [+*adv. / prep.*] to put sb/sth into a small space where there is very little room to move: [VN] *Six of us were jammed into one small car.* ◊ *We were jammed together like sardines in a can.* ◊ *The cupboards were jammed full of old newspapers.* ◊ [V] *Nearly 1000 students jammed into the hall.*—see also JAM-PACKED

FILL WITH PEOPLE/THINGS | **4** [VN] ~ **sth (up) (with sb/sth)** to fill sth with a large number of people or things so that it is unable to function as it should: *Viewers jammed the switchboard with complaints.*

RADIO BROADCAST | **5** [VN] (*technical*) to send out radio signals to prevent another radio broadcast from being heard

PLAY MUSIC | **6** [V, VN] to play music with other musicians in an informal way without preparing or practising first

IDM **jam on the brake(s) | jam the brake(s) on** to operate the BRAKES on a vehicle suddenly and with force: *The car skidded as he jammed on the brakes.*

jamb /dʒæm/ *noun* a vertical post at the side of a door or window

jam·bo·ree /ˌdʒæmbəˈriː/ *noun* **1** a large party or celebration: *the movie industry's annual jamboree at Cannes* **2** a large meeting of SCOUTS or GUIDES

'jam jar *noun* (*BrE*) a glass container for jam, etc.

jammed /dʒæmd/ *adj.* **1** [not before noun] not able to move SYN STUCK: *I can't get the door open—it's completely jammed.* **2** (*especially AmE*) very full; crowded SYN JAM-PACKED: *Hundreds more people were waiting outside the jammed stadium.*

jammy /'dʒæmi/ *adj.* **1** covered with jam: *jammy fingers* **2** (*BrE, slang*) lucky, especially because sth good has happened to you without you making any effort: *'What did you get for Maths?' 'A.' 'You jammy bastard.'*

jam-'packed *adj.* [not usually before noun] ~ **(with sb/sth)** (*informal*) very full or crowded: *The train was jam-packed with commuters.*

'jam session *noun* an occasion when musicians perform in an informal way without practising first

Jane Doe /ˌdʒeɪn ˈdəʊ; *AmE* ˈdoʊ/ *noun* [sing.] (*AmE*) **1** used to refer to a woman whose name is not known or is kept secret, especially in a court of law **2** an average woman—compare JOHN DOE

jan·gle /'dʒæŋgl/ *noun, verb*
■ *verb* **1** to make a harsh sound, like two pieces of metal hitting each other; to make sth do this: [V] *The shop bell jangled loudly.* ◊ *jangling pianos* ◊ [VN] *He jangled the keys in his pocket.* **2** if your nerves **jangle**, or if sb/sth **jangles** them, you feel anxious or upset: [V] *She was suddenly wide awake, her nerves jangling.* [also VN]
■ *noun* [usually sing.] a hard noise like that of metal hitting metal

jani·tor /'dʒænɪtə(r)/ *noun* (*AmE, ScotE*) = CARETAKER

Janu·ary /'dʒænjuəri; *AmE* -jueri/ *noun* [U, C] (*abbr.* Jan.) the 1st month of the year, between December and February. **HELP** To see how **January** is used, look at the examples at **April**.

Jap /dʒæp/ *noun* (⚠, *slang*) an offensive word for a Japanese person

jape /dʒeɪp/ *noun* (*old-fashioned, BrE*) a trick or joke that is played on sb

jar /dʒɑː(r)/ *noun, verb*
■ *noun* **1** [C] a round glass container, with a lid, used for storing food, especially jam, HONEY, etc: *a storage jar*—see also JAM JAR—picture at PACKAGING **2** [C] a jar and what it contains: *a jar of coffee* **3** [C] a tall container with a wide mouth, with or without handles, used in the past for carrying water, etc: *a water jar* **4** [C] (*BrE, informal*) a glass of beer: *Do you fancy a jar after work?* **5** [sing.] an unpleasant shock, especially from two things being suddenly shaken or hit: *The fall gave him a nasty jar.*
■ *verb* (-rr-) **1** ~ **(sth)** (**on sth**) to give or receive a sudden sharp painful knock: [VN] *The jolt seemed to jar every bone in her body.* ◊ [V] *The spade jarred on something metal.* **2** ~ **(on sth)** to have an unpleasant or annoying effect: [V] *His constant moaning was beginning to jar on her nerves.* ◊ *There was a jarring note of triumph in his voice.* [also VN] **3** [V] ~ **(with sth)** to be different from sth in a strange or unpleasant way SYN CLASH: *Her brown shoes jarred with the rest of the outfit.* ◊ *The only jarring note was the cheap modern furniture.*

jar·gon /'dʒɑːgən; *AmE* 'dʒɑːrgən/ *noun* [U] (*often disapproving*) words or expressions that are used by a particular profession or group of people, and are difficult for others to understand: *medical/legal/computer jargon*

jas·mine /'dʒæzmɪn/ *noun* [U, C] a plant with white or yellow flowers with a sweet smell, sometimes used to make PERFUME and to flavour tea

jaun·dice /'dʒɔːndɪs/ *noun* [U] a medical condition in which the skin and the white parts of the eyes become yellow

jaun·diced /'dʒɔːndɪst/ *adj.* **1** not expecting sb/sth to be good or useful, especially because of experiences that you have had in the past: *He had a jaundiced view of life.* ◊ *She looked on politicians with a jaundiced eye.* **2** suffering from jaundice: *a jaundiced patient/liver*

jaunt /dʒɔːnt/ *noun* (*old-fashioned* or *humorous*) a short journey that you make for pleasure

jaunty /'dʒɔːnti/ *adj.* **1** showing that you are feeling confident and pleased with yourself: *a jaunty smile* ◊ *a hat set at a jaunty angle* **2** lively: *a jaunty tune* ▶ **jaunt·ily** *adv.*: *He set off jauntily, whistling to himself.* **jaunti·ness** *noun* [U]

jav·elin /'dʒævlɪn/ *noun* **1** [C] a light SPEAR (= a long stick with a pointed end) which is thrown in a sporting event **2** (**the javelin**) [sing.] the event or sport of throwing a javelin as far as possible—picture on page 1251

jaw /dʒɔː/ *noun, verb*
■ *noun* **1** [C] either of the two bones at the bottom of the face that contain the teeth and move when you talk or eat: *the top/upper jaw* ◊ *the bottom/lower jaw* **2** [sing.] the lower part of the face; the lower jaw: *He has a strong square jaw.* ◊ *The punch broke my jaw.*—picture at BODY **3** (**jaws**) [pl.] the mouth and teeth of a person or an animal: *The alligator's jaws snapped shut.* **4** (**jaws**) [pl.] the parts of a tool or machine that are used to hold things

æ	ɑː	e	ɜː	ə	ɪ	iː	i	ɒ	ɔː	ʌ	ʊ	u	uː
cat	father	ten	bird	about	sit	see	many	got	saw	cup	put	actual	too
								(BrE)					

tightly: *the jaws of a vice*—picture at VICE **IDM** sb's ˈjaw dropped/fell/sagged used to say that sb suddenly looked surprised, shocked or disappointed **the jaws of a tunnel, etc.** the narrow entrance to a tunnel, etc., especially one that looks dangerous **the jaws of ˈdeath, deˈfeat, etc.** (*literary*) used to describe an unpleasant situation that almost happens: *The team snatched victory from the jaws of defeat.*

■ *verb* [V] (*informal, often disapproving*) to talk, especially to talk a lot or for a long time

jaw·bone /ˈdʒɔːbəʊn; *AmE* -boʊn/ *noun* the bone that forms the lower jaw **SYN** MANDIBLE—picture at BODY

jaw·line /ˈdʒɔːlaɪn/ *noun* the outline of the lower jaw

jay /dʒeɪ/ *noun* a European bird of the CROW family, with bright feathers and a noisy call—see also BLUEJAY

jay·walk /ˈdʒeɪwɔːk/ *verb* [V] to walk along or across a street illegally or without paying attention to the traffic ▶ **jay·walk·er** *noun* **jay·walk·ing** *noun* [U]

jazz /dʒæz/ *noun, verb*
■ *noun* [U] a type of music with strong rhythms, in which the players often IMPROVISE (= make up the music as they are playing), originally created by African American musicians: *a jazz band/club ◇ traditional/modern jazz ◇ jazz musicians* **IDM** **and all that ˈjazz** (*spoken, informal*) and things like that: *How's it going? You know—love, life and all that jazz.*
■ *verb* **PHRV** **jazz sth↔ˈup** (*informal*) **1** to make sth more interesting, exciting or attractive **2** to make a piece of music sound more modern, or more like popular music or jazz: *It's a jazzed up version of an old tune.*

jazzy /ˈdʒæzi/ *adj.* (*informal*) **1** in the style of jazz: *a jazzy melody/tune* **2** (*sometimes disapproving*) brightly coloured and likely to attract attention: *That's a jazzy tie you're wearing.*

JCB™ /ˌdʒeɪ siː ˈbiː/ *noun* (*BrE*) a powerful motor vehicle with a long arm for digging and moving earth

jeal·ous /ˈdʒeləs/ *adj.* **1** feeling angry or unhappy because sb you like or love is showing interest in sb else: *a jealous wife/husband ◇ He's only talking to her to make you jealous.* **2** ~ (**of sb/sth**) feeling angry or unhappy because you wish you had sth that sb else has **SYN** ENVIOUS: *She's jealous of my success. ◇ Children often feel jealous when a new baby arrives.* **3** ~ (**of sth**) wanting to keep or protect sth that you have because it makes you feel proud: *They are very jealous of their good reputation* (= they do not want to lose it). ▶ **jeal·ous·ly** *adv.*: *She eyed Natalia jealously. ◇ a jealously guarded secret*

jeal·ousy /ˈdʒeləsi/ *noun* (*pl.* **-ies**) **1** [U] a feeling of being jealous: *I felt sick with jealousy. ◇ sexual jealousy* **2** [C] an action or a remark that shows that a person is jealous: *I'm tired of her petty jealousies.*

jeans /dʒiːnz/ *noun* [pl.] trousers/pants made of strong cotton, especially DENIM: *a faded pair of blue jeans*—see also DENIMS —picture on page A4 **ORIGIN** From *Janne*, the Old French name for Genoa, where the heavy cotton now used for jeans was first made.

Jeep™ /dʒiːp/ *noun* a small strong motor vehicle used, especially by the army, for driving over rough ground—picture at TRUCK

jeer /dʒɪə(r); *AmE* dʒɪr/ *verb, noun*
■ *verb* ~ (**at sb**) to laugh at sb or shout rude remarks at them to show that you do not respect them: [V] *a jeering crowd ◇ The police were jeered at by the waiting crowd.* ◇ [VN] *The players were jeered by disappointed fans.* [also V speech]
■ *noun* [usually pl.] a rude remark that sb shouts at sb else to show that they do not respect or like them: *He walked on to the stage to be greeted with jeers and whistles.*

jeez /dʒiːz/ *exclamation* (*informal, especially AmE*) used to express anger, surprise, etc.

Je·ho·vah /dʒɪˈhəʊvə; *AmE* -ˈhoʊ-/ (also **Yah·weh**) *noun* [U] the name of God that is used in the Old Testament of the Bible

Jeˌhovah's ˈWitness *noun* a member of a religious organization based on Christianity, which believes that the end of the world is near and that only its members will be saved from being DAMNED

je·june /dʒɪˈdʒuːn/ *adj.* (*rare, formal*) **1** too simple **SYN** NAIVE **2** (of a speech, etc.) not interesting

Jek·yll and Hyde /ˌdʒekl ən ˈhaɪd/ *noun* [sing.] a person who is sometimes very pleasant (*Jekyll*) and sometimes very unpleasant (*Hyde*) or who leads two very separate lives **ORIGIN** From the story by Robert Louis Stevenson, *Dr Jekyll and Mr Hyde*, in which Dr Jekyll takes a drug which separates the good and bad sides of his personality into two characters. All the negative aspects go into the character of Mr Hyde.

jell *verb* [V] (*especially AmE*) = GEL (1, 2, 3)

jel·lied /ˈdʒelid/ *adj.* [only before noun] (*especially BrE*) prepared or cooked in jelly: *jellied eels*

jelly /ˈdʒeli/ (*pl.* **-ies**) *noun* **1** [U, C] (*BrE*) (*AmE* **jello**, **Jell-O**™ [U]) a cold sweet transparent food made from GELATIN, sugar and fruit juice, that shakes when it is moved: *jelly and ice cream ◇ a raspberry jelly*—picture on page A1 **2** [U] a substance like jelly made from GELATIN and meat juices, served around meat, fish, etc. **SYN** ASPIC: *chicken in jelly* **3** [U, C] a type of jam that does not contain any pieces of fruit: *blackcurrant jelly*—compare JAM **4** [U] any thick sticky substance, especially a type of cream used on the skin—see also PETROLEUM JELLY **5** [C] **jelly shoe** a light plastic shoe designed for wearing on the beach and in the sea **IDM** **be/feel like ˈjelly | turn to ˈjelly** (of legs or knees) to feel weak because you are nervous

ˈjelly baby *noun* (*BrE*) a small soft sweet/candy in the shape of a baby, made from GELATIN and flavoured with fruit

ˈjelly bean *noun* a small sweet/candy shaped like a bean, with a hard outside and a centre like jelly

jel·ly·fish /ˈdʒelifɪʃ/ *noun* (*pl.* **jel·ly·fish**) a sea creature with a body like jelly and long thin parts called TENTACLES that can give a sharp sting

ˈjelly roll *noun* (*AmE*) = SWISS ROLL

jemmy /ˈdʒemi/ (*BrE*) (*AmE* **jimmy**) *noun* (*pl.* **-ies**) a short heavy metal bar used by thieves to force open doors and windows

je ne sais quoi /ˌʒə nə seɪ ˈkwɑː/ *noun* [U] (from French, often *humorous*) a good quality that is difficult to describe: *He has that je ne sais quoi that distinguishes a professional from an amateur.*

jeop·ard·ize (*BrE* also **-ise**) /ˈdʒepədaɪz; *AmE* -pərd-/ *verb* [VN] (*written*) to risk harming or destroying sth/sb: *He would never do anything to jeopardize his career.*

jeop·ardy /ˈdʒepədi; *AmE* -pərdi/ *noun* **IDM** **in ˈjeopardy** in a dangerous position or situation and likely to be lost or harmed—see also DOUBLE JEOPARDY

jerk /dʒɜːk; *AmE* dʒɜːrk/ *verb, noun*
■ *verb* [usually +*adv.*/*prep.*] to move or to make sth move with a sudden short sharp movement: [VN] *He jerked the phone away from her. ◇ She jerked her head up. ◇* [V] *The bus jerked to a halt. ◇ He grabbed a handful of hair and jerked at it.* [also VN-ADJ] **PHRV** **jerk sb aˈround** (*informal, especially AmE*) to make things difficult for sb, especially by not being honest with them: *Consumers are often jerked around by big companies.* **jerk ˈoff** (△, *slang*) (of a man) to MASTURBATE **jerk ˈout | jerk sth↔ˈout** to say sth in a quick and awkward way because you are nervous
■ *noun* **1** a sudden quick sharp movement: *She sat up with a jerk.* **2** (*informal*) a stupid person who often says or does the wrong thing

jer·kin /ˈdʒɜːkɪn; *AmE* ˈdʒɜːrkɪn/ *noun* (*BrE*) a short jacket without sleeves, especially one worn by men in the past

jerky /ˈdʒɜːki; *AmE* ˈdʒɜːrki/ *adj., noun*
■ *adj.* making sudden starts and stops and not moving smoothly ▶ **jerk·ily** /-ɪli/ *adv.*: *The car moved off jerkily.*
■ *noun* [U] (*AmE*) meat that has been cut into long strips and smoked or dried: *beef jerky*

Jerry /ˈdʒeri/ *noun* (*pl.* **-ies**) (△, *BrE, slang*) an offensive word for a person from Germany, used especially during the First and Second World Wars

ˈjerry-built *noun* (*old-fashioned, disapproving*) built quickly and cheaply without caring about quality or safety

jer·ry·can /'dʒerɪkæn/ noun (old-fashioned) a large metal or plastic container with flat sides, used for carrying petrol/gas or water

Jer·sey /'dʒɜːzi; AmE 'dʒɜːrzi/ noun a type of light brown cow that produces high quality milk

jer·sey /'dʒɜːzi; AmE 'dʒɜːrzi/ noun 1 [C] a knitted woollen or cotton piece of clothing for the upper part of the body, with long sleeves and no buttons 2 [C] a shirt worn by sb playing football, rugby, etc. 3 [U] a soft fine knitted fabric used for making clothes: made from 100% cotton jersey

Je·ru·sa·lem ar·ti·choke /dʒəˌruːsələm 'ɑːtɪtʃəʊk; AmE 'ɑːrtətʃoʊk/ noun (BrE also **ar·ti·choke**) a light brown root vegetable that looks like a potato

jest /dʒest/ noun, verb
■ noun (old-fashioned or formal) something said or done to amuse people SYN JOKE IDM in 'jest as a joke: The remark was made half in jest. ◊ 'Many a true word is spoken in jest,' thought Rosie. (= people often say things as a joke that are actually true)
■ verb (formal or humorous) ~ (about sth) to say things that are not serious or true, especially in order to make sb laugh SYN JOKE: [V] Would I jest about such a thing? [also V speech]

jest·er /'dʒestə(r)/ noun a man employed in the past at the COURT of a king or queen to amuse people by telling jokes and funny stories: the court jester

Jes·uit /'dʒezjuit; AmE 'dʒeʒəwət/ noun a member of the Society of Jesus, a Roman Catholic religious group: a Jesuit priest/college

Jesus /'dʒiːzəs/ (also ˌJesus 'Christ) = CHRIST

jet /dʒet/ noun, verb
■ noun 1 [C] a plane driven by JET ENGINES: a jet aircraft/fighter/airliner ◊ The accident happened as the jet was about to take off.—see also JUMBO (JET) 2 [C] a strong narrow stream of gas, liquid, steam or flame that comes very quickly out of a small opening. The opening is also called a jet: The pipe burst and jets of water shot across the room. ◊ to clean the gas jets on the cooker 3 [U] a hard black mineral that can be polished and is used in jewellery: jet beads
■ verb (-tt-) [V+adv./prep.] (informal) to fly somewhere in a plane

ˌjet-'black adj. deep shiny black in colour: jet-black eyes/hair

ˌjet 'engine noun an engine that drives an aircraft forwards by pushing out a stream of gases behind it—picture at PLANE

ˈjet lag noun [U] the feeling of being tired and slightly confused after a long plane journey, especially when there is a big difference in the time at the place you leave and that at the place you arrive in ▶ **ˈjet-lagged** adj.

ˌjet-pro'pelled adj. driven by JET ENGINES

ˌjet pro'pulsion noun [U] the use of JET ENGINES for power

jet·sam /'dʒetsəm/ noun things that are thrown away, especially from a ship at sea and that float towards the shore—compare FLOTSAM

the ˈjet set noun [sing.+ sing./pl. v.] rich and fashionable people who travel a lot

ˈjet-setter noun a rich, fashionable person who travels a lot ▶ **ˈjet-setting** adj. [usually before noun]: her jet-setting millionaire boyfriend

ˈJet Ski™ noun a vehicle with an engine, like a motorcycle, for riding across water ▶ **ˈjet-skiing** noun [U]

ˈjet stream noun 1 (usually the jet stream) [sing.] a strong wind that blows high above the earth and that has an effect on the weather 2 [C] the flow of gases from a plane's engine

jet·ti·son /'dʒetɪsn/ verb [VN] 1 to throw sth out of a moving plane or ship to make it lighter: to jettison fuel 2 to get rid of sth/sb that you no longer need or want SYN DISCARD: He was jettisoned as team coach after the defeat. 3 to reject an idea, belief, plan, etc. that you no longer think is useful or likely to be successful SYN ABANDON

jetty /'dʒeti/ noun (pl. -ies) (AmE also **dock**) a wall or platform built out into the sea, a river, etc., where boats can be tied and where people can get on and off boats

Jew /dʒuː/ noun a member of the people and cultural community whose traditional religion is Judaism and who are descended from the ancient Hebrew people of Israel; a person who believes in and practises Judaism ▶ **Jew·ish** /'dʒuːɪʃ/ adj.: We're Jewish. ◊ the local Jewish community

jewel /'dʒuːəl/ noun 1 a precious stone such as a diamond, RUBY, etc. 2 [usually pl.] pieces of jewellery or ornaments that contain precious stones: The family jewels are locked away in a safe. ◊ a jewel box/case—see also CROWN JEWELS 3 a small precious stone or piece of special glass that is used in the machinery of a watch 4 (informal) a person or thing that is very important or valuable: Alice, you are a jewel. ◊ Venice is the jewel of the Adriatic.—compare GEM IDM the jewel in the 'crown the most attractive or valuable part of sth

ˈjewel case noun a plastic box for holding a CD

jew·elled (BrE) (AmE **jew·eled**) /'dʒuːəld/ adj. decorated with jewels

jew·el·ler (AmE **jew·el·er**) /'dʒuːələ(r)/ noun 1 a person who makes, repairs or sells jewellery and watches 2 (jeweller's) (pl. jew·el·lers) a shop/store that sells jewellery and watches: I bought it at the jeweller's near my office.

jew·el·lery (AmE **jew·el·ry**) /'dʒuːəlri/ noun [U] objects such as rings and NECKLACES that people wear as decoration: silver/gold jewellery—see also COSTUME JEWELLERY—picture on page 696

Jew·ess /'dʒuːəs/ noun (often offensive) an old-fashioned word for a Jewish woman

Jewry /'dʒʊəri; AmE 'dʒuː-/ noun [U] (formal) Jewish people as a group: British Jewry

jib /dʒɪb/ noun, verb
■ noun 1 a small sail in front of the large sail on a boat—picture at YACHT 2 the arm of a CRANE that lifts things
■ verb (-bb-) [V] ~ (at sth/at doing sth) (old-fashioned, informal) to be unwilling to do or accept sth: She agreed to attend but jibbed at making a speech.

jibe (also **gibe**) /dʒaɪb/ noun, verb
■ noun 1 ~ (at sb/sth) an unkind or insulting remark about sb: He made several cheap jibes at his opponent during the interview. 2 (AmE) = GYBE
■ verb 1 to say sth that is intended to embarrass sb or make them look silly: [V] He jibed repeatedly at the errors they had made. [also V speech, V that] 2 [V] ~ (with sth) (AmE, informal) to be the same as sth or to match it: Your statement doesn't jibe with the facts. 3 (AmE) = GYBE

jiffy /'dʒɪfi/ noun [usually sing.] (informal) a moment: I'll be with you in a jiffy (= very soon).

ˈJiffy bag™ noun (BrE) a thick soft envelope for sending things that might break or tear easily

jig /dʒɪg/ noun, verb
■ noun 1 a quick lively dance; the music for this dance: an Irish jig 2 a device that holds sth in position and guides the tools that are working on it
■ verb (-gg-) [usually +adv./prep.] to move or to make sb/sth move up and down with short quick movements: [V] He jigged up and down with excitement. [also V N]

jiggery-pokery /ˌdʒɪgəri 'pəʊkəri; AmE 'poʊk-/ noun [U] (informal, especially BrE) dishonest behaviour

jig·gle /'dʒɪgl/ verb (informal) to move or make sth move up and down or from side to side with short quick movements: [V] Stop jiggling around! ◊ She jiggled with the lock. ◊ [VN] He stood jiggling his car keys in his hand.

jig·saw /'dʒɪgsɔː/ noun 1 (also 'jigsaw puzzle) (both BrE) (also **puz·zle** AmE, BrE) a picture printed on cardboard or wood, that has been cut up into a lot of small pieces of different shapes that you have to fit together again: to do a jigsaw—picture on page A8 2 a mysterious situation in which it is not easy to understand all the causes of what is happening; a complicated problem: If Hollis was a double agent then the Crabb affair fits neatly into the jigsaw. 3 a SAW (= a type of tool) with a fine blade for cutting designs in thin pieces of wood or metal

J

b	d	f	g	h	k	l	m	n	p	r
bad	**did**	**fall**	**get**	**hat**	**cat**	**leg**	**man**	**now**	**pen**	**red**

jewellery (*BrE*)/ **jewelry** (*AmE*)

clasp · pearl necklace · charm bracelet · bangle · bracelet · brooch/ pin · charm · chain · bead · string of beads · anklet · watch · watch strap (*BrE*)/ watchband (*AmE*) · locket · medallion · pendant · signet ring · cuff · stud · wedding ring/ wedding band · ring · cuff links · clip-on earring · hoop earring · ring finger

jihad /dʒɪˈhɑːd/ *noun* a holy war fought by Muslims against those who reject Islam

jilt /dʒɪlt/ *verb* [VN] [often passive] to end a romantic relationship with sb in a sudden and unkind way: *He was jilted by his fiancée.* ◇ *a jilted bride/lover*

jimmy /ˈdʒɪmi/ (*AmE*) = JEMMY

jin·gle /ˈdʒɪŋɡl/ *noun, verb*
■ *noun* **1** [sing.] a sound like small bells ringing that is made when metal objects are shaken together: *the jingle of coins in his pocket* **2** [C] a short song or tune that is easy to remember and is used in advertising on radio or television
■ *verb* to make a pleasant gentle sound like small bells ringing; to make sth do this: [V] *The chimes jingled in the breeze.* ◇ [VN] *She jingled the coins in her pocket.*

jin·go·ism /ˈdʒɪŋɡəʊɪzəm; *AmE* -ɡoʊ-/ *noun* [U] (*disapproving*) a strong belief that your own country is best, especially when this is expressed in support of war with another country ▶ **jin·go·is·tic** /ˌdʒɪŋɡəʊˈɪstɪk; *AmE* -ɡoʊ-/ *adj.*

jink /dʒɪŋk/ *verb* [V] [usually +*adv./prep.*] (*BrE, informal*) to move quickly while changing direction suddenly and often, especially in order to avoid sb/sth

jinks /dʒɪŋks/ *noun* ⇨ HIGH JINKS

jinx /dʒɪŋks/ *noun* [sing.] ~ (on sb/sth) bad luck; sb/sth that is thought to bring bad luck in a mysterious way: *I'm convinced there's a jinx on this car.*

jinxed /dʒɪŋkst/ *adj.* (*informal*) having or bringing more bad luck than is normal: *The whole family seemed to be jinxed.*

jit·ters /ˈdʒɪtəz; *AmE* -tərz/ (often **the jitters**) *noun* [pl.] (*informal*) feelings of being anxious and nervous, especially before an important event or before having to do sth difficult: *I always get the jitters before exams.* ◇ *Louise had pre-wedding jitters.*

jit·tery /ˈdʒɪtəri/ *adj.* (*informal*) anxious and nervous

jiu-jitsu = JU-JITSU

jive /dʒaɪv/ *noun, verb*
■ *noun* **1** [U, sing.] a fast dance to music with a strong beat, especially popular in the 1950s **2** [U] (*AmE, slang*) nonsense: *to talk jive*
■ *verb* **1** [V] to dance to jazz or ROCK AND ROLL music **2** [V, VN] (*AmE, informal*) to try to make sb believe sth that is not true **SYN** KID

Jnr (*BrE*) (also **Jr.** especially in *AmE*) *abbr.* JUNIOR: *John F Davis Jnr*

job /dʒɒb; *AmE* dʒɑːb/ *noun*
PAID WORK | **1** work for which you receive regular payment: *He's trying to get a job.* ◇ *She took a job as a waitress.* ◇ *His brother's just lost his job.* ◇ *a summer/holiday/Saturday/vacation job* ◇ *I'm thinking of applying for a new job.* ◇ *The takeover of the company is bound to mean more job losses.* ◇ *Many women are in part-time jobs.* ◇ *Did they offer you the job?* ◇ *He certainly knows his job* (= is very good at his job). ◇ *I'm only doing my job* (= I'm doing what I am paid to do). ◇ *He's been out of a job* (= unemployed) *for six months now.* ◇ *She's never had a steady job* (= a job that is not going to end suddenly).
TASK | **2** a particular task or piece of work that you have to do: *I've got various jobs around the house to do.* ◇ *Sorting these papers out is going to be a long job.* ◇ *The builder has a couple of jobs on at the moment.*—see also BLOW JOB, NOSE JOB
DUTY | **3** [usually sing.] a responsibility or duty: *It's not my job to lock up!*
CRIME | **4** (*informal*) a crime, especially stealing: *a bank job* ◇ *He got six months for that last job he did.* ◇ *an inside job* (= done by sb in the organization where the crime happens)
OBJECT | **5** (*spoken*) a particular kind of thing: *It's real wood—not one of those plastic jobs.*
COMPUTING | **6** an item of work which is PROCESSED by a computer as a single unit
IDM **do the 'job** (*informal*) to be effective or successful in doing what you want: *This extra strong glue should do the job.* **do a good, bad, etc. 'job. do a good, bad, etc. job of sth** to do sth well, badly, etc: *They did a very professional job.* ◇ *You've certainly made an excellent job of the kitchen* (= for example, painting it). **give sb/sth up as a bad 'job** (*informal*) to decide to stop trying to help sb or to do sth because there is no hope of success **Good 'job!** (*AmE, spoken*) used to tell sb that they have done well at sth **a good 'job** (*spoken*) used to say that you are pleased about a situation or that sb is lucky that sth happened: *It's a good job you were there to help.* **have a (hard/difficult) job doing/to do sth** to have difficulty doing sth: *You'll have a job convincing them that you're right.* ◇ *He had a hard job to make himself heard.* **a job of 'work** (*BrE, old-fashioned* or *formal*) work that you are

paid to do or that must be done: *There was a job of work waiting for him that he was not looking forward to.* **jobs for the 'boys** (*BrE, informal, disapproving*) people use the expression **jobs for the boys** when they are criticizing the fact that sb in power has given work to friends or relatives **just the 'job** (*BrE*) (also **just the 'ticket** *AmE, BrE*) (*spoken, approving*) exactly what is needed in a particular situation: *That cup of tea was just the job.* **more than your 'job's worth (to do sth)** (*BrE, spoken*) not worth doing because it is against the rules or because it might cause you to lose your job—see also JOBSWORTH **on the 'job 1** while doing a particular job: *No sleeping on the job!* ◇ *on-the-job training* **2** (*BrE, slang*) having sex—more at BEST *n.*, DEVIL, WALK *v.*

VOCABULARY BUILDING
jobs and **employment**

job [C] *'What's his job?' 'He's a teacher.'* ◇ *I start my new job on Monday.*

work [U] *I'm going back to work tomorrow.* ◇ *She is now looking for work.*

post/position [C] *He resigned from his post as finance director.* ◇ *She holds a high-level position.*

occupation [C] (*formal or written*) *Please state your name, age and occupation.*

profession [C] *the medical profession* or [U] *She's a lawyer by profession.*

trade [C] *the building trade* or [U] *He was a carpenter by trade.*

vocation [C] *She found her true vocation as a nurse.*

career [C] *a distinguished career as a lawyer* ◇ *a career woman.*

employment [U] *a contract of employment* ◇ *employment opportunities for graduates.*

⇨ note at WORK

---

job·bing /'dʒɒbɪŋ; *AmE* 'dʒɑːb-/ *adj.* [only before noun] (*BrE*) doing pieces of work for different people rather than a regular job: *a jobbing actor/builder*

job·centre /'dʒɒbsentə(r); *AmE* 'dʒɑːb-/ *noun* (*BrE*) a government office where people can get advice in finding work and where jobs are advertised

'job creation *noun* [U] the process of providing opportunities for paid work, especially for people who are unemployed

'job description *noun* a written description of the exact work and responsibilities of a job

job·less /'dʒɒbləs; *AmE* 'dʒɑːb-/ *adj.* **1** unemployed; without a job: *The closure left 500 people jobless.* **2** (**the jobless**) *noun* [pl.] people who are unemployed ▶ **job·less·ness** *noun* [U]

,job 'lot *noun* (*BrE, informal*) a collection of different things, especially of poor quality, that are sold together

'job seeker *noun* often used in official language in Britain to describe a person without a job who is trying to find one

'job-sharing *noun* [U] an arrangement for two people to share the hours of work and the pay of one job ▶ **'job-share** *noun*: *The company encourages job-shares and part-time working.* **'job-share** *verb* [V]

jobs·worth /'dʒɒbzwɜːθ; *AmE* 'dʒɑːbzwɜːrθ/ *noun* (*BrE, informal, disapproving*) a person who follows the rules of a job exactly, even when this causes problems for other people, or when the rules are not sensible

Jock /dʒɒk; *AmE* dʒɑːk/ *noun* (*informal*) a way of describing a person from Scotland, that can be offensive

jockey /'dʒɒki; *AmE* 'dʒɑːki/ *noun, verb*
■ *noun* a person who rides horses in races, especially as a job
■ *verb* ~ (**for sth**) to try all possible ways of gaining an advantage over other people: [V] *The runners jockeyed for position at the start.* ◇ *The bands are constantly jockeying with each other for the number one spot.* [also V to inf]

jock·strap /'dʒɒkstræp; *AmE* 'dʒɑːk-/ (also **ath,letic sup'porter** especially in *AmE*) *noun* a piece of men's

underwear worn to support or protect the sexual organs while playing sports

jocu·lar /'dʒɒkjələ(r); *AmE* 'dʒɑːk-/ *adj.* (*formal*) **1** humorous: *a jocular comment* **2** (of a person) enjoying making people laugh—see also JOKE ▶ **jocu·lar·ity** /,dʒɒkjə-'lærəti; *AmE* ,dʒɑːk-/ *noun* [U] **jocu·lar·ly** *adv.*

jodh·purs /'dʒɒdpəz; *AmE* 'dʒɑːdpərz/ *noun* [pl.] trousers/pants that are loose above the knee and tight from the knee to the ankle, worn when riding a horse: *a pair of jodhpurs*

Joe Bloggs /,dʒəʊ 'blɒgz; *AmE* ,dʒoʊ 'blɔːgz; 'blɑːgz/ (*BrE*) (*AmE* **John 'Doe**) *noun* [sing.] (*informal*) a way of referring to a typical ordinary person

,Joe 'Public (*BrE*) (*AmE* ,**John ,Q. 'Public**) *noun* [U] (*informal*) people in general; the public

joey /'dʒəʊi; *AmE* 'dʒoʊi/ *noun* a young KANGAROO, WALLABY or POSSUM—picture on page A6

jog /dʒɒg; *AmE* dʒɑːg/ *verb, noun*
■ *verb* (**-gg-**) **1** (also **go jogging**)[V] to run slowly and steadily for a long time, especially for exercise: *I go jogging every evening.* **2** [VN] to hit sth lightly and accidentally: *Someone jogged her elbow, making her spill her coffee.* **IDM** **jog sb's 'memory** to say or do sth that makes sb remember sth **PHRV** **jog a'long** (*BrE, informal*) to continue as usual with little or no excitement, change or progress
■ *noun* [sing.] **1** a slow run, especially one done for physical exercise: *I like to go for a jog after work.* **2** a light push or knock

jog·ger /'dʒɒgə(r); *AmE* 'dʒɑːg-/ *noun* a person who jogs regularly for exercise

jog·ging /'dʒɒgɪŋ; *AmE* 'dʒɑːg-/ *noun* [U] the activity of running slowly and steadily as a form of exercise: *to go jogging*

'jogging suit *noun* = TRACKSUIT

jog·gle /'dʒɒgl; *AmE* 'dʒɑːgl/ *verb* [V, VN] (*informal*) to move or to make sb/sth move quickly up and down or from one side to another

john /dʒɒn; *AmE* dʒɑːn/ *noun* (*informal, especially AmE*) a toilet

John 'Bull *noun* [U, C] (*old-fashioned*) a word that is used to refer to England or the English people, or to a typical Englishman

John 'Doe *noun* [usually sing.] (*AmE*) **1** a name used for a person whose name is not known or is kept secret, especially in a court of law **2** an average man—compare JANE DOE

,John ,Q. 'Public *noun* [U] (*AmE*) = JOE PUBLIC

joie de vivre /,ʒwɑː də 'viːvrə/ *noun* [U] (from *French, written*) a feeling of great happiness and enjoyment of life

join /dʒɔɪn/ *verb, noun*
■ *verb*
CONNECT | **1** ~ **A to B** | ~ **A and B** (**together/up**) to fix or connect two or more things together: [VN] *Join one section of pipe to the next.* ◇ *Join the two sections of pipe together.* ◇ *The island is joined to the mainland by a bridge.* ◇ *Draw a line joining (up) all the crosses.* ◇ [V] *How do these two pieces join?*

BECOME ONE | **2** if two things or groups **join**, or if one thing or group **joins** another, they come together to form one thing or group: [V] *the place where the two paths join* ◇ [VN] *The path joins the road near the trees.*

CLUB/COMPANY | **3** to become a member of an organization, a company, a club, etc: [VN] *I've joined an aerobics class.* ◇ *She joined the company three months ago.* ◇ (*figurative*) *to join the ranks of the unemployed* ◇ [V] *It costs £20 to join.*

DO STH WITH SB ELSE | **4** [VN] to take part in sth that sb else is doing or to go somewhere with them: *Will you join us for lunch?* ◇ *Do you mind if I join you?* ◇ *Over 200 members of staff joined the strike.* ◇ *Members of the public joined 'the search for the missing boy.* ◇ *I'm sure you'll all join me in wishing Ted and Laura a very happy marriage.*

TRAIN/PLANE | **5** [VN] (*BrE*) if you **join** a train, plane, etc. you get on it

---

æ	ɑː	e	ɜː	ə	ɪ	iː	i	ɒ	ɔː	ʌ	ʊ	u	uː
cat	father	ten	bird	about	sit	see	many	got	saw	cup	put	actual	too
								(BrE)					

J

ROAD/PATH | **6** [VN] (*BrE*) if you **join** a road or a path, you start to travel along it

IDM **join 'battle (with sb)** (*formal*) to begin fighting sb: (*figurative*) *Local residents have joined battle with the council over the lack of parking facilities.* **join the 'club** used when sth bad that has happened to sb else has also happened to you: *So you didn't get a job either? Join the club!* **join 'hands (with sb)** **1** if two people **join hands**, they hold each other's hands **2** to work together in doing sth: *Education has been reluctant to join hands with business.*—more at BEAT *v.*, FORCE *n.*

PHRV **,join 'in (sth/doing sth)| ,join 'in (with sb/sth)** to take part in an activity with other people: *She listens but she never joins in.* ◊ *I wish he would join in with the other children.* **,join 'up** (*BrE*) to become a member of the armed forces SYN ENLIST: *Her grandfather joined up in 1914.* **,join 'up (with sb)** to combine with sb else to do sth: *We'll join up with the other groups later.*

■ *noun*

CONNECTION | a place where two things are fixed together: *The two pieces were stuck together so well that you could hardly see the join.*

join·er /'dʒɔɪnə(r)/ *noun* (*BrE*) a person whose job is to make the wooden parts of a building, especially window frames, doors, etc.—compare CARPENTER

join·ery /'dʒɔɪnəri/ *noun* [U] the work of a joiner or things made by a joiner

joint /dʒɔɪnt/ *adj., noun, verb*
■ *adj.* [only before noun] involving two or more people together: *a joint account* (= a bank account in the name of more than one person, for example a husband and wife) ◊ *a joint venture/statement* ◊ *The report was a joint effort* (= we worked on it together). ◊ *They finished in joint first place.* ◊ *They were joint owners of the house* (= they owned it together). ▶ **joint·ly** *adv.*: *The event was organized jointly by students and staff.*
■ *noun* **1** a place where two bones are joined together in the body in a way that enables them to bend and move: *inflammation of the knee joint* ◊ *My joints are really stiff this morning.* **2** a place where two or more parts of an object are joined together, especially to form a corner **3** (*BrE*) a piece of ROAST meat: *a joint of beef* ◊ *the Sunday joint* (= one traditionally eaten on a Sunday) **4** (*informal*) a place where people meet to eat, drink, dance, etc., especially one that is cheap: *a fast-food joint* **5** (*informal*) a cigarette containing MARIJUANA (= an illegal drug) **IDM** **out of 'joint** **1** (of a bone) pushed out of its correct position **2** not working or behaving in the normal way: *Time is thrown completely out of joint in the opening chapters.*—more at CASE *v.*, NOSE *n.*
■ *verb* [VN] to cut meat into large pieces, usually each containing a bone

,Joint ,Chiefs of 'Staff *noun* [pl.] (in the US) the leaders of the Army, Navy, Air Force and Marines who advise the President on military matters

,joint de'gree *noun* (in Britain and some other countries) a university course in which you study two subjects to the same standard

joint·ed /'dʒɔɪntɪd/ *adj.* [usually before noun] having parts that fit together and can move: *a doll with jointed arms/legs*

,joint-'stock company *noun* (*business*) a company that is owned by all the people who have shares in it

joist /dʒɔɪst/ *noun* a long thick piece of wood or metal that is used to support a floor or ceiling in a building

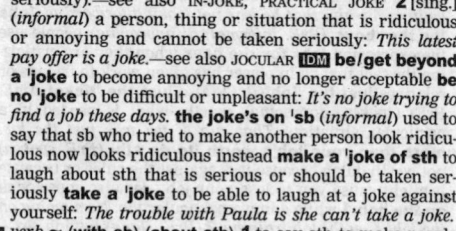
floorboard
joist

joke /dʒəʊk; *AmE* dʒoʊk/ *noun, verb*
■ *noun* **1** something that you say or do to make people laugh, for example a funny story that you tell: *I can't tell jokes.* ◊ *She's always cracking jokes.* ◊ *They often make jokes at each other's expense.* ◊ *I didn't get the joke* (= understand it). ◊ *I wish he wouldn't tell dirty jokes* (= about sex). ◊ *I only did it as a joke* (= it was not meant

seriously).—see also IN-JOKE, PRACTICAL JOKE **2** [sing.] (*informal*) a person, thing or situation that is ridiculous or annoying and cannot be taken seriously: *This latest pay offer is a joke.*—see also JOCULAR **IDM** **be/get beyond a 'joke** to become annoying and no longer acceptable **be no 'joke** to be difficult or unpleasant: *It's no joke trying to find a job these days.* **the joke's on 'sb** (*informal*) used to say that sb who tried to make another person look ridiculous now looks ridiculous instead **make a 'joke of sth** to laugh about sth that is serious or should be taken seriously **take a 'joke** to be able to laugh at a joke against yourself: *The trouble with Paula is she can't take a joke.*
■ *verb* ~ (with sb) (about sth) **1** to say sth to make people laugh; to tell a funny story: [V] *She was laughing and joking with the children.* ◊ *They often joked about all the things that could go wrong.* ◊ [V+speech] *'I cooked it myself, so be careful!' he joked.* **2** to say sth that is not true because you think it is funny: [V] *I didn't mean that—I was only joking.* ◊ [V that] *She joked that she only loved him for his money.* **IDM** **joking a'part/a'side** (*BrE*) used to show that you are now being serious after you have said sth funny **you're 'joking | you must be 'joking** (*spoken*) used to show that you are very surprised at what sb has just said: *No way am I doing that. You must be joking!* ◊ *She's going out with Dan? You're joking!*

joker /'dʒəʊkə(r); *AmE* 'dʒoʊk-/ *noun* **1** a person who likes making jokes or doing silly things to make people laugh: *He's always been a bit of a joker.* ◊ (*informal*) *Some joker's been using my computer.* **2** an extra playing card that is used in some card games, usually as a WILD CARD—picture on page A8 **IDM** **the joker in the 'pack** a person or thing who could change the way that things will happen in a way that cannot be predicted

jokey (also **joky**) /'dʒəʊki; *AmE* 'dʒoʊki/ *adj.* (*informal*) amusing; making people laugh

jok·ing·ly /'dʒəʊkɪŋli; *AmE* 'dʒoʊk-/ *adv.* in a way that is intended to be amusing and not serious

jolly /'dʒɒli; *AmE* 'dʒɑːli/ *adj., adv., verb*
■ *adj.* (jol·lier, jol·li·est) **1** happy and cheerful: *a jolly crowd/face/mood* **2** (*old-fashioned*) enjoyable: *a jolly evening/party/time* ▶ **jol·lity** /'dʒɒləti; *AmE* 'dʒɑːl-/ *noun* [U] (*old-fashioned*): *scenes of high-spirits and jollity*
■ *adv.* (*old-fashioned, BrE, informal*) very: *That's a jolly good idea.* **IDM** **jolly 'good!** (*old-fashioned, BrE, spoken*) used to show that you approve of sth that sb has just said **'jolly well** (*old-fashioned, BrE*) used to emphasize a statement when you are annoyed about sth: *If you don't come now, you can jolly well walk home!*
■ *verb* (jol·lies, jolly·ing, jol·lied, jol·lied) (*BrE*) **PHRV** **,jolly sb a'long** to encourage sb in a cheerful way **,jolly sb 'into sth/into 'doing sth** to persuade or encourage sb to do sth by making them feel happy about it **,jolly sb/sth 'up** to make sb/sth more cheerful

jolt /dʒəʊlt; *AmE* dʒoʊlt/ *verb, noun*
■ *verb* **1** to move or to make sb/sth move suddenly and roughly: [V] *The truck jolted and rattled over the rough ground.* ◊ *The bus jolted to a halt.* ◊ (*figurative*) *Her heart jolted when she saw him.* ◊ [VN] *He was jolted forwards as the bus moved off.* **2** ~ sb (into sth) | ~ sb (out of sth) to give sb a sudden shock, especially so that they start to take action or deal with a situation: [VN] *His remark jolted her into action.* ◊ *The sound jolted my memory, and I suddenly remembered what had happened.* ◊ *a method of jolting the economy out of recession* [also VN-ADJ]
■ *noun* [usually sing.] **1** a sudden rough movement SYN JERK: *The plane landed with a jolt.* **2** a sudden strong feeling, especially of shock or surprise: *a jolt of dismay*

Joneses /'dʒəʊnzɪz; *AmE* 'dʒoʊn-/ *noun* [pl.] **IDM** **,keep up with the 'Joneses** /'dʒəʊnzɪz/ (*informal, often disapproving*) to try to have all the possessions and social achievements that your friends and NEIGHBOURS have

josh /dʒɒʃ; *AmE* dʒɑːʃ/ *verb* [V, VN, V+speech] (*informal*) to gently make fun of sb or talk to them in a joking way

joss stick /'dʒɒstɪk; *AmE* 'dʒɑːs-/ *noun* a thin wooden stick covered with a substance that burns slowly and produces a sweet smell

jos·tle /'dʒɒsl; *AmE* 'dʒɑːsl/ *verb* to push roughly against sb in a crowd: [VN] *The visiting president was jostled by angry demonstrators.* ◊ [V] *People were jostling, arguing and complaining.* **PHRV** '**jostle for sth** to compete strongly and forcefully with other people for sth: *People in the crowd were jostling for the best positions.*

jot /dʒɒt; *AmE* dʒɑːt/ *verb, noun*

■ *verb* (**-tt-**) **PHRV** **jot sth** ↔ **down** to write sth quickly: *I'll just jot down the address for you.*

■ *noun* [sing.] (**not·a/one jot**) used to mean 'not even a small amount' when you are emphasizing a negative statement: *There's not a jot of truth in what he says* (= none *at all*).

jot·ter /'dʒɒtə(r); *AmE* 'dʒɑːt-/ *noun* (*BrE*) **1** a small book used for writing notes in **2** (*ScotE*) an exercise book

jot·tings /'dʒɒtɪŋz; *AmE* 'dʒɑːt-/ *noun* [pl.] short notes that are written down quickly

joule /dʒuːl/ *noun* (*abbr.* **J**) (*physics*) a unit of energy or work

jour·nal /'dʒɜːnl; *AmE* 'dʒɜːrnl/ *noun* **1** a newspaper or magazine that deals with a particular subject or profession: *a scientific/trade journal* ◊ *the British Medical Journal* **2** used in the title of some newspapers: *the Wall Street Journal* **3** a written record of the things you do, see, etc. every day: *He kept a journal of his travels across Asia.*—compare DIARY

jour·nal·ese /ˌdʒɜːnəˈliːz; *AmE* ˌdʒɜːrn-/ *noun* [U] (*usually disapproving*) a style of language that is thought to be typical of that used in newspapers

jour·nal·ism /'dʒɜːnəlɪzəm; *AmE* 'dʒɜːrn-/ *noun* [U] the work of collecting and writing news stories for newspapers, magazines, radio or television

jour·nal·ist /'dʒɜːnəlɪst; *AmE* 'dʒɜːrn-/ *noun* a person whose job is to collect and write news stories for newspapers, magazines, radio or television—compare REPORTER

jour·nal·is·tic /ˌdʒɜːnəˈlɪstɪk; *AmE* ˌdʒɜːrn-/ *adj.* [only before noun] connected with the work of a journalist: *journalistic skills* ◊ *his journalistic background*

jour·ney /'dʒɜːni; *AmE* 'dʒɜːrni/ *noun, verb*

■ *noun* an act of travelling from one place to another, especially when they are far apart: *They went on a long train journey across India.* ◊ *Did you have a good journey?* ◊ *We broke our journey* (= stopped for a short time) *in Madrid.* ◊ (*especially BrE*) *Don't use the car for short journeys.* ◊ (*especially BrE*) *It's a day's journey by car.* ◊ (*especially BrE*) *I'm afraid you've had a wasted journey* (= you cannot do what you have come to do). ◊ (*BrE, spoken*) *Bye! Safe journey!* (= used when sb is beginning a journey) ◊ (*figurative*) *The book describes a spiritual journey from despair to happiness.*

■ *verb* [V, usually +*adv./prep.*] (*formal* or *literary*) to travel, especially a long distance: *They journeyed for seven long months.*

jour·ney·man /'dʒɜːnimən; *AmE* 'dʒɜːrn-/ *noun* (*pl.* **-men** /-mən/) **1** (in the past) a person who was trained to do a particular job and who then worked for sb else **2** a person who has training and experience in a job but who is only average at it

journo /'dʒɜːnəʊ; *AmE* 'dʒɜːrnoʊ/ (*pl.* **-os**) *noun* (*BrE, AustralE, slang*) a journalist

joust /dʒaʊst/ *verb* [V] **1** to fight on horses using a long stick (= a LANCE) to try to knock the other person off their horse, especially as part of a formal contest in the past **2** (*formal*) to argue with sb, especially as part of a formal or public debate ▶ **joust** *noun*

Jove /dʒəʊv; *AmE* dʒoʊv/ *noun* **IDM** **by Jove** (*old-fashioned spoken, especially BrE*) used to express surprise or to emphasize a statement

jo·vial /'dʒəʊviəl; *AmE* 'dʒoʊ-/ *adj.* (*written*) very cheerful and friendly: *He was in a jovial mood.* ▶ **jovi·al·ity** /ˌdʒəʊviˈæləti; *AmE* ˌdʒoʊ-/ *noun* [U] **jo·vial·ly** /-iəli/ *adv.*

jowl /dʒaʊl/ *noun* [usually pl.] (*written*) the lower part of sb's cheek when it is fat and hangs down below their chin: *a man with heavy jowls* **IDM** see CHEEK *n.*

joy /dʒɔɪ/ *noun* **1** [U] a feeling of great happiness **SYN** DELIGHT: *the sheer joy of being with her again* ◊ *to dance for/with joy* ◊ *I didn't expect them to jump for joy at the*

WHICH WORD?
journey / travel / trip

Nouns

Journey = an act of travelling from one place to another. In *BrE* it can be long, or short but regular: *to go on a 6 000-mile journey* ◊ *How long is your journey to work?*

Trip = a journey to a place and back, especially for a short visit: *to go on a trip to Disneyland* ◊ *a business trip.*

In *AmE* **trip** is used instead of **journey** for a short distance: *The trip takes about 45 minutes.*

Travel is an uncountable noun that means the general act of travelling: *She loves travel.* ◊ *The price includes air travel.*

Travels [pl] means several journeys to other places or countries, especially far away.

Verbs

To travel puts emphasis on the journey itself: *to travel abroad* ◊ *I usually travel by air.*

If you are thinking more about the place you are going to than the journey itself, use **to go**: *I'm going to Italy on Friday.* ◊ *Do you go to New York often?* ◊ ~~I'm travelling to Italy on Friday.~~ ◊ ~~Do you travel to New York often?~~

— see also EXCURSION, TOUR, VOYAGE.

news (= to be very pleased). ◊ *To his great joy, she accepted.* **2** [C] a person or thing that causes you to feel very happy: *the joys of fatherhood* ◊ *The game was a joy to watch.* **3** [U] (*BrE, informal*) (in questions and negative sentences) success or satisfaction: *We complained about our rooms but got no joy from the manager.* ◊ *'Any joy at the shops?' 'No, they didn't have what I wanted.'* **IDM** **full of the joys of 'spring** very cheerful—more at PRIDE *n.*

joy·ful /'dʒɔɪfl/ *adj.* (*written*) very happy; causing people to be happy: *She gave a joyful laugh.* ◊ *It was a joyful reunion of all the family.* ▶ **joy·ful·ly** /-fəli/ *adv.*

joy·less /'dʒɔɪləs/ *adj.* (*written*) bringing no happiness; without joy: *a joyless marriage/childhood*

joy·ous /'dʒɔɪəs/ *adj.* (*literary*) very happy; causing people to be happy **SYN** JOYFUL: *joyous laughter* ▶ **joy·ous·ly** *adv.*

joy·pad /'dʒɔɪpæd/ *noun* a device used with some computer games, with buttons that you use to move images on the screen

joy·rid·ing /'dʒɔɪraɪdɪŋ/ *noun* [U] the crime of stealing a car and driving it for pleasure, usually in a fast and dangerous way ▶ **joy·ride** *noun* **joy·rider** *noun*

joy·stick /'dʒɔɪstɪk/ *noun* **1** an upright handle used with some computer games to move images on the screen **2** (*informal*) an upright handle used in an aircraft that is used to control direction or height

JP /ˌdʒeɪ ˈpiː/ *abbr.* JUSTICE OF THE PEACE: *Helen Alvey JP*

Jr. (*especially AmE*) *abbr.* JUNIOR—compare SR

ju·bi·lant /'dʒuːbɪlənt/ *adj.* (*written*) feeling or showing great happiness because of a success: *The fans were in jubilant mood after the victory.* ▶ **ju·bi·lant·ly** *adv.*

jubi·la·tion /ˌdʒuːbɪˈleɪʃn/ *noun* [U] a feeling of great happiness because of a success: *There were scenes of jubilation among her supporters.*

ju·bi·lee /'dʒuːbɪliː/ *noun* a special anniversary of an event, especially one that took place 25 or 50 years ago; the celebrations connected with it—see also DIAMOND JUBILEE, GOLDEN JUBILEE, SILVER JUBILEE

Ju·da·ism /'dʒuːdeɪɪzəm; *AmE* -dəɪzəm/ *noun* [U] the religion of the Jewish people, based mainly on the Bible (= the Christian Old Testament) and the Talmud ▶ **Ju·da·ic** /dʒuːˈdeɪɪk/ *adj.* [only before noun]: *Judaic tradition/law*

Judas /'dʒuːdəs/ *noun* a person who betrays a friend **SYN** TRAITOR

jud·der /'dʒʌdə(r)/ *verb* [V] to shake violently: *He slammed on the brakes and the car juddered to a halt.*

b	d	f	g	h	k	l	m	n	p	r
bad	**did**	**fall**	**get**	**hat**	**cat**	**leg**	**man**	**now**	**pen**	**red**

judge /dʒʌdʒ/ *noun, verb*

■ *noun*

IN COURT OF LAW | **1** a person in a court of law who has the authority to decide how criminals should be punished or to make legal decisions: *a High Court judge* ◊ *a federal judge* ◊ *The case comes before Judge Cooper next week.* ◊ *The judge sentenced him to five years in prison.*—compare JUSTICE OF THE PEACE, MAGISTRATE

IN COMPETITION | **2** a person who decides who has won a competition: *the panel of judges at the flower show* ◊ *The judges' decision is final.*

SB WHO GIVES OPINION | **3** [usually sing.] a person who has the necessary knowledge or skills to give their opinion about the value or quality of sb/sth: *She's a good judge of character.*

■ *verb*

FORM OPINION | **1** to form an opinion about sb/sth, based on the information you have: [V] *As far as I can judge, all of them are to blame.* ◊ *Judging by her last letter, they are having a wonderful time.* ◊ *To judge from what he said, he was very disappointed.* ◊ [VN] *Schools should not be judged only on exam results.* ◊ *Each painting must be judged on its own merits.* ◊ [VN-N, VNto inf] *The tour was judged a great success.* ◊ *The tour was judged to have been a great success.* ◊ [VN-ADJ] *They judged it wise to say nothing.* [also V that, VN that, V wh-]

ESTIMATE | **2** to guess the size, amount, etc. of sth: [V wh-] *It's difficult to judge how long the journey will take.* ◊ [VN to inf] *I judged him to be about 50.*

IN COMPETITION | **3** to decide the result of a competition; to be the judge in a competition: [VN] *She was asked to judge the essay competition.* [also V]

GIVE OPINION | **4** to give your opinion about sb, especially when you disapprove of them: [VN] *What gives you the right to judge other people?* [also V]

IN COURT OF LAW | **5** to decide whether sb is guilty or innocent in a court of law: [VN] *to judge a case* ◊ [VN-ADJ] *to judge sb guilty/not guilty*

IDM don't judge a ˌbook by its ˈcover (*saying*) used to say that you should not form an opinion about sb/sth from their appearance only

judge·ment (also **judg·ment** especially in *AmE*) /ˈdʒʌdʒmənt/ *noun* **1** [U] the ability to make sensible decisions after carefully considering the best thing to do: *good/poor/sound judgement* ◊ *She showed a lack of judgement when she gave Mark the job.* ◊ *It's not something I can give you rules for; you'll have to use your judgement.* ◊ *He achieved his aim more by luck than judgement.* ◊ *The accident was caused by an error of judgement on the part of the pilot.* **2** [C, U] ~ (of/about/on sth) an opinion that you form about sth after thinking about it carefully; the act of making this opinion known to others: *He refused to make a judgement about the situation.* ◊ *Who am I to pass judgement on her behaviour?* (= to criticize it) ◊ *I'd like to reserve judgement until I see the report.* ◊ *It was, in her judgement, the wrong thing to do.* ◊ *I did it against my better judgement* (= although I thought it was perhaps the wrong thing to do). **3** (usually **judgment**) [C, U] the decision of a court of law or a judge: *a judgment from the European Court of Justice* ◊ *The judgment will be given tomorrow.* ◊ *The court has yet to pass judgment* (= say what its decision is) *in this case.* **4** [C, usually sing.] ~ (on sth) (*formal*) something bad that happens to sb that is thought to be a punishment from God **IDM** see SIT

judge·ment·al (*BrE*) (also **judg·ment·al** *AmE, BrE*) /dʒʌdʒˈmentl/ *adj.* **1** (*disapproving*) judging people and criticizing them too quickly: *Stop always being so judgemental!* **2** (*formal*) connected with the process of judging things: *the judgemental process*

ˈ**Judgement Day** (also the ˌDay of ˈJudgement, the ˌLast ˈJudgement) *noun* [sing.] the day at the end of the world when, according to some religions, God will judge everyone who has ever lived

ju·di·ca·ture /ˈdʒuːdɪkətʃə(r)/ *noun* (*law*) **1** [U] the system and ADMINISTRATION of justice in a country **2** (the **judicature**) [sing.+ sing./pl. *v.*] judges when they are considered as a group

ju·di·cial /dʒuˈdɪʃl/ *adj.* [usually before noun] connected with a court of law, a judge or legal judgement: *judicial powers* ◊ *the judicial process/system* ▶ **ju·di·cial·ly** /-ʃəli/ *adv.*

ju·di·ciary /dʒuˈdɪʃəri; *AmE* -ʃieri/ *noun* (usually **the judiciary**) [C+sing./pl. *v.*] (*pl.* -**ies**) the judges of a country or a state, when they are considered as a group: *an independent judiciary*—compare EXECUTIVE *n.* (3), LEGISLATURE

ju·di·cious /dʒuˈdɪʃəs/ *adj.* (*formal, approving*) careful and sensible; showing good judgement: *It is curable with judicious use of antibiotics* **OPP** INJUDICIOUS ▶ **ju·di·cious·ly** *adv.*: *The letter was judiciously worded.*

judo /ˈdʒuːdəʊ; *AmE* -doʊ/ *noun* [U] a sport in which two people fight and try to throw each other to the ground

jug /dʒʌg/ *noun* **1** (*BrE*) (*AmE* **pitch·er**) a container with a handle and a LIP, for holding and pouring liquids: *a milk/water jug* **2** (*AmE*) a large round container with a small opening and a handle, for holding liquids: *a five-gallon jug of beer* **3** the amount of liquid contained in a jug: *She spilled a jug of water.*

pitcher (*BrE*)/
jug (*AmE*)

jug (*BrE*)/
pitcher (*AmE*)

jug·ger·naut /ˈdʒʌgənɔːt; *AmE* -gərn-/ *noun* **1** (*BrE*, often *disapproving*) a very large lorry/truck: *juggernauts roaring through country villages* **2** (*written*) a large and powerful force or institution that cannot be controlled: *a bureaucratic juggernaut*

jug·gle /ˈdʒʌgl/ *verb* **1** ~ (**with sth**) to throw a set of three or more objects such as balls into the air and catch and throw them again quickly, one at a time: [V] *to juggle with balls/clubs* ◊ [VN] (*figurative*) *I was juggling books, shopping bags and the baby* (= I was trying to hold them all without dropping them). **2** ~ **sth** (**with sth**) to try to deal with two or more important jobs or activities at the same time so that you can fit all of them into your life: [VN] *Working mothers are used to juggling their jobs, their children's needs and their housework.* [also V] **3** [VN] to organize information, figures, the money you spend, etc. in the most useful or effective way

jug·gler /ˈdʒʌglə(r)/ *noun* a person who juggles, especially an entertainer

jugu·lar /ˈdʒʌgjələ(r)/ (also ˌjugular ˈvein) *noun* any of the three large VEINS in the neck that carry blood from the head to the heart **IDM** go for the ˈjugular (*informal*) to attack sb's weakest point during a discussion, in an aggressive way

juice /dʒuːs/ *noun* **1** [U, C] the liquid that comes from fruit or vegetables; a drink made from this: *Add the juice of two lemons.* ◊ *a carton of apple juice* ◊ *Two orange juices, please.* **2** [C, usually pl., U] the liquid that comes out of a piece of meat when it is cooked **3** [C, usually pl.] the liquid in the stomach that helps you to DIGEST food: *digestive/gastric juices* **4** [U] (*informal, especially BrE*) petrol/gas **5** [U] (*AmE, informal*) electricity **IDM** see STEW *v.*

juicer /ˈdʒuːsə(r)/ *noun* **1** a piece of electrical equipment for getting the juice out of fruit or vegetables **2** (*AmE*) LEMON SQUEEZER

juicy /ˈdʒuːsi/ *adj.* (**juici·er**, **juici·est**) **1** (*approving*) containing a lot of juice and good to eat: *soft juicy pears* ◊ *The meat was tender and juicy.* **2** (*informal*) interesting because you find it shocking or exciting: *juicy gossip* **3** (*informal*) attractive because it will bring you a lot of money or satisfaction: *a juicy prize*

ju-jitsu (also **jiu-jitsu**) /dʒuːˈdʒɪtsuː/ *noun* [U] a Japanese system of fighting from which the sport of JUDO was developed

juke·box /ˈdʒuːkbɒks; *AmE* -bɑːks/ *noun* a machine in a pub, bar, etc. that plays music when you put coins into it

July /dʒuˈlaɪ/ *noun* [U, C] (*abbr.* **Jul.**) the 7th month of the year, between June and August **HELP** To see how **July** is used, look at the examples at **April**.

s	t	v	z	ʃ	ʒ	tʃ	dʒ	θ	ð	ŋ
see	tea	van	zoo	shoe	vision	chain	jam	thin	this	sing

jum·ble /'dʒʌmbl/ *verb, noun*

■ *verb* [VN] [usually passive] ~ **sth (together/up)** to mix things together in a confused or untidy way: *Books, shoes and clothes were jumbled together on the floor.* ► **jum·bled** *adj.*: *a jumbled collection of objects* ◇ *jumbled thoughts*

■ *noun* **1** [sing.] ~ **(of sth)** an untidy or confused mixture of things: *a jumble of books and paper* ◇ *The essay was a meaningless jumble of ideas.* **2** [U] (*BrE*) a collection of old or used clothes, etc. that are no longer wanted and are going to be taken to a jumble sale

'jumble sale (*BrE*) (also **'rummage sale** *AmE, BrE*) *noun* a sale of old or used clothes, etc. to make money for a church, school or other organization

jumbo /'dʒʌmbəʊ; *AmE* -boʊ/ *noun, adj.*

■ *noun* (*pl.* **-os**) (also **jumbo 'jet**) a large plane that can carry several hundred passengers, especially a Boeing 747

■ *adj.* [only before noun] (*informal*) very large; larger than usual: *a jumbo pack of cornflakes*

jump /dʒʌmp/ *verb, noun*

■ *verb*

MOVE OFF/TO GROUND | **1** to move quickly off the ground or away from a surface by pushing yourself with your legs and feet: [V] *to jump into the air/over a wall/into the water* ◇ *'Quick, jump!' he shouted.* ◇ *The children were jumping up and down with excitement.* ◇ *She jumped down from the chair.* ◇ *The pilot jumped from the burning plane* (= with a PARACHUTE). ◇ [VN] *She has jumped 2.2 metres.*

PASS OVER STH | **2** [VN] to pass over sth by jumping: *Can you jump that gate?* ◇ *His horse fell· as it jumped the last hurdle.* ◇ *I jumped my horse over all the fences.*

MOVE QUICKLY | **3** [V+*adv./prep.*] to move quickly and suddenly: *He jumped to his feet when they called his name.* ◇ *She jumped up and ran out of the room.* ◇ *Do you want a ride? Jump in.* **4** [V] to make a sudden movement because of surprise, fear or excitement: *A loud bang made me jump.* ◇ *Her heart jumped when she heard the news.*

INCREASE | **5** [V] to rise suddenly by a large amount: *Prices jumped by 60% last year.* ◇ *Sales jumped from $2.7 billion to $3.5 billion.*

CHANGE SUDDENLY | **6** [V] ~ **(about) (from sth to sth)** to change suddenly from one subject to another: *I couldn't follow the talk because he kept jumping about from one topic to another.* ◇ *The story then jumps from her childhood in New York to her first visit to London.*

LEAVE OUT | **7** [VN] to leave out sth and pass to a further point or stage: *You seem to have jumped several steps in the argument.*

OF MACHINE/DEVICE | **8** [V] to move suddenly and unexpectedly, especially out of the correct position: *The needle jumped across the dial.* ◇ *The film jumped during projection.*

ATTACK | **9** ~ **(on) sb** (*informal*) to attack sb suddenly: [VN] *The thieves jumped him in a dark alleyway.* [also V]

VEHICLE | **10** [VN] (*AmE*) to get on a vehicle very quickly: *to jump a bus* **11** [VN] (*AmE*) = JUMP-START

BE LIVELY | **12** (**be jumping**) (*informal*) to be very lively: *The bar's jumping tonight.*

IDM **jump down sb's 'throat** (*informal*) to react very angrily to sb **jump the 'gun** to do sth too soon, before the right time **jump the 'lights** (*informal*) to fail to stop at a red traffic light **jump out of your 'skin** (*informal*) to move violently because of a sudden shock **jump the 'queue** (*BrE*) (*AmE* **jump the 'line**) to go to the front of a line of people without waiting for your turn **jump the 'rails** (of a train) to leave the rails suddenly **jump 'ship 1** to leave the ship on which you are serving, without permission **2** to leave an organization that you belong to, suddenly and unexpectedly **jump through 'hoops** to do sth difficult or complicated in order to achieve sth **jump 'to it** (*AmE* also **hop 'to it**) (*informal*) used to tell sb to hurry and do something quickly—more at BANDWAGON, CONCLUSION, DEEP *adj.*

PHR V **'jump at sth** to enthusiastically accept an opportunity, offer, etc. ◇ **jump 'in 1** to interrupt a conversation: *Before she could reply Peter jumped in with an objection.*

2 to start to do sth very quickly without spending a long time thinking first **'jump on sb** (*AmE* also **'jump at sb**) (*informal*) to criticize sb/sth ◇ **jump 'out at sb** to be very obvious and easily noticed: *The mistake in the figures jumped out at me.*

■ *noun*

MOVEMENT | **1** an act of jumping: *a jump of over six metres* ◇ *The story takes a jump back in time.* ◇ *Somehow he survived the jump from the third floor of the building.* ◇ *to make/do a parachute jump* ◇ *a ski jump champion* ◇ *I sat up with a jump* (= quickly and suddenly). ◇ *The negotiations took a jump forward yesterday* (= they made progress).—see also HIGH JUMP, LONG JUMP, SKI JUMP, TRIPLE JUMP

BARRIER | **2** a barrier like a narrow fence that a horse or a runner has to jump over in a race or competition: *The horse fell at the last jump.*

INCREASE | **3** ~ **(in sth)** a sudden increase in amount, price or value: *a 20 per cent jump in pre-tax profits* ◇ *unusually large price jumps*

IDM **to keep, etc. one jump ahead (of sb)** to keep your advantage over sb, especially your competitors, by taking action before they do or by making sure you know more than they do—more at RUNNING *adj.*, HIGH JUMP

'jumped-up *adj.* [only before noun] (*BrE, informal, disapproving*) thinking you are more important than you really are, particularly because you have risen in social status

jump·er /'dʒʌmpə(r)/ *noun* **1** (*BrE*) a knitted woollen or cotton piece of clothing for the upper part of the body, with long sleeves and no buttons: *a woolly jumper* **2** (*AmE*) = PINAFORE—picture on page A5 **3** a person, an animal or an insect that jumps: *He's a good jumper.*

'jumper cable *noun* (*AmE*) = JUMP LEAD

'jumping-'off point (also **'jumping-'off place**) *noun* a place from which to start a journey or new activity

jump lead /'dʒʌmp liːd/ (*BrE*) (*AmE* **'jumper cable**) *noun* [usually pl.] one of two cables that are used to start a car when it has no power in its battery. The jump leads connect the battery to the battery of another car.

'jump-off *noun* (in the sport of SHOWJUMPING) an extra part of a competition in which horses that have the same score jump again to decide the winner

'jump rope *noun*, **'jump 'rope** *verb* (*AmE*) = SKIPPING ROPE, SKIP *v.* (2)

'jump-start (*AmE* also **jump**) *verb* [VN] **1** to start the engine of a car by connecting the battery to the battery of another car with JUMP LEADS. **2** to put a lot of energy into starting a process or an activity or into making it start more quickly

jump·suit /'dʒʌmpsuːt; *BrE* also -sjuːt/ *noun* a piece of clothing that consists of trousers/pants and a jacket or shirt sewn together in one piece, worn especially by women

jumpy /'dʒʌmpi/ *adj.* (*informal*) nervous and anxious, especially because you think that sth bad is going to happen

junc·tion /'dʒʌŋkʃn/ *noun* **1** (*especially BrE*) (*AmE* usually **inter·sec·tion**) the place where two or more roads or railway/railroad lines meet: *Come off the motorway at junction 6.* ◇ *It was near the junction of City Road and Old Street.* **2** a place where two or more cables, etc. meet or are joined: *a telephone junction box*

junc·ture /'dʒʌŋktʃə(r)/ *noun* (*formal*) a particular point or stage in an activity or a series of events: *The battle had reached a crucial juncture.* ◇ *At this juncture, I would like to make an important announcement.*

June /dʒuːn/ *noun* [U, C] (*abbr.* **Jun.**) the 6th month of the year, between May and July HELP To see how **June** is used, look at the examples at **April.**

jun·gle /'dʒʌŋgl/ *noun* **1** [U, C] an area of tropical forest where trees and plants grow very thickly: *The area was covered in dense jungle.* ◇ *the jungles of South-East Asia* ◇ *jungle warfare* ◇ *Our garden is a complete jungle.* **2** [sing.] an unfriendly or dangerous place or situation, especially one where it is very difficult to be successful or to trust

æ	ɑː	e	ɜː	ə	ɪ	iː	i	ɒ	ɔː	ʌ	ʊ	u	uː
cat	father	ten	bird	about	sit	see	many	got	saw	cup	put	actual	too
								(BrE)					

anyone: *It's a jungle out there—you've got to be strong to succeed.*—see also CONCRETE JUNGLE **3** (also ˈjungle music) [U] a type of popular dance music developed in Britain in the early 1990s, with fast music and spoken words about life in cities **IDM** see LAW

ˈjungle gym *noun* (*AmE*) = CLIMBING FRAME

jun·ior /ˈdʒuːniə(r)/ *adj., noun*
■ *adj.*
OF LOW RANK | **1** [usually before noun] ~ (**to sb**) having a low rank in an organization or a profession: *junior employees* ◊ *She is junior to me.*
IN SPORT | **2** [only before noun] connected with young people below a particular age, rather than with adults, especially in sports: *the world junior tennis championships*
SON | **3** (**Junior**) (*abbr.* **Jnr, Jr.**) (especially in US) used after the name of a man who has the same name as his father, to avoid confusion—compare THE YOUNGER at YOUNG *adj.* (6)
SCHOOL/COLLEGE | **4** [only before noun] (*BrE*) (of a school or part of a school) for children under the age of 11 or 13 **5** [only before noun] (*AmE*) connected with the year before the last year in a high school or college: *I spent my junior year in France.*
—compare SENIOR
■ *noun*
LOW LEVEL JOB | **1** [C] (*especially BrE*) a person who has a job at a low level within an organization: *office juniors*
IN SPORT | **2** [C] a young person below a particular age, rather than an adult: *She has coached many of our leading juniors.*
IN SCHOOL/COLLEGE | **3** [C] (*BrE*) a child who goes to JUNIOR SCHOOL **4** [C] (*AmE*) a student in the year before the last year at high school or college—compare SOPHOMORE
SON | **5** [sing.] (*AmE, informal*) a person's young son: *I leave junior with Mom when I'm at work.*
IDM be ...years sb's ˈjunior | be sb's junior (by ...) to be younger than sb, by the number of years mentioned: *She's four years his junior.* ◊ *She's his junior by four years.*

ˌjunior ˈcollege *noun* (in the US) a college that offers programmes that are two years long. Some students go to a university or a college offering four-year programmes after they have finished studying at a junior college.

ˈjunior doctor *noun* (in Britain) a doctor who has finished medical school and who is working at a hospital to get further practical experience—compare HOUSE OFFICER, INTERN

ˌjunior ˈhigh school (also **ˌjunior ˈhigh**) *noun* [C, U] (in the US) a school for young people between the ages of 12 and 14—compare SENIOR HIGH SCHOOL

ˈjunior school *noun* [C, U] (in Britain) a school for children between the ages of 7 and 11

ju·ni·per /ˈdʒuːnɪpə(r)/ *noun* [U, C] a bush with purple berries that are used in medicine and to flavour GIN

junk /dʒʌŋk/ *noun, verb*
■ *noun* **1** [U] things that are considered useless or of little value: *I've cleared out all that old junk in the attic.* ◊ *This china came from a junk shop.* ◊ *There's nothing but junk on the TV.* **2** [U] = JUNK FOOD **3** [C] a Chinese boat with a square sail and a flat bottom
■ *verb* [VN] (*informal*) to get rid of sth because it is no longer valuable or useful

ˈjunk bond *noun* (*business*) a type of BOND that pays a high rate of interest because there is a lot of risk involved, often used to raise money quickly in order to buy the shares of another company

jun·ket /ˈdʒʌŋkɪt/ *noun* (*informal disapproving, especially AmE*) a trip that is made for pleasure by sb who works for the government, etc. and that is paid for using public money

ˈjunk food (also **junk**) *noun* [U] (also **junk foods** [pl.]) (*informal, disapproving*) food that is quick and easy to prepare and eat but that is thought to be bad for your health

junkie /ˈdʒʌŋki/ *noun* (*informal*) a drug ADDICT (= a person who is unable to stop taking dangerous drugs)

ˈjunk mail *noun* [U] (*disapproving*) advertising material that is sent to people who have not asked for it—compare SPAM

junky /ˈdʒʌŋki/ *adj.* (*informal, especially AmE*) of poor quality or of little value

junk·yard /ˈdʒʌŋkjɑːd; *AmE* -jɑːrd/ *noun* (*especially AmE*) = SCRAPYARD

junta /ˈdʒʌntə; *AmE* ˈhʊntə/ *noun* a military government that has taken power by force

Ju·pi·ter /ˈdʒuːpɪtə(r)/ *noun* the largest planet of the SOLAR SYSTEM, fifth in order of distance from the sun

jur·id·ic·al /dʒʊəˈrɪdɪkl; *AmE* dʒʊˈr-/ *adj.* [usually before noun] (*formal*) connected with the law, judges or legal matters

jur·is·dic·tion /ˌdʒʊərɪsˈdɪkʃn; *AmE* ˌdʒʊr-/ *noun* (*formal*) **1** [U, C] ~ (**over sb/sth**) | ~ (**of sb/sth**) (**to do sth**) the authority that an official organization has to make legal decisions about sb/sth **2** [C] an area or a country in which a particular system of laws has authority

jur·is·pru·dence /ˌdʒʊərɪsˈpruːdns; *AmE* ˌdʒʊr-/ *noun* [U] (*technical*) the scientific study of law: *a professor of jurisprudence*

jur·ist /ˈdʒʊərɪst; *AmE* ˈdʒʊr-/ *noun* (*formal*) a person who is an expert in law

juror /ˈdʒʊərə(r); *AmE* ˈdʒʊr-/ *noun* a member of a jury

jury /ˈdʒʊəri; *AmE* ˈdʒʊri/ *noun* (*pl.* **-ies**) [C+sing./pl. *v.*] **1** (also **panel**, **ˈjury panel** especially in *AmE*) a group of members of the public who listen to the facts of a case in a court of law and decide whether or not sb is guilty of a crime: *members of the jury* ◊ *to be/sit/serve on a jury* ◊ *The jury has/have returned a verdict of guilty.* ◊ *the right to trial by jury*—see also GRAND JURY **2** a group of people who decide who is the winner of a competition **IDM** the jury is (still) ˈout on sth used when you are saying that sth is still not certain

ˈjury service (*BrE*) (also **ˈjury duty** *AmE, BrE*) *noun* [U] a period of time spent as a member of a jury in a court of law

just /dʒʌst/ *adv., adj.*
■ *adv.* **1** ~ (**like/what/as ...**) exactly: *This jacket is just my size.* ◊ *This gadget is just the thing for getting those nails out.* ◊ *Just my luck* (= the sort of bad luck I usually have). *The phone's not working.* ◊ *You're just in time.* ◊ *She looks just like her mother.* ◊ *It's just what I wanted!* ◊ *It's just as I thought.* ◊ (*BrE*) *It's just on six* (= exactly six o'clock). **2** ~ as ... at the same moment as: *The clock struck just as I arrived.* **3** ~ as good, nice, easily, etc. no less than; equally: *She's just as smart as her sister.* ◊ *You can get there just as cheaply by plane.* **4** (only) ~| ~ after, before, under, etc. sth by a small amount: *I got here just after nine.* ◊ *I only just caught the train.* ◊ *Inflation fell to just over 4 per cent.* **5** used to say that you/sb did sth very recently: *I've just heard the news.* ◊ *When you arrived they had only just left.* ◊ *She has just been telling us about her trip to Rome.* ◊ (*especially AmE*) *I just saw him a moment ago.* ⇨ note at ALREADY **6** at this/that moment; now: *I'm just finishing my book.* ◊ *I was just beginning to enjoy myself when we had to leave.* ◊ *I'm just off* (= I am leaving now). **7** ~ about/going to do sth going to do sth only a few moments from now or then: *The water's just about to boil.* ◊ *I was just going to tell you when you interrupted.* **8** simply: *It was just an ordinary day.* ◊ *I can't just drop all my commitments.* ◊ *This essay is just not good enough.* ◊ *I didn't mean to upset you. It's just that I had to tell somebody.* ◊ *This is not just another disaster movie—it's a masterpiece.* ◊ (*spoken*) *Just because you're older than me doesn't mean you know everything.* **9** (*informal*) really; completely: *The food was just wonderful!* ◊ *I can just imagine his reaction.* **10** ~ (**for sth**) | ~ (**to do sth**) only: *I decided to learn Japanese just for fun.* ◊ *I waited an hour just to see you.* ◊ *There is just one method that might work.* ◊ *'Can I help you?' 'No thanks, I'm just looking.'* (= in a shop/store) **11** used in orders to get sb's attention, give permission, etc: *Just listen to what I'm saying, will you!* ◊ *Just help yourselves.* **12** used to make a polite request, excuse, etc: *Could you just help me with this box, please?* ◊ *I've just got a few things to do first.*

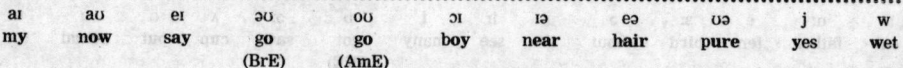

J

13 could/might/may ~ used to show a slight possibility that sth is true or will happen: *Try his home number—he might just be there.* **14** used to agree with sb: *'He's very pompous.' 'Isn't he just?'* IDM **could/might just as well ...** used to say that you/sb would have been in the same position if you had done sth else, because you got little benefit or enjoyment from what you did do: *The weather was so bad we might just as well have stayed at home.* **it is just as 'well (that ...)** it is a good thing: *It is just as well that we didn't leave any later or we'd have missed him.* **just about** (*informal*) **1** almost; very nearly: *I've met just about everyone.* ◊ *'Did you reach your sales target?' 'Just about.'* **2** approximately: *She should be arriving just about now.* **just a 'minute/ 'moment/ 'second** (*informal*) used to ask sb to wait for a short time: *'Is Mr Burns available?' 'Just a second, please, I'll check.'* **just like 'that** suddenly, without warning or explanation **just 'now 1** at this moment: *Come and see me later—I'm busy just now.* **2** during this present period: *Business is good just now.* **3** only a short time ago: *I saw her just now.* **just 'so** done or arranged very accurately or carefully: *He liked polishing the furniture and making everything just so.* **just 'then** at that moment: *Just then, someone knocked at the front door.* **not just 'yet** not now but probably quite soon: *I can't give you the money just yet.* **I, etc. would just as soon do sth** used to say that you would equally well like to do sth, as do sth else that has been suggested: *I'd just as soon stay at home as go out tonight.*—more at CASE *n.*, JOB
■ *adj.* [usually before noun] **1** that most people consider to be morally fair and reasonable: *a just decision/law/society* **2 (the just)** *noun* [pl.] people who are just **3** appropriate in a particular situation: *a just reward/punishment* ◊ *I think she got her just deserts* (= what she deserved). OPP UNJUST ► **just·ly** *adv.*: *to be treated justly* ◊ *to be justly proud of sth*

just·ice /ˈdʒʌstɪs/ *noun* **1** [U] the fair treatment of people: *laws based on the principles of justice* ◊ *They are demanding equal rights and justice.* OPP INJUSTICE—see also POETIC JUSTICE, ROUGH JUSTICE **2** [U] the quality of being fair or reasonable: *Who can deny the justice of their cause?* OPP INJUSTICE **3** [U] the legal system used to punish people who have committed crimes: *the criminal justice system* ◊ *The European Court of Justice*—see also MISCARRIAGE OF JUSTICE **4** (also **Just·ice**) [C] (*AmE*) a judge in a court of law (also used before the name of a judge): *Supreme Court Justice Sandra Day O'Connor*—see also CHIEF JUSTICE **5** (**Just·ice**) [C] (*BrE*) used before the name of a judge in the HIGH COURT: *Mr Justice Davies* IDM **bring sb to 'justice** to arrest sb for a crime and put them on trial in a court of law **do justice to 'sb/'sth; do sb/sth 'justice 1** to treat or represent sb/sth fairly, especially in a way that shows how good, attractive, etc. they are: *That photo doesn't do you justice.* **2** to deal with sb/sth correctly and completely: *You cannot do justice to such a complex situation in just a few pages.* **do yourself 'justice** to do sth as well as you can in order to show other people how good you are: *She didn't do herself justice in the exam.*—more at PERVERT *v.*

Justice of the 'Peace *noun* (*pl.* **Justices of the Peace**) (*abbr.* **JP**) an official who acts as a judge in the lowest courts of law SYN MAGISTRATE

jus·ti·fi·able /ˈdʒʌstɪfaɪəbl; ˌdʒʌstɪˈfaɪəbl/ *adj.* existing or done for a good reason, and therefore acceptable SYN LEGITIMATE: *justifiable criticism/pride* ◊ *justifiable homicide* ► **jus·ti·fi·ably** /-əbli/ *adv.*: *The university can be justifiably proud of its record.*

jus·ti·fi·ca·tion /ˌdʒʌstɪfɪˈkeɪʃn/ *noun* [U, C] ~ (for sth/ doing sth) a good reason why sth exists or is done: *I can see no possible justification for any further tax increases.* ◊ *He was getting angry—and with some justification.* IDM **in justifi'cation (of sb/sth)** as an explanation of why sth exists or why sb has done sth: *All I can say in justification of her actions is that she was under a lot of pressure at work.*

jus·ti·fied /ˈdʒʌstɪfaɪd/ *adj.* **1** ~ (in doing sth) having a good reason for doing sth: *She felt fully justified in asking for her money back.* **2** existing or done for a good reason: *His fears proved justified.*

jus·tify /ˈdʒʌstɪfaɪ/ *verb* (**jus·ti·fies, jus·ti·fy·ing, jus·ti·fied, jus·ti·fied**) **1** to show that sb/sth is right or reasonable: [V-ing] *How can they justify paying such huge salaries?* ◊ [VN] *Her success had justified the faith her teachers had put in her.* [also VN-ing] **2** ~ sth (to sb) to give an explanation or excuse for sth or for doing sth: [VN] *The Prime Minister has been asked to justify the decision to Parliament.* ◊ *You don't need to justify yourself to me.* [also V-ing, VN-ing] **3** [VN] (*technical*) to arrange lines of printed text so that one or both edges are straight IDM see END *n.*

,just-,in-'time *adj.* (*business*) used to describe a system in which parts or materials are only delivered to a factory just before they are needed

jut /dʒʌt/ *verb* (**-tt-**) ~ (out) (from, into, over sth) to stick out further than the surrounding surface, objects, etc.; to make sth stick out SYN PROJECT: [V] *A row of small windows jutted out from the roof.* ◊ *A rocky headland jutted into the sea.* ◊ *a jutting chin* ◊ [VN] *She jutted her chin out stubbornly.*

jute /dʒuːt/ *noun* [U] FIBRES (= thin threads) from a plant, also called **jute**, used for making rope and rough fabric

ju·ven·ile /ˈdʒuːvənaɪl; *AmE* -vənl/ *adj., noun*
■ *adj.* **1** [only before noun] (*formal or law*) connected with young people who are not yet adults: *juvenile crime/ employment* ◊ *juvenile offenders* **2** (*disapproving*) silly and more typical of a child than an adult SYN CHILDISH: *juvenile behaviour* ◊ *Don't be so juvenile!*
■ *noun* (*formal or law*) a young person who is not yet an adult

,juvenile 'court *noun* a court of law that deals with young people who are not yet adults

,juvenile de'linquent *noun* a young person who is not yet an adult and who is guilty of committing a crime, for example damaging property ► **,juvenile de'linquency** *noun* [U]

juxta·pose /ˌdʒʌkstəˈpəʊz; *AmE* -ˈpoʊz/ *verb* [VN] [usually passive] ~ A and/with B (*formal*) to put people or things together, especially in order to show a contrast or a new relationship between them: *In the exhibition, abstract paintings are juxtaposed with shocking photographs.* ► **juxta·pos·ition** /ˌdʒʌkstəpəˈzɪʃn/ *noun* [U, C]: *the juxtaposition of realistic and surreal situations in the novel*

Kk

K /keɪ/ *noun, abbr.*

■ *noun* (also **k**) [C, U] (*pl.* **K's**, **k's** /keɪz/) the 11th letter of the English alphabet: *'King' begins with (a) K/'K'.*

■ *abbr.* (*pl.* **K**) **1** (*informal*) one thousand: *She earns 40K (= £40000) a year.* **2** kilometre(s): *a 10K race* **3** (*computing*) KILOBYTE(S) **4** KELVIN(S)

kaf·tan (also **caf·tan**) /'kæftæn/ *noun* **1** a long loose piece of clothing, usually with a belt at the waist, worn by men in Arab countries **2** a woman's long loose dress with long wide sleeves

kale /keɪl/ *noun* [U] (*AmE* also **'collard greens** [pl.]) a dark green vegetable like a CABBAGE

kal·eido·scope /kə'laɪdəskəʊp; *AmE* -skoʊp/ *noun* **1** [C] a toy consisting of a tube that you look through with loose pieces of coloured glass and mirrors at the end. When the tube is turned, the pieces of glass move and form different patterns **2** [sing.] a situation, pattern, etc. containing a lot of different parts that are always changing ▶ **kal·eido·scop·ic** /kə,laɪdə'skɒpɪk; *AmE* -'skɑːpɪk/ *adj.*

kami·kaze /,kæmɪ'kɑːzi/ *adj.* [only before noun] (from *Japanese*) used to describe the way soldiers attack the enemy, knowing that they too will be killed: *a kamikaze pilot/attack* ◊ (*figurative*) *He made a kamikaze run across three lanes of traffic.*

kan·ga·roo /,kæŋgə'ruː/ *noun* (*pl.* **-oos**) a large Australian animal with a strong tail and back legs, that moves by jumping. The female carries its young in a pocket of skin (called a POUCH) on the front of its body.—picture on page A6

,kangaroo 'court *noun* (*disapproving*) an illegal court of law that punishes people unfairly

kao·lin /'keɪəlɪn/ (also **,china 'clay**) *noun* [U] a type of fine white clay used in some medicines and in making PORCELAIN for cups, plates, etc.

kapok /'keɪpɒk; *AmE* -pɑːk/ *noun* [U] a soft white material used for filling cushions, soft toys, etc.

kaput /kə'pʊt/ *adj.* [not before noun] (*spoken*) not working correctly; broken: *The truck's kaput.*

kara·oke /,kæri'əʊki; *AmE* -'oʊki/ *noun* (from *Japanese*) a type of entertainment in which a machine plays only the music of popular songs so that people can sing the words themselves: *a karaoke machine/night/bar*

karat (*AmE*) = CARAT

kar·ate /kə'rɑːti/ *noun* [U] a Japanese system of fighting in which you use your hands and feet as weapons: *a karate chop* (= a blow with the side of the hand)

karma /'kɑːmə; *AmE* 'kɑːrmə/ *noun* (in Buddhism and Hinduism) the sum of sb's good and bad actions in one of their lives, believed to decide their fate in the next

kayak /'kaɪæk/ *noun* a light CANOE in which the part where you sit is covered over—picture at BOAT

KC /,keɪ 'siː/ *noun* the highest level of BARRISTER, who can speak for the government in a court of law in Britain. KC is an abbreviation for 'King's Counsel' and is used when there is a king in Britain.—compare QC

kebab /kɪ'bæb/ (also **'shish kebab** especially in *AmE*) *noun* small pieces of meat and vegetables cooked on a wooden or metal stick

kedg·eree /'kedʒəriː/ *noun* [U] a hot dish of rice, fish and eggs cooked together

keel /kiːl/ *noun, verb*

■ *noun* the long piece of wood or steel along the bottom of a ship, on which the frame is built, and which helps it to keep upright in the water **IDM** see EVEN *adj.*—picture at YACHT

■ *verb* [V, VN] if a ship or boat **keels**, or sth **keels** it, it falls over onto its side **SYN** CAPSIZE **PHR V** **,keel 'over** to fall over sideways or forwards: *Several of them keeled over in the heat.*

keen /kiːn/ *adj., verb*

■ *adj.* (**keen·er**, **keen·est**)

EAGER/ENTHUSIASTIC | **1** (*especially BrE*) ~ (to do sth)| ~ (that …)| ~ (on doing sth) wanting to do sth or wanting sth to happen very much **SYN** EAGER: *John was very keen to help.* ◊ *We are keen that Britain should get involved too.* ◊ *I wasn't too keen on going to the party.* **2** [usually before noun] enthusiastic about an activity or idea, etc: *a keen sportsman* ◊ *one of the keenest supporters of the team*

LIKING SB/STH | **3** ~ **on sb/sth/on doing sth** (*BrE, informal*) liking sb/sth very much; very interested in sb/sth: *Tom's very keen on Anna.* ◊ *She's not keen on being told what to do.*

CLEVER | **4** [only before noun] quick to understand: *a keen mind/intellect*

IDEAS/FEELINGS | **5** [usually before noun] strong or deep: *a keen sense of tradition* ◊ *He took a keen interest in his grandson's education.*

SENSES | **6** [only before noun] highly developed; sharp: *Dogs have a keen sense of smell.* ◊ *My friend has **a keen eye for** (= is good at noticing) a bargain.*

COMPETITION | **7** involving people competing very hard with each other for sth: *There is keen competition for places at the college.*

PRICES | **8** (*especially BrE*) kept low in order to compete with other prices

WIND | **9** (*literary*) extremely cold

KNIFE | **10** [usually before noun] (*literary*) having a sharp edge or point

▶ **keen·ly** *adv.*: *a keenly fought contest* ◊ *We were keenly aware of the danger.* **keen·ness** *noun* [U]

IDM (as) **,keen as 'mustard** (*BrE, informal*) wanting very much to do well at sth; enthusiastic—more at MAD

■ *verb* [V] (usually used in the progressive tenses) (*old-fashioned*) to make a loud high sad sound, when sb has died

keep /kiːp/ *verb, noun*

■ *verb* (**kept, kept** /kept/)

STAY | **1** to stay in a particular condition or position; to make sb/sth do this: [V-ADJ] *We huddled together to keep warm.* ◊ [V+adv./prep.] *The notice said 'Keep off* (= Do not walk on) *the grass'.* ◊ *Keep left along the wall.* ◊ [VN-ADJ] *She kept the children amused for hours.* ◊ [VN] [usually+adv./prep.] *He kept his coat on.* ◊ *Don't keep us in suspense—what happened next?* ◊ *She had trouble keeping her balance.* ◊ [VN-ing] *I'm very sorry to keep you waiting.*

CONTINUE | **2** [V-ing] ~ **(on) doing sth** to continue doing sth; to do sth repeatedly: *Keep smiling!* ◊ *I wish you wouldn't keep on interrupting me!*

DELAY | **3** [VN] to delay sb: *You're an hour late—what kept you?*

NOT GIVE BACK | **4** [VN] to continue to have sth and not give it back or throw it away: *Here's a five dollar bill—please keep the change.* ◊ *I keep all her letters.*

SAVE FOR SB | **5** ~ **sth (for sb)**| ~ **sb sth** (*especially BrE*) to save sth for sb: [VN, VNN] *Please keep a seat for me.* ◊ *Please keep me a seat.*

PUT/STORE | **6** [VN+adv./prep.] to put or store sth in a particular place: *Keep your passport in a safe place.*

SHOP/RESTAURANT | **7** [VN] (*especially BrE*) to own and manage a shop/store or restaurant: *Her father kept a grocer's shop.*

s	t	v	z	ʃ	ʒ	tʃ	dʒ	θ	ð	ŋ
see	tea	van	zoo	shoe	vision	chain	jam	thin	this	sing

ANIMALS | 8 [VN] to own and care for animals: *to keep bees/ goats/hens*

ABOUT HEALTH | 9 [V+*adv./prep.*] (*spoken*) used to ask or talk about sb's health: *How is your mother keeping?* ◇ *We're all keeping well.*

OF FOOD | 10 [V] to remain in good condition: *Finish off the pie—it won't keep.* ◇ (*spoken, figurative*) *'I'd love to hear about it, but I'm late already.' 'That's OK—it'll keep* (= I can tell you about it later).

SECRET | 11 ~ a secret | ~ sth secret (from sb) to know sth and not tell it to anyone: [VN] *Can you keep a secret?* ◇ [VN-ADJ] *She kept her past secret from us all.*

PROMISE/APPOINTMENT | 12 [VN] **~ your promise/word | ~ an appointment** to do what you have promised to do; to go where you have agreed to go: *She kept her promise to visit them.* ◇ *He failed to keep his appointment at the clinic.*

DIARY/RECORD | 13 [VN] **~ a diary, an account, a record, etc.** to write down sth as a record: *She kept a diary for over twenty years.* ◇ *Keep a note of where each item can be found.*

SUPPORT SB | 14 [VN] to provide what is necessary for sb to live; to support sb financially: *He scarcely earns enough to keep himself and his family.*

PROTECT | 15 ~ sb (from sth) (*formal*) to protect sb from sth: *May the Lord bless you and keep you* (= used in prayers in the Christian Church). ◇ *His only thought was to keep the boy from harm.*

IN SPORT | 16 [VN] **~ goal/wicket** (*BrE*) (in football, hockey, cricket, etc.) to guard or protect the goal or WICKET—see also GOALKEEPER, WICKETKEEPER

IDM Most idioms containing **keep** are at the entries for the nouns and adjectives in the idioms, for example **keep house** is at **house**. **,keep 'going 1** to make an effort to live normally when you are in a difficult situation or when you have experienced great suffering: *You just have to keep yourself busy and keep going.* **2** (*spoken*) used to encourage sb to continue doing sth: *Keep going, Sarah, you're nearly there.* **,keep sb 'going** (*informal*) to be enough for sb until they get what they are waiting for: *Have an apple to keep you going till dinner time.*

PHRV ,keep sb 'after (*AmE*) = KEEP SB BACK (1)

,keep 'at sth to continue working at sth: *Come on, keep at it, you've nearly finished!* **,keep sb 'at sth** to make sb continue working at sth: *He kept us at it all day.*

,keep a'way (from sb/sth) to avoid going near sb/sth: *Keep away from the edge of the cliff.* **,keep sb/sth a'way (from sb/sth)** to prevent sb/sth from going somewhere: *Her illness kept her away from work for several weeks.*

,keep 'back (from sb/sth) to stay at a distance from sb/sth: *Keep well back from the road.* **,keep sb↔'back 1** (*BrE*) (*AmE* **,keep sb 'after**) to make a student stay at school after normal hours as a punishment **2** (*AmE*) to make a student repeat a year at school because of poor marks/grades **,keep sb↔'back (from sb/sth)** to make sb stay at a distance from sb/sth: *Barricades were erected to keep back the crowds.* **,keep sth↔'back 1** to prevent a feeling, etc. from being expressed **SYN** RESTRAIN: *She was unable to keep back her tears.* **2** to continue to have a part of sth: *He kept back half the money for himself.* **,keep sth↔'back (from sb)** to refuse to tell sb sth: *I'm sure she's keeping something back from us.*

,keep 'down to hide yourself by not standing up straight: *Keep down! You mustn't let anyone see you.* **,keep sb↔'down** to prevent a person, group, etc. from expressing themselves freely: *The people have been kept down for years by a brutal regime.* **,keep sth↔'down 1** to make sth stay at a low level; to avoid increasing sth: *to keep down wages/prices/the cost of living* ◇ *Keep your voice down—I don't want anyone else to hear.* ◇ *Keep the noise down* (= be quiet), *will you?* **2** to not bring sth back through the mouth from the stomach; to not VOMIT: *She's had some water but she can't keep any food down.*

'keep from sth| 'keep yourself from sth to prevent yourself from doing sth: [+-ing] *She could hardly keep from laughing.* ◇ *I just managed to keep myself from falling.* **'keep sb from sth** to prevent sb from doing sth: *I hope I'm not keeping you from your work.* ◇[+-ing] *The church*

bells keep me from sleeping. **'keep sth from sb** to avoid telling sb sth: *I think we ought to keep the truth from him until he's better.* **'keep sth from sth** to make sth stay out of sth: *She could not keep the dismay from her voice.*

,keep 'in with sb (*BrE, informal*) to make sure that you stay friendly with sb, because you will get an advantage from doing so **,keep sth↔'in** to avoid expressing an emotion **SYN** RESTRAIN: *He could scarcely keep in his indignation.* **,keep sb 'in** to make sb stay indoors or in a particular place **'keep sb/yourself in sth** to provide sb/yourself with a regular supply of sth: *The money should keep him in cigarettes for a week.*

,keep 'off if rain, snow, etc. keeps off, it does not fall **,keep 'off sth 1** to avoid eating, drinking or smoking sth: *I'm trying to keep off fatty foods.* **2** to avoid mentioning a particular subject: *It's best to keep off politics when my father's around.* **,keep sb/sth↔'off| ,keep sb/sth 'off sb/sth** to prevent sb/sth from coming near, touching, etc. sb/sth: *They lit a fire to keep off wild animals.* ◇ *Keep your hands off* (= do not touch) *me!*

,keep 'on to continue: *The rain kept on all night.* ◇ *Keep on until you get to the church.* **,keep sb↔'on** to continue to employ sb **,keep sth 'on** to continue to rent a house, flat/apartment, etc. **,keep 'on (at sb) (about sb/sth)** (*especially BrE*) to speak to sb often and in an annoying way about sb/sth **SYN** NAG: *He does keep on so!* ◇ *I'll do it—just don't keep on at me about it!*

,keep 'out (of sth) to not enter a place; to stay outside: *The sign said 'Ministry of Defence—Keep Out!'.* **,keep sb/ sth↔'out (of sth)** to prevent sb/sth from entering a place: *Keep that dog out of my study!* **,keep 'out of sth| ,keep sb 'out of sth** to avoid sth; to prevent sb from being involved in sth or affected by sth: *That child seems incapable of keeping out of mischief.* ◇ *Keep the baby out of the sun.*

'keep to sth 1 to avoid leaving a path, road, etc: *Keep to the track—the land is very boggy around here.* **2** to talk or write only about the subject that you are supposed to talk or write about: *Nothing is more irritating than people who do not keep to the point.* **3** to do what you have promised or agreed to do: *to keep to an agreement/an undertaking/ a plan* **4** to stay in and not leave a particular place or position: *She's nearly 90 and mostly keeps to her room.* **,keep yourself to your'self| ,keep sth to your'self** to avoid meeting people socially or becoming involved in their affairs: *Nobody knows much about him; he keeps himself very much to himself.* **,keep sth to your'self** to not tell other people about sth: *I'd be grateful if you kept this information to yourself.* ◇ *Kindly keep your opinions to yourself in future!*

,keep sb 'under to control or OPPRESS sb: *The local people are kept under by the army.*

,keep 'up if particular weather keeps up, it continues without stopping: *The rain kept up all afternoon.* **,keep 'up (with sb/sth)** to move, make progress or increase at the same rate as sb/sth: *Slow down—I can't keep up!* ◇ *I can't keep up with all the changes.* ◇ *Wages are not keeping up with inflation.* **,keep 'up with sb** to continue to be in contact with sb: *How many of your old school friends do you keep up with?* **,keep 'up with sth 1** to learn about or be aware of the news, current events, etc: *She likes to keep up with the latest fashions.* **2** to continue to pay or do sth regularly: *If you do not keep up with the payments you could lose your home.* **,keep sb 'up** to prevent sb from going to bed: *I hope we're not keeping you up.* **,keep sth↔'up 1** to make sth stay at a high level: *The high cost of raw materials is keeping prices up.* **2** to continue sth at the same, usually high, level: *The enemy kept up the bombardment day and night.* ◇ *We're having difficulty keeping up our mortgage payments.* ◇ *Well done! Keep up the good work/Keep it up!* **3** to make sth remain at a high level: *They sang songs to keep their spirits up.* **4** to continue to use or practise sth: *to keep up old customs/ traditions* ◇ *Do you still keep up your Spanish?* **5** to take care of a house, garden/yard, etc. so that it stays in good condition **SYN** MAINTAIN—related noun UPKEEP

■ *noun* **1** [U] food, clothes and all the other things that a person needs to live; the cost of these things: *It's about*

K

time you got a job to **earn your keep. 2** [C] a large strong tower, built as part of an old castle
IDM for 'keeps (*informal*) for ever: *Is it yours for keeps or does he want it back?*—more at EARN

keep·er /ˈkiːpə(r)/ *noun* **1** (especially in compounds) a person whose job is to look after a building, its contents or sth valuable: *the keeper of geology at the museum*—see also SHOPKEEPER **2** a person whose job is to look after animals, especially in a ZOO—see also GAMEKEEPER, ZOO-KEEPER **3** (*BrE, informal*) = GOALKEEPER, WICKETKEEPER

keep·ing /ˈkiːpɪŋ/ *noun* **IDM in sb's 'keeping** being taken care of by sb—see also SAFE KEEPING **in 'keeping (with sth)** appropriate or expected in a particular situation; in agreement with sth: *The latest results are in keeping with our earlier findings.* **out of 'keeping (with sth)** not appropriate or expected in a particular situation; not in agreement with sth: *The painting is out of keeping with the rest of the room.*

keep·sake /ˈkiːpseɪk/ *noun* a small object that sb gives you so that you will remember them **SYN** MEMENTO

keg /keg/ *noun* **1** [C] a round wooden or metal container with a flat top and bottom, used especially for storing beer, like a BARREL but smaller **2** [U] (*BrE*) = KEG BEER

'keg beer (*BrE also* **keg**) *noun* [U, C] (in Britain) beer served from metal containers, using gas pressure

kelp /kelp/ *noun* [U] a type of brown SEAWEED, sometimes used as a FERTILIZER to help plants grow

kel·vin /ˈkelvɪn/ *noun* [C, U] (*abbr.* **K**) a unit for measuring temperature. One degree kelvin is equal to one degree Celsius.

ken /ken/ *noun, verb*
■ *noun* **IDM beyond your ken** (*old-fashioned*) if sth is **beyond your ken**, you do not know enough about it to be able to understand it
■ *verb* (**-nn-**) [V, VN, V(**that**), V**wh-**] (*ScotE, NorthE*) to know **HELP** Kent is the usual form of the past tense used in Scotland.

ken·nel /ˈkenl/ *noun* **1** (*AmE* **dog·house**) a small hut for a dog to sleep in **2** (usually **kennels**) [C+sing./pl. *v.*] a place where people can leave their dogs to be looked after when they go on holiday/vacation; a place where dogs are bred: *We put the dog in kennels when we go away.*—see also BOARDING KENNEL

kept *pt, pp* of KEEP

kept 'woman *noun* (*old-fashioned*, usually *humorous*) a woman who is given money and a home by a man who visits her regularly to have sex

kerb (*BrE*) (*AmE* **curb**) /kɜːb; *AmE* kɜːrb/ *noun* the edge of the raised path at the side of a road, usually made of long pieces of stone: *The bus mounted the kerb* (= went onto the pavement/sidewalk) *and hit a tree.*

'kerb-crawling *noun* [U] (*BrE*) the crime of driving slowly along a road in order to find a prostitute ► **'kerb-crawler** *noun*

kerb·side (*BrE*) (*AmE* **curb·side**) /ˈkɜːbsaɪd; *AmE* ˈkɜːrb-/ *noun* [U] the side of the street or path near the kerb: *to stand at the kerbside*

ker·chief /ˈkɜːtʃɪf; *AmE* ˈkɜːrtʃɪf/ *noun* (*old-fashioned*) a square piece of fabric worn on the head or around the neck

ker·fuf·fle /kəˈfʌfl; *AmE* kərˈf-/ *noun* [sing.] (*BrE, informal*) unnecessary excitement or activity **SYN** COMMOTION: *What's all the kerfuffle about?*

ker·nel /ˈkɜːnl; *AmE* ˈkɜːrnl/ *noun* **1** the inner part of a nut or seed, or of the stone/pit of a fruit **2** the central, most important part of an idea or a subject: *the kernel of her argument*

kero·sene (*also* **kero·sine**) /ˈkerəsiːn/ *noun* [U] (*especially AmE*) = PARAFFIN: *a kerosene lamp*

kes·trel /ˈkestrəl/ *noun* a small BIRD OF PREY (= a bird that kills other creatures for food) of the FALCON family

ketch /ketʃ/ *noun* a sailing boat with two MASTS (= posts to support the sails)

ketchup /ˈketʃəp/ *noun* [U] a thick cold sauce made from tomatoes, usually sold in bottles

ket·tle /ˈketl/ *noun* a container with a lid, handle and a

SPOUT, used for boiling water: *an electric kettle* ◊ (*BrE*) *I'll put the kettle on* (= start boiling some water) *and make some tea.*—picture on page 274 **IDM** see DIFFERENT, POT *n.*

kettle·drum /ˈketldrʌm/ *noun* a large metal drum with a round bottom and a thin plastic top that can be made looser or tighter to produce different musical notes. A set of kettledrums is usually called TIMPANI.

key /kiː/ *noun, verb, adj.*
■ *noun*
TOOL FOR LOCK **1** a specially shaped piece of metal used for locking a door, starting a car, etc: *to insert/turn the key in the lock* ◊ *the car keys* ◊ *a bunch of keys* ◊ *the spare key to the front door* ◊ *We'll have a duplicate key cut* (= made). ◊ *There's a special key for winding up this clock.*
MOST IMPORTANT THING **2** [usually sing.] **~ (to sth)** a thing that makes you able to understand or achieve sth: *The key to success is preparation.* ◊ *The driver of the car probably holds the key to solving the crime.* ◊ (*especially AmE*) *The key is, how long can the federal government control the inflation rate?*
ON COMPUTER **3** any of the buttons that you press to operate a computer or TYPEWRITER: *Press the return key to enter the information.*
ON MUSICAL INSTRUMENT **4** any of the wooden or metal parts that you press to play a piano and some other musical instruments—picture on page 840
MUSIC **5** a set of related notes, based on a particular note. Pieces of music are usually written mainly using a particular key: *a sonata in the key of E flat major* ◊ *This piece changes key many times.*—compare SCALE *n.* (7)
ANSWERS **6** a set of answers to exercises or problems: *Check your answers in the key at the back of the book.*
ON MAP **7** an explanation of the symbols used on a map or plan
—see also LOW-KEY **IDM** see LOCK *n.*
■ *verb* [VN] **~ sth (in)** | **~ sth (into sth)** to put information into a computer using a keyboard **SYN** ENTER: *Key (in) your password.*
PHRV 'key sb/sth to sth [usually passive] (*especially AmE*) to make sb/sth suitable or appropriate for a particular purpose: *The classes are keyed to the needs of advanced students.*
■ *adj.* [only before noun] most important; essential: *the key issue/factor/point* ◊ *He was a key figure in the campaign.* ◊ *She played a key role in the dispute.*

key·board /ˈkiːbɔːd; *AmE* -bɔːrd/ *noun, verb*
■ *noun* **1** the set of keys for operating a computer or TYPE-WRITER—picture on page 250 **2** the set of black and white keys on a piano or other musical instrument—picture at PIANO **3** an electronic musical instrument that has keys like a piano and can be made to play in different styles or to sound like different instruments—compare SYNTHE-SIZER—picture on page 841
■ *verb* [VN, V] to type information into a computer ► **key·board·ing** *noun* [U]

key·board·er /ˈkiːbɔːdə(r); *AmE* -bɔːrd-/ *noun* a person whose job is to type data into a computer

keyed 'up *adj.* [not before noun] nervous and excited, especially before an important event

key·hole /ˈkiːhəʊl; *AmE* -hoʊl/ *noun* the hole in a lock that you put a key in

keyhole 'surgery *noun* [U] a medical operation which involves only a very small cut being made in the patient's body

key·note /ˈkiːnəʊt; *AmE* -noʊt/ *noun* [usually sing.] the central idea of a book, a speech, etc: *Choice is the keynote of the new education policy.* ◊ *a keynote speech/speaker* (= a very important one, introducing a meeting or its subject) ► **key·noter** *noun*: *For the first time, a woman will be the keynoter at the convention this year.*

key·pad /ˈkiːpæd/ *noun* a small set of buttons with numbers on used to operate a telephone, television, etc.; the buttons on the right of a computer keyboard

'key ring *noun* a small ring that you put keys on to keep them together

aɪ	aʊ	eɪ	əʊ	oʊ	ɔɪ	ɪə	eə	ʊə	j	w
my	now	say	go	go	boy	near	hair	pure	yes	wet
			(BrE)	(AmE)						

'key signature noun (music) the set of marks at the beginning of a printed piece of music to show what KEY the piece is in—picture at MUSIC

key·stone /'ki:stəʊn; AmE -stoʊn/ noun **1** (architecture) the central stone at the top of an arch that keeps all the other stones in position **2** [usually sing.] (written) the most important part of a plan or argument that the other parts depend on

kg abbr. (pl. **kg** or **kgs**) (in writing) kilogram(s): *10kg*

khaki /'kɑːki/ noun [U] **1** a strong greenish or yellowish brown fabric, used especially for making military uniforms **2** a dull greenish or yellowish brown colour ▶ **khaki** adj.: *khaki uniforms*

kHz abbr. (in writing) KILOHERTZ

kib·butz /kɪ'bʊts/ noun (pl. **kib·butz·im** /ˌkɪbʊt'siːm/) (in Israel) a type of farm or factory where a group of people live together and share all the work, decisions and income

kick /kɪk/ verb, noun

■ verb **1** [often +adv. / prep.] to hit sb/sth with your foot: [VN] *She was punched and kicked by her attackers.* ◊ *The boys were kicking a ball around in the yard.* ◊ *Vandals had kicked the door down.* ◊ [V] *Stop kicking—it hurts!* [also VN-ADJ] **2** to move your legs as if you were kicking sth: [VN] *The dancers kicked their legs in the air.* ◊ [V] *The child was dragged away, kicking and screaming.* **3** [VN] **~ yourself** (informal) to be annoyed with yourself because you have done sth stupid, missed an opportunity, etc: *He'll kick himself when he finds out he could have had the job.* **4** [VN] (in sports such as football and rugby) to score points by kicking the ball: *to kick a penalty/goal* **IDM** **kick (some/sb's) 'ass** (slang, especially AmE) to punish or defeat sb **kick the 'bucket** (informal or humorous) to die **kick the 'habit, 'drug, 'booze, etc.** to stop doing sth harmful that you have done for a long time **kick your 'heels** (BrE) to have nothing to do while you are waiting for sb/sth: *We were kicking our heels, waiting for some customers.* **kick sb in the 'teeth** to treat sb badly or fail to give them help when they need it **kick over the 'traces** (old-fashioned, BrE) to start to behave badly and refuse to accept any discipline or control **kick up a 'fuss, 'stink, etc.** (informal) to complain loudly about sth **kick up your 'heels** (informal, especially AmE) to be relaxed and enjoy yourself **kick sb up'stairs** (informal) to move sb to a job that seems to be more important but which actually has less power or influence **kick sb when they're 'down** to continue to hurt sb when they are already defeated, etc.—more at ALIVE, HELL **PHR V** **ˌkick aˈbout/aˈround** (informal) **1** (usually used in the progressive tenses) to be lying somewhere not being used: *There's a pen kicking around on my desk somewhere.* **2** to go from one place to another with no particular purpose: *They spent the summer kicking around Europe.* **ˌkick sb aˈround** (informal) to treat sb in a rough or unfair way **ˌkick sth aˈbout/aˈround** (informal) to discuss a plan, a plan, etc. in an informal way **ˈkick against sth** to protest about or resist sth: *Young people often kick against the rules.* **ˌkick ˈback** (especially AmE) to relax: *Kick back and enjoy the summer.* **ˌkick ˈin** (informal) **1** to begin to take effect: *Reforms will kick in later this year.* **2** (also **ˌkick ˈin sth**) (both AmE) to give your share of money or help **ˌkick ˈoff** when a football game or a team, etc. **kicks off**, the game starts—related noun KICK-OFF **ˌkick ˈoff (with sth)** (informal) to start: *What time shall we kick off?* ◊ *Tom will kick off with a few comments.*—related noun KICK-OFF **ˌkick sth↔ˈoff** to remove sth by kicking: *to kick off your shoes* **ˌkick ˈoff sth** to start a discussion, a meeting, an event, etc. **ˌkick ˈout (at sb/sth)** **1** to try to hit sb/sth with your legs because you are angry or upset **2** to react violently to sb/sth that makes you angry or upset **ˌkick sb ˈout (of sth)** (informal) to make sb leave or go away (from somewhere) **ˌkick ˈup** (especially AmE) (of wind or a storm) to become stronger **ˌkick sth↔ˈup** to make sth, especially dust, rise from the ground

■ noun **1** a movement with the foot or the leg, usually to hit sth with the foot: *the first kick of the game* ◊ *She gave him a kick on the shin.* ◊ *He aimed a kick at the dog.* ◊ *If the*

door won't open, give it a kick. ◊ (slang) *She needs a kick up the backside* (= she needs to be strongly encouraged to do sth or to behave better).—see also FREE KICK **2** (informal) a strong feeling of excitement and pleasure: *I get a kick out of driving fast cars.* ◊ *He gets his kicks from skiing.* ◊ *What do you do for kicks?* **3** [usually sing.] (informal) the strong effect that a drug or an alcoholic drink has: *This drink has quite a kick.* **IDM** **a kick in the 'teeth** (informal) a great disappointment; sth that hurts sb/sth

kick·back /'kɪkbæk/ noun [often pl.] (informal, especially AmE) money paid illegally to sb in return for work or help **SYN** BRIBE

'kick-boxing noun [U] a form of boxing in which the people fighting each other can kick as well as PUNCH (= hit with their hands)

kick·er /'kɪkə(r)/ noun **1** a person who kicks, especially the player in a sports team who kicks the ball to try to score points, for example in rugby **2** (AmE, informal) a surprising end to a series of events

kick·ing /'kɪkɪŋ/ adj. (informal) full of life and excitement: *The club was really kicking last night.*

'kick-off noun **1** [C, U] the start of a game of football: *The kick-off is at 3.* **2** [sing.] (informal) the start of an activity

kick·stand /'kɪkstænd/ noun a metal rod fixed to a bicycle or a motorcycle, which is kept horizontal while the bicycle is being ridden but which can be moved to a vertical position when you need to stand the bicycle somewhere

'kick-start verb, noun

■ verb [VN] **1** to start a motorcycle by pushing down a LEVER with your foot **2** to do sth to help a process or project start more quickly: *The government's attempt to kick-start the economy has failed.*

■ noun **1** (also **'kick-starter**) the part of a motorcycle that you push down with your foot in order to start it **2** a quick start that you give to sth by taking some action

kid /kɪd/ noun, verb, adj.

■ noun **1** [C] (informal) a child or young person: *A bunch of kids were hanging around outside.* ◊ *a kid of 15* ◊ *She's a bright kid.* ◊ *How are the kids* (= your children)*?* ◊ *Do you have any kids?* **HELP** **Kid** is much more common than **child** in informal and spoken AmE. **2** [C] (spoken) used when speaking to a person who is younger than you: *Hey, kid, what's wrong?* **3** [C] a young goat **4** [U] soft leather made from the skin of a young goat: *a pair of white kid gloves* **IDM** **handle/treat, etc. sb with kid 'gloves** to deal with sb in a very careful way so that you do not offend or upset them **'kids' stuff** (BrE) (AmE **'kid stuff**) something that is easy to do or understand, especially when this means that it is boring

■ verb (-dd-) (informal) **1** (usually used in the progressive tenses) to tell sb sth that is not true, especially as a joke **SYN** JOKE: [V] *I thought he was kidding when he said he was going out with a rock star.* ◊ *I didn't mean it. I was only kidding.* ◊ [VN] *I'm not kidding you. It does work.* **2** **~ sb/yourself** to allow sb/yourself to believe sth that is not true **SYN** DECEIVE: [VN] *They're kidding themselves if they think its going to be easy.* ◊ [VN(that)] *I tried to kid myself (that) everything was normal.* **IDM** **ˌno 'kidding** (spoken) **1** used to emphasize that sth is true or that you agree with sth that sb has just said: *'It's cold!' 'No kidding!'* **2** used to show that you mean what you are saying: *I want the money back tomorrow. No kidding.* **you're 'kidding | you must be 'kidding** (spoken) used to show that you are very surprised at sth that sb has just said **PHR V** **ˌkid aˈround** (especially AmE) to behave in a silly way

■ adj. **~ sister/brother** (informal, especially AmE) a person's younger sister/brother

kid·die /'kɪdi/ (also **kiddy**) (pl. -ies) noun (informal) a young child: *a kiddies' party*

kid·nap /'kɪdnæp/ verb (-pp-, AmE also -p-) [VN] to take sb away illegally and keep them as a prisoner, especially in order to get money or sth else for returning them: *Two businessmen have been kidnapped by terrorists.* ▶ **kid·napper** noun: *The kidnappers are demanding a ransom of $1 million.* **kid·nap·ping** (also **kid·nap**) noun [U, C]: *He*

K

b	d	f	g	h	k	l	m	n	p	r
bad	**did**	**fall**	**get**	**hat**	**cat**	**leg**	**man**	**now**	**pen**	**red**

admitted the charge of kidnap. ◊ the kidnapping of 12 US citizens

kid·ney /'kɪdni/ noun **1** [C] either of the two organs in the body that remove waste products from the blood and produce URINE: a kidney infection—picture at BODY **2** [U, C] the kidneys of some animals that are cooked and eaten: steak and kidney pie

'kidney bean noun a type of reddish-brown bean shaped like a kidney that is usually dried before it is sold and then soaked before cooking—picture on page A3

'kidney machine noun a machine that does the work of a KIDNEY for sb whose kidneys are damaged or have been removed

kike /kaɪk/ noun (⚠ slang, especially AmE) a very offensive word for a Jew

kill /kɪl/ verb, noun
■ verb **1** to make sb/sth die: [VN] Cancer kills thousands of people every year. ◊ Three people were killed in the crash. ◊ He tried to kill himself with sleeping pills. ◊ I bought a spray to kill the weeds. ◊ (informal) My mother will kill me (= be very angry with me) when she finds out what I've done. ◊ Don't kill yourself trying to get the work done by tomorrow. It can wait. ◊ [V] Excessive tiredness while driving can kill. **2** [VN] to destroy or spoil sth or make it stop: to kill a rumour/story ◊ Do you agree that television kills conversation? ◊ The defeat last night killed the team's chances of qualifying. **3** (informal) (usually used in the progressive tenses and not used in the passive) to cause sb pain or suffering: [VN] My feet are killing me. [also VN to inf] **4** [VN] to make sb laugh a lot: (BrE) He was killing himself laughing. ◊ (AmE) Stop it! You're killing me! **IDM kill the goose that lays the golden 'egg/'eggs** (saying) to destroy sth that would make you rich, successful, etc. ,**kill or 'cure** (BrE) used to say that what you are going to do will either be very successful or fail completely **kill 'time | kill an 'hour, a couple of 'hours, etc.** to spend time doing sth that is not important while you are waiting for sth else to happen: We killed time playing cards. **kill two birds with one 'stone** to achieve two things at the same time with one action ,**kill sb/sth with 'kindness** to be so kind to sb/sth that you in fact harm them—more at DRESSED, TIME n. **PHRV** ,**kill sb/sth↔'off 1** to make a lot of plants, animals, etc. die: Some drugs kill off useful bacteria in the user's body. **2** to stop or get rid of sth: He has effectively killed off any political opposition.
■ noun [usually sing.] **1** an act of killing, especially when an animal is hunted or killed: A cat often plays with a mouse before the kill. ◊ The plane prepared to move in for the kill. ◊ I was in at the kill when she finally lost her job (= present at the end of an unpleasant process). **2** an animal that has been hunted and killed: lions feeding on their kill

kill·er /'kɪlə(r)/ noun **1** a person, an animal or a thing that kills: Police are hunting his killer. ◊ Heart disease is the biggest killer in Scotland. ◊ an electric insect killer ◊ The players lacked the killer instinct.—see also LADY-KILLER, SERIAL KILLER **2** (informal) something that is very difficult, very exciting or very skilful: The exam was a real killer. ◊ The new movie is a killer.

'killer whale noun a small black and white WHALE that eats meat

kill·ing /'kɪlɪŋ/ noun, adj.
■ noun an act of killing sb deliberately; a murder: brutal killings—see also MERCY KILLING **IDM** ,**make a 'killing** (informal) to make a lot of money very quickly
■ adj. making you very tired: a killing schedule

kill·joy /'kɪldʒɔɪ/ noun (disapproving) a person who likes to spoil other people's enjoyment

kiln /kɪln/ noun a large oven for baking clay and bricks, drying wood and grain, etc.

kilo /'kiːləʊ; AmE 'kiːloʊ/ noun (pl. -os) = KILOGRAM

kilo- /'kɪləʊ; AmE 'kɪloʊ/ combining form (in nouns; often used in units of measurement) one thousand: kilojoule

kilo·byte /'kɪləbaɪt/ noun (abbr. K) a unit for measuring computer memory or information equal to 1024 BYTES

kilo·gram (BrE also **kilo·gramme**) /'kɪləgræm/ (also

kilo) noun (abbr. **kg**) a unit for measuring weight; 1000 grams: 2 kilograms of rice ◊ Flour is sold by the kilogram.

kilo·hertz /'kɪləhɜːts; AmE -hɜːrts/ noun (abbr. **kHz**) (pl. **kilo·hertz**) a unit for measuring radio waves

kilo·metre (BrE) (AmE **kilo·meter**) /'kɪləmiːtə(r); BrE also kɪ'lɒmɪtə(r); AmE also kɪ'lɑːm-/ noun (abbr. **k, km**) a unit for measuring distance; 1000 metres

kilo·watt /'kɪləwɒt; AmE -wɑːt/ noun (abbr. **kW, kw**) a unit for measuring electrical power; 1000 WATTS

,**kilowatt-'hour** noun (abbr. **kWh**) a unit for measuring electrical energy equal to the power provided by one kilowatt in one hour

kilt /kɪlt/ noun a skirt made of TARTAN fabric that reaches to the knees and is traditionally worn by Scottish men; a similar skirt worn by women—picture on page A5

kilt·ed /'kɪltɪd/ adj. wearing a kilt

ki·mono /kɪ'məʊnəʊ; AmE kɪ'moʊnoʊ/ noun (pl. -os) a traditional Japanese piece of clothing like a long loose dress with wide sleeves, worn on formal occasions; a DRESSING GOWN or ROBE in this style

kin /kɪn/ noun [pl.] (old-fashioned or formal) your family or your relatives—compare KINDRED—see also NEXT OF KIN **IDM** see KITH

GRAMMAR POINT

kind / sort

Use the singular (**kind/sort**) or plural (**kinds/sorts**) depending on the word you use before them:
each/one/every kind of animal ◊ all/many/other sorts of animals.

Kind/sort of is followed by a singular or uncountable noun: This kind of question often appears in the exam. ◊ That sort of behaviour is not acceptable.

Kinds/sorts of is followed by a plural or uncountable noun: These kinds of questions often appear in the exam. ◊ These sorts of behaviour are not acceptable.

Other variations are possible but less common: These kinds of question often appear in the exam. ◊ These sort of things don't happen in real life. (This example is very informal and is considered incorrect by some people.)

Note also that these examples are possible, especially in spoken English: The shelf was full of the sort of books I like to read. ◊ He faced the same kind of problems as his predecessor. ◊ There are many different sorts of animal on the island. ◊ What kind of camera is this? ◊ What kind/kinds of cameras do you sell? ◊ There were three kinds of cakes / cake on the plate.

---

kind /kaɪnd/ noun, adj.
■ noun [C, U] a group of people or things that are the same in some way; a particular variety or type: three kinds of cakes/cake ◊ music of all/various/different kinds ◊ Exercises of this kind are very popular. ◊ What kind of house do you live in? ◊ They sell all kinds of things. ◊ The school is the first of its kind in Britain. ◊ She isn't that kind of girl. ◊ The regions differ in size, but not in kind. ◊ I need to buy paper and pencils, that kind of thing. ◊ I'll never have that kind of money (= as much money as that). ◊ (formal) Would you like a drink of some kind? **IDM** in 'kind **1** (of a payment) consisting of goods or services, not money **2** (formal) with the same thing: She insulted him and he responded in kind. **a 'kind of** (informal) used to show that sth you are saying is not exact: I had a kind of feeling this might happen. **'kind of** (informal) (also spoken **'kinda**) slightly; in some ways: That made me feel kind of stupid. ◊ I like him, kind of. **nothing of the 'kind/'sort** used to emphasize that the situation is very different from what has been said: 'I was terrible!' 'You were nothing of the kind.' **of a 'kind 1** (disapproving) not as good as it could be: You're making progress of a kind. **2** very similar: They're two of a kind—both workaholics! **one of a 'kind** the only one like this: My father was one of a kind—I'll never be like him. **something of the/that 'kind** some-

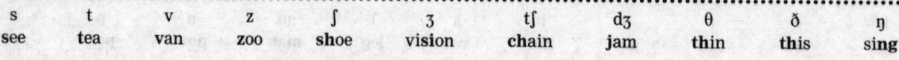

thing like what has been said: *'He's resigning.' 'I'd suspected something of the kind.'*

■ *adj.* (**kind·er**, **kind·est**) **1** ~ (**to sb/sth**)| ~ (**of sb**) (**to do sth**) caring about others; gentle, friendly and generous: *a very kind and helpful person* ◊ *a kind heart/face* ◊ *a kind action/gesture/comment* ◊ *kind to animals* ◊ *You've been very kind.* ◊ *It was really kind of you to help me.* ◊ (*figurative*) *Soft water is kinder to your hair.* ◊ (*figurative*) *The weather was very kind to us.* ◊ (*formal*) *Thank you for your kind invitation.* ◊ (*formal*) *'Do have another.' 'That's very kind of you* (= thank you).' OPP UNKIND **2** (*formal*) used to make a polite request or give an order: *Would you be kind enough to close the window.*—see also KINDLY, KINDNESS

kin·der·gar·ten /ˈkɪndəgɑːtn; *AmE* -dərgɑːrtn/ *noun* (from *German*) **1** (*especially AmE*) a school or class to prepare children aged five for school **2** (*BrE, AustralE*) a NURSERY school

,kind-'hearted *adj.* kind and generous

kin·dle /ˈkɪndl/ *verb* (*written*) **1** to start burning; to make a fire start burning: [V] *We watched as the fire slowly kindled.* ◊ [VN] *to kindle a fire/flame* **2** to make sth such as an interest, emotion, etc. start to grow in sb; to start to be felt by sb: [VN] *It was her teacher who kindled her interest in music.* ◊ [V] *Suspicion kindled within her.*

kind·ling /ˈkɪndlɪŋ/ *noun* [U] small dry pieces of wood, etc. used to start a fire

kind·ly /ˈkaɪndli/ *adv., adj.*

■ *adv.* **1** in a kind way: *She spoke kindly to them.* ◊ *He has kindly agreed to help.* **2** (*old-fashioned, formal*) used to ask or tell sb to do sth, especially when you are annoyed: *Kindly leave me alone!* ◊ *Visitors are kindly requested to sign the book.* IDM **not take 'kindly to sth/sb** to not like sth/sb: *She doesn't take kindly to sudden change.* **look 'kindly on/upon sth/sb** (*formal*) to approve of sth/sb: *He hoped they would look kindly on his request.*

■ *adj.* [only before noun] (*old-fashioned* or *literary*) kind and caring ▶ **kind·li·ness** *noun* [U]

kind·ness /ˈkaɪndnəs/ *noun* **1** [U] the quality of being kind: *to treat sb with kindness and consideration* **2** [C] a kind act: *I can never repay your many kindnesses to me.* IDM see KILL *v.*, MILK *n.*

kin·dred /ˈkɪndrəd/ *noun, adj.*

■ *noun* (*old-fashioned* or *formal*) **1** [pl.] your family and relatives—compare KIN **2** [U] the fact of being related to another person: *ties of kindred*

■ *adj.* [only before noun] (*formal*) very similar; related: *food and kindred products* ◊ *I knew I'd found* **a kindred spirit** (= a person with similar ideas, opinions, etc.)

kin·et·ic /kɪˈnetɪk; *BrE* also kaɪ-/ *adj.* [usually before noun] (*technical*) of or produced by movement: *kinetic energy*

king /kɪŋ/ *noun* **1** the male ruler of an independent state that has a royal family: *the kings and queens of England* ◊ *to become/be crowned king* ◊ *King George V* **2** ~ (**of sth**) a person, an animal or a thing that is thought to be the best or most important of a particular type: *the king of comedy* ◊ *The lion is the king of the jungle.* **3** used in compounds with the names of animals or plants to describe a very large type of the thing mentioned: *a king penguin* **4** the most important piece used in the game of CHESS, that can move one square in any direction—picture on page A8 **5** a playing card with the picture of a king on it—picture on page A8 IDM **a ,king's 'ransom** (*literary*) a very large amount of money—more at ENGLISH, EVIDENCE, UNCROWNED

king·dom /ˈkɪŋdəm/ *noun* **1** a country ruled by a king or queen: *the United Kingdom* ◊ *the kingdom of God* (= heaven) **2** an area controlled by a particular person or where a particular thing or idea is important **3** one of the three traditional divisions of the natural world: *the animal, vegetable and mineral kingdoms*—compare GENUS IDM **blow sb/sth to kingdom 'come** (*informal*) to completely destroy sb/sth with an explosion **till/until kingdom 'come** (*old-fashioned*) for ever

king·fish·er /ˈkɪŋfɪʃə(r)/ *noun* a bird with a long beak, that catches fish in rivers. The European kingfisher is

small and brightly coloured and the American kingfisher is larger and blue-grey in colour.

king·ly /ˈkɪŋli/ *adj.* (*literary*) like a king; connected with or good enough for a king SYN REGAL

king·pin /ˈkɪŋpɪn/ *noun* the most important person in an organization or activity

King's 'Counsel *noun* = KC

king·ship /ˈkɪŋʃɪp/ *noun* [U] the state of being a king; the official position of a king

'king-size (also **'king-sized**) *adj.* [usually before noun] very large; larger than normal when compared with a range of sizes: *a king-size bed* ◊ *a king-sized headache*

kink /kɪŋk/ *noun, verb*

■ *noun* **1** a bend or twist in sth that is usually straight: *a dog with a kink in its tail* ◊ (*figurative*) *We need to iron out the kinks in the new system.* **2** (*informal, disapproving*) an unusual feature in a person's character or mind, especially one that does not seem normal **3** (*AmE*) = CRICK

■ *verb* [V, VN] to develop or make sth develop a bend or twist

kinky /ˈkɪŋki/ *adj.* (*informal, usually disapproving*) used to describe sexual behaviour that most people would consider strange or unusual

kin·ship /ˈkɪnʃɪp/ *noun* (*written*) **1** [U] the fact of being related in a family: *the ties of kinship* **2** [U, sing.] a feeling of being close to sb because you have similar origins or attitudes

kins·man /ˈkɪnzmən/, **kins·woman** /ˈkɪnzwʊmən/ *nouns* (*pl.* **-men** /-mən/, **-women** /-wɪmɪn/) (*old-fashioned* or *literary*) a relative

kiosk /ˈkiːɒsk; *AmE* -ɑːsk/ *noun* **1** a small shop/store, open at the front, where newspapers, drinks, etc. are sold **2** (*old-fashioned, BrE*) a public telephone box

kip /kɪp/ *noun, verb*

■ *noun* [U, C, usually sing.] (*BrE, informal*) sleep: *I must get some kip.* ◊ *Why don't you have a quick kip?*

■ *verb* (**-pp-**) [V] (*BrE, informal*) to sleep: *You can kip on the sofa, if you like.*

kip·per /ˈkɪpə(r)/ *noun* a HERRING (= a type of fish) that has been preserved using salt, then smoked

kirk /kɜːk; *AmE* kɜːrk/ *noun* **1** [C] (*ScotE*) church: *the parish kirk* **2** (**the Kirk**) [sing.] a name often used for the official Church of Scotland

kirsch /kɪəʃ; *AmE* kɪrʃ/ *noun* [U] a strong alcoholic drink made from CHERRIES

kiss /kɪs/ *verb, noun*

■ *verb* **1** to touch sb with your lips as a greeting or as a sign of love, affection, sexual desire, etc: [V] *They stood in a doorway kissing* (= kissing each other). ◊ *Do people in Britain kiss when they meet?* ◊ [VN] *Go and kiss your mother good night.* ◊ *She kissed him on both cheeks.* ◊ *He lifted the trophy up and kissed it.* **2** (*literary*) to gently move or touch sth: *The sunlight kissed the warm stones.* IDM **,kiss and 'tell** a way of referring to sb talking publicly, usually for money, about a past sexual relationship with sb famous **kiss sb's 'arse** (*BrE*) (*AmE* **kiss sb's 'ass**) (△, *slang*) to be very nice to sb in order to persuade them to help you or to give you sth HELP A more polite way to express this is **lick sb's boots**. **,kiss sth 'better** (*spoken*) to take away the pain of an injury by kissing it: *Come here and let me kiss it better.* **kiss sth good'bye | kiss good'bye to sth** (*informal*) to accept that you will lose sth or be unable to do sth: *Well, you can kiss goodbye to your chances of promotion.* PHRV **,kiss sth ↔ a'way** to stop sb feeling sad or angry by kissing them: *He kissed away her tears.*

■ *noun* the act of kissing sb/sth: *Come here and give me a kiss!* ◊ *a kiss on the cheek* ◊ *We were greeted with hugs and kisses.* IDM **the kiss of 'death** (*informal, especially humorous*) an event that seems good, but is certain to make sth else fail: *An award can be the kiss of death for a writer.* **the kiss of 'life** (*BrE*) a method of helping sb who has stopped breathing to breathe again by placing your mouth on theirs and forcing air into their lungs—more at STEAL *v.*

kisso·gram /ˈkɪsəɡræm/ *noun* a humorous greeting on

æ	ɑː	e	ɜː	ə	ɪ	iː	i	ɒ	ɔː	ʌ	ʊ	u	uː
cat	father	ten	bird	about	sit	see	many	got	saw	cup	put	actual	too
								(BrE)					

K

your birthday, etc., delivered by sb dressed in a special COSTUME who kisses you, arranged as a surprise by your friends

kit /kɪt/ *noun, verb*

■ *noun* **1** [C] a set of parts ready to be made into sth: *a kit for a model plane* ◇ *She built the doll's house from a kit.* **2** [C, U] a set of tools or equipment that you use for a particular purpose: *a first-aid kit* ◇ *a drum kit* ◇ *a tool kit* **3** [U] (*BrE*) a set of clothes and equipment that you use for a particular activity: *sports kit* **IDM** get your 'kit off (*BrE, slang*) to take your clothes off—more at CABOODLE

■ *verb* (-tt-) **PHRV** ,kit sb 'out/'up (in/with sth) [usually passive] (*BrE*) to give sb the correct clothes and/or equipment for a particular activity: *They were all kitted out in brand-new ski outfits.*

kit-bag /'kɪtbæg/ *noun* (*especially BrE*) a long narrow bag, usually made of CANVAS in which soldiers, etc. carry their clothes and other possessions

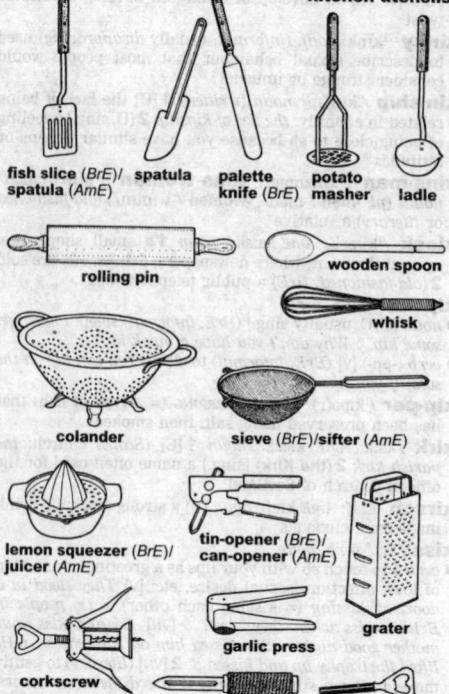

kitchen utensils

fish slice (*BrE*)/ **spatula** (*AmE*) | **spatula** | **palette knife** (*BrE*) | **potato masher** | **ladle**

rolling pin | **wooden spoon**

whisk

colander | **sieve** (*BrE*)/**sifter** (*AmE*)

lemon squeezer (*BrE*)/ **juicer** (*AmE*) | **tin-opener** (*BrE*)/ **can-opener** (*AmE*) | **grater**

corkscrew | **garlic press**

peeler | **bottle-opener**

kit·chen /'kɪtʃɪn/ *noun* a room in which meals are cooked or prepared: *She's in the kitchen.* ◇ *We ate at the kitchen table.*—see also SOUP KITCHEN **IDM** everything but the kitchen 'sink (*informal, humorous*) a very large number of things, probably more than is necessary: *We seem to take everything but the kitchen sink when we go camping.*—more at HEAT *n.*

kit·chen·ette /,kɪtʃɪ'net/ *noun* a small room or part of a room used as a kitchen, for example in a flat/apartment

kitchen 'garden *noun* (*BrE*) a part of a garden/yard where you grow vegetables and fruit for your own use

kitchen paper (also **'kitchen roll**, **'kitchen towel**) (all *BrE*) (*AmE* ,**paper 'towel**) *noun* [U] thick paper on a roll, used for cleaning up liquid, food, etc.

kit·chen·ware /'kɪtʃɪnweə(r); *AmE* -wer/ *noun* [U] used in shops/stores to describe objects that you use in a kitchen, such as pans, bowls, etc.

kite /kaɪt/ *noun, verb*

■ *noun* **1** a toy made of a light frame covered with paper or fabric, that you fly in the air at the end of one or more long strings: *to fly a kite*—picture on page A8 **2** a BIRD OF

PREY (= a bird that kills other creatures for food) of the HAWK family **IDM** see FLY *v.*, HIGH *adj.*

■ *verb* [VN] (*AmE, informal*) to use an illegal cheque to obtain money or to dishonestly change the amount written on a cheque: *to kite checks* ◇ *check kiting*

Kite·mark™ /'kaɪtmɑːk; *AmE* -mɑːrk/ *noun* [usually sing.] in Britain, an official mark, like a small KITE, that shows that goods reach particular standards of quality and safety

kith /kɪθ/ *noun* **IDM** kith and kin (*old-fashioned*) friends and relatives

kitsch /kɪtʃ/ *noun* [U] (*disapproving*) works of art or objects that are popular but that are considered to have no real artistic value and to be lacking in good taste, for example because they are SENTIMENTAL ▶ **kitsch** (also **kitschy**) *adj.*

kit·ten /'kɪtn/ *noun* a young cat **IDM** have 'kittens (*BrE, informal*) to be very anxious or nervous about sth

kitty /'kɪti/ *noun* (*pl.* **-ies**) **1** (*informal*) if money is put in a **kitty**, a group of people all give an amount and the money is spent on sth they all agree on: *We each put £20 in the kitty to cover the bills.* **2** (in card games, etc.) the sum of money that all the players bet, which is given to the winner **3** (*informal*) a way of referring to a cat

kitty-'corner(ed) *adj., adv.* (*AmE, informal*) = CATTY-CORNER(ED)

kiwi /'kiːwiː/ *noun* **1** (**Kiwi**) (*informal*) a person from New Zealand **2** a New Zealand bird with a long beak, short wings and no tail, that cannot fly **3** = KIWI FRUIT

'kiwi fruit *noun* (*pl.* **kiwi fruit**) (also **kiwi**) a small fruit with thin hairy brown skin, soft green flesh and black seeds, originally from New Zealand—picture on page A2

Klaxon™ /'klæksn/ *noun* (*BrE*) a horn, originally on a motor vehicle, that makes a very loud sound as a warning

Klee·nex™ /'kliːneks/ *noun* [U, C] (*pl.* **Klee·nex**) a paper HANDKERCHIEF; a tissue: *a box of Kleenex* ◇ *Here, have a Kleenex to dry your eyes.*

klep·to·mania /,kleptə'meɪniə/ *noun* [U] a mental illness in which sb has a strong desire, which they cannot control, to steal things ▶ **klep·to·maniac** /,kleptə'meɪniæk/ *noun*: *She's a kleptomaniac.*

km *abbr.* (*pl.* **km** or **kms**) (in writing) kilometre(s)

knack /næk/ *noun* [sing.] **1** ~ (of/for sth)| ~ (of/for doing sth) a special skill or ability that you have naturally or can learn: *It's easy, once you've got the knack.* ◇ *He's got a real knack for making money.* **2** ~ of doing sth (*BrE*) a habit of doing sth: *She has the unfortunate knack of always saying the wrong thing.*

knacker /'nækə(r)/ *verb* [VN] (*BrE, slang*) **1** to make sb very tired **SYN** EXHAUST **2** to injure sb or damage sth: *I knackered my ankle playing football.* ▶ **knacker·ing** *adj.* [not usually before noun] (*BrE, informal*): *I don't do aerobics any more—it's too knackering.*

knackered /'nækəd; *AmE* -kərd/ *adj.* (*BrE, slang*) **1** [not usually before noun] extremely tired: *I was knackered after the game.* **2** too old or broken to use: *The car's knackered.*

'knacker's yard (also **the knackers**) *noun* [usually sing.] (*old-fashioned, BrE*) a place where old and injured horses are taken to be killed

knap·sack /'næpsæk/ *noun* (*old-fashioned* or *AmE*) a small RUCKSACK

knave /neɪv/ *noun* **1** (*old-fashioned*) = JACK (3): *the knave of clubs*—picture on page A8 **2** (*old use*) a dishonest man or boy

knead /niːd/ *verb* [VN] **1** to press and stretch DOUGH, wet clay, etc. with your hands to make it ready to use **2** to rub and squeeze muscles, etc. especially to relax them or to make them less painful

knee /niː/ *noun, verb*

■ *noun* **1** the joint between the top and bottom parts of the leg where it bends in the middle: *a knee injury* ◇ *I grazed my knee when I fell.* ◇ *He went down on one knee and asked her to marry him.* ◇ *She was on her knees scrubbing the kitchen floor.*—picture at BODY **2** the part of a

aɪ	aʊ	eɪ	əʊ	oʊ	ɔɪ	ɪə	eə	ʊə	j	w
my	now	say	go (BrE)	go (AmE)	boy	near	hair	pure	yes	wet

piece of clothing that covers the knee: *These jeans are torn at the knee.* ◊ *a knee patch* **3** the top surface of the upper part of the legs when you are sitting down: *Come and sit on Daddy's knee.* **IDM** **bring sb to their 'knees** to defeat sb, especially in a war **bring sth to its 'knees** to badly affect an organization, etc. so that it can no longer function: *The strikes brought the industry to its knees.* **put sb over your 'knee** to punish sb by making them lie on top of your knee and hitting their bottom—more at BEE, BEND *v.*, MOTHER *n.*, WEAK
- *verb* (**kneed, kneed**) [VN] to hit or push sb/sth with your knee: *He kneed his attacker in the groin.*

knee·cap /'niːkæp/ *noun, verb*
- *noun* the small bone that covers the front of the knee **SYN** PATELLA—picture at BODY
- *verb* (**-pp-**) [VN] to shoot or break sb's kneecaps as a form of punishment that is not official and is illegal ▶ **knee·cap·ping** *noun* [C, U]

knee-'deep *adj.* up to your knees: *The snow was knee-deep in places.* ◊ (*figurative*) *I was knee-deep in work.* ▶ **knee-'deep** *adv.*: *I waded in knee-deep.*

knee-'high *adj.* high enough to reach your knees **IDM** **knee-high to a 'grasshopper** (*informal, humorous*) very small; very young

knee-jerk *adj.* [only before noun] (*disapproving*) produced automatically, without any serious thought: *It was a knee-jerk reaction on her part.*

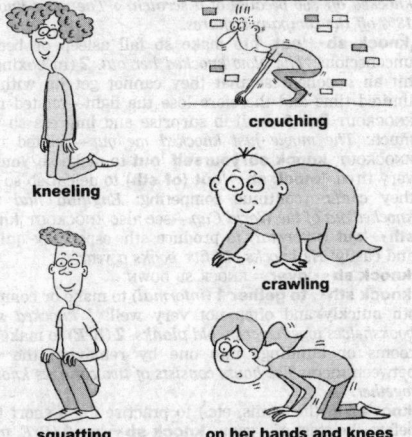

kneeling

crouching

crawling

squatting

on her hands and knees

kneel /niːl/ *verb* (**knelt, knelt** /nelt/) (*AmE also* **kneeled, kneeled**) [V] **~ (down)** to be in or move into a position where your body is supported on your knees, with the lower legs bent back: *a kneeling figure* ◊ *We knelt (down) on the ground to examine the tracks.* ◊ *People sometimes kneel to pray.*

knee-length *adj.* long enough to reach your knees: *knee-length shorts/socks*

knees-up *noun* [usually sing.] (*BrE, informal*) a noisy party, with dancing

knell /nel/ *noun* [sing.] = DEATH KNELL

knew *pt of* KNOW

knick·er·bockers /'nɪkəbɒkəz; *AmE* 'nɪkərbɑːkərz/ (*AmE also* **knick·ers**) *noun* [pl.] short loose trousers/pants that fit tightly just below the knee, worn especially in the past

knick·ers /'nɪkəz; *AmE* -kərz/ *noun* [pl.] **1** (*BrE*) (*also* **pan·ties** *AmE, BrE*) a piece of women's underwear that covers the body from the waist to the tops of the legs: *a pair of knickers* **2** (*AmE*) = KNICKERBOCKERS ▶ **knick·er** *adj.* [only before noun]: *knicker elastic* **IDM** **get your 'knickers in a twist** (*BrE, slang*) to become angry, confused or upset—more at WET *v.*

knick-knack /'nɪk næk/ *noun* [usually pl.] (sometimes *disapproving*) a small decorative object in a house

knife /naɪf/ *noun, verb*

- *noun* (*pl.* **knives** /naɪvz/) a sharp blade with a handle, used for cutting or as a weapon: *knives and forks* ◊ *a sharp knife* ◊ *a bread knife* (= one for cutting bread) ◊ *He had been stabbed repeatedly with a kitchen knife.* ◊ *She was murdered in a frenzied knife attack.*—see also FLICK KNIFE, JACKKNIFE, PALETTE KNIFE, PENKNIFE, STANLEY KNIFE—picture at CUTLERY **IDM** **the 'knives are out (for sb)** the situation has become so bad that people are preparing to make one person take the blame, for example by taking away their job: *The knives are out for the chancellor.* **like a knife through 'butter** (*informal*) easily; without meeting any difficulty **put/stick the 'knife in | put/stick the 'knife into sb** to be very unfriendly to sb and try to harm them **turn/twist the 'knife (in the wound)** to say or do sth unkind deliberately; to make sb who is unhappy feel even more unhappy **under the 'knife** (*informal*) having a medical operation
- *verb* [VN] to injure or kill sb with a knife: *She knifed him in the back.*

knife-edge *noun* [usually sing.] the sharp edge of a knife **IDM** **on a 'knife-edge 1** (of a situation, etc.) finely balanced between success and failure: *The economy is balanced on a knife-edge.* **2** (of a person) very worried or anxious about the result of sth

knife-point /'naɪfpɔɪnt/ *noun* **IDM** **at 'knifepoint** while being threatened, or threatening sb, with a knife: *She was raped at knifepoint.*

knight /naɪt/ *noun, verb*
- *noun* **1** (in the Middle Ages) a man of high social rank who had a duty to fight for his king. Knights are often shown in pictures riding horses and wearing ARMOUR. **2** (in Britain) a man who has been given a special honour by the king or queen and has the title *Sir* before his name—compare BARONET **3** a piece used in the game of CHESS that is shaped like a horse's head—picture at page A8—see also WHITE KNIGHT **IDM** **a knight in shining 'armour** (usually *humorous*) a man who saves sb, especially a woman, from a dangerous situation
- *verb* [VN] [usually passive] to give sb the rank and title of a knight: *He was knighted by the Queen for his services to industry.*

knight·hood /'naɪthʊd/ *noun* (in Britain) the rank or title of a KNIGHT: *He received a knighthood in the New Year's Honours list.*

knight·ly /'naɪtli/ *adj.* [usually before noun] (*literary*) consisting of knights; typical of a knight

knit /nɪt/ *verb, noun*
- *verb* (**knit·ted, knit·ted**) **HELP** In senses 3 and 4 **knit** is usually used for the past tense and past participle. **1** to make clothes, etc. from woollen or cotton thread using two long thin KNITTING NEEDLES or a machine: [VN] *I knitted this cardigan myself.* ◊ [VNN] *She's knitting the baby a shawl.* ◊ [V] *Lucy was sitting on the sofa, knitting.* **2** to use a basic stitch in knitting: [VN] *Knit one row, purl one row.* [also V] **3 ~ (sb/sth) (together)** to join people or things closely together or to be joined closely together: [VN] *a closely/tightly knit community* (= one in which relationships are very close) ◊ *Society is knit together by certain commonly held beliefs.* [also V] **4** (of broken bones) to grow together again to form one piece; to make broken bones grow together again: [V] *The bone failed to knit correctly.* [also VN] **IDM** **knit your 'brow(s)** to move your EYEBROWS together, to show that you are thinking hard, feeling angry, etc.
- *noun* [usually pl.] a piece of clothing that has been knitted: *winter knits*

knit·ted /'nɪtɪd/ (*also* **knit**) *adj.* made by knitting wool or thread: *knitted gloves* ◊ *a white knit dress* ◊ *a hand-knitted sweater* ◊ *a cotton-knit shirt*

knit·ter /'nɪtə(r)/ *noun* a person who knits

knit·ting /'nɪtɪŋ/ *noun* [U] **1** an item that is being knitted: *Where's my knitting?* **2** the activity of knitting—picture at SEW

knitting needle *noun* a long thin stick with a round end that you use for knitting by hand—picture at SEW

b	d	f	g	h	k	l	m	n	p	r
bad	**did**	**fall**	**get**	**hat**	**cat**	**leg**	**man**	**now**	**pen**	**red**

K

knit·wear /'nɪtweə(r); AmE -wer/ noun [U] items of clothing that have been knitted

knives pl. of KNIFE

knob /nɒb; AmE nɑːb/ noun **1** a round switch on a machine such as a television that you use to turn it on and off, etc: *the volume control knob* **2** a round handle on a door or a drawer **3** a round lump on the surface or end of sth **4** (*especially BrE*) a small lump of sth such as butter **5** (*BrE*, △, *slang*) a PENIS **IDM** **with 'knobs on** (*BrE, slang*) used to say that sth is a more complicated version of what you mention: *It isn't art—it's just a horror movie with knobs on!*

knob·bly /'nɒbli; AmE 'nɑːbli/ (also **knobby** /'nɒbi; AmE 'nɑːbi/) adj. having small hard lumps: *knobbly knees*

knock /nɒk; AmE nɑːk/ verb, noun

■ verb

AT DOOR/WINDOW | **1** [V] ~ (**at/on sth**) to hit a door, etc. firmly in order to attract attention: *He knocked three times and waited.* ◇ *Somebody was knocking on the window.*

HIT | **2** ~ (**sth**) (**against/on sth**) to hit sth, often accidentally, with a short, hard blow: [VN] *Be careful you don't knock your head on this low beam.* ◇ [V] *Her hand knocked against the glass.* **3** to put sb/sth into a particular state by hitting them/it: [VN-ADJ] *The blow knocked me flat.* ◇ *He was knocked senseless by the blow.* ◇ [VN-ing] *She knocked my drink flying.* ◇ [VN+adv./prep.] *The two rooms had been knocked into one* (= the wall between them had been knocked down). **4** [VN usually+adv./prep.] to hit sth so that it moves or breaks: *He'd knocked over a glass of water.* ◇ *I knocked the nail into the wall.* ◇ *They had to knock the door down to get in.* ◇ *The boys were knocking* (= kicking) *a ball around in the back yard.* ◇ (*figurative*) *The criticism had knocked* (= damaged) *her self-esteem.* **5** [VN+adv./prep.] to make a hole in sth by hitting it hard: *They managed to knock a hole in the wall.*

OF HEART/KNEES | **6** [V] if your heart **knocks**, it beats hard; if your knees **knock**, they shake, for example from fear: *My heart was knocking wildly.*

OF ENGINE/PIPES | **7** [V] to make a regular sound of metal hitting metal, especially because there is sth wrong

CRITICIZE | **8** [VN] (*informal*) to criticize sb/sth, especially when it happens unfairly: *The newspapers are always knocking the England team.* ◇ *'Plastics?'* ' *Don't knock it—there's a great future in plastics.'*

IDM **I'll knock your 'block/'head off!** (*BrE, spoken*) used to threaten sb that you will hit them **knock sb 'dead** (*spoken*) to impress sb very much: *You look fabulous—you'll knock 'em dead tonight.* **knock sb/sth into a cocked 'hat** (*BrE*) to be very much better than sb/sth **knock it 'off!** (*spoken*) used to tell sb to stop making a noise, annoying you, etc: *Knock it off, kids—I'm trying to work.* **knock sb off their 'pedestal/'perch** to make sb lose their position as sb/sth successful or admired **knock sth on the 'head** (*BrE, informal*) to stop sth from happening; to stop doing sth: *The recession knocked on the head any idea of expanding the company.* ◇ *By eleven o'clock we were all tired so we knocked it on the head.* **knock on 'wood** (*AmE*) = TOUCH WOOD at TOUCH v. **knock sb 'sideways** (*informal*) to surprise or shock sb so much that they are unable to react immediately **knock 'spots off sb/sth** (*BrE, informal*) to be very much better than sb/sth: *She knocks spots off all the other candidates.* **knock the 'stuffing out of sb** (*informal*) to make sb lose their confidence and enthusiasm **you could have knocked me down with a 'feather** (*informal*) used to express surprise—more at DAYLIGHTS, HEAD n., HELL, SENSE n., SHAPE n., SIX, SOCK n.

PHR V **knock a'round ...** (*BrE* also **knock a'bout ...**) (*informal*) **1** to travel and live in various places: *He spent a few years knocking around Europe.* **2** used to say that sth is in a place but you do not know exactly where: *It must be knocking around here somewhere.* **knock a'round with sb/together** (*BrE* also **knock a'bout with sb/together**) (*informal*) to spend a lot of time with sb/together **knock sb/sth a'round** (*BrE* also **knock sb/sth**

a'bout) (*informal*) to hit sb/sth repeatedly; to treat sb/sth roughly **knock sb 'back** (*BrE, informal*) **1** to cost sb a lot of money: *That house must have knocked them back a bit.* **2** to prevent sb from achieving sth or making progress, especially by rejecting them or sth that they suggest or ask—related noun KNOCK-BACK **3** to surprise or shock sb: *Hearing the news really knocked me back.* **knock sth↔'back** (*informal*) to drink sth quickly, especially an alcoholic drink **knock sb↔'down/'over** to hit sb and make them fall to the ground: *She was knocked down by a bus.* ◇ *He knocked his opponent down three times in the first round.* **knock sth↔'down** to destroy a building by breaking its walls **SYN** DEMOLISH: *These old houses are going to be knocked down.* **knock sb/sth 'down (from sth) (to sth)** (*informal*) to persuade sb to reduce the price of sth: *I managed to knock him down to $400.* ◇ *He knocked down the price.*—see also KNOCK-DOWN

knock 'off | knock 'off sth (*informal*) to stop doing sth, especially work: *Do you want to knock off early today?* ◇ *What time do you knock off work?* ◇ *Let's knock off for lunch.* **knock sb↔'off** (*slang*) to murder sb **knock sth↔'off 1** (*informal*) to complete sth quickly and without much effort: *He knocks off three novels a year.* **2** (*BrE, slang*) to steal sth; to rob a place: *to knock off a video recorder* ◇ *to knock off a bank* **knock sth↔'off | knock sth↔'off sth** to reduce the price or value of sth: *They knocked off $60 because of a scratch.* ◇ *The news knocked 13% off the company's shares.*

knock sb↔'out 1 to make sb fall asleep or become unconscious: *The blow knocked her out.* **2** (in boxing) to hit an opponent so that they cannot get up within a limited time and therefore lose the fight—related noun KNOCKOUT **3** (*informal*) to surprise and impress sb very much: *The movie just knocked me out.*—related noun KNOCKOUT **knock sb/yourself 'out** to make sb/yourself very tired **knock sb↔'out (of sth)** to defeat sb so that they cannot continue competing: *England had been knocked out of the World Cup.*—see also KNOCKOUT **knock sth↔'out** (*informal*) to produce sth, especially quickly and easily: *He knocks out five books a year.* **knock sb↔'over** = KNOCK SB DOWN

knock sth↔to'gether 1 (*informal*) to make or complete sth quickly and often not very well: *I knocked some bookshelves together from old planks.* **2** (*BrE*) to make two rooms or buildings into one by removing the wall between them: *The house consists of two cottages knocked together.*

knock 'up (in tennis, etc.) to practise for a short time before the start of a game **knock sb↔'up 1** (*BrE, informal*) to wake sb by knocking on their door **2** (*informal, especially AmE*) to make a woman pregnant **knock sth↔'up** to prepare or make sth quickly and without much effort: *She knocked up a fantastic meal in ten minutes.*

■ noun

AT DOOR/WINDOW | **1** the sound of sb hitting a door, window, etc. with their hand or with sth hard to attract attention: *There was a knock on/at the door.*

HIT | **2** a sharp blow from sth hard: *He got a nasty knock on the head.*

IDM **take a (hard, nasty, etc.) 'knock** to have an experience that makes sb/sth less confident or successful; to be damaged

knock·about /'nɒkəbaʊt; AmE 'nɑːk-/ adj. [usually before noun] (*BrE*) **knockabout** entertainment involves people acting in a deliberately silly way, for example falling over or hitting other people, in order to make the audience laugh

'knock-back noun (*informal*) a difficulty or problem that makes you feel less confident that you will be successful in sth that you are doing, especially when sb rejects you or sth you suggest or ask

'knock-down adj. [only before noun] (*informal*) **1** (of prices, etc.) much lower than usual **2** using a lot of force: *a knock-down punch*

knock·er /'nɒkə(r); AmE 'nɑːk-/ noun **1** (also **'door**

s	t	v	z	ʃ	ʒ	tʃ	dʒ	θ	ð	ŋ
see	tea	van	zoo	shoe	vision	chain	jam	thin	this	sing

K

knocker) [C] a metal object attached to the outside of the door of a house, etc. which you hit against the door to attract attention: *a polished brass knocker* **2** [C] (*informal*) a person who is always criticizing sb/sth **3** (**knockers**) [pl.] (⚠, *slang*) an offensive word for a woman's breasts

,knock-'kneed *adj.* having legs that turn inwards at the knees

,knock-'on *adj.* (*especially BrE*) causing other events to happen one after another in a series: *The increase in the price of oil had **a knock-on effect** on the cost of many other goods.*

knock·out /'nɒkaʊt; *AmE* 'nɑːk-/ *noun, adj.*
- *noun* **1** (*abbr.* **KO**) (in boxing) a blow that makes an opponent fall to the ground and be unable to get up, so that he or she loses the fight **2** (*informal*) a person or thing that is very attractive or impressive: *She's an absolute knockout.*
- *adj.* [only before noun] **1** (*especially BrE*) a **knockout** competition is one in which the winning player/team at each stage competes in the next stage and the losing one no longer takes part in the competition: *the knockout stages of the tournament* **2** a **knockout** blow is one that hits sb so hard that they can no longer get up: *a knockout punch*

'knock-up *noun* (*BrE*) a short practice before a game, especially of tennis

knoll /nəʊl; *AmE* noʊl/ *noun* a small round hill

knot /nɒt; *AmE* nɑːt/ *noun, verb*
- *noun*
  IN STRING/ROPE | **1** a join made by tying together two pieces or ends of string, rope, etc: *to tie a knot* ◊ *Tie the two ropes together with a secure knot.* ◊ *Make a knot at the end of the string.* ◊ (*figurative*) *hair full of knots and tangles* (= twisted in a way that is difficult to comb)
  OF HAIR | **2** a way of twisting hair into a small round shape at the back of the head: *She had her hair in a loose knot.*
  IN WOOD | **3** a hard round spot in a piece of wood where there was once a branch
  GROUP OF PEOPLE | **4** (*written*) a small group of people standing close together: *Little knots of people had gathered at the entrance.*
  OF MUSCLES | **5** a tight, hard feeling in the stomach, throat, etc. caused by nerves, anger, etc: *My stomach was in knots.* ◊ *I could feel a knot of fear in my throat.*
  SPEED OF BOAT/PLANE | **6** a unit for measuring the speed of boats and aircraft; one NAUTICAL MILE per hour
  IDM see RATE *n.*, TIE *v.*
- *verb* (**-tt-**)
  TIE WITH KNOT | **1** [VN] to fasten sth with a knot or knots: *He carefully knotted his tie.* ◊ *She wore a scarf loosely knotted around her neck.*
  TWIST | **2** [V] to become twisted into a knot [SYN] TANGLE **3** [VN] to twist hair into a particular shape: *She wore her hair loosely knotted on top of her head.*
  MUSCLES | **4** if muscles, etc. knot or sth **knots** them, they become hard and painful because of fear, excitement, etc: [V] *She felt her stomach knot with fear.* [also VN]
  IDM get 'knotted (*BrE*, *spoken*, *slang*) a rude way of telling sb to go away or of telling them that you are annoyed with them

knotty /'nɒti; *AmE* 'nɑːti/ *adj.* (**knot·tier, knot·ti·est**) **1** complicated and difficult to solve: *a knotty problem* **2** having parts that are hard and twisted together: *the knotty roots of the old oak tree*

know /nəʊ; *AmE* noʊ/ *verb, noun*
- *verb* (**knew** /njuː; *AmE* nuː/ **known** /nəʊn; *AmE* noʊn/) (not used in the progressive tenses)
  HAVE INFORMATION | **1** ~ (of/about sth) to have information in your mind as a result of experience or because you have learned or been told it: [VN] *Do you know his address?* ◊ *The cause of the fire is not yet known.* ◊ *All I know is that she used to work in a bank* (= I have no other information about her). ◊ [V(that)] *I know (that) people's handwriting changes as they get older.* ◊ [VN that] *It is widely known that CFCs can damage the ozone layer.* ◊

[V wh-] *I knew where he was hiding.* ◊ *I didn't know what he was talking about.* ◊ [V] *'You've got a flat tyre.' 'I know.'* ◊ *'What's the answer?' 'I don't know.'* ◊ *'There's no one in.'* **How do you know?** ' ◊ *You know about Amanda's baby, don't you?* ◊ (*spoken*) **I don't know about you, but** *I'm ready for something to eat.* ◊ **I know of** *at least two people who did the same thing.* ◊ (*spoken*) *'Is anyone else coming?' ' Not that I know of. '* ◊ (*spoken*) *'Isn't that his car?' ' I wouldn't know. / How should I know? '* (= I don't know and I am not the person you should ask). ◊ (*spoken*) *'What are you two whispering about?' ' **You don't want to know*** (= because you would be shocked or wouldn't approve).' ◊ [V to inf] *Does he know to come here* (= that he should come here) *first?* ◊ [VN to inf] *We know her to be honest.* ◊ *Two women are known to have died.* ⇨ note at DISCOVER

REALIZE | **2** to realize, understand or be aware of sth: [V(that)] *As soon as I walked in the room I knew (that) something was wrong.* ◊ *She knew she was dying.* ◊ [V wh-] *I knew perfectly well what she meant.* ◊ *I know exactly how you feel.* ◊ [VN] *This case is hopeless and he knows it* (= although he will not admit it). ◊ [V] *'Martin was lying all the time.' ' I should have known.'*

FEEL CERTAIN | **3** to feel certain about sth: [V(that)] *He knew (that) he could trust her.* ◊ *I know it's here somewhere!* ◊ *I don't know that I can finish it by next week.* ◊ [VN] (*spoken*) *'You were right—someone's been spreading rumours about you.' 'I knew it!'* ◊ [V] (*spoken*) *'She's the worst player in the team.' 'Oh, I don't know* (= I am not sure that I agree)— *she played well yesterday.'*

BE FAMILIAR | **4** [VN] to be familiar with a person, place, thing, etc: *I've known David for 20 years.* ◊ *Do you two know each other* (= have you met before)? ◊ *She's very nice when you get to know her.* ◊ **Knowing Ben,** *we could be waiting a long time* (= it is typical of him to be late). ◊ *This man **is known to the police*** (= as a criminal). ◊ *I know Paris well.* ◊ *Do you know the play* (= have you seen or read it before)? ◊ *The new rules could mean the end of football **as we know it*** (= in the form that we are familiar with).

REPUTATION | **5** ~ sb/sth as sth | ~ sb/sth for sth [usually passive] to think that sb/sth is a particular type of person or thing or has particular characteristics: [VN] *It's known as the most dangerous part of the city.* ◊ *She is best known for her work on the human brain.* ◊ [VN to inf] *He's known to be an outstanding physicist.*

GIVE NAME | **6** [VN] ~ sb/sth as sth [usually passive] to give sb/sth a particular name or title: *The drug is commonly known as Ecstasy.* ◊ *Peter Wilson, also known as 'the Tiger'.*

RECOGNIZE | **7** [VN] to be able to recognize sb/sth: *I couldn't see who was speaking, but I knew the voice.* ◊ *She knows a bargain when she sees one.*

DISTINGUISH | **8** [VN] ~ sb/sth from sb/sth to be able to distinguish one person or thing from another: *I hope we have taught our children to know right from wrong.*

SKILL/LANGUAGE | **9** to have learned a skill or language and be able to use it: [VN] *Do you know any Japanese?* ◊ [V wh-] *Do you know how to use spreadsheets?*

EXPERIENCE | **10** (only used in the perfect tenses) to have seen, heard or experienced sth: [VN inf, VN to inf] *I've never known it (to) snow in July before.* ◊ [VN to inf] *He has been known to spend all morning in the bathroom.* **11** [VN] to have personal experience of sth: *He has known both poverty and wealth.* ◊ *She may be successful now, but she has known what it is like to be poor.*

IDM before you know where you 'are very quickly or suddenly: *We were whisked off in a taxi before we knew where we were.* be not to 'know to have no way of realizing or being aware that you have done sth wrong: *'I'm sorry, I called when you were in bed.' 'Don't worry— you weren't to know.'* for all you, I, they, etc. know (*spoken*) used to emphasize that you do not know sth and that it is not important to you: *She could be dead for all I know.* God/goodness/Heaven knows (*spoken*) **1** used to emphasize that you do not know sth: *God knows what else they might find.* ◊ *'Where are they?' 'Goodness knows.'*

æ	ɑː	e	ɜː	ə	ɪ	iː	i	ɒ	ɔː	ʌ	ʊ	u	uː
cat	father	ten	bird	about	sit	see	many	got	saw	cup	put	actual	too
								(BrE)					

HELP Some people may find the use of **God knows** offensive. **2** used to emphasize the truth of what you are saying: *She ought to pass the exam—goodness knows she's been working hard enough.* **I don't know how, why, etc. ...** (*spoken*) used to criticize sb's behaviour: *I don't know how you can speak like that to your mother.* ◇ *I don't know what you think you're doing.* **I know** (*spoken*) **1** used to agree with sb or to show sympathy: *'What a ridiculous situation!' 'I know.'* **2** used to introduce a new idea or suggestion: *I know, let's see what's on at the theatre.* **know sth as well as 'I do** used to criticize sb by saying that they should realize or understand sth: *You know as well as I do that you're being unreasonable.* **know sb/sth 'backwards** (*informal, especially BrE*) to know sb/sth extremely well: *She must know the play backwards by now.* **know 'best** to know what should be done, etc. better than other people: *The doctor told you to stay in bed, and she knows best.* **know better (than that/than to do sth)** to be sensible enough not to do sth: *You left the car unlocked? I thought you'd know better.* ◇ *He knows better than to judge by appearances.* **know sb by 'sight** to recognize sb without knowing them well **know 'different/'otherwise** (*informal*) to have information or evidence that the opposite is true: *He says he doesn't care about what the critics write, but I know different.* **know full 'well** to be very aware of a fact and unable to deny or ignore it: *He knew full well what she thought of it.* **know sb/sth inside 'out | know sb/sth like the back of your 'hand** (*informal*) to be very familiar with sth: *This is where I grew up. I know this area like the back of my hand.* **know your own 'mind** to have very firm ideas about what you want to do **know your 'stuff** (*informal*) to know a lot about a particular subject or job **know your way a'round** to be familiar with a place, subject, etc. **know what you're 'talking about** (*informal*) to have knowledge about sth from your own experience: *I've lived in China, so I know what I'm talking about.* **know which side your 'bread is buttered** (*informal*) to know where you can get an advantage for yourself **let it be known/ make it known that ...** (*formal*) to make sure that people are informed about sth, especially by getting sb else to tell them: *The President has let it be known that he does not intend to run for election again.* **let sb 'know** to tell sb about sth: *I don't know if I can come, but I'll let you know tomorrow.* ◇ *Let me know how I can help.* **make yourself 'known to sb** to introduce yourself to sb: *I made myself known to the hotel manager.* **not know any 'better** to behave badly, usually because you have not been taught the correct way to behave: *Don't blame the children—they don't know any better.* **not know you are 'born** (*BrE, informal, spoken*) to have an easy life without realizing how easy it is: *You people without kids don't know you're born.* **not know your ‚arse from your 'elbow** (*BrE, △, slang*) to be very stupid or completely lacking in skill **not know the first thing a'bout sb/sth** to know nothing at all about sb/sth: *I'm afraid I don't know the first thing about cars.* **not know sb from 'Adam** (*informal*) to not know at all who sb is **not know what 'hit you** (*informal*) to be so surprised by sth that you do not know how to react **not know where to 'look** (*informal*) to feel great embarrassment **not know whether you're 'coming or 'going** (*informal*) to be so excited or confused that you cannot behave or think in a sensible way **there's no 'knowing** used to say that it is impossible to say what might happen: *There's no knowing how he'll react.* **what does ...know?** used to say that sb knows nothing about the subject you are talking about: *What does he know about football, anyway?* **what do you 'know (about 'that)?** (*informal*) used to express surprise: *Well, what do you know? Look who's here!* ‚you 'know (*spoken*) **1** used when you are thinking of what to say next: *Well, you know, it's difficult to explain.* **2** used to show what you are referring to is known or understood by the person you are speaking to: *Guess who I've just seen? Maggie! You know—Jim's wife.* ◇ *You know that restaurant round the corner? It's closed down.* **3** used to emphasize sth that you are saying: *That road is very dangerous, you know.* ◇ *I'm not stupid, you know.* **you**

'know something/'what? (*spoken*) used to introduce an interesting or surprising opinion, piece of news, etc: *You know something? I've never really enjoyed Christmas.* **you know 'who/'what** (*spoken*) used to refer to sb/sth without mentioning a name **you never know** (*spoken*) used to say that you can never be certain about what will happen in the future, especially when you are suggesting that sth good might happen—more at ANSWER *n.*, COST *n.*, DAY, DEVIL, FAR *adv.*, LORD *n.*, OLD, PAT *adv.*, ROPE *n.*, THING, TRUTH

■ *noun*

IDM **in the 'know** (*informal*) having more information about sth than most people: *Somebody in the know told me he's going to resign.*

'know-all (*BrE*) (also **'know-it-all** *AmE, BrE*) *noun* (*informal, disapproving*) a person who behaves as if they know everything

'know-how *noun* [U] (*informal*) knowledge of how to do sth and experience in doing it: *We need skilled workers and technical know-how.*

know·ing /'nəʊɪŋ; *AmE* 'noʊ-/ *adj.* [usually before noun] showing that you know or understand about sth that is supposed to be secret: *a knowing smile*—compare UNKNOWING

know·ing·ly /'nəʊɪŋli; *AmE* 'noʊ-/ *adv.* **1** while knowing the truth or likely result of what you are doing **SYN** DELIBERATELY: *She was accused of knowingly making a false statement to the police.* **2** in a way that shows that you know or understand about sth that is supposed to be secret: *He glanced at her knowingly.*

'know-it-all *noun* (*especially AmE*) = KNOW-ALL

know·ledge /'nɒlɪdʒ; *AmE* 'nɑːl-/ *noun* ~ **(of/about sth)** **1** [U, sing.] the information, understanding and skills that you gain through education or experience: *practical/ medical/scientific knowledge* ◇ *He has a wide knowledge of painting and music.* ◇ *There is a lack of knowledge about the tax system.* **2** [U] the state of knowing about a particular fact or situation: *She sent the letter without my knowledge.* ◇ *The film was made with the Prince's full knowledge and approval.* ◇ *She was impatient in the knowledge that time was limited.* ◇ *I went to sleep secure in the knowledge that I was not alone in the house.* ◇ *They could relax safe in the knowledge that they had the funding for the project.* ◇ *He denied all knowledge of the affair.* **IDM** **be common/public 'knowledge** to be sth that everyone knows, especially in a particular community or group **come to sb's 'knowledge** (*formal*) to become known by sb: *It has come to our knowledge that you have been taking time off without permission.* **to your 'knowledge** from the information you have, although you may not know everything: *'Are they divorced?' 'Not to my knowledge.'*

know·ledge·able /'nɒlɪdʒəbl; *AmE* 'nɑːl-/ *adj.* ~ **(about sth)** knowing a lot: *She is very knowledgeable about plants.* ► **know·ledge·ably** /-əbli/ *adv.*

known /nəʊn; *AmE* noʊn/ *adj.* [only before noun] known about, especially by a lot of people: *He's a known thief.* ◇ *The disease has no known cure.*—see also KNOW *v.*

knuckle /'nʌkl/ *noun, verb*

■ *noun* **1** any of the joints in the fingers, especially those connecting the fingers to the rest of the hand—picture at BODY **2** (also **hock** especially in *AmE*) [U, C] a piece of meat from the lower part of an animal's leg, especially a pig: *knuckle of pork* **IDM** **near the 'knuckle** (*BrE, informal*) (of a remark, joke, etc.) concerned with sex in a way that is likely to offend people or make them feel embarrassed—more at RAP *n.*, RAP *v.*

■ *verb* **PHRV** ‚knuckle 'down (to sth) (*informal*) to begin to work hard at sth: *I'm going to have to knuckle down to some serious study.* ‚knuckle 'under (to sb/sth) (*informal*) to accept sb else's authority

knuckle·dust·er /'nʌkldʌstə(r)/ *noun* (*AmE* also ‚brass 'knuckles [pl.]) a metal cover that is put on the fingers and used as a weapon

KO /‚keɪ 'əʊ; *AmE* 'oʊ/ *abbr.* KNOCKOUT

koala /kəʊ'ɑːlə; *AmE* koʊ-/ (also ko‚ala 'bear) *noun* an Australian animal with thick grey fur, large ears and no

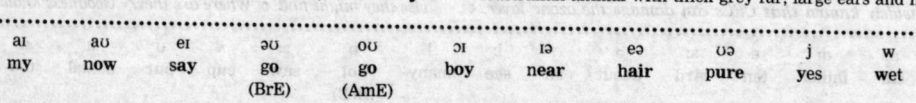

aɪ	aʊ	eɪ	əʊ	oʊ	ɔɪ	ɪə	eə	ʊə	j	w
my	now	say	go	go	boy	near	hair	pure	yes	wet
			(BrE)	(AmE)						

tail. Koalas live in trees and eat leaves.—picture on page A6

kohl /kəʊl; *AmE* koʊl/ *noun* [U] a black powder used, especially in eastern countries, around the eyes to make them more attractive

kohl·rabi /ˌkəʊlˈrɑːbi; *AmE* ˌkoʊl-/ *noun* [U] a vegetable of the CABBAGE family whose thick round white stem is eaten

kook /kuːk/ *noun* (*informal, especially AmE*) a person who acts in a strange or crazy way ► **kooky** *adj.*

kooka·burra /ˈkʊkəbʌrə; *AmE* -bɜːrə/ *noun* an Australian bird that makes a strange laughing cry

Koran (also **Qur'an**) /kəˈrɑːn/ *noun* (**the Koran**) [sing.] the holy book of the Islamic religion, written in Arabic, containing the word of Allah as REVEALED to the Prophet Muhammad ► **Kor·an·ic** /kəˈrænɪk/ *adj.*

ko·sher /ˈkəʊʃə(r); *AmE* ˈkoʊ-/ *adj.* **1** (of food) prepared according to the rules of Jewish law **2** (*informal*) honest or legal: *Their business deals are not always completely kosher.*

kow·tow /ˌkaʊˈtaʊ/ *verb* [V] ~ (**to sb/sth**) (*informal, disapproving*) to show sb in authority too much respect and be too willing to obey them

kph /ˌkeɪ piː ˈeɪtʃ/ *abbr.* kilometres per hour

Kraut /kraʊt/ *noun* (⚠, *slang*) an offensive word for a person from Germany

krill /krɪl/ *noun* [pl.] very small shellfish that live in the sea around the Antarctic and are eaten by WHALES

krona /ˈkrəʊnə; *AmE* ˈkroʊnə/ *noun* (*pl.* **kro·nor** /-nɔː(r); -nə(r)/) the unit of money in Sweden and Iceland

krone /ˈkrəʊnə; *AmE* ˈkroʊnə/ *noun* (*pl.* **kro·ner** /-nə(r)/) the unit of money in Denmark and Norway

kryp·ton /ˈkrɪptɒn; *AmE* -tɑːn/ *noun* [U] (*symb* **Kr**) a chemical element. Krypton is a colourless gas that does not react with anything, used in FLUORESCENT lights and LASERS.

kudos /ˈkjuːdɒs; *AmE* ˈkuːdɑːs/ *noun* [U] the admiration and respect that goes with a particular achievement or position: *the kudos of playing for such a famous team*

Ku Klux Klan /ˌkuː kluːks ˈklæn/ *noun* [sing.+ sing./pl. v.] a secret organization of white men in the southern states of the US who use violence to oppose social change and equal rights for black people

kum·quat /ˈkʌmkwɒt; *AmE* -kwɑːt/ *noun* a fruit like a very small orange with sweet skin that is eaten, and sour flesh

kung fu /ˌkʌŋ ˈfuː/ *noun* [U] a Chinese system of fighting without weapons, similar to KARATE

kvetch /kvetʃ/ *verb* [V] (*AmE, informal*) to complain about sth all the time SYN WHINE

kW *abbr.* (in writing) KILOWATT(S): *a 2kW electric fire*

kWh *abbr.* (*pl.* **kWh**) (in writing) KILOWATT-HOUR(S)

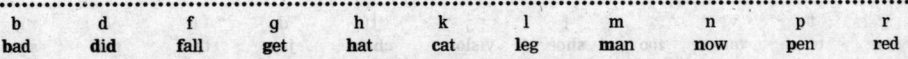

Ll

L /el/ *noun, abbr., symbol*
- *noun* (also **I**) [C, U] (*pl.* **L's, I's** /elz/) the 12th letter of the English alphabet: *'Lion' begins with (an) L/'L'.*—see also L-PLATE
- *abbr.* **1** (**L.**) (especially on maps) Lake: *L. Windermere* **2** (especially for sizes of clothes) large: *S M and L* (= small, medium and large)
- *symbol* (also **I**) the number 50 in ROMAN NUMERALS

l *abbr.* **1** (*pl.* **l**) (in writing) litre(s) **2** (also **l.**) (*pl.* **ll**) (in writing) line (= on a page in a book)

LA (also **L.A.**) /ˌel ˈeɪ/ *abbr.* the city of Los Angeles

la = LAH—see also À LA

Lab *abbr.* (in British politics) Labour: *Chris Hart (Lab)*

lab /læb/ *noun* (*informal*) = LABORATORY: *science labs* ◊ *a lab technician*

label /ˈleɪbl/ *noun, verb*
- *noun* **1** a piece of paper, etc. that is attached to sth and gives information about it: *The washing instructions are on the label.* ◊ *price/address labels* ◊ *We tested various supermarkets' own label pasta sauces* (= those marked with the name of the shop/store where they are sold). ◊ *He'll only wear clothes with a designer label.*—picture at PACKAGING **2** (*disapproving*) a word or phrase that is used to describe sb/sth in a way that seems too general, unfair or not correct: *I hated the label 'housewife'.* **3** a company that produces and sells records, CDs, etc: *the Virgin record label* ◊ *It's his first release for a major label.*
- *verb* (**-ll-**, *AmE* **-l-**) [often passive] **1** [VN] to fix a label on sth or write information on sth: *We carefully labelled each item with the contents and the date.* ◊ *The file was labelled 'Private'.* **2** ~ **sb/sth** (**as**) **sth** to describe sb/sth in a particular way, especially unfairly: [VN-N] *He was labelled*

(*as*) *a traitor by his former colleagues.* ◊ [VN-ADJ] *It is unfair to label a small baby as naughty.*

labia /ˈleɪbiə/ *noun* [pl.] the four folds of skin at the entrance to a woman's VAGINA

la·bial /ˈleɪbiəl/ *noun* (*phonetics*) a speech sound made with the lips, for example /m, p, v/ ▶ **la·bial** *adj.*

labor (*AmE*) = LABOUR

la·bora·tory /ləˈbɒrətri; *AmE* ˈlæbrətɔːri/ (also *informal* **lab**) *noun* (*pl.* **-ies**) a room or building used for scientific research, experiments, testing, etc: *a research laboratory* ◊ *laboratory experiments/tests*—see also LANGUAGE LABORATORY

'Labor Day *noun* [U, C] a public holiday in the US and Canada on the first Monday of September, in honour of working people—compare MAY DAY

la·bor·er (*AmE*) = LABOURER

la·bori·ous /ləˈbɔːriəs/ *adj.* taking a lot of time and effort: *a laborious task/process* ◊ *Checking all the information will be slow and laborious.* ▶ **la·bori·ous·ly** *adv.*

'labor union *noun* (*AmE*) = TRADE UNION

la·bour (*BrE*) (*AmE* **labor**) /ˈleɪbə(r)/ *noun, verb*
- *noun*
  - WORK **1** [U] work, especially physical work: *manual labour* (= work using your hands) ◊ *The price will include the labour and materials.* ◊ *The company wants to keep down labour costs.* ◊ *The workers voted to withdraw their labour* (= to stop work as a means of protest). ◊ *He was sentenced to two years in a labour camp* (= a type of prison where people have to do hard physical work). **2** [C, usually pl.] (*formal*) a task or period of work: *He was so exhausted from the day's labours that he went straight to bed.*

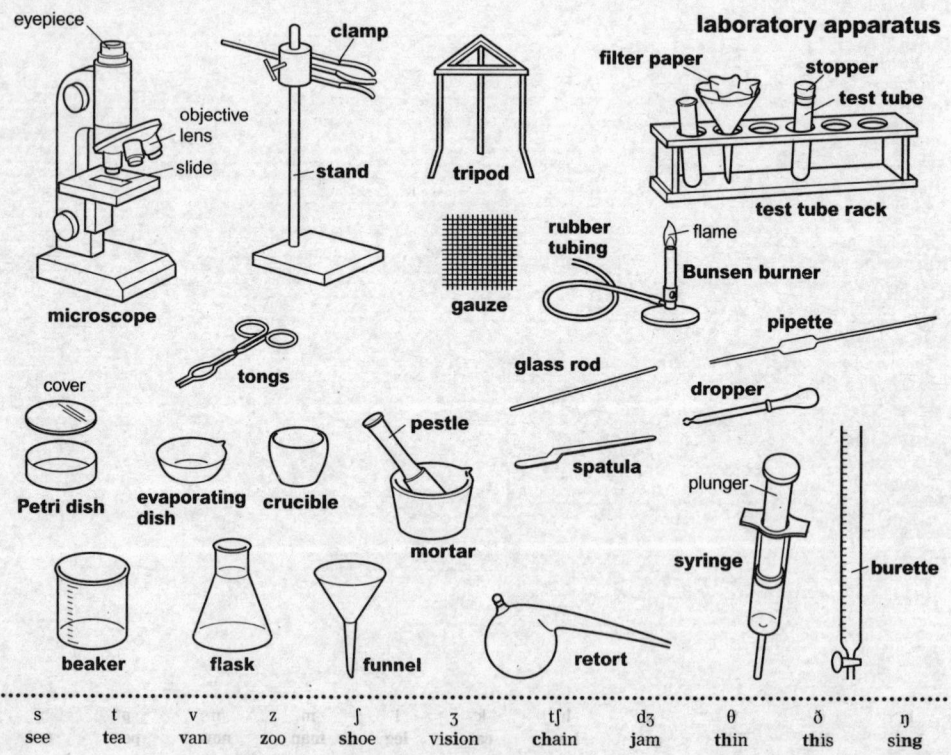

laboratory apparatus

eyepiece, clamp, objective lens, slide, stand, tripod, filter paper, stopper, test tube, test tube rack, rubber tubing, flame, Bunsen burner, pipette, gauze, glass rod, dropper, microscope, tongs, cover, pestle, spatula, plunger, Petri dish, evaporating dish, crucible, mortar, syringe, burette, beaker, flask, funnel, retort

PEOPLE WHO WORK | **3** [U] the people who work or are available for work in a country or a company: *a shortage of labour* ◇ *Employers are using immigrants as* **cheap labour.** ◇ *Repairs involve* **skilled labour,** *which can be expensive.* ◇ *good* **labour relations** (= the relationship between workers and employers)

HAVING BABY | **4** [U, C, usually sing.] the period of time or the process of giving birth to a baby: *Jane was* **in labour** *for ten hours.* ◇ *She* **went into labour** *early.* ◇ *labour pains*

POLITICS | **5** (**Labour**) [sing.+ sing./ pl. *v.*] (*abbr.* **Lab**) the British Labour Party: *He always votes Labour.* ◇ *Labour has/ have been in power for five years.*

IDM **a labour of 'love** a hard task that you do because you want to, not because it is necessary

■ *verb*

STRUGGLE | **1 ~** (**away**) to try very hard to do sth difficult: [V] *He was in his study labouring away over some old papers.* ◇ [Vto inf] *They laboured for years to clear their son's name.*

WORK HARD | **2** [V] to do hard physical work: *We laboured all day in the fields.* ◇ (*old-fashioned*) *the labouring classes* (= the working class)

MOVE WITH DIFFICULTY | **3** [V] to move with difficulty and effort: *The horses laboured up the steep slope.*

IDM **labour the 'point** to continue to repeat or explain sth that has already been said and understood

PHRV **'labour under sth** (*formal*) to believe sth that is not true: *to labour under a misapprehension/ delusion* ◇ *He's still labouring under the impression that he's written a great book.*

la·boured (*BrE*) (*AmE* **la·bored**) /ˈleɪbəd; *AmE* -bərd/ *adj.* **1** (of breathing) slow and taking a lot of effort **2** (of writing, speaking, etc.) not natural and seeming to take a lot of effort: *The movie looks laboured and slow by today's standards.*

la·bour·er (*BrE*) (*AmE* **la·bor·er**) /ˈleɪbərə(r)/ *noun* a person whose job involves hard physical work that is not skilled, especially work that is done outdoors: *an agricultural labourer*

'labour force (*BrE*) (*AmE* **'labor force**) *noun* all the people who work for a company or country: *a skilled/ an unskilled labour force*

la·bour·ing (*BrE*) (*AmE* **la·bor·ing**) /ˈleɪbərɪŋ/ *noun* [U] hard physical work that is not skilled: *a labouring job*

labour-in'tensive (*BrE*) (*AmE* **labor-in'tensive**) *adj.* (of work) needing a lot of people to do it: *labour-intensive methods*—compare CAPITAL-INTENSIVE

'labour market (*BrE*) (*AmE* **'labor market**) *noun* the number of people who are available for work in relation to the number of jobs available: *young people about to enter the labour market*

the 'Labour Party (also **Labour**) *noun* [sing.+ sing./ pl. *v.*] one of the main British political parties, on the political left, that has traditionally represented the interests of working people: *the Labour Party leader*

'labour-saving (*BrE*) (*AmE* **'labor-saving**) *adj.* [usually before noun] designed to reduce the amount of work or effort needed to do sth: *modern labour-saving devices such as washing machines and dishwashers*

Lab·ra·dor /ˈlæbrədɔː(r)/ *noun* a large dog that can be yellow, black or brown in colour, often used by blind people as a guide: *a black/ golden Labrador*

la·bur·num /ləˈbɜːnəm; *AmE* -ˈbɜːrn-/ *noun* [C, U] a small tree with hanging bunches of yellow flowers

laby·rinth /ˈlæbərɪnθ/ *noun* (*formal*) a complicated series of paths, which it is difficult to find your way through: *We lost our way in the labyrinth of streets.* ◇ (*figurative*) *a labyrinth of rules and regulations*—compare MAZE ▶ **laby·rin·thine** /ˌlæbəˈrɪnθaɪn/ *adj.* (*formal*): *labyrinthine corridors* ◇ *labyrinthine legislation*

lace /leɪs/ *noun, verb*

■ *noun* **1** [U] a delicate fabric made from threads of cotton, silk, etc. that are woven into a pattern of holes: *a lace handkerchief* ◇ *a tablecloth edged with lace*—see also LACY—picture at page A5 **2** [C] = SHOELACE: *Your laces are undone.*—picture at SHOE, FASTENER

■ *verb* **1 ~** (**sth**) (**up**) to be fastened with laces; to fasten sth with laces: [V] *She was wearing a dress that laced up at the side.* ◇ [VN] *He was sitting on the bed lacing up his shoes.*—see also LACE-UP **2** [V] to put a lace through the holes in a shoe, a boot, etc.—related noun LACE-UP **3** [VN] **~ sth** (**with sth**) to add a small amount of alcohol, a drug, poison, etc. to a drink: *He had laced her milk with rum.* **4** [VN] **~ sth** (**with sth**) to add a particular quality to a book, speech, etc: *Her conversation was laced with witty asides.* **5** [VN] to weave or twist sth together with another thing: *They sat with their fingers laced.*

la·cer·ate /ˈlæsəreɪt/ *verb* [VN] (*formal*) **1** to cut skin or flesh with sth sharp: *His hand had been badly lacerated.* **2** to criticize sb very severely ▶ **la·cer·ation** /ˌlæsəˈreɪʃn/ *noun* [C, U]: *She suffered multiple lacerations to the face.*

'lace-up *noun* [usually pl.] (*especially BrE*) a shoe that is fastened with laces: *a pair of lace-ups* ◇ *lace-up boots*—picture at SHOE

lach·ry·mose /ˈlækrɪməʊs; *AmE* -moʊs/ *adj.* (*formal*) having a tendency to cry easily **SYN** TEARFUL

lack /læk/ *noun, verb*

■ *noun* [U, sing.] **~** (**of sth**) the state of not having sth or not having enough of sth: *a lack of food/ money/ skills* ◇ *The trip was cancelled* **through lack of** (= because there was not enough) *interest.* ◇ *There was* **no lack of** *volunteers.* **IDM** see TRY V.

■ *verb* [VN] [no passive] to have none or not enough of sth: *Some houses still lack basic amenities such as bathrooms.* ◇ *He lacks confidence.* ◇ *She has the determination that her brother lacks.*—see also LACKING **IDM** **lack (for) 'nothing** (*formal*) to have everything that you need—more at COURAGE

lacka·dai·si·cal /ˌlækəˈdeɪzɪkl/ *adj.* (*written*) not showing enough care or enthusiasm

lackey /ˈlæki/ *noun* **1** (*old-fashioned*) a servant **2** (*disapproving*) a person who is treated like a servant or who behaves like one

lack·ing /ˈlækɪŋ/ *adj.* [not before noun] **1 ~** (**in sth**) having none or not enough of sth: *She's not usually lacking in confidence.* ◇ *The book is completely lacking in originality.* ◇ *He was taken on as a teacher but was* **found lacking** (= was thought not to be good enough). **2** not present or not available **SYN** MISSING: *I feel there is something lacking in my life.*

lack·lustre (*BrE*) (*AmE* **lack·lus·ter**) /ˈlæklʌstə(r)/ *adj.* not interesting or exciting; dull: *a lacklustre performance/ campaign* ◇ *lacklustre hair*

la·con·ic /ləˈkɒnɪk; *AmE* -ˈkɑːn-/ *adj.* using only a few words to say sth: *a laconic comment/ manner* ▶ **la·con·ic·al·ly** /-kli/ *adv.*

lac·quer /ˈlækə(r)/ *noun, verb*

■ *noun* [U] **1** a liquid that is used on wood or metal to give it a hard shiny surface **2** (*old-fashioned*) a liquid that is sprayed on the hair so that it stays in place

■ *verb* [VN] **1** to cover sth such as wood or metal with lacquer: *a lacquered Chinese table* **2** (*old-fashioned, BrE*) to put lacquer on your hair

la·crosse /ləˈkrɒs; *AmE* -ˈkrɔːs/ *noun* [U] a game played on a field by two teams of ten players who use sticks with curved nets on them to catch, carry, and throw the ball

lac·tate /lækˈteɪt/ *verb* [V] (*technical*) (of a woman or female animal) to produce milk from the breasts to feed a baby or young animal ▶ **lac·ta·tion** /lækˈteɪʃn/ *noun* [U]: *the period of lactation*

lac·tic acid /ˌlæktɪk ˈæsɪd/ *noun* [U] an acid that forms in sour milk and is also produced in the muscles during hard exercise

lac·tose /ˈlæktəʊs; -təʊz; *AmE* -toʊs; -toʊz/ *noun* [U] (*chemistry*) a type of sugar found in milk and used in some baby foods

la·cuna /ləˈkjuːnə; *AmE* also -ˈkuː-/ *noun* (*pl.* **-nae** /-niː/ or **la·cu·nas**) (*formal*) a place where sth is missing in a piece of writing or in an idea, a theory, etc. **SYN** GAP

lacy /ˈleɪsi/ *adj.* made of or looking like LACE: *lacy underwear*

lad /læd/ *noun* **1** [C] (*old-fashioned* or *informal*) a boy or

L

æ	ɑː	e	ɜː	ə	ɪ	iː	i	ɒ	ɔː	ʌ	ʊ	u	uː
cat	father	ten	bird	about	sit	see	many	got	saw	cup	put	actual	too
								(BrE)					

young man: *Things have changed since I was a lad.* ◊ *He's a nice lad.* ◊ *Hurry up, lad.*—compare LASS **2 (the lads)** [pl.] (*BrE, spoken*) a group of friends that a man works with or spends free time with: *to go to the pub with the lads* **3** [C, usually sing.] (*BrE, informal*) a lively young man, especially one who is very interested in women: *Tony was a bit of a lad—always had an eye for the women.*—see also LADDISH **4** [C] (*BrE*) a person who works in a STABLE—see also STABLE BOY

lad·der /'lædə(r)/ *noun, verb*
■ *noun* **1** a piece of equipment for climbing up and down a wall, the side of a building, etc., consisting of two lengths of wood or metal that are joined together by steps or RUNGS: *to climb up/fall off a ladder*—see also STEPLADDER **2** [usually sing.] a series of stages by which you can make progress in a career or an organization: *to move up or down the social ladder* ◊ *the career ladder* **3** (*BrE*) (*AmE* **run**) a long thin hole in TIGHTS or STOCKINGS where some threads have broken
■ *verb* [V, VN] (*BrE*) if TIGHTS or STOCKINGS **ladder** or you **ladder** them, a long thin hole appears in them

lad·die /'lædi/ *noun* (*informal, especially ScotE*) a boy—compare LASS

lad·dish /'lædɪʃ/ *adj.* (*informal*) behaving in a way that is supposed to be typical of a young man

laden /'leɪdn/ *adj.* ~ **(with sth) 1** heavily loaded with sth: *passengers laden with luggage* ◊ *The trees were laden with apples.* ◊ *a heavily/fully laden truck*—compare UNLADEN **2** (*literary*) full of sth, especially sth unpleasant: *His voice was soft, yet laden with threat.* **3** (-laden) used to form adjectives showing that sth is full of, or loaded with, the thing mentioned: *calorie-laden cream cakes*

la-di-da /ˌlɑː di 'dɑː/ *adj.* (*informal, disapproving, especially BrE*) used to describe a way of speaking or behaving that is typical of upper-class people but that is not natural or sincere: *I can't stand Jane or her la-di-da friends.*

'ladies' man (also **'lady's man**) *noun* a man who enjoys spending time with women and thinks he is attractive to them

'ladies' room *noun* (*AmE*) a women's toilet

ladle /'leɪdl/ *noun, verb*
■ *noun* a large deep spoon with a long handle, used especially for serving soup—picture at KITCHEN
■ *verb* [VN] to place food on a plate with a large spoon or in large quantities **PHRV** **ˌladle sth↔'out** (sometimes *disapproving*) to give sb a lot of sth, especially money or advice

lady /'leɪdi/ (*pl.* **-ies**) *noun* **1** [C] a word used to mean 'woman' that some people, especially older people, consider is more polite: *There's a lady waiting to see you.* ◊ *He was with an attractive young lady.* ◊ *the ladies' golf championship* ◊ *a tea lady* (= a woman who serves tea in an office) ◊ *a lady doctor/golfer* ◊ (*AmE, approving*) *She's a tough lady.* **HELP** Some women object to the way **lady** is used in some of these examples and prefer it to be avoided if possible: *a doctor/a woman doctor* ◊ *There's someone waiting to see you.*—see also BAG LADY, CLEANING LADY, FIRST LADY, LEADING LADY, OLD LADY **2** [C] a woman who is polite and well educated, has excellent manners and always behaves well: *His wife was a real lady.*—compare GENTLEMAN **3** [C, usually pl.] (*formal*) used when speaking to or about a girl or woman, especially sb you do not know: *Can I take your coats, ladies?* ◊ *Could I have your attention, ladies and gentlemen?* **HELP** Some women do not like **ladies** used on its own, as in the first example, and prefer it to be left out. **4** [sing.] (*especially AmE*) an informal way to talk to a woman, showing a lack of respect: *Listen, lady, don't shout at me.* **5** [C] (*old-fashioned*) (in Britain) a woman belonging to a high social class: *the lords and ladies of the court* ◊ *a lady's maid* **6 (Lady)** [C] (in Britain) a title used by women who are members of the NOBILITY or by the wives and daughters of some members of the NOBILITY, or by the wife of a KNIGHT: *Lady Thatcher* ◊ *Lady Jane Grey*—compare LORD, SIR **7 (a/the ladies)** [U] (*BrE*) (*AmE* **ladies' room** [C]) a toilet/bathroom for women in a public building or place:

Could you tell me where the ladies is? **8 (Our Lady)** a title used to refer to Mary, the mother of Christ, especially in the Roman Catholic Church: *Our Lady of Lourdes*

lady·bird /'leɪdibɜːd; *AmE* -bɜːrd/ (*BrE*) (*AmE* **lady·bug** /'leɪdibʌg/) *noun* a small flying insect, usually red with black spots—picture on page A7

ˌlady-in-'waiting *noun* (*pl.* **ladies-in-waiting**) a woman who goes to places with, and helps, a queen or princess

lady·kill·er /'leɪdikɪlə(r)/ *noun* (*old-fashioned or informal*) a man who is sexually attractive and successful with women, but who does not stay in a relationship with anyone for long

lady·like /'leɪdilaɪk/ *adj.* (*old-fashioned*) polite and quiet; typical of what is supposed to be socially acceptable for a woman: *ladylike behaviour* ◊ *Her language was not very ladylike.*

ˌlady 'mayor *noun* = MAYORESS

lady·ship /'leɪdiʃɪp/ *noun* **1 (Her/Your Ladyship)** a title used when talking to or about a woman who is a member of the NOBILITY: *Does Your Ladyship require anything?* **2** (*BrE, spoken*) a way of talking to or about a girl or woman that you think is trying to be too important: *Perhaps her ladyship would like to hang up her own clothes today!*—compare LORDSHIP

'lady's man *noun* = LADIES' MAN

lag /læg/ *verb, noun*
■ *verb* (**-gg-**) **1** ~ **(behind sb/sth)** | ~ **(behind)** to move or develop slowly or more slowly than other people, organizations, etc: *The little boy lagged behind his parents.* ◊ *We still lag far behind many of our competitors in using modern technology.* **2** [VN] ~ **sth (with sth)** to cover pipes, etc. with a special material to stop the water in them from freezing, or to save heat
■ *noun* = TIME LAG—see also JET LAG, OLD LAG

lager /'lɑːgə(r)/ *noun* (*BrE*) **1** [U, C] a type of light pale beer that usually has a lot of bubbles: *a pint of lager* ◊ *German lagers* **2** [C] a glass, can or bottle of this: *Two lagers, please.*

'lager lout *noun* (*BrE*) a young man who drinks too much alcohol and then behaves in a noisy and unpleasant way

lag·gard /'lægəd; *AmE* -gərd/ *noun* (*old-fashioned*) a slow and lazy person, organization, etc.

la·goon /lə'guːn/ *noun* **1** a lake of salt water that is separated from the sea by a REEF or an area of rock or sand **2** (*AmE*) a small area of fresh water near a lake or river **3** (*technical*) an artificial area built to hold waste water before it is treated at a SEWAGE WORKS

lah (also **la**) /lɑː/ *noun* (*music*) the 6th note of a MAJOR scale

laid *pt, pp* of LAY

ˌlaid-'back *adj.* (*informal*) calm, and relaxed; seeming not to worry about anything: *a laid-back attitude to life*

lain *pt* of LIE

lair /leə(r); *AmE* ler/ *noun* [usually sing.] **1** a place where a wild animal sleeps or hides **2** a place where sb goes to hide or to be alone

laird /leəd; *AmE* lerd/ *noun* (in Scotland) a person who owns a large area of land

laissez-faire /ˌleseɪ 'feə(r); *AmE* 'fer/ *noun* [U] (from French) the policy of allowing private businesses to develop without government control ► **laissez-faire** *adj.*: *a laissez-faire economy* ◊ *They have a laissez-faire approach to bringing up their children* (= they give them a lot of freedom).

laity /'leɪəti/ *noun* (**the laity**) [sing.+ sing./pl. *v.*] all the members of a Church who are not CLERGY—see also LAYMAN

lake /leɪk/ *noun* (*abbr.* **L.**) a large area of water that is surrounded by land: *We swam in the lake.* ◊ *Lake Ontario* ◊ (*figurative*) *a wine lake* (= a large supply of wine that is not being used)

lake·side /'leɪksaɪd/ *noun* [sing.] the area around the edge of a lake: *We went for a walk by the lakeside.* ◊ *a lakeside hotel*

la·la land /'lɑ: lɑ: lænd/ *noun* (*AmE*) = CLOUD-CUCKOO-LAND

lam /læm/ *noun* **IDM** **on the 'lam** (*AmE, informal*) escaping from sb, especially from the police

lamb /læm/ *noun, verb*
■ *noun* **1** [C] a young sheep **2** [U] meat from a young sheep: *a leg of lamb ◊ lamb chops*—compare MUTTON **3** [C] (*informal*) used to describe or address sb with affection or pity: *You poor lamb!* **IDM** **(like) a lamb/lambs to the 'slaughter** used to describe people who are going to do sth dangerous without realizing it—more at MUTTON
■ *verb* [V] (of a sheep) to give birth to a lamb: *She's due to lamb in two weeks' time.*

lam·bada /læm'bɑːdə/ *noun* a fast modern dance originally from Brazil

lam·baste (also **lam·bast**) /læm'beɪst/ *verb* [VN] (*formal*) to attack or criticize sb very severely, especially in public

lambs·wool /'læmzwʊl/ *noun* [U] soft fine wool from lambs, used for knitting clothes: *a lambswool sweater*

lame /leɪm/ *adj.* **1** (of people or animals) unable to walk well because of an injury to the leg or foot **2** (of an excuse, explanation, etc.) weak and difficult to believe ▶ **lame·ness** *noun* [U]: *The disease has left her with permanent lameness.*

lamé /'lɑːmeɪ; *AmE* lɑː'meɪ/ *noun* [U] a fabric into which gold or silver thread has been woven: *a silver lamé evening gown*

,lame 'duck *noun* **1** a person or an organization that is not very successful and that needs help **2** (*informal, especially AmE*) a politician or a government whose period of office will soon end and who will not be elected again: *a lame duck president/administration*

lame·ly /'leɪmli/ *adv.* in a way that does not sound very confident, or that does not persuade other people: *'I must have made a mistake,' she said lamely.*

lam·ent /lə'ment/ *verb, noun*
■ *verb* (*formal*) to feel or express great sadness or disappointment about sb/sth: [VN] *In the poem he laments the destruction of the countryside. ◊ She sat alone weeping, lamenting her fate.* [also V that, V speech]
■ *noun* (*formal*) a song, poem or other expression of great sadness for sb who has died or for sth that has ended: *a nostalgic lament for lost love*

lam·ent·able /'læməntəbl; lə'ment-/ *adj.* (*formal*) very disappointing **SYN** REGRETTABLE: *She shows a lamentable lack of understanding.* ▶ **lam·ent·ably** /-əbli/ *adv.*

lam·en·ta·tion /,læmən'teɪʃn/ *noun* [C, U] (*formal*) an expression of great sadness or disappointment

la·mented /lə'mentɪd/ *adj.* (*formal or humorous*) (of sb/sth that has died or disappeared) missed very much: *her late lamented husband ◊ the last edition of the much lamented newspaper*

lamin·ate /'læmɪnət/ *noun* [U, C] a material that is laminated

lamin·ated /'læmɪneɪtɪd/ *adj.* **1** (of wood, plastic, etc.) made by sticking several thin layers together: *laminated glass/timber ◊ a laminated table top* **2** covered with thin transparent plastic for protection: *laminated membership cards*

lamp /læmp/ *noun* **1** a device that uses electricity, oil or gas to produce light: *a table/desk/bicycle lamp ◊ to switch on/turn off a lamp ◊ She could see the rain in the light of the street lamps.*—see also FOG LAMP, HURRICANE LAMP, STANDARD LAMP—picture at LANTERN **2** an electrical device that produces rays of heat and that is used for medical or scientific purposes: *an infra-red/ultraviolet lamp*—see also BLOWLAMP, SUNLAMP

lamp·light /'læmplaɪt/ *noun* [U] light from a lamp: *Her face looked pale in the lamplight.*

lamp·lit /'læmplɪt/ *adj.* [usually before noun] given light by lamps; seen by the light from lamps: *a lamplit room ◊ a lamplit figure in the chair*

lam·poon /læm'puːn/ *verb, noun*
■ *verb* [VN] (*written*) to criticize sb/sth publicly in an amusing way that makes them or it look ridiculous: *His cartoons mercilessly lampooned the leading politicians of his time.*

■ *noun* (*written*) a piece of writing that criticizes sb/sth and makes them or it look silly

'lamp post *noun* (*especially BrE*) a tall post in the street with a lamp at the top: *The car skidded and hit a lamp post.*—compare STREET LIGHT

lamp·shade /'læmpʃeɪd/ *noun* a decorative cover for a lamp that is used to soften the light or to direct it—picture at LANTERN

LAN /læn/ *noun* (*computing*) the abbreviation for 'local area network' (a system for communicating by computer within a large building)—compare WAN

lance /lɑːns; *AmE* læns/ *noun, verb*
■ *noun* a weapon with a long wooden handle and a pointed metal end that was used by people fighting on horses in the past
■ *verb* [VN] to cut open an infected place on sb's body with a sharp knife in order to let out the PUS (= a yellow substance produced by infection): *to lance an abscess*

,lance 'corporal *noun* a member of one of the lower ranks in the British army: *Lance Corporal Alan Jackson*

lan·cet /'lɑːnsɪt; *AmE* 'læn-/ *noun* a knife with a sharp point and two sharp edges, used by doctors for cutting skin and flesh

land /lænd/ *noun, verb*
■ *noun*
SURFACE OF EARTH | **1** [U] the surface of the earth that is not sea: *It was good to be back on land. ◊ We made the journey by land, though flying would have been cheaper. ◊ In the distance the crew sighted land. ◊ The elephant is the largest living land animal.*—see also DRY LAND ⇨ note at EARTH
AREA OF GROUND | **2** [U] (also **lands** [pl.]) an area of ground, especially of a particular type or used for a particular purpose: *fertile/arid/stony land ◊ flat/undulating/hilly land ◊ agricultural/arable/industrial land ◊ The land was very dry and hard after the long, hot summer. ◊ The land rose to the east. ◊ a piece of waste/derelict land ◊ Some of the country's richest grazing lands are in these valleys.* **3** [U] (also *formal* **lands** [pl.]) the area of ground that sb owns, especially when you think of it as property that can be bought or sold: *The price of land is rising rapidly. ◊ He owns 500 acres of land in Scotland. ◊ During the war their lands were occupied by the enemy.*—see also NO-MAN'S-LAND
COUNTRYSIDE | **4** (**the land**) [U] used to refer to the countryside and the way people live in the country as opposed to in cities: *At the beginning of the 20th century almost a third of the population lived off the land* (= grew or produced their own food). *◊ Many people leave the land to find work in towns and cities. ◊ His family had always farmed the land.*
COUNTRY/REGION | **5** [C] (*literary*) used to refer to a country or region in an emotional or imaginative way: *She longed to return to her native land. ◊ They dreamed of travelling to foreign lands. ◊ America is the land of freedom and opportunity.*—see also CLOUD-CUCKOO-LAND, CLUBLAND, DOCKLAND, DREAMLAND, FAIRYLAND, NEVER-NEVER LAND, THE PROMISED LAND, WONDERLAND
HELP There are many other compounds ending in **land**. You will find them at their place in the alphabet.
IDM **(back) in the land of the 'living** used to emphasize that sb is still living or that sb is alive and well after an illness or accident: *I'm glad to see you're back in the land of the living. We were worried about you.* **the land of ,milk and 'honey** a place where life is pleasant and easy and people are very happy **see, etc. how the 'land lies** (*BrE*) to find out about a situation: *Let's wait and see how the land lies before we do anything.*—more at LIE *n.*, LIVE[1], SPY *v.*
■ *verb*
OF BIRD/PLANE/INSECT | **1** [V] to come down through the air onto the ground or another surface: *The plane landed safely. ◊ A fly landed on his nose.* **OPP** TAKE OFF
OF PILOT | **2** [VN] to bring a plane down to the ground in a controlled way: *The pilot landed the plane safely.*
ARRIVE IN PLANE/BOAT | **3** [V] to arrive somewhere in a plane or a boat: *We shall be landing shortly. Please fasten your*

seatbelts. ◊ *The troops landed at dawn.* ◊ *They were the first men to land on the moon.* ◊ *The ferry is due to land at 3 o'clock.* **4** [VN] to put sb/sth on land from an aircraft, a boat, etc: *The troops were landed by helicopter.*

FALL TO GROUND | **5** [V] to come down to the ground after jumping, falling or being thrown: *I fell and landed heavily at the bottom of the stairs.* ◊ *A large stone landed right beside him.*

DIFFICULTIES | **6** [V+*adv./prep.*] to arrive somewhere and cause difficulties that have to be dealt with: *Why do complaints always **land on my desk*** (= why do I always have to deal with them)?

JOB | **7** (*informal*) to succeed in getting a job, etc., especially one that a lot of other people want: [VN] *He's just landed a starring role in Spielberg's next movie.* ◊ [VNN] *She's just **landed herself** a company directorship.*

FISH | **8** [VN] to catch a fish and bring it out of the water on to the land

IDM **land a 'blow, 'punch, etc.** to succeed in hitting sb/sth: *She landed a punch on his chin.*—more at FOOT *n.*
PHRV **'land in sth | 'land sb/yourself in sth** (*informal*) to get sb/yourself into a difficult situation: *She was arrested and landed in court.* ◊ *His hot temper has landed him in trouble before.* ◊ *Now you've really **landed me in it!*** (= got me into trouble) **,land 'up in, at …** (*informal*) to reach a final position or situation, sometimes after other things have happened: *We travelled around for a while and landed up in Seattle.* ◊ *He landed up in a ditch after he lost control of his car.* **'land sb/yourself with sth/sb** (*informal*) to give sb/yourself sth unpleasant to do, especially because nobody else wants to do it: *As usual, I got landed with all the boring jobs.*

'land agent *noun* (*especially BrE*) a person whose job is to manage land, farms, etc. for sb else

'land-based *adj.* [usually before noun] situated on or living on the land: *land-based missiles* ◊ *land-based animals*

land·ed /'lændɪd/ *adj.* [only before noun] **1** owning a lot of land: *the landed gentry* **2** including a large amount of land: *landed estates*

land·fall /'lændfɔːl/ *noun* **1** [U, C] (*literary*) the land that you see or arrive at first after a journey by sea or by air: *After three weeks crossing the Atlantic, they made **landfall** on the coast of Ireland.* **2** [C] = LANDSLIDE

land·fill /'lændfɪl/ *noun* **1** [C, U] an area of land where large amounts of waste material are buried under the earth: *The map shows the position of the new landfills.* ◊ *a landfill site* **2** [U] the process of burying large amounts of waste material: *the choice of landfill or incineration* **3** [U] waste material that will be buried

land·form /'lændfɔːm; *AmE* -fɔːrm/ *noun* (*geology*) a natural feature of the earth's surface

land·hold·ing /'lændhəʊldɪŋ; *AmE* -hoʊld-/ *noun* [C, U] (*technical*) a piece of land that sb owns or rents; the act of owning or renting land ▶ **land·hold·er** *noun*: *farmers and landholders*

land·ing /'lændɪŋ/ *noun* **1** [C] the area at the top of a staircase where you arrive before you go into an upstairs room or move onto another staircase **2** [C, U] an act of bringing an aircraft or a spacecraft down to the ground after a journey: *a perfect/smooth/safe landing* ◊ *the first Apollo moon landing* ◊ *The pilot was forced to make **an emergency landing**.* ◊ *a landing site* OPP TAKE-OFF—see also CRASH LANDING **3** [C] an act of bringing soldiers to land in an area that is controlled by the enemy **4** = LANDING STAGE

'landing craft *noun* (*pl.* **landing craft**) a boat with a flat bottom, carried on a ship. Landing craft open at one end so soldiers and equipment can be brought to the shore.

'landing gear *noun* [U] = UNDERCARRIAGE

'landing stage (*BrE*) (also **landing** *AmE, BrE*) *noun* a flat wooden platform on the water where boats let people get on and off, and load and unload goods SYN JETTY

'landing strip *noun* = AIRSTRIP

land·lady /'lændleɪdi/ *noun* (*pl.* **-ies**) **1** a woman from whom you rent a room, a house, etc. **2** (*BrE*) a woman

who owns or manages a pub or a GUEST HOUSE—compare LANDLORD

land·less /'lændləs/ *adj.* [usually before noun] not owning land for farming; not allowed to own land: *landless peasants/labourers*

land·locked /'lændlɒkt; *AmE* -lɑːkt/ *adj.* almost or completely surrounded by land: *Switzerland is completely landlocked.*

land·lord /'lændlɔːd; *AmE* -lɔːrd/ *noun* **1** a man from whom you rent a room, a house, etc. **2** (*BrE*) a man who owns or manages a pub or a GUEST HOUSE—compare LANDLADY

land·mark /'lændmɑːk; *AmE* -mɑːrk/ *noun* **1** something, such as a large building, that you can see clearly from a distance and that will help you to know where you are: *The Empire State Building is a familiar landmark on the New York skyline.* **2 ~** (**in sth**) an event, a discovery, an invention, etc. that marks an important stage in sth: *The ceasefire was seen as a major landmark in the fight against terrorism.* ◊ *a landmark decision/ruling in the courts* **3** (*especially AmE*) a building or a place that is very important because of its history, and that should be preserved

'land mass *noun* (*technical*) a large area of land, for example a continent

land·mine /'lændmaɪn/ *noun* a bomb placed on or under the ground, which explodes when vehicles or people move over it

'land office *noun* (*AmE*) = LAND REGISTRY

land·owner /'lændəʊnə(r); *AmE* -oʊn-/ *noun* a person who owns land, especially a large area of land ▶ **land·owner·ship** (also **land·owning**) *noun* [U]: *private land-ownership* **land·owning** *adj.* [only before noun]: *the great landowning families*

'land reform *noun* [U, C] the principle of dividing land for farming into smaller pieces so that more people can own some

'land registry (*BrE*) (*AmE* **'land office**) *noun* a government office that keeps a record of areas of land and who owns them

'Land Rover™ (also **'Land-Rover**™) *noun* a strong motor vehicle used for travelling over rough ground

---

WHICH WORD?

landscape / scenery / countryside　　(?)

The following adjectives are frequently used with these nouns:

~ landscape	~ scenery	~ countryside
English	beautiful	surrounding
rural	mountain	English
natural	spectacular	open
flat	dramatic	beautiful
bleak	breathtaking	rolling
urban	coastal	unspoilt

The **landscape** [C] of an area is the way its physical features are arranged: *Mountains dominate the Welsh landscape.* ◊ *an urban landscape.*

You use **scenery** [U] when you are saying that these physical features are attractive to look at: *We stopped to admire the scenery.*

The **country/countryside** [U] describes land that is away from towns and cities: *When I was a child, I spent a lot of time in the country.* ◊ *a country house/park/road* ◊ *the surrounding countryside.* The **country** is more common in this sense but **countryside** is used especially in official language or when it would not be clear which sense of **country** is meant: *the Wildlife and Countryside Act.*

---

land·scape /'lændskeɪp/ *noun, verb*
■ *noun* **1** [C, usually sing.] everything you can see when you look across a large area of land, especially in the country: *the rugged/mountainous/dramatic landscape of Bolivia* ◊ *the woods and fields that are typical features of*

L

s	t	v	z	ʃ	ʒ	tʃ	dʒ	θ	ð	ŋ
see	tea	van	zoo	shoe	vision	chain	jam	thin	this	sing

the English landscape ◊ *an urban/industrial landscape* ◊ *(figurative) We can expect changes in the political landscape.* **2** [C, U] a painting of a view of the countryside; this style of painting: *a British artist famous for his landscapes*—compare TOWNSCAPE **3** [U] *(technical)* the way of printing a document in which the top of the page is one of the longer sides: *Select the landscape option when printing the file.*—compare PORTRAIT—picture on page 251 **IDM** see BLOT *n.*

■ *verb* [VN] to improve the appearance of an area of land by changing the design and planting trees, flowers, etc: *landscaped gardens*

landscape architect *noun* a person whose job is planning and designing the environment, especially so that roads, buildings, etc. combine with the landscape in an attractive way ▶ **landscape architecture** *noun* [U]

landscape gardener *noun* a person whose job is designing and creating attractive parks and gardens ▶ **landscape gardening** *noun* [U]

land·slide /ˈlændslaɪd/ *noun* **1** (also **land·fall**) a mass of earth, rock, etc. that falls down the slope of a mountain or a cliff: *The house was buried beneath a landslide.*—see also LANDSLIP **2** an election in which one person or party gets very many more votes than the other people or parties: *She was expected to win by a landslide.* ◊ *Labour's landslide victory of 1997*

land·slip /ˈlændslɪp/ *noun* a mass of rock and earth that falls down a slope, usually smaller than a landslide

land·ward /ˈlændwəd; *AmE* -wərd/ *adj.* [only before noun] facing the land; away from the sea: *on the landward side of the road* ▶ **land·ward** (also **land·wards**) *adv.*: *After an hour, the ship turned landward.*

lane /leɪn/ *noun* **1** a narrow road in the country: *winding country lanes* ◊ *We drove along a muddy lane to reach the farmhouse.*—see also MEMORY LANE **2** (especially in place names) a street, often a narrow one with buildings on both sides: *The quickest way is through the back lanes behind the bus station.* ◊ *Park Lane* **3** a section of a wide road, that is marked by painted white lines, to keep lines of traffic separate: *the inside/middle/outside lane* ◊ *the northbound/southbound lane* ◊ *to change lanes* ◊ *She signalled and pulled over into the slow lane.* ◊ *a four-lane highway*—see also BUS LANE, CYCLE LANE, FAST LANE **4** a narrow marked section of a track or a swimming pool that is used by one competitor in a race: *The Australian in lane four is coming up fast from behind.*—picture on page 1251 **5** a route used by ships or aircraft on regular journeys: *one of the world's busiest shipping/sea lanes* **IDM** see FAST LANE

lan·guage /ˈlæŋɡwɪdʒ/ *noun*

OF A COUNTRY **1** [C] the system of communication in speech and writing that is used by people of a particular country: *the Japanese language* ◊ *How many languages do you speak?* ◊ *Italian is my **first language**.* ◊ *All the children must learn a **foreign language**.* ◊ *She **has a good command** of the Spanish language.* ◊ *a qualification in language teaching* ◊ *They fell in love in spite of the **language barrier** (= the difficulty of communicating when people speak different languages).*—see also MODERN LANGUAGE

COMMUNICATION **2** [U] the use by humans of a system of sounds and words to communicate: *theories about the origins of language* ◊ *a study of language acquisition in two-year-olds*

STYLE OF SPEAKING/WRITING **3** [U] a particular style of speaking or writing: *bad/foul/strong language* (= words that people may consider offensive) ◊ *literary/poetic language* ◊ *the language of the legal profession* ◊ *Give your instructions in everyday language.*—see also BAD LANGUAGE

MOVEMENTS/SYMBOLS/SOUND **4** [C, U] a way of expressing ideas and feelings using movements, symbols and sound: *the language of mime* ◊ *the language of dolphins/bees*—see also BODY LANGUAGE, SIGN LANGUAGE

COMPUTING **5** [C, U] a system of symbols and rules that is used to operate a computer: *a programming language*

IDM **mind/watch your language** to be careful about

what you say in order not to upset or offend sb: *Watch your language, young man!* **speak/talk the same language** to be able to communicate easily with another person because you share similar opinions and experience

language laboratory *noun* a room in a school or college that contains special equipment to help students learn foreign languages by listening to tapes, watching videos, recording themselves, etc.

lan·guid /ˈlæŋɡwɪd/ *adj.* *(written)* moving slowly in a graceful manner, not needing energy or effort: *a languid wave of the hand* ◊ *a languid afternoon in the sun* ▶ **languid·ly** *adv.*: *He moved languidly across the room.*

lan·guish /ˈlæŋɡwɪʃ/ *verb* [V] *(formal)* **1** ~ (in sth) to be forced to stay somewhere or suffer sth unpleasant for a long time: *She continues to languish in a foreign prison.* **2** to become weaker or fail to make progress: *Share prices languished at 102p.*

lan·guor /ˈlæŋɡə(r)/ *noun* [U, sing.] *(literary)* the state of feeling lazy and without energy: *A delicious languor was stealing over him.* ▶ **lan·guor·ous** /ˈlæŋɡərəs/ *adj.*: *a languorous pace of life* **lan·guor·ous·ly** *adv.*

lank /læŋk/ *adj.* (of hair) straight, dull and not attractive

lanky /ˈlæŋki/ *adj.* (of a person) having long thin limbs and moving in an awkward way: *a tall, lanky teenager*

lano·lin /ˈlænəlɪn/ *noun* [U] an oil that comes from sheep's wool and is used to make skin creams

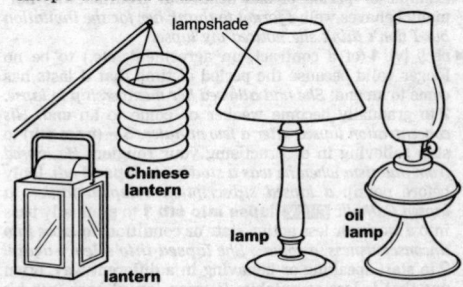

lampshade

Chinese lantern

oil lamp

lamp

lantern

lan·tern /ˈlæntən; *AmE* -tərn/ *noun* a lamp in a container, often a metal case with glass sides, that has a handle, so that you can carry it outside: *Chinese/paper lanterns*

lap /læp/ *noun, verb*

■ *noun* [C] **1** [usually sing.] the top part of your legs that forms a flat surface when you are sitting down: *There's only one seat so you'll have to sit on my lap.* ◊ *She sat with her hands in her lap.* **2** one journey from the beginning to the end of a track used for running, etc: *the fastest lap on record* ◊ *She has completed six laps.* ◊ *He was overtaken on the final lap.* ◊ *to do a **lap of honour** (= go around the track again to celebrate winning)* ◊ *(AmE) to do a **victory lap*** **3** a section of a journey or trip: *They're off on the first lap of their round-the-world tour.* **IDM** **drop/dump sth in sb's lap** *(informal)* to make sth the responsibility of another person: *They dropped the problem firmly back in my lap.* **sth drops/falls into sb's lap** somebody has the opportunity to do sth pleasant without having made any effort: *My dream job just fell into my lap.* **in the lap of the gods** if the result of sth is in the lap of the gods, you do not know what will happen because it depends on luck or things you cannot control **in the lap of luxury** in easy, comfortable conditions, and enjoying the advantages of being rich

■ *verb* (-pp-) **1** [V] (of water) to touch sth gently and regularly, often making a soft sound: *The waves lapped around our feet.* ◊ *the sound of water lapping against the boat* **2** [VN] (of animals) to drink sth with quick movements of the tongue **3** [VN] (in a race) to pass another competitor on a track who is one or more laps behind you: *She had already lapped most of the other runners.* **PHRV** **lap sth↔up 1** *(informal)* to accept or receive sth with great enjoyment, without thinking about whether it is good, true or sincere: *It's a terrible movie but audiences everywhere are lapping it up.* ◊ *She simply lapped up all*

æ	ɑː	e	ɜː	ə	ɪ	iː	i	ɒ	ɔː	ʌ	ʊ	u	uː
cat	father	ten	bird	about	sit	see	many	got	saw	cup	put	actual	too

(BrE)

L

the compliments. **2** to drink all of sth with great enjoyment: *The calf lapped up the bucket of milk.*

ˈlap belt *noun* a type of SEAT BELT that goes across your waist

ˈlap dancing *noun* [U] sexually exciting dancing or STRIPTEASE which is performed close to, or sitting on, a customer in a bar or club

lap-dog /ˈlæpdɒg; *AmE* -dɔːg/ *noun* **1** a pet dog that is small enough to be carried **2** (*disapproving*) a person who is under the control of another person or group

lapel /ləˈpel/ *noun* one of the two front parts of the top of a coat or jacket that are joined to the collar and are folded back: *to wear a flower in your lapel* ◇ *He grabbed him by the lapels of his jacket.*—picture on page A4

lapi·dary /ˈlæpɪdəri; *AmE* -deri/ *adj.* **1** (*formal*) (especially of written language) elegant and exact: *in lapidary style* **2** (*technical*) connected with stones and the work of cutting and polishing them

lapis laz·uli /ˌlæpɪs ˈlæzjuli; *AmE* ˈlæzəli/ *noun* [U] a bright blue stone, used in making jewellery and ornaments

lapse /læps/ *noun, verb*

■ *noun* **1** a small mistake, especially one that is caused by forgetting sth or by being careless: *a lapse of concentration/memory* ◇ *A momentary lapse in the final set cost her the match.* **2** a period of time between two things that happen: *After a lapse of six months we met up again.* **3** an example or period of bad behaviour from sb who normally behaves well: *I forgot to thank her for the invitation but I don't think she noticed my lapse.*

■ *verb* [V] **1** (of a contract, an agreement, etc.) to be no longer valid because the period of time that it lasts has come to an end: *She had allowed her membership to lapse.* **2** to gradually become weaker or come to an end: *His concentration lapsed after a few minutes.* **3** ~ (from sth) to stop believing in or practising your religion: *He lapsed from Judaism when he was a student.* ▶ **lapsed** *adj.* [only before noun]: *a lapsed subscription* ◇ *lapsed faith* ◇ *a lapsed Catholic* PHRV **lapse into sth 1** to gradually pass into a worse or less active state or condition: *to lapse into unconsciousness/a coma* ◇ *She lapsed into silence again.* **2** to start speaking or behaving in a different way, often one that is less acceptable: *He soon lapsed back into his old ways.*

lap-top /ˈlæptɒp; *AmE* -tɑːp/ *noun* a small computer that can work with a battery and be easily carried—compare DESKTOP COMPUTER, NOTEBOOK

lap·wing /ˈlæpwɪŋ/ (also **pee·wit**) *noun* a black and white bird with a row of feathers (called a CREST) standing up on its head

lar·ceny /ˈlɑːsəni; *AmE* ˈlɑːrs-/ *noun* [U, C] (*pl.* **-ies**) (*AmE* or *old-fashioned, BrE*) (*law*) the crime of stealing sth from sb; an occasion when this takes place SYN THEFT: *The couple were charged with grand/petty larceny* (= stealing things that are valuable/not very valuable).

larch /lɑːtʃ; *AmE* lɑːrtʃ/ *noun* [C, U] a tree with sharp pointed leaves that fall in winter and hard dry fruit called CONES

lard /lɑːd; *AmE* lɑːrd/ *noun, verb*

■ *noun* [U] a firm white substance made from the melted fat of pigs that is used in cooking

■ *verb* [VN] to put small pieces of fat on or into sth before cooking it PHRV **lard sth with sth** [usually passive] (*often disapproving*) to include a lot of a particular kind of word or expressions in a speech or in a piece of writing: *His conversation was larded with Russian proverbs.*

lar·der /ˈlɑːdə(r); *AmE* ˈlɑːrd-/ *noun* (*especially BrE*) a cupboard/closet or small room in a house, used for storing food, especially in the past SYN PANTRY

large /lɑːdʒ; *AmE* lɑːrdʒ/ *adj.* (**larger**, **larg·est**) **1** big in size or quantity: *a large area/family/house/car/appetite* ◇ *a large number of people* ◇ *very large sums of money* ◇ *He's a very large child for his age.* ◇ *A large proportion of old people live alone.* ◇ *Women usually do the larger share of the housework.* ◇ *Brazil is the world's largest producer of coffee.* ◇ *Who's the rather large* (= fat) *lady in the hat?*

2 (*abbr.* **L**) used to describe one size in a range of sizes of clothes, food, products used in the house, etc: *small, medium, large* ◇ *It's better value if you buy a large box.* **3** wide in range and involving many things: *a large and complex issue* ◇ *Some drugs are being used on a much larger scale than previously.* ◇ *If we look at the larger picture of the situation, the differences seem slight.* ⇨ note at BIG ▶ **large·ness** *noun* [U] IDM **at ˈlarge 1** (used after a noun) as a whole; in general: *the opinion of the public at large* **2** (of a dangerous person or animal) not captured; free: *Her killer is still at large.* **by and ˈlarge** (*informal*) used when you are saying something that is generally, but not completely, true: *By and large, I enjoyed my time at school.* **in ˈlarge part** | **in large ˈmeasure** (*formal*) to a great extent: *Their success is due in large part to their determination.* **(as) large as ˈlife** (*humorous*) used to show surprise at seeing sb/sth: *I hadn't seen her for fifteen years and then there she was, (as) large as life.* **ˌlarger than ˈlife** looking or behaving in a way that is more interesting or exciting than other people, and so is likely to attract attention: *He's a larger than life character—noisy, very friendly, and always joking.*—more at LOOM *v.*, WRIT *v.*

large·ly /ˈlɑːdʒli; *AmE* ˈlɑːrdʒli/ *adv.* to a great extent; mostly or mainly: *the manager who is largely responsible for the team's victory* ◇ *It was largely a matter of trial and error.* ◇ *He resigned largely because of the stories in the press.*

ˈlarge-scale *adj.* [usually before noun] **1** involving many people or things, especially over a wide area: *large-scale development* ◇ *the large-scale employment of women* **2** (of a map, model, etc.) drawn or made to a scale that shows a small area of land or a building in great detail OPP SMALL-SCALE

lar·gesse (also **lar·gess**) /lɑːˈdʒes; *AmE* lɑːrˈdʒes/ *noun* [U] (*formal* or *humorous*) the act or quality of being generous with money; money that you give to people who have less than you: *She is not noted for her largesse* (= she is not generous). ◇ *to dispense largesse to the poor*

lar·gish /ˈlɑːdʒɪʃ; *AmE* ˈlɑːrdʒɪʃ/ *adj.* fairly large

lark /lɑːk; *AmE* lɑːrk/ *noun, verb*

■ *noun* **1** a small brown bird with a pleasant song—see also SKYLARK **2** [usually sing.] (*informal*) a thing that you do for fun or as a joke: *The boys didn't mean any harm—they just did it for a lark.* **3** (*BrE, informal*) (used after another noun) an activity that you think is a waste of time or that you do not take seriously: *Perhaps this riding lark would be more fun than she'd thought.* IDM **be/get up with the ˈlark** (*old-fashioned, BrE*) to get out of bed very early in the morning **ˈblow/sod that for a lark** (*BrE, slang*) used by sb who does not want to do sth because it involves too much effort: *Sod that for a lark! I'm not doing any more tonight.*

■ *verb* PHRV **ˌlark aˈbout/aˈround** (*old-fashioned informal, especially BrE*) to enjoy yourself by behaving in a silly way

larva /ˈlɑːvə; *AmE* ˈlɑːrvə/ *noun* (*pl.* **lar·vae** /ˈlɑːviː; *AmE* ˈlɑːrviː/) an insect at the stage when it has just come out of an egg and looks like a short fat worm ▶ **lar·val** /ˈlɑːvl; *AmE* ˈlɑːrvl/ *adj.* [only before noun]: *an insect in its larval stage*—picture on page A7

laryn·gi·tis /ˌlærɪnˈdʒaɪtɪs/ *noun* [U] an infection of the larynx that makes speaking painful

lar·ynx /ˈlærɪŋks/ *noun* (*anatomy*) the area at the top of the throat that contains the VOCAL CORDS SYN VOICE BOX—picture at BODY

la·sagne (also **la·sagna**) /ləˈzænjə/ *noun* **1** [U] large flat pieces of PASTA **2** [U, C] an Italian dish made from layers of lasagne, finely chopped meat and/or vegetables and white sauce

la·scivi·ous /ləˈsɪviəs/ *adj.* (*formal, disapproving*) feeling or showing strong sexual desire: *a lascivious person* ◇ *lascivious thoughts* ▶ **la·scivi·ous·ly** *adv.* **la·scivi·ous·ness** *noun* [U]

laser /ˈleɪzə(r)/ *noun* a device that makes a very strong beam of controlled light (= with rays that are parallel and of the same WAVELENGTH): *a laser beam* ◇ *a laser naviga-*

aɪ	aʊ	eɪ	əʊ	oʊ	ɔɪ	ɪə	eə	ʊə	j	w
my	now	say	go (BrE)	go (AmE)	boy	near	hair	pure	yes	wet

tion device ◊ *The bar codes on the products are read by lasers.* ◊ *a laser show* (= lasers used as entertainment)

'laser printer *noun* a printer that produces good quality printed material by means of a laser beam

lash /læʃ/ *verb, noun*

■ *verb* **1** to hit sb/sth with great force: [V+adv./prep.] *The rain lashed at the windows.* ◊ [VN] *Huge waves lashed the shore.* **2** [VN] to hit a person or an animal with a whip, rope, stick, etc. **3** [VN] to criticize sb/sth in a very angry way **4** [VN+adv./prep.] to fasten sth tightly to sth else with ropes: *Several logs had been lashed together to make a raft.* ◊ *During the storm everything on deck had to be lashed down.* **5** to move or to move sth quickly and violently from side to side: [V] *The crocodile's tail was lashing furiously from side to side.* [also VN] **PHRV** **,lash 'out (at sb/sth) 1** to suddenly try to hit sb: *She suddenly lashed out at the boy.* **2** to criticize sb in an angry way: *In a bitter article he lashed out at his critics.*

■ *noun* **1** = EYELASH: *her long dark lashes* **2** a hit with a whip, given as a form of punishment: *They each received 20 lashes for stealing.* ◊ *(figurative)* to feel the lash of sb's tongue (= to be spoken to in an angry and critical way) **3** the thin leather part at the end of a whip

lash·ing /'læʃɪŋ/ *noun* **1** (**lashings**) [pl.] (*BrE, informal*) a large amount of sth, especially of food and drink: *a bowl of strawberries with lashings of cream* **2** [C] an act of hitting sb with a whip as a punishment: *(figurative)* He *was given a severe tongue lashing* (= angry criticism). **3** [C, usually pl.] a rope used to fasten sth tightly to sth else

lass /læs/ (also **las·sie** /'læsi/) *noun* (*ScotE, NorthE*) a girl; a young woman—compare LAD, LADDIE

las·si·tude /'læsɪtjuːd; *AmE* -tuːd/ *noun* [U] (*formal*) a state of feeling very tired in mind or body; lack of energy

lasso /læ'suː; 'læsəu; *AmE* 'læsoʊ/ *noun, verb*

■ *noun* (*pl.* **-os** or **-oes**) a long rope with one end tied into a LOOP that is used for catching horses, cows, etc.

■ *verb* [VN] to catch an animal using a lasso

last¹ /lɑːst; *AmE* læst/ *det., adv., noun, verb*—see also LAST²

■ *det.* **1** happening or coming after all other similar things or people: *We caught the last bus home.* ◊ *It's the last house on the left.* ◊ *She was last to arrive.* **2** [only before noun] most recent: *last night / Tuesday / month / summer / year* ◊ *her last book* ◊ *This last point is crucial.* **3** [only before noun] only remaining **SYN** FINAL: *This is our last bottle of wine.* ◊ *He knew this was his last hope of winning.* **4** used to emphasize that sb/sth is the least likely or suitable: *The last thing she needed was more work.* ◊ *He's the last person I'd trust with a secret.* **IDM** **be on your/its last 'legs** to be going to die or stop functioning very soon; to be very weak or in bad condition **the day, week, month, etc. before 'last** the day, week, etc. just before the most recent one; two days, weeks, etc. ago: *I haven't seen him since the summer before last.* **every last ...** every person or thing in a group: *We spent every last penny we had on the house.* **have the last 'laugh** to be successful when you were not expected to be, making your opponents look stupid **in the last re'sort** when there are no other possible courses of action: *In the last resort we can always walk home.* **your/the last 'gasp** the point at which you/sth can no longer continue living, fighting, existing, etc. **the ,last 'minute/'moment** the latest possible time before an important event: *They changed the plans at the last minute.* ◊ *Don't leave your decision to the last moment.* **a/your last re'sort** the person or thing you rely on when everything else has failed: *I've tried everyone else and now you're my last resort.* **the ,last 'word (in sth)** the most recent, fashionable, advanced, etc. thing: *These apartments are the last word in luxury.*—more at ANALYSIS, BREATH, LONG *adj.*, MAN *n.*, STRAW, THING, WEEK, WORD *n.*

■ *adv.* **1** after anyone or anything else; at the end: *He came last in the race.* ◊ *They arrived last of all.* **2** most recently: *When did you see him last?* ◊ *I saw him last / I last saw him in New York two years ago.* ◊ *They last won the cup in 1995.* **IDM** **,last but not 'least** used when mentioning the last person or thing of a group, in order to say that they are not less important than the others: *Last but not least,*

I'd like to thank all the catering staff. **,last 'in, ,first 'out** used, for example in a situation when people are losing their jobs, to say that the last people to be employed will be the first to go—more at FIRST *adv.*

■ *noun* (**the last**) (*pl.* **the last**) **1** the person or thing that comes or happens after all other similar people or things: *Sorry I'm late—am I the last?* ◊ *They were the last to arrive.* **2 ~ of sth** the only remaining part or items of sth: *These are the last of our apples.* **IDM** **at (long) 'last** after much delay, effort, etc.; in the end **SYN** FINALLY: *At last we're home!* ◊ *At long last the cheque arrived.* ⇨ note at LASTLY **hear/see the 'last of sb/sth** to hear/see sb/sth for the last time: *That was the last I ever saw of her.* ◊ *Unfortunately, I don't think we've heard the last of this affair.* **the last I 'heard** (*spoken*) used to give the most recent news you have about sb/sth: *The last I heard he was still working at the garage.* **to/till the 'last** until the last possible moment, especially until death: *He died protesting his innocence to the last.*—more at BREATHE, FIRST *n.*

■ *verb* **1** *linking verb* [V] (not used in the progressive tenses) to continue for a particular period of time: *The meeting only lasted (for) a few minutes.* ◊ *Each game lasts about an hour.* ◊ *How long does the play last?* **2** to continue to exist or to function well: [V] *This weather won't last.* ◊ *He's making a big effort now, and I hope it lasts.* ◊ [VN] *These shoes should last you till next year.* **3 ~ (sth) (out)** to survive sth or manage to stay in the same situation, in spite of difficulties: [V] *She won't last long in that job.* ◊ *Can you last (out) until I can get help?* ◊ [VN] *Doctors say that she probably won't last out the night* (= she will probably die before the morning). ◊ *He was injured early on and didn't last the match.* **4 ~ (sb) (out)** to be enough for sb to use, especially for a particular period of time: [V] *Will the coffee last out till next week?* ◊ *We've got enough food to last (for) three days.* ◊ [VN] *We've got enough food to last us (for) three days.*

WHICH WORD?
last / take

Last and **take** are both used to talk about the length of time that something continues.

Last is used to talk about the length of time that an event continues: *How long do you think this storm will last? ◊ The movie lasted over two hours.* **Last** does not always need an expression of time: *His annoyance won't last.* **Last** is also used to say that you have enough of something: *We don't have enough money to last until next month.*

Take is used to talk about the amount of time you need in order to go somewhere or do something. It must be used with an expression of time: *It takes (me) at least an hour to get home from work. ◊ How long will the flight take? ◊ The water took ages to boil.*

---

last² /lɑːst; *AmE* læst/ *noun* a block of wood or metal shaped like a foot, used in making and repairing shoes—see also LAST¹

,last 'call *noun* **1** (*especially AmE*) = LAST ORDERS **2** the final request at an airport for passengers to get on their plane

,last-'ditch *adj.* used to describe a final attempt to achieve sth, when there is not much hope of succeeding: *She underwent a heart transplant in a last-ditch attempt to save her.*

last·ing /'lɑːstɪŋ; *AmE* 'læstɪŋ/ *adj.* [usually before noun] continuing to exist or to have an effect for a long time: *Her words left a lasting impression on me.* ◊ *I formed several lasting friendships at college.* ◊ *The training was of no lasting value.*—see also LONG-LASTING ▶ **last·ing·ly**

the ,Last 'Judgement *noun* [sing.] = JUDGEMENT DAY

last·ly /'lɑːstli; *AmE* 'læstli/ *adv.* **1** used to introduce the final point that you want to make: *Lastly, I'd like to ask you about your plans.* **2** at the end; after all the other things that you have mentioned: *Lastly, add the lemon juice.* ⇨ note on page 724

---

b	d	f	g	h	k	l	m	n	p	r
bad	did	fall	get	hat	cat	leg	man	now	pen	red

L

L

WHICH WORD?
lastly / at last

Lastly is used to introduce the last in a list of things or the final point you are making: *Lastly, I would like to thank my parents for all their support.*

At last is used when something happens after a long time, especially when there has been some difficulty or delay: *At last, after twenty hours on the boat, they arrived at their destination.* You can also use **finally**, **eventually** or **in the end** with this meaning, but not *lastly*.

'last name *noun* your family name—compare SURNAME

,last 'orders *noun* [pl.] (*BrE*) (also **,last 'call** *AmE, BrE*) the last opportunity for people to buy drinks in a pub or a bar before it closes: *'Last orders, please!'*

the ,last 'post *noun* [sing.] (*BrE*) a tune played on a BUGLE at military funerals and at the end of the day in military camps

the ,last 'rites *noun* [pl.] a Christian religious ceremony that a priest performs for and in the presence of a dying person: *to administer the last rites to sb* ◊ *to receive the last rites*

lat. *abbr.* (in writing) LATITUDE

latch /lætʃ/ *noun, verb*
■ *noun* **1** a small metal bar that is used to fasten a door or a gate. You raise it to open the door, and lower it into a metal hook to fasten it: *He lifted the latch and opened the door.* **2** (*especially BrE*) a type of lock on a door that can only be opened from the outside with a key: *She listened for his key in the latch.* **IDM** **on the 'latch** (*BrE*) closed but not locked: *Can you leave the door on the latch so I can get in?*
■ *verb* [VN] to fasten sth with a latch: *He closed the window and latched it.* **PHRV** **,latch 'on (to sth)** | **,latch 'onto sth** (*informal*) to understand an idea or what sb is saying: *It was a difficult concept to grasp, but I soon latched on.* **,latch 'on (to sb/sth)** | **,latch 'onto sb/sth** (*informal*) **1** to become attached to sb/sth: *antibodies that latch onto germs* **2** to join sb and stay in their company, especially when they would prefer you not to be with them **3** to develop a strong interest in sth: *She always latches on to the latest craze.*

latch·key /'lætʃkiː/ *noun* a key for the front or the outer door of a house, etc.

'latchkey child (also **'latchkey kid**) *noun* (usually *disapproving*) a child who is at home alone after school because both parents are at work

late /leɪt/ *adj., adv.*
■ *adj.* (**later**, **lat·est**) **1** [only before noun] near the end of a period of time, a person's life, etc: *in the late afternoon* ◊ *in late summer* ◊ *She married in her late twenties* (= when she was 28 or 29). ◊ *In later life he started playing golf.* ◊ *The school was built in the late 1970s.* **OPP** EARLY **2** [not usually before noun] arriving, happening or done after the expected, arranged or usual time: *I'm sorry I'm late.* ◊ *She's late for work every day.* ◊ *My flight was an hour late.* ◊ *We apologize for the late arrival of this train.* ◊ *Because of the cold weather the crops are later this year.* ◊ *Interest will be charged for late payment.* ◊ *Here is a late news flash.* **OPP** EARLY **3** near the end of the day: *Let's go home—it's getting late.* ◊ *Look at the time—it's much later than I thought.* ◊ *What are you doing up at this late hour?* ◊ *What is the latest time I can have an appointment?* ◊ *I've had too many late nights recently* (= when I've gone to bed very late). **OPP** EARLY **4** [only before noun] (of a person) no longer alive: *her late husband* ◊ *the late Freddie Mercury* ▶ **late·ness** /'leɪtnəs/ *noun* [U]: *They apologized for the lateness of the train.* ◊ *Despite the lateness of the hour, the children were not in bed.*—see also LATER, LATEST **IDM** **be too 'late** happening after the time when it is possible to do sth: *It's too late to save her now.* ◊ *Buy now before it's too late.*
■ *adv.* (comparative **later**, no superlative) **1** after the expected, arranged or usual time: *I got up late.* ◊ *Can I stay up late tonight?* ◊ *She has to work late tomorrow.* ◊

The big stores are open later on Thursdays. ◊ *She married late.* ◊ *The birthday card arrived three days late.* **2** near the end of a period of time, a person's life, etc: *late in March/the afternoon* ◊ *It happened late last century—in 1895 to be exact.* ◊ *As late as* (= as recently as) *the 1950s, tuberculosis was still a fatal illness.* ◊ *He became an author late in life.* **3** near the end of the day: *There's a good film on late.* ◊ *Late that evening, there was a knock at the door.* ◊ *Share prices fell early on but rose again late in the day.*—see also LATER **OPP** EARLY **IDM** **,better ,late than 'never** (*saying*) used especially when you, or sb else, arrive late, or when sth such as success happens late, to say that this is better than not coming or happening at all ,**late in the 'day** (*disapproving*) after the time when an action could be successful: *He started working hard much too late in the day—he couldn't possibly catch up.* **late of ...** (*formal*) until recently working or living in the place mentioned: *Professor Jones, late of Oxford University* **of 'late** (*formal*) recently: *I haven't seen him of late.* **too 'late** after the time when it is possible to do sth successfully: *She's left it too late to apply for the job.* ◊ *I realized the truth too late.*—more at SOON

GRAMMAR POINT
late / lately

Late and **lately** are both adverbs, but **late** is used with similar meanings to the adjective **late**, whereas **lately** can only mean 'recently': *We arrived two hours late.* ◊ *I haven't heard from him lately.* **Lately** is usually used with a perfect tense of the verb.
Look also at the idioms **be too late** (at the adjective) and **too late** (at the adverb).

late·comer /'leɪtkʌmə(r)/ *noun* a person who arrives late

late·ly /'leɪtli/ *adv.* recently; in the recent past: *Have you seen her lately?* ◊ *It's only lately that she's been well enough to go out.* ◊ (*BrE*) *I haven't been sleeping well just lately.* ◊ *She had lately returned from India.*

'late-night *adj.* [only before noun] happening late at night; available after other things finish: *a late-night movie* ◊ *late-night shopping*

la·tent /'leɪtnt/ *adj.* [usually before noun] existing, but not yet very noticeable, active or well developed: *latent defects/disease* ◊ *These children have a huge reserve of latent talent.* ▶ **la·tency** /'leɪtənsi/ *noun* [U]

later /'leɪtə(r)/ *adv., adj.*
■ *adv.* **1** at a time in the future; after the time you are talking about: *See you later.* ◊ *I met her again three years later.* ◊ *His father died later that year.* ◊ *We're going to Rome later in the year.* ◊ *She later became a doctor.* **OPP** EARLIER **2** (**Later!**) (*spoken*) a way of saying goodbye, used by young people: *Later, guys!* **IDM** **later 'on** (*informal*) at a time in the future; after the time you are talking about: *I'm going out later on.* ◊ *Much later on, she realized what he had meant.* **not/no later than ...** by a particular time and not after it: *Entries must arrive no later than 12 June.*
■ *adj.* [only before noun] **1** coming after sth else or at a time in the future: *This is discussed in more detail in a later chapter.* ◊ *The match has been postponed to a later date.* **2** near the end of a period of time, life, etc: *the later part of the seventeenth century* ◊ *She found happiness in her later years.* **OPP** EARLIER **IDM** see SOON

lat·eral /'lætərəl/ *adj.* [usually before noun] connected with the side of sth or with movement to the side: *the lateral branches of a tree* ◊ *lateral eye movements* ▶ **lat·eral·ly** /'lætərəli/ *adv.*

,lateral 'thinking *noun* [U] (*especially BrE*) a way of solving problems by using your imagination to find new ways of looking at the problem

lat·est /'leɪtɪst/ *adj., noun*
■ *adj.* [only before noun] the most recent or newest: *the latest unemployment figures* ◊ *the latest craze/fashion/trend* ◊ *her latest novel* ◊ *Have you heard the latest news?*
■ *noun* (**the latest**) (*informal*) the most recent or the newest thing or piece of news: *This is the latest in robot technology.* ◊ *Have you heard the latest?* **IDM** **at the 'latest** no

s	t	v	z	ʃ	ʒ	tʃ	dʒ	θ	ð	ŋ
see	tea	van	zoo	shoe	vision	chain	jam	thin	this	sing

later than the time or the date mentioned: *Applications should be in by 31 October at the latest.*

latex /'leɪteks/ *noun* [U] **1** a thick white liquid that is produced by some plants and trees, especially rubber trees **2** an artificial substance similar to this that is used to make paints, glues and fabrics: *latex gloves*

lath /lɑːθ; *AmE* læð/ *noun* (*pl.* **laths** /lɑːðz; *AmE* læðz/) a thin narrow strip of wood that is used to support PLASTER (= material used for covering walls) on the inside walls and the ceilings of buildings

lathe /leɪð/ *noun* a machine that shapes pieces of wood or metal by holding and turning them against a fixed cutting tool

la·ther /'lɑːðə(r); *AmE* 'læð-/ *noun, verb*
■ *noun* [U, sing.] a white mass of small bubbles that is produced by mixing soap with water **IDM get into a 'lather | work yourself into a 'lather** (*BrE, informal*) to get anxious or angry about sth, especially when it is not necessary **in a 'lather** (*BrE, informal*) in a nervous, angry or excited state
■ *verb* **1** [VN] to cover sth with lather: *I lathered my face and started to shave.* **2** [V] to produce lather: *Soap does not lather well in hard water.*

Latin /'lætɪn; *AmE* 'lætn/ *noun, adj.*
■ *noun* **1** [U] the language of ancient Rome and the official language of its empire **2** [C] a person from countries where languages that have developed from Latin, such as Spanish, Portuguese, Italian or French, are spoken
■ *adj.* **1** of or in the Latin language: *Latin poetry* **2** connected with or typical of the countries or peoples using languages developed from Latin, such as Spanish, Portuguese, Italian or French: *a Latin temperament*

,**Latin A'merica** *noun* [U] the parts of central and S America in which Spanish or Portuguese is the main language ⇨ note at AMERICAN

La·tino /læ'tiːnəʊ; *AmE* -noʊ/ *noun* (*pl.* **-os**) a person living in the US whose family came from Central or S America where Spanish or Portuguese is spoken—compare CHICANO ▶ **La·tino** *adj.* [only before noun]

lati·tude /'lætɪtjuːd; *AmE* -tuːd/ *noun* **1** (*abbr.* **lat.**) [U] the distance of a place north or south of the EQUATOR (= the line around the world dividing north and south), measured in degrees—compare LONGITUDE **2** (**latitudes**) [pl.] a region of the world that is a particular distance from the EQUATOR: *the northern latitudes* **3** [U] ~ (in/for sth/to do sth) (*formal*) freedom to choose what you do or the way that you do it: *They allow their children far too much latitude.*

la·trine /lə'triːn/ *noun* a toilet in a camp, etc., especially one made by digging a hole in the ground

latte /'lɑːteɪ/ *noun* = CAFFÈ LATTE

lat·ter /'lætə(r)/ *adj., noun*
■ *adj.* **1** being the second of two things, people or groups that have just been mentioned, or the last in a list: *The latter point is the most important.* **2** nearer to the end of a period of time than the beginning: *the latter half of the year* ◊ *during the latter stages of the tournament*—compare FORMER
■ *noun* (**the latter**) (*pl.* **the latter**) the second of two things, people or groups that have just been mentioned, or the last in a list: *He presented two solutions. The latter seems much better.* ◊ *The town has a concert hall and two theatres. The latter were both built in the 1950s.*

'**latter-day** *adj.* [only before noun] being a modern version of a person or thing in the past: *a latter-day Robin Hood*

lat·ter·ly /'lætəli; *AmE* -tərli/ *adv.* (*formal*) **1** most recently: *Latterly his painting has shown a new freedom of expression.* **2** towards the end of a period of time: *Her health declined rapidly and latterly she never left the house.*

lat·tice /'lætɪs/ *noun* [U, C] (also '**lat·tice·work** [U]) a structure that is made of strips of wood or metal that cross over each other with spaces shaped like a diamond between them, used as a fence or a support for climbing plants; any structure or pattern like this: *a low wall of*

lattice

lattice   lattice window   trellis

stone lattice-work ◊ *a lattice of branches* ▶ **lat·ticed** /'lætɪst/ *adj.*

,**lattice 'window** (also ,**lat·ticed 'window**) *noun* a window with small pieces of glass shaped like diamonds in a FRAMEWORK of metal strips—picture at LATTICE

laud /lɔːd/ *verb* [VN] (*formal*) to praise sb/sth: *He was lauded for his courage.*

laud·able /'lɔːdəbl/ *adj.* (*formal*) deserving to be praised or admired, even if not really successful: *a laudable aim/ attempt* ▶ **laud·ably** /-əbli/ *adv.*

laud·anum /'lɔːdənəm/ *noun* [U] a drug made from OPIUM. In the past, people used to take laudanum to reduce pain and anxiety, and to help them sleep.

laud·atory /'lɔːdətəri; *AmE* -tɔːri/ *adj.* (*rare, formal*) expressing praise or admiration

laugh /lɑːf; *AmE* læf/ *verb, noun*
■ *verb* **1** ~ (at/about) to make the sounds and movements of your face that show you are happy or think sth is funny: [V] *to laugh loudly/aloud/out loud* ◊ *You never laugh at my jokes!* ◊ *The show was hilarious—I couldn't stop laughing.* ◊ *She always makes me laugh.* ◊ *He burst out laughing* (= suddenly started laughing). ◊ *She laughed to cover her nervousness.* ◊ *I told him I was worried but he laughed scornfully.* ◊ [V speech] *'You're crazy!' she laughed.* **2** [V] (**be laughing**) (*spoken, informal*) used to say that you are in a very good position, especially because you have done sth successfully: *If we win the next game we'll be laughing.* **IDM Don't make me 'laugh** (*spoken*) used to show that you think what sb has just said is impossible or stupid: *'Will your dad lend you the money?' 'Don't make me laugh!'* **laugh all the way to the 'bank** (*informal*) to make a lot of money easily and feel very pleased about it **laugh in sb's 'face** to show in a very obvious way that you have no respect for sb **laugh like a 'drain** (*BrE*) to laugh very loudly **laugh on the other side of your 'face** (*BrE, informal*) to be forced to change from feeling pleased or satisfied to feeling disappointed or annoyed **laugh sb/sth out of 'court** (*BrE, informal*) to completely reject an idea, a story, etc. that you think is not worth taking seriously at all **laugh till/ until you 'cry** to laugh so long and hard that there are tears in your eyes **laugh up your 'sleeve (at sb/sth)** (*informal*) to be secretly amused about sth **laugh your 'head off** to laugh very loudly and for a long time **not know whether to ,laugh or 'cry** (*informal*) to be unable to decide how to react to a bad or unfortunate situation **you ,have/you've ,got to 'laugh** (*spoken*) used to say that you think there is a funny side to a situation: *Well, I'm sorry you've lost your shoes, but you've got to laugh, haven't you?*—more at PISS *v.* **PHR V 'laugh at sb/sth** to make sb/sth seem stupid or not serious by making jokes about them/it: *Everybody laughs at my accent.* ◊ *She is not afraid to laugh at herself* (= not be too serious about herself). ,**laugh sth↔'off** (*informal*) to try to make people think that sth is not serious or important, especially by making a joke about it: *He laughed off suggestions that he was going to resign.*
■ *noun* [C] **1** the sound you make when you are amused or happy: *to give a laugh* ◊ *a short/harsh/bitter/nervous/ hearty laugh* ◊ *His first joke got the biggest laugh of the night.* **2** (**a laugh**) [sing.] (*informal*) an enjoyable and amusing occasion or thing that happens: *Come to the karaoke night—it should be a good laugh.* ◊ *And he didn't realize it was you? What a laugh!* **3** (**a laugh**) [sing.] a person who is amusing and fun to be with: *Paula's a good laugh, isn't she?* **IDM do sth for a 'laugh/for 'laughs** to do sth for fun or as a joke: *I just did it for a laugh, but it*

got out of hand. **have a (good) ˈlaugh (about sth)** to find sth amusing: *I was angry at the time but we had a good laugh about it afterwards.*—more at BARREL *n.*, LAST *det.*

> **VOCABULARY BUILDING**
> different ways of **laughing**
>
> **cackle** to laugh in a loud, unpleasant way, especially in a high voice
>
> **chuckle** to laugh quietly, especially because you are thinking about something funny
>
> **giggle** to laugh in a silly way because you are amused, embarrassed or nervous
>
> **guffaw** to laugh noisily
>
> **roar** to laugh very loudly
>
> **snigger/snicker** to laugh in a quiet unpleasant way, especially at something rude or at someone's problems or mistakes
>
> **titter** to laugh quietly, especially in a nervous or embarrassed way
>
> You can also **be convulsed with laughter** or **dissolve into laughter** when you find something very funny. In *BrE* people also **shriek with laughter** or **howl with laughter.**

---

laugh·able /ˈlɑːfəbl; *AmE* ˈlæf-/ *adj.* silly or ridiculous, and not worth taking seriously: *He was a laughable figure.* ◊ *The whole incident would be laughable if it were not so serious.* ▶ **laugh·ably** /-əbli/ *adv.*

laugh·ing /ˈlɑːfɪŋ; *AmE* ˈlæfɪŋ/ *adj.* showing amusement or happiness: *his laughing blue eyes* ◊ *laughing faces* **IDM** **be no laughing ˈmatter** to be sth serious that you should not joke about—more at DIE *v.*

ˈlaughing gas *noun* [U] (*informal*) = NITROUS OXIDE

laugh·ing·ly /ˈlɑːfɪŋli; *AmE* ˈlæf-/ *adv.* **1** in an amused way: *He laughingly agreed.* **2** used to show that you think a particular word is not at all a suitable way of describing something and therefore seems ridiculous: *I finally reached what we laughingly call civilization.*

ˈlaughing stock *noun* [usually sing.] a person that everyone laughs at because they have done sth stupid: *I can't wear that! I'd be a laughing stock.*

laugh·ter /ˈlɑːftə(r); *AmE* ˈlæf-/ *noun* [U] the act or sound of laughing: *to roar with laughter* ◊ *tears/gales/peals/shrieks of laughter* ◊ *to burst/dissolve into laughter* ◊ *a house full of laughter* (= with a happy atmosphere)

launch /lɔːntʃ/ *verb, noun*
■ *verb* [VN] **1** to start an activity, especially an organized one: *to launch an appeal/an inquiry/an investigation/a campaign* ◊ *to launch an attack/invasion* **2** to make a product available to the public for the first time: *a party to launch his latest novel* ◊ *The new model will be launched in July.* **3** to put a ship or boat into the water, especially one that has just been built: *The Navy is to launch a new warship today.* ◊ *The lifeboat was launched immediately.* **4** to send sth such as a spacecraft, weapon, etc. into space, into the sky or through water: *to launch a communications satellite* ◊ *to launch a missile/rocket/torpedo* **5** ~ **yourself at, from, etc. sth** | ~ **yourself forwards, etc.** to jump forwards with a lot of force: *Without warning he launched himself at me.* **PHRV** **ˈlaunch into sth**| **ˈlaunch yourself into sth** to begin sth in an enthusiastic way, especially sth that will take a long time: *He launched into a lengthy account of his career.* **ˌlaunch ˈout (into sth)** to do sth new in your career, especially sth more exciting: *It's time I launched out on my own.*
■ *noun* **1** [usually sing.] the action of launching sth; an event at which sth is launched: *the successful launch of the Ariane rocket* ◊ *a product launch* ◊ *The official launch date is in May.* **2** a large motor boat.

launch·er /ˈlɔːntʃə(r)/ *noun* (often in compounds) a device that is used to send a rocket, a MISSILE, etc. into the sky: *a rocket launcher*

ˈlaunch pad (also **ˈlaunching pad**) *noun* a platform from which a spacecraft, etc. is sent into the sky: (*figurative*) *She regards the job as a launch pad for her career in the media.*

laun·der /ˈlɔːndə(r)/ *verb* [VN] **1** (*formal*) to wash, dry and IRON clothes, etc: *freshly laundered sheets* **2** to move money that has been obtained illegally into foreign bank accounts or legal businesses so that it is difficult for people to know where the money came from

laun·der·ette (also **laun·drette**) /lɔːnˈdret/ (both *BrE*) (*AmE* **Laun·dro·mat**™) *noun* a place where you can wash and dry your clothes in machines that you operate by putting in coins

Laun·dro·mat™ /ˈlɔːndrəmæt/ *noun* (*AmE*) = LAUNDER-ETTE

laun·dry /ˈlɔːndri/ *noun* (*pl.* **-ies**) **1** [U] clothes, sheets, etc. that need washing, that are being washed, or that have been washed recently: *a pile of clean/dirty laundry* ◊ *a laundry basket/room* **2** [U, sing.] the process or the job of washing clothes, sheets, etc: *to do the laundry* ◊ *The hotel has a laundry service.* **3** [C] a business or place where you send sheets, clothes, etc. to be washed: *the hospital laundry* ◊ *a laundry van*

laure·ate /ˈlɒriət; *AmE* ˈlɔːr-/ *noun* **1** a person who has been given an official honour or prize for sth important they have achieved: *a Nobel laureate* **2** = POET LAUREATE

laurel /ˈlɒrəl; *AmE* ˈlɔːr-; ˈlɑːr-/ *noun* **1** [U, C] a bush with dark smooth shiny leaves that remain on the bush and stay green through the year: *a laurel hedge* **2** (**laurels**) [pl.] honour and praise given to sb because of sth that they have achieved: *She won laurels for her first novel.* **IDM** **look to your ˈlaurels** to be careful that you do not lose the success or advantage that you have over other people: *With so many good new actors around the older ones are having to look to their laurels.* **rest/sit on your ˈlaurels** (usually *disapproving*) to feel so satisfied with what you have already achieved that you do not try to do any more

ˈlaurel wreath *noun* a ring of laurel leaves that were worn on the head in the past as a sign of victory

lava /ˈlɑːvə/ *noun* [U] **1** hot liquid rock that comes out of a VOLCANO: *molten lava*—picture at VOLCANO **2** this type of rock when it has cooled and become hard

lava·tor·ial /ˌlævəˈtɔːriəl/ *adj.* (*especially BrE*) lavatorial humour refers in a rude way to parts of the body, going to the toilet, etc.

lav·atory /ˈlævətri; *AmE* -tɔːri/ *noun* (*pl.* **-ies**) (*old-fashioned or formal*) **1** (*especially BrE*) a toilet, or a room with a toilet in it: *There's a bathroom and a lavatory upstairs.* **2** (*BrE*) a public building or part of a building, with toilets in it: *The nearest public lavatory is at the station.* **3** (*AmE*) a SINK in a bathroom

lav·en·der /ˈlævəndə(r)/ *noun* [U] **1** a garden plant or bush with bunches of purple flowers with a sweet smell **2** the flowers of the lavender plant that have been dried, used for making sheets, clothes, etc. smell nice: *lavender oil* **3** a pale purple colour

lav·ish /ˈlævɪʃ/ *adj., verb*
■ *adj.* **1** large in amount, or impressive, and usually costing a lot of money [SYN] EXTRAVAGANT: *lavish gifts/costumes/celebrations* ◊ *They lived a very lavish lifestyle.* **2** ~ **(with/in sth)** giving or doing sth generously: *He was lavish in his praise for her paintings.* ▶ **lav·ish·ly** *adv.*: *lavishly decorated/illustrated*
■ *verb* **PHRV** **ˈlavish sth on/upon sb/sth** (*written*) to give a lot of sth, often too much, to sb/sth: *She lavishes most of her attention on her youngest son.*

law /lɔː/ *noun*
SYSTEM OF RULES | **1** (also **the law**) [U] the whole system of rules that everyone in a country or society must obey: *If they entered the building they would be breaking the law.* ◊ *In Sweden it is against the law to hit a child.* ◊ *Defence attorneys can use any means within the law to get their client off.* ◊ *British schools are now required by law to publish their exam results.* ◊ *The reforms have recently become law.* ◊ *Do not think you are above the law* (= think that you cannot be punished by the law). ◊ *the need for better law enforcement* ◊ (*humorous*) *Kate's word was law in the Brown household.* **2** [U] a particular branch of the law: *company/tax law* ◊ *He specializes in*

---

aɪ	aʊ	eɪ	əʊ	oʊ	ɔɪ	ɪə	eə	ʊə	j	w
my	now	say	go	go	boy	near	hair	pure	yes	wet
			(BrE)	(AmE)						

international law.—see also CANON LAW, CASE LAW, CIVIL LAW, COMMON LAW, PRIVATE LAW, STATUTE LAW

ONE RULE | **3** [C] ~ **(on sth)**| ~ **(against sth)** a rule that deals with a particular crime, agreement, etc: *the 1996 law against the hiring of illegal immigrants* ◇ *The government has introduced some tough new laws on food hygiene.* ◇ *strict gun/licensing laws* ◇ *a federal/state law* ◇ *to pass a law* (= officially make it part of the law) ◇ *(spoken) There ought to be a law against it!*—see also BY-LAW, LICENSING LAWS

SUBJECT/PROFESSION | **4** [U] the study of the law as a subject at university, etc.; the profession of being a lawyer: *Jane is studying law.* ◇ *(AmE) He's in law school.* ◇ *(BrE) He's at law school.* ◇ *What made you go into law?* ◇ *a law firm*

POLICE | **5 (the law)** [sing.] used to refer to the police and the legal system: *Jim is always getting into trouble with the law.* ◇ *She was well known for her brushes with the law.*

OF ORGANIZATION/ACTIVITY | **6** [C] one of the rules which controls an organization or activity: *the laws of the Church* ◇ *The first law of kung fu is to defend.* ◇ *the laws of cricket*

OF GOOD BEHAVIOUR | **7** [C] a rule for good behaviour or how you should behave in a particular place or situation: *moral laws* ◇ *the unspoken laws of the street*

IN BUSINESS/NATURE/SCIENCE | **8** [C] the fact that sth always happens in the same way in an activity or in nature: *the laws of supply and demand* ◇ *the law of gravity* **9** [C] a scientific rule that sb has stated to explain a natural process: *the first law of thermodynamics*—see also MURPHY'S LAW, PARKINSON'S LAW, SOD'S LAW, LEGAL, LEGALIZE, LEGISLATE

IDM **be a law unto your'self** to behave in an independent way and ignore rules or what other people want you to do: *Boys of that age are a law unto themselves.* **go to 'law** (*BrE*) to ask a court of law to settle a problem or disagreement: *They went to law to get back their property.* **,law and 'order** a situation in which people obey the law and behave in a peaceful way: *The government struggled to maintain law and order.* ◇ *After the riots, the military was brought in to restore law and order.* ◇ *They claim to be the party of law and order.* **the ,law of 'averages** the principle that one thing will happen as often as another if you try enough times: *Keep applying and by the law of averages you'll get a job sooner or later.* **the ,law of the 'jungle** a situation in which people are prepared to harm other people in order to succeed **lay down the 'law** to tell sb what they should or should not do, in a forceful way **take the law into your own 'hands** to do sth illegal in order to punish sb for doing sth wrong, instead of letting the police deal with them **there's no 'law against sth** (*spoken*) used to tell sb who is criticizing you that you are not doing anything wrong: *I'll sing if I want to—there's no law against it.*—more at LETTER *n.*, RULE *n.*, WRONG *adj.*

'law-abiding *adj.* obeying and respecting the law: *law-abiding citizens*

law·break·er /'lɔːbreɪkə(r)/ *noun* a person who does not obey the law ▶ **law·break·ing** *noun* [U]

'law court *noun* (*BrE*) = COURT OF LAW ⇨ note at COURT

law·ful /'lɔːfl/ *adj.* (*formal*) allowed or recognized by law; legal: *his lawful heir/wife* ◇ *Can an act that causes death ever be lawful?* **OPP** UNLAWFUL ▶ **law·ful·ly** /-fəli/ *adv.*: *a lawfully elected government*

WHICH WORD?
lawful / legal (?)

Lawful and legal can both mean 'allowed by law': *by lawful/legal means.* **Lawful** tends to be used in technical or literary contexts. The same is true of the opposites, **unlawful** and **illegal**, but **illegal** is used especially about criminal activities. **Legal** also means 'connected with the law': *the US legal system.*

law·less /'lɔːləs/ *adj.* **1** (of a country or an area) where laws do not exist or are not obeyed: *lawless streets* ◇ *the lawless days of the revolution* **2** (of people or their actions)

without respect for the law: *lawless gangs* ▶ **law·less·ness** *noun* [U]

'law lord *noun* (*BrE*) a member of the British House of Lords who is qualified to perform its legal work

law·maker /'lɔːmeɪkə(r)/ *noun* a person in government who makes the laws of a country

lawn /lɔːn/ *noun* **1** [C] an area of ground covered in short grass in a garden/yard or park, or used for playing a game: *In summer we have to mow the lawn twice a week.* ◇ *a croquet lawn*—picture at HOUSE **2** [U] a fine cotton or LINEN fabric used for making clothes

'lawn bowling *noun* [U] (*AmE*) = BOWLS

lawn·mow·er /'lɔːnməʊə(r)/; *AmE* -moʊ-/ (also **mower**) *noun* a machine for cutting the grass on LAWNS

,lawn 'tennis *noun* [U] (*formal*) = TENNIS

law·suit /'lɔːsuːt; *BrE* also -sjuːt/ (also **suit**) *noun* a claim or complaint against sb that a person or an organization can make in a court of law: *He filed a lawsuit against his record company.*

law·yer /'lɔːjə(r)/ *noun* a person who is trained and qualified to advise people about the law and to represent them in a court of law, and to write legal documents

WHICH WORD?
lawyer / barrister / advocate / attorney / solicitor (?)

Lawyer is a general term for a person who is qualified to advise people about the law, to prepare legal documents for them and/or to represent them in a court of law.

In England and Wales, a **lawyer** who is qualified to speak in the higher courts of law is called a **barrister**. In Scotland a **barrister** is called an **advocate**.

In *AmE* **attorney** is a more formal word used for a **lawyer** and is used especially in job titles: *district attorney*.

Counsel is the formal legal word used for a lawyer who is representing someone in court: *counsel for the prosecution.*

Solicitor is the *BrE* term for a lawyer who gives legal advice and prepares documents, for example when you are buying a house, and sometimes has the right to speak in a court of law.

In *AmE* **solicitor** is only used in the titles of some lawyers who work for the government: *Solicitor General.*

lax /læks/ *adj.* (*disapproving*) not strict, severe or careful enough about work, rules or standards of behaviour: *lax security/discipline* ◇ *a lax attitude to health and safety regulations* ▶ **lax·ity** /'læksəti/ *noun* [U]

laxa·tive /'læksətɪv/ *noun* a medicine, food or drink that makes sb empty their bowels easily ▶ **laxa·tive** *adj.*

lay /leɪ/ *verb, adj., noun*—see also LIE *v.*
■ *verb* (**laid**, **laid** /leɪd/)

PUT DOWN/SPREAD | **1** [usually +*adv. / prep.*] to put sb/sth in a particular position, especially when it is done gently or carefully: [VN] *She laid the baby down gently on the bed.* ◇ *He laid a hand on my arm.* ◇ *The horse laid back its ears.* ◇ *Relatives laid wreaths on the grave.* ◇ [VN-ADJ] *The cloth should be laid flat.* **HELP** Some speakers confuse this sense of **lay** with **lie**, especially in the present and progressive tenses. However, **lay** has an object and **lie** does not: *She was lying on the beach.* ◇ ~~She was laying on the beach.~~ ◇ *Why don't you lie on the bed?* ◇ ~~Why don't you lay on the bed?~~ In the past tenses **laid** (from *lay*) is often wrongly used for **lay** or **lain** (from *lie*): *She had lain there all night.* ◇ ~~She had laid there all night.~~ **2** [VN] ~ sth **(down)** to put sth down, especially on the floor, ready to be used: *to lay a carpet/cable/pipe* ◇ *The foundations of the house are being laid today.* ◇ *(figurative) They had laid the groundwork for future development.* **3** [VN] ~ A (on/over B) | ~ B with A to spread sth on sth; to cover sth with a layer of sth: *Before they started they laid newspaper on* *the floor.* ◊ *The floor was laid with newspaper.* ◊ *The grapes were laid to dry on racks.*

EGGS | **4** if a bird, an insect, a fish, etc. **lays** eggs, it produces them from its body: [VN] *The cuckoo lays its eggs in other birds' nests.* ◊ *new-laid eggs* ◊ [V] *The hens are not laying well* (= not producing many eggs).

TABLE | **5** [VN] (*BrE*) to arrange knives, forks, plates, etc. on a table ready for a meal SYN SET: *to lay the table*

PRESENT PROPOSAL | **6** [VN] to present a proposal, some information, etc. to sb for them to think about and decide on: *The bill was laid before Parliament.*

DIFFICULT SITUATION | **7** [VN] (*formal*) to put sb/sth in a particular position or state, especially a difficult or unpleasant one: *to lay a responsibility/burden on sb* ◊ *to lay sb under an obligation to do sth*

WITH NOUNS | **8** [VN] used with a noun to form a phrase that has the same meaning as the verb related to the noun: *to lay the blame on sb* (= to blame sb) ◊ *Our teacher lays great stress on good spelling* (= stresses it strongly).

PLAN/TRAP | **9** [VN] to prepare sth in detail: *to lay a trap for sb* ◊ *She began to **lay her plans** for her escape.* ◊ *Bad weather can upset even the best-laid plans.*

HAVE SEX | **10** [VN] (*often passive*) (⚠, *slang*) to have sex with sb: *He went out hoping to **get laid** that night.*

FIRE | **11** [VN] to prepare a fire by arranging wood, sticks or coal

BET | **12** to bet money on sth; to place a bet: [VN] *to lay a bet* ◊ *She had laid $100 on the favourite.* ◊ [VNN, VN(that)] [no passive] *I'll lay you any money you like (that) he won't come.*

IDM Idioms containing **lay** are at the entries for the nouns and adjectives in the idioms, for example **lay sth bare** is at **bare**.

PHRV **,lay a'bout sb (with sth)** (*BrE*) to attack sb violently: *The gang laid about him with sticks.* **,lay a'bout you/yourself (with sth)** (*BrE*) to hit sb/sth without control or move your arms or legs violently in all directions: *She laid about herself with her stick to keep the dogs off.* **,lay sth ↔ a'side** (*formal*) **1** to put sth on one side and not use it or think about it: *He laid aside his book and stood up.* ◊ (*figurative*) *Doctors have to lay their personal feelings aside.* **2** (also **,lay sth 'by**) to keep sth to use, or deal with later: *They had laid money aside for their old age.* **,lay sth ↔ 'down** to put sth down or stop using it: *She laid the book down on the table.* ◊ *Both sides were urged to lay down their arms* (= stop fighting). **,lay sth 'down 1** (*formal*) to stop doing a job, etc: *to lay down your office/duties* **2** if you **lay down** a rule or a principle, you state officially that people must obey it or use it: *You can't lay down hard and fast rules.* ◊ [+that] *It is laid down that all candidates must submit three copies of their dissertation.* **3** [usually passive] to produce sth that is stored and gradually increases: *If you eat too much, the surplus is laid down as fat.* **,lay sth ↔ 'in/'up** to collect and store sth to use in the future: *to lay in food supplies* **,lay 'into sb/sth** (*informal*) to attack sb violently with blows or words: *His parents really laid into him for wasting so much money.* **,lay 'off | ,lay 'off sb/sth** (*informal, spoken*) used to tell sb to stop doing sth: *Lay off me will you—it's nothing to do with me.* ◊ [+-ing] *Lay off bullying Jack.* **,lay 'off sth** (*informal*) to stop using sth: *I think you'd better lay off fatty foods for a while.* **,lay sb ↔ 'off** to stop employing sb because there is not enough work for them to do SYN MAKE SB REDUNDANT—related noun LAY-OFF **,lay sth ↔ 'on** (*BrE, informal*) to provide sth for sb, especially food or entertainment: *to lay on food and drink* ◊ *A bus has been laid on to take guests to the airport.* **,lay sth 'on sb** to make sb have to deal with sth unpleasant or difficult: *Stop laying a guilt trip on me* (= making me feel guilty). **,lay sb ↔ 'out 1** to knock sb unconscious **2** to prepare a dead body to be buried **,lay sth ↔ 'out 1** to spread sth out so that it can be seen easily or is ready to use: *He laid the map out on the table.* ◊ [+ADJ] *Lay the material out flat.* **2** [often passive] to plan how sth should look and arrange it in this way: *The gardens were laid out with lawns, flower beds and fountains.* ◊ *a well laid out magazine*—related noun LAYOUT

3 to present a plan, an argument, etc. clearly and carefully SYN SET OUT: *All the terms and conditions are laid out in the contract.* **4** (*informal*) to spend money: *I had to lay out a fortune on a new car.*—related noun OUTLAY **,lay 'over (at/in ...)** (*AmE*) to stay somewhere for a short time during a long journey—related noun LAYOVER—see also STOP OVER **,lay sb 'up** [usually passive] if sb is **laid up**, they are unable to work, etc. because of an illness or injury: *She's laid up with a broken leg.* **,lay sth ↔ 'up 1** = LAY STH IN **2** if you **lay up** problems or trouble for yourself, you do sth that will cause you problems later **3** to stop using a ship or other vehicle while it is being repaired

■ *adj.* [only before noun] **1** not having expert knowledge or professional qualifications in a particular subject: *His book explains the theory for the lay public.* **2** not in an official position in the Church: *a lay preacher*—see also LAYMAN, LAYWOMAN, LAYPERSON

■ *noun* **1** (⚠, *slang*) a partner in sex, especially a woman: *an easy lay* (= a person who is ready and willing to have sex) ◊ *to be a great lay* **2** (*old use*) a poem that was written to be sung, usually telling a story

IDM **the ,lay of the 'land** (*AmE*) = THE LIE OF THE LAND

lay·about /'leɪəbaʊt/ *noun* (*old-fashioned, BrE, informal*) a lazy person who does not do much work

lay·away /'leɪəweɪ/ *noun* [U] (*AmE*) a system of buying goods in a store, where the customer pays a small amount of the price for an article and the store keeps the goods until the full price has been paid: *I'll put it on layaway.*

'lay-by *noun* (*BrE*) an area at the side of a road where vehicles may stop for a short time—compare REST AREA

layer /'leɪə(r); 'leə(r); *AmE* 'ler/ *noun, verb*
■ *noun* **1** a quantity or thickness of sth that lies over a surface or between surfaces: *A thin layer of dust covered everything.* ◊ *How many layers of clothing are you wearing?* **2** a level or part within a system or set of ideas: *There were too many layers of management in the company.* ◊ *the layers of meaning in the poem*
■ *verb* [VN] [often passive] to arrange sth in layers: *Layer the potatoes and onions in a dish.* ◊ *Her hair had been layered* (= cut to several different lengths).—picture at HAIR

lay·ette /leɪ'et/ *noun* a set of clothes and other things for a new baby

lay·man /'leɪmən/ *noun* (*pl.* **-men** /-mən/) (also **lay·per·son**) **1** a person who does not have expert knowledge of a particular subject: *a book written for professionals and laymen alike* ◊ *to explain sth in layman's terms* (= in simple language) **2** a person who is a member of a Church but is not a priest or member of the CLERGY—see also LAYWOMAN

'lay-off *noun* **1** an act of making people unemployed because there is no more work left for them to do: *lay-offs in the factory* **2** a period of time when sb is not working or not doing sth that they normally do regularly: *an eight-week lay-off with a broken leg*

lay·out /'leɪaʊt/ *noun* [usually sing.] the way in which the parts of sth such as the page of a book, a garden or a building are arranged: *the layout of streets* ◊ *the magazine's attractive new page layout*

lay·over /'leɪəʊvə(r); *AmE* -oʊ-/ *noun* (*AmE*) = STOPOVER

lay·per·son /'leɪpɜːsn; *AmE* -pɜːrsn/ *noun* (also **'lay per·son**) (*pl.* **lay people** or **lay·persons**) a LAYMAN or LAYWOMAN: *The layperson cannot really understand mental illness.*

lay·woman /'leɪwʊmən/ *noun* (*pl.* **-women** /-wɪmɪn/) (*rare*) a woman who is a member of a Church but is not a priest or a member of the CLERGY—see also LAYMAN, LAYPERSON

laze /leɪz/ *verb* [V] **~ (about/around)** to relax and do very little: *We lazed by the pool all day.* ◊ *I've spent the afternoon just lazing around.* PHRV **'laze sth ↔ away** to spend time relaxing and doing very little: *They lazed away the long summer days.*

lazy /'leɪzi/ *adj.* (**lazi·er**, **lazi·est**) **1** (*disapproving*) unwilling to work or be active; doing as little as possible: *He*

L

was not stupid, just lazy. ◊ *I was feeling too lazy to go out.* **2** not involving much energy or activity; slow and relaxed: *We spent a lazy day on the beach.* **3** (*disapproving*) showing a lack of effort or care: *a lazy piece of work* **4** (*literary*) moving slowly: *the lazy river* ▸ **lazi·ly** *adv.*: *She woke up and stretched lazily.* **lazi·ness** *noun* [U]

lazy·bones /ˈleɪzibəʊnz; *AmE* -boʊnz/ *noun* [sing.] (*old-fashioned, informal*) used to refer to a lazy person: *Come on, lazybones, get up!*

lb (*AmE* **lb.**) *abbr.* (*pl.* **lb** or **lbs**) a pound in weight, equal to about 454 grams (from Latin 'libra').

lbw /ˌel biː ˈdʌbljuː/ *abbr.* (in cricket) leg before wicket (a reason for a BATSMAN being out (= having to stop BATTING), because the ball has hit his or her leg instead of hitting the bat, and would have hit the WICKET if the leg had not stopped it)

LCD /ˌel siː ˈdiː/ *abbr.* **1** liquid crystal display (a way of showing information in electronic equipment. An electric current is passed through a special liquid and numbers and letters can be seen on a small screen.): *a pocket calculator with LCD* **2** LOWEST COMMON DENOMINATOR

LEA /ˌel iː ˈeɪ/ *abbr.* Local Education Authority (a department responsible for education in British local government)

leach /liːtʃ/ *verb* (*technical*) **1** [V] ~ (**from sth**) (**into sth**)| ~ **out/away** (of chemicals, minerals, etc.) to be removed from soil, etc. by water passing through it: *Nitrates leach from the soil into rivers.* **2** [VN] ~ **sth** (**from sth**) (**into sth**)| ~ **sth out/away** (of a liquid) to remove chemicals, minerals, etc. from soil: *The nutrient is quickly leached away.*

lead¹ /liːd/ *verb, noun*—see also LEAD²
■ *verb* (**led**, **led** /led/)
SHOW THE WAY | **1** to go with or in front of a person or an animal to show the way or to make them go in the right direction: [VN+*adv./prep.*] *He led us out into the grounds.* ◊ *The receptionist led the way to the boardroom.* ◊ *She led the horse back into the stable.* ◊ (*figurative*) *I tried to lead the discussion back to the main issue.* ◊ [V] *If you lead, I'll follow.*
CONNECT TWO THINGS | **2** [V] ~ **from/to sth** (**to/from sth**) to connect one object or place to another: *the pipe leading from the top of the water tank* ◊ *The wire led to a speaker.*
OF ROAD/PATH/DOOR | **3** [+*adv./prep.*] to go in a particular direction or to a particular place: [V] *A path led up the hill.* ◊ *Which door leads to the yard?* ◊ [VN] *The track led us through a wood.*
CAUSE | **4** [V] ~ **to sth** to have sth as a result: *Eating too much sugar can lead to health problems.* **5** ~ **sb** (**to sth**) to be the reason why sb does or thinks sth: [VN] *What led you to this conclusion?* ◊ *He's too easily led* (= easily persuaded to do or think sth). ◊ [VN to inf] *This has led scientists to speculate on the existence of other galaxies.* ◊ *The situation is far worse than we had been led to believe.*
LIFE | **6** [VN] ~ **a particular type of life**: *to lead a quiet life/a life of luxury/a miserable existence*
BE BEST/FIRST | **7** ~ (**sb/sth**) (**in sth**) to be the best at sth; to be in first place: [VN] *The department led the world in cancer research.* ◊ *We lead the way in space technology.* ◊ [V, VN] *The champion is leading* (*her nearest rival*) *by 18 seconds.*
BE IN CONTROL | **8** to be in control of sth; to be the leader of sth: [VN] *to lead an army/an expedition* ◊ *to lead a discussion* ◊ *Who will lead the party in the next election?* [also V]
IN CARD GAMES | **9** to play first; to play sth as your first card: [V] *It's your turn to lead.* ◊ [VN] *to lead trumps/the ten of clubs*
IDM **lead sb by the ˈnose** to make sb do everything you want; to control sb completely **lead** (**sb**) **ˈnowhere** to have no successful result for sb: *This discussion is leading us nowhere.* **lead sb a** (**merry**) **ˈdance** (*BrE*) to cause sb a lot of trouble or worry **lead from the ˈfront** to take an active part in what you are telling or persuading others to do **lead sb up/down the garden ˈpath** to deceive sb—more at BLIND *adj.*, THING
PHRV ˌ**lead ˈoff** (**from**) **sth** to start at a place and go away from it: *narrow streets leading off from the main square* ˌ**lead ˈoff**| ˌ**lead sth ↔ ˈoff** to start sth: *Who would*

like to lead off the debate? ˌ**lead sb ˈon** (*informal*) to deceive sb and make them believe sth, especially that you love them or find them attractive ˌ**lead ˈup to sth** to be an introduction to or the cause of sth: *the weeks leading up to the exam* ◊ *the events leading up to the strike* ˈ**lead with sth 1** (of a newspaper) to have sth as the main item of news **2** (in boxing) to use a particular hand to begin an attack: *to lead with your right/left*
■ *noun*
FIRST PLACE | **1** (**the lead**) [sing.] the position ahead of everyone else in a race or competition: *She took the lead in the second lap.* ◊ *He has gone into the lead.* ◊ *The Democrats now appear to be in the lead.* ◊ *to hold/lose the lead* ◊ *The lead car is now three minutes ahead of the rest of the field.* **2** [sing.] ~ (**over sb/sth**) the amount or distance that sb/sth is in front of sb/sth else: *He managed to hold a lead of two seconds over his closest rival.* ◊ *The polls have given Labour a five-point lead.* ◊ *a commanding/comfortable lead* ◊ *to increase/widen your lead* ◊ *Manchester lost their early two-goal lead.*
EXAMPLE | **3** [sing.] an example or action for people to copy: *If one bank raises interest rates, all the others will follow their lead.* ◊ *If we take the lead in this* (= start to act), *others may follow.* ◊ *You go first, I'll take my lead from you.*
INFORMATION | **4** [C] a piece of information that may help to find out the truth or facts about a situation, especially a crime: *The police will follow up all possible leads.*
ACTOR/MUSICIAN | **5** [C] the main part in a play, film/movie, etc.; the person who plays this part: *Who is playing the lead?* ◊ *the male/female lead* ◊ *a lead role* ◊ *the lead singer in a band*
FOR DOG | **6** (*BrE*) (also **leash** *AmE*, *BrE*) [C] a long piece of leather, chain or rope used for holding and controlling a dog: *Dogs must be kept on a lead in the park.*
FOR ELECTRICITY | **7** [C] (*BrE*) a long piece of wire, usually covered in plastic, that is used to connect a piece of electrical equipment to a source of electricity—see also EXTENSION LEAD, JUMP LEAD

lead² /led/ *noun*—see also LEAD¹ **1** [U] (*symb* **Pb**) a chemical element. Lead is a heavy soft grey metal, used especially in the past for water pipes or to cover roofs. **2** [C, U] the thin black part of a pencil that marks paper—picture at STATIONERY IDM **go ˌdown like a lead balˈloon** (*informal*) to be very unsuccessful; to not be accepted by people

lead·ed /ˈledɪd/ *adj.* [usually before noun] **1** (of petrol, metal, etc.) with lead added to it OPP UNLEADED **2** with a cover or a frame of lead: *a leaded door/roof*

ˌ**leaded ˈlight** (also ˌ**leaded ˈwindow**) *noun* [usually pl.] (*BrE*) a window made from small pieces of glass that are arranged in diamond shapes and are separated by strips of LEAD

lead·en /ˈledn/ *adj.* (*literary*) **1** dull grey in colour, like LEAD: *leaden skies* **2** dull, heavy or slow: *a leaden heart* (= because you are sad) ◊ *On leaden feet he made his way down the stairs.*

lead·er /ˈliːdə(r)/ *noun* **1** a person who leads a group of people, especially the head of a country, an organization, etc: *a political/spiritual leader* ◊ *the leader of the Conservative party* ◊ *union leaders* ◊ *He was not a natural leader.* ◊ *She's a born leader.* **2** a person or thing that is the best, or in first place in a race, business, etc: *She was among the leaders of the race from the start.* ◊ *The company is a world leader in electrical goods.*—see also MARKET LEADER **3** (*BrE*) (also **con·cert·master** *AmE*, *BrE*) the most important violin player in an orchestra **4** (*BrE*) = EDITORIAL

lead·er·less /ˈliːdələs; *AmE* -dərl-/ *adj.* without a leader: *Her sudden death left the party leaderless.*

lead·er·ship /ˈliːdəʃɪp; *AmE* -dərʃ-/ *noun* **1** [U] the state or position of being a leader: *a leadership contest* ◊ *The party thrived under his leadership.* **2** [U] the ability to be a leader or the qualities a good leader should have: *leadership qualities/skills* ◊ *Strong leadership is needed to captain the team.* **3** [C+sing./pl. *v.*] a group of leaders of a

L

æ	ɑː	e	ɜː	ə	ɪ	iː	i	ɒ	ɔː	ʌ	ʊ	u	uː
cat	father	ten	bird	about	sit	see	many	got	saw	cup	put	actual	too

(BrE)

particular organization, etc: *The party leadership is/are divided.*

lead-free /ˌled ˈfriː/ *adj.* (of petrol, paint, etc.) without any of the metal LEAD added to it

lead-in /ˈliːd ɪn/ *noun* an introduction to a subject, story, show, etc.

lead·ing /ˈliːdɪŋ/ *adj.* [only before noun] most important or most successful SYN MAIN: *leading politicians/experts* ◇ *She was offered the leading role in the new TV series.*

ˌleading ˈarticle (also **lead·er**) *noun* (both *BrE*) = EDI-TORIAL.

ˌleading ˈedge *noun* **1** [sing.] the most important and advanced position in an area of activity, especially technology: *at the leading edge of scientific research* **2** [C] (*technical*) the front or forward edge of sth, especially an aircraft—picture at PLANE ▸ ˌleading-ˈedge *adj.* [only before noun]: *leading-edge technology*

ˌleading ˈlady, ˌleading ˈman *noun* the actor with the main female or male part in a play or film/movie

ˌleading ˈlight *noun* an important, active or respected person in a particular area of activity: *She's one of the leading lights in the opera world.*

ˌleading ˈquestion *noun* a question that you ask in a particular way in order to get the answer you want

lead shot /ˌled ˈʃɒt; *AmE* -ˈʃɑːt/ *noun* = SHOT

lead story /ˈliːd stɔːri/ *noun* the main or first item of news in a newspaper, magazine or news broadcast

lead time /ˈliːd taɪm/ *noun* the time between starting and completing a production process

leaf /liːf/ *noun, verb*
■ *noun* (*pl.* **leaves** /liːvz/) **1** [C] a flat green part of a plant, growing from a stem or branch or from the root: *lettuce/cabbage/oak leaves* ◇ *The trees are just coming into leaf.* ◇ *the dead leaves of autumn/the fall*—see also BAY LEAF, FIG LEAF—picture at PLANT **2** (*-leaf, -leafed, -leaved*) (in adjectives) having leaves of the type or number mentioned: *a four-leaf clover* ◇ *a broad-leaved plant* **3** [C] a sheet of paper, especially a page in a book—see also FLYLEAF, LOOSE-LEAF, OVERLEAF **4** [U] metal, especially gold or silver, in the form of very thin sheets: *gold leaf* **5** [C] a part of a table that can be lifted up or pulled into position in order to make the table bigger IDM **take a leaf from/out of sb's ˈbook** to copy sb's behaviour and do things in the same way that they do, because they are successful—more at NEW
■ *verb* PHRV ˈleaf through sth to quickly turn over the pages of a book, etc. without reading them or looking at them carefully

leaf·less /ˈliːfləs/ *adj.* having no leaves

leaf·let /ˈliːflət/ *noun, verb*
■ *noun* a printed sheet of paper or a few printed pages that are given free of charge to advertise or give information about sth: *a leaflet on local places of interest*
■ *verb* to give out leaflets to people: [V] *We did a lot of leafleting in the area.* [also VN]

ˈleaf mould (*BrE*) (*AmE* ˈleaf mold) *noun* [U] soil consisting mostly of dead, decayed leaves

leafy /ˈliːfi/ *adj.* **1** having a lot of leaves: *Eat plenty of leafy green vegetables.* **2** (*approving*) (of a place) having a lot of trees and plants: *leafy suburbs* **3** made by a lot of leaves or trees: *We sat in the leafy shade of an oak tree.*

league /liːɡ/ *noun* **1** a group of people, or nations who have combined for a particular purpose: *the League of Nations* ◇ *a meeting of the Women's League for Peace*—see also IVY LEAGUE **2** a group of sports teams who all play each other to earn points and find which team is best: *major league baseball* ◇ *United were league champions last season.* **3** (*informal*) a level of quality, ability, etc: *As a painter, he is in a league of his own* (= much better than others). ◇ *They're in a different league from us.* ◇ *When it comes to cooking, I'm not in her league* (= she is much better than me). ◇ *A house like that is out of our league* (= too expensive for us). **4** (*old use*) a unit for measuring distance, equal to about 3 miles or 4000 metres IDM **in ˈleague (with sb)** making secret plans with sb

leak /liːk/ *verb, noun*

■ *verb* **1** to allow liquid or gas to get in or out through a small hole or crack: [V] *a leaking pipe* ◇ *The roof was leaking.* ◇ [VN] *The tank had leaked a small amount of water.* **2** [V] (of a liquid or gas) to get in or out through a small hole or crack in sth: *Water had started to leak into the cellar.* **3** [VN] ~ sth (to sb) to give secret information to the public, for example by telling a newspaper: *The contents of the report were leaked to the press.* ◇ *a leaked document* PHRV ˌleak ˈout (of secret information) to become known to the public: *Details of the plan soon leaked out.*
■ *noun* **1** a small hole or crack that lets liquid or gas flow in or out of sth by accident: *a leak in the roof* ◇ *a leak in the gas pipe* **2** liquid or gas that escapes through a hole in sth: *a gas/radiation leak* ◇ *oil leaks/leaks of oil* **3** a deliberate act of giving secret information to the newspapers, etc: *a leak to the press about the government plans on tax* **4** (*slang*) an act of passing URINE from the body: *to have/take a leak* IDM see SPRING *v.*

leak·age /ˈliːkɪdʒ/ *noun* [C, U] an amount of liquid or gas escaping through a hole in sth; an occasion when there is a leak: *a leakage of toxic waste into the sea* ◇ *Check bottles for leakage before use.*

leaky /ˈliːki/ *adj.* having holes or cracks that allow liquid or gas to escape: *a leaky roof/tent/tap*

lean /liːn/ *verb, adj., noun*
■ *verb* (**leaned, leaned**) (*BrE also* **leant, leant** /lent/) **1** [V] [usually +adv./prep.] to bend or move from an upright position: *I leaned back in my chair.* ◇ *The tower is leaning dangerously.* ◇ *A man was leaning out of the window.* **2** [V] ~ against/on sth to rest on or against sth for support: *A shovel was leaning against the wall.* ◇ *She walked slowly, leaning on her son's arm.* **3** [VN] ~ sth against/on sth to make sth rest against sth in a sloping position: *Can I lean my bike against the wall?* IDM see BACKWARDS PHRV ˈlean on sb/sth **1** to depend on sb/sth for help and support: *He leans heavily on his family.* **2** to try to influence sb by threatening them: *The government has been leaning on the TV company not to broadcast the show.* ˈlean to/towards/toward sth to have a tendency to prefer sth, especially a particular opinion or interest: *The UK leant towards the US proposal.*
■ *adj.* (**lean·er, lean·est**) **1** (usually *approving*) (of people, especially men, or animals) without much flesh; thin and fit: *a lean, muscular body* ◇ *He was tall, lean and handsome.* **2** (of meat) containing little or no fat **3** [usually before noun] (of a period of time) difficult and not producing much money, food, etc: *a lean period/spell* ◇ *The company recovered well after going through several lean years.* **4** (of organizations, etc.) strong and efficient because the number of employees has been reduced: *The changes made the company leaner and more competitive.* ▸ **lean·ness** /ˈliːnnəs/ *noun* [U]
■ *noun* [U] the part of meat that has little or no fat

lean·ing /ˈliːnɪŋ/ *noun* [usually pl.] ~ (towards(s) sth) a tendency to prefer sth or to believe in particular ideas, opinions, etc. SYN INCLINATION: *a leaning towards comedy rather than tragedy* ◇ *a person with socialist leanings*

ˈlean-to *noun* (*pl.* **-tos** /-tuːz/) a small building with its roof leaning against the side of a large building, wall or fence: *a lean-to garage*

leap /liːp/ *verb, noun*
■ *verb* (**leapt, leapt** /lept/) *or* (**leaped, leaped**) **1** to jump high or a long way: [V+adv./prep.] *A dolphin leapt out of the water.* ◇ *We leapt over the stream.* ◇ [VN] *The horse leapt a five-foot wall.* **2** [V+adv./prep.] to move or do sth suddenly and quickly: *She leapt out of bed.* ◇ *He leapt across the room to answer the door.* ◇ *I leapt to my feet* (= stood up quickly). ◇ *They leapt into action immediately.* ◇ (*figurative*) *She was quick to leap to my defence* (= speak in support of me). ◇ *The photo seemed to leap off the page* (= it got your attention immediately). ◇ *His name leapt out at me* (= I saw it immediately). **3** [V] to increase suddenly and by a large amount: *Shares leapt in value from 476p to close at 536p.* IDM **look before you ˈleap** (*saying*) used to advise sb to think about the possible results or dangers of sth before doing it—more at CONCLUSION, HEART PHRV ˈleap at sth to accept a chance or an

opportunity quickly and with enthusiasm: *I leapt at the chance to go to France.* ■ *noun* **1** a long or high jump: *a leap of six metres* ◊ *She took a flying leap and landed on the other side of the stream.* ◊ *(figurative) His heart gave a sudden leap when he saw her.* ◊ *(figurative) Few people successfully make the leap from television to the movies.* **2** a sudden large change or increase in sth: *a leap in profits/productivity*—see also QUANTUM LEAP **IDM** **by/in ˌleaps and ˈbounds** very quickly; in large amounts: *Her health has improved in leaps and bounds.* **a leap in the ˈdark** an action or a risk that you take without knowing anything about the activity or what the result will be

leap·frog /ˈliːpfrɒg; *AmE* -frɔːg; -frɑːg/ *noun, verb*

leapfrog
■ *noun* [U] a children's game in which players take turns to jump over the backs of other players who are bending down
■ *verb* (**-gg-**) to get to a higher position or rank by going past sb else or by missing out some stages: [VN] *The win allowed Newcastle to leapfrog three teams to gain second place.* [also V]

ˈleap year *noun* one year in every four years when February has 29 days instead of 28

learn /lɜːn; *AmE* lɜːrn/ *verb* (**learnt, learnt** /lɜːnt; *AmE* lɜːrnt/) or (**learned, learned**) **1** ~ (**sth**) | ~ (**from sb/sth**) to gain knowledge or skill by studying, from experience, from being taught, etc: [VN] *to learn a language/a musical instrument/a skill* ◊ *I learned a lot from my father.* ◊ *You can learn a great deal just from watching other players.* ◊ [V] *She's very keen to learn about Japanese culture.* ◊ *The book is about how children learn.* ◊ [Vtoinf, Vwh-] *He's learning to dance.* ◊ *He's still learning how to dance.* ◊ [Vwh-] *Today we learnt how to use the new software.* ⇨ note at DISCOVER **2** ~ (**of/about**) **sth** to become aware of sth by hearing about it from sb else: [V] *I learnt of her arrival from a close friend.* ◊ [V(that)] *We were very surprised to learn (that) she had got married again.* ◊ [Vwh-] *We only learned who the new teacher was a few days ago.* ◊ [VN] *How did they react when they learned the news?* [also VNthat] **3** [VN] to study and repeat sth in order to be able to remember it **SYN** MEMORIZE: *We have to learn one of Hamlet's speeches for school tomorrow.* **4** ~ (**from sth**) to gradually change your attitudes about sth so that you behave in a different way: [V] *I'm sure she'll learn from her mistakes.* ◊ [V(that)] *He'll just have to learn (that) he can't always have his own way.* ◊ [Vtoinf] *I soon learned not to ask too many questions.* **IDM** **ˌlearn (sth) the ˈhard way** to find out how to behave by learning from your mistakes or from unpleasant experiences, rather than from being told **learn your ˈlesson** to learn what to do or not to do in the future because you have had a bad experience in the past—more at COST *n.*, LIVE[1], ROPE *n.*

VOCABULARY BUILDING
learning

learn *He's learning Spanish/ to swim / how to drive.*
study *She studied chemistry for three years.*
cram *I can't go out tonight — I'm cramming for the exam.*
revise *(BrE)* *(AmE* **review***)* *In this class we'll revise/ review what we did last week.*
practise *(BrE)* *(AmE* **practice***)* *If you practise speaking English, you'll soon improve.*
rehearse *We only had two weeks to rehearse the play.*

---

learn·ed /ˈlɜːnɪd; *AmE* ˈlɜːrnɪd/ *adj.* [usually before noun] **1** *(formal)* having a lot of knowledge because you have studied and read a lot: *a learned professor*—see also FRIEND (5) **2** *(formal)* connected with or for learned people; showing and expressing deep knowledge

SYN SCHOLARLY: *a learned journal* **3** /lɜːnd; *AmE* lɜːrnd/ developed by training or experience; not existing at birth: *a learned skill* ◊ *We all have different learned responses to anger.*

learn·er /ˈlɜːnə(r); *AmE* ˈlɜːrn-/ *noun* **1** a person who is finding out about a subject or how to do sth: *a slow/quick learner* ◊ *a dictionary for learners of English* ◊ *learner-centred teaching methods* **2** (also **ˌlearner ˈdriver**) a person who is learning to drive a car: *Learners are not allowed on the motorway.*

ˈlearner's permit *noun* (*AmE*) = PROVISIONAL LICENCE

learn·ing /ˈlɜːnɪŋ; *AmE* ˈlɜːrnɪŋ/ *noun* [U] **1** the process of learning sth: *computer-assisted learning* **2** knowledge that you get from reading and studying: *a woman of great learning*

ˈlearning curve *noun* the rate at which you learn a new subject or a new skill; the process of learning from the mistakes you make

ˈlearning difficulties *noun* [pl.] mental problems that people may have from birth, or that may be caused by illness or injury, that affect their ability to learn things

lease /liːs/ *noun, verb*
■ *noun* a legal agreement that allows you to use a building, a piece of equipment or some land for a period of time, usually in return for rent: *to take out a lease on a flat* ◊ *The lease expires/runs out next year.* ◊ *Under the terms of the lease, you have to pay maintenance charges.* **IDM** **a (ˌnew) lease of ˈlife** (*BrE*) (*AmE* **a (ˌnew) lease on ˈlife**) the chance to live or last longer, or with a better quality of life: *Since her hip operation she's had a new lease of life.*
■ *verb* ~ **sth** (**from sb**) | ~ **sth** (**out**) (**to sb**) to use or let sb use sth, especially property or equipment, in exchange for rent or a regular payment: [VN] *They lease the land from a local farmer.* ◊ *We lease all our photocopy equipment.* ◊ *Parts of the building are leased out to tenants.* [also VNN] ▶ **leas·ing** *noun* [U]: *car leasing* ◊ *a leasing company*

lease·back /ˈliːsbæk/ (*AmE* also **re·ver·sion**) *noun* [U] *(law)* the process of allowing the former owner of a property to continue to use it if they pay rent to the new owner; a legal agreement where this happens

lease·hold /ˈliːshəʊld; *AmE* -hoʊld/ *adj., noun*
■ *adj.* (*especially BrE*) (of property or land) that can be used for a limited period of time, according to the arrangements in a LEASE: *a leasehold property* ▶ **lease·hold** *adv.*: *to purchase land leasehold*—compare FREEHOLD
■ *noun* [U] (*especially BrE*) the right to use a building or a piece of land according to the arrangements in a LEASE: *to obtain/own the leasehold of a flat*—compare FREEHOLD

lease·hold·er /ˈliːshəʊldə(r); *AmE* -hoʊld-/ *noun* (*especially BrE*) a person who is allowed to use a building or a piece of land according to the arrangements in a LEASE—compare FREEHOLDER

leash /liːʃ/ *noun, verb*
■ *noun* (*especially AmE*) = LEAD (6): *All dogs must be kept on a leash in public places.* **IDM** see STRAIN *v.*
■ *verb* [VN] to control an animal, especially a dog, with a LEAD/LEASH

least /liːst/ *det., pron., adv.*
■ *det., pron.* (usually **the least**) smallest in size, amount, degree, etc: *He's the best teacher, even though he has the least experience.* ◊ *She never had the least idea what to do about it.* ◊ *He gave (the) least of all towards the wedding present.* ◊ *How others see me is the least of my worries* (= I have more important things to worry about). ◊ *It's the least I can do to help* (= I feel I should do more). **IDM** **at the (very) ˈleast** used after amounts to show that the amount is the lowest possible: *It'll take a year, at the very least.* **ˌnot in the ˈleast** not at all: *Really, I'm not in the least tired.* ◊ *'Do you mind if I put the television on?' 'No, not in the least.'*—more at SAY *v.*
■ *adv.* to the smallest degree: *He always turns up just when you least expect him.* ◊ *She chose the least expensive of the hotels.* ◊ *I never hid the truth, least of all from you.* **IDM** **at ˈleast 1** not less than: *It'll cost at least 500 dollars.* ◊ *She must be at least 40.* ◊ *Cut the grass at least once a week in summer.* ◊ *I've known her at least as long as you have.*

L

b	d	f	g	h	k	l	m	n	p	r
bad	did	fall	get	hat	cat	leg	man	now	pen	red

2 used to add a positive comment about a negative situation: *She may be slow but at least she's reliable.* **3** even if nothing else is true or you do nothing else: *You could at least listen to what he says.* ◇ *Well, at least they weren't bored.* **4** used to limit or make what you have just said less definite SYN ANYWAY: *They seldom complained—officially at least.* ◇ *It works, at least I think it does.* **not 'least** (*written*) especially: *The documentary caused a lot of bad feeling, not least among the workers whose lives it described.*—more at LAST *adv.*, LINE *n.*, SAY *v.*

lea·ther /ˈleðə(r)/ *noun* **1** [U, C] material made by removing the hair or fur from animal skins and preserving the skins using special processes: *a leather jacket / briefcase* ◇ *The soles are made of leather.* ◇ *a leather-bound book* **2** (**leathers**) [pl.] clothes made from leather, especially those worn by people riding motorcycles—see also CHAMOIS LEATHER, PATENT LEATHER IDM see HELL

lea·ther·ette /ˌleðəˈret/ *noun* [U] an artificial material that looks and feels like leather

lea·thery /ˈleðəri/ *adj.* that looks or feels hard and TOUGH like leather: *leathery skin*

leave /liːv/ *verb, noun*
■ *verb* (**left**, **left** /left/)
PLACE/PERSON | **1** to go away from a person or a place: [V] *Come on, it's time we left.* ◇ *The plane leaves for Dallas at 12.35.* ◇ [VN] *I hate leaving home.* ◇ *The plane leaves Heathrow at 12.35.*
HOME/JOB/SCHOOL | **2** to stop living at a place, belonging to a group, working for an employer, etc: [V] *My secretary has threatened to leave.* ◇ [VN] *Some children leave school at 16.*
WIFE/HUSBAND | **3** [VN] **~ sb (for sb)** to leave your wife, husband or partner permanently: *She's leaving him for another man.*
STH TO DO LATER | **4** [VN] to not do sth or deal with sth immediately: *Leave the dishes—I'll wash them up later.* ◇ *Why do you always leave everything until the last moment?*
SB/STH IN CONDITION/PLACE | **5** to make or allow sb/sth to remain in a particular condition, place, etc: [VN-ADJ] *Leave the door open, please.* ◇ *The bomb blast left 25 people dead.* ◇ [VN-ing] *Don't leave her waiting outside in the rain.* ◇ [VNto inf] *Leave the rice to cook for 20 minutes.* [also VN] **6** to make sth happen or remain as a result: [VN] *Red wine leaves a stain.* ◇ *The puppy left a trail of destruction behind it.* ◇ *She left me with the impression that she was unhappy with her job.* ◇ [VNN] *I'm afraid you leave me no choice.* **7** (**be left**) [VN] to remain to be used, sold, etc: *Is there any coffee left?* ◇ *How many tickets do you have left?* ◇ (*figurative*) *They are fighting to save what is left of their business.* ◇ *The only course of action left to me was to notify her employer.* **8** [VN] **~ sth/sb (behind)** to go away from a place without taking sth/sth with you: *I've left my bag on the bus.* ◇ *Don't leave any of your belongings behind.* ◇ *He wasn't well, so we had to leave him behind.*
MATHEMATICS | **9** [VN] to have a particular amount remaining: *Seven from ten leaves three.*
AFTER DEATH | **10** [VN] to have family remaining after your death: *He leaves a wife and two children.* **11** to give sth to sb when you die: [VN, VNN] *She left £1 million to her daughter.* ◇ *She left her daughter £1 million.*
RESPONSIBILITY TO SB | **12** to allow sb to take care of sth: [VN+adv. / prep.] *You can leave the cooking to me.* ◇ *She left her assistant in charge.* ◇ **Leave it with me**—*I'm sure I can sort it out.* ◇ *'Where shall we eat?' 'I'll leave it entirely (up) to you (= you can decide).'* ◇ *They left me with all the clearing up.* ◇ [VNto inf] *I was left to cope on my own.*
DELIVER | **13** **~ sth (for sb)** | **~ (sb) sth** to deliver sth and then go away: [VN, VNN] *Someone left this note for you.* ◇ *Someone left you this note.*
IDM Most idioms containing **leave** are at the entries for the nouns and adjectives in the idioms, for example **leave sb in the lurch** is at **lurch**. **leave 'go (of sth)** (*BrE, informal*) to stop holding on to sth: *Leave go of my arm—you're hurting me!* **leave it at 'that** (*informal*) to say or do nothing more about sth: *We'll never agree, so*

let's just leave it at that. **leave it 'out** (*BrE, spoken*) used to tell sb to stop doing sth
PHRV **leave sth↔a'side** to not consider sth: *Leaving the expense aside, do we actually need a second car?* **leave sb/sth be'hind 1** [usually passive] to make much better progress than sb: *Britain is being left behind in the race for new markets.* **2** to leave a person, place or state permanently: *She knew that she had left childhood behind.*—see also LEAVE (8) **leave 'off** (*informal*) to stop doing sth: *Start reading from where you left off last time.* ◇ [+-ing] *He left off playing the piano to answer the door.* **leave sb/sth↔'off (sth)** to not include sb/sth on a list, etc: *You've left off a zero.* ◇ *We left him off the list.* **leave sb/sth 'out (of sth)** to not include or mention sb/sth in sth: *Leave me out of this quarrel, please.* ◇ *He hadn't been asked to the party and was feeling very left out.* ◇ *She left out an 'm' in 'accommodation'.* **be ,left 'over (from sth)** to remain when all that is needed has been used: *There was lots of food left over.*—related noun LEFTOVER
■ *noun* [U] **1** a period of time when you are allowed to be away from work for a holiday/vacation or for a special reason: *to take a month's paid / unpaid leave* ◇ *soldiers home on leave* ◇ *to be on maternity / study leave* ◇ *How much annual leave do you get?*—see also COMPASSIONATE LEAVE, SICK LEAVE **2 ~ (to do sth)** (*formal*) official permission to do sth: *to be absent without leave* ◇ *The court granted him leave to appeal against the sentence.* ◇ *She asked for leave of absence (= permission to be away from work) to attend a funeral.*
IDM **by/ ,with your 'leave** (*formal*) with your permission **take (your) 'leave (of sb)** (*formal*) to say goodbye: *With a nod and a smile, she took leave of her friends.* **without a ,by your 'leave; without so much as a ,by your 'leave** (*old-fashioned*) without asking permission; rudely—more at BEG, FRENCH

-leaved /-liːvd/ ⟿ LEAF

leaven /ˈlevn/ *noun, verb*
■ *noun* [U] a substance, especially YEAST, that is added to bread before it is cooked to make it rise: (*figurative*) *A few jokes add leaven to a boring speech.*
■ *verb* [VN] [often passive] **~ sth (with sth)** (*formal*) to make sth more interesting or cheerful by adding sth to it: *Her speech was leavened with a touch of humour.*

leav·er /ˈliːvə(r)/ *noun* (often in compounds) a person who is leaving a place: *school-leavers*

leaves *pl.* of LEAF

'leave-taking *noun* [U, C, usually sing.] (*formal*) the act of saying goodbye

lech·er /ˈletʃə(r)/ *noun* (*disapproving*) a man who is always thinking about sex and looking for sexual pleasure ▶ **lech·ery** *noun* [U]

lech·er·ous /ˈletʃərəs/ *adj.* (*disapproving*) having too much interest in sexual pleasure

lec·tern /ˈlektən; AmE -tərn/ (*AmE also* **po·dium**) *noun* a stand for holding a book, notes, etc. when you are reading in church, giving a talk, etc.

lec·ture /ˈlektʃə(r)/ *noun, verb*
■ *noun* **~ (to sb) (on/about sth) 1** a talk that is given to a group of people to teach them about a particular subject, often as part of a university or college course: *to deliver / give a lecture to first-year students* ◇ *to attend a series of lectures on Jane Austen* ◇ *a lecture room / hall* **2** a long angry talk that sb gives to one person or a group of people because they have done sth wrong: *I know I should stop smoking—don't give me a lecture about it.*
■ *verb* **1 ~ (in/on sth)** [V] to give a talk or a series of talks to a group of people on a subject, especially as a way of teaching in a university or college: *She lectures in Russian literature.* **2** [VN] **~ sb (about/on sth)** | **~ sb (about doing sth)** to criticize sb or tell them how you think they should behave, especially when it is done in an annoying way: *Don't start lecturing me!* ◇ *He's always lecturing me about the way I dress.*

lec·tur·er /ˈlektʃərə(r)/ *noun* **1** a person who gives a lecture: *She's a superb lecturer.* **2** (especially in Britain) a person who teaches at a university or college: *He's a lecturer in French at Oxford.*

lec·ture·ship /ˈlektʃəʃɪp; AmE -tʃərʃ-/ noun the position of lecturer at a British university or college: *to take up a three-year lectureship in media studies*

ˈlecture theatre (BrE) (AmE **ˈlecture theater**) noun a large room with rows of seats on a slope, where lectures are given

LED /ˌel iː ˈdiː/ abbr. light emitting diode (a device that produces a light on electrical and electronic equipment): *A single red LED shows that the power is switched on.*

led /led/ **1** pt, pp of LEAD **2** (-**led**) (in adjectives) influenced or organized by: *a consumer-led society* ◊ *student-led activities*

ledge /ledʒ/ noun **1** a narrow flat piece of rock that sticks out from a cliff: *seabirds nesting on rocky ledges* **2** a narrow flat shelf fixed to a wall, especially one below a window: *She put the vase of flowers on the window ledge.*—see also SILL

ledger /ˈledʒə(r)/ noun a book in which a bank, a business, etc. records the money it has paid and received: *to enter figures in the purchase/sales ledger*

lee /liː/ noun **1** [sing.] the side or part of sth that provides shelter against the wind: *We built the house in the lee of the hill.*—compare LEEWARD, WINDWARD **2** (**lees**) [pl.] the substance that is left at the bottom of a bottle of wine, a container of beer, etc.

leech /liːtʃ/ noun **1** a small worm that usually lives in water and that attaches itself to other creatures and sucks their blood. Leeches were used in the past by doctors to remove blood from sick people. **2** (disapproving) a person who depends on sb else for money, or takes the profit from sb else's work

leek /liːk/ noun a vegetable like a long onion with many layers of wide flat leaves that are white at the bottom and green at the top. Leeks are eaten cooked.—picture on page A3

leer /lɪə(r); AmE lɪr/ verb, noun
■ verb [V] ~ (**at sb**) to look or smile at sb in an unpleasant way that shows an evil or a sexual interest in them
■ noun an unpleasant look or smile that shows sb is interested in a person in an evil or a sexual way: *He looked at her with an evil leer.*

leery /ˈlɪəri; AmE ˈlɪri/ adj. (informal) suspicious about sth, and trying to avoid it SYN WARY

lee·ward /ˈliːwəd; AmE -wərd; or, in nautical use, ˈluːəd; AmE -ərd/ adj., noun
■ adj. on the side of sth that is sheltered from the wind: *a harbour on the leeward side of the island* ▶ **lee·ward** adv. —compare WINDWARD
■ noun [U] the side or direction that is sheltered from the wind: *to steer leeward*—compare WINDWARD

lee·way /ˈliːweɪ/ noun [U] the amount of freedom that you have to change sth or to do sth in the way you want to: *How much leeway should parents give their children?* IDM **make up ˈleeway** (BrE) to get out of a bad position that you are in, especially because you have lost a lot of time

left /left/ adj., adv., noun—see also LEAVE v.
■ adj. [only before noun] on the side of your body which is towards the west when you are facing north: *Fewer people write with their left hand than with their right.* ◊ *I broke my left leg.* ◊ *There is a path along the left side of the field.* ◊ *The university is on the left bank of the river.* ◊ *Take a left turn at the intersection.* ◊ *(sport) a left back/wing* ◊ *a left hook* OPP RIGHT ▶ **left** adv.: *Turn left at the intersection.* ◊ *Look left and right before you cross the road.* IDM **have two left ˈfeet** (informal) to be very awkward in your movements, especially when you are dancing or playing a sport **,left, right and ˈcentre** (also **,right, left and ˈcentre**) (informal) in all directions; everywhere: *He's giving away money left, right and centre.*—more at RIGHT adv.
■ noun **1** (**the/sb's left**) [sing.] the left side or direction: *She was sitting on my left.* ◊ *Twist your body to the left, then to the right.* ◊ *Take the next road on the left.* ◊ *To the left of the library is the bank.* **2** [sing.] (**the first, second, etc. left**) the first, second, etc. road on the left side: *Take the first left.* **3** (**a left**) [sing.] a turn to the left: (BrE) *to take a*

left ◊ (AmE) *to hang/make a left* **4** (**the left, the Left**) [sing.+ sing./pl. v.] political groups who support the ideas and beliefs of SOCIALISM: *The Left only has/have a small chance of winning power.* ◊ *a left-leaning newspaper* **5** (**the left**) [sing.+ sing./pl. v.] the part of a political party whose members are most in favour of social change: *She is on the far left of the party.* **6** [C] (in boxing) a blow that is made with your left hand: *He hit him with two sharp lefts.* OPP RIGHT

ˈleft field noun [sing.] **1** (in baseball) the left part of the field, or the position played by the person who is there **2** (AmE, informal) an opinion or a position that is strange or unusual and a long way from the normal position: *The governor is way out/over in left field.*

ˈleft-hand adj. [only before noun] **1** on the left side of sth: *the left-hand side of the street* ◊ *the top left-hand corner of the page* **2** connected with a person's left hand: *a tennis player with a left-hand grip* ◊ *a left-hand glove* OPP RIGHT-HAND

ˌleft-hand ˈdrive adj. (of a vehicle) with the STEERING WHEEL on the left side OPP RIGHT-HAND DRIVE

ˌleft-ˈhanded adj. **1** (of a person) finding it easier to use the left hand to write, hit a ball, etc. than the right: *a left-handed golfer* ◊ *I'm left-handed.* **2** (of tools, etc.) designed to be used by sb who finds it easier to use their left hand: *left-handed scissors* **3** (of actions, etc.) done with your left hand: *a left-handed serve* ▶ **ˌleft-ˈhanded** adv.: *She writes left-handed.* **ˌleft-ˈhanded·ness** noun [U] IDM **ˌleft-handed ˈcompliment** (AmE) = BACKHANDED COMPLIMENT

ˌleft-ˈhander noun a person who finds it easier to use their left hand to write, hit a ball, etc. than their right OPP RIGHT-HANDER

leftie = LEFTY

left·ist /ˈleftɪst/ noun a person who supports LEFT-WING political parties and their ideas OPP RIGHTIST ▶ **left·ism** noun [U] **left·ist** adj.: *leftist groups/views*

ˌleft-ˈluggage office (also **ˌleft ˈluggage**) noun (both BrE) a place where you can pay to leave bags or suitcases for a short time, for example at a station

left·over /ˈleftəʊvə(r); AmE -oʊv-/ noun **1** [usually pl.] food that has not been eaten at the end of a meal: *Everyone was hungry so there were no leftovers.* **2** an object, a custom or a way of behaving that remains from an earlier time: *He's a leftover from the hippies in the 1960s.* ▶ **left·over** adj. [only before noun]: *Use any leftover meat to make a curry.*

left·ward /ˈleftwəd; AmE -wərd/ (BrE also **left·wards**) adj. [only before noun] towards the left: *a leftward swing in public opinion* ◊ *to move your eyes in a leftward direction* ▶ **left·ward** (BrE also **left·wards**) adv.

ˌleft ˈwing noun **1** [sing.+ sing./pl. v.] the part of a political party whose members are most in favour of social change: *He's on the left wing of the Conservative Party.* **2** [C, U] an attacking player or position on the left side of the field in a game of football, etc.

ˌleft-ˈwing adj. strongly supporting the ideas of SOCIALISM: *left-wing groups/politics*

ˌleft-ˈwinger noun **1** a person on the LEFT WING of a political party: *a Labour left-winger* **2** a person who plays on the left side of the field in a game of football, etc. OPP RIGHT-WINGER

lefty (also **leftie**) /ˈlefti/ noun (pl. -**ies**) (informal) **1** (disapproving, especially BrE) a person who has SOCIALIST views **2** (especially AmE) a person who uses their left hand to write, hit a ball, etc. ▶ **lefty** adj.: *a lefty feminist lecturer*

leg /leg/ noun, verb
■ noun
PART OF BODY **1** [C] one of the long parts that connect the feet to the rest of the body: *I broke my leg playing football.* ◊ *How many legs does a centipede have?* ◊ *front/back legs* ◊ *forelegs/hind legs* ◊ *a wooden leg*—see also BOW LEGS, DADDY-LONG-LEGS, LEGGY, LEGROOM, PEG LEG, SEA LEGS—picture at BODY
MEAT **2** [C, U] ~ (**of sth**) the leg of an animal, especially

æ	ɑː	e	ɜː	ə	ɪ	iː	i	ɒ	ɔː	ʌ	ʊ	u	uː
cat	father	ten	bird	about	sit	see	many	got	saw	cup	put	actual	too
								(BrE)					

the top part, cooked and eaten: *frogs' legs* ◊ *chicken legs* ◊ *roast leg of lamb*

OF TROUSERS/PANTS | **3** [C] the part of a pair of trousers/pants that covers the leg: *a trouser/pant leg* ◊ *These jeans are too long in the leg.*

OF TABLE/CHAIR | **4** [C] one of the long thin parts on the bottom of a table, chair, etc. that support it: *a chair/table leg*

-LEGGED | **5** /'legɪd; legd/ (in adjectives) having the number or type of legs mentioned: *a three-legged stool* ◊ *a long-legged insect* HELP When **-legged** is used with numbers, it is nearly always pronounced /'legɪd/ ; in other adjectives it can be pronounced /'legɪd/ or /legd/ .—see also CROSS-LEGGED

OF JOURNEY/RACE | **6** [C] ~ (of sth) one part of a journey or race: *The final leg of the trip was by donkey.*

SPORTS GAME | **7** [C] one of a series of matches played between the same opponents in a sports competition

IDM **break a 'leg!** (*spoken*) used to wish sb good luck **get your 'leg over** (*BrE, informal*) to have sex **not have a ˌleg to 'stand on** (*informal*) to be in a position where you are unable to prove sth or explain why sth is reasonable: *Without written evidence, we don't have a leg to stand on.*—more at ARM *n.*, FAST *adv.*, LAST *adj.*, PULL *v.*, SHAKE *v.*, STRETCH *v.*, TAIL *n.*, TALK *v.*—see also LEG-UP

■ *verb* (-gg-)

IDM **'leg it** (*informal, especially BrE*) to run, especially in order to escape from sb: *We saw the police coming and legged it down the road.*

leg·acy /'legəsi/ *noun* (*pl.* **-ies**) **1** money or property that is given to you by sb when they die: *They each received a legacy of £5000.* **2** a situation that exists now because of events, actions, etc. that took place in the past: *The problems were made worse by the legacy of centuries of neglect.* ◊ *Future generations will be left with a legacy of pollution and destruction.*

legal /'li:gl/ *adj.* **1** [only before noun] connected with the law: *the legal profession/system* ◊ *to take/seek legal advice* ◊ *a legal adviser* ◊ *legal costs/expenses* **2** allowed or required by law: *The driver was more than three times over the legal limit* (= the amount of alcohol you are allowed to have in your body when you are driving). ◊ *Should euthanasia be made legal?* OPP ILLEGAL ⇨ note at LAWFUL ▶ **le·gal·ly** /'li:gəli/ *adv.*: *a legally binding agreement* ◊ *to be legally responsible for sb/sth*

ˌlegal 'action *noun* [U] (also ˌlegal pro'ceedings [pl.]) the act of using the legal system to settle a disagreement, etc: *to take/begin legal action against sb* ◊ *They have threatened us with legal action.*

ˌlegal 'aid *noun* [U] money that is given by the government or another organization to sb who needs help to pay for legal advice or a lawyer

le·gal·ese /ˌli:gə'li:z/ *noun* (*informal*) the sort of language used in legal documents that is difficult to understand

ˌlegal 'holiday *noun* (in the US) a public holiday that is fixed by law—compare BANK HOLIDAY

le·gal·is·tic /ˌli:gə'lɪstɪk/ *adj.* (*disapproving*) obeying the law very strictly: *a legalistic approach to family disputes*

le·gal·ity /li:'gæləti/ *noun* (*pl.* **-ies**) **1** [U] the fact of being legal: *They intended to challenge the legality of his claim in the courts.* ◊ *The arrangement is of doubtful legality.* **2** [C, usually pl.] the legal aspect of an action or a situation: *You need a lawyer to explain all the legalities of the contracts.*—compare ILLEGALITY

le·gal·ize (*BrE also* **-ise**) /'li:gəlaɪz/ *verb* [VN] to make sth legal: *the campaign to legalize marijuana* ▶ **le·gal·iza·tion, -isa·tion** *noun* [U]

ˌlegal pro'ceedings *noun* [pl.] = LEGAL ACTION

ˌlegal 'tender *noun* [U] money that can be legally used to pay for things in a particular country: *These coins are no longer legal tender.*

leg·ate /'legət/ *noun* the official representative of the Pope in a foreign country: *a papal legate*

lega·tee /ˌlegə'ti:/ *noun* (*law*) a person who receives money or property (= a LEGACY) when sb dies

le·ga·tion /lɪ'geɪʃn/ *noun* **1** a group of DIPLOMATS representing their government in a foreign country in an office that is below the rank of an EMBASSY **2** the building where these people work

le·gato /lɪ'gɑːtəʊ; *AmE* -toʊ/ *adj.* (*music*) to be played or sung in a smooth, even manner ▶ **le·gato** *adv.* OPP STACCATO

le·gend /'ledʒənd/ *noun* **1** [C, U] a story from ancient times about people and events, that may or may not be true; this type of story: *the legend of Robin Hood* ◊ *the heroes of Greek legend* ◊ *Legend has it that the lake was formed by the tears of a god.* **2** [C] a very famous person, especially in a particular field, who is admired by other people: *a jazz/tennis legend* ◊ *She was a legend in her own lifetime.* ◊ *Many of golf's living legends were playing.* **3** [C] (*technical*) the explanation of a map or a diagram in a book **4** [C] (*formal*) a piece of writing on a sign, a label, a coin, etc.

le·gend·ary /'ledʒəndri; *AmE* -deri/ *adj.* **1** very famous and talked about a lot by people, especially in a way that shows admiration: *a legendary figure* ◊ *the legendary Orson Welles* ◊ *Her patience and tact are legendary.* **2** [only before noun] mentioned in stories from ancient times: *legendary heroes*—compare FABLED

leg·gings /'legɪŋz/ *noun* [pl.] **1** trousers/pants for women that fit tightly over the legs, made of fabric that stretches easily: *a pair of leggings*—picture on page A4 **2** protective outer coverings for the legs

leggy /'legi/ *adj.* (*informal*) (especially of girls and women) having long legs: *a tall leggy schoolgirl*

le·gible /'ledʒəbl/ *adj.* (of written or printed words) clear enough to read: *legible handwriting* ◊ *The signature was still legible.* OPP ILLEGIBLE ▶ **le·gi·bil·ity** /ˌledʒə'bɪləti/ *noun* [U] **le·gibly** /-əbli/ *adv.*

le·gion /'li:dʒən/ *noun, adj.*
■ *noun* **1** a large group of soldiers that forms part of an army, especially the one that existed in ancient Rome: *the French Foreign Legion* ◊ *Caesar's legions* **2** (*formal*) a large number of people of one particular type: *legions of photographers*
■ *adj.* [not before noun] (*formal*) very many: *The medical uses of herbs are legion.*

le·gion·ary /'li:dʒənəri; *AmE* -neri/ *noun* (*pl.* **-ies**) a soldier who is part of a legion ▶ **le·gion·ary** *adj.* [only before noun]

le·gion·naire /ˌli:dʒə'neə(r); *AmE* -'ner/ *noun* a member of a LEGION, especially the French Foreign Legion

ˌlegion'naires' disease *noun* [U] a serious lung disease caused by bacteria, especially spread by AIR CONDITIONING and similar systems

le·gis·late /'ledʒɪsleɪt/ *verb* [V] ~ (for/against/on sth) (*formal*) to make a law affecting sth: *The government has been urged to legislate against discrimination in the workplace.* ◊ (*figurative*) *You can't legislate against bad luck!* ◊ *They promised to legislate to protect people's right to privacy.*

le·gis·la·tion /ˌledʒɪs'leɪʃn/ *noun* [U] **1** a law or a set of laws passed by a parliament: *an important piece of legislation* ◊ *New legislation on the sale of drugs will be introduced next year.* **2** the process of making and passing laws: *Legislation will be difficult and will take time.*

le·gis·la·tive /'ledʒɪslətɪv; *AmE* -leɪtɪv/ *adj.* [only before noun] (*formal*) connected with the act of making and passing laws: *a legislative assembly/body/council* ◊ *legislative powers/changes*

le·gis·la·tor /'ledʒɪsleɪtə(r)/ *noun* (*formal*) a member of a group of people that has the power to make laws

le·gis·la·ture /'ledʒɪsleɪtʃə(r)/ *noun* (*formal*) a group of people who have the power to make and change laws: *a democratically elected legislature* ◊ *the national/state legislature*—compare EXECUTIVE, JUDICIARY

legit /lɪ'dʒɪt/ *adj.* (*informal*) legal, or acting according to the law or the rules: *The business seems legit.*

le·git·im·ate /lɪ'dʒɪtɪmət/ *adj.* **1** for which there is a fair and acceptable reason SYN VALID: *a legitimate expect-*

aɪ	aʊ	eɪ	əʊ	oʊ	ɔɪ	ɪə	eə	ʊə	j	w
my	now	say	go	go	boy	near	hair	pure	yes	wet
			(BrE)	(AmE)						

ation/concern/grievance/excuse ◇ *It seemed a perfectly legitimate question.* ◇ *Politicians are legitimate targets for satire.* **2** allowed and acceptable according to the law [SYN] LEGAL: *the legitimate government of the country* ◇ *Is his business strictly legitimate?* [OPP] ILLEGITIMATE **3** (of a child) born when its parents are legally married to each other [OPP] ILLEGITIMATE ▶ **le·git·im·acy** /lɪˈdʒɪtɪməsi/ *noun* [U]: *the dubious legitimacy of his argument* ◇ *I intend to challenge the legitimacy of his claim.* **le·git·im·ate·ly** *adv.*: *She can now legitimately claim to be the best in the world.*

le·git·im·ize (*BrE* also **-ise**) /lɪˈdʒɪtəmaɪz/ *verb* [VN] (*formal*) **1** to make sth that is wrong or unfair seem acceptable: *The movie has been criticized for apparently legitimizing violence.* **2** to make sth legal **3** to give a child whose parents are not married to each other the same rights as those whose parents are

leg·less /ˈleɡləs/ *adj.* **1** without legs **2** (*BrE, informal*) very drunk

leg·room /ˈleɡruːm; ˈleɡrʊm/ *noun* [U] the amount of space available for your legs when you are sitting in a vehicle, theatre, etc.

leg·ume /ˈleɡjuːm; lɪˈɡjuːm/ *noun* (*technical*) any plant that has seeds in long PODS. Peas and beans are legumes.

leg-up *noun* [IDM] **give sb a ˈleg-up** (*BrE, informal*) **1** to help sb to get on a horse, over a wall, etc. by allowing them to put their foot in your hands and lifting them up **2** to help sb to improve their situation

leg·work /ˈleɡwɜːk; *AmE* -wɜːrk/ *noun* [U] (*informal*) difficult or boring work that takes a lot of time and effort, but that is thought to be less important

lei·sure /ˈleʒə(r)/ *AmE* /ˈliːʒər/ *noun* [U] time that is spent doing what you enjoy when you are not working or studying: *These days we have more money and more leisure to enjoy it.* ◇ *leisure activities/interests/pursuits* [IDM] **at ˈleisure 1** with no particular activities; free: *Spend the afternoon at leisure in the town centre.* **2** without hurrying: *Let's have lunch so we can talk at leisure.* **at your ˈleisure** (*formal*) when you have the time to do sth without hurrying: *I suggest you take the forms away and read them at your leisure.*

leisure centre (*BrE*) *noun* a public building where people can go to do sports and other activities in their free time

leis·ured /ˈleʒəd; *AmE* ˈliːʒərd/ *adj.* **1** [only before noun] not having to work and therefore having a lot of time to do what you enjoy: *the leisured classes* **2** = LEISURELY

leis·ure·ly /ˈleʒəli; *AmE* ˈliːʒərli/ (also **leis·ured**) *adj.* [usually before noun] done without hurrying: *a leisurely bath/meal/stroll* ◇ *They set off at a leisurely pace.* ▶ **leis·ure·ly** *adv.*: *Couples strolled leisurely along the beach.*

leis·ure·wear /ˈleʒəweə(r); *AmE* ˈliːʒərwer/ *noun* [U] (used especially by shops/stores and clothes companies) informal clothes worn for relaxing or playing sports in

leit·motif (also **leit·motiv**) /ˈlaɪtməʊtiːf; *AmE* -moʊ-/ *noun* (from *German*) **1** (*music*) a short tune in a piece of music that is often repeated and is connected with a particular person, thing or idea **2** an idea or a phrase that is repeated often in a book or work of art, or is typical of a particular person or group

lem·ming /ˈlemɪŋ/ *noun* a small animal like a mouse, that lives in cold northern countries. Sometimes large groups of lemmings MIGRATE (= move from one place to another) in search of food. Many of them die on these journeys and there is a popular belief that lemmings kill themselves by jumping off cliffs: *Lemming-like we rushed into certain disaster.*

lemon /ˈlemən/ *noun, adj.*
■ *noun* **1** [C, U] a yellow CITRUS fruit with a lot of sour juice. Slices of lemon and lemon juice are used in cooking and drinks: *lemon tea* ◇ *A gin and tonic with ice and lemon, please.* ◇ *Squeeze the juice of half a lemon over the fish.* ◇ *a lemon tree*—picture on page A2 **2** [U] lemon juice or a drink made from lemon—see also BITTER LEMON **3** (also ˌlemon ˈyellow) [U] a pale yellow colour **4** [C] (*informal, especially AmE*) a thing that is useless because it does not work as it should **5** [C] (*BrE*) a stupid person
■ *adj.* (also ˌlemon ˈyellow) pale yellow in colour

lem·on·ade /ˌleməˈneɪd/ *noun* **1** [U] (*BrE*) a sweet FIZZY drink (= with bubbles) with a lemon flavour **2** [U] a drink made from lemon juice, sugar and water **3** [C] a glass or bottle of lemonade—compare ORANGEADE

ˌlemon ˈcurd *noun* [U] (*BrE*) a thick sweet yellow substance made from lemon, sugar, eggs and butter, spread on bread, etc. or used to fill cakes

ˈlemon grass *noun* [U] a type of grass with a lemon flavour that grows in hot countries and is used especially in SE Asian cooking

ˈlemon squeezer (*BrE*) (*AmE* **juicer**) *noun* a kitchen UTENSIL (= a tool) for squeezing juice out of a fruit—picture at KITCHEN

lem·ony /ˈleməni/ *adj.* tasting or smelling of lemon: *a lemony flavour/perfume*

lemur /ˈliːmə(r)/ *noun* an animal like a monkey, with thick fur and a long tail, that lives in trees in Madagascar

lend /lend/ *verb* (**lent, lent** /lent/) **1** ~ (**out**) **sth** (**to sb**)| ~ (**sb**) **sth** to give sth to sb or allow them to use sth that belongs to you, which they have to return to you later: [VN, VNN] *I've lent the car to a friend.* ◇ *Can you lend me your car this evening?* ◇ [VNN] *Has he returned that book you lent him?* ⇨ note at BORROW **2** ~ **sth** (**to sb**)| ~ (**sb**) **sth** (of a bank or financial institution) to give money to sb on condition that they pay it back over a period of time and pay interest on it: [VN, VNN] *The bank refused to lend the money to us.* ◇ *They refused to lend us the money.* [also V]—compare BORROW **3** ~ **sth** (**to sb/sth**)| ~ (**sb/sth**) **sth** (*written*) to give a particular quality to a person or a situation: [VN] *The setting sun lent an air of melancholy to the scene.* ◇ [VNN] *Her presence lent the occasion a certain dignity.* **4** ~ **sth** (**to sb/sth**)| ~ (**sb/sth**) **sth** to give or provide help, support, etc: [VN] *I was more than happy to lend my support to such a good cause.* ◇ [VNN] *He came along to lend me moral support.* [IDM] **lend an ˈear (to sb/sth)** to listen in a patient and sympathetic way to sb **lend (sb) a (helping) ˈhand (with sth)** (*informal*) to help sb with sth: *I went over to see if I could lend a hand.* **lend your name to sth** (*formal*) **1** to let it be known in public that you support or agree with sth: *I am more than happy to lend my name to this campaign.* **2** to have a place named after you **lend supˈport, ˈweight, ˈcredence, etc. to sth** to make sth seem more likely to be true or genuine: *This latest evidence lends support to her theory.*—more at HELP *v.* [PHRV] **ˈlend itself to sth** to be suitable for sth: *Her voice doesn't really lend itself well to blues singing.*

lend·er /ˈlendə(r)/ *noun* (*finance*) a person or an organization that lends money—compare BORROWER—see also MONEYLENDER

lend·ing /ˈlendɪŋ/ *noun* [U] (*finance*) the act of lending money: *Lending by banks and building societies rose to £4.9 billion last year.*

ˈlending library *noun* a public library from which you can borrow books and take them away to read at home—compare REFERENCE LIBRARY

ˈlending rate *noun* (*finance*) the rate of interest that you must pay when you borrow money from a bank or another financial organization

length /leŋθ/ *noun*
SIZE/MEASUREMENT | **1** [U, C] the size or measurement of sth from one end to the other: *This room is twice the length of the kitchen.* ◇ *The river is 300 miles in length.* ◇ *The snake usually reaches a length of 100cm.* ◇ *He ran the entire length of the beach* (= from one end to the other). ◇ *Did you see the length of his hair?*—compare BREADTH, WIDTH
TIME | **2** [U, C] the amount of time that sth lasts: *We discussed shortening the length of the course.* ◇ *He was disgusted at the length of time he had to wait.* ◇ *She got a headache if she had to read for any length of time* (= for a long time). ◇ *Size of pension depends partly on length of service with the company.* ◇ *Each class is 45 minutes in length.*
OF BOOK/MOVIE | **3** [U, C] the amount of writing in a book, or a document, etc.; the amount of time that a film/movie lasts: *Her novels vary in length.*
-LENGTH | **4** (in adjectives) having the length mentioned: *shoulder-length hair*—see also FULL-LENGTH, KNEE-LENGTH

L

OF SWIMMING POOL | **5** [C] the distance from one end of a swimming pool to the other: *He swims 50 lengths a day.*—compare WIDTH

IN RACE | **6** [C] the size of a horse or boat from one end to the other, when it is used to measure the distance between two competitors in a race: *The horse won by two clear lengths.*

LONG THIN PIECE | **7** [C] a long thin piece of sth: *a length of rope/string/wire*

—see also LONG *adj.*

IDM at 'length | at ...length **1** for a long time and in detail: *He quoted at length from the report.* ◊ *We have already discussed this matter at great length.* **2** (*literary*) after a long time: *'I'm still not sure,' he said at length.* **go to any, some, great, etc. 'lengths (to do sth)** to put a lot of effort into doing sth, especially when this seems extreme: *She goes to extraordinary lengths to keep her private life private.* **the length and 'breadth of ...** in or to all parts of a place: *They have travelled the length and breadth of Europe giving concerts.*—more at ARM *n.*

length·en /ˈleŋθən/ *verb* to become longer; to make sth longer: [V] *The afternoon shadows lengthened.* ◊ [VN] *I need to lengthen this skirt.* **OPP** SHORTEN

length·ways /ˈleŋθweɪz/ (also **length·wise** /ˈleŋθwaɪz/) *adv.* in the same direction as the longest side of sth: *Cut the banana in half lengthways.*—compare WIDTHWAYS

lengthy /ˈleŋθi/ *adj.* (**length·ier, lengthi·est**) very long, and often too long, in time or size: *lengthy delays/discussions* ◊ *the lengthy process of obtaining a visa* ◊ *a lengthy report/explanation*

le·ni·ent /ˈliːniənt/ *adj.* not as strict as expected when punishing sb or when making sure that rules are obeyed: *a lenient sentence/fine* ◊ *The judge was far too lenient with him.* ▶ **le·ni·ency** /-ənsi/ *noun* [U]: *She appealed to the judge for leniency.* **le·ni·ent·ly** *adv.*: *to treat sb leniently*

lens /lenz/ *noun* **1** a curved piece of glass or plastic that makes things look larger, smaller or clearer when you look through it: *a pair of glasses with tinted lenses* ◊ *a camera with an adjustable lens* ◊ *a lens cap/cover*—see also FISHEYE LENS, TELEPHOTO LENS, WIDE-ANGLE LENS, ZOOM LENS—picture at GLASS **2** (*informal*) = CONTACT LENS: *Have you got your lenses in?* **3** (*anatomy*) the transparent part of the eye, behind the PUPIL, that FOCUSES light so that you can see clearly—picture at BODY

Lent /lent/ *noun* [U] in the Christian Church, the period of 40 days from Ash Wednesday to the day before Easter, during which some Christians give up food or activities that they enjoy in memory of Christ's suffering

lent *pt, pp* of LEND

len·til /ˈlentl/ *noun* a small green, orange or brown seed that is usually dried and used in cooking, for example in soup or STEW

Leo /ˈliːəʊ; *AmE* ˈliːoʊ/ *noun* **1** [U] the fifth sign of the ZODIAC, the Lion **2** [C] (*pl.* **-os**) a person born under the influence of this sign, that is between 23 July and 22 August, approximately

leo·nine /ˈliːənaɪn/ *adj.* like a lion

leop·ard /ˈlepəd; *AmE* -ərd/ *noun* a large animal of the cat family, that has yellowish-brown fur with black spots. Leopards live in Africa and southern Asia. **IDM** **a leop·ard cannot change its 'spots** (*saying*) a person cannot change their character, especially if they have a bad character

leo·tard /ˈliːətɑːd; *AmE* -tɑːrd/ *noun* a piece of clothing that fits tightly over the body from the neck down to the tops of the legs, usually covering the arms, worn by dancers, women doing physical exercises, etc.

leper /ˈlepə(r)/ *noun* **1** a person suffering from LEPROSY **2** a person that other people avoid because they have done sth that these people do not approve of

lep·re·chaun /ˈleprəkɔːn/ *noun* (in Irish stories) a creature like a little man, with magic powers

lep·rosy /ˈleprəsi/ *noun* [U] an infectious disease that causes painful white areas on the skin and can destroy nerves and flesh—see also LEPER

les·bian /ˈlezbiən/ *noun* a woman who is sexually attracted to other women: *lesbians and gays*—compare GAY, HOMOSEXUAL ▶ **les·bian** *adj.*: *the lesbian and gay community* ◊ *a lesbian relationship* **les·bian·ism** *noun* [U]

le·sion /ˈliːʒn/ *noun* (*medical*) damage to the skin or part of the body caused by injury or by illness: *skin/brain lesions*

less /les/ *det., pron., adv., prep.*

■ *det., pron.* used with uncountable nouns to mean 'a smaller amount of': *less butter/time/importance* ◊ *He was advised to smoke fewer cigarettes and drink less beer.* ◊ *We have less to worry about now.* ◊ *It is less of a problem than I'd expected.* ◊ *We'll be there in less than no time* (= very soon). ◊ *The victory was nothing less than a miracle.* **IDM** **less and 'less** smaller and smaller amounts: *As time passed, she saw less and less of all her old friends at home.* **no 'less** (often *ironic*) used to suggest that sth is surprising or impressive: *She's having lunch with the Director, no less.* **no less than ...** used to emphasize a large amount: *The guide contains details of no less than 115 hiking routes.*

■ *adv.* to a smaller degree; not so much: *less expensive/likely/intelligent* ◊ *less often/enthusiastically* ◊ *I read much less now than I used to.* ◊ *The receptionist was less than* (= not at all) *helpful.* ◊ *She wasn't any the less happy for* (= she was perfectly happy) *being on her own.* ◊ *That this is a positive stereotype makes it no less a stereotype, and therefore unacceptable.* **IDM** **even/much/still 'less** and certainly not: *No explanation was offered, still less an apology.* **less and 'less** continuing to become smaller in amount: *She found the job less and less attractive.*—more at MORE *adv.*

■ *prep.* used before a particular amount that must be taken away from the amount just mentioned **SYN** MINUS: *a monthly salary of £1200 less tax and insurance*

-less /-ləs/ *suffix* (in adjectives) **1** without: *treeless* ◊ *meaningless* **2** not doing; not affected by: *tireless* ◊ *selfless* ▶ **-less·ly** (in adverbs): *hopelessly* **-less·ness** (in nouns): *helplessness*

les·see /leˈsiː/ *noun* (*law*) a person who has use of a building, an area of land, etc. on a LEASE

less·en /ˈlesn/ *verb* to become or make sth become smaller, weaker, less important, etc. (*written*): [V] *The noise began to lessen.* ◊ [VN] *to lessen the risk/impact/effect of sth* ▶ **less·en·ing** *noun* [sing., U]: *a lessening of tension*

less·er /ˈlesə(r)/ *adj.* [only before noun] **1** not as great in size, amount or importance as sth else: *people of lesser importance* ◊ *They were all involved to a greater or lesser degree* (= some were more involved than others). ◊ *The law was designed to protect wives, and, to a lesser extent, children.* ◊ *He was encouraged to plead guilty to the lesser offence.* **2** used in the names of some types of animals, birds and plants which are smaller than similar kinds **OPP** GREATER ▶ **less·er** *adv.*: *one of the lesser-known Caribbean islands* **IDM** **the ,lesser of two 'evils | the ,lesser 'evil** the less unpleasant of two unpleasant choices

les·son /ˈlesn/ *noun* **1** a period of time in which sb is taught sth: *She gives piano lessons.* ◊ *All new students are given lessons in/on how to use the library.* ◊ *I'm having/taking driving lessons.* ◊ (*especially BrE*) *Our first lesson on Tuesdays is French.* ◊ (*especially BrE*) *What did we do last lesson?*—compare CLASS **2** something that is intended to be learned: *The course book is divided into 30 lessons.* **3** ~ **(to sb)** an experience, especially an unpleasant one, that sb can learn from so that it does not happen again in the future: *a salutary/valuable lesson* ◊ *Let that be a lesson to you!* ◊ *The accident taught me a lesson I'll never forget.*—see also OBJECT LESSON **4** a passage from the Bible that is read aloud during a church service **IDM** see LEARN

les·sor /leˈsɔː(r)/ *noun* (*law*) a person who gives sb the use of a building, an area of land, etc. on a LEASE

lest /lest/ *conj.* (*formal* or *literary*) **1** in order to prevent sth from happening: *He gripped his brother's arm lest he be trampled by the mob.* **2** used to introduce the reason for the particular emotion mentioned **SYN** IN CASE: *She was afraid lest she had revealed too much.*

let /let/ *verb, noun*

s	t	v	z	ʃ	ʒ	tʃ	dʒ	θ	ð	ŋ
see	tea	van	zoo	shoe	vision	chain	jam	thin	this	sing

■ *verb* (**let·ting**, **let**, **let**)

ALLOW | **1** [no passive] to allow sb to do sth or sth to happen without trying to stop it: [VNinf] *Let them splash around in the pool for a while.* ◊ *Don't let her upset you.* ◊ *Let your body relax.* ◊ [VN] *He'd eat chocolate all day long if I let him.* **2** to give sb permission to do sth: [VNinf] *They won't let him leave the country.* ◊ [VN] *She wanted to lend me some money but I wouldn't let her.* **3** [VN+*adv.*/*prep.*] to allow sb/sth to go somewhere: *to let sb into the house* ◊ *I'll give you a key so that you can let yourself in.* ◊ *Please let me past.* ◊ *The cat wants to be let out.* ⟹ note at ALLOW

MAKING SUGGESTIONS | **4** (**let's**) [no passive] used for making suggestions: [VNinf] *Let's go to the beach.* ◊ *Let's not tell her what we did.* ◊ (*BrE*) *Don't let's tell her what we did.* ◊ *I don't think we'll make it, but let's try anyway.* ◊ [VN] *'Shall we check it again?' 'Yes, let's.'*

OFFERING HELP | **5** [VNinf] [no passive] used for offering help to sb: *Here, let me do it.* ◊ *Let us get those boxes down for you.*

MAKING REQUESTS | **6** [VNinf] [no passive] used for making requests or giving instructions: *Let me have your report by Friday.*

CHALLENGING | **7** [VNinf] [no passive] used to show that you are not afraid or worried about sb doing sth: *If he thinks he can cheat me, just let him try!*

WISHING | **8** [VNinf] [no passive] (*literary*) used to express a strong wish for sth to happen: *Let her come home safely!*

INTRODUCING STH | **9** [VNinf] [no passive] used to introduce what you are going to say or do: *Let me give you an example.* ◊ *Let me just finish this and then I'll come.*

IN CALCULATING | **10** [VNinf] [no passive] (*technical*) used to say that you are supposing sth to be true when you calculate sth: *Let line AB be equal to line CD.*

HOUSE/ROOM | **11** [VN] **~ sth (out) (to sb)** (*especially BrE*) to allow sb to use a house, room, etc. in return for regular payments: *I let the spare room.* ◊ *They decided to let out the smaller offices at low rents.* ⟹ note at RENT

IDM Most idioms containing **let** are at the entries for the nouns and adjectives in the idioms, for example **let alone** is at **alone**. ˌlet ˈfall sth to mention sth in a conversation, by accident or as if by accident: *She let fall a further heavy hint.* ˌlet sb ˈgo **1** to allow sb to be free: *Will they let the hostages go?* **2** to make sb have to leave their job: *They're having to let 100 employees go because of falling profits.* ˌlet sb/sth ˈgo | ˌlet ˈgo (of sb/sth) **1** to stop holding sb/sth: *Don't let the rope go.* ◊ *Don't let go of the rope.* ◊ *Let go! You're hurting me!* **2** to give up an idea or an attitude, or control of sth: *It's time to let the past go.* ◊ *It's time to let go of the past.* ˌlet yourself ˈgo **1** to behave in a relaxed way without worrying about what people think of your behaviour: *Come on, enjoy yourself, let yourself go!* **2** to stop being careful about how you look and dress, etc: *He has let himself go since he lost his job.* **let sb ˈhave it** (*spoken, informal*) to attack sb physically or with words **let it ˈgo (at ˈthat)** to say or do no more about sth: *I don't entirely agree, but I'll let it go at that.* ◊ *I thought she was hinting at something, but I let it go.* ˌlet me ˈsee/ˈthink used when you are thinking or trying to remember sth: *Now let me see—where did he say he lived?* **let us ˈsay** used when making a suggestion or giving an example: *I can let you have it for, well let's say £100.*

PHR V ˌlet sb↔ˈdown to fail to help or support sb as they had hoped or expected: *I'm afraid she let us down badly.* ◊ *This machine won't let you down.* ◊ *He trudged home feeling lonely and let down.*—related noun LET-DOWN, ˌlet sb/sth↔ˈdown to make sb/sth less successful than they/it should be: *She speaks French very fluently, but her pronunciation lets her down.* ˌlet sth↔ˈdown **1** to lower sth: *We let the bucket down by a rope.* **2** to make a dress, skirt, coat, etc. longer, by lowering the bottom edge: *This skirt needs letting down.* **OPP** TAKE UP **3** (*BrE*) to allow the air to escape from sth deliberately: *Some kids had let my tyres down.* ˌlet sb/yourself ˈin for sth (*informal*) to involve sb/yourself in sth that is likely to be unpleasant or difficult: *I volunteered to help, and then I thought 'Oh no, what have I let myself in for!'* ˌlet sb ˈin on sth, ˌlet sb ˈinto sth (*informal*) to allow sb to share a secret: *Are you*

going to *let them in on your plans?* ˌlet sth ˈinto sth to put sth into the surface of sth so that it does not stick out from it: *a window let into a wall* ˌlet sb ˈoff (with sth) to not punish sb for sth they have done wrong, or to give them only a light punishment: *They let us off lightly.* ◊ *She was let off with a warning.* ˌlet sb ˈoff sth to allow sb not to do sth or not to go somewhere: *He let us off homework today.* ˌlet sth ˈoff to fire a gun or make a bomb, etc. explode: *The boys were letting off fireworks.* ˌlet ˈon (to sb) (*informal*) to tell a secret: *I'm getting married next week, but please don't let on to anyone.* ◊ [+that] *She let on that she was leaving.* ˌlet sb ˈout to make sb stop feeling that they are involved in sth or have to do sth: *They think the attacker was very tall—so that lets you out.*—related noun LET-OUT, ˌlet sth ˈout **1** to give a cry, etc: *to let out a scream of terror/a gasp of delight* **OPP** HOLD IN **2** to make a shirt, coat, etc. looser or larger **OPP** TAKE IN ˌlet ˈup (*informal*) **1** to become less strong: *The pain finally let up.* **2** to make less effort: *We mustn't let up now.*—related noun LET-UP

■ *noun*

IN TENNIS | **1** a SERVE that lands in the correct part of the court but must be taken again because it has touched the top of the net

HOUSE/ROOM | **2** (*BrE*) an act of renting a home, etc: *a long-term/short-term let*

IDM **without ˌlet or ˈhindrance** (*formal* or *law*) without being prevented from doing sth; freely

-let *suffix* (in nouns) small; not very important: *booklet* ◊ *piglet* ◊ *starlet*

ˈlet-down *noun* [C usually sing., U] something that is disappointing because it is not as good as you expected it to be **SYN** DISAPPOINTMENT

le·thal /ˈliːθl/ *adj.* **1** causing or able to cause death **SYN** DEADLY: *a lethal dose of poison* ◊ *a lethal weapon* ◊ (*figurative*) *The closure of the factory dealt a lethal blow to the town.* **2** (*informal*) causing or able to cause a lot of harm or damage: *You and that car—it's a lethal combination!* ◊ *This wine's pretty lethal!* (= very strong) ▶ **le·thal·ly** /ˈliːθəli/ *adv.*

leth·argy /ˈleθədʒi; AmE ˈleθərdʒi/ *noun* [U] the state of not having any energy or enthusiasm for doing things: *bouts of lethargy and depression* ▶ **leth·ar·gic** /ləˈθɑːdʒɪk; AmE ˌ-ˈθɑːrdʒ-/ *adj.*: *The weather made her listless and lethargic.*

ˈlet-out *noun* [sing.] (*BrE*) an event or a statement that allows sb to avoid having to do sth: *Good—we have a let-out now.* ◊ *a let-out clause* (= in a contract)

let's *short form* of LET US: *Let's break for lunch.*

let·ter /ˈletə(r)/ *noun, verb*

■ *noun* **1** a message that is written down or printed on paper and usually put in an envelope and sent to sb: *a business/thank-you letter* ◊ *a letter of complaint/sympathy* ◊ (*BrE*) *to post a letter* ◊ (*AmE*) *to mail a letter* ◊ *There's a letter for you from your mother.* ◊ *You will be notified by letter.* **HELP** You will find compounds ending in **letter** at their place in the alphabet. **2** a written or printed sign representing a sound used in writing: *'B' is the second letter of the alphabet.* ◊ *Write your name in capital/block letters.* **3** (*AmE*) a sign in the shape of a letter that is sewn onto clothes to show that a person plays in a school or college sports team **IDM** **the ˈletter of the ˈlaw** (often *disapproving*) the exact words of a law or rule rather than its general meaning: *They insist on sticking to the letter of the law.* **to the ˈletter** exactly what sb/sth says, paying attention to every detail: *I followed your instructions to the letter.*

■ *verb* **1** [usually passive] to give a letter to sth as part of a series or list: [VN-N] *Curiously, the stars lettered Alpha and Beta are relatively faint.* [also VN] **2** [VN] [usually passive] **~ sth (in sth)** to print, paint, etc. letters onto sth: *a black banner lettered in white* **3** [V] (*AmE*) to receive a letter made of cloth that you sew onto your clothes for playing in a school or college sports team

ˈletter bomb *noun* a small bomb that is sent to sb hidden in a letter that explodes when the envelope is opened—see also PARCEL BOMB

æ	ɑː	e	ɜː	ə	ɪ	iː	i	ɒ	ɔː	ʌ	ʊ	u	uː
cat	father	ten	bird	about	sit	see	many	got	saw	cup	put	actual	too
								(BrE)					

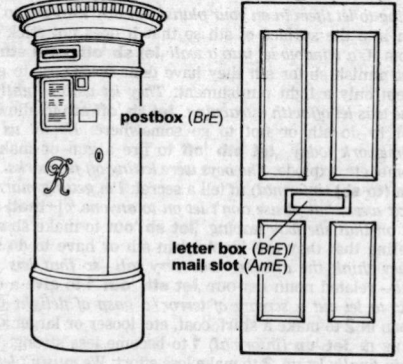

postbox (BrE)

letter box (BrE)/
mail slot (AmE)

mailboxes (AmE)

US. MAIL

The SMITHS

UNITED STATES POSTAL SERVICE
U.S MAIL

'letter box *noun* (*BrE*) **1** (*AmE* **'mail slot**) a narrow opening in a door or wall through which mail is delivered **2** (*AmE* **'mail·box**) a small box near the main door of a building or by the road, which mail is delivered to **3** = POSTBOX—compare PILLAR BOX

'letter carrier *noun* (*AmE*) = MAIL CARRIER

let·ter·head /'letəhed; *AmE* -tərh-/ *noun* the name and address of a person, company or organization printed at the top of their writing paper

let·ter·ing /'letərɪŋ/ *noun* [U] **1** letters or words that are written or printed in a particular style: *bold/Gothic lettering* **2** the process of writing, drawing or printing letters or words

,letter of 'credit *noun* (*pl.* **letters of credit**) (*finance*) a letter from a bank that allows you to get a particular amount of money from another bank

'letter opener *noun* (*AmE*) = PAPER KNIFE

,letter-'perfect *adj.* (*AmE*) **1** correct in all details **2** = WORD-PERFECT

let·ting /'letɪŋ/ *noun* (*BrE*) a period of time when you let a house or other property to sb else: *holiday lettings*

let·tuce /'letɪs/ *noun* [U, C] a plant with large green leaves that are eaten raw, especially in salad. There are many types of lettuce: *a bacon, lettuce and tomato sandwich* ◊ *Buy a lettuce and some tomatoes.*—picture on page A3

'let-up *noun* [U, sing.] ~ (**in sth**) a period of time during which sth stops or becomes less strong, difficult, etc.; a reduction in the strength of sth SYN LULL: *There is no sign of a let-up in the recession.*

leu·kae·mia (*BrE*) (*AmE* **leu·ke·mia**) /luːˈkiːmiə/ *noun* [U] a serious disease in which too many white blood cells are produced, causing weakness and sometimes death

levee /'levi/ *noun* (*AmE*) **1** a low wall built at the side of a river to prevent it from flooding **2** a place on a river where boats can let passengers on or off, etc.

level /'levl/ *noun, adj., verb*
■ *noun*

AMOUNT | **1** [C] the amount of sth that exists in a particular situation at a particular time: *relatively low levels of unemployment/crime* ◊ *a test that checks the level of alcohol in the blood* ◊ *high stress/pollution levels*

STANDARD | **2** [C, U] a particular standard or quality: *a high level of achievement/intelligence* ◊ *a computer game with 15 levels* ◊ *What is the level of this course?* ◊ *He studied French to degree level.* ◊ *Both players are on a level* (= of the same standard). ◊ *I refuse to sink to their level* (= behave as badly as them).—see also A LEVEL

RANK IN SCALE | **3** [U, C] a position or rank in a scale of size or importance: *a decision taken at board/cabinet level* ◊ *Discussions are currently being held at national level.*

POINT OF VIEW | **4** [C] a particular way of looking at, reacting to or understanding sth: *On a more personal level, I would like to thank Jean for all the help she has given me.* ◊ *Fables can be understood on various levels.*

HEIGHT | **5** [C, U] the height of sth in relation to the ground or to what it used to be: *the level of water in the bottle* ◊ *The cables are buried one metre below ground level.* ◊ *The flood water nearly reached roof level.* ◊ *The tables are not on a level* (= the same height).—see also EYE LEVEL, SEA LEVEL

FLOOR/LAYER | **6** [C] a floor of a building; a layer of ground: *The library is all on one level.* ◊ *Archaeologists found pottery in the lowest level of the site.* ◊ *a multi-level parking lot*—see also SPLIT-LEVEL

TOOL | **7** [C] = SPIRIT LEVEL

IDM **on the 'level** (*AmE* also **on the ,up and 'up**) (*informal*) honest; legal: *I'm not convinced he's on the level.* ◊ *Are you sure this deal is on the level?*

■ *adj.*

FLAT | **1** having a flat surface that does not slope: *Pitch the tent on level ground.* ◊ *Add a level tablespoon of flour* (= enough to fill the spoon but not so much that there is ⸰ round heap on the spoon).—compare HEAPED

EQUAL | **2** ~ (**with sth**) having the same height, position, value, etc. as sth: *Are these pictures level?* ◊ *This latest rise is intended to keep wages level with inflation.* ◊ *She drew level with* (= came beside) *the police car.* **3** ~ (**with sb**) (*especially BrE, sport*) having the same score as sb: *A good second round brought him level with the tournament leader.* ◊ *France took an early lead but Wales soon drew level* (= scored the same number of points).

VOICE/LOOK | **4** not showing any emotion; steady SYN EVEN: *a level gaze*—see also LEVELLY

IDM **be ,level 'pegging** (*BrE*) having the same score: *The contestants were level pegging after round 3.* **do/try your level 'best (to do sth)** to do as much as you can to try to achieve sth **a ,level 'playing field** a situation in which everyone has the same opportunities

■ *verb* (**-ll-**, *AmE* **-l-**)

MAKE FLAT | **1** [VN] ~ **sth** (**off/out**) to make sth flat or smooth: *If you're laying tiles, the floor will need to be levelled first.*

DESTROY | **2** [VN] to destroy a building or a group of trees completely by knocking it down: *The blast levelled several buildings in the area.*

MAKE EQUAL | **3** to make sth equal or similar: [VN] (*BrE*) *Davies levelled the score at 2 all.* [also V]

POINT | **4** [VN] ~ **sth** (**at sb**) to point sth, especially a gun, at sb: *I had a gun levelled at my head.*

IDM **,level the 'playing field** to create a situation where everyone has the same opportunities

PHRV **'level sth against/at sb** to say publicly that sb is to blame for sth, especially a crime or a mistake: *The speech was intended to answer the charges levelled against him by his opponents.* **,level sth↔'down** to make standards, amounts, etc. be of the same low or lower level: *Teachers are accused of levelling standards down to suit the needs of less able students.* **,level 'off/'out 1** to stop rising or falling and remain horizontal: *The plane levelled off at 1500 feet.* ◊ *After the long hill, the road levelled out.* **2** to stay at a steady level of development or progress after a period of sharp rises or falls: *Sales have levelled off after a period of rapid growth.* **,level sth↔'up** to make standards, amounts, etc. be of the same high or higher

L

aɪ	aʊ	eɪ	əʊ	oʊ	ɔɪ	ɪə	eə	ʊə	j	w
my	now	say	go (BrE)	go (AmE)	boy	near	hair	pure	yes	wet

level **'level with sb** (*informal*) to tell sb the truth and not hide any unpleasant facts from them

'level 'crossing (*BrE*) (*AmE* **'railroad crossing**) *noun* a place where a road crosses a railway/railroad line

'level-'headed *adj.* calm and sensible; able to make good decisions even in difficult situations

lev·el·ler (*BrE*) (*AmE* **lev·el·er**) /ˈlevələ(r)/ *noun* [usually sing.] an event or a situation that makes everyone equal whatever their age, importance, etc: *death, the great leveller*

lev·el·ly /ˈlevəli/ *adv.* in a calm and steady way: *She looked at him levelly.*

lever /ˈliːvə(r)*; AmE* ˈlevər/ *noun, verb*

lever

■ *noun* **1** a handle used to operate a vehicle or piece of machinery: *Pull the lever towards you to adjust the speed.*—see also GEAR LEVER **2** a long piece of wood, metal, etc. used for lifting or opening sth by sb placing one end of it under an object and pushing down on the other end **3** ~ (for/against sth) an action that is used to put pressure on sb to do sth they do not want to do: *The threat of sanctions is our most powerful lever for peace.*

She levered the top off the pot with a screwdriver.

■ *verb* to move sth with a lever: [VN+*adv./prep.*] *I levered the lid off the pot with a knife.* ◊ [VN-ADJ] *They managed to lever the door open.*

le·ver·age /ˈliːvərɪdʒ*; AmE* ˈlev-/ *noun* [U] **1** (*formal*) the ability to influence what people do: *diplomatic/political leverage* **2** (*technical*) the act of using a lever to open or lift sth; the force used to do this **3** (*AmE, finance*) = GEARING (1)

'leveraged 'buyout *noun* (*business*) (*especially AmE*) the act of a small company buying a larger company using money that is borrowed based on the value of this larger company

le·via·than /ləˈvaɪəθən/ *noun* **1** (in the Bible) a very large sea MONSTER **2** (*literary*) a very large and powerful thing: *the leviathan of government bureaucracy*

levi·tate /ˈlevɪteɪt/ *verb* [V, VN] to rise and float in the air with no physical support, especially by means of magic or by using special mental powers; to make sth rise in this way ▶ **levi·ta·tion** /ˌlevɪˈteɪʃn/ *noun* [U]

lev·ity /ˈlevəti/ *noun* [U] (*written*) behaviour that shows a lack of respect for sth serious and that treats it in an amusing way [SYN] FRIVOLITY

levy /ˈlevi/ *noun, verb*

■ *noun* (*pl.* **-ies**) ~ (on sth) an extra amount of money that has to be paid, especially as a tax to the government: *to put/impose a levy on oil imports*

■ *verb* (**lev·ies, levy·ing, lev·ied, lev·ied**) [VN] ~ sth (on sb/sth) to use official authority to demand and collect a payment, tax, etc: *a tax levied by the government on excess company profits*

lewd /luːd*; BrE* also ljuːd/ *adj.* referring to sex in a rude and offensive way [SYN] OBSCENE: *lewd behaviour/jokes/suggestions* ▶ **lewd·ly** *adv.* **lewd·ness** *noun* [U]

lex·ic·al /ˈleksɪkl/ *adj.* [usually before noun] (*linguistics*) connected with the words of a language: *lexical items/units* (= words and phrases) ▶ **lex·ic·al·ly** /-kli/ *adv.*

lexi·cog·raph·er /ˌleksɪˈkɒɡrəfə(r)*; AmE* -ˈkɑːɡ-/ *noun* a person who writes or EDITS dictionaries

lexi·cog·raphy /ˌleksɪˈkɒɡrəfi*; AmE* -ˈkɑːɡ-/ *noun* [U] the theory and practice of writing dictionaries

lexi·con /ˈleksɪkən*; AmE* -kɑːn/ *noun* **1** (also **the lexicon**) [sing.] (*linguistics*) all the words and phrases used in a particular language or subject; all the words and phrases used and known by a particular person or group of people: *the lexicon of finance and economics* **2** [C] a list of words on a particular subject or in a language in alphabetical order: *a lexicon of technical scientific terms*

3 [C] a dictionary, especially one of an ancient language, such as Greek or Hebrew

lexis /ˈleksɪs/ *noun* [U] (*linguistics*) all the words and phrases of a particular language [SYN] VOCABULARY

ley /leɪ/ *noun* **1** (also **'ley line**) an imaginary line that is believed to follow the route of an ancient track and to have special powers **2** (*technical*) an area of land where grass is grown temporarily instead of crops

li·abil·ity /ˌlaɪəˈbɪləti/ *noun* (*pl.* **-ies**) **1** [U] ~ (for sth) | ~ (to do sth) the state of being legally responsible for sth: *The company cannot accept liability for any damage caused by natural disasters.* **2** [C, usually sing.] (*informal*) a person or thing that causes you a lot of problems: *Since his injury, Jones has become more of a liability than an asset to the team.* **3** [C, usually pl.] the amount of money that a person or company owes: *The company is reported to have liabilities of nearly $90000.*—compare ASSET

li·able /ˈlaɪəbl/ *adj.* [not before noun] **1** ~ (for sth) legally responsible for paying the cost of sth: *You will be liable for any damage caused.* ◊ *The court ruled he could not be held personally liable for his wife's debts.* **2** ~ to do sth likely to do sth: *We're all liable to make mistakes when we're tired.* ◊ *The bridge is liable to collapse at any moment.* **3** ~ to sth likely to be affected by sth [SYN] PRONE: *You are more liable to injury if you exercise infrequently.* **4** ~ to sth likely to be punished by law for sth: *Offenders are liable to fines of up to £500.* **5** ~ for/to sth | ~ to do sth having to do sth by law: *People who earn under a certain amount are not liable to pay tax.*

li·aise /liˈeɪz/ *verb* [V] **1** ~ (with sb) (*especially BrE*) to work closely with sb and exchange information with them: *He had to liaise directly with the police while writing the report.* **2** ~ (between A and B) to act as a link between two or more people or groups: *Her job is to liaise between students and teachers.*

li·aison /liˈeɪzn*; AmE* liˈeɪzɑːn; ˈliːəzɑːn/ *noun* **1** [U, sing.] ~ (between A and B) a relationship between two organizations or different departments in an organization, involving the exchange of information or ideas: *Our role is to ensure liaison between schools and parents.* ◊ *We work in close liaison with the police.* **2** [C] ~ (to/with sb/sth) a person whose job is to make sure there is a good relationship between two groups or organizations: *the White House liaison to organized labor* **3** [C] ~ (with sb) a secret sexual relationship, especially if one or both partners are married

li'aison officer *noun* a person whose job is to make sure that there is a good relationship between two groups of people, organizations, etc.—see also LIAISON (2)

liar /ˈlaɪə(r)/ *noun* a person who tells lies

lib /lɪb/ *noun* (*informal*) (used in the names of organizations demanding greater freedom, equal rights, etc.) the abbreviation for LIBERATION: *women's/gay lib*

li·ba·tion /laɪˈbeɪʃn/ *noun* (*formal*) (in the past) a gift of wine to a god

Lib Dem /ˌlɪb ˈdem/ *abbr.* (in British Politics) LIBERAL DEMOCRAT: *I voted Lib Dem.*

libel /ˈlaɪbl/ *noun, verb*

■ *noun* [U, C] the act of printing a statement about sb that is not true and that gives people a bad opinion of them; a printed statement about sb that is not true: *He sued the newspaper for libel.* ◊ *a libel action* (= a case in a court of law)—compare SLANDER

■ *verb* (**-ll-**, *AmE* **-l-**) [VN] to publish a written statement about sb that is not true: *He claimed he had been libelled in an article the magazine had published.*—compare SLANDER

li·bel·lous (*BrE*) (*AmE* **li·bel·ous**) /ˈlaɪbələs/ *adj.* containing a LIBEL about sb: *a libellous statement*

lib·eral /ˈlɪbərəl/ *adj., noun*

■ *adj.*

RESPECTING OTHER OPINIONS **1** willing to understand and respect other people's behaviour, opinions, etc., especially when they are different from your own; believing people should be able to choose how they behave: *liberal*

L

attitudes towards religion/sex ◇ *Her parents are very liberal and allow her a lot of freedom.* ◇ *liberal views/opinions*

POLITICS | **2** wanting or allowing a lot of political and economic freedom and supporting gradual social, political or religious change: *Some politicians want more liberal trade relations with Europe.* ◇ *the spread of liberal democracy following the Cold War* ◇ *liberal theories/reform* ◇ *a liberal politician/policy* **3** (**Liberal**) connected with the British Liberal Party in the past, or of a Liberal Party in another country

GENEROUS | **4** ~ (**with sth**) generous; given in large amounts: *She is very liberal with her money.* ◇ *I think Sam is too liberal with his criticism* (= he criticizes people too much).

EDUCATION | **5** concerned with increasing sb's general knowledge and experience rather than particular skills: *liberal arts* ◇ *a liberal education*

NOT EXACT | **6** not completely accurate or exact [SYN] FREE: *a liberal translation of the text* ◇ *a liberal interpretation of history/the law*
▶ **lib·er·al·ly** /-rəli/ *adv.*: *Apply the cream liberally.* ◇ *The word 'original' is liberally interpreted in copyright law.*
■ *noun*

SB WHO RESPECTS OTHERS | **1** a person who understands and respects other people's opinions and behaviour, especially when they are different from their own: *He liked to think of himself as a liberal.*

POLITICS | **2** a person who supports political, social and religious change: *Reform is popular with middle-class liberals.* **3** (**Liberal**) (*politics*) a member of the British Liberal Party in the past, or of a Liberal Party in another country

,**liberal 'arts** *noun* [pl.] (*especially AmE*) subjects of study that develop students' general knowledge and ability to think, rather than their technical skills: *a liberal arts college*

,**Liberal 'Democrat** *noun* (*abbr.* **Lib Dem**) a member or supporter of the Liberal Democrats

the ,Liberal 'Democrats *noun* [pl.] (*abbr.* **Lib Dems**) one of the main British political parties, in favour of some political and social change, but not extreme—compare THE CONSERVATIVE PARTY, THE LABOUR PARTY

lib·er·al·ism /ˈlɪbərəlɪzəm/ *noun* [U] liberal opinions and beliefs, especially in politics

lib·er·al·ity /ˌlɪbəˈræləti/ *noun* [U] (*formal*) **1** respect for political, religious or moral views, even if you do not agree with them **2** the quality of being generous

lib·er·al·ize (*BrE also* **-ise**) /ˈlɪbrəlaɪz/ *verb* [VN] (*written*) to make sth such as a law or a political or religious system less strict ▶ **lib·er·al·iz·ation, -isa·tion** /ˌlɪbrəlaɪˈzeɪʃn; *AmE* -ləˈz-/ *noun* [U]

lib·er·ate /ˈlɪbəreɪt/ *verb* [VN] **1** ~ sb/sth (**from sb/sth**) to free a country or a person from the control of sb else: *The city was liberated by the advancing army.* **2** ~ sb (**from sth**) to free sb from sth that restricts their enjoyment of life: *Writing poetry liberated her from the routine of everyday life.* ▶ **lib·er·ation** /ˌlɪbəˈreɪʃn/ *noun* [U, sing.]: *a war of liberation* ◇ *liberation from poverty* ◇ *women's liberation* **lib·er·ator** *noun*

lib·er·ated /ˈlɪbəreɪtɪd/ *adj.* free from the restrictions of traditional ideas about social and sexual behaviour: *a liberated woman*

lib·er·tar·ian /ˌlɪbəˈteəriən; *AmE* -bərˈter-/ *noun* a person who strongly believes that people should have the freedom to do and think as they like

lib·er·tine /ˈlɪbətiːn; *AmE* -bərt-/ *noun* (*formal, disapproving*) a person, usually a man, who leads an immoral life and is interested in pleasure, especially sexual pleasure

lib·erty /ˈlɪbəti; *AmE* -bərti/ *noun* (*pl.* **-ies**) **1** [U] freedom to live as you choose without too many restrictions from government or authority: *the fight for justice and liberty* **2** [U] the state of not being a prisoner or a slave: *He had to endure six months' loss of liberty.* **3** [C] the legal right and freedom to do sth: *The right to vote should be a liberty enjoyed by all.* ◇ *People fear that security cameras could*

infringe personal liberties.—see also CIVIL LIBERTY **4** [sing.] an act or statement that may offend or annoy sb, especially because it is done without permission or does not show respect: *He took the liberty of reading my files while I was away.* ◇ *They've got a liberty, not even sending me a reply.* [IDM] **at liberty** (*formal*) (of a prisoner or an animal) no longer in prison or in a cage **at liberty to do sth** (*formal*) having the right or freedom to do sth: *You are at liberty to say what you like.* **take 'liberties with sb/sth 1** to make important and unreasonable changes to sth, especially a book: *The movie takes considerable liberties with the novel that it is based on.* **2** (*old-fashioned*) to be too friendly with sb, especially in a sexual way

li·bid·in·ous /lɪˈbɪdɪnəs/ *adj.* (*formal*) having or expressing strong sexual feelings

li·bido /lɪˈbiːdəʊ; ˈlɪbɪdəʊ; *AmE* -doʊ/ *noun* (*pl.* **-os**) [U, C, usually sing.] (*technical*) sexual desire: *loss of libido*

Libra /ˈliːbrə/ *noun* **1** [U] the 7th sign of the ZODIAC, the SCALES **2** [C] a person born under the influence of this sign, that is between 23 September and 22 October, approximately ▶ **Libran** *noun, adj.*

li·brar·ian /laɪˈbreəriən/ *noun* a person who is in charge of or works in a library ▶ **li·brar·ian·ship** *noun* [U]: *a degree in librarianship*

li·brary /ˈlaɪbrəri; ˈlaɪbri; *AmE* -breri/ *noun* (*pl.* **-ies**) **1** a building in which collections of books, tapes, newspapers, etc. are kept for people to read, study or borrow: *a public/reference/university library* ◇ *library books* ◇ *a toy library* (= for borrowing toys) **2** a room in a large house where most of the books are kept **3** (*formal*) a personal collection of books, CDs, etc: *a new edition to add to your library* **4** a series of books, recordings, etc. produced by the same company and similar in appearance: *a library of children's classics*

li·bret·tist /lɪˈbretɪst/ *noun* a person who writes the words for an opera or a musical play

li·bretto /lɪˈbretəʊ; *AmE* -toʊ/ *noun* (*pl.* **-os** *or* **li·bretti** /-tiː/) (*music*) the words that are sung or spoken in an opera or a MUSICAL

lice *pl.* of LOUSE

li·cence (*BrE*) (*AmE* **li·cense**) /ˈlaɪsns/ *noun* **1** [C] ~ (**for sth**) | ~ (**to do sth**) an official document that shows that permission has been given to do, own or use sth: (*BrE*) *a driving licence* ◇ (*AmE*) *a driver's license* ◇ *a licence for the software* ◇ *Is there a licence fee?* ◇ *James lost his licence for six months* (= had his licence taken away by the police as a punishment). ◇ *You need a licence to fish in this river.* ◇ *a licence holder* (= a person who has been given a licence) **2** [U, sing.] ~ (**to do sth**) (*formal*) freedom to do or say whatever you want, often sth bad or unacceptable: *Lack of punishment seems to give youngsters licence to break the law.* **3** [U] (*formal*) freedom to behave in a way that is considered sexually immoral [IDM] **artistic/poetic 'licence** the freedom of artists or writers to change facts in order to make a story, painting, etc. more interesting or beautiful **a licence to print 'money** (*disapproving*) used to describe a business which makes a lot of money with little effort **under 'licence** (of a product) made with the permission of a company or an organization

li·cense (*BrE also less frequent* **li·cence**) /ˈlaɪsns/ *verb* to give sb official permission to do, own, or use sth: [VN] *The new drug has not yet been licensed in the UK.* ◇ (*BrE*) *licensing hours* (= the times when alcohol can be sold at a pub, etc.) ◇ [VN to inf] *They had licensed the firm to produce the drug.*

li·censed /ˈlaɪsnst/ *adj.* **1** (*BrE*) having official permission to sell alcoholic drinks: *a licensed restaurant* **2** that you have official permission to own: *Is that gun licensed?* **3** having official permission to do sth: *She is licensed to fly solo.*

li·cen·see /ˌlaɪsənˈsiː/ *noun* **1** (*BrE*) a person who has a licence to sell alcoholic drinks **2** a person or company that has a licence to make sth or to use sth

'**license number** *noun* (*AmE*) = REGISTRATION NUMBER

'**license plate** *noun* (*AmE*) = NUMBER PLATE

'**licensing laws** *noun* [pl.] British laws that state where and when alcoholic drinks can be sold

li·cen·ti·ate /laɪˈsenʃiət/ *noun* (*technical*) a person with official permission to work in a particular profession

li·cen·tious /laɪˈsenʃəs/ *adj.* (*formal, disapproving*) behaving in a way that is considered sexually immoral ▶ **li·cen·tious·ness** *noun* [U]

li·chen /ˈlaɪkən; ˈlɪtʃən/ *noun* [U, C] a very small grey or yellow plant that spreads over the surface of rocks, walls and trees and does not have any flowers—compare MOSS

lick /lɪk/ *verb, noun*
- *verb* **1** to move your tongue over the surface of sth in order to eat it, make it wet or clean it: [VN] *He licked his fingers.* ◊ *I'm tired of licking envelopes.* ◊ *The cat sat licking its paws.* ◊ [VN-ADJ] *She licked the spoon clean.* **2** [VN+adv./prep.] to eat or drink sth by licking it: *The cat licked up the milk.* ◊ *She licked the honey off the spoon.* **3** (of flames) to touch sth lightly: [VN] *Flames were soon licking the curtains.* ◊ [V] *The flames were now licking at their feet.* **4** [VN] (*informal*) to easily defeat sb or deal with sth: *We thought we **had them licked**.* ◊ *It was a tricky problem but I think we've licked it.* IDM **lick sb's 'boots** (also ⚠, *slang* **lick sb's 'arse**) (*disapproving*) to show too much respect for sb in authority because you want to please them **lick your 'wounds** to spend time trying to get your strength or confidence back after a defeat or disappointment—more at LIP, SHAPE *n.*
- *noun* **1** [C] an act of licking sth with the tongue: *Can I have a lick of your ice cream?* **2** [sing.] **a ~ of paint** (*informal*) a small amount of paint, used to make a place look better: *What this room needs is a lick of paint.* **3** [C] (*informal*) a short piece of music which is part of a song and is played on a guitar: *a guitar/blues lick* IDM **at a (fair) 'lick** (*informal*) fast; at a high speed

lick·ing /ˈlɪkɪŋ/ *noun* [sing.] (*informal*) a severe defeat in a battle, game, etc: *to give sb/get a licking*

lic·orice *noun* [U] (*especially AmE*) = LIQUORICE

lid /lɪd/ *noun* **1** a cover over a container that can be removed or opened by turning it or lifting it: *a dustbin lid* ◊ *I can't get the lid off this jar.*—picture at PACKAGING **2** = EYELID IDM **keep a/the 'lid on sth 1** to keep sth secret or hidden **2** to keep sth under control: *The government is keeping the lid on inflation.* **lift the 'lid on sth | take/ blow the 'lid off sth** to tell people unpleasant or shocking facts about sth: *Her article lifts the lid on child prostitution.* **put the (tin) 'lid on sth/things** (*BrE, informal*) to be the final act or event that spoils your plans or hopes—more at FLIP *v.*

lid·ded /ˈlɪdɪd/ *adj.* [usually before noun] **1** (of containers) having a lid **2** (*literary*) used to describe a person's expression when their EYELIDS appear large or their eyes are almost closed: *heavily-lidded eyes* ◊ *his lidded gaze*

lido /ˈliːdəʊ; AmE -doʊ/ *noun* (*pl.* **-os**) (*BrE*) a public outdoor swimming pool or part of a beach used by the public for swimming, water sports, etc.

lie¹ /laɪ/ *verb, noun*—see also LIE²
- *verb* (**lies, lying, lay** /leɪ/ **lain** /leɪn/) **1** (of a person or an animal) to be or put yourself in a flat or horizontal position so that you are not standing or sitting: [V+adv./ prep.] *to lie on your back/side/front* ◊ [V-ADJ] *The cat was lying fast asleep by the fire.* **2** (of a thing) to be or remain in a flat position on a surface: [V+adv./prep.] *Clothes were lying all over the floor.* ◊ [V-ADJ] *The book lay open on his desk.* **3** to be, remain or be kept in a particular state: [V-ADJ] *Snow was lying thick on the ground.* ◊ *These machines have lain idle since the factory closed.* ◊ [V+adv./ prep.] *a ship lying at anchor* ◊ *I'd rather use my money than leave it lying in the bank.* **4** [V+adv./prep.] (of a town, natural feature, etc.) to be situated in a particular place: *The town lies on the coast.* **5** [V+adv./prep.] to be spread out in a particular place: *The valley lay below us.* **6** [V] **~ (in sth)** (of ideas, qualities, problems, etc.) to exist or be found: *The problem lies in deciding when to intervene.* **7** (*BrE*) to be in a particular position during a competition: [V+adv./prep.] *Thompson is lying in fourth place.* ◊ [V-ADJ] *After five games the German team are lying second.*—compare LAY IDM **lie in 'state** (of the dead body of an important person) to be placed on view in a public place before being buried **lie in 'wait (for sb)** to hide,

waiting to surprise, attack or catch sb: *He was surrounded by reporters who had been lying in wait for him.* **lie 'low** (*informal*) to try not to attract attention to yourself **take sth lying 'down** to accept an insult or offensive act without protesting or reacting—more at BED *n.*, BOTTOM *n.*, HEAVY *adv.*, LAND *n.*, SLEEP *v.* PHRV **lie a'round/ a'bout 1** (of a number of things) to be spread in an untidy way somewhere: *Don't leave toys lying around— someone might trip over them.* **2** (of a person) to spend time doing nothing and being lazy—related noun LAY-ABOUT **lie 'back** to do nothing except relax: *You don't have to do anything—just lie back and enjoy the ride.* **lie be'hind sth** to be the real reason for sth, often hidden: *What lay behind this strange outburst?* **lie 'down** to be or get into a flat position, especially in bed, in order to sleep or rest: *Go and lie down for a while.* ◊ *He lay down on the sofa and soon fell asleep.*—related noun LIE-DOWN **lie 'in** (*BrE*) (also **sleep 'in** *AmE, BrE*) (*informal*) to stay in bed after the time you usually get up: *It's a holiday tomorrow, so you can lie in.*—related noun LIE-IN **lie with sb (to do sth)** (*formal*) to be sb's duty or responsibility: *It lies with you to accept or reject the proposals.*
- *noun* IDM **the ˌlie of the 'land** (*BrE*) (*AmE* **the ˌlay of the 'land**) **1** the way the land in an area is formed and what physical characteristics it has **2** the way a situation is now and how it is likely to develop: *Check out the lie of the land before you make a decision.*

lie² /laɪ/ *verb, noun*—see also LIE¹
- *verb* (**lies, lying, lied, lied**) [V] **~ (to sb) (about sth)** to say or write sth that you know is not true: *You could see from his face that he was lying.* ◊ *Don't lie to me!* ◊ *She lies about her age.* ◊ *The camera cannot lie* (= give a false impression).—see also LIAR IDM **lie through your 'teeth** (*informal*) to say sth that is not true at all: *The witness was clearly lying through his teeth.* **lie your way into/out of sth** to get yourself into or out of a situation by lying
- *noun* a statement made by sb knowing that it is not true: *to tell a lie* ◊ *The whole story is nothing but a pack of lies.* ◊ *a barefaced lie* (= a lie that is deliberate and shocking)—see also WHITE LIE IDM **give the lie to sth** (*formal*) to show that sth is not true: *These new figures give the lie to the belief that unemployment is going down.* **I tell a 'lie** (*BrE, spoken*) used to say that sth you have just said is not true or correct: *We first met in 1982, no, I tell a lie, it was 1983.*—more at LIVE¹, TISSUE

lied /liːd/ *noun* (*pl.* **lieder** /ˈliːdə(r)/) (from *German*) a German song for one singer and piano

'lie detector (also *formal* **poly·graph**) *noun* a piece of equipment that is used, for example by the police, to find out if sb is telling the truth

ˌlie-'down *noun* [sing.] (*BrE, informal*) a short rest, especially on a bed

ˌlie-'in *noun* (*BrE, informal*) a time when you stay in bed longer than normal in the morning: *a Sunday morning lie-in*

lien /ˈliːən/ *noun* [U] **~ (in/over sth)** (*law*) the right to keep sb's property until a debt is paid

lieu /luː; BrE also ljuː/ *noun* (*formal*) IDM **in lieu (of sth)** instead of: *They took cash in lieu of the prize they had won.* ◊ *We work on Saturdays and have a day off in lieu during the week.*

Lieut. (also **Lt**) (both *BrE*) (*AmE* **Lt.**) *abbr.* (in writing) LIEUTENANT

lieu·ten·ant /lefˈtenənt; AmE luːˈt-/ *noun* (*abbr.* **Lieut., Lt**) **1** an officer of middle rank in the army, navy, or air force: *Lieutenant Paul Fisher*—see also FLIGHT LIEUTENANT, SECOND LIEUTENANT, SUB LIEUTENANT **2** (in compounds) an officer just below the rank mentioned: *a lieutenant colonel* ◊ *Lieutenant Commander Browning* **3** (in the US) a police officer of fairly high rank **4** a person who helps sb who is above them in rank or who carries out their duties when that person is unable to

life /laɪf/ *noun* (*pl.* **lives** /laɪvz/)
STATE OF LIVING | **1** [U] the ability to breathe, grow, reproduce, etc. which people, animals and plants have before they die and which objects do not have: *life and death* ◊ *The body was cold and showed no signs of life.* ◊ *My*

æ	ɑː	e	ɜː	ə	ɪ	iː	i	ɒ	ɔː	ʌ	ʊ	u	uː
cat	father	ten	bird	about	sit	see	many	got	saw	cup	put	actual	too
								(BrE)					

father died last year—I wish I could bring him back to life. ◇ *In spring the countryside bursts into life.* **2** [U, C] the state of being alive as a human being; an individual person's existence: *The floods caused a massive loss of life* (= many people were killed). ◇ *He risked his life to save his daughter from the fire.* ◇ *Hundreds of lives were threatened when the building collapsed.* ◇ *The operation saved her life.* ◇ *My grandfather lost his life* (= was killed) *in the Second World War.* ◇ *Several attempts have been made on the President's life* (= several people have tried to kill him).

LIVING THINGS | **3** [U] living things: *plant/animal life* ◇ *marine/pond life* ◇ *Is there intelligent life on other planets?*

PERIOD OF TIME | **4** [C, U] the period between sb's birth and their death; a part of this period: *He's lived here all his life.* ◇ *I've lived in England for most of my life.* ◇ *to have a long/short life* ◇ *He became very weak towards the end of his life.* ◇ *Brenda took up tennis late in life.* ◇ *He will spend the rest of his life* (= until he dies) *in a wheelchair.* ◇ *There's no such thing as a job for life any longer.* ◇ *She is a life member of the club.* ◇ *in early/adult life* **5** [C] (used with an adjective) a period of sb's life when they are in a particular situation or job: *She has been an accountant all her working life.* ◇ *He met a lot of interesting people during his life as a student.* ◇ *They were very happy throughout their married life.* **6** [C] the period of time when sth exists or functions: *The International Stock Exchange started life as a London coffee shop.* ◇ *They could see that the company had a limited life* (= it was going to close). ◇ *In Italy the average life of a government is eleven months.*—see also SHELF LIFE

PUNISHMENT | **7** [U] the punishment of being sent to prison for life; life IMPRISONMENT: *The judge gave him life.*

EXPERIENCE/ACTIVITIES | **8** [U] the experience and activities that are typical of all people's existences: *the worries of everyday life* ◇ *He is young and has little experience of life.* ◇ *Commuting is a part of daily life for many people.* ◇ *Jill wants to travel and see life for herself.* ◇ *We bought a dishwasher to make life easier.* ◇ *In Africa life can be hard.* ◇ *In real life* (= when she met him) *he wasn't how she had imagined him at all.* ◇ *Life isn't like in the movies, you know.* **9** [U, C] the activities and experiences that are typical of a particular way of living: *country/city life* ◇ *She enjoyed political life.* ◇ *family/married life* ◇ *How do you find life in America?* **10** [C] a person's experiences during their life, the activities that form a particular part of a person's life: *He has had a good life.* ◇ *a hard/an easy life* ◇ *My day-to-day life is not very exciting.* ◇ *a life of luxury/crime* ◇ *Her daily life involved meeting lots of people.* ◇ *Many of these children have led very sheltered lives* (= they have not had many different experiences). ◇ *They emigrated to start a new life in America.* ◇ *He doesn't like to talk about his private life.* ◇ *She has a full social life.* ◇ *articles about the love lives of the stars*—see also SEX LIFE

ENERGY/EXCITEMENT | **11** [U] the quality of being active and exciting: *This is a great holiday resort that is full of life.* ◇ *We need to inject some new life into this project.*

IN ART | **12** [U] a living model or a real object or scene that people draw or paint: *She had lessons in drawing from life.* ◇ *a life class* (= one in which art students draw a naked man or woman)—see also STILL LIFE

STORY OF LIFE | **13** [C] a story of sb's life [SYN] BIOGRAPHY: *She wrote a life of Mozart.*

IN CHILDREN'S GAMES | **14** [C] one of a set number of chances before a player is out of a game: *He's lost two lives, so he's only got one left.*

IDM **be sb's 'life** be the most important person or thing to sb: *My children are my life.* ◇ *Writing is his life.* **bring sb/sth to 'life** to make sb/sth more interesting or exciting: *The new teacher really brought French to life for us.* ◇ *Flowers can bring a dull room back to life.* **come to 'life 1** to become more interesting, exciting or full of activity: *The match finally came to life in the second half.* **2** to start to act or move as if alive: *In my dream all my toys came to life.* **for dear 'life | for your 'life** as hard or as fast as possible: *She was holding on to the rope for dear life.* ◇

Run for your life! **for the 'life of you** (*informal*) however hard you try: *I cannot for the life of me imagine why they want to leave.* **frighten/scare the 'life out of sb** to frighten sb very much **full of 'beans/'life** having a lot of energy **get a 'life** (*spoken*) used to tell sb to stop being boring and to do sth more interesting **lay down your 'life (for sb/sth)** (*literary*) to die in order to save sb/sth: *They were prepared to lay down their lives for their country.* **life after 'death** the possibility or belief that people continue to exist in some form after they die: *Do you believe in life after death?* **the life and 'soul of the party, etc.** (*BrE*) the most amusing and interesting person at a party, etc. **life is 'cheap** (*disapproving*) used to say that there is a situation in which it is not thought to be important if people somewhere die or are treated badly **(have) a life of its 'own** (of an object) seeming to move or function by itself without a person touching or working it **make life 'difficult (for sb)** to cause problems for sb: *She does everything she can to make life difficult for him.* **the 'man/'woman in your life** (*informal*) the man or woman that you are having a sexual or romantic relationship with **not on your 'life** (*spoken*) used to refuse very firmly to do sth **take sb's 'life** to kill sb **take your (own) 'life** to kill yourself **take your life in your 'hands** to risk being killed: *You take your life in your hands just crossing the road here.* **that's 'life** (*spoken*) used when you are disappointed about sth but know that you must accept it: *It's a shame I can't go on the trip to France, but that's life.*—more at BET *v.*, BREATH, BREATHE, CHANGE *n.*, DEPART, DOG *n.*, END *v.*, FACT, FEAR *n.*, FIGHT *v.*, INCH *n.*, KISS *n.*, LARGE, LEASE, LIGHT *n.*, MATTER *n.*, MISERY, NINE, RISK *v.*, SAVE *v.*, SLICE *n.*, SPRING *v.*, STAFF *n.*, STORY, TIME *n.*, TRUE *adj.*, VARIETY, WALK *n.*, WAY *n.*

,life-and-'death (also **,life-or-'death**) *adj.* [only before noun] extremely serious, especially when there is a situation in which people might die: *a life-and-death decision/struggle*

'life assurance *noun* [U] (*BrE*) = LIFE INSURANCE

life·belt /'laɪfbelt/ *noun* a large ring made of material that floats well, that is used to rescue sb who has fallen into water, to prevent them from DROWNING

life·blood /'laɪfblʌd/ *noun* [U] **1** ~ (of sth) the thing that keeps sth strong and healthy and is necessary for successful development: *Tourism is the lifeblood of the city.* **2** (*literary*) a person's blood, when it is thought of as the thing that is necessary for life

life·boat /'laɪfbəʊt; *AmE* -boʊt/ *noun* **1** a special boat that is sent out to rescue people who are in danger at sea: *a lifeboat crew/station* **2** a small boat carried on a ship in order to save the people on board if the ship sinks

life·buoy /'laɪfbɔɪ; *AmE* also 'buːi/ *noun* a piece of material that floats well, used to rescue sb who has fallen into water, by keeping them above water

'life cycle *noun* (*biology*) the series of forms into which a living thing changes as it develops: *the life cycle of the butterfly*

'life-enhancing *adj.* making you feel happier and making life more enjoyable

'life expectancy (also **,expectation of 'life**) *noun* [U, C] the number of years that a person is likely to live; the length of time that sth is likely to exist or continue for: *Life expectancy for both men and women has improved greatly in the past 20 years.*

'life form *noun* (*technical*) a living thing such as a plant or an animal

'life-giving *adj.* [usually before noun] (*written*) that gives life or keeps sth alive

life·guard /'laɪfɡɑːd; *AmE* -ɡɑːrd/ (also **life·saver**) *noun* a person who is employed at a beach or a swimming pool to rescue people who are in danger in the water

,life 'history *noun* all the events that happen in the life of a person, animal or plant: *the life history of an insect*

'life insurance (*BrE* also **'life assurance**) *noun* [U] a type of insurance in which you make regular payments so that you receive a sum of money when you are a particular age, or so that your family will receive a sum of money when you die: *a life insurance policy*

'life jacket (*AmE* also **'life vest**) *noun* a jacket without sleeves, that can be filled with air, designed to help you float if you fall in water

life·less /'laɪfləs/ *adj.* **1** (*formal*) dead or appearing to be dead **2** not living; not having living things growing on or in it: *lifeless machines* ◊ *a lifeless planet* **3** dull; lacking the qualities that make sth or sb interesting and full of life: *his lifeless performance on stage*

life·like /'laɪflaɪk/ *adj.* exactly like a real person or thing: *a lifelike statue/drawing/toy*

life·line /'laɪflaɪn/ *noun* **1** a line or rope thrown to rescue sb who is in difficulty in the water **2** a line attached to sb who goes deep under the sea **3** something that is very important for sb and that they depend on: *The extra payments are a lifeline for most single mothers.*

life·long /'laɪflɒŋ; *AmE* -lɔːŋ/ *adj.* [only before noun] lasting or existing all through your life

life-or-'death *adj.* = LIFE-AND-DEATH

life 'peer *noun* (in Britain) a person who is given the title of PEER (= 'Lord' or 'Lady') but who cannot pass it on to their son or daughter

'life preserver *noun* (*AmE*) a piece of material that floats well, or a jacket made of such material, used to rescue a person who has fallen into water, by keeping them above water

lifer /'laɪfə(r)/ *noun* (*slang*) a person who has been sent to prison for their whole life

'life raft *noun* an open rubber boat filled with air, used for rescuing people from sinking ships or planes

life·saver /'laɪfseɪvə(r)/ *noun* **1** a thing that helps sb in a difficult situation; sth that saves sb's life: *The new drug is a potential lifesaver.* **2** = LIFEGUARD

'life-saving *adj.*, *noun*
■ *adj.* [usually before noun] that is going to save sb's life: *a life-saving heart operation*
■ *noun* [U] the skills needed to save sb who is in water and is DROWNING: *a life-saving qualification*

'life sciences *noun* [pl.] the sciences concerned with studying humans, animals or plants—compare EARTH SCIENCE, NATURAL SCIENCE, PHYSICAL SCIENCE ▶ **'life science** *adj.*: *life science experiments/research*

'life sentence *noun* the punishment by which sb spends the rest of their life in prison

'life-size (also **'life-sized**) *adj.* the same size as a person or thing really is: *a life-size statue*

life·span /'laɪfspæn/ *noun* the length of time that sth is likely to live, continue or function: *Worms have a lifespan of a few months.*

'life story *noun* the story that sb tells you about their whole life

life·style /'laɪfstaɪl/ *noun* [C, U] the way in which a person or a group of people lives and works: *a comfortable/healthy/lavish lifestyle* ◊ *It was a big change in lifestyle when we moved to the country.* ◊ *the lifestyle section of the newspaper* (= the part which deals with clothes, furniture, hobbies, etc.)

life sup'port *noun* [U] the fact of sb being on a life-support machine: *Families want the right to refuse life support.* ◊ *She's critically ill, on life support.*

life-sup'port machine (also **life-sup'port system**) *noun* a piece of equipment that keeps sb alive when they are extremely ill and cannot breathe without help: *He was put on a life-support machine in intensive care.*

life's 'work (*AmE* **life-work** /ˌlaɪf'wɜːk; *AmE* 'wɜːrk/) *noun* [sing.] the main purpose or activity in a person's life, or their greatest achievement

'life-threatening *adj.* that is likely to kill sb: *His heart condition is not life-threatening.*

life·time /'laɪftaɪm/ *noun* the length of time that sb lives or that sth lasts: *His diary was not published during his lifetime.* ◊ *a lifetime of experience* ◊ *in the lifetime of the present government* **IDM** **the chance, etc. of a 'lifetime** a wonderful opportunity, etc. that you are not likely to get again

'life vest *noun* (*AmE*) = LIFE JACKET

lift /lɪft/ *verb*, *noun*
■ *verb*
RAISE | **1** ~ sb/sth (**up**) to raise sb/sth or be raised to a higher position or level: [VN, usually +*adv.* / *prep.*] *He stood there with his arms lifted above his head.* ◊ *I lifted the lid of the box and peered in.* ◊ (*figurative*) *John lifted his eyes* (= looked up) *from his book.* ◊ [V] *Her eyebrows lifted. 'Apologize? Why?'*

MOVE SB/STH | **2** [VN, usually +*adv.* / *prep.*] to take hold of sb/sth and move them/it to a different position: *I lifted the baby out of the chair.* ◊ *He lifted the suitcase down from the rack.* **3** [VN] to transport people or things by air: *The survivors were lifted to safety by helicopter.*—see also AIR-LIFT

REMOVE LAW/RULE | **4** [VN] to remove or end restrictions: *to lift a ban/curfew/blockade* ◊ *Martial law has now been lifted.*

HEART/SPIRITS | **5** to become or make sb more cheerful: [V] *His heart lifted at the sight of her.* ◊ [VN] *The news lifted our spirits.*

OF MIST/CLOUDS | **6** [V] to rise and disappear: *The fog began to lift.* ◊ (*figurative*) *Gradually my depression started to lift.*

STEAL | **7** ~ sth (**from sb/sth**) [VN] (*informal*) to steal sth: *He had been lifting electrical goods from the store where he worked.*—see also SHOPLIFT

COPY IDEAS/WORDS | **8** [VN] to use sb's ideas or words without asking permission or without saying where they come from: *She lifted most of the ideas from a book she had been reading.*

VEGETABLES | **9** [VN] to dig up vegetables or plants from the ground: *to lift potatoes/turnips*

INCREASE | **10** to make the amount or level of sth greater; to become greater in amount or level: [VN] *Interest rates were lifted yesterday.* [also V]

IDM **not lift/raise a finger/hand (to do sth)** (*informal*) to do nothing to help sb: *The children never lift a finger to help around the house.* **PHRV** **lift 'off** (of a rocket or, less frequently, an aircraft) to leave the ground and rise into the air—related noun LIFT-OFF

■ *noun*
MACHINE | **1** (*BrE*) (*AmE* **ele·va·tor**) [C] a machine that carries people or goods up and down to different levels in a building or a mine: *It's on the sixth floor—let's take the lift.*—see also CHAIRLIFT, SKI LIFT

FREE RIDE | **2** (*BrE*) (*AmE* **ride**) [C] a free ride in a car, etc. to a place you want to get to: *I'll give you a lift to the station.* ◊ *She hitched a lift on a truck.*

HAPPIER FEELING | **3** [sing.] a feeling of being happier or more confident than before: *Passing the exam gave him a real lift.*

RISING MOVEMENT | **4** [sing.] a movement in which sth rises or is lifted up: *the puzzled lift of his eyebrows*

ON AIRCRAFT | **5** [U] the upward pressure of air on an aircraft when flying—compare DRAG

'lift-off *noun* [C, U] the act of a spacecraft leaving the ground and rising into the air: *Ten minutes to lift-off.*

liga·ment /'lɪgəmənt/ *noun* a strong band of tissue in the body that connects bones, supports muscles, etc: *I've torn a ligament.*

liga·ture /'lɪgətʃə(r)/ *noun* (*technical*) something that is used for tying sth very tightly, for example to stop bleeding

light /laɪt/ *noun*, *adj.*, *verb*, *adv.*
■ *noun*
FROM SUN/LAMPS | **1** [U] the energy from the sun, a lamp, etc. that makes it possible to see things: *bright/dim light* ◊ *a room with good/poor natural light* ◊ *in the fading light of a summer's evening* ◊ *The light was beginning to fail* (= it was beginning to get dark). ◊ *She could just see by the light of the candle.* ◊ *Bring it into the light so I can see it.* ◊ *a beam/ray of light*—see also FIRST LIGHT **2** [C] a particular type of light with its own colour and qualities: *A cold grey light crept under the curtains.*—see also THE NORTHERN LIGHTS

b	d	f	g	h	k	l	m	n	p	r
bad	did	fall	get	hat	cat	leg	man	now	pen	red

<u>LAMP</u> | **3** [C] a thing that produces light, especially an electric light: *to turn/switch the lights on/off* ◊ *to turn out the lights* ◊ *Suddenly all the lights went out.* ◊ *to turn down/dim the lights* ◊ *A light was still burning in the bedroom.* ◊ *ceiling/wall lights* ◊ *Keep going—the lights* (= traffic lights) *are green.* ◊ *Check your car before you drive to make sure that your lights are working.*—see also BRAKE LIGHT, GREEN LIGHT, HEADLIGHT, LEADING LIGHT, RED LIGHT—picture at BICYCLE

<u>FOR CIGARETTE</u> | **4** [sing.] a match or device with which you can light a cigarette: (*BrE*) *Have you got a light?* ◊ (*AmE, BrE*) *Do you have a light?*

<u>EXPRESSION IN EYES</u> | **5** [sing.] an expression in sb's eyes which shows what they are thinking or feeling: *There was a soft light in her eyes as she looked at him.*

<u>IN PICTURE</u> | **6** [U] light colours in a picture, which contrast with darker ones: *the artist's use of light and shade*

<u>WINDOW</u> | **7** [C] (*architecture*) a window or an opening to allow light in: *leaded lights*—see also SKYLIGHT

WHICH WORD?
light / lighting

The noun **light** has several different meanings and is used in many phrases. **Lighting** can only be used to talk about the type of light in a place or how lights are used to achieve a particular effect: *the lighting system* ◊ *the movie's interesting lighting effects* ◊ *The lighting at the disco was fantastic.*

IDM **according to sb's/sth's 'lights** (*formal*) according to the standards which sb sets for him or herself **be/go out like a 'light** (*informal*) to go to sleep very quickly **be in sb's 'light** to be between sb and a source of light: *Could you move—you're in my light.* **bring sth to 'light** to make new information known to people: *These facts have only just been brought to light.* **cast/shed/throw 'light on sth** to make a problem, etc. easier to understand: *Recent research has thrown new light on the causes of the disease.* **come to 'light** to become known to people: *New evidence has recently come to light.* **in ¡a good, bad, favourable, etc. 'light** if you see sth or put sth in a good, bad, etc. light, it seems good, bad, etc: *You must not view what happened in a negative light.* ◊ *They want to present their policies in the best possible light.* **in the light of sth** (*BrE*) (*AmE* **in light of sth**) after considering sth: *He rewrote the book in the light of further research.* **light at the end of the 'tunnel** something that shows you are nearly at the end of a long and difficult time or situation **(the) light 'dawned (on sb)** somebody suddenly understood or began to understand sth: *I puzzled over the problem for ages before the light suddenly dawned.* **the light of sb's 'life** the person sb loves more than any other **see the 'light 1** to finally understand or accept sth, especially sth obvious **2** to begin to believe in a religion **see the 'light (of 'day)** to begin to exist or to become publicly known about: *He's written a lot of good material that has never seen the light of day.* **set 'light to sth** (*especially BrE*) to make sth start burning: *A spark from the fire had set light to a rug.*—more at BRIGHT *adj.*, COLD *adj.*, HIDE *v.*, JUMP *v.*, SWEETNESS

■ *adj.* (**light·er, light·est**)

<u>WITH NATURAL LIGHT</u> | **1** full of light; having the natural light of day: *We'll leave in the morning as soon as it's light.* ◊ *It gets light at about 5 o'clock.* ◊ *It was a light spacious apartment at the top of the building.* **OPP** DARK

<u>COLOURS</u> | **2** pale in colour: *light blue eyes* ◊ *Lighter shades suit you best.* ◊ *People with pale complexions should avoid wearing light colours.* **OPP** DARK

<u>WEIGHT</u> | **3** easy to lift or move; not weighing very much: *Modern video cameras are light and easy to carry.* ◊ *Carry this bag—it's the lightest.* ◊ *He's lost a lot of weight—he's three kilos lighter than he was.* ◊ *The little girl was as light as a feather.* ◊ *The aluminium body is 12% lighter than if built with steel.* **OPP** HEAVY **4** [usually before noun] of less than average or usual weight: *light summer clothes* ◊ *Only light vehicles are allowed over the old bridge.* **OPP** HEAVY **5** used with a unit of weight to say

that sth weighs less than it should do: *The delivery of potatoes was several kilos light.*

<u>GENTLE</u> | **6** [usually before noun] gentle or delicate; not using much force: *She felt a light tap on her shoulder.* ◊ *the sound of quick light footsteps* ◊ *You only need to apply light pressure.* ◊ *As a boxer, he was always light on his feet* (= quick and graceful in the way he moved). **OPP** HEAVY

<u>WORK/EXERCISE</u> | **7** [usually before noun] easy to do; not making you tired: *After his accident he was moved to lighter work.* ◊ *some light housework* ◊ *You are probably well enough to take a little light exercise.*

<u>NOT GREAT</u> | **8** not great in amount, degree, etc: *light traffic* ◊ *The forecast is for light showers.* ◊ *light winds* ◊ *Trading on the stock exchange was light today.* **OPP** HEAVY

<u>NOT SEVERE/SERIOUS</u> | **9** not severe: *He was convicted of assaulting a police officer but he got off with a light sentence.* **10** entertaining rather than serious and not needing much mental effort: *light reading for the beach* ◊ *a concert of light classical music* **11** not serious: *She kept her tone light.* ◊ *This programme looks at the lighter side of politics.* ◊ *We all needed a little light relief at the end of a long day* (= something amusing or entertaining that comes after sth serious or boring). ◊ *On a lighter note, we end the news today with a story about a duck called Quackers.*

<u>CHEERFUL</u> | **12** [usually before noun] free from worry; cheerful: *I left the island with a light heart.*

<u>FOOD</u> | **13** (of a meal) small in quantity: *a light supper/snack.* ◊ *I just want something light for lunch.* **OPP** HEAVY **14** (also **lite**) not containing much fat or not having a strong flavour and therefore easy for the stomach to DIGEST: *Stick to a light diet.* **15** containing a lot of air: *This pastry is so light.*

<u>DRINK</u> | **16** low in alcohol: *a light beer*

<u>SLEEP</u> | **17** [only before noun] a person in a **light** sleep is easy to wake: *She drifted into a light sleep.* ◊ *I've always been a light sleeper.* **OPP** DEEP

▶ **light·ness** *noun* [U]—see also LIGHTLY

IDM **be light on** (*BrE*) to not have enough of sth: *We seem to be light on fuel.* **a light touch** the ability to deal with sth in a delicate and relaxed way: *She handles this difficult subject with a light touch.* **make 'light of sth** to treat sth as not being important and not serious: *I didn't mean to make light of your injuries.* **make light 'work of sth** to do sth quickly and with little effort—more at HAND *n.*

■ *verb* (**lit, lit** /lɪt/ **HELP** **Lighted** is also used for the past tense and past participle, especially in front of nouns.)

<u>START TO BURN</u> | **1** [VN] to make sth start to burn: *She lit a candle.* ◊ *The candles were lit.* ◊ *I put a lighted match to the letter and watched it burn.* **2** [V] to start to burn: *The fire wouldn't light.*

<u>GIVE LIGHT</u> | **3** [VN] [usually passive] to give light to sth or to a place: *The stage was lit by bright spotlights.* ◊ *well/badly lit streets* **4** [VN] (*literary*) to guide sb with a light: *Our way was lit by a full moon.*

PHRV **'light on/upon sth** (*literary*) to see or find sth by accident: *His eye lit upon a small boat on the horizon.* **,light 'up** | **,light sth↔'up 1** (*informal*) to begin to smoke a cigarette: *They all lit up as soon as he left the room.* ◊ *He sat back and lit up a cigarette.* **2** to become or to make sth become bright with light or colour: *There was an explosion and the whole sky lit up.* ◊ *The night sky was lit up with fireworks.* **3** if sb's eyes or face **light up**, or sth **lights them up**, they show happiness or excitement: *His eyes lit up when she walked into the room.* ◊ *A smile lit up her face.*

■ *adv.* **IDM** see TRAVEL *v.*

,light 'aircraft *noun* (*pl.* **light aircraft**) a small plane with seats for no more than about six passengers

'light bulb *noun* = BULB

,light-'coloured (*BrE*) (*AmE* **,light-'colored**) *adj.* pale in colour; not dark

light·ed /'laɪtɪd/ *adj.* **1** a **lighted** candle, cigarette, match, etc. is burning **2** a **lighted** window is bright because there are lights on inside the room **OPP** UNLIT

light·en /ˈlaɪtn/ *verb* **1** [VN] to reduce the amount of work, debt, worry, etc. that sb has: *equipment to lighten the load of domestic work* ◊ *The measures will lighten the tax burden on small businesses.* **2** to become or make sth become brighter or lighter in colour: [V] *The sky began to lighten in the east.* ◊ [VN] *Use bleach to lighten the wood.* **3** ~ (sth) (up) to feel or make sb feel less sad, worried or serious: [V] *My mood gradually lightened.* ◊ [VN] *She told a joke to lighten the atmosphere.* **4** [VN] to make sth lighter in weight PHRV **,lighten 'up** (*spoken*) used to tell sb to become less serious or worried about sth: *Come on, John. Lighten up!*

light·er /ˈlaɪtə(r)/ *noun* **1** (also **ciga'rette lighter**) a small device that produces a flame for lighting cigarettes, etc. **2** a boat with a flat bottom used for carrying goods to and from ships in harbour

,light-'fingered *adj.* (*informal*) likely to steal things

,light-'headed *adj.* not completely in control of your thoughts or movements; slightly FAINT: *After four glasses of wine he began to feel light-headed.*

,light-'hearted *adj.* **1** intended to be amusing or easily enjoyable rather than too serious: *a light-hearted speech* **2** cheerful and without problems: *She felt light-hearted and optimistic.* ▶ **,light-'hearted·ly** *adv.*

,light 'heavyweight *noun* a boxer weighing between 72.5 and 79.5 kilograms, between a MIDDLEWEIGHT and a HEAVYWEIGHT: *a light heavyweight champion*

light·house /ˈlaɪthaʊs/ *noun* a tower or other building that contains a strong light to warn and guide ships near the coast

,light 'industry *noun* [U, C] industry that produces small or light objects such as things used in the house—compare HEAVY INDUSTRY

light·ing /ˈlaɪtɪŋ/ *noun* [U] **1** the arrangement or type of light in a place: *electric/natural lighting* ◊ *good/poor lighting* ◊ *The play had excellent sound and lighting effects.* **2** the use of electric lights in a place: *the cost of heating and lighting* ◊ *street lighting* ⇨ note at LIGHT

'lighting engineer *noun* a person who works in television, the theatre, etc. and whose job is to control and take care of the lights

light·ly /ˈlaɪtli/ *adv.* **1** gently; with very little force or effort: *He kissed her lightly on the cheek.* **2** to a small degree; not much: *It began to snow lightly.* ◊ *She tended to sleep lightly nowadays* (= it was easy to disturb her). ◊ *I try to eat lightly* (= not to eat heavy or greasy food). **3** in a way that sounds as though you are not particularly worried or interested: *'I'll be all right,' he said lightly.* **4** without being seriously considered: *This is not a problem we should take lightly.* IDM **get off/be let off 'lightly** (*informal*) to be punished or treated in a way that is less harsh than you deserve or may have expected

'light meter *noun* a device used to measure how bright the light is before taking a photograph

light·ning /ˈlaɪtnɪŋ/ *noun, adj.*
■ *noun* [U] a flash, or several flashes, of very bright light in the sky caused by electricity: *a flash of lightning* ◊ *a violent storm with thunder and lightning* ◊ *He was struck by lightning and killed.* ◊ (*AmE*) *Lightning strikes caused scores of fires across the state.* IDM **lightning never strikes (in the same place) twice** (*saying*) an unusual or unpleasant event is not likely to happen in the same place or to the same people twice **like (greased) 'lightning** very fast
■ *adj.* very fast or sudden

'lightning conductor (*BrE*) (*AmE* **'lightning rod**) *noun* a metal rod or wire leading from the highest part of a building to the ground, put there to prevent lightning damaging the building

'lightning rod *noun* **1** (*AmE*) = LIGHTNING CONDUCTOR **2** (*especially AmE*) a person or thing that attracts criticism, especially if the criticism is then not directed at sb/sth else

,lightning 'strike *noun* (*BrE*) a strike by a group of workers that is sudden and without warning

'light pen *noun* **1** a piece of equipment, shaped like a pen, that is sensitive to light and that can be used to pass

information to a computer when it touches the screen **2** a similar piece of equipment that is used for reading BAR CODES

light·ship /ˈlaɪtʃɪp/ *noun* a small ship that stays at a particular place at sea and that has a powerful light on it to warn and guide other ships

'light show *noun* a display of changing coloured lights, for example at a pop concert

light·weight /ˈlaɪtweɪt/ *adj., noun*
■ *adj.* **1** made of thinner material and less heavy than usual: *lightweight jackets/boots* **2** (*disapproving*) not very serious or impressive: *a lightweight book* ◊ *He was considered too lightweight for the job.*
■ *noun* **1** a boxer weighing between 57 and 61 kilograms, heavier than a FEATHERWEIGHT: *a lightweight champion* **2** a person or thing that weighs less than is usual **3** (*informal, disapproving*) a person or thing of little importance or influence: *a political lightweight* ◊ *He's an intellectual lightweight* (= he does not think very deeply or seriously).

'light year *noun* **1** (*astronomy*) the distance that light travels in one year, 9.4607×10^{12} kilometres: *The nearest star to earth is about 4 light years away.* **2** (**light years**) [pl.] a very long time: *Full employment still seems light years away.*

lig·nite /ˈlɪgnaɪt/ *noun* [U] a soft brown type of coal

lik·able (*especially AmE*) = LIKEABLE

like /laɪk/ *prep., verb, conj., noun, adj., adv.*
■ *prep.* **1** similar to sb/sth: *She's wearing a dress like mine.* ◊ *He's very like his father.* ◊ *She looks **nothing** like* (= not at all like) *her mother.* ◊ *That sounds like* (= I think I can hear) *him coming now.* **2** used to ask sb's opinion of sb/sth: *What's it like studying in Spain?* ◊ *This new girlfriend of his—what's she like?* **3** used to show what is usual or typical for sb: *It's just like her to tell everyone about it.* **4** in the same way as sb/sth: *Students were angry at being treated like children.* ◊ *He ran like the wind* (= very fast). ◊ *You do it like this.* ◊ *I, like everyone else, have read these stories in the press.* ◊ *Don't look at me like that.* ◊ (*spoken*) *The candles are arranged like so* (= in this way). **5** for example: *Utopian novels like 'Animal Farm' and '1984'* ⇨ note at AS IDM **more like …** used to give a number or an amount that is more accurate than one previously mentioned: *He believes the figure should be more like $10 million.* **more 'like (it)** (*informal*) **1** better; more satisfactory: *This is more like it! Real food—not that canned muck.* **2** used to give what you think is a better description of sth: *Just talking? Arguing more like it.*
■ *verb* (not usually used in the progressive tenses) **1** to find sb/sth pleasant, attractive or satisfactory; to enjoy sth: [VN] *She's nice. I like her.* ◊ *Do you like their new house?* ◊ *Which tie do you like best?* ◊ *How did you like Japan* (= did you find it pleasant)? ◊ *I don't like the way he's looking at me.* ◊ *You've got to go to school, whether you like it or not.* ◊ [V-ing] *She's never liked swimming.* ◊ [VN-ing] *I didn't like him taking all the credit.* ◊ (*formal*) *I didn't like his taking all the credit.* ◊ [Vto inf] *I like to see them enjoying themselves.* ◊ [VN wh-] *I like it when you do that.* **2** [no passive] to prefer to do sth; to prefer sth to be made or to happen in a particular way: [Vto inf] *At weekends I like to sleep late.* ◊ [VN-ADJ] *I like my coffee strong.* **3** [VN] [no passive] to want: *Do what you like—I don't care.* ◊ *You can dye your hair whatever colour you like.* **4** used in negative sentences to mean 'to be unwilling to do sth': [Vto inf] *I didn't like to disturb you.* ◊ [V-ing] *He doesn't like asking his parents for help.* **5** used with *would* or *should* as a polite way to say what you want or to ask what sb wants: [VN] *Would you like a drink?* ◊ [Vto inf] *I'd like to think it over.* ◊ *Would you like to come with us?* ◊ (*formal*) *We would like to apologize for the delay.* ◊ *How can they afford it? That's what I'd like to know.* ◊ [VN to inf] *We'd like you to come and visit us.* ◊ [V] (*AmE*) *I'd like for us to work together.* ⇨ note at WANT IDM **how would 'you like it?** used to emphasize that sth bad has happened to you and you want some sympathy: *How would you like it if someone called you a liar?* **if you 'like** (*spoken*) **1** used to politely agree to sth or to suggest sth: *'Shall we stop now?' 'If you like.'* ◊ *If you like, we could go out this evening.* **2** used

L

when you express sth in a new way or when you are not confident about sth: *It was, if you like, the dawn of a new era.* **I like 'that!** (*old-fashioned, spoken*) used to protest that sth that has been said is not true or fair: *'She called you a cheat.' 'Well, I like that!'* **I/I'd like to think** used to say that you hope or believe that sth is true: *I like to think I'm broad-minded.*

■ *conj.* (*informal*) **1** in the same way as: *No one sings the blues like she did.* ◊ *It didn't turn out like I intended.* ◊ **Like I said** (= as I said before), *you're always welcome to stay.* **2** as if: *She acts like she owns the place.* **HELP** You will find more information about this use of **like** at the entries for the verbs **act, behave, feel, look** and **sound** and in the note at **as.**

■ *noun* **1** (**likes**) [pl.] the things that you like: *We all have different **likes and dislikes**.* **2** [sing.] a person or thing that is similar to another: *jazz, rock **and the like** (= similar types of music)* ◊ *a man whose like we shall not see again* ◊ *You're not comparing like with like.* **3** (**the likes of sb/sth**) (*informal*) used to refer to sb/sth that is considered as a type, especially one that is considered not as good as sb/sth else: *She didn't want to associate with the likes of me.*

■ *adj.* [only before noun] (*formal*) having similar qualities to another person or thing: *a chance to meet people of like mind* (= with similar interests and opinions) ◊ *She responded in like manner.*

■ *adv.* **1** used in very informal speech, for example when you are thinking what to say next, explaining sth, or giving an example of sth: *It was, like, weird.* ◊ *It was kind of scary, like.* ◊ *It's really hard. Like I have no time for my own work.* **2** I'm, he's, she's, etc. ~ (*AmE*) used in very informal speech, to mean 'I say', 'he/she says', etc: *And then I'm like 'No Way!'* **3** used in informal speech instead of *as* to say that sth happens in the same way: *There was silence, but not like before.* ⇨ note at **AS** **IDM** **(as) like as 'not | like e'nough | most/very 'like** (*old-fashioned*) quite probably: *She would be in bed by now, as like as not.*

-like *combining form* (in adjectives) similar to; typical of: *childlike* ◊ *shell-like*

like·able (*especially BrE*) (also **lik·able** *AmE, BrE*) /ˈlaɪkəbl/ *adj.* pleasant and easy to like: *a very likeable man*

like·li·hood /ˈlaɪklihʊd/ *noun* [U, sing.] the chance of sth happening; how likely sth is to happen: *There is very little likelihood of that happening.* ◊ **In all likelihood** (= very probably) *the meeting will be cancelled.* ◊ *The likelihood is that* (= it is likely that) *unemployment figures will continue to fall.*

like·ly /ˈlaɪkli/ *adj., adv.*

■ *adj.* (**like·li·er, like·li·est**) **HELP** more likely and most likely are the usual forms **1** ~ **(to do sth)| ~ (that ...)** probable or expected: *the most likely cause/outcome* ◊ *Tickets are likely to be expensive.* ◊ *It's **more than likely** that the thieves don't know how much it is worth.* ◊ *They might refuse to let us do it, but it's **hardly likely**.* **2** seeming suitable for a purpose: *She seems the most likely candidate for the job.* **IDM** **a 'likely story** (*spoken, ironic*) used to show that you do not believe what sb has said

■ *adv.* **IDM** **as ,likely as 'not | most/very 'likely** very probably: *As likely as not she's forgotten all about it.* **not 'likely!** (*spoken, especially BrE*) used to disagree strongly with a statement or suggestion: *Me? Join the army? Not likely!*

GRAMMAR POINT

likely

In standard *BrE* the adverb **likely** must be used with a word such as *most, more* or *very*: *We will most likely see him later.* In informal *AmE* **likely** is often used on its own: *We will likely see him later.* ◊ *He said that he would likely run for President.*

---

like-'minded *adj.* having similar ideas and interests

liken /ˈlaɪkən/ *verb* **PHRV** **'liken sth/sb to sth/sb** (*formal*) to compare one person or thing to another and say they are similar: *Life is often likened to a journey.*

like·ness /ˈlaɪknəs/ *noun* **1** [C, U] the fact of being similar to another person or thing, especially in appearance; an example of this **SYN** RESEMBLANCE: *Joanna bears a strong likeness to her father.* ◊ *Do you notice any family likeness between them?* **2** [C, usually sing.] a painting, drawing, etc. of a person, especially one that looks very like them: *The drawing is said to be **a good likeness** of the girl's attacker.*

likes *noun* ⇨ LIKE (1)

like·wise /ˈlaɪkwaɪz/ *adv.* **1** (*formal*) the same; in a similar way: *He voted for the change and he expected his colleagues to **do likewise**.* **2** (*formal*) also: *Her second marriage was likewise unhappy.* **3** (*spoken*) used to show that you feel the same towards sb or about sth: *'Let me know if you ever need any help.' 'Likewise.'*

lik·ing /ˈlaɪkɪŋ/ *noun* [sing.] ~ **(for sb/sth)** the feeling that you like sb or sth; the enjoyment of sth: *He had a liking for fast cars.* ◊ *She had **taken a liking to him** on their first meeting.* **IDM** **for your 'liking** if you say, for example, that sth is too hot **for your liking**, you mean that you would prefer it to be less hot: *The town was too crowded for my liking.* **to sb's 'liking** (*formal*) suitable, and how sb likes sth: *The coffee was just to his liking.*

lilac /ˈlaɪlək/ *noun* **1** [U, C] a bush or small tree with purple or white flowers with a sweet smell that grow closely together in the shape of a CONE **2** [U] a pale purple colour ▸ **lilac** *adj.*: *a lilac dress*

Lil·li·pu·tian /ˌlɪlɪˈpjuːʃn/ *adj.* (*formal*) extremely small **ORIGIN** From the land of **Lilliput**, in Jonathan Swift's *Gulliver's Travels*, where the people are only 15 cm high.

lilo (also **Li-Lo**™) /ˈlaɪləʊ; *AmE* -loʊ/ *noun* (*pl.* **-os**) (*BrE*) a plastic or rubber bed that is filled with air and used when camping or for floating on water

lilt /lɪlt/ *noun* [sing.] **1** the pleasant way in which a person's voice rises and falls: *Her voice had a soft Welsh lilt to it.* **2** a regular rising and falling pattern in music, with a strong rhythm ▸ **lilt·ing** *adj.*: *a lilting voice/song*

lily /ˈlɪli/ *noun* (*pl.* **-ies**) a large white or brightly coloured flower with PETALS that curl back from the centre. There are many types of lily: *tiger lilies*—see also WATER LILY **IDM** see GILD

lily of the 'valley *noun* [C, U] (*pl.* **lilies of the valley**) a plant with small white flowers shaped like bells

lily-'white *adj.* **1** almost pure white in colour: *lily-white skin* **2** morally perfect: *They want me to conform, to be lily-white.*

lima bean /ˈliːmə biːn/ *noun* (*AmE*) a type of round, pale green bean. Several lima beans grow together inside a flat POD.

limb /lɪm/ *noun* **1** an arm or a leg; a similar part of an animal, such as a wing: *an artificial limb* ◊ *For a while, she lost the use of her limbs.* **2** (**-limbed**) (in adjectives) having the type of limbs mentioned: *long-limbed* ◊ *loose-limbed* **3** a large branch of a tree **IDM** **out on a 'limb** (*informal*) not supported by other people: *Are you prepared to **go out on a limb** (= risk doing sth that other people are not prepared to do) and make your suspicions public?* **tear/rip sb ,limb from 'limb** (often *humorous*) to attack sb very violently—more at RISK *v.*

lim·ber /ˈlɪmbə(r)/ *verb* **PHRV** **,limber 'up** to do physical exercises in order to stretch and prepare your muscles before taking part in a race, sporting activity, etc.

limbo /ˈlɪmbəʊ; *AmE* -boʊ/ *noun* **1** [sing.] a West Indian dance in which you lean backwards and go under a bar which is made lower each time you go under it **2** [U, sing.] a situation in which you are not certain what to do next, cannot take action, etc., especially because you are waiting for sb else to make a decision: *the limbo of the stateless person* ◊ *His life seemed stuck **in limbo**; he could not go forward and he could not go back.*

lime /laɪm/ *noun, verb*

■ *noun* **1** (also **quick·lime**) [U] a white substance obtained by heating LIMESTONE, used in building materials and to help plants grow **2** [C, U] a small green fruit, like a lemon, with a lot of sour juice, used in cooking and in drinks; the juice of this fruit: *lime juice* ◊ *slices of lime*—picture on page A2 **3** (also **'lime tree**) [C] a tree on which

---

aɪ	aʊ	eɪ	əʊ	oʊ	ɔɪ	ɪə	eə	ʊə	j	w
my	now	say	go	go	boy	near	hair	pure	yes	wet
			(BrE)	(AmE)						

limes grow **4** (also **'lime tree, 'linden tree, linden**) [C] a large tree with light green heart-shaped leaves and yellow flowers: *an avenue of limes*

■ *verb* [VN] to add the substance lime to soil, especially in order to control the acid in it

lime 'green *adj.* (also **lime**) bright pale green in colour ▶ **,lime 'green** (also **lime**) *noun* [U]: *The contrast between the lime green and the rose pink was striking.*

lime-light /'laɪmlaɪt/ (usually **the limelight**) *noun* [U] the centre of public attention: *to be in the limelight* ◊ *to stay out of the limelight* ◊ *to steal / hog the limelight* (= take attention away from other people) ◊ *to be brought / pushed / thrust into the limelight*

lim-er-ick /'lɪmərɪk/ *noun* a humorous short poem, with two long lines that RHYME with each other, followed by two short lines that RHYME with each other and ending with a long line that RHYMES with the first two

lime-scale /'laɪmskeɪl/ *noun* [U] (*BrE*) the hard white substance that is left by water on the inside of pipes, etc.

lime-stone /'laɪmstəʊn/; *AmE* -stoʊn/ *noun* [U] a type of white stone that contains CALCIUM, used in building and in making CEMENT

Limey /'laɪmi/ *noun* (*old-fashioned*, *AmE*) a slightly insulting word for a British person

limit /'lɪmɪt/ *noun, verb*
■ *noun* **1** ~ (**to sth**) a point at which sth stops being possible or existing: *There is a limit to the amount of pain we can bear.* ◊ *The team performed to the limit of its capabilities.* ◊ *She knew the limits of her power.* ◊ *to push / stretch / test sb/sth to the limit* ◊ *His arrogance knew* (= had) *no limits.* **2** ~ (**on sth**) the greatest or smallest amount of sth that is allowed: *a time / speed / age limit* ◊ *The EU has set strict limits on levels of pollution.* ◊ *They were travelling at a speed that was double the legal limit.* ◊ *You can't drive—you're over the limit* (= you have drunk more alcohol than is legal when driving). **3** the furthest edge of an area or a place: *We were reaching the limits of civilization.* ◊ *the city limits* (= the official boundary of the city) **IDM** **be the 'limit** (*old-fashioned*, *spoken*) to be extremely annoying **,off 'limits** (*especially AmE*) = OUT OF BOUNDS **within 'limits** to some extent; with some restrictions: *I'm willing to help, within limits.*—more at SKY
■ *verb* [VN] **1** ~ **sth** (**to sth**) to stop sth from increasing beyond a particular amount or level: *measures to limit carbon dioxide emissions from cars* ◊ *The amount of money you have to spend will limit your choice.* **2** ~ **yourself / sb** (**to sth**) to restrict or reduce the amount of sth that you or sb can have or use: *Families are limited to four free tickets each.* ◊ *I've limited myself to 1000 calories a day to try and lose weight.* **PHRV** **'limit sth to sb/sth** [usually passive] to make sth exist or happen only in a particular place or within a particular group: *Violent crime is not limited to big cities.* ◊ *The teaching of history should not be limited to dates and figures.*

limi·ta·tion /ˌlɪmɪ'teɪʃn/ *noun* **1** [U] the act or process of limiting or controlling sb/sth: *They would resist any limitation of their powers.*—see also DAMAGE LIMITATION **2** [C] ~ (**on sth**) a rule, fact or condition that limits sth: *to impose limitations on imports* ◊ *Disability is a physical limitation on your life.*—see also STATUTE OF LIMITATIONS **3** [C, usually pl.] a limit on what sb/sth can do or how good they or it can be: *This technique is useful but it has its limitations.*

limit·ed /'lɪmɪtɪd/ *adj.* **1** not very great in amount or extent: *We are doing our best with the limited resources available.* **2** ~ (**to sth**) restricted to a particular limit of time, numbers, etc: *This offer is for a limited period only.*

,limited 'company (also **,limited lia'bility company**) *noun* (in Britain) a company whose owners only have to pay a limited amount of its debts—see also LTD

,limited e'dition *noun* a fixed, usually small, number of copies of a book, picture, etc. produced at one time

,limited lia'bility *noun* [U] (*law*) the legal position of having to pay only a limited amount of your or your company's debts

limit·ing /'lɪmɪtɪŋ/ *adj.* putting limits on what is possible: *Lack of cash is a limiting factor.*

limit·less /'lɪmɪtləs/ *adv.* (*written*) without a limit; very great: *the limitless variety of consumer products* ◊ *The possibilities were almost limitless.*

limo /'lɪməʊ; *AmE* 'lɪmoʊ/ *noun* (*pl.* **-os**) (*informal*) = LIMOUSINE

lim·ou·sine /'lɪməziːn; ˌlɪmə'ziːn/ (also *informal* **limo**) *noun* **1** a large expensive comfortable car: *a long black chauffeur-driven limousine*—see also STRETCH LIMO **2** (*especially AmE*) a van or small bus that takes people to and from an airport

limp /lɪmp/ *adj., verb, noun*
■ *adj.* **1** lacking strength or energy: *His hand went limp and the knife clattered to the ground.* ◊ *She felt limp and exhausted.* **2** not stiff or firm: *The hat had become limp and shapeless.* ▶ **limp·ly** *adv.*: *Her hair hung limply over her forehead.*
■ *verb* [V] **1** to walk slowly or with difficulty because one leg is injured: *She had twisted her ankle and was limping.* ◊ *Matt limped painfully off the field.* **2** [+adv. / prep.] to move slowly or with difficulty after being damaged: *The plane limped back to the airport.* ◊ (*figurative*) *The government was limping along in its usual way.*
■ *noun* [usually sing.] a way of walking in which one leg is used less than normal because it is injured or stiff: *to walk with a slight / pronounced limp*

lim·pet /'lɪmpɪt/ *noun* a small shellfish that sticks very tightly to rocks: *The Prime Minister clung to his job like a limpet, despite calls for him to resign.*

lim·pid /'lɪmpɪd/ *adj.* (*literary*) (of liquids, etc.) clear **SYN** TRANSPARENT: *limpid eyes / water*

linch·pin (also **lynch·pin**) /'lɪntʃpɪn/ *noun* a person or thing that is the most important part of an organization, a plan, etc., because everything else depends on them or it: *Nurses are the linchpin of the health service.*

linc·tus /'lɪŋktəs/ *noun* [U] (*BrE*) thick liquid medicine that you take for a sore throat or a cough: *cough linctus*

lin·den /'lɪndən/ (also **'linden tree**) *noun* = LIME

line /laɪn/ *noun, verb*
■ *noun*
LONG THIN MARK | **1** [C] a long thin mark on a surface: *a straight / wavy / dotted / diagonal line* ◊ *parallel / vertical / horizontal lines* ◊ *Draw a thick black line across the page.* **2** [C] a long thin mark on the ground to show the limit or border of sth, especially of a playing area in some sports: *The ball went over the line.* ◊ *Be careful not to cross the line* (= the broken line painted down the middle of the road). ◊ *Your feet must be behind the line when you serve* (= in tennis). ◊ *They were all waiting on the starting line.*—see also FINISHING LINE, GOAL LINE, SIDELINE, TOUCHLINE **3** [C] a mark like a line on sb's skin that people usually get as they get older **SYN** WRINKLE: *He has fine lines around his eyes.*
DIVISION | **4** [C] an imaginary limit or border between one place or thing and another: *He was convicted of illegally importing weapons across state lines.* ◊ *a district / county line* ◊ *lines of longitude and latitude*—see also COASTLINE, DATE LINE, DIVIDING LINE, PICKET LINE, TREELINE, WATERLINE **5** [C] the division between one area of thought or behaviour and another: *We want to cut across lines of race, sex and religion.* ◊ *There is a fine line between showing interest in what someone is doing and interfering in it.*
SHAPE | **6** [C] the edge, outline or shape of sth: *I prefer simple lines in skirts and trousers.* ◊ *He traced the line of her jaw with his finger.* ◊ *a beautiful sports car with sleek lines*
ROW | **7** [C] a row of people or things next to each other or behind each other: *a long line of trees* ◊ *The children all stood in a line.* ◊ *They were stuck in a line of traffic.* ◊ *to stand / wait in line for sth* ◊ *A line formed at each teller window.*
IN FACTORY | **8** [C] a system of making sth, in which the product moves from one worker to the next until it is finished—see also ASSEMBLY LINE, PRODUCTION LINE
SERIES | **9** [C, usually sing.] a series of people, things or events that follow one another in time: *She came from a long line of doctors.* ◊ *to pass sth down through the male / female line* ◊ *This novel is the latest of a long line of*

L

thrillers that he has written. **10** [C, usually sing.] a series of people in order of importance: *Orders came down the line from the very top.* ◇ *a line of command* ◇ *He is second in line to the chairman.* ◇ *to be next in line to the throne*—see also LINE MANAGER

WORDS | **11** [C] (*abbr.* l) a row of words on a page or the empty space where they can be written; the words of a song or poem: *Look at line 5 of the text.* ◇ *Write the title of your essay on the top line.* ◇ *I can only remember the first two lines of that song.*—see also BOTTOM LINE **12** [C] the words spoken by an actor in a play or film/movie: *to study/learn your lines* ◇ *a line from the film 'Casablanca'* **13** (lines) [pl.] (*BrE*) (in some schools) a punishment in which a child has to write out a particular sentence a number of times **14** [C] (*informal*) a remark, especially when sb says it to achieve a particular purpose: *Don't give me that line about having to work late again.* ◇ (*BrE*) *That's the worst chat-up line I've ever heard.*

ROPE/WIRE/PIPE | **15** [C] a long piece of rope, thread, etc., especially when it is used for a particular purpose: *a fishing line* ◇ *He hung the towels out on the line* (= clothes line). ◇ *They dropped the sails and threw a line to a man on the dock.*—see also LIFELINE **16** [C] a pipe or thick wire that carries water, gas or electricity from one place to another—see also POWER LINE

TELEPHONE | **17** [C] a telephone connection; a particular telephone number: *Your bill includes line rental.* ◇ *The company's lines have been jammed* (= busy) *all day with people making complaints.* ◇ *I was talking to John when the line suddenly went dead.* ◇ *If you hold the line* (= stay on the telephone and wait), *I'll see if she is available.*—see also HELPLINE, HOTLINE, OFF-LINE, ONLINE

RAILWAY/RAILROAD | **18** [C] a railway/railroad track; a section of a railway/railroad system: *The train was delayed because a tree had fallen across the line.* ◇ *a branch line* ◇ *the East Coast line to Edinburgh*—see also MAIN LINE

ROUTE/DIRECTION | **19** [C, usually sing.] the direction that sb/sth is moving or situated in: *Just keep going in a straight line; you can't miss it.* ◇ *The town is in a direct line between London and the coast.* ◇ *Please move; you're right in my line of vision* (= the direction I am looking in). ◇ *They followed the line of the river for three miles.* ◇ *Be careful to stay out of the line of fire* (= the direction sb is shooting in). **20** [C] a route from one place to another especially when it is used for a particular purpose: *Their aim was to block guerrilla supply lines.*

ATTITUDE/ARGUMENT | **21** [C, usually sing.] an attitude or a belief, especially one that sb states publicly: *The government is taking a firm line on terrorism.* ◇ *The MP supported the official line on education.*—see also HARD LINE, PARTY LINE **22** [C] a method or way of doing or thinking about sth: *I don't follow your line of reasoning.* ◇ *She decided to try a different line of argument* (= way of persuading sb of sth). ◇ *sb's first line of attack/defence* ◇ *The police are pursuing a new line of enquiry/inquiry* (= way of finding out information).

ACTIVITY | **23** [sing.] a type or area of business, activity or interest: *My line of work pays pretty well.* ◇ *You can't do much in the art line without training.*—see also SIDELINE

PRODUCT | **24** [C] a type of product: *We are starting a new line in casual clothes.* ◇ *Some lines sell better than others.*

TRANSPORT | **25** [C] (often used in names) a company that provides transport for people or goods: *a shipping/bus line*—see also AIRLINE

SOLDIERS | **26** [C] a row or series of military defences where the soldiers are fighting during a war: *The regiment was sent to fight in the front line* (= the position nearest the enemy). ◇ *They were trapped behind enemy lines* (= in the area controlled by the enemy).

DRUGS | **27** [C] (*slang*) an amount of COCAINE that is spread out in a thin line, ready to take

IDM along/down the 'line (*informal*) at some point during an activity or a process: *Somewhere along the line a large amount of money went missing.* ◇ *We'll make a decision on that further down the line.* along/on (the) ... 'lines **1** (*informal*) in the way that is mentioned:

The new system will operate along the same lines as the old one. ◇ *They voted along class lines.* **2** (*informal*) similar to the way or thing that is mentioned: *Those aren't his exact words, but he said something along those lines.* ◇ *The hotel was built along the lines of a French chateau.* be on 'line **1** to be working or functioning: *The new working methods will come on line in June.* ◇ *It took five hours to get all the computer terminals back on line.* **2** using a computer; communicating with other people by computer: *Most schools will be on line by the year 2000.*—see also ONLINE bring sb/sth, come, get, fall, etc. into 'line (with sb/sth) to behave or make sb/sth behave in the same way as other people or how they should behave: *Britain must be brought into line with the rest of Europe on taxes.* in (a) 'line (with sth) in a position that forms a straight line with sth: *An eclipse happens when the earth and moon are in line with the sun.* in 'line for sth likely to get sth: *She is in line for promotion.* in the ˌline of 'duty while doing a job: *A policeman was injured in the line of duty yesterday.* in 'line with sth similar to sth or so that one thing is closely connected with another: *Annual pay increases will be in line with inflation.* ˌlay it on the 'line (*informal*) to tell sb clearly what you think, especially when they will not like what you say: *The manager laid it on the line—some people would have to lose their jobs.* (choose, follow, take, etc.) the line of least re'sistance (to choose, etc.) the easiest way doing sth (put sth) on the 'line (*informal*) at risk: *If we don't make a profit, my job is on the line.* out of 'line (with sb/sth) **1** not forming a straight line **2** different from sth: *London prices are way out of line with the rest of the country.* **3** (*AmE*) = OUT OF ORDER walk/tread a fine/thin line to be in a difficult or dangerous situation where you could easily make a mistake: *He was walking a fine line between being funny and being rude.*—more at BATTLE *n.*, DRAW *v.*, END *n.*, FIRING LINE, FRONT LINE, HARD *adj.*, HOOK *n.*, JUMP *v.*, OVERSTEP, PITCH *v.*, READ *v.*, SIGN *v.*, STEP *v.*, TOE *v.*

■ *verb* [VN]

COVER INSIDE | **1** [often passive] ~ sth (with sth) to cover the inside of sth with a layer of another material to keep it clean, make it stronger, etc: *Line the pan with grease-proof paper.* **2** to form a layer on the inside of sth: *the membranes that line the nose*

FORM ROWS | **3** [often passive] ~ sth (with sth) to form lines or rows along sth: *Crowds of people lined the streets to watch the race.* ◇ *The walls were lined with books.*—see also LINED

IDM line your (own)/sb's 'pockets to get richer or make sb richer, especially by taking unfair advantage of a situation or by being dishonest

PHRV ˌline 'up to stand in a line or row; to form a QUEUE/LINE: *Line up, children!* ◇ *Cars lined up waiting to board the ship.* ˌline sb/sth↔'up **1** to arrange people or things in a straight line or row: *The suspects were lined up against the wall.* ◇ *He lined the bottles up along the shelf.* **2** to arrange for an event or activity to happen, or arrange for sb to be available to do sth: *Mark had a job lined up when he left college.* ◇ *I've got a lot lined up this week* (= I'm very busy). ◇ *She's lined up a live band for the party.* ˌline sth↔'up (with sth) to move one thing into a correct position in relation to another thing

lin·eage /ˈlɪniɪdʒ/ *noun* [U, C] (*formal*) the series of families that sb is descended from: *a French nobleman of ancient lineage*

lin·eal /ˈlɪniəl/ *adj.* [only before noun] (*rare, formal*) descended directly from sb: *a lineal descendant of the company's founder*

lin·ea·ments /ˈlɪniəmənts/ *noun* [pl.] (*rare, formal*) the typical features of sth

lin·ear /ˈlɪniə(r)/ *adj.* **1** of or in lines: *In his art he broke the laws of scientific linear perspective.* **2** going from one thing to another in a single series of stages: *Students do not always progress in a linear fashion.* **OPP** NON-LINEAR **3** of length: *linear measurement* (= for example metres, feet, etc.) ▶ **lin·ear·ity** /ˌlɪniˈærəti/ *noun* [U]: *She abandoned the linearity of the conventional novel.* **lin·ear·ly** *adv.*

s	t	v	z	ʃ	ʒ	tʃ	dʒ	θ	ð	ŋ
see	tea	van	zoo	shoe	vision	chain	jam	thin	this	sing

line·back·er /ˈlaɪnbækə(r)/ *noun* (in American football) a DEFENSIVE player who tries to TACKLE members of the other team

lined /laɪnd/ *adj.* **1** (of skin, especially on the face) having folds or lines because of age, worry, etc: *a deeply lined face* **2** (of paper) having lines printed or drawn across it: *Lined paper helps keep handwriting neat.* **3** (of clothes) having a LINING inside them: *a lined skirt* **4** (-**lined**) having the object mentioned along an edge or edges, or as a LINING: *a tree-lined road*

'**line dancing** *noun* [U] a type of dancing originally from the US, in which people dance in lines, all doing a complicated series of steps at the same time

'**line drawing** *noun* a drawing that consists only of lines

line·man /ˈlaɪnmən/ *noun* (*pl.* -**men** /-mən/) (*AmE*) a player in the front line of an American football team

'**line management** *noun* [U] (*BrE*) the system of organizing a company, etc. in which information and instructions are passed from each employee and manager to the person one rank above or below them ▶ '**line manager** *noun*: *Review your training needs with your line manager.*

linen /ˈlɪnɪn/ *noun* [U] **1** a fabric made from FLAX, used to make high quality clothes, sheets, etc: *a linen shirt/ tablecloth* **2** sheets, TABLECLOTHS, PILLOWCASES, etc. made of linen or cotton: (*BrE*) *a linen cupboard* ◊ (*AmE*) *a linen closet*—see also BEDLINEN **IDM** see WASH *v.*

'**line printer** *noun* a machine that prints very quickly, producing a complete line of print at a time

liner /ˈlaɪnə(r)/ *noun* **1** a large ship that carries passengers: *an ocean liner* ◊ *a luxury cruise liner*—picture at BOAT **2** (especially in compounds) a piece of material used to cover the inside surface of sth: *bin/nappy liners* **3** = EYELINER—see also HARDLINER

'**liner note** *noun* [usually pl.] information about the music or the performers that comes with a CD or is printed on the cover of a record

lines·man /ˈlaɪnzmən/ *noun* (*pl.* -**men** /-mən/) an official who helps the REFEREE in some games, for example football, especially in deciding whether or where a ball crosses one of the lines (now officially called **referee's assistant** in football)

'**line-up** *noun* [usually sing.] **1** the people who are going to take part in a particular event: *an impressive line-up of speakers* ◊ *the starting line-up* (= the players who will begin the game) **2** a set of items, events etc. arranged to follow one another: *A horror movie completes this evening's TV line-up.* **3** (*especially AmE*) = IDENTIFICATION PARADE

ling /lɪŋ/ *noun* [U] a low plant that is a type of HEATHER and that grows on areas of wild open land (= MOORLAND)

-**ling** /lɪŋ/ *suffix* (in nouns) (sometimes *disapproving*) small; not important: *duckling* ◊ *princeling*

lin·ger /ˈlɪŋɡə(r)/ *verb* [V] **1 ~ (on)** to continue to exist for longer than expected: *The faint smell of her perfume lingered in the room.* ◊ *The civil war lingered on well into the 1930s.* **2** [usually +adv./prep.] to stay somewhere for longer because you do not want to leave; to spend a long time doing sth: *She lingered for a few minutes to talk to Nick.* ◊ *We lingered over breakfast on the terrace.* **3 ~ (on sb/sth)** to continue to look at sb/sth or think about sth for longer than usual: *His eyes lingered on the diamond ring on her finger.* **4 ~ (on)** to stay alive but become weaker: *He lingered on for several months after the heart attack.*

lin·ge·rie /ˈlænʒəri; *AmE* ˌlɑːndʒəˈreɪ/ *noun* [U] (used especially by shops/stores) women's underwear

lin·ger·ing /ˈlɪŋɡərɪŋ/ *adj.* slow to end or disappear: *a painful and lingering death* ◊ *a last lingering look* ◊ *lingering doubts/hopes* ◊ *a lingering smell of machine oil* ▶ **lin·ger·ing·ly** *adv.*

lingo /ˈlɪŋɡəʊ; *AmE* -ɡoʊ/ *noun* [sing.] (*informal*) **1** a language, especially a foreign language: *He doesn't speak the lingo.* **2** (*especially AmE*) expressions used by a particular group of people **SYN** JARGON: *baseball/aviation lingo*

lin·gua franca /ˌlɪŋɡwə ˈfræŋkə/ *noun* [usually sing.] (*technical*) a shared language of communication used by people whose main languages are different

lin·guist /ˈlɪŋɡwɪst/ *noun* **1** a person who knows several foreign languages well: *She's an excellent linguist.* ◊ *I'm afraid I'm no linguist* (= I find foreign languages difficult). **2** a person who studies languages or LINGUISTICS

lin·guis·tic /lɪŋˈɡwɪstɪk/ *adj.* connected with language or the scientific study of language: *linguistic and cultural barriers* ◊ *a child's innate linguistic ability* ◊ *new developments in linguistic theory* ▶ **lin·guis·tic·al·ly** *adv.*

lin·guis·tics /lɪŋˈɡwɪstɪks/ *noun* [U] the scientific study of language or of particular languages: *a course in applied linguistics*

lini·ment /ˈlɪnəmənt/ *noun* [C, U] a liquid, especially one made with oil, that you rub on a painful part of your body to reduce the pain

lin·ing /ˈlaɪnɪŋ/ *noun* **1** [C] a layer of material used to cover the inside surface of sth: *a pair of leather gloves with fur linings* **2** [U] the covering of the inner surface of a part of the body: *the stomach lining* **IDM** see CLOUD *n.*

link /lɪŋk/ *noun, verb*
■ *noun* **1 ~** (**between A and B**) a connection between two or more people or things: *Police suspect there may be a link between the two murders.* ◊ *evidence for a strong causal link between exposure to sun and skin cancer*—see also MISSING LINK **2 ~** (**between A and B**)| **~** (**with sth**) a relationship between two or more people, countries or organizations: *to establish/maintain trade links with Asia* ◊ *Social customs provide a vital link between generations.* **3** a means of travelling or communicating between two places: *a high-speed rail link* ◊ *a link road* ◊ *a telephone/ video link* **4** each ring of a chain—see also CUFFLINK—picture at CHAIN **IDM** **a link in the 'chain** one of the stages in a process or a line of argument—more at WEAK
■ *verb* [VN] [often passive] **~ A to/with B| ~ A and B** (**together**) **1** to make a physical connection between one object, machine, place, etc. and another: *The video cameras are linked to a powerful computer.* ◊ *The Channel Tunnel links Britain with the rest of Europe.* **2** if sth **links** two things, facts or situations, or they **are linked**, they are connected in some way: *Exposure to ultraviolet light is closely linked to skin cancer.* ◊ *The two factors are directly linked.* ◊ *The personal and social development of the child are inextricably linked* (= they depend on each other). **3** to state that there is a connection or relationship between two things or people: *Detectives have linked the break-in to a similar crime in the area last year.* ◊ *Newspapers have linked his name with the singer.* **4** to join two things by putting one through the other: *The two girls linked arms as they strolled down the street.* **PHR V** **link 'up (with sb/sth)** to join or become joined with sb/sth: *The two spacecraft will link up in orbit.* ◊ *The bands have linked up for a charity concert.*—related noun LINK-UP

link·age /ˈlɪŋkɪdʒ/ *noun* **1** [U, C] **~** (**between A and B**) the act of linking things; a link or system of links: *This chapter explores the linkage between economic development and the environment.* **2** [C] a device that links two or more things

'**linking verb** (also **cop·ula**) *noun* (*grammar*) a verb such as *be* or *become* that connects a subject with the adjective or noun (called the COMPLEMENT) that describes it: *In 'She became angry', the verb 'became' is a linking verb.*

link·man /ˈlɪŋkmæn/ *noun* (*pl.* -**men** /-men/) (*BrE*) **1** a person who helps two people or groups of people to communicate with each other **2** a person who works on the radio or television introducing the programmes or telling people about future programmes

links /lɪŋks/ *noun* = GOLF LINKS

'**link-up** *noun* a connection formed between two things, for example two companies or two broadcasting systems: *a live satellite link-up with the conference*

lin·net /ˈlɪnɪt/ *noun* a small brown and grey bird of the FINCH family

lino /ˈlaɪnəʊ; *AmE* -noʊ/ *noun* [U] (*BrE, informal*) = LINOLEUM

li·no·leum /lɪˈnəʊliəm; *AmE* -ˈnoʊ-/ (also *BrE informal*

lino) *noun* [U] a type of strong material with a hard shiny surface, used for covering floors

lin·seed oil /ˌlɪnsiːd ˈɔɪl/ *noun* [U] an oil made from FLAX seeds, used in paint or to protect wood, etc.

lint /lɪnt/ *noun* [U] **1** (*especially BrE*) a soft cotton fabric used for covering and protecting wounds **2** (*technical*) short fine FIBRES that come off the surface of fabric when it is being made **3** (*especially AmE*) (*BrE* usually **fluff**) small soft pieces of wool, cotton, etc. that stick on the surface of fabric

lin·tel /ˈlɪntl/ *noun* (*architecture*) a piece of wood or stone over a door or window, that forms part of the frame

lion /ˈlaɪən/ *noun* a large powerful animal of the cat family, that hunts in groups and lives in parts of Africa and southern Asia. Lions have yellowish-brown fur and the male has a MANE (= long thick hair round its neck).— see also MOUNTAIN LION—compare LIONESS—picture on page A6 **IDM** the **'lion's den** a difficult situation in which you have to face a person or people who are unfriendly or aggressive towards you **the 'lion's share (of sth)** (*BrE*) the largest or best part of sth when it is divided—more at BEARD *v.*

lion·ess /ˈlaɪənes/ *noun* a female lion

lion·ize (*BrE also* **-ise**) /ˈlaɪənaɪz/ *verb* [VN] (*written*) to treat sb as a famous or important person

lip /lɪp/ *noun* **1** [C] either of the two soft edges at the opening to the mouth: *The assistant pursed her lips.* ◇ *your upper/lower/top/bottom lip* ◇ *She kissed him on the lips.* ◇ *Not a drop of alcohol passed my lips* (= I didn't drink any).—picture at BODY **2** (**-lipped**) (in adjectives) having the type of lips mentioned: *thin-lipped* ◇ *thick-lipped*—see also TIGHT-LIPPED **3** [C] ~ **(of sth)** the edge of a container or a hollow place in the ground: *He ran his finger around the lip of the cup.* ◇ *Lava bubbled a few feet below the lip of the crater.*—picture at JUG **4** [U] (*informal*) words spoken to sb that are rude and show a lack of respect for that person **SYN** CHEEK: *Don't let him give you any lip!* **IDM** **lick/smack your 'lips 1** to move your tongue over your lips, especially before eating sth good **2** (*informal*) to show that you are excited about sth and want it to happen soon: *They were licking their lips at the thought of clinching the deal.* **my lips are 'sealed** used to say that you will not repeat sb's secret to other people **on everyone's 'lips** if sth is on everyone's lips, they are all talking about it—more at BITE *v.*, PASS *v.*, READ *v.*, STIFF *adj.*

lipo·suc·tion /ˈlɪpəʊsʌkʃn; ˈlaɪ-; *AmE* ˈlaɪpoʊ-; ˈlɪ-/ *noun* [U] a way of removing fat from sb's body by using SUCTION

lippy /ˈlɪpi/ *adj.* (*BrE, informal*) showing a lack of respect in the way that you speak to sb

'lip-read *verb* [V, VN] to understand what sb is saying by watching the way their lips move ▶ **'lip-reading** *noun* [U]

'lip-service *noun* if sb pays **lip-service** to sth, they say that they approve of it or support it, without proving their support by what they actually do: *All the parties pay lip-service to environmental issues.*

lip·stick /ˈlɪpstɪk/ *noun* [U, C] a substance made into a small stick, used for colouring the lips; a small stick of this substance: *She was wearing bright red lipstick.*— picture at STICK

lip-sync (*also* **lip-synch**) /ˈlɪp sɪŋk/ *verb* to move your mouth, without speaking or singing, so that its movements match the sound on a recorded song, etc: [V] *She lip-synced to a Beatles song.* ◇ [VN] *He lip-synced 'Return to Sender'.*

li·quefy /ˈlɪkwɪfaɪ/ *verb* (**li·que·fies**, **li·que·fy·ing**, **li·que·fied**, **li·que·fied**) [V, VN] (*formal*) to become liquid; to make sth liquid

li·queur /lɪˈkjʊə(r); *AmE* -ˈkɜːr/ (*AmE also* **cor·dial**) *noun* **1** [U, C] a strong sweet alcoholic drink, sometimes flavoured with fruit. It is usually drunk in very small glasses after a meal. **2** [C] a glass of liqueur

li·quid /ˈlɪkwɪd/ *noun, adj.*
■ *noun* [U, C] a substance that flows freely and is not a solid or a gas, for example water or oil: *She poured the dark*

brown liquid down the sink. ◇ *the transition from liquid to vapour*—see also WASHING-UP LIQUID
■ *adj.* **1** in the form of a liquid; not a solid or a gas: *liquid fertilizer/soap* ◇ *liquid nitrogen* ◇ *The detergent comes in powder or liquid form.* ◇ *a bar selling snacks and liquid refreshment* (= drinks) **2** (*finance*) that can easily be changed into cash: *liquid assets* **3** (*literary*) clear, like water: *liquid blue eyes* **4** (*literary*) (of sounds) clear, pure and flowing: *the liquid song of a blackbird*

li·quid·ate /ˈlɪkwɪdeɪt/ *verb* **1** [V, VN] to close a business and sell everything it owns in order to pay debts **2** [VN] (*finance*) to sell sth in order to get money: *to liquidate assets* **3** [VN] (*finance*) to pay a debt **4** [VN] to destroy or remove sb/sth that causes problems: *The government tried to liquidate the rebel movement and failed.*

li·quid·ation /ˌlɪkwɪˈdeɪʃn/ *noun* [U] the action of liquidating sb/sth: *The company has gone into liquidation.*

li·quid·ator /ˈlɪkwɪdeɪtə(r)/ *noun* a person responsible for closing down a business and using any profits from the sale to pay its debts

liquid crystal dis'play *noun* = LCD

li·quid·ity /lɪˈkwɪdəti/ *noun* [U] (*finance*) the state of owning things of value that can easily be exchanged for cash: *Financial institutions must maintain sufficient liquidity to meet the demands of depositors.*

li·quid·ize (*BrE also* **-ise**) /ˈlɪkwɪdaɪz/ *verb* [VN] (*especially BrE*) to crush fruit, vegetables, etc. into a thick liquid

li·quid·izer (*BrE also* **-iser**) /ˈlɪkwɪdaɪzə(r)/ *noun* (*BrE*) = BLENDER

li·quor /ˈlɪkə(r)/ *noun* [U] **1** (*especially AmE*) strong alcoholic drink **SYN** SPIRITS: *hard liquor* ◇ *She drinks wine and beer but no liquor.* **2** (*BrE, technical*) any alcoholic drink: *intoxicating liquor*

li·quor·ice (*especially BrE*) (*AmE usually* **lic·orice**) /ˈlɪkərɪʃ; -rɪs/ *noun* [U, C] a firm black substance with a strong flavour, obtained from the root of a plant, used in medicine and to make sweets/candy; a sweet/candy made from this substance

li·quor·ice all·sorts /ˌlɪkərɪʃ ˈɔːlsɔːts; -rɪs; *AmE* -sɔːrts/ *noun* [pl.] (*BrE*) brightly coloured sweets/candy made with liquorice

'liquor store *noun* (*AmE*) = OFF-LICENCE

lira /ˈlɪərə; *AmE* ˈlɪrə/ *noun* (*pl.* **lire** /ˈlɪərə; *AmE* ˈlɪreɪ/) (*abbr.* **l.**) the unit of money in Italy and Turkey (to be replaced in Italy by the euro)

lisp /lɪsp/ *noun, verb*
■ *noun* [usually sing.] a speech fault in which the sound 's' is pronounced 'th': *She spoke with a slight lisp.*
■ *verb* [V, V speech] to speak with a lisp

lis·som (*also* **lis·some**) /ˈlɪsəm/ *adj.* (*literary*) (of sb's body) thin and graceful

list /lɪst/ *noun, verb*
■ *noun* **1** [C] a series of names, items, figures, etc., especially when they are written or printed: *a shopping/wine/price list* ◇ *to make a list of things to do* ◇ (*formal*) *to draw up a list* ◇ *Is your name on the list?* ◇ *Having to wait hours came high on the list of complaints.*—see also HIT LIST, MAILING LIST, SHORTLIST, WAITING LIST **2** [sing.] the fact of a ship leaning to one side **IDM** see DANGER
■ *verb* **1** [VN] to write a list of things in a particular order: *We were asked to list our ten favourite songs.* ◇ *Towns in the guide are listed alphabetically.* **2** [VN] to mention or include sth in a list: *The koala is listed among Australia's endangered animals.* ◇ *soldiers listed as missing* **3** (*AmE*) to be put or put sth in a list of things for sale: [V] *This CD player lists at $200.* [also VN] **4** [V] (of a ship) to lean to one side

listed 'building *noun* (*BrE*) a building that is officially protected because it has artistic or historical value—see also LANDMARK

lis·ten /ˈlɪsn/ *verb, noun*
■ *verb* [V] **1** ~ **(to sb/sth)** to pay attention to sb/sth that you can hear: *to listen to music/the radio* ◇ *Listen! What's that noise? Can you hear it?* ◇ *Sorry, I wasn't really listening.* ◇ *I listened carefully to her story.* **HELP** You cannot 'listen

aɪ	aʊ	eɪ	əʊ	oʊ	ɔɪ	ɪə	eə	ʊə	j	w
my	now	say	go (BrE)	go (AmE)	boy	near	hair	pure	yes	wet

sth' (without 'to'): *I'm fond of listening to classical music.* ◊ *I'm fond of listening classical music.* **2 ~ (to sb/sth)** to take notice of what sb says to you so that you follow their advice or believe them: *None of this would have happened if you'd listened to me.* ◊ *Why won't you listen to reason?* **3** (*spoken*) used to tell sb to take notice of what you are going to say: *Listen, there's something I have to tell you.* **PHRV** **'listen ('out) for sth** to be prepared to hear a particular sound: *Can you listen out for the doorbell?* **,listen 'in (on/to sth) 1** to listen to a conversation that you are not supposed to hear: *You shouldn't listen in on other people's conversations.* **2** to listen to a radio broadcast **,listen 'up** (*spoken, especially AmE*) used to tell people to listen carefully because you are going to say sth important

■ *noun* [usually sing.] an act of listening: *Have a listen to this.*

lis·ten·able /ˈlɪsnəbl/ *adj.* (*informal*) pleasant to listen to: *Their new album is surprisingly listenable.*

lis·ten·er /ˈlɪsənə(r)/ *noun* **1** a person who listens: *a good listener* (= sb who you can rely on to listen with attention or sympathy) **2** a person listening to a radio programme

lis·teria /lɪˈstɪəriə; *AmE* -ˈstɪr-/ *noun* [U] a type of bacteria that makes people sick if they eat infected food

list·ing /ˈlɪstɪŋ/ *noun* **1** [C] a list, especially an official or published list of people or things, often arranged in alphabetical order: *a comprehensive listing of all airlines* **2 (listings)** [pl.] information in a newspaper or magazine about what films/movies, plays, etc. are being shown in a particular town or city: *a London listings magazine* **3** [C] a position or an item on a list: (*business*) *The company is seeking a stock exchange listing* (= for trading shares).

list·less /ˈlɪstləs/ *adj.* having no energy or enthusiasm: *The illness left her feeling listless and depressed.* ▶ **list·less·ly** *adv.* **list·less·ness** *noun* [U]

'list price *noun* [usually sing.] (*business*) the price at which goods are advertised for sale, for example in a CATALOGUE: *8% off the manufacturer's list price*

lit *pt, pp* of LIGHT

lit·any /ˈlɪtəni/ *noun* (*pl.* **-ies**) **1** a series of prayers to God for use in church services, spoken by a priest, etc., with set responses by the people **2 ~ (of sth)** (*written*) a long boring account of a series of events, reasons, etc: *a litany of complaints*

lite /laɪt/ *adj.* [usually before noun] (*informal, especially AmE*) (of food or drink) containing fewer CALORIES than other types of food, so less likely to make you fat (a way of spelling 'light'): *lite ice cream* ◊ *lite beer*

liter (*AmE*) = LITRE

lit·er·acy /ˈlɪtərəsi/ *noun* [U] the ability to read and write: *a campaign to promote adult literacy* ◊ *basic literacy skills* **OPP** ILLITERACY—see also COMPUTER LITERACY

lit·eral /ˈlɪtərəl/ *adj.* **1** [usually before noun] being the basic or usual meaning of a word or phrase: *His story is incredible in the literal sense of the word* (= it is impossible to believe it). ◊ *What is the literal meaning of this word?*—compare FIGURATIVE, METAPHORICAL **2** [usually before noun] that follows the original words exactly: *a literal translation* ◊ *a literal transcript of a speech*—compare FREE **3** (*disapproving*) lacking imagination: *Her interpretation of the music was too literal.* ▶ **lit·er·al·ness** *noun* [U]

lit·er·al·ly /ˈlɪtərəli/ *adv.* **1** in a literal way **SYN** EXACTLY: *The word 'planet' literally means 'wandering body'.* ◊ *When I told you to 'get lost' I didn't expect to be taken literally.* **2** used to emphasize the truth of sth that may seem surprising: *There are literally hundreds of prizes to win.* **3** (*informal*) used to emphasize a word or phrase that is being used in a FIGURATIVE way: *I literally jumped out of my skin.*

lit·er·ary /ˈlɪtərəri; *AmE* -reri/ *adj.* **1** connected with literature: *literary criticism/theory* **2** (of a language or style of writing) suitable for or typical of a work of literature: *It was Chaucer who really turned English into a literary language.* **3** liking literature very much; studying or writing literature: *a literary man*

lit·er·ate /ˈlɪtərət/ *adj.* able to read and write **OPP** ILLITERATE—see also NUMERATE, COMPUTER-LITERATE

lit·er·ati /ˌlɪtəˈrɑːti/ **(the literati)** *noun* [pl.] (*formal*) educated and intelligent people who enjoy literature

lit·era·ture /ˈlɪtrətʃə(r); *AmE also* -tʃʊr/ *noun* [U] **1** pieces of writing that are valued as works of art, especially novels, plays and poems (in contrast to technical books and newspapers, magazines, etc.): *to read/study French literature* ◊ *great works of literature* **2 ~ (on sth)** pieces of writing or printed information on a particular subject: *I've read all the available literature on keeping rabbits.* ◊ *sales/promotional literature*

lithe /laɪð/ *adj.* (of a person or their body) moving or bending easily, in a way that is graceful ▶ **lithe·ly** *adv.*

lith·ium /ˈlɪθiəm/ *noun* [U] (*symb* Li) a chemical element. Lithium is a soft, very light, silver-white metal used in batteries and ALLOYS.

litho·graph /ˈlɪθəɡrɑːf; *AmE* -ɡræf/ *noun* a picture printed by lithography

lith·og·raphy /lɪˈθɒɡrəfi; *AmE* -ˈθɑːɡ-/ *noun* (also *informal* **litho** /ˈlaɪθəʊ; *AmE* -θoʊ/) [U] the process of printing from a smooth surface, for example a metal plate, that has been specially prepared so that ink only sticks to the design to be printed ▶ **litho·graph·ic** /ˌlɪθəˈɡræfɪk/ *adj.*

liti·gant /ˈlɪtɪɡənt/ *noun* (*law*) a person who is making or defending a claim in a court of law

liti·gate /ˈlɪtɪɡeɪt/ *verb* [V, VN] (*law*) to take a claim or dispute to a court of law ▶ **liti·ga·tor** *noun*

liti·ga·tion /ˌlɪtɪˈɡeɪʃn/ *noun* [U] (*law*) the process of making or defending a claim in a court of law: *litigation costs/procedures* ◊ *The company has been in litigation with its previous auditors for a full year.*

li·ti·gious /lɪˈtɪdʒəs/ *adj.* (*formal, disapproving*) too ready to take disputes to a court of law ▶ **li·ti·gious·ness** *noun* [U]

lit·mus /ˈlɪtməs/ *noun* [U] a substance that turns red when it touches an acid and blue when it touches an ALKALI: *litmus paper*

'litmus test *noun* **1** (*especially AmE*) = ACID TEST: *The outcome will be seen as a litmus test of government concern for conservation issues.* **2** a test using litmus

litre (*BrE*) (*AmE* **liter**) /ˈliːtə(r)/ *noun* (*abbr.* l) a unit for measuring volume, equal to 1.76 British PINTS or 2.11 American pints: *3 litres of water* ◊ *a litre bottle of wine* ◊ *a car with a 3.5 litre engine*

lit·ter /ˈlɪtə(r)/ *noun, verb*

■ *noun* **1** [U] small pieces of rubbish/garbage such as paper, cans and bottles, that people have left lying in a public place: *There will be fines for people who drop litter.* **2** [sing.] **~ of sth** a number of things that are lying in an untidy way: *The floor was covered with a litter of newspapers, clothes and empty cups.* **3** [U] a dry substance that is put in a shallow open box for pets, especially cats, to use as a toilet when they are indoors: *cat litter* ◊ (*BrE*) *a litter tray* ◊ (*AmE*) *a litter box* **4** [C] a number of baby animals that one mother gives birth to at the same time: *a litter of puppies/kittens* ◊ *the runt* (= the smallest and weakest baby) *of the litter* **5** [U] the substance, especially STRAW, that is used for farm animals to sleep on **6** [C] a kind of chair or bed that was used in the past for carrying important people

■ *verb* **1** [VN] to be spread around a place, making it look untidy: *Piles of books and newspapers littered the floor.* ◊ *Broken glass littered the streets.* **2 ~ (sth) (with sth)** [usually passive] to leave things in a place, making it look untidy: [VN] *The floor was littered with papers.* ◊ [V] (*AmE*) *He was arrested for littering.* **3** [VN] **(be littered with sth)** to contain or involve a lot of a particular type of thing usually sth bad: *Your essay is littered with spelling mistakes.*

'litter bin (*BrE*) (*AmE* **'trash can**) *noun* a container for people to put rubbish/garbage in, in the street or in a public building

'litter lout (*BrE*) (also **'lit·ter·bug** *AmE, BrE*) *noun* (*informal, disapproving*) a person who leaves LITTER in public places

lit·tle /ˈlɪtl/ *adj., det., pron., adv.*

L

b	d	f	g	h	k	l	m	n	p	r
bad	did	fall	get	hat	cat	leg	man	now	pen	red

■ *adj.* [usually before noun] **HELP** The forms **littler** /ˈlɪtlə(r)/ and **littlest** /ˈlɪtlɪst/ are rare. It is more common to use **smaller** and **smallest**. **1** not big; small; smaller than others: *a little house* ◊ *a little group of tourists* ◊ *a little old lady* ◊ *the classic little black dress* ◊ *'Which do you want?' 'I'll take the little one.'* ◊ *She gave a little laugh.* ◊ *(BrE) We should manage, with* **a little bit** *of luck.* ◊ *Here's* **a little something** *(= a small present) for your birthday.* **2** used after an adjective to show affection or dislike, especially in a PATRONIZING way (= one that suggests that you think you are better than sb): *The poor little thing! It's lost its mother.* ◊ *What a nasty little man!* ◊ *She's a good little worker.* ◊ *He'd become* **quite the little** *gentleman.* **3** young: *a little boy/girl* ◊ *My little sister (= younger sister) is 21 today.* ◊ *I lived in America when I was little.* **4** (of distance or time) short: *A little while later the phone rang.* ◊ *Shall we walk a little way?* **5** not important; not serious: *I can't remember every little detail.* ◊ *You soon get used to the little difficulties.* ⇨ note at SMALL ▶ **little·ness** *noun* [U] *(rare)* **IDM** **a little 'bird told me** *(spoken)* used to say that sb told you sth but you do not want to say who it was—more at WONDER *n.*

■ *det., pron.* **1** used with uncountable nouns to mean 'not much': *There was little doubt in my mind.* ◊ *Students have little or no choice in the matter.* ◊ *I understood little of what he said.* ◊ *She said* **little or nothing** *(= hardly anything) about her experience.* ◊ *Tell him* **as little as possible.** **2** **(a little)** used with uncountable nouns to mean 'a small amount', 'some': *a little milk/sugar/tea* ◊ *If you have any spare milk, could you give me a little?* ◊ *I've only read a little of the book so far.* ◊ *(formal) It caused* **not a little/no little** *(= a lot of) confusion.* ◊ *After* **a little** *(= a short time) he got up and left.* **IDM** **little by 'little** slowly; gradually: *Little by little the snow disappeared.* ◊ *His English is improving little by little.*

■ *adv.* **(less, least)** **1** not much; only slightly: *He is little known as an artist.* ◊ *I slept very little last night.* ◊ *(written) Little did I know that this spelled the end of my career.* **2** **a little (bit)** to a small degree: *She seemed a little afraid of going inside.* ◊ *These shoes are a little (bit) too big for me.* ◊ *(informal) Everything has become* **just that little bit** *harder.* ◊ *(formal) She felt tired and* **more than a little** *worried.* ⇨ note at BIT

,little 'finger *noun* the smallest finger of the hand SYN PINKIE—picture at BODY **IDM** **twist/ wrap/ wind sb around your little 'finger** *(informal)* to persuade sb to do anything that you want: *She has always been able to twist her parents around her little finger.*

'Little League *noun* [sing., U] (in the US) a baseball LEAGUE for children

'little people *noun* [pl.] **1** all the people in a country who have no power: *the helplessness of little people facing vast political forces* **2** **(the little people)** *(BrE)* small imaginary people with magic powers SYN FAIRIES

lit·toral /ˈlɪtərəl/ *noun* (technical) the part of a country that is near the coast ▶ **lit·toral** *adj.* [only before noun]: *littoral states*

lit·urgy /ˈlɪtədʒi; AmE ˈlɪtərdʒi/ *noun* (pl. -ies) a fixed form of public worship used in churches ▶ **li·tur·gic·al** /lɪˈtɜːdʒɪkl; AmE -ˈtɜːrdʒ-/ *adj.* **li·tur·gic·al·ly** /-kli/ *adv.*

liv·able *adj.* = LIVEABLE

live¹ /lɪv/ *verb*—see also LIVE²
IN A PLACE | **1** [V+adv. / prep.] to have your home in a particular place: *to live in a house/an apartment* ◊ *Where do you live?* ◊ *She needs to find somewhere to live.* ◊ *We used to live in London.* ◊ *Both her children still live at home.* ◊ *(BrE, informal) Where do these plates live (= where are they usually kept)?*
BE ALIVE | **2** to remain alive: [V] *The doctors said he only had six months to live.* ◊ *Spiders can live for several days without food.* ◊ *[V to inf] She lived to see her first grandchild.* **3** [V] to be alive, especially at a particular time: *When did Handel live?* ◊ *He's the greatest player who ever lived.*
TYPE OF LIFE | **4** to spend your life in a particular way: [VN] *She lived a very peaceful life.* ◊ *[V] He lived in poverty most of his life.* ◊ *[V-N] She lived and died a single woman.*

BE REMEMBERED | **5** [V] to continue to exist or be remembered: *This moment will live in our memory for many years to come.* ◊ *Her words have lived with me all my life.*
HAVE EXCITEMENT | **6** [V] to have a full and exciting life: *I don't want to be stuck in an office all my life—I want to live!*
IDM ,live and 'breathe sth to be very enthusiastic about sth: *He just lives and breathes football.* **live and 'let live** *(saying)* used to say that you should accept other people's opinions and behaviour even though they are different from your own **live by your 'wits** to earn money by clever or sometimes dishonest means **live (from) ,hand to 'mouth** to spend all the money you earn on basic needs such as food without being able to save any money **live in the 'past** to behave as though society, etc. has not changed, when in fact it has **live in 'sin** *(old-fashioned* or *humorous)* to live together and have a sexual relationship without being married **live it 'up** *(informal)* to enjoy yourself in an exciting way, usually spending a lot of money **live a 'lie** to keep sth important about yourself a secret from other people, so that they do not know what you really think, what you are really like, etc. **live off the fat of the 'land** to have enough money to be able to afford expensive things, food, drink, etc. **live off the 'land** to eat whatever food you can grow, kill or find yourself **,live to fight another 'day** *(saying)* used to say that although you have failed or had a bad experience, you will continue **you haven't 'lived** used to tell sb that if they have not had a particular experience their life is not complete: *You've never been to New York? You haven't lived!* **you live and 'learn** used to express surprise at sth new or unexpected you have been told—more at BORROW, CLOVER, HALF *n.*, PEOPLE *n.*, POCKET *n.*, ROUGH *adv.*
PHRV 'live by sth to follow a particular belief or set of principles: *That's a philosophy I could live by.* 'live by doing sth to earn money or to get the things you need by doing a particular thing: *a community that lives by fishing* ,live sth↔'down to be able to make people forget about sth embarrassing you have done: *She felt so stupid. She'd never be able to live it down.* 'live for sb/sth to think that sb/sth is the main purpose of or the most important thing in your life: *She lives for her work.* ◊ *After his wife died, he had nothing to live for.* ,live 'in to live at the place where you work or study: *They have an au pair living in.*—see also LIVE-IN 'live off sb/sth (often *disapproving*) to receive the money you need to live from sb/sth because you do not have any yourself: *She's still living off her parents.* ◊ *to live off welfare* 'live off sth to have one particular type of food as the main thing you eat in order to live: *He seems to live off junk food.* ,live 'on to continue to live or exist: *She died ten years ago but her memory lives on.* 'live on sth **1** to eat a particular type of food to live: *Small birds live mainly on insects.* **2** (often *disapproving*) to eat only or a lot of a particular type of food: *She lives on burgers.* **3** to have enough money for the basic things you need to live: *You can't live on forty pounds a week.* ,live 'out to live away from the place where you work or study: *Some college students will have to live out.* ,live sth↔'out **1** to actually do what you have only thought about doing before: *to live out your dreams/fantasies* **2** to spend the rest of your life in a particular way: *He lived out his days alone.* ,live 'through sth to experience a disaster or other unpleasant situation and survive it: *He has lived through two world wars.* 'live together (also 'live with sb) **1** to live in the same house **2** to share a home and have a sexual relationship without being married ,live 'up to sth to do as well as or be as good as other people expect you to: *He failed to live up to his parents' expectations.* ◊ *The team called 'The No-Hopers' certainly lived up to its name.* 'live with sb = LIVE TOGETHER 'live with sth to accept sth unpleasant: *I just had to learn to live with the pain.*

live² /laɪv/ *adj., adv.*—see also LIVE¹
■ *adj.* [usually before noun]
NOT DEAD | **1** living; not dead: *live animals* ◊ *the number of live births (= babies born alive)* ◊ *We saw a* **real live** *rattlesnake!*
NOT RECORDED | **2** (of a broadcast) sent out while the event

s	t	v	z	ʃ	ʒ	tʃ	dʒ	θ	ð	ŋ
see	tea	van	zoo	shoe	vision	chain	jam	thin	this	sing

is actually happening, not recorded first and broadcast later: *live coverage of the World Cup*—compare PRE-RECORDED **3** (of a performance) given or made when people are watching, not recorded: *The club has live music most nights.* ◇ *a live recording made at Wembley Arena in 1999* ◇ *the band's new live album* ◇ *It was the first interview I'd done in front of a live audience* (= with people watching).—compare PRE-RECORDED

ELECTRICITY | **4** (of a wire or device) connected to a source of electrical power: *That terminal is live.*

BULLETS/MATCHES | **5** still able to explode or light; ready for use: *live ammunition*

COALS | **6** live coals are burning or are still hot and red

YOGURT | **7** live YOGURT still contains the bacteria needed to turn milk into YOGURT

QUESTION/SUBJECT | **8** (of a question or subject) of interest or importance at the present time: *Pollution is still very much a live issue.*

IDM **a live 'wire** a person who is lively and full of energy
■ *adv.* broadcast at the time of an actual event; played or recorded at an actual performance: *The show is going out live.*

IDM **go 'live** (*computing*) (of a computer system) to become OPERATIONAL (= ready to be used)

live·able (also **liv·able**) /ˈlɪvəbl/ *adj.* **1** (*BrE* also **live·able in** [not before noun]) (of a house, etc.) fit to live in SYN HABITABLE: *safer and more liveable residential areas* ◇ *The place looks liveable in.* **2** (of life) worth living SYN ENDURABLE **3** [not before noun] ~ **with** that can be dealt with: *The problem is paying the mortgage—everything else is liveable with.* **4** [only before noun] (of a wage, etc.) enough to live on: *a liveable salary/pension*

'lived-in *adj.* (of a place) that has been used so continuously for so long that it does not look new: (*approving*) *The room had a comfortable, lived-in feel about it.*

'live-in *adj.* **1** (of an employee) living in the house where they work: *a live-in nanny* **2** ~ **lover, boyfriend, girlfriend, etc.** a person who lives with their sexual partner but is not married to them

live·li·hood /ˈlaɪvlihʊd/ *noun* [C usually sing, U] a means of earning money in order to live: *Communities on the island depended on whaling for their livelihood.* ◇ *a means/source of livelihood*

live·ly /ˈlaɪvli/ *adj.* (**live·lier, live·li·est**) **1** full of life and energy, active and enthusiastic: *an intelligent and lively young woman* ◇ *a lively and enquiring mind* ◇ *He showed a lively interest in politics.* **2** (of a place, an event, etc.) full of interest or excitement: *a lively bar/resort/atmosphere* ◇ *a lively debate/discussion* **3** (of colours) strong and definite: *a lively shade of pink* **4** (*especially BrE*) busy and active: *They do a lively trade in souvenirs and gifts.*
▶ **live·li·ness** *noun* [U]

liven /ˈlaɪvn/ *verb* PHRV **liven 'up**, **liven sb/sth 'up** to become or to make sb/sth more interesting or exciting: *The game didn't liven up till the second half.* ◇ *Let's put some music on to liven things up.* ◇ *You look as if you need livening up!*

liver /ˈlɪvə(r)/ *noun* **1** [C] a large organ in the body that produces BILE and cleans the blood—picture at BODY **2** [U, C] the liver of some animals that is cooked and eaten: *liver and onions* ◇ *chicken livers*

liv·er·ied /ˈlɪvərid/ *adj.* **1** (*BrE*) painted in a LIVERY: *liveried aircraft* **2** wearing LIVERY: *liveried servants*

Liv·er·pud·lian /ˌlɪvəˈpʌdliən; *AmE* ˌlɪvərˈpʌd-/ *noun* a person from Liverpool in NW England ▶ **Liv·er·pud·lian** *adj.*

'liver sausage (*BrE*) (*AmE* **liv·er·wurst** /ˈlɪvəwɜːst; *AmE* ˈlɪvərwɜːrst/) *noun* [U] a type of soft sausage made from finely chopped LIVER, usually spread cold on bread

liv·ery /ˈlɪvəri/ *noun* [U, C] (*pl.* **-ies**) **1** (*BrE*) the colours in which the vehicles, aircraft, etc. of a particular company are painted **2** a special uniform worn by servants or officials, especially in the past

'livery stable *noun* a place where people can pay to keep their horses or can hire a horse

lives *pl.* of LIFE

live·stock /ˈlaɪvstɒk; *AmE* -stɑːk/ *noun* [U, pl.] the animals kept on a farm, for example cows or sheep

livid /ˈlɪvɪd/ *adj.* **1** extremely angry SYN FURIOUS: *Dad will be livid when he finds out.* **2** dark bluish-grey in colour: *a livid bruise*

liv·ing /ˈlɪvɪŋ/ *adj., noun*
■ *adj.* **1** alive now: *all living things* ◇ *living creatures/organisms/cells* ◇ *the finest living pianist* **2** [only before noun] used or practised now: *living languages* (= those still spoken) ◇ *a living faith* IDM **be living 'proof of sth/that ...** to show by your actions or qualities that a particular fact is true: *These figures are living proof of the government's incompetence.* ◇ *He is living proof that not all engineers are boring.* **within/in ,living 'memory** at a time, or during the time, that is remembered by people still alive: *the coldest winter in living memory*—more at DAYLIGHTS, IMAGE
■ *noun* **1** [C, usually sing.] money to buy the things that you need in life: *She earns her living as a freelance journalist.* ◇ *to make a good/decent/meagre living* ◇ *What do you do for a living?* ◇ *to scrape/scratch a living from part-time tutoring* **2** [U] a way or style of life: *daily/everyday living* ◇ *communal/family living* ◇ *healthy/plain living* ◇ *Their standard of living is very low.* ◇ *The cost of living has risen sharply.* ◇ *poor living conditions/standards* **3** (**the living**) [pl.] people who are alive now: *the living and the dead* **4** [C] (*BrE*) (especially in the past) a position in the Church as a priest and the income and house that go with this SYN BENEFICE IDM see LAND *n.*

,living 'death *noun* [sing.] a life that is worse than being dead

,living 'hell *noun* [sing.] a very unpleasant situation that causes a lot of suffering and lasts a long time

'living room (*BrE* also **'sitting room**) *noun* a room in a house where people sit together, watch television, etc.

,living 'wage *noun* [sing.] a wage that is high enough for sb to buy the things they need in order to live

,living 'will *noun* a document stating your wishes concerning medical treatment in the case that you become so ill that you can no longer make decisions about it, in particular asking doctors to stop treating you and let you die

liz·ard /ˈlɪzəd; *AmE* -ərd/ *noun* a small reptile with a rough skin, four short legs and a long tail

ll *abbr.* the abbreviation for 'lines', the plural form of 'l'

llama /ˈlɑːmə/ *noun* a S American animal kept for its soft wool or for carrying loads

lo /ləʊ; *AmE* loʊ/ *exclamation* (*old use* or *humorous*) used for calling attention to a surprising thing IDM **,lo and be'hold** (*humorous*) used for calling attention to a surprising or an annoying thing: *As soon as we went out, lo and behold, it began to rain.*

load /ləʊd; *AmE* loʊd/ *noun, verb*
■ *noun*
STH CARRIED | **1** [C] something that is being carried (usually in large amounts) by a person, vehicle, ship: *The trucks waited at the warehouse to pick up their loads.* ◇ *The women came down the hill with their loads of firewood.* ◇ *These backpacks are designed to carry a heavy load.* ◇ *A lorry shed its load* (= accidentally dropped its load) *on the motorway.* **2** [C] (often in compounds) the total amount of sth that sth can carry or contain: *a busload of tourists* ◇ *They ordered three truckloads of sand.* ◇ *He put half a load of washing in the machine.* ◇ *The plane took off with a full load.*
WEIGHT | **3** [C, usually sing.] the amount of weight that is pressing down on sth: *a load-bearing wall* ◇ *Modern backpacks spread the load over a wider area.*
LARGE AMOUNT | **4** [sing.] (*BrE* also **loads** [pl.]) ~ **(of sth)** (*informal*) a large number or amount of sb/sth; plenty: *She's got loads of friends.* ◇ *There's loads to do today.* ◇ *He wrote loads and loads of letters to people.* ◇ *Uncle Jim brought a whole load of presents for the kids.*
RUBBISH/NONSENSE | **5** [sing.] ~ **of rubbish, garbage, nonsense, etc.** (*spoken, especially BrE*) used to emphasize that sth is wrong, stupid, bad, etc: *You're talking a load of rubbish.*

æ	ɑː	e	ɜː	ə	ɪ	iː	i	ɒ	ɔː	ʌ	ʊ	u	uː
cat	father	ten	bird	about	sit	see	many	got	saw	cup	put	actual	too
								(BrE)					

WORK | **6** [C] an amount of work that a person or machine has to do: *Teaching loads have increased in all types of school.* ◇ *Extra warmth from sunlight can put an additional load on the air-conditioning system.*—see also CASE-LOAD, WORKLOAD

RESPONSIBILITY/WORRY | **7** [C, usually sing.] a feeling of responsibility or worry that is difficult to deal with: *She thought she would not be able to **bear the load** of bringing up her family alone.* ◇ *Knowing that they had arrived safely **took a load** off my mind.*

ELECTRICAL POWER | **8** [C] the amount of electrical power that is being supplied at a particular time

IDM **get a load of sb/sth** (*spoken*) used to tell sb to look at or listen to sb/sth: *Get a load of that dress!*
■ *verb*

GIVE/RECEIVE LOAD | **1** ~ (up)| ~ (up with sth)| ~ (up) (with sth)| ~ sth/sb (into/onto sth) to put a large quantity of sth onto or into sth: [VN] *We loaded the car in ten minutes.* ◇ *Can you help me load the dishwasher?* ◇ *Men were loading up a truck with timber.* ◇ *Sacks were being loaded onto the truck.* ◇ [V] *We finished loading and set off.* [OPP] UNLOAD **2** [V] to receive a load: *The ship was still loading.* [OPP] UNLOAD **3** [VN] ~ sb (up) (with sth)| ~ sth (onto sb) to give sb a lot of things, especially things they have to carry: *They loaded her with gifts.*

GUN/CAMERA | **4** ~ sth (into sth)| ~ sth (with sth) to put sth into a weapon, camera or other piece of equipment so that it can be used: [VN] *She loaded film into the camera.* ◇ *She loaded the camera with film.* ◇ *Is the gun loaded?* [also V] [OPP] UNLOAD

COMPUTING | **5** to put data or a program into the memory of a computer: [VN] *Have you loaded the software?* ◇ [V] *Wait for the game to load.*—compare DOWNLOAD

IDM **load the 'dice (against sb)** [usually passive] to put sb at a disadvantage: *He has always felt that the dice were loaded against him in life.* **PHRV** **,load sb/sth 'down (with sth)** [usually passive] to give sb/sth a lot of heavy things to carry: *She was loaded down with bags of groceries.*

load·ed /'ləʊdɪd; *AmE* 'loʊd-/ *adj.*

FULL | **1** ~ (with sth) carrying a load; full and heavy: *a fully loaded truck* ◇ *a truck loaded with supplies* ◇ *She came into the room carrying a loaded tray.* **2** ~ with sth (*informal*) full of a particular thing, quality or meaning: *cakes loaded with calories*

RICH | **3** [not before noun] (*informal*) very rich: *Let her pay—she's loaded.*

ADVANTAGE/DISADVANTAGE | **4** ~ in favour of sb/sth| ~ against sb/sth acting either as an advantage or a disadvantage to sb/sth in a way that is unfair: *a system that is loaded in favour of the young* (= gives them an advantage)

WORD/STATEMENT | **5** having more meaning than you realize at first and intended to make you think in a particular way: *It was a **loaded question** and I preferred not to comment.*

GUN/CAMERA | **6** containing bullets, film, etc: *a loaded shotgun*

DRUNK | **7** (*informal, especially AmE*) very drunk

load·star *noun* = LODESTAR

load·stone *noun* = LODESTONE

loaf /ləʊf; *AmE* loʊf/ *noun, verb*
■ *noun* (*pl.* **loaves** /ləʊvz; *AmE* loʊvz/) an amount of bread that has been shaped and baked in one piece: *a loaf of bread* ◇ *Two white loaves, please.* ◇ *a sliced loaf*—see also FRENCH LOAF—picture on page A5 **IDM** see USE *v.*
■ *verb* [V] ~ (about/around) (*informal*) to spend your time not doing anything, especially when you should be working: *A group of kids were loafing around outside.*

loaf·er /'ləʊfə(r); *AmE* 'loʊf-/ *noun* **1** a person who wastes their time rather than working **2** (**Loafer**™) a flat leather shoe that you can put on your foot without fastening it—picture at SHOE

loam /ləʊm; *AmE* loʊm/ *noun* [U] (*technical*) good quality soil containing sand, clay and decayed vegetable matter ▶ **loamy** *adj.*

loan /ləʊn; *AmE* loʊn/ *noun, verb*

■ *noun* **1** [C] money that an organization such as a bank lends and sb borrows: *to **take out**/**repay a loan*** (= to borrow money/pay it back) ◇ *bank loans with low interest rates* ◇ *It took three years to repay my **student loan*** (= money lent to a student). ◇ *a car loan* (= a loan to buy a car) **2** [sing.] ~ (of sth) the act of lending sth; the state of being lent: *I even gave her the loan of my car.* ◇ *an exhibition of paintings **on loan*** (= borrowed) *from private collections*

■ *verb* **1** ~ sth (to sb)| ~ (sb) sth (*especially AmE*) to lend sth to sb, especially money: [VN] *The bank is happy to loan money to small businesses.* ◇ [VNN] *A friend loaned me $1000.* **2** ~ sth (out) (to sb/sth)| ~ (sb) sth (*especially BrE*) to lend a valuable object to a museum, etc: [VN] *This exhibit was kindly loaned by the artist's family.* ◇ [VNN] *He loaned the museum his entire collection.*

'loan shark *noun* (*disapproving*) a person who lends money at very high rates of interest

loath (*also less frequent* **loth**) /ləʊθ; *AmE* loʊθ/ *adj.* ~ to do sth (*formal*) not willing to do sth: *He was loath to admit his mistake.*

loathe /ləʊð; *AmE* loʊð/ *verb* (not used in the progressive tenses) to dislike sb/sth very much: [VN] *I loathe modern art.* ◇ *They loathe each other.* [also V -ing]

loath·ing /'ləʊðɪŋ; *AmE* 'loʊð-/ *noun* [sing., U] ~ (for/of sb/sth) (*formal*) a strong feeling of hatred: *She looked at her attacker with **fear and loathing**.* ◇ *Many soldiers returned with a **deep loathing** of war.*

loath·some /'ləʊðsəm; *AmE* 'loʊð-/ *adj.* (*formal*) extremely unpleasant; disgusting

loaves *pl.* of LOAF

lob /lɒb; *AmE* lɑːb/ *verb* (-bb-) ~ **1** [+adv./prep.] (*informal*) to throw sth so that it goes quite high through the air: *Stones were lobbed over the wall.* **2** (*sport*) to hit or kick a ball in a high curve through the air, especially so that it lands behind the person you are playing against: *He lobbed the ball over the defender's head.* ▶ **lob** *noun*: *to play a lob*

lobby /'lɒbi; *AmE* 'lɑːbi/ *noun, verb*
■ *noun* (*pl.* **-ies**) **1** [C] a large area inside the entrance of a public building where people can meet and wait [SYN] FOYER: *a hotel lobby* **2** [C] (in the British Parliament) a large hall that is open to the public and used for people to meet and talk to Members of Parliament **3** [C+sing./pl. *v.*] a group of people who try to influence politicians on a particular issue: *The gun lobby is/are against any change in the law.*
■ *verb* (**lob·bies**, **lobby·ing**, **lob·bied**, **lob·bied**) ~ (sb) (for/against sth) to try to influence a politician or the government and, for example, persuade them to support or oppose a change in the law: [VN] *Farmers will lobby Congress for higher subsidies.* ◇ [V] *Women's groups are lobbying to get more public money for children.* ▶ **lobby·ist** /-ɪst/ *noun*: *political lobbyists*

lobe /ləʊb; *AmE* loʊb/ *noun* **1** = EAR LOBE **2** a part of an organ in the body, especially the lungs or brain

lo·belia /ləʊ'biːliə; *AmE* loʊ-/ *noun* [C, U] a small garden plant with small blue, red or white flowers

lob·ot·omy /ləʊ'bɒtəmi; lə-; *AmE* loʊ'bɑːt-/ *noun* (*pl.* **-ies**) a rare medical operation that cuts into part of a person's brain in order to treat mental illness

lob·ster /'lɒbstə(r); *AmE* 'lɑːb-/ *noun* **1** [C] a sea creature with a hard shell, a long body divided into sections, eight legs and two large CLAWS (= curved and pointed limbs for catching and holding things). Its shell is black but turns bright red when it is boiled. **2** [U] meat from a lobster, used for food

'lobster pot *noun* a trap for lobsters that is shaped like a basket

local /'ləʊkl; *AmE* 'loʊkl/ *adj., noun*
■ *adj.* [usually before noun] **1** belonging to or connected with the particular place or area that you are talking about or with the place where you live: *a local farmer/hairdresser* ◇ *A local man was accused of the murder.* ◇ *Our children go to the local school.* ◇ *a local newspaper* (= one that gives local news) ◇ *local radio* (= a radio station that broadcasts to one area only) ◇ *decisions made*

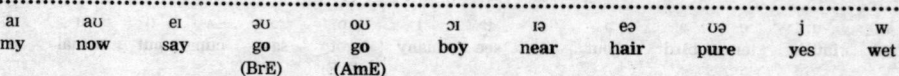

aɪ	aʊ	eɪ	əʊ	oʊ	ɔɪ	ɪə	eə	ʊə	j	w
my	now	say	go	go	boy	near	hair	pure	yes	wet
			(BrE)	(AmE)						

at local rather than national level ◊ *It was difficult to understand the way the local dialect.* **2** affecting only one part of the body: *Her tooth was extracted under local anaesthetic.* ▶ **lo·cal·ly** /-kəli/ *adv.*: *to advertise/shop/work locally* ◊ *Do you live locally* (= in this area)? ◊ *locally grown fruit*
■ *noun* **1** [usually pl.] a person who lives in a particular place or district: *The locals are very friendly.* **2** (*BrE, informal*) a pub near where you live: *I called in at my local on the way home.* **3** (*AmE*) a branch of a trade union **4** (*AmE*) a bus or train that stops at all places on the route

ˌlocal ˌarea ˈnetwork *noun* = LAN

ˌlocal auˈthority *noun* (*pl.* **-ies**) (*BrE*) the group of people which is responsible for the government of an area in Britain

ˈlocal call *noun* a telephone call to a place that is near

ˌlocal ˈcolour (*BrE*) (*AmE* **ˌlocal ˈcolor**) *noun* [U] the typical things, customs, etc. in a place that make it interesting, and that are used in a picture, story or film/movie to make it seem real

lo·cale /ləʊˈkɑːl; *AmE* loʊˈkæl/ *noun* (*formal* or *technical*) a place where sth happens: *the employment structure of the two locales*

ˌlocal ˈgovernment *noun* **1** [U] (*especially BrE*) the system of government of a town or an area by elected representatives of the people who live there **2** [C] (*AmE*) the organization that is responsible for the government of a local area and for providing services, etc: *state and local governments*

lo·cal·ity /ləʊˈkæləti; *AmE* loʊ-/ *noun* (*pl.* **-ies**) (*formal*) **1** the area that surrounds the place you are in or are talking about: *people living in the locality of the power station* ◊ *There is no airport in the locality.* **2** the place where sb/sth exists: *We talk of the brain as the locality of thought.* ◊ *The birds are found in over 70 different localities.*

lo·cal·ize (*BrE* also **-ise**) /ˈləʊkəlaɪz; *AmE* ˈloʊ-/ *verb* [VN] **1** to limit sth or its effects to a particular area **2** (*formal*) to find out where sth is: *animals' ability to localize sounds* ▶ **lo·cal·iza·tion**, **-isa·tion** /ˌləʊkəlaɪˈzeɪʃn; *AmE* ˌloʊkələˈz-/ *noun* [U]

lo·cal·ized (*BrE* also **-ised**) /ˈləʊkəlaɪzd/ *adj.* (*formal*) happening within one small area: *a localized infection* (= in one part of the body) ◊ *localized fighting*

ˈlocal time *noun* [U] the time of day in the particular part of the world that you are talking about: *We reach Delhi at 2 o'clock local time.*

lo·cate /ləʊˈkeɪt; *AmE* ˈloʊkeɪt/ *verb* **1** [VN] to find the exact position of sb/sth: *The mechanic located the fault immediately.* ◊ *Rescue planes are trying to locate the missing sailors.* **2** [VN] to put or build sth in a particular place: *They located their headquarters in Swindon.*—compare RELOCATE **3** [V +*adv./prep.*] (*especially AmE*) to start a business in a particular place: *There are tax breaks for businesses that locate in rural areas.*

lo·cated /ləʊˈkeɪtɪd; *AmE* ˈloʊkeɪt-/ *adj.* [not before noun] (*written*) if sth is **located** in a particular place, it exists there or has been put there SYN SITUATED: *a small town located 30 miles south of Chicago* ◊ *The offices are conveniently located just a few minutes from the main station.*

lo·ca·tion /ləʊˈkeɪʃn; *AmE* loʊ-/ *noun* **1** [C] a place where sth happens or exists; the position of sth: *a honeymoon to a secret location* ◊ *What is the exact location of the ship?* **2** [C, U] a place outside a film STUDIO where scenes of a film/movie are made: *A mountain in the Rockies became the location for a film about Everest.* ◊ *The movie was shot entirely on location in Italy.* **3** [U] the act of finding the position of sb/sth

loch /lɒk; lɒx; *AmE* lɑːk; lɑːx/ *noun* (in Scotland) a lake or a narrow strip of sea almost surrounded by land—see also LOUGH

loci *pl.* of LOCUS

lock /lɒk; *AmE* lɑːk/ *verb, noun*
■ *verb* **1** to fasten sth with a lock; to be fastened with a lock: [VN] *Did you lock the door?* ◊ [V] *This suitcase doesn't lock.* **2** [VN +*adv./prep.*] to put sth in a safe place and lock it:

She locked her passport and money in the safe. **3** ~ (sth) (in/into/around, etc. sth) | ~ (sth) (together) to become or make sth become fixed in one position and unable to move: [V] *The brakes locked and the car skidded.* ◊ [VN] *He locked his helmet into position with a click.* **4** [VN] (be locked in/into sth) to be involved in a difficult situation, an argument, a disagreement, etc: *The two sides are locked into a bitter dispute.* ◊ *She felt locked in a loveless marriage.* **5** [VN] (be locked together/in sth) to be held very tightly by sb: *They were locked in a passionate embrace.* **IDM** ˌlock ˈhorns (with sb) (over sth) to get involved in an argument or a dispute with sb: *The company has locked horns with the unions over proposed pay cuts.* **PHRV** ˌlock sb/sth aˈway = LOCK SB/STH UP ˌlock sb/yourself ˈin (…) to prevent sb from leaving a place by locking the door: *At 9 p.m. the prisoners are locked in for the night.* ˌlock ˈonto sth (of a MISSILE, etc.) to find the thing that is being attacked and follow it ˌlock sb/yourself ˈout (of sth) to prevent sb from entering a place by locking the door: *I'd locked myself out of the house and had to break a window to get in.* ˌlock sb ˈout (of an employer) to refuse to allow workers into their place of work until they agree to particular conditions—related noun LOCKOUT ˌlock ˈup|ˌlock sth↔ˈup to make a building safe by locking the doors and windows: *Don't forget to lock up at night.* ◊ *He locked up the shop and went home.* ˌlock sth↔ˈup/aˈway **1** to put sth in a safe place that can be locked **2** to put money into an INVESTMENT that you cannot easily turn into cash: *Their capital is all locked up in property.* ˌlock sb↔ˈup/aˈway (*informal*) to put sb in prison—related noun LOCK-UP
■ *noun* **1** [C] a device that keeps a door window, lid, etc. shut, usually needing a key to open it: *She turned the key in the lock.*—see also COMBINATION LOCK **2** [C] a device with a key that prevents a vehicle or machine from being used: *a bicycle lock* ◊ *a steering lock*—picture at BICYCLE **3** [U] a state in which the parts of a machine, etc. do not move **4** [U, sing.] (*BrE*) (on a car, etc.) the amount that the front wheels can be turned in one direction or the other in order to turn the vehicle: *I had the steering wheel on full lock* (= I had turned it as far as it would turn). **5** [C] a section of canal or river with a gate at either end, in which the water level can be raised or lowered so that boats can move from one level of the canal or river to another **6** [C] a few hairs that hang or lie together on your head: *John brushed a lock of hair from his eyes.* **7** (**locks**) [pl.] (*literary*) a person's hair: *She shook her long, flowing locks.* **8** [C] (in rugby) a player in the second row of the SCRUM **9** [sing.] **a ~ (on sth)** (*AmE*) total control of sth: *One company had a virtual lock on all orange juice sales in the state.*—see also ARMLOCK, HEADLOCK **IDM** ˌlock, stock and ˈbarrel including everything: *He sold the business lock, stock and barrel.* (**keep sth/put sth/be) under ˌlock and ˈkey** locked up safely somewhere; in prison: *We keep our valuables under lock and key.* ◊ *I will not rest until the murderer is under lock and key.*—more at PICK v.

lock·able /ˈlɒkəbl; *AmE* ˈlɑːk-/ *adj.* that you can lock with a key

lock·er /ˈlɒkə(r); *AmE* ˈlɑːk-/ *noun* a small cupboard that can be locked, where you can leave your clothes, bags, etc. while you play a sport or go somewhere

ˈlocker room *noun* (*especially AmE*) a room with lockers in it, at a school, GYM, etc., where people can change their clothes—compare CHANGING ROOM

locket /ˈlɒkɪt; *AmE* ˈlɑːk-/ *noun* a piece of jewellery in the form of a small case that you wear on a chain around your neck and in which you can put a picture, piece of hair, etc.—picture at JEWELLERY

lock·jaw /ˈlɒkdʒɔː; *AmE* ˈlɑːk-/ *noun* [U] (*old-fashioned, informal*) a form of the disease TETANUS in which the jaws become stiff and closed

ˈlock-keeper *noun* a person who is in charge of a lock on a canal or river, and opens and closes the gates

lock·out /ˈlɒkaʊt; *AmE* ˈlɑːk-/ *noun* a situation when an employer refuses to allow workers into their place of work until they agree to various conditions

b	d	f	g	h	k	l	m	n	p	r
bad	**did**	**fall**	**get**	**hat**	**cat**	**leg**	**man**	**now**	**pen**	**red**

lock·smith /ˈlɒksmɪθ; AmE ˈlɑːk-/ noun a person whose job is making, fitting and repairing locks

'lock-up noun **1** a small prison where prisoners are kept for a short time **2** (BrE) a small shop that the owner does not live in; a GARAGE that is usually separate from other buildings and that is rented to sb ▸ **'lock-up** adj. [only before noun]: a lock-up garage/shop/warehouse

loco /ˈləʊkəʊ; AmE ˈloʊkoʊ/ noun, adj.
■ noun (pl. -os) (informal) = LOCOMOTIVE—see also IN LOCO PARENTIS
■ adj. [not before noun] (slang, especially AmE) crazy

loco·mo·tion /ˌləʊkəˈməʊʃn; AmE ˌloʊkəˈmoʊʃn/ noun [U] (formal) movement or the ability to move

loco·mo·tive /ˌləʊkəˈməʊtɪv; AmE ˌloʊkəˈmoʊ-/ (also informal **loco**) noun, adj.
■ noun a railway engine that pulls a train: steam/diesel/electric locomotives = ENGINE
■ adj. (formal) connected with movement

locum /ˈləʊkəm; AmE ˈloʊ-/ noun a doctor or priest who does the work of another doctor or priest while they are ill, on holiday, etc.

locus /ˈləʊkəs; AmE ˈloʊ-/ noun (pl. **loci** /ˈləʊsaɪ; AmE ˈloʊ-/) (formal or technical) the exact place where sth happens or which is thought to be the centre of sth: the external locus of control

lo·cust /ˈləʊkəst; AmE ˈloʊ-/ noun a large insect that lives in hot countries and flies in large groups, destroying all the plants and crops of an area: a swarm of locusts

lo·cu·tion /ləˈkjuːʃn/ noun (technical) **1** [U] a style of speaking **2** [C] a particular phrase, especially one used by a particular group of people

lode /ləʊd; AmE loʊd/ noun a line of ORE (= metal in the ground or in rocks)

lode·star (also **load·star**) /ˈləʊdstɑː(r); AmE ˈloʊd-/ noun **1** the POLE STAR (= a star that is used by sailors to guide a ship) **2** (formal) a principle that guides sb's behaviour or actions

lode·stone (also **load·stone**) /ˈləʊdstəʊn; AmE ˈloʊd-stoʊn/ noun a piece of iron that acts as a MAGNET

lodge /lɒdʒ; AmE lɑːdʒ/ noun, verb
■ noun **1** [C] a small house in the country where people stay when they want to take part in some types of outdoor sport: a hunting/shooting/ski lodge **2** [C] a small house at the gates of a park or in the land belonging to a large house **3** [C] a room at the main entrance to a building for the person whose job is to see who enters and leaves the building: All visitors should report to the porter's lodge. **4** [C+sing./pl. v.] the members of a branch of a society such as the Freemasons; the building where they meet: a masonic lodge **5** [C] the home of a BEAVER or an OTTER **6** [C] a Native American's tent or home built of LOGS
■ verb **1** [VN] ~ (sth) (with sb) (against sb/sth) to make a formal statement about sth to a public organization or authority: They lodged a compensation claim against the factory. ◇ Portugal has lodged a complaint with the International Court of Justice. **2** [V+adv./prep.] (old-fashioned) to pay to live in a room in sb's house: He lodged with Mrs Brown when he arrived in the city. **3** [VN] to provide sb with a place to sleep or live: The refugees are being lodged at an old army base. **4** ~ (sth) in sth to become fixed or stuck somewhere; to make sth become fixed or stuck somewhere: [V] One of the bullets lodged in his chest. ◇ [VN] She lodged the number firmly in her mind. **5** [VN] ~ sth with sb/in sth to leave money or sth valuable in a safe place: Your will should be lodged with your lawyer.

lodg·er /ˈlɒdʒə(r); AmE ˈlɑːdʒ-/ noun (especially BrE) a person who pays rent to live in sb's house

lodg·ing /ˈlɒdʒɪŋ; AmE ˈlɑːdʒ-/ noun (especially BrE) **1** [U] temporary accommodation: full board and lodging (= a room to stay in and all meals provided) **2** [C, usually pl.] (old-fashioned) a room or rooms in sb else's house that you rent to live in: It was cheaper to live in lodgings than in a hotel.

'lodging house noun (old-fashioned, BrE) a house in which lodgings can be rented

loft /lɒft; AmE lɔːft/ noun, verb

■ noun **1** (especially BrE) a space just below the roof of a house, often used for storing things and sometimes made into a room: a **loft conversion** (= one that has been made into a room or rooms for living in)—compare ATTIC, GARRET **2** an upper level in a church, or a farm or factory building: the organ loft **3** a flat/apartment in a former factory, etc., that has been made suitable for living in: They lived in a SoHo loft. **4** (AmE) a part of a room that is on a higher level than the rest: The children slept in a loft in the upstairs bedroom.
■ verb [VN] (sport) to hit, kick or throw a ball very high into the air

lofty /ˈlɒfti; AmE ˈlɔːfti/ adj. (**loft·ier**, **lofti·est**) (formal) **1** (of buildings, mountains, etc.) very high and impressive: lofty ceilings/rooms/towers **2** [usually before noun] (approving) (of a thought, an aim, etc.) deserving praise because of its high moral quality: lofty ambitions/ideals/principles **3** (disapproving) showing a belief that you are worth more than other people: her lofty disdain for other people ▸ **loft·ily** /-ɪli/ adv. **lofti·ness** noun [U]

log /lɒg; AmE lɔːg; lɑːg/ noun, verb
■ noun **1** a thick piece of wood that is cut from or has fallen from a tree: logs for the fire **2** (also **log·book**) an official record of events during a particular period of time, especially a journey on a ship or plane: The captain keeps a log. ◇ (computing) to open a log file **3** (informal) = LOGARITHM IDM see EASY adj., SLEEP v.
■ verb (-gg-) [VN] **1** to put information in an official record or write a record of events SYN RECORD: The police log all phone calls. **2** to travel a particular distance or for a particular length of time: The pilot has logged 1000 hours in the air. **3** to cut down trees in a forest for their wood PHRV **,log 'in/'on** (computing) to perform the actions that allow you to begin using a computer system: You need a password to log on. **,log 'off/'out** (computing) to perform the actions that allow you to finish using a computer system

-log (AmE) = -LOGUE

lo·gan·berry /ˈləʊgənbəri; AmE ˈloʊgənberi/ noun (pl. -ies) a soft dark red fruit, like a large RASPBERRY, that grows on a bush

loga·rithm /ˈlɒgərɪðəm; AmE ˈlɔːg-; ˈlɑːg-/ (also informal **log**) noun (mathematics) any of a series of numbers set out in lists which make it possible to work out problems by adding and SUBTRACTING instead of multiplying and dividing ▸ **loga·rith·mic** /ˌlɒgəˈrɪðmɪk; AmE ˌlɔːg-; ˌlɑːg-/ adj.

log·book /ˈlɒgbʊk; AmE ˈlɔːg-; ˈlɑːg-/ noun **1** (BrE, becoming old-fashioned) a document that records official details about a vehicle, especially a car, and its owner—compare REGISTRATION **2** = LOG (2)

,log 'cabin noun a small house built of logs

log·ger /ˈlɒgə(r); AmE ˈlɔːg-/ noun = LUMBERJACK

log·ger·heads /ˈlɒgəhedz; AmE ˈlɔːg-gər-; ˈlɑːg-/ noun IDM **at loggerheads (with sb) (over sth)** in strong disagreement: The two governments are still at loggerheads over the island.

log·gia /ˈləʊdʒə; ˈlɒdʒiə; AmE ˈloʊdʒə; ˈlɑːdʒiə/ noun (BrE) a room or GALLERY with one or more open sides, especially one that forms part of a house and has one side open to the garden

log·ging /ˈlɒgɪŋ; AmE ˈlɔːg-; ˈlɑːg-/ noun [U] the work of cutting down trees for their wood: illegal logging

logic /ˈlɒdʒɪk; AmE ˈlɑːdʒɪk/ noun **1** [U] a way of thinking or explaining sth: I fail to see the logic behind his argument. ◇ The two parts of the plan were governed by the same logic. **2** [U, sing.] sensible reasons for doing sth: Linking the proposals in a single package did have a certain logic. ◇ a strategy based on sound commercial logic ◇ There is **no logic to/in** any of their claims. **3** [U] (philosophy) the science of thinking about or explaining the reason for sth using formal methods: the rules of logic **4** [U] (computing) a system or set of principles used in preparing a computer to perform a particular task

lo·gic·al /ˈlɒdʒɪkl; AmE ˈlɑːdʒ-/ adj. **1** (of an action, event, etc.) seeming natural, reasonable or sensible: a logical thing to do in the circumstances ◇ It was a logical conclu-

Study pages

Linking words together

Words used with prepositions and adverbs

■ Many verbs, nouns and adjectives are followed by a particular preposition:

*She is a very active person with a great **zest for** life.*
*I felt **nervous about** meeting him.*

> The correct preposition to use is shown in **bold type** before the definition.

> Where the preposition is optional, it is given in brackets.

ner·vous /'nɜːvəs; AmE 'nɜːrvəs/ adj. **1** ~ **(about/of sth)** anxious about sth or afraid of sth: *Consumers are very nervous about the future.* ◇ *He had been nervous about inviting us.* ◇ *The horse may be nervous of cars.* ◇ *I felt really nervous before the interview.* ◇ *a nervous glance/smile/voice* (= one that shows that you feel anxious) ◇ *By the time the police arrived, I was a nervous wreck.* OPP CONFIDENT

> The example sentences show the prepositions in use.

■ Sometimes, instead of a preposition, a verb will be followed by a particular adverb:

*We **lazed around** by the pool all day.*
*The paintwork was dirty and **peeling off** in places.*

These adverbs are shown in the same way as the prepositions:

peel /piːl/ verb, noun
■ verb **1** [VN] to take the skin off fruit, vegetables, etc: *to peel an orange/a banana* ◇ *Have you peeled the potatoes?*—picture on page A2 **2** ~ **(sth) away/off/back** to remove a layer, covering, etc. from the surface of sth; to come off the surface of sth: [VN] *Carefully peel away the lining paper.* ◇ [V] *The label will peel off if you soak it in water.*

■ Some verbs change their meaning when they are used with a particular preposition or adverb. These verb + preposition/adverb combinations are considered to be a special type of verb called a PHRASAL VERB. Common phrasal verbs include **care for sb** and **hold sb/sth up**:

*She **cares for** her elderly mother.*
*Traffic **was held up** for over two hours.*

■ Phrasal verbs are treated separately in the dictionary. For more information about them see study pages **B10–11**.

Words used with phrases and clauses

■ Very often, a verb, a noun or an adjective will be followed by a whole phrase or clause that includes another verb. This verb may be in its infinitive (**to-**) form or its **-ing** form, or it may follow a word like **that, what, how,** etc:

*I was all packed and **ready to leave**.*
*I'd appreciate your **cooperation in clearing** the hall.*
*It was **obvious that** he was not well.*

> The structures that you can use are shown in **bold type** before the definition.

> Structures or parts of structures that are optional are given in brackets.

ob·vi·ous /'ɒbviəs; AmE 'ɑːb-/ adj. **1** ~ **(to sb) (that...)** easy to see or understand: *It was obvious to everyone that the child had been badly treated.* ◇ *It's obvious from what she said that something is wrong.* ◇ *I know you don't like her but try not to make it so obvious.* ◇ *with obvious annoyance/distress/pleasure* ◇ ***For obvious reasons**, I'd prefer not to give my name.* ◇ *The reasons for this decision were **not immediately obvious**.*

> The example sentences show the structures in use.

■ Not all of the patterns in which verbs are used can be shown at the beginning of the entry. In order to give fuller information about verb patterns a system of verb pattern codes is used with the examples at verb entries. These codes are explained on study pages **B6–9**.

Nouns used together

■ Sometimes a noun is used like an adjective before another noun:

the chair back (= the back of the chair)
a family business (= a business belonging to one family)
garden flowers (= flowers grown in a garden)

■ The first noun is nearly always singular in form, even if it normally takes a plural form:

a pyjama jacket
a billiard ball

■ But a few plural nouns do keep their plural form when used in this way:

a clothes peg
a glasses case

■ Where a noun is often used in this way, examples are given at the dictionary entry.

Collocation

What is collocation?

■ COLLOCATION is the way in which particular words tend to occur or belong together. For example, you can say:
Meals will be served outside on the terrace, **weather permitting**.
but not ~~Meals will be served outside on the terrace, **weather allowing**~~.

■ Both these sentences seem to mean the same thing ('They'll bring us our meals outside if the weather is good enough.'): **allow** and **permit** have very similar meanings. But in this combination only **permitting** is correct. It COLLOCATES with **weather** and **allowing** does not.

Types of collocation

■ In order to write and speak natural and correct English, you need to know, for example, which adjectives are used with a particular noun:
Can you say '**pink** wine'?

which nouns a particular adjective is used with:
Which words can be used with the adjective **heady**?

which verbs are used with a particular noun:
A **mortgage** is a sum of money that you borrow to buy a house, but which verbs are used with **mortgage**?

which adverbs are used to intensify a particular adjective:
Would you be **strongly** or **bitterly** disappointed about something?

Collocation in this dictionary

■ To find out which adjectives to use with a particular noun, look at the examples at the entry for the noun. Typical adjectives used with the noun are separated by a slash (/):

pink wine?

wine /waɪn/ *noun, verb*
■ *noun* **1** [U, C] an alcoholic drink made from the juice of grapes that has been left to FERMENT. There are many different kinds of wine: *a bottle of wine ◇ a glass of dry/sweet wine ◇ red/rosé/white wine ◇ dessert/sparkling wine* **2** [U, C] an alcoholic drink made from plants or fruits other than grapes: *elderberry/rice wine* **3** [U] (also **wine ˈred**) a dark red colour: *a wine velvet jacket*

(No, rosé)

■ If you look up an adjective you will see what nouns are commonly used with it:

heady what?

heady /ˈhedi/ *adj.* (**head·ier**, **headi·est**) **1** [usually before noun] having a strong effect on your senses; making you feel excited and hopeful: *the heady days of youth ◇ the heady scent of hot spices ◇ a heady mixture of desire and fear ◇ House-buying is like drinking wine—it can be heady stuff.*

(days, scent, mixture, stuff)

■ Look at the examples in a noun entry to find out what verbs can be used with it:

verbs with **mortgage**?

mort·gage /ˈmɔːɡɪdʒ; *AmE* ˈmɔːrɡ-/ *noun, verb*
■ *noun* (also *informal* ˌhome ˈloan) a legal agreement by which a bank or similar organization lends you money to buy a house, etc., and you pay the money back over a particular number of years; the sum of money that you borrow: *to apply for/take out/pay off a mortgage ◇ mortgage rates (= of interest) ◇ a mortgage on the house ◇ a mortgage of £60 000 ◇ monthly mortgage repayments*

(apply for, take out, pay off)

■ If you look up an adjective, you will see which adverbs you can use to intensify it:

strongly or bitterly disappointed?

dis·ap·point·ed /ˌdɪsəˈpɔɪntɪd/ *adj.* ~ (**at/by sth**)| ~ (**in/with sb/sth**)| ~ (**to see, hear, etc.**)| ~ (**that … **)| ~ (**not**) **to be …** upset because sth you hoped for has not happened or been as good, successful, etc. as you expected: *They were **bitterly disappointed** at the result of the game. ◇ I was disappointed by the quality of the wine. ◇ I'm disappointed in you—I really thought I could trust you! ◇ I was very disappointed with myself. ◇ He was disappointed to see she wasn't at the party. ◇ I'm disappointed (that) it was sold out.*

(bitterly)

■ Important collocations are printed in **bold type** within the examples. If the meaning of the collocation is not obvious there is a short explanation after it in brackets.

hoping someone else will be lucky

hoping you will be lucky

luck /lʌk/ *noun, verb*
■ *noun* [U] **1** good things that happen to you by chance, not because of your own efforts or abilities: **With (any) luck**, *we'll be home before dark.* ◇ (*BrE*) **With a bit of luck**, *we'll finish on time.* ◇ *So far I have had no luck with finding a job.* ◇ *I could hardly believe my luck when he said yes.* ◇ *It was **a stroke of luck** that we found you.* ◇ *By **sheer luck** nobody was hurt in the explosion.* ◇ *We **wish her luck** in her new career.* ◇ *You're **in luck** (= lucky)—there's one ticket left.* ◇ *You're **out of luck**. She's not here.* ◇ *What a piece of*

being lucky

not being lucky

having unexpected luck

Nouns and adjectives

Nouns

- You say **too much sugar** but **too many chairs**.

  Nouns are of different types according to whether they have both a singular and a plural form, whether they must be used with a DETERMINER such as:

  a   both   each   the

  and whether a verb should be singular or plural in order to agree with the noun.

Countable and uncountable

- The two biggest groups of nouns are COUNTABLE NOUNS (or COUNT nouns) and UNCOUNTABLE NOUNS (also called UNCOUNT nouns or MASS nouns). Most countable nouns are words for separate things that can be counted, like **apples**, **books** or **teachers**. Uncountable nouns are usually words for things that are thought of as a quantity or mass, like **water** or **time**.

- However, there are some nouns in English that you might expect to be countable but which are not. For example, **furniture**, **information** and **equipment** are all uncountable nouns in English, although they are countable in some other languages.

Countable nouns [C]

- A countable noun has a singular form and a plural form. When it is singular, it must always have a determiner in front of it. In the plural it can be used with or without a determiner:

  *I'm having **a** driving **lesson** this afternoon.*
  *She's learning to play golf – she's had **several lessons** already.*
  ***Lessons** cost £20 an hour.*

- Countable nouns are the most common type of noun. If they have only one meaning, or if all the meanings are countable, they are just marked *noun*. For nouns that have a number of meanings, some of which are not countable, each meaning that is countable is marked [C].

Uncountable nouns [U]

- An uncountable noun has only one form, not a separate singular and plural. It can be used with or without a determiner:

  *Can we make **space** for an extra chair?*
  *There isn't **much space** in this room.*

- If an uncountable noun is the subject of a verb, the verb is singular:

  *Extra **money has been found** for this project.*
  ***Sadness is** not the same as depression.*

- With nouns such as **furniture**, **information** and **equipment**, as with many other uncountable nouns, you can talk about amounts of the thing or separate parts of the thing by using phrases like **a piece of**, **three items of**, **some bits of**. Nouns like **piece**, **item** and **bit** are called PARTITIVES when used in this way:

  *I picked up **some information** that might interest you.*
  *I picked up **two pieces of information** that might interest you.*

Plural nouns [pl.]

- Some nouns are always plural and have no singular form. Nouns that refer to things that have two parts joined together, for example **glasses**, **jeans** and **scissors** are plural nouns. You can usually also talk about **a pair of jeans**, **a pair of scissors**, etc.

  *I'm going to buy **some** new **jeans**.*
  *I'm going to buy **a** new **pair of jeans**.*

  An example is given in the entry for the noun to show that it can be used in this way.

- Some plural nouns, such as **police** and **cattle**, look as if they are singular. Nouns like this usually refer to a group of people or animals of a particular type, when they are considered together as one unit. They also take a plural verb:

  ***Police are searching** for a man who escaped from Pentonville prison today.*
  *The **cattle are fed** on barley and grass.*

Singular nouns [sing.]

- Some nouns are always singular and have no plural form. Many nouns like this can be used in only a limited number of ways. For example, some singular nouns must be or are often used with a particular determiner in front of them or with a particular preposition after them. The correct determiner or preposition is shown before the definition. In the case of **fillip** the pattern given is
  a ~ (to/for sth):

---

fil·lip /ˈfɪlɪp/ *noun* [sing.] **a ~ (to/for sth)** (*formal*) a thing or person that causes sth to improve suddenly **SYN** BOOST: *A drop in interest rates gave a welcome fillip to the housing market.*

Nouns + singular or plural verbs

[sing.+sing./pl. *v.*] [C+sing./pl. *v.*]

■ In British English some singular nouns (or countable nouns in their singular form) can be used with a plural verb as well as a singular one. Nouns like this usually refer to a group of people, an organization or a place and can be thought of either as the organization, place or group (singular) or as many individual people (plural). In the dictionary an example is usually given to show agreement with a singular and a plural verb:

The **Vatican has/have issued** a further statement this morning.
The **committee has/have decided** to dismiss him.

■ These nouns are marked [sing.+sing./pl. *v.*] if they are always singular in form and [C+sing./pl. *v.*] if they also have a plural form. The plural form always agrees with a plural verb.

■ In American English the singular form of these nouns must take a singular verb:

The government **says it is** committed to tax reform.

[U + sing./pl. *v.*]

■ Some uncountable nouns can be used with a plural verb as well as a singular one. These include some nouns that end in 's' and therefore look as though they are plural:

His **whereabouts are/is** still unknown.

and some nouns that refer to a group of people or things and can be thought of either as a group (singular) or as many individual people or things (plural):

Personnel is/are currently reviewing pay scales.

Adjectives

■ Many adjectives can be used both before a noun:

a serious expression
grey hair

and after a linking verb, for example **be**, **become**, **seem**, **turn**:

She looked serious.
His hair had turned grey.

[only before noun]
[usually before noun]

■ Some adjectives, or particular meanings of adjectives, are always used before a noun, and cannot be used after a linking verb. These are labelled [only before noun]. The label [usually before noun] is used when it is rare but possible to use the adjective after a verb.

> Senses **1** and **3** can only be used before a noun.

sunk·en /'sʌŋkən/ *adj.* **1** [only before noun] that has fallen to the bottom of the sea, or the ocean, or of a lake or river: *a sunken ship* ◊ *sunken treasure.* **2** (of eyes or cheeks) hollow and falling inwards as a result of disease, hunger or age: *His eyes were dark and sunken.* **3** [only before noun] at a lower level than the area around: *a sunken bath / garden*

> Sense **2** has no grammar label because it can be used both before a noun and after a linking verb.

[not before noun]
[not usually before noun]

■ Adjectives labelled [not before noun] are used only after a linking verb, never before a noun. The label [not usually before noun] is used when it is rare but possible to use the adjective before a noun.

> The grammar label straight after the *adj.* label shows that both meanings must be used after a linking verb.

rife /raɪf/ *adj.* [not before noun] **1** if sth bad or unpleasant is **rife** in a place, it is very common there: *It is a country where corruption is rife.* ◊ *Rumours are rife that he is going to resign.* **2** ~ (**with sth**) full of sth bad or unpleasant: *Los Angeles is rife with gossip about the stars' private lives.*

[after noun]

■ A few adjectives always follow the noun they describe. This is shown in the dictionary by the label [after noun]:

gal·ore /gəˈlɔː(r)/ *adv.* [after noun] (*informal*) in large quantities: *There will be games and prizes galore.*

Verbs

■ *He sighed.*
She cut her hand.
The soup tastes salty.

Each of these sentences has a subject (**he, she, the soup**) and a verb (**sigh, cut, taste**). In the first sentence **sigh** stands alone. Verbs like this are called INTRANSITIVE. In the second sentence, **cut** is TRANSITIVE because it is used with an object (**her hand**). In the third sentence, **taste** has no object but it cannot be used alone without an adjective. An adjective like **salty** that gives more information about the subject of a verb is called a COMPLEMENT. Verbs that take complements are called LINKING VERBS.

■ Compare the following sentences:
She can drive.
She drives a fast car.

In the first sentence the verb **drive** is used intransitively, without an object. In the second it is used transitively with the noun phrase **a fast car** as the object.

■ In the dictionary, grammatical codes and examples show you exactly how each verb is used in each of its meanings:

> The code [V] shows you that **drive** can be used without an object as an intransitive verb. The following examples show **drive** used intransitively.

drive /draɪv/ *verb, noun*
■ *verb* (**drove** /drəʊv/; *AmE* drəʊv/, **driven** /ˈdrɪvn/)
VEHICLE| **1** to operate a vehicle so that it goes in a particular direction: [V] *Can you drive? ◇ Don't drive so fast! ◇ I drove to work this morning. ◇ Shall we drive* (= go there by car) *or go by train? ◇* [VN] *He drives a taxi* (= that is his job).

> The code [VN] shows you that **drive** can also be a transitive verb with a noun phrase as the object. The next example shows **drive** used transitively.

> The code [V] given straight after the *verb* label shows that both meanings of **bask** are always intransitive.

bask /bɑːsk; *AmE* bæsk/ *verb* [V] ~ (**in** sth) **1** to enjoy sitting or lying in the heat or light of sth, especially the sun: *We sat basking in the warm sunshine.* **2** to enjoy the good feelings that you have when other people praise or admire you, or when they give you a lot of attention: *He had always basked in his parents' attention, but now things were different. ◇ I never minded **basking** in my wife's **reflected glory*** (= enjoying the praise, attention, etc. she got).

> The code [VN] given straight after the sense number shows that the first meaning of **pelt** is always transitive. Sense **2** is always intransitive.

pelt /pelt/ *verb, noun*
■ *verb* **1** [VN] ~ **sb** (**with** sth) to attack sb by throwing things at them: *The children pelted him with snowballs. ◇ We were pelted with rotten tomatoes.* **2** [V] ~ (**down**) (of rain) to fall very heavily: *By now the rain was pelting down.*

Intransitive verbs
[V] [V+*adv./prep.*]

■ Intransitive verbs do not take an object. When they are used alone after a subject, they are coded [V]:
*A large dog **appeared**.*

■ Some intransitive verbs are always used with a prepositional phrase or an adverb. These are often verbs showing movement in a particular direction. They are coded [V+*adv./prep.*]:
*A runaway car came **hurtling towards** us.*
*A group of swans **floated by**.*

Transitive verbs
[VN] [VN+*adv./prep.*]

■ Transitive verbs must have an object. The object can be a noun or a pronoun, a noun phrase or a clause. Pages **B8–9** explain verbs that take a clause as the object.

■ The code used to show a transitive verb with a noun, pronoun or noun phrase as object is [VN]:
*Jill's behaviour **annoyed me**.*

■ Most transitive verbs can be used in the PASSIVE:
***I was annoyed** by Jill's behaviour.*

> The label [no passive] shows when a transitive verb **cannot** be used in the passive.

af·ford /əˈfɔːd; *AmE* əˈfɔːrd/ *verb* **1** [no passive] (usually used with *can, could* or *be able to*, especially in negative sentences or questions) to have enough money or time to be able to buy or to do sth: [VN] *Can we afford a new car? ◇ None of them could afford £50 for a ticket. ◇ She felt she couldn't afford any more time off work. ◇* [V to inf] *We can't afford to go abroad this summer. ◇ She never took a taxi, even though she could afford to. ◇* [VN to inf] *He couldn't then afford the money to go on the trip.*

■ Like intransitive verbs, some transitive verbs are always used with a prepositional phrase or an adverb that is closely connected with the verb. They are coded [VN+adv./prep.]:

*He **wedged the phone under** his chin.*
*She **was bundled off** to boarding school.*

[+adv./prep.]

> The code [+adv./prep.] straight after the sense number shows that this meaning of **wind** is always used with a prepositional phrase or an adverb, whether it is transitive or intransitive.

wind² /waɪnd/ *verb*—see also WIND¹ (**wound, wound** /waʊnd/) **1** [+adv./prep.] (of a road, river, etc.) to have many bends and twists: [V] *The path wound down to the beach.* ◊ [VN] *The river **winds its way** between two meadows.*—see also WINDING

> The examples with their codes, [V] for instransitive and [VN] for transitive, show the verb in use with a prepositional phrase or an adverb.

Transitive verbs + two objects
[VNN]

■ Some verbs, like **sell** and **buy**, can be used with two objects. This is shown by the code [VNN]:

I sold Jim a car.
I bought Mary a book.

■ You can often express the same idea by using the verb as an ordinary transitive verb and adding a prepositional phrase starting with **to** or **for**:

*I **sold** a car **to** Jim.*
*I **bought** a book **for** Mary*

> The words in **bold type** before the definition show you which preposition you can use.

bake /beɪk/ *verb* **1** ~ **sth (for sb)**| ~ **(sb) sth** to cook food in an oven without extra fat or liquid; to be cooked in this way: [VN] *baked potatoes* ◊ [VN, VNN] *I'm baking a birthday cake for Alex.* ◊ *I'm baking Alex a cake.* ◊ [V] *the delicious smell of baking bread* ⇨ vocabulary notes on page 274

> A pair of examples shows the same idea expressed in two different ways.

Linking verbs
[V-ADJ] [V-N] [VN-ADJ] [VN-N]

■ *His voice sounds hoarse.*
Elena became a doctor.

In these sentences the linking verb (**sound, become**) is followed by a complement, an adjective (**hoarse**) or a noun phrase (**a doctor**) that tells you more about the subject.

■ Verbs that have an adjective as the complement have the code [V-ADJ], and verbs with a noun phrase as the complement have the code [V-N].

> The linking verb **become** can be used with either an adjective or a noun phrase.

be·come /bɪˈkʌm/ *verb* (**be·came** /bɪˈkeɪm/, **be·come**) **1** *linking verb* to start to be sth: [V-ADJ] *It was becoming more and more difficult to live on his salary.* ◊ *It soon became apparent that no one was going to come.* ◊ *She was becoming confused.* ◊ [V-N] *She became queen in 1952.* ◊ *The bill will become law next year.*

■ There are also verbs that take both an object and a complement:

She considered herself lucky.
They elected him president.

The complement (**lucky, president**) tells you more about the object (**herself, him**) of the verb. The code [VN-ADJ] shows you that a verb is transitive and takes an adjective as the complement, while the code [VN-N] indicates a transitive verb that takes a noun phrase as the complement:

deem /diːm/ *verb* (*formal*) (not usually used in the progressive tenses) to have a particular opinion about sth [SYN] CONSIDER: [VN-N] *The evening was deemed a great success.* ◊ [VN-ADJ] *She **deemed** it prudent not to say anything.* ◊ *They would take any action **deemed necessary**.* [also V (that), VN to inf]

Verbs used with clauses

- *George complained that it was too hot.*
Did you hear what he said?
Don't forget to lock the door.
He enjoys working with children.
Jane asked, 'Are you OK?'

All these sentences contain a verb
(**complain**, **hear**, **forget**, **enjoy**, **ask**) that is
used with a clause or phrase containing
another verb (**that it was … , what he
said … , to lock … , working…**). In this
dictionary, the types of clause or phrase that
can be used with verbs are called '**that
clause**', '**wh- clause**', '**infinitive phrase**',
'**-ing phrase**' and '**direct speech**'.

Verbs + that *clause*
[V that] [V (that)] [VN that] [VN (that)]

- The code [V that] shows that a verb is
followed by a clause beginning with **that**:
*She **answered that** she would prefer to walk.*

- However, it is not always necessary to use
the word **that** itself:
*I **said that** he would come.*
*I **said** he would come.*

These two sentences mean the same.
In the dictionary they are shown by the code
[V (that)] and a single example is given, using
brackets:
*I **said (that)** he would come.*

- Some verbs can be used with both a noun
phrase and a '*that* clause'. The code for verbs
used like this is [VN that] or [VN (that)]:
*Can you **remind me that** I need to buy some
milk?*
*I **told her (that)** I would be late.*

Verbs + wh- *clause*
[V wh-] [VN wh-]

- A 'wh- clause' (or phrase) is a clause or
phrase beginning with one of the following
words: **which, what, whose, why, where,
when, who, whom, how, if, whether**. The
code used in this dictionary for a verb that
takes a 'V wh- clause' is [V wh-]:
*I **wonder what** the new job will be like.*
*He doesn't **care how** he looks.*
*Did you **see which** way they went?*

- Some verbs can be used with both a noun
phrase and a 'wh- clause'. The code for verbs
used like this is [VN wh-]:

*I **asked him where** the library was.*
*I **told her when** the baby was due.*
*He **teaches his students how** to research a
subject thoroughly.*

Verbs + infinitive phrase
[V to inf] [VN+ to inf] [VN inf]

- **Eat** and **to eat** are both the infinitive form of
the verb. **Eat** is called a **bare infinitive** and **to
eat** is called a **to-infinitive**. Most verbs that
take an infinitive are used with the *to*-infinitive.
The code for these verbs is [V to inf]:
*The goldfish **need to be fed**.*
*She never **learned to read**.*

- Some verbs can be used with both a noun
phrase and a *to*-infinitive. The code for this is
[VN to inf]. The noun phrase can be the object
of the main verb:
*Can you **persuade Sheila** to chair the
meeting?*
*He **was forced** to hand over the keys.*

or the noun phrase and the infinitive phrase
together can be the object:
*I expected **her to pass** her driving test first
time.*
*We'd love **you to come** and visit us.*

- Only two groups of verbs are used with a bare
infinitive (without 'to'). One is the group of
MODAL VERBS (or MODAL AUXILIARIES).
These are the special verbs like **can**, **must**
and **will** that go before a main verb and show
that an action is possible, necessary, etc.
These verbs have special treatment in the
dictionary and are labelled *modal verb*.

- A small group of ordinary verbs, for example
see and **hear**, can be used with a noun
phrase and a bare infinitive. The code for
these is [VN inf]:
*Did you **hear the phone ring** just then?*
*She **watched him eat** his lunch.*

Verbs + -ing phrase
[V -ing] [VN -ing]

- An '-ing phrase' is a phrase containing a
PRESENT PARTICIPLE (or GERUND). The
present participle is the form of the verb that
ends in -ing, for example **doing**, **eating** or
catching. Sometimes the '-ing phrase'
consists of a present participle on its own.
The code for a verb that takes an '-ing phrase'
is [V -ing]:

*She never **stops talking**!*
*I **started looking** for a job two years ago.*

- Some verbs can be used with both a noun phrase and an '-ing phrase'. The code for this is [VN **-ing**].The noun phrase can be the object of the main verb:

*His comments **set me** thinking.*
*I can **smell something** nice cooking.*

or the noun phrase and the '-ing phrase' *together* can be the object:

*I hate **him joking** (= the fact that he jokes) about serious things.*

- In this pattern, you can replace **him** with the possessive pronoun **his**:

*I hate **his joking** about serious things.*

However, sentences with a possessive pronoun sound very formal and the object pronoun is more common, especially in American English. In cases where the verb itself is formal and the possessive pronoun may well be used, this is shown in the dictionary entry:

pre·clude /prɪˈkluːd/ *verb* ~ **sth| ~ sb from doing sth** *(formal)* to prevent sth from happening or sb from doing sth; to make sth impossible: [VN] *Lack of time precludes any further discussion.* ◇ [VN-ing] *His religious beliefs precluded him/his serving in the army.* [also V-ing]

Verbs + direct speech
[V **speech**] [VN **speech**]

- Verbs like **say**, **answer** and **demand** can be used either to report what somebody has said using a 'that clause' or to give their exact words in DIRECT SPEECH, using quotation marks (' '). Verbs that can be used with direct speech have the code [V **speech**]. Compare:

[V **speech**] *'It's snowing,' she said.* and
[V **(that)**]   *She said that it was snowing.*

- Writers often make a story more interesting by using verbs like **laugh** or **gulp**, that are not actually ways of speaking, as speech verbs, in order to show how something is said or what the speaker is doing while speaking.

*'I'd love to come,' she **beamed**.*
*'I can't believe you did that!' he **exploded**.*

- Some verbs can be used with both direct speech and a noun phrase, to show who is being spoken to. The code for this pattern is [VN **speech**]:

*'Tom's coming to lunch,' she **told him**.*

Verbs in different patterns

- Many verbs, for example **watch**, can be used in a number of different ways:

[VN inf]   *I watched him eat.*
[VN **-ing**] *I watched him eating.*
[VN]   *I watched the pianist's left hand.*
[V **wh-**] *I watched how the pianist used her left hand.*

- The dictionary entry for each verb shows the different ways in which it can be used by giving a range of example sentences. The code before each example shows what type of grammatical pattern is being used. When an example follows another one illustrating the same pattern, the code is not repeated.

- Some patterns are possible after a particular verb but are less common. These are not shown in example sentences but the codes for them are given at the end of the entry or at the end of a particular sense:

sus·pect *verb, noun, adj.*
- *verb* /səˈspekt/ (not used in the progressive tenses) **1** to have an idea that sth is probably true or likely to happen, especially sth bad, but without having definite proof: [VN] *If you suspect a gas leak, do not strike a match or even turn on an electric light.* ◇ *Suspecting nothing, he walked right into the trap.* ◇ [V **(that)**] *I began to suspect (that) they were trying to get rid of me.* ◇ [V] *As I had suspected all along, he was not a real policeman.* [also VN **to** inf, VN **that**]

Verb patterns with example sentences.

Extra verb patterns.

Phrasal verbs

What are phrasal verbs?

■ Jan **turned down** the chance to work abroad.
Buying that new car has really **eaten into** my savings.
I don't think I can **put up with** his behaviour much longer.

Phrasal verbs (sometimes called multi-word verbs) are verbs that consist of two, or sometimes three, words. The first word is a verb and it is followed by an adverb (turn **down**) or a preposition (eat **into**) or both (put **up with**). These adverbs or prepositions are sometimes called PARTICLES.

■ In this dictionary, phrasal verbs are listed at the end of the entry for the main verb in a section marked **PHR V**. They are listed in alphabetical order of the particles following them:

> **PHR V** ˌfight 'back (against sb/sth) to resist strongly or attack sb who has attacked you: *Don't let them bully you. Fight back!* ◊ *It is time to fight back against street crime.* ˌfight sth↔'back/'down to try hard not to do or show sth, especially not to show your feelings: *She fought back the urge to run.* ◊ *He fought down his disgust.* ˌfight sb/sth↔'off to resist sb/sth by fighting against them/it: *The jeweller was stabbed as he tried to fight the robbers off.* ˌfight 'out sth│ˌfight it 'out to fight or argue until an argument has been settled: *The conflict is still being fought out.* ◊ *They still hadn't reached any agreement so we left them to fight it out.*

Meaning of phrasal verbs

■ He **sat down** on the bed.

The meaning of some phrasal verbs, such as **sit down**, is easy to guess because the verb and the particle keep their usual meaning. However, many phrasal verbs have idiomatic meanings that you need to learn. The separate meanings of **put**, **up** and **with**, for example, do not add up to the meaning of **put up with** (= tolerate).

■ Some particles have particular meanings that are the same when they are used with a number of different verbs:
I didn't see the point of **hanging around** waiting for him, so I went home.
I wish you wouldn't leave all those books **lying around**.

Around adds the meaning of 'with no particular purpose or aim' and is also used in a similar way with many other verbs, such as **play**, **sit** and **wait**.

■ The meaning of a phrasal verb can sometimes be explained with a one-word verb. However, phrasal verbs are frequently used in spoken English and, if there is a one-word equivalent, it is usually more formal in style:
I wish my ears didn't **stick out** so much.
The garage **projects** 5 metres beyond the front of the house.

Both **stick out** and **project** have the same meaning – 'to extend beyond a surface' – but they are very different in style. **Stick out** is used in informal contexts, and **project** in formal or technical contexts.

Grammar of phrasal verbs

■ Phrasal verbs can be TRANSITIVE (they take an object) or INTRANSITIVE (they have no object). Some phrasal verbs can be used in both ways:
For heaven's sake **shut** her **up**. (transitive)
He told me to **shut up**. (intransitive)

■ INTRANSITIVE phrasal verbs are written in the dictionary without **sb** (somebody) or **sth** (something) after them. This shows that they do not have an object:

> ˌeat 'out to have a meal in a restaurant, etc. rather than at home: *Do you feel like eating out tonight?*

Eat out is intransitive, and the two parts of the verb cannot be separated by any other word. You can say:

> Shall we eat out tonight?

but not ~~Shall we eat tonight out?~~

■ In order to use TRANSITIVE phrasal verbs correctly, you need to know where to put the object. With some phrasal verbs (often called SEPARABLE verbs), the object can go either between the verb and the particle or after the particle:
She **tore** the letter **up**.
She **tore up** the letter.

■ When the object is a long phrase, it usually comes after the particle:
She **tore up** all the letters he had sent her.

■ When the object is a pronoun (for example **it** standing for 'the letter'), it must **always** go between the verb and the particle:
She read the letter and then **tore** it **up**.

■ In the dictionary, verbs that are separable are written like this:
tear sth↔up

■ The double arrow between the object and the particle shows that the object may come either before or after the particle:

_¡**call sth**↔**off** to cancel sth; to decide that sth will not happen: *to call off a deal / trip / strike* ◇ *They have called off their engagement* (= decided not to get married). ◇ *The game was called off because of bad weather*

You can say:
> They **called** the deal **off**.
and They **called off** the deal.

■ With other phrasal verbs (sometimes called INSEPARABLE verbs), the two parts of the verb cannot be separated by an object:
> I didn't really **take to** her husband.
not *I didn't really take her husband to.*
> I didn't really **take to** him.
not *I didn't really take him to.*

■ In the dictionary, verbs that are inseparable are written like this:
> **take to sb**

When you see **sb** or **sth** after the two parts of a phrasal verb, and there is no double arrow, you know that they cannot be separated by an object:

_¡**run** '**into sb** to meet sb by chance: *Guess who I ran into today!*

You can say:
> I **ran into Joe** yesterday.
but not *I ran Joe into.*

■ There are a few phrasal verbs in which the two parts of the verb must be separated by the object. You can say:
> They changed the plans and **messed** everyone **around**.
but not *They changed the plans and messed around everyone.*

■ In the dictionary, these verbs are written like this:
> **mess sb around**

When you see **sb** or **sth** between the two parts of a phrasal verb and there is no double arrow, you know that they must be separated by the object.

■ Some transitive phrasal verbs can be made passive:
> The deal **has been called off**.

When this is common, you will find an example at the dictionary entry.

Phrasal verbs used with phrases and clauses

■ Like other verbs some phrasal verbs can be used with another phrase or clause. The different types of clause and phrase are explained on study pages B8–9. When a phrasal verb can be used with a particular type of clause or phrase an example is given in the dictionary entry, labelled with a special code:

[+ that] *Suddenly it **dawned on me that** they couldn't possibly have met before.*

[+ wh] *I can't **figure out how** to do this.*

[+ to inf] *I'm **counting on you to help** me.*

[+ -ing] *I didn't **bargain on finding** Matthew there as well.*

[+ speech] *'Help!' he **cried out**.*

Related nouns

■ A particular phrasal verb may have a noun related to it. This noun will be mentioned at the verb entry:

_¡**break** '**in** to enter a building by force: *Burglars had broken in while we were away.*—related noun BREAK-IN
_¡**break sb/sth** '**in 1** to train sb/sth in sth new that they must do: *to break in new recruits* ◇ *The young horse was not yet broken in* (= trained to carry a rider). **2** to wear sth, especially new shoes, until they become comfortable _¡**break** '**in (on sth)** to interrupt or disturb sth: *She longed to break in on their conversation but didn't want to appear rude.* ◇ [+ speech] *'I didn't do it!' she broke in.*
_¡**break** '**into sth 1** to enter a building by force; to open a car, etc. by force: *We had our car broken into last week.*—related noun BREAK-IN **2** to begin laughing, singing, etc. suddenly: *As the President's car drew up, the crowd broke into loud applause.*

_¡**break** '**out** (of war, fighting or other unpleasant events), to start suddenly: *They had escaped to America shortly before war broke out in 1939.* ◇ *Fighting had broken out between rival groups of fans.* ◇ *Fire broke out during the night.*—related noun OUTBREAK _¡**break** '**out (of sth)** to escape from a place or situation: *Several prisoners broke out of the jail.* ◇ *She needed to break out of her daily routine and do something exciting.*—related noun BREAKOUT

■ A noun is often related in meaning to only one or two of the phrasal verbs using a particle. **Break-in** is related to **break in** and the first meaning of **break into sth**, but not to **break sb/sth in** or **break in (on sth)**. **Breakout** is related to **break out (of sth)**, whereas the noun **outbreak** relates to **break out**.

Idioms

What are idioms?

■ An idiom is a phrase whose meaning is difficult or sometimes impossible to guess by looking at the meanings of the individual words it contains. For example, the phrase **be in the same boat** has a literal meaning that is easy to understand, but it also has a common idiomatic meaning:

I found the job difficult at first. But we were all in the same boat; we were all learning.

Here, **be in the same boat** means 'to be in the same difficult or unfortunate situation'.

■ Some idioms are imaginative expressions such as proverbs and sayings:

Too many cooks spoil the broth.
(If too many people are involved in something, it will not be well done.)

■ If the expression is well known, part of it may be left out:

Well, I knew everything would go wrong – it's the usual story of too many cooks!

■ Other idioms are short expressions that are used for a particular purpose:

Hang in there! (used to encourage somebody in a difficult situation)

Get lost! (a rude way of saying 'go away')

■ Many idioms, however, are not vivid in this way. They are considered as idioms because their form is fixed:

for certain   in any case

Looking up idioms

■ Idioms are defined at the entry for the first 'full' word (a noun, a verb, an adjective or an adverb) that they contain. This means ignoring any grammatical words such as articles and prepositions. Idioms follow the main senses of a word, in a section marked **IDM**:

> **IDM in the blink of an 'eye** very quickly; in a short time **on the 'blink** (*informal*) (of a machine) no longer working correctly

The words **in**, **the**, and **on** in these idioms do not count as 'full' words, and so the idioms are not listed at the entries for these words.

■ Deciding where idioms start and stop is not always easy. If you hear the expression:

They decided to bury the hatchet and try to be friends again

you might think that **hatchet** is the only word you do not know and look that up. In fact,

bury the hatchet is an idiomatic expression and it is defined at **bury**. At **hatchet** you will find a cross-reference directing you to **bury**:

> **hatchet** /ˈhætʃɪt/ *noun* a small AXE (= a tool with a heavy blade for chopping things) with a short handle—picture at AXE **IDM** see BURY

■ Sometimes one 'full' word of an idiom can be replaced by another. For example, in the idiom **be a bag of nerves**, **bag** can be replaced by **bundle**. This is shown as **be a bag/bundle of nerves** and the idiom is defined at the first full fixed word, **nerve**. If you try to look the phrase up at either **bag** or **bundle** you will find a cross-reference to **nerve** at the end of the idioms section.

> **IDM not go a bundle on sb/sth** (*BrE*, *informal*) to not like sb/sth very much—more at NERVE *n.*

■ A few very common verbs and the adjectives **bad** and **good** have so many idioms that they cannot all be listed in the entry. Instead, there is a note telling you to look at the entry for the next noun, verb, adjective, etc. in the idiom:

> **IDM** Most idioms containing **go** are at the entries for the nouns and adjectives in the idioms, for example **go it alone** is at **alone**.

■ In some idioms, many alternatives are possible. In the expression **disappear into thin air**, you could replace **disappear** with **vanish, melt** or **evaporate**. In the dictionary this is shown as **disappear, vanish, etc. into thin air**, showing that you can use other words with a similar meaning to **disappear** in the idiom. Since the first 'full' word of the idiom is not fixed, the expression is defined at **thin** with a cross-reference only at **air**.

■ If you cannot find an idiom in the dictionary, look it up at the entry for one of the other main words in the expression.

■ Some idioms only contain grammatical words such as **one**, **it**, or **in**. These idioms are defined at the first word that appears in them. For example, the idiom **one up on sb** is defined at the entry for **one**.

■ Idioms are given in alphabetical order within the idioms sections. Grammatical words such as **a/an** or **the**, **sb/sth**, and the possessive forms **your**, **sb's**, **his**, **her**, etc. as well as words in brackets ( ) or after the symbol (/), are ignored.

Letter writing

Informal letters

- **Your address** (but **not** your name) usually goes in the top right-hand corner, if it is included, but it is often left out altogether in informal letters.

- There is no need to put the address of the person you are writing to.

- There are many different ways of ending an informal letter. These are some of the most common:

  To family members and close friends:
  Love
  Love from
  Lots of love

  To friends and acquaintances:
  Best wishes
  All the best
  Take care

> 2 South Street
> Liverpool L17 6HS
>
> 11 August
>
> Dear Liz
>
> Just a quick note to thank you for the wonderful day we spent with you on Sunday. The kids really enjoyed themselves and it was a rare treat for me to sit back, glass in hand, while you and John did all the hard work of entertaining them.
>
> Anyway, the two of you must come and have dinner with me sometime soon. I'll put the kids to bed and we'll have a really civilized evening. I'll give you a call during the week and we can arrange something.
>
> Love,
>
> Rachel

Faxes, memos and e-mails

- The format is similar for faxes, memos and e-mails. You do not have to write *Dear Sir / Madam / Mr Smith* at the beginning or use a particular formula at the end: you can just sign your name. Memos and e-mails between colleagues can be very informal in style. Business faxes to clients, suppliers, etc. should use the language of a formal letter (see p **B14**). It is also common for normal business letters to be sent as faxes.

FAX from: 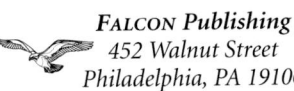 **FALCON Publishing**
452 Walnut Street
Philadelphia, PA 19106
Fax : 215 925 8722

Fax to: Charles H. Reed, Badger Books
Fax no: 202 736 5412
Date: May 22, 2000
Subject: Publicity material
No. of pages including this one: 1
From: Amy Cavadino, Publicity Assistant
Children's Books, cavada@falcpub.com

Following our phone conversation last Friday, I am sorry to say that the publicity material for *The Magic Pineapple* will not be available until next week. I will arrange for it to be sent to you as soon as we receive it from the printers.

Amy Cavadino

MEMORANDUM  *FALCON Publis[...]*
Children's Boo[...]

To: All editors
Subject: Sales figures
From: Robert Parker
Date: July 3, 2000

Attached are the sales figures for June. Enjoy!

Bob

Formal letters

**Asking for information
American style**

179 San Jacinto Blvd
San Antonio, TX 78210

September 3, 2000

Denver Chamber of Commerce
124 Highfield Road
Denver, CO 80201-1023

To whom it may concern:

We are planning to spend our vacation in Denver over Christmas and would like some information on available lodging in the area.

We would appreciate it if you could send us information about inexpensive hotels in the Denver area. A city map and brochures about activities and sights in the city would also be appreciated.

Thank you.

Sincerely,

Laura Jensen

Laura Jensen

- **Your address** (but **not** your name) usually goes in the top right-hand corner, but may alternatively go on the left.

- **The date:** this can go on either the right or the left.

- **The name and / or job title** (if you know them) and address of the person you are writing to.

- **To address someone whose name you do not know you can write**:
Dear Sir
Dear Madam
Dear Sirs
Dear Sir / Madam
Dear Sir or Madam (all especially BrE)
To whom it may concern:
  (especially AmE)

- **To address someone by name, use their title and surname:**
Dear Dr Smith (BrE) /
Dear Dr. Smith: (AmE)
(**not** Dear James Smith or
Dear Dr James Smith)

- **To end formal letters in American English you use:**
Sincerely
Sincerely Yours
Yours Truly
In British English you should write:
Yours sincerely if you have addressed the person by name,
Yours faithfully if you have begun the letter Dear Sir / Madam, etc.

**Applying for a job
British style**

26 Windmill Road
Bristol BS2 6DP

24 May 2000

Ms Emma Campbell
Personnel Manager
Multimedia Design
4 Kennington Road
London SE1 8DD

Dear Ms Campbell

I am writing to apply for the position of assistant designer advertised in the Evening Post of 23 May. Please find enclosed a copy of my CV.

I have a degree in Graphic Design from Anglia Polytechnic University. Since graduation last summer I have been working for EMS Corporate Imaging on a contract basis. I have become particularly interested in interactive and multimedia work and now wish to develop my career in that direction. I would welcome the chance to work as part of a small, dynamic team where I could make a significant contribution while developing my skills yet further. I would be happy to show you a portfolio of my work.

I look forward to hearing from you.

Yours sincerely

Peter Green

Peter Green

Writing a CV or resumé

<table>
<tr><td>**American style**</td><td colspan="2">**RESUMÉ**</td></tr>
<tr><td></td><td>Jennifer Roberts
1320 Forest Drive
Palo Alto, CA94309
tel: (650) 498-129
e-mail: jlroberts@mailbox.com</td><td>Married
No children</td></tr>
<tr><td>**Objective**</td><td colspan="2">To obtain a position as a German–English translator with a firm in the Bay Area.</td></tr>
<tr><td>**Education**
1996–98
1990–94</td><td colspan="2">Master of Arts in Translation, Stanford University
Bachelor of Arts (cum laude)
Major: German; Minor: Russian, Georgetown University</td></tr>
<tr><td>**Experience**
1998–present

1996–98
1994–96</td><td colspan="2">Freelance technical translator, German–English, mostly for hi-tech industries in California
Teaching Assistant (German), Stanford University
English Teacher, Cambridge Institute, Heidelberg, Germany</td></tr>
<tr><td>**Languages**</td><td colspan="2">Fluent German and Russian</td></tr>
<tr><td>**Personal**</td><td colspan="2">Interests include sailing, cooking and entertaining friends.</td></tr>
<tr><td>**Reference**</td><td colspan="2">Dr. M. Rosen, Chair, Department of Modern Languages, Stanford University, Palo Alto, CA94305</td></tr>
</table>

- **On a British CV it is usual to put your date of birth.** On an American resumé you may choose whether or not to include your birth date, marital status, children, etc.
- **One or more references may be included on the CV/resumé** or they may be included in the letter of application instead.

Other useful phrases

- *Near-native command of English*
- *Adequate spoken Dutch and German*
- *Native French speaker*
- *Baccalauréat, série C (equivalent of A levels in Maths and Physics)*
- *The qualifications described below do not have exact equivalents in the American system.*
- *I enclose photocopies of my certificates with English translations.*

<table>
<tr><td>**British style**</td><td colspan="2">**CURRICULUM VITAE**</td></tr>
<tr><td>**Name**</td><td colspan="2">Peter James Green</td></tr>
<tr><td>**Address**</td><td colspan="2">26 Windmill Road, Bristol BS2 6DP</td></tr>
<tr><td>**Telephone**</td><td colspan="2">0117 945649</td></tr>
<tr><td>**Nationality**</td><td colspan="2">British</td></tr>
<tr><td>**Date of birth**</td><td colspan="2">11 March 1977</td></tr>
<tr><td>**Marital status**</td><td colspan="2">Single</td></tr>
<tr><td colspan="3">**Education/Qualifications**</td></tr>
<tr><td>1996–99</td><td colspan="2">Anglia Polytechnic University: BA in Graphic Design (First Class Hons)</td></tr>
<tr><td>1988–95</td><td colspan="2">Clifton School, 3 A levels: Art (A); Design and Technology (A); Mathematics (C) 10 GCSEs</td></tr>
<tr><td colspan="3">**Employment to date**</td></tr>
<tr><td>1999–present</td><td colspan="2">EMS Corporate Imaging, Design Department, Riverside House, 22 Charles St, Bristol</td></tr>
<tr><td>**Skills**</td><td colspan="2">Computer literate: familiar with a number of design and DTP packages; Clean driving licence</td></tr>
<tr><td>**Interests**</td><td colspan="2">Tennis, swimming, jazz</td></tr>
</table>

New words

■ The world is changing all the time and so is the English language. New technology and products (**DVDs**), new sports and leisure activities (**line dancing**), new fashions (**body piercing**), attitudes (**in-your-face**) and ways of working (**multi-skilling**): these are just some of the new words explained in this dictionary.

■ If you know how new words are formed, you may be able to work out what they mean.

■ PREFIXES AND SUFFIXES (= beginnings and endings) are added to existing words to give a new meaning and sometimes a new part of speech. *Profile* (= a description of sb/sth that gives useful information) + *-ing* gives us **profiling** ...

Customer profiling is an important part of any marketing campaign.

... while the new prefixes *cyber-* and *e-* (both meaning 'relating to electronic communication networks') produce **cybercafe** and **cyberspace**, **e-business** and **e-commerce**.

■ PHRASAL VERBS are formed by adding an adverb or a preposition to an existing verb ...

*She has been appointed to **head up** the research team.*

... or a completely new verb may be formed by adding the adverb to a noun or an adjective:

*The network has been accused of **dumbing down** its news bulletins.*

■ COMPOUNDS are the commonest type of new word, when two existing words are combined to give a new meaning. It is not hard to guess what a **helpdesk** is, or **voice mail**. One new combination sometimes inspires another. After **road rage** there has come **air rage**, **phone rage** and **store rage**:

*Overcrowding in supermarkets has resulted in a recent spate of **trolley rage** incidents.*

■ PORTMANTEAU WORDS are similar to compounds but may include only part of one or both of the original words in the new word: **alco**hol + **pop** = **alcopop** (*BrE*)

*The documentary turned out to be the world's longest **infomercial**, plugging reissues of all the band's albums.*
(**info**rmation + com**mercial**).

*the latest **edutainment** videos*
(**edu**cation + enter**tainment**)

trolley rage

■ LOAN WORDS are words that are borrowed from other languages. They usually refer to foreign things – food, sports – that become popular in Britain or the US. **Caffè latte** (= hot milky coffee) is from Italian and **feng shui** (= a Chinese system for arranging buildings and furniture) from Chinese.

■ NEW MEANINGS for old words: sometimes the need for a new word can be filled by extending the meaning of a word that already exists. Language changes when people see or make a connection between things that may seem very different: ice cream and computer software, for example:

*This is just the plain **vanilla** version of the software* (= the version without any extra features, like plain vanilla ice cream).

Work out the meanings of these new words, or look them up in the dictionary:

*Politicians put their own **spin** on the economic situation.*

***Canyoning** has become a popular activity in alpine resorts.*

*It was the archetypal **dysfunctional** family: harassed mother, absent father, delinquent kids.*

*There'll be a certain amount of **hot-desking** required as the office move is managed in stages.*

*This new **docu-soap** follows the day-to-day lives of vets at London Zoo.*

*The public seems unconvinced by the party's latest **charm offensive**.*

*The bar's **kicking** tonight.*

sion from the child's point of view. **2** following or able to follow the rules of logic in which ideas or facts are based on other true ideas or facts: *a logical argument* ◊ *Computer programming needs someone with a logical mind.* OPP ILLOGICAL ▶ **logic·al·ly** /-kli/ *adv.*: *to argue/think logically*

-logical (*BrE* also **-logic**) ⇨ -OLOGY

lo·gi·cian /ləˈdʒɪʃn/ *noun* a person who studies or is skilled in LOGIC

-logist ⇨ -OLOGY

lo·gis·tics /ləˈdʒɪstɪks/ *noun* [U+sing./pl. *v.*] **~ (of sth)** the practical organization that is needed to make a complicated plan successful when a lot of people and equipment is involved: *the logistics of moving the company to a new building* ▶ **lo·gis·tic** (also **lo·gis·tic·al** /ləˈdʒɪstɪkl/) *adj.*: *logistic support* ◊ *Organizing famine relief presents huge logistical problems.* **lo·gis·tic·al·ly** /-kli/ *adv.*

log·jam /ˈlɒɡdʒæm; *AmE* ˈlɔːɡ-; ˈlɑːɡ-/ *noun* **1** a mass of LOGS floating on a river, that are blocking it **2** a difficult situation in which you cannot make progress easily because there are too many things to do

logo /ˈləʊɡəʊ; *AmE* ˈloʊɡoʊ/ *noun* (*pl.* **-os**) a printed design or symbol that a company or an organization uses as its special sign

-logue (*AmE* also **-log**) *combining form* (in nouns) talk or speech: *a monologue*

-logy ⇨ -OLOGY

loin /lɔɪn/ *noun* **1** [U, C] a piece of meat from the back or sides of an animal, near the tail: *loin of pork* **2** (**loins**) [pl.] (*old-fashioned*) the part of the body around the hips between the waist and the tops of the legs **3** (**loins**) [pl.] (*literary*) a person's sex organs IDM see GIRD

loin·cloth /ˈlɔɪnklɒθ; *AmE* -klɔːθ/ *noun* a piece of fabric worn around the body at the hips by men in some hot countries, sometimes as the only piece of clothing worn

loi·ter /ˈlɔɪtə(r)/ *verb* [V] to stand or wait somewhere especially with no obvious reason SYN HANG AROUND: *Teenagers were loitering in the street outside.*

loll /lɒl; *AmE* lɑːl/ *verb* [V+*adv./prep.*] **1** to lie, sit or stand in a lazy, relaxed way: *He lolled back in his chair by the fire.* **2** (of your head, tongue, etc.) to move or hang in a relaxed way: *My head lolled against his shoulder.*

lol·li·pop /ˈlɒlipɒp; *AmE* ˈlɑːlipɑːp/ (also *BrE informal* **lolly**) (also *AmE informal* **suck·er**) *noun* a hard round or flat sweet/candy made of boiled sugar on a small stick

ˈlollipop man, **ˈlollipop lady** *noun* (*BrE, informal*) a person whose job is to help children cross a busy road on their way to and from school by holding up a sign on a stick telling traffic to stop

lol·lop /ˈlɒləp; *AmE* ˈlɑːləp/ *verb* [V] [usually+*adv./prep.*] (*informal, especially BrE*) to walk or run with long awkward steps: *The dog came lolloping towards them.*

lolly /ˈlɒli; *AmE* ˈlɑːli/ *noun* (*pl.* **-ies**) (*BrE, informal*) **1** [C] = LOLLIPOP **2** [C] = ICE LOLLY **3** [U] (*old-fashioned*) money

lone /ləʊn; *AmE* loʊn/ *adj.* [only before noun] **1** without any other people or things SYN SOLITARY: *a lone sailor crossing the Atlantic* **2** (*especially BrE*) without a husband, wife or partner to share the care of children: *a lone mother/parent/father* ⇨ note at ALONE IDM **a ˌlone ˈwolf** a person who prefers to be alone

lone·ly /ˈləʊnli; *AmE* ˈloʊn-/ *adj.* (**lone·lier**, **lone·li·est**) **1** unhappy because you have no friends or people to talk to: *She lives alone and often feels lonely.* **2** (of a situation or period of time) sad and spent alone: *all those lonely nights at home watching TV* **3** [only before noun] (of places) where only a few people ever come or visit: *a lonely beach/farmhouse/road* ⇨ note at ALONE ▶ **lone·li·ness** *noun* [U]: *a period of loneliness in his life*

ˌlonely ˈhearts *adj.* [only before noun] a **lonely hearts column** in a newspaper is where people can advertise for a new lover or friend: *He placed a lonely hearts ad in a magazine.*

ˌlone-parent ˈfamily *noun* = ONE-PARENT FAMILY

loner /ˈləʊnə(r); *AmE* ˈloʊn-/ *noun* a person who is often alone or who prefers to be alone, rather than with other people

lone·some /ˈləʊnsəm; *AmE* ˈloʊn-/ *adj.* (*especially AmE*) **1** unhappy because you are alone and do not want to be or because you have no friends: *I felt so lonesome after he left.* **2** (of a place) where not many people go; a long way from where people live: *a lonesome road* ⇨ note at ALONE

long /lɒŋ; *AmE* lɔːŋ/ *adj., adv., verb*

■ *adj.* (**long·er** /ˈlɒŋɡə(r); *AmE* ˈlɔːŋ-/ **long·est** /ˈlɒŋɡɪst; *AmE* ˈlɔːŋ-/)

DISTANCE | **1** measuring or covering a great length or distance, or a greater length or distance than usual: *She had long dark hair.* ◊ *He walked down the long corridor.* ◊ *It was the world's longest bridge.* ◊ *a long journey/walk/drive/flight* ◊ *We're a long way from anywhere here.* ◊ *It's a long way away.* OPP SHORT **2** used for asking or talking about particular lengths or distances: *How long is the River Nile?* ◊ *The table is six feet long.* ◊ *The report is only three pages long.*

TIME | **3** lasting or taking a great amount of time or more time than usual: *He's been ill (for) a long time.* ◊ *There was a long silence before she spoke.* ◊ *I like it now the days are getting longer* (= it stays light for more time each day). ◊ *a long book/film/list* (= taking a lot of time to read/watch/deal with) ◊ *Nurses have to work long hours* (= for more hours in the day than is usual). ◊ (*AmE*) *He stared at them for the longest time* (= for a very long time) *before answering.* OPP SHORT **4** used for asking or talking about particular periods of time: *How long is the course?* ◊ *I think it's only three weeks long.* ◊ *How long a stay did you have in mind?* **5** seeming to last or take more time than it really does because, for example, you are very busy or not happy: *I'm tired. It's been a long day.* ◊ *We were married for ten long years.* OPP SHORT

CLOTHES | **6** covering all or most of your legs or arms: *She usually wears long skirts.* ◊ *a long-sleeved shirt*

VOWEL SOUNDS | **7** (*phonetics*) taking more time to make than a short vowel sound in the same position OPP SHORT

—see also LENGTH

IDM **as long as your ˈarm** (*informal*) very long: *There's a list of repairs as long as your arm.* **at long last** after a long time SYN FINALLY: *At long last his prayers had been answered.* **at the ˈlongest** not longer than the particular time given: *It will take an hour at the longest.* **by a ˈlong way** by a great amount **go back a long ˈway** (of two or more people) to have known each other for a long time: *We go back a long way, he and I.* **go a long ˈway** (of money, food, etc.) to last a long time: *She seems to make her money go a long way.* ◊ *A small amount of this paint goes a long way* (= covers a large area). ◊ (*ironic*) *I find that a little of Jerry's company can go a long way* (= I quickly get tired of being with him). **have come a long ˈway** to have made a lot of progress: *We've come a long way since the early days of the project.* **have a long way to ˈgo** to need to make a lot of progress before you can achieve sth: *She still has a long way to go before she's fully fit.* **How long is a piece of ˈstring?** (*BrE, spoken*) used to say that there is no definite answer to a question: 'How long will it take?' 'How long's a piece of string?' **in the ˈlong run** concerning a longer period in the future: *This measure inevitably means higher taxes in the long run.* **It's a ˌlong ˈstory.** (*informal*) used to say that the reasons for sth are complicated and you would prefer not to give all the details **the long arm of sth** the power and/or authority of sth: *There is no escape from the long arm of the law.* **the long and (the) ˈshort of it** used when you are telling sb the essential facts about sth or what effect it will have, without explaining all the details (**pull, wear, etc.) a long ˈface** (to have) an unhappy or disappointed expression **ˌlong in the ˈtooth** (*humorous, especially BrE*) old or too old **a ˈlong shot** an attempt or a guess that is not likely to be successful but is worth trying: *It's a long shot, but it just might work.* **long time no ˈsee** (*spoken*) used to greet sb you have not seen for a long time **not by a ˈlong chalk** (*BrE*) (also **not by a ˈlong shot** *AmE, BrE*) not nearly; not at all: *It's not over yet—not by a long chalk.* **take a long (cool/hard) ˈlook at sth** to consider a problem or possibility very carefully and without hurrying: *We need to take a long hard look at all the options.* **take the ˈlong view (of sth)** to consider

L

æ	ɑː	e	ɜː	ə	ɪ	iː	i	ɒ	ɔː	ʌ	ʊ	u	uː
cat	father	ten	bird	about	sit	see	many	got	saw	cup	put	actual	too
								(BrE)					

what is likely to happen or be important over a long period of time rather than only considering the present situation: *As pension funds are investing for members' retirements, they can take the long view.* **to cut a long story 'short** (*BrE*) (*AmE* **to make a long story 'short**) (*spoken*) used when you are saying that you will get to the point of what you are saying quickly, without including all the details—more at BROAD *adj.*, TERM *n.*, WAY *n.*

■ *adv.* (**long·er** /'lɒŋgə(r); *AmE* 'lɔːŋ-/, **long·est** /'lɒŋgɪst; *AmE* 'lɔːŋ-/) **1** for a long time: *Have you been here long?* ◇ *Stay as long as you like.* ◇ *The party went on long into the night.* ◇ *This may take longer than we thought.* ◇ *I won't be long* (= I'll return, be ready, etc. soon). ◇ *How long have you been waiting?* ◇ *These reforms are long overdue.* **2** a long time before or after a particular time or event: *He retired long before the war.* ◇ *It wasn't long before she had persuaded him* (= it only took a short time). ◇ *We'll be home before long* (= soon). ◇ *The house was pulled down long ago.* ◇ *They had long since* (= a long time before the present time) *moved away.* **3** used after a noun to emphasize that sth happens for the whole of a particular period of time: *We had to wait all day long.* ◇ *They stayed up the whole night long.*

IDM **as/so 'long as 1** only if: *We'll go as long as the weather is good.* **2** since; to the extent that: *So long as there is a demand for these drugs, the financial incentive for drug dealers will be there.* **for (so) 'long** for (such) a long time: *Will you be away for long?* ◇ *I'm sorry I haven't written to you for so long.* **no/any 'longer** used to say that sth which was possible or true before, is not now: *I can't wait any longer.* ◇ *He no longer lives here.* **so 'long** (*informal*) goodbye

■ *verb* ~ **for sb/sth** | ~ **(for sb) to do sth** to want sth very much especially if it does not seem likely to happen soon: [V] *Lucy had always longed for a brother.* ◇ *He longed for Pat to phone.* ◇ [V **to** inf] *I'm longing to see you again.*—see also LONGED-FOR

WHICH WORD?
(for) long / (for) a long time

Both **(for) long** and **(for) a long time** are used as expressions of time. In positive sentences **(for) a long time** is used: *We've been friends a long time.* **(For) long** is not used in positive sentences unless it is used with *too, enough, as, so, seldom*, etc.: *I stayed out in the sun for too long.* ◇ *You've been waiting long enough.* Both **(for) long** and **(for) a long time** can be used in questions, but **(for) long** is usually preferred: *Have you been waiting long?*

In negative sentences **(for) a long time** sometimes has a different meaning from **(for) long**: Compare: *I haven't been here for a long time* (= It is a long time since the last time I was here) and *I haven't been here long* (= I arrived here only a short time ago).

---

long. *abbr.* (in writing) LONGITUDE

long-a'waited *adj.* that people have been waiting for for a long time: *her long-awaited new novel*

long·boat /'lɒŋbəʊt; *AmE* 'lɔːŋboʊt/ *noun* a large rowing boat, used especially for travelling on the sea

long·bow /'lɒŋbəʊ; *AmE* 'lɔːŋboʊ/ *noun* a large BOW made of a long thin curved piece of wood that was used in the past for shooting arrows

long-'distance *adj.* [only before noun] **1** travelling or involving travel between places that are far apart: *a long-distance commuter* ◇ *long-distance flights* **2** operating between people and places that are far apart: *a long-distance phone call* ▶ **long 'distance** *adv.*: *It's a relaxing car to drive long distance.* ◇ *to call long distance*

long di'vision *noun* [U] (*mathematics*) a method of dividing one number by another in which all the stages involved are written down

long-drawn-'out (also *less frequent* **long-drawn**) *adj.* lasting a very long time, often too long: *long-drawn-out negotiations*

long 'drink *noun* a cold drink that fills a tall glass, such as LEMONADE or beer

'longed-for *adj.* [only before noun] that sb has been wanting or hoping for very much: *the birth of a longed-for baby*

lon·gev·ity /lɒn'dʒevəti; *AmE* lɑːn-; lɔːn-/ *noun* [U] (*formal*) long life; the fact of lasting a long time: *We wish you both health and longevity.* ◇ *He prides himself on the longevity of the company.*

long·hand /'lɒŋhænd; *AmE* 'lɔːŋ-/ *noun* [U] ordinary writing, not typed or written in SHORTHAND

long-haul *adj.* [only before noun] involving the transport of goods or passengers over long distances: *long-haul flights/routes* OPP SHORT-HAUL

long-horn /'lɒŋhɔːn; *AmE* -hɔːrn/ *noun* a cow with long horns

long·house /'lɒŋhaʊs; *AmE* 'lɔːŋ-/ *noun* **1** (in Britain) an old type of house in which people and animals lived together **2** (in the US) a traditional house used by some NATIVE AMERICANS

long·ing /'lɒŋɪŋ; *AmE* 'lɔːŋ-/ *noun, adj.*
■ *noun* [C, U] ~ **(for sb/sth)** | ~ **(to do sth)** a strong feeling of wanting sth/sb: *a longing for home/peace* ◇ *She was filled with longing to hear his voice again.* ◇ *romantic longings* ◇ *His voice was husky with longing* (= sexual desire).
■ *adj.* [only before noun] feeling or showing that you want sth very much: *He gave a longing look at the ice cream.* ▶ **long·ing·ly** *adv.*: *We looked longingly towards the hills.*

long·ish /'lɒŋɪʃ; *AmE* 'lɔːŋ-/ *adj.* [only before noun] fairly long: *longish hair* ◇ *There was a longish pause.*

lon·gi·tude /'lɒŋgɪtjuːd; 'lɒndʒɪ-; *AmE* 'lɑːndʒətuːd/ *noun* [U] (*abbr.* **long.**) the distance of a place east or west of the Greenwich MERIDIAN, measured in degrees: *the longitude of the island*—compare LATITUDE

lon·gi·tu·din·al /ˌlɒŋgɪ'tjuːdɪnl; ˌlɒndʒɪ-; *AmE* ˌlɑːndʒə'tuːdnl/ *adj.* (*technical*) **1** going downwards rather than across: *The plant's stem is marked with thin green longitudinal stripes.* **2** concerning the development of sth over a period of time: *a longitudinal study of aging* **3** connected with longitude: *the town's longitudinal position* ▶ **lon·gi·tu·din·al·ly** /-nəli/ *adv.*

'long johns *noun* [pl.] (*informal*) warm UNDERPANTS with long legs down to the ankles: *a pair of long johns*

the 'long jump (*AmE* also **the 'broad jump**) *noun* [sing.] a sporting event in which people try to jump as far forward as possible after running up to a line—picture on page 1251

long-'lasting *adj.* that can or does last for a long time: *long-lasting effects* ◇ *a long-lasting relationship*

long-'life *adj.* [especially of milk or batteries) made to remain fresh or to last longer than the ordinary type

long-'lived *adj.* having a long life; lasting for a long time

long-'lost *adj.* [only before noun] that you have not seen or received any news of for a long time: *a long-lost friend*

'long-range *adj.* [only before noun] **1** travelling a long distance: *long-range missiles* **2** made for a period of time that will last a long way into the future: *a long-range weather forecast* ◇ *long-range plans*—compare SHORT-RANGE

'long-running *adj.* [only before noun] that has been continuing for a long time: *a long-running campaign/debate/dispute* ◇ *a long-running TV series*

'long-serving *adj.* [only before noun] having had the job or position mentioned for a long time: *long-serving employees*

long·shore·man /'lɒŋʃɔːmən; *AmE* 'lɔːŋʃɔːrmən/ *noun* (*pl.* **-men** /-mən/) (*AmE*) a man whose job is moving goods on and off ships

long-'sighted (*especially BrE*) (also **far-'sighted** especially in *AmE*) *adj.* [not usually before noun] not able to see things that are close to you clearly OPP SHORT-SIGHTED

long-'standing *adj.* [usually before noun] that has existed or lasted for a long time: *a long-standing relationship*

'long-stay *adj.* [usually before noun] **1** likely to need treatment or care for a long time: *long-stay patients* ◇ *long-stay hospitals/institutions/wards* (= for long-stay

aɪ	aʊ	eɪ	əʊ	oʊ	ɔɪ	ɪə	eə	ʊə	j	w
my	now	say	go (BrE)	go (AmE)	boy	near	hair	pure	yes	wet

patients) **2** for people who wish to park their cars for a long period: *long-stay parking*

,long-'suffering *adj.* bearing problems or another person's unpleasant behaviour with patience: *his long-suffering wife*

,long-'term *adj.* [usually before noun] **1** that will last or have an effect over a long period of time: *a long-term strategy/solution* ◇ *the long-term effects of fertilizers* ◇ *a long-term aim/investment* **2** that is not likely to change or be solved quickly: *long-term debt/injury/unemployment*—compare SHORT-TERM

'long-time *adj.* [only before noun] having been the particular thing mentioned for a long time: *his long-time colleague/friend/rival*

'long wave *noun* [U, C] (*abbr.* **LW**) a radio wave with a length of more than 1000 metres: *to broadcast on long wave*—compare SHORT WAVE

,long week'end *noun* a holiday/vacation of three or four days from Friday or Saturday to Sunday or Monday: *to have a long weekend in Amsterdam*

,long-'winded *adj.* (*disapproving*) (especially of talking or writing) continuing for too long and therefore boring: *a long-winded speaker* ◇ *a long-winded process*

loo /luː/ *noun* (*pl.* **loos**) (*BrE, informal*) a toilet: *She's gone to the loo.* ◇ *Can I use your loo, please?*

loo·fah /ˈluːfə/ *noun* a long rough bath SPONGE made from the dried fruit of a tropical plant

look /lʊk/ *verb, noun, exclamation*

■ *verb*

USE EYES | **1** [V] ~ **(at sb/sth)** to turn your eyes in a particular direction: *If you look carefully you can just see our house from here.* ◇ *She looked at me and smiled.* ◇ *'Has the mail come yet?' 'I'll look and see.* ◇ *Look! I'm sure that's Brad Pitt!* ◇ *Don't look now, but there's someone staring at you!*—see also FORWARD-LOOKING

SEARCH | **2** [V] ~ **(for sb/sth)** to try to find sb/sth: *I can't find my book—I've looked everywhere.* ◇ *Where have you been? We've been looking for you.* ◇ *Are you still looking for a job?*

PAY ATTENTION | **3** ~ **(at sth)** to pay attention to sth: [V] *Look at the time! We're going to be late.* ◇ [Vwh-] *Can't you look where you're going?*

APPEAR/SEEM | **4** *linking verb* ~ **(to sb) like sb/sth** to seem; to appear: [V-ADJ] *to look pale/puzzled/sad/tired* ◇ *That book looks interesting.* ◇ [V] *That looks like an interesting book.* ◇ [V-N] *That looks an interesting book.* ◇ *You made me look a complete fool!*—see also GOOD-LOOKING **5** [V] ~ **(to sb) like sb/sth | ~ (to sb) as if …/as though …** (not usually used in the progressive tenses) to have a similar appearance to sb/sth; to have an appearance that suggests that sth is true or will happen: *That photograph doesn't look like her at all.* ◇ *It looks like rain (= it looks as if it's going to rain).* ◇ *You look as though you slept badly.* **HELP** In spoken English people often use **like** instead of **as if** or **as though** in this meaning, especially in *AmE*: *You look like you slept badly.* This is considered incorrect in written *BrE*. **6** [V] ~ **(to sb) as if …/as though … | ~ (to sb) like …** to seem likely: *It doesn't look as if we'll be moving after all.* ◇ (*informal*) *It doesn't look like we'll be moving after all.* **HELP** This use of **like** instead of **as if** or **as though** is considered incorrect in written *BrE*.

FACE | **7** [V+*adv./prep.*] to face a particular direction: *The house looks east.* ◇ *The hotel looks out over the harbour.*

IDM Most idioms containing **look** are at the entries for the nouns and adjectives in the idioms, for example **look daggers at sb** is at **dagger**. **be just 'looking** used in a shop/store to say that you are not ready to buy sth: *'Can I help you?' 'I'm just looking, thank you.'* **be looking to do sth** to try to find ways of doing sth: *The government is looking to reduce inflation.* **look 'bad | not look 'good** to be considered bad behaviour or bad manners: *It looks bad not going to your own brother's wedding.* **look 'bad (for sb)** to show that sth bad might happen: *He's had another heart attack; things are looking bad for him, I'm afraid.* **look 'good** to show success or that sth good might happen: *This year's sales figures are looking good.* **look 'here** (*old-fashioned*) used to protest about sth: *Now*

look here, it wasn't my fault. **look sb ,up and 'down** to look at sb in a careful or critical way **(not) look your'self** to not have your normal healthy appearance: *You're not looking yourself today (= you look tired or ill/sick).* **never/not look 'back** (*informal*) to become more and more successful: *Her first novel was published in 1998 and since then she hasn't looked back.* **not much to 'look at** (*informal*) not attractive **to 'look at sb/sth** judging by the appearance of sb/sth: *To look at him you'd never think he was nearly fifty.*

PHR V **,look 'after yourself/sb/sth** (*especially BrE*) **1** to be responsible for or to take care of sb/sth: *Who's going to look after the children while you're away?* ◇ *I'm looking after his affairs while he's in hospital.* ◇ *Don't worry about me—I can look after myself (= I don't need any help).* ⇨ note at CARE **2** to make sure that things happen to sb's advantage: *He's good at looking after his own interests.*

,look a'head (to sth) to think about what is going to happen in the future

,look a'round/'round to turn your head so that you can see sth: *People came out of their houses and looked around.* **,look a'round/'round for sth** to search for sth in a number of different places: *We're looking around for a house in this area.* **,look a'round/'round (sth)** to visit a place or building, walking around it to see what is there: *Let's look round the town this afternoon.*

'look at sth 1 to examine sth closely: *Your ankle's swollen—I think the doctor ought to look at it.* ◇ *I haven't had time to look at (= read) the papers yet.* **2** to think about, consider or study sth: *The implications of the new law will need to be looked at.* **3** to view or consider sth in a particular way: *Looked at from that point of view, his decision is easier to understand.*

,look 'back (on sth) to think about sth in your past: *to look back on your childhood*

,look 'down on sb/sth to think that you are better than sb/sth: *She looks down on people who haven't been to college.*

'look for sth to hope for sth; to expect sth: *We shall be looking for an improvement in your work this term.*

,look 'forward to sth to be thinking with pleasure about sth that is going to happen (because you expect to enjoy it): *I'm looking forward to the weekend.* ◇[+-ing] *We're really looking forward to seeing you again.* ⇨ note at EXPECT

,look 'in (on sb) (*BrE*) to make a short visit to a place, especially sb's house: *Why don't you look in on me next time you're in town?*

,look 'into sth to examine sth: *A working party has been set up to look into the problem.*

,look 'on to watch sth without becoming involved in it yourself: *Passers-by simply looked on as he was attacked.*—related noun ONLOOKER **'look on sb/sth as sb/sth** to consider sb/sth to be sb/sth: *She's looked on as the leading authority on the subject.* **'look on sb/sth with sth** to consider sb/sth in a particular way: *They looked on his behaviour with contempt.*

,look 'out used to warn sb to be careful, especially when there is danger: *Look out! There's a car coming.* **,look 'out for sth/sb 1** to try to avoid sth bad happening or doing sth bad: *You should look out for pickpockets.* ◇ *Do look out for spelling mistakes in your work.* **2** to keep trying to find sth or meet sb: *I'll look out for you at the conference.*—related noun LOOKOUT **,look 'out for sb/yourself** to think of sb's/your own advantage: *We should look out for each other.* **,look sth↔'out (for sb/sth)** (*BrE*) to search for sth from among your possessions: *I'll look out those old photographs you wanted to see.*

,look sth↔'over to examine sth to see how good, big, etc. it is: *We looked over the house again before we decided to rent it.*

,look 'round (*BrE*) to turn your head to see sb/sth behind you: *She looked round when she heard the noise.*

,look 'through sb [no passive] to ignore sb by pretending not to see them: *She just looked straight through me.* **'look through sth** [no passive] to examine or read sth quickly: *She looked through her notes before the exam.*

'look to sb for sth | 'look to sb to do sth (*formal*) to rely

L

on or expect sb to provide sth or do sth: *We are looking to you for help.* **look 'to sth** (*formal*) to consider sth and think about how to make it better: *We need to look to ways of improving our marketing.*

look 'up (*informal*) (of business, sb's situation, etc.) to become better: *At last things were beginning to look up.* **look 'up (from sth)** to raise your eyes when you are looking down at sth: *She looked up from her book as I entered the room.* **look sb ‹ ›'up** [no passive] (*informal*) to visit or make contact with sb, especially when you have not seen them for a long time: *Do look me up the next time you're in London.* **look sth ‹ ›'up** to look for information in a dictionary or REFERENCE BOOK: *Can you look up the time of the next train?* ◊ *I looked it up in the dictionary.* **look 'up to sb** to admire or respect sb

■ *noun*

USING EYES | **1** [C, usually sing.] ~ (**at sb/sth**) an act of looking at sb/sth: *Here, have a look at this.* ◊ *Take a look at these figures!* ◊ *Make sure you get a good look at their faces.* ◊ *One look at his face and Jenny stopped laughing.* ◊ *A look passed between them* (= they looked at each other). ◊ *It's an interesting place. Do you want to take a look around?* ◊ *We'll be taking a close look at these proposals* (= examining them carefully).

SEARCH | **2** [C, usually sing.] ~ (**for sth/sb**) an act of trying to find sth/sb: *I've had a good look for it, but I can't find it.*

EXPRESSION | **3** [C] an expression in your eyes or face: *a look of surprise/anger* ◊ *He didn't like the look in her eyes.*

APPEARANCE | **4** [C, usually sing.] the way sb/sth looks; the appearance of sb/sth: *It's going to rain today by the look of it* (= judging by appearances). ◊ *Looks can be deceptive.* ◊ *I don't like the look of that guy* (= I don't trust him, judging by his appearance). **5** (**looks**) [pl.] a person's appearance, especially when the person is attractive: *She has her father's good looks.* ◊ *He lost his looks* (= became less attractive) *in later life.*—see also GOOD-LOOKING

FASHION | **6** [sing.] a fashion; a style: *The punk look is back in fashion this year.* ◊ *They've given the place a completely new look.*

IDM see DIRTY *adj.*, LONG *adj.*

■ *exclamation* used to interrupt sb or make them listen to sth you are saying: *Look, I have to go now.*

VOCABULARY BUILDING
different ways of looking

gaze	*He gazed dreamily out of the window.*
stare	*She stared at him in disbelief.*
glare	*They glared angrily at each other.*
peer	*I peered into the dark room.*
squint	*I squinted at the target and took aim.*
glance	*She glanced quickly at her watch.*
eye	*They eyed each other suspiciously.*
scan	*He scanned the crowd anxiously but couldn't see her.*
examine	*Scientists are examining the wreckage.*
study	*I spent a few minutes studying the map.*
inspect	*New buildings have to be inspected by the Fire Department.*

⇨ note at SEE

---

look·alike /'lʊkəlaɪk/ *noun* (often used after a person's name) a person who looks very similar to the person mentioned: *an Elvis lookalike*

look·er /'lʊkə(r)/ *noun* (*informal*) a way of describing an attractive person, usually a woman: *She's a real looker!*

'look-in *noun* **IDM** (not) **get/have a 'look-in** (*BrE, informal*) (not) to get a chance to take part or succeed in sth: *She talks so much that nobody else can get a look-in.*

'looking glass *noun* (*old-fashioned*) a mirror

look·out /'lʊkaʊt/ *noun* **1** a place for watching from, especially for danger or an enemy coming towards you: *a lookout point/tower* **2** a person who has the responsibility of watching for sth, especially danger, etc: *One of the men stood at the door to act as a lookout.* **IDM** be '**your (own) lookout** (*BrE, informal*) used to say that you do not think sb's actions are sensible, but that it is their

own problem or responsibility: *If he wants to waste his money, that's his lookout.* be on the '**lookout (for sb/sth)** | keep a '**lookout (for sb/sth)** (*informal*) to watch carefully for sb/sth in order to avoid danger, etc. or in order to find sth you want: *The public should be on the lookout for symptoms of the disease.*

look-'see *noun* [sing.] (*informal, especially AmE*) a quick look at sth: *Come and have a look-see.*

loom /luːm/ *verb, noun*

■ *verb* [V] **1** [usually +*adv./prep.*] to appear as a large shape that is not clear, especially in a frightening or threatening way: *A dark shape loomed up ahead of us.* **2** to appear important or threatening and likely to happen soon: *Food shortages loom in some parts of Africa.* **IDM** **loom 'large** to be worrying or frightening and seem hard to avoid: *The prospect of war loomed large.*

■ *noun* a machine for weaving fabric

loon /luːn/ *noun* **1** a large N American bird that eats fish and has a cry like a laugh **2** = LOONY

loony /'luːni/ *adj., noun*

■ *adj.* (*informal*) crazy or strange: *He does have some pretty loony ideas.*

■ *noun* (*pl.* **-ies**) (also **loon**) (*informal*) a person who has strange ideas or who behaves in a strange way

loop /luːp/ *noun, verb*

■ *noun* **1** a shape like a curve or circle made by a line curving right round and crossing itself: *The road went in a huge loop around the lake.* **2** a piece of rope, wire, etc. in the shape of a curve or circle: *He tied a loop of rope around his arm.* ◊ *Make a loop in the string.* ◊ *a belt loop* (= on trousers/pants, etc. for holding a belt in place) **3** a strip of film or tape on which the pictures and sound are repeated continuously: *The film is on a loop.* ◊ (*figurative*) *His mind kept turning in an endless loop.* **4** (*computing*) a set of instructions that is repeated again and again until a particular condition is satisfied **5** a complete CIRCUIT for electrical current **6** (*BrE*) a railway line or road that leaves the main track or road and then joins it again **IDM** be in the '**loop** | be out of the '**loop** (both *AmE, informal*) to be part of a group of people that is dealing with sth important; to not be part of this group: *A lot of people want to be in the loop on this operation.* ◊ *Lawton had gradually been cut out of the loop on legal reviews.* **knock/throw sb for a 'loop** (*AmE, informal*) to shock or surprise sb: *The result of the election knocked most people for a loop.*

■ *verb* [+*adv./prep.*] **1** [VN] to form or bend sth into a loop: *He looped the strap over his shoulder.* **2** [V] to move in a way that makes the shape of a loop: *The river loops around the valley.* ◊ *The ball looped high up in the air.* **IDM** **loop the 'loop** to fly or make a plane fly in a circle going up and down

loop·hole /'luːphəʊl; *AmE* -hoʊl/ *noun* ~ (**in sth**) a mistake in the way a law, contract, etc. has been written which enables people to legally avoid doing sth that the law, contract, etc. had intended them to do: *a legal/tax loophole* ◊ *to close/plug existing loopholes*

loopy /'luːpi/ *adj.* (*informal*) **1** not sensible; strange **SYN** CRAZY **2** (*BrE*) very angry: *He'll go loopy when he sees that!*

loose /luːs/ *adj., verb, noun*

■ *adj.* (**loos·er, loos·est**)

NOT FIXED/TIED | **1** not firmly fixed where it should be; able to become separated from sth: *a loose button/tooth* ◊ *Check that the plug has not come loose.* **2** not tied together; not held in position by anything or contained in anything: *She usually wears her hair loose.* ◊ *The potatoes were sold loose, not in bags.* **3** [not usually before noun] free to move around without control; not tied up or shut in somewhere: *The sheep had got out and were loose on the road.* ◊ *The horse had broken loose* (= escaped) *from its tether.* ◊ *During the night, somebody had cut the boat loose from its moorings.*

CLOTHES | **4** not fitting closely: *a loose jacket/shirt* **OPP** TIGHT

NOT SOLID/HARD | **5** not tightly packed together; not solid or hard: *loose soil* ◊ *a fabric with a loose weave*

---

s	t	v	z	ʃ	ʒ	tʃ	dʒ	θ	ð	ŋ
see	tea	van	zoo	shoe	vision	chain	jam	thin	this	sing

NOT STRICT/EXACT | **6** not strictly organized or controlled: *a loose alliance/coalition/federation* **7** not exact; not very careful: *a loose translation* ◇ *loose thinking*

IMMORAL | **8** [usually before noun] (*old-fashioned*) having or involving an attitude to sexual relationships that people consider to be immoral: *a young man of loose morals*

BALL | **9** (*sport*) not in any player's control: *He pounced on a loose ball.*

BODY WASTE | **10** having too much liquid in it: *a baby with loose bowel movements*

▶ **loose·ness** *noun* [U]

IDM **break/cut/tear (sth) 'loose from sb/sth** to separate yourself or sb/sth from a group of people or their influence, etc: *The organization broke loose from its sponsors.* ◇ *He cut himself loose from his family.* **hang/stay 'loose** (*informal, especially AmE*) to remain calm; to not worry: *It's OK—hang loose and stay cool.* **have a loose 'tongue** to talk too much, especially about things that are private **let 'loose** (*BrE*) (*AmE* **cut 'loose**) (*informal*) to do sth or to happen in a way that is not controlled: *Teenagers need a place to let loose.* **let 'loose sth** to make a noise or remark, especially in a loud or sudden way: *She let loose a stream of abuse.* **let sb/sth 'loose 1** to free sb/sth from whatever holds them/it in place: *She let her hair loose and it fell around her shoulders.* ◇ *Who's let the dog loose?* **2** to give sb complete freedom to do what they want in a place or situation: *He was at last let loose in the kitchen.* ◇ *A team of professionals were* **let loose on** *the project*—more at FAST *adv.*, HELL, SCREW *n.*

■ *verb* [VN] (*formal*)

RELEASE | **1 ~ sth (on/upon sb/sth)** to release sth or let it happen or be expressed in an uncontrolled way: *His speech loosed a tide of nationalist sentiment.*

MAKE STH LOOSE | **2** to make sth loose, especially sth that is tied or held tightly: *He loosed the straps that bound her arms.*

FIRE BULLETS | **3 ~ sth (off) (at sb/sth)** to fire bullets, arrows, etc.

HELP Do not confuse this verb with **to lose** = 'to be unable to find sth'.

■ *noun*

IDM **on the 'loose** (of a person or an animal) having escaped from somewhere; free: *Three prisoners are still on the loose.*

'loose box *noun* (*BrE*) a small area in a building or a vehicle where a horse can move freely

loose 'cannon *noun* a person, usually a public figure, who often behaves in a way that nobody can predict

loose 'change *noun* [U] coins that you have in a pocket or a bag

loose 'cover (*BrE*) (*AmE* **'slip cover**) *noun* [usually pl.] a cover for a chair, etc. that you can take off, for example to wash it

loose 'end *noun* [usually pl.] a part of sth such as a story that has not been completely finished or explained: *The play has too many loose ends.* ◇ *There are still a few loose ends to tie up* (= a few things to finish). **IDM** **at a loose 'end** (*BrE*) (*AmE* **at loose 'ends**) having nothing to do and not knowing what you want to do: *Come and see us, if you're at a loose end.*

loose-'fitting *adj.* (of clothes) not fitting the body tightly

loose-'leaf *adj.* [usually before noun] (of a book, file, etc.) having pages that can be taken out and put in separately: *a loose-leaf binder*

loose-'limbed *adj.* (*written*) (of a person) moving in an easy, not stiff, way

loose·ly /ˈluːsli/ *adv.* **1** in a way that is not firm or tight: *She fastened the belt loosely around her waist.* **2** in a way that is not exact: *to use a term loosely* ◇ *The play is loosely based on his childhood in Russia.*

loos·en /ˈluːsn/ *verb* **1** to make sth less tight or firmly fixed; to become less tight or firmly fixed: [VN] *First loosen the nuts, then take off the wheel.* ◇ [V] *The rope holding the boat loosened.* **2** [VN] to make a piece of clothing, hair, etc. loose, when it has been tied or fastened **3** [VN] **~ your hands, hold, etc.** to hold sb/sth less tightly: *He loosened*

his grip and let her go. ◇ (*figurative*) *The military regime has not loosened its hold on power.* **4** [VN] to make sth weaker or less controlled than before: *The party has loosened its links with trade unions.* **OPP** TIGHTEN **IDM** **loosen sb's 'tongue** to make sb talk more freely than usual: *A bottle of wine had loosened Harry's tongue.* **PHRV** **loosen 'up** to relax and stop worrying: *Come on, Jo. Loosen up.* **loosen 'up|** **loosen sb/sth··'up** to relax your muscles or parts of the body or to make them relax, before taking exercise, etc: *Dancers were loosening up before going on stage.*

loot /luːt/ *verb, noun*
■ *verb* to steal things from shops/stores or buildings after a RIOT, fire, etc: [VN] *More than 20 shops were looted.* [also V] ▶ **loot·er** /ˈluːtə(r)/ *noun* **loot·ing** *noun* [U]
■ *noun* [U] **1** money and valuable objects taken by soldiers from the enemy after winning a battle **2** (*informal*) money and valuable objects that have been stolen by thieves **3** (*informal*) money

lop /lɒp; *AmE* lɑːp/ *verb* (**-pp-**) [VN] to cut down a tree, or cut some large branches off it **PHRV** **lop sth··'off (sth)** **1** to remove part of sth by cutting it, especially to remove branches from a tree **2** to make sth smaller or less by a particular amount: *They lopped 20p off the price of each unit.*

lope /ləʊp; *AmE* loʊp/ *verb* [V+*adv./prep.*] to run taking long relaxed steps: *The dog loped along beside her.* ◇ *He set off with a loping stride.* ▶ **lope** *noun* [usually sing.]

lop·sided /ˌlɒpˈsaɪdɪd; *AmE* ˌlɑːp-/ *adj.* having one side lower, smaller, etc. than the other: *a lopsided grin/mouth* ◇ (*figurative*) *The article presents a somewhat lopsided view of events.*

lo·qua·cious /ləˈkweɪʃəs/ *adj.* (*formal*) talking a lot TALKATIVE ▶ **lo·qua·city** /ləˈkwæsəti/ *noun* [U]

lord /lɔːd; *AmE* lɔːrd/ *noun, verb*
■ *noun* **1** [C] (in Britain) a NOBLEMAN: *She's married to a lord.*—compare LADY **2** (**Lord**) (in Britain) the title used by some high ranks of NOBLEMEN (= men of high social class): *Lord Beaverbrook* **3** (**Lord**) a title used for some high official positions in Britain: *the Lord Chancellor* ◇ *the Lord Mayor* **4** (**My Lord**) (in Britain) a title of respect used when speaking to a judge, BISHOP or some male members of the NOBILITY (= people of high social class)—compare LADY **5** a powerful man in MEDIEVAL Europe, who owned a lot of land and property: *a feudal lord* ◇ *the lord of the manor*—see also OVERLORD, WARLORD **6** (usually **the Lord**) [sing.] a title used to refer to God or Christ: *Love the Lord with all your heart.* **7** (**Our Lord**) [sing.] a title used to refer to Christ **8** (**the Lords**) [sing.+ sing./pl. *v.*] = HOUSE OF LORDS: *The Lords has/have not yet reached a decision.*—compare COMMONS—see also LAW LORD **IDM** **(good) 'Lord!| oh 'Lord!** *exclamation* used to show that you are surprised, annoyed or worried about sth: *Good Lord, what have you done to your hair!* **'Lord knows ...** used to emphasize what you are saying: *Lord knows, I tried to teach her.* **'Lord ('only) knows (what, where, why, etc.) ...** (*spoken*) used to say that you do not know the answer to sth: *'Why did she say that?' 'Lord knows!'* **HELP** Some people may find the use of **Lord** in these expressions offensive. **IDM** see DRUNK *adj.*, YEAR
■ *verb* **IDM** **lord it over sb** (*disapproving*) to act as if you are better or more important than sb: *A good manager does not try to lord it over his or her team.*

lord·ly /ˈlɔːdli; *AmE* ˈlɔːrd-/ *adj.* **1** behaving in a way that suggests that you think you are better than other people **SYN** HAUGHTY: *He dismissed us with a lordly gesture.* **2** large and impressive; suitable for a LORD: *a lordly mansion*

lord·ship /ˈlɔːdʃɪp; *AmE* ˈlɔːrd-/ *noun* **1** (**His/Your Lordship**) a title of respect used when speaking to or about a judge, a BISHOP or a NOBLEMAN: *His Lordship is away on business.*—compare LADYSHIP **2** (*BrE, spoken*) a humorous way of talking to or about a boy or man that you think is trying to be too important: *Can his lordship manage to switch off the TV?* **3** [U] the power or position of a LORD

the ˌLord's 'Prayer *noun* [sing.] the prayer that Jesus

æ	ɑː	e	ɜː	ə	ɪ	iː	i	ɒ	ɔː	ʌ	ʊ	u	uː
cat	father	ten	bird	about	sit	see	many	got (BrE)	saw	cup	put	actual	too

Christ taught the people who followed him, that begins 'Our Father ...'

lore /lɔː(r)/ *noun* [U] knowledge and information related to a particular subject, especially when this is not written down; the stories and traditions of a particular group of people: *weather lore* ◊ *Celtic lore*—see also FOLKLORE

lor·gnette /lɔːˈnjet; *AmE* lɔːrˈnjet/ *noun* an old-fashioned pair of glasses that you hold to your eyes on a long handle

lorry /ˈlɒri; *AmE* ˈlɔːri/ (*BrE*) (also **truck** *AmE, BrE*) *noun* (*pl.* **-ies**) a large motor vehicle for carrying heavy loads by road: *a lorry driver* ◊ *Emergency food supplies were brought in by lorry.* ◊ *a lorry load of frozen fish* **IDM** see BACK *n.*—picture at TRUCK

lose /luːz/ *verb* (**lost, lost** /lɒst; *AmE* lɑːst; lɔːst/)

NOT FIND | **1** [VN] to be unable to find sth/sb: *I've lost my keys.* ◊ *The tickets seem to have got lost.* ◊ *She lost her husband in the crowd.*

HAVE STH TAKEN AWAY | **2** [VN] to have sth/sb taken away from you by accident, old age, death, etc: *She lost a leg in a car crash.* ◊ *to lose your hair/teeth* (= as a result of getting old) ◊ *He's lost his job.* ◊ *Some families lost everything* (= all they owned) *in the flood.* ◊ *They lost both their sons* (= they were killed) *in the war.* ◊ *The ship was lost at sea.* ◊ *Many people lost their lives* (= were killed). **3** [VN] **~ sth** (**to sb**) to have sth taken away by sb/sth: *The company has lost a lot of business to its competitors.* **4** [VN] to have to give up sth; to fail to keep sth: *You will lose your deposit if you cancel the order.* ◊ *Sit down or you'll lose your seat.*

HAVE LESS | **5** [VN] to have less and less of sth, especially until you no longer have any of it: *to lose your confidence* ◊ *He lost his nerve at the last minute.* ◊ *She seemed to have lost interest in food.* ◊ *At that moment he lost his balance and fell.* ◊ *I've lost ten pounds since I started this diet.* ◊ *The train was losing speed.*

NOT UNDERSTAND/HEAR | **6** [VN] to fail to get, hear or understand sth: *His words were lost* (= could not be heard) *in the applause.* **7** [VN] (*informal*) to be no longer understood by sb: *I'm afraid you've lost me there.*

ESCAPE | **8** [VN] to escape from sb/sth: *We managed to lose our pursuers in the darkness.*

NOT WIN | **9** **~ (sth) (to sb)|~ (sth) (by sth)** to be defeated; to fail to win a competition, a court case, an argument, etc: [VN] *to lose a game/a race/an election/a battle* ◊ [V] *We lost to a stronger team.* ◊ *He lost by less than 100 votes.*

NOT KEEP | **10** **~ (sth) (on sth/by doing sth)|~ sb sth** to fail to keep sth you want or need, especially money; to cause sb to fail to keep sth: [VN] *The business is losing money.* ◊ *Poetry always loses something in translation.* ◊ *You have nothing to lose by telling the truth.* ◊ [V] *We lost on that deal.* ◊ [VNN] *His carelessness lost him the job.*

TIME | **11** [VN] to waste time or an opportunity: *We lost twenty minutes changing a tyre.* ◊ *Hurry—there's no time to lose!* ◊ *He lost no time in setting out for London.* **12** if a watch or clock **loses** or **loses time**, it goes too slowly or becomes a particular amount of time behind the correct time: [VN] *This clock loses two minutes a day.* [also V] **OPP** GAIN

IDM Most idioms containing **lose** are at the entries for the nouns and adjectives in the idioms, for example **lose your bearings** is at **bearing**. **ˈlose it** (*spoken*) to be unable to stop yourself from crying, laughing, etc.; to become crazy: *Then she just lost it and started screaming.* **PHR V** **ˌlose yourself in sth** to become so interested in sth that it takes all your attention **ˌlose ˈout (on sth)** (*informal*) to not get sth you wanted or feel you should have: *While the stores make big profits, it's the customer who loses out.* **ˌlose ˈout to sb/sth** (*informal*) to not get business, etc. that you expected or used to get because sb/sth else has taken it: *Small businesses are losing out to the large chains.*

loser /ˈluːzə(r)/ *noun* **1** a person who is defeated in a competition: *winners and losers* ◊ *He's a good/bad loser* (= he accepts defeat well/badly). **2** a person who is regularly unsuccessful, especially when you have a low opinion of them: *She's one of life's losers.* ◊ *He's a born*

loser. **3** a person who suffers because of a particular action, decision, etc: *The real losers in all of this are the students.*

loss /lɒs; *AmE* lɔːs/ *noun* **1** [U, C, usually sing.] the state of no longer having sth or as much of sth; the process that leads to this: *loss of blood/sleep/self-control* ◊ *hair/weight loss* ◊ *I want to report the loss of a package.* ◊ *The closure of the factory will lead to a number of job losses.* ◊ *When she died I was filled with a sense of loss.* **2** [C] money that has been lost by a business or an organization: *The company has announced net losses of $1·5 million.* ◊ *We made a loss on* (= lost money on) *the deal.* ◊ *We are now operating at a loss.* **OPP** PROFIT **3** [C, U] the death of a person: *The loss of his wife was a great blow to him.* ◊ *Enemy troops suffered heavy losses.* ◊ *The drought has led to widespread loss of life.* **4** [sing.] the disadvantage that is caused when sb leaves or when a useful or valuable object is taken away; a person who causes a disadvantage by leaving: *Her departure is a big loss to the school.* ◊ *She will be a great loss to the school.* ◊ *If he isn't prepared to accept this money, then that's his loss.*—see also DEAD LOSS **IDM at a ˈloss** not knowing what to say or do: *His comments left me at a loss for words.* ◊ *I'm at a loss what to do next.* **cut your ˈlosses** to stop doing sth that is not successful before the situation becomes even worse

ˈloss adjuster (*BrE*) (*AmE* **inˈsurance adjuster**) *noun* a person who works for an insurance company and whose job is to calculate how much money sb should receive after they have lost sth or had sth damaged

ˈloss-leader *noun* an item that a shop/store sells at a very low price to attract customers

ˈloss-making *adj.* (of a company or business) not making a profit; losing money

lost /lɒst; *AmE* lɔːst/ *adj.* **1** unable to find your way; not knowing where you are: *We always get lost in London.* ◊ *We're completely lost.* **2** that cannot be found or brought back: *I'm still looking for that lost file.* ◊ *Your cheque must have got lost in the post.* **3** [usually before noun] that cannot be obtained; that cannot be found or created again: *The strike cost them thousands of pounds in lost business.* ◊ *She's trying to recapture her lost youth.* ◊ *He regretted the lost* (= wasted) *opportunity to apologize to her.* **4** [not before noun] unable to deal successfully with a particular situation; unable to understand sb/sth: *We would be lost without your help.* ◊ *I felt so lost after my mother died.* ◊ *He's a lost soul* (= a person who does not seem to know what to do, and seems unhappy). ◊ *They spoke so quickly I just got lost.*—see also LOSE *v.* **IDM** **ˌall is not ˈlost** there is still some hope of making a bad situation better **be lost for ˈwords** to be so surprised, confused, etc. that you do not know what to say **be ˈlost in sth** to be giving all your attention to sth so that you do not notice what is happening around you: *to be lost in thought/admiration* **be ˈlost on sb** not understood or noticed by sb: *His jokes were completely lost on most of the students.* **be lost to the ˈworld** to be giving all your attention to sth so that you do not notice what is happening around you **get ˈlost** (*informal*) a rude way of telling sb to go away, or of refusing sth **give sb up for ˈlost** (*formal*) to stop expecting to find sb alive **make up for lost ˈtime** to do sth quickly or very often because you wish you had started doing it sooner—more at LOVE *n.*

ˌlost and ˈfound *noun* [U] (*AmE*) = LOST PROPERTY (2)

ˌlost ˈcause *noun* something that has failed or that cannot succeed

ˌlost ˈproperty *noun* [U] (*BrE*) **1** items that have been found in public places and are waiting to be collected by the people who lost them: *a lost-property office* **2** (*AmE* **ˌlost and ˈfound**) the place where items that have been found are kept until they are collected

lot /lɒt; *AmE* lɑːt/ *pron., det., adv., noun*
■ *pron.* **(a lot)** (also *informal* **lots**) **~ (to do)** a large number or amount: *'How many do you need?' 'A lot.'* ◊ *Have some more cake. There's lots left.* ◊ *She still has an awful lot* (= a very large amount) *to learn.* ◊ *He has invited nearly a hundred people but a lot aren't able to come.* ⇨ note at MANY, MUCH

L

■ *det.* (a lot of) (also *informal* lots of) a large number or amount of sb/sth: *What a lot of presents!* ◊ *A lot of people are coming to the meeting.* ◊ *black coffee with lots of sugar* ◊ *I saw a lot of her* (= I saw her often) *last summer.* ⇨ note at MANY, MUCH

■ *adv.* (*informal*) **1** (a lot) (also *informal* lots) used with adjectives and adverbs to mean 'much': *I'm feeling a lot better today.* ◊ *I eat lots less than I used to.* **2** (a lot) used with verbs to mean 'a great amount': *I care a lot about you.* ◊ *Thanks a lot for your help.* ◊ *I play tennis quite a lot* (= often) *in the summer.* ⇨ note at MUCH

■ *noun*
WHOLE AMOUNT/NUMBER **1** (the lot, the whole lot) [sing.+ sing./pl. *v.*] (*informal*) the whole number or amount of people or things: *She's got a PC, colour printer, scanner— the lot.* ◊ *Get out of my house, the lot of you!* ◊ *That's the lot!* (= that includes everything) ◊ *That's your lot!* (= that's all you're getting)
GROUP/SET **2** [C+sing./pl. *v.*] (*especially BrE*) a group or set of people or things: *The first lot of visitors has/have arrived.* ◊ *I have several lots of essays to mark this weekend.* ◊ (*informal*) *What do you lot want?*
ITEMS SOLD **3** [C] an item or a number of items sold, especially at an AUCTION: *Lot 46: six chairs*
AREA OF LAND **4** [C] an area of land used for a particular purpose: *a parking lot* ◊ *a vacant lot* (= one available to be built on or used for sth)
LUCK/SITUATION **5** [sing.] a person's luck or situation in life: *She was feeling very dissatisfied with her lot.*
IDM all 'over the lot (*AmE*) = ALL OVER THE PLACE a bad 'lot (*old-fashioned, BrE*) a person who is dishonest by 'lot using a method of choosing sb to do sth in which each person takes a piece of paper, etc. from a container and the one whose paper has a special mark is chosen draw/ cast 'lots (for sth/to do sth) to choose sb/sth by lot: *They drew lots for the right to go first.* fall to sb's 'lot (to do sth) (*formal*) to become sb's task or responsibility throw in your 'lot with sb to decide to join sb and share their successes and problems

loth (*rare*) = LOATH

lo·tion /ˈləʊʃn; *AmE* ˈloʊʃn/ *noun* [C, U] a liquid used for cleaning, protecting or treating the skin: *a body/hand lotion* ◊ *suntan lotion*

lot·tery /ˈlɒtəri; *AmE* ˈlɑːt-/ *noun* (*pl.* -ies) **1** [C] a way of raising money for a government, charity, etc. by selling tickets that have different numbers on them that people have chosen. Numbers are then chosen by chance and the people who have those numbers on their tickets win prizes: *the national/state lottery* ◊ *a lottery ticket*—compare DRAW, RAFFLE **2** [sing.] (*often disapproving*) a situation whose success or result is based on luck rather than on effort or careful organization: *Some people think that marriage is a lottery.*

lotto /ˈlɒtəʊ; *AmE* ˈlɑːtoʊ/ *noun* **1** [U] a game of chance similar to BINGO but with the numbers drawn from a container by the players instead of being called out **2** [C] (*informal, especially AmE*) a lottery

lotus /ˈləʊtəs; *AmE* ˈloʊ-/ *noun* **1** a tropical plant with white or pink flowers that grows on the surface of lakes in Africa and Asia: *a lotus flower* **2** a picture in the shape of the lotus plant, used in art and architecture, especially in ancient Egypt **3** (in ancient Greek stories) a fruit that is supposed to make you feel happy and relaxed when you have eaten it, as if in a dream

'lotus position *noun* [sing.] a way of sitting with your legs crossed, used especially when people do YOGA

louche /luːʃ/ *adj.* (*formal*) not socially acceptable, but often still attractive in spite of this

loud /laʊd/ *adj., adv.*
■ *adj.* (loud·er, loud·est) **1** making a lot of noise: *a deafeningly loud bang/explosion* ◊ *loud applause/laughter* ◊ *She spoke in a very loud voice.* ◊ *That music's too loud—please turn it down.* **2** (of a person or their behaviour) talking very loudly, too much and in a way that is annoying **3** (of colours, patterns, etc.) too bright and lacking good taste **SYN** GAUDY ▶ loud·ly *adv.*: *She screamed as loudly as she could.* loud·ness *noun* [U]

■ *adv.* (loud·er, loud·est) (*informal*) in a way that makes a lot of noise or can be easily heard **SYN** LOUDLY: *Do you have to play that music so loud?* ◊ *You'll have to speak louder—I can't hear you.* **IDM** ,loud and 'clear in a way that is very easy to understand: *The message is coming through loud and clear.* ,out 'loud in a voice that can be heard by other people: *I almost laughed out loud.* ◊ *Please read the letter out loud.*—compare ALOUD—more at ACTION, CRY *v.*

loud·hail·er /ˌlaʊdˈheɪlə(r)/ (*BrE*) (*AmE* bull·horn) *noun* an electronic device, shaped like a horn, with a MICROPHONE at one end, that you speak into in order to make your voice louder so that it can be heard at a distance— compare MEGAPHONE

loud·mouth /ˈlaʊdmaʊθ/ *noun* (*informal*) a person who is annoying because they talk too loudly or too much in an offensive or stupid way ▶ loud-mouthed *adj.*

loud·speak·er /ˌlaʊdˈspiːkə(r)/ (also speak·er) *noun* a piece of equipment, especially part of a radio, cassette player, etc., that changes electrical signals into sound; a similar piece of equipment used in public places for announcing things, playing music, etc: *Their names were called over the loudspeaker.*—see also PUBLIC ADDRESS SYSTEM, TANNOY

lough /lɒk; lɒx; *AmE* lɑːk; lɑːx/ *noun* (in Ireland) a lake or a long strip of sea that is almost surrounded by land: *Lough Corrib*—see also LOCH

lounge /laʊndʒ/ *noun, verb*
■ *noun* **1** a room for waiting in at an airport, etc: *the departure lounge* **2** a public room in a hotel, club, etc. for waiting or relaxing in: *the television lounge* **3** (*BrE*) a room in a private house for sitting and relaxing in **4** (*AmE*) = LOUNGE BAR—see also SUN LOUNGE
■ *verb* [V] [usually+*adv./prep.*] to stand, sit or lie in a lazy way: *Several students were lounging around, reading newspapers.*

'lounge bar (also sal·oon) (both *BrE*) (*AmE* lounge) *noun* a bar in a pub, hotel, etc. which is more comfortable than the other bars and where the drinks are usually more expensive—compare PUBLIC BAR

loun·ger /ˈlaʊndʒə(r)/ *noun* = SUNLOUNGER

'lounge suit *noun* (*BrE*) a man's suit of matching jacket and trousers/pants, worn especially in offices and on fairly formal occasions

lour *verb* [V] = LOWER[2]

louse /laʊs/ *noun, verb*
■ *noun* **1** (*pl.* lice /laɪs/) a small insect that lives on the bodies of humans and animals: *head lice*—see also WOODLOUSE **2** (*pl.* louses) (*informal, disapproving*) a very unpleasant person
■ *verb* **PHRV** ,louse sth↔'up (*slang*) to spoil sth or do it very badly

lousy /ˈlaʊzi/ *adj.* **1** (*informal*) very bad **SYN** AWFUL: *What lousy weather!* ◊ *She felt lousy* (= ill). **2** [only before noun] (*informal*) used to show that you feel annoyed or insulted because you do not think that sth is worth very much: *All she bought me was this lousy T-shirt.*

lout /laʊt/ *noun* (*BrE*) a man or boy who behaves in a rude and aggressive way—see also LAGER LOUT, LITTER LOUT ▶ **lout·ish** adj.: *loutish behaviour*

louvre (also **lou·ver**) /ˈluːvə(r)/ noun one of a set of narrow strips of wood, plastic, etc. in a door or a window that are designed to let air and some light in, but to keep out strong sunlight or rain; a door or a window that has these strips across it ▶ **louvred** adj.

lov·able (also **love·able**) /ˈlʌvəbl/ adj. having qualities that people find attractive and easy to love, often in spite of any faults: *a lovable child ◊ a lovable rogue*

love /lʌv/ noun, verb

■ noun

UNDERLINE AFFECTION | **1** [U] a strong feeling of deep affection for sb/sth, especially a member of your family or a friend: *a mother's love for her children ◊ love of your country ◊ He seems incapable of love.*

ROMANTIC | **2** [U] a strong feeling of affection for sb that you are sexually attracted to: *a love song/story ◊ We're **in love**! ◊ She was in love with him. ◊ They fell in love with each other. ◊ It was **love at first sight** (= they were attracted to each other the first time they met). ◊ They're **madly in love**. ◊ Their love grew with the years.*

ENJOYMENT | **3** [U, sing.] the strong feeling of enjoyment that sth gives you: *a love of learning/nature/music ◊ He's **in love with** his work. ◊ I fell in love with the house.*

SB/STH YOU LIKE | **4** [C] a person, a thing or an activity that you like very much: *Take care, my love. ◊ He was the love of my life (= the person I loved most). ◊ I like most sports but tennis is my first love.*

FRIENDLY NAME | **5** [C] (BrE, spoken, informal) a word used as a friendly way of addressing sb: *Can I help you, love?*—compare DUCK

IN TENNIS | **6** [U] a score of zero (points or games): *40–love! ◊ She won the first set six–love/six games to love.*

IDM **(just) for 'love | (just) for the 'love of sth** without receiving payment or any other reward: *They're all volunteers, working for the love of it.* **for the love of 'God** (old-fashioned, spoken) used when you are expressing anger and the fact that you are impatient: *For the love of God, tell me what he said!* **give/send my love to sb** (informal) used to send friendly greetings to sb: *Give my love to Mary when you see her. ◊ Bob sends his love.* **'love from | lots of 'love (from)** (written, informal) used at the end of a letter to a person or to sb you love, followed by your name: *Lots of love, Jenny* ➪ Study page B13 **make 'love (to sb)** to have sex: *It was the first time they had made love.* **not for love or/nor 'money** if you say you cannot do sth **for love nor money**, you mean it is completely impossible to do it **there's little/no 'love lost between A and B** they do not like each other: *There's no love lost between her and her in-laws.*—more at CUPBOARD, FAIR adj., HEAD n., LABOUR n.

■ verb

FEEL AFFECTION | **1** [VN] (not used in the progressive tenses) to have very strong feelings of affection for sb: *I love you. ◊ If you love each other, why not get married? ◊ Her much-loved brother lay dying of Aids. ◊ He had become a well-loved and respected member of staff. ◊ Relatives need time to grieve over **loved ones** they have lost. ◊ to love your country*

LIKE/ENJOY | **2** to like or enjoy sth very much: [VN] *I really love summer evenings. ◊ I just love it when you bring me presents! ◊ He loved the way she smiled. ◊ I love it in Spain (= I like the life there). ◊ It was one of his best-loved songs. ◊ (ironic) You're going to love this. They've changed their minds again. ◊* [V-ing] (especially in BrE) *My dad loves going to football games. ◊* [Vtoinf] (especially AmE) *I love to go out dancing. ◊* [VNtoinf] *He loved her to sing to him.* **3** (**would love**) used to say that you would very much like sth: [Vtoinf] *Come on Rory, the kids would love to hear you sing. ◊ I haven't been to Brazil, but I'd love to. ◊* [VNtoinf] *I'd love her to come and live with us. ◊* [VN] *'Cigarette?' 'I'd love one, but I've just given up.'*

IDM **,love you and 'leave you** (spoken, humorous) used to say that you must go, although you would like to stay longer: *Well, time to love you and leave you.*

'love affair noun **1** a romantic and/or sexual relationship between two people who are in love and not married to each other **2** great enthusiasm for sth: *the English love affair with gardening*

love·bird /ˈlʌvbɜːd; AmE -bɜːrd/ noun **1** [C] a small African PARROT (= a bird with brightly-coloured feathers) **2** (**lovebirds**) [pl.] (humorous) two people who love each other very much and show this in their behaviour

'love bite (BrE) (AmE **hickey**) noun a red mark on the skin that is caused by sb biting their partner's skin when they are kissing

'love child noun (used especially in newspapers, etc.) a child born to parents who are not married to each other

,love-'hate relationship noun [usually sing.] a relationship in which your feelings for sb/sth are a mixture of love and hatred

love·less /ˈlʌvləs/ adj. without love: *a loveless marriage*

'love letter noun a letter that you write to sb telling them that you love them

'love life noun the part of your life that involves your romantic and sexual relationships

love·li·ness /ˈlʌvlinəs/ noun [U] (written) the state of being very attractive

love·lorn /ˈlʌvlɔːn; AmE -lɔːrn/ adj. (literary) unhappy because the person you love does not love you

love·ly /ˈlʌvli/ adj., noun

■ adj. (**love·lier**, **love·li·est**) HELP You can also use **more lovely** and **most lovely**. (especially BrE) **1** beautiful; attractive: *lovely countryside/eyes/flowers ◊ She looked particularly lovely that night. ◊ He has a lovely voice.* **2** (informal) very enjoyable and pleasant; wonderful: *'Can I get you anything?' 'A cup of tea would be lovely' ◊ What a lovely surprise! ◊ How lovely to see you! ◊ Isn't it a lovely day? ◊ We've had a lovely time. ◊ It's a lovely old farm. ◊ It's been lovely having you here. ◊ (ironic) You've got yourself into a lovely mess, haven't you? ◊* **3** (informal) (of a person) very kind, generous and friendly: *Her mother was a lovely woman.* HELP **Very lovely** is not very common and is only used about the physical appearance of a person or thing. IDM **lovely and 'warm, 'cold, 'quiet,** etc. (BrE, spoken) used when you are emphasizing that sth is good because of the quality mentioned: *It's lovely and warm in here.*

■ noun (pl. **-ies**) (old-fashioned) a beautiful woman

love·mak·ing /ˈlʌvmeɪkɪŋ/ noun [U] sexual activity between two lovers, especially the act of having sex

'love match noun a marriage of two people who are in love with each other

'love nest noun [usually sing.] (informal) a house or an apartment where two people who are not married but are having a sexual relationship can meet

lover /ˈlʌvə(r)/ noun **1** a partner in a sexual relationship outside marriage: *He denied that he was her lover. ◊ We were lovers for several years. ◊ The park was full of young lovers holding hands.* **2** (often in compounds) somebody who likes or enjoys a particular thing: *a lover of music ◊ an art-lover ◊ a nature-lover*

'love seat noun (AmE) a comfortable seat with a back and arms, for two people to sit on

love·sick /ˈlʌvsɪk/ adj. (written) unable to think clearly or behave in a sensible way because you are in love with sb, especially sb who is not in love with you

lovey (also **luvvy**) /ˈlʌvi/ noun (BrE, spoken) used as a friendly way of addressing sb: *Ruth, lovey, are you there?*

lov·ing /ˈlʌvɪŋ/ adj. **1** feeling or showing love and affection for sb/sth: *a warm and loving family ◊ She chose the present with loving care.* **2** (**-loving**) (in adjectives) enjoying the object or activity mentioned: *fun-loving young people* ▶ **lov·ing·ly** adv.: *He gazed lovingly at his children. ◊ The house has been lovingly restored.*

low /ləʊ; AmE loʊ/ adj., adv., noun, verb

■ adj. (**lower**, **low·est**)

NOT HIGH/TALL | **1** not high or tall; not far above the ground: *a low wall/building/table ◊ a low range of hills ◊ low clouds ◊ flying at low altitude ◊ The sun was low in the sky.* OPP HIGH

NEAR BOTTOM | **2** at or near the bottom of sth: *low back pain* ◊ *the lower slopes of the mountain* ◊ *temperatures in the low 20s* (= no higher than 21–23°) OPP HIGH

CLOTHING | **3** not high at the neck: *a dress with a low neckline*—see also LOW-CUT

LEVEL/VALUE | **4** (often in compounds) below the usual or average amount, level or value: *low prices/wages* ◊ *low-income families* ◊ *the lowest temperature ever recorded* ◊ *a low level of unemployment* ◊ *Yogurt is usually very low in fat.* ◊ *low-fat yogurt* OPP HIGH **5** having a reduced amount or not enough of sth: *The reservoir was low after the long drought.* ◊ *Our supplies are running low* (= we only have a little left). ◊ *They were low on fuel.*

SOUND | **6** not high; not loud: *The cello is lower than the violin.* ◊ *They were speaking in low voices.* OPP HIGH

STANDARD | **7** below the usual or expected standard: *students with low marks/grades in their exams* ◊ *a low standard of living* OPP HIGH

STATUS | **8** below other people or things in importance or status: *low forms of life* (= creatures with a very simple structure) ◊ *jobs with low status* ◊ *Training was given a very low priority.* ◊ *the lower classes of society* OPP HIGH

DEPRESSED | **9** weak or depressed; with very little energy: *I'm feeling really low.* ◊ *They were in low spirits.*

OPINION | **10** [usually before noun] not very good SYN POOR: *She has a very low opinion of her own abilities.* OPP HIGH

NOT HONEST | **11** (of a person) not honest: *He mixes with some pretty low types.* ◊ *low cunning*

LIGHT | **12** not bright SYN DIM: *The lights were low and romance was in the air.*

IN VEHICLE | **13** if a vehicle is in **low gear**, it travels at a slower speed in relation to the speed of the engine

IDM **at a low 'ebb** a poor state; worse than usual: *Morale among teachers is at a low ebb.* **be brought 'low** (*old-fashioned*) to lose your wealth or your high position in society **lay sb 'low** if sb is **laid low** by/with an injury or illness, they feel very weak and are unable to do much **the ˌlowest of the 'low** people who are not respected at all because they are dishonest, immoral or not at all important—more at PROFILE *n.*

■ *adv.* (**lower, low·est**)

NOT HIGH | **1** in or into a low position, not far above the ground: *to crouch/bend low* ◊ *a plane flying low over the town* ◊ *low-flying aircraft* ◊ *The sun sank lower towards the horizon.*

NEAR BOTTOM | **2** in or into a position near the bottom of sth: *a window set low in the wall* ◊ *The candles were burning low.*

LEVEL | **3** (especially in compounds) at a level below what is usual or expected: *low-priced goods* ◊ *a low-powered PC* ◊ *a very low-scoring game*

SOUND | **4** not high; not loudly: *He's singing an octave lower than the rest of us.* ◊ *Can you turn the music lower—you'll wake the baby.*

IDM see HIGH *adv.*, LIE *v.*, SINK *v.*, STOOP *v.*

■ *noun*

LEVEL/VALUE | **1** a low level or point; a low figure: *The yen has fallen to* **an all-time low** *against the dollar.* ◊ *The temperature reached a record low in London last night.* ◊ *The government's popularity has hit a new low.*

DIFFICULT TIME | **2** a very difficult time in sb's life or career: *The break-up of her marriage marked* **an all-time low** *in her life.*

WEATHER | **3** an area of low pressure in the atmosphere: *Another low is moving in from the Atlantic.*

■ *verb* [V] (*literary*) when a cow **lows**, it makes a deep sound

low·brow /ˈləʊbraʊ; AmE ˈloʊ-/ *adj.* (usually *disapproving*) having no connection with or interest in serious artistic or cultural ideas: *lowbrow newspapers/readers* OPP HIGHBROW—compare MIDDLEBROW

ˌLow 'Church *adj.* connected with the part of the Anglican Church that is least similar to the Roman Catholic Church in its beliefs and practices

ˌlow-'class *adj.* **1** of poor quality **2** connected with a low social class OPP HIGH-CLASS

ˌlow-'cut *adj.* (of dresses etc.) with the top very low so that you can see the neck and the top of the chest

'low-down *adj., noun*
■ *adj.* [only before noun] (*informal*) not fair or honest: *What a dirty, low-down trick!*
■ *noun* (**the low-down**) [sing.] ~ **on** (**sb/sth**) (*informal*) the true facts about sb/sth, especially those considered most important to know: *Jane gave me the low-down on the other guests at the party.*

lower¹ /ˈləʊə(r); AmE ˈloʊ-/ *adj., verb*—see also LOWER²
■ *adj.* [only before noun] **1** situated below sth else, especially sth of the same type, or the other of a pair: *the lower deck of a ship* ◊ *His lower lip trembled.* **2** at or near the bottom of sth: *the mountain's lower slopes* ◊ *I have problems with my lower back.* **3** (of a place) situated towards the coast, on low ground or towards the south of an area: *the lower reaches of the Nile* OPP UPPER
■ *verb* **1** to let or make sth/sb go down: [VN] *He had to lower his head to get through the door.* ◊ *She lowered her newspaper and looked around.* ◊ *They lowered him down the cliff on a rope.* OPP RAISE **2** to reduce sth or to become less in value, quality, etc: [VN] *He lowered his voice to a whisper.* ◊ *This drug is used to lower blood pressure.* ◊ [V] *Her voice lowered as she spoke.* IDM **'lower yourself (by doing sth)** (usually used in negative sentences) to behave in a way that makes other people respect you less: *I wouldn't lower myself by working for him.*—more at SIGHT *n.*, TEMPERATURE

lower² (also **lour**) /ˈlaʊə(r)/ *verb* [V] (*literary*) (of the sky or clouds) to be dark and threatening: *Huge clouds lowered over the bay.*—see also LOWER¹

ˌlower 'case *noun* [U] (in printing and writing) small letters: *The text is all in lower case.* ◊ *lower-case letters*—compare CAPITAL *adj.*, UPPER CASE

the ˌlower 'classes *noun* [pl.] (also **the ˌlower 'class** [sing.]) the groups of people who are considered to have the lowest social status and who have less money and/or power than other people in society ▶ **ˌlower 'class** *adj.*: *The new bosses were condemned as 'too lower-class'.* ◊ *a lower-class accent*—compare UPPER CLASS

ˌlower 'house (also ˌlower 'chamber) *noun* [sing.] the larger group of people who make laws in a country, usually consisting of elected representatives, such as the House of Commons in Britain or the House of Representatives in the US—compare UPPER HOUSE

the ˌlower 'orders *noun* [pl.] (*old-fashioned*) people who are considered to be less important because they belong to groups with a lower social status

'lower school *noun* a school, or the classes in a school, for younger students, usually between the ages of 11 and 14—compare UPPER SCHOOL

ˌlowest ˌcommon de'nominator *noun* **1** (*mathematics*) (*abbr.* LCD) the smallest number that the bottom numbers of a group of FRACTIONS can be divided into exactly **2** (*disapproving*) something that is simple enough to seem interesting to, or to be understood by, the highest number of people in a particular group; the sort of people who are least intelligent or accept sth that is of low quality: *The school syllabus seems aimed at the lowest common denominator.*

ˌlow-'fat *adj.* [usually before noun] containing only a very small amount of fat

ˌlow-'key *adj.* not intended to attract a lot of attention: *Their wedding was a very low-key affair.*

low·land /ˈləʊlənd; AmE ˈloʊ-/ *adj., noun*
■ *adj.* [only before noun] connected with an area of land that is fairly flat and not very high above sea level: *lowland areas/farmers*—compare HIGHLAND
■ *noun* [usually pl.] an area of land that is fairly flat and not very high above sea level: *the lowlands of Scotland* ◊ *Much of the region is lowland.*—compare HIGHLAND

low·land·er /ˈləʊləndə(r); AmE ˈloʊ-/ *noun* a person who comes from an area which is flat and low—compare HIGHLANDER

L

æ	ɑː	e	ɜː	ə	ɪ	iː	i	ɒ	ɔː	ʌ	ʊ	u	uː
cat	father	ten	bird	about	sit	see	many	got (BrE)	saw	cup	put	actual	too

low-'level *adj.* [usually before noun] **1** close to the ground: *low-level bombing attacks* **2** of low rank; involving people of junior rank: *a low-level job* ◊ *low-level negotiations* **3** not containing much of a particular substance especially RADIOACTIVITY: *low-level radioactive waste* **4** (*computing*) (of a computer language) similar to MACHINE CODE in form OPP HIGH-LEVEL

'low life *noun* [U] the life and behaviour of people who are outside normal society, especially criminals ▶ **'low-life** *adj.*: *a low-life bar*

lowly /'ləʊli; *AmE* 'loʊli/ *adj.* (**low·lier, low·li·est**) (often *humorous*) low in status or importance SYN HUMBLE: *a lowly government clerk*

low-'lying *adj.* (of land) not high, and usually fairly flat

low-'paid *adj.* earning or providing very little money: *low-paid workers* ◊ *It is one of the lowest-paid jobs.*

low-'pitched *adj.* (of sounds) deep; low: *a low-pitched voice* OPP HIGH-PITCHED

'low point *noun* the least interesting, enjoyable or worst part of sth OPP HIGH POINT

low 'pressure *noun* [U] **1** the condition of air, gas or liquid that is kept in a container with little force: *Water supplies to the house are at low pressure.* **2** a condition of the air which affects the weather when the pressure is lower than average—compare HIGH PRESSURE

low-'profile *adj.* [only before noun] receiving or involving very little attention: *a low-profile campaign*—see also PROFILE

low-rise *adj.* [only before noun] (of a building) low, with only a few floors: *low-rise housing* ▶ **'low-rise** *noun* —compare HIGH-RISE

low-'risk *adj.* [usually before noun] involving only a small amount of danger and little risk of injury, death, damage, etc.: *a low-risk investment* ◊ *low-risk patients* (= who are very unlikely to get a particular illness) OPP HIGH-RISK

'low season (also **'off season**) *noun* [U, sing.] (*especially BrE*) the time of year when a hotel or tourist area receives fewest visitors OPP HIGH SEASON

'low slung *adj.* very low and close to the ground

low-'tech *adj.* (*informal*) not involving the most modern technology or methods OPP HIGH-TECH

low 'tide (also **,low 'water**) *noun* [U, C] the time when the sea is at its lowest level; the sea at this time: *The island can only be reached at low tide.* OPP HIGH TIDE

low-'water mark *noun* a line or mark showing the lowest point that the sea reaches at low tide OPP HIGH-WATER MARK

lox /lɒks; *AmE* lɑːks/ *noun* [U] (*AmE*) smoked SALMON (= a type of fish)

loyal /'lɔɪəl/ *adj.* ~ **(to sb/sth)** remaining faithful to sb/sth and supporting them or it: *a loyal friend/supporter* ◊ *She has always remained loyal to her political principles.* ▶ **loy·al·ly** /'lɔɪəli/ *adv.*

loyal·ist /'lɔɪəlɪst/ *noun* **1** a person who is loyal to the ruler or government, or to a political party, especially during a time of change: *party loyalists* **2** (**Loyalist**) a person who supports the union between Great Britain and Northern Ireland—compare REPUBLICAN

loy·alty /'lɔɪəlti/ *noun* (*pl.* **-ies**) **1** ~ **(to/towards sb/sth)** [U] the quality of being faithful in your support of sb/sth: *They swore their loyalty to the king.* ◊ *Can I count on your loyalty?* **2** [C, often pl.] a strong feeling that you want to be loyal to sb/sth: *a case of divided loyalties* (= with strong feelings of support for two different causes, people, etc.)

loz·enge /'lɒzɪndʒ; *AmE* 'lɑːz-/ *noun* **1** (*geometry*) a figure with four sides in the shape of a diamond that has two opposite angles more than 90° and the other two less than 90° **2** a small sweet/candy, often in a lozenge shape, especially one that contains medicine and that you dissolve in your mouth: *throat/cough lozenges*

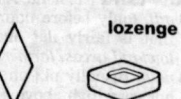
lozenge

LP /ˌel 'piː/ *noun* the abbreviation for 'long-playing record' (a record that plays for about 25 minutes each side and turns 33 times per minute)

'L-plate *noun* a white sign with a large red letter L on it, that you put on a car when you are learning to drive in Britain and some other countries

L-plate

LPN /ˌel piː 'en/ *abbr.* (in the US) licensed practical nurse

LSD /ˌel es 'diː/ (also *slang* **acid**) *noun* [U] a powerful illegal drug that affects people's minds and makes them see and hear things that are not really there

Lt (*BrE*) (*AmE* **Lt.**) *abbr.* (in writing) LIEUTENANT: *Lt (Helen) Brown*

Ltd *abbr.* Limited (used after the name of a British company or business): *Pearce and Co. Ltd*

lu·bri·cant /'luːbrɪkənt/ *noun* [U, C] a substance, for example oil, that you put on surfaces or parts of a machine so that they move easily and smoothly

lu·bri·cate /'luːbrɪkeɪt/ *verb* [VN] to put a lubricant on sth such as the parts of a machine, to help them move smoothly ▶ **lu·bri·ca·tion** /ˌluːbrɪ'keɪʃn/ *noun* [U]

lu·bri·cious /luː'brɪʃəs/ *adj.* (*formal*) showing a great interest in sex in a way that is considered unpleasant or unacceptable

lucid /'luːsɪd/ *adj.* **1** clearly expressed; easy to understand SYN CLEAR: *a lucid style/explanation* **2** able to think clearly, especially during or after a period of illness or confusion ▶ **lu·cid·ity** /luː'sɪdəti/ *noun* [U] **lu·cid·ly** *adv.*

luck /lʌk/ *noun, verb*

■ *noun* [U] **1** good things that happen to you by chance, not because of your own efforts or abilities: *With (any) luck, we'll be home before dark.* ◊ (*BrE*) *With a bit of luck, we'll finish on time.* ◊ *So far I have had no luck with finding a job.* ◊ *I could hardly believe my luck when he said yes.* ◊ *It was a stroke of luck that we found you.* ◊ *By sheer luck nobody was hurt in the explosion.* ◊ *We wish her luck in her new career.* ◊ *You're in luck* (= lucky)—*there's one ticket left.* ◊ *You're out of luck. She's not here.* ◊ *What a piece of luck!* **2** chance; the force that causes good or bad things to happen to people: *to have good/bad luck*—see also HARD-LUCK STORY IDM **Any 'luck?** (*spoken*) used to ask sb if they have been successful with sth: '*Any luck?*' '*No, they're all too busy to help.*' **as luck would 'have it** in the way that chance decides what will happen: *As luck would have it, the train was late.* **bad, hard, etc. luck (on sb)** used to express sympathy for sb: *Bad luck, Helen, you played very well.* ◊ *It's hard luck on him that he wasn't chosen.* **be down on your 'luck** (*informal*) to have no money because of a period of bad luck **the best of 'luck (with sth)** | **good 'luck (with sth)** (*spoken*) used to wish sb success with sth: *The best of luck with your exams.* ◊ *Good luck! I hope it goes well.* **,better luck 'next time** (*spoken*) used to encourage sb who has not been successful at sth **do sth for 'luck 1** to do sth because you believe it will bring you good luck, or because this is a traditional belief: *Take something blue. It's for luck.* **2** to do sth for no particular reason: *I hit him once more for luck.* **good 'luck to sb** (*spoken*) used to say that you do not mind what sb does as it does not affect you, but you hope they will be successful: *It's not something I would care to try myself but if she wants to, good luck to her.* **just my/sb's 'luck** (*informal*) used to show you are not surprised sth bad has happened to you, because you are not often lucky: *Just my luck to arrive after they had left.* **your/sb's 'luck is in** used to say that sb has been lucky or successful: *On a Sunday I didn't expect to find him at his desk but my luck was in.* **the luck of the 'draw** the fact that chance decides sth, in a way that you cannot control **no such 'luck** used to show disappointment that sth you were hoping for did not happen—more at BEGIN-

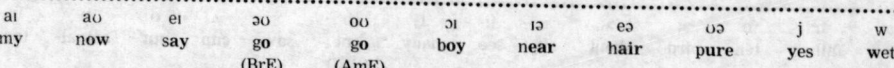

aɪ	aʊ	eɪ	əʊ	oʊ	ɔɪ	ɪə	eə	ʊə	j	w
my	now	say	go (BrE)	go (AmE)	boy	near	hair	pure	yes	wet

NER, POT *n.*, PUSH *v.*, TOUGH *adj.*, TRY *v.*, WORSE *adj.*

■ *verb* PHRV ˌluck 'out (*AmE, informal*) to be lucky

luck·less /ˈlʌkləs/ *adj.* (*written*) having bad luck; SYN UNLUCKY: *the luckless victim of the attack*

lucky /ˈlʌki/ *adj.* (**luck·ier, lucki·est**) **1** ~ (**to do sth**) | ~ (**that …**) having good luck SYN FORTUNATE: *His friend was killed and he knows he is lucky to be alive.* ◊ *She was lucky enough to be chosen for the team.* ◊ *You were lucky (that) you spotted the danger in time.* ◊ *Mark is one of the lucky ones—he at least has somewhere to sleep.* ◊ *the lucky winners* ◊ *You can think yourself lucky you didn't get mugged.* ◊ *She counted herself lucky that she still had a job.* **2** ~ (**for sb**) (**that …**) being the result of good luck: *It was lucky for us that we were able to go.* ◊ *That was the luckiest escape of my life.* ◊ *a lucky guess* **3** bringing good luck: *a lucky charm* ▶ **luck·ily** /ˈlʌkɪli/ *adv.* ~ (**for sb**): *Luckily for us, the train was late.* ◊ *Luckily, I am a good swimmer.* IDM **lucky 'you, 'me, etc.** (*spoken*) used to show that you think sb is lucky to have sth, be able to do sth, etc: *'I'm off to Paris.' 'Lucky you!'* **you'll be 'lucky** (*spoken*) used to tell sb that sth that they are expecting probably will not happen: *'I was hoping to get a ticket for Saturday.' 'You'll be lucky.'* ˌyou, etc. **should be so 'lucky** (*spoken*) used to tell sb that they will probably not get what they are hoping for, and may not deserve it— more at STRIKE *v.*, THANK, THIRD

ˌlucky 'dip (*BrE*) (*AmE* **ˈgrab bag**) *noun* [usually sing.] a game in which people choose a present from a container of presents without knowing what it is going to be

lu·cra·tive /ˈluːkrətɪv/ *adj.* producing a large amount of money; making a large profit: *a lucrative business/contract/market* ▶ **lu·cra·tive·ly** *adv.*

lucre /ˈluːkə(r)/ *noun* [U] (*disapproving*) money, especially when it has been obtained in a way that is dishonest or immoral: *the lure of filthy lucre*

Lud·dite /ˈlʌdaɪt/ *noun* (*BrE, disapproving*) a person who is opposed to new technology or working methods ORIGIN Named after Ned *Lud,* one of the workers who destroyed machinery in the cotton and woollen mills in the early 19th century, because they believed it would take away their jobs.

ludi·crous /ˈluːdɪkrəs/ *adj.* ridiculous and unreasonable; that you cannot take seriously: *a ludicrous idea/suggestion/situation* ◊ *It was ludicrous to think that the plan could succeed.* ▶ **ludi·crous·ly** *adv.*: *ludicrously expensive* **ludi·crous·ness** *noun* [U]

ludo /ˈluːdəʊ; *AmE* -doʊ/ (*BrE*) (*AmE* **Par·cheesi**™) *noun* [U] a simple game played with DICE and COUNTERS on a special board

lug /lʌg/ *verb, noun*
■ *verb* (**-gg-**) [VN+*adv./prep.*] (*informal*) to carry or drag sth heavy with a lot of effort: *I had to lug my bags up to the fourth floor.*
■ *noun* **1** (*technical*) a part of sth that sticks out, used as a handle or support **2** (also **ˈlug·hole**) (both *BrE, humorous*) an ear

lug·gage /ˈlʌɡɪdʒ/ (*especially BrE*) (also **bag·gage** especially in *AmE*) *noun* [U] bags, cases, etc. that contain sb's clothes and things when they are travelling: *There's room for one more piece of luggage.* ◊ *You stay there with the luggage while I find a cab.*—see also HAND LUGGAGE, LEFT-LUGGAGE OFFICE ⇨ note at BAGGAGE

ˈluggage rack *noun* a shelf for luggage above the seats in a train, bus, etc.

ˈluggage van *noun* (*BrE*) (*AmE* **ˈbaggage car**) a carriage on a train for carrying passengers' luggage

lug·hole /ˈlʌɡhəʊl; *AmE* -hoʊl/ *noun* (*BrE, humorous*) = LUG (2)

lu·gu·bri·ous /ləˈɡuːbriəs/ *adj.* (*written*) sad and serious: *a lugubrious expression/face* ▶ **lu·gu·bri·ous·ly** *adv.*

lug·worm /ˈlʌɡwɜːm; *AmE* -wɜːrm/ *noun* a large worm that lives in the sand by the sea. Lugworms are often used as BAIT on a hook to catch fish.

luke·warm /ˌluːkˈwɔːm; *AmE* -ˈwɔːrm/ *adj.* (often *disapproving*) **1** slightly warm SYN TEPID: *Our food was only*

lukewarm. **2** ~ (**about sb/sth**) not interested or enthusiastic: *a lukewarm response* ◊ *She was lukewarm about the plan.*

lull /lʌl/ *noun, verb*
■ *noun* [usually sing.] ~ (**in sth**) a quiet period between times of activity: *a lull in the conversation/fighting* ◊ *Just before an attack everything would go quiet but we knew it was just the lull before the storm* (= before a time of noise or trouble).
■ *verb* (*written*) **1** [VN] to make sb relaxed and calm: *The vibration of the engine lulled the children to sleep.* **2** to make sth, or to become, less strong: [VN] *His father's arrival lulled the boy's anxiety.* [also V] PHRV ˌlull sb 'into sth to make sb feel confident and relaxed, especially so that they do not expect it when sb does sth bad or dishonest: *His friendly manner lulled her into a false sense of security* (= made her feel safe with him when she should not have).

lul·laby /ˈlʌləbaɪ/ *noun* (*pl.* **-ies**) a soft gentle song sung to make a child go to sleep

lum·bago /lʌmˈbeɪɡəʊ; *AmE* -goʊ/ *noun* [U] pain in the muscles and joints of the lower back

lum·bar /ˈlʌmbə(r)/ *adj.* [only before noun] (*medical*) relating to the lower part of the back: *pain in the lumbar region*

ˌlumbar 'puncture (*BrE*) (*AmE* **ˈspinal tap**) *noun* the removal of liquid from the lower part of the SPINE with a hollow needle

lum·ber /ˈlʌmbə(r)/ *noun, verb*
■ *noun* [U] **1** (*especially AmE*) = TIMBER **2** (*BrE*) pieces of furniture, and other large objects that you do not use any more
■ *verb* **1** [V+*adv./prep.*] to move in a slow, heavy and awkward way: *A family of elephants lumbered by.* **2** [VN] [usually passive] ~ **sb** (**with sb/sth**) (*informal*) to give sb a responsibility, etc., that they do not want and that they cannot get rid of: *When our parents went out, my sister got lumbered with me for the evening.*

lum·ber·jack /ˈlʌmbədʒæk; *AmE* -bərdʒ-/ (also **ˈlog·ger**) *noun* (*especially in the US and Canada*) a person whose job is cutting down trees or cutting or transporting wood

lu·mi·nary /ˈluːmɪnəri; *AmE* -neri/ (*pl.* **-ies**) *noun* a person who is an expert or a great influence in a special area or activity: *leading luminaries of the arts*

lu·mi·nes·cence /ˌluːmɪˈnesns/ *noun* [U] (*technical* or *literary*) a quality in sth that produces light: *the fading luminescence of the sky* ▶ **lu·mi·nes·cent** *adj.*

lu·mi·nous /ˈluːmɪnəs/ *adj.* **1** shining in the dark; giving out light: *luminous paint* ◊ *luminous hands on a clock* ◊ *staring with huge luminous eyes* ◊ (*figurative*) *the luminous quality of the music* **2** very bright in colour: *They painted the door a luminous green.* ▶ **lu·mi·nous·ly** *adv.* **lu·mi·nos·ity** /ˌluːmɪˈnɒsəti; *AmE* -ˈnɑːs-/ *noun* [sing., U]

lump /lʌmp/ *noun, verb*
■ *noun* **1** a piece of sth hard or solid, usually without a particular shape: *a lump of coal/cheese/wood* ◊ *This sauce has lumps in it.* **2** (*BrE*) = SUGAR LUMP: *One lump or two?* **3** a swelling under the skin, sometimes a sign of serious illness: *He was unhurt apart from a lump on his head.* ◊ *Check your breasts for lumps every month.* **4** (*informal, especially BrE*) a heavy, lazy or stupid person IDM **have, etc. a lump in your throat** to feel pressure in the throat because you are very angry or emotional **take your 'lumps** (*AmE, informal*) to accept bad things that happen to you without complaining
■ *verb* [VN] ~ **A and B together** | ~ **A** (**in**) **with B** to put or consider different things together in the same group: *You can't lump all Asian languages together.* IDM **ˈlump it** (*informal*) to accept sth unpleasant because there's no other choice: *I'm sorry you're not happy about it but you'll just have to lump it.* ◊ *That's the situation—like it or lump it!*

lump·en /ˈlʌmpən/ *adj.* (*BrE, literary*) looking heavy and awkward or stupid

lump·ish /ˈlʌmpɪʃ/ *adj.* heavy and awkward; stupid

b	d	f	g	h	k	l	m	n	p	r
bad	did	fall	get	hat	cat	leg	man	now	pen	red

lump 'sum (also **,lump ,sum 'payment**) *noun* an amount of money that is paid at one time and not on separate occasions

lumpy /'lʌmpi/ *adj.* full of lumps; covered in lumps: *lumpy sauce ◊ a lumpy mattress*

lu·na·cy /'luːnəsi/ *noun* [U] **1** behaviour that is stupid or crazy: *It's sheer lunacy driving in such weather.* **2** (*old-fashioned*) mental illness **SYN** MADNESS

lunar /'luːnə(r)/ *adj.* [usually before noun] connected with the moon: *a lunar eclipse/landscape*

,lunar 'month *noun* the average time between one new moon and the next (about 29½ days)—compare CALENDAR MONTH

lu·na·tic /'luːnətɪk/ *noun, adj.*
- *noun* **1** a person who does crazy things that are often dangerous: *This lunatic in a white van pulled out right in front of me!* **2** (*old-fashioned*) a person who is severely mentally ill (the use of this word is now offensive): *a dangerous/homicidal lunatic* **ORIGIN** Originally from the Latin *lunaticus* (*luna* = moon), because people believed that the changes in the moon caused temporary madness.
- *adj.* crazy, ridiculous or extremely stupid: *lunatic ideas ◊ a lunatic smile* **IDM** **the ,lunatic 'fringe** *noun* [sing.+ sing./pl. v.] (*disapproving*) those members of a political or other group whose views are considered to be very extreme and crazy

'lunatic asylum *noun* (*old-fashioned, especially BrE*) an institution where mentally ill people live

lunch /lʌntʃ/ *noun, verb*
- *noun* [U, C] a meal eaten in the middle of the day: *She's gone to lunch. ◊ I'm ready for some lunch. ◊ What shall we have for lunch? ◊ We serve hot and cold lunches. ◊ a one-hour lunch break* ◆ **Let's do lunch** (= have lunch together).—see also PACKED LUNCH, PLOUGHMAN'S LUNCH ▷ note at MEAL **IDM** see FREE *adj.*
- *verb* [V] (*formal*) to have lunch, especially at a restaurant: *He lunched with a client at the Ritz.*

'lunch box *noun* a container to hold a meal that you take away from home to eat

lunch·eon /'lʌntʃən/ *noun* [C, U] a formal lunch or a formal word for lunch: *a charity luncheon ◊ Luncheon will be served at one, Madam.*

'luncheon meat *noun* [U] finely chopped cooked meat that has been pressed together in a container, usually sold in cans and served cold in slices

'luncheon voucher *noun* a ticket given by some employers in Britain that sb can exchange for food at some restaurants and shops/stores

'lunch hour *noun* the time around the middle of the day when you stop work or school to eat lunch: *I usually go to the gym during my lunch hour.*

lunch·room /'lʌntʃruːm; -rʊm/ *noun* (*AmE*) a large room in a school where students eat lunch

lunch·time /'lʌntʃtaɪm/ *noun* [U, C] the time around the middle of the day when people usually eat lunch: *The package still hadn't arrived by lunchtime. ◊ a lunchtime concert ◊ The sandwich bar is generally packed at lunchtimes.*

lung /lʌŋ/ *noun* either of the two organs in the chest that you use when breathing: *lung cancer*—picture at BODY

lunge /lʌndʒ/ *verb, noun*
- *verb* [V] **~ (at/towards/for sb/sth)|~ (forward)** to make a sudden powerful forward movement in order to attack sb
- *noun* [usually sing.] **1 ~ (at sb)|~ (for sb/sth)** a sudden powerful forward movement of the body and arm that a person makes towards another person or thing, especially when attacking them: *He made a lunge for the phone.* **2** (in the sport of FENCING) a THRUST made by putting the right foot forward and making the back leg straight

lung·ful /'lʌŋfʊl/ *noun* the amount of sth such as air or smoke that is breathed in at one time

lupin (*BrE*) (*AmE* **lu·pine**) /'luːpɪn/ *noun* a tall garden plant with many small flowers growing up its thick stem

lurch /lɜːtʃ; *AmE* lɜːrtʃ/ *verb, noun*
- *verb* [V] **1** to make a sudden, unsteady movement forward or sideways: *Suddenly the horse lurched to one side and*

the child fell off. ◊ *The man lurched drunkenly out of the pub. ◊* (*figurative*) *Their relationship seems to lurch from one crisis to the next.* **2** if your heart or stomach **lurches**, you have a sudden feeling of fear or excitement
- *noun* [usually sing.] a sudden strong movement that moves you forward or sideways and nearly makes you lose your balance: *The train gave a violent lurch. ◊ His heart gave a lurch when he saw her.* **IDM** **leave sb in the 'lurch** (*informal*) to fail to help sb when they are relying on you to do so

lurch·er /'lɜːtʃə(r); *AmE* 'lɜːrtʃ-/ *noun* (*BrE*) a dog that is a mixture of two different breeds of dog, one of which is usually a GREYHOUND

lure /lʊə(r); ljʊə(r); *AmE* lʊr/ *verb, noun*
- *verb* [VN] [usually +*adv./prep.*] (*disapproving*) to persuade or trick sb to go somewhere or to do sth by promising them a reward: *The child was lured into a car but managed to escape. ◊ Young people are lured to the city by the prospect of a job and money.*
- *noun* **1** [usually sing.] the attractive qualities of sth: *Few can resist the lure of adventure.* **2** a thing that is used to attract fish or animals, so that they can be caught

Lurex™ /'lʊəreks; 'ljʊə-; *AmE* 'lʊr-/ *noun* [U] a type of thin metal thread; a fabric containing this thread, used for making clothes

lurid /'lʊərɪd; 'ljʊər-; *AmE* 'lʊr-/ *adj.* (*disapproving*) **1** bright in colour, in a way that is not attractive: *She was wearing a lurid orange and green blouse.* **2** (especially of a story or piece of writing) shocking and violent in a way that is deliberate: *lurid headlines ◊ The paper gave all the lurid details of the murder.* ▶ **lur·id·ly** *adv.*

lurk /lɜːk; *AmE* lɜːrk/ *verb* [V] **1** [usually +*adv./prep.*] to wait somewhere secretly, especially because you are going to do sth bad or illegal: *Why are you lurking around outside my house? ◊ A crocodile was lurking just below the surface.* **2** when sth unpleasant or dangerous **lurks**, it is present but not in an obvious way: *At night, danger lurks in these streets. ◊ a lurking doubt/suspicion*

lus·cious /'lʌʃəs/ *adj.* **1** having a strong pleasant taste **SYN** DELICIOUS: *luscious fruit* **2** (of fabric, colours or music) soft and deep or heavy in a way that is pleasing to feel, look at or hear: *luscious silks and velvets ◊ luscious harmonies/colours* **3** (especially of a woman) sexually attractive: *a luscious young girl*

lush /lʌʃ/ *adj., noun*
- *adj.* **1** (of plants, gardens, etc.) growing thickly and strongly in a way that is attractive; covered in healthy grass and plants: *lush vegetation ◊ the lush green countryside* **2** beautiful, and making you feel pleasure; seeming expensive: *a lush apartment*
- *noun* (*AmE, informal*) = ALCOHOLIC

lust /lʌst/ *noun, verb*
- *noun* (often *disapproving*) [U, C] **1 ~ (for sb)** very strong sexual desire, especially when love is not involved: *Their affair was driven by pure lust.* **2 ~ (for sth)** very strong desire for sth or enjoyment of sth: *to satisfy his lust for power/revenge ◊ She has a real lust for life* (= she really enjoys life).—see also BLOODLUST
- *verb* **PHRV** **'lust after/for sb/sth** (often *disapproving*) to feel an extremely strong, especially sexual, desire for sb/sth

lust·ful /'lʌstfl/ *adj.* (often *disapproving*) feeling or showing strong sexual desire

lustre (*BrE*) (*AmE* **lust·er**) /'lʌstə(r)/ *noun* [U] **1** the shining quality of a surface: *Her hair had lost its lustre. ◊ The shell had a beautiful pearly lustre.* **2** the quality of being special in a way that is exciting: *The presence of the prince added lustre to the occasion.*—compare LACKLUSTRE

lus·trous /'lʌstrəs/ *adj.* (*written*) soft and shining: *thick lustrous hair ◊ the smooth lustrous surface of the fabric*

lusty /'lʌsti/ *adj.* healthy and strong: *a lusty young man ◊ lusty singing* ▶ **lust·ily** /-ɪli/ *adv.*: *singing/cheering lustily*

lute /luːt/ *noun* an early type of musical instrument with strings, played like a guitar

lu·ten·ist (also **lu·tan·ist**) /'luːtənɪst/ *noun* a person who plays the lute

s	t	v	z	ʃ	ʒ	tʃ	dʒ	θ	ð	ŋ
see	tea	van	zoo	shoe	vision	chain	jam	thin	this	sing

luv /lʌv/ *noun* **1** (*BrE*) a way of spelling 'love', when used as an informal way of addressing sb: *Never mind, luv.* **2** an informal way of spelling 'love', for example when ending a letter: *See you soon, lots of luv, Sue.*

luvvy (also **luv·vie**) /ˈlʌvi/ *noun* (*BrE, informal*) **1** (*disapproving*) an actor, especially when they behave in a way that seems exaggerated and not sincere **2** = LOVEY

lux·uri·ant /lʌɡˈʒʊəriənt; *AmE* -ˈʒʊr-/ *adj.* **1** (of plants or hair) growing thickly and strongly in a way that is attractive: *luxuriant vegetation/foliage* ◊ *thick, luxuriant hair* **2** (especially of art or the atmosphere of a place) rich in sth that is pleasant or beautiful: *the poet's luxuriant imagery* ▶ **lux·uri·ance** /-əns/ *noun* [U]: *the luxuriance of the tropical forest*

lux·uri·ant·ly /lʌɡˈʒʊəriəntli; *AmE* -ˈʒʊr-/ *adv.* (*written*) **1** in a way that is thick and attractive: *a tall, luxuriantly bearded man* **2** (especially of a way of moving your body) in a way that is comfortable and enjoyable: *She turned luxuriantly on her side, yawning.*

lux·uri·ate /lʌɡˈʒʊərieɪt; *AmE* -ˈʒʊr-/ *verb* **PHRV** **luˈxuriate in sth** (*written*) to relax while enjoying sth very pleasant: *She luxuriated in all the attention she received.*

lux·uri·ous /lʌɡˈʒʊəriəs; *AmE* -ˈʒʊr-/ *adj.* very comfortable; containing expensive and enjoyable things: *a luxurious hotel* ◊ *luxurious surroundings* **OPP** SPARTAN ▶ **lux·uri·ous·ly** *adv.*: *luxuriously comfortable* ◊ *a luxuriously furnished apartment* ◊ *She stretched luxuriously on the bed.*

lux·ury /ˈlʌkʃəri/ *noun* (*pl.* **-ies**) **1** [U] the enjoyment of special and expensive things, particularly food and drink, clothes and surroundings: *Now we'll be able to live in luxury for the rest of our lives.* ◊ *to lead/live a* **life of luxury** ◊ *a luxury hotel/cruise* ◊ *luxury goods/items* **2** [C] a thing that is expensive but not essential: *small luxuries like chocolate and cigarettes* ◊ *There's no brandy. I can't afford such luxuries.* ◊ *I love having a long, hot bath—it's one of life's little luxuries.* ◊ *It was a luxury if you had a washing machine in those days.* **3** [U, sing.] a pleasure or an advantage that you do not often have: *I allow myself the luxury of a sauna once a week.* ◊ *We had the luxury of being able to choose from four good candidates for the job.* **IDM** see LAP *n.*

LW *abbr.* (*especially BrE*) LONG WAVE: *1500m LW*

-ly *suffix* **1** (in adverbs) in the way mentioned: *happily* ◊ *stupidly* **2** (in adjectives) having the qualities of: *cowardly* ◊ *scholarly* **3** (in adjectives and adverbs) at intervals of: *hourly* ◊ *daily*

ly·chee /ˌlaɪˈtʃiː; ˈlaɪtʃiː/ *noun* a small Chinese fruit with thick rough reddish skin, white flesh and a large stone/pit—picture on page A2

lych-gate /ˈlɪtʃ ɡeɪt/ *noun* a gate with a roof at the entrance to a CHURCHYARD

Lycra™ /ˈlaɪkrə/ (also **Span·dex**™) *noun* [U] an artificial fabric that stretches, used for making clothes that fit close to the body: *All our swimwear contains Lycra.*

lying *pres part* of LIE

lying-in *noun* [sing.] (*old-fashioned*) the period of time during which a woman in the past stayed in bed before and after giving birth to a child

lymph /lɪmf/ *noun* [U] a colourless liquid containing white blood cells that cleans the tissues of the body and helps to prevent infections from spreading: *lymph glands/nodes* ▶ **lymph·at·ic** /lɪmˈfætɪk/ *adj.* [only before noun]: *the lymphatic system*

lynch /lɪntʃ/ *verb* [VN] if a crowd of people **lynch** sb whom they consider guilty of a crime, they capture them, do not allow them to have a trial in a court of law, and kill them illegally, usually by hanging ▶ **lynch·ing** *noun* [C, U]

ˈlynch mob *noun* a crowd of people who gather to lynch sb

lynch·pin *noun* = LINCHPIN

lynx /lɪŋks/ *noun* (*pl.* **lynx** or **lynxes**) a wild animal of the cat family, with spots on its fur and a very short tail

lyre /ˈlaɪə(r)/ *noun* an ancient musical instrument with strings fastened in a frame shaped like a U. It was played with the fingers.

lyric /ˈlɪrɪk/ *adj., noun*
■ *adj.* **1** (of poetry) expressing a person's personal feelings and thoughts—compare EPIC **2** connected with, or written for, singing
■ *noun* **1** [C] a lyric poem—compare EPIC **2** (**lyrics**) [pl.] the words of a song: *music and lyrics by Rodgers and Hart*

lyr·ic·al /ˈlɪrɪkl/ *adj.* expressing strong emotion in an imaginative way: *a lyrical melody* ◊ *He began to wax lyrical* (= talk enthusiastically) *about his new car.*

lyr·ic·al·ly /ˈlɪrɪkli/ *adv.* **1** in a way that expresses strong emotion **2** connected with the words of a song: *Both musically and lyrically it is very effective.*

lyri·cism /ˈlɪrɪsɪzəm/ *noun* [U] the expression of strong emotion in poetry, art, music, etc.

lyri·cist /ˈlɪrɪsɪst/ *noun* a person who writes the words of songs

L

æ	ɑː	e	ɜː	ə	ɪ	iː	i	ɒ	ɔː	ʌ	ʊ	uː
cat	father	ten	bird	about	sit	see	many	got	saw	cup	put	actual	too
								(BrE)				

Mm

M /em/ *noun, abbr., symbol*

▪ *noun* (also **m**) [C, U] (*pl.* **M's**, **m's** /emz/) the 13th letter of the English alphabet: *'Milk' begins with* (*an*) *M /'M'*.

▪ *abbr.* **1** (also **med.**) (especially for sizes of clothes) medium: *S M and L* (= small, medium and large) **2** (used with a number to show the name of a British motorway): *heavy traffic on the M25*

▪ *symbol* (also **m**) the number 1000 in ROMAN NUMERALS

m (*BrE*) (also **m.** *AmE, BrE*) *abbr.* **1** male **2** married **3** metre(s): *800m medium wave* **4** million(s): *population: 10m*

MA (*BrE*) (*AmE* **M.A.**) /ˌem ˈeɪ/ *noun* the abbreviation for 'Master of Arts' (a second university degree in an ARTS subject, or, in Scotland, a first university degree in an arts subject): *to be/have/do an MA ◇ Julie Bell MA*

ma /mɑː/ *noun* (*informal*) mother: *I'm going now, ma. ◇ 'I want my ma,' sobbed the little girl.*

ma'am /mæm; mɑːm/ *noun* [sing.] **1** (*AmE*) used as a polite way of addressing a woman: *'Can I help you, ma'am?'*—compare SIR **2** (*BrE*) used when addressing the Queen or senior women officers in the police or army = MADAM

Mac /mæk/ *noun* [sing.] (*AmE, informal*) used to address a man whose name you do not know

mac (also **mack**) /mæk/ *noun* (*BrE, informal*) = MACKINTOSH

ma·cabre /məˈkɑːbrə/ *adj.* unpleasant and strange because connected with death and frightening things: *a macabre tale/joke/ritual*

mac·adam /məˈkædəm/ *noun* [U] a road surface made of layers of broken stones

maca·da·mia /ˌmækəˈdeɪmiə/ (also **maca'damia nut**) *noun* the round nut of an Australian tree

maca·roni /ˌmækəˈrəʊni; *AmE* -ˈroʊni/ *noun* [U] PASTA in the shape of hollow tubes

ˌmacaroni ˈcheese (*BrE*) (*AmE* ˌmacaroni and ˈcheese) *noun* [U] a hot dish of macaroni in a cheese sauce

maca·roon /ˌmækəˈruːn/ *noun* a soft round sweet biscuit/cookie made with ALMONDS or COCONUT

macaw /məˈkɔː/ *noun* a large South and Central American tropical bird of the PARROT family, with bright feathers and a long tail

Mace™ /meɪs/ *noun* [U] a chemical that makes your eyes and skin sting, that some people, including police officers, carry in spray cans so that they can defend themselves against people attacking them

mace /meɪs/ *noun* **1** [C] a decorative stick, carried as a sign of authority by an official such as a MAYOR—compare SCEPTRE **2** [C] a large heavy stick that has a head with metal points on it, used in the past as a weapon **3** [U] the dried outer covering of NUTMEGS (= the hard nuts of an E Indian tree), used in cooking as a spice

ma·cer·ate /ˈmæsəreɪt/ *verb* [V, VN] (*technical*) to make sth (especially food) soft by soaking it in a liquid; to become soft in this way

Mach /mɑːk; mæk/ *noun* [U] (often followed by a number) a measurement of speed, used especially for aircraft. Mach 1 is the speed of sound: *a fighter plane with a top speed of Mach 3* (= 3 times the speed of sound)

ma·chete /məˈʃeti/ *noun* a broad heavy knife used as a cutting tool and as a weapon

Ma·chia·vel·lian /ˌmækiəˈveliən/ *adj.* (*formal, disapproving*) using clever plans to achieve what you want, without people realizing what you are doing ‖ORIGIN‖ Named after **Niccolò Machiavelli**, an Italian statesman (1469-1527), who explained in his book *The Prince*, that it was often necessary for rulers to use immoral methods in order to achieve power and success.

ma·chin·ation /ˌmæʃɪˈneɪʃn/ *noun* [usually pl.] (*disapproving*) a secret and complicated plan: *political machinations*

ma·chine /məˈʃiːn/ *noun, verb*

▪ *noun* **1** (often in compounds) a piece of equipment with moving parts that is designed to do a particular job. The power used to work a machine may be electricity, steam, gas, etc. or human power: *Machines have replaced human labour in many industries. ◇ to operate/run a machine ◇ How does this machine work? ◇ a washing/sewing machine ◇ a machine for making plastic toys ◇ I left a message on her answering machine. ◇ The potatoes are planted by machine.* **2** (*informal*) a particular machine, for example in the home, when you do not refer to it by its full name: *Just put those clothes in the machine* (= the washing machine). *◇ The new machines* (= computers) *will be shipped next month.* **3** a group of people that control an organization or part of an organization: *the president's propaganda machine* **4** (often *disapproving*) a person who acts automatically, without allowing their feelings to show or to affect their work—see also MECHANICAL, FRUIT MACHINE, SLOT MACHINE, TIME MACHINE ‖HELP‖ You will find other compounds ending in **machine** at their place in the alphabet. ‖IDM‖ see COG

▪ *verb* (*technical*) to make or shape sth with a machine: [VN] *This material can be cut and machined easily.* [also V]

ma·chine code (also **ma·chine language**) *noun* (*computing*) a CODE in which instructions are written in the form of numbers so that a computer can understand and act on them

ma·chine gun *noun* a gun that automatically fires many bullets one after the other very quickly: *a burst/ hail of machine-gun fire*

ma·chine-gun *verb* (**-nn-**) [VN] to shoot at sb/sth with a machine gun

ma·chine-ˈmade *adj.* made by a machine—compare HANDMADE

ma·chine-ˈreadable *adj.* (of data) in a form that a computer can understand

ma·chin·ery /məˈʃiːnəri/ *noun* **1** [U] machines as a group, especially large ones: *agricultural/industrial machinery ◇ a piece of machinery* **2** [U] the parts of a machine that make it work **3** [U, sing.] **~ (of sth)** | **~ (for doing sth)** the organization or structure of sth; the system for doing sth: *the machinery of government ◇ There is no machinery for resolving disputes.*

ma·chine tool *noun* a tool for cutting or shaping metal, wood, etc., driven by a machine

ma·chine transˈlation *noun* [U] the process of translating language by computer

ma·chin·ist /məˈʃiːnɪst/ *noun* **1** a person whose job is operating a machine, especially machines used in industry for cutting and shaping things, or a sewing machine **2** a person whose job is to make or repair machines

mach·ismo /məˈtʃɪzməʊ; *AmE* mɑːˈtʃiːzmoʊ/ *noun* [U] (from *Spanish*, usually *disapproving*) aggressive male behaviour that emphasizes the importance of being strong rather than being intelligent and sensitive

macho /ˈmætʃəʊ; *AmE* ˈmɑːtʃoʊ/ *adj.* (usually *disapproving*) male in an aggressive way: *He's too macho to ever admit he was wrong. ◇ macho pride/posturing*

mack = MAC

mack·erel /ˈmækrəl/ *noun* [C, U] (*pl.* **mack·erel**) a sea fish with greenish-blue bands on its body, that is used for food: *smoked mackerel*

mack·in·tosh /ˈmækɪntɒʃ; *AmE* -tɑːʃ/ (also *informal* **mac, mack**) (all *BrE*) *noun* a coat made of material that keeps you dry in the rain

mac·ramé /məˈkrɑːmi/ *noun* [U] the art of tying knots in string in a decorative way, to make things

macro- /ˈmækrəʊ/ *combining form* (in nouns, adjectives and adverbs) large; on a large scale: *macroeconomics* OPP MICRO-

macro·bi·ot·ic /ˌmækrəʊbaɪˈɒtɪk; *AmE* -krəʊbaɪˈɑːt-/ *adj.* consisting of whole grains and vegetables grown without chemical treatment: *a macrobiotic diet*

macro·cosm /ˈmækrəʊkɒzəm; *AmE* -krəʊkɑːz-/ *noun* any large complete structure that contains smaller structures, for example the universe—compare MICROCOSM

macro·eco·nom·ics /ˌmækrəʊˌiːkəˈnɒmɪks; *AmE* -krəʊˌekəˈnɑːm-/ *noun* [U] the study of large economic systems, such as those of whole countries or areas of the world ▶ **macro·eco·nom·ic** *adj.*: *macroeconomic policy*

mad /mæd/ *adj.* (**mad·der, mad·dest**) **1** (*especially BrE*) (also **crazy** *AmE*, *BrE*) having a mind that does not work normally; mentally ill: *They realized that he had gone mad.* ◊ *Inventors are not mad scientists.* ◊ *She seemed to have gone* **stark raving mad**.—see also BARKING MAD **2** (*informal, especially BrE*) (also **crazy** *AmE*, *BrE*) very stupid; not at all sensible: *You must be* **mad** *to risk it.* ◊ *It was a mad idea.* ◊ *'I'm going to buy some new clothes.' 'Well, don't go mad* (= spend more than is sensible).' **3** [not before noun] **~ (at/with sb)| ~ (about sth)** (*informal, especially AmE*) very angry: *He got mad and walked out.* ◊ *She's mad at me for being late.* ◊ *That noise is* **driving me mad**. **4** [not usually before noun] **~ (about/on sth/sb)** (*informal*) liking sth/sb very much; very interested in sth: *to be mad on tennis* ◊ *He's always been mad about kids.* ◊ *football-mad boys* ◊ *She's completely power-mad.* **5 ~ (with sth)** done without thought or control; wild and excited: *The crowd made a* **mad** *rush for the exit.* ◊ *Only a mad dash got them to the meeting on time.* ◊ *to be mad with anger/excitement/grief/love* ◊ *The team won and the fans went mad.* IDM **like 'crazy/'mad** (*informal*) very fast, hard, much, etc: *I had to run like mad to catch the bus.* **(as) mad as a 'hatter/a March 'hare** (*informal*) (of a person) mentally ill; very silly ORIGIN From the Mad Hatter, a character in Lewis Carroll's *Alice's Adventures in Wonderland*. Because of the chemicals used in hat-making, workers often suffered from mercury poisoning, which can cause loss of memory and damage to the nervous system. A **March hare** was called mad because of the strange behaviour of hares during the mating season. **mad 'keen (on sth/sb)** (*BrE, informal*) liking sth/sb very much; very interested in sth: *He's mad keen on planes.*—more at HOP *v.*

madam /ˈmædəm/ *noun* **1** [sing.] (*formal*) used when speaking or writing to a woman in a formal or business situation: *Can I help you, madam?* ◊ *Dear Madam* (= used like *Dear Sir in a letter*)—see also MA'AM ⇨ Study page B14 **2** [C] (*informal, disapproving, especially BrE*) a girl or young woman who expects other people to do what she wants: *She's a proper little madam.* **3** [C] a woman who is in charge of the prostitutes in a BROTHEL

mad·cap /ˈmædkæp/ *adj.* [usually before noun] (*informal*) (of people, plans etc.) crazy and not caring about danger; not sensible SYN RECKLESS: *madcap schemes/escapades*

mad 'cow disease *noun* [U] (*informal*) = BSE

mad·den /ˈmædn/ *verb* [VN] [usually passive] to make sb very angry or crazy: *Maddened with pain, the wounded bull ran at them.* ▶ **mad·den·ing** /ˈmædnɪŋ/ *adj.*: *maddening delays* **mad·den·ing·ly** *adv.*: *Progress is maddeningly slow.*

made /meɪd/ **1** *pt, pp* of MAKE **2** (-**made**) (in adjectives) made in the way, place, etc. mentioned: *well-made* ◊ *home-made*—see also SELF-MADE IDM **have (got) it made** (*informal*) to be sure of success; to have everything that you want **(be) made for sb/each other** to be completely

suited to sb/each other: *Peter and Judy seem made for each other, don't they?*

Ma·deira /məˈdɪərə; *AmE* məˈdɪrə/ (also ˌMadeira 'wine) *noun* **1** [U, C] a strong sweet white wine from the island of Madeira **2** [C] a glass of Madeira

Ma'deira cake (*BrE*) (*AmE* 'pound cake) *noun* [U, C] a plain yellow cake made with eggs, fat, flour and sugar

ˌmade-to-'measure *adj.* (of clothes, curtains/drapes, etc.) made specially to fit a particular person, window, etc.

ˌmade-to-'order *adj.* (*especially AmE*) (of clothes, furniture, etc.) made specially for a particular customer

ˈmade-up *adj.* **1** wearing MAKE-UP: *a heavily made-up face/woman* **2** not true or real; invented: *a made-up story/word/name*

mad·house /ˈmædhaʊs/ *noun* **1** [usually sing.] (*informal*) a place where there is confusion and noise: *Don't work in that department; it's a madhouse.* **2** (*old use*) a hospital for people who are mentally ill

madly /ˈmædli/ *adv.* **1** (only used *after* a verb) in a way that shows a lack of control: *She was rushing around madly trying to put out the fire.* ◊ *His heart thudded madly against his ribs.* **2** (*informal*) very, extremely: *madly excited/jealous* ◊ *She's* **madly in love** *with him.*

mad·man /ˈmædmən/ *noun* (*pl.* **-men** /-mən/) a man who has a serious mental illness: *The killing was the act of a madman.* ◊ *He drove* **like a madman**. ◊ *Some madman* (= stupid person) *deleted all the files.*—see also MAD-WOMAN

mad·ness /ˈmædnəs/ *noun* [U] **1** (*old-fashioned*) the state of having a serious mental illness SYN INSANITY: *There may be a link between madness and creativity.* **2** crazy or stupid behaviour that could be dangerous: *It would be sheer madness to trust a man like that.* ◊ *In a* **moment of madness** *she had agreed to go out with him.* IDM see METHOD

ma·donna /məˈdɒnə; *AmE* məˈdɑːnə/ *noun* **1** (**the Madonna**) [sing.] the Virgin Mary, mother of Jesus Christ **2** [C] a statue or picture of the Virgin Mary

mad·ri·gal /ˈmædrɪɡl/ *noun* a song for several singers, usually without musical instruments, popular in the 16th century

mad·woman /ˈmædwʊmən/ *noun* (*pl.* **-women** /-wɪmɪn/) a woman who has a serious mental illness—see also MADMAN

mael·strom /ˈmeɪlstrɒm; *AmE* -strɑːm/ *noun* [usually sing.] **1** (*literary*) a situation full of strong emotions or confusing events, that is hard to control and makes you feel frightened: *a maelstrom of conflicting emotions* ◊ *They were being sucked into the maelstrom of war.* **2** a very strong current of water that moves in circles SYN WHIRL-POOL

maes·tro /ˈmaɪstrəʊ; *AmE* -stroʊ/ *noun* (*pl.* **-os**) (often used as a way of addressing sb, showing respect) a great performer, especially a musician: *Maestro Giulini* ◊ *The winning goal was scored by the maestro himself.*

Mafia /ˈmæfiə; *AmE* ˈmɑːf-/ *noun* **1** (**the Mafia**) [sing.+ sing./pl. *v.*] a secret organization of criminals, that is active especially in Sicily, Italy and the US **2** (**mafia**) [C+sing./pl. *v.*] a group of people within an organization or a community who use their power to get advantages for themselves: *a member of the local mafia* ◊ *Politics is still dominated by the middle-class mafia.*

Mafi·oso /ˌmæfiˈəʊsəʊ; *AmE* ˌmɑːfiˈoʊsoʊ/ *noun* (*pl.* **Mafi·osi** /-siː/) a member of the Mafia

maga·zine /ˌmæɡəˈziːn; *AmE* ˈmæɡəziːn/ *noun* **1** (also *informal* **mag** /mæɡ/) a type of large thin book with a paper cover that you can buy every week or month, containing articles, photographs, etc., often on a particular topic: *a weekly/monthly magazine* ◊ *a magazine article/interview* ◊ *Her designer clothes were from the pages of a glossy fashion magazine.* **2** a radio or television programme that is about a particular topic: *a regional news magazine on TV* ◊ *a magazine programme/program* **3** the part of a gun that holds the bullets before they are fired **4** a room or building where weapons, explosives and bullets are stored

M

ma·genta /məˈdʒentə/ adj. reddish-purple in colour ▶ **ma·genta** noun [U]

mag·got /ˈmæɡət/ noun a creature like a small short worm, that is the young form of a fly and is found in decaying meat and other food. Maggots are often used as BAIT on a hook to catch fish.

Magi /ˈmeɪdʒaɪ/ (**the Magi**) noun [pl.] (in the Bible) the three wise men from the East who are said to have brought presents to the baby Jesus

magic /ˈmædʒɪk/ noun, adj., verb

■ noun [U] **1** the secret power of appearing to make impossible things happen by saying special words or doing special things: *Do you believe in magic?* ◊ *He suddenly appeared as if by magic.* ◊ *A passage was cleared through the crowd like magic.*—see also BLACK MAGIC **2** the art of doing tricks that seem impossible in order to entertain people [SYN] CONJURING **3** a special quality or ability that sb/sth has, that seems too wonderful to be real: *dance and music which capture the magic of India* ◊ *Like all truly charismatic people he can **work his magic** on both men and women.* ◊ *Our year in Italy was pure/sheer magic.* [IDM] see WEAVE v.

■ adj. **1** having or using special powers to make impossible things happen or seem to happen: *a magic spell/charm/potion/trick* ◊ *There is no magic formula for passing exams—only hard work.* **2** (*informal*) having a special quality that makes sth seem wonderful: *It was a magic moment when the two sisters were reunited after 30 years.* ◊ *She has a **magic touch** with the children and they do everything she asks.* ◊ *Trust is the magic ingredient in our relationship.* **3** [not before noun] (*BrE, informal*) very good or enjoyable: *'What was the trip like?' 'Magic!'*

■ verb (**-ck-**) [VN+*adv.*/*prep.*] to make sb/sth appear somewhere, disappear or turn into sth, by magic, or as if by magic: *Three goal scoring chances were conjured up by Swindon, only to be magicked away by Leicester.*

magic·al /ˈmædʒɪkl/ adj. **1** containing magic; used in magic: *magical powers* ◊ *Her words had a magical effect on us.* **2** (*informal*) wonderful; very enjoyable: *a truly magical feeling* ◊ *We spent a magical week in Paris.* ▶ **ma·gic·al·ly** /-kli/ adv.

ˌmagic 'carpet noun (in stories) a carpet that can fly and carry people

ma·gi·cian /məˈdʒɪʃn/ noun **1** a person who can do magic tricks [SYN] CONJUROR **2** (in stories) a person who has magic powers [SYN] SORCERER

ˌmagic 'lantern noun a piece of equipment used in the past to make pictures appear on a white wall or screen

ˌmagic 'mushroom noun a type of MUSHROOM that has an effect like some drugs and that may make people who eat it HALLUCINATE (= see things that are not there)

ˌmagic 'realism (also **ˌmagical 'realism**) noun [U] a style of writing that mixes realistic events with FANTASY

ˌmagic 'wand noun = WAND: *I wish I could **wave a magic wand** and make everything all right again.*

magis·ter·ial /ˌmædʒɪˈstɪəriəl; AmE -ˈstɪr-/ adj. (*formal*) **1** (especially of a person or their behaviour) having or showing power or authority: *He talked with the magisterial authority of the head of the family.* ◊ *a magisterial forehead* **2** (of a book or piece of writing) showing great knowledge or understanding: *his magisterial work 'The Roman Wall in Scotland'* **3** [only before noun] connected with a magistrate ▶ **magis·teri·al·ly** /-iəli/ adv.

the magis·tracy /ˈmædʒɪstrəsi/ noun [sing.+ sing./pl. v.] magistrates as a group

magis·trate /ˈmædʒɪstreɪt/ noun an official who acts as a judge in the lowest courts of law [SYN] JUSTICE OF THE PEACE: *a magistrate's court* ◊ *to come up before the magistrates*

magma /ˈmæɡmə/ noun [U] (*technical*) very hot liquid rock found below the earth's surface—picture at VOLCANO

magna cum laude /ˌmæɡnə kʊm ˈlɔːdi; ˈlaʊdeɪ/ adv., adj. (from *Latin*) (in the US) at the second of the three highest levels of achievement that students can reach when they finish their studies at college: *She graduated magna cum laude from UCLA.*—compare CUM LAUDE, SUMMA CUM LAUDE

mag·nani·mous /mæɡˈnænɪməs/ adj. (*formal*) kind, generous and forgiving, especially towards an enemy or a RIVAL: *a magnanimous gesture* ◊ *He was magnanimous in defeat and praised his opponent's skill.* ▶ **mag·na·nim·ity** /ˌmæɡnəˈnɪməti/ noun [U]: *She accepted the criticism with magnanimity.* **mag·nani·mous·ly** adv.

mag·nate /ˈmæɡneɪt/ noun a person who is rich, powerful and successful, especially in business: *a media/property/shipping magnate*

mag·ne·sium /mæɡˈniːziəm/ noun [U] (*symb* **Mg**) a chemical element. Magnesium is a light, silver-white metal that burns with a bright white flame.

mag·net /ˈmæɡnət/ noun

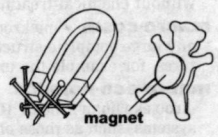
magnet

1 a piece of iron that attracts objects made of iron towards it, either naturally or because of an electric current that is passed through it **2** [usually sing.] ~ (**for sb/sth**) a person, place or thing that sb/sth is attracted to or that: *In the 1980s the area became a magnet for new investment.* **3** an object with a magnetic surface that you can stick onto a metal surface: *fridge magnets of your favourite cartoon characters*

mag·net·ic /mæɡˈnetɪk/ adj. [usually before noun] **1** behaving like a magnet (1): *magnetic materials* ◊ *The block becomes magnetic when the current is switched on.* **2** connected with or produced by magnetism: *magnetic properties/forces* ◊ *a **magnetic disk** (= one containing magnetic tape that stores information to be used by a computer)* **3** that people find very powerful and attractive: *a magnetic smile/personality* ▶ **mag·net·ic·al·ly** /-kli/ adv.

magˌnetic 'compass noun = COMPASS (1)

magˌnetic 'field noun an area around a MAGNET or MAGNETIC materials, where there is a force that will attract some metals towards it

magˌnetic 'media noun [pl., U] the different methods, for example MAGNETIC TAPE, that are used to store information for computers

magˌnetic 'north noun [U] the direction that is approximately north as it is shown on a magnetic compass—compare TRUE NORTH

magˌnetic 'strip noun a line of magnetic material on a plastic card, containing information

magˌnetic 'tape noun [U] a type of plastic tape that is used for recording sound, pictures or computer information

mag·net·ism /ˈmæɡnətɪzəm/ noun [U] **1** a physical PROPERTY (= characteristic) of some metals such as iron, produced by electric currents, that causes forces between objects, either pulling them towards each other or pushing them apart **2** the qualities of sth, especially a person's character, that people find powerful and attractive: *She exudes sexual magnetism.*

mag·net·ize (*BrE* also **-ise**) /ˈmæɡnətaɪz/ verb [VN] **1** [usually passive] (*technical*) to make sth metal behave like a MAGNET **2** (*written*) to strongly attract sb: *Cities have a powerful magnetizing effect on young people.*

mag·neto /mæɡˈniːtəʊ; AmE -ˈniːtoʊ/ noun (*pl.* **-os**) a small piece of equipment that uses MAGNETS (1) to produce the electricity that lights the fuel in the engine of a car, etc.

ˈmagnet school noun (*AmE*) a school in a large city that offers extra courses in some subjects in order to attract students from other areas of the city

mag·ni·fi·ca·tion /ˌmæɡnɪfɪˈkeɪʃn/ noun **1** [U] the act of making sth look larger: *The insects were examined under magnification.* **2** [C, U] the degree to which sth is made to look larger; the degree to which sth is able to make things look larger: *a magnification of 10 times the actual size* ◊ *high/low magnification* ◊ *The telescope has a magnification of 50.*

mag·nifi·cent /mæɡˈnɪfɪsnt/ adj. extremely attractive and impressive; deserving praise: *The Taj Mahal is a magnificent building.* ◊ *She looked magnificent in her*

s	t	v	z	ʃ	ʒ	tʃ	dʒ	θ	ð	ŋ
see	tea	van	zoo	shoe	vision	chain	jam	thin	this	sing

wedding dress. ◊ *You've all done a magnificent job.*
► **mag·nifi·cence** /-sns/ *noun* [U]: *the magnificence of the scenery* **mag·nifi·cent·ly** *adv.*: *The public have responded magnificently to our appeal.*

mag·ni·fier /'mægnɪfaɪə(r)/ *noun* a piece of equipment that is used to make things look larger

mag·nify /'mægnɪfaɪ/ *verb* (**mag·ni·fies**, **mag·ni·fy·ing**, **mag·ni·fied**, **mag·ni·fied**) [VN] **1** to make sth look bigger than it really is, for example by using a LENS or MICROSCOPE: *bacteria magnified to 1000 times their actual size* ◊ *an image magnified by a factor of 4* **2** to make sth bigger, louder or stronger: *The sound was magnified by the high roof.* ◊ *The dry summer has magnified the problem of water shortages.* **3** to make sth seem more important or serious than it really is [SYN] EXAGGERATE

'magnifying glass *noun* a round piece of glass, usually with a handle, that you look through and that makes things look bigger than they really are—picture at GLASS

mag·ni·tude /'mægnɪtjuːd/; *AmE* -tuːd/ *noun* ~ (**of sth**) **1** [U] (*formal*) the great size or importance of sth; the degree to which sth is large or important: *We did not realize the magnitude of the problem.* ◊ *a discovery of the first magnitude* **2** [C, U] (*astronomy*) the degree to which a star is bright: *The star varies in brightness by about three magnitudes.* **3** [C, U] (*geology*) the size of an earthquake

mag·no·lia /mæg'nəʊliə/; *AmE* -'noʊ-/ *noun* **1** [C] a tree with large white, pink or purple flowers that smell sweet **2** [U] a very pale cream colour

mag·num /'mægnəm/ *noun* a bottle containing 1.5 litres of wine, etc.

ˌmagnum 'opus *noun* [sing.] (from *Latin*) a work of art, music or literature that people think is the best that the artist, etc. has ever produced

mag·pie /'mægpaɪ/ *noun* a black and white bird with a long tail and a noisy cry. There is a popular belief that magpies like to steal small bright objects.

maha·raja (also **maha·ra·jah**) /ˌmɑːhə'rɑːdʒə/ *noun* an Indian prince, especially one who ruled over one of the states of India in the past

maha·rani (also **maha·ra·nee**) /ˌmɑːhə'rɑːni/ *noun* the wife of a maharaja

mah·jong /mɑː'dʒɒŋ; *AmE* -'ʒɑːŋ/ *noun* [U] a Chinese game played with small pieces of wood with symbols on them

ma·hog·any /mə'hɒgəni/; *AmE* -'hɑːg-/ *noun* [U] **1** the hard reddish-brown wood of a tropical tree, used for making furniture: *a mahogany table* **2** a reddish-brown colour: *skin tanned to a deep mahogany*

maid /meɪd/ *noun* **1** (often in compounds) a female servant in a house or hotel: *There is a maid to do the housework.*—see also BARMAID, CHAMBERMAID, DAIRYMAID, HOUSEMAID, MILKMAID, NURSEMAID **2** (*old use*) a young woman who is not married—see also OLD MAID

maid·en /'meɪdn/ *noun, adj.*
■ *noun* **1** (*literary*) a young girl or woman who is not married: *stories of knights and fair maidens* **2** (also **ˌmaiden 'over**) (in cricket) an OVER in which no points are scored
■ *adj.* [only before noun] being the first of its kind: *a maiden flight/voyage* (= the first journey made by a plane/ship) ◊ *a maiden speech* (= the first speech made by an MP in the British Parliament)

ˌmaiden 'aunt *noun* (*old-fashioned*) an aunt who has not married

maid·en·hair fern /ˌmeɪdnheə(r) 'fɜːn; *AmE* ˌmeɪdnher 'fɜːrn/ *noun* (also **maid·en·hair** [U]) a type of FERN with long thin stems and delicate pale green leaves that are shaped like FANS

maid·en·head /'meɪdnhed/ *noun* (*old use*) **1** the state of being a VIRGIN **2** = HYMEN

'maiden name *noun* a woman's family name before marriage: *Kate kept her maiden name when she got married* (= did not change her SURNAME to that of her husband).

ˌmaid of 'honour (*BrE*) (*AmE* ˌmaid of 'honor) (*pl.* **maids of honour/honor**) (especially in the US) a young woman or girl who is not married and who is the main BRIDESMAID at a wedding—compare MATRON OF HONOUR

mail /meɪl/ *noun, verb*
■ *noun* [U] **1** (*BrE* also **post**) the official system used for sending and delivering letters, packages, etc: *a mail service/train/van* ◊ *the Royal Mail* ◊ *Your cheque is in the mail.* ◊ *We do our business by mail.*—see also AIRMAIL, SNAIL MAIL, VOICEMAIL **2** (*BrE* also **post**) letters, packages, etc. that are sent and delivered: *There isn't much mail today.* ◊ *I sat down to open the mail.* ◊ *Is there a letter from them in the mail?* ◊ *hate mail* (= letters containing insults and threats)—see also JUNK MAIL, SURFACE MAIL **3** messages that are sent or received on a computer: *Check regularly for new mail.*—see also ELECTRONIC MAIL, E-MAIL **4** used in the title of some newspapers: *the Mail on Sunday* **5** = CHAIN MAIL: *a coat of mail* ⇨ note at POST
■ *verb* ~ **sth (to sb/sth)** | ~ **(sb) sth** (*especially AmE*) to send sth to sb using the POSTAL system: [VN, VNN] *Don't forget to mail that letter to your mother.* ◊ *Don't forget to mail your mother that letter.* ◊ [VN] *The company intends to mail 50000 households in the area.* ⇨ note at POST [PHRV] ˌmail **sth↔'out** to send out a large number of letters, etc. at the same time: *The brochures were mailed out last week.*

mail·bag /'meɪlbæg/ *noun* **1** (*BrE* also **post·bag**) a large strong bag that is used for carrying letters and parcels/packages **2** (*BrE*) = POSTBAG (1)

mail·box /'meɪlbɒks; *AmE* -bɑːks/ *noun* **1** (*AmE*) = LETTER BOX (2) **2** (*AmE*) = POSTBOX—picture at LETTER BOX **3** the area of a computer's memory where electronic mail messages are stored

'mail carrier (also **'letter carrier**) (both *AmE*) *noun* = MAILMAN

mail·er /'meɪlə(r)/ *noun* (*AmE*) **1** = MAILING (2) **2** an envelope, box, etc. for sending small things by mail

mail·ing /'meɪlɪŋ/ *noun* **1** [U] the act of sending items by mail: *The strike has delayed the mailing of tax reminders.* ◊ *a mailing address* **2** (*AmE* also **mailer**) [C] a letter or parcel/package that is sent by mail, especially one that is sent to a large number of people: *An order form is included in the mailing.*

'mailing list *noun* a list of the names and addresses of people who are regularly sent information, advertising material, etc. by an organization: *I am already on your mailing list.*

mail·man /'meɪlmæn/ *noun* (*pl.* **-men** /-men/) (also **'mail carrier**, **'letter carrier**) (all *AmE*) a person whose job is to collect and deliver letters, etc.—see also POSTMAN

ˌmail 'order *noun* [U] a system of buying and selling goods through the mail: *All our products are available by mail order.* ◊ *a mail-order company* ◊ *a mail-order catalogue*

mail·shot /'meɪlʃɒt; *AmE* -ʃɑːt/ *noun* advertising or information that is sent to a large number of people at the same time by mail

'mail slot *noun* (*AmE*) = LETTER BOX (1)

maim /meɪm/ *verb* [VN] to injure sb seriously, causing permanent damage to their body: *Hundreds of people are killed or maimed in car accidents every week.*

main /meɪn/ *adj., noun*
■ *adj.* [only before noun] being the largest or most important of its kind: *Be careful crossing the main road.* ◊ *the main course* (= of a meal) ◊ *We have our main meal at lunchtime.* ◊ *Reception is in the main building.* ◊ *Poor housing and unemployment are the main problems.* ◊ (*spoken*) *The main thing is to stay calm.* [IDM] see EYE *n.*
■ *noun* **1** [C] a large pipe that carries water or gas to a building; a large cable that carries electricity to a building: *a leaking gas main*—see also WATER MAIN **2** a large pipe that carries waste/water and SEWAGE (= human waste, etc.) away from a building **3** (**the mains**) [pl.] (*BrE*) the place where the supply of water, gas or electricity to a building or an area starts; the system of providing gas, water and electricity to a building or of carrying it away from a building: *The house is not yet connected to the mains.* ◊ *The electricity supply has been cut off at the mains.* ◊ *Plug the transformer into the mains* (= the place

M

æ	ɑː	e	ɜː	ə	ɪ	iː	i	ɒ	ɔː	ʌ	ʊ	u	uː
cat	father	ten	bird	about	sit	see	many	got	saw	cup	put	actual	too
							(BrE)						

on a wall where electricity is brought into a room). ◊ *mains gas/water/electricity* ◊ *The shaver will run off batteries or mains.* ◊ *mains drainage* **IDM** **in the ˈmain** used to say that a statement is true in most cases: *The service here is, in the main, reliable.*

ˌmain ˈclause *noun* (*grammar*) a group of words that includes a subject and a verb and can form a sentence—compare SUBORDINATE CLAUSE

the ˌmain ˈdrag *noun* [sing.] (*AmE, informal*) the most important or the busiest street in a town

main·frame /ˈmeɪnfreɪm/ (also **ˌmainframe com-ˈputer**) *noun* a large powerful computer, usually the centre of a NETWORK and shared by many users—compare MICROCOMPUTER, MINICOMPUTER, PERSONAL COMPUTER

main·land /ˈmeɪnlænd/ *noun* [sing.] (**the mainland**) the main area of land of a country, not including any islands near to it: *a boat to/from the mainland* ◊ *The Hebrides are to the west of the Scottish mainland.* ▶ **main·land** *adj.* [only before noun]: *mainland Greece*

ˌmain ˈline *noun* an important railway/railroad line between two cities: *the main line from London to Edin-burgh* ▶ **ˌmain-ˈline** *adj.*: *a main-line station*

main-line /ˈmeɪnlaɪn/ *adj., verb*
■ *adj.* (*especially AmE*) belonging to the system, or con-nected with the ideas that most people accept or believe in **SYN** MAINLINE: *mainline churches/faiths*
■ *verb* (*slang*) to take an illegal drug by INJECTING it into a VEIN: [VN] *At 18 he was mainlining heroin.* [also V]

main·ly /ˈmeɪnli/ *adv.* used to show that a statement is true to a large degree: *The people in the hotel were mainly foreign tourists.* ◊ *an advertising campaign aimed mainly at teenagers* ◊ *The population almost doubles in summer, mainly because of the jazz festival.* ◊ *'Where do you export to?' 'France, mainly.'*

main·sail /ˈmeɪnseɪl/ ˈmeɪnsl/ *noun* the largest and most important sail on a boat or ship—picture at YACHT

main·spring /ˈmeɪnsprɪŋ/ *noun* **1** [usually sing.] **~ (of sth)** (*written*) the most important part of sth; the most important influence on sth: *Small companies are the mainspring of the British economy.* **2** the most important spring in a watch, clock, etc.

main·stay /ˈmeɪnsteɪ/ *noun* [usually sing.] **~ (of sth)** a person or thing that is the most important part of sth and enables it to exist or be successful: *He is the mainstay of our theatre group.* ◊ *Cocoa is the country's economic main-stay.*

main·stream /ˈmeɪnstriːm/ *noun* (**the mainstream**) [sing.] the ideas and opinions that are thought to be normal because they are shared by most people; the people whose ideas and opinions are most accepted: *His radical views place him outside the mainstream of Ameri-can politics.* ◊ *He was never part of the literary mainstream as a writer.* ▶ **main·stream** *adj.* [usually before noun]: *mainstream education*

ˈmain street *noun* (*AmE*) **1** [C] = HIGH STREET **2** (**Main Street**) [U] typical middle-class Americans: *Main Street won't be happy with this new program.*

main·tain /meɪnˈteɪn/ *verb* **1** [VN] to make sth continue at the same level, standard, etc. **SYN** PRESERVE: *to main-tain law and order/standards/a balance* ◊ *The two coun-tries have always maintained close relations.* ◊ (*formal*) *She maintained a dignified silence.* ◊ *to maintain prices* (= prevent them falling or rising) **2** [VN] to keep a building, a machine, etc. in good condition by checking or repairing it regularly: *The house is large and difficult to maintain.* **3** to keep stating that sth is true, even though other people do not agree or do not believe it: [V (that)] *The men maintained (that) they were out of the country when the crime was committed.* ◊ [VN] *She has always maintained her innocence.* [also V speech] **4** [VN] to support sb/sth financially over a long period of time **SYN** KEEP: *Her income was barely enough to maintain one child, let alone three.*

main·ten·ance /ˈmeɪntənəns/ *noun* [U] **1** **~ (of sth)** the act of keeping sth in good condition by checking or repairing it regularly: *The school pays for heating and the maintenance of the buildings.* ◊ *car maintenance* **2** **~ (of**

sth) the act of making a state or situation continue: *the maintenance of international peace* **3** (*BrE, law*) money that sb must pay regularly to their former wife, husband or partner, especially when they have had children together: *He has to pay maintenance to his ex-wife.* ◊ *child maintenance* ◊ *a maintenance order* (= given by a court of law)—see also ALIMONY

mai·son·ette /ˌmeɪzəˈnet/ *noun* (*BrE*) a flat/apartment with rooms on two floors within a building, usually with a separate entrance

maize /meɪz/ *noun* [U] **1** (*BrE*) (*AmE* **corn**) a tall plant grown for its large yellow grains that are used for mak-ing flour or eaten as a vegetable; the grains of this plant—see also CORN ON THE COB, SWEETCORN—picture at CEREAL **2** (*especially AmE*) = INDIAN CORN

Maj. *abbr.* (in writing) MAJOR: *Maj. (Tony) Davies* ◊ *Maj. Gen.* (= Major General)

ma·jes·tic /məˈdʒestɪk/ *adj.* impressive because of size or beauty: *a majestic castle/river/view* ▶ **ma·jes·tic·al-ly** /-kli/ *adv.*

maj·esty /ˈmædʒəsti/ *noun* (*pl.* **-ies**) **1** [U] (*written*) the impressive and attractive quality that sth has: *the sheer majesty of St Peter's in Rome* ◊ *the majesty of the music* **2** [C] (**His/Her/Your Majesty**) a title of respect used when speaking about or to a king or queen **3** [U] royal power

major /ˈmeɪdʒə(r)/ *adj., noun, verb*
■ *adj.* **1** [usually before noun] very large or important: *a major road* ◊ *major international companies* ◊ *to play a major role in sth* ◊ *We have encountered major problems.* ◊ *There were calls for major changes to the welfare system.* **OPP** MINOR **2** [not before noun] (*AmE, spoken*) serious: *Never mind—it's not major.* **3** (*music*) based on a SCALE (= a series of eight notes) in which the third note is two whole TONES/STEPS higher than the first note: *the key of D major*—compare MINOR **4** (*AmE*) related to sb's main sub-ject of study in college
■ *noun* **1** [C] (*abbr.* **Maj.**) an officer of fairly high rank in the army or the US air force: *Major Smith* ◊ *He's a major in the US army.*—see also DRUM MAJOR, SERGEANT MAJOR **2** [C] (*AmE*) the main subject or course of a student at college or university: *Her major is French.*—compare MINOR **3** [C] (*AmE*) a student studying a particular subject as the main part of their course: *She's a French major.* **4** [U] (*music*) a major key or scale: *to change from major to minor* **5** (**the majors**) [pl.] (*AmE, sport*) the MAJOR LEAGUES
■ *verb* **PHRV** **ˈmajor in sth** (*AmE*) to study sth as your main subject at a university or college: *She majored in History at Stanford.* **ˈmajor on sth** (*BrE*) to pay particu-lar attention to one subject, issue, etc.

ma·jor·ette /ˌmeɪdʒəˈret/ *noun* (*especially AmE*) = DRUM MAJORETTE

ˌmajor ˈgeneral *noun* an officer of very high rank in the army or the US air force: *Major General William Hunt*

ma·jor·ity /məˈdʒɒrəti; *AmE* -ˈdʒɔːr-; -ˈdʒɑːr-/ *noun* (*pl.* **-ies**) **1** [sing.+ sing./pl.v.] **~ (of sb/sth)** the largest part of a group of people or things: *The majority of people inter-viewed prefer TV to radio.* ◊ *The majority was/were in favour of banning smoking.* ◊ *This treatment is not avail-able in the vast majority of hospitals.* ◊ *a majority deci-sion* (= one that is decided by what most people want) ◊ *In the nursing profession, women are in a/the majority.* **OPP** MINORITY—see also MORAL MAJORITY, THE SILENT MAJORITY **2** [C] **~ (over sb)** the number of votes by which one political party wins an election; the number of votes by which one side in a discussion, etc. wins: *She was elected by/with a majority of 749.* ◊ *They had a large majority over their nearest rivals.* ◊ *a clear* (= large) *majority* ◊ *The government does not have an overall majority* (= more members than all the other parties added together). ◊ *The resolution was carried by a huge majority.*—see also ABSOLUTE MAJORITY **3** [C] (*AmE*) the difference between the number of votes given to the candidate who wins the election and the total number of votes of all the other candidates—see also PLURALITY **4** [U] (*law*) the age at which you are legally considered to be an adult

aɪ	aʊ	eɪ	əʊ	oʊ	ɔɪ	ɪə	eə	ʊə	j	w
my	now	say	go	go	boy	near	hair	pure	yes	wet
			(BrE)	(AmE)						

ma'jority leader *noun* the leader of the political party that has the majority in either the House of Representatives or the Senate in the US

majority 'rule *noun* [U] a system in which power is held by the group that has the largest number of members

majority 'verdict *noun* (*law*) a decision made by a JURY in a court of law that most members, but not all, agree with

major 'league *adj.* [only before noun] (*AmE*) **1** (*sport*) connected with baseball teams in the Major Leagues (= the most important groups of teams that compete against each other): *a major league team/game/player* **2** very important and having a lot of influence: *a major league business*

major·ly /ˈmeɪdʒəli; *AmE* -dʒərli/ *adv.* (used before an adjective) (*informal, especially AmE*) very; extremely: *majorly disappointed*

make /meɪk/ *verb, noun*
■ *verb* (**made, made** /meɪd/)
  CREATE | **1** ~ sth (from/(out) of sth)| ~ sth into sth| ~ sth (for sb)| ~ sb sth to create or prepare sth by combining materials or putting parts together: [VN] *to make a table/dress/cake* ◊ *to make bread/cement/paper* ◊ *She makes her own clothes.* ◊ *Wine is made from grapes.* ◊ *The grapes are made into wine.* ◊ *What's your shirt made of?* ◊ *made in France* (= on a label) ◊ [VN, VNN] *She made coffee for us all.* ◊ *She made us all coffee.* ⇨ note at DO **2** [VN] to write, create or prepare sth for use: *These regulations were made to protect children.* ◊ *My lawyer has been urging me to make a will.* ◊ *She has made* (= directed or acted in) *several movies.*
  A BED | **3** [VN] to arrange a bed so that it is neat and ready for use
  CAUSE TO APPEAR/HAPPEN/BECOME/DO | **4** [VN] to cause sth to appear as a result of breaking, tearing, hitting or removing material: *The stone made a dent in the roof of the car.* ◊ *The holes in the cloth were made by moths.* **5** [VN] to cause sth to exist, happen or be done: *to make a noise/mess/fuss* ◊ *She tried to make a good impression on the interviewer.* ◊ *I keep making the same mistakes.* **6** [VN-ADJ] to cause sb/sth to be or become sth: *The news made him very happy.* ◊ *She made her objections clear.* ◊ *He made it clear that he objected.* ◊ *The full story was never made public.* ◊ *Can you make yourself understood in Russian?* ◊ *She couldn't make herself heard above the noise of the traffic.* ◊ *The terrorists made it known that tourists would be targeted.* **7** [VNinf] to cause sb/sth to do sth: *She always makes me laugh.* ◊ *This dress makes me look fat.* ◊ *What makes you say that* (= why do you think so)? ◊ *Nothing will make me change my mind.* **8** ~ sth of sb/sth| ~ sth sth to cause sb/sth to be or become sth: [VN] *This isn't very important—I don't want to make an issue of it.* ◊ *Don't make a habit of it.* ◊ *You've made a terrible mess of this job.* ◊ *It's important to try and make something of* (= achieve sth in) *your life.* ◊ *We'll make a tennis player of you yet.* ◊ [VN-N] *I made painting the house my project for the summer.* ◊ *She made it her business to find out who was responsible.*
  A DECISION/GUESS/COMMENT, etc. | **9** [VN] ~ a decision, guess, comment, etc. to decide, guess, etc. sth: *Come on! It's time we made a start.* **HELP** Make can be used in this way with a number of different nouns. These expressions are included at the entry for each noun.
  FORCE | **10** to force sb to do sth: [VNinf] *They made me repeat the whole story.* ◊ [VNtoinf] *She must be made to comply with the rules.* **HELP** This pattern is only used in the passive. [VN] *He never cleans his room and his mother never tries to make him.*
  REPRESENT | **11** to represent sb/sth as being or doing sth: [VN-ADJ] *You've made my nose too big* (for example in a drawing). ◊ [VN-N] *He makes King Lear a truly tragic figure.*
  APPOINT | **12** [VN-N] to elect or choose sb as sth: *She made him her assistant.*
  BE SUITABLE | **13** *linking verb* [V-N] to become or develop into sth; to be suitable for sth: *She would have made an excellent teacher.* ◊ *This room would make a nice office.*
  EQUAL | **14** *linking verb* [V-N] to add up to or equal sth: *5 and 7 make 12.* ◊ *A hundred cents make one euro.* **15** *linking verb* [V-N] to be a total of sth: *That makes the third time he's failed his driving test!*
  MONEY | **16** [VN] to earn or gain money: *She makes $100000 a year.* ◊ *to make a profit/loss* ◊ *We need to think of ways to make money.* ◊ *He made a fortune on the stock market.* ◊ *He makes a living as a stand-up comic.*
  CALCULATE | **17** [VN-N] [no passive] to think or calculate sth to be sth: *What time do you make it?* ◊ *I make that exactly $50.*
  REACH | **18** [VN] [no passive] to manage to reach or go to a place or position: *Do you think we'll make Dover by 12?* ◊ *I'm sorry I couldn't make your party last night.* ◊ *He'll never make* (= get a place in) *the team.* ◊ *The story made* (= appeared on) *the front pages of the national newspapers.* ◊ *We just managed to make the deadline* (= to finish sth in time).
  STH SUCCESSFUL | **19** [VN] to cause sth to be a success: *Good wine can make a meal.* ◊ *The news really made my day.*
  IDM Most idioms containing **make** are at the entries for the nouns and adjectives in the idioms, for example **make merry** is at **merry**. **make as if to do sth** (*written*) to make a movement that makes it seem as if you are just going to do sth: *He made as if to speak.* **make 'do (with sth)** to manage with sth that is not really satisfactory: *We were in a hurry so we had to make do with a quick snack.* **make 'good** to become rich and successful **make sth 'good 1** to pay for, replace or repair sth that has been lost or damaged: *She promised to make good the damage.* **2** to carry out a promise, threat, etc. **SYN** FULFIL **'make it 1** to be successful in your career: *He never really made it as an actor.* **2** to succeed in reaching a place in time, especially when this is difficult: *The flight leaves in twenty minutes—we'll never make it.* **3** to be able to be present at a place: *I'm sorry I won't be able to make it* (for example, to a party) *on Saturday.* **4** to survive after a serious illness or accident; to deal successfully with a difficult experience: *The doctors think he's going to make it.* ◊ *I don't know how I made it through the week.* **'make it with sb** (*AmE, slang*) to have sex with sb **make like ...** (*AmE, informal*) to pretend to be, know or have sth in order to impress people: *He makes like he's the greatest actor of all time.* **make the 'most of sth/sb/yourself** to gain as much advantage, enjoyment, etc. as you can from sb/sth: *It's my first trip abroad so I'm going to make the most of it.* ◊ *She doesn't know how to make the most of herself* (= make herself appear in the best possible way). **make 'much of sth/sb** (*written*) to treat sth/sb as very important: *He always makes much of his humble origins.* **make or 'break sth** to be the thing that makes sb/sth either a success or a failure: *This movie will make or break him as a director.* ◊ *It's make-or-break time for the company.* **'make something of yourself** to be successful in your life
  PHRV 'make for sth 1 to move towards sth **2** to help to make sth possible: *Constant arguing doesn't make for a happy marriage.*—see also BE MADE FOR SB/EACH OTHER at MADE
  'make sb/sth into sb/sth to change sb/sth into sb/sth: *We're making our attic into an extra bedroom.*
  'make sth of sb/sth to understand the meaning or character of sb/sth: *What do you make of it all?* ◊ *I can't make anything of this note.* ◊ *I don't know what to make of* (= think of) *the new manager.*
  make 'off to hurry away, especially in order to escape **make 'off with sth** to steal sth and hurry away with it **make 'out** (*informal*) **1** used to ask if sb managed well or was successful in a particular situation: *How did he make out while his wife was away?* **2** (*AmE*) ~ **(with sb)** to kiss and touch sb in a sexual way; to have sex with sb **make sb 'out** to understand sb's character **make sb/sth↔'out 1** to manage to see sb/sth or read or hear sth: *I could just make out a figure in the darkness.* ◊ [+wh-] *I could hear voices but I couldn't make out what they were saying.* **2** to say that sth is true when it may not be **SYN** CLAIM: *She's*

M

not as rich as people make out. ◊[+that] *He made out that he had been robbed.* ◊[+to inf] *She makes herself out to be smarter than she really is.* ,make sth↔'out 1 to write out or complete a form or document: *He made out a cheque for £100.* ◊ *The doctor made out a prescription for me.* 2 (used in negative sentences and questions) to understand sth; to see the reasons for sth: *How do you make that out* (= what are your reasons for thinking that)*?* ◊[+wh-] *I can't make out what she wants.*

,make sth↔'over (to sb/sth) 1 to legally give sth to sb: *He made over the property to his eldest son.* 2 to change sth in order to make it look different or use it for a different purpose; to give sb a different appearance by changing their clothes, hair, etc.—related noun MAKEOVER

'make towards sth to start moving towards sth: *He made towards the door.*

,make 'up | ,make yourself/sb↔'up to put powder, LIP-STICK, etc. on your/sb's face to make it more attractive or to prepare for an appearance in the theatre, on television, etc.—related noun MAKE-UP (1) ,make sth↔'up 1 to form sth SYN CONSTITUTE: *Women make up 56% of the student numbers.*—related noun MAKE-UP ⇨ note at COMPRISE 2 to put sth together from several different things—related noun MAKE-UP 3 to invent a story, etc., especially in order to deceive or entertain sb: *He made up some excuse about his daughter being sick.* ◊ *I told the kids a story, making it up as I went along.* ◊ *You made that up!* 4 to complete a number or an amount required: *We need one more person to make up a team.* 5 to replace sth that has been lost; to COMPENSATE for sth: *Can I leave early this afternoon and make up the time tomorrow?* 6 to prepare a medicine by mixing different things together 7 to prepare a bed for use; to create a temporary bed: *We made up the bed in the spare room.* ◊ *They made up a bed for me on the sofa.* ,make 'up for sth to do sth that corrects a bad situation: *Nothing can make up for the loss of a child.* ◊ *After all the delays, we were anxious to make up for lost time.* ◊ *Her enthusiasm makes up for her lack of experience.* ,make 'up (to sb) for sth to to do sth for sb or give them sth because you have caused them trouble, suffering or disappoint-ment and wish to show that you are sorry SYN COMPEN-SATE: *How can I make up for the way I've treated you?* ◊ (*informal*) *I'll make it up to you, I promise.* ,make 'up to sb (*BrE, informal, disapproving*) to be pleasant to sb, praise them, etc. especially in order to get an advantage for yourself ,make 'up (with sb) (*BrE* also ,make it 'up) to end a quarrel with sb and become friends again: *Why don't you two kiss and make up?* ◊ *Has he made it up with her yet?* ◊ *Have they made it up yet?*

■ *noun* ~ (of sth) the name or type of a machine, piece of equipment, etc. that is made by a particular company: *What make of car does he drive?* ◊ *There are so many different makes to choose from.* ◊ *a Swiss make of watch* IDM on the 'make (*informal, disapproving*) trying to get money or an advantage for yourself

'make-believe *noun* [U] 1 (*disapproving*) imagining or pretending things to be different or more exciting than they really are: *They live in a world of make-believe.* 2 imagining that sth is real, or that you are sb else, for example in a child's game: *'Let's play make-believe,' said Sam.*

make·over /'meɪkəʊvə(r); *AmE* -oʊ-/ *noun* [C, U] the pro-cess of improving the appearance of a person or a place

maker /'meɪkə(r)/ *noun* 1 [C] ~ (of sth) (often in com-pounds) a person, company, or piece of equipment that makes or produces sth: *a decision/law/policy maker* ◊ *programme makers* ◊ *a new film/movie from the makers of 'Terminator'* ◊ *If it doesn't work, send it back to the maker.* ◊ *an electric coffee-maker* ◊ *one of the best winemakers is France*—see also HOLIDAYMAKER, PEACEMAKER, TROUBLE-MAKER 2 (the, his, your, etc. Maker) [sing.] God IDM see MEET *v.*

make·shift /'meɪkʃɪft/ *adj.* [usually before noun] used temporarily for a particular purpose because the real thing is not available: *A few cushions formed a makeshift bed.*

'make-up *noun* 1 [U] substances used especially by women to make their faces look more attractive, or used by actors to change their appearance: *eye make-up* ◊ *to put on your make-up* ◊ *She never wears make-up.* ◊ *a make-up artist* (= a person whose job is to put make-up on the faces of actors and models) 2 [sing.] the different qual-ities that combine to form sb's character: *Jealousy is not part of his make-up.* ◊ *a person's genetic make-up* 3 [sing.] ~ (of sth) the different things, people, etc. that combine to form sth; the way in which they combine: *the make-up of a TV audience* ◊ (*technical*) *the page make-up of a text* (= the way in which the words and pictures are arranged on a page) 4 [C] (*AmE*) a special exam taken by students who missed or failed an earlier one

make·weight /'meɪkweɪt/ *noun* an unimportant person or thing that is only added or included in sth in order to make it the correct number, quantity, size, etc.

mak·ing /'meɪkɪŋ/ *noun* [U] ~ (of sth) (often in com-pounds) the act or process of making or producing sth: *strategic decision making* ◊ *film-making* ◊ *dressmaking* ◊ *tea and coffee making facilities* ◊ *the making of social policy*—see also HAYMAKING, NON-PROFIT IDM be the 'mak-ing of sb to make sb become a better or more successful person: *University was the making of Joe.* have the 'mak-ings of sth to have the qualities that are necessary to become sth: *Her first novel has all the makings of a classic.* ◊ *He has the makings of a first-rate lawyer.* in the 'making in the process of becoming sth or of being made: *This model was two years in the making.* ◊ *These events are history in the making.* of your own 'making (of a problem, difficulty, etc.) created by you rather than by sb/sth else

mal- /mæl/ *combining form* (in nouns, verbs and adjec-tives) bad or badly; not correct or correctly: *malpractice* ◊ *malodorous* ◊ *malfunction*

mal·ach·ite /'mæləkaɪt/ *noun* [U] a green mineral that can be polished and used in making ornaments

mal·adjust·ed /ˌmælə'dʒʌstɪd/ *adj.* (especially of chil-dren) having mental and emotional problems that lead to unacceptable behaviour—compare WELL ADJUSTED ▶ mal·adjust·ment /ˌmælə'dʒʌstmənt/ *noun* [U]

mal·admin·is·tra·tion /ˌmæləd,mɪnɪ'streɪʃn/ *noun* [U] (*formal*) the fact of managing a business or an organ-ization in a bad or dishonest way

mal·adroit /ˌmælə'drɔɪt/ *adj.* (*formal*) done without skill, especially in a way that annoys or offends people

mal·ady /'mælədi/ *noun* (*pl.* -ies) 1 (*formal*) a serious problem: *Violent crime is only one of the maladies afflict-ing modern society.* 2 (*old use*) an illness

mal·aise /mə'leɪz/ *noun* [U, sing.] (*formal*) 1 the prob-lems affecting a particular situation or group of people that are difficult to explain or identify: *economic/finan-cial/social malaise* 2 a general feeling of being ill, unhappy or not satisfied, without signs of any particular problem: *a serious malaise among the staff*

mala·prop·ism /'mæləprɒpɪzəm; *AmE* -prɑːp-/ *noun* an amusing mistake sb makes when they use a word which sounds similar to the word they wanted to use, but means sth different

mal·aria /mə'leəriə; *AmE* -'ler-/ *noun* [U] a disease that causes fever and SHIVERING (= shaking of the body) caused by the bite of some types of MOSQUITO ▶ mal·ar·ial /-iəl/ *adj.*: *malarial insects/patients/regions*

ma·lar·key /mə'lɑːki; *AmE* mə'lɑːrki/ *noun* [U] (*infor-mal, disapproving*) behaviour or an idea that you think is nonsense or has no meaning

mal·con·tent /'mælkəntent; *AmE* ˌmælkən'tent/ *noun* [usually pl.] (*formal, disapproving*) a person who is not satisfied with a situation and who complains about it, or causes trouble in order to change it

male /meɪl/ *adj., noun*

■ *adj.* 1 (*abbr.* m) belonging to the sex that does not give birth to babies; connected with this sex: *A male bird* ◊ *All the attackers were male, aged between 25 and 30.* ◊ *a male nurse/model/colleague* ◊ *male attitudes to women* ◊ *male bonding* (= the act of forming close friendships between men) ◊ *the male menopause* (= emotional and physical problems that affect some men at about the age of 50)—compare MASCULINE 2 (*biology*) (of a plant) producing POL-

s	t	v	z	ʃ	ʒ	tʃ	dʒ	θ	ð	ŋ
see	tea	van	zoo	shoe	vision	chain	jam	thin	this	sing

LEN rather than seeds and fruit: *a male flower* **3** (*technical*) (of electrical PLUGS, parts of tools, etc.) having a part that sticks out which is designed to fit into a hole, SOCKET, etc. ▶ **male·ness** *noun* [U]: *the chromosome that determines maleness*

■ *noun* a male person, animal or plant: *The body is that of a white male aged about 40.* ◊ *The male of the species has a white tail.* ◊ *a male-dominated profession* ◊ *Haemophilia is a condition that affects mostly males.*

,male 'chauvinism (also **chauvinism**) *noun* [U] (*disapproving*) the belief held by some men that men are more important, intelligent, etc. than women

,male 'chauvinist (also **chauvinist**) *noun* (*disapproving*) a man who believes men are more important, intelligent, etc. than women: *He's just another male chauvinist who is jealous of his wife's success.* ◊ *I hate working for that male chauvinist pig Steve.*

mal·efac·tor /'mælɪfæktə(r)/ *noun* (*formal*) a person who does wrong, illegal or wicked things

ma·levo·lent /mə'levələnt/ *adj.* [usually before noun] having or showing a desire to harm other people: *malevolent intentions / thoughts* ◊ *his dark malevolent eyes* [OPP] BENEVOLENT ▶ **ma·levo·lence** /-əns/ *noun* [U]: *an act of pure malevolence* **ma·levo·lent·ly** *adv.*

mal·for·ma·tion /,mælfɔː'meɪʃn; *AmE* -fɔːr'm-/ *noun* **1** [C] a part of the body that is not formed correctly: *Some foetal malformations cannot be diagnosed until late in pregnancy.* **2** [U] the state of not being correctly formed

mal·formed /,mæl'fɔːmd; *AmE* -'fɔːrmd/ *adj.* (*technical*) badly formed or shaped

mal·func·tion /,mæl'fʌŋkʃn/ *verb* [V] (of a machine, etc.) to fail to work correctly ▶ **mal·func·tion** *noun* [C, U]: *The drug caused a malfunction in the brain.*

mal·ice /'mælɪs/ *noun* [U] a feeling of hatred for sb that causes a desire to harm them: *He sent the letter out of malice.* ◊ *She is entirely without malice.* ◊ *He certainly bears you no malice* (= does not want to harm you). [IDM] **with ,malice a'forethought** (*law*) with the deliberate intention of committing a crime or harming sb

ma·li·cious /mə'lɪʃəs/ *adj.* having or showing hatred and a desire to harm sb or hurt their feelings: *malicious gossip / lies / rumours* ◊ *He took malicious pleasure in telling me what she had said.* ▶ **ma·li·cious·ly** *adv.*

ma·lign /mə'laɪn/ *verb, adj.*
■ *verb* [VN] (*written*) to say bad things about sb/sth publicly: *She feels she has been much maligned by the press.*
■ *adj.* [usually before noun] (*formal*) causing harm: *a malign force / influence / effect*—compare BENIGN

ma·lig·nancy /mə'lɪgnənsi/ *noun* (*pl.* **-ies**) (*formal*) **1** [C] a malignant mass of tissue in the body [SYN] TUMOUR **2** [U] the state of being malignant

ma·lig·nant /mə'lɪgnənt/ *adj.* **1** (of a TUMOUR or disease) that cannot be controlled and is likely to cause death: *malignant cells*—compare BENIGN **2** (*formal*) having or showing a strong desire to harm sb

ma·lin·ger /mə'lɪŋgə(r)/ *verb* [V] (usually **be malingering**) (*disapproving*) to pretend to be ill/sick, especially in order to avoid work ▶ **ma·lin·ger·er** *noun*

mall /mɔːl; *BrE* also mæl/ *noun* (*especially AmE*) = SHOPPING MALL: *Let's go to the mall.*

mal·lard /'mælɑːd; *AmE* 'mælərd/ *noun* (*pl.* **mal·lards** or **mal·lard**) a common wild duck

mal·le·able /'mæliəbl/ *adj.* **1** (*technical*) (of metal, etc.) that can be hit or pressed into different shapes easily without breaking or cracking **2** (of people, ideas, etc.) easily influenced or changed ▶ **mal·le·abil·ity** /,mæliə-'bɪləti/ *noun* [U]

mal·let /'mælɪt/ *noun* **1** a hammer with a large wooden head—picture at TOOL **2** a hammer with a long handle and a wooden head, used for hitting the ball in the games of CROQUET and POLO

mal·nour·ished /,mæl'nʌrɪʃt; *AmE* -'nɜːr-/ *adj.* in bad health because of a lack of food or a lack of the right type of food

mal·nu·tri·tion /,mælnju:'trɪʃn; *AmE* -nuː-/ *noun* [U] a poor condition of health caused by a lack of food or a lack of the right type of food—compare NUTRITION

mal·odor·ous /,mæl'əʊdərəs; *AmE* -'oʊdərəs/ *adj.* (*formal or literary*) having an unpleasant smell

mal·prac·tice /,mæl'præktɪs/ *noun* [U, C] (*law*) careless, wrong or illegal behaviour while in a professional job: *medical malpractice* ◊ *a malpractice suit* ◊ *He is currently standing trial for alleged malpractices.*

malt /mɔːlt; *BrE* also mɒlt/ *noun* **1** [U] grain, usually BARLEY, that has been soaked in water for a period of time and then dried, used for making beer, whisky, etc. **2** [U, C] = MALT WHISKY **3** [U, C] (*AmE*) = MALTED MILK

malt·ed /'mɔːltɪd/ *adj.* [only before noun] **1** having been made into malt: *malted barley* **2** having had malt added to it

,malted 'milk (*AmE* also **malt**) *noun* [U, C] a hot or cold drink made from MALT and dried milk mixed with water or milk and usually sugar, sometimes with ice cream and/or chocolate added

mal·treat /,mæl'triːt/ *verb* [VN] (*written*) to be very cruel to a person or an animal: *Officers were accused of maltreating prisoners.* ▶ **mal·treat·ment** *noun* [U]

,malt 'whisky (also **malt**) *noun* [U, C] high quality whisky from Scotland; a glass of this

mam /mæm/ *noun* (*BrE, dialect, informal*) mother

mama (also **mamma**) /'mæmə; *BrE* also mə'mɑː/ *noun* (*AmE* or *old-fashioned, BrE*) mother—see also MUMMY

mamba /'mæmbə/ *noun* a black or green poisonous African snake

mam·mal /'mæml/ *noun* any animal that gives birth to live babies, not eggs, and feeds its young on milk. Cows, humans and WHALES are all mammals. ▶ **mam·ma·lian** /mæ'meɪliən/ *adj.*: *mammalian species*—picture on page A6

mam·mary /'mæməri/ *adj.* [only before noun] (*biology*) connected with the breasts: *mammary glands* (= parts of the breast that produce milk)

mam·mo·gram /'mæməgræm/ *noun* an examination of a woman's breasts using X-RAYS to check for CANCER ▶ **mam·mog·raphy** /mæ'mɒgrəfi; *AmE* -'mɑːg-/ *noun* [U]

Mam·mon /'mæmən/ *noun* [U] (*formal, disapproving*) a way of talking about money and wealth when it has become the most important thing in sb's life and as important as a god: *gamblers worshipping at the temple of Mammon*

mam·moth /'mæməθ/ *noun, adj.*
■ *noun* an animal like a large hairy elephant, that lived thousands of years ago and is now EXTINCT
■ *adj.* [usually before noun] extremely large: *a mammoth task* ◊ *a financial crisis of mammoth proportions*

mammy /'mæmi/ *noun* (*pl.* **-ies**) (*dialect, informal*) mother

man /mæn/ *noun, verb, exclamation*
■ *noun* (*pl.* **men** /men/)

MALE PERSON | **1** [C] an adult male human being: *a good-looking young man* ◊ *the relationships between men and women*—see also DIRTY OLD MAN, LADIES' MAN, MEN'S ROOM

HUMAN BEINGS | **2** [U] human beings as a group or from a particular period of history: *the damage caused by man to the environment* ◊ *early / modern / Prehistoric man* ⇨ note at GENDER **3** [C] (*literary* or *old-fashioned*) a person, either male or female: *All men must die.*

PARTICULAR TYPE OF MAN | **4** [C] (in compounds) a man who comes from the place mentioned or whose job or interest is connected with the thing mentioned: *a Frenchman* ◊ *a businessman* ◊ *a medical man* ◊ *a sportsman* ⇨ note at GENDER **5** [C] a man who likes or who does the thing mentioned: *a betting / drinking / fighting man*—see also FAMILY MAN **6** [C] a man who works for or supports a particular organization, comes from a particular town, etc: *the BBC's man in Moscow* (= the man who reports on news from Moscow) ◊ *a loyal Republican Party man*—see also RIGHT-HAND MAN, YES-MAN

SOLDIER / WORKER | **7** [C, usually pl.] a soldier or a male worker who obeys the instructions of a person of higher rank: *The officer refused to let his men take part in the operation.* **8** [C] a man who comes to your house to do a

æ	ɑː	e	ɜː	ə	ɪ	iː	i	ɒ	ɔː	ʌ	ʊ	u	uː
cat	father	ten	bird	about	sit	see	many	got	saw	cup	put	actual	too

(BrE)

job: *the gas man* ◊ *The man's coming to repair the TV today.*

FORM OF ADDRESS | **9** [sing.] (*informal spoken, especially AmE*) used for addressing a male person: *Nice shirt, man!* ◊ *Hey man. Back off!* **10** [sing.] (*old-fashioned, spoken*) used for addressing a male person in an angry or impatient way: *Don't just stand there, man—get a doctor!*

HUSBAND/BOYFRIEND | **11** [C] (*sometimes disapproving*) a husband or sexual partner: *What's her new man like?* ◊ *I now pronounce you man and wife* (= you are now officially married).—see also OLD MAN

STRONG/BRAVE PERSON | **12** [C] a person who is strong and brave or has other qualities that some people think are particularly male: *Come on, now—be a man.* ◊ *She's more of a man than he is.*—see also HE-MAN, MUSCLEMAN, SUPERMAN

SERVANT | **13** [sing.] (*old-fashioned, formal*) a male servant: *My man will drive you home.*

IN CHESS | **14** [C] one of the figures or objects that you play with in a game such as CHESS—see also CHESSMAN

IDM **as one 'man** with everyone doing or thinking the same thing at the same time; in agreement **be sb's 'man** to be the best or most suitable person to do a particular job, etc: *For a superb haircut, David's your man.* **be 'man enough (to do sth/for sth)** to be strong or brave enough: *He was not man enough to face up to his responsibility.* **every man for him'self** (*saying*) people must look after themselves and not give or expect any help: *In business, it's every man for himself.* **make a 'man (out) of sb** to make a young man develop and become more adult **a/the ˌman about 'town** a man who frequently goes to fashionable parties, clubs, theatres, etc. **ˌman and 'boy** from when sb was young to when they were old or older: *He's been doing the same job for 50 years—man and boy.* **the ˌman (and/or ˌwoman) in the 'street** an average or ordinary person, either male or female: *Politicians often don't understand the views of the man in the street.* **a ˌman of 'God/the 'cloth** (*old-fashioned, formal*) a religious man, especially a priest or a CLERGYMAN **the ˌman of the 'match** (*BrE, sport*) the member of a team who plays the best in a particular game: *Cole was named man of the match.* **a ˌman of the 'people** (especially of a politician) a man who understands and is sympathetic to ordinary people **man's best 'friend** a way of describing a dog **a ˌman's ˌhome is his 'castle** (*AmE*) = AN ENGLISHMAN'S HOME IS HIS CASTLE at ENGLISHMAN **a 'man's man** a man who is more popular with men than with women **be your own 'man/'woman** to act or think independently, not following others or being ordered: *Working for himself meant that he could be his own man.* **ˌman to 'man** between two men who are treating each other honestly and equally: *I'm telling you all this man to man.* ◊ *a man-to-man talk* **separate/sort out the ˌmen from the 'boys** to show or prove who is brave, skilful, etc. and who is not **to a 'man | to the last 'man** (*written*) used to emphasize that sth is true of all the people being described: *They answered 'Yes,' to a man.* ◊ *They were all destroyed, to the last man.*—more at GRAND *adj.*, HEART, MARKED, NEXT *adj.*, ODD *adj.*, PART *n.*, POOR, POSSESSED, SUBSTANCE, THING, WORD *n.*, WORLD

■ *verb* (**-nn-**) [VN] to work at a place or be in charge of a place or a machine; to supply people to work somewhere: *Soldiers manned barricades around the city.* ◊ *The telephones are manned 24 hours a day by volunteers.* ◊ *a manned space flight*

■ *exclamation* (*informal, especially AmE*) used to express surprise, anger, etc.: *Man, that was great!*

man·acle /ˈmænəkl/ *noun, verb*

■ *noun* [usually pl.] one of two metal bands joined by a chain, used for fastening a prisoner's ankles or wrists together

■ *verb* [VN] [usually passive] to put manacles on sb's wrists or ankles, to stop them from escaping

man·age /ˈmænɪdʒ/ *verb*

DO STH DIFFICULT | **1** to succeed in doing sth, especially sth difficult: [VN] *In spite of his disappointment, he managed a weak smile.* ◊ *I don't know exactly how we'll manage it,* but we will, somehow. ◊ *Can you manage another piece of cake?* (= eat one) ◊ [V to inf] *We managed to get to the airport in time.* ◊ *How did you manage to persuade him?* ◊ (*humorous*) *He always manages to say the wrong thing.* ◊ [V] *We couldn't have managed without you.* ◊ *'Need any help?' 'No, thanks. I can manage.'* ⇨ note at CAN[1]

DEAL WITH PROBLEMS | **2** [V] **~ (with/without sb/sth)** to be able to solve your problems, deal with a difficult situation, etc. **SYN** COPE: *I don't know how she manages on her own with four kids.* ◊ *How do you manage without a car?* ◊ *She's 82 and can't manage on her own any more.*

MONEY/TIME/INFORMATION | **3** [V] **~ (on sth)** to be able to live without having much money: *He has to manage on less than £100 a week.* **4** [VN] to use money, time, information, etc. in a sensible way: *Don't tell me how to manage my affairs.* ◊ *a computer program that helps you manage data efficiently* **5** [VN] to be able to do sth at a particular time: *Let's meet up again—can you manage next week sometime?*

BUSINESS/TEAM | **6** to control or be in charge of a business, a team, an organization, etc: [VN] *to manage a factory/bank/hotel/soccer team* ◊ *to manage a department/project* ◊ [V] *We need people who are good at managing.*

CONTROL | **7** [VN] to keep sb/sth under control; to be able to deal with sb/sth: *It's like trying to manage an unruly child.* ◊ *Can you manage that suitcase?*

man·age·able /ˈmænɪdʒəbl/ *adj.* possible to deal with or control: *Use conditioner regularly to make your hair soft and manageable.* ◊ *The debt has been reduced to a more manageable level.* **OPP** UNMANAGEABLE

man·aged /ˈmænɪdʒd/ *adj.* [only before noun] carefully looked after and controlled: *The money will be invested in managed funds.* ◊ *Only wood from managed forests is used in our furniture.*

man·age·ment /ˈmænɪdʒmənt/ *noun* **1** [U] the act of running and controlling a business or similar organization: *a career in management* ◊ *hotel/project management* ◊ *a management training course* ◊ *The report blames bad management.* **2** [C+sing./pl. v., U] the people who run and control a business or similar organization: *The management is/are considering closing the factory.* ◊ *The shop is now under new management.* ◊ *junior/middle/senior management* ◊ *a management decision/job* ◊ *My role is to act as a mediator between employees and management.* ◊ *Most managements are keen to avoid strikes.* **3** [U] the act or skill of dealing with people or situations in a successful way: *classroom management* ◊ *time management* (= the way in which you organize how you spend your time) ◊ *management of staff* ◊ *Diet plays an important role in the management of heart disease.*

man·ager /ˈmænɪdʒə(r)/ *noun* **1** a person who is in charge of running a business, a shop/store or a similar organization or part of one: *a bank/hotel manager* ◊ *the sales/marketing/personnel manager* ◊ *a meeting of area managers*—see also MIDDLE MANAGER **2** a person who deals with the business affairs of an actor, a musician, etc. **3** a person who trains and organizes a sports team: *the new manager of Italy*

man·ager·ess /ˌmænɪdʒəˈres/ *noun* (*BrE, becoming old-fashioned*) a woman who is in charge of a small business, for example, a shop/store, restaurant or hotel

man·ager·ial /ˌmænəˈdʒɪəriəl; *AmE* -ˈdʒɪr-/ *adj.* [usually before noun] connected with the work of a manager: *Does she have any managerial experience?*

ˌmanaging diˈrector *noun* (*abbr.* MD) (*especially BrE*) the person who is in charge of a business

mana·tee /ˈmænəti/ *noun* a large water animal with front legs and a strong tail but no back legs, that lives in America and Africa

Man·cu·nian /mænˈkjuːniən/ *noun* a person from Manchester in NW England ▶ **Man·cu·nian** *adj.*

man·dala /ˈmændələ/ *noun* a circular picture that represents the universe in some eastern religions

man·da·rin /ˈmændərɪn/ *noun* [C] **1** (*BrE*) a powerful official of high rank, especially in the CIVIL SERVICE **2** a government official of high rank in China in the past **3** (also ˌmandarin 'orange) a type of small orange with loose skin that comes off easily

man·date *noun, verb*

■ *noun* /ˈmændeɪt/ **1** ~ **(to do sth)** | ~ **(for sth)** the authority to do sth, given to a government or other organization by the people who vote for it in an election: *The election victory gave the party a clear mandate to continue its programme of reform.* ◊ *a mandate for an end to the civil war* **2** the period of time for which a government is given power: *The presidential mandate is limited to two terms of four years each.* **3** ~ **(to do sth)** *(formal)* an official order given to sb to perform a particular task: *The bank had no mandate to honour the cheque.* **4** the power given to a country to govern another country or region, especially in the past

■ *verb* /ˈmændeɪt; ˌmænˈdeɪt/ [often passive] *(formal)* **1** *(especially AmE)* to order sb to behave, do sth or vote in a particular way: [Vthat] *The law mandates that imported goods should be identified as such.* [also VN to inf, VN] **2** [VN to inf] to give sb, especially a government or a committee, the authority to do sth: *The assembly was mandated to draft a constitution.*

man·dated /ˈmændeɪtɪd/ *adj.* [only before noun] *(formal)* **1** (of a country or state) placed under the rule of another country: *mandated territories* **2** required by law: *a mandated curriculum* **3** having a mandate to do sth: *a mandated government*

man·da·tory /ˈmændətəri; AmE -tɔːri BrE also mænˈdeɪtəri/ *adj.* ~ **(for sb) (to do sth)** *(formal)* required by law [SYN] COMPULSORY: *It is mandatory for blood banks to test all donated blood for the virus.* ◊ *The offence carries a mandatory life sentence.*

man·dible /ˈmændɪbl/ *noun (anatomy)* **1** the JAWBONE—picture at BODY **2** the upper or lower part of a bird's beak **3** either of the two parts that are at the front and on either side of an insect's mouth, used especially for biting and crushing food—picture on page A7

man·do·lin /ˈmændəlɪn; ˌmændəˈlɪn/ *noun* a musical instrument with metal strings (usually eight) arranged in pairs, and a curved back, played with a PLECTRUM/PICK

man·drake /ˈmændreɪk/ *noun* [C, U] a poisonous plant used to make drugs, especially ones to make people sleep, thought in the past to have magic powers

mane /meɪn/ *noun* **1** the long hair on the neck of a horse or a lion—picture on page A6 **2** *(informal or literary)* a person's long or thick hair

ˈman-eater *noun* **1** a wild animal that attacks and eats human beings **2** *(humorous)* a woman who has many sexual partners ▶ **ˈman-eating** *adj.* [only before noun]: *a man-eating shark/tiger*

man·eu·ver, man·eu·ver·able, man·eu·ver·ing *(AmE)* = MANOEUVRE, MANOEUVRABLE, MANOEUVRING

man·ful·ly /ˈmænfəli/ *adv.* using a lot of effort in a brave and determined way ▶ **man·ful** *adj.* [only before noun] *(rare)*

man·ga·nese /ˈmæŋɡəniːz/ *noun* [U] *(symb Mn)* a chemical element. Manganese is a grey-white metal that breaks easily, used in making glass and steel.

mange /meɪndʒ/ *noun* [U] a skin disease of hairy animals, caused by a PARASITE—see also MANGY

man·ger /ˈmeɪndʒə(r)/ *noun* a long open box that horses and cows can eat from [IDM] see DOG *n.*

mange·tout /ˌmɑːnʒ ˈtuː/ *(BrE)* *(AmE* **ˈsnow pea***) noun* [usually pl.] a type of very small pea that grows in long, flat green PODS that are cooked and eaten whole

man·gle /ˈmæŋɡl/ *verb, noun*

■ *verb* [VN] [usually passive] **1** to crush or twist sth so that it is badly damaged: *His hand was mangled in the machine.* **2** to spoil sth, for example a poem or a piece of music, by saying it wrongly or playing it badly ▶ **mangled** *adj.*: *mangled bodies/remains*

■ *noun* (also **wring·er**) a machine with two ROLLERS (1) used especially in the past for squeezing the water out of clothes that had been washed

mango /ˈmæŋɡəʊ; AmE -ɡoʊ/ *noun* [C, U] *(pl.* **-oes)** a tropical fruit with smooth yellow or red skin, soft orange flesh and a large stone/pit inside—picture on page A2

man·grove /ˈmæŋɡrəʊv; AmE -ɡroʊv/ *noun* a tropical tree that grows in mud or at the edge of rivers and sends roots down from its branches: *mangrove swamps*

mangy /ˈmeɪndʒi/ *adj.* [usually before noun] **1** (of an animal) suffering from MANGE: *a mangy dog* **2** *(informal)* dirty and in bad condition: *a mangy old coat*

man·handle /ˈmænhændl/ *verb* **1** [VN] to push, pull or handle sb roughly: *Bystanders claim they were manhandled by security guards.* **2** [VN+adv./prep.] to move or lift a heavy object using a lot of effort: *They were trying to manhandle an old sofa across the road.*

man·hole /ˈmænhəʊl; AmE -hoʊl/ *noun* a hole in the street that is covered with a lid, used when sb needs to go down to examine the pipes or SEWERS below the street

man·hood /ˈmænhʊd/ *noun* **1** [U] the state or time of being an adult man rather than a boy: *to reach manhood* ◊ *His youth and early manhood were spent in America.* **2** [U] the qualities that a man is supposed to have, for example courage, strength and sexual power: *Her new-found power was a threat to his manhood.* **3** [sing.] *(written or humorous)* a man's PENIS. People use 'manhood' to avoid saying 'penis'. **4** [U] *(literary)* all the men of a country: *The nation's manhood died on the battlefields of World War I.*—compare WOMANHOOD

ˈman-hour *noun* [usually pl.] the amount of work done by one person in one hour

man·hunt /ˈmænhʌnt/ *noun* an organized search by a lot of people for a criminal or a prisoner who has escaped

mania /ˈmeɪniə/ *noun* **1** [C usually sing, U] ~ **(for sth/for doing sth)** an extremely strong desire or enthusiasm for sth, often shared by a lot of people at the same time: *He had a mania for fast cars.* ◊ *Football mania is sweeping the country.* **2** [U] *(psychology)* a mental illness in which sb has an OBSESSION about sth that makes them extremely anxious, violent or confused

-mania *combining form* (in nouns) mental illness of a particular type: *kleptomania* ▶ **-maniac** (in nouns): *a pyromaniac*

ma·niac /ˈmeɪniæk/ *noun* **1** *(informal)* a person who behaves in an extremely dangerous, wild, or stupid way: *He was driving like a maniac.* **2** a person who has an extremely strong desire or enthusiasm for sth, to an extent that other people think is not normal: *a football/ religious/sex maniac* **3** *(psychology)* a person suffering from mania: *a homicidal maniac* ▶ **ma·niac** *adj.* [only before noun]: *a maniac driver/fan/killer*

ma·ni·acal /məˈnaɪəkl/ *adj.* wild or violent: *maniacal laughter*

manic /ˈmænɪk/ *adj.* **1** *(informal)* full of activity, excitement and anxiety; behaving in a busy, excited, anxious way: *Things are manic in the office at the moment.* ◊ *Martha's pretty manic.* ◊ *The performers had a manic energy and enthusiasm.* **2** *(psychology)* connected with MANIA (2): *manic mood swings* ▶ **man·ic·al·ly** *adv.*: *I rushed around manically, trying to finish the housework.*

ˌmanic deˈpression *noun (psychology)* a mental illness causing sb to change quickly from being extremely happy to being extremely depressed

ˌmanic-deˈpressive *noun (psychology)* a person suffering from manic depression ▶ **ˌmanic-deˈpressive** *adj.*

mani·cure /ˈmænɪkjʊə(r); AmE -kjʊr/ *noun, verb*

■ *noun* [C, U] the care and treatment of a person's hands and nails: *to have a manicure*—compare PEDICURE

■ *verb* [VN] to care for and treat your hands and nails

mani·cured /ˈmænɪkjʊəd; AmE -kjʊrd/ *adj.* **1** (of hands or fingers) with nails that are neatly cut and polished **2** (of gardens, a LAWN, etc.) very neat and well cared for

mani·cur·ist /ˈmænɪkjʊərɪst; AmE -kjʊr-/ *noun* a person whose job is the care and treatment of the hands and nails

mani·fest /ˈmænɪfest/ *verb, adj., noun*

■ *verb* *(formal)* **1** [VN] ~ **sth (in sth)** to show sth clearly, especially a feeling, an attitude or a quality [SYN] DEMONSTRATE: *Social tensions were manifested in the recent political crisis.* **2** [VN] ~ **itself (in sth)** to appear or become noticeable [SYN] APPEAR: *The symptoms of the disease manifested themselves ten days later.*

M

b	d	f	g	h	k	l	m	n	p	r
bad	did	fall	get	hat	cat	leg	man	now	pen	red

■ *adj.* ~ **(to sb) (in sth)**| ~ **(in sth)** (*formal*) easy to see or understand: *His nervousness was manifest to all those present.* ◊ *The anger he felt is manifest in his paintings.*
▶ **mani·fest·ly** *adv.*: *manifestly unfair* ◊ *The party has manifestly failed to achieve its goal.*

■ *noun* (*technical*) a list of goods or passengers on a ship or an aircraft

mani·fest·ation /ˌmænɪfeˈsteɪʃn/ *noun* (*formal*) **1** [C, U] ~ **(of sth)** an event, action or thing that is a sign that sth exists or is happening; the act of appearing as a sign that sth exists or is happening: *The riots are a clear manifestation of the people's discontent.* ◊ *Some manifestation of your concern would have been appreciated.* **2** [C] an appearance of a ghost or spirit: *The church is the site of a number of supernatural manifestations.*

mani·festo /ˌmænɪˈfestəʊ; *AmE* -ˈfestoʊ/ *noun* (*pl.* **-os**) a written statement in which a group of people, especially a political party, explain their beliefs and say what they will do if they win an election: *an election manifesto* ◊ *the party manifesto*

mani·fold /ˈmænɪfəʊld; *AmE* -foʊld/ *adj.*, *noun*

■ *adj.* (*formal*) many; of many different types: *The possibilities were manifold.*

■ *noun* (*technical*) a pipe or an enclosed space with several openings for taking gases in and out of a car engine: *the exhaust manifold*

mani·kin (also **man·ni·kin**) /ˈmænɪkɪn/ *noun* **1** a model of the human body that is used for teaching art or medicine **2** (*old-fashioned*) a very small man [SYN] DWARF

Ma·nila (also **Ma·nilla**) /məˈnɪlə/ *noun* [U] strong brown paper, used especially for making envelopes

ma·nipu·late /məˈnɪpjuleɪt/ *verb* [VN] **1** ~ **(sb into sth/ into doing sth)** (*disapproving*) to control or influence sb/sth, often in a dishonest way so that they do not realize it: *She uses her charm to manipulate people.* ◊ *As a politician, he knows how to manipulate public opinion.* ◊ *They managed to manipulate us into agreeing to help.* **2** to control or use sth in a skilful way: *to manipulate the gears and levers of a machine* ◊ *Computers are very efficient at manipulating information.* **3** (*technical*) to move a person's bones or joints into the correct position ▶ **ma·nipu·la·tion** /məˌnɪpjuˈleɪʃn/ *noun* [U, C]: *Advertising like this is a cynical manipulation of the elderly.* ◊ *data manipulation* ◊ *manipulation of the bones of the back*

ma·nipu·la·tive /məˈnɪpjələtɪv; *AmE* -leɪtɪv/ *adj.* **1** (*disapproving*) skilful at influencing sb or forcing sb to do what you want, often in an unfair way: *manipulative behaviour* ◊ *He's extremely manipulative, so don't let him persuade you.* **2** (*formal*) connected with the ability to handle objects skilfully: *manipulative skills such as typing and knitting*

ma·nipu·la·tor /məˈnɪpjuleɪtə(r)/ *noun* (often *disapproving*) a person who is skilful at influencing people or situations in order to get what they want

man·kind /mænˈkaɪnd/ *noun* [U] all human beings thought about as one large group; the human race: *the history of mankind* ◊ *an invention for the good of all mankind*—see also HUMANKIND—compare WOMANKIND

manky /ˈmæŋki/ *adj.* (*BrE, informal*) dirty and unpleasant: *a manky old coat*

manly /ˈmænli/ *adj.* (often *approving*) having the qualities or physical features that are admired or expected in a man: *the manly virtues of courage and strength* ◊ *He looked so manly in his uniform.* ▶ **man·li·ness** *noun* [U]

man-'made *adj.* made by people; not natural [SYN] ARTIFICIAL: *a man-made lake* ◊ *man-made fibres such as nylon and polyester*

manna /ˈmænə/ *noun* [U] (in the Bible) the food that God provided for the people of Israel during their 40 years in the desert: (*figurative*) *To the refugees, the food shipments were manna from heaven* (= an unexpected and very welcome gift).

man·ne·quin /ˈmænɪkɪn/ *noun* (*old-fashioned*) **1** a person whose job is to wear and display new styles of clothes [SYN] MODEL **2** a model of a human body, used for displaying clothes in shops/stores

man·ner /ˈmænə(r)/ *noun* **1** [sing.] (*formal*) the way that sth is done or happens: *She answered in a businesslike manner.* ◊ *The manner in which the decision was announced was extremely regrettable.* **2** [sing.] the way that sb behaves and speaks towards other people: *to have an aggressive/a friendly/a relaxed manner* ◊ *His manner was polite but cool.*—see also BEDSIDE MANNER **3** (**manners**) [pl.] behaviour that is considered to be polite in a particular society or culture: *to have good/bad manners* ◊ *It is bad manners to talk with your mouth full.* ◊ *He has no manners* (= behaves very badly).—see also TABLE MANNERS **4** (**manners**) [pl.] (*formal*) the habits and customs of a particular group of people: *the social morals and manners of the seventeenth century* [IDM] **all 'manner of sb/sth** many different types of people or things: *The problem can be solved in all manner of ways.* **in a manner of 'speaking** if you think about it in a particular way; true in some but not all ways: *The warring governments could be seen as terrorists too, in a manner of speaking.* **in the manner of sb/sth** (*formal*) in a style that is typical of sb/sth: *a painting in the manner of Raphael* (**as/as if) to the manner 'born** (*formal*) as if sth is natural for you and you have done it many times in the past **what manner of ...** (*formal* or *literary*) what kind of ...: *What manner of man could do such a terrible thing?*

man·nered /ˈmænəd; *AmE* -nərd/ *adj.* **1** (*disapproving*) (of behaviour, art, writing, etc.) trying to impress people by being formal and not natural **2** (-**mannered**) (in compounds) having the type of manners mentioned: *a well-mannered child* ◊ *a mild-mannered person*—see also ILL-MANNERED

man·ner·ism /ˈmænərɪzəm/ *noun* **1** [C] a particular habit or way of speaking or behaving that sb has but is not aware of: *nervous/odd/irritating mannerisms* **2** [U] too much use of a particular style in painting or writing **3** (**Mannerism**) a style in 16th century Italian art that did not show things in a natural way but made them look strange or out of their usual shape

man·ner·ist /ˈmænərɪst/ (usually **Mannerist**) *adj.* (of painting or writing) in the style of Mannerism

man·ni·kin = MANIKIN

man·nish /ˈmænɪʃ/ *adj.* (usually *disapproving*) (of a woman or of sth belonging to a woman) having qualities that are thought of as typical of or suitable for a man

man·oeuvr·able (*BrE*) (*AmE* **man·euv·er·able**) /məˈnuːvrəbl/ *adj.* that can easily be moved into different positions: *a small, highly manoeuvrable vehicle* ▶ **man·oeuv·ra·bil·ity** (*AmE* **man·eu·ver·abil·ity**) *noun* [U]

man·oeuvre (*BrE*) (*AmE* **man·eu·ver**) /məˈnuːvə(r)/ *noun*, *verb*

■ *noun* **1** [C] a movement performed with care and skill: *a complicated/skilful manoeuvre* ◊ *You will be asked to perform some standard manoeuvres during your driving test.* **2** [C, U] a clever plan, action or movement that is used to give sb an advantage: *diplomatic manoeuvres* ◊ *a complex manoeuvre in a game of chess* **3** (**manoeuvres**) [pl.] military exercises involving a large number of soldiers, ships, etc: *The army is on manoeuvres in the desert.* [IDM] **freedom of/room for ma'noeuvre** the chance to change the way that sth happens and influence decisions that are made: *Small farmers have limited room for manoeuvre.*

■ *verb* **1** to move or turn skilfully or carefully; to move or turn sth skilfully or carefully: [V] *The yachts manoeuvred for position.* ◊ *There was very little room to manoeuvre.* ◊ [VN] *She manoeuvred the car carefully into the garage.* **2** to control or influence a situation in a skilful but sometimes dishonest way: [V] *The new laws have left us little room to manoeuvre* (= not much opportunity to change or influence a situation). ◊ [VN+adv./prep.] *She manoeuvred her way to the top of the company.*

man·oeuv·ring (*BrE*) (*AmE* **man·eu·ver·ing**) /məˈnuːvərɪŋ/ *noun* [U, C] clever, skilful, and often dishonest ways of achieving your aims

man of 'letters *noun* a man who is a writer, or who writes about literature

man-of-'war *noun* (*pl.* **men-of-'war**) a sailing ship

M

manor /'mænə(r)/ *noun* (*BrE*) **1** (also **'manor house**) a large country house surrounded by land that belongs to it **2** an area of land with a manor house on it **3** (*slang*) an area in which sb works or for which they are responsible, especially officers at a police station

man·orial /mə'nɔːriəl/ *adj.* typical of or connected with a manor, especially in the past

man·power /'mænpaʊə(r)/ *noun* [U] the number of workers needed or available to do a particular job: *a need for trained/skilled manpower ◊ a manpower shortage*

man·qué /'mɒŋkeɪ; *AmE* mɑːŋ'keɪ/ *adj.* (following nouns) (from French, *formal* or *humorous*) used to describe a person who hoped to follow a particular career but who failed in it or never tried it: *He's really an artist manqué.*

man·sard /'mænsɑːd; *AmE* -sɑːrd/ (also ,**mansard 'roof**) *noun* (*technical*) a roof with a double slope in which the upper part is less steep than the lower part

manse /mæns/ *noun* the house of a Christian minister, especially in Scotland

man·ser·vant /'mænsɜːvənt; *AmE* -sɜːrv-/ *noun* (*pl.* **men·ser·vants**) (*old-fashioned*) a male servant, especially a man's personal servant

man·sion /'mænʃn/ *noun* **1** [C] a large impressive house: *an 18th century country mansion* **2** (**Mansions**) [pl.] (*BrE*) used in the names of blocks of flats: *2 Moscow Mansions, Cromwell Road*

'**man-sized** *adj.* [only before noun] suitable or large enough for a man: *a man-sized breakfast*

man·slaugh·ter /'mænslɔːtə(r)/ *noun* [U] (*law*) the crime of killing sb illegally but not deliberately: *The charge has been reduced to manslaughter.*—compare HOMI-CIDE, MURDER

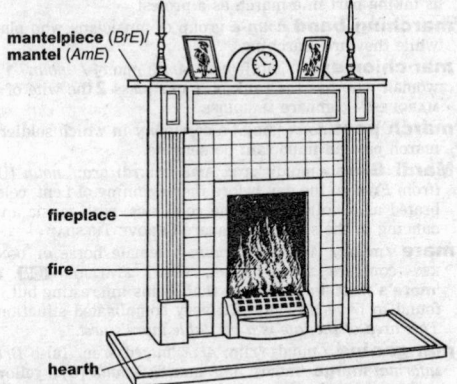

mantelpiece (*BrE*)/
mantel (*AmE*)

fireplace

fire

hearth

man·tel·piece /'mæntlpiːs/ (also **man·tel** especially in *AmE* /'mæntl/) *noun* a shelf above a FIREPLACE

man·tis /'mæntɪs/ *noun* (*pl.* **man·tises** or **man·tids** /'mæntɪdz/) = PRAYING MANTIS

man·tle /'mæntl/ *noun, verb*
■ *noun* **1** [sing.] **the ~ of sb/sth** (*literary*) the role and responsibilities of an important person or job, especially when they are passed on from one person to another: *The vice-president must now* **take on the mantle** *of supreme power.* **2** [C] (*literary*) a layer of sth that covers a surface: *hills with a mantle of snow* **3** [C] a loose piece of clothing without sleeves, worn over other clothes, especially in the past **4** (also '**gas mantle**) [C] a cover around the flame of a gas lamp that becomes very bright when it is heated **5** [sing.] (*geology*) the part of the earth below the CRUST and surrounding the CORE
■ *verb* [VN] (*literary*) to cover the surface of sth

man·tra /'mæntrə/ *noun* a word, phrase or sound that is repeated again and again, especially during prayer or MEDITATION: *a Buddhist mantra*

man·ual /'mænjuəl/ *adj., noun*
■ *adj.* **1** (of work, etc.) involving using the hands or physical strength: *manual labour/jobs/skills ◊ manual and non-manual workers* **2** operated or controlled by hand

rather than automatically or using electricity, etc: *a manual gearbox ◊ My camera has manual and automatic functions.* **3** connected with using the hands: *manual dexterity* ▶ **manu·al·ly** /-juəli/ *adv.*: *manually operated*
■ *noun* a book that tells you how to do or operate sth, especially one that comes with a machine, etc. when you buy it: *a computer/car/instruction manual*—compare HANDBOOK **IDM on 'manual** not being operated automatically: *Leave the controls on manual.*

manu·fac·ture /,mænju'fæktʃə(r)/ *verb, noun*
■ *verb* [VN] **1** to make or produce goods in large quantities, using machinery: *manufactured goods* **2** to invent a story, an excuse, etc: *a news story manufactured by an unscrupulous journalist* **3** (*technical*) to produce a substance: *Vitamins cannot be manufactured by our bodies.*
■ *noun* **1** [U] the process of producing goods in large quantities: *the manufacture of cars* **2** (**manufactures**) [pl.] (*technical*) manufactured goods: *a major importer of cotton manufactures*

manu·fac·turer /,mænju'fæktʃərə(r)/ *noun* (also **the manu·fac·tur·ers** [pl.]) a person or company that produces goods in large quantities: *a car/computer manufacturer ◊ Always follow the manufacturer's instructions. ◊ Faulty goods should be returned to the manufacturers.*

manu·fac·tur·ing /,mænju'fæktʃərɪŋ/ *noun* [U] the business or industry of producing goods in large quantities in factories, etc: *Many jobs in manufacturing were lost during the recession.*

ma·nure /mə'njʊə(r); *AmE* mə'nʊr/ *noun, verb*
■ *noun* [U] the waste matter from animals that is spread over or mixed with the soil to help plants and crops grow
■ *verb* [VN] to put manure on or in soil to help plants grow

manu·script /'mænjuskrɪpt/ *noun* **1** a copy of a book, piece of music, etc. before it has been printed: *an unpublished/original manuscript ◊ I read her poems* **in manuscript**. **2** a very old book or document that was written by hand before printing was invented: *medieval illuminated manuscripts*

Manx /mæŋks/ *adj.* of or connected with the Isle of Man, its people or the language once spoken there

,**Manx 'cat** *noun* a breed of cat with no tail

many /'meni/ *det., pron.* **1** used with plural nouns and verbs, especially in negative sentences or in more formal English, to mean 'a large number of'. Also used in questions to ask about the size of a number, and with 'as' and 'too': *We don't have very many copies left. ◊ You can't have one each. We haven't got many. ◊ Many people feel that the law should be changed. ◊ Many of those present disagreed. ◊* **How many** *children do you have? ◊ There are too many mistakes in this essay. ◊ He made ten mistakes* **in as many** (= in ten) *lines. ◊ New drivers have* **twice as many** *accidents as experienced drivers. ◊ I've known her for* **a great many** (= very many) *years. ◊ Even if one person is hurt that is* **one too many**. *◊ It was one of my many mistakes. ◊ a many-headed monster* ⇨ note on page 782 **2** (**the many**) used with a plural verb to mean 'most people': *a government which improves conditions for the many* **3** (**many a**) (*formal*) used with a singular noun and verb to mean 'a large number of': *Many a good man has been destroyed by drink.* **IDM as many as ...** used to show surprise that the number of people or things involved is so large: *There were as many as 200 people at the lecture.* **have had ,one too 'many** (*informal*) to be slightly drunk **many's the ...** (*formal*) used to show that sth happens often: *Many's the time I heard her use those words.*

Maori /'maʊri/ *noun* **1** [C] a member of a race of people who were the original people living in New Zealand **2** [U] the language of the Maori people ▶ **Maori** *adj.*

map /mæp/ *noun, verb*
■ *noun* a drawing or plan of the earth's surface or part of it, showing countries, towns, rivers, etc: *a map of France ◊ a street map of Miami ◊ to read a/the map* (= understand the information on a map) *◊ large-scale maps ◊ Can you find Black Hill* **on the map**? *◊ I'll draw you a map of how to get to my house.* **IDM put sb/sth on the 'map** to make sb/sth famous or important: *The exhibition has helped put the city on the map.*—more at WIPE *v.*

M

æ	ɑː	e	ɜː	ə	ɪ	iː	i	ɒ	ɔː	ʌ	ʊ	u	uː
cat	father	ten	bird	about	sit	see	many	got	saw	cup	put	actual	too

(BrE)

Many is used only with countable nouns. It is used mainly in questions and negative sentences: *Do you go to many concerts?* ◇ *How many people came to the meeting?* ◇ *I don't go to many concerts.* Although it is not common in statements, it is used after *so*, *as* and *too*: *You :nade too many mistakes.*

In statements **a lot of** or **lots of** (*informal*) are much more common: *I go to a lot of concerts.* ◇ *'How many CDs have you got?' 'Lots!'* However, they are not used with measurements of time or distance: *I stayed in England many/quite a few/ten weeks.* ◇ *I stayed in England a lot of weeks.* When **a lot of/lots of** means 'many', it takes a plural verb: *Lots of people like Italian food.* You can also use **plenty of** (*informal*): *Plenty of stores stay open late.* These phrases can also be used in questions and negative sentences.

A lot of/lots of is still felt to be informal, especially in *BrE*, so in formal writing it is better to use **many** or **a large number of** in statements.

▷ note at **MUCH**

■ *verb* (**-pp-**) [VN] **1** to make a map of an area: *an unexplored region that has not yet been mapped* **2** to discover or give information about sth, especially the way it is arranged or organized: *It is now possible to map the different functions of the brain.* ▶ **map·ping** *noun* [U]: *the mapping of the Indian subcontinent* ◇ *gene mapping* **PHRV** ,**map sth on/onto sth** to link a group of qualities, items, etc. with their source, cause, position on a scale, etc: *Grammar information enables students to map the structure of a foreign language onto their own.* ,**map sth**↔'**out** to plan or arrange sth in a careful or detailed way: *He has his career path clearly mapped out.*

maple /'meɪpl/ *noun* **1** [C, U] (also ,**maple 'tree**) a tall tree with leaves that have five points and turn bright red or yellow in the autumn/fall. Maples grow in northern countries: *The maple leaf is Canada's national emblem.* **2** [U] the wood of the maple tree

,**maple 'syrup** *noun* [U] a sweet sticky sauce made with liquid obtained from some types of maple tree, often eaten with PANCAKES—picture on page A1

mar /mɑː(r)/ *verb* (**-rr-**) [VN] to damage or spoil sth good: *The game was marred by the behaviour of drunken fans.*

mara·thon /'mærəθən; *AmE* -θɑːn/ *noun* **1** a long running race of about 42 kilometres or 26 miles: *the London marathon* ◇ *to run a marathon* **2** an activity or a piece of work that takes a long time and requires a lot of effort and patience: *My job interview was a real marathon.* **ORIGIN** From the story that in ancient Greece a messenger ran from Marathon to Athens (22 miles) with the news of a victory over the Persians. ▶ **mara·thon** *adj.* [only before noun]: *a marathon journey lasting 56 hours* ◇ *a marathon legal battle*

ma·raud·ing /mə'rɔːdɪŋ/ *adj.* [only before noun] (*written*) (of people or animals) going around a place in search of things to steal or people to attack: *marauding wolves* ▶ **ma·raud·er** /mə'rɔːdə(r)/ *noun*

mar·ble /'mɑːbl; *AmE* 'mɑːrbl/ *noun* **1** [U] a type of hard stone that is usually white and often has coloured lines in it. It can be polished and is used in building and for making statues, etc: *a slab/block of marble* ◇ *a marble floor/sculpture* **2** [C] a small ball of coloured glass that children roll along the ground in a game **3** (**marbles**) [U] a game played with marbles: *Three boys were playing marbles.*—picture on page A8 **4** (**marbles**) [pl.] (*informal*) a way of referring to sb's intelligence or mental ability: *He's losing his marbles* (= he's not behaving in a sensible way).

mar·bled /'mɑːbld; *AmE* 'mɑːrbld/ *adj.* having the colours and/or patterns of marble: *marbled wallpaper*

marb·ling /'mɑːblɪŋ; *AmE* 'mɑːrb-/ *noun* [U] the method of decorating sth with a pattern that looks like MARBLE

March /mɑːtʃ; *AmE* mɑːrtʃ/ *noun* [U, C] (*abbr.* **Mar.**) the 3rd month of the year, between February and April **HELP** To see how **March** is used, look at the examples at **April**. **IDM** see MAD

march /mɑːtʃ; *AmE* mɑːrtʃ/ *verb, noun*

■ *verb* **1** [usually +*adv.*/*prep.*] to walk with stiff regular steps like a soldier: [V] *Soldiers were marching up and down outside the government buildings.* ◇ *Quick march!* (= the order to start marching) ◇ [VN] *They marched 20 miles to reach the capital.* **2** [V+*adv.*/*prep.*] to walk somewhere quickly in a determined way: *She marched over to me and demanded an apology.* **3** [VN+*adv.*/*prep.*] to force sb to walk somewhere with you: *The guards marched the prisoner away.* **4** [V] to walk through the streets in a large group in order to protest about sth **SYN** DEMONSTRATE **IDM** **get your 'marching orders** (*BrE*, *informal*) to be ordered to leave a place, a job, etc. **give sb their 'marching orders** (*informal*) to order sb to leave a place, their job, etc. **PHRV** ,**march 'on** to move on or pass quickly: *Time marches on and we still have not made a decision.* '**march on ...** to march to a place to protest about sth or to attack it: *Several thousand people marched on City Hall.*

■ *noun* **1** [C] an organized walk by many people from one place to another, in order to protest about sth, or to express their opinions: *protest marches* ◇ *to go on a march*—compare DEMONSTRATION **2** [C] an act of marching; a journey made by marching: *The army began their long march to the coast.* **3** [sing.] **the ~ of sth** the steady development or forward movement of sth: *the march of progress/technology/time* **4** [C] a piece of music written for marching to: *a funeral march* **IDM** **on the 'march** marching somewhere: *The enemy are on the march*—more at STEAL *v.*

march·er /'mɑːtʃə(r); *AmE* 'mɑːrtʃ-/ *noun* a person who is taking part in a march as a protest

'**marching band** *noun* a group of musicians who play while they are marching

mar·chion·ess /,mɑːʃə'nes; *AmE* ,mɑːrʃ-/ *noun* **1** a woman who has the rank of a MARQUESS **2** the wife of a MARQUESS—compare MARQUISE

'**march past** *noun* [sing.] a ceremony in which soldiers march past an important person, etc.

Mardi Gras /,mɑːdi 'grɑː; *AmE* 'mɑːrdi grɑː/ *noun* [U] (from *French*) the day before the beginning of Lent, celebrated as a holiday in some countries, with music and dancing in the streets—compare SHROVE TUESDAY

mare /meə(r); *AmE* mer/ *noun* a female horse or DONKEY—compare BROOD MARE, FILLY, STALLION **IDM** **a 'mare's nest 1** a discovery that seems interesting but is found to have no value **2** a very complicated situation: *This area of the law is a veritable mare's nest.*

mar·gar·ine /,mɑːdʒə'riːn; *AmE* 'mɑːrdʒərən/ (also *BrE informal* **marge** /mɑːdʒ; *AmE* mɑːrdʒ/) *noun* [U] a yellow substance like butter made from animal or vegetable fats, used in cooking or spread on bread, etc.

mar·gin /'mɑːdʒɪn; *AmE* 'mɑːrdʒən/ *noun* **1** [C] the empty space at the side of a written or printed page: *the left-hand/right-hand margin* ◇ *a narrow/wide margin* ◇ *notes scribbled in the margin* **2** [C, usually sing.] the amount of time, or number of votes, etc. by which sb wins sth: *He won by a narrow margin.* ◇ *She beat the other runners by a margin of ten seconds.* **3** [C] (*business*) = PROFIT MARGIN: *What are your average operating margins?* ◇ *a gross margin of 45%* **4** [C, usually sing.] an extra amount of sth such as time, space, money, etc. that you include in order to make sure that sth is successful: *a safety margin* ◇ *The narrow gateway left me little margin for error as I reversed the car.*—see also MARGIN OF ERROR **5** [C] (*formal*) the extreme edge or limit of a place: *the eastern margin of the Indian Ocean* **6** [C, usually pl.] the part that is not included in the main part of a group or situation: *people living on the margins of society*

mar·gin·al /'mɑːdʒɪnl; *AmE* 'mɑːrdʒ-/ *adj., noun*

■ *adj.* **1** small and not important: *a marginal improvement in weather conditions* ◇ *The story will only be of marginal interest to our readers.* **2** not part of a main or important group or situation: *marginal groups in society* **3** (*politics*) (*especially BrE*) won or lost by a very small number of

M

votes and therefore very important or interesting politically: *a marginal seat/constituency* **4** [only before noun]
written in the margin of a page: *marginal notes/com-
ments* **5** (of land) that cannot produce enough good crops
to make a profit
■ *noun* (*BrE*) a seat in a parliament, on a local council, etc.
that was won by a very small number of votes: *a Labour
marginal*

mar·gin·al·ize (*BrE* also **-ise**) /ˈmɑːdʒɪnəlaɪz; *AmE*
ˈmɑːrdʒ-/ *verb* [VN] to make sb feel as if they are not
important and cannot influence decisions or events; to
put sb in a position in which they have no power ▶ **mar-
gin·al·iza·tion, -isa·tion** *noun* [U]: *the marginalization of
the elderly*

mar·gin·al·ly /ˈmɑːdʒɪnəli; *AmE* ˈmɑːrdʒ-/ *adv.* very
slightly; not very much: *They now cost marginally more
than they did last year.*

margin of ˈerror *noun* [usually sing.] an amount that
you allow when you calculate sth, for the possibility that
a number is not completely accurate: *The survey has a
margin of error of 2.5%*

mari·gold /ˈmærɪɡəʊld; *AmE* -ɡoʊld/ *noun* an orange or
yellow garden flower. There are several types of mari-
gold.

ma·ri·juana (also **ma·ri·huana**) /ˌmærəˈwɑːnə/ (also
informal **pot**) *noun* [U] a drug (illegal in many countries)
made from the dried leaves and flowers of the HEMP plant,
which gives a feeling of being relaxed when it is smoked
SYN CANNABIS

ma·rimba /məˈrɪmbə/ *noun* a musical instrument like a
XYLOPHONE

mar·ina /məˈriːnə/ *noun* a specially designed harbour for
small boats and YACHTS

mar·in·ade /ˌmærɪˈneɪd/ *noun* [C, U] a mixture of oil,
wine, spices, etc., used for soaking meat or fish in before
it is cooked in order to make it softer or to give it a
particular flavour

marin·ate /ˈmærɪneɪt/ (also **mar·in·ade**) *verb* [VN, V] if
you **marinate** food or it **marinates**, you soak it in a
marinade before cooking it

mar·ine /məˈriːn/ *adj.*, *noun*
■ *adj.* [only before noun] **1** connected with the sea and the
creatures and plants that live there: *marine life ◊ a marine biologist* (= a scientist who studies life in the sea)
2 connected with ships or trade at sea
■ *noun* a soldier who is trained to serve on land or at sea,
especially one in the US Marine Corps or the British
Royal Marines

mari·ner /ˈmærɪnə(r)/ *noun* (*old-fashioned* or *literary*) a
sailor

mar·io·nette /ˌmæriəˈnet/ *noun* a PUPPET whose arms,
legs and head are moved by strings

mari·tal /ˈmærɪtl/ *adj.* [only before noun] connected with
marriage or with the relationship between a husband and
wife: *marital difficulties/breakdown*

marital ˈstatus *noun* [U] (*formal*) (used especially on
official forms) the fact of whether you are single, married, etc: *questions about age, sex and marital status*

mari·time /ˈmærɪtaɪm/ *adj.* **1** connected with the sea or
ships: *a maritime museum* **2** (*formal*) near the sea: *maritime Antarctica*

mar·joram /ˈmɑːdʒərəm; *AmE* ˈmɑːrdʒ-/ *noun* [U] a plant
with leaves that smell sweet and are used in cooking as a
herb, often when dried

mark /mɑːk; *AmE* mɑːrk/ *verb*, *noun*
■ *verb*
WRITE/DRAW | **1** ~ **A (with B)** | ~ **B on A** to write or draw a
symbol, line, etc. on sth in order to give information
about it: [VN] *Items marked with an asterisk can be omitted.* ◊ *Prices are marked on the goods.* ◊ [VN-ADJ] *The
teacher marked her absent* (= made a mark by her name
to show that she was absent). ◊ *Do not open any mail
marked 'Confidential'.*
SPOIL/DAMAGE | **2** to make a mark on sth in a way that
spoils or damages it; to become spoilt or damaged in this
way: [VN] *A large purple scar marked his cheek.* ◊ [V] *The
surfaces are made from a material that doesn't mark.*

SHOW POSITION | **3** [VN] to show the position of sth: *The cross
marks the spot where the body was found.* ◊ *The route has
been marked in red.*
CELEBRATE | **4** [VN] to celebrate or officially remember an
event that you consider to be important: *a ceremony to
mark the 50th anniversary of the end of the war*
BE SIGN | **5** [VN] to be a sign that sth new is going to
happen: *This speech may* **mark a change in** *government
policy.* ◊ *The agreement marks a new phase in international relations.*
GIVE MARK/GRADE | **6** (*BrE*) to give marks to students' work:
[VN] *I hate marking exam papers.* ◊ [VN-ADJ] *Why have you
marked this wrong?* ◊ [V] *I spend at least six hours a week
marking.*—compare GRADE
GIVE PARTICULAR QUALITY | **7** [VN] [usually passive] ~ **sb/sth
(as sth)** (*formal*) to give sb/sth a particular quality or
character SYN CHARACTERIZE: *a life marked by suffering* ◊
He was marked as an enemy of the poor.
PAY ATTENTION | **8** (*old-fashioned, spoken*) used to tell sb to
pay careful attention to sth: [VN] *There'll be trouble over
this,* **mark my words**. ◊ [Vwh-] *You mark what I say,
John.*
IN SPORT | **9** [VN] (in a team game) to stay close to an
opponent in order to prevent them from getting the ball:
Hughes was marking Taylor. ◊ *Our defence had him
closely marked.*—see also MARKING
IDM **mark ˈtime 1** to pass the time while you wait for sth
more interesting: *I'm just marking time in this job—I'm
hoping to get into journalism.* **2** (of soldiers) to make
marching movements without moving forwards **mark
ˈyou** (*old-fashioned spoken, especially BrE*) used to remind
sb of sth they should consider in a particular case: *She
hasn't had much success yet. Mark you, she tries hard.*
PHRV **mark sb ˈdown** (*BrE*) to reduce the mark/grade
given to sb in an exam, etc: *She was marked down because
of poor grammar.* **mark sb ˈdown as sth** (*especially BrE*)
to recognize sb as a particular type: *I hadn't got him
marked down as a liberal.* **mark sth ↔ ˈdown 1** to reduce
the price of sth: *All goods have been marked down by 15%.*
OPP MARK UP—related noun MARKDOWN **2** to make a note
of sth for future use or action: *The factory is already
marked down for demolition.* **mark sb/sth ˈoff (from
sb/sth)** to make sb/sth seem different from other people
or things: *Each of London's districts had a distinct character that marked it off from its neighbours.* **mark sth ↔ ˈoff**
to separate sth by marking a line between it and sth else:
The playing area was marked off with a white line. **mark
sb ˈout as/for sth** to make people recognize sb as special
in some way: *She was marked out for early promotion.*
mark sth ↔ ˈout to draw lines to show the edges of sth:
They marked out a tennis court on the lawn. **mark
sth ↔ ˈup 1** to increase the price of sth: *Share prices were
marked up as soon as trading started.* OPP MARK DOWN—
related noun MARK-UP **2** (*technical*) to mark or correct a
text, etc., for example for printing: *to mark up a manuscript*
■ *noun*
SPOT/DIRT | **1** a small area of dirt, a spot or a cut on a
surface that spoils its appearance: *The children left dirty
marks all over the kitchen floor.* ◊ *a burn/scratch mark* ◊
Detectives found no marks on the body. **2** a noticeable spot
or area of colour on the body of a person or an animal
which helps you to recognize them: *a horse with a white
mark on its head* ◊ *He was about six feet tall, with no
distinguishing marks.*—see also BIRTHMARK, MARKING
SYMBOL | **3** a written or printed symbol that is used as a
sign of sth, for example the quality of sth or who made or
owns it: *punctuation marks* ◊ *Any piece of silver bearing
his mark is extremely valuable.* ◊ *I put a mark in the
margin to remind me to check the figure.*—see also QUES-
TION MARK, EXCLAMATION MARK, TRADEMARK
SIGN | **4** a sign that a quality or feeling exists: *On the day
of the funeral businesses remained closed as* **a mark of
respect**. ◊ *Such coolness under pressure is the mark of a
champion.*
STANDARD/GRADE | **5** (*especially BrE*) a number or letter

M

that is given to show the standard of sb's work or performance or is given to sb for answering sth correctly: *to get a good/poor mark in English* ◊ *to give sb a high/low mark* ◊ *What's the **pass mark*** (= the mark you need in order to pass)? ◊ *I got **full marks*** (= the highest mark possible) *in the spelling test.* ◊ (*ironic*) '*You're wearing a tie!*' ' *Full marks for observation.*'—see also BLACK MARK, GRADE

LEVEL | **6** a level or point that sth reaches that is thought to be important: *Unemployment has passed the four million mark.* ◊ *She was leading at the half-way mark.*

MACHINE/VEHICLE | **7** (**Mark**) (followed by a number) a particular type or model of a machine or vehicle: *the Mark II engine*

IN GAS OVEN | **8** (**Mark**) (*BrE*) (followed by a number) a particular level of temperature in a gas oven: *Preheat the oven to gas Mark 6.*

SIGNATURE | **9** a cross made on a document instead of a signature by sb who is not able to write their name

TARGET | **10** (*formal*) a TARGET (sth/sb you aim at when attacking): *Of the blows delivered, barely half found their mark.* ◊ *to hit/miss the mark*

GERMAN MONEY | **11** = DEUTSCHMARK

IDM **be close to/near the 'mark** to be fairly accurate in a guess, statement, etc. **be off the 'mark** not to be accurate in a guess, statement, etc: *No, you're way off the mark.* **get off the 'mark** to start scoring, especially in cricket: *Stewart got off the mark with a four.* **,hit/,miss the 'mark** to succeed/fail in achieving or guessing sth: *He blushed furiously and Robyn knew she had hit the mark.* **,leave your/its/a 'mark (on sth/sb)** to have an effect on sth/sb, especially a bad one, that lasts for a long time: *Such a traumatic experience was bound to leave its mark on the children.* **,make your/a 'mark (on sth)** to become famous and successful in a particular area **not be/feel ,up to the 'mark** (*old-fashioned, BrE*) to not feel as well or lively as usual **on your ,marks, get ,set, 'go!** used to tell runners in a race to get ready and then to start **quick/slow off the 'mark** fast/slow in reacting to a situation **,up to the 'mark** as good as it/they should be: *Your work isn't really up to the mark.*—more at OVERSTEP, TOE *v.*, WIDE *adj.*

mark·down /ˈmɑːkdaʊn; *AmE* ˈmɑːrk-/ *noun* [usually sing.] a reduction in price

marked /mɑːkt; *AmE* mɑːrkt/ *adj.* easy to see; noticeable: *a marked difference/improvement* ◊ *a marked increase in profits* ◊ *She is quiet and studious, in marked contrast to her sister.*—compare UNMARKED ▶ **mark·ed·ly** /ˈmɑːkɪdli; *AmE* ˈmɑːrk-/ *adv.*: *Her background is markedly different from her husband's.* ◊ *This year's sales have risen markedly.* **IDM** **a marked 'man** a man who is in danger because his enemies want to harm him

mark·er /ˈmɑːkə(r); *AmE* ˈmɑːrk-/ *noun* **1** [C] an object or a sign that shows the position of sth: *a boundary marker* ◊ *He placed a marker where the ball had landed.* **2** [sing.] **a ~ (of/for sth)** a sign that sth exists or that shows what it is like: *Price is not always an accurate marker of quality.* **3** (*BrE* also **'marker pen**) a pen with a thick FELT tip—picture at STATIONERY **4** (*BrE*) (*AmE* **grader**) a person who marks/grades students' work or exam papers **5** (*BrE*) (in team games, especially football) a player who stays close to a player on the other team in order to stop them getting the ball

mar·ket /ˈmɑːkɪt; *AmE* ˈmɑːrk-/ *noun, verb*

■ *noun* **1** [C] an occasion when people buy and sell goods; the open area or building where they meet to do this: *a fruit/flower/antiques market* ◊ *an indoor/a street market* ◊ *market stalls/traders* ◊ *We buy our fruit and vegetables at the market.* ◊ *Thursday is market day in Poitiers.* ◊ *a market town* (= a town in Britain where a regular market is or was held) **2** [sing.] business or trade, or the amount of trade in a particular type of goods: *the world market in coffee* ◊ *They have increased their share of the market by 10%.* ◊ *the property/job market* (= the number and type of houses, jobs, etc. that are available) ◊ *They have **cornered the market** in sportswear.* (= sell the most) **3** [C] a particular area, country or section of the

population that might buy goods: *the US/Japanese market* ◊ *the global/domestic market* **4** [sing.] **~ (for sth)** the number of people who want to buy sth SYN DEMAND: *a growing/declining market for second-hand cars* **5** (often **the market**) [sing.] people who buy and sell goods in competition with each other: *The market will decide if the TV station has any future.* ◊ *a market-based/market-driven/market-led economy*—see also BLACK MARKET, MARKET FORCES **6** [C] = STOCK MARKET: *the futures market* ◊ *the market crash of 1987* **HELP** There are many other compounds ending in **market**. You will find them at their place in the alphabet. **IDM** **in the 'market for sth** interested in buying sth: *I'm not in the market for a new car at the moment.* **on the 'market** available for people to buy: *to put your house on the market* ◊ *The house came on the market last year.* ◊ *There are hundreds of different brands on the market.* **on the open 'market** available to buy without any restrictions: *Firearms are not freely available on the open market.* **play the 'market** to buy and sell STOCKS and shares in order to make a profit—more at BUYER, PRICE *v.*, SELLER

■ *verb* [VN] **~ sth (to sb) (as sth)** to advertise and offer a product for sale; to present sth in a particular way and make people want to buy it: *It is marketed as a low-alcohol wine.* ◊ *School meals need to be marketed to children in the same way as other food.*—see also MARKETING

mar·ket·able /ˈmɑːkɪtəbl; *AmE* ˈmɑːrk-/ *adj.* easy to sell; attractive to customers or employers: *marketable products/skills/qualifications* ▶ **mar·ket·abil·ity** /ˌmɑːkɪtə-ˈbɪləti; *AmE* ˌmɑːrk-/ *noun* [U]

mar·ket·eer /ˌmɑːkɪˈtɪə(r); *AmE* ˌmɑːrkəˈtɪr/ *noun* (usually in compounds) a person who is in favour of a particular system of buying and selling: *a free marketeer* (= a person who believes in a FREE MARKET *system of trade*)—see also BLACK MARKETEER

,market 'forces *noun* [pl.] a free system of trade in which prices and wages rise and fall without being controlled by the government

,market 'garden (*BrE*) (*AmE* **'truck farm**) *noun* a type of farm where vegetables are grown for sale ▶ **,market 'gardener** *noun* **,market 'gardening** *noun* [U]

mar·ket·ing /ˈmɑːkɪtɪŋ; *AmE* ˈmɑːrk-/ *noun* [U] the activity of presenting, advertising and selling a company's products in the best possible way: *a marketing campaign* ◊ *She works in **sales and marketing**.*—see also DIRECT MARKETING ▶ **mar·ket·er** *noun*: *a company that is a developer and marketer of software*

,market 'leader *noun* **1** the company that sells the largest quantity of a particular kind of product: *We are the market leader in hi-fi.* **2** a product that is the most successful of its kind

mar·ket·place /ˈmɑːkɪtpleɪs; *AmE* ˈmɑːrk-/ *noun* **1** (**the marketplace**) [sing.] the activity of competing with other companies to buy and sell goods, services, etc: *Companies must be able to survive in the marketplace.* ◊ *the education marketplace* **2** (also **,market 'square**) [C] an open area in a town where a market is held

,market 'price *noun* the price that people are willing to pay for sth at a particular time

,market re'search (also **,market 'research**) *noun* [U] the work of collecting information about what people buy and why

,market 'share *noun* [U, sing.] (*business*) the amount that a company sells of its products or services compared with other companies selling the same things: *They claim to have a 40% worldwide market share.*

,market 'value *noun* [U, sing.] what sth would be worth if it were sold

mark·ing /ˈmɑːkɪŋ; *AmE* ˈmɑːrk-/ *noun* **1** [usually pl.] a pattern of colours or marks on animals, birds or wood **2** [usually pl.] lines, colours or shapes painted on roads, vehicles, etc: *Road markings indicate where you can stop.* **3** [U] (*especially BrE*) (*AmE* usually **grad·ing**) the activity of checking and correcting the written work or exam papers of students: *She does her marking in the evenings.* **4** [U] (in team games, especially football) the practice of

M

staying close to a player on the other team in order to stop them getting the ball

marks·man /ˈmɑːksmən; *AmE* ˈmɑːrk-/ *noun* (*pl.* **-men** /-mən/) a person who is skilled in accurate shooting

marks·man·ship /ˈmɑːksmənʃɪp; *AmE* ˈmɑːrk-/ *noun* [U] skill in shooting

mark-up *noun* [usually sing.] an increase in the price of sth based on the difference between the cost of producing it and the price it is sold at: *an average mark-up of 10%*

marl /mɑːl; *AmE* mɑːrl/ *noun* **1** [U, C] soil consisting of clay and LIME (1) **2** [U] a type of fabric with threads in it that are not of an even colour: *blue marl leggings*

mar·lin /ˈmɑːlɪn; *AmE* ˈmɑːrlɪn/ *noun* (*pl.* **mar·lin**) a large sea fish with a long sharp nose, that people catch for sport

mar·ma·lade /ˈmɑːməleɪd; *AmE* ˈmɑːrm-/ *noun* [U] jam/jelly made from oranges, lemons, etc., eaten especially for breakfast—compare JAM (1)

Mar·mite™ /ˈmɑːmaɪt; *AmE* ˈmɑːrm-/ *noun* [U] (*BrE*) a dark substance made from YEAST, spread on bread, etc. [SYN] YEAST EXTRACT: *Marmite sandwiches*

mar·mo·set /ˈmɑːməzet; *AmE* ˈmɑːrm-/ *noun* a small monkey with a long thick tail, that lives in Central and S America

mar·mot /ˈmɑːmət; *AmE* ˈmɑːrmət/ *noun* a small European or American animal that lives in holes in the ground

ma·roon /məˈruːn/ *adj., noun, verb*
■ *adj.* dark brownish-red in colour
■ *noun* **1** [U] a dark brownish-red colour **2** [C] a large FIREWORK that shoots into the air and makes a loud noise, used to attract attention, especially at sea
■ *verb* [VN] [usually passive] to leave sb in a place that they cannot escape from, for example an island: *'Lord of the Flies' is a novel about English schoolboys marooned on a desert island.*

marque /mɑːk; *AmE* mɑːrk/ *noun* (*formal*) a well-known MAKE of a product, especially a car, that is expensive and fashionable: *the Porsche marque*

mar·quee /mɑːˈkiː; *AmE* mɑːrˈkiː/ *noun* **1** a large tent used at social events **2** (*AmE*) a covered entrance to a theatre, hotel, etc. often with a sign on or above it

mar·quess (also **mar·quis**) /ˈmɑːkwɪs; *AmE* ˈmɑːrk-/ *noun* (in Britain) a NOBLEMAN of high rank: *the Marquess of Bath*—compare MARCHIONESS

mar·quet·ry /ˈmɑːkɪtri; *AmE* ˈmɑːrk-/ *noun* [U] patterns or pictures made of pieces of wood on the surface of furniture, etc.; the art of making these patterns

mar·quis /ˈmɑːkwɪs; *AmE* ˈmɑːrk-/ *noun* **1** (in some European countries but not Britain) a NOBLEMAN of high rank **2** = MARQUESS

mar·quise /mɑːˈkiːz; *AmE* mɑːrˈkiːz/ *noun* the wife of a marquis **2** a woman who has the rank of a marquis—compare MARCHIONESS

mar·ram grass /ˈmærəm grɑːs; *AmE* græs/ (also **marram**) *noun* [U] a type of grass that grows in sand, often planted to prevent sand DUNES from being destroyed by the wind, rain, etc.

mar·riage /ˈmærɪdʒ/ *noun* **1** [C] the legal relationship between a husband and wife: *a good/happy marriage* ◇ *All of her children's marriages ended in divorce.* ◇ *an arranged marriage* (= one in which the parents choose a husband or wife for their child) ◇ *She has two children by a previous marriage.*—see also MIXED **2** [U] the state of being married: *They don't believe in marriage.* ◇ *My parents are celebrating 30 years of marriage.* **3** [C] the ceremony in which two people become husband and wife: *Their marriage took place in a local church.* [HELP] Wedding is more common in this meaning. [IDM] **by marriage** when sb is related to you by marriage, they are married to sb in your family, or you are married to sb in their family—more at HAND *n.*

mar·riage·able /ˈmærɪdʒəbl/ *adj.* (*old-fashioned*) suitable for marriage: *She had reached marriageable age.*

marriage bureau *noun* (*old-fashioned*, *BrE*) an organization that introduces people who are looking for sb to marry

marriage certificate (*BrE*) (*AmE* **marriage license**) *noun* a legal document that proves two people are married

marriage guidance *noun* [U] (*BrE*) advice that is given by specially trained people to couples with problems in their marriage

marriage licence (*BrE*) (*AmE* **marriage license**) *noun* **1** a document that allows two people to get married **2** (*AmE*) = MARRIAGE CERTIFICATE

marriage of convenience *noun* a marriage that is made for practical, financial or political reasons and not because the two people love each other

mar·ried /ˈmærid/ *adj.* **1** (*abbr.* **m**) having a husband or wife: *a married man/woman* ◇ *Is he married?* ◇ *a happily married couple* ◇ *She's married to John.* ◇ *Rachel and David are getting married on Saturday.* ◇ *How long have you been married?* [OPP] UNMARRIED **2** [only before noun] connected with marriage: *Are you enjoying married life?* ◇ *Her married name* (= the family name of her husband) *is Jones—Mary Jones.* **3 ~ to sth** very involved in sth so that you have no time for other activities or interests: *My brother is married to his job.*

mar·row /ˈmærəʊ; *AmE* -roʊ/ *noun* **1** [U] = BONE MARROW **2** (*BrE*) [U, C] a large vegetable that grows on the ground. Marrows are long and thick with dark green skin and white flesh—picture on page A3

marry /ˈmæri/ *verb* (**mar·ries**, **marry·ing**, **mar·ried**, **mar·ried**) **1** to become the husband or wife of sb; to get married to sb: [VN] *She married a German.* ◇ [V] *He never married.* ◇ *I guess I'm not the marrying kind* (= the kind of person who wants to get married). ◇ [V-ADJ] *They married young.* [HELP] It is more common to say *They're getting married next month.* than *They're marrying next month.* **2** [VN] to perform a ceremony in which a man and woman become husband and wife: *They were married by the local priest.* **3** [VN] **~ sb (to sb)** to find a husband or wife for sb, especially your daughter or son **4** [VN] **~ sth and/to/with sth** (*formal*) to combine two different things, ideas, etc. successfully: *The music business marries art and commerce.* [IDM] **marry money** to marry a rich person [PHRV] **marry into sth** to become part of a family or group because you have married sb who belongs to it: *She married into the aristocracy.* **marry sb⇔off (to sb)** (*disapproving*) to find a husband or wife for sb, especially your daughter or son **marry sth⇔up (with sth)** to combine two things, people or parts of sth successfully

> **WORD FAMILY**
> marry *v.*
> marriage *n.*
> married *adj.* (≠ unmarried)
> marital *adj.*

Mars /mɑːz; *AmE* mɑːrz/ *noun* the planet in the SOLAR SYSTEM that is fourth in order of distance from the sun, between the Earth and Jupiter

marsh /mɑːʃ; *AmE* mɑːrʃ/ *noun* [C, U] an area of low land that is always soft and wet because there is nowhere for the water to flow away to: *Cows were grazing on the marshes.* ▶ **marshy** *adj.*: *marshy ground/land*

mar·shal /ˈmɑːʃl; *AmE* ˈmɑːrʃl/ *noun, verb*
■ *noun* **1** (usually in compounds) an officer of the highest rank in the British army or air force: *Field Marshal Lord Haig* ◇ *Marshal of the Royal Air Force*—see also AIR CHIEF MARSHAL, AIR MARSHAL, AIR VICE-MARSHAL, FIELD MARSHAL **2** a person responsible for making sure that public events, especially sports events, take place without any problems, and for controlling crowds **3** (in the US) an officer whose job is to carry out court orders: *a federal marshal* **4** (in some US cities) an officer of high rank in a police or fire department
■ *verb* (**-ll-**, *AmE* **-l-**) [VN] (*written*) **1** to gather together and organize the people, things, ideas, etc. that you need for a particular purpose: *to marshal your arguments/thoughts/facts* ◇ *They have begun marshalling forces to*

æ	ɑː	e	ɜː	ə	ɪ	iː	i	ɒ	ɔː	ʌ	ʊ	u	uː
cat	father	ten	bird	about	sit	see	many	got	saw	cup	put	actual	too
								(BrE)					

send relief to the hurricane victims. **2** to control or organize a large group of people: *Police were brought in to marshal the crowd.*

'marshalling yard *noun* (*BrE*) a place where railway WAGONS are connected, prepared, etc. to form trains

marsh·land /'mɑːʃlænd; *AmE* 'mɑːrʃ-/ *noun* [U, C] an area of soft wet land: *low-lying areas that used to be marshland*

marsh·mal·low /ˌmɑːʃ'mæləʊ; *AmE* 'mɑːrʃmeloʊ/ *noun* [C, U] a pink or white sweet/candy that feels soft and elastic when you chew it

mar·su·pial /mɑː'suːpiəl; *AmE* mɑːr's-/ *noun* any Australian animal that carries its young in a pocket of skin (called a POUCH) on the mother's stomach. KANGAROOS and KOALAS are marsupials.—picture on page A6. ► **mar·su·pial** *adj.*

mart /mɑːt; *AmE* mɑːrt/ *noun* (*especially AmE*) a place where things are bought and sold: *a used car mart*

mar·ten /'mɑːtɪn; *AmE* 'mɑːrtn/ *noun* a small wild animal with a long body, short legs and sharp teeth. Martens live in forests and eat smaller animals: *a pine marten*

mar·tial /'mɑːʃl; *AmE* 'mɑːrʃl/ *adj.* (*formal*) [only before noun] connected with fighting or war: *martial discipline/skill*

ˌmartial 'art *noun* [usually pl.] any of the fighting sports that include JUDO and KARATE

ˌmartial 'law *noun* [U] a situation where the army of a country controls an area instead of the police during a time of trouble: *to declare/impose/lift martial law* ◊ *The city remains firmly under martial law.*

Mar·tian /'mɑːʃn; *AmE* 'mɑːrʃn/ *noun* an imaginary creature from the planet Mars

mar·tinet /ˌmɑːtɪ'net; *AmE* ˌmɑːrtn'et/ *noun* (*formal*) a very strict person who demands that other people obey orders or rules completely

mar·tini /mɑː'tiːni; *AmE* mɑːr't-/ *noun* **1** (**Martini**™) [U] a type of VERMOUTH **2** [U] an alcoholic drink made with GIN and VERMOUTH **3** [C] a glass of martini: *a dry martini*

mar·tyr /'mɑːtə(r); *AmE* 'mɑːrt-/ *noun, verb*

- *noun* **1** a person who suffers very much or is killed because of their religious or political beliefs: *the early Christian martyrs* ◊ *a martyr to the cause of freedom* **2** (usually *disapproving*) a person who tries to get sympathy from other people by telling them how much he or she is suffering **3** ~ **to sth** (*informal*) a person who suffers very much because of an illness, problem or situation: *She's a martyr to her nerves.*
- *verb* [VN] [usually passive] to kill sb because of their religious or political beliefs

mar·tyr·dom /'mɑːtədəm; *AmE* 'mɑːrtərdəm/ *noun* [U] the suffering or death of a martyr: *the martyrdom of Joan of Arc*

mar·tyred /'mɑːtəd; *AmE* 'mɑːrtərd/ *adj.* [usually before noun] (*disapproving*) showing pain or suffering so that people will be kind and sympathetic towards you: *She wore a perpetually martyred expression.*

mar·vel /'mɑːvl; *AmE* 'mɑːrvl/ *noun, verb*

- *noun* **1** a wonderful and surprising person or thing: *the marvels of nature/technology* **2** (**marvels**) [pl.] wonderful results or things that have been achieved: *The doctors have done marvels for her.*
- *verb* (-ll-, *AmE* -l-) ~ (**at sth**) to be very surprised or impressed by sth:[V] *Everyone marvelled at his courage.* [also Vthat, Vspeech]

mar·vel·lous (*BrE*) (*AmE* **mar·vel·ous**) /'mɑːvələs; *AmE* 'mɑːrv-/ *adj.* extremely good; wonderful: *This will be a marvellous opportunity for her.* ◊ *The weather was marvellous.* ◊ *It's marvellous what modern technology can do.* ► **mar·vel·lous·ly** (*BrE*) (*AmE* **mar·vel·ous·ly**) *adv.*

Marx·ism /'mɑːksɪzəm; *AmE* 'mɑːrks-/ *noun* [U] the political and economic theories of Karl Marx (1818-83) which explain the changes and developments in society as the result of opposition between the social classes ► **Marx·ist** /'mɑːksɪst; *AmE* 'mɑːrks-/ *noun* **Marx·ist** *adj.*: *Marxist theory/doctrine/ideology*

mar·zi·pan /'mɑːzɪpæn; ˌmɑːzɪ'pæn; *AmE* 'mɑːrtsəpæn;

'mɑːrz-/ *noun* [U] a sweet firm substance, sometimes with yellow colour added, made from ALMONDS, sugar and eggs and used to make sweets/candy and cover cakes—picture on page A1

mas·cara /mæ'skɑːrə; *AmE* -'skærə/ *noun* [U] a substance that is put on EYELASHES to make them look dark and thick

mas·cot /'mæskət; *AmE* -skɑːt/ *noun* an animal, a toy, etc. that people believe will bring them good luck, or that represents an organization, etc: *The team's mascot is a giant swan.* ◊ *Misha, the bear—the official mascot of the 1980 Moscow Olympics*

mas·cu·line /'mæskjəlɪn/ *adj., noun*

- *adj.* **1** having the qualities or appearance considered to be typical of men; connected with or like men: *He was handsome and strong, and very masculine.* ◊ *a bold masculine design* ◊ *That suit makes her look very masculine.*—compare FEMININE, MALE **2** (*grammar*) belonging to a class of words that refer to male people or animals and often have a special form: *'He' and 'him' are masculine pronouns.* **3** (*grammar*) (in some languages) belonging to a class of nouns, pronouns or adjectives that have masculine GENDER not FEMININE or NEUTER: *The French word for 'sun' is masculine.*
- *noun* **1** (**the masculine**) [sing.] the masculine GENDER (= form of nouns, adjectives and pronouns) **2** [C] a masculine word or word form—compare FEMININE, NEUTER

mas·cu·lin·ity /ˌmæskju'lɪnəti/ *noun* [U] the quality of being masculine: *He felt it was a threat to his masculinity.*

mash /mæʃ/ *noun, verb*

- *noun* **1** (also **ˌmashed po'tato**, **ˌmashed po'tatoes**) (all *BrE*) [U] potatoes that have been boiled and crushed into a soft mass, often with butter and milk: *bangers and mash* **2** [U] grain cooked in water until soft, used to feed farm animals **3** [U] a mixture of MALT grains and hot water, used for making beer, etc. **4** [sing.] **a ~ (of sth)** any food that has been crushed into a soft mass: *The soup was a mash of grain and vegetables.*—see also MISHMASH
- *verb* [VN] ~ **sth (up)** to crush food into a soft mass: *Mash the fruit up with a fork.* ► **mashed** *adj.*: *mashed banana*

mask /mɑːsk; *AmE* mæsk/ *noun, verb*

- *noun* **1** a covering for part or all of the face, worn to hide or protect it: *a gas/surgical mask* ◊ *The robbers were wearing stocking masks.*—see also OXYGEN MASK—picture at HOCKEY, SNORKELLING **2** something that covers your face and has another face painted on it: *The kids were all wearing animal masks.*—see also DEATH MASK **3** a thick cream made of various substances that you put on your face and neck in order to improve the quality of your skin: *a face mask* **4** [usually sing.] a manner or an expression that hides your true character or feelings: *He longed to throw off the mask of respectability.* ◊ *Her face was a cold blank mask.*
- *verb* [VN] to hide a feeling, smell, fact, etc. so that it cannot be easily seen or noticed: *She masked her anger with a smile.*

surgical mask   **Halloween mask**

masked /mɑːskt; *AmE* mæskt/ *adj.* wearing a MASK: *a masked gunman*

ˌmasked 'ball *noun* a formal party at which guests wear masks

'masking tape *noun* [U] sticky tape that you use to keep an area clean or protected when you are painting around or near it

maso·chism /'mæsəkɪzəm/ *noun* [U] **1** the practice of getting sexual pleasure from being physically hurt—compare SADISM **2** (*informal*) the enjoyment of sth that most people would find unpleasant or painful: *You spent the whole weekend in a tent in the rain? That's masochism!* ► **maso·chist** /-kɪst/ *noun* **maso·chis·tic** /ˌmæsə'kɪstɪk/ *adj.*: *masochistic behaviour/tendencies*

mason /'meɪsn/ *noun* **1** a person who builds using stone, or works with stone **2** (**Mason**) = FREEMASON

M

Ma·son·ic /məˈsɒnɪk; AmE -ˈsɑːn-/ adj. connected with FREEMASONS

ma·son·ry /ˈmeɪsənri/ noun [U] the parts of a building that are made of stone: *She was injured by falling masonry.* ◊ *He acquired a knowledge of carpentry and masonry* (= building with stone).

masque /mɑːsk; AmE mæsk/ noun a play written in verse, often with music and dancing, popular in England in the 16th and 17th centuries

mas·quer·ade /ˌmæskəˈreɪd; BrE also ˌmɑːsk-/ noun, verb
■ noun **1** (formal) a way of behaving that hides the truth or a person's true feelings **2** (especially AmE) a type of party where people wear special COSTUMES and MASKS over their faces, to hide their identities
■ verb [V] ~ **as sth** to pretend to be sth that you are not: *commercial advertisers masquerading as private individuals*

Mass /mæs/ noun **1** (sometimes **mass**) [U, C] (especially in the Roman Catholic Church) a ceremony held in memory of the last meal that Christ had with his DISCIPLES: *to go to/hear Mass* ◊ *a priest celebrating/saying Mass*—see also EUCHARIST, COMMUNION **2** [C] a piece of music that is written for the prayers, etc. of this ceremony: *Bach's Mass in B minor*

mass /mæs/ noun, adj., verb
■ noun **1** [C] ~ **(of sth)** a large amount of a substance that does not have a definite shape or form: *a mass of snow and rocks falling down the mountain* ◊ *The hill appeared as a black mass in the distance.* ◊ *The sky was full of dark masses of clouds.* **2** [C, usually sing.] ~ **of sth** a large amount or quantity of sth: *a mass of blonde hair* ◊ *I began sifting through the mass of evidence.* **3** [sing.] ~ **of sth** a large number of people or things grouped together, often in a confused way: *I struggled through the mass of people to the exit.* ◊ *The page was covered with a mass of figures.* **4** (**masses** (**of sth**)) [pl.] (informal) a large number or amount of sth: *There were masses of people in the shops yesterday.* ◊ *I've got masses of work to do.* ◊ *Don't give me any more. I've eaten masses!* **5** (**the masses**) [pl.] the ordinary people in society who are not leaders or who are considered to be not very well educated: *government attempts to suppress dissatisfaction among the masses* ◊ *a TV programme that brings science to the masses* **6** (**the mass of sth**) [sing.] the most; the MAJORITY: *The reforms are unpopular with the mass of teachers and parents.* **7** [U] (physics) the quantity of material that sth contains: *calculating the mass of a planet* HELP **Weight** is used in non-technical language for this meaning.—see also BIOMASS, CRITICAL MASS, LAND MASS IDM **be a ˈmass of** to be full of or covered with sth: *The rose bushes are a mass of flowers in June.* ◊ *Her arm was a mass of bruises.*
■ adj. [only before noun] affecting or involving a large number of people or things: *mass unemployment/production* ◊ *weapons of mass destruction* ◊ *Their latest product is aimed at the mass market.*—see also MASS-MARKET
■ verb to come together in large numbers; to gather people or things together in large numbers: [V] [usually +adv./prep.] *Demonstrators had massed outside the embassy.* ◊ *Dark clouds massed on the horizon.* ◊ [VN] *The general massed his troops for a final attack.* ▶ **massed** adj.: *the massed ranks of his political opponents*

mas·sacre /ˈmæsəkə(r)/ noun, verb
■ noun [C, U] **1** the killing of a large number of people especially in a cruel way: *the bloody massacre of innocent civilians* ◊ *Nobody survived the massacre.* **2** (informal) a very big defeat in a game or competition: *The game was a 10–0 massacre for our team.*
■ verb [VN] **1** to kill a large number of people, especially in a cruel way: *Hundreds of innocent women and children were massacred.* **2** (informal) to defeat sb very badly in a game or competition: *Our team was massacred in the final.*

mas·sage /ˈmæsɑːʒ; AmE məˈsɑːʒ/ noun, verb
■ noun [U, C] the action of rubbing and pressing a person's body with the hands to reduce pain in the muscles and joints: *Massage will help the pain.* ◊ *a back massage* ◊ *to give sb a massage* ◊ *massage oils*

■ verb [VN] **1** to rub and press a person's body with the hands to reduce pain in the muscles and joints: *He massaged the aching muscles in her feet.* ◊ *(figurative)* to massage sb's ego (= to make sb feel better, more confident, attractive, etc.) **2** to rub a substance into the skin, hair, etc: *Massage the cream into your skin.* **3** (disapproving) to change facts, figures, etc. in order to make them seem better than they really are: *The government was accused of massaging the unemployment figures.*

ˈmassage parlour (BrE) (AmE **ˈmassage parlor**) noun **1** a place where you can pay to have a massage **2** a place that is supposed to offer the service of massage, but is also where men go to pay for sex with prostitutes

mas·seur /mæˈsɜː(r)/ noun a person whose job is giving people massage

mas·seuse /mæˈsɜːz/ noun a woman whose job is giving people massage

mas·sif /mæˈsiːf/ noun (technical) a group of mountains that form a large mass

mas·sive /ˈmæsɪv/ adj. **1** very large, heavy and solid: *a massive rock* ◊ *the massive walls of the castle* **2** extremely large or serious: *The explosion made a massive hole in the ground.* ◊ *a massive increase in spending* ◊ *He suffered a massive heart attack.* ◊ *(BrE, spoken, informal) Their house is massive.* ◊ *They have a massive great house.* ▶ **mas·sive·ly** adv.

ˌmass-ˈmarket adj. [only before noun] (of goods etc.) produced for very large numbers of people

the ˌmass ˈmedia noun [pl.] sources of information and news such as newspapers, magazines, radio and television, that reach and influence large numbers of people

ˌmass-proˈduce verb [VN] to produce goods in large quantities, using machinery ▶ **ˌmass-proˈduced** adj.: *mass-produced goods* **ˌmass proˈduction** noun [U]: *the mass production of consumer goods*

mast /mɑːst; AmE mæst/ noun **1** a tall pole on a boat or ship that supports the sails—picture at YACHT **2** a tall metal tower with an AERIAL that sends and receives radio or television signals **3** a tall pole that is used for holding a flag—see also HALF MAST IDM see NAIL v.

mast·ec·tomy /mæˈstektəmi/ noun (pl. **-ies**) a medical operation to remove a woman's breast

mas·ter /ˈmɑːstə(r); AmE ˈmæs-/ noun, verb, adj.
■ noun
OF SERVANTS | **1** (old-fashioned) a man who has people working for him, often as servants in his home: *I'm afraid the master is away on business.* ◊ *They lived in fear of their master.*
PERSON IN CONTROL | **2** ~ **of sth** (written) a person who is able to control sth: *She was no longer master of her own future.*
SKILLED PERSON | **3** ~ **(of sth)** a person who is skilled at sth: *a master of disguise* ◊ *a master of the serve-and-volley game*—see also PAST MASTER
DOG OWNER | **4** the male owner of a dog: *The dog saved its master's life.*—compare MISTRESS
TEACHER | **5** (BrE, becoming old-fashioned) a male teacher at a school, especially a private school: *the physics master*—compare SCHOOLMASTER, MISTRESS
UNIVERSITY DEGREE | **6** (**master's**) (also **ˈmaster's degree**) a second university degree, or, in Scotland, a first university degree, such as an MA: *He has a Master's in Business Administration.*—see also MA, MB, MBA, MSc **7** (usually **Master**) a person who has a master's degree: *a Master of Arts/Science*
CAPTAIN OF SHIP | **8** the captain of a ship that transports goods
FAMOUS PAINTER | **9** a famous painter who lived in the past: *an exhibition of work by the French master, Monet*—see also OLD MASTER
ORIGINAL RECORD/TAPE/MOVIE | **10** (often used as an adjective) a version of a record, tape, film/movie, etc. from which copies are made: *the master copy*
TITLE | **11** (**Master**) (rather old-fashioned) a title used when speaking to or about a boy who is too young to be called

M

b	d	f	g	h	k	l	m	n	p	r
bad	did	fall	get	hat	cat	leg	man	now	pen	red

Mr (also used in front of the name on an envelope, etc.) **12 (Master)** (in Britain) the title of the head of some schools and university colleges: *the Master of Wolfson College* **13 (Master)** a title used for speaking to or about some religious teachers or leaders

HELP There are many other compounds ending in **master**. You will find them at their place in the alphabet.

IDM **be your own 'master/'mistress** to be free to make your own decisions rather than being told what to do by sb else—more at LORD, SERVE *v.*

■ *verb* [VN]

LEARN/UNDERSTAND | **1** to learn or understand sth completely: *to master new skills/techniques* ◇ *French was a language he had never mastered.*

CONTROL | **2** to manage to control an emotion: *She struggled hard to master her temper.* **3** to gain control of an animal or a person

■ *adj.* [only before noun]

SKILLED | **1 ~ baker/chef/mason**, etc. used to describe a person who is very skilled at the job mentioned: *a master builder/craftsman*

MOST IMPORTANT | **2** the largest and/or most important: *the master bedroom* ◇ *a master file/switch*

mas·ter·class /ˈmɑːstəklɑːs; AmE ˈmæstərklæs/ *noun* a lesson, especially in music, given by a famous expert to very skilled students

mas·ter·ful /ˈmɑːstəfl; AmE ˈmæstərfl/ *adj.* **1** (of a person, especially a man) able to control people or situations in a way that shows confidence as a leader **2** = MASTERLY: *a masterful performance* ▶ **mas·ter·ful·ly** /-fəli/ *adv.*: *He took her arm masterfully and led her away.*

'master key (also **'pass key**) *noun* a key that can be used to open many different locks in a building

mas·ter·ly /ˈmɑːstəli; AmE ˈmæstərli/ (also **mas·ter·ful**) *adj.* showing great skill or understanding: *a masterly performance* ◇ *Her handling of the situation was masterly.*

mas·ter·mind /ˈmɑːstəmaɪnd; AmE ˈmæstərm-/ *noun, verb*

■ *noun* [usually sing.] an intelligent person who plans and directs a complicated project or activity (often one that involves a crime): *The mastermind behind the robbery was never caught.*

■ *verb* [VN] to plan and direct a complicated project or activity

master of 'ceremonies *noun* (*abbr.* **MC**) a person who introduces guests or entertainers at a formal occasion

mas·ter·piece /ˈmɑːstəpiːs; AmE ˈmæstərp-/ (also **mas·ter·work**) *noun* a work of art such as a painting, film/movie, book, etc. that is an excellent, or the best, example of the artist's work: *The museum houses several of his Cubist masterpieces.* ◇ *Her work is a masterpiece of* (= excellent example of) *simplicity.*

'master plan *noun* [sing.] a detailed plan that will make a complicated project successful

'master's degree (also **master's**) *noun* a further university degree that you study for after a first degree

'master stroke *noun* [usually sing.] something clever that you do that gives a successful result: *a master stroke that established his career*

mas·ter·work /ˈmɑːstəwɜːk; AmE ˈmæstərwɜːrk/ *noun* = MASTERPIECE

mas·tery /ˈmɑːstəri; AmE ˈmæst-/ *noun* **1** [U, sing.] **~ (of sth)** great knowledge about or understanding of a particular thing: *She has mastery of several languages.* **2** [U] **~ (of/over sb/sth)** control or power: *human mastery of the natural world*

mast·head /ˈmɑːsthed; AmE ˈmæst-/ *noun* **1** the top of a MAST on a ship **2** the name of a newspaper at the top of the front page

mas·tic /ˈmæstɪk/ *noun* [U] **1** a substance that comes from the bark of a tree and is used in making VARNISH **2** a substance that is used in building to fill holes and keep out water

mas·ti·cate /ˈmæstɪkeɪt/ *verb* [V] (*technical*) to chew food ▶ **mas·ti·ca·tion** /ˌmæstɪˈkeɪʃn/ *noun* [U]

mas·tiff /ˈmæstɪf/ *noun* a large strong dog with short hair, often used to guard buildings

mas·titis /mæˈstaɪtɪs/ *noun* [U] (*medical*) painful swelling of the breast or UDDER usually because of infection

mas·tur·bate /ˈmæstəbeɪt; AmE -stɑːrb-/ *verb* **1** [V] to give yourself sexual pleasure by rubbing your sexual organs **2** [VN] to give sb sexual pleasure by rubbing their sexual organs ▶ **mas·tur·ba·tion** /ˌmæstəˈbeɪʃn; AmE -stər'b-/ *noun* [U] **mas·tur·ba·tory** /ˌmæstəˈbeɪtəri; AmE ˈmæstərbətɔːri/ *adj.*

mat /mæt/ *noun, adj.*

■ *noun* **1** a small piece of thick carpet or strong material that is used to cover part of a floor: *Wipe your feet on the mat before you come in, please.*—see also BATH MAT, DOORMAT, MOUSE MAT **2** a piece of thick material such as rubber or plastic used especially in some sports for people to lie on or fall onto: *a judo/exercise mat* **3** a small piece of wood or fabric used on a table for decoration or to protect the surface from heat or damage: *a beer mat*—see also TABLE MAT **4** a thick mass of sth that is stuck together: *a mat of hair*—see also MATTED

■ *adj.* (*AmE*) = MATT

mata·dor /ˈmætədɔː(r)/ *noun* a person who fights and kills the BULL in a BULLFIGHT

match /mætʃ/ *noun, verb*

■ *noun*

FOR LIGHTING FIRES | **1** [C] a small stick made of wood or cardboard that is used for lighting a fire, cigarette, etc: *a box of matches* ◇ *to strike a match* (= to make it burn) ◇ *to put a match to sth* (= set fire to sth)

IN SPORT | **2** [C] (*especially BrE*) a sports event where people or teams compete against each other: (*BrE*) *a football match* ◇ (*AmE, BrE*) *a tennis match* ◇ *They are playing an important match against Liverpool on Saturday.*—see also SLANGING MATCH

AN EQUAL | **3** [sing.] **a ~ for sb/sb's match** a person who is equal to sb else in strength, skill, intelligence, etc: *I was no match for him at tennis.* ◇ *I was his match at tennis.*

SB/STH THAT COMBINES WELL | **4** [sing.] a person or thing that combines well with sb/sth else: *The curtains and carpet are a good match.* ◇ *Jo and Ian are a perfect match for each other.*

STH THE SAME | **5** [C] a thing that looks exactly the same as or very similar to sth else: *I've found a vase that is an exact match of the one I broke.*

MARRIAGE | **6** [C] (*old-fashioned*) a marriage or a marriage partner—see also LOVE MATCH

IDM **find/meet your 'match (in sb)** to meet sb who is equal to, or even better than you in strength, skill or intelligence—more at MAN *n.*, WHOLE

■ *verb*

COMBINE WELL | **1** if two things **match**, or if one thing **matches** another, they have the same colour, pattern, or style and therefore look attractive together: [VN] *The doors were painted blue to match the walls.* ◇ *a scarf with gloves to match* ◇ [V] *None of these glasses match* (= they are all different).—see also MATCHING

BE THE SAME | **2** if two things **match** or if one thing **matches** another, they are the same or very similar: [VN] *Her fingerprints match those found at the scene of the crime.* ◇ *As a couple they are not very well matched* (= they are not very suitable for each other). ◇ [V] *The two sets of figures don't match.*

FIND STH SIMILAR/CONNECTED | **3** [VN] **~ sb/sth (to/with sb/sth)** to find sb/sth that goes together with or is connected with another person or thing: *The aim of the competition is to match the quote to the person who said it.*

BE EQUAL/BETTER | **4** [VN] to be as good, interesting, successful, etc. as sb/sth else [SYN] EQUAL: *The profits made in the first year have never been matched.* ◇ *The teams were evenly matched.* **5** [VN] to make sth the same or better than sth else: *The company was unable to match his current salary.*

PROVIDE STH SUITABLE | **6** [VN] to provide sth that is suitable for or enough for a particular situation: *Investment in* *hospitals is needed now to match the future needs of the country.*

IDM see MIX *v.*

PHRV '**match sth against sth** to compare sth with sth else in order to find things that are the same or similar: *New information is matched against existing data in the computer.* '**match sb/sth against/with sb/sth** to arrange for sb to compete in a game or competition against sb else: *We are matched against last year's champions in the first round.* ,**match** '**up (with sth)** to be the same or similar **SYN** TALLY: *The suspects' stories just don't match up.* ,**match sth ‹ › 'up (with sth)** to find things that belong together or that look attractive together: *She spent the morning matching up orders with invoices.* ,**match** '**up (to sb/sth)** (usually used in negative sentences) to be as good, interesting, successful as sb/sth **SYN** MEASURE UP: *The trip failed to match up to her expectations.*

match·box /'mætʃbɒks; *AmE* -baːks/ *noun* a small box for holding matches—picture at PACKAGING

match·ing /'mætʃɪŋ/ *adj.* [only before noun] (of clothing, fabric, objects, etc.) having the same colour, pattern, style, etc. and therefore looking attractive together: *a pine table with four matching chairs*

match·less /'mætʃləs/ *adj.* (*written*) so good that nothing can be compared with it: *matchless beauty/skill*

match·maker /'mætʃmeɪkə(r)/ *noun* a person who tries to arrange marriages or relationships between others ▶ **match·mak·ing** *noun* [U]

,**match** '**point** *noun* [U, C] (especially in tennis) a point that, if won by a player, will also win them the match

match·stick /'mætʃstɪk/ *noun* a single wooden match: *starving children with legs like matchsticks*—picture at STICK

matchstick figure (*BrE*)/ **stick figure** (*AmE*)

matchstick man

matchstick woman

'**matchstick figure** (*BrE*) (*AmE* '**stick figure**) *noun* a picture of a person drawn only with thin lines for the arms and legs, a circle for the head, etc.

match·wood /'mætʃwʊd/ *noun* [U] very small pieces of wood

mate /meɪt/ *noun, verb*

■ *noun*

FRIEND | **1** [C] (*BrE, informal*) a friend: *They've been best mates since school.* ◊ *I was with a mate.*

FRIENDLY NAME | **2** [C] (*BrE, informal*) used as a friendly way of addressing sb, especially between men: *Sorry mate, you'll have to wait.* ◊ *All right, mate?*

SB YOU SHARE WITH | **3** [C] (in compounds) a person you share an activity or accommodation with: *workmates/ teammates/playmates/classmates* ◊ *my room-mate/flat-mate*—see also RUNNING MATE, SOUL MATE

BIRD/ANIMAL | **4** [C] either of a pair of birds or animals: *A male bird sings to attract a mate.*

SEXUAL PARTNER | **5** [C] (*informal*) a husband, wife or other sexual partner

JOB | **6** [C] (*BrE*) a person whose job is to help a skilled worker: *a builder's/plumber's mate*

ON SHIP | **7** [C] an officer in a commercial ship below the rank of captain or MASTER—see also FIRST MATE

IN CHESS | **8** [U] = CHECKMATE

■ *verb*

ANIMALS/BIRDS | **1** [V] ~ (**with sth**) (of two animals or birds) to have sex in order to produce young: *Do foxes ever mate with dogs?*—see also MATING **2** [VN] ~ **sth (to/with sth)** to put animals or birds together so that they will have sex and produce young

IN CHESS | **3** [VN] = CHECKMATE

ma·ter·ial /mə'tɪəriəl; *AmE* -'tɪr-/ *noun, adj.*

■ *noun* **1** [U, C] cloth used for making clothes, curtains, etc. **SYN** FABRIC: *a piece of material* ◊ '*What material is this dress made of?*' '*Cotton.*'—picture at SEW **2** [C, U] a substance that things can be made from: *building materials* (= bricks, sand, glass, etc.) ◊ *Oil is the raw material for plastic.* **3** [C, usually pl., U] things that are needed in order to do a particular activity: *teaching materials* ◊ *The company produces its own training material.* ◊ (*figurative*) *The teacher saw her as good university material* (= good enough to go to university). **4** [U] information or ideas used in books, etc: *She's collecting material for her latest novel.* **5** [U] items used in a performance: *The band played all new material at the gig.*

■ *adj.* **1** [only before noun] connected with money, possessions, etc. rather than with the needs of the mind or spirit: *material comforts* ◊ *changes in your material circumstances* **OPP** SPIRITUAL **2** [only before noun] connected with the physical world rather than with the mind or spirit: *the material world* **OPP** IMMATERIAL **3** ~ (**to sth**) (*formal* or *law*) important and needing to be considered: *material evidence* ◊ *She omitted information that was material to the case.*—see also IMMATERIAL ▶ **ma·teri·ally** /-iəli/ *adv.*: *Materially they are no better off.* ◊ *Their comments have not materially affected our plans* (= in a noticeable or important way).

ma·teri·al·ism /mə'tɪəriəlɪzəm; *AmE* -'tɪr-/ *noun* [U] **1** (usually *disapproving*) the belief that money, possessions and physical comforts are more important than spiritual values: *the greed and materialism of modern society* **2** (*philosophy*) the belief that only material things exist—compare IDEALISM

ma·teri·al·ist /mə'tɪəriəlɪst; *AmE* -'tɪr-/ *noun* **1** a person who believes that money, possessions and physical comforts are more important than spiritual values in life **2** a person who believes in the philosophy of materialism

ma·teri·al·is·tic /mə,tɪəriə'lɪstɪk; *AmE* -,tɪr-/ *adj.* (*disapproving*) caring more about money and possessions than anything else: *Children today are so materialistic.*

ma·teri·al·ize (*BrE* also **-ise**) /mə'tɪəriəlaɪz; *AmE* -'tɪr-/ *verb* [V] **1** (usually used in negative sentences) to take place or start to exist as expected or planned: *The promotion he had been promised failed to materialize.* **2** to appear suddenly and/or in a way that cannot be explained: *A tall figure suddenly materialized at her side.* ◊ (*informal*) *The train failed to materialize* (= it did not come). ▶ **ma·teri·al·iza·tion, -isa·tion** /mə,tɪəriəl-aɪ'zeɪʃn; *AmE* -,tɪriələ'z-/ *noun* [U]

ma·ter·nal /mə'tɜːnl; *AmE* mə'tɜːrnl/ *adj.* **1** having feelings that are typical of a caring mother towards a child: *maternal love* ◊ *I'm not very maternal.* ◊ *She didn't have any maternal instincts.* **2** connected with being a mother: *Maternal age affects the baby's survival rate.* **3** [only before noun] related through the mother's side of the family: *my maternal grandfather* (= my mother's father) ▶ **ma·ter·nal·ly** /-nəli/ *adv.*: *She behaved maternally towards her students.*—compare PATERNAL

ma·ter·nity /mə'tɜːnəti; *AmE* -'tɜːrn-/ *noun* [U] the state of being or becoming a mother: *maternity clothes* (= clothes for women who are pregnant) ◊ *a maternity ward/ hospital* (= one where women go to give birth to their babies)

ma'ternity leave *noun* [U] a period of time when a woman temporarily leaves her job to have a baby

matey /'meɪti/ *adj., noun*

■ *adj.* ~ (**with sb**) (*BrE, informal*) friendly, sometimes in a way that is not completely sincere: *She started off being quite matey with everyone.*

■ *noun* (*BrE*) used by men as an informal way of addressing another man

math·em·at·ician /,mæθəmə'tɪʃn/ *noun* a person who is an expert in mathematics

math·emat·ics /,mæθə'mætɪks/ (also *BrE informal* **maths** /mæθs/) (also *AmE informal* **math** /mæθ/) *noun* **1** [U] the science of numbers and shapes. Branches of mathematics include ARITHMETIC, ALGEBRA, GEOMETRY and TRIGONOMETRY: *the core subjects of English, Maths and*

M

æ	ɑː	e	ɜː	ə	ɪ	iː	i	ɒ	ɔː	ʌ	ʊ	u	uː
cat	father	ten	bird	about	sit	see	many	got	saw	cup	put	actual	too

(BrE)

Science.◇ a maths teacher ◇ the school mathematics curriculum **2** [U+sing./pl. *v.*] the process of calculating using numbers: *If my maths is/are right, the answer is 142. ◇ Is your math correct?* ▶ **math·emat·ic·al** /ˌmæθəˈmætɪkl/ *adj.: mathematical calculations/problems/models ◇ to assess children's mathematical ability* **math·emat·ic·al·ly** /ˌmæθəˈmætɪkli/ *adv.: It's mathematically impossible. ◇ Some people are very mathematically inclined* (= interested in and good at mathematics).

mat·inee (also **mat·inée**) /ˈmætɪneɪ; *AmE* ˌmætnˈeɪ/ *noun* an afternoon performance of a play, etc.; an afternoon showing of a film/movie

mat·ing /ˈmeɪtɪŋ/ *noun* [U, C] sex between animals: *the mating season*

mat·ins (also **mat·tins**) /ˈmætɪnz; *AmE* ˈmætnz/ *noun* [U] the service of morning prayer, especially in the Anglican Church—compare EVENSONG, VESPERS

ma·tri·arch /ˈmeɪtriɑːk; *AmE* -ɑːrk/ *noun* a woman who is the head of a family or social group—compare PATRIARCH

ma·tri·arch·al /ˌmeɪtriˈɑːkl; *AmE* -ˈɑːrkl/ *adj.* (of a society or system) controlled by women rather than men; passing power, property, etc. from mother to daughter rather than from father to son: *The animals live in matriarchal groups.*—compare PATRIARCHAL

ma·tri·archy /ˈmeɪtriɑːki; *AmE* -ɑːrki/ *noun* (*pl.* **-ies**) a social system that gives power and authority to women rather than men—compare PATRIARCHY

matri·ces *pl.* of MATRIX

matri·cide /ˈmætrɪsaɪd/ *noun* [U, C] (*formal*) the crime of killing your mother; a person who is guilty of this crime—compare FRATRICIDE, PARRICIDE, PATRICIDE

ma·tric·ulate /məˈtrɪkjuleɪt/ *verb* [V] (*formal*) to officially become a student at a university: *She matriculated in 1968.* ▶ **ma·tricu·la·tion** /məˌtrɪkjuˈleɪʃn/ *noun* [U]

matri·mo·nial /ˌmætrɪˈməʊniəl; *AmE* -ˈmoʊ-/ *adj.* [usually before noun] (*formal or technical*) connected with marriage or with being married: *matrimonial problems ◇ the matrimonial home*

matri·mony /ˈmætrɪməni; *AmE* -moʊni/ *noun* [U] (*formal or technical*) marriage; the state of being married: *holy matrimony*

mat·rix /ˈmeɪtrɪks/ *noun* (*pl.* **matri·ces** /ˈmeɪtrɪsiːz/) **1** (*mathematics*) an arrangement of numbers, symbols, etc. in rows and columns, treated as a single quantity **2** (*formal*) the formal social, political, etc. situation from which a society or person grows and develops: *the European cultural matrix* **3** (*formal or literary*) a system of lines, roads, etc. that cross each other, forming a series of squares or shapes in between [SYN] NETWORK: *a matrix of paths* **4** (*technical*) a MOULD in which sth is shaped **5** (*computing*) a group of electronic CIRCUIT elements arranged in rows and columns like a GRID—see also DOT MATRIX PRINTER **6** (*geology*) a mass of rock in which minerals, precious stones, etc. are found in the ground

ma·tron /ˈmeɪtrən/ *noun* **1** (*BrE*) a woman who works as a nurse in a school **2** (*old-fashioned, BrE*) a senior female nurse in charge of the other nurses in a hospital (now usually called a **senior nursing officer**) **3** (*becoming old-fashioned*) an older married woman

ma·tron·ly /ˈmeɪtrənli/ *adj.* (*disapproving*) (of a woman) no longer young, and rather fat

matron of honour (*BrE*) (*AmE* **matron of honor**) *noun* [sing.] a married woman who is the most important BRIDESMAID at a wedding—compare MAID OF HONOUR

matt (*BrE*) (*AmE* **mat**) (also **matte** *AmE, BrE*) /mæt/ *adj.* (of a colour, surface, or photograph) not shiny: *a matt finish ◇ matt white paint ◇ Prints are available on matt or glossy paper.*

mat·ted /ˈmætɪd/ *adj.* (of hair, etc.) forming a thick mass, especially because it is wet and dirty: *the dog's matted fur*

mat·ter /ˈmætə(r)/ *noun, verb*
■ *noun*
  SUBJECT/SITUATION | **1** [C] a subject or situation that you must consider or deal with [SYN] AFFAIR: *It's a private*

matter. ◇ They had important matters to discuss. ◇ She may need your help with some business matters. ◇ I always consulted him on matters of policy. ◇ It's a matter for the police (= for them to deal with). *◇ That's a matter for you to take up with your boss. ◇ Let's get on with the matter in hand* (= what we need to deal with now). *◇ I wasn't prepared to let the matter drop* (= stop discussing it). *◇ It was no easy matter getting him to change his mind. ◇ It should have been a simple matter to check. ◇* (*ironic*) *And then there's the little matter of the fifty pounds you owe me. ◇* (*formal*) *It was a matter of some concern to most of those present* (= something they were worried about). *◇ I did not feel that we had got to the heart of the matter* (= the most important part). *◇ And that is the crux of the matter* (= the most important thing about the situation). **2** (**matters**) [pl.] the present situation, or the situation that you are talking about [SYN] THINGS: *Unfortunately, there is nothing we can do to improve matters. ◇ I'd forgotten the keys, which didn't help matters. ◇ Matters were made worse by a fire in the warehouse. ◇ And then, to make matters worse, his parents turned up. ◇ I decided to take matters into my own hands* (= deal with the situation myself). *◇ Matters came to a head* (= the situation became very difficult) *with his resignation.*
  PROBLEM | **3** (**the matter**) [sing.] **~** (**with sb/sth**) used (to ask) if sb is upset, unhappy, etc. or if there is a problem: *What's the matter? Is there something wrong? ◇ Is anything the matter? ◇ Is something the matter with Bob? He seems very down. ◇ There's something the matter with my eyes. ◇ 'We've bought a new TV.' 'What was the matter with the old one?' ◇ What's the matter with you today* (= why are you behaving like this)*?*
  A MATTER OF STH/OF DOING STH | **4** [sing.] a situation that involves sth or depends on sth [SYN] QUESTION: *Learning to drive is all a matter of coordination. ◇ Planning a project is just a matter of working out the right order to do things in. ◇ That's not a problem. It's simply a matter of letting people know in time. ◇ Some people prefer the older version to the new one. It's a matter of taste. ◇ She resigned over a matter of principle. ◇ The government must deal with this as a matter of urgency. ◇* (*spoken*) *Just as a matter of interest* (= because it is interesting, not because it is important), *how much did you pay for it? ◇ 'I think this is the best so far.' 'Well, that's a matter of opinion* (= other people may think differently).
  SUBSTANCE | **5** [U] (*technical*) physical substance in general that everything in the world consists of; not mind or spirit: *to study the properties of matter* **6** [U] a substance or things of a particular sort: *Add plenty of organic matter to improve the soil. ◇ elimination of waste matter from the body ◇ She didn't approve of their choice of reading matter.*—see also SUBJECT MATTER
  [IDM] **as a matter of 'fact 1** used to add a comment on sth that you have just said, usually adding sth that you think the other person will be interested in: *It's a nice place. We've stayed there ourselves, as a matter of fact.* **2** used to disagree with sth that sb has just said: *'I suppose you'll be leaving soon, then?' 'No, as a matter of fact I'll be staying for another two years.'* **be another/a different 'matter** to be very different: *I know which area they live in, but whether I can find their house is a different matter.* **for 'that matter** (*spoken*) used to add a comment on sth that you have just said: *I didn't like it much. Nor did the kids, for that matter.* **it's just/only a matter of 'time (before …)** used to say that sth will definitely happen, although you are not sure when: *It's only a matter of time before they bring out their own version of the software.* **(as) a matter of 'course** the usual and correct thing that is done: *We always check people's addresses as a matter of course.* **a matter of 'hours, 'minutes, etc. | a matter of 'inches, 'metres, etc.** only a few hours, minutes, etc: *It was all over in a matter of minutes. ◇ The bullet missed her by a matter of inches.* **a ˌmatter of ˌlife and 'death** used to describe a situation that is very important or serious **a ˌmatter of 'record** (*formal*) something that has been recorded as being true **no matter** (*spoken*) used to say that sth is not important **no matter who, what, where, etc.** used to say that sth

aɪ	aʊ	eɪ	əʊ	oʊ	ɔɪ	ɪə	eə	ʊə	j	w
my	now	say	go	go	boy	near	hair	pure	yes	wet
			(BrE)	(AmE)						

is always true, whatever the situation is, or that sb should certainly do sth: *They don't last long no matter how careful you are.* ◊ *Call me when you get there, no matter what the time is.*—more at FACT, LAUGHING

■ *verb* **~ (to sb)** (not used in the progressive tenses) to be important or have an important effect on sb/sth: [V] *The children matter more to her than anything else in the world.* ◊ *It doesn't matter to me what you do.* ◊ *'What did you say?' 'Oh, it doesn't matter'* (= it is not important enough to repeat).' ◊ *'I'm afraid I forgot that book again.' 'It doesn't matter* (= it is not important enough to worry about).' ◊ *What does it matter if I spent $100 on it—it's my money!* ◊ *As long as you're happy, that's* **all that matters.** ◊ *After his death, nothing seemed to matter any more.* ◊ *He's been in prison, you know—not that it matters* (= that information does not affect my opinion of him).* ◊ [V**wh-**] *Does it really matter who did it?* ◊ [V**that**] *It didn't matter that the weather was bad.*

,**matter-of-'fact** *adj.* said or done without showing any emotion, especially in a situation in which you would expect sb to express their feelings: *She told us the news of his death in a very matter-of-fact way.* ▶ ,**matter-of-'factly** *adv.*

mat·ting /'mætɪŋ/ *noun* rough, woven material for making MATS: *coconut matting*

mat·tins *noun* [U] = MATINS

mat·tress /'mætrəs/ *noun* the soft part of a bed, that you lie on: *a soft/hard mattress*—picture at BED

mat·ur·ation /ˌmætʃu'reɪʃn/ *noun* [U] (*formal*) **1** the process of becoming or being made mature (= ready to eat or drink after being left for a period of time) **2** the process of becoming adult

ma·ture /mə'tʃʊə(r)/ *; AmE* -'tʃʊr/ *adj., verb*
■ *adj.* **HELP** **maturer** is occasionally used instead of **more mature**
SENSIBLE | **1** (of a child or young person) behaving in a sensible way, like an adult: *Jane is very mature for her age.* ◊ *a mature and sensible attitude* **OPP** IMMATURE
FULLY GROWN | **2** (of a person, a tree, a bird or an animal) fully grown and developed: *sexually mature* ◊ *a mature oak/eagle/elephant* **OPP** IMMATURE
WINE/CHEESE | **3** developed over a period of time to produce a strong, rich flavour
NO LONGER YOUNG | **4** used as a polite or humorous way of saying that sb is no longer young: *clothes for the mature woman* ◊ *a man of mature years*
WORK OF ART | **5** created late in an artist's life and showing great understanding and skill
INSURANCE POLICY | **6** (*business*) ready to be paid
▶ **ma·ture·ly** *adv.*
IDM **on mature re'flection/conside'ration** (*formal*) after thinking about sth carefully and for a long time
■ *verb*
BECOME FULLY GROWN | **1** [V] to become fully grown or developed: *This particular breed of cattle matures early.* ◊ *Technology in this field has matured considerably over the last decade.*
BECOME SENSIBLE | **2** [V] to develop emotionally and start to behave like a sensible adult: *He has matured a great deal over the past year.*
DEVELOP SKILL | **3** [V] **~ (into sth)** to fully develop a particular skill or quality: *She has matured into one of the country's finest actresses.*
WINE/CHEESE | **4** [V, VN] if wine, cheese, etc. **matures** or **is matured**, it develops over a period of time to produce a strong, rich flavour
INSURANCE POLICY | **5** [V] (*business*) to reach the date when it must be paid

ma·ture 'student *noun* (*BrE*) an adult student who goes to college or university some years after leaving school

ma·tur·ity /mə'tʃʊərəti; -'tʃɔː-; *AmE* -'tʃʊr-; -'tʊr-/ *noun* [U] **1** the quality of thinking and behaving in a sensible, adult manner: *He has maturity beyond his years.* ◊ *Her poems show great maturity.*—compare IMMATURITY **2** (of a person, an animal, or a plant) the state of being fully

grown or developed: *The forest will take 100 years to reach maturity.*—compare IMMATURITY **3** (*business*) (of an insurance policy, etc.) the time when money you have invested is ready to be paid

matzo /'mætsəʊ; *AmE* 'mɑːtsoʊ/ *noun* [U, C] (*pl.* **-os**) a type of bread in the form of a large flat biscuit, traditionally eaten by Jews during Passover; one of these biscuits

maud·lin /'mɔːdlɪn/ *adj.* **1** talking in a silly, emotional way, often full of pity for yourself, especially when drunk **2** (of a book, film/movie, or song) expressing or causing exaggerated emotions, especially in way that is not sincere

maul /mɔːl/ *verb* [VN] **1** (of an animal) to attack and injure sb by tearing their flesh **2** to touch sb/sth in an unpleasant and/or violent way: *She was mauled by guards at the border.* **3** to criticize sth/sb severely and publicly **4** (*informal*) to defeat sb easily ▶ **maul·ing** *noun* [sing.]: *The play received a mauling from the critics.* ◊ *They face a mauling by last year's winners.*

Maundy Thurs·day /ˌmɔːndi 'θɜːzdeɪ; -di; *AmE* 'θɜːrz-/ *noun* [U, C] (in the Christian Church) the Thursday before Easter

mau·so·leum /ˌmɔːsə'liːəm/ *noun* a special building made to hold the dead body of an important person or the dead bodies of a family: *the royal mausoleum*

mauve /məʊv; *AmE* moʊv/ *adj.* pale purple in colour ▶ **mauve** *noun* [U]

maven /'meɪvn/ *noun* (*AmE*) an expert on sth

mav·er·ick /'mævərɪk/ *noun* a person who does not behave or think like everyone else, but who has independent, unusual opinions: *a political maverick* ▶ **mav·er·ick** *adj.* [only before noun]: *a maverick film director*

maw /mɔː/ *noun* **1** (*literary*) something that seems like a big mouth that swallows things up completely **2** (*old-fashioned*) an animal's stomach or throat

mawk·ish /'mɔːkɪʃ/ *adj.* (*disapproving*) expressing or sharing emotion in a way that is exaggerated or embarrassing: *a mawkish poem* ▶ **mawk·ish·ness** *noun* [U]

max /mæks/ *abbr., verb*
■ *abbr.* **1** (also **max.** especially in *AmE*) MAXIMUM: *max temperature 18°C* **2** at the most: (*informal*) *It'll cost £50 max.* **OPP** MIN.
■ *verb* **PHRV** ,**max 'out** (*AmE, informal*) to reach the limit at which nothing more is possible: *The car maxed out at 150 mph.*

maxim /'mæksɪm/ *noun* a well-known phrase that expresses sth that is usually true or that people think is a rule for sensible behaviour

max·imal /'mæksɪml/ *adj.* [usually before noun] (*technical*) as great or as large as possible: *It takes several weeks for the treatment to have maximal effect.*—compare MINIMAL

maxi·mize (*BrE* also **-ise**) /'mæksɪmaɪz/ *verb* [VN] **1** to increase sth as much as possible: *to maximize efficiency/fitness/profits* ◊ (*computing*) *Maximize the window to full screen.* **2** to make the best use of sth: *to maximize opportunities/resources* **OPP** MINIMIZE ▶ **maxi·miza·tion, -isa·tion** /ˌmæksɪmaɪ'zeɪʃn; *AmE* -mə'z-/ *noun* [U]

max·imum /'mæksɪməm/ *adj., noun*
■ *adj.* [only before noun] (*abbr.* **max**) as large, fast, etc. as is possible, or the most that is possible or allowed: *the maximum speed/temperature/volume* ◊ *For maximum effect do the exercises every day.* ◊ *a maximum security prison*—compare MINIMUM
■ *noun* [usually sing.] (*pl.* **max·ima** /'mæksɪmə/) (*abbr.* **max**) the greatest amount, size, speed, etc. that is possible, recorded or allowed: *a maximum of 30 children in a class* ◊ *The job will require you to use all your skills* **to the maximum.** ◊ *The July maximum* (= the highest temperature recorded in July) *was 30°C* ◊ *What is the absolute maximum you can afford to pay?*—compare MINIMUM

May /meɪ/ *noun* [U, C] the fifth month of the year, between April and June **HELP** To see how **May** is used, look at the examples at **April.**

may /meɪ/ *modal verb, noun*
■ *modal verb* (*negative* **may not**, *rare short form* **mayn't** /'meɪənt/, *pt* **might** /maɪt/, *negative* **might not**, *rare short*

M

form **mightn't** /'maɪtnt/) **1** used to say that sth is possible: *That may or may not be true.* ◊ *He may have* (= perhaps he has) *missed his train.* ◊ *They may well win.* ◊ *There is a range of programs on the market which may be described as design aids.* **2** used when admitting that sth is true before introducing another point, argument, etc: *He may be a good father but he's a terrible husband.* **3** (*formal*) used to ask for or give permission: *May I come in?* ◊ *You may come in if you wish.* ⇨ note at CAN¹ **4** (*formal, spoken*) used as a polite way of making a comment, asking a question, etc: *You look lovely, if I may say so.* ◊ *May I ask why you took that decision?* ◊ *If I may just add one thing …* **5** (*formal*) used to express wishes and hopes: *May she rest in peace.* ◊ *Business has been thriving in the past year. Long may it continue to do so.* **6** (*formal*) used to say what the purpose of sth is: *There is a need for more resources so that all children may have a decent education.* ⇨ note at MODAL **IDM be that as it 'may** (*formal*) in spite of that SYN NEVERTHELESS: *I know that he has tried hard; be that as it may, his work is just not good enough.*

■ *noun* [U] the white or pink flowers of the HAWTHORN

maybe /'meɪbi/ *adv.* **1** used when you are not certain that sth will happen or that sth is true or is a correct number: *Maybe he'll come, maybe he won't.* ◊ *'Are you going to sell your house?' 'Maybe.'* ◊ *It will cost two, maybe three hundred pounds.* ◊ *We go there maybe once or twice a month.* **2** used when making a suggestion: *I thought maybe we could go together.* ◊ *Maybe you should tell her.* **3** used to agree with sb, and to add more information that should be thought about: *'You should stop work when you have the baby.' 'Maybe, but I can't afford to.'* **4** used when replying to a question or an idea, when you are not sure whether to agree or disagree: *'I think he should resign.' 'Maybe.'*

'May Day *noun* [U, C] the first day of May, celebrated as a spring festival and, in some countries, as a holiday in honour of working people—compare LABOR DAY

May·day /'meɪdeɪ/ *noun* [sing.] an international radio signal used by ships and aircraft needing help when they are in danger ORIGIN From the French *venez m'aider* 'come and help me'.

may·fly /'meɪflaɪ/ *noun* (*pl.* **-ies**) a small insect that lives near water and only lives for a very short time

may·hem /'meɪhem/ *noun* [U] confusion and fear, usually caused by violent behaviour or by some sudden shocking event: *There was absolute mayhem when everyone tried to get out at once.*

may·on·naise /ˌmeɪə'neɪz; *AmE* 'meɪəneɪz/ (also *informal* **mayo** /'meɪəʊ; *AmE* 'meɪoʊ/) *noun* [U] a thick cold white sauce made from eggs, oil and VINEGAR, used to add flavour to sandwiches, salads, etc: *egg mayonnaise* (= a dish made with HARD-BOILED eggs and mayonnaise)

mayor /meə(r); *AmE* 'meɪər/ *noun* **1** (in England, Wales and N Ireland) the head of a town, BOROUGH or county council, chosen by other members of the council to represent them at official ceremonies, etc: *the Lord Mayor of London*—compare PROVOST **2** the head of the government of a town or city, etc., elected by the public: *the Mayor of New York* ◊ *Mayor Bob Anderson* ◊ *London has elected its new mayor.* ► **may·oral** /'meərəl; *AmE* 'meɪə-/ *adj.* [only before noun]: *mayoral robes/duties*

may·or·alty /'meərəlti; *AmE* 'meɪər-/ *noun* (*pl.* **-ies**) (*formal*) **1** the title or position of a mayor **2** the period of time during which a person is a mayor

may·or·ess /meə'res; *AmE* 'meɪərəs/ *noun* **1** (also ˌlady 'mayor) a woman who has been elected MAYOR ⇨ note at GENDER **2** (in England, Wales and N Ireland) the wife of a MAYOR or a woman who helps a MAYOR at official ceremonies

may·pole /'meɪpəʊl; *AmE* -poʊl/ *noun* a decorated pole that people dance round in ceremonies on MAY DAY

maze /meɪz/ *noun* **1** a system of paths separated by walls or HEDGES built in a park or garden, that is designed so that it is difficult to find your way through: *We got lost in the maze.* ◊ (*figurative*) *The building is a maze of corridors.*—compare LABYRINTH **2** [usually sing.] a large number of complicated rules or details that are difficult to understand: *a maze of regulations* **3** (*AmE*) a printed PUZZLE in which you have to draw a line that shows a way through a complicated pattern of lines

MB /ˌem 'bi:/ *abbr.* **1** /ˌem 'bi:/ (in Britain) Bachelor of Medicine (a university degree in medicine): *Philip Watt MB* **2** (also **Mb**) MEGABYTE: *24MB of memory*

MBA /ˌem bi: 'eɪ/ *noun* the abbreviation for 'Master of Business Administration' (a second university degree in business): *to do/have an MBA*

MBE /ˌem bi: 'i:/ *noun* the abbreviation for 'Member (of the Order) of the British Empire' (an award given to some people in Britain for a special achievement): *He was made an MBE in 1995.* ◊ *Tracey Edwards MBE*

MC /ˌem 'si:/ *noun* **1** the abbreviation for MASTER OF CEREMONIES **2** (**M.C.**) the abbreviation for Member of Congress

MCC /ˌem si: 'si:/ *abbr.* Marylebone Cricket Club (the organization which is responsible for English cricket)

McCoy /mə'kɔɪ/ *noun* IDM **the real Mc'Coy** (*informal*) something that is genuine and that has value, not a copy: *It's an American flying jacket, the real McCoy.*

MD /ˌem 'di:/ *noun* **1** the abbreviation for 'Doctor of Medicine': *Paul Clark MD* **2** the abbreviation for MANAGING DIRECTOR: *Where's the MD's office?*

ME /ˌem 'i:/ *noun, abbr.*

■ *noun* (*BrE*) (also ˌchronic fa'tigue syndrome *AmE, BrE*) *noun* [U] the abbreviation for MYALGIC ENCEPHALOMYELITIS (an illness that makes people feel extremely weak and tired and that can last a long time): *She's had ME for six months.*

■ *abbr.* (*AmE*) MEDICAL EXAMINER

me *pron., noun*

■ *pron.* /mi; *strong form* mi:/ the form of *I* that is used when the speaker or writer is the object of a verb or preposition: *Don't hit me.* ◊ *Excuse me!* ◊ *Give it to me.* ◊ *Hello, it's me.* ◊ *You're taller than me.* ◊ *'Who's there?' 'Only me.'* HELP The use of **me** in the last three examples is correct in modern standard English. **I** in these sentences would be considered much too formal for almost all contexts, especially in *BrE*.

■ *noun* (also **mi**) /mi:/ (*music*) the third note of a MAJOR scale

mea culpa /ˌmeɪə 'kʊlpə/ *exclamation* (from *Latin*, often *humorous*) used when you are admitting that sth is your fault

mead /mi:d/ *noun* [U] a sweet alcoholic drink made from HONEY and water, drunk especially in the past

meadow /'medəʊ; *AmE* -doʊ/ *noun* a field covered in grass, used especially for HAY: *water meadows* (= near a river)

meagre (*BrE*) (*AmE* **mea·ger**) /'mi:gə(r)/ *adj.* small in quantity and poor in quality: *a meagre diet of bread and water* ◊ *She supplements her meagre income by cleaning at night.*

meal /mi:l/ *noun* **1** [C] an occasion when people sit down to eat food, especially breakfast, lunch or dinner: *Try not to eat between meals.* ◊ *Lunch is his main meal of the day.* ◊ *What time would you like your evening meal?* ⇨ note on page 793 **2** [C] the food that is eaten at a meal: *Enjoy your meal.* ◊ *a three-course meal* **3** [U] (often in compounds) grain that has been crushed to produce a powder, used as food for animals and for making flour—see also BONEMEAL, OATMEAL, WHOLEMEAL **IDM make a 'meal of sth** (*informal*) to spend a lot of time, energy, etc. doing sth in a way that other people think is unnecessary and/or annoying: *Why do you have to make such a meal of everything?*—more at SQUARE *adj.*

ˌmeals on 'wheels *noun* [pl.] a service that takes meals to old or sick people in their homes

'meal ticket *noun* **1** (*informal*) a person or thing that you see only as a source of money and food: *He suspected that he was just a meal ticket for her.* **2** (*AmE*) a card or ticket that gives you the right to have a cheap or free meal, for example at school

meal·time /'mi:ltaɪm/ *noun* a time in the day when you eat a meal

mealy /'mi:li/ *adj.* (especially of vegetables or fruit) that feel soft and dry when you eat them

s	t	v	z	ʃ	ʒ	tʃ	dʒ	θ	ð	ŋ
see	tea	van	zoo	shoe	vision	chain	jam	thin	this	sing

MORE ABOUT
meals

People use the words **dinner**, **lunch**, **supper** and **tea** in different ways depending on which English-speaking country they come from. In Britain it may also depend on which part of the country or which social class a person comes from.

A meal eaten in the middle of the day is usually called **lunch**. If it is the main meal of the day it may also be called **dinner** in *BrE*, especially in the north of the country.

A main meal eaten in the evening is usually called **dinner**, especially if it is a formal meal. **Supper** is also an evening meal, but more informal than **dinner** and usually eaten at home. It can also be a late meal or something to eat and drink before going to bed.

In *BrE*, **tea** is a light meal in the afternoon with sandwiches, cakes, etc. and a cup of tea: *a cream tea*. It can also be a main meal eaten early in the evening, especially by children: *What time do the kids have their tea?*

As a general rule, if **dinner** is the word someone uses for the meal in the middle of the day, they probably call the meal in the evening **tea** or **supper**. If they call the meal in the middle of the day **lunch**, they probably call the meal in the evening **dinner**.

Brunch, a combination of breakfast and lunch, is becoming more common, especially as a meal you eat outside or one where your guests serve themselves.

,**mealy-'mouthed** *adj.* (*disapproving*) not willing or honest enough to speak in a direct or open way about what you really think: *mealy-mouthed politicians*

mean /miːn/ *verb, adj., noun*
■ *verb* (**meant**, **meant** /ment/)
‣ HAVE AS MEANING | **1** (not used in the progressive tenses) ~ **sth (to sb)** to have sth as a meaning SYN SIGNIFY: [VN] *What does this sentence mean?* ◇ *What is meant by 'batch processing'?* ◇ *Does the name 'David Berwick' mean anything to you* (= do you know who he is)? ◇ [V(**that**)] *The flashing light means (that) you must stop.*
‣ INTEND AS MEANING | **2** (not used in the progressive tenses) to intend to say sth on a particular occasion: [VN] *What did you mean by that remark?* ◇ *'Perhaps we should try another approach.' ' What do you mean?* (= I don't understand what you are suggesting.) *' What do you mean, you thought I wouldn't mind?* (= of course I mind and I am very angry.) ◇ *What she means is that there's no point in waiting here.* ◇ *I always found him a little strange, if you know what I mean* (= if you understand what I mean by 'strange'). ◇ *I know what you mean* (= I understand and feel sympathy). *I hated learning to drive too.* ◇ (*spoken*) *It was like—weird. Know what I mean?* ◇ *I see what you mean* (= I understand although I may not agree), *but I still think it's worth trying.* ◇ *See what I mean* (= I was right and this proves it, doesn't it?) *She never agrees to anything I suggest.* ◇ *'But Pete doesn't know we're here!' ' That's what I mean!* (= that's what I have been trying to tell you.) *' Do you mean Ann Smith or Mary Smith?* ◇ [V(**that**)] *Did he mean (that) he was dissatisfied with our service?* ◇ *You mean* (= are you telling me) *we have to start all over again?*
‣ HAVE AS PURPOSE | **3** ~ **sth (as sth)** | ~ **what ...** | ~ **sth for sb** to have sth as a purpose or intention SYN INTEND: [VN] *What did she mean by leaving so early* (= why did she do it)? ◇ *Don't be upset—I'm sure she meant it as a compliment.* ◇ *He means what he says* (= is not joking, exaggerating, etc.). ◇ *Don't laugh! I mean it* (= I am serious). ◇ *Don't be angry. I'm sure she meant it for the best* (= intended to be helpful). ◇ *He means trouble* (= to cause trouble). ◇ *The chair was clearly meant for a child.* ◇ [V**toinf**] *She means to succeed.* ◇ *I'm sorry I hurt you. I didn't mean to.* ◇ [VN**toinf**] *I didn't mean you to read the letter.* ◇ *I'm feeling very guilty—I've been meaning to call my parents for days, but still haven't got around to it.* ◇

You're meant to (= you are supposed to) *pay before you go in.* ◇ [V(**that**)] (*formal*) *I never meant (that) you should come alone.*
‣ INTEND SB TO BE/DO STH | **4** [often passive] ~ **sb for sth** | ~ **sb to be sth** to intend sb to be or do sth: [VN] *I was never meant for the army* (= did not have the qualities needed to become a soldier). ◇ *Philip and Kim were meant for each other* (= are very suitable as partners). ◇ [VN**toinf**] *His father meant him to be an engineer.* ◇ *She did everything to get the two of them together, but I guess it just wasn't meant to be.*
‣ HAVE AS RESULT | **5** to have sth as a result or a likely result SYN ENTAIL: [VN] *Spending too much now will mean a shortage of cash next year.* ◇ [VN**toinf**] *Do you have any idea what it means to be poor?* ◇ [V(**that**)] *We'll have to be careful with money but that doesn't mean (that) we can't enjoy ourselves.* ◇ [V-**ing**] *This new order will mean working overtime.* ◇ [VN-**ing**] *The injury could mean him missing next week's game.*
‣ BE IMPORTANT | **6** [VN] [no passive] ~ **sth to sb** to be of value or importance to sb: *Your friendship means a great deal to me.* ◇ *$20 means a lot* (= represents a lot of money) *when you live on $100 a week.* ◇ *Money means nothing to him.* ◇ *Her children mean the world to her.*
IDM **be meant to be sth** to be generally considered to be sth: *This restaurant is meant to be excellent.* **I mean** (*spoken*) used to explain or correct what you have just said: *It was so boring—I mean, nothing happened for the first hour!* ◇ *She's English—Scottish, I mean.* **mean 'business** (*informal*) to be serious in your intentions: *He has the look of a man who means business.* **mean (sb) no 'harm** | **not mean (sb) any 'harm** to not have any intention of hurting sb **mean to 'say** used to emphasize what you are saying or to ask sb if they really mean what they say: *I mean to say, you should have known how he would react!* ◇ *Do you mean to say you've lost it?* '**mean well** (usually *disapproving*) to have good intentions, although their effect may not be good
■ *adj.* (**mean·er**, **mean·est**)
‣ NOT GENEROUS | **1** (*BrE*) (*AmE* **cheap**) not willing to give or share things, especially money: *She's always been mean with money.* OPP GENEROUS—see also STINGY
‣ UNKIND | **2** ~ **(to sb)** (of people or their behaviour) unkind, for example by not letting sb have or do sth: *Don't be so mean to your little brother!*
‣ ANGRY/VIOLENT | **3** (*especially AmE*) likely to become angry or violent: *That's a mean-looking dog.*
‣ SKILFUL | **4** (*informal approving, especially AmE*) very good and skilful: *He's a mean tennis player.* ◇ *She plays a mean game of chess.*
‣ AVERAGE | **5** [only before noun] (*technical*) average; between the highest and the lowest, etc: *the mean temperature*
‣ INTELLIGENCE | **6** (*formal*) (of a person's understanding or ability) not very great: *This should be clear even to the meanest intelligence.*
‣ POOR | **7** (*literary*) poor and dirty in appearance: *mean houses/streets* **8** (*old-fashioned*) born into or coming from a low social class
IDM **be no mean ...** (*approving*) used to say that sb is very good at doing sth: *His mother was a painter, and he's no mean artist himself.*
■ *noun*—see also MEANS
‣ MIDDLE WAY | **1** ~ **(between A and B)** a quality, condition, or way of doing sth that is in the middle of two extremes and better than either of them: *He needed to find a mean between frankness and rudeness.*
‣ AVERAGE | **2** (also **arith,metic 'mean**) (*mathematics*) the value found by adding together all the numbers in a group, and dividing the total by the number of numbers **3** (also **geo'metric mean**) (*mathematics*) a value between two extreme values, found by adding them together and dividing the total by 2
IDM **the happy/golden 'mean** (*approving*) a course of action that is not extreme

me·ander /mi'ændə(r)/ *verb* [V] [usually +*adv.*/*prep.*]
1 (of a river, road, etc.) to curve a lot rather than being in

M

æ	ɑː	e	ɜː	ə	ɪ	iː	i	ɒ	ɔː	ʌ	ʊ	u	uː
cat	father	ten	bird	about	sit	see	many	got	saw	cup	put	actual	too

(BrE)

a straight line: *The stream meanders slowly down to the sea.* **2** to walk slowly and change direction often, especially without a particular aim: *They meandered around the old town admiring the architecture.* **3** (of a conversation, discussion, etc.) to develop slowly and change subject often, in a way that makes it boring or difficult to understand ▶ **me·ander** *noun*: *the meanders of a river*—picture at COAST

me·ander·ings /miˈændrɪŋz/ *noun* [pl.] **1** a course that does not follow a straight line: *the meanderings of a river/path* **2** walking or talking without any particular aim: *his philosophical meanderings*

meanie /ˈmiːni/ *noun* (*spoken*) used especially by children to describe an unkind person who will not give them what they want: *Don't be such a meanie!*

mean·ing /ˈmiːnɪŋ/ *noun, adj.*
■ *noun*
OF SOUND/WORD/SIGN | **1** ~ (of sth) [U, C] the thing or idea that a sound, word, sign, etc. represents: *What's the meaning of this word?* ◊ *Words often have several meanings.* ◊ *'Honesty'? He doesn't* **know the meaning of the word!**
OF WHAT SB SAYS/DOES | **2** [U, C] the things or ideas that sb wishes to communicate to you by what they say or do: *I don't quite* **get your meaning** (= understand what you mean to say). ◊ *What's the meaning of this? I explicitly told you not to leave the room.*
OF FEELING/EXPERIENCE | **3** the real importance of a feeling or experience: *With Anna she learned the meaning of love.*
OF BOOK/PAINTING | **4** [U, C] the ideas that a writer, artist, etc. wishes to communicate through a book, painting, etc: *several layers of meaning* ◊ *There are, of course, deeper meanings in the poem.*
SENSE OF PURPOSE | **5** [U] the quality or sense of purpose that makes you feel that your life is valuable: *Her life seemed to have lost all meaning.* ◊ *Having a child gave new meaning to their lives.*
■ *adj.* [usually before noun] (*rare*) = MEANINGFUL

mean·ing·ful /ˈmiːnɪŋfl/ *adj.* **1** serious and important: *a meaningful relationship/discussion/experience* **2** (also *less frequent* **mean·ing**) intended to communicate or express sth to sb, without any words being spoken: *She gave me a* **meaningful look.** **3** having a meaning that is easy to understand: *These statistics are not very meaningful.* ▶ **mean·ing·ful·ly** /-fəli/ *adv.* **mean·ing·ful·ness** *noun* [U]

mean·ing·less /ˈmiːnɪŋləs/ *adj.* **1** without any purpose or reason and therefore not worth doing or having: *a meaningless existence* ◊ *meaningless violence on TV* ◊ *We fill up our lives with meaningless tasks.* **2** not considered important: *Fines are meaningless to a huge company like that.* **3** not having a meaning that is easy to understand: *To me that painting is completely meaningless.* ▶ **mean·ing·less·ly** *adv.* **mean·ing·less·ness** *noun* [U]

means /miːnz/ *noun* (*pl.* **means**) **1** [C] ~ (of doing sth/sth) an action, an object or a system by which a result is achieved; a way of achieving or doing sth: *Television is an effective means of communication.* ◊ *Is there any means of contacting him?* ◊ *Have you any* **means of identification?** ◊ *We needed to get to London but we had no* **means of transport.** **2** [pl.] the money that a person has: *People should pay* **according to their means.** ◊ *He doesn't have the means to support a wife and child.* ◊ *Private school fees are* **beyond the means of most people** (= more than they can afford). ◊ *Are the monthly repayments* **within your means** (= can you afford them)? ◊ *Try to* **live within your means** (= not spend more money than you have). ◊ *a man* **of means** (= a rich man) **IDM** **by 'all means** (*spoken*) used to say that you are very willing for sb to have sth or do sth: *'Do you mind if I have a look?' 'By all means.'* **by means of sth** (*formal*) with the help of sth: *The load was lifted by means of a crane.* **by 'no means | not by 'any (manner of) means** not at all: *She is by no means an inexperienced teacher.* ◊ *We haven't won yet, not by any means.* **a ,means to an 'end** a thing or action that is not interesting or important in itself but is a way of achieving sth else: *He doesn't particularly like the work but he*

sees it as a means to an end.—more at END *n.*, FAIR *adj.*, WAY *n.*

'means test *noun* an official check of sb's wealth or income in order to decide if they are poor enough to receive money from the government for a particular purpose ▶ **'means-test** *verb* [VN]

'means-tested *adj.* paid to sb according to the results of a means test: *means-tested benefits*

meant *pt, pp* of MEAN

mean·time /ˈmiːntaɪm/ *noun, adv.*
■ *noun* **IDM** **in the 'meantime** in the period of time between two times or two events **SYN** MEANWHILE: *My first novel was rejected by six publishers. In the meantime I had written a play.*
■ *adv.* (*informal*) = MEANWHILE: *I'll contact them soon. Meantime don't tell them I'm back.*

mean·while /ˈmiːnwaɪl/ *adv., noun*
■ *adv.* (also *informal* **mean·time**) **1** while sth else is happening: *Bob spent fifteen months alone on his yacht. Ann, meanwhile, took care of the children on her own.* **2** in the period of time between two times or two events: *The doctor will see you again next week. Meanwhile, you must rest as much as possible.* **3** used to compare two aspects of a situation: *Stress can be extremely damaging to your health. Exercise, meanwhile, can reduce its effects.*
■ *noun* **IDM** **in the 'meanwhile** in the period of time between two times or two events: *I hope to go to medical school eventually. In the meanwhile, I am going to study chemistry.*

mea·sles /ˈmiːzlz/ *noun* [U] an infectious disease, especially of children, that causes fever and small red spots that cover the whole body—see also GERMAN MEASLES

measly /ˈmiːzli/ *adj.* (*informal, disapproving*) very small in size or quantity; not enough: *I get a measly £4 an hour.*

meas·ur·able /ˈmeʒərəbl/ *adj.* **1** that can be measured **2** [usually before noun] large enough to be noticed or to have a clear and noticeable effect: *measurable improvements* ▶ **meas·ur·ably** /-əbli/ *adv.*: *Working conditions have changed measurably in the last ten years.*

meas·ure /ˈmeʒə(r)/ *verb, noun*
■ *verb*
SIZE/QUANTITY | **1** ~ sb/sth (for sth) to find the size, quantity, etc. of sth in standard units: [VN] *A ship's speed is measured in knots.* ◊ *a device that measures the level of radiation in the atmosphere* ◊ *He's gone to be measured for a new suit.* ◊ *measuring equipment/instruments* ◊ [V wh-] *A dipstick is used to measure how much oil is left in an engine.* **2** linking verb [V-N] (not used in the progressive tenses) to be a particular size, length, amount, etc: *The main bedroom measures 12ft by 15ft.* ◊ *The pond measures about 2 metres across.*
JUDGE | **3** to judge the importance, value or effect of sth **SYN** ASSESS: [VN] *It is difficult to measure the success of the campaign at this stage.* [also V wh-]
PHRV **'measure sb/sth against sb/sth** to compare sb/sth with sb/sth: *The figures are not very good when measured against those of our competitors.* **,measure sth↔'out** to take the amount of sth that you need from a larger amount: *He measured out a cup of milk and added it to the mixture.* **,measure 'up | ,measure sb/sth↔'up** to measure sb/sth: *We spent the morning measuring up and deciding where the furniture would go.* **,measure 'up (to sth/sb)** (usually used in negative sentences and questions) to be as good, successful, etc. as expected or needed **SYN** MATCH UP: *Last year's intake just didn't measure up.* ◊ *The job failed to measure up to her expectations.*
■ *noun*
OFFICIAL ACTION | **1** [C] ~ (to do sth) an official action that is done in order to achieve a particular aim: *safety/security/austerity measures* ◊ *a temporary/an emergency measure* ◊ *We must take* **preventive measures** *to reduce crime in the area.* ◊ *The government is introducing tougher measures to combat crime.* ◊ *measures against racism* ◊ *Police in riot gear were in attendance as a* **precautionary measure.**—see also HALF MEASURES
AMOUNT | **2** [sing.] a particular amount of sth, especially a fairly large amount **SYN** DEGREE: *A measure of technical*

aɪ	aʊ	eɪ	ɔʊ	oʊ	ɔɪ	ɪə	eə	ʊə	j	w
my	now	say	go (BrE)	go (AmE)	boy	near	hair	pure	yes	wet

M

knowledge is desirable in this job. ◊ *She achieved some measure of success with her first book.*

WAY OF SHOWING/JUDGING | **3** [sing.] a sign of the size or the strength of sth: *Sending flowers is a measure of how much you care.* **4** [C] a way of judging or measuring sth: *an accurate measure of ability* ◊ *Is this test a good measure of reading comprehension?*

UNIT OF SIZE/QUANTITY | **5** [C, U] a unit used for stating the size, quantity or degree of sth; a system or a scale of these units: *weights and measures* ◊ *The Richter Scale is a measure of ground motion.* ◊ *liquid/dry measure* ◊ *Which measure of weight do pharmacists use?* **6** [C] (especially of alcohol) a standard quantity: *a generous measure of whisky*

INSTRUMENT FOR MEASURING | **7** [C] an instrument such as a stick, a long tape or a container that is marked with standard units and is used for measuring—see also TAPE MEASURE

IN MUSIC | **8** [C] (*AmE*) = BAR (9)

IDM **beyond 'measure** (*formal*) very much: *He irritated me beyond measure.* **for good 'measure** as an extra amount of sth in addition to what has already been done or given: *Use 50g of rice per person and an extra spoonful for good measure.* **full/short 'measure** the whole of sth or less of sth than you expect or should have: *We experienced the full measure of their hospitality.* ◊ *The concert only lasted an hour, so we felt we were getting short measure.* **in full 'measure** (*written*) to the greatest possible degree: *My expectations had been met in full measure.* **get/take/have the 'measure of sb | get/have/take sb's 'measure** (*formal*) to form an opinion about sb's character or abilities so that you can deal with them: *After only one game, the chess champion had the measure of his young opponent.* **in no small 'measure | in some, equal, etc. 'measure** (*formal*) to a large extent or degree; to some, etc. extent or degree: *The introduction of a new tax accounted in no small measure for the downfall of the government.* ◊ *Our thanks are due in equal measure to every member of the team.* **,made to 'measure** (*BrE*) made especially for one person according to particular measurements: *You'll need to get a suit made to measure.* ◊ *a made-to-measure suit*—more at LARGE

meas·ured /'meʒəd; *AmE* -ərd/ *adj.* [only before noun] slow and careful; controlled: *She replied in a measured tone to his threat.* ◊ *He walked down the corridor with measured steps.*

meas·ure·ment /'meʒəmənt; *AmE* 'meʒərm-/ *noun* **1** [U] the act or the process of finding the size, quantity or degree of sth: *the metric system of measurement* ◊ *Accurate measurement is very important in science.* **2** [C, usually pl.] the size, length or amount of sth: *to take sb's chest/waist measurement* ◊ *Do you know your measurements* (= the size of parts of your body)*?* ◊ *The exact measurements of the room are 3 metres 20 by 2 metres 84.* ➪ Appendix 3

'**measuring jug** (*BrE*), '**measuring cup** (*AmE*) *noun* a glass or plastic container for measuring liquids when cooking

'**measuring tape** *noun* = TAPE MEASURE

meat /miːt/ *noun* **1** [U, C] the flesh of an animal or a bird eaten as food; a particular type of this: *a piece/slice of meat* ◊ *horse meat* (= from a horse) ◊ *dog meat* (= for a dog) ◊ *meat-eating animals* ◊ *There's not much meat on this chop.* ◊ (*figurative, humorous*) *There's not much meat on her* (= she is very thin).—see also LUNCHEON MEAT, MINCE-MEAT, RED MEAT, SAUSAGE MEAT, WHITE MEAT **2** [U] ~ (of sth) the important or interesting part of sth: *This chapter contains the real meat of the writer's argument.* **IDM** ,**meat and 'drink to sb** something that sb enjoys very much: *Dealing with difficult customers is meat and drink to her.* ,**meat-and-po'tatoes** (*AmE*) dealing with or interested in the most basic and important aspects of sth: *a meat-and-potatoes argument* ◊ *a meat-and-potatoes man* (= a person who likes simple things)—more at DEAD

meat·ball /'miːtbɔːl/ *noun* a small ball of finely chopped meat, usually eaten hot with a sauce

'**meat grinder** *noun* (*AmE*) = MINCER

'**meat packing** *noun* [U] (*AmE*) the process of killing animals and preparing the meat for sale

meaty /'miːti/ *adj.* (**meat·ier**, **meati·est**) **1** containing a lot of meat: *meaty sausages* **2** smelling, or tasting like meat: *a meaty taste* **3** (*approving*) containing a lot of important or interesting ideas: *a meaty discussion* **4** (*informal*) large and fat; with a lot of flesh: *a meaty hand* ▶ *big, meaty tomatoes*

Mecca /'mekə/ *noun* **1** a city in Saudi Arabia that is the holiest city of Islam, being the place where the Prophet Muhammad was born **2** (usually **mecca**) a place that many people like to visit, especially for a particular reason: *The coast is a mecca for tourists.*

mech·an·ic /mə'kænɪk/ *noun* **1** a person whose job is repairing machines, especially the engines of motor vehicles: *a car mechanic* **2** (**mechanics**) [U] the science of movement and force—see also QUANTUM MECHANICS **3** (**mechanics**) [U] the practical study of machinery: *the school's car maintenance department where students learn basic mechanics* **4** (**the mechanics**) [pl.] the way sth works or is done: *The exact mechanics of how payment will be made will be decided later.*

mech·an·ic·al /mə'kænɪkl/ *adj.* **1** operated by power from an engine: *a mechanical device/toy/clock* ◊ *mechanical parts* **2** connected with machines and engines: *mechanical problems/defects* ◊ *The breakdown was due to a mechanical failure.* **3** (*disapproving*) (of people's behaviour and actions) done without thinking, like a machine: *a mechanical gesture/response* ◊ *My work has become mechanical—I could do it in my sleep.* **4** connected with the physical laws of movement and cause and effect (= with MECHANICS): *mechanical processes* **5** (of a person) good at understanding how machines work ▶ **mech·an·ic·al·ly** /-kli/ *adv.*: *a mechanically powered vehicle* ◊ *She spoke mechanically, as if thinking of something else.* ◊ *He's always been mechanically minded.*

me,chanical engi'neering *noun* [U] the study of how machines are designed, built and repaired ▶ **me,chanical engi'neer** *noun* [U]

mech·an·ism /'mekənɪzəm/ *noun* **1** a set of moving parts in a machine that performs a task: *a delicate watch mechanism* **2** a method or a system for achieving sth: *mechanisms for dealing with complaints from the general public*—see also ERM **3** a system of parts in a living thing that together perform a particular function: *the balance mechanism in the ears* ◊ *Pain acts as a natural defence mechanism.*

mech·an·is·tic /,mekə'nɪstɪk/ *adj.* (often *disapproving*) connected with the belief that all things in the universe can be explained as if they were machines; based on this belief: *the mechanistic philosophy that compares the brain to a computer* ▶ **mech·an·is·ti·cal·ly** /,mekə'nɪstɪkli/ *adv.*

mech·an·ize (*BrE* also **-ise**) /'mekənaɪz/ *verb* [VN] [usually passive] to change a process, so that the work is done by machines rather than people: *The production process is now highly mechanized.* ▶ **mech·an·iza·tion**, **-isa·tion** /,mekənaɪ'zeɪʃn; *AmE* -nə'z-/ *noun* [U]: *the increasing mechanization of farm work*

Med /med/ (**the Med**) *noun* [sing.] (*informal*) the Mediterranean Sea

med /med/ *adj.* (*informal, especially AmE*) = MEDICAL: *a med student* ◊ *She's in med school.*

medal /'medl/ *noun* a flat piece of metal, usually shaped like a coin, that is given to the winner of a competition or to sb who has been brave, for example in war: *to win a gold medal in the Olympics* ◊ *to award a medal for bravery* **IDM** SEE DESERVE

med·al·lion /mə'dæliən/ *noun* a piece of jewellery in the shape of a large flat coin worn on a chain around the neck—picture at JEWELLERY

med·al·list (*BrE*) (*AmE* **med·al·ist**) /'medəlɪst/ *noun* a person who has received a medal, usually for winning a competition in a sport: *an Olympic medallist* ◊ *a gold/silver/bronze medallist*

M

b	d	f	g	h	k	l	m	n	p	r
bad	did	fall	get	hat	cat	leg	man	now	pen	red

,**Medal of 'Freedom** *noun* the highest award that the US gives to a CIVILIAN who has achieved sth very important

,**Medal of 'Honor** *noun* the highest award that the US gives to a member of the armed forces who has shown very great courage in a war

med·dle /'medl/ *verb* [V] (*disapproving*) **1 ~ (in/with sth)** (*disapproving*) to become involved in sth that does not concern you: *He had no right to meddle in her affairs.* **2 ~ (with sth)** to touch sth in a careless way, especially when it is not yours or when you do not know how to use it correctly: *Somebody had been meddling with her computer.* ▶ **med·dling** *noun* [U]

med·dler /'medlə(r)/ *noun* (*disapproving*) a person who tries to get involved in sth that does not concern them [SYN] BUSYBODY

meddle·some /'medlsəm/ *adj.* (*written, disapproving*) (of people) enjoying getting involved in situations that do not concern them: *meddlesome politicians*

media /'miːdiə/ *noun* **1 (the media)** [sing.+ sing./pl. *v.*] the main ways that large numbers of people receive information and entertainment, that is television, radio and the newspapers: *the news/broadcasting/national media* ◇ *The trial was fully reported in the media.* ◇ *The media was/were accused of influencing the final decision.* ◇ *Any event attended by the actor received widespread media coverage.*—see also MASS MEDIA **2** *pl.* of MEDIUM

medi·aeval *adj.* = MEDIEVAL

me·dian /'miːdiən/ *adj., noun*
■ *adj.* [only before noun] (*technical*) **1** having a value in the middle of a series of values: *the median age/price* **2** situated in or passing through the middle: *a median point/line*
■ *noun* **1** (*mathematics*) the middle value of a series of numbers arranged in order of size **2** (*geometry*) a straight line passing from a point of a triangle to the centre of the opposite side. **3** (also **'median strip**) (both *AmE*) = CENTRAL RESERVATION

'**media studies** *noun* [U, pl.] the study of newspapers, television, radio, etc.

me·di·ate /'miːdieɪt/ *verb* **1 ~ (in sth)| ~ (between A and B)** to try to end a disagreement between two or more people or groups by talking to them and trying to find things that everyone can agree on: [V] *The Secretary-General was asked to mediate in the dispute.* ◇ *An independent body was brought in to mediate between staff and management.* ◇ [VN] *to mediate differences/disputes/problems* **2** [VN] to succeed in finding a solution to a disagreement between people or groups: *They mediated a settlement.* **3** [VN] [usually passive] (*formal* or *technical*) to influence sth and/or make it possible for it to happen: *Educational success is mediated by economic factors.* ▶ **me·di·ation** /ˌmiːdiˈeɪʃn/ *noun* [U]

me·di·ator /'miːdieɪtə(r)/ *noun* a person or an organization that tries to get agreement between people or groups who disagree with each other

medic /'medɪk/ *noun* **1** (*BrE, informal*) a medical student **2** (*informal*) a doctor **3** (*AmE*) a person in the armed forces who can give medical treatment

Me·dic·aid /'medɪkeɪd/ *noun* [U] (in the US) the system that provides medical care for poor people and that is paid for by taxes

med·ic·al /'medɪkl/ *adj., noun*
■ *adj.* [usually before noun] **1** connected with illness and injury and their treatment: *medical advances/care/research* ◇ *her medical condition/history/records* ◇ *the medical profession* ◇ *a medical student/school* ◇ *a medical certificate* (= a statement by a doctor that gives details of your state of health)—see also MED **2** connected with ways of treating illness that do not involve cutting the body: *medical or surgical treatment* ▶ **med·ic·al·ly** /-kli/ *adv.*: *medically fit/unfit*
■ *noun* (also ,**medical exami'nation**) (*informal*) a thorough examination of your body that a doctor does, for example, before you start a particular job

,**medical e'xaminer** *noun* (*abbr.* ME) (*AmE*) a doctor whose job is to examine a dead body in order to find out the cause of death—compare PATHOLOGIST

'**medical officer** *noun* (*abbr.* MO) a person, usually a doctor, employed in an organization to deal with medical and health matters

Medi·care /'medɪkeə(r); *AmE* -ker/ *noun* [U] (in the US) the system that provides medical care for old people and that is paid for by taxes

medi·cated /'medɪkeɪtɪd/ *adj.* containing a substance for preventing or curing infections of your skin or hair: *medicated shampoo/soap*

medi·ca·tion /ˌmedɪˈkeɪʃn/ *noun* [U, C] a drug or another form of medicine that you take to prevent or to treat an illness: *to be on medication* ◇ *Are you currently taking any medication?* ◇ *Many flu medications are available without a prescription.*

me·di·cin·al /məˈdɪsɪnl/ *adj.* helpful in the process of healing illness or infection: *medicinal herbs/plants* ◇ *medicinal properties/use* ◇ (*humorous*) *He claims he keeps a bottle of brandy only for medicinal purposes.*

medi·cine /'medsn; -dɪsn/ *noun* **1** [U] the study and treatment of diseases and injuries: *advances in modern medicine* ◇ *to study/practise medicine* ◇ *traditional/conventional/orthodox medicine* ◇ *alternative medicine* **2** [U, C] a substance, especially a liquid that you drink or swallow in order to cure an illness: *Did you take your medicine?* ◇ *cough medicine* ◇ *Chinese herbal medicines*—picture on page 599 [IDM] **the best 'medicine** the best way of improving a situation, especially of making you feel happier: *Laughter is the best medicine.* **a taste/dose of your own 'medicine** the same bad treatment that you have given to others: *Let the bully have a taste of his own medicine.*

'**medicine man** *noun* a person who is believed to have special magic powers of healing, especially among Native Americans—compare WITCH DOCTOR

med·ico /'medɪkəʊ; *AmE* -koʊ/ *noun* (*pl.* **-os**) (*informal*) a doctor

medi·eval (also **medi·aeval**) /ˌmediˈiːvl; *AmE* also ˌmiːd-/ *adj.* [usually before noun] connected with the Middle Ages (about AD 1000 to AD 1450): *medieval architecture/castles/manuscripts* ◇ *the literature of the late medieval period*

me·di·ocre /ˌmiːdiˈəʊkə(r); *AmE* -ˈoʊkər/ *adj.* (*disapproving*) not very good; of only average standard: *a mediocre musician/talent/performance* ◇ *I thought the play was only mediocre.*

me·di·oc·rity /ˌmiːdiˈɒkrəti; *AmE* -ˈɑːk-/ *noun* (*pl.* **-ies**) (*disapproving*) **1** [U] the quality of being average or not very good: *His acting career started brilliantly, then sank into mediocrity.* **2** [C] a person who is not very good at sth: *a brilliant leader, surrounded by mediocrities*

medi·tate /'medɪteɪt/ *verb* **1** [V] **~ (on/upon sth)** to think deeply, usually in silence, especially for religious reasons or in order to make your mind calm **2** [VN] (*written*) to plan sth in your mind; to consider doing sth: *They were meditating revenge.*

medi·ta·tion /ˌmedɪˈteɪʃn/ *noun* **1** [U] the practice of thinking deeply in silence, especially for religious reasons or in order to make your mind calm: *She found peace through yoga and meditation.* ◇ *He was deep in meditation and didn't see me come in.* **2** [C, usually pl.] **~ (on sth)** (*formal*) serious thoughts on a particular subject that sb writes down or speaks: *his meditations on life and art*

medi·ta·tive /'medɪtətɪv; *AmE* -teɪt-/ *adj.* (*formal*) thinking very deeply; involving deep thought: *She found him in a meditative mood.* ◇ *a meditative poem*

Medi·ter·ra·nean /ˌmedɪtəˈreɪniən/ *adj.* [only before noun] connected with the Mediterranean Sea or the countries and regions that surround it; typical of this area: *a Mediterranean country* ◇ *a Mediterranean climate*

me·dium /'miːdiəm/ *adj., noun*
■ *adj.* [usually before noun] (*abbr.* M) in the middle between two sizes, amounts, lengths, temperatures, etc. [SYN] AVERAGE: *a medium size car/business/town* ◇ *a man of medium height/build* ◇ *There are three sizes—small, medium and large.* ◇ *Cook over a medium heat for 15*

s	t	v	z	ʃ	ʒ	tʃ	dʒ	θ	ð	ŋ
see	tea	van	zoo	shoe	vision	chain	jam	thin	this	sing

minutes. ◇ a **medium dry white wine** ◇ Choose **medium to large** tomatoes. **IDM** see TERM
■ noun (pl. **media** /ˈmiːdiə/ or **me·diums**) **1** a way of communicating information, etc. to people: the medium of radio/television ◇ electronic/audio-visual media ◇ Television is the modern medium of communication. ◇ A T-shirt can be an excellent medium for getting your message across. **HELP** The plural in this meaning is usually **media.**—see also MEDIA, MASS MEDIA **2** something that is used for a particular purpose: English is the **medium of instruction** (= the language used to teach other subjects). ◇ Video is a good medium for practising listening to a foreign language. **3** the material or the form that an artist, a writer or a musician uses: the medium of paint/poetry/drama ◇ Watercolour is his favourite medium. **4** (biology) a substance that sth exists or grows in or that it travels through: The bacteria were growing in a sugar medium. **5** (pl. **me·diums**) a person who claims to be able to communicate with the spirits of dead people **IDM** see HAPPY

ˈmedium-sized adj. of average size: a medium-sized saucepan

ˈmedium-term adj. used to describe a period of time that is a few weeks or months into the future: the government's medium-term financial strategy

ˈmedium wave (abbr. **MW**) noun [U] (also **the medium wave** [sing.]) a band of radio waves with a length of between 100 and 1000 metres: 648 m on (the) medium wave—compare SHORT WAVE

med·ley /ˈmedli/ noun **1** a piece of music consisting of several songs or tunes played or sung one after the other: a medley of Beatles hits **2** a mixture of people or things of different kinds: a medley of flavours/smells **3** a swimming race in which each member of a team uses a different stroke: the 4×100 metres medley

meek /miːk/ adj. (**meek·er**, **meek·est**) **1** quiet, gentle, and always ready to do what other people want without expressing your own opinion: They called her Miss Mouse because she was so **meek and mild**. **2** (**the meek**) noun [pl.] people who are meek ▶ **meek·ly** adv.: He meekly did as he was told. **meek·ness** noun [U]

meet /miːt/ verb, noun
■ verb (**met**, **met** /met/)
BY CHANCE | **1** [no passive] to be in the same place as sb by chance and talk to them: [V] I hope we'll meet again soon. ◇ [VN] Did you meet anyone in town?

BY ARRANGEMENT | **2** [no passive] to come together formally in order to discuss sth: [V] The committee meets on Fridays. ◇ [VN] The Prime Minister met other European leaders for talks. **3** [no passive] to come together socially after you have arranged it: [V] Let's meet for a drink after work. ◇ [VN] We're meeting them outside the theatre at 7. **4** [VN] to go to a place and wait there for a particular person to arrive: Will you meet me at the airport? ◇ The hotel bus meets all incoming flights.

FOR THE FIRST TIME | **5** [no passive] to see and know sb for the first time; to be introduced to sb: [VN] Where did you first meet your husband? ◇ (especially BrE) **Pleased to meet you.** ◇ (AmE) **Nice meeting you.** ◇ There's someone I want you to meet. ◇ [V] I don't think we've met.

IN CONTEST | **6** [no passive] to play, fight, etc. together as opponents in a competition: [V, VN] Sampras and Agassi met in last year's final. ◇ Sampras met Agassi in last year's final.

EXPERIENCE STH | **7** [VN] to experience sth, often sth unpleasant **SYN** COME ACROSS, ENCOUNTER: Others have met similar problems. ◇ How she **met her death** will probably never be known.

TOUCH/JOIN | **8** to touch sth; to join: [V] The curtains don't meet in the middle. ◇ [VN] That's where the river meets the sea. ◇ His hand met hers.

SATISFY | **9** [VN] to do or satisfy what is needed or what sb asks for: How can we best **meet the needs** of all the different groups? ◇ Until these **conditions are met** we cannot proceed with the sale. ◇ I can't possibly meet that deadline.

PAY | **10** [VN] to pay sth: The cost will be met by the company.

IDM **meet sb's ˈeye(s)** **1** (also **meet sb's ˈgaze, ˈlook,** etc.; **people's ˈeyes meet**) if you meet sb's eye(s), you look directly at them as they look at you; if two people's eyes meet, they look directly at each other: She was afraid to meet my eye. ◇ Their eyes met across the crowded room. ◇ She met his gaze without flinching. **2** if a sight meets your eyes, you see it: A terrible sight met their eyes. **meet sb halfˈway** to reach an agreement with sb by giving them part of what they want: If he was prepared to apologize, the least she could do was meet him halfway and accept some of the blame. **meet your ˈMaker** (especially humorous) to die **there is more to sb/sth than meets the ˈeye** a person or thing is more complicated or interesting than you might think at first—more at END n., MATCH n., TWAIN

PHRV **ˌmeet ˈup (with sb)** to meet sb, especially by arrangement: They met up again later for a drink. **ˈmeet with sb** (especially AmE) to meet sb, especially for discussions: The President met with senior White House aides. **ˈmeet with sth** (written) **1** to be received or treated by sb in a particular way: Her proposal met with resistance from the Left. ◇ to meet with success/failure **2** to experience sth unpleasant: She was worried that he might have met with an accident. **ˈmeet sth with sth** to react to sth in a particular way: His suggestion was met with howls of protest.
■ noun **1** (especially AmE) a sports competition: a track meet **2** (BrE) an event at which horse riders and dogs hunt FOXES

meet·ing /ˈmiːtɪŋ/ noun **1** [C] an occasion when people come together to discuss or decide sth: to have/hold/call/attend a meeting ◇ a committee/staff meeting ◇ What time is the meeting? ◇ Helen will **chair the meeting** (= be in charge of it). ◇ I'll be **in a meeting** all morning—can you take my calls? ◇ a meeting of the United Nations Security Council **2** (the meeting) [sing.] the people at a meeting: The meeting voted to accept the pay offer. **3** [C] a situation in which two or more people meet together, because they have arranged it or by chance: At our first meeting I was nervous. ◇ It was a **chance meeting** that would change my life. ◇ He remembered their childhood meetings with nostalgia. **4** [C] a sports event or set of races, especially for horses: an athletics meeting **IDM** a **meeting of ˈminds** a close understanding between people with similar minds, especially when they meet to do sth or meet for the first time

ˈmeeting house noun a place where Quakers meet for worship

ˈmeeting place noun a place where people often meet: The cafe is a popular meeting place for students.

mega /ˈmegə/ adj. [usually before noun] (slang) very large or impressive: The song was a mega hit last year. ▶ **mega** adv.: They're mega rich.

mega- /ˈmegə-/ combining form (in nouns) **1** (especially informal) very large or great: a megastore **2** (in units of measurement) one million: a megawatt **3** (computing) 1048576 (= 2²⁰): megabyte

mega·bucks /ˈmegəbʌks/ noun [pl.] (informal) a very large amount of money: He earns megabucks.

mega·byte /ˈmegəbaɪt/ noun (abbr. **MB**) a unit of computer memory, equal to 2²⁰ (or about 1 million) BYTES: a 40-megabyte hard disk

mega·hertz /ˈmegəhɜːts/ AmE -hɜːrts/ noun (pl. **mega·hertz**) (abbr. **MHz**) a unit for measuring radio waves; 1000000 HERTZ

mega·lith /ˈmegəlɪθ/ noun a very large stone, especially one put in a place that was used for ceremonies in ancient times ▶ **mega·lith·ic** /ˌmegəˈlɪθɪk/: megalithic monuments

meg·alo·mania /ˌmegələˈmeɪniə/ noun [U] a mental illness or condition in which sb has an exaggerated belief in their own importance or power

meg·alo·maniac /ˌmegələˈmeɪniæk/ noun a person suffering from megalomania ▶ **meg·alo·maniac** adj.

M

æ	ɑː	e	ɜː	ə	ɪ	iː	i	ɒ	ɔː	ʌ	ʊ	u	uː
cat	father	ten	bird	about	sit	see	many	got	saw	cup	put	actual	too

(BrE)

mega·phone /'megəfəʊn; *AmE* -foʊn/ *noun* a device for making your voice sound louder, that is wider at one end, like a CONE, and is often used at outside events—compare LOUD-HAILER

megaphone

mega·star /'megəstɑː(r)/ *noun* (*informal*) a very famous singer, actor or entertainer

mega·ton (also **mega·tonne**) /'megətʌn/ *noun* a unit for measuring the power of an explosive, equal to one million TONS of TNT: *a one megaton nuclear bomb*

mega·watt /'megəwɒt; *AmE* -wɑːt/ *noun* (*abbr.* **MW**) a unit for measuring electrical power; one million WATTS

mela·mine /'meləmiːn/ *noun* [U] a hard plastic material, used especially for covering other materials

mel·an·cho·lia /ˌmelən'kəʊliə; *AmE* -'koʊ-/ *noun* (*old-fashioned*) a mental illness in which the patient is depressed and worried by unnecessary fears

mel·an·chol·ic /ˌmelən'kɒlɪk; *AmE* -'kɑːl-/ *adj.* (*old-fashioned* or *literary*) feeling or expressing sadness, especially when the sadness is like an illness

mel·an·choly /'melənkəli; -kɒli; *AmE* -kɑːli/ *noun, adj.*
■ *noun* [U] (*formal*) a deep feeling of sadness that lasts for a long time and often cannot be explained: *A mood of melancholy descended on us.*
■ *adj.* very sad or making you feel sadness: *melancholy thoughts/memories* ◊ *The melancholy song died away.*

mel·anin /'melənɪn/ *noun* [U] (*technical*) a dark substance in the skin and hair that causes the skin to change colour in the sun's light

mela·noma /ˌmelə'nəʊmə; *AmE* -'noʊmə/ *noun* [C,U] (*medical*) a type of CANCER that appears as a dark spot or TUMOUR on the skin

meld /meld/ *verb* (*formal*) to combine with sth else; to make sth combine with sth else: [V] *The restored stonework melds beautifully with the original architecture.* [also VN]

melee /'meleɪ; *AmE* 'meɪleɪ/ *noun* [sing.] (from *French*) a situation in which a crowd of people are rushing or pushing each other in a confused way: *Several people were hurt in the melee.*

mel·lif·lu·ous /me'lɪfluəs/ *adj.* (*formal*) (of music or of sb's voice) sounding sweet and smooth; very pleasant to listen to

mel·low /'meləʊ; *AmE* -loʊ/ *adj., verb*
■ *adj.* (**mel·low·er, mel·low·est**) **1** (of colour or sound) soft, rich and pleasant: *mellow autumn colours* ◊ *Mellow music and lighting helped to create the right atmosphere.* **2** (of a taste or flavour) smooth and pleasant: *a mellow, fruity wine* **3** (of people) calm, gentle and reasonable because of age or experience: *Dad's certainly grown mellower with age.* **4** (*informal*) (of people) relaxed, calm and happy, especially after drinking alcohol: *After two glasses of wine, I was feeling mellow.*
■ *verb* **1** to become or make sb become less extreme in their attitudes, behaviour, etc., especially as a result of growing older: [V] *She had mellowed a great deal since their days at college.* ◊ [VN] *A period spent working abroad had done nothing to mellow him.* **2** [V, VN] to become, or make a colour become less bright, especially over a period of time **3** [V, VN] to develop or make wine develop a pleasant and less bitter taste over a period of time **PHRV** ˌmellow 'out (*informal, especially AmE*) to enjoy yourself by relaxing and not doing much: *We just listened to music and mellowed out all afternoon.*

me·lod·ic /mə'lɒdɪk; *AmE* -'lɑːd-/ *adj.* **1** [only before noun] connected with the main tune in a piece of music: *The melodic line is carried by the two clarinets.* **2** = MELODIOUS

me·lo·di·ous /mə'ləʊdiəs; *AmE* -'loʊ-/ (also **me·lod·ic**) *adj.* pleasant to listen to, like music: *a rich melodious voice* ▶ **me·lo·di·ous·ly** *adv.*

melo·drama /'melədrɑːmə/ *noun* [U,C] **1** a story, play or novel that is full of exciting events and in which the characters and emotions seem too exaggerated to be real; the action in such a play, etc: *a gripping Victorian melodrama* ◊ *Instead of tragedy, we got melodrama.* **2** events, behaviour, etc. which are exaggerated or extreme: *Her love of melodrama meant that any small problem became a crisis.*

melo·dra·mat·ic /ˌmelədrə'mætɪk/ *adj.* (often *disapproving*) full of exciting and extreme emotions or events; behaving or reacting to sth in an exaggerated way: *a melodramatic plot full of deceit and murder* ▶ **melo·dra·mat·ic·al·ly** /-kli/ *adv.*

mel·ody /'melədi/ *noun* (*pl.* **-ies**) **1** [C] a tune, especially the main tune in a piece of music written for several instruments or voices: *a haunting melody* ◊ *The melody is then taken up by the flutes.* **2** [C] a piece of music or a song with a clear or simple tune: *old Irish melodies* **3** [U] the arrangement of musical notes in a tune: *a few bars of melody drifted towards us*

melon /'melən/ *noun* [C,U] a large fruit with hard green, yellow or orange skin, sweet flesh and juice and a lot of seeds: *a slice of melon*—see also HONEYDEW MELON, WATERMELON

melt /melt/ *verb* **1** to become or make sth become liquid as a result of heating: [V] *The snow showed no sign of melting.* ◊ *melting ice* ◊ [VN] *The sun had melted the snow.* ◊ *First, melt two ounces of butter.*—compare DEFROST, DE-ICE **2** to become or to make a feeling, an emotion, etc. become gentler and less strong: [V] *The tension in the room began to melt.* ◊ [VN] *Her trusting smile melted his heart.* **IDM** ˌmelt in your 'mouth (of food) to be soft and very good to eat: *They serve steaks that just melt in your mouth.*—more at BUTTER *n.* **PHRV** ˌmelt a'way| ˌmelt sth↔a'way to disappear or make sth disappear gradually: *At the first sign of trouble, the supporters melted away.* ˌmelt sth↔'down to heat a metal or WAX object until it is liquid, especially so that the metal or wax can be used to make sth else—related noun MELTDOWN 'melt into sth to gradually become part of sth and therefore become difficult to see

melt·down /'meltdaʊn/ *noun* [U,C] a serious accident in which the central part of a nuclear REACTOR melts, causing harmful RADIATION to escape: (*figurative*) *meltdown on the New York Stock Exchange*

melt·ing /'meltɪŋ/ *adj.* [usually before noun] persuading you to feel love, pity or sympathy: *his melting eyes*

'melting point *noun* [U,C] the temperature at which a substance will melt

'melting pot *noun* [usually sing.] a place or situation in which large numbers of people, ideas, etc. are mixed together: *the vast melting pot of American society* **IDM in the 'melting pot** (*especially BrE*) likely to change; in the process of changing

mem·ber /'membə(r)/ *noun* **1** ~ (of sth) a person, an animal or a plant that belongs to a particular group: *a member of staff/society/the family* ◊ *characteristics common to all members of the species* **2** ~ (of sth) a person, a country or an organization that has joined a particular group, club or team: *party/union members* ◊ *a meeting of member countries/states* ◊ *How much does it cost to become a member?* ◊ *an active member of the local church* **3** (*old use* or *literary*) a part of the body, especially an arm or a leg **4** a PENIS. People say 'member' to avoid saying 'PENIS'. **5** (**Member**) (in Britain) a Member of Parliament: *the Hon. Member for Brent North*—see also PRIVATE MEMBER

ˌMember of 'Parliament = MP

mem·ber·ship /'membəʃɪp; *AmE* -bərʃ-/ *noun* **1** [U] (*BrE*) ~ (of sth)| (*AmE*) ~ (in sth) the state of being a member of a group, a club, an organization, etc: *Who is eligible to apply for membership of the association?* ◊ *a membership card/fee* **2** [C+sing./pl. *v.*] the members, or the number of members, of a group, a club, an organization, etc: *The membership has/have not yet voted.* ◊ *The club has a membership of more than 500.*

mem·brane /'membreɪn/ *noun* [C,U] **1** a thin layer of skin that connects or covers parts inside the body—see

M

also MUCOUS MEMBRANE **2** a thin layer of tissue that covers cells in a plant **3** a thin layer of material used to prevent air, liquid, etc. from entering a particular part of sth: *a waterproof membrane* ▶ **mem·bran·ous** /ˈmembrənəs/ *adj.*

me·men·to /məˈmentəʊ; *AmE* -toʊ/ *noun* (*pl.* **-oes** or **-os**) a thing that you keep or give to sb to remind you or them of a person or place: *a memento of our trip to Italy*

memo /ˈmeməʊ; *AmE* -moʊ/ (*also formal* **memo·ran·dum**) *noun* (*pl.* **-os**) **~** (**to sb**) an official note from one person to another in the same organization: *to write/send/circulate a memo* ⇨ Study page B13

mem·oir /ˈmemwɑː(r)/ *noun* **1** (**memoirs**) [pl.] an account written by sb, especially sb famous, about their life and experiences: *The retired actress is writing her memoirs.* **2** [C] (*formal*) a written account of sb's life, a place, or an event, written by sb who knows it well

mem·ora·bilia /ˌmemərəˈbɪliə/ *noun* [pl.] things that people collect because they once belonged to a famous person, or because they are connected with a particular interesting place, event or activity: *football/Beatles memorabilia*

mem·or·able /ˈmemərəbl/ *adj.* **~** (**for sth**) special, good or unusual and therefore worth remembering or easy to remember: *a truly memorable occasion* ▶ **mem·or·ably** /-əbli/ *adv.*

memo·ran·dum /ˌmeməˈrændəm/ *noun* (*pl.* **memo·randa** /ˌmeməˈrændə/) **1** (*formal*) = MEMO: *an internal memorandum* **2** (*law*) a record of a legal agreement which has not yet been formally prepared and signed **3** a proposal or report on a particular subject for a person, an organization, a committee, etc: *a detailed memorandum to the commission on employment policy*

me·mor·ial /məˈmɔːriəl/ *noun, adj.*
▪ *noun* **~** (**to sb/sth**) **1** [C] a statue, stone, etc. that is built in order to remind people of an important past event or of a famous person who has died: *a war memorial* (= in memory of soldiers who died in a war) ◊ *a memorial to victims of the Holocaust* **2** [sing.] a thing that will continue to remind people of sb/sth: *The painting will be a lasting memorial to a remarkable woman.*
▪ *adj.* [only before noun] created or done in order to remember sb who has died: *a memorial statue/plaque/prize* ◊ *The memorial service will be held at a local church.* ◊ *the John F Kennedy Memorial Hospital*

Me·morial Day *noun* [U, C] a holiday in the US, usually the last Monday in May, in honour of members of the armed forces who have died in war—see also REMEMBRANCE SUNDAY, VETERANS DAY

me·mor·ial·ize (*BrE also* **-ise**) /məˈmɔːriəlaɪz/ *verb* (*formal*) [VN] to produce sth that will continue to exist and remind people of sb who has died or sth that has gone

me·mor·iam /məˈmɔːriəm/ ⇨ IN MEMORIAM

mem·or·ize (*BrE also* **-ise**) /ˈmeməraɪz/ *verb* [VN] to learn sth carefully so that you can remember it exactly: *to memorize a poem*

mem·ory /ˈmeməri/ (*pl.* **-ies**) *noun*
ABILITY TO REMEMBER **1** [C, U] **~** (**for sth**) your ability to remember things: *I have a bad memory for names.* ◊ *People have short memories* (= they soon forget). ◊ *He had a long memory for people who had disappointed him.* ◊ *She can recite the whole poem from memory.* ◊ *He suffered loss of memory for weeks after the accident.* ◊ *Are you sure? Memory can play tricks on you.* **2** [U] the period of time that sb is able to remember events: *There hasn't been peace in the country in/within my memory.* ◊ *It was the worst storm in recent memory.* ◊ *This hasn't happened in living memory* (= nobody alive now can remember it happening).
STH YOU REMEMBER **3** [C] a thought of sth that you remember from the past: *childhood memories* ◊ *I have vivid memories of my grandparents.* ◊ *What is your earliest memory?* ◊ *The photos bring back lots of good memories.* **4** [U] (*formal*) what is remembered about sb after they have died: *Her memory lives on* (= we still remember her).
COMPUTING **5** [C, U] the part of a computer where information is stored; the amount of space in a computer for storing information: *a computer with 8 megabytes of memory*—see also RAM

IDM **if (my) memory serves me well, correctly, etc.** if I remember correctly **in memory of sb** | **to the memory of sb** intended to show respect and remind people of sb who has died: *He founded the charity in memory of his late wife.*—more at ETCH, JOG *v.*, REFRESH, SIEVE *n.*

memory 'lane *noun* [U] **IDM** **a trip/walk down ˌmemory 'lane** time that you spend thinking about and remembering the past or going to a place again in order to remind yourself of past experiences

men *pl.* of MAN

men·ace /ˈmenəs/ *noun, verb*
▪ *noun* **1** [C, usually sing.] **~** (**to sb/sth**) a person or thing that will probably cause serious damage, harm or danger **SYN** THREAT: *a new initiative aimed at beating the menace of illegal drugs* **2** [U] an atmosphere that makes you feel threatened or frightened: *a sense/an air/a hint of menace in his voice* **3** [C, usually sing.] (*informal*) a person or thing that is annoying or causes trouble **SYN** NUISANCE: *Slugs can be a menace in the greenhouse in winter.* **4** (**menaces**) [pl.] (*BrE, law*) threats that sb will cause harm if they do not get what they are asking for: *to demand money with menaces*
▪ *verb* [VN] (*formal*) to be a possible danger to sth/sb **SYN** THREATEN: *The forests are being menaced by major development projects.*

men·acing /ˈmenəsɪŋ/ *adj.* seeming likely to cause you harm or danger **SYN** THREATENING: *a menacing face/tone* ◊ *At night, the dark streets become menacing.* ▶ **men·acing·ly** *adv.*: *The thunder growled menacingly.*

mé·nage /meɪˈnɑːʒ/ *noun* [usually sing.] (from *French, formal* or *humorous*) all the people who live together in one house **SYN** HOUSEHOLD

ménage à trois /ˌmeɪnɑːʒ ɑː ˈtrwɑː/ *noun* (*pl.* **ménages à trois** /ˌmeɪnɑːʒ ɑː ˈtrwɑː/) [usually sing.] (from *French*) a situation where three people, especially a husband, wife and lover, live together and have sexual relationships with each other

men·agerie /məˈnædʒəri/ *noun* a collection of wild animals

mend /mend/ *verb, noun*
▪ *verb* (*especially BrE*) **1** [VN] to repair sth that has been damaged or broken so that it can be used again: *He mended shoes for a living.* ◊ *Could you mend my bike for me?* **2** [VN] to find a solution to a problem or disagreement: *They tried to mend their differences.* **3** [V] (of a person) to improve in health after being ill/sick **SYN** RECOVER: *He's mending slowly after the operation.* **4** [V] (of a broken bone) to heal **IDM** **mend (your) fences (with sb)** to find a solution to a disagreement with sb **mend your 'ways** to stop behaving badly—more at SAY *v.*
▪ *noun* **IDM** **on the 'mend** (*informal, especially BrE*) getting better after an illness or injury; improving after a difficult situation: *My leg is definitely on the mend now.* ◊ *Does he believe the economy's really on the mend?*

men·da·cious /menˈdeɪʃəs/ *adj.* (*formal*) not telling the truth **SYN** LYING

men·da·city /menˈdæsəti/ *noun* [U] (*formal*) the act of not telling the truth **SYN** LYING: *politicians accused of hypocrisy and mendacity*

mend·er /ˈmendə(r)/ *noun* (*BrE*) (usually in compounds) a person who mends sth: *road menders*

men·di·cant /ˈmendɪkənt/ *adj.* (*formal*) (especially of members of religious groups) living by asking people for money and food ▶ **men·di·cant** *noun*

men·folk /ˈmenfəʊk; *AmE* -foʊk/ *noun* [pl.] (*old-fashioned*) men of a particular family or community: *a society sending its menfolk off to war*—compare WOMENFOLK

me·nial /ˈmiːniəl/ *adj., noun*
▪ *adj.* (usually *disapproving*) (of work) not skilled or important, and often boring or badly paid: *menial jobs/work* ◊ *menial tasks like cleaning the floor*
▪ *noun* (*old-fashioned*) a person with a menial job

men·in·gi·tis /ˌmenɪnˈdʒaɪtɪs/ *noun* [U] a serious disease in which the tissues enclosing the brain and SPINAL CORD

M

become infected and swollen, causing severe HEADACHE, fever and sometimes death

meno·pause /ˈmenəpɔːz/ (also informal **the ˈchange (of life)**) noun [U] (often **the menopause**) [sing.] the time during which a woman gradually stops MENSTRUATING, usually at around the age of 50: *to reach (the) menopause* ▶ **meno·pausal** /ˌmenəˈpɔːzl/ adj.: *menopausal women/ symptoms*

me·norah /mɪˈnɔːrə/ noun a traditional Jewish object to hold seven or nine candles

men·ses /ˈmensiːz/ noun (often **the menses**) [pl.] (technical) the flow of blood each month from a woman's body

ˈmen's room noun (AmE) a public toilet for men

men·strual /ˈmenstruəl/ adj. connected with the time when a woman menstruates each month: *The average length of a woman's menstrual cycle is 28 days.* ◊ *menstrual blood* ◊ (formal) *a menstrual period*—compare PREMENSTRUAL

men·stru·ate /ˈmenstrueɪt/ verb [V] (formal) when a woman **menstruates**, there is a flow of blood from her womb, usually once a month

men·stru·ation /ˌmenstruˈeɪʃn/ noun [U] (formal) the process or time of menstruating—compare PERIOD

mens·wear /ˈmenzweə(r); AmE -wer/ noun [U] used especially in shops/stores to describe clothes for men: *the menswear department*

-ment suffix (in nouns) the action or result of: *bombardment* ◊ *development* ▶ **-mental** (in adjectives): *governmental* ◊ *judgemental*

men·tal /ˈmentl/ adj. **1** [usually before noun] connected with or happening in the mind; involving the process of thinking: *the mental process of remembering* ◊ *Do you have a mental picture of what it will look like?* ◊ *I must make a mental note to talk to her about it.* ◊ *He has a complete mental block* (= difficulty in understanding or remembering) *when it comes to physics.* **2** [usually before noun] connected with the state of health of the mind or with the treatment of illnesses of the mind: *mental health* ◊ *a mental disorder/illness/hospital* ◊ *She was suffering from physical and mental exhaustion.*—compare PSYCHIATRIC **3** [not usually before noun] (BrE, slang) crazy: *Watch him. He's mental.* ◊ *My dad will go mental* (= be very angry) *when he finds out.*

ˌmental ˈage noun [C, usually sing.] the level of sb's ability to think, understand, etc. that is judged by comparison with the average ability for children of a particular age: *She is sixteen but has a mental age of five.*—compare CHRONOLOGICAL

ˌmental aˈrithmetic noun [U] adding, multiplying, etc. numbers in your mind without writing anything down or using a CALCULATOR

men·tal·ity /menˈtæləti/ noun [usually sing.] (pl. -ies) the particular attitude or way of thinking of a person or group: *I cannot understand the mentality of football hooligans.* ◊ *a criminal/ghetto mentality*—see also SIEGE MENTALITY

men·tal·ly /ˈmentəli/ adv. connected with or happening in the mind: *mentally ill* ◊ *The baby is very mentally alert.* ◊ *Mentally, I began making a list of things I had to do.* ◊ *a mentally handicapped child*

men·thol /ˈmenθɒl; AmE -θɔːl; -θɑːl/ noun [U] a substance that tastes and smells of MINT, that is used in some medicines for colds and to give a strong cool flavour to cigarettes, TOOTHPASTE, etc.

men·tion /ˈmenʃn/ verb, noun
■ verb ~ sth/sb **(to sb)** to write or speak about sth/sb, especially without giving much information: [VN] *Nobody mentioned anything to me about it.* ◊ *Sorry, I won't mention it again.* ◊ *Now that you mention it, she did seem to be in a strange mood.* ◊ *His name has been mentioned as a future MP.* ◊ [V wh-] *Did she mention where she was going?* ◊ [V that] *You mentioned in your letter that you might be moving abroad.* ◊ *He failed to mention that he was the one who started the fight.* [also V -ing]—see also ABOVE-MENTIONED, AFOREMENTIONED **IDM** **don't ˈmention it** (spoken) used as a polite answer when sb has thanked you for sth: *'Thanks for all your help.' 'Don't mention it.'* **not to**

mention used to introduce extra information and emphasize what you are saying: *He has two big houses in this country, not to mention his villa in France.*
■ noun [U, C, usually sing.] an act of referring to sb/sth in speech or writing: *He made no mention of her work.* ◊ *The concert didn't even get a mention in the newspapers.* ◊ *Richard deserves (a) special mention for all the help he gave us.*

men·tor /ˈmentɔː(r)/ noun an experienced person who advises and helps sb with less experience over a period of time ▶ **men·tor·ing** noun [U]: *a mentoring programme*

menu /ˈmenjuː/ noun **1** a list of the food that is available at a restaurant or to be served at a meal: *to ask for/look at the menu* ◊ *What's on the menu* (= for dinner) *tonight?* **2** (computing) a list of possible choices that are shown on a computer screen: *a pull-down menu*

meow (especially AmE) = MIAOW

MEP /ˌem iː ˈpiː/ noun the abbreviation for 'Member of the European Parliament': *the Labour MEP for South East Wales*

mer·can·tile /ˈmɜːkəntaɪl; AmE ˈmɜːrk-; -tiːl/ adj. (formal) connected with trade and commercial affairs

mer·cen·ary /ˈmɜːsənəri; AmE ˈmɜːrsəneri/ noun, adj.
■ noun (pl. -ies) a soldier who will fight for any country or group that offers payment: *foreign mercenaries* ◊ *mercenary soldiers*
■ adj. (disapproving) only interested in making or getting money: *a mercenary society/attitude* ◊ *She's interested in him for purely mercenary reasons.*

mer·chan·dise noun, verb
■ noun /ˈmɜːtʃəndaɪs; -daɪz; AmE ˈmɜːrtʃ-/ [U] **1** (formal) goods that are bought or sold; goods that are for sale in a shop/store: *a wide selection of merchandise* **2** things you can buy that are connected with or that advertise a particular event or organization: *official Olympic merchandise*
■ verb /ˈmɜːtʃəndaɪz; AmE ˈmɜːrtʃ-/ [VN] (written) to sell sth using advertising, etc.

mer·chan·dis·ing /ˈmɜːtʃəndaɪzɪŋ; AmE ˈmɜːrtʃ-/ noun [U] **1** (especially AmE) the activity of selling goods, or of trying to sell them, by advertising or displaying them **2** products connected with a popular film/movie, person or event; the process of selling these goods: *millions of pounds' worth of Batman merchandising*

mer·chant /ˈmɜːtʃənt; AmE ˈmɜːrtʃ-/ noun, adj.
■ noun **1** a person who buys and sells goods in large quantities, especially one who imports and exports goods: *builders' merchants* (= who sell supplies to the building trade) ◊ *a coal/wine merchant* ◊ *Venice was once a city of rich merchants.* **2** (informal, disapproving) a person who likes a particular activity: *a speed merchant* (= sb who likes to drive fast) ◊ *noise merchants* (= for example, a band who make a lot of noise) **IDM** see DOOM n.
■ adj. [only before noun] connected with the transport of goods by sea: *merchant navy/ships/seamen*

mer·chant·able /ˈmɜːtʃəntəbl; AmE ˈmɜːrtʃ-/ adj. (law) in a good enough condition to be sold

ˌmerchant ˈbank noun (BrE) a bank that deals with large businesses ▶ **ˌmerchant ˈbanker** noun **ˌmerchant ˈbanking** noun [U]

ˌmerchant ˈnavy (BrE) (AmE **ˌmerchant maˈrine**) noun [C+sing./pl. v.] a country's commercial ships and the people who work on them

mer·ci·ful /ˈmɜːsɪfl; AmE ˈmɜːrs-/ adj. **1** ready to forgive people and show them kindness: *a merciful God* ◊ *They asked her to be merciful to the prisoners.* **2** (of an event) seeming to be lucky, especially because it brings an end to sb's problems or suffering: *Death came as a merciful release.*—see also MERCY

mer·ci·ful·ly /ˈmɜːsɪfəli; AmE ˈmɜːrs-/ adv. **1** used to show that you feel sb/sth is lucky because a situation could have been much worse: *Deaths from the disease are mercifully rare.* ◊ *Mercifully, everyone arrived on time.* **2** in a merciful way: *He was treated mercifully.*

mer·ci·less /ˈmɜːsɪləs; AmE ˈmɜːrs-/ adj. showing no kindness or pity **SYN** CRUEL: *a merciless killer/attack* ◊

s	t	v	z	ʃ	ʒ	tʃ	dʒ	θ	ð	ŋ
see	tea	van	zoo	shoe	vision	chain	jam	thin	this	sing

the merciless heat of the sun—see also MERCY ▶ **mer·ci·less·ly** *adv.*

mer·cur·ial /mɜːˈkjʊəriəl; *AmE* mɜːrˈkjʊr-/ *adj.* **1** (*literary*) often changing or reacting in a way that is unexpected: *Emily's mercurial temperament made her difficult to live with.* **2** (*literary*) lively and quick: *a brilliant, mercurial mind* **3** (*technical*) containing MERCURY

Mer·cury /ˈmɜːkjəri; *AmE* ˈmɜːrk-/ *noun* the smallest planet in the SOLAR SYSTEM, nearest to the sun

mer·cury /ˈmɜːkjəri; *AmE* ˈmɜːrk-/ *noun* [U] (*symb* **Hg**) a chemical element. Mercury is a poisonous silver-white liquid metal, used in THERMOMETERS.

mercy /ˈmɜːsi; *AmE* ˈmɜːrsi/ *noun* (*pl.* **-ies**) **1** [U] a kind or forgiving attitude towards sb that you have the power to harm or right to punish: *to ask/beg/plead for mercy* ◇ *They showed no mercy to their hostages.* ◇ *God have mercy on us.* ◇ *The troops are on a mercy mission* (= a journey to help people) *in the war zone.* **2** [C, usually sing.] (*informal*) an event or a situation to be grateful for, usually because it stops sth unpleasant: *It's a mercy she wasn't seriously hurt.*—see also MERCIFUL, MERCILESS **IDM** **at the mercy of sb/sth** not able to stop sb/sth harming you because they have power or control over you: *I'm not going to put myself at the mercy of the bank.* ◇ *We were at the mercy of the weather.* **leave sb/sth to the mercy/ mercies of sb/sth** to leave sb/sth in a situation that may cause them to suffer or to be treated badly **throw yourself on sb's mercy** (*formal*) to put yourself in a situation where you must rely on sb to be kind to you and not harm or punish you—more at SMALL *adj.*

'mercy killing *noun* [C, U] the act of killing sb out of pity, for example because they are in severe pain **SYN** EUTHANASIA

mere /mɪə(r); *AmE* mɪr/ *adj., noun*
■ *adj.* [only before noun] (*superlative* **mer·est**, no *comparative*) **1** used when you want to emphasize how small, unimportant, etc. sb/sth is: *It took her a mere 20 minutes to win.* ◇ *A mere 2% of their budget has been spent on publicity.* ◇ *He seemed so young, a mere boy.* ◇ *You've got the job. The interview will be a mere formality.* **2** used when you are saying that the fact that a particular thing is present in a situation is enough to have an influence on that situation: *His mere presence* (= just the fact that he was there) *made her feel afraid.* ◇ *The mere fact that they were prepared to talk was encouraging.* ◇ *The mere thought of eating made him feel sick.* ◇ *The merest* (= the slightest) *noise is enough to wake her.*
■ *noun* (*BrE*) (*literary*) (also used in names) a small lake

mere·ly /ˈmɪəli; *AmE* ˈmɪrli/ *adv.* used meaning 'only' or 'simply' to emphasize a fact or sth that you are saying: *It is not merely a job, but a way of life.* ◇ *He said nothing, merely smiled and watched her.* ◇ *They agreed to go merely because they were getting paid for it.* ◇ *I'm merely stating what everybody knows anyway.*

mere·tri·cious /ˌmerəˈtrɪʃəs/ *adj.* (*formal*) seeming attractive, but in fact having no real value

merge /mɜːdʒ; *AmE* mɜːrdʒ/ *verb* **1** ~ (**with/into**) **sth**|~ **A with B**|~ **A and B** (**together**) to combine or make two or more things combine to form a single thing: [V] *The banks are set to merge next year.* ◇ *His department will merge with mine.* ◇ *The villages expanded and merged into one large town.* ◇ *Fact and fiction merge together in his latest thriller.* ◇ *The two groups have merged to form a new party.* ◇ [VN] *His department will be merged with mine.* ◇ *The company was formed by merging three smaller firms.* **2** [V] if two things **merge**, or if one thing **merges** into another, the differences between them gradually disappear so that it is impossible to separate them: *The hills merged into the dark sky behind them.* **IDM** **merge into the 'background** (of a person) to behave quietly when you are with a group of people so that they do not notice you

mer·ger /ˈmɜːdʒə(r); *AmE* ˈmɜːrdʒ-/ *noun* [C] ~ (**between/ of A and B**)|~ (**with sth**) the act of joining two or more organizations or businesses into one: *a merger between the two banks* ◇ *our proposed merger with the university*

me·rid·ian /məˈrɪdiən/ *noun* one of the lines that is drawn from the North Pole to the South Pole on a map of the world

mer·ingue /məˈræŋ/ *noun* [U, C] a sweet white mixture made from egg whites and sugar, usually baked until crisp and used to make cakes; a small cake made from this mixture: *a lemon meringue pie*—picture on page A1

me·rino /məˈriːnəʊ; *AmE* -noʊ/ *noun* (*pl.* **-os**) **1** [C] a breed of sheep with long fine wool **2** [U] the wool of the merino sheep or a fabric made from this wool, used for making clothes

merit /ˈmerɪt/ *noun, verb*
■ *noun* **1** [U] (*formal*) the quality of being good and of deserving praise, reward or admiration: *a work of outstanding artistic merit.* ◇ *The plan is entirely without merit.* ◇ *I want to get the job on merit.* **2** [C, usually pl.] a good feature that deserves praise, reward or admiration: *We will consider each case on its (own) merits* (= without considering any other issues, feelings, etc.). ◇ *They weighed up the relative merits of the four candidates.*
■ *verb* (not used in the progressive tenses) (*formal*) to do sth to deserve praise, attention, etc. **SYN** DESERVE [VN] *He claims that their success was not merited.* ◇ *The case does not merit further investigation.* [also V-ing]

mer·it·oc·racy /ˌmerɪˈtɒkrəsi; *AmE* -ˈtɑːk-/ *noun* (*pl.* **-ies**) **1** [C, U] a country or social system where people get power or money on the basis of their ability **2** (**the meritocracy**) [sing.] the group of people with power in this kind of social system ▶ **mer·ito·crat·ic** /ˌmerɪtəˈkrætɪk/ *adj.*

meri·tori·ous /ˌmerɪˈtɔːriəs/ *adj.* (*formal*) deserving praise

mer·maid /ˈmɜːmeɪd; *AmE* ˈmɜːrm-/ *noun* (in stories) a creature with a woman's head and body, and a fish's tail instead of legs

mer·rily /ˈmerəli/ *adv.* **1** in a happy, cheerful way: *They chatted merrily.* **2** without thinking about the problems that your actions might cause: *She carried on merrily, not realizing the offence she was causing.*

mer·ri·ment /ˈmerimənt/ *noun* [U] (*formal*) happy talk, laughter and enjoyment

merry /ˈmeri/ *adj.* (**mer·rier**, **mer·ri·est**) **1** happy and cheerful: *a merry grin* **2** (**Merry Christmas**) used as a greeting at Christmas to say that you hope that sb has an enjoyable holiday **3** (*informal, especially BrE*) slightly drunk **IDM** **make 'merry** (*old-fashioned*) to enjoy yourself by singing, laughing, drinking, etc. **the ˌmore the 'merrier** the more people or things there are the better the situation will be or the more fun people will have: *'Can I bring a friend to your party?' 'Sure—the more the merrier!'*—more at HELL, LEAD *v.*

'merry-go-round *noun* **1** (also **car·ou·sel** especially in *AmE*) (*BrE* also **round·about**) a circular platform with model horses, cars, etc. that turns around and around and that children ride on at a FAIRGROUND **2** (*AmE*) = ROUNDABOUT (2) **3** continuous busy activity or a continuous series of changing events: *He was tired of the merry-go-round of romance and longed to settle down.*

merry·mak·ing /ˈmerimeɪkɪŋ/ *noun* [U] (*literary*) fun and enjoyment with singing, laughing, drinking, etc.

mesa /ˈmeɪsə/ *noun* (*pl.* **mesas**) a hill with a flat top and steep sides that is common in the south-west of the US

mes·ca·line (also **mes·ca·lin**) /ˈmeskəlɪn/ *noun* [U] a drug obtained from a type of CACTUS, that affects people's minds and makes them see and hear things that are not really there

mesh /meʃ/ *noun, verb*
■ *noun* **1** [U, C] material made of threads of plastic rope or wire that are woven together like a net: *wire mesh over the door of the cage* **2** [C, usually sing.] a complicated situation or system that it is difficult to escape from
■ *verb* (*written*) **1** ~ (**sth**) (**with sth**)|~ (**sth**) (**together**) to fit together or match closely, especially in a satisfactory way; to make things fit together successfully: [V] *This evidence meshes with earlier reports of an organized riot.* ◇ [VN] *His theories mesh together various political and religious beliefs.* **2** [V] (*technical*) (of parts of a machine) to fit

æ	ɑː	e	ɜː	ə	ɪ	iː	i	ɒ	ɔː	ʌ	ʊ	u	uː
cat	father	ten	bird	about	sit	see	many	got	saw	cup	put	actual	too

(BrE)

M

together as they move: *If the cogs don't mesh correctly, the gears will keep slipping.*

mes·mer·ic /mez'merɪk/ *adj.* [usually before noun] (*formal*) having such a strong effect on people that they cannot give their attention to anything else: *She gave a mesmeric performance.*

mes·mer·ize (*BrE also* **-ise**) /'mezməraɪz/ *verb* [VN] [usually passive] to have such a strong effect on you that you cannot give your attention to anything else: *They were mesmerized by her performance.* ▶ **mes·mer·iz·ing,** **-is·ing** *adj.*: *Her performance was mesmerizing.*

mess /mes/ *noun, verb*
■ *noun*
UNTIDY STATE | **1** [C, usually sing.] a dirty or untidy state: *The room was in a mess. ◊ The kids made a mess in the bathroom. ◊ ' What a mess!' she said, surveying the scene after the party. ◊ My hair's a real mess!*

DIFFICULT SITUATION | **2** [C, usually sing.] a situation that is full of problems, usually because of a lack of organization or because of mistakes that sb has made: *The economy is in a mess. ◊ I feel I've made a mess of things. ◊ The whole situation is a mess. ◊ Let's try to sort out the mess. ◊ The biggest question is how they got into this mess in the first place.*

UNTIDY PERSON | **3** [sing.] a person who is dirty or whose clothes and hair are not tidy: *You're a mess!*

ANIMAL WASTE | **4** [U, C] (*informal*) the EXCREMENT (= solid waste matter) of an animal, usually a dog or cat

A LOT | **5 a ~ of sth** (*AmE, informal*) a lot of sth: *There's a mess of fish down there, so get your lines in the water.*

ARMED FORCES | **6** (also **'mess hall** especially in *AmE*) a building or room in which members of the armed forces have their meals: *the officers' mess*

■ *verb*
MAKE UNTIDY | **1** [VN] (*informal, especially AmE*) to make sth dirty or untidy: *Careful—you're messing my hair.*

OF AN ANIMAL | **2** [V] to empty its bowels somewhere that it should not

IDM **,no 'messing** (*spoken*) used to say that sth has been done easily: *We finished in time, no messing.*

PHR V **,mess a'round** (*BrE also* **,mess a'bout**) **1** to behave in a silly and annoying way, especially instead of doing sth useful **SYN** FOOL AROUND: *Will you stop messing around and get on with some work?* **2** to spend time doing sth for pleasure in a relaxed way: *We spent the day messing around on the river.* **,mess a'round with sb** (*BrE also* **,mess a'bout with sb**) to have a sexual relationship with sb, especially when you should not **,mess a'round with sth** (*BrE also* **,mess a'bout with sth**) **1** to touch or use sth in a careless and/or annoying way: *Who's been messing around with my computer?* **2** to spend time playing with sth, repairing sth, etc. **,mess sb a'bout/a'round** (*BrE*) to treat sb in an unfair and annoying way, especially by changing your mind a lot or not doing what you said you would: *I'm sorry to mess you about but there are a few last-minute changes.* **,mess 'up** | **,mess sth↔'up** to spoil sth or do it badly: *I've really messed up this time. ◊ If you cancel now you'll mess up all my arrangements.* **,mess sb↔'up 1** (*informal*) to cause sb to have serious emotional or mental problems **2** (*AmE, especially spoken*) to physically hurt sb, especially by hitting them: *He was messed up pretty bad by the other guy.* **,mess sth↔'up to** make sth dirty or untidy: *I don't want you messing up my nice clean kitchen.* **'mess with sb/sth** (usually used in negative sentences) to get involved with sb/sth that may be harmful: *I wouldn't mess with him if I were you.*

mes·sage /'mesɪdʒ/ *noun ~ (from sb) (to sb)* **1** a written or spoken piece of information, etc. that you send to sb or leave for sb when you cannot speak to them yourself: *There were no messages for me at the hotel. ◊ I left a message on your answering machine. ◊ Jenny's not here at the moment. Can I take a message? ◊ We've had an urgent message saying that your father's ill. ◊ a televised message from the President to the American people ◊ an e-mail message* **2** [usually sing.] an important moral, social or political idea that a book, speech, etc. is trying

to communicate: *a film with a strong religious message ◊ The campaign is trying to get the message across to young people that drugs are dangerous.* **3** (**messages**) [pl.] (*ScotE*) shopping: *to do the messages ◊ to go for the messages ◊ You can leave your messages* (= the things that you have bought) *here.* **IDM** **get the 'message** (*informal*) to understand what sb is trying to tell you indirectly: *When he started looking at his watch, I got the message and left.* **on/off 'message** (of a politician) stating/not stating the official point of view of their political party

mes·sen·ger /'mesɪndʒə(r)/ *noun* a person who gives a message to sb or who delivers messages to people as a job: *He sent the order by messenger. ◊ a motorcycle messenger*

Mes·siah /mə'saɪə/ *noun* **1** (**the Messiah**) [sing.] (in Christianity) Jesus Christ who was sent by God into the world to save people from evil and SIN **2** (**the Messiah**) [sing.] (in Judaism) a king who will be sent by God to save the Jewish people **3** (**messiah**) a leader who people believe will solve the problems of a country or the world: *He's seen by many as a political messiah.* ▶ **mes·si·an·ic** /,mesi'ænɪk/ *adj.*: *a messianic prophecy ◊ a political leader who speaks with messianic fervour*

Messrs (*BrE*) (*AmE* **Messrs.**) /'mesəz; *AmE* -sərz/ *abbr.* (used as the plural of 'Mr' before a list of names and before names of business companies): *Messrs Smith, Brown and Jones ◊ Messrs T Brown and Co*

messy /'mesi/ *adj.* (**mess·ier, messi·est**) **1** dirty and/or untidy: *The house was always messy.* **2** making sb/sth dirty and/or untidy: *It was a messy job.* **3** (of a situation) unpleasant, confused or difficult to deal with: *The divorce was painful and messy.*

Met /met/ *abbr.* (*informal*) **1** METEOROLOGICAL: *the Met Office weather forecast service* **2** (**the Met**) the Metropolitan Opera House (in New York) **3** (**the Met**) the Metropolitan Police (the police force in London)

met *pt, pp of* MEET

meta- /'metə/ *combining form* (in nouns, adjectives and verbs) **1** connected with a change of position or state: *metamorphosis ◊ metabolism* **2** higher; beyond: *metaphysics ◊ metalanguage*

me·tab·ol·ism /mə'tæbəlɪzəm/ *noun* [U, sing.] (*biology*) the chemical processes in living things that change food, etc. into energy and materials for growth: *The body's metabolism is slowed down by extreme cold.* ▶ **meta·bol·ic** /,metə'bɒlɪk; *AmE* -'bɑːl-/ *adj.* [usually before noun]: *a metabolic process/disorder ◊ a high/low metabolic rate*

me·tab·ol·ize (*BrE also* **-ise**) /mə'tæbəlaɪz/ *verb* [VN] (*biology*) to turn food, minerals, etc. in the body into new cells, energy and waste products by means of chemical processes

metal /'metl/ *noun* [C, U] a type of solid mineral substance that is usually hard and shiny and that heat and electricity can travel through, for example tin, iron, and gold: *a piece of metal ◊ a metal pipe/bar/box ◊ The frame is made of metal.*—see also HEAVY METAL, PRECIOUS METAL

meta·lan·guage /'metəlæŋgwɪdʒ/ *noun* [C, U] (*linguistics*) the words and phrases that people use to talk about or describe language or a particular language

'metal detector *noun* **1** an electronic device that you use to look for metal objects that are buried under the ground **2** an electronic machine that is used, for example at an airport, to see if people are hiding metal objects such as weapons

'metal fatigue *noun* [U] weakness in metal that is frequently put under pressure that makes it likely to break

met·alled /'metld/ *adj.* (of a road or track) made or repaired with small pieces of broken stone

me·tal·lic /mə'tælɪk/ *adj.* [usually before noun] **1** that looks, tastes or sounds like metal: *metallic paint/colours/ blue ◊ a metallic taste ◊ a metallic sound/click ◊ a metallic voice* (= harsh and unpleasant) **2** made of or containing metal: *a metallic object ◊ metallic compounds*

me·tal·lur·gist /mə'tælədʒɪst; *AmE* 'metlɜːrdʒɪst/ *noun* a scientist who studies metallurgy

me·tal·lurgy /mə'tælədʒi; *AmE* 'metlɜːrdʒi/ *noun* [U] the

aɪ	aʊ	eɪ	əʊ	oʊ	ɔɪ	ɪə	eə	ʊə	j	w
my	now	say	go	go	boy	near	hair	pure	yes	wet
			(BrE)	(AmE)						

M

scientific study of metals and their uses ▶ **me·tal·lur·gical** /ˌmetəˈlɜːdʒɪkl; AmE ˌmetlˈɜːrdʒ-/ adj.

met·al·work /ˈmetlwɜːk; AmE -wɜːrk/ noun [U] **1** the activity of making objects out of metal in an artistic and skilful way; objects that are made in this way **2** the metal parts of sth: cracks in the metalwork

meta·morph·ose /ˌmetəˈmɔːfəʊz; AmE -ˈmɔːrfoʊz/ verb ~ (sth/sb) (from sth) (into sth) (formal) to change or make sth/sb change into sth completely different, especially over a period of time: [V] The caterpillar will eventually metamorphose into a butterfly. [also VN]

meta·mor·phosis /ˌmetəˈmɔːfəsɪs; AmE -ˈmɔːrf-/ noun (pl. meta·mor·phoses /-əsiːz/) [C, U] (formal) a process in which sb/sth changes completely into sth different: the metamorphosis of a caterpillar into a butterfly ◊ She had undergone an amazing metamorphosis from awkward schoolgirl to beautiful woman.

meta·phor /ˈmetəfə(r)/ noun [C, U] a word or phrase used in an imaginative way to describe sb/sth else, in order to show that the two things have the same qualities and to make the description more powerful, for example She has a heart of stone; the use of such words and phrases: a game of football used as a metaphor for the competitive struggle of life ◊ The writer's striking use of metaphor.—compare SIMILE

meta·phor·ical /ˌmetəˈfɒrɪkl; AmE -ˈfɔːr-; -ˈfɑːr-/ adj. connected with or containing metaphors: metaphorical language—compare FIGURATIVE, LITERAL ▶ **meta·phor·ic·al·ly** /-kli/ adv.: I'll leave you in Robin's capable hands—metaphorically speaking, of course!

meta·phys·ics /ˌmetəˈfɪzɪks/ noun [U] the branch of philosophy that deals with the nature of existence, truth and knowledge ▶ **meta·phys·ic·al** /ˌmetəˈfɪzɪkl/ adj.: metaphysical problems/speculation

mete /miːt/ verb PHR V ˌmete sth↔ˈout (to sb) (formal) to give sb a punishment; to make sb suffer bad treatment: Severe penalties were meted out by the court. ◊ the violence meted out to the prisoners

me·teor /ˈmiːtiə(r); -iɔː(r)/ noun a piece of rock from outer space that makes a bright line across the night sky as it burns up while falling through the earth's atmosphere: a meteor shower—see also SHOOTING STAR

me·teor·ic /ˌmiːtiˈɒrɪk; AmE -ˈɔːr-; -ˈɑːr-/ adj. **1** achieving success very quickly: a meteoric rise to fame ◊ a meteoric career **2** connected with meteors: meteoric craters

me·teor·ite /ˈmiːtiəraɪt/ noun a piece of rock from outer space that hits the earth's surface

me·teor·olo·gist /ˌmiːtiəˈrɒlədʒɪst; AmE -ˈrɑːl-/ noun a scientist who studies meteorology

me·teor·ology /ˌmiːtiəˈrɒlədʒi; AmE -ˈrɑːl-/ noun [U] the scientific study of the earth's atmosphere and its changes, used especially in FORECASTING the weather (= saying what it will be like) ▶ **me·teoro·logic·al** /ˌmiːtiərəˈlɒdʒɪkl; AmE -ˈlɑːdʒ-/ adj.: meteorological conditions

meter /ˈmiːtə(r)/ noun, verb
■ noun **1** (especially in compounds) a device that measures and records the amount of electricity, gas, water, etc. that you have used or the time and distance you have travelled, etc: A man came to read the gas meter. ◊ The cab driver left the meter running while he waited for us.—see also LIGHT METER **2** = PARKING METER **3** (-meter) (in compounds) a device for measuring the thing mentioned: speedometer ◊ altimeter ◊ calorimeter **4** (AmE) = METRE
■ verb [VN] to measure sth (for example how much gas, electricity, etc. has been used) using a meter

metha·done /ˈmeθədəʊn; AmE -doʊn/ noun [U] a drug that is used to treat people who are trying to stop taking the illegal drug HEROIN

me·thane /ˈmiːθeɪn/ noun [U] (symb CH₄) a gas without colour or smell, that burns easily and is used as fuel. Natural gas consists mainly of methane.

me·thinks /mɪˈθɪŋks/ verb (pt me·thought) (not used in the perfect tenses) [V, V(that)] (old use or humorous) I think

method /ˈmeθəd/ noun **1** [C] ~ (of sth/of doing sth)| ~ (for sth/for doing sth) a particular way of doing sth: a reliable/effective/scientific method of data analysis ◊ a new method of solving the problem ◊ traditional/alternative methods ◊ the best method for arriving at an accurate prediction of the costs **2** [U] the quality of being well planned and organized IDM there is (a) method in your madness there is a reason for your behaviour and it is not as strange or as stupid as it seems

meth·od·ic·al /məˈθɒdɪkl; AmE -ˈθɑːd-/ adj. **1** done in a careful and logical way: a methodical approach/study **2** (of a person) doing things in a careful and logical way: to have a methodical mind ▶ **meth·od·ic·al·ly** /-kli/ adv.: They sorted slowly and methodically through the papers.

Meth·od·ist /ˈmeθədɪst/ noun a member of a Christian Protestant Church that broke away from the Church of England in the 18th century ▶ **Meth·od·ism** /ˈmeθədɪzəm/ noun [U] **Meth·od·ist** adj.: a Methodist church/preacher

meth·od·ology /ˌmeθəˈdɒlədʒi; AmE -ˈdɑːl-/ noun (pl. -ies) [C, U] (formal) a set of methods and principles used to perform a particular activity: recent changes in the methodology of language teaching ▶ **meth·odo·logic·al** /ˌmeθədəˈlɒdʒɪkl; AmE -ˈlɑːdʒ-/ adj. [usually before noun]: methodological problems **meth·odo·logic·al·ly** /ˌmeθədəˈlɒdʒɪkli; AmE -ˈlɑːdʒ-/ adv.

meths /meθs/ noun [U] (informal, especially BrE) = METHYLATED SPIRIT

meth·yl·ated spirit /ˌmeθəleɪtɪd ˈspɪrɪt/ (also **meth·yl·ated spirits**) (also informal **meths**) noun [U] a type of alcohol that is not fit for drinking, used as a fuel for lighting and heating and for cleaning off dirty marks

me·ticu·lous /məˈtɪkjələs; AmE -kjəl-/ adj. ~ (in sth/doing sth)| ~ (about sth/in doing sth) paying careful attention to every detail: meticulous planning/records/research ◊ He's always meticulous in keeping the records up to date. ◊ Their room had been prepared with meticulous care. ▶ **me·ticu·lous·ly** adv.: a meticulously planned schedule ◊ meticulously clean **me·ticu·lous·ness** noun [U]

mé·tier /ˈmetieɪ; AmE ˈmeɪt-/ noun [usually sing.] (from French, formal) a person's work, especially when they have a natural skill or ability for it

me·ton·ymy /məˈtɒnəmi; AmE -ˈtɑːn-/ noun [U] (technical) the act of referring to sth by the name of sth else that is closely connected with it, for example using the White House for the US president

metre (BrE) (AmE **meter**) /ˈmiːtə(r)/ noun (abbr. m) **1** [C] a unit for measuring length; a hundred CENTIMETRES **2** (metres) used in the name of races: She came second in the 200 metres. ◊ the 4×100 metres relay **3** [U, C] the arrangement of strong and weak stresses in lines of poetry that produces the rhythm; a particular example of this

met·ric /ˈmetrɪk/ adj. **1** based on the metric system: metric units/measurements/sizes ◊ British currency went metric in 1971. **2** made or measured using the metric system: These screws are metric.—compare IMPERIAL **3** = METRICAL

met·ric·al /ˈmetrɪkl/ (also **met·ric**) adj. connected with the rhythm of a poem, produced by the arrangement of stress on the syllables in each line

met·ri·ca·tion /ˌmetrɪˈkeɪʃn/ noun [U] the process of changing to using the metric system

the ˈmetric system noun [sing.] the system of measurement that uses the metre, the kilogram and the litre as basic units

ˌmetric ˈton (also **tonne**) noun a unit for measuring weight, equal to 1000 kilograms

metro /ˈmetrəʊ; AmE ˈmetroʊ/ noun, adj.
■ noun (also **the Metro**) [sing.] an underground train system, especially the one in Paris: to travel on the metro/by metro ◊ the Paris Metro ◊ a metro station ⇨ note at UNDERGROUND
■ adj. (AmE, informal) = METROPOLITAN: the New York metro areas

met·ro·nome /ˈmetrənəʊm; AmE -noʊm/ noun a device that makes a regular sound like a clock and is used by musicians to help them keep the correct rhythm when

M

playing a piece of music ▶ **met·ro·nom·ic** /ˌmetrə-ˈnɒmɪk; *AmE* -ˈnɑːm-/ *adj.*: *His financial problems hit the headlines with almost metronomic regularity.*

me·trop·olis /məˈtrɒpəlɪs; *AmE* məˈtrɑːp-/ *noun* a large important city (often the capital city of a country or region)

met·ro·pol·itan /ˌmetrəˈpɒlɪtən; *AmE* -ˈpɑːl-/ *adj.* [only before noun] **1** (also *AmE informal* **metro**) connected with a large or capital city: *the New York metropolitan area* ◊ *metropolitan districts/regions* **2** connected with a particular country rather than with the other regions of the world that the country controls: *metropolitan France/Spain*

met·tle /ˈmetl/ *noun* [U] the ability and determination to do sth successfully in spite of difficult conditions: *The next game will be a real test of their mettle.* **IDM** **on your ˈmettle** prepared to use all your skills, knowledge, etc. because you are being tested

mew /mjuː/ *noun* the soft high noise that a cat makes ▶ **mew** *verb*: [V] *The kitten mewed pitifully.*

mews /mjuːz/ *noun* (*pl.* **mews**) (*BrE*) a short, narrow street with a row of STABLES (= buildings used to keep horses in) that have been made into small houses

ˈmews house (*BrE*) (*AmE* **ˈcarriage house**) *noun* a house in a mews

ˌMexican ˈwave (*BrE*) (*AmE* **the ˈwave**) *noun* a continuous movement that looks like a wave on the sea, made by a large group of people, especially people watching a football game, when one person after another stands up, raises their arms, and then sits down again

mez·za·nine /ˈmezəniːn; ˈmetsə-/ *noun* **1** a floor that is built between two floors of a building and is smaller than the other floors: *a bedroom on the mezzanine* ◊ *a mezzanine floor* **2** (*AmE*) the first area of seats above the ground floor in a theatre; the first few rows of these seats—see also DRESS CIRCLE

mezzo-soprano /ˌmetsəʊ səˈprɑːnəʊ; *AmE* ˌmetsoʊ səˈprɑːnoʊ; -ˈpræn-/ (also **mezzo**) *noun* (*pl.* **mezzo-sopranos** or **mezzos**) a singing voice with a range between SOPRANO and ALTO; a woman with a mezzo-soprano voice

mg *abbr.* (in writing) MILLIGRAM(S): *Each tablet contains 250mg aspirin.*

Mgr (also **Mgr.** especially in *AmE*) *abbr.* (in writing) MONSIGNOR

MHz *abbr.* (in writing) MEGAHERTZ: *frequencies from 108 to 120 MHz*

MIA /ˌem aɪ ˈeɪ/ *abbr.* (*especially AmE*) (of a soldier) missing in action (missing after a battle)

mi = ME *n*

miaow (*BrE*) (also **meow** *AmE, BrE*) /miˈaʊ/ *noun* the crying sound made by a cat—see also MEW ▶ **miaow** (*BrE*) (also **meow** *AmE, BrE*) *verb* [V]

mi·asma /miˈæzmə; maɪˈæ-/ *noun* [C usually sing, U] (*literary*) a mass of air that is dirty and smells unpleasant: *A miasma of stale alcohol hung around him.* ◊ (*figurative*) *the miasma of depression*

mic /maɪk/ *noun* (*informal*) = MICROPHONE

mica /ˈmaɪkə/ *noun* [U] a clear mineral that splits easily into thin flat layers and is used to make electrical equipment

mice *pl.* of MOUSE

Mich·ael·mas /ˈmɪklməs/ *noun* [U, C] (in the Christian Church) the holy day in honour of St Michael, 29 September

ˌMichaelmas ˈdaisy *noun* a plant that has blue, white, pink or purple flowers with dark centres, that appear in the autumn/fall

mickey /ˈmɪki/ *noun* **IDM** **take the ˈmickey (out of sb)** (*BrE, informal*) to make sb look or feel silly by copying the way they talk, behave, etc. or by making them believe sth that is not true, often in a way that is not intended to be unkind

ˌMickey ˈMouse *adj.* (*disapproving*) not of high quality; too easy: *It's only a Mickey Mouse job.*

micro /ˈmaɪkrəʊ; *AmE* -kroʊ/ *noun* (*pl.* **-os**) = MICROCOMPUTER

micro- /ˈmaɪkrəʊ; *AmE* -kroʊ/ *combining form* (in nouns, adjectives and adverbs) small; on a small scale: *microchip* ◊ *micro-organism* OPP MACRO-

mi·crobe /ˈmaɪkrəʊb; *AmE* -kroʊb/ *noun* an extremely small living thing that you can only see under a MICROSCOPE and that may cause disease

micro·biolo·gist /ˌmaɪkrəʊbaɪˈɒlədʒɪst; *AmE* -kroʊbaɪˈɑːl-/ *noun* a scientist who studies microbiology

micro·biol·ogy /ˌmaɪkrəʊbaɪˈɒlədʒi; *AmE* -kroʊbaɪˈɑːl-/ *noun* [U] the scientific study of very small living things, such as bacteria ▶ **micro·bio·logic·al** /ˌmaɪkrəʊˌbaɪəˈlɒdʒɪkl; *AmE* -kroʊˌbaɪəˈlɑːdʒ-/ *adj.*

micro·chip /ˈmaɪkrəʊtʃɪp; *AmE* -kroʊ-/ (also **chip**) *noun* a very small piece of a material that is a SEMICONDUCTOR, used to carry a complicated electronic CIRCUIT

micro·com·puter /ˈmaɪkrəʊkəmpjuːtə(r); *AmE* -kroʊ-/ (also **micro**) *noun* a small computer that contains a MICROPROCESSOR—compare MAINFRAME, MINICOMPUTER, PERSONAL COMPUTER

micro·cosm /ˈmaɪkrəʊkɒzəm; *AmE* -kroʊkɑːz-/ *noun* a thing, a place or a group that has all the features and qualities of sth much larger: *The family is a microcosm of society.*—compare MACROCOSM **IDM** **in microcosm** on a small scale: *The developments in this town represent in microcosm what is happening in the country as a whole.*

micro·elec·tron·ics /ˌmaɪkrəʊɪˌlekˈtrɒnɪks; *AmE* -kroʊɪˌlekˈtrɑːn-/ *noun* [U] the design, production and use of very small electronic CIRCUITS ▶ **micro·elec·tron·ic** *adj.* [only before noun]

micro·fiche /ˈmaɪkrəʊfiːʃ; *AmE* -kroʊ-/ *noun* [U, C] a piece of film with written information on it in print of very small size. Microfiches can only be read with a special machine: *The directory is available on microfiche.*

micro·film /ˈmaɪkrəʊfɪlm; *AmE* -kroʊ-/ *noun* [U, C] film used for storing written information on in print of very small size

micro·light /ˈmaɪkrəʊlaɪt; *AmE* -kroʊ-/ *noun* a very small light aircraft for one or two people

micro·metre (*BrE*) (*AmE* **micro·meter**) /ˈmaɪkrəʊmiːtə(r); *AmE* -kroʊ-/ *noun* a unit for measuring length, equal to one MILLIONTH of a metre

mi·cron /ˈmaɪkrɒn; *AmE* -krɑːn/ *noun* (*old-fashioned*) = MICROMETRE

micro-ˈorganism *noun* (*technical*) a very small living thing that you can only see under a MICROSCOPE

micro·phone /ˈmaɪkrəfəʊn; *AmE* -foʊn/ (also *informal* **mic**, **mike**) *noun* a device that is used for recording sounds or for making your voice louder when you are speaking or singing to an audience: *a cassette recorder with a built-in microphone* ◊ *to speak into the microphone* ◊ *Their remarks were picked up by the hidden microphones.*

micro·pro·ces·sor /ˈmaɪkrəʊˈprəʊsesə(r); *AmE* -kroʊˈproʊ-/ *noun* (*computing*) a small unit of a computer that contains all the functions of the CENTRAL PROCESSING UNIT

micro·scope /ˈmaɪkrəskəʊp; *AmE* -skoʊp/ *noun* an instrument used in scientific study for making very small things look larger so that you can examine them carefully: *a microscope slide* ◊ *The bacteria were then examined under a/the microscope.* ◊ (*figurative*) *In the play, love and marriage are put under the microscope.*—see also ELECTRON MICROSCOPE—picture at LABORATORY

micro·scop·ic /ˌmaɪkrəˈskɒpɪk; *AmE* -ˈskɑːpɪk/ *adj.* **1** [usually before noun] extremely small and difficult or impossible to see without a microscope: *a microscopic creature/particle* ◊ (*humorous*) *The sandwiches were microscopic!* **2** [only before noun] using a microscope: *a microscopic analysis/examination* ▶ **micro·scop·ic·al·ly** /-kli/ *adv.*: *microscopically small creatures* ◊ *All samples are examined microscopically.*

micro·wave /ˈmaɪkrəweɪv/ *noun, verb*
■ *noun* **1** (also *formal* **ˌmicrowave ˈoven**) a type of oven that cooks or heats food very quickly using ELECTROMAGNETIC waves rather than heat: *Reheat the soup in the microwave.* ◊ *microwave cookery/meals*—compare OVEN—picture on page 275 **2** (*technical*) an ELECTROMAGNETIC

s	t	v	z	ʃ	ʒ	tʃ	dʒ	θ	ð	ŋ
see	tea	van	zoo	shoe	vision	chain	jam	thin	this	sing

wave that is shorter than a radio wave but longer than a light wave

■ *verb* [VN] to cook or heat sth in a microwave ⇨ vocabulary notes on page 275 ▶ **micro·wave·able** (also **micro·wav·able**) *adj.*: *microwaveable meals*

mid /mɪd/ *prep.* (*literary*) = AMID

mid- /mɪd/ *combining form* (in nouns and adjectives) in the middle of: *mid-morning coffee* ◇ *She's in her mid-thirties.*

mid-'air *noun* [U] a place in the air or the sky, not on the ground: *The bird caught the insects in mid-air* ▶ **mid-'air** *adj.*: *a mid-air collision*

Midas touch /ˈmaɪdəs tʌtʃ/ *noun* (usually **the Midas touch**) [sing.] the ability to make a financial success of everything you do ORIGIN From the Greek myth in which King Midas was given the power to turn everything he touched into gold.

mid-At'lantic *adj.* [only before noun] **1** connected with the area on the east coast of the US, that is near New York and immediately to the south of it: *the mid-Atlantic states/coast* **2** in the middle of the Atlantic ocean: (*figurative*) *a mid-Atlantic accent* (= a form of English that uses a mixture of British and American sounds)

mid·day /ˌmɪdˈdeɪ/ *noun* [U] 12 o'clock in the middle of the day; the period around this time SYN NOON: *The train arrives at midday.* ◇ *a midday meal* ◇ *the heat of the midday sun*

mid·dle /ˈmɪdl/ *noun, adj.*
■ *noun* **1** (**the middle**) [sing.] the part of sth that is at an equal distance from all its edges or sides; a point or a period of time between the beginning and the end of sth: *a lake with an island in the middle* ◇ *He was standing in the middle of the room.* ◇ *The phone rang in the middle of the night.* ◇ *This chicken isn't cooked in the middle.* ◇ *His picture was right/bang* (= exactly) *in the middle of the front-page.* ◇ *Take a sheet of paper and draw a line down the middle.* ◇ *I should have finished by the middle of the week.* **2** [C, usually sing.] (*informal*) a person's waist: *He grabbed her around the middle.* ◇ *I've put on weight around the middle.* IDM **be in the middle of sth/of doing sth** to be busy doing sth: *They were in the middle of dinner when I called* ◇ *I'm in the middle of writing a difficult letter.* **the middle of 'nowhere** (*informal*) a place that is a long way from other buildings, towns, etc: *She lives on a small farm in the middle of nowhere.* **split/divide sth down the 'middle** to divide sth into two equal parts: *The country was split down the middle over the strike* (= half supported it, half did not).—more at PIG *n.*
■ *adj.* [only before noun] in a position in the middle of an object, group of objects, people, etc. between the beginning and the end of sth: *Pens are kept in the middle drawer.* ◇ *She's the middle child of three.* ◇ *He was very successful in his middle forties.* ◇ *a middle-sized room* ◇ *the middle-income groups in society* IDM **(steer, take, etc.) a middle 'course | (find, etc.) a/the middle 'way** (to take/find) a course of action that is a COMPROMISE between two extreme positions

middle 'age *noun* [U] the period of your life when you are neither young nor old, between the ages of about 45 and 60: *a pleasant woman in early/late middle age*

middle-'aged *adj.* **1** (of a person) neither young nor old **2** (**the middle aged**) *noun* [pl.] people who are middle-aged **3** (*disapproving*) (of a person's attitudes or behaviour) rather boring and old-fashioned

the Middle 'Ages *noun* [pl.] in European history, the period from about AD 1000 to AD 1450

middle-age 'spread (also **middle-aged 'spread**) *noun* [U] (*humorous*) the fat around the stomach that some people develop in middle age

Middle A'merica *noun* [U] the middle class in the US, especially those people who represent traditional social and political values, and who come from small towns and SUBURBS rather than cities

middle-brow /ˈmɪdlbraʊ/ *adj.* [usually before noun] (usually *disapproving*) (of books, music, art, etc.) of good quality but not needing a lot of thought to understand—compare HIGHBROW, LOWBROW

middle 'C *noun* [U] the musical note C near the middle of the piano keyboard

middle 'class *noun* [C+sing./pl. *v.*] the social class whose members are neither very rich nor very poor and that includes professional and business people: *the upper/lower middle class* ◇ *the growth of the middle classes*—compare UPPER CLASS, WORKING CLASS

middle-'class *adj.* **1** connected with the middle social class: *a middle-class background/family/suburb* **2** (*disapproving*) typical of people from the middle social class, for example having traditional views: *a middle-class attitude* ◇ *The magazine is very middle-class.*

middle 'distance *noun* (**the middle distance**) [sing.] the part of a painting or a view that is neither very close nor very far away: *His eyes were fixed on a small house in the middle distance.*

middle-'distance *adj.* [only before noun] (*sport*) connected with running a race over a distance that is neither very short nor very long: *a middle-distance runner* (= for example, somebody who runs 800 or 1500 metre races)

middle 'ear *noun* [sing.] the central part of the ear behind the EARDRUM

the Middle 'East (also *less frequent* **the Near 'East**) *noun* [sing.] an area that covers SW Asia and NE Africa—compare THE FAR EAST ▶ **Middle 'Eastern** (also *less frequent* **Near 'Eastern**) *adj.*

middle 'finger *noun* the longest finger in the middle of each hand—picture at BODY

middle ground *noun* [U] a set of opinions, decisions, etc. that two or more groups who oppose each other can agree on; a position that is not extreme: *Negotiations have failed to establish any middle ground.* ◇ *The ballet company now occupies the middle ground between classical ballet and modern dance.*

middle·man /ˈmɪdlmæn/ *noun* (*pl.* **-men** /-men/) **1** a person or a company that buys goods from the company that makes them and sells them to sb else: *Buy direct from the manufacturer and cut out the middleman.* **2** a person who helps to arrange things between people who do not want to talk directly to each other SYN INTERMEDIARY, GO-BETWEEN

middle 'management *noun* [U+sing./pl. *v.*] the people who are in charge of small groups of people and departments within a business organization but who are not involved in making important decisions that will affect the whole organization ▶ **middle 'manager** *noun*

middle 'name *noun* a name that comes between your first name and your family name IDM **be sb's middle 'name** (*informal*) used to say that sb has a lot of a particular quality: *'Patience' is my middle name!*

middle-of-the-'road *adj.* (of people, policies, etc.) not extreme; acceptable to most people: *a middle-of-the-road newspaper* ◇ *Their music is very middle-of-the-road.*

middle-'ranking *adj.* [only before noun] having a responsible job or position, but not one of the most important: *a middle-ranking officer*

middle school *noun* **1** (in Britain) a school for children between the ages of about 9 and 13 **2** (in the US) a school for children between the ages of about 11 and 14—compare UPPER SCHOOL

middle·weight /ˈmɪdlweɪt/ *noun* a boxer weighing between 67 and 72.5 kilograms, heavier than a WELTERWEIGHT: *a middleweight champion*

the Middle 'West *noun* [sing.] = MIDWEST

mid·dling /ˈmɪdlɪŋ/ *adj.* [usually before noun] of average size, quality, status, etc: *a golfer of middling talent*

mid·field /ˈmɪdfiːld; ˌmɪdˈfiːld/ *noun* [U, C, sing.] the central part of a sports field in football, etc.; the group of players in this position: *He plays (in) midfield.* ◇ *The team's midfield looks strong.* ◇ *a midfield player* ▶ **mid·field·er** /ˈmɪdfiːldə(r)/ *noun*

midge /mɪdʒ/ *noun* a small flying insect that lives especially in damp places and that bites humans and animals: *clouds of midges*

M

æ	ɑː	e	ɜː	ə	ɪ	iː	i	ɒ	ɔː	ʌ	ʊ	u	uː
cat	father	ten	bird	about	sit	see	many	got	saw	cup	put	actual	too
								(BrE)					

midget /ˈmɪdʒɪt/ *noun, adj.*
■ *noun* **1** (⚠, *offensive*) an extremely small person, who will never grow to a normal size because of a physical problem; a person suffering from DWARFISM **2** (*informal*, sometimes *offensive*) a very small person or animal
■ *adj.* [only before noun] very small

Mid·lands /ˈmɪdləndz/ *noun* (**the Midlands**) [sing.+ sing./pl. *v.*] the central part of a country, especially the central counties of England ▶ **Mid·land** *adj.* [only before noun]

mid·life /ˈmɪdlaɪf/ *noun* [U] the middle part of your life when you are neither young nor old: *It is not difficult to take up a new career in midlife* ◊ *midlife stresses*

midlife 'crisis *noun* [usually sing.] the feelings of worry, disappointment or lack of confidence that a person may feel in the middle part of their life

mid·night /ˈmɪdnaɪt/ *noun* [U] **1** 12 o'clock at night: *They had to leave at midnight.* ◊ *on the stroke of midnight/ shortly after midnight* ◊ *She heard the clock strike midnight.* ◊ *We have to catch the midnight train.* **2** (*especially AmE*) = MIDNIGHT BLUE **IDM** see BURN *v.*, FLIT *n.*

midnight 'blue (also **mid·night** especially in *AmE*) *noun* [U] a very dark blue colour ▶ **midnight 'blue** *adj.*

the midnight 'sun *noun* [sing.] the sun that you can see in the middle of the summer near the North and South Poles

mid-point *noun* [usually sing.] the point that is halfway through sth or through a period of time; the point that is halfway between two things: *the mid-point of the decade* ◊ *At its mid-point, the race had no clear winner.* ◊ *the mid-point between the first number and the last*

mid-'range *adj.* [only before noun] (especially of a product for sale) neither the best nor the worst that is available: *a mid-range computer*

mid·riff /ˈmɪdrɪf/ *noun* the middle part of the body between the chest and the waist: *a bare midriff*

mid·ship·man /ˈmɪdʃɪpmən/ *noun* (*pl.* **-men** /-mən/) a person training to be an officer in the navy: *Midshipman Paul Brooks*

mid-'sized (also **mid-'size**) *adj.* (*especially AmE*) of average size, neither large nor small

midst /mɪdst/ *noun* (*formal*) (used after a preposition) the middle part of sth: *Such beauty was unexpected in the midst of the city.* ◊ *She appeared from the midst of the crowd.* **IDM in the midst of sth/of doing sth** while sth is happening or being done; while you are doing sth: *a country in the midst of a recession* ◊ *She discovered it in the midst of sorting out her father's things.* **in their/our/its/ your midst** (*formal*) among or with them/us/it/you: *There is a traitor in our midst.*

mid·stream /ˌmɪdˈstriːm/ *noun* [U] the middle part of a river, stream, etc: *We anchored in midstream* **IDM** (**in**) **midstream** in the middle of doing sth; while sth is still happening: *Their conversation was interrupted in midstream by the baby crying.*—more at CHANGE *v.*

mid·sum·mer /ˌmɪdˈsʌmə(r)/ *noun* [U] the middle of summer, especially the period in June in northern parts of the world, in December in southern parts: *a midsummer evening*

Midsummer's 'Day (*BrE*) (also **Midsummer 'Day** *AmE, BrE*) *noun* 24 June, in northern parts of the world

mid-term /ˌmɪdˈtɜːm/ *AmE* -'tɜːrm/ *adj.* [only before noun] **1** in the middle of the period that a government, a council, etc. is elected for: *midterm elections* **2** for or connected with a period of time that is neither long nor short; in the middle of a particular period: *a midterm solution* ◊ *midterm losses*—see also LONG-TERM, SHORT-TERM **3** in the middle of one of the main periods of the academic year: *a midterm examination / break*—see also HALF-TERM

mid·town /ˈmɪdtaʊn/ *noun* (*AmE*) the part of a city that is between the central business area and the outer parts: *a house in midtown* ◊ *midtown Manhattan*—compare DOWNTOWN, UPTOWN

mid·way /ˌmɪdˈweɪ/ *adv.* in the middle of a period of time; between two places **SYN** HALFWAY: *The goal was scored midway through the first half.* ▶ **mid·way** *adj.*: *to reach the midway point*

mid·week /ˌmɪdˈwiːk/ *noun* [U] the middle of the week: *to play a match in midweek* ◊ *By midweek he was too tired to go out.* ◊ *a midweek defeat for the team* ▶ **mid·week** *adv.*: *It's cheaper to travel midweek.*

Mid·west /ˌmɪdˈwest/ (**the Midwest**) (also **the Middle 'West**) *noun* [sing.] the northern central part of the US ▶ **Mid·west·ern** /ˌmɪdˈwestən; *AmE* -ərn/ *adj.*

mid·wife /ˈmɪdwaɪf/ *noun* (*pl.* **mid·wives** /-waɪvz/) a person, especially a woman, who is trained to help women give birth to babies—compare DOULA

mid·wif·ery /ˌmɪdˈwɪfəri/ *noun* [U] the profession and work of a midwife

mid·win·ter /ˌmɪdˈwɪntə(r)/ *noun* [U] the middle of winter, around December in northern parts of the world, June in southern parts: *midwinter weather*

mien /miːn/ *noun* [sing.] (*formal* or *literary*) a person's appearance or manner that shows how they are feeling

miffed /mɪft/ *adj.* [not before noun] (*informal*) slightly angry or upset

might /maɪt/ *modal verb, noun*
■ *modal verb* (*negative* **might not**, *short form* **mightn't** /ˈmaɪtnt/) **1** used as the past tense of *may* when reporting what sb has said: *He said he might come tomorrow.* **2** used when showing that sth is or was possible: *He might get there in time, but I can't be sure.* ◊ *I know Vicky doesn't like the job, but I mightn't find it too bad.* ◊ *The pills might have helped him, if only he'd taken them regularly.* ◊ *He might say that now* (= it is true that he does), *but he can soon change his mind.* **3** used to make a polite suggestion: *You might try calling the help desk.* ◊ *I thought we might go to the zoo on Saturday.* **4** (*BrE*) used to ask permission politely: *Might I use your phone?* ◊ *If I might just say something ...* **5** (*formal*) used to ask for information: *How might the plans be improved upon?* ◊ *And who might she be?* **6** used to show that you are annoyed about sth that sb could do or could have done: *I think you might at least offer to help!* ◊ *Honestly, you might have told me!* **7** used to say that you are not surprised by sth: *I might have guessed it was you!* **8** used to emphasize that an important point has been made: '*And where is the money coming from?*' '*You might well ask!*' ⇨ note at MODAL **IDM** see WELL
■ *noun* [U] (*formal* or *literary*) great strength, energy or power: *America's military might* ◊ *I pushed the rock with all my might.*

might·ily /ˈmaɪtɪli/ *adv.* (*old-fashioned*) **1** very; very much: *mightily impressed / relieved* **2** (*formal*) with great strength or effort: *We have struggled mightily to win back lost trade.*

mighty /ˈmaɪti/ *adj., adv.*
■ *adj.* (**might·ier**, **mighti·est**) **1** (especially *literary*) very strong and powerful: *a mighty warrior* ◊ *He struck him with a mighty blow across his shoulder.* **2** large and impressive: *the mighty Mississippi river* **IDM** see HIGH *adj.*
■ *adv.* (*informal, especially AmE*) (with adjectives and adverbs) very: *mighty difficult* ◊ *driving mighty fast*

mi·graine /ˈmiːɡreɪn; ˈmaɪɡ-; *AmE* ˈmaɪɡ-/ *noun* [U, C] a very severe type of HEADACHE which often makes a person feel sick and have difficulty in seeing: *severe migraine* ◊ *I'm getting a migraine.*

mi·grant /ˈmaɪɡrənt/ *noun* **1** a person who moves from one place to another, especially in order to find work: *They claimed they were political refugees and not economic migrants.* ◊ *migrant workers*—compare EMIGRANT, IMMIGRANT **2** a bird or an animal that moves from one place to another according to the season

mi·grate /maɪˈɡreɪt; *AmE* ˈmaɪɡreɪt/ *verb* [V] **1** (of birds, animals, etc.) to move from one part of the world to another according to the season: *Swallows migrate south in winter.* **2** (of a lot of people) to move from one town, country, etc. to go and live and/or work in another **SYN** EMIGRATE: *Thousands were forced to migrate from rural to urban areas in search of work.* **3** (*technical*) to move from one place to another: *The infected cells then migrate to other areas of the body.*

mi·gra·tion /maɪˈɡreɪʃn/ *noun* [U, C] the movement of

aɪ	aʊ	eɪ	əʊ	oʊ	ɔɪ	ɪə	eə	ʊə	j	w
my	now	say	go (BrE)	go (AmE)	boy	near	hair	pure	yes	wet

large numbers of people, birds or animals from one place to another: *seasonal migrations* ◇ *mass migrations*

mi·gra·tory /'maɪɡrətri; maɪ'ɡreɪtəri; *AmE* 'maɪɡrətɔːri/ *adj.* (*technical*) connected with, or having the habit of, regular migration: *migratory flights / birds*

mike /maɪk/ *noun* (*informal*) = MICROPHONE

mild /maɪld/ *adj.*, *noun*
■ *adj.* (**mild·er**, **mild·est**) **1** not severe or harsh: *a mild form of the disease* ◇ *a mild punishment / criticism* ◇ *It's safe to take a mild sedative.* ◇ *Use a soap that is mild on the skin.* **2** (of weather) not very cold, and therefore pleasant: *the mildest winter since records began* ◇ *a mild climate*—compare HARD **3** (of feelings) not great or extreme [SYN] SLIGHT: *mild irritation / amusement / disapproval* ◇ *She looked at him in mild surprise.* **4** (of people or their behaviour) gentle and kind; not usually getting angry or violent: *a mild woman, who never shouted* **5** (of a flavour) not strong, spicy or bitter: *a mild curry* ◇ *mild cheese* [OPP] HOT ▶ **mild·ness** *noun* [U]: *the mildness of a sunny spring day* ◇ *her mildness of manner*
■ *noun* [U] (*BrE*) a type of clear dark beer with a mild flavour: *Two pints of mild, please.*—compare BITTER

mil·dew /'mɪldjuː; *AmE* -duː/ *noun* [U] a very small white FUNGUS that grows on walls, plants, food, etc. in warm wet conditions

mil·dewed /'mɪldjuːd; *AmE* -duːd/ *adj.* with MILDEW growing on it

mild·ly /'maɪldli/ *adv.* **1** slightly; not very much: *mildly surprised / irritated / interested* **2** in a gentle manner: *'I didn't mean to upset you' he said mildly.* [IDM] **to put it ¦mildly** (*spoken*) used to show that what you are talking about is much more extreme, etc. than your words suggest: *The result was unfortunate, to put it mildly* (= it was extremely unfortunate).

mile /maɪl/ *noun* **1** [C] a unit for measuring distance equal to 1609 metres or 1760 YARDS: *a 20-mile drive to work* ◇ *an area of four square miles* ◇ *a mile-long procession* ◇ *The nearest bank is about half a mile down the road.* ◇ *We did about 30 miles a day on our cycling trip.* ◇ *The car must have been doing at least 100 miles an hour.* ◇ *My car does 35 miles to the gallon.*—see also MPH, NAUTICAL MILE **2** (**miles**) [pl.] a large area or a long distance: *miles and miles of desert* ◇ *There isn't a house for miles around here.* ◇ *I'm not walking—it's **miles away**.* **3** [C, usually pl.] (*informal*) very much; far: *I'm feeling miles better today, thanks.* ◇ *I'm miles behind with my work.* ◇ *She's taller than you by a mile.* **4** (**the mile**) [sing.] a race over one mile: *He ran the mile in less than four minutes.* ◇ *a four-minute mile* [IDM] **be ¦miles away** (*informal*) to be thinking deeply about sth and not aware of what is happening around you **go the ¦extra ¦mile (for sb/sth)** to make a special effort to achieve sth, help sb, etc. **¦miles from ¦anywhere** (*informal*) in a place that is a long way from a town and surrounded only by a lot of open country, sea, etc: *We broke down miles from anywhere.* **run a ¦mile (from sb/sth)** (*informal*) to show that you are very frightened of doing sth **see, spot, tell, smell, etc. sth a ¦mile off** (*informal*) to see or realize sth very easily and quickly: *He's wearing a wig—you can see it a mile off.* **stand / stick out a ¦mile** to be very obvious or noticeable: *It stood out a mile that she was lying.*—more at INCH *n.*

mile·age /'maɪlɪdʒ/ *noun* **1** [U, C, usually sing.] the distance that a vehicle has travelled, measured in miles: *My annual mileage is about 10000.* ◇ *a used car with one owner and a low mileage* ◇ *The price of the car included unlimited mileage, but not fuel.* ◇ *I get a **mileage allowance** if I use my car for work* (= an amount of money paid for each mile I travel). **2** [U, C] the number of miles that a vehicle can travel using a particular amount of fuel: *If you drive carefully you can get better mileage from your car.* **3** [U] (*informal*) the amount of advantage or use that you can get from a particular event or situation: *I don't think the press can get any more mileage out of that story.*

mile·om·eter *noun* = MILOMETER

mile·post /'maɪlpəʊst; *AmE* -poʊst/ *noun* (*especially*

AmE) **1** a post by the side of the road that shows how far it is to the next town, and to other places **2** = MILESTONE

mile·stone /'maɪlstəʊn; *AmE* -stoʊn/ *noun* **1** (also **mile·post** especially in *AmE*) a very important stage or event in the development of sth **2** a stone by the side of a road that shows how far it is to the next town and to other places

mi·lieu /miːˈljɜː/ *noun* [C, usually sing.] (*pl.* **mi·lieux** or **mi·lieus** /-ˈljɜːz/) (from French, *formal*) the social environment that you live or work in

mili·tant /'mɪlɪtənt/ *adj.* using, or willing to use, force or strong pressure to achieve your aims, especially to achieve social or political change: *militant groups / leaders* ▶ **mili·tancy** /-ənsi/ *noun* [U]: *a growing militancy amongst the unemployed* **mili·tant** *noun*: *Student militants were fighting with the police.* **mili·tant·ly** *adv.*

mili·tar·ism /'mɪlɪtərɪzəm/ *noun* [U] (usually *disapproving*) the belief that a country should have great military strength in order to be powerful ▶ **mili·tar·ist** *noun*: *Militarists ran the country.* **mili·tar·is·tic** /ˌmɪlɪtəˈrɪstɪk/ *adj.*: *militaristic government*

mili·tar·ize (*BrE* also **-ise**) /'mɪlɪtəraɪz/ *verb* [VN] (usually *passive*) **1** to send armed forces to an area: *a militarized zone* [OPP] DEMILITARIZE **2** to make sth similar to an army: *a militarized police force* ▶ **mili·tar·iza·tion, -isa·tion** /ˌmɪlɪtəraɪˈzeɪʃn; *AmE* -rəˈz-/ *noun* [U]

mili·tary /'mɪlətri; *AmE* -teri/ *adj.*, *noun*
■ *adj.* [usually before noun] connected with soldiers or the armed forces: *military training / intelligence* ◇ *a military coup* ◇ *military uniform* ◇ *We may have to take military action.*—compare CIVILIAN ▶ **mili·tar·ily** *adv.*: *a militarily superior country* ◇ *We may have to intervene militarily in the area.*
■ *noun* (**the military**) [sing.+ sing. / pl. *v.*] soldiers; the armed forces: *The military was / were called in to deal with the riot.*

¦military ¦service *noun* [U] **1** a period during which young people train in the armed forces: *to be **called up** for military service* ◇ *She has to **do her military service**.* **2** the time sb spends in the armed forces: *He's completed 30 years of active military service.*

mili·tate /'mɪlɪteɪt/ *verb* [PHRV] **¦militate against sth** (*formal*) to prevent sth; to make it difficult for sth to happen or exist: *The supervisor's presence militated against a relaxed atmosphere.*

mili·tia /məˈlɪʃə/ *noun* [sing.+ sing. / pl. *v.*] a group of people who are not professional soldiers but who have had military training and can act as an army

mili·tia·man /məˈlɪʃəmən/ *noun* (*pl.* **-men** /-mən/) a member of a militia

milk /mɪlk/ *noun*, *verb*
■ *noun* [U] **1** the white liquid produced by cows, goats and some other animals as food for their young and used as a drink by humans: *a pint / litre of milk* ◇ *a bottle / carton of milk* ◇ *fresh / dried / powdered milk* ◇ *Do you take milk in your tea?* ◇ *milk products* (= butter, cheese, etc.)—see also BUTTERMILK, CONDENSED MILK, EVAPORATED MILK, MALTED MILK, SKIMMED MILK **2** the white liquid that is produced by women and female MAMMALS for feeding their babies: *breast milk* **3** the white juice of some plants and trees, especially the COCONUT—picture on page A2 [IDM] **the milk of human ¦kindness** (*literary*) kind behaviour, considered to be natural to human beings—more at CRY *v.*, LAND *n.*
■ *verb* [VN] **1** to take milk from a cow, goat, etc. **2 ~ A (of B) | ~ B (from A)** (*disapproving*) to obtain as much money, advantage, etc. for yourself as you can from a particular situation, especially in a dishonest way: *She's milked a small fortune from the company over the years.* ◇ *She's milked the company of a small fortune.* ◇ *I know he's had a hard time lately, but he's certainly **milking it for all it's worth*** (= using it as an excuse to do things that people would normally object to). [IDM] see DRY *n.*

¦milk ¦chocolate *noun* [U] light brown chocolate made with extra milk—compare PLAIN CHOCOLATE

¦milk float *noun* (*BrE*) a small electric vehicle used for delivering milk to people's houses

b	d	f	g	h	k	l	m	n	p	r
bad	did	fall	get	hat	cat	leg	man	now	pen	red

M

milk·ing /'mɪlkɪŋ/ noun [U] the process of taking milk from a cow, etc: *milking machines/sheds*

milk·maid /'mɪlkmeɪd/ noun (in the past) a woman whose job was to take milk from cows and make butter and cheese

milk·man /'mɪlkmən/ noun (pl. **-men** /-mən/) (especially in Britain) a person whose job is to deliver milk to customers each morning

'milk round noun **1** (in Britain) the job of going from house to house regularly, delivering milk; the route taken by sb doing this job **2** (also **the milk round**) (in Britain) a series of visits that large companies make each year to colleges and universities, to talk to students who are interested in working for them

milk·shake /'mɪlkʃeɪk/ (also **shake**) noun a drink made of milk, and sometimes ice cream, with an added flavour of fruit or chocolate, which is mixed or shaken until it is full of bubbles: *a banana milkshake*

'milk tooth (BrE) (also **'baby tooth** AmE, BrE) noun any of the first set of teeth in young children that drop out and are replaced by others

mil·ky /'mɪlki/ adj. **1** made of milk; containing a lot of milk: *a hot milky drink ◇ milky tea/coffee* **2** like milk: *milky* (= not clear) *blue eyes ◇ milky* (= white) *skin*

the ˌMilky 'Way noun [sing.] = THE GALAXY

mill /mɪl/ noun, verb

▪ noun **1** a building fitted with machinery for GRINDING grain into flour—see also WATERMILL, WINDMILL **2** (often in compounds) a factory that produces a particular type of material: *a cotton/cloth/steel/paper mill ◇ mill owners/workers*—see also ROLLING MILL, SAWMILL **3** (often in compounds) a small machine for crushing or GRINDING a solid substance into powder: *a pepper mill*—see also RUN-OF-THE-MILL, TREADMILL **IDM** **go through the 'mill | put sb through the 'mill** to have or make sb have a difficult time: *They really put me through the mill in my interview.*—more at GRIST

▪ verb [VN] [often passive] to crush or GRIND sth in a mill **PHRV** ˌmill a'round (BrE also ˌmill a'bout) (especially of a large group of people) to move around an area without seeming to be going anywhere in particular: *Hundreds of fans were milling around outside the hotel.*—see also MILLING

mil·len·nium /mɪ'leniəm/ noun (pl. **mil·len·nia** /-niə/ or **mil·len·niums**) **1** a period of 1000 years, especially as calculated before or after the birth of Christ: *the second millennium AD* **2** (**the millennium**) the time when one period of 1000 years ends and another begins: *How did you celebrate the millennium?*

the mil'lennium bug noun [sing.] a problem that threatened to make computer systems all over the world stop working in the year 2000 because they could not recognize a date ending in two zeros

mill·er /'mɪlə(r)/ noun a person who owns or works in a MILL for making flour

mil·let /'mɪlɪt/ noun [U] a type of plant producing very small grain, grown mainly as food for animals but also eaten by people in parts of Africa and Asia—picture at CEREAL

milli- /'mɪli/ combining form (in nouns; used in units of measurement) one THOUSANDTH: *milligram*

milli·bar /'mɪlibɑː(r)/ (also informal **bar**) noun a unit for measuring the pressure of the atmosphere

milli·gram (BrE also **milli·gramme**) /'mɪligræm/ noun (abbr. **mg**) a unit for measuring weight; a 1000th of a gram

milli·litre (BrE) (AmE **milli·liter**) /'mɪlilɪːtə(r)/ noun (abbr. **ml**) a unit for measuring the volume of liquids and gases; a 1000th of a litre

milli·metre (BrE) (AmE **milli·meter**) /'mɪlimiːtə(r)/ noun (abbr. **mm**) a unit for measuring length; a 1000th of a metre

mill·iner /'mɪlɪnə(r)/ noun a person whose job is making and/or selling women's hats

mill·in·ery /'mɪlɪnəri; AmE 'mɪlɪneri/ noun [U] **1** the work of a milliner **2** the things made by a milliner: *the millinery department* (= in a large store)

mill·ing /'mɪlɪŋ/ adj. [only before noun] **1** connected with the work of GRINDING grain, etc. to make flour: *milling machines* **2** (of people) moving around in a large mass: *I had to fight my way through the milling crowd.*

mil·lion /'mɪljən/ number (plural verb) **1** (abbr. **m**) 1000000 **HELP** You say *a*, *one*, *two*, *several*, etc. **million** without a final 's' on 'million'. **Millions** (of…) can be used if there is no number or quantity before it. Always use a plural verb with **million** or **millions**.: *a population of half a million ◇ tens of millions of dollars ◇ It must be worth a million* (= pounds, dollars, etc.) **2** *a million* or *millions* (**of**…) (informal) a very large amount: *I still have a million things to do. ◇ He made his millions* (= all his money) *on currency deals.* **HELP** There are more examples of how to use numbers at the entry for **hundred**. **IDM** **look/feel like a million 'dollars/'bucks** (informal) to look/feel extremely good **one**, etc. **in a 'million** a person or thing that is very unusual or special: *He's a man in a million.*

mil·lion·aire /ˌmɪljə'neə(r); AmE -'ner/ noun a person who has a million pounds, dollars, etc.; a very rich person: *an oil millionaire ◇ She's a millionaire several times over. ◇ a millionaire businessman*

mil·lion·air·ess /ˌmɪljə'neərəs; AmE -'ner-/ noun (old-fashioned) a woman who is a millionaire

mil·lionth /'mɪljənθ/ ordinal number, noun

▪ ordinal number 1000000th

▪ noun each of one million equal parts of sth: *a/one millionth of a second*

milli·pede /'mɪlipiːd/ noun a small creature like an insect, with a long thin body divided into many sections, each with two pairs of legs

milli·sec·ond /'mɪlisekənd/ noun (technical) a 1000th of a second: (figurative) *I hesitated a millisecond too long.*

mill·pond /'mɪlpɒnd; AmE -pɑːnd/ noun a small area of water used especially in the past to make the wheel of a MILL turn

mill·stone /'mɪlstəʊn; AmE -stoʊn/ noun one of two flat circular stones used, especially in the past, to crush grain to make flour **IDM** **a millstone around/round your 'neck** a difficult problem or responsibility that it seems impossible to solve or get rid of: *My debts are a millstone around my neck.*

'mill wheel noun a large wheel that is turned by water and that makes the machinery of a MILL work

mil·om·eter (also **mile·ometer**) /maɪ'lɒmɪtə(r); AmE -'lɑːm-/ (both BrE) (AmE **odom·eter**) (also informal **the clock** AmE, BrE) noun an instrument in a vehicle that measures the number of miles it has travelled—picture at CAR

mime /maɪm/ noun, verb

▪ noun [U, C] (especially in the theatre) the use of movements of your hands or body and the expressions on your face to tell a story or to act sth without speaking; a performance using this method of acting: *The performance consisted of dance, music and mime. ◇ a mime artist ◇ She performed a brief mime.*

▪ verb **1** to act, tell a story, etc. by moving your body and face but without speaking: [VN] *the title of a movie, play or book. ◇* [V-ing] *He mimed climbing a mountain.* [also V] **2** ~ (**to**) **sth** to pretend to sing a song that is actually being sung by sb else on a record, tape, etc: [V] *The band was miming to a backing tape.* [also VN]

mi·met·ic /mɪ'metɪk/ adj. (technical or formal) copying the behaviour or appearance of sb/sth else

mimic /'mɪmɪk/ verb, noun

▪ verb (**-ck-**) **1** to copy the way sb speaks, moves, behaves, etc., especially in order to make other people laugh: [VN] *She's always mimicking the teachers. ◇ He mimicked her southern accent.* [also V **speech**] **2** [VN] to look or behave like sth else **SYN** IMITATE: *The robot was programmed to mimic a series of human movements.*

▪ noun a person or an animal that can copy the voice, movements, etc. of others

mim·ic·ry /'mɪmɪkri/ noun [U] the action or skill of

M

being able to copy the voice, movements, etc. of others: *a talent for mimicry*

mi·mosa /mɪˈməʊzə; -ˈməʊsə; *AmE* -ˈmoʊ-/ *noun* **1** [C, U] a tropical bush or tree with balls of yellow flowers and leaves that are sensitive to touch and light **2** [C] (*AmE*) a drink made with CHAMPAGNE and orange juice

min. *abbr.* **1** (in writing) minute(s): *Cook for 8–10 min. until tender.* **2** (in writing) MINIMUM: *min. charge £4.50* [OPP] MAX

min·aret /ˌmɪnəˈret/ *noun* a tall thin tower, usually forming part of a MOSQUE, from which Muslims are called to prayer

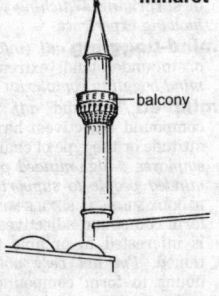

minaret

— balcony

mince /mɪns/ *verb, noun*
- *verb* **1** [VN] to cut food, especially meat, into very small pieces using a special machine (= called a MINCER): *minced beef* **2** [V+adv./ prep.] (*disapproving*) to walk with quick short steps, in a way that is not natural: *He minced over to serve us.* [IDM] **not mince (your) words** to say sth in a direct way even though it might offend other people
- *noun* (*BrE*) (*AmE* ˌground ˈbeef, ˈham·burg·er, ˈhamburger meat**) [U] meat, especially beef, that has been finely chopped in a special machine: *a pound of mince*

mince·meat /ˈmɪnsmiːt/ *noun* [U] (*especially BrE*) a mixture of dried fruit, spices, etc. used especially for making pies [IDM] **make ˈmincemeat of sb** (*informal*) to defeat sb completely in a fight, an argument or a competition

ˌmince ˈpie *noun* a small round pie filled with mincemeat, traditionally eaten at Christmas, especially in Britain

min·cer /ˈmɪnsə(r)/ (*especially BrE*) (*AmE* usually ˈmeat grinder**) *noun* a machine for cutting food, especially meat, into very small pieces

min·cing /ˈmɪnsɪŋ/ *adj.* (*disapproving*) (of a way of walking or speaking) very delicate, and not natural: *short mincing steps*

mind /maɪnd/ *noun, verb*
- *noun*

ABILITY TO THINK | **1** [C, U] the part of a person that makes them able to be aware of things, to think and to feel: *the conscious/subconscious mind* ◊ *There were all kinds of thoughts running through my mind.* ◊ *There was no doubt in his mind that he'd get the job.* ◊ *'Drugs' are associated in most people's minds with drug abuse.* ◊ *She was in a disturbed state of mind.* ◊ *I could not have complete peace of mind before they returned.*—see also FRAME OF MIND, PRESENCE OF MIND **2** [C] your ability to think and reason; your intelligence; the particular way that sb thinks [SYN] INTELLECT: *to have a brilliant/good/keen mind* ◊ *a creative/evil/suspicious mind* ◊ *She had a lively and enquiring mind.* ◊ *His mind is as sharp as ever.* ◊ *I've no idea how her mind works!* ◊ *He had the body of a man and the mind of a child.* ◊ *insights into the criminal mind*—see also ONE-TRACK MIND

INTELLIGENT PERSON | **3** [C] a person who is very intelligent: *She was one of the greatest minds of her generation.*—see also MASTERMIND

THOUGHTS | **4** [C] your thoughts, interest, etc: *Keep your minds on your work!* ◊ *Her mind is completely occupied by the new baby.* ◊ *The lecture dragged on and my mind wandered.* ◊ *She gave her mind to the arrangements for the next day.* ◊ *As for avoiding you, nothing could be further from my mind* (= I was not thinking of it at all).

MEMORY | **5** [C, usually sing.] your ability to remember things: *When I saw the exam questions my mind just went blank* (= I couldn't remember anything). ◊ *Sorry—your name has gone right out of my mind.*

[IDM] **be all in sb's/the ˈmind** to be sth that only exists in sb's imagination: *These problems are all in your mind,*

you know. **bear/keep sb/sth in ˈmind | bear/keep in ˈmind that …** to remember sb/sth; to remember or consider that … **be bored, frightened, pissed, stoned, etc. out of your ˈmind** (*informal*) to be extremely bored, etc. **be/go ˌout of your ˈmind** to be unable to think or behave in a normal way; to become crazy: (*informal*) *You're lending them money? You must be out of your tiny mind!* **be in two ˈminds about sth/about doing sth** (*BrE*) (*AmE* **be of two ˈminds about sth/about doing sth**) to be unable to decide what you think about sb/sth, or whether to do sth or not: *I was in two minds about the book* (= I didn't know if I liked it or not). ◊ *She's in two minds about accepting his invitation.* **be of one/the same ˈmind (about sb/sth)** to have the same opinion about sb/sth **be ˌout of your ˈmind with worry, etc.** to be extremely worried, etc. **bring/call sb/sth to ˈmind** (*formal*) **1** to remember sb/sth: *She couldn't call to mind where she had seen him before.* **2** to remind you of sb/sth: *The painting brings to mind some of Picasso's early works.* **come/spring to ˈmind** if sth comes/springs to mind, you suddenly remember or think of it: *When discussing influential modern artists, three names immediately come to mind.* **have a good mind to do sth | have half a mind to do sth 1** used to say that you think you will do sth, although you are not sure: *I've half a mind to come with you tomorrow.* **2** used to say that you disapprove of what sb has done and should do sth about it, although you probably will not: *I've a good mind to write and tell your parents about it.* **have sb/sth in ˈmind (for sth)** to be thinking of sb/sth, especially for a particular job, etc: *Do you have anyone in mind for this job?* ◊ *Watching TV all evening wasn't exactly what I had in mind!* **have it in mind to do sth** (*formal*) to intend to do sth **have a mind of your ˈown** to have your own opinion and make your own decisions without being influenced by other people: *She has a mind of her own and isn't afraid to say what she thinks.* ◊ (*humorous*) *My computer seems to have a mind of its own!* **lose your ˈmind** to become mentally ill **make up your ˈmind** to decide sth: *They're both beautiful—I can't make up my mind.* ◊ *Have you made up your minds where to go for your honeymoon?* ◊ *You'll never persuade him to stay—his mind's made up* (= he has definitely decided to go). ◊ *Come on—it's make your mind up time!* ˌmind over ˈmatter** the use of the power of your mind to deal with physical problems **your mind's ˈeye** your imagination: *He pictured the scene in his mind's eye.* **on your ˈmind** if sb/sth is on your mind, you are thinking and worrying about them/it a lot: *You've been on my mind all day.* ◊ *Don't bother your father tonight—he's got a lot on his mind.* **put/get sth out of your ˈmind** to stop thinking about sb/sth; to deliberately forget sb/sth: *I just can't get her out of my mind.* **put sb in mind of sb/sth** (*old-fashioned*) to make sb think of sb/sth; to remind sb of sb/sth **put/set sb's ˈmind at ease/rest** to do or say sth to make sb stop worrying about sth **put/set/turn your ˈmind to sth | set your ˈmind on sth** to decide you want to achieve sth and give this all your attention: *She could have been a brilliant pianist if she'd put her mind to it.* **take your mind off sth** to make you forget about sth unpleasant for a short time: *Painting helped take her mind off her troubles.* **to ˈmy mind** (*spoken*) in my opinion: *It was a ridiculous thing to do, to my mind.*—more at BACK *n.*, BEND *v.*, BLOW *v.*, BOGGLE, CAST *v.*, CHANGE *v.*, CHANGE *n.*, CLOSE[1] *v.*, CROSS *v.*, ETCH, KNOW *v.*, MEETING, OPEN *adj.*, OPEN *v.*, PIECE *n.*, PREY *v.*, PUSH *v.*, RIGHT *adj.*, SIEVE *n.*, SIGHT *n.*, SLIP *v.*, SPEAK, STICK *v.*, TURN *n.*, UNSOUND

- *verb*

BE UPSET/ANNOYED | **1** (used especially in questions or with negatives; not used in the passive) to be upset, annoyed or worried by sth: [VN] *I don't mind the cold—it's the rain I don't like.* ◊ *I hope you don't mind the noise.* ◊ [V, V-**ing**] *Did she mind about not getting the job?* ◊ *Did she mind not getting the job?* ◊ [V] *He wouldn't have minded so much if she'd told him the truth.* ◊ [VN-**ing**] *Do your parents mind you leaving home?* ◊ (*formal*) *Do your parents mind your leaving home?* ◊ [V**wh-**] *She never minded how hot it was.* ◊ [V**that**] *He minded that he hadn't been asked.*

ASKING PERMISSION | **2** used to ask for permission to do sth,

æ	ɑː	e	ɜː	ə	ɪ	iː	i	ɒ	ɔː	ʌ	ʊ	u	uː
cat	father	ten	bird	about	sit	see	many	got	saw	cup	put	actual	too
								(BrE)					

M

or to ask sb in a polite way to do sth: [V] *Do you mind if I open the window?* ◊ [VN-**ing**] *Are you married, if you don't mind me asking?* ◊ (*formal*) *Are you married, if you don't mind my asking?* ◊ [V-**ing**] *Would you mind explaining that again, please?* ◊ *Do you mind driving? I'm feeling pretty tired.*

NOT CARE/WORRY | **3** (**not mind**) [no passive] to not care or not be concerned about sth: [V] *'Would you like tea or coffee?' 'I don't mind—either's fine.'* ◊ [VN] *Don't mind her—she didn't mean what she said.* ◊ *Don't mind me* (= don't let me disturb you)—*I'll just sit here quietly.*

BE WILLING | **4** (**not mind doing sth**) [VN-**ing**] to be willing to do sth: *I don't mind helping if you can't find anyone else.*

WARNING | **5** (*BrE*) (also **watch** *AmE, BrE*) (*spoken*) used to tell sb to be careful about sth or warn them about a danger: [VN] *Mind* (= Don't fall on) *that step!* ◊ *Mind your head!* (= for example, be careful you don't hit it on a low ceiling) ◊ *Mind your language!* (= don't speak in a rude or offensive way) ◊ [V**wh**-] *Mind how you go!* (= often used when you say goodbye to sb) ◊ *Mind where you're treading!* ◊ [V(**that**)] *Mind you don't cut yourself—that knife's very sharp.* ◊ *You must be home for dinner, mind.* **HELP** 'That' is nearly always left out in this pattern.

TAKE CARE OF | **6** (*especially BrE*) (*AmE* usually **watch**) [VN] to take care of sb/sth: *Who's minding the children this evening?* ◊ *Could you mind my bags for a moment?*

IDM ,do you 'mind? (*ironic*) used to show that you are annoyed about sth that sb has just said or done: *Do you mind? I was here before you.* **I don't mind ad'mitting, 'telling you…, etc.** used to emphasize what you are saying, especially when you are talking about sth that may be embarrassing for you: *I was scared, I don't mind telling you!* **I don't mind if I 'do** (*spoken, informal*) used to say politely that you would like sth you have been offered: *'Cup of tea, Brian?' 'I don't mind if I do.'* **if you ,don't 'mind | if you ,wouldn't 'mind** (*spoken*) **1** used to check that sb does not object to sth you want to do, or to ask sb politely to do sth: *I'd like to ask you a few questions, if you don't mind.* ◊ *Can you read that form carefully, if you wouldn't mind, and then sign it.* **2** (often *ironic*) used to show that you object to sth that sb has said or done: *I give the orders around here, if you don't mind.* **3** used to refuse an offer politely: *'Will you come with us tonight?' 'I won't, if you don't mind—I've got a lot of work to do.'* **if you ,don't mind me/my 'saying so …** (*spoken*) used when you are going to criticize sb or say sth that might upset them: *That colour doesn't really suit you, if you don't mind my saying so.* **I wouldn't mind sth/doing sth** (*spoken*) used to say politely that you would very much like sth/to do sth: *I wouldn't mind a cup of coffee, if it's no trouble.* ◊ *I wouldn't mind having his money!* ,mind your ,own 'business (*spoken, informal*) to think about your own affairs and not ask questions about or try to get involved in other people's lives: *'What are you reading?' 'Mind your own business!'* ◊ *I was just sitting there, minding my own business, when a man started shouting at me.* mind the 'shop (*BrE*) (*AmE* mind the 'store) to be in charge of sth for a short time while sb is away: *Who's minding the shop while the boss is abroad?* ,mind 'you (*spoken*) used to add sth to what you have just said especially sth that makes it less strong: *I've heard they're getting divorced. Mind you, I'm not surprised—they were always arguing.* ,never 'mind **1** (*especially BrE*) used to tell sb not to worry or be upset: *Have you broken it? Never mind, we can buy another one.* **2** used to suggest that sth is not important: *This isn't where I intended to take you—but never mind, it's just as good.* **3** used to emphasize that what is true about the first thing you have said is even more true about the second **SYN** LET ALONE: *I never thought she'd win once, never mind twice!* never mind (about) (doing) sth used to tell sb they shouldn't think about sth or do sth because it is not as important as sth else, or because you will do it: *Never mind your car—what about the damage to my fence?* ◊ *Never mind washing the dishes—I'll do them later.* ,never you 'mind (*informal*) used to tell sb not to ask about sth because you are not going to tell them: *'Who told you about it?' 'Never*

you mind!' ◊ *Never you mind how I found out—it's true, isn't it?*—more at STEP *n.*

PHR V ,mind 'out (*BrE, spoken, informal*) used to tell sb to move so that you can pass: *Mind out—you're in the way there!* ,mind 'out (for sb/sth) (*BrE*) used to warn sb of danger: *Have some of my plum jam—but mind out for the stones.*

'**mind-bending** *adj.* (*informal*) (especially of drugs) having a strong effect on your mind

'**mind-blowing** *adj.* (*informal*) very exciting, impressive or surprising: *Watching your baby being born is a mind-blowing experience.*

'**mind-boggling** *adj.* (*informal*) very difficult to imagine or to understand; extremely surprising: *a problem of mind-boggling complexity*—compare BOGGLE

mind·ed /ˈmaɪndɪd/ *adj.* **1** (used with adjectives to form compound adjectives) having the way of thinking, the attitude or the type of character mentioned: *a fair-minded employer* ◊ *high-minded principles* ◊ *I appeal to all like-minded people to support me.*—see also ABSENT-MINDED, BLOODY-MINDED, SINGLE-MINDED **2** (used with adverbs to form compound adjectives) having the type of mind that is interested in or able to understand the areas mentioned: *I'm not very politically minded.* **3** (used with nouns to form compound adjectives) interested in or enthusiastic about the thing mentioned: *a reform-minded government* **4** [not before noun] **~** (to do sth) (*formal*) wishing or intending to do sth **SYN** INCLINED: *She was minded to accept their offer.* ◊ *The government could change the law if they were so minded.*

mind·er /ˈmaɪndə(r)/ *noun* (*especially BrE*) a person whose job is to take care of and protect another person: *a star surrounded by her minders*—see also CHILDMINDER

mind·ful /ˈmaɪndfl/ *adj.* **~** of sb/sth | **~** that … (*formal*) remembering sb/sth and considering them or it when you do sth **SYN** CONSCIOUS: *mindful of our responsibilities* ◊ *Mindful of the danger of tropical storms, I decided not to go out.*

mind·less /ˈmaɪndləs/ *adj.* **1** done or acting without thought and for no particular reason or purpose; **SYN** SENSELESS: *mindless violence* ◊ *mindless vandals* **2** not needing thought or intelligence **SYN** DULL: *a mindless and repetitive task* ▶ **mind·less·ly** *adv.*: *There is no excuse for mindlessly destroying public property.*

'**mind-reader** *noun* (often *humorous*) a person who knows what sb else is thinking without being told

mind·set /ˈmaɪndset/ *noun* a set of attitudes or fixed ideas that sb has and that are often difficult to change: *a conservative/old-fashioned mindset* ◊ *the mindset of the computer generation*

mine /maɪn/ *pron., noun, verb*
▪ *pron.* (the POSSESSIVE form of *I*) of or belonging to the person writing or speaking: *That's mine.* ◊ *He's a friend of mine* (= one of my friends).
▪ *noun* **1** a deep hole or holes under the ground where minerals such as coal, gold, etc. are dug: *a copper/diamond mine*—see also MINING, COAL MINE, GOLD MINE—compare PIT, QUARRY **2** a type of bomb that is hidden under the ground or in the sea and that explodes when sb/sth touches it—see also LANDMINE **IDM a mine of infor'mation (about/on sb/sth)** a person, book, etc. that can give you a lot of information on a particular subject
▪ *verb* **1** to dig holes in the ground in order to find and obtain coal, diamonds, etc: [VN] *The area has been mined for slate for centuries.* ◊ [V] *They were mining for gold.* **2** [VN] to place mines below the surface of an area of land or water; to destroy a vehicle with mines: *The coastal route had been mined.* ◊ *The UN convoy was mined on its way to the border.*

mine·field /ˈmaɪnfiːld/ *noun* **1** an area of land or water where bombs that explode when they are touched (= MINES) have been hidden **2** a situation that contains hidden dangers or difficulties: *a legal minefield* ◊ *Tax can be a minefield for the unwary.*

miner /ˈmaɪnə(r)/ *noun* a person who works in a mine taking out coal, gold, diamonds, etc.—see also COAL MINER

min·eral /ˈmɪnərəl/ *noun* **1** [C, U] a substance that is

aɪ	aʊ	eɪ	əʊ	oʊ	ɔɪ	ɪə	eə	ʊə	j	w
my	now	say	go	go	boy	near	hair	pure	yes	wet
			(BrE)	(AmE)						

naturally present in the earth and is not formed from animal or vegetable matter, for example gold and salt. Some minerals are also present in food and drink and in the human body and are essential for good health: *mineral deposits/extraction* ◊ *the recommended intake of vitamins and minerals*—compare VEGETABLE **2** [C, usually pl.] (*BrE, formal*) (*AmE* **soda**) a sweet drink in various flavours that has bubbles of gas in it and does not contain alcohol: *Soft drinks and minerals sold here.*

min·er·al·ogist /ˌmɪnəˈrælədʒɪst/ *noun* a scientist who studies mineralogy

min·er·al·ogy /ˌmɪnəˈrælədʒi/ *noun* [U] the scientific study of minerals ▶ **min·er·al·ogic·al** /ˌmɪnərəˈlɒdʒɪkl; *AmE* -ˈlɑːdʒ-/ *adj.*

mineral water *noun* **1** [U, C] water from a SPRING in the ground that contains mineral salts or gases: *A glass of mineral water, please.* **2** [C] a glass or bottle of mineral water

mine·shaft /ˈmaɪnʃɑːft; *AmE* -ʃæft/ *noun* a deep narrow hole that goes down to a mine

min·es·trone /ˌmɪnəˈstrəʊni; *AmE* -ˈstroʊ-/ *noun* [U] an Italian soup containing small pieces of vegetables and PASTA

mine·sweeper /ˈmaɪnswiːpə(r)/ *noun* a ship used for finding and clearing away MINES (= a type of bomb)

mine·work·er /ˈmaɪnwɜːkə(r); *AmE* -wɜːrk-/ *noun* a person who works in a mine

min·gle /ˈmɪŋɡl/ *verb* **1** ~ (A) (with B)| ~ A and B (**together**) (*written*) to combine or make one thing combine with another: [V] *The sounds of laughter and singing mingled in the evening air.* ◊ *Her tears mingled with the blood on her face.* ◊ *The flowers mingle together to form a blaze of colour.* ◊ [VN] *He felt a kind of happiness mingled with regret.* **2** [V] to move among people and talk to them, especially at a social event: *The princess was not recognized and mingled freely with the crowds.* ◊ *If you'll excuse me, I must go and mingle* (= talk to other guests).

mingy /ˈmɪndʒi/ *adj.* (*BrE, informal*) small, not generous

mini- /ˈmɪni/ *combining form* (in nouns) small: *minibreak* (= a short holiday/vacation) ◊ *minigolf*

mini·ature /ˈmɪnətʃə(r); *AmE* also -tʃʊr/ *adj., noun*
■ *adj.* [only before noun] very small; much smaller than usual: *miniature roses* ◊ *a rare breed of miniature horses* ◊ *It looks like a miniature version of James Bond's car.*
■ *noun* **1** a very small detailed painting, often of a person **2** a very small copy or model of sth; a very small version of sth: *brandy miniatures* (= very small bottles) **IDM in miniature** on a very small scale: *a doll's house with everything in miniature* ◊ *Through play, children act out in miniature the dramas of adult life.*

mini·atur·ize (*BrE* also **-ise**) /ˈmɪnətʃəraɪz/ *verb* [VN] to make a much smaller version of sth ▶ **mini·atur·iza·tion, -isa·tion** /ˌmɪnətʃəraɪˈzeɪʃn; *AmE* -rəˈzeɪ-/ *noun* [U] **mini·atur·ized, -ised** *adj.* [only before noun]: *a miniaturized listening device*

mini·bar /ˈmɪnibɑː(r)/ *noun* a small FRIDGE in a hotel room, with drinks in it for guests to use—picture at BAR

mini·bus /ˈmɪnibʌs/ *noun* a small vehicle with seats for about twelve people—picture at BUS

mini·cab /ˈmɪnikæb/ *noun* (*BrE*) a taxi that you have to order by telephone and cannot stop in the street

mini·com·puter /ˈmɪnikəmpjuːtə(r)/ *noun* a computer that is smaller and slower than a MAINFRAME but larger and faster than a MICROCOMPUTER

mini·disc /ˈmɪnidɪsk/ *noun* a disc like a small CD that can record and play sound or data

minim /ˈmɪnɪm/ (*BrE*) (*AmE* **half note**) *noun* (*music*) a note that lasts twice as long as a CROTCHET/QUARTER NOTE—picture at MUSIC

min·imal /ˈmɪnɪml/ *adj.* very small in size or amount; as small as possible: *The work was carried out at minimal cost.* ◊ *There's only a minimal amount of risk involved.* ◊ *The damage to the car was minimal.*—compare MAXIMAL ▶ **min·im·al·ly** *adv.*: *minimally invasive surgery* ◊ *The episode was reported minimally in the press.*

min·im·al·ist /ˈmɪnɪməlɪst/ *noun* an artist, a musician,

etc. who uses very simple ideas or a very small number of simple things in their work ▶ **min·im·al·ism** *noun* [U] **min·im·al·ist** *adj.*: *a minimalist style* ◊ *minimalist paintings/sculptures*

min·im·ize (*BrE* also **-ise**) /ˈmɪnɪmaɪz/ *verb* [VN] **1** to reduce sth, especially sth bad, to the lowest possible level: *Good hygiene helps to minimize the risk of infection.* OPP MAXIMIZE **2** to try to make sth seem less important than it really is SYN PLAY DOWN: *He always tried to minimize his own faults, while exaggerating those of others.* **3** to make sth small, especially on a computer screen: *Minimize any windows you have open.* OPP MAXIMIZE

min·imum /ˈmɪnɪməm/ *adj., noun*
■ *adj.* [usually before noun] (*abbr.* **min.**) the smallest that is possible or allowed; extremely small: *a minimum charge/price* ◊ *the minimum age for retirement* ◊ *The work was done with the minimum amount of effort.* OPP MAXIMUM ▶ **min·imum** *adv.*: *You'll need £200 minimum for your holiday expenses.*
■ *noun* (*pl.* **min·ima** /-mə/) [C, usually sing.] **1** (*abbr.* **min.**) the smallest or lowest amount that is possible, required or recorded: *costs should be kept to a minimum.* ◊ *The class needs a minimum of six students to continue.* ◊ *As an absolute minimum, you should spend two hours in the evening studying.* ◊ *Temperatures will fall to a minimum of 10 degrees.* **2** [sing.] an extremely small amount: *He passed the exams with the minimum of effort.* OPP MAXIMUM

minimum se'curity prison *noun* (*AmE*) = OPEN PRISON

minimum 'wage *noun* [sing.] the lowest wage that an employer is allowed to pay by law

min·ing /ˈmaɪnɪŋ/ *noun* [U] the process of getting coal and other minerals from under the ground; the industry involved in this: *coal/diamonds/gold/tin mining* ◊ *a mining company/community/engineer*—see also MINE

min·ion /ˈmɪniən/ *noun* (*disapproving* or *humorous*) an unimportant person in an organization who has to obey orders; a servant: *While I was waiting to see him, a minion brought me some tea.*

mini·ser·ies /ˈmɪnisɪəriːz; *AmE* -sɪriːz/ *noun* (*pl.* **mini·ser·ies**) a television play that is divided into a number of parts and shown on different days

mini·skirt /ˈmɪniskɜːt; *AmE* -skɜːrt/ *noun* a very short skirt

min·is·ter /ˈmɪnɪstə(r)/ *noun, verb*
■ *noun* **1** (often **Minister**) (*BrE*) (in Britain and many other countries) a senior member of the government who is in charge of a government department or a branch of one: *the Minister of Education* ◊ *a meeting of EU Foreign Ministers* ◊ *senior ministers in the Cabinet* ◊ *cabinet ministers*—see also PRIME MINISTER **2** (in some Protestant Christian Churches) a trained religious leader: *a Methodist minister*—compare PASTOR, PRIEST, VICAR **3** a person, lower in rank than an AMBASSADOR, whose job is to represent their government in a foreign country
■ *verb* PHRV **'minister to sb/sth** (*formal*) to care for sb, especially sb who is sick or old, and make sure that they have everything they need

min·is·ter·ial /ˌmɪnɪˈstɪəriəl; *AmE* -ˈstɪr-/ *adj.* connected with a government minister or ministers: *decisions taken at ministerial level* ◊ *to hold ministerial office* (= to have the job of a government minister)

min·is·ter·ing /ˈmɪnɪstərɪŋ/ *adj.* [only before noun] (*written*) caring for people: *She could not see herself in the role of ministering angel.*

Minister of 'State *noun* a British government minister but not one who is in charge of a department

min·is·tra·tions /ˌmɪnɪˈstreɪʃnz/ *noun* [pl.] (*formal* or *humorous*) the act of helping or caring for sb especially when they are ill or in trouble: *He recovered swiftly under the nurse's expert ministrations.*

min·is·try /ˈmɪnɪstri/ *noun* (*pl.* **-ies**) **1** [C] (*BrE*) a government department that has a particular area of responsibility: *the Ministry of Defence* ◊ *a ministry spokesperson* **2** (**the Ministry**) [sing.+ sing./pl. *v.*] ministers of religion, especially Protestant ministers, when they are mentioned

M

as a group: *He was an excellent candidate for the Baptist ministry.* **3** [C, usually sing.] the work and duties of a minister in the Church; the period of time spent working as a minister in the Church

mini·van /ˈmɪnivæn/ *noun* (*AmE*) = PEOPLE CARRIER

mink /mɪŋk/ *noun* (*pl.* **mink** or **minks**) **1** [C] a small wild animal with thick shiny fur, a long body and short legs. Mink are often kept on farms for their fur: *a mink farm* **2** [U] the skin and shiny brown fur of the mink, used for making expensive coats, etc: *a mink jacket* **3** [C] a coat or jacket made of mink

min·now /ˈmɪnəʊ; *AmE* -noʊ/ *noun* **1** a very small FRESH-WATER fish **2** a company or sports team that is small or unimportant: *These two companies are both minnows in the international market.*

minor /ˈmaɪnə(r)/ *adj., noun, verb*
- *adj.* **1** [usually before noun] not very large, important or serious: *a minor road ◇ minor injuries ◇ to undergo minor surgery ◇ youths imprisoned for minor offences ◇ There may be some minor changes to the schedule. ◇ Women played a relatively minor role in the organization.* OPP MAJOR **2** (*music*) based on a SCALE (= a series of eight notes) in which the third note is a SEMITONE/HALF-TONE higher than the second note: *the key of C minor*—compare MAJOR
- *noun* **1** (*law*) a person who is under the age at which you legally become an adult and are responsible for your actions: *It is an offence to serve alcohol to minors.* **2** (*especially AmE*) a subject that you study at university in addition to your MAJOR
- *verb* PHRV **ˈminor in sth** (*AmE*) to study sth at college, but not as your main subject—compare MAJOR

mi·nor·ity /maɪˈnɒrəti; *AmE* -ˈnɔːr-; -ˈnɑːr-/ *noun* (*pl.* **-ies**) **1** [sing.+ sing./pl. *v.*] the smaller part of a group; less than half of the people or things in a large group: *Only a small minority of students is/are interested in politics these days. ◇ For a minority, the decision was a disappointment. ◇ minority shareholders in the bank* OPP MAJORITY **2** [C] a small group within a community or country that is different because of race, religion, language, etc: *the rights of ethnic/racial minorities ◇ minority languages ◇ a large German-speaking minority in the east of the country ◇ (AmE) The school is 95 per cent minority* (= 95 per cent of children are not white Americans but from different racial groups). ◇ (*AmE*) *minority neighborhoods* (= where no or few white people live) **3** (*law*) the state of being under the age at which you are legally an adult IDM **be in a/the miˈnority** to form much less than half of a large group: *Men are in the minority in this profession.* **be in a minority of ˈone** (often *humorous*) to be the only person to have a particular opinion or to vote a particular way

miˌnority ˈgovernment *noun* [C, U] a government that has fewer seats in parliament than the total number held by all the other parties

min·ster /ˈmɪnstə(r)/ *noun* (*BrE*) a large or important church: *York Minster*

min·strel /ˈmɪnstrəl/ *noun* a musician or singer in the Middle Ages

mint /mɪnt/ *noun, verb*
- *noun* **1** [U] a plant with dark green leaves that have a fresh smell and taste and are added to food and drinks to give flavour, and used in cooking as a herb and to decorate food: *mint-flavoured toothpaste ◇ I decorated the fruit salad with a sprig of mint. ◇ roast lamb with mint sauce* **2** [C] a sweet/candy flavoured with a type of mint called PEPPERMINT: *after-dinner mints* **3** a place where money is made: *the Royal Mint* (= the one where British money is made) **4** (**a mint**) [sing.] (*informal*) a large amount of money: *to make/cost a mint* IDM **in mint conˈdition** new or as good as new; in perfect condition
- *verb* [VN] to make a coin from metal

mint·ed /ˈmɪntɪd/ *adj.* **1** freshly/newly ~ recently produced, invented, etc: *a newly minted expression* **2** (of food) flavoured with mint

minty /ˈmɪnti/ *adj.* tasting or smelling of MINT: *a minty flavour/smell*

min·uet /ˌmɪnjuˈet/ *noun* a slow graceful dance that was popular in the 17th and 18th centuries; a piece of music for this dance

minus /ˈmaɪnəs/ *prep., noun, adj.*
- *prep.* **1** used when you SUBTRACT one number or thing from another one: *Seven minus three is four* (7 − 3 = 4). ◇ *the former Soviet Union, minus the Baltic republics and Georgia* **2** used to express temperature below zero degrees: *It was minus ten.* ◇ *The temperature dropped to minus 28 degrees centigrade* (−28°C). **3** (*informal*) without sth that was there before: *We're going to be minus a car for a while.* OPP PLUS IDM see PLUS *prep.*
- *noun* **1** (also **ˈminus sign**) The symbol (−), used in mathematics **2** (*informal*) a negative quality; a disadvantage: *Let's consider the pluses and minuses of changing the system.* OPP PLUS
- *adj.* **1** (*mathematics*) lower than zero: *a minus figure/number* **2** making sth seem negative and less attractive or good: *What are the car's minus points* (= the disadvantages)? ◇ *On the minus side rented property is expensive and difficult to find.* **3** [not before noun] (used in a system of marks/grades) slightly lower than the mark/grade A, B, etc: *I got (a) B minus* (B−) *in the test.* OPP PLUS

min·us·cule /ˈmɪnəskjuːl/ *adj.* extremely small: *minuscule handwriting*

min·ute¹ /ˈmɪnɪt/ *noun, verb*—see also MINUTE²
- *noun*
  PART OF HOUR | **1** [C] (*abbr.* **min.**) each of the 60 parts of an hour, that are equal to 60 seconds: *It's four minutes to six. ◇ I'll be back in a few minutes. ◇ Boil the rice for 20 minutes. ◇ a ten-minute bus ride ◇ I enjoyed every minute of the party.*
  VERY SHORT TIME | **2** [sing.] (*spoken*) a very short time: *It only takes a minute to make a salad.* ◇ **Hang on a minute**—*I'll just get my coat. ◇ I just have to finish this*—*I won't be a minute. ◇ Could I see you for a minute? ◇ I'll be with you in a minute, Jo. ◇ Typical English weather—one minute it's raining and the next minute the sun is shining!*
  EXACT MOMENT | **3** [sing.] an exact moment in time: *At that very minute, Tom walked in.*
  ANGLES | **4** [C] each of the 60 equal parts of a degree, used in measuring angles: *37 degrees 30 minutes* (37° 30′)
  RECORD OF MEETING | **5** (usually **the minutes**) [pl.] a summary or record of what is said or decided at a formal meeting: *We read through the minutes of the last meeting.* ◇ *Who is going to take the minutes* (= write them)?
  IDM **(at) any ˈminute/ˈmoment (ˈnow)** very soon: *Hurry up! He'll be back any minute now.* **the minute/moment (that) ...** as soon as ...: *I want to see him the minute he arrives.* **ˌnot for a/one ˈminute/ˈmoment** certainly not; not at all: *I don't think for a minute that she'll accept but you can ask her.* **this minute** immediately; now: *Come down from there this minute! ◇ I don't know what I'm going to do yet*—*I've just this minute found out.* **to the ˈminute** exactly: *The train arrived at 9.05 to the minute.* **ˌup to the ˈminute** (*informal*) **1** fashionable and modern: *Her styles are always up to the minute.* **2** having the latest information: *The traffic reports are up to the minute.*—see also UP-TO-THE-MINUTE—more at BORN, JUST *adv.*, LAST *det.*, WAIT *v.*
- *verb* to write down sth that is said at a meeting in the official record (= the MINUTES): [VN] *I'd like that last remark to be minuted.* [also VN]

min·ute² /maɪˈnjuːt; *AmE* also -ˈnuːt/ *adj.*—see also MINUTE¹ (*superlative* **minut·est**, no *comparative*) **1** extremely small: *minute amounts of chemicals in the water ◇ The kitchen on the boat is minute.* **2** very detailed, careful and thorough: *a minute examination/inspection ◇ She remembered everything in minute detail/in the minutest detail(s).* ▶ **mi·nute·ly** *adv.*: *The agreement has been examined minutely.*

ˈminute hand *noun* [usually sing.] the hand on a watch or clock that points to the minutes

mi·nu·tiae /maɪˈnjuːʃiiː; *AmE* mɪˈnuːʃiiː/ *noun* [pl.] very small details: *the minutiae of the contract*

minx /mɪŋks/ *noun* [sing.] (*old-fashioned* or *humorous*) a girl who is CUNNING and does not show respect

mir·acle /ˈmɪrəkl/ *noun* **1** [C] an act or event that does not follow the laws of nature and is believed to be caused by God **2** [sing.] (*informal*) a lucky thing that happens that you did not expect or think was possible: *an economic miracle* ◊ *It's a miracle (that) nobody was killed in the crash.* ◊ *It would take a miracle to make this business profitable.* ◊ *a miracle cure/drug* **3** [C] **~ of sth** a very good example or product of sth: *The car is a miracle of engineering.* IDM **work/perform 'miracles** to achieve very good results: *Her exercise programme has worked miracles for her.*

mi·rac·u·lous /mɪˈrækjələs/ *adj.* like a miracle; completely unexpected and very lucky: *miraculous powers of healing* ◊ *She's made a miraculous recovery.* ▶ **mi·rac·u·lous·ly** *adv.*: *They miraculously survived the plane crash.*

mir·age /ˈmɪrɑːʒ; mɪˈrɑːʒ; AmE məˈrɑːʒ/ *noun* **1** an effect caused by hot air in deserts or on roads, that makes you think you can see sth, such as water, which is not there **2** a hope or wish that you cannot make happen because it is not realistic: *His idea of love was a mirage.*

mire /ˈmaɪə(r)/ *noun* [U] (*written*) an area of deep mud: *The wheels sank deeper into the mire.* ◊ (*figurative*) *My name had been dragged through the mire* (= my reputation was ruined). ◊ (*figurative*) *The government was sinking deeper and deeper into the mire* (= getting further into a difficult situation).

mired /ˈmaɪəd; AmE ˈmaɪərd/ *adj.* [not before noun] **~ in sth** (*written*) **1** in a difficult or unpleasant situation that you cannot escape from: *The country was mired in recession.* **2** stuck in deep mud

mir·ror /ˈmɪrə(r)/ *noun, verb*
■ *noun* **1** [C] a piece of special flat glass that reflects images, so that you can see yourself when you look in it: *He looked at himself in the mirror.* ◊ *a rear-view mirror* (= in a car, so that the driver can see what is behind) ◊ (*BrE*) *a wing mirror* (= on the side of a car) ◊ (*AmE*) *a side mirror* **2 a ~ of sth** [sing.] something that shows what sth else is like: *The face is the mirror of the soul.* ◊ *Dickens' novels are a mirror of his times.*
■ *verb* [VN] (*written*) **1** to have features that are similar to sth else and which show what it is like: *The music of the time mirrored the feeling of optimism in the country.* **2** to show the image of sb/sth on the surface of water, glass, etc. SYN REFLECT: *She saw herself mirrored in the shiny wood panelling.*

mir·rored /ˈmɪrəd; AmE -rərd/ *adj.* [only before noun] having a mirror or mirrors or behaving like a mirror: *mirrored doors/sunglasses*

mirror 'image *noun* an image of sth that is like a REFLECTION of it, either because it is exactly the same or because the right side of the original object appears on the left and the left side appears on the right

mirth /mɜːθ; AmE mɜːrθ/ *noun* [U] (*written*) happiness, fun and laughter: *The performance produced much mirth among the audience.*

mirth·less /ˈmɜːθləs; AmE ˈmɜːrθ-/ *adj.* (*written*) showing no real enjoyment or amusement: *a mirthless laugh/smile* ▶ **mirth·less·ly** *adv.*

mis- /mɪs/ *prefix* (in verbs and nouns) bad or wrong; badly or wrongly: *misinterpret* ◊ *misbehaviour*

mis·ad·ven·ture /ˌmɪsədˈventʃə(r)/ *noun* **1** [U] (*BrE, law*) death caused by accident, rather than as a result of a crime: *a verdict of death by misadventure* **2** [C, U] (*formal*) bad luck or a small accident

mis·an·thrope /ˈmɪsənθrəʊp; AmE -θroʊp/ *noun* (*formal*) a person who hates and avoids other people

mis·an·throp·ic /ˌmɪsənˈθrɒpɪk; AmE -ˈθrɑːp-/ *adj.* (*formal*) hating and avoiding other people ▶ **mis·an·thropy** /mɪˈsænθrəpi/ *noun* [U]

mis·ap·pli·ca·tion /ˌmɪsæplɪˈkeɪʃn/ *noun* [U, C] (*formal*) the use of sth for the wrong purpose or in the wrong way

mis·ap·ply /ˌmɪsəˈplaɪ/ *verb* (**mis·ap·plies, mis·ap·ply·ing, mis·ap·plied, mis·ap·plied**) [VN] [usually passive] (*formal*) to use sth for the wrong purpose or in the wrong way: *The company admitted that their system of penalties had been misapplied.*

mis·ap·pre·hen·sion /ˌmɪsæprɪˈhenʃn/ *noun* [U, C]

(*formal*) a wrong idea about sth, or sth you believe to be true that is not true: *I was under the misapprehension that the course was for complete beginners.*

mis·ap·pro·pri·ate /ˌmɪsəˈprəʊprieɪt; AmE -ˈproʊ-/ *verb* [VN] (*formal*) to take sb else's money or property for yourself, especially when they have trusted you to take care of it SYN EMBEZZLE—compare APPROPRIATE *v.* ▶ **mis·ap·pro·pri·ation** /ˌmɪsəˌprəʊpriˈeɪʃn; AmE -ˌproʊ-/ *noun* [U]

mis·be·got·ten /ˌmɪsbɪˈɡɒtn; AmE -ˈɡɑːtn/ *adj.* [usually before noun] (*rare, formal*) badly designed or planned

mis·be·have /ˌmɪsbɪˈheɪv/ *verb* **~ (yourself)** to behave badly: [V] *Any child caught misbehaving was made to stand at the front of the class.* ◊ [VN] *I see the dog has been misbehaving itself again.* OPP BEHAVE ▶ **mis·be·hav·iour** (*AmE* **mis·be·hav·ior**) /ˌmɪsbɪˈheɪvjə(r)/ *noun* [U]

mis·cal·cu·late /ˌmɪsˈkælkjuleɪt/ *verb* **1** to estimate an amount, a figure, a measurement, etc. wrongly: [VN] *They had seriously miscalculated the effect of inflation.* ◊ [V wh-] *He had miscalculated how long the trip would take.* [also V] **2** to judge a situation wrongly: [VN] *She miscalculated the level of opposition to her proposals.* [also V wh-, V] ▶ **mis·cal·cu·la·tion** /ˌmɪskælkjuˈleɪʃn/ *noun* [C, U]: *to make a miscalculation*

mis·car·riage /ˈmɪskærɪdʒ; BrE also ˌmɪsˈk-/ *noun* [C, U] the process of giving birth to a baby before it is fully developed and able to survive; an occasion when this happens: *to have a miscarriage* ◊ *The pregnancy ended in miscarriage at 11 weeks.*—compare ABORTION

mis,carriage of 'justice *noun* [U, C] (*law*) a situation in which a court of law makes a wrong decision, especially when sb is punished when they are innocent

mis·carry /ˌmɪsˈkæri/ *verb* (**mis·car·ries, mis·carry·ing, mis·car·ried, mis·car·ried**) **1** to give birth to a baby before it is fully developed and able to live: [V] *The shock caused her to miscarry.* [also VN] **2** [V] (*formal*) (of a plan) to fail

mis·cast /ˌmɪsˈkɑːst; AmE -ˈkæst/ *verb* (**mis·cast, mis·cast**) [VN] [usually passive] **~ sb (as sb/sth)** to choose an actor to play a role for which they are not suitable: *He was hopelessly miscast as the romantic hero.*

mis·ce·gen·ation /ˌmɪsɪdʒəˈneɪʃn/ *noun* [U] (*formal*) the fact of children being produced by parents who are of different races, especially when one parent is white

mis·cel·lan·eous /ˌmɪsəˈleɪniəs/ *adj.* [usually before noun] consisting of many different kinds of things that are not connected and do not easily form a group: *a sale of miscellaneous household items* ◊ *She gave me some money to cover any miscellaneous expenses.*

mis·cel·lany /mɪˈseləni; AmE ˈmɪsəleɪni/ *noun* [sing.] (*written*) a group or collection of different kinds of things: *a miscellany of objects in the room*

mis·chance /ˌmɪsˈtʃɑːns; AmE -ˈtʃæns/ *noun* [U, C] (*formal*) bad luck

mis·chief /ˈmɪstʃɪf/ *noun* [U] **1** bad behaviour (especially of children) that is annoying but does not cause any serious damage or harm: *Those children are always getting into mischief.* ◊ *I try to keep out of mischief.* ◊ *It's very quiet upstairs; they must be up to some mischief!* **2** the wish or tendency to behave or play in a way that causes trouble: *Her eyes were full of mischief.* **3** (*formal*) harm or injury that is done to sb or to their reputation: *The incident caused a great deal of political mischief.* IDM **,do yourself a 'mischief** (*BrE, informal*) to hurt yourself physically: *Watch how you use those scissors—you could do yourself a mischief!* **make 'mischief** to do or say sth deliberately to upset other people, or cause trouble between them

'mischief-making *noun* [U] the act of deliberately causing trouble for people, such as harming their reputation

mis·chiev·ous /ˈmɪstʃɪvəs/ *adj.* **1** enjoying playing tricks and annoying people: *a mischievous boy* ◊ *a mischievous grin/smile/look* **2** (*formal*) (of an action or a statement) causing trouble, such as damaging sb's reputation: *mischievous lies/gossip* ▶ **mis·chiev·ous·ly** *adv.*

mis·con·ceive /ˌmɪskənˈsiːv/ *verb* [VN] (*rare, formal*) to understand sth in the wrong way SYN MISUNDERSTAND

M

æ	ɑː	e	ɜː	ə	ɪ	iː	i	ɒ	ɔː	ʌ	ʊ	u	uː
cat	father	ten	bird	about	sit	see	many	got	saw	cup	put	actual	too
								(BrE)					

mis·con·ceived /ˌmɪskən'siːvd/ adj. badly planned or judged; not carefully thought about: a misconceived education policy ◊ their misconceived expectations of country life

mis·con·cep·tion /ˌmɪskən'sepʃn/ noun [C, U] ~ (about sth) a belief or an idea that is not based on correct information, or that is not understood by people: frequently held misconceptions about the disease ◊ A popular misconception (= a lot of people have it) is that plastic is a hazard to the environment. ◊ Let me deal with some common misconceptions. ◊ views based on misconception and prejudice—compare PRECONCEPTION

mis·con·duct /ˌmɪs'kɒndʌkt; AmE -'kɑːn-/ noun [U] (formal) 1 unacceptable behaviour, especially by a professional person: a doctor accused of gross misconduct (= very serious misconduct) ◊ professional misconduct 2 bad MANAGEMENT of a company, etc: misconduct of the company's financial affairs

mis·con·struc·tion /ˌmɪskən'strʌkʃn/ noun [U, C] (formal) a completely wrong understanding of sth

mis·con·strue /ˌmɪskən'struː/ verb [VN] ~ sth (as sth) (formal) to understand sb's words or actions wrongly SYN MISINTERPRET: He deliberately misconstrued everything I said. ◊ It is easy to misconstrue confidence as arrogance.

mis·cre·ant /'mɪskriənt/ noun (literary) a person who has done sth wrong or illegal

mis·deed /ˌmɪs'diːd/ noun [usually pl.] (formal) a bad or evil act: He will have to answer for his misdeeds in a court of law.

mis·de·meanour (BrE) (AmE **mis·de·meanor**) /ˌmɪsdɪ'miːnə(r)/ noun 1 (formal) an action that is bad or unacceptable, but not very serious: youthful misdemeanours 2 (especially AmE, law) a crime that is not considered to be very serious—compare FELONY

mis·diag·nose /ˌmɪs'daɪəgnəʊz; AmE -noʊz/ verb [VN] ~ sth (as sth) to give an explanation of the nature of an illness or a problem that is not correct: Her depression was misdiagnosed as stress. ▶ **mis·diag·nosis** /ˌmɪsdaɪəg'nəʊsɪs; AmE -'noʊ-/ noun (pl. **mis·diag·noses** /-siːz/)

mis·dir·ect /ˌmɪsdə'rekt; -daɪ'rekt/ verb [VN] 1 [usually passive] (written) to use sth in a way that is not appropriate to a particular situation: Their efforts over the past years have been largely misdirected. ◊ misdirected aggression/concern 2 (written) to send sb/sth in the wrong direction or to the wrong place: Several passengers were misdirected to the wrong airport. 3 (law) (of a judge) to give a JURY (= the group of people who decide if sb is guilty of a crime) wrong information about the law ▶ **mis·dir·ec·tion** /ˌmɪsdə'rekʃn; -daɪ'rek-/ noun [U]

miser /'maɪzə(r)/ noun (disapproving) a person who loves money and hates spending it

mis·er·able /'mɪzrəbl/ adj. 1 very unhappy or uncomfortable: We were cold, wet and thoroughly miserable. ◊ Don't look so miserable! ◊ She knows how to make life miserable for her employees. 2 making you feel very unhappy or uncomfortable SYN DEPRESSING: miserable housing conditions ◊ I spent a miserable weekend alone at home. ◊ What a miserable day (= cold and wet)! ◊ The play was a miserable failure. 3 [only before noun] (disapproving) (of a person) always unhappy, bad-tempered and unfriendly: He was a miserable old devil. 4 too small in quantity: How can anyone live on such a miserable wage? ▶ **mis·er·ably** /-əbli/ adv.: They wandered around miserably. ◊ a miserably cold day ◊ He failed miserably as an actor. IDM see SIN n.

miser·ly /'maɪzəli; AmE -ərli/ adj. (disapproving) 1 (of a person) hating to spend money SYN MEAN 2 (of a quantity or amount) too small SYN PALTRY

mis·ery /'mɪzəri/ noun (pl. -ies) 1 [U] great suffering of the mind or body SYN DISTRESS: Fame brought her nothing but misery. 2 [U] very poor living conditions SYN POVERTY: The vast majority of the country live in utter misery. 3 [C] something that causes great suffering of mind or body: the miseries of unemployment 4 [C] (BrE, informal) a person who is always unhappy and complaining: Don't be such an old misery! IDM **make sb's life a misery** to behave in a way that makes sb else feel very

unhappy **put an animal, a bird, etc. out of its misery** to kill a creature because it has an illness or injury that cannot be treated **put sb out of their misery** (informal) to stop sb worrying by telling them sth that they are anxious to know: Put me out of my misery—did I pass or didn't I?

mis·fire /ˌmɪs'faɪə(r)/ verb [V] 1 (of a plan or joke) to fail to have the effect that you had intended 2 (also **miss**) (of an engine) to not work correctly because the petrol/gas does not burn at the right time 3 (of a gun, etc.) to fail to send out a bullet, etc. when fired—compare BACKFIRE

mis·fit /'mɪsfɪt/ noun a person who is not accepted by a particular group of people, especially because their behaviour or their ideas are very different: a social misfit

mis·for·tune /ˌmɪs'fɔːtʃuːn; AmE -'fɔːrtʃ-/ noun (written) 1 [U] bad luck: He has known great misfortune in his life. ◊ We **had the misfortune to** run into a violent storm. 2 [C] an unfortunate accident, condition or event: She bore her misfortunes bravely.

mis·giv·ing /ˌmɪs'gɪvɪŋ/ noun [C, often pl., U] ~ about sth/about doing sth feelings of doubt or anxiety about what might happen, or about whether or not sth is the right thing to do: I had grave misgivings about making the trip. ◊ She decided to go despite her misgivings. ◊ I read the letter with a sense of misgiving.

mis·guided /ˌmɪs'gaɪdɪd/ adj. wrong because you have understood or judged a situation badly: The new proposals are, in our opinion, totally misguided. ◊ She only did it in a misguided attempt to help. ▶ **mis·guided·ly** adv.

mis·handle /ˌmɪs'hændl/ verb [VN] (written) 1 to deal badly with a problem or situation SYN MISMANAGE: The entire campaign had been badly mishandled. 2 to touch or treat sb/sth in a rough and careless way: The equipment could be dangerous if mishandled. ▶ **mis·hand·ling** noun [U]: the government's mishandling of the economy

mis·hap /'mɪshæp/ noun [C, U] a small accident or piece of bad luck that does not have serious results: a slight mishap ◊ a series of mishaps ◊ I managed to get home without (further) mishap.

mis·hear /ˌmɪs'hɪə(r); AmE -'hɪr/ verb (mis·heard, mis·heard /-'hɜːd; AmE -'hɜːrd/) to fail to hear correctly what sb says, so that you think they said sth else: [VN] You may have misheard her—I'm sure she didn't mean that. ◊ [V] I thought he said he was coming today, but I must have misheard. [also∨wh-]

mis·hit /ˌmɪs'hɪt/ verb (mis·hit·ting, mis·hit, mis·hit) [VN] (in cricket, golf, etc.) to hit the ball badly so that it does not go where you had intended ▶ **mis·hit** /'mɪshɪt/ noun

mish·mash /'mɪʃmæʃ/ noun [sing.] (informal, usually disapproving) a confused mixture of different kinds of things, styles, etc.

mis·in·form /ˌmɪsɪn'fɔːm; AmE -'fɔːrm/ verb [VN] [often passive] ~ sb (about sth) (written) to give sb wrong information about sth: They were deliberately misinformed about their rights. ◊ a misinformed belief (= based on wrong information) ▶ **mis·in·for·ma·tion** /ˌmɪsɪnfə'meɪʃn/ noun [U]: a campaign of misinformation

mis·in·ter·pret /ˌmɪsɪn'tɜːprɪt; AmE -'tɜːrp-/ verb [VN] ~ sth (as sth/doing sth) to understand sth/sb wrongly SYN MISCONSTRUE, MISREAD: His comments were misinterpreted as a criticism of the project.—compare INTERPRET ▶ **mis·in·ter·pret·ation** /ˌmɪsɪntɜːprɪ'teɪʃn; AmE -'tɜːrp-/ noun [U, C]: A number of these statements could be open to misinterpretation (= could be understood wrongly).

mis·judge /ˌmɪs'dʒʌdʒ/ verb 1 to form a wrong opinion about a person or situation, especially in a way that makes you deal with them or it unfairly: [VN] She now realizes that she misjudged him. [also∨wh-] 2 to estimate sth such as time or distance wrongly: [VN] He misjudged the distance and his ball landed in the lake. [also∨wh-] ▶ **mis·judge·ment** (also **mis·judg·ment**) noun [C, U]

mis·lay /ˌmɪs'leɪ/ verb (mis·laid, mis·laid /-'leɪd/) (especially BrE) to put sth somewhere and then be unable to find it again, especially for only a short time: I seem to have mislaid my keys.

mis·lead /ˌmɪs'liːd/ verb (mis·led, mis·led /-'led/) [VN] ~

aɪ	aʊ	eɪ	əʊ	oʊ	ɔɪ	ɪə	eə	ʊə	j	w
my	now	say	go	go	boy	near	hair	pure	yes	wet
			(BrE)	(AmE)						

sb (about sth)| ~ sb (into doing sth) to give sb the wrong idea or impression and make them believe sth that is not true: *He deliberately misled us about the nature of their relationship.* ◊ *Misleading the court in a trial is a serious offence.*

mis·lead·ing /ˌmɪsˈliːdɪŋ/ *adj.* giving the wrong idea or impression and making you believe sth that is not true SYN DECEPTIVE: *misleading information/advertisements* ▶ **mis·lead·ing·ly** *adv.*: *These bats are sometimes misleadingly referred to as 'flying foxes'.*

mis·man·age /ˌmɪsˈmænɪdʒ/ *verb* [VN] to deal with or manage sth badly SYN MISHANDLE: *The department's budget was badly mismanaged.* ▶ **mis·man·age·ment** *noun* [U]: *accusations of corruption and financial mismanagement*

mis·match /ˈmɪsmætʃ/ *noun* ~ (between A and B) a combination of things or people that do not go together well or are not suitable for each other: *a mismatch between people's real needs and the available facilities* ▶ **mis·match** /ˌmɪsˈmætʃ/ *verb* [VN] [often passive]: *They made a mismatched couple.*

mis·name /ˌmɪsˈneɪm/ *verb* [VN] [usually passive] (*written*) to give sb/sth a name that is wrong or not appropriate

mis·nomer /ˌmɪsˈnəʊmə(r); *AmE* -ˈnoʊ-/ *noun* a name or a word that is not appropriate or accurate: *'Villa' was something of a misnomer; the place was no more than an old farmhouse.*

mis·ogyn·ist /mɪˈsɒdʒɪnɪst; *AmE* -ˈsɑːdʒ-/ *noun* (*formal*) a man who hates women ▶ **mis·ogyn·is·tic** /mɪˌsɒdʒɪˈnɪstɪk/ (also **mis·ogyn·ist**) *adj.*: *misogynistic attitudes* **mis·ogyny** *noun* [U]

mis·place /ˌmɪsˈpleɪs/ *verb* [VN] (*written*) to put sth somewhere and then be unable to find it again, especially for a short time SYN MISLAY

mis·placed /ˌmɪsˈpleɪst/ *adj.* **1** not appropriate or correct in the situation: *misplaced confidence/optimism/fear* **2** (of love, trust, etc.) given to a person who does not deserve or return those feelings: *misplaced loyalty*

mis·print /ˈmɪsprɪnt/ *noun* a mistake such as a spelling mistake that is made when a book, etc. is printed

mis·pro·nounce /ˌmɪsprəˈnaʊns/ *verb* [VN] to pronounce a word wrongly: *People are always mispronouncing my name.* ▶ **mis·pro·nun·ci·ation** /ˌmɪsprənʌnsiˈeɪʃn/ *noun* [C, U]

mis·quote /ˌmɪsˈkwəʊt; *AmE* -ˈkwoʊt/ *verb* [VN] to repeat what sb has said or written in a way that is not correct: *The senator claims to have been misquoted in the article.* ▶ **mis·quo·ta·tion** /ˌmɪskwəʊˈteɪʃn; *AmE* -kwoʊ-/ *noun* [C, U]

mis·read /ˌmɪsˈriːd/ *verb* (**mis·read, mis·read** /-ˈred/) [VN] ~ sth (as sth) **1** to understand sb/sth wrongly SYN MISINTERPRET: *I'm afraid I completely misread the situation.* ◊ *His confidence was misread as arrogance.* **2** to read sth wrongly: *I misread the 1 as a 7.*

mis·re·port /ˌmɪsrɪˈpɔːt; *AmE* -ˈpɔːrt/ *verb* to give a report of an event, etc. that is not correct: [VN] *The newspapers misreported the facts of the case.* [also ∨ wh-, ∨N that]

mis·rep·re·sent /ˌmɪsˌreprɪˈzent/ *verb* [often passive] ~ sb/sth (as sth) to give information about sb/sth that is not true or complete so that other people have the wrong impression about them/it: [VN] *He felt that the book misrepresented his opinions.* ◊ *In the article she was misrepresented as an uncaring mother.* [also ∨ wh-] ▶ **mis·rep·re·sen·ta·tion** /ˌmɪsˌreprɪzenˈteɪʃn/ *noun* [C, U]: *a deliberate misrepresentation of the facts*

mis·rule /ˌmɪsˈruːl/ *noun* [U] (*formal*) bad government: *The regime finally collapsed after 25 years of misrule.*

miss /mɪs/ *verb, noun*

▪ *verb*

NOT HIT | **1** to fail to hit, catch, reach, etc. sth: [VN] *How many goals has he missed this season?* ◊ *The bullet missed her by about six inches.* ◊ [V] *She threw a plate at him and only narrowly missed.* ◊ [V-ing] *She narrowly missed hitting him.*

NOT HEAR/SEE | **2** [VN] to fail to hear, see or notice sth: *The*

hotel is the only white building on the road—*you can't miss it.* ◊ *Don't miss next week's issue!* ◊ *I missed her name.* ◊ *Your mother will know who's moved in—she doesn't miss much.*

NOT UNDERSTAND | **3** [VN] to fail to understand sth: *He completely missed the joke.* ◊ *You're missing the point* (= failing to understand the main part) *of what I'm saying.*

NOT BE/GO SOMEWHERE | **4** [VN] to fail to be or go somewhere: *She hasn't missed a game all year.* ◊ *You missed a good party last night* (= because you did not go). ◊ *'Are you coming to the school play?' ' I wouldn't miss it for the world '.*

NOT DO STH | **5** [VN] to fail to do sth: *You can't afford to miss meals* (= not eat meals) *when you're in training.* ◊ *to miss a turn* (= to not play when it is your turn in a game) **6** to not take the opportunity to do sth: [VN] *The sale prices were too good to miss.* ◊ *It was an opportunity not to be missed.* [also ∨-ing]

BE LATE | **7** to be or arrive too late for sth: [VN] *If I don't leave now I'll miss my plane.* ◊ *Sorry I'm late—have I missed anything?* ◊ *'Is Ann there?' 'You've just missed her* (= she has just left).' [also ∨-ing]

FEEL SAD | **8** to feel sad because you can no longer see sb or do sth that you like: [VN] *She will be greatly missed when she leaves.* ◊ *What did you miss most when you lived abroad?* ◊ [V-ing] *I don't miss getting up at six every morning!* [also ∨N-ing]

NOTICE STH NOT THERE | **9** [VN] to notice that sb/sth is not where they/it should be: *When did you first miss the necklace?* ◊ *We seem to be missing some students this morning.*

AVOID STH BAD | **10** to avoid sth unpleasant: [VN] *If you go now you should miss the crowds.* ◊ [V-ing] *He fell and just missed knocking the whole display over.*

OF ENGINE | **11** [V] = MISFIRE

IDM **he, she, etc. doesn't miss a 'trick** (*spoken*) used to say that sb notices every opportunity to gain an advantage ˌmiss the 'boat (*informal*) to be unable to take advantage of sth because you are too late: *If you don't buy now, you may find that you've missed the boat.*—more at HEART, MARK *n.*

PHR V ˌmiss sb/sth↔'out (*BrE*) to fail to include sb/sth in sth: *I'll just read through the form again to make sure I haven't missed anything out.* ˌmiss 'out (on sth) to fail to benefit from sth useful or enjoyable by not taking part in it: *Of course I'm coming—I don't want to miss out on all the fun!*

▪ *noun*

TITLE/FORM OF ADDRESS | **1** (**Miss**) used before the family name, or the first and family name, of a woman who is not married, in order to speak or write to her politely: *That's all, thank you, Miss Lipman.* ◊ (*old-fashioned* or *formal*) *the Misses Hill*—compare MRS, MS **2** (**Miss**) a title given to the winner of a beauty contest in a particular country, town, etc: *Miss America/Miss Brighton* ◊ *the Miss World contest* **3** (**Miss**) (*informal, spoken*) used especially by men to address a young woman when they do not know her name: *Will that be all, Miss?* **4** (**Miss**) (*BrE, spoken*) used as a form of address by children in some schools to a woman teacher, whether she is married or not: *Good morning, Miss!*—compare SIR **5** (*old-fashioned*) a girl or young woman

NOT HIT | **6** a failure to hit, catch or reach sth: *He scored two goals and had another two near misses.*

IDM **give sth a 'miss** (*informal, especially BrE*) to decide not to do sth, eat sth, etc: *I think I'll give badminton a miss tonight.*

mis·sal /ˈmɪsl/ *noun* a book that contains the prayers etc. that are used at MASS in the Roman Catholic Church

mis·sha·pen /ˌmɪsˈʃeɪpən/ *adj.* with a shape that is not normal or natural: *misshapen feet*

mis·sile /ˈmɪsaɪl; *AmE* ˈmɪsl/ *noun* **1** a weapon that is sent through the air and that explodes when it hits the thing that it is aimed at: *nuclear missiles* ◊ *a missile base/site*—see also BALLISTIC MISSILE, CRUISE MISSILE, GUIDED MISSILE **2** an object that is thrown at sb to hurt them:

M

b	d	f	g	h	k	l	m	n	p	r
bad	did	fall	get	hat	cat	leg	man	now	pen	red

Missiles including stones and bottles were thrown at the police.

miss·ing /ˈmɪsɪŋ/ *adj.* **1** that cannot be found or that is not in its usual place, or at home [SYN] LOST: *I never found the missing piece.* ◊ *My gloves have been missing for ages.* ◊ *Two files have gone missing.* ◊ *They still hoped to find their missing son.* ◊ (*especially BrE*) *Our cat's gone missing again.* **2** that has been removed, lost or destroyed and has not been replaced: *The book has two pages missing/missing pages.* ◊ *He didn't notice there was anything missing from his room until later on.* **3** (of a person) not present after an accident, battle, etc. but not known to have been killed: *He was reported missing, presumed dead.* ◊ *Many soldiers were listed as missing in action.* **4** not included, often when it should have been: *Fill in the missing words in this text.* ◊ *There were several candidates missing from the list.*

missing 'link *noun* **1** [C] something, such as a piece of information, that is necessary to be able to understand a problem or to make sth complete **2** (**the missing link**) [sing.] an animal similar to humans that was once thought to exist at the time that APES were developing into human beings

missing 'person *noun* (*pl.* **missing persons**) a person who has disappeared from their home and whose family are trying to find them with the help of the police

mis·sion /ˈmɪʃn/ *noun*

OFFICIAL JOB/GROUP | **1** [C] an important official job that a person or group of people is given to do, especially when they are sent to another country: *a trade mission to China* ◊ *a fact-finding mission* ◊ *a mercy mission to aid homeless refugees* **2** [C] a group of people doing such a job; the place where they work: *the head of the British mission in Berlin*

TEACHING CHRISTIANITY | **3** [C, U] the work of teaching people about Christianity, especially in a foreign country; a group of people doing such work: *a Catholic mission in Africa* ◊ *Gandhi's attitude to mission and conversion* **4** [C] a building or group of buildings used by a Christian mission

YOUR DUTY | **5** [C] particular work that you feel it is your duty to do: *Her mission in life was to work with the homeless.*

OF ARMED FORCES | **6** [C] an important job that is done by a soldier, group of soldiers, etc: *The squadron flew on a reconnaissance mission.*

SPACE FLIGHT | **7** [C] a flight into space: *a US space mission* ◊ *mission control* (= the people on earth who control and communicate with the people on the mission)

[IDM] **,mission ac'complished** used when you have successfully completed what you have had to do: *Mission accomplished. Let's go and have a drink.*

mis·sion·ary /ˈmɪʃənri; *AmE* -neri/ *noun* (*pl.* **-ies**) a person who is sent to a foreign country to teach people about Christianity: *Baptist missionaries* ◊ *missionary work* ◊ (*figurative*) *She spoke about her new project with missionary zeal* (= with great enthusiasm).

'mission statement *noun* an official statement of the aims of a company or an organization

mis·sis *noun* = MISSUS

mis·sive /ˈmɪsɪv/ *noun* (*formal* or *humorous*) a letter, especially a long or an official one

mis·spell /ˌmɪsˈspel/ *verb* (**mis·spelled, mis·spelled**) or (**mis·spelt, mis·spelt** /ˌmɪsˈspelt/) [VN] to spell a word wrongly ► **mis·spell·ing** *noun* [C, U]

mis·spend /ˌmɪsˈspend/ *verb* (**mis·spent, mis·spent** /-ˈspent/) [VN] [usually passive] to spend time or money in a careless rather than a useful way: *He joked that being good at cards was the sign of a misspent youth* (= having wasted his time when he was young).

mis·step /ˌmɪsˈstep/ *noun* (*AmE*) a mistake; a wrong action

mis·sus (also **mis·sis**) /ˈmɪsɪz/ *noun* (becoming *old-fashioned*) **1** (*informal, spoken*) (used after 'the', 'my', 'your', 'his') a man's wife: *How's the missus* (= your wife)? **2** (*slang, especially BrE*) used by some people as a form of address to a woman whose name they do not know: *Is this your bag, missus?*

mist /mɪst/ *noun, verb*

■ *noun* **1** [U, C] a cloud of very small drops of water in the air just above the ground, that make it difficult to see: *The hills were shrouded in mist.* ◊ *Early morning mist patches will soon clear.* ◊ *The origins of the story are lost in the mists of time* (= forgotten because it happened such a long time ago). ◊ (*figurative*) *She gazed at the scene through a mist of tears.*––compare FOG––see also MISTY **2** [sing.] a fine spray of liquid, for example, from an AEROSOL can

■ *verb* **1** ~ (**sth**) (**up**) | ~ (**over**) when sth such as glass **mists** or is **misted**, it becomes covered with very small drops of water, so that it is impossible to see through it: [VN] *The windows were misted up with condensation.* ◊ [V] *As he came in from the cold, his glasses misted up.* **2** ~ (**sth**) (**up**) | ~ (**over**) if your eyes **mist** or sth **mists** them, they fill with tears: [V] *Her eyes misted over as she listened to the speech.* ◊ [VN] *Tears misted his eyes.* **3** [VN] to spray the leaves of a plant with very small drops of water

mis·take /mɪˈsteɪk/ *noun, verb*

■ *noun* **1** an action or an opinion that is not correct, or that produces a result that you did not want: *It's easy to make a mistake.* ◊ *This letter is addressed to someone else––there must be some mistake.* ◊ *It would be a mistake to ignore his opinion.* ◊ *Don't worry, we all make mistakes.* ◊ *You must try to learn from your mistakes.* ◊ *Leaving school so young was the biggest mistake of my life.* ◊ *I made the mistake of giving him my address.* ◊ *It was a big mistake on my part to have trusted her.* **2** a word, figure, etc. that is not said or written down correctly: *It's a common mistake among learners of English.* ◊ *The waiter made a mistake* (in) *adding up the bill.* ◊ *Her essay is full of spelling mistakes.* [IDM] **and 'no mistake** (*old-fashioned spoken, especially BrE*) used to show that you are sure about the truth of what you have just said: *This is a strange business and no mistake.* **by mi'stake** accidentally; without intending to: *I took your bag instead of mine by mistake.* **,make no mi'stake (about sth)** (*spoken*) used to emphasize what you are saying, especially when you want to warn sb about sth: *Make no mistake (about it), this is one crisis that won't just go away.* **in mi'stake for sth** thinking that sth is sth else: *Children may eat pills in mistake for sweets.*

■ *verb* (**mis·took** /mɪˈstʊk/, **mis·taken** /mɪˈsteɪkən/) ~ **sb/sth** (**as sb/sth**) to not understand or judge sb/sth correctly: [VN] *I admit that I mistook his intentions.* ◊ *I mistook her offer as a threat.* ◊ *There was no mistaking* (= it was impossible to mistake) *the bitterness in her voice.* [also V *wh*-] [PHRV] **mi'stake sb/sth for sb/sth** to think wrongly that sb/sth is sb/sth else: *I think you must be mistaking me for someone else.*

mis·taken /mɪˈsteɪkən/ *adj.* **1** [not usually before noun] ~ (**about sb/sth**) wrong in your opinion or judgement: *You are completely mistaken about Jane.* ◊ *Unless I'm very much mistaken, that's Paul's wife over there.* ◊ *I thought I saw someone I knew, but I must have been mistaken.* **2** based on a wrong opinion or bad judgement: *mistaken views/ideas* ◊ *I told her my secret in the mistaken belief that I could trust her.* ► **mis·taken·ly** *adv.*: *He mistakenly believed that his family would stand by him.*

mi,staken i'dentity *noun* [U] a situation in which you think wrongly that you recognize sb or have found the person you are looking for: *He was shot in what seems to have been a case of mistaken identity.*

mis·ter /ˈmɪstə(r)/ *noun* **1** (**Mister**) the full form, not often used in writing, of the abbreviation *Mr* **2** (*spoken*) used, especially by children, to address a man whose name they do not know: *Please, mister, can we have our ball back?*

mis·time /ˌmɪsˈtaɪm/ *verb* [VN] to do sth at the wrong time, especially when this makes sth bad or unpleasant happen: *The horse completely mistimed the jump and threw its rider.* ► **mis·tim·ing** *noun* [U]: *The failure of the talks was mainly due to insensitivity and mistiming.*

mistle·toe /ˈmɪsltəʊ; ˈmɪzl-; *AmE* -toʊ/ *noun* [U] a plant with small shiny white berries that grows on other trees and is often used as a decoration at Christmas: *the tradition of kissing under the mistletoe*

mis·took *pt of* MISTAKE

mis·treat /ˌmɪsˈtriːt/ *verb* [VN] to treat a person or an animal in a cruel, unkind or unfair way SYN ILL-TREAT, MALTREAT: *animals that have been mistreated by their owners* ▶ **mis·treat·ment** *noun* [U]

mis·tress /ˈmɪstrəs/ *noun* **1** a man's (usually a married man's) **mistress** is a woman that he is having a regular sexual relationship with and who is not his wife **2** (*BrE*, becoming *old-fashioned*) a female teacher in a school, especially a private school: *the Biology mistress* **3** (in the past) the female head of a house, especially one who employed servants: *the mistress of the house* **4** the female owner of a dog or other animal **5** (*formal*) a woman who is in a position of authority or control, or who is highly skilled in sth: *She wants to be mistress of her own affairs* (= to organize her own life).—compare MASTER

mis·trial /ˌmɪsˈtraɪəl/ *noun* (*law*) **1** a trial that is not considered valid because of a mistake in the way it has been carried out **2** (*AmE*) a trial in which the JURY cannot reach a decision

mis·trust /ˌmɪsˈtrʌst/ *verb, noun*
■ *verb* [VN] to have no confidence in sb/sth because you think they may be harmful; to not trust sb/sth SYN DISTRUST: *She mistrusts anyone in a position of authority.* ⇨ note at DISTRUST
■ *noun* [U, sing.] a feeling that you cannot trust sb/sth SYN SUSPICION: *a climate of mistrust and fear* ◊ *She has a deep mistrust of strangers.* ▶ **mis·trust·ful** /-fl/ *adj.* ~ (**of sb/sth**): *Some people are very mistrustful of computers.* **mis·trust·ful·ly** /-fəli/ *adv.*

misty /ˈmɪsti/ *adj.* **1** with a lot of MIST: *a misty morning* **2** not clear or bright: *misty memories* ◊ (*literary*) *His eyes grew misty* (= full of tears) *as he talked.*

misty-'eyed *adj.* feeling full of emotion, as if you are going to cry: *I get very misty-eyed over our wedding pictures.*

mis·un·der·stand /ˌmɪsʌndəˈstænd; *AmE* -dərˈs-/ *verb* (**mis·un·der·stood**, **mis·un·der·stood** /-ˈstʊd/) to fail to understand sb/sth correctly: [VN] *I completely misunderstood her intentions.* ◊ *Don't misunderstand me—I am grateful for all you've done.* ◊ [V] *I thought he was her husband—I must have misunderstood.* [also V **wh-**]

mis·un·der·stand·ing /ˌmɪsʌndəˈstændɪŋ; *AmE* -dərˈs-/ *noun* **1** [U, C] ~ (**of/about sth**)| ~ (**between A and B**) a situation in which a comment, an instruction, etc. is not understood correctly: *There must be some misunderstanding—I thought I ordered the smaller model.* ◊ *There is still a fundamental misunderstanding about the real purpose of this work.* ◊ *All contracts are translated to avoid any misunderstanding between the companies.* **2** [C] a slight disagreement or argument: *We had a little misunderstanding over the bill.*

mis·un·der·stood /ˌmɪsʌndəˈstʊd/ *adj.* having qualities that people do not see or fully understand: *a much misunderstood illness* ◊ *She felt very alone and misunderstood.*

mis·use *noun, verb*
■ *noun* /ˌmɪsˈjuːs/ [U, C, usually sing.] the act of using sth in a dishonest way or for the wrong purpose: *alcohol/drug misuse* ◊ *the misuse of power/authority*
■ *verb* /ˌmɪsˈjuːz/ [VN] **1** to use sth in the wrong way or for the wrong purpose: *individuals who misuse power for their own ends* **2** to treat sb badly and/or unfairly

mite /maɪt/ *noun* **1** a very small creature like a spider that lives on plants, animals, carpets, etc: *house dust mites* **2** a small child or animal, especially one that you feel sorry for: *Poor little mite!* **3** (*old-fashioned*) a small amount of sth: *The place looked a mite* (= a little) *expensive.*

miter (*AmE*) = MITRE

miti·gate /ˈmɪtɪgeɪt/ *verb* [VN] (*formal*) to make sth less harmful, serious, etc. SYN ALLEVIATE: *action to mitigate poverty* ◊ *Soil erosion was mitigated by the planting of trees.*

miti·gat·ing /ˈmɪtɪgeɪtɪŋ/ *adj.* [only before noun] ~ **cir-**

cumstances/factors (*formal* or *law*) circumstances or FACTORS that provide a reason that explains sb's actions or a crime, and make them easier to understand so that the punishment may be less severe

miti·ga·tion /ˌmɪtɪˈgeɪʃn/ *noun* [U] (*formal*) a reduction in how unpleasant, serious, etc. sth is: *the mitigation of a problem/punishment* IDM **in miti'gation** (*law*) with the aim of making a crime seem less serious or easier to forgive: *In mitigation, the defence lawyer said his client was seriously depressed at the time of the assault.*

mitre (*BrE*) (*AmE* **mi·ter**) /ˈmaɪtə(r)/ *noun, verb*
■ *noun* **1** a tall pointed hat worn by BISHOPS at special ceremonies as a symbol of their position and authority **2** (also **'mitre joint**) a corner joint, formed by two pieces of wood each cut at an angle, as in a picture frame
■ *verb* [VN] (*technical*) to join two pieces of wood together with a mitre joint

mitt /mɪt/ *noun* **1** = MITTEN **2** (in baseball) a large thick leather glove worn for catching the ball **3** [usually pl.] (*slang*) a hand: *I'd love to get my mitts on one of those.*

mit·ten /ˈmɪtn/ (also **mitt**) *noun* a type of glove that covers the four fingers together and the thumb separately

mix /mɪks/ *verb, noun*
■ *verb*
COMBINE | **1** ~ **A with B** | ~ **A and B (together)** if two or more substances **mix** or you **mix** them, they combine, usually in a way that means they cannot easily be separated: [V] *Oil and water do not mix.* ◊ *Oil does not mix with water.* ◊ [VN] *Mix all the ingredients together in a bowl.* ◊ *If you mix blue and yellow, you get green.* ◊ *I don't like to mix business with pleasure* (= combine social events with doing business). **2** ~ **sth (for sb)** | ~ **sb sth** to prepare sth by combining two or more different substances: [VN] *With this range of paints, you can mix your own colours.* ◊ [VN, VNN] *Why don't you mix a cocktail for our guests?* ◊ *Why don't you mix our guests a cocktail?* **3** [V] if two or more things, people or activities **do not mix**, they are likely to cause problems or danger if they are combined: *Children and fireworks don't mix.*

MEET PEOPLE | **4** [V] ~ (**with sb**) to meet and talk to different people, especially at social events SYN SOCIALIZE: *They don't mix much with the neighbours.*

MUSIC/ SOUNDS | **5** [VN] (*technical*) to combine different recordings of voices and/or instruments to produce a single piece of music

IDM **be/get mixed 'up in sth** to be/become involved in sth, especially sth illegal or dishonest **be/get mixed 'up with sb** to be/become friendly with or involved with sb that other people do not approve of **mix and 'match** to combine things in different ways for different purposes: *You can mix and match courses to suit your requirements.* **'mix it (with sb)** (*BrE*) (*AmE* **mix it 'up (with sb)**) (*informal*) to argue with sb or cause trouble
PHR V **mix sth↔'in (with sth)** to add one substance to others, especially in cooking: *Mix the remaining cream in with the sauce.* **'mix sth into sth** to combine one substance with others, especially in cooking: *Mix the fruit into the rest of the mixture.* **'mix sth into/to sth** to produce sth by combining two or more substances, especially in cooking: *Add the milk and mix to a smooth dough.* **mix sth↔'up** to change the order or arrangement of a group of things, especially by mistake or in a way that you do not want: *Someone has mixed up all the application forms.*—related noun MIX-UP **mix sb/sth 'up (with sb/sth)** to think wrongly that sb/sth is sb/sth else SYN CONFUSE: *I think you must be mixing me up with someone else.*—see also MIXED-UP
■ *noun*
COMBINATION | **1** [C, usually sing.] a combination of different people or things: *a school with a good social mix of children* ◊ *The town offers a fascinating mix of old and new.* ◊ *a pair of wool mix socks* (= made of wool and other materials) **2** [C, U] a combination of things that you need to make sth, often sold as a powder that you add water, etc. to: *a cake mix* ◊ *cement mix*

IN POPULAR MUSIC | **3** [C] = REMIX **4** [sing.] the particular way that instruments and voices are arranged in a piece

M

æ	ɑː	e	ɜː	ə	ɪ	iː	i	ɒ	ɔː	ʌ	ʊ	u	uː
cat	father	ten	bird	about	sit	see	many	got	saw	cup	put	actual	too
								(BrE)					

of music **5** [C] an arrangement of several songs or pieces of music into one continuous piece, especially for dancing

mixed /mɪkst/ *adj.* **1** having both good and bad qualities or feelings: *The weather has been very mixed recently.* ◊ *I still have mixed feelings about going to Brazil* (= I am not sure what to think). ◊ *The play was given a mixed reception by the critics* (= some liked it, some did not). ◊ *British athletes had mixed fortunes in yesterday's competition.* **2** [only before noun] consisting of different kinds of people, for example, people from different races and cultures: *a mixed community* ◊ *people of mixed race* ◊ *a mixed marriage* (= between two people of different races or religions) **3** [only before noun] consisting of different types of the same thing: *a mixed salad* **4** [usually before noun] of or for both males and females: *a mixed school* ◊ *I'd rather not talk about it in mixed company.*

mixed-a·bil·ity *adj.* [usually before noun] with or for students who have different levels of ability: *a mixed-ability class* ◊ *mixed-ability teaching*

mixed 'bag *noun* [sing.] (*informal*) a collection of things or people of very different types

mixed 'blessing *noun* [usually sing.] something that has advantages and disadvantages

mixed 'doubles *noun* [U, C] (*pl.* **mixed 'doubles**) (in tennis, etc.) a game in which a man and a woman play together against another man and woman

mixed e'conomy *noun* an economic system in a country in which some companies are owned by the state and some are private

mixed 'grill *noun* (*BrE*) a hot dish of different types of meat and vegetables that have been GRILLED: *a mixed grill of fried eggs, bacon, sausages, tomatoes and mushrooms*

mixed 'metaphor *noun* a combination of two or more METAPHORS or IDIOMS that produces a ridiculous effect, for example, 'He put his foot down with a firm hand.'

mixed-'up *adj.* (*informal*) confused because of mental, emotional or social problems: *a mixed-up kid / teenager*

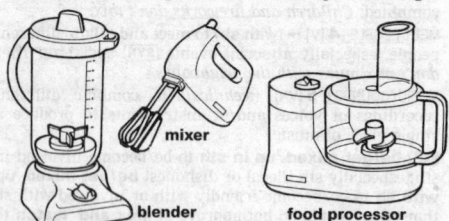

mixer

blender   food processor

mixer /ˈmɪksə(r)/ *noun* **1** a machine or device used for mixing things: *a food mixer* ◊ (*BrE*) *a mixer tap* (= one in which hot and cold water can be mixed together before it comes out of the pipe)—see also CEMENT MIXER **2** a drink such as fruit juice that is not alcoholic and that can be mixed with alcohol: *low-calorie mixers* **3** (*technical*) a device used for mixing together different sound or picture signals in order to produce a single sound or picture; a person whose job is to operate this device: *a sound / vision mixer* **IDM** **a good/bad 'mixer** a person who finds it easy/difficult to talk to people they do not know, for example at a party

mixing bowl *noun* a large bowl for mixing food in

mix·ture /ˈmɪkstʃə(r)/ *noun* **1** [C, usually sing.] a combination of different things: *The city is a mixture of old and new buildings.* ◊ *We listened to the news with a mixture of surprise and horror.* **2** [C, U] a substance made by mixing other substances together: *cake mixture* ◊ *Add the eggs to the mixture and beat well.*—see also COUGH MIXTURE **3** [C] (*technical*) a combination of two or more substances that mix together without any chemical reaction taking place—compare COMPOUND *n.* **4** [U] the act of mixing different substances together

mix-up *noun* (*informal*) a situation that is full of confusion, especially because sb has made a mistake **SYN** MUDDLE: *There has been a mix-up over the dates.*

ml *abbr.* (*pl.* **ml** or **mls**) MILLILITRE(S): *25ml water*

mm *abbr., exclamation*
■ *abbr.* MILLIMETRE(S): *rainfall 6mm* ◊ *a 35mm camera*
■ *exclamation* (also **mmm**) the way of writing the sound /m/ that people make to show that they are listening to sb or that they agree, they are thinking, they like sth, they are not sure, etc: *Mm, I know what you mean.* ◊ *Mm, what lovely cake!* ◊ *Mmm, I'm not so sure that's a good idea.*

mne·mon·ic /nɪˈmɒnɪk; *AmE* -ˈmɑːn-/ *noun* a word, sentence, poem, etc. that helps you to remember sth ▶ **mne·mon·ic** *adj.* [only before noun]: *a mnemonic device*

MO (*BrE*) (also **M.O.** *AmE, BrE*) /ˌem ˈəʊ; *AmE* ˈoʊ/ *abbr.* MEDICAL OFFICER

mo /məʊ; *AmE* moʊ/ *noun* [sing.] (*BrE, informal, spoken*) a very short period of time **SYN** MOMENT: *See you in a mo!*

moan /məʊn; *AmE* moʊn/ *verb, noun*
■ *verb* **1** (of a person) to make a long deep sound, usually expressing unhappiness, suffering or sexual pleasure **SYN** GROAN: [V] *to moan in / with pain* ◊ *The injured man was lying on the ground, moaning.* ◊ [V speech] *'I might never see you again,' she moaned.* **2** ~ (on) (about sth) (to sb) | ~ (at sb) (*BrE, informal*) to complain about sth in a way that other people find annoying: [V] *What are you moaning on about now?* ◊ *They're always moaning and groaning about how much they have to do.* ◊ [V that] *Bella moaned that her feet were cold.* **3** [V] (*literary*) (especially of the wind) to make a long deep sound: *The wind was moaning through the trees.* ▶ **moan·er** *noun*
■ *noun* **1** [C] a long deep sound, usually expressing unhappiness, suffering or sexual pleasure: *a low moan of despair / anguish* **2** [C] (*BrE, informal*) a complaint about sth: *We had a good moan about work.* ◊ *His letters are full of the usual moans and groans.* **3** [sing.] (*literary*) a long deep sound, especially the sound that is made by the wind: *She lay listening to the moan of the wind in the trees behind the house.*

moat /məʊt; *AmE* moʊt/ *noun* a deep wide channel that was dug around a castle, etc. and filled with water to make it more difficult for enemies to attack ▶ **moat·ed** *adj.* [usually before noun]: *a moated manor house*

mob /mɒb; *AmE* mɑːb/ *noun, verb*
■ *noun* **1** [C, sing.+ sing./pl. *v.*] a large crowd of people, especially one that may become violent or cause trouble: *an angry / unruly mob* ◊ *The mob was / were preparing to storm the building.* ◊ *an excited mob of fans* ◊ *mob rule* (= a situation in which a mob has control, rather than people in authority)—see also LYNCH MOB **2** [C, usually sing.] (*informal*) a group of people who are similar in some way **SYN** GANG: *All the usual mob were there.* **3** (**the Mob**) [sing.] (*informal*) the people involved in organized crime; the MAFIA **IDM** see HEAVY *adj.*
■ *verb* (**-bb-**) [VN] [usually passive] **1** if a crowd of birds or animals **mob** another bird or animal, they gather round it and attack it **2** if a person is **mobbed** by a crowd of people, the crowd gathers round them in order to see them and try and get their attention

mob cap *noun* a light cotton cap covering all the hair, worn by women in the 18th and 19th centuries

mo·bile /ˈməʊbaɪl; *AmE* ˈmoʊbl/ *adj., noun*
■ *adj.* **1** [usually before noun] that is not fixed in one place and can be moved easily and quickly: *mobile equipment* ◊ *a mobile shop / library* (= one inside a vehicle)—compare STATIONARY **2** [not usually before noun] (of a person) able to move or travel around easily: *a kitchen especially designed for the elderly or people who are less mobile* ◊ *You really need to be mobile* (= have a car) *if you live in the country.* **OPP** IMMOBILE **3** (of people) able to change your social class, your job or the place where you live easily: *a highly mobile workforce* (= people who can move easily from place to place)—see also UPWARDLY MOBILE **4** (of a face or its features) changing shape or expression easily and often
■ *noun* **1** a decoration made from wire, etc. that is hung from the ceiling and that has small objects hanging from it which move when the air around them moves **2** (*BrE*) = MOBILE PHONE: *Call me on my mobile.*

aɪ	aʊ	eɪ	əʊ	oʊ	ɔɪ	ɪə	eə	ʊə	j	w
my	now	say	go	go	boy	near	hair	pure	yes	wet
			(BrE)	(AmE)						

mobile 'home *noun* (*especially AmE*) a building that can be moved, sometimes with wheels, that is usually parked in one place and used for living in

mobile 'phone (also **mo·bile**) (both *BrE*) (also **'cellular phone**, **cell·phone** *AmE*, *BrE*) *noun* a telephone that does not have wires and works by radio, that you can carry with you and use anywhere

mo·bil·ity /məʊˈbɪləti; *AmE* moʊ-/ *noun* [U] **1** the ability to move easily from one place, social class, or job to another: *social/geographical/career mobility*—see also UPWARD MOBILITY **2** the ability to move or travel around easily: *An electric wheelchair has given her greater mobility.*

mo·bil·ize (*BrE* also **-ise**) /ˈməʊbəlaɪz; *AmE* ˈmoʊ-/ *verb* **1** to work together in order to achieve a particular aim; to organize a group of people to do this: [VN] *The unions mobilized thousands of workers in a protest against the cuts.* [also V] **2** [VN] to find and start to use sth that is needed for a particular purpose SYN MARSHAL: *They were unable to mobilize the resources they needed.* **3** if a country **mobilizes** its army, or if a country or army **mobilizes**, it makes itself ready to fight in a war: [V] *The troops were ordered to mobilize.* [also VN] —compare DEMOBILIZE ▶ **mo·bil·iza·tion, -isa·tion** /ˌməʊbɪlaɪˈzeɪʃn; *AmE* ˌmoʊbələˈz-/ *noun* [U]

mob·ster /ˈmɒbstə(r); *AmE* ˈmɑːb-/ *noun* a member of a group of people who are involved in organized crime

moc·ca·sin /ˈmɒkəsɪn; *AmE* ˈmɑːk-/ *noun* a flat shoe that is made from soft leather and has large stitches around the front, of a type originally worn by Native Americans—picture at SHOE

mocha /ˈmɒkə; *AmE* ˈmoʊkə/ *noun* [U] **1** a type of coffee of very good quality **2** a drink made or flavoured with this, often with chocolate added

mock /mɒk; *AmE* mɑːk/ *verb, adj., noun*
- *verb* **1** to laugh at sb/sth in an unkind way, especially by copying what they say or do: [VN] *He's always mocking my French accent.* ◊ *The other children mocked her, laughing behind their hands.* ◊ [V] *You can mock, but at least I'm willing to have a try!* [also V speech, VN speech] **2** [VN] (*formal*) to show no respect for sth: *The new exam mocked the needs of the majority of children.* ▶ **mock·er** *noun*
- *adj.* [only before noun] **1** not sincere: *mock horror/surprise* **2** that is a copy of sth; not real: *a mock election* ◊ *a mock interview/examination* (= used to practise for the real one)
- *noun* (*informal*) (in Britain) a practice exam that you do before the official one: *The mocks are in November.* ◊ *What did you get in the mock?*

mock·ery /ˈmɒkəri; *AmE* ˈmɑːk-/ *noun* **1** [U] comments or actions that are intended to make sb/sth seem ridiculous: *She couldn't stand any more of their mockery.* **2** [sing.] (*disapproving*) an action, a decision, etc. that is a failure and that is not as it is supposed to be: *It was a mockery of a trial.* IDM **make a 'mockery of sth** to make sth seem ridiculous or useless: *The trial made a mockery of justice.*

mock·ing /ˈmɒkɪŋ; *AmE* ˈmɑːk-/ *adj.* (of behaviour, an expression, etc.) showing that you think sb/sth is ridiculous: *a mocking smile* ◊ *Her voice was faintly mocking.* ▶ **mock·ing·ly** *adv.*

mock·ing·bird /ˈmɒkɪŋbɜːd; *AmE* ˈmɑːkɪŋbɜːrd/ *noun* a black and white American bird that can copy the songs of other birds

'mock-up *noun* a model or a copy of sth, often the same size as it, that is used for testing, or for showing people what the real thing will look like

MOD /ˌem əʊ ˈdiː; *AmE* oʊ/ *abbr.* Ministry of Defence (the government department in Britain that is responsible for defence)

mod /mɒd; *AmE* mɑːd/ *noun* a member of a group of young people, especially in Britain in the 1960s, who wore neat, fashionable clothes and rode MOTOR SCOOTERS—compare ROCKER

modal /ˈməʊdl; *AmE* ˈmoʊdl/ (also **modal 'verb**, **modal au'xiliary**, **modal au'xiliary verb**) *noun* (*grammar*) a

verb such as *can*, *may* or *will* that is used with another verb (not a modal) to express possibility, permission, intention, etc. ▶ **modal** *adj.* —compare AUXILIARY

> **GRAMMAR POINT**
> **modal verbs**
>
> The **modal verbs** are **can**, **could**, **may**, **might**, **must**, **ought to**, **shall**, **should**, **will** and **would**. **Dare**, **need**, **have to** and **used to** also share some of the features of modal verbs.
>
> Modal verbs have only one form. They have no *-ing* or *-ed* forms and do not add *-s* to the 3rd person singular form: *He can speak three languages.* ◊ *She will try and visit tomorrow.*
>
> Modal verbs are followed by the infinitive of another verb without **to**. The exceptions are **ought to** and **used to**: *You must find a job.* ◊ *You ought to stop smoking.* ◊ *I used to smoke but I gave up two years ago.*
>
> Questions are formed without **do/does** in the present, or **did** in the past: *Can I invite Mary?* ◊ *Should I have invited Mary?*
>
> Negative sentences are formed with **not** or the short form **-n't** and do not use **do/does** or **did**.
>
> You will find more help with how to use modal verbs at the dictionary entries for each verb.

mod cons /ˌmɒd ˈkɒnz; *AmE* ˌmɑːd ˈkɑːnz/ *noun* [pl.] (*BrE*, *informal*) (especially in advertisements) the things in a house or flat/apartment that make living there easier and more comfortable

mode /məʊd; *AmE* moʊd/ *noun* **1** (*formal*) a particular way of doing sth; a particular type of sth: *a mode of production/operation/communication* ◊ *a mode of life/behaviour/dress* ◊ *environment-friendly modes of transport* **2** the way in which a piece of equipment is set to perform a particular task: *Switch the camera into the automatic mode.* **3** [sing.] (*informal*) a particular way of feeling or behaving: *to be in holiday/work mode* **4** [usually sing.] a particular style or fashion in clothes, art, etc: *narrative mode* ◊ *a pop video made by a director who really understands the mode*—see also À LA MODE, MODISH **5** (*technical*) a particular arrangement of notes in music for example the musical SCALE system: *major/minor mode*

model /ˈmɒdl; *AmE* ˈmɑːdl/ *noun, verb*
- *noun*
  SMALL COPY ┃ **1** a copy of sth, usually smaller than the original object: *a working model* (= one in which the parts move) *of a fire engine* ◊ *to make/build model aeroplanes* ◊ *The architect had produced a **scale model** of the proposed shopping complex.*
  DESIGN ┃ **2** a particular design or type of product: *The latest models will be on display at the motor show.*
  DESCRIPTION OF SYSTEM ┃ **3** a simple description of a system, used for explaining how sth works or calculating what might happen, etc: *a mathematical model for determining the safe level of pesticides in food* ◊ *a realistic model of evolution*
  EXAMPLE TO COPY ┃ **4** something such as a system that can be copied by other people: *The nation's constitution provided a model that other countries followed.* **5** (*approving*) a person or thing that is considered an excellent example of sth: *It was a model of clarity.* ◊ *a model student* ◊ *a model farm* (= one that has been specially designed to work well)—see also ROLE MODEL
  FASHION ┃ **6** a person whose job is to wear and show new styles of clothes and be photographed wearing them: *a fashion model* ◊ *a male model*
  FOR ARTIST ┃ **7** a person who is employed to be painted, drawn, photographed, etc. by an artist or photographer
- *verb* (**-ll-**, *AmE* **-l-**)
  WORK AS MODEL ┃ **1** [V] to work as a model for an artist or in the fashion industry
  CLOTHES ┃ **2** [VN] to wear clothes in order to show them to

M

b	d	f	g	h	k	l	m	n	p	r
bad	did	fall	get	hat	cat	leg	man	now	pen	red

people who might want to buy them: *The wedding gown is being modelled for us by the designer's daughter.*

CREATE COPY | **3** [VN] to create a copy of an activity, a situation, etc. so that you can study it before dealing with the real thing: *The program can model a typical home page for you.*

CLAY etc. | **4** [VN] to shape clay, etc. in order to make sth: *a statue modelled in bronze*

PHRV '**model yourself on sb** to copy the behaviour, style, etc. of sb you like and respect in order to be like them: *As a politician, he modelled himself on Churchill.* '**model sth on/after sth** to make sth so that it looks, works, etc. like sth else: *The country's parliament is modelled on the British system.*

'**model home** *noun* (*AmE*) = SHOW HOUSE

mod·el·ler (*BrE*) (*AmE* **mod·el·er**) /ˈmɒdələ(r); *AmE* ˈmɑːd-/ *noun* **1** a person who makes models of objects **2** a person who makes a simple description of a system or a process that can be used to explain it, etc.

mod·el·ling (*BrE*) (*AmE* **mod·el·ing**) /ˈmɒdəlɪŋ; *AmE* ˈmɑːd-/ *noun* [U] **1** the work of a fashion model: *a career in modelling ◊ a modelling agency* **2** the activity of making models of objects: *clay modelling* **3** the work of making a simple description of a system or a process that can be used to explain it, etc: *mathematical/statistical/computer modelling*

modem /ˈməʊdem; *AmE* ˈmoʊ-/ *noun* a device that connects one computer system to another using a telephone line so that data can be sent

mod·er·ate *adj., verb, noun*
■ *adj.* /ˈmɒdərət; *AmE* ˈmɑːd-/ **1** that is neither very good, large, hot, etc. nor very bad, small, cold, etc: *students of moderate ability ◊ Even moderate amounts of the drug can be fatal. ◊ The team enjoyed only moderate success last season. ◊ Cook over a moderate heat.* **2** having or showing opinions, especially about politics, that are not extreme: *moderate views/policies ◊ a moderate socialist* **3** staying within limits that are considered to be reasonable by most people: *a moderate drinker ◊ moderate wage demands* OPP IMMODERATE
■ *verb* /ˈmɒdəreɪt; *AmE* ˈmɑːd-/ **1** to become or make sth become less extreme, severe, etc: [V] *By evening the wind had moderated slightly.* ◊ [VN] *We agreed to moderate our original demands.* **2** [VN, V] (*BrE*) to check that an exam has been marked fairly and in the same way by different people
■ *noun* /ˈmɒdərət; *AmE* ˈmɑːd-/ a person who has opinions, especially about politics, that are not extreme

mod·er·ate·ly /ˈmɒdərətli; *AmE* ˈmɑːd-/ *adv.* **1** to an average extent; fairly but not very SYN REASONABLY: *a moderately successful career ◊ She only did moderately well in the exam. ◊ Cook in a moderately hot oven.* **2** within reasonable limits: *He only drinks (alcohol) moderately.*

mod·er·ation /ˌmɒdəˈreɪʃn; *AmE* ˌmɑːd-/ *noun* [U] **1** the quality of being reasonable and not being extreme: *There was a call for moderation on the part of the trade unions. ◊ Alcohol is usually not harmful if it is taken in moderation* (= in small quantities). **2** (*BrE*) (in education) the process of making sure that the same standards are used by different people in marking exams, etc.

mod·er·ator /ˈmɒdəreɪtə(r); *AmE* ˈmɑːd-/ *noun* **1** a person whose job is to help the two sides in a dispute to reach an agreement—see also MEDIATOR **2** (*especially AmE*) a person whose job is to make sure that a discussion or a debate is fair **3** (*BrE*) a person whose job is to make sure that an exam is marked fairly **4** (**Moderator**) a religious leader in the Presbyterian Church who is in charge of the Church council

mod·ern /ˈmɒdn; *AmE* ˈmɑːdərn/ *adj.* **1** [only before noun] of the present time or recent times SYN CONTEMPORARY: *the modern industrial world ◊ Modern European history ◊ modern Greek ◊ Stress is a major problem of modern life.* **2** [only before noun] (of styles in art, music, fashion, etc.) new and intended to be different from traditional styles SYN CONTEMPORARY: *modern art/architecture/drama/jazz* **3** (usually *approving*) using the latest technology, designs, materials, etc. SYN UP-TO-DATE: *a*

modern computer system ◊ modern methods of farming ◊ the most modern, well-equipped hospital in London **4** (of ways of behaving, thinking, etc.) new and not always accepted by most members of society: *She has very modern ideas about educating her children.*

'**modern-day** *adj.* [only before noun] **1** of the present time SYN CONTEMPORARY: *modern-day America* **2** used to describe a modern form of sb/sth, usually sb/sth bad or unpleasant, that existed in the past: *It has been called modern-day slavery.*

mod·ern·ism /ˈmɒdənɪzəm; *AmE* ˈmɑːdərn-/ *noun* [U] **1** modern ideas or methods **2** a style and movement in art, architecture and literature popular in the middle of the 20th century in which modern ideas, methods and materials were used rather than traditional ones—compare POSTMODERNISM ▶ **mod·ern·ist** /ˈmɒdənɪst; *AmE* ˈmɑːdərn-/ *adj.* [only before noun]: *modernist art* **mod·ern·ist** *noun*

mod·ern·is·tic /ˌmɒdəˈnɪstɪk; *AmE* ˌmɑːdər'n-/ *adj.* (of a painting, building, piece of furniture, etc.) painted, designed, etc. in a very modern style

mod·ern·ity /məˈdɜːnəti; *AmE* -ˈdɜːrn-/ *noun* [U] (*written*) the condition of being new and modern

mod·ern·ize (*BrE* also **-ise**) /ˈmɒdənaɪz; *AmE* ˈmɑːdərn-/ *verb* **1** [VN] to make a system, methods, etc. more modern and more suitable for use at the present time SYN UPDATE: *The company is investing $9 million to modernize its factories. ◊ a campaign to modernize the voting system* **2** [V] to start using modern equipment, ideas, etc: *Unfortunately we lack the resources to modernize.* ▶ **mod·ern·iza·tion, -isa·tion** /ˌmɒdənaɪˈzeɪʃn; *AmE* ˌmɑːdərnəˈz-/ *noun* [U]

,**modern 'language** *noun* (*especially BrE*) a language that is spoken or written now, especially a European language, such as French or Spanish, that you study at school, university or college: *the department of modern languages ◊ a degree in modern languages ◊ a modern language teacher*

mod·est /ˈmɒdɪst; *AmE* ˈmɑːd-/ *adj.* **1** not very large, expensive, important, etc: *modest improvements/reforms ◊ He charged a relatively modest fee. ◊ a modest little house ◊ The research was carried out on a modest scale.* **2** (*approving*) not talking much about your own abilities or possessions: *She's very modest about her success. ◊ You're too modest!* OPP IMMODEST **3** (of people, especially women, or their clothes) shy about showing much of the body; not intended to attract attention, especially in a sexual way: *a modest dress* OPP IMMODEST ▶ **mod·est·ly** *adv.*

mod·esty /ˈmɒdəsti; *AmE* ˈmɑːd-/ *noun* [U] **1** the fact of not talking much about your abilities or possessions: *He accepted the award with characteristic modesty. ◊ I hate false* (= pretended) *modesty.* **2** the action of behaving or dressing so that you do not show your body or attract sexual attention **3** the state of being not very large, expensive, important, etc: *They tried to disguise the modesty of their achievements.*

modi·cum /ˈmɒdɪkəm; *AmE* ˈmɑːd-/ *noun* [sing.] (*formal*) a fairly small amount, especially of sth good or pleasant: *They should win, given a modicum of luck.*

modi·fi·ca·tion /ˌmɒdɪfɪˈkeɪʃn; *AmE* ˌmɑːd-/ *noun* [U, C] ~ (of/to/in sth) the act or process of changing sth in order to improve it or make it more acceptable; a change that is made: *Considerable modification of the existing system is needed. ◊ It might be necessary to make a few slight modifications to the design.*

modi·fier /ˈmɒdɪfaɪə(r); *AmE* ˈmɑːd-/ *noun* (*grammar*) a word, such as an adjective or adverb, that describes another word or group of words, or restricts its/their meaning in some way: *In 'speak quietly', the adverb 'quietly' is a modifier.*

modi·fy /ˈmɒdɪfaɪ; *AmE* ˈmɑːd-/ *verb* (**modi·fies, modi·fy·ing, modi·fied, modi·fied**) [VN] **1** to change sth slightly, especially in order to make it more suitable for a particular purpose SYN ADAPT: *The office software has been modified over the years. ◊ Patients are taught how to modify their diet.* ⇨ note at CHANGE **2** to make sth less extreme: *to modify your behaviour / language / views* **3** (*grammar*) a word, such as an adjective or adverb, that **modifies** another word or group of words describes it or restricts its meaning in some way: *In 'walk slowly', the adverb 'slowly' modifies the verb 'walk'.*

mod·ish /'məʊdɪʃ; *AmE* 'moʊ-/ *adj.* (sometimes *disapproving*) fashionable

modu·lar /'mɒdjələ(r); *AmE* 'mɑːdʒə-/ *adj.* **1** (of a course of study, especially at a British university or college) consisting of separate units from which students may choose several: *a modular course* **2** (of machines, buildings, etc.) consisting of separate parts or units that can be joined together

modu·late /'mɒdjuleɪt; *AmE* 'mɑːdʒə-/ *verb* **1** [VN] (*formal*) to change the quality of your voice in order to create a particular effect by making it louder, softer, lower, etc. **2** [V] ~ (**from sth**) (**to / into sth**) (*music*) to change from one musical KEY (= set of notes) to another **3** [VN] (*technical*) to affect sth so that it becomes more regular, slower, etc: *drugs that effectively modulate the disease process* **4** [VN] (*technical*) to change the rate at which a sound wave or radio signal VIBRATES (= the FREQUENCY) so that it is able to carry information ▶ **modu·la·tion** /ˌmɒdju-'leɪʃn; *AmE* ˌmɑːdʒə-/ *noun* [U, C]

mod·ule /'mɒdjuːl; *AmE* 'mɑːdʒuːl/ *noun* **1** a unit that can form part of a course of study, especially at a college or university in Britain: *The course consists of ten core modules and five optional modules.* **2** (*computing*) a unit of a computer system or program that has a particular function: *software modules* ◊ *a tutorial module* **3** one of a set of separate parts or units that can be joined together to make a machine, a piece of furniture, a building, etc. **4** a unit of a spacecraft that can function independently of the main part: *the lunar module*

modus op·er·andi /ˌməʊdəs ˌɒpə'rændiː; *AmE* ˌmoʊdəs ˌɑːpə-/ *noun* [sing.] (from *Latin*, *formal*) a particular method of working

modus vi·vendi /ˌməʊdəs vɪ'vendiː; *AmE* ˌmoʊdəs-/ *noun* [sing.] (from *Latin*, *formal*) an arrangement that is made between people, institutions or countries who have very different opinions or ideas, so that they can live or work together without quarrelling

mog·gie (also **moggy**) /'mɒgi; *AmE* 'mɔːgi; 'mɑːgi/ *noun* (*pl.* **-ies**) (*BrE*, *informal*) a cat

mogul /'məʊgl; *AmE* 'moʊgl/ *noun* a very rich, important and powerful person: *a movie / media mogul*

mo·hair /'məʊheə(r); *AmE* 'moʊher/ *noun* [U] soft wool or fabric made from the fine hair of the ANGORA goat, used for making clothes: *a mohair sweater*

Mo·ham·med *noun* = MUHAMMAD

Mo·hi·can /məʊ'hiːkən; *AmE* moʊ-/ *noun* a way of cutting the hair in which the head is shaved except for a strip of hair in the middle that is made to stick up ▶ **Mo·hi·can** *adj.*: *a punk with a Mohican haircut*

moist /mɔɪst/ *adj.* slightly wet: *warm moist air* ◊ *a rich moist cake* ◊ *Water the plants regularly to keep the soil moist.* ◊ *Her eyes were moist* (= with tears). ▶ **moist·ness** *noun* [U]

mois·ten /'mɔɪsn/ *verb* to become or make sth slightly wet: [VN] *He moistened his lips before he spoke.* [also V]

mois·ture /'mɔɪstʃə(r)/ *noun* [U] very small drops of water that are present in the air, on a surface or in a substance: *the skin's natural moisture* ◊ *a material that is designed to absorb / retain moisture*

mois·tur·ize (*BrE* also **-ise**) /'mɔɪstʃəraɪz/ *verb* to put a special cream on your skin to make it less dry: [VN] *a moisturizing cream / lotion* ◊ [V] *a product that soothes and moisturizes*

mois·tur·izer (*BrE* also **-iser**) /'mɔɪstʃəraɪzə(r)/ *noun* [C, U] a cream that is used to make the skin less dry

molar /'məʊlə(r); *AmE* 'moʊ-/ *noun* any of the twelve large teeth at the back of the mouth used for crushing and chewing food—compare CANINE, INCISOR

mo·las·ses /mə'læsɪz/ *noun* [U] (*AmE*) = TREACLE

mold, mol·der, mold·ing, moldy (*AmE*) = MOULD, MOULDER, MOULDING, MOULDY

mole /məʊl; *AmE* moʊl/ *noun* **1** a small animal with dark grey fur, that is almost blind and digs tunnels under the ground to live in—see also MOLEHILL **2** a small dark brown mark on the skin, sometimes slightly higher than the skin around it—compare FRECKLE **3** a person who works within an organization and secretly passes important information to another organization or country **4** (*chemistry*) a unit for measuring the amount of a substance

mol·ecule /'mɒlɪkjuːl; *AmE* 'mɑːl-/ *noun* the smallest unit, usually consisting of a group of atoms, into which a substance can be divided without a change in its chemical nature: *A molecule of water consists of two atoms of hydrogen and one atom of oxygen.* ▶ **mo·lecu·lar** /mə'lekjələ(r)/ *adj.* [only before noun]: *molecular structure / biology*

mole·hill /'məʊlhɪl; *AmE* 'moʊl-/ *noun* a small pile of earth that a MOLE leaves on the surface of the ground when it digs underground IDM see MOUNTAIN

mole·skin /'məʊlskɪn; *AmE* 'moʊl-/ *noun* [U] a strong cotton fabric with a soft surface, used for making clothes

mo·lest /mə'lest/ *verb* [VN] **1** to attack sb, especially a child, sexually **2** (*old-fashioned*) to attack sb physically: *The couple were molested while walking through the park.* ▶ **mo·lest·ation** /ˌmɒle'steɪʃn; *AmE* ˌmoʊ-/ *noun* [U] **mo·lest·er** /mə'lestə(r)/ *noun*: *a child molester*

moll /mɒl; *AmE* mɑːl/ *noun* (*old-fashioned*, *slang*) the female friend of a criminal

mol·lify /'mɒlɪfaɪ; *AmE* 'mɑːl-/ *verb* (**mol·li·fies, mol·li·fying, mol·li·fied, mol·li·fied**) [VN] (*formal*) to make sb feel less angry or upset SYN PLACATE: *His explanation failed to mollify her.*

mol·lusc (*BrE*) (*AmE* **mol·lusk**) /'mɒləsk; *AmE* 'mɑːl-/ *noun* (*technical*) any creature with a soft body that is not divided into different sections, and usually a hard outer shell. SNAILS and SLUGS are molluscs.—compare BIVALVE, SHELLFISH—picture on page A7

molly·cod·dle /'mɒlikɒdl; *AmE* 'mɑːl-/ *verb* [VN] (*disapproving*, becoming *old-fashioned*) to protect sb too much and make their life too comfortable and safe: *She was mollycoddled as a child.*—compare CODDLE

Molo·tov cock·tail /ˌmɒlətɒf 'kɒkteɪl; *AmE* ˌmɑːlətɔːf 'kɑːk-; ˌmoʊl-/ (*BrE* also **petrol bomb**) *noun* a simple bomb that consists of a bottle filled with petrol / gas and a piece of fabric in the end that is made to burn just before the bomb is thrown

molt (*AmE*) = MOULT

mol·ten /'məʊltən; *AmE* 'moʊl-/ *adj.* (of metal, rock, or glass) heated to a very high temperature so that it becomes liquid

mom /mɒm; *AmE* mɑːm/ *noun* (*AmE*, *informal*) = MUM: *Where's my mom?* ◊ *Mom and Dad* ◊ *Are you listening, Mom?*

mo·ment /'məʊmənt; *AmE* 'moʊ-/ *noun* **1** a very short period of time: *Could you wait a moment, please?* ◊ *One moment, please* (= Please wait a short time). ◊ *He thought for a moment before replying.* ◊ *I'll be back in a moment.* ◊ *We arrived not a moment too soon* (= almost too late). ◊ *Moments later* (= a very short time later), *I heard a terrible crash.* **2** [sing.] an exact point in time: *We're busy at the moment* (= now). ◊ *I agreed in a moment of weakness.* ◊ *At that very moment, the phone rang.* ◊ *From that moment on, she never felt really well again.* **3** [C] a particular occasion; a time for doing sth: *I haven't finished. I'm still waiting for a quiet moment.* ◊ *I'm waiting for the right moment to tell him the bad news.* ◊ *That was one of the happiest moments of my life.* ◊ *Have I caught you at a bad moment?* IDM **for the 'moment / 'present** for now; for a short time: *This house is big enough for the moment, but we'll have to move if we have children.* **have it's / your 'moments** to have short times that are better, more interesting, etc. than others **the ˌmoment of 'truth** a time when sb / sth is tested, or when important decisions are made **of 'moment** very important: *matters of great moment* **of the 'moment** (of a person, a job, an issue, etc.) famous, important and talked about a lot now: *She's the fashion designer of the moment.*—more at

M

æ	ɑː	e	ɜː	ə	ɪ	iː	i	ɒ	ɔː	ʌ	ʊ	u	uː
cat	father	ten	bird	about	sit	see	many	got	saw	cup	put	actual	too

(BrE)

JUST *adv.*, LAST *det.*, MINUTE¹ *n.*, NOTICE *n.*, PSYCHOLOGICAL, SPUR *n.*, WAIT *v.*

mo·ment·ar·ily /ˈməʊməntrəli; *AmE* ˌməʊmənˈterəli/ *adv.* **1** for a very short time $\boxed{\text{SYN}}$ BRIEFLY: *He paused momentarily.* **2** (*AmE*, *spoken*) very soon; in a moment: *I'll be with you momentarily.*

mo·ment·ary /ˈməʊməntri; *AmE* ˈməʊmənteri/ *adj.* lasting for a very short time $\boxed{\text{SYN}}$ BRIEF: *a momentary lapse of concentration* ◇ *momentary confusion*

mo·men·tous /məˈmentəs; *AmE* moʊˈm-/ *adj.* very important or serious, especially because there may be important results: *a momentous decision/event/occasion*

mo·men·tum /məˈmentəm; *AmE* moʊˈm-/ *noun* [U] **1** the ability to keep increasing or developing: *The fight for his release gathers momentum each day.* ◇ *They began to lose momentum in the second half of the game.* **2** a force that is gained by movement: *The vehicle gained momentum as the road dipped.* **3** (*technical*) the quantity of movement of a moving object, measured as its MASS (= weight) multiplied by its speed

mommy /ˈmɒmi; *AmE* ˈmɑːmi/ (also **momma** /ˈmɒmə; *AmE* ˈmɑːmə/) (both *AmE*) *noun* = MUMMY

mon- ⇨ MONO-

mon·arch /ˈmɒnək; *AmE* ˈmɑːnərk; -ɑːrk/ *noun* a person who rules a country or an empire, for example a king or a queen

mo·nar·chic·al /məˈnɑːkɪkl; *AmE* -ˈnɑːrk-/ *adj.* [usually before noun] (*formal*) connected with a ruler such as a king or a queen or with the system of government by a king or queen: *monarchical rule/power*

mon·arch·ist /ˈmɒnəkɪst; *AmE* ˈmɑːnərk-/ *noun* a person who believes that a country should be ruled by a king or queen ▸ **mon·arch·ist** *adj.*

mon·archy /ˈmɒnəki; *AmE* ˈmɑːnərki/ *noun* (*pl.* **-ies**) **1** (**the monarchy**) a system of government by a king or a queen: *plans to abolish the monarchy* **2** a country that is ruled by a king or a queen: *There are several constitutional monarchies in Europe.*—compare REPUBLIC **3** (**the monarchy**) the king or queen of a country and their family

mon·as·tery /ˈmɒnəstri; *AmE* ˈmɑːnəsteri/ *noun* (*pl.* **-ies**) a building in which MONKS (= members of a male religious community) live together

mo·nas·tic /məˈnæstɪk/ *adj.* **1** connected with MONKS or monasteries **2** (of a way of life) simple and quiet and possibly CELIBATE

mo·nas·ti·cism /məˈnæstɪsɪzəm/ *noun* [U] the way of life of MONKS in MONASTERIES

Mon·day /ˈmʌndeɪ; -di/ *noun* [C, U] (*abbr.* **Mon.**) the day of the week after Sunday and before Tuesday, the first day of the working week: *It's Monday today, isn't it?* ◇ *She started work last Monday.* ◇ *Are you busy next Monday?* ◇ *Monday morning/afternoon/evening* ◇ *We'll discuss this at Monday's meeting.* ◇ *Do we still have Monday's paper?* ◇ *I work Monday to Friday.* ◇ *I work Mondays to Fridays.* ◇ *On Monday(s)* (= Every Monday) *I do yoga.* ◇ *I always do yoga on a Monday.* ◇ *He was born on a Monday.* ◇ *I went to Paris on Thursday, and came back the following Monday.* ◇ *We'll meet on Monday.* ◇ (*BrE*) *'When did the accident happen?' 'It was the Monday* (= the Monday of the week we are talking about).' ◇ (*BrE*) *Come back Monday week* (= a week after next Monday). ◇ (*informal* or *AmE*) *We'll meet Monday.* $\boxed{\text{ORIGIN}}$ From the Old English for 'day of the moon', translated from Latin *lunae dies.*

mon·et·ar·ism /ˈmʌnɪtərɪzəm/ *noun* [U] the policy of controlling the amount of money available in a country as a way of keeping the economy strong

mon·et·ar·ist /ˈmʌnɪtərɪst/ *noun* a person who supports monetarism ▸ **mon·et·ar·ist** *adj.*: *a monetarist economic policy*

mon·et·ary /ˈmʌnɪtri; *AmE* -teri/ *adj.* [only before noun] connected with money, especially all the money in a country: *monetary policy/growth* ◇ *an item of little monetary value* ◇ *closer European political, monetary and economic union*

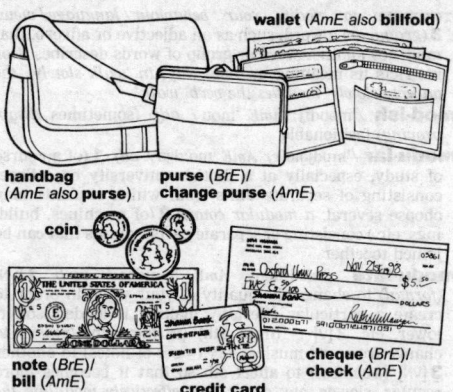

wallet (*AmE* also **billfold**)

handbag (*AmE* also **purse**)

purse (*BrE*)/ **change purse** (*AmE*)

coin

note (*BrE*)/ **bill** (*AmE*)

credit card

cheque (*BrE*)/ **check** (*AmE*)

money /ˈmʌni/ *noun* **1** [U] what you earn by working or selling things, and use to buy things: *to borrow/save/spend/earn money* ◇ *How much money is there in my account?* ◇ *The money is much better in my new job.* ◇ *If the item is not satisfactory, you will get your money back.* ◇ *We'll need to raise more money* (= collect or borrow it) *next year.* ◇ *Can you lend me some money until tomorrow?* **2** [U] coins or paper notes: *I counted the money carefully.* ◇ *Where can I change my money into dollars?*—see also PAPER MONEY, READY MONEY ⇨ Appendix 3 **3** [U] a person's wealth including their property: *He lost all his money.* ◇ *The family made their money in the 18th century.* **4** (**moneys** or **monies**) [pl.] (*old use* or *law*) sums of money: *a statement of all monies paid into your account* $\boxed{\text{HELP}}$ You will find other compounds ending in **money** at their place in the alphabet. $\boxed{\text{IDM}}$ **be in the 'money** (*informal*) to have a lot of money to spend **for 'my money** (*informal*) in my opinion: *For my money, he's one of the greatest comedians of all time.* **get your 'money's worth** to get enough value or enjoyment out of sth, considering the amount of money, time, etc. that you are spending on it **good 'money** a lot of money; money that you earn with hard work: *Thousands of people paid good money to watch the band perform.* ◇ *Don't waste good money on that!* **have money to 'burn** to have so much money that you do not have to be careful with it **made of money** (*informal*) very rich **make 'money** to earn a lot of money; to make a profit: *The movie should make money.* ◇ *There's money to be made from tourism.* **make/lose money, hand over 'fist** to make/lose money very fast and in large quantities **money for 'jam/old 'rope** (*BrE*, *informal*) money that is earned very easily, for sth that needs little effort **money is no 'object** money is not sth that needs to be considered, because there is plenty of it available: *She travels around the world as if money is no object.* **money 'talks** (*saying*) people who have a lot of money have more power and influence than others **on the 'money** (*AmE*) correct; accurate: *His prediction was right on the money.* **put 'money into sth** to invest money in a business or a particular project: *We would welcome interest from anyone prepared to put money into the club.* **put your 'money on sb/sth 1** to bet that a particular horse, dog, etc. will win a race **2** to feel very sure that sth is true or that sb will succeed: *He'll be there tonight. I'd put money on it.* **put your money where your 'mouth is** (*informal*) to support what you say by doing sth practical; to show by your actions that you really mean sth **throw your 'money about/around** (*informal*) to spend money in a careless and obvious way **throw good money after 'bad** (*disapproving*) to spend more money on sth, when you have wasted a lot on it already **throw 'money at sth** (*disapproving*) to try to deal with a problem or improve a situation by spending money on it, when it would be better to deal with it in other ways: *It is inappropriate simply to throw money at these problems.*—more at CAREFUL, COIN *v.*, COLOUR *n.*, EASY *adj.*, GROW, LICENCE *n.*, LOVE *n.*, MARRY, OBJECT, POT *n.*, ROLL *v.*, RUN *n.*

aɪ	aʊ	eɪ	əʊ	oʊ	ɔɪ	ɪə	eə	ʊə	j	w
my	now	say	go (BrE)	go (AmE)	boy	near	hair	pure	yes	wet

money box noun (especially BrE) a small closed box with a narrow opening and sometimes with a lock and key, into which children put coins as a way of saving money—compare PIGGY BANK

mon·eyed (also **mon·ied**) /ˈmʌnid/ adj. [only before noun] (formal) having a lot of money: the moneyed classes

money-grubbing (also **money-grabbing**) adj. [only before noun] (informal, disapproving) trying to get a lot of money ▶ **money-grubber** (also **money-grabber**) noun

money·lend·er /ˈmʌnilendə(r)/ noun (old-fashioned) a person whose business is lending money, usually at a very high rate of interest

money·maker /ˈmʌnimeɪkə(r)/ noun a product, business, etc. that produces a large profit ▶ **money·mak·ing** adj.: a moneymaking movie **money·mak·ing** noun [U]

money market noun the banks and other institutions that lend or borrow money, and buy and sell foreign money

money order noun (especially AmE) = POSTAL ORDER

money-saving adj. [only before noun] that helps you spend less money: money-saving offers/tips

money-spinner noun (BrE, informal) something that earns a lot of money

money supply noun [sing., U] (economics) the total amount of money that exists in the economy of a country at a particular time: to control/increase/reduce the money supply ◊ a rapid growth in (the) money supply

mon·gol /ˈmɒŋgəl; AmE ˈmɑːŋ-/ noun (old-fashioned) an offensive word for a person with DOWN'S SYNDROME ▶ **mon·gol·ism** noun [U]

mon·goose /ˈmɒŋguːs; AmE ˈmɑːŋ-/ noun (pl. **mon-gooses** /-siːz/) a small tropical animal with fur, that kills snakes, rats, etc.

mon·grel /ˈmʌŋgrəl/ (especially BrE) (also **mutt** especially in AmE) noun a dog that is a mixture of different breeds

mon·ied adj. = MONEYED

moni·ker /ˈmɒnɪkə(r); AmE ˈmɑːn-/ noun (humorous) a name

moni·tor /ˈmɒnɪtə(r); AmE ˈmɑːn-/ noun, verb
■ noun **1** a television screen used to show particular kinds of information; a screen that shows information from a computer: The details of today's flights are displayed on the monitor. ◊ a PC with a 17 inch colour monitor—see also VDU—picture on page 250 **2** a piece of equipment used to check or record sth: a heart monitor **3** a student in a school who carries out special duties, such as helping the teacher **4** a person whose job is to check that sth is done fairly and honestly, especially in a foreign country: UN monitors declared the referendum fair.
■ verb **1** to watch and check sth over a period of time in order to see how it develops, so that you can make any necessary changes: [VN] Each student's progress is closely monitored. [also V wh-] **2** [VN] to listen to telephone calls, foreign radio broadcasts, etc. in order to find out information that might be useful

monk /mʌŋk/ noun a member of a religious group of men who often live apart from other people in a MONASTERY and who do not marry or have personal possessions: Benedictine/Buddhist monks—compare FRIAR, NUN

mon·key /ˈmʌŋki/ noun **1** an animal with a long tail, that climbs trees and lives in hot countries. There are several types of monkey and they are related to APES and humans. **2** (informal) a child who is active and likes playing tricks on people: Come here, you cheeky little monkey! **IDM** **I don't/couldn't give a 'monkey's** (BrE, slang) used to say, in a way that is not very polite, that you do not care about sth, or are not at all interested in it **make a 'monkey (out) of sb** to make sb seem stupid—more at BRASS

monkey business noun [U] (informal) dishonest or silly behaviour

monkey wrench noun = ADJUSTABLE SPANNER

mono /ˈmɒnəʊ; AmE ˈmɑːnoʊ/ adj., noun
■ adj. recording or producing sound which comes from only one direction: a mono recording—compare STEREO
■ noun [U] **1** a system of recording or producing sound which comes from only one direction: recorded in mono—compare STEREO **2** (AmE, informal) = GLANDULAR FEVER

mono- /ˈmɒnəʊ; AmE ˈmɑːnoʊ/ (also **mon-**) combining form (in nouns and adjectives) one; single: monorail ◊ monogamy

mono·chrome /ˈmɒnəkrəʊm; AmE ˈmɑːnəkroʊm/ adj. **1** (of photographs, etc.) using only black, white and shades of grey: monochrome illustrations/images ◊ (figurative) a dull monochrome life **2** using different shades of one colour: monochrome furnishings ▶ **mono·chro·mat·ic** /ˌmɒnəkrəˈmætɪk; AmE ˌmɑːnəkroʊm-/ adj.: a monochromatic colour scheme **mono·chrome** noun [U]: an artist who works in monochrome

mon·ocle /ˈmɒnəkl; AmE ˈmɑːn-/ noun a single glass LENS for one eye, held in place by the muscles around the eye and used by people in the past to help them see clearly

mon·og·amy /məˈnɒgəmi; AmE məˈnɑːg-/ noun [U] **1** the fact or custom of being married to only one person at a particular time—compare BIGAMY, POLYGAMY **2** the practice or custom of having a sexual relationship with only one partner at a particular time ▶ **mon·og·am·ous** /məˈnɒgəməs; AmE məˈnɑːg-/ adj.: a monogamous marriage ◊ Most birds are monogamous.

mono·gram /ˈmɒnəgræm; AmE ˈmɑːn-/ noun two or more letters, usually the first letters of sb's names, that are combined in a design and marked on items of clothing, etc. that they own ▶ **mono·grammed** adj.: a monogrammed handkerchief

mono·graph /ˈmɒnəgrɑːf; AmE ˈmɑːnəgræf/ noun (technical) a detailed written study of a single subject, usually in the form of a short book

mono·lin·gual /ˌmɒnəˈlɪŋgwəl; AmE ˌmɑːnə-/ adj. speaking or using only one language: a monolingual dictionary—compare BILINGUAL, MULTILINGUAL

mono·lith /ˈmɒnəlɪθ; AmE ˈmɑːn-/ noun **1** a large single upright block of stone, especially one that was shaped into a column by people living in ancient times, and that may have had some religious meaning **2** (often disapproving) a single, very large organization, etc. that is very slow to change and not interested in individual people: the monolith of the state ▶ **mono·lith·ic** /ˌmɒnəˈlɪθɪk; AmE ˌmɑːnə-/ adj.: a monolithic block ◊ the monolithic structure of the state

mono·logue (AmE also **mono·log**) /ˈmɒnəlɒg; AmE ˈmɑːnəlɔːg; -lɑːg/ noun **1** [C] a long speech by one person during a conversation that stops other people from speaking or expressing an opinion: He went into a long monologue about life in America. **2** [U, C] a long speech in a play, film/movie, etc. spoken by one actor, especially when alone **3** [C, U] a dramatic story, especially in verse, told or performed by one person: a dramatic monologue—compare DIALOGUE, SOLILOQUY

mono·nucle·osis /ˌmɒnəʊˌnjuːkliˈəʊsɪs; AmE ˌmɑːnoʊˌnuːkliˈoʊsɪs/ noun [U] (AmE or BrE medical) = GLANDULAR FEVER

mono·plane /ˈmɒnəpleɪn; AmE ˈmɑː-/ noun an early type of plane with one set of wings—compare BIPLANE

mon·op·ol·ist /məˈnɒpəlɪst; AmE məˈnɑːp-/ noun (technical) a person or company that has a MONOPOLY

mon·op·ol·is·tic /məˌnɒpəˈlɪstɪk; AmE məˌnɑːpə-/ adj. (written) controlling or trying to get complete control over sth, especially an industry or a company: monopolistic corporations

mon·op·ol·ize (BrE also **-ise**) /məˈnɒpəlaɪz; AmE məˈnɑːp-/ verb [VN] **1** to have or take control of the largest part of sth so that other people are prevented from sharing it: Men traditionally monopolized jobs in the printing industry. ◊ As usual, she completely monopolized the conversation. **2** to have or take a large part of sb's attention or time so that they are unable to speak to or deal with other people: Don't let him monopolize you like he did at the last party. ▶ **mon·op·ol·iza·tion, -isa·tion** /məˌnɒpəlaɪˈzeɪʃn; AmE məˌnɑːpələˈz-/ noun [U]

M

b	d	f	g	h	k	l	m	n	p	r
bad	did	fall	get	hat	cat	leg	man	now	pen	red

mon·op·oly /mə'nɒpəli; *AmE* mə'nɑːp-/ *noun* (*pl.* **-ies**)
1 ~ (in/of/on sth) (*business*) the complete control of trade in particular goods or the supply of a particular service; a type of goods or a service that is controlled in this way: *In the past central government had a monopoly on television broadcasting.* ◇ *Electricity, gas and water were considered to be natural monopolies.* **2** [usually sing.] ~ in/of/on sth the complete control, possession or use of sth; a thing that belongs only to one person or group and that other people cannot share: *Managers do not have a monopoly on stress.* ◇ *A good education should not be the monopoly of the rich.*—compare DUOPOLY

mono·rail /'mɒnəʊreɪl; *AmE* 'mɑːnoʊ-/ *noun* **1** [U] a railway/railroad system in which trains travel along a track consisting of a single rail, usually one placed high above the ground **2** [C] a train used in a monorail system

mono·so·dium glu·ta·mate /ˌmɒnəˌsəʊdiəm 'gluːtəmeɪt; *AmE* ˌmɑːnəˌsoʊ-/ *noun* [U] (*abbr.* **MSG**) a chemical compound that is sometimes added to food to improve its flavour

mono·syl·lab·ic /ˌmɒnəsɪ'læbɪk; *AmE* ˌmɑːn-/ *adj.* **1** having only one syllable: *a monosyllabic word/reply* **2** (of a person or their way of speaking) saying very little, in a way that appears rude to other people: *Ralph grew increasingly monosyllabic as the evening progressed.*

mono·syl·lable /'mɒnəsɪləbl; *AmE* 'mɑːnoʊ-/ *noun* a word with only one syllable, for example, 'it' or 'no'

mono·the·ism /'mɒnəʊθiːɪzəm; *AmE* 'mɑːnoʊ-/ *noun* [U] the belief that there is only one God—compare POLYTHEISM ▶ **mono·the·ist** /'mɒnəʊθiːɪst; *AmE* 'mɑːnoʊ-/ *noun* **mono·the·is·tic** /ˌmɒnəʊθi'ɪstɪk; *AmE* ˌmɑːnoʊ-/ *adj.*

mono·tone /'mɒnətəʊn; *AmE* 'mɑːnətoʊn/ *noun, adj.*
■ *noun* [sing.] a dull sound or way of speaking in which the tone and volume remain the same and therefore seem boring: *He spoke in a flat monotone.*
■ *adj.* [only before noun] without any changes or differences in sound or colour: *He spoke in a monotone drawl.* ◇ *monotone engravings*

mon·ot·on·ous /mə'nɒtənəs; *AmE* mə'nɑːt-/ *adj.* never changing and therefore boring: *a monotonous voice/diet/routine* ◇ *monotonous work* ◇ *New secretaries came and went with monotonous regularity.* ▶ **mon·ot·on·ous·ly** *adv.*

mon·ot·ony /mə'nɒtəni; *AmE* mə'nɑːt-/ *noun* [U] boring lack of variety: *She watches television to relieve the monotony of everyday life.*

Mon·si·gnor /mɒn'siːnjə(r); *AmE* mɑːn-/ *noun* (*abbr.* **Mgr**) used as a title when speaking to or about a priest of high rank in the Roman Catholic Church

mon·soon /ˌmɒn'suːn; *AmE* ˌmɑːn-/ *noun* **1** a period of heavy rain in summer in S Asia; the rain that falls during this period **2** a wind in S Asia that blows from the south-west in summer, bringing rain, and the north-east in winter

mon·ster /'mɒnstə(r); *AmE* 'mɑːn-/ *noun, adj.*
■ *noun* **1** (in stories) an imaginary creature that is very large, ugly and frightening: *a monster with three heads* ◇ *prehistoric monsters* **2** an animal or a thing that is very large or ugly: *Their dog's an absolute monster!* **3** a person who is very cruel and evil **4** (*humorous*) a child who behaves badly
■ *adj.* [only before noun] (*informal*) unusually large: *monster mushrooms*

mon·stros·ity /mɒn'strɒsəti; *AmE* mɑːn'strɑːs-/ *noun* (*pl.* **-ies**) something that is very large and very ugly, especially a building: *a concrete monstrosity*

mon·strous /'mɒnstrəs; *AmE* 'mɑːn-/ *adj.* **1** considered to be shocking and unacceptable because it is morally wrong or unfair: *a monstrous lie/injustice* **2** very large: *a monstrous wave* **3** very large, ugly and frightening: *a monstrous figure/creature* ▶ **mon·strous·ly** *adv.*: *monstrously unfair* ◇ *a monstrously fat man*

mont·age /ˌmɒn'tɑːʒ; 'mɒn-; *AmE* ˌmɑːn'tɑːʒ/ *noun* **1** [C] a picture, film/movie or piece of music or writing that consists of many separate items put together, especially in an interesting or unusual combination: *a photographic montage* **2** [U] the process of making a montage

Mon·terey Jack /ˌmɒntəreɪ 'dʒæk; *AmE* ˌmɑːn-/ (*AmE* also '**Jack cheese**) *noun* [U] a type of white American cheese with a mild flavour

month /mʌnθ/ *noun* **1** [C] any of the twelve periods of time into which the year is divided, for example May or June: *the month of August* ◇ *We're moving house next month.* ◇ *She earns $1000 a month.* ◇ *The rent is £300 per month.* ◇ *Have you read this month's 'Physics World'?* ◇ *Prices continue to rise* **month after month** (= over a period of several months). ◇ *Her anxiety mounted* **month by month** (= as each month passed).—see also CALENDAR MONTH **2** [C] a period of about 30 days, for example, 3 June to 3 July: *The baby is three months old.* ◇ *a three-month-old baby* ◇ *They lived in Toronto during their first few months of marriage.* ◇ *several months later* ◇ *a six-month contract* ◇ *a month-long strike* ◇ *He visits Paris once or twice a month.*—see also LUNAR MONTH **3** (**months**) [pl.] a long time, especially a period of several months: *He had to wait for months for the visas to come through.* ◇ *It will be months before we get the results.* **IDM in a ,month of 'Sundays** (*spoken*) used to emphasize that sth will never happen: *You won't find it, not in a month of Sundays.*—more at FLAVOUR *n.*

month·ly /'mʌnθli/ *adj., adv., noun*
■ *adj.* **1** happening once a month or every month: *a monthly meeting/visit/magazine* **2** paid, valid or calculated for one month: *a monthly salary of £1000* ◇ *a monthly season ticket* ◇ *Summers are hot, with monthly averages above 22°C.*
■ *adv.* every month or once a month: *She gets paid monthly.*
■ *noun* (*pl.* **-ies**) a magazine published once a month: *the fashion monthlies*

monty /'mɒnti; *AmE* 'mɑːnti/ *noun* **IDM the ,full 'monty** the full amount that people expect or want: *They'll do the full monty* (= take off all their clothes) *if you pay them enough.*

monu·ment /'mɒnjumənt; *AmE* 'mɑːn-/ *noun* **1** ~ (to sb/sth) a building, column, statue, etc. built to remind people of a famous person or event: *A monument to him was erected in St Paul's Cathedral.* **2** a building that has special historical importance: *an ancient monument* **3** ~ to sth a thing that remains as a good example of sb's qualities or of what they did: *These recordings are a monument to his talent as a pianist.*

monu·men·tal /ˌmɒnju'mentl; *AmE* ˌmɑːn-/ *adj.* **1** [usually before noun] very important and having a great influence, especially as the result of years of work: *a monumental achievement* ◇ *Gibbon's monumental work 'The Rise and Fall of the Roman Empire'* **2** [only before noun] very large, good, bad, stupid, etc: *a book of monumental significance* ◇ *We have a monumental task ahead of us.* ◇ *It seems like an act of monumental folly.* **3** [only before noun] appearing in or serving as a monument: *a monumental inscription/tomb* ◇ *a monumental mason* (= a person who makes monuments)

monu·men·tal·ly /ˌmɒnju'mentəli; *AmE* ˌmɑːn-/ *adv.* (used to describe negative qualities) extremely: *monumentally difficult/stupid*

moo /muː/ *noun* (*pl.* **moos**) the long deep sound made by a cow ▶ **moo** *verb* [V]

mooch /muːtʃ/ *verb* (*informal*) **1** [V+adv./prep.] (*BrE*) to walk slowly with no particular purpose; to be somewhere not doing very much: *He's happy to mooch around the house all day.* **2** ~ (sth) (off sb) (*AmE*) to get money, food, etc. from sb else instead of paying for it yourself: [V] *He's always mooching off his friends.* [also VN]

mood /muːd/ *noun* **1** [C] the way you are feeling at a particular time: *She's in a good mood today* (= happy and friendly). ◇ *He's always in a bad mood* (= unhappy, or angry and impatient). ◇ *to be in a foul/filthy mood* ◇ *Some addicts suffer violent mood swings* (= changes of mood) *if deprived of the drug.* ◇ *I'm just not in the mood for a party tonight.* ◇ *He was in no mood for being polite to visitors.* **2** [C] a period of being angry or impatient: *I wonder why he's in such a mood today.* ◇ *She was in one of her moods* (= one of her regular periods of being angry or impatient). **3** [sing.] the way a group of people feel about sth; the atmosphere in a place or among a group of people: *The mood of the meeting was distinctly pessimistic.* ◊ *The movie captures the mood of the interwar years perfectly.* **4** [C] (*grammar*) any of the sets of verb forms that show whether what is said or written is certain, possible, necessary, etc. **5** [C] (*grammar*) one of the categories of verb use that expresses facts, orders, questions, wishes or conditions: *the indicative/imperative/subjunctive mood*

'**mood music** *noun* [U] popular music intended to create a particular atmosphere, especially a relaxed or romantic one

moody /'muːdi/ *adj.* (**mood·ier**, **moodi·est**) **1** having moods that change quickly and often: *Moody people are very difficult to deal with.* **2** bad-tempered or upset, often for no particular reason: *Why are you so moody today?* **3** (of a film/movie, piece of music or place) suggesting particular emotions, especially sad ones: *She gazed out at the moody grey sea.* ▶ **mood·ily** /-ɪli/ *adv.*: *He stared moodily into the fire.* **moodi·ness** *noun* [U]

moon /muːn/ *noun, verb*
■ *noun* **1** (usually **the moon**) (also **the Moon**) [sing.] the round object that moves around the earth once every 28 days and shines at night by light reflected from the sun: *the surface of the moon* ◊ *a moon landing* **2** [sing.] the moon as it appears in the sky at a particular time: *a crescent moon* ◊ *There's no moon tonight* (= no moon can be seen). ◊ *By the light of the moon I could just make out shapes and outlines.*—see also FULL MOON, HALF-MOON, NEW MOON **3** [C] a natural SATELLITE that moves around a planet other than the earth: *How many moons does Jupiter have?* **IDM ask, cry, etc. for the 'moon** (*BrE, informal*) to ask for sth that is difficult or impossible to get or achieve **many 'moons ago** (*literary*) a very long time ago **over the 'moon** (*informal, especially BrE*) extremely happy and excited—more at ONCE *adv.*, PROMISE *v.*
■ *verb* [V] (*informal*) to show your bottom to people in a public place as a joke or an insult **PHRV** ,**moon a'bout/a'round** (*BrE, informal*) to spend time doing nothing or walking around with no particular purpose, especially because you are unhappy '**moon over sb** (*informal*) to spend time thinking about sb that you love, especially when other people think this is silly or annoying

moon·beam /'muːnbiːm/ *noun* a ray of light from the moon

'**moon boot** *noun* a thick warm boot made of fabric or plastic, worn in snow or cold weather

moon·less /'muːnləs/ *adj.* without a moon that can be seen: *a moonless night/sky*

moon·light /'muːnlaɪt/ *noun, verb*
■ *noun* [U] the light of the moon: *to go for a walk by moonlight/in the moonlight* **IDM** see FLIT *n.*
■ *verb* (**moon·lighted**, **moon·lighted**) [V] (*informal*) to have a second job that you do secretly, usually without paying tax on the extra money that you earn

moon·lit /'muːnlɪt/ *adj.* lit by the moon: *a moonlit night/beach*

moon·scape /'muːnskeɪp/ *noun* **1** a view of the surface of the moon **2** an area of land that is bare and empty and looks like the surface of the moon

moon·shine /'muːnʃaɪn/ *noun* [U] **1** (*old-fashioned, AmE*) whisky or other strong alcoholic drinks made and sold illegally **2** (*informal*) silly talk **SYN** NONSENSE

moon·struck /'muːnstrʌk/ *adj.* slightly crazy, especially because you are in love

Moor /mɔː(r); mʊə(r); *AmE* mʊr/ *noun* a member of a race of Muslim people living in NW Africa who entered and took control of part of Spain in the 8th century ▶ **Moor·ish** /'mɔːrɪʃ; 'mʊə-; *AmE* 'mʊrɪʃ/ *adj.*: *the Moorish architecture of Cordoba in Spain*

moor /mɔː(r); mʊə(r); *AmE* mʊr/ *noun, verb*
■ *noun* **1** [C, usually pl.] (*especially BrE*) a high open area of land that is not used for farming, especially an area covered with rough grass and HEATHER: *the North York moors* ◊ *to go for a walk on the moors* **2** [U] = MOORLAND: *moor and rough grassland*

■ *verb* ~ **sth (to sth)** to attach a boat, ship, etc. to a fixed object or to the land with a rope, or ANCHOR it: [V] *We moored off the north coast of the island.* ◊ [VN] *A number of fishing boats were moored to the quay.*

moor·hen /'mɔːhen; 'mʊə-; *AmE* 'mʊrhen/ *noun* a small black bird with a short reddish-yellow beak that lives on or near water

moor·ing /'mɔːrɪŋ; 'mʊər-; *AmE* 'mʊr-/ *noun* **1** (**moorings**) [pl.] the ropes, chains, etc. by which a ship or boat is MOORED: *The boat slipped its moorings and drifted out to sea.* **2** [C] the place where a ship or boat is MOORED: *private moorings* ◊ *to find a mooring* ◊ *mooring ropes*

moor·land /'mɔːlənd; 'mʊə-; *AmE* 'mʊrlənd/ (also **moor**) *noun* [U, C, usually pl.] (*especially BrE*) land that consists of MOORS: *walking across open moorland*

moose /muːs/ *noun* (*pl.* **moose**) a large deer that lives in N America. In Europe and Asia it is called an ELK.

moot /muːt/ *adj., verb*
■ *adj.* (*AmE*) unlikely to happen and therefore not worth considering: *He argued that the issue had become moot since the board had changed its policy.* **IDM a moot** '**point/question** (*BrE, AmE*) a matter about which there may be disagreement or uncertainty
■ *verb* [VN] [usually passive] (*formal*) to suggest an idea for people to discuss **SYN** PROPOSE, PUT FORWARD

'**moot court** *noun* (*especially AmE*) a MOCK court in which law students practise trials

mop /mɒp; *AmE* mɑːp/ *noun, verb*
■ *noun* **1** a tool for washing floors that has a long handle with a bunch of thick strings or soft material at the end: *a mop and bucket* **2** a kitchen UTENSIL (= a tool) for washing dishes, that has a short handle with soft material at one end **3** a mass of thick, often untidy, hair: *a mop of curly red hair*
■ *verb* (-pp-) [VN] **1** to clean sth with a mop: *She wiped all the surfaces and mopped the floor.* **2** ~ **sth (from sth)** to remove liquid from the surface of sth using a cloth: *He took out a handkerchief to **mop his brow** (= to remove the sweat).* **PHRV** ,**mop sth/sb↔'up** to remove the liquid from sth using sth that absorbs it: *Do you want some bread to mop up that sauce?* ◊ (*figurative*) *A number of smaller companies were mopped up* (= taken over) *by the American multinational.* ◊ (*figurative*) *New equipment mopped up* (= used up) *what was left of this year's budget.* ,**mop sb/sth↔'up 1** to complete or end sth by dealing with the final parts: *There are a few things that need mopping up before I can leave.* **2** to get rid of the last few people who continue to oppose you, especially by capturing or killing them: *Troops combed the area to mop up any remaining resistance.*

mope /məʊp; *AmE* moʊp/ *verb* [V] to spend your time doing nothing and feeling sorry for yourself: *Moping won't do any good!* **PHRV** ,**mope a'bout/a'round** (…) (*disapproving*) to spend time walking around a place with no particular purpose, especially because you feel sorry for yourself: *Instead of moping around the house all day, you should be out there looking for a job.*

moped /'məʊped; *AmE* 'moʊ-/ *noun* a motorcycle with a small engine and also PEDALS—picture at MOTORCYCLE

mop·pet /'mɒpɪt; *AmE* 'mɑːp-/ *noun* (*informal*) an attractive small child, especially a girl

mo·raine /mə'reɪn; *BrE also* mɒ'reɪn/ *noun* [U, C] (*technical*) a mass of earth, stones, etc., carried along by a GLACIER and left when it melts—picture at MOUNTAIN

moral /'mɒrəl; *AmE* 'mɔːr-; 'mɑːr-/ *adj., noun*
■ *adj.* **1** [only before noun] concerned with principles of right and wrong behaviour: *a moral issue/dilemma/question* ◊ *traditional moral values* ◊ *a decline in moral standards* ◊ *moral philosophy* ◊ *a deeply religious man with a highly developed moral sense* ◊ *British newspapers were full of **moral outrage** at the weakness of other countries.* **2** [only before noun] based on your own sense of what is right and fair, not on legal rights or duties: *moral responsibility/duty* ◊ *Governments have at least a **moral obligation** to answer these questions.* ◊ (*BrE*) *The job was to call on all her diplomatic skills and **moral courage*** (= the courage to do what you think is right). **3** following the

æ	ɑː	e	ɜː	ə	ɪ	iː	i	ɒ	ɔː	ʌ	ʊ	u	uː
cat	father	ten	bird	about	sit	see	many	got	saw	cup	put	actual	too
								(BrE)					

standards of behaviour considered acceptable and right by most people: *He led a very moral life.* ◊ *a very moral person*—compare AMORAL, IMMORAL **4** [only before noun] able to understand the difference between right and wrong: *Children are not naturally moral beings.* **IDM** **take, claim, seize, etc. the moral ˈhigh ground** to claim that your side of an argument is morally better than your opponents' side; to argue in a way that makes your side seem morally better

■ *noun* **1** (**morals**) [pl.] standards or principles of good behaviour, especially in matters of sexual relationships: *Young people these days have no morals.* ◊ *The play was considered an affront to public morals.* ◊ *The question is one of manners rather than morals.* ◊ (*old-fashioned*) *a woman of loose morals* (= with a low standard of sexual behaviour) **2** [C] a practical lesson that a story, an event or an experience teaches you: *And the moral is that crime doesn't pay.*

mor·ale /məˈrɑːl; *AmE* -ˈræl/ *noun* [U] the amount of confidence and enthusiasm, etc. that a person or a group has at a particular time: *to boost/raise/improve morale* ◊ *Morale amongst the players is very high at the moment.* ◊ *Staff are suffering from low morale.*

ˌmoral ˈfibre (*BrE*) (*AmE* ˌmoral ˈfiber) *noun* [U] the inner strength to do what you believe to be right in difficult situations

mor·al·ist /ˈmɒrəlɪst; *AmE* ˈmɔːr-; ˈmɑːr-/ *noun* **1** (often *disapproving*) a person who has strong ideas about moral principles, especially one who tries to tell other people how they should behave **2** a person who teaches or writes about moral principles

mor·al·is·tic /ˌmɒrəˈlɪstɪk; *AmE* ˌmɔːr-; ˌmɑːr-/ *adj.* (usually *disapproving*) having or showing very fixed ideas about what is right and wrong, especially when this causes you to judge other people's behaviour

mor·al·ity /məˈræləti/ *noun* **1** [U] principles concerning right and wrong or good and bad behaviour: *matters of public/private morality* ◊ *Standards of morality seem to be dropping.* **2** [U] the degree to which sth is right or wrong, good or bad, etc. according to moral principles: *a debate on the morality of abortion* **3** [U] a system of moral principles followed by a particular group of people: *Christian morality*—compare IMMORALITY

mor·al·ize (*BrE* also **-ise**) /ˈmɒrəlaɪz; *AmE* ˈmɔːr-; ˈmɑːr-/ *verb* [V] (usually *disapproving*) to tell other people what is right and wrong especially in order to emphasize that your opinions are correct: *He's always moralizing about 'young people today'.*

mor·al·ly /ˈmɒrəli; *AmE* ˈmɔːr-; ˈmɑːr-/ *adv.* according to principles of good behaviour and what is considered to be right or wrong: *to act morally* ◊ *morally right/wrong/justified/unacceptable* ◊ *He felt morally responsible for the accident.*

the ˌmoral maˈjority *noun* [sing.+ sing./pl. *v.*] the largest group of people in a society, considered as having very traditional ideas about moral matters, religion, sexual behaviour, etc.

ˌmoral supˈport *noun* [U] the act of giving encouragement by showing your approval and interest, rather than by giving financial or practical support: *My sister came along just to give me some moral support.*

ˌmoral ˈvictory *noun* a situation in which your ideas or principles are proved to be right and fair, even though you may not have succeeded where practical results are concerned

mor·ass /məˈræs/ *noun* [usually sing.] (*written*) **1** an unpleasant and complicated situation that is difficult to escape from: *a morass of lies and deceit* **2** a dangerous area of low soft wet land

mora·tor·ium /ˌmɒrəˈtɔːriəm; *AmE* ˌmɔːr-/ *noun* (*pl.* **-riums** or **-toria** /-riə/) **~** (**on sth**) a temporary stopping of an activity, especially by official agreement: *The convention called for a two-year moratorium on commercial whaling.*

mor·bid /ˈmɔːbɪd; *AmE* ˈmɔːrbɪd/ *adj.* **1** having or expressing a strong interest in sad or unpleasant things, especially disease or death: *He had a morbid fascination*

with blood. ◊ *'He might even die.' 'Don't be so morbid.'* **2** (*medical*) connected with disease ▶ **mor·bid·ity** /mɔːrˈbɪdəti; *AmE* mɔːrˈb-/ *noun* [U] **mor·bid·ly** *adv.*

mor·dant /ˈmɔːdnt; *AmE* ˈmɔːrdnt/ *adj.* (*formal*) critical and unkind, but funny: *His mordant wit appealed to students.* ▶ **mor·dant·ly** *adv.*

more /mɔː(r)/ *det., pron., adv.*

■ *det., pron.* (used as the comparative of 'much', 'a lot of', 'many') **~** (**sth/of sth**) (**than ...**) a larger number or amount of: *more bread/cars* ◊ *Only two more days to go!* ◊ *people with more money than sense* ◊ *I can't stand much more of this.* ◊ *She earns a lot more than I do.* ◊ *There is room for no more than three cars.* ◊ *I hope we'll see more of you* (= see you again or more often). **IDM** ˌmore and ˈmore continuing to become larger in number or amount: *More and more people are using the Internet.* ◊ *She spends more and more time alone in her room.*

■ *adv.* **~** (**than ...**) **1** used to form the comparative of adjectives and adverbs with two or more syllables: *She was far more intelligent than her sister.* ◊ *He read the letter more carefully the second time.* **2** to a greater degree than sth else; to a greater degree than usual: *I like her more than her husband.* ◊ *a course for more advanced students* ◊ *It had more the appearance of a deliberate crime than of an accident.* ◊ *Could you repeat that once more* (= one more time)? ◊ *I had no complaints and no more* (= neither) *did Tom.* ◊ *Signing the forms is little more than* (= only) *a formality.* ◊ *I'm more than happy* (= extremely happy) *to take you there in my car.* ◊ *She was more than a little shaken* (= extremely shaken) *by the experience.* ◊ (*formal*) *I will torment you no more* (= no longer).—see also ANY MORE **IDM** ˌmore and ˈmore continuing to become larger in number or amount **SYN** INCREASINGLY: *I was becoming more and more irritated by his behaviour.* ˌmore or ˈless **1** almost: *I've more or less finished the book.* **2** approximately: *She could earn $200 a night, more or less.* **what is ˈmore** used to add a point that is even more important: *You're wrong, and what's more you know it!*

more·over /mɔːrˈəʊvə(r); *AmE* -ˈoʊvər/ *adv.* (*formal*) used to introduce some new information that adds to or supports what you have said previously **SYN** IN ADDITION: *A talented artist, he was, moreover, a writer of some note.*

mores /ˈmɔːreɪz/ *noun* [pl.] (*formal*) the customs and behaviour that are considered typical of a particular social group or community

morgue /mɔːɡ; *AmE* mɔːrɡ/ *noun* **1** (*BrE*) a building in which dead bodies are kept before they are buried or CREMATED (= burned)—compare MORTUARY **2** a place where dead bodies that have been found are kept until they can be identified

mori·bund /ˈmɒrɪbʌnd; *AmE* ˈmɔːr-; ˈmɑːr-/ *adj.* (*formal*) **1** (of an industry, an institution, a custom, etc.) no longer effective and about to come to an end completely: *a moribund company/economy* **2** in a very bad condition; dying: *a moribund patient/tree*

Mor·mon /ˈmɔːmən; *AmE* ˈmɔːrmən/ *noun* a member of a religion formed by Joseph Smith in the US in 1830, officially called 'the Church of Jesus Christ of Latter-day Saints': *a Mormon church/chapel*

morn /mɔːn; *AmE* mɔːrn/ *noun* [usually sing.] (*literary*) morning

morn·ing /ˈmɔːnɪŋ; *AmE* ˈmɔːrnɪŋ/ *noun* **1** the early part of the day from the time when people wake up until midday or before lunch: *They left for Spain early this morning.* ◊ *See you tomorrow morning.* ◊ *I prefer coffee in the morning.* ◊ *She woke every morning at the same time.* ◊ *Our group meets on Friday mornings.* ◊ *I walk to work most mornings.* ◊ *We got the news on the morning of the wedding.* ◊ *He's been in a meeting all morning.* ◊ *the morning papers* **2** the part of the day from midnight to midday: *I didn't get home until two in the morning!* ◊ *He died in the early hours of Sunday morning.* **3** (**mornings**) *adv.* in the morning of each day: *I only work mornings.* **IDM** **Good ˈmorning** used as a polite greeting when people first see each other in the morning; sometimes also used formally when people leave each other in the morning; in informal use people often just say *Morning:*

M

aɪ	aʊ	eɪ	əʊ	oʊ	ɔɪ	ɪə	eə	ʊə	j	w
my	now	say	go	go	boy	near	hair	pure	yes	wet
			(BrE)	(AmE)						

Good morning, Mr Dixon. ◊ *Morning, Mike.* **in the 'morning** **1** during the morning of the next day; tomorrow morning: *I'll give you a call in the morning.* **2** between midnight and midday: *It must have happened at about five o'clock in the morning.* **morning, noon and 'night** at all times of the day and night (used to emphasize that sth happens very often or that it happens continuously): *She talks about him morning, noon and night.* ◊ *The work continues morning, noon and night.*—more at OTHER *adj.*

morning-'after *adj.* [only before noun] **1** happening the next day, after an exciting or important event: *After his election victory, the president held a morning-after news conference.* **2** used to describe how sb feels the next morning, after an occasion when they have drunk too much alcohol: *a morning-after headache*

morning-'after pill *noun* a drug that a woman can take some hours after having sex in order to avoid becoming pregnant

'morning coat (*BrE*) (*AmE* **cut·away**) *noun* a black or grey jacket for men, short at the front and very long at the back, worn as part of morning dress—compare TAILS (6)

'morning dress *noun* [U] clothes worn by a man on very formal occasions, for example a wedding, including a morning coat and dark trousers/pants

'morning room *noun* (*old-fashioned, especially BrE*) (in some large houses, especially in the past) a room that you sit in in the morning

'morning sickness *noun* [U] the need to VOMIT that some women feel, often only in the morning, when they are pregnant, especially in the first months

mo·rocco /məˈrɒkəʊ; *AmE* məˈrɑːkoʊ/ *noun* [U] fine soft leather made from the skin of a goat, used especially for making shoes and covering books

moron /ˈmɔːrɒn; *AmE* -rɑːn/ *noun* (*informal*) an offensive way of referring to sb that you think is very stupid: *They're a bunch of morons.* ◊ *You moron—now look what you've done!* ► **mor·on·ic** /məˈrɒnɪk; *AmE* -ˈrɑːn-/ *adj.*: *a moronic stare* ◊ *a moronic TV programme*

mor·ose /məˈrəʊs; *AmE* məˈroʊs/ *adj.* unhappy, bad-tempered and not talking very much: *She just sat there looking morose.* ► **mor·ose·ly** *adv.*: *He was staring morosely out of the window.*

mor·pheme /ˈmɔːfiːm; *AmE* ˈmɔːrf-/ *noun* (*grammar*) the smallest unit of meaning that a word can be divided into: *The word 'like' contains one morpheme but 'un-like-ly' contains three.*

mor·phia /ˈmɔːfiə; *AmE* ˈmɔːrf-/ *noun* [U] (*old-fashioned*) the drug morphine

mor·phine /ˈmɔːfiːn; *AmE* ˈmɔːrf-/ *noun* [U] a powerful drug that is made from OPIUM and used to reduce pain

morph·ology /mɔːˈfɒlədʒi; *AmE* mɔːrˈfɑːl-/ *noun* [U] **1** (*biology*) the form and structure of animals and plants, studied as a science **2** (*linguistics*) the forms of words, studied as a branch of linguistics—compare GRAMMAR, SYNTAX ► **mor·pho·logic·al** /ˌmɔːfəˈlɒdʒɪkl; *AmE* ˌmɔːrfə-ˈlɑːdʒ-/ *adj.*

mor·ris dance /ˈmɒrɪs dɑːns; *AmE* ˈmɔːrɪs dæns/ *noun* a traditional English dance that is performed by people wearing special clothes decorated with bells and carrying sticks that they hit together ► **'morris dancer** *noun* **'morris dancing** *noun* [U]

mor·row /ˈmɒrəʊ; *AmE* ˈmɑːroʊ; ˈmɔːr-/ *noun* (**the morrow**) [sing.] (*old-fashioned, literary*) the next day; tomorrow: *We had to leave on the morrow.* ◊ *Who knows what the morrow* (= the future) *will bring?*

Morse code /ˌmɔːs ˈkəʊd; *AmE* ˌmɔːrs ˈkoʊd/ *noun* [U] a system for sending messages, using combinations of long and short sounds or flashes of light to represent letters of the alphabet and numbers

mor·sel /ˈmɔːsl; *AmE* ˈmɔːrsl/ *noun* a small amount or a piece of sth, especially food: *a tasty morsel of food* ◊ *He ate it all, down to the last morsel.*

mor·tal /ˈmɔːtl; *AmE* ˈmɔːrtl/ *adj., noun*
■ *adj.* **1** that cannot live for ever and must die: *We are all mortal.* OPP IMMORTAL **2** (*literary*) causing death or likely to cause death; very serious: *a mortal blow/wound* ◊ *to be in mortal danger* ◊ (*figurative*) *Her reputation suffered a mortal blow as a result of the scandal.*—compare FATAL **3** [only before noun] (*formal*) lasting until death SYN DEADLY: *mortal enemies* ◊ *They were locked in mortal combat* (= a fight that will only end with the death of one of them). **4** [only before noun] (*formal*) (of fear, terror, etc.) extreme: *We lived in mortal dread of him discovering our secret.*
■ *noun* (often *humorous*) a human being, especially an ordinary person with little power or influence SYN HUMAN BEING: *old stories about gods and mortals* ◊ (*humorous*) *Such things are not for mere mortals like ourselves.* ◊ (*humorous*) *She can deal with complicated numbers in her head, but we lesser mortals need calculators!*

mor·tal·ity /mɔːˈtæləti; *AmE* mɔːrˈt-/ *noun* (*pl.* **-ies**) **1** [U] the state of being human and not living for ever: *After her mother's death, she became acutely aware of her own mortality.* **2** [U] the number of deaths in a particular situation or period of time: *the infant mortality rate* (= the number of babies that die at or just after birth) ◊ *Mortality from lung cancer is still increasing.* **3** [C] (*technical*) a death: *hospital mortalities* (= deaths in hospital)

mor·tal·ly /ˈmɔːtəli; *AmE* ˈmɔːrt-/ *adv.* (*literary*) **1** causing or resulting in death SYN FATALLY: *mortally wounded/ill* **2** extremely: *mortally afraid/offended*

'mortal 'sin *noun* [C, U] (in the Roman Catholic Church) a very serious SIN for which you can be sent to HELL unless you CONFESS and are forgiven

mor·tar /ˈmɔːtə(r); *AmE* ˈmɔːrt-/ *noun, verb*
■ *noun* **1** [U] a mixture of sand, water, LIME and CEMENT used in building for holding bricks and stones together **2** [C] a heavy gun that fires bombs and SHELLS high into the air; the bombs that are fired by this gun: *to come under mortar fire/attack* **3** [C] a small hard bowl in which you can crush substances such as seeds and grains into powder with a special object (called a PESTLE)—picture at LABORATORY **IDM** SEE BRICK *n.*
■ *verb* [V, VN] to attack sb/sth using a mortar

'mortar board *noun* a black hat with a stiff square top, worn by some university teachers and students at special ceremonies—compare CAP (4)

mort·gage /ˈmɔːɡɪdʒ; *AmE* ˈmɔːrɡ-/ *noun, verb*
■ *noun* (also *informal* **home 'loan**) a legal agreement by which a bank or similar organization lends you money to buy a house, etc., and you pay the money back over a particular number of years; the sum of money that you borrow: *to apply for/take out/pay off a mortgage* ◊ *mortgage rates* (= of interest) ◊ *a mortgage on the house* ◊ *a mortgage of £60000* ◊ *monthly mortgage repayments*
■ *verb* [VN] to give a bank, etc. the legal right to own your house, land, etc. if you do not pay the money back that you have borrowed from the bank to buy the house or land: *He had to mortgage his house to pay his legal costs.*

mort·ga·gee /ˌmɔːɡɪˈdʒiː; *AmE* ˌmɔːrɡ-/ *noun* (*technical*) a person or an organization that lends money to people to buy houses, etc.

mort·ga·gor /ˈmɔːɡɪdʒɔː(r); *AmE* ˈmɔːrɡ-/ *noun* (*technical*) a person who borrows money from a bank or a similar organization to buy a house, etc.

mor·ti·cian /mɔːˈtɪʃn; *AmE* mɔːrˈt-/ *noun* (*AmE*) = UNDERTAKER

mor·tify /ˈmɔːtɪfaɪ; *AmE* ˈmɔːrt-/ *verb* (**mor·ti·fies, mor·ti·fy·ing, mor·ti·fied, mor·ti·fied**) [usually passive] to make sb feel very ashamed or embarrassed: *She was mortified to realize he had heard every word she said.* [also VN, VN that] ► **mor·ti·fi·ca·tion** /ˌmɔːtɪfɪˈkeɪʃn; *AmE* ˌmɔːrt-/ *noun* [U] **mor·ti·fy·ing** *adj.*: *How mortifying to have to apologize to him!*

mor·tise (also **mor·tice**) /ˈmɔːtɪs; *AmE* ˈmɔːrtɪs/ *noun* (*technical*) a hole cut in a piece of wood, etc. to receive the end of another piece of wood, so that the two are held together—see also TENON

'mortise lock *noun* a lock that is fitted inside a hole cut into the edge of a door, not one that is screwed onto the surface of one side

mor·tu·ary /ˈmɔːtʃəri; *AmE* ˈmɔːrtʃueri/ *noun* (*pl.* **-ies**)

M

1 (*AmE*) a room or building, for example part of a hospital, in which dead bodies are kept before they are buried or CREMATED (= burned) **2** (*AmE*) = FUNERAL PARLOUR—compare MORGUE

mo·saic /məʊˈzeɪk; *AmE* moʊ-/ *noun* [C, U] a picture or pattern made by placing together small pieces of glass, stone, etc. of different colours: *a Roman mosaic* ◊ *a design in mosaic* ◊ *mosaic tiles* ◊ (*figurative*) *A mosaic of fields, rivers and woods lay below us.*

mosey /ˈməʊzi; *AmE* ˈmoʊzi/ *verb* [V+adv./prep.] (*informal*) to go in a particular direction slowly and with no definite purpose: *He moseyed on over to the bar.*

mosh /mɒʃ; *AmE* mɑːʃ/ *verb* [V] to dance and jump up and down violently or without control at a concert where ROCK music is played

Mos·lem /ˈmɒzləm; *AmE* ˈmɑːz-/ *noun* = MUSLIM ▶ **Mos·lem** *adj.* = MUSLIM HELP The form **Moslem** is sometimes considered offensive. Use **Muslim.**

mosque /mɒsk; *AmE* mɑːsk/ *noun* a building in which Muslims worship

mos·quito /məˈskiːtəʊ; *AmE* -toʊ *BrE* also mɒs-/ *noun* (*pl.* **-oes** or *less frequent* **-os**) a flying insect that bites humans and animals and sucks their blood. One type of mosquito can spread the disease MALARIA: *a mosquito bite*—picture on page A7

mosˈquito net *noun* a net that you hang over a bed, etc. to keep mosquitoes away from you

moss /mɒs; *AmE* mɔːs/ *noun* [U, C] a very small green or yellow plant without flowers that spreads over damp surfaces, rocks, trees, etc: *moss-covered walls*—compare LICHEN—see also SPANISH MOSS

mossy /ˈmɒsi; *AmE* ˈmɔːsi/ *adj.* covered with moss: *mossy walls/tree trunks*

most /məʊst; *AmE* moʊst/ *det., pron., adv.*
■ *det., pron.* (used as the superlative of 'much', 'a lot of', 'many') **1** the largest in number or amount: *Who do you think will get (the) most votes?* ◊ *She had the most money of all of them.* ◊ *I spent most time on the first question.* ◊ *Who ate the most?* ◊ *The director has* **the most to lose.** HELP The can be left out in informal *BrE.* **2** more than half of sb/sth; almost all of sb/sth: *I like most vegetables.* ◊ *Most classical music sends me to sleep.* ◊ *As most of you know, I've decided to resign.* ◊ *Most of the people I had invited turned up.* ◊ *There are thousands of verbs in English and most (of them) are regular.* HELP The is not used with **most** in this meaning. IDM **at (the) ˈmost** not more than: *As a news item it merits a short paragraph at most.* ◊ *There were 50 people there, at the very most.*
■ *adv.* **1** used to form the superlative of adjectives and adverbs of two or more syllables: *the most boring/beautiful part* ◊ *It was the people with the least money who gave most generously.* HELP When **most** is followed only by an adverb, the is not used: *This reason is mentioned most frequently,* but *the most frequently mentioned reason.* **2** to the greatest degree: *What did you enjoy (the) most?* ◊ *It was what she wanted most of all.* HELP The is often left out in informal English. **3** (*formal*) very; extremely; completely: *It was most kind of you to meet me.* ◊ *We shall most probably never meet again.* ◊ *This technique looks easy, but it most certainly is not.* **4** (*AmE, informal*) almost: *I go to the store most every day.*

-most *suffix* (in adjectives) the furthest: *inmost* (= the furthest in) ◊ *southernmost* ◊ *topmost* (= the furthest up/nearest to the top)

most·ly /ˈməʊstli; *AmE* ˈmoʊ-/ *adv.* mainly; generally: *The sauce is mostly cream.* ◊ *We're mostly out on Sundays.*

MOT /ˌem əʊ ˈtiː; *AmE* oʊ/ (also **MOT test**) *noun* a test that any vehicle in Britain over three years old must take in order to make sure that it is safe and in good condition (abbreviation for 'Ministry of Transport'): *I've got to take the car in for its MOT.* ◊ *to pass/fail the MOT*

mote /məʊt; *AmE* moʊt/ *noun* (*old-fashioned*) a very small piece of dust SYN SPECK

motel /məʊˈtel; *AmE* moʊ-/ *noun* a hotel for people who are travelling by car, with space for parking cars near the rooms

motet /məʊˈtet; *AmE* moʊ-/ *noun* a short piece of church music, usually for voices only—compare CANTATA

moth /mɒθ; *AmE* mɔːθ/ *noun* a flying insect with a long thin body and four large wings, like a BUTTERFLY, but less brightly coloured. Moths fly mainly at night and are attracted to bright lights.—picture on page A7

moth·ball /ˈmɒθbɔːl; *AmE* ˈmɔːθ-/ *noun, verb*
■ *noun* a small white ball made of a chemical with a strong smell, used for keeping moths away from clothes IDM **in ˈmothballs** stored and not in use, often for a long time
■ *verb* [VN] [usually passive] to decide not to use or develop sth, for a period of time, especially a piece of equipment or a plan: *The original proposal had been mothballed years ago.*

ˈmoth-eaten *adj.* **1** (of clothes, etc.) damaged or destroyed by moths **2** (*informal, disapproving*) very old and in bad condition

mother /ˈmʌðə(r)/ *noun, verb*
■ *noun* **1** a female parent of a child or animal; a person who is acting as a mother to a child: *I want to buy a present for my mother and father.* ◊ *the relationship between mother and baby* ◊ *She's the mother of twins.* ◊ *a mother of three* (= with three children) ◊ *an expectant* (= pregnant) *mother* ◊ *She was a wonderful mother to both her natural and adopted children.* ◊ *the mother chimpanzee caring for her young* **2** the title of a woman who is head of a CONVENT (= a community of NUNS)—see also MOTHER SUPERIOR IDM **at your ˌmother's ˈknee** when you were very young: *I learnt these songs at my mother's knee.* **the ˈmother of (all) sth** (*informal*) used to emphasize that sth is very large, unpleasant, important, etc: *I got stuck in the mother of all traffic jams.*—more at OLD
■ *verb* [VN] to care for sb/sth because you are their mother, or as if you were their mother: *He was a disturbed child who needed mothering.* ◊ *Stop mothering me!*

mother·board /ˈmʌðəbɔːd; *AmE* ˈmʌðərbɔːrd/ *noun* (*computing*) the main board of a computer, containing all the CIRCUITS

ˈmother country *noun* [sing.] **1** the country where you or your family were born and which you feel a strong emotional connection with **2** the country that controls or used to control the government of another country

ˈmother figure *noun* an older woman that you go to for advice, support, help, etc., as you would to a mother—see also FATHER FIGURE

mother·fuck·er /ˈmʌðəfʌkə(r); *AmE* -ðərf-/ *noun* (△ *slang, especially AmE*) an offensive word used to insult sb, especially a man, and to show anger or dislike

ˌmother ˈhen *noun* (*usually disapproving*) a woman who likes to care for and protect people and who worries about them a lot

mother·hood /ˈmʌðəhʊd; *AmE* -ðərh-/ *noun* [U] the state of being a mother: *Motherhood suits her.*

mother·ing /ˈmʌðərɪŋ/ *noun* [U] the act of caring for and protecting children or other people: *an example of good/poor mothering*

ˈMother·ing Sun·day *noun* [U, C] (*BrE, becoming old-fashioned*) = MOTHER'S DAY

ˈmother-in-law *noun* (*pl.* **mothers-in-law**) the mother of your husband or wife—compare FATHER-IN-LAW

mother·land /ˈmʌðəlænd; *AmE* -ðərl-/ *noun* (*formal*) the country that you were born in and that you feel a strong emotional connection with—see also FATHERLAND

mother·less /ˈmʌðələs; *AmE* -ðərl-/ *adj.* having no mother because she has died or does not live with you: *children left motherless*

ˈmother lode *noun* [usually sing.] (*especially AmE*) a very rich source of gold, silver, etc. in a mine: (*figurative*) *Her own experiences have provided her with a mother lode of material for her songs.*

mother·ly /ˈmʌðəli; *AmE* -ðərli/ *adj.* having the qualities of a good mother; typical of a mother SYN MATERNAL: *motherly love/advice/instincts* ◊ *She was a kind, motherly woman.*

ˌMother ˈNature *noun* [U] the natural world, when you consider it as a force that affects the world and human beings

s	t	v	z	ʃ	ʒ	tʃ	dʒ	θ	ð	ŋ
see	tea	van	zoo	shoe	vision	chain	jam	thin	this	sing

mother-of-'pearl (also **pearl**) *noun* [U] the hard smooth shiny substance in various colours that forms a layer inside the shells of some types of shellfish and is used in making buttons, ornaments, etc.

'Mother's Day *noun* [U, C] a day on which mothers traditionally receive cards and gifts from their children, celebrated in Britain on the fourth Sunday in Lent and in the US on the 2nd Sunday in May

Mother Su'perior *noun* a woman who is the head of a female religious community, especially a CONVENT (= a community of NUNS)

mother-to-'be *noun* (*pl.* **mothers-to-be**) a woman who is pregnant

mother 'tongue *noun* the language that you first learn to speak when you are a child

motif /məʊ'tiːf; *AmE* moʊ-/ *noun* **1** a design or a pattern used as a decoration: *wallpaper with a flower motif* **2** a subject, an idea or a phrase that is repeated and developed in a work of literature or a piece of music—see also LEITMOTIF

mo·tion /'məʊʃn; *AmE* 'moʊʃn/ *noun, verb*
■ *noun* **1** [U, sing.] the act or process of moving or the way sth moves: *Newton's laws of motion* ◊ *The swaying motion of the ship was making me feel seasick.* ◊ (*formal*) *Do not alight while the train is still in motion* (= moving). ◊ *Rub the cream in with a circular motion.*—see also SLOW MOTION **2** [C] a particular movement made usually with your hand or your head, especially to communicate sth [SYN] GESTURE: *At a single motion of his hand, the room fell silent.* **3** [C] a formal proposal that is discussed and voted on at a meeting: *to table/put forward a motion* ◊ *to propose a motion* (= to be the main speaker in favour of a motion) ◊ *The motion was adopted/carried by six votes to one.* **4** [C] (*BrE, formal*) an act of emptying the bowels; the waste matter that is emptied from the bowels [IDM] **go through the 'motions (of doing sth)** to do or say sth because you have to, not because you really want to **set/ put sth in 'motion** to start sth moving: *They set the machinery in motion.* ◊ (*figurative*) *The wheels of change have been set in motion.*
■ *verb* **~ to sb (to do sth)| ~ (for) sb to do sth** to make a movement, usually with your hand or head to show sb what you want them to do: [V] *I motioned to the waiter.* ◊ *She motioned him into her office.* ◊ *He motioned for us to follow him.* [also VN to inf]

mo·tion·less /'məʊʃnləs; *AmE* 'moʊʃn-/ *adj.* not moving; still: *She stood absolutely motionless.*

motion 'picture *noun* (*especially AmE*) a film/movie that is made for the cinema

'motion sickness *noun* [U] the unpleasant feeling that you are going to VOMIT, that some people have when they are moving, especially in a vehicle

mo·tiv·ate /'məʊtɪveɪt; *AmE* 'moʊ-/ *verb* **1** [VN] [often passive] to be the reason why sb does sth or behaves in a particular way: *He is motivated entirely by self-interest.* **2** to make sb want to do sth, especially sth that involves hard work and effort: [VN] *She's very good at motivating her students.* ◊ [VN to inf] *The plan is designed to motivate employees to work more efficiently.* ► **mo·tiv·ated** *adj.*: *a racially motivated attack* ◊ *a highly motivated student* (= one who is very interested and works hard) **mo·tiv·ation** /ˌməʊtɪ'veɪʃn; *AmE* ˌmoʊ-/ *noun* [C, U]: *What is the motivation behind this sudden change?* ◊ *Most people said that pay was their main motivation for working.* ◊ *He's intelligent enough but he lacks motivation.* **mo·tiv·ation·al** *adj.* (*formal*): *an important motivational factor* **mo·tiv·ator** *noun*: *Desire for status can be a powerful motivator.*

mo·tive /'məʊtɪv; *AmE* 'moʊ-/ *noun, adj.*
■ *noun* **~ (for sth)** a reason for doing sth: *There seemed to be no motive for the murder.* ◊ *I'm suspicious of his motives.* ◊ *the profit motive* (= the desire to make a profit) ◊ *I have an ulterior motive in offering to help you.* ► **mo·tive·less** *adj.*: *an apparently motiveless murder/attack*
■ *adj.* [only before noun] (*technical*) causing movement or action: *motive power/force* (for example, electricity, to operate machinery)

mot·ley /'mɒtli; *AmE* 'mɑːtli/ *adj.* (*disapproving*) consist-

ing of many different types of people or things that do not seem to belong together: *She had a motley group of friends at college.* ◊ *The room was filled with a motley collection of furniture and paintings.* ◊ *The audience was a motley crew of students and tourists.*

moto·cross /'məʊtəkrɒs; *AmE* 'moʊtoʊkrɔːs/ (*BrE* also **scram·bling**) *noun* [U] the sport of racing motorcycles over rough ground

motor /'məʊtə(r); *AmE* 'moʊ-/ *noun, adj., verb*
■ *noun* **1** a device that uses electricity, petrol/gas, etc. to produce movement and makes a machine, a vehicle, a boat, etc. work: *an electric motor* ◊ *He started the motor.*—see also OUTBOARD MOTOR **2** (*BrE, old-fashioned* or *humorous*) a car
■ *adj.* [only before noun] **1** having an engine; using the power of an engine: *motor vehicles* **2** (*especially BrE*) connected with vehicles that have engines: *the motor industry/trade* ◊ *a motor accident* ◊ *motor insurance* ◊ *motor fuel/oil* **3** (*technical*) connected with movement of the body that is produced by muscles; connected with the nerves that control movement: *uncoordinated motor activity* ◊ *Both motor and sensory functions are affected.*
■ *verb* [V + adv. / prep.] (*old-fashioned, BrE*) to travel by car, especially for pleasure: *We motored down to Oxford for the day.* ► **motor·ing** *noun* [U]: *They're planning a motoring holiday to France this year.*

motor·bike /'məʊtəbaɪk; *AmE* 'moʊtərb-/ *noun* **1** (*BrE*) = MOTORCYCLE: *Ben drove off on his motorbike.* **2** (*AmE*) a small light motorcycle

'motor boat *noun* a small fast boat driven by an engine—picture at BOAT

motor·cade /'məʊtəkeɪd; *AmE* 'moʊtərk-/ *noun* a line of motor vehicles including one or more that famous or important people are travelling in: *The President's motorcade glided by.*

'motor car *noun* (*BrE, formal*) a car

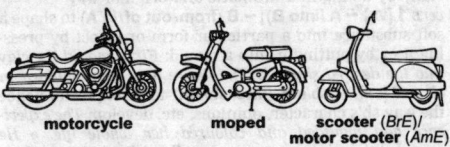

motorcycle   **moped**   **scooter** (*BrE*)/ **motor scooter** (*AmE*)

motor·cycle /'məʊtəsaɪkl; *AmE* 'moʊtərs-/ (*BrE* also **motor·bike**) *noun* a road vehicle with two wheels, driven by an engine, with one seat for the driver and a seat for a passenger behind the driver: *motorcycle racing* ◊ *a motorcycle accident*

motor·cyc·ling /'məʊtəsaɪklɪŋ; *AmE* 'moʊtərs-/ *noun* [U] the sport of riding motorcycles

motor·cyc·list /'məʊtəsaɪklɪst; *AmE* 'moʊtərs-/ *noun* a person riding a motorcycle: *a police motorcyclist* ◊ *leather-clad motorcyclists*

motor·home /'məʊtəhəʊm; *AmE* 'moʊtərhoʊm/ *noun* = CAMPER (2)

motor·ing /'məʊtərɪŋ; *AmE* 'moʊ-/ *adj.* [only before noun] connected with driving a car: *a motoring offence*

motor·ist /'məʊtərɪst; *AmE* 'moʊ-/ *noun* a person driving a car: *The accident was reported by a passing motorist.*—compare PEDESTRIAN

motor·ized (*BrE* also **-ised**) /'məʊtəraɪzd; *AmE* 'moʊ-/ *adj.* [only before noun] **1** having an engine: *motorized vehicles* ◊ *a motorized wheelchair* **2** (of groups of soldiers, etc.) using motor vehicles: *motorized forces/divisions*

motor·mouth /'məʊtəmaʊθ; *AmE* 'moʊtərm-/ *noun* (*pl.* **motor·mouths** /-maʊðz/) (*informal*) a person who talks loudly and too much

motor neur·one dis·ease /ˌməʊtə 'njʊərəʊn dɪziːz; *AmE* ˌmoʊtər 'nʊroʊn/ *noun* [U] a disease in which the nerves and muscles become gradually weaker until the person dies

'motor pool *noun* (*especially AmE*) = CAR POOL (2)

'motor racing *noun* [U] the sport of racing fast cars on a special track

'motor scooter *noun* (*especially AmE*) = SCOOTER (1)

M

æ	ɑː	e	ɜː	ə	ɪ	iː	i	ɒ	ɔː	ʌ	ʊ	u	uː
cat	father	ten	bird	about	sit	see	many	got	saw	cup	put	actual	too
								(BrE)					

'motor vehicle *noun* any road vehicle driven by an engine

motor·way /'məʊtəweɪ; *AmE* 'moʊtərweɪ/ *noun* [C, U] (in Britain) a wide road, with at least two LANES in each direction, where traffic can travel fast for long distances between large towns. You can only enter and leave motorways at special JUNCTIONS: *busy/congested motorways* ◇ *Join the motorway at Junction 19.* ◇ *Leave the motorway at the next exit.* ◇ *A nine-mile stretch of motorway has been closed.* ◇ *a motorway service area/station*—compare FREEWAY

mot·tled /'mɒtld; *AmE* 'mɑːtld/ *adj.* marked with shapes of different colours without a regular pattern: *the mottled skin of a snake*

motto /'mɒtəʊ; *AmE* 'mɑːtoʊ/ *noun* (*pl.* **-oes** or **-os**) a short sentence or phrase that expresses the aims and beliefs of a person, a group, an institution, etc. and is used as a rule of behaviour: *The school's motto is: 'Duty, Honour, Country'.* ◇ *'Live and let live.' That's my motto.*

mould (*BrE*) (*AmE* **mold**) /məʊld; *AmE* moʊld/ *noun, verb*
■ *noun* **1** [C] a container that you pour a soft liquid or substance into, which then becomes solid in the same shape as the container, for example when it is cooled or cooked: *A clay mould is used for casting bronze statues.* ◇ *Pour the chocolate into a heart-shaped mould.* ◇ *They broke the mould when they made you* (= there is nobody like you). **2** [C, usually sing.] a particular style showing the characteristics, attitudes or behaviour that are typical of sb/sth: *a hero in the 'Superman' mould* ◇ *He is cast in a different mould from his predecessor.* ◇ *She doesn't fit (into) the traditional mould of an academic.* **3** [U, C] a fine soft green, grey or black substance like fur that grows on old food or on objects that are left in warm wet air: *There's mould on the cheese.* ◇ *moulds and fungi* ◇ *mould growth*—see also LEAF MOULD **IDM** **break the 'mould (of sth)** to change what people expect from a situation, especially by acting in a dramatic and original way
■ *verb* [VN] **~ A (into B)|~ B (from/out of/in A)** to shape a soft substance into a particular form or object by pressing it or by putting it into a mould: *First, mould the clay into the desired shape.* ◇ *The figure had been moulded in clay.* **2** [VN] **~ sb/sth (into sb/sth)** to strongly influence the way sb's character, opinions, etc. develop: *The experience had moulded and coloured her whole life.* ◇ *He moulded them into a superb team.* **3 ~ (sth) to sth** to fit or make sth fit tightly around the shape of sth: [V] *The fabric moulds to the body.* [alsoVN]

mould·er (*AmE* **mol·der**) /'məʊldə(r); *AmE* 'moʊ-/ *verb* [V] to decay slowly and steadily: *The room smelt of disuse and mouldering books.*

mould·ing (*BrE*) (*AmE* **mold·ing**) /'məʊldɪŋ; *AmE* 'moʊ-/ *noun* a decorative strip of plastic, stone, wood, etc. around the top edge of a wall, on a door, etc.

mouldy (*BrE*) (*AmE* **moldy**) /'məʊldi; *AmE* 'moʊ-/ *adj.* **1** covered with or containing MOULD: *mouldy bread/cheese* ◇ *Strawberries go mouldy very quickly.* **2** old and not in good condition

moult (*BrE*) (*AmE* **molt**) /məʊlt; *AmE* moʊlt/ *verb* [V] (of a bird or an animal) to lose feathers or hair before new feathers or hair grow

mound /maʊnd/ *noun* **1** a large pile of earth or stones; a small hill: *a Bronze Age burial mound* ◇ *The castle was built on top of a natural grassy mound.* **2** a pile: *a small mound of rice/sand* **3 ~ of sth** (*informal*) a large amount of sth: *I've got a mound of paperwork to do.* **4** (in baseball) the small hill where the player who throws the ball (called the PITCHER) stands

mount /maʊnt/ *verb, noun*
■ *verb*
ORGANIZE | **1** [VN] to organize and begin sth: *to mount a protest/campaign/an exhibition*
INCREASE | **2** [V] to increase gradually: *Pressure is mounting on the government to change the law.* ◇ *The death toll continues to mount.*—see also MOUNTING
GO UP STH | **3** [VN] (*formal*) to go up sth, or up on to sth that is raised: *She slowly mounted the steps.* ◇ *He mounted the platform and addressed the crowd.*

BICYCLE/HORSE | **4** to get on a bicycle, horse, etc. in order to ride it: [VN] *He mounted his horse and rode away.* [alsoV]—see also MOUNTED **OPP** DISMOUNT

PICTURE/JEWEL, etc. | **5** [VN] **~ sth (on/onto/in sth)** to fix sth into position on sth, so that you can use it, look at it or study it: *The specimens were mounted on slides.* ◇ *The diamond is mounted in gold.*

OF MALE ANIMAL | **6** [VN] to get onto the back of a female animal in order to have sex **IDM** see GUARD *n.*

PHRV **,mount 'up** to increase gradually in size and quantity: *Meanwhile, my debts were mounting up.*
■ *noun*
MOUNTAIN | **1** (**Mount**) (*abbr.* **Mt**) (used in modern English only in place names) a mountain or a hill: *Mt. Everest* ◇ *St Michael's Mount*

HORSE | **2** (*formal* or *literary*) a horse that you ride on

FOR DISPLAYING/SUPPORTING STH | **3** something such as a piece of card or glass that you put sth on or attach sth to, to display it: *Choose a blue mount for this picture.* **4** (also **mount·ing**) something that an object stands on or is attached to for support: *an engine/gun mount*

moun·tain /'maʊntən; *AmE* 'maʊntn/ *noun* **1** a very high hill, often with rocks near the top: *a chain/range of mountains* ◇ *to climb a mountain* ◇ *We spent a week walking **in the mountains**.* ◇ *to enjoy the mountain air/scenery* ◇ *mountain roads/streams/villages* ◇ *a mountain rescue team* **2** [often pl.] **~ of sth** (*informal*) a very large amount or number of sth: *a mountain of work* ◇ *We made mountains of sandwiches.* ◇ *the problem of Europe's butter mountain* (= the large amount of butter that has to be stored because it is not needed) **IDM** **make a ,mountain out of a 'molehill** (*disapproving*) to make an unimportant matter seem important

,mountain 'ash *noun* = ROWAN

'mountain bike *noun* a bicycle with a strong frame, wide tyres and many GEARS, designed for riding on rough ground

moun·tain·eer /,maʊntə'nɪə(r); *AmE* -tn'ɪr/ *noun* a person who climbs mountains as a sport

moun·tain·eer·ing /,maʊntə'nɪərɪŋ; *AmE* -tn'ɪrɪŋ/ *noun* [U] the sport or activity of climbing mountains: *to go mountaineering* ◇ *a mountaineering expedition*

'mountain lion *noun* (*AmE*) = PUMA

moun·tain·ous /'maʊntənəs/ *adj.* **1** having many mountains: *a mountainous region/terrain* **2** very large in size or amount; like a mountain: *a mountainous plateful of food* ◇ *mountainous waves*

moun·tain·side /'maʊntənsaɪd/ *noun* the side or slope of a mountain: *Tracks led up the mountainside.*

moun·tain·top /'maʊntəntɒp; *AmE* 'maʊntntɑːp/ *noun* the top of a mountain: *to reach the mountaintop* ▶ **moun·tain·top** *adj.* [only before noun]: *a mountaintop ranch*

mount·ed /'maʊntɪd/ *adj.* [only before noun] **1** (of a person, especially a soldier or a police officer) riding a horse: *mounted policemen* **2** placed on sth or attached to sth for display or support: *a mounted photograph* **3** (**-mounted**) (in compounds) attached to the thing mentioned for support: *a ceiling-mounted fan*—see also WALL-MOUNTED

Moun·tie /'maʊnti/ *noun* (*informal*) a member of the Royal Canadian Mounted Police

mount·ing /'maʊntɪŋ/ *adj., noun*
■ *adj.* [only before noun] increasing, often in a manner that causes or expresses anxiety **SYN** GROWING: *mounting excitement/concern/tension* ◇ *There is mounting evidence of serious effects on people's health.*
■ *noun* = MOUNT: *The engine came loose from its mountings.*

mourn /mɔːn; *AmE* mɔːrn/ *verb* **~ (for sb/sth)** to feel and show sadness because sb has died; to feel sad because sth no longer exists or is no longer the same **SYN** GRIEVE FOR: [VN] *He was still mourning his brother's death.* ◇ *They mourn the passing of a simpler way of life.* ◇ [V] *Today we mourn for all those who died in two world wars.* ◇ *She mourned for her lost childhood.*

mourn·er /'mɔːnə(r); *AmE* 'mɔːrn-/ *noun* a person who

M

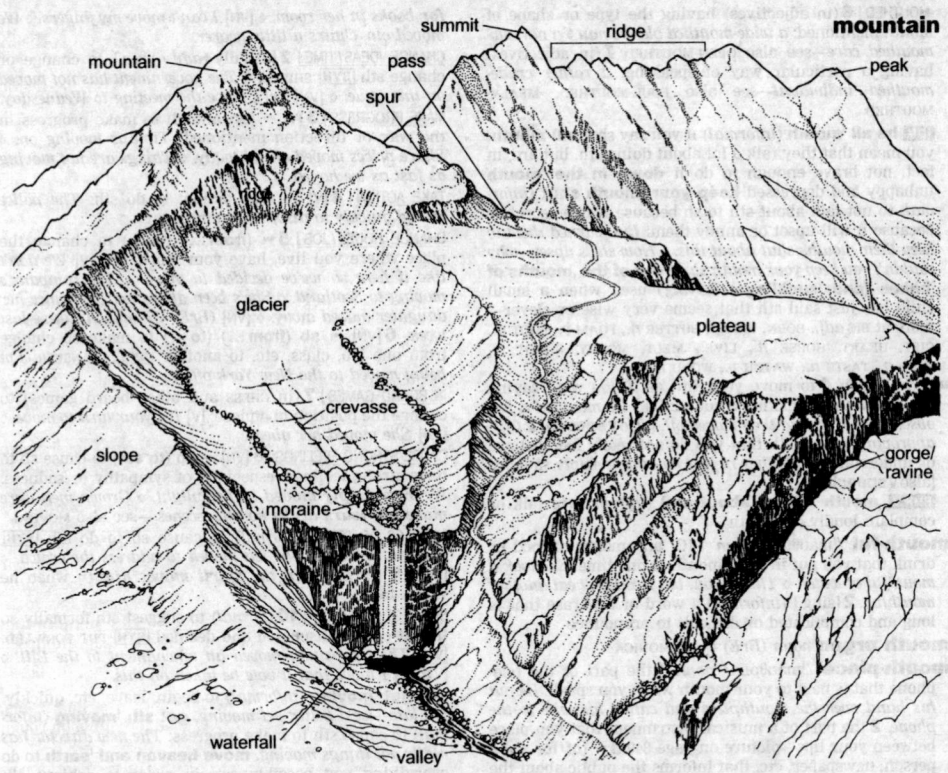

mountain

summit — ridge — peak

mountain — pass

spur

ridge

glacier — plateau

crevasse

slope — gorge/ravine

moraine

waterfall — valley

---

attends a funeral, especially a friend or a relative of the dead person

mourn·ful /ˈmɔːnfl; *AmE* ˈmɔːrnfl/ *adj.* (*written*) very sad: *mournful eyes ◊ mournful music ◊ I couldn't bear the mournful look on her face.* ▶ **mourn·ful·ly** /-fəli/ *adv.*: *The dog looked mournfully after its owner.*

mourn·ing /ˈmɔːnɪŋ; *AmE* ˈmɔːrn-/ *noun* [U] **1** sadness that you show and feel because sb has died: *The government announced a day of national mourning for the victims. ◊ She was still in mourning for her husband.* **2** clothes that people wear to show their sadness at sb's death

mouse /maʊs/ *noun* (*pl.* **mice** /maɪs/) **1** a small animal that is covered in fur and has a long thin tail. Mice live in fields, in people's houses or where food is stored: *a field mouse ◊ a house mouse ◊ The stores were overrun with rats and mice. ◊ She crept upstairs, quiet as a mouse. ◊ He was a weak little mouse of a man.*—see also DORMOUSE **2** (*pl.* also **mouses**) (*computing*) a small device that is moved by hand across a surface to control the movement of the CURSOR on a computer screen: *Click the left mouse button twice to highlight the program. ◊ Use the mouse to drag the icon to a new position.*—picture on page 250 **IDM** see CAT

ˈmouse mat (*BrE*) (*AmE* **ˈmouse pad**) *noun* a small square of plastic that is the best kind of surface on which to use a computer mouse—picture on page 250

mouse·trap /ˈmaʊstræp/ *noun* a trap with a powerful spring that is used, for example in a house, for catching mice

mousey = MOUSY

mous·saka /muːˈsɑːkə/ *noun* [U, C] a Greek dish made from layers of AUBERGINE and finely chopped meat with cheese on top

mousse /muːs/ *noun* [C, U] **1** a cold DESSERT (= a sweet dish) made with cream and egg whites and flavoured with fruit, chocolate, etc.; a similar dish flavoured with fish, vegetables, etc: *a chocolate/strawberry mousse ◊ sal-*

mon/mushroom mousse **2** a substance that is sold in AEROSOLS, for example the light white substance that is used on hair to give it a particular style or to improve its condition

mous·tache /məˈstɑːʃ/ (*BrE*) (*AmE* **mus·tache** /ˈmʌstæʃ; məˈstæʃ/) *noun* **1** a line of hair that a man allows to grow on his upper lip—picture at HAIR **2** (**moustaches**) [pl.] a very long moustache—compare BEARD

mous·tached /məˈstɑːʃt/ (*BrE*) (*AmE* **mus·tached** /ˈmʌstæʃt/) *adj.* [usually before noun] having a moustache—compare MUSTACHIOED

mous·tachi·oed = MUSTACHIOED

mousy (also **mousey**) /ˈmaʊsi/ *adj.* (*disapproving*) **1** (of hair) of a dull brown colour **2** (of people) shy and quiet; without a strong personality: *He was accompanied by his mousy little wife.*

mouth *noun, verb*

■ *noun* /maʊθ/ (*pl.* **mouths** /maʊðz/)

PART OF FACE | **1** the opening in the face used for speaking, eating, etc.; the area inside the head behind this opening: *She opened her mouth to say something. ◊ His mouth twisted into a wry smile. ◊ Their mouths fell open (= they were surprised). ◊ Don't talk with your mouth full (= when eating). ◊ The creature was foaming at the mouth.*—see also FOOT-AND-MOUTH DISEASE

PERSON NEEDING FOOD | **2** a person considered only as sb who needs to be provided with food: *Now there would be another mouth to feed. ◊ The world will not be able to support all these extra hungry mouths.*

ENTRANCE/OPENING | **3** ~ (of sth) the entrance or opening of sth: *the mouth of a cave/pit*—see also GOALMOUTH

OF RIVER | **4** the place where a river joins the sea: *A number of industries sprang up around the mouth of the river.*

WAY OF SPEAKING | **5** a particular way of speaking: *He has a foul mouth on him! ◊ Watch your mouth! (= stop saying things that are rude and/or offensive)*—see also LOUDMOUTH

M

---

b	d	f	g	h	k	l	m	n	p	r
bad	did	fall	get	hat	cat	leg	man	now	pen	red

-MOUTHED | **6** (in adjectives) having the type or shape of mouth mentioned: *a wide-mouthed old woman* ◊ *a narrow-mouthed cave*—see also OPEN-MOUTHED **7** (in adjectives) having a particular way of speaking: *a rather crude-mouthed individual*—see also FOUL-MOUTHED, MEALY-MOUTHED

IDM **be all 'mouth** (*informal*) if you say sb is **all mouth**, you mean that they talk a lot about doing sth, but are, in fact, not brave enough to do it **down in the 'mouth** unhappy and depressed **keep your 'mouth shut** (*informal*) to not talk about sth to sb because it is a secret or because it will upset or annoy them: *I've warned them to keep their mouths shut about this.* ◊ *Now she's upset—why couldn't you keep your mouth shut?* **out of the ‚mouths of 'babes (and 'sucklings)** (*saying*) used when a small child has just said sth that seems very wise or clever—more at BIG *adj.*, BORN, BREAD, BUTTER *n.*, FOAM *v.*, FOOT *n.*, GIFT, HEART, HORSE *n.*, LIVE¹, MELT, MONEY, SHOOT *v.*, SHUT *v.*, TASTE *v.*, WATCH *v.*, WORD *n.*

▪ *verb* /maʊð/ **1** to move your lips as if you were saying sth, but without making a sound: [VN] *He mouthed a few obscenities at us and then moved off.* [also v **speech**] **2** (*disapproving*) to say sth that you do not really feel, believe or understand: [VN] *They're just mouthing empty slogans.* [also v **speech**]

PHR V ‚mouth 'off (at/about sth) (*informal*) to talk or complain loudly about sth

mouth·ful /'maʊθfʊl/ *noun* **1** [C] an amount of food or drink that you put in your mouth at one time: *She took a mouthful of water.* ◊ *Thank you, but I couldn't eat another mouthful.* **2** [sing.] (*informal*) a word or a phrase that is long and complicated or difficult to pronounce

'**mouth organ** *noun* (*BrE*) = HARMONICA

mouth·piece /'maʊθpi:s/ *noun* **1** the part of the telephone that is next to your mouth when you speak: *He put his hand over the mouthpiece and called his wife to the phone.* **2** the part of a musical instrument that you place between your lips—picture on page 840 **3** ~ (of/for sb) a person, newspaper, etc. that informs the public about the opinions of a group of people or a political organization: *The newspaper has become the official mouthpiece of the opposition party.*

‚mouth-to-‚mouth re‚susci'tation (also ‚mouth-to-'mouth) *noun* [U] the act of breathing air into the mouth of an unconscious person to make them start breathing again—compare ARTIFICIAL RESPIRATION

'**mouth ulcer** (*BrE*) (*AmE* '**canker sore**) *noun* a small sore area in the mouth

mouth·wash /'maʊθwɒʃ; *AmE* -wɑːʃ; -wɔːʃ/ *noun* [C, U] a liquid used to make the mouth fresh and healthy

'**mouth-watering** *adj.* (*approving*) **mouth-watering** food looks or smells so good that you want to eat it immediately: *a mouth-watering display of cakes* ◊ (*figurative*) *mouth-watering travel brochures*

mouthy /'maʊθi; -ði/ *adj.* (*informal, disapproving*) used to describe a person who talks a lot, sometimes expressing their opinions strongly and in a rude way: *mouthy teenagers*

mov·able (also **move·able**) /'mu:vəbl/ *adj., noun*
▪ *adj.* **1** that can be moved from one place or position to another: *movable partitions* ◊ *a doll with a movable head* **2** (*law*) (of property) able to be taken from one house, etc. to another
▪ *noun* [C, usually pl.] (*law*) a thing that can be moved from one house, etc. to another; a personal possession

‚movable 'feast *noun* a religious festival, such as Easter, whose date changes from year to year

move /mu:v/ *verb, noun*
▪ *verb*
CHANGE POSITION | **1** to change position or make sb/sth change position in a way that can be seen, heard or felt: [V] *Don't move—stay perfectly still.* ◊ *The bus was already moving when I jumped onto it.* ◊ *He could hear someone moving around in the room above.* ◊ *Phil moved towards the window.* ◊ *You can hardly move in this pub on Saturdays* (= because it is so crowded). ◊ *You can't move*

for books in her room. ◊ [VN] *I can't move my fingers.* ◊ *We moved our chairs a little nearer.*

CHANGE IDEAS/TIME | **2** [usually +*adv.* / *prep.*] to change or change sth **SYN** SHIFT: [V] *The government has not moved on this issue.* ◊ [VN] *Let's move the meeting to Wednesday.*

MAKE PROGRESS | **3** [V] ~ (on/ahead) to make progress in the way or direction mentioned: *Time is moving on.* ◊ *Share prices moved ahead today.* ◊ *Things are not moving as fast as we hoped.*

TAKE ACTION | **4** [V] to take action; to do sth: *The police moved quickly to dispel the rumours.*

CHANGE HOUSE/JOB | **5** ~ (from …) (to …) to change the place where you live, have your work, etc: [V] *We don't like it here so we've decided to move.* ◊ *The company's moving to Scotland.* ◊ *She's been all on her own since her daughter moved away.* ◊ [VN] (*BrE*) *We moved house last week.* **6** [VN] ~ sb (from …) (to …) to make sb change from one job, class, etc. to another **SYN** TRANSFER: *I'm being moved to the New York office.*

IN BOARD GAMES | **7** (in CHESS and other board games) to change the position of a piece: [V] *It's your turn to move.* ◊ [VN] *She moved her queen.*

CAUSE STRONG FEELINGS | **8** [VN] ~ sb (to sth) to cause sb to have strong feelings, especially of sympathy or sadness: *We were deeply moved by her plight.* ◊ *Grown men were moved to tears at the horrific scenes.*—see also MOVING

MAKE SB DO STH | **9** (*formal*) to cause sb to do sth **SYN** PROMPT: [VN to inf] *She felt moved to address the crowd.* ◊ [VN] *He works when the spirit moves him* (= when he wants to).

SUGGEST FORMALLY | **10** (*formal*) to suggest sth formally so that it can be discussed and decided **SYN** PUT FORWARD: [VN] *The Opposition moved an amendment to the Bill.* ◊ [V that] *I move that a vote be taken on this.*

IDM **get 'moving** (*informal*) to begin, leave, etc. quickly: *It's late—we'd better get moving.* **get sth 'moving** (*informal*) to cause sth to make progress: *The new director has really got things moving.* **move heaven and 'earth** to do everything you possibly can in order to achieve sth **move with the 'times** to change the way you think and behave according to changes in society—more at ASS
PHR V ‚move a'long to go to a new position, especially in order to make room for other people: *The bus driver asked them to move along.* ‚move 'in | ‚move 'into sth to start to live in your new home: *Our new neighbours moved in yesterday.* **OPP** MOVE OUT 'move in sth to live, spend your time, etc. in a particular social group: *She only moves in the best circles.* ‚move 'in (on sb/sth) to move towards sb/sth from all directions, especially in a threatening way: *The police moved in on the terrorists.* ‚move 'off (especially of a vehicle) to start moving; to leave: *The signal was given and the procession moved off.* ‚move 'on (to sth) to start doing or discussing sth new: *I've been in this job long enough—it's time I moved on.* ◊ *Can we move on to the next item on the agenda?* ‚move sb 'on (of police, etc.) to order sb to move away from the scene of an accident, etc. ‚move 'out to leave your old home **OPP** MOVE IN ‚move 'over/'up to change your position in order to make room for sb: *There's room for another one if you move up a bit.*
▪ *noun*
ACTION | **1** ~ (towards/to sth) | ~ (to do sth) an action that you do or need to do to achieve sth: *This latest move by the government has aroused fierce opposition.* ◊ *The management have made no move to settle the strike.* ◊ *Getting a job in marketing was a good career move.*—see also FALSE MOVE

CHANGE OF POSITION | **2** [usually sing.] a change of place or position: *Don't make a move!* ◊ *Every move was painful.* ◊ *She felt he was watching her every move.*

CHANGE OF IDEAS/BEHAVIOUR | **3** ~ to/away from sth a change in ideas, attitudes or behaviour: *There has been a move away from nuclear energy.*

CHANGE OF HOUSE/JOB | **4** an act of changing the place where you live or work: *What's the date of your move?* ◊ *Their move from Italy to the US has not been a success.* ◊ *Her new job is just a sideways move.*

M

IN BOARD GAMES | **5** an act of changing the position of a piece in CHESS or other games that are played on a board; the way you can do this: *The game was over in only six moves.* ◊ *It's your move.* ◊ *There are far too many possible chess moves.*

IDM **be on the 'move 1** to be travelling between one place and another: *I need a mobile phone as I'm always on the move.* **2** to be moving; to be going somewhere: *The car was already on the move.* ◊ *The firm is on the move to larger offices.* **3** to become active: *Student power is on the move again.* **4** = BE ON THE GO **get a 'move on** (*spoken*) you tell sb to **get a move on** when you want them to hurry **make the first 'move** to do sth before sb else, for example in order to end an argument or to begin sth: *If he wants to see me, he should make the first move.* **make a 'move** (*BrE, informal*) to begin a journey or a task: *It's getting late—we'd better make a move.* **make a, your, etc. 'move** to do the action that you intend to do or need to do in order to achieve sth: *The rebels waited until nightfall before they made their move.*

move·able *adj.* = MOVABLE

move·ment /'muːvmənt/ *noun*

CHANGING POSITION | **1** [C, U] an act of moving the body or part of the body: *hand/eye movements* ◊ *She observed the gentle movement of his chest as he breathed.* ◊ *Loose clothing gives you greater freedom of movement.* ◊ *There was a sudden movement in the undergrowth.* **2** [C, U] an act of moving from one place to another or of moving sth from one place to another: *enemy troop movements* ◊ *laws to allow free movement of goods and services*

GROUP OF PEOPLE | **3** [C+sing./pl. v.] a group of people who share the same ideas or aims: *the women's/peace movement* ◊ *the Romantic movement* (= for example in literature) ◊ *a mass movement for change*

PERSON'S ACTIVITIES | **4** (**movements**) [pl.] a person's activities over a period of time, especially as watched by sb else: *The police are keeping a close watch on the suspect's movements.*

CHANGE OF IDEAS/BEHAVIOUR | **5** [sing.] ~ (**away from/towards sth**) a gradual change in what people in society do or think: *a movement towards greater sexual equality*

PROGRESS | **6** [U] ~ (**in sth**) progress, especially in a particular task: *It needs cooperation from all the powers to get any movement in arms control.*

CHANGE IN AMOUNT | **7** [U, C] ~ (**in sth**) a change in amount: *There has been no movement in oil prices.*

MUSIC | **8** [C] any of the main parts that a long piece of music is divided into: *the slow movement of the First Concerto*

OF BOWELS | **9** [C] (*technical*) = BOWEL MOVEMENT

mover /'muːvə(r)/ *noun* **1** a person or a thing that moves in a particular way: *a great mover on the dance floor* **2** a machine or a person that moves things from one place to another, especially sb who moves furniture from one house to another: *an earth mover* ◊ *professional furniture movers*—see also REMOVER—see also PRIME MOVER **IDM** **,movers and 'shakers** people with power in important organizations

movie /'muːvi/ *noun* (*especially AmE*) **1** [C] a series of moving pictures recorded with sound that tells a story, shown at the cinema/movie theater **SYN** FILM: *to make a horror movie* ◊ *Have you seen the latest Tarantino movie?* ◊ *a famous movie director/star* **2** (**the movies**) [pl.] = THE CINEMA (2): *Let's go to the movies.* **3** (**the movies**) [pl.] = CINEMA (3): *I've always wanted to work in the movies.*

movie·goer /'muːviɡəʊə(r); AmE -ɡoʊ-/ *noun* (*especially AmE*) = FILM-GOER

'movie star *noun* (*especially AmE*) = FILM STAR

'movie theater (also **theater**) *noun* (*AmE*) = CINEMA

mov·ing /'muːvɪŋ/ *adj.* **1** causing you to have deep feelings of sadness or sympathy: *a deeply moving experience* ◊ *His performance was very moving.* **2** [only before noun] (of things) changing from one place or position to another: *the moving parts of a machine* ◊ *fast-moving water* ◊ *a moving target* ▶ **mov·ing·ly** *adv.*: *She described her experiences in Africa very movingly.*

'moving van *noun* (*AmE*) = REMOVAL VAN

mow /məʊ; AmE moʊ/ *verb* (**mowed, mown** /məʊn; AmE moʊn/ or **mowed**) to cut grass, etc. using a machine or tool with a special blade or blades: [VN] *I mow the lawn every week in summer.* ◊ *the smell of new-mown hay* [also V] **PHRV** **,mow sb↔'down** to kill sb using a vehicle or a gun, especially when several people are all killed at the same time: *The gunmen opened fire, mowing down at least seven people.*

mower /'məʊə(r); AmE 'moʊ-/ *noun* (especially in compounds) a machine that cuts grass: *You should clean your mower each time you use it.* ◊ *a lawnmower* ◊ *a motor/rotary mower*

moxie /'mɒksi; AmE 'mɑːksi/ *noun* [U] (*AmE, informal*) courage, energy and determination

moz·za·rel·la /ˌmɒtsəˈrelə; AmE ˌmɑːts-/ *noun* [U] a type of soft white Italian cheese with a mild flavour

MP /ˌem ˈpiː/ *noun* **1** the abbreviation for 'Member of Parliament' (a person who has been elected to represent the people of a particular area in a parliament): *Paul Lewis MP* ◊ *Write to your local MP to protest.* ◊ *Conservative/Labour MPs* ◊ *the MP for Oxford East* ◊ *a Euro-MP* **2** a member of the military police

mpg /ˌem piː ˈdʒiː/ *abbr.* miles per gallon (used for saying how much petrol/gas a vehicle uses): *It does 40 mpg* ◊ *(AmE) It gets 40 mpg.*

mph /ˌem piː ˈeɪtʃ/ *abbr.* miles per hour: *a 60 mph speed limit*

MPV /ˌem piː ˈviː/ *noun* the abbreviation for 'multi-purpose vehicle', a large car like a van **SYN** PEOPLE CARRIER

Mr (*BrE*) (also **Mr.** *AmE, BrE*) /'mɪstə(r)/ *abbr.* **1** a title that comes before a man's family name, or before his first and family names together: *Mr Brown* ◊ *Mr John Brown* ◊ *Mr and Mrs Brown* **2** a title used to address a man in some official positions: *Thank you, Mr Chairman.* ◊ *Mr. President*—see also MISTER **IDM** **,Mr 'Nice Guy** (*informal*) a way of describing a man who is very honest and thinks about the wishes and feelings of other people **Mr 'Right** (*informal*) the man who would be the right husband for a particular woman: *I'm not getting married in a hurry—I'm waiting for Mr Right to come along.*

Mrs (*BrE*) (also **Mrs.** *AmE, BrE*) /'mɪsɪz/ *abbr.* a title that comes before a married woman's family name or before her first and family names together: *Mrs Hill* ◊ *Mrs Susan Hill* ◊ *Mr and Mrs Hill*—compare MISS, Ms

MS /ˌem ˈes/ *abbr.* MULTIPLE SCLEROSIS

Ms (*BrE*) (also **Ms.** *AmE, BrE*) /mɪz; məz/ *abbr.* a title that comes before a woman's family name or before her first and family names together, and that can be used when you do not want to state whether she is married or not: *Ms Murphy* ◊ *Ms Jean Murphy*—compare MISS, MRS

MSc (also **M.Sc.** especially in *AmE*) /ˌem es ˈsiː/ *noun* the abbreviation for 'Master of Science' (a second university degree in science): *to be/have/do an MSc* ◊ *(BrE) J Stevens MSc*

MSG /ˌem es ˈdʒiː/ *abbr.* MONOSODIUM GLUTAMATE

MSP /ˌem es ˈpiː/ *noun* the abbreviation for 'Member of the Scottish Parliament': *Donald Dewar MSP* ◊ *Write to your local MSP to protest.* ◊ *Labour MSPs*

Mt (also **Mt.** especially in *AmE*) *abbr.* (especially on maps) MOUNT: *Mt Kenya*

MTV™ /ˌem tiː ˈviː/ *abbr.* music television (a television channel that shows videos of popular music and other light entertainment programmes)

much /mʌtʃ/ *det., pron., adv.*

■ *det., pron.* used with uncountable nouns, especially in negative sentences to mean 'a large amount of sth', or after 'how' to ask about the amount of sth. It is also used with 'as', 'so' and 'too': *I don't have much money with me.* ◊ *'Got any money?' 'Not much.'* ◊ *How much water do you need?* ◊ *How much is it* (= What does it cost)? ◊ *Take as much time as you like.* ◊ *There was so much traffic that we were an hour late.* ◊ *I've got far too much to do.* ◊ *'Is there any mail?' 'Not much.'* ◊ *(formal) I lay awake for much of the night.* ◊ *(formal) There was much discussion about the reasons for the failure.* **IDM** **as 'much** the same:

M

æ	ɑː	e	ɜː	ə	ɪ	iː	i	ɒ	ɔː	ʌ	ʊ	u	uː
cat	father	ten	bird	about	sit	see	many	got	saw	cup	put	actual	too
								(BrE)					

Please help me get this job—you know I would do as much for you. ◊ *'Roger stole the money.' 'I thought as much.'* as much as sb can do used to say that sth is difficult to do: *No dessert for me, thanks. It was as much as I could do to finish the main course.* not much 'in it used to say that there is little difference between two things: *I won, but there wasn't much in it* (= our scores were nearly the same). 'not much of a ... not a good ...: *He's not much of a tennis player.* 'this much used to introduce sth positive or definite: *I'll say this much for him—he never leaves a piece of work unfinished.*

■ *adv.* (**more, most**) to a great degree: *Thank you very much for the flowers.* ◊ *I would very much like to see you again.* ◊ *He isn't in the office much* (= often). ◊ *You worry too much.* ◊ *My new job is much the same as the old one.* ◊ *Much to her surprise he came back the next day.* ◊ *She's much better today.* ◊ *The other one was much too expensive.* ◊ *Nikolai's English was much the worst.* ◊ *We are very much aware of the lack of food supplies.* ◊ *I'm not much good at tennis.* ◊ *He was much loved by all who knew him.* ◊ *an appeal to raise much-needed cash* **IDM** 'much as although: *Much as I would like to stay, I really must go home.*—more at LESS *adv.*

much·ness /'mʌtʃnəs/ *noun* **IDM** ,much of a 'muchness very similar; almost the same: *The two candidates are much of a muchness—it's hard to choose between them.*

muck /mʌk/ *noun, verb*
■ *noun* **1** waste matter from farm animals **SYN** MANURE: *to spread muck on the fields* **2** (*informal, especially BrE*) dirt or mud: *My face and hands were covered in muck.* ◊ *Can you wipe the muck off the windows?* **3** (*informal, especially BrE*) something very unpleasant: *I can't eat this muck!* **IDM** where there's ,muck there's 'brass (*BrE, saying*) used to say that sb has made a lot of money from an unpleasant or dirty business activity
■ *verb* **PHRV** ,muck a'bout/a'round (*BrE, informal*) to behave in a silly way, especially when you should be working or doing sth else **SYN** MESS ABOUT/AROUND ,muck a'bout/a'round with sth (*BrE, informal, disapproving*) to do sth, especially to a machine, so that it does not work correctly **SYN** MESS ABOUT/AROUND: *Who's mucking around with my radio?* ,muck sb a'bout/a'round (*BrE, informal*) to treat sb badly, especially by changing your mind a lot, or by not being honest **SYN** MESS SB ABOUT/AROUND: *They've really mucked us about over our car insurance.* ,muck 'in (*BrE, informal*) **1** to work with other people in order to complete a task: *If we all muck in, we could have the job finished by the end of the week.* **2** to share food, accommodation etc. with other people: *We didn't have much money, but everyone just mucked in together.* ,muck 'out | ,muck sth↔'out to clean out the place where an animal lives: *Part of her job was to muck out the stables.* ,muck sth↔'up (*informal, especially BrE*) **1** to do sth badly so that you fail to achieve what you wanted or hoped to achieve **SYN** MESS

STH UP: *He completely mucked up his English exam.* **2** to spoil a plan or an arrangement **SYN** MESS STH UP **3** to make sth dirty: *I don't want you mucking up my nice clean floor.*

muck·rak·ing /'mʌkreɪkɪŋ/ *noun* [U] (*informal, disapproving*) the activity of looking for information about people's private lives that they do not wish to make public

mucky /'mʌki/ *adj.* (*informal, especially BrE*) **1** dirty: *mucky hands* **2** sexually offensive: *mucky books/jokes*

,mucous 'membrane *noun* (*anatomy*) a thin layer of skin that covers the inside of the nose and mouth and the outside of other organs in the body, producing mucus to prevent these parts from becoming dry

mucus /'mju:kəs/ *noun* [U] a thick liquid that is produced in parts of the body, such as the nose, by a mucous membrane: *a handkerchief stained with blood and mucus* ▶ **mu·cous** /'mju:kəs/ *adj.*: *mucous glands*

mud /mʌd/ *noun* [U] wet earth that is soft and sticky: *The car wheels got stuck in the mud.* ◊ *Your boots are covered in mud.* ◊ *mud bricks/huts* (= made of dried mud) **IDM** fling, sling, etc. 'mud (at sb) to criticize sb or accuse sb of bad or shocking things in order to damage their reputation, especially in politics—see also MUD-SLINGING—more at CLEAR *adj.*, NAME *n.*

mud·dle /'mʌdl/ *verb, noun*
■ *verb* [VN] (*especially BrE*) **1** ~ sth (up) to put things in the wrong order or mix them up: *Don't do that—you're muddling my papers.* ◊ *Their letters were all muddled up together in a drawer.* **2** ~ sb (up) to confuse sb: *Slow down a little—you're muddling me.* **3** ~ sb/sth (up) | ~ A (up) with B to confuse one person or thing with another: *I muddled the dates and arrived a week early.* ◊ *He got all muddled up about what went where.* ◊ *They look so alike, I always get them muddled up.* **PHRV** ,muddle a'long (*especially BrE*) to continue doing sth without any clear plan or purpose: *We can't just keep muddling along like this.* ,muddle 'through to achieve your aims even though you do not know exactly what you are doing and do not have the correct equipment, knowledge, etc: *We'll muddle through somehow.*
■ *noun* (*especially BrE*) **1** [C, usually sing.] a state of mental confusion: *Can you start from the beginning again—I'm in a muddle.* **2** [C, usually sing., U] ~ (about/over sth) a situation in which there is confusion about arrangements, etc. and things get done wrong: *There was a muddle over the theatre tickets.* ◊ *There followed a long period of confusion and muddle.* **3** [C usually sing, U] a state of disorder in which things are untidy: *My papers are all in a muddle.*

mud·dled /'mʌdld/ *adj.* (*especially BrE*) confused: *He gets muddled when the teacher starts shouting.* ◊ *muddled thinking* ◊ *a muddled* (= badly organized) *attempt to rescue the situation*

mud·dling /'mʌdlɪŋ/ *adj.* (*especially BrE*) causing confusion; difficult to understand: *These tax forms are very muddling.*

muddy /'mʌdi/ *adj., verb*
■ *adj.* (**mud·dier, mud·di·est**) **1** full of or covered in mud: *a muddy field/track* ◊ *muddy boots/knees* **2** (of a liquid) containing mud; not clear: *muddy water* ◊ *a muddy pond* **3** (of colours) not clear or bright: *muddy green/brown*
■ *verb* (**mud·dies, muddy·ing, mud·died, mud·died**) [VN] to make sth muddy **IDM** muddy the 'waters, 'issue, etc. (*disapproving*) to make a simple situation confused and more complicated than it really is

mud·flat /'mʌdflæt/ *noun* [usually pl.] an area of flat muddy land that is covered by the sea when it comes in at HIGH TIDE

mud·guard /'mʌdɡɑːd; *AmE* -ɡɑːrd/ (*BrE*) (*AmE* **fender**) *noun* a curved cover over a wheel of a bicycle

mud·slide /'mʌdslaɪd/ *noun* (*especially AmE*) a large amount of mud sliding down a mountain, often destroying buildings and injuring or killing people below

'mud-slinging *noun* [U] (*disapproving*) the act of criticizing sb and accusing them of sth in order to damage their reputation: *This election campaign has seen all the usual mud-slinging we have come to expect.*

aɪ	aʊ	eɪ	əʊ	oʊ	ɔɪ	ɪə	eə	ʊə	j	w
my	now	say	go	go	boy	near	hair	pure	yes	wet
			(BrE)	(AmE)						

muesli /ˈmjuːzli/ *noun* [U] (*BrE*) a mixture of grains, nuts, dried fruit, etc. served with milk and eaten for breakfast

muez·zin /muːˈezɪn; mjuː-/ *noun* a man who calls Muslims to prayer, usually from the tower of a MOSQUE

muff /mʌf/ *noun, verb*
- *noun* a short tube of fur or other warm material that you put your hands into to keep them warm in cold weather—see also EARMUFF
- *verb* [VN] (*informal, disapproving*) to miss an opportunity to do sth well: *He muffed his lines* (= he forgot them or said them wrongly). ◊ *It was a really simple shot, and I muffed it.*

muf·fin /ˈmʌfɪn/ *noun* **1** (*BrE*) (*AmE* ˌEnglish ˈmuffin) a type of round flat bread roll, usually TOASTED and eaten hot with butter **2** a small cake in the shape of a cup, often containing small pieces of fruit, etc: *a blueberry muffin*—picture on page A1

muf·fle /ˈmʌfl/ *verb* [VN] **1** to make a sound quieter or less clear: *He tried to muffle the alarm clock by putting it under his pillow.* **2** ~ sb/sth (up) (in sth) to wrap or cover sb/sth in order to keep them/it warm: *She muffled the child up in a blanket.*

muf·fled /ˈmʌfld/ *adj.* (of sounds) not heard clearly because sth is in the way that stops the sound from travelling easily: *muffled voices from the next room*

muf·fler /ˈmʌflə(r)/ *noun* **1** (*old-fashioned*) a thick piece of fabric worn around the neck for warmth SYN SCARF **2** (*AmE*) = SILENCER (1)

mufti /ˈmʌfti/ *noun* **1** [C] (also **Mufti**) a Muslim who is an expert in legal matters connected with Islam **2** [U] (*old-fashioned*) ordinary clothes worn by people such as soldiers who wear uniform in their job: *officers in mufti*

mug /mʌɡ/ *noun, verb*
- *noun* **1** a tall cup for drinking from, usually with straight sides and a handle, used without a SAUCER: *a coffee mug* ◊ *a beer mug* (= a large glass with a handle)—picture at CUP, GLASS **2** a mug and what it contains: *a mug of coffee* **3** (*slang*) a person's face: *I never want to see his ugly mug again.* **4** (*informal*) a person who is stupid and easy to trick: *They made me look a complete mug.* ◊ *He's no mug.* IDM a ˈmug's game (*disapproving, especially BrE*) an activity that is unlikely to be successful or make a profit
- *verb* (-gg-) **1** [VN] to attack sb violently in order to steal their money, especially in a public place: *She had been mugged in the street in broad daylight.* **2** [V] ~ (for sb/sth) (*informal, especially AmE*) to make silly expressions with your face or behave in a silly, exaggerated way, especially on the stage or before a camera: *to mug for the cameras* PHRV ˌmug sth↔ˈup, ˌmug ˈup on sth (*BrE, informal*) to learn sth, especially in a short time for a particular purpose, for example an exam

mug·ger /ˈmʌɡə(r)/ *noun* a person who threatens or attacks sb in order to steal their money, especially in a public place

mug·ging /ˈmʌɡɪŋ/ *noun* [U, C] the crime of attacking sb violently, or threatening to do so, in order to steal their money, especially in a public place: *Mugging is on the increase.* ◊ *There have been several muggings here recently.*

mug·gins /ˈmʌɡɪnz/ *noun* [sing.] (*BrE, informal, humorous*) used without 'a' or 'the' to refer to yourself when you feel stupid because you have let yourself be treated unfairly: *And muggins here had to clean up all the mess.*

muggy /ˈmʌɡi/ *adj.* (of weather) warm and damp in an unpleasant way: *a muggy August day*

ˈ**mug shot** *noun* (*informal*) a photograph of sb's face kept by the police in their records to identify criminals

Mu·ham·mad (also **Mo·ham·med**) /məˈhæmɪd/ *noun* the Arab PROPHET who FOUNDED the religion of Islam

mu·ja·he·din (also **mu·ja·hi·din, mu·ja·hed·din, mu·ja·hi·deen**) /ˌmuːdʒəhəˈdiːn/ *noun* [pl.] (in some Muslim countries) soldiers fighting in support of their strong Muslim beliefs

mu·latto /mjuˈlætəʊ; məˈl-; *AmE* -toʊ/ *noun* (*pl.* -os or -oes) (*offensive*) a person with one black parent and one white parent

mul·berry /ˈmʌlbəri; *AmE* -beri/ *noun* (*pl.* -ies) **1** (also

ˈ**mulberry tree**) [C] a tree with broad dark green leaves and berries that can be eaten. SILKWORMS (that make silk) eat the leaves of the white mulberry. **2** [C] the small purple or white berries of the mulberry tree **3** [U] a deep reddish-purple colour

mulch /mʌltʃ/ *noun, verb*
- *noun* [C, U] material, for example, decaying leaves, that you put around a plant to protect its base and its roots, to improve the quality of the soil or to stop WEEDS growing
- *verb* [VN] to cover the soil or the roots of a plant with a mulch

mule /mjuːl/ *noun* **1** an animal that has a horse and a DONKEY as parents, used especially for carrying loads: *He's as stubborn as a mule.* **2** (*slang*) a person who is paid to take drugs illegally from one country to another **3** a woman's SLIPPER (= a soft shoe for wearing indoors) that is open around the heel

mull /mʌl/ *verb* PHRV ˌmull sth↔ˈover to spend time thinking carefully about a plan or proposal: *I need some time to mull it over before making a decision.*

mul·lah /ˈmʌlə; ˈmʊlə/ *noun* a Muslim teacher of religion and holy law

mulled /mʌld/ *adj.* [only before noun] **mulled** wine has been mixed with sugar and spices and heated

mul·let /ˈmʌlɪt/ *noun* [C, U] (*pl.* **mul·let**) a sea fish that is used for food. The two main types are **red mullet** and **grey mullet**.

mul·lion /ˈmʌliən/ *noun* (*architecture*) a solid upright piece of stone, wood or metal between two parts of a window ▶ **mul·lioned** /ˈmʌliənd/ *adj.* [only before noun]: *mullioned windows*

multi- /ˈmʌlti/ *combining form* (in nouns and adjectives) more than one; many: *multicoloured* ◊ *a multimillionaire* ◊ *a multi-ethnic society*

multi·cul·tural /ˌmʌltiˈkʌltʃərəl/ *adj.* for or including people of several different races, religions, languages and traditions: *We live in a multicultural society.* ◊ *a multicultural approach to education* ▶ **multi·cul·tural·ism** /-ɪzəm/ *noun* [U]

ˌ**multi·disciˈplinary** *adj.* involving several different subjects of study: *a multi-disciplinary course*

multi·fac·et·ed /ˌmʌltiˈfæsɪtɪd/ *adj.* (*written*) having many different aspects to be considered: *a complex and multifaceted problem*

multi·fari·ous /ˌmʌltiˈfeəriəs; *AmE* -ˈfer-/ *adj.* (*formal*) of many different kinds; having great variety: *the multifarious life forms in the coral reef* ◊ *a vast and multifarious organization*

multi·lat·eral /ˌmʌltiˈlætərəl/ *adj.* **1** in which three or more groups, nations, etc. take part: *multilateral negotiations* **2** having many sides or parts—compare BILATERAL, UNILATERAL

multi·lin·gual /ˌmʌltiˈlɪŋɡwəl/ *adj.* **1** speaking or using several different languages: *multilingual translators/communities/societies* ◊ *a multilingual classroom* **2** written or printed in several different languages: *a multilingual phrase book*—compare BILINGUAL, MONOLINGUAL

multi·media /ˌmʌltiˈmiːdiə/ *adj.* [only before noun] **1** (in computing) using sound, pictures and film in addition to text on a screen: *multimedia systems/products* ◊ *the multimedia industry* (= producing CD-ROMs etc.) **2** (in teaching) using several different ways of giving information: *a multimedia approach to learning*

multi·nation·al /ˌmʌltiˈnæʃnəl/ *adj., noun*
- *adj.* existing in or involving many countries: *multinational companies/corporations* ◊ *A multinational force is being sent to the trouble spot.*
- *noun* a company that operates in several different countries, especially a large and powerful company: *The country's industry is largely controlled by the multinationals.*

multi·party /ˌmʌltiˈpɑːti; *AmE* -ˈpɑːrti/ *adj.* [only before noun] involving several different political parties: *These are the country's first multiparty elections.*

mul·tiple /ˈmʌltɪpl/ *adj., noun*
- *adj.* [only before noun] many in number; involving many different people or things: *multiple copies of documents* ◊ *a*

M

multiple entry visa ◊ to suffer multiple injuries (= in many different places in the body) ◊ a multiple birth (= several babies born to a mother at one time) ◊ a multiple pile-up (= a crash involving many vehicles) ◊ a house in multiple ownership/occupancy (= owned/occupied by several different people or families)
■ noun **1** (*mathematics*) a quantity that contains another quantity an exact number of times: *14, 21 and 28 are all multiples of 7.* ◊ *16 is the lowest **common multiple** of 8 and 4.* ◊ *Traveller's cheques are available in multiples of £10 (=* to the value of £10, £20, £30, etc.). **2** (also ,multiple 'store) (both *BrE*) = CHAIN STORE

,multiple-'choice *adj.* (of questions in an exam) showing several possible answers from which you must choose the correct one

,multiple scle'rosis *noun* [U] (*abbr.* **MS**) a disease of the nervous system that gets worse over a period of time with loss of feeling and loss of control of movement and speech

multi·plex /'mʌltɪpleks/ (*BrE also* ,multiplex 'cinema) *noun* a large cinema/movie theater with several separate screens

multi·pli·ca·tion /ˌmʌltɪplɪ'keɪʃn/ *noun* [U] the act or process of multiplying: *the multiplication sign (×)* ◊ *Multiplication of cells leads to rapid growth of the organism.*— compare DIVISION

,multipli'cation table (also **table**) *noun* a list showing the results when a number is multiplied by a set of other numbers, especially 1 to 12, in turn

multi·pli·city /ˌmʌltɪ'plɪsəti/ *noun* [sing., U] (*formal*) a great number and variety of sth: *This situation can be influenced by a multiplicity of different factors.*

multi·ply /'mʌltɪplaɪ/ *verb* (multi·plies, multi·ply·ing, multi·plied, multi·plied) **1** ~ (A by B)| ~ A and B (together) to add a number to itself a particular number of times: [V] *The children are already learning to multiply and divide.* ◊ [VN] *2 multiplied by 4 is/equals/makes 8 (=* 2×4 = 8) ◊ *Multiply 2 and 6 together and you get 12.* **2** to increase or make sth increase very much in number or amount: [V] *Our problems have multiplied since last year.* ◊ [VN] *Cigarette smoking multiplies the risk of cancer.* **3** (*biology*) to reproduce in large numbers; to make sth do this: [V] *Rabbits multiply rapidly.* ◊ [VN] *It is possible to multiply these bacteria in the laboratory.*

,multi-'purpose *adj.* able to be used for several different purposes: *a multi-purpose tool/machine*—see also MPV

multi·racial /ˌmʌlti'reɪʃl/ *adj.* including or involving several different races of people: *We live in a multiracial society.*

,multi-'skilling *noun* [U] (*business*) the fact of a person being trained in several different jobs which require different skills: *In the future there will be more flexible working and multi-skilling.*

,multi-storey 'car park (also ,multi-'storey) (both *BrE*) (*AmE* 'parking garage) *noun* a large building with several floors for parking cars in

multi·task·ing /ˌmʌlti'tɑːskɪŋ; *AmE* -tæsk-/ *noun* [U] (*computing*) the ability of a computer to operate several programs at the same time

multi·tude /'mʌltɪtjuːd; *AmE* -tuːd/ *noun* (*formal*) **1** [C] ~ (of sth/sb) an extremely large number of things or people: *a multitude of problems/possibilities/reasons* ◊ *a multitude of birds/people/pedestrians* ◊ *These elements can be combined in a multitude of different ways.* ◊ *The region attracts tourists in their multitudes.* **2** (the multitude) [sing.+ sing./pl. *v.*] (also **the multitudes** [pl.]) (sometimes *disapproving*) the mass of ordinary people: *It was an elite that believed its task was to enlighten the multitude.* ◊ *to feed the starving multitudes* **3** [C] (*literary*) a large crowd of people: *He preached to the assembled multitude.* **IDM** **cover/hide a multitude of sins** (often *humorous*) to hide the real situation or facts when these are not good or pleasant

multi·tu·di·nous /ˌmʌlti'tjuːdɪnəs; *AmE* -'tuːdɪnəs/ *adj.* (*formal*) extremely large in number

mum /mʌm/ *noun, adj.*

■ noun (*BrE*) (*AmE* **mom**) (*informal*) a mother: *My mum says I can't go.* ◊ *Happy Birthday, Mum.* ◊ *A lot of mums and dads have the same worries.*
■ adj. **IDM** **keep mum** (*informal*) to say nothing about sth; to stay silent: *He kept mum about what he'd seen.* ,mum's the 'word! (*informal*) used to tell sb to say nothing about sth and keep it secret

mum·ble /'mʌmbl/ *verb, noun*
■ verb to speak or say sth in a quiet voice in a way that is not clear **SYN** MUTTER: [V] *I could hear him mumbling to himself.* ◊ [VN] *She mumbled an apology and left.* ◊ [Vspeech] *'Sorry,' she mumbled.* [also Vthat]
■ noun [usually sing.] (also **mum·bling** [C, usually pl., U]) speech or words that are spoken in a quiet voice in a way that is not clear: *He spoke in a low mumble, as if to himself.* ◊ *They tried to make sense of her mumblings.*

mumbo-jumbo /ˌmʌmbəʊ 'dʒʌmbəʊ; *AmE* ˌmʌmboʊ 'dʒʌmboʊ/ *noun* [U] (*informal, disapproving*) language or a ceremony that seems complicated and important but is actually without real sense or meaning; nonsense: *religious/medical/bureaucratic mumbo-jumbo* ◊ *I won't have anything to do with spiritualism, ghosts and all that mumbo-jumbo.*

mum·mify /'mʌmɪfaɪ/ *verb* (mum·mi·fies, mum·mi·fy·ing, mum·mi·fied, mum·mi·fied) [VN] [usually passive] to preserve a dead body by treating it with special oils and wrapping it in cloth **SYN** EMBALM

mummy /'mʌmi/ *noun* (*pl.* **-ies**) **1** (*BrE*) (*AmE* **mommy, momma**) (*informal*) a child's word for a mother: *'I want my mummy!' he wailed.* ◊ *It hurts, Mummy!* ◊ *Mummy and Daddy will be back soon.* **2** a body of a human being or an animal that has been mummified: *an Egyptian mummy*

mumps /mʌmps/ *noun* [U] a disease, especially of children, that causes painful swellings in the neck

munch /mʌntʃ/ *verb* ~ (on/at) sth to eat sth steadily and often noisily, especially sth crisp: [V] *She munched on an apple.* ◊ [VN] *He sat in a chair munching his toast.* ◊ *I munched my way through a huge bowl of cereal.*

munch·ies /'mʌntʃɪz/ *noun* [pl.] (*AmE, informal*) small pieces of food for eating with drinks at a party **IDM** **have the 'munchies** (*informal*) to feel hungry

mun·dane /mʌn'deɪn/ *adj.* (often *disapproving*) not interesting or exciting: *a mundane task/job* ◊ *I lead a pretty mundane existence.* ◊ *On a more mundane level, can we talk about the timetable for next week?*

mu·ni·ci·pal /mjuː'nɪsɪpl/ *adj.* [usually before noun] connected with or belonging to a town, city or district that has its own local government: *municipal elections/councils* ◊ *municipal workers* ◊ *the Los Angeles Municipal Art Gallery*

mu·ni·ci·pal·ity /mjuːˌnɪsɪ'pæləti/ *noun* (*pl.* **-ies**) a town, city or district with its own local government; the group of officials who govern it

mu·nifi·cent /mjuː'nɪfɪsnt/ *adj.* (*formal*) extremely generous: *a munificent patron/gift/gesture* ▶ mu·nifi·cence /-sns/ *noun* [U]

mu·ni·tions /mjuː'nɪʃnz/ *noun* [pl.] military weapons, AMMUNITION, and equipment: *a shortage of munitions* ◊ *a munitions factory* ▶ mu·ni·tion *adj.* [only before noun]: *a munition store*

munt·jac (also **munt·jak**) /'mʌntdʒæk/ *noun* a type of small deer, originally from SE Asia

mural /'mjʊərəl; *AmE* 'mjʊrəl/ *noun* a painting, usually a large one, done on a wall, sometimes on an outside wall of a building ▶ mural *adj.*: *mural paintings*

mur·der /'mɜːdə(r); *AmE* 'mɜːrd-/ *noun, verb*
■ noun **1** [U, C] the crime of killing sb deliberately **SYN** HOMICIDE: *He was found guilty of murder.* ◊ *She has been charged with the attempted murder of her husband.* ◊ *to commit (a) murder* ◊ *a murder case/investigation/trial* ◊ *The rebels were responsible for the mass murder of 400 civilians.* ◊ *What was the murder weapon?* ◊ *The play is a murder mystery.*—compare MANSLAUGHTER **2** [U] (*spoken*) used to describe sth that is difficult or unpleasant: *It's murder trying to get to the airport at this time of day.* ◊ *It was murder (= very busy and unpleasant) in the office today.* **IDM** **get away with 'murder** (*informal*, often

M

humorous) to do whatever you want without being stopped or punished—more at SCREAM *v.*

■ *verb* [VN] **1** to kill sb deliberately and illegally: *He denies murdering his wife's lover.* ◇ *The murdered woman was well known in the area.* **2** to spoil sth because you do not do it very well: *Critics accused him of murdering the English language* (= writing or speaking it very badly). **3** (*BrE, informal*) to defeat sb completely, especially in a team sport SYN THRASH IDM **I could murder a…** (*spoken*) used to say that you very much want to eat or drink sth: *I could murder a beer.* **sb will 'murder you** (*spoken*) used to warn sb that another person will be very angry with them

mur·der·er /'mɜːdərə(r); AmE 'mɜːrd-/ *noun* a person who has killed sb deliberately and illegally: *a convicted murderer* ◇ *a mass murderer* (= who has killed a lot of people)

mur·der·ess /'mɜːdərəs; AmE 'mɜːrd-/ *noun* (*old-fashioned*) a woman who has killed sb deliberately and illegally

mur·der·ous /'mɜːdərəs; AmE 'mɜːrd-/ *adj.* intending or likely to murder: *a murderous villain/tyrant* ◇ *a murderous attack* ◇ *She gave him **a murderous look*** (= a very angry one). ▶ **mur·der·ous·ly** *adv.*

murk /mɜːk; AmE mɜːrk/ *noun* (usually **the murk**) [U] (*literary*) darkness caused by smoke, FOG, etc. SYN GLOOM

murky /'mɜːki; AmE 'mɜːrki/ *adj.* (**murk·ier, murki·est**) **1** (of a liquid) not clear; dark or dirty with mud or another substance: *She gazed into the murky depths of the water.* **2** (of air, light, etc.) dark and unpleasant because of smoke, FOG, etc: *a murky night* **3** (*disapproving* or *humorous*) (of people's actions or character) not clearly known and suspected of not being honest: *He had a somewhat murky past.* ◇ *the murky world of arms dealing* IDM see WATER *n.*

mur·mur /'mɜːmə(r); AmE 'mɜːrm-/ *verb, noun*

■ *verb* **1** to say sth in a soft quiet voice that is difficult to hear or understand: [VN] *She murmured her agreement.* ◇ *He murmured something in his sleep.* ◇ [V] *She was murmuring in his ear.* [also V speech, V that] **2** [V] to make a quiet continuous sound: *The wind murmured in the trees.* **3** [V] ~ (**against sb/sth**) (*literary*) to complain about sb/sth, but not openly: *The people murmured against the new regime.*

■ *noun* **1** [C] a quietly spoken word or words: *She answered in a faint murmur.* ◇ *Murmurs of 'Praise God' went around the circle.* **2** [C] (also **mur·mur·ings** [pl.]) a quiet expression of feeling: *a murmur of agreement/approval/complaint* ◇ *He paid the extra cost **without a murmur*** (= without complaining at all). ◇ *polite murmurings of gratitude* **3** (also **mur·mur·ing**) [sing.] a low continuous sound in the background: *the distant murmur of traffic* **4** [C] (*medical*) a faint sound in the chest, usually a sign of damage or disease in the heart: *a heart murmur*

Murphy's Law /ˌmɜːfiz 'lɔː; AmE ˌmɜːrfiz/ *noun* (*humorous*) a statement of the fact that, if anything can possibly go wrong, it will go wrong

muscle /'mʌsl/ *noun, verb*

■ *noun* **1** [C, U] a piece of body tissue that you tighten and relax in order to move a particular part of the body; the tissue that forms the muscles of the body: *a calf/neck/thigh muscle* ◇ *to pull/tear/strain a muscle* ◇ *This exercise will work the muscles of the lower back.* ◇ *He **didn't move a muscle*** (= stood completely still). **2** [U] physical strength: *He's an intelligent player but lacks the muscle of older competitors.* **3** [U] the power and influence to make others do what you want: *to exercise political/industrial/financial muscle* ▶ **muscled** *adj.*: *heavily muscled shoulders* IDM see FLEX *v.*

■ *verb* PHRV **muscle 'in (on sb/sth)** (*informal, disapproving*) to involve yourself in a situation when you have no right to do so, in order to get sth for yourself

'muscle-bound *adj.* having large stiff muscles as a result of too much exercise

muscle·man /'mʌslmæn/ *noun* (*pl.* **-men** /-men/) a big strong man, especially one employed to protect sb/sth

mus·cu·lar /'mʌskjələ(r)/ *adj.* **1** connected with the muscles: *muscular tension/power/tissue* **2** (also *informal* **muscly** /'mʌsli/) having large strong muscles: *a muscular body/build/chest* ◇ *He was tall, lean and muscular.*

muscular dystrophy /ˌmʌskjələ 'dɪstrəfi; AmE -lər/ *noun* [U] a medical condition that some people are born with in which the muscles gradually become weaker

mus·cu·lat·ure /'mʌskjələtʃə(r)/ *noun* [U, sing.] (*biology*) the system of muscles in the body or part of the body

muse /mjuːz/ *noun, verb*

■ *noun* **1** a person or spirit that gives a writer, painter, musician, etc. ideas and the desire to create things: *He felt that his muse had deserted him* (= that he could no longer write, paint, etc.). **2** (**Muse**) (in ancient Greek and Roman stories) one of the nine GODDESSES who encouraged poetry, music and other branches of art and literature

■ *verb* (*written*) **1** [V] ~ (**about/on/over/upon sth**) to think carefully about sth for a time, ignoring what is happening around you: *I sat quietly, musing on the events of the day.* **2** to say sth to yourself in a way that shows you are thinking carefully about it: [V speech] *'I wonder why?' she mused.* [also V that]

mu·seum /mjuˈziːəm/ *noun* a building in which objects of artistic, cultural, historical or scientific interest are kept and shown to the public: *a museum of modern art* ◇ *a science museum*

mu'seum piece *noun* **1** an object that is of enough historical or artistic value to have in a museum **2** (*humorous*) a thing or person that is old-fashioned, or old and no longer useful: *That car of his is a real museum piece.*

mush /mʌʃ/ *noun* **1** [U, sing.] (usually *disapproving*) a soft thick mass or mixture: *The vegetables had turned to mush.* ◇ *The ground was a mush of wet leaves.* ◇ *His insides suddenly felt like mush.* **2** [U] (*AmE*) a type of thick PORRIDGE made from corn

musher /'mʌʃə(r)/ *noun* (*AmE*) a person who drives a dog SLED

mush·room /'mʌʃrʊm; -ruːm/ *noun, verb*

■ *noun* a FUNGUS with a round flat head and short stem. Many mushrooms can be eaten: *a field mushroom* (= the most common type that is eaten, often just called a 'mushroom', and often grown to be sold) ◇ *fried mushrooms* ◇ *cream of mushroom soup*—see also BUTTON MUSHROOM, TOADSTOOL—picture on page A3

■ *verb* [V] **1** to rapidly grow or increase in number: *We expect the market to mushroom in the next two years.*—picture on page A3 **2** (usually **go mushrooming**) to gather mushrooms in a field or wood

'mushroom cloud *noun* a large cloud, shaped like a mushroom, that forms in the air after a nuclear explosion

mushy /'mʌʃi/ *adj.* **1** soft and thick, like mush: *Cook until the fruit is soft but not mushy.* **2** (*informal, disapproving*) too emotional in a way that is embarrassing SYN SENTIMENTAL: *mushy romantic novels*

ˌmushy 'peas *noun* [pl.] (*BrE*) soft cooked peas, eaten especially in the north of England

music /'mjuːzɪk/ *noun* [U] **1** sounds that are arranged in a way that is pleasant or exciting to listen to. People sing music or play it on instruments: *pop/dance/classical/church music* ◇ *to listen to music* ◇ *She could hear music playing somewhere.* ◇ *It was a charming **piece of music**.* ◇ *the popularity of Mozart's music* ◇ *He wrote the music but I don't know who wrote the words.* ◇ *The poem has been set to music.* ◇ *Every week they get together to **make music** (= to play music or sing).*—see also CHAMBER MUSIC, COUNTRY MUSIC, ROCK MUSIC, SOUL MUSIC **2** the art of writing or playing music: *to study music* ◇ *a career in music* ◇ *music lessons* ◇ *the music business/industry* **3** the written or printed signs that represent the sounds to be played or sung in a piece of music: *Can you **read music*** (= understand the signs in order to play or sing a piece of music)? ◇ *I had to play it without the music.*—see also SHEET MUSIC—picture on page 838 IDM **music to your 'ears** news or information that you are very pleased to hear—more at FACE *v.*

æ	ɑː	e	ɜː	ə	ɪ	iː	i	ɒ	ɔː	ʌ	ʊ	u	uː
cat	father	ten	bird	about	sit	see	many	got	saw	cup	put	actual	too
							(BrE)						

M

musical notation

notes		rests
𝅝	semibreve (*BrE*)/ whole note (*AmE*)	▬
𝅗𝅥	minim (*BrE*)/ half note (*AmE*)	▬
𝅘𝅥	crotchet (*BrE*)/ quarter note (*AmE*)	𝄽
𝅘𝅥𝅮	quaver (*BrE*)/ eighth note (*AmE*)	𝄾
𝅘𝅥𝅯	semiquaver (*BrE*)/ sixteenth note (*AmE*)	𝄿

sharp	natural	flat
♯	♮	♭

treble clef — time signature — tie — key signature — bar (*BrE*)/ measure (*AmE*)

bass clef — stave (*BrE*)/ staff (*AmE*)

mu·sic·al /ˈmjuːzɪkl/ *adj., noun*

■ *adj.* **1** [only before noun] connected with music; containing music: *the musical director of the show ◊ musical talent/ability/skill ◊ musical styles/tastes ◊ a musical production/entertainment* **2** (of a person) with a natural skill or interest in music: *She's very musical.* [OPP] UNMUSICAL **3** (of a sound) pleasant to listen to, like music: *a musical voice* [OPP] UNMUSICAL

■ *noun* (also *old-fashioned* ˌmusical ˈcomedy) a play or a film/movie in which part or all of the story is told using songs and often dancing: *the latest Andrew Lloyd Webber musical*

ˈmusical box *noun* (*especially BrE*) = MUSIC BOX

ˌmusical ˈchairs *noun* [U] **1** a children's game in which players run round a row of chairs while music is playing. Each time the music stops, players try to sit down on one of the chairs, but there are always more players than chairs. **2** (often *disapproving*) a situation in which people frequently exchange jobs or positions

ˌmusical ˈinstrument (also in·stru·ment) *noun* an object used for producing musical sounds, for example a piano or a drum: *Most pupils learn (to play) a musical instrument. ◊ the instruments of the orchestra* ⇨ vocabulary notes and pictures on pages 840 and 841

mu·sic·al·ity /ˌmjuːzɪˈkæləti/ *noun* [U] (*formal*) skill and understanding in performing music

music·al·ly /ˈmjuːzɪkli/ *adv.* **1** in a way that is connected with music: *musically gifted ◊ Musically speaking, their latest album is nothing special.* **2** with musical skill: *He plays really musically.* **3** in a way that is pleasant to listen to, like music: *to laugh/speak musically*

ˈmusic box (also ˈmusical box *especially in BrE*) *noun* a box containing a device that plays a tune when the box is opened

ˈmusic hall *noun* (*BrE*) **1** (also vaude·ville *AmE, BrE*) [U] a type of entertainment popular in the late 19th and early 20th centuries, including singing, dancing and COMEDY: *an old music hall song* **2** (*AmE* ˈvaudeville theater) [C] a theatre used for popular entertainment in the late 19th and early 20th centuries

mu·si·cian /mjuˈzɪʃn/ *noun* a person who plays a musical instrument or writes music, especially as a job: *a jazz/rock musician*

mu·si·cian·ship /mjuˈzɪʃnʃɪp/ *noun* [U] skill in performing or writing music

mu·sic·ology /ˌmjuːzɪˈkɒlədʒi; *AmE* -ˈkɑːl-/ *noun* [U] the study of the history and theory of music ▶ **mu·sic·olo·gist** /ˌmjuːzɪˈkɒlədʒɪst; *AmE* -ˈkɑːl-/ *noun*

ˈmusic stand *noun* a metal frame, especially one that you can fold, that is used for holding sheets of music while you play a musical instrument

musk /mʌsk/ *noun* [U] a substance with a strong smell that is used in making some PERFUMES. It is produced naturally by a type of male deer. ▶ **musky** *adj.*: *a musky perfume* (= smelling of or like musk)

mus·ket /ˈmʌskɪt/ *noun* an early type of long gun that was used by soldiers in the past

mus·ket·eer /ˌmʌskəˈtɪə(r)/; *AmE* -ˈtɪr/ *noun* a soldier who uses a musket

musk·rat /ˈmʌskræt/ *noun* a N American water animal that has a strong smell and is hunted for its fur

Mus·lim /ˈmʊzlɪm; ˈmʌz-; -ləm/ *noun* a person whose religion is Islam ▶ **Mus·lim** *adj.*—see also MOSLEM

mus·lin /ˈmʌzlɪn/ *noun* [U] a fine cotton fabric that is almost transparent, used, especially in the past, for making clothes and curtains

mus·sel /ˈmʌsl/ *noun* a small shellfish that can be eaten, with a black shell in two parts

---

> **GRAMMAR POINT**
> **must / have (got) to / must not / don't have to**
>
> **Necessity and Obligation**
> **Must** and **have (got) to** are used in the present to say that something is necessary or should be done.
> **Have to** is more common in *AmE*, especially in speech: *You must be home by 11 o'clock. ◊ I must wash the car tomorrow. ◊ I have to collect the children from school at 3 o'clock. ◊ Nurses have to wear a uniform.*
> In *BrE* there is a difference between them. **Must** is used to talk about what the speaker or listener wants, and **have (got) to** about rules, laws and other people's wishes: *I'd love to stay, but I must go now – I've got to write an assignment for my tutor this evening.*
> There are no past or future forms of **must**. To talk about the past you use **had to** and **has had to**: *I had to wait half an hour for a bus.* **Will have to** is used to talk about the future, or **have to** if an arrangement has already been made: *We'll have to borrow the money we need. ◊ I have to go to the dentist tomorrow.*
> Questions with **have to** are formed using **do**: *Do the children have to wear a uniform?* In negative sentences both **must not** and **don't have to** are used, but with different meanings. **Must not** is used to tell somebody not to do something: *Passengers must not smoke until the signs have been switched off.* The short form **mustn't** is used especially in *BrE*: *You mustn't leave the gate open.* **Don't have to** is used when it is not necessary to do something: *You don't have to pay for the tickets in advance. ◊ She doesn't have to work at weekends.*
> ⇨ note at NEED
>
> **Certainty**
> Both **must** and **have to** are used to say that you are certain about something. **Have to** is the usual verb used in *AmE* and this is becoming more frequent in *BrE* in this meaning: *He has (got) to be the worst actor on TV! ◊ This must be the most boring party I've ever been to (BrE).* If you are talking about the past, use **must have**: *Your trip must have been fun!*

must *modal verb, noun*

■ *modal verb* /məst; *strong form* mʌst/ (*negative* **must not**, *short form* **mustn't** /ˈmʌsnt/) **1** used to say that sth is necessary or very important (sometimes involving a rule or a law): *All visitors must report to reception. ◊ Cars must not park in front of the entrance* (= it is not allowed). *◊ I must ask you not to do that again. ◊ You mustn't say things like that. ◊ I must go to the bank and get some*

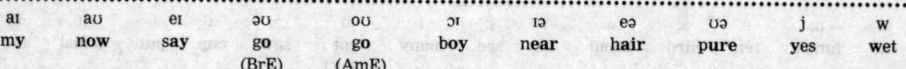

aɪ	aʊ	eɪ	əʊ	oʊ	ɔɪ	ɪə	eə	ʊə	j	w
my	now	say	go (BrE)	go (AmE)	boy	near	hair	pure	yes	wet

money. ◊ *I must admit* (= I feel that I should admit) *I was surprised it cost so little.* ◊ *Must you always question everything I say?* (= it is annoying) ◊ *'Do we have to finish this today?' 'Yes, you must.'* **HELP** Note that the negative for the last example is *'No, you don't have to.* **2** used to say that sth is likely or logical: *You must be hungry after all that walking.* ◊ *He must have known* (= surely he knew) *what she wanted.* ◊ *I'm sorry she's not here. She must have left already* (= that must be the explanation). **3** used to recommend that sb does sth because you think it is a good idea: *You simply must read this book.* ◊ *We must get together soon for lunch.* ⇨ note at MODAL **IDM** **if you 'must (do sth)** used to say that sb may do sth but you do not really want them to: *'Can I smoke?' 'If you must.'* ◊ *It's from my boyfriend, if you must know.*

■ *noun* /mʌst/ [usually sing.] (*informal*) something that you must do, see, buy, etc: *His new novel is a must for all lovers of crime fiction.*

mus·tache, **mus·tached** (*AmE*) = MOUSTACHE, MOUS-TACHED

mus·tachi·oed (also **mous·tachi·oed**) /məˈstæʃiəʊd; *AmE* -ʃiəʊd/ *adj.* (*written*) having a large moustache with curls at the ends

mus·tang /ˈmʌstæŋ/ *noun* a small American wild horse

mus·tard /ˈmʌstəd; *AmE* -tərd/ *noun* [U] **1** a thick cold yellow or brown sauce that tastes hot and spicy and is usually eaten with meat: *a jar of mustard* ◊ *mustard powder* ◊ *French/English mustard* **2** a small plant with yellow flowers, grown for its seeds that are crushed to make mustard **3** a brownish-yellow colour ▶ **mus·tard** *adj.*: *a mustard sweater* **IDM** **(not) cut the 'mustard** to (not) be as good as expected or required: *I didn't cut the mustard as a hockey player.*—more at KEEN *adj.*

mus·ter /ˈmʌstə(r)/ *verb, noun*
■ *verb* **1** [VN] ~ **sth (up)** to find as much support, courage, etc. as you can **SYN** SUMMON: *We mustered what support we could for the plan.* ◊ *She left the room with all the dignity she could muster.* **2** to come together, or bring people, especially soldiers, together for example for military action **SYN** GATHER: [V] *The troops mustered.* ◊ [VN] *to muster an army*
■ *noun* a group of people, especially soldiers, that have been brought together: *muster stations/areas* (= parts of a building, a ship, etc. that people must go to if there is an emergency) **IDM** see PASS *v.*

musty /ˈmʌsti/ *adj.* smelling damp and unpleasant because of a lack of fresh air: *a musty room*

mut·able /ˈmjuːtəbl/ *adj.* (*formal*) that can change; likely to change ▶ **mut·abil·ity** /ˌmjuːtəˈbɪləti/ *noun* [U]

mu·tant /ˈmjuːtənt/ *adj., noun*
■ *adj.* (*biology*) (of a living thing) different in some way from others of the same kind because of a change in its GENETIC structure: *a mutant gene*
■ *noun* **1** (*biology*) a living thing with qualities that are different from its parents' qualities because of a change in its GENETIC structure **2** (*informal*) (in stories about space, the future, etc.) a living thing with an unusual and frightening appearance because of a change in its GEN-ETIC structure

mu·tate /mjuːˈteɪt; *AmE* ˈmjuːteɪt/ *verb* ~ **(into sth)** **1** to develop or make sth develop a new form or structure, because of a GENETIC change: [V] *the ability of the virus to mutate into new forms* ◊ [VN] *mutated genes* **2** [V] to change into a new form: *Rhythm and blues mutated into rock and roll.*—see also MUTATION

mu·ta·tion /mjuːˈteɪʃn/ *noun* **1** [U, C] (*biology*) a process in which the GENETIC material of a person, a plant or an animal changes in structure when it is passed on to children, etc., causing different physical characteristics to develop; a change of this kind: *cells affected by muta-tion* ◊ *genetic/colour mutations* **2** [U, C] a change in the form or structure of sth: (*linguistics*) *vowel mutation*

mute /mjuːt/ *adj., noun, verb*
■ *adj.* **1** (*written*) not speaking **SYN** SILENT: *a look of mute appeal* ◊ *The child sat mute in the corner of the room.* **2** (*old-fashioned*) (of a person) unable to speak **SYN** DUMB

■ *noun* **1** (*music*) a device made of metal, rubber or plastic that you use to make the sound of a musical instrument softer—picture on page 840 **2** (*old-fashioned*) a person who is not able to speak
■ *verb* [VN] **1** to make the sound of sth, especially a musical instrument, quieter or softer, sometimes using a mute: *He muted the strings with his palm.* ◊ *The traffic noise was muted by the heavy drapes.* **2** to make sth weaker or less severe: *She thought it better to mute her criticism.*

muted /ˈmjuːtɪd/ *adj.* (*written*) **1** (of sounds) quiet; not as loud as usual: *the muted sound of traffic outside* ◊ *They spoke in muted voices.* **2** (of emotions, opinions, etc.) not strongly expressed: *The proposals received only a muted response.* **3** (of colours, light, etc.) not bright: *a dress in muted shades of blue* **4** (of musical instruments) used with a mute: *muted trumpets*

mute·ly /ˈmjuːtli/ *adv.* without speaking **SYN** SILENTLY

mu·ti·late /ˈmjuːtɪleɪt/ *verb* [VN] **1** to damage sb's body very severely, especially by cutting or tearing off part of it: *The body had been badly mutilated.* **2** to damage sth very badly: *Intruders slashed and mutilated several paint-ings.* ▶ **mu·ti·la·tion** /ˌmjuːtɪˈleɪʃn/ *noun* [U, C]: *Thou-sands suffered death or mutilation in the bomb blast.*

mu·tin·eer /ˌmjuːtɪˈnɪə(r); *AmE* -ˈnɪr/ *noun* a person who takes part in a MUTINY

mu·tin·ous /ˈmjuːtənəs/ *adj.* **1** refusing to obey the orders of sb in authority; wanting to do this **SYN** REBELLI-OUS: *mutinous workers* ◊ *a mutinous expression* **2** taking part in a mutiny ▶ **mu·tin·ous·ly** *adv.*

mu·tiny /ˈmjuːtəni/ *noun, verb*
■ *noun* (*pl.* **-ies**) [U, C] the act of refusing to obey the orders of sb in authority, especially by soldiers or sailors: *Dis-content among the ship's crew finally led to the outbreak of mutiny.* ◊ *the famous movie 'Mutiny on the Bounty'* ◊ *We have a family mutiny on our hands!*
■ *verb* (**mu·tin·ies, mu·tiny·ing, mu·tin·ied, mu·tin·ied**) [V] (especially of soldiers or sailors) to refuse to obey the orders of sb in authority

mutt /mʌt/ *noun* (*informal, especially AmE*) a dog, espe-cially one that is not of a particular breed **SYN** MONGREL

mut·ter /ˈmʌtə(r)/ *verb, noun*
■ *verb* **1** ~ **(sth) (to sb/yourself) (about sth)** to speak or say sth in a quiet voice that is difficult to hear, especially because you are annoyed about sth: [V+speech] *'How dare she,' he muttered under his breath.* ◊ [V] *She just sat there muttering to herself.* ◊ [VN] *I muttered something about needing to get back to work.* [also V that] **2** ~ **(about sth)** to complain about sth, without saying publicly what you think: [V] *Workers continued to mutter about the manage-ment.* [also V that]
■ *noun* [usually sing.] a quiet sound or words that are difficult to hear: *the soft mutter of voices*

mut·ter·ing /ˈmʌtərɪŋ/ *noun* [U] **1** (also **mutterings** [pl.]) complaints that you express privately rather than openly: *There have been mutterings about his leadership.* **2** words that you speak very quietly to yourself

mut·ton /ˈmʌtn/ *noun* [U] meat from a fully grown sheep—compare LAMB **IDM** **mutton dressed as 'lamb** (*BrE, informal, disapproving*) used to describe a woman who is trying to look younger than she really is, espe-cially by wearing clothes that are designed for young people

mu·tual /ˈmjuːtʃuəl/ *adj.* **1** used to describe feelings that two or more people have for each other equally, or actions that affect two or more people equally: *mutual respect/understanding* ◊ *mutual support/aid* ◊ *I don't like her, and I think the feeling is mutual* (= she doesn't like me either). **2** [only before noun] shared by two or more people: *We met at the home of a mutual friend.* ◊ *They soon discovered a mutual interest in music.* ▶ **mu·tu·al·ity** /ˌmjuːtʃuˈæləti/ *noun* [U, C] (*formal*): *mutuality of respect/feeling*

'mutual fund *noun* (*AmE*) = UNIT TRUST

mu·tu·al·ly /ˈmjuːtʃuəli/ *adv.* felt or done equally by two or more people: *a mutually beneficial/supportive relation-ship* ◊ *Can we find a mutually convenient time to meet?* ◊

M

🎼 *Musical instruments*

Playing an instrument

When talking generally about playing musical instruments, **the** is usually used before the name of the instrument:

- He played **the** trumpet in a jazz band.
- She decided to take up (= start learning to play) **the** flute.

The is not usually used when two or more instruments are mentioned:
She teaches violin, cello and piano.

The preposition **on** is used to say who is playing which instrument:

- The CD features James Galway **on the** flute.
- She sang and he accompanied her **on the** piano.

The is not usually used when you are talking about pop or jazz musicians:

- John Squire on guitar
- Miles Davis played trumpet.

Describing instruments

There are four **sections** of instruments in an **orchestra: strings**, **woodwind**, **brass** and **percussion**.

Different bands or **ensembles** can be formed when instruments from the different sections play separately:

- a brass band
- a string quartet
- a wind band
- a jazz trio

Particular adjectives are used before the names of musical instruments to describe the type of instrument it is:

- a tenor saxophone
- a bass drum
- a classical guitar

> **GRAMMAR POINT**
>
> The names of instruments can be used like adjectives before other nouns:
> - a clarinet lesson
> - Chopin's Piano Concerto No 1
> - She's going to do her cello practice.

Orchestral instruments

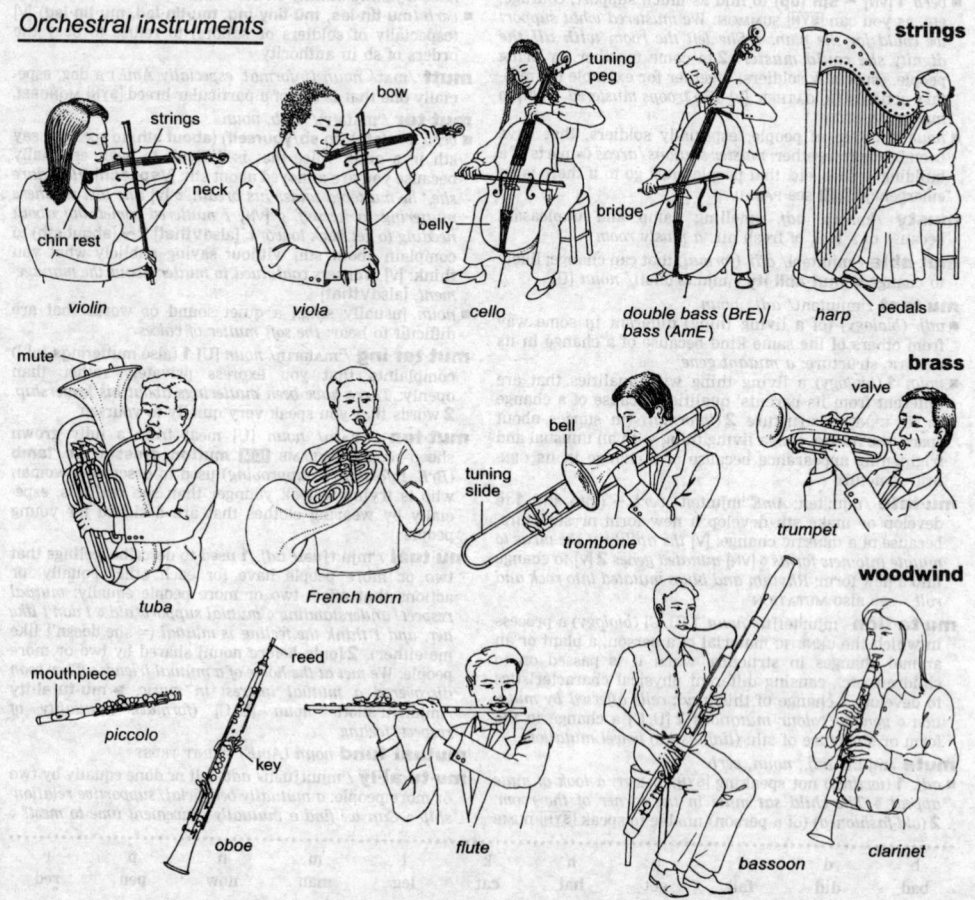

strings

chin rest · strings · bow · neck · belly · tuning peg · bridge · pedals

violin · viola · cello · double bass (BrE)/ bass (AmE) · harp

brass

mute · valve · bell · tuning slide

tuba · French horn · trombone · trumpet

woodwind

mouthpiece · reed · key

piccolo · oboe · flute · bassoon · clarinet

People who play instruments

Some musical instruments have a special name, ending in **-ist** or **-er** for the people who play them:

- *The violinist lifted his bow.*
- *the South African drummer, Louis Moholo*

Check near the entry for each instrument to find the correct word. If there is no special word, you use **player** after the name of the instrument:

- *the quartet's viola player*

When talking about pop or jazz, people often use **player** even when there is a word for the person like **saxophonist** or **bassist**:

- *a brilliant young sax player*
- *We're looking for a new bass player.*

In an orchestra playing classical music, **principal, deputy principal** (*BrE*), **associate principal** (*AmE*) and **assistant principal** (*AmE*) are used with the names of instruments to describe a player's position or importance.

- *He became principal cellist within a few years.*

A person who directs (or **conducts**) an orchestra is a **conductor**. The principal violinist (who **leads** the orchestra) is the **leader** (*BrE*) or the **concertmaster** (*AmE*).

Music for instruments

Music is **composed** or **written for** an instrument. In a piece of music written for a group of instruments, each has a different **part** to play:

- *There are parts for oboe and bassoon.*

If there is more than one part for the same type of instrument, the terms **first** and **second** and sometimes **third** and **fourth** are used:

- *She's a second violin* (= plays the second violin part).
- *the deep low notes of the third horn*

A **solo** is a part for one instrument playing alone. A **soloist** plays it:

- *She performs regularly as a soloist and in chamber music.*
- *I love the saxophone solo on this song.*

More illustrations at MUSIC and PIANO.

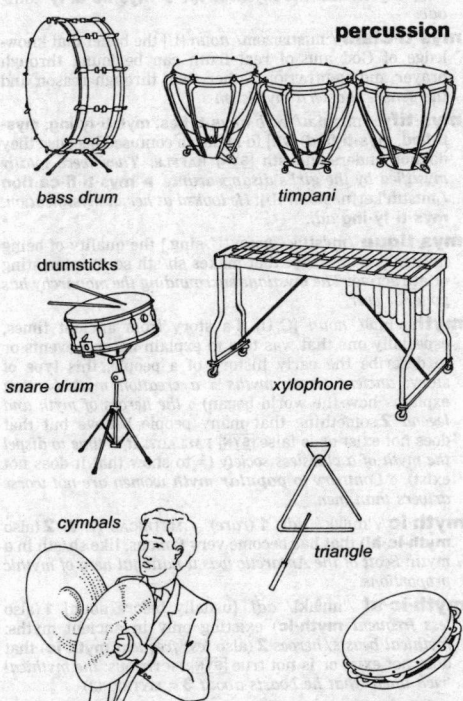

percussion

bass drum

timpani

drumsticks

snare drum

xylophone

cymbals

triangle

tambourine

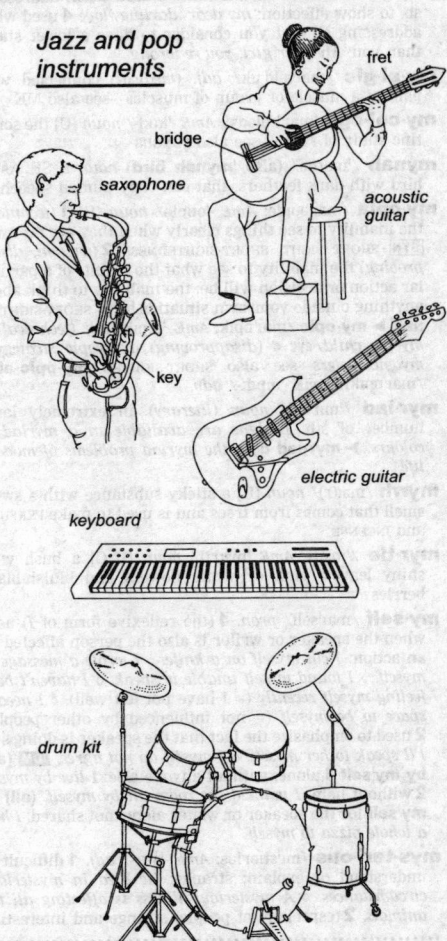

Jazz and pop instruments

fret

bridge

saxophone

acoustic guitar

key

electric guitar

keyboard

drum kit

*The two views are not **mutually exclusive*** (= both can be true at the same time).

Muzak™ /'mjuː.zæk/ *noun* [U] (often *disapproving*) continuous recorded music that is played in shops, restaurants, airports, etc.—compare PIPE *v.*

muz·zle /'mʌzl/ *noun, verb*
■ *noun* **1** the nose and mouth of an animal, especially a dog or a horse—compare SNOUT—picture on page A6 **2** a device made of leather or plastic that you put over the nose and mouth of an animal, especially a dog, to prevent it from biting people **3** the open end of a gun, where the bullets come out
■ *verb* [VN] **1** [usually passive] to put a muzzle over a dog's head to prevent it from biting people **2** to prevent sb from expressing their opinions in public as they want to SYN GAG: *They accused the government of muzzling the press.*

muzzy /'mʌzi/ *adj.* (*BrE, informal*) **1** unable to think in a clear way: *a muzzy head* ◇ *Those drugs made me feel muzzy.* **2** not clear: *a muzzy voice* ◇ *muzzy plans*

MV /ˌem 'viː/ *abbr.* (*BrE*) (used before the name of a ship) motor vessel: *the MV Puma*

MVP /ˌem viː 'piː/ *abbr.* (*AmE*) most valuable player (the best player in a team): *He has just earned his fourth MVP award this season.*

MW *abbr.* **1** MEDIUM WAVE **2** (*pl.* **MW**) MEGAWATT(S)

my /maɪ/ *det.* (the possessive form of *I*) **1** of or belonging to the speaker or writer: *Where's my passport?* ◇ *My feet are cold.* **2** used in exclamations to express surprise, etc: *My goodness! Look at the time!* **3** used when addressing sb, to show affection: *my dear/darling/love* **4** used when addressing sb that you consider to have a lower status than you: *My dear girl, you're wrong.*

my·al·gic /maɪ'ældʒɪk/ *adj.* (*medical*) connected with pain in a muscle or group of muscles—see also ME

my·col·ogy /maɪ'kɒlədʒi; *AmE* -'kɑː.l-/ *noun* [U] the scientific study of FUNGI—see also FUNGUS

mynah /'maɪnə/ (also **'mynah bird**) *noun* a SE Asian bird with dark feathers, that can copy human speech

my·opia /maɪ'əʊpiə; *AmE* -'oʊpiə/ *noun* [U] **1** (*technical*) the inability to see things clearly when they are far away SYN SHORT SIGHT, SHORT-SIGHTEDNESS **2** (*written, disapproving*) the inability to see what the results of a particular action or decision will be; the inability to think about anything outside your own situation SYN SHORT-SIGHTEDNESS ▶ **my·opic** /maɪ'ɒpɪk; *AmE* -'ɑː.pɪk/ *adj.* (*technical*): *a myopic child/eye* ◇ (*disapproving*) *a myopic strategy* ◇ *myopic voters*—see also SHORT-SIGHTED **my·opic·al·ly** /maɪ'ɒpɪkli; *AmE* -'ɑː.pɪk-/ *adv.*

myr·iad /'mɪriəd/ *noun* (*literary*) an extremely large number of sth: *Designs are available in a myriad of colours.* ▶ **myr·iad** *adj.*: *the myriad problems of modern life*

myrrh /mɜː(r)/ *noun* [U] a sticky substance with a sweet smell that comes from trees and is used to make PERFUME and INCENSE

myr·tle /'mɜːtl; *AmE* 'mɜːrtl/ *noun* [U, C] a bush with shiny leaves, pink or white flowers and bluish-black berries

my·self /maɪ'self/ *pron.* **1** (the reflexive form of *I*) used when the speaker or writer is also the person affected by an action: *I cut myself on a knife.* ◇ *I wrote a message to myself.* ◇ *I found myself unable to speak.* ◇ *I haven't been feeling myself recently* (= I have not felt well). ◇ *I needed space to be myself* (= not influenced by other people). **2** used to emphasize the fact that the speaker is doing sth: *I'll speak to her myself.* ◇ *I myself do not agree.* IDM **(all) by my'self 1** alone; without anyone else: *I live by myself* **2** without help: *I painted the room all by myself.* **(all) to my'self** for the speaker or writer alone; not shared: *I had a whole pizza to myself.*

mys·teri·ous /mɪ'stɪəriəs; *AmE* -'stɪr-/ *adj.* **1** difficult to understand or explain; strange: *He died in mysterious circumstances.* ◇ *A mysterious illness is affecting all the animals.* **2** (especially of people) strange and interesting

because you do not know much about them: *A mysterious young woman is living next door.* **3** (of people) not saying much about sth, especially when other people want to know more: *He was being very mysterious about where he was going.* ▶ **mys·teri·ous·ly** *adv.*: *My watch had mysteriously disappeared.* ◇ *Mysteriously, the streets were deserted.* ◇ *She was silent, smiling mysteriously.*

mys·tery /'mɪstri/ *noun* (*pl.* **-ies**) **1** [C] something that is difficult to understand or to explain: *It is one of the great unsolved mysteries of this century.* ◇ *Their motives remain a mystery.* ◇ *It's a complete mystery to me why they chose him.* **2** [C] (often used as an adjective) a person or a thing that is strange and interesting because you do not know much about them or it: *He's a bit of a mystery.* ◇ *There was a mystery guest on the programme.* ◇ *The band was financed by a mystery backer.* ◇ (*BrE*) *a mystery tour* (= when you do not know where you are going) **3** [U] the quality of being difficult to understand or to explain, especially when this makes sb/sth seem interesting and exciting: *Mystery surrounds her disappearance.* ◇ *His past is shrouded in mystery* (= not much is known about it). ◇ *The dark glasses give her an air of mystery.* **4** [C] a story, a film/movie or a play in which crimes and strange events are only explained at the end: *I enjoy murder mysteries.* **5** (**mysteries**) [pl.] secret religious ceremonies; secret knowledge: (*figurative*) *the teacher who initiated me into the mysteries of mathematics* **6** [C] a religious belief that cannot be explained or proved in a scientific way: *the mystery of creation*

'mystery play *noun* a type of play that was popular between the 11th and 14th centuries and was based on events in the Bible or the lives of the Christian saints

mys·tic /'mɪstɪk/ *noun* a person who tries to become united with God through prayer and MEDITATION and so understand important things that are beyond normal human understanding

mys·tic·al /'mɪstɪkl/ (also *less frequent* **mys·tic** /'mɪstɪk/) *adj.* **1** having spiritual powers or qualities that are difficult to understand or to explain: *mystical forces/ powers* ◇ *mystic beauty* ◇ *Watching the sun rise over the mountain was an almost mystical experience.* **2** connected with mysticism: *the mystical life* ▶ **mys·tic·al·ly** /-kli/ *adv.*

mys·ti·cism /'mɪstɪsɪzəm/ *noun* [U] the belief that knowledge of God and of real truth can be found through prayer and MEDITATION rather than through reason and the senses: *Eastern mysticism*

mys·tify /'mɪstɪfaɪ/ *verb* (**mys·ti·fies**, **mys·ti·fy·ing**, **mys·ti·fied**, **mys·ti·fied**) [VN] to make sb confused because they do not understand sth SYN BAFFLE: *They were totally mystified by the girl's disappearance.* ▶ **mys·ti·fi·ca·tion** /ˌmɪstɪfɪ'keɪʃn/ *noun* [U]: *He looked at her in mystification.* **mys·ti·fy·ing** *adj.*

mys·tique /mɪ'stiːk/ *noun* [U, sing.] the quality of being mysterious or secret that makes sb/sth seem interesting or attractive: *The mystique surrounding the monarchy has gone for ever.*

myth /mɪθ/ *noun* [C, U] **1** a story from ancient times, especially one that was told to explain natural events or to describe the early history of a people; this type of story: *ancient Greek myths* ◇ *a creation myth* (= that explains how the world began) ◇ *the heroes of myth and legend* **2** something that many people believe but that does not exist or is false SYN FALLACY: *It is time to dispel the myth of a classless society* (= to show that it does not exist). ◇ *Contrary to popular myth women are not worse drivers than men.*

myth·ic /'mɪθɪk/ *adj.* **1** (*rare*) = MYTHICAL (1, 2) **2** (also **myth·ic·al**) that has become very famous, like sb/sth in a myth: *Scott of the Antarctic was a national hero of mythic proportions.*

myth·ic·al /'mɪθɪkl/ *adj.* [usually before noun] **1** (also *less frequent* **myth·ic**) existing only in ancient myths: *mythical beasts/heroes* **2** (also *less frequent* **myth·ic**) that does not exist or is not true SYN FICTITIOUS: *the mythical 'rich uncle' that he boasts about* **3** = MYTHIC (2)

mytho·logic·al /ˌmɪθəˈlɒdʒɪkl; *AmE* -ˈlɑːdʒ-/ *adj.* [usually before noun] connected with ancient MYTHS: *mythological subjects/figures/stories*

myth·ology /mɪˈθɒlədʒi; *AmE* -ˈθɑːl-/ *noun* (*pl.* **-ies**) [U, C] **1** ancient MYTHS in general; the ancient MYTHS of a particular culture, society, etc: *Greek mythology* ◊ *a study of the religions and mythologies of ancient Rome* **2** ideas or facts that many people think are true but that do not exist or are false: *the popular mythology that life begins at forty*

myxo·ma·tosis /ˌmɪksəməˈtəʊsɪs; *AmE* -ˈtoʊ-/ *noun* [U] an infectious disease of rabbits that usually causes death

M

b	d	f	g	h	k	l	m	n	p	r
bad	did	fall	get	hat	cat	leg	man	now	pen	red

Nn

N /en/ *noun, abbr.*

■ *noun* (also **n**) (*pl.* **N's, n's** /enz/) **1** [C, U] the 14th letter of the English alphabet: *'Night' begins with (an) N/'N'.* **2** [U] (*mathematics*) used to represent a number whose value is not mentioned: *The equation is impossible for any value of n greater than 2.*—see also NTH

■ *abbr.* (*AmE* also **No.**) north; northern: *N Ireland*

n. *abbr. noun*

NAACP /ˌen dʌbəl ˌeɪ si: ˈpi:/ *abbr.* National Association for the Advancement of Colored People (an organization in the US that works for the rights of African Americans)

NAAFI /ˈnæfi/ *noun* [sing.] the abbreviation for 'Navy, Army and Air Force Institutes' (an organization which provides shops and places to eat for British soldiers)

naan *noun* [U] = NAN²

nab /næb/ *verb* (**-bb-**) ~ (**at sb**) **1** to catch or arrest sb who is doing sth wrong [SYN] COLLAR: *He was nabbed by the police for speeding.* **2** to take or get sth: *Who's nabbed my drink?*

nachos /ˈnætʃəʊz; *AmE* -tʃoʊz/ *noun* [pl.] (from *Spanish*) a Mexican dish of crisp pieces of TORTILLA served with beans, cheese, spices, etc.

nadir /ˈneɪdɪə(r); *AmE* -dɪr/ *noun* [sing.] (*written*) the worst moment of a particular situation: *the nadir of his career* ◇ *Company losses reached their nadir in 1992.* [OPP] ZENITH

nae /neɪ/ *det.* (*ScotE, spoken*) no: *We have nae money.* ▶ **nae** *adv.*: *It's nae (= not) bad.*

naff /næf/ *adj.* (*BrE, informal*) lacking style, taste, quality, etc: *There was a naff band playing.*

nag /næg/ *verb, noun*

■ *verb* (**-gg-**) ~ (**at sb**) **1** to keep complaining to sb about their behaviour or keep asking them to do sth: [V] *Stop nagging—I'll do it as soon as I can.* ◇ [VN **to** inf] *She had been nagging him to paint the fence.* [also VN] **2** to worry or irritate you continuously: [V] *A feeling of unease nagged at her.* ◇ [VN] *Doubts nagged me all evening.*

■ *noun* (*old-fashioned, informal*) a horse

nag·ging /ˈnægɪŋ/ *adj.* [only before noun] **1** continuing for a long time and difficult to cure or remove: *a nagging pain/doubt* **2** complaining: *a nagging voice*

nah /nɑː/ *exclamation* (*spoken, slang*) = NO

nail /neɪl/ *noun, verb*

■ *noun* **1** a thin hard layer covering the outer tip of the fingers or toes: *Stop biting your nails!* ◇ *nail clippers*—see also FINGERNAIL, TOENAIL—picture at BODY **2** a small thin pointed piece of metal with a flat head, used for hanging things on a wall or for joining pieces of wood together: *She hammered the nail in.*—compare SCREW (1), TACK (3)—picture at TOOL [IDM] **a nail in sb's/sth's ˈcoffin** something that makes the end or failure of an organization, sb's plans, etc. more likely to happen **on the ˈnail** (*informal*) (of payment) without delay: *They're good customers who always pay on the nail.*—more at FIGHT *v.*, HARD *adj.*, HIT *v.*, TOUGH *adj.*

■ *verb* [VN] **1** to fasten sth to sth with a nail or nails: *I nailed the sign to a tree.* **2** (*informal*) to catch sb and prove they are guilty of a crime or of doing sth bad: *The police haven't been able to nail the killer.* **3** (*informal*) to prove that sth is not true: *We must nail this lie.* [IDM] **nail your colours to the ˈmast** (*especially BrE*) to say publicly and firmly what you believe or who you support [PHRV] ˌ**nail sth↔ˈdown 1** to fasten sth down with a nail or nails **2** to reach an agreement or a decision, usually after a lot of discussion: *All the parties seem anxious to nail down a ceasefire.* ˌ**nail sb↔ˈdown (to sth)** to force sb to give you a definite promise or tell you exactly what they intend to do: *She says she'll come, but I can't nail her down to a specific time.* ˌ**nail sth↔ˈup 1** to fasten sth to a wall, post, etc. with a nail or nails **2** to put nails into a door or window so that it cannot be opened

ˈ**nail-biting** *adj.* [usually before noun] making you feel very excited or anxious because you do not know what is going to happen: *a nail-biting finish* ◇ *It's been a nail-biting couple of weeks waiting for my results.*

ˈ**nail brush** *noun* a small stiff brush for cleaning the fingernails

ˈ**nail file** *noun* a small metal tool with a rough surface for shaping the fingernails—see also EMERY BOARD

ˈ**nail scissors** *noun* [pl.] small scissors that are usually curved, used for cutting the nails on your fingers and toes: *a pair of nail scissors*

ˈ**nail varnish** (*BrE*) (also ˈ**nail polish** *AmE, BrE*) *noun* [U] clear or coloured liquid that you paint on your nails to make them look attractive: *nail varnish/polish remover*

naive (also **naïve**) /naɪˈiːv/ *adj.* **1** (*disapproving*) lacking experience of life, knowledge or good judgement and willing to believe that people always tell you the truth: *a naive question/remark* ◇ *to be politically naive* ◇ *I can't believe you were so naive as to trust him!* ◇ *It would be naive of us to think that football is only a game.* **2** (*approving*) (of people and their behaviour) innocent and simple: *Their approach to life is refreshingly naive.*—compare SOPHISTICATED ▶ **naive·ly** (also **naïve·ly**) *adv.*: *I naively assumed that I would be paid for the work.* **naiv·ety** (also **naïv·ety**) /naɪˈiːvəti/ *noun* [U]: *They laughed at the naivety of his suggestion.* ◇ *She has lost none of her naivety.*

WHICH WORD?
naked / bare

Both these words can be used to mean 'not covered with clothes' and are frequently used with the following nouns:

naked ~	bare ~
body	feet
man	arms
fear	walls
aggression	branches
flame	essentials

Naked is more often used to describe a person or their body and **bare** usually describes a part of the body.

Bare can also describe other things with nothing on them: *bare walls* ◇ *a bare hillside.* **Naked** can mean 'without a protective covering': *a naked sword.*

Bare can also mean 'just enough': *the bare minimum.* **Naked** can be used to talk about strong feelings that are not hidden: *naked fear.* Note also the idiom: *(visible) to/with the naked eye.*

---

naked /ˈneɪkɪd/ *adj.* **1** not wearing any clothes [SYN] BARE: *a naked body* ◇ *naked shoulders* ◇ *They often wandered around the house stark naked (= completely naked).* ◇ *They found him half naked and bleeding to death.* ◇ *The prisoners were stripped naked.*—see also BUCK NAKED **2** [usually before noun] without the usual covering [SYN] BARE: *a naked bulb/light* ◇ *a naked flame* ◇ *a naked sword* ◇ *Mice are born naked (= without fur).* **3** [only before noun] (of emotions, attitudes, etc.) expressed strongly and not hidden: *naked aggression/ambition* ◇ *the naked truth* **4** [not usually before noun] unable to protect yourself from being harmed, criticized, etc. SYN HELPLESS: *He still felt naked and drained after his ordeal.* ▶ **naked·ly** *adv.*: *nakedly aggressive* **naked·ness** *noun* [U] IDM **the naked 'eye** the normal power of your eyes without the help of an instrument: *The planet should be visible with/to the naked eye.*

namby-pamby /ˌnæmbi ˈpæmbi/ *adj.* (*informal, disapproving*) weak and too emotional

name /neɪm/ *noun, verb*
■ *noun* **1** a word or words that a particular person, animal, place or thing is known by: *What's your name?* ◊ *What is/was the name, please?* (= a polite way of asking sb's name) ◊ *Please write your full name and address below.* ◊ *Do you know the name of this flower?* ◊ *Rubella is just another name for German measles.* ◊ (*computing*) *a user/file name* ◊ *Are you changing your name when you get married?*— see also ASSUMED NAME, BRAND NAME, CODE NAME, FAMILY NAME, FIRST NAME, FORENAME, MAIDEN NAME, MIDDLE NAME, NICKNAME, PEN-NAME, PET NAME, PLACE NAME, SURNAME, TRADE NAME **2** [usually sing.] a reputation that sb/sth has; the opinion that people have about sb/sth: *She first made her name as a writer of children's books.* ◊ *He's made quite a name for himself* (= become famous). ◊ *The college has a good name for languages.* ◊ *This kind of behaviour gives students a bad name.* **3** (in compound adjectives) having a name or a reputation of the kind mentioned, especially one that is known by a lot of people: *a big-name company/celebrity* ◊ *brand-name goods*—see also HOUSEHOLD NAME **4** a famous person: *Some of the biggest names in the art world were at the party.* IDM **by 'name** using the name of sb/sth: *She asked for you by name.* ◊ *The principal knows all the students by name.* ◊ *I only know her by name* (= I have heard about her but I have not met her). **by the name of …** (*written*) who is called: *a young actor by the name of Tom Rees* **enter sb's/your 'name (for sth) | put sb's/your 'name down (for sth)** to apply for a place at a school, in a competition, etc. for sb or yourself: *Have you entered your name for the quiz yet?* **give your 'name to sth** to invent sth which then becomes known by your name **go by the name of …** to use a name that may not be your real one **in ˌall but 'name** used to describe a situation which exists in reality but that is not officially recognized: *He runs the company in all but name.* **in 'God's/'Heaven's name | in the name of 'God/'Heaven** used especially in questions to show that you are angry, surprised or shocked: *What in God's name was that noise?* ◊ *Where in the name of Heaven have you been?* **in the name of 'sb/'sth | in sb's/sth's 'name 1** for sb; showing that sth officially belongs to sb: *We reserved two tickets in the name of Brown.* ◊ *The car is registered in my name.* **2** using the authority of sb/sth; as a representative of sb/sth: *I arrest you in the name of the law.* **3** used to give a reason or an excuse for doing sth, often when what you are doing is wrong: *crimes committed in the name of religion* **in 'name only** officially recognized but not existing in reality: *He's party leader in name only.* **sb's name is 'mud** (*informal, usually humorous*) used to say that sb is not liked or popular because of sth they have done **the name of the 'game** (*informal*) the most important aspect of an activity; the most important quality needed for an activity: *Hard work is the name of the game if you want to succeed in business.* **put a 'name to sb/sth** to know or remember what sb/sth is called: *I recognize the tune but I can't put a name to it.* **take sb's name in 'vain** to show a lack of respect when using sb's name: (*humorous*) *Have you been taking my name in vain again?* **(have sth) to your 'name** to have or own sth: *an Olympic athlete with five gold medals to his name* ◊ *She doesn't have a penny/cent to her name* (= she is very poor). **under the name (of) …** using a name that may not be your real name—more at ANSWER *v.*, BIG *adj.*, CALL *v.*, DROP *v.*, LEND, MIDDLE NAME, NAME *v.*, REJOICE
■ *verb* **1** ~ **sb/sth (after sb) |** (*AmE* also) ~ **sb/sth (for sb)** to give a name to sb/sth: [VN] *He was named after his father* (= given his father's first name). ◊ [VN-N] *They named their son John.* **2** [VN] to say the name of sb/sth SYN IDENTIFY: *The victim has not yet been named.* ◊ *The missing*

man has been named as James Kelly. ◊ *Can you name all the American states?* **3** [VN] to state sth exactly SYN SPECIFY: *Name your price.* ◊ *They're engaged, but they haven't yet named the day* (= chosen the date for their wedding). ◊ *Activities available include squash, archery and swimming* **to name but a few.** ◊ *Chairs, tables, cabinets—you name it, she makes it* (= she makes anything you can imagine). **4** ~ **sb (as) sth | ~ sb (to sth)** to choose sb for a job or position: [VN-N] *I had no hesitation in naming him* (as) *captain.* ◊ [VN] *When she resigned, he was named to the committee in her place.* IDM **name 'names** to give the names of the people involved in sth, especially sth wrong or illegal

---

MORE ABOUT
names and titles

Names

Your **name** is either your whole name or one part of your name: *My name is Maria.* ◊ *His name is Tom Smith.* ◊ *The name's Bond.*

Your **last name** or **family name**, (also called **surname** in *BrE*)
= the name that all members of your family share.

Your **first name/names** (*formal* **forename**)
= the name(s) your parents gave you when you were born.

In *BrE* some people use the expression **Christian name(s)** to refer to a person's first name(s).

Your **middle name(s)**
= any name your parents gave you other than the one that is placed first. The initial of this name is often used as part of your name, especially in America: *John T. Harvey*

Your **full name**
= all your names usually in the order: first + middle + last name

A woman's **maiden name**
= the family name she had before she got married. Some women keep this name after they are married, and do not use their husband's name. In America, married women often use their maiden name followed by their husband's family name: *Hillary Rodham Clinton.*

Titles

Mr (for both married and unmarried men)

Mrs (for married women)

Miss (for unmarried women)

Ms (a title that some women prefer to use as it does not distinguish between married and unmarried women)

Doctor, Professor, President, Vice-President, Reverend (or **Rev**), etc.

The correct way to talk to someone is:
  first name, if you know them well: *Hello, Maria.*
  or title + surname: *Hello, Mr Brown.*
  or *Doctor* (medical), *Professor*, etc. on its own: *Thank you, Doctor.* This is only used for a very limited number of titles.

For information on ways of addressing people in writing see Study Page B14.

'name-calling *noun* [U] the act of using rude or insulting words about sb: *They were subjected to name-calling and jokes at their expense.*

'name-dropping *noun* [U] (*disapproving*) the act of mentioning the names of famous people you know or have met in order to impress other people ▶ **'name-drop** *verb* [V] —see also DROP NAMES

name·less /ˈneɪmləs/ *adj.* **1** [usually before noun] having no name; whose name you do not know: *a nameless grave* ◊ *thousands of nameless and faceless workers* **2** whose name is kept secret SYN ANONYMOUS: *a nameless source in the government* ◊ *a well-known public figure who*

æ	ɑː	e	ɜː	ə	ɪ	iː	i	ɒ	ɔː	ʌ	ʊ	u	uː
cat	father	ten	bird	about	sit	see	many	got	saw	cup	put	actual	too
								(BrE)					

N

shall remain nameless **3** [usually before noun] (*literary*) difficult or too unpleasant to describe: *nameless horrors/ fears* ◊ *a nameless longing*

name·ly /ˈneɪmli/ *adv.* used to introduce more exact and detailed information about sth that you have just mentioned: *We need to concentrate on our target audience, namely women aged between 20 and 30.*

name·plate /ˈneɪmpleɪt/ *noun* **1** a sign on the door or the wall of a building showing the name of a company or the name of a person who is living or working there **2** a piece of metal or plastic on an object showing the name of the person who owns it, made it or presented it

name·sake /ˈneɪmseɪk/ *noun* a person or a thing that has the same name as sb/sth else: *Unlike his more famous namesake, this Bill Clinton has little interest in politics.*

'name tag *noun* a small piece of plastic, paper or metal that you wear, with your name on it

'name tape *noun* a small piece of fabric that is sewn or stuck onto a piece of clothing and that has the name of the owner on it

nan[1] /næn/ *noun* (*BrE*) = NANNY

nan[2] (also **naan**) /nɑːn/ *noun* (also **'nan bread**, **'naan bread**) [U] a type of soft flat Indian bread

nanny /ˈnæni/ *noun* (*pl.* **-ies**) **1** a woman whose job is to take care of young children in the children's own home **2** (also **nan**) (both *BrE*) (used by children, especially as a form of address) a grandmother: *When is Nanny coming to stay?* ◊ *my nan and grandad*—see also GRANNY **IDM** **the 'nanny state** (*BrE*) a disapproving way of talking about the fact that government seems to get too much involved in people's lives and to protect them too much, in a way that limits their freedom

'nanny goat *noun* a female goat—compare BILLY GOAT

nano- /ˈnænəʊ/ *combining form* (*technical*) (in nouns and adjectives; used especially in units of measurement) one BILLIONTH: *nanosecond* ◊ *nanometre*

nap /næp/ *noun, verb*

■ *noun* **1** [C] a short sleep, especially during the day: *to take/have a nap*—see also CATNAP—compare SIESTA **2** [sing.] the short fine threads on the surface of some fabrics, usually lying in the same direction

■ *verb* (**-pp-**) [V] to sleep for a short time, especially during the day **IDM** see CATCH *v.*

na·palm /ˈneɪpɑːm/ *noun* [U] a substance like jelly, made from petrol/gas, that burns and is used in making bombs

nape /neɪp/ *noun* [sing.] **~ (of sb's neck)** the back of the neck: *Her hair was cut short at the nape of her neck.*—picture at BODY

naph·tha /ˈnæfθə/ *noun* [U] a type of oil that catches fire very easily, used as fuel or in making chemicals

nap·kin /ˈnæpkɪn/ *noun* **1** (also **'table napkin**) a piece of fabric or paper used at meals for protecting your clothes and cleaning your lips and fingers **SYN** SERVIETTE **2** (*AmE*) = SANITARY NAPKIN **3** (*BrE, old-fashioned* or *formal*) = NAPPY

nappy /ˈnæpi/ *noun* (*pl.* **-ies**) (*BrE*) (*AmE* **di·aper**) a piece of soft fabric or paper that is folded around a baby's bottom and between its legs to absorb and hold its body waste: *I'll change her nappy.* ◊ *a disposable nappy* (= one that is made to be used once only) ◊ *nappy rash*

nar·cis·sism /ˈnɑːsɪsɪzəm; *AmE* ˈnɑːrs-/ *noun* [U] (*formal, disapproving*) the habit of admiring yourself too much, especially your appearance ► **nar·cis·sis·tic** /ˌnɑːsɪˈsɪstɪk; *AmE* ˌnɑːrs-/ *adj.* **ORIGIN** From the Greek myth in which Narcissus fell in love with his own reflection in a pool.

nar·cis·sus /nɑːˈsɪsəs; *AmE* nɑːr's-/ *noun* (*pl.* **nar·cissi** /nɑːˈsɪsaɪ; *AmE* nɑːr's-/) a plant with white or yellow flowers that appear in spring. There are many types of narcissus, including the DAFFODIL.

nar·cot·ic /nɑːˈkɒtɪk; *AmE* nɑːrˈkɑː-/ *noun, adj.*

■ *noun* **1** a powerful illegal drug that affects the mind in a harmful way. HEROIN and COCAINE are narcotics: *a narcotics agent* (= a police officer investigating the illegal trade in drugs) **2** (*medical*) a substance that relaxes you, reduces pain or makes you sleep: *a mild narcotic*

■ *adj.* **1** (of a drug) that affects your mind in a harmful way **2** (of a substance) making you sleep: *a mild narcotic effect*

nark /nɑːk; *AmE* nɑːrk/ *noun* (*BrE, slang*) a person who is friendly with criminals and who gives the police information about them

narked /nɑːkt; *AmE* nɑːrkt/ *adj.* [not usually before noun] (*old-fashioned, BrE, informal*) annoyed about sth: *I could see he was getting narked with me.*

nar·rate /nəˈreɪt; *AmE* also ˈnæreɪt/ *verb* [VN] **1** (*formal*) to tell a story **SYN** RELATE: *She entertained them by narrating her adventures in Africa.* **2** to speak the words that form the text of a DOCUMENTARY film or programme: *The film was narrated by Andrew Sachs.*

nar·ra·tion /nəˈreɪʃn; *AmE* næˈr-/ *noun* (*formal*) **1** [U, C] the act or process of telling a story, especially in a novel, a film/movie or a play **2** [C] a description of events that is spoken during a film/movie, a play, etc. or with music: *He has recorded the narration for the production.*

nar·ra·tive /ˈnærətɪv/ *noun* (*formal*) **1** [C] a description of events, especially in a novel **SYN** STORY: *a gripping narrative of their journey up the Amazon* **2** [U] the act, process or skill of telling a story: *a master of narrative* ◊ *The novel contains too much dialogue and not enough narrative.* ► **nar·ra·tive** *adj.* [only before noun]: *narrative fiction/structure*

nar·ra·tor /nəˈreɪtə(r)/ *noun* a person who tells a story, especially in a book, play or film/movie; the person who speaks the words in a television programme but who does not appear in it: *a first-person narrator*

nar·row /ˈnærəʊ; *AmE* -roʊ/ *adj., verb*

■ *adj.* (**nar·row·er**, **nar·row·est**) **1** measuring a short distance from one side to the other, especially in relation to length: *narrow streets* ◊ *a narrow bed/doorway/shelf* ◊ *narrow shoulders/hips* ◊ *There was only a narrow gap between the bed and the wall.* ◊ (*figurative*) *the narrow confines of prison life* **OPP** BROAD, WIDE **2** [usually before noun] only just achieved or avoided: *a narrow victory* ◊ *He lost the race by the narrowest of margins.* ◊ *She was elected by a narrow majority.* ◊ *He had a narrow escape when his car skidded on the ice.* **3** limited in a way that ignores important issues or the opinions of other people: *narrow interests* ◊ *She has a very narrow view of the world.* **OPP** BROAD **4** limited in variety or numbers **SYN** RESTRICTED: *The shop sells only a narrow range of goods.* ◊ *a narrow circle of friends* **OPP** WIDE **5** limited in meaning; exact: *I am using the word 'education' in the narrower sense.* **OPP** BROAD ⇨ note on page 847 ► **nar·row·ness** *noun* [U]: *The narrowness of the streets caused many traffic problems.* ◊ *We were surprised by the narrowness of our victory.* ◊ *His attitudes show a certain narrowness of mind.* **IDM** see STRAIGHT *n.*

■ *verb* to become or make sth narrower: [V] *This is where the river narrows.* ◊ *The gap between the two teams has narrowed to three points.* ◊ *Her eyes narrowed* (= almost closed) *menacingly.* ◊ [VN] *He narrowed his eyes at her.* ◊ *We need to narrow the health divide between rich and poor.* **PHRV** **,narrow sth↔'down (to sth)** to reduce the number of possibilities or choices: *We have narrowed down the list to four candidates.*

nar·row·boat /ˈnærəʊbəʊt; *AmE* ˈnæroʊboʊt/ *noun* (*BrE*) a long narrow boat, used on canals

'narrow gauge *noun* [U] a size of railway/railroad track that is not as wide as the standard track that is used in Britain and the US: *a narrow-gauge railway*

nar·row·ly /ˈnærəʊli; *AmE* -roʊ-/ *adv.* **1** only by a small amount: *The car narrowly missed a cyclist.* ◊ *She narrowly escaped injury.* ◊ *The team lost narrowly.* **2** (*sometimes disapproving*) in a way that is limited: *a narrowly defined task* ◊ *a narrowly specialized education* **3** closely; carefully: *She looked at him narrowly.*

,narrow-'minded *adj.* (*disapproving*) not willing to listen to new ideas or to the opinions of others: *a narrow-minded attitude* ◊ *a narrow-minded nationalist* **OPP** BROAD-MINDED, OPEN-MINDED ► **,narrow-'mindedness** *noun* [U]

nar·rows /ˈnærəʊz; *AmE* -roʊz/ *noun* [pl.] a narrow channel that connects two larger areas of water

nar·whal /ˈnɑːwəl; *AmE* ˈnɑːrwɑːl/ *noun* a small white

aɪ	aʊ	eɪ	əʊ	oʊ	ɔɪ	ɪə	eə	ʊə	j	w
my	now	say	go	go	boy	near	hair	pure	yes	wet
			(BrE)	(AmE)						

WHALE from the Arctic region. The male narwhal has a long TUSK (= outer tooth).

NASA /'næsə/ abbr. National Aeronautics and Space Administration. NASA is a US government organization that carries out research into space and organizes space travel.

nasal /'neɪzl/ adj. **1** connected with the nose: *the nasal passages* ◊ *a nasal spray* **2** produced partly through the nose: *a nasal voice* ◊ *(phonetics) nasal consonants*

nas·cent /'næsnt/ adj. (formal) beginning to exist; not yet fully developed

na·stur·tium /nə'stɜːʃəm; AmE -'stɜːrʃ-/ noun a garden plant with round flat leaves and red, orange or yellow flowers that are sometimes eaten in salads

nasty /'nɑːsti; AmE 'næsti/ adj. (**nas·tier, nas·ti·est**) **1** very bad or unpleasant: *a nasty accident* ◊ *The news gave me a nasty shock.* ◊ *I had a nasty feeling that he would follow me.* ◊ *He had a nasty moment when he thought he'd lost his passport.* ◊ *This coffee has a nasty taste.* ◊ *Don't buy that coat—it looks cheap and nasty.* **2** unkind; unpleasant: *to make nasty remarks about sb* ◊ *the nastier side of her character* ◊ *to have a nasty temper* ◊ *Don't be so nasty to your brother.* ◊ *That was a nasty little trick.* ◊ *Life has a nasty habit of repeating itself.* **3** dangerous or serious: *a nasty bend* (= dangerous for cars going fast) ◊ *He had a nasty look in his eye.* ◊ *a nasty injury/cough* **4** offensive; in bad taste: *to have a nasty mind* ◊ *nasty jokes*—see also VIDEO NASTY ▶ **nas·tily** adv.: *'I hate you,' she said nastily.* **nas·ti·ness** noun [U] **IDM** **to get/turn 'nasty 1** to become threatening and violent: *You'd better do what he says or he'll turn nasty.* **2** to become bad or unpleasant: *It looks as though the weather is going to turn nasty again.* **a nasty piece of 'work** (BrE, informal) a person who is unpleasant, unkind or dishonest—more at TASTE n.

natch /nætʃ/ adv. (slang) used to say that sth is obvious or exactly as you would expect [SYN] NATURALLY: *He was wearing the latest T-shirt, natch.*

na·tion /'neɪʃn/ noun **1** [C] a country considered as a group of people with the same language, culture and history, who live in a particular area under one government: *an independent nation* ◊ *the African nations* **2** [sing.] all the people in a country: *The entire nation, it seemed, was watching TV.* ▶ **na·tion·hood** /'neɪʃnhʊd/ noun [U]: *Citizenship is about the sense of nationhood.*

na·tion·al /'næʃnəl/ adj., noun
■ adj. [usually before noun] **1** connected with a particular nation; shared by a whole nation: *national and local newspapers* ◊ *national and international news* ◊ *national and regional politics* ◊ *a national debate/campaign/election* ◊ *These buildings are part of our national heritage.* ◊ *They are afraid of losing their national identity.* **2** owned, controlled or financially supported by the FEDERAL government: *a national airline/museum/theatre*

■ noun (technical) a citizen of a particular country: *Polish nationals living in Germany* ⇨ note at CITIZEN

national 'anthem noun the official song of a nation that is sung on special occasions

national con'vention noun a meeting held by a political party, especially in the US, to choose a candidate to take part in the election for President

the national cur'riculum noun [sing.] (in Britain) a programme of study in all the main subjects that children aged 5 to 16 in state schools must follow

national 'debt noun [usually sing.] the total amount of money that the government of a country owes

the National 'Front noun [sing.+ sing./pl. v.] (in Britain) a small political party with extreme views, especially on issues connected with race

national 'grid noun [sing.] (BrE) the system of power lines that joins the places where electricity is produced, and takes electricity to all parts of the country

the National 'Guard noun [sing.] **1** a small army, often used to protect a political leader **2** the army in each state of the US that can be used by the FEDERAL government if needed

the National 'Health Service noun [sing.] (abbr. NHS) the public health service in Britain that provides medical care and is paid for by taxes: *I got my glasses on the National Health (Service).*

National In'surance noun [U] (abbr. NI) (in Britain) a system of payments that have to be made by employers and employees to provide help for people who are sick, old or unemployed

na·tion·al·ism /'næʃnəlɪzəm/ noun [U] **1** the desire by a group of people who share the same race, culture, language, etc. to form an independent country: *Scottish nationalism* **2** (sometimes disapproving) a feeling of love for and pride in your country; a feeling that your country is better than any other

na·tion·al·ist /'næʃnəlɪst/ noun **1** a person who wants their country to become independent: *Scottish nationalists* **2** (sometimes disapproving) a person who has a great love for and pride in their country; a person who has a feeling that their country is better than any other ▶ **na·tion·al·ist** adj.: *nationalist demands/sentiments*

na·tion·al·is·tic /ˌnæʃnə'lɪstɪk/ adj. (usually disapproving) having very strong feelings of love for and pride in your country, so that you think that it is better than any other

na·tion·al·ity /ˌnæʃə'næləti/ noun (pl. -ies) **1** [U, C] the legal right of belonging to a particular nation: *to take/have/hold French nationality* ◊ *All applicants will be considered regardless of age, sex, religion or nationality.* ◊ *The college attracts students of all nationalities.* ◊ *She has dual nationality* (= is a citizen of two countries). **2** [C] a group of people with the same language, culture and history who form part of a political nation: *Kazakhstan alone contains more than a hundred nationalities.*

na·tion·al·ize (BrE also **-ise**) /'næʃnəlaɪz/ verb [VN] to put an industry or a company under the control of the government, which becomes its owner: *The government announced plans to nationalize the public transport system.* ◊ *nationalized industries* [OPP] DENATIONALIZE, PRIVATIZE ▶ **na·tion·al·iza·tion, -isa·tion** /ˌnæʃnəlaɪ'zeɪʃn; AmE -ələ'z-/ noun [U, C]

na·tion·al·ly /'næʃnəli/ adv. relating to a country as a whole; relating to a particular country: *The programme was broadcast nationally.* ◊ *Meetings were held locally and nationally.* ◊ *He's a talented athlete who competes nationally and internationally.*

national 'park noun an area of land that is protected by the government for people to visit because of its natural beauty and historical or scientific interest

national 'service noun [U] the system in some countries in which young people have to do military training for a period of time [SYN] MILITARY SERVICE: *to do your national service*

nation 'state noun a group of people with the same culture, language, etc. who have formed an independent country

N

na·tion·wide /ˌneɪʃn'waɪd/ *adj.* happening or existing in all parts of a particular country: *a nationwide campaign* ▶ **na·tion·wide** *adv.*: *The company has over 500 stores nationwide.*

na·tive /'neɪtɪv/ *adj., noun*
■ *adj.* **1** [only before noun] connected with the place where you were born and lived for the first years of your life: *your native land/country/city* ◊ *It is a long time since he has visited his native Poland.* ◊ *Her native language is German.*—see also NATIVE SPEAKER **2** [only before noun] connected with the place where you have always lived or have lived for a long time: *native Berliners/Texans* **3** [only before noun] (sometimes *offensive*) connected with the people who originally lived in a country before other people, especially white people, came there: *native peoples/traditions* ◊ *native art/dance* **4** ~ (**to ...**) (of animals and plants) existing naturally in a place: *the native plants of America* ◊ *The tiger is native to India.* ◊ *When planting trees, stick to native species.* **5** [only before noun] that you have naturally without having to learn it SYN INNATE: *native cunning/wit/intelligence* IDM **go 'native** (often *humorous*) (of a person staying in another country) to try to live and behave like the local people
■ *noun* **1** a person who was born in a particular country or area: *a native of New York/Greece* **2** a person who lives in a particular place, especially sb who has lived there a long time SYN LOCAL: *You can always tell the difference between the tourists and the natives.* ◊ *She speaks Italian like a native.* **3** (*old-fashioned, offensive*) a word used in the past by Europeans to describe a person who lived in a place originally, before white people arrived there: *disputes between early settlers and natives* **4** an animal or a plant that lives or grows naturally in a particular area: *The kangaroo is a native of Australia.*

Native A'merican (also **A,merican 'Indian**) *noun* a member of any of the races of people who were the original people living in America ▶ **Native A'merican** *adj.*: *Native American culture/languages*

native 'speaker *noun* a person who speaks a language as their first language and has not learned it as a foreign language

na·tiv·ity /nə'tɪvəti/ *noun* **1** (**the Nativity**) [sing.] the birth of Jesus Christ, celebrated by Christians at Christmas **2** a picture or a model of the baby Jesus Christ and the place where he was born

na'tivity play *noun* a play about the birth of Jesus Christ, usually performed by children at Christmas

NATO (also **Nato**) /'neɪtəʊ; *AmE* -toʊ/ *abbr.* North Atlantic Treaty Organization. NATO is an organization to which many European countries and the US and Canada belong. They agree to give each other military help if necessary.

nat·ter /'nætə(r)/ *verb* [V] ~ (**away/on**) (**about sth**) (*BrE, informal*) to talk for a long time, especially about unimportant things SYN CHAT ▶ **nat·ter** *noun* [sing.] (*BrE, informal*): *to have a good natter*

natty /'næti/ *adj.* (*old-fashioned, informal*) **1** neat and fashionable: *a natty suit* **2** well designed; clever: *a natty little briefcase* ▶ **nat·tily** *adv.*

nat·ural /'nætʃrəl/ *adj., noun*
■ *adj.*
IN NATURE **1** [only before noun] existing in nature; not made or caused by human beings: *natural phenomena/disasters* ◊ *the natural world* (= of trees, rivers, animals and birds) ◊ *a country's natural resources* (= its coal, oil, forests, etc.) ◊ *wildlife in its natural habitat* ◊ *natural yogurt* (= with no flavour added) ◊ *My hair soon grew back to its natural colour* (= after being dyed). ◊ *The clothes are available in warm natural colours.*—compare SUPERNATURAL
EXPECTED **2** normal; as you would expect: *to die of natural causes* (= not by violence, but normally, of old age) ◊ *He thought social inequality was all part of the natural order of things.* ◊ *She was the natural choice for the job.*—compare UNNATURAL
BEHAVIOUR **3** used to describe behaviour that is part of the character that a person or an animal was born with: *the*

natural agility of a cat ◊ *the natural processes of language learning* ◊ *It's only natural to worry about your children.*
ABILITY **4** [only before noun] having an ability that you were born with: *He's a natural leader.*
RELAXED **5** relaxed and not pretending to be sb/sth different: *It's difficult to look natural when you're feeling nervous.*
PARENTS/CHILDREN **6** [only before noun] (of parents or their children) related by blood: *His natural mother was unable to care for him so he was raised by an aunt.* **7** [only before noun] (*old use* or *formal*) (of a son or daughter) born to parents who are not married SYN ILLEGITIMATE: *She was a natural daughter of King James II.*
BASED ON HUMAN REASON **8** [only before noun] based on human reason alone: *natural justice/law*
IN MUSIC **9** used after the name of a note to show that the note is neither SHARP nor FLAT. The written symbol is (♮): *B natural*—see also picture at MUSIC
■ *noun*
PERSON **1** ~ (**for sth**) a person who is very good at sth without having to learn how to do it, or who is perfectly suited for a particular job: *She took to flying like a natural.* ◊ *He's a natural for the role.*
IN MUSIC **2** a normal musical note, not its SHARP or FLAT form. The written symbol is (♮).

'natural-born *adj.* [only before noun] having a natural ability or skill that you have not had to learn

natural 'childbirth *noun* [U] a method of giving birth to a baby in which a woman chooses not to take drugs and does special exercises to make her relaxed

natural 'gas *noun* [U] gas that is found under the ground or the sea, and that is used as a fuel

natural 'history *noun* [U, C] the study of plants and animals; an account of the plant and animal life of a particular place: *the Natural History Museum* ◊ *He has written a natural history of Scotland.*

nat·ur·al·ism /'nætʃrəlɪzəm/ *noun* [U] **1** a style of art or writing that shows people, things and experiences as they really are **2** (*philosophy*) the theory that everything in the world and life is based on natural causes and laws, and not on spiritual or SUPERNATURAL ones

nat·ur·al·ist /'nætʃrəlɪst/ *noun* a person who studies animals, plants, birds and other living things

nat·ur·al·is·tic /ˌnætʃrə'lɪstɪk/ *adj.* **1** (of artists, writers, etc. or their work) showing things as they appear in the natural world: *a naturalistic painter/style* **2** copying the way things are in the natural world: *to study behaviour in laboratory and naturalistic settings*

nat·ur·al·ize (*BrE* also **-ise**) /'nætʃrəlaɪz/ *verb* [usually passive] **1** [VN] to make sb who was not born in a particular country a citizen of that country: *a naturalized American who was born in Poland* **2** [VN] to introduce a plant or an animal to a country where it is not native: *The grey squirrel is now naturalized in Britain.* **3** [V] (of a plant or an animal) to start growing or living naturally in a country where is it not native: *The grass* ▶ **nat·ur·al·iza·tion, -isa·tion** /ˌnætʃrəlaɪ'zeɪʃn; *AmE* -lə'z-/ *noun* [U]

nat·ur·al·ly /'nætʃrəli/ *adv.* **1** SYN OF COURSE: *Naturally, I get upset when things go wrong.* ◊ *After a while, we naturally started talking about the children.* ◊ *'Did you complain about the noise?' 'Naturally.'* **2** without special help, treatment or action by sb: *naturally occurring chemicals* ◊ *plants that grow naturally in poor soils* **3** as a normal, logical result of sth: *This leads naturally to my next point.* **4** in a way that shows or uses abilities or qualities that a person or an animal is born with: *to be naturally shy/artistic* ◊ *a naturally gifted athlete* **5** in a relaxed and normal way: *Just act naturally.* IDM **come 'naturally (to sb/sth)** if sth comes naturally to you, you are able to do it very easily and very well: *Making money came naturally to him.*

nat·ur·al·ness /'nætʃrəlnəs/ *noun* [U] **1** the state or quality of being like real life: *The naturalness of the dialogue made the book so true to life.* **2** the quality of behaving in a normal, relaxed or innocent way: *Teenagers lose their childhood simplicity and naturalness.*

3 the style or quality of happening in a normal way that you would expect: *the naturalness of her reaction*

natural 'science *noun* [C, U] a science concerned with studying the physical world. Chemistry, biology and physics are all natural sciences.—compare EARTH SCIENCE, LIFE SCIENCES

natural se'lection *noun* [U] the process by which plants, animals, etc. that can adapt to their environment survive and reproduce, while the others disappear

natural 'wastage (*BrE*) (also **at·tri·tion** *AmE, BrE*) *noun* [U] the process of reducing the number of people who are employed by an organization by, for example, not replacing the people who leave their jobs

na·ture /ˈneɪtʃə(r)/ *noun*

PLANTS, ANIMALS | **1** (often **Nature**) [U] all the plants, animals and things that exist in the universe that are not made by people: *the beauties of nature* ◊ *man-made substances not found in nature* ◊ *nature conservation* HELP You cannot use 'the nature' in this meaning: *the beauties of the nature*. It is often better to use another appropriate word, for example **the countryside**, **the scenery** or **wildlife**: *We stopped to admire the scenery.* ◊ *We stopped to admire the nature.*. **2** (often **Nature**) [U] the way that things happen in the physical world when it is not controlled by people: *the forces/laws of nature* ◊ *Just let nature take its course.* ◊ *Her illness was Nature's way of telling her to do less.*—see also MOTHER NATURE

CHARACTER | **3** [C, U] the usual way that a person or an animal behaves that is part of their character: *It's not in his nature to be unkind.* ◊ *She is very sensitive by nature.* ◊ *We appealed to his better nature* (= his kindness).—see also GOOD NATURE, HUMAN NATURE, SECOND NATURE

BASIC QUALITIES | **4** [sing.] the basic qualities of a thing: *the changing nature of society* ◊ *It's difficult to define the exact nature of the problem.* ◊ *My work is very specialized in nature.*

TYPE/KIND | **5** [sing.] a type or kind of sth: *books of a scientific nature* ◊ *Don't worry about things of that nature.*

-NATURED | **6** (in adjectives) having the type of character or quality mentioned: *a good-natured man*

IDM **against 'nature** not natural; not moral: *Murder is a crime against nature.* **(get, go, etc.) back to 'nature** to return to a simple kind of life in the country, away from cities **in the nature of 'sth** similar to sth; a type of sth; in the style of sth: *His speech was in the nature of an apology.* **in the 'nature of things** in the way that things usually happen: *In the nature of things, young people often rebel against their parents.*—more at CALL *n.*, FORCE *n.*

'nature reserve *noun* an area of land where the animals and plants are protected

'nature trail *noun* a path through countryside which you can follow in order to see the interesting plants and animals that are found there

na·tur·ism /ˈneɪtʃərɪzəm/ *noun* [U] (*especially BrE*) = NUDISM

na·tur·ist /ˈneɪtʃərɪst/ *noun* (*especially BrE*) = NUDIST

naught *noun* = NOUGHT

naughty /ˈnɔːti/ *adj.* (**naugh·tier**, **naugh·ti·est**) **1** (*especially BrE*) (especially of children) behaving badly; not willing to obey: *a naughty boy/girl* ◊ (*humorous*) *I'm being very naughty—I've ordered champagne!* **2** (*informal, often humorous*) slightly rude; connected with sex: *a naughty joke/word* ▶ **naugh·tily** *adv.* **naugh·ti·ness** *noun* [U]

nau·sea /ˈnɔːziə; ˈnɔːsiə/ *noun* [U] the feeling that you have when you want to VOMIT, for example because you are ill/sick or are disgusted by sth: *A wave of nausea swept over her.* ◊ *Nausea and vomiting are common symptoms.*—see also AD NAUSEAM

nau·se·ate /ˈnɔːzieɪt; ˈnɔːsieɪt/ *verb* [VN] **1** to make sb feel that they want to VOMIT: *The smell of meat nauseates me.* **2** to make sb feel disgusted: *I was nauseated by the violence in the movie.* ▶ **nau·se·at·ing** *adj.*: *a nauseating smell* ◊ *his nauseating behaviour* **nau·se·at·ing·ly** *adv.*

nau·se·ous /ˈnɔːziəs; ˈnɔːsiəs; *AmE* ˈnɔːʃəs/ *adj.* **1** feeling as if you want to VOMIT: *She felt dizzy and nauseous.*

2 making you feel as if you want to VOMIT: *a nauseous smell*

naut·ical /ˈnɔːtɪkl/ *adj.* connected with ships, sailors and sailing: *nautical terms*

nautical 'mile (also **'sea mile**) *noun* a unit for measuring distance at sea; 1852 metres

naval /ˈneɪvl/ *adj.* connected with the navy of a country: *a naval base/officer/battle*

nave /neɪv/ *noun* the long central part of a church where most of the seats are—compare TRANSEPT

navel /ˈneɪvl/ (also *informal* **'belly button**) *noun* the small hollow part or lump in the middle of the stomach where the UMBILICAL CORD was cut at birth—picture at BODY

nav·ig·able /ˈnævɪgəbl/ *adj.* (of rivers, etc.) wide and deep enough for ships and boats to sail on ▶ **nav·ig·abil·ity** /ˌnævɪgəˈbɪləti/ *noun* [U]

navi·gate /ˈnævɪgeɪt/ *verb* **1** to find your position or the position of your ship, plane, car etc. and the direction you need to go in, for example by using a map: [V] *to navigate by the stars* ◊ *I'll drive, and you can navigate.* ◊ [VN] *How do you navigate your way through a forest?* **2** [VN] (*written*) to sail along, over or through a sea, river etc: *The river became too narrow and shallow to navigate.* **3** [VN] to find the right way to deal with a difficult or complicated situation: *We next had to navigate a complex network of committees.*

navi·ga·tion /ˌnævɪˈgeɪʃn/ *noun* [U] **1** the skill or the process of planning a route for a ship or other vehicle and taking it there: *navigation aids/lights/systems* ◊ *an expert in navigation* **2** the movement of ships or aircraft: *the right of navigation through international waters* ▶ **nav·iga·tion·al** *adj.*: *navigational aids*

navi·ga·tor /ˈnævɪgeɪtə(r)/ *noun* a person who navigates, for example on a ship or an aircraft

navvy /ˈnævi/ *noun* (*pl.* -**ies**) (*BrE*) a person employed to do hard physical work, especially building roads, etc.

navy /ˈneɪvi/ *noun* (*pl.* -**ies**) **1** [C+sing./pl. *v.*] the part of a country's armed forces that fights at sea, and the ships that it uses: *the British and German navies* ◊ *He's joined the navy/the Navy.* ◊ *an officer in the navy/the Navy* ◊ *The Navy is/are considering buying six new warships.*—see also NAVAL **2** [U] = NAVY BLUE

'navy bean *noun* (*AmE*) = HARICOT

navy 'blue (also **navy**) *adj.* very dark blue in colour: *a navy blue suit* ▶ **navy 'blue** (also **navy**) *noun* [U]: *She was dressed in navy blue.*

nay /neɪ/ *adv.* **1** (*old-fashioned*) used to emphasize sth you have just said by introducing a stronger word or phrase: *Such a policy is difficult, nay impossible.* **2** (*old use* or *dialect*) no—compare YEA

Nazi /ˈnɑːtsi/ *noun* **1** a member of the National Socialist party which controlled Germany from 1933 to 1945 **2** (*disapproving*) a person who uses their power in a cruel way; a person with extreme and unreasonable views about race ▶ **Nazi** *adj.* **Naz·ism** /ˈnɑːtsɪzəm/ *noun* [U]

NB (*BrE*) (also **N.B.** *AmE, BrE*) /ˌen ˈbiː/ *abbr.* used in writing to make sb take notice of a particular piece of information that is important (from Latin 'nota bene'): *NB The office will be closed from 1 July.*

NBC /ˌen biː ˈsiː/ *abbr.* National Broadcasting Company (an American company that produces television and radio programmes): *NBC News*

NCO /ˌen si: ˈəʊ; *AmE* ˈoʊ/ *abbr.* non-commissioned officer (a soldier who has a rank such as CORPORAL or SERGEANT)

NE *abbr.* north-east; north-eastern: *NE England*

Ne·an·der·thal (also **ne·an·der·thal**) /niˈændətɑːl; *AmE* -dərt-/ *adj.* **1** used to describe a type of human being who used stone tools and lived in Europe during the early period of human history **2** (*disapproving*) very old-fashioned and not wanting any change: *neanderthal attitudes* **3** (*disapproving*) (of a man) unpleasant, rude and not behaving in a socially acceptable way ▶ **Ne·an·der·thal** *noun*

æ	ɑː	e	ɜː	ə	ɪ	iː	i	ɒ	ɔː	ʌ	ʊ	u:
cat	father	ten	bird	about	sit	see	many	got	saw	cup	put	actual	too
								(BrE)				

N

neap tide /ˈniːp taɪd/ (also **neap**) *noun* a TIDE in the sea in which there is only a very small difference between the level of the water at HIGH TIDE and that at LOW TIDE

near /nɪə(r); *AmE* nɪr/ *adj., adv., prep., verb*

■ *adj.* (**near·er, near·est**) HELP In senses 1 to 4 **near** and **nearer** do not usually go before a noun; **nearest** can go either before or after a noun. **1** a short distance away SYN CLOSE: *His house is very near.* ◇ *Where's the nearest bank?* ⇨ note at NEXT **2** a short time away in the future: *The conflict is unlikely to be resolved in the near future* (= very soon). **3** coming next after sb/sth: *She has a 12-point lead over her nearest rival.* **4** (usually *near*) similar; most similar: *He was the nearest thing to* (= the person most like) *a father she had ever had.*—see also O.N.O. **5** [only before noun] (no comparative or superlative) close to being sb/sth: *The election proved to be a near disaster for the party.* ◇ *a near impossibility/certainty* **6** ~ **relative/relation** used to describe a close family connection: *Only the nearest relatives were present at the funeral.* ▶ **near·ness** *noun* [U]: *the nearness of death* IDM **your ˌnearest and ˈdearest** (*informal*) your close family and friends **a ˌnear ˈthing** a situation in which you are successful, but which could also have ended badly: *Phew! That was a near thing! It could have been a disaster.* ◇ *We won in the end but it was a near thing.* **to the nearest ...** followed by a number when counting or measuring approximately: *We calculated the cost to the nearest 50 dollars.*

■ *adv.* (**near·er, near·est**) **1** at a short distance away: *A bomb exploded somewhere near.* ◇ *She took a step nearer.* **2** a short time away in the future: *The exams are drawing near.* **3** (especially in compounds) almost: *a near-perfect performance* ◇ *I'm as near certain as can be.* IDM **as near as** as accurately as: *There were about 3000 people there, as near as I could judge.* **as ˌnear as ˈdamn it/ ˈdammit** (*BrE, spoken*) used to say that an amount is so nearly correct that the difference does not matter: *It will cost £350, or as near as dammit.* **near eˈnough** (*BrE, spoken*) used to say that sth is so nearly true that the difference does not matter: *We've been here twenty years, near enough.* **not anywhere near/nowhere near** far from; not at all: *The job doesn't pay anywhere near enough for me.* **so ˌnear and ˌyet so ˈfar** used to comment on sth that was almost successful but in fact failed—more at PRETTY *adv.*

■ *prep.* (also **near to, near·er (to), near·est (to)**) HELP **Near to** is not usually used before the name of a place, person, festival, etc. **1** at a short distance away from sb/sth: *Do you live near here?* ◇ *Go and sit nearer (to) the fire.* ⇨ note at NEXT **2** a short period of time from sth: *My birthday is very near Christmas.* ◇ *I'll think about it nearer (to) the time* (= when it is just going to happen). **3** used before a number to mean 'approximately', 'just below or above': *Share prices are near their record high of last year.* ◇ *Profits fell from $11 million to nearer $8 million.* **4** similar to sb/sth in quality, size, etc: *Nobody else comes near her in intellect.* ◇ *He's nearer 70 than 60.* ◇ *This colour is nearest (to) the original.* **5** ~ **(doing)** sth close to a particular state: *a state near (to) death* ◇ *She was near to tears* (= almost crying). ◇ *We came near to being killed.* IDM see HAND *n.*, HEART, MARK *n.*

■ *verb* (rather *formal*) to come close to sth in time or space SYN APPROACH [VN] *The project is nearing completion.* ◇ *She was nearing the end of her life.* ◇ *We neared the top of the hill.* ◇ [V] *As Christmas neared, the children became more and more excited.*

WHICH WORD?
near / close

The adjectives **near** and **close** are often the same in meaning, but in some phrases only one of them may be used: *the near future* ◇ *a near neighbour* ◇ *a near miss* ◇ *a close contest* ◇ *a close encounter* ◇ *a close call*. **Close** is more often used to describe a relationship between people: *a close friend* ◇ *close family* ◇ *close links*. You do not usually use **near** in this way.

---

near·by /ˌnɪəˈbaɪ; *AmE* ˌnɪrˈbaɪ/ *adj., adv.*
■ *adj.* [usually before noun] near in position; not far away: *Her mother lived in a nearby town.* ◇ *There were complaints from nearby residents.*
■ *adv.* a short distance from sb/sth; not far away: *They live nearby.* ◇ *The car is parked nearby.*

the ˌNear ˈEast *noun* [sing.] = THE MIDDLE EAST

near·ly /ˈnɪəli; *AmE* ˈnɪrli/ *adv.* almost; not quite; not completely: *The bottle's nearly empty.* ◇ *I've worked here for nearly two years.* ◇ *It's nearly time to leave.* ◇ *The audience were nearly all men.* ◇ *He's nearly as tall as you are.* ◇ *They're nearly always late.* ◇ *She very nearly died.* ⇨ note at ALMOST IDM **not ˈnearly** much less than; not at all: *It's not nearly as hot as last year.* ◇ *There isn't nearly enough time to get there now.*—more at PRETTY *adv.*

ˌnear ˈmiss *noun* **1** a situation when a serious accident or a disaster very nearly happens **2** a bomb or a shot that nearly hits what it is aimed at but misses it: (*figurative*) *He should have won the match—it was a near miss.*—see also CLOSE/NEAR THING at THING

near·side /ˈnɪəsaɪd; *AmE* ˈnɪrs-/ *adj.* [only before noun] (*BrE*) (for a driver) on the side that is nearest the edge of the road: *the car's nearside doors* ◇ *Keep to the nearside lane.* ▶ **the near·side** *noun* [sing.]: *The driver lost control and veered to the nearside.*—compare OFFSIDE

ˌnear-ˈsighted *adj.* (especially *AmE*) = SHORT-SIGHTED

neat /niːt/ *adj.* (**neat·er, neat·est**) **1** tidy and in order; carefully done or arranged: *a neat desk* ◇ *neat handwriting* ◇ *neat rows of books* ◇ *She was wearing a neat black suit.* ◇ *They sat in their neat and tidy kitchen.* **2** (of people) liking to keep things tidy and in order; looking tidy or doing things in a tidy way: *Try and be neater!* **3** small, with a pleasing shape or appearance: *her neat figure* **4** simple but clever: *a neat explanation/idea/trick* ◇ *a neat solution to the problem* ◇ *People don't often fit into neat categories.* **5** (*AmE, informal*) good; excellent: *It's a really neat movie.* ◇ *We had a great time—it was pretty neat.* **6** (*BrE*) (*AmE* **straight**) (especially of alcoholic drinks) not mixed with water or anything else: *neat whisky* ◇ *The weedkiller was applied to the lawn neat.* ▶ **neat·ly** *adv.*: *neatly folded clothes* ◇ *The box fitted neatly into the drawer.* ◇ *She summarized her plan very neatly.* **neat·ness** *noun* [U]

neat·en /ˈniːtn/ *verb* [VN] (*rare*) to make sth tidy

neb·ula /ˈnebjələ/ *noun* (*pl.* **nebu·lae** /-liː/) (*astronomy*) a mass of dust or gas that can be seen in the night sky, often appearing very bright; a bright area in the night sky caused by a large cloud of stars that are far away

nebu·lous /ˈnebjələs/ *adj.* (*formal*) not clear SYN VAGUE: *a nebulous idea/concept/description*

ne·ces·sar·ies /ˈnesəsəriz; *AmE* ˈnesəseriz/ *noun* [pl.] (*old-fashioned*) the things that you need, especially in order to live

ne·ces·sar·ily /ˌnesəˈserəli; *BrE* also ˈnesəsərəli/ *adv.* used to say that sth cannot be avoided: *The number of places available is necessarily limited.* IDM **ˌnot ˈneces·sarily** used to say that sth is possibly true but not definitely or always true: *The more expensive articles are not necessarily better.* ◇ *Biggest doesn't necessarily mean best.* ◇ (*spoken*) 'We're going to lose.' 'Not necessarily.'

ne·ces·sary /ˈnesəsəri; *AmE* -seri/ *adj.* **1** ~ **(for sb/sth) (to do sth)** that is needed for a purpose or a reason SYN ESSENTIAL: *It may be necessary to buy a new one.* ◇ *It doesn't seem necessary for us to meet.* ◇ *Only use your car when absolutely necessary.* ◇ *If necessary, you can contact me at home.* ◇ *I'll make the necessary arrangements.* **2** [only before noun] (*written*) that must exist or happen and cannot be avoided: *This is a necessary consequence of progress.* IDM **a ˌnecessary ˈevil** a thing that is bad or that you do not like but which you must accept for a particular reason

ne·ces·si·tate /nəˈsesɪteɪt/ *verb* (*formal*) to make sth necessary: [VN] *Recent financial scandals have necessitated changes in parliamentary procedures.* ◇ [V-ing] *Increased traffic necessitated widening the road.* ◇ [VN-ing] *His new job necessitated him/his getting up at six.*

ne·ces·sity /nəˈsesəti/ *noun* **1** [U] ~ **(for sth)** | ~ **(of sth/**

---

aɪ	aʊ	eɪ	əʊ	oʊ	ɔɪ	ɪə	eə	ʊə	j	w
my	now	say	go	go	boy	near	hair	pure	yes	wet
			(BrE)	(AmE)						

of doing sth)|~ (to do sth) the fact that sth must happen or be done; the need for sth: *We recognize the necessity for a written agreement.* ◊ *We were discussing the necessity of employing more staff.* ◊ *There had never been any necessity for her to go out to work.* ◊ *This is,* **of necessity,** *a brief and incomplete account.* **2** [C] a thing that you must have and cannot manage without: *Many people cannot even afford* **basic necessities** *such as food and clothing.* ◊ *Air-conditioning is an absolute necessity in this climate.* **3** [C, usually sing.] a situation that must happen and that cannot be avoided: *Living in London he felt, was an unfortunate necessity.* **IDM** see VIRTUE

neck /nek/ *noun, verb*
■ *noun* **1** [C] the part of the body between the head and the shoulders: *He tied a scarf around his neck.* ◊ *Giraffes have very long necks.* ◊ *She* **craned** (= stretched) *her neck to get a better view.* ◊ *He broke his neck in the fall.* ◊ *Somebody's going to* **break their neck** (= injure themselves) *on these steps.*—picture at BODY **2** [C] the part of a piece of clothing that fits around the neck: *What neck size do you take?*—see also CREW NECK, POLO NECK, TURTLENECK, V-NECK **3** (-**necked**) (in adjectives) having the type of neck mentioned: *a round-necked sweater*—see also OPEN-NECKED, STIFF-NECKED **4** [C] ~ (**of sth**) a long narrow part of sth: *the neck of a bottle* ◊ *a neck of land* **5** [U] ~ (**of sth**) the neck of an animal, cooked and eaten: *neck of lamb*—see also BOTTLENECK, REDNECK, ROUGHNECK **IDM** **be up to your neck in sth** to have a lot of sth to deal with: *We're up to our neck in debt.* ◊ *He's in it* (= trouble) *up to his neck.* **by a ˈneck** if a person or an animal wins a race **by a neck,** they win it by a short distance ˌ**get it in the ˈneck** (*BrE, informal*) to be shouted at or punished because of sth that you have done ˌ**neck and ˈneck (with sb/sth)** (also ˌ**nip and ˈtuck (with sb)** especially in *AmE*) level with sb in a race or competition ˌ**neck of the ˈwoods** (*informal*) a particular place or area: *He's from your neck of the woods* (= the area where you live).—more at BLOCK *n.,* BRASS, BREATHE, MILLSTONE, PAIN *n.,* RISK *v.,* SAVE *v.,* SCRUFF, STICK *v.,* WRING
■ *verb* [V] (usually **be necking**) (*old-fashioned, informal*) when two people **are necking,** they are kissing each other in a sexual way

neck·lace /ˈnekləs/ *noun, verb*
■ *noun* a piece of jewellery consisting of a chain, string of BEADS, etc. worn around the neck: *a diamond necklace*
■ *verb* [VN] to kill sb by putting a burning car tyre around their neck ▶ **neck·lacing** *noun* [U]

neck·line /ˈneklaɪn/ *noun* the edge of a piece of clothing, especially a woman's, which fits around or below the neck: *a dress with a low/round/plunging neckline*

neck·tie /ˈnektaɪ/ *noun* (*old-fashioned* or *AmE*) = TIE

necro·man·cer /ˈnekrəʊmænsə(r)*; AmE* ˈnekroʊ-/ *noun* a person who claims to communicate by magic with people who are dead

necro·mancy /ˈnekrəʊmænsi*; AmE* ˈnekroʊ-/ *noun* [U] **1** the practice of claiming to communicate by magic with the dead in order to learn about the future **2** the use of magic powers, especially evil ones

necro·philia /ˌnekrəˈfɪliə/ *noun* [U] sexual interest in dead bodies ▶ **necro·phil·iac** *noun*

ne·crop·olis /nəˈkrɒpəlɪs*; AmE* -ˈkrɑːp-/ *noun* (*pl.* ne·crop·olises /-lɪsɪz/) a place where dead people are buried, especially a large ancient one

nec·tar /ˈnektə(r)/ *noun* [U] **1** a sweet liquid that is produced by flowers and collected by bees for making HONEY **2** the thick juice of some fruits as a drink: *apricot/peach nectar*

nec·tar·ine /ˈnektəriːn/ *noun* a round red and yellow fruit, like a PEACH with smooth skin

née /neɪ/ *adj.* (from *French*) a word used after a married woman's name to introduce the family name that she had when she was born: *Jane Smith, née Brown*

need /niːd/ *verb, modal verb, noun*
■ *verb* **1** to require sth/sb because they are essential or very important, not just because you would like to have them: [VN] *Do you need any help?* ◊ *It's here if you need it.* ◊ *Don't go—I might need you.* ◊ *They* **badly needed** *a change.* ◊ *Food aid is urgently needed.* ◊ *What do you need*

your own computer for? You can use ours.* ◊ (*spoken*) *I don't need your comments, thank you.* ◊ [Vtoinf] *I need to get some sleep.* ◊ *He needs to win this game to stay in the match.* ◊ *You don't need to leave yet, do you?* ◊ [V-ing, Vtoinf] *This shirt needs washing.* ◊ *This shirt needs to be washed.* **2** [Vtoinf] used to show what you should or have to do: *All you need to do is complete this form.* ◊ *I didn't need to go to the bank after all—Mary lent me the money.* ⇨ note at MODAL **IDM** **need (to have) your ˈhead examined** (*informal*) to be crazy
■ *modal verb* (*negative* **need not,** *short form* **needn't** /ˈniːdnt/) (*BrE*) ~ (**not**) **do sth** | ~ (**not**) **have done sth** used to state that sth is/was not necessary or that only very little is/was necessary; used to ask if sth is/was necessary: *You needn't finish that work today.* ◊ *You needn't have hurried* (= it was not necessary for you to hurry, but you did). ◊ *I* **need hardly** *tell you* (= you must already know) *that the work is dangerous.* ◊ *If she wants anything, she* **need only** *ask.* ◊ *All you need bring are sheets.* ◊ *Need you have paid so much?*
■ *noun* **1** [sing., U] ~ (**for sth**) | ~ (**for sb/sth**) **to do sth** a situation when sth is necessary or must be done: *to satisfy/meet/identify a need* ◊ *There is an urgent need for qualified teachers.* ◊ *There is* **no need** *for you to get up early tomorrow.* ◊ *I* **had no need** *to open the letter—I knew what it would say.* ◊ *The house is* **in need** *of a thorough clean.* ◊ *We will contact you again if the* **need arises.** ◊ (*spoken*) *There's* **no need** *to cry* (= stop crying). **2** [C, U] a strong feeling that you want sb/sth or must have sth: *to fulfil an emotional need* ◊ *She felt the need to talk to someone.* ◊ *I'm* **in need** *of some fresh air.* ◊ *She had* **no more need** *of me.* **3** [C, usually pl.] the things that sb requires in order to live in a comfortable way or achieve what they want: *financial/physical needs* ◊ *a programme to suit your individual needs* ◊ *to meet children's special educational needs* **4** [U] the state of not having enough food, money or support: *The charity aims to provide assistance to people* **in need.** ◊ *He helped me in my* **hour of need.**—see also NEEDY **IDM** **if need ˈbe** if necessary: *There's always food in the freezer if need be.*—more at CRYING *adj.,* FRIEND

GRAMMAR POINT
need

In *BrE* there are two separate verbs **need.**

Need as a main verb has the question form **do you need?,** the negative **you don't need** and the past forms **needed, did you need?** and **didn't need.** It has two meanings: 1. to require something or to think that something is necessary: *Do you need any help?* ◊ *I needed to get some sleep.* 2. to have to or to be obliged to do sth: *Will we need to show our passports?*

Need as a modal verb has **need** for all forms of the present tense, **need you?** as the question form and **need not (needn't)** as the negative. The past is **need have, needn't have.** It is used to say that something is or is not necessary: *Need I pay the whole amount now?*

In *AmE* only the main verb is used. This leads to some important differences in the use and meaning of **need** in British and American English.

In *AmE* it is more common for **need** to be used to speak about what is necessary, rather than about what you must do: *I don't need to go home yet — it's still early.* (*BrE* and *AmE* = it isn't necessary) ◊ *You don't need to go home yet — we never go to bed before midnight.* (*BrE* = you don't have to.)

The difference is even more noticeable in the past tenses: *He* **didn't need to** *go to hospital, but he went just to reassure himself.* (*AmE*) ◊ *He* **needn't have** *gone to hospital, but he went just to reassure himself.* (*BrE* = he did something that wasn't necessary.) ◊ *He* **didn't need to** *go to hospital after all — he only had a few bruises.* (*BrE* = he didn't go.)

---

need·ful /ˈniːdfl/ *adj.* (*old-fashioned*) necessary

nee·dle /ˈniːdl/ *noun, verb*

N

■ *noun* [C]

FOR SEWING | **1** a small thin piece of steel that you use for sewing, with a point at one end and a hole for the thread at the other: *a **needle and thread** ◊ the eye* (= hole) *of a needle*—see also PINS AND NEEDLES—picture at SEW

FOR KNITTING | **2** a long thin piece of plastic or metal with a point at one end that you use for knitting. You usually use two together: *knitting needles*

FOR DRUGS | **3** a very thin, pointed piece of steel used on the end of a SYRINGE for putting a drug into sb's body, or for taking blood out of it: *a hypodermic needle*

ON INSTRUMENT | **4** a thin piece of metal on a scientific instrument that moves to point to the correct measurement or direction: *The compass needle was pointing north.*

ON PINE TREE | **5** [usually pl.] the thin, hard pointed leaf of a PINE tree

ON RECORD PLAYER | **6** the very small pointed piece of metal that touches a record that is being played in order to produce the sound SYN STYLUS

IDM **a needle in a 'haystack** a thing that is almost impossible to find: *Searching for one man in this city is like looking for a needle in a haystack.*

■ *verb* [VN] (*informal*) to deliberately annoy sb, especially by criticizing them continuously: *Don't let her needle you.*

need·less /ˈniːdləs/ *adj.* **needless** death or suffering is not necessary because it could have been avoided: *needless anxiety/suffering ◊ Banning smoking would save needless deaths.* ▶ **need·less·ly** *adv.*: *Many soldiers died needlessly. ◊ The process was needlessly slow.* IDM **,needless to 'say** used to emphasize that the information you are giving is obvious: *The problem, needless to say, is the cost involved.*

needle·woman /ˈniːdlwʊmən/ *noun* (*pl.* **-women** /-wɪmɪn/) a woman who sews well

needle·work /ˈniːdlwɜːk; *AmE* -wɜːrk/ *noun* [U] things that are sewn by hand, especially for decoration; the activity of making things by sewing

needn't /ˈniːdnt/ *short form of* NEED NOT

needy /ˈniːdi/ *adj.* (**need·ier, needi·est**) **1** (of people) not having enough money, food, clothes, etc. **2** (**the needy**) *noun* [pl.] people who do not have enough money, food, etc: *help for the homeless and the needy*

neep /niːp/ *noun* (*ScotE, informal*) a SWEDE (= a large round yellow root vegetable): *neeps and tatties*

ne'er-do-well /ˈneə duː wel; *AmE* ˈner/ *noun* (*old-fashioned*) a useless or lazy person

ne·fari·ous /nɪˈfeəriəs; *AmE* -ˈfer-/ *adj.* (*rare, formal*) wicked; not moral: *nefarious activities*

neg. *abbr.* NEGATIVE

neg·ate /nɪˈɡeɪt/ *verb* [VN] (*formal*) **1** to stop sth from having any effect SYN NULLIFY: *Alcohol negates the effects of the drug.* **2** to state that sth does not exist

neg·ation /nɪˈɡeɪʃn/ *noun* (*formal*) **1** [C usually sing, U] the exact opposite of sth; the act of causing sth not to exist or to become its opposite: *This political system was the negation of democracy.* **2** [U] disagreement or refusal: *She shook her head in negation.*

nega·tive /ˈneɡətɪv/ *adj., noun, verb*

■ *adj.*

BAD | **1** bad or harmful: *The crisis had a **negative effect on** trade. ◊ The whole experience was definitely more positive than negative.* OPP POSITIVE

NOT HOPEFUL | **2** considering only the bad side of sth/sb; lacking enthusiasm or hope: *Scientists have a fairly **nega-tive attitude** to the theory. ◊ 'He probably won't show up.' 'Don't be so negative.'* OPP POSITIVE

NO | **3** expressing the answer 'no': *His response was negative. ◊ They received a negative reply.* OPP AFFIRMATIVE

GRAMMAR | **4** containing a word such as 'no', 'not', 'never', etc: *a negative form/sentence*

SCIENTIFIC TEST | **5** (*abbr.* **neg.**) not showing any evidence of a particular substance or medical condition: *Her pregnancy test was negative.* OPP POSITIVE

ELECTRICITY | **6** (*technical*) containing or producing the type

of electricity that is carried by an ELECTRON: *a negative charge/current ◊ the negative terminal of a battery* OPP POSITIVE

NUMBER/QUANTITY | **7** less than zero: *a negative trade balance* OPP POSITIVE

▶ **nega·tive·ly** *adv.*: *to react negatively to stress ◊ to answer/respond negatively ◊ negatively charged electrons*

■ *noun*

NO | **1** a word or statement that means 'no'; a refusal or DENIAL: (*formal*) *She answered **in the negative** (= said 'no').* OPP AFFIRMATIVE

PHOTOGRAPHIC FILM | **2** a developed photographic film showing the dark areas of an actual scene as light and light areas as dark—compare POSITIVE

IN SCIENTIFIC TEST | **3** the result of a test or an experiment that shows that a substance or condition is not present: *The percentage of false negatives generated by the cancer test is of great concern.* OPP POSITIVE

■ *verb* [VN] (*formal*) **1** to refuse to agree to a proposal or a request **2** to prove that sth is not true

negative 'equity *noun* [U] the situation in which the value of sb's house is less than the amount of money that is still owed to a MORTGAGE company, such as a bank

nega·tiv·ity /ˌneɡəˈtɪvəti/ *noun* (*formal*) a tendency to consider only the bad side of sth/sb; a lack of enthusiasm or hope: *feelings of negativity*

neg·lect /nɪˈɡlekt/ *verb, noun*

■ *verb* **1** [VN] to fail to take care of sb/sth: *She denies neglecting her baby. ◊ The buildings had been neglected for years.* **2** [VN] to not give enough attention to sth: *Dance has been neglected by television. ◊ She has neglected her studies.* **3** [Vto inf] (*formal*) to fail or forget to do sth that you ought to do: *You neglected to mention the name of your previous employer.*—see also NEGLIGENCE

■ *noun* [U] **~ (of sth/sb)** the fact of not giving enough care or attention to sth/sb; the state of not receiving enough care or attention: *The law imposed penalties for the neglect of children. ◊ The buildings are crumbling from years of neglect. ◊ The place smelled of decay and neglect.*

neg·lect·ed /nɪˈɡlektɪd/ *adj.* not receiving enough care or attention: *neglected children ◊ a neglected area of research*

neg·lect·ful /nɪˈɡlektfl/ *adj.* **~ (of sth/sb)** (*formal*) not giving enough care or attention to sb/sth: *neglectful parents ◊ She became neglectful of her appearance.*

neg·ligee (also **neg·ligée**) /ˈneɡliʒeɪ; *AmE* ˌneɡliˈʒeɪ/ *noun* a woman's DRESSING GOWN made of very thin fabric

neg·li·gence /ˈneɡlɪdʒəns/ *noun* [U] (*formal or law*) the failure to give sb/sth enough care or attention: *The accident was caused by negligence on the part of the driver. ◊ The doctor was sued for medical negligence.*

neg·li·gent /ˈneɡlɪdʒənt/ *adj.* **1** (*formal or law*) failing to give sb/sth enough care or attention, especially when this has serious results: *The school had been negligent in not informing the child's parents about the incident. ◊ grossly negligent* **2** (*literary*) (of a person or their manner) relaxed; not formal or awkward SYN NONCHALANT: *He waved his hand in a negligent gesture.* ▶ **neg·li·gent·ly** *adv.*: *The defendant drove negligently and hit a lamp post. ◊ She was leaning negligently against the wall.*

neg·li·gible /ˈneɡlɪdʒəbl/ *adj.* of very little importance or size and not worth considering SYN INSIGNIFICANT: *The cost was negligible. ◊ a negligible amount*

ne·go·ti·able /nɪˈɡəʊʃiəbl; *AmE* -ˈɡoʊ-/ *adj.* **1** that you can discuss or change before you make an agreement or a decision: *The terms of employment are negotiable. ◊ The price was not negotiable.* **2** (*business*) that you can exchange for money or give to another person in exchange for money OPP NON-NEGOTIABLE

ne·go·ti·ate /nɪˈɡəʊʃieɪt; *AmE* -ˈɡoʊ-/ *verb* **1** [V] **~ (with sb)** **(for/about sth)** to try to reach an agreement by formal discussion: *The government will not negotiate with terrorists. ◊ We have been negotiating for more pay. ◊ a strong negotiating position ◊ negotiating skills* **2** [VN] to arrange or agree sth by formal discussion: *to negotiate a deal/contract/treaty/settlement ◊ We successfully negotiated the release of the hostages.* **3** [VN] to successfully get

N

over or past a difficult part on a path or route: *The climbers had to negotiate a steep rock face.*

the ne·'gotiating table *noun* [sing.] (used mainly in newspapers) a formal discussion to try and reach an agreement: *We want to get all the parties back to the negotiating table.*

ne·go·ti·ation /nɪˌɡəʊʃi'eɪʃn; *AmE* -ˌɡoʊʃi-/ *noun* [C, often pl., U] formal discussion between people who are trying to reach an agreement: *peace / trade / wage negoti-ations* ◇ *They begin another **round of negotiations** today.* ◇ *to enter into / open / conduct negotiations with sb* ◇ *The rent is a **matter for negotiation** between the landlord and the tenant.* ◇ *A contract is prepared **in negotiation with** our clients* ◇ *The issue is still **under negotiation**.* ◇ *The price is generally **open to negotiation**.*

ne·go·ti·ator /nɪ'ɡəʊʃieɪtə(r); *AmE* -'ɡoʊʃi-/ *noun* a per-son who is involved in formal political or financial dis-cussions, especially because it is their job: *the union's chief negotiator* ◇ *a skilled negotiator*

Ne·gress /'niːɡres/ *noun* (*old-fashioned*, often *offensive*) a Negro woman or girl

Negro /'niːɡrəʊ; *AmE* -ɡroʊ/ *noun* (*pl.* **-oes**) (*old-fash-ioned*, often *offensive*) a member of a race of people with dark skin who originally came from Africa

ˌNegro 'spiritual *noun* = SPIRITUAL

neigh /neɪ/ *verb* [V] when a horse **neighs** it makes a long high sound ▶ **neigh** *noun*

neigh·bour (*BrE*) (*AmE* **neigh·bor**) /'neɪbə(r)/ *noun* **1** a person who lives next to you or near you: *We've had a lot of support from all our **friends and neighbours**.* ◇ *Our **next-door neighbours** are very noisy.* **2** a country that is next to or near another country: *Britain's nearest neigh-bour is France.* ◇ *peace treaties between Israel and its neighbours* **3** a person or thing that is standing or situ-ated next to another person or thing: *Stand quietly, chil-dren, and try not to talk to your neighbour.* ◇ *The tree fell slowly, its branches caught in those of its neighbours.* **4** (*literary*) any other human being: *We should all love our neighbours.*

neigh·bour·hood (*BrE*) (*AmE* **neigh·bor·hood**) /'neɪbəhʊd; *AmE* 'neɪbər-/ *noun* **1** a district or an area of a town; the people who live there: *We grew up in the same neighbourhood.* ◇ *a poor / quiet / residential neighbourhood* ◇ *Manhattan is divided into distinct neighborhoods.* ◇ *the neighbourhood police / residents / services* ◇ *He shouted so loudly that the whole neighbourhood could hear him.* **2** the area that you are in or the area near a particular place: *We searched the surrounding neighbourhood for the miss-ing boy.* ◇ *Houses in the **neighbourhood of** Paris are extremely expensive.* **IDM in the neighbourhood of** (of a number or an amount) approximately; not exactly: *It cost in the neighbourhood of £500.*

ˌneighbourhood 'watch (*BrE*) (*AmE* **ˌneighborhood 'watch**) *noun* [U] an arrangement by which a group of people in an area watch each other's houses regularly as a way of preventing crime

neigh·bour·ing (*BrE*) (*AmE* **neigh·bor·ing**) /'neɪbərɪŋ/ *adj.* [only before noun] situated or living near or next to a place or person: *a neighbouring house* ◇ *neighbouring towns* ◇ *a neighbouring farmer*

neigh·bour·ly (*BrE*) (*AmE* **neigh·bor·ly**) /'neɪbəli; *AmE* -bərli/ *adj.* **1** involving people, countries, etc. that live or are situated near each other: *the importance of good neighbourly relations between the two states* ◇ *neighbourly help / support / cooperation* ◇ *a neighbourly dispute* **2** friendly and helpful: *It was a neighbourly gesture of theirs.* ▶ **neigh·bour·li·ness** (*BrE*) (*AmE* **neighbor·li·ness**) *noun* [U]: *good neighbourliness* ◇ *a sense of commu-nity and neighbourliness*

nei·ther /'naɪðə(r); 'niːðə(r)/ *det., pron., adv.*
■ *det., pron.* not one nor the other of two things or people: *Neither answer is correct.* ◇ *Neither of them has / have a car.* ◇ *They produced two reports, neither of which con-tained any useful suggestions.* ◇ *'Which do you like?' 'Nei-ther. I think they're both ugly.'*
■ *adv.* **1** used to show that a negative statement is also true of sb / sth else: *He didn't remember and neither did I.* ◇ *I*

*hadn't been to New York before and **neither had Jane**.* ◇ *'I can't understand a word of it.' 'Neither can I.'* ◇ (*infor-mal*) *'I don't know.' 'Me neither.'* **2** (**neither ... nor ...**) used to show that a negative statement is true of two things: *I neither knew nor cared what had happened to him.* ◇ *Their house is neither big nor small.* ◇ *Neither the TV nor the video actually work / works.*

> **GRAMMAR POINT**
> **neither / either**
>
> After **neither** and **either** you use a singular verb:
> *Neither candidate was selected for the job.*
>
> **Neither of** and **either of** are followed by a plural noun
> or pronoun and a singular or plural verb. A plural verb
> is more informal: *Neither of my parents speaks / speak
> a foreign language.*
>
> When **neither... nor...** or **either... or...** are used with
> two singular nouns, the verb can be singular or
> plural. A plural verb is more informal.

nem·esis /'neməsɪs/ *noun* [U, sing.] (*formal*) punishment or defeat that is deserved and cannot be avoided

neo- /'niːəʊ; *AmE* 'niːoʊ/ *combining form* (in adjectives and nouns) new; in a later form: *neo-Georgian* ◇ *neo-fascist*

neo·clas·sic·al /ˌniːəʊ'klæsɪkl; *AmE* ˌniːoʊ-/ *adj.* [usu-ally before noun] used to describe art and architecture that is based on the style of Ancient Greece or Rome, or music, literature, etc. that uses traditional ideas or styles

Neo·lith·ic /ˌniːə'lɪθɪk/ *adj.* of the later part of the STONE AGE: *Neolithic stone axes* ◇ *Neolithic settlements*

neo·lo·gism /ni'ɒlədʒɪzəm; *AmE* -'ɑːl-/ *noun* (*formal*) a new word or expression or a new meaning of a word

neon /'niːɒn; *AmE* 'niːɑːn/ *noun* [U] (*symb* **Ne**) a chemical element. Neon is a colourless gas that does not react with anything and that shines with a bright light when electri-city is passed through it: *neon lights / signs*

neo·natal /ˌniːəʊ'neɪtl; *AmE* ˌniːoʊ-/ *adj.* (*technical*) con-nected with a child that has just been born: *the hospital's neonatal unit* ◇ *neonatal care / screening / mortality*

nephew /'nefjuː; 'nevjuː/ *noun* the son of your brother or sister; the son of your husband's or wife's brother or sister—compare NIECE

nepo·tism /'nepətɪzəm/ *noun* [U] (*disapproving*) giving unfair advantages to your own family if you are in a position of power, especially by giving them jobs

Nep·tune /'neptjuːn; *AmE* -tuːn/ *noun* a planet in the SOLAR SYSTEM that is 8th in order of distance from the sun

nerd /nɜːd; *AmE* nɜːrd/ *noun* (*informal, disapproving*) **1** a person who is boring, stupid and not fashionable: *I feel like a nerd in these shoes.* **2** a person who is very inter-ested in computers ▶ **nerdy** *adj.*: *He looked kind of nerdy.*

nerve /nɜːv; *AmE* nɜːrv/ *noun, verb*
■ *noun* **1** [C] any of the long thin threads that carry mes-sages between the brain and parts of the body, enabling you to move, feel pain, etc: *the optic nerve* ◇ *nerve cells* ◇ *nerve endings* ◇ *Every nerve in her body was tense.* **2** (**nerves**) [pl.] feelings of worry or anxiety: *Even after years as a singer, he still suffers from nerves before a performance.* ◇ *I need something to **calm / steady my nerves.*** ◇ *Everyone's **nerves were on edge** (= everyone felt tense).* ◇ *He **lives on his nerves** (= is always worried).* **3** [U] the courage to do sth difficult or dangerous: *It took a lot of nerve to take the company to court.* ◇ *I was going to have a go at parachuting but **lost my nerve** at the last minute.* ◇ *He **kept his nerve** to win the final set 6–4.* **4** [sing., U] (*informal*) a way of behaving that other people think is rude or not appropriate: *I don't know how you **have the nerve** to show your face after what you said! ◇ He's **got a nerve** asking us for money!* ◇ *'Then she demanded to see the manager!' 'What a nerve!'* **IDM be a bag / bundle of 'nerves** (*informal*) to be very nervous **get on sb's 'nerves** (*informal*) to annoy sb: *That music is starting to get on my nerves.* **have nerves of steel** to be able to remain calm in a difficult or dangerous situation **hit / touch a (raw / sensitive) 'nerve** to mention a subject

æ   ɑː   e   ɜː   ə   ɪ   iː   i   ɒ   ɔː   ʌ   ʊ   u   uː
cat   father   ten   bird   about   sit   see   many   got   saw   cup   put   actual   too
(BrE)

N

that makes sb feel angry, upset, embarrassed, etc: *You touched a raw nerve when you mentioned his first wife.*—more at BRASS, STRAIN *v.*, WAR *n.*

■ *verb* ~ **yourself for sth/to do sth** (*written*) to give yourself the courage or strength to do sth: [VN to inf] *He nerved himself to ask her out.* [also VN]

'nerve centre (*AmE* **'nerve center**) *noun* the place from which an activity or organization is controlled and instructions are sent out: *Frankfurt is the economic nerve centre of Germany.*

'nerve gas *noun* a poisonous gas used in war that attacks your CENTRAL NERVOUS SYSTEM

nerve·less /'nɜːvləs; *AmE* 'nɜːrv-/ *adj.* **1** having no strength or feeling: *The knife fell from her nerveless fingers.* **2** having no fear: *She is a nerveless rider.* OPP NERVOUS

'nerve-racking (also **'nerve-wracking**) *adj.* making you feel very nervous and worried: *It was a nerve-racking drive up the mountain.*

ner·vous /'nɜːvəs; *AmE* 'nɜːrvəs/ *adj.* **1** ~ **(about/of sth)** anxious about sth or afraid of sth: *Consumers are very nervous about the future.* ◇ *He had been nervous about inviting us.* ◇ *The horse may be nervous of cars.* ◇ *I felt really nervous before the interview.* ◇ *a nervous glance/smile/voice* (= one that shows that you feel anxious) ◇ *By the time the police arrived, I was a nervous wreck.* OPP CONFIDENT **2** easily worried or frightened: *She was a thin, nervous girl.* ◇ *He's not the nervous type.* ◇ *She was of a nervous disposition.* OPP NERVELESS **3** connected with the body's nerves and often affecting you mentally or emotionally: *a nervous condition/disorder/disease* ◇ *She was in a state of nervous exhaustion.* ⇨ note at WORRIED IDM see SHADOW *n.* ▸ **ner·vous·ly** *adv.*: *She smiled nervously.* **ner·vous·ness** *noun* [U]: *He tried to hide his nervousness.*

,nervous 'breakdown (also **break·down**) *noun* a period of mental illness in which sb becomes very depressed, anxious and tired, and cannot deal with normal life: *to have a nervous breakdown*

'nervous system *noun* the system of all the nerves in the body—see also CENTRAL NERVOUS SYSTEM

nervy /'nɜːvi; *AmE* 'nɜːrvi/ *adj.* (*informal*) **1** (*BrE*) anxious and nervous **2** (*AmE*) rude in a way that shows a lack of respect: *a nervy kid*

-ness *suffix* (in nouns) the quality, state or character of: *dryness* ◇ *blindness* ◇ *silliness*

nest /nest/ *noun, verb*
■ *noun* **1** [C] a hollow place or structure that a bird makes or chooses for laying its eggs and sheltering its young—picture on page A6 **2** [C] a place where insects or other small creatures live and produce their young **3** [sing.] a secret place which is full of bad people and their activities: *a nest of thieves* **4** [sing.] the home, thought of as the safe place where parents bring up their children: *to leave the nest* (= leave your parents' home) **5** [C, usually sing.] a group or set of similar things that are made to fit inside each other: *a nest of tables* IDM see EMPTY *adj.*, FEATHER *v.*, FLY *v.*, HORNET, MARE
■ *verb* [V] to make and use a nest: *Thousands of seabirds are nesting on the cliffs.*

'nest egg *noun* (*informal*) a sum of money that you save to use in the future

nes·tle /'nesl/ *verb* [+*adv./prep.*] **1** [V] to sit or lie down in a warm or soft place: *He hugged her and she nestled against his chest.* **2** [VN] to put or hold sb/sth in a comfortable position in a warm or soft place: *He nestled the baby in his arms.* **3** [V] to be situated in a position that is protected, sheltered or partly hidden: *The little town nestles snugly at the foot of the hill.*

nest·ling /'nestlɪŋ/ *noun* a bird that is too young to leave the nest

net /net/ *noun, adj., verb*
■ *noun* **1** [U] a type of material that is made of string, thread or wire woven or tied together, with small spaces in between: *net curtains*—see also FISHNET, NETTING **2** [C] (especially in compounds) a piece of net used for a particular purpose, such as catching fish or covering sth:

fishing nets ◇ *a mosquito net* (= used to protect you from mosquitoes)—see also HAIRNET, SAFETY NET **3** (**the net**) [sing.] (in football, etc.) the frame covered in net that forms the goal: *to kick/hit the ball into the back of the net*—picture on page 1250 **4** (**the net**) [sing.] (in tennis, etc.) the piece of net between the two players that the ball goes over **5** (**the Net**) (*informal*) = THE INTERNET IDM see CAST *v.*, SLIP *v.*, SPREAD *v.*
■ *adj.* (*BrE* also **nett**) **1** [usually before noun] a **net** amount of money is the amount that remains when nothing more is to be taken away: *a net profit of £500* ◇ *net income/earnings* (= after tax has been paid)—compare GROSS **2** [only before noun] the **net** weight of sth is the weight without its container or the material it is wrapped in: *450 gms net weight*—compare GROSS **3** [only before noun] final, after all the important facts have been included: *The net result is that small shopkeepers are being forced out of business.* ◇ *Canada is now a substantial net importer of medicines* (= it imports more than it exports). ◇ *c. net gain* ▸ **net** *adv.*: *a salary of $50000 net* ◇ *Interest on the investment will be paid net* (= tax will already have been taken away).—compare GROSS
■ *verb* (**-tt-**) [VN] **1** to earn an amount of money as a profit after you have paid tax on it: *The sale of paintings netted £17000.* **2** to catch sth, especially fish, in a net **3** to catch sb or obtain sth in a skilful way: *A swoop by customs officers netted a large quantity of drugs.* **4** (*especially BrE*) to kick or hit a ball into the goal SYN SCORE: *He has netted 21 goals so far this season.* **5** to cover sth with a net or nets: *It is a good idea to net the strawberry plants.*

net·ball /'netbɔːl/ *noun* [U] a game played by two teams of seven players, especially women or girls. Players score by throwing a ball through a high net hanging from a ring on a post.

,net 'curtain (*BrE*) (*AmE* **curtain**) *noun* a very thin piece of fabric that you hang at a window, and that stops people outside from being able to see inside

nether /'neðə(r)/ *adj.* [only before noun] (*literary* or *humorous*) lower: *the nether world* (= the world of the dead; hell) ◇ *a person's nether regions* (= their GENITALS)

'net surfer *noun* = SURFER (2)

nett *adj.* (*BrE*) = NET

net·ting /'netɪŋ/ *noun* [U] material that is made of string, thread or wire woven or tied together, with spaces in between: *wire netting*

net·tle /'netl/ *noun, verb*
■ *noun* (also **'stinging nettle**) a wild plant with leaves that have pointed edges, are covered in fine hairs and sting if you touch them IDM see GRASP *v.*
■ *verb* [usually passive] (*informal, especially BrE*) to make sb slightly angry SYN ANNOY: [VN] *My remarks clearly nettled her.* [also VN that]

net·work /'netwɜːk; *AmE* -wɜːrk/ *noun, verb*
■ *noun* **1** a complicated system of roads, lines, tubes, nerves, etc. that cross each other and are connected to each other: *a rail/road/canal network* ◇ *a network of veins* **2** a closely connected group of people, companies, etc. that exchange information, etc: *a communications/distribution network* ◇ *a network of friends* **3** (*computing*) a number of computers and other devices that are connected together so that equipment and information can be shared: *The office network allows users to share files and software, and to use a central printer.*—see also LAN, WAN **4** a group of radio or television stations in different places that are connected and that broadcast the same programmes at the same time: *the four big US television networks* IDM see OLD BOY
■ *verb* **1** [VN] (*computing*) to connect a number of computers and other devices together so that equipment and information can be shared: *networked computer systems* **2** [VN] to broadcast a television or radio programme on stations in several different areas at the same time: *nationally networked TV* **3** [V] to try to meet and talk to people who may be useful to you in your work: *Conferences are a good place to network.*

net·work·ing /'netwɜːkɪŋ; *AmE* -wɜːrk-/ *noun* [U] a system of trying to meet and talk to other people who may be useful to you in your work

neur·al /'njʊərəl; AmE 'nʊrəl/ adj. (technical) connected with a nerve or the NERVOUS SYSTEM: neural processes

neur·al·gia /njʊə'rældʒə; AmE nʊ'r-/ noun [U] (medical) a sharp pain felt along a nerve, especially in the head or face ▶ **neur·al·gic** /njʊə'rældʒɪk; AmE nʊ'r-/ adj.

neuro- /'njʊərəʊ; AmE 'nʊroʊ/ combining form (in nouns, adjectives and adverbs) connected with the nerves: neuroscience ◇ a neurosurgeon

neuro·logic·al /ˌnjʊərə'lɒdʒɪkl; AmE ˌnʊrə'lɑːdʒ-/ adj. relating to nerves or to the science of NEUROLOGY: neurological damage/disease

neurolo·gist /njʊə'rɒlədʒɪst; AmE nʊ'rɑːl-/ noun a doctor who studies and treats diseases of the nerves

neurol·ogy /njʊə'rɒlədʒi; AmE nʊ'rɑːl-/ noun [U] the scientific study of nerves and their diseases

neuron /'njʊərɒn; AmE 'nʊrɑːn/ (also **neur·one** /'njʊərəʊn; AmE 'nʊroʊn/) noun (biology) a cell that carries information between the brain and the other parts of the body; a nerve cell—see also MOTOR NEURONE DISEASE

neur·osis /njʊə'rəʊsɪs; AmE nʊ'roʊ-/ noun [C, U] (pl. **neur·oses** /-əʊsiːz; AmE -oʊ-/) **1** (medical) a mental illness in which a person suffers strong feelings of fear and worry **2** any strong worry or fear

neur·ot·ic /njʊə'rɒtɪk; AmE nʊ'rɑː-/ adj., noun
■ adj. **1** caused by or suffering from neurosis: neurotic fears/obsessions **2** not behaving in a reasonable, calm way, because you are worried about sth: She became neurotic about keeping the house clean. ◇ a brilliant but neurotic actor ▶ **neur·ot·ic·al·ly** /-kli/ adv.
■ noun a neurotic person

neu·ter /'njuːtə(r); AmE 'nuːtə(r)/ adj., verb
■ adj. (grammar) (in some languages) belonging to a class of nouns, pronouns or adjectives whose GENDER is not FEMININE OR MASCULINE: The Polish word for 'window' is neuter.
■ verb [VN] **1** to remove part of the sex organs of an animal so that it cannot produce young: Has your cat been neutered? **2** (written, disapproving) to prevent sth from having the effect that it ought to have

neu·tral /'njuːtrəl; AmE 'nuː-/ adj., noun
■ adj.
IN DISAGREEMENT/CONTEST | **1** not supporting or helping either side in a disagreement, competition, etc: Journalists are supposed to be politically neutral. ◇ I didn't take my father's or my mother's side; I tried to remain neutral.
IN WAR | **2** not belonging to any of the countries that are involved in a war; not supporting any of the countries involved in a war: neutral territory/waters ◇ Switzerland was neutral during the war.
WITHOUT STRONG FEELING | **3** deliberately not expressing any strong feeling: 'So you told her?' he said in a neutral tone of voice. ◇ Is there a neutral word for 'terrorist'?
COLOUR | **4** not very bright or strong, such as grey or light brown: a neutral colour scheme ◇ neutral tones
CHEMISTRY | **5** neither acid nor ALKALINE
ELECTRICAL | **6** (abbr. N) having neither a positive nor a negative electrical CHARGE: the neutral wire in a plug
▶ **neu·tral·ly** /-rəli/ adv.
IDM **on neutral ground/territory** in a place that has no connection with either of the people or sides who are meeting and so does not give an advantage to either of them: We decided to meet on neutral ground.
■ noun
IN VEHICLE | **1** [U] the position of the GEARS of a vehicle in which no power is carried from the engine to the wheels: to leave/put the car in neutral
IN DISAGREEMENT/WAR | **2** [C] a person or country that does not support either side in a disagreement, competition or war
COLOUR | **3** [C] a colour that is not bright or strong, such as grey or light brown: The room was decorated in pale neutrals.

neu·tral·ist /'njuːtrəlɪst; AmE 'nuː-/ noun (especially AmE) a person who does not support either side in a war ▶ **neu·tral·ist** adj.: a neutralist state/policy

neu·tral·ity /njuː'træləti; AmE nuː-/ noun [U] the state of not supporting either side in a disagreement, competition or war: political neutrality ◇ a position of neutrality

neu·tral·ize (BrE also **-ise**) /'njuːtrəlaɪz; AmE 'nuː-/ verb [VN] **1** to stop sth from having any effect: The latest figures should neutralize the fears of inflation. **2** (chemistry) to make a substance NEUTRAL (5): Lime was used to neutralize the acidity of the soil. **3** to make a country or an area NEUTRAL (2): The treaty neutralized the Black Sea. ▶ **neu·tral·iza·tion**, **-isa·tion** /ˌnjuːtrəlaɪ'zeɪʃn; AmE ˌnuːtrələ'z-/ noun [U]

neu·tron /'njuːtrɒn; AmE 'nuːtrɑːn/ noun (physics) a very small piece of MATTER (= a substance) that carries no electric CHARGE and that forms part of the NUCLEUS (= central part) of an ATOM—see also ELECTRON, PROTON

never /'nevə(r)/ adv., exclamation
■ adv. **1** not at any time; not on any occasion: You never help me. ◇ He has never been abroad. ◇ 'Would you vote for him?' 'Never.' ◇ 'I work for a company called Orion Technology.' 'Never heard of them.' ◇ **Never in all my life** have I seen such a horrible thing. ◇ Never ever tell anyone your password. **2** used to emphasize a negative statement instead of 'not': I never knew ◇ (= didn't know until now) you had a twin sister. ◇ (especially BrE) Someone might find out and that **would never do** (= that is not acceptable). ◇ He **never so much as smiled** (= did not smile even once). ◇ (especially BrE) 'I told my boss exactly what I thought of her.' 'You never did!' (= 'Surely you didn't!') ◇ (BrE, slang) 'You took my bike.' 'No, I never.' ◇ (old-fashioned or humorous) **Never fear** (= Do not worry), everything will be all right. **IDM** **on the never-never** (BrE, informal) on HIRE PURCHASE (= by making payments over a long period): to buy a new car on the never-never **Well, I never (did)!** (old-fashioned) used to express surprise or disapproval
■ exclamation (spoken) used to show that you are very surprised about sth because you do not believe it is possible: 'I got the job.' 'Never!'

never-ending adj. seeming to last for ever: Housework is a never-ending task.

never·more /ˌnevə'mɔː(r); AmE ˌnevər'm-/ adv. (old use) never again

never-never land noun [sing.] an imaginary place where everything is wonderful

never·the·less /ˌnevəðə'les; AmE -vərðə-/ adv. in spite of sth that you have just mentioned: There is little chance that we will succeed in changing the law. Nevertheless, it is important that we try. ◇ Our defeat was expected but it is disappointing nevertheless.

new /njuː; AmE nuː/ adj. (newer, new·est)
NOT EXISTING BEFORE | **1** not existing before; recently made, invented, introduced, etc: Have you read her new novel? ◇ new ways of doing things ◇ This idea isn't new. ◇ The latest model has over 100 new features.—see also BRAND-NEW **OPP** OLD **2** (the new) noun [U] something that is new: It was a good mix of the old and the new.
RECENTLY BOUGHT | **3** recently bought: Let me show you my new dress.
NOT USED BEFORE | **4** not used or owned by anyone before: A second-hand car costs a fraction of a new one.
DIFFERENT | **5** different from the previous one: I like your new hairstyle. ◇ When do you start your new job? ◇ He's made a lot of new friends. **OPP** OLD
NOT FAMILIAR | **6** ~ (to sb) already existing but not seen, experienced, etc. before; not familiar: This is a new experience for me. ◇ I'd like to learn a new language. ◇ Our system is probably new to you. ◇ the discovery of a new star
RECENTLY ARRIVED | **7** ~ (to sth) not yet familiar with sth because you have only just started, arrived, etc: I should tell you, I'm completely new to this kind of work. ◇ I am new to the town. ◇ a new arrival/recruit ◇ You're new here, aren't you?
NEW- | **8** used in compounds to describe sth that has recently happened: He was enjoying his new-found freedom.
MODERN | **9** (usually with the) modern; of the latest type: the new morality ◇ the new breed of civil servant ◇ Comedy is the new rock and roll. ◇ They called themselves the New Romantics.

N

JUST BEGINNING | **10** [usually before noun] just beginning or beginning again: *a new day* ◇ *It was a new era in the history of our country.* ◇ *She went to Australia to start a new life.*

WITH FRESH ENERGY | **11** having fresh energy, courage or health: *Since he changed jobs he's looked like a new man.*

RECENTLY PRODUCED | **12** only recently produced or developed: *The new buds are appearing on the trees now.* ◇ *new potatoes* (= ones dug from the soil early in the season)

▶ **new·ness** *noun* [U] —see also NEWLY

IDM **,break new 'ground** to make a new discovery or do sth that has not been done before—see also GROUNDBREAKING **(as) ,good as 'new | like 'new** in very good condition, as it was when it was new: *I've had your coat cleaned—it's as good as new now.* **a new one on 'me** used to say that you have not heard a particular idea, piece of information, joke, etc. before: *'Have you come across this before?' 'No, it's a new one on me.'* **turn over a new 'leaf** to change your way of life to become a better, more responsible person **what's 'new?** (*spoken*) used as a friendly greeting: *Hi! What's new?*—more at COMPLEXION, BLOOD, BRAVE *adj.*, BREATHE, TEACH

,New 'Age *adj.* connected with a way of life that rejects modern Western values and is based on spiritual ideas and beliefs, ASTROLOGY, etc: *a New Age festival* ◇ *New Age travellers* (= people in Britain who reject the values of modern society and travel from place to place, living in their vehicles) ▶ **,New 'Age** *noun* [U]

new·born /ˈnjuːbɔːn; *AmE* ˈnuːbɔːrn/ *adj.* [only before noun] recently born: *a newborn baby*

,new 'broom *noun* (*BrE*) a person who has just started to work for an organization, especially in a senior job, and who is likely to make a lot of changes

New·cas·tle /ˈnjuːkɑːsl; *AmE* ˈnuːkæsl/ *noun* [U] IDM see COAL

new·comer /ˈnjuːkʌmə(r); *AmE* ˈnuː-/ *noun* ~ **(to sth)** a person who has only recently arrived in a place or started an activity

new·fan·gled /ˌnjuːˈfæŋgld; *AmE* ˌnuːˈf-/ *adj.* [usually before noun] (*disapproving*) used to describe sth that has recently been invented or introduced, but that you do not like because it is not what you are used to, or is too complicated

newly /ˈnjuːli; *AmE* ˈnuːli/ *adv.* (usually before a past participle) recently: *a newly qualified doctor* ◇ *a newly created job* ◇ *a newly independent republic*

'newly-wed *noun* [usually pl.] a person who has recently got married ▶ **'newly-wed** *adj.*

,new 'man *noun* (*BrE*) a man who shares the work in the home that is traditionally done by women, such as cleaning, cooking and taking care of children. New men are considered sensitive and not aggressive.

,new 'moon *noun* **1** the moon when it looks like a thin curved shape (= a CRESCENT) **2** the time of the month when the moon has this shape—compare FULL MOON, HALF-MOON

news /njuːz; *AmE* nuːz/ *noun* **1** [U] new information about sth that has happened recently: *What's the latest news?* ◇ *Have you heard the news? Pat's leaving!* ◇ *That's great news.* ◇ *Tell me all your news.* ◇ *Have you had any news of Patrick?* ◇ *Any news on the deal?* ◇ *Messengers brought news that the battle had been lost.* ◇ *Do you want the good news or the bad news first?* ◇ *a piece/bit of news* ◇ (*spoken*) *It's news to me* (= I haven't heard it before). **2** [U] reports of recent events that appear in newspapers or on television or radio: *national/international news* ◇ *a news story/item/report* ◇ *News of a serious road accident is just coming in.* ◇ *She is always in the news.* ◇ *The wedding was front-page news.* **3** (**the news**) [sing.] a regular television or radio broadcast of the latest news: *to listen to/watch the news* ◇ *Can you put the news on?* ◇ *I saw it on the news.* ◇ *the nine o'clock news* **4** [U] a person, thing or event that is considered to be interesting enough to be reported as news: *Pop stars are always news.*—see also NEWSY IDM **be bad 'news (for sb/sth)** to be likely to cause problems: *Central heating is bad news for indoor*

plants. **break the 'news (to sb)** to be the first to tell sb some bad news **be good news (for sb/sth)** to be likely to be helpful or give an advantage: *The cut in interest rates is good news for homeowners.* **,no news is 'good news** (*saying*) if there were bad news we would hear it, so as we have heard nothing, it is likely that nothing bad has happened

'news agency (also **'press agency**) *noun* an organization that collects news and supplies it to newspapers and television and radio companies

news·agent /ˈnjuːzeɪdʒənt; *AmE* ˈnuːz-/ (*BrE*) (*AmE* **news·deal·er**) *noun* **1** a person who owns or works in a shop selling newspapers and magazines, and often sweets/candy and cigarettes **2** (**news·agent's**) (*pl.* **news·agents**) (*BrE* also **'paper shop**) a shop/store that sells newspapers, magazines, sweets/candy, etc: *I'll go to the newsagent's on my way home.*

news·cast /ˈnjuːzkɑːst; *AmE* ˈnuːzkæst/ *noun* (*especially AmE*) a news programme on radio or television

news·cast·er /ˈnjuːzkɑːstə(r); *AmE* ˈnuːzkæstər/ (*BrE* also **news·read·er**) *noun* a person who reads the news on television or radio

'news conference *noun* (*especially AmE*) = PRESS CONFERENCE

news·deal·er /ˈnjuːzdiːlə(r); *AmE* ˈnuːz-/ *noun* (*AmE*) = NEWSAGENT

news·flash /ˈnjuːzflæʃ; *AmE* ˈnuːz-/ (also **flash**) *noun* (*especially BrE*) a short item of important news that is broadcast on radio or television, often interrupting a programme

news·let·ter /ˈnjuːzletə(r); *AmE* ˈnuːz-/ *noun* a printed report containing news of the activities of a club or organization that is sent regularly to all its members

news·paper /ˈnjuːzpeɪpə(r); *AmE* ˈnuːz-/ *noun* **1** [C] a set of large printed sheets of paper containing news, articles, advertisements, etc. and published every day or every week: *a daily/weekly newspaper* ◇ *a local/national newspaper* ◇ *a newspaper article* ◇ *I read about it in the newspaper.* ◇ *a newspaper cutting* ◇ *She works for the local newspaper* (= the company that produces it). ◇ *newspaper proprietors*—see also PAPER **2** [U] paper taken from old newspapers: *Wrap all your glasses in newspaper.*

news·paper·man /ˈnjuːzpeɪpəmæn; *AmE* ˈnuːzperpərmæn/ *noun* (*pl.* **-men** /-men/) a journalist, usually a man, who works for a newspaper

news·print /ˈnjuːzprɪnt; *AmE* ˈnuːz-/ *noun* [U] the cheap paper that newspapers are printed on

news·read·er /ˈnjuːzriːdə(r); *AmE* ˈnuːz-/ *noun* (*BrE*) = NEWSCASTER

news·reel /ˈnjuːzriːl; *AmE* ˈnuːz-/ *noun* a short film of news that was shown in the past in cinemas/movie theaters: *old newsreel footage of the 1936 Olympics*

'news room *noun* the room at a newspaper office or a radio or television station where news is received and prepared for printing or broadcasting

'news-sheet *noun* a small newspaper with only a few pages

'news-stand *noun* a place on the street, at a station, etc. where you can buy newspapers and magazines: *The first issue of the magazine hit the news-stands* (= went on sale) *today.*

news·worthy /ˈnjuːzwɜːði; *AmE* ˈnuːzwɜːrði/ *adj.* interesting and important enough to be reported as news

newsy /ˈnjuːzi; *AmE* ˈnuːzi/ *adj.* (*informal*) full of interesting and entertaining news: *a newsy letter*

newt /njuːt; *AmE* nuːt/ *noun* a small animal with short legs, a long tail and cold blood, that lives both in water and on land (= is an AMPHIBIAN) IDM see PISSED

the ,New 'Testament *noun* [sing.] the second part of the Bible, that describes the life and teachings of Jesus Christ—compare THE OLD TESTAMENT

'new town *noun* one of the complete towns that were planned and built in Britain after 1946

,new 'wave *noun* [U, sing.] **1** a group of people who together introduce new styles and ideas in art, music, cinema, etc: *one of the most exciting directors of the Aus-*

tralian new wave ◊ *new wave films* **2** a style of ROCK music popular in the 1970s

the ˌNew 'World *noun* [sing.] a way of referring to North, Central and South America, used especially in the past—compare THE OLD WORLD

ˌnew 'year (also **ˌNew 'Year**) *noun* [U, sing.] the beginning of the year: *Happy New Year!* ◊ *We're going to Germany for Christmas and New Year.* ◊ *I'll see you in the new year.*—see also RESOLUTION

ˌNew Year's 'Day (*AmE* also **ˌNew Year's**) *noun* [U] 1 January

ˌNew Year's 'Eve (*AmE* also **ˌNew Years**) *noun* [U] 31 December, especially the evening of that day

next /nekst/ *adj., adv., noun*
■ *adj.* [only before noun] **1** (usually with *the*) coming straight after sb/sth in time, order or space: *The next train to Baltimore is at ten.* ◊ *The next six months will be the hardest.* ◊ *the next chapter* ◊ *Who's next?* ◊ *the woman in the next room* ◊ *I fainted and **the next thing I knew** I was in the hospital.* ◊ (*informal*) *Round here, you leave school at sixteen and **next thing you know**, you're married with three kids.* **2** (used without *the*) **~ Monday, week, summer, year, etc.** the Monday, week, etc. immediately following: *Next Thursday is 12 April.* ◊ *Next time I'll bring a book.* **IDM** **the 'next man** the average person: *I can enjoy a joke **as well as the next man**, but this is going too far.*—more at DAY, LUCK *n.*
■ *adv.* **1** after sth else; then; afterwards: *What happened next?* ◊ *Next, I heard the sound of voices.* **2 ~ best, biggest, most important, etc. ... (after/to sb/sth)** coming in the order mentioned: *Jo was the next oldest after Martin.* ◊ *The next best thing to flying is gliding.* **3** used in questions to express surprise or confusion: *You're going bungee jumping? **Whatever next?***
■ *noun* (usually **the next**) [sing.] a person or thing that is next: *One moment he wasn't there, the next he was.* ◊ *the week after next*

> **WHICH WORD?** ⊘
> **next / nearest**
>
> **(The) next** means 'after this/that one' in time or in a series of events, places or people: *When is your next appointment?* ◊ *Turn left at the next traffic lights.* ◊ *Who's next?* **(The) nearest** means 'closest' in space: *Where's the nearest supermarket?*
>
> Notice the difference between the prepositions **nearest to** and **next to**: *Janet's sitting nearest to the window* (= of all the people in the room). *Sarah's sitting next to the window* (= right beside it). In informal *BrE* **nearest** can be used instead of **nearest to**: *Who's sitting nearest the door?*

ˌnext 'door *adv., adj., noun*
■ *adv.* in the next room, house or building: *The cat is from the house next door.* ◊ *The manager's office is just next door.* ◊ *We live **next door to** the pub.* ▶ **ˌnext-'door** *adj.* [only before noun]: *our next-door neighbours* ◊ *the next-door house*
■ *noun* [U+sing./pl. *v.*] (*BrE, spoken*) the people who live in the house or flat/apartment next to yours: *Is that next door's dog?*

ˌnext of 'kin *noun* [C, U] (*pl.* **next of kin**) your closest living relative or relatives: *I'm her next of kin.* ◊ *Her next of kin have been informed.* ◊ *The form must be signed by next of kin.*

'next to *prep.* **1** in or into a position right beside sb/sth: *We sat next to each other.* ⇨ note at NEXT **2** following in order or importance after sb/sth: *Next to skiing my favourite sport is skating.* **3** almost: *Charles knew **next to nothing** about farming.* ◊ *The horse came **next to last** (= the one before the last one) in the race.* **4** in comparison with sb/sth: *Next to her I felt like a fraud.*

nexus /'neksəs/ *noun* [sing.] (*formal*) a complicated series of connections between different things

NFL /ˌen ef 'el/ *abbr.* (in the US) National Football League
NGO /ˌen dʒiː 'əʊ; *AmE* 'oʊ/ *abbr.* non-governmental

organization (a CHARITY, association, etc. that is independent of government and business)

NHS /ˌen eɪtʃ 'es/ *noun* [sing.] The NHS is the public health service in Britain that provides medical treatment and is paid for by taxes (abbreviation for 'National Health Service'): *an NHS hospital* ◊ *I had the operation done **on the NHS** (= paid for by the NHS).*

NI *abbr.* (in Britain) NATIONAL INSURANCE

nib /nɪb/ *noun* the metal point of a pen—picture at STATIONERY

nib·ble /'nɪbl/ *verb, noun*
■ *verb* **1 ~ (at sth)** to take small bites of sth, especially food: [VN] *We sat drinking wine and nibbling olives.* ◊ *He nibbled her ear playfully.* ◊ [V] *She took some cake from the tray and nibbled at it.* **2** [V] **~ (at sth)** to show a slight interest in an offer, idea, etc: *He nibbled at the idea, but would not make a definite decision.* **PHRV** **ˌnibble a'way at sth** to take away small amounts of sth, so that the total amount is gradually reduced: *Inflation is nibbling away at spending power.*
■ *noun* **1** [C] a small bite of sth: *I took a nibble from the biscuit.* **2** (**nibbles**) [pl.] small things to eat with a drink before a meal or at a party: *wine and nibbles*

nibs /nɪbz/ *noun* **IDM** **his nibs** (*old-fashioned, BrE, informal*) used to refer to a man who is, or thinks he is, more important than other people

nice /naɪs/ *adj.* (**nicer, nicest**)
▸ PLEASANT/ATTRACTIVE | **1 ~ (to do sth)| ~ (doing sth)| ~ (that ...)** pleasant, enjoyable or attractive: *a nice day/smile/place* ◊ *nice weather* ◊ *Did you have a nice time?* ◊ *You look very nice.* ◊ *'Do you want to come, too?' 'Yes, that would be nice.'* ◊ *The nicest thing about her is that she never criticizes us.* ◊ *Nice to meet you!* (= a friendly greeting) ◊ *It's been nice meeting you.* ◊ *It's nice that you can come with us.* ◊ *It would be nice if he moved to London.* ◊ *It's nice to know that somebody appreciates what I do.* ◊ *We all had the flu last week—it wasn't very nice.* **2** used before adjectives or adverbs to emphasize how pleasant sth is: *a nice hot bath* ◊ *a nice long walk* ◊ *It was nice and warm yesterday.* ◊ *Everyone arrived nice and early.* **HELP** **Nice and** with another adjective cannot be used before a noun: ~~*a nice and quiet place.*~~
▸ KIND/FRIENDLY | **3 ~ (to sb)| ~ of sb (to do sth)| ~ (about sth)** kind; friendly: *Our new neighbours are very nice.* ◊ *He's a really nice guy.* ◊ *Be nice to me. I'm not feeling well.* ◊ *It was nice of them to invite us.* ◊ *I complained to the manager and he was very nice about it.* ◊ *I asked him in the nicest possible way to put his cigarette out.* **OPP** NASTY
▸ NOT NICE | **4** (*ironic*) bad or unpleasant: *That's a nice thing to say!* ◊ *That's a nice way to speak to your mother!*
▸ SMALL DETAILS | **5** (*formal*) involving a very small detail or difference **SYN** SUBTLE: *a nice point of law* (= one that is difficult to decide)
⇨ note on page 858
▸ **nice·ness** *noun* [U]: *In some professions, niceness does not get you very far.*
IDM **as ˌnice as 'pie** (*informal*) very kind and friendly, especially when you are not expecting it **Have a nice 'day!** (*spoken, especially AmE*) a friendly way of saying goodbye, especially to customers **'Nice one!** (*BrE, spoken*) used to show you are pleased when sth good has happened or sb has said sth amusing: *You got the job? Nice one!* **Nice 'work!** (*spoken, especially BrE*) used to show you are pleased when sb has done sth well: *You did a good job today. Nice work, James!* **nice work if you can 'get it** (*informal*) used when you wish that you had sb's success or good luck and think they have achieved it with little effort—more at MR

ˌnice-'looking *adj.* attractive: *What a nice-looking young man!*

nice·ly /'naɪsli/ *adv.* **1** in an attractive or satisfactory way; well: *The room was nicely furnished.* ◊ *The plants are **coming along nicely** (= growing well).* **2** in a kind, friendly or polite way: *If you ask her nicely she might say yes.* **3** (*formal*) carefully; exactly: *His novels nicely describe life in Britain between the wars.* **IDM** **do 'nicely 1** (usually **be doing nicely**) to be making good progress: *Her new*

æ	ɑː	e	ɜː	ə	ɪ	iː	i	ɒ	ɔː	ʌ	ʊ	u	uː
cat	father	ten	bird	about	sit	see	many	got	saw	cup	put	actual	too
							(BrE)						

N

business is doing very nicely. **2** to be satisfactory: *Tomorrow at ten will do nicely* (= will be a good time).

ni·cety /ˈnaɪsəti/ *noun* (*pl.* **-ies**) (*written*) **1** [C, usually pl.]
the small details or points of difference, especially con-
cerning the correct way of behaving or of doing things:
legal niceties ◇ *He has no time for social niceties.* **2** [U]
(*formal*) the quality of being very detailed or careful
about sth: *The nicety of his argument.*

niche /niːtʃ; niːʃ/ *noun* **1** a comfortable or suitable role,
job, way of life, etc: *He eventually found his niche in sports
journalism.* **2** (*business*) an opportunity to sell a particular product to a particular group of people: *They spotted a
niche in the market, with no serious competition.* ◇ *a niche
market* ◇ *the development of* **niche marketing** (= aiming
products at particular groups) **3** a small hollow place,
especially in a wall to contain a statue, etc., or in the side
of a hill **4** (*biology*) the conditions in which a type of
living thing can live successfully

nick /nɪk/ *noun, verb*
■ *noun* **1** (**the nick**) [sing.] (*BrE, slang*) a prison or a police
station: *He'll end up in the nick.* **2** a small cut in the edge
or surface of sth [IDM] **in good, etc.** ˈnick (*BrE, informal*)
in good, etc. condition or health **in the** ˌnick of ˈtime
(*informal*) at the very last moment; just in time before sth
bad happens
■ *verb* [VN] **1** to make a small cut in sth: *He nicked himself
while shaving.* **2** ~ sth (**from sb/sth**) (*BrE, informal*) to
steal sth [SYN] PINCH: *Who nicked my pen?* **3** ~ **sb** (**for sth**)
(*BrE, informal*) to arrest sb for committing a crime:
You're nicked!

nickel /ˈnɪkl/ *noun* **1** [U] (*symb* **Ni**) a chemical element.
Nickel is a hard silver-white metal used in making some
types of steel and other ALLOYS. **2** [C] a coin of the US and
Canada worth 5 cents

ˌnickel-and-ˈdime *adj.* (*AmE, informal*) involving only
a small amount of money; not important: *a nickel-and-
dime job*

nick·name /ˈnɪkneɪm/ *noun, verb*
■ *noun* an informal, often humorous, name for a person
that is connected with their real name, their personality
or appearance, or with sth they have done
■ *verb* [VN-N] [often passive] to give a nickname to sb/sth:
She was nicknamed 'The Ice Queen'.

nico·tine /ˈnɪkətiːn/ *noun* [U] a poisonous substance in
tobacco that people become ADDICTED to, so that it is
difficult to stop smoking: *fingers stained with nicotine*

niece /niːs/ *noun* the daughter of your brother or sister;
the daughter of your husband's or wife's brother or sister—compare NEPHEW

nifty /ˈnɪfti/ *adj.* (*informal*) **1** skilful and accurate: *There's
some nifty guitar work on his latest CD.* **2** practical; working well: *a nifty little gadget for slicing cucumbers*

nig·gard·ly /ˈnɪɡədli; *AmE* -ɡərd-/ *adj.* (*written, disapproving*) **1** unwilling to be generous with money, time,
etc: *a niggardly attitude* **2** (of a gift or an amount of
money) not worth much and given unwillingly: *a niggardly allowance*

nig·ger /ˈnɪɡə(r)/ *noun* (⚠, *slang*) a very offensive word
for a black person

nig·gle /ˈnɪɡl/ *noun, verb*
■ *noun* **1** a small criticism or complaint **2** a slight feeling
such as worry, doubt, etc. that does not go away: *a niggle
of doubt/jealousy* **3** a slight pain: *He gets the occasional
niggle in his right shoulder.*
■ *verb* **1** ~ (**at sb**) to irritate or annoy sb slightly; to make
sb slightly worried [SYN] BOTHER: [V] *A doubt niggled at
her.* ◇ [VNthat] *It niggled him that she had not phoned
back.* ◇ [VN] *Something was niggling her.* **2** [V] ~ (**about/
over sth**)|~ (**at sb**) (**for sth**) to argue about sth unimport-
ant; to criticize sb for sth that is not important

nig·gling /ˈnɪɡlɪŋ/ (*also less frequent* **nig·gly** /-li/) *adj.*
1 used to describe a slight feeling of worry or pain that
does not go away: *She had niggling doubts about their
relationship.* ◇ *As a player he suffered from a series of
niggling injuries.* **2** not important: *niggling details*

nigh /naɪ/ *adv.* **1** ~ **on** (*old-fashioned*) almost; nearly:
They've lived in that house for nigh on 30 years.—see also
WELL-NIGH **2** (*old use or literary*) near: *Winter was draw-
ing nigh.*

night /naɪt/ *noun* [U, C] **1** the time of darkness between
one day and the next, usually when people sleep: *These
animals only come out at night.* ◇ *They sleep by day and
hunt by night.* ◇ *The accident happened on Friday night.* ◇
on the night of 10 January/January 10 ◇ *Did you hear the
storm last night?* ◇ *I lay awake all night.* ◇ *Where did you
spend the night?* ◇ *You're welcome to stay the night here.*
◇ *What is he doing calling at this time of night?* ◇ *You'll
feel better after you've had a good night's sleep.* ◇ *The
trip was for ten nights.* ◇ *The hotel costs £65 per person per
night.* ◇ *the night train/boat/flight* ◇ (*written*) *Night fell*
(= it became dark). **2** the evening until you go to bed:
Let's go out on Saturday night. ◇ *Bill's parents came for
dinner last night.* ◇ *She doesn't like to walk home late at
night.* ◇ *I saw her in town the other night* (= a few nights
ago). ◇ *I'm working late tomorrow night.* **3** an evening
when a special event happens: *the first/opening night* (=
of a play, film/movie, etc.) ◇ *a karaoke night* ◇ *an Irish/
Scottish night* (= with Irish/Scottish music, entertainment, etc.)—see also STAG NIGHT ▶ **nights** *adv.* (*especially
AmE*): *He can't get used to working nights* (= at night).
[IDM] **Good** ˈnight (*also* **Good**ˈnight) used when you are
saying goodbye to sb late in the evening, or when they or
you are going to bed; in informal use people often just say
Night: *Good night. See you in the morning.* ◇ *Night! Sleep
well.* **have an early/a late** ˈnight to go to bed earlier or
later than usual: *I've had a lot of late nights recently.*
have a good/bad ˈnight to sleep well/badly during the
night **have a night on the** ˈtiles (*BrE, informal*) to stay
out late enjoying yourself ˌnight and ˈday | ˌday and
ˈnight all the time; continuously: *The machines are kept
running night and day.* **night** ˈnight used by children or
to children, to mean 'Good night': *'Night night, sleep
tight!'* **a night** ˈout an evening that you spend enjoying
yourself away from home: *They enjoy a night out occasionally.*—more at ALL RIGHT *adj.*, DANCE *v.*, DEAD *n.*, MORN-
ING, SPEND *v.*, STILL *n.*, THING

night·cap /ˈnaɪtkæp/ *noun* **1** a drink, usually containing
alcohol, taken before going to bed **2** (in the past) a soft
cap worn in bed

night·clothes /ˈnaɪtkləʊðz; *AmE* -kloʊðz/ *noun* [pl.]
clothes that you wear in bed

night·club /ˈnaɪtklʌb/ *noun* a place that is open late in
the evening where people can go to dance, drink, etc.

ˈnight depository *noun* (*AmE*) = NIGHT SAFE

night·dress /ˈnaɪtdres/ (*BrE*) (*AmE or old-fashioned*
night·gown /ˈnaɪtɡaʊn/) (*also informal* **nightie** /ˈnaɪti/,
BrE, AmE) *noun* a long loose piece of clothing like a thin
dress, worn by a woman or girl in bed: *I prefer pyjamas to
nightdresses.*—picture on page A5

ˈnight duty *noun* [U] work that people have to do at
night, for example in a hospital: *to be on night duty*

night·fall /ˈnaɪtfɔːl/ *noun* [U] (*formal or literary*) the time
in the evening when it becomes dark [SYN] DUSK: *He
wanted to be home before nightfall.*

night·gown /ˈnaɪtɡaʊn/ *noun* (*AmE or old-fashioned*) =
NIGHTDRESS—picture on page A5

aɪ	aʊ	eɪ	əʊ	oʊ	ɔɪ	ɪə	eə	ʊə	j	w
my	now	say	go	go	boy	near	hair	pure	yes	wet
			(BrE)	(AmE)						

N

nightie /'naɪti/ *noun* (*informal*) = NIGHTDRESS

night·in·gale /'naɪtɪŋgeɪl/ *noun* a small brown bird, the male of which has a beautiful song

night·life /'naɪtlaɪf/ *noun* [U] entertainment that is available in the evening and at night

night·ly /'naɪtli/ *adj.* happening every night: *a nightly news bulletin* ▶ **night·ly** *adv.*: *The programme is broadcast nightly.*

night·mare /'naɪtmeə(r); *AmE* -mer/ *noun* **1** a dream that is very frightening or unpleasant: *He still has nightmares about the accident.* **2** ~ (for sb) an experience that is very frightening and unpleasant, or very difficult to deal with: *The trip turned into a nightmare when they both got sick.* ◊ (*informal*) *Nobody knows what's going on—it's a nightmare!* ◊ (*informal*) *Filling in all those forms was a nightmare.* ◊ *Losing a child is most people's worst nightmare.* ◊ *If it goes ahead it will be the nightmare scenario* (= the worst thing that could happen). ◊ *a nightmare situation / ordeal* ▶ **night·mar·ish** /'naɪtmeərɪʃ; *AmE* -mer-/ *adj.*: *nightmarish living conditions*

'night owl *noun* (*informal*) a person who enjoys staying up late at night

'night safe (*BrE*) (*AmE* **'night depository**) *noun* a SAFE in the outside wall of a bank where money, etc. can be left when the bank is closed

'night school *noun* [U, C] (*old-fashioned*) classes for adults, held in the evening

night·shirt /'naɪtʃɜːt; *AmE* -ʃɜːrt/ *noun* a long loose shirt worn in bed

night·spot /'naɪtspɒt; *AmE* -spaːt/ *noun* (*informal*) a place people go to for entertainment at night SYN NIGHTCLUB: *top London nightspots*

night·stand /'naɪtstænd/ (also **'night table**) (both *AmE*) *noun* = BEDSIDE TABLE

night·stick /'naɪtstɪk/ *noun* (*AmE*) = TRUNCHEON

'night·time *noun* [U] the time when it is dark: *This area can be very noisy at night-time.*

night·watch·man /naɪt'wɒtʃmən; *AmE* -'wɔːtʃ-; -'wɑːtʃ-/ *noun* (*pl.* **-men** /-mən/) a man whose job is to guard a building such as a factory at night

night·wear /'naɪtweə(r); *AmE* -wer/ *noun* [U] a word used by shops/stores for clothes that are worn in bed

ni·hil·ism /'naɪɪlɪzəm/ *noun* [U] (*philosophy*) the belief that nothing has any value, especially that religious and moral principles have no value ▶ **ni·hil·is·tic** /,naɪɪ'lɪstɪk/ *adj.*: *Her latest play is a nihilistic vision of the world of the future.*

ni·hil·ist /'naɪɪlɪst/ *noun* a person who believes in nihilism

nil /nɪl/ *noun* [U] **1** (*especially BrE*) the number 0, especially as the score in some games SYN ZERO: *Newcastle beat Leeds four nil / by four goals to nil.* **2** nothing: *The doctors rated her chances as nil* (= they did not exist). ⇨ Appendix 3

nim·ble /'nɪmbl/ *adj.* (**nim·bler** /'nɪmblə(r)/, **nim·blest** /'nɪmblɪst/) **1** able to move quickly and easily: *You need nimble fingers for that job.* ◊ *She was extremely nimble on her feet.* **2** (of the mind) able to think and understand quickly ▶ **nim·bly** /'nɪmbli/ *adv.*

nim·bus /'nɪmbəs/ *noun* (*technical*) **1** [C usually sing, U] a large grey rain cloud **2** [C, usually sing.] a circle of light

nimby /'nɪmbi/ *noun* (*pl.* **-ies**) (*humorous, disapproving*) a person who claims to be in favour of a new development or project, but objects if it is too near their home and will disturb them in some way ORIGIN Formed from the first letters of 'not in my back yard'.

nin·com·poop /'nɪŋkəmpuːp/ *noun* (*old-fashioned, informal*) a stupid person

nine /naɪn/ *number* 9 HELP There are examples of how to use numbers at the entry for **nine**. IDM **have nine 'lives** (especially of a cat) to be very lucky in dangerous situations **a ,nine days' 'wonder** a person or thing that makes people excited for a short time but does not last very long **,nine to 'five** the normal working hours in an

office: *I work nine to five.* ◊ *a nine-to-five job*—more at DRESSED

nine·pins /'naɪnpɪnz/ *noun* IDM **,go down, ,drop, etc. like 'ninepins** (*BrE, informal*) to fall down or become ill in great numbers

nine·teen /,naɪn'tiːn/ *number* 19 ▶ **nine·teenth** /,naɪn'tiːnθ/ *ordinal number* IDM **talk, etc. nineteen to the 'dozen** (*BrE, informal*) to talk, etc. without stopping: *She was chatting away, nineteen to the dozen.*

ninety /'naɪnti/ **1** *number* 90 **2** (*noun*) (**the nineties**) [pl.] numbers, years or temperatures from 90 to 99: *The temperature must be in the nineties today.* ▶ **nine·ti·eth** /'naɪntiəθ/ *ordinal number*: *her ninetieth birthday* IDM **in your nineties** between the ages of 90 and 99 **,ninety-nine times out of a 'hundred** almost always

ninny /'nɪni/ *noun* (*pl.* **-ies**) (*informal*) a stupid person

ninth /naɪnθ/ *ordinal number, noun*
■ *ordinal number* 9th HELP There are examples of how to use ordinal numbers at the entry for **fifth**.
■ *noun* each of nine equal parts of sth

nip /nɪp/ *verb, noun*
■ *verb* (**-pp-**) **1** ~ (at sth) to give sb/sth a quick painful bite or PINCH: [VN] *He winced as the dog nipped his ankle.* ◊ [V] *She nipped at my arm.* **2** ~ (at sth) (of cold, wind, etc.) to harm or damage sth: [V] *The icy wind nipped at our faces.* ◊ [VN] *growing shoots nipped by frost* **3** [V+adv. / prep.] (*BrE, informal*) to go somewhere quickly and/or for only a short time: *He's just nipped out to the bank.* ◊ *A car nipped in* (= got in quickly) *ahead of me.* IDM **nip sth in the 'bud** to stop sth when it has just begun because you can see that problems will come from it PHR V **,nip sth↔'off** to remove a part of sth with your finger or with scissors, etc.
■ *noun* **1** the act of giving sb a small bite or PINCH (= squeezing their skin between your finger and thumb) **2** (*informal*) a feeling of cold: *There was a real nip in the air.*—see also NIPPY **3** (*informal*) a small drink of strong alcohol: *a nip of brandy* IDM **,nip and 'tuck** (*especially AmE*) = NECK AND NECK

nip·per /'nɪpə(r)/ *noun* (*BrE, informal*) a small child

nip·ple /'nɪpl/ *noun* **1** either of the two small round dark parts on a person's chest. Babies can suck milk from their mother's breasts through the nipples.—picture at BODY **2** (*AmE*) = TEAT (1) **3** a small metal, plastic or rubber object that is shaped like a nipple with a small hole in the end, especially one that is used as part of a machine to direct oil, etc. into a particular place: *a grease nipple*

nippy /'nɪpi/ *adj.* **1** (*BrE*) able to move quickly and easily: *a nippy little sports car* **2** (*informal*) (of the weather) cold

nir·vana /nɪə'vɑːnə; *AmE* nɪr'v-/ *noun* [U] (in the religion of Buddhism) the state of peace and happiness that a person achieves after giving up all personal desires

Nis·sen hut /'nɪsn hʌt/ (*BrE*) (*AmE* **Quonset hut**™) *noun* a hut made of metal with curved walls and roof

nit /nɪt/ *noun* **1** the egg or young form of a LOUSE (= a small insect that lives in human hair) **2** (*BrE, informal*) a stupid person

'nit-picking *noun* [U] (*informal, disapproving*) the habit of finding small mistakes in sb's work or paying too much attention to small details that are not important ▶ **'nit-picker** *noun* **'nit-picking** *adj.*

ni·trate /'naɪtreɪt/ *noun* [U, C] (*chemistry*) a compound containing NITROGEN. There are several different nitrates and they are used especially to make soil better for growing crops: *We need to cut nitrate levels in water.*

ni·tric acid /,naɪtrɪk 'æsɪd/ *noun* [U] (*chemistry*) (*symb* HNO_3) a powerful colourless acid that can destroy most substances and is used to make explosives and other chemical products

ni·tro·gen /'naɪtrədʒən/ *noun* [U] (*symb* N) a chemical element. Nitrogen is a colourless gas that is found in large quantities in the earth's atmosphere. ▶ **ni·tro·gen·ous** /naɪ'trɒdʒənəs; *AmE* -'trɑːdʒ-/ *adj.*

nitro·gly·cer·ine /,naɪtrəʊ'glɪsəriːn; -rɪn; *AmE* ,naɪtroʊ'glɪsərən/ (*especially BrE*) (also **nitro·gly·cerin** /-rɪn; *AmE* -rən/ *especially in AmE*) *noun* [U] a powerful liquid explosive

b	d	f	g	h	k	l	m	n	p	r
bad	did	fall	get	hat	cat	leg	**man**	now	pen	red

ni·trous oxide /ˌnaɪtrəs ˈɒksaɪd; *AmE* ˈɑːk-/ (also *informal* **ˈlaughing gas**) *noun* [U] a gas used especially in the past by dentists to prevent you from feeling pain

the nitty-gritty /ˌnɪti ˈɡrɪti/ *noun* [sing.] (*informal*) the basic or most important details of an issue or a situation: *Time ran out before we could get down to the real nitty-gritty.*

nit·wit /ˈnɪtwɪt/ *noun* (*informal*) a stupid person

nix /nɪks/ *verb* [VN] (*AmE, informal*) to prevent sth from happening by saying 'no' to it

No. *abbr.* **1** (also **no.**) (*pl.* **Nos, nos**) number: *Room No. 145* **2** (*AmE*) north; northern

no /nəʊ; *AmE* noʊ/ *exclamation, det., adv., noun*

■ *exclamation* **1** used to give a negative reply or statement: *Just say yes or no.* ◊ *'Are you ready?' 'No, I'm not.'* ◊ *Sorry, the answer's no.* ◊ *'Another drink?' 'No, thanks.'* ◊ *It's about 70—no, I'm wrong—80 kilometres from Rome.* ◊ *No! Don't touch it! It's hot.* ◊ *'It was Tony.' 'No, you're wrong. It was Ted.'* ◊ *'It's not very good, is it?' 'No, you're right, it isn't (= I agree).'* **2** used to express shock or surprise at what sb has said: *'I'm leaving!' 'No!'* ◊ *'She's had an accident.' 'Oh, no!'* **IDM** **not take no for an answer** to refuse to accept that sb does not want sth, will not do sth, etc: *You're coming and I won't take no for an answer!*—more at YES *exclam.*

■ *det.* **1** not one; not any; not a: *No student is to leave the room.* ◊ *There were no letters this morning.* ◊ *There's no bread left.* ◊ *No two days are the same.*—see also NO ONE **2** used, for example on notices, to say that sth is not allowed: *No smoking!* **3 there's ~ doing sth** used to say that it is impossible to do sth: *There's no telling what will happen next.* **4** used to express the opposite of what is mentioned: *She's no fool (= she's intelligent).* ◊ *It was no easy matter (= it was difficult).*

■ *adv.* used before adjectives and adverbs to mean 'not': *She's feeling no better this morning.* ◊ *Reply by no later than 21 July.*

■ *noun* (*pl.* **noes** /nəʊz; *AmE* noʊz/) **1** an answer that shows you do not agree with an idea, a statement, etc.; a person who says 'no': *Can't you give me a straight yes or no?* ◊ *When we took a vote there were nine yesses and 3 noes.* ◊ *I'll put you down as a no.* **2** (**the noes**) [pl.] the total number of people voting 'no' in a formal debate, for example in a parliament: *The noes have it (= more people have voted against sth than for it).* **OPP** AYES

Noah's ark /ˌnəʊəz ˈɑːk; *AmE* ˌnoʊəz ˈɑːrk/ *noun* = ARK

nob /nɒb; *AmE* nɑːb/ *noun* (*old-fashioned, BrE, informal*) a person who has a high social position; a member of the upper class

no-ˈball *noun* (in cricket) a ball that is BOWLED (= thrown) in a way that is not allowed and which means that a RUN (= a point) is given to the other team

nob·ble /ˈnɒbl; *AmE* ˈnɑːbl/ *verb* [VN] (*BrE, informal*) **1** to prevent a horse from winning a race, for example by giving it drugs **2** to persuade sb to do what you want, especially illegally, by offering them money: *his attempts to nobble the jury* **3** to prevent sb from achieving what they want **SYN** THWART **4** to catch sb or get their attention, especially when they are unwilling: *He was nobbled by the press who wanted details of the affair.* ▶ **nob·bling** *noun* [U]

no·bil·ity /nəʊˈbɪləti; *AmE* noʊ-/ *noun* **1** (**the nobility**) [sing.+ sing./ pl. v.] people of high social position who have titles such as that of DUKE or DUCHESS **SYN** THE ARISTOCRACY **2** [U] (*formal*) the quality of being noble in character: *The bravery and nobility of these men who died for their country.*

noble /ˈnəʊbl; *AmE* ˈnoʊbl/ *adj., noun*

■ *adj.* (**no·bler** /ˈnəʊblə(r); *AmE* ˈnoʊ-/ **nob·lest** /ˈnəʊblɪst; *AmE* ˈnoʊ-/) **1** having fine personal qualities that people admire, such as courage, HONESTY and care for others: *a noble leader* ◊ *noble ideals/actions* ◊ *He died for a noble cause.*—compare IGNOBLE **2** very impressive in size or quality **SYN** SPLENDID: *a noble building* **3** belonging to a family of high social rank (= belonging to the nobility): *a man of noble birth* ▶ **nobly** /ˈnəʊbli; *AmE* ˈnoʊbli/ *adv.*: *She bore the disappointment nobly.* ◊ *to be nobly born*

■ *noun* a person who comes from a family of high social rank; a member of the nobility

noble·man /ˈnəʊblmən; *AmE* ˈnoʊbl-/, **noble·woman** /-wʊmən/ *nouns* (*pl.* **-men** /-mən/, **-women** /-wɪmɪn/) a person from a family of high social rank; a member of the NOBILITY

no·blesse ob·lige /nəʊˌbles əˈbliːʒ; *AmE* noʊ-/ *noun* [U] (from *French*) the idea that people who have special advantages of wealth, etc. should help other people who do not have these advantages

no·body /ˈnəʊbədi; *AmE* ˈnoʊ-/ *pron., noun*

■ *pron.* = NO ONE: *Nobody knew what to say.* **HELP** Nobody is more common than **no one** in spoken English. **OPP** SOMEBODY

■ *noun* (*pl.* **-ies**) a person who has no importance or influence **SYN** NONENTITY: *She rose from being a nobody to become a superstar.*—compare SOMEONE

no-ˈclaims bonus (also **no-ˈclaim bonus, no-ˈclaim(s) discount**) *noun* (all *BrE*) a reduction in the cost of your insurance because you made no claims in the previous year

noc·tur·nal /nɒkˈtɜːnl; *AmE* nɑːkˈtɜːrnl/ *adj.* **1** (of animals) active at night **OPP** DIURNAL **2** (*written*) happening during the night: *a nocturnal visit*

noc·turne /ˈnɒktɜːn; *AmE* ˈnɑːktɜːrn/ *noun* a short piece of music in a romantic style, especially for the piano

nod /nɒd; *AmE* nɑːd/ *verb, noun*

■ *verb* (**-dd-**) **1** if you **nod, nod** your head or your head **nods**, you move your head up and down to show agreement, understanding, etc: [V] *I asked him if he would help me and he nodded.* ◊ *Her head nodded in agreement.* ◊ [VN] *He nodded his head sympathetically.* ◊ *She nodded approval.* **2 ~ (sth) (at/to sb)** to move your head down and up once to greet sb or to give them a sign to do sth: [V] *The president nodded to the crowd as he passed in the motorcade.* ◊ *She nodded at him to begin speaking* ◊ [VN] *to nod a greeting* **3** [V+adv./prep.] to move your head in the direction of sb/sth to show that you are talking about them/it: *I asked where Steve was and she nodded in the direction of the kitchen.* **4** [V] to let your head fall forward when you are sleeping in a chair: *He sat nodding in front of the fire.* **IDM** **have a nodding acˈquaintance with sb/sth** to only know sb/sth slightly **PHRV** ˌnod ˈoff (*informal*) to fall asleep for a short time while you are sitting in a chair: *I was practically nodding off in that meeting.*

■ *noun* a small quick movement of the head down and up again: *to give a nod of approval/agreement/encouragement* **IDM** **get the ˈnod** (*informal*) to be chosen for sth; to be given permission or approval to do sth: *He got the nod from the team manager (= he was chosen for the team).* ◊ *The proposal should get the nod.* **give sb/sth the ˈnod** (*informal*) **1** to give permission for sth; to agree to sth: *We've been given the nod to expand the business.* ◊ *I hope he'll give the nod to the plan.* **2** to choose sb for sth **a ˌnod and a ˈwink | a ˌnod is as good as a ˈwink** used to say that a suggestion or a HINT will be understood, without anything more being said: *Everything could be done by a nod and a wink.* **on the ˈnod** (*BrE, informal*) if a proposal is accepted **on the nod**, it is accepted without any discussion

node /nəʊd; *AmE* noʊd/ *noun* **1** (*biology*) a place on the stem of a plant from which a branch or leaf grows **2** (*biology*) a small swelling on a root or branch **3** (*technical*, especially *computing*) a point at which two lines or systems meet or cross: *a data/network node* **4** (*anatomy*) a small hard mass of tissue, especially near a joint in the human body: *a lymph/sinus node* ▶ **nodal** *adj.*

nod·ule /ˈnɒdjuːl; *AmE* ˈnɑːdʒuːl/ *noun* a small round lump or swelling, especially on a plant

Noel /nəʊˈel; *AmE* noʊ-/ *noun* [C, U] a word for 'Christmas' used especially in songs or on cards: *Joyful Noel*

noes *pl.* of NO

no-ˈfault *adj.* [only before noun] (*especially AmE, law*) not involving a decision as to who is to blame for sth: *no-fault insurance (= in which the insurance company pays for damage, etc. without asking whose fault it was)*

s	t	v	z	ʃ	ʒ	tʃ	dʒ	θ	ð	ŋ
see	tea	van	zoo	shoe	vision	chain	jam	thin	this	sing

,no-'fly zone *noun* an area above a country where planes from other countries are not allowed to fly

,no-'go area *noun* (*especially BrE*) an area, especially in a city, which is dangerous for people to enter, or that the police or army do not enter, often because it is controlled by a violent group: (*figurative*) *Some clubs are no-go areas for people over 30.* ◊ (*figurative*) *This subject is definitely a no-go area* (= we must not discuss it).

'no-good *adj.* [only before noun] (*slang*) (of a person) bad or useless

,no-'hoper *noun* (*informal*) a person or an animal that is considered useless or very unlikely to be successful: *a team of complete no-hopers*

noise /nɔɪz/ *noun* **1** [C, U] a sound, especially when it is loud, unpleasant or disturbing: *a rattling noise* ◊ *What's that noise?* ◊ *Don't make so much noise.* ◊ *I was woken by the noise of a car starting up.* ◊ *We had to shout above the noise of the traffic.* ◊ *to monitor/reduce noise levels* **2** [U] (*technical*) extra electrical or electronic signals that are not part of the signal that is being broadcast or TRANSMITTED and which may damage it **IDM make a 'noise (about sth)** (*informal*) to complain loudly **make 'noises (about sth)** (*informal*) **1** to talk in an indirect way about sth that you think you might do: *The company has been making noises about closing several factories.* **2** to complain about sth **make soothing, encouraging, reassuring, etc. noises** to make remarks of the kind mentioned, even when that is not what you really think: *He made all the right noises at the meeting yesterday* (= said what people wanted to hear).—more at BIG *adj.*

> **WHICH WORD?** ❓
> **noise / sound**
>
> **Sound** is a general word for anything you hear: *strange sounds and smells* ◊ *She could hear the sound of children laughing.* Do not use words like *much* or *a lot of* with **sound**.
>
> **Noise** is usually loud and unpleasant: *What a terrible noise!* It can be uncountable: *Try not to make so much noise.*
>
> **Racket** and **din** (especially *BrE*) are informal words for a loud unpleasant noise that continues for a time: *Who's making all that racket?* ◊ *What a terrible din!*

noise·less /'nɔɪzləs/ *adj.* (*written*) making little or no noise: *He moved with noiseless steps.* ▶ **noise·less·ly** *adv.*

noi·some /'nɔɪsəm/ *adj.* (*rare, formal*) extremely unpleasant or offensive: *noisome smells/sights*

noisy /'nɔɪzi/ *adj.* (**nois·ier, noisi·est**) **1** making a lot of noise: *noisy children/traffic/crowds* ◊ *a noisy protest* (= when people shout) ◊ *The engine is very noisy at high speed.* **2** full of noise: *a noisy classroom* ▶ **nois·ily** /-ɪli/ *adv.*: *The children were playing noisily upstairs.*

nomad /'nəʊmæd; *AmE* 'noʊ-/ *noun* a member of a tribe that moves with its animals from place to place ▶ **no·mad·ic** /nəʊ'mædɪk; *AmE* noʊ-/ *adj.*: *nomadic tribes* ◊ *the nomadic life of a foreign correspondent*

'no-man's-land *noun* [U, sing.] an area of land between the borders of two countries or between two armies, that is not controlled by either

nom de plume /ˌnɒm də 'pluːm; *AmE* ˌnɑːm/ *noun* (*pl.* **noms de plume** /ˌnɒm də 'pluːm; *AmE* ˌnɑːm/*) (from *French*) a name used by a writer instead of their real name **SYN** PEN-NAME, PSEUDONYM

no·men·cla·ture /nə'menklətʃə(r); *AmE* also 'noʊmənkleɪtʃər/ *noun* [U, C] (*formal*) a system of naming things, especially in a branch of science: *chemical/zoological nomenclature*

nom·in·al /'nɒmɪnl; *AmE* 'nɑːm-/ *adj.* **1** being sth in name only, and not in reality: *the nominal leader of the party* ◊ *He remained in nominal control of the business for another ten years.* **2** (of a sum of money) very small and much less than the normal cost or change: *We only pay a nominal rent.* **3** (*grammar*) connected with a noun or nouns ▶ **nom·in·al·ly** /-nəli/ *adv.*: *He was nominally in charge of the company.*

nom·in·ate /'nɒmɪneɪt; *AmE* 'nɑːm-/ *verb* **1** ~ **sb (for/as sth)** to formally suggest that sb should be chosen for an important role, prize, position, etc: [VN] *She has been nominated for the presidency.* ◊ [VN-N] *He was nominated (as) best actor.* [also VN to inf] **2** ~ **sb (to/as sth)** to choose sb to do a particular job **SYN** APPOINT: [VN] *I have been nominated to the committee.* ◊ [VN to inf] *She was nominated to speak on our behalf.* **3** [VN] ~ **sth (as sth)** to choose a time, date or title for sth: *1 December has been nominated as the day of the election.*

nom·in·ation /ˌnɒmɪ'neɪʃn; *AmE* ˌnɑːm-/ *noun* [U, C] the act of suggesting or choosing sb as a candidate in an election, or for a job or an award; the fact of being suggested for this: *Membership of the club is by nomination only.* ◊ *He won the nomination as Democratic candidate for the presidency.* ◊ *They opposed her nomination to the post of Deputy Director.* ◊ *Meryl Streep has had nine Oscar nominations.*

nom·ina·tive /'nɒmɪnətɪv; *AmE* 'nɑːm-/ *noun* (*grammar*) (in some languages) the form of a noun, a pronoun or an adjective when it is the subject of a verb—compare ACCUSATIVE, DATIVE, GENITIVE, VOCATIVE ▶ **nom·ina·tive** *adj.*: *nominative pronouns*

nom·inee /ˌnɒmɪ'niː; *AmE* ˌnɑːm-/ *noun* **1** a person who has been formally suggested for a job, a prize, etc: *a presidential nominee* ◊ *an Oscar nominee* **2** (*business*) a person in whose name money is invested in a company, etc.

non- /nɒn; *AmE* nɑːn/ *prefix* (in nouns, adjectives and adverbs) not: *nonsense* ◊ *non-fiction* ◊ *non-alcoholic* ◊ *non-profit-making* ◊ *non-committally* **HELP** Most compounds with **non** are written with a hyphen in *BrE* but are written as one word with no hyphen in *AmE*.

nona·gen·ar·ian /ˌnɒnədʒə'neəriən; ˌnəʊn-; *AmE* ˌnɑːnədʒə'ner-; ˌnoʊn-/ *noun* a person who is between 90 and 99 years old ▶ **nona·gen·ar·ian** *adj.*

,non-ag'gres·sion *noun* [U] (often used as an adjective) a relationship between two countries that have agreed not to attack each other: *a policy of non-aggression* ◊ *a non-aggression pact/treaty*

,non-alco'hol·ic *adj.* (of a drink) not containing any alcohol: *a non-alcoholic drink* ◊ *Can I have something non-alcoholic?*

,non-a'ligned *adj.* not providing support for or receiving support from any of the powerful countries in the world: *the non-aligned countries/states* ▶ **,non-a'lignment** *noun* [U]: *a policy of non-alignment*

,non-ap'pear·ance *noun* [U] (*formal*) failure to be in a place where people expect to see you

,non-at'tend·ance *noun* [U] failure to go to a place at a time or for an event where you are expected: *the problems of children's non-attendance at school*

non-cha·lant /'nɒnʃələnt; *AmE* ˌnɑːnʃə'lɑːnt/ *adj.* behaving in a calm and relaxed way; giving the impression that you are not feeling any anxiety: *to appear/look/sound nonchalant* ◊ *'It'll be fine,' she replied, with a nonchalant shrug.* ▶ **non-cha·lance** /-ləns; *AmE* -'lɑːns/ *noun* [U]: *an air of nonchalance* **non-cha·lant·ly** *adv.*: *He was leaning nonchalantly against the wall.*

,non-'citizen *noun* (*AmE*) = ALIEN(1)

,non-'combat·ant *noun* **1** a member of the armed forces who does not actually fight in a war, for example an army doctor **2** in a war, a person who is not a member of the armed forces **SYN** CIVILIAN—compare COMBATANT

,non-commis·sioned 'officer *noun* (*abbr.* NCO) a soldier in the army, etc. who has a rank such as SERGEANT or CORPORAL, but not a high rank—compare COMMISSIONED OFFICER

,non-co'mmit·tal *adj.* not giving an opinion; not showing which side of an argument you agree with: *a non-committal reply/tone* ◊ *The doctor was non-committal about when I could drive again.*—see also COMMIT (5) ▶ **,non-com'mit·tal·ly** *adv.*

,non-com'pli·ance *noun* [U] ~ **(with sth)** the fact of failing or refusing to obey a rule: *There are penalties for non-compliance with the fire regulations.* **OPP** COMPLIANCE

non·con·form·ist /ˌnɒnkən'fɔːmɪst; *AmE* ˌnɑːn-

æ	ɑː	e	ɜː	ə	ɪ	iː	i	ɒ	ɔː	ʌ	ʊ	u	uː
cat	father	ten	bird	about	sit	see	many	got	saw	cup	put	actual	too
								(BrE)					

N

kən'fɔːrm-/ *noun* **1 (Nonconformist)** a member of a Protestant Church that does not follow the beliefs and practices of the Anglican Church—compare DISSENTER **2** a person who does not follow normal ways of thinking or behaving ► **non·con·form·ist, Non·con·form·ist** *adj.*

non·con·form·ity /ˌnɒnkən'fɔːmɪti; *AmE* ˌnɑːnkən-'fɔːrm-/ (also **non·con·form·ism**) *noun* [U] **1** the fact of not following normal ways of thinking and behaving **2 (Nonconformity)** the beliefs and practices of Nonconformist Churches

non·con'tribu·tory *adj.* (of an insurance or pension plan) paid for by the employer and not the employee: *non-contributory benefits* OPP CONTRIBUTORY

non·contro·'ver·sial *adj.* not causing, or not likely to cause, any disagreement OPP CONTROVERSIAL HELP This is not as strong as **uncontroversial**, which is more common.

non·co,ope'r·ation *noun* [U] refusal to help a person in authority by doing what they have asked you to do, especially as a form of protest: *A strike is unlikely, but some forms of non-cooperation are being considered.*

non·cu'stod·ial *adj.* [only before noun] (*law*) **1** (of a punishment) that does not involve a period of time in prison: *a non-custodial sentence/penalty* **2** (of a parent) not having CUSTODY of a child OPP CUSTODIAL

non-'dairy *adj.* [only before noun] not made with milk or cream: *a non-dairy whipped topping*

non·de·script /'nɒndɪskrɪpt; *AmE* 'nɑːn-/ *adj.* (*disapproving*) having no interesting or unusual features or qualities SYN DULL: *a nondescript person/building/town*

none /nʌn/ *pron., adv.*
■ *pron.* **~ (of sb/sth)** not one of a group of people or things; not any: *None of these pens works/work.* ◊ *We have three sons but none of them lives/live nearby.* ◊ *We saw several houses but none we really liked.* ◊ *Tickets for Friday? Sorry we've got none left.* ◊ *He told me all the news but none of it was very exciting.* ◊ *'Is there any more milk?' 'No, none at all.'* ◊ (*formal*) *Everybody liked him but none* (= nobody) *more than I.* IDM **'none but** (*literary*) only: *None but he knew the truth.* **none 'other than** used to emphasize who or what sb/sth is, when this is surprising: *Her first customer was none other than Mrs Blair.* **have/want none of sth** to refuse to accept sth: *I offered to pay but he was having none of it.* **none the 'less** = NONETHELESS
■ *adv.* **1** used with *the* and a comparative to mean 'not at all': *She told me what it meant at great length but I'm afraid I'm none the wiser.* ◊ *He seems none the worse for the experience.* **2** used with *too* and an adjective or adverb to mean 'not at all' or 'not very': *She was looking none too pleased.*

> **GRAMMAR POINT**
> **none of**
>
> When you use **none** with an uncountable noun, the verb is in the singular: *None of the work was done.*
> When you use **none of** with a plural noun or pronoun, or a singular noun referring to a group of people or things, you can use either a singular or a plural verb. The singular form is used in a formal style in *BrE*: *None of the trains is/are going to London.* ◊ *None of her family has/have been to college.*

non·en·tity /nɒ'nentəti; *AmE* nɑː'n-/ *noun* (*pl.* **-ies**) (*disapproving*) a person without any special qualities, who has not achieved anything important SYN NOBODY

non-es'sential *adj.* [usually before noun] not completely necessary—compare ESSENTIAL HELP This is not as strong as **inessential** and is more common. **Inessential** can suggest disapproval. ► **,non-es'sential** *noun* [usually pl.]: *I have no money for non-essentials.*

none·the·less /ˌnʌnðə'les/ (also **,none the 'less**) *adv.* (*written*) in spite of this fact SYN NEVERTHELESS: *The book is too long but, nonetheless, informative and entertaining.* ◊ *The problems are not serious. Nonetheless, we shall need to tackle them soon.*

,non-e'vent *noun* (*informal*) an event that was expected to be interesting, exciting and popular but is in fact very disappointing

,non-ex'ecutive *adj.* [only before noun] (*BrE, business*) a **non-executive** DIRECTOR of a company can give advice at a high level but does not have the power to make decisions about the company

,non-e'xistent *adj.* not existing; not real: *a non-existent danger/problem* ◊ *'How's your social life?' 'Non-existent, I'm afraid.'*—compare EXISTENT ► **,non-e'xistence** *noun* [U]

,non-'fiction *noun* [U] books, articles or texts about real facts, people and events: *I prefer reading non-fiction.* ◊ *the non-fiction section of the library* OPP FICTION

,non-'finite *adj.* (*grammar*) a **non-finite** verb form or CLAUSE does not show a particular tense, PERSON OR NUMBER OPP FINITE

,non-'flammable *adj.* not likely to catch fire easily: *non-flammable nightwear* OPP FLAMMABLE

,non-'human *adj.* not human: *similarities between human and non-human animals*—compare HUMAN, INHUMAN

,non-inter'ven·tion (also **,non-inter'fer·ence**) *noun* [U] the policy or practice of not becoming involved in other people's disputes, especially those of foreign countries: *a policy of non-intervention in the internal affairs of other countries* ► **,non-inter'ven·tion·ism** *noun* [U] **,non-inter'ven·tion·ist** *adj.*

,non-'linear *adj.* (*technical*) that does not develop from one thing to another in a single smooth series of stages OPP LINEAR

,non-ne'gotiable *adj.* **1** that cannot be discussed or changed: *non-negotiable demands* **2** (of a cheque, etc.) that cannot be changed for money by anyone except the person whose name is on it OPP NEGOTIABLE

'no-no *noun* [sing.] (*informal*) a thing or a way of behaving that is not acceptable in a particular situation

,non-ob'servance *noun* [U] (*formal*) the failure to keep or to obey a rule, custom, etc. OPP OBSERVANCE

,no-'nonsense *adj.* [only before noun] simple and direct; only paying attention to important and necessary things: *a no-nonsense approach/style*

,non-parti'san *adj.* [usually before noun] not supporting the ideas of one particular political party or group of people strongly

,non-'payment *noun* [U] (*formal*) failure to pay a debt, a tax, rent, etc.

non·plussed (*AmE* also **non·plused**) /ˌnɒn'plʌst; *AmE* ˌnɑːn-/ *adj.* so surprised and confused that you do not know what to do or say

,non-pre'scrip·tion *adj.* [only before noun] (of drugs) that you can buy directly without a special form from a doctor

,non-pro'fes·sion·al *adj.* **1** having a job that does not need a high level of education or special training; connected with a job of this kind: *training for non-professional staff* **2** doing sth as a hobby rather than as a paid job: *non-professional actors/drivers*—compare PROFESSIONAL, UNPROFESSIONAL—see also AMATEUR

,non-'profit (*BrE* also **,non-'profit-making**) *adj.* (of an organization) without the aim of making a profit: *an independent non-profit organization/body* ◊ *The centre is run on a non-profit basis.* ◊ *The charity is non-profit-making.*

,non-pro,life'r·ation *noun* [U] a limit to the increase in the number of nuclear and chemical weapons that are produced

,non-re'fund·able (also **,non-re'turnable**) *adj.* (of a sum of money) that cannot be returned: *a non-refundable deposit* ◊ *a non-refundable ticket* (= you cannot return it and get your money back)

,non-'renewable *adj.* (of natural RESOURCES such as gas or oil) **1** that cannot be replaced after use **2** that cannot be continued or repeated for a further period of time after it has ended: *a non-renewable contract/lease* OPP RENEWABLE

,non-'resident *adj., noun*

aɪ	aʊ	eɪ	əʊ	oʊ	ɔɪ	ɪə	eə	ʊə	j	w
my	now	say	go	go	boy	near	hair	pure	yes	wet
			(BrE)	(AmE)						

■ *adj.* (*formal*) **1** (of a person or company) not living or situated permanently in a particular place or country **2** not living in the place where you work or in a house that you own **3** not staying at a particular hotel

■ *noun* **1** a person who does not live permanently in a particular country **2** a person not staying at a particular hotel

non-resi'dent·ial *adj.* **1** that is not used for people to live in **2** that does not require you to live in the place where you work or study: *a non-residential course*

non-re'turn·able *adj.* **1** = NON-REFUNDABLE **2** that you cannot give back, for example to a shop/store, to be used again; that will not be given back to you: *non-returnable bottles ◇ a non-returnable deposit* OPP RETURNABLE

non-scien'ti·fic *adj.* not involving or connected with science or scientific methods: *scientific and non-scientific subjects*—compare SCIENTIFIC, UNSCIENTIFIC

non·sense /'nɒnsns; *AmE* 'nɑːnsens; -sns/ *noun* **1** [U, C] ideas, statements or beliefs that you think are ridiculous or not true SYN RUBBISH: *Reports that he has resigned are nonsense. ◇ You're talking nonsense! ◇ 'I won't go.' 'Nonsense! You must go!' ◇ It's nonsense to say they don't care. ◇ The idea is an economic nonsense.* **2** [U] silly or unacceptable behaviour: *The new teacher won't stand for any nonsense.*—see also NO-NONSENSE **3** [U] spoken or written words that have no meaning or make no sense: *a book of children's nonsense poems ◇ Most of the translation he did for me was complete nonsense.* IDM **make (a) 'nonsense of sth** to reduce the value of sth by a lot; to make sth seem ridiculous: *If people can bribe police officers, it makes a complete nonsense of the legal system.*

non·sens·ical /nɒn'sensɪkl; *AmE* nɑːn-/ *adj.* ridiculous; with no meaning SYN ABSURD: *a nonsensical argument/theory*

non sequi·tur /ˌnɒn 'sekwɪtə(r); *AmE* ˌnɑːn/ *noun* (from Latin, *formal*) a statement that does not seem to follow what has just been said in any natural or logical way

non-'slip *adj.* that helps to prevent sb/sth from slipping; that does not slip: *a non-slip bath mat*

non-'smoker *noun* a person who does not smoke OPP SMOKER

non-'smoking (also ˌno-'smoking) *adj.* [usually before noun] **1** (of a place) where people are not allowed to smoke: *a non-smoking area in a restaurant* **2** (of a person) who does not smoke: *She's a non-smoking, non-drinking fitness fanatic.* ▶ **non-'smoking** (also ˌno-'smoking) *noun* [U]: *Non-smoking is now the norm in most workplaces.*

non-spe'cific *adj.* [usually before noun] **1** not definite or clearly defined; general: *The candidate's speech was non-specific.* **2** (*medical*) (of pain, a disease, etc.) with more than one possible cause

non-'standard *adj.* **1** (of language) not considered correct by most educated people: *non-standard dialects ◇ non-standard English*—compare STANDARD **2** not the usual size, type, etc: *The paper was of non-standard size.*

non-'starter *noun* (*informal*) a thing or a person that has no chance of success: *As a business proposition, it's a non-starter.*

non-'stick *adj.* [usually before noun] (of a pan or a surface) covered with a substance that prevents food from sticking to it

non-'stop *adj.* **1** (of a train, a journey, etc.) without any stops SYN DIRECT: *a non-stop flight to Tokyo ◇ a non-stop train/service* **2** without any pauses or stops SYN CONTINUOUS: *non-stop entertainment/work* ▶ **non-'stop** *adv.*: *We flew non-stop from Paris to Chicago. ◇ It rained non-stop all week.*

non-'union (also *less frequent* ˌnon-'unionized, -ised) *adj.* [usually before noun] **1** not belonging to a trade union: *non-union labour/workers* **2** (of a business, company, etc.) not accepting trade unions or employing trade union members

non-'verbal *adj.* [usually before noun] not involving words or speech: *non-verbal communication/behaviour*

non-'violence *noun* [U] the policy of using peaceful methods, not force, to bring about political or social change

non-'violent *adj.* **1** using peaceful methods, not force, to bring about political or social change: *non-violent action/opposition/resistance* **2** not involving force, or injury to sb: *non-violent crimes*

non-'white *noun* a person who is not a member of a race of people who have white skin ▶ **non-'white** *adj.*

noo·dle /'nuːdl/ *noun* [usually pl.] a long thin strip of PASTA, used especially in Chinese and Italian cooking: *chicken noodle soup ◇ Would you prefer rice or noodles?*

nook /nʊk/ *noun* a small quiet place or corner that is sheltered or hidden from other people: *a cosy little nook by the fire ◇ a shady nook in the garden ◇ dark woods full of secret nooks and crannies* IDM **every ˌnook and 'cranny** (*informal*) every part of a place; every aspect of a situation

nooky (also **nookie**) /'nʊki/ *noun* [U] (*slang*) sexual activity

noon /nuːn/ *noun* [U] 12 o'clock in the middle of the day SYN MIDDAY: *We should be there by noon. ◇ The conference opens at 12 noon on Saturday. ◇ the noon deadline for the end of hostilities ◇ I'm leaving on the noon train. ◇ the glaring light of high noon* IDM see MORNING

noon·day /'nuːndeɪ/ *adj.* [only before noun] (*old-fashioned* or *literary*) happening or appearing at noon: *the noonday sun*

'no one (also ˌno-'body) *pron.* not anyone; no person: *No one was at home. ◇ There was no one else around. ◇ We were told to speak to no one.* HELP **No one** is much more common than **nobody** in written English.

noose /nuːs/ *noun* a circle that is tied in one end of a rope with a knot that allows the circle to get smaller as the other end of the rope is pulled: *a hangman's noose ◇* (*figurative*) *His debts were a noose around his neck.*

nope /nəʊp; *AmE* noʊp/ *exclamation* (*informal*) used to say 'no': *'Have you seen my pen?' 'Nope.'*

'no place *adv.* (*informal, especially AmE*) = NOWHERE: *I have no place else to go.*

nor /nɔː(r)/ *conj., adv.* **1 neither ... nor ... | not ... nor ...** and not: *She seemed neither surprised nor worried. ◇ He wasn't there on Monday. Nor on Tuesday, for that matter. ◇* (*formal*) *Not a building nor a tree was left standing.* **2** used before a positive verb to agree with sth negative that has just been said: *She doesn't like them and nor does Jeff. ◇ 'I'm not going.' 'Nor am I.'*

Nor·dic /'nɔːdɪk; *AmE* 'nɔːrdɪk/ *adj.* **1** of or connected with the countries of Scandinavia, Finland and Iceland **2** typical of a member of a European race of people who are tall and have blue eyes and BLONDE hair: *Nordic features*

norm /nɔːm; *AmE* nɔːrm/ *noun* **1** (often **the norm**) [sing.] a situation or a pattern of behaviour that is usual or expected: *a deviation/departure from the norm ◇ Single parents seem to be the norm rather than the exception nowadays.* **2** (**norms**) [pl.] standards of behaviour that are typical of or accepted within a particular group or society: *social/cultural norms* **3** [C] a required or agreed standard, amount, etc: *detailed education norms for children of particular ages*

nor·mal /'nɔːml; *AmE* 'nɔːrml/ *adj., noun*

■ *adj.* **1** typical, usual or ordinary; what you would expect: *quite/perfectly* (= completely) *normal ◇ Her temperature is normal. ◇ It's normal to feel tired after such a long trip. ◇ Divorce is complicated enough in normal circumstances, but this situation is even worse. ◇ Under normal circumstances, I would say 'yes'. ◇ He should be able to lead a perfectly normal life. ◇ In the normal course of events I wouldn't go to that part of town. ◇ We are open during normal office hours.* **2** not suffering from any mental disorder: *People who commit such crimes aren't normal.* OPP ABNORMAL ⇨ note on page 864 IDM see PER

■ *noun* [U] the usual or average state, level or standard: *above/below normal ◇ Things soon returned to normal.*

nor·mal·ity /nɔːˈmæləti; *AmE* nɔːrˈm-/ (also **nor·malcy** /ˈnɔːmlsi; *AmE* ˈnɔːrm-/ especially in *AmE*) noun [U] a situation where everything is normal or as you would expect it to be: *They are hoping for a return to normality now that the war is over.*

nor·mal·ize (*BrE* also **-ise**) /ˈnɔːməlaɪz; *AmE* ˈnɔːrm-/ verb (*written*) to fit or make sth fit a normal pattern or condition: [VN] *a lotion to normalize oily skin* ◊ *The two countries agreed to normalize relations* (= return to a normal, friendly relationship, for example after a disagreement or war). ◊ [V] *It took time until the political situation had normalized.* ▶ **nor·mal·iza·tion, -isa·tion** /ˌnɔːməlaɪˈzeɪʃn; *AmE* ˌnɔːrmələˈz-/ noun [U]: *the normalization of relations*

nor·mal·ly /ˈnɔːməli; *AmE* ˈnɔːrm-/ adv. **1** usually; in normal circumstances: *I'm not normally allowed to stay out late.* ◊ *It's normally much warmer than this in July.* ◊ *It normally takes 20 minutes to get there.* **2** in the usual or ordinary way: *Her heart is beating normally.* ◊ *Just try to behave normally.*

Nor·man /ˈnɔːmən; *AmE* ˈnɔːrm-/ adj. **1** used to describe the style of architecture in Britain in the 11th and 12th centuries that developed from the ROMANESQUE style: *a Norman church/castle* **2** connected with the Normans (= the people from northern Europe who defeated the English in 1066 and then ruled the country): *the Norman Conquest*

nor·ma·tive /ˈnɔːmətɪv; *AmE* ˈnɔːrm-/ adj. (*formal*) describing or setting standards or rules of behaviour: *a normative approach*

north /nɔːθ; *AmE* nɔːrθ/ noun, adj., adv.
■ noun [U, sing.] (*abbr.* **N, No.**) **1** (usually **the north**) the direction that is on your left when you watch the sun rise; one of the four main points of the COMPASS: *Which way is north?* ◊ *cold winds coming from the north.* ◊ *Mount Kenya is to the north of* (= further north than) *Nairobi.*—compare EAST, SOUTH, WEST—see also MAGNETIC NORTH, TRUE NORTH—picture at COMPASS **2** (**the north, the North**) the northern part of a country, a region or the world: *birds migrating from the north* ◊ *Houses are less expensive in the North* (= of England) *than in the South.* **3** (**the North**) the NE states of the US which fought against the South in the American Civil War **4** (**the North**) the richer and more developed countries of the world, especially in Europe and N America
■ adj. [only before noun] **1** (*abbr.* **N, No.**) in or towards the north: *North London* ◊ *the north bank of the river* **2** a **north wind** blows from the north—compare NORTHERLY
■ adv. towards the north: *The house faces north.* **IDM up 'north** (*informal*) to or in the north of a country, especially England: *They've gone to live up north.*

north·bound /ˈnɔːθbaʊnd; *AmE* ˈnɔːrθ-/ adj. travelling or leading towards the north: *northbound traffic* ◊ *the northbound carriageway of the motorway*

'north-country adj. [only before noun] connected with the northern part of England: *a north-country accent*

,north-'east noun (usually **the north-east**) [sing.] (*abbr.* **NE**) the direction or region halfway between north and east—picture at COMPASS ▶ **,north-'east** adv., adj.

,north-'easterly adj. **1** [only before noun] in or towards the north-east: *travelling in a north-easterly direction* **2** [usually before noun] (of winds) blowing from the north-east

,north-'eastern adj. [only before noun] (*abbr.* **NE**) connected with the north-east

,north-'eastwards (also **,north-'eastward**) adv. towards the north-east ▶ **,north-'eastward** adj.

north·er·ly /ˈnɔːðəli; *AmE* ˈnɔːrðərli/ adj., noun
■ adj. **1** [only before noun] in or towards the north: *travelling in a northerly direction* **2** [usually before noun] (of winds) blowing from the north: *a northerly breeze*—compare NORTH
■ noun (*pl.* **-ies**) a wind that blows from the north

north·ern /ˈnɔːðən; *AmE* ˈnɔːrðərn/ adj. (also **Northern**) [usually before noun] (*abbr.* **N, No.**) situated in the north or facing north; connected with or typical of the north part of the world or a region: *the northern slopes of the mountains* ◊ *northern Scotland* ◊ *a northern accent/climate*

north·ern·er /ˈnɔːðənə(r); *AmE* ˈnɔːrðən-/ noun a person who comes from or lives in the northern part of a country

the ,northern 'lights noun [pl.] (also **aurora bore'alis**) bands of coloured light, mainly green and red, that are sometimes seen in the sky at night in the most northern countries of the world

north·ern·most /ˈnɔːðənməʊst; *AmE* ˈnɔːrðərnmoʊst/ adj. [usually before noun] furthest north: *the northernmost city in the world*

the ,North 'Pole noun [sing.] the point on the surface of the earth that is furthest north

north·wards /ˈnɔːθwədz; *AmE* ˈnɔːrθwərdz/ (also **north-ward**) adv. towards the north: *to go/look/turn northwards* ▶ **north·ward** adj.: *in a northward direction*

,north-'west noun (usually **the north-west**) [sing.] (*abbr.* **NW**) the direction or region halfway between north and west—picture at COMPASS ▶ **,north-'west** adv., adj.

,north-'westerly adj. **1** [only before noun] in or towards the north-west **2** (of winds) blowing from the north-west

,north-'western adj. [only before noun] (*abbr.* **NW**) connected with the north-west

,north-'westwards (also **,north-'westward**) adv. towards the north-west ▶ **,north-'westward** adj.

nose /nəʊz; *AmE* noʊz/ noun, verb
■ noun **1** [C] the part of the face that sticks out above the mouth, used for breathing and smelling things: *He broke his nose in the fight.* ◊ *She wrinkled her nose in disgust.* ◊ *He blew his nose* (= cleared it by blowing strongly into a HANDKERCHIEF). ◊ *a blocked/runny nose* ◊ *Stop picking your nose!* (= removing dirt from it with your finger)—see also NASAL, ROMAN NOSE—picture at BODY **2** (**-nosed**) (in adjectives) having the type of nose mentioned: *red-nosed* ◊ *large-nosed*—see also HARD-NOSED, TOFFEE-NOSED **3** [C] the front part of a plane, spacecraft, etc.—picture at PLANE **4** [sing.] a **~ for sth** a special ability for finding or recognizing sth: *As a journalist, she has always had a nose for a good story.* **5** [sing.] a sense of smell: *a dog with a good nose* **6** [sing.] (of wine) a characteristic smell [SYN] BOUQUET—see also PARSON'S NOSE [IDM] **cut off your nose to spite your 'face** (*informal*) to do sth when you are angry that is meant to harm sb else but which also harms you **get up sb's 'nose** (*BrE, informal*) to annoy sb **have your nose in 'sth** (*informal*) to be reading sth and giving it all your attention **have a nose 'round** (*BrE, informal*) to look around a place; to look for sth in a place **keep your 'nose clean** (*informal*) to avoid doing anything wrong or illegal: *Since leaving prison, he's managed to keep his nose clean.* **keep your nose out of sth** to try not to become involved in things that do not concern you **keep your nose to the 'grindstone** (*informal*) to work hard for a long period of time without stopping **look down your 'nose at sb/sth** (*informal, especially BrE*) to behave in a way that suggests that you think that you are better than sb or that sth is not good enough for you **,nose to 'tail** (*BrE*) if cars, etc. are nose to tail, they are moving slowly in a long line with little space between

N

them **on the ˈnose** (*informal, especially AmE*) exactly: *The budget should hit the $136 billion target on the nose.* **poke/stick your nose into** ˈsth (*informal*) to try to become involved in sth that does not concern you **put sb's ˈnose out of joint** (*informal*) to upset or annoy sb, especially by not giving them enough attention **turn your ˈnose up at sth** (*informal*) to refuse sth, especially because you do not think that it is good enough for you **under sb's ˈnose** (*informal*) **1** if sth is **under sb's nose**, it is very close to them but they cannot see it: *I searched everywhere for the letter and it was under my nose all the time!* **2** if sth happens **under sb's nose**, they do not notice it even though it is not being done secretly: *The police didn't know the drugs ring was operating right under their noses.* **with your nose in the air** (*informal*) in a way that is unfriendly and suggests that you think that you are better than other people—more at FOLLOW, LEAD *v.*, PAY *v.*, PLAIN *adj.*, POWDER *v.*, RUB *v.*, SKIN *n.*, THUMB *v.*

▪ *verb* **1** [+*adv./prep.*] to move forward slowly and carefully: [V] *The plane nosed down through the thick clouds.* ◊ [VN] *The taxi nosed its way back into the traffic.* **2** [V+*adv./prep.*] (of an animal) to search for sth or push sth with its nose: *Dogs nosed around in piles of refuse.* **PHRV** ˌnose aˈbout/aˈround (for sth) to look for sth, especially information about sb: *We found a man nosing around in our backyard.* ˌnose sth↔ˈout (*informal*) to discover information about sb/sth by searching for it: *Reporters nosed out all the details of the affair.*

nose·bag /ˈnəʊzbæg; *AmE* ˈnoʊz-/ (*BrE*) (*AmE* **feed·bag**) *noun* a bag containing food for a horse, that you hang from its head

nose·bleed /ˈnəʊzbliːd; *AmE* ˈnoʊz-/ *noun* a flow of blood that comes from the nose

ˈnose-cone *noun* the pointed front end of a rocket, an aircraft, etc.

nose·dive /ˈnəʊzdaɪv; *AmE* ˈnoʊz-/ *noun, verb*
▪ *noun* **1** a sudden steep fall or drop; a situation where sth suddenly becomes worse or begins to fail: *Oil prices took a nosedive in the crisis.* ◊ *These policies have sent the construction industry into an abrupt nosedive.* **2** the sudden sharp fall of an aircraft towards the ground with its front part pointing down
▪ *verb* [V] **1** (of prices, costs, etc.) to fall suddenly SYN PLUMMET: *Building costs have nosedived.* **2** (of an aircraft) to fall suddenly with the front part pointing towards the ground

nose·gay /ˈnəʊzgeɪ; *AmE* ˈnoʊz-/ *noun* (*old-fashioned*) a small bunch of flowers

ˈnose job *noun* (*informal*) a medical operation on the nose to improve its shape

ˈnose ring *noun* **1** a ring that is put in an animal's nose for leading it **2** a ring worn in the nose as a piece of jewellery

nosey = NOSY

nosh /nɒʃ; *AmE* nɑːʃ/ *noun, verb*
▪ *noun* **1** [U, sing.] (*old-fashioned, BrE, slang*) food; a meal: *She likes her nosh.* ◊ *Did you have a good nosh?* **2** (*especially AmE*) a small meal that you eat quickly between main meals
▪ *verb* [V, VN] (*informal*) to eat

ˌno-ˈshow *noun* (*informal*) a person who is expected to be somewhere and does not come; a situation where this happens: *No-shows are a great problem in the hotel trade.* ◊ *Fans were disappointed by his no-show at the festival.*

ˈnosh-up *noun* (*slang, especially BrE*) a very large meal: *We went for a nosh-up at that new restaurant in town.*

ˌno-ˈsmoking *adj.* = NON-SMOKING

nos·tal·gia /nɒˈstældʒə; *AmE* nəˈs-; nɑːˈs-/ *noun* [U] a feeling of sadness mixed with pleasure and affection when you think of happy times in the past: *a sense/wave/pang of nostalgia* ◊ *She is filled with nostalgia for her own college days.* ▸ **nos·tal·gic** /nɒˈstældʒɪk; *AmE* nəˈs-; nɑːˈs-/ *adj.*: *nostalgic memories* ◊ *I feel quite nostalgic for the place where I grew up.* **nos·tal·gic·al·ly** /-kli/ *adv.*: *to look back nostalgically to your childhood*

nos·tril /ˈnɒstrəl; *AmE* ˈnɑːs-/ *noun* either of the two openings at the end of the nose that you breathe through—picture at BODY

nos·trum /ˈnɒstrəm; *AmE* ˈnɑːs-/ *noun* **1** (*formal, disapproving*) an idea that is intended to solve a problem but that will probably not succeed **2** (*old-fashioned*) a medicine that is not made in a scientific way, and that is not effective

nosy (also **nosey**) /ˈnəʊzi; *AmE* ˈnoʊzi/ *adj.* (*informal, disapproving*) too interested in things that do not concern you, especially other people's affairs SYN INQUISITIVE: *nosy neighbours* ◊ *Don't be so nosy—it's none of your business.* ▸ **nosi·ness** *noun* [U]

ˌnosy ˈparker *noun* (*BrE, informal, becoming old-fashioned*) a person who is too interested in other people's affairs

not /nɒt; *AmE* nɑːt/ *adv.* **1** used to form the negative of the verbs *be*, *do* and *have* and modal verbs like *can* or *must* and often shortened to *n't*: *She did not/didn't see him.* ◊ *It's not/it isn't raining.* ◊ *I can't see from here.* ◊ *He must not go.* ◊ *Don't you eat meat?* ◊ *It's cold, isn't it?* **2** used to give the following word or phrase a negative meaning, or to reply in the negative: *He warned me not to be late.* ◊ *I was sorry not to have seen them.* ◊ *Not everybody agrees.* ◊ *'Who's next?' 'Not me.'* ◊ *'What did you do at school?' ' Not a lot.'* ◊ *It's not easy being a parent* (= it's difficult). **3** used after *hope*, *expect*, *believe*, etc. to give a negative reply: *'Will she be there?' 'I hope not.'* ◊ *'Is it ready?' 'I'm afraid not.'* ◊ (*formal*) *'Does he know?' 'I believe not.'* **4** or **~** used to show a negative possibility: *I don't know if he's telling the truth or not.* **5** used to say that you do not want sth or will not allow sth: *'Some more?' 'Not for me, thanks.'* ◊ *'Can I throw this out?' 'Certainly not.'* **IDM** **not a ...** | **not one ...** used for emphasis to mean 'no thing or person': *He didn't speak to me—not one word.* ˌnot at ˈall used to politely accept thanks or to agree to sth: *'Thanks a lot.' 'Not at all.'* ◊ *'Will it bother you if I smoke?' 'Not at all.'* **not only ...(but) also ...** used to emphasize that sth else is also true: *She not only wrote the text but also selected the illustrations.* ˈnot that used to state that you are not suggesting sth: *She hasn't written—not that she said she would.*

not·able /ˈnəʊtəbl; *AmE* ˈnoʊ-/ *adj., noun*
▪ *adj.* **~** (for sth) deserving to be noticed or to receive attention; important: *a notable success/achievement/example* ◊ *His eyes are his most notable feature.* ◊ *The town is notable for its ancient harbour.* ◊ *With a few notable exceptions, everyone gave something.*
▪ *noun* [usually pl.] (*written*) a famous or important person: *All the usual local notables were there.*

not·ably /ˈnəʊtəbli; *AmE* ˈnoʊ-/ *adv.* **1** used for giving a good or the most important example of sth SYN ESPECIALLY: *The house had many drawbacks, most notably its location and price.* **2** to a great degree SYN REMARKABLY: *This has not been a notably successful project.*

no·tary /ˈnəʊtəri; *AmE* ˈnoʊ-/ *noun* (*pl.* **-ies**) (also *technical* ˌnotary ˈpublic *pl.* ˌnotaries ˈpublic) a person, especially a lawyer, with official authority to be a WITNESS when sb signs a document and to make this document valid in law

no·ta·tion /nəʊˈteɪʃn; *AmE* noʊ-/ *noun* [U, C] a system of signs or symbols used to represent information, especially in mathematics, science and music

notch /nɒtʃ; *AmE* nɑːtʃ/ *noun, verb*
▪ *noun* **1** a level on a scale, often marking quality or achievement: *The quality of the food here has dropped a notch recently.* ◊ *My spirits lifted a few notches when I heard the news.*—see also TOP-NOTCH **2** a V-shaped or circular cut in an edge or a surface, sometimes used to keep a record of sth: *For each day he spent on the island, he cut a new notch in his stick.* ◊ *She tightened her belt an extra notch.*
▪ *verb* [VN] **1** (*informal*) **~** sth (up) to achieve sth such as a win or a high score: *The team has notched up 20 goals already this season.* **2** to make a small V-shaped cut in an edge or a surface

note /nəʊt; *AmE* noʊt/ *noun, verb*
▪ *noun*

æ	ɑː	e	ɜː	ə	ɪ	iː	i	ɒ	ɔː	ʌ	ʊ	u	uː
cat	father	ten	bird	about	sit	see	many	got	saw	cup	put	actual	too

(BrE)

N

TO REMIND YOU | **1** [C] a short piece of writing to help you remember sth: *Please make a note of the dates.* ◊ *He sat taking notes of everything that was said.* ◊ *She made a mental note* (= decided that she must remember) *to ask Alan about it.* ◊ *Can I borrow your lecture notes?*

SHORT LETTER | **2** [C] a short informal letter: *Just a quick note to say thank you for a wonderful evening.* ◊ *She left a note for Ben on the kitchen table.* ◊ *a suicide note*

IN BOOK | **3** [C] a short comment on a word or passage in a book: *a new edition of 'Hamlet', with explanatory notes* ◊ *See note 3, page 259.*—see also FOOTNOTE

INFORMATION | **4** [C, usually pl.] information about a performance, an actor's career, a piece of music, etc. printed in a special book or on a record cover, CD case, etc: *The sleeve notes include a short biography of the performers on this recording.*

MONEY | **5** (also **bank·note**) (both *especially BrE*) (*AmE* usually **bill**) [C] a piece of paper money: *a £5 note* ◊ *We only exchange notes and traveller's cheques.*—picture at MONEY

IN MUSIC | **6** [C] a single sound of a particular length and PITCH (= how high or low a sound is), made by the voice or a musical instrument; the written or printed sign for a musical note: *He played the first few notes of the tune.* ◊ *high/low notes*—picture at MUSIC

QUALITY | **7** [sing.] **~ (of sth)** a particular quality in sth, for example in sb's voice or the atmosphere at an event: *There was a note of amusement in his voice.* ◊ *On a more serious note* (= speaking more seriously)...

OFFICIAL DOCUMENT | **8** [C] an official document with a particular purpose: *a sick note from your doctor* ◊ *The buyer has to sign a delivery note as proof of receipt.*—see also CREDIT NOTE, PROMISSORY NOTE **9** [C] (*technical*) an official letter from the representative of one government to another: *an exchange of diplomatic notes*

IDM **of 'note** of importance or of great interest: *a scientist/composer of note* ◊ *The museum contains nothing of great note.* **hit/strike the right/wrong 'note** (*especially BrE*) to do, say or write sth that is suitable/not suitable for a particular occasion **sound/strike a 'note (of 'sth)** to express feelings or opinions of a particular kind: *She sounded a note of warning in her speech.* **take 'note (of sth)** to pay attention to sth and be sure to remember it: *Take note of what he says.*—more at COMPARE *v.*

■ *verb* (rather *formal*) **1** to notice or pay careful attention to sth: [VN] *Note the fine early Baroque altar inside the chapel.* ◊ [V(that)] *Please note (that) the office will be closed on Monday.* ◊ [Vwh-] *Note how these animals sometimes walk with their tails up in the air.* ◊ [VNthat] *It should be noted that dissertations submitted late will not be accepted.* **2** to mention sth because it is important or interesting: [Vthat] *It is worth noting that the most successful companies had the lowest prices.* [also VN, also Vwh-, VNthat]

PHR V ,**note sth** ↔ '**down** to write down sth important so that you will not forget it

note·book /'nəʊtbʊk; *AmE* 'noʊt-/ *noun* **1** a small book of plain paper for writing notes in **2** (*AmE*) = EXERCISE BOOK **3** (also ,**notebook com'puter**) a very small computer that you can carry with you and use anywhere—compare DESKTOP COMPUTER, LAPTOP

noted /'nəʊtɪd; *AmE* 'noʊt-/ *adj.* **~ (for/as sth)** well known because of a special skill or feature SYN FAMOUS: *a noted dancer* ◊ *He is not noted for his sense of humour.* ◊ *The lake is noted as a home to many birds.*

note·let /'nəʊtlət; *AmE* 'noʊt-/ *noun* (*BrE*) a small folded sheet of paper or card with a picture on the front that you use for writing a short letter on

note·pad /'nəʊtpæd; *AmE* 'noʊt-/ *noun* sheets of paper that are held together at the top and used for writing notes on: *a notepad by the phone for messages*

note·paper /'nəʊtpeɪpə(r); *AmE* 'noʊt-/ (also '**writing paper**) *noun* [U] paper for writing letters on

note·worthy /'nəʊtwɜːði; *AmE* 'noʊtwɜːrði/ *adj.* deserving to be noticed or to receive attention because it is unusual, important or interesting: *a noteworthy feature/aspect* ◊ *It is noteworthy that only 15% of senior managers are women.*

noth·ing /'nʌθɪŋ/ *pron.* **1** not anything; no single thing: *There was nothing in her bag.* ◊ *There's nothing you can do to help.* ◊ *The doctor said there was nothing wrong with me.* ◊ *Nothing else matters to him apart from his job.* ◊ *It cost us nothing to go in.* ◊ (*BrE*) *He's five foot nothing* (= exactly five feet tall). **2** something that is not at all important or interesting: *'What's that in your pocket?' 'Oh, nothing.'* ◊ *We did nothing at the weekend.* IDM **be 'nothing to sb** to be a person for whom sb has no feelings: *I used to love her but she's nothing to me any more.* **be/have nothing to do with sb/sth** to have no connection with sb/sth: *Get out! It's nothing to do with you* (= you have no right to know about it). ◊ *That has nothing to do with what we're discussing.* **for 'nothing 1** without payment SYN FREE: *We could have got in for nothing—nobody was collecting tickets.* **2** with no reward or result: *All that preparation was for nothing because the visit was cancelled.* **have nothing on sb** (*informal*) **1** to have much less of a particular quality than sth/sb: *I'm quite a fast worker, but I've got nothing on her!* **2** (of the police, etc.) to have no information that could show sb to be guilty of sth **not for 'nothing** for a very good reason: *Not for nothing was he called the king of rock and roll.* '**nothing but** only; no more/less than: *Nothing but a miracle can save her now.* ◊ *I want nothing but the best for my children.* '**nothing if not** extremely; very: *The trip was nothing if not varied.* '**nothing less than** used to emphasize how great or extreme sth is: *It was nothing less than a disaster.* **nothing 'like** (*informal*) **1** not at all like: *It looks nothing like a horse.* **2** not nearly; not at all: *I had nothing like enough time to answer all the questions.* ,**nothing 'much** not a great amount of sth; nothing of great value or importance: *There's nothing much in the fridge.* ◊ *I got up late and did nothing much all day.* **(there's) ,nothing 'to it** (it's) very easy: *You'll soon learn. There's nothing to it really.* **there is/was nothing (else) 'for it (but to do sth)** there is no other action to take except the one mentioned: *There was nothing else for it but to resign.* **there is/was nothing in sth** something is/was not true: *There was a rumour she was going to resign, but there was nothing in it.* **there's nothing like sth** used to say that you enjoy sth very much: *There's nothing like a brisk walk on a cold day!*—more at ALL *det.*, STOP *v.*, SWEET *adj.*

noth·ing·ness /'nʌθɪŋnəs/ *noun* [U] a situation where nothing exists; the state of not existing

no·tice /'nəʊtɪs; *AmE* 'noʊ-/ *noun, verb*
■ *noun*

PAYING ATTENTION | **1** [U] the fact of sb paying attention to sb/sth or knowing about sth: *Don't take any notice of what you read in the papers.* ◊ *Take no notice of what he says.* ◊ *These protests have really made the government sit up and take notice* (= realize the importance of the situation). ◊ *It was Susan who brought the problem to my notice* (= told me about it). ◊ *Normally, the letter would not have come to my notice* (= I would not have known about it). ◊ (*formal*) *It will not have escaped your notice that there have been some major changes in the company.*

GIVING INFORMATION | **2** [C] a sheet of paper giving written or printed information, usually put in a public place: *There was a notice on the board saying the class had been cancelled.* **3** [C] a board or sign giving information, an instruction or a warning: *a notice saying 'Keep off the Grass'*

ANNOUNCING STH | **4** [C] a small advertisement or ANNOUNCEMENT in a newspaper or magazine: *notices of births, marriages and deaths* **5** [C] a short ANNOUNCEMENT made at the beginning or end of a church service, a meeting, etc: *There are just two notices this week.*

WARNING | **6** [U] information or a warning given in advance of sth that is going to happen: *You must give one month's notice.* ◊ *Prices may be altered without notice.* ◊ *The bar is closed until further notice* (= until you are told that it is open again). ◊ *You are welcome to come and stay as long as you give us plenty of notice.*

WHEN LEAVING JOB/HOUSE | **7** [U] a formal letter or state-

aɪ	aʊ	eɪ	əʊ	oʊ	ɔɪ	ɪə	eə	ʊə	j	w
my	now	say	go (BrE)	go (AmE)	boy	near	hair	pure	yes	wet

ment saying that you will or must leave your job or house at the end of a particular period of time: *He has handed in his notice.* ◊ *They gave her two weeks' notice.*

REVIEW OF BOOK/PLAY | **8** [C] a short article in a newspaper or magazine, giving an opinion about a book, play, etc.

IDM at short 'notice | at a moment's 'notice not long in advance; without warning or time for preparation: *This was the best room we could get at such short notice.* ◊ *You must be ready to leave at a moment's notice.* **on short 'notice** (*AmE*) = AT SHORT NOTICE

■ *verb* (not usually used in the progressive tenses)

SEE/HEAR | **1** to see or hear sb/sth; to become aware of sb/sth: [VN] *The first thing I noticed about the room was the smell.* ◊ [V] *People were making fun of him but he didn't seem to notice.* ◊ [V (that)] *I couldn't help noticing (that) she was wearing a wig.* ◊ [VWh-] *Did you notice how Rachel kept looking at her watch?* ◊ [VN inf] *I noticed them come in.* ◊ [VN-ing] *I didn't notice him leaving.*

PAY ATTENTION | **2** [VN] to pay attention to sb/sth: *She wears those strange clothes just to get herself noticed.* ◊ *My husband hardly seems to notice me any more.*

no·tice·able /ˈnəʊtɪsəbl; *AmE* ˈnoʊ-/ *adj.* ~ (**in sb/sth**) | ~ (**that …**) easy to see or notice; clear or definite: *a noticeable feature/improvement/difference* ◊ *This effect is particularly noticeable in younger patients.* ◊ *It was noticeable that none of the family were present.* ▶ **no·tice·ably** /-əbli/ *adv.*: *Her hand was shaking noticeably.* ◊ *Marks were noticeably higher for girls than for boys.*

no·tice·board /ˈnəʊtɪsbɔːd; *AmE* ˈnoʊtɪsbɔːrd/ (*BrE*) (*AmE* **'bulletin board**) (also **board** *BrE*, *AmE*) *noun* a board for putting notices on

no·ti·fi·able /ˈnəʊtɪfaɪəbl; *AmE* ˈnoʊ-/ *adj.* [usually before noun] (*formal*) (of a disease or a crime) so dangerous or serious that it must by law be reported officially to the authorities

no·ti·fi·ca·tion /ˌnəʊtɪfɪˈkeɪʃn; *AmE* ˌnoʊ-/ *noun* [U, C] (*formal*) the act of giving or receiving official information about sth: *advance/prior notification* (= telling sb in advance about sth) ◊ *written notification* ◊ *You should receive (a) notification of our decision in the next week.*

no·tify /ˈnəʊtɪfaɪ; *AmE* ˈnoʊ-/ *verb* (**no·ti·fies, no·ti·fy·ing, no·ti·fied, no·ti·fied**) ~ **sb (of sth)** | ~ **sth to sb** to formally or officially tell sb about sth **SYN INFORM**: [VN] *Competition winners will be notified by post.* ◊ *The police must be notified of the date of the demonstration.* ◊ *The date of the demonstration must be notified to the police.* [also VN that]

no·tion /ˈnəʊʃn; *AmE* ˈnoʊʃn/ *noun* ~ (**that …**) | ~ (**of sth**) an idea, a belief or an understanding of sth: *a political system based on the notions of equality and liberty* ◊ *I have to reject the notion that greed can be a good thing.* ◊ *She had only a vague notion of what might happen.*

no·tion·al /ˈnəʊʃənl; *AmE* ˈnoʊ-/ *adj.* (*formal*) based on a guess, estimate or theory; not existing in reality: *My calculation is based on notional figures, since the actual figures are not yet available.* ▶ **no·tion·al·ly** /ˈnəʊʃənəli; *AmE* ˈnoʊ-/ *adv.*

no·tori·ety /ˌnəʊtəˈraɪəti; *AmE* ˌnoʊ-/ *noun* [U, sing.] ~ (**for/as sth**) fame for being bad in some way: *She achieved notoriety for her affair with the senator.* ◊ *He gained a certain notoriety as a gambler.*

no·tori·ous /nəʊˈtɔːriəs; *AmE* noʊ-/ *adj.* ~ (**for sth/for doing sth**) | ~ (**as sth**) well known for being bad: *a notorious criminal* ◊ *The country is notorious for its appalling prison conditions.* ◊ *The bar has become notorious as a meeting-place for drug dealers.* ▶ **no·tori·ous·ly** *adv.*: *Mountain weather is notoriously difficult to predict.*

not·with·stand·ing /ˌnɒtwɪθˈstændɪŋ; -wɪð-; *AmE* ˌnɑːt-/ *prep., adv.*

■ *prep.* (*formal*) (also used following the noun it refers to) without being affected by sth; in spite of sth: *Notwithstanding some major financial problems, the school has had a successful year.* ◊ *The bad weather notwithstanding, the event was a great success.*

■ *adv.* (*formal*) in spite of this **SYN HOWEVER, NEVERTHELESS**: *Notwithstanding, the problem is a significant one.*

nou·gat /ˈnuːɡɑː; *AmE* ˈnuːɡət/ *noun* [U] a hard sweet/candy that has to be chewed a lot, often containing nuts, CHERRIES, etc. and pink or white in colour

nought /nɔːt/ *noun* **1** [C, U] (*BrE*) (also **zero** especially in *AmE*) the figure 0: *A million is written with six noughts.* ◊ *nought point one* (= written 0·1) ◊ *I give the programme nought out of ten for humour.* ⇨ Appendix 3 **2** (also **naught**) [U] (*literary*) used in particular phrases to mean 'nothing': *All our efforts have come to nought* (= have not been successful).

,noughts and 'crosses (*BrE*) (*AmE* **,tic-tac-'toe**) *noun* [U] a simple game in which two players take turns to write Os or Xs in a set of nine squares. The first player to complete a row of three Os or three Xs is the winner.

noughts and crosses (*BrE*)/ **tic-tac-toe** (*AmE*)

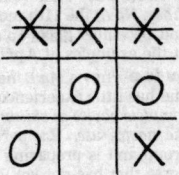

noun /naʊn/ *noun* (*grammar*) (*abbr.* **n.**) a word that refers to a person, (such as *Ann* or *doctor*), a place (such as *Paris* or *city*) or a thing, a quality or an activity (such as *plant, sorrow* or *tennis*)—see also ABSTRACT NOUN, COMMON NOUN, PROPER NOUN

'noun phrase *noun* (*grammar*) a group of words in a sentence that behaves in the same way as a noun, that is as a subject, an object, a COMPLEMENT, or as the object of a preposition: *In the sentence 'I spoke to the driver of the car', 'the driver of the car' is a noun phrase.*

nour·ish /ˈnʌrɪʃ; *AmE* ˈnɜːrɪʃ/ *verb* [VN] **1** to keep a person, an animal or a plant alive and healthy with food, etc: *All the children were well nourished and in good physical condition.* ◊ *Most plants are nourished by water drawn up through their roots.* **2** (*formal*) to allow a feeling, an idea, etc. to develop or grow stronger: *By investing in education, we nourish the talents of our children.* ▶ **nour·ish·ing** *adj.*: *nourishing food*

nour·ish·ment /ˈnʌrɪʃmənt; *AmE* ˈnɜːr-/ *noun* [U] (*formal* or *technical*) food that is needed to stay alive, grow and stay healthy: *Can plants obtain adequate nourishment from such poor soil?* ◊ (*figurative*) *As a child, she was starved of intellectual nourishment.*

nous /naʊs/ *noun* [U] (*BrE, informal*) intelligence and the ability to think and act in a practical way **SYN COMMON SENSE**

nou·veau riche /ˌnuːvəʊ ˈriːʃ; *AmE* ˌnuːvoʊ/ *noun* (*pl.* **nou·veaux riches** /ˌnuːvəʊ ˈriːʃ; *AmE* ˌnuːvoʊ/ or **the nou·veau riche**) (from *French, disapproving*) a person who has recently become rich and likes to show how rich they are in a very obvious way ▶ **nou·veau riche** *adj.*

nou·velle cuis·ine /ˌnuːvel kwɪˈziːn/ *noun* [U] (from *French*) a modern style of cooking that avoids heavy foods and serves small amounts of different dishes arranged in an attractive way on the plate

nova /ˈnəʊvə; *AmE* ˈnoʊvə/ *noun* (*pl.* **novae** /-viː/ or **novas**) (*astronomy*) a star that suddenly becomes much brighter for a short period—compare SUPERNOVA

novel /ˈnɒvl; *AmE* ˈnɑːvl/ *noun, adj.*

■ *noun* a story long enough to fill a complete book, in which the characters and events are usually imaginary: *to write/publish/read a novel* ◊ *detective/historical/romantic novels* ◊ *the novels of Jane Austen*

■ *adj.* (often *approving*) different from anything known before; new, interesting and often seeming slightly strange: *a novel idea/feature/design*

nov·el·ette /ˌnɒvəˈlet; *AmE* ˌnɑːv-/ *noun* a short novel, especially a romantic novel that is considered to be badly written

nov·el·ist /ˈnɒvəlɪst; *AmE* ˈnɑːv-/ *noun* a person who writes novels: *a romantic/historical novelist*

nov·el·is·tic /ˌnɒvəˈlɪstɪk; *AmE* ˌnɑːv-/ *adj.* (*formal*) typical of or used in novels

nov·ella /nəˈvelə/ *noun* a short novel

nov·elty /ˈnɒvlti; *AmE* ˈnɑːv-/ *noun, adj.*

b	d	f	g	h	k	l	m	n	p	r
bad	**did**	**fall**	**get**	**hat**	**cat**	**leg**	**man**	**now**	**pen**	**red**

N

noun (pl. **-ies**) **1** [U] the quality of being new, different and interesting: *It was fun working there at first but the novelty soon wore off* (= it became boring). ◊ *There's a certain novelty value in this approach.* **2** [C] a thing, person or situation that is interesting because it is new, unusual, or has not been known before: *Electric-powered cars are still something of a novelty.* **3** [C] a small cheap object sold as a toy or an ornament: *chocolate novelties sold at Easter*

■ adj. [only before noun] different and unusual; intended to be amusing and to catch people's attention: *a novelty teapot*

No·vem·ber /nəʊˈvembə(r); AmE noʊ-/ noun [U, C] (abbr. **Nov.**) the 11th month of the year, between October and December **HELP** To see how **November** is used, look at the examples at **April**.

nov·ice /ˈnɒvɪs; AmE ˈnɑːv-/ noun **1** a person who is new and has little experience in a skill, job or situation: *I'm a complete novice at skiing.* ◊ *computer software for novices/ the novice user* **2** a person who has joined a religious group and is preparing to become a MONK or a NUN **3** a horse that has not yet won an important race

now /naʊ/ adv., conj.

■ adv. **1** (at) the present time: *Where are you living now?* ◊ *It's been two weeks now since she called.* ◊ *It's too late now.* ◊ *From now on I'll be more careful.* ◊ *He'll be home by now.* ◊ *I've lived at home up till now.* ◊ *That's all for now.* **2** at or from this moment, but not before: *Start writing now.* ◊ *I am now ready to answer your questions.* **3** (spoken) used to show that you are annoyed about sth: *Now they want to tax food!* ◊ *What do you want now?* ◊ *It's broken. Now I'll have to get a new one.* **4** (spoken) used to get sb's attention before changing the subject or asking them to do sth: *Now, listen to what she's saying.* ◊ *Now, the next point is quite complex.* ◊ *Now come and sit down.* ◊ *Now let me think …* **IDM** **(every) now and aˈgain/ˈthen** from time to time; occasionally: *Every now and again she checked to see if he was still asleep.* **now for ˈsb/ˈsth** used when turning to a fresh activity or subject: *And now for some travel news.* ˌ**now, ˈnow** (also ˌ**now ˈthen**) used to show in a mild way that you do not approve of sth: *Now then, that's enough noise.* **now … now** … at one time … at another time …: *Her moods kept changing—now happy, now sad.* **(it's) ˌnow or ˈnever** this is the only opportunity sb will have to do sth **ˈnow then 1** = NOW, NOW **2** used when making a suggestion or an offer: *Now then, who wants to come for a walk?* **ˈNow what?** (spoken) **1** (also **What is it ˈnow?**) used when you are annoyed because sb is always asking questions or interrupting you: *'Yes, but Dad …' 'Now what?'* **2** used to say that you do not know what to do next in a particular situation

■ conj. ~ **(that)** … because the thing mentioned is happening or has just happened: *Now that the kids have left home we've got a lot of extra space.*

now·adays /ˈnaʊədeɪz/ adv. at the present time, in contrast with the past: *Nowadays most kids prefer watching TV to reading.*

no·where /ˈnəʊweə(r); AmE ˈnoʊwer/ (also **ˈno place** especially in AmE) adv. not in or to any place: *This animal is found in Australia, and nowhere else.* ◊ *There was nowhere for me to sit.* ◊ *'Where are you going this weekend?' 'Nowhere special.'* ◊ (written) *Nowhere is the effect of government policy more apparent than in agriculture.* **IDM** **get/go ˈnowhere | get sb ˈnowhere** to make no progress or have no success; to allow sb to do this: *We discussed it all morning but got nowhere.* ◊ *Talking to him will get you nowhere.* **nowhere to be ˈfound/ˈseen | nowhere in ˈsight** impossible for anyone to find or see: *The children were nowhere to be seen.* ◊ *A peace settlement is nowhere in sight* (= is not likely in the near future).—more at LEAD¹v., MIDDLE n., NEAR adv.

ˌ**no-ˈwin** adj. [only before noun] (of a situation, policy, etc.) that will end badly whatever you decide to do: *We are considering the options available to us in this no-win situation.*

nowt /naʊt/ pron. (BrE, dialect, informal) nothing: *There's nowt wrong with it.*

nox·ious /ˈnɒkʃəs; AmE ˈnɑːk-/ adj. (formal) **1** poisonous or harmful: *noxious gases/chemicals/fumes* **2** very unpleasant: *a noxious problem*

noz·zle /ˈnɒzl; AmE ˈnɑːzl/ noun a narrow piece that is attached to the end of a pipe or tube to direct the stream of liquid, air or gas passing through—picture at GARDEN

nr abbr. (BrE) near (used, for example, in the address of a small village): *Howden, nr Goole*

nth /enθ/ adj. (informal) [only before noun] used when you are stating that sth is the last in a long series and emphasizing how often sth has happened: *It's the nth time I've explained it to you.* **IDM** **to the nth ˈdegree** extremely; to an extreme degree

nu·ance /ˈnjuːɑːns; AmE ˈnuː-/ noun [C, U] a very slight difference in meaning, sound, colour or sb's feelings that is not usually very obvious: *He watched her face intently to catch every nuance of expression.* ▸ **nu·anced** /ˈnjuːɑːnst; AmE ˈnuːɑːnst/ adj. (rare): *subtle and finely nuanced*

nub /nʌb/ noun [sing.] **the ~ (of sth)** the central or essential point of a situation, problem, etc: *The nub of the matter is that business is declining.*

nu·bile /ˈnjuːbaɪl; AmE ˈnuː-; ˈnuːbl/ adj. (written) (of a girl or young woman) sexually attractive

nu·clear /ˈnjuːkliə(r); AmE ˈnuː-/ adj. [usually before noun] **1** using, producing or resulting from nuclear energy: *a nuclear power station* ◊ *the nuclear industry* ◊ *nuclear-powered submarines* **2** connected with weapons that use nuclear energy: *a nuclear weapon/bomb/missile* ◊ *a nuclear explosion/attack/war* ◊ *the country's nuclear capability* (= the fact that it has nuclear weapons) ◊ *nuclear capacity* (= the number of nuclear weapons a country has) **3** (physics) of the NUCLEUS (= central part) of an atom: *nuclear particles/physics* ◊ *a nuclear reaction*

ˌ**nuclear ˈenergy** (also ˌ**nuclear ˈpower**) noun [U] a powerful form of energy produced by splitting the NUCLEI (= central parts) of atoms and used to produce electricity

ˌ**nuclear ˈfamily** noun (technical) a family that consists of father, mother and children, when it is thought of as a unit in society: *Not everybody nowadays lives in the conventional nuclear family.*—compare EXTENDED FAMILY

ˌ**nuclear ˈfission** noun [U] = FISSION

ˌ**nuclear-ˈfree** adj. [usually before noun] (of a country or a region) not having or allowing nuclear energy, weapons or materials: *a nuclear-free zone*

ˌ**nuclear ˈfusion** noun [U] = FUSION

ˌ**nuclear ˈpower** noun [U] = NUCLEAR ENERGY

ˌ**nuclear reˈactor** noun = REACTOR

ˌ**nuclear ˈwaste** noun [U] waste material which is RADIOACTIVE, especially used fuel from nuclear power stations

nu·cle·ic acid /njuːˌkliːɪk ˈæsɪd; -ˌkleɪɪk; AmE nuː-/ noun [U] (chemistry) either of two acids, DNA and RNA, that are present in all living cells

nu·cleus /ˈnjuːkliəs; AmE ˈnuː-/ noun (pl. **nu·clei** /-kliaɪ/) **1** (physics) the central part of an atom, that contains most of its MASS (= weight) and that carries a positive electric CHARGE—see also PROTON, NEUTRON **2** (biology) the central part of some cells, containing the GENETIC material **3** the central part of sth around which other parts are situated or collected: *These paintings will form the nucleus of a new collection.*

nude /njuːd; AmE nuːd/ adj., noun

■ adj. **1** (especially of a human figure in art) not wearing any clothes **SYN** NAKED: *a nude model* ◊ *He asked me to pose nude for him.* **2** involving people who are naked: *a nude photograph* ◊ *Are there any nude scenes in the movie?* **3** (AmE) (of TIGHTS/PANTYHOSE, etc.) skin-coloured

■ noun a work of art consisting of a naked human figure; a naked human figure in art: *a bronze nude by Rodin* ◊ *a reclining nude* **IDM** **in the ˈnude** not wearing any clothes **SYN** NAKED: *She refuses to be photographed in the nude.*

nudge /nʌdʒ/ verb, noun

■ verb **1** [VN] to push sb gently, especially with your elbow, in order to get their attention: *He nudged me and whispered, 'Look who's just come in.'* **2** [VN+adv./prep.] to

push sb/sth gently or gradually in a particular direction: *He nudged the ball past the goalie and into the net.* ◊ *She nudged me out of the way.* ◊ (*figurative*) *He nudged the conversation towards the subject of money.* ◊ (*figurative*) *She tried to nudge him into changing his mind* (= persuade him to do it). **3** [+*adv./prep.*] to move forward by pushing with your elbow: [VN] *He* **nudged his way** *through the crowd.* [also V] **4** [VN] to reach or make sth reach a particular level: *Inflation is nudging 20%.* ◊ *This afternoon's sunshine could nudge the temperature above freezing.*
■ *noun* a slight push, usually with the elbow: *She gave me a gentle nudge in the ribs to tell me to shut up.* ◊ (*figurative*) *He can work hard but he needs a nudge now and then.* **IDM** ,**nudge 'nudge**, ,**wink 'wink** | a ,**nudge and a 'wink** used to suggest sth to do with sex without actually saying it: *They've been spending a lot of time together, nudge nudge, wink wink.*

nud·ism /'nju:dɪzəm; *AmE* 'nu:-/ (*also* **na·tur·ism** especially in *BrE*) *noun* [U] the practice of not wearing any clothes because you believe this is more natural and healthy

nud·ist /'nju:dɪst; *AmE* 'nu:-/ (*also* **na·tur·ist** especially in *BrE*) *noun* a person who does not wear any clothes because they believe this is more natural and healthy: *a nudist beach/camp*

nud·ity /'nju:dəti; *AmE* 'nu:-/ *noun* [U] the state of being naked: *The committee claimed that there was too much nudity on television.*

nu·ga·tory /'nju:gətəri; *AmE* 'nu:gətɔ:ri/ *adj.* (*rare, formal*) having no purpose or value **SYN** WORTHLESS

nug·get /'nʌgɪt/ *noun* **1** a small lump of a valuable metal or mineral, especially gold, that is found in the earth **2** a small round piece of some types of food: *chicken nuggets* **3** a small thing such as an idea or a fact that people think of as valuable: *a useful nugget of information*

nuis·ance /'nju:sns; *AmE* 'nu:-/ *noun* **1** [C, usually sing.] a thing, person or situation that is annoying or causes trouble or problems: *I don't want to* **be a nuisance** *so tell me if you want to be alone.* ◊ *I hope you're not* **making a nuisance of yourself.** ◊ *It's a nuisance having to go back tomorrow.* ◊ *What a nuisance!* **2** [C, U] (*law*) behaviour by sb that annoys other people and that a court of law can order the person to stop: *He was charged with causing a public nuisance.*

nuke /nju:k/ *verb, noun*
■ *verb* [VN] (*informal*) to attack a place with nuclear weapons
■ *noun* (*informal*) a nuclear weapon

null /nʌl/ *adj.* (*technical*) having the value zero: *a null result/output* **IDM** ,**null and 'void** (*law*) (of an election, agreement, etc.) having no legal force; not valid: *The contract was declared null and void.*

nul·lify /'nʌlɪfaɪ/ *verb* (**nul·li·fies**, **nul·li·fy·ing**, **nul·li·fied**, **nul·li·fied**) [VN] (*formal*) **1** to make sth such as an agreement or order lose its legal force **SYN** INVALIDATE: *Judges were unwilling to nullify government decisions.* **2** to make sth lose its effect or power **SYN** NEGATE: *An unhealthy diet will nullify the effects of training.*

null·ity /'nʌləti/ *noun* [sing.] (*formal or law*) the fact of sth, for example a marriage, having no legal force or no longer being valid; something which is no longer valid

numb /nʌm/ *adj., verb*
■ *adj.* **1** if a part of your body is **numb**, you cannot feel anything in it, for example because of cold: *to be/go numb* ◊ *numb with cold* ◊ *I've just been to the dentist and my face is still numb.* **2** unable to feel, think or react in the normal way: *He felt numb with shock.*—see also NUMB·ING ▶ **numb·ly** *adv.*: *Her life would never be the same again, she realized numbly.* **numb·ness** *noun* [U]: *pain and numbness in my fingers* ◊ *He was still in a state of numbness and shock from the accident.*
■ *verb* **1** [VN] to make a part of your body unable to feel anything, for example because of cold: *His fingers were numbed with the cold.* **2** [VN] to make sb unable to feel, think or react in a normal way, for example because of an

emotional shock **SYN** STUN: *We sat there in silence, numbed by the shock of her death.*

num·ber /'nʌmbə(r)/ *noun, verb*
■ *noun*
WORD/SYMBOL | **1** [C] a word or symbol that represents an amount or a quantity: *Think of a number and multiply it by two.* ◊ *a high/low number* ◊ *even numbers* (= 2, 4, 6, etc.) ◊ *odd numbers* (= 1, 3, 5, etc.) ◊ *You owe me 27 dollars? Make it 30, that's a good* **round number.**—see also CARDINAL NUMBER, ORDINAL, PRIME NUMBER, WHOLE NUMBER ⇨ Appendix 3
POSITION IN SERIES | **2** [C] (*abbr.* **No.**) (*symb* **#**) used before a figure to show the position of sth in a series: *They live at number 26.* ◊ *The song reached number 5 in the charts.*
TELEPHONE, etc. | **3** [C] (often in compounds) a number used to identify sth or communicate by telephone, FAX, etc: *My phone number is 266998* ◊ *I'm sorry, I think you have the* **wrong number** (= wrong telephone number). ◊ *What is your account number, please?*—see also BOX NUMBER, E-NUMBER, PIN, REGISTRATION NUMBER, SERIAL NUMBER
QUANTITY | **4** [C] ~ (**of sb/sth**) a quantity of people or things: *The number of homeless people has increased dramatically.* ◊ *Huge numbers of* (= very many) *animals have died.* ◊ *A number of* (= some) *problems have arisen.* ◊ *I could give you* **any number of** (= a lot of) *reasons for not going.* ◊ *We were eight* **in number** (= there were eight of us). ◊ *Nurses are leaving the profession in increasing numbers.* ◊ *Sheer weight of numbers* (= the large number of soldiers) *secured them the victory.* ◊ *staff/student numbers* **HELP** A plural verb is needed after **a/an** (large, small, etc.) **number of ...**: *A large number of people have applied for the job.*
GROUP OF PEOPLE | **5** [sing.] (*formal*) a group or quantity of people: *one of our number* (= one of us) ◊ *The prime minister is elected by MPs from among their number.*
MAGAZINE | **6** [C] (*BrE*) the version of a magazine, etc. published on a particular day, in a particular month, etc. **SYN** ISSUE: *the October number of 'Vogue'*—see also BACK NUMBER
SONG/DANCE | **7** [C] a song or dance, especially one of several in a performance: *They sang a slow romantic number.*
THING ADMIRED | **8** [sing.] (*informal*) (following one or more adjectives) a thing, such as a dress or a car, that is admired: *She was wearing a black velvet number.*
GRAMMAR | **9** [U] the form of a word, showing whether one or more than one person or thing is being talked about: *The word 'men' is plural in number.* ◊ *The subject of a sentence and its verb must agree in number.*
IDM **by 'numbers** following a set of simple instructions identified by numbers: *painting by numbers* **have (got) sb's 'number** (*informal*) to know what sb is really like and what they plan to do: *He thinks he can fool me but I've got his number.* **your 'number is up** (*informal*) the time has come when you will die or lose everything ,**number 'one** (*informal*) **1** the most important or best person or thing: *We're number one in the used car business.* ◊ *the world's number one athlete* ◊ *the number one priority* **2** yourself: *Looking after number one is all she thinks about.* '**numbers game** a way of considering an activity, etc. that is concerned only with the number of people doing sth, things achieved, etc., not with who or what they are: *MPs were playing the numbers game as the crucial vote drew closer.*—more at CUSHY, OPPOSITE *adj.*, SAFETY, WEIGHT *n.*
■ *verb*
MAKE A SERIES | **1** to give a number to sth as part of a series or list: [VN] *All the seats in the stadium are numbered.* ◊ *Number the car's features from 1 to 10 according to importance.* ◊ [V] *I couldn't work out the numbering system for the hotel rooms.* [also VN-N]
MAKE STH AS TOTAL | **2** [V-N] to make a particular number when added together **SYN** ADD UP TO STH: *The crowd numbered more than a thousand.* ◊ *We numbered 20* (= there were 20 of us in the group).
INCLUDE | **3** ~ (**sb/sth**) **among sth** (*formal*) to include sb/sth in a particular group; to be included in a particular

æ	ɑː	e	ɜː	ə	ɪ	iː	i	ɒ	ɔː	ʌ	ʊ	u	uː
cat	father	ten	bird	about	sit	see	many	got	saw	cup	put	actual	too
								(BrE)					

N

group: [VN] *I number her among my closest friends.* ◊ [V] *He numbers among the best classical actors in Britain.* **IDM** see DAY

'number crunching *noun* [U] (*informal*) the process of calculating numbers, especially when a large amount of data is involved and the data is processed in a short space of time

num·ber·less /'nʌmbələs; *AmE* -bərl-/ *adj.* (*literary*) too many to be counted **SYN** INNUMERABLE

'number plate (*BrE*) (*AmE* '**license plate**) *noun* a metal or plastic plate on the front and back of a vehicle that shows its REGISTRATION NUMBER—picture at CAR

Number 'Ten *noun* [U+sing./pl. *v.*] (**No 10**) number 10 Downing Street, London, the official home of the British PRIME MINISTER, often used to refer to the government: *Number Ten had nothing to say on the matter.*

numb·ing /'nʌmɪŋ/ *adj.* (of an experience or a situation) making you unable to feel anything: *numbing cold/fear* ◊ *Watching television had a numbing effect on his mind.*

numb·skull (also **num·skull**) /'nʌmskʌl/ *noun* (*informal*) a stupid person

nu·mer·acy /'nju:mərəsi; *AmE* 'nu:-/ *noun* [U] a good basic knowledge of mathematics; the ability to understand and work with numbers: *standards of literacy and numeracy* ▶ **nu·mer·ate** /'nju:mərət; *AmE* 'nu:-/ *adj.*: *All students should be numerate and literate when they leave school.* **OPP** INNUMERATE

nu·meral /'nju:mərəl; *AmE* 'nu:-/ *noun* a sign or symbol that represents a number—see also ARABIC NUMERAL, ROMAN NUMERAL

nu·mer·ator /'nju:məreɪtə(r); *AmE* 'nu:-/ *noun* (*mathematics*) the number above the line in a FRACTION, for example 3 in the FRACTION ¾—compare DENOMINATOR

nu·mer·ic·al /nju:'merɪkl; *AmE* nu:-/ (also *less frequent* **nu·mer·ic** /-ɪk/) *adj.* relating to numbers; expressed in numbers: *numerical data* ◊ *The results are expressed in descending numerical order.* ▶ **nu·mer·ic·al·ly** /-kli/ *adv.*: *to express the results numerically*

nu·mer·ous /'nju:mərəs; *AmE* 'nu:-/ *adj.* (*formal*) existing in large numbers **SYN** MANY: *He has been late on numerous occasions.* ◊ *The advantages of this system are too numerous to mention.*

nu·min·ous /'nju:mɪnəs; *AmE* 'nu:-/ *adj.* (*formal*) having a strong religious and spiritual quality that makes you feel that God is present

nu·mis·mat·ics /ˌnju:mɪz'mætɪks; *AmE* ˌnu:-/ *noun* [U] the study of coins and medals ▶ **nu·mis·mat·ic** *adj.*

nu·mis·ma·tist /nju:'mɪzmətɪst; *AmE* nu:-/ *noun* a person who collects or studies coins or medals

num·skull = NUMBSKULL

nun /nʌn/ *noun* a member of a religious community of women who promise to serve God all their lives and often live together in a CONVENT—compare MONK

nun·cio /'nʌnsiəʊ; *AmE* -sioʊ/ *noun* (*pl.* **-os**) a representative of the POPE (= the leader of the Roman Catholic Church) in a foreign country

nun·nery /'nʌnəri/ *noun* (*pl.* **-ies**) (*old-fashioned* or *literary*) = CONVENT

nup·tial /'nʌpʃl/ *adj.* [only before noun] (*formal*) connected with marriage or a wedding: *nuptial bliss* ◊ *a nuptial mass*

nup·tials /'nʌpʃlz/ *noun* [pl.] (*old-fashioned*) a wedding

nurse /nɜːs; *AmE* nɜːrs/ *noun, verb*
■ *noun* **1** a person whose job is to take care of sick or injured people, usually in a hospital: *a qualified/registered nurse* ◊ *student nurse* ◊ *a male nurse* ◊ *a dental nurse* (= one who helps a dentist) ◊ *a psychiatric nurse* (= one who works in a hospital for people with mental illnesses) ◊ *Nurse Bennett* ◊ *Nurse, come quickly!*—see also CHARGE NURSE, DISTRICT NURSE, PRACTICAL NURSE, REGISTERED NURSE, STAFF NURSE ⇨ note at GENDER **2** (also **nurse·maid**) (*old-fashioned*) (in the past) a woman or girl whose job was to take care of babies or small children in their own homes—see also NURSERY NURSE, WET NURSE
■ *verb* **1** [VN] to care for sb who is ill/sick or injured: *He worked in a hospital for ten years nursing cancer patients.*

◊ *She nursed her daughter back to health.* **2** [VN] to take care of an injury or illness: *Several weeks after the match, he was still nursing a shoulder injury.* ◊ *You'd better go to bed and nurse that cold.* ◊ (*figurative*) *She was nursing her hurt pride.* **3** [VN] (*formal*) to have a strong feeling or idea in your mind for a long time **SYN** HARBOUR: *to nurse an ambition/a grievance/a grudge* ◊ *She had been nursing a secret desire to see him again.* **4** [VN] to give special care or attention to sb/sth: *to nurse tender young plants* **5** [VN] to hold sb/sth carefully in your arms or close to your body: *He sat nursing his cup of coffee.* **6** (of a woman or female animal) **a** to feed a baby with milk from the breast **SYN** SUCKLE: [V] *a nursing mother* ◊ [VN] *The lioness is still nursing her cubs.*—compare BREASTFEED **7** [V] (of a baby) to suck milk from its mother's breast **SYN** SUCKLE

nurse·maid /'nɜːsmeɪd; *AmE* 'nɜːrs-/ *noun* (*old-fashioned*) = NURSE (2)

,nurse prac'titioner *noun* a nurse who is trained to do many of the tasks usually done by a doctor

nur·sery /'nɜːsəri; *AmE* 'nɜːrs-/ *noun, adj.*
■ *noun* (*pl.* **-ies**) **1** = DAY NURSERY **2** = NURSERY SCHOOL: *Her youngest child is at nursery now.* **3** (*AmE* or *old-fashioned*) a room in a house where a baby sleeps **4** (*old-fashioned*) a room in a house where young children can play **5** a place where young plants and trees are grown for sale or for planting somewhere else
■ *adj.* [only before noun] (*BrE*) connected with the education of children from 2 to 5 years old: *nursery education* ◊ *a nursery teacher*

nur·sery·man /'nɜːsərimən; *AmE* 'nɜːrs-/ *noun* (*pl.* **-men** /-mən/) a person who owns or works in a nursery

'nursery nurse *noun* (*BrE*) a person whose job involves taking care of small children in a DAY NURSERY

'nursery rhyme *noun* a simple traditional poem or song for children

'nursery school *noun* (*BrE*) a school for children between the ages of two and five—compare KINDERGARTEN, PLAYGROUP

'nursery slope (*BrE*) (*AmE* '**bunny slope**) *noun* [usually pl.] a slope that is not very steep and is used by people who are learning to ski

nurs·ing /'nɜːsɪŋ; *AmE* 'nɜːrs-/ *noun* [U] the job or skill of caring for people who are sick or injured: *a career in nursing* ◊ *nursing care* ◊ *the nursing profession*

'nursing home *noun* a small private hospital, especially one where old people live and are cared for: *Eventually she had to give up her house and go into a nursing home.*

nur·ture /'nɜːtʃə(r); *AmE* 'nɜːrtʃ-/ *verb, noun*
■ *verb* [VN] (*formal*) **1** to care for and protect sb/sth while they are growing and developing: *These delicate plants need careful nurturing.* ◊ *children nurtured by loving parents* **2** to help sb/sth to develop and be successful: *It's important to nurture a good working relationship.* **3** to have a feeling, an idea, a plan, etc. for a long time and encourage it to develop: *She secretly nurtured a hope of becoming famous.*
■ *noun* [U] (*formal*) care, encouragement and support given to sb/sth while they are growing

nut /nʌt/ *noun, verb*

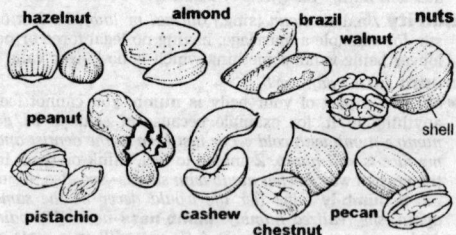

hazelnut · almond · brazil · nuts · walnut · peanut · shell · pistachio · cashew · pecan · chestnut

■ *noun* **1** (often in compounds) a small hard fruit with a very hard shell that grows on some trees: *to crack a nut* (= open it) ◊ *a Brazil nut* ◊ *a hazelnut* ◊ *nuts and raisins* **2** a small piece of metal with a hole through the centre that is screwed onto a BOLT to hold pieces of wood,

machinery, etc. together: *to tighten a nut* ◇ *a wheel nut*—picture at TOOL **3** (*BrE*, *slang*) a person's head or brain **4** (*informal*) (*BrE* also **nut·ter**) a strange or crazy person: *He's a complete nut, if you ask me.*—see also NUTS, NUTTY **5** (*informal*) (in compounds) a person who is extremely interested in a particular subject, activity, etc: *a fitness/ tennis/computer nut* **6** (**nuts**) [pl.] (*slang*) a man's TESTICLES **IDM** **do your 'nut** (*BrE*, *informal*, *spoken*) to become very angry: *She'll do her nut when she finds out!* **a hard/tough 'nut** (*informal*) a person who is difficult to deal with or to influence **a hard/tough 'nut (to 'crack)** a difficult problem or situation to deal with **the ,nuts and 'bolts (of sth)** (*informal*) the basic practical details of a subject or an activity ,**off your 'nut** (*BrE*, *informal*, *spoken*) crazy—more at SLEDGEHAMMER
■ *verb* [VN] (**-tt-**) (*BrE*, *informal*) to deliberately hit sb hard with your head: *He grabbed my tie and I thought he was going to nut me in the face.*

,**nut-'brown** *adj.* dark brown in colour: *nut-brown eyes/ hair*

nut·case /ˈnʌtkeɪs/ *noun* (*informal*) a crazy person: *She's a complete nutcase.*

nut·crack·er /ˈnʌtkrækə(r)/ *noun* (*BrE* also **nut·crack·ers**) [pl.] a tool for cracking open the shells of nuts

nut·meg /ˈnʌtmeg/ *noun* [U, C] the hard seed of an E Indian tree, used in cooking as a spice, especially to give flavour to cakes and sauces: *freshly grated nutmeg*

nu·tri·ent /ˈnjuːtriənt; *AmE* ˈnuː-/ *noun* (*technical*) a substance that is needed to keep a living thing alive and to help it to grow: *a lack/supply of essential nutrients* ◇ *Plants draw minerals and other nutrients from the soil.* ◇ *children suffering from a serious nutrient deficiency*

nu·tri·tion /njuˈtrɪʃn; *AmE* nuː-/ *noun* [U] the process by which living things receive the food necessary for them to grow and be healthy: *advice on diet and nutrition* ◇ *to study food science and nutrition*—compare MALNUTRITION ▶ **nu·tri·tion·al** /-ʃənl/ (*also less frequent* **nu·tri·tive**) *adj.*: *the nutritional value of milk* **nu·tri·tion·al·ly** /-ʃənəli/ *adv.*: *a nutritionally balanced menu*

nu·tri·tion·ist /njuˈtrɪʃənɪst; *AmE* nuː-/ *noun* a person who is an expert on the relationship between food and health—see also DIETICIAN

nu·tri·tious /njuˈtrɪʃəs; *AmE* nuː-/ *adj.* (*approving*) (of food) very good for you; containing many of the substances which help the body to grow **SYN** NOURISHING: *tasty and nutritious meals*

nuts /nʌts/ *adj.* [not before noun] (*informal*) **1** crazy: *My friends think I'm nuts for saying yes.* ◇ *That phone ringing all the time is driving me nuts!* **2 ~ about sb/sth** very much in love with sb; very enthusiastic about sth: *He's absolutely nuts about her.*

nut·shell /ˈnʌtʃel/ *noun* **IDM** **(put sth) in a nutshell** (to say or express sth) in a very clear way, using few words: *To put it in a nutshell, we're bankrupt.*

nut·ter /ˈnʌtə(r)/ *noun* (*BrE*, *informal*) = NUT (4)

nutty /ˈnʌti/ **1** tasting of or containing nuts: *a nutty taste* **2** (*informal*) slightly crazy: *She's got some nutty friends.* ◇ *He's as nutty as a fruitcake* (= completely crazy).

nuz·zle /ˈnʌzl/ *verb* to touch or rub sb/sth with the nose or mouth, especially to show affection: [VN] *She nuzzled his ear.* ◇ [V+adv./prep.] *The child nuzzled up against his mother.*

NVQ /ˌen viː ˈkjuː/ *noun* a British qualification that shows that you have reached a particular standard in the work that you do (the abbreviation for 'National Vocational Qualification'): *NVQ Level 3 in Catering*

NW *abbr.* north-west; north-western: *NW Australia*

NY *abbr.* New York

NYC *abbr.* New York City

nylon /ˈnaɪlɒn; *AmE* -lɑːn/ *noun* **1** [U] a very strong artificial material, used for making clothes, rope, brushes, etc: *a nylon fishing line* ◇ *This material is 45% nylon.* **2** (**nylons**) [pl.] (*old-fashioned*) women's STOCKINGS or TIGHTS/PANTYHOSE made of nylon

nymph /nɪmf/ *noun* **1** (in ancient Greek and Roman stories) a spirit of nature in the form of a young woman, that lives in rivers, woods, etc. **2** (*biology*) a young insect that has a similar form to the adult: *a dragonfly nymph*

nymph·et /ˈnɪmfet; nɪmˈfet/ *noun* (*written*) a young girl who is very sexually attractive

nym·pho·maniac /ˌnɪmfəˈmeɪniæk/ (*also informal* **nym·pho** /ˈnɪmfəʊ; *AmE* -foʊ/) *noun* (*disapproving*) a woman who has sex or wants to have sex very often

NZ (*BrE*) (also **N.Z.** *AmE*, *BrE*) *abbr.* New Zealand

O /əʊ; AmE oʊ/ noun, exclamation
■ noun (also **o**) (pl. **O's, o's** /əʊz; AmE oʊz/) **1** [C, U] the 15th letter of the English alphabet: *'Orange' begins with (an) O/'O'.* **2** (*spoken*) used to mean 'zero' when saying telephone numbers, etc: *My number is six o double three* (= 6033). ⇨ Appendix 3—see also O GRADE, O LEVEL
■ exclamation (*rare*, especially *literary*) = OH

o' /ə/ prep. used in written English to represent an informal way of saying *of: a couple o' times*—see also O'CLOCK, WILL-O'-THE-WISP

oaf /əʊf; AmE oʊf/ noun a stupid, unpleasant or awkward person, especially a man: *Mind that cup, you clumsy oaf!* ▶ **oaf·ish** adj.

oak /əʊk; AmE oʊk/ noun **1** [C, U] (also **'oak tree**) a large tree that produces small nuts called ACORNS, often eaten by animals. Oaks are common in northern countries and can live to be hundreds of years old: *a gnarled old oak tree ◊ forests of oak and pine*—see also POISON OAK **2** [U] the hard wood of the oak tree: *oak beams ◊ a carved oak door ◊ This table is made of solid oak.*

oaken /'əʊkən; AmE 'oʊkən/ adj. [only before noun] (*literary*) made of oak

oakum /'əʊkəm; AmE 'oʊkəm/ noun [U] a material obtained by pulling old rope to pieces, a job done in the past by prisoners

OAP /ˌəʊ eɪ 'piː; AmE ˌoʊ-/ noun (*BrE*, becoming *old-fashioned*) the abbreviation for OLD-AGE PENSIONER: *adults £4.50, children and OAPs £3*

oar /ɔː(r)/ noun a long pole with a flat blade at one end that is used to move a boat through water: *He pulled as hard as he could on the oars.*—compare PADDLE—picture at BOAT **IDM** **put/stick your 'oar in** (*BrE*, *informal*) to give your opinion, advice, etc. without being asked and when it is probably not wanted **SYN** INTERFERE

oar·lock /'ɔːlɒk; AmE 'ɔːrlɑːk/ noun (*AmE*) = ROWLOCK

oars·man /'ɔːzmən; AmE 'ɔːrz-/ noun (pl. **-men** /-mən/) a person who rows a boat, especially as a member of a CREW (= team)

oasis /əʊ'eɪsɪs; AmE oʊ-/ noun (pl. **oases** /-siːz/) **1** an area in the desert where there is water and where plants grow **2** a pleasant place or period of time in the middle of sth unpleasant or difficult: *an oasis of calm ◊ a green oasis in the heart of the city*

oat /əʊt; AmE oʊt/ adj. [only before noun] made from or containing OATS: *oat cakes ◊ oat bran*—see also OATMEAL

oath /əʊθ; AmE oʊθ/ noun (pl. **oaths** /əʊðz; AmE oʊðz/) **1** a formal promise to do sth or a formal statement that sth is true: *to take/swear an oath of allegiance ◊ Before giving evidence, witnesses in court have to take the oath* (= promise to tell the truth). **2** (*old-fashioned*) an offensive word or phrase used to express anger, surprise, etc.; a swear word: *She heard the sound of breaking glass, followed by a muttered oath.* **IDM** **on/under 'oath** (*law*) having made a formal promise to tell the truth in a court of law: *Is she prepared to give evidence on oath? ◊ The judge reminded the witness that he was still under oath.*

oat·meal /'əʊtmiːl; AmE 'oʊt-/ noun [U] **1** flour made from crushed oats, used to make biscuits/cookies, PORRIDGE, etc. **2** (*AmE*) = PORRIDGE **3** a pale brown colour ▶ **oat·meal** adj.: *an oatmeal carpet*

oats /əʊts; AmE oʊts/ noun [pl.] grain grown in cool countries and used as food for animals and for making flour, PORRIDGE/OATMEAL, etc.—see also OAT—picture at CEREAL **IDM** see SOW v.

ob·dur·ate /'ɒbdjərət; AmE 'ɑːbdər-/ adj. (*rare*, *formal*) (usually *disapproving*) refusing to change your mind or your actions in any way **SYN** STUBBORN ▶ **ob·dur·acy** /'ɒbdjərəsi; AmE 'ɑːbdər-/ noun [U] **ob·dur·ate·ly** adv.

OBE /ˌəʊ biː 'iː; AmE ˌoʊ-/ noun the abbreviation for 'Officer of the Order of the British Empire' (an award given in Britain for a special achievement): *She was made an OBE. ◊ Matthew Silk OBE*

obedi·ent /ə'biːdiənt/ adj. ~ (**to sb/sth**) doing what you are told to do; willing to obey: *an obedient child ◊ He was always obedient to his father's wishes.* **OPP** DISOBEDIENT ▶ **obedi·ence** /-əns/ noun [U] ~ (**to sb/sth**): *blind/complete/unquestioning/total obedience ◊ He has acted in obedience to the law.* **obedi·ent·ly** adv. **IDM** **your obedi·ent servant** (*old use*) used to end a formal letter

obei·sance /əʊ'beɪsns; AmE oʊ'biːsns/ noun (*rare*, *formal*) **1** [U] respect for sb/sth or willingness to obey sb **2** [C] the act of bending your head or the upper part of your body in order to show respect for sb/sth

ob·el·isk /'ɒbəlɪsk; AmE 'ɑːb-; 'oʊb-/ noun a tall pointed stone column with four sides, put up in memory of a person or an event

obese /əʊ'biːs; AmE oʊ-/ adj. (*formal* or *medical*) (of people) very fat, in a way that is not healthy ▶ **obes·ity** /əʊ'biːsəti; AmE oʊ-/ noun [U]: *Obesity can increase the risk of heart disease.*

obey /ə'beɪ/ verb to do what you are told or expected to do: [VN] *to obey a command/an order/rules/the law ◊ Had always obeyed his parents without question.* ◊ [V] *'Sit down!' Meekly, she obeyed.* **OPP** DISOBEY

ob·fus·cate /'ɒbfʌskeɪt; AmE 'ɑːb-/ verb (*rare*, *formal*) to make sth less clear and more difficult to understand, usually deliberately: [VN] *He accused the government of obfuscating the issue.* [also V] ▶ **ob·fus·ca·tion** noun [U, C]

ob·gyn /ˌəʊ biː ˌdʒiː waɪ'en; AmE ˌoʊ-/ noun (*AmE*, *informal*) **1** [U] the branches of medicine concerned with the birth of children (= OBSTETRICS) and the diseases of women (= GYNAECOLOGY) **2** [C] a doctor who is trained in this type of medicine

ob·itu·ary /ə'bɪtʃuəri; AmE oʊ'bɪtʃueri/ noun (pl. **-ies**) an article about sb's life and achievements, that is printed in a newspaper soon after they have died

ob·ject noun, verb
■ noun /'ɒbdʒɪkt; AmE 'ɑːbdʒekt; -dʒɪkt/ **1** a thing that can be seen and touched, but is not alive: *everyday/household objects ◊ Glass and plastic objects lined the shelves.*—see also UFO ⇨ note on page 873 **2** ~ **of desire, study, attention, etc.** a person or thing that sb DESIRES, studies, pays attention to, etc: *the urge to possess the objects of our desire*—see also SEX OBJECT **3** an aim or a purpose: *Her sole object in life is to become a travel writer. ◊ The object is to educate people about road safety. ◊ If you're late, you'll defeat the whole object of the exercise.* **4** (*grammar*) a noun, noun phrase or pronoun that refers to a person or thing that is affected by the action of the verb (called the DIRECT OBJECT), or that the action is done to or for (called the INDIRECT OBJECT)—compare SUBJECT (5) **IDM** **expense, money, etc. is no 'object** used to say that you are willing to spend a lot of money: *He always travels first class—expense is no object.*
■ verb /əb'dʒekt/ **1** [V] ~ (**to sb/sth**) | ~ (**to doing sth/to sb doing sth**) to say that you disagree with, disapprove of or oppose sth: *Many local people object to the building of the new airport. ◊ If nobody objects, we'll postpone the meeting till next week. ◊ I really object to being charged for parking.* **2** to give sth as a reason for opposing sth: [V that] *He objected that the police had arrested him without sufficient evidence.* [also V speech]

s	t	v	z	ʃ	ʒ	tʃ	dʒ	θ	ð	ŋ
see	tea	van	zoo	shoe	vision	chain	jam	thin	this	sing

ob·jec·tification /ˌəbˌdʒektɪfɪˈkeɪʃn/ *noun* [U] (*formal*) the act of treating people as if they are objects, without rights or feelings of their own

ob·jec·tion /əbˈdʒekʃn/ *noun* ~ (to sth/to doing sth)| ~ (that ...) a reason why you do not like or are opposed to sth; a statement about this: *I have no objection to him coming to stay.* ◊ *I'd like to come too, if you have no objection.* ◊ *The main objection to the plan was that it would cost too much.* ◊ *to raise an objection to sth* ◊ *No objections were raised at the time.* ◊ *The proposal will go ahead despite strong objections from the public.*

ob·jec·tion·able /əbˈdʒekʃənəbl/ *adj.* (*formal*) unpleasant or offensive: *objectionable people/odours* ◊ *Why are you being so objectionable today?* ◊ *I myself didn't find his behaviour objectionable.*

ob·ject·ive /əbˈdʒektɪv/ *noun, adj.*
■ *noun* **1** something that you are trying to achieve: *the main/primary/principal objective* ◊ *to meet/achieve your objectives* ◊ *You must set realistic aims and objectives for yourself.* ◊ *The main objective of this meeting is to give more information on our plans.* **2** (also **ob,jective 'lens**) (*technical*) the LENS in a TELESCOPE or MICROSCOPE that is nearest to the object being looked at—picture at LABORATORY
■ *adj.* **1** not influenced by personal feelings or opinions; considering only facts: *an objective analysis/assessment/ report* ◊ *objective criteria* ◊ *I find it difficult to be objective where he's concerned.* **2** (*philosophy*) existing outside the mind; based on facts that can be proved: *objective reality* OPP SUBJECTIVE ▶ **ob·ject·ive·ly** *adv.*: *Looked at objectively, the situation is not too bad.* ◊ *Can these effects be objectively measured?* **ob·ject·iv·ity** /ˌɒbdʒekˈtɪvəti; *AmE* ˌɑːb-/ *noun* [U]: *There was a lack of objectivity in the way the candidates were judged.* ◊ *scientific objectivity*

'object lesson *noun* [usually sing.] a practical example of what you should or should not do in a particular situation

ob·ject·or /əbˈdʒektə(r)/ *noun* ~ (to sth) a person who objects to sth: *There were no objectors to the plan.*—see also CONSCIENTIOUS OBJECTOR

objet d'art /ˌɒbʒeɪ ˈdɑː; *AmE* ˌɔːbʒeɪ ˈdɑːr/ *noun* (*pl.* **objets d'art** /ˌɒbʒeɪ ˈdɑː; *AmE* ˌɔːbʒeɪ ˈdɑːr/) (from *French*) a small artistic object, used for decoration

ob·li·gated /ˈɒblɪgeɪtɪd; *AmE* ˈɑːb-/ *adj.* ~ (to do sth)

(*AmE* or *formal, BrE*) having a moral or legal duty to do sth SYN OBLIGED: *He felt obligated to help.*

ob·li·ga·tion /ˌɒblɪˈgeɪʃn; *AmE* ˌɑːb-/ *noun* **1** [U, C, usually sing.] the state of being forced to do sth because it is your duty, or because of a law, etc: *You are under no obligation to buy anything.* ◊ *She did not feel under any obligation to tell him the truth.* ◊ *I don't want people coming to see me out of a sense of obligation.* ◊ *We have a moral obligation to protect the environment.* ◊ *We will send you an estimate for the work without obligation* (= you do not have to accept it). **2** [C] something which you must do because you have promised, because of a law, etc: *to fulfil your legal/professional/financial obligations* ◊ *They reminded him of his contractual obligations.*

ob·liga·tory /əˈblɪgətri; *AmE* -tɔːri/ *adj.* **1** ~ (for sb) (to do sth) (*formal*) that you must do because of the law, rules, etc. SYN COMPULSORY: *It is obligatory for all employees to wear protective clothing.* **2** (often *humorous*) that you do because you always do it, or other people in the same situation always do it: *In the mid 60s he took the almost obligatory trip to India.*

ob·lige /əˈblaɪdʒ/ *verb* **1** [VN to inf] [usually passive] to force sb to do sth, by law, because it is a duty, etc: *Parents are obliged by law to send their children to school.* ◊ *I felt obliged to ask them to dinner.* ◊ *He suffered a serious injury that obliged him to give up work.* **2** ~ sb (by doing sth)| ~ sb (with sth) to help sb by doing what they ask or what you know they want: [V] *Call me if you need any help—I'd be happy to oblige.* ◊ [VN] (*formal*) *Would you oblige me with some information?*

ob·liged /əˈblaɪdʒd/ *adj.* [not before noun] ~ (to sb) (for sth/for doing sth) (*formal*) used when you are expressing thanks or asking politely for sth, to show that you are grateful to sb: *I'm much obliged to you for helping us.* ◊ *I'd be obliged if you would keep this to yourself.*

ob·li·ging /əˈblaɪdʒɪŋ/ *adj.* very willing to help: *They were very obliging and offered to wait for us.* ▶ **ob·li·ging·ly** *adv.*

ob·lique /əˈbliːk/ *adj., noun*
■ *adj.* **1** not expressed or done in a direct way SYN INDIRECT: *an oblique reference/approach/comment* **2** (of a line) sloping at an angle **3** ~ **angle** an angle that is not an angle of 90° ▶ **ob·lique·ly** *adv.*: *He referred only obliquely to their recent problems.* ◊ *Always cut stems obliquely to enable flowers to absorb more water.*
■ *noun* (*BrE*) = SLASH (3)

ob·lit·er·ate /əˈblɪtəreɪt/ *verb* [VN] [often passive] to remove all signs of sth, either by destroying or covering it completely: *The building was completely obliterated by the bomb.* ◊ *The snow had obliterated their footprints.* ◊ *Everything that happened that night was obliterated from his memory.* ▶ **ob·lit·er·ation** /əˌblɪtəˈreɪʃn/ *noun* [U]

ob·liv·ion /əˈblɪviən/ *noun* [U] **1** a state in which you are not aware of what is happening around you, usually because you are unconscious or asleep: *He often drinks himself into oblivion.* ◊ *Sam longed for the oblivion of sleep.* **2** the state in which sb/sth has been forgotten and is no longer famous or important: *An unexpected victory saved him from political oblivion.* ◊ *Most of his inventions have been consigned to oblivion.* **3** a state in which sth has been completely destroyed: *Hundreds of homes were bombed into oblivion during the first weeks of the war.*

ob·livi·ous /əˈblɪviəs/ *adj.* [not usually before noun] ~ (of/to sth) not aware of sth: *He drove off, oblivious of the damage he had caused.* ◊ *You eventually become oblivious to the noise.* ▶ **ob·livi·ous·ly** *adv.*

ob·long /ˈɒblɒŋ; *AmE* ˈɑːblɔːŋ/ *adj.* **1** an oblong shape has four straight sides, two of which are longer than the other two, and four angles of 90°: *an oblong patch of grass* **2** (*AmE*) used to describe any shape that is longer than it is wide: *an oblong melon* ▶ **ob·long** *noun*: *a tiny oblong of glass in the roof*—see also RECTANGLE

ob·lo·quy /ˈɒbləkwi; *AmE* ˈɑːb-/ *noun* [U] (*rare, formal*) **1** strong public criticism **2** loss of respect and honour

ob·nox·ious /əbˈnɒkʃəs; *AmE* -ˈnɑːk-/ *adj.* extremely unpleasant, especially in a way that offends people:

obnoxious behaviour ◊ *a thoroughly obnoxious little man* ◊ *obnoxious odours* ▶ **ob·nox·ious·ly** *adv.*

oboe /ˈəʊbəʊ; *AmE* ˈoʊboʊ/ *noun* a musical instrument of the WOODWIND group. It is shaped like a pipe and has a double REED at the top that you blow into.—picture on page 840

obo·ist /ˈəʊbəʊɪst; *AmE* ˈoʊbəʊɪst/ *noun* a person who plays the oboe

ob·scene /əbˈsiːn/ *adj.* **1** connected with sex in a way that most people find offensive: *obscene gestures/language/books* ◊ *an obscene phone call* (= made by sb saying obscene things) **2** extremely large in size or amount in a way that most people find unacceptable and offensive: *He earns an obscene amount of money.* ◊ *It's obscene to spend so much on food when millions are starving.* ▶ **ob·scene·ly** *adv.: to behave obscenely* ◊ *obscenely fat/rich*

ob·scen·ity /əbˈsenəti/ *noun* (*pl.* **-ies**) **1** [U] obscene language or behaviour: *The editors are being prosecuted for obscenity.* ◊ *the laws on obscenity* **2** [C, usually pl.] an obscene word or act: *She screamed a string of obscenities at the judge.*

ob·scur·ant·ism /ˌɒbskjuˈræntɪzəm; *AmE* ɑːbˈskjʊr-/ *noun* [U] (*formal*) the practice of deliberately preventing sb from understanding or discovering sth ▶ **ob·scur·ant·ist** *adj.*

ob·scure /əbˈskjʊə(r); *AmE* əbˈskjʊr/ *adj., verb*
■ *adj.* **1** not well known: *an obscure German poet* ◊ *He was born around 1650 but his origins remain obscure.* **2** difficult to understand: *I found her lecture very obscure.* ◊ *For some obscure reason, he failed to turn up.* ▶ **ob·scure·ly** *adv.: They were making her feel obscurely worried* (= for reasons that were difficult to understand).
■ *verb* [VN] to make it difficult to see, hear or understand sth: *The view was obscured by fog.* ◊ *Symptoms of the disease can easily be obscured.* ◊ *We mustn't let these minor details obscure the main issue.*

ob·scur·ity /əbˈskjʊərəti; *AmE* -ˈskjʊr-/ *noun* (*pl.* **-ies**) **1** [U] the state in which sb/sth is not well known or has been forgotten: *The actress was only 17 when she was plucked from obscurity and made a star.* ◊ *He spent most of his life working in obscurity.* **2** [U, C, usually pl.] the quality of being difficult to understand; something that is difficult to understand: *The course teaches students to avoid ambiguity and obscurity of expression.* ◊ *a speech full of obscurities* **3** [U] (*literary*) darkness

ob·se·quies /ˈɒbsəkwiz; *AmE* ˈɑːb-/ *noun* [pl.] (*rare, formal*) funeral ceremonies: *royal/state obsequies*

ob·se·qui·ous /əbˈsiːkwiəs/ *adj.* (*formal, disapproving*) trying too hard to please sb, especially sb who is important: *an obsequious manner/smile* ▶ **ob·se·qui·ous·ly** *adv.: smiling obsequiously* **ob·se·qui·ous·ness** *noun* [U]

ob·serv·able /əbˈzɜːvəbl; *AmE* -ˈzɜːrv-/ *adj.* that can be seen or noticed: *observable differences/effects* ◊ *Similar trends are observable in mainland Europe.* ▶ **ob·serv·ably** /əbˈzɜːvəbli; *AmE* -ˈzɜːrv-/ *adv.*

ob·ser·vance /əbˈzɜːvəns; *AmE* -ˈzɜːrv-/ *noun* **1** [U, sing.] the practice of obeying a law, celebrating a festival or behaving according to a particular custom: *observance of the law* ◊ *a strict observance of the Sabbath* [OPP] NON-OBSERVANCE **2** [C, usually pl.] an act performed as part of a religious or traditional ceremony: *religious/ritual observances*

ob·ser·vant /əbˈzɜːvənt; *AmE* -ˈzɜːrv-/ *adj.* **1** good at noticing things around you: *Observant walkers may see red deer along this stretch of the road.* ◊ *How very observant of you!* **2** (*formal*) careful to obey religious laws and customs

ob·ser·va·tion /ˌɒbzəˈveɪʃn; *AmE* ˌɑːbzərˈv-/ *noun* **1** [U, C] the act of watching sb/sth carefully for a period of time, especially to learn sth: *Most information was collected by direct observation of the animals' behaviour.* ◊ *results based on scientific observations* ◊ *We managed to escape observation* (= we were not seen). ◊ *The suspect is being kept under observation* (= watched closely by the police). ◊ *She has outstanding powers of observation* (= the ability to notice things around her). ◊ *an observation post/tower* (= a place from where sb, especially an

enemy, can be watched) **2** [C] ~ (**about/on sth**) a comment, especially based on sth you have seen, heard or read: *He began by making a few general observations about the report.* ◊ *She has some interesting observations on possible future developments.*

ob·ser·va·tory /əbˈzɜːvətri; *AmE* əbˈzɜːrvətɔːri/ *noun* (*pl.* **-ies**) a special building from which scientists watch the stars, the weather, etc.

ob·serve /əbˈzɜːv; *AmE* əbˈzɜːrv/ *verb* (not used in the progressive tenses) (*formal*) **1** to see or notice sb/sth: [VN] *Have you observed any changes lately?* ◊ *All the characters in the novel are closely observed* (= seem like people in real life). ◊ [VN inf] *The police observed a man enter the bank.* ◊ [VN] *They observed him entering the bank.* ◊ [V that] *She observed that all the chairs were already occupied.* ◊ [VN to inf] *He was observed to follow her closely.* [HELP] This pattern is only used in the passive. **2** to watch sb/sth carefully, especially to learn more about them: [VN] *I felt he was observing everything I did.* ◊ *The patients were observed over a period of several months.* ◊ [V wh-] *They observed how the parts of the machine fitted together.* ◊ [V] *He observes keenly, but says little.* **3** (*formal*) to make a remark: [V that] *She observed that it was getting late.* [also V speech] **4** [VN] to obey rules, laws, etc: *Will the rebels observe the ceasefire?* **5** [VN] (*formal*) to celebrate festivals, birthdays, etc: *Do they observe Christmas?*

ob·ser·ver /əbˈzɜːvə(r); *AmE* -ˈzɜːrv-/ *noun* **1** a person who watches sb/sth: *To the casual observer, the system appears confusing.* ◊ *According to observers, the plane exploded shortly after take-off.* **2** a person who attends a meeting, lesson, etc. to listen and watch but not to take part: *A team of British officials were sent as observers to the conference.* **3** a person who watches and studies particular events, situations, etc. and is therefore considered to be an expert on them: *a royal/political observer*

ob·sess /əbˈses/ *verb* **1** [VN] [usually passive] to completely fill your mind so that you cannot think of anything else: *He's obsessed by computers.* ◊ *She's completely obsessed with him.* ◊ *The need to produce the most exciting newspaper story obsesses most journalists.* **2 be obsessing (about sth)** [V] to be always talking or worrying about a particular thing, especially when this annoys other people: *I think you should try to stop obsessing about food.*

ob·ses·sion /əbˈseʃn/ *noun* ~ (**with sth/sb**) **1** [U] the state in which a person's mind is completely filled with thoughts of one particular thing or person so that they cannot think of anything else: *Her fear of flying is bordering on obsession.* ◊ *The media's obsession with the young prince continues.* **2** [C] a person or thing that sb thinks about too much: *Fitness has become an obsession with him.*

ob·ses·sion·al /əbˈseʃənl/ *adj.* thinking too much about one particular person or thing; showing this: *She is obsessional about cleanliness.* ◊ *obsessional behaviour* ▶ **ob·ses·sion·al·ly** *adv.*

ob·ses·sive /əbˈsesɪv/ *adj., noun*
■ *adj.* thinking too much about one particular person or thing; showing this: *He's becoming more and more obsessive about punctuality.* ◊ *an obsessive attention to detail* ◊ *obsessive behaviour/love* ▶ **ob·ses·sive·ly** *adv.: obsessively jealous* ◊ *He worries obsessively about his appearance.*
■ *noun* (*psychology*) a person whose mind is filled with thoughts of one particular thing or person so that they cannot think of anything else

ob·sid·ian /əbˈsɪdiən/ *noun* [U] a type of dark rock that looks like glass and comes from VOLCANOES

ob·so·les·cence /ˌɒbsəˈlesns; *AmE* ˌɑːb-/ *noun* [U] (*formal*) the state of becoming old-fashioned and no longer useful (= becoming OBSOLETE): *products with built-in/planned obsolescence* (= designed not to last long so that people will have to buy new ones) ▶ **ob·so·les·cent** /ˌɒbsəˈlesnt; *AmE* ˌɑːb-/ *adj.*

ob·so·lete /ˈɒbsəliːt; *AmE* ˌɑːbsəˈliːt/ *adj.* no longer used because sth new has been invented [SYN] OUT OF DATE:

obsolete technology ◊ *With technological changes many traditional skills have become obsolete.*

obs·tacle /ˈɒbstəkl; *AmE* ˈɑːb-/ *noun* **1** ~ **(to sth/to doing sth)** a situation, an event, etc. that makes it difficult for you to do or achieve sth: *A lack of qualifications can be a major obstacle to finding a job.* ◊ *So far, we have managed to overcome all the obstacles that have been placed in our path.* **2** an object that is in your way and that makes it difficult for you to move forward: *The area was full of streams and bogs and other natural obstacles.* **3** (in SHOWJUMPING) a fence, etc. for a horse to jump over

obstacle course *noun* **1** a series of objects that competitors in a race have to climb over, under, through, etc. **2** a series of difficulties that people have to deal with in order to achieve a particular aim **3** (*AmE*) = ASSAULT COURSE

obstacle race *noun* a race in which the competitors have to climb over, under, through, etc. various objects

ob·stet·ri·cian /ˌɒbstəˈtrɪʃn; *AmE* ˌɑːb-/ *noun* a doctor who is trained in obstetrics

ob·stet·rics /əbˈstetrɪks/ *noun* [U] the branch of medicine concerned with the birth of children ▸ **ob·stet·ric** /əbˈstetrɪk/ *adj.*: *obstetric medicine*

ob·stin·ate /ˈɒbstɪnət; *AmE* ˈɑːb-/ *adj.* **1** (often *disapproving*) refusing to change your opinions, way of behaving, etc. when other people try to persuade you to; showing this SYN STUBBORN: *He can be very obstinate when he wants to be!* ◊ *her obstinate refusal to comply with their request* **2** [usually before noun] difficult to get rid of or deal with SYN STUBBORN: *the obstinate problem of unemployment* ◊ *an obstinate stain* ▸ **ob·stin·acy** /ˈɒbstɪnəsi; *AmE* ˈɑːb-/ *noun* [U]: *an act of sheer obstinacy* **ob·stin·ate·ly** *adv.*: *He obstinately refused to consider the future.*

ob·strep·er·ous /əbˈstrepərəs/ *adj.* (*formal* or *humorous*) noisy and difficult to control

ob·struct /əbˈstrʌkt/ *verb* [VN] **1** to block a road, an entrance, a passage, etc. so that people cannot get through, see past, etc: *You can't park here, you're obstructing my driveway.* ◊ *First check that the accident victim doesn't have an obstructed airway.* ◊ *The pillar obstructed our view of the stage.* **2** to prevent sb/sth from doing sth or making progress, especially when this is done deliberately: *They were charged with obstructing the police in the course of their duty.* ◊ *terrorists attempting to obstruct the peace process*

ob·struc·tion /əbˈstrʌkʃn/ *noun* **1** [U, C] the fact of trying to prevent sth/sb from making progress: *the obstruction of justice* ◊ *He was arrested for obstruction of a police officer in the execution of his duty.* **2** [U, C] the fact of blocking a road, an entrance, a passage, etc: *obstruction of the factory gates* ◊ *The abandoned car was causing an obstruction.* **3** [C] something that blocks a road, an entrance, etc: *It is my job to make sure that all pathways are clear of obstructions.* **4** [C, U] something that blocks a passage or tube in your body; a medical condition resulting from this: *He had an operation to remove an obstruction in his throat.* ◊ *bowel/intestinal obstruction* **5** [U] (*sport*) the offence of unfairly preventing a player of the other team from moving to get the ball

ob·struc·tion·ism /əbˈstrʌkʃənɪzəm/ *noun* [U] (*formal*) the practice of trying to prevent a parliament or committee from making progress, passing laws, etc. ▸ **ob·struc·tion·ist** /-ɪst/ *noun, adj.*

ob·struct·ive /əbˈstrʌktɪv/ *adj.* **1** trying to prevent sb/sth from making progress: *Of course she can do it. She's just being deliberately obstructive.*—compare CONSTRUCTIVE **2** [only before noun] (*medical*) connected with a passage, tube, etc. in your body that has become blocked: *obstructive lung disease*

ob·tain /əbˈteɪn/ *verb* (*formal*) **1** [VN] (rather *formal*) to get sth, especially by making an effort: *to obtain advice/information/permission* ◊ *I finally managed to obtain a copy of the report.* ◊ *To obtain the overall score, add up the totals in each column.* **2** [V] (not used in the progressive tenses) (*formal*) (of rules, systems, customs, etc.) to exist: *These conditions no longer obtain.*

ob·tain·able /əbˈteɪnəbl/ *adj.* [not usually before noun] that can be obtained: *Full details are obtainable from any post office.*

ob·trude /əbˈtruːd/ *verb* ~ **(sth/yourself) (on/upon sb)** (*formal*) to become or make sth/yourself noticed, especially in a way that is not wanted: [V] *Music from the next room obtruded upon his thoughts.* [also VN]

ob·tru·sive /əbˈtruːsɪv/ *adj.* noticeable in an unpleasant way: *The sofa would be less obtrusive in a paler colour.* ◊ *They tried to ensure that their presence was not too obtrusive.* ▸ **ob·tru·sive·ly** *adv.*

ob·tuse /əbˈtjuːs; *AmE* -ˈtuːs/ *adj.* (*formal, disapproving*) slow or unwilling to understand sth: *Are you being deliberately obtuse?* ▸ **ob·tuse·ness** *noun* [U]

ob,tuse 'angle *noun* an angle between 90° and 180°—compare ACUTE ANGLE, REFLEX ANGLE, RIGHT ANGLE

ob·verse /ˈɒbvɜːs; *AmE* ˈɑːbvɜːrs/ *noun* (usually **the obverse**) [sing.] **1** (*formal*) the opposite of sth: *The obverse of love is hate.* ◊ *Nobody liked his conclusions but the obverse was equally unattractive.* **2** (*technical*) the side of a coin or medal that has the head or main design on it

ob·vi·ate /ˈɒbvieɪt; *AmE* ˈɑːb-/ *verb* [VN] (*formal*) to remove a problem or the need for sth: *This new evidence obviates the need for any further enquiries.*

ob·vi·ous /ˈɒbviəs; *AmE* ˈɑːb-/ *adj.* **1** ~ **(to sb) (that…)** easy to see or understand: *It was obvious to everyone that the child had been badly treated.* ◊ *It's obvious from what she said that something is wrong.* ◊ *I know you don't like her but try not to make it so obvious.* ◊ *with obvious annoyance/distress/pleasure* ◊ *For obvious reasons, I'd prefer not to give my name.* ◊ *The reasons for this decision were **not immediately obvious.*** **2** that most people would think of or agree to: *She was the obvious choice for the job.* ◊ *There's no obvious solution to the problem.* ◊ *This seemed the most obvious thing to do.* **3** (*disapproving*) not interesting, new or imaginative; unnecessary because it is clear to everyone: *an obvious comment/statement* ◊ *The ending was pretty obvious.* ◊ *I may be **stating the obvious** but without more money the project cannot survive.* ▸ **ob·vi·ous·ness** *noun* [U]

ob·vi·ous·ly /ˈɒbviəsli; *AmE* ˈɑːb-/ *adv.* **1** used when giving information that you expect other people to know already or agree with: *Obviously, we don't want to spend too much money.* ◊ *Diet and exercise are obviously important.* **2** used to say that a particular situation or fact is easy to see or understand: *He was obviously drunk.* ◊ *They're obviously not coming.* ◊ *'I didn't realise it was a formal occasion.' 'Obviously!'* (= I can see by the way you are dressed)

oc·ca·sion /əˈkeɪʒn/ *noun, verb*
■ *noun* **1** [C] a particular time when sth happens: *on this/that occasion* ◊ *I've met him on several occasions.* ◊ *I can remember very few occasions when he had to cancel because of ill health.* ◊ *They have been seen together on two separate occasions.* ◊ *On one occasion, she called me in the middle of the night.* ◊ *He used the occasion to announce further tax cuts.* **2** [C] a special event, ceremony or celebration: *a great/memorable/happy occasion* ◊ *Turn every meal into **a special occasion.*** ◊ *They marked the occasion* (= celebrated it) *with an open-air concert.* ◊ *Their wedding turned out to be quite an occasion.* ◊ *He was presented with the watch **on the occasion of** his retirement.* **3** [sing.] ~ **(for sth/doing sth)** a suitable time for sth: *It should have been an occasion for rejoicing, but she could not feel any real joy.* ◊ *I'll speak to him about it **if the occasion arises** (= if I get a chance).* ⇨ note at POSSIBILITY **4** [U, sing.] ~ **(to do sth)** | ~ **(of/for sth)** (*formal*) a reason or cause: *I've had no occasion to visit him recently.* ◊ *Her death was the occasion of mass riots.* ◊ *I'm willing to go to court over this **if the occasion arises** (= if it becomes necessary).* IDM **on oc'casion(s)** sometimes but not often: *He has been known on occasion to lose his temper.*—more at SENSE *n.*
■ *verb* (*formal*) to cause sth: [VN] *The flight delay was occasioned by the need for a further security check.* ◊ [VNN] *The decision occasioned us much anxiety.*

oc·ca·sion·al /əˈkeɪʒənl/ adj. [only before noun] happening or done sometimes but not often: *He works for us on an occasional basis.* ◊ *I enjoy the occasional glass of wine.* ◊ *He spent five years in Paris, with occasional visits to Italy.* ◊ *an occasional smoker* (= a person who smokes, but not often)

oc·ca·sion·al·ly /əˈkeɪʒnəli/ adv. sometimes but not often: *We occasionally meet for a drink after work.* ◊ *This type of allergy can very occasionally be fatal.*

Oc·ci·dent /ˈɒksɪdənt; AmE ˈɑːk-/ noun (the Occident) [sing.] (formal) the western part of the world, especially Europe and America—compare ORIENT ▶ **oc·ci·den·tal** /ˌɒksɪˈdentl; AmE ˌɑːk-/ adj.

oc·cult /əˈkʌlt; ˈɒkʌlt; AmE ˈɑːk-/ adj. **1** [only before noun] connected with magic powers and things that cannot be explained by reason or science: *occult powers/practices* **2** (the occult) noun [sing.] everything connected with occult practices, etc: *He's interested in witchcraft and the occult.*

oc·cult·ist /əˈkʌltɪst; ˈɒkʌltɪst; AmE ˈɑːk-/ noun a person who is involved in the occult

oc·cu·pancy /ˈɒkjəpənsi; AmE ˈɑːk-/ noun [U] (formal, written) the act of living in or using a building, room, piece of land, etc: *Prices are based on full occupancy of an apartment.* ◊ *to be in sole occupancy*

oc·cu·pant /ˈɒkjəpənt; AmE ˈɑːk-/ noun (especially written) **1** a person who lives or works in a particular house, room, building, etc: *All outstanding bills will be paid by the previous occupants.* **2** a person who is in a vehicle, seat, etc. at a particular time: *The car was badly damaged but the occupants were unhurt.*

oc·cu·pa·tion /ˌɒkjuˈpeɪʃn; AmE ˌɑːk-/ noun **1** [C] (especially written) a job or profession: *Please state your name, age and occupation below.* **2** [C] the way in which you spend your time, especially when you are not working: *Her main occupation seems to be shopping.* **3** [U] the act of moving into a country, town, etc. and taking control of it using military force; the period of time during which a country, town, etc. is controlled in this way: *the Roman occupation of Britain* ◊ *The areas under occupation contained major industrial areas.* ◊ *occupation forces* **4** [U] (written) the act of living in or using a building, room, piece of land, etc: *The offices will be ready for occupation in June.* ◊ *The following applies only to tenants in occupation after January 1 1997.* ◊ *The level of owner occupation* (= people owning their homes) *has increased rapidly in the last 30 years.*

oc·cu·pa·tion·al /ˌɒkjuˈpeɪʃənl; AmE ˌɑːk-/ adj. [only before noun] connected with a person's job or profession: *occupational health* ◊ *an occupational risk/hazard* ◊ *an occupational pension scheme* ▶ **oc·cu·pa·tion·al·ly** adv.: *occupationally induced disease*

occu·pational 'therapist noun a person whose job is to help people get better after illness or injury by giving them special activities to do

occu·pational 'therapy noun [U] the work of an occupational therapist

oc·cu·pied /ˈɒkjupaɪd; AmE ˈɑːk-/ adj. **1** [not before noun] being used by sb: *Only half of the rooms are occupied at the moment.*—see also OWNER-OCCUPIED **2** [not before noun] ~ (doing sth/in doing sth/in sth)| ~ (with sth/with doing sth) busy: *He's fully occupied looking after three small children.* ◊ *Only half her time is occupied with politics.* ◊ *The most important thing is to keep yourself occupied.* **3** (of a country, etc.) controlled by people from another country, etc., using military force: *He spent his childhood in occupied Europe.* OPP UNOCCUPIED

oc·cu·pier /ˈɒkjupaɪə(r); AmE ˈɑːk-/ noun **1** ~ (of sth) (formal) a person who lives in or uses a building, room, piece of land, etc. SYN OCCUPANT: *The letter was addressed to the occupier of the house.*—see also OWNER-OCCUPIER **2** [usually pl.] a member of an army that is occupying a foreign country, etc: *the Nazi occupiers of Poland*

oc·cupy /ˈɒkjupaɪ; AmE ˈɑːk-/ verb (oc·cu·pies, oc·cu·py·ing, oc·cu·pied, oc·cu·pied) **1** [VN] to fill or use a space, an area or an amount of time SYN TAKE UP: *The*

bed seemed to occupy most of the room. ◊ *How much memory does the program occupy?* ◊ *Administrative work occupies half of my time.* **2** [VN] (formal) to live or work in a room, house or building: *He occupies an office on the 12th floor.* **3** [VN] to enter a place in a large group and take control of it, especially by military force: *The capital has been occupied by the rebel army.* ◊ *Protesting students occupied the TV station.* **4** ~ sb/yourself (in doing sth/with sb/sth) to fill your time or keep you busy doing sth: [VN] *a game that will occupy the kids for hours* ◊ *She occupied herself with routine office tasks.* ◊ *Problems at work continued to occupy his mind for some time.* [also VN -ing] **5** [VN] to have an official job or position SYN HOLD: *The president occupies the position for four years.*

occur /əˈkɜː(r)/ verb (-rr-) **1** [V] (formal) to happen: *When exactly did the incident occur?* ◊ *Something unexpected occurred.* ⇨ note at HAPPEN **2** [V+adv./prep.] to exist or be found somewhere: *Sugar occurs naturally in fruit.* PHRV

oc'cur to sb (of an idea or a thought) to come into your mind: *The idea occurred to him in a dream.* ◊ [+that] *It didn't occur to him that his wife was having an affair.* ◊ [+to inf] *It didn't occur to her to ask for help.*

oc·cur·rence /əˈkʌrəns; AmE əˈkɜːr-/ noun **1** [C] something that happens or exists: *a common/everyday/frequent/regular occurrence* ◊ *Vandalism used to be a rare occurrence here.* ◊ *The program counts the number of occurrences of any word, or group of words, within the text.* ⇨ note at EVENT **2** [U] ~ (of sth) the fact of sth happening or existing: *a link between the occurrence of skin cancer and the use of computer monitors*

ocean /ˈəʊʃn; AmE ˈoʊʃn/ noun **1** (usually the ocean) [sing.] (especially AmE) the mass of salt water that covers most of the earth's surface: *the depths of the ocean* ◊ *People were swimming in the ocean despite the hurricane warning.* ◊ *The plane hit the ocean several miles offshore.* ◊ *Our beach house is just a couple of miles from the ocean.* ◊ *an ocean liner/voyage* ◊ *Ocean levels are rising.*—picture at COAST **2** (usually Ocean) [C] one of the five large areas that the ocean is divided into: *the Antarctic/Arctic/Atlantic/Indian/Pacific Ocean* ⇨ note at SEA IDM **an ocean of sth** (BrE also **oceans of sth**) (informal) a large amount of sth: *oceans of food*—more at DROP n.

ocean·front /ˈəʊʃnfrʌnt; AmE ˈoʊ-/ adj. (AmE) situated on land near the ocean: *an oceanfront hotel*

'ocean-going adj. [only before noun] (of ships) made for crossing the sea or ocean, not for journeys along the coast or up rivers

ocean·ic /ˌəʊʃiˈænɪk; AmE ˌoʊʃi-/ adj. [usually before noun] (technical) connected with the ocean: *oceanic islands/birds/fish*

ocean·og·raphy /ˌəʊʃəˈnɒɡrəfi; AmE ˌoʊʃəˈnɑːɡ-/ noun [U] the scientific study of the ocean ▶ **ocean·og·raph·er** noun

oce·lot /ˈɒsəlɒt; AmE ˈɑːsəlɑːt; ˈoʊs-/ noun a wild animal of the cat family, that has yellow fur with black lines and spots, found in Central and S America

och /ɒk; ɒx; AmE ɑːk; ɑːx/ exclamation (ScotE, IrishE) used to express the fact that you are surprised, sorry, etc: *Och, aye* (= Oh, yes).

ochre (AmE also **ocher**) /ˈəʊkə(r); AmE ˈoʊ-/ noun [U] **1** a type of red or yellow earth used in some paints and DYES **2** the red or yellow colour of ochre

o'clock /əˈklɒk; AmE əˈklɑːk/ adv. used with the numbers 1 to 12 when telling the time, to mean an exact hour: *He left between five and six o'clock.* ◊ *at/after/before eleven o'clock*

OCR abbr. (computing) OPTICAL CHARACTER RECOGNITION

octa·gon /ˈɒktəɡən; AmE ˈɑːktəɡɑːn/ noun (geometry) a flat shape with eight straight sides and eight angles ▶ **oc·tag·on·al** /ɒkˈtæɡənl; AmE ɑːkˈt-/ adj.: *an octagonal tower/coin*

oc·tane /ˈɒkteɪn; AmE ˈɑːk-/ noun a chemical substance in petrol/gas, used as a way of measuring its quality: *high-octane fuel*

oct·ave /ˈɒktɪv; AmE ˈɑːk-/ noun (music) the difference (called the INTERVAL) between the first and last notes in a

s	t	v	z	ʃ	ʒ	tʃ	dʒ	θ	ð	ŋ
see	tea	van	zoo	shoe	vision	chain	jam	thin	this	sing

series of eight notes on a musical SCALE: *to play an octave higher* ◊ *Orbison's vocal range spanned three octaves.*

octet /ɒkˈtet; *AmE* ɑːk-/ *noun* **1** [C+sing./pl. *v.*] a group of eight singers or musicians, playing classical music **2** [C] a piece of music for eight singers or musicians

octo- /ˈɒktəʊ; *AmE* ˈɑːktoʊ-/ (also **oct-**) *combining form* (in nouns, adjectives and adverbs) eight; having eight: *octagon*

Oc·to·ber /ɒkˈtəʊbə(r); *AmE* ɑːkˈtoʊ-/ *noun* [U, C] (*abbr.* Oct.) the 10th month of the year, between September and November **HELP** To see how **October** is used, look at the examples at **April**.

oc·to·gen·ar·ian /ˌɒktədʒəˈneəriən; *AmE* ˌɑːktədʒəˈner-/ *noun* a person between 80 and 89 years old

octo·pus /ˈɒktəpəs; *AmE* ˈɑːk-/ *noun* [C, U] (*pl.* **octo-puses**) a sea creature with a soft round body and eight long TENTACLES (= long thin parts like arms), that is sometimes used for food—picture on page A7

ocu·lar /ˈɒkjələ(r); *AmE* ˈɑːk-/ *adj.* [only before noun] **1** (*technical*) connected with the eyes: *ocular muscles* **2** (*formal*) that can be seen: *ocular proof*

ocu·list /ˈɒkjəlɪst; *AmE* ˈɑːk-/ *noun* (*old-fashioned*) a doctor who examines and treats people's eyes

OD /ˌəʊ diː; *AmE* ˌoʊ/ *verb* (**OD's, OD'ing, OD'd, OD'd**) [V] ~ **(on sth)** (*informal*) = OVERDOSE

odd /ɒd; *AmE* ɑːd/ *adj.* (**odder, oddest**)
STRANGE | **1** strange or unusual: *They're very odd people.* ◊ *There's something odd about that man.* ◊ *It's most odd that* (= very odd that) *she hasn't written.* ◊ *The odd thing was that he didn't recognize her.* ◊ *She had the oddest feeling that he was avoiding her.*—compare PECULIAR
ODD- | **2** (in compounds) strange or unusual in the way mentioned: *an odd-looking house* ◊ *an odd-sounding name*
NOT REGULAR/OFTEN | **3** (**the odd**) [only before noun] (no comparative or superlative) happening or appearing occasionally; not very regular or frequent [SYN] OCCASIONAL: *He makes the odd mistake—nothing too serious.*
VARIOUS | **4** [only before noun] (no comparative or superlative) of no particular type or size; various: *decorations made of odd scraps of paper*
NOT MATCHING | **5** [usually before noun] (no comparative or superlative) not with the pair or set that it belongs to; not matching: *You're wearing odd socks!*
NUMBERS | **6** (no comparative or superlative) (of numbers) that cannot be divided exactly by the number two: *1, 3, 5 and 7 are odd numbers.* [OPP] EVEN
AVAILABLE | **7** [only before noun] available; that sb can use: *Could I see you when you've got an odd moment?* ◊ *Have you got an odd 20p?*
APPROXIMATELY | **8** (no comparative or superlative; usually placed immediately after a number) approximately or a little more than the number mentioned: *How old is she—seventy odd?* ◊ *He's worked there for twenty-odd years.*
▶ **odd·ness** *noun* [U]: *the oddness of her appearance* ◊ *His oddness frightened her.*
[IDM] **the odd man/one 'out** a person or thing that is different from others or does not fit easily into a group or set: *At school he was always the odd man out.* ◊ *Dog, cat, horse, shoe—which is the odd one out?*—more at FISH *n.*

odd·ball /ˈɒdbɔːl; *AmE* ˈɑːd-/ *noun* (*informal*) a person who behaves in a strange or unusual way ▶ **odd·ball** *adj.*: *oddball characters*

odd·ity /ˈɒdəti; *AmE* ˈɑːd-/ *noun* (*pl.* **-ies**) **1** [C] a person or thing that is strange or unusual: *The book deals with some of the oddities of grammar and spelling.* **2** [U] the quality of being strange or unusual: *She suddenly realized the oddity of her remark and blushed.*

odd-'job man *noun* (*especially BrE*) a person paid to do odd jobs

odd 'jobs *noun* [pl.] small jobs of various types: *to do odd jobs around the house*

oddly /ˈɒdli; *AmE* ˈɑːd-/ *adv.* **1** in a strange or unusual way: *She's been behaving very oddly lately.* ◊ *oddly coloured clothes* ◊ *He looked at her in a way she found oddly disturbing.* **2** used to show that sth is surprising: *She felt, oddly, that they had been happier when they had no*

money. ◊ *Oddly enough, the most expensive tickets sold fastest.*

odd·ments /ˈɒdmənts; *AmE* ˈɑːd-/ *noun* [pl.] (*especially BrE*) **1** small pieces of fabric, wood, etc. that are left after a larger piece has been used to make sth **2** small items that are not valuable or are not part of a larger set

odds /ɒdz; *AmE* ɑːdz/ *noun* [pl.] **1** (usually **the odds**) the degree to which sth is likely to happen: *The odds are very much in our favour* (= we are likely to succeed). ◊ *The odds are heavily against him* (= he is not likely to succeed). ◊ *The odds are that* (= it is likely that) *she'll win.* ◊ *What are the odds* (= how likely is it) *he won't turn up?* **2** something that makes it seem impossible to do or achieve sth: *They secured a victory in the face of overwhelming odds.* ◊ *Against all* (*the*) *odds, he made a full recovery.* **3** (in betting) the connection between two numbers that shows how much money sb will receive if they win a bet: *odds of ten to one* (= ten times the amount of money that has been bet by sb) *will be paid to them if they win* ◊ *They are offering **long/short odds*** (= the winnings will be high/low because there is a high/low risk of losing) *on the defending champion.* ◊ (*figurative*) *I'll **lay odds** on him getting the job* (= I'm sure he will get it). [IDM] **be at 'odds (with sth)** to be different from sth, when the two things should be the same: *These findings are at odds with what is going on in the rest of the country.* **be at 'odds (with sb) (over/on sth)** to disagree with sb about sth: *He's always at odds with his father over politics.* **it makes no 'odds** (*spoken, especially BrE*) used to say that sth is not important: *It makes no odds to me whether you go or stay.* **over the 'odds** (*BrE, informal*) more money than you would normally expect: *Many collectors are willing to pay over the odds for early examples of his work.*—more at STACKED

odds and 'ends (*BrE also* ˌodds and 'sods) *noun* [pl.] (*informal*) small items that are not valuable or are not part of a larger set: *She spent the day sorting through a box full of odds and ends.* ◊ *I've got a few odds and ends* (= small jobs) *to do before leaving.*

odds-'on *adj.* very likely to happen, win, etc: *the odds-on favourite* (= the person, horse, etc. that is most likely to succeed, to win a race, etc.) ◊ *It's odds-on that he'll be late.* ◊ *Arazi is odds-on to win the Kentucky Derby.*

ode /əʊd; *AmE* oʊd/ *noun* a poem that speaks to a person or thing or celebrates a special event: *Keats's 'Ode to a Nightingale'*

odi·ous /ˈəʊdiəs; *AmE* ˈoʊ-/ *adj.* (*formal*) extremely unpleasant: *What an odious man!*

odium /ˈəʊdiəm; *AmE* ˈoʊ-/ *noun* [U] (*rare, formal*) a feeling of hatred that a lot of people have towards sb, because of sth they have done

odom·eter /əʊˈdɒmɪtə(r); *AmE* oʊˈdɑːm-/ *noun* (*AmE*) = MILOMETER

odor·ous /ˈəʊdərəs; *AmE* ˈoʊ-/ *adj.* (*literary or technical*) having a smell: *odorous gases*

odour (*BrE*) (*AmE* **odor**) /ˈəʊdə(r); *AmE* ˈoʊ-/ *noun* [C, U] (*formal*) a smell, especially one that is unpleasant: *a fishy/musty/pungent odour* ◊ *the stale odour of cigarette smoke* ◊ (*figurative*) *the odour of suspicion*—see also BODY ODOUR [IDM] **be in good/bad 'odour (with sb)** (*formal*) to have/not have sb's approval and support

odour·less (*BrE*) (*AmE* **odor·less**) /ˈəʊdələs; *AmE* ˈoʊdərləs/ *adj.* without a smell: *an odourless liquid*

odys·sey /ˈɒdəsi; *AmE* ˈɑːd-/ *noun* [sing.] (*literary*) a long journey full of experiences [ORIGIN] From the **Odyssey**, a Greek poem that is said to have been written by Homer, about the adventures of **Odysseus**. After a battle in Troy Odysseus had to spend ten years travelling before he could return home.

OECD /ˌəʊ iː siː 'diː; *AmE* ˌoʊ/ *abbr.* Organization for Economic Cooperation and Development (an organization of industrial countries that encourages trade and economic growth)

Oedi·pal /ˈiːdɪpl; *AmE* usually 'ed-/ *adj.* [usually before noun] connected with an Oedipus complex

Oedi·pus com·plex /ˈiːdɪpəs kɒmpleks; *AmE* usually 'edɪpəs kɑːm-/ *noun* [sing.] (*psychology*) feelings of sexual

æ	ɑː	e	ɜː	ə	ɪ	iː	i	ɒ	ɔː	ʌ	ʊ	u	uː
cat	father	ten	bird	about	sit	see	many	got	saw	cup	put	actual	too
								(BrE)					

desire that a boy has for his mother and the jealous feelings towards his father that this causes **ORIGIN** From the Greek story of **Oedipus**, whose father Laius had been told by the oracle that his son would kill him. Laius left Oedipus on a mountain to die, but a shepherd rescued him. Oedipus returned home many years later but did not recognize his parents. He killed his father and married his mother Jocasta.

o'er /ɔː(r)/ adv., prep. (old use) over

oe·soph·a·gus (BrE) (AmE **eso·pha·gus**) /iˈsɒfəgəs; AmE iˈsɑː-/ noun (pl. **-phag·uses** or **-phagi** /-gaɪ/) (anatomy) the tube through which food passes from the mouth to the stomach **SYN** GULLET—picture at BODY

oes·tro·gen /ˈiːstrədʒən/ (BrE) (AmE **es·tro·gen** /ˈes-/) noun [U] a HORMONE produced in women's OVARIES that causes them to develop the physical and sexual features that are characteristic of females and that causes them to prepare their body to have babies—compare PROGESTERONE, TESTOSTERONE

oeuvre /ˈɜːvrə/ noun [sing.] (from French, formal) all the works of a writer, artist, etc: Picasso's oeuvre

of /əv; strong form ɒv; AmE ʌv/ prep. **1** belonging to sb; relating to sb: a friend of mine ◊ the love of a mother for her child ◊ the role of the teacher ◊ Can't you throw out that old bike of Tommy's? ◊ the paintings of Monet **HELP** When you are talking about everything someone has painted, written, etc. use **of**. When you are referring to one or more examples of somebody's work, use **by**: a painting by Monet **2** belonging to sth; being part of sth; relating to sth: the lid of the box ◊ the director of the company ◊ a member of the team ◊ the result of the debate **3** coming from a particular background or living in a place: a woman of Italian descent ◊ the people of Wales **4** concerning or showing sb/sth: a story of passion ◊ a photo of my dog ◊ a map of India **5** used to say what sb/sth is, consists of, or contains: the city of Dublin ◊ the issue of housing ◊ a crowd of people ◊ a glass of milk **6** used with measurements and expressions of time, age, etc: 2 kilos of potatoes ◊ an increase of 2% ◊ a girl of 12 ◊ the fourth of July ◊ the year of his birth ◊ (old-fashioned) We would often have a walk of an evening. **7** used to show sb/sth belongs to a group, often after some, a few, etc: some of his friends ◊ a few of the problems ◊ the most famous of all the stars **8** used to show the position of sth/sb in space or time: just north of Detroit ◊ at the time of the revolution ◊ (AmE) at a quarter of eleven tonight (= 10.45 p.m.) **9** used after nouns formed from verbs. The noun after 'of' can be either the object or the subject of the action: the arrival of the police (= they arrive) ◊ criticism of the police (= they are criticized) ◊ fear of the dark ◊ the howling of the wind **10** used after some verbs before mentioning sb/sth involved in the action: to rob/deprive sb of sth ◊ He was cleared of all blame. ◊ Think of a number, any number. **11** used after some adjectives before mentioning sb/sth that a feeling relates to: to be ashamed/proud of sth **12** used to give your opinion of sb's behaviour: It was kind of you to offer. **13** used when one noun describes a second one: Where's that idiot of a boy? (= the boy that you think is an idiot) **IDM** of **'all** used before a noun to say that sth is very surprising: I'm surprised that you of all people should say that. **of all the ...** used to express anger: Of all the nerve!

off /ɒf; AmE ɔːf; ɑːf/ adv., prep., adj., noun

■ adv. **HELP** For the special uses of **off** in phrasal verbs, look at the entries for the verbs. For example **come off** is in the phrasal verb section at **come**. **1** away from a place; at a distance in space or time: I called him but he ran off. ◊ Sarah's off in India somewhere. ◊ I must be off soon (= leave). ◊ Off you go! ◊ Summer's not far off now. ◊ A solution is still some way off. **2** used to say that sth has been removed: He's had his beard shaved off. ◊ Take your coat off. ◊ Don't leave the toothpaste with the top off. **3** starting a race: They're off (= the race has begun). **4** no longer going to happen; cancelled: The wedding is off. **5** not connected or functioning: The water is off. ◊ Make sure the TV is off. **6** (especially BrE) (of an item on a menu) no longer available or being served: Sorry, the duck is off. **7** away from work or duty: She's off today. ◊

I've got three days off next week. ◊ How many days did you take off? ◊ I need some time off. **8** taken from the price: shoes with £5 off ◊ All shirts have/are 10% off. **9** behind or at the sides of the stage in a theatre **SYN** OFFSTAGE **IDM** be better **'off** to have more money: Families will be better off under the new law. ◊ Her promotion means she's $100 a week better off. **be better off (doing sth)** used to say that sb is/would be happier or more satisfied if they were in a particular position or took a particular action: She's better off without him. ◊ The weather was so bad we'd have been better off staying at home. **be ,off for 'sth** (informal) to have a particular amount of sth: How are we off for coffee (= how much have we got)?—see also BADLY OFF **,off and 'on/,on and 'off** from time to time; now and again: It rained on and off all day.

■ prep. **HELP** For the special uses of **off** in phrasal verbs, look at the entries for the verbs. For example **take sth off sth** is in the phrasal verb section at **take**. **1** down or away from a place or at a distance in space or time: I fell off the ladder. ◊ Keep off the grass! ◊ an island off the coast of Spain ◊ They were still 100 metres off the summit. ◊ Scientists are still a long way off finding a cure. ◊ We're getting right off the subject. **2** leading away from sth, for example a road or room: We live off Main Street. ◊ There's a bathroom off the main bedroom. **3** used to say that sth has been removed: You need to take the top off the bottle first! ◊ I want about an inch off the back of my hair. **4** away from work or duty: He's had ten days off school. **5** away from a price: They knocked £500 off the car. **6** (**off of**) (non-standard or AmE, informal) off; from: I got it off of my brother. **7** not wanting or liking sth that you usually eat or use: I'm off (= not drinking) alcohol for a week. ◊ He's finally off drugs (= he no longer takes them).

■ adj. [not before noun] **1** (of food) no longer fresh enough to eat or drink: This fish has gone off. ◊ The milk smells off. ◊ It's off. **2 ~ (with sb)** (informal, especially BrE) not polite or friendly: He was a bit off with me this morning. **3** (informal, especially BrE) not acceptable: It's a bit off expecting us to work on Sunday.

■ noun [sing.] (**the off**) the start of a race: They're ready for the off.

off- /ɒf; AmE ɔːf; ɑːf/ prefix (in nouns, adjectives, verbs and adverbs) not on; away from: offstage ◊ offload

,off-'air adj. (in radio and television) not being broadcast: off-air recording **OPP** ON-AIR ► **,off-'air** adv.: to record off-air

offal /ˈɒfl; AmE ˈɔːfl; ˈɑːfl/ noun [U] the inside parts of an animal, such as the heart and LIVER, cooked and eaten as food

off·beat /ˌɒfˈbiːt; AmE ˌɔːf-; ˌɑːf-/ adj. [usually before noun] (informal) different from what most people expect: offbeat humour ◊ an offbeat approach to interviewing

off-Broadway /ˌɒf ˈbrɔːdweɪ; AmE ˌɔːf-; ˌɑːf-/ adj. (AmE) **1** (of a theatre) not on Broadway, New York's main theatre district **2** (of a play) unusual in some way and often by new writers—compare FRINGE THEATRE

,off-'centre (BrE) (AmE **,off-'center**) adv., adj. not exactly in the centre of sth: She wore a beret, set slightly off-centre.

'off chance noun **IDM** do sth on the **'off chance** to do sth even though you think that there is only a small possibility of it being successful: She scanned the crowd on the off chance of seeing someone she knew. ◊ I called in at the office on the off chance that you would still be there.

off·cut /ˈɒfkʌt; AmE ˈɔːf-; ˈɑːf-/ noun (especially BrE) a piece of wood, paper, etc. that remains after the main piece has been cut

'off day noun (informal) a day when you do not do things as well as usual: Even the best players sometimes have an off day.

,off-'duty adj. not at work: an off-duty policeman

of·fence (BrE) (AmE **of·fense**) /əˈfens/ noun **1** [C] **~ (against sb/sth)** an illegal act **SYN** CRIME: a criminal/serious/minor/sexual offence ◊ a first offence (= the first time that sb has been found guilty of a crime) ◊ **a capital offence** (= one for which sb may be punished by death) ◊ He was not aware that he had **committed an offence**. ◊ an

aɪ	aʊ	eɪ	əʊ	oʊ	ɔɪ	ɪə	eə	ʊə	j	w
my	now	say	go (BrE)	go (AmE)	boy	near	hair	pure	yes	wet

offence against society/humanity/the state ◇ *New legislation makes it an offence to carry guns.* **2** [U] the act of upsetting or insulting sb: *I'm sure he meant no offence when he said that.* ◇ *The photo on the cover of the book may cause offence to some people.* ◇ *No one will take offence* (= feel upset or insulted) *if you leave early.* ◇ *Don't be so quick to take offence.* **IDM** **no of'fence** *(spoken)* used to say that you do not mean to upset or insult sb by sth you say or do: *No offence, but I'd really like to be on my own.*

of·fend /ə'fend/ *verb* **1** [often passive] to make sb feel upset because of sth you say or do that is rude or embarrassing: [VN] *They'll be offended if you don't go to their wedding.* ◇ *Neil did not mean to offend anybody with his joke.* ◇ [V] *A TV interviewer must be careful not to offend.* **2** [VN] to seem unpleasant to sb: *The smell from the farm offended some people.* ◇ *an ugly building that offends the eye* **3** [V] *(formal)* to commit a crime or crimes: [V] *He started offending at the age of 16.* **4** [V] **~ (against sb/sth)** *(formal)* to be against what people believe is morally right: *comments that offend against people's religious beliefs* ▶ **of·fend·ed** *adj.: Alice looked rather offended.*

of·fend·er /ə'fendə(r)/ *noun* **1** a person who commits a crime: *a persistent/serious/violent offender* ◇ *a young offender institution*—see also FIRST OFFENDER, SEX OFFENDER **2** a person or thing that does sth wrong: *The report on sexual discrimination at work shows that some of the worst offenders are women.* ◇ *When it comes to pollution, the chemical industry is a major offender.*

of·fend·ing /ə'fendɪŋ/ *adj.* [only before noun] **1** causing you to feel annoyed or upset; causing problems: *The offending paragraph was deleted.* ◇ *The traffic jam soon cleared once the offending vehicle had been removed.* **2** guilty of a crime: *The offending driver received a large fine.*

of·fense /ə'fens/ *noun (AmE)* **1** [C, U] = OFFENCE **2** (usually **the offense**) [sing., U] *(BrE* **at·tack** [sing.]*) (sport)* the members of a team whose main aim is to score points against the other team; a method of attack: *The Redskins' offense is stronger than their defense.* ◇ *He played offense for the Chicago Bulls.*—compare DEFENCE

of·fen·sive /ə'fensɪv/ *adj., noun*
■ *adj.* **1 ~ (to sb)** rude in a way that causes you to feel upset, insulted or annoyed: *offensive behaviour/remarks* ◇ *His comments were deeply offensive to a large number of single mothers.* ◇ *The programme contains language which some viewers may find offensive.* **2** *(formal)* extremely unpleasant: *an offensive smell* **3** [only before noun] connected with the act of attacking sb/sth: *an offensive war* ◇ *offensive action* ◇ *He was charged with carrying an offensive weapon.*—compare DEFENSIVE **4** *(AmE, sport)* connected with the team that has control of the ball; connected with the act of scoring points: *offensive play*—compare DEFENSIVE ▶ **of·fen·sive·ly** *adv.* **of·fen·sive·ness** *noun* [U]
■ *noun* **1** a military operation in which large numbers of soldiers, etc. attack another country: *an air/a bombing offensive* ◇ *The final offensive was launched on January 10.* **2** a series of actions aimed at achieving sth in a way that attracts a lot of attention: *The government has launched a new offensive against crime.* ◇ *a sales offensive* ◇ *The public seems unconvinced by their latest charm offensive* (= their attempt to make people like them). **IDM** **be on the of'fensive** to be attacking sb/sth rather than waiting for them to attack you: *The Scots were on the offensive for most of the game.* ◇ *The government is very much on the offensive in the fight against drugs.* **go on (to) the of'fensive** | **take the of'fensive** to start attacking sb/sth before they start attacking you

offer /'ɒfə(r); *AmE* 'ɔ:f-; 'ɑ:f-/ *verb, noun*
■ *verb* **1 ~ sth (to sb) (for sth)** | **~ sb sth** to say that you are willing to do sth for sb or give sth to sb: [VN] *He offered £4000 for the car.* ◇ *Josie had offered her services as a guide* ◇ *He offered some useful advice.* ◇ [VN, VNN] *They decided to offer the job to Jo.* ◇ *They decided to offer Jo the job.* ◇ [VNN] *I gratefully took the cup of coffee she offered me.* ◇ *Taylor offered him 500 dollars to do the work.* ◇ [V to inf] *The kids offered to do the dishes.* ◇ [V speech] *'I'll do it,' she offered.*

2 [VN] to make sth available or to provide the opportunity for sth: *The hotel offers excellent facilities for families.* ◇ *The job didn't offer any prospects for promotion.* ◇ *He did not offer any explanation for his behaviour.* **3** [VN] **~ sth/sb (up) (to sb)** *(formal)* to give sth to God: *We offered up our prayers for the men's safe return.* **IDM** **have sth to offer** to have sth available that sb wants: *Oxford has a lot to offer its visitors in the way of entertainment.* ◇ *a young man with a great deal to offer* (= who is intelligent, has many skills, etc.) **offer your 'hand** *(formal)* to hold out your hand for sb to shake
■ *noun* **1 ~ (of sth/to do sth)** an act of saying that you are willing to do sth for sb or give sth to sb: *Thank you for your kind offer of help.* ◇ *I accepted her offer to pay.* ◇ *to accept/refuse/decline an offer* ◇ *I took him up on his offer of a loan.* ◇ *You can't just turn down offers of work like that.* ◇ *an offer of marriage* **2 ~ (for sth)** an amount of money that sb is willing to pay for sth: *I've had an offer of £2500 for the car.* ◇ *They've decided to accept our original offer.* ◇ *The offer has been withdrawn.* ◇ *They made me an offer I couldn't refuse.* ◇ *The original price was £3000, but I'm open to offers* (= willing to consider offers that are less than that).—see also O.N.O. **3** a reduction in the normal price of sth, usually for a short period of time: *This special offer is valid until the end of the month.* ◇ *See next week's issue for details of more free offers.* ◇ *They have an offer on beer at the moment.* **IDM** **on 'offer 1** that can be bought, used, etc: *The following is a list of courses currently on offer.* ◇ *Prizes worth more than £20000 are on offer to the winner.* **2** *(especially BrE)* on sale at a lower price than normal for a short period of time: *Italian wines are on (special) offer this week.* **under 'offer** *(BrE)* if a house or other building is **under offer**, sb has agreed to buy it at a particular price

of·fer·ing /'ɒfərɪŋ; *AmE* 'ɔ:f-; 'ɑ:f-/ *noun* **1** something that is produced for other people to use, watch, enjoy etc: *This is the latest offering from the Canadian-born writer.* **2** something that is given to a god as part of religious worship: *All these sacrifices are essentially offerings to the gods.*—see also PEACE OFFERING

of·fer·tory /'ɒfətri; *AmE* 'ɔ:fərtɔ:ri; 'ɑ:f-/ *noun (pl. -ies)* **1** the offering of bread and wine to God at a church service **2** an offering or a collection of money during a church service

off·hand /ˌɒf'hænd; *AmE* ˌɔ:f-; ˌɑ:f-/ *adj., adv.*
■ *adj. (disapproving)* not showing much interest in sb/sth: *an offhand manner/voice* ◇ *He was very offhand with me.* ◇ *She seemed offhand about the danger involved.* ▶ **off·hand·ed·ly** /ˌɒf'hændɪdli; *AmE* ˌɔ:f-; ˌɑ:f-/ *adv.: He spoke offhandedly, making it clear I had no say in the matter.*
■ *adv.* without being able to check sth or think about it: *I don't know offhand how much we made last year.*

of·fice /'ɒfɪs; *AmE* 'ɔ:f-; 'ɑ:f-/ *noun*
ROOM/BUILDING | **1** [C] a room, set of rooms or building where people work, usually sitting at desks: *The company is moving to new offices on the other side of town.* ◇ *Are you going to the office today?* ◇ *We ought to inform head office.* ◇ *an office job* ◇ *office workers* **2** [C] a room in which a particular person works, usually at a desk: *Some people have to share an office.* ◇ *Come into my office.* **3** *(AmE)* = SURGERY: *a doctor's/dentist's office* **4** [C] (often in compounds) a room or building used for a particular purpose, especially to provide information or a service: *the local tourist office* ◇ *a ticket office*—see also BOX OFFICE, REGISTRY OFFICE

GOVERNMENT DEPARTMENT | **5 (Office)** [C] used in the names of some British government departments: *the Foreign Office* ◇ *the Home Office*

IMPORTANT POSITION | **6** [U, C] an important position of authority, especially in government; the work and duties connected with this: *She held office as a cabinet minister for ten years.* ◇ *How long has he been in office?* ◇ *The party has been out of office* (= has not formed a government) *for many years.* ◇ *The present government took office in 1997.* ◇ *to seek/run for office* ◇ *(BrE) to stand for office* ◇ *the office of treasurer*

IDM **through sb's good 'offices** *(formal)* with sb's help

'office block (*BrE*) (also **'office building** *AmE, BrE*) *noun* a large building that contains offices, usually belonging to more than one company: *high-rise office blocks*

'office boy, 'office girl *noun* (*old-fashioned*) a young person employed to do simple tasks in an office

'office-holder (also **'office-bearer**) *noun* a person who is in a position of authority, especially in the government or a government organization

'office hours *noun* [pl.] the time when people in offices are normally working: *Our telephone lines are open during normal office hours.*

of·fi·cer /'ɒfɪsə(r); *AmE* 'ɔːf-; 'ɑːf-/ *noun* **1** a person who is in a position of authority in the armed forces: *army/airforce/naval officers* ◊ *a* **commissioned**/**non-commissioned** *officer* ◊ *The matter was passed on to me, as your* **commanding** *officer.*—see also FLYING OFFICER, PETTY OFFICER, PILOT OFFICER, WARRANT OFFICER **2** (often in compounds) a person who is in a position of authority in the government or a large organization: *an environmental health officer* ◊ *a customs/prison/welfare officer* ◊ *officers of state* (= ministers in the government)—see also CHIEF EXECUTIVE OFFICER, MEDICAL OFFICER, PRESS OFFICER, PROBATION OFFICER, RETURNING OFFICER **3** (often used as a form of address) = POLICE OFFICER: *the officer in charge of the case* ◊ *the investigating officer* ◊ *Yes, officer, I saw what happened.* **4** (*AmE*) a title for a police officer: *Officer Dibble*

'office worker *noun* a person who works in the offices of a business or company

of·fi·cial /ə'fɪʃl/ *adj., noun*
■ *adj.* **1** [only before noun] connected with the job of sb who is in a position of authority: *official responsibilities* ◊ *the Prime Minister's official residence* ◊ *He attended in his official capacity as mayor.* ◊ *This was her first official engagement.* ◊ *He made an official visit to Tokyo in March.* **2** [usually before noun] agreed to, said, done, etc. by sb who is in a position of authority: *an official announcement/decision/statement* ◊ *according to official statistics/figures* ◊ *An official inquiry has been launched into the cause of the accident.* ◊ *The country's official language is Spanish.* ◊ *I intend to lodge an official complaint* (= to complain to sb in authority). ◊ *The news is not yet official.* **3** [only before noun] that is told to the public but may not be true: *I only knew the official version of events.* ◊ *The official story has always been that they are just good friends.* **4** [only before noun] formal and attended by people in authority: *an official function/reception* ◊ *The official opening is planned for October.* [OPP] UNOFFICIAL
■ *noun* (often in compounds) a person who is in a position of authority in a large organization: *a bank/company/court/government official* ◊ *a senior official in the State Department* ◊ *Palace officials are refusing to comment on the royal divorce.*

of·fi·cial·dom /ə'fɪʃldəm/ *noun* [U] (*disapproving*) people who are in positions of authority in large organizations when they seem to be more interested in following rules than in being helpful: *The report is critical of attempts by officialdom to deal with the problem of homelessness.*

of·fi·cial·ese /ə,fɪʃə'liːz/ *noun* [U] (*disapproving*) language used in official documents that is thought by many people to be too complicated and difficult to understand

of·fi·cial·ly /ə'fɪʃəli/ *adv.* **1** publicly and by sb who is in a position of authority: *The library will be officially opened by the local MP.* ◊ *We haven't yet been told officially about the closure.* ◊ *The college is not an officially recognized English language school.* **2** according to a particular set of rules, laws, etc: *Many of those living on the streets are not officially homeless.* ◊ *I'm not officially supposed to be here.* **3** according to information that has been told to the public but that may not be true: *Officially, he resigned because of bad health.* [OPP] UNOFFICIALLY

of·ficial re'ceiver *noun* = RECEIVER

of·ficial 'secret *noun* (in Britain) a piece of information known only to the government and its employees,

which it is illegal for them to tell anyone under the **Official Secrets Act**

of·fi·ci·ate /ə'fɪʃieɪt/ *verb* [V] ~ **(at sth)** (*formal*) to do the official duties at a public or religious ceremony

of·fi·cious /ə'fɪʃəs/ *adj.* (*disapproving*) too ready to tell people what to do or to use the power you have to give orders: *a nasty officious little man* ▶ **of·fi·cious·ly** *adv.*: *'You can't park here,' he said officiously.* **of·fi·cious·ness** *noun* [U]

off·ing /'ɒfɪŋ; *AmE* 'ɔːf-; 'ɑːf-/ *noun* [IDM] **in the offing** (*informal*) likely to appear or happen soon: *I hear there are more staff changes in the offing.*

off-'key *adj.* **1** (of a voice or a musical instrument) not in tune **2** not suitable or correct in a particular situation: *Some of his remarks were very off-key.* ▶ **off-'key** *adv.*: *to sing off-key*

off-licence (*BrE*) (*AmE* **'liquor store**) *noun* a shop that sells alcoholic drinks in bottles and cans to take away

off-'line *adj.* (*computing*) not directly controlled by or connected to a computer or to the Internet—see also ONLINE

off·load /,ɒf'ləʊd; *AmE* ,ɔːf'loʊd; ,ɑːf-/ *verb* [VN] ~ **sth/sb (on/onto sb)** to get rid of sth/sb that you do not need or want by passing it/them to sb else: *They should stop offloading waste from oil tankers into the sea.* ◊ *It's nice to have someone you can offload your problems onto.*

off-'peak *adj.* [only before noun] happening or used at a time that is less popular or busy, and therefore cheaper: *off-peak electricity/travel* ▶ **off-'peak** *adv.*: *Phone calls cost 20p per unit off-peak.*—compare PEAK

off-putting *adj.* (*informal, especially BrE*) not pleasant, in a way that prevents you from liking sb/sth: *I find his manner very off-putting.*

off-road *adj.* [usually before noun] not on the public road: *an off-road vehicle* (= one for driving on rough ground)

off-'screen *adj.* [only before noun] in real life, not in a film/movie: *They were off-screen lovers.* ▶ **off-'screen** *adv.*: *She looks totally different off-screen.*—compare ON-SCREEN

off season *noun* [sing.] **1** the time of the year that is less busy in business and travel [SYN] LOW SEASON: *We don't get many tourists in the off season.* **2** (*AmE, sport*) = CLOSE SEASON ▶ **off-'season** *adj.* [only before noun]: *off-season prices* **off-'season** *adv.*: *We prefer to travel off-season.*

off·set /'ɒfset; *AmE* 'ɔːf-; 'ɑːf-/ *verb, adj.*
■ *verb* (**off·set·ting, off·set, off·set**) [VN] ~ **sth (against sth)** to use one cost, payment or situation in order to cancel or reduce the effect of another: *Prices have risen in order to offset the increased cost of materials.* ◊ (*BrE*) *What expenses can you offset against tax?*
■ *adj.* [only before noun] used to describe a method of printing in which ink is put onto a metal plate, then onto a rubber surface and only then onto the paper

off·shoot /'ɒfʃuːt; *AmE* 'ɔːf-; 'ɑːf-/ *noun* **1** a thing that develops from sth, especially a small organization that develops from a larger one **2** (*technical*) a new stem that grows on a plant

off·shore /,ɒf'ʃɔː(r); *AmE* ,ɔːf-; ,ɑːf-/ *adj.* [usually before noun] **1** happening or existing in the sea, not far from the land: *offshore drilling* ◊ *an offshore island* **2** (of winds) blowing from the land towards the sea: *offshore breezes* **3** (*business*) (of money, companies, etc.) kept or situated in a country that has more generous tax laws than other places: *offshore investments* ▶ **off·shore** *adv.*: *a ship anchored offshore* ◊ *profits earned offshore*—compare INSHORE, ONSHORE

off·side *adj., noun*
■ *adj.* /,ɒf'saɪd; *AmE* ,ɔːf-; ,ɑːf-/ *adj.* [usually before noun] **1** (*AmE* also **off·sides**) in some sports, for example football or hockey, a player is **offside** if he or she is in a position, usually ahead of the ball, that is not allowed: *He was offside when he scored.* ◊ *the offside rule*—compare ONSIDE **2** (*BrE*) on the side of a vehicle that is furthest from the edge of the road: *the offside mirror*—compare NEARSIDE
■ *noun* [U] **1** /,ɒf'saɪd; *AmE* ,ɔːf-; ,ɑːf-/ (*AmE* also **off·sides**)

	s	t	v	z	ʃ	ʒ	tʃ	dʒ	θ	ð	ŋ
	see	tea	van	zoo	shoe	vision	chain	jam	thin	this	sing

the fact of being offside in a game such as football or hockey: *The goal was disallowed for offside.* **2** /'ɒfsaɪd; *AmE* 'ɔːf-; 'ɑːf-/ (*BrE*) the side of a vehicle that is furthest from the edge of the road: *The offside was damaged.*—compare NEARSIDE

off·spring /'ɒfsprɪŋ; *AmE* 'ɔːf-; 'ɑːf-/ *noun* (*pl.* **off·spring**) (*formal* or *humorous*) **1** a child of a particular person or couple: *the problems parents have with their teenage offspring* ◇ *to produce/raise offspring* **2** the young of an animal or plant

off·stage /ˌɒf'steɪdʒ; *AmE* ˌɔːf-; ˌɑːf-/ *adj.* **1** not on the stage in a theatre; not where the audience can see: *offstage sound effects* **2** happening to an actor in real life, not on the stage: *The stars were having an offstage relationship.* ▶ **off·stage** *adv.*: *The hero dies offstage.*—compare ONSTAGE

'off-street *adj.* [usually before noun] not on the public road: *an apartment with off-street parking*

ˌoff-the-'cuff ⇨ CUFF *n.* **HELP** You will also find other compounds beginning **off-the-** at the entry for the last word in the compound.

ˌoff-'white *adj.* very pale yellowish-white in colour: *The walls were painted off-white.* ▶ **ˌoff-'white** *noun* [U]

oft /ɒft; *AmE* ɔːft/ *adv.* (*old use*) (often in compounds) often: *an oft-repeated claim*

often /'ɒfn; 'ɒftən; *AmE* 'ɔːfn; 'ɔːftən; 'ɑːf-/ *adv.* **1** many times [SYN] FREQUENTLY: *We often go there.* ◇ *I've often wondered what happened to him.* ◇ *How often do you go to the theatre?* ◇ *I see her quite often.* ◇ *Try to exercise as often as possible.* ◇ *We should meet for lunch more often.* ◇ *It is not often that you get such an opportunity.* **2** in many cases [SYN] COMMONLY: *Old houses are often damp.* ◇ *People are often afraid of things they don't understand.* ◇ (*written*) *All too often the animals die through neglect.* **IDM** **as ˌoften as 'not | more ˌoften than 'not** usually; in a way that is typical of sb/sth: *As often as not, he's late for work.* **ˌevery so 'often** occasionally; sometimes—more at ONCE *adv.*

often·times /'ɒfntaɪmz; 'ɒftən-; *AmE* 'ɔːfn-; 'ɔːftən-; 'ɑːf-/ *adv.* (*old use* or *AmE*) often

ogle /'əʊɡl; *AmE* 'oʊɡl/ *verb* to look hard at sb in an offensive way, usually showing sexual interest: [VN] *He was not in the habit of ogling women.* [also V]

'O grade (also **ˌordinary 'grade**) *noun* [C, U] (in Scotland in the past) an exam in a particular subject, at a lower level than HIGHERS, usually taken at the age of 16. In 1988 it was replaced by the STANDARD GRADE.

ogre /'əʊɡə(r); *AmE* 'oʊ-/ *noun* **1** (in stories) a cruel and frightening GIANT (= a very large strong person) who eats people **2** a very frightening person: *My boss is a real ogre.*

oh (also *less frequent* **O**) /əʊ; *AmE* oʊ/ *exclamation* **1** used when you are reacting to sth that has been said, especially if you did not know it before: *'I saw Ben yesterday.' 'Oh yes, how is he?'* ◇ *'Emma has a new job.' 'Oh, has she?'* **2** used to express surprise, fear, joy, etc: *Oh, how wonderful!* ◇ *Oh no, I've broken it!* **3** used to attract sb's attention: *Oh, Sue! Could you help me a moment?* **4** used when you are thinking of what to say next: *I've been in this job for, oh, about six years.*

ohm /əʊm; *AmE* oʊm/ *noun* (*physics*) a unit for measuring electrical RESISTANCE

OHP /ˌəʊ eɪtʃ 'piː; *AmE* ˌoʊ eɪtʃ 'piː/ *noun* the abbreviation for 'overhead projector': *Will you be using an OHP?*

oi /ɔɪ/ *exclamation* (*BrE, informal*) used to attract sb's attention, especially in an angry way: *Oi, you! What do you think you're doing?*

-oid *suffix* (in adjectives and nouns) similar to: *humanoid* ◇ *rhomboid*

oik /ɔɪk/ *noun* (*BrE, slang*) an offensive way of referring to a person that you consider rude or stupid, especially a person of a lower social class

oil /ɔɪl/ *noun, verb*
■ *noun* **1** [U] a thick liquid that is found in rock underground [SYN] PETROLEUM: *drilling for oil* **2** [U] a form of PETROLEUM that is used as fuel and to make parts of machines move smoothly: *engine oil* ◇ *an oil lamp/heater*

◇ *Put some oil in the car.* **3** [U, C] a smooth thick liquid that is made from plants or animals and is used in cooking: *olive oil* ◇ *vegetable oils* **4** [U, C] a smooth thick liquid that is made from plants, minerals, etc. and is used on the skin or hair: *lavender bath oil* ◇ *suntan oil*—see also ESSENTIAL OIL **5** [U] (also **oils** [pl.]) coloured paint containing oil used by artists: *a painting done in oils* ◇ *landscapes in oil*—see also OIL PAINT **6** [C] = OIL PAINTING: *Among the more important Turner oils was 'Venus and Adonis'.*—see also OILY, CASTOR OIL, COD LIVER OIL, LINSEED OIL **IDM** see BURN *v.*, POUR
■ *verb* [VN] to put oil onto or into sth, for example a machine, in order to protect it or make it work smoothly: *He oiled his bike and pumped up the tyres.* **IDM** **oil the 'wheels** (*BrE*) **grease the 'wheels** (*AmE*) to help sth to happen easily and without problems, especially in business or politics

oil·can /'ɔɪlkæn/ *noun* a metal container for oil, especially one with a long thin SPOUT, used for putting oil onto machine parts

oil·cloth /'ɔɪlklɒθ; *AmE* -klɔːθ/ *noun* [U] a cotton fabric that has been COATED (= covered) on one side with a layer of oil so that water cannot pass through it, used especially in the past for covering tables

'oil colour (*BrE*) (*AmE* **'oil color**) *noun* [C, U] = OIL PAINT

oiled /ɔɪld/ *adj.* **well ~** (*BrE, informal*) drunk

oil·field /'ɔɪlfiːld/ *noun* an area where oil is found in the ground or under the sea

ˌoil-'fired *adj.* (of a heating system, etc.) burning oil as fuel

oil·man /'ɔɪlmæn/ *noun* (*pl.* **-men** /-men/) a man who owns an oil company or works in the oil industry

'oil paint (also **'oil colour**) *noun* [C, U] a type of paint that contains oil

'oil painting *noun* **1** (also **oil**) [C] a picture painted in OIL PAINT **2** [U] the art of painting in OIL PAINT **IDM** **be no 'oil painting** (*BrE, humorous*) used when you are saying that a person is not attractive to look at

'oil pan *noun* (*AmE*) = SUMP

'oil rig (also **'oil platform** especially in *AmE*) *noun* a large structure with equipment for getting oil from under the ground or under the sea

ˌoilseed 'rape *noun* [U] = RAPE (2)

oil·skin /'ɔɪlskɪn/ *noun* **1** [U] a cotton fabric that has had oil put on it in a special process so that water cannot pass through it, used for making WATERPROOF clothing: *an oilskin coat* **2** [C] a coat or jacket made of oilskin **3** (**oilskins**) [pl.] a set of clothes made of oilskin, worn especially by sailors

'oil slick *noun* = SLICK

'oil tanker *noun* a large ship with containers for carrying oil—picture at BOAT

'oil well (also **well**) *noun* a hole made in the ground to obtain oil

oily /'ɔɪli/ *adj.* (**oil·ier**, **oili·est**) **1** containing or covered with oil: *oily fish* ◇ *an oily rag* **2** feeling, tasting, smelling or looking like oil: *an oily substance* **3** (*disapproving*) (of a person or their behaviour) trying to be too polite, in a way that is annoying: *an oily smile* ▶ **oili·ness** *noun* [U]

oink /ɔɪŋk/ *exclamation, noun* used to represent the sound a pig makes

oint·ment /'ɔɪntmənt/ *noun* [U, C] a smooth substance that you rub on the skin to heal a wound or sore place: *antiseptic ointment*—picture on page 598 **IDM** see FLY *n.*

OK (also **okay**) /əʊ'keɪ; *AmE* oʊ-/ *exclamation, adj., adv., noun, verb*
■ *exclamation* (*informal*) **1** yes; all right: *'Shall we go for a walk?' 'OK.'* **2** used to attract sb's attention or to introduce a comment: *Okay, let's go.* **3** used to check that sb agrees with you or understands you: *The meeting's at 2, OK?* ◇ *I'll do it my way, OK?* **4** used to stop people arguing with you or criticizing you: *OK, so I was wrong. I'm sorry.*

æ	ɑː	e	ɜː	ə	ɪ	iː	i	ɒ	ɔː	ʌ	ʊ	u	uː
cat	father	ten	bird	about	sit	see	many	got (BrE)	saw	cup	put	actual	too

- *adj., adv.* (*spoken*) **1** safe and well; in a calm or happy state: *Are you OK?* **2 ~ (for sb) (to do sth)** all right; satisfactory; in a satisfactory way: *Is it OK if I leave now?* ◊ *Is it OK for me to come too?* ◊ *Does my hair look okay?* ◊ *I think I did OK in the exam.* ◊ *Whatever you decide, it's okay by me.* ◊ *an okay movie*
- *noun* [sing.] (*informal*) permission: *I'm still waiting for the boss to give me the OK.*
- *verb* (**OK's, OK'ing, OK'd, OK'd**) [VN] (*informal*) to officially agree to sth or allow it to happen: *She filled in an expenses claim and her manager OK'd it.*

okey-doke /ˌəʊki ˈdəʊk; AmE ˌoʊki ˈdoʊk/ (also **okey-dokey** /ˌəʊki ˈdəʊki; AmE ˌoʊki ˈdoʊki/) *exclamation* (*BrE, informal*) used to express agreement [SYN] OK

okra /ˈəʊkrə; ˈɒkrə; AmE ˈoʊkrə/ *noun* [U] the green seed cases of the **okra** plant, eaten as a vegetable—picture on page A3

old /əʊld; AmE oʊld/ *adj.* (**old·er, old·est**)

AGE | **1** be … years, months, etc. ~ of a particular age: *The baby was only a few hours old.* ◊ *In those days most people left school when they were only fifteen years old.* ◊ *At thirty years old, he was already earning £40000 a year.* ◊ *two fourteen-year-old boys* ◊ *a class for five-year-olds* (= children who are five) ◊ *I didn't think she was old enough for the responsibility.* ◊ *How old is this building?*

NOT YOUNG | **2** having lived for a long time; no longer young: *to get/grow old* ◊ *The old man lay propped up on cushions.* ◊ *She was a woman grown old before her time* (= who looked older than she was). [OPP] YOUNG **3** (**the old**) *noun* [pl.] old people: *The old feel the cold more than the young.*

NOT NEW | **4** having existed or been used for a long time: *old customs/beliefs/habits* ◊ *He always gives the same old excuses.* ◊ *This carpet's getting pretty old now.* [OPP] NEW **5** [only before noun] former; belonging to past times or a past time in your life: *Things were different in the old days.* ◊ *I went back to visit my old school.* ◊ *Old and Middle English* **6** [only before noun] used to refer to sth that has been replaced by sth else: *We had more room in our old house.* [OPP] NEW **7** [only before noun] known for a long time: *She's an old friend of mine* (= I have known her for a long time). ◊ *We're old rivals.*—compare RECENT

GOOD OLD/POOR OLD | **8** [only before noun] (*spoken*) used to show affection or a lack of respect: *Good old Dad!* ◊ *You poor old thing!* ◊ *I hate her, the silly old cow!*

[IDM] **'any old how** (*spoken*) in a careless or untidy way: *The books were piled up all over the floor any old how.* **as old as the 'hills** very old; ancient **'any old …** (*spoken*) any item of the type mentioned (used when it is not important which particular item is chosen): *Any old room would have done.* **for 'old times' sake** if you do sth **for old times' sake**, you do it because it is connected with sth good that happened to you in the past **the 'good/'bad old days** an earlier period of time in your life or in history that is seen as better/worse than the present: *That was in the bad old days of rampant inflation.* **of 'old** (*formal* or *literary*) in or since past times: *in days of old* ◊ *We know him of old* (= we have known him for a long time). **old 'boy, 'chap, 'man, etc.** (*old-fashioned, BrE, informal*) used by older men of the middle and upper classes as a friendly way of addressing another man **old enough to be sb's 'father/'mother** (*disapproving*) very much older than sb (especially used to suggest that a romantic or sexual relationship between the two people is not appropriate) **old enough to know 'better** old enough to behave in a more sensible way than you actually did **(have) an old head on young 'shoulders** used to describe a young person who acts in a more sensible way than you would expect for a person of their age **the (ˌsame) old 'story** what usually happens: *It's the same old story of a badly managed project with inadequate funding.* **an old 'wives' tale** (*disapproving*) an old idea or belief that has been proved not to be scientific: *the old wives' tale that make-up ruins the skin* **one of the 'old school** an old-fashioned person who likes to do things as they were done in the past—more at CHIP *n.,* GRAND *adj.,* HEAVE-HO, HIGH *adj.,* MONEY, RIPE, SETTLE *v.,* TEACH, TOUGH *adj.,* TRICK *n.*

ˌold 'age *noun* [U] the time of your life when you are old: *Old age can bring many problems.* ◊ *He lived alone in his old age.*

ˌold-age 'pension *noun* (*BrE*) a regular income paid by the state to people above a particular age

ˌold-age 'pensioner *noun* (*abbr.* OAP) (*BrE, becoming old-fashioned*) a person who receives an old-age pension—see also SENIOR CITIZEN

ˌold 'bat *noun* (*BrE, informal, disapproving*) a silly or annoying old person

the ˌOld 'Bill *noun* [sing.] (*BrE, informal*) the police

ˌold 'boy *noun* **1** ('old boy) (*BrE*) a man who used to be a student at a particular school, usually a private one **2** (ˌold 'boy) (*spoken, especially BrE*) an old man: *The old boy next door has died.*—see also OLD GIRL [IDM] **the ˌold 'boy network** (*BrE, informal*) the practice of men who went to the same school using their influence to help each other at work or socially

the 'old country *noun* [sing.] the country where you were born, especially when you have left it to live somewhere else

olde /əʊld; ˈəʊldi; AmE oʊld; ˈoʊldi/ *adj.* [only before noun] (*old use*) a way of spelling 'old' that was used in the past and is now sometimes used in names and advertisements to give the impression that sth is traditional: *a pub that tries to recreate the flavour of olde England*

olden /ˈəʊldən; AmE ˈoʊldən/ *adj.* [only before noun] existing a long time ago in the past: *What was life like in the olden days, Gran?*

ˌOld 'English (also ˌAnglo-'Saxon) *noun* [U] the English language before about 1150, very different from modern English

ˌOld ˌEnglish 'sheepdog *noun* a very large dog with very long grey and white hair

ˌold-e'stablished *adj.* [only before noun] that has existed for a long time: *old-established customs/industries/families*

olde worlde /ˌəʊldi 'wɜːldi; AmE ˌoʊldi 'wɜːrldi/ *adj.* [usually before noun] (*BrE, humorous*) (of a place or its atmosphere) trying deliberately to seem old-fashioned: *the olde worlde atmosphere of the tea room with its log fire*

ˌold-'fashioned *adj.* (sometimes *disapproving*) **1** not modern; no longer fashionable: *old-fashioned clothes/styles/methods/equipment*—compare FASHIONABLE **2** (of a person) believing in old or traditional ways; having traditional ideas: *My parents are old-fashioned about relationships and marriage.*

ˌold 'flame *noun* a former lover: *She met an old flame at the party.*

ˌold 'girl *noun* **1** ('old girl) (*BrE*) a woman who used to be a student at a particular school, usually a private one **2** (ˌold 'girl) (*spoken, especially BrE*) an old woman: *The old girl next door has died.*

ˌOld 'Glory *noun* (*AmE*) a name for the flag of the US

the ˌold 'guard *noun* [sing.+ sing./pl. v.] the original members of a group or an organization, who are often against change

ˌold 'hand *noun* ~ (at sth/at doing sth) a person with a lot of experience and skill in a particular activity: *She's an old hand at dealing with the press.*

ˌold 'hat *noun* [U] something that is old-fashioned and no longer interesting: *Today's hits rapidly become old hat.*

aɪ	aʊ	eɪ	əʊ	oʊ	ɔɪ	ɪə	eə	ʊə	j	w
my	now	say	go	go	boy	near	hair	pure	yes	wet
			(BrE)	(AmE)						

oldie /ˈəʊldi; *AmE* ˈoʊldi/ *noun* (*informal*) an old person or thing—see also GOLDEN OLDIE

old·ish /ˈəʊldɪʃ; *AmE* ˈoʊldɪʃ/ *adj.* fairly old

,**old ˈlady** *noun* (*informal*) a person's wife or mother

,**old ˈlag** *noun* (*BrE, informal*) a person who has been in prison many times

,**old ˈmaid** *noun* (*old-fashioned, disapproving*) a woman who has never married and is now no longer young

,**old ˈman** *noun* (*informal*) a person's husband or father

,**old ˈmaster** *noun* **1** a famous painter, especially of the 13th–17th centuries in Europe **2** a picture painted by an old master: *They have a collection of priceless old masters.*

,**Old ˈNick** *noun* (*old-fashioned, humorous*) the devil

,**old ˈpeople's home** (*BrE*) (also re'tirement home *AmE, BrE*) *noun* a place where old people live and are cared for

,**old school ˈtie** *noun* (*BrE*) a tie worn by former students of a particular school, especially a private one; the respect for the school and traditional attitudes that this represents: *Systems based on social class and the old school tie are more common in Britain than in the US.*

old·ster /ˈəʊldstə(r); *AmE* ˈoʊld-/ *noun* (*informal*) an old person

'**old-style** *adj.* [only before noun] typical of past fashions or times: *an old-style dress shop* ◊ *old-style socialism*

the ˌOld ˈTestament *noun* [sing.] the first part of the Bible, that tells the history of the Jews, their beliefs and their relationship with God before the birth of Christ—compare THE NEW TESTAMENT

'**old-time** *adj.* [only before noun] typical of the past: *old-time dancing*

,**old-ˈtimer** *noun* **1** a person who has been connected with a club or an organization, or who has lived in a place, for a long time **2** (*AmE*) an old man

,**old ˈwoman** *noun* **1** (*informal, especially BrE*) a person's wife or mother **2** (*BrE, disapproving*) a man who worries too much about things that are not important

the ˌOld ˈWorld *noun* [sing.] Europe, Asia and Africa—compare THE NEW WORLD

'**old-world** *adj.* [only before noun] (*approving*) belonging to past times; not modern: *an old-world hotel with character and charm*

ole /əʊl; *AmE* oʊl/ *adj.* used in written English to represent how some people say the word 'old': *My ole man used to work there.*

ole·an·der /ˌəʊliˈændə(r); *AmE* ˌoʊli-/ *noun* [C, U] a Mediterranean bush or tree with purple, white or pink flowers and long pointed thick leaves

'**O level** (also '**ordinary level**) *noun* [C, U] (in England and Wales in the past) an exam in a particular subject, at a lower level than A LEVEL, usually taken at the age of 16. In 1988 it was replaced by the GCSE: *O level French/chemistry* ◊ *She took six subjects at O level.* ◊ *He's got an O level in Russian.*—compare GCE

ol·fac·tory /ɒlˈfæktəri; *AmE* ɑːl-; oʊl-/ *adj.* [only before noun] (*technical*) connected with the sense of smell: *olfactory cells/nerves/organs*

oli·garch /ˈɒlɪɡɑːk; *AmE* ˈɑːləɡɑːrk/ *noun* a member of an oligarchy

oli·garchy /ˈɒlɪɡɑːki; *AmE* ˈɑːləɡɑːrki/ *noun* (*pl.* **-ies**) **1** [U] a form of government in which only a small group of people hold all the power **2** [C+sing./pl. *v.*] the people who hold power in an oligarchy **3** [C] a country governed by an oligarchy

olive /ˈɒlɪv; *AmE* ˈɑːlɪv/ *noun, adj.*
■ *noun* **1** [C] a small green or black fruit with a strong taste, used in cooking and for its oil: *olive oil*—see also VIRGIN OLIVE OIL **2** (also '**olive tree**) [C] a tree on which olives grow: *olive groves* **3** (also ,**olive ˈgreen**) [U] a yellowish-green colour
■ *adj.* **1** (also ,**olive-ˈgreen**) yellowish-green in colour **2** (of skin) yellowish-brown in colour: *an olive complexion*

'**olive branch** *noun* [usually sing.] a symbol of peace; sth you say or do to show that you wish to make peace with sb: *Management is holding out an olive branch to the strikers.*

-ology (*BrE* also **-logy**) *combining form* (in nouns) **1** a subject of study: *sociology* ◊ *genealogy* **2** a characteristic of speech or writing: *phraseology* ◊ *trilogy* ▶ **-ological, -logical** (also **-ologic, -logic**) (in adjectives): *pathological* **-ologist, -logist** (in nouns): *biologist*

Olym·piad /əˈlɪmpiæd/ *noun* **1** an occasion when the modern Olympic games are held: *The 26th Olympiad took place in Atlanta, Georgia.* **2** an international competition in a particular subject, especially a science: *the 14th International Physics Olympiad*

Olym·pian /əˈlɪmpiən/ *adj.* (*formal*) like a god; powerful and impressive: *He viewed the problem with Olympian detachment.*

Olym·pic /əˈlɪmpɪk/ *adj.* [only before noun] connected with the Olympic Games: *an Olympic athlete/medallist* ◊ *the British Olympic team*

the Oˌlympic ˈGames (also **the Olym·pics**) *noun* [pl.] an international sports festival held every four years in a different country: *the Sydney Olympics in 2000*

om·buds·man /ˈɒmbʊdzmən; -mæn; *AmE* ˈɑːm-/ *noun* (*pl.* **-men** /-mən/) a government official whose job is to examine and report on complaints made by ordinary people about the government or public authorities

omega /ˈəʊmɪɡə; *AmE* oʊˈmeɡə/ *noun* the last letter of the Greek alphabet (Ω, ω)

om·elette (*AmE* also **om·elet**) /ˈɒmlət; *AmE* ˈɑːm-/ *noun* a hot dish of eggs mixed together and fried, often with cheese, meat, vegetables, etc. added: *a cheese and mushroom omelette* **IDM** **you can't make an ˌomelette without breaking ˈeggs** (*saying*) you cannot achieve sth important without causing a few small problems

omen /ˈəʊmən; *AmE* ˈoʊ-/ *noun* ~ (**for sth**) a sign of what is going to happen in the future: *a good/bad omen* ◊ *an omen of death/disaster* ◊ *The omens for their future success are not good.*

om·in·ous /ˈɒmɪnəs; *AmE* ˈɑːm-/ *adj.* suggesting that sth bad is going to happen in the future: *There were ominous dark clouds gathering overhead.* ◊ *She picked up the phone but there was an ominous silence at the other end.* ▶ **om·in·ous·ly** *adv.*

omis·sion /əˈmɪʃn/ *noun* **1** [U] ~ (**from sth**) the act of not including sb/sth or not doing sth; the fact of not being included/done: *Everyone was surprised at her omission from the squad.* ◊ *The play was shortened by the omission of two scenes.* ◊ (*formal*) *sins of omission* (= not doing things that should be done) **2** [C] a thing that has not been included or done: *There were a number of errors and omissions in the article.*

omit /əˈmɪt/ *verb* (**-tt-**) [VN] (*formal*) **1** ~ **sth/sb (from sth)** to not include sth/sb either deliberately or because you have forgotten it/them **SYN** LEAVE OUT: *If you are a student, you can omit questions 16–18.* ◊ *People were surprised that Smith was omitted from the team.* **2** [V to inf] to not do or fail to do sth: *She omitted to mention that they were staying the night.*

omni- /ˈɒmni-; *AmE* ˈɑːm-/ *combining form* (in nouns, adjectives and adverbs) of all things; in all ways or places: *omnivore* ◊ *omnipresent*

omni·bus /ˈɒmnɪbəs; *AmE* ˈɑːm-/ *noun, adj.*
■ *noun* **1** (*BrE*) a television or radio programme that combines several recent programmes in a series: *the 90-minute Sunday omnibus edition* **2** a large book that contains a number of books, for example novels by the same author **3** (*old-fashioned*) a bus
■ *adj.* (*AmE*) including many things or different types of thing: *an omnibus law*

om·nipo·tent /ɒmˈnɪpətənt; *AmE* ɑːm-/ *adj.* (*formal*) having total power; able to do anything: *an omnipotent God* ▶ **om·nipo·tence** /-təns/ *noun* [U]: *the omnipotence of God*

omni·pres·ent /ˌɒmnɪˈpreznt; *AmE* ˌɑːm-/ *adj.* (*formal*) present everywhere: *These days the media are omnipresent.* ▶ **omni·pres·ence** /ˌɒmnɪˈprezns; *AmE* ˌɑːm-/ *noun* [U]

om·nis·ci·ent /ɒmˈnɪsiənt; *AmE* ɑːm-/ *adj.* (*formal*) knowing everything: *The novel has an omniscient narrator.* ▶ **om·nis·ci·ence** /-siəns/ *noun* [U]

b	d	f	g	h	k	l	m	n	p	r
bad	did	fall	get	hat	cat	leg	man	now	pen	red

0

om·ni·vore /ˈɒmnɪvɔː(r); AmE ˈɑːm-/ noun an animal or a person that eats all types of food, especially both plants and meat—compare CARNIVORE, HERBIVORE, INSECTIVORE

om·niv·or·ous /ɒmˈnɪvərəs; AmE ɑːm-/ adj. **1** (technical) eating all types of food, especially both plants and meat: an omnivorous diet / animal—compare CARNIVOROUS, HERBIVOROUS **2** (formal) having wide interests in a particular area or activity: She has always been an omnivorous reader.

on /ɒn; AmE ɑːn; ɔːn/ prep., adv.
- prep. **HELP** For the special uses of **on** in phrasal verbs, look at the entries for the verbs. For example **turn on sb** is in the phrasal verb section at **turn**. **1** in or into a position covering, touching or forming part of a surface: a picture on a wall ◊ There's a mark on your skirt. ◊ the diagram on page 5 ◊ Put it down on the table. ◊ He had been hit on the head. ◊ She climbed on to the bed. **HELP** This could also be written: onto the bed **2** supported by sb/sth: She was standing on one foot. ◊ Try lying on your back. ◊ Hang your coat on that hook. **3** used to show a means of transport: He was on the plane from New York. ◊ to travel on the bus / tube / coach ◊ I came on my bike. ◊ a woman on horseback **4** used to show a day or date: He came on Sunday. ◊ We meet on Tuesdays. ◊ on May the first / the first of May ◊ on the evening of May the first ◊ on one occasion ◊ on your birthday **5** immediately after sth: On arriving home I discovered they had gone. ◊ Please report to reception on arrival. ◊ There was a letter waiting for him on his return. **6** about sth: a book on South Africa ◊ She tested us on irregular verbs. **7** being carried by sb; in the possession of sb: Have you got any money on you? **8** used to show that sb belongs to a group or an organization: to be on the committee / staff / jury / panel ◊ Whose side are you on (= which of two or more different views do you support)? **9** eating or drinking sth; using a drug or a medicine regularly: He lived on a diet of junk food. ◊ The doctor put me on antibiotics. **10** used to show direction: on the left / right ◊ He turned his back on us. **11** at or near a place: a town on the coast ◊ a house on the Thames ◊ We lived on an estate. **12** used to show the basis or reason for sth: a story based on fact ◊ On their advice I applied for the job. **13** supported financially by sth: to live on a pension / a student grant ◊ to be on a low wage ◊ You can't feed a family on £50 a week. ◊ Drinks are on me (= I am paying). **14** by means of sth; using sth: She played a tune on her guitar. ◊ The information is available on the Internet. ◊ We spoke on the phone. ◊ What's on TV? ◊ The programme's on Channel 4. **15** used with some nouns or adjectives to say who or what is affected by sth: a ban on smoking ◊ He's hard on his kids. ◊ Go easy on the mayo! (= do not give me too much) **16** compared with sb/sth: Sales are up on last year. **17** used to describe an activity or a state: to be on business / holiday / vacation ◊ The book is currently on loan. **18** used when giving a telephone number: You can get me on 0181 530 3906. ◊ She's on extension 2401.
- adv. **HELP** For the special uses of **on** in phrasal verbs, look at the entries for the verbs. For example **get on** is in the phrasal verb section at **get**. **1** used to show that sth continues: He worked on without a break. ◊ If you like a good story, read on. **2** used to show that sb/sth moves or is sent forward: She stopped for a moment, then walked on. ◊ Keep straight on for the beach. ◊ From then on he never trusted her again. ◊ Please send the letter on to my new address. **HELP** This cannot be written: onto my new address **3** on sb's body; being worn: Put your coat on. ◊ I didn't have my glasses on. ◊ What did she have on (= what was she wearing)? **4** covering, touching or forming part of sth: Make sure the lid is on. **5** connected or operating; being used: The lights were all on. ◊ The TV is always on in their house. ◊ We were without electricity for three hours but it's on again now. **6** happening: There was a war on at the time. ◊ What's on at the movies? ◊ The band are on (= performing) in ten minutes. **7** planned to take place in the future: The game is still on (= it has not been cancelled). ◊ I don't think we've got anything on this weekend. ◊ I'm sorry we can't come—we've got a lot on. **8** on duty; working: I'm on now till 8 tomorrow morning. **9** in or into a

vehicle: The bus stopped and four people got on. ◊ They hurried on to the plane.—see also ONTO **IDM be 'on about sth** (informal) to talk about sth; to mean sth: I didn't know what he was on about. It didn't make sense. **be / go / keep 'on about sth** (informal, disapproving) to talk in a boring or complaining way about sth: Stop keeping on about it! **be / go / keep 'on at sb (to do sth)** (informal, disapproving) to keep asking or telling sb sth so that they become annoyed or tired: He was on at me again to lend him money. **it isn't 'on** (informal) used to say that sth is not acceptable ˌon and 'on without stopping; continuously: She went on and on about her trip. **What are you 'on?** (informal) used when you are very surprised at sb's behaviour and are suggesting that they are acting in a similar way to sb using drugs **you're 'on** (informal) used when you are accepting a bet—more at OFF adv.

ˌon-'air adj. (in radio and television) being broadcast: She explains how she deals with on-air technical problems. **OPP** OFF-AIR ► ˌon-'air adv.

once /wʌns/ adv., conj.
- adv. **1** on one occasion only; one time: I've only been there once. ◊ He cleans his car once a week. ◊ She only sees her parents once every six months. ◊ (informal) He only did it **the once**. **2** at some time in the past: I once met your mother. ◊ He once lived in Zambia. ◊ This book was famous once, but nobody reads it today. **3** used in negative sentences and questions, and after if to mean 'ever' or 'at all': He never once offered to help. ◊ If she once decides to do something, you won't change her mind. **IDM** ˌall at 'once **1** suddenly: All at once she lost her temper. **2** all together; at the same time: I can't do everything all at once—you'll have to be patient. **at 'once 1** immediately; without delay: Come here at once! **2** at the same time: Don't all speak at once! ◊ I can't do two things at once. **(just) for 'once | just this 'once** (spoken) on this occasion (which is in contrast to what happens usually): Just for once he arrived on time. ◊ Can't you be nice to each other just this once? **going 'once, going 'twice, 'sold** (especially AmE) = GOING, GOING, GONE **once a'gain | once 'more** one more time; another time: Once again the train was late. ◊ Let me hear it just once more. **once a …, always a …** used to say that sb cannot change: Once an actor, always an actor. **once and for 'all** now and for the last time; finally or completely: We need to settle this once and for all. ˌonce 'bitten, ˌtwice 'shy (saying) after an unpleasant experience you are careful to avoid sth similar **once in a blue 'moon** (informal) very rarely **(every) ˌonce in a 'while** occasionally ˌonce or 'twice a few times: I don't know her well, I've only met her once or twice. ˌonce too 'often used to say that sb has done sth wrong or stupid again, and this time they will suffer because of it: You've tried that trick once too often. ˌonce upon a 'time used, especially at the beginning of stories, to mean 'a long time in the past': Once upon a time there was a beautiful princess.
- conj. as soon as; when: We didn't know how we would cope once the money had gone. ◊ The water is fine once you're in!

'once-over noun **IDM give sb/sth a/the 'once-over** (informal) **1** to look at sb/sth quickly to see what they or it are like **2** to clean sth quickly: She gave the room a quick once-over before the guests arrived.

on·col·ogy /ɒŋˈkɒlədʒi; AmE ɑːnˈkɑː-/ noun [U] the scientific study of and treatment of TUMOURS in the body ► **on·colo·gist** /ɒŋˈkɒlədʒɪst; AmE ɑːnˈkɑːl-/

on·com·ing /ˈɒnkʌmɪŋ; AmE ˈɑːn-; ˈɔːn-/ adj. [only before noun] coming towards you **SYN** APPROACHING: Always walk facing the oncoming traffic.

one /wʌn/ number, det., pron.
- number, det. **1** the number 1: Do you want one or two? ◊ There's only room for one person. ◊ One more, please! ◊ a one-bedroomed apartment ◊ I'll see you at one (= one o'clock). **2** used in formal language or for emphasis before hundred, thousand, etc., or before a unit of measurement: It cost one hundred and fifty pounds. ◊ He lost by less than one second. **3** used for emphasis to mean 'a single' or 'just one': There's only one thing we can do. **4** a person or thing, especially when they are part of a group: One of my friends lives in Brighton. ◊ One place I'd really

s	t	v	z	ʃ	ʒ	tʃ	dʒ	θ	ð	ŋ
see	tea	van	zoo	shoe	vision	chain	jam	thin	this	sing

like to visit is Bali. **5** used for emphasis to mean 'the only one' or 'the most important one': *He's the one person I can trust.* ◊ *Her one concern was for the health of her baby.* ◊ *It's the one thing I can't stand about him.* **6** used when you are talking about a time in the past or the future, without actually saying which one: *I saw her one afternoon last week.* ◊ *One day* (= at some time in the future) *you'll understand.* **7** the same: *They all went off in one direction.* **8** (*spoken, especially AmE*) used for emphasis instead of *a* or *an*: *That was one hell of a game!* ◊ *She's one snappy dresser.* **9** used with a person's name to show that the speaker does not know the person SYN A CERTAIN: *He worked as an assistant to one Mr Ming.* IDM **as ˈone** (*formal*) in agreement; all together: *We spoke as one on this matter.* **(be) at ˈone (with sb/sth)** (*formal*) to feel that you completely agree with sb/sth, or that you are part of sth: *a place where you can feel at one with nature* **for ˈone** used to emphasize that a particular person does sth and that you believe other people do too: *I, for one, would prefer to postpone the meeting.* **get sth in ˈone** to understand or guess sth immediately: *'Oh, so she's his sister!' 'Got it in one!'* **get one ˈover (on) sb/sth** (*informal*) to get an advantage over sb/sth: *I'm not going to let them get one over on me!* **go one ˈbetter (than sb/sth)** to do sth better than sb else or than you have done before SYN OUTDO: *She did well this year and next year she hopes to go one better.* **in ˈone** used to say that sb/sth has different roles, contains different things or is used for different purposes: *She's a mother and company director in one.* ◊ *It's a public relations office, a press office and a private office all in one.*—see also ALL-IN-ONE ˌone after aˈnother/the ˈother first one person or thing, and then another, and then another, up to any number or amount: *The bills kept coming in, one after another.* ˌone and ˈall (*old-fashioned, informal*) everyone: *Happy New Year to one and all!* ˌone and ˈonly used to emphasize that sb is famous: *Here he is, the one and only Van Morrison!* ˌone and the ˈsame used for emphasis to mean 'the same': *I never realized Ruth Rendell and Barbara Vine were one and the same* (= the same person). ˌone by ˈone separately and in order: *I went through the items on the list one by one.* ˌone or ˈtwo a few: *We've had one or two problems—nothing serious.* ˌone ˈup (on sb) having an advantage over sb—more at ALL *pron.*, MINORITY, NUMBER *n.*, SQUARE *n.*

■ *pron.* **1** used to avoid repeating a noun, when you are referring to sb/sth that you have already been mentioned, or that the person you are speaking to knows about: *I'd like an ice cream. Are you having one, too?* ◊ *Our car's always breaking down. But we're getting a new one soon.* ◊ *She was wearing her new dress, the red one.* ◊ *My favourite band? Oh, that's a hard one* (= a hard question). ◊ *What made you choose the one rather than the other?* ◊ (*BrE*) *How about those ones over there?* **2** used when you are identifying the person or thing you are talking about: *Our house is the one next to the school.* ◊ *The students who are most successful are usually the ones who come to all the classes.* **3 ~ of** a person or thing belonging to a particular group: *It's a present for one of my children.* ◊ *We think of you as one of the family.* **4 ~ (to do sth)** a person of the type mentioned: *10 o'clock is too late for the little ones.* ◊ *He ached to be home with his loved ones.* ◊ *She was never one to criticize.* **5** (*formal*) used to mean 'people in general' or 'I', when the speaker is referring to himself or herself: *One should never criticize if one is not sure of one's facts.* ◊ *One gets the impression that they disapprove.* HELP This use of one is very formal and now sounds old-fashioned. It is much more usual to use **you** for 'people in general' and **I** when you are talking about yourself. **6 (a ˈone)** (*old-fashioned, especially BrE*) a person whose behaviour is amusing or surprising: *Oh, you are a one!* **7 the ~ about sth** the joke: *Have you heard the one about the Englishman, the Irishman and the Scotsman?* IDM **(a) one for (doing) sth** to be a person who enjoys sth, or who does sth often or well: *I've never been a great one for fish and chips.*

ˌone aˈnother *pron.* one another is used when you are saying that each member of a group does sth to or for the

other people in the group: *We all try and help one another.* ◊ *I think we've learned a lot about one another in this session.*

ˌone-armed ˈbandit *noun* = FRUIT MACHINE

ˌone-ˈliner *noun* (*informal*) a short joke or funny remark: *He came out with some good one-liners.*

ˌone-ˈman *adj.* [only before noun] done or controlled by one person only; suitable for one person: *a one-man show/business* ◊ *a one-man tent*—see also ONE-WOMAN

ˌone-man ˈband *noun* a street musician who plays several instruments at the same time: (*figurative*) *He runs the business as a one-man band* (= one person does everything).

one·ness /ˈwʌnnəs/ *noun* [U] (*formal*) the state of being completely united with sb/sth, or of being in complete agreement with sb: *a sense of oneness with the natural world*

ˌone-night ˈstand *noun* (*informal*) a sexual relationship that lasts for a single night; a person that sb has this relationship with: *I wanted it to be more than a one-night stand.* ◊ *For her I was just a one-night stand.*

ˌone-ˈoff *adj., noun*
■ *adj.* (*BrE*) (*AmE* ˈone-shot) [only before noun] made or happening only once and not regularly: *a one-off payment*
■ *noun* [sing.] (*BrE*) a thing that is made or that happens only once and not regularly: *It was just a one-off; it won't happen again.*

ˌone-on-ˈone *adj.* [usually before noun] (*AmE*) = ONE-TO-ONE

ˌone-parent ˈfamily (also ˌlone-parent ˈfamily) *noun* a family in which the children live with one parent rather than two—see also SINGLE PARENT

ˈone-piece *adj.* [only before noun] (especially of clothes) consisting of one piece, not separate parts: *a one-piece swimsuit*

oner·ous /ˈəʊnərəs; *AmE* ˈɑːn-; ˈoʊ-/ *adj.* (*formal*) needing great effort; causing trouble or worry: *an onerous duty/task/responsibility*

one·self /wʌnˈself/ *pron.* (*formal*) **1** (the reflexive form of *one*) used as the object of a verb or preposition when 'one' is the subject of the verb or is understood as the subject: *One has to ask oneself what the purpose of the exercise is.* ◊ *One cannot choose freedom for oneself without choosing it for others.* ◊ *It is difficult to make oneself concentrate for long periods.* **2** used to emphasize *one*: *One likes to do it oneself.* HELP One and oneself are very formal words and now sound old-fashioned. It is much more usual to use **you** and **yourself** for referring to people in general and **I** and **myself** when the speaker is

æ	ɑː	e	ɜː	ə	ɪ	iː	i	ɒ	ɔː	ʌ	ʊ	u	uː
cat	father	ten	bird	about	sit	see	many	got	saw	cup	put	actual	too
								(BrE)					

referring to himself or herself. **IDM** **be one'self** to be in a normal state of body and mind, not influenced by other people: *One needs space to be oneself.* **(all) by one'self 1** alone; without anyone else **2** without help **(all) to one'self** not shared with anyone

'one-shot *adj.* [only before noun] (*AmE*) = ONE-OFF

one-'sided *adj.* **1** (*disapproving*) (of an argument, opinion, etc.) showing only one point of view; not balanced: *The press were accused of presenting a very one-sided picture of the issue.* **2** (of a competition or a relationship) involving people who have different abilities; involving one person more than another: *a totally one-sided match ◇ a one-sided conversation* (= in which one person talks most of the time)

'one-stop *adj.* in which you can buy or do everything you want in one place: *Our agency is a one-stop shop for all your travel needs.*

'one-time *adj.* [only before noun] **1** former: *her one-time best friend, Anna* **2** not to be repeated **SYN** ONE-OFF: *a one-time fee of $500*

one-to-'one (*especially BrE*) (*AmE* usually **one-on-'one**) *adj.* [usually before noun] **1** between two people only: *a one-to-one meeting* **2** matching sth else in an exact way: *There is no one-to-one correspondence between sounds and letters.* ▶ **one-to-'one** *adv.*: *He teaches one-to-one.*

one-track 'mind *noun* if sb has a **one-track mind**, they can only think about one subject

one-upmanship /ˌwʌnˈʌpmənʃɪp/ *noun* [U] (*disapproving*) the skill of getting an advantage over other people

one-'way *adj.* [usually before noun] **1** moving or allowing movement in only one direction: *one-way traffic ◇ a one-way street ◇ a one-way valve* **2** (*especially AmE*) = SINGLE (5) **3** operating in only one direction: *Theirs was a one-way relationship* (= one person made all the effort). ◇ *They observed the prisoners through a one-way mirror* (= a mirror that allows a person standing behind it to see through it).

one-'woman *adj.* [only before noun] done or controlled by one woman only: *a one-woman show*

on-going /ˈɒnɡəʊɪŋ; *AmE* ˈɑːn-/ *adj.* [usually before noun] continuing to exist or develop: *an ongoing debate/discussion/process ◇ The police investigation is ongoing.*

onion /ˈʌnjən/ *noun* [C, U] a round vegetable with many layers inside each other and a brown, red or white skin. Onions have a strong smell and flavour: *Chop the onions finely.* ◇ *French onion soup*—picture on page A3

on-line /ˌɒnˈlaɪn; *AmE* ˌɑːn-; ˌɔːn-/ *adj.* controlled by or connected to a computer or to the Internet: *an online ticket booking system ◇ The data entry terminal is connected to an online database while editing is taking place.* ▶ **on·line** *adv.*

on·look·er /ˈɒnlʊkə(r); *AmE* ˈɑːn-; ˈɔːn-/ *noun* a person who watches sth that is happening but is not involved in it: *A crowd of onlookers gathered at the scene of the crash.*

only /ˈəʊnli; *AmE* ˈoʊnli/ *adj., adv., conj.*

■ *adj.* [only before noun] **1** used to say that no other or others of the same group exist or are there: *She's their only daughter. ◇ We were the only people there. ◇ His only answer was a grunt. ◇ Only five people turned up.* **2** used to say that sb/sth is the best and you would not choose any other: *She's the only person for the job.* **IDM** **the only thing 'is ...** (*spoken*) used before mentioning a worry or problem you have with sth: *I'd love to come—the only thing is I might be late.*—more at NAME *n.*, ONE *det.*

■ *adv.* **1** nobody or nothing except: *There are only a limited number of tickets available. ◇ The bar is for members only. ◇ You only have to look at her to see she doesn't eat enough. ◇ Only five people turned up.* **2** in no other situation, place, etc: *I agreed, but only because I was frightened. ◇ Children are admitted only if accompanied by an adult.* **HELP** In formal written English **only**, or **only if** and its clause, can be placed first in the sentence. In the second part of the sentence, **be**, **do**, **have**, etc. come before the subject and the main part of the verb: *Only in Paris do you find bars like this. ◇ Only if these conditions are fulfilled can the application proceed to the next stage.*

3 no more important, interesting, serious, etc. than: *It was only a suggestion. ◇ Don't blame me, I'm only the messenger! ◇ He was only teasing you.* **4** no more than; no longer than: *She's only 21 and she runs her own business. ◇ It only took a few seconds. ◇ It took only a few seconds.* **5** not until: *We only got here yesterday. ◇* (*written*) *Only then did she realize the stress he was under.* **HELP** When **only** begins a sentence like **be**, **do**, **have**, etc. come before the subject and the main part of the verb. **6** used to say that sb can do no more than what is mentioned, although this is probably not enough: *We can only guess what happened. ◇ He could only watch helplessly as the car plunged into the ravine. ◇ I only hope that she never finds out.* **7** used to say that sth will have a bad effect: *If you do that, it will only make matters worse. ◇ Trying to reason with him only enrages him even more.* **8** ~ **to do sth** (*written*) used to mention sth that happens immediately afterwards, especially sth that causes surprise, disappointment, etc: *She turned up the driveway, only to find her way blocked.* **IDM** **not only...but (also)... both ...and ...**: *He not only read the book, but also remembered what he had read.* **only 'just 1** not long ago/before: *We've only just arrived.* **2** almost not: *He only just caught the train. ◇ I can afford it, but only just.* **only too ...** very: *I was only too pleased to help. ◇ Children can be difficult as we know only too well.* **you're only young 'once** (*saying*) young people should enjoy themselves as much as possible, because they will have to work and worry later in their lives—more at EYE *n.*, IF *conj.*

■ *conj.* (*informal*) except that; but: *I'd love to come, only I have to work. ◇ It tastes like chicken, only stronger.*

only 'child *noun* a child who has no brothers or sisters: *I'm an only child. ◇ Only children often relate well to adults.*

o.n.o. *abbr.* (*BrE, written*) (used in small advertisements to show that sth may be sold at a lower price than the price that has been asked) or near/nearest offer: *Guitar £200 o.n.o.*

ono·mato·poeia /ˌɒnəˌmætəˈpiːə; *AmE* ˌɑːn-/ *noun* [U] (*technical*) the fact of words containing sounds similar to the noises they describe, for example *hiss* or *thud*; the use of words like this in a piece of writing ▶ **ono·mato·poe·ic** /-ˈpiːɪk/ *adj.*: *Bang and pop are onomatopoeic words.*

on·rush /ˈɒnrʌʃ; *AmE* ˈɑːn-; ˈɔːn-/ *noun* [sing.] (*written*) a strong movement forward; the sudden development of sth: *She was seized by an onrush of nerves.*

on-'screen *adj.* [only before noun] **1** appearing or written on the screen of a computer, television or cinema/movie theater: *on-screen courtroom dramas ◇ on-screen instructions/messages* **2** connected with the imaginary story of a film/movie and not with real life: *His on-screen father is also his father in real life.*—compare OFF-SCREEN ▶ **on-'screen** *adv.*

onset /ˈɒnset; *AmE* ˈɑːn-; ˈɔːn-/ *noun* [sing.] the beginning of sth, especially sth unpleasant: *the onset of disease/old age/winter*

on·shore /ˈɒnʃɔː(r); *AmE* ˈɑːn-; ˈɔːn-/ *adj.* [usually before noun] **1** on the land rather than at sea: *the largest onshore oil field in Europe* **2** (of wind) blowing from the sea towards the land ▶ **on·shore** *adv.*—compare OFFSHORE

on·side /ˌɒnˈsaɪd; *AmE* ˌɑːn-; ˌɔːn-/ *adj.* (in sports such as football) in a position on the field where you are allowed to play the ball ▶ **on·side** *adv.* —compare OFFSIDE

on·slaught /ˈɒnslɔːt; *AmE* ˈɑːn-; ˈɔːn-/ *noun* ~ **(against/ on sb/sth)|~ (of sth)** (*written*) a strong or violent attack: *the enemy onslaught on our military forces ◇ The town survives the onslaught of tourists every summer. ◇ an onslaught of abuse*

on·stage /ˌɒnˈsteɪdʒ; *AmE* ˌɑːn-; ˌɔːn-/ *adj.* on the stage in a theatre; in front of an audience: *onstage fights* ▶ **on·stage** *adv.* —compare OFFSTAGE

onto (also **on to**) /ˈɒntə; *before vowels* ˈɒntu; *AmE* ˈɑːn-; ˈɔːn-/ *prep.* used with verbs to express movement on or to a particular place or position: *Move the books onto the second shelf. ◇ She stepped down from the train onto the platform.* **PHRV** **be 'onto sb 1** (*informal*) to know about what sb has done wrong: *She knew the police would be* *onto them.* **2** to be talking to sb, usually in order to ask or tell them sth: *They've been onto me for ages to get a job.* **be ˈonto sth** to know about sth or be in a situation that could lead to a good result for you: *Scientists believe they are onto something big.* ◊ *She's onto a good thing with that new job.*

ontol·ogy /ɒnˈtɒlədʒi; *AmE* ɑːnˈtɑːl-/ *noun* [U] a branch of philosophy that deals with the nature of existence ▶ **onto·logic·al** /ˌɒntəˈlɒdʒɪkl; *AmE* ˌɑːntəˈlɑːdʒ-/ *adj.*

onus /ˈəʊnəs; *AmE* ˈoʊnəs/ *noun* (usually **the onus**) [sing.] (*formal*) the responsibility for sth: *The onus is on employers to follow health and safety laws.*

on·ward /ˈɒnwəd; *AmE* ˈɑːnwərd; ˈɔːn-/ *adj.* [only before noun] (*formal*) continuing or moving forward: *Ticket prices include your flight and onward rail journey.*

on·wards /ˈɒnwədz; *AmE* ˈɑːnwərdz; ˈɔːn-/ (*especially BrE*) (*AmE* usually **on·ward** /ˈɒnwəd; *AmE* ˈɑːnwərd; ˈɔːn-/) *adv.* **1** from…**onwards** continuing from a particular time: *They lived there from the 1980s onwards.* ◊ *The pool is open from 7 a.m. onwards.* **2** (*formal*) forward: *We drove onwards towards the coast.*

onyx /ˈɒnɪks; *AmE* ˈɑːn-/ *noun* [U] a type of stone that has layers of different colours in it, usually used for ornaments: *an onyx paperweight*

oo·dles /ˈuːdlz/ *noun* [pl.] ~ **(of sth)** (*old-fashioned, informal*) a large amount of sth

oomph /ʊmf/ *noun* [U] (*informal*) energy; a special quality: *a styling product to give your hair more oomph*

ooze /uːz/ *verb, noun*
■ *verb* **1** ~ **from/out of/through sth | ~ out | ~ (with) sth** if a thick liquid **oozes** from a place, or if sth **oozes** a thick liquid, the liquid flows from the place slowly: [V] *Blood oozed out of the wound.* ◊ *an ugly swelling oozing with pus* ◊ [VN] *The wound was oozing blood.* ◊ *a plate of toast oozing butter* **2** ~ **(with) sth** if sb/sth **oozes** a particular characteristic, quality, etc., they show it strongly: [VN] *She walked into the party oozing confidence.* ◊ [V] *His voice oozed with sex appeal.*
■ *noun* **1** [U] very soft mud, especially at the bottom of a lake or river **2** [sing.] the very slow flow of a thick liquid ▶ **oozy** *adj.*

op /ɒp; *AmE* ɑːp/ *noun* (*BrE, informal*) = OPERATION (1): *I'm going in for my op on Monday.*

op. *abbr.* OPUS: *Webern's Five Pieces, op. 10*

opa·city /əʊˈpæsəti; *AmE* oʊ-/ *noun* [U] **1** (*technical*) the fact of being difficult to see through; the fact of being OPAQUE **2** (*formal*) the fact of being difficult to understand; the fact of being OPAQUE

opal /ˈəʊpl; *AmE* ˈoʊpl/ *noun* [C, U] a white or almost clear precious stone in which changes of colour are seen, used in jewellery: *an opal ring*

opal·es·cent /ˌəʊpəˈlesnt; *AmE* ˌoʊpə-/ *adj.* (*formal* or *literary*) changing colour like an opal

opaque /əʊˈpeɪk; *AmE* oʊ-/ *adj.* **1** (of glass, liquid, etc.) not clear enough to see through or allow light through: *opaque glass* ◊ *opaque tights* **2** (of speech or writing) difficult to understand; not clear: *The jargon in his talk was opaque to me.* OPP TRANSPARENT

ˈop art *noun* [U] a style of modern art that uses patterns and colours in a way that makes the images seem to move as you look at them

op. cit. *abbr.* used in formal writing to refer to a book or an article that has already been mentioned

OPEC /ˈəʊpek; *AmE* ˈoʊ-/ *abbr.* Organization of Petroleum Exporting Countries (an organization of countries that produce and sell oil)

open /ˈəʊpən; *AmE* ˈoʊ-/ *adj., verb, noun*
■ *adj.*
NOT CLOSED | 1 allowing things or people to go through: *A wasp flew in the open window.* ◊ *She had left the door wide open.* ◊ *The door flew open and the children rushed in.* OPP CLOSED **2** (of sb's eyes, mouth, etc.) with lips apart: *She had difficulty keeping her eyes open* (= because she was very tired). ◊ *He was breathing through his open mouth.* OPP CLOSED **3** spread out; with the edges apart: *The flowers are all open now.* ◊ *The book lay open on the table.* OPP CLOSED **4** not blocked by anything: *The pass is kept open all the year.* OPP CLOSED
NOT FASTENED | 5 not fastened or covered, so that things can easily come out or be put in: *Leave the envelope open.* ◊ *The bag burst open and everything fell out.* **6** (of clothes) not fastened: *Her coat was open.* ◊ *a tie knotted below the open collar of a shirt*
NOT ENCLOSED | 7 not surrounded by anything; not enclosed: *open country* (= without forests, buildings, etc.) ◊ *a city with a lot of parks and open spaces* ◊ *driving along the open road* (= part of a road in the country, where you can drive fast)
NOT COVERED | 8 with no cover or roof on: *an open drain* ◊ *people working in the open air* (= not in a building) ◊ *The hall of the old house was open to the sky.* ◊ *an open wound* (= with no skin covering it)
FOR CUSTOMERS/VISITORS | 9 [not usually before noun] if a shop/store, bank, business, etc. is **open**, it is ready for business and will admit customers or visitors: *Is the museum open on Sundays?* ◊ *The new store will be open in the spring.* ◊ *The house had been thrown open to the public.* ◊ *I declare this festival open.* OPP CLOSED
OF COMPETITION/BUILDING | 10 if a competition, etc. is **open**, anyone can enter it SYN PUBLIC: *an open debate/championship/scholarship* ◊ *She was tried in open court* (= the public could go and listen to the trial). ◊ *The debate was thrown open to the audience.* **11** [not before noun] ~ **to sb** if a competition, building, etc. is **open** to particular people, those people can enter it: *The competition is open to young people under the age of 18.* ◊ *The house is not open to the public.* OPP CLOSED
AVAILABLE | 12 [not before noun] ~ **(to sb)** to be available and ready to use: *What options are open to us?* ◊ *Is the offer still open?* ◊ *I want to keep my Swiss bank account open.* OPP CLOSED
NOT PROTECTED | 13 ~ **(to sth)** likely to suffer sth such as criticism, injury, etc. SYN VULNERABLE: *The system is open to abuse.* ◊ *He has laid himself wide open to political attack.*
NOT HIDDEN | 14 known to everyone; not kept hidden: *an open quarrel* ◊ *open government* ◊ *their open display of affection* ◊ *His eyes showed open admiration as he looked at her.* OPP SECRET
PERSON'S CHARACTER | 15 honest; not keeping thoughts and feelings hidden: *She was always open with her parents.* ◊ *He was quite open about his reasons for leaving.* **16** ~ **to sth** (of a person) willing to listen to and think about new ideas: *I'm open to suggestions for what you would like to do in our classes.*
NOT YET DECIDED | 17 ~ **(to sth)** not yet finally decided or settled: *The race is still wide open* (= anyone could win). ◊ *The price is not open to negotiation.* ◊ *Some phrases in the contract are open to interpretation.* ◊ *Which route is better remains an open question* (= it is not decided). ◊ *In an interview try to ask open questions* (= to which the answer is not just 'yes' or 'no').
FABRIC | 18 with wide spaces between the threads: *an open weave*

IDM **be an ˌopen ˈsecret** if sth is **an open secret**, many people know about it, although it is supposed to be a secret **have/keep an ˌopen ˈmind (about/on sth)** to be willing to listen to or accept new ideas or suggestions **keep your ˈears/ˈeyes open (for sth)** to be quick to notice or hear things **an ˌopen ˈbook** if you describe sb or their life as **an open book**, you mean that you can easily understand them and know everything about them **an ˌopen inviˈtation (to sb)** **1** an invitation to sb to visit you at any time **2** if sth is **an open invitation** to criminals, etc., it encourages them to commit a crime by making it easier: *Leaving your camera on the seat in the car is an open invitation to thieves.* **with ˌopen ˈarms** if you welcome sb **with open arms**, you are extremely happy and pleased to see them—more at BURST *v.*, DOOR, EYE *n.*, MARKET *n.*, OPTION
■ *verb*
DOOR/WINDOW/LID | 1 [VN] to move a door, window, lid, etc. so that it is no longer closed: *Mr Chen opened the car door*

b	d	f	g	h	k	l	m	n	p	r
bad	did	fall	get	hat	cat	leg	man	now	pen	red

for his wife. OPP CLOSE **2** [V] to move or be moved so that it is no longer closed: *The door opened and Alan walked in.* OPP CLOSE

CONTAINER/PACKAGE | **3** [VN] to remove the lid, undo the FASTENING, etc. of a container, etc. in order to see or get what is inside: [V] *Shall I open another bottle?* ◇ *He opened the letter and read it.*

EYES | **4** [VN, V] if you **open** your eyes or your eyes **open**, you move your EYELIDS upwards so that you can see OPP CLOSE

MOUTH | **5** if you **open** your mouth or your mouth **opens**, you move your lips, for example in order to speak: [VN] *He hardly ever opens his mouth* (= speaks). [also V]

BOOK | **6** [VN] to turn the cover or the pages of a book so that it is no longer closed: *Open your books at page 25.* OPP CLOSE

SPREAD OUT | **7** to spread out or UNFOLD; to spread sth out or UNFOLD it: [V] *What if the parachute doesn't open?* ◇ *The flowers are starting to open.* ◇ [VN] *Open the map on the table.* ◇ *He opened his arms wide to embrace her.*

BORDER/ROAD | **8** [VN] to make it possible for people, cars, goods, etc. to pass through a place: *When did the country open its borders to Western business?* ◇ *The road will be opened again in a few hours after police have cleared it.* OPP CLOSE

FOR CUSTOMERS/VISITORS | **9** (of a shop/store, business, etc.) to start business for the day; to start business for the first time: [V] *What time does the bank open?* ◇ [VN] *The company opened its doors for business a month ago.* OPP CLOSE **10** [V] to be ready for people to go to: *The new hospital opens on July 1st.* ◇ *When does the play open?* OPP CLOSE

START STH | **11** [VN] ~ **sth (with sth)** to start an activity or event: *You need just one pound to open a bank account with us.* ◇ *The police have opened an investigation into the death.* ◇ *They will open the new season with a performance of 'Carmen'.* ◇ *Troops opened fire on* (= started shooting) *the crowds.* **12** [V] ~ **(with sth)** (of a story, film/movie, etc.) to start in a particular way: *The story opens with a murder.*

WITH CEREMONY | **13** [VN] to perform a ceremony showing that a building can start being used: *The bridge was opened by the Queen.*

COMPUTING | **14** [VN, V] to start a computer program or file so that you can use it on the screen

IDM **open 'doors for sb** to provide opportunities for sb to do sth and be successful **open your/sb's 'eyes (to sth)** to realize or make sb realize the truth about sth: *Travelling really opens your eyes to other cultures.* **open your/sb's mind to sth** to become or make sb aware of new ideas or experiences **open the way for sb/sth (to do sth)** to make it possible for sb to do sth or for sth to happen—more at HEART, HEAVEN

PHR V **'open into/onto sth** to lead to another room, area or place **,open 'out** to become bigger or wider: *The street opened out into a small square.* **,open 'out (to sb)** to become less shy and more willing to communicate **,open 'up 1** to talk about what you feel and think: *It helps to discuss your problems but I find it hard to open up.* **2** to begin shooting: *Anti-aircraft guns opened up.* **3** (often used in orders) to open a door, container, etc: *Open up or we'll break the door down!* **,open sth↔'up** | **,open 'up 1** to become or make sth possible, available or able to be reached: *The railway opened up the east of the country.* ◇ *Exciting possibilities were opening up for her in the new job.* **2** to open for business for the day; to start a new business: *I open up the store for the day at around 8.30.* OPP CLOSE UP **3** to start a new business: *There's a new Thai restaurant opening up in town.* OPP CLOSE DOWN **4** to develop or start to happen or exist; to develop or start sth: *A division has opened up between the two ministers over the single European currency.* ◇ *Scott opened up a 3-point lead in the final game.* **5** to appear and become wider; to make sth wider when it is narrow or closed: *The wound opened up and started bleeding.* ◇ *The operation will open up the blocked passages around his heart.* OPP

CLOSE UP **,open sth↔'up** to make sth open that is shut, locked, etc: *She laid the book flat and opened it up.*

■ noun **(the open)** [sing.]

OUTDOORS | **1** outdoors; in the countryside: *Children need to play out in the open.*

NOT HIDDEN | **2** not hidden or secret: *Government officials do not want these comments in the open.* ◇ *They intend to bring their complaints out into the open.*

,open-'air *adj.* [only before noun] happening or existing outside rather than inside a building: *an open-air swimming pool*

,open-and-shut 'case *noun* a legal case or other matter that is easy to decide or solve: *The murder was an open-and-shut case.*

open·cast /ˈəʊpənkɑːst; *AmE* ˈoʊpənkæst/ *adj.* [usually before noun] in **opencast** mines coal is taken out of the ground near the surface: *opencast mines/mining*—see also STRIP MINING

'open day *noun* (*BrE*) (*AmE* **,open 'house**) a day when people can visit a school, an organization, etc. and see the work that is done there

,open-'door *adj.* [only before noun] (of a policy, system, principle, etc.) allowing people or goods freedom to come into a country; allowing people to go to a place or get information without restrictions: *the country's open-door policy for refugees*

,open-'ended *adj.* without any limits, aims or dates fixed in advance: *an open-ended discussion* ◇ *The contract is open-ended.*

open·er /ˈəʊpnə(r); *AmE* ˈoʊ-/ *noun* **1** (usually in compounds) a tool that is used to open things: *a can-opener* ◇ *a bottle-opener*—see also EYE-OPENER **2** the first in a series of things such as sports games; the first action in an event, a game, etc: *They won the opener 4–2.* ◇ *Jones scored the opener.* ◇ *a good conversation opener* **3** (in cricket) either of the two BATSMEN who start play IDM **for 'openers** (*informal, especially AmE*) as a beginning or first part of a process

,open-'handed *adj.* **1** generous and giving willingly: *an open-handed host* **2** using the flat part of the hand: *an open-handed blow*

,open-'hearted *adj.* kind and friendly

,open-heart 'surgery *noun* [U] a medical operation on the heart, during which the patient's blood is kept flowing by a machine

,open 'house *noun* **1** [U, sing.] a place or a time at which visitors are welcome: *It's always open house at their place.* **2** [C] (*AmE*) = OPEN DAY **3** [C] (*AmE*) a time when people who are interested in buying a particular house or apartment can look around it

open·ing /ˈəʊpnɪŋ; *AmE* ˈoʊ-/ *noun, adj.*
■ noun **1** [C] a space or hole that sth/sb can pass through: *We could see the stars through an opening in the roof.* **2** [C, usually sing.] the beginning or first part of sth: *The movie has an exciting opening.* OPP ENDING **3** [C, usually sing.] a ceremony to celebrate the start of a public event or the first time a new building, road, etc. is used: *the opening of the Olympic Games* ◇ *the official opening of the new hospital* **4** [C, U] the act or process of making sth open or of becoming open: *the opening of a flower* ◇ *the opening of the new play* ◇ *Late opening of supermarkets is common in Britain now.* OPP CLOSING **5** [C] a job that is available: *There are several openings in the sales department.* **6** [C] a good opportunity for sb: *Winning the competition was the opening she needed for her career.* **7** [C] part of a piece of clothing that is made to open and close so that it can be put on easily: *The skirt has a side opening.*
■ adj. [only before noun] first; beginning: *his opening remarks* ◇ *the opening chapter of the book* OPP CLOSING

'opening hours *noun* [pl.] the time during which a shop/store, bank, etc. is open for business

,opening 'night *noun* [usually sing.] the first night that, for example, a play is performed or a film/movie is shown to the public

'opening time *noun* [U] (*BrE*) the time when pubs can legally open and begin to serve drinks

,opening 'up noun [sing.] **1** the process of removing restrictions and making sth such as land or jobs available to more people: *the opening up of new opportunities for women in business* **2** the process of making sth ready for use: *the opening up of a new stretch of highway*

,open 'letter noun a letter of complaint or protest to an important person or group that is printed in a newspaper so that the public can read it

open·ly /'əʊpənli; *AmE* 'oʊ-/ adv. without having any feelings, opinions or information: *Can you talk openly about sex with your parents?* ◊ *The men in prison would never cry openly* (= so that other people could see).

,open 'market noun [sing.] a situation in which companies can trade without restrictions, and prices depend on the amount of goods and the number of people buying them: *to buy/sell/trade* **on the open market**

,open-'minded adj. willing to listen to, think about or accept different ideas: *an open-minded attitude* OPP NARROW-MINDED ▶ **,open-'minded·ness** noun [U]

,open-'mouthed adj. with your mouth open because you are surprised or shocked

,open-'necked (also **,open-'neck**) adj. [only before noun] (of a shirt) worn without a tie and with the top button undone

open·ness /'əʊpənnəs; *AmE* 'oʊ-/ noun [U] **1** the quality of being honest and not hiding information or feelings **2** the quality of being able to think about, accept or listen to different ideas or people: *a child's openness to life* **3** the quality of not being enclosed or covered

,open-'plan adj. an **open-plan** building or area does not have inside walls dividing it up into rooms: *an open-plan office*

,open 'prison (*BrE*) (*AmE* **,minimum se'curity prison**) noun a prison with fewer restrictions on prisoners' freedom than ordinary prisons

'open season noun [sing.] **1 ~ (for sth)** the time in the year when it is legal to hunt and kill particular animals or birds, or to catch fish, for sport OPP CLOSE SEASON **2 ~ for/on sb/sth** a time when there are no restrictions on criticizing particular groups of people or treating them unfairly: *It seems to be open season on teachers now.*

,open 'sesame noun [sing.] an easy way to gain or achieve sth that is usually very difficult to get: *Academic success is not always an open sesame to a well-paid job.* ORIGIN From the fairy-tale *Ali Baba and the Forty Thieves*, in which the magic words **open sesame** had to be said to open the cave where the thieves kept their treasure.

,open 'verdict noun an official decision in a British court stating that the exact cause of a person's death is not known

opera /'ɒprə; *AmE* 'ɑːprə/ noun **1** [C, U] a dramatic work in which all or most of the words are sung to music; works of this type as an art form or entertainment: *Puccini's operas* ◊ *to go to the opera* ◊ *an opera singer* ◊ *light/grand opera*—see also SOAP OPERA **2** [C] a company that performs opera; a building in which operas are performed: *the Vienna State Opera* ▶ **op·er·at·ic** /,ɒpə'rætɪk; *AmE* ,ɑːp-/ adj.: *operatic arias/composers*

op·er·able /'ɒpərəbl; *AmE* 'ɑːp-/ adj. **1** that functions; that can be used: *When will the single currency be operable?* **2** (of a medical condition) that can be treated by an operation OPP INOPERABLE

'opera house noun a theatre where operas are performed

op·er·ate /'ɒpəreɪt; *AmE* 'ɑːp-/ verb

MACHINE | **1** [V] to work in a particular way SYN FUNCTION: *Most domestic freezers operate at below –18°C.* ◊ *Solar panels can only operate in sunlight.* ◊ (*figurative*) *Some people can only operate well under pressure.* **2** [VN] to use or control a machine or make it work: *What skills are needed to operate this machinery?*

SYSTEM/PROCESS/SERVICE | **3** to be used or working; to use sth or make it work: [V] *A new late-night service is now operating.* ◊ *The regulation operates in favour of married couples.* ◊ [VN] *The airline operates flights to 25 countries.* ◊

France operates a system of subsidized loans to dairy farmers.

OF BUSINESS/ORGANIZATION | **4** [V] to work in a particular way or from a particular place: *They plan to operate from a new office in Edinburgh.* ◊ *Illegal drinking clubs continue to operate in the city.*

MEDICAL | **5** [V] **~ (on sb)** (**for sth**) to cut open sb's body in order to remove a part that has a disease or to repair a part that is damaged: *The doctors operated last night.* ◊ *We will have to operate on his eyes.*

OF SOLDIERS | **6** [V] to be involved in military activities in a place: *Troops are operating from bases in the north.*

'operating system noun a set of programs that controls the way a computer works and runs other programs

'operating table noun a special table that you lie on to have a medical operation in a hospital: *The patient died on the operating table* (= during an operation).

'operating theatre (also **theatre**) (both *BrE*) (*AmE* **'operating room**) noun a room in a hospital used for medical operations

op·er·ation /,ɒpə'reɪʃn; *AmE* ,ɑːp-/ noun

MEDICAL | **1** (also *BrE informal* **op**) [C] **~ (on sb)** (**for sth**) | **~ (to do sth)** the process of cutting open a part of a person's body in order to remove or repair a damaged part: *an operation on her lung to remove a tumour* ◊ *Will I need to have an operation?* ◊ *He underwent a three-hour heart operation.* ◊ *Doctors performed an emergency operation for appendicitis last night.*

ORGANIZED ACTIVITY | **2** [C] an organized activity that involves several people doing different things: *a rescue/security operation* ◊ *The police have launched a major operation against drug suppliers.* ◊ *the UN peacekeeping operations*

BUSINESS | **3** [C] a business or company involving many parts: *a huge multinational operation* **4** [C] the activity or work done in an area of business or industry: *the firm's banking operations overseas*

COMPUTER | **5** [C, U] an act performed by a machine, especially a computer: *The whole operation is performed in less than three seconds.*

MACHINE/SYSTEM | **6** [U] the way that parts of a machine or a system work; the process of making sth work: *Regular servicing guarantees the smooth operation of the engine.* ◊ *Operation of the device is extremely simple.*

MILITARY ACTIVITY | **7** [C, usually pl.] military activity: *He was the officer in charge of operations.*

IDM **in ope'ration** working, being used or having an effect: *The system needs to be in operation for six months before it can be assessed.* ◊ *Temporary traffic controls are in operation on New Road.* **come into ope'ration** to start working; to start having an effect: *The new rules come into operation from next week.* **put sth into ope'ration** to make sth start working; to start using sth: *It's time to put our plan into operation.*

op·er·ation·al /,ɒpə'reɪʃənl; *AmE* ,ɑːp-/ adj. **1** [usually before noun] connected with the way in which a business, machine, system, etc. works: *operational activities/costs/difficulties* **2** [not usually before noun] ready to be used: *The new airport should be* **fully operational** *by the end of the year.* **3** [only before noun] connected with a military operation: *operational headquarters* ▶ **op·er·ation·al·ly** adv.

,operational 're·search (also **'operations research**) noun [U] (*technical*) the study of how businesses are organized, in order to make them more efficient

op·era·tive /'ɒpərətɪv; *AmE* 'ɑːpərətɪv; -reɪt-/ noun, adj.

■ noun **1** (*technical*) a worker, especially one who works with their hands: *a factory operative* ◊ *skilled/unskilled operatives* **2** (*especially AmE*) a person who does secret work, especially for a government organization: *an intelligence operative*

■ adj. **1** [not usually before noun] ready to be used; in use: *This law becomes operative immediately.* ◊ *The station will be* **fully operative** *again in January.* **2** [only before noun] (*medical*) connected with a medical operation: *operative mortality/treatment*—see also POST-OPERATIVE IDM **the**

æ	ɑː	e	ɜː	ə	ɪ	iː	i	ɒ	ɔː	ʌ	ʊ	u	uː
cat	father	ten	bird	about	sit	see	many	got	saw	cup	put	actual	too
								(BrE)					

operative word used to emphasize that a particular word or phrase is the most important one in a sentence: *I was in love with her—'was' being the operative word.*

op·er·ator /ˈɒpəreɪtə(r); AmE ˈɑːp-/ noun **1** (often in compounds) a person who operates equipment or a machine: *a computer/machine operator* **2** (BrE also **tel·eph·on·ist**) a person who works on the telephone SWITCHBOARD of a large company or organization, especially at a TELEPHONE EXCHANGE: *Dial 100 and ask for the operator.* **3** (often in compounds) a person or company that runs a particular business: *a tour operator ◇ a bus/ferry operator* **4** (*informal*, especially *disapproving*) a person who is skilful at getting what they want, especially when this involves behaving in a dishonest way: *a smooth/slick/shrewd operator*

op·er·etta /ˌɒpəˈretə; AmE ˌɑːpə-/ noun a short opera, usually with a humorous subject

oph·thal·mic /ɒfˈθælmɪk; AmE ɑːf-/ adj. (*medical*) connected with the eye: *ophthalmic surgery*

oph·thalmic op·ti·cian noun (BrE) = OPTICIAN

oph·thal·molo·gist /ˌɒfθælˈmɒlədʒɪst; AmE ˌɑːfθæl-ˈmɑːl-/ noun a doctor who studies and treats the diseases of the eye

oph·thal·mol·ogy /ˌɒfθælˈmɒlədʒi; AmE ˌɑːfθælˈmɑːl-/ noun [U] the scientific study of the eye and its diseases

opi·ate /ˈəʊpiət; AmE ˈoʊ-/ noun (*formal*) a drug containing OPIUM

opin·ion /əˈpɪnjən/ noun **1** [C] ~ (about/of/on sb/sth)| ~ (that...) your feelings or thoughts about sb/sth, rather than a fact: *We were invited to give our opinions about how the work should be done. ◇ I've recently changed my opinion of her. ◇ Everyone had a different opinion on the subject. ◇ The chairman expressed the opinion that job losses were inevitable. ◇ He has very strong political opinions.* **In my opinion**, *it's a very sound investment. ◇* (*formal*) *It is our opinion that he should resign. ◇* (*spoken*) *If you want my opinion, I think you'd be crazy not to accept.* **2** [U] the beliefs or views of a group of people: *Public opinion is shifting in favour of change. ◇ legal/medical/political opinion* (= the beliefs of people working in the legal, etc. profession) *◇ There is **a difference of opinion*** (= people disagree) *as to the merits of the plan. ◇* **Opinion is divided** *on the issue. ◇ There is a wide body of opinion that supports this proposal. ◇ Which is the better is **a matter of opinion*** (= people have different opinions about it). **3** [C] advice from a professional person: *They called in a psychologist to give an independent opinion. ◇ I'd like a **second opinion*** (= advice from another person) *before I make a final decision.* **IDM** **be of the opinion that ...** (*formal*) to believe or think that ... **have a good, bad, high, low, etc. opinion of sb/sth** to think that sb/sth is good, bad, etc: *The boss has a very high opinion of her.*—more at CONSIDER

opin·ion·ated /əˈpɪnjəneɪtɪd/ (also ˌself-oˈpinion·ated) adj. (*disapproving*) having very strong opinions that you are not willing to change

oˈpinion poll noun = POLL

opium /ˈəʊpiəm; AmE ˈoʊ-/ noun [U] a powerful drug made from the juice of a type of POPPY (= a kind of flower), used in the past in medicines to reduce pain and help people sleep. Some people take opium illegally for pleasure and can become ADDICTED to it: *opium poppies ◇ the opium trade*

opos·sum /əˈpɒsəm; AmE əˈpɑːs-/ (also **pos·sum**) noun a small American or Australian animal that lives in trees and carries its young in a POUCH (= a pocket of skin on the front of the mother's body)

op·pon·ent /əˈpəʊnənt; AmE əˈpoʊ-/ noun **1** a person that you are playing or fighting against in a game, competition, argument, etc: *a political opponent ◇ a dangerous/worthy/formidable opponent ◇ The team's opponents are unbeaten so far this season.* **2** ~ **(of sth)** a person who is against sth and tries to change or stop it: *opponents of abortion ◇ opponents of the regime*

op·por·tune /ˈɒpətjuːn; AmE ˌɑːpərˈtuːn/ adj. (*formal*) **1** (of a time) suitable for doing a particular thing, so that it is likely to be successful: *The offer could not have come at a more opportune moment.* **2** (of an action or event) done or happening at the right time to be successful: *an opportune remark* **OPP** INOPPORTUNE ▶ **op·por·tune·ly** adv.

op·por·tun·ism /ˌɒpəˈtjuːnɪzəm; AmE ˌɑːpərˈtuː-/ noun [U] (*disapproving*) the practice of using situations unfairly to gain advantage for yourself without thinking about how your actions will affect other people: *political opportunism*

op·por·tun·ist /ˌɒpəˈtjuːnɪst; AmE ˌɑːpərˈtuː-/ (also **op·por·tun·is·tic**) [usually before noun] (often *disapproving*) making use of an opportunity, especially to get an advantage for yourself; not done in a planned way: *an opportunist crime ◇ Smith marked his debut match with an opportunist goal.* ▶ **op·por·tun·ist** noun: *80% of burglaries are committed by casual opportunists.*

op·por·tun·is·tic /ˌɒpətjuːˈnɪstɪk; AmE ˌɑːpərtuːˈn-/ adj. **1** (*disapproving*) = OPPORTUNIST **2** [only before noun] (*medical*) harmful to people whose IMMUNE SYSTEM has been made weak by disease or drugs: *an opportunistic infection*

op·por·tun·ity /ˌɒpəˈtjuːnəti; AmE ˌɑːpərˈtuː-/ noun [C, U] (*pl.* **-ies**) ~ **(to do sth)**| ~ **(for sth/for doing sth)**| ~ **(of doing sth)** a time when a particular situation makes it possible to do or achieve sth: *You'll have the opportunity to ask any questions at the end. ◇ There was no opportunity for further discussion. ◇ At least give him the opportunity of explaining what happened. ◇ Our company promotes **equal opportunities** for women* (= women are given the same jobs, pay, etc. as men). *◇ career/employment/job opportunities ◇ I'd like to **take this opportunity** to thank my colleagues for their support. ◇ He is rude to me **at every opportunity*** (= whenever possible). *◇ They intend to close the school **at the earliest opportunity*** (= as soon as possible). *◇ a **window of opportunity*** (= a period of time when the circumstances are right for doing sth)—see also PHOTO OPPORTUNITY ⇨ note at POSSIBILITY

op·pose /əˈpəʊz; AmE əˈpoʊz/ verb to disagree strongly with sb's plan, policy, etc. and try to change it or prevent it from succeeding: [VN] *This party would bitterly oppose the re-introduction of the death penalty. ◇ He found himself opposed by his own deputy.* ◇ [V-ing] *I would oppose changing the law.* [also VN -ing] —compare PROPOSE

op·posed /əˈpəʊzd; AmE əˈpoʊzd/ adj. [not usually before noun] ~ **(to sth)** **1** (of a person) disagreeing strongly with sth and trying to stop it: *She remained bitterly opposed to the idea of moving abroad. ◇ They are totally opposed to abortion.* **2** (of ideas, opinions, etc.) very different from sth: *Our views are **diametrically opposed** on this issue.* **IDM** **as opposed to** (*written*) used to make a contrast between two things: *200 attended, as opposed to 300 the previous year. ◇ This exercise develops suppleness as opposed to* (= rather than) *strength.*

op·pos·ing /əˈpəʊzɪŋ; AmE əˈpoʊzɪŋ/ adj. [only before noun] **1** (of teams, armies, forces, etc.) playing, fighting, working, etc. against each other: *a player from the opposing side ◇ It is time for opposing factions to unite and work towards a common goal.* **2** (of attitudes, views etc.) very different from each other

op·pos·ite /ˈɒpəzɪt; -sɪt; AmE ˈɑːpəzət/ adj., adv., noun, prep.

■ adj. **1** [only before noun] on the other side of a particular area from sb/sth and usually facing them: *Answers are given on the opposite page. ◇ We live further down on the opposite side of the road. ◇ It's not easy having a relationship when you live at opposite ends of the country.* **2** (used after the noun) facing the speaker or sb/sth that has been mentioned: *I could see smoke coming from the windows of the house directly opposite. ◇ He sat down in the chair opposite.* **3** [usually before noun] as different as possible from sth: *I watched them leave and then drove off in the opposite direction. ◇ She tried calming him down but it seemed to be having the opposite effect. ◇ students at opposite ends of the ability range* ▶ **op·pos·ite** adv.: *There's a newly married couple living opposite* (= on the other side of the road). *◇ See opposite* (= on the opposite page) *for further details.* **IDM** **your ˌopposite ˈnumber** a person who does the same job as you in another organization: *The Foreign Secretary is currently having talks with his opposite number in the White House.* **the ˌopposite ˈsex** the other sex: *He found it difficult to talk to members of the opposite sex.*

■ *noun* [often sing.] a person or thing that is as different as possible from sb/sth else: *Hot and cold are opposites.* ◊ *What is the opposite of heavy?* ◊ *I thought she would be small and blonde but she's* **the complete opposite.** ◊ *Exactly the opposite is true.* ◊ *'Is it better now?' ' Quite the opposite, I'm afraid.'* **IDM** ˌopposites at'tract used to say that people who are very different are often attracted to each other

■ *prep.* **1** on the other side of a particular area from sb/sth, and usually facing them: *I sat opposite him during the meal* (= on the other side of the table). ◊ *The bank is opposite the supermarket* (= on the other side of the road). ◊ *Write your address opposite* (= next to) *your name*—picture at FRONT *n.* **2** acting in a film/movie or play as the partner of sb: *She starred opposite Tom Hanks.*

op·pos·ition /ˌɒpəˈzɪʃn; *AmE* ˌɑːpə-/ *noun* **1** [U] ~ (to sb/sth) the act of strongly disagreeing with sb/sth, especially with the aim of preventing sth from happening: *Delegates expressed strong opposition to the plans.* ◊ *The army met with fierce opposition in every town.* ◊ *He spent five years in prison for his opposition to the regime.* ◊ *opposition forces* (= people who are arguing, fighting, etc. with another group) **2** (the opposition) [sing.+ sing./pl. *v.*] the people you are competing against in business, a competition, a game, etc: *He's gone to work for the opposition.* ◊ *The opposition is/are mounting a strong challenge to our business.* ◊ *Liverpool couldn't match the opposition in the final and lost 2–0.* **3** (the Opposition) [sing.+ sing./pl. *v.*] the main political party that is opposed to the government; the political parties that are in a parliament but are not part of the government: *the leader of the Opposition* ◊ *Opposition MPs/parties* ◊ *the Opposition spokesman on education* **4** [U,C] (*formal*) the state of being as different as possible; two things that are as different as possible: *the opposition between good and evil* ◊ *His poetry is full of oppositions and contrasts.* ▶ **op·pos·ition·al** /ˌɒpəˈzɪʃənl; *AmE* ˌɑːpə-/ *adj.* [usually before noun] (*formal*): *oppositional groups/tactics* **IDM** in oppo'sition **1** (of a political party) forming part of a parliament but not part of the government in oppo'sition to sb/sth **1** disagreeing strongly with sb/sth, especially with the aim of preventing sth from happening: *Protest marches were held in opposition to the proposed law.* **2** contrasting two people or things that are very different: *Leisure is often defined in opposition to work.*

op·press /əˈpres/ *verb* [VN] (*written*) **1** to treat sb in a cruel and unfair way, especially by not giving them the same freedom, rights, etc. as other people: *The regime is accused of oppressing religious minorities.* **2** to make sb only able to think about sad or worrying things: *The gloomy atmosphere in the office oppressed her.* ▶ **op·pres·sion** /əˈpreʃn/ *noun* [U]: *victims of oppression*

op·pressed /əˈprest/ *adj.* **1** treated in a cruel and unfair way and not given the same freedom, rights, etc. as other people: *oppressed groups/minorities* **2** (the oppressed) *noun* [pl.] people who are oppressed

op·pres·sive /əˈpresɪv/ *adj.* **1** treating people in a cruel and unfair way and not giving them the same freedom, rights, etc. as other people: *oppressive laws* ◊ *an oppressive regime* **2** (of the weather) extremely hot and unpleasant and lacking fresh air: *oppressive heat* **3** making you feel unhappy and anxious: *an oppressive relationship* ▶ **op·pres·sive·ly** *adv.*: *to behave oppressively* ◊ *oppressively hot* ◊ *He suffered from an oppressively dominant mother.*

op·pres·sor /əˈpresə(r)/ *noun* a person or group of people that treats sb in a cruel and unfair way, especially by not giving them the same freedom, rights, etc. as other people

op·pro·brium /əˈprəʊbriəm; *AmE* əˈproʊ-/ *noun* [U] (*formal*) severe criticism of a person, country, etc. by a large group of people ▶ **op·pro·bri·ous** /əˈprəʊbriəs; *AmE* əˈproʊ-/ *adj.* (*rare*): *an opprobrious remark*

opt /ɒpt; *AmE* ɑːpt/ *verb* ~ (for/against sth) to choose to take or not to take a particular course of action: [V] *After graduating she opted for a career in music.* ◊ [Vto inf] *Many workers opted to leave their jobs rather than take a pay cut.* **PHRV** ˌopt ˈin (to sth) to choose to be part of a system or an agreement ˌopt ˈout (of sth) **1** to choose not to take part in sth: *Employees may opt out of the company's pension plan.* **2** (of a school or hospital in Britain) to choose not to be under the control of the local authority—related noun OPT-OUT

optic /ˈɒptɪk; *AmE* ˈɑːp-/ *adj.* [usually before noun] (*technical*) connected with the eye or the sense of sight: *the optic nerve* (= from the eye to the brain)

op·tic·al /ˈɒptɪkl; *AmE* ˈɑːp-/ *adj.* [usually before noun] **1** connected with the sense of sight or the relationship between light and sight: *optical effects* **2** used to help you see sth more clearly: *optical aids* ◊ *optical instruments such as microscopes and telescopes* **3** (*computing*) using light for reading or storing information: *optical storage* ◊ *an optical disk* ▶ **op·tic·al·ly** /-kli/ *adv.*

ˌoptical ˈcharacter recognition *noun* [U] (*abbr.* OCR) (*computing*) the process of using light to record printed information onto disks for use in a computer system

ˌoptical ˈfibre (*BrE*) (*AmE* ˌoptical ˈfiber) *noun* [C,U] a thin glass thread through which light can be TRANSMITTED (= sent)

ˌoptical il'lusion *noun* something that tricks your eyes and makes you think that you can see sth that is not there

op·ti·cian /ɒpˈtɪʃn; *AmE* ɑːp-/ *noun* **1** (also oph,thalmic op'tician) (both *BrE*) (also op·tom·etrist *AmE*, *BrE*) a person whose job is to examine people's eyes and to recommend and sell glasses **2** (op·ti·cian's) (*pl.* op·ti·cians) the shop/store where an optician works: *to go to the optician's* **3** a person who makes LENSES, glasses, etc.

op·tics /ˈɒptɪks; *AmE* ˈɑːp-/ *noun* [U] the scientific study of sight and light—see also FIBRE OPTICS

op·ti·mal /ˈɒptɪml; *AmE* ˈɑːp-/ *adj.* = OPTIMUM

op·ti·mism /ˈɒptɪmɪzəm; *AmE* ˈɑːp-/ *noun* [U] ~ (about/for sth) a feeling that good things will happen and that sth will be successful; the tendency to have this feeling: *optimism about/for the future* ◊ *We may now look forward with optimism.* ◊ *a mood of cautious optimism* ◊ *There are very real grounds for optimism.* **OPP** PESSIMISM

op·ti·mist /ˈɒptɪmɪst; *AmE* ˈɑːp-/ *noun* a person who always expects good things to happen or things to be successful: *He's an incurable optimist.* **OPP** PESSIMIST

op·ti·mis·tic /ˌɒptɪˈmɪstɪk; *AmE* ˌɑːp-/ *adj.* ~ (about sth)| ~ (that ...) expecting good things to happen or sth to be successful; showing this feeling: *She's not very optimistic about the outcome of the talks.* ◊ *They are cautiously optimistic that the reforms will take place.* ◊ *We are now taking a more optimistic view.* ◊ *in an optimistic mood* ◊ *I think you're being a little over-optimistic.* **OPP** PESSIMISTIC ▶ **op·ti·mis·tic·al·ly** /-kli/ *adv.*

op·ti·mize (*BrE* also -ise) /ˈɒptɪmaɪz; *AmE* ˈɑːp-/ *verb* [VN] to make sth as good as it can be; to use sth in the best possible way: *to optimize the use of resources*

op·ti·mum /ˈɒptɪməm; *AmE* ˈɑːp-/ *adj.* [only before noun] **1** (also op·ti·mal) the best possible; producing the best possible results: *optimum efficiency/growth/health* ◊ *the optimum use of resources* ◊ *the optimum conditions for effective learning* **2** (the optimum) *noun* [sing.] the best possible result, set of conditions, etc.

op·tion /ˈɒpʃn; *AmE* ˈɑːp-/ *noun* **1** [C,U] ~ (of doing sth)| ~ (to do sth) something that you can choose to have or do; the freedom to choose what you do: *As I see it, we have two options ...* ◊ *There are various options open to you.* ◊ *Going to college was not an option for me.* ◊ *I had no option but to* (= I had to) *ask him to leave.* ◊ *Students have the option of studying abroad in their second year.* ◊ *A savings plan that gives you the option to vary your monthly payments.* ◊ *This particular model comes with a wide range of options* (= things you can choose to have when buying sth but which you will have to pay extra for) **2** [C] a subject that a student can choose to study, but

b	d	f	g	h	k	l	m	n	p	r
bad	did	fall	get	hat	cat	leg	man	now	pen	red

that they do not have to do: *The course offers options in design and computing.* **3** [C] ~ **(on sth)** | ~ **(to do sth)** the right to buy or sell sth at some time in the future: *We have an option on the house.* ◊ *The property is for rent with an option to buy at any time.* ◊ *He has promised me first option on his car* (= the opportunity to buy it before anyone else). ◊ *share options* (= the right to buy shares in a company) **4** [C] (*computing*) one of the choices you can make when using a computer program: *Choose the 'Cut' option from the Edit menu.* **IDM** **keep/leave your options open** to avoid making a decision now so that you still have a choice in the future **the ˌsoft/ˌeasy ˈoption** (often *disapproving*) a choice which is thought to be easier because it involves less effort, difficulty, etc: *They are anxious that the new course should not be seen as a soft option.* ◊ *He decided to take the easy option and give them what they wanted.*

op·tion·al /ˈɒpʃənl; *AmE* ˈɑːp-/ *adj.* that you can choose to do or have if you want to: *Certain courses are compulsory, others are optional.* ◊ *This model comes with a number of optional extras* (= things you can choose to have but which you will have to pay extra for).

op·tom·etrist /ɒpˈtɒmətrɪst; *AmE* ɑːpˈtɑːm-/ *noun* = OPTICIAN ▶ **op·tom·etry** /ɒpˈtɒmətri; *AmE* ɑːpˈtɑːm-/ *noun* [U]

ˈopt-out *noun* (often used as an adjective) **1** (in Britain) the action of a school or hospital that decides to manage its own money and is therefore no longer controlled by a LOCAL AUTHORITY or similar organization: *Nurses and health workers voted against the opt-out.* ◊ *an opt-out school/hospital* **2** the act of choosing not to be involved in an agreement: *an opt-out clause* ◊ *MPs hoped to reverse Britain's opt-out from the treaty.*

opu·lent /ˈɒpjələnt; *AmE* ˈɑːp-/ *adj.* (*formal*) **1** made or decorated using expensive materials: *opulent fabrics/surroundings* **2** (of people) extremely rich: *the opulent elite of Europe* ▶ **opu·lence** /-ləns/ *noun* [U] **opu·lent·ly** *adv.*

opus /ˈəʊpəs; *AmE* ˈoʊ-/ *noun* (*pl.* **opera** /ˈɒpərə; *AmE* ˈɑːp-/) (usually *sing.*) **1** (*abbr.* **op.**) a piece of music written by a famous COMPOSER and usually followed by a number that shows when it was written: *Beethoven's Opus 18* **2** (*formal*) an important piece of literature, music, etc., especially one that is on a large scale—see also MAGNUM OPUS

or /ɔː(r)/ *conj.* **1** used to introduce another possibility: *Is your sister older or younger than you?* ◊ *Are you coming or not?* ◊ *Is it a boy or a girl?* ◊ *It can be black, white or grey.*—compare EITHER…OR… **2** used in negative sentences when mentioning two or more things: *He can't read or write.* ◊ *There are people without homes, jobs or family.*—compare NEITHER…NOR… **3** (also **or else**) used to warn or advise sb that sth bad could happen; otherwise: *Turn the heat down or it'll burn.* **4** used between two numbers to show approximately how many: *There were six or seven of us there.* **5** used to introduce a word or phrase that explains or means the same as another: *geology, or the science of the earth's crust* ◊ *It weighs a kilo, or just over two pounds.* **6** used to say why sth must be true: *He must like her, or he wouldn't keep calling her.* **7** used to introduce a contrasting idea: *He was lying—or was he?* **IDM** **or so** about: *It'll cost £100 or so.* **or somebody/ something/ somewhere** | **somebody/ something/somewhere or other** (*informal*) used when you are not exactly sure about a person, thing or place: *He's a factory supervisor or something.* ◊ *'Who said so?' 'Oh, somebody or other. I can't remember who it was.'*

-or *suffix* (in nouns) a person or thing that: *actor*—compare -EE, -ER

or·acle /ˈɒrəkl; *AmE* ˈɔːr-; ˈɑːr-/ *noun* [C] **1** (in ancient Greece) a place where people could go to ask the gods for advice or information about the future; the priest or PRIESTESS through whom the gods were thought to give their message: *They consulted the oracle at Delphi.* **2** (in ancient Greece) the advice or information that the gods gave, which often had a hidden meaning **3** (usually *sing.*) a person or book that gives valuable advice or information: *My sister's the oracle on investment matters.*

or·acu·lar /əˈrækjələ(r)/ *adj.* (*formal* or *humorous*) of or like an oracle; with a hidden meaning

oral /ˈɔːrəl/ *adj., noun*
■ *adj.* **1** [usually before noun] spoken rather than written: *a test of both oral and written French* ◊ *oral evidence*—compare VERBAL **2** [only before noun] connected with the mouth: *oral hygiene* ◊ *oral sex* (= using the mouth to STIMULATE sb's sex organs) ▶ **or·al·ly** /ˈɔːrəli/ *adv.*: *Answers can be written or presented orally on tape.* ◊ *not to be taken orally* (= a warning on some medicines to show that they must not be swallowed)
■ *noun* **1** (especially *BrE*) a spoken exam, especially in a foreign language: *a French oral* ◊ *He failed the oral.* **2** (*AmE*) a spoken exam in a university

or·ange /ˈɒrɪndʒ; *AmE* ˈɔːr-; ˈɑːr-/ *noun, adj.*
■ *noun* **1** [C, U] a round CITRUS fruit with thick reddish-yellow skin and a lot of sweet juice: *orange peel* ◊ *an orange tree* ◊ *freshly squeezed orange juice* ◊ *orange groves* (= groups of orange trees) ◊ *orange blossom*—see also BLOOD ORANGE—picture on page A2 **2** [U, C] (*BrE*) orange juice, or a drink made from or tasting of oranges: *Would you like some orange?* ◊ *A vodka and orange, please.* **3** [U, C] a bright reddish-yellow colour
■ *adj.* bright reddish-yellow in colour: *yellow and orange flames*

or·ange·ade /ˌɒrɪndʒˈeɪd; *AmE* ˌɔːr-; ˌɑːr-/ *noun* **1** [U] a sweet drink with an orange flavour. In Britain it always has bubbles in it; in the US it can be with or without bubbles. **2** [C] a glass of orangeade—compare LEMONADE

or·an·gery /ˈɒrɪndʒəri; *AmE* ˈɔːr-; ˈɑːr-/ *noun* (*pl.* **-ies**) a place, especially a glass building, where orange trees are grown

ˌorange ˈsquash *noun* (*BrE*) **1** [U] a thick sweet liquid made with orange juice and sugar; a drink made from this with water added: *a bottle of orange squash* **2** [C] a glass of orange squash: *Two orange squashes, please.*

orang-utan /ɔːˌræŋuːˈtæn; əˈræŋuːtæn; *AmE* əˈræŋətæn/ *noun* a large APE (= an animal like a large monkey with no tail) with long arms and reddish hair, that lives in Borneo and Sumatra **ORIGIN** From Malay *orang huan*, meaning 'forest person'.

ora·tion /ɔːˈreɪʃn/ *noun* (*formal*) a formal speech made on a public occasion, especially as part of a ceremony

ora·tor /ˈɒrətə(r); *AmE* ˈɔːr-; ˈɑːr-/ *noun* (*formal*) a person who makes formal speeches in public or is good at public speaking: *a fine political orator*

ora·tor·ic·al /ˌɒrəˈtɒrɪkl; *AmE* ˌɔːrəˈtɔːr-; ˌɑːrəˈtɑːr-/ *adj.* (*formal*, sometimes *disapproving*) connected with the art of public speaking: *oratorical skills/technique*

ora·torio /ˌɒrəˈtɔːriəʊ; *AmE* ˌɔːrəˈtɔːrioʊ; ˌɑːrə-/ *noun* (*pl.* **-os**) a long piece of music for singers and an orchestra, usually based on a story from the Bible—compare CANTATA

ora·tory /ˈɒrətri; *AmE* ˈɔːrətɔːri; ˈɑːr-/ *noun* (*pl.* **-ies**) **1** [U] the skill of making powerful and effective speeches in public: *The crowd was held spellbound by her oratory.* **2** [C] a room or small building that is used for private prayer or worship

orb /ɔːb; *AmE* ɔːrb/ *noun* **1** (*literary*) an object shaped like a ball, especially the sun or moon **2** a gold ball with a cross on top, carried by a king or queen at formal ceremonies as a symbol of power—compare SCEPTRE

orbit /ˈɔːbɪt; *AmE* ˈɔːrbɪt/ *noun, verb*
■ *noun* **1** [C, U] a curved path followed by a planet or an object as it moves around another planet, star, moon, etc: *the earth's orbit around the sun* ◊ *a space station in orbit round the moon* ◊ *A new satellite has been put into orbit around the earth.* **2** [sing.] an area that a particular person, organization, etc. deals with or is able to influence: *to come/fall/be within sb's orbit*
■ *verb* ~ **(around sth)** to move in an orbit (= a curved path) around a much larger object, especially a planet, star, etc: [VN] *The earth takes a year to orbit the sun.* [also V]

or·bit·al /ˈɔːbɪtl; *AmE* ˈɔːrb-/ *adj., noun*
■ *adj.* [only before noun] **1** connected with the orbit of a planet or object in space **2** (*BrE*) (of a road) built around

s	t	v	z	ʃ	ʒ	tʃ	dʒ	θ	ð	ŋ
see	tea	van	zoo	shoe	vision	chain	jam	thin	this	sing

the edge of a town or city to reduce the amount of traffic travelling through the centre
- *noun* (*BrE*) a very large RING ROAD, especially if it is a motorway: *the M25 London orbital*

orch·ard /'ɔːtʃəd; *AmE* 'ɔːrtʃərd/ *noun* a piece of land, normally enclosed, in which fruit trees are grown

or·ches·tra /'ɔːkɪstrə; *AmE* 'ɔːrk-/ *noun* **1** [C+sing./ pl. *v.*] a large group of people who play various musical instruments together, led by a CONDUCTOR: *She plays the flute in the school orchestra.* ◊ *the Scottish Symphony Orchestra*—see also CHAMBER ORCHESTRA **2** (**the orchestra**) [sing.] (*AmE*) = THE STALLS

or·ches·tral /ɔː'kestrəl; *AmE* ɔːr'k-/ *adj.* connected with an orchestra: *orchestral music/works*

'orchestra pit (also **pit**) *noun* the place in a theatre just in front of the stage where the orchestra sits and plays for an opera, a ballet, etc.

or·ches·trate /'ɔːkɪstreɪt; *AmE* 'ɔːrk-/ *verb* [VN] **1** to arrange a piece of music in parts so that it can be played by an orchestra **2** (*written*) to organize a complicated plan or event very carefully or secretly SYN STAGE-MAN-AGE: *a carefully orchestrated publicity campaign* ◊ *The group is accused of orchestrating violence at demonstrations.* ► **or·ches·tra·tion** /ˌɔːkɪ'streɪʃn; *AmE* ˌɔːrk-/ *noun* [C, U]

or·chid /'ɔːkɪd; *AmE* 'ɔːrkɪd/ *noun* a plant with brightly coloured flowers of unusual shapes. There are many different types of orchid and some of them are very rare.

or·dain /ɔː'deɪn; *AmE* ɔːr'd-/ *verb* **1** ~ **sb (as) (sth)** to make sb a priest or minister of a Church: [VN-N] *He was ordained (as) a priest last year.* [also VN] —see also ORDIN-ATION **2** (*formal*) (of God, the law or fate) to order or command sth; to decide sth in advance: [Vthat] *Fate had ordained that they would never meet again.* [also VN]

or·deal /ɔː'diːl; 'ɔːdiːl; *AmE* ɔːr'd-/ *noun* [usually sing.] ~ (**of sth/of doing sth**) a difficult or unpleasant experience: *They are to be spared the ordeal of giving evidence in court.* ◊ *The hostages spoke openly about the terrible ordeal they had been through.* ◊ *The interview was less of an ordeal than she'd expected.*

order /'ɔːdə(r); *AmE* 'ɔːrd-/ *noun, verb*
- *noun*
ARRANGEMENT | **1** [U, C] the way in which people or things are placed or arranged in relation to each other: *The names are listed in alphabetical order.* ◊ *in chrono-logical/numerical order* ◊ *arranged in order of priority/importance/size* ◊ *The results, ranked in descending/ascending order are as follows:* ◊ *All the procedures must be done in the correct order.* ◊ *Let's take the problems in a different order.* **2** [U] the state of being carefully and neatly arranged: *It was time she put her life in order.* ◊ *The house had been kept in good order.* ◊ *Get your ideas into some sort of order before beginning to write.* ◊ *It is one of the functions of art to bring order out of chaos.* OPP DISORDER
CONTROLLED STATE | **3** [U] the state that exists when people obey laws, rules or authority: *The army has been sent in to maintain order in the capital.* ◊ *Some teachers find it difficult to keep their classes in order.* ◊ *The police are trying to restore public order.* ◊ *The argument continued until the chairman called them both to order* (= ordered them to obey the formal rules of the meeting).—compare DISORDER (2)—see also POINT OF ORDER
INSTRUCTIONS | **4** [C] ~ (**for sb to do sth**)| ~ (**to do sth**) something that sb is told to do by sb in authority: *He gave orders for the work to be started.* ◊ *The general gave the order to advance.* ◊ *Dogs can be trained to obey orders.* ◊ *She takes orders only from the president.* ◊ *I'm under orders not to let anyone in.* ◊ (*informal*) *No sugar for me—doctor's orders.* ◊ *Interest rates can be controlled by order of the central bank.*
GOODS | **5** [C, U] ~ (**for sth**) a request to make or supply goods: *I would like to place an order for ten copies of this book.* ◊ *an order form* ◊ *The machine parts are still on order* (= they have been ordered but have not yet been received) ◊ *These items can be made to order* (= produced especially for a particular customer)—see also MAIL

ORDER **6** [C] goods supplied in response to a particular order that sb has placed: *The stationery order has arrived.*
FOOD/DRINKS | **7** [C] a request for food or drinks in a res-taurant, bar etc.; the food or drinks that you ask for: *May I take your order?* ◊ *Last orders at the bar now please!* (= because the bar is going to close) ◊ *an order for steak and fries* ◊ *a side order* (= for example, vegetables or salad that you eat with your main dish)
MONEY | **8** [C] a formal written instruction for sb to be paid money or to do sth—see also BANKER'S ORDER, COURT ORDER, MONEY ORDER, POSTAL ORDER, STANDING ORDER
SYSTEM | **9** [C, usually sing.] (*formal*) the way that a soci-ety, the world, etc. is arranged, with its system of rules and customs: *a change in the political and social order* ◊ *the natural order of things* ◊ *He was seen as a threat to the established order.* ◊ *A new order seems to be emerging.*
SOCIAL CLASS | **10** [C, usually sing.] (*disapproving* or *humorous*) a social class: *the lower orders*
BIOLOGY | **11** [C] a group into which animals, plants, etc. that have similar characteristics are divided, smaller than a CLASS and larger than a FAMILY: *the order of primates*—compare GENUS
RELIGIOUS COMMUNITY | **12** [C+sing./pl. *v.*] a group of people living in a religious community, especially MONKS or NUNS: *religious orders* ◊ *the Benedictine order*
SPECIAL HONOUR | **13** [C+sing./pl. *v.*] a group of people who have been given a special honour by a queen, king, president, etc: *The Order of the Garter is an ancient order of chivalry.* **14** [C] a BADGE or RIBBON worn by members of an order who have been given a special honour
SECRET SOCIETY | **15** [C+sing./pl. *v.*] a secret society whose members meet for special ceremonies: *the Ancient Order of Druids*
IDM **be in/take (holy) 'orders** to be/become a priest **in 'order 1** (of an official document) that can be used because it is all correct and legal SYN VALID: *Is your work permit in order?* **2** (*formal*) as it should be: *Is everything in order, sir?* **3** if sth is **in order**, it is a suitable thing to do or say on a particular occasion: *I think a drink would be in order.* **in 'order (to do sth)** (*formal*) allowed accord-ing to the rules of a meeting, etc: *Is it in order to speak now?* **in order that** (*formal*) so that sth can happen: *All those concerned must work together in order that agree-ment can be reached on this issue.* **in order to do sth** with the purpose or intention of doing or achieving sth: *She arrived early in order to get a good seat.* ◊ *In order to get a complete picture, further information is needed.* **in run-ning/working 'order** (especially of machines) working well: *The engine is now in perfect working order.* **of a high order | of the highest/first order** of a high quality or degree; of the highest quality or greatest degree: *The job requires diplomatic skills of a high order.* ◊ *She was a snob of the first order.* **of/in the order of sth** (*BrE*) (*AmE* **on the order of**) (*formal*) about sth; approximately sth: *She earns something in the order of £80000 a year.* **the ˌorder of the 'day** common, popular or suitable at a particular time or for a particular occasion: *Pessimism seems to be the order of the day.* **Order! Order!** used to remind people to obey the rules of a formal meeting or debate **ˌout of 'order 1** (of a machine, etc.) not working correctly: *The phone is out of order.* **2** not arranged cor-rectly or neatly: *I checked the files and some of the papers were out of order.* **3** (*BrE*) (*AmE* **ˌout of 'line**) (*informal*) behaving in a way that is not acceptable or right: *You were well out of order taking it without asking.* **4** (*formal*) not allowed by the rules of a formal meeting or debate: *His objection was ruled out of order.*—more at CALL *v.*, HOUSE *n.*, LAW, MARCH *v.*, PECK *v.*, SHORT *n.*, STARTER, TALL
- *verb*
GIVE INSTRUCTIONS | **1** to use your position of authority to tell sb to do sth or say that sth must happen: [VN to inf] *The company was ordered to pay compensation to its former employees.* ◊ *The officer ordered them to fire.* ◊ [VN] *They were ordered out of the class for fighting.* ◊ *The government has ordered an investigation into the accident.* ◊ [Vthat] *They ordered that for every tree cut down two more be planted.* ◊ (*BrE* also) *They ordered that for every*

0

æ	ɑː	e	ɜː	ə	ɪ	iː	i	ɒ	ɔː	ʌ	ʊ	u	uː
cat	father	ten	bird	about	sit	see	many	got	saw	cup	put	actual	too
								(BrE)					

tree cut down two more should be planted. ◊ [V speech] *'Sit down and be quiet,' she ordered.* [also VN **speech**]

GOODS/SERVICE | **2 ~** (sb) sth | **~** sth (for sb) to ask for goods to be made or supplied; to ask for a service to be provided: [VN] *These boots can be ordered direct from the manufacturer.* ◊ [VNN, VN] *Shall I order you a taxi?* ◊ *Shall I order a taxi for you?*

FOOD/DRINK | **3 ~** (sb sth) | **~** (sth) (for sb) to ask for sth to eat or drink in a restaurant, bar, etc: [VN] *I ordered a beer and a sandwich.* ◊ [VNN] *He ordered himself a double whisky.* ◊ [V] *Have you ordered yet?*

ORGANIZE/ARRANGE | **4** [VN] (*formal*) to organize or arrange sth: *I need time to order my thoughts*—see also ORDERED, DISORDERED

PHRV **,order sb a'bout/a'round** (*disapproving*) to keep telling sb what to do in a way that is annoying or unpleasant: *It was obvious he was used to ordering people around.*

WHICH WORD?

order / tell / instruct / command (?)

When you are talking about wanting somebody to do something, the usual word to use is **tell**: *He told me to phone back today.* ◊ *I was told to get my hair cut.* ◊ *How many times have I told you to hang up your clothes?* ◊ *We told the builder to finish the job as quickly as possible.* **Ask** sounds a little more polite: *He asked me to phone back. We asked the builders to finish the job as quickly as possible.*

Instruct is more formal and is often used in official situations: *Patients were instructed to follow the diet exactly.*

Order is a stronger word and used when people in a position of authority or power expect you to obey them: *A police officer ordered me to get out of the car.*

Command is used mainly in military situations.

'order book *noun* a record kept by a business of the products it has agreed to supply to its customers, often used to show how well the business is doing: *We have a full order book for the coming year.*

or·dered /ˈɔːdəd; AmE ˈɔːrdərd/ *adj.* [usually before noun] carefully arranged or organized: *an ordered existence* ◊ *a well-ordered society* OPP DISORDERED

'order form *noun* a document filled in by customers when ordering goods

order·ing /ˈɔːdərɪŋ; AmE ˈɔːrdər-/ *noun* [C, U] the way in which sth is ordered or arranged; the act of putting sth into an order: *Many possible orderings may exist.* ◊ *the successful ordering of complex data*

or·der·ly /ˈɔːdəli; AmE ˈɔːrdərli/ *adj., noun*
- *adj.* **1** arranged or organized in a neat, careful and logical way: *a calm and orderly life* ◊ *vegetables planted in orderly rows* ◊ *a woman with an orderly mind* **2** behaving well; peaceful: *an orderly demonstration* OPP DISORDERLY ▶ **or·der·li·ness** /ˈɔːdəlinəs; AmE ˈɔːrdər-/ *noun* [U]
- *noun* (*pl.* **-ies**) **1** a person who works in a hospital, usually doing jobs that do not need any special training **2** a soldier who does jobs that do not need any special training

,order of 'magnitude *noun* (*mathematics*) a level in a system of ordering things by size or amount, where each level is higher by a FACTOR of ten: *The actual measurement is two orders of magnitude* (= a hundred times) *greater than we expected.* ◊ (*figurative*) *The problem is of the same order of magnitude for all concerned.*

'Order Paper *noun* (*BrE*) a list of the subjects to be discussed by Parliament on a particular day

or·din·al /ˈɔːdɪnl; AmE ˈɔːrdənl/ (also **,ordinal 'number**) *noun* a number that refers to the position of sth in a series, for example 'first', 'second', etc.—compare CARDINAL ⇨ Appendix 3 ▶ **or·din·al** *adj.*

or·din·ance /ˈɔːdɪnəns; AmE ˈɔːrd-/ *noun* [C, U] (*formal*) an order or a rule made by a government or sb in a position of authority

or·din·and /ˈɔːdɪnænd; AmE ˈɔːrd-/ *noun* a person who is preparing to become a priest

or·din·ar·ily /ˈɔːdnrəli; AmE ˌɔːrdn'erəli/ *adv.* **1** in a normal way: *To the untrained eye, the children were behaving ordinarily.* **2** used to say what normally happens in a particular situation, especially because sth different is happening this time: *Ordinarily, she wouldn't have bothered arguing with him.* ◊ *We do not ordinarily carry out this type of work.*

or·din·ary /ˈɔːdnri; AmE ˈɔːrdneri/ *adj.* **1** [usually before noun] not unusual or different in any way: *an ordinary sort of day* ◊ *in the ordinary course of events* ◊ *ordinary people like you and me* ◊ *This was no ordinary meeting.* ⇨ note at NORMAL **2** (*disapproving*) having no unusual or interesting features: *The meal was very ordinary.*—compare EXTRAORDINARY **IDM** **in the ordinary way** (*BrE*) used to say what normally happens in a particular situation: *In the ordinary way, she's not a nervous person.* **out of the 'ordinary** unusual or different: *I'm looking for something a little more out of the ordinary.*

'ordinary grade *noun* = O GRADE

'ordinary level *noun* = O LEVEL

,ordinary 'seaman *noun* (*abbr.* OS) a sailor of the lowest rank in the British navy

,ordinary 'share *noun* a fixed unit of a company's CAPITAL. People who own ordinary shares have voting rights in the company.

or·din·ation /ˌɔːdɪˈneɪʃn; AmE ˌɔːrdnˈeɪʃn/ *noun* [U, C] the act or ceremony of making sb a priest or minister of a Church—see also ORDAIN

ord·nance /ˈɔːdnəns; AmE ˈɔːrd-/ *noun* [U] **1** large guns on wheels SYN ARTILLERY **2** military supplies and materials: *an ordnance depot*

,Ordnance 'Survey map *noun* a very detailed map of an area of Britain or Ireland, prepared by an organization called the Ordnance Survey, which is supported by the government

ord·ure /ˈɔːdjʊə(r); AmE ˈɔːrdʒər/ *noun* [U] (*rare, formal*) solid waste from the body of a person or an animal SYN FAECES

ore /ɔː(r)/ *noun* [U, C] rock, earth, etc. from which metal can be obtained: *iron ore*

ore·gano /ˌɒrɪˈɡɑːnəʊ; AmE əˈreɡənoʊ/ *noun* [U] a plant with leaves that have a sweet smell and are used in cooking as a herb

organ /ˈɔːɡən; AmE ˈɔːrɡən/ *noun* **1** a part of the body that has a particular purpose, such as the heart or the brain; part of a plant with a particular purpose: *the internal organs* ◊ *the sense organs* (= the eyes, ears, nose, etc.) ◊ *the sexual/reproductive organs* ◊ *an organ transplant/donor*—picture at BODY **2** (*especially humorous*) a PENIS: *the male organ* **3** (also **'pipe organ**) a large musical instrument with keys like a piano. Sounds are produced by air forced through pipes: *She plays the organ in church.* ◊ *organ music*—compare HARMONIUM **4** a musical instrument similar to a pipe organ, but without pipes: *an electric organ*—see also BARREL ORGAN, MOUTH ORGAN **5** (*formal*) an official organization that is part of a larger organization and has a special purpose: *the organs of government* **6** (*formal*) a newspaper or magazine that gives information about a particular group or organization; a means of communicating the views of a particular group: *The People's Daily is the official organ of the Chinese Communist Party.* ◊ *the organs of public opinion* (= for example, newspapers, television, radio)

'organ-grinder *noun* a person who plays a BARREL ORGAN (= a large musical instrument played by turning a handle)

or·gan·ic /ɔːˈɡænɪk; AmE ɔːrˈɡ-/ *adj.* [usually before noun] **1** (of food, farming methods, etc.) produced or practised without using artificial chemicals: *organic cheese/vegetables/wine* ◊ *an organic farmer/gardener* ◊ *organic farming/horticulture* **2** produced by or from living things: *Improve the soil by adding organic matter.* ◊ *organic compounds* OPP INORGANIC **3** (*technical*) connected with the organs of the body: *organic disease* **4** (*formal*) consisting of different parts that are all con-

aɪ	aʊ	eɪ	əʊ	oʊ	ɔɪ	ɪə	eə	ʊə	j	w
my	now	say	go (BrE)	go (AmE)	boy	near	hair	pure	yes	wet

nected to each other: *the view of society as an organic whole* **5** (*formal*) happening in a slow and natural way, rather than suddenly: *the organic growth of foreign markets* ▸ **or·gan·ic·al·ly** /-kli/ *adv.*: *organically grown fruit* ◇ *The cardboard disintegrates organically.* ◇ *Doctors could find nothing organically wrong with her.* ◇ *The organization should be allowed to develop organically.*

or·ganic 'chemistry *noun* [U] the branch of chemistry that deals with substances that contain CARBON—compare INORGANIC CHEMISTRY

or·gan·ism /'ɔːɡənɪzəm; *AmE* 'ɔːrɡ-/ *noun* **1** a living thing, especially one that is extremely small: *a living/marine organism*—see also MICRO-ORGANISM **2** a system consisting of parts that are dependent on each other: *the social organism* (= society)

or·gan·ist /'ɔːɡənɪst; *AmE* 'ɔːrɡ-/ *noun* a person who plays the organ

or·gan·iza·tion (*BrE* also **-isa·tion**) /ˌɔːɡənaɪ'zeɪʃn; *AmE* ˌɔːrɡənə'z-/ *noun* **1** [C] a group of people who form a business, club, etc. together in order to achieve a particular aim: *to work for a business/political/voluntary organization* ◇ *the World Health Organization* ◇ *He's the president of a large international organization.* **2** [U] the act of making arrangements or preparations for sth: *I leave most of the organization of these conferences to my assistant.* ◇ *A wedding on that scale takes a lot of organization.* **3** [U] the way in which the different parts of sth are arranged: *The report studies the organization of labour within the company.* **4** [U] the quality of being arranged in a neat, careful and logical way: *She is highly intelligent but her work lacks organization.* ▸ **or·gan·iza·tion·al, -isa·tion·al** /-ʃənl/ *adj.* [only before noun]: *organizational skills/ability* ◇ *organizational change/problems/structure*

or·gan·ize (*BrE* also **-ise**) /'ɔːɡənaɪz; *AmE* 'ɔːrɡ-/ *verb* **1** [VN] to arrange for sth to happen or to be provided: *to organize a meeting/party/trip* ◇ *I'll invite people if you can organize food and drinks.* **2** [VN] to arrange sth or the parts of sth into a particular order or structure: *Modern computers can organize large amounts of data very quickly.* ◇ *You should try and organize your time better.* ◇ *We do not fully understand how the brain is organized.* **3** [VN] **~ yourself/sb** to plan your/sb's work and activities in an efficient way: *I'm sure you don't need me to organize you.* **4 ~ sb (into sth)** to form a group of people with a shared aim especially a union or political party: [VN] *the right of workers to organize themselves into unions* [also V]—see also DISORGANIZED ▸ **or·gan·izer, -iser** *noun: the organizers of the festival*—see also PERSONAL ORGANIZER

or·gan·ized (*BrE* also **-ised**) /'ɔːɡənaɪzd; *AmE* 'ɔːrɡ-/ *adj.* **1** [only before noun] involving large numbers of people who work together to do sth in a way that has been carefully planned: *an organized body of workers* ◇ *an organized system of childcare* ◇ *organized religion* (= traditional religion with large numbers of followers who obey a fixed set of rules) ◇ *organized crime* (= committed by professional criminals working in large groups)—compare UNORGANIZED **2** arranged or planned in the way mentioned: *a carefully organized campaign* ◇ *a well-organized office* ◇ *a badly organized event*—compare DISORGANIZED **3** (of a person) able to plan your work, life, etc. well and in an efficient way: *a very organized person* ◇ *Isn't it time you started to get organized?*—compare DISORGANIZED

or·gasm /'ɔːɡæzəm; *AmE* 'ɔːrɡ-/ *noun* [U, C] the moment during sexual activity when feelings of sexual pleasure are at their strongest: *to achieve/reach orgasm* ◇ *to have an orgasm*

or·gas·mic /ɔː'ɡæzmɪk; *AmE* ɔːr'ɡ-/ *adj.* [only before noun] connected with or like an orgasm

or·gi·as·tic /ˌɔːdʒi'æstɪk; *AmE* ˌɔːrdʒ-/ *adj.* [usually before noun] (*formal*) typical of an orgy

orgy /'ɔːdʒi; *AmE* 'ɔːrdʒi/ *noun* (*pl.* **-ies**) **1** a party at which there is a lot of eating, drinking and sexual activity: *a drunken orgy* **2 ~ (of sth)** (*disapproving*) an extreme amount of a particular activity: *The rebels went on an orgy of killing and destruction.* ◇ *an orgy of spending*

oriel /'ɔːriəl/ *noun* (*architecture*) a part of a building, like a small room with windows, that sticks out from a wall above the ground: *an oriel window*

Ori·ent /'ɔːriənt/ **(the Orient)** *noun* [sing.] (*literary*) the eastern part of the world, especially China and Japan—compare OCCIDENT

ori·ent /'ɔːrient/ (*BrE* also **orien·tate**) *verb* [VN] **1** [usually passive] **~ sb/sth (to/towards sb/sth)** to direct sb/sth towards sth; to make or adapt sb/sth for a particular purpose: *Our students are oriented towards science subjects.* ◇ *We run a commercially oriented operation.* ◇ *profit-orientated organizations* ◇ *Neither of them is politically oriented* (= interested in politics). ◇ *policies oriented to the needs of working mothers* **2 ~ yourself** to find your position in relation to your surroundings: *The mountaineers found it hard to orient themselves in the fog.* **3 ~ yourself** to make yourself familiar with a new situation: *It took him some time to orient himself in his new school.*—compare DISORIENTATE

Orien·tal /ˌɔːri'entl/ *noun* (*old-fashioned*, often *offensive*) a person from China, Japan or other countries in E Asia

orien·tal /ˌɔːri'entl/ *adj.* connected with or typical of the eastern part of the world, especially China and Japan, and the people who live there: *oriental languages*

orien·tal·ist /ˌɔːri'entəlɪst/ *noun* a person who studies the languages, arts, etc. of oriental countries

orien·tate /'ɔːriənteɪt/ *verb* [VN] (*BrE*) = ORIENT

orien·ta·tion /ˌɔːriən'teɪʃn/ *noun* **1** [U, C] **~ (of sb/sth) (to/towards sth)** the type of aims or interests that a person or an organization has; the act of directing your aims towards a particular thing: *The course is essentially theoretical in orientation.* ◇ *Companies have been forced into a greater orientation to the market.* **2** [U, C] a person's basic beliefs or feelings about a particular subject: *religious/political orientation* ◇ *a person's sexual orientation* (= whether they are attracted to men, women or both) **3** [U] training or information that you are given before starting a new job, course, etc: *an orientation course* **4** [C] (*technical*) the direction in which an object faces: *The orientation of the planet's orbit is changing continuously.*

orien·teer·ing /ˌɔːriən'tɪərɪŋ; *AmE* -'tɪr-/ *noun* [U] the sport of following a route across country on foot, as quickly as possible, using a map and COMPASS

ori·fice /'ɒrɪfɪs; *AmE* 'ɔːr-; 'ɑːr-/ *noun* (*formal* or *humorous*) a hole or opening, especially one in the body: *the nasal/anal orifice*

ori·gami /ˌɒrɪ'ɡɑːmi; *AmE* ˌɔːr-/ *noun* [U] the Japanese art of folding paper into attractive shapes

ori·gin /'ɒrɪdʒɪn; *AmE* 'ɔːr-; 'ɑːr-/ *noun* [C, U] (also **ori·gins** [pl.]) **1** the point from which sth starts; the cause of sth: *the origins of life on earth* ◇ *Most coughs are viral in origin* (= caused by a virus). ◇ *The origin of the word remains obscure.* ◇ *This particular custom has its origins in Wales.* **2** a person's social and family background: *She has risen from humble origins to immense wealth.* ◇ *children of various ethnic origins* ◇ *people of German origin* ◇ *a person's country of origin* (= where they were born)

ori·gin·al /ə'rɪdʒənl/ *adj., noun*

▪ *adj.* **1** [only before noun] existing at the beginning of a particular period, process or activity: *The room still has many of its original features.* ◇ *I think you should go back to your original plan.* **2** new and interesting in a way that is different from anything that has existed before; able to produce new and interesting ideas: *an original design/idea* ◇ *That's not a very original suggestion.* ◇ *an original thinker/writer/painter* ◇ *the product of a highly original mind* **3** [usually before noun] painted, written, etc. by the artist rather than copied: *an original painting by local artist Graham Tovey* ◇ *The original manuscript has been lost.* ◇ *Only original documents* (= not photocopies) *will be accepted as proof of status.*

▪ *noun* **1** a document, work of art, etc. produced for the first time, from which copies are later made: *This painting is a copy; the original is in Madrid.* ◇ *Send out the photocopies and keep the original.* **2** (*formal*) a person who thinks, behaves, dresses, etc. in an unusual way **IDM in the o'riginal** in the language in which a book, etc. was

b	d	f	g	h	k	l	m	n	p	r
bad	did	fall	get	hat	cat	leg	man	now	pen	red

first written, before being translated: *I studied Italian so that I would be able to read Dante in the original.*

ori·gin·al·ity /əˌrɪdʒəˈnæləti/ *noun* [U] the quality of being new and interesting in a way that is different from anything that has existed before: *This latest collection lacks style and originality.*

ori·gin·al·ly /əˈrɪdʒənəli/ *adv.* used to describe the situation that existed at the beginning of a particular period or activity, especially before sth was changed: *The school was originally very small.* ◊ *She comes originally from York.* ◊ *Originally, we had intended to go to Italy, but then we won the trip to Greece.*

oˌriginal ˈsin *noun* [U] (in Christianity) the tendency to be evil that is believed to be present in everyone from birth

ori·gin·ate /əˈrɪdʒɪneɪt/ *verb* (*formal*) **1** [V] [usually +adv. / prep.] to happen or appear for the first time in a particular place or situation: *The disease is thought to have originated in the tropics.* ◊ *The word originated as a marketing term.* **2** [VN] to create sth new: *Locke originated this theory in the 17th century.* ▶ **ori·gin·ator** *noun*

ori·ole /ˈɔːriəʊl; *AmE* -oʊl/ *noun* **1** a N American bird: the male is black and orange and the female is yellow-green **2** a European bird, the male of which is bright yellow with black wings

or·molu /ˈɔːməluː; *AmE* ˈɔːrm-/ *noun* [U] a gold metal made of a mixture of other metals, used to decorate furniture, make ornaments, etc.

or·na·ment *noun, verb*
■ *noun* /ˈɔːnəmənt; *AmE* ˈɔːrn-/ (*formal*) **1** [C] an object that is used as decoration in a room, garden/yard, etc. rather than for a particular purpose: *a china / glass ornament* **2** [C] (*formal*) an object that is worn as jewellery **3** [U] (*formal*) the use of objects, designs, etc. as decoration: *The clock is simply for ornament; it doesn't work any more.*
■ *verb* /ˈɔːnəment; *AmE* ˈɔːrn-/ [VN] [usually passive] (*formal*) to add decoration to sth [SYN] DECORATE: *a room richly ornamented with carving*

or·na·men·tal /ˌɔːnəˈmentl; *AmE* ˌɔːrn-/ *adj.* used as decoration rather than for a practical purpose: *an ornamental fountain / lake / plant*

or·na·men·ta·tion /ˌɔːnəmenˈteɪʃn; *AmE* ˌɔːrn-/ *noun* [U] the use of objects, designs, etc. to decorate sth: *The architect was instructed to keep ornamentation to a minimum.*

or·nate /ɔːˈneɪt; *AmE* ɔːrˈn-/ *adj.* covered with a lot of decoration, especially when this involves very small or complicated designs: *a mirror in an ornate gold frame* ▶ **or·nate·ly** *adv.*: *ornately carved chairs*

or·nery /ˈɔːnəri; *AmE* ˈɔːrn-/ *adj.* (*AmE, informal*) bad-tempered and difficult to deal with

or·ni·tholo·gist /ˌɔːnɪˈθɒlədʒɪst; *AmE* ˌɔːrnɪˈθɑːl-/ *noun* a person who studies birds

or·ni·thol·ogy /ˌɔːnɪˈθɒlədʒi; *AmE* ˌɔːrnɪˈθɑːl-/ *noun* [U] the scientific study of birds ▶ **or·ni·tho·logic·al** /ˌɔːnɪθəˈlɒdʒɪkl; *AmE* ˌɔːrnɪθəˈlɑːdʒ-/ *adj.*

orphan /ˈɔːfn; *AmE* ˈɔːrfn/ *noun, verb*
■ *noun* a child whose parents are dead: *He was an orphan and lived with his uncle.* ◊ *orphan boys / girls*
■ *verb* [VN] [usually passive] to make a child an orphan: *She was orphaned in the war.*

or·phan·age /ˈɔːfənɪdʒ; *AmE* ˈɔːrf-/ *noun* a home for children whose parents are dead

ortho- /ˈɔːθəʊ; *AmE* ˈɔːrθoʊ/ *combining form* (in nouns, adjectives and adverbs) correct; standard: *orthodox* ◊ *orthography*

ortho·don·tics /ˌɔːθəˈdɒntɪks; *AmE* ˌɔːrθəˈdɑːn-/ *noun* [U] the treatment of problems concerning the position of the teeth and jaws ▶ **ortho·don·tic** *adj.*: *orthodontic treatment*

ortho·don·tist /ˌɔːθəˈdɒntɪst; *AmE* ˌɔːrθəˈdɑːn-/ *noun* a dentist who treats problems concerning the position of the teeth and jaws

ortho·dox /ˈɔːθədɒks; *AmE* ˈɔːrθədɑːks/ *adj.* **1** (especially of beliefs or behaviour) generally accepted or approved

of; following generally accepted beliefs: *orthodox medicine* ◊ *He is very orthodox in his views.* [OPP] UNORTHODOX—compare HETERODOX **2** following closely the traditional beliefs and practices of a religion: *an orthodox Jew* **3** (**Orthodox**) belonging to or connected with the Orthodox Church

the ˌOrthodox ˈChurch (also **the ˌEastern ˌOrthodox ˈChurch**) *noun* [sing.] a branch of the Christian Church in Eastern Europe and Greece

ortho·doxy /ˈɔːθədɒksi; *AmE* ˈɔːrθədɑːksi/ *noun* (*pl.* -ies) **1** [C, U] (*formal*) an idea or view that is generally accepted: *an economist arguing against the current financial orthodoxy* **2** [U, C, usually pl.] the traditional beliefs or practices of a religion, etc. **3** (**Orthodoxy**) [U] the Orthodox Church, its beliefs and practices

orth·og·raphy /ɔːˈθɒɡrəfi; *AmE* ɔːrˈθɑːɡ-/ *noun* [U] (*formal*) the system of spelling in a language ▶ **or·tho·graph·ic** /ˌɔːθəˈɡræfɪk; *AmE* ˌɔːrθ-/ *adj.*

ortho·paed·ics (*BrE*) (*AmE* **ortho·ped·ics**) /ˌɔːθəˈpiːdɪks; *AmE* ˌɔːrθə-/ *noun* [U] the branch of medicine concerned with injuries and diseases of the bones or muscles ▶ **ortho·paed·ic** (*BrE*) (*AmE* **ortho·ped·ic**) *adj.*: *an orthopaedic surgeon / hospital* ◊ *orthopaedic surgery*

-ory *suffix* **1** (in adjectives) that does: *explanatory* **2** (in nouns) a place for: *observatory*

OS /ˌəʊ ˈes; *AmE* ˌoʊ-/ *abbr.* (in Britain) ORDNANCE SURVEY

Oscar /ˈɒskə(r); *AmE* ˈɑːs-/ *noun* = ACADEMY AWARD: *The movie was nominated for an Oscar.* ◊ *an Oscar nomination / winner*

os·cil·late /ˈɒsɪleɪt; *AmE* ˈɑːs-/ *verb* [V] **1** ~ (**between A and B**) (*formal*) to keep changing from one extreme of feeling or behaviour to another, and back again: *Her moods oscillated between depression and elation.* **2** (*physics*) to keep moving from one position to another and back again: *Watch how the needle on the dial oscillates.* **3** (*physics*) (of an electric current, radio waves, etc.) to change in strength or direction at regular intervals

os·cil·la·tion /ˌɒsɪˈleɪʃn; *AmE* ˌɑːs-/ *noun* (*formal*) ~ (**between A and B**) **1** [U, sing.] a regular movement between one position and another or between one amount and another: *the oscillation of the compass needle / of radio waves* ◊ *the economy's continual oscillation between growth and recession* **2** [C] a single movement from one position to another of sth that is oscillating: *the oscillations of the pound against foreign currency* **3** [U, C] a repeated change between different feelings, types of behaviour or ideas: *his oscillation, as a teenager, between science and art*

os·cil·la·tor /ˈɒsɪleɪtə(r); *AmE* ˈɑːs-/ *noun* (*physics*) a piece of equipment for producing OSCILLATING electric currents

os·cil·lo·scope /əˈsɪləskəʊp; *AmE* -skoʊp/ *noun* (*physics*) a piece of equipment that shows changes in electrical current as waves in a line on the screen of a CATHODE RAY TUBE

osier /ˈəʊziə(r); *AmE* ˈoʊzər/ *noun* a type of WILLOW tree, with thin branches that bend easily and are used for making baskets

os·mo·sis /ɒzˈməʊsɪs; *AmE* ɑːzˈmoʊ-/ *noun* [U] **1** (*biology* or *chemistry*) the gradual passing of a liquid through a MEMBRANE (= a thin layer of material): *Water passes into the roots of a plant by osmosis.* **2** the gradual process of learning or being influenced by sth, as a result of being in close contact with it ▶ **os·mot·ic** /ɒzˈmɒtɪk; *AmE* ɑːzˈmɑːtɪk/ *adj.*: *osmotic pressure*

os·prey /ˈɒspreɪ; *AmE* ˈɑːs-/ *noun* a large BIRD OF PREY (= a bird that kills other creatures for food) that eats fish

os·sify /ˈɒsɪfaɪ; *AmE* ˈɑːs-/ *verb* [usually passive] (**os·si·fies, os·si·fy·ing, os·si·fied, os·si·fied**) (*formal, disapproving*) **1** to become or make sth fixed and unable to change: [VN] *an ossified political system* [also V] **2** [VN] (*technical*) to become or make sth hard like bone ▶ **os·si·fi·ca·tion** *noun* [U] (*formal*)

os·ten·sible /ɒˈstensəbl; *AmE* ɑːˈst-/ *adj.* [only before noun] seeming or stated to be real or true, when this is perhaps not the case: *The ostensible reason for his absence* *was illness.* ▶ **os·ten·sibly** /-əbli/ *adv.*: *Troops were sent in, ostensibly to protect the civilian population.*

os·ten·ta·tion /ˌɒstenˈteɪʃn; *AmE* ˌɑːs-/ *noun* [U] (*disapproving*) an exaggerated display of wealth, knowledge or skill that is made in order to impress people: *The house was spacious but without any trace of ostentation.*

os·ten·ta·tious /ˌɒstenˈteɪʃəs; *AmE* ˌɑːs-/ *adj.* **1** (*disapproving*) expensive or noticeable in a way that is intended to impress people: *ostentatious gold jewellery* **2** (*disapproving*) behaving in a way that is meant to impress people by showing how rich, important, etc. you are **3** (of an action) done in a very obvious way so that people will notice it: *He gave an ostentatious yawn.* ▶ **os·ten·ta·tious·ly** *adv.*: *ostentatiously dressed*

osteo- /ˈɒstiəʊ; *AmE* ˈɑːstioʊ-/ *combining form* (in nouns and adjectives) connected with bones: *osteopath*

osteo·arth·ritis /ˌɒstiəʊɑːˈθraɪtɪs; *AmE* ˌɑːstioʊɑːrˈθ-/ *noun* [U] (*medical*) a disease that causes painful swelling and permanent damage in the joints of the body, especially the hips, knees and thumbs

osteo·path /ˈɒstiəpæθ; *AmE* ˈɑːs-/ *noun* a person whose job involves treating some diseases and physical problems by pressing and moving the bones and muscles— compare CHIROPRACTOR

oste·op·athy /ˌɒstiˈɒpəθi; *AmE* ˌɑːstiˈɑːp-/ *noun* [U] the treatment of some diseases and physical problems by pressing and moving the bones and muscles ▶ **osteo·path·ic** /ˌɒstiəˈpæθɪk; *AmE* ˌɑːs-/ *adj.*

osteo·por·osis /ˌɒstiəʊpəˈrəʊsɪs; *AmE* ˌɑːstioʊpəˈroʊ-/ *noun* [U] (*medical*) a condition in which the bones become weak and are easily broken

ost·ler /ˈɒslə(r); *AmE* ˈɑːs-/ (*AmE also* **host·ler**) *noun* (in the past) a man who took care of guests' horses at an INN

os·tra·cism /ˈɒstrəsɪzəm; *AmE* ˈɑːs-/ *noun* [U] (*formal*) the act of deliberately not including sb in a group or activity; the state of not being included: *social ostracism*

os·tra·cize (*BrE also* **-ise**) /ˈɒstrəsaɪz; *AmE* ˈɑːs-/ *verb* [VN] (*formal*) to refuse to let sb be a member of a social group; to refuse to meet or talk to sb: *He was ostracized by his colleagues for refusing to support the strike.*

os·trich /ˈɒstrɪtʃ; *AmE* ˈɑːs-; ˈɔːs-/ *noun* **1** a very large African bird with a long neck and long legs, that cannot fly but can run very fast **2** (*informal*) a person who prefers to ignore problems rather than try and deal with them

other /ˈʌðə(r)/ *adj., pron.* **1** used to refer to people or things that are additional or different to people or things that have been mentioned or are known about: *Mr Harris and Mrs Bate and three other teachers were there.* ◊ *Are there any other questions?* ◊ *I can't see you now—some other time, maybe.* ◊ *Two buildings were destroyed and many others damaged in the blast.* ◊ *This option is preferable to any other.* ◊ *Some designs* **are better than** *others.*—compare ANOTHER **2 the, my, your, etc.** ~ used to refer to the second of two people or things: *My other sister is a doctor.* ◊ *One son went to live in Australia and* **the other one** *was killed in a car crash.* ◊ *He raised one arm and then the other.* ◊ *You must ask* **one** *or* **other** *of your parents.* ◊ (*humorous*) *You'll have to ask* **my other half** (= husband, wife or partner). **3 the, my, your, etc.** ~ used to refer to the remaining people or things in a group: *I'll wear my other shoes—these are dirty.* ◊ *'I like this one.' 'What about the other ones?'* ◊ *I went swimming while the others played tennis.* **4 the** ~ used to refer to a place, direction, etc. that is the opposite to where you are, are going, etc: *I work on the other side of town.* ◊ *He crashed into a car coming the other way.* ◊ *He found me, not the other way round/around.* **IDM** Most idioms containing **other** are at the entries for the nouns and verbs in the idioms, for example **in other words** is at **word.** **the ¡other ˈday/ˈmorning/ˈevening/ˈweek** recently: *I saw Jack the other day.* **other than** (usually used in negative sentences) **1** except: *I don't know any French people other than you.* ◊ *We're going away in June but other than that I'll be here all summer.* **2** (*written*) different or differently from; not: *I have never known him to behave other than selfishly.*

other·ness /ˈʌðənəs; *AmE* ˈʌðərnəs/ *noun* [U] (*formal*) the quality of being different or strange: *the otherness of an alien culture*

other·wise /ˈʌðəwaɪz; *AmE* ˈʌðərwaɪz/ *adv.* **1** used to state what the result would be if sth did not happen or if the situation were different: *My parents lent me the money. Otherwise, I couldn't have afforded the trip.* ◊ *Shut the window, otherwise it'll get too cold in here.* ◊ *We're committed to the project. We wouldn't be here otherwise.* **2** apart from that: *There was some music playing upstairs. Otherwise the house was silent.* ◊ *He was slightly bruised but otherwise unhurt.* **3** in a different way to the way mentioned; differently: *Bismarck,* **otherwise known as** *'the Iron Chancellor'* ◊ *It is not permitted to sell or otherwise distribute copies of past examination papers.* ◊ *You know what this is about. Why* **pretend otherwise** (= that you don't)? ◊ *I wanted to see him but he was* **otherwise engaged** (= doing sth else). **IDM** **or otherwise** used to refer to sth that is different from or the opposite of what has just been mentioned: *It was necessary to discover the truth or otherwise of these statements.* ◊ *We insure against all damage, accidental or otherwise.*—more at KNOW *v.*

¡other ˈwoman *noun* [usually sing.] a woman with whom a man is having a sexual relationship, although he already has a wife or partner

¡other-ˈworldly *adj.* concerned with spiritual thoughts and ideas rather than with ordinary life ▶ **¡otherˈworldli·ness** *noun* [U]

oti·ose /ˈəʊtiəʊs; *AmE* ˈoʊʃioʊs/ *adj.* (*formal*) having no useful purpose **SYN** UNNECESSARY: *an otiose round of meetings*

OTT /ˌəʊ tiː ˈtiː; *AmE* ˌoʊ/ *adj.* (*BrE*, *informal*) the abbreviation for OVER THE TOP: *Her make-up was a bit OTT.*

otter /ˈɒtə(r); *AmE* ˈɑːtər/ *noun* a small animal that has four WEBBED feet (= feet with skin between the toes), a flat tail and thick brown fur. Otters live in rivers and eat fish.

ot·to·man /ˈɒtəmən; *AmE* ˈɑːt-/ *noun* a piece of furniture like a large box with a soft top, used for storing things and sitting on

OU /ˌəʊ ˈjuː; *AmE* ˌoʊ/ *abbr.* (in Britain) Open University

ouch /aʊtʃ/ *exclamation* used to express sudden pain: *Ouch! That hurt!*

ought to /ˈɔːt tə; *before vowels and finally* ˈɔːt tu/ *modal verb* (*negative* **ought not to**, *short form especially BrE* **oughtn't to**) **1** used to say what is the right thing to do: *They ought to apologize.* ◊ *'Ought I to write to say thank you?' 'Yes, I think you ought (to).'* ◊ *They ought to have apologized* (= but they didn't). ◊ *Such things ought not to be allowed.* ◊ *He oughtn't to have been driving so fast.* ⇨ note at SHOULD **2** used to say what you expect or would like to happen: *Children ought to be able to read by the age of 7.* ◊ *Nurses ought to earn more.* **3** used to say what you advise or recommend: *We ought to be leaving now.* ◊ *This is delicious. You ought to try some.* ◊ *You ought to have come to the meeting. It was interesting.* **4** used to say what has probably happened or is probably true: *If he started out at nine, he ought to be here by now.* ◊ *That ought to be enough food for the four of us.* ◊ *Oughtn't the water to have boiled by now?* ⇨ note at MODAL

Ouija board™ /ˈwiːdʒə bɔːd; *AmE* bɔːrd/ *noun* a board marked with letters of the alphabet and other signs, used in SEANCES to receive messages said to come from people who are dead

ounce /aʊns/ *noun* **1** [C] (*abbr.* **oz**) a unit for measuring weight, ¹⁄₁₆ of a pound, equal to 28.35 grams—see also FLUID OUNCE **2** [sing.] **~ of sth** (*informal*) (used especially with negatives) a very small quantity of sth: *There's not an ounce of truth in her story.* **IDM** see PREVENTION

our /ɑː(r); ˈaʊə(r)/ *det.* (the possessive form of *we*) **1** belonging to us; connected with us: *our daughter/dog/house* ◊ *We showed them some of our photos.* ◊ *Our main export is rice.* ◊ *And now, over to our Rome correspondent ... .* **2** (**Our**) used to refer to or address God or a holy person: *Our Father* (= God) ◊ *Our Lady* (= the Virgin Mary)

ours /ɑːz; ˈaʊəz; *AmE* ɑːrz; ˈaʊərz/ *pron.* the one or ones

æ	ɑː	e	ɜː	ə	ɪ	iː	i	ɒ	ɔː	ʌ	ʊ	u	uː
cat	father	ten	bird	about	sit	see	many	got	saw	cup	put	actual	too
							(BrE)						

O

that belong to us: *Their house is very similar to ours, but ours is bigger.* ◊ *No, those are Ellie's kids. Ours are upstairs.* ◊ *He's a friend of ours.*

our·selves /ɑːˈselvz; ˌaʊəˈs-; *AmE* ɑːrˈs-; ˌaʊərˈs-/ *pron.* **1** the reflexive form of *we*; used when you and another person or other people together cause and are affected by an action: *We shouldn't blame ourselves for what happened.* ◊ *Let's just relax and enjoy ourselves.* ◊ *We'd like to see it for ourselves.* **2** used to emphasize *we* or *us*; sometimes used instead of these words: *We've often thought of going there ourselves.* ◊ *The only people there were ourselves.* **IDM** **(all) by our'selves 1** alone; without anyone else **2** without help **(all) to our'selves** for us alone; not shared with anyone: *We had the pool all to ourselves.*

-ous *suffix* (in adjectives) having the nature or quality of: *poisonous* ◊ *mountainous* ▶**-ously** (in adverbs): *gloriously* **-ousness** (in nouns): *spaciousness*

oust /aʊst/ *verb* [VN] ~ **sb (from sth/as sth)** (*written*) to force sb out of a job or position of power, especially in order to take their place: *He was ousted as chairman.* ◊ *The rebels finally managed to oust the government from power.*

ouster /ˈaʊstə(r)/ *noun* (*AmE*) the act of removing sb from a position of authority in order to put sb else in their place; the fact of being removed in this way: *a resolution condemning the president's ouster by the military*

out /aʊt/ *adv., prep., noun, verb*
■ *adv., prep.* **HELP** For the special uses of **out** in phrasal verbs, look at the entries for the verbs. For example **burst out** is in the phrasal verb section at **burst**. **1** ~ **(of sth)** away from the inside of a place or thing: *She ran out into the corridor.* ◊ *She shook the bag and some coins fell out.* ◊ *I got out of bed.* ◊ *He opened the box and out jumped a frog.* ◊ *Out you go!* (= used to order sb to leave a room) ◊ (*spoken, non-standard*) *He ran out the door.* **2** ~ **(of sth)** (of people) away from or not at home or their place of work: *I called Liz but she was out.* ◊ *Let's go out this evening* (= for example to a restaurant or club). ◊ *We haven't had a night out for weeks.* ◊ *Mr Green is out of town this week.* **3** ~ **(of sth)** away from the edge of a place: *The boy dashed out into the road.* ◊ *Don't lean out of the window.* **4** ~ **(of sth)** a long or a particular distance away from a place or from land: *She's working out in Australia.* ◊ *He lives right out in the country.* ◊ *The boats are all out at sea.* ◊ *The ship sank ten miles out of Stockholm.* **5** ~ **(of sth)** used to show that sth/sb is removed from a place, job, etc: *This detergent is good for getting stains out.* ◊ *We want this government out.* ◊ *He got thrown out of the restaurant.* **6** ~ **of sth** used to show that sth comes from or is obtained from sth/sb: *He drank his beer out of the bottle.* ◊ *a statue made out of bronze* ◊ *a romance straight out of a fairy tale* ◊ *I paid for the damage out of my savings.* ◊ *We'll get the truth out of her.* **7** ~ **of sth** used to show that sb/sth does not have any of sth: *We're out of milk.* ◊ *He's been out of work for six months.* ◊ *You're out of luck—she left ten minutes ago.* **8** ~ **of sth** used to show that sb/sth is not or no longer in a particular state or condition: *Try and stay out of trouble.* ◊ *I watched the car until it was out of sight.* **9** ~ **(of sth)** used to show that sb is no longer involved in sth: *It was an awful job and I'm glad to be out of it.* ◊ *He gets out of the army in a few weeks.* ◊ *They'll be out* (= of prison) *on bail in no time.* ◊ *Brown goes on to the semi-finals but Lee is out.* **10** ~ **of sth** used to show the reason why sth is done: *I asked out of curiosity.* ◊ *She did it out of spite.* **11** ~ **of sth** from a particular number or set: *You scored six out of ten.* ◊ *Two out of three people think the President should resign.* **12** (of a book, etc.) not in the library; borrowed by sb else: *The book you wanted is out on loan.* **13** (of the TIDE) at or towards its lowest point on land: *I like walking on the wet sand when the tide is out.* **14** if the sun, moon or stars are or come **out**, they can be seen from the earth and are not hidden by clouds **15** (of flowers) fully open: *There should be some snowdrops out by now.* **16** available to everyone; known to everyone: *When does her new book come out?* ◊ *Word always gets out* (= people find out about things) *no matter how careful you are.* ◊ *Out with it!* (= say what

you know) **17** clearly and loudly so that people can hear: *to call/cry/shout out* ◊ *Read it out loud.* ◊ *Nobody spoke out in his defence.* **18** (*informal*) having told other people that you are HOMOSEXUAL: *I had been out since I was 17.* **19** (in cricket, baseball, etc.) if a team or team member is **out**, it is no longer their turn with the bat: *The West Indies were all out for 364* (= after scoring 364 RUNS in cricket). **20** (in tennis, etc.) if the ball is **out**, it landed outside the line: *The umpire said the ball was out.* **21** ~ **(in sth)** not correct or exact; wrong: *I was slightly out in my calculations.* ◊ *Your guess was a long way out* (= completely wrong). ◊ *The estimate was out by more than $100.* **22** not possible or not allowed: *Swimming is out until the weather gets warmer.* **23** not fashionable: *Is rap out yet?* **24** (of fire, lights or burning materials) not or no longer burning or lit: *Suddenly all the lights went out.* ◊ *The fire had burnt itself out.* ◊ *He stubbed his cigarette out.* **25** at an end: *It was summer and school was out.* ◊ *She was to regret her words before the day was out.* **26** unconscious: *He was out for more than an hour and came round in the hospital.* ◊ *She was knocked out cold.* **27** (*BrE, informal*) on strike **28** to the end; completely: *Hear me out before you say anything.* ◊ *We left them to fight it out* (= settle a dispute by fighting or arguing).—see also ALL-OUT **IDM** **be out for sth/to do sth** to be trying to get or do sth: *I'm not out for revenge.* ◊ *She's out for what she can get* (= trying to get something for herself). ◊ *The company is out to capture the Canadian market.* ˌout and aˈbout (*BrE*) **1** able to go outside again after an illness **2** travelling around a place: *We've been out and about talking to people all over the country.* ˈout of it (*informal*) **1** sad because you are not included in sth: *We've only just moved here so we feel a little out of it.* **2** not aware of what is happening, usually because of drinking too much alcohol, or taking drugs: *He looks completely out of it.*
■ *noun* **IDM** see IN *n.*
■ *verb* [VN] to say publicly that sb is HOMOSEXUAL, especially when they would prefer to keep the fact a secret: *He is the latest politician to be outed by gay activists.*

out- /aʊt/ *prefix* **1** (in verbs) greater, better, further, longer, etc: *outnumber* ◊ *outwit* ◊ *outgrow* ◊ *outlive* **2** (in nouns and adjectives) outside; OUTWARD; away from: *outbuildings* ◊ *outpatient* ◊ *outlying* ◊ *outgoing*

out·age /ˈaʊtɪdʒ/ *noun* (*AmE*) a period of time when the supply of electricity, etc. is not working: *a power outage*

out-and-ˈout *adj.* [only before noun] in every way SYN COMPLETE: *What she said was an out-and-out lie.*

out·back /ˈaʊtbæk/ *noun* (**the outback**) [sing.] the area of Australia that is a long way from the coast and the towns, where few people live

out·bid /ˌaʊtˈbɪd/ *verb* (**out·bid·ding, out·bid, out·bid**) [VN] ~ **sb (for sth)** to offer more money than sb else in order to buy sth, for example at an AUCTION

out·board /ˈaʊtbɔːd; *AmE* -bɔːrd/ *adj.* (*technical*) on, towards or near the outside of a ship or an aircraft: *outboard wing panels*

ˌoutboard ˈmotor (also ˌoutboard ˈengine, ˈout·board) *noun* an engine that you can fix to the back of a small boat—picture at BOAT

out·bound /ˈaʊtbaʊnd/ *adj.* (*formal*) travelling from a place rather than arriving in it: *outbound flights/passengers* OPP INBOUND

out·break /ˈaʊtbreɪk/ *noun* the sudden start of sth unpleasant, especially violence or a disease: *the outbreak of war* ◊ *an outbreak of hostilities/typhoid* ◊ *Outbreaks of rain are expected in the afternoon.*

out·build·ing /ˈaʊtbɪldɪŋ/ *noun* [usually pl.] a building such as a SHED or STABLE that is built near to, but separate from, a main building: *a large farmhouse with several outbuildings*

out·burst /ˈaʊtbɜːst; *AmE* -bɜːrst/ *noun* **1** a sudden strong expression of an emotion: *an outburst of anger/laughter* ◊ *She was alarmed by his violent outburst.* **2** a sudden increase in a particular activity or attitude: *an outburst of racism*

out·cast /ˈaʊtkɑːst; *AmE* -kæst/ *noun* a person who is not

aɪ	aʊ	eɪ	əʊ	oʊ	ɔɪ	ɪə	eə	ʊə	j	w
my	now	say	go (BrE)	go (AmE)	boy	near	hair	pure	yes	wet

accepted by other people and who sometimes has to leave their home and friends: *People with the disease were often treated as social outcasts.* ▶ **out·cast** *adj.*

out·class /ˌaʊtˈklɑːs; *AmE* -ˈklæs/ *verb* [VN] [often passive] to be much better than a competitor: *Kennedy was outclassed 0–6 0–6 in the final.*

out·come /ˈaʊtkʌm/ *noun* the result or effect of an action or event: *We are waiting to hear the final outcome of the negotiations.* ◊ *These costs are payable whatever the outcome of the case.* ◊ *We are confident of a successful outcome.* ◊ *Four possible outcomes have been identified.*

out·crop /ˈaʊtkrɒp; *AmE* -krɑːp/ *noun* a large mass of rock that stands above the surface of the ground

out·cry /ˈaʊtkraɪ/ *noun* [C, U] (*pl.* **-ies**) ~ (**at/ over/ against sth**) a reaction of anger or strong protest shown by people in public: *an outcry over the proposed change* ◊ *The new tax provoked a **public outcry**.* ◊ *There was outcry at the judge's statement.*

out·dated /ˌaʊtˈdeɪtɪd/ *adj.* no longer useful because of being old-fashioned: *outdated equipment / laws / methods* ◊ *These figures are now outdated.*—compare OUT-OF-DATE

out·dis·tance /ˌaʊtˈdɪstəns/ *verb* [VN] (*written*) to leave sb/sth behind by going faster, further, etc.; to be better than sb/sth SYN OUTSTRIP: *She easily outdistanced the other runners.*

outdo /ˌaʊtˈduː/ *verb* (**out·does** /-ˈdʌz/ **out·did** /-ˈdɪd/ **out·done** /-ˈdʌn/) [VN] (*written*) to do more or better than sb else: *Sometimes small firms can outdo big business when it comes to customer care.* ◊ *Not to be outdone* (= not wanting to let sb else do better)*, she tried again.*

out·door /ˈaʊtdɔː(r)/ *adj.* [only before noun] used, happening or situated outside rather than in a building: *outdoor clothing / activities* ◊ *an outdoor swimming pool* ◊ *I'm not really the outdoor type* (= I prefer indoor activities)*.* OPP INDOOR

out·doors /ˌaʊtˈdɔːz; *AmE* -ˈdɔːrz/ *adv., noun*
■ *adv.* outside, rather than in a building: *The rain prevented them from eating outdoors.* ◊ *The seeds may be sown outdoors in the spring.* OPP INDOORS
■ *noun* (**the outdoors**) [sing.] the open air and the countryside, away from busy places: *They both have a love of the outdoors.* ◊ *Come to Canada and enjoy the great outdoors.*

outer /ˈaʊtə(r)/ *adj.* [only before noun] **1** on the outside of sth: *the outer layers of the skin* **2** furthest from the inside or centre of sth: *I walked along the outer edge of the track.* ◊ *the outer suburbs of the city* ◊ *Outer London / Mongolia* ◊ (*figurative*) *to explore the outer* (= most extreme) *limits of human experience* OPP INNER

ˈouter belt *noun* (*AmE*) = RING ROAD

outer·most /ˈaʊtəməʊst; *AmE* ˈaʊtərmoʊst/ *adj.* [only before noun] furthest from the inside or centre: *the outermost planet* ◊ *He fired and hit the outermost ring of the target.* OPP INNERMOST

ˌouter ˈspace *noun* [U] = SPACE (4): *radio waves from outer space*

outer·wear /ˈaʊtəweə(r); *AmE* ˈaʊtərwer/ *noun* [U] clothes such as coats, hats, etc. that you wear outside

out·face /ˌaʊtˈfeɪs/ *verb* [VN] (*formal*) to defeat an enemy or opponent by being brave and remaining confident

out·fall /ˈaʊtfɔːl/ *noun* (*technical*) the place where a river, pipe, etc. flows out into the sea: *a sewage outfall*

out·field /ˈaʊtfiːld/ *noun* (**the outfield**) [sing.] (in cricket and baseball) the part of the field that is furthest from the person who is hitting the ball

out·field·er /ˈaʊtfiːldə(r)/ *noun* (in cricket and baseball) a player in the outfield

out·fit /ˈaʊtfɪt/ *noun, verb*
■ *noun* **1** [C] a set of clothes that you wear together, especially for a particular occasion or purpose: *She was wearing an expensive new outfit.* ◊ *a wedding outfit* ◊ *a cowboy / Superman outfit* (= one that you wear for fun in order to look like the type of person mentioned) **2** [C+sing./ pl. *v.*] (*informal*) a group of people working together as an organization, business, team, etc: *a market research outfit* ◊ *The team were beaten by Dave Bassett's outfit last season.*

◊ *This was the fourth album by the top rock outfit.* **3** [C] a set of equipment that you need for a particular purpose: *a bicycle repair outfit*
■ *verb* (**-tt-**) [VN] [often passive] ~ **sth/sb** (**with sth**) (especially *AmE*) to provide sb/sth with equipment or clothes for a special purpose: *The ship was outfitted with a 12-bed hospital.*

out·fit·ter (also **out·fit·ters**) /ˈaʊtfɪtə(r)/ *noun* **1** (*old-fashioned, BrE*) a shop/store that sells men's clothes or school uniforms **2** (*AmE*) a shop/store that sells equipment for camping and other outdoor activities

out·flank /ˌaʊtˈflæŋk/ *verb* [VN] **1** to move around the side of an enemy or opponent, especially in order to attack them from behind **2** to gain an advantage over sb, especially by doing sth unexpected: *They found themselves outflanked by the rival takeover bid.*

out·flow /ˈaʊtfləʊ; *AmE* -floʊ/ *noun* ~ (**of sth/sb**) (**from sth**) the movement of ‘a large amount of money, liquid, people, etc. out of a place: *There was a capital outflow of $22 billion in 1998.* ◊ *a steady outflow of oil from the tank* ◊ *the outflow of refugees* OPP INFLOW

out·going /ˈaʊtɡəʊɪŋ; *AmE* -ɡoʊ-/ *adj.* **1** liking to meet other people, enjoying their company and being friendly towards them: *an outgoing personality* **2** [only before noun] leaving the position of responsibility mentioned: *the outgoing president / government* OPP INCOMING **3** [only before noun] going away from a particular place rather than arriving in it: *This telephone should be used for outgoing calls.* ◊ *outgoing flights / passengers* ◊ *the outgoing tide* OPP INCOMING

out·goings /ˈaʊtɡəʊɪŋz; *AmE* -ɡoʊ-/ *noun* [pl.] (*BrE*) the amount of money that a person or a business has to spend regularly, for example every month: *to have low / high outgoings* ◊ *Write down your incomings and outgoings.*

out·grow /ˌaʊtˈɡrəʊ; *AmE* -ˈɡroʊ/ *verb* (**out·grew** /-ˈɡruː/ **out·grown** /-ˈɡrəʊn; *AmE* -ˈɡroʊn/) [VN] **1** to grow too big to be able to wear or fit into sth SYN GROW OUT OF: *She's already outgrown her school uniform.* ◊ *The company has outgrown its offices.* **2** to grow taller, larger or more quickly than another person: *He's already outgrown his older brother.* **3** to stop doing sth or lose interest in sth as you become older SYN GROW OUT OF: *He's outgrown his passion for rock music.*

out·growth /ˈaʊtɡrəʊθ; *AmE* -ɡroʊθ/ *noun* **1** (*technical*) a thing that grows out of sth else: *The eye first appears as a cup-shaped outgrowth from the brain.* **2** (*formal*) a natural development or result of sth: *The law was an outgrowth of the 1996 presidential election.*

out·gun /ˌaʊtˈɡʌn/ *verb* (**-nn-**) [V] [often passive] to have greater military strength than sb: (*figurative*) *The England team was completely outgunned.*

out·house /ˈaʊthaʊs/ *noun* **1** (*BrE*) a small building, such as a SHED, outside a main building **2** (*AmE*) a toilet in a small building of its own

out·ing /ˈaʊtɪŋ/ *noun* **1** [C] ~ (**to ...**) a trip that you go on for pleasure or education, usually with a group of people and lasting no more than one day: *We went on an outing to London.* ◊ *a family outing* **2** [C] (*sport*) (*informal*) an occasion when a competitor takes part in a competition **3** [U, C] the practice of naming people as HOMOSEXUALS in public, when they do not want anyone to know, done especially by other HOMOSEXUALS

out·land·ish /aʊtˈlændɪʃ/ *adj.* (*usually disapproving*) strange or extremely unusual: *outlandish costumes / ideas* ▶ **out·land·ish·ly** *adv.*

out·last /ˌaʊtˈlɑːst; *AmE* -ˈlæst/ *verb* [VN] to continue to exist or take part in an activity for a longer time than sb/sth: *He can outlast anyone on the dance floor.*

out·law /ˈaʊtlɔː/ *verb, noun*
■ *verb* [VN] **1** to make sth no longer legal: *plans to outlaw the carrying of knives* ◊ *the outlawed nationalist party* **2** (in the past) to make sb an outlaw
■ *noun* (used especially about people in the past) a person who has done sth illegal and is hiding to avoid being caught; a person who is not protected by the law: *Robin Hood, the world's most famous outlaw*

b	d	f	g	h	k	l	m	n	p	r
bad	**did**	**fall**	**get**	**hat**	**cat**	**leg**	**man**	**now**	**pen**	**red**

out·lay /ˈaʊtleɪ/ noun [C, U] ~ (on sth) the money that you have to spend in order to start a new project or to save yourself money or time later: *The business quickly repaid the initial outlay on advertising.* ◇ *a massive financial/capital outlay*

out·let /ˈaʊtlet/ noun ~ (for sth) **1** a way of expressing or making good use of strong feelings, ideas or energy: *She needed to find an outlet for her many talents and interests.* ◇ *Sport became the perfect outlet for his aggression.* **2** (*business*) a shop/store or an organization that sells goods made by a particular company or of a particular type: *The business has 34 retail outlets in this state alone.* **3** (*especially AmE*) a shop/store that sells goods of a particular make at reduced prices: *the Nike outlet in the outlet mall* **4** a pipe or hole through which liquid or gas can flow out: *a sewage outlet* ◇ *an outlet hose/pipe* OPP INLET **5** (*AmE*) = SOCKET (1)

out·line /ˈaʊtlaɪn/ verb, noun
■ verb **1** ~ sth (to sb) to give a description of the main facts or points involved in sth: [VN] *We outlined our proposals to the committee.* [also V wh-] **2** [VN] [usually passive] to show or mark the outer edge of sth: *They saw the huge building outlined against the sky.*
■ noun **1** a description of the main facts or points involved in sth: *This is a brief outline of the events.* ◇ *You should draw up a plan or outline for the essay.* ◇ *The book describes* in outline *the main findings of the research.* ◇ *an outline agreement/proposal* **2** the line that goes around the edge of sth, showing its main shape but not the details: *At last we could see the dim outline of an island.* ◇ *an outline map/sketch* ◇ *She drew the figures* in outline.

out·live /ˌaʊtˈlɪv/ verb [VN] **1** to live longer than sb: *He outlived his wife by three years.* **2** to continue to exist after sth else has ended or disappeared: *The machine had* outlived its usefulness (= was no longer useful).

out·look /ˈaʊtlʊk/ noun **1** ~ (on sth) the attitude to life and the world of a particular person, group or culture: *He had a practical outlook on life.* ◇ *Most western societies are liberal in outlook.* **2** [usually sing.] ~ (for sth) the probable future for sb/sth; what is likely to happen: *The outlook for jobs is bleak.* ◇ *the country's economic outlook* ◇ *The outlook* (= the probable weather) *for the weekend is dry and sunny.* **3** a view from a particular place: *The house has a pleasant outlook over the valley.*

out·ly·ing /ˈaʊtlaɪɪŋ/ adj. [only before noun] far away from the cities of a country or from the main part of a place: *outlying areas/islands/farms*

out·man·oeuvre (*BrE*) (*AmE* **out·ma·neu·ver**) /ˌaʊtməˈnuːvə(r)/ verb [VN] (*written*) to do better than an opponent by acting in a way that is cleverer or more skilful: *The president has so far managed to outmanoeuvre his critics.*

out·moded /ˌaʊtˈməʊdɪd; *AmE* -ˈmoʊd-/ adj. (*disapproving*) no longer fashionable or useful: *an outmoded attitude* ◇ *This organizational structure was now outmoded.*

out·num·ber /ˌaʊtˈnʌmbə(r)/ verb [VN] to be greater in number than sb/sth: *The demonstrators were heavily outnumbered by the police.* ◇ *In this profession, women outnumber men by two to one* (= there are twice as many women as men).

out of 'date adj. **1** old-fashioned or without the most recent information and therefore no longer useful: *These figures are very out of date.* ◇ *Suddenly she felt old and out of date.* ◇ *an out-of-date technology*—compare OUTDATED **2** no longer valid: *an out-of-date driving licence*—see also UP TO DATE

out-of-'state adj. [only before noun] (*AmE*) coming from or happening in a different state: *out-of-state license plates*

out-of-'town adj. [only before noun] **1** situated away from the centre of a town or city: *out-of-town superstores/sites* **2** coming from or happening in a different place: *an out-of-town guest* ◇ *an out-of-town performance*

out-of-'work adj. [only before noun] unemployed: *an out-of-work actor*

out·pace /ˌaʊtˈpeɪs/ verb [VN] (*written*) to go, rise, improve, etc. faster than sb/sth SYN OUTSTRIP: *He easily* outpaced *the other runners.* ◇ *Demand is outpacing production.*

out·pa·tient /ˈaʊtpeɪʃnt/ noun a person who goes to a hospital for treatment but does not stay there: *an outpatient clinic/department*—compare INPATIENT

out·per·form /ˌaʊtpəˈfɔːm; *AmE* -pərˈfɔːrm/ verb [VN] to achieve better results than sb/sth: *The company has consistently outperformed its larger rivals.* ▶ **out·per·form·ance** noun [U]

out·place·ment /ˈaʊtpleɪsmənt/ noun [U] (*business*) the process of helping people to find new jobs after they have been made unemployed

out·play /ˌaʊtˈpleɪ/ verb [VN] to play much better than a competitor: *We were totally outplayed and lost 106–74.*

out·point /ˌaʊtˈpɔɪnt/ verb [VN] (especially in boxing) to defeat sb by scoring more points

out·post /ˈaʊtpəʊst; *AmE* -poʊst/ noun **1** a small military camp away from the main army, used for watching an enemy's movements, etc. **2** a small town or group of buildings in a lonely part of a country: *a lonely/remote outpost* ◇ *the last outpost of civilization*

out·pour·ing /ˈaʊtpɔːrɪŋ/ noun **1** [usually pl.] a strong and sudden expression of feeling: *spontaneous outpourings of praise* **2** a large amount of sth produced in a short time: *a remarkable outpouring of new ideas*

out·put /ˈaʊtpʊt/ noun, verb
■ noun [U, sing.] **1** the amount of sth that a person, a machine or an organization produces: *Manufacturing output has increased by 8%.* **2** (*computing*) the information, results, etc. produced by a computer: *data output* ◇ *an output device*—compare INPUT **3** the power, energy, etc. produced by a piece of equipment: *an output of 100 watts* **4** a place where energy, power, information, etc. leaves a system: *Connect a cable to the output.*
■ verb (**out·put·ting**, **out·put**, **out·put**) [VN] (*computing*) to supply or produce information, results, etc: *Computers can now output data much more quickly.*—compare INPUT

out·rage /ˈaʊtreɪdʒ/ noun, verb
■ noun [U] **1** a strong feeling of shock and anger: *The judge's remarks caused public outrage.* ◇ *She was filled with an overwhelming sense of outrage.* ◇ *Environmentalists have expressed outrage at the ruling.* **2** [C] an act or event that is violent, cruel or very wrong and that shocks people or makes them very angry: *No one has yet claimed responsibility for this latest bomb outrage.*
■ verb [VN] [often passive] to make sb very shocked and angry: *He was outraged at the way he had been treated.*

out·ra·geous /aʊtˈreɪdʒəs/ adj. **1** very shocking and unacceptable: *outrageous behaviour* ◇ *'That's outrageous!'* *he protested.* **2** very unusual and slightly shocking: *She says the most outrageous things sometimes.* ◇ *outrageous clothes* ▶ **out·ra·geous·ly** adv.: *an outrageously expensive meal* ◇ *They behaved outrageously.*

out·rank /ˌaʊtˈræŋk/ verb [VN] to be of higher rank, quality, etc. than sb: *Colonel Jones outranks everyone here.*

outré /ˈuːtreɪ; *AmE* uːˈtreɪ/ adj. (from *French*, *written*) very unusual and slightly shocking

out·reach /ˈaʊtriːtʃ/ noun [U] the activity of an organization that provides a service or advice to people in the community, especially those who cannot or are unlikely to come to an office, a hospital, etc. for help: *an outreach and education programme* ◇ *outreach workers* ◇ *efforts to expand the outreach to black voters*

out·rider /ˈaʊtraɪdə(r)/ noun a person who rides a motorcycle or a horse in front of or beside the vehicle of an important person in order to give protection

out·rig·ger /ˈaʊtrɪgə(r)/ noun a wooden structure that is fixed to the side of a boat or ship in order to keep it steady in the water; a boat fitted with such a structure

out·right /ˈaʊtraɪt/ adj., adv.
■ adj. [only before noun] **1** complete and total: *an outright ban/rejection/victory* ◇ *She was the outright winner.* ◇ *No one party is expected to gain an outright majority.* **2** open and direct: *There was outright opposition to the plan.*
■ adv. **1** in a direct way and without trying to hide anything: *Why don't you ask him outright if it's true?* ◇ *She*

s	t	v	z	ʃ	ʒ	tʃ	dʒ	θ	ð	ŋ
see	tea	van	zoo	shoe	vision	chain	jam	thin	this	sing

couldn't help herself and she laughed outright. **2** clearly and completely: *Neither candidate won outright.* ◊ *The group rejects outright any negotiations with the government.* **3** not gradually; immediately: *Most of the crash victims were **killed outright**.* ◊ *We had saved enough money to buy the house outright.*

out·run /ˌaʊtˈrʌn/ *verb* (**out·run·ning**, **out·ran** /-ˈræn/ **out·run**) [VN] (*written*) **1** to run faster or further than sb/sth: *He couldn't outrun his pursuers.* **2** to develop faster than sth: *Demand for the new model is outrunning supply.*

out·sell /ˌaʊtˈsel/ *verb* (**out·sold**, **out·sold** /-ˈsəʊld/ *AmE* -ˈsoʊld/) [VN] to sell more or to be sold in larger quantities than sb/sth: *We are now outselling all our competitors.* ◊ *This year the newspaper has outsold its main rival.*

out·set /ˈaʊtset/ *noun* IDM **at/from the ˈoutset (of sth)** at/from the beginning of sth: *I made it clear right from the outset that I disapproved.*

out·shine /ˌaʊtˈʃaɪn/ *verb* (**out·shone**, **out·shone** /-ˈʃɒn/ *AmE* -ˈʃoʊn/) [VN] (*written*) to be more impressive than sb/sth; to be better than sb/sth: *He far outshone the rest of the class.*

out·side *noun, adj., prep., adv.*
■ *noun* /ˌaʊtˈsaɪd/ **1** (usually **the outside**) [C, usually sing.] the outer side or surface of sth: *The outside of the house needs painting.* ◊ *You can't open the door from the outside.* **2** [sing.] the area that is near or around a building, etc: *I walked around the outside of the building.* ◊ *I didn't go into the church—I only saw it from the outside.* **3** [sing.] the part of a road nearest to the middle: *Always overtake **on the outside**.* **4** [sing.] the part of a curving road or track furthest from the inner or shorter side of the curve OPP THE INSIDE IDM **at the outside** at the most; as a MAXIMUM: *There was room for 20 people at the outside.* **on the outside 1** used to describe how sb appears or seems: *On the outside she seems calm, but I know she's worried.* **2** not in prison: *Life on the outside took some getting used to again.*
■ *adj.* /ˈaʊtsaɪd/ [only before noun] **1** of, on or facing the outer side SYN EXTERNAL: *The outside walls are damp.* **2** not situated in the main building; going out of the main building SYN EXTERNAL: *an outside toilet* ◊ *You have to pay to make outside calls.* ◊ *I can't get an outside line.* **3** not included in or connected with your group, organization, country, etc: *We plan to use an outside firm of consultants.* ◊ *She has a lot of **outside interests** (= not connected with her work).* ◊ *They felt cut off from the **outside world** (= from other people and from other things that were happening).* **4** used to say that sth is very unlikely: *They have only an **outside chance** of winning.* ◊ *150 is an outside estimate (= it is very likely to be less).*
■ *prep.* /ˌaʊtˈsaɪd/ (also **out·side of** especially in *AmE*) **1** on or to a place on the outside of sth: *You can park your car outside our house.* OPP INSIDE **2** away from or not in a particular place: *It's the biggest theme park outside the United States.* ◊ *We live in a small village **just outside** Leeds.* **3** not part of sth: *The matter is outside my area of responsibility.* ◊ *You may do as you wish outside working hours.* OPP WITHIN **4** (**outside of**) apart from: *There was nothing they could do, outside of hoping things would get better.*
■ *adv.* /ˌaʊtˈsaɪd/ **1** not in a room, building or container but on or to the outside of it: *I'm seeing a patient—please wait outside.* ◊ *The house is painted green outside.* **2** not inside a building: *It's warm enough to eat outside.* ◊ *Go outside and see if it's raining.* OPP INSIDE

ˌoutside ˈbroadcast *noun* (*BrE*) a programme filmed or recorded away from the main STUDIO

out·sider /ˌaʊtˈsaɪdə(r)/ *noun* **1** a person who is not accepted as a member of a society, group, etc: *Here she felt she would always be an outsider.* **2** a person who is not part of a particular organization or profession: *They have decided to hire outsiders for some of the key positions.* ◊ *To an outsider it may appear to be a glamorous job.* **3** a person or an animal taking part in a race or competition that is not expected to win: *The race was won by a 20–1*

outsider. ◊ *To everyone's surprise, the post went to **a rank outsider** (= a complete outsider).*

out·size /ˈaʊtsaɪz/ (also **out·sized** /ˈaʊtsaɪzd/) *adj.* [usually before noun] **1** larger than the usual size: *an outsize desk* **2** designed for large people: *outsize clothes*

out·skirts /ˈaʊtskɜːts; *AmE* -skɜːrts/ *noun* [pl.] the parts of a town or city that are furthest from the centre: *They live **on the outskirts** of Milan.*

out·smart /ˌaʊtˈsmɑːt; *AmE* -ˈsmɑːrt/ *verb* [VN] to gain an advantage over sb by acting in a clever way SYN OUTWIT: *She always managed to outsmart her political rivals.*

out·source /ˈaʊtsɔːs; *AmE* -sɔːrs/ *verb* (*business*) to arrange for a company to do work or provide goods for that company: [VN] *We outsource all our computing work.* [also V] ▸ **out·sourc·ing** *noun* [U]

out·spoken /aʊtˈspəʊkən; *AmE* -ˈspoʊkən/ *adj.* ~ (**in sth**) saying exactly what you think, even if this shocks or offends people: *an outspoken opponent of the leadership* ◊ *outspoken comments/views* ◊ *She was outspoken in her criticism of the plan.* ▸ **out·spoken·ly** *adv.* **out·spoken·ness** *noun* [U]

out·spread /ˌaʊtˈspred/ *adj.* (*written*) spread out completely: *The bird soared high, with outspread wings.*

out·stand·ing /aʊtˈstændɪŋ/ *adj.* **1** extremely good; excellent: *an outstanding player/achievement/success* ◊ *an area of outstanding natural beauty* **2** [usually before noun] very obvious or important: *the outstanding features of the landscape* **3** (of payment, work, problems, etc.) not yet paid, done, solved, etc: *She has outstanding debts of over £500.* ◊ *A lot of work is still outstanding.*

out·stand·ing·ly /aʊtˈstændɪŋli/ *adv.* **1** used to emphasize the good quality of sth: *outstandingly successful* **2** extremely well: *He performed well but not outstandingly.*

out·stay /ˌaʊtˈsteɪ/ *verb* [VN] IDM see WELCOME *n.*

out·stretched /ˌaʊtˈstretʃt/ *adj.* (of parts of the body) stretched or spread out as far as possible: *He ran towards her with arms outstretched/with outstretched arms.*

out·strip /ˌaʊtˈstrɪp/ *verb* (**-pp-**) [VN] **1** to become larger, more important, etc. than sb/sth: *Demand is outstripping supply.* **2** to be faster, better or more successful than a competitor SYN SURPASS: *Their latest computer outstrips all its rivals.* **3** to run faster than sb in a race so that you pass them: *She soon outstripped the slower runners.*

ˈout·take *noun* a piece of a film that is removed before the film/movie is shown, for example because it contains a mistake

ˈout tray *noun* (in an office) a container on your desk for letters or documents that are waiting to be sent out or passed to sb else—compare IN TRAY

out·vote /ˌaʊtˈvəʊt; *AmE* -ˈvoʊt/ *verb* [VN] [usually passive] to defeat sb/sth by winning a larger number of votes SYN VOTE SB/STH DOWN: *Britain was heavily outvoted on the issue.* ◊ *His proposal was outvoted by 10 votes to 8.*

out·ward /ˈaʊtwəd; *AmE* -wərd/ *adj.* [only before noun] **1** connected with the way people or things seem to be rather than with what is actually true: *Mark showed no outward signs of distress.* ◊ *She simply observes the outward forms of religion.* ◊ ***To all outward appearances** (= as far as it was possible to judge from the outside) they were perfectly happy.* OPP INWARD **2** going away from a particular place, especially one that you are going to return to: *the outward voyage/journey* **3** away from the centre or a particular point: *outward pressure/movement* ◊ *outward investment* (= in other countries) ◊ *Managers need to become more **outward-looking** (= more open to new ideas).* OPP INWARD

ˌoutward ˈbound *adj.* going away from home or a particular place

out·ward·ly /ˈaʊtwədli; *AmE* -wərd-/ *adv.* on the surface; in appearance: *Though badly frightened, she remained outwardly composed.* ◊ *Outwardly, the couple seemed perfectly happy.* OPP INWARDLY

out·wards /ˈaʊtwədz; *AmE* -wərdz/ (*BrE*) (also **out·ward** *AmE, BrE*) *adv.* ~ (**from sth**) towards the outside; away

O

æ	ɑː	e	ɜː	ə	ɪ	iː	i	ɒ	ɔː	ʌ	ʊ	u	uː
cat	father	ten	bird	about	sit	see	many	got	saw	cup	put	actual	too
									(BrE)				

from the centre or from a particular point: *The door opens outwards.* ◇ *Factories were spreading outwards from the old heart of the town.* OPP INWARD

out·weigh /ˌaʊtˈweɪ/ *verb* [VN] to be greater or more important than sth: *The advantages far outweigh the disadvantages.*

out·wit /ˌaʊtˈwɪt/ *verb* (-tt-) [VN] to defeat sb/sth or gain an advantage over them by doing sth clever SYN OUT-SMART: *the amusing story of a bird outwitting a cat* ◇ *Somehow he always manages to outwit his opponents.*

out·with /ˌaʊtˈwɪθ/ *prep.* (*ScotE*) outside of sth; not within sth

out·work /ˈaʊtwɜːk; *AmE* -ˈwɜːrk/ *noun* (*BrE, business*) work that is done by people at home ▸ **out·work·er** *noun*

out·worn /ˌaʊtˈwɔːn; *AmE* -ˈwɔːrn/ *adj.* [usually before noun] (*rare, written*) old-fashioned and no longer useful: *outworn institutions*—compare WORN OUT

ouzo /ˈuːzəʊ; *AmE* ˈuːzoʊ/ *noun* [U] a strong alcoholic drink from Greece, made from ANISEED and usually drunk with water

ova *pl.* of OVUM

oval /ˈəʊvl; *AmE* ˈoʊvl/ *adj.* shaped like an egg: *an oval face/window* ▸ **oval** *noun*

ovals

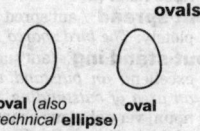

oval (*also technical* **ellipse**)   oval

ovary /ˈəʊvəri; *AmE* ˈoʊ-/ *noun* (*pl.* **-ies**) **1** either of the two organs in a woman's body that produce eggs; a similar organ in female animals, birds and fish **2** (*technical*) the part of a plant that produces seeds ▸ **ovar·ian** /əʊˈveəriən; *AmE* oʊˈver-/ *adj.* [only before noun]: *ovarian cancer*

ova·tion /əʊˈveɪʃn; *AmE* oʊ-/ *noun* enthusiastic CLAPPING by an audience as a sign of their approval: *to give sb a huge/rapturous/rousing ovation* ◇ *The soloist got a ten-minute* **standing ovation** (= in which people stand up from their seats).

oven /ˈʌvn/ *noun* the part of a cooker/stove shaped like a box with a door on the front, in which food is cooked or heated: *Take the cake out of the oven.* ◇ *a gas/an electric oven* ◇ *a cool/hot/moderate oven* ◇ (*spoken*) *Open a window, it's* **like an oven** *in here!*—picture on page 274—compare MICROWAVE IDM see BUN

'oven glove (*also* **'oven mitt**) *noun* a glove made of thick material, used for holding hot dishes from an oven—picture on page 275

oven·proof /ˈʌvnpruːf/ *adj.* suitable for use in a hot oven: *an ovenproof dish*

oven-'ready *adj.* [usually before noun] (of food) bought already prepared and ready for cooking: *an oven-ready turkey*

over /ˈəʊvə(r); *AmE* ˈoʊ-/ *adv., prep., noun*

■ *adv.* HELP For the special uses of **over** in phrasal verbs, look at the entries for the verbs. For example **take sth over** is in the phrasal verb section at **take**. **1** downwards and outwards from an upright position: *Try not to knock that vase over.* ◇ *The wind must have blown it over.* **2** from one side to another side: *She turned over onto her front.* ◇ *The car skidded off the road and rolled over and over.* **3** across a street, an open space, etc: *I stopped and crossed over.* ◇ *He rowed us over to the other side of the lake.* ◇ *They have gone over to France.* ◇ *This is my aunt who's over from Canada.* ◇ *I went over* (= across the room) *and asked her name.* ◇ *Let's ask some friends over* (= to our home). ◇ *Put it down* **over there**. **4** so as to cover sb/sth completely: *The lake was frozen over.* ◇ *Cover her over with a blanket.* **5** above; more: *children of 14 and over* ◇ *You get an A grade for scores of 75 and over.* **6** remaining; not used or needed: *If there's any food left over, put it in the fridge.* **7** again: *He repeated it several times over until he could remember it.* ◇ (*AmE*) *It's all wrong—you'll have to do it over.* **8** ended: *By the time we arrived the meeting was over.* ◇ *Thank goodness that's over!* ◇ *I was glad when it was* **over and done with**. **9** used to talk about sb/sth changing position: *He's gone over to the enemy* (= joined them). ◇ *Please change the wheels over* (= for example, put the front wheels at the back). ◇ *Hand over the money!*

10 used when communicating by radio: *Message received. Over* (= it is your turn to speak). ◇ *Message understood.* **Over and out**. IDM **(all) over a'gain** a second time from the beginning: *He did the work so badly that I had to do it all over again myself.* **over against sth** in contrast with sth ˌover and ˈover (a'gain) many times; repeatedly: *I've told you over and over again not to do that.* ˌover to 'you used to say that it is sb's turn to do sth

■ *prep.* HELP For the special uses of **over** in phrasal verbs, look at the entries for the verbs. For example **get over sth** is in the phrasal verb section at **get**. **1** resting on the surface of sb/sth and partly or completely covering them/it: *She put a blanket over the sleeping child.* ◇ *He wore an overcoat over his suit.* ◇ *She put her hand over her mouth to stop herself from screaming.* **2** in or to a position higher than but not touching sb/sth; above sb/sth: *They held a large umbrella over her.* ◇ *The balcony juts out over the street.* ◇ *There was a lamp hanging over the table.* **3** from one side of sth to the other; across sth: *a bridge over the river* ◇ *They ran over the grass.* ◇ *They had a wonderful view over the park.* **4** on the far or opposite side of sth: *He lives over the road.* **5** so as to cross sth and be on the other side: *She climbed over the wall.* **6** falling from or down from a place: *The car had toppled over the cliff.* ◇ *He didn't dare look over the edge.* **7** (all) **~** in or on all or most parts of sth: *Snow is falling all over the country.* ◇ *They've travelled all over the world.* ◇ *There were papers lying around all over the place.* **8** more than a particular time, amount, cost, etc: *over 3 million copies sold* ◇ *She stayed in Lagos for over a month.* ◇ *He's over sixty.* **9** used to show that sb has control or authority: *She has only the director over her.* ◇ *He ruled over a great empire.* ◇ *She has editorial control over what is included.* **10** during sth: *We'll discuss it over lunch.* ◇ *Over the next few days they got to know the town well.* ◇ *We're away over* (= until after) *the New Year.* **11** past a particular difficult stage or situation: *We're over the worst of the recession.* ◇ *It took her ages to get over her illness.* **12** because of or concerning sth; about sth: *an argument over money* ◇ *a disagreement over the best way to proceed* **13** using sth; by means of sth: *We heard it over the radio.* ◇ *She wouldn't tell me over the phone.* **14** louder than sth: *I couldn't hear what he said over the noise of the traffic.* ⇨ note at ABOVE IDM ˌover and a'bove in addition to sth: *There are other factors over and above those we have discussed.*

■ *noun* (in cricket) a series of six balls BOWLED by the same person

over- /ˈəʊvə(r); *AmE* ˈoʊ-/ *prefix* (in nouns, verbs, adjectives and adverbs) **1** more than usual; too much: *overproduction* ◇ *overload* ◇ *over-optimistic* ◇ *overconfident* ◇ *overanxious* **2** completely: *overjoyed* **3** upper; outer; extra: *overcoat* ◇ *overtime* ◇ *over* **4** over; above: *overcast* ◇ *overhang*

over·all *adj., adv., noun*

■ *adj.* /ˌəʊvərˈɔːl; *AmE* ˌoʊ-/ [only before noun] including all the things or people that are involved in a particular situation; general: *the person with overall responsibility for the project* ◇ *There will be winners in each of three age groups, and one overall winner.* ◇ *an overall improvement in standards of living* (= affecting everyone) ◇ *When she finished painting, she stepped back to admire the overall effect.*

■ *adv.* /ˌəʊvərˈɔːl; *AmE* ˌoʊ-/ **1** including everything or everyone; in total: *The company will invest $1.6m overall in new equipment.* **2** generally; when you consider everything: *Overall, this is a very useful book.*

■ *noun* /ˈəʊvərɔːl; *AmE* ˈoʊ-/ **1** (*BrE*) [C] a loose coat worn over other clothes to protect them from dirt, etc: *The lab assistant was wearing a white overall.* **2** (**overalls**) (*BrE*) (*AmE* **cov·er·alls**) [pl.] a loose piece of clothing like a shirt and trousers/pants in one piece, made of heavy fabric and usually worn over other clothing by workers doing dirty work: *The mechanic was wearing a pair of blue overalls.*—compare BOILER SUIT **3** (**overalls**) [pl.] (*AmE*) = DUNGAREES

ˌoverall ma'jority *noun* [usually sing.] **1** more votes in an election or vote than all the other people or parties together **2** the difference between the number of members that the government has in a parliament and the number that all the other political parties have together: *The Conservatives had a huge 101-seat overall majority.*

over·arch·ing /ˌəʊvər'ɑːtʃɪŋ; *AmE* ˌoʊvər'ɑːrtʃɪŋ/ *adj.* [usually before noun] (*formal*) very important, because it includes or influences many things

over·arm /'əʊvərɑːm; *AmE* 'oʊvərɑːrm/ (*especially BrE*) (also **over·hand** especially in *AmE*) *adv.* if you throw a ball **overarm**, you throw it with your arm swung backwards and then lifted high above your shoulder ▶ **over·arm** (*especially BrE*) (also **over·hand** especially in *AmE*) *adj.*: *an overarm throw*—compare UNDERARM

over·awe /ˌəʊvər'ɔː; *AmE* ˌoʊ-/ *verb* [VN] [usually passive] to impress sb so much that they feel nervous or frightened: *The younger players were overawed by the occasion and played badly.*

over·bal·ance /ˌəʊvə'bæləns; *AmE* ˌoʊvər'b-/ *verb* (*especially BrE*) to lose your balance and fall; to make sb/sth lose their balance and fall: [V] *He overbalanced and fell into the water.* [also VN]

over·bear·ing /ˌəʊvə'beərɪŋ; *AmE* ˌoʊvər'ber-/ *adj.* (*disapproving*) trying to control other people in an unpleasant way SYN DOMINEERING: *an overbearing manner*

over·bite /'əʊvəbaɪt; *AmE* 'oʊvər-/ *noun* (*technical*) a condition in which a person or animal's upper jaw is too far forward in relation to their lower jaw

over·blown /ˌəʊvə'bləʊn; *AmE* ˌoʊvər'bloʊn/ *adj.* **1** that is made to seem larger, more impressive or more important than it really is SYN EXAGGERATED: *overblown ambitions/egos* **2** (of flowers) past the best, most beautiful stage

over·board /'əʊvəbɔːd; *AmE* 'oʊvərbɔːrd/ *adv.* over the side of a boat or a ship into the water: *to fall/jump overboard* ◊ *Huge waves washed him overboard.* **go 'overboard** (*informal*) to be too excited or enthusiastic about sth or about doing sth: *Don't go overboard on fitness.* **throw sb/sth 'overboard** to get rid of sb/sth that you think is useless

over·book /ˌəʊvə'bʊk; *AmE* ˌoʊvər'bʊk/ *verb* to sell more tickets on a plane or RESERVE more rooms in a hotel than there are places available: [VN] *The flight was heavily overbooked.* [also V] —compare DOUBLE-BOOK

over·bur·den /ˌəʊvə'bɜːdn; *AmE* ˌoʊvər'bɜːrdn/ *verb* [VN] [usually passive] **~ sb/sth (with sth)** to give sb/sth more work, worry, etc. than they can deal with

over·cap·acity /ˌəʊvəkə'pæsəti; *AmE* ˌoʊvərkə-/ *noun* [U, sing.] (*business*) the situation in which an industry or a factory cannot sell as much as it is designed to produce

over·cast /ˌəʊvə'kɑːst; *AmE* ˌoʊvər'kæst/ *adj.* covered with clouds; dull: *an overcast sky/day* ◊ *Today it will be dull and overcast.*

over·charge /ˌəʊvə'tʃɑːdʒ; *AmE* ˌoʊvər'tʃɑːrdʒ/ *verb* **~ (sb) (for sth)** to make sb pay too much for sth: [VN] *Make sure they don't overcharge you for the drinks.* ◊ *We were overcharged by £5.* [also V] OPP UNDERCHARGE

over·coat /'əʊvəkəʊt; *AmE* 'oʊvərkoʊt/ *noun* a long warm coat worn in cold weather—picture on page A5

over·come /ˌəʊvə'kʌm; *AmE* ˌoʊvər'kʌm/ *verb* (**overcame** /-'keɪm/ **over·come**) [VN] **1** to succeed in dealing with or controlling a problem that has been preventing you from achieving sth: *She overcame injury to win the Olympic gold medal.* ◊ *The two parties managed to overcome their differences on the issue.* **2** (*written*) to defeat sb: *In the final game Sweden easily overcame France.* **3** [usually passive] to be extremely strongly affected by sth: *Her parents were overcome with grief at the funeral.* ◊ *The dead woman had been overcome by smoke.*

over·com·pen·sate /ˌəʊvə'kɒmpenseɪt; *AmE* ˌoʊvər'kɑːm-/ *verb* [V] **~ (for sth) (by doing sth)** (*written*) to do too much when trying to correct a problem and so cause a different problem: *She overcompensated for her shyness by talking too much and laughing too loud.*

over·cook /ˌəʊvə'kʊk; *AmE* ˌoʊvər'kʊk/ *verb* [VN] to cook food for too long

over·crowd·ed /ˌəʊvə'kraʊdɪd; *AmE* ˌoʊvər'k-/ *adj.* (of a place) with too many people or things in it: *overcrowded cities/prisons* ◊ *Too many poor people are living in overcrowded conditions.*

over·crowd·ing /ˌəʊvə'kraʊdɪŋ; *AmE* ˌoʊvər'k-/ *noun* [U] the situation when there are too many people or things in one place: *overcrowding in prisons/prison overcrowding*

over·de·veloped /ˌəʊvədɪ'veləpt; *AmE* ˌoʊvərd-/ *adj.* that has grown too large: *overdeveloped muscles* ◊ *an overdeveloped sense of humour* ▶ **over·de·velop** *verb* [VN]

over·do /ˌəʊvə'duː; *AmE* ˌoʊvər'duː/ *verb* (**over·does** /-'dʌz/, **over·did** /-'dɪd/, **over·done** /-'dʌn/) [VN] **1** to do sth too much; to exaggerate sth: *She really overdid the sympathy* (= and so did not seem sincere). **2** to use too much of sth: *Don't overdo the salt in the food.* ◊ *Use illustrations where appropriate but don't overdo it.* **3** [usually passive] to cook sth for too long: *The fish was overdone and very dry.* IDM **over'do it/things** to work, study, etc. too hard or for too long: *He's been overdoing things recently.* ◊ *I overdid it in the gym and hurt my back.*

over·dose /'əʊvədəʊs; *AmE* 'oʊvərdoʊs/ *noun, verb*
■ *noun* too much of a drug taken at one time: *a drug/drugs overdose* ◊ *She took a massive overdose of sleeping pills.*
■ *verb* (also *informal* **OD**) [V] **~ (on sth)** to take too much of a drug at one time, so that it is dangerous: *He had overdosed on heroin.*

over·draft /'əʊvədrɑːft; *AmE* 'oʊvərdræft/ *noun* the amount of money that you owe to a bank when you have spent more money than is in your bank account; an arrangement that allows you to do this: *to run up/pay off an overdraft*

over·draw /ˌəʊvə'drɔː; *AmE* ˌoʊvər'drɔː/ *verb* (**over·drew** /-'druː/ **over·drawn** /-'drɔːn/) (*especially BrE*) to take out more money from a bank account than it contains: [VN] *Customers who overdraw their accounts will be charged a fee.* [also V]

over·drawn /ˌəʊvə'drɔːn; *AmE* ˌoʊvər'd-/ *adj.* **1** [not usually before noun] (of a person) having taken more money out of your bank account than you have in it: *I'm overdrawn by £100.* **2** (of a bank account) with more money taken out than was paid in or left in: *an overdrawn account* ◊ *Your account is £200 overdrawn.*

over·dressed /ˌəʊvə'drest; *AmE* ˌoʊvər'd-/ *adj.* (usually *disapproving*) wearing clothes that are too formal or too elegant for a particular occasion

over·drive /'əʊvədraɪv; *AmE* 'oʊvərd-/ *noun* [C, U] an extra high GEAR in a vehicle, that you use when you are driving at high speeds: *to be in overdrive* IDM **go into 'overdrive** to start being very active and working very hard: *As the wedding approached, the whole family went into overdrive.*

over·due /ˌəʊvə'djuː; *AmE* ˌoʊvər'duː/ *adj.* **1** not paid, done, returned, etc. by the required or expected time: *an overdue payment/library book* ◊ *The rent is now overdue.* ◊ *Her baby is two weeks overdue.* ◊ *This car is overdue for a service.* **2** that should have happened or been done before now: *overdue reforms* ◊ *A book like this is long overdue.*

over 'easy *adj.* (*AmE*) (of fried eggs) turned over when almost cooked and fried for a short time on the other side

over·eat /ˌəʊvər'iːt; *AmE* ˌoʊ-/ *verb* (**over·ate** /-'et; *AmE* -'eɪt/ **over·eaten** /-'iːtn/) [V] to eat more than you need or more than is healthy ▶ **over·eat·ing** *noun* [U]: *She went through periods of compulsive overeating.*

over 'egg *verb* IDM **over-egg the 'pudding** used to say that you think sb has done more than is necessary, or has added unnecessary details to make sth seem better or worse than it really is: *If you're telling lies, keep it simple—never over-egg the pudding.*

over·empha·sis /ˌəʊvər'emfəsɪs; *AmE* ˌoʊ-/ *noun* [U, sing.] **~ (on sth)** too much emphasis or importance: *an overemphasis on curing illness rather than preventing it* ▶ **over·empha·size, -ise** /ˌəʊvər'emfəsaɪz; *AmE* ˌoʊ-/ *verb*: [VN] *The importance of preparation cannot be overemphasized.*

over·esti·mate *verb, noun*
■ *verb* /ˌəʊvər'estɪmeɪt; *AmE* ˌoʊ-/ [VN] to estimate sth to be larger, better, more important, etc. than it really is: *They overestimated his ability when they promoted him.* ◊ *The importance of these findings **cannot be overestimated*** (=

b	d	f	g	h	k	l	m	n	p	r
bad	did	fall	get	hat	cat	leg	man	now	pen	red

is very great). OPP UNDERESTIMATE ► **over·esti·mation** noun [U, C]

■ noun /ˌəʊvər'estɪmət; AmE ˌoʊ-/ [usually sing.] an estimate about the size, cost, etc. of sth that is too high OPP UNDERESTIMATE

over·ex·cited /ˌəʊvərɪk'saɪtɪd; AmE ˌoʊ-/ adj. too excited and not behaving in a calm or sensible way: *Don't get the children overexcited just before bedtime.*

over·ex·pose /ˌəʊvərɪk'spəʊz; AmE ˌoʊvərɪk'spoʊz/ verb [VN] [usually passive] **1** to affect the quality of a photograph or film by allowing too much light to enter the camera OPP UNDEREXPOSE **2** to allow sb/sth to be seen too much on television, in the newspapers, etc. ► **over·exposure** /ˌəʊvərɪk'spəʊʒə(r); AmE ˌoʊvərɪk'spoʊ-/ noun [U]

over·ex·tend·ed /ˌəʊvərɪk'stendɪd; AmE ˌoʊ-/ adj. [not usually before noun] involved in more work or activities, or spending more money, than you can manage without problems ► **over·ex·tend** verb [VN] ~ **yourself**: *They should not overextend themselves on the mortgage.*

over·feed /ˌəʊvə'fiːd; AmE ˌoʊvər'fiːd/ verb (**over·fed**, **over·fed** /ˌəʊvə'fed; AmE ˌoʊvər'fed/) [VN] to give sb/sth too much food ► **over·fed** adj. OPP UNDERFED

over·fish·ing /ˌəʊvə'fɪʃɪŋ; AmE ˌoʊvər'f-/ noun [U] the process of taking so many fish from the sea, a river, etc. that the number of fish in it becomes very low

over·flow verb, noun
■ verb /ˌəʊvə'fləʊ; AmE ˌoʊvər'floʊ/ **1** ~ (**with sth**)| ~ **sth** to be so full that the contents go over the sides: [V] *Plates overflowed with party food.* ◊ *The bath is overflowing* ◊ (*figurative*) *Her heart overflowed with love.* ◊ [VN] *The river overflowed its banks.* **2** [V] ~ (**with sth**) (of a place) to have too many people in it: *The streets were overflowing with the crowds.* ◊ *The hospitals are filled to overflowing* (= with patients). **3** ~ (**into sth**) to spread beyond the limits of a place or container that is too full: [V] *The meeting overflowed into the street.* [also VN]
■ noun /ˈəʊvəfləʊ; AmE ˈoʊvərfloʊ/ **1** [U, sing.] a number of people or things that do not fit into the space available: *A new office block was built to accommodate the overflow of staff.* ◊ *an overflow car park* **2** [U, sing.] the action of liquid flowing out of a container that is already full; the liquid that flows out: *Stop the overflow from the cistern.* ◊ *an overflow of water from the lake* ◊ (*figurative*) *an overflow of powerful emotions* **3** (also **'overflow pipe**) [C] a pipe that allows extra liquid to escape **4** [C, usually sing.] (*computing*) a fault that happens because a number or data item (for example, the result of a calculation) is too large for the computer to represent it exactly

over·fly /ˌəʊvə'flaɪ; AmE ˌoʊvər'f-/ verb (**over·flies**, **over·fly·ing**, **over·flew**, /-'fluː/ **over·flown** /-'fləʊn; AmE -'floʊn/) to fly over a place: [VN] *We overflew the war zone, taking photographs.* ◊ [V] *the noise from overflying planes* ► **over·flight** noun

over·ground /ˈəʊvəɡraʊnd; AmE ˈoʊvərɡ-/ adv. (*BrE*) on or above the surface of the ground, rather than under it: *The new railway line will run overground.* ► **over·ground** adj.: *overground trains/routes*—compare UNDERGROUND

over·grown /ˌəʊvə'ɡrəʊn; AmE ˌoʊvər'ɡroʊn/ adj. **1** ~ (**with sth**) (of gardens, etc.) covered with plants that have been allowed to grow wild and have not been controlled: *an overgrown path* ◊ *The garden's completely overgrown with weeds.* **2** (often *disapproving*) that has grown too large: *an overgrown village* ◊ *They act like a pair of overgrown children* (= they are adults but they behave like children).

over·growth /ˈəʊvəɡrəʊθ; AmE ˈoʊvərɡroʊθ/ noun [U, sing.] (*technical*) too much growth of sth, especially sth that grows on or over sth else

over·hand /ˈəʊvəhænd; AmE ˈoʊvərh-/ adj., adv. (*especially AmE*) = OVERARM

over·hang verb, noun
■ verb /ˌəʊvə'hæŋ; AmE ˌoʊvər'h-/ (**over·hung**, **over·hung** /-'hʌŋ/) to stick out over and above sth else: [VN] *His fat belly overhung his belt.* ◊ [V] *The path was cool and dark with overhanging trees.*—picture at OVERLAP

■ noun /ˈəʊvəhæŋ; AmE ˈoʊvərh-/ **1** the part of sth that sticks out over and above sth else: *The roof has an overhang to protect the walls from the rain.* **2** the amount by which sth hangs over and above sth else **3** [usually sing.] (*especially AmE, business*) the state of being extra to what is required; the things that are extra: *attempts to reduce the overhang of unsold goods*

over·haul noun, verb
■ noun /ˈəʊvəhɔːl; AmE ˈoʊvərh-/ an examination of a machine or system, including doing repairs on it or making changes to it: *a complete/major overhaul* ◊ *A radical overhaul of the tax system is necessary.*
■ verb /ˌəʊvə'hɔːl; AmE ˌoʊvər'h-/ **1** to examine every part of a machine, system, etc. and make any necessary changes or repairs: *The engine has been completely overhauled.* **2** to come from behind a competitor and go past them SYN OVERTAKE: *He managed to overhaul the leader on the final lap.*

over·head adv., adj., noun
■ adv. /ˌəʊvə'hed; AmE ˌoʊvər'hed/ above your head; in the sky: *Planes flew overhead constantly.* ◊ *Thunder boomed in the sky overhead.*
■ adj. /ˈəʊvəhed; AmE ˈoʊvərhed/ **1** above your head; raised above the ground: *overhead power lines* **2** [only before noun] connected with the general costs of running a business or an organization, for example paying for rent or electricity: *overhead costs*
■ noun [U] (*especially AmE*) = OVERHEADS

overhead pro'jector noun (*abbr.* OHP) a piece of equipment that PROJECTS an image onto a wall or screen so that many people can see it

over·heads /ˈəʊvəhedz; AmE ˈoʊvərh-/ noun [pl.] (*especially BrE*) (also **over·head** [U] especially in *AmE*) regular costs that you have when you are running a business or an organization, such as rent, electricity, wages, etc.

over·hear /ˌəʊvə'hɪə(r); AmE ˌoʊvər'hɪr/ verb (**over·heard**, **over·heard** /-'hɜːd; AmE -'hɜːrd/) to hear, especially by accident, a conversation in which you are not involved: [VN] *We talked quietly so as not to be overheard.* ◊ *I overheard a conversation between two boys on the bus.* ◊ [VN-ing] *We overheard them arguing.* ◊ [VNinf] *I overheard him say he was going to France.*—compare EAVESDROP

over·heat /ˌəʊvə'hiːt; AmE ˌoʊvər'h-/ verb **1** to become or to make sth become too hot: *The engine is overheating.* ◊ [VN] *It's vital not to overheat the liquid.* **2** [V] (of a country's economy) to be too active, with rising prices ► **over·heat·ing** noun [U]

over·heated /ˌəʊvə'hiːtɪd; AmE ˌoʊvər'h-/ adj. **1** too hot: *Don't sleep in an overheated room.* **2** too interested or excited: *the figment of an overheated imagination* **3** (of a country's economy) too active in a way that may cause problems

over·joyed /ˌəʊvə'dʒɔɪd; AmE ˌoʊvər'dʒ-/ adj. [not before noun] ~ (**at sth/to do sth**)| ~ (**that ...**) extremely happy or pleased: *He was overjoyed at my success.* ◊ *We were overjoyed to hear their good news.* ◊ *She was overjoyed that her article had been published.*

over·kill /ˈəʊvəkɪl; AmE ˈoʊvərkɪl/ noun [U] (*disapproving*) too much of sth that reduces the effect it has: *There is a danger of overkill if you plan everything too carefully.*

over·land /ˈəʊvəlænd; AmE ˈoʊvərl-/ adj. across the land; by land, not by sea or by air: *an overland route* ► **over·land** adv.: *to travel overland*

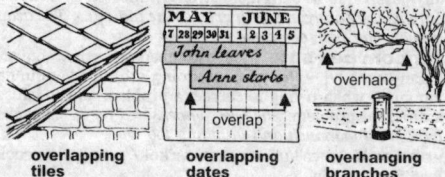

overlapping tiles   **overlapping dates**   **overhanging branches**

over·lap verb, noun
■ verb /ˌəʊvə'læp; AmE ˌoʊvər'læp/ (**-pp-**) **1** if one thing **overlaps** another, or the two things **overlap**, part of one thing covers part of the other: [VN] *A fish's scales overlap*

each other ◊ [V] *The floor was protected with overlapping sheets of newspaper.* **2** [VN] to make two or more things overlap: *You will need to overlap the pieces of wood slightly.* **3** [V, VN] if two events **overlap** or **overlap** each other, the second one starts before the first one has finished **4** ~ **(with sth)** to cover part of the same area of interest, knowledge, responsibility, etc: [V] *Our jobs overlap slightly, which sometimes causes difficulties.* ◊ *The language of science overlaps with that of everyday life.* [also VN]

■ *noun* /ˈəʊvəlæp; *AmE* ˈoʊvərlæp/ **1** [C, U] ~ **(between sth and sth)** a shared area of interest, knowledge, responsibility, etc: *There is (a) considerable overlap between the two subjects.* **2** [C, U] the amount by which one thing covers another thing: *an overlap of 5 cm on each roof tile* **3** [sing.] a period of time in which two events or activities happen together: *There will be an overlap of a week while John teaches Ann the job.*

over·lay *verb, noun*
■ *verb* /ˌəʊvəˈleɪ; *AmE* ˌoʊvərˈleɪ/ **(over·laid, over·laid** /-ˈleɪd/) [VN] [usually passive] ~ **(with sth) 1** *(technical)* to put sth on top of a surface so as to cover it completely; to lie on top of a surface: *wood overlaid with gold* **2** *(literary)* to add sth, especially a feeling or quality, to sth else so that it seems to cover it: *The place was overlaid with memories of his childhood.*
■ *noun* /ˈəʊvəleɪ; *AmE* ˈoʊvərleɪ/ **1** a transparent sheet with drawings, figures, etc. on it that can be placed on top of another sheet in order to change it: *An overlay showing population can be placed on top of the map.* **2** a thing that is laid on top of or covers sth else: *an overlay of fibreglass insulation*

over·leaf /ˌəʊvəˈliːf; *AmE* ˌoʊvərˈliːf/ *adv.* *(written)* on the other side of the page of a book, etc: *Complete the form overleaf.* ◊ *The changes are explained in detail overleaf.*

over·lie /ˌəʊvəˈlaɪ; *AmE* ˌoʊvərˈlaɪ/ *verb* **(over·ly·ing, over·lay** /-ˈleɪ/ **over·lain** /-ˈleɪn/) *(technical)* to lie over sth: [V] *overlying rock* [also VN]

over·load *verb, noun*
■ *verb* /ˌəʊvəˈləʊd; *AmE* ˌoʊvərˈloʊd/ [VN] [often passive] **1** to put too great a load on sth: *an overloaded truck* **2** ~ **sb (with sth)** to give sb too much of sth: *He's overloaded with responsibilities.* ◊ *Don't overload the students with information.* **3** to put too great a demand on a computer, an electrical system, etc. causing it to fail: *The lights went out because the system was overloaded.*
■ *noun* /ˈəʊvələʊd; *AmE* ˈoʊvərloʊd/ [U, sing.] too much of sth: *In these days of technological change we all suffer from information overload.*

over·long /ˌəʊvəˈlɒŋ; *AmE* ˌoʊvərˈlɔːŋ/ *adj.* *(BrE)* *(AmE* ˈoverly long**)** too long: *an overlong agenda*

over·look /ˌəʊvəˈlʊk; *AmE* ˌoʊvərˈlʊk/ *verb* [VN] **1** to fail to see or notice sth [SYN] MISS: *He seems to have overlooked one important fact.* **2** to see sth wrong or bad but decide to ignore it: *We could not afford to overlook such a serious offence.* **3** if a building, etc. **overlooks** a place, you can see that place from the building: *a restaurant overlooking the lake* ◊ *Our back yard is overlooked by several houses.* **4** ~ **sb (for sth)** to not consider sb for a job or position, even though they might be suitable: *She's been overlooked for promotion several times.*

over·lord /ˈəʊvəlɔːd; *AmE* ˈoʊvərlɔːrd/ *noun* (especially in the past) a person who has power over many other people: *feudal/imperial overlords*

over·ly /ˈəʊvəli; *AmE* ˈoʊvərli/ *adv.* (before an adjective) too; very: *I'm not overly fond of pasta.* ◊ *We think you are being overly optimistic.*

over·manned /ˌəʊvəˈmænd; *AmE* ˌoʊvərˈm-/ *adj.* (of a company, office, etc.) having more workers than are needed [SYN] OVERSTAFFED [OPP] UNDERMANNED ▶ **over·man·ning** /ˌəʊvəˈmænɪŋ; *AmE* ˌoʊvərˈm-/ *noun* [U]: *the problems of overmanning in industry*

over·much /ˌəʊvəˈmʌtʃ; *AmE* ˌoʊvərˈm-/ *adv.* *(BrE)* *(AmE* ˈoverly much**)** (especially with a negative verb) too much; very much: *She didn't worry overmuch about it.* ◊ *Details did not concern him overmuch.* ▶ **over·much** *adj.*

over·night *adv., adj.*

■ *adv.* /ˌəʊvəˈnaɪt; *AmE* ˌoʊvərˈn-/ **1** during or for the night: *We stayed overnight in London after the theatre.* **2** suddenly or quickly: *Don't expect it to improve overnight.*
■ *adj.* /ˈəʊvənaɪt; *AmE* ˈoʊvərn-/ [only before noun] **1** happening during the night; for a night: *an overnight flight* ◊ *overnight accommodation* ◊ *She took only an overnight bag* (= containing the things needed for a night spent away from home). **2** happening suddenly or quickly: *The play was an overnight success.*

over·pass /ˈəʊvəpɑːs; *AmE* ˈoʊvərpæs/ *noun* *(AmE)* = FLYOVER—compare UNDERPASS

over·pay /ˌəʊvəˈpeɪ; *AmE* ˌoʊvərˈpeɪ/ *verb* **(over·paid, over·paid** /-ˈpeɪd/) [VN] [usually passive] to pay sb too much; to pay sb more than their work is worth: *I think he's grossly overpaid for what he does.* [OPP] UNDERPAY ▶ **over·pay·ment** /-ˈpeɪmənt/ *noun* [C, U]

over·play /ˌəʊvəˈpleɪ; *AmE* ˌoʊvərˈp-/ *verb* [VN] to give too much importance to sth: *His role in the negotiations has been overplayed.* [OPP] UNDERPLAY [IDM] **overplay your ˈhand** to spoil your chance of success by judging your position to be stronger than it really is

over·popu·lated /ˌəʊvəˈpɒpjuleɪtɪd; *AmE* ˌoʊvərˈpɑːp-/ *adj.* (of a country or city) with too many people living in it ▶ **over·popu·la·tion** /ˌəʊvəˌpɒpjuˈleɪʃn; *AmE* ˌoʊvərˌpɑːp-/ *noun* [U]: *the problems of overpopulation*

over·power /ˌəʊvəˈpaʊə(r); *AmE* ˌoʊvərˈp-/ *verb* [VN] **1** to defeat or gain control over sb completely by using greater strength: *Police finally managed to overpower and arrest the gunman.* **2** to be so strong or great that it affects or disturbs sb/sth seriously: *Her beauty overpowered him.* ◊ *The flavour of the garlic overpowered the meat.*

over·power·ing /ˌəʊvəˈpaʊərɪŋ; *AmE* ˌoʊvərˈp-/ *adj.* very strong or powerful: *an overpowering smell of fish* ◊ *an overpowering personality* ◊ *The heat was overpowering.* ▶ **over·power·ing·ly** *adv.*

over·priced /ˌəʊvəˈpraɪst; *AmE* ˌoʊvərˈp-/ *adj.* too expensive; costing more than it is worth

over·print /ˌəʊvəˈprɪnt; *AmE* ˌoʊvərˈp-/ *verb* [VN] ~ **A (on B)** | ~ **B with A** to print sth on a document, etc. that already has printing on it

over·pro·tect·ive /ˌəʊvəprəˈtektɪv; *AmE* ˌoʊvərp-/ *adj.* too anxious to protect sb from being hurt, in a way that restricts their freedom: *overprotective parents*

over·quali·fied /ˌəʊvəˈkwɒlɪfaɪd; *AmE* ˌoʊvərˈkwɑːl-/ *adj.* having more experience or training than is necessary for a particular job, so that people do not want to employ you

over·rate /ˌəʊvəˈreɪt; *AmE* ˌoʊvərˈr-/ *verb* [VN] [usually passive] to have too high an opinion of sb/sth; to put too high a value on sb/sth: *In my opinion, Hirst's work has been vastly overrated.* [OPP] UNDERRATE

over·reach /ˌəʊvəˈriːtʃ; *AmE* ˌoʊvərˈr-/ *verb* ~ **(yourself)** to fail by trying to achieve more than is possible: [VN] *In making these promises, the company had clearly overreached itself.* [also V]

over·react /ˌəʊvəriˈækt; *AmE* ˌoʊ-/ *verb* [V] ~ **(to sth)** to react too strongly, especially to sth unpleasant: *The financial markets overreacted to the news.* ▶ **over·reac·tion** /-ˈækʃn/ *noun* [sing., U] ~ **(to sth)**

over·ride /ˌəʊvəˈraɪd; *AmE* ˌoʊvərˈr-/ *verb* **(over·rode** /-ˈrəʊd; *AmE* -ˈroʊd/ **over·rid·den** /-ˈrɪdn/) [VN] **1** to use your authority to reject sb's decision, order, etc. [SYN] OVERRULE: *The chairman overrode the committee's objections and signed the agreement.* **2** to be more important than sth: *Considerations of safety override all other concerns.* **3** to stop a process that happens automatically and control it yourself: *A special code is needed to override the time lock.*

over·rid·ing /ˌəʊvəˈraɪdɪŋ; *AmE* ˌoʊvərˈr-/ *adj.* [only before noun] more important than anything else in a particular situation: *the overriding factor/consideration/concern* ◊ *Their overriding aim was to keep costs low.* ◊ *Time was of overriding importance.*

over·rule /ˌəʊvəˈruːl; *AmE* ˌoʊvərˈr-/ *verb* [VN] [often passive] to change a decision or reject an idea from a position of greater power: *to overrule a decision/an objection* ◊ *The verdict was overruled by the Supreme Court.*

æ	ɑː	e	ɜː	ə	ɪ	iː	i	ɒ	ɔː	ʌ	ʊ	u	uː
cat	father	ten	bird	about	sit	see	many	got	saw	cup	put	actual	too

(BrE)

over·run /ˌəʊvəˈrʌn; *AmE* ˌoʊ-/ *verb* (**over·ran** /-ˈræn/ **over·run**) **1** [VN] [often passive] (especially of sth bad or not wanted) to fill or spread over an area quickly, especially in large numbers: *The house was completely overrun with mice.* ◇ *Enemy soldiers had overrun the island.* **2** to take more time or money than was intended: [V] *Her lectures never overrun.* ◇ [VN] *You've overrun your time by 10 minutes.* ▶ **over·run** /ˈəʊvərʌn; *AmE* ˈoʊ-/ *noun: a cost overrun*

over·seas /ˌəʊvəˈsiːz; *AmE* ˌoʊvərˈs-/ *adj., adv.*
■ *adj.* connected with foreign countries, especially those separated from your country by the sea or ocean: *overseas development/markets/trade* ◇ *overseas students/visitors*—compare HOME
■ *adv.* to or in a foreign country, especially those separated from your country by the sea or ocean [SYN] ABROAD: *to live/work/go overseas* ◇ *The product is sold both at home and overseas.*

over·see /ˌəʊvəˈsiː; *AmE* ˌoʊvərˈsiː/ *verb* (**over·saw** /-ˈsɔː/ **over·seen** /-ˈsiːn/) [VN] to watch sb/sth and make sure that a job or an activity is done correctly [SYN] SUPERVISE: *United Nations observers oversaw the elections.*

over·seer /ˈəʊvəsɪə(r); *AmE* ˈoʊvərsɪr/ *noun* **1** (*old-fashioned*) a person whose job is to make sure that other workers do their work **2** a person or an organization that is responsible for making sure that a system is working as it should

over·sell /ˌəʊvəˈsel; *AmE* ˌoʊvərˈsel/ *verb* (**over·sold**, **over·sold** /-ˈsəʊld; *AmE* ˌoʊvərˈsoʊld/) [VN] [often passive] **1** to say that sb/sth is better than they really are: *He has a tendency to oversell himself.* **2** (*business*) to sell too much or more of sth than is available: *The seats on the plane were oversold.*

over·sen·si·tive /ˌəʊvəˈsensɪtɪv; *AmE* ˌoʊvərˈs-/ *adj.* too easily upset or offended

over·sexed /ˌəʊvəˈsekst; *AmE* ˌoʊvərˈs-/ *adj.* having stronger sexual desire than is usual

over·shadow /ˌəʊvəˈʃædəʊ; *AmE* ˌoʊvərˈʃædoʊ/ *verb* [VN] [often passive] **1** to make sb/sth seem less important, or successful: *He had always been overshadowed by his elder sister.* **2** to make an event less enjoyable than it should be: *News of the accident overshadowed the day's events.* **3** to throw a shadow over sth: *The garden is overshadowed by tall trees.*

over·shoot /ˌəʊvəˈʃuːt; *AmE* ˌoʊvərˈʃ-/ *verb* (**over·shot**, **over·shot** /-ˈʃɒt; *AmE* -ˈʃɑːt/) **1** to go further than the place you intended to stop or turn: [VN] *The aircraft overshot the runway.* ◇ [V] *She had overshot by 20 metres.* **2** [VN] to do more or to spend more money than you originally planned: *The department may overshoot its cash limit this year.*

over·sight /ˈəʊvəsaɪt; *AmE* ˈoʊvərs-/ *noun* **1** [C, U] the fact of making a mistake because you forget to do sth or you do not notice sth: *I didn't mean to leave her name off the list; it was an oversight.* ◇ *You can never entirely eliminate human error and oversight.* **2** [U] (*formal*) the state of being in charge of sb/sth: *The committee has oversight of finance and general policy.*

over·sim·plify /ˌəʊvəˈsɪmplɪfaɪ; *AmE* ˌoʊvərˈs-/ *verb* (**over·sim·pli·fies**, **over·sim·pli·fy·ing**, **over·sim·pli·fied**, **over·sim·pli·fied**) to describe a situation, a problem, etc. in a way that is too simple and ignores some of the facts: [VN] *It's easy to oversimplify the issues involved.* ◇ *an oversimplified view of human nature* [also V] ▶ **over·sim·pli·fi·ca·tion** /ˌəʊvəˌsɪmplɪfɪˈkeɪʃn; *AmE* ˌoʊvərˌs-/ *noun* [C usually sing, U]: *This is a gross oversimplification of the facts.*—compare SIMPLIFICATION

over·sized /ˈəʊvəsaɪzd; *AmE* ˈoʊvərs-/ (also *less frequent* **over·size** /-saɪz/) *adj.* bigger than the normal size; too big

over·sleep /ˌəʊvəˈsliːp; *AmE* ˌoʊvərˈs-/ *verb* (**over·slept**, **over·slept** /-ˈslept/) [V] to sleep longer than you intended: *I overslept and missed the bus.*

over·spend /ˌəʊvəˈspend; *AmE* ˌoʊvərˈs-/ *verb* (**over·spent**, **over·spent** /-ˈspent/) ~ (**on sth**) to spend too much money or more than you planned: [V] *The company has overspent on marketing.* ◇ [VN] *Many departments have*

overspent their budgets this year. ▶ **over·spend** /ˈəʊvəspend; *AmE* ˈoʊvərs-/ *noun* [sing.] (*BrE*): *a £1 million overspend* **over·spent** /ˌəʊvəˈspent; *AmE* ˌoʊvərs-/ *adj.*: *The organization is heavily overspent.*

over·spill /ˈəʊvəspɪl; *AmE* ˈoʊvərs-/ *noun* [U, sing.] (*BrE*) people who move out of a city because it is too crowded to an area where there is more space: *New towns were designed to house London's overspill.*

over·staffed /ˌəʊvəˈstɑːft; *AmE* ˌoʊvərˈstæft/ *adj.* (of a company, office, etc.) having more workers than are needed [SYN] OVERMANNED [OPP] UNDERSTAFFED

over·state /ˌəʊvəˈsteɪt; *AmE* ˌoʊvərˈs-/ *verb* [VN] to say sth in a way that makes it seem more important than it really is [SYN] EXAGGERATE: *He tends to overstate his case when talking politics.* ◇ *The seriousness of the crime cannot be overstated.* [OPP] UNDERSTATE ▶ **over·state·ment** /ˈəʊvəsteɪtmənt; *AmE* ˈoʊvərs-/ *noun* [C, U]: *It is not an overstatement to say a crisis is imminent.*

over·stay /ˌəʊvəˈsteɪ; *AmE* ˌoʊvərˈs-/ *verb* [VN] to stay longer than the length of time you are expected or allowed to stay: *They overstayed their visa.* [IDM] see WELCOME *n.*

over·step /ˌəʊvəˈstep; *AmE* ˌoʊvərˈs-/ *verb* (**-pp-**) [VN] to go beyond what is normal or allowed: *to overstep your authority* ◇ *He tends to overstep the boundaries of good taste.* [IDM] **overstep the 'mark/'line** to behave in a way that people think is not acceptable

over·stock /ˌəʊvəˈstɒk; *AmE* ˌoʊvərˈstɑːk/ *verb* [VN, V] **1** to buy or make more of sth than you need or can sell **2** to put too many animals in a place where there is not enough room or food for them

over·stretch /ˌəʊvəˈstretʃ; *AmE* ˌoʊvərˈs-/ *verb* [VN] ~ **sb/sth/yourself** (*especially BrE*) to do more than you are capable of; to make sb/sth do more than they are capable of: *The prison service is badly overstretched.* ◇ *Credit cards can tempt you to overstretch yourself* (= spend more money than you can afford). ▶ **over·stretched** *adj.*: *overstretched muscles* ◇ *overstretched services*

over·sub·scribed /ˌəʊvəsəbˈskraɪbd; *AmE* ˌoʊvərs-/ *adj.* if an activity, service, etc. is **oversubscribed**, there are fewer places, tickets, etc. than the number of people who are asking for them

overt /əʊˈvɜːt; ˈəʊvɜːt; *AmE* oʊˈvɜːrt; ˈoʊvɜːrt/ *adj.* [usually before noun] (*formal*) done in an open way and not secretly: *There was little overt support for the project.*—compare COVERT ▶ **overt·ly** *adv.*: *overtly political activities*

over·take /ˌəʊvəˈteɪk; *AmE* ˌoʊvərˈt-/ *verb* (**over·took** /-ˈtʊk/ **over·taken** /-ˈteɪkən/) **1** (*especially BrE*) to go past a moving vehicle or person ahead of you because you are going faster than they are: [VN] *He pulled out to overtake a truck.* ◇ [V] *It's dangerous to overtake on a bend.* **2** [VN] to become greater in number, amount or importance than sth else: *In the next century, nuclear energy could overtake oil as the main fuel.* ◇ *We mustn't let ourselves be overtaken by our competitors.* **3** [VN] [often passive] if sth unpleasant **overtakes** a person, it unexpectedly starts to happen and to affect them: *The climbers were overtaken by bad weather.* ◇ *Sudden panic overtook her.* ◇ *Our original plan was overtaken by events* (= the situation changed very rapidly) *and we had to make a new one.*

over·tax /ˌəʊvəˈtæks; *AmE* ˌoʊvərˈt-/ *verb* [VN] ~ **sb/sth/yourself 1** to do more than you are able or want to do; to make sb/sth do more than they are able or want to do: *to overtax your strength/heart/voice* ◇ *Take it easy. Don't overtax yourself.* **2** to make a person or an organization pay too much tax

over-the-'counter *adj.* [only before noun] **1** (of drugs and medicines) that can be obtained without a PRESCRIPTION (= a written order from a doctor) **2** (*AmE, business*) (of stocks and shares) not appearing in an official STOCK EXCHANGE list

over·throw *verb, noun*
■ *verb* /ˌəʊvəˈθrəʊ; *AmE* ˌoʊvərˈθroʊ/ (**over·threw** /-ˈθruː/ **over·thrown** /-ˈθrəʊn; *AmE* -ˈθroʊn/) [VN] to remove a leader or a government from a position of power by force: *The president was overthrown in a military coup.*

aɪ	aʊ	eɪ	əʊ	oʊ	ɔɪ	ɪə	eə	ʊə	j	w
my	now	say	go	go	boy	near	hair	pure	yes	wet
			(BrE)	(AmE)						

■ *noun* /ˈəʊvəθrəʊ; *AmE* ˈoʊvərθroʊ/ [usually sing.] the act of taking power by force from a leader or government

over·time /ˈəʊvətaɪm; *AmE* ˈoʊvərt-/ *noun* [U] **1** time that you spend working at your job after you have worked the normal hours: *to do/work overtime* ◇ *overtime pay/earnings/hours* ◇ *The union announced a ban on overtime.* **2** the money sb earns for doing overtime: *They pay £58 a day plus overtime.* **3** (*AmE, sport*) = EXTRA TIME **IDM be working ˈovertime** (*informal*) to be very active or too active: *There was nothing to worry about. It was just her imagination working overtime.*

over·tired /ˌəʊvəˈtaɪəd; *AmE* ˌoʊvərˈtaɪərd/ *adj.* extremely tired, so that you become irritated easily

over·tone /ˈəʊvətəʊn; *AmE* ˈoʊvərtoʊn/ *noun* [usually pl.] an attitude or an emotion that is suggested and is not expressed in a direct way: *There were political overtones to the point he was making.*—compare UNDERTONE

over·ture /ˈəʊvətʃʊə(r), -tjʊə(r); *AmE* ˈoʊvərtʃər; -tʃʊr/ *noun* **1** a piece of music written as an introduction to an opera or a ballet: *Prokofiev's overture to 'Romeo and Juliet'* **2** [usually pl.] **~ (to sb)** a suggestion or an action by which sb tries to make friends, start a business relationship, have discussions, etc. with sb else: *He began making overtures to a number of merchant banks.*

over·turn /ˌəʊvəˈtɜːn; *AmE* ˌoʊvərˈtɜːrn/ *verb* **1** if sth **overturns**, or if sb **overturns** it, it turns upside down or on its side: [V] *The car skidded and overturned.* ◇ [VN] *He stood up quickly, overturning his chair.* **2** [VN] to officially decide that a legal decision etc. is not correct, and to make it no longer valid: *to overturn a decision/conviction/verdict* ◇ *His sentence was overturned by the appeal court.*

over·use /ˌəʊvəˈjuːz; *AmE* ˌoʊvərˈj-/ *verb* [VN] to use sth too much or too often: *'Nice' is a very overused word.* ▶ **over·use** /ˌəʊvəˈjuːs; *AmE* ˌoʊvərˈj-/ *noun* [U, sing.]

over·value /ˌəʊvəˈvæljuː; *AmE* ˌoʊvərˈv-/ *verb* [VN] [often passive] to put too high a value on sth: *Intelligence can be overvalued.* ◇ (*business*) *overvalued currencies/stocks*

over·view /ˈəʊvəvjuː; *AmE* ˈoʊvərv-/ *noun* a general description or an outline of sth

over·ween·ing /ˌəʊvəˈwiːnɪŋ; *AmE* ˌoʊvərˈw-/ *adj.* [only before noun] (*formal, disapproving*) showing too much confidence or pride

over·weight /ˌəʊvəˈweɪt; *AmE* ˌoʊvərˈw-/ *adj.* (of people) too heavy and fat: *She was only a few pounds overweight.* **OPP** UNDERWEIGHT

over·whelm /ˌəʊvəˈwelm; *AmE* ˌoʊvərˈw-/ *verb* [VN] [often passive] **1** to have such a strong emotional effect on sb that it is difficult for them to resist or know how to react: *She was overwhelmed by feelings of guilt.* ◇ *He felt completely overwhelmed by their kindness.* ◇ *The beauty of the landscape overwhelmed me.* **2** to defeat sb completely: *The army was overwhelmed by the rebels.* **3** to be so bad or so great that a person cannot deal with it; to give too much of a thing to a person: *We were overwhelmed by requests for information.* **4** (*literary*) (of water) to cover sb/sth completely **SYN** FLOOD

over·whelm·ing /ˌəʊvəˈwelmɪŋ; *AmE* ˌoʊvərˈw-/ *adj.* very great or very strong; so powerful that you cannot resist it or decide how to react: *The evidence against him was overwhelming.* ◇ *The overwhelming majority of those present were in favour of the plan.* ◇ *an overwhelming sense of loss/relief* ◇ *She had the almost overwhelming desire to tell him the truth.* ◇ *You may find it somewhat overwhelming at first.* ▶ **over·whelm·ing·ly** *adv.*: *They voted overwhelmingly against the proposal.*

over·winter /ˌəʊvəˈwɪntə(r); *AmE* ˌoʊvərˈw-/ *verb* [V, VN] (of animals, birds and plants) to spend the winter months in a place; to stay alive or to keep sth alive during the winter—compare WINTER

over·work /ˌəʊvəˈwɜːk; *AmE* ˌoʊvərˈwɜːrk/ *verb, noun*
■ *verb* to work too hard; to make a person or an animal work too hard: [V] *You look tired. Have you been overworking?* ◇ [VN] *The staff are grossly overworked.*
■ *noun* [U] the fact of working too hard: *His illness was brought on by money worries and overwork.*

over·worked /ˌəʊvəˈwɜːkt; *AmE* ˌoʊvərˈwɜːrkt/ *adj.*

1 made to work too hard or too much: *overworked nurses* **2** (of words or phrases) used too often so that the meaning or effect has become weaker

over·write /ˌəʊvəˈraɪt; *AmE* ˌoʊvərˈr-/ *verb* (**over·wrote** /-ˈrəʊt; *AmE* -ˈroʊt/ **over·writ·ten** /-ˈrɪtn/) [VN] (*computing*) to replace information on the screen or in a file by putting new information over it

over·wrought /ˌəʊvəˈrɔːt; *AmE* ˌoʊvərˈr-/ *adj.* very worried and upset; excited in a nervous way

ovoid /ˈəʊvɔɪd; *AmE* ˈoʊ-/ *adj.* (*formal*) shaped like an egg ▶ **ovoid** *noun*

ovu·late /ˈɒvjuleɪt; *AmE* ˈɑːv-/ *verb* [V] (of a woman or a female animal) to produce an egg (= called an OVUM), from the OVARY ▶ **ovu·la·tion** /ˌɒvjuˈleɪʃn; *AmE* ˌɑːv-/ *noun* [U]: *methods of predicting ovulation*

ovum /ˈəʊvəm; *AmE* ˈoʊ-/ *noun* (*pl.* **ova** /ˈəʊvə; *AmE* ˈoʊvə/) (*biology*) a female cell of an animal or a plant that can develop into a young animal or plant when FERTILIZED

ow /aʊ/ *exclamation* used to express sudden pain: *Ow! That hurt!*

owe /əʊ; *AmE* oʊ/ *verb* (not used in the progressive tenses) **1 ~ sth (to sb) (for sth)| ~ (sb) sth (for sth)** to have to pay sb for sth that you have already received or return money that you have borrowed: [VNN, VN] *She still owes her father £3000.* ◇ *She still owes £3000 to her father* ◇ [VN] *The country owes billions of dollars to foreign creditors.* ◇ [VNN] *How much do I owe you for the groceries?* ◇ (*figurative*) *I'm still owed three days' leave.* **2 ~ sth to sb| ~ sb sth** to feel that you ought to do sth for sb or give them sth, especially because they have done sth for you: [VN] *I owe a debt of gratitude to all my family.* ◇ *You owe it to your staff to be honest with them.* ◇ [VNN] *You owe me a favour!* ◇ *Thanks for sticking up for me—I owe you one* (= I owe you a favour). ◇ *I think you owe us an explanation.* ◇ *I think we're owed an apology.* **HELP** The passive is not used in this meaning except with a person as the subject: *An apology is owed to us.* **3 ~ sth to sb/sth| ~ sb sth** to exist or be successful because of the help or influence of sb/sth: [VN] *He owes his success to hard work.* ◇ *The play owes much to French tragedy.* ◇ [VN, VNN] *I owe everything to him.* ◇ *I owe him everything.* ◇ [VNN] *I knew that I owed the surgeon my life.* **4** [VN] **~ allegiance/loyalty/obedience (to sb)** (*formal*) to have to obey or be loyal to sb who is in a position of authority or power

owing /ˈəʊɪŋ; *AmE* ˈoʊɪŋ/ *adj.* [not before noun] (*BrE*) money that is **owing** has not been paid yet: *£100 is still owing on the loan.*

ˈowing to *prep.* because of: *The game was cancelled owing to torrential rain.*

owl /aʊl/ *noun* a BIRD OF PREY (= a bird that kills other creatures for food) with large round eyes, that hunts at night. Owls are traditionally thought to be wise: *a little/short-eared/snowy owl* ◇ *An owl hooted nearby.*—see also BARN OWL, NIGHT OWL, TAWNY OWL

owl·ish /ˈaʊlɪʃ/ *adj.* looking like an owl, especially because you are wearing round glasses, and therefore seeming serious and intelligent ▶ **owl·ish·ly** *adv.*: *She blinked at them owlishly.*

own /əʊn; *AmE* oʊn/ *adj., pron., verb*
■ *adj., pron.* **1** used to emphasize that sth belongs to or is connected with sb: *It was her own idea.* ◇ *I saw it with my own eyes* (= I didn't hear about it from somebody else). ◇ *Is the car your own?* ◇ *Your day off is your own* (= you can spend it as you wish). ◇ *Our children are grown up and have children of their own.* ◇ *For reasons of his own* (= particular reasons that perhaps only he knew about), *he refused to join the club.* ◇ *The accident happened through no fault of her own.* ◇ *He wants to come into the business on his own terms.* ◇ *I need a room of my own.* ◇ *I have my very own room at last.* **HELP** Own cannot be used after an article: *I need my own room.* ◇ *I need an own room.* ◇ *It's good to have your own room.* ◇ *It's good to have the own room.* **2** done or produced by and for yourself: *She makes all her own clothes.* ◇ *He has to cook his own meals.* **IDM come into your/its ˈown** to have the opportunity to show how good or useful you are or sth is: *When the*

traffic's this bad, a bicycle really comes into its own. **get your 'own back (on sb)** (*informal*) to do sth to sb in return for harm they have done to you; to get REVENGE: *I'll get my own back on him one day, I swear!* **hold your 'own (against sb/sth) (in sth)** to remain in a strong position when sb is attacking you, competing with you, etc: *Business isn't good but we're managing to hold our own.* ◇ *She can hold her own against anybody in an argument.* ◇ *The patient is holding her own although she is still very sick.* **(all) on your 'own 1** alone; without anyone else: *I'm all on my own today.* ◇ *She lives on her own.* **2** without help: *He did it on his own.*—more at MIND *n.*, SAKE¹, SOUND *n.*

■ *verb* (not used in the progressive tenses) **1** [VN] to have sth that belongs to you, especially because you have bought it: *Do you own your house or do you rent it?* ◇ *I don't own anything of any value.* ◇ *Most of the apartments are privately owned.* ◇ *an American owned company* **2 ~ to sth/to doing sth** (*old-fashioned*) to admit that sth is true: [V] *He owned to a feeling of guilt.* ◇ [V(that)] *She owned (that) she had been present.* **IDM** **,behave/,act as if you 'own the place | think you 'own the place** (*disapproving*) to behave in a very confident way that annoys other people, for example by telling them what to do **PHRV** **,own 'up (to sth/to doing sth)** to admit that you are responsible for sth bad or wrong **SYN** CONFESS: *I'm still waiting for someone to own up to the breakages.*

,own-'brand (also **,own-'label**) (both *BrE*) (*AmE* **'store-brand**) *adj.* used to describe goods that are marked with the name of the shop/store in which they are sold rather than with the name of the company that produced them

owner /'əʊnə(r); *AmE* 'oʊ-/ *noun* a person who owns sth: *a boat/dog/factory owner* ◇ *The painting has now been returned to its rightful owner.* ◇ *He's now the proud owner of a cottage in Wales.*—see also HOMEOWNER, LANDOWNER

,owner-'occupied *adj.* (of a house, etc.) lived in by the owner rather than rented to sb else

,owner-'occupier *noun* a person who owns the house, flat/apartment, etc. that they live in

own·er·ship /'əʊnəʃɪp; *AmE* 'oʊnərʃɪp/ *noun* [U] the fact of owning sth: *a growth in home ownership* ◇ *Ownership of the land is currently being disputed.* ◇ *to be in joint/private/public ownership* ◇ *The restaurant is under new ownership.*

,own 'goal *noun* [usually sing.] (*BrE*) **1** (in football and some other sports) a goal that is scored by mistake by a player against his or her own team **2** something that you do that achieves the opposite of what you wanted and that brings you a disadvantage

,own-'label *adj.* (*BrE*) = OWN-BRAND

ox /ɒks; *AmE* ɑːks/ *noun* (*pl.* **oxen** /'ɒksn; *AmE* 'ɑːksn/) **1** a BULL (= a male cow) that has been CASTRATED (= had part of its sex organs removed), used, especially in the past, for pulling farm equipment, etc.—compare BULLOCK,

STEER **2** (*old-fashioned*) any cow or BULL on a farm—see also CATTLE

Ox·bridge /'ɒksbrɪdʒ; *AmE* 'ɑːks-/ *noun* [U] the universities of Oxford and Cambridge, when they are thought of together: *an Oxbridge education/graduate*—compare IVY LEAGUE, RED-BRICK

ox·ford /'ɒksfəd; *AmE* 'ɑːksfərd/ *noun* **1** (**oxfords**) [pl.] (*especially AmE*) leather shoes that fasten with LACES—picture at SHOE **2** [U] (*AmE*) a thick cotton fabric: *an oxford shirt*

oxide /'ɒksaɪd; *AmE* 'ɑːk-/ *noun* [U, C] (*chemistry*) a compound of OXYGEN and another chemical element: *iron oxide* ◇ *an oxide of tin*

oxi·dize (*BrE* also **-ise**) /'ɒksɪdaɪz; *AmE* 'ɑːk-/ *verb* [VN] (*technical*) to combine or to make sth combine with OXYGEN, especially when this causes metal to become covered with RUST ► **oxi·diza·tion, -isa·tion** /,ɒksɪdaɪ'zeɪʃn; *AmE* ,ɑːksɪdɪ'z-/ (also **oxi·da·tion** /,ɒksɪ'deɪʃn; *AmE* ,ɑːk-/) *noun* [U]

Oxon /'ɒksɒn; *AmE* 'ɑːksɑːn/ *abbr.* (used after degree titles) of Oxford University: *Alice Tolley MA (Oxon)*

ox·tail /'ɒksteɪl; *AmE* 'ɑːks-/ *noun* [U, C] meat from the tail of a cow, used especially for making soup: *oxtail soup*

oxy·gen /'ɒksɪdʒən; *AmE* 'ɑːk-/ *noun* [U] (*symb* O) a chemical element. Oxygen is a colourless gas that is present in air and water and is necessary for people, animals and plants to live.

oxy·gen·ate /'ɒksɪdʒəneɪt; *AmE* 'ɑːk-/ *verb* [VN] (*technical*) to supply sth with oxygen ► **oxy·gen·ation** *noun* [U]

'oxygen mask *noun* a device placed over the nose and mouth through which a person can breathe OXYGEN, for example in an aircraft or a hospital

oxy·moron /,ɒksɪ'mɔːrɒn; *AmE* ,ɑːksɪ'mɔːrɑːn/ *noun* (*technical*) a phrase that combines two words that seem to be the opposite of each other, for example *a deafening silence*

oys·ter /'ɔɪstə(r)/ *noun* a large flat shellfish. Some types of oyster can be eaten and others produce shiny white jewels called PEARLS: *Oyster beds, on the mudflats, are a form of fish farming.* **IDM** see WORLD

Oz /ɒz; *AmE* ɑːz/ *noun* [U] (*BrE, AustralE, informal*) Australia

oz *abbr.* OUNCE(S): *4oz sugar*

ozone /'əʊzəʊn; *AmE* 'oʊzoʊn/ *noun* [U] **1** (*chemistry*) a poisonous gas with a strong smell that is a form of OXYGEN **2** (*BrE, informal*) air near the sea that smells fresh and pure

,ozone-'friendly *adj.* not containing substances that will damage the OZONE LAYER

'ozone hole *noun* an area in the ozone layer where the amount of OZONE has been very much reduced so that harmful rays from the sun can pass through it

'ozone layer *noun* [sing.] a layer of OZONE high above the earth's surface that helps to protect the earth from the sun's harmful rays

Pp

P (also **p**) /piː/ noun [C, U] (pl. **P's**, **p's** /piːz/) the 16th letter of the English alphabet: *'Pizza' begins with (a) P/ 'P'.*

p (also **p.**) abbr. **1** (pl. **pp.**) page: *See p.34 and pp.63-72.* **2** PENNY, PENCE: *a 30p stamp* **3** (*music*) quietly (from Italian 'piano')—see also P. AND P., P. AND H.

PA /ˌpiː ˈeɪ/ abbr. **1** PUBLIC ADDRESS (SYSTEM): *Announcements were made over the PA.* **2** (*especially BrE*) PERSONAL ASSISTANT: *She's the Managing Director's PA.* **3** Press Association

pa /pɑː/ noun (*old-fashioned, informal*) father: *I used to know your pa.*

p.a. abbr. per year (from Latin 'per annum'): *an increase of 3% p.a.*

pace¹ /peɪs/ noun, verb—see also PACE²
■ noun **1** [sing., U] the speed at which sb/sth walks, runs or moves: *to set off at a steady/gentle/leisurely pace* ◊ *Congestion frequently reduces traffic to walking pace.* ◊ *The ball gathered pace as it rolled down the hill.* ◊ *The runners have noticeably quickened their pace.* **2** [sing., U] ~ (**of sth**) the speed at which sth happens: *It is difficult to keep up with the rapid pace of change.* ◊ *We encourage all students to work at their own pace* (= as fast or as slow as they can). ◊ *I prefer the relaxed pace of life in the country.* ◊ *Rumours of corruption and scandal gathered pace* (= increased in number). **3** [C] an act of stepping once when walking or running; the distance travelled when doing this: *She took two paces forward.* **4** [U] the fact of sth happening, changing, etc. quickly: *He gave up his job in advertising because he couldn't stand the pace.* ◊ *The novel lacks pace* (= it develops too slowly).—see also PACY **IDM** **go through your 'paces** | **show your 'paces** to perform a particular activity in order to show other people what you are capable of doing **keep 'pace (with sb/sth)** to move, increase, change, etc. at the same speed as sb/sth: *She found it hard to keep pace with him as he strode off.* ◊ *Until now, wage increases have always kept pace with inflation.* **put sb/sth through their/its 'paces** to give sb/sth a number of tasks to perform in order to see what they are capable of doing **set the 'pace 1** to do sth at a particular speed or to a particular standard so that other people are then forced to copy it if they want to be successful: *The company is no longer setting the pace in the home computer market.* **2** (in a race) to run faster than the other competitors, at a speed that they then try to copy—more at FORCE *v.*, SNAIL
■ verb **1** to walk up and down in a small area many times, especially because you are feeling nervous or angry: [V+adv./prep.] *She paced up and down outside the room.* ◊ [VN] *Ted paced the floor restlessly.* **2** [VN] to set the speed at which sth happens or develops: *He paced his game skilfully.* **3** [VN] ~ **yourself** to find the right speed or rhythm for your work or an activity so that you have enough energy to do what you have to do: *He'll have to learn to pace himself in this job.* **PHRV** **pace sth↔off/out** to measure the size of sth by walking across it with regular steps

pace² /ˈpɑːkeɪ; ˈpɑːtʃeɪ; ˈpeɪsi/ prep. (from Latin, *formal*) used before a person's name to express polite disagreement with what they have said: *The evidence suggests, pace Professor Jones, that…* (= Professor Jones has a different opinion).—see also PACE¹

pace·maker /ˈpeɪsmeɪkə(r)/ noun **1** an electronic device that is put inside a person's body to help their heart beat regularly **2** (also **pace·setter** especially in *AmE*) a person or an animal that begins a race quickly so that the other competitors will try to copy the speed and run a fast race: (*figurative*) *The big banks have been the pacesetters in developing the system.* **3** (also **pace·setter** especially in *AmE*) a person or team that is winning in a sports competition: *The local club are now only one point off the pacemakers.*

pace·setter /ˈpeɪssetə(r)/ noun (*especially AmE*) = PACE-MAKER

pachy·derm /ˈpækidɜːm; *AmE* -dɜːrm/ noun (*technical*) a type of animal with a very thick skin, for example, an elephant—picture on page A6

pa·cif·ic /pəˈsɪfɪk/ adj. [usually before noun] (*literary*) peaceful or loving peace

the Pa·cific 'Rim noun [sing.] the countries around the Pacific Ocean, especially the countries of Eastern Asia, considered as an economic group

paci·fier /ˈpæsɪfaɪə(r)/ noun (*AmE*) = DUMMY

paci·fism /ˈpæsɪfɪzəm/ noun [U] the belief that war and violence are always wrong

paci·fist /ˈpæsɪfɪst/ noun a person who believes in pacifism and who refuses to fight in a war—compare CONSCIENTIOUS OBJECTOR ▶ **paci·fist** adj. [usually before noun]: *pacifist beliefs/groups/views*

pacify /ˈpæsɪfaɪ/ verb (**paci·fies**, **paci·fy·ing**, **paci·fied**, **paci·fied**) **1** to make sb who is angry or upset become calm and quiet: *The baby could not be pacified.* ◊ *The announcement was designed to pacify the irate crowd.* **2** to bring peace to an area where there is fighting or a war ▶ **paci·fi·ca·tion** /ˌpæsɪfɪˈkeɪʃn/ noun [U]

pack /pæk/ verb, noun
■ verb
PUT INTO CONTAINER | **1** to put clothes, etc. into a bag in preparation for a trip away from home: [V] *I haven't packed yet.* ◊ [VN] *I haven't packed my suitcase yet.* ◊ *He packed a bag with a few things and was off.* ◊ *He packed a few things into a bag.* ◊ *Did you pack the camera?* ◊ [VNN] *I've packed you some food for the journey.* **OPP** UNPACK **2** [VN] ~ **sth (up) (in/into sth)** to put sth into a container so that it can be stored, transported or sold: *The pottery was packed in boxes and shipped to the US.* ◊ *I carefully packed up the gifts.* ◊ *He found a part-time job packing eggs.* **OPP** UNPACK
PROTECT | **3** [VN] ~ **sth (in/with sth)** to protect sth that breaks easily by surrounding it with soft material: *The paintings were carefully packed in newspaper.*
PRESERVE FOOD | **4** [VN] ~ **sth (in sth)** to preserve food in a particular substance: *fish packed in ice*
FILL | **5** to fill sth with a lot of people or things: [V+adv./prep.] *We all packed together into one car.* ◊ [VN] *Fans packed the hall to see the band.*—see also PACKED OUT, PACKED
SNOW/SOIL | **6** [VN] ~ **sth (down)** to press sth such as snow or soil to form a thick hard mass: *Pack the earth down around the plant.* ◊ *a patch of packed snow*
CARRY GUN | **7** [VN] (*AmE, informal*) to carry sth dangerous, especially a gun: *to pack a gun* ◊ *A storm packing 75 mph winds swept across the area last night.*
IDM **pack a (powerful, real, etc.) 'punch** (*informal*) **1** (of a boxer) to be capable of hitting sb very hard **2** to have a powerful effect on sb: *The advertising campaign packs quite a punch.* **pack your 'bags** (*informal*) to leave a person or place permanently, especially after a disagreement—more at SEND
PHRV **pack 'away** to be capable of being folded up small when it is not being used: *The tent packs away in a small bag.* **pack sth↔'away** to put sth in a box, etc. when you have finished using it: *We packed away the summer clothes.* **pack sb↔'in** [no passive] (of plays, performers, etc.) to attract a lot of people to see it/them: *The show is*

æ	ɑː	e	ɜː	ə	ɪ	iː	i	ɒ	ɔː	ʌ	ʊ	u	uː
cat	father	ten	bird	about	sit	see	many	got	saw	cup	put	actual	too
								(BrE)					

still **packing them in**. **₁pack sth↔'in** (*informal*) to stop
doing sth: *She decided to pack in her job.* ◊ (*especially BrE*)
Pack it in (= stop behaving badly or annoying me), *you
two!* **₁pack sb/sth 'in/'into sth 1** to do a lot of things in a
limited period of time: *You seem to have packed a lot into
your life!* **2** to put a lot of things or people into a limited
space: *They've managed to pack a lot of information into a
very small book.* **₁pack 'into sth** to go somewhere in large
numbers so that all available space is filled: *Over 80000
fans packed into the stadium to watch the final.*—see also
PACK (5) **₁pack sb↔'off (to …)** (*informal*) to send sb
somewhere, especially because you do not want them
with you: *My parents always packed me off to bed early.*
₁pack sth↔'out (of shows, performers, etc.) to attract
enough people to completely fill a theatre, etc: *The band
can still pack out concert halls.*—see also PACKED OUT
₁pack 'up (*informal, especially BrE*) (of a machine) to stop
working: *The fax machine's packed up again.* **₁pack 'up** |
₁pack (sth)↔'up **1** to put your possessions into a bag,
etc. before leaving a place: *Are you packing up already?
It's only 4 o'clock.* ◊ *We arrived just as the musicians were
packing up their instruments.* **2** (*BrE, informal*) to stop
doing sth, especially a job: *What made you pack up a good
job like that?*—see also PACK (2)

■ *noun*

CONTAINER | **1** [C] (*especially AmE*) a container, usually
made of paper, that holds a number of the same thing or
an amount of sth, ready to be sold: *a pack of cigarettes/
gum* ◊ *You can buy the disks in packs of ten.*—compare
PACKAGE, PACKET—see also FLAT-PACK, SIX-PACK

SET | **2** [C] a set of different things that are supplied
together for a particular purpose: *Send for your free
information pack today.*

THINGS TIED FOR CARRYING | **3** [C] A number of things that are
wrapped or tied together, especially for carrying: *donkeys
carrying packs of wool* ◊ (*figurative*) *Everything she told us
is a pack of lies* (= a story that is completely false).

LARGE BAG | **4** [C] a large bag that you carry on your back,
with straps that fit over your shoulders: *We passed a
group of walkers, carrying huge packs.*—see also BACK-
PACK, FANNY PACK

OF ANIMALS | **5** [C+sing./pl. *v.*] a group of animals that hunt
together or are kept for hunting: *packs of savage dogs* ◊
wolves hunting in packs ◊ *a pack of hounds*

OF PEOPLE | **6** [C+sing./pl. *v.*] a group of similar people or

things, especially one that you do not like or approve of:
We avoided a pack of journalists waiting outside. ◊ *He's the
leader of the pack.* **7** [C+sing./pl. *v.*] all the people who
are behind the leaders in a race, competition, etc: *measures aimed at keeping the company ahead of the pack*

OF CARDS | **8** (*BrE*) (also **deck** *AmE, BrE*) [C] a complete
set of 52 playing cards: *a pack of cards*—picture on page
A8

OF CUBS/BROWNIES | **9** [C+sing./pl. *v.*] an organized group
of CUBS or BROWNIES: *to join a Brownie pack*

FOR WOUND | **10** [C] a hot or cold piece of soft material that
absorbs liquid, used for treating a wound—see also ICE
PACK, FACE PACK

IDM see JOKER

pack·age /'pækɪdʒ/ *noun, verb*

■ *noun* **1** (*especially AmE*) = PARCEL: *A large package has
arrived for you.*—compare PACK **2** (*AmE*) a box, bag, etc.
in which things are wrapped or packed; the contents of a
box etc: *Check the list of ingredients on the side of the
package.* ◊ *a package of hamburger buns*—compare
PACKET **3** (also **'package deal**) a set of items or ideas that
must be bought or accepted together: *a benefits package* ◊
an aid package ◊ *a package of measures to help small
businesses* **4** (also **'software package**) (*computing*) a set
of related programs for a particular type of task such as
WORD PROCESSING, sold and used as a single unit: *The
system came with a database software package.*

■ *verb* [VN] [often passive] **1 ~ sth (up)** to put sth into a box,
bag, etc. to be sold or transported: *packaged food/goods* ◊
We package our products in recyclable materials. ◊ *The
orders were already packaged up, ready to be sent.* **2 ~
sb/sth** (**as sth**) to present sb/sth in a particular way: *an
attempt to package news as entertainment*

'package tour (*BrE* also **'package holiday**) *noun* a
holiday/vacation that is organized by a company at a
fixed price and that includes the cost of travel, hotels, etc.

pack·aging /'pækɪdʒɪŋ/ *noun* [U] **1** materials used to
wrap or protect goods that are sold in shops/stores:
Attractive packaging can help to sell products. **2** the process of wrapping goods: *His company offers a flexible
packaging service for the food industry.*

'pack animal *noun* an animal used for carrying loads,
for example a horse

packed /pækt/ *adj.* **1** extremely full of people: *The res-*

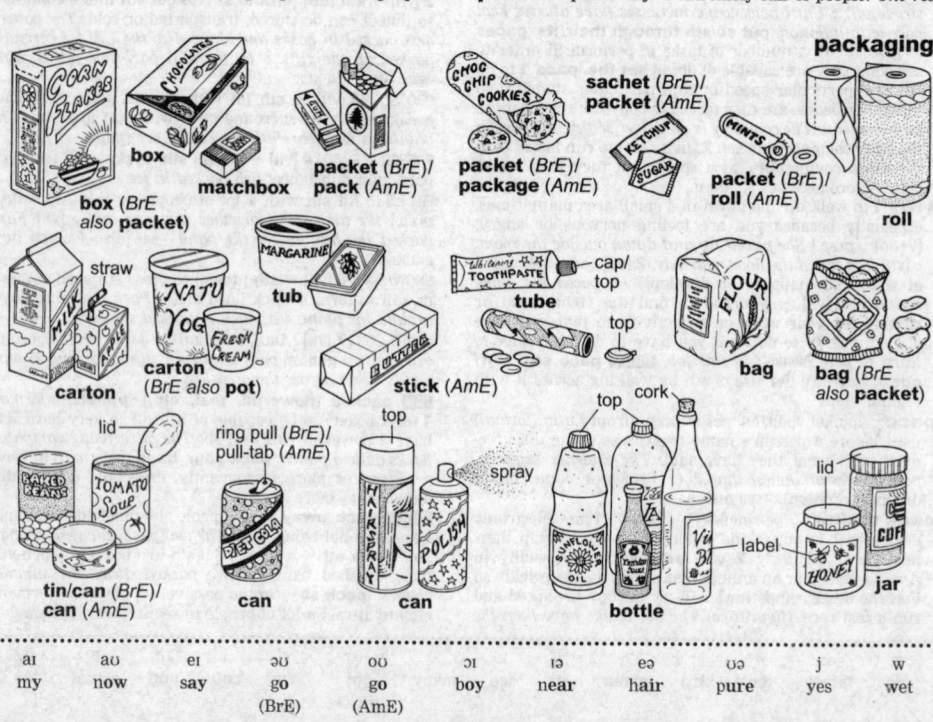

packaging

box

CORN FLAKES · CHOCOLATES

box *(BrE
also* **packet**)   **matchbox**   **packet** *(BrE)/*
pack *(AmE)*   CHOC CHIP COOKIES · KETCHUP   **packet** *(BrE)/*
package *(AmE)*   KETCHUP · SUGAR   **sachet** *(BrE)/*
packet *(AmE)*   MINTS   **packet** *(BrE)/*
roll *(AmE)*   **roll**

straw   MILK · APPLE · NATU YOG · FRESH CREAM   MARGARINE   **tub**   BUTTER   TOOTHPASTE   cap/
top   FLOUR   bag

carton   **carton**
(BrE also **pot**)   **stick** *(AmE)*   **tube**   top   **bag**   **bag** *(BrE
also* **packet**)

lid   BAKED BEANS · TOMATO Soup   ring pull *(BrE)/*
pull-tab *(AmE)*   top   HAIR SPRAY · POLISH   top   cork   SUNFLOWER OIL · Vin B   spray   label   lid   HONEY · COFFEE

tin/can *(BrE)/*
can *(AmE)*   **can**   **can**   **bottle**   **jar**

aɪ	aʊ	eɪ	əʊ	oʊ	ɔɪ	ɪə	eə	ʊə	j	w
my	now	say	go (BrE)	go (AmE)	boy	near	hair	pure	yes	wet

taurant was packed. ◇ *The show played to **packed houses*** (= large audiences). **2 ~ with sth** containing a lot of a particular thing: *The book is packed with information.* **3 tightly ~** pressed closely together: *The birds' nests are lined with tightly packed leaves.* **4** [not before noun] (*informal*) having put everything you need into cases, boxes, etc. before you go somewhere: *I'm all packed and ready to go.*

ˌpacked ˈlunch (*BrE*) (*AmE* ˈbag lunch) *noun* a meal of sandwiches, fruit, etc. that is prepared at home and eaten at school, work, etc.

ˌpacked ˈout *adj.* [not before noun] (*informal, especially BrE*) completely full of people or things: *Opera houses are packed out wherever she sings.*

pack·er /ˈpækə(r)/ *noun* a person, machine or company that puts food, goods, etc. into containers to be sold or sent to sb

packet /ˈpækɪt/ *noun* **1** (*BrE*) a small paper or cardboard container in which goods are packed for selling: *a packet of biscuits/cigarettes/crisps*—compare PACKAGE, PACK *n.* (1)—picture at PACKAGING **2** a small object wrapped in paper or put into a thick envelope so that it can be sent by mail, carried easily or given as a present: *A packet of photographs arrived with the mail.* **3** (*AmE*) = SACHET: *a packet of instant cocoa mix* **4** [sing.] (*informal*) a large amount of money: *That car must have cost a packet.* **5** (*computing*) a piece of information that forms part of a message sent through a computer NETWORK—see also PAY PACKET

ˈpack horse *noun* a horse used for carrying heavy loads

ˈpack ice *noun* [U] a large mass of ice floating in the sea, formed from smaller pieces that have frozen together

pack·ing /ˈpækɪŋ/ *noun* [U] **1** the act of putting your possessions, clothes, etc. into bags or boxes in order to take or send them somewhere: *Have you finished your packing?* **2** material for wrapping around delicate objects in order to protect them, especially before sending them somewhere: (*BrE*) *The price includes postage and packing.*

ˈpacking case *noun* (*BrE*) a large strong box for packing or transporting goods in

ˈpack rat *noun* (*AmE*) a person who collects and stores things that they do not really need

pact /pækt/ *noun* **~ (between A and B)** | **~ (with sb)** (**to do sth**) a formal agreement between two or more people, groups or countries, especially one in which they agree to help each other: *a non-aggression pact* ◇ *They have **made a pact** with each other not to speak about their differences in public.* ◇ *a suicide pact* (= an agreement by two or more people to kill themselves at the same time)

pacy /ˈpeɪsi/ *adj.* (*informal*) **1** (of a book, film/movie, etc.) having a story that develops quickly **2** able to run quickly: *a pacy winger who can also score goals*

pad /pæd/ *noun, verb*
■ *noun*
OF SOFT MATERIAL | **1** a thick piece of soft material that is used, for example, for absorbing liquid, cleaning or protecting sth: *medicated cleansing pads for sensitive skin* ◇ *sanitary pads* (= that a woman uses during her PERIODS)—see also SHOULDER PAD
OF PAPER | **2** a number of pieces of paper for writing or drawing on, that are fastened together at one edge: *a sketch/writing pad* ◇ *She always kept a pad and pencil by the phone.*—see also NOTEPAD, SCRATCH PAD
OF ANIMAL'S FOOT | **3** the soft part under the foot of a cat, dog, etc.
FOR CLEANING | **4** [C] a small piece of rough material used for cleaning pans, surfaces, etc: *a scouring pad*
FOR SPACECRAFT/HELICOPTER | **5** a flat surface where a spacecraft or a HELICOPTER takes off and lands—see also HELI-PAD, LAUNCH PAD
FOR PROTECTION | **6** [usually pl.] a piece of thick material that you wear in some sports, for example football and cricket, to protect your legs, elbows, etc.—picture at HOCKEY

OF WATER PLANTS | **7** the large flat leaf of some water plants, especially the WATER LILY: *floating lily pads*
FLAT/APARTMENT | **8** [usually sing.] (*old-fashioned, informal*) the place where sb lives, especially a flat/apartment: *He moved back into his old bachelor pad.*
—see also INK-PAD, KEYPAD
■ *verb* (**-dd-**)
ADD SOFT MATERIAL | **1** [VN] [often passive] **~ sth (with sth)** to put a layer of soft material in or on sth in order to protect it, make it thicker or change its shape: *All the sharp corners were padded with foam.* ◇ *a padded jacket* ◇ *a padded envelope* (= for sending delicate objects)
WALK QUIETLY | **2** [V+adv./prep.] to walk with quiet steps: *She padded across the room to the window.*
BILLS | **3** [VN] (*AmE*) to dishonestly add items to bills to obtain more money: *to pad bills/expense accounts*
PHRV ˌpad sth↔ˈout **1** to put soft material into a piece of clothing in order to change its shape **2** to make sth such as an article, seem longer or more impressive by adding things that are unnecessary: *The report was padded out with extracts from previous documents.*

ˌpadded ˈcell *noun* a room in a hospital for mentally ill people, with soft walls to prevent violent patients from injuring themselves

pad·ding /ˈpædɪŋ/ *noun* [U] **1** soft material that is placed inside sth to make it more comfortable or to change its shape **2** words that are used to make a speech, piece of writing, etc. longer, but that do not contain any interesting information

pad·dle /ˈpædl/ *noun, verb*
■ *noun* **1** [C] a short pole with a flat wide part at one or both ends, that you hold in both hands and use for moving a small boat, especially a CANOE, through water—compare OAR—picture at BOAT **2** [C] a tool or part of a machine shaped like a paddle, especially one used for mixing food **3** (**a paddle**) [sing.] (*BrE*) an act or period of walking in shallow water with bare feet: *Let's go for a paddle.*—see also DOG-PADDLE **4** (*AmE*) a bat used for playing TABLE TENNIS **5** (*AmE*) a bat of wood with a handle, used for hitting children as a punishment IDM see CREEK
■ *verb* **1** [usually +adv./prep.] to move a small boat through water using a paddle: [V] *We paddled downstream for about a mile.* ◇ [VN] *We paddled the canoe along the coast.* **2** (*BrE*) (*AmE* **wade**) [V] to walk or stand with bare feet in shallow water in the sea, a lake, etc: *The children have gone paddling.* **3** [V] to swim with short movements of your hands or feet up and down **4** [VN] (*AmE*) to hit a child with a flat piece of wood as a punishment

ˈpaddle steamer (*BrE*) (also **paddle·boat** *AmE, BrE*) *noun* an old-fashioned type of boat driven by steam and moved forward by a large wheel or wheels at the side

ˈpaddling pool (*BrE*) (*AmE* ˈwading pool) *noun* a shallow swimming pool for children to play in, especially a small plastic one that you fill with water

pad·dock /ˈpædək/ *noun* **1** a small field in which horses are kept **2** (in horse racing or motor racing) an enclosed area where horses or cars are taken before a race and shown to the public

paddy /ˈpædi/ *noun* (*pl.* **-ies**) **1** (also ˈpaddy field) a field in which rice is grown: *a rice paddy* **2** [usually sing.] (*BrE, informal*) a state of being angry or in a bad mood: *The news put him in a bit of a paddy.*

Paddy /ˈpædi/ *noun* (*pl.* **-ies**) (*informal*) an offensive word for a person from Ireland

ˈpaddy wagon *noun* (*informal, AmE*) = PATROL WAGON

pad·lock /ˈpædlɒk; *AmE* -lɑːk/ *noun, verb*
■ *noun* a type of lock that is used to fasten two things together or to fasten one thing to another. Padlocks are used with chains on gates, bicycles, etc.—picture at CHAIN
■ *verb* [VN] **~ sth (to sth)** to lock sth with a padlock: *She always padlocked her bike to the railings.* ◇ *The doors were padlocked.*

padre /ˈpɑːdreɪ/ *noun* (often used as a form of address) a priest, or other Christian MINISTER, especially in the armed forces—compare CHAPLAIN

b	d	f	g	h	k	l	m	n	p	r
bad	did	fall	get	hat	cat	leg	man	now	pen	red

paean /ˈpiːən/ noun (literary) a song of praise or victory

paed- (BrE) (AmE **ped-**) /piːd-/ combining form (in nouns and adjectives) connected with children: *paediatrician*

paedi·at·ri·cian (BrE) (AmE **pedi·at·ri·cian**) /ˌpiːdiəˈtrɪʃn/ noun a doctor who studies and treats the diseases of children

paedi·at·rics (BrE) (AmE **pedi·at·rics**) /ˌpiːdiˈætrɪks/ noun [U] the branch of medicine concerned with children and their diseases ▶ **paedi·at·ric** (BrE) (AmE **pedi·**) adj.: *paediatric surgery*

paedo·phile (BrE) (AmE **pedo·phile**) /ˈpiːdəʊfaɪl; AmE -doʊ-/ noun a person who is sexually attracted to children

paedo·philia (BrE) (AmE **pedo-**) /ˌpiːdəˈfɪliə/ noun [U] the condition of being sexually attracted to children; sexual activity with children

pa·ella /paɪˈelə/ noun [U, C] a Spanish dish of rice, chicken, fish and vegetables, cooked and served in a large shallow pan

pagan /ˈpeɪɡən/ noun (often disapproving) **1** a person who holds religious beliefs that are not part of any of the world's main religions **2** used in the past by Christians to describe a person who did not believe in Christianity ▶ **pagan** adj.: *a pagan festival/religion* **pa·gan·ism** /ˈpeɪɡənɪzəm/ noun [U]

page /peɪdʒ/ noun, verb
■ noun **1** (abbr. **p**) one side or both sides of a sheet of paper in a book, magazine, etc: *Turn to page 64.* ◊ *Someone has torn a page out of this book.* ◊ *a blank/new page* ◊ *the sports/financial pages of the newspaper* ◊ *on the opposite/facing page* ◊ *over the page* (= on the next page)— see also FRONT-PAGE, FULL-PAGE, YELLOW PAGES **2** a section of data or information that can be shown on a computer screen at any one time—see also HOME PAGE **3** (literary) an important event or period of history: *a glorious page of Arab history* **4** (BrE) = PAGEBOY **5** (in the Middle Ages) a boy or young man who worked for a KNIGHT while training to be a knight himself **6** (AmE) a student who works as an assistant to a member of the US Congress **IDM** see PRINT v.
■ verb [VN] **1** to call sb's name over a PUBLIC ADDRESS SYSTEM in order to find them and give them a message: *Why don't you have him paged at the airport?* **2** to contact sb by sending a message to their PAGER: *Page Dr Green immediately.*

pa·geant /ˈpædʒənt/ noun **1** a public entertainment in which people dress in historical COSTUMES and give performances of scenes from history **2** (AmE) a competition for young women in which their beauty, personal qualities and skills are judged: *a beauty pageant*—compare BEAUTY CONTEST **3** ~ (of sth) (literary) something that is considered as a series of interesting and different events: *life's rich pageant*

pa·geant·ry /ˈpædʒəntri/ noun [U] impressive and colourful events and ceremonies involving a lot of people wearing special clothes: *the pageantry of royal occasions*

page·boy /ˈpeɪdʒbɔɪ/ noun **1** (also **page**) (both BrE) (also **bell·boy** AmE, BrE) (AmE also **bell·hop**) a boy or young man, usually in uniform, employed in a hotel to carry cases, open doors for people, etc. **2** (also **page**) (both BrE) a small boy who helps or follows a BRIDE during a marriage ceremony—compare BRIDESMAID **3** a woman's hairstyle in which the hair is shoulder-length and turned under at the ends

pager /ˈpeɪdʒə(r)/ noun a small electronic device that you carry around with you and that shows a message or lets you know when sb is trying to contact you, for example by making a sound: *Try to contact him on his pager.* ◊ *Suddenly a pager went off.*—see also BEEPER, BLEEPER

pa·gin·ate /ˈpædʒɪneɪt/ verb [VN] (technical) to give a number to each page of a book, piece of writing, etc.

pa·gin·ation /ˌpædʒɪˈneɪʃn/ noun [U] (technical) the process of giving a page number to each page of a book; the page numbers given

pa·goda /pəˈɡəʊdə; AmE -ˈɡoʊ-/ noun a TEMPLE (= religious building) in India or E Asia in the form of a tall tower with several levels, each of which has its own roof which stretches over the floor below

pagoda

pah /pɑː/ exclamation used to represent the sound that people make when they disagree with sth or disapprove of sth strongly

paid /peɪd/ adj. [usually before noun] **1** (of work, etc.) for which people receive money: *Neither of them is currently in paid employment.* ◊ *a well-paid job* **2** (of a person) receiving money for doing work: *Men still outnumber women in the paid workforce.* ◊ *I'm just a poorly paid teacher.* **OPP** UNPAID—see also PAY v.

paid-up adj. [only before noun] **1** having paid all the money necessary to be a member of a club or an organization: *a fully paid-up member* **2** (informal) strongly supporting sb/sth: *a fully paid-up environmental campaigner*

pail /peɪl/, **pail·ful** /ˈpeɪlfʊl/ noun (AmE or old-fashioned) = BUCKET

pain /peɪn/ noun, verb
■ noun—see also PAINS **1** [U, C] the feelings that you have in your body when you have been hurt or when you are ill: *a cry of pain* ◊ *She was clearly in a lot of pain.* ◊ *He felt a sharp pain in his knee.* ◊ *patients suffering from acute back pain* ◊ *stomach/chest pains* ◊ *You get more aches and pains as you get older.* ◊ *The booklet contains information on pain relief during labour.* ◊ *This cream should help to relieve the pain.*—see also GROWING PAINS **2** [U, C] mental or emotional suffering: *the pain of separation/loss* ◊ *I never meant to cause her pain.* ◊ *the pleasures and pains of growing old* **3** [C] (informal) a person or thing that is very annoying: *She can be a real pain when she's in a bad mood.* ◊ *It's a pain having to go all that way for just one meeting.* **IDM** **on/under pain of sth** (formal) with the threat of having sth done to you as a punishment if you do not obey: *They were required to cut pollution levels, on pain of a £10 000 fine if they disobeyed.* **a pain in the ˈneck** (BrE) also **a pain in the ˈarse/ˈbackside** (AmE also **a pain in the ˈass/ˈbutt**) (informal) a person or thing that is very annoying
■ verb (not used in the progressive tenses) (formal) to cause sb pain or make them unhappy **SYN** HURT: [VN] *She was deeply pained by the accusation.* ◊ *(old use) The wound still pained him occasionally.* ◊ [VN to inf] *It pains me to see you like this.* [also VN that]

pained /peɪnd/ adj. showing that sb is feeling annoyed or upset: *a pained expression/voice*

pain·ful /ˈpeɪnfl/ adj. **1** causing you pain: *Is your back still painful?* ◊ *a painful death* ◊ *My ankle is still too painful to walk on.* **2** ~ (for sb) (to do sth) | ~ (doing sth) causing you to feel upset or embarrassed: *a painful experience/memory* ◊ *Their efforts were painful to watch.* **3** unpleasant or difficult to do: *Applying for jobs can be a long and painful process.*

pain·ful·ly /ˈpeɪnfəli/ adv. **1** extremely, and in a way that makes you feel annoyed, upset, etc: *painfully shy/thin* ◊ *He was painfully aware of his lack of experience.* ◊ *Progress has been painfully slow.* **2** in a way that causes you physical or emotional pain: *He banged his knee painfully against the desk.* **3** with a lot of effort and difficulty: *painfully acquired experience*

pain·kill·er /ˈpeɪnkɪlə(r)/ noun a drug that reduces pain: *She's on* (= taking) *painkillers.* ▶ **pain·kill·ing** adj.: *painkilling drugs/injections*

pain·less /ˈpeɪnləs/ adj. **1** causing you no pain: *a painless death* ◊ *The treatment is painless.* **2** not unpleasant or difficult to do: *The interview was relatively painless.* ▶ **pain·less·ly** adv.

pains /peɪnz/ noun [pl.] **IDM** **be at pains to do sth** to put a lot of effort into doing sth correctly: *She was at great pains to stress the advantages of the new system.* **for**

your '**pains** (*especially BrE*, often *ironic*) as payment, reward or thanks for sth you have done: *I told her what I thought and got a mouthful of abuse for my pains!* **take (great) pains (to do sth) | go to great pains (to do sth)** to put a lot of effort into doing sth: *The couple went to great pains to keep their plans secret.* **take (great) pains with/over sth** to do sth very carefully: *He always takes great pains with his lectures.*

pains·tak·ing /'peɪnzteɪkɪŋ/ *adj.* [usually before noun] needing a lot of care, effort and attention to detail: *painstaking research* ◊ *The event had been planned with painstaking attention to detail.* ▶ **pains·tak·ing·ly** *adv.*

paint /peɪnt/ *noun, verb*
■ *noun* **1** [U] a liquid that is put on surfaces to give them a particular colour; a layer of this liquid when it has dried on a surface: *white/yellow paint* ◊ *gloss/matt/acrylic paint* ◊ *The woodwork has recently been given a fresh coat of paint.* ◊ *Wet paint!* (= used as a sign) ◊ *The paint is starting to peel off.*—see also GREASEPAINT, OIL PAINT, WARPAINT **2** (**paints**) [pl.] tubes or blocks of paint used for painting pictures: *oil paints*
■ *verb* **1** ~ **sth** (**with sth**) to cover a surface or object with paint: [VN] *We've decided to have the house painted.* ◊ *Paint the shed with weather-resistant paint.* ◊ *a brightly painted barge* ◊ *The walls were painted yellow.* [also VN-N, V] **2** ~ (**in sth**) | ~ **sth** (**on sth**) to make a picture or design using paints: [VN] *to paint landscapes/portraits* ◊ *A friend painted the children for me* (= painted a picture of the children). ◊ *Slogans had been painted on the walls.* ◊ [V] *She paints in oils.* ◊ *My mother paints well.* **3** [VN] ~ **sb/sth** (**as sth**) to give a particular impression of sb/sth SYN PORTRAY: *The article paints them as a bunch of petty criminals.* ◊ *The documentary painted her in a bad light.* **4** [VN] to put coloured MAKE-UP on your nails, lips, etc. IDM **paint a (grim, gloomy, rosy, etc.) 'picture of sb/sth** to describe sth in a particular way; to give a particular impression of sb/sth: *The report paints a vivid picture of life in the city.* ◊ *Journalists paint a grim picture of conditions in the camps.* **paint the town 'red** (*informal*) to go to a lot of different bars, clubs, etc. and enjoy yourself **paint sth with a ,broad 'brush** to describe sth in a general way, ignoring the details—more at BLACK *adj.* PHRV **,paint sth↔'out** to cover part of a picture, sign, etc. with another layer of paint **,paint 'over sth** to cover sth with a layer of paint: *We painted over the dirty marks on the wall.*

paint·ball /'peɪntbɔːl/ *noun* [U] a game in which people shoot balls of paint at each other

paint·box /'peɪntbɒks; *AmE* -bɑːks/ *noun* a box containing a set of paints

paint·brush /'peɪntbrʌʃ/ *noun* a brush that is used for painting

paint·er /'peɪntə(r)/ *noun* **1** a person whose job is painting buildings, walls, etc: *He works as a painter and decorator.* **2** an artist who paints pictures: *a famous painter* ◊ *a portrait/landscape painter* **3** a rope fastened to the front of a boat, used for tying it to a post, ship, etc.

paint·er·ly /'peɪntəli; *AmE* -ərli/ *adj.* (*written*) typical of artists or painting

paint·ing /'peɪntɪŋ/ *noun* **1** [C] a picture that has been painted: *a collection of paintings by American artists* ◊ *cave paintings*—see also OIL PAINTING **2** [U] the act or art of using paint to produce pictures: *Her hobbies include music and painting.* **3** [U] the act of putting paint onto the surface of objects, walls, etc: *painting and decorating*

'**paint stripper** *noun* [U] a liquid used to remove old paint from surfaces

paint·work /'peɪntwɜːk; *AmE* -wɜːrk/ *noun* [U] the layer of paint on the surface of a door, wall, car, etc: *The paintwork is beginning to peel.*

pair /peə(r); *AmE* per/ *noun, verb*
■ *noun*
TWO THINGS THE SAME | **1** [C] two things of the same type, especially when they are used or worn together: *a pair of gloves/shoes/earrings* ◊ *a huge pair of eyes* ◊ *The vase is one of a matching pair.*
TWO PARTS JOINED | **2** [C] an object consisting of two parts

that are joined together: *a pair of trousers/pants/jeans* ◊ *a pair of glasses/binoculars/scissors*

HELP A plural verb is sometimes used with **pair** in the singular in senses 1 and 2. In informal *AmE* some people use **pair** as a plural form: *three pair of shoes*. This is not considered correct in written English.
TWO PEOPLE | **3** [C+sing./pl. *v.*] two people who are doing sth together or who have a particular relationship: *Get pairs of students to act out the dialogue in front of the class.* ◊ (*informal*) *I've had enough of the pair of you!* HELP In *BrE* a plural verb is usually used: *A pair of children were kicking a ball about.* ◊ *The pair are planning a trip to India together.*
TWO ANIMALS/BIRDS | **4** [C+sing./pl. *v.*] two animals or birds of the same type that are breeding together: *a breeding pair* ◊ *a pair of swans*
TWO HORSES | **5** [C] two horses working together to pull a carriage: *a carriage and pair*
—see also AU PAIR
IDM **a pair of 'hands** (*informal*) a person who can do, or is doing, a job: *We need an extra pair of hands if we're going to finish on time.* ◊ *Colleagues regard him as a safe pair of hands* (= sb who can be relied on to do a job well). **in 'pairs** in groups of two objects or people: *Students worked in pairs on the project.* **I've only got one pair of 'hands** (*spoken*) used to say that you are too busy to do anything else
■ *verb*
MAKE GROUPS OF TWO | **1** [VN] [usually passive] ~ **A with B | ~ A and B** (**together**) to put people or things into groups of two: *Each blind student was paired with a sighted student.* ◊ *All the shoes on the floor were neatly paired.*
OF ANIMALS/BIRDS | **2** [V] (*technical*) to come together in order to breed: *Many of the species pair for life.*
PHRV **,pair 'off (with sb) | ,pair sb↔'off (with sb)** to come together, especially in order to have a romantic relationship; to bring two people together for this purpose: *It seemed that all her friends were pairing off.* ◊ *He's always trying to pair me off with his cousin.* **,pair 'up (with sb) | ,pair sb↔'up (with sb)** to come together or to bring two people together to work, play a game, etc.

pair·ing /'peərɪŋ; *AmE* 'per-/ *noun* two people or things that work together or are placed together; the act of placing them together: *Tonight they take on a Chinese pairing in their bid to reach the final tomorrow.*

pais·ley /'peɪzli/ *noun* a detailed pattern of curved shapes that look like feathers: *a paisley tie*—picture on page A4

pa·ja·mas (*AmE*) = PYJAMAS

pak choi /ˌpæk 'tʃɔɪ/ (*BrE*) [U] = CHINESE CABBAGE

Paki /'pæki/ *noun* (*BrE, informal*) an offensive word for a person from Pakistan, especially one living in Britain

pal /pæl/ *noun, verb*
■ *noun* **1** (*informal, becoming old-fashioned*) a friend: *We've been pals for years.*—see also PEN PAL **2** (*spoken*) used to address a man in an unfriendly way: *If I were you, pal, I'd stay away from her!* ▶ **pally** *adj.*: *I got very pally* (= friendly) *with him.*
■ *verb* (**-ll-**) PHRV **,pal a'round (with sb)** (*informal, especially AmE*) to do things with sb as a friend: *I palled around with him and his sister at school.* **,pal 'up (with sb)** (*BrE*) (*AmE* ,**buddy 'up (to/with sb)**) (*informal*) to become sb's friend: *They palled up while they were at college.*

pal·ace /'pæləs/ *noun* **1** [C] the official home of a king, queen, president, etc: *Buckingham Palace* ◊ *the royal/presidential palace* **2** (often **the Palace**) [sing.] the people who live in a palace, especially the British royal family: *The Palace last night refused to comment on the reports.* ◊ *a Palace spokesman* **3** [C] any large impressive house: *The Old Town has a whole collection of churches, palaces and mosques.* **4** [C] (*old-fashioned*) (sometimes used in the names of buildings) a large public building, such as a hotel or cinema/movie theater: *the Strand Palace Hotel* ◊ *old movie palaces*

æ	ɑː	e	ɜː	ə	ɪ	iː	i	ɒ	ɔː	ʌ	ʊ	u	uː
cat	father	ten	bird	about	sit	see	many	got	saw	cup	put	actual	too

(BrE)

palace 'coup (also ˌpalace revoˈlution) *noun* a situation in which a ruler or leader has their power taken away from them by sb within the same party, etc.

palaeo- (*especially BrE*) (*AmE* usually **paleo-**) /ˈpæliəʊ; ˈpeɪl-; *AmE* -ioʊ/ *combining form* (in nouns, adjectives and adverbs) connected with ancient times: *palaeography* (= the study of ancient writing)

palaeo·lith·ic (*especially BrE*) (*AmE* usually **paleo-**) /ˌpæliəˈlɪθɪk; ˌpeɪl-/ *adj.* from or connected with the early part of the Stone Age

palae·on·tolo·gist (*especially BrE*) (*AmE* usually **paleo-**) /ˌpæliɒnˈtɒlədʒɪst; ˌpeɪl-; *AmE* ˌpeɪliɑːnˈtɑːl-/ *noun* a person who studies FOSSILS

palae·on·tology (*especially BrE*) (*AmE* usually **paleo-**) /ˌpæliɒnˈtɒlədʒi; ˌpeɪl-; *AmE* ˌpeɪliɑːnˈtɑːl-/ *noun* [U] the study of FOSSILS (= the remains of animals or plants in rocks) as a guide to the history of life on earth

pal·at·able /ˈpælətəbl/ *adj.* **1** (of food or drink) having a pleasant or acceptable taste **2 ~** (**to sb**) pleasant or acceptable to sb: *Some of the dialogue has been changed to make it more palatable to an American audience.* OPP UNPALATABLE

pal·atal /ˈpælətl/ *noun* (*phonetics*) a speech sound made by placing the tongue against or near the hard palate of the mouth, for example /dʒ/ ▶ **pal·atal** *adj.*

pal·ate /ˈpælət/ *noun* **1** the top part of the inside of the mouth: *the hard/soft palate* (= the hard/soft part at the front/back of the palate)—see also CLEFT PALATE **2** [usually sing.] the ability to recognize and/or enjoy good food and drink: *a menu to tempt even the most jaded palate*

pa·la·tial /pəˈleɪʃl/ *adj.* [usually before noun] (of a room or building) extremely large and impressive, like a PALACE

pa·la·ver /pəˈlɑːvə(r); *AmE* also -ˈlæv-/ *noun* (*informal*) **1** [U, sing.] (*BrE*) a lot of unnecessary activity, excitement or trouble, especially caused by sth that is unimportant: *What's all the palaver about?* ◇ *What a palaver it is, trying to get a new visa!* **2** [U] (*AmE*) talk that does not have any meaning; nonsense: *He's talking palaver.*

pale /peɪl/ *adj., verb, noun*
■ *adj.* (**paler, pal·est**) **1** (of a person, their face, etc.) having skin that is almost white; having skin that is whiter than usual because of illness, a strong emotion, etc: *a pale complexion* ◇ *pale with anger/fear/shock* ◇ *to go/turn pale* ◇ *You look pale. Are you OK?* ◇ *The ordeal left her looking pale and drawn.*—see also PALLOR **2** light in colour; containing a lot of white: *pale blue eyes* ◇ *a paler shade of green* ◇ *a pale sky* OPP DARK, DEEP **3** (of light) not strong or bright: *the cold pale light of dawn*—see also PALLID ▶ **pale·ly** /ˈpeɪlli/ *adv.*: *Mark stared palely* (= with a pale face) *at his plate.* **pale·ness** *noun* [U]
■ *verb* [V] **~** (**at sth**) (*written*) to become paler than usual: *She* (= her face) *paled visibly at the sight of the police car.* ◇ *The blue of the sky paled to a light grey.* IDM **pale beside/next to sth** | **pale in/by comparison** (**with/to sth**) | **pale into insignificance** to seem less important when compared with sth else: *Last year's riots pale in comparison with this latest outburst of violence.*
■ *noun* IDM **be·yond the 'pale** considered by most people to be unacceptable or unreasonable: *His remarks were clearly beyond the pale.*

paleo- (*AmE*) = PALAEO-

pal·ette /ˈpælət/ *noun* **1** a thin board with a hole in it for the thumb to go through, used by an artist for mixing colours on when painting **2** [usually sing.] (*technical*) the colours used by a particular artist: *Greens and browns are typical of Ribera's palette.*

'palette knife *noun* a knife with a blade that bends easily and has a round end, used by artists and in cooking—picture at KITCHEN

pali·mony /ˈpælɪməni/ *noun* [U] (*informal, especially AmE*) money that a court of law orders sb to pay regularly to a former partner when they have lived together without being married—compare ALIMONY

pal·imp·sest /ˈpælɪmpsest/ *noun* **1** an ancient document from which some or all of the original text has been removed and replaced by a new text **2** (*formal*) something that has many different layers of meaning or detail

pal·in·drome /ˈpælɪndrəʊm; *AmE* -droʊm/ *noun* a word or phrase that reads the same backwards as forwards, for example *madam* or *nurses run*

pal·ing /ˈpeɪlɪŋ/ *noun* [C, usually pl., U] a metal or wooden post that is pointed at the top; a fence made of these posts: *He leaned against the paling.*

pal·is·ade /ˌpælɪˈseɪd/ *noun* **1** a fence made of strong wooden or metal posts that are pointed at the top, especially used to protect a building in the past: *a wooden palisade* **2** (**palisades**) [pl.] (*AmE*) a line of high steep cliffs, especially along a river or by the sea or ocean

pall /pɔːl/ *noun, verb*
■ *noun* **1** [usually sing.] **~ of sth** a thick dark cloud of sth: *a pall of smoke/dust* ◇ (*figurative*) *News of her death cast a pall over the event.* **2** a cloth spread over a COFFIN (= a box used for burying a dead person in)
■ *verb* [V] (not used in the progressive tenses) **~** (**on sb**) to become less interesting to sb over a period of time because they have done or seen it too much: *Even the impressive scenery began to pall on me after a few hundred miles.*

'pall-bearer *noun* a person who walks beside or helps to carry the COFFIN at a funeral

pal·let /ˈpælət/ *noun* **1** a heavy wooden or metal base that can be used for moving or storing goods **2** a fabric bag filled with STRAW, used for sleeping on

pal·lia·tive /ˈpæliətɪv/ *noun* **1** (*medical*) a medicine or medical treatment that reduces pain without curing its cause **2** (*formal, usually disapproving*) an action, a decision, etc. that is designed to make a difficult situation seem better without actually solving the cause of the problems ▶ **pal·lia·tive** *adj.* [usually before noun]: *palliative treatment* ◇ *short-term palliative measures*

pal·lid /ˈpælɪd/ *adj.* (*written*) **1** (of a person, their face, etc.) pale, especially because of illness: *a pallid complexion/face* **2** (of colours or light) not strong or bright, and therefore not attractive: *a pallid sun/sky*

pal·lor /ˈpælə(r)/ *noun* [U] pale colouring of the face, especially because of illness or fear: *Her cheeks had an unhealthy pallor.*

pally /ˈpæli/ *adj.* ⇨ PAL

palm /pɑːm/ *noun, verb*
■ *noun* **1** the inner surface of the hand between the wrist and the fingers: *He held the bird gently in the palm of his hand.* ◇ *sweaty palms* ◇ *to read sb's palm* (= to say what will happen to sb by looking at the lines on their palm)—picture at BODY **2** (also **'palm tree**) a straight tree with a mass of long leaves at the top, growing in tropical countries. There are several types of palm tree, some of which produce fruit: *a date palm* ◇ *a coconut palm* ◇ *palm leaves/fronds/groves* IDM **have sb in the ˌpalm of your 'hand** to have complete control or influence over sb—more at CROSS v., GREASE v.
■ *verb* [VN] to hide a coin, card, etc. in your hand, especially when performing a trick PHRV **ˌpalm sb↔'off** (**with sth**) (*informal*) to persuade sb to believe an excuse or an explanation that is not true, in order to stop them asking questions or complaining **ˌpalm sth↔'off** (**on/onto sb**) | **ˌpalm sb↔'off** (**with sth**) (*informal*) to persuade sb to accept sth that has no value or that you do not want, especially by deceiving them: *She's always palming the worst jobs off on her assistant.* ◇ *Make sure he doesn't try to palm you off with faulty goods.* **ˌpalm sth 'off as sth** (*informal*) to tell sb that sth is better than it is, especially in order to sell it: *They were trying to palm the table off as a genuine antique.*

palm·ist /ˈpɑːmɪst/ *noun* a person who claims to be able to tell what a person is like and what will happen to them in the future, by looking at the lines on the PALM of their hand

palm·is·try /ˈpɑːmɪstri/ *noun* [U] the art of telling what a person is like and what will happen to them by looking at the lines on the PALM of their hand

aɪ	aʊ	eɪ	əʊ	oʊ	ɔɪ	ɪə	eə	ʊə	j	w
my	now	say	go	go	boy	near	hair	pure	yes	wet
			(BrE)	(AmE)						

'palm oil *noun* [U] oil obtained from the fruit of some types of PALM tree, used in cooking and in making soap, candles, etc.

,Palm 'Sunday *noun* [U, C] (in the Christian Church) the Sunday before Easter

palm·top /'pɑːmtɒp; *AmE* -tɑːp/ *noun* a small computer that can be held in the PALM of one hand

palo·mino /ˌpælə'miːnəʊ; *AmE* -noʊ/ *noun* (pl. -os) a horse that is a cream or gold colour with a white MANE and tail

palp·able /'pælpəbl/ *adj.* that is easily noticed by the mind or the senses: *a palpable sense of loss/relief* ◊ *The tension in the room was almost palpable.* ► **palp·ably** /-əbli/ *adv.*: *It was palpably clear what she really meant.*

pal·pate /pæl'peɪt/ *verb* [VN] (*medical*) to examine part of the body by touching it ► **pal·pa·tion** *noun* [U]

pal·pi·tate /'pælpɪteɪt/ *verb* [V] (of the heart) to beat rapidly and/or in an irregular way especially because of fear or excitement

pal·pi·ta·tions /ˌpælpɪ'teɪʃnz/ *noun* [pl.] a physical condition in which your heart beats very quickly and in an irregular way: *Just the thought of flying gives me palpitations* (= makes me very nervous).

palsy /'pɔːlzi/ *noun* [U] (*old-fashioned*) PARALYSIS (= loss of control or feeling in part or most of the body), especially when the limbs shake without control—see also CEREBRAL PALSY ► **pal·sied** /'pɔːlzid/ *adj.*

pal·try /'pɔːltri/ *adj.* [usually before noun] **1** (of an amount) too small to be considered as important or useful: *This account offers a paltry 1% return on your investment.* ◊ *a paltry sum* **2** having no value or useful qualities: *a paltry excuse/gesture*

pam·pas /'pæmpəs; *AmE* also -pəz/ *noun* (usually **the pampas**) [sing.+ sing./pl. *v.*] the large area of land in S America that has few trees and is covered in grass

pam·per /'pæmpə(r)/ *verb* [VN] (sometimes *disapproving*) to take care of sb very well and make them feel as comfortable as possible: *Pamper yourself with our new range of beauty treatments.* ◊ *a spoilt and pampered child*

pamph·let /'pæmflət/ *noun* a very thin book with a paper cover, containing information about a particular subject

pamph·let·eer /ˌpæmflə'tɪə(r); *AmE* -'tɪr/ *noun* a person who writes pamphlets on particular subjects

pan /pæn/ *noun, verb*

pots and pans

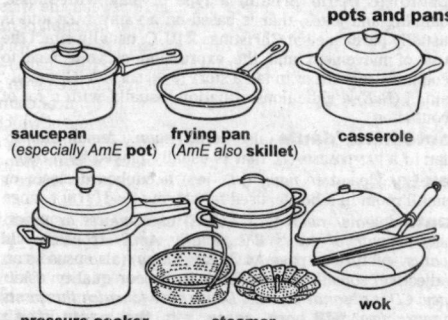

saucepan   frying pan   casserole
(especially *AmE* **pot**) (*AmE* also **skillet**)

pressure cooker   steamer   wok

■ *noun* **1** a container, usually made of metal, with a handle or handles, used for cooking food in: *pots and pans* ◊ *a large stainless steel pan*—see also FRYING PAN, SAUCEPAN **2** the amount contained in a pan: *a pan of boiling water* **3** (*AmE*) = TIN (5): *a cake pan* **4** either of the dishes on a pair of SCALES that you put things into in order to weigh them **5** (*BrE*) the bowl of a toilet—see also BEDPAN, DUSTPAN, SKIDPAN **IDM** **go down the 'pan** (*BrE, slang*) to be wasted or spoiled: *That's another brilliant idea down the pan.*—more at FLASH *n.*

■ *verb* (-nn-) **1** [VN] [usually passive] (*informal*) to severely criticize sth such as a play or a film/movie: *The television series was panned by critics and viewers alike.* **2** if a television or video camera **pans** somewhere, or a person

pans or **pans** a camera, the camera moves in a particular direction, to follow an object or to film a wide area:[V, +adv./prep.] *The camera panned back to the audience.* ◊ [VN] *He panned the camera along the row of faces.* **3 ~** (**for sth**) to wash soil or small stones in a pan to find gold or other valuable minerals: [V] *panning for gold* [alsoVN] **PHRV** **,pan 'out** (*informal*) (of events or a situation) to develop in a particular way: *I'm happy with the way things have panned out.*

pan- /pæn/ *combining form* (in adjectives and nouns) including all of sth; connected with the whole of sth: *pan-African* ◊ *pandemic*

pana·cea /ˌpænə'siːə/ *noun* **~** (**for sth**) something that will solve all the problems of a particular situation

pan·ache /pə'næʃ; pæ'n-/ *noun* [U] the quality of being able to do things in a confident and elegant way that other people find attractive

pan·ama /'pænəmɑː/ (also **,panama 'hat**) *noun* a man's hat made from fine woven STRAW—picture at HAT

pan·cake /'pænkeɪk/ *noun* **1** [C] a thin flat round cake made from a mixture of flour, eggs and milk that is fried on both sides, usually eaten hot for breakfast in the US, and in Britain either as a DESSERT with sugar, jam, etc. or as a main course with meat, cheese, etc: *pancakes with maple syrup* ◊ *a selection of savoury pancakes*—picture on page A1 **2** [U] thick make-up for the face, used especially in the theatre **IDM** see FLAT *adj.*

'Pancake Day *noun* [U, C] (*informal*) the day before the beginning of Lent, when people in Britain traditionally eat PANCAKES—compare SHROVE TUESDAY

pan·creas /'pæŋkriəs/ *noun* an organ near the stomach that produces INSULIN and a liquid that helps the body to DIGEST food—picture at BODY ► **pan·cre·at·ic** /ˌpæŋkri'ætɪk/ *adj.* [only before noun]: *pancreatic juices/cancer*

panda /'pændə/ *noun* **1** (also **,giant 'panda**) a large black and white animal like a bear, that lives in China and is very rare **2** (also **,red 'panda**) an Indian animal like a RACCOON, with reddish-brown fur and a long thick tail

'panda car *noun* (*BrE, informal*) a small police car

pan·dem·ic /pæn'demɪk/ *noun* a disease that spreads over a whole country or the whole world: *the Aids pandemic in Asia* ► **pan·dem·ic** *adj.*: *a pandemic disease*—compare ENDEMIC, EPIDEMIC

pan·de·mon·ium /ˌpændə'məʊniəm; *AmE* -'moʊ-/ *noun* [U] a situation in which there is a lot of noise, activity and confusion, especially because people are feeling angry or frightened: *Pandemonium broke out when the news was announced.*

pan·der /'pændə(r)/ *verb* **PHRV** **'pander to sth/sb** (*disapproving*) to do what sb wants, or try to please them, especially when this is not acceptable or reasonable: *to pander to sb's whims/wishes* ◊ *The speech was just pandering to racial prejudice.*

p. and h. (also **p. & h.**) /ˌpiː ənd 'eɪtʃ/ *abbr.* (*AmE*) postage and handling—compare P. AND P.

Pandora's box /pænˌdɔːrəz 'bɒks; *AmE* 'bɑːks/ *noun* [sing., U] a process that, if started, will cause many problems that cannot be solved: *This court case could open a Pandora's box of similar claims.* **ORIGIN** From the Greek myth in which **Pandora** was created by the god Zeus and sent to the earth with a box containing many evils. When she opened the box, the evils came out and infected the earth.

p. and p. (also **p. & p.**) /ˌpiː ən 'piː/ *abbr.* (*BrE*) postage and packing (the cost of packing sth and sending it by post): *Add £2 for p. and p.*—compare P. AND H., S AND H

pane /peɪn/ *noun* a single sheet of glass in a window: *a pane of glass* ◊ *a windowpane*

pan·egyr·ic /ˌpænə'dʒɪrɪk/ *noun* (*formal*) a speech or piece of writing praising sb/sth

panel /'pænl/ *noun, verb*

■ *noun* **1** [C] a square or RECTANGULAR piece of wood, glass or metal that forms part of a larger surface such as a door or wall: *One of the glass panels in the front door was cracked.*—see also SOLAR PANEL **2** [C] a piece of metal that

forms part of the outer frame of a vehicle **3** [C] a piece of fabric that forms part of a piece of clothing: *The trousers have double thickness knee panels for extra protection.* **4** [C+sing./pl. *v.*] a group of specialists who give their advice or opinion about sth; a group of people who discuss topics of interest on television or radio: *an advisory/ interview panel* ◊ *a panel of experts* ◊ *We have two politicians on tonight's panel.* ◊ *a panel discussion* **5** [C] (also '**jury panel**') (both *especially AmE*) = JURY **6** [C] a flat board in a vehicle or on a piece of machinery where the controls and instruments are fixed: *an instrument panel* ◊ *a control/display panel*
■ *verb* (**-ll-**, *AmE* **-l-**) [VN] [usually passive] to cover or decorate a surface with flat strips of wood, glass, etc: *The walls were panelled in oak.* ◊ *a glass-/wood-panelled door*

'**panel beater** *noun* (*BrE*) a person whose job is to remove the DENTS from the outer frame of a vehicle that has been in an accident

pan·el·ling (*BrE*) (*AmE* **pan·el·ing**) /'pænəlɪŋ/ *noun* [U] square or RECTANGULAR pieces of wood used to cover and decorate walls, ceilings, etc: *The room still has all its original oak panelling.*

pan·el·list (*BrE*) (*AmE* **pan·el·ist**) /'pænəlɪst/ *noun* a person who is a member of a PANEL answering questions during a discussion, for example on radio or television

'**pan-fry** *verb* (**pan-fries**, **pan-frying**, **pan-fried**, **pan-fried**) [VN] to fry food in a pan in shallow fat: *pan-fried chicken*

pang /pæŋ/ *noun* a sudden strong feeling of physical or emotional pain: *hunger pangs/pangs of hunger* ◊ *a sudden pang of jealousy*

pan·han·dler /'pænhændlə(r)/ *noun* (*AmE, informal*) a person who asks other people for money in the street ▶ **pan·han·dle** *verb* [V]

panic /'pænɪk/ *noun, verb*
■ *noun* [U, C, usually sing.] **1** a sudden feeling of great fear that cannot be controlled and prevents you from thinking clearly: *a moment of panic* ◊ *They were in a state of panic.* ◊ *Office workers fled **in panic** as the fire took hold.* ◊ *There's no point **getting into a panic** about the exams.* ◊ *a **panic attack** (= a condition in which you suddenly feel very anxious, causing your heart to beat faster, etc.)* ◊ *a **panic decision** (= one that is made when you are in a state of panic)* **2** a situation in which people are made to feel very anxious, causing them to act quickly and without thinking carefully: *News of the losses caused (a) panic among investors.* ◊ *Careful planning at this stage will help to avoid a last-minute panic.* ◊ ***There's no panic** (= we do not need to rush), we've got plenty of time.* ▣ '**panic stations** (*BrE, informal*) a situation in which people feel anxious and there is a lot of confused activity, especially because there is a lot to do in a short period of time
■ *verb* (**-ck-**) to suddenly feel frightened so that you cannot think clearly and you say or do sth stupid, dangerous, etc.; to make sb do this: [V] *I panicked when I saw smoke coming out of the engine.* ◊ [VN] *The gunfire panicked the horses.* ▣ '**panic sb into doing sth** [usually passive] to make sb act too quickly because they are afraid of sth

'**panic button** *noun* a button that sb working in a shop, bank, etc. can press to call for help if they are in danger ▣ **press/push the 'panic button** (*BrE*) to react in a sudden or extreme way to sth unexpected that has frightened you

pan·icky /'pænɪki/ *adj.* (*informal*) anxious about sth; feeling or showing panic: *He was feeling panicky.* ◊ *a panicky voice*

'**panic-stricken** *adj.* extremely anxious about sth, in a way that prevents you from thinking clearly: *He sounded panic-stricken on the phone.*

pan·nier /'pæniə(r)/ *noun* each of a pair of bags or boxes carried on either side of the back wheel of a bicycle or motorcycle; each of a pair of baskets carried on either side of its back by a horse or DONKEY—picture at BAG

pan·oply /'pænəpli/ *noun* [sing., U] (*formal*) a large and impressive number or collection of sth

pan·or·ama /ˌpænə'rɑːmə; *AmE* -'ræmə/ *noun* **1** a view of a wide area of land: *There is a superb panorama of the mountains from the hotel.* **2** a description, study or set of

pictures that presents all the different aspects or stages of a particular subject, event, etc. ▶ **pan·or·am·ic** /ˌpænə-'ræmɪk/ *adj.* [usually before noun]: *a panoramic view over the valley*

'**pan pipes** *noun* [pl.] (*BrE*) (*AmE* '**pan·pipe** [C]) a musical instrument made of a row of pipes of different lengths that you play by blowing across the open ends

pansy /'pænzi/ *noun* (*pl.* **-ies**) **1** a small garden plant with brightly coloured flowers **2** (⚠) an offensive word for a HOMOSEXUAL man

pant /pænt/ *verb* to breathe quickly with short breaths, usually with your mouth open, because you have been doing some physical exercise, or because it is very hot: [V] *She finished the race panting heavily.* ◊ *She could hear him panting up the stairs (= running up and breathing quickly).* ◊ *He found her panting for breath at the top of the hill.* [also V speech] ▶ **pant** *noun* [usually pl.]: *His breath came in short pants.*—see also PANTS ▣ see PUFF *v.* ▣ '**pant for/after sb/sth** to want sth/sb very much: *The end of the novel leaves you panting for more.*

pan·ta·loons /ˌpæntə'luːnz/ *noun* [pl.] **1** women's loose trousers/pants with wide legs that fit tightly at the ankles **2** (in the past) men's tight trousers/pants fastened at the foot

pan·tech·nicon /pæn'teknɪkən/ *noun* (*old-fashioned, BrE*) = REMOVAL VAN

pan·the·ism /'pænθiɪzəm/ *noun* [U] **1** the belief that God is present in all natural things **2** belief in many or all gods ▶ **pan·the·ist** /-θiɪst/ *noun* **pan·the·ist·ic** /ˌpænθi'ɪstɪk/ *adj.*

pan·theon /'pænθiən; *AmE* -θiɑːn/ *noun* **1** (*technical*) all the gods of a nation or people: *the ancient Egyptian pantheon* **2** (*formal*) a group of people who are famous within a particular area of activity: *She has won her place in the pantheon of popular culture.* **3** a TEMPLE (= religious building) built in honour of all the gods of a nation; a building in which famous dead people of a nation are buried or HONOURED

pan·ther /'pænθə(r)/ *noun* **1** a black LEOPARD (= a large wild animal of the cat family) **2** (*AmE*) = PUMA

pan·ties /'pæntiz/ *noun* (*especially AmE*) = KNICKERS

pan·tile /'pæntaɪl/ *noun* a curved TILE used for roofs

panto /'pæntəʊ; *AmE* -toʊ/ *noun* (*pl.* **pantos** /'pæntəʊz; *AmE* -toʊz/) (*BrE, informal*) = PANTOMIME

panto·mime /'pæntəmaɪm/ *noun* **1** (also *BrE informal* **panto**) [C, U] (in Britain) a type of play with music, dancing and jokes, that is based on a FAIRY TALE and is usually performed at Christmas **2** [U, C, usually sing.] the use of movement and the expression of your face to communicate sth or to tell a story SYN MIME **3** [C, usually sing.] (*BrE*) a ridiculous situation, usually with a lot of confusion

ˌpantomime '**dame** (also **dame**) *noun* a female character in a PANTOMIME (1), that is usually played by a man

pan·try /'pæntri/ *noun* (*pl.* **-ies**) a cupboard/closet or small room in a house, used for storing food SYN LARDER

pants /pænts/ *noun* [pl.] **1** (*BrE*) UNDERPANTS or KNICKERS: *a pair of pants* **2** (*especially AmE*) trousers: *ski pants*—picture on page A4 **3** (*BrE, slang*) (also used as an adjective) something you think is of poor quality: *Their new CD is absolute pants!* ◊ *Do we have to watch this pants programme?* ▣ **bore, scare, etc. the 'pants off sb** (*informal*) to make sb extremely bored, frightened, etc.—more at ANT, CATCH *v.*, SEAT *n.*, WEAR *v.*, WET *v.*

'**pant·suit** /'pæntsuːt; *BrE* also -sjuːt/ *noun* (*AmE*) = TROUSER SUIT

'**panty·hose** /'pæntihəʊz; *AmE* -hoʊz/ *noun* [pl.] (*AmE*) = TIGHTS

pap /pæp/ *noun* [U] **1** (*disapproving*) books, magazines, television programmes, etc. that have no real value **2** soft or almost liquid food eaten by babies or people who are ill

papa /pə'pɑː; *AmE* 'pɑːpə/ *noun* (*old-fashioned*) used by children to talk about or to address their father

pap·acy /'peɪpəsi/ *noun* **1** (**the papacy**) [sing.] the position or the authority of the POPE **2** [C, usually sing.] the period of time when a particular POPE is in power: *during the papacy of Pope John Paul II*

papal /'peɪpl/ *adj.* [only before noun] connected with the POPE: *papal authority* ◇ *a papal visit to Mexico*

pap·ar·azzo /ˌpæpə'rætsəʊ; *AmE* -'rætsoʊ/ *noun* (*pl.* **pap·ar·azzi** /-tsi/) [usually *pl.*] a photographer who follows famous people around in order to get interesting photographs of them to sell to a newspaper

pa·paya /pə'paɪə/ (*BrE* also **paw-paw**) *noun* a tropical fruit with yellow and green skin, sweet orange or red flesh and round black seeds

paper /'peɪpə(r)/ *noun, verb*

■ *noun*

FOR WRITING/WRAPPING 1 [U] (often in compounds) the thin material that you write and draw on and that is also used for wrapping and packing things: *a piece/sheet of paper* ◇ *a package wrapped in brown paper* ◇ *recycled paper* ◇ *She wrote her name and address on a slip* (= a small piece) *of paper.* ◇ *Experience is more important for this job than paper qualifications* (= that exist on paper, but may not have any real value). ◇ *paper losses/profits* (= that are shown in accounts but which may not exist in reality)—see also NOTEPAPER, WRAPPING PAPER, WRITING PAPER

NEWSPAPER 2 [C] a newspaper: *a local/national paper* ◇ *a daily/evening/Sunday paper* ◇ *I read about it in the paper.* ◇ *Have you seen today's paper?* ◇ *The papers* (= newspapers in general) *soon got hold of the story.*

DOCUMENTS 3 (papers) [pl.] pieces of paper with writing on them, such as letters, pieces of work or private documents: *His desk was covered with books and papers.* 4 (papers) [pl.] official documents that prove your identity, give you permission to do sth, etc: *divorce/identification papers*—see also WALKING PAPERS, WORKING PAPER

EXAM 5 [C] (*BrE*) a set of exam questions on a particular subject; the answers that people write to the questions: *The Geography paper was hard.* ◇ *She spent the evening marking exam papers.*

ARTICLE 6 [C] an academic article about a particular subject that is written by and for specialists: *a recent paper in the Journal of Medicine* ◇ *She was invited to give a paper* (= a talk) *on the results of her research.*—see also GREEN PAPER, ORDER PAPER, POSITION PAPER, WHITE PAPER, WORKING PAPER (1) 7 [C] (*AmE*) a piece of written work done by a student: *Your grade will be based on four papers and a final exam.*—see also TERM PAPER

ON WALLS 8 [C, U] paper that you use to cover and decorate the walls of a room SYN WALLPAPER: *The room was damp and the paper was peeling off.*

HELP There are many other compounds ending in **paper**. You will find them at their place in the alphabet.

IDM **on paper 1** when you put sth **on paper**, you write it down **2** judged from written information only, but not proved in practice: *The idea looks good on paper.*—more at PEN *n.*, WORTH *adj.*

■ *verb* [VN] to decorate the walls of a room by covering them with WALLPAPER

PHRV ˌpaper 'over sth **1** to cover a wall with WALLPAPER in order to hide sth: *The previous owners had obviously papered over any damp patches.* = WALLPAPER **2** to try to hide a problem or disagreement in a way that is temporary and not likely to be successful: *The government is trying to paper over the cracks in the cabinet.* ◇ *We can't just paper over the problem.*

paper·back /'peɪpəbæk; *AmE* -pərb-/ *noun* [C, U] a book that has a thick paper cover: *a cheap paperback* ◇ *When is it coming out in paperback?* ◇ *a paperback book/edition*—compare HARDBACK

'**paper boy**, '**paper girl** *noun* a boy or girl who delivers newspapers to people's houses

pa·per·chase /'peɪpətʃeɪs; *AmE* -pərtʃ-/ *noun* (*BrE*) a game in which one runner drops pieces of paper for the other runners to follow

'**paper clip** *noun* a piece of bent wire or plastic that is designed to hold loose sheets of paper together—picture at STATIONERY

'**paper cutter** *noun* (*AmE*) = GUILLOTINE (2)

'**paper knife** *noun* (*especially BrE*) (*AmE* usually '**letter opener**) a knife used for opening envelopes

paper·less /'peɪpələs; *AmE* -pərləs/ *adj.* using computers, telephones, etc. rather than paper to exchange information: *the paperless office* ◇ *a system of paperless business transactions*

ˌpaper '**money** *noun* [U] money that is made of paper, not coins SYN NOTES

'**paper round** *noun* (*BrE*) (*AmE* '**paper route**) *noun* the job of delivering newspapers to houses; the route taken when doing this

'**paper shop** *noun* (*BrE*) = NEWSAGENT

ˌpaper-'thin *adj.* (of objects) very thin and delicate: *paper-thin slices of meat*—compare WAFER-THIN

ˌpaper '**tiger** *noun* a person, a country or a situation that seems or claims to be powerful or dangerous but is not really

ˌpaper '**towel** *noun* **1** [C] a thick sheet of paper that you use to dry your hands or to absorb water **2** [U] (*AmE*) = KITCHEN PAPER

'**paper trail** *noun* (*informal, especially AmE*) a series of documents that provide evidence of what you have done or what has happened: *He was a shrewd lawyer with a talent for uncovering paper trails of fraud.*

paper·weight /'peɪpəweɪt; *AmE* -pərw-/ *noun* a small heavy object that you put on top of loose papers to keep them in place

paper·work /'peɪpəwɜːk; *AmE* 'peɪpərwɜːrk/ *noun* [U] **1** the written work that is part of a job, such as filling in forms or writing letters and reports: *We're trying to cut down on the amount of paperwork involved.* ◇ *I spent the afternoon doing routine paperwork.* **2** all the documents that you need for sth, such as a court case or buying a house: *How quickly can you prepare the paperwork?*

pa·pery /'peɪpəri/ *adj.* like paper; thin and dry: *papery skin*

pa·pier mâché /ˌpæpieɪ 'mæʃeɪ; *AmE* ˌpeɪpər mə'ʃeɪ; ˌpæpjeɪ/ *noun* [U] (from *French*) paper mixed with glue or flour and water, that is used to make ornaments, etc.

pap·ist /'peɪpɪst/ *noun* (△) an offensive word for a Roman Catholic, used by some Protestants ▶ **pap·ist** *adj.*

pap·rika /pə'priːkə; *BrE* also /'pæprɪkə/ *noun* [U] a red powder made from a type of PEPPER, used in cooking as a spice

'**Pap smear** *noun* (*AmE*) = SMEAR TEST

pa·pyrus /pə'paɪrəs/ *noun* (*pl.* **pa·pyri** /pə'paɪriː/) **1** [U] a tall plant with thick stems that grows in water **2** [U] paper made from the stems of the papyrus plant, used in ancient Egypt for writing and drawing on **3** [C] a document or piece of paper made of papyrus

par /pɑː(r)/ *noun* [U] **1** (in golf) the number of strokes a good player should need to complete a course or to hit the ball into a particular hole: *a par five hole* ◇ *Par for the course is 72.* **2** (also '**par value**) (*business*) the value that a share in a company had originally: *to be redeemed at par* IDM **below/under 'par** less well, good, etc. than is usual or expected: *I may take tomorrow off if I'm still feeling under par.* ◇ *Teaching in some subjects has been well below par.* **be ˌpar for the 'course** (*disapproving*) to be just what you would expect to happen or expect sb to do in a particular situation: *Starting early and working long hours is par for the course in this job.* **on a par with sb/sth** as good, bad, important, etc. as sb/sth else **up to 'par** as good as usual or as good as it should be: *I didn't think her performance was up to par.*

par. (also **para.**) *abbr.* (in writing) PARAGRAPH: *See par. 3.*

para /'pærə/ *noun* (*informal*) = PARATROOPER

para- /'pærə/ *prefix* (in nouns and adjectives) **1** beyond: *paranormal* **2** similar to but not official or not fully qualified: *paramilitary* ◇ *a paramedic*

par·able /'pærəbl/ *noun* a short story that teaches a moral or spiritual lesson, especially one of those told by Jesus as recorded in the Bible

æ	ɑː	e	ɜː	ə	ɪ	iː	i	ɒ	ɔː	ʌ	ʊ	u	uː
cat	father	ten	bird	about	sit	see	many	got	saw	cup	put	actual	too
								(BrE)					

para·bola /pəˈræbələ/ noun (geometry) a curve like the path of an object thrown into the air and falling back to earth ▶ **para·bol·ic** /ˌpærəˈbɒlɪk; AmE -ˈbɑːlɪk/ adj.: parabolic curves

parabola

para·ceta·mol /ˌpærəˈsetəmɒl; -ˈsiːtə-; AmE -mɑːl; -mɔːl/ noun [U, C] (pl. **para·ceta·mol** or **para·ceta·mols**) a drug used to reduce pain and fever: Do you have any paracetamol? ◇ Take two paracetamol(s) and try to sleep.

para·chute /ˈpærəʃuːt/ noun, verb
■ noun (also informal **chute**) a device that is attached to people or objects to make them fall slowly and safely when they are dropped from an aircraft. It consists of a large piece of thin cloth that opens out in the air to form an umbrella shape: Planes dropped supplies by parachute. ◇ a parachute drop/jump ◇ a parachute regiment
■ verb 1 [V, usually +adv./prep.] to jump from an aircraft using a parachute: The pilot was able to parachute to safety. ◇ She regularly **goes parachuting**. 2 [VN+adv./prep.] to drop sb/sth from an aircraft by parachute: Supplies were parachuted into the region.

para·chut·ist /ˈpærəʃuːtɪst/ noun a person who jumps from a plane using a parachute

par·ade /pəˈreɪd/ noun, verb
■ noun
PUBLIC CELEBRATION | 1 [C] a public celebration of a special day or event, usually with bands in the streets and decorated vehicles: the Lord Mayor's parade ◇ St Patrick's Day parade in New York
OF SOLDIERS | 2 [C, U] a formal occasion when soldiers march or stand in lines so that they can be examined by their officers or other important people: a military parade ◇ They stood as straight as soldiers **on parade**. ◇ (figurative) The latest software will be on parade at the exhibition.—see also IDENTIFICATION PARADE
SERIES | 3 [C] a series of things or people: Each generation passes through a similar parade of events.
WEALTH/ KNOWLEDGE | 4 [C, usually sing.] ~ **of wealth, knowledge, etc.** (often disapproving) an obvious display of sth, particularly in order to impress other people
ROW OF SHOPS | 5 [C] (especially BrE) (often in names) a street with a row of small shops: a shopping parade
IDM see RAIN v.
■ verb
WALK TO CELEBRATE/PROTEST | 1 [V, usually +adv./prep.] to walk somewhere in a formal group of people, in order to celebrate or protest about sth: The victorious team will parade through the city tomorrow morning.
SHOW IN PUBLIC | 2 [V+adv./prep.] to walk around in a way that makes other people notice you: People were parading up and down showing off their finest clothes. 3 [VN+adv./prep.] to show sb/sth in public so that people can see them/it: The trophy was paraded around the stadium. ◇ The prisoners were paraded in front of the crowd. ◇ (figurative) He is not one to parade his achievements.
OF SOLDIERS | 4 [+adv./prep.] to come together, or to bring soldiers together, in order to march in front of other people: [V] The crowds applauded as the guards paraded past. ◇ [VN] The colonel paraded his men before the Queen.
PRETEND | 5 ~ **(sb/sth) as sth** to pretend to be, or to make sb/sth seem to be, good or important when they are not: [V] myth parading as fact ◇ [VN] He paraded himself as a loyal supporter of the party.

pa·rade ground noun a place where soldiers gather to march or to be INSPECTED by an officer or an important visitor

para·digm /ˈpærədaɪm/ noun 1 (formal or technical) a typical example or pattern of sth: a paradigm for students to copy ◇ The war was a paradigm of the evil and destructive side of human nature. 2 (grammar) a set of all the different forms of a word: verb paradigms ▶ **para·dig·mat·ic** /ˌpærədɪɡˈmætɪk/ adj.

para·dise /ˈpærədaɪs/ noun 1 (often Paradise) [U] (in some religions) a perfect place where people go when

they die **SYN** HEAVEN: The Ancient Egyptians saw paradise as an idealized version of their own lives. 2 [C] a place that is extremely beautiful and that seems perfect, like heaven: a tropical paradise 3 [C] a perfect place for a particular activity or kind of person: The area is a bird-watcher's paradise. 4 [U] a state of perfect happiness: Being alone is his idea of paradise. 5 (Paradise) [U] (in the Bible) the garden of Eden, where Adam and Eve lived

para·dox /ˈpærədɒks; AmE -dɑːks/ noun 1 [C] a person, thing or situation that has two opposite features and therefore seems strange: He was a paradox—a loner who loved to chat to strangers. ◇ It is a curious paradox that professional comedians often have unhappy personal lives. 2 [C, U] a statement containing two opposite ideas that make it seem impossible or unlikely, although it is probably true; the use of this in writing: 'More haste, less speed' is a well-known paradox. ◇ It's a work full of paradox and ambiguity. ▶ **para·dox·ical** /ˌpærəˈdɒksɪkl; AmE -ˈdɑːks-/ adj.: It is paradoxical that some of the poorest people live in some of the richest areas of the country. **para·dox·ic·al·ly** /-kli/ adv.: Paradoxically, the less she ate, the fatter she got.

par·af·fin /ˈpærəfɪn/ (also **ˈparaffin oil**) (both especially BrE) (also **kero·sene** especially in AmE) noun [U] a type of oil obtained from PETROLEUM, coal, etc. and used as a fuel for heat and light: a paraffin heater/lamp/stove

para·glid·ing /ˈpærəɡlaɪdɪŋ/ noun [U] a sport in which you wear a special structure like a PARACHUTE, jump from a plane or a high place and are carried along by the wind before coming down to earth: to go paragliding

para·gon /ˈpærəɡən; AmE -ɡɑːn/ noun a person who is perfect or who is a perfect example of a particular good quality: I make no claim to be a paragon. ◇ He wasn't the **paragon of virtue** she had expected.

para·graph /ˈpærəɡrɑːf; AmE -ɡræf/ noun (abbr. **par.**, **para.**) a section of a piece of writing, usually consisting of several sentences dealing with a single subject. The first sentence of a paragraph starts on a new line: an opening/introductory paragraph ◇ Write a paragraph on each of the topics given below. ◇ See paragraph 15 of the handbook.

para·keet /ˈpærəkiːt/ noun a small bird of the PARROT family, usually with a long tail

para·legal /ˌpærəˈliːɡl/ noun (AmE) a person who is trained to help a lawyer ▶ **para·legal** adj.

par·al·lel /ˈpærəlel/ adj., noun, verb
■ adj. 1 ~ **(to/with sth)** two or more lines that are **parallel** to each other are the same distance apart at every point: parallel lines ◇ The road and the canal are parallel to each other. 2 very similar or taking place at the same time: a parallel career/case/development ◇ parallel trends 3 (computing) involving several computer operations at the same time: parallel processing ▶ **par·al·lel** adv.: The road and the canal **run parallel** to each other. ◇ The plane flew parallel to the coast.
■ noun 1 [C, U] a person, a situation, an event, etc. that is very similar to another, especially one in a different place or time **SYN** EQUIVALENT: These ideas have parallels in Freud's thought too. ◇ This is an achievement **without parallel** in modern times. ◇ This tradition **has no parallel** in our culture. 2 [C, usually pl.] similar features: There are interesting parallels between the 1960s and the late 1990s. ◇ It is possible to **draw a parallel between** (= find similar features in) their experience and ours. 3 (also **ˌparallel of ˈlatitude**) [C] an imaginary line around the earth that is always the same distance from the EQUATOR; this line on a map: the 49th parallel **IDM in ˈparallel (with sth/sb)** with and at the same time as sth/sb else: The new degree and the existing certificate courses would run in parallel. ◇ Ann wanted to pursue her own career in parallel with her husband's.
■ verb [VN] (written) 1 to be similar to sth; to happen at the same time as sth: Their legal system parallels our own. ◇ The rise in unemployment is paralleled by an increase in petty crime. 2 to be as good as sth: a level of achievement that has never been paralleled—compare UNPARALLELED

aɪ	aʊ	eɪ	əʊ	oʊ	ɔɪ	ɪə	eə	ʊə	j	w
my	now	say	go	go	boy	near	hair	pure	yes	wet
			(BrE)	(AmE)						

,parallel 'bars *noun* [pl.] two bars on posts that are used for doing GYMNASTIC exercises

par·al·lel·ism /ˈpærəlelɪzəm/ *noun* [U, C] (*formal*) the state of being similar; a similar feature: *I think he exaggerates the parallelism between the two cases.*

parallelograms

square   rectangle   rhombus   rhomboid

par·al·lelo·gram /ˌpærəˈleləgræm/ *noun* (*geometry*) a flat shape with four straight sides, the opposite sides being parallel and equal to each other

para·lyse (*BrE*) (*AmE* **para·lyze**) /ˈpærəlaɪz/ *verb* [VN] [often passive] **1** to make sb unable to feel or move all or part of their body: *The accident left him paralysed from the waist down.* ◊ (*figurative*) *paralysing pain/heat* ◊ (*figurative*) *She stood there, paralysed with fear.* **2** to prevent sth from functioning normally: *The airport is still paralysed by the strike.*

par·aly·sis /pəˈræləsɪs/ *noun* [U, C] (*pl.* **par·aly·ses** /-siːz/) **1** a loss of control of, and sometimes feeling in, part or most of the body, caused by disease or an injury to the nerves: *paralysis of both legs* **2** [U] a total inability to move, act, function, etc: *The strike caused total paralysis in the city*

para·lyt·ic /ˌpærəˈlɪtɪk/ *adj.* **1** [not before noun] (*BrE*, *informal*) very drunk **2** [usually before noun] (*formal*) suffering from PARALYSIS; making sb unable to move: *a paralytic illness* ◊ *paralytic fear*

para·med·ic /ˌpærəˈmedɪk/ *noun* a person whose job is to help people who are sick or injured, but who is not a doctor or a nurse: *Paramedics treated the injured at the roadside before taking them to the hospital.*—compare AMBULANCE MAN ▶ **para·med·ic·al** /-ɪkl/ *adj.*: *paramedical skills/staff*

par·am·eter /pəˈræmɪtə(r)/ *noun* [usually pl.] something that decides or limits the way in which sth can be done: *to set/define the parameters* ◊ *We had to work within the parameters that had already been established.*

para·mili·tary /ˌpærəˈmɪlətri; *AmE* -teri/ *adj., noun*
■ *adj.* [usually before noun] **1** a **paramilitary** organization is an illegal group that is organized like an army: *a right-wing paramilitary group* **2** helping the official army of a country: *paramilitary police, such as the CRS in France*
■ *noun* [usually pl.] (*pl.* **-ies**) **1** a member of an illegal paramilitary group or organization **2** a member of an organization that helps the official army of a country

para·mount /ˈpærəmaʊnt/ *adj.* **1** more important than anything else: *This matter is of paramount importance.* ◊ *Safety is paramount.* **2** (*formal*) having the highest position or the greatest power: *China's paramount leader* ▶ **para·mount·cy** /-maʊntsi/ *noun* [U]

par·amour /ˈpærəmʊə(r); *AmE* -mʊr/ *noun* (*old-fashioned* or *literary*) a person that sb is having a romantic or sexual relationship with SYN LOVER

para·noia /ˌpærəˈnɔɪə/ *noun* [U] **1** (*medical*) a mental illness in which a person may wrongly believe that other people are trying to harm them, that they are sb very important, etc. **2** (*informal*) fear or suspicion of other people when there is no evidence or reason for this

para·noid /ˈpærənɔɪd/ *adj., noun*
■ *adj.* (also *less frequent* **para·noiac** /ˌpærəˈnɔɪɪk; -ˈnɔɪæk/) **1** afraid or suspicious of other people and believing that they are trying to harm you, in a way that is not reasonable: *She's getting really paranoid about what other people say about her.* **2** suffering from a mental illness in which you wrongly believe that other people are trying to harm you or that you are very important: *paranoid delusions* ◊ *paranoid schizophrenia* ◊ *a paranoid killer*
■ *noun* (also **para·noiac** /ˌpærəˈnɔɪk; -ˈnɔɪæk/) a person who suffers from paranoia

para·nor·mal /ˌpærəˈnɔːml; *AmE* -ˈnɔːrml/ *adj.* **1** that cannot be explained by science or reason and that seems to involve mysterious forces SYN SUPERNATURAL: *para-*

normal phenomena/events **2** (**the paranormal**) *noun* [sing.] events or subjects that are paranormal SYN THE SUPERNATURAL: *an interest in the paranormal*

para·pet /ˈpærəpɪt; -pet/ *noun* a low protective wall along the edge of a bridge, a roof, etc: (*figurative*) *He was not prepared to put his head above the parapet and say what he really thought* (= he did not want to risk doing it).

para·pher·na·lia /ˌpærəfəˈneɪliə; *AmE* also -fərˈn-/ *noun* [U] a large number of objects or personal possessions, especially the equipment that you need for a particular activity: *skiing paraphernalia* ◊ *an electric kettle and all the paraphernalia for making tea and coffee* ◊ (*figurative*, *disapproving*) *the legal paraphernalia of court hearings and appeals*

para·phrase /ˈpærəfreɪz/ *verb, noun*
■ *verb* to express what sb has said or written using different words, especially in order to make it easier to understand: [VN] *Try to paraphrase the question before you answer it.* [also V]
■ *noun* a statement that expresses sth that sb has written or said using different words, especially in order to make it easier to understand

para·ple·gia /ˌpærəˈpliːdʒə/ *noun* [U] PARALYSIS (= loss of control or feeling) in the legs and lower body

para·ple·gic /ˌpærəˈpliːdʒɪk/ *noun* a person who suffers from paraplegia ▶ **para·ple·gic** *adj.*

para·psych·ology /ˌpærəsaɪˈkɒlədʒi; *AmE* -ˈkɑːl-/ *noun* [U] the study of mental powers that seem to exist but that cannot be explained by scientific knowledge

para·quat /ˈpærəkwɒt; *AmE* -kwɑːt/ *noun* [U] an extremely poisonous liquid used to kill plants that are growing where they are not wanted

par·as·cend·ing /ˈpærəsendɪŋ/ *noun* [U] a sport in which you wear a PARACHUTE and are pulled along behind a boat so that you rise up into the air: *to go parascending*

para·site /ˈpærəsaɪt/ *noun* **1** a small animal or plant that lives on or inside another animal or plant and gets its food from it **2** (*disapproving*) a person who always relies on or benefits from other people and gives nothing back: *He regards students as parasites on society.*

para·sit·ic /ˌpærəˈsɪtɪk/ (also *less frequent* **para·sit·ical** /ˌpærəˈsɪtɪkl/) *adj.* **1** caused by a parasite: *a parasitic disease/infection* **2** living on another animal or plant and getting its food from it: *a parasitic mite/worm* **3** (*disapproving*) (of a person) always relying on or benefiting from other people and giving nothing back ▶ **para·sit·ic·al·ly** /-kli/ *adv.*

para·sol /ˈpærəsɒl; *AmE* -sɔːl; -sɑːl/ *noun* **1** a type of light umbrella that women in the past carried to protect themselves from the sun **2** a large umbrella that is used for example on beaches or outside cafes to protect people from hot sun—compare SUNSHADE

para·troop·er /ˈpærətruːpə(r)/ (also *informal* **para**) *noun* a member of the paratroops

para·troops /ˈpærətruːps/ *noun* [pl.] soldiers who are trained to jump from planes using a PARACHUTE ▶ **para·troop** *adj.* [only before noun]: *a paratroop regiment*

par·boil /ˈpɑːbɔɪl; *AmE* ˈpɑːrb-/ *verb* [VN] to boil food, especially vegetables, until it is partly cooked

par·cel /ˈpɑːsl; *AmE* ˈpɑːrsl/ *noun, verb*
■ *noun* **1** (*especially BrE*) (*AmE usually* **pack·age**) something that is wrapped in paper or put into a thick envelope so that it can be sent by mail, carried easily, or given as a present: *There's a parcel and some letters for you.* ◊ *She was carrying a parcel of books under her arm.* ◊ *The prisoners were allowed food parcels.* **2** a piece of land: *50 five-acre parcels have already been sold.* IDM see PART *n.*
■ *verb* (*especially BrE*) (**-ll-**, *AmE* **-l-**) [VN] ~ **sth** (**up**) to wrap sth up and make it into a parcel: *She parcelled up the books to send.* PHRV **,parcel sth↔'out** to divide sth into parts or between several people: *The land was parcelled out into small lots.*

'parcel bomb *noun* a bomb that is sent to sb in a parcel/package and that explodes when the parcel is opened

b	d	f	g	h	k	l	m	n	p	r
bad	did	fall	get	hat	cat	leg	man	now	pen	red

parch /pɑːtʃ; AmE pɑːrtʃ/ verb [VN] (especially of hot weather) to make an area of land very dry: *A drought is parching much of the country.*

parched /pɑːtʃt; AmE pɑːrtʃt/ adj. **1** very dry, especially because the weather is hot: *large areas of dry parched land* ◊ *soil parched by drought* ◊ *She licked her parched lips.* **2** (informal) very thirsty: *Let's get a drink—I'm parched.*

Par·cheesi™ /pɑːˈtʃiːzi; AmE pɑːrˈtʃiː-/ noun [U] (AmE) = LUDO

parch·ment /ˈpɑːtʃmənt; AmE ˈpɑːrtʃ-/ noun **1** [U] material made from the skin of a sheep or goat, used in the past for writing on: *parchment scrolls* **2** [U] a thick yellowish type of paper: *a sheet of non-stick baking parchment* **3** [C] a document written on a piece of parchment

par·don /ˈpɑːdn; AmE ˈpɑːrdn/ exclamation, noun, verb
■ exclamation **1** (also ˌpardon ˈme especially in AmE) used to ask sb to repeat sth because you did not hear it or did not understand it: *'You're very quiet today.' 'Pardon?' 'I said you're very quiet today.'* **2** (also ˌpardon ˈme) used by some people to say 'sorry' when they have accidentally made a rude noise, or said or done sth wrong
■ noun **1** (also BrE, law ˌfree ˈpardon) [C] an official decision not to punish sb for a crime, or to say that sb is not guilty of a crime: *to ask/grant/receive a pardon* ◊ *a royal/presidential pardon* **2** [U] (formal) ~ (for sth) the action of forgiving sb for sth: *He asked her pardon for having deceived her.* **IDM** see BEG
■ verb (not usually used in the progressive tenses) **1** [VN] to officially allow sb who has been found guilty of a crime to leave prison and/or avoid punishment: *She was pardoned after serving ten years of a life sentence.* **2** ~ sb (for sth/ for doing sth) to forgive sb for sth they have said or done (used in many expressions when you want to be polite) **SYN** EXCUSE: [VN] *Pardon my ignorance, but what is a 'duplex'?* ◊ *The place was, if you'll pardon the expression, a dump.* ◊ (BrE) *You could be pardoned for thinking* (= it is easy to understand why people think) *that education is not the government's priority.* ◊ *Pardon me for interrupting you.* ◊ [VN-ing] *Pardon my asking, but is that your husband?* [also VNN] **IDM** ˌpardon ˈme (spoken) **1** (especially AmE) used to ask sb to repeat sth because you did not hear it or do not understand it **2** used by some people to say 'sorry' when they have accidentally made a rude noise or done sth wrong—see also I BEG YOUR PARDON, ˌpardon me for ˈdoing sth used to show that you are upset or offended by the way that sb has spoken to you: *'Oh, just shut up!' 'Well, pardon me for breathing!'*

par·don·able /ˈpɑːdnəbl; AmE ˈpɑːrdn-/ adj. (written) that can be forgiven or excused: *a pardonable error* **OPP** UNPARDONABLE

pare /peə(r); AmE per/ verb [VN] **1** ~ sth (off/away) to remove the thin outer layer of sth: *First, pare the rind from the lemon.* ◊ *She pared the apple.* ◊ *He pared away the excess glue with a razor blade.* **2** ~ sth (back/down) to gradually reduce the size or amount: *The training budget has been pared back to a minimum.* ◊ *The workforce has been pared to the bone* (= reduced to the lowest possible level). **3** (especially BrE) to cut away the edges of sth, especially your nails, in order to make them smooth and neat—see also PARINGS

par·ent /ˈpeərənt; AmE ˈper-/ noun **1** [usually pl.] a person's father or mother: *He's still living with his parents.* ◊ *her adoptive parents* ◊ *Sue and Ben have recently become parents.*—see also ONE-PARENT FAMILY, SINGLE PARENT, STEP-PARENT **2** an animal or a plant which produces other animals or plants: *the parent bird/tree* **3** (often used as an adjective) an organization that produces and owns or controls smaller organizations of the same type: *a parent bank and its subsidiaries* ◊ *the parent company*

par·ent·age /ˈpeərəntɪdʒ; AmE ˈper-/ noun [U] the origin of a person's parents and who they are: *a young American of German parentage* ◊ *Nothing is known about her parentage and background.*

par·en·tal /pəˈrentl/ adj. [usually before noun] connected with a parent or parents: *parental responsibility/ rights* ◊ *parental choice in education* ◊ *the parental home*

par·en·thesis /pəˈrenθəsɪs/ noun (pl. par·en·theses /-əsiːz/) **1** a word, sentence, etc. that is added to a speech or piece of writing, especially in order to give extra information. In writing, it is separated from the rest of the text using BRACKETS, COMMAS or DASHES. **2** [usually pl.] (AmE or formal) = BRACKET

par·en·thet·ic /ˌpærənˈθetɪk/ (also par·en·thet·ical /-ɪkl/) adj. [usually before noun] (formal) given as extra information in a speech or piece of writing: *parenthetic remarks* ▶ **par·en·thet·ic·al·ly** /-kli/ adv.

par·ent·hood /ˈpeərənthʊd; AmE ˈper-/ noun [U] the state of being a parent: *the responsibilities/joys of parent-hood*

par·ent·ing /ˈpeərəntɪŋ; AmE ˈper-/ noun [U] the process of caring for your child or children: *good/poor parenting* ◊ *parenting skills*

par·en·tis ⇨ IN LOCO PARENTIS

ˈparents-in-law noun [pl.] the parents of your husband or wife—see also IN-LAWS

ˌparent-ˈteacher association noun = PTA

par excellence /ˌpɑːr ˈeksəlɑːns; AmE ˌeksəˈlɑːns/ adj. (from French) (only used after the noun it describes) better than all the others of the same kind; a very good example of sth: *She turned out to be an organizer par excellence.* ▶ **par excellence** adv.: *Chemistry was par excellence the laboratory science of the early nineteenth century.*

par·iah /pəˈraɪə/ noun a person who is not acceptable to society and is avoided by everyone **SYN** OUTCAST

par·ings /ˈpeərɪŋz; AmE ˈper-/ noun [pl.] thin pieces that have been cut off sth: *cheese parings*—see also PARE

par·ish /ˈpærɪʃ/ noun **1** an area that has its own church and that a priest is responsible for: *a parish church/ priest* ◊ *He is vicar of a large rural parish.* **2** (in England) a small country area that has its own elected local government: *the parish council* **3** [sing.+ sing./pl. v.] the people living in a particular area, especially those who go to church

ˌparish ˈclerk noun an official who does administrative work for a church in a particular area

pa·rish·ion·er /pəˈrɪʃənə(r)/ noun a person living in a parish, especially one who goes to church regularly

ˌparish-ˈpump adj. [only before noun] (BrE, disapproving) connected with local affairs only (and therefore not thought of as being very important): *parish-pump politics*

ˌparish ˈregister noun a book that has a list of all the BAPTISMS, marriages and funerals that have taken place at a particular PARISH church

par·ity /ˈpærəti/ noun (pl. -ies) **1** [U] ~ (with sb/sth) | ~ (between A and B) (formal) the state of being equal, especially the state of having equal pay or status: *Prison officers are demanding pay parity with the police force.* **2** [U, C] (finance) the fact of the units of money of two different countries being equal: *to achieve parity with the dollar*

park /pɑːk; AmE pɑːrk/ noun, verb
■ noun **1** [C] an area of public land in a town or a city where people go to walk, play and relax: *Hyde Park* ◊ *We went for a walk in the park.* ◊ *a park bench* **2** [C] (in compounds) an area of land used for a particular purpose: *a business/science park* ◊ *a wildlife park*—see also AMUSEMENT PARK, CAR PARK, NATIONAL PARK, SAFARI PARK, THEME PARK **3** [C] (in Britain) an enclosed area of land, usually with fields and trees, attached to a large country house **4** [C] (AmE) a piece of land for playing sports, especially baseball —see also BALLPARK **5** (the park) [sing.] (BrE) a football or rugby field: *the fastest man on the park*
■ verb **1** to leave a vehicle that you are driving in a particular place for a period of time: [V, VN] *You can't park here.* ◊ *You can't park the car here.* ◊ (VN) *He's parked very badly.* ◊ [VN] *a badly parked truck* ◊ *A red van was parked in front of the house.* ◊ *a parked car* ◊ (informal, figurative) *Just park your bags in the hall until your room is ready.*—see also DOUBLE-PARK **2** [VN+adv./prep.] ~ yourself (informal) to sit or stand in a particular place for a period of time: *She parked herself on the edge of the bed.*

s	t	v	z	ʃ	ʒ	tʃ	dʒ	θ	ð	ŋ
see	tea	van	zoo	shoe	vision	chain	jam	thin	this	sing

parka /ˈpɑːkə; *AmE* ˈpɑːrkə/ *noun* a very warm jacket or coat with a HOOD that often has fur inside

‚park and ˈride *noun* a system designed to reduce traffic in towns in which people park their cars on the edge of a town and then take a special bus to the town centre; the area where people park their cars before taking the bus: *Use the park and ride.* ◊ *I've left my car in the park and ride.* ◊ *a park-and-ride service*

park·ing /ˈpɑːkɪŋ; *AmE* ˈpɑːrk-/ *noun* [U] **1** the act of stopping a vehicle at a place and leaving it there for a period of time: *There is no parking here between 9 a.m. and 6 p.m.* ◊ *I managed to find a **parking space**.* ◊ *a parking fine* (= for parking illegally) **2** a space or an area for leaving vehicles: *The hotel is centrally situated with ample free parking.*

ˈparking brake *noun* (*AmE*) = HANDBRAKE

ˈparking garage *noun* (*AmE*) = MULTI-STOREY CAR PARK

ˈparking lot *noun* (*AmE*) an area where people can leave their cars—compare CAR PARK

ˈparking meter (also **meter**) *noun* a machine beside the road that you put money into when you park your car next to it

ˈparking ticket (also **ticket**) *noun* an official notice that is put on your car when you have parked illegally, ordering you to pay money

Par·kin·son's dis·ease /ˈpɑːkɪnsnz dɪziːz; *AmE* ˈpɑːrk-/ (also **Par·kin·son·ism** /ˈpɑːkɪnsənɪzəm; *AmE* ˈpɑːrk-/) *noun* [U] a disease of the nervous system that gets worse over a period of time and causes the muscles to become weak and the limbs to shake

ˈParkinson's law *noun* [U] (*humorous*) the idea that work will always take as long as the time available for it

park·land /ˈpɑːklænd; *AmE* ˈpɑːrk-/ *noun* [U] open land with grass and trees, for example around a large house in the country

park·way /ˈpɑːkweɪ; *AmE* ˈpɑːrk-/ *noun* (*AmE*) a wide road with trees and grass along the sides or middle

par·lance /ˈpɑːləns; *AmE* ˈpɑːrl-/ *noun* [U] (*formal*) a particular way of using words or expressing yourself, for example one used by a particular group: *in common/ legal/modern parlance* ◊ *A Munro, in climbing parlance, is a Scottish mountain exceeding 3000 feet.*

par·lay /ˈpɑːleɪ; *AmE* ˈpɑːrleɪ/ *verb* PHRV **parlay sth into sth** (*AmE*) to use or develop sth such as money or a skill to make it more successful or worth more: *She hopes to parlay her success as a model into an acting career.*

par·ley /ˈpɑːli; *AmE* ˈpɑːrli/ *noun, verb*
■ *noun* (*old-fashioned*) a discussion between enemies or people who disagree, in order to try and find a way of solving a problem
■ *verb* [V] ~ (**with sb**) (*old-fashioned*) to discuss sth with sb in order to solve a disagreement

par·lia·ment /ˈpɑːləmənt; *AmE* ˈpɑːrl-/ *noun* **1** [C, sing.+ sing./pl. *v.*] the group of people who are elected to make and change the laws of a country: *The German parliament is called the 'Bundestag'.* **2** (**Parliament**) [U+sing./pl. *v.*] the parliament of the United Kingdom, consisting of the House of Commons and the House of Lords: *a Member of Parliament* ◊ *the issue was debated in Parliament* ◊ *an Act of Parliament* ◊ *to have/win a seat in Parliament* ◊ *to be elected to Parliament* **3** (also **Parliament**) [C, U] a particular period during which a parliament is working; Parliament as it exists between one GENERAL ELECTION and the next: *We are now into the second half of the parliament.* ◊ *to dissolve Parliament* (= formally end its activities) *and call an election*—see also HOUSES OF PARLIAMENT, HUNG

par·lia·men·tar·ian /ˌpɑːləmənˈteəriən; *AmE* ˌpɑːrləmənˈter-/ *noun* a member of a parliament, especially one with a lot of skill and experience

par·lia·men·tary /ˌpɑːləˈmentri; *AmE* ˌpɑːrl-/ *adj.* [usually before noun] connected with a parliament; having a parliament: *parliamentary elections* ◊ *a parliamentary democracy*—compare UNPARLIAMENTARY

par·lour (*BrE*) (*AmE* **par·lor**) /ˈpɑːlə(r); *AmE* ˈpɑːrl-/ *noun* **1** (*old-fashioned*) a room in a private house for sitting in, entertaining visitors, etc. **2** (in compounds) (*especially AmE*) a shop/store that provides particular goods or services: *a beauty/an ice-cream parlour*—see also FUNERAL PARLOUR, MASSAGE PARLOUR

ˈparlour game (*BrE*) (*AmE* ˈparlor game) *noun* a game played in the home, especially a word game or guessing game

par·lous /ˈpɑːləs; *AmE* ˈpɑːrləs/ *adj.* (*formal*) (of a situation) very bad and very uncertain; dangerous: *the parlous state of the economy*

Par·mesan /ˌpɑːmɪˈzæn; ˌpɑːmɪˈzæn; *AmE* ˈpɑːrməzɑːn; -zæn/ (also ‚Parmesan ˈcheese) *noun* [U] a type of very hard Italian cheese that is usually GRATED and eaten on Italian food

pa·ro·chial /pəˈrəʊkiəl; *AmE* -ˈroʊ-/ *adj.* **1** [usually before noun] (*formal*) connected with a church PARISH: *parochial schools* ◊ *a member of the parochial church council* **2** (*disapproving*) only concerned with small issues that happen in your local area and not interested in more important things ▶ **pa·ro·chial·ism** /-ɪzəm/ *noun* [U]: *the parochialism of a small community*

par·od·ist /ˈpærədɪst/ *noun* a person who writes parodies

par·ody /ˈpærədi/ *noun, verb*
■ *noun* (*pl.* **-ies**) ~ (**of sth**) **1** [C, U] a piece of writing, music, acting, etc. that deliberately copies the style of sb/sth in order to be amusing: *a parody of a horror film* **2** [C] (*disapproving*) something that is such a bad or unfair example of sth that it seems ridiculous: *The trial was a parody of justice.*
■ *verb* (**par·odies, par·ody·ing, par·odied, par·odied**) [VN] to copy the style of sb/sth in an exaggerated way, especially in order to make people laugh: *to parody an author/a style/an accent*

par·ole /pəˈrəʊl; *AmE* pəˈroʊl/ *noun* [U] permission that is given to a prisoner to leave prison before the end of their SENTENCE on condition that they behave well: *to be eligible for parole* ◊ *She was released on parole.* ▶ **par·ole** *verb* [VN] [usually passive]: *She was paroled after two years.*

par·ox·ysm /ˈpærəksɪzəm/ *noun* ~ (**of sth**) (*written*) **1** a sudden strong feeling or expression of an emotion that cannot be controlled: *paroxysms of hate* ◊ *a paroxysm of laughter* **2** (*medical*) a sudden short attack of pain, causing physical shaking that cannot be controlled

par·quet /ˈpɑːkeɪ; *AmE* pɑːrˈkeɪ/ *noun* [U] a floor covering made of flat pieces of wood fixed together in a pattern: *parquet flooring*—compare WOODBLOCK

parri·cide /ˈpærɪsaɪd/ *noun* [U, C] (*formal*) the crime of killing your father, mother or a close relative; a person who is guilty of this crime—compare FRATRICIDE, MATRICIDE, PATRICIDE

par·rot /ˈpærət/ *noun, verb*
■ *noun* a tropical bird with a curved beak. There are several types of parrot, most of which have bright feathers. Some are kept as pets and can be trained to copy human speech. IDM see SICK *adj.*
■ *verb* [VN] (*disapproving*) to repeat what sb else has said without thinking about what it means

ˈparrot-fashion *adv.* (*BrE, disapproving*) if sb learns or repeats sth **parrot-fashion**, they do it without thinking about it or understanding what it means

parry /ˈpæri/ *verb* (**par·ries, parry·ing, par·ried, par·ried**) **1** to defend yourself against sb who is attacking you by pushing their hand, arm, weapon, etc. to one side SYN DEFLECT: [VN] *He parried a blow to his head.* ◊ *The shot was parried by the goalie.* [also V] **2** to avoid having to answer a difficult question, criticism, etc., especially by replying in the same way: [VN] *She parried all questions about their relationship.* [also V speech] ▶ **parry** *noun* (*pl.* **-ies**)

parse /pɑːz; *AmE* pɑːrs/ *verb* [VN] (*grammar*) to divide a sentence into parts and describe the grammar of each word or part

æ	ɑː	e	ɜː	ə	ɪ	iː	i	ɒ	ɔː	ʌ	ʊ	u	uː
cat	father	ten	bird	about	sit	see	many	got	saw	cup	put	actual	too
								(BrE)					

P

Par·see (also **Parsi**) /ˌpɑːˈsiː; *AmE* ˌpɑːrˈsiː/ *noun* a member of a religious group in India whose ancestors originally came from Persia and whose religion is Zoroastrianism

par·si·mo·ni·ous /ˌpɑːsɪˈməʊniəs; *AmE* ˌpɑːrsəˈmoʊ-/ *adj.* (*formal*) extremely unwilling to spend money SYN MEAN ▶ **par·si·mo·ni·ous·ly** *adv.*

par·si·mony /ˈpɑːsɪməni; *AmE* ˈpɑːrsəmoʊni/ *noun* [U] (*formal*) the fact of being extremely unwilling to spend money

pars·ley /ˈpɑːsli; *AmE* ˈpɑːrsli/ *noun* [U] a plant with curly green leaves that are used in cooking as a herb and to decorate food: *fish with parsley sauce*—see also COW PARSLEY

pars·nip /ˈpɑːsnɪp; *AmE* ˈpɑːrs-/ *noun* [C, U] a long pale yellow root vegetable—picture on page A3

par·son /ˈpɑːsn; *AmE* ˈpɑːrsn/ *noun* (*old-fashioned*) **1** an Anglican VICAR or PARISH priest **2** (*informal*) a Protestant CLERGYMAN

par·son·age /ˈpɑːsənɪdʒ; *AmE* ˈpɑːrs-/ *noun* a parson's house

parson's 'nose (*AmE* also **pope's 'nose**) *noun* the piece of flesh at the tail end of a cooked bird, usually a chicken

part /pɑːt; *AmE* pɑːrt/ *noun, verb, adv.*

■ *noun*

SOME | **1** [U] ~ **of sth** some but not all of a thing: *We spent part of the time in the museum.* ◊ *Part of the building was destroyed in the fire.* ◊ *Voters are given **only part of the story** (= only some of the information).* ◊ *Part of me feels sorry for him (= I feel partly, but not entirely, sorry for him).*

PIECE | **2** [C] a section, piece or feature of sth: *The early part of her life was spent in Paris.* ◊ *The novel is good **in parts**.* ◊ *We've done the difficult part of the job.* ◊ *The procedure can be divided into two parts.* ◊ *The worst part was having to wait three hours in the rain.*

MEMBER | **3** [U] a member of sth; a person or thing that, together with others, makes up a single unit: *You need to be able to work as part of a team.*

OF MACHINE | **4** [C] a piece of a machine or structure: *aircraft parts* ◊ *the working parts of the machinery* ◊ **spare parts**

OF BODY/PLANT | **5** [C] a separate piece or area of a human or animal body or of a plant: *the parts of the body*—see also PRIVATE PARTS

REGION/AREA | **6** [C] an area or a region of the world, a country, a town, etc: *the northern part of the country* ◊ *a plant that grows in many parts of the world* ◊ *Which part of London do you come from?* ◊ *Come and visit us if you're ever in our part of the world.* **7** (**parts**) [pl.] (*old-fashioned, informal*) a region or an area: *She's not from these parts.* ◊ *He's just arrived back from foreign parts.*

OF BOOK/SERIES | **8** [C] (*abbr.* **pt**) a section of a book, television series, etc., especially one that is published or broadcast separately: *an encyclopedia published in 25 weekly parts* ◊ *Henry IV, Part II* ◊ *The final part will be shown next Sunday evening.*

FOR ACTOR | **9** [C] a role played by an actor in a play, film/movie, etc.; the words spoken by an actor in a particular role: *She was very good in the part.* ◊ *Have you learned your part yet?* ◊ (*figurative*) *He's always **playing a part** (= pretending to be sth that he is not).*

IN MUSIC | **10** [C] music for a particular voice or instrument in a group singing or playing together: *the clarinet part* ◊ *four-part harmony*

EQUAL PORTION | **11** [C] a unit of measurement that allows you to compare the different amounts of substances in sth: *Add three parts wine to one part water.* ◊ *fluoride levels of 0.2 parts per million*

IN HAIR | **12** [C] (*AmE*) = PARTING

IDM **the best/better part of sth** most of sth, especially a period of time; more than half of sth: *He drank the best part of a bottle of Scotch waiting for her to get home.* ◊ *The journey took her the better part of an hour.* **for the 'most part** mostly; usually: *The contributors are, for the most part, professional scientists.* **for 'my, 'his, 'their, etc. part** speaking for myself, etc. SYN PERSONALLY **have a part to 'play (in sth)** to be able to help sth: *We all have a part to play in the fight against crime.* **have/play a 'part (in sth)** to be involved in sth: *She plays an active part in local politics.* **have/play/take/want no 'part in/of sth** to not be involved or refuse to be involved in sth, especially because you disapprove of it: *He had no part in the decision.* ◊ *I want no part of this sordid business.* **in 'part** partly; to some extent: *Her success was due in part to luck.* **look/dress the 'part** to have an appearance or wear clothes suitable for a particular job, role or position **a man/woman of (many) 'parts** a person with many skills **on the part of sb/on sb's part** made or done by sb: *It was an error on my part.* **part and parcel of sth** an essential part of sth: *Keeping the accounts is part and parcel of my job.* **part of the 'furniture** a person or thing that you are so used to seeing that you no longer notice them: *I worked there so long that I became part of the furniture.* **take sth in good 'part** (*BrE*) to accept sth slightly unpleasant without complaining or being offended: *He took the teasing in good part.* **take 'part (in sth)** to be involved in sth SYN PARTICIPATE: *to take part in a discussion/demonstration/fight/celebration* ◊ *Many countries took part in the last Olympic Games?* **take sb's 'part** (*BrE*) to support sb, for example in an argument: *His mother always takes his part.*—more at DISCRETION, LARGE, SUM *n.*

■ *verb*

LEAVE SB | **1** [V] ~ **(from sb)** (*formal*) if a person **parts** from another person, or two people **part**, they leave each other: *We parted at the airport.* ◊ *I hate to part on such bad terms.* ◊ *He has recently parted from his wife (= they have started to live apart).* ◊ *I never forgot his parting words (= what he said as he left)*—see also PARTING *adj.*

KEEP APART | **2** [VN] [often passive] ~ **sb (from sb)** (*formal*) to prevent sb from being with sb else: *I hate being parted from the children.* ◊ *The puppies were parted from their mother at birth.*

MOVE AWAY | **3** if two things or parts of things **part** or you **part** them, they move away from each other: [V] *The crowd parted in front of them.* ◊ *The elevator doors parted and out stepped the President.* ◊ [VN] *Her lips were slightly parted.* ◊ *She parted the curtains a little and looked out.*

HAIR | **4** [VN] to divide your hair into two sections with a comb, creating a line that goes from the back of your head to the front: *He parts his hair in the middle.*—see also PARTING *n.*

IDM **part 'company (with/from sb)** **1** to leave sb; to end a relationship with sb: *This is where we part company (= go in different directions).* ◊ *The band have parted company with their manager.* ◊ *The band and their manager have parted company.* **2** to disagree with sb about sth: *Weber parted company with Marx on a number of important issues.*

PHRV **'part with sth** to give sth to sb else, especially sth that you would prefer to keep: *Make sure you read the contract before parting with any money.*

■ *adv.* (often in compounds) consisting of two things; to some extent but not completely: *She's part French, part English.* ◊ *His feelings were part anger, part relief.* ◊ *The course is part funded by the European Commission.* ◊ *He is part owner of a farm in France.*

par·take /pɑːˈteɪk; *AmE* pɑːrˈt-/ *verb* (**par·took** /-ˈtʊk/ **par·taken** /-ˈteɪkən/) [V] (*formal*) **1** ~ **(of sth)** (*old-fashioned* or *humorous*) to eat or drink sth especially sth that is offered to you: *Would you care to partake of some refreshment?* **2** ~ **(in sth)** (*old-fashioned*) to take part in an activity: *They preferred not to partake in the social life of the town.* PHRV **par'take of sth** (*formal*) to have some of a particular quality: *His work partakes of the aesthetic fashions of his time.*

part ex'change *noun* [U] (*BrE*) a way of buying sth, such as a car, in which you give the old one as part of the payment for a more expensive one: *We'll take your car **in part-exchange**.* ▶ **part-ex'change** *verb* [VN]

par·tial /ˈpɑːʃl; *AmE* ˈpɑːrʃl/ *adj.* **1** not complete or whole: *It was only a partial solution to the problem.* ◊ *a partial*

aɪ	aʊ	eɪ	əʊ	oʊ	ɔɪ	ɪə	eə	ʊə	j	w
my	now	say	go	go	boy	near	hair	pure	yes	wet
			(BrE)	(AmE)						

eclipse of the sun ◊ *Our success was only partial.* **2** [not before noun] **~ to sb/sth** (*old-fashioned*) liking sb/sth very much: *I'm not partial to mushrooms.* **3** [not usually before noun] **~ (towards sb/sth)** (*disapproving*) showing or feeling too much support for one person, team, idea, etc., in a way that is unfair OPP IMPARTIAL

par·ti·al·ity /ˌpɑːʃiˈæləti; *AmE* ˌpɑːrʃ-/ *noun* (*formal*) **1** [U] (*disapproving*) the unfair support of one person, team, idea, etc. OPP IMPARTIALITY **2** [sing.] **~ for sb/sth** a feeling of liking sth/sb very much: *She has a partiality for exotic flowers.*

par·tial·ly /ˈpɑːʃəli; *AmE* ˈpɑːrʃ-/ *adv.* partly; not completely: *The road was partially blocked by a fallen tree.* ◊ *a society for the blind and* **partially sighted** (= people who can see very little). ⟹ note at PARTLY

par·tici·pant /pɑːˈtɪsɪpənt; *AmE* pɑːrˈt-/ *noun* **~ (in sth)** a person who is taking part in an activity or event: *He has been an active participant in the discussion.*

par·tici·pate /pɑːˈtɪsɪpeɪt; *AmE* pɑːrˈt-/ *verb* [V] **~ (in sth)** to take part in or become involved in an activity: *She didn't participate in the discussion.* ◊ *We want to encourage students to participate fully in the running of the college.* ◊ *Details of the competition are available at all participating stores.* ⟹ note at HELP

par·tici·pa·tion /pɑːˌtɪsɪˈpeɪʃn; *AmE* pɑːrˌt-/ *noun* [U] **~ (in sth)** the act of taking part in an activity or event: *a show with lots of audience participation* ◊ *A back injury prevented active participation in any sports for a while.*

par·ti·ciple /ˈpɑːtɪsɪpl; *AmE* ˈpɑːrt-/ *noun* (*grammar*) (in English) a word formed from a verb, ending in *-ing* (= the PRESENT PARTICIPLE) or *-ed*, *-en*, etc. (= the PAST PARTICIPLE) ▶ **par·ti·ci·pial** /ˌpɑːtɪˈsɪpiəl; *AmE* ˌpɑːrt-/ *adj.*

par·ticle /ˈpɑːtɪkl; *AmE* ˈpɑːrt-/ *noun* **1** a very small piece of sth: *particles of dust* ◊ *dust particles* ◊ *There was* **not a particle of evidence** (= no evidence at all) *to support the case.* **2** (*physics*) a very small piece of matter, such as an ELECTRON or PROTON, that is part of an atom—see also ELEMENTARY PARTICLE **3** (*grammar*) an adverb or a preposition that can combine with a verb to make a PHRASAL VERB: *In 'She tore up the letter', the word 'up' is a particle.*—see also ADVERBIAL PARTICLE

par·ticu·lar /pəˈtɪkjələ(r); *AmE* pərˈt-/ *adj., noun*

■ *adj.* **1** [only before noun] used to emphasize that you are referring to one individual person, thing or type of thing and not others: *There is one particular patient I'd like you to see.* ◊ *Is there a particular type of book he enjoys?* **2** [only before noun] greater than usual; special: *We must pay particular attention to this point.* ◊ *These documents are of particular interest.* **3** **~ (about/over sth)** very definite about what you like and careful about what you choose SYN FUSSY: *She's very particular about her clothes.* IDM **in particular 1** especially or particularly: *He loves science fiction in particular.* **2** special or SPECIFIC: *Peter was lying on the sofa doing* **nothing in particular.** ◊ *Is there anything in particular you'd like for dinner?* ◊ *She directed the question at* **no one in particular.**

■ *noun* (*formal*) **1** [usually pl.] a fact or detail especially one that is officially written down: *The police officer took down all the particulars of the burglary.* ◊ *The nurse asked me for my particulars* (= personal details such as your name, address, etc.). ◊ *The new contract will be the same in every particular as the old one.* **2** (**particulars**) [pl.] written information and details about a property, business, job, etc: *Application forms and further particulars are available from the Personnel Office.* ◊ *the particulars of a house in Bury*

par·ticu·lar·ity /pəˌtɪkjuˈlærəti; *AmE* pərˈt-/ *noun* (*pl.* **-ies**) (*formal*) **1** [U] the quality of being individual or UNIQUE: *the particularity of each human being* **2** [U] attention to detail; being exact **3** (**particularities**) [pl.] the special features or details of sth

par·ticu·lar·ize (*BrE* also **-ise**) /pəˈtɪkjələraɪz; *AmE* pərˈt-/ *verb* [V, VN] (*formal*) to give details of sth, especially one by one; to give particular examples of sth

par·ticu·lar·ly /pəˈtɪkjələli; *AmE* pərˈtɪkjələrli/ *adv.* especially; more than usual or more than others: *particularly good/important/useful* ◊ *Traffic is bad, particularly*

in the city centre. ◊ *I enjoyed the play, particularly the second half.* ◊ *The lecture was* **not particularly** (= not very) *interesting.* ◊ (*spoken*) *'Did you enjoy it?' 'No,* **not particularly** (= not very much).'

part·ing /ˈpɑːtɪŋ; *AmE* ˈpɑːrt-/ *noun, adj.*

■ *noun* **1** [U, C] the act or occasion of leaving a person or place: *the pain/misery/moment of parting* ◊ *We had a tearful parting at the airport.* **2** (*BrE*) (*AmE* **part**) [C] a line on a person's head where the hair is divided with a comb: *a side/centre parting*—picture at HAIR **3** [U, C] the act or result of dividing sth into parts: *the parting of the clouds* IDM **a/the ˌparting of the ˈways** a point at which two people or groups of people decide to separate

■ *adj.* [only before noun] said or done by sb as they leave: *a parting kiss* ◊ *His parting words were 'I love you.'* IDM **ˌparting ˈshot** a final remark, especially an unkind one, that sb makes as they leave

par·ti·san /ˌpɑːtɪˈzæn; ˈpɑːtɪzæn; *AmE* ˈpɑːrtəzn/ *adj., noun*

■ *adj.* (often *disapproving*) showing too much support for one person, group or idea, especially without considering it carefully: *Most newspapers are politically partisan.*

■ *noun* **1** a person who strongly supports a particular leader, group or idea **2** a member of an armed group that is fighting secretly against enemy soldiers who have taken control of its country ▶ **par·ti·san·ship** /-ʃɪp/ *noun* [U]

par·ti·tion /pɑːˈtɪʃn; *AmE* pɑːrˈt-/ *noun, verb*

■ *noun* **1** [C] a wall or screen that separates one part of a room from another: *a glass partition* ◊ *partition walls* **2** [U] the division of one country into two or more countries: *the partition of Germany after the war*

■ *verb* [VN] (often *passive*) to divide sth into two parts: *to partition a country* ◊ *The room is partitioned into three sections.* PHRV **parˌtition sth↔ˈoff** to separate one area, one part of a room, etc. from another with a wall or screen

par·ti·tive /ˈpɑːtətɪv; *AmE* ˈpɑːrt-/ *noun* (*grammar*) a word or phrase that shows a part or quantity of sth: *In 'a spoonful of sugar', the word 'spoonful' is a partitive.* ▶ **par·ti·tive** *adj.*

part·ly /ˈpɑːtli; *AmE* ˈpɑːrt-/ *adv.* to some extent; not completely: *Some people are unwilling to attend the classes* **partly because** *of the cost involved.* ◊ *He was only partly responsible for the accident.*

> **WHICH WORD?** ❓
> **partly / partially**
>
> **Partly** and **partially** both mean 'not completely': *The road is partly/partially finished.* **Partly** is especially used to talk about the reason for something, often followed by *because* or *due to*: *I didn't enjoy the trip very much, partly because of the weather.* **Partially** should be used when you are talking about physical conditions: *His mother is partially blind.*

---

part·ner /ˈpɑːtnə(r); *AmE* ˈpɑːrt-/ *noun, verb*

■ *noun* **1** the person that you are married to or having a sexual relationship with: *Come to the New Year disco and bring your partner!* ◊ *a marriage partner* **2** one of the people who owns a business and shares the profits, etc: *a partner in a law firm* ◊ *a junior/senior partner* **3** a person that you are doing an activity with, such as dancing or playing a game: *a dancing/tennis partner* **4** a country or an organization that has an agreement with another country: *a trading partner*—see also SLEEPING PARTNER, SPARRING PARTNER

■ *verb* [VN] to be sb's partner in a dance, game, etc: *Gerry offered to partner me at tennis.*

part·ner·ship /ˈpɑːtnəʃɪp; *AmE* ˈpɑːrtnərʃɪp/ *noun* **1** [U] **~ (with sb)** the state of being a partner in business: *to be in/to go into partnership* ◊ *He developed his own program in partnership with an American expert.* **2** [C, U] **~ (with sb)** a relationship between two people, organizations, etc.; the state of having this relationship: *Marriage should be an equal partnership.* ◊ *the school's partnership with parents* ◊ *a partnership between the United States and*

---

b	d	f	g	h	k	l	m	n	p	r
bad	**did**	**fall**	**get**	**hat**	**cat**	**leg**	**man**	**now**	**pen**	**red**

P

Europe **3** [C] a business owned by two or more people who share the profits: *a junior member of the partnership*

,part of 'speech *noun* (*grammar*) one of the classes into which words are divided according to their grammar, such as noun, verb, adjective, etc.

par·took *pt of* PARTAKE

par·tridge /'pɑːtrɪdʒ; *AmE* 'pɑːrt-/ *noun* [C, U] (*pl.* **par·tridges** or **par·tridge**) a brown bird with a round body and a short tail, that people hunt for sport or food; the meat of this bird

,part-'time *adj.* (*abbr.* **PT**) for part of the day or week in which people work: *She's looking for a part-time job.* ◊ *to study on a part-time basis* ◊ *part-time workers* ◊ *I'm only part-time at the moment.* ▶ ,part-'time *adv.*: *Liz works part-time from 10 till 2.*—compare FULL-TIME

,part-'timer *noun* a person who works part-time

'part-way *adv.* some of the way: *They were part-way through the speeches when he arrived.*

'part-work *noun* (*BrE*) a book that is published in several parts that people can collect over a period of time

party /'pɑːti; *AmE* 'pɑːrti/ *noun, verb*

■ *noun* (*pl.* **-ies**) **1** (also **Party**) [C+sing./pl. *v.*] a political organization that you can vote for in elections and whose members have the same aims and ideas: *the Democratic and Republican Parties in the United States* ◊ *She belongs to the Labour Party.* ◊ *the ruling/opposition party* ◊ *the party leader/manifesto/policy* **2** [C] (especially in compounds) a social occasion, often in a person's home, at which people eat, drink, talk, dance and enjoy themselves: *a birthday/dinner/garden party* ◊ *to give/have/throw a party* ◊ *Did you go to their party?* ◊ *party games*—see also HEN PARTY, HOUSE PARTY, STAG PARTY **3** [C+sing./pl. *v.*] a group of people who are doing sth together such as travelling or visiting somewhere: *The school is taking a party of 40 children to France.* ◊ *The theatre gives a 10% discount to parties of more than ten.*—see also SEARCH PARTY, WORKING PARTY **4** [C] (*formal*) one of the people or groups of people involved in a legal agreement or dispute: *the guilty/innocent party* ◊ *The contract can be terminated by either party with three months' notice.*—see also INJURED PARTY, THIRD PARTY **IDM** **be (a) party to sth** (*formal*) to be involved in an agreement or action: *to be party to a decision* ◊ *He refused to be a party to any violence.*

■ *verb* (**par·ties**, **party·ing**, **par·tied**, **par·tied**) [V] (*informal*) to enjoy yourself, especially by eating, drinking alcohol and dancing: *They were out partying every night.*

,party 'favors (also **favors**) (both *AmE*) *noun* [pl.] small gifts that are often given to children at a party

'party-goer *noun* a person who enjoys going to parties or who is a guest at a particular party

,party 'line *noun* the official opinions and policies of a political party, which members are expected to support **IDM** see TOE *v.*

'party piece *noun* (*BrE, informal*) a thing that sb does to entertain people, especially at parties, for example singing a song

,party po'litical *adj.* [only before noun] (*especially BrE*) made by or related to a political party: *a party political broadcast*

,party 'politics *noun* [U+sing./pl. *v.*] political activity that involves political parties: *The President should spread above party politics.* ◊ *Many people think that party politics should not enter into local government.*

party-pooper /'pɑːti puːpə(r)/ *noun* (*informal*) a person who does not want to take part in an enjoyable activity and spoils the fun for other people

,party 'spirit *noun* [U] the sort of mood in which you can enjoy a party and have fun

,party 'wall *noun* a wall that divides two buildings or rooms and belongs to both owners

par·venu /'pɑːvənjuː; *AmE* 'pɑːrvənuː/ *noun* (*pl.* **-us**) (*formal, disapproving*) a person from a low social or economic position who has suddenly become rich or powerful

pass /pɑːs; *AmE* pæs/ *verb, noun*

■ *verb*

MOVE | **1** to move past or to the other side of sb/sth: [V] *Several people were passing but nobody offered to help.* ◊ *I hailed a passing taxi.* ◊ *The road was so narrow that cars were unable to pass.* ◊ [VN] *to pass a barrier/sentry/checkpoint* ◊ *She passed me in the street without even saying hello.* **2** [V+*adv./prep.*] to go or move in the direction mentioned: *The procession passed slowly along the street.* ◊ *A plane passed low overhead.* **3** [VN+*adv./prep.*] to make sth move in the direction or into the position mentioned: *He passed the rope around the post three times to secure it.*

GIVE | **4** ~ sth (**to sb**)|~ sb sth to give sth to sb by putting it into their hands or in a place where they can easily reach it: [VN] *Pass the salt, please.* ◊ [VN, VNN] *Pass that book over.* ◊ *Pass me over that book.*

BALL | **5** ~ (**sth**) (**to sb**) (in football, hockey, etc.) to kick, hit or throw the ball to a player of your own side: [VN] *He passed the ball to Owen.* ◊ [V] *Why do they keep passing back to the goalie?*—picture on page 1250

AFTER DEATH | **6** [V] ~ **to sb** to be given to another person after first belonging to sb else, especially after the first person has died: *On his death, the title passed to his eldest son.*

BECOME GREATER | **7** [VN] (of an amount) to become greater than a particular total **SYN** EXCEED: *Unemployment has now passed the three million mark.*

CHANGE | **8** [V] ~ **from sth to/into sth** to change from one state or condition to another: *She had passed from childhood to early womanhood.*

TIME | **9** [V] when time **passes**, it goes by: *Six months passed and we still had no news of them.* ◊ *We grew more anxious with every passing day.* **10** [VN] to spend time, especially when you are bored or waiting for sth: *We sang songs to pass the time.* ◊ *How did you pass the evening?*

END | **11** [V] to come to an end; to be over: *They waited for the storm to pass.*

TEST/EXAM | **12** to achieve the required standard in an exam, a test, etc: [V] *I'm not really expecting to pass first time.* ◊ [VN] *She hasn't passed her driving test yet.* **OPP** FAIL **13** [VN] to test sb and decide that they are good enough, according to an agreed standard: *The examiners passed all the candidates.* **OPP** FAIL

LAW/PROPOSAL | **14** [VN] to accept a proposal, law, etc. by voting: *The bill was passed by 360 votes to 280.*

HAPPEN | **15** [V] to be allowed: *I don't like it, but I'll let it pass* (= will not object). ◊ *Her remarks passed without comment* (= people ignored them). **16** ~ (**between A and B**) to happen; to be said or done: [V] *They'll never be friends again after all that has passed between them.* ◊ [V-ADJ] *His departure passed unnoticed.*

NOT KNOW | **17** [V] ~ (**on sth**) to say that you do not know the answer to a question, especially during a QUIZ: *'What's the capital of Peru?' 'I'll have to pass on that one.'* ◊ *'Who wrote 'Catch-22'?' 'Pass* (= I don't know).'

NOT WANT | **18** [V] ~ (**on sth**) to say that you do not want sth that is offered to you: *Thanks. I'm going to pass on dessert, if you don't mind.*

SAY/STATE STH | **19** [VN] ~ **sth** (**on sb/sth**) to say or state sth, especially officially: *The court waited in silence for the judge to pass sentence.* ◊ *It's not for me to pass judgement on your behaviour.* ◊ *The man smiled at the girl and passed a friendly remark.*

BELIEF/UNDERSTANDING | **20** [VN] ~ **belief, understanding,** etc. (*formal*) to go beyond the limits of what you can believe, understand, etc: *It passes belief* (= is impossible to believe) *that she could do such a thing.*

IN CARD GAMES | **21** [V] to refuse to play a card or make a BID when it is your turn

FROM THE BODY | **22** [VN] to send sth out from the body as or with waste matter: *If you're passing blood you ought to see a doctor.*

IDM ,come to 'pass (*old use*) to happen **not pass your 'lips 1** if words do **not pass your lips**, you say nothing **2** if food or drink does **not pass your lips**, you eat or drink nothing **pass the 'hat round/around** (*informal*) to

s	t	v	z	ʃ	ʒ	tʃ	dʒ	θ	ð	ŋ
see	tea	van	zoo	shoe	vision	chain	jam	thin	this	sing

collect money from a number of people, for example to buy a present for sb **pass 'muster** to be accepted as satisfactory **pass the time of 'day (with sb)** to greet sb and have a short conversation with them **pass 'water** (*formal*) to URINATE

PHR V **'pass as sb/sth** = PASS FOR SB/STH **,pass a'way** 1 (also **,pass 'on**) to die. People say 'pass away' to avoid saying 'die': *His mother passed away last year.* 2 to stop existing: *civilizations that have passed away.* **,pass 'by (sb/sth)** to go past: *The procession passed right by my front door.* **,pass sb/sth 'by** to happen without affecting sb/sth: *She feels that life is passing her by* (= that she is not enjoying the opportunities and pleasures of life). **,pass sth↔'down** [often passive] to give or teach sth to your children or people younger than you, who will then give or teach it to those who live after them, and so on **'pass for/as sb/sth** to be accepted as sb/sth: *He speaks the language so well he could easily pass for a German.* ◊ *We had some wine—or what passes for wine in that area.* **'pass into sth** to become a part of sth: *Many foreign words have passed into the English language.* **,pass 'off** (*BrE*) (of an event) to take place and be completed in a particular way: *The demonstration passed off peacefully.* **,pass sb/yourself/sth 'off as sb/sth** to pretend that sb/sth is sth they are not: *He escaped by passing himself off as a guard.* **,pass 'on** = PASS AWAY **,pass sth↔'on (to sb)** to give sth to sb else, especially after receiving it or using it yourself: *Pass the book on to me when you've finished with it.* ◊ *I passed your message on to my mother.* ◊ *Much of the discount is pocketed by retailers instead of being passed on to customers.* **,pass 'out** to lose consciousness SYN FAINT **,pass 'out (of sth)** (*BrE*) to leave a military college after finishing a course of training: *a passing-out ceremony* **,pass sb↔'over** to not consider sb for promotion in a job, especially when they deserve it or think that they deserve it: *He was passed over in favour of a younger man.* **,pass 'over sth** to ignore or avoid sth: *They chose to pass over her rude remarks.* **,pass 'through ...** to go through a town, etc., stopping there for a short time but not staying: *We were passing through, so we thought we'd come and say hello.* **,pass sth↔'up** (*informal*) to choose not to make use of a chance, an opportunity, etc: *Imagine passing up an offer like that!*

■ *noun*

IN EXAM | 1 (*especially BrE*) a successful result in an exam: *She got a pass in French.* ◊ *12 passes and 3 fails* ◊ *Two A-level passes are needed for this course.* ◊ *The pass mark is 50%.* ◊ *The school has a 90% pass rate* (= 90% of students pass their exams).

OFFICIAL DOCUMENT | 2 an official document or ticket that shows that you have the right to enter or leave a place, to travel on a bus or train, etc: *a bus pass* ◊ *a boarding pass* (= for a plane) ◊ *There is no admittance without a security pass.*

OF BALL | 3 (in some sports) an act of hitting or throwing the ball to another player in your team: *a short/long pass to Anelka* ◊ *a back pass to the goalkeeper*

THROUGH MOUNTAINS | 4 a road or way over or through mountains: *a mountain pass*—picture at MOUNTAIN

MOVING PAST/OVER | 5 an act of going or moving past or over sth: *The helicopter made several passes over the village before landing.*

STAGE IN PROCESS | 6 a stage in a process, especially one that involves separating things from a larger group: *In the first pass all the addresses are loaded into the database.*

IDM **come to such a 'pass | come to a pretty 'pass** (*old-fashioned* or *humorous*) to reach a sad or difficult state **make a pass at sb** (*informal*) to try to start a sexual relationship with sb

pass·able /ˈpɑːsəbl; *AmE* ˈpæs-/ *adj.* 1 fairly good but not excellent SYN SATISFACTORY: *She put on a passable imitation of a Scottish accent.* 2 [not usually before noun] if a road or a river is **passable**, it is not blocked and you can travel along or across it OPP IMPASSABLE

pass·ably /ˈpɑːsəbli; *AmE* ˈpæs-/ *adv.* in an acceptable or satisfactory way: *He speaks passably good French.*

pas·sage /ˈpæsɪdʒ/ *noun*

LONG NARROW WAY | 1 (also **pas·sage·way** /ˈpæsɪdʒweɪ/) [C] a long narrow area with walls on either side that connects one room or place with another SYN CORRIDOR: *a secret underground passage* ◊ *A dark narrow passage led to the main hall.*

IN THE BODY | 2 [C] a tube in the body through which air, liquid, etc. passes: *blocked nasal passages* ◊ *the back passage* (= between the bowels and the ANUS)

SECTION FROM BOOK | 3 [C] a short section from a book, piece of music, etc. SYN EXCERPT, EXTRACT: *Read the following passage and answer the questions below.*

OF TIME | 4 [sing.] **the ~ of time** (*literary*) the process of time passing: *Her confidence grew with the passage of time.*

OF BILL IN PARLIAMENT | 5 [sing.] the process of discussing a BILL in a parliament so that it can become law: *The bill is now guaranteed an easy passage through the House of Representatives.*

JOURNEY BY SHIP | 6 [sing.] a journey from one place to another by ship: *Her grandfather had worked his passage* (= worked on a ship to pay for the journey) *to America.*

GOING THROUGH | 7 [sing.] **a ~ (through sth)** a way through sth: *The officers forced a passage through the crowd.* 8 [U] (*formal*) the action of going across, through or past sth: *Large trees may obstruct the passage of light.* 9 [U, C, usually sing.] the permission to travel across a particular area of land: *We were promised (a) safe passage through the occupied territory.*

—see also BIRD OF PASSAGE, RITE OF PASSAGE

pas·sant ⊳ EN PASSANT

pass·book /ˈpɑːsbʊk; *AmE* ˈpæs-/ *noun* a small book containing a record of the money you put into and take out of an account at a BUILDING SOCIETY or a bank

passé /ˈpæseɪ; ˈpɑːs-; *AmE* pæˈseɪ/ *adj.* [not usually before noun] (from *French*, *disapproving*) no longer fashionable: *Her ideas on food are distinctly passé.*

pas·sen·ger /ˈpæsɪndʒə(r)/ *noun* 1 a person who is travelling in a car, bus, train, plane or ship and who is not driving it or working on it: *a passenger train* (= carrying passengers, not goods) 2 (*informal*, *disapproving*, *especially BrE*) a member of a group or team who does not do as much work as the others: *The firm cannot afford to carry passengers.*

passer-'by *noun* (*pl.* **passers-by**) a person who is going past sb/sth by chance, especially when sth unexpected happens: *Police asked passers-by if they had seen the accident.*

pass-'fail *adj.* (*AmE*) connected with a grading system for school classes, etc. in which a student passes or fails rather than receiving a grade as a letter (for example, A or B) ▶ **,pass-'fail** *adv.*: *to take a class pass-fail*

pas·sim /ˈpæsɪm/ *adv.* (from *Latin*) used in the notes to a book or an article to show that a particular name or subject appears in several places in it

pass·ing /ˈpɑːsɪŋ; *AmE* ˈpæs-/ *noun, adj.*

■ *noun* [U] 1 **the ~ of time/the years** the process of time going by 2 (*formal*) the fact of sth ending or of sb dying: *When the government is finally brought down, no one will mourn its passing.* ◊ *the passing of the old year* (= on New Year's Eve) ◊ *Many will mourn her passing* (= her death, when you do not want to say this directly). 3 **the ~ of sth** the act of making sth law: *the passing of a resolution/statute/law* IDM **in passing** done or said while you are giving your attention to sth else SYN CASUALLY: *He only mentioned it in passing and didn't give any details.*

■ *adj.* [only before noun] 1 lasting only for a short period of time and then disappearing SYN BRIEF: *a passing phase/thought/interest* ◊ *He makes only a passing reference to the theory in his book.* ◊ *She bears more than a passing resemblance to* (= looks very like) *your sister.* 2 going past: *I love him more with each passing day.* ◊ *the noise of passing cars*

pas·sion /ˈpæʃn/ *noun* 1 [C, U] a very strong feeling of love, hatred, anger, enthusiasm, etc: *He's a man of violent passions.* ◊ *a crime of passion* ◊ *She argued her case with*

æ	ɑː	e	ɜː	ə	ɪ	iː	i	ɒ	ɔː	ʌ	ʊ	u	uː
cat	father	ten	bird	about	sit	see	many	got	saw	cup	put	actual	too

(BrE)

P

considerable passion. ◊ *Passions were running high* (= people were angry and emotional) *at the meeting.* **2** [sing.] (*formal*) a state of being very angry: *She flies into a passion if anyone even mentions his name.* **3** [U] ~ **(for sb)** a very strong feeling of sexual love: *His passion for her made him blind to everything else.* **4** [sing.] ~ **(for sth)** a very strong feeling of liking sth; a hobby, an activity, etc. that you like very much: *The English have a passion for gardens.* ◊ *Music is a passion with him.* **5** (**the Passion**) [sing.] (in Christianity) the suffering and death of Jesus Christ

pas·sion·ate /ˈpæʃənət/ *adj.* **1** having or showing strong feelings of sexual love or of anger, etc: *to have a passionate nature* **2** having or showing strong feelings of enthusiasm for sth or belief in sth: *a passionate interest in music* ◊ *a passionate defender of civil liberties* ▶ **pas·sion·ate·ly** *adv.*: *He took her in his arms and kissed her passionately.* ◊ *They are all passionately interested in environmental issues.*

ˈ**passion flower** *noun* a tropical climbing plant with large brightly coloured flowers

ˈ**passion fruit** *noun* [C, U] (*pl.* **passion fruit**) a small tropical fruit with a thick purple skin and many seeds inside, produced by some types of passion flower—picture on page A2

pas·sion·less /ˈpæʃnləs/ *adj.* (*rare*) without emotion or enthusiasm

ˈ**passion play** *noun* a play about the suffering and death of Jesus Christ

pas·sive /ˈpæsɪv/ *adj., noun*
■ *adj.* **1** accepting what happens or what people do without trying to change anything or oppose them: *He played a passive role in the relationship.* ◊ *a passive observer of events* **2** (*grammar*) connected with the form of a verb used when the subject is affected by the action of the verb as in *He was bitten by a dog.: a passive sentence*—compare ACTIVE ▶ **pas·sive·ly** *adv.*
■ *noun* (also ˌ**passive** ˈ**voice**) [sing.] (*grammar*) the form of a verb used when the subject is affected by the action of the verb—compare ACTIVE

ˌ**passive re**ˈ**sistance** *noun* [U] a way of opposing a government or an enemy by peaceful means, often by refusing to obey laws or orders

ˌ**passive** ˈ**smoking** *noun* [U] the act of breathing in smoke from other people's cigarettes

pas·siv·ity /pæˈsɪvəti/ *noun* [U] the state of accepting what happens without reacting or trying to fight against it

ˈ**pass key** *noun* = MASTER KEY

Pass·over /ˈpɑːsəʊvə(r); *AmE* ˈpæsoʊ-/ *noun* [U, C] the Jewish religious festival and holiday in memory of the escape of the Jews from Egypt

pass·port /ˈpɑːspɔːt; *AmE* ˈpæspɔːrt/ *noun* **1** an official document that identifies you as a citizen of a particular country, and that you may have to show when you enter or leave a country: *a valid passport* ◊ *a South African passport* ◊ *I was stopped as I went through* **passport control** (= where passports are checked). ◊ *a passport photo* **2** ~ **to sth** a thing that makes sth possible or enables you to achieve sth: *The only passport to success is hard work.*

pass·word /ˈpɑːswɜːd; *AmE* ˈpæswɜːrd/ *noun* **1** a secret word or phrase that you need to know in order to be allowed into a place **2** (*computing*) a series of letters or numbers that you must type into a computer or computer system in order to be able to use it: *Enter a user name and password to get into the system.*

past /pɑːst; *AmE* pæst/ *adj., noun, prep., adv.*
■ *adj.* **1** gone by in time: *in past years/centuries/ages* ◊ *in times past* ◊ *The time for discussion is past.* **2** [only before noun] gone by recently; just ended: *I haven't seen much of her in the past few weeks.* ◊ *The past month has been really busy at work.* **3** [only before noun] belonging to an earlier time: *past events* ◊ *From past experience I'd say he'd probably forgotten the time.* ◊ *past and present students of the college* ◊ *Let's forget about who was more to blame—it's all* **past history.** **4** [only before noun] (*grammar*) con-

nected with the form of a verb used to express actions in the past
■ *noun* **1** (**the past**) [sing.] the time that has gone by; things that happened in an earlier time: *I used to go there often in the past.* ◊ *the recent/distant past* ◊ *She looked back on the past without regret.* ◊ *Writing letters seems to be a* **thing of the past. 2** [C] a person's past life or career: *We don't know anything about his past.* ◊ *They say she has a* '*past*' (= bad things in her past life that she wishes to keep secret). **3** (**the past**) [sing.] (*grammar*) = PAST TENSE **IDM** see DISTANT, LIVE¹
■ *prep.* **1** (*AmE* also **after**) later than sth: *half past two* ◊ *ten (minutes) past six* ◊ *There's a bus at twenty minutes past the hour* (= at 1.20, 2.20, etc.). ◊ *We arrived at two o'clock and left at ten past* (= ten minutes past two). ◊ *It was past midnight when we got home.* **2** on or to the other side of sb/sth: *We live in the house just past the church.* ◊ *He hurried past them without stopping.* ◊ *He just walked* **straight past us!** **3** above or further than a particular point or stage: *Unemployment is now past the 3 million mark.* ◊ *The flowers are past their best.* ◊ *He's past his prime.* ◊ *She's long past retirement age.* ◊ *Honestly, I'm* **past caring** what happens (= I can no longer be bothered to care). **IDM** ˈ**past it** (*BrE, informal*) too old to do what you used to be able to do; too old to be used for its normal function: *In some sports you're past it by the age of 25.* ◊ *That coat is looking decidedly past it.*
■ *adv.* **1** from one side of sth to the other: *I called out to him as he ran past.* **2** used to describe time passing: *A week went past and nothing had changed.*

pasta /ˈpæstə; *AmE* ˈpɑːstə/ *noun* [U] an Italian food made from flour, eggs and water, formed into different shapes and usually served with a sauce. It is often sold in packets and is hard when dry and soft when cooked.

paste /peɪst/ *noun, verb*
■ *noun* **1** [sing.] a soft wet mixture, usually made of a powder and a liquid: *She mixed the flour and water to a smooth paste.* **2** [C] (especially in compounds) a smooth mixture of crushed meat, fish, etc. that is spread on bread or used in cooking **3** [U] a type of glue that is used for sticking paper to things: *wallpaper paste* **4** [U] a substance like glass, that is used for making artificial jewels, for example DIAMONDS
■ *verb* **1** [VN+*adv./prep.*] to stick sth to sth else using glue or paste: *He pasted the pictures into his scrapbook.* ◊ *Paste the two pieces together.* ◊ *Paste down the edges.* **2** [VN] to make sth by sticking pieces of paper together: *The children were busy cutting and pasting paper hats.* **3** (*computing*) to copy or move text into a document from another place or another document: [VN] *This function allows you to* **cut and paste** *text.* ◊ [V] *It's quicker to cut and paste than to retype.*

paste·board /ˈpeɪstbɔːd; *AmE* -bɔːrd/ *noun* [U] a type of thin board made by sticking sheets of paper together

pas·tel /ˈpæstl; *AmE* pæˈstel/ *noun* **1** [U] soft coloured chalk, used for drawing pictures: *landscapes in pastel and oil* **2** (**pastels**) [pl.] small sticks of chalk: *a box of pastels* **3** [C] a picture drawn with pastels: *an exquisite pastel of a riverside scene* **4** [C] a pale delicate colour: *The whole house was painted in soft pastels.*

pas·teur·ize (*BrE* also **-ise**) /ˈpɑːstʃəraɪz; *AmE* ˈpæs-/ *verb* [VN] to heat a liquid, especially milk, to a particular temperature and then cool it, in order to kill harmful bacteria: *pasteurized milk* ▶ **pas·teur·iza·tion, -isa·tion** /ˌpɑːstʃəraɪˈzeɪʃn; *AmE* ˌpæstʃərəˈzeɪʃn/ *noun* [U]

pas·tiche /pæˈstiːʃ/ *noun* **1** [C] a work of art, piece of writing, etc. that is created by deliberately copying the style of sb/sth else: *a pastiche of the classic detective story* **2** [C] a work of art, etc. that consists of a variety of different styles **3** [U] the art of creating a pastiche

pas·tille /ˈpæstl; *AmE* pæˈstiːl/ *noun* (*especially BrE*) a small sweet/candy that you suck, especially one that is flavoured with fruit or that contains medicine for a sore throat: *fruit pastilles* ◊ *throat pastilles*

pas·time /ˈpɑːstaɪm; *AmE* ˈpæs-/ *noun* something that you enjoy doing when you are not working **SYN** HOBBY

past·ing /ˈpeɪstɪŋ/ *noun* **1** [sing.] (*especially BrE*) a heavy

aɪ	aʊ	eɪ	əʊ	oʊ	ɔɪ	ɪə	eə	ʊə	j	w
my	now	say	go (BrE)	go (AmE)	boy	near	hair	pure	yes	wet

defeat in a game or competition **2** [sing.] (*especially BrE*) an instance of being hit very hard as a punishment for sth

,past 'master *noun* **~ (at sth/at doing sth)** a person who is very good at sth because they have a lot of experience in it SYN EXPERT: *She's a past master at getting what she wants.*

pas·tor /'pɑːstə(r); *AmE* 'pæs-/ *noun* a MINISTER in charge of a Christian church or group, especially in some NON-CONFORMIST churches

pas·tor·al /'pɑːstərəl; *AmE* 'pæs-/ *adj.* **1** relating to the work of a priest or teacher in giving help and advice on personal matters, not just those connected with religion or education: *pastoral care/counselling/duties/work* **2** showing country life or the countryside, especially in a romantic way: *a pastoral scene/poem/symphony* **3** relating to the farming of animals: *agricultural and pastoral practices*

,past 'participle *noun* (*grammar*) the form of a verb that in English ends in -*ed*, -*en*, etc. and is used with the verb *have* to form PERFECT tenses such as *I have eaten*, with the verb *be* to form PASSIVE sentences such as *It was destroyed*, or sometimes as an adjective as in *an upset stomach*—compare PRESENT PARTICIPLE

the ,past 'perfect (also **the ,past ,perfect 'tense**, **the plu·per·fect**) *noun* [sing.] (*grammar*) the form of a verb that expresses an action completed before a particular point in the past, formed in English with *had* and the past participle

pas·trami /pæ'strɑːmi/ *noun* [U] cold spicy smoked beef

pas·try /'peɪstri/ *noun* (*pl.* -**ies**) **1** [U] a mixture of flour, fat and water or milk that is rolled out flat and baked as a base or covering for pies, etc: *a pastry case*—see also FILO PASTRY, PUFF PASTRY, SHORTCRUST PASTRY **2** [C] a small cake made using pastry—see also DANISH PASTRY—picture on page A1

the ,past 'tense (also **the past**) *noun* [sing.] (*grammar*) the form of a verb used to describe actions in the past: *The past tense of 'take' is 'took'.*

pas·ture /'pɑːstʃə(r); *AmE* 'pæs-/ *noun, verb*
- *noun* **1** [U, C] land covered with grass that is suitable for feeding animals on: *an area of permanent/rough/rich pasture* ◇ *high mountain pastures* ◇ *The cattle were put out to pasture.* **2** (**pastures**) [pl.] the circumstances of your life, work, etc: *I felt we were off to greener pastures* (= a better way of life). ◇ (*BrE*) *She decided it was time to move on to pastures new* (= a new job, place to live, etc.).
- *verb* [VN] to put animals in a field to feed on grass: *The cattle were pastured on rich meadow grass.*

pas·ture·land /'pɑːstʃələænd; *AmE* 'pæstʃərl-/ *noun* [U, pl.] (also **pas·tur·age** [U]) land where animals can feed on grass

pasty¹ /'pæsti/ *noun* (*pl.* -**ies**) (*BrE*) a small pie containing meat and vegetables—see also CORNISH PASTY

pasty² /'peɪsti/ *adj.* pale and not looking healthy: *a pasty face/complexion*

pat /pæt/ *verb, noun, adj., adv.*
- *verb* (-**tt**-) to touch sb/sth gently several times with your hand flat, especially as a sign of affection: [VN] *She patted the dog on the head.* ◇ *He patted his sister's hand consolingly.* ◇ [VN-ADJ] *Pat your face dry with a soft towel.* IDM **pat sb/yourself on the 'back** to praise sb or yourself for doing sth well
- *noun* **1** a gentle friendly touch with your open hand or with a flat object: *a pat on the head* ◇ *He gave her knee an affectionate pat.* **2 ~ of butter** a small, soft, flat lump of butter—see also COWPAT IDM **a ,pat on the 'back (for sth/for doing sth)** praise or approval for sth that you have done well: *He deserves a pat on the back for all his hard work.*
- *adj.* (usually *disapproving*) (of an answer, a comment, etc.) too quick, easy or simple; not seeming natural or realistic SYN GLIB: *The ending of the novel is a little too pat to be convincing.* ◇ *There are no pat answers to these questions.*
- *adv.* IDM **have/know sth off 'pat** (*BrE*) (*AmE* **have/know sth down 'pat**) to know sth perfectly so that you

can repeat it at any time without having to think about it: *He had all the answers off pat.* **stand 'pat** (*especially AmE*) to refuse to change your mind about a decision you have made or an opinion you have

patch /pætʃ/ *noun, verb*

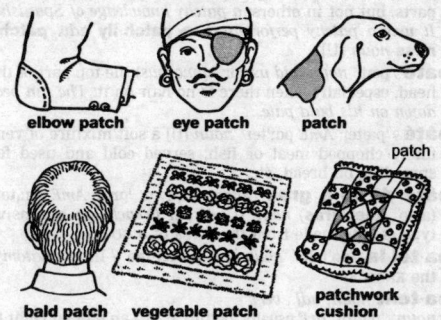

elbow patch   **eye patch**   **patch**

patch

bald patch   **vegetable patch**   **patchwork cushion**

- *noun*

SMALL AREA | **1** a small area of sth, especially one which is different from the area around it: *a black dog with a white patch on its back* ◇ *a bald patch on the top of his head* ◇ *damp patches on the wall* ◇ *patches of dense fog*

PIECE OF MATERIAL | **2** a small piece of material that is used to cover a hole in sth or to strengthen a weak area: *I sewed patches on the knees of my jeans.* **3** a piece of material that you wear over an eye, usually because the eye is damaged: *He had a black patch over one eye.*—see also EYEPATCH **4** (*especially AmE*) (*BrE* usually **badge**) a piece of material that you sew onto clothes, etc. as a decoration or as part of a uniform **5** a piece of material that people can wear on their skin to help them to stop smoking: *nicotine patches*

PIECE/AREA OF LAND | **6** a small piece of land, especially one used for growing vegetables or fruit: *a vegetable patch*—picture at HOUSE **7** (*BrE*, *informal*) an area that sb works in, knows well or comes from: *He knows every house in his patch.* ◇ *She has had a lot of success in her home patch.*

DIFFICULT TIME | **8** (*informal, especially BrE*) a period of time of the type mentioned, usually a difficult or unhappy one: *to go through a bad/difficult/sticky patch*—see also PURPLE PATCH

IDM **be not a 'patch on sb/sth** (*informal, especially BrE*) to be much less good, attractive, etc. than sb/sth else: *This book isn't a patch on her others.*

- *verb* [VN] **~ sth (with sth)** to cover a hole or a worn place, especially in clothes, with a piece of cloth or other material: *patched jeans* ◇ *to patch a hole in the roof*
PHRV **,patch sb/sth 'through (to sb/sth)** to connect telephone or electronic equipment temporarily: *She was patched through to London on the satellite link.* **,patch sth↔to'gether** to make sth from several different parts, especially in a quick careless way: *They hope to be able to patch together a temporary settlement.* **,patch sth/sb↔'up 1** to repair sth especially in a temporary way by adding a new piece of material or patch: *Just to patch the boat up will cost £10000.* **2** to treat sb's injuries, especially quickly or temporarily: *The doctor will soon patch you up.* **3** to try to stop quarrelling with sb and be friends again: *They've managed to patch up their differences.* ◇ *Have you tried patching things up with her?* **4** to agree on sth, especially after long discussions and even though the agreement is not completely satisfactory: *They managed to patch up a deal.*

patch·ouli /'pætʃuli; pə'tʃuːli/ *noun* [C] a PERFUME made with oil from the leaves of a SE Asian bush

patch·work /'pætʃwɜːk; *AmE* -wɜːrk/ *noun* **1** [U] a type of NEEDLEWORK in which small pieces of fabric of different colours or designs are sewn together: *a patchwork quilt*—picture at PATCH **2** [sing.] a thing that is made up of many different pieces or parts: *a patchwork of different styles*

b	d	f	g	h	k	l	m	n	p	r
bad	**did**	**fall**	**get**	**hat**	**cat**	**leg**	**man**	**now**	**pen**	**red**

and cultures ◇ *From the plane, the landscape was just a patchwork of fields.*

patchy /'pætʃi/ *adj.* **1** existing or happening in some places and not others: *patchy fog* ◇ *The grass was dry and patchy.* **2** (*AmE* also **spotty**) not complete; good in some parts, but not in others: *a patchy knowledge of Spanish* ◇ *It was a patchy performance.* ▶ **patch·ily** *adv.* **patchi·ness** *noun* [U]

pate /peɪt/ *noun* (*old use* or *humorous*) the top part of the head, especially when there is no hair on it: *The sun beat down on his bald pate.*

pâté /'pæteɪ; *AmE* pɑː'teɪ/ *noun* [U] a soft mixture of very finely chopped meat or fish, served cold and used for spreading on bread, etc.

pâté de foie gras /ˌpæteɪ də fwɑː 'grɑː; *AmE* pɑːˌteɪ/ (also ˌfoie 'gras) *noun* [U] (from *French*) an expensive type of pâté made from the LIVER of a GOOSE

pa·tel·la /pə'telə/ *noun* (*pl.* **pa·tel·lae** /-liː/) (*anatomy*) the KNEECAP

pa·tent *noun, adj., verb*
■ *noun* /'pætnt; *BrE* usually 'peɪtnt/ [C, U] an official right to be the only person to make, use or sell a product or an invention; a document that proves this: *to apply for/ obtain a patent on an invention* ◇ *The device was protected by patent.*
■ *adj.* /'peɪtnt; *AmE* usually 'pætnt/ [only before noun] **1** connected with a patent: *patent applications/laws* ◇ *the US Patent Office* **2** (of a product) made or sold by a particular company: *patent medicines* **3** (*formal*) used to emphasize that sth bad is very clear and obvious: *It was a patent lie.*
■ *verb* /'pætnt; *BrE* usually 'peɪtnt/ [VN] to obtain a patent for an invention or a process

patent leather /ˌpeɪtnt 'leðə(r); *AmE* usually 'pætnt/ *noun* [U] a type of leather with a hard shiny surface, used especially for making shoes and bags

pa·tent·ly /'peɪtntli; 'pætntli; *AmE* 'pæt-/ *adv.* (*formal*) without doubt; clearly: *Her explanation was patently ridiculous.* ◇ *It was patently obvious that she was lying.*

pater·famil·ias /ˌpeɪtəfə'mɪliæs; *AmE* ˌpætərf-/ *noun* [sing.] (*formal* or *humorous*) the man who is the head of a family

pa·ter·nal /pə'tɜːnl; *AmE* -'tɜːrnl/ *adj.* **1** connected with being a father; typical of a kind father: *paternal instincts/ love* ◇ *He gave me a piece of paternal advice.* **2** related through the father's side of the family: *my paternal grandmother* (= my father's mother) ▶ **pa·ter·nal·ly** *adv.*: *He smiled paternally at them.*—compare MATERNAL

pa·ter·nal·ism /pə'tɜːnəlɪzəm; *AmE* -'tɜːrn-/ *noun* [U] (sometimes *disapproving*) the system in which a government or an employer protects the people who are governed or employed by providing them with what they need, but does not give them any responsibility or freedom of choice ▶ **pa·ter·nal·is·tic** /pəˌtɜːnə'lɪstɪk; *AmE* -ˌtɜːrn-/ (also **pa·ter·nal·ist**) *adj.*: *a paternalistic employer/state*

pa·ter·nity /pə'tɜːnəti; *AmE* -'tɜːrn-/ *noun* [U] (*written*) the fact of being the father of a child: *He refused to admit paternity of the child.*—compare MATERNITY

pa'ternity leave *noun* time that the father of a new baby is allowed to have away from work

pa'ternity suit (also **pa'ternity case**) *noun* a court case that is intended to prove who a child's father is, especially so that he can be ordered to give the child financial support

path /pɑːθ; *AmE* pæθ/ *noun* (also **path·way**) **1** a way or track that is built or is made by the action of people walking: *a concrete path* ◇ *the garden path* ◇ *Follow the path through the woods.* ◇ *to walk along a path* ◇ *The path led up a steep hill.* ◇ *a coastal path*—see also FOOTPATH—picture at HOUSE **2** a line along which sb/sth moves; the space in front of sb/sth as they move: *He threw himself into the path of an oncoming vehicle.* ◇ *The avalanche forced its way down the mountain, crushing everything in its path.* ◇ *Three men blocked her path.*—see also FLIGHT PATH **3** a plan of action or a way of achieving sth: *a career*

path ◇ *the path to freedom/success/victory* **IDM** see BEAT *v.*, CROSS *v.*, LEAD¹ *v.*, PRIMROSE, SMOOTH *v.*

path·et·ic /pə'θetɪk/ *adj.* **1** making you feel pity or sadness: *a pathetic and lonely old man* ◇ *The starving children were a pathetic sight.* **2** (*informal, disapproving*) weak, useless and not successful: *a pathetic excuse/joke* ◇ *She made a pathetic attempt to smile.* ◇ *I know it sounds pathetic, but I can't ride a bike.* ◇ *You're pathetic!* ▶ **path·et·ic·al·ly** /-kli/ *adv.*: *He cried pathetically.* ◇ *a pathetically shy woman*

pa·thetic 'fallacy *noun* [U, sing.] (in art and literature) the act of describing animals and things as having human feelings: *the poet's use of pathetic fallacy in showing nature mourning the death of the shepherd*

path·find·er /'pɑːθfaɪndə(r); *AmE* 'pæθ-/ *noun* **1** a person, group or thing that goes before others and shows the way over unknown land **2** a person, group or thing that finds a new way of doing sth: *The company is a pathfinder in computer technology.*

patho- /'pæθəʊ; *AmE* -θoʊ/ *combining form* (in nouns, adjectives and adverbs) connected with disease: *pathogenesis* (= the development of a disease) ◇ *pathophysiology*

patho·gen /'pæθədʒən/ *noun* (*technical*) a thing that causes disease ▶ **patho·gen·ic** /ˌpæθə'dʒenɪk/ *adj.*

patho·logic·al /ˌpæθə'lɒdʒɪkl; *AmE* -'lɑːdʒ-/ *adj.* **1** not reasonable or sensible; impossible to control: *pathological fear/hatred/violence* ◇ *a pathological liar* (= a person who cannot stop telling lies) **2** caused by, or connected with, disease or illness: *pathological depression* **3** (*technical*) connected with PATHOLOGY ▶ **patho·logic·al·ly** /-kli/ *adv.*: *pathologically jealous*

path·olo·gist /pə'θɒlədʒɪst; *AmE* -'θɑːl-/ *noun* a doctor who studies pathology and examines dead bodies to find out the cause of death—compare MEDICAL EXAMINER

path·ology /pə'θɒlədʒi; *AmE* -'θɑːl-/ *noun* **1** [U] the scientific study of diseases **2** [C] an aspect of sb's behaviour that is extreme and unreasonable and that they cannot control

pathos /'peɪθɒs; *AmE* -θɑːs/ *noun* [U] (in writing, speech and plays) the power of a performance, description, etc. to produce feelings of sadness and sympathy: *The scene was full of pathos.*

path·way /'pɑːθweɪ; *AmE* 'pæθ-/ *noun* = PATH

pa·tience /'peɪʃns/ *noun* [U] **1** ~ (with sb/sth) the ability to stay calm and accept a delay or sth annoying without complaining: *She has little patience with* (= will not accept or consider) *such views.* ◇ *People have lost patience with* (= have become annoyed about) *the slow pace of reform.* ◇ *My patience is wearing thin.* ◇ *I have run out of patience with her.* ◇ *Teaching children with special needs requires patience and understanding.* **2** the ability to spend a lot of time doing sth difficult that needs a lot of attention and effort: *It takes time and patience to photograph wildlife.* ◇ *I don't have the patience to do jigsaw puzzles.* **3** (*BrE*) (*AmE* **soli·taire**) a card game for only one player **IDM** see TRY *v.*

pa·tient /'peɪʃnt/ *noun, adj.*
■ *noun* **1** a person who is receiving medical treatment, especially in a hospital: *cancer patients* **2** a person who receives treatment from a particular doctor, dentist, etc: *He's one of Dr Shaw's patients.*
■ *adj.* ~ (with sb/sth) able to wait for a long time or accept annoying behaviour or difficulties without becoming angry: *She's very patient with young children.* ◇ *You'll just have to be patient and wait till I'm finished.* ▶ **pa·tient·ly** *adv.*: *to listen/sit/wait patiently* ◇ *She sat patiently waiting for her turn.*

pat·ina /'pætɪnə; *AmE* pə'tiːnə/ *noun* [usually sing.] **1** a green, black or brown layer that forms on the surface of some metals **2** a thin layer that forms on other materials; the shiny surface that develops on wood or leather when it is polished: (*figurative*) *He looked relaxed and elegant and had the patina of success.*

patio /'pætiəʊ; *AmE* -oʊ/ *noun* (*pl.* **-os** /-əʊz; *AmE* -oʊz/) a flat hard area outside, and usually behind, a house where people can sit: *Let's have lunch out on the patio.*

pa·tis·serie /pə'tiːsəri/ *noun* (from *French*) **1** [C] a shop/store that sells cakes, etc. **2** [U] (also **pa·tis·series** [pl.]) (*formal*) cakes

pat·ois /ˈpætwɑː/ *noun* (*pl.* **pat·ois** /-twɑːz/) a form of a language, spoken by people in a particular area, that is different from the standard language of the country

patri·arch /ˈpeɪtriɑːk; *AmE* -ɑːrk/ *noun* **1** the male head of a family or tribe—compare MATRIARCH **2** an old man that people have a lot of respect for **3** (**Patriarch**) the title of a most senior BISHOP (= a senior priest) in the Orthodox or Roman Catholic Church: *the Patriarch of Constantinople* ◇ *the Orthodox Patriarch*

patri·arch·al /ˌpeɪtriˈɑːkl; *AmE* -ˈɑːrkl/ *adj.* **1** ruled or controlled by men; giving power and importance only to men: *a patriarchal society* **2** connected with a patriarch—compare MATRIARCHAL

patri·arch·ate /ˈpeɪtriɑːkət; *AmE* -ɑːrk-/ *noun* (*formal*) **1** the title, position or period of office of a patriarch (3) **2** the area governed by a patriarch (3)

patri·archy /ˈpeɪtriɑːki; *AmE* -ɑːrki/ *noun* [C, U] a society, system or country that is ruled or controlled by men—compare MATRIARCHY

pa·tri·cian /pəˈtrɪʃn/ *adj.* (*formal*) typical of the highest social class SYN ARISTOCRATIC: *She comes from an old patrician family.* ▸ **pa·tri·cian** *noun*—compare PLEBEIAN

patri·cide /ˈpætrɪsaɪd/ *noun* [U, C] (*formal*) the crime of killing your father; a person who is guilty of this crime—compare FRATRICIDE, MATRICIDE, PARRICIDE

patri·mony /ˈpætrɪməni; *AmE* -mouni/ *noun* [sing.] (*formal*) **1** property that is given to sb when their father dies SYN INHERITANCE **2** the works of art and TREASURES of a nation, church, etc. SYN HERITAGE

pat·riot /ˈpeɪtriət; *BrE* also ˈpæt-/ *noun* a person who loves their country and who is ready to defend it against an enemy

pat·ri·ot·ic /ˌpeɪtriˈɒtɪk; ˌpæt-; *AmE* ˌpeɪtriˈɑːtɪk/ *adj.* having or expressing a great love of your country: *a patriotic man who served his country well* ◇ *patriotic music/songs*

pat·ri·ot·ism /ˈpeɪtriətɪzəm; *BrE* also ˈpæt-/ *noun* [U] love of your country and willingness to defend it: *a wave of patriotism*

pa·trol /pəˈtrəʊl; *AmE* pəˈtroʊl/ *verb, noun*
■ *verb* (**-ll-**) **1** to go around an area or a building at regular times to check that it is safe and that there is no trouble: [VN] *Troops patrolled the border day and night.* ◇ [V] *Guards can be seen patrolling everywhere.* **2** [VN] to drive or walk around a particular area, especially in a threatening way: *Gangs of youths patrol the streets at night.*
■ *noun* **1** [C, U] the act of going to different parts of a building, an area, etc. to make sure that there is no trouble or crime: *Security guards make regular patrols at night.* ◇ *a police car on patrol* **2** [C] a group of soldiers, vehicles, etc. that patrol an area: *a naval/police patrol* ◇ *a patrol car/boat* **3** a group of about six BOY SCOUTS or GIRL GUIDES/SCOUTS that forms part of a larger group

pa·trol·man /pəˈtrəʊlmən/, **pa·trol·woman** /pəˈtrəʊlwʊmən/ *noun* (*pl.* **-men** /-mən/, *pl.* **-women** /-wɪmɪn/) **1** (in the US) a police officer who walks or drives around an area to make sure that there is no trouble or crime: *Patrolman Don Lilly* **2** (in Britain) an official of an association for car owners who goes to give help to drivers who have trouble with their cars

pa·trol wagon (also *informal* **ˈpaddy wagon**) (both *AmE*) *noun* a police van for transporting prisoners in

pat·ron /ˈpeɪtrən/ *noun* **1** a person who gives money and support to artists and writers: *Frederick the Great was the patron of many artists.* **2** a famous person who supports an organization such as a charity and whose name is used in the advertisements, etc. for the organization: *Diana, Princess of Wales was patron of the charity Birthright.* **3** (*formal*) a person who uses a particular shop/store, restaurant, theatre, etc: *Patrons are requested not to smoke.*

pat·ron·age /ˈpætrənɪdʒ; ˈpeɪt-/ *noun* [U] **1** the support, especially financial, that is given to a person or an organization by a patron: *Patronage of the arts comes mostly from businesses and private individuals.* **2** the system by which an important person gives help or a job to sb in

return for their support **3** (*especially AmE*) the support that a person gives a shop/store, restaurant, etc. by spending money there

pat·ron·ess /ˌpeɪtrənˈes/ *noun* a female PATRON (1)

pat·ron·ize (*BrE* also **-ise**) /ˈpætrənaɪz; *AmE* ˈpeɪt-/ *verb* **1** (*disapproving*) to treat sb in a way that seems friendly, but which shows that you think that they are not very intelligent, experienced, etc: [VN] *Some television programmes tend to patronize children.* [also V] **2** [VN] (*formal*) to be a regular customer of a shop/store, restaurant, etc: *The club is patronized by students and locals alike.* **3** [VN] to help a particular person, organization or activity by giving them money: *She patronizes many contemporary British artists.*

pat·ron·iz·ing (*BrE* also **-is·ing**) /ˈpætrənaɪzɪŋ; *AmE* ˈpeɪtrənaɪzɪŋ/ *adj.* (*disapproving*) showing that you feel better, or more intelligent than sb else: *a patronizing manner/smile* ◇ *I was only trying to explain; I didn't want to sound patronizing.* ▸ **pat·ron·iz·ing·ly, -is·ing·ly** *adv.*: *He patted her hand patronizingly.*

ˌpatron ˈsaint *noun* a Christian saint who is believed to protect a particular place or group of people: *St Patrick, Ireland's patron saint* ◇ *St Christopher, patron saint of travellers*

patsy /ˈpætsi/ *noun* (*pl.* **-ies**) (*informal disapproving, especially AmE*) a weak person who is easily cheated or deceived, or who is forced to take the blame for sth that sb else has done wrong

pat·ter /ˈpætə(r)/ *noun, verb*
■ *noun* **1** [sing.] the sound that is made by sth repeatedly hitting a surface quickly and lightly: *the patter of feet/footsteps* ◇ *the patter of rain on the roof* **2** [U, sing.] fast continuous talk by sb who is trying to sell you sth or entertain you: *sales patter* IDM **the patter of tiny feet** (*informal* or *humorous*) a way of referring to children when sb wants, or is going to have, a baby: *We can't wait to hear the patter of tiny feet.*
■ *verb* [V+adv./prep.] **1** to make quick, light sounds as a surface is being hit several times: *Rain pattered against the window.* **2** to walk with light steps in a particular direction: *I heard her feet pattering along the corridor.*

pat·tern /ˈpætn; *AmE* -tərn/ *noun, verb*
■ *noun* **1** the regular way in which sth happens or is done: *changing patterns of behaviour/work/weather* ◇ *an irregular sleeping pattern* ◇ *The murders all seem to follow a (similar) pattern* (= happen in the same way). **2** [usually sing.] an excellent example to copy: *This system sets the pattern for others to follow.* **3** a regular arrangement of lines, shapes, colours, etc. as a design on material, carpets, etc: *a pattern of diamonds and squares* ◇ *a shirt with a floral pattern* **4** a design, set of instructions or shape to cut around that you use in order to make sth: *a knitting pattern* ◇ *She bought a dress pattern and some material.* **5** a small piece of material, paper, etc. that helps you choose the design of sth SYN SAMPLE: *wallpaper patterns*
■ *verb* [VN] **1** (*written*) to form a regular arrangement of lines or shapes on sth: *Frost patterned the window.* ◇ *a landscape patterned by vineyards* **2** (*technical*) to cause a particular type of behaviour to develop: *Adult behaviour is often patterned by childhood experiences.* PHRV **ˈpattern sth on sth** (*BrE*) (*AmE* **ˈpattern sth after sth**) [usually passive] to use sth as a model for sth; to copy sth: *a new approach patterned on Japanese ideas*

pat·terned /ˈpætənd; *AmE* -tərnd/ *adj.* ~ (**with sth**) decorated with a pattern: *patterned wallpaper* ◇ *cups patterned with yellow flowers*

pat·tern·ing /ˈpætənɪŋ; *AmE* -tərn-/ *noun* [U] **1** (*technical*) the forming of fixed ways of behaving by copying or repeating sth: *cultural patterning* ◇ *the patterning of husband-wife roles* **2** the arrangement of shapes or colours to make patterns: *a red fish with black patterning*

patty /ˈpæti/ *noun* (*pl.* **-ies**) (*especially AmE*) finely chopped meat, fish, etc. formed into a small round flat shape: *a hamburger patty*

pau·city /ˈpɔːsəti/ *noun* [sing.] (*formal*) ~ (**of sth**) a small

P

æ	ɑː	e	ɜː	ə	ɪ	iː	i	ɒ	ɔː	ʌ	ʊ	u	uː
cat	father	ten	bird	about	sit	see	many	got	saw	cup	put	actual	too
								(BrE)					

amount of sth; less than enough of sth: *a paucity of knowledge/information/research*

paunch /pɔːntʃ/ *noun* a fat stomach on a man ▶ **paunchy** *adj.*

pau·per /ˈpɔːpə(r)/ *noun* (*old use*) a very poor person: *He died a pauper.*

pause /pɔːz/ *verb, noun*
- *verb* **1** [V] to stop talking or doing sth for a short time before continuing: *Anita paused for a moment, then said: 'All right'.* ◇ *The woman spoke almost without pausing for breath* (= very quickly). ◇ *I paused at the door and looked back.* ◇ *Pausing only to pull on a sweater, he ran out of the house.* **2** [VN] to stop a tape, CD, etc. for a short time using the pause button: *She paused the video and went to answer the phone.*
- *noun* **1** ~ (**in sth**) a period of time during which sb stops talking or stops what they are doing: *There was a long pause before she answered.* ◇ *David waited for a pause in the conversation so he could ask Joe his question.* ◇ *After a brief pause, they continued climbing.* ◇ *The rain fell without pause.* ⇨ note at BREAK **2** (*especially BrE*) (also **fer·mata** especially in *AmE*) (*music*) a sign (⌢) over a note or a REST to show that it should be longer than usual **3** [U] (also **'pause button**) a control that allows you to stop a TAPE RECORDER, CD player, etc. for a short time: *Press pause to stop the tape.* IDM **give (sb) 'pause** (*BrE* also **give (sb) pause for 'thought**) (*formal*) to make sb think seriously about sth or hesitate before doing sth: *Popular resistance to the measures should give the government pause.*—more at PREGNANT

pave /peɪv/ *verb* [VN] [often passive] ~ **sth** (**with sth**) to cover a surface with flat stones or bricks: *a paved area near the back door* IDM **,pave the 'way (for sb/sth)** to create a situation in which sb will be able to do sth or sth can happen: *This decision paved the way for changes in employment rights for women.*—more at STREET

pave·ment /ˈpeɪvmənt/ *noun* **1** [C] (*BrE*) (*AmE* **side·walk**) a flat part at the side of a road for people to walk on: *a pavement cafe* **2** [C, U] (*BrE*) any area of flat stones on the ground: *a mosaic pavement* **3** [U] (*AmE*) the surface of a road: *Two cars skidded on the icy pavement.*

pa·vil·ion /pəˈvɪliən/ *noun* **1** a temporary building used at public events and EXHIBITIONS: *the US pavilion at the Trade Fair* **2** (*BrE*) a building next to a sports ground, used by players and people watching the game: *a cricket pavilion* **3** (*AmE*) a large building used for sports or entertainment: *the Pauley Pavilion, home of the university's basketball team* **4** a building that is meant to be more beautiful than useful, built as a shelter in a park or used for concerts and dances: *his first show at the Winter Gardens Pavilion, Blackpool*

pav·ing /ˈpeɪvɪŋ/ *noun* [U] **1** a surface of flat stones or material like stone on the ground: *Weeds grew through the cracks in the paving.*—see also CRAZY PAVING **2** the stones or material that are used to make a flat surface on the ground: *We'll use concrete paving.*

'paving stone *noun* a flat, usually square, piece of stone that is used to make a hard surface for walking on

paw /pɔː/ *noun, verb*
- *noun* **1** the foot of an animal that has CLAWS or nails—picture on page A6 **2** (*informal*) a person's hand: *Take your filthy paws off me!*
- *verb* ~ (**at**) **sth 1** (of an animal) to scratch or touch sth repeatedly with a paw: [V] *The dog pawed at my sleeve.* ◇ [VN] *The stallion pawed the ground impatiently.* **2** [VN] (sometimes *humorous*) to touch sb in a rough sexual way that they find offensive

pawn /pɔːn/ *noun, verb*
- *noun* **1** a CHESS piece of the smallest size and least value. Each player has eight pawns at the start of a game.—picture on page A8 **2** a person or group whose actions are controlled by more powerful people: *The hostages are being used as political pawns.* IDM **in pawn** if sth is in pawn, it has been pawned: *All her jewellery was in pawn.*
- *verb* [VN] to leave an object with a pawnbroker in exchange for money. The object is returned to the owner

if he or she pays back the money within an agreed period of time. If not, it can be sold.

pawn·broker /ˈpɔːnbrəʊkə(r); *AmE* -broʊ-/ *noun* a person who lends money in exchange for articles left with them. If the money is not paid back by a particular time, the pawnbroker can sell the article.

pawn·shop /ˈpɔːnʃɒp; *AmE* -ʃɑːp/ *noun* a pawnbroker's shop/store

paw·paw /ˈpɔːpɔː/ *noun* (*BrE*) = PAPAYA

pay /peɪ/ *verb, noun*
- *verb* (**paid, paid** /peɪd/) **1** ~ (**sb**) (**for sth**) to give sb money for work, goods, services, etc: [V] *I'll pay for the tickets.* ◇ *Are you paying in cash or by credit card?* ◇ *Her parents paid for her to go to Canada.* ◇ *My company pays well* (= pays high salaries). ◇ [VN] *to pay cash* ◇ *Would you mind paying the taxi driver?* ◇ *She pays £200 a week for this apartment.* ◇ [VNN] *He still hasn't paid me the money he owes me.* ◇ *I'm paid $100 a day.* ◇ [VN to inf] *I don't pay you to sit around all day doing nothing!*—see also LOW-PAID **2** ~ **sth (to sb)** | ~ (**sb**) **sth** to give sb money that you owe them: [VN] *Membership fees should be paid to the secretary.* ◇ *to pay a bill/debt/fine/ransom* ◇ [VNN] *Have you paid him the rent yet?* **3** [V] (of a business, etc.) to produce a profit: *It's hard to make farming pay.* **4** to result in some advantage or profit for sb: [V] *Crime doesn't pay.* ◇ [V to inf] *It pays to keep up to date with your work.* ◇ [VN to inf] *It would probably pay you to hire an accountant.* **5** [V] ~ (**for sth**) to suffer or be punished for your beliefs or actions: *You'll pay for that remark!* ◇ *Many people paid with their lives* (= they died). **6** used with some nouns to show that you are giving or doing the thing mentioned [VN, VNN] *I'll pay a call on* (= visit) *my friends.* ◇ *I'll pay you a call when I'm in town.* ◇ [VN] *I didn't pay attention to what she was saying.* ◇ *The director paid tribute to all she had done for the charity.* ◇ [VNN] *He's always paying me compliments.* IDM **the 'devil/'hell to pay** a lot of trouble: *There'll be hell to pay when he finds out.* **he who pays the piper calls the 'tune** (*saying*) the person who provides the money for sth can also control how it is spent **pay 'court to sb** (*old-fashioned*) to treat sb with great respect in order to gain favour with them **pay 'dividends** to produce great advantages or profits: *Exercising regularly will pay dividends in the end.* **,pay for it'self** (of a new system, sth you have bought, etc.) to save as much money as it cost: *The rail pass will pay for itself after only about two trips.* **pay its 'way** (of a business, etc.) to make enough money to pay what it costs to keep it going: *The bridge is still not paying its way.* **pay the 'penalty (for sth/for doing sth)** | **pay a/the 'price (for sth/for doing sth)** to suffer because of bad luck, a mistake or sth you have done: *He looked terrible this morning. I think he's paying the penalty for all those late nights.* ◇ *They're now paying the price for past mistakes.* **pay your re'spects (to sb)** (*formal*) to visit sb or to send greetings as a sign of respect for them: *Many came to pay their last respects* (= by attending sb's funeral). **pay through the 'nose (for sth)** (*informal*) to pay much too much money for sth **pay your 'way** to pay for everything yourself without having to rely on anyone else's money **put 'paid to sth** (*informal*) to stop or destroy sth, especially what sb plans or wants to do—more at ARM *n.*, HEED *n.*, ROB PHR V **,pay sb 'back (sth)** | **,pay sth ↤↦'back (to sb)** to return money that you borrowed from sb: *I'll pay you back next week.* ◇ *You can pay back the loan over a period of three years.* ◇ *Did he ever pay you back that $100 he owes you?* **,pay sb 'back (for sth)** to punish sb for making you or sb else suffer: *I'll pay him back for making me look like a fool in front of everyone.*—related noun PAYBACK **,pay sth ↤↦'in** | **'pay sth into sth** to put money into a bank account: *I paid in a cheque this morning.* ◇ *I'd like to pay some money into my account.* **,pay 'off** (*informal*) (of a plan or an action, especially one that involves risk) to be successful and bring good results: *The gamble paid off.* **,pay sb ↤↦'off 1** to pay sb what they have earned and tell them to leave their job: *The crew were paid off as soon as the ship docked.* **2** (*informal*) to give sb money to prevent them from doing sth or talking about sth illegal or

dishonest that you have done: *All the witnesses had been paid off.*—related noun PAY-OFF ,**pay sth**‹›'**off** to finish paying money owed for sth: *We paid off our mortgage after fifteen years.* ,**pay sth**‹›'**out 1** to pay a large sum of money for sth: *I had to pay out £500 to get my car repaired*—related noun PAYOUT **2** to pass a length of rope through your hands ,**pay 'up** to pay all the money that you owe to sb, especially when you do not want to or when the payment is late: *I had a hard time getting him to pay up.*

■ *noun* [U] the money that sb gets for doing regular work: *Her job is hard work, but the pay is good.* ◊ *a pay increase* ◊ *(BrE) a pay rise* ◊ *(AmE) a pay raise* ◊ *a 3% pay offer* ◊ *holiday pay* ◊ *to make a **pay claim** (= to officially ask for an increase in pay)*—see also SICK PAY **IDM in the pay of sb/sth** (usually *disapproving*) working for sb or for an organization, often secretly

pay·able /'peɪəbl/ *adj.* [not before noun] **1** that must be paid or can be paid: *A 10% deposit is payable in advance.* ◊ *The price is payable in monthly instalments.* **2** when a cheque, etc. is made **payable to** sb, their name is written on it and they can then pay it into their bank account

,**pay as you 'earn** *noun* [U] = PAYE—compare WITHHOLDING TAX

pay·back /'peɪbæk/ *noun* [C, U] **1** the money that you receive back on money that you have invested (especially when this is equal to the amount that you invested to start with); the time that it takes to get your money back: *a 10-year payback* **2** the advantage or REWARD that sb receives for sth they have done; the act of paying sth back: *His victory was seen as payback for all the hard work he'd put in during training.* ◊ *(informal) It's payback time! (= a person will have to suffer for what they have done)*

'**pay cheque** (*BrE*) (*AmE* **pay·check** /'peɪtʃek/) *noun* **1** the cheque that you are given when your wages are paid to you **2** (*especially AmE*) a way of referring to the amount of money that you earn: *a huge paycheck*

'**pay day** *noun* [U] the day on which you get your wages or SALARY: *Friday is pay day.*

'**pay dirt** *noun* [U] (*especially AmE*) earth that contains valuable minerals or metal such as gold **IDM hit/strike** '**pay dirt** (*informal*) to suddenly be in a successful situation, especially one that makes you rich

PAYE /,piː eɪ waɪ 'iː/ *abbr.* pay as you earn (a British system of paying income tax in which money is taken from your wages by your employer and paid to the government)

payee /,peɪ'iː/ *noun* (*technical*) a person that money or a cheque is paid to

payer /'peɪə(r)/ *noun* a person who pays or who has to pay for sth: *mortgage payers* ◊ *The company are not very good payers (= they are slow to pay their bills, or they do not pay their employees well).*

,**paying 'guest** *noun* a person who pays to live in sb's house with them, usually for a short time

pay·load /'peɪləʊd; *AmE* -loʊd/ *noun* (*technical*) **1** the passengers and goods on a ship or an aircraft for which payment is received **2** the goods that a vehicle, for example a lorry/truck, is carrying; the amount it is carrying **3** the explosive power of a bomb or a MISSILE **4** the equipment carried by a spacecraft or satellite

pay·mas·ter /'peɪmɑːstə(r); *AmE* -mæs-/ *noun* **1** (usually *disapproving*) a person or group of people that pays another person or organization and therefore can control their actions **2** an official who pays the wages in the army, a factory, etc.

pay·ment /'peɪmənt/ *noun* ~ (**for sth**) **1** [U] the act of paying sb/sth or of being paid: *payment in instalments/in advance/by cheque* ◊ *There will be a penalty for late payment of bills.* **2** [C] a sum of money paid or expected to be paid: *a cash payment* ◊ *They are finding it difficult to meet the payments on their car.* ◊ *He agreed to make ten monthly payments of £50.*—see also BALANCE OF PAYMENTS **3** [U, sing.] a reward or an act of thanks for sth you have done: *We'd like you to accept this gift in payment for your kindness.* ◊ *Is this all the payment I get for my efforts?*

'**pay-off** *noun* (*informal*) **1** a payment of money to sb so that they will not cause you any trouble or to make them keep a secret **SYN** BRIBE: *The police are accused of receiving secret pay-offs from the drug barons.* **2** a payment of money to sb to persuade them to leave their job **3** an advantage or a reward from sth you have done

pay·ola /peɪ'əʊlə; *AmE* -'oʊlə/ *noun* [U] (*AmE, informal*) the practice of giving or taking payments for doing sth illegal, especially for illegally influencing the sales of a particular product **SYN** BRIBERY

pay·out /'peɪaʊt/ *noun* a large amount of money that is given to sb: *an insurance payout* ◊ *a lottery payout*

'**pay packet** (also '**wage packet**) (both *BrE*) *noun* an envelope containing your wages; the amount sb earns

pay·phone /'peɪfəʊn; *AmE* -foʊn/ *noun* a telephone, usually in a public place, that is operated using coins or a card

pay·roll /'peɪrəʊl; *AmE* -roʊl/ *noun* **1** a list of people employed by a company showing the amount of money to be paid to each of them: *We have 500 people on the payroll.* **2** [usually sing.] the total amount paid in wages by a company

pay·slip /'peɪslɪp/ *noun* (*BrE*) a piece of paper given to an employee that shows how much money they have been paid and how much has been taken away for tax, etc.

PC /,piː 'siː/ *abbr.* **1** the abbreviation for 'personal computer' (a small computer that is designed for one person to use at work or at home): *software for PCs*—picture on page 250 **2** (*BrE*) the abbreviation for 'Police Constable' (a police officer of the lowest rank): *PC Tom March*—see also WPC **3** the abbreviation for POLITICALLY CORRECT

p.d.q. /,piː diː 'kjuː/ *abbr.* pretty damn/damned quick: *Make sure you get here p.d.q.*

PE (*BrE*) (*AmE* **P.E.**) /,piː 'iː/ *noun* [U] the abbreviation for 'physical education' (sport and exercise that is taught in schools): *a PE lesson/class*

pea /piː/ *noun* a small round green seed, eaten as a vegetable. Several peas grow together inside a long thin POD on a climbing plant also called a **pea**: *frozen peas* ◊ *pea soup*—picture on page A3—see also CHICKPEA, MUSHY PEAS, SWEET PEA

peace /piːs/ *noun* **1** [U, sing.] a situation or a period of time in which there is no war or violence in a country or an area: *war and peace* ◊ *peace talks/negotiations* ◊ *The negotiators are trying to **make peace** between the warring factions.* ◊ *A UN force has been sent to **keep the peace** (= to prevent people from fighting).* ◊ *After years of war, the people long for a lasting peace.* ◊ *the Peace of Utrecht, 1713 (= the agreement ending the war)* ◊ *The two communities live together **in peace**.* ◊ *The countries have been **at peace** for more than a century.* ◊ *the peace movement (= that tries to prevent war by protesting, persuading politicians, etc.)* **2** [U] the state of being calm or quiet: *She lay back and enjoyed the peace of the summer evening.* ◊ *I would work better if I had some **peace and quiet**.* ◊ *He just wants to be **left in peace** (= not to be disturbed).* ◊ *I need to check that she is all right, just for my own **peace of mind** (= so that I do not have to worry).* ◊ *He never felt really **at peace** with himself.* **3** [U] the state of living in friendship with sb without arguing: *They simply can't seem to live in peace with each other.* ◊ *She felt **at peace** with the world.*—see also BREACH, JUSTICE OF THE PEACE **IDM hold your** '**peace/'tongue** (*old-fashioned*) to remain silent although you would like to give your opinion **make (your) peace with sb** to end an argument with sb, usually by saying you are sorry—more at WICKED *n.*

WHICH WORD? ❓

peace / peacefulness

The noun **peace** can be used to talk about a peaceful state or situation: *world peace* ◊ *I just need some peace and quiet.* **Peacefulness** is not a common word. It means 'the quality of being peaceful'.

---

peace·able /'piːsəbl/ *adj.* **1** not involving or causing argument or violence **SYN** PEACEFUL: *A peaceable settlement has been reached.* ◊ *A peaceable crowd gathered*

P

---

b	d	f	g	h	k	l	m	n	p	r
bad	did	fall	get	hat	cat	leg	man	now	pen	red

P

outside the White House. **2** not liking to argue; wishing to live in peace with others SYN PEACEFUL, CALM: *a peaceable nature/character* ▶ **peace·ably** /-əbli/ *adv.*

peace dividend *noun* [usually sing.] money previously spent on weapons and the defence of a country and now available to be used for other things because of a reduction in a country's military forces

peace·ful /'piːsfl/ *adj.* **1** not involving a war, violence or argument: *a peaceful protest/demonstration/solution* ◊ *They hope for a peaceful settlement of the dispute.* **2** quiet and calm; not worried or disturbed in any way: *a peaceful atmosphere/evening* ◊ *a peaceful sleep* ◊ *It's so peaceful out here in the country.* ◊ *He had a peaceful life.* **3** trying to create peace or to live in peace; not liking violence or disagreement SYN PEACEABLE: *a peaceful society* ◊ *The aims of the organization are wholly peaceful.* ▶ **peace·ful·ly** /-fəli/ *adv.*: *The siege has ended peacefully.* ◊ *The baby slept peacefully.* **peace·ful·ness** *noun* [U] ⇨ note at PEACE

peace·keep·ing /'piːskiːpɪŋ/ *adj.* [only before noun] intended to help keep the peace and prevent war or violence in a place where this is likely: *peacekeeping operations* ◊ *a United Nations peacekeeping force*

peace-loving *adj.* preferring to live in peace and to avoid arguments and fighting

peace·maker /'piːsmeɪkə(r)/ *noun* a person who tries to persuade people or countries to stop arguing or fighting and to make peace

peace offering *noun* a present given to sb to show that you are sorry for sth or want to make peace after an argument

peace·time /'piːstaɪm/ *noun* [U] a period of time when a country is not at war—compare WARTIME

peach /piːtʃ/ *noun, adj.*
■ *noun* **1** [C] a round fruit with soft red and yellow skin, yellow flesh and a rough stone/pit inside: *a peach tree*—compare NECTARINE—picture on page A2 **2** [sing.] ~ (of a ...) (*old-fashioned, informal*) a particularly good or attractive person or thing **3** [U] a pinkish-orange colour
■ *adj.* pinkish-orange in colour

peachy /'piːtʃi/ *adj.* **1** like a peach in colour or appearance: *pale peachy skin* **2** (*AmE, informal*) fine; very nice: *Everything is just peachy.*

pea·cock /'piːkɒk; *AmE* -kɑːk/ *noun* a large male bird with long blue and green tail feathers that it can spread out like a FAN: *as proud as a peacock*—see also PEAHEN

pea-'green *adj.* bright green in colour, like peas

pea·hen /'piːhen/ *noun* a large brown bird, the female of the peacock

peak /piːk/ *noun, verb, adj.*
■ *noun* **1** [usually sing.] the point when sb/sth is best, most successful, strongest, etc: *Traffic reaches its peak between 8 and 9 in the morning.* ◊ *She's at the peak of her career.* ◊ *the peaks and troughs of married life*—compare OFF-PEAK **2** the pointed top of a mountain; a mountain with a pointed top: *a mountain peak* ◊ *snow-capped/jagged peaks* ◊ *The climbers made camp halfway up the peak.* **3** any narrow and pointed shape, edge, etc: *Whisk the egg whites into stiff peaks.* **4** (*BrE*) (*AmE* **bill**, **visor**) the stiff front part of a cap that sticks out above your eyes—picture at HAT
■ *verb* [V] to reach the highest point or value: *Oil production peaked in the early 1980s.* ◊ *Unemployment peaked at 17%.* ◊ *an athlete who peaks* (= produces his or her best performance) *at just the right time*
■ *adj.* [only before noun] used to describe the highest level of sth, or a time when the greatest number of people are doing sth or using sth: *It was a time of peak demand for the product.* ◊ *March is one of the peak periods for our business.* ◊ *The athletes are all in peak condition.* ◊ *We need extra help during the peak summer season.* ◊ (*BrE*) *peak viewing time* (= when the greatest number of people are watching television) ◊ (*BrE*) *peak rate telephone calls* (= made during the busiest period and charged at the highest rate)—compare OFF-PEAK

peaked /piːkt/ *adj.* **1** having a peak **2** (*AmE*) = PEAKY

peaky /'piːki/ (*BrE, informal*) (*AmE* **peaked**) *adj.* ill or pale: *You're looking a little peaky. Are you OK?*

peal /piːl/ *noun, verb*
■ *noun* **1** ~ (**of sth**) a loud sound or series of sounds: *She burst into peals of laughter.* **2** the loud ringing sound of a bell: *a peal of bells rang out* ◊ *a set of bells that all have different notes; a musical pattern that can be rung on a set of bells*
■ *verb* **1** [V] ~ (**out**) (of bells) to ring loudly: *The bells of the city began to peal out.* **2** to suddenly laugh loudly: *Ellen pealed with laughter.*

pea·nut /'piːnʌt/ *noun* **1** (*BrE* also **ground·nut**) [C] a nut that grows underground in a thin shell: *a packet of salted peanuts* ◊ *peanut oil*—picture at NUT **2** (**peanuts**) [pl.] (*informal*) a very small amount of money: *I won't work for peanuts.* ◊ *He gets paid peanuts for doing that job.*

peanut 'butter *noun* [U] a thick soft substance made from very finely chopped PEANUTS, usually eaten spread on bread: (*AmE*) *a peanut butter and jelly sandwich*

pear /peə(r); *AmE* per/ *noun* a yellow or green fruit that is narrow at the top and wide at the bottom: *a pear tree*—see also PRICKLY PEAR

pearl /pɜːl; *AmE* pɜːrl/ *noun* **1** [C] a small hard shiny white ball that forms inside the shell of an OYSTER and is of great value as a jewel: *a string of pearls* ◊ *a pearl necklace* ◊ *She was wearing her pearls* (= a necklace of pearls).—see also SEED PEARL **2** [C] a copy of a pearl that is made artificially **3** [U] = MOTHER-OF-PEARL: *pearl buttons* **4** [C, usually sing.] a thing that looks like a pearl in shape or colour: *pearls of dew on the grass* **5** [C] a thing that is very precious or highly valued: *She is a pearl among women.* IDM **cast, throw, etc. pearls before 'swine** to give or offer valuable things to people who do not understand their value **a ,pearl of 'wisdom** (usually *ironic*) a wise remark: *Thank you for those pearls of wisdom.*

pearly /'pɜːli; *AmE* 'pɜːrli/ *adj.* of or like a pearl: *pearly white teeth*

the ,Pearly 'Gates *noun* [pl.] (*humorous*) the gates of heaven

pear-shaped *adj.* **1** shaped like a pear **2** a pear-shaped person is wider around their waist and hips than around the top part of their body IDM **go 'pear-shaped** (*BrE, informal*) if things go pear-shaped, they go wrong

peas·ant /'peznt/ *noun* **1** (especially in the past, or in poorer countries) a farmer who owns or rents a small piece of land: *peasant farmers/communities/agriculture* **2** (*informal, disapproving*) a person who is rude, behaves badly, or has little education

peas·ant·ry /'pezntri/ *noun* [sing.+ sing./pl. *v.*] all the peasants in a region or country: *the local peasantry*

pea·shoot·er /'piːʃuːtə(r)/ *noun* (*BrE*) a small tube that children use to blow small objects such as dried peas at sb/sth, in order to hit them or it

peat /piːt/ *noun* [U] a soft black or brown substance formed from decaying plants just under the surface of the ground, especially in cool wet areas. It can be burned as a fuel or used to improve garden soil: *peat bogs* ▶ **peaty** *adj.*: *peaty soils*

peb·ble /'pebl/ *noun* a smooth, round stone that is found in or near water

pebble-dash *noun* [U] (*BrE*) CEMENT mixed with small stones used for covering the outside walls of houses

pebbly /'pebli/ *adj.* covered with pebbles: *a pebbly beach*

pecan /'piːkən; pɪ'kæn; *AmE* pɪ'kɑːn/ *noun* the nut of the American **pecan** tree with a smooth pinkish-brown shell—picture at NUT

pecca·dillo /,pekə'dɪləʊ; *AmE* -'dɪloʊ/ *noun* (*pl.* **-oes** or **-os**) (*written*) a small unimportant thing that sb does wrong

peck /pek/ *verb, noun*
■ *verb* **1** ~ (**at sth**) (of birds) to move the beak forward quickly and hit or bite sth: *A robin was pecking at crumbs on the ground.* ◊ [VN] *A bird had pecked a hole in the sack.* ◊ *Vultures had pecked out the dead goat's eyes.* **2** [VN] ~ **sb** (**on sth**) (*informal*) to kiss sb lightly and

quickly: *He pecked her on the cheek as he went out.* ◊ *She pecked his cheek.* **IDM** **a/the 'pecking order** (*informal, often humorous*) the order of importance in relation to one another among the members of a group: *New Zealand is at the top of the pecking order of rugby nations.* **PHR V** **'peck at sth** to eat only a very small amount of a meal because you are not hungry

■ *noun* **1** (*informal*) a quick kiss: *He gave her a friendly peck on the cheek.* **2** an act of pecking sb/sth: *The budgerigar gave a quick peck at the seed.*

peck·er /'pekə(r)/ *noun* (*slang, especially AmE*) a PENIS **IDM** **,keep your 'pecker up** (*BrE, informal*) to remain cheerful in spite of difficulties

peck·ish /'pekɪʃ/ *adj.* (*BrE, informal*) slightly hungry

pec·tin /'pektɪn/ *noun* [U] (*chemistry*) a substance similar to sugar that forms in ripe fruit and is used to make jam/jelly firm as it is cooked

pec·toral /'pektərəl/ *adj.* (*anatomy*) relating to or connected with the chest or breast: *pectoral muscles*

pec·torals /'pektərəlz/ (also *informal* **pecs** /peks/) *noun* [pl.] the muscles of the chest

pe·cu·liar /pɪˈkjuːliə(r)/ *adj.* **1** strange or unusual, especially in a way that is unpleasant or worrying: *a peculiar smell/taste* ◊ *There was something peculiar in the way he smiled.* ◊ *I had a peculiar feeling we'd met before.*—compare ODD **2** ~ (**to sb/sth**) belonging or relating to one particular place, situation, person, etc., and not to others: *a humour that is peculiar to American sitcoms* ◊ *a species of bird peculiar to Asia* ◊ *He has his own peculiar style which you'll soon get used to.* ◊ *the peculiar properties of mercury* **3** (*BrE, informal*) slightly ill

pe·cu·li·ar·ity /pɪˌkjuːliˈærəti/ *noun* (*pl.* **-ies**) **1** [C] a strange or unusual feature or habit: *a physical peculiarity* **2** [C] a feature that only belongs to one particular person, thing, place, etc: *the cultural peculiarities of the English* **3** [U] the quality of being strange or unusual

pe·cu·li·ar·ly /pɪˈkjuːliəli; *AmE* -ərli/ *adv.* (*especially written*) **1** very; more than usually **SYN** PARTICULARLY, ESPECIALLY: *These plants are peculiarly prone to disease.* **2** in a way that relates to or is especially typical of one particular person, thing, place, etc: *He seemed to believe that it was a peculiarly British problem.* **3** in a strange or unusual way

pe·cu·ni·ary /pɪˈkjuːniəri; *AmE* -ieri/ *adj.* (*formal*) relating to or connected with money: *pecuniary advantage/ interest/gain*

ped- (*AmE*) = PAED-

peda·gogic /ˌpedəˈɡɒdʒɪk; *AmE* -ˈɡɑːdʒ-/ (also **peda·gogic·al** /-ɪkl/) *adj.* (*formal*) concerning teaching methods: *pedagogic practice/principles* ▶ **peda·gogic·al·ly** /ˌpedəˈɡɒdʒɪkli; *AmE* -ˈɡɑːdʒ-/ *adv.*

peda·gogue /'pedəɡɒɡ; *AmE* -ɡɑːɡ/ *noun* (*old use or formal*) a teacher; a person who likes to teach people things, especially because they think they know more than other people

peda·gogy /'pedəɡɒdʒi; *AmE* -ɡoʊdʒi/ *noun* [U] (*technical*) the study of teaching methods

pedal /'pedl/ *noun, verb*
■ *noun* **1** a flat bar on a machine such as a bicycle, car, etc. that you push down with your foot in order to make parts of the machine move or work: *I couldn't reach the pedals on her bike.* ◊ *She pressed her foot down sharply on the brake pedal.*—picture at BICYCLE **2** a bar on a musical instrument such as a piano or an organ that you push with your foot in order to produce or control the sound—picture at PIANO
■ *verb* (**-ll-**, *AmE* also **-l-**) **1** [+*adv./prep.*] to ride a bicycle somewhere: [V] *I saw her pedalling along the towpath.* ◊ *He jumped on his bike and pedalled off.* ◊ [VN] *She pedalled her bicycle up the track.* **2** to turn or press the pedals on a bicycle or other machine: [V] *You'll have to pedal hard up this hill.* ◊ [VN] *She had been pedalling her exercise bike all morning.*—see also BACK-PEDAL, SOFT-PEDAL

'pedal bin *noun* (*BrE*) a container for rubbish, usually in a kitchen, with a lid that opens when a pedal is pressed

ped·alo /'pedæləʊ; *AmE* -loʊ/ *noun* (*pl.* **-oes** or **-os**) (*BrE*) a small pleasure boat that you move through the water by pushing PEDALS with your feet

ped·ant /'pednt/ *noun* (*disapproving*) a person who is too concerned with small details or rules especially when learning or teaching

pe·dan·tic /pɪˈdæntɪk/ *adj.* (*disapproving*) too worried about small details or rules: *a pedantic insistence on the correct way of doing things* ▶ **pe·dan·tic·al·ly** /-kli/ *adv.*

ped·ant·ry /'pedntri/ *noun* [U] (*disapproving*) too much attention to small details or rules

ped·dle /'pedl/ *verb* [VN] **1** to try to sell goods by going from house to house or from place to place: *He worked as a door-to-door salesman peddling cloths and brushes.* ◊ *to peddle illegal drugs* **2** to spread an idea or story in order to get people to accept it: *to peddle malicious gossip* ◊ *This line* (= publicly stated opinion) *is being peddled by all the government spokesmen.*

ped·dler /'pedlə(r)/ *noun* **1** (also **'drug peddler**) (both *BrE*) a person who sells illegal drugs **2** (*AmE*) = PEDLAR

ped·es·tal /'pedɪstl/ *noun* the base that a column, statue, etc. rests on: *a pedestal basin* (= a washbasin supported by a column) ◊ *I replaced the vase carefully on its pedestal* **IDM** **to put/place sb on a 'pedestal** to admire sb so much that you do not see their faults—more at KNOCK *v.*

ped·es·trian /pəˈdestriən/ *noun, adj.*
■ *noun* a person walking in the street and not travelling in a vehicle—compare MOTORIST
■ *adj.* **1** [only before noun] used by or for the use of pedestrians; connected with pedestrians: *pedestrian areas* ◊ *Pedestrian accidents are down by 5%.* **2** without any imagination or excitement; dull

pe,destrian 'crossing (*BrE*) (*AmE* **cross·walk**) *noun* a part of a road where vehicles must stop to allow people to cross—see also ZEBRA CROSSING

ped·es·tri·an·ize (*BrE* also **-ise**) /pəˈdestriənaɪz/ *verb* [VN] to make a street or part of a town into an area that is only for people who are walking, not for vehicles: *Most of the city streets have been pedestrianized.* ▶ **ped·es·tri·an·iza·tion, -isa·tion** *noun* [U]

pe,destrian 'precinct *noun* (*BrE*) a part of a town, especially a shopping area, that vehicles are not allowed to enter

pedi·at·ri·cian (*AmE*) = PAEDIATRICIAN

pedi·at·rics (*AmE*) = PAEDIATRICS

pedi·cure /'pedɪkjʊə(r); *AmE* -kjʊr/ *noun* [C, U] care and treatment of the feet and TOENAILS—compare MANICURE

pedi·gree /'pedɪɡriː/ *noun, adj.*
■ *noun* **1** [C] knowledge of or an official record of the animals from which an animal has been bred: *dogs with good pedigrees* (= their ancestors are known and of the same breed) **2** [C, U] a person's family history or the background of sth, especially when this is impressive: *She was proud of her long pedigree.* ◊ *The product has a pedigree going back to the last century.*
■ *adj.* (*BrE*) (*AmE* **pedi·greed**) [only before noun] (of an animal) descended from a family of the same breed that has been officially recorded for a long time and is thought to be of a good quality: *pedigree sheep*

pedi·ment /'pedɪmənt/ *noun* (*architecture*) the part in the shape of a triangle above the entrance of a building in the ancient Greek style

ped·lar (*BrE*) (*AmE* **ped·dler**) /'pedlə(r)/ *noun* a person who in the past travelled from place to place trying to sell small objects

ped·ometer /peˈdɒmɪtə(r); *AmE* -ˈdɑːm-/ *noun* an instrument for measuring how far you have walked

pedo·phile, pedo·philia (*AmE*) = PAEDOPHILE, PAEDOPHILIA

pee /piː/ *verb, noun*
■ *verb* (**peed, peed**) [V] (*informal*) to pass waste liquid from your body **SYN** URINATE: *I need to pee.*
■ *noun* (*informal*) **1** [sing.] an act of passing liquid waste from your body: (*BrE*) *to go for a pee* ◊ *to have a pee* ◊ (*AmE*) *to take a pee* **2** [U] liquid waste passed from your body; URINE

peek /piːk/ *verb* [V] **1** ~ (**at sth**) to look at sth quickly and

æ	ɑː	e	ɜː	ə	ɪ	iː	i	ɒ	ɔː	ʌ	ʊ	u	uː
cat	father	ten	bird	about	sit	see	many	got	saw	cup	put	actual	too
								(BrE)					

secretly because you should not be looking at it: *No peeking! ◊ I couldn't resist peeking in the drawer. ◊ She peeked at the audience from behind the curtain.* **2 ~ out/ over/through, etc.** to be just visible: *Her feet peeked out from the end of the blanket. ◊ A toe peeked through the hole in his sock.* ▶ **peek** *noun* [sing.]: *I took a quick peek inside.*

peek·aboo /ˌpiːkəˈbuː/ (*BrE* also **peep-bo**) *noun* [U] a simple game played to amuse young children, in which you keep hiding your face and then showing it again, saying 'Peekaboo!' or 'Peep-bo!'

peel /piːl/ *verb, noun*

■ *verb* **1** [VN] to take the skin off fruit, vegetables, etc: *to peel an orange/a banana ◊ Have you peeled the potatoes?*—picture on page A2 **2 ~ (sth) away/off/back** to remove a layer, covering, etc. from the surface of sth; to come off the surface of sth: [VN] *Carefully peel away the lining paper. ◊* [V] *The label will peel off if you soak it in water.* **3** [V] **~ (off)** (of a covering) to come off in strips or small pieces: *The wallpaper was beginning to peel. ◊ If I stay in the sun too long my skin peels.* **4** [V] (of a surface) to lose strips or small pieces of its covering: *Put on some cream to stop your nose from peeling. ◊ The walls have begun to peel.* **IDM** see EYE *n.* **PHRV** ˌpeel **'off** to ˈleave a group of vehicles, aircraft, etc. and turn to one side: *The leading car in the motorcade peeled off to the right.* ˌpeel **'off**| ˌpeel **(sth)** ↔ **'off** (*informal*) to remove some or all of your clothes: *You look hot—why don't you peel off? ◊ He peeled off his shirt.*

■ *noun* **1** [U, C] the skin of some fruits and vegetables: *orange/lemon peel ◊* (*AmE* also) *an orange/a lemon peel*—compare RIND, SKIN, ZEST **2 (peels)** [pl.] (*AmE*) = PEELINGS

peel·er /ˈpiːlə(r)/ *noun* (usually in compounds) a special type of knife for taking the skin off fruit and vegetables: *a potato peeler*—picture at KITCHEN

peel·ings /ˈpiːlɪŋz/ (*AmE* also **peels**) *noun* [pl.] the skin of fruit or vegetables that has been removed

peep /piːp/ *verb, noun*

■ *verb* **1** [V] **~ (at sth)** to look quickly and secretly at sth, especially through a small opening: *We caught her peeping through the keyhole. ◊ He was peeping at her through his fingers. ◊ Could I just peep inside?* **2** [V+adv./prep.] (*written*) to be just visible: *The tower peeped above the trees. ◊ The sun peeped out from behind the clouds.* **3** [V, VN] to make a short high sound; to make sth make this sound.

■ *noun* **1** [C, usually sing.] a quick or secret look at sth: *Dave took a quick peep at the last page.* **2** [sing.] (*informal*) something that sb says or a sound that sb makes: *We did not hear a peep out of the baby all night.* **3** [C] a short high sound like the one made by a young bird or by a whistle **4** (also **peep 'peep**) [C] a word for the sound of a car's horn, used especially by children

peep-bo /ˈpiːpbəʊ; ˈpiːpəʊ; *AmE* -boʊ; -poʊ/ *noun* [U] (*BrE*) = PEEKABOO

peep·hole /ˈpiːphəʊl; *AmE* -hoʊl/ *noun* a small opening in a wall, door, etc. that you can look through

ˌPeeping **'Tom** *noun* (*disapproving*) a person who likes to watch people secretly when they are taking off their clothes **SYN** VOYEUR

ˈpeep show *noun* **1** a series of moving pictures in a box that you look at through a small opening **2** a type of show in which a man pays to watch a woman take off her clothes

peer /pɪə(r); *AmE* pɪr/ *noun, verb*

■ *noun* **1** [usually pl.] a person who is the same age or who has the same social status as you: *She enjoys the respect of her peers. ◊ Children are worried about failing in front of their peers. ◊ Peer pressure is strong among young people* (= they want to be like other people of the same age). **2** (in Britain) a member of the NOBILITY—see also LIFE PEER, PEERESS

■ *verb* [V, usually+*adv./prep.*] to look closely or carefully at sth, especially when you cannot see it clearly: *We peered into the shadows. ◊ He went to the window and peered out. ◊ She kept peering over her shoulder. ◊ He peered closely at the photograph.*

peer·age /ˈpɪərɪdʒ; *AmE* ˈpɪr-/ *noun* **1** [sing.] all the peers (2) as a group: *a member of the peerage* **2** [C] the rank of a peer (2) or peeress

peer·ess /ˈpɪəres; *AmE* ˈpɪrəs/ *noun* a female PEER (2)

ˈpeer group *noun* a group of people of the same age or social status: *She gets on well with her peer group. ◊ peer-group pressure*

peer·less /ˈpɪələs; *AmE* ˈpɪrləs/ *adj.* (*written*) better than all others of its kind: *a peerless performance*

peeve /piːv/ *noun* **IDM** *sb's pet* **'peeve** (*AmE*) = SB'S PET HATE at PET *adj.*

peeved /piːvd/ *adj.* **~ (about sth)** (*informal*) annoyed: *He sounded peeved about not being told.*

peev·ish /ˈpiːvɪʃ/ *adj.* easily annoyed by unimportant things; bad-tempered ▶ **peev·ish·ly** *adv.*

pee·wit /ˈpiːwɪt/ *noun* = LAPWING

peg /peg/ *noun, verb*

■ *noun* **1** a short piece of wood, metal or plastic used for holding things together, hanging things on, marking a position, etc: *There's a peg near the door to hang your coat on.* **2** (also **'tent peg**) a small pointed piece of wood or metal that you attach to the ropes of a tent and push into the ground in order to hold the tent in place **3** (also **'clothes peg**) (both *BrE*) (*AmE* **clothes·pin**) a piece of wood or plastic used for attaching wet clothes to a clothes line **4** (also **'tuning peg**) a wooden screw for making the strings of a musical instrument tighter or looser **IDM** ˌoff the **'peg** (*BrE*) (*AmE* ˌoff the **'rack**) (of clothes) made to a standard average size and not made especially to fit you: *He buys his clothes off the peg. ◊ off-the-peg fashions* ˌbring/ˌtake sb **'down a peg (or two)** to make sb realize that they are not as good, important, etc. as they think they are: *He needed to be taken down a peg or two.* **a peg to 'hang sth on** something that gives you an excuse or opportunity to discuss or explain sth—more at SQUARE *adj.*

■ *verb* (-**gg**-) **1** [VN] **~ sth (out)** to fasten sth with pegs: *All their wet clothes were pegged out on the line. ◊ She was busy pegging her tent to the ground.* **2** [VN] [usually passive] **~ sth (at/to sth)** to fix or keep prices, wages, etc. at a particular level: *Pay increases will be pegged at 5%. ◊ Loan repayments are pegged to your income.* **3** [VN] **~ sb as sth** (*AmE, informal*) to think of sb in a particular way: *She pegged him as a big spender.* **IDM** see LEVEL *adj.* **PHRV** ˌpeg a'**way (at sth)** (*informal, especially BrE*) to continue working hard at sth or trying to achieve sth difficult ˌpeg sb/sth ↔ **'back** (*especially in sport*) to stop sb/sth from winning or increasing the amount by which they are ahead: *Each time we scored we were pegged back minutes later.* ˌpeg **'out** (*BrE, informal*) to die

ˈpeg leg *noun* (*informal*) an artificial leg, especially one made of wood

pe·jora·tive /pɪˈdʒɒrətɪv; *AmE* -ˈdʒɔːr-; -ˈdʒɑːr-/ *adj.* (*formal*) a word or remark that is **pejorative** expresses disapproval or criticism: *I'm using the word 'academic' here in a pejorative sense.* ▶ **pe·jora·tive·ly** *adv.*

Pe·kin·ese (also **Pe·king·ese**) /ˌpiːkɪˈniːz/ *noun* (*pl.* **Pe·kin·ese** or **Pe·kin·eses**) a very small dog with long soft hair, short legs and a flat nose

pe·la·gic /pəˈlædʒɪk/ *adj.* (*technical*) connected with, or living in, the parts of the sea that are far from the shore: *pelagic fish*

peli·can /ˈpelɪkən/ *noun* a large waterbird with a bag of skin under its long beak, for storing food

ˌpelican **'crossing** *noun* (in Britain) a place on a road where you can stop the traffic and cross by operating a set of TRAFFIC LIGHTS

pel·let /ˈpelɪt/ *noun* **1** a small hard ball of any substance, often of soft material that has become hard: *food pellets for chickens* **2** a very small metal ball that is fired from a gun

pel·let·ed /ˈpelɪtɪd/ *adj.* (*technical*) formed into pellets

pell-mell /ˌpelˈmel/ *adv.* (*old-fashioned*) very quickly and in a way that is not controlled

pel·lu·cid /pəˈluːsɪd/ *adj.* (*literary*) extremely clear **SYN** TRANSPARENT

aɪ	aʊ	eɪ	əʊ	oʊ	ɔɪ	ɪə	eə	ʊə	j	w
my	now	say	go	go	boy	near	hair	pure	yes	wet
			(BrE)	(AmE)						

pel·met /ˈpelmɪt/ (also **val·ance** especially in *AmE*) *noun* a strip of wood or fabric above a window that hides the curtain rail

pelt /pelt/ *verb, noun*
- *verb* **1** [VN] ~ **sb** (**with sth**) to attack sb by throwing things at them: *The children pelted him with snowballs.* ◊ *We were pelted with rotten tomatoes.* **2** [V] ~ (**down**) (of rain) to fall very heavily: *By now the rain was pelting down.* **3** [V+adv./prep.] (*informal*) to run somewhere very fast: *We pelted down the hill after the car.*
- *noun* the skin of an animal, especially with the fur or hair still on it IDM **(at) full ˈpelt/ˈtilt** as fast as possible

pel·vis /ˈpelvɪs/ *noun* the wide curved set of bones at the bottom of the body that the legs and SPINE are connected to—picture at BODY ▶ **pel·vic** /ˈpelvɪk/ *adj.* [only before noun]: *the pelvic bones*

pen /pen/ *noun, verb*
- *noun* **1** (often in compounds) an instrument made of plastic or metal used for writing with ink: *pen and ink* ◊ (*written*) *a new book from the pen of Martin Amis*—see also BALLPOINT PEN, FELT-TIP PEN, FOUNTAIN PEN **2** a small piece of land surrounded by a fence in which farm animals are kept: *a sheep pen* **3** (*AmE, slang*) = PENITENTIARY IDM **put pen to ˈpaper** to write or start to write sth—more at SLIP *n.*
- *verb* (**-nn-**) [VN] **1** (*formal*) to write sth: *He penned a letter to the local paper.* **2** ~ **sb/sth** (**in/up**) to shut an animal or a person in a small space: *At clipping time sheep need to be penned.* ◊ *The whole family were penned up in one room for a month.*

penal /ˈpiːnl/ *adj.* [usually before noun] **1** connected with or used for punishment, especially by law: *penal laws/reforms* ◊ *the penal system* ◊ *Criminals could at one time be sentenced to penal servitude* (= prison with hard physical work). ◊ *a penal colony* (= a place where criminals were sent as a punishment in the past) **2** that can be punished by law: *a penal offence* **3** very severe: *penal rates of interest*

ˈpenal code *noun* a system of laws connected with crime and punishment

pen·al·ize (*BrE* also **-ise**) /ˈpiːnəlaɪz/ *verb* [VN] **1** ~ **sb** (**for sth**) to punish sb for breaking a rule or law by making them suffer a disadvantage: *You will be penalized for poor spelling.* **2** ~ **sb** (**for sth**) to punish sb for breaking a rule in a sport or game by giving an advantage to their opponent: *He was penalized for time-wasting.* ◊ *Foul play will be severely penalized.* **3** to put sb at a disadvantage by treating them unfairly: *The new law appears to penalize the poorest members of society.*

pen·alty /ˈpenlti/ *noun* (*pl.* **-ies**) **1** ~ (**for sth**) a punishment for breaking a law, rule or contract: *to impose a penalty* ◊ *Assault carries a maximum penalty of seven years' imprisonment.* ◊ *The penalty for travelling without a ticket is £200.* ◊ *Contractors who fall behind schedule incur heavy financial penalties.* ◊ *a penalty clause in a contract* ◊ *You can withdraw money from the account at any time without penalty.*—see also DEATH PENALTY **2** ~ (**of sth**) a disadvantage suffered as a result of sth: *One of the penalties of fame is loss of privacy.* **3** (in sports and games) an advantage given to a player or a team when the other side breaks a rule: *The referee awarded a penalty to the home team.* **4** (in football) a chance to kick the ball into the goal without any defending players, except the GOALKEEPER, trying to stop it; the goal that is given if the kick is successful: *Two minutes later Ford equalized with a penalty.* IDM see PAY *v.*

ˈpenalty area (*BrE* also **ˈpenalty box**) *noun* (in football) the area in front of the goal. If the defending team breaks the rules within this area, the other team is given a penalty.

ˈpenalty point *noun* (*BrE*) a note on sb's DRIVING LICENCE showing they have committed an offence while driving

ˈpenalty ˈshoot-out *noun* (in football) a way of deciding the winner when both teams have the same score at the end of a game. Each team is given a number of chances to kick the ball into the goal and the team that scores the most goals wins.

pen·ance /ˈpenəns/ *noun* **1** [C usually sing, U] ~ (**for sth**) (especially in particular religions) an act that you give yourself to do, or that a priest gives you to do in order to show that you are sorry for sth you have done wrong: *an act of penance* ◊ *to do penance for your sins* **2** [sing.] something that you have to do even though you do not like doing it: *She regards living in New York as a penance; she hates big cities.*

ˌpen-and-ˈink *adj.* [usually before noun] drawn with a pen: *pen-and-ink drawings*

pence /pens/ (*BrE*) (*abbr.* **p**) *pl.* of PENNY

pen·chant /ˈpɒ̃ʃɒ̃; *AmE* ˈpentʃənt/ *noun* ~ **for sth** (*written*) a special liking for sth: *She has a penchant for champagne.*

pen·cil /ˈpensl/ *noun, verb*
- *noun* [C, U] a narrow piece of wood, or a metal or plastic case, containing a black or coloured substance, used for drawing or writing: *a pencil drawing* ◊ *I'll get a pencil and paper.* ◊ *She scribbled a note in pencil* ◊ *coloured pencils*
- *verb* (**-ll-**, *AmE* **-l-**) [VN] to write, draw or mark sth with a pencil: *a pencilled portrait* ◊ *A previous owner has pencilled 'First Edition' inside the book's cover.* PHRV **ˌpencil sth/sb↔ˈin** to write down sb's name or details of an arrangement with them that you know might have to be changed later: *We've pencilled in a meeting for Tuesday afternoon.* ◊ *Shall I pencil you in for Friday?* (= for a meeting)

ˈpencil case *noun* a small bag, etc. for holding pencils and pens

ˈpencil-pusher *noun* (*AmE*) = PEN-PUSHER

ˈpencil sharpener *noun* a small device with a blade inside, used for making pencils sharp—picture at STATIONERY

pen·dant /ˈpendənt/ *noun* a piece of jewellery that you wear around your neck on a chain—picture at CHAIN, JEWELLERY

pend·ing /ˈpendɪŋ/ *prep., adj.*
- *prep.* (*formal*) while waiting for sth to happen; until sth happens: *He was released on bail pending further inquiries.*
- *adj.* (*formal*) **1** [not before noun] waiting to be decided or settled: *Nine cases are still pending.* ◊ *a pending file/tray* (= where you put letters, etc. you are going to deal with soon) **2** going to happen soon: *An election is pending in Italy.* ◊ *his pending departure*

pen·du·lous /ˈpendjələs; *AmE* -dʒələs/ *adj.* (*formal*) hanging down loosely and swinging from side to side

pen·du·lum /ˈpendjələm; *AmE* -dʒələm/ *noun* a rod with a weight at the end that moves regularly from side to side to control the mechanism of a clock: (*figurative*) *In education, the pendulum has swung back to traditional teaching methods.* ◊ *the pendulum of public opinion*—picture at GRANDFATHER CLOCK

pene·trable /ˈpenɪtrəbl/ *adj.* (*rare, formal*) that allows sth to be pushed into or through it; that can have a way made through it: *soil that is easily penetrable with a fork* OPP IMPENETRABLE

pene·trate /ˈpenɪtreɪt/ *verb* **1** ~ (**into/through/to**) sth to go into or through sth: [VN] *The knife had penetrated his chest.* ◊ *The sun's radiation penetrates the skin.* ◊ (*figurative*) *The war penetrates every area of the nation's life.* ◊ [V] *These fine particles penetrate deep into the lungs.* **2** to succeed in entering or joining an organization, a group, etc. especially when this is difficult to do: [VN] *They had penetrated airport security.* ◊ *The party has been penetrated by extremists.* ◊ *This year the company has been trying to penetrate new markets* (= start selling their products there). ◊ [V] *The troops had penetrated deep into enemy lines.* **3** [VN] to see or show a way into or through sth: *Our eyes could not penetrate the darkness.* ◊ *The flashlights barely penetrated the gloom.* **4** [VN] to understand or discover sth that is difficult to understand or is hidden: *Science can penetrate many of nature's mysteries.*

5 to be understood or realized by sb: [V] *I was at the door before his words penetrated.* ◊ [VN] *None of my advice seems to have penetrated his thick skull* (= he has not listened to any of it). **6** [VN] (of a man) to put the PENIS into the VAGINA or ANUS of a sexual partner

pene·trat·ing /ˈpenɪtreɪtɪŋ/ *adj.* **1** (of sb's eyes or the way they look at you) making you feel uncomfortable because the person seems to know what you are thinking: *penetrating blue eyes* ◊ *a penetrating gaze/look/stare* **2** (of a sound or voice) loud and hard: *Her voice was shrill and penetrating.* **3** showing that you have understood sth quickly and completely: *a penetrating comment/criticism/question* **4** spreading deeply or widely: *a penetrating smell* ◊ *the penetrating cold/damp*

pene·tra·tion /ˌpenɪˈtreɪʃn/ *noun* [U] **1** the act or process of making a way into or through sth: *The floor is sealed to prevent water penetration.* ◊ *the company's successful penetration of overseas markets* **2** the act of a man putting his PENIS into his partner's VAGINA or ANUS

pene·tra·tive /ˈpenɪtrətɪv; *AmE* -treɪtɪv/ *adj.* **1** (of sexual activity) involving putting the PENIS into sb's VAGINA or ANUS: *penetrative sex* **2** able to make a way into or through sth: *penetrative weapons* **3** deep and thorough: *a penetrative survey*

pen·friend /ˈpenfrend/ (*BrE*) (also **ˈpen pal** *AmE, BrE*) *noun* a person that you make friends with by writing letters, often sb you have never met

pen·guin /ˈpeŋɡwɪn/ *noun* a black and white seabird that lives in the Antarctic. Penguins cannot fly but use their wings for swimming. There are several types of penguin, some of them very large but some of them quite small.

peni·cil·lin /ˌpenɪˈsɪlɪn/ *noun* [U] a substance obtained from MOULD, used as a drug to treat or prevent infections caused by bacteria; a type of ANTIBIOTIC

pen·ile /ˈpiːnaɪl/ *adj.* [only before noun] (*technical*) relating to the PENIS

pen·in·sula /pəˈnɪnsjələ; *AmE* -sələ/ *noun* an area of land that is almost surrounded by water but is joined to a larger piece of land: *the Iberian peninsula* (= Spain and Portugal)

pen·in·su·lar /pəˈnɪnsjələ(r); *AmE* -sələr/ *adj.* on or connected with a peninsula: *peninsular Spanish* (= that is spoken in Spain, not Latin America)

penis /ˈpiːnɪs/ *noun* the organ on the body of a man or male animal, used for URINATING and sex

peni·tence /ˈpenɪtəns/ *noun* [U] (*written*) a feeling of being sorry because you have done sth wrong: *He expressed suitable penitence for what he had done.*

peni·tent /ˈpenɪtənt/ *adj., noun*
■ *adj.* (*written*) feeling or showing that you are sorry for having done sth wrong
■ *noun* a person who shows that they are sorry for doing sth wrong, especially a religious person who wants God to forgive them

peni·ten·tial /ˌpenɪˈtenʃl/ *adj.* (*formal*) showing that you are sorry for having done sth wrong: *to be in a penitential mood*

peni·ten·tiary /ˌpenɪˈtenʃəri/ *noun* (*pl.* -ies) (also *informal* **pen**) (both *AmE*) a prison

pen·knife /ˈpennaɪf/ *noun* (*pl.* -knives /-naɪvz/) (also **ˈpocket knife** especially in *AmE*) a small knife with one or more blades that fold down into the handle

pen·man·ship /ˈpenmənʃɪp/ *noun* [U] (*formal*) the art of writing by hand; skill in doing this

ˈpen-name *noun* a name used by a writer instead of their real name **SYN** NOM DE PLUME—compare PSEUDONYM

pen·nant /ˈpenənt/ *noun* **1** a long narrow pointed flag, for example one used on a ship to give signals **2** (in the US) a flag given to the winning team in a sports LEAGUE, especially in baseball

pen·ni·less /ˈpeniləs/ *adj.* having no money; very poor

penn'orth /ˈpenəθ; *AmE* -nərθ/ *noun* [usually sing.] (*old-fashioned, BrE*) = PENNYWORTH

penny /ˈpeni/ *noun* (*pl.* **pen·nies** or **pence**) **HELP** In senses 1 and 2, **pennies** is used to refer to the coins, and **pence** to refer to an amount of money. In sense 3, the plural is **pennies**. **1** (*abbr.* p) a small British coin and unit of money. There are 100 pence in one pound (£1): *He had a few pennies in his pocket.* ◊ *That will be 45 pence, please.* ◊ *They cost 20p each.* **2** (*abbr.* d) a British coin in use until 1971. There were twelve pennies in one SHILLING. **3** (*AmE*) a cent **IDM** ,every 'penny all of the money: *We collected £700 and every penny went to charity.* ,in for a 'penny, ,in for a 'pound (*BrE, saying*) used to say that since you have started to do sth, it is worth spending as much time or money as you need to in order to complete it not a 'penny no money at all: *It didn't cost a penny.* the 'penny drops (*informal, especially BrE*) used to say that sb has finally understood or realized sth that they had not understood or realized before a ,penny for your 'thoughts | a penny for them (*saying*) used to ask sb what they are thinking about turn up like a bad 'penny (*informal*) (of a person) to appear when they are not welcome or not wanted, especially when this happens regularly ,two/,ten a 'penny (*BrE*) (*AmE* a ,dime a 'dozen) very common and therefore not valuable—more at PINCH *v.*, PRETTY *adj.*, SPEND *v.*

,penny-'farthing *noun* (*BrE*) an early type of bicycle with a very large front wheel and a very small back wheel

ˈpenny-pinching *adj.* (*disapproving*) unwilling to spend money on things: *this penny-pinching government* ◊ *a penny-pinching approach* ▶ **ˈpenny-pinching** *noun* [U]

,penny 'whistle *noun* = TIN WHISTLE

penny·worth /ˈpeniwɜːθ; *AmE* -wɜːrθ/ *noun* [sing.] (*old-fashioned, BrE*) as much as you can buy with a PENNY; a small amount of sth

pen·ology /piːˈnɒlədʒi; pɪ-; *AmE* -ˈnɑːl-/ *noun* [U] the scientific study of the punishment of criminals and the operation of prisons ▶ **pen·olo·gist** /piːˈnɒlədʒɪst; pɪ-; *AmE* -ˈnɑːl-/ *noun*

ˈpen pal *noun* (*especially AmE*) = PENFRIEND

ˈpen-pusher (*especially BrE*) (*AmE* usually **ˈpencil-pusher**) *noun* (*informal, disapproving*) a person with a boring job, especially in an office, that involves a lot of writing

pen·sion¹ /ˈpenʃn/ *noun, verb*—see also PENSION²
■ *noun* an amount of money paid regularly by a government or company to sb who is considered to be too old or too ill to work: *to receive an old-age/a retirement pension* ◊ *a disability/widow's pension* ◊ *a state pension* ◊ *to live on a pension* ◊ *to take out a personal/private pension* ◊ *a pension fund*
■ *verb* **PHRV** ,pension sb 'off (*especially BrE*) [usually passive] to allow or force sb to RETIRE (= leave their job and stop regular work) and to pay them a pension: *He was pensioned off and his job given to a younger man.* ◊ (*informal, figurative*) *That car of yours should have been pensioned off years ago.*

pension² /ˈpɒ̃sjɒ̃; *AmE* pɑːˈsjoʊn/ *noun* (from *French*) a small, usually cheap, hotel in some European countries, especially France—see also PENSION¹

pen·sion·able /ˈpenʃənəbl/ *adj.* giving sb the right to receive a pension: *people of pensionable age* ◊ *pensionable pay/earnings*

pen·sion·er /ˈpenʃənə(r)/ *noun* (*especially BrE*) a person who is receiving a PENSION, especially from the government: *an old-age pensioner*—see also OAP, SENIOR CITIZEN

ˈpension scheme (*BrE*) (also **ˈpension plan** *AmE, BrE*) *noun* a system in which you, and usually your employer, pay money regularly into a PENSION FUND while you are employed. You are then paid a PENSION when you RETIRE.

pen·sive /ˈpensɪv/ *adj.* thinking deeply about sth, especially because you are sad or worried: *a pensive expression/mood* ◊ *to look pensive* ▶ **pen·sive·ly** *adv.*

penta- /ˈpentə/ *combining form* (in nouns, adjectives and adverbs) five; having five: *pentagon* ◊ *pentathlon*

penta·gon /'pentəgən; AmE -gɑːn/ noun **1** [C] (geometry) a flat shape with five straight sides and five angles **2** (**the Pentagon**) [sing.] the building near Washington DC that is the HEADQUARTERS of the US Department of Defence and the military leaders: *a spokesman for the Pentagon*

pen·tag·on·al /pen'tægənl/ adj. (geometry) having five sides

penta·gram /'pentəgræm/ noun a flat shape of a star with five points, formed by five straight lines. Pentagrams are often used as magic symbols.

pen·tam·eter /pen'tæmɪtə(r)/ noun [C, U] (technical) a line of poetry with five stressed syllables; the rhythm of poetry with five stressed syllables to a line

pent·ath·lon /pen'tæθlən/ noun [sing., U] a sporting event in which people compete in five different sports (running, riding, swimming, shooting and FENCING)—compare BIATHLON, DECATHLON, HEPTATHLON, TRIATHLON

Pente·cost /'pentɪkɒst; AmE -kɔːst; -kɑːst/ noun [U, C] **1** (BrE also ,Whit 'Sunday) (in the Christian Church) the 7th Sunday after Easter when Christians celebrate the Holy Spirit coming to the APOSTLES **2** a Jewish festival that takes place 50 days after the second day of Passover

Pente·cos·tal /ˌpentɪ'kɒstl; AmE -'kɔːs-; -'kɑːs-/ adj. connected with a group of Christian Churches that emphasize the gifts of the Holy Spirit, such as the power to heal the sick ▶ **Pente·cos·talist** noun

pent·house /'penthaʊs/ noun an expensive and comfortable flat/apartment or set of rooms at the top of a tall building: *a luxury penthouse suite*

pent up /ˌpent 'ʌp/ adj. **1** (of feelings, energy, etc.) that cannot be expressed or released: *pent-up frustration/ energy* **2** having feelings that you cannot express: *She was too pent up to speak.*

pen·ul·ti·mate /pen'ʌltɪmət/ adj. [only before noun] (written) just before the last one; last but one: *the penultimate chapter/day/stage*

pen·uri·ous /pə'njʊəriəs; AmE -'nʊr-/ adj. (rare, formal) very poor

pen·ury /'penjəri/ noun [U] (formal) the state of being very poor SYN POVERTY

peon /'piːən/ noun **1** a worker on a farm in Latin America **2** (AmE, humorous) a person with a hard or boring job that is not well paid and not considered important

peony /'piːəni/ noun (pl. **-ies**) a garden plant with large round white, pink or red flowers

people /'piːpl/ noun, verb
- noun **1** [pl.] persons; men, women and children: *At least ten people were killed in the crash.* ◊ *There were a lot of people at the party.* ◊ *Many young people are out of work.* **2** [pl.] persons in general or everyone: *He doesn't care what people think of him.* ◊ *She tends to annoy people.* HELP Use **everyone** or **everybody** instead of 'all people'. **3** [C] all the persons who live in a particular place or belong to a particular country, race, etc: *the French people* ◊ *the native peoples of Siberia*—see also TOWNSPEOPLE **4** (**the people**) [pl.] the ordinary men and women of a country rather than those who govern or have a special position in society: *the life of the common people* ◊ *It was felt that the government was no longer in touch with the people.*—see also LITTLE PEOPLE **5** [pl.] men and women who work in a particular type of job or are involved in a particular area of activity: *a meeting with business people and bankers* ◊ *These garments are intended for professional sports people.* **6** [pl.] (literary) the men, women and children that a person leads: *The king urged his people to prepare for war.* **7** [pl.] the men and women who work for you or support you: *I've had my people watching the house for a few days.* **8** [pl.] (BrE, informal) guests or friends: *I'm having people to dinner this evening.* **9** [pl.] (old-fashioned) the men, women and children that you are closely related to, especially your parents, grandparents, etc: *She's spending the holidays with her people.*—see also BOAT PEOPLE, STREET PEOPLE, TRADESPEOPLE IDM **of 'all people** when you say of all people, you are emphasizing that sb is the person you would most or least expect to do sth: *She of all people should know the answer to that.* **people (who live) in glass houses shouldn't throw**

'stones (saying) you should not criticize other people, because they will easily find ways of criticizing you—more at MAN n., THING
- verb [VN] [usually passive] **~ sth (with sth)** (written) to live in a place or fill it with people: *The town was peopled largely by workers from the car factory and their families.* ◊ *The ballroom was peopled with guests.*

'people carrier (also **'people mover**) (both BrE) (AmE **mini·van**) noun a large car, like a van, designed to carry up to eight people—picture at CAR

pep /pep/ verb, noun
- verb (-pp-) PHRV ,pep sb/sth↔'up (informal) to make sb/sth more interesting or full of energy: *Pep up meals by adding more unusual spices.* ◊ *A walk in the fresh air will pep you up.*
- noun [U] energy and enthusiasm

pep·per /'pepə(r)/ noun, verb
- noun **1** [U] a grey or pale yellow powder made from dried berries (called PEPPERCORNS), used to give a hot flavour to food: *Season with salt and pepper* ◊ *freshly ground pepper* ◊ *black/white pepper*—see also CAYENNE **2** [C, U] (BrE) (AmE **'bell pepper**) a hollow fruit, usually red, green or yellow, eaten as a vegetable either raw or cooked—picture on page A3
- verb [VN] to put pepper on food: *peppered steak* ◊ *Salt and pepper the potatoes.* PHRV **'pepper sb/sth with sth** [usually passive] to hit sb/sth with a series of small objects, especially bullets **'pepper sth with sth** [often passive] to include large numbers of sth in sth: *He peppered his speech with jokes.*

pep·per·corn /'pepəkɔːn; AmE -pərkɔːrn/ noun a dried berry from a tropical plant, that is crushed to make pepper

,peppercorn 'rent noun (BrE) a very low rent

pep·per·mint /'pepəmɪnt; AmE -pərm-/ noun **1** [U] a type of MINT (= a plant used to give flavour to food that produces an oil with a strong flavour)—compare SPEARMINT **2** [C] a sweet/candy flavoured with peppermint oil

pep·per·oni /ˌpepə'rəʊni; AmE -'roʊ-/ noun [U] a type of spicy Italian sausage: *a pepperoni pizza*

'pepper pot (especially BrE) (AmE usually **'pepper shaker**) noun a small container with holes in the top, used for putting pepper on food

pep·pery /'pepəri/ adj. **1** tasting of pepper **2** bad-tempered: *a peppery old man*

'pep pill noun (informal) a PILL containing a drug that gives you more energy or makes you happy for a short time

'pep rally noun (AmE, informal) a meeting of school students before a sports event to encourage support for the team: *(figurative) The Democrats held a pep rally on Capitol Hill yesterday.*

'pep talk noun (informal) a short speech intended to encourage sb to work harder, try to win, have more confidence, etc.

pep·tic ulcer /ˌpeptɪk 'ʌlsə(r)/ noun an ULCER in the DIGESTIVE SYSTEM, especially in the stomach

per /pə(r); strong form pɜː(r)/ prep. used to express the cost or amount of sth for each person, number used, distance travelled, etc: *Rooms cost £50 per person, per night.* ◊ *60 miles per hour* IDM **as per sth** following sth that has been decided: *The work was carried out as per instructions.* **as per 'normal/'usual** (spoken) in the way that is normal or usual; as often happens: *Everyone blamed me as per usual.*

per·am·bu·la·tion /pəˌræmbju'leɪʃn/ noun [C] (formal or humorous) a slow walk or journey around a place, especially one made for pleasure ▶ **per·am·bu·late** verb [V, VN]

per annum /pər 'ænəm/ adv. (abbr. **p.a.**) (from Latin) for each year: *earning £30000 per annum*

per cap·ita /pə 'kæpɪtə; AmE pər/ adj. (from Latin) for each person: *Per capita income rose sharply last year.* ▶ **per cap·ita** adv.: *average earnings per capita*

æ	ɑː	e	ɜː	ə	ɪ	iː	i	ɒ	ɔː	ʌ	ʊ	uː
cat	father	ten	bird	about	sit	see	many	got	saw	cup	put	actual	too
								(BrE)				

per·ceive /pəˈsiːv; *AmE* pərˈs-/ *verb* (*written*) **1** to notice or become aware of sth: [VN] *I perceived a change in his behaviour.* ◊ [V that] *She perceived that all was not well.* ◊ [VN to inf] *The patient was perceived to have difficulty in breathing.* **HELP** This pattern is usually used in the passive. **2** ~ sth (**as sth**) to understand or think of sth in a particular way: [VN] *This discovery was perceived as a major breakthrough.* ◊ *She did not perceive herself as disabled.* ◊ [VN to inf] *They were widely perceived to have been unlucky.* **HELP** This pattern is usually used in the passive.

> **WORD FAMILY**
> **perceive** *v.*
> **perception** *n.*
> **perceptive** *adj.*
> **perceptible** *adj.* (≠ imperceptible)

per cent (*especially BrE*) (*AmE* usually **per·cent**) /pəˈsent; *AmE* pərˈsent/ *noun, adj., adv.*

■ *noun* (*pl.* **per cent, per·cent**) one part in every hundred: *Poor families spend about 80 to 90 per cent of their income on food.* ◊ *It is often stated that we use only 10 per cent of our brain.* ◊ *What per cent of the population is/are overweight?*

■ *adj., adv.* by in or for every hundred: *a 15 per cent rise in price* ◊ *House prices rose five per cent last year.*

> **GRAMMAR POINT**
> **expressing percentages**
>
> Percentages (= numbers of per cent) are written in words as *twenty-five per cent* and in figures as *25%*.
>
> If a percentage is used with an uncountable or a singular noun the verb is generally singular: *90% of the land is cultivated.*
>
> If the noun is singular but represents a group of people, the verb is singular in *AmE* but in *BrE* it may be singular or plural: *Eighty per cent of the work force is/are against the strike.*
>
> If the noun is plural, the verb is plural: *65% of children play computer games.*

per·cent·age /pəˈsentɪdʒ; *AmE* pərˈs-/ *noun* **1** [C+sing./ pl. *v.*] the number, amount, rate of sth, expressed as if it is part of a total which is 100; a part or share of a whole: *What percentage of the population is/are overweight?* ◊ *A high percentage of the female staff are part-time workers.* ◊ *Interest rates are expected to rise by one* **percentage point** (= one per cent). ◊ *The figure is* **expressed as a percentage.** ◊ *The results were analysed* **in percentage terms.** **2** [C, usually sing.] a share of the profits of sth: *He gets a percentage for every car sold.*

per·cent·ile /pəˈsentaɪl; *AmE* pərˈs-/ *noun* (*technical*) one of the 100 equal groups that a larger group of people can be divided into, according to their place on a scale measuring a particular value: *Overall these students rank in the 21st percentile on the tests—that is, they did worse than 79 per cent of all children taking the test.*

per·cep·tible /pəˈseptəbl; *AmE* pərˈs-/ *adj.* (*formal*) **1** great enough for you to notice it: *a perceptible change/increase/decline/impact* ◊ *The price increase has had no perceptible effect on sales.* ◊ *Her foreign accent was barely perceptible.* **2** (*technical*) that you can notice or feel with your senses: *the perceptible world* **OPP** IMPERCEPTIBLE ► **per·cep·tibly** /-əbli/ *adv.*: *Income per head rose perceptibly.* ◊ *It was perceptibly colder.*

per·cep·tion /pəˈsepʃn; *AmE* pərˈs-/ *noun* (*formal*) **1** [U] (*formal* or *technical*) the way you notice things, especially with the senses: *our perception of reality* ◊ *colour/visual perception*—see also EXTRASENSORY PERCEPTION **2** [U] (*formal*) the ability to understand the true nature of sth **SYN** INSIGHT: *She showed great perception in her assessment of the family situation.* **3** [C] ~ (**that …**) (*formal*) an idea, a belief or an image you have as a result of how you see or understand sth: *a campaign to change public perception of the police* ◊ *There is a general public perception that standards in schools are falling.*

per·cep·tive /pəˈseptɪv; *AmE* pərˈs-/ *adj.* **1** (*approving*) having or showing the ability to see or understand things quickly, especially things that are not obvious: *a highly perceptive analysis/observation/comment* ◊ *It was very perceptive of you to notice that.* **2** connected with seeing, hearing and understanding: *our innate perceptive abilities* ► **per·cep·tive·ly** *adv.* **per·cep·tive·ness** *noun* [U]

per·cep·tual /pəˈseptʃuəl; *AmE* pərˈs-/ *adj.* [only before noun] (*technical*) relating to the ability to PERCEIVE things or the process of PERCEIVING: *perceptual skills/problems*

perch /pɜːtʃ; *AmE* pɜːrtʃ/ *verb, noun*

■ *verb* [V+adv./prep.] **1** [V] ~ (**on sth**) (of a bird) to land and stay on a branch, etc: *A robin was perching on the fence.* **2** ~ (**sb/yourself**) (**on sth**) (*informal*) to sit or to make sb sit on sth, especially on the edge of it: [V] *We perched on a couple of high stools at the bar.* ◊ [VN] *She perched herself on the edge of the bed.* **3** [V] ~ (**on sth**) to be placed on the top or the edge of sth: *The hotel perched precariously on a steep hillside.*

■ *noun* **1** a place where a bird rests, especially a branch or bar for this purpose, for example in a bird's cage **2** a high seat or position: *He watched the game from his precarious perch on top of the wall.* **3** (*pl.* **perch**) a FRESHWATER fish that is sometimes used for food **IDM** see KNOCK *v.*

per·chance /pəˈtʃɑːns; *AmE* pərˈtʃæns/ *adv.* (*old use*) perhaps

perched /pɜːtʃt; *AmE* pɜːrtʃt/ *adj.* ~ **on, etc. sth 1** (especially of a bird) sitting or resting on sth: *There was a bird perched on the roof.* **2** placed in a high and/or dangerous position: *a hotel perched high on the cliffs*

per·cipi·ent /pəˈsɪpiənt; *AmE* pərˈs-/ *adj.* (*formal*) having or showing the ability to understand things, especially things that are not obvious **SYN** PERCEPTIVE: *percipient comments*

per·co·late /ˈpɜːkəleɪt; *AmE* ˈpɜːrk-/ *verb* **1** [V] (of a liquid, gas, etc.) to move gradually through a surface that has very small holes or spaces in it: *Water had percolated down through the rocks.* **2** [V] to gradually become known or spread through a group or society: *It had percolated through to us that something interesting was about to happen.* **3** [VN, V] to make coffee in a percolator; to be made in this way

per·co·la·tor /ˈpɜːkəleɪtə(r); *AmE* ˈpɜːrk-/ *noun* a pot for making coffee, in which boiling water is forced up a central tube and then comes down again through the coffee

per·cus·sion /pəˈkʌʃn; *AmE* pərˈk-/ *noun* **1** [U] musical instruments that you play by hitting them with your hand or with a stick, for example drums: *percussion instruments* ◊ *The track features Joey Langton on percussion.*—picture on page 841 **2** (**the percussion**) [sing.] (also **per·cussion section** [C]) the players of percussion instruments in an orchestra—compare BRASS, STRINGS, WOODWIND

per·cus·sion·ist /pəˈkʌʃənɪst; *AmE* pərˈk-/ *noun* a person who plays percussion instruments

per·cus·sive /pəˈkʌsɪv; *AmE* pərˈk-/ *adj.* (*technical*) connected with sounds made by hitting things, especially PERCUSSION instruments

per diem /ˌpɜː ˈdiːem; *AmE* ˌpɜːr/ *noun* [U, C] (from *Latin, especially AmE*) money paid, for example to employees, for things they need to buy every day: *He will get $14000 a year in per diem to help with the higher costs of living in Washington.* ◊ *a per diem allowance*

per·di·tion /pəˈdɪʃn; *AmE* pɜːrˈd-/ *noun* [U] (*formal*) punishment that lasts for ever after death

pere·grin·ation /ˌperəɡrɪˈneɪʃn/ *noun* [usually pl.] (*literary* or *humorous*) a journey, especially a long slow one

pere·grine /ˈperɪɡrɪn/ (also **peregrine ˈfalcon**) *noun* a grey and white BIRD OF PREY (= a bird that kills other creatures for food) that can be trained to hunt for sport

per·emp·tor·ily /pəˈremptrəli/ *adv.* (*formal*) in a way that allows no discussion or refusal: *She peremptorily rejected the request.*

per·emp·tory /pəˈremptəri/ *adj.* (*formal, disapproving*) (especially of sb's manner or behaviour) expecting to be obeyed immediately and without question or refusal: *a peremptory summons/order/command* ◊ *The letter was peremptory in tone.*

per·en·nial /pəˈreniəl/ *adj., noun*

■ *adj.* **1** continuing for a very long time; happening again and again: *the perennial problem of water shortage ◇ that perennial favourite, hamburgers* **2** (of plants) living for two years or more ▶ **per·en·ni·al·ly** /-niəli/ *adv.: a perennially popular subject*

■ *noun* any plant that lives for more than two years— compare ANNUAL, BIENNIAL

per·fect *adj., verb*

■ *adj.* /ˈpɜːfɪkt; *AmE* ˈpɜːrf-/ **1** having everything that is necessary; complete and without faults or weaknesses: *in perfect condition ◇ a perfect set of teeth ◇ Well I'm sorry—but nobody's perfect* (= used when sb has criticized you). **2** completely correct; exact and accurate: *She speaks perfect English. ◇ a perfect copy/fit/match ◇ What perfect timing!*—see also WORD-PERFECT **3** the best of its kind: *a perfect example of the painter's early style ◇ the perfect crime* (= one in which the criminal is never discovered) **4** excellent; very good: *The weather was perfect.* **5 ~ for sb/sth** exactly right for sb/sth SYN IDEAL: *It was a perfect day for a picnic. ◇ She's the perfect candidate for the job. ◇ 'Will 2.30 be OK for you?' 'Perfect, thanks.'* **6** [only before noun] total; complete: *I don't know him—he's a perfect stranger.* **7** (*grammar*) connected with the form of a verb that consists of part of the verb *have* with the past participle of the main verb, used to express actions completed by the present or a particular point in the past or future: *'I have eaten' is the present perfect tense of the verb 'to eat', 'I had eaten' is the past perfect and 'I will have eaten' is the future perfect.* IDM see PRACTICE, WORLD

■ *verb* /pəˈfekt; *AmE* pərˈf-/ [VN] to make sth perfect or as good as you can: *As a musician, she has spent years perfecting her techniques. ◇ They have perfected the art of winemaking.*

per·fec·tion /pəˈfekʃn; *AmE* pərˈf-/ *noun* **1** [U, sing.] the state of being perfect: *technical/physical perfection ◇ The fish was cooked to perfection. ◇ The novel achieves a perfection of form that is quite new. ◇ His performance was perfection* (= sth perfect). **2** [U, sing.] the act of making sth perfect by doing the final improvements: *They have been working on the perfection of the new model.* IDM see COUNSEL *n.*

per·fec·tion·ist /pəˈfekʃənɪst; *AmE* pərˈf-/ *noun* (sometimes *disapproving*) a person who likes to do things perfectly and is not satisfied with anything less. ▶ **per·fec·tion·ism** /pəˈfekʃənɪzəm; *AmE* pərˈf-/ *noun* [U]

per·fect·ly /ˈpɜːfɪktli; *AmE* ˈpɜːrf-/ *adv.* **1** completely: *It's perfectly normal to feel like this. ◇ It's perfectly good as it is* (= it doesn't need changing). ◇ *You know perfectly well what I mean. ◇ To be perfectly honest, I didn't want to go anyway. ◇ He stood perfectly still until the danger had passed. ◇ 'Do you understand?' 'Perfectly.' ◇ (old-fashioned) How perfectly awful!* **2** in a perfect way: *The TV works perfectly now. ◇ It fits perfectly.*

ˌperfect ˈpitch *noun* [U] (*music*) the ability to identify or sing a musical note correctly without the help of an instrument

per·fidi·ous /pəˈfɪdiəs; *AmE* pərˈf-/ *adj.* (*literary*) that cannot be trusted SYN TREACHEROUS

per·fidy /ˈpɜːfədi; *AmE* ˈpɜːrf-/ *noun* [U] (*literary*) actions that betray sb/sth SYN TREACHERY: *In Act 2 he learns of Giovanni's perfidy and swears revenge.*

per·for·ate /ˈpɜːfəreɪt; *AmE* ˈpɜːrf-/ *verb* [VN] to make a hole or holes through sth: *The explosion perforated his eardrum. ◇ a perforated line* (= a row of small holes in paper, made so that a part can be torn off easily)

per·for·ation /ˌpɜːfəˈreɪʃn; *AmE* ˌpɜːrf-/ *noun* **1** [C, usually pl., U] a small hole in a surface, often one of a series of small holes: *Tear the sheet of stamps along the perforations.* **2** [U] (*medical*) the process of splitting or tearing in such a way that a hole is left: *Excessive pressure can lead to perforation of the stomach wall.*

per·force /pəˈfɔːs; *AmE* pərˈfɔːrs/ *adv.* (*old use* or *formal*) because it is necessary or cannot be avoided

per·form /pəˈfɔːm; *AmE* pərˈfɔːrm/ *verb* **1** [VN] to do sth, such as a piece of work, task or duty: *to perform an experiment/a miracle/a ceremony ◇ She performs an*

important role in our organization. ◇ *This operation has never been performed in this country. ◇ A computer can perform many tasks at once.* **2** to entertain an audience by playing a piece of music, acting in a play, etc: [VN] *to perform somersaults/magic tricks ◇ The play was first performed in 1987. ◇ I'd like to hear it performed live. ◇* [V] *to perform on the flute ◇ I'm looking forward to seeing you perform.* **3** [V] **~** (**well/badly/poorly**) to work or function well or badly: *The engine seems to be performing well. ◇ The company has been performing poorly over the past year.* IDM see MIRACLE

per·form·ance /pəˈfɔːməns; *AmE* pərˈfɔːrm-/ *noun* **1** [C] the act of performing a play, concert or some other form of entertainment: *The performance starts at seven. ◇ an evening performance ◇ a performance of Ravel's String Quartet ◇ a series of performances by the Kirov Ballet ◇ one of the band's rare live performances* **2** [C] the way a person performs in a play, concert, etc: *She gave the greatest performance of her career. ◇ an Oscar-winning performance from Al Pacino* **3** [U, C] how well or badly you do sth; how well or badly sth works: *the country's economic performance ◇ It was an impressive performance by the French team. ◇ The new management techniques aim to improve performance. ◇ He criticized the recent poor performance of the company. ◇ high-performance* (= very powerful) *cars/aircraft ◇ performance indicators* (= things that show how well or badly sth is working) ◇ *performance-related pay* (= money that you earn that depends on how well you do your job) **4** [U, sing.] (*formal*) the act or process of performing a task, an action, etc: *She has shown enthusiasm in the performance of her duties. ◇ He did not want a repeat performance of the humiliating defeat he had suffered.* **5** [sing.] (*informal, especially BrE*) an act that involves a lot of effort or trouble, sometimes when it is not necessary: *It's such a performance getting the children off to school in the morning.*

per·form·er /pəˈfɔːmə(r); *AmE* pərˈfɔːrm-/ *noun* **1** a person who performs for an audience in a show, concert, etc: *a brilliant/polished/seasoned performer* **2** a person or thing that behaves or works in the way mentioned: *He was a poor performer at school and left with no qualifications. ◇ VW is the star performer of the motor industry this year.*

the perˌforming ˈarts *noun* [pl.] arts such as music, dance and DRAMA which are performed for an audience

per·fume /ˈpɜːfjuːm; *AmE* pərˈfjuːm/ *noun, verb*

■ *noun* [C, U] **1** a liquid, often made from flowers, that you put on your skin to make yourself smell nice: *a bottle of expensive perfume ◇ We stock a wide range of perfumes. ◇ the perfume counter of the store* **2** a pleasant, often sweet, smell: *the sweet/heady perfume of the roses*

■ *verb* [VN] [often passive] **~ sth** (**with sth**) **1** (*literary*) (especially of flowers) to make the air in a place smell pleasant: *The garden was perfumed with the smell of roses.* **2** to put perfume in or on sth: *She perfumed her bath with fragrant oils.* ▶ **per·fumed** *adj.: perfumed soap/paper/candles*

per·fumery /pəˈfjuːməri; *AmE* pərˈf-/ *noun* (*pl.* **-ies**) **1** [C] a place where perfumes are made and/or sold **2** [U] the process of making perfume

per·func·tory /pəˈfʌŋktəri; *AmE* pərˈf-/ *adj.* (*formal*) (of an action) done as a duty or habit, without real interest, attention or feeling: *a perfunctory smile/nod ◇ They only made a perfunctory effort.* ▶ **per·func·tor·ily** /-trəli/ *adv.: to nod/smile perfunctorily*

per·gola /ˈpɜːɡələ; *AmE* ˈpɜːrɡ-/ *noun* an arch in a garden/yard with a frame for plants to grow over and through

per·haps /pəˈhæps; præps; *AmE* pərˈh-/ *adv.* **1** possibly SYN MAYBE: *'Are you going to come?' 'Perhaps. I'll see how I feel.' ◇ Perhaps he's forgotten.* **2** used when you want to make a statement or opinion less definite: *This is perhaps his best novel to date.* **3** used when making a rough estimate: *a change which could affect perhaps 20% of the population.* **4** used when you agree or accept sth unwillingly, or do not want to say strongly that you disapprove: *'You could do it yourself.' 'Yeah, perhaps.'* **5** used when making a polite request, offer or suggestion: *Perhaps it* would be better if you came back tomorrow. ◊ I think perhaps you've had enough to drink tonight.

per·il /'perəl/ noun (formal or literary) **1** [U] serious danger: The country's economy is now in grave peril. **2** [C, usually pl.] ~ (of sth) the fact of sth being dangerous or harmful: a warning about the perils of drug abuse **IDM** **do sth at your (own) 'peril** used to warn sb that if they do sth, it may be dangerous or cause them problems: Teachers ignore the importance of these results at their peril.

per·il·ous /'perələs/ adj. (formal or literary) very dangerous: a perilous adventure/journey ► **per·il·ous·ly** adv.: We came perilously close to disaster.

per·im·eter /pə'rɪmɪtə(r)/ noun **1** the outside edge of an enclosed area of land: Guards patrol the perimeter of the estate. ◊ a perimeter fence/track/wall **2** (mathematics) the total length of the outside edge of an area or a shape—compare CIRCUMFERENCE

peri·natal /ˌperɪ'neɪtl/ adj. (technical) at or around the time of birth: perinatal care/deaths

period /'pɪəriəd; AmE 'pɪr-/ noun, adv., adj.
■ noun
LENGTH OF TIME | **1** a particular length of time: a period of consultation/mourning/uncertainty ◊ The factory will be closed down over a 2-year period/a period of two years. ◊ This compares with a 4% increase for the same period last year. ◊ This offer is available for a limited period only. ◊ The aim is to reduce traffic at peak periods. ◊ You can have it for a trial period (= in order to test it).—see also COOLING-OFF PERIOD **2** a length of time in the life of a particular person or in the history of a particular country: Which period of history would you most like to have lived in? ◊ the post-war period ◊ Like Picasso, she too had a blue period. ◊ Most teenagers go through a period of rebelling. **3** a particular length of time during which rocks are formed: the Jurassic period
LESSON | **4** any of the parts that a day is divided into at a school, college, etc. for study: 'What do you have next period?' 'French.' ◊ a free/study period (= for private study)
WOMAN | **5** the flow of blood each month from the body of a woman who is not pregnant: period pains ◊ monthly periods ◊ When did you last have a period?—compare MENSTRUATION
PUNCTUATION | **6** (AmE) = FULL STOP noun
■ adv. (spoken, especially AmE) = FULL STOP adv.: The answer is no, period!
■ adj. [only before noun] having a style typical of a particular time in history: period costumes/furniture

peri·od·ic /ˌpɪəri'ɒdɪk; AmE ˌpɪri'ɑːdɪk/ (also less frequent **peri·od·ical** /-kl/) adj. [usually before noun] happening fairly often and regularly: Periodic checks are carried out on the equipment. ► **peri·od·ic·al·ly** /-kli/ adv.: Mailing lists are updated periodically.

peri·od·ical /ˌpɪəri'ɒdɪkl; AmE ˌpɪri'ɑːd-/ noun a magazine that is published every week, month, etc., especially one that is concerned with an academic subject

the ˌperiodic 'table noun [sing.] (chemistry) a list of all the chemical elements, arranged according to their ATOMIC NUMBER

'period piece noun **1** a play, film/movie, etc. that is set in a particular period of history **2** an ornament, piece of furniture, etc. that was made during a particular period of history and is typical of that period

peri·pat·et·ic /ˌperɪpə'tetɪk/ adj. (formal) going from place to place, for example on order to work: a peripatetic music teacher

per·iph·eral /pə'rɪfərəl/ adj., noun
■ adj. **1** ~ (to sth) (formal) not as important as the main aim, part, etc. of sth: peripheral information ◊ Fundraising is peripheral to their main activities. **2** (technical) connected with the outer edge of a particular area: the peripheral nervous system ◊ peripheral vision **3** (computing) (of equipment) connected to a computer: a peripheral device ► **per·iph·er·al·ly** /pə'rɪfərəli/ adv.
■ noun (computing) a piece of equipment that is connected to a computer: monitors, printers and other peripherals

per·iph·ery /pə'rɪfəri/ noun [usually sing.] (pl. -ies)

(formal) **1** the outer edge of a particular area: industrial development on the periphery of the town ◊ The condition makes it difficult for patients to see objects at the periphery of their vision. **2** the less important part of sth, for example of a particular activity or of a social or political group: minor parties on the periphery of American politics

peri·scope /'perɪskəʊp; AmE -skoʊp/ noun a device like a long tube, containing mirrors which enable the user to see over the top of sth, used especially in a SUBMARINE (= a ship that can operate underwater) to see above the surface of the sea

per·ish /'perɪʃ/ verb **1** [V] (formal or literary) (of people or animals) to die, especially in a sudden violent way: A family of four perished in the fire. **2** [V] (formal) to be lost or destroyed: Early buildings were made of wood and have perished. **3** [V, VN] (BrE) if a material such as rubber perishes or is perished, it becomes damaged, weaker or full of holes **IDM** **perish the 'thought** (spoken) used to say that you find a suggestion unacceptable or that you hope that sth will never happen: Me get married? Perish the thought!

per·ish·able /'perɪʃəbl/ adj. (especially of food) likely to decay or go bad quickly: perishable goods/foods

per·ish·ables /'perɪʃəblz/ noun [pl.] (technical) types of food that decay or go bad quickly

per·ished /'perɪʃt/ adj. [not before noun] (BrE, informal) (of a person) very cold: We were perished.

per·ish·ing /'perɪʃɪŋ/ adj. (BrE, informal) **1** extremely cold: It's perishing outside! ◊ I'm perishing! **2** [only before noun] (old-fashioned) used to show that you are annoyed about sth: I've had enough of this perishing job!

peri·ton·itis /ˌperɪtə'naɪtɪs/ noun [U] (medical) a serious condition in which the inside wall of the body becomes swollen and infected

peri·win·kle /'periwɪŋkl/ noun **1** [C, U] a small plant that grows along the ground **2** [C] = WINKLE

per·jure /'pɜːdʒə(r); AmE 'pɜːrdʒ-/ verb [VN] ~ yourself (law) to tell a lie in a court of law after you have sworn to tell the truth: She admitted that she had perjured herself. ► **per·jurer** /'pɜːdʒərə(r); AmE 'pɜːrdʒ-/ noun

per·jury /'pɜːdʒəri; AmE 'pɜːrdʒ-/ noun [U] (law) the crime of telling a lie in a court of law: The defence witnesses were found guilty of perjury. ◊ to commit perjury

perk /pɜːk; AmE pɜːrk/ noun, verb
■ noun (also formal **per·quis·ite**) [usually pl.] something you receive as well as your wages for doing a particular job: Perks offered by the firm include a car and free health insurance. ◊ (figurative) Not having to get up early is just one of the perks of being retired.
■ verb [V] **PHRV** **ˌperk 'up|ˌperk sb↔'up** (informal) to become or to make sb become more cheerful or lively, especially after they have been ill/sick or sad: He soon perked up when his friends arrived. **ˌperk 'up|ˌperk sth↔'up** (informal) to increase, or to make sth increase in value, etc: Share prices had perked up slightly by close of trading. **ˌperk sth↔'up** (informal) to make sth more interesting, more attractive, etc: ideas for perking up bland food

perky /'pɜːki; AmE 'pɜːrki/ adj. (perk·ier, perki·est) (informal) cheerful and full of energy: She hasn't been her usual perky self lately. ► **perki·ness** noun [U]

perm /pɜːm; AmE pɜːrm/ noun, verb
■ noun a way of changing the style of your hair by using chemicals to create curls that last for several months: to have a perm
■ verb [VN] to give sb's hair a perm: to have your hair permed ◊ a shampoo for permed or damaged hair—picture at HAIR

perma·frost /'pɜːməfrɒst; AmE 'pɜːrməfrɔːst/ noun [U] (technical) a layer of soil that is permanently frozen, in very cold regions of the world

per·man·ence /'pɜːmənəns; AmE 'pɜːrm-/ (also less frequent **per·man·ency** /-nənsi/) noun [U] the state of lasting for a long time or for all time in the future: The spoken word is immediate but lacks permanence. ◊ We no longer talk of the permanence of marriage.

s	t	v	z	ʃ	ʒ	tʃ	dʒ	θ	ð	ŋ
see	tea	van	zoo	shoe	vision	chain	jam	thin	this	sing

per·man·ent /'pɜːmənənt; *AmE* 'pɜːrm-/ *adj., noun*
■ *adj.* lasting for a long time or for all time in the future; existing all the time: *a permanent job* ◊ *permanent/temporary staff* ◊ *They are now living together on a permanent basis.* ◊ *The accident has not done any permanent damage.* ◊ *a permanent fixture* (= a person or an object that is always in a particular place) OPP IMPERMANENT, TEMPORARY ▶ **per·man·ent·ly** *adv.*: *The stroke left his right side permanently damaged.* ◊ *She had decided to settle permanently in France.*
■ *noun* (*old-fashioned, AmE*) = PERM
ˌPermanent ˈUndersecretary (also **ˌPermanent ˈSecretary**) *noun* (in Britain) a person of high rank in the CIVIL SERVICE, who advises a SECRETARY OF STATE—compare UNDERSECRETARY
ˌpermanent ˈwave *noun* (*old-fashioned*) = PERM
per·me·able /'pɜːmiəbl; *AmE* 'pɜːrm-/ *adj.* ~ (**to sth**) (*technical*) allowing a liquid or gas to pass through: *The skin of amphibians is permeable to water.* ◊ *permeable rocks* OPP IMPERMEABLE ▶ **per·mea·bil·ity** /ˌpɜːmiə-ˈbɪləti; *AmE* ˌpɜːrm-/ *noun* [U]
per·me·ate /'pɜːmieɪt; *AmE* 'pɜːrm-/ *verb* (*formal*) **1** (of a liquid, gas, etc.) to spread to every part of an object or a place: [VN] *The smell of leather permeated the room.* ◊ [V+*adv./prep.*] *rainwater permeating through the ground* **2** (of an idea, an influence, a feeling, etc.) to affect every part of sth: [VN] *a belief that permeates all levels of society* ◊ [V+*adv./prep.*] *Dissatisfaction among the managers soon permeated down to members of the workforce.* ▶ **per·me·ation** /ˌpɜːmieɪʃn; *AmE* ˌpɜːrm-/ *noun* [U] (*formal*)
per·mis·sible /pəˈmɪsəbl; *AmE* pər'm-/ *adj.* ~ (**for sb**) (**to do sth**) (*formal*) acceptable according to the law or a particular set of rules: *permissible levels of nitrates in water* ◊ *It is not permissible for employers to discriminate on grounds of age.*
per·mis·sion /pəˈmɪʃn; *AmE* pər'm-/ *noun* **1** [U] ~ (**for sth**) | ~ (**for sb/sth**) (**to do sth**) the act of allowing sb to do sth, especially when this is done by sb in a position of authority: *You must **ask** permission for all major expenditure.* ◊ *The school has been refused permission to expand.* ◊ *No official **permission** has been **given** for the event to take place.* ◊ *She took the car **without permission**.* ◊ *poems reprinted **by kind permission** of the author* ◊ (*formal, spoken*) *With your permission, I'd like to say a few words.* **2** [C, usually pl.] an official written statement allowing sb to do sth: *The publisher is responsible for obtaining the necessary permissions to reproduce illustrations.*—see also PLANNING PERMISSION
per·mis·sive /pəˈmɪsɪv; *AmE* pər'm-/ *adj.* allowing or showing a freedom of behaviour that many people do not approve of, especially in sexual matters: *permissive attitudes* ◊ *permissive parents* (= who allow their children a lot of freedom) ▶ **per·mis·sive·ness** *noun* [U]
per·mit *verb, noun*
■ *verb* /pəˈmɪt; *AmE* pər'm-/ (**-tt-**) (*formal*) **1** to allow sb to do sth or to allow sth to happen: [VN] *Radios are not permitted in the library.* ◊ *There are substantial fines for exceeding permitted levels of noise pollution.* ◊ [VNN] *We were not permitted any contact with each other.* ◊ *Jim permitted himself a wry smile.* ◊ [VNto inf] *Visitors are not permitted to take photographs.* ◊ *She would not permit herself to look at them.* ◊ (*formal, spoken*) *Permit me to offer you some advice.* [alsoV+*-ing*] ⇨ note at ALLOW **2** to make sth possible: [V] *We hope to visit the cathedral, if time permits.* ◊ *I'll come tomorrow, **weather permitting*** (= if the weather is fine). ◊ [VN] *The password permits access to all files on the hard disk.* ◊ [VNto inf] *Cash machines permit you to withdraw money at any time.* [alsoV+*-ing*]
■ *noun* /'pɜːmɪt; *AmE* 'pɜːrmɪt/ an official document that gives sb the right to do sth, especially for a limited period of time: *a fishing/work/residence/parking permit* ◊ *to apply for a permit* ◊ *to issue a permit*
per·mu·ta·tion /ˌpɜːmjuˈteɪʃn; *AmE* ˌpɜːrm-/ *noun* (usually pl.) any of the different ways in which a set of things can be ordered: *The possible permutations of x, y and z are xyz, xzy, yxz, yzx, zxy and zyx.*
per·ni·cious /pəˈnɪʃəs; *AmE* pər'n-/ *adj.* (*formal*) having

a very harmful effect on sb/sth, especially in a way that is gradual and not easily noticed: *the pernicious influence of TV violence on children*
per·nick·ety /pəˈnɪkəti; *AmE* pər'n-/ (*especially BrE*) (*AmE* usually **per·snick·ety**) *adj.* (*informal, disapproving*) worrying too much about unimportant details; showing this SYN FUSSY
per·or·ation /ˌperəˈreɪʃn/ *noun* (*formal*) **1** the final part of a speech in which the speaker gives a summary of the main points **2** (*disapproving*) a long speech that is not very interesting
per·ox·ide /pəˈrɒksaɪd; *AmE* -ˈrɑːk-/ (also **hydrogen peˈroxide**) *noun* [U] a colourless liquid used to kill bacteria and to BLEACH hair (= make it lighter): *a woman with peroxide blonde hair*
per·pen·dicu·lar /ˌpɜːpənˈdɪkjələ(r); *AmE* ˌpɜːrp-/ *adj., noun*
■ *adj.* **1** ~ (**to sth**) (usually *technical*) forming an angle of 90° with another line or surface; upright and going straight up: *Are the lines perpendicular to each other?* ◊ *The staircase was almost perpendicular* (= very steep). **2** (**Perpendicular**) (*architecture*) connected with a style of architecture common in England in the 14th and 15th centuries, that makes use of vertical lines and wide arches
■ *noun* (**the perpendicular**) [sing.] a line, position or direction that is exactly perpendicular: *The wall is a little out of the perpendicular.*
per·pet·rate /'pɜːpətreɪt; *AmE* 'pɜːrp-/ *verb* [VN] ~ **sth** (**against/upon/on sb**) (*formal*) to commit a crime or do sth wrong or evil: *to perpetrate a crime/fraud/massacre* ◊ *violence perpetrated against women and children* ◊ *security breaches perpetrated by people working for the company* ▶ **per·pet·ra·tion** /ˌpɜːpəˈtreɪʃn; *AmE* ˌpɜːrp-/ *noun* [U]
per·pet·ra·tor /'pɜːpətreɪtə(r); *AmE* 'pɜːrp-/ *noun* a person who commits a crime or does sth that is wrong or evil: *the perpetrators of the attack/crime/offence*
per·pet·ual /pəˈpetʃuəl; *AmE* pər'p-/ *adj.* **1** [usually before noun] continuing for a long period of time without interruption SYN CONTINUOUS: *the perpetual noise of traffic* ◊ *We lived for years in a perpetual state of fear.* ◊ *We're all in a state of **perpetual motion** in this office* (= we're always moving round or changing things). **2** [usually before noun] frequently repeated, in a way that is annoying SYN CONTINUAL: *How can I work with these perpetual interruptions?* **3** [only before noun] (of a job or position) lasting for the whole of sb's life: *He was elected perpetual president.* ◊ (*humorous*) *She's a perpetual student.* ▶ **per·petu·al·ly** /-tʃuəli/ *adv.*
per·petu·ate /pəˈpetʃueɪt; *AmE* pər'p-/ *verb* [VN] (*formal*) to make sth such as a bad situation, a belief, etc. continue for a long time: *to perpetuate inequality/injustice/conflict* ◊ *This system perpetuated itself for several centuries.* ◊ *Comics and books for children tend to perpetuate the myth that 'boys don't cry'.* ▶ **per·petu·ation** /pəˌpetʃuˈeɪʃn; *AmE* pər'p-/ *noun* [U]
per·petu·ity /ˌpɜːpəˈtjuːəti; *AmE* ˌpɜːrpəˈtuː-/ *noun* [U] IDM **in perpetuity** (*formal*) for all time in the future SYN FOREVER: *They do not own the land in perpetuity.*
per·plex /pəˈpleks; *AmE* pər'p-/ *verb* [usually passive] if sth **perplexes** you, it makes you confused or worried because you do not understand it SYN PUZZLE: [VN] *They were perplexed by her response.* [alsoVN that] ▶ **per·plex·ing** *adj.*: *a perplexing problem/question* ◊ *I found the whole thing extremely perplexing.*
per·plexed /pəˈplekst; *AmE* pər'p-/ *adj.* confused and anxious because you are unable to understand sth; showing this: *a perplexed expression/look/voice* ◊ *She looked perplexed.* ▶ **per·plex·ed·ly** /-ɪdli/ *adv.* (*rare*)
per·plex·ity /pəˈpleksəti; *AmE* pər'p-/ *noun* (*pl.* **-ies**) (*formal*) **1** [U] the state of feeling confused and anxious because you do not understand sth: *Most of them just stared at her in perplexity.* **2** [C, usually pl.] something that is difficult to understand: *the perplexities of life*
per·quis·ite /'pɜːkwɪzɪt; *AmE* 'pɜːrk-/ *noun* (*formal*) **1** [usually pl.] = PERK **2** ~ (**of sb**) something to which sb

æ	ɑː	e	ɜː	ə	ɪ	iː	i	ɒ	ɔː	ʌ	ʊ	u	uː
cat	father	ten	bird	about	sit	see	many	got	saw	cup	put	actual	too
								(BrE)					

ics used to be the perquisite of the property-owning classes.

perry /'peri/ *noun* [U] a slightly sweet alcoholic drink made from the juice of PEARS—compare CIDER

per se /ˌpɜː 'seɪ; *AmE* ˌpɜːr/ *adv.* (from *Latin*) used meaning 'by itself' to show that you are referring to sth on its own, rather than in connection with other things: *The drug is not harmful per se, but is dangerous when taken with alcohol.*

per·se·cute /'pɜːsɪkjuːt; *AmE* 'pɜːrs-/ *verb* [VN] [often passive] **1** ~ **sb (for sth)** to treat sb in a cruel and unfair way, especially because of their race, religion or political beliefs: *Throughout history, people have been persecuted for their religious beliefs.* ◊ *persecuted minorities* **2** to deliberately annoy sb all the time and make their life unpleasant: *Why are the media persecuting him like this?* ▶ **per·se·cu·tion** /ˌpɜːsɪ'kjuːʃn; *AmE* ˌpɜːrs-/ *noun* [U, C]: *the victims of religious persecution*

perse'cution complex *noun* a type of mental illness in which sb believes that other people are trying to harm them

per·se·cu·tor /'pɜːsɪkjuːtə(r); *AmE* 'pɜːrs-/ *noun* a person who treats another person or group of people in a cruel and unfair way

per·se·ver·ance /ˌpɜːsɪ'vɪərəns; *AmE* ˌpɜːrsə'vɪr-/ *noun* [U] (*approving*) the quality of continuing to try to achieve a particular aim in spite of difficulties: *They showed great perseverance in the face of difficulty.* ◊ *The only way to improve is through hard work and dogged perseverance.*

per·se·vere /ˌpɜːsɪ'vɪə(r); *AmE* ˌpɜːrsə'vɪr/ *verb* [V] ~ **(in sth/in doing sth)** | ~ **(with sth/sb)** (*approving*) to continue trying to do or achieve sth in spite of difficulties: *Despite a number of setbacks, they persevered in their attempts to fly around the world in a balloon.* ◊ *She persevered with her violin lessons.* ◊ *You have to persevere with difficult students.*

per·se·ver·ing /ˌpɜːsɪ'vɪərɪŋ; *AmE* ˌpɜːrsə'vɪrɪŋ/ *adj.* [usually before noun] (*approving*) showing determination to achieve a particular aim in spite of difficulties

Per·sian /'pɜːʃn; -ʒn; *AmE* 'pɜːrʒn/ *noun* **1** [C] a person from ancient Persia, or modern Persia, now called Iran **2** (also **Farsi**) [U] the official language of Iran **3** [C] = PERSIAN CAT ▶ **Per·sian** *adj.*

ˌPersian 'carpet (also **ˌPersian 'rug**) *noun* a carpet of traditional design from the Near East, made by hand from silk or wool

ˌPersian 'cat (also **Per·sian**) *noun* a breed of cat with long hair, short legs and a round face

per·sim·mon /pə'sɪmən; *AmE* pər's-/ *noun* a sweet tropical fruit that looks like a large orange tomato

per·sist /pə'sɪst; *AmE* pər's-/ *verb* **1** ~ **(in sth/in doing sth)** | ~ **(with sth)** to continue to do sth in spite of difficulties or opposition, in a way that can seem unreasonable: [V] *Why do you persist in blaming yourself for what happened?* ◊ *She persisted in her search for the truth.* ◊ *He persisted with his questioning.* ◊ [V speech] *'So, did you agree or not?' he persisted.* **2** [V] to continue to exist: *The belief that the earth was flat persisted for many centuries.* ◊ *If the symptoms persist, consult your doctor.*

per·sist·ence /pə'sɪstəns; *AmE* pər's-/ *noun* [U] **1** the fact of continuing to try to do sth in spite of difficulties, especially when other people are against you and think that you are being annoying or unreasonable: *His persistence was finally rewarded when the insurance company agreed to pay for the damage.* ◊ *It was her sheer persistence that wore them down in the end.* **2** the state of continuing to exist for a long period of time: *the persistence of unemployment in the 1970s and 1980s*

per·sist·ent /pə'sɪstənt; *AmE* pər's-/ *adj.* **1** determined to do sth in spite of difficulties, especially when other people are against you and think that you are being annoying or unreasonable: *How do you deal with persistent salesmen who won't take no for an answer?* ◊ *a persistent offender* (= a person who continues to commit crimes after they have been caught and punished) **2** continuing for a long period of time without interruption, or repeated frequently, especially in a way that is annoying

and cannot be stopped: *persistent rain/pain* ◊ *a persistent cough* ◊ *I can't take much more of this persistent criticism.* ▶ **per·sist·ent·ly** *adv.*: *They have persistently denied claims of illegal dealing.* ◊ *persistently high interest rates*

perˌsistent ˌvegetative 'state *noun* (*medical*) a condition in which a person's body is kept working by medical means but the person shows no sign of other brain activity

per·snick·ety /pə'snɪkəti; *AmE* pər's-/ *adj.* (*AmE*) = PERNICKETY

per·son /'pɜːsn; *AmE* 'pɜːrsn/ *noun* (*pl.* **people** /'piːpl/ or, especially in formal use, **per·sons**) **1** a human being as an INDIVIDUAL: *What sort of person would do a thing like that?* ◊ *He's a fascinating person.* ◊ *What is she like as a person?* ◊ *He's just the person we need for the job.* ◊ *I had a letter from the people who used to live next door.* ◊ *I'm not really a city person* (= I don't really like cities). **HELP** Use **everyone** or **everybody** instead of 'all people'. **2** (*formal* or *disapproving*) a human being, especially one who is not identified: *A certain person* (= somebody that I do not wish to name) *told me about it.* ◊ *The price is $40 per person.* ◊ *This vehicle is licensed to carry 4 persons.* (= in a notice) ◊ (*law*) *The verdict was murder by a person or persons unknown.*—see also VIP **3** (**-person**) (in compounds) a person working in the area of business mentioned; a person concerned with the thing mentioned: *a salesperson* ◊ *a spokesperson* **4** (*grammar*) any of the three classes of personal pronouns. The **first person** (*I/we*) refers to the person(s) speaking; the **second person** (*you*) refers to the person(s) spoken to; the **third person** (*he/she/it/they*) refers to the person(s) or thing(s) spoken about. **IDM** **about/on your 'person** if you have or carry sth **about/on your person**, you carry it about with you, for example in your pocket **in 'person** if you do sth **in person**, you go somewhere and do it yourself, instead of doing it by letter, asking sb else to do it, etc. **in the person of sb** (*formal*) in the form or shape of sb: *Help arrived in the person of his mother.*—more at RESPECTER

per·sona /pə'səʊnə; *AmE* pər'soʊnə/ *noun* (*pl.* **per·son·ae** /-niː; -naɪ/ or **per·so·nas**) (*formal*) the aspects of a person's character that they show to other people, especially when their real character is different: *His public persona is quite different from the private family man described in the book.*

per·son·able /'pɜːsənəbl; *AmE* 'pɜːrs-/ *adj.* (of a person) attractive to other people because of having a pleasant appearance and character

per·son·age /'pɜːsənɪdʒ; *AmE* 'pɜːrs-/ *noun* (*formal*) an important or famous person: *a royal personage*

per·son·al /'pɜːsənl; *AmE* 'pɜːrs-/ *adj.*
YOUR OWN | **1** [only before noun] your own; not belonging to or connected with anyone else: *personal effects/belongings/possessions* ◊ *personal details* (= your name, age, etc.) ◊ *Of course, this is just a personal opinion.* ◊ *Coogan has run a **personal best** of just under four minutes.* ◊ *The novel is written from **personal experience**.* ◊ *Use stencils to add a few **personal touches** to walls and furniture.* ◊ *All hire cars are for personal use only.*
FEELINGS/CHARACTER/RELATIONSHIPS | **2** [only before noun] connected with individual people, especially their feelings, characters and relationships: *Having good **personal relationships** is the most important thing for me.* ◊ *He was popular as much for his personal qualities as for his cricketing skills.*
NOT OFFICIAL | **3** not connected with a person's job or official position: *The letter was marked 'Personal'.* ◊ *I'd like to talk to you about a personal matter.* ◊ *I try not to let work interfere with my **personal life**.* ◊ *She's a personal friend of mine* (= not just somebody I know because of my job).
DONE BY PERSON | **4** [only before noun] done by a particular person rather than by sb who is acting for them: *The President made a personal appearance at the event.* ◊ *I shall give the matter my personal attention.*
DONE FOR PERSON | **5** [only before noun] made or done for a particular person rather than for a large group of people or people in general: *We offer a **personal service** to all*

aɪ	aʊ	eɪ	əʊ	oʊ	ɔɪ	ɪə	eə	ʊə	j	w
my	now	say	go (BrE)	go (AmE)	boy	near	hair	pure	yes	wet

our customers. ◊ *a **personal pension plan** (= a pension organized by a private company for one particular person)*

OFFENSIVE | **6** referring to a particular person's character, appearance, opinions, etc. in a way that is offensive: *Try to avoid making personal remarks.* ◊ *There's no need to get personal!* ◊ *Nothing personal (= I do not wish to offend you), but I do have to go now.*

CONNECTED WITH BODY | **7** [only before noun] connected with a person's body: *personal cleanliness/hygiene*

,personal al'lowance (*BrE*) *noun* the amount of money you are allowed to earn each year before you have to pay INCOME TAX

,personal as'sistant *noun* (*abbr.* PA) a person who works as a secretary or an assistant for one person

'personal column *noun* a part of a newspaper or magazine for private messages or small advertisements

,personal com'puter *noun* (*abbr.* PC) a small computer that is designed for one person to use at work or at home—compare MAINFRAME, MICROCOMPUTER, MINICOMPUTER

per·son·al·ity /ˌpɜːsəˈnæləti; *AmE* ˌpɜːrs-/ *noun* (*pl.* -ies) **1** [C, U] the various aspects of a person's character that combine to make them different from other people: *His wife has a strong personality.* ◊ *The children all have very different personalities.* ◊ *He maintained order by sheer force of personality.* ◊ *There are likely to be tensions and **personality clashes** in any social group.* **2** [U] the qualities of a person's character that make them interesting and attractive: *We need someone with lots of personality to head the project.* **3** [C] a famous person, especially one who works in entertainment or sport: *personalities from the world of music* ◊ *a TV/sports personality* **4** [C] a person whose strong character makes them noticeable: *Their son is a real personality.* **5** [U] the qualities of a place or thing that make it interesting and different: *The problem with many modern buildings is that they lack personality.*

perso'nality cult *noun* (*disapproving*) a situation in which people are encouraged to show extreme love and admiration for a famous person, especially a political leader

per·son·al·ize (*BrE* also -ise) /ˈpɜːsənəlaɪz; *AmE* ˈpɜːrs-/ *verb* [VN] **1** [usually passive] to mark sth in some way to show that it belongs to a particular person: *All the towels were personalized with their initials.* **2** to design or change sth so that it is suitable for the needs of a particular person: *All our courses are personalized to the needs of the individual.* **3** to refer to particular people when discussing a general subject: *The mass media tends to personalize politics.* ▶ per·son·al·ized, -ised *adj.*: *a highly personalized service* ◊ (*BrE*) *a personalized number plate (= on a car)*

per·son·al·ly /ˈpɜːsənəli; *AmE* ˈpɜːrs-/ *adv.* **1** used to show that you are giving your own opinion about sth: *Personally, I prefer the second option.* ◊ *'Is it worth the effort?' 'Speaking personally, yes.'* **2** by a particular person rather than by sb acting for them: *All letters will be answered personally.* ◊ *Do you know him personally (= have you met him, rather than just knowing about him from other people)?* **3** in a way that is connected with one particular person rather than a group of people: *He was personally criticized by inspectors for his incompetence.* ◊ *You will be held personally responsible for any loss or breakage.* **4** in a way that is intended to be offensive: *I'm sure she didn't mean it personally.* **5** in a way that is connected with sb's personal life rather than with their job or official position: *Have you had any dealings with any of the suspects, either personally or professionally?* IDM **take sth 'personally** to be offended by sth: *I'm afraid he took your remarks personally.*

,personal 'orga'nizer (*BrE* also **-iser**) *noun* a small file with loose sheets of paper in which you write down information, addresses, what you have arranged to do, etc.; a very small computer for the same purpose—see also FILOFAX™

,personal 'pronoun *noun* (*grammar*) any of the pronouns *I, you, he, she, it, we, they, me, him, her, us, them*

,personal 'space *noun* [U] the space directly around where you are standing or sitting: *He leaned towards her and she stiffened at this invasion of her personal space.*

,personal 'stereo *noun* = WALKMAN™

persona non grata /pɜːˌsəʊnə nɒn ˈɡrɑːtə; nəʊn; *AmE* pɜːrˌsoʊnə nɑːn; noʊn/ *noun* [U] (from *Latin*) a person who is not welcome in a particular place because of sth they have said or done, especially one who is told to leave a country by the government

per·soni·fi·ca·tion /pəˌsɒnɪfɪˈkeɪʃn; *AmE* pərˌsɑːn-/ *noun* **1** [C, usually sing.] ~ of sth a person who has a lot of a particular quality or characteristic: *She was the personification of elegance.* **2** [U, C] the practice of representing objects, qualities, etc. as human beings, in art and literature; an object, quality, etc. that is represented in this way: *the personification of autumn in Keats's poem*

per·son·ify /pəˈsɒnɪfaɪ; *AmE* pərˈsɑːn-/ *verb* (per·soni·fies, per·soni·fy·ing, per·soni·fied, per·soni·fied) [VN] **1** to be an example of a quality or characteristic, or to have a lot of it: *These children personify all that is wrong with the education system.* ◊ *He is kindness personified.* **2** [usually passive] ~ sth (as sb) to show or think of an object, quality, etc. as a person: *The river was personified as a goddess.*

per·son·nel /ˌpɜːsəˈnel; *AmE* ˌpɜːrs-/ *noun* **1** [pl.] the people who work for an organization or one of the armed forces: *skilled/trained personnel* ◊ *sales/technical/medical/security personnel* ◊ *army/military personnel* **2** [U+sing./pl. v.] the department in a company that deals with employing and training people SYN HUMAN RESOURCES: *the personnel department/manager* ◊ *She works in personnel.* ◊ *Personnel is/are currently reviewing pay scales.*

,person'nel carrier *noun* a military vehicle for carrying soldiers

,person-to-'person *adj.* [usually before noun] **1** happening between two or more people who deal directly with each other rather than through another person: *Technical support is offered on a person-to-person basis.* **2** (*especially AmE*) (of a telephone call) made by calling the OPERATOR (= a person who works at a telephone exchange) and asking to speak to a particular person. If that person is not available, the call does not have to be paid for: *a person-to-person call*

per·spec·tive /pəˈspektɪv; *AmE* pərˈs-/ *noun* **1** [C] ~ (on sth) a particular attitude towards sth; a way of thinking about sth: *a global perspective* ◊ *Try to see the issue from a different perspective.* ◊ *a report that looks at the education system from the perspective of deaf people* ◊ *His experience abroad provides a wider perspective on the problem.* **2** [U] the ability to think about problems and decisions in a reasonable way without exaggerating their importance: *She was aware that she was losing all sense of perspective.* ◊ *Try to keep these issues in perspective.* ◊ *Talking to others can often help to put your own problems into perspective.* ◊ *It is important not to let things get out of perspective.* **3** [U] the art of creating an effect of depth and distance in a picture by representing people and things that are far away as being smaller than those that are nearer the front: *The artist plays with perspective to confuse the eye.* ◊ *We learnt how to draw buildings in perspective.* ◊ *The tree on the left is out of perspective.* **4** [C] a view, especially one in which you can see far into the distance: *a perspective of the whole valley*

Per·spex™ /ˈpɜːspeks; *AmE* ˈpɜːrs-/ *noun* [U] a strong transparent plastic material that is often used instead of glass

per·spi·ca·cious /ˌpɜːspɪˈkeɪʃəs; *AmE* ˌpɜːrs-/ *adj.* (*formal*) able to understand sb/sth quickly and accurately; showing this: *a perspicacious remark* ▶ per·spi·ca·city /ˌpɜːspɪˈkæsəti; *AmE* ˌpɜːrs-/ *noun* [U]

per·spir·ation /ˌpɜːspəˈreɪʃn; *AmE* ˌpɜːrs-/ *noun* [U] **1** drops of liquid that form on your skin when you are hot SYN SWEAT: *Beads of perspiration stood out on his*

b	d	f	g	h	k	l	m	n	p	r
bad	did	fall	get	hat	cat	leg	man	now	pen	red

P

forehead. ◊ *Her skin was damp with perspiration.* **2** the act of perspiring: *Perspiration cools the skin in hot weather.*

per·spire /pə'spaɪə(r); *AmE* pər's-/ *verb* [V] (*formal*) to produce sweat on your body [SYN] SWEAT: *The game of squash left me perspiring profusely.*

per·suade /pə'sweɪd; *AmE* pər's-/ *verb* **1 ~ sb (into sth/ into doing sth)** to make sb do sth by giving them good reasons for doing it: [VN to inf] *Try to persuade him to come.* ◊ [VN] *Please try and persuade her.* ◊ *She's always easily persuaded.* ◊ *I allowed myself to be persuaded into entering the competition.* ◊ *I'm sure he'll come with a bit of persuading.* **2** to make sb believe that sth is true [SYN] CONVINCE: [VN that] *It will be difficult to persuade them that there's no other choice.* ◊ *She had persuaded herself that life was not worth living.* ◊ [VN] *No one was persuaded by his arguments.* ◊ (*formal*) *I am still not fully persuaded of the plan's merits.*

WHICH WORD?

persuade / convince

The main meaning of **persuade** is to make someone agree to do something by giving them good reasons for doing it: *I tried to persuade her to see a doctor.* The main meaning of **convince** is to make someone believe that something is true: *He convinced me he was right.*

It is quite common, however, for each of these words to be used with both meanings, especially for **convince** to be used as a synonym for **persuade**: *I persuaded/ convinced her to see a doctor.* Some speakers of *BrE* think that this is not correct.

---

per·sua·sion /pə'sweɪʒn; *AmE* pər's-/ *noun* **1** [U] the act of persuading sb to do sth or to believe sth: *It didn't take much persuasion to get her to tell us where he was.* ◊ *After a little gentle persuasion, he agreed to come.* ◊ *She has great powers of persuasion.* **2** [C, U] a particular set of beliefs, especially about religion or politics: *politicians of all persuasions* ◊ *every shade of religious persuasion* [IDM] **of the ... persuasion** (*formal or humorous*) of the type mentioned: *peers of the Liberal persuasion*

per·sua·sive /pə'sweɪsɪv; *AmE* pər's-/ *adj.* able to persuade sb to do or believe sth: *persuasive arguments/ evidence* ◊ *He can be very persuasive.* ▶ **per·sua·sive·ly** *adv.*: *They argue persuasively in favour of a total ban on handguns.* **per·sua·sive·ness** *noun* [U]

pert /pɜːt; *AmE* pɜːrt/ *adj.* **1** (especially of a girl or young woman) showing a lack of respect, especially in a cheerful and amusing way: *a pert reply* **2** (of a part of the body) small, firm and attractive: *a pert nose* ◊ *pert features* ▶ **pert·ly** *adv.*

per·tain /pə'teɪn; *AmE* pər't-/ *verb* [V] (*formal*) to exist or to apply in a particular situation or at a particular time: *Living conditions are vastly different from those pertaining in their country of origin.* ◊ *Those laws no longer pertain.* [PHR V] **per'tain to sth/sb** (*formal*) to be connected with sth/sb: *the laws pertaining to adoption*

per·tin·acious /ˌpɜːtɪ'neɪʃəs; *AmE* ˌpɜːrtn'eɪ-/ *adj.* (*formal*) determined to achieve a particular aim in spite of difficulties or opposition ▶ **per·tin·acity** /ˌpɜːtɪ'næsəti; *AmE* ˌpɜːrtn'æ-/ *noun* [U]

per·tin·ent /'pɜːtɪnənt; *AmE* 'pɜːrtnənt/ *adj.* **~ (to sth)** (*formal*) appropriate to a particular situation: *a pertinent question/fact* ◊ *Please keep your comments pertinent to the topic under discussion.* ▶ **per·tin·ent·ly** *adv.* **per·tin·ence** /-əns/ *noun* [U]

per·turb /pə'tɜːb; *AmE* pər'tɜːrb/ *verb* [VN] (*formal*) to make sb worried or anxious [SYN] ALARM: *Her sudden appearance did not seem to perturb him in the least.* ◊ *I was perturbed by his lack of interest.* ▶ **per·turbed** /-'tɜːbd; *AmE* -'tɜːrbd/ *adj.* **~ (at/about sth)**: *a perturbed young man* ◊ *She didn't seem perturbed at the change of plan.* [OPP] UNPERTURBED

per·turb·ation /ˌpɜːtə'beɪʃn; *AmE* ˌpɜːrtər'b-/ *noun* **1** [U] (*formal*) the state of feeling anxious about sth that has happened **2** [C, U] (*technical*) a small change in the qual-

ity, behaviour or movement of sth: *climatic/temperature perturbations*

per·use /pə'ruːz/ *verb* [VN] (*formal or humorous*) to read sth, especially in a careful way: *A copy of the report is available for you to peruse at your leisure.* ▶ **per·usal** /pə'ruːzl/ *noun* [U, sing.]: *a brief/casual perusal of a document* ◊ *The agreement was signed after careful perusal.*

per·vade /pə'veɪd; *AmE* pər'v-/ *verb* [VN] (*formal*) to spread through and be noticeable in every part of sth: *a pervading mood of fear* ◊ *the sadness that pervades most of her novels* ◊ *The entire house was pervaded by a sour smell.*

per·va·sive /pə'veɪsɪv; *AmE* pər'v-/ *adj.* existing in all parts of a place or thing; spreading gradually to affect all parts of a place or thing: *a pervasive smell of damp* ◊ *A sense of social change is pervasive in her novels.* ▶ **per·va·sive·ly** *adv.* **per·va·sive·ness** *noun* [U]

per·verse /pə'vɜːs; *AmE* pər'vɜːrs/ *adj.* showing deliberate determination to behave in a way that most people think is wrong, unacceptable or unreasonable: *a perverse decision/judgement/result* (= one that most people do not expect and think is wrong) ◊ *She finds a perverse pleasure in upsetting her parents.* ◊ *Do you really mean that or are you just being deliberately perverse?* ▶ **per·verse·ly** *adv.*: *She seemed perversely proud of her criminal record.* **per·vers·ity** *noun* [U]: *He refused to attend out of sheer perversity.*

per·ver·sion /pə'vɜːʃn; *AmE* pər'vɜːrʒn/ *noun* [U, C] **1** behaviour that most people think is not normal or acceptable, especially when it is connected with sex; an example of this type of behaviour: *sexual perversion* ◊ *sadomasochistic perversions* **2** the act of changing sth that is good or right into sth that is bad or wrong; the result of this: *the perversion of innocence/justice* ◊ *Her account was a perversion of the truth.*

per·vert *verb, noun*

■ *verb* /pə'vɜːt; *AmE* pər'vɜːrt/ [VN] **1** to change a system, process, etc. in a bad way so that it is not what it used to be or what it should be: *Some scientific discoveries have been perverted to create weapons of destruction.* **2** to affect sb in a way that makes them act or think in an immoral or unacceptable way [SYN] CORRUPT: *Some people believe that television can pervert the minds of children.* [IDM] **per,vert the course of 'justice** (*law*) to tell a lie or do sth in order to prevent the police, etc. from finding out the truth about a crime

■ *noun* /'pɜːvɜːt; *AmE* 'pɜːrvɜːrt/ a person whose sexual behaviour is not thought to be normal or acceptable by most people: *a sexual pervert*

per·verted /pə'vɜːtɪd; *AmE* pər'vɜːrtəd/ *adj.* not thought to be normal or acceptable by most people: *sexual acts, normal and perverted* ◊ *She was having difficulty following his perverted logic.* ◊ *They clearly take a perverted delight in watching others suffer.*

pe·seta /pə'seɪtə/ *noun* the unit of money in Spain (to be replaced by the euro)

pesky /'peski/ *adj.* [only before noun] (*informal, especially AmE*) annoying: *pesky insects*

peso /'peɪsəʊ; *AmE* -soʊ/ *noun* (*pl.* **pesos**) the unit of money in many Latin American countries and the Philippines

pes·sary /'pesəri/ *noun* (*pl.* **-ies**) **1** a small piece of solid medicine that is placed inside a woman's VAGINA and left to dissolve, used to cure an infection or to prevent her from becoming pregnant—see also SUPPOSITORY **2** a device that is placed inside a woman's VAGINA to support the WOMB

pes·sim·ism /'pesɪmɪzəm/ *noun* [U] **~ (about/over sth)** a feeling that bad things will happen and that sth will not be successful; the tendency to have this feeling: *There is a mood of pessimism in the company about future job prospects.* [OPP] OPTIMISM

pes·sim·ist /'pesɪmɪst/ *noun* a person who always expects bad things to happen: *You don't have to be a pessimist to realize that we're in trouble.* [OPP] OPTIMIST

pes·sim·is·tic /ˌpesɪ'mɪstɪk/ *adj.* **~ (about sth)** expecting bad things to happen or sth not to be successful;

---

showing this: *They appeared surprisingly pessimistic about their chances of winning.* ◊ *a pessimistic view of life* ◊ *I think you're being far too pessimistic.* OPP OPTIMISTIC ▶ **pes·sim·is·tic·al·ly** /-kli/ *adv.*

pest /pest/ *noun* **1** an insect or animal that destroys plants, food, etc: *pest control* ◊ *insect/plant/garden pests* **2** (*informal*) an annoying person or thing: *That child is being a real pest.*

pes·ter /ˈpestə(r)/ *verb* ~ **sb** (**for/with sth**) to annoy sb, especially by asking them sth many times: [VN] *Journalists pestered neighbours for information.* ◊ *He has been pestering her with phone calls for over a week.* ◊ *The horses were continually pestered by flies.* ◊ [VN to inf] *The kids kept pestering me to read to them.* [also V]

pesti·cide /ˈpestɪsaɪd/ *noun* [C, U] a chemical used for killing pests, especially insects: *vegetables grown without the use of pesticides* ◊ *crops sprayed with pesticide*—see also HERBICIDE, INSECTICIDE

pesti·lence /ˈpestɪləns/ *noun* [U, sing.] (*old use* or *literary*) any infectious disease that spreads quickly and kills a lot of people

pesti·len·tial /ˌpestɪˈlenʃl/ *adj.* **1** [only before noun] (*literary*) extremely annoying **2** (*old use*) connected with or causing a pestilence

pes·tle /ˈpesl/ *noun* a small heavy tool with a round end used for crushing things in a special bowl called a MORTAR—picture at LABORATORY

pet /pet/ *noun, verb, adj.*
▪ *noun* **1** an animal, a bird, etc. that you have at home for pleasure, rather than one that is kept for work or food: *Do you have any pets?* ◊ *a pet dog/hamster* ◊ *a family/domestic pet* ◊ *pet food* ◊ *a pet shop* (= where animals are sold as pets) **2** (usually *disapproving*) a person who is given special attention by sb, especially in a way that seems unfair to other people: *She's the teacher's pet.* **3** (*BrE, spoken*) used when speaking to a child or young woman to show affection: *What's wrong, pet?* ◊ *Be a pet* (= be kind) *and post this letter for me.*
▪ *verb* (-tt-) **1** [VN] (*especially AmE*) to touch or move your hand gently over an animal or a child in a kind and loving way **2** [V] (*informal*) (of two people) to kiss and touch each other in a sexual way—see also PETTING
▪ *adj.* [only before noun] that you are very interested in: *his pet subject/theory/project*—see also PET NAME **IDM** **sb's pet ˈhate** (*BrE*) (*AmE* **sb's pet ˈpeeve**) something that you particularly dislike

petal /ˈpetl/ *noun* a delicate coloured part of a flower. The head of a flower is usually made up of several petals around a central part.—picture at PLANT

pe·tard /pəˈtɑːd; *AmE* pəˈtɑːrd/ *noun* **IDM** see HOIST *v.*

Peter /ˈpiːtə(r)/ *noun* **IDM** see ROB

peter /ˈpiːtə(r)/ *verb* **PHRV** ˌpeter ˈout to gradually become smaller, quieter, etc. and then end: *The campaign petered out for lack of support.* ◊ *The road petered out into a dirt track.*

peth·id·ine /ˈpeθədiːn/ *noun* [U] a drug used to reduce severe pain, especially for women giving birth

petit bourgeois /ˌpeti ˈbʊəʒwɑː; *AmE* ˈbʊrʒ-/ (also ˌpetty ˈbourgeois) *noun* (*pl.* petits/petty bourgeois) (*disapproving*) a member of the lower middle class in society, especially one who thinks that money, work and social position are very important ▶ ˌpetit ˈbourgeois (also ˌpetty ˈbourgeois) *adj.* [usually before noun]

pe·tite /pəˈtiːt/ *adj.* (*approving*) (of a girl, woman or her figure) small and thin: *a petite blonde*

the pe·tite ˌbourgeoiˈsie (also ˌpetty ˌbourgeoiˈsie) *noun* [sing.] the lower middle class in society

petit four /ˌpeti ˈfɔː(r)/ *noun* [usually pl.] (*pl.* petits fours /ˌpeti ˈfɔː(r)/) (from *French*) a very small decorated cake or biscuit/cookie that is served with coffee or tea—picture on page A1

pe·ti·tion /pəˈtɪʃn/ *noun, verb*
▪ *noun* **1** ~ (**against/for sth**) a written document signed by a large number of people that asks sb in a position of authority to do or change sth: *a petition against experiments on animals* ◊ *The workers are getting up* (= starting)

a petition for tighter safety standards. **2** (*law*) an official document asking a court of law to take a particular course of action **3** (*formal*) a formal prayer to God or request to sb in authority
▪ *verb* **1** ~ **for/against sth** | ~ **sb** (**for sth**) to make a formal request to sb in authority, especially by sending them a petition: [V] *Local residents have successfully petitioned against the siting of a prison in their area.* ◊ [VN] *The group intends to petition Parliament for reform of the law.* ◊ [VN to inf] *Parents petitioned the school to review its admission policy.* **2** ~ (**sb**) (**for sth**) to formally ask for sth in a court of law: [V] *to petition for divorce* [also VN, VN to inf]

pe·ti·tion·er /pəˈtɪʃənə(r)/ *noun* **1** a person who organizes or signs a petition **2** (*law*) a person who asks a court of law to take a particular course of action **3** (*formal*) a person who makes a formal request to sb in authority

ˈpet name *noun* a name you use for sb instead of their real name, as a sign of affection

pet·rel /ˈpetrəl/ *noun* a black and white seabird that can fly a long way from land

Petri dish /ˈpetri dɪʃ; ˈpiːtri/ *noun* a shallow covered dish used for growing bacteria, etc. in—picture at LABORATORY

petri·fied /ˈpetrɪfaɪd/ *adj.* **1** ~ (**of sth**)| ~ (**that …**) extremely frightened SYN TERRIFIED: *a petrified expression* ◊ *I'm petrified of snakes.* ◊ *They were petrified with fear* (= so frightened that they were unable to move or think). **2** [only before noun] **petrified** trees, insects, etc. have died and been changed into stone over a very long period of time: *a petrified forest*

pet·rify /ˈpetrɪfaɪ/ *verb* (**petri·fies, petri·fy·ing, petri·fied, petri·fied**) **1** [VN] to make sb feel extremely frightened SYN TERRIFY: *Just the thought of making a speech petrifies me.* **2** [V, VN] to change or to make sth change into a substance like stone

petro- /ˈpetrəʊ; *AmE* ˈpetroʊ/ *combining form* (in nouns, adjectives and adverbs) **1** connected with rocks: *petrology* **2** connected with petrol/gas: *petrochemical*

petro·chem·ical /ˌpetrəʊˈkemɪkl; *AmE* ˌpetroʊ-/ *noun* any chemical substance obtained from PETROLEUM oil or natural gas: *the petrochemical industry*

petro·dol·lar /ˈpetrəʊdɒlə(r); *AmE* ˈpetroʊdɑːlər/ *noun* a unit of money that is used for calculating the money earned by countries that produce and sell oil

pet·rol /ˈpetrəl/ (*BrE*) (*AmE* **gas·oline, gas**) *noun* [U] a liquid obtained from PETROLEUM, used as fuel in car engines, etc: *to fill a car up with petrol* ◊ *the petrol tank of a car* ◊ *an increase in petrol prices* ◊ *leaded/unleaded petrol*—compare DIESEL

ˈpetrol bomb *noun* (*BrE*) = MOLOTOV COCKTAIL

pet·rol·eum /pəˈtrəʊliəm; *AmE* -ˈtroʊ-/ *noun* [U] mineral oil that is found under the ground or the sea and is used to produce petrol/gas, PARAFFIN, DIESEL oil, etc.

peˌtroleum ˈjelly (*AmE* also **pet·rol·atum** /ˌpetrəˈleɪtəm/) *noun* [U] a soft clear substance obtained from petroleum, used to heal injuries on the skin or to make machine parts move together more smoothly SYN VASELINE

pet·rology /pəˈtrɒlədʒi; *AmE* -ˈtrɑːl-/ *noun* [U] the scientific study of rocks

ˈpetrol station (*BrE*) (*AmE* ˈgas station) (also ˈfilling station, ˈservice station *AmE, BrE*) *noun* a place at the side of a road where you take your car to buy petrol/gas, oil, etc.

petti·coat /ˈpetɪkəʊt; *AmE* -koʊt/ *noun* (*old-fashioned*) a piece of women's underwear like a thin dress or skirt, worn under a dress or skirt SYN SLIP

petti·fog·ging /ˈpetɪfɒgɪŋ; *AmE* -fɑːg-; -fɔːg-/ *adj.* [only before noun] (*rare, old-fashioned*) paying too much attention to unimportant details; concerned with unimportant things

pet·ting /ˈpetɪŋ/ *noun* [U] the activity of kissing and touching sb, especially in a sexual way: *heavy* (= very intense) *petting*

ˈpetting zoo *noun* (*AmE*) a zoo with animals that children can touch

æ	ɑː	e	ɜː	ə	ɪ	iː	i	ɒ	ɔː	ʌ	ʊ	u	uː
cat	father	ten	bird	about	sit	see	many	got	saw	cup	put	actual	too

(BrE)

petty /'peti/ *adj.* (usually *disapproving*) **1** [usually before noun] small and unimportant: *petty squabbles/restrictions* ◊ *petty crime/theft* (= that is not very serious) ◊ *a petty criminal/thief* ◊ *a petty bureaucrat/official* (= who does not have much power or authority) **2** concerned with small and unimportant matters, especially when this is unkind to other people: *How could you be so petty?* ▶ **petti·ness** *noun* [U]

,**petty** '**bourgeois** *noun, adj.* = PETIT BOURGEOIS

the ,**petty** ,**bourgeoi·sie** *noun* [sing.] = PETITE BOURGEOISIE

,**petty** '**cash** *noun* [U] a small amount of money kept in an office for small payments

,**petty** '**officer** *noun* (*abbr.* PO) a sailor of middle rank in the navy

petu·lant /'petjulənt; *AmE* 'petʃə-/ *adj.* (*written*) bad-tempered and unreasonable, especially because you cannot do or have what you want: *He behaved like a petulant child and refused to cooperate.* ▶ **petu·lant·ly** *adv.* **petu·lance** /-əns/ *noun* [U]

pe·tu·nia /pə'tju:niə; *AmE* -'tu:-/ *noun* a garden plant with white, pink, purple or red flowers

pew /pju:/ *noun* a long wooden seat in a church—picture at CHAIR **IDM** ,**Take a** '**pew!** (*BrE, spoken, humorous*) used to tell sb to sit down

pew·ter /'pju:tə(r)/ *noun* [U] a grey metal made by mixing TIN with LEAD, used especially in the past for making cups, dishes, etc.; objects made from pewter: *a pewter tankard* ◊ *a fine collection of old pewter*

PG /ˌpiː 'dʒiː/ *abbr.* (*BrE*) parental guidance. A film that has the label 'PG' is not suitable for children to watch without an adult.

PGCE /ˌpiː dʒiː siː 'iː/ *noun* the abbreviation for 'Postgraduate Certificate of Education' (a British teaching qualification taken by people with a degree in another subject)

pH /ˌpiː 'eɪtʃ/ *noun* [sing.] (*chemistry*) a measurement of the level of acid or ALKALI in a solution or substance. In the pH range of 0 to 14 a reading of below 7 shows an acid and of above 7 shows an ALKALI: *a pH of 7.5* ◊ *to test the pH level of the soil*

phal·anx /'fælæŋks/ *noun* (*formal*) a group of people or things standing very close together: *The protesters ran into a solid phalanx of riot police.*

phal·lic /'fælɪk/ *adj.* of or like a phallus: *phallic imagery/symbols*

phal·lus /'fæləs/ *noun* **1** (*technical*) the male sexual organ, especially when it is ERECT **2** a model or an image of the male sexual organ that represents power and FERTILITY

phan·tasm /'fæntæzəm/ *noun* (*formal*) a thing seen in the imagination **SYN** ILLUSION

phan·tas·ma·goria /ˌfæntæzmə'ɡɒriə; *AmE* -'ɡɔːr-/ *noun* [sing.] (*formal*) a changing scene of real or imagined figures, for example as seen in a dream or created as an effect in a film/movie ▶ **phan·tas·ma·gor·ical** /-'ɡɒrɪkl; *AmE* -'ɡɔːr-; -'ɡɑːr-/ *adj.*

phan·tasy *noun* [C, U] (*old use*) = FANTASY

phantom /'fæntəm/ *noun, adj.*
■ *noun* **1** a ghost: *the phantom of his dead father* **2** a thing that exists only in your imagination
■ *adj.* [only before noun] **1** like a ghost: *a phantom horseman* **2** existing only in your imagination: *phantom fears/illnesses* ◊ *a phantom pregnancy* (= a condition in which a woman seems to be pregnant but in fact is not) **3** that people think exists but that in fact does not: *phantom assets/profits*

phar·aoh /'feərəʊ; *AmE* 'feroʊ/ *noun* a ruler of ancient Egypt

Phari·see /'færɪsiː/ *noun* **1** a member of an ancient Jewish group who followed religious laws and teaching very strictly **2** (*disapproving*) a person who is very proud of the fact that they have high religious and moral standards, but who does not care enough about other people **SYN** HYPOCRITE

pharma·ceut·ical /ˌfɑːmə'suːtɪkl; -'sjuː-; *AmE* ˌfɑːrmə-'suː-/ *adj., noun*
■ *adj.* [only before noun] connected with making and selling drugs and medicines: *pharmaceutical companies/products* ◊ *the pharmaceutical industry*
■ *noun* [usually pl.] (*technical*) a drug or medicine: *the development of new pharmaceuticals* ◊ *the pharmaceuticals industry*

pharma·cist /'fɑːməsɪst; *AmE* 'fɑːrm-/ *noun* **1** (*AmE also* **drug·gist**) a person whose job is to prepare medicines and sell or give them to the public in a shop/store or in a hospital: *We had to wait for the pharmacist to make up her prescription.*—compare CHEMIST **2** (**pharma·cist's**) (*pl.* **pharma·cists**) (*BrE*) a shop that sells medicines: *They sell vitamin supplements at the pharmacist's.*—compare CHEMIST—see also PHARMACY

pharma·colo·gist /ˌfɑːmə'kɒlədʒɪst; *AmE* ˌfɑːrmə'kɑːl-/ *noun* a scientist who studies pharmacology

pharma·col·ogy /ˌfɑːmə'kɒlədʒi; *AmE* ˌfɑːrmə'kɑːl-/ *noun* [U] the scientific study of drugs and their use in medicine ▶ **pharma·co·logic·al** /ˌfɑːməkə'lɒdʒɪkl; *AmE* ˌfɑːrməkə'lɑːdʒ-/ *adj.*: *pharmacological research*

pharma·co·poeia (*AmE also* **pharma·co·peia**) /ˌfɑːmə-kə'piːə; *AmE* ˌfɑːrmə-/ *noun* (*technical*) an official book containing a list of medicines and drugs and instructions for their use

phar·macy /'fɑːməsi; *AmE* 'fɑːrm-/ *noun* (*pl.* **-ies**) **1** [C] a shop/store, or part of one, that sells medicines and drugs—compare CHEMIST, DRUGSTORE **2** [C] a place in a hospital where medicines are prepared—see also DISPENSARY **3** [U] the study of how to prepare medicines and drugs

phar·ynx /'færɪŋks/ *noun* (*pl.* **pha·ryn·ges** /fə'rɪndʒiːz/) (*anatomy*) the soft area at the top of the throat where the passages to the nose and mouth connect with the throat—picture at BODY

phase /feɪz/ *noun, verb*
■ *noun* **1** a stage in a process of change or development: *during the first/next/last phase* ◊ *the initial/final phase of the project* ◊ *a critical/decisive phase* ◊ *the design phase* ◊ *His anxiety about the work was just a passing phase.* ◊ *She's going through a difficult phase.* ◊ *The wedding marked the beginning of a new phase in Emma's life.* **2** each of the shapes of the moon as we see it from the earth at different times of the month: *the phases of the moon* **IDM** **in phase/out of phase (with sth)** (*BrE*) working/not working together in the right way: *The traffic lights were out of phase.*
■ *verb* [VN] [usually passive] to arrange to do sth gradually in stages over a period of time: *the phased withdrawal of troops from the area* ◊ *Closure of the hospitals was phased over a three-year period.* **PHRV** ,**phase sth** ↔ '**in** to introduce or start using sth gradually in stages over a period of time: *The new tax will be phased in over two years.* ,**phase sth** ↔ '**out** to stop using sth gradually in stages over a period of time: *Subsidies to farmers will be phased out by the year 2000.*

PhD (*also* **Ph.D.** especially in *AmE*) /ˌpiː eɪtʃ 'diː/ *noun* the abbreviation for 'Doctor of Philosophy' (a university degree of a very high level that is given to sb who has done research in a particular subject): *to be/have/do a PhD* ◊ (*BrE*) *Anne Thomas PhD*

phea·sant /'feznt/ *noun* [C, U] (*pl.* **phea·sants** *or* **phea·sant**) a large bird with a long tail, the male of which is brightly coloured. People sometimes shoot pheasants for sport or food. Meat from this bird is also called **pheasant**: (*BrE*) *to shoot pheasant* ◊ (*AmE*) *to hunt pheasant* ◊ *roast pheasant*—picture on page A6

phe·nol /'fiːnɒl; *AmE* -nɑːl/ *noun* [U] (*chemistry*) a poisonous white chemical compound. When dissolved in water it is used as an ANTISEPTIC and DISINFECTANT, usually called CARBOLIC

phe·nom /fə'nɒm; *AmE* fə'nɑːm/ *noun* (*AmE, informal*) a person or thing that is very successful or impressive **SYN** PHENOMENON

phe·nom·enal /fə'nɒmɪnl; *AmE* -'nɑːm-/ *adj.* very great or impressive: *The product has been a phenomenal success.* ◊ *The response to the appeal has been phenomenal.*

phe·nom·en·al·ly /fə'nɒmɪnəli; *AmE* -'nɑːm-/ *adv.* **1** in a very great or impressive way: *This product has been phenomenally successful* **2** extremely; very: *phenomenally bad weather*

phe·nom·en·ology /fɪˌnɒmɪ'nɒlədʒi; *AmE* -ˌnɑːmə'nɑːl-/ *noun* [U] the branch of philosophy that deals with what you see, hear, feel, etc. in contrast to what may actually be real or true about the world ▶ **phe·nom·en·olo·gic·al** /fɪˌnɒmɪnə'lɒdʒɪkl; *AmE* -ˌnɑːmənə'lɑːdʒ-/ *adj.*: *a phenomenological approach to language*

phe·nom·enon /fə'nɒmɪnən; *AmE* fə'nɑːm-/ *noun* (*pl.* **phe·nom·ena** /-ɪnə/) **1** a fact or an event in nature or society, especially one that is not fully understood: *cultural/natural/social phenomena* ◊ *Terrorism is a phenomenon of the 20th century.* **2** (*pl.* **phe·nom·enons** in *AmE*) a person or thing that is very successful or impressive

phero·mone /'ferəməʊn; *AmE* -moʊn/ *noun* (*biology*) a substance produced by an animal as a chemical signal, to attract another animal of the same SPECIES

phew /fjuː/ (*BrE*) *exclamation* a sound that people make to show that they are hot, tired, or happy that something bad has finished or did not happen: *Phew, it's hot in here!* ◊ *Phew, I'm glad that's all over.*—compare WHEW

phial /'faɪəl/ (also **vial** especially in *AmE*) *noun* (*formal*) a small glass container, for medicine or PERFUME

Phi Beta Kappa /ˌfaɪ ˌbiːtə 'kæpə/ *noun* (in the US) a society for college and university students who are very successful in their studies

phil·an·der·er /fɪ'lændərə(r)/ *noun* (*old-fashioned, disapproving*) a man who has sexual relationships with many different women

phil·an·dering /fɪ'lændərɪŋ/ *noun* [U] (*old-fashioned, disapproving*) (of a man) the fact of having sexual relationships with many different women [SYN] WOMANIZING ▶ **phil·an·dering** *adj.* [only before noun]: *a philandering husband*

phil·an·throp·ist /fɪ'lænθrəpɪst/ *noun* a rich person who helps the poor and those in need, especially by giving money

phil·an·thropy /fɪ'lænθrəpi/ *noun* [U] the practice of helping the poor and those in need, especially by giving money ▶ **phil·an·throp·ic** /ˌfɪlən'θrɒpɪk; *AmE* -'θrɑːp-/ *adj.*: *philanthropic work* **phil·an·throp·ic·al·ly** /ˌfɪlən'θrɒpɪkli; *AmE* -'θrɑːp-/ *adv.*

phila·tel·ist /fɪ'lætəlɪst/ *noun* (*technical*) a person who collects or studies stamps

phil·ately /fɪ'lætəli/ *noun* [U] (*technical*) the collection and study of POSTAGE STAMPS ▶ **phila·tel·ic** /ˌfɪlə'telɪk/ *adj.*

-phile *combining form* (in nouns and adjectives) liking a particular thing; a person who likes a particular thing: *Anglophile* ◊ *bibliophile*—compare -PHOBE

phil·har·mon·ic /ˌfɪlə'mɒnɪk; *AmE* ˌfɪlər'mɑːnɪk/ *adj.* used in the names of orchestras, music societies, etc: *the Berlin Philharmonic (Orchestra)*

-philia *combining form* (in nouns) love of sth, especially connected with a sexual attraction that is not considered normal: *paedophilia*—compare -PHOBIA

phil·is·tine /'fɪlɪstaɪn; *AmE* -stiːn/ *noun* (*disapproving*) a person who does not like or understand art, literature, music, etc: *In artistic matters he's a complete philistine* ▶ **phil·is·tine** *adj.*: *philistine attitudes* **phil·is·tin·ism** /-tɪnɪzəm/ *noun* [U]: *the philistinism of the tabloid press*

philo- /'fɪləʊ; *AmE* 'fɪloʊ/ (also **phil-**) *combining form* (in nouns, adjectives, verbs and adverbs) liking: *philanthropy*

phil·olo·gist /fɪ'lɒlədʒɪst; *AmE* -'lɑːl-/ *noun* a person who studies philology

phil·ology /fɪ'lɒlədʒi; *AmE* -'lɑːl-/ *noun* [U] the scientific study of the development of language or of a particular language ▶ **phil·olo·gic·al** /ˌfɪlə'lɒdʒɪkl; *AmE* -'lɑːdʒ-/ *adj.*

phil·oso·pher /fə'lɒsəfə(r); *AmE* -'lɑːs-/ *noun* **1** a person who studies or writes about philosophy: *the Greek phil-*

osopher Aristotle **2** a person who thinks deeply about things: *He seems to be a bit of a philosopher.*

philo·soph·ical /ˌfɪlə'sɒfɪkl/ (also **philo·soph·ic** /-'sɒfɪk; *AmE* -'sɑːfɪk/) *adj.* **1** connected with philosophy: *the philosophical writings of Kant* ◊ *philosophic debate/discussion/enquiry* **2** ~ (**about sth**) (*approving*) having a calm attitude towards a difficult or disappointing situation: *He was philosophical about losing and said that he'd be back next year to try again.* ▶ **philo·soph·ic·al·ly** /-kli/ *adv.*: *This kind of evidence is philosophically unconvincing.* ◊ *She took the bad news philosophically.*

philo·so·phize (*BrE* also **-ise**) /fə'lɒsəfaɪz; *AmE* -'lɑːs-/ *verb* [V] ~ (**about/on sth**) to talk about sth in a serious way, especially when other people think this is boring: *He spent the evening philosophizing on the meaning of life.* ▶ **philo·oso·phiz·ing, -is·ing** *noun* [U]

philo·sophy /fə'lɒsəfi; *AmE* -'lɑːs-/ *noun* **1** [U] the study of nature and meaning of the universe and of human life: *moral philosophy* ◊ *the philosophy of science* ◊ *a professor of philosophy* ◊ *a degree in philosophy* **2** [C] a particular set or system of beliefs resulting from the search for knowledge about life and the universe: *the philosophy of Jung* ◊ *the development of different philosophies* **3** [C] a set of beliefs or an attitude to life that guides sb's behaviour: *Her philosophy of life is to take every opportunity that presents itself.*

phil·tre (*BrE*) (*AmE* **phil·ter**) /'fɪltə(r)/ *noun* (*literary*) a magic drink that is supposed to make people fall in love

phlegm /flem/ *noun* [U] **1** the thick yellowish-green substance that forms in the nose and throat, especially when you have a cold **2** (*written*) the ability to remain calm in a situation that is difficult or upsetting

phleg·mat·ic /fleg'mætɪk/ *adj.* not easily made angry or upset [SYN] CALM: *a phlegmatic man/temperament*

-phobe *combining form* (in nouns) a person who dislikes a particular thing or particular people: *Anglophobe* ◊ *xenophobe*—compare -PHILE

pho·bia /'fəʊbiə; *AmE* 'foʊ-/ *noun* **1** a strong unreasonable fear or hatred of sth: *He has a phobia about flying.* **2** (**-phobia**) (in nouns) a strong unreasonable fear or hatred of a particular thing: *claustrophobia* ◊ *xenophobia*—compare -PHILIA

pho·bic /'fəʊbɪk; *AmE* 'foʊ-/ *noun* **1** a person who has a strong unreasonable fear or hatred of sth: *cat phobics* **2** (**-phobic**) (in adjectives) having a strong unreasonable fear or hatred of a particular thing: *claustrophobic* ◊ *xenophobic* ▶ **pho·bic** *adj.*: *phobic anxiety*

phoe·nix /'fiːnɪks/ *noun* (in stories) a magic bird that lives for several hundred years before burning itself and then being born again from its ashes: *to rise like a phoenix from the ashes* (= to be powerful or successful again)

phone /fəʊn; *AmE* foʊn/ *noun, verb*
■ *noun* **1** (also **tele·phone**) [U, C] a system for talking to sb else over long distances using wires or radio; a machine used for this: *I have to make a phone call.* ◊ *The phone rang and Pat answered it.* ◊ *They like to do business by phone/ on the phone.* ◊ *a phone bill*—see also CAR PHONE, CELLULAR PHONE, ENTRYPHONE, MOBILE PHONE, PAY-PHONE **2** (also **tele·phone**) [C] the part of the telephone that you hold in your hand and speak into: *to pick up the phone* ◊ *to put the phone down* ◊ *He left the phone off the hook as he didn't want to be disturbed.*—see also ANSWER-PHONE **3** (**-phone**) (in nouns) an instrument that uses or makes sound: *dictaphone* ◊ *xylophone* **4** (**-phone**) (in adjectives and nouns) speaking a particular language; a person who does this: *anglophone* ◊ *francophone* [IDM] **be on the 'phone 1** to be using the telephone: *He's been on the phone to Kate for more than an hour.* **2** (*BrE*) to have a telephone in your home or place of work: *They're not on the phone at the holiday cottage.*
■ *verb* (*especially BrE*) (*BrE* also **phone 'up**) to make a telephone call to sb: [V] *I was just phoning up for a chat.* ◊ *He phoned to invite me out for dinner.* ◊ *Someone phone for an ambulance!* ◊ *Could you phone back later?* ◊ *He phoned home, but there was no reply.* ◊ [VN] *Don't forget to phone New York.* ◊ *For reservations, phone 0171 281 3964.* ◊ *Phone them up and find out when they are coming.* [PHR V] **,phone**

b	d	f	g	h	k	l	m	n	p	r
bad	did	fall	get	hat	cat	leg	**man**	now	pen	red

P

'in (*especially BrE*) **1** to make a telephone call to the place where you work: [+ADJ] *Three people have **phoned** in sick already this morning.* **2** to make a telephone call to a radio or television station: *Listeners are invited to phone in with their comments.*—related noun PHONE-IN ,**phone sth** ↔ **'in** (*especially BrE*) to make a telephone call to the place where you work in order to give sb some information: *I need you to phone the story in before five.*

BRITISH / AMERICAN
phone / call / ring

Verbs

In *BrE*, **to phone, to ring** and **to call** are the usual ways of saying **to telephone**. In *AmE* the most common word is **call**, but **phone** is also used. Speakers of *AmE* do not say **ring**. **Telephone** is very formal and is used mainly in *BrE*.

Nouns

You can use **call** or **phone call** (more formal) in both *BrE* and *AmE*: *Were there any phone calls for me?* ◇ *How do I make a local call?* The idiom **give sb a call** is also common: *I'll give you a call tonight.* In informal *BrE* you could also say: *I'll give you a ring tonight.*

'phone book *noun* = TELEPHONE DIRECTORY

'phone booth (also **'telephone booth**) *noun* a place that is partly enclosed, containing a public telephone, in a hotel, restaurant, in the street, etc.

'phone box (also **'telephone box, 'telephone kiosk, 'call box**) (all *BrE*) *noun* a small unit that is completely enclosed, containing a public telephone, in the street, at a station, etc.

'phone call *noun* = CALL

phone·card /'fəʊnkɑːd; *AmE* 'foʊnkɑːrd/ *noun* (*BrE*) a plastic card that you can use in some public telephones instead of money

'phone-in (*BrE*) (*AmE* **'call-in**) *noun* a radio or television programme in which people can telephone and make comments or ask questions about a particular subject: *a phone-in/call-in show*

phon·eme /'fəʊniːm; *AmE* 'foʊ-/ *noun* (*phonetics*) any one of the set of smallest units of sound in a language that distinguish one word from another. In English, the 's' in 'sip' and the 'z' in 'zip' represent two different phonemes. ▶ **phon·em·ic** /fə'niːmɪk/ *adj.*

'phone number *noun* = TELEPHONE NUMBER

'phone tapping *noun* = TELEPHONE TAPPING

phon·et·ic /fə'netɪk/ *adj.* **1** using special symbols to represent each different speech sound: *the International Phonetic Alphabet* ◇ *a phonetic symbol/transcription* **2** (of a spelling or spelling system) that closely matches the sounds represented: *Spanish spelling is phonetic, unlike English spelling.* **3** connected with the sounds of human speech ▶ **phon·et·ic·al·ly** /-kli/ *adv.*

phon·et·ics /fə'netɪks/ *noun* [U] the study of speech sounds and how they are produced ▶ **phon·et·ician** /,fəʊnə'tɪʃn; ,fɒn-; *AmE* ,foʊn-; ,fɑːn-/ *noun*

pho·ney (also **phony** especially in *AmE*) /'fəʊni; *AmE* 'foʊni/ *adj., noun*
■ *adj.* (**pho·nier, pho·ni·est**) (*informal, disapproving*) not real or true; false, and trying to deceive people: *She spoke with a phoney Russian accent.*
■ *noun* (*pl.* **-neys** or **-nies**) (*formal*) a person who is not •honest or sincere; a thing that is not real or true

,**phoney 'war** *noun* [sing.] (*BrE*) a period of time when two groups are officially at war but not actually fighting

phon·ic /'fɒnɪk; *AmE* 'fɑːnɪk/ *adj.* **1** (*technical*) relating to sound; relating to sounds made in speech **2** (**-phonic**) (in adjectives) connected with an instrument that uses or makes sound: *telephonic*

phon·ics /'fɒnɪks; *AmE* 'fɑːn-/ *noun* [U] a method of teaching people to read based on the sounds that letters represent

phono- /'fəʊnəʊ; *AmE* 'foʊnoʊ/ (also **phon-**) *combining form* (in nouns, adjectives and adverbs) connected with sound or sounds: *phonetic*

phon·ology /fə'nɒlədʒi; *AmE* -'nɑːl-/ *noun* [U] (*linguistics*) the speech sounds of a particular language; the study of these sounds ▶ **phono·logic·al** /,fəʊnə'lɒdʒɪkl; *AmE* ,foʊnə'lɑːdʒ-; ,fɑːn-; *fɒn-*/ *adj.*: *phonological analysis* **phon·olo·gist** /fə'nɒlədʒɪst; *AmE* fə'nɑːl-/ *noun*

phony (*especially AmE*) = PHONEY

phos·phate /'fɒsfeɪt; *AmE* 'fɑːs-/ *noun* [C, U] (*chemistry*) any salt or compound containing phosphorus, used in industry or for helping plants to grow: *phosphate-free washing powder* ◇ *the use of nitrates and phosphates to fertilize the soil*

phos·phor·es·cent /,fɒsfə'resnt; *AmE* ,fɑːs-/ *adj.* (*technical*) **1** producing a faint light in the dark—compare FLUORESCENT **2** producing light without heat or with so little heat that it cannot be felt ▶ **phos·phor·es·cence** /-sns/ *noun* [U]

phos·phorus /'fɒsfərəs; *AmE* 'fɑːs-/ *noun* [U] (*symb* P) a chemical element found in several different forms, including as a poisonous, pale yellow substance that shines in the dark and starts to burn as soon as it is placed in air

photo /'fəʊtəʊ; *AmE* 'foʊtoʊ/ *noun* (*pl.* **-os** /-təʊz; *AmE* -toʊz/) = PHOTOGRAPH: *a colour/black-and-white/passport photo* ◇ *I'll take a photo of you.* HELP The usual phrase in *AmE* is **take a picture**.

photo- /'fəʊtəʊ; *AmE* 'foʊtoʊ/ *combining form* (in nouns, adjectives, verbs and adverbs) **1** connected with light: *photosynthesis* **2** connected with photography: *photogenic*

'photo booth *noun* a small enclosed structure where you can put money in a machine and get a photograph of yourself in a few minutes

'photo call *noun* a time that is arranged in advance when photographers or television cameras are invited to take pictures of a famous person

photo·cell /'fəʊtəʊsel; *AmE* 'foʊtoʊ-/ *noun* = PHOTOELEC-TRIC CELL

photo·copier /'fəʊtəʊkɒpiə(r); *AmE* 'foʊtoʊkɑːp-/ (also **copier** especially in *AmE*) *noun* a machine that makes copies of documents, etc. by photographing them

photo·copy /'fəʊtəʊkɒpi; *AmE* 'foʊtoʊkɑːpi/ *noun, verb*
■ *noun* (also **copy**) (*pl.* **-ies**) a photographic copy of a document, etc: *Make as many photocopies as you need.*
■ *verb* (**photo·cop·ies, photo·copy·ing, photo·cop·ied, photo·cop·ied**) (*especially BrE* **copy**) **1** to make a photocopy of sth: [VN] *a photocopied letter* ◇ *Can you get these photocopied for me by 5 o'clock?* ◇ [V] *I seem to have spent most of the day photocopying.* **2** [V] ~ **well/badly** (of printed material) to produce a good/bad photocopy: *The comments in pencil haven't photocopied very well.*

photo·elec·tric /,fəʊtəʊɪ'lektrɪk; *AmE* ,foʊtoʊ-/ *adj.* using an electric current that is controlled by light

,**photoelectric 'cell** (also **photo·cell**) *noun* an electric device that uses a beam of light. When the beam is broken it shows that sb/sth is present, and can be used to control ALARMS, machinery, etc.

,**photo 'finish** *noun* [usually sing.] the end of a race in which the leading runners or horses are so close together that only a photograph of them passing the finishing line can show which is the winner

'Photo-Fit™ *noun* (*BrE*) a picture of a person who is wanted by the police, made by putting together photographs of different features of faces from information that is given by sb who has seen the person—compare E-FIT, IDENTIKIT

photo·gen·ic /,fəʊtəʊ'dʒenɪk; *AmE* ,foʊtoʊ-/ *adj.* looking attractive in photographs: *I'm not very photogenic.*

photo·graph /'fəʊtəɡrɑːf; *AmE* 'foʊtəɡræf/ *noun, verb*
■ *noun* (also **photo**) a picture that is made by using a camera that has a film sensitive to light inside it: *aerial/satellite photographs* ◇ *colour photographs* ◇ *Please enclose a recent passport-sized photograph of yourself.* ◇ *I spent the day **taking photographs** of the city.* HELP The usual phrase in *AmE* is **take pictures**.
■ *verb* **1** to take a photograph of sb/sth: [VN] *He has photographed some of the world's most beautiful women.* ◇ *a*

---

beautifully photographed book (= with good photographs in it) ◊ [VN-ADJ] *She refused to be photographed nude.* ◊ [VN-ing] *They were photographed playing with their children.* **2** [V] **~ well, badly, etc.** to look or not look attractive in photographs: *Some people just don't photograph well.*

pho·tog·raph·er /fəˈtɒɡrəfə(r); AmE fəˈtɑːɡ-/ noun a person who takes photographs, especially as a job: *a wildlife/fashion/portrait photographer*

photo·graph·ic /ˌfəʊtəˈɡræfɪk; AmE ˌfoʊ-/ adj. connected with photographs or photography: *photographic equipment/film/images* ◊ *They produced a photographic record of the event.* ◊ *His paintings are almost photographic in detail.* ▶ **photo·graph·ic·al·ly** /-kli/ adv.

photographic 'memory noun [usually sing.] the ability to remember things accurately and in great detail after seeing them

pho·tog·raphy /fəˈtɒɡrəfi; AmE fəˈtɑːɡ-/ noun [U] the art, process or job of taking photographs or filming sth: *colour/flash/aerial photography* ◊ *fashion photography by David Burn* ◊ *Her hobbies include hiking and photography.* ◊ *the director of photography* (= the person who is in charge of the actual filming of a film/movie, programme, etc.) ◊ *Did you see the film about Antarctica? The photography was superb!*

photo·jour·nal·ism /ˌfəʊtəʊˈdʒɜːnəlɪzəm; AmE ˌfoʊtoʊ-ˈdʒɜːrn-/ noun [U] the work of giving news using mainly photographs, especially in a magazine

pho·ton /ˈfəʊtɒn; AmE ˈfoʊtɑːn/ noun (physics) a unit of ELECTROMAGNETIC energy

photo opportunity noun an occasion when a famous person arranges to be photographed doing sth that will impress the public

photo·sensi·tive /ˌfəʊtəʊˈsensətɪv; AmE ˌfoʊtoʊ-/ adj. reacting to light, for example by changing colour or producing an electrical signal

photo session (also **photo shoot**) noun an occasion when a photographer takes pictures of a famous person, fashion model, etc. for use in a magazine, etc.

Photo·stat™ /ˈfəʊtəstæt; AmE ˈfoʊ-/ noun a PHOTOCOPY or a machine that produces them

photo·syn·thesis /ˌfəʊtəʊˈsɪnθəsɪs; AmE ˌfoʊtoʊ-/ noun [U] (biology) the process by which green plants turn CARBON DIOXIDE and water into food using energy from sunlight

phrasal /ˈfreɪzl/ adj. of or connected with a phrase

phrasal 'verb noun (grammar) a verb combined with an adverb or a preposition, or sometimes both, to give a new meaning, for example *go in for, win over* and *see to* ⇨ Study pages B10–11

phrase /freɪz/ noun, verb
■ noun **1** (grammar) a group of words without a FINITE verb, especially one that forms part of a sentence. 'the green car' and 'on Friday morning' are phrases.—see also NOUN PHRASE **2** a group of words which have a particular meaning when used together: *a memorable/famous phrase* ◊ *She was, in her own favourite phrase, 'a woman without a past'.*—see also CATCHPHRASE **3** (music) a short series of notes that form a unit within a longer passage in a piece of music **IDM** see COIN v., TURN n.
■ verb **1** [VN] **~ sth (as sth)** to say or write sth in a particular way: *a carefully phrased remark* ◊ *I agree with what he says, but I'd have phrased it differently.* ◊ *Her order was phrased as a suggestion.* **2** [V, VN] to divide a piece of music into small groups of notes; to play or sing these in a particular way, especially in an effective way

phrase book noun a book containing lists of common expressions translated into another language, especially for people visiting a foreign country

phrase·ology /ˌfreɪziˈɒlədʒi; AmE -ˈɑːlə-/ noun [U] (formal) the particular way in which words and phrases are arranged when saying or writing sth

phras·ing /ˈfreɪzɪŋ/ noun [U] **1** the words used to express sth: *The phrasing of the report is ambiguous.* **2** (music) the way in which a musician or singer divides a piece of music into phrases by pausing in suitable places

phren·ology /frəˈnɒlədʒi; AmE -ˈnɑːl-/ noun [U] the study of the shape of the human head, which some people think is a guide to a person's character ▶ **phren·olo·gist** /frəˈnɒlədʒɪst; AmE -ˈnɑːl-/ noun

phylum /ˈfaɪləm/ noun (pl. **phyla** /-lə/) (biology) a group into which animals, plants, etc. are divided, smaller than a KINGDOM and larger than a CLASS—compare GENUS

phys·ic·al /ˈfɪzɪkl/ adj., noun
■ adj.
THE BODY | **1** [usually before noun] connected with a person's body rather than their mind: *physical fitness/strength/disabilities* ◊ *physical appearance/beauty* ◊ *The ordeal has affected both her mental and physical health.* ◊ *He tends to avoid all physical contact.*
REAL THINGS | **2** [only before noun] connected with things that actually exist or are present and can be seen, felt, etc. rather than things that only exist in a person's mind: *the physical world/universe/environment* ◊ *the physical properties* (=the colour, weight, shape, etc.) *of copper*
NATURE/SCIENCE | **3** [only before noun] according to the laws of nature: *It is a physical impossibility to be in two places at once.* **4** [only before noun] connected with the scientific study of forces such as heat, light, sound, etc. and how they affect objects: *physical chemistry/laws*
SEX | **5** involving sex: *physical love* ◊ *They are having a physical relationship.*
PERSON | **6** (informal) (of a person) liking to touch other people a lot: *She's not very physical.*
VIOLENT | **7** (informal) violent (used to avoid saying this in a direct way): *Are you going to cooperate or do we have to get physical?*
■ noun (also **physical exami'nation**) a medical examination of a person's body, for example, to check that they are fit enough to do a particular job

physical edu'cation noun = PE

physical ge'ography noun [U] **1** the scientific study of the natural features on the surface of the earth, for example mountains and rivers **2** the way in which the natural features of a place are arranged: *the physical geography of Scotland*

phys·ic·al·ity /ˌfɪzɪˈkæləti/ noun [U] (formal) the quality of being physical rather than emotional or spiritual

phys·ic·al·ly /ˈfɪzɪkli/ adv. **1** in a way that is connected with a person's body rather than their mind: *mentally and physically handicapped* ◊ *physically and emotionally exhausted* ◊ *I felt physically sick before the exam.* ◊ *I don't find him physically attractive.* ◊ *They were physically prevented from entering the building.* **2** according to the laws of nature or what is probable: *It's physically impossible to finish by the end of the week.*

physical 'science noun [U] (also **the physical 'sciences** [pl.]) the areas of science concerned with studying natural forces and things that are not alive, for example physics and chemistry—compare LIFE SCIENCES

physical 'therapist noun (AmE) = PHYSIOTHERAPIST

physical 'therapy noun (AmE) = PHYSIOTHERAPY

physical 'training noun = PT

phys·ician /fɪˈzɪʃn/ noun (formal, especially AmE) a doctor, especially one who is a specialist in general medicine and not SURGERY—compare SURGEON **HELP** This word is now old-fashioned in BrE. Doctor or GP is used instead.

physi·cist /ˈfɪzɪsɪst/ noun a scientist who studies physics: *a nuclear physicist*

phys·ics /ˈfɪzɪks/ noun [U] the scientific study of forces such as heat, light, sound, etc., of relationships between them, and how they affect objects: *a degree in physics* ◊ *particle/nuclear/theoretical physics* ◊ *the laws of physics* ◊ *a school physics department* ◊ *to study the physics of the electron*—see also ASTROPHYSICS, GEOPHYSICS

physio /ˈfɪziəʊ; AmE ˈfɪzioʊ/ noun (pl. **-os**) (BrE, informal) **1** [U] = PHYSIOTHERAPY **2** [C] = PHYSIOTHERAPIST

physio- /ˈfɪziəʊ; AmE ˈfɪzioʊ/ combining form (in nouns, adjectives and adverbs) **1** connected with nature **2** connected with PHYSIOLOGY

physi·ognomy /ˌfɪziˈɒnəmi; AmE -ˈɑːnə-/ noun (pl. **-ies**) (formal) the shape and features of a person's face

æ	ɑː	e	ɜː	ə	ɪ	iː	i	ɒ	ɔː	ʌ	ʊ	u	uː
cat	father	ten	bird	about	sit	see	many	got	saw	cup	put	actual	too

(BrE)

physi·olo·gist /ˌfɪziˈɒlədʒɪst; *AmE* -ˈɑːlə-/ *noun* a scientist who studies physiology

physi·ology /ˌfɪziˈɒlədʒi; *AmE* -ˈɑːlə-/ *noun* **1** [U] the scientific study of the normal functions of living things: *the department of anatomy and physiology* **2** [U, sing.] the way in which a particular living thing functions: *plant physiology* ◊ *the physiology of the horse* ▶ **physio·logic·al** /ˌfɪziəˈlɒdʒɪkl; *AmE* -ˈlɑːdʒ-/ *adj.*: *the physiological effect of space travel* **physio·lo·gic·al·ly** /-ɪkli/ *adv.*

physio·ther·ap·ist /ˌfɪziəʊˈθerəpɪst; *AmE* ˌfɪzioʊ-/ (also *informal* **physio**) (both *BrE*) (*AmE* ˌphysical ˈtherapist) *noun* a person whose job is to give patients physiotherapy

physio·ther·apy /ˌfɪziəʊˈθerəpi; *AmE* ˌfɪzioʊ-/ (also *informal* **physio**) (both *BrE*) (*AmE* ˌphysical ˈtherapy) *noun* [U] the treatment of disease, injury or weakness in the joints or muscles by exercises, MASSAGE and the use of light and heat

phys·ique /fɪˈziːk/ *noun* [U] the size and shape of a person's body: *He has the physique of a rugby player.* ◊ *a good/strong/youthful physique*

pi /paɪ/ *noun* (*geometry*) the symbol π used to show the RATIO of the CIRCUMFERENCE of (= distance around) a circle to its DIAMETER (= distance across), that is about 3.14159

pi·an·is·simo /ˌpiəˈnɪsɪməʊ; *AmE* -moʊ/ *adv.* (*abbr.* pp) (*music*) played or sung very quietly [OPP] FORTISSIMO ▶ **pi·an·is·simo** *adj.*

pi·an·ist /ˈpiənɪst/ *noun* a person who plays the piano: *a concert/jazz pianist*

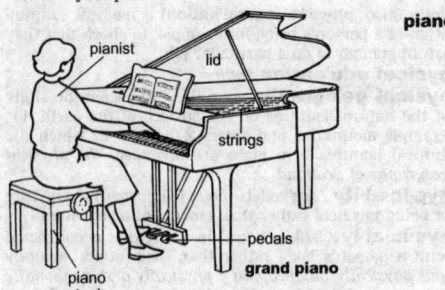

piano

pianist
lid
strings
pedals
grand piano
piano stool

upright piano

keyboard

piano *noun, adv.*

■ *noun* /piˈænəʊ; *AmE* -noʊ/ (*pl.* **-os**) (also *old-fashioned, formal* **pi·ano·forte** /piˌænəʊˈfɔːti; *AmE* piˌænoʊˈfɔːr-/) a large musical instrument played by pressing the black and white keys on the keyboard. The sound is produced by small hammers hitting the metal strings inside the piano: *to play the piano* ◊ *playing jazz* **on the piano** ◊ *piano music* ◊ *a piano teacher/lesson* ◊ *Ravel's piano concerto in G*—see also GRAND PIANO, UPRIGHT PIANO

■ *adv.* /ˈpjɑːnəʊ; *AmE* -noʊ/ (*abbr.* p) (*music*) played or sung quietly [OPP] FORTE ▶ **piano** *adj.*

pi·ano ac·cordion *noun* (*BrE*) = ACCORDION

pi·azza /piˈætsə; *AmE* piˈɑːzə/ *noun* a public square, especially in an Italian town

pic /pɪk/ *noun* (*informal*) a picture

pic·ar·esque /ˌpɪkəˈresk/ *adj.* (*formal*) connected with literature that describes the adventures of a person who

is sometimes dishonest but easy to like: *a picaresque novel*

pic·colo /ˈpɪkələʊ; *AmE* -loʊ/ *noun* (*pl.* **-os**) a musical instrument of the WOODWIND group, like a small FLUTE that plays high notes—picture on page 840

pick /pɪk/ *verb, noun*

■ *verb* **1** to choose sb/sth from a group of people or things: [VN] *Pick a number from one to twenty.* ◊ *She picked the best cake for herself.* ◊ *He picked his words carefully.* ◊ *Have I picked a bad time to talk to you?* ◊ [VN to inf] *He has been picked to play in this week's game.*—see also HAND-PICKED **2** [VN] to take flowers, fruit, etc. from the plant or the tree where they are growing: *to pick grapes/cotton* ◊ *flowers freshly picked from the garden* ◊ *to go blackberry picking* **3** to pull or remove sth or small pieces of sth from sth else, especially with your fingers: [VN+adv. / prep.] *She picked bits of fluff from his sweater.* ◊ *He picked the nuts off the top of the cake.* ◊ [VN] **to pick your nose** (= put your finger inside your nose to remove dried MUCUS) ◊ **to pick your teeth** (= use a small sharp piece of wood to remove pieces of food from your teeth) ◊ [VN-ADJ] *The dogs picked the bones clean* (= ate all the meat from the bones). **4** [V, VN] (*AmE*) = PLUCK (3) [IDM] **pick and 'choose** to choose only those things that you like or want very much: *You have to take any job you can get—you can't pick and choose.* **pick sb's 'brains** (*informal*) to ask sb a lot of questions about sth because they know more about the subject than you do **pick a 'fight/'quarrel (with sb)** to deliberately start a fight or an argument with sb **pick 'holes in sth** to find the weak points in sth such as a plan, suggestion, etc: *It was easy to pick holes in his arguments.* **pick a 'lock** to open a lock without a key, using sth such as a piece of wire **pick sb's 'pocket** to steal sth from sb's pocket without them noticing—related noun PICKPOCKET **pick up the 'bill, 'tab, etc. (for sth)** (*informal*) to pay for sth: *The company picked up the tab for his hotel room.* ◊ *The government will continue to pick up college fees for some students.* **pick up the 'pieces** to return or to help sb return to a normal situation, particularly after a shock or a disaster: *You cannot live your children's lives for them; you can only be there to pick up the pieces when things go wrong.* **pick up 'speed** to go faster **pick up the 'threads** to return to an earlier situation or way of life after an interruption **pick your 'way (across, along, among, over, through sth)** to walk carefully, choosing the safest, driest, etc. place to put your feet: *She picked her way delicately over the rough ground.* **pick a 'winner 1** to choose a horse, etc. that you think is most likely to win a race **2** (*informal*) to make a very good choice—more at BONE *n.*, PIECE *n.*, SHRED *n.* [PHR V] **'pick at sth 1** to eat food slowly, taking small amounts or bites because you are not hungry **2** to pull or touch sth several times: *He tried to undo the knot by picking at it with his fingers.*

ˌ**pick sb**↔'**off** (*informal*) to aim carefully at a person, an animal or an aircraft, especially one of a group, and then shoot them: *Snipers were picking off innocent civilians.* ˌ**pick sth**↔'**off** to remove sth from sth such as a tree, a plant, etc: *Pick off all the dead leaves.*

'**pick on sb/sth 1** to treat sb unfairly, by blaming, criticizing or punishing them: *She was picked on by the other girls because of her size.* **2** to choose sb/sth: *He picked on two of her statements which he said were untrue.*

ˌ**pick sb/sth**↔'**out 1** to choose sb/sth carefully from a group of people or things: *She was picked out from dozens of applicants for the job.* ◊ *He picked out the ripest peach for me.* **2** to recognize sb/sth from among other people or things: *See if you can pick me out in this photo.* ◊ *We couldn't pick out any familiar landmarks.* ˌ**pick sth**↔'**out 1** to play a tune on a musical instrument slowly without using written music: *He picked out the tune on the piano with one finger.* **2** to discover or recognize sth after careful study: *Read the play again and pick out the major themes.* **3** to make sth easy to see or hear: *a sign painted cream, with the lettering picked out in black* ◊ *The car lights picked out a cat running across the road.*

ˌ**pick sth**↔'**over**, ˌ**pick 'through sth** to examine a group of things carefully, especially to choose the ones you want: *Pick over the lentils and remove any little stones.* ◇ *I picked over the facts of the case.*

,**pick** '**up 1** to get better, stronger, etc.; to improve: *Trade usually picks up in the spring.* ◇ *The wind is picking up now.* ◇ *Sales have picked up 14% this year.*—related noun PICKUP **2** (*informal*) to start again; to continue: *Let's pick up where we left off yesterday.* **3** (*informal, especially AmE*) to put things away and make things neat, especially for sb else: *All I seem to do is cook, wash and pick up after the kids.* ,**pick sb** ↔ '**up 1** to go somewhere in your car and collect sb who is waiting for you [SYN] COLLECT: *I'll pick you up at five.* **2** to allow sb to get into your vehicle and take them somewhere: *The bus picks up passengers outside the airport.* **3** to rescue sb from the sea or from a dangerous place, especially one that is difficult to reach: *A lifeboat picked up survivors.* **4** (*informal*, often *disapproving*) to start talking to sb you do not know because you want to have a sexual relationship with them: *He goes to clubs to pick up girls.*—related noun PICKUP **5** (*informal*) (of the police) to arrest sb: *He was picked up by police and taken to the station for questioning.* **6** to make sb feel better: *Try this—it will pick you up.*—related noun PICK-ME-UP ,**pick sb/sth** ↔ '**up 1** to take hold of sb/sth and lift them/it up: *She went over to the crying child and picked her up.* ◇ *He picked up the phone and dialled the number.* **2** to receive an electronic signal, sound or picture: *We were able to pick up the BBC World Service.* ,**pick sth** ↔ '**up 1** to get information or a skill by chance rather than by making a deliberate effort: *to pick up bad habits* ◇ *Here's a tip I picked up from my mother.* ◇ *She picked up Spanish when she was living in Mexico.* **2** to identify or recognize sth: *Scientists can now pick up early signs of the disease.* **3** to collect sth from a place: *I picked up my coat from the cleaners.*—related noun PICKUP **4** to buy sth, especially cheaply or by chance: *We managed to pick up a few bargains at the auction.* **5** to get or obtain sth: *I seem to have picked up a terrible cold from somewhere.* ◇ *I picked up £30 in tips today.* **6** to find and follow a route: *to pick up the scent/trail of an animal* ◇ *We can pick up the motorway in a few miles.* **7** to return to an earlier subject or situation in order to continue it: *He picks up this theme again in later chapters of the book.* **8** to notice sth that is not very obvious; to see sth that you are looking for: *I picked up the faint sound of a car in the distance.* **9** (*especially AmE*) to put things away neatly: *Will you pick up all your toys?* **10** (*AmE*) to put things away and make a room neat: *to pick up a room/an apartment* ,**pick** '**up on sth 1** to notice sth and perhaps react to it: *She failed to pick up on the humour in his remark.* **2** to return to a point that has already been mentioned or discussed: *If I could just pick up on a question you raised earlier.* ,**pick sb** '**up on sth** to mention sth that sb has said or done that you think is wrong: *I knew he would pick me up on that slip sooner or later.* ,**pick yourself** '**up** to stand up again after you have fallen: *He just picked himself up and went on running.* ◇ (*figurative*) *She didn't waste time feeling sorry for herself— she just picked herself up and carried on.*

▪ *noun* **1** [sing.] an act of choosing sth: *Take your pick* (= choose). ◇ *The winner gets first pick of the prizes.* **2** [sing.] (*especially AmE*) a person or thing that is chosen: *She was his pick for best actress.* **3** [sing.] **the ~ of sth** the best thing or things in a group: *We're reviewing the pick of this month's new books.* ◇ *I think we got the pick of the bunch* (= the best in the group). **4** = PICKAXE: *picks and shovels*— see also ICE PICK, TOOTHPICK

'**pick-and-mix** *adj.* (*BrE*) used to describe a way of putting sth together by choosing things from among a large variety of different items: *a pick-and-mix programme of study*

pick·axe (*AmE* also **pick·ax**) /ˈpɪkæks/ (also **pick**) *noun* a large heavy tool that has a curved metal bar with sharp ends fixed at the centre to a wooden handle. It is used for breaking rocks or hard ground.—picture at AXE

pick·er /ˈpɪkə(r)/ *noun* a person or machine that picks flowers, vegetables, etc. ~~cotton~~ *pickers*

picket /ˈpɪkɪt/ *noun, verb*

▪ *noun* **1** a person or group of people who stand outside the entrance to a building in order to protest about sth, especially in order to stop people from entering a factory, etc. during a strike; an occasion at which this happens: *Five pickets were arrested by police.* ◇ *I was on picket duty at the time.* ◇ *We are organizing a mass picket of the abortion clinic.*—see also PICKETER **2** a soldier or group of soldiers guarding a military base **3** a piece of wood that is pointed at the bottom so that it can be fixed in the ground, especially as part of a fence: *a picket fence*— picture at HOUSE

▪ *verb* to stand outside somewhere such as your place of work to protest about sth or to try and persuade people to join a strike: [VN] *200 workers were picketing the factory.* ◇ [V] *Striking workers picketed outside the plant.*

pick·et·er /ˈpɪkɪtə(r)/ *noun* (*AmE*) a person who takes part in a picket

picket·ing /ˈpɪkɪtɪŋ/ *noun* [U] the activity of standing outside the entrance to a building in order to protest about sth and stop people from entering the building: *mass picketing of the factory*

'**picket line** *noun* a line or group of PICKETS: *Fire crews refused to cross the picket line.*

pick·ings /ˈpɪkɪŋz/ *noun* [pl.] something, especially money, that can be obtained from a particular situation in an easy or a dishonest way: *easy/slim pickings* ◇ *There are rich pickings to be had by investing in this sort of company.*

pickle /ˈpɪkl/ *noun, verb*

▪ *noun* **1** [C, usually pl.] (*BrE*) a vegetable that has been preserved in VINEGAR or salt water and has a strong flavour, served cold with meat, salads, etc. **2** [U] (*BrE*) a cold thick spicy sauce made from fruit and vegetables that have been boiled, often sold in JARS and served with meat, cheese, etc. **3** [U, C] (*AmE*) = GHERKIN [IDM] **in a** '**pickle** (*informal*) in a difficult or unpleasant situation

▪ *verb* [VN] to preserve food in VINEGAR or salt water

pickled /ˈpɪkld/ *adj.* **1** (of food) preserved in VINEGAR: *pickled cabbage/herring/onions* **2** (*old-fashioned, informal*) drunk

'**pick-me-up** *noun* (*informal*) something that makes you feel better, happier, healthier, etc., especially medicine or an alcoholic drink: (*figurative*) *This deal would offer the best possible pick-me-up to the town's ailing economy.*

pick·pocket /ˈpɪkpɒkɪt; *AmE* -pɑːkɪt/ *noun* a person who steals money, etc. from other people's pockets, especially in crowded places

pick·up /ˈpɪkʌp/ *noun* **1** (also '**pickup truck**) [C] a motor vehicle with low sides and no roof at the back used, for example, by farmers—picture at TRUCK **2** [C] a person sb meets for the first time, for example in a bar, with whom they start a sexual relationship: *casual pickups* **3** [C] **~ (in sth)** an improvement: *a pickup in the housing market* **4** [U, C] an occasion when sb/sth is collected: *Goods are delivered not later than noon on the day after pickup.* **5** [C] the part of a record player or musical instrument that changes electrical signals into sound, or sound into electrical signals **6** [U] (*AmE*) a vehicle's ability to ACCELERATE (= increase in speed)

picky /ˈpɪki/ *adj.* (*informal*) (of a person) liking only particular things and difficult to please

pic·nic /ˈpɪknɪk/ *noun, verb*

▪ *noun* **1** an occasion when people pack a meal and take it to eat outdoors, especially in the countryside: *It's a nice day. Let's go for a picnic.* **2** the meal, usually consisting of sandwiches, salad and fruit, etc. that you take with you when you go on a picnic: *Let's eat our picnic by the lake.* ◇ *a picnic lunch/supper/basket* [IDM] **be no** '**picnic** (*informal*) to be difficult and cause a lot of problems: *Bringing up a family when you're unemployed is no picnic.*

▪ *verb* (**-ck-**) [V] to have a picnic: *No picnicking allowed* (= on a sign)

pic·nick·er /ˈpɪknɪkə(r)/ *noun* a person who is having a picnic

picto·gram /ˈpɪktəɡræm/ *noun* **1** a picture representing a word or phrase **2** a diagram that uses pictures to ~~represent~~ amounts or numbers of a particular thing

b	d	f	g	h	k	l	m	n	p	r
bad	**did**	**fall**	**get**	**hat**	**cat**	**leg**	**man**	**now**	**pen**	**red**

pic·tor·ial /pɪk'tɔːriəl/ adj. [usually before noun] **1** using or containing pictures: *a pictorial account/record of the expedition* **2** connected with pictures: *pictorial traditions* ▶ **pic·tor·ial·ly** /-əli/ adv.

pic·ture /'pɪktʃə(r)/ noun, verb
■ noun
PAINTING/DRAWING | **1** [C] a painting or drawing, etc. that shows a scene, a person or a thing: *A picture of flowers hung on the wall.* ◊ *The children were drawing pictures of their pets.* ◊ *She wanted a famous artist to paint her picture* (= a picture of herself). ◊ *a book with lots of pictures in it*
PHOTOGRAPH | **2** [C] a photograph: *We had our **picture** **taken** in front of the hotel.* ◊ *The picture shows the couple together on their yacht.* ◊ *Have you got any pictures of your trip?*
ON TV | **3** [C] an image on a television screen: *harrowing television pictures of the famine* ◊ *satellite pictures* ◊ *The picture isn't very clear tonight.*
DESCRIPTION | **4** [C, usually sing.] a description that gives you an idea in your mind of what sth is like: *The writer paints a gloomy picture of the economy.* ◊ *The police are trying **to build up a picture** of what happened.*
MENTAL IMAGE | **5** [C, usually sing.] a mental image or memory of sth: *I have a vivid picture of my grandfather smiling down at me when I was very small.*
GENERAL SITUATION | **6** (**the picture**) [sing.] the general situation concerning sb/sth: *Just a few years ago the picture was very different.* ◊ *The overall picture for farming is encouraging.*
MOVIES | **7** [C] a film/movie: *The movie won nine Academy Awards, including Best Picture.* ◊ (*especially AmE*) *I believe her husband's **in pictures** (= he acts in movies or works in the industry).*—see also MOTION PICTURE **8** (**the pictures**) [pl.] (*old-fashioned, informal*) the cinema/the movies: *Shall we go to the pictures tonight?*
IDM **be/look a 'picture** to look very beautiful or special: *The garden looks a picture in the summer.* **be the picture of 'health/ 'guilt/ 'misery, etc.** (*informal*) to look extremely healthy, guilty, etc. **get the 'picture** (*spoken*) to understand a situation, especially one that sb is describing to you: *'I pretended that I hadn't heard.' 'I get the picture.'* **in/out of the 'picture** involved/ not involved in a situation: *Morris is likely to win, with Jones out of the picture now.* **put/keep sb in the 'picture** (*informal*) to give sb the information they need in order to understand a situation: *Just to put you in the picture— there have been a number of changes here recently.*—more at BIG adj., PAINT v., PRETTY adj.
■ verb
IMAGINE | **1** ~ sb (**as sth**) to imagine sb/sth; to create an image of sb/sth in your mind: [VN] *I can still picture the house I grew up in.* ◊ *We found it hard to picture him as the father of teenage sons.* ◊ [VN-ing] *When he did not come home she pictured him lying dead on the roadside somewhere.* ◊ [V wh-] *I tried to picture what it would be like to live alone.*
DESCRIBE | **2** [VN] [often passive] ~ sb/sth **as sth** to describe or present sb/sth in a particular way [SYN] PORTRAY: *Before the trial Liz had been pictured as a frail woman dominated by her husband.*
SHOW IN PHOTOGRAPH | **3** [usually passive] to show sb/sth in a photograph or picture: [VN] *She is pictured here with her parents.* ◊ [VN-ing] *The team is pictured setting off on their European tour.* [also VN-ADJ]

'picture book noun a book with a lot of pictures, especially one for children

picture-'perfect adj. (*AmE*) exactly right in appearance or in the way things are done: *Her wedding day was picture-perfect.*

picture 'postcard noun (*old-fashioned*) a POSTCARD with a picture on one side

picture-'postcard adj. [only before noun] (*especially BrE*) (of places) very pretty: *a picture-postcard village*

'picture rail noun a narrow strip of wood attached to the walls of a room below the ceiling and used for hanging pictures from

pic·tur·esque /ˌpɪktʃə'resk/ adj. **1** (of a place, building, scene, etc.) pretty, especially in a way that looks old-fashioned: *a picturesque cottage/setting/village* **2** (of language) producing strong mental images by using unusual words: *a picturesque description of life at sea* ▶ **pic·tur·esque·ly** adv.: *The inn is picturesquely situated on the banks of the river.*

'picture window noun a very large window made of a single piece of glass

pid·dle /'pɪdl/ verb [V] (*old-fashioned, informal*) to URINATE

pid·dling /'pɪdlɪŋ/ adj. [only before noun] (*informal, disapproving*) small and unimportant: *I spent all day doing piddling little jobs.*

pidgin /'pɪdʒɪn/ noun [U] **1** a simple form of a language, especially English, Portuguese or Dutch, with a limited number of words, that are used together with words from a local language. It is used when people who do not speak the same language need to talk to each other. **2** (**Pidgin**) = TOK PISIN **3** ~ **English, French, Japanese, etc.** a way of speaking a language that uses simple words and forms, used when a person does not speak the language well, or when he or she is talking to sb who does not speak the language well: *I tried to get my message across in my pidgin Italian.*

pie /paɪ/ noun [C, U] **1** fruit baked in a dish with pastry on the bottom, sides and top: *a slice of apple pie* ◊ *Help yourself to some more pie.* ◊ *a pie dish*—picture on page A1 **2** (*especially BrE*) meat, vegetables, etc. baked in a dish with pastry on the bottom, sides and top: *a steak and kidney pie*—see also MINCE PIE, PORK PIE, SHEPHERD'S PIE—see also CUSTARD PIE IDM **a ,piece/,slice/,share of the 'pie** (*AmE*) a share of sth such as money, profits, etc. **,pie in the 'sky** (*informal*) an event that sb talks about that seems very unlikely to happen: *This talk of moving to Australia is all just pie in the sky.*—more at AMERICAN adj., EASY adj., EAT, FINGER n., NICE

pie·bald /'paɪbɔːld/ adj. (of a horse) with areas on it of two colours, usually black and white

piece /piːs/ noun, verb
■ noun
SEPARATE AMOUNT | **1** [C] ~ (**of sth**) (used especially with *of* and uncountable nouns) an amount of sth that has been cut or separated from the rest of it; a standard amount of sth: *a piece of string/wood* ◊ *She wrote something on a small piece of paper.* ◊ *a large piece of land* ◊ *a piece of cake/cheese/meat* ◊ *He cut the pizza into bite-sized pieces.* ◊ *I've got a piece of grit in my eye.* ⇨ note on page 953
PART | **2** [C, usually pl.] one of the bits or parts that sth breaks into: *There were tiny pieces of glass all over the road.* ◊ *The boat had been smashed **to pieces** on the rocks.* ◊ *The vase lay **in pieces** on the floor.* **3** [C] one of the parts that sth is made of: *He took the clock **to pieces**.* ◊ *a missing piece of the puzzle* ◊ *The bridge was taken down **piece by piece**.* ◊ *a 500 piece jigsaw*—see also ONE-PIECE, TWO-PIECE, THREE-PIECE
SINGLE ITEM | **4** [C] (used especially with *of* and uncountable nouns) a single item of a particular type, especially one that forms part of a set: *a piece of clothing/furniture/ luggage* ◊ *a piece of equipment/machinery* ◊ *a 28-piece dinner service* **5** [C] ~ **of sth** used with many uncountable nouns to describe a single example or an amount of sth: *a piece of advice/information/news* ◊ *an interesting piece of research* ◊ *Isn't that a piece of luck?* **6** [C] ~ (**of sth**) a single item of writing, art, music, etc. that sb has produced or created: *a piece of art/music/poetry* ◊ *They performed pieces by Bach and Handel.* ◊ (*formal*) *They have some beautiful pieces* (= works of art, etc.) *in their home.*—see also MASTERPIECE, MUSEUM PIECE, PARTY PIECE, PERIOD PIECE, SHOWPIECE ⇨ note on page 953
NEWS ARTICLE | **7** [C] an article in a newspaper or magazine or a broadcast on television or radio: *Did you see her piece about the Internet in the paper today?*—see also SET PIECE
COIN | **8** [C] a coin of the value mentioned: *a 50p piece* ◊ *a five-cent piece*
IN CHESS, etc. | **9** [C] one of the small figures or objects that you move around in games such as CHESS

SHARE OF STH | **10** [sing.] **~ of sth** (*especially AmE*) a part or share of sth: *companies seeking a piece of the market* GUN | **11** [C] (*AmE, slang*) a gun

HELP You will find other compounds ending in **piece** at their place in the alphabet.

IDM fall to 'pieces 1 (usually used in the progressive tenses) (of things) to become very old and in bad condition because of long use: *Our car is falling to pieces, we've had it so long.* **2** (of a person, an organization, a plan, etc.) to stop working; to be destroyed: *He's worried that the business will fall to pieces without him.* **give sb a piece of your 'mind** (*informal*) to tell sb that you disapprove of their behaviour or are angry with them **go to 'pieces** (*informal*) (of a person) to be so upset or afraid that you cannot manage to live or work normally **(all) in one 'piece** (*informal*) safe; not damaged or hurt, especially after a journey or dangerous experience: *They were lucky to get home in one piece.* **(all) of a 'piece** (*formal*) **1** all the same or similar: *The houses are all of a piece.* **2** all at the same time: *The house was built all of a piece in 1754.* **pick/pull/tear sb/sth to 'pieces/'shreds** (*informal*) to criticize sb, or their work or ideas, very severely **a ,piece of 'cake** (*informal*) a thing that is very easy to do **a ,piece of 'piss** (*BrE*, △, *slang*) a thing that is very easy to do—more at ACTION, BIT, LONG *adj.*, NASTY, PICK *v.*, PIE, SAY *v.*, VILLAIN

■ *verb*

PHRV ,piece sth↔to'gether 1 to understand a story, situation, etc. by taking all the facts and details about it and putting them together: *Police are trying to piece together the last hours of her life.* **2** to put all the separate parts of sth together to make a complete whole: *to piece together a jigsaw*

VOCABULARY BUILDING
pieces

If you want to talk about a small amount or one example of something that is normally an uncountable noun, there is a range of words you can use. You must choose the right one to go with the substance you are talking about.

Piece and (*BrE, informal*) **bit** are very general words and can be used with most uncountable nouns: *a piece of paper / wood / string / cake / fruit / meat / work / research / advice* ◊ *a bit of paper / work / chocolate / luck.*

A **slice** is a thin flat piece: *a slice of bread / cake / salami / cheese / pie /apple* ◊ (figurative) *a slice of life.*

A **chunk** is a thick, solid piece: *a chunk of cheese / bread / rock* ◊ *a chunk of land* (= a fairly large piece).

A **lump** is a piece of something solid without any particular shape: *a lump of coal / rock / mud.*

A **fragment** is a very small piece of something that is broken or damaged: *fragments of glass* ◊ (figurative) *fragments of conversation.* It can also be used with countable nouns to mean a small part of something: *a fragment of the story.*

A **speck** is a tiny piece of powder: *a speck of dust / dirt.* You can also say: *a speck of light.*

Drop is used with liquids: *a drop of water / rain / blood / milk / whisky.*

A **pinch** is as much as you can hold between your finger and thumb: *a pinch of salt / cinnamon.*

A **portion** is enough for one person: *a portion of chicken / fish and chips.* It can also be used with some countable nouns to mean a part of something.

---

pièce de ré·sist·ance /ˌpjes də reˈzɪstɒs; *AmE* -stɑːns/ *noun* [usually sing.] (*pl.* **pièces de ré·sist·ance** /ˌpjes də reˈzɪstɒs; *AmE* ˌrezi:ˈstɑːns/) (from *French, written*) the most important or impressive part of a group or series of things

piece·meal /ˈpiːsmiːl/ *adj.* [usually before noun] (often *disapproving*) done or happening gradually at different times and often in different ways, rather than carefully planned at the beginning: *a piecemeal approach to dealing with the problem* ◊ *piecemeal changes/reforms* ▶ **piecemeal** *adv.*: *The reforms were implemented piecemeal.*

'piece rate *noun* an amount of money paid for each thing or amount of sth that a worker produces

piece·work /ˈpiːswɜːk; *AmE* -wɜːrk/ *noun* [U] work that is paid for by the amount done and not by the hours worked

'pie chart *noun* a diagram consisting of a circle that is divided into sections to show the size of particular amounts in relation to the whole—picture at CHART

pied /paɪd/ *adj.* (especially of birds) of two or more different colours, especially black and white

pied-à-terre /ˌpjeɪd ɑː ˈteə(r); *AmE* ˈter/ *noun* (*pl.* **pieds-à-terre** /ˌpjeɪd ɑː/) (from *French*) a small flat/apartment, usually in a town, that you do not live in as your main home but keep for use when necessary

pier /pɪə(r); *AmE* pɪr/ *noun* **1** a long structure built in the sea and joined to the land at one end, often with places of entertainment on it **2** a long low structure built in a lake, river or the sea and joined to the land at one end, used by boats to allow passengers to get on and off: *The river bus leaves from Pier 4.* **3** (*technical*) a large strong piece of wood, metal or stone that is used to support a roof, wall, bridge, etc.

pierce /pɪəs; *AmE* pɪrs/ *verb* **1 ~ (through) sth** to make a small hole in sth, or to go through sth, with a sharp object: [VN] *The arrow pierced his shoulder.* ◊ *He pierced another hole in his belt with his knife.* ◊ *to have your ears/ nose pierced* (= to have a small hole made in your ears/ nose so that you can wear jewellery there) ◊ (figurative) *She was pierced to the heart with guilt.* ◊ [V] *The knife pierced through his coat.* **2 ~ (through) sth** (*literary*) (of light, sound, etc.) to be suddenly seen or heard: [VN] *Sirens pierced the silence of the night.* ◊ *Shafts of sunlight pierced the heavy mist.* [also V] **3 ~ (through) sth** to force a way through a barrier: [VN] *They failed to pierce the Liverpool defence.* [also V]

pier·cing /ˈpɪəsɪŋ; *AmE* ˈpɪrsɪŋ/ *adj.* **1** [usually before noun] (of eyes or the way they look at sb) seeming to notice things about another person that would not normally be noticed, especially in a way that makes that person feel anxious or embarrassed: *She looked at me with piercing blue eyes.* ◊ *a piercing look/gaze* **2** [usually before noun] (of sounds) very high, loud and unpleasant: *a piercing shriek/scream/whistle* ◊ *She has such a piercing voice.* **3** [only before noun] (of feelings) affecting you very strongly, especially in a way that causes you pain: *piercing sadness/fear/nostalgia* **4** (of the wind or cold) very strong and feeling as if it can pass through your clothes and skin **5** [only before noun] sharp and able to make a hole in sth: *The belly of the animal is covered in long piercing spikes.* ▶ **pier·cing·ly** *adv.*: *His eyes were piercingly blue.* ◊ *The weather remained piercingly cold.*

piety /ˈpaɪəti/ *noun* [U] the state of having or showing a deep respect for sb/sth, especially for God and religion; the state of being PIOUS **OPP** IMPIETY

pif·fle /ˈpɪfl/ *noun* [U] (*old-fashioned, informal*) nonsense: *That's absolute piffle!*

pif·fling /ˈpɪflɪŋ/ *adj.* (*informal, disapproving*) small and unimportant: *piffling amounts*

pig /pɪg/ *noun, verb*

■ *noun* **1** (also **hog** especially in *AmE*) an animal with pink, black or brown skin, short legs, a broad nose and a short curly tail. Pigs are kept on farms for their meat (called PORK) or live in the wild: *a pig farmer* ◊ *Pigs were grunting and squealing in the yard.*—see also BOAR, SOW, PIGLET, SWINE, GUINEA PIG **2** (*informal, disapproving*) an unpleasant or offensive person; a person who is dirty or GREEDY: *Arrogant pig!* ◊ *Don't be such a pig!* ◊ *The greedy pig's eaten all the biscuits!* ◊ *She made a pig of herself with the ice cream* (= ate too much). ◊ *He's a real male chauvinist pig* (= a man who does not think women are equal to men). **3** (*slang*) an offensive word for a police

æ	ɑː	e	ɜː	ə	ɪ	iː	i	ɒ	ɔː	ʌ	ʊ	u	uː
cat	father	ten	bird	about	sit	see	many	got	saw	cup	put	actual	too
								(BrE)					

officer **IDM** **make a ¹pig's ear (out) of sth** (*BrE, informal*) to do sth badly; to make a MESS of sth **(buy) a pig in a ¹poke** if you **buy a pig in a poke**, you buy sth without seeing it or knowing if it is satisfactory **a pig of a sth** (*BrE, informal*) a difficult or unpleasant thing or task: *I've had a pig of a day.* **pig/piggy in the ¹middle 1** a children's game where two people throw a ball to each other over the head of another person who tries to catch it **2** a person who is caught between two people or groups who are fighting or arguing **pigs might ¹fly** (*BrE*) (*AmE* **when pigs ¹fly**) (*ironic, saying*) used to show that you do not believe sth will ever happen: *'With a bit of luck, we'll be finished by the end of the year.' 'Yes, and pigs might fly!'*
▪ *verb* (**-gg-**) [VN] **~ sth | ~ yourself (on sth)** (*BrE, informal*) to eat too much of sth: *I had a whole box of chocolates and pigged the lot!* ◊ *Don't give me cakes—I'll just pig myself.* **PHRV** **,pig ¹out (on sth)** (*informal*) to eat too much food: *They pigged out on pizza.*

pi·geon /ˈpɪdʒɪn/ *noun* a fat grey and white bird with short legs. Pigeons are common in cities and also live in woods and fields where people shoot them for sport or food: *the sound of pigeons cooing*—compare DOVE—see also CARRIER PIGEON, CLAY PIGEON, HOMING PIGEON, WOOD PIGEON **IDM** **be sb's pigeon** (*old-fashioned, BrE*) to be sb's responsibility or business—more at CAT

¹pigeon-hole *noun, verb*
▪ *noun* one of a set of small boxes that are fixed on a wall and open at the front, used for putting letters, messages, etc. in; one of a similar set of boxes that are part of a desk, used for keeping papers, documents, etc. in: *If you can't come, leave a note in my pigeon-hole.*
▪ *verb* **1** [VN] **~ sb (as sth)** to decide that sb belongs to a particular group or type without thinking deeply enough about it and considering what other qualities they might have [SYN] CATEGORIZE, LABEL: *He has been pigeon-holed as a youth writer.* **2** [VN] to decide to deal with sth later or to forget it: *Plans to build a new school have been pigeon-holed.*

,pigeon-¹toed *adj.* having feet that turn inwards and not straight forward

pig·gery /ˈpɪgəri/ *noun* (*pl.* **-ies**) a place where pigs are kept or bred

piggy /ˈpɪgi/ *noun, adj.*
▪ *noun* (*pl.* **-ies**) a child's word for a pig **IDM** see = PIG IN THE MIDDLE
▪ *adj.* [only before noun] (*informal, disapproving*) (of a person's eyes) like those of a pig

pig·gy·back /ˈpɪgibæk/ *noun, verb*
▪ *noun* a ride on sb's back, while he or she is walking: *Give me a piggyback, Daddy!* ◊ *a piggyback ride* ► **pig·gy·back** *adv.*: *to ride piggyback*
▪ *verb* **PHRV** **¹piggyback on sb/sth** to use sth that already exists as a support for your own work; to use a larger organization, etc. for your own advantage

¹piggy bank *noun* a container in the shape of a pig, with a narrow opening in the top for putting coins in, used by children to save money—compare MONEY BOX

,pig-¹headed *adj.* unwilling to change your opinion about sth, in a way that other people think is annoying and unreasonable ► **pig-headed·ness** *noun* [U]

¹pig iron *noun* [U] a form of iron that is not pure

pig·let /ˈpɪglət/ *noun* a young pig

pig·ment /ˈpɪgmənt/ *noun* [U, C] **1** a substance that exists naturally in people, animals and plants and gives their skin, leaves, etc. a particular colour **2** a coloured powder that is mixed with a liquid to produce paint, etc.

pig·men·ta·tion /ˌpɪgmenˈteɪʃn/ *noun* [U] the presence of pigments in skin, hair, leaves, etc. that causes them to be a particular colour

pig·ment·ed /ˈpɪgmentɪd/ *adj.* (especially of skin) having a natural colour

pigmy *noun, adj.* = PYGMY

pig·skin /ˈpɪgskɪn/ *noun* **1** [U] leather made from the skin of a pig: *a pigskin suitcase* **2** [sing.] (*AmE, informal*) the ball used in American football

pig·sty /ˈpɪgstaɪ/ (also **sty**) *noun* (*pl.* **-ies**) (*AmE* also **¹pig-**

pen /ˈpɪgpen/) **1** [C] a small building or an enclosed area where pigs are kept **2** [sing.] (*informal*) a very dirty or untidy place

pig·swill /ˈpɪgswɪl/ *noun* [U] = SWILL

pig·tail /ˈpɪgteɪl/ (*BrE*) (also **braid** *AmE, BrE*) *noun* hair that is tied together into one or two bunches and twisted into a PLAIT or PLAITS, worn either at the back of the head or one on each side of the head: *She wore her hair in pigtails.*—compare PONYTAIL—picture at HAIR

pike /paɪk/ *noun* **1** (*pl.* **pike**) a large FRESHWATER fish with very sharp teeth **2** a weapon with a sharp blade on a long wooden handle, used in the past by soldiers on foot **3** (*AmE*) = TURNPIKE **4** (*dialect*) a pointed top of a hill in N England: *the Langdale Pikes* **IDM** **come down the ¹pike** (*AmE, informal*) to happen; to become noticeable: *We're hearing a lot about new inventions coming down the pike.*

pike·staff /ˈpaɪkstɑːf; *AmE* -stæf/ *noun* **IDM** see PLAIN *adj.*

pilaf /ˈpiːlæf; *AmE* pɪˈlɑːf/ (also **pilau** /ˈpiːlaʊ/) *noun* [U, C] a hot spicy Eastern dish of rice and vegetables and often pieces of meat or fish

pi·las·ter /pɪˈlæstə(r)/ *noun* (*technical*) a flat column that sticks out from the wall of a building, used as decoration

pil·chard /ˈpɪltʃəd; *AmE* -tʃərd/ *noun* a small sea fish that is used for food

pile /paɪl/ *noun, verb*
▪ *noun*—see also PILES **1** [C] a number of things that have been placed on top of each other: *a pile of books / clothes / bricks* ◊ *He arranged the documents in neat piles.* ◊ *She looked in horror at the mounting pile of letters on her desk.* **2** [C] a mass of sth that is high in the middle and wider at the bottom than at the top: *a pile of sand* ◊ *piles of dirty washing* **3** [C] **~ of sth** (*informal*) a lot of sth: *I have got piles of work to do.* ◊ *He walked out leaving a pile of debts behind him.* **4** [U, sing.] the short threads, pieces of wool, etc. that form the soft surface of carpets and some fabrics such as VELVET: *a deep-pile carpet* **5** [C] a large wooden, metal or stone post that is fixed into the ground and used to support a building, bridge etc. **6** [C] (*formal or humorous*) a large impressive building **IDM** **(at the) bottom/ top of the ¹pile** in the least/most important position in a group of people or things **make a/your ¹pile** (*informal*) to make a lot of money
▪ *verb* **1** [VN] **~ sth (up)** to put things one on top of another; to form a pile: *She piled the boxes one on top of the other.* ◊ *The clothes were piled high on the chair.* ◊ *Snow was piled up against the door.* **2** [VN+adv. / prep.] **~ A in(to)/on(to) B | ~ B with A** to put sth on/into sth; to load sth with sth: *The sofa was piled high with cushions.* ◊ *She piled everything into her suitcase.* ◊ *He piled as much food as he could onto his plate.* ◊ *He piled his plate with as much food as he could.*—see also STOCKPILE **3** [V+adv. / prep.] (*informal*) (of a number of people) to go somewhere quickly without order or control: *The coach finally arrived and we all piled on.* **IDM** **pile on the ¹agony/ ¹gloom** (*informal, especially BrE*) to make an unpleasant situation worse: *Bosses piled on the agony with threats of more job losses.* **PHRV** **,pile ¹on** (especially of a person's weight) to increase quickly: *The weight just piled on while I was abroad.* **,pile sth↔¹on 1** to make sth increase rapidly: *The team piled on the points in the first half of the game.* ◊ *I've been piling on the pounds* (= I have put on weight) *recently.* **2** to express a feeling in a much stronger way than is necessary: *Don't pile on the drama!* ◊ *Things aren't really that bad—she does tend to pile it on.* **3** to give sb more or too much of sth: *The German team piled on the pressure in the last 15 minutes.* **,pile sth ¹on(to) sb** to give sb a lot of sth to do, carry, etc: *He felt his boss was piling too much work on him.* **,pile ¹up** to become larger in quantity or amount: *Work always piles up at the end of the year.*

pile-driver /ˈpaɪldraɪvə(r)/ *noun* **1** (*BrE, informal*) a very heavy kick or blow **2** a machine for forcing heavy posts into the ground

piles /paɪlz/ *noun* [U] painful swollen VEINS at or near the ANUS [SYN] HAEMORRHOIDS

aɪ	aʊ	eɪ	əʊ	oʊ	ɔɪ	ɪə	eə	ʊə	j	w
my	now	say	go (BrE)	go (AmE)	boy	near	hair	pure	yes	wet

'pile-up *noun* a road accident involving several vehicles crashing into each other: *Three people died in a multiple pile-up in freezing fog.*

pil·fer /ˈpɪlfə(r)/ *verb* ~ (sth) (from sb/sth) to steal things of little value or in small quantities, especially from the place where you work: [V] *He was caught pilfering.* ◊ [VN] *She regularly pilfered stamps and stationery from work.* ▶ **pil·fer·age** /ˈpɪlfərɪdʒ/ *noun* [U] (*formal*): *pilferage of goods* **pil·fer·ing** *noun* [U]: *We know that pilfering goes on.*

pil·grim /ˈpɪlgrɪm/ *noun* a person who travels to a holy place for religious reasons: *Muslim pilgrims on their way to Mecca* ◊ *Christian pilgrims visiting Lourdes*

pil·grim·age /ˈpɪlgrɪmɪdʒ/ *noun* [C, U] **1** a journey to a holy place for religious reasons: *to go on / make a pilgrimage* **2** a journey to a place that is connected with sb/sth that you admire or respect: *His grave has become a place of pilgrimage.*

pill /pɪl/ *noun, verb*
- *noun* **1** [C] a small flat round piece of medicine that you swallow without chewing it: *a vitamin pill*—see also PEP PILL, SLEEPING PILL—picture on page 599 **2** (**the pill** or **the Pill**) [sing.] a pill that some women take to prevent them becoming pregnant: *the contraceptive pill* ◊ *to be / go on the pill*—see also MORNING-AFTER PILL **3** [C] (*AmE*) an annoying person **IDM** **sugar / sweeten the pill** to do sth that makes an unpleasant situation seem less unpleasant **SYN** SUGAR-COAT—more at BITTER *adj.*
- *verb* [V] (of a piece of clothing, especially one made of wool) to become covered in very small balls of FIBRE

pil·lage /ˈpɪlɪdʒ/ *verb* to steal things from a place or region, especially in a war, using violence: [V] *The rebels went looting and pillaging.* ◊ [VN] *The town had been pillaged and burned.* ▶ **pil·lage** *noun* [U] (*formal*): *They brought back horrific accounts of murder and pillage.*—compare LOOT, PLUNDER

pil·lar /ˈpɪlə(r)/ *noun* **1** a large round stone, metal or wooden post that is used to support a bridge, the roof of a building, etc., especially when it is also decorative **2** a large round stone, metal or wooden post that is built to remind people of a famous person or event **SYN** COLUMN **3** ~ of sth a mass of sth that is shaped like pillar: *a pillar of smoke / rock* **4** ~ of sth a strong supporter of sth; an important member of sth: *a pillar of the Church* ◊ *a pillar of society* **5** ~ of sth a person who has a lot of a particular quality: *She is a pillar of strength in a crisis.* **6** a basic part or feature of a system, organization, belief, etc: *the central pillar of this theory* **IDM** **be driven, pushed, etc. from ,pillar to 'post** to be forced to go from one person or situation to another without achieving anything

'pillar box *noun* (*old-fashioned, BrE*) a tall red metal box in the street, used for putting letters in which are being sent by post—compare LETTER BOX, POSTBOX

pil·lared /ˈpɪləd; *AmE* -ərd/ *adj.* [only before noun] (of a building or part of a building) having PILLARS

pill·box /ˈpɪlbɒks; *AmE* -bɑːks/ *noun* a small shelter for soldiers, often partly underground, from which a gun can be fired

pil·lion /ˈpɪliən/ *noun* a seat for a passenger behind the driver of a motorcycle: *a pillion passenger / seat* ▶ **pil·lion** *adv.*: *to ride pillion*

pil·lock /ˈpɪlək/ *noun* (*BrE, slang*) a stupid person

pil·lory /ˈpɪləri/ *verb, noun*
- *verb* (**pil·lor·ies**, **pil·lory·ing**, **pil·lor·ied**, **pil·lor·ied**) [VN] [often passive] (*written*) to criticize sb strongly in public: *He was regularly pilloried by the press for his radical ideas.*
- *noun* (*pl.* -**ies**) a wooden frame, with holes for the head and hands, which people were locked into in the past as a punishment—compare STOCKS (9)

pil·low /ˈpɪləʊ; *AmE* -loʊ/ *noun, verb*
- *noun* **1** a square or RECTANGULAR piece of fabric filled with soft material, used to rest your head on in bed: *She lay back against the pillows.* ◊ *pillow talk* (= conversations in bed between lovers) ◊ *He lay back on the grass using his backpack as a pillow.*—picture at BED **2** (*AmE*) = CUSHION

- *verb* [VN] (*literary*) to rest sth, especially your head, on an object: *She lay on the grass, her head pillowed on her arms.*

pil·low·case /ˈpɪləʊkeɪs; *AmE* -loʊ-/ (*also* **'pil·low·slip** /ˈpɪləʊslɪp; *AmE* -loʊ-/*)* *noun* a fabric cover for a PILLOW, that can be removed

pilot /ˈpaɪlət/ *noun, verb, adj.*
- *noun* **1** a person who operates the controls of an aircraft, especially as a job: *an airline pilot* ◊ *a fighter pilot* ◊ *The accident was caused by pilot error.*—see also AUTOMATIC PILOT, AUTOPILOT, CO-PILOT, TEST PILOT **2** a person with special knowledge of a difficult area of water, for example, a canal, the entrance to a harbour, etc., whose job is to guide ships through it **3** a single television programme that is made in order to find out whether people will like it and want to watch further programmes **4** = PILOT LIGHT
- *verb* [VN] **1** to fly an aircraft or guide a ship: to act as a pilot: *The plane was piloted by the instructor.* ◊ *The captain piloted the boat into a mooring.* **2** ~ sth (through sth) to guide sb/sth somewhere, especially through a complicated place or system: *She piloted a bill on the rights of part-time workers through parliament.* **3** to test a new product, idea, etc. with a few people or in a small area before it is introduced everywhere
- *adj.* [only before noun] done on a small scale in order to see if sth is successful enough to do on a large scale: *a pilot project / study / survey* ◊ *a pilot episode* (= of a radio or television series)

'pilot light (*also* **pilot**) *noun* a small flame that burns all the time, for example on a gas BOILER, and lights a larger flame when the gas is turned on

'pilot officer *noun* (*abbr.* **PO**) an officer of the lowest rank in the British air force

'pilot whale *noun* a small WHALE that lives in warm seas

pi·mento /pɪˈmentəʊ; *AmE* -toʊ/ *noun* (*pl.* -**os**) a small red PEPPER with a mild taste

pimp /pɪmp/ *noun, verb*
- *noun* a man who controls prostitutes and lives on the money that they earn
- *verb* [V] ~ (for sb) to get customers for a prostitute

pim·ple /ˈpɪmpl/ *noun* a small raised spot on the skin: *a pimple on her chin*—compare SPOT—see also GOOSE PIMPLES ▶ **pim·ply** /ˈpɪmpli/ *adj.*: *pimply skin* ◊ *a pimply youth*

PIN /pɪn/ (*also* **'PIN number**) *noun* the abbreviation for 'personal identification number' (a number given to you, for example by a bank so that you can use a plastic card to take out money from a cash machine)

pin /pɪn/ *noun, verb*
- *noun*

FOR FASTENING / JOINING | **1** a short thin piece of stiff wire with a sharp point at one end and a round head at the other, used especially for fastening together pieces of fabric when sewing—see also BOBBY PIN, DRAWING PIN, HAIRPIN, LINCHPIN, PINS AND NEEDLES, SAFETY PIN—picture at SEW

JEWELLERY | **2** a short thin piece of stiff wire with a sharp point at one end and an item of decoration at the other, worn as jewellery: *a diamond pin*—see also TIEPIN **3** (*especially AmE*) = BROOCH

BADGE | **4** (*especially AmE*) a type of BADGE that is fastened with a pin at the back: *He supports the group and wears its pin on his lapel.*

MEDICAL | **5** a piece of steel used to support a bone in your body when it has been broken

ELECTRICAL | **6** one of the metal parts that stick out of an electric PLUG and fit into a SOCKET: *a 2-pin plug*—picture at PLUG

IN GAMES | **7** a wooden or plastic object that is shaped like a bottle and that players try to knock down in games such as BOWLING—see also NINEPINS, TENPIN

IN GOLF | **8** a stick with a flag on top of it, placed in a hole so that players can see where they are aiming for—see also LINCHPIN

LEGS | **9** (**pins**) [pl.] (*informal*) a person's legs

P

ON SMALL BOMB | **10** a small piece of metal on a HAND GRENADE that stops it from exploding and is pulled out just before the HAND GRENADE is thrown

IDM for two '**pins** (*old-fashioned, BrE*) used to say that you would like to do sth, even though you know that it would not be sensible: *I'd kill him for two pins.*—more at HEAR

■ *verb* (-nn-) [VN+*adv. / prep.*]
FASTEN/JOIN | **1** to attach sth onto another thing or fasten things together with a pin, etc: *She pinned the badge onto her jacket.* ◊ *A message had been pinned to the notice board.* ◊ *Pin all the pieces of material together.* ◊ *She always wears her hair pinned back.*

PREVENT MOVEMENT | **2** to make sb unable to move by holding them or pressing them against sth: *They pinned him against a wall and stole his wallet.* ◊ *He grabbed her arms and pinned them to her sides.* ◊ *They found him pinned under the wreckage of the car.*

IDM ,pin (all) your '**hopes on sb/sth** | ,pin your '**faith on sb/sth** to rely on sb/sth completely for success or help: *The company is pinning its hopes on the new project.* **PHRV** ,pin sb↔'**down 1** to make sb unable to move by holding them firmly: *Two men pinned him down until the police arrived.* **2** to find sb and make them answer a question or tell you sth you need to know: *I need the up-to-date sales figures but I can never pin him down at the office.* ,pin sb↔'**down (to sth/doing sth)** to make sb make a decision or say clearly what they think or what they intend to do: *It's difficult to pin her down to fixing a date for a meeting.* ,pin sth↔'**down** to explain or understand sth exactly: *The cause of the disease is difficult to pin down precisely.* '**pin sth on sb** to make sb be blamed for sth, especially for sth they did not do: *No one would admit responsibility. They all tried to pin the blame on someone else.* ◊ *You can't pin this one on me—I wasn't even there!*

pina·fore /'pɪnəfɔː(r)/ *noun* **1** (also *informal* **pinny**) (both *BrE*) a loose piece of clothing without sleeves, worn over the front of your clothes to keep them clean, for example when cooking—compare APRON **2** (also '**pinafore dress**) (both *especially BrE*) (*AmE usually* **jumper**) a loose dress with no sleeves, usually worn over a shirt or BLOUSE

pin·ball /'pɪnbɔːl/ *noun* [U] a game played on a **pinball machine**, in which the player sends a small metal ball up a sloping board and scores points as it bounces off objects. The player tries to prevent the ball from reaching the bottom of the machine by pressing two buttons at the side.

pince-nez /ˌpæs 'neɪ/ *noun* (*pl.* **pince-nez**) (from *French*) a pair of glasses, worn in the past, with a spring that fits on the nose, instead of parts at the sides that fit over the ears

pin·cer /'pɪnsə(r)/ *noun* **1** (**pincers**) [pl.] a tool made of two crossed pieces of metal, used for holding things firmly and pulling things, for example nails out of wood: *a pair of pincers* **2** [C] one of a pair of curved CLAWS of some types of shellfish—picture on page A7

'**pincer movement** *noun* [usually sing.] a military attack in which an army attacks the enemy from two sides at the same time

pinch /pɪntʃ/ *verb, noun*
■ *verb*
WITH THUMB AND FINGER | **1** [VN] to take a piece of sb's skin between your thumb and first finger and squeeze hard, especially to hurt the person: *My sister's always pinching me and it really hurts.* ◊ *He pinched the baby's cheek playfully.* ◊ (*figurative*) *She had to pinch herself to make sure she was not dreaming.* **2** [VN] to hold sth tightly between the thumb and finger or between two things that are pressed together: *Pinch the nostrils together with your thumb and finger to stop the bleeding.* ◊ *a pinched nerve in the neck*
OF A SHOE | **3** if sth such as a shoe **pinches** part of your body, it hurts you because it is too tight: [V] *These new shoes pinch.* [also VN]
STEAL | **4** [VN] ~ **sth (from sb/sth)** (*BrE, informal*) to steal sth, especially sth small and not very valuable: *Kids have been pinching our apples again.* ◊ *Who's pinched my pen?*

COST TOO MUCH | **5** [VN] to cost a person or an organization a lot of money or more than they can spend: *Higher interest rates are already pinching the housing industry.*
ARREST | **6** [VN] (*old-fashioned, BrE, informal*) to arrest sb: *I was pinched for dangerous driving.*

IDM pinch '**pennies** (*informal*) to try to spend as little money as possible
PHRV ,pinch sth↔'**off/**'**out** to remove sth by pressing your fingers together and pulling: *Pinch off the dead flowers.*

■ *noun*
WITH THUMB AND FINGER | **1** an act of squeezing a part of sb's skin tightly between your thumb and finger, especially in order to hurt them: *She gave him a pinch on the arm to wake him up.*
SMALL AMOUNT | **2** the amount of sth that you can hold between your finger and thumb: *a pinch of salt*

IDM at a '**pinch** (*BrE*) (*AmE* in a '**pinch**) used to say that sth could be done or used in a particular situation if it is really necessary: *We can get six people round this table at a pinch.* take sth with a pinch of '**salt** to be careful about believing that sth is completely true—more at FEEL *v.*

pinched /pɪntʃt/ *adj.* (of a person's face) pale and thin, especially because of illness, cold or worry

'**pinch-hit** *verb* [V] (*AmE*) **1** (in baseball) to hit the ball for another player **2** ~ (**for sb**) (*informal*) to do sth for sb else who is suddenly unable to do it

pin·cush·ion /'pɪnkʊʃn/ *noun* a small thick PAD made of fabric, used for sticking pins in when they are not being used

pine /paɪn/ *noun, verb*
■ *noun* **1** [C, U] (also '**pine tree**) a tall forest tree with leaves like needles. Pine trees are EVERGREEN and grow in cool northern countries: *pine forests* ◊ *pine needles* ◊ *a Scots pine* **2** (also **pine-wood**) [U] the pale soft wood of the pine tree, used in making furniture, etc: *a pine table*
■ *verb* [V] to become very sad because sb has died or gone away: *She pined for months after he'd gone.* **PHRV** ,pine a'**way** to become very sick and weak because you miss sb/sth very much: *After his wife died, he just pined away.* '**pine for sb/sth** to want or miss sb/sth very much: *She was pining for the mountains of her native country.*

pine·apple /'paɪnæpl/ *noun* [C, U] a large tropical fruit with thick rough skin, sweet yellow flesh with a lot of juice and stiff leaves on top: *fresh pineapple* ◊ *a tin of pineapple chunks* ◊ *pineapple juice*—picture on page A2

'**pine cone** *noun* the hard dry fruit of the PINE tree

'**pine marten** *noun* a small wild animal with a long body, short legs and sharp teeth. Pine martens live in forests and eat smaller animals.

'**pine nut** (*BrE* also '**pine kernel**) *noun* the white seed of some PINE trees, used in cooking

pine·wood /'paɪnwʊd/ *noun* = PINE

ping /pɪŋ/ *noun, verb*
■ *noun* a short high sound made when a hard object hits sth that is made of metal or glass
■ *verb* **1** [V, VN] to make a short, high ringing sound; to make sth produce this sound **2** [V] (*AmE*) = PINK

'**ping-pong** (*informal*) *noun* [U] = TABLE TENNIS

pin·head /'pɪnhed/ *noun* the very small flat surface at one end of a pin

pin·hole /'pɪnhəʊl; *AmE* -hoʊl/ *noun* a very small hole, especially one made by a pin

pin·ion /'pɪnjən/ *verb* [VN+*adv. / prep.*] to hold or tie sb, especially by their arms, so that they cannot move: *His arms were pinioned to his sides.* ◊ *They were pinioned against the wall.*

pink /pɪŋk/ *adj., noun, verb*
■ *adj.* **1** pale red in colour: *pale pink roses* ◊ *She went bright pink with embarrassment.* **2** [only before noun] connected with HOMOSEXUAL people: *the pink pound/dollar* (= money spent by HOMOSEXUALS as an influence in the economy) **3** (*politics*) (*informal, disapproving*) having or showing slightly LEFT-WING political views: *pale pink politics*—compare RED *adj.* ▸ **pink·ness** *noun* [U] **IDM** see TICKLE *v.*

s	t	v	z	ʃ	ʒ	tʃ	dʒ	θ	ð	ŋ
see	tea	van	zoo	shoe	vision	chain	jam	thin	this	sing

■ *noun* **1** [U, C] a pale red colour: *She was dressed in pink at the wedding.* ◊ *The bedroom was decorated in pale pinks.* **2** [C] a garden plant with pink, red or white flowers that have a sweet smell **IDM** **in the ˈpink** (*old-fashioned, informal*) in good health

■ *verb* (*BrE*) (*AmE* **ping**) [V] (of a car engine) to make knocking sounds because the fuel is not burning correctly

ˌpink ˈgin *noun* **1** [U] an alcoholic drink made from GIN mixed with ANGOSTURA that gives it a bitter flavour **2** [C] a glass of pink gin

pinkie (also **pinky**) /ˈpɪŋki/ *noun* (*AmE, ScotE*) the smallest finger of the hand: *a pinkie ring* (= worn on the smallest finger) **SYN** LITTLE FINGER

ˈpink·ing shears *noun* [pl.] special scissors used for cutting fabric so that it will not FRAY at the edges

pink·ish /ˈpɪŋkɪʃ/ *adj.* fairly pink in colour: *a pinkish colour/glow*

pinko /ˈpɪŋkəʊ; *AmE* -koʊ/ *noun* **1** (*AmE, informal, disapproving*) a COMMUNIST or a SOCIALIST **2** (*BrE, informal*) a person who is slightly LEFT-WING in their ideas, but not very—compare RED *n.* (3) ▶ **pinko** *adj.*

ˌpink ˈslip *noun* (*AmE, informal*) a letter given to sb to say that they must leave their job

ˈpin money *noun* [U] a small amount of money that you earn, especially when this is used to buy things that you want rather than things that you need

pin·na·cle /ˈpɪnəkl/ *noun* **1** [usually sing.] **~ cf sth** the most important or successful part of sth: *the pinnacle of her career* **2** a small pointed stone ornament built on the roof of a building **3** a high pointed piece of rock, especially at the top of a mountain

pinny /ˈpɪni/ *noun* (*pl.* **-ies**) (*BrE, informal*) = PINAFORE

pin·point /ˈpɪnpɔɪnt/ *verb, adj., noun*

■ *verb* [VN] **1** to find and show the exact position of sb/sth or the exact time that sth happened: *He was able to pinpoint on the map the site of the medieval village.* **2** to be able to give the exact reason for sth or to describe sth exactly: *The report pinpointed the areas most in need of help.*

■ *adj.* if sth is done with **pinpoint accuracy**, it is done exactly and in exactly the right position: *The pilots bombed strategic targets with pinpoint accuracy.*

■ *noun* a very small area of sth, especially light

pin·prick /ˈpɪnprɪk/ *noun* **1** a very small area of sth, especially light: *His eyes narrowed to two small pinpricks of black.* **2** a very small hole in sth, especially one that has been made by a pin **3** something that annoys you even though it is small and unimportant

ˌpins and ˈneedles *noun* [U] an uncomfortable feeling in a part of your body, caused when a normal flow of blood returns after it has been partly blocked, especially because you have been sitting or lying in an awkward position: *to have pins and needles* **IDM** **be on ˌpins and ˈneedles** (*AmE*) = BE ON TENTERHOOKS

pin·stripe /ˈpɪnstraɪp/ *noun* **1** [C] one of the white vertical lines printed on dark fabric that is used especially for making business suits. **2** [U, C] dark fabric with white vertical lines printed on it; a suit made from this cloth: *a tall man in grey pinstripe* ◊ *Without a pinstripe, you'd be underdressed.* ◊ *a pinstripe suit* ▶ **pin-striped** *adj.* [only before noun]: *a pinstriped suit* ◊ *a pinstriped official* (= who is wearing a pinstriped suit)—picture on page A4

pint /paɪnt/ *noun* **1** (*abbr.* **pt**) a unit for measuring liquids and some dry goods. There are 8 pints in a GALLON, equal to 0.568 of a litre in the UK and 0.473 of a litre in the US: *a pint of beer/milk* ◊ *We'd better get a couple of extra pints* (= of milk) *tomorrow.* ◊ *Add half a pint of cream.* **2** (*BrE*) a pint of beer (especially in a pub): *Do you want to go for a pint later?* **IDM** see QUART

ˈpint-sized *adj.* (*informal*) (of people) very small

ˈpin-up *noun* **1** a picture of an attractive person, especially one who is not wearing many clothes, that is put on a wall for people to look at: *Pin-ups have been banned from the factory.* **2** a person who appears in a pin-up

pin·wheel /ˈpɪnwiːl/ *noun* (*AmE*) = CATHERINE WHEEL

pi·on·eer /ˌpaɪəˈnɪə(r); *AmE* -ˈnɪr/ *noun, verb*

■ *noun* **1 ~ (in/of sth)** a person who is the first to study and develop a particular area of knowledge, culture, etc. that other people then continue to develop: *a pioneer in the field of microsurgery* ◊ *a computer pioneer* ◊ *a pioneer aviator* ◊ *a pioneer design* (= one that introduces new ideas, methods, etc.) **2** one of the first people to go to a particular area in order to live and work there: *the pioneer spirit*

■ *verb* [VN] when sb **pioneers** sth, they are one of the first people to do, discover or use sth new: *a new technique pioneered by surgeons in a London hospital*

pi·on·eer·ing /ˌpaɪəˈnɪərɪŋ; *AmE* -ˈnɪr-/ *adj.* [usually before noun] introducing ideas and methods that have never been used before: *pioneering work on infant mortality* ◊ *the pioneering days of radio*

pious /ˈpaɪəs/ *adj.* **1** having or showing a deep respect for God and religion: *pious acts* **OPP** IMPIOUS—see also PIETY **2** (*disapproving*) pretending to be religious, moral or good in order to impress other people: *pious sentiments* **3 ~ hope** something that you want to happen but is unlikely to be achieved: *Such reforms seem likely to remain little more than pious hopes.* ▶ **pi·ous·ly** *adv.*

pip /pɪp/ *noun, verb*

■ *noun* **1** (*especially BrE*) (*AmE usually* **seed**) the small hard seed that is found in some types of fruit: *an apple/ orange pip*—picture on page A2 **2** (**the pips**) [pl.] (*old-fashioned, BrE*) a series of short high sounds, especially those used when giving the exact time on the radio **3** (*AmE*) one of the dots showing the value on DICE and DOMINOES; one of the marks showing the value and SUIT of a playing card

■ *verb* (**-pp-**) [VN] (*BrE, informal*) to beat sb in a race, competition, etc. by only a small amount or at the last moment: *She pipped her rival for the gold medal.* ◊ *He was pipped at/to the post for the top award.*

pipe /paɪp/ *noun, verb*

■ *noun* **1** [C, U] a tube through which liquids and gases can flow: *hot and cold water pipes* ◊ *lead/plastic pipes* ◊ *a leaking gas pipe* ◊ *Copper pipe is sold in lengths.* ◊ *a burst pipe*—see also DRAINPIPE, EXHAUST, WINDPIPE **2** [C] a narrow tube with a bowl at one end, used for smoking tobacco: *to smoke a pipe* ◊ *He puffed on his pipe.* ◊ *pipe tobacco* **3** [C] a musical instrument in the shape of a tube, played by blowing—see also PAN PIPES **4** [C] any of the tubes from which sound is produced in an ORGAN **5** (**pipes**) [pl.] = BAGPIPES

■ *verb* **1** [VN] to send water, gas, oil, etc. through a pipe from one place to another: *to pipe oil across the desert* ◊ *Water is piped from the reservoir to the city.* **2** [VN] [usually passive] to send sounds or signals through a wire or cable from one place to another: *The speech was piped over a public address system.* ◊ *piped music* **3** to play music on a pipe or the BAGPIPES, especially to welcome sb who has arrived: [VN] *Passengers were piped aboard ship at the start of the cruise.* ◊ [V] *a prize for piping and drumming* **4** to speak or sing in a high voice or with a high sound: [V] *Outside a robin piped.* [also V **speech**] **5** [VN] to decorate food, especially a cake, with thin lines of ICING, etc. by squeezing it out of a special bag or tube: *The cake had 'Happy Birthday' piped on it.* **6** [VN] to decorate the edge of a cushion, a piece of clothing, etc. using thin strips of fabric, especially of a different colour **PHRV** **ˌpipe ˈdown** (*informal, spoken*) used especially in orders, to tell sb to stop talking or to be less noisy **ˌpipe ˈup (with sth)** (*informal*) to begin to speak: *The person next to me piped up with a silly comment.* ◊ [+ **speech**] *'I know the answer,' piped up a voice at the back of the room.*

ˈpipe-cleaner *noun* a short piece of wire, covered with soft material, used for cleaning inside a pipe (= the kind used for smoking tobacco)

ˈpipe-dream /ˈpaɪpdriːm/ *noun* a hope or plan that is impossible to achieve or not practical

ˈpipe·line /ˈpaɪplaɪn/ *noun* a series of pipes that are usually underground and are used for carrying oil, gas, etc. over long distances: *a gas/an oil pipeline* **IDM** **in the ˈpipeline** something that is **in the pipeline** is being

æ	ɑː	e	ɜː	ə	ɪ	iː	i	ɒ	ɔː	ʌ	ʊ	u	uː
cat	father	ten	bird	about	sit	see	many	got	saw	cup	put	actual	too
								(BrE)					

discussed, planned or prepared and will happen or exist soon

'pipe organ *noun* = ORGAN

piper /'paɪpə(r)/ *noun* a person who plays music on a pipe or the BAGPIPES **IDM** see PAY *v.*

pip·ette /pɪ'pet/ *noun* (*technical*) a narrow tube used in a LABORATORY for measuring or TRANSFERRING small amounts of liquids—picture at LABORATORY

pipe·work /'paɪpwɜːk; *AmE* -wɜːrk/ *noun* [U] the pipes used for carrying oil, gas or water around a machine, building, etc.

pip·ing /'paɪpɪŋ/ *noun, adj.*
- *noun* [U] **1** a pipe or pipes of the type or length mentioned: *ten metres of lead piping* **2** a folded strip of fabric, often with a length of string inside, used to decorate a piece of clothing, a cushion, etc: *a uniform with gold piping* **3** lines of cream or ICING/FROSTING as decoration on a cake **4** the sound of a pipe or pipes being played
- *adj.* (of a person's voice) high

,piping 'hot *adj.* (of liquids or food) very hot

pipit /'pɪpɪt/ *noun* (often in compounds) a small brown bird with a pleasant song: *a meadow/rock/tree pipit*

pip·squeak /'pɪpskwiːk/ *noun* (*old-fashioned, informal*) a person that you think is unimportant or does not deserve respect because they are small or young

pi·quancy /'piːkənsi/ *noun* [U] (*written*) the quality of being piquant: *The situation has an added piquancy since the two men are also rivals in love.* ◊ *The tart flavour of the cranberries adds piquancy.*

pi·quant /'piːkənt/ *adj.* (*written*) **1** having a pleasantly strong or spicy taste **2** exciting and interesting

pique /piːk/ *noun, verb*
- *noun* [U] (*formal*) annoyed or bitter feelings that you have, usually because your pride has been hurt: *When he realized nobody was listening to him, he left in a fit of pique.*
- *verb* [VN] (*formal*) to make sb annoyed or upset: *The incident piqued his pride.* ▶ **piqued** *adj.* [not before noun]: *She couldn't help feeling a little piqued by his lack of interest.* **IDM** **,pique sb's 'interest, curi'osity, etc.** (*especially AmE*) to make sb very interested in sth

pir·acy /'paɪrəsi/ *noun* [U] **1** the crime of attacking ships at sea in order to steal from them **2** the act of making illegal copies of video tapes, computer programs, books, etc., in order to sell them: *software piracy*—see also PIRATE

pi·ranha /pɪ'rɑːnə/ *noun* a small S American FRESHWATER fish that attacks and eats live animals

pir·ate /'paɪrət/ *noun, verb*
- *noun* **1** (especially in the past) a person on a ship who attacks other ships at sea in order to steal from them: *a pirate ship* **2** (often used as an adjective) a person who makes illegal copies of video tapes, computer programs, books, etc., in order to sell them: *a pirate edition/recording* ◊ *software pirates* **3** (often used as an adjective) a person or an organization that broadcasts illegally: *a pirate radio station*—see also PIRACY ▶ **pir·at·ical** /paɪ'rætɪkl/ *adj.*
- *verb* [VN] to copy and use or sell sb's work or a product without permission and without having the right to do so: *pirated computer games/books/videos*

pirou·ette /,pɪru'et/ *noun* a fast turn or SPIN that a person, especially a ballet dancer, makes on one foot ▶ **pirou·ette** *verb*: [V] *She pirouetted across the stage.*

Pis·ces /'paɪsiːz/ *noun* **1** [U] the 12th sign of the ZODIAC, the Fishes **2** [sing.] a person born under the influence of this sign, that is between 20 February and 20 March ▶ **Pis·cean** /'paɪsiən/ *noun, adj.*

piss /pɪs/ *verb, noun*
- *verb* (⚠, *slang*) [V] to URINATE **HELP** A more polite way of expressing this is 'go to the toilet/loo' (*BrE*), 'go to the bathroom' (*AmE*) or 'to go'. **IDM** **'piss yourself (laughing)** to laugh very hard **PHRV** **,piss a'bout/a'round** (*BrE*) to waste time by behaving in a silly way **HELP** A more polite, informal way of saying this is **mess about** (*BrE*) or **mess around** (*AmE, BrE*). **,piss sb a'bout/**

a'round (*BrE*) to treat sb in a way that is deliberately not helpful to them or wastes their time **HELP** A more polite, informal way of saying this is **mess sb about/around** (*BrE*). **'piss down** (*BrE*) to rain heavily **,piss 'off** (*especially BrE*) (usually used in orders) to go away: *Why don't you just piss off and leave me alone?* **,piss sb↔'off** to make sb annoyed or bored: *Her attitude really pisses me off.* ◊ *I'm pissed off with the way they've treated me.*
- *noun* (⚠, *slang*) **1** [U] = URINE **2** [sing.] an act of URINATING: *to go for a piss* **IDM** **be on the 'piss** (*BrE*) to be out at a pub, club, etc. and drinking a large amount of alcohol **take the 'piss (out of sb/sth)** (*BrE*) to make fun of sb, especially by copying them or laughing at them for reasons they do not understand—more at PIECE *n.*

'piss artist *noun* (*BrE*, ⚠, *slang*) **1** a person who drinks too much alcohol **SYN** ALCOHOLIC **2** a person who behaves in a stupid way

pissed /pɪst/ *adj.* **1** (*BrE*, ⚠, *slang*) drunk **2** (*AmE, slang*) very angry or annoyed **IDM** **(as) pissed as a 'newt** (*BrE*) very drunk

'piss-up *noun* (*BrE*, ⚠, *slang*) an occasion when a large amount of alcohol is drunk **HELP** A more polite, informal word for this is **booze-up**.

pis·ta·chio /pɪ'stæʃiəʊ; -'stɑːʃiəʊ; *AmE* -ʃiəʊ/ *noun* (*pl.* -os) **1** (also **pi'stachio nut**) [C] the small green nut of an Asian tree—picture at NUT **2** [U] a pale green colour

piste /piːst/ *noun* a track of firm snow prepared for skiing on: *He enjoys skiing off piste* (= away from the track). ◊ *off-piste snowboarding*

pistil /'pɪstɪl/ *noun* (*biology*) the female organs of a flower, which receive the POLLEN and produce seeds

pis·tol /'pɪstl/ *noun* a small gun that you can hold and fire with one hand: *an automatic pistol* ◊ *a starting pistol* (= used to signal the start of a race)—see also WATER PISTOL

'pistol-whip *verb* [VN] to hit sb with the BUTT of a pistol many times

pis·ton /'pɪstən/ *noun* a part of an engine that consists of a short CYLINDER that fits inside a tube and moves up and down or backwards and forwards to make other parts of the engine move

pit /pɪt/ *noun, verb*
- *noun*
  DEEP HOLE | **1** [C] a large deep hole in the ground: *We dug a deep pit in the yard.* ◊ *The body had been dumped in a pit.* **2** [C] (especially in compounds) a deep hole in the ground from which minerals are dug out: *a chalk/gravel pit*
  MINE | **3** [C] = COAL MINE: *pit closures* ◊ (*BrE*) *He went down the pit* (= started work as a miner) *when he left school.*
  IN SKIN | **4** a small shallow hole in the surface of sth, especially a mark left on the surface of the skin by some disease, such as CHICKENPOX—see also PITTED
  IN FRUIT | **5** (*especially AmE*) = STONE (5): *a peach pit*
  IN MOTOR RACING | **6** (**the pits**) [pl.] (*BrE*) (*AmE* **the pit** [C]) a place near the track where cars can stop for fuel, new tyres, etc. during a race—see also PIT STOP
  IN THEATRE | **7** = ORCHESTRA PIT
  PART OF BODY | **8** (*AmE, informal*) = ARMPIT
  IN BUSINESS | **9** (*AmE*) the area of a STOCK EXCHANGE where a particular product is traded: *the corn pit*—compare FLOOR (6)
  —see also SANDPIT
  IDM **be the 'pits** (*informal*) to be very bad or the worst example of sth **the pit of your/the 'stomach** the bottom of the stomach where people say they feel strong feelings, especially fear: *He had a sudden sinking feeling in the pit of his stomach.*—more at BOTTOMLESS
- *verb* (-tt-) [VN] [usually passive]
  MAKE HOLES | **1** to make marks or holes on the surface of sth: *The surface of the moon is pitted with craters.* ◊ *Smallpox scars had pitted his face.*
  FRUIT | **2** = STONE (2): *pitted dates/olives*
  PHRV **'pit sb/sth against sth** to test sb or their strength, intelligence, etc. in a struggle or contest against sb/sth else: *Lawyers and accountants felt that they were being pitted against each other.* ◊ *a chance to pit your wits*

aɪ	aʊ	eɪ	əʊ	oʊ	ɔɪ	ɪə	eə	ʊə	j	w
my	now	say	go (BrE)	go (AmE)	boy	near	hair	pure	yes	wet

against the world champions (= in a test of your intelligence)

pita, **'pita bread** *noun* [U] (*AmE*) = PITTA

pit-a-pat /ˌpɪtəˈpæt/ (also **'pitter-patter**) *adv.* with quick light steps or beats: *Her heart went pit-a-pat.* ▶ **pit-a-pat** (also **pitter-patter**) *noun* [sing.]: *I could hear the pit-a-pat of feet in the corridor.*

pit ˌbull 'terrier (also **'pit ˌbull**) *noun* a small strong fierce dog, sometimes used in dog fights where people bet on which dog will win

pitch /pɪtʃ/ *noun, verb*
■ *noun*
* FOR SPORT | **1** (*BrE*) (also **field** *AmE*, *BrE*) [C] an area of ground specially prepared and marked for playing a game such as football: *a football/cricket/rugby pitch* ◊ *The rugby tour was a disaster both on and off the pitch.*
* DEGREE/STRENGTH | **2** [sing., U] the degree or strength of a feeling or activity; the highest point of sth: *a frenetic pitch of activity* ◊ *Speculation has reached such a pitch that a decision will have to be made immediately.*
* OF SOUND | **3** [sing., U] how high or low a sound is, especially a musical note: *A basic sense of rhythm and pitch is essential in a music teacher.*—see also PERFECT PITCH
* TO SELL STH | **4** [C, usually sing.] talk or arguments used by a person trying to sell things or persuade people to do sth: *an aggressive sales pitch* ◊ *the candidate's campaign pitch* ◊ *Each company was given ten minutes to make its pitch.*
* IN BASEBALL | **5** [C] an act of throwing the ball; the way in which it is thrown
* BLACK SUBSTANCE | **6** [U] a black sticky substance made from oil or coal, used on roofs or the wooden boards of a ship to stop water from coming through
* IN STREET/MARKET | **7** [C] (*BrE*) a place in a street or market where sb sells things, or where a street entertainer usually performs
* OF SHIP/AIRCRAFT | **8** [U] (*technical*) the movement of a ship up and down in the water or of an aircraft in the air—compare ROLL *n.* (5)
* OF ROOF | **9** [sing., U] (*technical*) the degree to which a roof slopes
* **IDM** **make a 'pitch for sb/sth** | **make a 'pitch to sb** (*especially AmE*) to make a determined effort to get sth or to persuade sb of sth—more at QUEER *v.*
■ *verb*
* THROW | **1** [VN+adv./prep.] to throw sb/sth in a rough or forceful way: *The explosion pitched her violently into the air.* ◊ (*figurative*) *The new government has already been pitched into a crisis.*
* IN SPORTS | **2** [V, VN] (in baseball) to throw the ball to the person who is BATTING—picture on page 1250 **3** [+adv./prep.] (of the ball in the games of cricket or golf) to hit the ground; to make the ball hit the ground: [V] *The ball pitched a yard short.* [also VN] **4** [VN, V] (in golf) to hit the ball in a high curve
* FALL | **5** [V+adv./prep.] to fall heavily in a particular direction: *With a cry she pitched forward.*
* OF SHIP/AIRCRAFT | **6** [V] to move up and down on the water or in the air: *The sea was rough and the ship pitched and rolled all night.*—compare PITCH *v.* (9)
* SET LEVEL | **7** [VN+adv./prep.] ~ **sth (at sth)** to set sth at a particular level: *They have pitched their prices too high.* ◊ *The test was pitched at too low a level for the students.*
* TRY TO SELL | **8** [VN] ~ **sth (at sb)** | ~ **sth (as sth)** to aim or direct a product or service at a particular group of people: *The new software is being pitched at banks.* ◊ *Orange juice is to be pitched as an athlete's drink.* **9** ~ **(for sth)** to try to persuade sb to buy sth, to give you sth or to make a business deal with you: [VN] *Representatives went to Japan to pitch the company's newest products.* ◊ [V] *We were pitching against a much larger company for the contract.*
* SOUND/MUSIC | **10** [VN] to produce a sound or piece of music at a particular level: *You pitched that note a little flat.* ◊ *The song was pitched too low for my voice.*—see also HIGH-PITCHED, LOW-PITCHED

TENT | **11** [VN] to set up a tent or a camp for a short time: *We could pitch our tent in that field.* ◊ *They pitched camp for the night near the river.*—see also PITCHED
IDM **pitch a 'story/'line/'yarn (to sb)** (*informal*) to tell sb a story or make an excuse that is not true
PHRV **ˌpitch 'in (with sb/sth)** (*informal*) to join in and help with an activity, by doing some of the work or by giving money, advice, etc: *Everyone pitched in with the work.* ◊ *Local companies pitched in with building materials and labour.* **ˌpitch sth↔'in** to give a particular amount of money in order to help with sth: *We all pitched in $10 to buy her a gift.* **ˌpitch 'into sb** (*informal*) to attack or criticize sb: *She started pitching into me as soon as I arrived.* **ˌpitch 'into sth** (*informal*) to start an activity with enthusiasm: [+-ing] *I rolled up my sleeves and pitched into cleaning the kitchen.*

ˌpitch and 'putt *noun* [U] (*BrE*) golf played on a very small course

pitch-'black *adj.* completely black or dark: *a pitch-black night*

pitch-'dark *adj.* completely dark: *It was pitch-dark in the shed.*

pitched /pɪtʃt/ *adj.* (of a roof) sloping; not flat

ˌpitched 'battle *noun* **1** a fight that involves a large number of people: *The demonstration escalated into a pitched battle with the police.* **2** a military battle fought with soldiers arranged in prepared positions

pitch-er /ˈpɪtʃə(r)/ *noun* **1** (*AmE*) = JUG (1): *a pitcher of water/wine*—picture at JUG **2** (*BrE*) a large clay container with a small opening and one or two handles, used, especially in the past, for holding liquids—picture at JUG **3** (in baseball) the player who throws the ball to the BATTER—picture on page 1250

pitch-fork /ˈpɪtʃfɔːk; *AmE* -fɔːrk/ *noun* a farm tool in the shape of a large fork with a long handle and two or three sharp metal points, used especially for lifting and moving HAY (= dried grass), etc.

pit-eous /ˈpɪtiəs/ *adj.* (*literary*) deserving or causing pity: *a piteous cry/sight* ▶ **pit-eous-ly** *adv.*

pit-fall /ˈpɪtfɔːl/ *noun* a danger or difficulty, especially one that is hidden or not obvious at first: *the potential pitfalls of buying a house*

pith /pɪθ/ *noun* [U] **1** a soft dry white substance inside the skin of oranges and some other fruits—picture on page A2 **2** the essential or most important part of sth: *the pith of her argument*

pit-head /ˈpɪthed/ *noun* the entrance to a coal mine and the offices, machinery, etc. in the area around it

'pith helmet *noun* a light hard hat worn to give protection from the sun in very hot countries

pithy /ˈpɪθi/ *adj.* (*approving*) (of a comment, piece of writing, etc.) short but expressed well and full of meaning: *a pithy observation* ▶ **pith-ily** /-ɪli/ *adv.*: *pithily expressed*

piti-able /ˈpɪtiəbl/ *adj.* (*formal*) **1** deserving pity or causing you to feel pity: *The refugees were in a pitiable state.* **2** not deserving respect: *a pitiable lack of talent* ▶ **piti-ably** /-əbli/ *adv.*

piti-ful /ˈpɪtɪfl/ *adj.* **1** deserving or causing you to feel pity: *The horse was a pitiful sight* (= because it was very thin or sick). **2** not deserving respect: *a pitiful effort/excuse/performance* ▶ **piti-fully** /-fəli/ *adv.*: *The dog was whining pitifully.* ◊ *She was pitifully thin.* ◊ *The fee is pitifully low.*

piti-less /ˈpɪtiləs/ *adj.* **1** showing no pity; cruel: *a pitiless killer/tyrant* **2** very harsh or severe, and never ending: *a scorching, pitiless sun* ▶ **piti-less-ly** *adv.*

piton /ˈpiːtɒn; *AmE* -tɑːn/ *noun* a short pointed piece of metal used in rock-climbing. The piton is fixed into the rock and has a rope attached to it through a ring at the other end.

'pit stop *noun* **1** (in motor racing) an occasion when a car stops during a race for more fuel, etc. **2** (*AmE, informal*) a short stop during a long trip for a rest, a meal, etc.

pitta (*BrE*) (*AmE* **pita**) /ˈpiːtə; *BrE* also ˈpɪtə/ (also **'pitta bread**, **'pita bread**) *noun* [U, C] a type of flat bread in the

b	d	f	g	h	k	l	m	n	p	r
bad	did	fall	get	hat	cat	leg	man	now	pen	red

shape of an OVAL that can be split open and filled—picture on page A1

pit·tance /ˈpɪtns/ *noun* [usually sing.] a very small amount of money that sb receives, for example as a wage, and that is hardly enough to live on: *to pay sb a pittance* ◊ *to work for a pittance* ◊ *She could barely survive on the pittance she received as a pension.*

pit·ted /ˈpɪtɪd/ *adj.* **1** having small marks or holes in the surface **2** (of fruit) having had the stone/pit removed: *pitted olives*

pitter-patter /ˈpɪtə pætə(r)/ *adv., noun* = PIT-A-PAT

pi·tu·it·ary /pɪˈtjuːɪtəri; *AmE* -ˈtuːəteri/ (also **pi'tuitary gland**) *noun* a small organ at the base of the brain that produces HORMONES that influence growth and sexual development

pity /ˈpɪti/ *noun, verb*

■ *noun* **1** [U] ~ (for sb/sth) a feeling of sympathy and sadness caused by the suffering and troubles of others: *I could only feel pity for what they were enduring.* ◊ *a look/feeling/surge of pity* ◊ *I took pity on her and lent her the money.* ◊ (*formal*) *I beg you to have pity on him.* ◊ *I don't want your pity.* **2** [sing.] **a ~ (that ...)** | **a ~ (to do sth)** used to show that you are disappointed about sth: *It's a pity that you can't stay longer.* ◊ *'I've lost it!' 'Oh, what a pity.'* ◊ *What a pity that she didn't tell me earlier.* ◊ *It seems a pity to waste this food.* ◊ *This dress is really nice. Pity it's so expensive.* ◊ *Oh, that's a pity.* ◊ *It would be a great pity if you gave up now.* **IDM** **more's the 'pity** (*BrE, informal*) unfortunately: *'Was the bicycle insured?' 'No, more's the pity!'*

■ *verb* (**pit·ies, pity·ing, pit·ied, pit·ied**) (not used in the progressive tenses) to feel sorry for sb because of their situation; to feel PITY for sb: [VN] *He pitied people who were stuck in dead-end jobs.* ◊ *Compulsive gamblers are more to be pitied than condemned.* ◊ [VN-ing] *I pity her having to work such long hours.*

> **WORD FAMILY**
> pity *n., v.*
> pitiful *adj.*
> pitiless *adj.*
> pitiable *adj.*
> piteous *adj.*

pity·ing /ˈpɪtiɪŋ/ *adj.* [usually before noun] showing pity for sb, often in a way that shows that you think you are better than them: *a pitying look/smile* ▶ **pity·ing·ly** *adv.*

pivot /ˈpɪvət/ *noun, verb*

■ *noun* **1** the central point, pin or column on which sth turns or balances **2** the central or most important person or thing: *West Africa was the pivot of the cocoa trade.* ◊ *The pivot on which the old system turned had disappeared.*

■ *verb* [usually +*adv./prep.*] to turn or balance on a central point (= a pivot); to make sth do this: [V] *Windows that pivot from a central point are easy to clean.* ◊ *She pivoted around and walked out.* [also VN] **PHRV** **'pivot on/around sth** (of an argument, a theory, etc.) to depend completely on sth

piv·otal /ˈpɪvətl/ *adj.* (*written*) of great importance because other things depend on it: *a pivotal role in European affairs*

pixel /ˈpɪksl/ *noun* (*computing*) any of the small individual areas on a computer screen, which together form the whole display

pixie /ˈpɪksi/ *noun* (in stories) a creature like a small person with pointed ears, who has magic powers

pizza /ˈpiːtsə/ *noun* [C, U] an Italian dish consisting of a flat round bread base with cheese, tomatoes, vegetables, meat, etc. on top: *a ham and mushroom pizza* ◊ *Is there any pizza left?*

pizz·azz /pɪˈzæz/ *noun* [U] (*formal*) a lively and exciting quality or style: *We need someone with youth, glamour and pizzazz.*

piz·zeria /ˌpiːtsəˈriːə/ (*AmE* also **'pizza parlor**) *noun* a restaurant that serves mainly pizzas

pizzi·cato /ˌpɪtsɪˈkɑːtəʊ; *AmE* -toʊ/ *adj., adv.* (*music*) played using the fingers instead of a BOW to pull at the strings of a musical instrument such as a violin

Pl. *abbr.* (used in written addresses) Place: *Grosvenor Pl.*

pl. *abbr.* (in writing) plural

plac·ard /ˈplækɑːd; *AmE* -kɑːrd/ *noun* a large written or printed notice that is put in a public place or carried on a stick in a march: *They were carrying placards and banners demanding that he resign.*

pla·cate /pləˈkeɪt; *AmE* ˈpleɪkeɪt/ *verb* [VN] to make sb feel less angry about sth **SYN** PACIFY: *a placating smile* ◊ *The concessions did little to placate the students.*

pla·ca·tory /pləˈkeɪtəri; *AmE* ˈpleɪkətɔːri/ *adj.* (*formal*) designed to make sb feel less angry by showing that you are willing to satisfy or please them: *a placatory remark/smile/gesture*

place /pleɪs/ *noun, verb*

■ *noun*

POSITION/POINT/AREA | **1** [C] a particular position, point or area: *Is this the place where it happened?* ◊ *This would be a good place for a picnic.* ◊ *I can't be in two places at once.* ⇨ note on page 961

CITY/TOWN/BUILDING | **2** [C] a particular city, town, building, etc: *I can't remember all the places we visited in Thailand.* ◊ *I used to live in York and I'm still fond of the place.* ◊ *The police searched the place.* ◊ *We were looking for a place to eat.* ◊ *Let's get out of this place!* **3** [C] (especially in compounds or phrases) a building or an area of land used for a particular purpose: *a meeting place* ◊ *The town has many excellent eating places.* ◊ *churches and other places of worship* ◊ *He can usually be contacted at his place of work.*—see also RESTING PLACE

AREA ON SURFACE | **4** [C] a particular area on a surface, especially on a person's body: *He broke his arm in three places.* ◊ *The paint was peeling off the wall in places.*

IN BOOK/SPEECH, etc. | **5** [C] a point in a book, speech, piece of music, etc., especially one that sb has reached at a particular time: *She had marked her place with a bookmark.* ◊ *Excuse me, I seem to have lost my place.*

SEAT | **6** [C] a position, seat, etc., especially one that is available for or being used by a person or vehicle: *Come and sit here—I've saved you a place.* ◊ *I don't want to lose my place in the line.* ◊ *Would you like to change places with me so you can see better?* ◊ *I've set a place for you at the table.*

ROLE/IMPORTANCE | **7** [sing.] ~ (in sth) the role or importance of sb/sth in a particular situation, usually in relation to others: *He is assured of his place in history.* ◊ *Accurate reporting takes second place to lurid detail.* ◊ *My father believed that people should know their place* (= behave according to their social position). ◊ *It's not your place* (= your role) *to give advice.* ◊ *Anecdotes have no place in* (= are not acceptable in) *an academic essay.*

AT UNIVERSITY/SCHOOL | **8** [C] an opportunity to take part in sth, especially to study at a school or university or on a course: *She's been offered a place at Bath to study Business.* ◊ *There are very few places left on the course.*

IN SPORTS TEAM | **9** [C] the position of being a member of a sports team: *She has won a place in the Olympic team.* ◊ *He lost his place in the first team.*

CORRECT POSITION | **10** [C] the natural or correct position for sth: *Is there a place on the form to put your address?* ◊ *Put it back in its place when you've finished with it.*

SAFE AREA | **11** [C] (usually with a negative) a suitable or safe area for sb to be: *These streets are no place for a child to be out alone at night.*

HOME | **12** [sing.] a house or flat/apartment; a person's home: *What about dinner at my place?* ◊ *I'm fed up with living with my parents, so I'm looking for a place of my own.*

IN RACE/COMPETITION | **13** [C, usually sing.] a position among the winning competitors in a race or competition: *He finished in third place.*

MATHEMATICS | **14** [C] the position of a figure after a DECIMAL POINT: *The number is correct to three decimal places.*

STREET/SQUARE | **15** (**Place**) [sing.] (*abbr.* **Pl.**) used as part of a name for a short street or square: *66 Portland Place* **IDM** **all 'over the place** (*BrE* also **all 'over the shop**) (*AmE* also **all 'over the lot**) (*informal*) **1** everywhere: *New restaurants are appearing all over the place.* **2** not neat or tidy; not well organized: *Your calculations are all over the place* (= completely wrong). **change/swap 'places (with sb)** (usually used in negative sentences) to

s	t	v	z	ʃ	ʒ	tʃ	dʒ	θ	ð	ŋ
see	tea	van	zoo	shoe	vision	chain	jam	thin	this	sing

be in sb else's situation: *I'm perfectly happy—I wouldn't change places with anyone.* **fall/slot into 'place** if sth complicated or difficult to understand **falls** or **slots into place**, it becomes organized or clear in your mind **give 'place to sb/sth** (*formal*) to be replaced by sb/sth: *Houses and factories gave place to open fields as the train gathered speed.* **be 'going places** to be getting more and more successful in your life or career: *a young architect who's really going places* **if ˌI was/were in 'your place** used to introduce a piece of advice you are giving to sb: *If I were in your place, I'd resign immediately.* **in the 'first place** used at the end of a sentence to talk about why sth was done or whether it should have been done or not: *I still don't understand why you chose that name in the first place.* ◇ *I should never have taken that job in the first place.* **in the 'first, 'second, etc. place** used at the beginning of a sentence to introduce the different points you are making in an argument: *Well, in the first place he has all the right qualifications.* **in 'my, 'your, etc. place** in my, your, etc. situation: *I wouldn't like to be in your place.* **in 'place | into 'place 1** in the correct position; ready for sth: *Carefully lay each slab in place.* ◇ *The receiver had already clicked into place.* **2** working or ready to work: *All the arrangements are now in place for their visit.* **in place of sb/sth | in sb's/sth's 'place** instead of sb/sth: *You can use milk in place of cream in this recipe.* ◇ *He was unable to come to the ceremony, but he sent his son to accept the award in his place.* **out of 'place 1** not in the correct place: *Some of these files seem to be out of place.* **2** not suitable for a particular situation: *Her remarks were out of place.* ◇ *I felt completely out of place among all these successful people.* **a place in the 'sun** a position of privilege or advantage **put yourself in sb else's/sb's 'place** to imagine that you are in sb else's situation: *Of course I was upset—just put yourself in my place.* **put sb in their 'place** to make sb feel stupid or embarrassed for showing too much confidence: *At first she tried to take charge of the meeting but I soon put her in her place.* **take 'place** to happen, especially after previously being arranged or planned: *The film festival takes place in October.* ◇ *We may never discover what took place that night.* ⇨ note at HAPPEN **take sb's/sth's 'place | take the place of sb/sth** to replace sb/sth: *She couldn't attend the meeting so her assistant took her place.* ◇ *Computers have taken the place of typewriters in most offices.* **take your 'place 1** to go to the physical position that is necessary for an activity: *Take your places for dinner.* **2** to take or accept the status in society that is correct or that you deserve—more at HAIR, HEART, PRIDE *n.*, ROCK *n.*

■ *verb*

IN POSITION | **1** [VN+*adv./prep.*] to put sth in a particular place, especially when you do it carefully or deliberately: *He placed his hand on her shoulder.* ◇ *A bomb had been placed under the seat.* ◇ *The parking areas in the town are few, but strategically placed.*

IN SITUATION | **2** [VN+*adv./prep.*] (more formal than *put*) to put sb/yourself in a particular situation: *to place sb in command/under arrest* ◇ *She was placed in the care of an uncle.* ◇ *His resignation placed us in a difficult position.* ◇ *The job places great demands on me.*

ATTITUDE | **3** [VN] ~ sth (on sth/doing sth) used to express the attitude sb has towards sb/sth: *Great emphasis is placed on education.* ◇ *They place a high value on punctuality.*

RECOGNIZE | **4** [VN] (usually used in negative sentences) to recognize sb/sth and be able to identify them/it: *I've seen her before but I just can't place her.* ◇ *His accent was impossible to place.*

BET/ORDER/ADVERTISEMENT | **5** [VN] to give instructions about sth or make a request for sth to happen: *to place a bet/an order* ◇ *We placed an advertisement for a cleaner in the local paper.*

FIND HOME/JOB | **6** [VN] ~ sb (in sth)|~ sb (with sb/sth) to find a suitable home, job, etc. for sb: *The children were placed with foster parents.* ◇ *The agency placed about 2000 secretaries last year.*

GIVE RANK | **7** [VN+*adv./prep.*] to decide that sb/sth has a particular position or rank compared with other people

or things: *I would place her among the top five tennis players in the world.* ◇ *Nursing attracts people who place relationships high on their list of priorities.*

IN RACE | **8** used to describe a person, a team or a horse, etc. finishing in a particular position in a race: [VN-ADJ] *He was placed fifth in last Saturday's race.* ◇ [VN] (*BrE*) *My horse has been placed several times* (= it was among the first three or four to finish the race). ◇ [V] (*AmE*) *His horse placed in the last race* (= it was among the first three to finish the race, usually in second place).

IDM **be well, ideally, uniquely, better, etc. placed for sth/to do sth 1** to be in a good, very good, etc. position or have a good, very good, etc. opportunity to do sth: *Engineering graduates are well placed for a wide range of jobs.* ◇ *The company is ideally placed to take advantage of the new legislation.* **2** to be situated in a pleasant or convenient place: *The hotel is well placed for restaurants, bars and clubs.*—more at PEDESTAL, PREMIUM *n.*, RECORD *n.*

WHICH WORD?

place / space / room

Place, **space**, and **room** all describe an area in a room, building, vehicle, etc. which can be occupied by somebody or something.

Place is a countable noun. It is used to talk about a particular area where you can sit, work, sleep, etc: *I'm looking for a place to stay.* ◇ *Will you save me a place in the classroom?*

In *BrE* **place** cannot be used with *no* or *any*, but in *AmE* it can. *There is nowhere to park.* (*BrE*, *AmE*) ◇ *There's no place to park.* (*AmE* only) ◇ *I couldn't find anywhere to stay.* (*BrE*, *AmE*) ◇ *I couldn't find any place to stay.* (*AmE* only)

Space and **room** are used as uncountable nouns to talk about an empty area: *The wardrobe takes up too much room.* ◇ *There isn't enough space for another chair.*

---

pla·cebo /pləˈsiːbəʊ; *AmE* -boʊ/ *noun* (*pl.* **-os**) a substance that has no physical effects, given to patients who do not need medicine but think that they do, or used when testing new drugs: *the **placebo effect** (= the effect of taking a placebo and feeling better)

placed /pleɪst/ *adj.* [after noun] (*BrE*) (of a horse, in a race) finishing among the winners (usually second or third)

'place mat *noun* a MAT on a table on which a person's plate is put

place·ment /ˈpleɪsmənt/ *noun* **1** [U] the act of finding sb a suitable job or place to live: *a job placement service* ◇ *placement with a foster family* **2** [U, C] (*BrE*) a job, often as part of a course of study, where you get some experience of a particular kind of work: *The third year is spent on placement in selected companies.* ◇ *The course includes a placement in Year 3.* **3** [U] the act of placing sth somewhere: *This procedure ensures correct placement of the catheter.*

'place name *noun* a name of a town or other place

pla·centa /pləˈsentə/ (usually **the placenta**) *noun* (*anatomy*) the material that comes out of a woman or female animal's body after a baby has been born, and which was necessary to feed and protect the baby **SYN** AFTERBIRTH

'place setting *noun* a set or an arrangement of knives, forks and spoons, and/or plates and dishes for one person

pla·cid /ˈplæsɪd/ *adj.* **1** (of a person or an animal) not easily excited or irritated: *a placid baby/horse* **OPP** HIGH-SPIRITED **2** calm and peaceful, with very little movement: *the placid waters of the lake* ▶ **pla·cid·ly** *adv.* **pla·cid·ity** /pləˈsɪdəti/ *noun* [U]

pla·cing /ˈpleɪsɪŋ/ *noun* the position of sb/sth in a race or a competition or in a list arranged in order of success: *He needs a high placing in today's qualifier to reach the final.*

pla·giar·ism /ˈpleɪdʒərɪzəm/ *noun* [U, C] (*disapproving*) an act of plagiarizing sth; sth that has been plagiarized:

æ	ɑː	e	ɜː	ə	ɪ	iː	i	ɒ	ɔː	ʌ	ʊ	u	uː
cat	father	ten	bird	about	sit	see	many	got	saw	cup	put	actual	too

(BrE)

P

p

There were accusations of plagiarism. ◊ *a text full of plagiarisms* ▶ **pla·giar·ist** /ˈpleɪdʒərɪst/ *noun*

pla·giar·ize (*BrE also* **-ise**) /ˈpleɪdʒəraɪz/ *verb* (*disapproving*) to copy another person's ideas, words or work and pretend that they are your own: [VN] *He was accused of plagiarizing his colleague's results.* [also V]

plague /pleɪg/ *noun, verb*

■ *noun* **1** (*also* **the plague**) [U] = BUBONIC PLAGUE: *an outbreak of plague* **2** [C] any infectious disease that kills a lot of people: *the new plague of Aids* **3** [C] ~ **of sth** large numbers of an animal or insect that come into an area and cause great damage: *a plague of locusts/rats* IDM see AVOID

■ *verb* [VN] ~ **sb/sth** (**with sth**) **1** to cause pain or trouble to sb/sth over a period of time: *to be plagued by doubts/jealousy* ◊ *Financial problems are plaguing the company.* ◊ *The team has been plagued by injury this season.* **2** to annoy sb or create problems, especially by asking for sth, demanding attention, etc: *Rock stars have to get used to being plagued by autograph hunters.*

plaice /pleɪs/ *noun* [C, U] (*pl.* **plaice**) a flat sea fish that is used for food

plaid /plæd/ *noun* **1** [U] a thick fabric with a pattern of lines and squares of different colours and widths, especially a TARTAN pattern—picture on page A5 **2** [C] a long piece of woollen plaid worn over the shoulders as part of the Scottish national dress

plain /pleɪn/ *adj., noun, adv.*

■ *adj.* (**plain·er**, **plain·est**) **1** easy to see or understand: *He made it plain that we should leave.* ◊ *She made her annoyance plain.* ◊ *The facts were plain to see.* **2** not trying to trick anyone; honest and direct: *The plain fact is that nobody really knows.* ◊ *a politician with a reputation for plain speaking* **3** not decorated or complicated; simple: *a plain but elegant dress* ◊ *plain food/cooking* ◊ *The interior of the church was plain and simple.* ◊ *plain yogurt* (= without sugar or fruit)—compare FANCY **4** without marks or a pattern on it: *covers in plain or printed cotton* ◊ *Write on plain paper* (= without lines). **5** [only before noun] used to emphasize that sth is very ordinary, not special in any way: *You don't need any special skills for this job, just plain common sense.* **6** (*especially of a woman*) not beautiful or attractive ▶ **plain·ness** *noun* [U] IDM **be plain ˈsailing** (*AmE also* **clear ˈsailing**) to be simple and free from trouble **in plain ˈEnglish** simply and clearly expressed, without using technical language **(as) plain as a ˈpikestaff** | **(as) plain as ˈday** | **(as) plain as the nose on your ˈface** very obvious

■ *noun* (*also* **plains** [pl.]) a large area of flat land: *the flat coastal plain of Thassos* ◊ *the Great Plains*

■ *adv.* (*informal*) used to emphasize how bad, stupid, etc. sth is: *plain stupid/wrong*

plain·chant /ˈpleɪntʃɑːnt; *AmE* -tʃænt/ *noun* [U] = PLAIN-SONG

ˌplain ˈchocolate *noun* [U] (*BrE*) dark brown chocolate with a slightly bitter taste, made without milk being added—compare MILK CHOCOLATE

ˌplain ˈclothes *noun* [pl.] ordinary clothes, not uniform, when worn by police officers on duty: *officers in plain clothes* ▶ **ˌplain-ˈclothes** *adj.* [only before noun]: *plain-clothes police officers*

ˌplain ˈflour *noun* [U] flour that does not contain BAKING POWDER—compare SELF-RAISING FLOUR

plain·ly /ˈpleɪnli/ *adv.* **1** in a way that is easy to see, hear, understand or believe SYN CLEARLY: *The sea was plainly visible in the distance.* ◊ *The lease plainly states that all damage must be paid for.* ◊ *She had no right to interfere in what was plainly a family matter.* ◊ *Plainly* (= obviously) *something was wrong.* **2** using simple words to say sth in a direct and honest way: *To put it plainly, he's a crook.* **3** in a simple way, without decoration: *She was plainly dressed and wore no make-up.*

plain·song /ˈpleɪnsɒŋ; *AmE* -sɔːŋ/ (*also* **plain·chant**) *noun* [U] a type of church music for voices alone, used since the Middle Ages

plaint /pleɪnt/ *noun* **1** (*BrE, law*) a complaint made against sb in a court of law **2** (*literary*) a sad cry or sound

plain·tiff /ˈpleɪntɪf/ (*BrE less frequent* **com·plain·ant**) *noun* (*law*) a person who makes a formal complaint against sb in a court of law—compare DEFENDANT

plaint·ive /ˈpleɪntɪv/ *adj.* (*written*) sounding sad, especially in a weak complaining way SYN MOURNFUL: *a plaintive cry/voice* ▶ **plaint·ive·ly** *adv.*

plait /plæt/ (*BrE*) (*also* **braid** *AmE, BrE*) *noun, verb*

■ *noun* a long piece of sth, especially hair, that is divided into three parts and woven together: *She wore her hair in plaits.*—picture at HAIR

■ *verb* [VN] to twist three or more long pieces of hair, rope, etc. together to make one long piece

plan /plæn/ *noun, verb*

■ *noun*

INTENTION | **1** ~ (**for sth**) | ~ (**to do sth**) something that you intend to do or achieve: *Do you have any plans for the summer?* ◊ *There are no plans to build new offices.* ◊ *Your best plan would be to go by car.* ◊ *There's been a change of plan.* ◊ *We can't change our plans now.*

ARRANGEMENT | **2** ~ (**for sth**) | ~ (**to do sth**) a set of things to do in order to achieve sth, especially one that has been considered in detail in advance: *Both sides agreed to a detailed plan for keeping the peace.* ◊ *The government has announced plans to create one million new training places.* ◊ *a development/business/peace plan* ◊ *a five-point/three-year plan* ◊ *We need to make plans for the future.* ◊ *a plan of action/campaign* ◊ *Let's hope everything will go according to plan.*—see also MASTER PLAN

MAP | **3** a detailed map of a building, town, etc: *a plan of the museum* ◊ *a street plan of the city*

DRAWING | **4** [especially pl.] ~ (**for/of sth**) (*technical*) a detailed drawing of a machine, building, etc. that shows its size, shape and measurements: *The architect is drawing up plans for the new offices.*—compare ELEVATION (4), GROUND PLAN **5** a diagram that shows how sth will be arranged: *a seating plan* (= showing where each person will sit, for example at a dinner) ◊ *a floor plan* (= showing how furniture is arranged)

MONEY | **6** (*especially in compounds*) a way of investing money for the future: *a savings plan*

■ *verb* (**-nn-**)

MAKE ARRANGEMENTS | **1** ~ (**sth**) (**for sth**) to make detailed arrangements for sth you want to do in the future: [VN] *to plan a trip/an expedition* ◊ *A meeting has been planned for early next year.* ◊ *Everything went exactly as planned.* ◊ *We planned the day down to the last detail.* ◊ [V] *to plan for the future* ◊ [Vwh-] *I've been planning how I'm going to spend the day.* ◊ [Vthat] *They planned that the two routes would connect.*

INTEND/EXPECT | **2** ~ (**on sth/on doing sth**) to intend or expect to do sth: [V] *We hadn't planned on going anywhere this evening.* ◊ [Vtoinf] *They plan to arrive some time after three.* ◊ [VN] *We're planning a trip to France in the spring—are you interested?*

DESIGN | **3** [VN] to make a design or an outline for sth: *to plan an essay/a garden* ◊ *a well-planned campaign*

PHRV **ˌplan sth↔ˈout** to plan carefully and in detail sth that you are going to do in the future: *Plan out your route before you go.* ◊ *She has her career all planned out.*

plane /pleɪn/ *noun, verb, adj., verb*

■ *noun* **1** (*BrE also* **aero·plane**) (*AmE also* **air·plane**) a flying vehicle with wings and one or more engines: *She left by plane for Berlin.* ◊ *a plane crash* ◊ *I caught the next plane to Dublin.* ◊ *The plane took off an hour late.* ◊ *The plane landed at Geneva.* **2** (*geometry*) any flat or level surface, or an imaginary flat surface through or joining material objects: *the horizontal/vertical plane* **3** a level of thought, existence or development: *to reach a higher plane of achievement* **4** a tool with a blade set in a flat surface, used for making the surface of wood smooth by shaving very thin layers off it—picture at TOOL

■ *adj.* [only before noun] (*technical*) completely flat; level: *a plane surface*

■ *verb* **1** to make a piece of wood smoother or flatter with a plane: [VN] *Plane the surface down first.* ◊ [VN-ADJ] *Then plane the wood smooth.* **2** [V] (*of a bird*) to fly without moving the wings, especially high up in the air: *Gulls*

aɪ	aʊ	eɪ	əʊ	oʊ	ɔɪ	ɪə	eə	ʊə	j	w
my	now	say	go (BrE)	go (AmE)	boy	near	hair	pure	yes	wet

plane

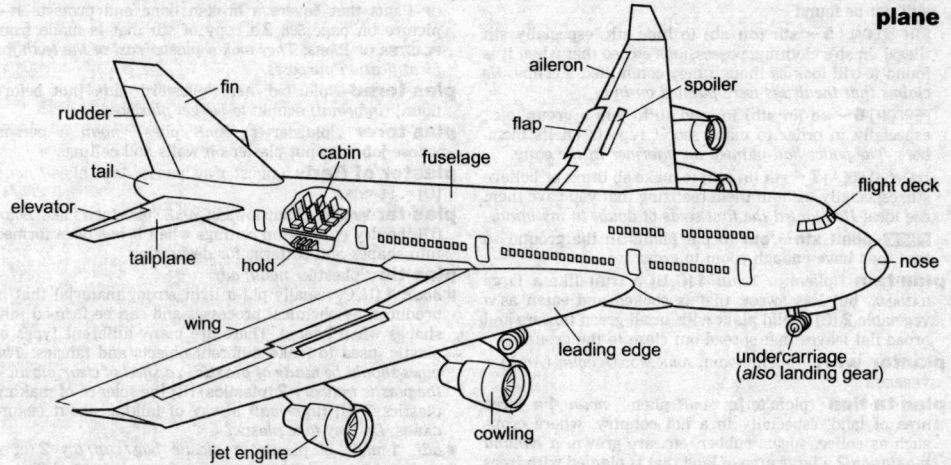

Labels: aileron, spoiler, flap, fin, rudder, cabin, fuselage, tail, flight deck, elevator, nose, tailplane, hold, wing, leading edge, undercarriage (*also* landing gear), jet engine, cowling

swooped and planed overhead. **3** [V] (of a boat, etc.) to move quickly across water, only just touching the surface

planer /ˈpleɪnə(r)/ *noun* an electric tool for making wooden surfaces smooth

planet /ˈplænɪt/ *noun* **1** [C] a large round object in space that moves around a star (such as the sun) and receives light from it: *the planets of our solar system* ◊ *the planet Earth/Venus/Mars* **2** (**the planet**) [sing.] used to mean 'the world', especially when talking about the environment: *the battle to save the planet* **IDM** **to be on another ˈplanet** | **what ˈplanet is sb on?** (*spoken, humorous*) used to suggest that sb's ideas are not realistic or practical

plan·et·arium /ˌplænɪˈteəriəm; *AmE* -ˈter-/ *noun* (*pl.* **-iums**) a building with a curved ceiling to represent the sky at night, with moving images of the planets and stars, used to educate and entertain people

plan·et·ary /ˈplænətri; *AmE* -teri/ *adj.* [only before noun] (*technical*) relating to a planet or planets: *planetary activity/motion* ◊ *a planetary system*

ˈplane tree *noun* a tree with spreading branches and broad leaves, that is often found in towns in northern countries

plan·gent /ˈplændʒənt/ *adj.* **1** (*formal*) (of sounds) loud, with a strong beat **2** (*literary*) (of sounds or images) expressing sadness: *the plangent sound of the harpsichord*

plank /plæŋk/ *noun* **1** a long narrow flat piece of wood that is used for making floors, etc: *a plank of wood* ◊ *a wooden plank*—picture at VICE **2** a main point in the policy of an organization, especially a political party: *The central plank of the bill was rural development.* **IDM** see THICK *adj.*, WALK *v.*

plank·ing /ˈplæŋkɪŋ/ *noun* [U] planks used to make a floor, etc.

plank·ton /ˈplæŋktən/ *noun* [U+sing./pl. *v.*] the very small forms of plant and animal life that live in seas, rivers, lakes, etc.

plan·ner /ˈplænə(r)/ *noun* **1** (also ˌtown ˈplanner) a person whose job is to plan the growth and development of a town **2** a person who makes plans for a particular area of activity: *curriculum/economic/media planners* **3** a book, computer program, etc. that contains dates and is used for recording information, arranging meetings, etc: *a year planner*

plan·ning /ˈplænɪŋ/ *noun* [U] **1** the act or process of making plans for sth: *curriculum/financial planning*—see also FAMILY PLANNING **2** = TOWN PLANNING

ˈplanning permission *noun* [U] official permission to build a new building or change one that already exists

plant /plɑːnt; *AmE* plænt/ *noun, verb*
■ *noun*

LIVING THING | **1** [C] a living thing that grows in the earth and usually has a stem, leaves and roots, especially one that is smaller than a tree or bush: *All plants need light and water.* ◊ *flowering/garden/indoor plants* ◊ *a tomato/potato plant* ◊ *the animal and plant life of the area*—see also BEDDING PLANT, HOUSE PLANT, POT PLANT, RUBBER PLANT

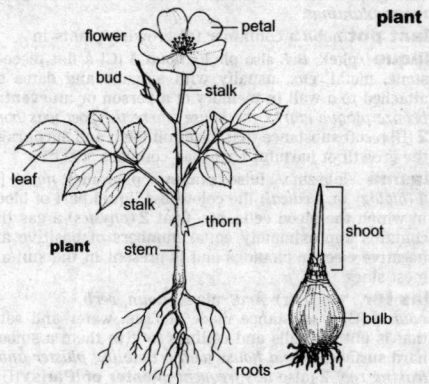

Labels: flower, petal, bud, stalk, leaf, stalk, thorn, shoot, plant, stem, bulb, roots

FACTORY | **2** [C] a factory or place where power is produced or an industrial process takes place: *a nuclear reprocessing plant* ◊ *Japanese car plants* ◊ *a chemical/manufacturing plant*—see also SEWAGE PLANT

MACHINERY | **3** [U] the large machinery that is used in industrial processes: *The company has been investing in new plant and equipment.*

STH ILLEGAL | **4** [C, usually sing.] (*informal*) something that sb has deliberately placed among another person's clothes or possessions to make them appear guilty of a crime

PERSON | **5** [C] a person who joins a group of criminals or enemies in order to get and secretly report information about their activities

■ *verb* [VN]

SEEDS/PLANTS | **1** to put plants, seeds, etc. in the ground to grow: *to plant and harvest rice* ◊ *Plant these shrubs in full sun.* **2** ~ sth (**with sth**) to cover or supply a garden/yard, area of land, etc. with plants: *a densely planted orange grove* ◊ *The field had been ploughed and planted with corn.*

PUT IN POSITION | **3** [+adv./prep.] to place sth or yourself firmly in a particular place or position: *They planted a flag on the summit.* ◊ *He planted himself squarely in front of us.*

P

BOMB | **4** to hide sth such as a bomb in a place where it will not be found

STH ILLEGAL | **5 ~ sth (on sb)** to hide sth, especially sth illegal, in sb's clothing, possessions etc. so that when it is found it will look as though they committed a crime: *He claims that the drugs were planted on him.*

PERSON | **6 ~ sb (in sth)** to send sb to join a group, etc., especially in order to make secret reports on its members: *The police had planted an informer in the gang.*

THOUGHT/IDEA | **7 ~ sth (in sth)** to make sb think or believe sth, especially without them realizing that you gave them the idea: *He planted the first seeds of doubt in my mind.*

PHRV **,plant sth↔'out** to put plants in the ground so that they have enough room to grow

plan·tain /'plæntɪn/ *noun* **1** [C, U] a fruit like a large BANANA, but less sweet, that is cooked and eaten as a vegetable **2** [C] a wild plant with small green flowers and broad flat leaves that spread out close to the ground

plantar wart /'plæntə wɔːt; *AmE* wɔːrt/ *noun* (*AmE*) = VERRUCA

plan·ta·tion /plɑːn'teɪʃn; *AmE* plæn-/ *noun* **1** a large area of land, especially in a hot country, where crops such as coffee, sugar, rubber, etc. are grown: *a banana plantation* **2** a large area of land that is planted with trees to produce wood: *conifer/forestry plantations*

plant·er /'plɑːntə(r); *AmE* 'plæn-/ *noun* **1** an attractive container to grow a plant in **2** a person who owns or manages a PLANTATION in a tropical country: *a tea planter* **3** a machine that plants seeds, etc.

plant·ing /'plɑːntɪŋ; *AmE* 'plæn-/ *noun* [U, C] an act of planting sth; sth that has just been planted: *The Tree Council promotes tree planting.* ◊ *These bushes are fairly recent plantings.*

'plant pot *noun* a container for growing plants in

plaque /plæk; *BrE also* plɑːk/ *noun* **1** [C] a flat piece of stone, metal, etc., usually with a name and dates on, attached to a wall in memory of a person or an event: *A bronze plaque marks the house where the poet was born.* **2** [U] a soft substance that forms on teeth and encourages the growth of harmful bacteria—compare SCALE

plasma /'plæzmə/ (*also* **plasm** /'plæzəm/) *noun* [U] **1** (*biology or medical*) the colourless liquid part of blood, in which the blood cells, etc. float **2** (*physics*) a gas that contains approximately equal numbers of positive and negative electric CHARGES and is present in the sun and most stars

plas·ter /'plɑːstə(r); *AmE* 'plæs-/ *noun, verb*
■ *noun* **1** [U] a substance made of LIME, water and sand, that is put on walls and ceilings to give them a smooth hard surface: *an old house with crumbling plaster and a leaking roof* **2** (*also less frequent* **,plaster of 'Paris**) [U] a white powder that is mixed with water and becomes very hard when it dries, used especially for making copies of statues or holding broken bones in place: *a plaster bust of Julius Caesar* ◊ (*BrE*) *She broke her leg a month ago and it's still in plaster.*—picture on page 598 **3** (*also* **'sticking plaster**) (*both BrE*) (*also* **'Band-Aid**™ *AmE, BrE*) [C, U] material that can be stuck to the skin to protect a small wound or cut; a piece of this—picture on page 598
■ *verb* [VN] **1** to cover a wall, etc. with plaster **2 ~ sb/sth in/with sth** to cover sb/sth with a wet or sticky substance: *She plastered herself in suntan lotion.* ◊ *We were plastered from head to foot with mud.* **3** [+*adv./prep.*] to make your hair flat and stick to your head: *His wet hair was plastered to his head.* **4** [+*adv./prep.*] to completely cover a surface with pictures or POSTERS: *She had plastered her bedroom wall with photos of him.* ◊ *She had photos of him plastered all over her bedroom wall.* ◊ *The next day their picture was plastered all over the newspapers.* PHRV **,plaster 'over sth** to cover sth such as a crack or an old wall with plaster: *The original brickwork has been plastered over.*

plas·ter·board /'plɑːstəbɔːd; *AmE* 'plæstərbɔːrd/ (*also* **'dry wall**) *noun* [U] a building material made of sheets of cardboard with plaster between them, used for inside walls and ceilings

'plaster cast *noun* **1** (*also* **cast**) a case made of PLASTER OF PARIS that covers a broken bone and protects it—picture on page 598 **2** a copy of sth that is made from PLASTER OF PARIS: *They took a plaster cast of the teeth for identification purposes.*

plas·tered /'plɑːstəd; *AmE* 'plæstərd/ *adj.* [not before noun] (*informal*) drunk: *to be/get plastered*

plas·terer /'plɑːstərə(r); *AmE* 'plæs-/ *noun* a person whose job is to put plaster on walls and ceilings

plaster of Paris /,plɑːstər əv 'pærɪs; *AmE* ,plæs-/ *noun* [U] = PLASTER

plas·ter·work /'plɑːstəwɜːk; *AmE* 'plæstərwɜːrk/ *noun* [U] the dry PLASTER on ceilings when it has been formed into shapes and patterns for decoration

plas·tic /'plæstɪk/ *noun, adj.*
■ *noun* **1** [U, C, usually *pl.*] a light strong material that is produced by chemical processes and can be formed into shapes when heated. There are many different types of plastic, used to make different objects and fabrics: *The pipes should be made of plastic.* ◊ *a sheet of clear plastic* ◊ *the plastic industry* **2** (**plastics**) [U] the science of making plastics **3** [U] (*informal*) a way of talking about CREDIT CARDS: *Do they take plastic?*
■ *adj.* **1** made of plastic: *a plastic bag/cup/toy* **2** (of a material or substance) easily formed into different shapes: *Clay is a plastic substance.* **3** (*disapproving*) that seems artificial; false; not real or sincere: *TV game show hosts with their banal remarks and plastic smiles*

,plastic 'bullet *noun* a bullet made of plastic, that is intended to injure but not to kill people

,plastic ex'plosive *noun* [U, C] an explosive substance that is used to make bombs

Plas·ti·cine™ /'plæstəsiːn/ *noun* [U] (*BrE*) a soft substance like clay that is made in different colours, used especially by children for making models

plas·ti·city /plæ'stɪsəti/ *noun* [U] (*technical*) the quality of being easily made into different shapes

,plastic 'surgeon *noun* a doctor who is qualified to perform plastic surgery

,plastic 'surgery *noun* [U] medical operations to repair injury to a person's skin, or to improve their appearance

'plastic wrap *noun* (*AmE*) = CLING FILM

plate /pleɪt/ *noun, verb*
■ *noun*
FOOD | **1** [C] a flat, usually round, dish that you put food on: *sandwiches on a plate* ◊ *a pile of dirty plates* ◊ *dinner/side plates* **2** [C] the amount of food that you can put on a plate: *a plate of sandwiches* ◊ *two large plates of pasta*—compare PLATEFUL **3** [C] (*especially AmE*) a whole main course of a meal, served on one plate: *Try the seafood plate.*

FOR STRENGTH | **4** [C] a thin flat piece of metal, used especially to join or strengthen sth: *The tanks were mainly constructed of steel plates.* ◊ *She had a metal plate inserted in her arm.*

FOR INFORMATION | **5** [C] a flat piece of metal with some information on it, for example sb's name: *A brass plate beside the door said 'Dr Alan Tate'.*—see also NAMEPLATE

ON VEHICLE | **6** [usually *pl.*] the pieces of metal or plastic at the front and back of a vehicle with numbers and letters on it—compare L-PLATE—see also LICENSE PLATE, NUMBER PLATE

SILVER/GOLD | **7** [U] ordinary metal that is covered with a thin layer of silver or gold: *The cutlery is plate, not solid silver.*—see also GOLD PLATE, SILVER PLATE, TINPLATE **8** [U] dishes, bowls, etc. that are made of silver or gold: *the family plate*

ON ANIMAL | **9** [C] (*biology*) one of the thin flat pieces of horn or bone that cover and protect an animal: *the armadillo's protective shell of bony plates*

GEOLOGY | **10** [C] one of the very large pieces of rock that form the earth's surface and move slowly: *the Pacific/Indian plate* ◊ *Earthquakes are caused by two tectonic plates bumping into each other.*—see also PLATE TECTONICS

PRINTING/PHOTOGRAPHY | **11** [C] a photograph that is used as

s	t	v	z	ʃ	ʒ	tʃ	dʒ	θ	ð	ŋ
see	tea	van	zoo	shoe	vision	chain	jam	thin	this	sing

a picture in a book, especially one that is printed on a separate page on high quality paper: *The book includes 55 colour plates.* ◊ *See plate 4.* **12** [C] a sheet of metal, plastic, etc. that has been treated so that words or pictures can be printed from it: *a printing plate* **13** [C] a thin sheet of glass, metal, etc. that is covered with chemicals so that it reacts to light and can form an image, used in larger or older cameras

IN MOUTH | **14** [C] a thin piece of plastic that fits inside your mouth, that has artificial teeth attached to it, or wire, etc. to make the teeth straight—compare BRACE, DENTURES

IN BASEBALL | **15** [sing.] (*AmE*) = HOME PLATE

—see also BOOKPLATE, BREASTPLATE, FOOTPLATE, HOTPLATE

IDM **have enough/a lot/too much on your 'plate** (*informal*) to have a lot of work or problems, etc. to deal with—more at HAND *v.*

■ *verb* [VN] [usually passive] **1** to cover a metal with a thin layer of another metal, especially gold or silver: *a silver ring plated with gold*—see also GOLD-PLATED, SILVER PLATE **2** to cover sth with sheets of metal or another hard substance: *The walls of the vault were plated with steel.*—see also ARMOUR-PLATED

plat·eau /'plætəʊ; *AmE* plæ'toʊ/ *noun* (*pl.* **plat·eaux** or **plat·eaus** /-təʊz; *AmE* -'toʊz/) **1** an area of flat land that is higher than the land around it—picture at MOUNTAIN **2** a time of little or no change after a period of growth or progress: *Inflation has reached a plateau.*

plate·ful /'pleɪtfʊl/ *noun* the amount that a plate holds: *She ate three platefuls of spaghetti.*—compare PLATE

,plate 'glass *noun* [U] very clear glass of good quality, made in thick sheets, used for doors, windows of shops/stores, etc.

plate·let /'pleɪtlət/ *noun* a very small blood cell, shaped like a disc. Platelets help to CLOT the blood when a person bleeds.

,plate tec'tonics *noun* [U] (*geology*) the movements of the large sheets of rock (called PLATES) that form the earth's surface; the scientific study of these movements

plat·form /'plætfɔːm; *AmE* -fɔːrm/ *noun*

AT TRAIN STATION | **1** the raised flat area beside the track at a train station where you get on or off the train: (*BrE*) *What platform does it go from?* ◊ (*BrE*) *The train now standing at platform 1 is for Leeds.*—compare TRACK

FOR PERFORMERS | **2** a flat surface raised above the level of the ground or floor, used by public speakers or performers so that the audience can see them: *Coming onto the platform now is tonight's conductor, Jane Glover.* ◊ *Representatives of both parties shared a platform* (= they spoke at the same meeting).

FOR EQUIPMENT | **3** a raised level surface for example one that equipment stands on or is operated from: *an oil/gas platform* ◊ *a launch platform* (= for spacecraft) ◊ *a viewing platform giving stunning views over the valley*

POLITICS/OPINIONS | **4** [usually sing.] the aims of a political party and the things that they say they will do if they are elected to power: *They are campaigning on an anti-immigration platform.* **5** an opportunity or a place for sb to express their opinions publicly or make progress in a particular area: *She used the newspaper column as a platform for her feminist views.*

COMPUTING | **6** the type of computer system or the SOFTWARE that is used: *an IBM platform* ◊ *a multimedia platform*

SHOES | **7** a high thick sole of a shoe: *platform shoes*

ON BUS | **8** (*BrE*) the open part at the back of a DOUBLE-DECKER bus where you get on or off

plat·ing /'pleɪtɪŋ/ *noun* [U] **1** a thin covering of a metal, especially silver or gold, on another metal: *gold plating* **2** a layer of coverings, especially of metal plates: *armour plating*

plat·inum /'plætɪnəm/ *noun* [U] (*symb* Pt) a chemical element. Platinum is a silver-grey precious metal, used in making expensive jewellery and in industry.

,platinum 'blonde *noun* (*informal*) a woman whose hair is a very pale silver colour, especially because it has

been coloured with chemicals; this colour of hair ▶ **,plat·inum 'blonde** *adj.*

plati·tude /'plætɪtjuːd; *AmE* -tuːd/ *noun* (*written, disapproving*) a comment or statement that has been made very often before and is therefore not interesting ▶ **plati·tud·in·ous** /,plætɪ'tjuːdɪnəs; *AmE* -'tuːdənəs/ *adj.* (*formal*)

pla·ton·ic /plə'tɒnɪk; *AmE* -'tɑːn-/ *adj.* (of a relationship) friendly but not involving sex: *platonic love* ◊ *Their relationship is strictly platonic.*

pla·toon /plə'tuːn/ *noun* a small group of soldiers that is part of a COMPANY and commanded by a LIEUTENANT

plat·ter /'plætə(r)/ *noun* a large plate that is used for serving food: *a silver platter* ◊ *I'll have the fish platter* (= several types of fish and other food served on a large plate). **IDM** see SILVER *n.*

platy·pus /'plætɪpəs/ (*also* ,duck-billed 'platypus) *noun* an Australian animal that is covered in fur and has a beak like a duck, WEBBED feet (= with skin between the toes) and a flat tail. Platypuses lay eggs but give milk to their young.

plau·dits /'plɔːdɪts/ *noun* [pl.] (*formal*) praise and approval: *His work won him plaudits from the critics.*

plaus·ible /'plɔːzəbl/ *adj.* **1** (of an excuse or explanation) reasonable and likely to be true: *Her story sounded perfectly plausible.* ◊ *The only plausible explanation is that he forgot.* **OPP** IMPLAUSIBLE **2** (*disapproving*) (of a person) good at sounding honest and sincere, especially when trying to trick people: *She was a plausible liar.* ▶ **plausi·bil·ity** /,plɔːzə'bɪləti/ *noun* [U] **plaus·ibly** /-əbli/ *adv.*: *He argued very plausibly that the claims were true.*

play /pleɪ/ *verb, noun*
■ *verb*

OF CHILDREN | **1** ~ (**with sb/sth**) to do things for pleasure, as children do; to enjoy yourself, rather than work: [V] *A group of kids were playing with a ball in the street.* ◊ *You'll have to play inside today.* ◊ *I haven't got anybody to play with!* ◊ *There's a time to work and a time to play.* ◊ [VN] *Let's play a different game.* **2** [no passive] ~ (**at doing**) **sth** to pretend to be or do sth for amusement: [V] *Let's play pirates.* ◊ [V] *They were playing at being cowboys.*

TRICK | **3** [VN] ~ **a trick/tricks** (**on sb**) to trick sb for amusement

SPORTS/GAMES | **4** ~ (**sth**) (**with/against sb**)| ~ **sb** (**at sth**) to be involved in a game; to compete against sb in a game: [VN] *to play football/chess/cards* ◊ *Have you played her at squash yet?* ◊ *France are playing Wales tomorrow.* ◊ [V] *He plays for Cleveland.* ◊ *France are playing against Wales on Saturday.* ◊ *Evans played very well.* **5** to take a particular position in a sports team: [V] *Who's playing on the wing?* ◊ [V-N] *I've never played right back before.* **6** [VN] to include sb in a sports team: *I think we should play Matt on the wing.* **7** [VN] to make contact with the ball and hit or kick it in the way mentioned: *She played the ball and ran forward.* ◊ *He played a backhand volley.* **8** [VN] (in CHESS) to move a piece in CHESS, etc: *She played her bishop.* **9** (in card games) to put a card face upwards on the table, showing its value: [VN] *to play your ace/a trump* ◊ [V] *He played out of turn!*

MUSIC | **10** ~ (**sth**) (**on sth**)| ~ **sth** (**to sb**)| ~ **sb sth** to perform on a musical instrument; to perform music: [VN] *to play the piano/violin/flute* ◊ *He played a tune on his harmonica.* ◊ [VN, VNN] *Play that new piece to us.* ◊ *Play us that new piece.* ◊ [V] *In the distance a band was playing.* **11** ~ **sth** (**for sb**)| ~ **sb sth** to make a tape, CD, etc. produce sound: [VN, VNN] *Play their new CD for me, please.*

æ	ɑː	e	ɜː	ə	ɪ	iː	i	ɒ	ɔː	ʌ	ʊ	u	uː
cat	father	ten	bird	about	sit	see	many	got	saw	cup	put	actual	too
								(BrE)					

◇ *Play me their new CD, please.* ◇ [V] *My favourite song was playing on the radio.*

ACT/PERFORM | **12** [VN] to act in a play, film/movie, etc.; to act the role of sb: *The part of Elizabeth was played by Cate Blanchett.* ◇ *He had always wanted to play Othello.* **13** to pretend to be sth that you are not: [V-ADJ] *I decided it was safer to play dead.* ◇ [V-N] *She enjoys playing the wronged wife.* **14** [V] ~ **(to sb)** to be performed: *A production of 'Carmen' was playing to packed houses.*

HAVE EFFECT | **15** [VN] ~ **a part/role (in sth)** to have an effect on sth: *The media played an important part in the last election.*

SITUATION | **16** [VN+adv./prep.] (*written*) to deal with a situation in the way mentioned: *He played the situation carefully for maximum advantage.*

OF LIGHT/A SMILE | **17** [V+adv./prep.] (*written*) to move or appear quickly and lightly, often changing direction or shape: *Sunlight played on the surface of the lake.*

OF FOUNTAIN | **18** [V] (*written*) when a FOUNTAIN **plays**, it produces a steady stream of water

IDM Most idioms containing **play** are at the entries for the nouns and adjectives in the idioms, for example **play the game** is at **game**. **have money, time, etc. to 'play with** (*informal*) to have plenty of money, time, etc. for doing sth **what is sb 'playing at?** used to ask in an angry way about what sb is doing: *What do you think you are playing at?*

PHRV ,play a'bout/a'round (with sb/sth) **1** to behave or treat sth in a careless way: *Don't play around with my tools!* **2** (*informal*) to have a sexual relationship with sb, usually with sb who is not your usual partner: *Her husband is always playing around.* ,play a'long (with sb/sth) to pretend to agree with sb/sth: *I decided to play along with her idea.* 'play at sth/at doing sth (often *disapproving*) to do sth without being serious about it or putting much effort into it ,play sth↔'back (to sb) to play music, film, etc. that has been recorded on a tape, video, etc: *Play that last section back to me again.*—related noun PLAYBACK ,play sth↔'down to try to make sth seem less important than it is [SYN] DOWNPLAY [OPP] PLAY UP **play A off against B** (*BrE*) (*AmE* **play A off B**) to put two people or groups in competition with each other, especially in order to get an advantage for yourself: *She played her two rivals off against each other and got the job herself.*—related noun PLAY-OFF ,play 'on (*sport*) to continue to play; to start playing again: *The home team claimed a penalty but the referee told them to play on.* 'play on/upon sth to take advantage of sb's feelings, etc. [SYN] EXPLOIT: *Advertisements often play on people's fears.* ,play sth↔'out (*written*) when an event is **played out**, it happens [SYN] ENACT: *Their love affair was played out against the backdrop of war.* ,play yourself/itself 'out (*written*) to become weak and no longer useful or important ,play 'up, ,play sb 'up (*informal, especially BrE*) to cause sb problems or pain: *The kids have been playing up all day.* ◇ *My shoulder is playing me up today.* ,play sth↔'up to try to make sth seem more important than it is [SYN] OVERPLAY [OPP] PLAY DOWN 'play with yourself (*informal*) to MASTURBATE

■ *noun*
CHILDREN | **1** [U] things that people, especially children, do for pleasure rather than as work: *the happy sounds of children at play* ◇ *the importance of learning through play* ◇ *a play area*

IN THEATRE | **2** [C] a piece of writing performed by actors in a theatre or on television or radio: *to put on* (= perform) *a play* ◇ *a play by Shakespeare* ◇ *a radio play*—see also MYSTERY PLAY, PASSION PLAY

IN SPORT | **3** [U] the playing of a game: *Rain stopped play.* ◇ *There was some excellent play in yesterday's match.*—see also FAIR PLAY, FOUL PLAY **4** [C] (*AmE*) an action or move in a game: *a defensive/passing play*

IN ROPE | **5** [U] the possibility of free and easy movement: *We need more play in the rope.*

ACTIVITY/INFLUENCE | **6** [U] the activity or operation of sth; the influence of sth on sth else: *the free play of market forces* ◇ *The financial crisis has brought new factors into*

play. ◇ *Personal feelings should not come into play when you are making business decisions.*

OF LIGHT/A SMILE | **7** [U] (*literary*) a light, quick movement that keeps changing: *the play of sunlight on water*

IDM in/out of 'play (*sport*) (of a ball) inside/outside the area allowed by the rules of the game: *She just managed to keep the ball in play.* **make a 'play for sb/sth** (*especially AmE*) to try to obtain sth; to do things that are intended to produce a particular result: *She was making a play for the sales manager's job.* **make great/much 'play of sth** to emphasize the importance of a particular fact: *He made great play of the fact that his uncle was a duke.* **a play on 'words** the humorous use of a word or phrase that can have two different meanings [SYN] PUN—more at CALL *v.*, CHILD, STATE *n.*

play·able /'pleɪəbl/ *adj.* **1** (of a piece of music or a computer game) easy to play **2** (of a sports field) in a good condition and suitable for playing on [OPP] UNPLAYABLE

'play-acting *noun* [U] behaviour that seems to be honest and sincere when in fact the person is pretending ▶ 'play-act *verb*: [V] *He thought she was play-acting but in fact she had really hurt herself.*

play·back /'pleɪbæk/ *noun* [U, C, usually sing.] the act of playing music, showing a film/movie or listening to a telephone message that has been recorded before; a recording that you listen to or watch again

play·bill /'pleɪbɪl/ *noun* **1** a printed notice advertising a play **2** (*AmE*) a theatre PROGRAMME

play·boy /'pleɪbɔɪ/ *noun* a rich man who spends his time enjoying himself

,play-by-'play *noun* [usually sing.] (*AmE*) a report on what is happening in a sports game, given as the game is being played

,played 'out *adj.* [not before noun] (*informal*) no longer having any influence or effect: *This country's world role is just about played out.*

play·er /'pleɪə(r)/ *noun* **1** a person who takes part in a game or sport: *a tennis/rugby/chess player* ◇ *a game for four players* ◇ *a midfield player*—picture on page A8 **2** (*written*) a company or person involved in a particular area of business or politics: *The company has emerged as a major player in the London property market.* **3** (in compounds) a machine for reproducing sound or pictures that have been recorded on cassettes, discs, etc: *a CD/cassette/record player* **4** (usually in compounds) a person who plays a musical instrument: *a trumpet player* **5** (old-fashioned) (especially in names) an actor: *Phoenix Players present 'Juno and the Paycock'.*

play·ful /'pleɪfl/ *adj.* **1** full of fun; wanting to play: *a playful puppy* **2** (of a remark, an action, etc.) made or done in fun; not serious: *He gave her a playful punch on the arm.* ▶ play·ful·ly /-fəli/ *adv.* play·ful·ness *noun* [U]

play·ground /'pleɪgraʊnd/ *noun* **1** an outdoor area where children can play, especially at a school or in a park—see also ADVENTURE PLAYGROUND **2** a place where a particular type of people go to enjoy themselves: *The resort is a playground of the rich and famous.*

play·group /'pleɪgruːp/ (also **play·school**) (both *BrE*) *noun* [C, U] a place where children who are below school age go regularly to play together and to learn through playing—compare NURSERY SCHOOL

play·house /'pleɪhaʊs/ *noun* **1** used in names of theatres: *the Liverpool Playhouse* **2** (*BrE* also **'Wendy house**) a model of a house large enough for children to play in

play·ing /'pleɪɪŋ/ *noun* **1** [U] the way in which sb plays sth, especially a musical instrument: *The orchestral playing is superb.* **2** [C] the act of playing a piece of music: *repeated playings of the National Anthem*

'playing card (also **card**) *noun* any one of a set of 52 cards with numbers and pictures printed on one side, which are used to play various card games: (*BrE*) *a pack of (playing) cards* ◇ (*AmE*) *a deck of (playing) cards*

'playing field *noun* a large area of grass, usually with lines marked on it, where people play sports and games: *the school playing fields* **IDM** see LEVEL *adj.*

aɪ	aʊ	eɪ	əʊ	oʊ	ɔɪ	ɪə	eə	ʊə	j	w
my	now	say	go (BrE)	go (AmE)	boy	near	hair	pure	yes	wet

play·mate /'pleɪmeɪt/ *noun* a friend with whom a child plays

play-off *noun* a match/game, or a series of them, between two players or teams with equal points or scores to decide who the winner is: *They lost to Chicago in the play-offs.*

play·pen /'pleɪpen/ *noun* a frame with wooden bars or NETTING that encloses a small area in which a baby or small child can play safely

play·room /'pleɪruːm; -rʊm/ *noun* a room in a house for children to play in

play·school /'pleɪskuːl/ *noun* (*BrE*) = PLAYGROUP

play·thing /'pleɪθɪŋ/ *noun* **1** a person or thing that you treat like a toy, without really caring about them: *She was an intelligent woman who refused to be a rich man's plaything.* **2** (*old-fashioned*) a toy: *The teddy bear was his favourite plaything.*

play·time /'pleɪtaɪm/ *noun* [U, C] **1** (*especially BrE*) a time at school when teaching stops for a short time and children can play **2** a time for playing and having fun: *With so much homework to do, her playtime is now very limited.*

play·wright /'pleɪraɪt/ *noun* a person who writes plays for the theatre, television or radio SYN DRAMATIST—compare SCREENWRITER, SCRIPTWRITER

plaza /'plɑːzə; *AmE* 'plæzə/ *noun* (*especially AmE*) **1** a public outdoor square especially in a town where Spanish is spoken **2** a small shopping centre, sometimes also with offices: *a downtown shopping plaza*

plc (also **PLC**) /ˌpiː el 'siː/ *abbr.* (*BrE*) public limited company (used after the name of a company or business): *Lloyd's Bank plc*

plea /pliː/ *noun* **1** (*formal*) ~ (**for sth**) an urgent emotional request: *She made an impassioned plea for help.* ◇ *a plea to industries to stop pollution* ◇ *He refused to listen to her tearful pleas.* **2** (*law*) a statement made by sb or for sb who is accused of a crime: *a plea of guilty/not guilty* ◇ *to enter/offer a guilty plea* **3** ~ **of sth** (*law*) a reason given to a court of law for doing or not doing sth: *He was charged with murder, but got off on a plea of insanity.*

plea bargaining *noun* [U] (*law*) an arrangement in a court of law by which a person admits to being guilty of a smaller crime in the hope of receiving less severe punishment for a more serious crime—compare COP A PLEA at COP *v.*, TURN KING'S/QUEEN'S EVIDENCE at EVIDENCE
▶ **'plea bargain** *noun*: *He reached a plea bargain with the authorities.*

plead /pliːd/ *verb* (**pleaded, pleaded** *AmE* also **pled, pled** /pled/) **1** ~ (**with sb**) (**for sth**) to ask sb for sth in a very strong and serious way: [V] *She pleaded with him not to go.* ◇ *I was forced to plead for my child's life.* ◇ *pleading eyes* ◇ [V to inf] *He pleaded to be allowed to see his mother one more time.* ◇ [V speech] *'Do something!' she pleaded.* **2** to state in a court of law that you are guilty or not guilty of a crime: [V-ADJ] *to plead guilty/not guilty* ◇ [V] *How do you plead?* (= said by the judge at the start of the trial) ◇ [VN] [no passive] *He advised his client to plead insanity* (= say that he/she was mentally ill and therefore not responsible for his/her actions). **3** [VN] to present a case to a court of law: *They hired a top lawyer to plead their case.* **4** ~ **sth** (**for sth**) to give sth as an explanation or excuse for sth: [VN] [no passive] *He pleaded family problems for his lack of concentration.* [also V that] **5** ~ (**for sb/sth**) to argue in support of sb/sth: [VN] *She appeared on television to plead the cause of political prisoners everywhere.* ◇ [V] *The United Nations has pleaded for a halt to the bombing.*

plead·ing /'pliːdɪŋ/ *noun* **1** [C, U] an act of asking for sth that you want very much, in an emotional way: *He refused to give in to her pleadings.* **2** [C, usually pl.] (*law*) a formal statement of sb's CASE (= their claims and the arguments they use to support them) in a court of law—see also SPECIAL PLEADING

plead·ing·ly /'pliːdɪŋli/ *adv.* in an emotional way that shows that you want sth very much but are not certain that sb will give it to you: *He looked pleadingly at her.*

pleas·ant /'pleznt/ *adj.* (**pleas·ant·er, pleas·ant·est**)

HELP **more pleasant** and **most pleasant** are more common **1** enjoyable, pleasing or attractive: *a pleasant climate/evening/place* ◇ *What a pleasant surprise!* ◇ *to live in pleasant surroundings* ◇ *music that is pleasant to the ear* ◇ *a pleasant environment to work in* ◇ *It was pleasant to be alone again.* **2** ~ (**to sb**) friendly and polite: *a pleasant young man* ◇ *a pleasant smile/voice/manner* ◇ *Please try to be pleasant to our guests.* OPP UNPLEASANT
▶ **pleas·ant·ly** *adv.*: *a pleasantly cool room* ◇ *I was pleasantly surprised by my exam results.* ◇ *'Can I help you?' he asked pleasantly.* **pleas·ant·ness** *noun* [U]: *She remembered the pleasantness of the evening.*

pleas·ant·ry /'plezntri/ *noun* [usually pl.] (*pl.* **-ies**) (*formal*) a friendly remark made in order to be polite: *After exchanging the usual pleasantries, they got down to serious discussion.*

please /pliːz/ *exclamation, verb*
▪ *exclamation* **1** used as a polite way of asking for sth or telling sb to do sth: *Please sit down.* ◇ *Two coffees, please.* ◇ *Quiet please!* ◇ *Please could I leave early today?* **2** used to add force to a request or statement: *Please don't leave me here alone.* ◇ *Please, please don't forget.* ◇ *Please, I don't understand what I have to do.* **3** used as a polite way of accepting sth: *'Would you like some help?' 'Yes, please.'* ◇ *'Coffee?' 'Please.'* **4** (**Please!**) (*informal*, often *humorous*) used to ask sb to stop behaving badly: *Children, please! I'm trying to work.* ◇ *John! Please!* **5** (**Please, P-lease**) /pə'liːz/ used when you are replying to sb who has said sth that you think is stupid: *Oh, please! You cannot be serious.*
▪ *verb* **1** to make sb happy: [VN] *You can't please everybody.* ◇ *He's a difficult man to please.* ◇ *There's just no pleasing some people* (= some people are impossible to please). ◇ *I did it to please my parents.* ◇ [V] *She's always very eager to please.* [also VN to inf] OPP DISPLEASE **2** [V] often used after **as** or **what, where**, etc. to mean 'to want', 'to choose' or 'to like' to do sth: *You may stay as long as you please.* ◇ *She always does exactly as she pleases.* ◇ *I'm free now to live wherever I please.* IDM **if you 'please 1** (*old-fashioned, formal*) (*spoken*) used when politely asking sb to do sth: *Take a seat, if you please.* **2** (*old-fashioned, especially BrE*) used to say that you are annoyed or surprised at sb's actions: *And now, if you please, he wants me to rewrite the whole thing!* ,**please the 'eye** to be very attractive to look at ,**please 'God** used to say that you very much hope or wish that sth will happen: *Please God, don't let him be dead.* ,**please your'self** (*spoken*) used to tell sb that you are annoyed with them and do not care what they do: *'I don't think I'll bother finishing this.' 'Please yourself.'* ,**please your'self** | ,**do as you 'please** to be able to do whatever you like: *There were no children to cook for, so we could just please ourselves.*

pleased /pliːzd/ *adj.* **1** ~ (**with sb/sth**) | ~ **that ...** feeling happy about sth: *She was very pleased with her exam results.* ◇ *The boss should be pleased with you.* ◇ *I'm really pleased that you're feeling better.* ◇ *I'm pleased to hear about your news.* ◇ *You're coming? I'm so pleased.* ◇ *He did not look too pleased when I told him.* **2** ~ **to do sth** happy or willing to do sth: *We are always pleased to be able to help.* ◇ *I was pleased to hear you've been promoted.* ◇ *Aren't you pleased to see me?* ◇ (*spoken, especially BrE*) **Pleased to meet you** (= said when you are introduced to sb) ◇ (*written*) *Thank you for your invitation which I am very pleased to accept.* ◇ (*written*) *I am pleased to inform you that the book you ordered has arrived.* IDM (**as**) ,**pleased as 'Punch** (*BrE*) very pleased **far from 'pleased** | **none too 'pleased** not pleased; angry: *She was none too pleased at having to do it all again.* **only too 'pleased (to do sth)** very happy or willing to do sth: *We're only too pleased to help.* **'pleased with yourself** (often *disapproving*) too proud of sth you have done: *He was looking very pleased with himself.*

pleas·ing /'pliːzɪŋ/ *adj.* ~ (**to sb/sth**) that gives you pleasure or satisfaction: *a pleasing design/effect* ◇ *The new building was pleasing to the eye.* ▶ **pleas·ing·ly** *adv.*: *She had a pleasingly direct manner.*

pleas·ur·able /'pleʒərəbl/ *adj.* giving pleasure SYN

P

b	d	f	g	h	k	l	m	n	p	r
bad	did	fall	get	hat	cat	leg	man	now	pen	red

ENJOYABLE: *a pleasurable activity/experience/sensation* ◊ *We do everything we can to make your trip pleasurable.*

pleas·ur·ably /ˈpleʒərəbli/ *adv.* with pleasure: *He sipped his coffee pleasurably.*

pleas·ure /ˈpleʒə(r)/ *noun* 1 [U] ~ (in sth/in doing sth)| ~ (of sth/of doing sth) a state of feeling or being happy or satisfied SYN ENJOYMENT: *to read for pleasure* ◊ *He takes no pleasure in his work.* ◊ *She had the pleasure of seeing him look surprised.* ◊ *(formal) It gives me great pleasure to introduce our guest speaker.* ◊ *(written) We request the pleasure of your company at the marriage of our daughter Lisa.* 2 [U] the activity of enjoying yourself, especially in contrast to working: *Are you in Paris on business or pleasure?* 3 [C] a thing that makes you happy or satisfied: *the pleasure and pains of everyday life* ◊ *the simple pleasures of the countryside* ◊ *It's a pleasure to meet you.* ◊ *'Thanks for doing that.' 'It's a pleasure.'*—compare DISPLEASURE IDM **at your/sb's ˈpleasure** *(formal)* as you want; as sb else wants: *The land can be sold at the owner's pleasure.* **with ˈpleasure** *(formal)* used as a polite way of accepting or agreeing to sth: *'May I sit here?' 'Yes, with pleasure.'*

ˈ**pleasure boat** (also ˈ**pleasure craft**) *noun* a boat used for short pleasure trips

pleat /pliːt/ *noun* a permanent fold in a piece of fabric, made by sewing the top or side of the fold

pleat·ed /ˈpliːtɪd/ *adj.* having pleats: *a pleated skirt*

plebe /pliːb/ *noun (AmE, informal)* a first-year student at a military or NAVAL college in the US

ple·beian /pləˈbiːən/ *adj., noun*
■ *adj.* 1 connected with ordinary people or people of the lower social classes 2 *(disapproving)* lacking in culture or education: *plebeian tastes*
■ *noun (usually disapproving)* a person from a lower social class (used originally in ancient Rome)—compare PATRI-CIAN

pleb·is·cite /ˈplebɪsɪt; -saɪt/ *noun* ~ (on sth) *(politics)* a vote by the people of a country or a region on an issue that is very important: *to hold a plebiscite on the country's future system of government*

plebs /plebz/ *noun (usually the plebs)* [pl.] *(informal)* an offensive way of referring to ordinary people, especially those of the lower social classes

plec·trum /ˈplektrəm/ *noun (pl.* plec·trums *or* plec·tra /-trə/) a small piece of metal, plastic, etc. used for PLUCK-ING the strings of a guitar or similar instrument

pled *(AmE)* pt, pp of PLEAD

pledge /pledʒ/ *noun, verb*
■ *noun* 1 ~ (to do sth) a serious promise: *a pledge of help/support/loyalty* ◊ *Will the government honour its election pledge not to raise taxes?* ◊ *Management has given a pledge that there will be no job losses this year.* 2 a sum of money or sth valuable that you leave with sb to prove that you will do sth or pay back money that you owe IDM **sign/take the ˈpledge**: *(old-fashioned)* to make a promise never to drink alcohol
■ *verb* 1 ~ sth (to sb/sth) to formally promise to give or do sth: [VN] *Japan has pledged $100 million in humanitarian aid.* ◊ *The government pledged their support for the plan.* ◊ *We all had to pledge allegiance to the flag* (= state that we are loyal to our country). ◊ [V to inf] *The group has pledged to continue campaigning.* ◊ [V(that)] *The group has pledged that they will continue campaigning.* 2 ~ sb/yourself (to sth) to make sb or yourself formally promise to do sth: [VN] *They were all pledged to secrecy.* ◊ [VN to inf] *The government has pledged itself to root out corruption.* 3 [VN] to leave sth with sb as a pledge(2) 4 *(AmE)* to promise to become a junior member of a FRATERNITY or SORORITY: [V] *Do you think you'll pledge this semester?* ◊ [VN] *My brother pledged Sigma NU.*

plen·ary /ˈpliːnəri/ *adj., noun*
■ *adj.* [only before noun] *(formal)* 1 (of meetings, etc.) to be attended by everyone who has the right to attend: *The new committee holds its first plenary session this week.* 2 without any limit; complete: *The Council has plenary powers to administer the agreement.*
■ *noun (pl.* -ies) a plenary meeting

pleni·po·ten·tiary /ˌplenɪpəˈtenʃəri; *AmE* also -ʃieri/ *noun (pl.* -ies) *(technical)* a person who has full powers to take action, make decisions, etc. on behalf of their government, especially in a foreign country ▶ **pleni·po·ten·tiary** *adj.: plenipotentiary powers*

pleni·tude /ˈplenɪtjuːd; *AmE* -tuːd/ *noun* [sing., U] *(formal)* a large amount of sth: *a plenitude of wealth and food*

plent·eous /ˈplentiəs/ *adj. (literary)* = PLENTIFUL

plen·ti·ful /ˈplentɪfl/ (also **plent·eous**) *adj.* available or existing in large amounts or numbers: *a plentiful supply of food* ◊ *In those days jobs were plentiful.* ▶ **plen·ti·ful·ly** /-fəli/ *adv.: Evidence is plentifully available.* ◊ *She kept them plentifully supplied with gossip.*

plenty /ˈplenti/ *pron., adv., noun, det.*
■ *pron.* ~ (of sth) a large amount; as much or as many as you need: *plenty of eggs/money/time* ◊ *'Do we need more milk?' 'No, there's plenty in the fridge.'* ◊ *They always gave us plenty to eat.* ◊ *We had plenty to talk about.* ⇨ notes at MANY, MUCH
■ *adv.* 1 ~ more (of) (sth) a lot: *We have plenty more of them in the warehouse.* ◊ *There's plenty more paper if you need it.* 2 ~ big, long, etc. enough (to do sth) *(informal)* more than big, long, etc. enough: *The rope was plenty long enough to reach the ground.* 3 *(AmE)* a lot; very: *We talked plenty about our kids.* ◊ *You can be married and still be plenty lonely.*
■ *noun* [U] *(formal)* a situation in which there is a large supply of food, money, etc: *Everyone is happier in times of plenty.* ◊ *We had food and drink in plenty.*
■ *det. (AmE or informal)* a lot of: *There's plenty room for all of you!*

plenum /ˈpliːnəm/ *noun* a meeting attended by all the members of a committee, etc.; a PLENARY meeting

pleth·ora /ˈpleθərə/ *noun* [sing.] *(formal)* an amount that is greater than is needed or can be used SYN EXCESS: *The report contained a plethora of detail.*

pleur·isy /ˈplʊərəsi; *AmE* ˈplʊr-/ *noun* [U] a serious illness that affects the inner covering of the chest and lungs, causing severe pain in the chest or sides

plexus ⇨ SOLAR PLEXUS

pli·able /ˈplaɪəbl/ *adj.* 1 easy to bend without breaking 2 (of people) easy to influence or control: *He'd always thought of her as pliable.*

pli·ant /ˈplaɪənt/ *adj. (written)* 1 (of a person or their body) soft and giving way to sb, especially in a sexual way: *her pliant body/lips* ◊ *She lay pliant in his arms.* 2 *(sometimes disapproving)* willing to accept change; easy to influence or control: *He was deposed and replaced by a more pliant successor.* ▶ **pli·ancy** /ˈplaɪənsi/ *noun* [U] **pli·ant·ly** *adv.*

pli·ers /ˈplaɪəz; *AmE* -ərz/ *noun* [pl.] a tool made of two pieces of metal with handles, used for holding things firmly and twisting and cutting wire: *a pair of pliers*—picture at SCISSORS, TOOL

plight /plaɪt/ *noun, verb*
■ *noun* [sing.] a difficult and sad situation: *the plight of the homeless* ◊ *The African elephant is in a desperate plight.*
■ *verb* IDM **plight your ˈtroth** *(old use or humorous)* to make a promise to a person saying that you will marry them; to marry sb

plim·soll /ˈplɪmsəl/ (also ˈ**gym shoe, pump**) (all *BrE*) *noun* a light simple sports shoe made of CANVAS (= strong cotton fabric) with a rubber sole: *a pair of plimsolls*

plinth /plɪnθ/ *noun* a block of stone on which a column or statue stands

plod /plɒd; *AmE* plɑːd/ *verb* (-dd-) [+adv./prep.] to walk slowly with heavy steps, especially because you are tired: [V] *Our horses plodded down the muddy track.* ◊ *We plodded on through the rain.* ◊ [VN] *I watched her plodding her way across the field.* ▶ **plod** *noun* [sing.] **plod·ding** *adj.: plodding donkeys* ◊ *(figurative, disapproving) The production was plodding and unimaginative.* PHRV ˌ**plod aˈlong/ˈon** to make very slow progress, especially with difficult or boring work

plod·der /ˈplɒdə(r); *AmE* ˈplɑːd-/ *noun* a person who works slowly and steadily but without imagination

s	t	v	z	ʃ	ʒ	tʃ	dʒ	θ	ð	ŋ
see	tea	van	zoo	shoe	vision	chain	jam	thin	this	sing

plonk /plɒŋk; *AmE* plɑːŋk; plɔːŋk/ *verb, noun*

■ *verb* (*especially BrE*) (*AmE* usually **plunk**) [VN] (*informal*) **1** [+*adv. / prep.*] to put sth down on sth, especially noisily or carelessly: *He plonked the books down on the table.* ◇ *Just plonk your bag anywhere.* **2 ~** (**yourself**) (**down**) to sit down heavily or carelessly: *He just plonked himself down and turned on the TV.*

■ *noun* (*informal, especially BrE*) **1** [U] cheap wine that is not of good quality **2** [C, usually sing.] a low sound like that of sth heavy falling and hitting a surface: *She sat down with a plonk.*

plonk·er /ˈplɒŋkə(r); *AmE* ˈplɑːŋk-; ˈplɔːŋk-/ *noun* (*BrE, slang*) a stupid person

plop /plɒp; *AmE* plɑːp/ *noun, verb*

■ *noun* [usually sing.] a short sound like that of a small object dropping into water

■ *verb* (-**pp**-) **1** [V+*adv. / prep.*] to fall, making a plop: *The frog plopped back into the water.* ◇ *A tear plopped down onto the page she was reading.* **2** [VN] to drop sth into sth, especially a liquid, so that it makes a plop: *Can you just plop some ice in my drink?* **3** [VN, V] **~** (**yourself**) (**down**) to sit or lie down heavily or in a relaxed way

plo·sive /ˈpləʊsɪv; *AmE* ˈploʊ-/ *noun* (*phonetics*) a speech sound made by stopping the flow of air coming out of the mouth and then suddenly releasing it, for example /t/ and /p/ in *top*—compare FRICATIVE ▶ **plo·sive** *adj.*

plot /plɒt; *AmE* plɑːt/ *noun, verb*

■ *noun* **1** [C, U] the series of events which form the story of a novel, play, film/movie, etc.: *a conventional plot about love and marriage* ◇ *The book is well organized in terms of plot.* **2** [C] **~** (**to do sth**) a secret plan made by a group of people to do sth wrong or illegal **3** [C] a small piece of land that is used or intended for a special purpose: *She bought a small plot of land to build a house on.* ◇ *a vegetable plot* **IDM** **lose the ˈplot** (*BrE, informal*) to lose your ability to understand or deal with what is happening **the plot ˈthickens** used to say that a situation is becoming more complicated and difficult to understand

■ *verb* (-**tt**-) **1 ~** (**with sb**) (**against sb**) to make a secret plan to harm sb, especially a government or its leader: [V] *They were accused of plotting against the state.* ◇ [VN] *Military officers were suspected of plotting a coup.* ◇ [V to inf] *They were plotting to overthrow the government.* **2** [VN] **~** **sth** (**on sth**) to mark sth on a map, for example the position or course of sth: *The earthquake centres had been plotted on a world map.* ◇ *He plotted a new route across the Atlantic.* **3** [VN] **~** **sth** (**on sth**) to make a diagram or CHART from some information: *We carefully plotted each patient's response to the drug on a chart.* **4** [VN] **~** **sth** (**on sth**) to mark points on a GRAPH and draw a line or curve connecting them: *First, plot the temperature curve on the graph.* **5** [VN] to write the plot of a novel, play, etc.: *a tightly-plotted thriller*

plot·ter /ˈplɒtə(r); *AmE* ˈplɑːtər/ *noun* **1** a person who makes a secret plan to harm sb **2** a device that turns data from a computer into a GRAPH, usually on paper

plough (*BrE*) (*AmE* **plow**) /plaʊ/ *noun, verb*

■ *noun* **1** [C] a large piece of farming equipment with one or several curved blades, pulled by a TRACTOR or by animals. It is used for digging and turning over soil, especially before seeds are planted.—see also SNOW-PLOUGH **2** (**the Plough**) (*BrE*) (*AmE* **the ˌBig ˈDipper**) [sing.] a group of seven bright stars that can only be seen from the northern half of the world **IDM** **under the ˈplough** (*BrE, formal*) (of land) used for growing crops, not for keeping animals on

■ *verb* to dig and turn over a field or other area of land with a plough: [VN] *ploughed fields* [also V] **IDM** **ˌplough a lonely, your own, etc, ˈfurrow** (*literary*) to do things that other people do not do, or be interested in things that other people are not interested in **PHR V** **ˌplough sth↔ˈback (in/into sth)** | **ˌplough sth↔back ˈin 1** to turn over growing crops, grass, etc. with a plough and mix them into the soil to improve its quality **2** to put money made as profit back into a business in order to improve it: *The money was all ploughed back into the company.* **ˈplough into sb/sth** (especially of a vehicle or its driver) to crash violently into sth especially because you are driving too fast or not paying enough attention: *A truck ploughed into the back of the bus.* **ˌplough sth ˈinto sth** to invest a large amount of money in a company or project: *The government has ploughed more than $20 billion into building new schools.* **ˌplough ˈon (with sth)** to continue doing sth that is difficult or boring: *No one was listening to her, but she ploughed on regardless.* **ˌplough (your way) ˈthrough sth 1** to force a way through sth: *She ploughed her way through the waiting crowds.* **2** (of a vehicle or an aircraft) to go violently through sth, out of control: *The plane ploughed through the trees.* **3** to make slow progress through sth difficult or boring especially a book, a report, etc: *I had to plough through dozens of legal documents.* **ˌplough sth↔ˈup 1** to turn over a field or other area of land with a plough to change it from grass, for example, to land for growing crops **2** to break up the surface of the ground by walking or driving across it again and again: *The paths get all ploughed up by motorbikes.*

plough·man (*BrE*) (*AmE* **plow·man**) /ˈplaʊmən/ *noun* (*pl.* -**men** /-mən/) a man whose job is guiding a plough, especially one pulled by animals

ˌploughman's ˈlunch (also **ˈploughman's**) *noun* (*BrE*) a cold meal of bread, cheese, PICKLE and salad, often served in pubs

plough·share (*BrE*) (*AmE* **plow·share**) /ˈplaʊʃeə(r); *AmE* -ʃer/ (*AmE* also **share**) *noun* the broad curved blade of a PLOUGH **IDM** see SWORD

plover /ˈplʌvə(r)/ *noun* a bird with long legs and a short tail that lives on wet ground

plow, plow·man, plow·share (*AmE*) = PLOUGH, PLOUGHMAN, PLOUGHSHARE

ploy /plɔɪ/ *noun* **~** (**to do sth**) words or actions that are carefully planned to get an advantage over sb else: *a clever marketing ploy* ◇ *It was all a ploy to distract attention from his real aims.*

pluck /plʌk/ *verb, noun*

■ *verb*

HAIR | **1** [VN] **~** **sth** (**out**) to pull out hairs with your fingers or with TWEEZERS: *She plucked out a grey hair.* ◇ *expertly plucked eyebrows*

CHICKEN, etc. | **2** [VN] to pull the feathers off a dead bird, for example a chicken, in order to prepare it for cooking

MUSICAL INSTRUMENT | **3** (*AmE* also **pick**) to play a musical instrument, especially a guitar, by pulling the strings with your fingers: [VN] *to pluck the strings of a violin* ◇ [V] *He picked up the guitar and plucked at the strings.*

REMOVE SB/STH | **4** [VN] **~** **sb** (**from sth**) (*written*) to remove sb from a place or situation, especially one that is unpleasant or dangerous: *Police plucked a drowning girl from the river yesterday.* ◇ *Survivors of the wreck were plucked to safety by a helicopter.* ◇ *She was plucked from obscurity to instant stardom.* **5** [VN] **~** **sth** (**from sth**) (*written*) to take hold of sth and remove it by pulling it: *He plucked the wallet from the man's grasp.*

FRUIT / FLOWER | **6** [VN] **~** **sth** (**from sth**) (*old-fashioned* or *literary*) to pick a fruit, flower, etc. from where it is growing: *I plucked an orange from the tree.*

IDM **pluck sth out of the ˈair** to say a name, number, etc. without thinking about it, especially in answer to a question: *I just plucked a figure out of the air and said: 'Would £1 000 seem reasonable to you?'* **pluck up ˈcourage (to do sth)** to make yourself do sth even though you are afraid to do it: *I finally plucked up the courage to ask her for a date.* **PHR V** **ˈpluck at sth** to hold sth with the fingers and pull it gently, especially more than once: *The child kept plucking at his mother's sleeve.* ◇ (*figurative*) *The wind plucked at my jacket.*

■ *noun* [U] (*old-fashioned, informal*) courage and determination: *It takes a lot of pluck to do what she did.*

plucky /ˈplʌki/ *adj.* (*informal*) having a lot of courage and determination

plug /plʌg/ *noun, verb*

æ	ɑː	e	ɜː	ə	ɪ	iː	i	ɒ	ɔː	ʌ	ʊ	u	uː
cat	father	ten	bird	about	sit	see	many	got	saw	cup	put	actual	too

(BrE)

P

tap *(BrE)*/
faucet *(AmE)*

socket *(BrE)*/
outlet *(AmE)*

plugs

plug

pin plug

sink

■ *noun*
UNDERLINE ELECTRICAL EQUIPMENT | **1** a small plastic object with two or three metal pins, that connects a piece of electrical equipment to the main supply of electricity: *a three-pin plug* ◊ *I'll have to change the plug on my hairdryer.* **2** (*informal, especially BrE*) a small opening in a wall, by which you connect a piece of electrical equipment to the main supply of electricity SYN SOCKET: *Can I use this plug for my iron?* **3** a small object that connects a wire from one piece of electrical equipment to an opening in another: *the plug from the computer to the printer*

IN ENGINE | **4** = SPARK PLUG

IN BATH/SINK | **5** a thick round piece of plastic or rubber that you put in the hole in a bath or a SINK to stop the water flowing out: *She pulled out the plug and let the water drain away.*

IN HOLE | **6** a round piece of material that fits into a hole and blocks it: *She took the plug of cotton wool from her ear.*—see also EARPLUG **7** (*AmE*) = STOPPER

FOR SCREW | **8** a small plastic tube that you put into a hole in a wall so that it will hold a screw

FOR BOOK/MOVIE | **9** (*informal*) praise or attention that sb gives to a new book, film/movie, etc. in order to encourage people to buy or see it: *He managed to get in a plug for his new book.*

IDM see PULL *v.*
■ *verb* (**-gg-**) [VN]
FILL HOLE | **1** ~ sth (**up**) to fill a hole with a substance or piece of material that fits tightly into it: *He plugged the hole in the pipe with an old rag.*

PROVIDE STH MISSING | **2** to provide sth that has been missing from a particular situation and is needed in order to improve it: *A cheaper range of products was introduced to plug the gap at the lower end of the market.*

BOOK/MOVIE | **3** to give praise or attention to a new book, film/movie, etc. in order to encourage people to buy it or see it SYN PROMOTE: *She came on the show to plug her latest album.*

SHOOT | **4** (*old-fashioned, AmE, informal*) to shoot sb

PHRV ˌplug aˈway (**at sth**) to continue working hard at sth, especially sth that you find difficult ˌplug sth↔ˈin| ˌplug sth ˈinto sth to connect a piece of electrical equipment to the main supply of electricity or to another piece of electrical equipment: *Is the printer plugged in?* OPP UNPLUG ˌplug sth ˈinto sth **1** = TO PLUG STH IN **2** to connect a computer to a computer system: *All our computers are plugged into the main network.* ˌplug ˈinto sth **1** (of a piece of electrical equipment) to be able to be connected to the main supply of electricity or to another piece of electrical equipment: *The VCR plugs into the back of the television.* **2** to become involved with a particular activity or group of people: *The company has doubled its profits since plugging into lucrative overseas markets.*

plug·hole /ˈplʌɡhəʊl; *AmE* -hoʊl/ (*BrE*) (*AmE* **drain**) *noun* a hole in a bath, SINK, etc. where the water flows away and into which a plug fits IDM **go down the ˈplughole** (*BrE*) = (GO) DOWN THE DRAIN at DRAIN *n.*

plum /plʌm/ *noun, adj.*
■ *noun* **1** [C] a soft round fruit with smooth red or purple skin, sweet flesh and a flat stone/pit inside: *a plum tree* **2** [U, C] a dark reddish-purple colour

■ *adj.* (*BrE*) (of a job, etc.) considered very good and worth having: *She's landed a plum job at the BBC.*

plum·age /ˈpluːmɪdʒ/ *noun* [U] the feathers covering a bird's body

plumb /plʌm/ *verb, adv.*
■ *verb* [VN] (*literary*) to try to understand or succeed in understanding sth mysterious SYN FATHOM: *She spent her life plumbing the mysteries of the human psyche.* IDM **plumb the depths of sth** to be or to experience an extreme example of sth unpleasant: *His latest novel plumbs the depths of horror and violence.* ◊ *The team's poor performances plumbed new depths last night when they lost 10-2.* PHRV ˌplumb sth↔ˈin (*especially BrE*) to connect a WASHING MACHINE, toilet, etc. to the water supply in a building
■ *adv.* **1** (used before prepositions) exactly: *He was standing plumb in the middle of the road.* **2** (*old-fashioned, AmE, informal*) completely: *He's plumb crazy.*

plumb·er /ˈplʌmə(r)/ *noun* a person whose job is to fit and repair things such as water pipes, toilets, etc.

plumb·ing /ˈplʌmɪŋ/ *noun* [U] **1** the system of pipes, etc. that supply water to a building **2** the work of a plumber

ˈplumb line *noun* a piece of thick string with a weight attached to one end, used to find the depth of water or to test whether a wall, etc. is straight

plume /pluːm/ *noun* **1** a cloud of sth that rises and curves upwards in the air: *a plume of smoke* **2** a large feather: *a black hat with an ostrich plume* **3** a group of feathers or long thin pieces of material tied together and often used as a decoration: *The red plume on the horse's head was nodding to the rhythm of its steps.*—see also NOM DE PLUME

plumed /pluːmd/ *adj.* having or decorated with a plume or plumes: *a plumed helmet*

plum·met /ˈplʌmɪt/ *verb* [V] to fall suddenly and quickly from a high level or position SYN PLUNGE: *Share prices plummeted to an all-time low.* ◊ *Her spirits plummeted at the thought of meeting him again.* ◊ *The jet plummeted into a row of houses.*

plummy /ˈplʌmi/ *adj.* **1** (*BrE, informal, usually disapproving*) (of a voice) having a sound that is typical of upper-class English people: *a plummy accent* **2** like a PLUM in colour, taste, etc.

plump /plʌmp/ *adj., verb*
■ *adj.* (**plump·er, plump·est**) **1** having a soft, round body; slightly fat: *a short, plump woman* ◊ *a plump body/face/figure* **2** looking soft, full and attractive to use or eat: *plump cushions* ◊ *plump tomatoes* ▶ **plump·ness** *noun* [U]
■ *verb* [VN] ~ sth (**up**) to make sth larger, softer and rounder: *He leaned forward while the nurse plumped up his pillows.* PHRV ˈplump for sb/sth (*informal*) to choose sb/sth from a number of people or things, especially after thinking carefully

ˌplum ˈpudding *noun* [U, C] (*old-fashioned, BrE*) = CHRISTMAS PUDDING

plun·der /ˈplʌndə(r)/ *verb, noun*
■ *verb* to steal things from a place, especially using force during a time of war: [V] *The troops crossed the country, plundering and looting as they went.* ◊ [VN] *The abbey had been plundered of its valuables.*—compare PILLAGE
■ *noun* [U] **1** the act of plundering **2** things that have been stolen, especially during a war, etc.—compare PILLAGE

plunge /plʌndʒ/ *verb, noun*
■ *verb* **1** [+adv. / prep.] to move or make sb/sth move suddenly forwards and/or downwards: [V] *She lost her balance and plunged 100 feet to her death.* ◊ [VN] *The earthquake plunged entire towns over the edge of the cliffs.* **2** [V] (of prices, temperatures, etc.) to decrease suddenly and quickly SYN PLUMMET: *Stock markets plunged at the news of the coup.* **3** [V+adv. / prep.] (of a road, surface, etc.) to slope steeply: *The track plunged down into the valley.* **4** [V] to move up and down suddenly and violently: *The horse plunged and reared.* ◊ (*figurative*) *His heart plunged* (= because of a strong emotion). PHRV ˌplunge ˈin ˌplunge ˈinto sth **1** to jump into sth, especially with force: *The pool was declared open and eager swimmers*

aɪ	aʊ	eɪ	əʊ	oʊ	ɔɪ	ɪə	eə	ʊə	j	w
my	now	say	go *(BrE)*	go *(AmE)*	boy	near	hair	pure	yes	wet

plunged in. **2** to start doing sth in an enthusiastic way, especially without thinking carefully about what you are doing: *She was about to plunge into her story when the phone rang.* ◊ *He's always plunging in at the deep end* (= becoming involved in difficult situations without being well enough prepared). ,**plunge sth 'in**|,**plunge sth 'into sth** to push sth quickly and with force into sth else: *She plunged the knife deep into his chest.* ,**plunge 'into sth 1** = PLUNGE IN **2** to experience sth unpleasant: *The country plunged deeper into recession.* ,**plunge sb/sth 'into sth** to make sb/sth experience sth unpleasant: *The news plunged them into deep depression.* ◊ *There was a flash of lightning and the house was plunged into darkness.*

■ *noun* [usually sing.] **1** a sudden movement downwards or away from sth: *The calm water ends there and the river begins a headlong plunge.* **2 ~ (in sth)** a sudden decrease in an amount or the value of sth: *a dramatic plunge in profits* **3 ~ into sth** the act of becoming involved in a situation or activity: *The company is planning a deeper plunge into the commercial market.* **4** an act of jumping or DIVING into water; a quick swim: *He took the plunge into the deep end.* ◊ *She went for a plunge.* **IDM** **take the 'plunge** (*informal*) to decide to do sth important or difficult, especially after thinking about it for a long time: *They finally decided to take the plunge and get married.*

plun·ger /'plʌndʒə(r)/ *noun* **1** a part of a piece of equipment that can be pushed down—picture at CAFETIERE, LABORATORY **2** a piece of equipment used for clearing kitchen and bathroom pipes, that consists of a rubber cup fixed to a handle

plun·ging /'plʌndʒɪŋ/ *adj.* (of a dress, BLOUSE, etc.) cut in a deep V shape at the front: *a plunging neckline*

plunk /plʌŋk/ *verb* [VN] (*informal*) **1** [+*adv./prep.*] (*AmE*) = PLONK: *He plunked the package down on the desk.* **2** to play a guitar, a keyboard, etc. with your fingers and produce a quick, harsh sound ▶ **plunk** *noun: the plunk, plunk of the banjo* **PHRV** '**plunk down sth** to pay money for sth, especially a large amount

plu·per·fect /ˌpluː'pɜːfɪkt; *AmE* -'pɜːrf-/ *noun* (*grammar*) = PAST PERFECT

plural /'plʊərəl; *AmE* 'plʊrəl/ *noun, adj.*
■ *noun* (*grammar*) (*abbr.* **pl.**) a form of a noun or verb that refers to more than one person or thing: *The plural of 'child' is 'children'.* ◊ *The verb should be* **in the plural.**—compare SINGULAR
■ *adj.* **1** (*grammar*) (*abbr.* **pl.**) connected with or having the plural form: *Most plural nouns in English end in 's'.* **2** relating to more than one: *a plural society* (= one with more than one RACIAL, religious, etc. group)

plur·al·ism /'plʊərəlɪzəm; *AmE* 'plʊr-/ *noun* [U] (*formal*) **1** the existence of many different groups of people in one society, for example people of different races or of different political or religious beliefs: *cultural/political pluralism* **2** the belief that it is possible and good for different groups of people to live together in peace in one society **3** (usually *disapproving*) the fact of having more than one job or position at the same time, especially in the Church

plur·al·ist /'plʊərəlɪst; *AmE* 'plʊr-/ *adj., noun*
■ *adj.* (also **plur·al·is·tic** /ˌplʊərə'lɪstɪk; *AmE* ˌplʊr-/) **1** (of a society) having many different groups of people and different political parties in it: *a pluralist democracy/system* **2** (*philosophy*) not based on a single set of principles or beliefs: *a pluralist approach to politics*
■ *noun* **1** a person who believes that it is possible and good for different groups of people to live together in peace in our society **2** a person who has more than one job or position at the same time, especially in the Church

plur·al·ity /plʊə'ræləti; *AmE* plʊ'r-/ *noun* (*pl.* **-ies**) **1** [C, usually sing.] (*formal*) a large number: *a plurality of influences* **2** [C, usually sing.] (*politics*) (*especially AmE*) the number of votes given to one person, political party, etc. when this number is less than 50% but more than any other single person, etc. receives: *In order to be elected, a candidate needs only a plurality of the votes cast.*—compare MAJORITY **3** [U] (*grammar*) the state of being plural

plus /plʌs/ *prep., noun, adj., conj.*
■ *prep.* **1** used when the two numbers or amounts mentioned are being added together: *Two plus five is seven.* ◊ *The cost is £22, plus £1 for postage.* **2** as well as sth/sb; and also: *We have to fit five of us plus all our gear in the car.* **OPP** MINUS **IDM** **plus or 'minus** used when the number mentioned may actually be more or less by a particular amount: *The margin of error was plus or minus three percentage points.*
■ *noun* **1** (*informal*) an advantage; a good thing: *Knowledge of French is a plus in her job.* ◊ *There were a lot of pluses in the performance.* **2** (also **'plus sign**) the symbol(+), used in mathematics: *He put a plus instead of a minus.* **OPP** MINUS
■ *adj.* **1** used after a number to show that the real number or amount is more than the one mentioned: *The work will cost £10000 plus.* **2** above zero: *The temperature is plus four degrees.* **OPP** MINUS **3** [only before noun] used to describe an aspect of sth that you consider to be a good thing: *One of the hotel's* **plus points** *is that it is very central.* ◊ **On the plus side,** *all the staff are enthusiastic.* **OPP** MINUS **4** [not before noun] (used in a system of marks/grades) slightly higher than the mark/grade A, B, etc: *I got B plus (B+) in the test.* **OPP** MINUS
■ *conj.* (*informal*) used to add more information **SYN** FURTHERMORE: *I've got too much on at work. Plus my father is not well.*

,**plus 'fours** *noun* [pl.] (*BrE*) wide loose trousers/pants that end just below the knees, where they fit closely, and that used to be worn, for example, by men playing golf: *a pair of plus fours*

plush /plʌʃ/ *noun, adj.*
■ *noun* [U] a silk or cotton fabric with a thick soft surface made of a mass of threads: *red plush armchairs*
■ *adj.* (*informal*) very comfortable; expensive and of good quality: *a plush hotel*

Pluto /'pluːtəʊ; *AmE* -toʊ/ *noun* the planet in the SOLAR SYSTEM that is furthest from the sun

plu·toc·racy /pluː'tɒkrəsi; *AmE* -'tɑːk-/ *noun* (*pl.* **-ies**) **1** [U] government by the richest people of a country **2** [C] a country governed by the richest people in it

plu·to·crat /'pluːtəkræt/ *noun* (often *disapproving*) a person who is powerful because of their wealth

plu·to·nium /pluː'təʊniəm; *AmE* -'toʊ-/ *noun* [U] (*symb* **Pu**) a chemical element. Plutonium is RADIOACTIVE and is used in nuclear weapons and in producing nuclear energy.

ply /plaɪ/ *verb, noun*
■ *verb* (**plies, ply·ing, plied, plied**) **1** (*literary*) (of ships, buses, etc.) to travel regularly along a particular route or between two particular places; [V, +*adv./prep.*] *Ferries ply across a narrow strait to the island.* ◊ [VN] *canals plied by gondolas and steam boats* **2** [VN] (*formal*) to use a tool, especially in a skilful way: *The tailor delicately plied his needle.* **IDM** **ply your 'trade** (*written*) to do your work or business: *This is the restaurant where he plied his trade as a cook.* **ply for 'hire/'trade/'business** (*BrE*) to look for customers, passengers, etc. in order to do business: *taxis plying for hire outside the theatre* **PHRV** '**ply sb with sth 1** to keep giving sb large amounts of sth, especially food and/or drink: *She plied us with tea and cake.* **2** to keep asking sb questions: *He plied me with questions from the moment he arrived.*
■ *noun* [U] (especially in compounds) a measurement of wool, rope, wood, etc. that tells you how thick it is: *four-ply knitting yarn*

ply·wood /'plaɪwʊd/ *noun* [U] board made by sticking thin layers of wood on top of each other: *plywood furniture*

PM /ˌpiː 'em/ *noun* (*informal, especially BrE*) the abbreviation for PRIME MINISTER: *an interview with the PM*

p.m. (*AmE* also **P.M.**) /ˌpiː 'em/ *abbr.* after 12 o'clock NOON (from Latin 'post meridiem'): *The appointment is at 3 p.m.*—compare A.M.

PMS /ˌpiː em 'es/ (*BrE*) (also **PMT** /ˌpiː em 'tiː/, *AmE*, *BrE*) *noun* [U] physical and emotional problems such as pain and feeling depressed that many women experience before their PERIOD (= flow of blood) each month. PMS/ PMT are abbreviations for 'premenstrual syndrome/ tension'.

pneu·mat·ic /njuːˈmætɪk; AmE nuː-/ adj. [usually before noun] **1** filled with air: a pneumatic tyre **2** worked by air under pressure: pneumatic tools

pneuˌmatic ˈdrill (BrE) (AmE **jack·ham·mer**) noun a large powerful tool, worked by air pressure, used especially for breaking up road surfaces

pneu·mo·nia /njuːˈməʊniə; AmE nuːˈmoʊ-/ noun [U] a serious illness affecting one or both lungs that makes breathing difficult

PO /ˌpiː ˈəʊ; AmE ˈoʊ/ abbr. **1** POST OFFICE—see also PO BOX **2** POSTAL ORDER

poach /pəʊtʃ; AmE poʊtʃ/ verb **1** [VN] to cook food, especially fish, gently in a small amount of liquid: poached salmon **2** [VN] to cook an egg gently in nearly boiling water after removing its shell **3** to illegally hunt birds, animals or fish on sb else's property or without permission: [VN] The elephants are poached for their tusks. [also V] **4** ~ (sb/sth) (from sb/sth) to take and use sb/sth that belongs to sb/sth else, especially in a secret, dishonest or unfair way: [VN] The company poached the contract from their main rivals. ◇ Several of our employees have been poached by a rival firm. ◇ [V] I hope I'm not **poaching on your territory** (= doing sth that is actually your responsibility).

poach·er /ˈpəʊtʃə(r); AmE ˈpoʊtʃ-/ noun **1** a person who illegally hunts birds, animals, or fish on sb's else's property **2** a special pan for POACHING eggs **IDM poacher turned ˈgamekeeper** (BrE) a person who has changed from one situation or attitude to the opposite one, especially sb who used to oppose people in authority but is now in a position of authority

ˌPˈO box (also **ˌpost office ˈbox**) noun used as a kind of address, so that mail can be sent to a post office where it is kept until it is collected: Radio Netherlands, PO Box 222, Hilversum

pocked /pɒkt; AmE pɑːkt/ adj. having holes or hollow marks on the surface

pocket /ˈpɒkɪt; AmE ˈpɑːk-/ noun, verb

■ noun

IN CLOTHING **1** a small piece of material like a small bag sewn into or onto a piece of clothing so that you can carry things in it: a coat pocket ◇ I put the note in my pocket. ◇ **Turn out your pockets** (= empty your pockets). ◇ Take your hands out of your pockets! ◇ a pocket dictionary (= one that is small enough to fit in your pocket)

SMALL CONTAINER **2** a small bag or container fastened to sth so that you can put things in it, for example, in a car door or in a handbag: Information about safety procedures is in the pocket in front of you (= on a plane).—picture at BAG

MONEY **3** [usually sing.] used to talk about the amount of money that you have to spend: We have holidays to suit every pocket. ◇ He had no intention of paying for the meal out of his own pocket. ◇ The Foundation is reputed to have very deep pockets (= to have a lot of money).

SMALL GROUP/AREA **4** a small group or area that is different from its surroundings: There are still a few isolated pockets of resistance to the new regime. ◇ a pocket of air—see also AIR POCKET

IN BILLIARDS, etc. **5** any of the holes or nets around the edges of the table used in the games of BILLIARDS, POOL or SNOOKER, which you have to hit the ball into—picture on page A8

IDM be in sb's **ˈpocket** to be controlled or strongly influenced by sb **be/live in each other's ˈpockets** (BrE) if two people are **in each other's pockets**, they are too close to each other or spend too much time with each other **have sb in your ˈpocket** to have influence or power over sb, for example, a police officer or a politician, especially by threatening them or by offering them money **to have sth in your ˈpocket** to be certain to win sth **ˌin/ˌout of ˈpocket** (especially BrE) having gained/ lost money as a result of sth: That one mistake left him

thousands of pounds out of pocket.—more at BURN v., DIP v., HAND n., LINE v., PICK v.

■ verb [VN]

PUT INTO POCKET **1** to put sth into your pocket: She paid for the drink and pocketed the change without counting it.

MONEY **2** to take or keep sth, especially an amount of money, that does not belong to you: He regularly charges passengers more than the normal fare and pockets the difference. **3** to earn or win an amount of money: Last year, she pocketed over $1 million in advertising contracts. IN BILLIARDS, etc. **4** (in the games of BILLIARDS, POOL and SNOOKER) to hit a ball into a pocket **SYN** POT

pock·et·book /ˈpɒkɪtbʊk; AmE ˈpɑːk-/ noun **1** (AmE) used to refer to the financial situation of a person or country. (In the past it was a small flat case for carrying papers or money.): Many foreign goods are too expensive for American pocketbooks. ◇ The increase is likely to hit the pocketbooks of consumers. **2** (especially BrE) a small book for writing in **SYN** NOTEBOOK **3** (old-fashioned, AmE) = HANDBAG

pock·et·ful /ˈpɒkɪtfʊl; AmE ˈpɑːk-/ noun the amount a pocket holds: a pocketful of coins

ˈpocket knife noun (especially AmE) = PENKNIFE

ˈpocket money noun [U] **1** (especially BrE) (also **alˈlowance** especially in AmE) a small amount of money that parents give their children, usually every week or every month **2** a small amount of money that you can spend on things you need or want—compare SPENDING MONEY

ˈpocket-sized (also **ˈpocket-size**) adj. small enough to fit into your pocket or to be carried easily

ˌpocket ˈveto noun (in the US) a method by which the President can stop a new law from being introduced by not signing it and keeping it until a SESSION of Congress has finished

pock·mark /ˈpɒkmɑːk; AmE ˈpɑːkmɑːrk/ noun a hollow mark on the skin, often caused by disease or infection

ˈpock-marked adj. covered with hollow marks or holes: a pock-marked face ◇ The district is pock-marked with caves.

pod /pɒd; AmE pɑːd/ noun **1** a long thin case filled with seeds that develops from the flowers of some plants, especially peas and beans: a pea pod ◇ a vanilla pod— picture on page A3 **2** a long narrow container that is hung under an aircraft and used to carry fuel, equipment, weapons, etc. **3** part of a spacecraft or a boat that can be separated from the main part

podgy /ˈpɒdʒi; AmE ˈpɑːdʒi/ (BrE) (also **pudgy** AmE, BrE) adj. (informal, usually disapproving) slightly fat: podgy arms/hands

po·dia·trist /pəˈdaɪətrɪst/ noun (especially AmE) = CHIROPODIST

po·dia·try /pəˈdaɪətri/ noun [U] (especially AmE) = CHIROPODY

po·dium /ˈpəʊdiəm; AmE ˈpoʊ-/ noun **1** a small platform that a person stands on when giving a speech or CONDUCTING an orchestra, etc. **2** (AmE) = LECTERN

poem /ˈpəʊɪm; AmE ˈpoʊəm/ noun a piece of writing in which the words are chosen for their sound and the images they suggest, not just for their obvious meanings. The words are arranged in separate lines, usually with a repeated rhythm, and sometimes the lines RHYME at the end.

poet /ˈpəʊɪt; AmE ˈpoʊət/ noun a person who writes poems

poet·ess /ˌpəʊɪˈtes; AmE ˌpoʊəˈtes/ noun (old-fashioned) a woman who writes poems

poet·ic /pəʊˈetɪk; AmE poʊ-/ (also less frequent **poet·ical** /-ɪkl/) adj. **1** [only before noun] connected with poetry; being poetry: poetic language ◇ Byron's Poetical Works **2** (approving) like or suggesting poetry, especially because it is imaginative and shows deep feeling: There is a poetic quality to her playing. ▶ **poet·ic·al·ly** /-kli/ adv.

poˌetic ˈjustice noun [U] a situation in which sth bad happens to sb, and you think that this is what they deserve

poˌetic ˈlicence noun [U] the freedom to change facts,

the normal rules of language, etc. in a special piece of writing or speech in order to achieve a particular effect: *He used a little poetic licence to embroider a good story.*

Poet 'Laureate (also **Laureate**) *noun* **1** (especially in Britain) a person who has been officially chosen to write poetry for the country's important occasions and is paid by the government or by the king or queen **2** (*especially AmE*) a person whose poetry is considered to be the best, or most typical of their country or region.

poet·ry /ˈpəʊətri; *AmE* ˈpoʊ-/ *noun* **1** [U] a collection of poems; poems in general SYN VERSE: *epic/lyric/pastoral poetry* ◊ *T.S. Eliot's poetry* ◊ *a poetry reading*—compare PROSE **2** [U, sing.] (*approving*) a beautiful and graceful quality: *There was poetry in all her gestures.*

po-faced /ˈpəʊ feɪst; *AmE* ˈpoʊ-/ *adj.* (*BrE, informal, disapproving*) looking very serious and as though you do not approve of sb/sth

pogo stick /ˈpəʊgəʊ stɪk; *AmE* ˈpoʊgoʊ/ *noun* a pole with a bar to stand on and a spring at the bottom, that you jump around on for fun

pog·rom /ˈpɒgrəm; *AmE* ˈpoʊg-/ *noun* the organized killing of large numbers of people, especially because of their race or religion (originally the killing of Jews in Russia)

poign·ant /ˈpɔɪnjənt/ *adj.* having a strong effect on your feelings, especially in a way that makes you feel sad SYN MOVING: *a poignant image/moment/memory* ▶ **poign·ancy** /-jənsi/ *noun* [U]: *the poignancy of parting and separation* ◊ *Of particular poignancy was the photograph of their son with his sisters, taken the day before he died.* **poign·ant·ly** /-jəntli/ *adv.*

poin·set·tia /ˌpɔɪnˈsetiə/ *noun* a tropical plant with large red or pink leaves that grow to look like flowers, often grown indoors in pots

point /pɔɪnt/ *noun, verb*
■ *noun*
OPINION/FACT | **1** [C] a thing that sb says or writes giving their opinion or stating a fact: *She made several interesting points in the article.* ◊ *I take your point* (= understand and accept what you are saying). ◊ *He's just saying that to prove a point* (= to show his idea is right). ◊ *OK, you've made your point!*—see also TALKING POINT

MAIN IDEA | **2** [C] (usually **the point**) the main or most important idea in sth that is said or done: *The point is you shouldn't have to wait so long to see a doctor.* ◊ *I wish he would get to the point* (= say it quickly). ◊ *I'll come straight to the point: we need more money.* ◊ *Do you see my point* (= understand)? ◊ *I think I missed the point* (= did not understand). ◊ *You have a point* (= your idea is right)—*it would be better to wait till this evening.* ◊ *'There won't be anywhere to park.' 'Oh, that's a (good) point.'* (= I had not thought of that) ◊ *It just isn't true. That's the whole point* (= the only important fact). ◊ *'He's been married before.' 'That's beside the point.* '(= not important) ◊ *I know it won't cost very much but that's not the point* (= not the important thing).

PURPOSE | **3** [U, sing.] the purpose or aim of sth: *What's the point of all this violence?* ◊ *There's no point in getting angry.* ◊ *I don't see the point of doing it all again.* ◊ *The point of the lesson is to compare the two countries.*

DETAIL | **4** [C] a particular detail or fact: *Here are the main points of the news.* ◊ *Can you explain that point again?*

QUALITY | **5** [C] a particular quality or feature that sb/sth has: *Tact is not one of her strong points.* ◊ *Read the manual to learn the program's finer points* (= small details). ◊ *Living in Scotland has its good points but the weather is not one of them.* ◊ *One of the hotel's plus points* (= good features) *is that it is very central.*—see also SELLING POINT

TIME | **6** [C] a particular time or stage of development: *The climber was at/on the point of death when they found him.* ◊ *We were on the point of giving up.* ◊ *Many people suffer from mental illness at some point in their lives.* ◊ *We had reached the point when there was no money left.* ◊ *At this point in time we just have to wait.* ◊ *At this point I don't care what you decide to do.*—see also HIGH POINT, LOW POINT, SATURATION POINT, STARTING POINT, STICKING POINT, TURNING POINT

PLACE | **7** [C] a particular place or area: *I'll wait for you at the meeting point in the arrivals hall.* ◊ *the point at which the river divides* ◊ *Draw a line from point A to point B.* ◊ *No parking beyond this point.*—see also FOCAL POINT, JUMPING-OFF POINT, THREE-POINT TURN, VANISHING POINT, VANTAGE POINT

DIRECTION | **8** [C] one of the marks of direction around a COMPASS: *the points of the compass* (= N, S, E, W, etc.)

IN COMPETITION | **9** [C] (*abbr.* **pt**) an individual unit that adds to a score in a game or sports competition: *to win/lose a point* ◊ *Australia finished 20 points ahead.* ◊ *They won on points* (= by scoring more points rather than by completely defeating their opponents).—see also BROWNIE POINT, MATCH POINT

MEASUREMENT | **10** [C] a mark or unit on a scale of measurement: *The party's share of the vote fell by ten percentage points.*—see also BOILING POINT, FREEZING POINT, MELTING POINT

PUNCTUATION | **11** [C] a small dot used in PUNCTUATION, especially the dot that separates a whole number from the part that comes after it: *two point six (2·6)* ◊ *a decimal point* ◊ *We broadcast on ninety-five point nine (95·9) FM.*

SHARP END | **12** [C] the sharp thin end of sth: *the point of a pencil/knife/pin*—see also BALLPOINT, GUNPOINT, KNIFE-POINT

LAND | **13** (also **Point**) a narrow piece of land that stretches into the sea: *The ship sailed around the point.* ◊ *Pagoda Point*

OF LIGHT/COLOUR | **14** [C] a very small dot of light or colour: *The stars were points of light in the sky.*

FOR ELECTRICITY | **15** [C] (*BrE*) a place in a wall, etc. where a piece of equipment can be connected to electricity: *a power/shaver/telephone point*

IN BALLET | **16** (**points**) [pl.] = POINTE

ON RAILWAY TRACK | **17** (**points**) [pl.] (*BrE*) (*AmE* **switch** [C]) a piece of track at a place where a railway/railroad line divides that can be moved to allow a train to change tracks

SIZE OF LETTERS | **18** [U] a unit of measurement for the size of letters in printing or on a computer screen, etc: *Change the text to 10 point.*

IDM **if/when it comes to the 'point** used when you have to decide sth or say what you really think: *When it comes to the point, he always changes his mind.* **in point of 'fact** used to say what is true in a situation: *In point of fact, she is their adopted daughter.* **make a 'point of doing sth** be or make sure you do sth because it is important or necessary: *I made a point of closing all the windows before leaving the house.* **,more to the 'point** used to say that sth is more important than sth else: *I couldn't do the job—I've never been to Spain and, more to the point, I don't speak Spanish.* **,point of 'contact** a place where you go or a person that you speak to when you are dealing with an organization: *The receptionist is the first point of contact most people have with the clinic.* **a ,point of de'parture 1** a place where a journey starts **2** (*formal*) an idea, a theory or an event that is used to start a discussion, an activity, etc. **a ,point of 'honour** a thing that sb considers to be very important for their honour or reputation **the ,point of ,no re'turn** the time when you must continue with what you have decided to do, because it is not possible to get back to an earlier situation **,point 'taken** used to say that you accept that sb else is right when they have disagreed with you or criticized you: *Point taken. Let's drop the subject.* **to the 'point** expressed in a simple, clear way without any extra information or feelings: *The letter was short and to the point.* **to the 'point of (doing) sth** to a degree that can be described as sth: *He was rude to the point of being aggressive.* **up to a (certain) 'point** to some extent; to some degree but not completely: *I agree with you up to a point.*—more at BELABOUR, CASE *n.*, FINE *adj.*, LABOUR *v.*, MOOT *adj.*, SCORE *v.*, SORE *adj.*, STRETCH *v.*

■ *verb*
SHOW WITH FINGER | **1** [no passive] **~ (at/to/towards sb/sth)** to stretch out your finger or sth held in your hand towards sb/sth in order to show sb where a person or

æ	ɑː	e	ɜː	ə	ɪ	iː	i	ɒ	ɔː	ʌ	ʊ	u	uː
cat	father	ten	bird	about	sit	see	many	got	saw	cup	put	actual	too
								(BrE)					

P

P

thing is: [V] *It's rude to point!* ◊ *He pointed to the spot where the house used to stand.* ◊ *'What's your name?' he asked, pointing at the child with his pen.* ◊ *She pointed in my direction.* ◊ [VN] *She pointed her finger in my direction.* AIM | **2** [VN] **~ sth (at sb/sth)** to aim sth at sb/sth: *He pointed the gun at her head.*

FACE DIRECTION | **3** [V+*adv./prep.*] to face in or be directed towards a particular direction: *The telescope was pointing in the wrong direction.* ◊ *The signpost pointed straight ahead.* ◊ *A compass needle points north.*

LEAD TO | **4** [+*adv./prep.*] to lead to or suggest a particular development or logical argument: [V] *The evidence seems to point in that direction.* ◊ [VN] *The fans are looking to the new players to* **point the way** *to victory.*

SHOW THE WAY | **5** [VN+*adv./prep.*] to show sb which way to go: *I wonder if you could point me in the right direction for the bus station.* ◊ *A series of yellow arrows* **pointed the way** *to reception.*

WALL | **6** [VN] to put MORTAR between the bricks of a wall IDM **point a/the 'finger (at sb)** to accuse sb of doing sth: *The article points an accusing finger at the authorities.* PHRV **,point sb/sth ↔ 'out (to sb)** to stretch your finger out towards sb/sth in order to show sb which person or thing you are referring to: *I'll point him out to you next time he comes in.* **,point 'out (to sb)** | **,point sth ↔ 'out (to sb)** to mention sth in order to give sb information about it or make them notice it: *She tried in vain to point out to him the unfairness of his actions.* ◊ *He pointed out the dangers of driving alone.* ◊ [+that] *I should point out that not one of these paintings is original.* ◊ *'It's not very far,' she pointed out.* **'point to sth 1** to mention sth that you think is important and/or the reason why a particular situation exists: *The board of directors pointed to falling productivity to justify their decision.* **2** to suggest that sth is true or likely: *All the signs point to a successful year ahead.* **,point sth ↔ 'up** (*formal*) to emphasize sth so that it becomes more noticeable: *The conference merely pointed up divisions in the party.*

,point-'blank *adj.* [only before noun] **1** (of a shot) fired with the gun touching or very close to the person or thing it is aimed at: *The officer was shot dead at point-blank range.* **2** (of sth that is said) very definite and direct and not very polite: *a point-blank refusal* ▶ **,point-'blank** *adv.*: *She fired point-blank at his chest.* ◊ *He refused point-blank to be photographed.*

'point duty *noun* [U] (*BrE*) the job of controlling traffic that is done by a police officer standing in the middle of the road: *to be on point duty*

pointe /pwæt/ *noun* [U] (also **pointes** /pwæt/ **points** [pl.]) the tops of the toes that a ballet dancer balances on

point·ed /'pɔɪntɪd/ *adj.* **1** having a sharp end: *a pointed chin* ◊ *pointed teeth* ◊ *the pointed arches used in medieval buildings* ◊ *a pointed instrument*—see also POINTY **2** aimed in a clear and often critical way against a particular person or their behaviour: *a pointed comment/remark* ◊ *His words were a pointed reminder of her position.*

point·ed·ly /'pɔɪntɪdli/ *adv.* in a way that is clearly intended to show what you mean or to express criticism: *She yawned and looked pointedly at her watch.*

point·er /'pɔɪntə(r)/ *noun* **1** (*informal*) a piece of advice: *Here are some pointers on how to go about the writing task.* **2 ~ (to sth)** a sign that sth exists; a sign that shows how sth may develop in the future: *The surge in car sales was regarded as an encouraging pointer to an improvement in the economy.* **3** a thin strip of metal that points to the numbers on a DIAL on a piece of equipment for measuring sth **4** a stick used to point to things on a map or picture on a wall **5** (*computing*) a small symbol, for example an arrow that marks a point on a computer screen **6** a large dog used in hunting, trained to stand still with its nose pointing towards the birds being hunted

poin·til·lism /'pɔɪntɪlɪzəm; 'pwænt-/ *noun* [U] a style of painting that was developed in France in the late 19th century in which very small dots of colour are used to build up the picture ▶ **poin·til·list** /-lɪst/ *adj.* **poin·til·list** *noun*: *Seurat, the French pointillist*

point·ing /'pɔɪntɪŋ/ *noun* [U] (*BrE*) the MORTAR that is put in the spaces between the bricks or stones in a wall; the method of filling in the spaces with MORTAR

point·less /'pɔɪntləs/ *adj.* having no purpose; not worth doing: *We searched until we knew it would be pointless to continue.* ▶ **point·less·ly** *adv.*: *He argued pointlessly with his parents.* **point·less·ness** *noun* [U]: *the pointlessness of war*

'point man *noun* a soldier who goes in front of the others to look for danger: (*figurative, AmE*) *the President's point man on education* (= the person who is responsible for it)

,point of 'order *noun* (*pl.* **points of order**) (*formal*) a question about whether the rules of behaviour in a formal discussion or meeting are being followed correctly

,point of 'reference *noun* (*pl.* **points of reference**) something that you already know that helps you understand a situation or explain sth to sb

,point of 'sale *noun* [sing.] the place where a product is sold: *More information on healthy foods should be provided at the point of sale.*

,point of 'use *noun* [sing.] the place where a product or a service is actually used: *Medical care is still free at the point of use.*

,point of 'view *noun* (*pl.* **points of view**) **1** the particular attitude or opinion that sb has about sth: *Why can't you ever see my point of view?* ◊ *There are a number of different points of view on this issue.* ◊ *From my point of view* (= as far as I was concerned) *the party was a complete success.* **2** a particular way of considering or judging a situation SYN ANGLE: *These statistics are important from an ecological point of view.* ◊ *From the point of view of higher education, the cuts will be a disaster.* ◊ *The book is written from the father's point of view.*

,point-to-'point *noun* (*BrE*) a race on horses that goes over a marked course across fields and has fences or walls for the horses to jump over

pointy /'pɔɪnti/ *adj.* (*informal*) with a point at one end SYN POINTED: *pointy ears*

poise /pɔɪz/ *noun, verb*
■ *noun* [U] **1** a calm and confident manner with control of your feelings or behaviour: *His performance was full of maturity and poise.* **2** the ability to move or stand in a graceful way with good control of your body
■ *verb* to be or hold sth steady in a particular position, especially above sth else: [V+*adv./prep.*] *The hawk poised in mid-air ready to swoop.* ◊ [VN to inf] *He was poising himself to launch a final attack.* ◊ [VN+*adv./prep.*] *She poised the javelin in her hand before the throw.*

poised /pɔɪzd/ *adj.* **1** [not before noun] **~ (on, above, over, etc. sth)** | **~ (to do sth)** in a position that is completely still but is ready to move at any moment: *Tina was tense, her hand poised over the telephone.* ◊ *He stopped writing and looked at me, pen poised.* ◊ *The cat crouched in the grass, poised to jump.* **2** [not before noun] **~ (in, on, above, etc. sth)** in a position that is balanced but likely to change in one direction or another: *The dancer was poised on one foot.* ◊ *The cup was poised on the edge of the chair.* ◊ (*figurative*) *The world stood poised between peace and war.* **3** [not before noun] **~ for sth** | **~ to do sth** completely ready for sth or to do sth SYN SET: *The economy is poised for recovery.* ◊ *The British team is poised to win the title.* ◊ *Kate is poised to become the highest-paid supermodel in the fashion world.* **4** having a calm and confident manner and in control of your feelings and behaviour: *He is a remarkably poised young man.*

poi·son /'pɔɪzn/ *noun, verb*
■ *noun* [C, U] **1** a substance that causes death or harm if it is swallowed or absorbed into the body: *Some mushrooms contain a deadly poison.* ◊ *How did he die? Was it poison?* ◊ *The dog was killed by rat poison* (= poison intended to kill rats). ◊ *to hunt with poison arrows* ◊ *bombs containing poison gas* **2** an idea, a feeling, etc. that is extremely harmful: *the poison of racial hatred* IDM **what's your 'poison?** (*spoken, humorous*) used to ask sb what alcoholic drink they would like
■ *verb* [VN] **1 ~ sb (with sth)** to harm or kill a person or an animal by giving them poison **2** to put poison in or on

sth: *a poisoned arrow* ◊ *Someone had been poisoning his food.* ◊ *Large sections of the river have been poisoned by toxic waste from factories.* **3** (*written*) to have a bad effect on sth: *His comment served only to poison the atmosphere still further.* ◊ *She succeeded in **poisoning their minds** against me.* **IDM** **a poisoned 'chalice** (*especially BrE*) a thing which seems attractive when it is given to sb but which soon becomes unpleasant: *He inherited a poisoned chalice when he took over the job as union leader.*

poi·son·er /'pɔɪzənə(r)/ *noun* a person who murders sb by using poison

poi·son·ing /'pɔɪzənɪŋ/ *noun* [U, C] **1** the fact or state of having swallowed or absorbed poison: *a series of deaths caused by carbon monoxide poisoning* ◊ *At least 10000 children are involved in accidental poisonings every year.* **2** the act of killing or harming sb/sth by giving them poison: *The police suspected poisoning.* ◊ *The rats were controlled by poisoning.*—see also BLOOD POISONING, FOOD POISONING

ˌpoison 'ivy *noun* [U] a N American climbing plant that causes painful spots on the skin when you touch it

ˌpoison 'oak *noun* [U] a N American bush that causes painful spots on the skin when you touch it

poi·son·ous /'pɔɪzənəs/ *adj.* **1** causing death or illness if swallowed or absorbed into the body **SYN** TOXIC: *poisonous chemicals/plants* ◊ *This gas is highly poisonous.* ◊ *The leaves of certain trees are poisonous to cattle.* **2** (of animals and insects) producing a poison that can cause death or illness if the animal or insect bites you **SYN** VENOMOUS: *poisonous snakes* ◊ *a tiny spider with a poisonous bite* **3** extremely unpleasant or unfriendly: *a poisonous person* ◊ *the poisonous atmosphere in the office*

ˌpoison 'pen letter *noun* an unpleasant letter which is not signed and is intended to upset the person who receives it

ˌpoison 'pill *noun* (*informal, business*) a form of defence used by a company to prevent, or to reduce the effect of, a TAKEOVER BID that they do not want, for example by selling some of their important possessions

poke /pəʊk; *AmE* poʊk/ *verb, noun*

▪ *verb* **1** [VN] ~ **sb/sth (with sth)** to quickly push your fingers or another object into sb/sth: *She poked him in the ribs with her elbow.* ◊ *She poked her elbow into his ribs.* ◊ *I'm sick of being poked and prodded by doctors.* ◊ *She got up and poked the fire* (= to make it burn more strongly). **2** [VN+adv./prep.] to push sth somewhere or move it in a particular direction with a small quick movement: *He poked his head around the corner to check that nobody was coming.* ◊ *Someone had poked a message under the door.* ◊ *Don't poke her eye out with that stick!* **3** [V+adv./prep.] if an object is **poking out of, through, etc.** sth, you can see a part of it that is no longer covered by sth else: *The end of the cable was left poking out of the wall.* ◊ *Clumps of grass poked up through the snow.* **4** [VN+adv./prep.] ~ **a hole in sth (with sth)** to make a hole in sth by pushing your finger or another object into it: *The kids poked holes in the ice with sticks.* **5** [VN] (*slang*, △) (of a man) to have sex with sb **IDM** **poke 'fun at sb/sth** to say unkind things about sb/sth in order to make other people laugh at them: *Her novels poke fun at the upper class.*—more at NOSE *n.* **PHRV** **ˌpoke a'bout/a'round** (*informal*) to look for sth, especially sth that is hidden among other things that you have to move: *The police spent the day poking around in his office but found nothing.* ◊ (*figurative*) *We've had journalists poking around and asking a lot of questions.* **'poke at sth** to push a pointed object, your finger, etc. at sth repeatedly with small quick movements: *He poked at the spaghetti with a fork.*

▪ *noun* **1** [C, usually sing.] the action of quickly pushing your fingers or another object into sb/sth: *to give the fire a poke* ◊ *He gave me a poke in the ribs to wake me up.* **2** [U] (*BrE*) power in a car: *I prefer something with a bit more poke.* **IDM** **have a ˌpoke a'round** (*informal*) to look carefully around a place to see what you can find; to try to find out information about sb/sth **take a 'poke at sb/sth** (*old-fashioned, AmE, informal*) to make an unkind remark about sb/sth; to laugh at sb/sth—more at PIG *n.*

poker /'pəʊkə(r); *AmE* 'poʊ-/ *noun* **1** [U] a card game for two or more people, in which the players bet on the values of the cards they hold **2** [C] a metal stick for moving or breaking up coal in a fire

'poker-faced *adj.* (*informal*) with an expression on your face that does not show what you are thinking or feeling: *Our passports were checked by poker-faced officials.* ◊ *a poker-faced expression* ▶ **'poker face** *noun*: *He maintained a poker face.*

poky /'pəʊki; *AmE* 'poʊki/ *adj.* (*informal*) **1** (of a room or a building) too small; without much space: *a poky little room* **2** (also **pokey**) (both *AmE*) extremely slow and annoying

pol /pɒl; *AmE* pɑːl/ *noun* (*AmE, informal*) = POLITICIAN

polar /'pəʊlə(r); *AmE* 'poʊ-/ *adj.* [only before noun] **1** connected with, or near the North or South Pole: *the polar regions* ◊ *polar ice* ◊ *polar explorers* **2** (*technical*) connected with the POLES (= the positive and negative ends) of a MAGNET: *polar attraction* **3** (*formal*) used to describe sth that is the complete opposite of sth else: *The parents' position is often the polar opposite of the child's.*

'polar bear *noun* a white bear that lives near the North Pole

po·lar·ity /pə'lærəti/ *noun* [U] **1** ~ **(between A and B)** (*formal*) the situation when two tendencies, opinions, etc. oppose each other: *the growing polarity between the left and right wings of the party* **2** [U, C] (*physics*) the condition of having two POLES with opposite qualities: *the polarity of a magnet*

po·lar·ize (*BrE* also **-ise**) /'pəʊləraɪz; *AmE* 'poʊ-/ *verb* **1** to separate or make people separate into two groups with completely opposite opinions: [V] *Public opinion has polarized on this issue.* ◊ [VN] *The issue has polarized public opinion.* **2** [VN] (*physics*) to make waves of light, etc. VIBRATE in a single direction **3** [VN] (*physics*) to give polarity to sth: *to polarize a magnet* ▶ **po·lar·iza·tion, -isa·tion** /ˌpəʊləraɪ'zeɪʃn; *AmE* ˌpoʊlərə'z-/ *noun* [U, C]

Po·lar·oid™ /'pəʊlərɔɪd; *AmE* 'poʊ-/ *noun* **1** [C] (also **ˌPolaroid 'camera**) a camera that can produce a photograph within a few seconds **2** [C] a photograph that has been taken with a Polaroid camera **3** [U] a transparent substance that is put on SUNGLASSES and car windows to make the sun seem less bright: *Polaroid sunglasses* **4** (**Polaroids**) [pl.] (also **ˌPolaroid 'sunglasses**) SUNGLASSES that have a layer of Polaroid on them

pole /pəʊl; *AmE* poʊl/ *noun, verb*

▪ *noun* **1** a long thin straight piece of wood or metal, especially one with the end placed in the ground, used as a support: *a tent/telegraph pole* ◊ *a ski pole*—see also BARGEPOLE, FLAGPOLE, TOTEM POLE **2** either of the two points at the opposite ends of the line on which the earth or any other planet turns: *the North/South Pole* **3** (*physics*) either of the two ends of a MAGNET, or the positive or negative points of an electric battery **4** either of two opposite or contrasting extremes: *Their opinions were at opposite poles of the debate.* **IDM** **be ˌpoles a'part** to be widely separated; to have no interests that you share: *Her own friends were poles apart from his.* **up the 'pole** (*old-fashioned, BrE, informal*) crazy—more at TOUCH *v.*

▪ *verb* [VN, V+adv./prep.] to move a boat by pushing on the bottom of a river, etc. with a pole

pole-axe (*BrE*) (*AmE* **pole-ax**) /'pəʊlæks; *AmE* 'poʊl-/ *verb* [VN] **1** to hit sb very hard so that they fall down and cannot stand up again **2** [usually passive] to surprise or shock you so much that you do not know what to say or do

pole·cat /'pəʊlkæt; *AmE* 'poʊl-/ *noun* **1** a small European wild animal with a long thin body, dark brown fur and a strong unpleasant smell **2** (*AmE*) = SKUNK

po·lem·ic /pə'lemɪk/ *noun* (*formal*) **1** [C] a speech or a piece of writing that argues very strongly for or against sth/sb **2** [U] (also **po·lem·ics** [pl.]) the practice or skill of arguing strongly for or against sth/sb: *Her speech was memorable for its polemic rather than its substance.*

po·lem·ic·al /pə'lemɪkl/ (also *less frequent* **po·lem·ic**) *adj.* (*formal*) involving strong arguments for or against sth, often in opposition to the opinion of others: *a polemical attack*

b	d	f	g	h	k	l	m	n	p	r
bad	did	fall	get	hat	cat	leg	man	now	pen	red

po·lemi·cist /pəˈlemɪsɪst/ *noun* (*formal*) a person who makes skilful use of POLEMIC

ˈpole position *noun* [U, C] the leading position at the start of a race involving cars or bicycles

the ˈPole Star *noun* [sing.] the star that is above the North Pole in the sky

the ˈpole vault *noun* [sing.] a sporting event in which people try to jump over a high bar, using a long pole to push themselves off the ground—picture on page 1251
▶ **ˈpole-vaulter** *noun* **ˈpole-vaulting** *noun* [U]

po·lice /pəˈliːs/ *noun, verb*
■ *noun* (often **the police**) [pl.] an official organization whose job is to make people obey the law and to prevent and solve crime; the people who work for this organization: *A man was arrested by the police and held for questioning.* ◊ *Get out of the house or I'll call the police.* ◊ *Police suspect a local gang.* ◊ *a police car/enquiry/warning* ◊ *Hundreds of police in riot gear struggled to control the violence.*—see also SECRET POLICE
■ *verb* [VN] **1** (of the police, army, etc.) to go around a particular area to make sure that nobody is breaking the law there: *The border will be policed by UN officials.* **2** (of a committee, etc.) to make sure that a particular set of rules is obeyed: *The profession is policed by its own regulatory body.*

po·lice commissioner *noun* (*especially AmE*) = COMMISSIONER

po·lice ˈconstable (also **constable**) *noun* (*abbr.* PC) (in Britain and some other countries) a police officer of the lowest rank: *Police Constable Jordan*

po·lice dog *noun* a dog that is trained to find or attack suspected criminals

po·lice force *noun* the police organization of a country, district or town

po·lice·man /pəˈliːsmən/ *noun* (*pl.* **-men** /-mən/) a male police officer ⇨ note at GENDER

po·lice officer (also **officer**) *noun* a member of the police

po·lice state *noun* (*disapproving*) a country where people's freedom, especially to travel and to express political opinions, is controlled by the government, with the help of the police

po·lice station (*AmE* also **ˈstation house**) *noun* the office of a local police force: *The suspect was taken to the nearest police station for questioning.*

po·lice·wo·man /pəˈliːswʊmən/ *noun* (*pl.* **-women** /-wɪmɪn/) a female police officer ⇨ note at GENDER

po·licing /pəˈliːsɪŋ/ *noun* [U] **1** the activity of keeping order in a place with police: *community policing* **2** the activity of controlling an industry, an activity, etc. to make sure that people obey the rules: *the policing of legislation*

pol·icy /ˈpɒləsi; *AmE* ˈpɑːl-/ *noun* (*pl.* **-ies**) **1** [C, U] ~ (on sth) a plan of action agreed or chosen by a political party, a business, etc: *the present government's policy on education* ◊ *The company has adopted a firm policy on shoplifting.* ◊ *US foreign/domestic policy* ◊ *They have had a significant change in policy on paternity leave.* ◊ *a policy document* **2** [C, U] (*formal*) a principle that you believe in that influences how you behave; a way in which you usually behave: *She is following her usual policy of ignoring all offers of help.* ◊ (*saying*) *Honesty is the best policy.* **3** [C] a written statement of a contract of insurance: *Check the terms of the policy before you sign.*

pol·icy·hold·er /ˈpɒləsihəʊldə(r); *AmE* ˈpɑːləsihoʊl-/ *noun* (*formal*) a person or group that holds an insurance policy

polio /ˈpəʊliəʊ; *AmE* ˈpoʊlioʊ/ (also *formal* **polio·my·el·itis** /ˌpəʊliəʊˌmaɪəˈlaɪtɪs; *AmE* ˌpoʊlioʊ-/) *noun* [U] an infectious disease that affects the central nervous system and can cause temporary or permanent PARALYSIS (= loss of control or feeling in part or most of the body)

pol·ish /ˈpɒlɪʃ; *AmE* ˈpɑːl-/ *noun, verb*
■ *noun* **1** [U, C] a substance used when rubbing a surface to make it smooth and shiny: *furniture/floor/shoe/silver polish* ◊ *wax polish*—see also FRENCH POLISH, NAIL POLISH

2 [sing.] an act of polishing sth: *I give it a polish now and again.* **3** [sing.] the shiny appearance of sth after it has been polished **4** [U] a high quality of performance achieved with great skill: *She played the cello with the polish of a much older musician.* **5** [U] high standards of behaviour; being polite: *She thought that her husband's family lacked polish.* **IDM** SEE SPIT *n.*
■ *verb* **1** ~ sth (up) (with sth) to make sth smooth and shiny by rubbing it with a piece of fabric, often with polish on it: [VN] *Polish shoes regularly to protect the leather.* ◊ *He polished his glasses with a handkerchief.* [also V]—see also FRENCH POLISH **2** [VN] ~ sth (up) to make changes to sth in order to improve it: *The statement was carefully polished and checked before release.* ◊ *The hotel has polished up its act* (= improved its service) *since last year.* **PHRV** ˌpolish sb↔ˈoff (*informal, especially AmE*) to kill sb ˌpolish sth↔ˈoff (*informal*) to finish sth, especially food, quickly: *He polished off the remains of the apple pie.*

pol·ished /ˈpɒlɪʃt; *AmE* ˈpɑːl-/ *adj.* **1** shiny as a result of polishing **2** elegant, confident and/or highly skilled: *polished manners* ◊ *She gave a polished performance on the piano.*

pol·ish·er /ˈpɒlɪʃə(r); *AmE* ˈpɑːl-/ *noun* a machine for polishing sth: *a floor polisher*

pol·it·buro /ˈpɒlɪtbjʊərəʊ; *AmE* ˈpɑːlɪtbjʊroʊ/ *noun* (*pl.* **-os**) the most important committee of a Communist party, with the power to decide on policy, especially in the former USSR

po·lite /pəˈlaɪt/ *adj.* (**po·liter, po·litest**) **HELP** more polite and most polite are also common **1** having or showing good manners and respect for the feelings of others **SYN** COURTEOUS: *Please be polite to our guests.* ◊ *We were all too polite to object.* **OPP** IMPOLITE **2** socially correct but not always sincere: *I don't know how to make polite conversation.* ◊ *The performance was greeted with polite applause.* **3** [only before noun] from a class of society that believes it is better than others: *'Bum' is not a word we use in polite company.* ▶ **po·lite·ly** *adv.* **po·lite·ness** *noun* [U]

pol·it·ic /ˈpɒlətɪk; *AmE* ˈpɑːl-/ *adj.* (*formal*) (of actions) based on good judgement **SYN** WISE, PRUDENT: *It seemed politic to say nothing.*—see also BODY POLITIC

pol·it·ical /pəˈlɪtɪkl/ *adj.* **1** connected with the state, government or public affairs: *a monarch without political power* ◊ *He was a political prisoner* (= one who was imprisoned because he was thought to be harmful to the state). **2** connected with the different groups working in politics, especially their policies and the competition between them: *a political debate/party/leader* ◊ *What are your political sympathies?* **3** (of people) interested in or active in politics: *She became very political at university.* ◊ *I'm not a political animal* (= person). **4** concerned with power, status, etc. within an organization, rather than with matters of principle: *I suspect that he was dismissed for political reasons.*—see also POLITICALLY

po·litical aˈsylum *noun* [U] (*formal*) = ASYLUM

po·litical corˈrectness *noun* [U] (sometimes *disapproving*) the principle of avoiding language and behaviour that may offend particular groups of people

po·litical eˈconomy *noun* [U] the study of how nations organize the production and use of wealth

po·litical geˈography *noun* [U] the way in which the world is divided into different countries, especially as a subject of study

pol·it·ic·al·ly /pəˈlɪtɪkli/ *adv.* in a way that is connected with politics: *a politically sensitive issue* ◊ *politically motivated crimes* ◊ *It makes sense politically as well as economically.*

po·litically corˈrect *adj.* (*abbr.* PC) used to describe language or behaviour that deliberately tries to avoid offending particular groups of people

po·litically incorˈrect *adj.* failing to avoid language or behaviour that may offend particular groups of people

po·litical ˈscience (also **pol·it·ics**) *noun* [U] the study of government and politics

po·litical ˈscientist *noun* an expert in political science

pol·it·ician /ˌpɒləˈtɪʃn; *AmE* ˌpɑːl-/ *noun* **1** (also *AmE*

P

informal **pol**) a person whose job is concerned with politics, especially as an elected member of parliament, etc. **2** (*disapproving*) a person who is good at using different situations in an organization to try to get power or advantage for himself or herself

pol·iti·cize (*BrE* also **-ise**) /pəˈlɪtɪsaɪz/ *verb* [VN] [often passive] **1** to make sth a political issue: *the highly politicized issue of unemployment* **2** to make sb/sth become more involved in politics: *The rural population has become increasingly politicized in recent years.* ▶ **pol·iti·ciza·tion, -isa·tion** /pəˌlɪtɪsaɪˈzeɪʃn/ *noun* [U]: *the politicization of education*

pol·it·ick·ing /ˈpɒlɪtɪkɪŋ; *AmE* ˈpɑːl-/ *noun* [U] (often *disapproving*) political activity, especially to win support for yourself

pol·it·ico /pəˈlɪtɪkəʊ; *AmE* -koʊ/ *noun* (*pl.* **-os**) (*informal, disapproving*) a politician; sb who is active in politics

pol·it·ics /ˈpɒlətɪks; *AmE* ˈpɑːl-/ *noun* **1** [U+sing./pl. *v.*] the activities involved in getting and using power in public life, and being able to influence decisions that affect a country or a society: *party politics ◊ local politics ◊ He's thinking of **going into politics** (= trying to become a Member of Parliament, Congress, etc.) ◊ a major figure in British politics* **2** [U+sing./pl. *v.*] (*disapproving*) matters concerned with getting or using power within a particular group or organization: *I don't want to get involved in office politics. ◊ the internal politics of the legal profession ◊ sexual politics* (= concerning relationships of power between the sexes) **3** [pl.] a person's political views or beliefs: *His politics are extreme.* **4** [U] = POLITICAL SCIENCE: *a degree in Politics* **5** [sing.] a system of political beliefs; a state of political affairs: *A politics of the future has to engage with new ideas.*

pol·ity /ˈpɒləti; *AmE* ˈpɑːl-/ *noun* (*pl.* **-ies**) (*technical*) **1** [C] a society as a politically organized state **2** [U] the form or process of government

polka /ˈpɒlkə; *AmE* ˈpoʊlkə/ *noun* a fast dance for two people together that was popular in the 19th century; a piece of music for this dance

'polka dot *noun* one of many dots that together form a pattern, especially on fabric: *a polka-dot tie*—compare SPOT—picture on page A4

poll /pəʊl; *AmE* poʊl/ *noun, verb*
■ *noun* **1** (also **o'pinion poll**) [C] the process of questioning people who are representative of a larger group in order to get information about the general opinion: *to carry out/conduct a poll ◊ A recent poll suggests some surprising changes in public opinion.* **2** [C] (also **the polls** [pl.]) the process of voting at an election; the process of counting the votes: *The final result of the poll will be known tomorrow. ◊ Thursday is traditionally the day when Britain **goes to the polls** (= when elections are held). ◊ Polls close* (= voting ends) *at 9 p.m.* **3** [sing.] the number of votes given in an election: *Labour is ahead in the poll. ◊ They gained 20% of the poll.*—see also DEED POLL, EXIT POLL, STRAW POLL
■ *verb* **1** to receive a particular number of votes in an election: [VN] *They polled 39% of the vote in the last election. ◊* [V] *The Republicans have polled well* (= received many votes) *in recent elections.* **2** [VN] [usually passive] to ask a large number of members of the public what they think about sth: *Over 50% of those polled were against the proposed military action.*

pol·lard /ˈpɒləd; *-lɑːd; AmE* ˈpɑːlərd/ *verb* [VN] [usually passive] (*technical*) to cut off the lower branches at the top of the tree so that the lower branches will grow more thickly

pol·len /ˈpɒlən; *AmE* ˈpɑːlən/ *noun* [U] fine powder, usually yellow, that is formed in flowers, and carried to other flowers of the same kind by the wind or by insects, to make those flowers produce seeds

'pollen count *noun* [usually sing.] a number that shows the amount of pollen in the air, used to warn people whose health is affected by it

pol·lin·ate /ˈpɒləneɪt; *AmE* ˈpɑːl-/ *verb* [VN] to put POLLEN into a flower or plant so that it produces seeds: *flowers*

pollinated by bees/the wind ▶ **pol·lin·ation** /ˌpɒləˈneɪʃn; *AmE* ˌpɑːl-/ *noun* [U]

poll·ing /ˈpəʊlɪŋ; *AmE* ˈpoʊ-/ *noun* [U] **1** the activity of voting: *Polling has been heavy since 8 a.m.* **2** the act of asking questions as part of an opinion POLL

'polling booth (*especially BrE*) (*AmE* usually **'voting booth**) *noun* a small, partly enclosed place in a POLLING STATION where people vote by marking a card, etc.

'polling day *noun* [U, C] (*BrE*) a day on which people vote in an election: *a week before polling day*

'polling station (*especially BrE*) (*AmE* usually **'polling place**) *noun* a building where people go to vote in an election

poll·ster /ˈpəʊlstə(r); *AmE* ˈpoʊl-/ *noun* a person who makes or asks the questions in an OPINION POLL

'poll tax *noun* a tax that must be paid at the same rate by every person or every adult in a particular area

pol·lu·tant /pəˈluːtənt/ *noun* (*formal*) a substance that pollutes sth, especially air and water

pol·lute /pəˈluːt/ *verb* [VN] **~ sth (by/with sth)** to add dirty or harmful substances to land, air, water, etc. so that it is no longer pleasant or safe to use: *the exhaust fumes that are polluting our cities ◊ The river has been polluted with toxic waste from local factories. ◊* (*figurative*) *a society polluted by racism*

pol·luter /pəˈluːtə(r)/ *noun* a person, company, country, etc. that causes pollution

pol·lu·tion /pəˈluːʃn/ *noun* [U] **1** the process of making air, water, soil, etc. dirty; the state of being dirty: *air/water pollution ◊ to reduce levels of environmental pollution* **2** substances that make air, water, soil, etc. dirty: *beaches covered with pollution* **3** **noise/light ~** harmful or annoying levels of noise, or of artificial light at night

polo /ˈpəʊləʊ; *AmE* ˈpoʊloʊ/ *noun* [U] a game in which two teams of players riding on horses try to hit a ball into a goal using long wooden hammers (called MALLETS)—see also WATER POLO

'polo neck (*BrE*) (*AmE* **turtle·neck**) *noun* a high round collar made when the neck of a piece of clothing is folded over; a piece of clothing with a polo neck: *You can wear a polo neck with that jacket. ◊ a polo-neck sweater*—picture on page A5

'polo shirt *noun* an informal shirt with short sleeves, a collar and a few buttons at the neck

pol·ter·geist /ˈpəʊltəgaɪst; ˈpɒl-; *AmE* ˈpoʊltərg-/ *noun* a ghost that makes loud noises and throws objects

poly /ˈpɒli; *AmE* ˈpɑːli/ *noun* (*pl.* **polys**) (*BrE, informal*) = POLYTECHNIC

poly- /ˈpɒli; *AmE* ˈpɑːli/ *combining form* (in nouns, adjectives and adverbs) many: *polygamy ◊ polyphonic*

poly·an·dry /ˌpɒliˈændri; *AmE* ˌpɑːl-/ *noun* [U] (*technical*) the custom of having more than one husband at the same time ▶ **poly·an·drous** /ˌpɒliˈændrəs; *AmE* ˌpɑːl-/ *adj.*

poly·es·ter /ˌpɒliˈestə(r); *AmE* ˌpɑːli-; ˈpɑːliestər/ *noun* [U, C] a strong artificial fabric, often mixed with other fabrics and used especially for making clothes: *a cotton and polyester shirt*

poly·ethyl·ene /ˌpɒliˈeθəliːn; *AmE* ˌpɑːl-/ *noun* [U] (*AmE*) = POLYTHENE

pol·yg·amy /pəˈlɪɡəmi/ *noun* [U] (*technical*) the custom of having more than one wife at the same time—compare BIGAMY, MONOGAMY ▶ **pol·yg·am·ous** /pəˈlɪɡəməs/ *adj.*: *a polygamous marriage/society*

poly·glot /ˈpɒliɡlɒt; *AmE* ˈpɑːliɡlɑːt/ *adj.* (*formal*) knowing, using or written in many languages: *a polyglot nation*

poly·gon /ˈpɒliɡən; *AmE* ˈpɑːliɡɑːn/ *noun* (*geometry*) a flat shape with at least three straight sides and angles, and usually five or more ▶ **pol·yg·on·al** /pəˈlɪɡənl/ *adj.*

poly·graph /ˈpɒliɡræf; *AmE* ˈpɑːli- BrE also -ɡrɑːf/ *noun* (*technical*) = LIE DETECTOR

poly·math /ˈpɒlimæθ; *AmE* ˈpɑːl-/ *noun* (*formal, approving*) a person who knows a lot about many different subjects

poly·mer /ˈpɒlimə(r); *AmE* ˈpɑːl-/ *noun* (*chemistry*) a natural or artificial compound consisting of large MOLECULES

æ	ɑː	e	ɜː	ə	ɪ	iː	i	ɒ	ɔː	ʌ	ʊ	u	uː
cat	father	ten	bird	about	sit	see	many	got	saw	cup	put	actual	too
								(BrE)					

P

(= groups of atoms) that are made from combinations of small simple MOLECULES

poly·morph·ous /ˌpɒliˈmɔːfəs; *AmE* ˌpɑːliˈmɔːrfəs/ (also **poly·morph·ic** /-fɪk/) *adj.* (*formal* or *technical*) having or passing through many stages of development

polyp /ˈpɒlɪp; *AmE* ˈpɑːlɪp/ *noun* **1** (*medical*) a small lump that grows inside the body, especially in the nose, that is caused by disease but is usually harmless **2** a small and very simple sea creature with a body shaped like a tube

pol·yph·ony /pəˈlɪfəni/ *noun* [U] (*music*) the combination of several different patterns of musical notes sung together to form a single piece of music SYN COUNTERPOINT ▶ **poly·phon·ic** /ˌpɒliˈfɒnɪk; *AmE* ˌpɑːliˈfɑːnɪk/ *adj.*

poly·pro·pyl·ene /ˌpɒliˈprəʊpəliːn; *AmE* ˌpɑːliˈprəʊ-/ *noun* [U] a strong plastic often used for objects such as toys or chairs that are made in a MOULD

poly·sem·ous /ˌpɒliˈsiːməs; *AmE* ˌpɑːl-/ *adj.* (*linguistics*) (of a word) having more than one meaning

poly·styr·ene /ˌpɒliˈstaɪriːn; *AmE* ˌpɑːl-/ (also **Styrofoam**™ especially in *AmE*) *noun* [U] a very light soft plastic that is usually white, used especially for making containers that prevent heat loss: *polystyrene cups/mugs*

poly·syl·lable /ˈpɒlisɪləbl; *AmE* ˈpɑːl-/ *noun* (*technical*) a word of several (usually more than three) syllables ▶ **poly·syl·lab·ic** /ˌpɒlisɪˈlæbɪk; *AmE* ˌpɑːl-/ *adj.*

poly·tech·nic /ˌpɒliˈteknɪk; *AmE* ˌpɑːl-/ (also *BrE informal* **poly**) *noun* (in Britain in the past) a college for higher education, especially in scientific and technical subjects. Most polytechnics are now called, and have the same status as, universities.

poly·the·ism /ˈpɒliθiːɪzəm; *AmE* ˈpɑːl-/ *noun* [U] the belief that there is more than one god—compare MONOTHEISM ▶ **poly·the·is·tic** /ˌpɒliθiˈɪstɪk; *AmE* ˌpɑːl-/ *adj.*

poly·thene /ˈpɒliθiːn; *AmE* ˈpɑːl-/ (*BrE*) (*AmE* **poly·ethyl·ene**) *noun* [U] a strong thin plastic material, used especially for making bags or for wrapping things: *a polythene bag*

poly·un·sat·ur·ated /ˌpɒliʌnˈsætʃəreɪtɪd; *AmE* ˌpɑːl-/ *adj.* (of many vegetable fats and some animal fats) having a chemical structure which does not encourage the harmful development of CHOLESTEROL: *polyunsaturated margarine*—see also SATURATED, UNSATURATED

poly·ur·eth·ane /ˌpɒliˈjʊərəθeɪn; *AmE* ˌpɑːliˈjʊr-/ *noun* [U] a type of plastic material used in making paints, glues, etc: *polyurethane gloss* (= a paint that dries with a hard shiny surface)

pom /pɒm; *AmE* pɑːm/ *noun* = POMMY

po·man·der /pəˈmændə(r); *AmE* ˈpoʊmændər/ *noun* a round container filled with dried flowers, leaves, etc. that is used to give a pleasant smell to rooms or clothes

pom·egran·ate /ˈpɒmɪɡrænɪt; *AmE* ˈpɑːm-/ *noun* a round fruit with thick smooth skin and red flesh full of large seeds—picture on page A2

pom·mel /ˈpɒml; *AmE* ˈpɑːml/ *noun* **1** the higher front part of a SADDLE on a horse **2** the round part on the end of the handle of a SWORD

pommy /ˈpɒmi; *AmE* ˈpɑːmi/ *noun* (*pl.* **-ies**) (also **pom**) (*AustralE*, *NZE*, *informal*, often *disapproving*) a British person

pomp /pɒmp/ *noun* [U] the impressive clothes, decorations, music, etc. and traditional customs that are part of an official occasion or ceremony: *all the pomp and ceremony of a royal wedding* IDM **pomp and 'circumstance** formal and impressive ceremony

pom-pom /ˈpɒmpɒm; *AmE* ˈpɑːmpɑːm/ (also **pon-pon** /ˈpɒmpɒn; *AmE* ˈpɑːmpɑːn/) *noun* **1** a small woollen ball used for decoration, especially on a hat SYN BOBBLE—picture at HAT **2** (especially in the US) a large round bunch of strips of plastic, tied to a handle, used by CHEERLEADERS

pom·pous /ˈpɒmpəs; *AmE* ˈpɑːm-/ *adj.* (*disapproving*) showing that you think you are more important than other people, especially by using long and formal words: *a pompous official* ◊ *His speech sounded very pompous and self-congratulatory.* ▶ **pom·pos·ity** /pɒmˈpɒsəti; *AmE*

pɑːmˈpɑːs-/ *noun* [U]: *The prince's manner was informal, without a trace of pomposity.* **pom·pous·ly** *adv.*

ponce /pɒns; *AmE* pɑːns/ *noun*, *verb*
■ *noun* (*BrE*, *informal*) **1** a man who controls one or several prostitutes and the money that they earn SYN PIMP **2** an offensive word for a man whose appearance and behaviour seem similar to a woman's, or who is thought to be HOMOSEXUAL
■ *verb* PHRV ˌponce aˈbout/aˈround (usually used in the progressive tenses) (*BrE*, *informal*) to waste time when you are doing sth so that you achieve nothing; to do silly things in a way that looks ridiculous

pon·cho /ˈpɒntʃəʊ; *AmE* ˈpɑːntʃoʊ/ *noun* (*pl.* **-os**) a type of coat without sleeves, made from one large piece of fabric with a hole in the middle for the head to go through

pond /pɒnd; *AmE* pɑːnd/ *noun* a small area of still water, especially one that is artificial: *a fish pond* IDM **across the 'pond** (*informal*) on the other side of the Atlantic Ocean from Britain/the US—more at BIG *adj.*

pon·der /ˈpɒndə(r); *AmE* ˈpɑːn-/ *verb* ~ (**about/on/over sth**) (*written*) to think about sth carefully for a period of time SYN CONSIDER: [V] *She pondered over his words.* ◊ *They were left to ponder on the implications of the announcement.* ◊ [VN] *The senator pondered the question for a moment.* ◊ [V wh-] *They are pondering whether the money could be better used elsewhere.* [also V speech]

pon·der·ous /ˈpɒndərəs; *AmE* ˈpɑːn-/ *adj.* (*written*) **1** (*disapproving*) (of speech and writing) too slow and careful; serious and boring: *He spoke in a slow ponderous voice.* **2** moving slowly and heavily; able to move only slowly: *She watched the cow's ponderous progress.* ▶ **pon·der·ous·ly** *adv.* **pon·der·ous·ness** *noun* [U]

pone /pəʊn; *AmE* poʊn/ *noun* [U] (*AmE*) = CORN PONE

pong /pɒŋ; *AmE* pɑːŋ/ *noun* (*BrE*, *informal*) a strong unpleasant smell: *What's that pong?* ▶ **pong** *verb*: [V] *That cheese pongs!*

pon·tiff /ˈpɒntɪf; *AmE* ˈpɑːn-/ *noun* (*formal*) the POPE (= the leader of the Roman Catholic Church)

pon·tif·ic·al /pɒnˈtɪfɪkl; *AmE* pɑːn-/ *adj.* (*formal*) connected with a POPE

pon·tifi·cate *verb*, *noun*
■ *verb* /pɒnˈtɪfɪkeɪt; *AmE* pɑːn-/ [V] ~ (**about/on sth**) (*disapproving*) to give your opinions about sth in a way that shows that you think you are right
■ *noun* /pɒnˈtɪfɪkət; *AmE* pɑːn-/ the official position or period in office of a POPE

pon·toon /pɒnˈtuːn; *AmE* pɑːn-/ *noun* **1** [C] a temporary floating platform built across several boats or hollow structures, especially one used for tying boats to **2** [C] a boat or hollow structure that is one of several used to support a floating platform or bridge: *a pontoon bridge* **3** [U] (*BrE*) = BLACKJACK

pony /ˈpəʊni; *AmE* ˈpoʊni/ *noun* (*pl.* **-ies**) **1** a type of small horse—see also SHETLAND PONY **2** (*BrE*, *slang*) £25 IDM see SHANK

pony·tail /ˈpəʊniteɪl; *AmE* ˈpoʊ-/ *noun* a bunch of hair tied at the back of the head so that it hangs like a horse's tail—compare PIGTAIL—picture at HAIR

'pony-trekking *noun* [U] (*BrE*) the activity of riding PONIES in the countryside for pleasure: *to go pony-trekking*

poo (also **pooh**) /puː/ (both *BrE*) *noun* [U, C] (also **poop** [U] *AmE*, *BrE*) a child's word for the solid waste that is passed through the bowels SYN FAECES: *dog poo* ◊ *I want to do a poo!* ▶ **poo** (also **pooh**) *verb* [V]

pooch /puːtʃ/ *noun* (*informal*, *especially AmE*) a dog

poo·dle /ˈpuːdl/ *noun* **1** a dog with thick, curly hair that is sometimes cut into special shapes **2** (*BrE*, *informal*) a person who is too willing to do what sb else tells them to do: *He has made himself appear a poodle of the Prime Minister.*

poof /pʊf/ *noun*, *exclamation*
■ *noun* (also **poof·ter** /ˈpʊftə(r)/) (*BrE*, ⚠, *slang*) an offensive word for a HOMOSEXUAL man

aɪ	aʊ	eɪ	əʊ	oʊ	ɔɪ	ɪə	eə	ʊə	j	w
my	now	say	go (BrE)	go (AmE)	boy	near	hair	pure	yes	wet

■ *exclamation* used when talking about sth disappearing suddenly: *He walked through—and vanished. Poof! Like that.*

pooh /puː/ *exclamation, noun, verb*
■ *exclamation* (*especially BrE*) **1** used to express disgust at a bad smell: *It stinks! Pooh!* **2** used to say that you think sb's idea, suggestion, etc. is not very good or that you do not believe what sb has said: *'I might lose my job for this.' 'Oh, pooh, nobody will care.'*
■ *noun, verb* = POO

,pooh-'pooh *verb* [VN] (*informal*) to say that a suggestion, an idea, etc. is not true or not worth thinking about: *They are pooh-poohing suggestions of a split in the party.*

pool /puːl/ *noun, verb*
■ *noun*
FOR SWIMMING | **1** [C] = SWIMMING POOL: *Does the hotel have a pool?* ◊ *relaxing by the pool*
OF WATER | **2** [C] a small area of still water, especially one that has formed naturally: *freshwater pools* ◊ *a rock pool* (= between rocks by the sea)
OF LIQUID/LIGHT | **3** [C] ~ (of sth) a small amount of liquid or light lying on a surface: *The body was lying in a pool of blood.* ◊ *a pool of light*
GROUP OF THINGS/PEOPLE | **4** [C] ~ (of sth) a supply of things or money that is shared by a group of people and can be used when needed: *a pool of cars used by the firm's salesmen* ◊ *a pool car* **5** [C] ~ (of sth) a group of people available for work when needed: *a large pool of software engineers* ◊ *a pool of cheap labour*
GAME | **6** [U] a game for two people played with 16 coloured balls on a table, often in pubs and bars. Players use CUES (= long sticks) to try to hit the balls into pockets at the edge of the table: *a pool table/hall* ◊ *to shoot* (= play) *pool*—compare BILLIARDS, SNOOKER—picture on page A8
FOOTBALL | **7** (the pools) = FOOTBALL POOLS: *He does the pools every week.* ◊ *a pools winner*
—see also GENE POOL
■ *verb* [VN] to collect money, information, etc. from different people so that it can be used by all of them: *The students work individually, then pool their ideas in groups of six.* ◊ *Police forces across the country are pooling resources in order to solve this crime.*

pool·side /'puːlsaɪd/ *noun* [sing.] the area around a swimming pool: *lazing at the poolside* ◊ *a poolside bar*

poop /puːp/ *noun, verb*
■ *noun* **1** (also **'poop deck**) [C] the raised part at the back end of a ship—compare STERN **2** [U] (*informal, especially AmE*) = POO: *dog poop on the sidewalk*
■ *verb* (*AmE, informal*) **1** [V] to pass solid waste from the bowels: *The dog just pooped in the kitchen!* **2** [VN] ~ sb (**out**) to make sb very tired: *That walk really pooped me out!* PHRV ,poop 'out to stop working or functioning

pooped /puːpt/ (also **,pooped 'out**) *adj.* [not before noun] (*informal, especially AmE*) very tired: *It's among the poorer*

pooper scoop·er /'puːpə skuːpə(r)/ (also **'poop scoop**) *noun* (*informal*) a tool used by dog owners for removing their dog's solid waste from the streets

poor /pɔː(r); puə(r); *AmE* pɔːr; pur/ *adj.* (**poor·er, poor·est**)
HAVING LITTLE MONEY | **1** having very little money; not having enough money for basic needs: *They were too poor to buy shoes for the kids.* ◊ *We aim to help the poorest families.* ◊ *It's among the poorer countries of the world.* OPP RICH **2** (the poor) *noun* [pl.] people who have very little money: *They provided food and shelter for the poor.* OPP RICH
UNFORTUNATE | **3** [only before noun] (*especially spoken*) deserving pity and sympathy: *Have you heard about poor old Harry? His wife's left him.* ◊ *It's hungry—the poor little thing.* ◊ *'I have stacks of homework to do.' 'Oh, you poor thing.'*
NOT GOOD | **4** not good; of a quality that is low or lower than expected: *the party's poor performance in the election* ◊ *to be in poor health/condition* ◊ *It was raining heavily and visibility was poor.* ◊ *poor food/light/soil* ◊ *to have a poor opinion of sb* (= to not think well of sb) **5** (of a person) not good or skilled at sth: *a poor swimmer* ◊ *a*

poor judge of character ◊ *She's a good teacher but a poor manager.* ◊ *a poor sailor* (= sb who easily gets sick at sea)
HAVING LITTLE OF STH | **6** ~ in sth having very small amounts of sth: *a country poor in natural resources* ◊ *soil poor in nutrients* OPP RICH
IDM **be/come a poor second, third, etc.** (*especially BrE*) to finish a long way behind the winner in a race, competition, etc. **the ,poor man's 'sb/'sth** a person or thing that is similar to but of a lower quality than a particular famous person or thing: *Sparkling white wine is the poor man's champagne.*—more at ACCOUNT *n.*

poor·house /'pɔːhaus; 'puə-; *AmE* 'purh-; 'pɔːr-/ *noun* = WORKHOUSE

poor·ly /'pɔːli; 'puəli; *AmE* 'purli; 'pɔːrli/ *adv., adj.*
■ *adv.* in a way that is not satisfactory SYN BADLY: *a poorly attended meeting* (= at which there are not many people) ◊ *poorly designed* ◊ *The job is relatively poorly paid.* ◊ *Our candidate fared poorly in the election* (= did not get many votes).
■ *adj.* [not usually before noun] (*BrE, informal*) ill: *She felt poorly.*

,poor re'lation *noun* something that is not treated with as much respect as other similar things because it is not thought to be as good, important or successful

pop /pɒp; *AmE* pɑːp/ *noun, verb, adj., adv.*
■ *noun*
MUSIC | **1** (also **'pop music**) [U] modern popular music of the sort that has been popular since the 1950s, usually with a strong rhythm and simple tunes: *rock, pop and soul*
FATHER | **2** [sing.] (*informal, especially AmE*) used as a word for 'father', especially as a form of address: *Hi, Pop!*
SOUND | **3** [C] a short sharp explosive sound: *The cork came out of the bottle with a loud pop.*
DRINK | **4** [U] (*old-fashioned, BrE, informal*) a sweet FIZZY drink (= with bubbles) that is not alcoholic
■ *verb* (**-pp-**)
MAKE SOUND | **1** to make a short explosive sound; to cause sth to make this sound: [V] *the sound of corks popping* [also VN] **2** to burst, or make sth burst, with a short explosive sound: [VN] *She jumped as someone popped a balloon behind her.* [also V]
GO QUICKLY | **3** [V+*adv. / prep.*] (*BrE, informal*) to go somewhere, suddenly or for a short time: *I'll pop over and see you this evening.* ◊ *Why don't you pop in* (= visit us) *for a drink next time you're in the area?*
PUT QUICKLY | **4** [VN+*adv. / prep.*] (*informal, especially BrE*) to put sth somewhere quickly, suddenly or for a short time: ◊ *He popped his head around the door and said hello.* ◊ *I'll pop the books in* (= deliver them) *on my way home.*
APPEAR SUDDENLY | **5** [V+*adv. / prep.*] to suddenly appear especially when not expected: *The window opened and a dog's head popped out.* ◊ *An idea suddenly popped into his head.* ◊ (*computing*) *The menu pops up when you click twice on the mouse.*
OF EARS | **6** [V] if your ears **pop**, the pressure in them suddenly changes when going up or down in a plane, etc.
OF EYES | **7** [V] if your eyes **pop** or **pop out**, they suddenly open fully because you are surprised or excited: *Her eyes nearly popped out of her head when she saw them.*
TAKE DRUGS | **8** [VN] (*informal*) to take a lot of a drug, regularly: *She's been popping pills for months.*
IDM **pop your 'clogs** (*BrE, humorous*) to die **pop the 'question** (*informal*) to ask sb to marry you
PHRV ,pop 'off (*informal*) to die ,pop sth↔'on (*BrE, informal*) **1** to put on a piece of clothing: *I'll just pop on a sweater and meet you outside.* **2** to turn on a piece of electrical equipment
■ *adj.* [only before noun]
MUSIC/STYLE | **1** connected with modern popular music: *a pop band/concert/group/singer/song/star/video* **2** made in a modern popular style: *pop culture*
■ *adv.*
IDM **go 'pop** (*BrE*) to burst or explode with a sudden short sound: *The balloon went pop.*

pop. *abbr.* population: *pop. 200000*

b	d	f	g	h	k	l	m	n	p	r
bad	did	fall	get	hat	cat	leg	man	now	pen	red

pop art (also **Pop Art**) *noun* [U] a style of art, developed in the 1960s, that was based on popular culture and that used material such as advertisements, film/movie images, etc.

pop·corn /'pɒpkɔːn; *AmE* 'pɑːpkɔːrn/ *noun* [U] a type of food, made from grains of MAIZE that are heated until they burst, forming light whitish balls that are then covered with salt or sugar

pope /pəʊp; *AmE* poʊp/ *noun* (often **the Pope**) *noun* the leader of the Roman Catholic Church, who is also the Bishop of Rome: *the election of a new pope* ◊ *Pope John Paul* ◊ *a visit from the Pope*—see also PAPACY, PAPAL

popery /'pəʊpəri; *AmE* 'poʊ-/ *noun* [U] (⚠, *offensive*) used by some people to refer to Roman Catholicism

pope's nose *noun* (*AmE*) = PARSON'S NOSE

pop-eyed *adj.* (*informal*) having eyes that are wide open, especially because you are very surprised, excited or frightened

pop·gun /'pɒpgʌn; *AmE* 'pɑːp-/ *noun* a toy gun that fires small objects such as CORKS and makes a short sharp noise

pop·ish /'pəʊpɪʃ; *AmE* 'poʊ-/ *adj.* [usually before noun] (⚠, *offensive*) used by some people to describe sb/sth that is connected with Roman Catholicism

pop·lar /'pɒplə(r); *AmE* 'pɑːp-/ *noun* a tall straight tree with soft wood

pop·lin /'pɒplɪn; *AmE* 'pɑːp-/ *noun* [U] a strong cotton fabric used for making clothes

poppa /'pɒpə; *AmE* 'pɑːpə/ *noun* (*AmE, informal*) used by children to talk about or to address their father—see also PAPA, POP

pop·pa·dom /'pɒpədəm; *AmE* 'pɑːp-/ *noun* a type of thin round crisp Indian bread that is fried in oil and often served with CURRY

pop·per /'pɒpə(r); *AmE* 'pɑːp-/ *noun* (*BrE*) = PRESS STUD

pop·pet /'pɒpɪt; *AmE* 'pɑːp-/ *noun* (*BrE, informal, spoken*) used to talk to or about sb you like or love, especially a child

poppy /'pɒpi; *AmE* 'pɑːpi/ *noun* (*pl.* **-ies**) a wild or garden plant, with a large delicate flower that is usually red, and small black seeds. Opium is obtained from one type of poppy: *poppy fields/seeds*

poppy·cock /'pɒpikɒk; *AmE* 'pɑːpikɑːk/ *noun* [U] (*old-fashioned, informal*) nonsense

pop quiz *noun* (*AmE*) a short test that is given to students without any warning

Pop·sicle™ /'pɒpsɪkl; *AmE* 'pɑːp-/ *noun* (*AmE*) = ICE LOLLY

popu·lace /'pɒpjələs; *AmE* 'pɑːp-/ *noun* (usually **the populace**) *noun* [sing.+ sing./pl. *v.*] (*formal*) all the ordinary people of a particular country or area: *He had the support of large sections of the local populace.* ◊ *The populace at large is/are opposed to sudden change.*

popu·lar /'pɒpjələ(r); *AmE* 'pɑːp-/ *adj.* **1** ~ (**with sb**) liked or enjoyed by a large number of people: *a hugely/immensely popular singer* ◊ *This is one of our most popular designs.* ◊ *Skiing has become very popular recently.* ◊ *These policies are unlikely to prove popular with middle-class voters.* ◊ *I'm not very popular with my parents* (= they are annoyed with me) *at the moment.* ◊ (*spoken, ironic*) *'Our dog got into the neighbour's garden again!'* *'You'll be popular.'* [OPP] UNPOPULAR **2** [only before noun] (sometimes *disapproving*) suited to the taste and knowledge of ordinary people: *popular music/culture/fiction* ◊ *the popular press* **3** [only before noun] (of ideas, beliefs and opinions) shared by a large number of people: *a popular misconception* ◊ *Contrary to popular belief, women cause fewer road accidents than men.* ◊ *Popular opinion was divided on the issue.* ◊ *By popular demand, the tour has been extended by two weeks.* **4** [only before noun] connected with the ordinary people of a country: *The party still has widespread popular support.*

popu·lar·ity /ˌpɒpjuˈlærəti; *AmE* ˌpɑːp-/ *noun* [U] ~ (**with/among sb**) the state of being liked, enjoyed or supported by a large number of people: *the increasing popularity of cycling* ◊ *to win/lose popularity with the students* ◊ *Her novels have gained in popularity over recent years.*

popu·lar·ize (*BrE* also **-ise**) /'pɒpjələraɪz; *AmE* 'pɑːp-/ *verb* [VN] (*written*) **1** to make a lot of people know about sth and enjoy it: *The programme did much to popularize little-known writers.* **2** to make a difficult subject easier to understand for ordinary people: *He spent his life popularizing natural history.* ▶ **popu·lar·iza·tion, -isa·tion** /ˌpɒpjələraɪˈzeɪʃn; *AmE* ˌpɑːpjələrəˈz-/ *noun* [U]

popu·lar·ly /'pɒpjələli; *AmE* 'pɑːpjələrli/ *adv.* **1** by a large number of people [SYN] COMMONLY: *a popularly held belief* ◊ *the UN Conference on Environment and Development, popularly known as the 'Earth Summit'* **2** by the ordinary people of a country [SYN] DEMOCRATICALLY: *a popularly elected government*

popu·late /'pɒpjuleɪt; *AmE* 'pɑːp-/ *verb* [VN] [often passive] **1** to live in an area and form its population [SYN] INHABIT: *a heavily/densely/sparsely/thinly populated country* ◊ *The island is populated largely by sheep.* ◊ (*figurative*) *the amazing characters that populate her novels* **2** to move people or animals to an area to live there: *The French began to populate the island in the 15th century.*

popu·la·tion /ˌpɒpjuˈleɪʃn; *AmE* ˌpɑːp-/ *noun* **1** [C+sing./pl.*v.*, U] all the people who live in a particular area, city or country; the total number of people who live there: *One third of the world's population consumes/consume two thirds of the world's resources.* ◊ *The entire population of the town was at the meeting.* ◊ *countries with ageing populations* ◊ *Muslims make up 55% of the population.* ◊ *an increase in population* ◊ *areas of dense/sparse population* (= where many/not many people live) ◊ *The population is increasing at about 6% per year.* ◊ *Nigeria has a population of nearly 100 million.* **2** [C+sing./pl.*v.*] a particular group of people or animals living in a particular area: *the adult/working/rural population of the country*

popu'lation explosion *noun* a sudden large increase in the number of people in an area

popu·lism /'pɒpjəlɪzəm; *AmE* 'pɑːp-/ *noun* [U] a type of politics that claims to represent the opinions and wishes of ordinary people ▶ **popu·list** /-ɪst/ *noun*: *a party of populists* **popu·list** *adj.* [usually before noun]: *a populist leader*

popu·lous /'pɒpjələs; *AmE* 'pɑːp-/ *adj.* (*formal*) where a large number of people live: *one of America's most populous states*

pop-up *adj.* [only before noun] **1** (of a book, etc.) containing a picture that stands up when the pages are opened: *a pop-up birthday card* **2** (of an electric toaster) that pushes the bread quickly upwards when it is ready **3** (of a computer MENU, etc.) that can be brought to the screen quickly while you are working on another document: *a pop-up menu/window*

por·cel·ain /'pɔːsəlɪn; *AmE* 'pɔːrs-/ *noun* [U, C] a hard white shiny substance made by baking clay and used for making delicate cups, plates and ornaments; objects that are made of this: *a porcelain figure*

porch /pɔːtʃ; *AmE* pɔːrtʃ/ *noun* **1** a small area at the entrance to a building, such as a house or a church, that is covered by a roof and often has walls—picture at HOUSE, THATCH **2** (*AmE*) = VERANDA

por·cine /'pɔːsaɪn; *AmE* 'pɔːrs-/ *adj.* (*formal*) like a pig; connected with pigs

por·cu·pine /'pɔːkjupaɪn; *AmE* 'pɔːrk-/ *noun* an animal covered with long stiff parts like needles (called QUILLS), which it can raise to protect itself when it is attacked

pore /pɔː(r)/ *noun, verb*
■ *noun* one of the very small holes in your skin that sweat can pass through; one of the similar small holes in the surface of a plant or a rock: *a blocked pore*—see also POROUS
■ *verb* [PHRV] **'pore over sth** to look at or read sth very carefully: *His lawyers are poring over the small print in the contract.*

pork /pɔːk; *AmE* pɔːrk/ *noun* [U] meat from a pig that has not been CURED (= preserved using salt or smoke): *roast* *pork* ◊ *pork chops* ◊ *a leg of pork*—compare BACON, GAM-MON, HAM (1)

'pork barrel *noun* [U] (*AmE, slang*) local projects that are given a lot of government money in order to win votes; the money that is used

porker /'pɔːkə(r); *AmE* 'pɔːrk-/ *noun* a pig that is made fat and used as food

pork 'pie *noun* [C, U] (*BrE*) a small pie filled with PORK and usually eaten cold

pork 'scratchings *noun* [pl.] (*BrE*) crisp pieces of pig skin that are fried and eaten cold, often sold in packets as a SNACK

porky /'pɔːki; *AmE* 'pɔːrki/ *noun, adj.*
■ *noun* (*pl.* **-ies**) (also **porky 'pie**) (*BrE, slang*) a statement that is not true; a lie: *to tell porkies*
■ *adj.* (*informal, disapproving*) (of people) fat

porn /pɔːn; *AmE* pɔːrn/ *noun* [U] (*informal*) = PORNOG-RAPHY—see also HARD PORN, SOFT PORN

porno /'pɔːnəʊ; *AmE* 'pɔːrnoʊ/ *adj.* [usually before noun] (*informal*) = PORNOGRAPHIC: *a porno movie/mag*

porn·og·raph·er /pɔː'nɒɡrəfə(r); *AmE* pɔːr'nɑːɡ-/ *noun* (*disapproving*) a person who produces or sells pornography

porno·graph·ic /ˌpɔːnə'ɡræfɪk; *AmE* ˌpɔːrn-/ (also *informal* **porno**) *adj.* [usually before noun] (*disapproving*) intended to make people feel sexually excited by showing naked people or sexual acts, usually in a way that many other people find offensive: *pornographic movies/magazines*

porn·og·raphy /pɔː'nɒɡrəfi; *AmE* pɔːr'nɑːɡ-/ (also *informal* **porn**) *noun* [U] (*disapproving*) books, videos, etc. that describe or show naked people and sexual acts in order to make people feel sexually excited, especially in a way that many other people find offensive: *child pornography* ◊ *the distribution of pornography* ◊ *measures to tighten the laws on pornography*

por·os·ity /pɔː'rɒsəti; *AmE* -'rɑːs-/ *noun* [U] (*technical*) the quality or state of being porous

por·ous /'pɔːrəs/ *adj.* having many small holes that allow water or air to pass through slowly: *porous material/rocks/surfaces*

por·poise /'pɔːpəs; *AmE* 'pɔːrpəs/ *noun* a sea animal that looks like a large fish with a pointed mouth. Porpoises are similar to DOLPHINS but smaller.

por·ridge /'pɒrɪdʒ; *AmE* 'pɔːr-; 'pɑːr-/ (*especially BrE*) (*AmE* usually **oat·meal**) *noun* [U] a type of soft thick white food made by boiling OATS in milk or water, eaten hot, especially for breakfast

port /pɔːt; *AmE* pɔːrt/ *noun* **1** [C] a town or city with a harbour, especially one where ships load and unload goods: *fishing ports* ◊ *Rotterdam is a major port.* **2** [C, U] (*abbr.* **Pt.**) a place where ships load and unload goods or shelter from storms: *a naval port* ◊ *The ship spent four days in port.* ◊ *They reached port at last.* ◊ *port of entry* (= a place where people or goods can enter a country)—see also AIRPORT, FREE PORT, HELIPORT, SEAPORT **3** [U] a strong sweet wine, usually dark red, that is made in Portugal. It is usually drunk at the end of a meal. **4** [C] a glass of port **5** [U] the side of a ship or aircraft that is on the left when you are facing forward: *the port side/engine*—compare STARBOARD **IDM any port in a 'storm** (*saying*) if you are in great trouble, you take any help that is offered

port·able /'pɔːtəbl; *AmE* 'pɔːrt-/ *adj., noun*
■ *adj.* that is easy to carry or to move: *a portable TV* ◊ (*figurative*) *a portable loan/pension* (= that can be moved if you change banks, jobs, etc.) ◊ *portable software* ▶ **port·abil·ity** /ˌpɔːtə'bɪləti; *AmE* ˌpɔːrt-/ *noun* [U]: *The new light cover increases this model's portability.*
■ *noun* a small type of machine that is easy to carry, especially a computer or a television

Porta·kabin™ /'pɔːtəkæbɪn; *AmE* 'pɔːrt-/ *noun* (*BrE*) a small building that can be moved from place to place by a vehicle, designed to be used as a temporary office, etc.

por·tal /'pɔːtl; *AmE* 'pɔːrtl/ *noun* [often pl.] (*formal or literary*) a large, impressive gate or entrance to a building

port·cul·lis /pɔːt'kʌlɪs; *AmE* pɔːrt-/ *noun* a strong, heavy iron gate that can be raised or lowered at the entrance to a castle

por·tend /pɔː'tend; *AmE* pɔːr't-/ *verb* [VN] (*formal*) to be a sign or warning of sth that is going to happen in the future, especially sth bad or unpleasant

por·tent /'pɔːtent; *AmE* 'pɔːrt-/ *noun* (*literary*) a sign or warning of sth that is going to happen in the future, especially when it is sth unpleasant SYN OMEN: *The event proved to be a portent of the disaster that was to come.*

por·tent·ous /pɔː'tentəs; *AmE* pɔːr't-/ *adj.* **1** (*literary*) important as a sign or a warning of sth that is going to happen in the future, especially when it is sth unpleasant: *a portentous dream/sign* **2** (*formal, disapproving*) very serious and intended to impress people: *a portentous remark/voice* ▶ **por·tent·ous·ly** *adv.*: *She frowned portentously to add weight to her suggestion.* **por·tent·ous·ness** *noun* [U]

por·ter /'pɔːtə(r); *AmE* 'pɔːrt-/ *noun* **1** a person whose job is carrying people's bags and other loads **2** (*especially BrE*) a person whose job is to move patients from one place to another in a hospital **3** (*BrE*) a person whose job is to be in charge of the entrance to a hotel, large building, college, etc: *the night porter* ◊ *The hotel porter will get you a taxi.*—compare DOORMAN **4** (*AmE*) a person whose job is helping passengers on a train, especially in a SLEEPING CAR

port·folio /pɔːt'fəʊliəʊ; *AmE* pɔːrt'foʊlioʊ/ *noun* (*pl.* **-os**) **1** a thin flat case used for carrying documents, drawings, etc. **2** a collection of photographs, drawings, etc. that you use as an example of your work, especially when applying for a job: *She spent most of last year getting her portfolio together.* **3** (*finance*) a set of shares owned by a particular person or organization: *an investment/share portfolio* **4** (*formal, especially BrE*) the particular area of responsibility of a government minister: *the defence portfolio* ◊ *She resigned her portfolio.* ◊ *He was asked to join as a* **minister without portfolio** (= one without responsibility for a particular government department). **5** the range of products or services offered by a particular company or organization: *a portfolio of wines/courses*

port·hole /'pɔːthəʊl; *AmE* 'pɔːrthoʊl/ *noun* a round window in the side of a ship or an aircraft

por·tico /'pɔːtɪkəʊ; *AmE* 'pɔːrtɪkoʊ/ *noun* (*pl.* **-oes** or **-os**) (*formal*) a roof that is supported by columns, especially one that forms the entrance to a large building

por·tion /'pɔːʃn; *AmE* 'pɔːrʃn/ *noun* **1** one part of sth larger: *a substantial/significant portion of the population* ◊ *Only a small portion of the budget is spent on books.* ◊ *The central portion of the bridge collapsed.* **2** an amount of food that is large enough for one person: *a generous portion of meat* ◊ *She cut the cake into six small portions.* ◊ *You should eat several portions of fruit a day.* **3** [usually sing.] a part of sth that is shared with other people: *You must accept a portion of the blame for this crisis.*

port·ly /'pɔːtli; *AmE* 'pɔːrt-/ *adj.* [usually before noun] (especially of an older man) rather fat

port·man·teau /pɔːt'mæntəʊ; *AmE* pɔːrt'mæntoʊ/ *noun, adj.*
■ *noun* (*pl.* **-eaus** or **-eaux**) (*old-fashioned*) a large heavy suitcase that opens into two parts
■ *adj.* [only before noun] consisting of a number of different items that are combined into a single thing: *a portmanteau course* ◊ *'Depression' is a portmanteau condition.*

port'manteau word *noun* a word that is invented by combining the beginning of one word and the end of another and keeping the meaning of each. For example *motel* is a portmanteau word that is a combination of *motor* and *hotel*.

port of 'call *noun* (*pl.* **ports of call**) **1** a port where a ship stops during a journey **2** (*informal*) a place where you go or stop for a short time, especially when you are going to several places: *My first port of call in town was the bank.*

por·trait /'pɔːtreɪt; -trət; *AmE* 'pɔːrtrət/ *noun, adj.*
■ *noun* **1** a painting, drawing or photograph of a person, especially of the head and shoulders: *He had his portrait*

æ	ɑː	e	ɜː	ə	ɪ	iː	i	ɒ	ɔː	ʌ	ʊ	u	uː
cat	father	ten	bird	about	sit	see	many	got	saw	cup	put	actual	too
								(BrE)					

P

painted in uniform. ◊ *a full-length portrait* ◊ *a portrait painter*—see also SELF-PORTRAIT **2** a detailed description of sb/sth: *a portrait of life at the French court*

■ *adj.* (*computing*) (of a page of a document) printed so that the top of the page is one of the shorter sides—compare LANDSCAPE—picture on page 251

por·trait·ist /ˈpɔːtreɪtɪst; -trət-; *AmE* ˈpɔːrtrət-/ *noun* a person who makes portraits

por·trait·ure /ˈpɔːtrətʃə(r); *AmE* ˈpɔːrt-/ *noun* [U] the art of making portraits; the portraits that are made

por·tray /pɔːˈtreɪ; *AmE* pɔːrˈt-/ *verb* [VN] **1** to show sb/sth in a picture; to describe sb/sth in a piece of writing SYN DEPICT: *The painting portrays the duke's third wife.* ◊ *His war poetry vividly portrays life in the trenches.* **2** ~ sb/sth (as sb/sth) to describe or show sb/sth in a particular way, especially when this does not give a complete or accurate impression of what they are like: *Throughout the trial, he portrayed himself as the victim.* **3** to act a particular role in a film/movie or play: *Her father will be portrayed by Sean Connery.*

por·tray·al /pɔːˈtreɪəl; *AmE* pɔːrˈt-/ *noun* [C, U] the act of showing or describing sb/sth in a picture, play, book, etc.; a particular way in which this is done: *The article examines the portrayal of gay men in the media.* ◊ *He is best known for his chilling portrayal of Hannibal Lecter.*

pose /pəʊz; *AmE* poʊz/ *verb, noun*

■ *verb* **1** [VN] to create a threat, problem, etc. that has to be dealt with: *to pose a threat/challenge/danger/risk* ◊ *The task poses no special problems.* **2** [VN] ~ a question (*formal*) to ask a question, especially one that needs serious thought **3** [V] ~ (for sb/sth) to sit or stand in a particular position in order to be painted, drawn or photographed: *The delegates posed for a group photograph.* ◊ *They posed briefly for photographs before driving off.* **4** [V] ~ as sb to pretend to be sb in order to deceive other people: *The gang entered the building posing as workmen.* **5** [V] (usually used in the progressive tenses) (*disapproving*) to dress or behave in a way that is intended to impress other people: *I saw him out posing in his new sports car.*

■ *noun* **1** a particular position in which sb stands, sits, etc., especially in order to be painted, drawn or photographed: *a stiff/dramatic pose* ◊ *He adopted a relaxed pose for the camera.* ◊ *I can't hold this pose much longer!* **2** (*disapproving*) a way of behaving that is not sincere and is only intended to impress other people: *This show of concern is just a pose.* IDM see STRIKE *v.*

poser /ˈpəʊzə(r); *AmE* ˈpoʊ-/ *noun* **1** (*informal*) a difficult question or problem **2** (also **pos·eur**) (*disapproving*) a person who behaves or dresses in a way that is intended to impress other people and is not sincere: *He's such a poser on the dance floor.*

pos·eur /pəʊˈzɜː(r); *AmE* poʊ-/ *noun* = POSER (2)

posh /pɒʃ; *AmE* pɑːʃ/ *adj.* (**posh·er, posh·est**) (*informal*) **1** elegant and expensive: *a posh hotel/restaurant* ◊ *You look very posh in your new suit.* **2** (*BrE*, sometimes *disapproving*) typical of or used by people who belong to a high social class: *a posh accent/voice* ◊ *They live in the posh part of town.* ▶ **posh** *adv.* (*BrE*): *to talk posh*

posit /ˈpɒzɪt; *AmE* ˈpɑːz-/ *verb* (*formal*) to suggest or accept that sth is true so that it can be used as the basis for an argument or discussion SYN POSTULATE: [VN] *Most religions posit the existence of life after death.* [also V that]

pos·ition /pəˈzɪʃn/ *noun, verb*

■ *noun*

PLACE | **1** [C] the place where sb/sth is situated: *From his position on the cliff top, he had a good view of the harbour.* ◊ *Where would be the best position for the lights?* **2** [U] the place where sb/sth is meant to be; the correct place: *Is everybody in position?* ◊ *He took up his position by the door.*

WAY OF SITTING/STANDING | **3** [C, U] the way in which sb is sitting or standing or the way in which sth is arranged: *a sitting/kneeling/lying position* ◊ *Keep the box in an upright position.* ◊ *Make sure that you are working in a comfortable position.* ◊ *My arms were aching so I shifted (my) position slightly.*

SITUATION | **4** [C, usually sing.] ~ (to do sth) the situation that sb is in, especially when it affects what they can and cannot do: *to be in a position of power/strength/authority* ◊ *What would you do in my position?* ◊ *This put him and his colleagues in a difficult position.* ◊ *The company's financial position is not certain.* ◊ *I'm afraid I am not in a position to help you.*

OPINION | **5** [C] ~ (on sth) an opinion on or an attitude towards a particular subject: *to declare/reconsider/shift/change your position* ◊ *the party's position on education reforms* ◊ *She has made her position very clear.*

LEVEL OF IMPORTANCE | **6** [C, U] a person or organization's level of importance when compared with others: *the position of women in society* ◊ *the company's dominant position in the world market* ◊ *Wealth and position* (= high social status) *were not important to her.*

JOB | **7** [C] (*formal*) a job: *He held a senior position in a large company.* ◊ *I should like to apply for the position of Sales Director.*

IN RACE/COMPETITION | **8** [C] a place in a race, competition, or test, when compared to others: *United's 3–0 win moved them up to third position.*

IN SPORT | **9** [C] the place where sb plays and the responsibilities they have in some team games: *What position does he play?*

IN WAR | **10** [C, usually pl.] a place where a group of people involved in fighting have put men and guns: *They attacked the enemy positions at dawn.*

■ *verb* [VN] [usually +*adv./prep.*] to put sb/sth in a particular position: *Large television screens were positioned at either end of the stadium.* ◊ *She quickly positioned herself behind the desk.* ◊ *The company is now well positioned to compete in foreign markets.* ▶ **pos·ition·ing** *noun* [U]

pos·ition·al /pəˈzɪʃənl/ *adj.* [only before noun] (*technical* or *sport*) connected with the position of sb/sth: *The team has made some positional changes because two players are injured.*

po'sition ˌpaper *noun* a written report from an organization or a government department that explains or recommends a particular course of action

posi·tive /ˈpɒzətɪv; *AmE* ˈpɑːz-/ *adj., noun*

■ *adj.*

FEELING HOPEFUL | **1** ~ (about sth) thinking about what is good in a situation; feeling confident and hopeful: *a positive attitude/outlook* ◊ *the power of positive thought* ◊ *She tried to be more positive about her new job.* ◊ *On the positive side, profits have increased.* ◊ *The report ended on a positive note.* OPP NEGATIVE

EFFECTIVE/USEFUL | **2** directed at dealing with sth or producing a successful result: *We must take positive steps to deal with the problem.* ◊ *It will require positive action by all in the industry.* OPP NEGATIVE **3** expressing agreement or support: *We've had a very positive response to the idea.* OPP NEGATIVE **4** good or useful: *to make a positive contribution to a discussion* ◊ *His family have been a very positive influence on him.* ◊ *Overseas investment has had a positive effect on exports.* OPP NEGATIVE

SURE/DEFINITE | **5** [not before noun] ~ (about sth) | ~ (that) ... (of a person) completely sure that sth is correct or true: *I can't be positive about what time it happened.* ◊ *She was positive that he had been there.* ◊ *'Are you sure?' 'Positive.'* **6** [only before noun] (*informal*) complete and definite: *He has a positive genius for upsetting people.* ◊ *It was a positive miracle that we survived.* **7** giving clear and definite proof or information: *We have no positive evidence that she was involved.* ◊ (*formal*) *This is proof positive that he stole the money.*

SCIENTIFIC TEST | **8** showing clear evidence that a particular substance or medical condition is present: *a positive pregnancy test* ◊ *The athlete tested positive for steroids.* ◊ *to be HIV positive* OPP NEGATIVE

NUMBER/QUANTITY | **9** greater than zero OPP NEGATIVE

ELECTRICITY | **10** (*technical*) containing or producing the type of electricity that is carried by a PROTON: *a positive charge* ◊ *the positive terminal of a battery* OPP NEGATIVE

■ *noun*

GOOD QUALITY | **1** [C, U] a good or useful quality or aspect:

Take your weaknesses and translate them into positives. ◊ *To manage your way out of recession, accentuate the positive.*

IN PHOTOGRAPHY **2** [C] (*technical*) a developed photographic film showing light and dark areas and colours as they actually were, especially one printed from a NEGATIVE

RESULT OF TEST **3** [C] the result of a test or an experiment that shows that a substance or condition is present **OPP** NEGATIVE

,positive dis,crimin'ation (*BrE*) (also **af,firmative 'action** *AmE*, *BrE*) *noun* [U] the practice or policy of making sure that a particular number of jobs, etc. are given to people from groups that are often treated unfairly because of their race, sex, etc.

posi·tive·ly /ˈpɒzətɪvli; *AmE* ˈpɑːz-/ *adv.* **1** used to emphasize the truth of a statement, especially when this is surprising or when it contrasts with a previous statement: *Some diets may be positively dangerous.* ◊ *The instructions were not just confusing, they were positively misleading.* **2** in a way that shows you are thinking of the good things about a situation, not the bad: *Very few of those interviewed spoke positively about their childhood.* ◊ *Thinking positively is one way of dealing with stress.* **OPP** NEGATIVELY **3** in a way that shows you approve of, or agree with sth/sb: *Investors reacted positively to news of the takeover.* **OPP** NEGATIVELY **4** in a way that leaves no possibility of doubt **SYN** CONCLUSIVELY: *Her attacker has now been positively identified by police.* **5** (*technical*) in a way that contains or produces the type of electricity that is opposite to that carried by an ELECTRON: *positively charged protons* **OPP** NEGATIVELY

,positive 'vetting *noun* [U, C] (*BrE*) the process of checking everything about a person's background and character when they apply for a job in which they will have to deal with secret information, especially in the CIVIL SERVICE

posi·tiv·ism /ˈpɒzətɪvɪzəm; *AmE* ˈpɑːz-/ *noun* [U] a system of philosophy based on things that can be seen or proved, rather than on ideas ▶ **posi·tiv·ist** /-vɪst/ *noun* **posi·tiv·ist** *adj.*: *a positivist approach*

poss /pɒs; *AmE* pɑːs/ *adj.* [not before noun] (*BrE*, *informal*) possible: *I'll be there if poss.* ◊ *as soon as poss*

posse /ˈpɒsi; *AmE* ˈpɑːsi/ *noun* **1** (*informal*) a group of people who are similar in some way: *a little posse of helpers* **2** (in the US in the past) a group of people who were brought together by a SHERIFF (= an officer of the law) in order to help him catch a criminal

pos·sess /pəˈzes/ *verb* (not used in the progressive tenses) **1** [VN] (*formal*) to have or own sth: *He was charged with possessing a shotgun without a licence.* ◊ *I'm afraid this is the only suitcase I possess.* ◊ *The gallery possesses a number of the artist's early works.* **2** [VN] (*formal*) to have a particular quality or feature: *I'm afraid he doesn't possess a sense of humour.* ◊ *He credited her with a maturity she did not possess.* **3** [VN] [usually passive] (*literary*) (of a feeling, an emotion, etc.) to have a powerful effect on sb and control the way that they think, behave, etc: *A terrible fear possessed her.* **4** [VN to inf] (used in negative sentences and questions) to make sb do sth that seems strange or unreasonable: *What possessed him to say such a thing?*

pos·sessed /pəˈzest/ *adj.* [not before noun] ~ **(by sth)** (of a person or their mind) controlled by an evil spirit: *She has convinced herself that she is possessed by the devil.* **IDM** **be possessed of sth** (*formal*) to have a particular quality or feature: *She was possessed of exceptional powers of concentration.* **like a man/woman pos'sessed | like one pos'sessed** with a lot of force or energy: *He flew out of the room like a man possessed.*

pos·ses·sion /pəˈzeʃn/ *noun*
HAVING/OWNING **1** [U] (*formal*) the state of having or owning sth: *The manuscript is just one of the treasures in their possession.* ◊ *The gang was caught in possession of stolen goods.* ◊ *The possession of a passport is essential for foreign travel.* ◊ *On her father's death, she came into possession of* (= received) *a vast fortune.* ◊ *You cannot legally*

take possession of the property (= start using it after buying it) *until three weeks after the contract is signed.*— see also VACANT POSSESSION **2** [C, usually pl.] something that you own or have with you at a particular time **SYN** BELONGINGS: *personal possessions* ◊ *The ring is one of her most treasured possessions.*

IN SPORT **3** [U] the state of having control of the ball: *to win/get/lose possession of the ball*

LAW **4** [U] the state of having illegal drugs or weapons with you at a particular time: *She was charged with possession.*

COUNTRY **5** [C] (*formal*) a country that is controlled or governed by another country: *The former colonial possessions are now independent states.*

BY THE DEVIL **6** [U] the situation when sb's mind is believed to be controlled by the devil or by an evil spirit **IDM** see FIELD *n.*

pos·ses·sive /pəˈzesɪv/ *adj.*, *noun*
■ *adj.* **1** ~ **(of/about sb/sth)** demanding total attention or love; not wanting sb to be independent: *Some parents are too possessive of their children.* **2** ~ **(of/about sth)** not liking to lend things or share things with others: *Jimmy's very possessive about his toys.* **3** (*grammar*) showing that sth belongs to sb/sth: *possessive pronouns* (= yours, his, etc.). ▶ **pos·ses·sive·ly** *adv.*: *'That's mine!' she said possessively.* **pos·ses·sive·ness** *noun* [U]: *I couldn't stand his jealousy and possessiveness.*
■ *noun* (*grammar*) **1** [C] an adjective, a pronoun or a form of a word that expresses the fact that sth belongs to sb/sth: *'Ours' and 'their' are possessives.* **2** (**the possessive**) *noun* [sing.] the special form of a word that expresses belonging—compare GENITIVE

pos·ses·sor /pəˈzesə(r)/ *noun* (*formal* or *humorous*) a person who owns or has sth **SYN** OWNER: *He is now the proud possessor of a driving licence.*

WHICH WORD? ⑦
possibility / occasion / opportunity / chance

Occasion, opportunity and **chance** all mean a time when it is possible to do something. **Possibility** and **chance** are used to suggest that something might happen.

Occasion suggests a time that is right or suitable for an activity: *A wedding is an occasion for celebration.*

Opportunity and **chance** suggest it is possible for you to do something because the circumstances are good or lucky at the time: *I had the opportunity to spend a year in Paris while I was a student.* ◊ *I hope you get the chance to relax this weekend.*

Possibility. Note that you cannot say **a/the possibility to do sth**: *I had the possibility to spend a year in Paris while I was a student.* **Possibility** means the fact that something might happen or be true and is used with **of** or **that**: *There is a possibility that I might go to Paris to study for a year.* **Chance** can also be used in this way: *I have a good chance of being promoted.*

---

pos·si·bil·ity /ˌpɒsəˈbɪləti; *AmE* ˌpɑːs-/ *noun* (*pl.* **-ies**) **1** [U, C] ~ **(of sth/of doing sth) | ~ (that …)** the fact that sth might exist or happen, but is not certain to: *There is now no possibility that she will make a full recovery.* ◊ *He refused to rule out the possibility of a tax increase.* ◊ *It is not beyond the bounds of possibility that we'll all meet again one day.* ◊ *Bankruptcy is a real possibility if sales don't improve.* ◊ *What had seemed impossible now seemed a distinct possibility.* **OPP** IMPOSSIBILITY **2** [C, often pl.] one of the different things that you can do in a particular situation **SYN** OPTION: *to explore/consider/investigate a wide range of possibilities* ◊ *to exhaust all the possibilities* ◊ *Selling the house is just one possibility that is open to us.* ◊ *The possibilities are endless.* **3** [C, usually pl.] something that gives you a chance to achieve sth **SYN** OPPORTUNITY: *The course offers a range of exciting possibilities for developing your skills.* **4** (**possibilities**) [pl.] if sth has

P

b	d	f	g	h	k	l	m	n	p	r
bad	did	fall	get	hat	cat	leg	man	now	pen	red

possibilities, it can be improved or made successful [SYN] POTENTIAL: *The house is in a bad state of repair but it has possibilities.*

pos·sible /ˈpɒsəbl; *AmE* ˈpɑːs-/ *adj., noun*

■ *adj.* **1** [not usually before noun] that can be done or achieved: *It is possible to get there by bus.* ◊ *Would it be possible for me to leave a message for her?* ◊ *This wouldn't have been possible without you.* ◊ *Try to avoid losing your temper if at all possible* (= if you can). ◊ *Use public transport whenever possible* (= when you can). ◊ *It's just not physically possible to finish all this by the end of the week.* ◊ *We spent every possible moment on the beach.* [OPP] IMPOSSIBLE **2** that might exist or happen but is not certain to: *a possible future president* ◊ *the possible side effects of the drug* ◊ *Frost is possible, although unlikely, at this time of year.* ◊ *It's just possible that I gave them the wrong directions.* ◊ *With the possible exception of the Beatles, no other band has become so successful so quickly.* **3** reasonable or acceptable in a particular situation: *There are several possible explanations.* **4** used after adjectives to emphasize that sth is the best, worst, etc. of its type: *It was the best possible surprise anyone could have given me.* ◊ *Don't leave your packing until the last possible moment.* [IDM] **as quickly, much, soon, etc. as ˈpossible** as quickly, much, soon, etc. as you can: *We will get your order to you as soon as possible.*—more at WORLD

■ *noun* a person or a thing that is suitable for a particular job, purpose, etc. and might be chosen: *Out of all the people interviewed, there are only five possibles.*

pos·sibly /ˈpɒsəbli; *AmE* ˈpɑːs-/ *adv.* **1** used to say that sth might exist, happen or be true, but you are not certain [SYN] PERHAPS: *This is possibly their worst performance ever.* ◊ *She found it difficult to get on with her, possibly because of the difference in their ages.* ◊ *'Will you be around next week?' 'Possibly.'* **2** (*spoken*) used to emphasize that you are surprised, annoyed, etc. about sth: *You can't possibly mean that!* **3** (*spoken*) used to ask sb politely to do sth: *Could you possibly open that window for me?* **4** used to say that sb will do or has done as much as they can in order to make sth happen: *I will come as soon as I possibly can.* ◊ *They tried everything they possibly could to improve the situation.* **5** (*especially spoken*) used with negatives, especially 'can't' and 'couldn't', to say strongly that you cannot do sth or that sth cannot or could not happen or be done: *I can't possibly tell you that!* ◊ *You can't possibly carry all those bags.* ◊ *'Let me buy it for you.' 'That's very kind of you, but I couldn't possibly* (= accept).'

pos·sum /ˈpɒsəm; *AmE* ˈpɑːsəm/ *noun* = OPOSSUM [IDM] **play ˈpossum** (*informal*) to pretend to be asleep or not aware of sth, in order to trick sb

post /pəʊst; *AmE* poʊst/ *noun, verb*

■ *noun*

LETTERS | **1** (*BrE*) (also **mail** *AmE, BrE*) [U] the official system used for sending and delivering letters, packages, etc: *I'll send the original to you by post.* ◊ *I'll put the information in the post to you tomorrow.* ◊ *My application got lost in the post.* **2** (*BrE*) (also **mail** *AmE, BrE*) [U] letters, packages, etc. that are sent and delivered: *There was a lot of post this morning.* ◊ *Have you opened your post yet?* **3** (*BrE*) [U, sing.] an occasion during the day when letters, etc. are collected or delivered: *to catch/miss the post* ◊ *The parcel came in this morning's post.* ◊ *Payment should be sent by return of post* (= immediately).

JOB | **4** [C] a job, especially an important one in a large organization: *an academic/administrative/government post* ◊ *to take up a post* ◊ *to resign (from) a post* ◊ *We will be creating 15 new posts next year.* ◊ *The company has been unable to fill the post.* ◊ *He has held the post for three years.*

FOR SOLDIER/GUARD | **5** [C] the place where sb, especially a soldier, does their job: *a police/customs/military post* ◊ *a command/an observation post* ◊ *The guards were ordered not to leave their posts.*—see also THE LAST POST, STAGING POST, TRADING POST

WOOD/METAL | **6** [C] (often in compounds) a piece of wood or metal that is set in the ground in an upright position, especially to support sth or to mark a position: *corner posts* (= that mark the corners of a sports field) ◊ *The team's 'net' was a piece of string tied to two posts.*—see also BEDPOST, GATEPOST, LAMP POST, SIGNPOST

END OF RACE | **7** (**the post**) [sing.] the place where a race finishes, especially in horse racing—see also FIRST-PAST-THE-POST, WINNING POST

FOOTBALL | **8** [C, usually sing.] = GOALPOST: *The ball hit the post and bounced in.*

[IDM] see DEAF, PILLAR

■ *verb*

LETTERS | **1** (*BrE*) (*AmE* **mail**) ~ sth (off) (to sb) | ~ sb sth to send a letter, etc. to sb by post/mail: [VN] *Have you posted off your order yet?* ◊ [VN, VNN] *Is it OK if I post the cheque to you next week?* ◊ *Is it OK if I post you the cheque next week?*—compare MAIL **2** [VN] (*BrE*) (*AmE* **mail**) to put a letter, etc. into a POSTBOX: *Could you post this letter for me?*

STH THROUGH HOLE | **3** [VN] to put sth through a hole into a container: *Let yourself out and post the keys through the letter box.*

SB FOR JOB | **4** [VN] [usually passive] to send sb to a place for a period of time as part of their job: *She's been posted to Washington for two years.* ◊ *Most employees get posted abroad at some stage.*

SOLDIER/GUARD | **5** [VN+*adv./prep.*] to put sb, especially a soldier, in a particular place so that they can guard a building or area: *Guards have been posted along the border.*

PUBLIC NOTICE | **6** [VN] [often passive] to put a notice, etc. in a public place so that people can see it: *A copy of the letter was posted on the noticeboard.* ◊ *The results will be posted on the Internet.*

GIVE INFORMATION | **7** (*especially AmE*) to announce sth publicly or officially, especially financial information or a warning: [VN] *The company posted a $1.1 billion loss.* ◊ *A snow warning was posted for Ohio.* ◊ [VN-ADJ] *The aircraft and its crew were posted missing.*

PAY MONEY TO COURT | **8** [VN] ~ bail/(a) bond (*especially AmE*) to pay money to a court of law so that a person accused of a crime can go free until their trial: *She was released after posting $100 cash bond and her driver's license.*

[IDM] **keep sb ˈposted (about/on sth)** to regularly give sb the most recent information about sth and how it is developing: *I'll keep you posted on his progress.*

BRITISH / AMERICAN
post / mail

Nouns

In *BrE* the official system used for sending and delivering letters, parcels/packages, etc. is usually called the **post**. In *AmE* it is usually called the **mail**: *I'll put an application form in the post/mail for you today.* ◊ *Send your fee by post/mail to this address.* **Mail** is sometimes used in *BrE* in such expressions as *the Royal Mail*. **Post** occurs in *AmE* in such expressions as *the US Postal Service*.

In *BrE* **post** is also used to mean the letters, parcels/packages, etc. that are delivered to you. **Mail** is the usual word in *AmE* and is sometimes also used in *BrE*: *Was there any post/mail this morning?* ◊ *I sat down to open my post/mail.*

Verbs

Compare: *I'll post the letter when I go out.* (*BrE*) and *I'll mail the letter when I go out.* (*AmE*)

Compounds

Note these words: **postman** (*BrE*), **mailman/mail carrier** (both *AmE*); **postbox** *BrE*, **mailbox** *AmE*. Some compounds are used in both *BrE* and *AmE*: **post office, postcard, mail order**.

Electronic

Mail, not **post**, is always used in connection with electronic messages: **e-mail, voicemail**.

---

	s	t	v	z	ʃ	ʒ	tʃ	dʒ	θ	ð	ŋ
	see	tea	van	zoo	shoe	vision	chain	jam	thin	this	sing

post- /pəʊst; *AmE* poʊst/ *prefix* (in nouns, verbs and adjectives) after: *a postgraduate* ◇ *a post-Impressionist* ◇ *the post-1945 period*—compare ANTE-, PRE-

post·age /ˈpəʊstɪdʒ; *AmE* ˈpoʊ-/ *noun* [U] the cost of sending a letter, etc. by post: *an increase in postage rates* ◇ *How much was the postage on that letter?* ◇ (*BrE*) *All prices include postage and packing.* ◇ (*AmE*) *All prices include postage and handling.*

'postage stamp *noun* (*formal*) = STAMP

pos·tal /ˈpəʊstl; *AmE* ˈpoʊstl/ *adj.* [only before noun] **1** connected with the official system for sending and delivering letters, etc: *your full postal address* ◇ *postal charges/rates/services/workers* ◇ *the postal service/system* **2** (*especially BrE*) involving things that are sent by post: *postal applications/bookings*

'postal ballot *noun* (*BrE*) a system of voting on a particular issue in which everyone sends their vote by post

'postal code *noun* = POSTCODE

'postal order (*BrE*) (also **'money order** *AmE, BrE*) *noun* (*abbr.* **PO**) an official document that you can buy at a bank or a post office and send to sb so that they can exchange it for money

'postal service *noun* **1** a system of collecting and delivering letters, etc: *a good postal service* **2** (**the Postal Service**) (*AmE*) = POST OFFICE (2)

'postal vote (*BrE*) (*AmE* **,absentee 'ballot**) *noun* a vote in an election that you can send when you cannot be present

post·bag /ˈpəʊstbæg; *AmE* ˈpoʊst-/ *noun* (*BrE*) **1** (also **mail·bag**) [usually sing.] all the letters received by a newspaper, a radio station, or an important person at a particular time or about a particular subject: *We had a huge postbag on the subject from our readers.* **2** = MAIL-BAG (1)

post·box /ˈpəʊstbɒks; *AmE* ˈpoʊstbɑːks/ (also **'letter box**) (both *BrE*) (*AmE* **mail·box**) *noun* a public box, for example in the street, that you put letters into when you send them—compare PILLAR BOX—picture at LETTER BOX

post·card /ˈpəʊstkɑːd; *AmE* ˈpoʊstkɑːrd/ (also **card**) *noun* a card used for sending messages by post without an envelope, especially one that has a picture on one side: *colourful postcards of California* ◇ *Send us a postcard from Venice!* ◇ *Send your answers on a postcard to the above address.*—see also PICTURE POSTCARD

post·code /ˈpəʊstkəʊd; *AmE* ˈpoʊstkoʊd/ (also **'postal code**) (both *BrE*) (*AmE* **'Zip code**) *noun* a group of letters and/or numbers that are used as part of an address so that post/mail can be separated into groups and delivered more quickly

post·date *verb* [VN] **1** to write a date on a cheque that is later than the actual date so that the cheque cannot be CASHED (= exchanged for money) until that date: *a post-dated cheque*—compare BACKDATE **2** to happen, exist or be made at a later date than sth else in the past OPP PRE-DATE

post·doc·tor·al /ˌpəʊstˈdɒktərəl; *AmE* ˌpoʊstˈdɑːk-/ *adj.* connected with advanced research or study that is done after a PhD has been completed

pos·ter /ˈpəʊstə(r); *AmE* ˈpoʊ-/ *noun* **1** a large notice, often with a picture on it, that is put in a public place to advertise sth: *election posters* ◇ *a poster campaign* (= an attempt to educate people about sth by using posters) **2** a large picture that is printed on paper and put on a wall as decoration: *posters of her favourite pop stars*

poste rest·ante /ˌpəʊst ˈrestɑːnt; *AmE* ˌpoʊst reˈstɑːnt/ (*BrE*) (*AmE* **,general deˈlivery**) *noun* [U] an arrangement in which a post office keeps a person's mail until they go to collect it, used especially when sb is travelling

pos·ter·ior /pɒˈstɪəriə(r); *AmE* pɑːˈstɪr-/ *adj., noun*
■ *adj.* [only before noun] (*technical*) situated behind sth or at the back of sth OPP ANTERIOR
■ *noun* (*humorous*) the part of your body that you sit on; your bottom

pos·teri·ori ⇨ A POSTERIORI

pos·ter·ity /pɒˈsterəti; *AmE* pɑːˈs-/ *noun* [U] (*formal*) all the people who will live in the future: *Their music has been preserved for posterity.* ◇ *Posterity will remember him as a great man.*

,post·ˈfree *adj.* [only before noun] (*BrE*) used to describe sth that you can send by post without having to pay anything ▶ **,post·ˈfree** *adv.*: *Information will be sent post-free to any interested readers.*

post·gradu·ate /ˌpəʊstˈgrædʒuət; *AmE* ˌpoʊst-/ (*especially BrE*) *noun* a person who already holds a first degree and who is doing advanced study or research; a GRADUATE student: *postgraduate students* ◇ *a postgraduate course* ⇨ note at STUDENT

,post·ˈhaste *adv.* (*literary*) as quickly as you can: *to depart post-haste*

post·hu·mous /ˈpɒstjʊməs; *AmE* ˈpɑːstʃəməs/ *adj.* [usually before noun] happening, done, published, etc. after a person has died: *a posthumous award for bravery* ▶ **post·hu·mous·ly** *adv.*

post·ie /ˈpəʊsti; *AmE* ˈpoʊ-/ *noun* (*BrE, informal*) = POST-MAN

,post·in·ˈdus·trial *adj.* [only before noun] (of a place or society) no longer relying on heavy industry (= the production of steel, large machinery, etc.): *the importance of information technology in post-industrial societies*

post·ing /ˈpəʊstɪŋ; *AmE* ˈpoʊ-/ *noun* (*especially BrE*) an act of sending sb to a particular place to do their job, especially for a limited period of time: *an overseas posting*

'Post·it ™ (also **'Post·it note**) *noun* a small piece of coloured, sticky paper that you use for writing a note on, and that can be easily removed—picture at STATIONERY

post·man /ˈpəʊstmən; *AmE* ˈpoʊst-/, **post·woman** /ˈpəʊstwʊmən; *AmE* ˈpoʊst-/ *noun* (*pl.* **-men** /-mən/) (**-women** /-wɪmɪn/) (also *informal* **post·ie**) (*especially BrE*) a person whose job is to collect and deliver letters, etc.—see also MAILMAN

,postman's ˈknock (*BrE*) (*AmE* **'post office**) *noun* [U] a children's game in which imaginary letters are exchanged for kisses

post·mark /ˈpəʊstmɑːk; *AmE* ˈpoʊstmɑːrk/ *noun* an official mark placed over the stamp on a letter, etc. that shows when and where it was posted and makes it impossible to use the stamp again ▶ **post·mark** *verb* [VN] (usually passive): *The card was postmarked Tokyo 9th March.* ◇ *an anonymous letter postmarked in Chicago*

post·mas·ter /ˈpəʊstmɑːstə(r); *AmE* ˈpoʊstmæstər/, **post·mist·ress** /ˈpəʊstmɪstrəs; *AmE* ˈpoʊst-/ *noun* a person who is in charge of a post office

post·mod·ern /ˌpəʊstˈmɒdn; *AmE* ˌpoʊstˈmɑːdərn/ *adj.* connected with or influenced by postmodernism: *postmodern culture/architecture*

post·mod·ern·ism /ˌpəʊstˈmɒdənɪzəm; *AmE* ˌpoʊstˈmɑːdərn-/ *noun* [U] a style and movement in art, architecture, literature, etc. in the late 20th century that reacts against modern styles, for example by mixing features from traditional and modern styles—compare MODERNISM ▶ **post·mod·ern·ist** *noun* **post·mod·ern·ist** *adj.* [usually before noun]: *postmodernist culture/writing/cinema*

post·mortem /ˌpəʊst ˈmɔːtəm; *AmE* ˌpoʊst ˈmɔːrtəm/ *noun* **1** (also **post-,mortem exami'nation**) ~ (**on sb**) a medical examination of the body of a dead person in order to find out how they died SYN AUTOPSY: *to do/conduct/carry out a post-mortem* ◇ *The post-mortem on the child revealed that she had been poisoned.* **2** ~ (**on sth**) a discussion or an examination of an event after it has happened, especially in order to find out why it failed: *to hold a post-mortem on the party's election defeat*

post·natal /ˌpəʊst ˈneɪtl; *AmE* ˌpoʊst-/ *adj.* [only before noun] connected with the period after the birth of a child: *post-natal care/depression*—compare ANTENATAL, PRE-NATAL

'post office *noun* **1** [C] a place where you can buy stamps, send letters, etc: *Where's the main post office?* ◇ *You can buy your stamps at the post office.* ◇ *a post office counter* **2** (**the 'Post Office**) [sing.] (*abbr.* **PO**) the national organization in many countries that is responsible for collecting and delivering letters, etc: *He works for the Post Office.* **3** [U] (*AmE*) = POSTMAN'S KNOCK

æ	ɑː	e	ɜː	ə	ɪ	iː	i	ɒ	ɔː	ʌ	ʊ	u	uː
cat	father	ten	bird	about	sit	see	many	got	saw	cup	put	actual	too
								(BrE)					

P

'post office box *noun* = PO BOX

post-'op·era·tive *adj.* [only before noun] (*medical*) connected with the period after a medical operation: *post-operative complications/pain/care*

post-'paid *adj.* [only before noun] that you can send free because the charge has already been paid: *a post-paid envelope* ▶ **post-'paid** *adv.*

post·pone /pə'spəʊn; *AmE* poʊ'spoʊn/ *verb* ~ **sth (to/until sth)** to arrange for an event, etc. to take place at a later time or date: [VN] *The game has already been postponed three times.* ◊ *We'll have to postpone the meeting until next week.* ◊ [V-ing] *It was an unpopular decision to postpone building the new hospital.*—compare CANCEL ▶ **post·pone·ment** *noun* [U, C]: *Riots 'ed to the postponement of local elections.*

post·pran·dial /ˌpəʊst'prændiəl; *AmE* ˌpoʊst-/ *adj.* [usually before noun] (*formal or humorous*) happening immediately after a meal

post·script /'pəʊstskrɪpt; *AmE* 'poʊst-/ *noun* ~ **(to sth)** **1** (*abbr.* PS) an extra message that you add at the end of a letter after your signature **2** extra facts or information about a story, an event, etc. that is added after it has finished: *News of the award comes as a fitting postscript to a long and successful career.*

post-traumatic 'stress disorder *noun* [U] (*medical*) a medical condition in which a person suffers mental and emotional problems resulting from an experience that shocked them very much

pos·tu·late *verb, noun*
■ *verb* /'pɒstjuleɪt; *AmE* 'pɑːstʃəl-/ (*formal*) to suggest or accept that sth is true so that it can be used as the basis for a theory, etc. [SYN] POSIT: [VN] *They postulated a 500-year lifespan for a plastic container.* [also V that]
■ *noun* /'pɒstjulət; *AmE* 'pɑːstʃəl-/ (*formal*) a statement that is accepted as true, that forms the basis of a theory, etc.

pos·tural /'pɒstʃərəl; *AmE* 'pɑːs-/ *adj.* (*formal*) connected with the way you hold your body when sitting or standing: *bad postural habits*

pos·ture /'pɒstʃə(r); *AmE* 'pɑːs-/ *noun, verb*
■ *noun* **1** [U, C] the position in which you hold your body when standing or sitting: *a comfortable/relaxed posture* ◊ *upright/sitting/supine postures* ◊ *Back pains can be the result of bad posture.* **2** [C, usually sing.] your attitude to a particular situation or the way in which you deal with it: *The government has adopted an aggressive posture on immigration.*
■ *verb* [V] ~ **(as sth)** (*formal*) to pretend to be sth that you are not by saying and doing things in order to impress or deceive people

pos·tur·ing /'pɒstʃərɪŋ; *AmE* 'pɑːs-/ *noun* [U, C] (*disapproving*) behaviour that is not natural or sincere but is intended to attract attention or to have a particular effect: *political posturing*

post-'war *adj.* [usually before noun] existing, happening or made in the period after a war, especially the Second World War: *the post-war years*

post·woman ⇨ POSTMAN

posy /'pəʊzi; *AmE* 'poʊzi/ *noun* (*pl.* **-ies**) a small bunch of flowers

pot /pɒt; *AmE* pɑːt/ *noun, verb*
■ *noun*
FOR COOKING | **1** [C] a deep round, usually metal, container used for cooking things in: *pots and pans*
CONTAINER | **2** [C] (*especially BrE*) a container made of glass, clay or plastic, used for storing food in: *a pot of jam/honey* ◊ *a yogurt pot*—picture at PACKAGING **3** [C] (especially in compounds) a container of various kinds, made for a particular purpose: *a coffee pot* ◊ *a pepper pot* ◊ *a teapot* ◊ *Is there any more tea in the pot?*—see also CHAMBER POT, CHIMNEY POT, FLOWERPOT, LOBSTER POT, MELTING POT, POTTED **4** [C] the amount contained in a pot: *They drank a pot of coffee.* **5** [C] a bowl, etc. that is made by a POTTER
MONEY | **6 (the pot)** [sing.] (*especially AmE*) the total amount of money that is bet in a card game **7 (the pot)** [sing.] (*especially AmE*) all the money given by a group of

pot

pots (*BrE*)

pot

clay

potter's wheel

teapot   flowerpot   pots

people in order to do sth together, for example to buy food—see also KITTY
DRUG | **8** [U] (*informal*) = MARIJUANA: *pot smoking*
SHOT | **9** [C] = POTSHOT: *He took a pot at the neighbour's cat with his air rifle.*
IN BILLIARDS, etc. | **10** [C] (in the game of BILLIARDS, POOL or SNOOKER) the act of hitting a ball into one of the pockets around the edge of the table
STOMACH | **11** [C] (*informal*) = POT BELLY
IDM **go to 'pot** (*informal*) to be spoiled because people are not working hard or taking care of things **the pot calling the kettle 'black** (*saying, informal*) used to say that you should not criticize sb for a fault that you have yourself **pot 'luck** when you take **pot luck**, you choose sth or go somewhere without knowing very much about it, but hope that it will be good, pleasant, etc: *It's pot luck whether you get good advice or not.* ◊ *You're welcome to stay to supper, but you'll have to take pot luck* (= eat whatever is available).—see also POTLUCK **'pots of money** (*BrE, informal*) a very large amount of money—more at GOLD *n.*, MELTING POT, QUART
■ *verb* (**-tt-**) [VN]
PLANT | **1** to put a plant into a FLOWERPOT filled with soil
IN BILLIARDS, etc. | **2** (in the games of BILLIARDS, POOL and SNOOKER) to hit a ball into one of the pockets (= holes at the corners and edges of the table) [SYN] POCKET: *He potted the black to take a 7–3 lead.*
SHOOT | **3** to kill an animal or a bird by shooting it—see also POTTED

pot·able /'pəʊtəbl; *AmE* 'poʊ-/ *adj.* (*formal*) (of water) safe to drink

pot·ash /'pɒtæʃ; *AmE* 'pɑːt-/ *noun* [U] a chemical compound of potassium used to improve soil for farming and in making soap

po·tas·sium /pə'tæsiəm/ *noun* [U] (*symb* K) a chemical element. Potassium is a soft silver-white metal that exists mainly in compounds which are used in industry and farming.

po·tato /pə'teɪtəʊ; *AmE* -toʊ/ *noun* [C, U] (*pl.* **-oes**) a round white vegetable with a brown or red skin that grows underground as the root of a plant also called a **potato** : *Will you peel the potatoes for me?* ◊ (*BrE*) *mashed potato* ◊ (*AmE*) *mashed potatoes* ◊ *roast/boiled/baked/fried potatoes*—see also COUCH POTATO, HOT POTATO, JACKET, SWEET POTATO—picture on page A3 **IDM** see MEAT

po,tato 'crisp (*BrE*), **po,tato 'chip** (*AmE*) *noun* = CRISP

po'tato masher *noun* a kitchen UTENSIL (= tool) for MASHING potatoes—picture at KITCHEN

pot-'bellied *adj.* (of people and animals) having a large stomach that sticks out ▶ **pot 'belly** (also *informal* **pot**) *noun*

pot-boil·er /'pɒtbɔɪlə(r); *AmE* 'pɑːt-/ *noun* (*disapproving*) a book, a play, etc. that is produced only to earn money quickly

po·tency /'pəʊtnsi; *AmE* 'poʊ-/ *noun* [U, C] (*pl.* **-ies**) **1** the

aɪ	aʊ	eɪ	əʊ	oʊ	ɔɪ	ɪə	eə	ʊə	j	w
my	now	say	go (BrE)	go (AmE)	boy	near	hair	pure	yes	wet

power that sb/sth has to affect your body or mind: *the potency of desire ◇ If you keep a medicine too long, it may lose its potency.* **2** the ability of a man to have sex

po·tent /ˈpəʊtnt; AmE ˈpoʊ-/ *adj.* **1** having a strong effect on your body or mind: *a potent drug ◇ a very potent alcoholic brew ◇ a potent argument/reason* **2** powerful: *a potent weapon/force*—see also IMPOTENT ▶ **po·tent·ly** *adv.*

po·ten·tate /ˈpəʊtnteɪt; AmE ˈpoʊ-/ *noun* (*literary,* often *disapproving*) a ruler who has a lot of power, especially when this is not restricted by a parliament, etc.

po·ten·tial /pəˈtenʃl/ *adj., noun*
■ *adj.* [only before noun] that can develop into sth or be developed in the future $\boxed{\text{SYN}}$ POSSIBLE: *potential customers ◇ a potential source of conflict ◇ the potential benefits of European integration ◇ a potential prime minister ◇ First we need to identify actual and potential problems.* ▶ **po·ten·tial·ly** /-ʃəli/ *adv.*: *a potentially dangerous situation*
■ *noun* **1** [U] ~ (**for/for doing sth**) the possibility of sth happening or being developed or used: *the potential for change ◇ The European marketplace offers excellent potential for increasing sales.* **2** [U] qualities that exist and can be developed: *All children should be encouraged to realize their full potential. ◇ She has great potential as an artist. ◇ He has the potential to become a world-class musician. ◇ The house has a lot of potential.* **3** [U, C] (*physics*) the difference in VOLTAGE between two points in an electric field or CIRCUIT

po·ten·ti·al·ity /pəˌtenʃiˈæləti/ *noun* (*pl.* **-ies**) (*formal*) a power or a quality that exists and is capable of being developed: *We often underestimate our potentialities.*

pot·hole /ˈpɒthəʊl; AmE ˈpɑːthoʊl/ *noun* **1** a large rough hole in the surface of a road that is formed by traffic and bad weather **2** a deep hole that is formed in rock, especially by the action of water

pot·hol·ing /ˈpɒthəʊlɪŋ; AmE ˈpɑːthoʊlɪŋ/ (*BrE*) *noun* [U] = CAVING: *to go potholing* ▶ **pot·holer** *noun* = CAVER

po·tion /ˈpəʊʃn; AmE ˈpoʊʃn/ *noun* (*literary*) a drink of medicine or poison; a liquid with magic powers: *a magic/love potion*

pot·luck /pɒtˈlʌk; AmE pɑːt-/ *noun* (*AmE*) a meal to which each guest brings some food, which is then shared out among the guests

'pot plant *noun* (*BrE*) = HOUSE PLANT

pot-pourri /ˌpəʊ puˈriː; AmE ˌpoʊ-/ *noun* (from *French*) **1** [U, C] a mixture of dried flowers and leaves used for making a room smell pleasant **2** [sing.] a mixture of various things that were not originally intended to form a group: *a pot-pourri of tunes*

pot·shot /ˈpɒtʃɒt; AmE ˈpɑːtʃɑːt/ (also **pot**) *noun* (*informal*) a shot that sb fires without aiming carefully: *Somebody took a potshot at him as he drove past. ◇ (figurative) The newspapers took constant potshots at* (= criticized) *the president.*

pot·ted /ˈpɒtɪd; AmE ˈpɑːt-/ *adj.* [only before noun] **1** planted in a pot: *potted plants/palms* **2** (*BrE*) (of a book, or a story) in a short simple form: *a potted history of England* **3** (*BrE*) **potted** meat or fish has been cooked and preserved in a small container

pot·ter /ˈpɒtə(r); AmE ˈpɑːt-/ *verb, noun*
■ *verb* (*BrE*) (*AmE* **putt·er**) [V+adv. / prep.] to do things or move without hurrying, especially when you are doing sth that you enjoy and that is not important: *I spent the day pottering around the house.*
■ *noun* a person who makes clay pots by hand

ˌpotter's 'wheel *noun* a piece of equipment with a flat disc that goes around, on which potters put wet clay in order to shape it into pots—picture at POT

pot·tery /ˈpɒtəri; AmE ˈpɑːt-/ *noun* (*pl.* **-ies**) **1** [U] pots, dishes, etc. made with clay that is baked in an oven, especially when they are made by hand: *Roman pottery ◇ a piece of pottery* **2** [U] the clay that some dishes and pots are made of: *a jug made of blue-glazed pottery* **3** [U] the skill of making pots and dishes from clay, especially by hand: *a pottery class* **4** [C] a place where clay pots and dishes are made

'potting shed *noun* (*BrE*) a small building where seeds and young plants are grown in pots before they are planted outside

potty /ˈpɒti; AmE ˈpɑːti/ *adj., noun*
■ *adj.* (*BrE, informal,* becoming *old-fashioned*) **1** crazy: *The kids are driving me potty!* **2** ~ **about sb/sth** liking sb/sth a lot: *She's potty about you!*
■ *noun* (*pl.* **-ies**) (*informal*) a bowl that very young children use when they are too small to use a toilet—compare CHAMBER POT

'potty-train *verb* [VN] to teach a small child to use a potty or toilet ▶ **'potty-trained** *adj.* **'potty-training** *noun* [U]

pouch /paʊtʃ/ *noun* **1** a small bag, usually made of leather, and often carried in a pocket or attached to a belt: *a tobacco pouch ◇ She kept her money in a pouch around her neck.* **2** a large bag for carrying letters, especially official ones **3** a pocket of skin on the stomach of some female animals, such as KANGAROOS, in which they carry their young—picture on page A6 **4** a pocket of skin in the cheeks of some animals, such as HAMSTERS, in which they store food

pouffe (also **pouf**) /puːf/ (both *BrE*) (*AmE* **has·sock**) *noun* a large thick cushion used as a seat or for resting your feet on

poult·ice /ˈpəʊltɪs; AmE ˈpoʊ-/ *noun* a soft substance spread on a cloth, sometimes heated, and put on the skin to reduce pain or swelling

poult·ry /ˈpəʊltri; AmE ˈpoʊ-/ *noun* **1** [pl.] chickens, ducks and GEESE, kept for their meat or eggs: *to keep poultry ◇ poultry farming*—picture on page A6 **2** [U] meat from chickens, ducks and GEESE: *Eat plenty of fish and poultry.*

pounce /paʊns/ *verb* [V] ~ (**on/upon sb/sth**) to move suddenly forwards in order to attack or catch sb/sth: *The lion crouched ready to pounce. ◇ The muggers pounced on her as she got out of the car. ◇ Owen pounced on the loose ball and scored.* $\boxed{\text{PHR V}}$ **pounce on/upon sth** to quickly notice sth that sb has said or done, especially in order to criticize it $\boxed{\text{SYN}}$ SEIZE ON/ UPON: *His comments were pounced upon by the press.*

pound /paʊnd/ *noun, verb*
■ *noun*
MONEY | **1** [C] (also *technical* ˌpound 'sterling) (*symb* £) [C] the unit of money in Britain, worth 100 pence: *a ten-pound note ◇ a pound coin ◇ I've spent £25 on food today. ◇ What would you do if you won a million pounds?*—see also STERLING **2** [C] the unit of money of several other countries **3** (**the pound**) [sing.] (*finance*) the value of the British pound compared with the value of the money of other countries: *the strength/ weakness of the pound (against other currencies) ◇ The pound closed slightly down at $1.534.*
WEIGHT | **4** [C] (*abbr.* **lb**) a unit for measuring weight, equal to 0.454 of a kilogram: *half a pound of butter ◇ They cost two dollars a pound. ◇ I've lost six and a half pounds since I started my diet.*
FOR CARS | **5** [C] a place where motor vehicles that have been parked illegally are kept until their owners pay to get them back
FOR DOGS | **6** [C] a place where dogs that have been found in the street without their owners are kept until their owners claim them
$\boxed{\text{IDM}}$ **(have, get, want, etc.) your pound of 'flesh** the full amount that sb owes you, even if this will cause them trouble or suffering $\boxed{\text{ORIGIN}}$ From Shakespeare's *Merchant of Venice,* in which the moneylender Shylock demanded a pound of flesh from Antonio's body if he could not pay back the money he borrowed.—more at PENNY, PREVENTION
■ *verb*
HIT | **1** ~ (**away**) (**at/against/on sth**) to hit sth/sb hard many times, especially in a way that makes a lot of noise: [V] *Heavy rain pounded on the roof. ◇ Someone was pounding at the door. ◇ The factory's machinery pounded away day and night. ◇* [VN] *She pounded him with her fists.*
WALK NOISILY | **2** [V+adv. / prep.] to move with noisy steps: *She pounded along the corridor after him.*
OF HEART/BLOOD | **3** [V] to beat quickly and loudly: *Her*

heart was pounding with excitement. ◊ *The blood was pounding* (= making a beating noise) *in his ears.* ◊ *Her head began to pound.* ◊ *a pounding headache*

BREAK INTO PIECES | **4** [VN] **~ sth (to/into sth)** to hit sth many times in order to break it into smaller pieces: *The seeds were pounded to a fine powder.*

ATTACK WITH BOMBS | **5** [VN] to attack an area with a large number of bombs over a period of time: *The area is still being pounded by rebel guns.*

OF MUSIC | **6** [V] **~ (out)** to be played loudly: *Rock music was pounding out from the jukebox.*

PHRV ˌpound sth↔ˈout to play music loudly on a musical instrument: *Nobody pounds out a tune on the piano quite like her.*

pound·age /ˈpaʊndɪdʒ/ *noun* [U] **1** (*technical*) a charge that is made for every pound in weight of sth, or for every £1 in value **2** (*informal*) weight: *to carry extra poundage*

ˈ**pound cake** *noun* [C, U] (*AmE*) = MADEIRA CAKE

pound·er /ˈpaʊndə(r)/ *noun* (in compounds) **1** something that weighs the number of pounds mentioned: *a three-pounder* (= a fish, for example, that weighs 3lb) **2** a gun that fires a SHELL that weighs the number of pounds mentioned: *an eighteen-pounder*

pound·ing /ˈpaʊndɪŋ/ *noun* **1** a very loud repeated noise, such as the sound of sth hitting sth else hard; the sound or the feeling of your heart beating strongly: *We were awoken by a pounding at the door.* ◊ *There was a pounding in his head.* **2** an occasion when sth is hit hard or attacked and severely damaged: *The boat took a pounding in the gale.* ◊ (*figurative*) *The team took a pounding* (= were badly defeated).

ˈ**pound sign** *noun* **1** the symbol (£) that represents a pound in British money **2** (*AmE*) = HASH (3)

pour /pɔː(r)/ *verb* **1** [VN] [usually+adv. / prep.] to make a liquid or other substance flow from a container in a continuous stream, especially by holding the container at an angle: *Pour the sauce over the pasta.* ◊ *Although I poured it carefully, I still managed to spill some.* **2** [V+adv. / prep.] (of liquid, smoke, light, etc.) to flow quickly in a continuous stream: *Tears poured down his cheeks.* ◊ *Thick black smoke was pouring out of the roof.* **3 ~ (sth) (out)** to serve a drink by letting it flow from a container into a cup or glass: [VN] *Will you pour the coffee?* ◊ *I was in the kitchen, pouring out drinks.* ◊ [VN, VNN] *I've poured a cup of tea for you.* ◊ *I've poured you a cup of tea.* ◊ [V] *Shall I pour?* **4** [V] when rain **pours** down or when it's **pouring with rain**, rain is falling heavily: *The rain continued to pour down.* ◊ *It's pouring outside.* ◊ *It's pouring with rain.* **5** [V+adv. / prep.] to come or go somewhere continuously in large numbers: *Letters of complaint continue to pour in.* ◊ *Commuters came pouring out of the station.* IDM **pour oil on troubled ˈwater(s)** to try to settle a disagreement or dispute—more at COLD adj., HEART, RAIN v., SCORN n. PHRV ˌpour sth ˈinto sth to provide a large amount of money for sth: *The government has poured millions into the education system.* ˌpour ˈout when feelings or sb's words **pour out** they are expressed, usually after they have been kept hidden for some time: *Wave after wave of pent-up emotion poured out.* ◊ *The whole story then came pouring out.* ˌpour sth↔ˈout to express your feelings or give an account of sth, especially after keeping them or it secret or hidden: *She poured out her troubles to me over a cup of coffee.*—related noun OUTPOURING

pout /paʊt/ *verb* if you **pout**, **pout** your lips or if your lips **pout**, you push out your lips, to show you are annoyed or to look sexually attractive: [V] *He pouted angrily.* ◊ *Her lips pouted invitingly.* ◊ [VN] *models pouting their lips for the camera* [also v**speech**] ▶ **pout** *noun*: *Her lips were set in a pout of annoyance.*

pov·erty /ˈpɒvəti; *AmE* ˈpɑːvərti/ *noun* **1** [U] the state of being poor: *conditions of abject / extreme poverty* ◊ *to alleviate / relieve poverty* ◊ *Many elderly people live in poverty.* **2** [U, sing.] a lack of sth; poor quality: *There is a poverty of colour in her work.*

the ˈpoverty line (also **the ˈpoverty level** especially in *AmE*) *noun* [sing.] the official level of income that is necessary to be able to buy the basic things you need such as food and clothes and to pay for somewhere to live: *A third of the population is living at or below the poverty line.*

ˈ**poverty-stricken** *adj.* extremely poor; with very little money

ˈ**poverty trap** *noun* [usually sing.] a situation in which sb stays poor even when they get a job because the money they receive from the government is reduced

POW /ˌpiː əʊ ˈdʌbljuː; *AmE* əʊ/ *noun* the abbreviation for PRISONER OF WAR: *a POW camp*

pow /paʊ/ *exclamation* used to express the sound of an explosion, a gun firing or sb hitting sb else

pow·der /ˈpaʊdə(r)/ *noun, verb*

■ *noun* **1** [U, C] a dry mass of very small fine pieces or grains: *chilli powder* ◊ *lumps of chalk crushed to (a) fine white powder* ◊ *The snow was like powder.* ◊ *A wide range of cleaning fluids and powders is available.* ◊ *The mustard is sold in powder form.*—see also BAKING POWDER, CURRY POWDER, SOAP POWDER, TALCUM POWDER, WASHING POWDER **2** [U] a very fine, soft, dry substance that you can put on your face to make it look smooth and dry **3** [U] = GUNPOWDER IDM **keep your ˈpowder dry** (*old-fashioned*) to remain ready for a possible emergency **take a ˈpowder** (*AmE, informal*) to leave suddenly; to run away

■ *verb* [VN] to put powder on sth: *She powdered her face and put on her lipstick.* IDM **powder your ˈnose** (*old-fashioned*) a polite way of referring to the fact that a woman is going to the toilet / bathroom: *I'm just going to powder my nose.*

ˌ**powder ˈblue** *adj.* very pale blue in colour ▶ ˌ**powder ˈblue** *noun* [U]

pow·dered /ˈpaʊdəd; *AmE* -dərd/ *adj.* **1** (of a substance that is naturally liquid) dried and made into powder: *powdered milk* **2** crushed and made into a powder: *powdered chalk* **3** covered with powder: *her powdered cheeks*

ˌ**powdered ˈsugar** *noun* [U] (*AmE*) = ICING SUGAR

ˈ**powder keg** *noun* a dangerous situation that may suddenly become very violent

ˈ**powder puff** *noun* a round thick piece of soft material that you use for putting powder on your face

ˈ**powder room** *noun* **1** a polite word for a women's toilet / bathroom in a public building **2** (*AmE*) a small room in a house, containing a WASHBASIN and a toilet, usually for guests to use SYN HALF-BATH

pow·dery /ˈpaʊdəri/ *adj.* like powder; covered with powder: *a light fall of powdery snow* ◊ *powdery cheeks*

power /ˈpaʊə(r)/ *noun, verb*

■ *noun*

CONTROL | **1** [U] **~ (over sb/sth)** | **~ (to do sth)** the ability to control people or things: *The aim is to give people more power over their own lives.* ◊ *He has the power to make things very unpleasant for us.* ◊ *to have sb in your power* (= to be able to do what you like with sb) **2** [U] political control of a country or an area: *to take / seize / lose power* ◊ *The present regime has been in power for two years.* ◊ *The party came to power at the last election.* ◊ *They are hoping to return to power.* ◊ *a power struggle between rival factions within the party*—see also BALANCE OF POWER

ABILITY | **3** [U] (in people) the ability or opportunity to do sth: *It is not within my power* (= I am unable or not in a position) *to help you.* ◊ *I will do everything in my power to help you.* **4** [U] (also **powers** [pl.]) a particular ability of the body or mind: *He had lost the power of speech.* ◊ *The drug may affect your powers of concentration.* ◊ *He had to use all his powers of persuasion.* **5** (**powers**) [pl.] all the abilities of a person's body or mind: *Sufferers from the disease have failing mental powers and poor memories.* ◊ *At 26, he is at the height of his powers and ranked fourth in the world.*

AUTHORITY | **6** [U, C, usually pl.] **~ (to do sth)** the right or authority of a person or group to do sth: *The Secretary of State has the power to approve the proposals.* ◊ *The powers of the police must be clearly defined.* ◊ *The president has*

s	t	v	z	ʃ	ʒ	tʃ	dʒ	θ	ð	ŋ
see	tea	van	zoo	shoe	vision	chain	jam	thin	this	sing

the power of veto over all new legislation.—see also POWER OF ATTORNEY

COUNTRY | **7** [C] a country with a lot of influence in world affairs, or with great military strength: *world powers ◊ an allied/enemy power*—see also SUPERPOWER

INFLUENCE | **8** [U] (in compounds) strength or influence in a particular area of activity: *military/economic power ◊ air/sea power* (= military strength in the air/at sea) ◊ *purchasing/earning power* **9** [U] the influence of a particular thing or group within society: *the power of television/the media ◊ parent power*

ENERGY | **10** [U] the strength or energy contained in sth: *The ship was helpless against the power of the storm. ◊ It was a performance of great power.*—see also FIREPOWER, STAYING POWER **11** [U] energy that can be collected and used to operate a machine, to make electricity, etc: *nuclear/wind/solar power ◊ engine power*—see also HORSEPOWER ⇨ note at STRENGTH

ELECTRICITY | **12** [U] the public supply of electricity: *They've switched off the power. ◊ a power failure*

MATHEMATICS | **13** [C, usually sing.] the number of times that an amount is to be multiplied by itself: *4 to the power of 3 is 4^3* (= $4 \times 4 \times 4 = 64$).

OF LENS | **14** [U] the amount by which a LENS can make objects appear larger: *the power of a microscope/telescope*

GOOD/EVIL SPIRIT | **15** [C] a good or evil spirit that controls the lives of others: *the powers of darkness* (= the forces of evil)

IDM do sb a '**power of good** (*old-fashioned, informal*) to be very good for sb's physical or mental health **more power to sb's 'elbow** (*old-fashioned, BrE, informal*) used to express support or encouragement for sb to do sth **the (real) power behind the 'throne** the person who really controls an organization, a country, etc. in contrast to the person who is legally in charge **the ¸powers that 'be** (often *ironic*) the people who control an organization, a country, etc.—more at CORRIDOR, SWEEP *v.*

■ *verb*

SUPPLY ENERGY | **1** [VN] [usually passive] to supply a machine or vehicle with the energy that makes it work: *The aircraft is powered by a jet engine.*

MOVE QUICKLY | **2** [+adv./prep.] to move or move sth very quickly and with great power in a particular direction: [V] *He powered through the water. ◊* [VN] *She powered her way into the lead. ◊ He powered his header past the goalie.*

PHR V ¸power sth↔'up to prepare a machine to start working by supplying it with electricity, etc.

¸power-assisted 'steering *noun* [U] (*BrE*) = POWER STEERING

'**power base** *noun* the area or the people that provide the main support for a politician or a political party

power-boat /'paʊəbəʊt; *AmE* 'paʊərboʊt/ *noun* a fast boat with a powerful engine that is used especially for racing

'**power broker** *noun* a person who has a strong influence on who has political power in an area

'**power cut** (*BrE*) (*AmE* '**power outage**) *noun* an interruption in the supply of electricity; a period of time when this happens

'**power dressing** *noun* [U] a style of dressing in which people in business wear formal and expensive clothes to emphasize how important they and their jobs are

powered /'paʊəd; *AmE* 'paʊərd/ *adj.* (usually in compounds) operated by a form of energy such as electricity or by the type of energy mentioned: *a powered wheelchair ◊ a solar-powered calculator*—see also HIGH-POWERED

power-ful /'paʊəfl; *AmE* 'paʊərfl/ *adj.* **1** (of people) being able to control and influence people and events **SYN** INFLUENTIAL: *an immensely powerful nation/group/organization ◊ one of the most powerful directors in Hollywood ◊ a rich and powerful man ◊ Only the intervention of powerful friends obtained her release.* **2** having great power or force; very effective: *powerful weapons/tools ◊ a powerful engine/car ◊ a powerful voice/smell* **3** having a strong effect on your mind or body: *a powerful image/drug/speech* **4** (of a person or an animal) physically strong: *a*

powerful body ◊ a powerful athlete ▶ **power-ful-ly** /-fəli/ *adv.*: *a powerfully emotive song ◊ He is powerfully built* (= he has a large strong body). *◊ She argued powerfully for reform.*

power-house /'paʊəhaʊs; *AmE* 'paʊərh-/ *noun* **1** a group or an organization that has a lot of power: *China has been described as an 'emerging economic powerhouse'.* **2** a person who is very strong and full of energy

power-less /'paʊələs; *AmE* 'paʊərləs/ *adj.* **1** without power to control or to influence sb/sth **SYN** HELPLESS: *powerless minorities ◊ When the enemy attacked, we were completely powerless against them.* **2** ~ **to do sth** completely unable to do sth: *I saw what was happening, but I was powerless to help.* ▶ **power-less-ness** *noun* [U]: *a feeling/sense of powerlessness*

'**power line** *noun* a thick wire that carries electricity: *overhead power lines*

¸power of at'torney *noun* [U, C] (*pl.* **powers of attorney**) (*law*) the right to act as the representative of sb in business or financial matters; a document that gives sb this right

'**power outage** *noun* (*AmE*) = POWER CUT

'**power plant** *noun* = POWER STATION

'**power point** *noun* (*BrE*) = SOCKET (1)

'**power politics** *noun* [U+sing./pl. *v.*] a situation in which a country tries to achieve its aims by using or threatening to use its military or economic power against another country

'**power-sharing** *noun* [U] a policy or system in which different groups or political parties share responsibility for making decisions, taking political action, etc.

'**power station** (*BrE*) (also '**power plant** *AmE, BrE*) *noun* a building or group of buildings where electricity is produced: *a coal-fired power station ◊ a nuclear power station*

'**power steering** (*BrE* also ¸power-assisted 'steering) *noun* [U] (in a vehicle) a system that uses power from the engine to help the driver change direction

pow-wow /'paʊwaʊ/ *noun* **1** a meeting of Native Americans **2** (*informal* or *humorous*) a meeting for discussion

pox /pɒks; *AmE* pɑːks/ *noun* (**the pox**) [sing.] (*old use*) **1** an infectious disease spread by sexual contact **SYN** SYPHILIS **2** = SMALLPOX

poxy /'pɒksi; *AmE* 'pɑːksi/ *adj.* [only before noun] (*BrE*) if sb describes sth as **poxy**, they think it has little value or importance

pp *abbr.* **1** (**pp.**) pages: *See pp. 100–117.* **2** (also **p.p.**) (*especially BrE*) used in front of a person's name when sb signs a business letter on his/her behalf: *pp Chris Baker* (= from Chris Baker, but signed by sb else because Chris Baker is away) **3** (*music*) very quietly (from Italian 'pianissimo')

PPS /¸piː piː 'es/ *noun* the abbreviation for 'Parliamentary Private Secretary' (a Member of Parliament in Britain who is given the job of helping a minister)

PR /¸piː 'ɑː(r)/ *noun* [U] **1** the abbreviation for PUBLIC RELATIONS: *a PR department/agency/campaign ◊ The article is very good PR for the theatre.* **2** the abbreviation for PROPORTIONAL REPRESENTATION

prac-tic-able /'præktɪkəbl/ *adj.* (*formal*) (of an idea, a plan or a suggestion) able to be done; likely to be successful **SYN** FEASIBLE, WORKABLE: *at the earliest practicable date/opportunity ◊ as soon as (is) practicable ◊ The only practicable alternative is to postpone the meeting.*—compare IMPRACTICABLE ▶ **prac-tic-abil-ity** /¸præktɪkə'bɪləti/ *noun* [U]: *We were doubtful about the practicability of the plan.* **prac-tic-ably** /-əbli/ *adv.*: *Please reply as soon as is practicably possible.*

prac-tical /'præktɪkl/ *adj., noun*
■ *adj.*

CONNECTED WITH REAL THINGS | **1** connected with real situations rather than with ideas or theories: *to have gained practical experience of the work ◊ practical advice/help/support ◊ practical problems/difficulties ◊ There are some obvious practical applications of the research. ◊ In practical terms, it means spending less. ◊ From a practical*

æ	ɑː	e	ɜː	ə	ɪ	iː	i	ɒ	ɔː	ʌ	ʊ	u	uː
cat	father	ten	bird	about	sit	see	many	got	saw	cup	put	actual	too
								(BrE)					

point of view, it isn't a good place to live.—compare THEOR-ETICAL

LIKELY TO WORK | **2** (of an idea, a method or a course of action) right or sensible; likely to be successful SYN WORKABLE: *It wouldn't be practical for us to go all that way just for the weekend.* OPP IMPRACTICAL

USEFUL | **3** (of things) useful or suitable: *a practical little car, ideal for the city* OPP IMPRACTICAL

SENSIBLE | **4** (of a person) sensible and realistic: *Let's be practical and work out the cost first.* OPP IMPRACTICAL

GOOD AT MAKING THINGS | **5** (of a person) good at making or repairing things: *Bob's very practical. He does all the odd jobs around the house.*

ALMOST TOTAL | **6** [only before noun] almost complete or total SYN VIRTUAL: *She married a practical stranger.*

IDM **for (all) 'practical purposes** used when you are stating what the reality of a situation is: *There's still another ten minutes of the game to go, but for practical purposes it's already over.*

■ *noun* (*BrE, informal*) a lesson or an exam in science or technology in which students have to do or make things, not just read or write about them

prac·ti·cal·ity /ˌpræktɪˈkæləti/ *noun* **1** [U] the quality of being suitable, or likely to be successful: *I have doubts about the practicality of their proposal.* **2** [U] the quality of being sensible and realistic: *I was impressed by her practicality.* **3** (**practicalities**) [pl.] the real facts and circumstances rather than ideas or theories: *It sounds like a good idea; let's look at the practicalities and work out the costs.*

ˌpractical 'joke *noun* a trick that is played on sb to make them look stupid and to make other people laugh ► ˌpractical 'joker *noun*

prac·tic·al·ly /ˈpræktɪkli/ *adv.* **1** (especially *spoken*) almost; very nearly SYN VIRTUALLY: *practically empty/ impossible* ◇ *I meet famous people practically every day.* ◇ *My essay is practically finished now.* ◇ *There's practically no difference between the two options.* ⇨ note at ALMOST **2** in a realistic or sensible way; in real situations: *Practically speaking, we can't afford it.* ◇ *It sounds like a good idea, but I don't think it will work practically.*—compare THEORETICALLY

ˌpractical 'nurse *noun* (*AmE*) a nurse with practical experience but less training than a REGISTERED NURSE

prac·tice /ˈpræktɪs/ *noun, verb*
■ *noun*
ACTION NOT IDEAS | **1** [U] action rather than ideas: *the theory and practice of teaching* ◇ *She's determined to put her new ideas into practice.*

WAY OF DOING STH | **2** [U, C] a way of doing sth that is the usual or expected way in a particular organization or situation: *common/current/standard practice* ◇ *guidelines for good/best practice* ◇ *a review of pay and working practices* ◇ *occult/religious practices*—see also CODE OF PRACTICE, RESTRICTIVE PRACTICES, SHARP PRACTICE

HABIT/CUSTOM | **3** [C] a thing that is done regularly; a habit or a custom: *the German practice of giving workers a say in how their company is run* ◇ *It is his practice to read several books a week.*

FOR IMPROVING SKILL | **4** [U, C] doing an activity or training regularly so that you can improve your skill; the time you spend doing this: *conversation practice* ◇ *piano/football practice* ◇ *It takes a lot of practice to play the violin well.* ◇ *There's a basketball practice every Friday evening.* ◇ *She does an hour's piano practice every day.*

OF DOCTOR/LAWYER | **5** [U, C] the work or the business of some professional people such as doctors, dentists and lawyers; the place where they work: *the practice of law/medicine* ◇ *Students should have prior experience of veterinary practice.* ◇ *My solicitor is no longer in practice.* ◇ *a successful medical/dental/law practice*—see also GENERAL PRACTICE, GROUP PRACTICE, PRIVATE PRACTICE

IDM **in 'practice** in reality: *Prisoners have legal rights, but in practice these rights are not always respected.* **be/get/ˌout of 'practice** to be/become less good at doing sth than you were because you have not spent time doing it recently: *Don't ask me to speak French! I'm out of practice.*

ˌpractice makes 'perfect (*saying*) a way of encouraging people by telling them that if you do an activity regularly and try to improve your skill, you will become very good at it
■ *verb* (*AmE*) = PRACTISE

prac·tise (*BrE*) (*AmE* **prac·tice**) /ˈpræktɪs/ *verb* **1** ~ (**for sth**) | ~ (**sth**) (**on sb/sth**) to do an activity or train regularly so that you can improve your skill: [V] *You need to practise every day.* ◇ *She's practising for her piano exam.* ◇ [VN] *I've been practising my serve for weeks.* ◇ *He usually wants to practise his English on me.* ◇ [V-ing] *Practise reversing the car into the garage.* **2** [VN] to do sth regularly as part of your normal behaviour: *to practise self-restraint/safe sex* ◇ *Do you still practise your religion?* **3** ~ (**as sth**) to work as a doctor, lawyer, etc: [V] *There are over 50000 solicitors practising in England and Wales.* ◇ *She practised as a barrister for many years.* ◇ [VN] *He was banned from practising medicine.* IDM **ˌpractise what you 'preach** to do the things yourself that you tell other people to do

prac·tised (*BrE*) (*AmE* **-ticed**) /ˈpræktɪst/ *adj.* ~ (**in sth**) good at doing sth because you have been doing it regularly: *She's only 18 but she's already a practised composer.* ◇ *It took a practised eye to spot the difference.* ◇ *He has good ideas but he isn't practised in the art of marketing.*

prac·tis·ing (*BrE*) (*AmE* **-ticing**) /ˈpræktɪsɪŋ/ *adj.* [only before noun] taking an active part in a particular religion, profession, etc: *a practising Christian/teacher*

prac·ti·tion·er /prækˈtɪʃənə(r)/ *noun* **1** (*technical*) a person who works in a profession, especially medicine or law: *dental/legal practitioners* ◇ *a qualified practitioner*—see also GENERAL PRACTITIONER **2** (*formal*) a person who regularly does a particular activity, especially one that requires skill: *one of the greatest practitioners of science fiction*

prae·sid·ium (especially *BrE*) = PRESIDIUM

prag·mat·ic /prægˈmætɪk/ *adj.* solving problems in a practical and sensible way rather than by having fixed ideas or theories SYN REALISTIC: *a pragmatic approach to management problems* ► **prag·mat·ic·al·ly** /-kli/ *adv.*

prag·mat·ics /prægˈmætɪks/ *noun* [U] (*linguistics*) the study of the way in which language is used to express what sb really means in particular situations, especially when the actual words used may appear to mean sth different

prag·ma·tism /ˈprægmətɪzəm/ *noun* [U] (*formal*) thinking about solving problems in a practical and sensible way rather than by having fixed ideas and theories ► **prag·ma·tist** /-tɪst/ *noun*

prairie /ˈpreəri; *AmE* ˈpreri/ *noun* [C, U] a flat wide area of land in N. America and Canada, without many trees and originally covered with grass

praise /preɪz/ *noun, verb*
■ *noun* [U] **1** (also *less frequent* **praises** [pl.]) words that show approval of or admiration for sb/sth: *His teachers are full of praise for the progress he's making.* ◇ *She wrote poems in praise of freedom.* ◇ *His latest movie has won high praise from the critics.* ◇ *We have nothing but praise for the way they handled the investigation.* ◇ *The team coach singled out two players for special praise.* ◇ *She left with their praises ringing in her ears.* ◇ *They always sing his praises* (= praise him very highly). **2** the expression of worship to God: *hymns/songs of praise* ◇ *Praise be (to God)!* (= expressing belief or joy) IDM see DAMN *v.*
■ *verb* [VN] **1** ~ **sb/sth (for sth)** | ~ **sb/sth (as sth)** to express your approval or admiration for sb/sth SYN COMPLIMENT: *She praised his cooking.* ◇ *He praised his team for their performance.* ◇ *Critics praised the work as highly original.* **2** to express your thanks to or your respect for God: *Praise the Lord.* ◇ *Allah be praised.* IDM **praise sb/sth to the 'skies** to praise sb/sth a lot

praise·worthy /ˈpreɪzwɜːði; *AmE* -wɜːrði/ *adj.* (*formal*) deserving praise: *a praiseworthy achievement/effort/attempt*

pram /præm/ (*BrE*) (*AmE* **baby carriage**) *noun* a small vehicle on four wheels for a baby to go out in, pushed by a person on foot—picture at PUSHCHAIR

aɪ	aʊ	eɪ	əʊ	oʊ	ɔɪ	ɪə	eə	ʊə	j	w
my	now	say	go	go	boy	near	hair	pure	yes	wet
			(BrE)	(AmE)						

prance /prɑːns; *AmE* præns/ *verb* [V] **1** [+*adv.*/*prep.*] to move quickly with exaggerated steps so that people will look at you: *The lead singer was prancing around with the microphone.* ◊ *She pranced out of the room.* **2** (of a horse) to move with high steps

prang /præŋ/ *verb* [VN] (*BrE, informal*) to damage a vehicle in an accident ▶ **prang** *noun*

prank /præŋk/ *noun* a trick that is played on sb as a joke: *a childish*/*silly prank* ▶ **prank·ster** /ˈpræŋkstə(r)/ *noun*: *Student pranksters have done considerable damage to the school buildings.*

prat /præt/ *noun* (*BrE, slang*) a stupid person: *He got drunk and made a complete prat of himself.*

prate /preɪt/ *verb* [V] ~ (**on**) (**about sth**) (*old-fashioned, disapproving*) to talk too much in a stupid or boring way

prat·fall /ˈprætfɔːl/ *noun* (*especially AmE*) **1** an embarrassing mistake **2** a fall on your bottom

prat·tle /ˈprætl/ *verb* [V] ~ (**on**/**away**) (**about sb/sth**) (*old-fashioned*, often *disapproving*) to talk a lot about unimportant things: *She prattled on about her children all evening.* ▶ **prat·tle** *noun* [U]

prawn /prɔːn/ *noun* (*especially BrE*) (*AmE* usually **shrimp**) a shellfish with ten legs and a long tail, that can be eaten. Prawns turn pink when cooked.—picture on page A7

praxis /ˈpræksɪs/ *noun* [U] (*philosophy*) a way of doing sth; the use of a theory or a belief in a practical way

pray /preɪ/ *verb, adv.*
■ *verb* **1** ~ (**to sb**) (**for sb/sth**) to speak to God, especially to give thanks or ask for help: [V] *They knelt down and prayed.* ◊ *I'll pray for you.* ◊ *to pray for peace*/*rain* ◊ *She prayed to God for an end to her sufferings.* ◊ [V(**that**)] *We prayed (that) she would recover from her illness.* ◊ [V **to** inf] *He prayed to be forgiven.* [also V **speech**] **2** ~ (**for sth**) to hope very much that sth will happen: [V] *We're praying for good weather on Saturday.* ◊ [V **that**] *I prayed that nobody would notice my mistake.*
■ *adv.* (*old use* or *ironic*) used to mean 'please' when you are asking a question or telling sb to do sth: *What, pray, is the meaning of this?* ◊ *Pray continue.*

pray·er /preə(r); *AmE* prer/ *noun* **1** [C] ~ (**for sb/sth**) words which you say to God giving thanks or asking for help: *to say your prayers* ◊ *prayers for the sick* ◊ *He arrived at that very moment, as if in answer to her prayer.* ◊ *Their prayers were answered and the child was found safe and well.* **2** [C] a fixed form of words that you can say when you speak to God: *It was a prayer she had learnt as a child.*—see also THE LORD'S PRAYER **3** [U] the act or habit of praying: *They knelt in prayer.* ◊ *We believe in the power of prayer.* **4** (**prayers**) [pl.] a religious meeting that takes place regularly, in which people say prayers **5** [usually sing.] a thing that you hope for very much: *My prayer is that one day he will walk again.* **IDM** see WING *n.*

'prayer book *noun* a book that contains prayers, for using in church services

'prayer rug (also **'prayer mat**) *noun* a small carpet that Muslims kneel on when they are saying prayers

praying 'mantis (also **mantis**) *noun* a large green insect that eats other insects. The female praying mantis often eats the male.

pre- /priː/ *prefix* (in verbs, nouns and adjectives) before: *preheat* ◊ *precaution* ◊ *pre-war* ◊ *preseason training* (= before a sports season starts)—compare ANTE-, POST-

preach /priːtʃ/ *verb* **1** to give a religious talk in a public place, especially in a church during a service: [V] *She preached to the congregation about forgiveness.* ◊ [VN] *The minister preached a sermon on the parable of the lost sheep.* **2** to tell people about a particular religion, way of life, system, etc. in order to persuade them to accept it: [VN] *to preach the word of God* ◊ *He preached the virtues of capitalism to us.* ◊ [V] *She preached about the benefits of a healthy lifestyle.* **3** [V] (*disapproving*) to give sb advice on morals, behaviour, etc., especially in a way that they find annoying or boring: *I'm sorry, I didn't mean to preach.* ◊ *You're preaching at me again!* **IDM** **preach to the con'verted** to speak to people in support of views that they already hold—more at PRACTISE

preach·er /ˈpriːtʃə(r)/ *noun* a Christian, often a member of the CLERGY, who preaches at a church service or a religious meeting: *a preacher famous for her inspiring sermons* ◊ *a lay preacher* (= who is not a priest, etc. but who has been trained to give religious talks)

preachy /ˈpriːtʃi/ *adj.* (*informal, disapproving*) trying to give advice or to persuade people to accept an opinion on what is right and wrong

pre·amble /priˈæmbl; ˈpriːæmbl/ *noun* [C, U] (*formal*) an introduction to a book or a written document; an introduction to sth you say: *The aims of the treaty are stated in its preamble.* ◊ *She gave him the bad news without preamble.*

pre-ar'ranged *adj.* planned or arranged in advance: *a pre-arranged signal*

pre·car·ious /prɪˈkeəriəs; *AmE* -ˈker-/ *adj.* **1** (of a situation) not safe or certain; dangerous: *He earned a precarious living as an artist.* ◊ *The museum is in a financially precarious position.* ◊ *The world is a precarious and unstable place.* **2** likely to fall or cause sb to fall: *That ladder looks very precarious.* ◊ *The path down to the beach is very precarious in wet weather.* ▶ **pre·car·ious·ly** *adv.*: *The economy is precariously close to recession.* ◊ *He balanced the glass precariously on the arm of his chair.* **pre·car·ious·ness** *noun* [U]

pre·cast /ˌpriːˈkɑːst; *AmE* -ˈkæst/ *adj.* (of some building materials) made into blocks ready to use: *precast concrete slabs*

pre·cau·tion /prɪˈkɔːʃn/ *noun* [often pl.] **1** ~ (**against sth**) something that is done in advance in order to prevent problems or to avoid danger: *safety precautions* ◊ *precautions against fire* ◊ *You must take all reasonable precautions to protect yourself and your family.* ◊ *I'll keep the letter as a precaution.* **2** (**precautions**) [pl.] a way of referring to CONTRACEPTION: *We didn't take any precautions and I got pregnant.* ▶ **pre·cau·tion·ary** /prɪˈkɔːʃənəri; *AmE* -neri/ *adj.*: *He was kept in hospital overnight as a precautionary measure.*

pre·cede /prɪˈsiːd/ *verb* (*written*) **1** to happen before sth or come before sth/sb in order: [VN] *the years preceding the war* ◊ *His resignation was preceded by weeks of speculation.* ◊ *She preceded me in the job.* ◊ [V] *See the preceding chapter.* **2** [VN+*adv.*/*prep.*] to go in front of sb: *She preceded him out of the room.* **PHRV** **pre'cede sth with sth** to do or say sth to introduce sth else: *She preceded her speech with a vote of thanks to the committee.*

pre·ce·dence /ˈpresɪdəns/ *noun* [U] ~ (**over sb/sth**) the condition of being more important than sb else and therefore coming or being dealt with first **SYN** PRIORITY: *She had to learn that her wishes did not take precedence over other people's needs.* ◊ *The speakers came on to the platform in order of precedence* (= the most important one first).

pre·ce·dent /ˈpresɪdənt/ *noun* **1** [C, U] an official action or decision that has happened in the past and that is seen as an example or a rule to be followed in a similar situation later: *The ruling set a precedent for future libel cases.* **2** [C, U] a similar action or event that happened earlier: *historical precedents* ◊ *There is no precedent for a disaster of this scale.* ◊ *Such protests are without precedent in recent history.* **3** [U] the way that things have always been done **SYN** TRADITION: *to break with precedent* (= to do sth in a different way)—see also UNPRECEDENTED

pre·cept /ˈpriːsept/ *noun* [C, U] (*formal*) a rule about how to behave or what to think **SYN** PRINCIPLE: *moral*/*ideological precepts*

pre·cinct /ˈpriːsɪŋkt/ *noun* **1** (*BrE*) a commercial area in a town where cars cannot go: *a pedestrian*/*shopping precinct* **2** (*AmE*) one of the parts into which a town or city is divided in order to organize elections: *voters in key precincts* **3** (*AmE*) a part of a city that has its own police station; the police station in this area: *Detective Hennessy of the 44th precinct* ◊ *The murder occurred just a block from the precinct.* **4** [usually pl.] the area around a place or a building, sometimes enclosed by a wall: *the cathedral*/*college precincts* ◊ *within the precincts of the castle*

b	d	f	g	h	k	l	m	n	p	r
bad	**did**	**fall**	**get**	**hat**	**cat**	**leg**	**man**	**now**	**pen**	**red**

pre·cious /ˈpreʃəs/ *adj., adv.*

■ *adj.* **1** rare and worth a lot of money: *a precious vase* ◊ *The crown was set with precious jewels—diamonds, rubies and emeralds.*—see also PRECIOUS METAL, PRECIOUS STONE **2** valuable or important and not to be wasted: *Clean water is a precious commodity in that part of the world.* ◊ *You're wasting precious time!* **3** loved or valued very much: *precious memories/possessions* **4** [only before noun] (*spoken*) used to show you are angry that another person thinks sth is very important: *I didn't touch your precious car!* **5** (*disapproving*) (especially of people and their behaviour) very formal, exaggerated and not natural in what you say and do ▶ **pre·cious·ness** *noun* [U]: *the preciousness of an old friendship* ◊ *His writings reveal an unattractive preciousness of style.*

■ *adv.* (*informal*) ~ **little/few** used to emphasize the fact that there is very little of sth or that there are very few of sth: *There's precious little to do in this town.*

precious 'metal *noun* [C, U] a very valuable metal such as gold or silver

precious 'stone (also **stone**) *noun* a rare valuable stone, such as a diamond, that is used in jewellery: *a ring set with a precious stone*—see also SEMI-PRECIOUS

preci·pice /ˈpresəpɪs/ *noun* a very steep side of a high cliff, mountain or rock: (*figurative*) *The country was now on the edge of a precipice* (= very close to disaster).—see also PRECIPITOUS

pre·cipi·tate *verb, adj., noun*

■ *verb* /prɪˈsɪpɪteɪt/ [VN] (*formal*) **1** to make sth, especially sth bad, happen suddenly or sooner than it should: *His resignation precipitated a leadership crisis.* **2** ~ **sb/sth into sth** to suddenly force sb/sth into a particular state or condition: *The assassination of the president precipitated the country into war.*

■ *adj.* /prɪˈsɪpɪtət/ (*formal*) (of an action or a decision) happening very quickly or suddenly and usually without enough care and thought: *the precipitate resignation of the director* ▶ **pre·cipi·tate·ly** *adv.*: *to act precipitately*

■ *noun* /prɪˈsɪpɪteɪt/ (*chemistry*) a solid substance that has been separated from a liquid in a chemical process: *A yellow precipitate should form immediately.*

pre·cipi·ta·tion /prɪˌsɪpɪˈteɪʃn/ *noun* **1** [U] (*technical*) rain, snow, etc. that falls; the amount of this that falls: *an increase in annual precipitation* **2** [U, C] (*chemistry*) a chemical process in which solid material is separated from a liquid

pre·cipit·ous /prɪˈsɪpɪtəs/ *adj.* (*formal*) **1** very steep, high and often dangerous: *precipitous cliffs/slopes* ◊ *a precipitous drop at the side of the road* **2** sudden and great: *a precipitous decline in exports* **3** done very quickly, without enough thought or care: *a precipitous action* ▶ **pre·cipit·ous·ly** *adv.*: *The land dropped precipitously down to the rocky shore.* ◊ *The dollar plunged precipitously.* ◊ *We don't want to act precipitously.*—see also PRECIPICE

pre·cis /ˈpreɪsiː; *AmE* preɪˈsiː/ *noun* [C, U] (*pl.* **pre·cis** /-siːz/) a short version of a speech or a piece of writing that gives the main points or ideas SYN SUMMARY: *to write/give/make a precis of a report* ▶ **pre·cis** *verb* (**pre·cises** /-siːz/ **pre·cis·ing** /-siːɪŋ/ **pre·cised, pre·cised** /-siːd/): [VN] *to precis a scientific report*

pre·cise /prɪˈsaɪs/ *adj.* **1** clear and accurate: *precise details/instructions/measurements* ◊ *Can you give a more precise definition of the word?* ◊ *I can be reasonably precise about the time of the incident.* **2** [only before noun] used to emphasize that sth happens at a particular time or in a particular way: *We were just talking about her when, at that precise moment, she walked in.* ◊ *Doctors found it hard to establish the precise nature of her illness.* **3** taking care to be exact and accurate, especially about small details: *a skilled and precise worker* ◊ *small, precise movements* ◊ (*disapproving*) *She's rather prim and precise.* IDM **to be (more) pre'cise** used to show that you are giving more detailed and accurate information about sth you have just mentioned: *The shelf is about a metre long—well, 98cm, to be precise.*

pre·cise·ly /prɪˈsaɪsli/ *adv.* **1** exactly: *They look precisely the same to me.* ◊ *That's precisely what I meant.* ◊ *It's not clear precisely how the accident happened.* ◊ *The meeting starts at 2 o'clock precisely.* **2** accurately; carefully: *to describe/define/time sth precisely* ◊ *She pronounced the word very slowly and precisely.* **3** used to emphasize that sth is very true or obvious: *It's precisely because I care about you that I don't like you staying out late.* **4** (*spoken*) used to emphasize that you agree with a statement, especially because you think it is obvious or is similar to what you have just said: 'It's not that easy, is it?' 'No, precisely.' IDM **more pre'cisely** used to show that you are giving more detailed and accurate information about sth you have just mentioned: *The problem is due to discipline, or, more precisely, the lack of discipline, in schools.*

pre·ci·sion /prɪˈsɪʒn/ *noun* [U] the quality of being exact, accurate and careful: *done with mathematical precision* ◊ *Her writing is imaginative but lacks precision.* ◊ *Historians can't estimate the date with any (degree of) precision.* ◊ *He chose his words with precision.* ◊ *precision instruments/tools* ◊ *precision engineering*

pre·clude /prɪˈkluːd/ *verb* ~ **sth** | ~ **sb from doing sth** (*formal*) to prevent sth from happening or sb from doing sth; to make sth impossible: [VN] *Lack of time precludes any further discussion.* ◊ [VN-ing] *His religious beliefs precluded him/his serving in the army.* [also V-ing]

pre·co·cious /prɪˈkəʊʃəs; *AmE* -ˈkoʊ-/ *adj.* (sometimes *disapproving*) (of a child) having developed particular abilities and ways of behaving at a much younger age than usual: *a precocious child who started her acting career at the age of 5* ◊ *sexually precocious* ◊ *From an early age she displayed a precocious talent for music.* ▶ **pre·co·cious·ly** *adv.*: *a precociously talented child* **pre·co·city**, **pre·co·cious·ness** *noun* [U]: *his unusual precocity*

pre·cog·ni·tion /ˌpriːkɒɡˈnɪʃn; *AmE* -kɑːɡ-/ *noun* [U] (*formal*) the knowledge that sth will happen in the future, that sb has because of a dream or a sudden feeling

pre·con·ceived /ˌpriːkənˈsiːvd/ *adj.* [only before noun] (of ideas, opinions, etc.) formed before you have enough information or experience of sth: *Before I started the job, I had no preconceived notions of what it would be like.*

pre·con·cep·tion /ˌpriːkənˈsepʃn/ *noun* [C, often pl., U] an idea or opinion that is formed before you have enough information or experience: *a book that will challenge your preconceptions about rural life*—compare MISCONCEPTION

pre·con·di·tion /ˌpriːkənˈdɪʃn/ *noun* ~ (**for/of sth**) (*written*) something that must happen or exist before sth else can exist or be done SYN PREREQUISITE: *A ceasefire is an essential precondition for negotiation.*

pre-'cooked *adj.* (of food) prepared and partly cooked in advance so that it can be quickly heated and eaten later

pre·cur·sor /priːˈkɜːsə(r); *AmE* -ˈkɜːrs-/ *noun* ~ (**of/to sth**) (*formal*) a person or a thing that comes before sb/sth similar and that leads to or influences its development SYN FORERUNNER

pre-'date (also **ante·date**) *verb* [VN] to be built or formed, or to happen, at an earlier date than sth else in the past: *Few of the town's fine buildings pre-date the earthquake of 1755.* OPP POST-DATE

pre·da·tion /prɪˈdeɪʃn/ *noun* [U] (*technical*) the act of an animal killing and eating other animals

preda·tor /ˈpredətə(r)/ *noun* **1** an animal that kills and eats other animals: *the relationship between predator and prey* ◊ *Some animals have no natural predators.* **2** (*disapproving*) a person or an organization that uses weaker people for their own advantage: *to protect domestic industry from foreign predators*

preda·tory /ˈpredətri; *AmE* -tɔːri/ *adj.* **1** (*technical*) (of animals) living by killing and eating other animals: *predatory birds/insects* **2** (*written*) (of people) using weaker people for their own financial or sexual advantage: *a predatory insurance salesman* ◊ *a predatory look/smile* ◊ *predatory young women*

pre·de·cease /ˌpriːdɪˈsiːs/ *verb* [VN] (*law*) to die before sb: *His wife predeceased him.*

pre·de·ces·sor /ˈpriːdɪsesə(r); *AmE* ˈpredəs-/ *noun* **1** a person who did a job before sb else: *The new president reversed many of the policies of his predecessor.* **2** a thing, such as a machine, that has been followed or replaced by sth else—compare SUCCESSOR

pre·des·tin·ation /ˌpriːdestɪˈneɪʃn/ *noun* [U] the theory or the belief that everything that happens has been decided or planned in advance by God or by fate and that humans cannot change it

pre·des·tined /ˌpriːˈdestɪnd/ *adj.* ~ (to do sth) (*formal*) already decided or planned by God or by fate: *It seems she was predestined to be famous.*

pre·de·ter·mine /ˌpriːdɪˈtɜːmɪn; *AmE* -ˈtɜːrm-/ *verb* [VN] (*formal*) to decide sth in advance so that it does not happen by chance: *The sex of the embryo is predetermined at fertilization.* ▶ **pre·de·ter·mined** *adj.*: *An alarm sounds when the temperature reaches a predetermined level.*

pre·de·ter·miner /ˌpriːdɪˈtɜːmɪnə(r); *AmE* -ˈtɜːrm-/ *noun* (*grammar*) a word that can be used before a DETERMINER, such as *all* in *all the students* or *twice* in *twice the price*

pre·dica·ment /prɪˈdɪkəmənt/ *noun* a difficult or unpleasant situation, especially one where it is difficult to know what to do: *the club's financial predicament* ◇ *I'm in a terrible predicament.*

predi·cate *noun, verb*
- *noun* /ˈpredɪkət/ (*grammar*) a part of a sentence containing a verb that makes a statement about the subject of the verb, such as *went home* in *John went home.*—compare OBJECT *n.* (5)
- *verb* /ˈpredɪkeɪt/ (*formal*) **1** [VN] [usually passive] ~ sth on/upon sth to base sth on a particular belief, idea or principle: *Democracy is predicated upon the rule of law.* **2** to state that sth is true: [VthT] *The article predicates that the market collapse was caused by weakness of the dollar.* [alsoVN]

pre·dica·tive /prɪˈdɪkətɪv; *AmE* ˈpredɪkeɪtɪv/ *adj.* (*grammar*) (of an adjective) coming after a verb such as *be, become, get, seem, look.* Many adjectives, for example *old* can be either predicative as in *The man is very old,* or ATTRIBUTIVE as in *an old man.* Some, like *asleep,* can only be predicative. ▶ **pre·dica·tive·ly** *adv.*

pre·dict /prɪˈdɪkt/ *verb* to say that sth will happen in the future SYN FORECAST: [VN] *a reliable method of predicting earthquakes* ◇ *Nobody could predict the outcome.* ◇ [Vwh-] *It is impossible to predict what will happen.* ◇ [V(that)] *She predicted (that) the election result would be close.* ◇ [VNthat] *It was predicted that inflation would continue to fall.* ◇ [VNtoinf] *The trial is predicted to last for months.* **HELP** This pattern is only used in the passive.

pre·dict·able /prɪˈdɪktəbl/ *adj.* **1** if sth is **predictable**, you know in advance that it will happen or what it will be like: *predictable responses/results* ◇ *The ending of the book was entirely predictable.* ◇ *The disease follows a highly predictable pattern.* ◇ *In March and April, the weather is much less predictable.* **2** (often *disapproving*) behaving or happening in a way that you would expect and therefore boring: *He's very nice, but I find him rather dull and predictable.* ◇ *Rock music is getting so predictable these days.* ▶ **pre·dict·abil·ity** /prɪˌdɪktəˈbɪləti/ *noun* [U] **pre·dict·ably** *adv.*: *Prices were predictably high.* ◇ *Predictably, the new regulations proved unpopular.*

pre·dic·tion /prɪˈdɪkʃn/ *noun* [C, U] a statement that says what you think will happen; the act of making such a statement: *Not many people agree with the government's prediction that the economy will improve.* ◇ *The results of the experiment confirmed our predictions.* ◇ *Skilled readers make use of context and prediction.* ◇ *It's difficult to make accurate predictions about the effects on the environment.*

pre·dict·ive /prɪˈdɪktɪv/ *adj.* [usually before noun] (*formal*) connected with the ability to show what will happen in the future: *the predictive power of science*

pre·dic·tor /prɪˈdɪktə(r)/ *noun* (*formal*) something that can show what will happen in the future: *Cholesterol level is not a strong predictor of heart disease in women.*

pre·digest·ed /ˌpriːdaɪˈdʒestɪd/ *adj.* (of information) put in a simple form that is easy to understand

pre·di·lec·tion /ˌpriːdɪˈlekʃn; *AmE* ˌpredlˈek-/ *noun* [usually sing.] ~ (for sth) (*formal*) if you have a predilection for sth, you like it very much: *an artist with a predilection for bright colours*

pre·dis·pose /ˌpriːdɪˈspəʊz; *AmE* -ˈspoʊz/ *verb* (*formal*) **1** ~ sb to sth/to do sth to influence sb so that they are likely to think or behave in a particular way: [VN] *He believes that some people are predisposed to criminal behaviour.* ◇ [VNtoinf] *Her good mood predisposed her to enjoy the play.* **2** [VN] ~ sb to sth to make it likely that you will suffer from a particular illness: *Stress can predispose people to heart attacks.*

pre·dis·pos·ition /ˌpriːdɪspəˈzɪʃn/ *noun* [C, U] ~ (to/ towards sth) | ~ (to do sth) (*formal*) a condition that makes sb/sth likely to behave in a particular way or to suffer from a particular disease: *a genetic predisposition to liver disease*

pre·dom·in·ance /prɪˈdɒmɪnəns; *AmE* -ˈdɑːm-/ *noun* **1** [sing.] the situation of being greater in number or amount than other things or people SYN PREPONDERANCE: *a predominance of female teachers in elementary schools* **2** [U] the state of having more power or influence than others SYN DOMINANCE: *the ongoing struggle for global predominance*

pre·dom·in·ant /prɪˈdɒmɪnənt; *AmE* -ˈdɑːm-/ *adj.* **1** most obvious or noticeable: *a predominant feature/factor* ◇ *Yellow is the predominant colour this spring in the fashion world.* **2** having more power or influence than others SYN DOMINANT: *a predominant culture* ◇ *a way of thinking that is predominant in modern social life*

pre·dom·in·ant·ly /prɪˈdɒmɪnəntli; *AmE* -ˈdɑːm-/ (also *less frequent* **pre·dom·in·ate·ly**) *adv.* mostly; mainly: *She works in a predominantly male environment.*

pre·dom·in·ate /prɪˈdɒmɪneɪt; *AmE* -ˈdɑːm-/ *verb* [V] **1** to be greater in amount or number than sth/sb else in a place, group, etc: *a colour scheme in which red predominates* ◇ *Women predominated in the audience.* **2** ~ (over sb/sth) to have the most influence or importance: *Private interest was not allowed to predominate over the public good.*

pree·mie /ˈpriːmi/ *noun* (*AmE, informal*) a PREMATURE baby

pre-'eminent *adj.* (*formal*) more important, more successful or of a higher standard than others: *a pre-eminent example of the artist's work* ◇ *Charles Dickens was pre-eminent among English writers of his day.* ▶ **pre-'eminence** *noun* [U]: *to achieve pre-eminence in public life*

pre-'eminently *adv.* to a very great degree; especially: *a subject that she was pre-eminently qualified to talk about*

pre-empt /prɪˈempt/ *verb* [VN] **1** to prevent sth from happening by taking action to stop it: *Her departure pre-empted any further questions.* ◇ *A good training course will pre-empt many problems.* **2** to do or say sth before sb else does: *She was just about to apologize when he pre-empted her.* **3** (*AmE*) to replace a planned programme on the television: *'Roseanne' will be pre-empted by a special news bulletin.*

pre-emption /prɪˈempʃn/ *noun* [U] (*business*) the opportunity given to one person or group to buy goods, shares, etc: *Existing shareholders will have pre-emption rights.*

pre-emptive /prɪˈemptɪv/ *adj.* done to stop sb taking action, especially action that will be harmful to yourself: *a pre-emptive attack/strike on the military base*

preen /priːn/ *verb* **1** ~ (yourself) (usually *disapproving*) to spend a lot of time making yourself look attractive and then admiring your appearance: [VN] *Will you stop preening yourself in front of the mirror?* [alsoV] **2** [VN] ~ yourself (on sth) (usually *disapproving*) to feel very pleased with yourself about sth and show other people how pleased you are **3** [V, VN] ~ (itself) (of a bird) to clean itself or make its feathers smooth with its beak

pre-e'xist *verb* [V] to exist from an earlier time: *a pre-existing medical condition* ▶ **pre-e'xistent** *adj.*

pre·fab /ˈpriːfæb/ *noun* (*informal*) a prefabricated building: *prefabs built after the war*

pre·fab·ri·cated /ˌpriːˈfæbrɪkeɪtɪd/ *adj.* (especially of a building) made in sections that can be put together later ▶ **pre·fab·ri·ca·tion** /ˌpriːfæbrɪˈkeɪʃn/ *noun* [U]

æ	ɑː	e	ɜː	ə	ɪ	iː	i	ɒ	ɔː	ʌ	ʊ	u	uː
cat	father	ten	bird	about	sit	see	many	got	saw	cup	put	actual	too

(BrE)

pref·ace /ˈprefəs/ *noun, verb*

■ *noun* an introduction to a book, especially one that explains the author's aims—compare FOREWORD

■ *verb* [VN] **1 ~** sth **(with** sth**)** to provide a book or other piece of writing with a preface: *He prefaced the diaries with a short account of how they were discovered.* **2 ~** sth **by/with** sth**|~** sth **by doing** sth *(formal)* to say sth before you start making a speech, answering a question, etc: *I must preface my remarks with an apology.*

pre·fect /ˈpriːfekt/ *noun* **1** (in some British schools) an older student with some authority over younger students and some other responsibilities and privileges **2** (also **Prefect**) an officer responsible for an area of local government in some countries, for example France, Italy and Japan

pre·fec·ture /ˈpriːfektʃə(r)/ *noun* an area of local government in some countries, for example France, Italy and Japan

pre·fer /prɪˈfɜː(r)/ *verb* **(-rr-)** (not used in the progressive tenses) to choose one thing rather than sth else because you like it better: [VN] *'Coffee or tea?' 'I'd prefer tea, thanks.'* ◊ *I prefer jazz to rock music.* ◊ *I would prefer it if you didn't tell anyone.* ◊ *A local firm is to be preferred.* ◊ [VN-ADJ] *I prefer my coffee black.* ◊ [V to inf] *The donor prefers to remain anonymous.* ◊ *I prefer not to think about it.* ◊ [VN to inf] *Would you prefer me to stay?* ◊ [V -ing] *I prefer playing in defence.* ◊ [V that] *(formal)* *I would prefer that you did not mention my name.* **IDM** see CHARGE *n.*

pref·er·able /ˈprefrəbl/ *adj.* **~ (to** sth/**to doing** sth**)|~ (to do** sth**)** more attractive or more suitable; to be preferred to sth: *Anything was preferable to the tense atmosphere at home.* ◊ *He finds country life **infinitely preferable** to living in the city.* ◊ *It would be preferable to employ two people, not one.* ▶ **pref·er·ably** /ˈprefrəbli/ *adv.*: *We're looking for a new house, preferably one near the school.*

pref·er·ence /ˈprefrəns/ *noun* **1** [U, sing.] **~ (for** sb/sth**)** a greater interest in or desire for sb/sth than sb/sth else: *It's a matter of **personal preference**.* ◊ *Many people expressed a **strong preference** for the original plan.* ◊ *I can't say that I have any particular preference.* ◊ *Let's make a list of possible speakers, **in order of preference**.* **2** [C] a thing that is liked better or best: *a study of consumer preferences* **IDM** **give (a) preference to** sb/sth to treat sb/sth in a way that gives them an advantage over other people or things: *Preference will be given to graduates of this university.* **in preference to** sb/sth rather than sb/sth: *She was chosen in preference to her sister.*

pref·er·en·tial /ˌprefəˈrenʃl/ *adj.* [only before noun] giving an advantage to a particular person or group: *Don't expect to get preferential treatment.* ◊ *Bank employees usually get preferential rates of interest.* ▶ **pref·er·en·tial·ly** /-ʃəli/ *adv.*

pre·fer·ment /prɪˈfɜːmənt; *AmE* ˈfɜːrm-/ *noun* [U] *(formal)* the fact of being given a more important job or a higher rank

pre·fig·ure /ˌpriːˈfɪgə(r); *AmE* -gjər/ *verb* [VN] *(formal)* to suggest or show sth that will happen in the future: *These early paintings clearly prefigure his later work.*

pre·fix /ˈpriːfɪks/ *noun, verb*

■ *noun* **1** *(grammar)* a letter or group of letters added to the beginning of a word to change its meaning, such as *un-* in *unhappy* and *pre-* in *preheat*—compare AFFIX, SUFFIX **2** a word, letter or number that is put before another: *Car insurance policies have the prefix MC (for motor car).* **3** *(old-fashioned)* a title such as *Dr* or *Mrs* used before a person's name

■ *verb* [VN] **~ A to B|~ B with A** to add letters or numbers to the beginning of a word or number: *American members have the letters US prefixed to their code numbers.* ◊ *Their code numbers are prefixed with US.*

preg·nancy /ˈpregnənsi/ *noun* [U, C] *(pl.* **-ies)** the state of being pregnant: *Many women experience sickness during pregnancy.* ◊ *a pregnancy test* ◊ *unplanned/unwanted pregnancies* ◊ *the increase in teenage pregnancies*

preg·nant /ˈpregnənt/ *adj.* **1** (of a woman or female animal) having a baby or young animal developing inside her/its body: *My wife is pregnant.* ◊ *I was pregnant with our third child at the time.* ◊ *a **heavily pregnant** woman* (= one whose baby is nearly ready to be born) ◊ *to get/ become pregnant* ◊ *Tom got his girlfriend pregnant and they're getting married.* ◊ *She's six months pregnant.* **2 ~ with** sth *(formal)* full of a quality or feeling: *Her silences were pregnant with criticism.* **IDM** **a pregnant 'pause/ 'silence** an occasion when nobody speaks, although people are aware that there are feelings or thoughts to express: *There was a pregnant pause before she replied.*

pre·heat /ˌpriːˈhiːt/ *verb* [VN] to heat an oven to a particular temperature before you put food in to cook

pre·hen·sile /prɪˈhensaɪl; *AmE* -sl/ *adj.* *(technical)* (of a part of an animal's body) able to hold things: *the monkey's prehensile tail*—picture on page A6

pre·his·toric /ˌpriːhɪˈstɒrɪk; *AmE* -ˈstɔːr-; -ˈstɑːr-/ *adj.* connected with the time in history before information was written down: *in prehistoric times* ◊ *prehistoric man/ remains/animals/burial sites*

pre·his·tory /ˌpriːˈhɪstri/ *noun* **1** [U] the period of time in history before information was written down: *These climate changes continued throughout prehistory.* **2** [sing.] the earliest stages of the development of sth: *the prehistory of capitalism*

pre·judge /ˌpriːˈdʒʌdʒ/ *verb* [VN] *(formal)* to make a judgement about a situation before you have all the necessary information: *They took care not to **prejudge** the issue.*

preju·dice /ˈpredʒudɪs/ *noun, verb*

■ *noun* [U, C] **~ (against** sb/sth**)** an unreasonable dislike of or PREFERENCE for a person, group, custom, etc., especially when it is based on their race, religion, sex, etc: *a victim of **racial prejudice**.* ◊ *Their decision was based on ignorance and prejudice.* ◊ *There is little prejudice against workers from other EU states.* ◊ *I must admit to a prejudice in favour of British universities.* **IDM** **without 'prejudice (to** sth**)** *(law)* without affecting any other legal matter: *They agreed to pay compensation without prejudice* (= without admitting guilt).

■ *verb* [VN] **1 ~** sb **(against** sb/sth**)** to influence sb so that they have an unfair or unreasonable opinion about sb/ sth: *The prosecution lawyers have been trying to prejudice the jury against her.* **2** *(formal)* to have a harmful effect on sth: *Any delay will prejudice the child's welfare.*

preju·diced /ˈpredʒədɪst/ *adj.* **~ (against** sb/sth**)** having an unreasonable dislike of or PREFERENCE for sb/sth, especially based on their race, religion, sex, etc: *Few people will admit to being racially prejudiced.* ◊ *They are prejudiced against older applicants.* ◊ *(humorous)* *I think it's an excellent article, but then I'm prejudiced—I wrote it.*

preju·di·cial /ˌpredʒuˈdɪʃl/ *adj.* **~ (to** sth**)** *(formal)* harming or likely to harm sb/sth: *developments prejudicial to the company's future*

prel·ate /ˈprelət/ *noun* *(formal)* a priest of high rank, such as a BISHOP or CARDINAL

pre·lim·in·ary /prɪˈlɪmɪnəri; *AmE* -neri/ *adj., noun*

■ *adj.* **~ (to** sth**)** happening before a more important action or event **SYN** INITIAL: *After a few preliminary remarks he announced the winners.* ◊ *preliminary results/findings/ enquiries* ◊ *the preliminary rounds of the contest* ◊ *pilot studies preliminary to a full-scale study*

■ *noun* *(pl.* **-ies) ~ (to** sth**)** a **preliminary** is an action or event that is done in preparation for sth: *Research will be needed as a preliminary to taking a decision.* ◊ *I'll skip the usual preliminaries and come straight to the point.* ◊ *England was lucky to get through the preliminaries* (= the preliminary stages in a sports competition).

prel·ude /ˈpreljuːd/ *noun* **1** a short piece of music, especially an introduction to a longer piece: *the prelude to Act II* ◊ *J S Bach's preludes and fugues* **2 ~ (to** sth**)** *(written)* an action or event that happens before another more important one and forms an introduction to it

pre·mar·ital /ˌpriːˈmærɪtl/ *adj.* [only before noun] happening before marriage: *premarital sex*

pre·ma·ture /ˈpremətʃə(r); *AmE* ˌpriːməˈtʃʊr; -ˈtʊr/ *adj.* **1** happening before the normal or expected time: *his*

aɪ	aʊ	eɪ	əʊ	oʊ	ɔɪ	ɪə	eə	ʊə	j	w
my	now	say	go (BrE)	go (AmE)	boy	near	hair	pure	yes	wet

premature death at the age of 37 **2** (of a birth or a baby) happening or being born before the normal length of pregnancy has been completed: *The baby was four weeks premature.* ◊ *a premature birth after only thirty weeks* **3** happening or made too soon: *a premature conclusion/decision/judgement* ◊ *It is premature to talk about success at this stage.* ▶ **pre·ma·ture·ly** *adv.*: *The child was born prematurely.* ◊ *Her hair became prematurely white.*

pre·medi·tated /ˌpriːˈmedɪteɪtɪd/ *adj.* (of a crime or bad action) planned in advance: *a premeditated attack* ◊ *The killing had not been premeditated.* OPP UNPREMEDITATED ▶ **pre·medi·ta·tion** /ˌpriːˌmedɪˈteɪʃn/ *noun* [U]

pre·men·strual /ˌpriːˈmenstruəl/ *adj.* happening or experienced before MENSTRUATION: *Many women suffer from premenstrual tension/syndrome, causing headaches and depression.*—see also PMS

prem·ier /ˈpremiə(r); *AmE* prɪˈmɪr; -ˈmjɪr/ *adj., noun*
■ *adj.* [only before noun] most important, famous or successful: *one of Britain's premier chefs* ◊ (*BrE, sport*) *the Premier League/Division* (= in football)
■ *noun* used especially in newspapers, etc. to mean 'prime minister'

premi·ere /ˈpremieə(r); *AmE* prɪˈmɪr; -ˈmjɪr/ *noun, verb*
■ *noun* the first public performance of a film/movie or play: *the world premiere of his new play* ◊ *The movie will have its premiere in July.*
■ *verb* to perform a play or piece of music or show a film/movie to an audience for the first time; to be performed or shown to an audience for the first time: [VN] *The play was premiered at the Birmingham Rep in 1999.* ◊ [V] *His new movie premieres in New York this week.*

prem·ier·ship /ˈpremiəʃɪp; *AmE* prɪˈmɪrʃɪp; -ˈmjɪr-/ *noun* [sing.] **1** the period or position of being PRIME MINISTER: *during Blair's premiership* **2** (often **the Premiership**) the football LEAGUE in England and Wales which has the best teams in it

prem·ise (*BrE* also *less frequent* **prem·iss**) /ˈpremɪs/ *noun* (*formal*) a statement or an idea that forms the basis for a reasonable line of argument: *the basic premise of her argument* ◊ *a false premise* ◊ *His reasoning is based on the premise that all people are equally capable of good and evil.*

prem·ised /ˈpremɪst/ *adj.* ~ **on/upon sth** (*formal*) based on a particular idea or belief that is considered to be true: *Traditional economic analysis is premised on the assumption that more is better.*

prem·ises /ˈpremɪsɪz/ *noun* [pl.] the building and land near to it that a business owns or uses: *business/commercial/industrial premises* ◊ *The company is looking for larger premises.* ◊ *No alcohol may be consumed **on the premises**.* ◊ *Police were called to escort her **off the premises**.*

pre·mium /ˈpriːmiəm/ *noun, adj.*
■ *noun* **1** an amount of money that you pay once or regularly for an insurance policy: *a monthly premium of £6.25* **2** an extra payment added to the basic rate: *You have to pay a high premium for express delivery.* ◊ *A premium of 10% is paid out after 20 years.* IDM **at a ˈpremium 1** if sth is at a premium, there is little of it available and it is difficult to get: *Space is at a premium in a one-bedroomed apartment.* **2** at a higher than normal price: *Shares are selling at a premium.* **put/place/set a premium on sb/sth** to think that sb/sth is particularly important or valuable
■ *adj.* [only before noun] very high (and higher than usual); of high quality: *premium prices/products*

pre·mon·ition /ˌpriːməˈnɪʃn; ˌprem-/ *noun* ~ (**of sth/that …**) a feeling that sth is going to happen, especially sth unpleasant: *a premonition of disaster* ◊ *He had a premonition that he would never see her again.* ▶ **pre·moni·tory** /prɪˈmɒnɪtəri; *AmE* -ˈmɑːnɪtɔːri/ *adj.* (*rare, formal*): *a premonitory dream*

pre·natal /ˌpriːˈneɪtl/ *adj.* (*especially AmE*) = ANTENATAL—compare POSTNATAL

pre·occu·pa·tion /priˌɒkjuˈpeɪʃn; *AmE* -ˌɑːk-/ *noun* **1** [U, C] ~ (**with sth**) a state of thinking about sth continu-

ously; sth that you think about frequently or for a long time: *She found his preoccupation with money irritating.* ◊ *His current preoccupation is the appointment of the new manager.* **2** [U] a mood created by thinking or worrying about sth and ignoring everything else: *She spoke slowly, in a state of preoccupation.*

pre·occu·pied /priˈɒkjupaɪd; *AmE* -ˈɑːk-/ *adj.* ~ (**with sth**) thinking and/or worrying continuously about sth so that you do not pay attention to other things: *He was too preoccupied with his own thoughts to notice anything wrong.*

pre·occupy /priˈɒkjupaɪ; *AmE* -ˈɑːk-/ *verb* (**pre·occu·pies, pre·occu·py·ing, pre·occu·pied, pre·occu·pied**) [VN] if sth is preoccupying you, you think or worry about it very often or all the time: *Thoughts of failure preoccupied him.*

pre·or·dained /ˌpriːɔːˈdeɪnd; *AmE* -ɔːrˈd-/ *adj.* ~ **to do sth** (*formal*) already decided or planned by God or by fate SYN PREDESTINED: *Is everything we do preordained?* ◊ *They seemed preordained to meet.*

prep /prep/ *noun, verb*
■ *noun* [U] (*BrE*) (in some private schools) school work that is done at the end of the day after lessons
■ *verb* [VN] **1** (*AmE, informal*) to prepare sb/sth **2** (*technical*) to prepare sb for a medical operation

pre·ˈpacked (also **ˌpre·ˈpackaged**) *adj.* (of goods, especially food) put into packages before being sent to shops/stores to be sold: *pre-packed sandwiches*

pre·paid /ˌpriːˈpeɪd/ *adj.* paid for in advance: *a prepaid envelope is enclosed* (= so you do not pay to have the cost of sending a letter)

prep·ar·ation /ˌprepəˈreɪʃn/ *noun* **1** [U] ~ (**for sth**) the act or process of getting ready for sth or making sth ready: *Preparation for the party started early.* ◊ *food preparation* ◊ *Careful preparation for the exam is essential.* ◊ *The third book in the series is currently in preparation.* ◊ *The team has been training hard in preparation for the big game.* **2** [C, usually pl.] ~ (**for sth**) | ~ (**to do sth**) things that you do to get ready for sth or make sth ready: *The country is **making preparations** for war.* ◊ *We made preparations to move to new offices.* ◊ *Christmas/wedding preparations* ◊ *Was going to college a good preparation for your career?* **3** [C] a substance that has been specially prepared for use as a medicine, COSMETIC, etc: *a pharmaceutical preparation* ◊ *preparations for the hair and skin*

pre·para·tory /prɪˈpærətri; *AmE* -tɔːri/ *adj.* [only before noun] (*formal*) done in order to prepare for sth: *preparatory meetings/studies/work* ◊ *After a few preparatory drawings, she completed the portrait in one session.* ◊ *Security checks had been carried out **preparatory to** (= to prepare for) the President's visit.*

pre·ˈparatory school (also **ˈprep school**) *noun* **1** (in Britain) a private school for children between the ages of 7 and 13—compare PUBLIC SCHOOL **2** (in the US) a school, usually a private one, that prepares students for college

pre·pare /prɪˈpeə(r); *AmE* -ˈper/ *verb* **1** [VN] ~ **sth/sb (for sb/sth)** to make sth or sb ready to be used or to do sth: *to prepare a report/the accounts* ◊ *A hotel room is being prepared for them.* ◊ *The college prepares students for a career in business.* **2** ~ (**yourself**) (**for sth**) to make yourself ready to do sth or for sth that you expect to happen: [V] *I had no time to prepare.* ◊ *The whole class is working hard preparing for the exams.* ◊ [VN] *The police are preparing themselves for trouble at the demonstration.* ◊ [VN to inf] *I was preparing to leave.* ◊ [VN to inf] *The troops prepared themselves to go into battle.* **3** [VN] to make food ready to be eaten: *He was in the kitchen preparing lunch.* **4** [VN] ~ **sth (from sth)** to make a medicine or chemical substance, for example by mixing other substances together: *remedies prepared from herbal extracts* IDM **prepare the ˈground (for sth)** to make it possible or easier for sth to be achieved: *The committee will prepare the ground for next month's meeting.*

pre·pared /prɪˈpeəd; *AmE* -ˈperd/ *adj.* **1** [not before noun] ~ (**for sth**) ready and able to deal with sth: *I was not prepared for all the problems it caused.* ◊ *We'll be better* *prepared next time.* ◊ *When they set out they were well prepared.* OPP UNPREPARED—see also ILL-PREPARED **2 ~ to do sth** willing to do sth: *We are not prepared to accept these conditions.* ◊ *How much are you prepared to pay?* OPP UNPREPARED **3** done, made, written, etc. in advance: *The police officer read out a prepared statement.*

pre·pared·ness /prɪˈpeərɪdnəs; AmE -ˈperd-/ *noun* [U] **~ to do sth** (*formal*) the state of being ready or willing to do sth: *I was surprised by his preparedness to break the law.* ◊ *The troops are in a state of preparedness.*

pre·pay·ment /ˌpriːˈpeɪmənt/ *noun* [U] payment in advance: *a prepayment meter/plan*

pre·pon·der·ance /prɪˈpɒndərəns; AmE -ˈpɑːn-/ *noun* [sing.] if there is a **preponderance** of one type of people or things in a group, there are more of them than others SYN PREDOMINANCE

pre·pon·der·ant /prɪˈpɒndərənt; AmE -ˈpɑːn-/ *adj.* [usually before noun] (*formal*) larger in number or more important than other people or things in a group ▶ **pre·pon·der·ant·ly** *adv.*

prep·os·ition /ˌprepəˈzɪʃn/ *noun* (*grammar*) a word or group of words, such as *in, from, to, out of* and *on behalf of*, used before a noun or pronoun to show place, position, time or method ▶ **prep·os·ition·al** /-ʃənl/ *adj.*: *a prepositional phrase* (= a preposition and the noun following it, for example *at night* or *after breakfast*)

pre·pos·sess·ing /ˌpriːpəˈzesɪŋ/ *adj.* (especially after a negative) (*formal*) attractive in appearance SYN APPEALING: *He was not a prepossessing sight.*—compare UNPREPOSSESSING

pre·pos·ter·ous /prɪˈpɒstərəs; AmE -ˈpɑːs-/ *adj.* (*formal*) **1** completely unreasonable, especially in a way that is shocking or annoying SYN OUTRAGEOUS: *These claims are absolutely preposterous!* **2** unusual in a silly or shocking way SYN OUTRAGEOUS: *The band were famous for their preposterous clothes and haircuts.* ▶ **pre·pos·ter·ous·ly** *adv.*: *a preposterously expensive bottle of wine*

prep·py (also **prep·pie**) /ˈprepi/ *noun* (*pl.* **-ies**) (*AmE, informal*) a young person who goes or went to an expensive private school and who dresses and acts in a way that is thought to be typical of such a school ▶ **prep·py** (also **prep·pie**) *adj.*: *a preppy image* ◊ *preppy clothes*

prep school *noun* = PREPARATORY SCHOOL

pre·quel /ˈpriːkwəl/ *noun* a book or a film/movie about events that happened before those in a popular book or film/movie: *Fans have been waiting for years for the first Star Wars prequel.*—compare SEQUEL

Pre-Raphael·ite /ˌpriː ˈræfəlaɪt/ *noun, adj.*
■ *noun* a member of a group of British 19th century artists who painted in a style similar to Italian artists of the 14th and 15th centuries, before the time of Raphael: *the Pre-Raphaelites*
■ *adj.* **1** connected with or in the style of the Pre-Raphaelites: *Pre-Raphaelite paintings* **2** (especially of a woman) looking like a person in a painting by one of the Pre-Raphaelites, for example with pale skin and long thick dark red hair

pre·re·cord /ˌpriːrɪˈkɔːd/ *verb* [VN] to record music, a television programme, etc. in advance, so that it can be broadcast or used later

pre·re·corded /ˌpriːrɪˈkɔːdɪd/ *adj.* [usually before noun] a **prerecorded** piece of music, film, or radio or television programme has been recorded in advance so that it can be played later: *a pre-recorded interview* ◊ *a pre-recorded tape/video*—compare LIVE *adj.* (2, 3)

pre·regis·ter /ˌpriːˈredʒɪstə(r)/ *verb* [V] (*especially AmE*) to REGISTER for sth before the usual time or before sth starts: *I went back to college a week early to preregister for classes.* ▶ **pre·regis·tra·tion** /ˌpriːredʒɪˈstreɪʃn/ *noun* [U]

pre·requis·ite /ˌpriːˈrekwəzɪt/ *noun* [usually sing.] **~ (for/of/to sth)** (*formal*) something that must exist or happen before sth else can happen or be done SYN PRECONDITION: *A degree is an essential prerequisite for employment at this level.*—compare REQUISITE ▶ **pre·requis·ite** *adj.* [only before noun]: *prerequisite knowledge/skills*

pre·roga·tive /prɪˈrɒɡətɪv; AmE -ˈrɑːɡ-/ *noun* (*formal*) a right or privilege belonging to a particular person or group because of their importance or social position: *It's a woman's prerogative to change her mind!* ◊ *In many countries education is still the prerogative of the rich.* ◊ *the royal prerogative* (= the special rights of a king or queen)

pres·age /ˈpresɪdʒ; prɪˈseɪdʒ/ *verb* [VN] (*literary*) to be a warning or sign that sth will happen, usually sth unpleasant: *Nothing had presaged the dreadful fate about to befall him.* ▶ **pre·sage** /ˈpresɪdʒ/ *noun*: *the first presages of winter*

Pres·by·ter·ian /ˌprezbɪˈtɪəriən; AmE -ˈtɪr-/ *noun* a member of a branch of the Christian Protestant Church that is the national Church of Scotland and one of the largest Churches in the US. It is governed by ELDERS who are all equal in rank ▶ **Pres·by·ter·ian** *adj.*: *a Presbyterian church/minister* **Pres·by·ter·ian·ism** /ˌprezbɪˈtɪəriənɪzəm; AmE -ˈtɪr-/ *noun* [U]

pres·by·tery /ˈprezbɪtri; AmE -teri/ *noun* (*pl.* **-ies**) **1** a local council of the Presbyterian Church **2** a house where a Roman Catholic priest lives **3** part of a church, near the east end, beyond the CHOIR

pre·school /ˈpriːskuːl/ *noun* (*especially AmE*) a school for children between the ages of about two and five SYN NURSERY SCHOOL ▶ **pre·schooler** *noun*: *a class of pre-schoolers*

pre·school *adj.* [only before noun] connected with the age when a child is too young to go to school: *children of pre-school age* ◊ *pre-school children/education*

pres·ci·ent /ˈpresiənt/ *adj.* (*formal*) knowing or appearing to know about things before they happen: *prescient remarks/warnings* ▶ **pres·ci·ence** /-əns/ *noun* [U]

pre·scribe /prɪˈskraɪb/ *verb* **1 ~ (sb) sth (for sth)** (of a doctor) to tell sb to take a particular medicine or have a particular treatment; to write a PRESCRIPTION for a particular medicine, etc: [VN] *Valium is usually prescribed to treat anxiety.* ◊ [VNN] *He may be able to prescribe you something for that cough.* **2** (used about a person or an organization with authority) to say what should be done or how sth should be done: [VN] *The prescribed form must be completed and returned to this office.* ◊ [Vthat] *Police regulations prescribe that an officer's number must be clearly visible.* ◊ [Vwh-] *The syllabus prescribes precisely which books should be studied.*

pre·scrip·tion /prɪˈskrɪpʃn/ *noun* **1** [C] (*abbr.* Rx) **~ (for sth)** an official piece of paper on which a doctor writes the type of medicine you should have, and which enables you to get it from a CHEMIST/PHARMACIST (= a person who has been trained to prepare medicines): *The doctor gave me a prescription for antibiotics.* ◊ *Antibiotics are only available on prescription.* ◊ *They are not available without a prescription.* ◊ *prescription drugs/medication(s)*—picture on page 599 **2** [C] medicine that your doctor has ordered for you: *The pharmacist will make up your prescription.* ◊ *prescription charges* (= in Britain, the money you must pay for a medicine your doctor has ordered for you) **3** [U] the act of prescribing medicine: *The prescription of drugs is a doctor's responsibility.* **4** [C] **~ (for sth)** (*formal*) a plan or a suggestion for making sth happen or for improving it: *a prescription for happiness*

pre·scrip·tive /prɪˈskrɪptɪv/ *adj.* **1** (*formal*) telling people what should be done: *prescriptive methods of teaching* **2** (*linguistics*) telling people how a language should be used, rather than describing how it is used: *a prescriptive grammar of English* OPP DESCRIPTIVE **3** (*technical*) (of rights and institutions) made legal or acceptable because they have existed for a long time: *prescriptive powers*

pres·ence /ˈprezns/ *noun* **1** [U] (of a person) the fact of being in a particular place: *He hardly seemed to notice my presence.* ◊ *Her presence during the crisis had a calming effect.* ◊ (*formal*) *Your presence is requested at the meeting.* OPP ABSENCE **2** [U] (of a thing or substance) the fact of being in a particular place or thing: *The test can identify the presence of abnormalities in the unborn child.* OPP ABSENCE **3** [sing.] a group of people, especially soldiers,

s	t	v	z	ʃ	ʒ	tʃ	dʒ	θ	ð	ŋ
see	tea	van	zoo	shoe	vision	chain	jam	thin	this	sing

who have been sent to a place to deal with a particular situation: *The government is maintaining a heavy police presence in the area.* ◊ *a military presence* **4** [C, usually sing.] (*literary*) a person or spirit that you cannot see but that you feel is near: *She felt a presence behind her.* **5** [U] (*approving*) the quality of making a strong impression on other people by the way you talk or behave: *a man of great presence* ◊ *She has a strong voice but absolutely no stage presence.* **IDM** in the 'presence of sb | in sb's 'presence with sb in the same place: *The document was signed in the presence of two witnesses.* ◊ *She asked them not to discuss the matter in her presence.* in the 'presence of sth when sth exists in a particular place: *Litmus paper turns red in the presence of an acid.* make your presence 'felt to do sth to make people very aware of the fact that you are there; to have a strong influence on a group of people or a situation

ˌpresence of 'mind *noun* [U] the ability to react quickly and stay calm in a difficult or dangerous situation: *The boy had the presence of mind to turn off the gas.*

pres·ent *adj., noun, verb*

■ *adj.* /ˈpreznt/ **1** [only before noun] existing or happening now **SYN** CURRENT: *in the present situation / case* ◊ *the present owner of the house* ◊ *a list of all club members, past and present* ◊ *We do not have any more information at the present time.* ◊ (*written*) *A few brief comments are sufficient for present purposes.* ⇨ note at ACTUAL **2** [not before noun] ~ (at sth) (of a person) being in a particular place: *Most fathers wish to be present at the birth of their child.* ◊ *There were 200 people present at the meeting.* **OPP** ABSENT ⇨ note at HELP **3** [not before noun] ~ (in sth) (of a thing or a substance) existing in a particular place or thing: *Levels of pollution present in the atmosphere are increasing.* ◊ *Analysis showed that traces of arsenic were present in the body.* **OPP** ABSENT **IDM** all ˌpresent and corˈrect (*BrE*) (*AmE* all present and acˈcounted for) (*spoken*) used to say that all the things or people who should be there are now there present company exˈcepted (*spoken*) used after being rude or critical about sb to say that the people you are talking to are not included in the criticism

■ *noun* /ˈpreznt/ **1** a thing that you give to sb as a gift: *Christmas / wedding presents* ◊ *What can I get him for a birthday present?* **2** (usually the present) [sing.] the time now: *You've got to forget the past and start living in the present.* ◊ *I'm sorry he's out at present* (= now). **3** (the present) [sing.] (*grammar*) = THE PRESENT TENSE **IDM** see MOMENT, TIME *n.*

■ *verb* /prɪˈzent/ [VN]
GIVE | **1** ~ sb with sth | ~ sth (to sb) to give sth to sb, especially formally at a ceremony: *The local MP will start the race and present the prizes.* ◊ *On his retirement, colleagues presented him with a set of golf clubs.* ◊ *The sword was presented by the family to the museum.*

STH TO BE CONSIDERED | **2** ~ sth (for sth) | ~ sth (to sb) to show or offer sth for other people to look at or consider: *The committee will present its final report to Parliament in June.* ◊ *Eight options were presented for consideration.* ◊ *Are you presenting a paper at the conference?*

STH IN PARTICULAR WAY | **3** ~ sth | ~ sth/sb/yourself as sth to show or describe sth/sb from a particular point of view or in a particular way: *They have decided it must present a more modern image.* ◊ *It is essential that we present a united front* (= show that we all agree). ◊ *You need to present yourself better.* ◊ *He likes to present himself as a radical politician.* ◊ *The article presents these proposals as misguided.*

SB WITH PROBLEM | **4** ~ sb with sth | ~ sth to cause sth to happen or be experienced: *Your request shouldn't present us with any problems.* ◊ *Use of these chemicals may present a fire risk.*

ITSELF | **5** ~ itself (to sb) (of an opportunity, a solution, etc.) to suddenly happen or become available: *One major problem did present itself, though.* ◊ *As soon as the opportunity presented itself, she would get another job.* ◊ *Thankfully, a solution presented itself to him surprisingly soon.*

RADIO/TV PROGRAMME | **6** to appear in a radio or television programme and introduce the different items in it: *She used to present a gardening programme on TV.*

PLAY/BROADCAST | **7** to produce a show, play, broadcast, etc. for the public: *Compass Theatre Company presents a new production of 'King Lear'.*

INTRODUCE SB | **8** ~ sb (to sb) (*formal*) to introduce sb formally, especially to sb of higher rank or status: *May I present my fiancé to you?*

YOURSELF | **9** ~ yourself at, for, in, etc. (*formal*) to officially appear somewhere: *You will be asked to present yourself for interview.* ◊ *She was ordered to present herself in court on 20 May.*

EXPRESS STH | **10** ~ sth (to sb) (*formal*) to offer or express sth in speech or writing: *Please allow me to present my apologies.*

CHEQUE/BILL | **11** to give sb a cheque or bill that they should pay: *A cheque presented by Mr Jackson was returned by the bank.* ◊ *The builders presented a bill for several hundred pounds.*

IDM preˌsent 'arms (of soldiers) to hold a RIFLE upright in front of the body as a mark of respect

pre·sent·able /prɪˈzentəbl/ *adj.* **1** looking clean and attractive and suitable to be seen in public: *I must go and make myself presentable before the guests arrive.* **2** acceptable: *You're going to have to do a lot more work on this essay before it's presentable.*

pre·sen·ta·tion /ˌpreznˈteɪʃn; *AmE* ˌpriːzen-/ *noun* **1** [U] the act of showing sth or of giving sth to sb: *The trial was adjourned following the presentation of new evidence to the court.* ◊ *The presentation of prizes began after the speeches.* ◊ *The Mayor will make the presentation* (= hand over the gift) *herself.* ◊ *Members will be admitted on presentation of a membership card.* **2** [U] the way in which sth is offered, shown, explained, etc. to others: *Improving the product's presentation* (= the way it is wrapped, advertised, etc.) *should increase sales.* ◊ *I admire the clear, logical presentation of her arguments.* **3** [C] a meeting at which sth, especially a new product or idea, or piece of work, is shown to a group of people: *The sales manager will give a presentation on the new products.* **4** [C] a ceremony or formal occasion during which a gift or prize is given **5** [C] a performance of a play, etc. in a theatre **6** [C, U] (*medical*) the position in which a baby is lying in the mother's body just before birth

pre·sen·ta·tion·al /ˌpreznˈteɪʃənl; *AmE* ˌpriːzen-/ *adj.* [only before noun] connected with the act of showing, explaining or offering sth to other people, especially a new product, a policy or a performance: *a course on developing presentational skills*

the ˌpresent 'day *noun* [sing.] the situation that exists in the world now, rather than in the past or the future: *a study of European drama, from Ibsen to the present day* ▶ ˌpresent-ˈday *adj.* [only before noun]: *present-day fashions* ◊ *present-day America*

pre·sent·er /prɪˈzentə(r)/ (*BrE*) (*AmE* an·noun·cer) *noun* a person who introduces the different sections of a radio or television programme: *a radio / sports / TV presenter*

pre·sen·ti·ment /prɪˈzentɪmənt/ *noun* (*formal*) a feeling that sth is going to happen, especially sth unpleasant: *I was filled with a presentiment of disaster.*

pres·ent·ly /ˈprezntli/ *adv.* **1** (*especially AmE*) at the time you are speaking or writing; now **SYN** CURRENTLY: *The crime is presently being investigated by the police.* ◊ *These are the courses presently available.* **HELP** In this meaning **presently** usually comes before the verb, adjective or noun that it refers to. **2** (*written*) used to show that sth happened after a short time: *Presently, the door opened again and three men stepped out.* **HELP** In this meaning **presently** usually comes at the beginning of a sentence. **3** used to show that sth will happen soon **SYN** SHORTLY: *She'll be here presently.* **HELP** In this meaning **presently** usually comes at the end of a sentence. ⇨ note on page 998

ˌpresent 'participle *noun* (*grammar*) the form of the verb that in English ends in *-ing* and is used with the

æ	ɑː	e	ɜː	ə	ɪ	iː	i	ɒ	ɔː	ʌ	ʊ	u	uː
cat	father	ten	bird	about	sit	see	many	got	saw	cup	put	actual	too
								(BrE)					

verb *to be* to form PROGRESSIVE tenses such as *I was running* or sometimes as an adjective as in *running water*—compare PAST PARTICIPLE

the ¦present ¦perfect *noun* [sing.] (*grammar*) the form of a verb that expresses an action done in a time period up to the present, formed in English with the present tense of *have* and the past participle of the verb, as in *I have eaten*

¦present ¦tense (also **the present**) *noun* [usually sing.] (*grammar*) the form of a verb that expresses an action that is happening now or at the time of speaking

pre·ser·va·tion /ˌprezəˈveɪʃn; *AmE* -zərˈv-/ *noun* [U] **1** the act of keeping sth in its original state or in good condition: *building/environmental/food preservation* ◊ *a preservation group/society* **2** the act of making sure that sth is kept: *The central issue in the strike was the preservation of jobs.* **3** the degree to which sth has not been changed or damaged by age, weather, etc: *The paintings were in an excellent state of preservation.*—see also SELF-PRESERVATION

pre·ser·va·tion·ist /ˌprezəˈveɪʃənɪst; *AmE* -zərˈv-/ *noun* a person who works to keep old buildings or areas of the countryside in their original condition and to prevent them from being destroyed

preser¦vation order *noun* (in Britain) a document that makes it illegal to change or destroy a building, a tree or part of the countryside, because of its beauty or historical interest

pre·ser·va·tive /prɪˈzɜːvətɪv; *AmE* -ˈzɜːrv-/ *noun* [C, U] a substance used to prevent food or wood from decaying: *The juice contains no artificial preservatives.* ◊ *(a) wood preservative* ▶ **pre·ser·va·tive** *adj.* [only before noun]

pre·serve /prɪˈzɜːv; *AmE* -ˈzɜːrv/ *verb, noun*
■ *verb* **1** [VN] to keep a particular quality, feature, etc.; to make sure that sth is kept: *He was anxious to preserve his reputation.* ◊ *Efforts to preserve the peace have failed.* **2** [often passive] to keep sth in its original state in good condition: [VN] *a perfectly preserved 14th-century house* ◊ (*humorous*) *Is he really 60? He's remarkably well preserved.* ◊ [VN-ADJ] *This vase has been preserved intact.* **3** [VN] to prevent sth, especially food, from decaying by treating it in a particular way: *olives preserved in brine* ◊ *Wax polish preserves wood and leather.* **4** [VN] ~ **sb/sth (from sth)** to keep sb/sth alive, or safe from harm or danger: *The society was set up to preserve endangered species from extinction.*—compare CONSERVE
■ *noun* **1** [sing.] ~ **(of sb)** an activity, a job, an interest, etc. that is thought to be suitable for one particular person or group of people: *Football is no longer the preserve of men.* ◊ *in the days when nursing was a female preserve* **2** [C, usually pl., U] a type of jam made by boiling fruit with a large amount of sugar **3** [C, usually pl., U] (*especially BrE*) a type of PICKLE made by cooking vegetables with salt or VINEGAR **4** [C] (*AmE*) = RESERVE (2) **5** [C] an area of private land or water where animals and fish are kept for people to hunt

pre·server /prɪˈzɜːvə(r); *AmE* -ˈzɜːrv-/ *noun* **1** [C] a person who makes sure that a particular situation does not change: *The police are the preservers of law and order.* **2** [C, U] a substance used to prevent wood from decaying—see also LIFE PRESERVER

pre·set /ˌpriːˈset/ *verb* (**pre·setting**, **pre·set**, **pre·set**) **1** to set the controls of a piece of electrical equipment so that

it will start to work at a particular time: [VN to inf] *You can preset the radiators to come on when you need them to.* ◊ [VN] *to preset TV channels/radio stations* (= to set the controls so that particular channels are selected when you press particular buttons) **2** [VN] [usually passive] to decide sth in advance: *They kept to the preset route.*

pre·side /prɪˈzaɪd/ *verb* [V] ~ **(at/over sth)** to lead or be in charge of a meeting, ceremony, etc: *the presiding officer/judge* ◊ *They asked if I would preside at the committee meeting.* ◊ (*figurative*) *The party presided over one of the worst economic declines in the country's history* (= it was in power when the decline happened).

presi·dency /ˈprezɪdənsi/ *noun* [usually sing.] (*pl.* **-ies**) the job of being president of a country or an organization; the period of time sb holds this job: *the current holder of the EU presidency* ◊ *He was a White House official during the Bush presidency.*

presi·dent /ˈprezɪdənt/ *noun* **1** (also **President**) the leader of a republic, especially the US: *Several presidents attended the funeral.* ◊ *the President of the United States* ◊ *President Clinton is due to visit the country next month.* ◊ *Do you have any comment, Mr President?* **2** (also **President**) the person in charge of some organizations, clubs, colleges, etc: *to be made president of the students' union* **3** (*especially AmE*) the person in charge of a bank or a commercial organization: *the bank president* ◊ *the president of Columbia Pictures* ▶ **presi·den·tial** /ˌprezɪˈdenʃl/ *adj.*: *a presidential campaign/candidate/election* ◊ *a presidential system of government*

¦president-eˈlect *noun* (*pl.* **presidents-elect**) a person who has been elected to be president but who has not yet begun the job

ˈPresidents' Day *noun* [U, C] (in the US) a legal holiday on the third Monday in February, in memory of the birthdays of George Washington and Abraham Lincoln

pre·sid·ium (also **prae·sid·ium** especially in *BrE*) /prɪˈsɪdiəm/ *noun* a permanent committee that makes important decisions as part of a government or large political organization, especially in COMMUNIST countries

press /pres/ *noun, verb*
■ *noun*
NEWSPAPERS | **1** (often **the Press**) [sing.+ sing./pl. *v.*] newspapers and magazines: *the local/national/foreign press* ◊ *the popular/tabloid press* (= smaller newspapers with a lot of pictures and stories of famous people) ◊ *The story was reported in the press and on television.* ◊ *the music/sporting press* (= newspapers and magazines about music/sport) ◊ *Unlike the American, the British press operates on a national scale.* ◊ *the freedom of the Press/press freedom* (= the freedom to report any events and express opinions) ◊ *The event is bound to attract wide press coverage* (= it will be written about in many newspapers).—see also GUTTER PRESS **2** (**the press, the Press**) [sing.+ sing./pl. *v.*] the journalists and photographers who work for newspapers and magazines: *The Press was/were not allowed to attend the trial.* **3** [sing., U] the type or amount of reports that newspapers write about sb/sth: *The airline has had a bad press recently* (= journalists have written unpleasant things about it).

PUBLISHING/PRINTING | **4** [C, U] a machine for printing books, newspapers, etc.; the process of printing them: *We were able to watch the books rolling off the presses.* ◊ *These prices are correct at the time of going to press.* ◊ *a story that is hot off the press* (= has just appeared in the newspapers)—see also PRINTING PRESS, STOP PRESS **5** [C] a business that prints and publishes books: *Oxford University Press*

EQUIPMENT FOR PRESSING | **6** [C] (especially in compounds) a piece of equipment that is used for creating pressure on things, to make them flat or to get liquid from them: *a trouser press* ◊ *a garlic press*

ACT OF PUSHING | **7** [C, usually sing.] an act of pushing sth with your hand or with a tool that you are holding: *He gave the bell another press.* ◊ *Those shirts need a press* (= with an iron).

CROWD | **8** [sing.] a large number of people or things com-

aɪ	aʊ	eɪ	əʊ	oʊ	ɔɪ	ɪə	eə	ʊə	j	w
my	now	say	go	go	boy	near	hair	pure	yes	wet
			(BrE)	(AmE)						

peting for space or movement: *the press of bodies all moving the same way*

CUPBOARD | **9** [C] (*IrishE, ScotE*) a large cupboard, usually with shelves, for holding clothes, books, etc.

■ *verb*

PUSH/SQUEEZE | **1** ~ (sth/sb/yourself) against sth| ~ sth to sth| ~ sth together to push sth closely and firmly against sth; to be pushed in this way: [VN] *She pressed her face against the window.* ◊ *He pressed a handkerchief to his nose.* ◊ *She pressed her lips together.* ◊ [V] *His body was pressing against hers.* **2** to push or squeeze part of a device, etc. in order to make it work: [VN] *to press a button/switch/key* ◊ [VN-ADJ] *He pressed the lid firmly shut.* ◊ [V] [usually+adv./prep.] *Press here to open.* ◊ *She pressed down hard on the gas pedal.* **3** [VN] ~ sth into/onto sth to put sth in a place by pushing it firmly: *He pressed a coin into her hand and moved on.* **4** [VN] to squeeze sb's hand or arm, especially as a sign of affection **5** [V+adv./prep.] (of people in a crowd) to move in the direction mentioned by pushing: *The photographers pressed around the royal visitors.* ◊ (*figurative*) *A host of unwelcome thoughts were pressing in on him.*

TRY TO PERSUADE | **6** ~ sb (for sth)| ~ sb (into sth/into doing sth) to make strong efforts to persuade or force sb to do sth: [VN] *If pressed, he will admit that he knew about the affair.* ◊ *The bank is pressing us for repayment of the loan.* ◊ [VNtoinf] *They are pressing us to make a quick decision.*

POINT/CLAIM/CASE | **7** [VN] to express or repeat sth in a forceful way: *I don't want to **press the point**, but you do owe me $200.* ◊ *She is still **pressing her claim** for compensation.* ◊ *They were determined to **press their case** at the highest level.*

MAKE FLAT/SMOOTH | **8** to make sth flat or smooth by using force or putting sth heavy on top: [VN] *pressed flowers* (= pressed between the pages of a book) ◊ [VN-ADJ] *Press the soil flat with the back of a spade.* **9** [VN] to make clothes smooth using a hot iron SYN IRON: *My suit needs pressing.*

FRUIT/VEGETABLES | **10** [VN] to squeeze the juice out of fruit or vegetables by using force or weight

METAL | **11** [VN] to make sth from a material, using pressure: *to press a CD* ◊ *The car bodies are pressed out of sheets of metal.*

IDM ,press (the) 'flesh (*informal*) (of a famous person or politician) to greet people by shaking hands ,press sth 'home to get as much advantage as possible from a situation by attacking or arguing in a determined way: *to press home an attack/an argument/a point* ◊ *Simon saw she was hesitating and pressed home his advantage.* ,press sb/sth into 'service to use sb/sth for a purpose that they were not trained or intended for because there is nobody or nothing else available: *Every type of boat was pressed into service to rescue passengers from the sinking ferry.*—more at CHARGE *n.*, PANIC BUTTON

PHRV ,press a'head/'on (with sth) to continue doing sth in a determined way; to hurry forward: *The company is pressing ahead with its plans for a new warehouse.* ◊ *'Shall we stay here for the night?' 'No, let's press on.'* 'press for sth to keep asking for sth: *They continued to press for a change in the law.* 'press sth on sb to try to make sb accept sth, especially food or drink, although they may not want it: *She kept pressing cake on us.*

'press agency *noun* = NEWS AGENCY

'press agent (also *AmE informal* flack) *noun* a person whose job is to supply information and advertising material about a particular actor, musician, theatre, etc. to newspapers, radio or television

'press box *noun* a special area or a room at a sports ground where sports journalists sit

'press conference (*especially BrE*) (*AmE* usually 'news conference) *noun* a meeting at which sb talks to a group of journalists in order to answer their questions or to make an official statement: *to hold/give a press conference*

'press corps *noun* (*pl.* press corps) a group of journalists who work in or go to a particular place to report on an event

'press cutting (*BrE*) (also 'press clipping *AmE, BrE*) *noun* = CUTTING

pressed /prest/ *adj.* **1** [not before noun] ~ (for sth) not having enough of sth, especially time or money: *I'm really pressed for cash at the moment.*—see also HARD-PRESSED **2** made flat using force or a heavy object: *pictures made with pressed flowers* ◊ *neatly pressed trousers*

'press gallery *noun* an area in a parliament building or a court of law for journalists to sit in

'press gang *noun* a group of people who were employed in the past to force men to join the army or navy

'press-gang *verb* [VN] ~ sb (into sth/into doing sth) (*informal*) to force sb to do sth that they do not want to do

pres·sie *noun* = PREZZIE

press·ing /'presɪŋ/ *adj.*, *noun*

■ *adj.* [usually before noun] **1** needing to be dealt with immediately SYN URGENT: *I'm afraid I have some pressing business to attend to.* **2** difficult to refuse or to ignore: *a pressing invitation*

■ *noun* an object, especially a record, made by using pressure or weight to shape a piece of metal, plastic, etc.; a number of such objects that are made at one time: *The initial pressing of the group's album has already sold out.*

press·man /'presmæn/ *noun* (*pl.* -men /-men/) (*BrE, informal*) a journalist

'press office *noun* the office of a large organization, political party or government department that answers questions from journalists and provides them with information

'press officer *noun* a person who is in charge of or works for a press office

'press release *noun* an official statement made to journalists by a large organization, a political party or a government department

'press secretary *noun* a person who works for a politician or a political organization and gives information about them to journalists, the newspapers, etc.

'press stud (also pop·per) (both *BrE*) (*AmE* snap) *noun* a type of button used for fastening clothes, consisting of two metal or plastic sections that can be pressed together—picture at FASTENER

'press-up (*BrE*) (also 'push-up *AmE, BrE*) *noun* [usually pl.] an exercise in which you lie on your stomach and raise your body off the ground by pressing down on your hands until your arms are straight—picture at SIT-UP

pres·sure /'preʃə(r)/ *noun*, *verb*

■ *noun*

WHEN STH PRESSES | **1** [U] the force or weight with which sth presses against sth else: *The nurse applied pressure to his arm to stop the bleeding.* ◊ *The barriers gave way under the pressure of the crowd.*

OF GAS/LIQUID | **2** [U, C] the force produced by a particular amount of gas or liquid in an enclosed space or container; the amount of this: *air/water pressure* ◊ *Check the tyre pressure* (= the amount of air in a tyre) *regularly.*—see also BLOOD PRESSURE

OF ATMOSPHERE | **3** [U] the force of the atmosphere on the earth's surface: *A band of high pressure is moving across the country.*—see also ATMOSPHERIC

PERSUASION/FORCE | **4** [U] ~ (for sth)| ~ (on sb) (to do sth) the act of trying to persuade or to force sb to do sth: *The pressure for change continued to mount.* ◊ *There is a great deal of pressure on young people to conform.* ◊ *The government eventually bowed to popular pressure* (= they agreed to do what people were trying to get them to do). ◊ *Teenagers may find it difficult to resist peer pressure.*

STRESS | **5** [U] (also pressures [pl.]) difficulties and feelings of anxiety that are caused by the need to achieve or to behave in a particular way: *She was unable to attend because of the pressure of work.* ◊ *You need to be able to*

b	d	f	g	h	k	l	m	n	p	r
bad	did	fall	get	hat	cat	leg	man	now	pen	red

P

handle pressure in this job. ◇ *How can anyone enjoy the pressures of city life?*

IDM **put 'pressure on sb (to do sth)** to force or to try to persuade sb to do sth: *Advertisements put pressure on girls to be thin.* **under 'pressure 1** if a liquid or a gas is kept **under pressure**, it is forced into a container so that when the container is opened, the liquid or gas escapes quickly **2** being forced to do sth: *The director is under increasing pressure to resign.* **3** made to feel anxious about sth you have to do: *The team performs well under pressure.*

■ *verb* [often passive] **~ sb (into sth/into doing sth)** (*especially AmE*) = PRESSURIZE [VN] *Don't let yourself be pressured into making a hasty decision.* [also VN to inf]

'pressure cooker *noun* a strong metal pot with a tight lid, that cooks food quickly by steam under high pressure—picture at PAN

'pressure group *noun* a group of people who try to influence the government and ordinary people's opinion in order to achieve the action they want, for example a change in a law: *the environmental pressure group 'Greenpeace'*

'pressure point *noun* **1** a place on the surface of the body that is sensitive to pressure, for example where an artery can be pressed against a bone to stop bleeding **2** a place or situation where there is likely to be trouble: *a new political pressure point*

pres·sur·ize (*BrE* also **-ise**) /ˈpreʃəraɪz/ *verb* **1** (*BrE*) (also **pres·sure** *AmE, BrE*) [often passive] **~ sb (into sth/ into doing sth)** to persuade sb to do sth, especially by making them feel that they have to or should do it: [VN] *Stop trying to pressurize me!* ◇ *She was pressurized into accepting the job.* ◇ [VN to inf] *He felt that he was being pressurized to resign.* **2** [VN] [usually passive] to keep the air pressure in a SUBMARINE, an aircraft, etc. the same as it is on earth: *a pressurized cabin* ▶ **pres·sur·iza·tion, -isa·tion** /ˌpreʃəraɪˈzeɪʃn; *AmE* -rəˈz-/ *noun* [U]

pres·tige /preˈstiːʒ/ *noun, adj.*
■ *noun* [U] the respect and admiration that sb/sth has because of their social position, or what they have done [SYN] STATUS: *social/personal/international prestige* ◇ *There is a lot of prestige attached to owning a car like this.* ◇ *jobs with low prestige*
■ *adj.* [only before noun] **1** that brings respect and admiration; important: *a prestige job/accent* **2** admired and respected because it looks important and expensive [SYN] LUXURY: *a prestige car* ◇ *prestige items such as jewellery and silver*

pres·ti·gious /preˈstɪdʒəs/ *adj.* [usually before noun] respected and admired as very important or of very high quality: *a prestigious award/event* ◇ *a prestigious university*

presto /ˈprestəʊ; *AmE* ˈprestoʊ/ *exclamation* (*AmE*) = HEY PRESTO at HEY

pre·sum·ably /prɪˈzjuːməbli; *AmE* -ˈzuː-/ *adv.* used to say that you think that sth is probably true: *Presumably this is where the accident happened.* ◇ *You'll be taking the car, presumably?* ◇ *I couldn't concentrate, presumably because I was so tired.*

pre·sume /prɪˈzjuːm; *AmE* -ˈzuːm/ *verb* **1** to suppose that sth is true, although you do not have actual proof [SYN] ASSUME: [V] *They are very expensive, I presume?* ◇ *'Is he still abroad?' ' I presume so.'* ◇ [V (that)] *I presumed (that) he understood the rules.* ◇ [VN that] *Little is known of the youngest son; it is presumed that he died young.* ◇ [VN to inf] *I presumed him to be her husband.* **2** to accept that sth is true until it is shown not to be true, especially in a court of law: [VN-ADJ] *Twelve passengers are missing, presumed dead.* ◇ *In English law, a person is presumed innocent until proved guilty.* ◇ [VN] *We must presume innocence until we have proof of guilt.* [also VN to inf] **3** (*formal*) to accept sth as true or existing and to act on that basis [SYN] PRESUPPOSE: *The course seems to presume some previous knowledge of the subject.* **4** [V to inf] (*formal*) to behave in a way that shows a lack of respect by doing sth that you have no right to do: *I wouldn't presume to tell you how to run your own business.* **PHRV** **pre'sume on/**

upon sb/sth (*formal*) to make use of sb's friendship by asking them for more than you should: [+to inf] *I felt it would be presuming on our personal relationship to keep asking her for help.*

pre·sump·tion /prɪˈzʌmpʃn/ *noun* **1** [C] something that is thought to be true or probable: *There is a general presumption that the doctor knows best.* **2** [U] (*formal*) behaviour that is too confident and shows a lack of respect for other people **3** [U, C] (*law*) the act of supposing that sth is true, although it has not yet been proved or is not certain: *Everyone is entitled to the presumption of innocence until they are proved to be guilty.*

pre·sump·tive /prɪˈzʌmptɪv/ *adj.* [usually before noun] (*formal or technical*) likely to be true, based on the facts that are available: *a presumptive diagnosis of bowel cancer*—see also HEIR PRESUMPTIVE

pre·sump·tu·ous /prɪˈzʌmptʃuəs/ *adj.* [not usually before noun] too confident, in a way that shows a lack of respect for other people: *Would it be presumptuous of me to ask to borrow your car?*

pre·sup·pose /ˌpriːsəˈpəʊz; *AmE* -ˈpoʊz/ *verb* (*formal*) **1** [VN] to accept sth as true or existing and act on that basis, before it has been proved to be true [SYN] PRESUME: *Teachers sometimes presuppose a fairly high level of knowledge by the students.* **2** to depend on sth in order to exist or be true: [V that] *His argument presupposes that it does not matter who is in power.* [also VN]

pre·sup·pos·ition /ˌpriːsʌpəˈzɪʃn/ *noun* [C, U] (*formal*) something that you believe to be true and use as the beginning of an argument even though it has not been proved; the act of believing it is true [SYN] ASSUMPTION: *theories based on presupposition and coincidence*

pre-'tax *adj.* [only before noun] before the tax is taken away: *pre-tax profits/losses/income*

pre-teen /ˌpriːˈtiːn/ *noun* a young person of about 11 or 12 years of age ▶ **pre-teen** *adj.* [usually before noun]: *the pre-teen years*

pre·tence (*BrE*) (*AmE* **pre·tense**) /prɪˈtens/ *noun* **1** [U, sing.] **~ (of sth/of doing sth)** | **~ (that …)** the act of behaving in a particular way, in order to make other people believe sth that is not true: *Their friendliness was only pretence.* ◇ *By the end of the evening she had abandoned all pretence of being interested.* ◇ *He made no pretence of great musical knowledge.* ◇ *She was unable to keep up the pretence that she loved him.* **2** [C, usually sing.] **~ (to sth/to doing sth)** (*formal or literary*) a claim that you have a particular quality or skill: *a woman with some pretence to beauty* ◇ *I make no pretence to being an expert on the subject.* **IDM** see FALSE

pre·tend /prɪˈtend/ *verb, adj.*
■ *verb* **1 ~ (to sb) (that …)** to behave in a particular way, in order to make other people believe sth that is not true: [V] *I'm tired of having to pretend all the time.* ◇ *Of course I was wrong; it would be hypocritical to pretend otherwise.* ◇ [V (that)] *He pretended to his family that everything was fine.* ◇ *We pretended (that) nothing had happened.* ◇ [V to inf] *He pretended not to notice.* ◇ *She didn't love him, though she pretended to.* ◇ [VN] (*formal*) *She pretended an interest she did not feel.* **2** (especially of children) to imagine that sth is true as part of a game: [V (that)] *Let's pretend (that) we're astronauts.* ◇ [V] *They didn't have any real money so they had to pretend.* **3 ~ (to sth)** (usually used in negative sentences and questions) to claim to be, do or have sth, especially when this is not true: [V] *I can't pretend to any great musical talent.* ◇ [V (that)] *I don't pretend (that) I know much about the subject, but …* ◇ [V to inf] *The book doesn't pretend to be a great work of literature.*
■ *adj.* [usually before noun] (*informal*) (often used by children) not real, imaginary: *pretend cakes/toys*

pre·tend·er /prɪˈtendə(r)/ *noun* **~ (to sth)** a person who claims they have a right to a particular title even though other people disagree with them

pre·tense (*AmE*) = PRETENCE

pre·ten·sion /prɪˈtenʃn/ *noun* [C, usually pl., U] **1** the act of trying to appear more important, intelligent, etc. than you are in order to impress other people: *artistic/*

s	t	v	z	ʃ	ʒ	tʃ	dʒ	θ	ð	ŋ
see	tea	van	zoo	shoe	vision	chain	jam	thin	this	sing

intellectual/social pretensions ◊ *The play mocks the pretensions of the new middle class.* ◊ *He spoke without pretension.* **2 ~ (to sth/to doing sth)|~ (to do sth)** a claim to be or to do sth: *a building with no pretensions to architectural merit* ◊ *The movie makes no pretension to reproduce life.*

pre·ten·tious /prɪˈtenʃəs/ *adj.* (*disapproving*) trying to appear important, intelligent, etc. in order to impress other people; trying to be sth that you are not, in order to impress: *That's a pretentious name for a dog!* ◊ *It was just an ordinary house—nothing pretentious.* ◊ *He's so pretentious!*—compare UNPRETENTIOUS ▶ **pre·ten·tious·ly** *adv.* **pre·ten·tious·ness** *noun* [U]

pre·ter·nat·ural /ˌpriːtəˈnætʃrəl; *AmE* -tərˈn-/ *adj.* [only before noun] (*formal*) that does not seem natural; that cannot be explained by natural laws ▶ **pre·ter·nat·ur·al·ly** *adv.*: *The city was preternaturally quiet.*

pre·text /ˈpriːtekst/ *noun* **~ (for sth/for doing sth)|~ (to do sth)** a false reason that you give for doing sth, usually sth bad, in order to hide the real reason; an excuse: *The incident was used as a pretext for intervention in the area.* ◊ *He left the party early **on the pretext of** having work to do.* ⇨ note at REASON

pret·tify /ˈprɪtɪfaɪ/ *verb* (**pret·ti·fies, pret·ti·fy·ing, pret·ti·fied, pret·ti·fied**) [VN] (usually *disapproving*) to try to make sth pretty, often with the result that it looks worse or false: *man's attempts to prettify nature*

pretty /ˈprɪti/ *adv., adj.*

■ *adv.* (especially *spoken*) (with adjectives and adverbs) **1** to some extent; fairly: *I'm pretty sure I'll be going.* ◊ *The game was pretty good.* ◊ *It's pretty hard to explain.* ◊ *I'm going to have to find a new apartment pretty soon.* ⇨ note at QUITE **2** very: *That performance was pretty impressive.* ◊ *Things are looking pretty good!* **IDM** **pretty ˈmuch/ˈwell** (*BrE* also **pretty ˈnearly**) (*AmE* also **pretty ˈnear**) (*spoken*) almost; almost completely: *One dog looks pretty much like another to me.*—more at SIT

■ *adj.* (**pret·tier, pret·ti·est**) **1** (especially of a woman, or a girl) attractive without being very beautiful: *a pretty face* ◊ *a pretty little girl* ◊ *You look so pretty in that dress!* **2** (of places or things) attractive and pleasant to look at or to listen to without being large, beautiful or impressive: *pretty clothes/flowers* ◊ *a pretty garden/village/room* ◊ *a pretty voice/name* ▶ **pret·tily** /ˈprɪtɪli/ *adv.* (especially *BrE*): *She laughed prettily.* ◊ *The rooms are simply but prettily furnished.* **pret·ti·ness** *noun* [U]: *the prettiness of youth* **IDM** **as ˌpretty as a ˈpicture** (*old-fashioned*) very pretty **not just a pretty ˈface** (*humorous*) used to emphasize that you have particular skills or qualities: *'I didn't know you could play the piano.' 'I'm not just a pretty face, you know!'* **ˌnot a pretty ˈsight** (*humorous*) not pleasant to look at: *You should have seen him in his swimming trunks—not a pretty sight!* **a pretty ˈpenny** (*old-fashioned*) a lot of money—more at PASS *n.*

pret·zel /ˈpretsl/ *noun* a crisp salty biscuit in the shape of a knot or stick, often served with drinks at a party

pre·vail /prɪˈveɪl/ *verb* [V] **1 ~ (in/among sth)** (*written*) to exist or be very common at a particular time or in a particular place: *We were horrified at the conditions prevailing in local prisons.* ◊ *Those beliefs still prevail among certain social groups.* **2 ~ (against/over sth)** (*formal*) (of ideas, opinions, etc.) to be accepted, especially after a struggle or an argument: *Justice will prevail over tyranny.* ◊ *Fortunately, common sense prevailed.* **3** [V] **~ (against/over sb)** (*formal*) to defeat an opponent, especially after a long struggle **PHRV** **preˈvail on/upon sb to do sth** (*formal*) to persuade sb to do sth: *I'm sure he could be prevailed upon to give a talk.*

pre·vail·ing /prɪˈveɪlɪŋ/ *adj.* [only before noun] **1** (*written*) existing or most common at a particular time **SYN** CURRENT, PREDOMINANT: *the prevailing economic conditions* ◊ *the attitude towards science prevailing at the time* ◊ *The prevailing view seems to be that they will find her guilty.* **2** the **prevailing wind** in an area is the one that blows over it most frequently

preva·lent /ˈprevələnt/ *adj.* **~ (among sb)|~ (in sb/sth)** that exists or is very common at a particular time or in a particular place **SYN** COMMON, WIDESPREAD: *a prevalent belief/view* ◊ *These prejudices are particularly prevalent among people living in the North.* ▶ **preva·lence** /-əns/ *noun* [U]

pre·vari·cate /prɪˈværɪkeɪt/ *verb* (*formal*) to avoid giving a direct answer to a question in order to hide the truth: [V] *Stop prevaricating and come to the point.* [also V speech] ▶ **pre·vari·ca·tion** /prɪˌværɪˈkeɪʃn/ *noun* [U, C]

pre·vent /prɪˈvent/ *verb* **~ sb/sth (from doing sth)** to stop sb from doing sth; to stop sth from happening: [VN] *The accident could have been prevented.* ◊ *He is prevented by law from holding a licence.* ◊ *Nothing would prevent him from speaking out against injustice.* ◊ [VN-ing] (*BrE*) *Nothing would prevent him/his speaking out against further injustices.* [also V-ing] ▶ **pre·vent·able** *adj.*: *preventable diseases/accidents*

pre·ven·tion /prɪˈvenʃn/ *noun* [U] the act of stopping sth bad from happening: *accident/crime prevention* ◊ *the prevention of disease* ◊ *a fire prevention officer* **IDM** **preˌvention is better than ˈcure** (*BrE*) (*AmE* **an ounce of preˌvention is better than a pound of ˈcure**) (*saying*) it is better to stop sth bad from happening rather than try to deal with the problems after it has happened

pre·vent·ive /prɪˈventɪv/ (also **pre·venta·tive** /prɪˈventətɪv/) *adj.* [only before noun] intended to try to stop sth that causes problems or difficulties from happening: *preventive medicine* ◊ *The police were able to take preventive action and avoid a possible riot.*—compare CURATIVE

pre·ver·bal /ˌpriːˈvɜːbl; *AmE* -ˈvɜːrbl/ *adj.* [usually before noun] (*technical*) connected with the time before a child learns to speak: *a preverbal communication*

pre·view /ˈpriːvjuː/ *noun, verb*

■ *noun* **1** an occasion at which you can see a film/movie, a show, etc. before it is shown to the general public: *a press preview* (= for journalists only) ◊ *a special preview of our winter fashion collection*—see also SNEAK PREVIEW **2** a description in a newspaper or a magazine that tells you about a film/movie, a television programme, etc. before it is shown to the general public: *Turn to page 12 for a preview of next week's programmes.*

■ *verb* [VN] **1** to see a film/movie, a television programme, etc. before it is shown to the general public and write an account of it for a newspaper or magazine: *The exhibition was previewed in last week's issue.* **2** (especially *AmE*) to give sb a short account of sth that is going to happen, be studied, etc: *The professor previewed the course for us.*

pre·vi·ous /ˈpriːviəs/ *adj.* [only before noun] **1** happening or existing before the event or object that you are talking about: *No previous experience is necessary for this job.* ◊ *The car has only had one previous owner.* ◊ *She is his daughter from a previous marriage.* ◊ *I was unable to attend because of a previous engagement.* ◊ *The judge will take into consideration any previous convictions.* **2** immediately before the time you are talking about **SYN** PRECEDING: *I couldn't believe it when I heard the news. I'd only seen him the previous day.* ▶ **pre·vi·ous·ly** *adv.*: *The building had previously been used as a hotel.* ◊ *I had visited them three days previously.* **pre·vi·ous to** *prep.* (*spoken*): *Previous to this, she'd always been well.*

ˌpre·ˈwar *adj.* [usually before noun] happening or existing before a war, especially before the Second World War: *the pre-war years* ◊ *pre-war Britain*

prey /preɪ/ *noun, verb*

■ *noun* [U, sing.] **1** an animal, a bird, etc. that is hunted, killed and eaten by another: *The lion will often stalk its prey for hours.* ◊ **birds of prey** (= birds that kill for food) **2** a person who is harmed or deceived by sb, especially for dishonest purposes: *Elderly people are easy prey for dishonest salesmen.* **IDM** **be/fall ˈprey to sth** (*formal*) **1** (of an animal) to be killed and eaten by another animal or bird **2** (of a person) to be harmed or affected by sth bad: *Since the attack, she had fallen prey to irrational fears.*

■ *verb* **IDM** **prey on sb's ˈmind** (of a thought, problem, etc.) to make sb think and worry about it all the time: *The*

æ	ɑː	e	ɜː	ə	ɪ	iː	i	ɒ	ɔː	ʌ	ʊ	u	uː
cat	father	ten	bird	about	sit	see	many	got	saw	cup	put	actual	too

(BrE)

P

thought that he could have helped more *preyed on his mind*. **PHRV** **'prey on/upon sb/sth** **1** (of an animal or a bird) to hunt and kill another animal for food: *Hawks prey on rodents and small birds.* **2** to harm sb who is weaker than you, or make use of them in a dishonest way to get what you want: *Bogus social workers have been preying on old people living alone.*

prez·zie (also **pres·sie**) /ˈprezi/ *noun* (*BrE, informal*) a present that you give sb, for example for their birthday

price /praɪs/ *noun, verb*
■ *noun* **1** [C, U] the amount of money that you have to pay for sth: *Rover 200 for sale, price £2000* ◇ *house/retail/oil/ share prices* ◇ *to charge a high/reasonable/low price for sth* ◇ *The price of cigarettes is set to rise again.* ◇ *He managed to get a good price for the car.* ◇ *rising/falling prices* ◇ *Can you give me a price for the work* (= tell me how much you will charge)? ◇ *I'm only buying it if it's the right price* (= a price that I think is reasonable). ◇ *Children over five must pay (the) full price for the ticket.* ◇ *How much are these? They don't have a price on them.* ◇ *It's amazing how much computers have come down in price over the past few years.* ◇ *price rises/increases/cuts* ◇ *a price list*—see also ASKING PRICE, COST PRICE, CUT-PRICE, HALF-PRICE, MARKET PRICE, LIST PRICE, PURCHASE PRICE, SELLING PRICE **2** [sing.] **~ (of sth)** | **~ (for sth/for doing sth)** the unpleasant things that you must do or experience in order to achieve sth or as a result of achieving sth: *Criticism is part of the price of leadership.* ◇ *Loneliness is a high price to pay for independence in your old age.* ◇ *Giving up his job was a small price to pay for his children's happiness.* **3** [C] (in horse racing) the numbers that tell you how much money you will receive if the horse that you bet on wins the race **SYN** ODDS: *Six to one is a good price for that horse.*—see also STARTING PRICE **IDM** **at 'any price** whatever the cost or the difficulties may be: *We want peace at any price.* **at a 'price 1** costing a lot of money: *You can buy strawberries all year round, but at a price.* **2** involving sth unpleasant: *He'll buy you—at a price!* **beyond 'price** (*formal* or *literary*) extremely valuable or important **everyone has their 'price** (*saying*) you can persuade anyone to do sth by giving them more money or sth that they want **not at 'any price** used to say that no amount of money would persuade you to do or to sell sth: *I wouldn't work for her again—not at any price!* **a 'price on sb's head** an amount of money that is offered for capturing or killing sb **put a 'price on sth** to say how much money sth valuable is worth: *They haven't yet put a price on the business.* ◇ *You can't put a price on that sort of loyalty.* **'what price …?** (*BrE, spoken*) **1** used to say that you think that sth you have achieved may not be worth all the problems and difficulties it causes: *What price fame and fortune?* **2** used to say that sth seems unlikely: *What price England winning the World Cup?*—more at CHEAP *adj.*, PAY *v.*
■ *verb* [VN] **1** [usually passive] **~ sth (at sth)** to fix the price of sth at a particular level: *a reasonably priced house* ◇ *The tickets are priced at $100 each.* ◇ *These goods are priced too high.* **2 ~ sth (up)** to write or stick tickets on goods to show how much they cost **3** to compare the prices of different types of the same thing: *We priced various models before buying this one.* **IDM** **price yourself/sth out of the 'market** to charge such a high price for your goods, services, etc. that nobody wants to buy them

'price-fixing *noun* [U] the practice of companies agreeing not to sell goods below a particular price

'price index *noun* = RETAIL PRICE INDEX

price·less /ˈpraɪsləs/ *adj.* **1** extremely valuable or important: *a priceless collection of antiques* ◇ *priceless information* ◇ *Our family photos are priceless.*—compare VALUABLE **2** (*informal*) extremely amusing: *You should have seen his face—it was priceless!*

'price tag *noun* a label on sth that shows how much you must pay: (*figurative*) *There is a £2 million price tag on the team's star player.*

'price war *noun* a situation in which companies or shops/stores keep reducing the prices of their products

and services in order to attract customers away from their competitors

pricey /ˈpraɪsi/ *adj.* (**prici·er, prici·est**) (*informal*) expensive

pri·cing /ˈpraɪsɪŋ/ *noun* [U] the act of deciding how much to charge for sth: *competitive pricing* ◇ *pricing strategy/ policy*

prick /prɪk/ *verb, noun*
■ *verb* **1** [VN] **~ sth (with sth)** to make a very small hole in sth with a sharp point: *Prick holes in the paper with a pin.* ◇ *He pricked the balloon and burst it.* **2** [VN] **~ sth (on sth)** to make a small hole in the skin so that it hurts or bleeds: *She pricked her finger on a needle.* **3** to make sb feel a slight pain as if they were being pricked: [V] *He felt a pricking sensation in his throat.* ◇ [VN] *Tears pricked her eyes.* **IDM** **prick your 'conscience | your 'conscience pricks you** to make you feel guilty about sth; to feel guilty about sth: *Her conscience pricked her as she lied to her sister.* **prick (up) your 'ears 1** (of an animal, especially a horse or dog) to raise the ears (also **your 'ears prick up**) **2** (of a person) to listen carefully, especially because you have just heard sth interesting: *Her ears pricked up at the sound of his name.*
■ *noun* **1** (⚠, *slang*) a PENIS **2** (⚠, *slang*) an offensive word for a stupid or unpleasant man: *Don't be such a prick!* **3** an act of making a very small hole in sth with a sharp point: *I'm going to give your finger a little prick with this needle.* **4** a slight pain caused by a sharp point or sth that feels like a sharp point: *You will feel a tiny prick in your arm.* ◇ (*figurative*) *He could feel the hot prick of tears in his eyes.*

prickle /ˈprɪkl/ *verb, noun*
■ *verb* **1** to give sb an unpleasant feeling on their skin, as if they were being pricked by sth sharp: [VN] *The rough cloth prickled my skin.* ◇ [V] *His moustache prickled when he kissed me.* **2** [V] (of skin, eyes, etc.) to sting or feel strange and unpleasant because you are frightened, angry, excited, etc: *Her eyes prickled with tears.* ◇ *The hairs on the back of my neck prickled when I heard the door open.* ◇ (*figurative*) *He prickled* (= became angry) *at the suggestion that it had been his fault.*
■ *noun* **1** a small sharp part on the stem or leaf of a plant or on the skin of some animals: *a cactus covered in prickles* **2** a slight stinging feeling on the skin: *a prickle of fear/ excitement*

prick·ly /ˈprɪkli/ *adj.* **1** covered with prickles: *a prickly bush/branch/leaf* **2** causing you to feel as if your skin is touching sth that is covered with prickles: *a prickly feeling/sensation* **3** (*informal*) (of a person) easily annoyed or offended **SYN** TOUCHY **4** (of a decision, an issue, etc.) difficult to deal with because people have very different ideas about it **SYN** THORNY: *Let's move on to the prickly subject of taxation reform.*

prickly 'pear *noun* **1** a type of CACTUS with PRICKLES (= sharp parts like needles), and yellow flowers **2** the reddish fruit of the prickly pear that is shaped like a PEAR and can be eaten

pride /praɪd/ *noun, verb*

■ *noun*

PLEASURE/SATISFACTION | **1** [U, sing.] ~ (**in sth/in doing sth**) a feeling of pleasure or satisfaction that you get when you or people who are connected with you have done sth well or own sth that other people admire: *The sight of her son graduating filled her with pride.* ◊ *I take (a) pride in my work.* ◊ *We take great pride in offering the best service in town.* ◊ *I looked with pride at what I had achieved.* ◊ *Success in sport is a source of national pride.* **2** [sing.] **the ~ of sth** a person or a thing that gives people a feeling of pleasure or satisfaction: *The new sports stadium is the pride of the town.*

RESPECT FOR YOURSELF | **3** [U] the feeling of respect that you have for yourself: *Pride would not allow him to accept the money.* ◊ *Her pride was hurt.* ◊ *Losing his job was a real blow to his pride.* ◊ *It's time to swallow your pride* (= hide your feelings of pride) *and ask for your job back.* **4** [U] (*disapproving*) the feeling that you are better or more important than other people: *Male pride forced him to suffer in silence.*—see also PROUD

LIONS | **5** [C+sing./pl. *v.*] a group of lions

IDM **sb's pride and 'joy** a person or a thing that causes sb to feel great pleasure or satisfaction **pride comes/ goes before a 'fall** (*saying*) if you have too high an opinion of yourself or your abilities, sth will happen to make you look stupid **pride of 'place** the position in which sth is most easily seen, that is given to the most important thing in a particular group

■ *verb*

PHRV **'pride yourself on sth/on doing sth** [no passive] to be proud of sth: *She had always prided herself on her appearance.*

priest /priːst/ *noun* **1** a person who is qualified to perform religious duties and ceremonies in the Roman Catholic, Anglican and Orthodox Churches: *a parish priest* ◊ *the ordination of women priests*—compare CHAPLAIN, CLERGYMAN, MINISTER, VICAR **2** (*feminine* **priest·ess** /ˈpriːstes/) a person who performs religious ceremonies in some religions that are not Christian

priest·hood /ˈpriːsthʊd/ (**the priesthood**) *noun* **1** [sing.] the job or position of being a priest: *to enter the priesthood* (= to become a priest) **2** all the priests of a particular religion or country

priest·ly /ˈpriːstli/ *adj.* [usually before noun] connected with a priest; like a priest

prig /prɪg/ *noun* (*disapproving*) a person who behaves in a morally correct way and who shows that they disapprove of what other people do ▶ **prig·gish** *adj.* **prig·gish·ness** *noun* [U]

prim /prɪm/ *adj.* (*disapproving*) **1** (of a person) always behaving in a careful and formal way, and easily shocked by anything that is rude: *You can't tell her that joke—she's much too prim and proper.* **2** formal and neat: *a prim suit with a high-necked collar* ▶ **prim·ly** *adv.*: *'You're not supposed to say that,' she said primly.*

prima ballerina /ˌpriːmə ˌbæləˈriːnə/ *noun* the main woman dancer in a ballet company

pri·macy /ˈpraɪməsi/ *noun* (*pl.* **-ies**) (*formal*) **1** [U] the fact of being the most important person or thing: *a belief in the primacy of the family* **2** [C] the position of an ARCHBISHOP

prima donna /ˌpriːmə ˈdɒnə; *AmE* ˈdɑːnə/ *noun* **1** the main woman singer in an opera performance or an opera company **2** (*disapproving*) a person who thinks they are very important because they are good at sth, and who behaves badly when they do not get what they want

prim·aeval *adj.* = PRIMEVAL

prima facie /ˌpraɪmə ˈfeɪʃi/ *adj.* [only before noun] (from *Latin*, especially *law*) based on what at first seems to be true, although it may be proved false later: *prima facie evidence* ▶ **prima facie** *adv.*: *Prima facie, there is a strong case against him.*

primal /ˈpraɪml/ *adj.* [only before noun] (*formal*) connected with the earliest origins of life; very basic **SYN** PRIMEVAL: *the primal hunter-gatherer* ◊ *a primal urge/fear*

pri·mar·ily /praɪˈmerəli; *BrE* also ˈpraɪmərəli/ *adv.* mainly: *a course designed primarily for specialists* ◊ *The problem is not primarily a financial one.*

pri·mary /ˈpraɪməri; *AmE* -meri/ *adj., noun*

■ *adj.* **1** [usually before noun] main; most important; basic: *The primary aim of this course is to improve your spoken English.* ◊ *Our primary concern must be the children.* ◊ *Good health care is of primary importance.* **2** [usually before noun] developing or happening first; earliest: *primary causes* ◊ *The disease is still in its primary stage.* **3** [only before noun] (*especially BrE*) connected with the education of children between the ages of about five and eleven: *primary teachers*—compare ELEMENTARY, SECONDARY, TERTIARY

■ *noun* (*pl.* **-ies**) (also **,primary e'lection**) (in the US) an election in which people in a particular area vote to choose a candidate for a future important election: *the Illinois primary* ◊ *the presidential primaries*

,primary 'colour (*BrE*) (*AmE* **,primary 'color**) *noun* one of the three colours, red, yellow and blue, that can be mixed together to make all other colours

,primary 'health care *noun* [U] the medical treatment that you receive first when you are ill/sick, for example from your family doctor

'primary school *noun* **1** (*BrE*) a school for children between the ages of 5 and 11 **2** (*old-fashioned, AmE*) = ELEMENTARY SCHOOL—compare SECONDARY SCHOOL

'primary source *noun* a document, etc. that contains information obtained by experience, research or OBSERVATION, not taken from other books, etc.—compare SECONDARY SOURCE

,primary 'stress *noun* [C, U] (*phonetics*) the strongest stress that is put on a syllable in a word or a phrase when it is spoken—compare SECONDARY STRESS

pri·mate /ˈpraɪmeɪt/ *noun* **1** any animal that belongs to the group of MAMMALS that includes human beings, APES and monkeys—picture on page A6 **2** an ARCHBISHOP (= a priest of very high rank in the Christian Church): *the Primate of all England* (= the Archbishop of Canterbury)

prime /praɪm/ *adj., noun, verb*

■ *adj.* [only before noun] main; most important; basic **SYN** PRIMARY: *My prime concern is to protect my property.* ◊ *Winning is not the prime objective in this sport.* ◊ *The care of the environment is of prime importance.* ◊ *He's the police's prime suspect in this case.* **2** of the best quality; excellent: *prime (cuts of) beef* ◊ *The store has a prime position in the mall.* **3** a **prime example** of sth is one that is typical of it: *The building is a prime example of 1960s architecture.* **4** most likely to be chosen for sth; most suitable: *The house is isolated and a prime target for burglars.* ◊ *He's a prime candidate to captain the team this season.*

■ *noun* [sing.] the time in your life when you are strongest or most successful: *a young woman in her prime* ◊ *He was barely 30 and in the prime of (his) life.* ◊ *These flowers are long past their prime.*

■ *verb* **1** ~ **sb** (**for/with sth**) to prepare sb for a situation so that they know what to do, especially by giving them special information **SYN** BRIEF: [VN] *They had been primed with good advice.* ◊ *She was ready and primed for action.* ◊ [VN to inf] *He had primed his friends to give the journalists as little information as possible.* **2** [VN] to make sth ready for use or action: *The bomb was primed, ready to explode.* **3** [VN] to prepare wood, metal, etc. for painting by covering it with a special paint that helps the next layer of paint to stay on **IDM** **prime the 'pump** to encourage the growth of a new or weak business or industry by putting money into it

,prime 'minister (also **,Prime 'Minister**) *noun* (*abbr.* **PM**) the main minister and leader of the government in some countries

,prime 'mover *noun* a person or a thing that starts sth and has an important influence on its development

---

	b	d	f	g	h	k	l	m	n	p	r
	bad	did	fall	get	hat	cat	leg	man	now	pen	red

prime number

prime 'number *noun* (*mathematics*) a number that can be divided exactly only by itself and 1, for example 7, 17 and 41

primer /'praɪmə(r)/ *noun* **1** [U, C] a type of paint that is put on wood, metal, etc. before it is painted to help the paint to stay on the surface **2** /'praɪmə(r); *AmE* 'prɪmər/ (*AmE*) a book that contains basic instructions: *The President doesn't need a primer on national security.* **3** /'praɪmə(r); *AmE* 'prɪmər/ (*AmE, old-fashioned*) a book for teaching children how to read, or containing basic facts about a school subject

'prime rate *noun* (*especially AmE*) the lowest rate of interest at which business customers can borrow money from banks—compare BASE RATE

'prime time *noun* [U] the time when the greatest number of people are watching television or listening to the radio: *prime-time television/viewing*

pri·meval (also **prim·aeval**) /praɪ'miːvl/ *adj.* [usually before noun] **1** from the earliest period of the history of the world, very ancient: *primeval rocks/forests* ◇ *primeval soup* (= the mixture of gases and substances that is thought to have existed when the earth was formed and from which life started) **2** (*formal*) (of a feeling, or a desire) very strong and not based on reason, as if from the earliest period of human life: *primeval instincts/urges*

primi·tive /'prɪmətɪv/ *adj., noun*
■ *adj.* **1** [usually before noun] belonging to a very simple society with no industry, etc: *primitive tribes* ◇ *primitive rituals/beliefs* **2** [usually before noun] belonging to an early stage in the development of humans or animals: *primitive man* **3** very simple and old-fashioned, especially when sth is also not convenient and comfortable: *The methods of communication used during the war were primitive by today's standards.* ◇ *The facilities on the campsite were very primitive.* **4** [usually before noun] (of a feeling or a desire) very strong and not based on reason, as if from the earliest period of human life: *a primitive instinct/desire* ▶ **primi·tive·ness** *noun* [U]
■ *noun* **1** an artist of the period before the Renaissance; an example of work from this period **2** an artist who paints in a very simple style like a child; an example of the work of such an artist

primo·geni·ture /ˌpraɪməʊ'dʒenɪtʃə(r); *AmE* -moʊ-/ *noun* [U] **1** (*formal*) the fact of being the first child born in a family **2** (*law*) the system in which the oldest son in a family receives all the property when his father dies

prim·or·dial /praɪ'mɔːdiəl; *AmE* -'mɔːrdiəl/ *adj.* [usually before noun] (*formal*) **1** existing at or from the beginning of the world SYN PRIMEVAL: *primordial gases/seas* **2** (*formal*) (of a feeling or a desire) very basic SYN PRIM-EVAL: *primordial impulses/fears*

primp /prɪmp/ *verb* (often *disapproving*) to make yourself look attractive by arranging your hair, putting on MAKE-UP, etc: [V] *She was busy primping in the bedroom.* [also VN]

prim·rose /'prɪmrəʊz; *AmE* -roʊz/ *noun* **1** [C] a small wild plant that produces pale yellow flowers in spring **2** (also ˌprimrose 'yellow) [U] a pale yellow colour ▶ **prim·rose** (also ˌprimrose 'yellow) *adj.*: *primrose paintwork* IDM **the primrose 'path** (*literary*) an easy life that is full of pleasure but that causes you harm in the end

prim·ula /'prɪmjələ/ *noun* a type of primrose that is often grown in gardens/yards

Pri·mus™ /'praɪməs/ (also **'Primus stove**) *noun* a small cooker/stove that you can move around that burns oil. It is used especially by people who are camping.

prince /prɪns/ *noun* **1** a male member of a royal family who is not king, especially the son or grandson of the king or queen: *the royal princes* ◇ *the Prince of Wales* **2** the male ruler of a small country or state that has a royal family; a male member of this family, especially the son or grandson of the ruler: *Prince Rainier of Monaco* **3** (in some European countries) a NOBLEMAN **4** ~ of/among sth (*literary*) a man who is thought to be one of the best in a particular field: *the prince of comedy* ◇ *a prince among men*

Prince 'Charming *noun* [sing.] (usually *humorous*) a man who seems to be a perfect boyfriend or husband because he is very attractive, kind, etc: *I'm still waiting for my Prince Charming!*

prince 'consort *noun* a title sometimes given to the husband of a queen who is himself a prince: *Prince Albert, the Prince Consort*

prince·ling /'prɪnslɪŋ/ *noun* (usually *disapproving*) a prince who rules a small or unimportant country

prince·ly /'prɪnsli/ *adj.* [usually before noun] **1** (usually *ironic*) if you say that an amount of money is **princely**, you are usually saying the opposite and that it is not very large: *I bought a bike for the princely sum of £20!* **2** (*old-fashioned, formal*) very grand; generous: *princely buildings* ◇ *a princely gift* **3** connected with a prince; like a prince: *a man of princely appearance*

prin·cess /ˌprɪn'ses; 'prɪnses/ *noun* **1** a female member of a royal family who is not queen, especially the daughter or granddaughter of the king or queen: *the royal princesses* ◇ *Princess Anne* **2** the wife of a prince: *the Princess of Wales* ◇ *Princess Michael of Kent*

Princess 'Royal *noun* a title often given to the eldest daughter of a British king or queen

prin·ci·pal /'prɪnsəpl/ *adj., noun*
■ *adj.* [only before noun] most important; main: *The principal reason for this omission is lack of time.* ◇ *New roads will link the principal cities of the area.*
■ *noun* **1** (*BrE*) the person who is in charge of a college or a university: *Peter Brown, principal of St John's college*—see also DEAN **2** (*AmE*) = HEAD TEACHER: *Principal Ray Smith* **3** [usually sing.] (*finance*) an amount of money that you lend to sb or invest to earn interest **4** the person who has the most important part in a play, an opera, etc: *The performance of the two principals is disappointing.*

prin·ci·pal·ity /ˌprɪnsɪ'pæləti/ *noun* (*pl.* -ies) **1** [C] a country that is ruled by a prince: *the principality of Monaco* **2** (**the Principality**) [sing.] (*BrE*) Wales

prin·ci·pal·ly /'prɪnsəpli/ *adv.* mainly: *The book is aimed principally at beginners.* ◇ *No new power stations have been built, principally because of the cost.*

principal 'parts *noun* [pl.] (*grammar*) the forms of a verb from which all the other forms can be made. In English these are the INFINITIVE (for example *swim*), the past tense (*swam*) and the past participle (*swum*).

prin·ciple /'prɪnsəpl/ *noun* **1** [C, usually pl., U] a moral rule or a strong belief that influences your actions: *He has high moral principles.* ◇ *I refuse to lie about it; it's against my principles.* ◇ *Stick to your principles and tell him you won't do it.* ◇ *She refuses to allow her family to help her as a matter of principle.* ◇ *He doesn't invest in the arms industry on principle.* **2** [C] a law, a rule or a theory that sth is based on: *the principles and practice of writing reports* ◇ *The principle behind it is very simple.* ◇ *There are three fundamental principles of teamwork.* ◇ *Discussing all these details will get us nowhere; we must get back to first principles* (= the most basic rules). **3** [C] a belief that is accepted as a reason for acting or thinking in a particular way: *the principle that free education should be available for all children* **4** [sing.] a general or scientific law that explains how sth works or why sth happens: *the principle that heat rises* IDM **in 'principle 1** if something can be done **in principle**, there is no good reason why it should not be done although it has not yet been done and there may be some difficulties: *In principle there is nothing that a human can do that a machine might not be able to do one day.* **2** in general but not in detail: *They have agreed to the proposal in principle but we still have to negotiate the terms.*

prin·cipled /'prɪnsəpld/ *adj.* **1** having strong beliefs about what is right and wrong; based on strong beliefs: *a principled woman* ◇ *to take a principled stand against abortion* OPP UNPRINCIPLED **2** based on rules or truths: *a principled approach to language teaching*

print /prɪnt/ *verb, noun*
■ *verb*
LETTERS/PICTURES **1** to produce letters, pictures, etc. on paper using a machine that puts ink on the surface: [VN]

s	t	v	z	ʃ	ʒ	tʃ	dʒ	θ	ð	ŋ
see	tea	van	zoo	shoe	vision	chain	jam	thin	this	sing

Do you want your address printed at the top of the letter? ◊ *I'm printing a copy of the document for you.* ◊ *Each card is printed with a different message.* ◊ [V] (*computing*) *Click on the icon when you want to print.*

BOOKS/NEWSPAPERS | **2** [VN] to produce books, newspapers, etc. by printing them in large quantities: *They printed 30000 copies of the book.*

PUBLISH | **3** [VN] to publish sth in printed form: *The photo was printed in all the national newspapers.*

PHOTOGRAPH | **4** [VN] to produce a photograph from photographic film: *I'm having the pictures developed and printed.*

WRITE | **5** to write without joining the letters together: [V] *In some countries children learn to print when they first go to school.* ◊ [VN] *Print your name and address clearly in the space provided.*

MAKE MARK | **6** [VN] ~ **sth (in/on sth)** to make a mark on a soft surface by pressing: *The tracks of the large animal were clearly printed in the sand.* ◊ (*figurative*) *The memory of that day was indelibly printed on his brain.*

MAKE DESIGN | **7** [VN] to make a design on a surface or fabric by pressing a surface against it which has been coloured with ink or DYE: *They had printed their own design on the T-shirt.*

IDM the ˌprinted ˈword/ˈpage what is published in books, newspapers, etc: *the power of the printed word*—more at LICENCE *n.*, WORTH *adj.*

PHRV ˌprint sth↔ˈoff/ˈout to produce a document or information from a computer in printed form—related noun PRINTOUT

■ *noun*

LETTERS/NUMBERS | **1** [U] letters, words, numbers, etc. that have been printed onto paper: *in large/small/bold print* ◊ *The print quality of the new laser printer is superb.*—see also THE SMALL PRINT

NEWSPAPERS/BOOKS | **2** [U] used to refer to the business of producing newspapers, magazines and books: *the print media* ◊ *print unions* ◊ *a print run* (= the number of copies of a book, etc. printed at one time)

MARK | **3** [C, usually pl.] a mark left by your finger, foot, etc. on the surface of sth: *His prints were found on the gun.*—see also FINGERPRINT, FOOTPRINT

PICTURE | **4** [C] a picture that is carved into metal or wood then covered with ink and printed onto paper; a picture that is copied from a painting using photography: *a framed set of prints*

PHOTOGRAPH | **5** [C] a photograph produced from film: *How many sets of prints would you like?* ◊ *a colour print*

FABRIC | **6** [U, C] cotton fabric that has a pattern printed on it; this pattern: *a cotton print dress* ◊ *a floral print*—picture on page A4—see also BLUEPRINT

IDM get into ˈprint to be published: *By the time this gets into print, they'll already have left the country.* in ˈprint **1** (of a book) still available from the company that publishes it: *Is this edition still in print?* **2** (of a person's work) printed in a book, newspaper, etc: *It was the first time he had seen his name in print.* ˌout of ˈprint (of a book) no longer available from the company that publishes it: *Her first novel is now out of print.*

print·able /ˈprɪntəbl/ *adj.* (usually used with a negative) suitable to be repeated in writing and read by people: *His comment when he heard the news was not printable* (= was very rude). **OPP** UNPRINTABLE

ˌprinted ˈcircuit *noun* a CIRCUIT for electricity that uses thin strips of metal instead of wires to carry the current

print·er /ˈprɪntə(r)/ *noun* **1** a machine for printing text on paper, especially one connected to a computer: *a colour/laser printer*—picture on page 251 **2** a person or a company whose job is printing books, etc. **3** (**printer's**) (*pl.* **printers**) a place where books, etc. are printed

print·ing /ˈprɪntɪŋ/ *noun* **1** [U] the act of producing letters, pictures, patterns, etc. on sth by pressing a surface covered with ink against it: *the invention of printing* ◊ *the printing trade* ◊ *fabric/colour printing* **2** [C] the act of printing a number of copies of a book at one time: *The book is in its sixth printing.* **3** [U] a type of writing when

you write all the letters separately and do not join them together

ˈprinting press *noun* a machine that produces books, newspapers, etc. by pressing a surface covered in ink onto paper

print·out /ˈprɪntaʊt/ *noun* [U, C] a page or set of pages containing information in printed form from a computer: *a printout of text downloaded from the Internet*—compare READ-OUT

prion /ˈpriːɒn; *AmE* -ɑːn/ *noun* (*biology*) a very small unit of PROTEIN that is believed to be the cause of brain diseases such as BSE, CJD and SCRAPIE

prior /ˈpraɪə(r)/ *adj., noun*

■ *adj.* [only before noun] **1** happening or existing before sth else or before a particular time **SYN** PREVIOUS: *Although not essential, some prior knowledge of statistics is desirable.* ◊ *This information must not be disclosed without prior written consent.* ◊ *Visits are by prior arrangement.* ◊ *Please give us prior notice if you need an evening meal.* ◊ *She will be unable to attend because of a prior engagement.* **2** already existing and therefore more important: *They have a prior claim to the property.* **3** (ˈprior to) (*formal*) before sth: *during the week prior to the meeting*

■ *noun* (*feminine* **pri·or·ess** /ˈpraɪərəs; *BrE* also ˌpraɪəˈres/) **1** a person who is in charge of a group of MONKS or NUNS living in a PRIORY **2** (in an ABBEY) a person next in rank below an ABBOT or ABBESS

pri·ori ⇨ A PRIORI

pri·ori·tize (*BrE* also **-ise**) /praɪˈɒrətaɪz; *AmE* -ˈɔːr-; -ˈɑːr-/ *verb* **1** to put problems, etc. in order of importance, so that you can deal with the most important first: [VN] *You should make a list of all the jobs you have to do and prioritize them.* [also V] **2** [VN] (*formal*) to treat sth as being more important than other things: *The organization was formed to prioritize the needs of older people.*

► **pri·ori·tiza·tion**, **-isa·tion** /praɪˌɒrətaɪˈzeɪʃn; *AmE* -ˌɔːrətə-ˈz-; -ˌɑːrə-/ *noun* [U]

pri·or·ity /praɪˈɒrəti; *AmE* -ˈɔːr-; -ˈɑːr-/ *noun* (*pl.* **-ies**) **1** [C] something that you think is more important than other things and should be dealt with first: *a high/low priority* ◊ *Education is a top priority.* ◊ *Our first priority is to improve standards.* ◊ *Financial security was high on his list of priorities.* ◊ *You need to get your priorities right* (= decide what is important to you). ◊ (*AmE*) *You need to get your priorities straight.* **2** [U] ~ (**over sth**) the most important place among various things that have to be done or among a group of people **SYN** PRECEDENCE: *Club members will be given priority.* ◊ *The search for a new vaccine will take priority over all other medical research.* ◊ *Priority cases, such as homeless families, get dealt with first.* **3** [U] (*BrE*) the right of a vehicle to go before other traffic at a particular place on a road: *Buses have priority at this junction.*

pri·ory /ˈpraɪəri/ *noun* (*pl.* **-ies**) a building where a community of MONKS or NUNS lives, which is smaller and less important than an ABBEY

prise (*BrE*) (*AmE* **prize**) /praɪz/ (also **pry** /praɪ/ especially in *AmE*) *verb* to use force to separate sth from sth else: [VN, +*adv.*/*prep.*] *He prised her fingers from the bag and took it from her.* ◊ [VN-ADJ] *She used a knife to prise open the lid.* **PHRV** ˌprise sth↔ˈout (of sb) | ˈprise sth from sb to force sb to give you information about sb/sth

prism /ˈprɪzəm/ *noun* **1** (*geometry*) a solid figure with ends that are parallel and of the same size and shape, and with sides whose opposite edges are equal and parallel—picture at SOLID **2** a transparent glass or plastic object, often with ends in the shape of a triangle, which separates light that passes through it into the colours of the RAINBOW

pris·mat·ic /prɪzˈmætɪk/ *adj.* **1** (*technical*) using or containing a prism; in the shape of a prism **2** (*literary*) (of colours) formed by a prism; very bright and clear

prison /ˈprɪzn/ *noun* **1** [C, U] a building where people are kept as a punishment for a crime they have committed, or while they are waiting for trial: *He was sent to prison for five years.* ◊ *She is in prison, awaiting trial.* ◊ *to be*

æ	ɑː	e	ɜː	ə	ɪ	iː	i	ɒ	ɔː	ˌʌ	ʊ	u	uː
cat	father	ten	bird	about	sit	see	many	got	saw	cup	put	actual	too

(BrE)

P

released from prison ◊ *a maximum-security prison* ◊ *the prison population* (= the total number of prisoners in a country) ◊ *the problem of overcrowding in prisons* ◊ *Ten prison officers and three inmates needed hospital treatment following the riot.* ⇨ note at SCHOOL **2** [U] the system of keeping people in prisons: *the prison service/system* ◊ *The government insists that 'prison works' and plans to introduce a tougher sentencing policy for people convicted of violent crime.* **3** [C] a place or situation from which sb cannot escape: *His hospital room had become a prison.*

'prison camp *noun* a guarded camp where prisoners, especially prisoners of war or political prisoners, are kept

pris·on·er /'prɪznə(r)/ *noun* **1** a person who is kept in prison as a punishment, or while they are waiting for trial: *The number of prisoners serving life sentences has fallen.* ◊ *They are demanding the release of all political prisoners.* **2** a person who has been captured, for example by an enemy, and is being kept somewhere: *He was taken prisoner by rebel soldiers.* ◊ *They are holding her prisoner and demanding a large ransom.* ◊ (*figurative*) *She is afraid to go out and has become a virtual prisoner in her own home.*

prisoner of 'conscience *noun* (*pl.* **prisoners of conscience**) a person who is kept in prison because of his or her political or religious beliefs

prisoner of 'war *noun* (*pl.* **prisoners of war**) (*abbr.* POW) a person, usually a member of the armed forces, who is captured by the enemy during a war and kept in a prison camp until the war has finished

prissy /'prɪsi/ *adj.* (*informal, disapproving*) too careful to always behave correctly and appearing easily shocked by rude behaviour, etc.

pris·tine /'prɪstiːn/ *adj.* **1** fresh and clean, as if new: *The car is in pristine condition.* **2** not developed or changed in any way; left in its original condition: *pristine, pollution-free beaches*

priv·acy /'prɪvəsi; *AmE* 'praɪv-/ *noun* [U] **1** the state of being alone and not watched or disturbed by other people: *She was longing for some peace and privacy.* ◊ *I value my privacy.* ◊ *He read the letter later in the privacy of his own room.* **2** the state of being free from the attention of the public: *freedom of speech and the right to privacy*

pri·vate /'praɪvət/ *adj., noun*
■ *adj.*
NOT PUBLIC | **1** [usually before noun] belonging to or for the use of a particular person or group; not for public use: *The sign said, 'Private property. Keep out.'* ◊ *Those are my father's private papers.* ◊ *The hotel has 110 bedrooms, all with private bathrooms.* OPP PUBLIC
CONVERSATION/MEETING | **2** intended for or involving a particular person or group of people, not for people in general or for others to know about: *a private conversation/letter* ◊ *They were sharing a private joke.* ◊ *Senior defence officials held private talks.*
FEELINGS/INFORMATION | **3** that you do not want other people to know about; SYN SECRET: *her private thoughts and feelings*
NOT OWNED/RUN BY STATE | **4** [usually before noun] owned or managed by an individual person or an independent company rather than by the state: *private banks/companies/schools* ◊ *a programme to return many of the state companies to private ownership* OPP PUBLIC **5** [only before noun] working or acting for yourself rather than for the state or for a group or company, especially in health or education: *private doctors* ◊ *to offer advice to private investors* ◊ (*BrE*) *If I can afford it, I think I'll go private* (= pay for medical care rather than use the government service).
NOT WORK | **6** [usually before noun] not connected with your work or official position: *a politician's private life*
QUIET | **7** where you are not likely to be disturbed; quiet: *Let's go somewhere a bit more private.* OPP PUBLIC
PERSON | **8** [usually before noun] not wanting to share thoughts and feelings with other people: *He's a very private person.*

LESSONS | **9** [usually before noun] given by a teacher, etc. to one person or a small group of people for payment: *She gives private English lessons at weekends.* ◊ *private students*

MONEY | **10** that you receive from property or other sources but do not have to earn: *He has a private income.*
▶ **pri·vate·ly** *adv.*: *Can we speak privately?* ◊ *In public he supported the official policy, but privately he was sure it would fail.* ◊ *a privately owned company* ◊ *Their children were educated privately.* ◊ *She smiled, but privately she was furious.*
■ *noun* **1** [C] (*abbr.* Pte) (*BrE*) a soldier of the lowest rank in the army: *Private (John) Smith* **2** (**privates**) [pl.] (*informal*) = PRIVATE PARTS
IDM in 'private with nobody else present: *Is there somewhere we can discuss this in private?*—compare IN PUBLIC

private 'company (also **private ,limited 'company**) *noun* (*business*) a business that may not offer its shares for sale to the public—compare PUBLIC COMPANY, PLC

private de'tective (also **private in'vestigator**) (also *informal* **private 'eye**) *noun* a DETECTIVE who is not in the police, but who can be employed to find out information, find a missing person, follow sb, etc.

private 'enterprise *noun* [U] the economic system in which industry or business is owned by independent companies or private people and is not controlled by the government—compare FREE ENTERPRISE

pri·vat·eer /,praɪvə'tɪə(r); *AmE* -'tɪr/ *noun* a ship used in the past for attacking and robbing other ships

private 'law *noun* [U] (*law*) the part of the law that concerns individual people and their property

private 'member *noun* (in Britain) a member of the House of Commons who is not a minister in the government

private 'parts (also *informal* **pri·vates**) *noun* [pl.] a polite way of referring to the sexual organs without saying their names

private 'patient *noun* (in Britain) a person who is treated by a doctor outside the National Health Service and who pays for their treatment

private 'practice *noun* **1** [U] (of a profession) the fact of working on your own or in a small independent company rather than as an employee of the government or a large company: *Most solicitors in England and Wales are in private practice.* **2** [U, C] (in Britain) the fact of providing medical care outside the National Health Service, which people must pay for; a place providing this care

private 'school (also **inde,pendent 'school**) *noun* a school that receives no money from the government and where the education of the students is paid for by their parents—compare PUBLIC SCHOOL, STATE SCHOOL

private 'secretary *noun* **1** a secretary whose job is to deal with the more important and personal affairs of a business person **2** a CIVIL SERVANT who acts as an assistant to a senior government official

the ,private 'sector *noun* [sing.] the part of the economy of a country that is not under the direct control of the government: *to work in the private sector* ◊ *private-sector pay rises*—compare THE PUBLIC SECTOR

private 'view (also **private 'viewing**) *noun* an occasion when a few people are invited to look at an EXHIBITION of paintings before it is open to the public

pri·va·tion /praɪ'veɪʃn/ *noun* [C, usually pl., U] (*formal*) a lack of the basic things that people need for living: *the privations of poverty* ◊ *They endured years of suffering and privation.*

pri·vat·ize (*BrE* also **-ise**) /'praɪvətaɪz/ *verb* [VN] to sell a business or an industry so that it is no longer owned by the government SYN DENATIONALIZE: *Air traffic control has been privatized.* OPP NATIONALIZE ▶ **pri·vat·iza·tion, -isa·tion** /,praɪvətaɪ'zeɪʃn; *AmE* -tə'z-/ *noun* [U]: *There were fears that privatization would lead to job losses.*

privet /'prɪvɪt/ *noun* [U] a bush with small dark green leaves that remain on the bush and stay green all year, often used for garden HEDGES: *a privet hedge*

priv·il·ege /'prɪvəlɪdʒ/ *noun, verb*

aɪ	aʊ	eɪ	əʊ	oʊ	ɔɪ	ɪə	eə	ʊə	j	w
my	now	say	go	go	boy	near	hair	pure	yes	wet
			(BrE)	(AmE)						

■ *noun* **1** [C] a special right or advantage that a particular person or group of people has: *Education should be a universal right and not a privilege.* ◊ *You can enjoy all the benefits and privileges of club membership.* **2** [U] (*disapproving*) the rights and advantages that rich and powerful people in a society have: *As a member of the nobility, his life had been one of wealth and privilege.* **3** [sing.] something that you are proud and lucky to have the opportunity to do SYN HONOUR: *I hope to have the privilege of working with them again.* ◊ *It was a great privilege to hear her sing.* **4** [C, U] (*technical*) a special right to do or say things without being punished: *parliamentary privilege* (= the special right of members of parliament to say particular things without risking legal action)
■ *verb* [VN] (*formal*) to give sb/sth special rights or advantages that others do not have: *education policies that privilege the children of wealthy parents*

priv·il·eged /ˈprɪvəlɪdʒd/ *adj.* **1** (sometimes *disapproving*) having special rights or advantages that most people do not have: *Those in authority were in a privileged position.* ◊ *She comes from a privileged background.* ◊ *In those days, only a privileged few had the vote.* **2** [not before noun] having an opportunity to do sth that makes you feel proud SYN HONOURED: *We are privileged to welcome you as our speaker this evening.* **3** (*law*) (of information) known only to a few people and legally protected so that it does not have to be made public SYN CONFIDENTIAL

privy /ˈprɪvi/ *adj.*, *noun*
■ *adj.* (*formal*) **~ to sth** allowed to know about sth secret: *She was not privy to any information contained in the letters.*
■ *noun* (*pl.* **-ies**) (*old-fashioned*) a toilet, especially an outdoor one

the ˌPrivy ˈCouncil *noun* [sing.+ sing./pl. *v.*] (in Britain) a group of people who advise the king or queen on political affairs ▶ **Privy ˈCouncillor** *noun*

the ˌprivy ˈpurse *noun* [sing.] (in Britain) an amount of money that the government gives to the king or queen for their own private use

prize /praɪz/ *noun*, *adj.*, *verb*
■ *noun* **1** an award that is given to a person who wins a competition, race, etc. or who does very good work: *She was awarded the Nobel Peace prize.* ◊ *He won first prize in the woodwind section.* ◊ *There are no prizes for guessing* (= it is very easy to guess) *who she was with.* ◊ *I won £500 in prize money.* ◊ *Win a car in our grand prize draw!*—see also CONSOLATION PRIZE **2** something very important or valuable that is difficult to achieve or obtain: *World peace is the greatest prize of all.*
■ *adj.* [only before noun] **1** (especially of an animal, a flower or a vegetable) good enough to win a prize in a competition: *prize cattle/blooms* **2** being a very good example of its kind: *a prize pupil/student* ◊ *a prize example* ◊ *He's a prize specimen of the human race!* ◊ (*informal*) *She's a prize idiot* (= very silly).
■ *verb* [VN] **1** [usually passive] **~ sth (for sth)** to value sth highly TREASURE: *an era when honesty was prized above all other virtues* ◊ *Oil of cedarwood is highly prized for its use in medicine and perfumery.* **2** (*AmE*) = PRISE

prized /praɪzd/ *adj.* [only before noun] very valuable to sb: *I lost some of my most prized possessions in the fire.*

prize·fight /ˈpraɪzfaɪt/ *noun* a boxing competition that is fought for money ▶ **prize·fight·er** *noun* **prize·fight·ing** *noun* [U]

ˈprize-giving *noun* (*BrE*) a ceremony at which prizes are given to people who have done very good work

prize·win·ner /ˈpraɪzwɪnə(r)/ *noun* a person who has won a prize ▶ **prize·win·ning** *adj.* [only before noun]: *a prizewinning story*

pro /prəʊ; *AmE* proʊ/ *noun*, *adj.*
■ *noun* (*pl.* **pros**) (*informal*) a person who works as a PROFESSIONAL, especially in a sport: *a golf pro* ◊ *a young boxer who's just turned pro* ◊ *He handled the situation like an old pro* (= sb who has a lot of experience). IDM **the ˌpros and ˈcons** the advantages and disadvantages of sth: *We weighed up the pros and cons.*

■ *adj.* [only before noun] (*especially AmE*) (in sport) professional: *a pro athlete/wrestler* ◊ *pro football*

pro- /prəʊ; *AmE* proʊ-/ *prefix* (in adjectives) in favour of; supporting: *pro-democracy* ◊ *pro-European*—compare ANTI-

pro·active /ˌprəʊˈæktɪv; *AmE* ˌproʊ-/ *adj.* (of a person or policy) controlling a situation by making things happen rather than waiting for things to happen and then reacting to them: *a proactive approach/role*—compare REACTIVE ▶ **pro·active·ly** *adv.*

ˌpro-ˈam *adj.* [only before noun] (in sport) involving both professional and AMATEUR players: *a pro-am golf tournament* ▶ **ˌpro-ˈam** *noun*: *to play in a pro-am*

prob·abil·ist·ic /ˌprɒbəbɪˈlɪstɪk; *AmE* ˌprɑːb-/ *adj.* [usually before noun] (*technical*) (of methods, arguments, etc.) based on the idea that, as we cannot be certain about things, we can base our beliefs or actions on what is probable

prob·abil·ity /ˌprɒbəˈbɪləti; *AmE* ˌprɑːb-/ *noun* (*pl.* **-ies**) **1** [U, C] how likely sth is to happen: *The probability is that prices will rise rapidly.* ◊ *There seemed to be a high probability of success.* **2** [C] a thing that is likely to happen: *A fall in interest rates is a strong probability in the present economic climate.* ◊ *It now seems a probability rather than just a possibility.* **3** [C] (*mathematics*) a RATIO showing the chances that a particular thing will happen: *There is a 60% probability that the population will be infected with the disease.* IDM **in ˌall probaˈbility ...** (*written*) it is very likely that: *In all probability he failed to understand the consequences of his actions.*—more at BALANCE *n.*

prob·able /ˈprɒbəbl; *AmE* ˈprɑːb-/ *adj.*, *noun*
■ *adj.* likely to happen, to exist or to be true: *the probable cause/explanation/outcome* ◊ *highly/quite/most probable* ◊ *It is probable that the disease has a genetic element.*—compare IMPROBABLE
■ *noun* **~ (for sth)** (*especially BrE*) a person or an animal that is likely to win a race or to be chosen for a team

prob·ably /ˈprɒbəbli; *AmE* ˈprɑːb-/ *adv.* used to say that sth is likely to happen or to be true: *You're probably right.* ◊ *It'll probably be OK.* ◊ *It was the best known and probably the most popular of her songs.* ◊ *'Is he going to be there?' 'Probably.'* ◊ *'Do we need the car?' 'Probably not.'* ◊ *As you probably know, I'm going to be changing jobs soon.* ◊ (*written*) *The two cases are most probably connected.*

pro·bate /ˈprəʊbeɪt; *AmE* ˈproʊ-/ *noun*, *verb*
■ *noun* [U] (*law*) the official process of proving that a WILL (= a legal document that says what is to happen to a person's property when they die) is valid
■ *verb* [VN] (*AmE*, *law*) to prove that a WILL is valid

pro·ba·tion /prəˈbeɪʃn; *AmE* proʊ-/ *noun* [U] **1** (*law*) a system that allows a person who has committed a crime not to go to prison if they behave well and if they see an official (called a PROBATION OFFICER) regularly for a fixed period of time: *The prisoner was put on probation.* ◊ *He was given two years' probation.* **2** a time of training and testing when you start a new job to see if you are suitable for the work: *a period of probation* **3** (*AmE*) a fixed period of time during which a student who has behaved badly or not worked hard must improve their work or their behaviour ▶ **pro·ba·tion·ary** /prəˈbeɪʃnri; *AmE* proʊˈbeɪʃəneri/ *adj.*: *a probationary period* ◊ *young probationary teachers* **pro·ba·tion·er** *noun*: *prisoners and probationers* ◊ *a young probationer nurse*

proˈbation officer *noun* a person whose job is to check on people who are on probation and help them

probe /prəʊb; *AmE* proʊb/ *verb*, *noun*
■ *verb* **1 ~ (into sth)** to ask questions in order to find out secret or hidden information about sb/sth: [V] *He didn't like the media probing into his past.* ◊ [VN] *a TV programme that probed government scandals in the 1990s* [also V speech] **2** [VN] to touch, examine or look for sth, especially with a long thin instrument: *The doctor probed the wound for signs of infection.* ◊ *Searchlights probed the night sky.*
■ *noun* **1 ~ (into sth)** (used especially in newspapers) a thorough and careful investigation of sth: *a police probe*

	b	d	f	g	h	k	l	m	n	p	r
	bad	did	fall	get	hat	cat	leg	man	now	pen	red

into the financial affairs of the company **2** (also **'space probe**) a spacecraft without people on board which obtains information and sends it back to earth **3** (*technical*) a long thin metal tool used by doctors for examining inside the body **4** (*technical*) a small device put inside sth and used by scientists to test sth or record information

prob·ing /ˈprəʊbɪŋ; *AmE* ˈproʊ-/ *adj.* **1** intended to discover the truth: *They asked a lot of probing questions.* **2** examining sb/sth closely: *She looked away from his dark probing eyes.* ▶ **prob·ing** *noun*: *the journalist's unwanted probings*

prob·ity /ˈprəʊbəti; *AmE* ˈproʊ-/ *noun* [U] (*formal*) the quality of being completely honest: *financial probity*

prob·lem /ˈprɒbləm; *AmE* ˈprɑːb-/ *noun, adj.*
■ *noun* **1** a thing that is difficult to deal with or to understand: *big / major / serious problems* ◊ *health / unemployment / family problems* ◊ *financial / practical / technical problems* ◊ *to address / tackle / solve a problem* ◊ (*especially AmE*) *to fix a problem* ◊ *the problem of drug abuse* ◊ *If he chooses Mary it's bound to cause problems.* ◊ *Let me know if you have any problems.* ◊ *Most students face the problem of funding themselves while they are studying.* ◊ *The problem first arose in 1993.* ◊ *Unemployment is a very real problem for graduates now.* ◊ *It's a nice table! The only problem is (that) it's a bit too big for our room.* ◊ *Stop worrying about their marriage—it isn't your problem.* ◊ *There's no history of heart problems* (= disease connected with the heart) *in our family.* ◊ *the magazine's problem page* (= containing letters about readers' problems and advice about how to solve them) **2** a question that can be answered by using logical thought or mathematics: *mathematical / philosophical problems* ◊ *to find the answer to the problem* **IDM** **Do you have a 'problem with that?** (*spoken*) used to show that you are impatient with sb who disagrees with you **no 'problem** (*spoken, informal*) **1** (also **not a 'problem**) used to show that you are happy to help sb or that sth will be easy to do: *'Can I pay by credit card?' 'Yes, no problem.'* **2** used after sb has thanked you or said they are sorry for sth: *'Thanks for the ride.' 'No problem.'* **it's / that's not 'my problem** (*spoken, informal*) used to show that you do not care about sb else's difficulties **that's 'her / 'his / 'their / 'your problem** (*spoken, informal*) used to show that you think a person should deal with their own difficulties **What's your problem?** (*spoken, informal*) used to show that you think sb is being unreasonable: *What's your problem?—I only asked if you could help me for ten minutes.*
■ *adj.* [only before noun] causing problems for other people: *She was a problem child, always in trouble with the police.*

prob·lem·at·ic /ˌprɒbləˈmætɪk; *AmE* ˌprɑːb-/ (also *less frequent* **prob·lem·at·ical** /-ɪkl/) *adj.* difficult to deal with or to understand; full of problems; not certain to be successful: *Providing the necessary care for elderly people can be problematic.* **OPP** UNPROBLEMATIC

'problem-solving *noun* [U] the act of finding ways of dealing with problems

pro·bos·cis /prəˈbɒsɪs; *AmE* -ˈbɑːs-/ *noun* (*pl.* **pro·bos·ces** /-siːz/ **pro·bos·cises**) (*technical*) **1** the long FLEXIBLE nose of some animals, such as an elephant **2** the long thin mouth, like a tube, of some insects **3** (*humorous*) the human nose

probs /prɒbz; *AmE* prɑːbz/ *noun* [pl.] **IDM** **no 'probs** (*spoken*) used to mean 'there is no problem': *I can let you have it by next week. No probs.*

pro·ced·ure /prəˈsiːdʒə(r)/ *noun* **1** [C, U] ~ **(for sth)** a way of doing sth, especially the usual or correct way: *maintenance procedures* ◊ *emergency / safety / disciplinary procedures* ◊ *to follow normal / standard / accepted procedure* ◊ *Making a complaint is quite a simple procedure.* **2** [U] the official or formal order or way of doing sth, especially in business, law or politics: *court / legal / parliamentary procedure* **3** [C] (*medical*) a medical operation: *to perform a routine surgical procedure* ▶ **pro·ced·ural** /prəˈsiːdʒərəl/ *adj.* (*formal*): *procedural matters / rules*

pro·ceed /prəˈsiːd; *AmE* proʊ-/ *verb* [V] ~ **(with sth)** to

continue doing sth that has already been started; to continue being done: *We're not sure whether we still want to proceed with the sale.* ◊ *Work is proceeding slowly.* **2** [Vtoinf] to do sth next, after having done sth else first: *He outlined his plans and then proceeded to explain them in more detail.* ◊ (*humorous*) *Having said she wasn't hungry, she then proceeded to order a three-course meal.* **3** [V+adv. / prep.] (*formal*) to move or travel in a particular direction: *The marchers proceeded slowly along the street.* ◊ *Passengers for Rome should proceed to Gate 32 for boarding.* **PHRV** **pro'ceed against sb** (*law*) to start a court case against sb **pro'ceed from sth** (*formal*) to be caused by or be the result of sth

pro·ceed·ing /prəˈsiːdɪŋ/ *noun* (*formal*) **1** [C, usually pl.] ~ **(against sb)** **(for sth)** the process of using a court of law to settle a dispute or to deal with a complaint: *bankruptcy / divorce / extradition proceedings* ◊ *to bring legal proceedings against sb* **2** (**proceedings**) [pl.] an event or series of actions: *The Mayor will open the proceedings at the City Hall tomorrow.* ◊ *We watched the proceedings from the balcony.* **3** (**proceedings**) [pl.] the official written report of a meeting, etc.

pro·ceeds /ˈprəʊsiːdz; *AmE* ˈproʊ-/ *noun* [pl.] ~ **(of / from sth)** the money that you receive when you sell sth or organize a performance, etc.; profits: *She sold her car and bought a piano with the proceeds.* ◊ *The proceeds of the concert will go to charity.*

pro·cess¹ /ˈprəʊses; *AmE* ˈprɑːses; ˈproʊ-/ *noun, verb*— see also PROCESS²
■ *noun* **1** a series of things that are done in order to achieve a particular result: *the Middle East peace process* ◊ *a consultation process* ◊ *to begin the difficult process of reforming the education system* ◊ *I'm afraid getting things changed will be a slow process.* ◊ *cognitive / mental processes* ◊ *Coming off the drug was a long and painful* (= difficult) *process for him.* ◊ *Find which food you are allergic to by a process of elimination.* ◊ *We're in the process of selling our house.* ◊ *I was moving some furniture and I twisted my ankle in the process* (= while I was doing it). **2** a series of things that happen, especially ones that result in natural changes: *the digestive / ageing process* ◊ *It's a normal part of the learning process.* **3** a method of doing or making sth, especially one that is used in industry: *manufacturing processes*
■ *verb* [VN] **1** to treat raw material, food, etc. in order to change it, preserve it, etc: *Most of the food we buy is processed in some way.* ◊ *processed cheese* ◊ *I sent three rolls of film away to be processed.* ◊ *a sewage processing plant* **2** to deal officially with a document, request, etc: *It will take a week for your application to be processed.* **3** (*computing*) to perform a series of operations on data in a computer ▶ **pro·cess·ing** *noun* [U]: *a course on colour photography and processing* ◊ *the food processing industry*—see also DATA PROCESSING, WORD PROCESSING

pro·cess² /prəˈses/ *verb* [V+adv. / prep.] (*formal*) to walk or move along slowly in, or as if in, a procession—see also PROCESS¹

pro·ces·sion /prəˈseʃn/ *noun* **1** [C, U] a line of people or vehicles that move along slowly, especially as part of a ceremony; the act of moving in this way: *a funeral procession* ◊ *a torchlight procession* ◊ *The procession made its way down the hill.* ◊ *Groups of unemployed people from all over the country marched in procession to the capital.* **2** [C] a number of people who come one after the other: *A procession of waiters appeared bearing trays of food.*

pro·ces·sion·al /prəˈseʃənl/ *adj.* [only before noun] used in a procession, especially a religious one; connected with a procession

pro·ces·sor /ˈprəʊsesə(r); *AmE* ˈprɑː-; ˈproʊ-/ *noun* **1** a machine or person that processes things **2** (*computing*) a part of a computer that controls all the other parts of the system **SYN** CENTRAL PROCESSING UNIT—see also FOOD PROCESSOR, MICROPROCESSOR, WORD PROCESSOR

pro-'choice *adj.* believing that a pregnant woman should be able to choose to have an ABORTION if she wants—compare ANTI-CHOICE, PRO-LIFE

pro·claim /prəˈkleɪm/ *verb* **1** to publicly and officially tell people about sth important [SYN] DECLARE: [VN] *The president proclaimed a state of emergency.* ◊ [V**that**] *The charter proclaimed that all states would have their own government.* ◊ [VN-N] *He proclaimed himself emperor.* [also VN**to**inf, also V**wh-**, V**speech**] **2** (*formal*) to show sth clearly; to be a sign of sth: [VN] *This building, more than any other, proclaims the character of the town.* ◊ [VN-N, VN**to**inf] *His accent proclaimed him a Scot.* ◊ *His accent proclaimed him to be a Scot.* [also V**that**]

pro·cla·ma·tion /ˌprɒkləˈmeɪʃn; *AmE* ˌprɑːk-/ *noun* [C, U] an official statement about sth important that is made to the public; the act of making an official statement

pro·cliv·ity /prəˈklɪvəti/ *noun* (*pl.* **-ies**) ~ (**for sth/for doing sth**) (*formal*) a natural tendency to do sth or to feel sth, often its bad: *his sexual/criminal proclivities* ◊ *the government's proclivity for spending money*

pro·cras·tin·ate /prəʊˈkræstɪneɪt; *AmE* prəʊ-/ *verb* [V] (*formal, disapproving*) to delay doing sth that you should do, usually because you do not want to do it: *People were dying of starvation while governments procrastinated.* ▶ **pro·cras·tin·ation** /prəʊˌkræstɪˈneɪʃn; *AmE* prəʊ-/ *noun* [U]

pro·cre·ate /ˈprəʊkrieɪt; *AmE* ˈprəʊ-/ *verb* (*formal*) to produce children or baby animals [SYN] REPRODUCE: [V] *the urge to procreate* [also VN] ▶ **pro·cre·ation** /ˌprəʊkriˈeɪʃn; *AmE* ˌprəʊ-/ *noun* [U]: *They believe that sex is primarily for procreation.*

proc·tor /ˈprɒktə(r); *AmE* ˈprɑːk-/ *noun, verb*
■ *noun* (*AmE*) = INVIGILATOR
■ *verb* [VN] (*AmE*) = INVIGILATE

proc·ur·ator fis·cal /ˌprɒkjʊreɪtə ˈfɪskl; *AmE* ˌprɑːkjəreɪtər/ *noun* (*pl.* **proc·ur·ators fis·cal**) (in Scotland) a public official whose job is to decide whether people who are suspected of a crime should be brought to trial

pro·cure /prəˈkjʊə(r); *AmE* -ˈkjʊr/ *verb* **1** ~ **sth** (**for sth**) (*formal*) to obtain sth, especially with difficulty: [VN] *She managed to procure a ticket for the concert.* ◊ [VNN, VN] *They procured us a copy of the report.* ◊ *They procured a copy of the report for us.* **2** to provide a prostitute for sb: [VN] *He was accused of procuring under-age girls.* [also V]

pro·cure·ment /prəˈkjʊəmənt; *AmE* -ˈkjʊrm-/ *noun* [U] (*formal*) the process of obtaining supplies of sth, especially for a government or an organization: *arms procurement*

prod /prɒd; *AmE* prɑːd/ *verb, noun*
■ *verb* (**-dd-**) **1** ~ (**at**) **sb/sth** to push sb/sth with your finger or with a pointed object [SYN] POKE: [VN] *She prodded him in the ribs to wake him up.* ◊ [V] *He prodded at his breakfast with a fork.* **2** [VN] ~ **sb** (**into sth/into doing sth**) to try to make sb do sth, especially when they are unwilling: *She finally prodded him into action.*
■ *noun* **1** the act of pushing sb with your finger or with a pointed object: *She gave him a sharp prod with her umbrella.* **2** (*informal*) 'an act of encouraging sb or of reminding sb to do sth: *If they haven't replied by next week, you'll have to call them and **give them a prod**.* **3** an instrument like a stick that is used for prodding animals

prod·ding /ˈprɒdɪŋ; *AmE* ˈprɑːd-/ *noun* [U] encouragement to do sth: *He needed no prodding.*

prod·igal /ˈprɒdɪɡl; *AmE* ˈprɑːd-/ *adj.* (*formal, disapproving*) too willing to spend money or waste time, energy or materials [SYN] EXTRAVAGANT: *a prodigal administration* ▶ **prod·ig·al·ity** /ˌprɒdɪˈɡæləti; *AmE* ˌprɑːd-/ *noun* [U] [IDM] **the/a prodigal ('son)** a person who leaves home and wastes their money and time on a life of pleasure, but who later is sorry about this and returns home

pro·di·gious /prəˈdɪdʒəs/ *adj.* [usually before noun] (*formal*) very large or powerful and causing surprise or admiration [SYN] COLOSSAL, ENORMOUS: *a prodigious achievement/memory/talent* ◊ *Laser discs can store prodigious amounts of information.* ▶ **pro·di·gious·ly** *adv.*: *a prodigiously talented musician*

prod·igy /ˈprɒdɪdʒi; *AmE* ˈprɑːd-/ *noun* (*pl.* **-ies**) a young person who is unusually intelligent or skilful for their age: *a child/an infant prodigy* ◊ *a musical/tennis prodigy*

pro·duce *verb, noun*
■ *verb* [VN] /prəˈdjuːs; *AmE* -ˈduːs/

<table>
<tr><td colspan="2">WORD FAMILY</td></tr>
<tr><td>produce</td><td>v.</td></tr>
<tr><td>produce</td><td>n.</td></tr>
<tr><td>producer</td><td>n.</td></tr>
<tr><td>production</td><td>n.</td></tr>
<tr><td colspan="2">productive adj. (≠ unproductive)</td></tr>
</table>

GOODS | **1** to make things to be sold, especially in large quantities [SYN] MANUFACTURE: *a factory that produces microchips*—see also MASS-PRODUCE

MAKE NATURALLY | **2** to grow or make sth as part of a natural process; to have a baby or young animal: *The region produces over 50% of the country's wheat.* ◊ *These shrubs produce bright red berries.* ◊ *Our cat produced kittens last week.* ◊ *Her duty was to produce an heir to the throne.*

CREATE WITH SKILL | **3** to create sth, especially when skill is needed: *She produced a delicious meal out of a few leftovers.*

RESULT/EFFECT | **4** to cause a particular result or effect: *A phone call to the manager produced the result she wanted.* ◊ *The drug produces a feeling of great happiness and excitement.*

SHOW/BRING OUT | **5** ~ **sth** (**from/out of sth**) to show sth or make sth appear from somewhere: *He produced a letter from his pocket.* ◊ *At the meeting the finance director produced the figures for the previous year.*

PERSON | **6** if a town, country, etc. **produces** sb with a particular skill or quality, the person comes from that town, country, etc: *He is the greatest athlete this country has ever produced.*

MOVIE/PLAY | **7** to be in charge of preparing a film/movie, play, etc. for the public to see: *She produced a TV series about adopted children.*

■ *noun* /ˈprɒdjuːs; *AmE* ˈprɑːduːs; ˈproʊ-/ [U] things that have been made or grown, especially things connected with farming: *farm produce* ◊ *The shop sells only fresh local produce.* ◊ *It says on the label 'Produce of France'.*

pro·du·cer /prəˈdjuːsə(r); *AmE* -ˈduː-/ *noun* **1** a person, a company or a country that grows or makes food, goods or materials: *French wine producers* ◊ *Libya is a major oil producer.*—compare CONSUMER **2** a person who is in charge of the practical and financial aspects of making a film/movie or a play: *Hollywood screenwriters, actors and producers*—compare DIRECTOR (2) **3** a person or company that arranges for sb to make a programme for radio or television, or a record: *an independent television producer*

prod·uct /ˈprɒdʌkt; *AmE* ˈprɑːd-/ *noun* **1** [C, U] a thing that is grown or produced, usually for sale: *dairy/meat/pharmaceutical products* ◊ *investment in product development* ◊ *to launch a new product on to the market* ◊ (*business*) *We need new product to sell (= a new range of products).*—see also END PRODUCT, GROSS NATIONAL PRODUCT **2** [C] a thing produced during a natural, chemical or industrial process: *the products of the reaction*—see also BY-PRODUCT, WASTE PRODUCT **3** ~ **of sth** a person or thing that is the result of sth: *The child is the product of a broken home.* **4** (*mathematics*) a quantity obtained by multiplying one number by another: *The product of 21 and 16 is 336.*

pro·duc·tion /prəˈdʌkʃn/ *noun* **1** [U] the process of growing or making food, goods or materials, especially large quantities: *wheat/oil/car production* ◊ *land available for food production* ◊ *The new model will be **in production** by the end of the year.* ◊ *Production of the new aircraft will start next year.* ◊ *The car **went out of production** in 1990.* ◊ *production costs/difficulties* ◊ *a production manager/process*—see also MASS PRODUCTION **2** [U] the quantity of goods that is produced: *a decline/fall in production* ◊ *an increase in production* ◊ *It is important not to let production levels fall.* **3** [U] the act or process of making sth naturally: *drugs to stimulate the body's production of hormones* **4** [C, U] a film/movie, a play or a broadcast that is prepared for the public; the act of preparing a film or a play, etc: *a new production of 'King Lear'* ◊ *Every year the school puts on a musical production.*

æ	ɑː	e	ɜː	ə	ɪ	iː	i	ɒ	ɔː	ʌ	ʊ	u	uː
cat	father	ten	bird	about	sit	see	many	got	saw	cup	put	actual	too

(BrE)

◊ *He wants a career in film production.* **IDM** **on production of sth** *(formal)* when you show sth: *Discounts only on production of your student ID card.*

pro·duction line (also **as·sembly line**) *noun* a line of workers and machines in a factory, along which a product passes, having parts made, put together or checked at each stage until the product is finished: *Cars are checked as they come off the production line.* ◊ *Education is not a production line.*

pro·duction number *noun* a scene in a musical play or a film/movie where a lot of people sing and dance

pro·duct·ive /prəˈdʌktɪv/ *adj.* **1** making goods or growing crops, especially in large quantities: *highly productive farming land/manufacturing methods* ◊ *productive farmers/workers* **OPP** UNPRODUCTIVE **2** doing or achieving a lot: *a productive meeting* ◊ *My time spent in the library was very productive.*—compare COUNTERPRODUCTIVE **3 ~ of sth** *(formal)* resulting in sth or causing sth: *a play productive of the strongest emotions* **OPP** UNPRODUCTIVE ▶ **pro·duct·ive·ly** *adv.*: *to use land more productively* ◊ *It's important to spend your time productively.*

prod·uct·iv·ity /ˌprɒdʌkˈtɪvəti; *AmE* ˌprɑːd-; ˌproʊd-/ *noun* [U] the rate at which a worker, a company or a country produces goods, and the amount produced, compared with how much time, work and money is needed to produce them: *high/improved/increased productivity* ◊ *Wage rates depend on levels of productivity.*

Prof. *abbr.* (in writing) PROFESSOR: *Prof. Mike Harrison*

prof /prɒf; *AmE* prɑːf/ *noun* *(informal)* = PROFESSOR: *a college prof*

pro·fane /prəˈfeɪn/ *adj., verb*
▪ *adj.* **1** *(formal)* having or showing a lack of respect for God or holy things: *profane language* **2** *(technical)* not connected with religion or holy things **SYN** SECULAR: *songs of sacred and profane love*
▪ *verb* [VN] *(rare, formal)* to treat sth holy with a lack of respect

pro·fan·ity /prəˈfænəti; *AmE* also proʊˈf-/ *noun* (*pl.* **-ies**) *(formal)* **1** [U] behaviour that shows a lack of respect for God or holy things **2** [C, usually pl.] swear words, or religious words used in a way that shows a lack of respect for God or holy things: *He uttered a stream of profanities.*

pro·fess /prəˈfes/ *verb* *(formal)* **1** to claim that sth is true or correct, especially when it is not: [VN] *She still professes her innocence.* ◊ [V to inf] *I don't profess to be an expert in this subject.* **2** to state openly that you have a particular belief, feeling, etc: [VN] *He professed his admiration for their work.* ◊ [VN-ADJ] *She professed herself satisfied with the progress so far.* **3** [VN] to belong to a particular religion: *to profess Christianity/Islam/Judaism*

pro·fessed /prəˈfest/ *adj.* [only before noun] *(formal)* **1** used to describe a belief or a position that sb has publicly made known: *a professed Christian/anarchist* **2** used to describe a feeling or an attitude that sb says they have but which may not be sincere: *These, at least, were their professed reasons for pulling out of the deal.*

pro·fes·sion /prəˈfeʃn/ *noun* **1** [C] a type of job that needs special training or skill, especially one that needs a high level of education: *the medical/legal/teaching profession* ◊ *to enter/go into/join the nursing profession* ◊ *(BrE)* the **caring professions** (= that involve looking after people) ◊ *He was an electrician by profession.* ◊ *She was at the very top of her profession.* **2** **(the profession)** [sing.+ sing./pl. *v.*] all the people who work in a particular type of profession: *The legal profession has/have always resisted change.* **3** **(the professions)** [pl.] the traditional jobs that need a high level of education and training, such as being a doctor or a lawyer: *employment in industry and the professions* **4** [C] **~ of sth** a statement about what you believe, feel or think about sth, that is sometimes made publicly: *a profession of faith* ◊ *His professions of love did not seem sincere.*

pro·fes·sion·al /prəˈfeʃənl/ *adj., noun*
▪ *adj.* **1** [only before noun] connected with a job that needs special training or skill, especially one that needs a high

level of education: *professional qualifications/skills* ◊ *professional standards/practice* ◊ *an opportunity for professional development* ◊ *If it's a legal matter you need to seek professional advice.* **2** (of people) having a job which needs special training and a high level of education: *Most of the people on the course were professional women.* **3** showing that sb is well trained and extremely skilled: *He dealt with the problem in a highly professional way.* **OPP** AMATEUR **4** suitable or appropriate for sb working in a particular profession: *professional conduct/misconduct* **OPP** UNPROFESSIONAL **5** doing sth as a paid job rather than as a hobby: *a professional golfer* ◊ *After he won the amateur championship he* **turned professional.** **OPP** AMATEUR **6** (of sport) done as a paid job rather than as a hobby: *the world of professional football* **OPP** AMATEUR—compare NON-PROFESSIONAL
▪ *noun* **1** a person who does a job that needs special training and a high level of education: *the terms that doctors and other health professionals use* **2** (also *informal* **pro**) a person who does a sport or other activity as a paid job rather than as a hobby: *a top golf professional* **OPP** AMATEUR **3** (also *informal* **pro**) a person who has a lot of skill and experience: *This was clearly a job for a real professional.* **OPP** AMATEUR

pro·fessional 'foul *noun* *(BrE)* (in sport, especially football) a rule that sb breaks deliberately so that their team can gain an advantage, especially to prevent a player from the other team from scoring a goal

pro·fes·sion·al·ism /prəˈfeʃənəlɪzəm/ *noun* [U] **1** the high standard that you expect from a person who is well trained in a particular job: *We were impressed by the professionalism of the staff.* **2** great skill and ability: *the power and professionalism of her performance* **3** the practice of using professional players in sport: *Increased professionalism has changed the game radically.*

pro·fes·sion·al·ize *(BrE also* **-ise***)* /prəˈfeʃənəlaɪz/ *verb* [VN] [usually passive] to make an activity more professional, for example by paying people who take part in it ▶ **pro·fes·sion·al·iza·tion, -isa·tion** /prəˌfeʃənəlaɪˈzeɪʃn/ *noun* [U]: *the increasing professionalization of sports*

pro·fes·sion·al·ly /prəˈfeʃənəli/ *adv.* **1** in a way that is connected with a person's job or training: *You need a complete change, both professionally and personally.* **2** in a way that shows skill and experience: *The product has been marketed very professionally.* **3** by a person who has the right skills and qualifications: *The burglar alarm should be professionally installed.* **4** as a paid job, not as a hobby: *After the injury, he never played professionally again.*

pro·fes·sor /prəˈfesə(r)/ (also *informal* **prof**) *noun* (*abbr.* **Prof.**) **1** *(especially BrE)* (*AmE* **'full professor**) a university teacher of the highest rank: *Professor (Ann) Williams* ◊ *a chemistry professor* ◊ *to be appointed Professor of French at Cambridge* ◊ *He was made (a) professor at the age of 40.* **HELP** **Full professor** is used to describe a rank of university teacher, and not as a title. **2** *(AmE)* a teacher at a university or college—compare ASSISTANT PROFESSOR, ASSOCIATE PROFESSOR

pro·fes·sor·ial /ˌprɒfəˈsɔːriəl; *AmE* ˌprɑːf-/ *adj.* connected with a professor; like a professor: *professorial duties/posts* ◊ *His tone was almost professorial.*

pro·fes·sor·ship /prəˈfesəʃɪp; *AmE* -sərʃ-/ *noun* the rank or position of a university PROFESSOR: *a visiting professorship* ◊ *She was appointed to a professorship in Economics at Princeton.*

prof·fer /ˈprɒfə(r); *AmE* ˈprɑːf-/ *verb* **~ sth (to sb)** | **~ sb sth** *(formal)* **1** to offer sth to sb, by holding it out to them: [VN] *'Try this,' she said, proffering a plate.* [also VNN] **2** to offer sth such as advice or an explanation: [VN, VNN] *What advice would you proffer to someone starting up in business?* ◊ *What advice would you proffer her?* ◊ [VN] *A solution proffered itself.*

pro·fi·cient /prəˈfɪʃnt/ *adj.* **~ (in/at sth)** | **~ (in/at doing sth)** *(written)* able to do sth well because of training and practice: *She's proficient in several languages.* ◊ *He's proficient at his job.* ◊ *I'm a reasonably proficient driver.* ▶ **pro-**

aɪ	aʊ	eɪ	əʊ	oʊ	ɔɪ	ɪə	eə	ʊə	j	w
my	now	say	go (BrE)	go (AmE)	boy	near	hair	pure	yes	wet

fi·ciency /-nsi/ *noun* [U] ~ (**in sth/in doing sth**): *to develop proficiency* ◊ *a high level of oral proficiency in English* ◊ *a certificate of language proficiency*

pro·file /ˈprəʊfaɪl; *AmE* ˈproʊ-/ *noun, verb*
■ *noun* **1** the outline of a person's face when you look from the side, not the front: *his strong profile* ◊ *a picture of the president* **in profile 2** a description of sb/sth that gives useful information: *a job/employee profile* ◊ *We first build up a detailed profile of our customers and their requirements.* **3** the general impression that sb/sth gives to the public and the amount of attention they receive: *The deal will certainly raise the company's international profile.* **4** the edge or outline of sth that you see against a background: *the profile of the tower against the sky* **IDM** **a ˌhigh/ˌlow ˈprofile** the amount of attention sb/sth has from the public: *This issue has had a high profile in recent months.* ◊ *I advised her to keep a low profile for the next few days* (= not to attract attention).
■ *verb* [VN] (*written*) to give or write a description of sb/sth that gives the most important information: *His career is profiled in this month's journal.*

pro·fil·ing /ˈprəʊfaɪlɪŋ; *AmE* ˈproʊ-/ *noun* [U] the act of collecting useful information about sb/sth so that you can give a description of them: *customer profiling* ◊ *offender profiling*

profit /ˈprɒfɪt; *AmE* ˈprɑːfɪt/ *noun, verb*
■ *noun* **1** [C, U] the money that you make in business or by selling things, especially after paying the costs involved: *a rise/an increase/a drop/a fall in profits* ◊ *The company* **made a healthy profit** *of $106m last year.* ◊ *Net profit* (= after you have paid costs and tax) *was up 16.1%.* ◊ *The sale generated record profits.* ◊ *We should be able to sell the house* **at a profit.** ◊ *The agency is voluntary and not run for profit.* **OPP** LOSS **2** [U] (*formal*) the advantage that you get from doing sth: *Future lawyers could study this text with profit.*
■ *verb* ~ (**by/from sth**) (*formal*) to get sth useful from a situation; to be useful to sb or give them an advantage:[V] *Farmers are profiting from the new legislation.* ◊ *We tried to profit by our mistakes* (= learn from them). ◊ [VN] *Many local people believe the development will profit them.*

prof·it·able /ˈprɒfɪtəbl; *AmE* ˈprɑːf-/ *adj.* **1** that makes or is likely to make money: *a highly profitable business* ◊ *a profitable investment* ◊ *It is usually more profitable to sell direct to the public.* **2** that gives sb an advantage or a useful result: *a profitable experience* ◊ *She spent a profitable afternoon in the library.* ▶ **prof·it·abil·ity** /ˌprɒfɪtəˈbɪləti; *AmE* ˌprɑːf-/ *noun* [U]: *to increase profitability* **prof·it·ably** /-əbli/ *adv.*: *to run a business profitably* ◊ *He spent the weekend profitably.*

prof·it·eer·ing /ˌprɒfɪˈtɪərɪŋ; *AmE* ˌprɑːfəˈtɪr-/ *noun* [U] (*disapproving*) the act of making a lot of money in an unfair way, for example by asking very high prices for things that are hard to get ▶ **prof·it·eer** *noun*

pro·fit·er·ole /prəˈfɪtərəʊl; *AmE* -roʊl/ (*especially BrE*) (*AmE* usually ˌcream ˈpuff) *noun* a small cake in the shape of a ball, made of light pastry, filled with cream and usually with chocolate on top—picture on page A1

prof·it·less /ˈprɒfɪtləs; *AmE* ˈprɑːf-/ *adj.* (*rare*) producing no useful result: *Further argument was profitless.*

ˈprofit-making *adj.* [usually before noun] (of a company or a business) that makes or will make a profit

ˈprofit margin (also **margin**) *noun* the difference between the cost of buying or producing sth and the price that it is sold for

ˈprofit-sharing *noun* [U] the system of dividing all or some of a company's profits among its employees

prof·li·gate /ˈprɒflɪgət; *AmE* ˈprɑːf-/ *adj.* (*formal, disapproving*) using money, time, materials, etc. in a careless way **SYN** WASTEFUL: *profligate spending* ▶ **prof·li·gacy** /ˈprɒflɪgəsi; *AmE* ˈprɑːf-/ *noun* [U]

pro forma /ˌprəʊ ˈfɔːmə; *AmE* ˌproʊ ˈfɔːrmə/ *adj.* (from *Latin*) [usually before noun] **1** (especially of a document) prepared in order to show the usual way of doing sth or to provide a standard method: *a pro forma letter* ◊ *pro forma instructions* **2** (of a document) sent in advance: *a pro forma invoice* (= a document that gives details of the goods being sent to a customer) **3** done because it is part of the usual way of doing sth, although it has no real meaning: *a pro forma debate* ▶ **pro forma** *noun*: *I enclose a pro forma for you to complete, sign and return.*

pro·found /prəˈfaʊnd/ *adj.* **1** very great; felt or experienced very strongly: *profound changes in the earth's climate* ◊ *My father's death had a profound effect on us all.* **2** showing great knowledge or understanding: *profound thought/understanding/insights* ◊ *a profound book/drama* **3** needing a lot of study or thought: *profound questions about life and death* **4** (*medical*) very serious; complete: *profound disability*

pro·found·ly /prəˈfaʊndli/ *adv.* **1** in a way that has a very great effect on sb/sth: *a profoundly disturbing programme* ◊ *We are profoundly affected by what happens to us in childhood.* **2** (*medical*) very seriously; completely: *profoundly deaf*

pro·fund·ity /prəˈfʌndəti/ *noun* (*pl.* **-ies**) (*formal*) **1** [U] the quality of understanding or dealing with a subject at a very serious level: *He lacked profundity and analytical precision.* **2** [U] the quality of being very great, serious or powerful: *the profundity of her misery* **3** [C, usually pl.] something that sb says that shows great understanding: *His profundities were lost on the young audience.*

pro·fuse /prəˈfjuːs/ *adj.* produced in large amounts: *profuse apologies/thanks* ◊ *profuse bleeding* ◊ *The flowers are profuse in spring.* ▶ **pro·fuse·ly** *adv.*: *to bleed profusely* ◊ *to apologize profusely*

pro·fu·sion /prəˈfjuːʒn/ *noun* [sing.+ sing./ pl. *v.*, U] (*formal* or *literary*) a very large quantity of sth: *a profusion of colours/flowers* ◊ *Roses grew* **in profusion** *against the old wall.*

prog /prɒg; *AmE* prɑːg/ *noun* (*informal*) = PROGRAMME

pro·geni·tor /prəʊˈdʒenɪtə(r); *AmE* proʊ-/ *noun* (*formal*) **1** a person or a thing from which sb/sth develops or is produced **SYN** ANCESTOR: *He was the progenitor of a distinguished family.* **2** a person who starts an idea or a development: *the progenitors of modern art*

pro·geny /ˈprɒdʒəni; *AmE* ˈprɑːdʒ-/ *noun* [pl.] (*formal* or *humorous*) a person's children; the young of animals and plants: *He was surrounded by his numerous progeny.* ◊ (*figurative*) *These stories have produced progeny of their own.*

pro·ges·ter·one /prəˈdʒestərəʊn; *AmE* -roʊn/ *noun* [U] a HORMONE produced in the bodies of women and female animals which prepares the body to become pregnant and is also used in CONTRACEPTION—compare OESTROGEN, TESTOSTERONE

prog·no·sis /prɒgˈnəʊsɪs; *AmE* prɑːgˈnoʊ-/ *noun* (*pl.* **prog·no·ses** /-siːz/) **1** (*medical*) an opinion, based on medical experience, of the likely development of a disease or an illness **2** (*formal*) a judgement about how sth is likely to develop in the future: *The prognosis is for more people to work part-time in the future.*

prog·nos·ti·ca·tion /prɒgˌnɒstɪˈkeɪʃn; *AmE* prɑːgˌnɑːs-/ *noun* (*formal*) a thing that sb says will happen in the future: *gloomy prognostications*

pro·gram /ˈprəʊgræm; *AmE* ˈproʊ-/ *noun, verb*
■ *noun* **1** (*computing*) a set of instructions in CODE that control the operations or functions of a computer: *Load the program into the computer.* **2** (*AmE*) = PROGRAMME
■ *verb* (**-mm-**, *AmE* also **-m-**) **1** (*computing*) to give a computer, etc. a set of instructions to make it perform a particular task: [V] *In this class, students will learn how to program.* ◊ [VNtoinf] *The computer is programmed to warn users before information is deleted.* [alsoVN] —compare PROGRAMME **2** (*AmE*) = PROGRAMME

pro·gram·mable /ˈprəʊgræməbl; prəʊˈgræm-; *AmE* ˈproʊ-; proʊˈg-/ *adj.* (of a computer or electrical device) able to accept instructions that control how it operates or functions: *a programmable CD player*

pro·gram·mat·ic /ˌprəʊgrəˈmætɪk; *AmE* ˌproʊ-/ *adj.* [usually before noun] (*formal*) connected with, suggesting or following a plan: *programmatic reforms*

pro·gramme (*BrE*) (*AmE* **pro·gram**) /ˈprəʊgræm; *AmE* ˈproʊ-/ *noun, verb*
■ *noun*

P

PLAN | **1** a plan of things that will be done or included in the development of sth: *to launch a research programme* ◊ *a training programme for new staff* ◊ *a programme for/of economic reform*

ON TV/RADIO | **2** (also *informal* **prog**) something that people watch on television or listen to on the radio: *a news programme* ◊ *Did you see that programme on India last night?*

FOR PLAY/CONCERT | **3** a thin book or a piece of paper that gives you information about a play, a concert, etc: *a theatre programme*

ORDER OF EVENTS | **4** an organized order of performances or events: *an exciting musical programme* ◊ *a week-long programme of lectures* ◊ (*spoken*) *What's the programme for* (= what are we going to do) *tomorrow?*

COURSE OF STUDY | **5** (*AmE*) a course of study: *a school programme* ⇨ note at COURSE

OF MACHINE | **6** a series of actions done by a machine, such as a WASHING MACHINE: *Select a cool programme for woollen clothes.*

■ *verb* [usually passive]

PLAN | **1** [VN] ~ **sth** (**for sth**) to plan for sth to happen, especially as part of a series of planned events: *The final section of road is programmed for completion next month.*

PERSON/ANIMAL | **2** [VN to inf] to make a person, an animal, etc. behave in a particular way, so that it happens automatically: *Human beings are genetically programmed to learn certain kinds of language.*

MACHINE | **3** to give a machine instructions to do a particular task: [VN to inf] *She programmed the VCR to come on at eight.* [also VN]

programmed 'learning *noun* [U] a method of study in which a subject is divided into very small parts and the student must be successful in one part before he or she can go on to the next

pro·gram·mer /ˈprəʊɡræmə(r); *AmE* ˈproʊ-/ *noun* a person whose job is writing programs for computers

pro·gram·ming /ˈprəʊɡræmɪŋ; *AmE* ˈproʊ-/ *noun* [U] **1** the process of writing and testing programs for computers: *a high-level programming language* **2** the planning of which television or radio programmes to broadcast: *politically balanced programming*

pro·gress *noun, verb*

■ *noun* /ˈprəʊɡres; *AmE* ˈprɑːɡ-; -ɡrəs/ [U] **1** the process of improving or developing, or of getting nearer to achieving or completing sth: *to make slow/steady/rapid/good progress* ◊ *economic/scientific/technical progress* ◊ *We have made great progress in controlling inflation.* ◊ *They asked for a progress report on the project.* **2** movement forwards or towards a place: *We watched his slow progress down the steep slope.* ◊ *There wasn't much traffic so we made good progress.* **IDM** **in progress** (*formal*) happening at this time: *Work on the new offices is now in progress.* ◊ *Please be quiet—examination in progress.*

■ *verb* /prəˈɡres/ [V] **1** to improve or develop over a period of time; to make progress: *The course allows students to progress at their own speed.* ◊ *Work on the new road is progressing slowly.* **2** [+adv./prep.] (*formal*) to move forward: *The line of traffic progressed slowly through the town.* ◊ (*figurative*) *Cases can take months to progress through the courts.* **3** to go forward in time: *The weather became colder as the day progressed.* **PHRV** **pro'gress to sth** to move on from doing one thing to doing sth else: *She started off playing the recorder and then progressed to the clarinet.*

pro·gres·sion /prəˈɡreʃn/ *noun* **1** [U, C] ~ (**from sth**) (**to sth**) the process of developing gradually from one stage or state to another: *opportunities for career progression* ◊ *the rapid progression of the disease* ◊ *a natural progression from childhood to adolescence* **2** [C] a number of things that come in a series: *a long progression of sunny days*—see also ARITHMETIC PROGRESSION, GEOMETRIC PROGRESSION

pro·gres·sive /prəˈɡresɪv/ *adj., noun*

■ *adj.* **1** in favour of new ideas, modern methods and change: *progressive schools* ◊ *The approach taken by US courts has been more progressive than that in Britain.*

OPP RETROGRESSIVE **2** happening or developing steadily: *a progressive reduction in the size of the workforce* ◊ *a progressive muscular disease* **3** (also **con·tinu·ous**) (*grammar*) connected with the form of a verb (for example *I am waiting* or *It is raining*) that is made from a part of *be* and the present participle. Progressive forms are used to express an action that continues for a period of time. ▶ **pro·gres·siv·ism** *noun* [U]: *political progressivism*

■ *noun* [usually pl.] a person who is in favour of new ideas, modern methods and change: *political battles between progressives and conservatives*

pro·gres·sive·ly /prəˈɡresɪvli/ *adv.* (often with a comparative) steadily and continuously: *The situation was becoming progressively more difficult.* ◊ *The pain got progressively worse.*

pro·hibit /prəˈhɪbɪt; *AmE also* proʊˈh-/ *verb* ~ **sth** | ~ **sb from doing sth** (*formal*) **1** [often passive] to stop sth from being done or used especially by law **SYN** FORBID: [VN] *a law prohibiting the sale of alcohol* ◊ *Soviet citizens were prohibited from travelling abroad.* [also V-ing, VN-ing] **2** to make sth impossible to do **SYN** PREVENT: *The high cost of equipment prohibits many people from taking up this sport.*

pro·hib·ition /ˌprəʊɪˈbɪʃn; *AmE* ˌproʊəˈb-/ *noun* **1** [U] the act of stopping sth being done or used, especially by law: *the prohibition of smoking in public areas* **2** [C] ~ (**against/on sth**) a law or a rule that stops sth being done or used: *a prohibition against selling alcohol to people under the age of 18* **3** (**Prohibition**) [U] (in the US) the period of time from 1920 to 1933 when it was forbidden by law to make and sell alcoholic drinks

pro·hibi·tive /prəˈhɪbətɪv; *AmE also* proʊˈh-/ *adj.* **1** (of a price or a cost) so high that it prevents people from buying sth or doing sth: *prohibitive costs* ◊ *a prohibitive tax on imported cars* ◊ *The price of property in the city is prohibitive.* **2** preventing people from doing sth by law: *prohibitive legislation* ▶ **pro·hibi·tive·ly** *adv.*: *Car insurance can be prohibitively expensive for young drivers.*

pro·ject *noun, verb*

■ *noun* /ˈprɒdʒekt; *AmE* ˈprɑːdʒ-/

PLANNED WORK | **1** a planned piece of work that is designed to find information about sth, to produce sth new, or to improve sth: *a research project* ◊ *a building project* ◊ *to set up a project to computerize the library system*

SCHOOL/COLLEGE WORK | **2** a piece of work involving careful study of a subject over a period of time, done by school or college students: *a history project* ◊ *The final term will be devoted to project work.*

SET OF AIMS/ACTIVITIES | **3** a set of aims, ideas or activities that sb is interested in or wants to bring to people's attention: *The party attempted to assemble its aims into a focussed political project.*

HOUSING | **4** (*AmE*) = HOUSING PROJECT: *Going into the projects alone is dangerous.*

■ *verb* /prəˈdʒekt/

PLAN | **1** [VN] [usually passive] to plan an activity, a project etc. for a time in the future: *The next edition of the book is projected for publication in March.* ◊ *The projected housing development will go ahead next year.*

ESTIMATE | **2** [usually passive] to estimate what the size, cost or amount of sth will be in the future based on what is happening now: [VN] *A growth rate of 4% is projected for next year.* ◊ [VN to inf] *The unemployment rate has been projected to fall.* **HELP** This pattern is usually used in the passive. [also VN that]

LIGHT/IMAGE | **3** [VN] ~ **sth** (**on/onto sth**) to make light, a photographic image, etc. fall onto a flat surface or screen: *Images are projected onto the retina of the eye.*

STICK OUT | **4** [V+adv./prep.] to stick out beyond an edge or a surface **SYN** PROTRUDE: *a building with balconies projecting out over the street*

PRESENT YOURSELF | **5** [VN] ~ (**yourself**) to present sb/sth/yourself to other people in a particular way, especially one that gives a good impression: *They sought advice on how to project a more positive image of their company.* ◊

s	t	v	z	ʃ	ʒ	tʃ	dʒ	θ	ð	ŋ
see	tea	van	zoo	shoe	vision	chain	jam	thin	this	sing

She projects an air of calm self-confidence. ◊ He projected himself as a man worth listening to.

SEND/THROW OUTWARDS | **6** [VN] to send or throw sth outwards or upwards: *Actors must learn to project their voices.* ◊ *(figurative) the powerful men who would project him into The White House*

PHRV **pro'ject sth onto sb** *(psychology)* to imagine that other people have the same feelings, problems, etc. as yourself, especially when this is not true

pro·ject·ile /prə'dʒektaɪl; *AmE* -tl/ *noun (formal or technical)* **1** an object, such as a bullet, that is fired from a gun or other weapon **2** any object that is thrown as a weapon

pro·jec·tion /prə'dʒekʃn/ *noun*

ESTIMATE | **1** [C] an estimate or a statement of what figures, amounts, or events will be in the future, or what they were in the past, based on what is happening now: *to make forward/backward projections of population figures* ◊ *Sales have exceeded our projections.*

OF IMAGE | **2** [U, C] the act of putting an image of sth onto a surface; an image that is shown in this way: *the projection of three-dimensional images on a computer screen* ◊ *film/holographic/laser/video projection*

OF SOLID SHAPE | **3** [C] *(technical)* a solid shape or object as represented on a flat surface: *map projections*

STH THAT STICKS OUT | **4** [C] something that sticks out from a surface: *tiny projections on the cell*

OF VOICE/SOUND | **5** [U] the act of making your voice, a sound, etc. AUDIBLE (= able to be heard) at a distance: *voice projection*

PSYCHOLOGY | **6** [U] *(technical)* the act of imagining that sb else is thinking the same as you and is reacting in the same way

OF THOUGHTS/FEELINGS | **7** [C, U] the act of giving a form and structure to inner thoughts and feelings: *The idea of God is a projection of humans' need to have something greater than themselves.*

pro·jec·tion·ist /prə'dʒekʃənɪst/ *noun* a person whose job is to show films/movies by operating a PROJECTOR

pro·ject·or /prə'dʒektə(r)/ *noun* a piece of equipment for PROJECTING photographs or films/movies onto a screen: *a slide projector*—see also OVERHEAD PROJECTOR

pro·lapse /'prəʊlæps; *AmE* 'proʊ-/ *noun (medical)* a condition in which an organ of the body has slipped forward or down from its normal position

prole /prəʊl; *AmE* proʊl/ *noun (old-fashioned, BrE, informal)* an offensive word for a WORKING CLASS person

pro·le·tar·ian /ˌprəʊlə'teəriən; *AmE* ˌproʊlə'ter-/ *adj.* (often *disapproving*) connected with ordinary people who earn money by working, especially those who do not own any property: *proletarian power/revolution/writers*—compare BOURGEOIS ▶ **pro·le·tar·ian** *noun*

the pro·le·tar·iat /ˌprəʊlə'teəriət; *AmE* ˌproʊlə'ter-/ *noun* [sing.+ sing./ pl. *v.*] *(technical)* (used especially when talking about the past) the class of ordinary people who earn money by working, especially those who do not own any property: *the industrial proletariat*—compare BOURGEOISIE

pro-'life *adj.* [usually before noun] opposed to ABORTION: *the pro-life movement* ◊ *a pro-life campaigner*—compare PRO-CHOICE

pro·lif·er·ate /prə'lɪfəreɪt/ *verb* [V] *(written)* to increase rapidly in number or amount SYN MULTIPLY: *Books and articles on the subject have proliferated over the last year.*

pro·lif·er·ation /prəˌlɪfə'reɪʃn/ *noun* [U, sing.] the sudden increase in the number or amount of sth; a large number of a particular thing: *attempts to prevent cancer cell proliferation* ◊ *a proliferation of personal computers*

pro·lif·ic /prə'lɪfɪk/ *adj.* **1** (of an artist, a writer, etc.) producing many works, etc: *a prolific author* ◊ *a prolific goalscorer* ◊ *one of the most prolific periods in her career* **2** (of plants, animals, etc.) producing a lot of fruit, flowers, young, etc: *a prolific harvest* **3** able to produce enough food, etc. to keep many animals and plants alive: *prolific rivers* **4** existing in large numbers: *a pop star with*

a prolific following of teenage fans ▶ **pro·lif·ic·al·ly** *adv.*: *to write prolifically* ◊ *animals that breed prolifically*

pro·lix /'prəʊlɪks; *AmE* 'proʊ-/ *adj.* *(rare, formal)* (of writing, a speech, etc.) using too many words and therefore boring ▶ **pro·lix·ity** /prəʊ'lɪksəti; *AmE* proʊ-/ *noun* [U]

pro·logue (*AmE* also **pro·log**) /'prəʊlɒg; *AmE* 'proʊlɔːg; -lɑːg/ *noun* a speech, etc. at the beginning of a play, book, or film/movie that introduces it—compare EPILOGUE

pro·long /prə'lɒŋ; *AmE* -'lɔːŋ; -'lɑːŋ/ *verb* [VN] to make sth last longer SYN EXTEND: *The operation could prolong his life by two or three years.* ◊ *Don't prolong the agony* (= of not knowing sth)—*just tell us who won!*

pro·longa·tion /ˌprəʊlɒŋ'geɪʃn; *AmE* ˌproʊlɔːŋ-; -lɑːŋ-/ *noun* [U, sing.] *(formal)* the act of making sth last longer: *the artificial prolongation of human life*

pro·longed /prə'lɒŋd; *AmE* -'lɔːŋd; -'lɑːŋd/ *adj.* [only before noun] continuing for a long time: *a prolonged illness* ◊ *a prolonged period of dry weather*

prom /prɒm; *AmE* prɑːm/ *noun* **1** (in the US) a formal dance, especially one that is held at a high school: *the senior prom* **2** (*BrE, informal*, becoming *old-fashioned*) = PROMENADE *n.* (1): *to walk along the prom* **3** (*BrE*) = PROMENADE CONCERT: *the last night of the proms*

prom·en·ade /ˌprɒmə'nɑːd; *AmE* ˌprɑːmə'neɪd/ *noun, verb*
■ *noun* **1** (also *informal* **prom**) (both *BrE*, becoming *old-fashioned*) a public place for walking, usually a wide path beside the sea **2** (*old-fashioned*) a walk that you take for pleasure or exercise, especially by the sea, in a public park, etc.
■ *verb* [V] *(old-fashioned)* to walk up and down in a relaxed way, by the sea, in a public park, etc.

prom·en·ade 'concert (also *informal* **prom**) (both *BrE*) *noun* a concert at which many of the audience stand up or sit on the floor

prom·in·ence /'prɒmɪnəns; *AmE* 'prɑːm-/ *noun* [U, sing.] the state of being important, well known or noticeable: *a young actor who has recently risen to prominence* ◊ *The newspapers have given undue prominence to the story.* ◊ *She has achieved a prominence she hardly deserves.*

prom·in·ent /'prɒmɪnənt; *AmE* 'prɑːm-/ *adj.* **1** important or well known: *a prominent leader/politician* ◊ *He played a prominent part in the campaign.* ◊ *She was prominent in the fashion industry.* **2** easily seen SYN NOTICEABLE: *The church tower was a prominent feature in the landscape.* ◊ *The story was given a prominent position on the front page.* **3** sticking out from sth: *a prominent nose* ◊ *prominent cheekbones/teeth* ▶ **prom·in·ent·ly** *adv.*: *The photographs were prominently displayed on her desk.* ◊ *Problems of family relationships feature prominently in her novels.*

pro·mis·cu·ous /prə'mɪskjuəs/ *adj.* *(disapproving)* **1** having many sexual partners: *a promiscuous man/woman* ◊ *promiscuous behaviour* ◊ *a promiscuous lifestyle* ◊ *to be sexually promiscuous* **2** *(formal)* taken from a wide range of sources, especially without careful thought: *promiscuous reading* ◊ *a stylistically promiscuous piece of music* ▶ **prom·is·cu·ity** /ˌprɒmɪs'kjuːəti; *AmE* ˌprɑːməs-/ *noun*: *sexual promiscuity* **prom·is·cu·ous·ly** *adv.*

prom·ise /'prɒmɪs; *AmE* 'prɑːm-/ *verb, noun*
■ *verb* **1** ~ sth (to sb)| ~ sb sth to tell sb that you will definitely do or not do sth, or that sth will definitely happen: [V to inf] *The college principal promised to look into the matter.* [V to inf, V] *'Promise not to tell anyone!' 'I promise.'* ◊ [V] *They arrived at 7.30 as they had promised.* ◊ [VN] *The government has promised a full investigation into the disaster.* ◊ *I'll see what I can do but I can't promise anything.* ◊ [V (that)] *The brochure promised (that) the local food would be superb.* ◊ [VN (that)] *You promised me (that) you'd be home early tonight.* ◊ [VN, VNN] *He promised the money to his grandchildren.* ◊ *He promised his grandchildren the money.* ◊ [VNN] *I've promised myself some fun when the exams are over.* ◊ [V speech] *'I'll be back soon,' she promised.* [also VN speech] **2** to make sth seem likely to happen; to show signs of sth: [V to inf] *It promises to be an exciting few days.* ◊ [VN] *There were*

æ	ɑː	e	ɜː	ə	ɪ	iː	i	ɒ	ɔː	ʌ	ʊ	u	uː
cat	father	ten	bird	about	sit	see	many	got	saw	cup	put	actual	too

(BrE)

dark clouds overhead promising rain. **IDM** **I (can) 'promise you** (*informal*) used as a way of encouraging or warning sb about sth: *I can promise you, you'll have a wonderful time.* ◊ *If you don't take my advice, you'll regret it, I promise you.* **promise (sb) the 'earth/'moon/'world** (*informal*) to make promises that will be impossible to keep: *Politicians promise the earth before an election, but things are different afterwards.*

■ *noun* **1** [C] ~ **(to do sth)** | ~ **(that ...)** a statement that tells sb that you will definitely do or not do sth: *to make/keep/break a promise* ◊ *to extract/win a promise from sb* ◊ *She kept her promise to visit her aunt regularly.* ◊ *The government failed to keep its promise of lower taxes.* ◊ *Do I have your promise that you won't tell anyone about this?* ◊ *You haven't gone back on your promise, have you?* **2** [U] a sign that sb/sth will be successful: *Her work shows great promise.* ◊ *He failed to fulfil his early promise.* ◊ *Their future was full of promise.* **3** [U, sing.] ~ **of sth** a sign, or a reason for hope that sth may happen, especially sth good: *The day dawned bright and clear, with the promise of warm, sunny weather.*

the ˌpromised 'land *noun* [sing.] a place or situation where you expect to be happy, safe, etc.

prom·is·ing /ˈprɒmɪsɪŋ; *AmE* ˈprɑːm-/ *adj.* showing signs of being good or successful: *He was voted the most promising newcomer for his part in the movie.* ◊ *The weather doesn't look very promising.* ▶ **prom·is·ing·ly** *adv.*: *The day began promisingly with bright sunshine.*

prom·is·sory note /ˈprɒmɪsəri nəʊt; *AmE* ˈprɑːm-; noʊt/ *noun* (*technical*) a signed document containing a promise to pay a stated amount of money before a particular date

promo /ˈprəʊməʊ; *AmE* ˈproʊmoʊ/ *adj.* [only before noun] (*informal*) connected with advertising (= PROMOTING) sb/sth, especially a new pop record: *a promo photo/video/poster* ▶ **promo** *noun* (*pl.* **-os**): *to make pop promos*

prom·on·tory /ˈprɒməntri; *AmE* ˈprɑːməntɔːri/ *noun* (*pl.* **-ies**) a long narrow area of high land that goes out into the sea: *a rocky promontory overlooking the bay*—picture at COAST

pro·mote /prəˈməʊt; *AmE* -ˈmoʊt/ *verb* [VN] **1** to help sth to happen or develop: *policies to promote economic growth* ◊ *a campaign to promote awareness of environmental issues* **2** ~ **sth (as sth)** to help sell a product, service, etc. or make it more popular by advertising it or offering it at a special price: *The band has gone on tour to promote their new album.* ◊ *The area is being promoted as a tourist destination.* **3** ~ **sb (from sth) (to sth)** [often passive] to move sb to a higher rank or more senior job: *She worked hard and was soon promoted.* ◊ *He has been promoted to sergeant.* **OPP** DEMOTE **4** ~ **sth (from sth) (to sth)** to move a sports team from playing with one group of teams to playing in a better group: *They were promoted to the First Division last season.* **OPP** RELEGATE

pro·moter /prəˈməʊtə(r); *AmE* -ˈmoʊ-/ *noun* **1** a person or company that organizes or provides money for an artistic performance or a sporting event **2** ~ **of sth** a person who tries to persuade others about the value or importance of sth: *She became a leading promoter of European integration.*

pro·mo·tion /prəˈməʊʃn; *AmE* -ˈmoʊʃn/ *noun* **1** [U, C] ~ **(to sth)** a move to a more important job or rank in a company or an organization: *Her promotion to Sales Manager took everyone by surprise.* ◊ *The new job is a promotion for him.* ◊ *a job with excellent promotion prospects* **2** [U] ~ **(to sth)** a move by a sports team from playing in one group of teams to playing in a better group: *the team's promotion to the First Division* **OPP** RELEGATION **3** [C, U] activities done in order to increase the sales of a product or service; a set of advertisements for a particular product or service: *Her job is mainly concerned with sales and promotion.* ◊ *We are doing a special promotion of Chilean wines.* **4** [U] ~ **of sth** (*formal*) activity that encourages people to believe in the value or importance of sth, or that helps sth to succeed: *a society for the promotion of religious tolerance*

pro·mo·tion·al /prəˈməʊʃənl; *AmE* -ˈmoʊ-/ *adj.* connected with advertising: *promotional literature/material/videos*

prompt /prɒmpt; *AmE* prɑːmpt/ *adj., verb, noun, adv.*

■ *adj.* **1** done without delay **SYN** IMMEDIATE: *Prompt action was required as the fire spread.* ◊ *Prompt payment of the invoice would be appreciated.* **2** [not before noun] (of a person) acting without delay; arriving at the right time: *Please be prompt when attending these meetings.* ▶ **prompt·ness** *noun* [U]

■ *verb* **1** to make sb decide to do sth; to cause sth to happen: [VN] *The discovery of the bomb prompted an increase in security.* ◊ *His speech prompted an angry outburst from a man in the crowd.* ◊ [VN to inf] *The thought of her daughter's wedding day prompted her to lose some weight.* **2** to encourage sb to speak by asking them questions or suggesting words that they could say: [VN] *She was too nervous to speak and had to be prompted.* ◊ (*computing*) *The program will prompt you to enter data where required.* ◊ [V speech] *'And then what happened?' he prompted.* [also VN speech] **3** [VN, V] to follow the text of a play and remind the actors what the words are if they forget their lines

■ *noun* **1** a word or words said to an actor, to remind them what to say next when they have forgotten **2** (*computing*) a sign on a computer screen that shows that the computer has finished doing sth and is ready for more instructions

■ *adv.* exactly at the time mentioned: *The meeting will begin at ten o'clock prompt.*

prompt·er /ˈprɒmptə(r); *AmE* ˈprɑːm-/ *noun* a person who prompts actors in a play

prompt·ing /ˈprɒmptɪŋ; *AmE* ˈprɑːm-/ *noun* [U] (also **promptings**) [pl.] an act of persuading sb to do sth: *He wrote the letter without further prompting.* ◊ *Never again would she listen to the promptings of her heart.*

prompt·ly /ˈprɒmptli; *AmE* ˈprɑːm-/ *adv.* **1** without delay: *She deals with all the correspondence promptly and efficiently.* **2** exactly at the correct time or at the time mentioned **SYN** PUNCTUALLY: *They arrived promptly at two o'clock.* **3** (always used before the verb) immediately: *She read the letter and promptly burst into tears.*

pro·mul·gate /ˈprɒmlɡeɪt; *AmE* ˈprɑːm-/ *verb* [VN] (*formal*) **1** [usually passive] to spread an idea, a belief, etc. among many people **2** to announce a new law or system officially or publicly ▶ **pro·mul·ga·tion** /ˌprɒmlˈɡeɪʃn; *AmE* ˌprɑːm-/ *noun* [U]

prone /prəʊn; *AmE* proʊn/ *adj.* **1** ~ **to sth/to do sth** likely to suffer from sth or to do sth bad **SYN** LIABLE: *prone to infection/injury* ◊ *Working without a break makes you more prone to error.* ◊ *Tired drivers were found to be particularly prone to ignore warning signs.* **2** (-prone) (in adjectives) likely to suffer or do the thing mentioned: *error-prone* ◊ *injury-prone*—see also ACCIDENT-PRONE **3** (*formal*) lying flat with the front of your body touching the ground **SYN** PROSTRATE: *The victim lay prone without moving.* ◊ *He was found lying in a prone position.*—compare SUPINE ▶ **prone·ness** /ˈprəʊnnəs; *AmE* ˈproʊn-/ *noun* [U]: *proneness to depression/injury*

prong /prɒŋ; *AmE* prɔːŋ; prɑːŋ/ *noun* **1** each of the two or more long pointed parts of a fork—picture at CUTLERY **2** each of the separate parts of an attack, argument, etc., that move towards a place, subject, etc. from different positions **3** (-pronged) (in adjectives) having the number or type of prongs mentioned: *a two-pronged fork* ◊ *a three-pronged attack*

pro·nom·inal /prəʊˈnɒmɪnl; *AmE* proʊˈnɑːm-/ *adj.* (*grammar*) relating to a pronoun: *a pronominal reference to an object* (= the use of the pronoun *it* to replace the name of the object)

pro·noun /ˈprəʊnaʊn; *AmE* ˈproʊ-/ *noun* (*grammar*) a word that is used instead of a noun or noun phrase, for example *he, it, hers, me, them,* etc: *demonstrative/interrogative/possessive/relative pronouns*—see also PERSONAL PRONOUN

aɪ	aʊ	eɪ	əʊ	oʊ	ɔɪ	ɪə	eə	ʊə	j	w
my	now	say	go	go	boy	near	hair	pure	yes	wet
			(BrE)	(AmE)						

pro·nounce /prə'naʊns/ *verb* **1** [VN] to make the sound of a word or letter in a particular way: *Very few people can pronounce my name correctly.* ◇ *The 'b' in lamb is not pronounced.*— see also PRONUNCIATION, UNPRONOUNCEABLE **2** to say or give sth formally, officially or publicly: [VN] *to pronounce an opinion* ◇ *The judge will pronounce sentence today.* ◇ [VN-N] *She pronounced him the winner of the competition.* ◇ *I now pronounce you man and wife* (= in a marriage ceremony). ◇ [VN-ADJ] *She was pronounced dead on arrival at the hospital.* ◇ [VN to inf] *He pronounced the country to be in a state of war.* [also V that, V speech] PHRV **pro'nounce for/against sb** (*law*) to give a judgement in a court of law for or against sb: *The judge pronounced for* (= in favour of) *the defendant.* **pro'nounce on/upon sth** (*formal*) to state your opinion on sth, or give a decision about sth: *He feels able to pronounce on all kinds of subjects.* ◇ *The minister will pronounce on further security measures later today.*

pro·nounce·able /prə'naʊnsəbl/ *adj.* (of sounds or words) that can be pronounced OPP UNPRONOUNCEABLE

pro·nounced /prə'naʊnst/ *adj.* very noticeable, obvious or strongly expressed SYN DEFINITE: *He walked with a pronounced limp.* ◇ *She has very pronounced views on art.*

pro·nounce·ment /prə'naʊnsmənt/ *noun* (*formal*) ~ (**on sth**) a formal public statement: *She made an official pronouncement on changes in government policy.*

pronto /'prɒntəʊ; *AmE* 'prɑːntoʊ/ *adv.* (*informal*) quickly; immediately: *I expect to see you back here, pronto!*

pro·nun·ci·ation /prə,nʌnsi'eɪʃn/ *noun* **1** [U, C] the way in which a language or a particular word or sound is pronounced: *a guide to English pronunciation* ◇ *There is more than one pronunciation of 'garage'.* **2** [sing.] the way in which a particular person pronounces the words of a language: *Your pronunciation is excellent.*

proof /pruːf/ *noun, adj., verb*
▪ *noun* **1** [U, C] ~ (**of sth/that …**) information, documents, etc. that show that sth is true: *positive/conclusive proof* ◇ *Can you provide any proof of identity?* ◇ *Keep the receipt as proof of purchase.* ◇ *There is no proof that the knife belonged to her.* ◇ *These results are a further proof of his outstanding ability.* **2** [U] the process of testing whether sth is true or a fact: *Is the claim capable of proof?*—see also BURDEN OF PROOF **3** [C] (*mathematics*) a way of proving that a statement is true or that what you have calculated is correct **4** [C, usually pl.] a copy of printed material which is produced so that mistakes can be corrected: *She was checking the proofs of her latest novel.* **5** [U] a standard used to measure the strength of alcoholic drinks: *What proof is this whisky?* ◇ (*BrE*) *The purest whisky is 80% proof.* ◇ (*AmE*) *It's 160* (= degrees) *proof.* IDM **the proof of the 'pudding (is in the 'eating)** (*saying*) you can only judge if sth is good or bad when you have tried it—more at LIVING *adj.*
▪ *adj.* **1** ~ **against sth** (*formal*) that can resist the damaging or harmful effects of sth: *The sea wall was not proof against the strength of the waves.* **2** (in compounds) that can resist or protect against the thing mentioned: *rainproof/windproof clothing* ◇ *The car has childproof locks on the rear doors.* ◇ *an inflation-proof pension plan*
▪ *verb* [VN] **1** to put a special substance on sth, especially fabric, to protect it against water, fire, etc: *proofed canvas* **2** to produce a test copy of a piece of printed work so that mistakes can be corrected: *colour proofing*

proof·read /'pruːfriːd/ *verb* (**proof·read, proof·read** /-red/) to read and correct a piece of written or printed work: [VN] *Has this document been proofread?* [also V] ▸ **proof·read·er** *noun*: *to work as a proofreader for a publishing company*

prop /prɒp; *AmE* prɑːp/ *noun, verb*
▪ *noun* **1** a piece of wood, metal, etc. used to support sth or keep it in position: *Rescuers used props to stop the roof of the tunnel collapsing.* ◇ *a pit prop* (= one used in a coal mine) **2** a person or thing that gives help or support to sb/sth that is weak: *After being the emotional prop he*

needed for so long, she dared not leave him. **3** [usually pl.] a small object used by actors during the performance of a play or in a film/movie: *He is responsible for all the stage props and lighting.* **4** (also **'prop forward**) (in rugby) a player on either side of the front row of a SCRUM
▪ *verb* (-**pp**-) ~ **sth/sb** (**up**) (**against sth**) to support an object by leaning it against sth, or putting sth under it etc.; to support a person in the same way: [VN, +adv./prep.] *She propped his bike against the wall.* ◇ *She propped herself up on one elbow.* ◇ *He lay propped against the pillows.* ◇ [VN-ADJ] *The door was propped open.* PHRV **,prop sth↔'up 1** to prevent sth from falling by putting sth under it to support it: *They had to prop up the tree with long poles under the branches.* **2** (often *disapproving*) to help sth that is having difficulties: *The government was accused of propping up declining industries.*

propa·ganda /,prɒpə'gændə; *AmE* ,prɑːpə-/ *noun* [U] (usually *disapproving*) ideas or statements that may be false or exaggerated and that are used in order to gain support for a political leader, party, etc: *enemy propaganda* ◇ *a propaganda campaign*

propa·gand·ist /,prɒpə'gændɪst; *AmE* ,prɑːpə-/ *noun* (*formal*, usually *disapproving*) a person who creates or spreads propaganda ▸ **propa·gand·ist** *adj.* [only before noun]: *a propagandist organization*

propa·gate /'prɒpəgeɪt; *AmE* 'prɑːp-/ *verb* **1** [VN] (*formal*) to spread an idea, a belief or a piece of information among many people: *Television advertising propagates a false image of the ideal family.* **2** (*technical*) to produce new plants from a parent plant: [VN] *The plant can be propagated from seed.* ◇ [V] *Plants won't propagate in these conditions.* ▸ **propa·ga·tion** /,prɒpə'geɪʃn; *AmE* ,prɑːp-/ *noun* [U]

pro·pane /'prəʊpeɪn; *AmE* 'proʊ-/ *noun* [U] a colourless gas found in natural gas and PETROLEUM and used as a fuel for cooking and heating: *a propane gas cylinder*

pro·pel /prə'pel/ *verb* (-**ll**-) [VN] (often *passive*) **1** to move, drive or push sth forward or in a particular direction: *mechanically propelled vehicles* ◇ *He succeeded in propelling the ball across the line.* **2** [+adv./prep.] to force sb to move in a particular direction or to get into a particular situation: *He was grabbed from behind and propelled through the door.* ◇ *Fury propelled her into action.*—see also PROPULSION

pro·pel·lant /prə'pelənt/ *noun* [C, U] **1** a gas that forces out the contents of an AEROSOL **2** a thing or substance that propels sth, for example the fuel that fires a rocket

pro·pel·ler /prə'pelə(r)/ *noun* a device with two or more blades that turn quickly and cause a ship or an aircraft to move forward

pro·pen·sity /prə'pensəti/ *noun* (*pl.* -**ies**) ~ (**for sth**) | ~ (**for doing sth**) | ~ (**to do sth**) (*formal*) a tendency to a particular kind of behaviour: *He showed a propensity for violence.* ◇ *She has a propensity to exaggerate.*

proper /'prɒpə(r); *AmE* 'prɑːp-/ *adj.* **1** [only before noun] (*especially BrE*) right, appropriate or correct; according to the rules: *We should have had a proper discussion before voting.* ◇ *Please follow the proper procedures for dealing with complaints.* ◇ *Nothing is in its proper place.* **2** [only before noun] (*BrE, spoken*) that you consider to be real and satisfactory: *Eat some proper food, not just toast and jam!* ◇ *When are you going to get a proper job?* **3** socially and morally acceptable: *It is right and proper that parents take responsibility for their children's attendance at school.* ◇ *The development was planned without proper regard to the interests of local people.* ◇ *He is always perfectly proper in his behaviour.* OPP IMPROPER—see also PROPRIETY **4** [after noun] according to the most exact meaning of the word: *The celebrations proper always begin on the last stroke of midnight.* **5** [only before noun] (*BrE, spoken*) complete: *We're in a proper mess now.* **6** ~ **to sth** (*formal*) belonging to a particular type of thing; natural in a particular situation or place: *They should be treated with the dignity proper to all individuals created by God.* IDM **,good and 'proper** (*BrE, spoken*) completely; thoroughly: *That's messed things up good and proper.*

prop·er·ly /'prɒpəli; *AmE* 'prɑːpərli/ *adv.* **1** (*especially*

b	d	f	g	h	k	l	m	n	p	r
bad	did	fall	get	hat	cat	leg	man	now	pen	red

BrE) in a way that is correct and/or appropriate: *How much money do we need to do the job properly?* ◊ *The television isn't working properly.* ◊ *Make sure the letter is properly addressed.* **2** in a way that is socially or morally acceptable: *You acted perfectly properly in approaching me first.* ◊ *When will these kids learn to behave properly?* [OPP] IMPROPERLY **3** really; in fact: *He had usurped powers that properly belonged to parliament.* ◊ *The subject is not, properly speaking* (= really), *a science.*

,proper 'noun (also **,proper 'name**) *noun* (*grammar*) a word that is the name of a person, a place, an institution, etc. and is written with a capital letter, for example *Tom, Mrs Jones, Rome, Europe, the Rhine, the Houses of Parliament*—compare ABSTRACT NOUN, COMMON NOUN

prop·er·tied /'prɒpətid; *AmE* 'prɑːpərtid/ *adj.* [only before noun] (*formal*) owning property, especially land

prop·erty /'prɒpəti; *AmE* 'prɑːpərti/ *noun* (*pl.* **-ies**) **1** [U] a thing or things that are owned by sb; a possession or possessions: *This building is government property.* ◊ *Be careful not to damage other people's property.*—see also INTELLECTUAL PROPERTY, LOST PROPERTY, PUBLIC PROPERTY **2** [U] land and buildings: *The price of property has risen enormously.* ◊ *property prices* ◊ *a property developer* **3** [C] a building or buildings and the surrounding land: *There are a lot of empty properties in the area.* **4** [C, usually pl.] (*formal*) a quality or characteristic that sth has: *Compare the physical properties of the two substances.* ◊ *a plant with medicinal properties*

proph·ecy /'prɒfəsi; *AmE* 'prɑːf-/ *noun* (*pl.* **-ies**) **1** [C] a statement that will happen in the future, especially one made by sb with religious or magic powers: *to fulfil a prophecy* (= make it come true) **2** [U] (*formal*) the power of being able to say what will happen in the future: *She was believed to have the gift of prophecy.*

proph·esy /'prɒfəsaɪ; *AmE* 'prɑːf-/ *verb* (**proph·es·ies**, **proph·esy·ing**, **proph·es·ied**, **proph·es·ied**) to say what will happen in the future (done in the past using religious or magic powers): [VN] *to prophesy war* ◊ *The event was prophesied in the Old Testament.* ◊ [V that] *She prophesied that she would win a gold medal.* [also V speech]

prophet /'prɒfit; *AmE* 'prɑːf-/ *noun* **1** [C] (in the Christian, Jewish and Muslim religions) a person sent by God to teach the people and give them messages from God: *an Old Testament prophet* ◊ *Hebrew prophets* **2** (**the Prophet**) [sing.] Muhammad, who FOUNDED the religion of Islam **3** a person who claims to know what will happen in the future **4** ~ (**of sth**) a person who teaches or supports a new idea, theory, etc: *William Morris was one of the early prophets of socialism.* **5** (**the Prophets**) [pl.] the name used for some books of the Old Testament and the Hebrew Bible [IDM] see DOOM *n.*

proph·et·ess /'prɒfites; ˌprɒfi'tes; *AmE* 'prɑːfətes/ *noun* a woman who is a prophet (1, 3, 4)

proph·et·ic /prə'fetɪk/ *adj.* (*formal*) **1** correctly stating or showing what will happen in the future: *Many of his warnings proved prophetic.* **2** like or connected with a prophet or prophets: *the prophetic books of the Old Testament* ◊ *prophetic zeal* ▶ **proph·et·ic·al·ly** /prə'fetɪkli/ *adv.*

prophy·lac·tic /ˌprɒfi'læktɪk; *AmE* ˌprɑːf-/ *adj.*, *noun*
■ *adj.* (*medical*) done or used in order to prevent a disease: *prophylactic treatment*
■ *noun* (*formal* or *technical*) **1** a medicine, device or course of action that prevents disease **2** (*AmE*) = CONDOM

pro·pin·quity /prə'pɪŋkwəti/ *noun* [U] (*formal*) the state of being near in space or time [SYN] PROXIMITY

pro·piti·ate /prə'pɪʃieɪt/ *verb* [VN] (*formal*) to stop sb from being angry by trying to please them [SYN] PLACATE: *Sacrifices were made to propitiate the gods.* ▶ **pro·piti·ation** /prəˌpɪʃi'eɪʃn/ *noun* [U]

pro·pi·tious /prə'pɪʃəs/ *adj.* ~ (**for sth/sb**) (*formal*) likely to produce a successful result: *It was not a propitious time to start a new business.*

pro·pon·ent /prə'pəʊnənt; *AmE* -'poʊ-/ *noun* ~ (**of sth**) (*formal*) a person who supports an idea or course of action [SYN] ADVOCATE

pro·por·tion /prə'pɔːʃn; *AmE* -'pɔːrʃn/ *noun*

PART OF WHOLE **1** [C+sing./pl. *v.*] a part or share of a whole: *Water covers a large proportion of the earth's surface.* ◊ *Loam is a soil with roughly equal proportions of clay, sand and silt.* ◊ *The proportion of regular smokers increases with age.* ◊ *A higher proportion of Americans go on to higher education than is the case in Britain.*

RELATIONSHIP **2** [U] ~ (**of sth to sth**) the relationship of one thing to another in size, amount, etc. [SYN] RATIO: *The proportion of men to women in the college has changed dramatically over the years.* ◊ *The basic ingredients are limestone and clay in the proportion 2:1.* ◊ *The room is very long in proportion to* (= relative to) *its width.* **3** [U, C, usually pl.] the correct relationship in size, degree, importance, etc. between one thing and another or between the parts of a whole: *You haven't drawn the figures in the foreground in proportion.* ◊ *The head is out of proportion with the body.* ◊ *an impressive building with fine proportions* ◊ *Always try to keep a sense of proportion* (= of the relative importance of different things).

SIZE/SHAPE **4** (**proportions**) [pl.] the measurements of sth; its size and shape: *This method divides the task into more manageable proportions.* ◊ *a food shortage that could soon reach crisis proportions* ◊ *a room of fairly generous proportions*

MATHEMATICS **5** [U] the equal relationship between two pairs of numbers, as in the statement '4 is to 8 as 6 is to 12'

[IDM] **,keep sth in pro'portion** to react to sth in a sensible way and not think it is worse or more serious than it really is **out of (all) pro'portion (to sth)** larger, more serious, etc. in relation to sth than is necessary or appropriate: *They earn salaries out of all proportion to their ability.* ◊ *The media have blown the incident up out of all proportion.*

> **GRAMMAR POINT**
> **proportion**
>
> If **proportion** is used with an uncountable or a singular noun, the verb is generally singular: *A proportion of the land is used for agriculture.*
>
> If **the proportion of** is used with a plural countable noun, or a singular noun that represents a group of people, the verb is usually singular, but with **a (large, small, etc.) proportion of** a plural verb is often used, especially in *BrE*: *The proportion of small cars on America's roads is increasing.* ◊ *A high proportion of five-year-olds have teeth in poor condition.*

pro·por·tion·al /prə'pɔːʃənl; *AmE* -'pɔːrʃ-/ *adj.* ~ (**to sth**) of an appropriate size, amount or degree in comparison with sth: *Salary is proportional to years of experience.* ◊ *to be directly/inversely proportional to sth* ▶ **pro·por·tion·al·ly** *adv.*: *Families with children spend proportionally less per person than families without children.*

pro·por·tion·al·ity /prəˌpɔːʃə'næləti; *AmE* -pɔːrʃ-/ *noun* [U] (*formal*) the principle that an action, a punishment, etc. should not be more severe than is necessary

pro,portional ,represen'tation *noun* [U] (*abbr.* PR) a system that gives each party in an election a number of seats in relation to the number of votes its candidates receive—compare FIRST-PAST-THE-POST

pro·por·tion·ate /prə'pɔːʃənət; *AmE* -'pɔːrʃ-/ *adj.* ~ (**to sth**) (*formal*) increasing or decreasing in size, amount or degree according to changes in sth else [SYN] PROPORTIONAL: *Increasing costs resulted in proportionate increases in prices.* ◊ *The number of accidents is proportionate to the increased volume of traffic.*—compare DISPROPORTIONATE ▶ **pro·por·tion·ate·ly** *adv.*: *Prices have risen but wages have not risen proportionately.*

pro·por·tioned /prə'pɔːʃənd; *AmE* -'pɔːrʃ-/ *adj.* (used especially after an adverb) having parts that relate in size to other parts in the way that is described: *a well-proportioned living room* ◊ *She was tall and perfectly proportioned.*

pro·posal /prə'pəʊzl; *AmE* -'poʊzl/ *noun* **1** [C, U] ~ (for sth)| ~ (to do sth)| ~ (that ...) a formal suggestion or plan; the act of making a suggestion: *to submit/consider/accept/reject a proposal* ◊ *a proposal to build more office accommodation* ◊ *His proposal that the system should be changed was rejected.* ◊ *They judged that the time was right for the proposal of new terms for the trade agreement.* **2** [C] an act of formally asking sb to marry you

pro·pose /prəˈpəʊz; *AmE* -ˈpoʊz/ *verb*
SUGGEST PLAN | **1** (*formal*) to suggest a plan, an idea, etc. for people to think about and decide on: [VN] *The government proposed changes to the voting system.* ◊ *What would you propose?* ◊ [Vthat] *She proposed that the book be banned.* ◊ (*BrE* also) *She proposed that the book should be banned.* ◊ [VNthat] *It was proposed that the president be elected for a period of two years.* ◊ [V-ing] *He proposed changing the name of the company.* ◊ [VNtoinf] *It was proposed to pay the money from public funds.* **HELP** This pattern is only used in the passive.
INTEND | **2** to intend to do sth: [Vtoinf] *What do you propose to do now?* ◊ [V-ing] *How do you propose getting home?*
MARRIAGE | **3** ~ (sth) (to sb) to ask sb to marry you: [V] *He was afraid that if he proposed she might refuse.* ◊ *She proposed to me!* ◊ [VN] *to propose marriage*
AT FORMAL MEETING | **4** [VN] ~ sth| ~ sb (for/as sth) to suggest sth at a formal meeting and ask people to vote on it: *I propose Tom Ellis for chairman.* ◊ *to propose a motion* (= to be the main speaker in support of an idea at a formal debate)—compare OPPOSE, SECOND
SUGGEST EXPLANATION | **5** [VN] (*formal*) to suggest an explanation of sth for people to consider SYN PROPOUND: *She proposed a possible solution to the mystery.*
IDM propose a 'toast (to sb) | propose sb's 'health to ask people to wish sb health, happiness and success by raising their glasses and drinking: *I'd like to propose a toast to the bride and groom.*

pro·poser /prəˈpəʊzə(r); *AmE* -ˈpoʊz-/ *noun* a person who formally suggests sth at a meeting—compare SECONDER

prop·os·ition /ˌprɒpəˈzɪʃn; *AmE* ˌprɑːp-/ *noun, verb*
▪ *noun* **1** an idea or a plan of action that is suggested, especially in business: *I'd like to put a business proposition to you.* ◊ *He was trying to make it look like an attractive proposition.* **2** a thing that you intend to do; a problem or task to be dealt with: *Getting a work permit in the UK is not always a simple proposition.* **3** (also **Proposition**) (in the US) a suggested change to the law that people can vote on: *How did you vote on Proposition 8?* **4** (*formal*) a statement that expresses an opinion: *Her assessment is based on the proposition that power corrupts.* **5** (*mathematics*) a statement of a THEOREM, and an explanation of how it can be proved
▪ *verb* [VN] to say in a direct way to sb that you would like to have sex with them: *She was propositioned by a strange man in the bar.*

pro·pound /prəˈpaʊnd/ *verb* [VN] (*formal*) to suggest an idea or explanation of sth for people to consider SYN PROPOSE: *the theory of natural selection, first propounded by Charles Darwin*

pro·pri·etary /prəˈpraɪətri; *AmE* -teri/ *adj.* [usually before noun] **1** (of goods) made and sold by a particular company and protected by a REGISTERED TRADEMARK: *a proprietary medicine* ◊ *proprietary brands* ◊ *a proprietary name* **2** relating to an owner or to the fact of owning sth: *The company has a proprietary right to the property.*

pro·pri·etor /prəˈpraɪətə(r)/ *noun* (*formal*) the owner of a business, a hotel, etc: *newspaper proprietors* ◊ *Enquiries must be made to the proprietor.* ▶ **pro·pri·etor·ship** /prəˈpraɪətəʃɪp; *AmE* -tərʃ-/ *noun* [U]—see also PROPRIETRESS

pro·pri·etor·ial /prəˌpraɪəˈtɔːriəl/ *adj.* (*formal*) relating to an owner or to the fact of owning sth: *proprietorial rights* ◊ *He laid a proprietorial hand on her arm* (= as if he owned her). ▶ **pro·pri·etor·ial·ly** *adv.*

pro·pri·etress /prəˈpraɪətres/ *noun* (*old-fashioned*) a woman who owns a business, hotel, etc.—see also PROPRIETOR

pro·pri·ety /prəˈpraɪəti/ *noun* (*formal*) **1** [U] moral and social behaviour that is considered to be correct and

acceptable: *Nobody questioned the propriety of her being there alone.* OPP IMPROPRIETY **2** (the proprieties) [pl.] the rules of correct behaviour: *They were careful to observe the proprieties.* ◊ *The company had acted in accordance with all legal proprieties.*

pro·pul·sion /prəˈpʌlʃn/ *noun* [U] (*technical*) the force that drives sth forward: *wind/steam/jet propulsion* ◊ *The fish uses its tail fins for propulsion through the water.*—see also PROPEL ▶ **pro·pul·sive** /prəˈpʌlsɪv/ *adj.*

pro rata /ˌprəʊ ˈrɑːtə; *AmE* ˌproʊ/ *adj.* (from Latin, *formal*) (of a payment or share of sth) calculated according to how much of sth has been used, the amount of work done, etc. SYN PROPORTIONATE: *If costs go up, there will be a pro rata increase in prices.* ▶ **pro rata** *adv.*: *Prices will increase pro rata.*

pro·sa·ic /prəˈzeɪɪk/ *adj.* (*written*, usually *disapproving*) **1** ordinary and not showing any imagination: *a prosaic style/writer* **2** dull; not romantic SYN MUNDANE: *the prosaic side of life* ▶ **pro·sa·ic·al·ly** /-kli/ *adv.*

pro·scen·ium /prəˈsiːniəm/ *noun* the part of the stage in a theatre that is in front of the curtain: *a traditional theatre with a proscenium arch* (= an arch that forms a frame for the stage where the curtain is opened)

pro·scribe /prəˈskraɪb; *AmE* proʊ's-/ *verb* [VN] (*formal*) to say officially that sth is forbidden: *proscribed organizations* ▶ **pro·scrip·tion** /prəˈskrɪpʃn; *AmE* proʊ's-/ *noun* [U, C]

prose /prəʊz; *AmE* proʊz/ *noun* [U] writing that is not poetry: *the author's clear elegant prose* (= style of writing)

pros·ecute /ˈprɒsɪkjuːt; *AmE* ˈprɑːs-/ *verb* **1** ~ sb (for sth/doing sth) to officially charge sb with a crime in a court of law: [VN] *The company was prosecuted for breaching the Health and Safety Act.* ◊ *Trespassers will be prosecuted* (= a notice telling people to keep out of a particular area). ◊ [V] *The police decided not to prosecute.* **2** to be a lawyer in a court of law for a person or an organization that is charging sb with a crime: [V] *the prosecuting counsel/lawyer/attorney* ◊ *James Spencer, prosecuting, claimed that the witness was lying.* [alsoVN] **3** [VN] (*formal*) to continue taking part in or doing sth: *They had overwhelming public support to prosecute the war.*

pros·ecu·tion /ˌprɒsɪˈkjuːʃn; *AmE* ˌprɑːs-/ *noun* **1** [U, C] the process of trying to prove in a court of law that sb is guilty of a crime (= of prosecuting them); the process of being officially charged with a crime in a court of law: *Prosecution for a first minor offence rarely leads to imprisonment.* ◊ *He threatened to bring a private prosecution against the doctor.* **2** (the prosecution) [sing.+ sing./pl. v.] a person or an organization that prosecutes sb in a court of law, together with the lawyers, etc: *He was a witness for the prosecution.* ◊ *The prosecution has/have failed to prove its/their case.* ◊ *defence and prosecution* ◊ *a prosecution lawyer* **3** [U] (*formal*) the act of making sth happen or continue

pros·ecu·tor /ˈprɒsɪkjuːtə(r); *AmE* ˈprɑːs-/ *noun* **1** a public official who charges sb officially with a crime and prosecutes them in a court of law: *the public/state prosecutor* **2** a lawyer who leads the case against a DEFENDANT in a court of law

pros·elyt·ize (*BrE* also **-ise**) /ˈprɒsələtaɪz; *AmE* ˈprɑːs-/ *verb* [V] (*formal*, often *disapproving*) to try to persuade other people to accept your beliefs, especially about religion or politics

pros·ody /ˈprɒsədi; *AmE* ˈprɑːs-/ *noun* [U] (*technical*) the patterns of sounds and rhythms in poetry and speech; the study of this

pros·pect *noun, verb*
▪ *noun* /ˈprɒspekt; *AmE* ˈprɑːs-/ **1** [U, sing.] ~ (of sth/of doing sth)| ~ (that ...) the possibility that sth will happen: *There is no immediate prospect of peace.* ◊ *A place in the semi-finals is in prospect* (= likely to happen). ◊ *There's a reasonable prospect that his debts will be paid.* **2** [sing.] ~ (of sth/of doing sth) an idea of what might or will happen in the future: *an exciting prospect* ◊ *Travelling alone around the world is a daunting prospect.* ◊ *The prospect of becoming a father filled him with alarm.* **3** (prospects) [pl.] ~ (for/of sth) the chances of being

æ	ɑː	e	ɜː	ə	ɪ	iː	i	ɒ	ɔː	ʌ	ʊ	u	uː
cat	father	ten	bird	about	sit	see	many	got	saw	cup	put	actual	too
								(BrE)					

successful: *good job/employment/career prospects* ◊ *At 25 he was an unemployed musician with no prospects.* ◊ *Long-term prospects for the economy have improved.* ◊ *What are the prospects of promotion in this job?* **4** [C] ~ **(for sth)** a person who is likely to be successful in a competition: *She is one of Britain's best prospects for a gold medal.* **5** [C] (*written*) a wide view of an area of land, etc: *a delightful prospect of the lake*

■ *verb* /prə'spekt; *AmE* 'prɑ:spekt/ [V] ~ **(for sth)** to search an area for gold, minerals, oil, etc: *Thousands moved to the area to prospect for gold.* ◊ (*figurative*) *to prospect for new clients*

pro·spect·ive /prə'spektɪv/ *adj.* [usually before noun] **1** expected to do sth or to become sth SYN POTENTIAL: *a prospective buyer/client* **2** expected to happen soon SYN FORTHCOMING: *They are worried about prospective changes in the law.*

pro·spect·or /prə'spektə(r); *AmE* 'prɑ:spektər/ *noun* a person who searches an area for gold, minerals, oil, etc.

pro·spec·tus /prə'spektəs/ *noun* **1** a book or printed document that gives information about a school, college, etc. in order to advertise it **2** (*business*) a document that gives information about a company's SHARES before they are offered for sale

pros·per /'prɒspə(r); *AmE* 'prɑ:s-/ *verb* [V] to develop in a successful way; to be successful, especially financially SYN THRIVE: *The economy prospered under his administration.* ◊ *She seems to be prospering since she moved out of the city.*

pros·per·ity /prɒ'sperəti; *AmE* prɑ:s-/ *noun* [U] the state of being successful, especially financially SYN AFFLUENCE: *Our future prosperity depends on economic growth.* ◊ *The country is enjoying a period of peace and prosperity.*

pros·per·ous /'prɒspərəs; *AmE* 'prɑ:s-/ *adj.* rich and successful SYN AFFLUENT: *prosperous countries/cities/economies* ◊ *Farmers are more prosperous in the south of the country.*

pro·state /'prɒsteɪt; *AmE* 'prɑ:s-/ (also **prostate gland**) *noun* a small organ in men, near the BLADDER, that produces a liquid in which SPERM is carried

pros·thesis /prɒs'θi:sɪs; *AmE* prɑ:s-/ *noun* (*pl.* **prostheses** /-'θi:si:z/) (*medical*) an artificial part of the body, for example a limb, an eye or a tooth ▶ **pros·thet·ic** /prɒs'θetɪk; *AmE* prɑ:s-/ *adj.*: *a prosthetic arm*

pros·ti·tute /'prɒstɪtju:t; *AmE* 'prɑ:stətu:t/ *noun, verb*
■ *noun* a person who has sex for money
■ *verb* [VN] **1** ~ **sth/yourself** to use your skills, abilities, etc. to do sth that earns you money but that other people do not respect because you are capable of doing sth better: *Many felt he was prostituting his talents by writing Hollywood scripts.* **2** ~ **yourself** to work as a prostitute

pros·ti·tu·tion /ˌprɒstɪ'tju:ʃn; *AmE* ˌprɑ:stə'tu:ʃn/ *noun* [U] **1** the work of a prostitute: *Many women were forced into prostitution.* ◊ *child prostitution* **2** ~ **of sth** (*formal*) the use of your abilities on sth of little value

pros·trate *adj., verb*
■ *adj.* /'prɒstreɪt; *AmE* 'prɑ:s-/ (*written*) **1** lying on the ground and facing downwards: *They fell prostrate in worship.* ◊ *He stumbled over Luke's prostrate body.* **2** ~ **(with sth)** so shocked, upset, etc. that you cannot do anything: *She was prostrate with grief after her son's death.*
■ *verb* /prɒ'streɪt; *AmE* 'prɑ:streɪt/ [VN] (*written*) **1** ~ **yourself** to lie on your front with your face looking downwards, especially as an act of worship **2** [usually passive] to make sb feel weak, shocked, and unable to do anything: *He was expecting to find her prostrated by the tragedy.* ◊ *For months he was prostrated with grief.*

pros·tra·tion /prɒ'streɪʃn; *AmE* prɑ:'s-/ *noun* [U] (*written*) **1** extreme physical weakness: *a state of prostration brought on by the heat* **2** the action of lying with your face downwards, especially in worship

prot·ag·on·ist /prə'tægənɪst/ *noun* (*formal*) **1** the main character in a play, film/movie or book **2** one of the main people in a real event, especially a competition, battle or struggle **3** an active supporter of a policy or movement, especially one that is trying to change sth: *a leading protagonist of the conservation movement*

pro·tean /'prəʊtiən; prəʊ'ti:ən; *AmE* 'proʊ-; proʊ't-/ *adj.* (*literary*) able to change quickly and easily: *a protean character*

pro·tect /prə'tekt/ *verb* **1** ~ **(sb/sth) (against/from sth)** to make sure that sb/sth is not harmed, injured, damaged, etc: [VN] *Troops have been sent to protect aid workers against attack.* ◊ *They huddled together to protect themselves from the wind.* ◊ *Each company is fighting to protect its own commercial interests.* ◊ [V] *a paint that helps protect against rust* **2** [VN] [usually passive] to introduce laws that make it illegal to kill, harm or damage a particular animal, area of land, building, etc: *a protected area/species* **3** [VN] [usually passive] to help an industry in your own country by taxing goods from other countries so that there is less competition: *protected markets* **4** ~ **(sb/sth) (against sth)** to provide sb/sth with insurance against fire, injury, damage, etc: [VN] *Many policies do not protect you against personal injury.* [also V]

pro·tec·tion /prə'tekʃn/ *noun* **1** [U] ~ **(for/ of sb/sth) (against/from sth)** the act of protecting sb/sth; the state of being protected: *Remember to bring clothes that provide adequate protection against the wind and rain.* ◊ *He asked to be put under police protection.* ◊ *the conservation and protection of the environment* ◊ *consumer/child/data protection laws* **2** [C] ~ **(against sth)** a thing that protects sb/sth against sth: *They wore the charm as a protection against evil spirits.* **3** [U] ~ **(against sth)** insurance against fire, injury, damage, etc: *Our policy offers complete protection against fire and theft.* **4** [U] the system of helping an industry in your own country by taxing foreign goods: *The government is ready to introduce protection for the car industry.* **5** [U] the system of paying criminals so that they will not attack your business or property: *to pay protection money* ◊ *to run a protection racket*

pro·tec·tion·ism /prə'tekʃənɪzəm/ *noun* [U] the principle or practice of protecting a country's own industry by taxing foreign goods ▶ **pro·tec·tion·ist** /-ʃənɪst/ *adj.*: *protectionist measures/policies*

pro·tect·ive /prə'tektɪv/ *adj.* **1** [only before noun] providing or intended to provide protection: *Workers should wear full protective clothing.* ◊ *a protective layer of varnish* ◊ *a protective barrier against the sun's rays* **2** ~ **(of/ towards sb/sth)** having or showing a wish to protect sb/sth: *She had been fiercely protective towards him as a teenager.* ◊ *He was extremely protective of his role as advisor.* ◊ *He put a protective arm around her shoulders.* ◊ *Parents can easily become over-protective of their children* (= want to protect them too much). **3** intended to give an advantage to your own country's industry: *protective legislation/tariffs* ▶ **pro·tect·ive·ly** *adv.*: *She clutched her bag protectively.* **pro·tect·ive·ness** *noun* [U]

pro,tective 'custody *noun* [U] the state of being kept in prison for your own safety

pro·tect·or /prə'tektə(r)/ *noun* a person, an organization or a thing that protects sb/sth: *I regarded him as my friend and protector.* ◊ *the company's image as a protector of the environment* ◊ *Hard hats and ear protectors are provided.*

pro·tect·or·ate /prə'tektərət/ *noun* **1** [C] a country that is controlled and protected by a more powerful country: *a British protectorate*—compare COLONY **2** [U] the state or period of being controlled and protected by another country

pro·tégé (*feminine* **pro·té·gée**) /'prɒtəʒeɪ; *AmE* 'proʊt-/ *noun* (from *French*) a young person who is helped in their career and personal development by a more experienced person: *a protégé of the great violinist Yehudi Menuhin*

pro·tein /'prəʊti:n; *AmE* 'proʊ-/ *noun* [C, U] a natural substance found in meat, eggs, fish, some vegetables, etc. There are many different proteins and they are an essential part of what humans and animals eat to help them grow and stay healthy: *essential proteins and vitamins* ◊ *protein deficiency* ◊ *Peas, beans and lentils are a good source of vegetable protein.*

pro tem /ˌprəʊ 'tem; *AmE* ˌproʊ/ *adv.* (from *Latin*) for now, but not for a long time SYN TEMPORARILY: *a new*

aɪ	aʊ	eɪ	əʊ	oʊ	ɔɪ	ɪə	eə	ʊə	j	w
my	now	say	go	go	boy	near	hair	pure	yes	wet
			(BrE)	(AmE)						

manager will be appointed pro tem ▶ **pro tem** *adj.*: *A pro tem committee was formed from existing members.*

pro·test *noun, verb*

■ *noun* /ˈprəʊtest; AmE ˈproʊ-/ [U, C] ~ **(against sth)** the expression of strong disagreement with or opposition to sth; a statement or an action that shows this: *The director resigned in protest at the decision.* ◊ *The announcement raised a storm of protest.* ◊ *a protest march* ◊ *She accepted the charge without protest.* ◊ *The workers staged a protest against the proposed changes in their contracts.* ◊ *The building work will go ahead, despite protests from local residents.* ◊ *The riot began as a peaceful protest.* IDM **under ˈprotest** unwillingly and after expressing disagreement: *She wrote a letter of apology but only under protest.*

■ *verb* /prəˈtest; AmE also ˈproʊ-/ **1** ~ **(about/against/at sth)** to say or do sth to show that you disagree with or disapprove of sth, especially publicly: [V] *Students took to the streets to protest against the decision.* ◊ *The victim's widow protested at the leniency of the sentence.* ◊ *There's no use protesting, I won't change my mind.* ◊ [VN] *(AmE) They fully intend to protest the decision.* **2** to say firmly that sth is true, especially when you have been accused of sth or when other people do not believe you: [VN] *She has always protested her innocence.* ◊ [V that] *He protested that the journey was too far by car.* ◊ [V speech] *'That's not what you said earlier!' Jane protested.*

Prot·est·ant /ˈprɒtɪstənt; AmE ˈprɑːt-/ *noun* a member of a part of the Western Christian Church that separated from the Roman Catholic Church in the 16th century: *He's a Protestant.* ▶ **Prot·est·ant** *adj.*: *The majority of the population is Protestant.* ◊ *a Protestant church/country* **Prot·est·ant·ism** /ˈprɒtɪstəntɪzəm; AmE ˈprɑːt-/ *noun* [U]

pro·test·ation /ˌprɒtəˈsteɪʃn; AmE ˌprɑːt-/ *noun* [C, U] *(formal)* a strong statement that sth is true, especially when other people do not believe you: *She repeated her protestation of innocence.* ◊ *Despite his protestation to the contrary, he was extremely tired.*

pro·test·er /prəˈtestə(r)/ *noun* a person who makes a public protest: *Thousands of protesters marched through the city.*

proto- /ˈprəʊtəʊ; AmE ˈproʊtoʊ/ *combining form* (in nouns and adjectives) original; from which others develop: *prototype* ◊ *proto-modernist painters*

proto·col /ˈprəʊtəkɒl; AmE ˈproʊtəkɔːl; -kɑːl/ *noun* **1** [U] a system of fixed rules and formal behaviour used at official meetings, usually between governments: *a breach of protocol* ◊ *the protocol of diplomatic visits* **2** [C] *(technical)* the first or original version of an agreement, especially a TREATY between countries, etc.; an extra part added to an agreement or TREATY: *the first Geneva Protocol* ◊ *It is set out in a legally binding protocol which forms part of the treaty.* **3** [C] *(computing)* a set of rules that control the way data is sent between computers **4** [C] *(technical)* a plan for carrying out a scientific experiment or medical treatment

pro·ton /ˈprəʊtɒn; AmE ˈproʊtɑːn/ *noun* (physics) a very small piece of MATTER (= a substance) that forms part of the NUCLEUS (= central part) of an atom—see also ELECTRON, NEUTRON

proto·plasm /ˈprəʊtəplæzəm; AmE ˈproʊ-/ *noun* [U] *(biology)* a colourless substance like jelly which forms the living part of an animal or plant cell

proto·type /ˈprəʊtətaɪp; AmE ˈproʊ-/ *noun* ~ **(for/of sth)** the first design of sth from which other forms are copied or developed: *the prototype of the modern bicycle* ▶ **proto·typ·ical** /ˌprəʊtəˈtɪpɪkl; AmE ˌproʊ-/ *adj.*

proto·zoan /ˌprəʊtəˈzəʊən; AmE ˌproʊtəˈzoʊən/ (also **proto·zoon** /-ˈzəʊɒn; AmE -ˈzoʊɑːn/) *noun* (pl. **proto·zoans** or **proto·zoa** /-ˈzəʊə; AmE -ˈzoʊə/) *(biology)* a very small living thing, usually with only one cell, that can only be seen under a MICROSCOPE ▶ **proto·zoan** *adj.*

pro·tract·ed /prəˈtræktɪd; AmE also proʊˈt-/ *adj.* (written) lasting longer than expected or longer than usual: *protracted delays/disputes/negotiations*

pro·tract·or /prəˈtræktə(r); AmE also proʊˈt-/ *noun* an instrument for measuring and drawing angles, usually

made from a half circle of clear plastic with degrees (0° to 180°) marked on it

pro·trude /prəˈtruːd; AmE proʊ-/ *verb* [V] ~ **(from sth)** *(formal)* to stick out from a place or a surface: *protruding eyes/teeth* ◊ *His stomach protruded slightly.* ◊ *He hung his coat on a nail protruding from the wall.*

pro·tru·sion /prəˈtruːʒn; AmE proʊˈt-/ *noun* [C, U] *(formal)* a thing that sticks out from a place or surface; the fact of doing this: *a protrusion on the rock face*

pro·tu·ber·ance /prəˈtjuːbərəns; AmE proʊˈtuː-/ *noun* *(formal)* a round part that sticks out from a surface: *The diseased trees are marked by protuberances on their trunks.*

pro·tu·ber·ant /prəˈtjuːbərənt; AmE proʊˈtuː-/ *adj.* *(formal)* curving or swelling out from a surface: *protuberant eyes*

proud /praʊd/ *adj., adv.*

■ *adj.* (**proud·er**, **proud·est**)
PLEASED | **1** ~ **(of sb/sth)** | ~ **(to do sth)** | ~ **(that …)** feeling pleased and satisfied about sth that you own or have done, or are connected with: *proud parents* ◊ *the proud owner of a new car* ◊ *Your achievements are something to be proud of.* ◊ *He was proud of himself for not giving up.* ◊ *I feel very proud to be a part of the team.* ◊ *She was proud that her daughter had so much talent.*—see also HOUSE-PROUD **2** [only before noun] causing sb to feel pride: *This is the proudest moment of my life.* ◊ *The car had been his proudest possession.*

FEELING TOO IMPORTANT | **3** *(disapproving)* feeling that you are better and more important than other people SYN ARROGANT: *She was too proud to admit she could be wrong.* ◊ *He is too proud now to be seen with his former friends.*

HAVING SELF-RESPECT | **4** having respect for yourself and not wanting to lose the respect of others: *They were a proud and independent people.* ◊ *Don't be too proud to ask for help.*

BEAUTIFUL/TALL | **5** *(literary)* beautiful, tall and impressive: *The sunflowers stretched tall and proud to the sun.*—see also PRIDE

■ *adv.*
IDM **do sb ˈproud** *(old-fashioned, BrE)* to treat sb very well by giving them a lot of good food, entertainment, etc. **do yourself/sb ˈproud** to do sth that makes you proud of yourself or that makes other people proud of you

proud·ly /ˈpraʊdli/ *adv.* **1** in a way that shows that sb is proud of sth: *She proudly displayed her prize.* **2** *(literary)* in a way that is large and impressive: *The Matterhorn rose proudly in the background.*

prov·able /ˈpruːvəbl/ *adj.* that can be shown to be true SYN VERIFIABLE

prove /pruːv/ *verb* (**proved**, **proved**) or (**proved**, **proven** /ˈpruːvn/ especially in *AmE*) HELP In *BrE* **proved** is the more common form. Look also at **proven**.

WORD FAMILY
prove v. (≠ disprove)
proof n.
proven adj. (≠ unproven)

SHOW STH IS TRUE | **1** ~ **sth (to sb)** to use facts, evidence, etc. to show that sth is true: [VN] *They hope this new evidence will prove her innocence.* ◊ *'I know you're lying.' 'Prove it!'* ◊ *Just give me a chance and I'll prove it to you.* ◊ *He felt he needed to prove his point* (= show other people that he was right). ◊ *Are you just doing this to prove a point?* ◊ *(spoken)* **What are you trying to prove?** ◊ *(spoken)* **I certainly don't have anything to prove**—*my record speaks for itself.* ◊ [V (that)] *This proves (that) I was right.* ◊ [VN-ADJ] *She was determined to prove everyone wrong.* ◊ *In this country, you are innocent until proved guilty.* ◊ [V wh-] *This just proves what I have been saying for some time.* ◊ [VN that] **Can it be proved that he did commit these offences?** [also VN-N, VN to inf] OPP DISPROVE—see also PROOF

BE | **2** *linking verb* if sth **proves** dangerous, expensive, etc. or if it **proves to be** dangerous, etc., you discover that it is dangerous, etc. over a period of time SYN TURN OUT: [V-ADJ] *The opposition proved too strong for him.* ◊ [V-N]

Shares in the industry proved a poor investment. ◊ [V to inf] *The promotion proved to be a turning point in his career.* **YOURSELF** | **3** [VN] **~ yourself (to sb)** to show other people how good you are at doing sth or that you are capable of doing sth: *He constantly feels he has to prove himself to others.* **4 ~ yourself sth/to be sth** to show other people that you are a particular type of person or that you have a particular quality: [VN-ADJ] *He proved himself determined to succeed.* [also VN-N, VN to inf] **OF BREAD** | **5** [V] to swell before being baked because of the action of YEAST **SYN** RISE

IDM see EXCEPTION

proven /ˈpruːvn; ˈprəʊvn; *AmE* ˈproʊ-/ *adj.* [only before noun] tested and shown to be true: *a student of proven ability* ◊ *It is a proven fact that fluoride strengthens growing teeth.*—see also PROVE *v.* **OPP** UNPROVEN **IDM** **not ˈproven** (in Scottish law) a VERDICT (= decision) at a trial that there is not enough evidence to show that sb is guilty or innocent, and that they must be set free

prov·en·ance /ˈprɒvənəns; *AmE* ˈprɑːv-/ *noun* [U, C] (*technical*) the place that sth originally came from **SYN** ORIGIN: *All the furniture is of English provenance.* ◊ *There's no proof about the provenance of the painting* (= whether it is genuine or not).

prov·erb /ˈprɒvɜːb; *AmE* ˈprɑːvɜːrb/ *noun* a well-known phrase or sentence that gives advice or says sth that is generally true, for example 'Waste not, want not'.

pro·verb·ial /prəˈvɜːbiəl; *AmE* -ˈvɜːrb-/ *adj.* **1** [only before noun] used to show that you are referring to a particular proverb or well-known phrase: *Let's not count our proverbial chickens.* **2** [not usually before noun] well known and talked about by a lot of people **SYN** FAMOUS: *Their hospitality is proverbial.* ▶ **pro·verb·ial·ly** /-biəli/ *adv.*

pro·vide /prəˈvaɪd/ *verb* **1** [VN] **~ sb (with sth)** | **~ sth (for sb)** to give sth to sb or make it available for them to use **SYN** SUPPLY: *The hospital has a commitment to provide the best possible medical care.* ◊ *We are here to provide a service for the public.* ◊ *We are here to provide the public with a service.* ◊ *Please answer questions in the space provided.* ◊ *The report was not expected to provide any answers.* **2** [V that] (*formal*) (of a law or rule) to state that sth will or must happen **SYN** STIPULATE: *The final section provides that any work produced for the company is thereafter owned by the company.*—see also PROVISION **PHRV** **proˈvide against sth** (*formal*) to make preparations to deal with sth bad or unpleasant that might happen in the future **proˈvide for sb** to give sb the things that they need to live, such as food, money and clothing **proˈvide for sth** (*formal*) **1** to make preparations to deal with sth that might happen in the future **2** (of a law, rule, etc.) to make it possible for sth to be done: *The legislation provides for the detention of suspected terrorists for up to seven days.*

pro·vid·ed /prəˈvaɪdɪd/ (also **pro·vid·ing**) *conj.* **~ (that…)** used to say what must happen or be done to make it possible for sth else to happen **SYN** IF: *We'll buy everything you produce, provided of course the price is right.* ◊ *Provided that you have the money in your account, you can withdraw up to £100 a day.*

provi·dence /ˈprɒvɪdəns; *AmE* ˈprɑːv-/ (also **Provi·dence**) *noun* [U] God, or a force that some people believe controls our lives and the things that happen to us, usually in a way that protects us **SYN** FATE: *to trust in divine providence* **IDM** see TEMPT

provi·dent /ˈprɒvɪdənt; *AmE* ˈprɑːv-/ *adj.* (*formal*) careful in planning for the future, especially by saving money **OPP** IMPROVIDENT

provi·den·tial /ˌprɒvɪˈdenʃl; *AmE* ˌprɑːv-/ *adj.* (*formal*) lucky because it happens at the right time, but without being planned: *A providential wind carried the raft to the shore.* ▶ **provi·den·tial·ly** /-ʃəli/ *adv.*

pro·vider /prəˈvaɪdə(r)/ *noun* a person or an organization that supplies sb with sth they need or want: *training providers* ◊ *We are one of the largest providers of employment in the area.* ◊ *The eldest son is the family's sole provider* (= the only person who earns money).

pro·vid·ing /prəˈvaɪdɪŋ/ *conj.* = PROVIDED

prov·ince /ˈprɒvɪns; *AmE* ˈprɑːv-/ *noun* **1** [C] one of the areas that some countries are divided into with its own local government: *the provinces of Canada* **2** (**the prov·inces**) [pl.] (*BrE*) all the parts of a country except the capital city: *The show will tour the provinces after it closes in London.* ◊ *a shy young man from the provinces* **3** [sing.] (*formal*) a person's particular area of knowledge, interest or responsibility: *Such decisions are normally the province of higher management.* ◊ *I'm afraid the matter is outside my province* (= I cannot or need not deal with it).

pro·vin·cial /prəˈvɪnʃl/ *adj., noun*
- *adj.* **1** [only before noun] connected with one of the large areas that some countries are divided into, with its own local government: *provincial assemblies/elections* **2** [only before noun] (sometimes *disapproving*) connected with the parts of a country that do not include the capital city: *a provincial town/theatre/newspaper* **3** (*disapproving*) unwilling to consider new or different ideas or things: *In spite of his education and travels, he has remained very provincial.* ▶ **pro·vin·cial·ly** /-ʃəli/ *adv.*
- *noun* (often *disapproving*) a person who lives in or comes from a part of the country that is not near the capital city

pro·vin·cial·ism /prəˈvɪnʃlɪzəm/ *noun* [U] (*disapproving*) the attitude of people who are unwilling to consider new or different ideas or things

ˈproving ground *noun* a place where sth such as a new machine, vehicle or weapon can be tested: *It's an ideal proving ground for the new car.* ◊ (*figurative*) *The club is the proving ground for young boxers.*

pro·vi·sion /prəˈvɪʒn/ *noun, verb*
- *noun* **1** [U, C, usually sing.] the act of supplying sb with sth that they need or want; sth that is supplied: *educational/housing provision* ◊ *The government is responsible for the provision of health care.* ◊ *There is no provision for anyone to sit down here.* ◊ *The provision of specialist teachers is being increased.* **2** [U, C] **~ for sb/sth** preparations that you make for sth that might or will happen in the future: *He had already made provisions* (= planned for the financial future of) *his wife and children before the accident.* ◊ *You should make provision for things going wrong.* **3** (**provisions**) [pl.] supplies of food and drink, especially for a long journey **4** [C] a condition or an arrangement in a legal document: *Under the provisions of the lease, the tenant is responsible for repairs.*—see also PROVIDE
- *verb* [VN] [often passive] **~ sb/sth (with sth)** (*formal*) to supply sb/sth with enough of sth, especially food, to last for a particular period of time

pro·vi·sion·al /prəˈvɪʒənl/ *adj.* **1** arranged for the present time only and likely to be changed in the future **SYN** TEMPORARY: *a provisional government* ◊ *provisional arrangements* **2** arranged, but not yet definite: *The booking is only provisional.* ▶ **pro·vi·sion·al·ly** /-nəli/ *adv.*: *The meeting has been provisionally arranged for 3 p.m. next Friday.*

proˌvisional ˈlicence (*BrE*) (*AmE* **ˈlearner's permit**) *noun* an official document that you must have when you start to learn to drive

pro·viso /prəˈvaɪzəʊ; *AmE* -zoʊ/ *noun* (*pl.* **-os**) a condition that must be accepted before an agreement can be made **SYN** PROVISION: *Their participation is subject to a number of important provisos.* ◊ *He agreed to their visit with the proviso that they should stay no longer than one week.*

pro·voca·teur /prəˌvɒkəˈtɜː(r); *AmE* -ˌvɑːkə-/ *noun* = AGENT PROVOCATEUR

provo·ca·tion /ˌprɒvəˈkeɪʃn; *AmE* ˌprɑːv-/ *noun* [U, C] the act of doing or saying sth deliberately in order to make sb angry or upset; something that is done or said to cause this: *He reacted violently only under provocation.* ◊ *The terrorists can strike at any time without provocation.* ◊ *She bursts into tears at the slightest provocation.* ◊ *So far the police have refused to respond to their provocations.*

pro·voca·tive /prəˈvɒkətɪv; *AmE* -ˈvɑːkə-/ *adj.* **1** intended to make people angry or upset; intended to make people argue about sth: *a provocative act/book/*

P

remark ◇ *He doesn't really mean that—he's just being deliberately provocative.* **2** intended to make sb sexually excited: *a provocative smile* ▶ **pro·vo·ca·tive·ly** *adv.*

pro·voke /prə'vəʊk; *AmE* -'voʊk/ *verb* **1** [VN] to cause a particular reaction or have a particular effect: *The announcement provoked a storm of protest.* ◇ *The article was intended to provoke discussion.* ◇ *Dairy products may provoke allergic reactions in some people.* **2** ~ **sb (into sth/ into doing sth)** to say or do sth that you know will annoy sb so that they react in an angry way [SYN] GOAD: [VN] *The lawyer claimed his client was provoked into acts of violence by the defendant.* ◇ *Be careful what you say—he's easily provoked.* [also VN to inf]

prov·ost /'prɒvəst; *AmE* 'proʊvoʊst/ (also **Provost**) *noun* **1** (in Britain) the person in charge of a college at some universities **2** (in the US) a senior member of the administrative staff at some universities **3** (in Scotland) the head of a council in some towns, cities and districts—compare MAYOR **4** the head of a group of priests belonging to a particular CATHEDRAL

prow /praʊ/ *noun* (*formal* or *literary*) the pointed front part of a ship or boat

prow·ess /'praʊəs/ *noun* [U] (*formal*) great skill at doing sth: *academic/sporting/technical prowess*

prowl /praʊl/ *verb, noun*
- *verb* **1** (of an animal) to move quietly and carefully around an area, especially when hunting:[V, usually +adv./prep.] *The tiger prowled through the undergrowth.* [also VN] **2** to move quietly and carefully around an area, especially with the intention of committing a crime:[V, usually +adv./prep.] *A man was seen prowling around outside the factory just before the fire started.* [also VN] **3** to walk around a room, an area, etc., especially because you are bored, anxious, etc., and cannot relax: [VN] *He prowled the empty rooms of the house at night.* [also V +adv./prep.]
- *noun* [IDM] **(be/go) on the 'prowl** (of an animal or a person) moving quietly and carefully, hunting or looking for sth: *There was a fox on the prowl near the chickens.* ◇ *an intruder on the prowl*

prowl·er /'praʊlə(r)/ *noun* a person who follows sb or who moves around quietly outside their house, especially at night, in order to frighten them, harm them or steal sth from them

prox·im·ate /'prɒksɪmət; *AmE* 'prɑːk-/ *adj.* [usually before noun] (*technical*) nearest in time, order, etc. to sth

prox·im·ity /prɒk'sɪməti; *AmE* prɑːk-/ *noun* [U] ~ **(of sb/sth) (to sb/sth)** (*formal*) the state of being near sb/sth in distance or time: *a house in the proximity of* (= near) *the motorway* ◇ *The proximity of the college to London makes it very popular.* ◇ *The area has a number of schools in close proximity to each other.* ◇ *the death of two members of her family in close proximity*

proxy /'prɒksi; *AmE* 'prɑːksi/ *noun* (*pl.* **-ies**) **1** [U] the authority that you give to sb to do sth for you, when you cannot do it yourself: *You can vote either in person or by proxy.* ◇ *a proxy vote* **2** [C, U] ~ **(for sb)** a person who has been given the authority to represent sb else: *Your proxy will need to sign the form on your behalf.* ◇ *She is acting as proxy for her husband.* ◇ *They were like proxy parents to me.* **3** [C] ~ **for sth** (*formal* or *technical*) something that you use to represent sth else that you are trying to measure or calculate: *The number of patients on a doctor's list was seen as a good proxy for assessing how hard they work.*

prude /pruːd/ *noun* (*disapproving*) a person that you think is too easily shocked by things connected with sex

pru·dent /'pruːdnt/ *adj.* sensible and careful when you make judgements and decisions; avoiding unnecessary risks: *a prudent businessman* ◇ *a prudent decision/investment* ◇ *It might be more prudent to get a second opinion before going ahead.* [OPP] IMPRUDENT ▶ **pru·dence** /-dns/ *noun* [U] **pru·dent·ly** *adv.*

prud·ery /'pruːdəri/ *noun* [U] (*formal, disapproving*) the attitude or behaviour of people who seem very easily shocked by things connected with sex

prud·ish /'pruːdɪʃ/ *adj.* (*disapproving*) very easily

shocked by things connected with sex ▶ **prud·ish·ness** *noun* [U]

prune /pruːn/ *noun, verb*
- *noun* a dried PLUM that is often eaten cooked: *stewed prunes*
- *verb* [VN] ~ **sth (back)** **1** to cut off some of the branches from a tree, bush, etc. so that it will grow better and stronger: *When should you prune apple trees?* ◇ *He pruned the longer branches off the tree.* ◇ *The hedge needs pruning back.* **2** to make sth smaller by removing parts; to cut out parts of sth: *Staff numbers have been pruned back to 175.* ◇ *The railway companies have pruned their timetables* (= there are fewer trains). ◇ *Prune out any unnecessary details.* ▶ **prun·ing** *noun* [U]: *All roses require annual pruning.* ◇ *The company would benefit from a little pruning here and there.*

pruri·ent /'prʊəriənt; *AmE* 'prʊr-/ *adj.* (*formal, disapproving*) having or showing too much interest in things connected with sex: *a prurient interest in the details of a rape case* ▶ **pruri·ence** /-əns/ *noun* [U]

Prus·sian blue /ˌprʌʃn 'bluː/ *noun* [U] a deep blue colour used in paints

pry /praɪ/ *verb* (**pries, pry·ing, pried, pried** /praɪd/) **1** [V] ~ **(into sth)** to try to find out information about other people's private lives in a way that is annoying or rude: *I'm sick of you prying into my personal life!* ◇ *I'm sorry. I didn't mean to pry.* ◇ *She tried to keep the children away from the prying eyes of the world's media.* **2** (*especially AmE*) = PRISE

PS /ˌpiː 'es/ *noun* something written at the end of a letter to introduce some more information or sth that you have forgotten. PS is an abbreviation for 'postscript': *PS Could you send me your fax number again?* ◇ *She added a PS asking me to water the plants.*

psalm /sɑːm/ *noun* a song, poem or prayer that praises God, especially one in the Bible: *the Book of Psalms*

pseph·ology /siˈfɒlədʒi; *AmE* -ˈfɑːl-/ *noun* [U] the study of how people vote in elections ▶ **pseph·olo·gist** /siˈfɒlədʒɪst; *AmE* -ˈfɑːl-/ *noun*

pseud /suːd; *BrE* also sjuːd/ *noun* (*BrE, informal, disapproving*) a person who pretends to know a lot about a particular subject in order to impress other people: *She's such a pseud!* ▶ **pseud** *adj.*

pseudo- /'suːdəʊ; 'sjuː-; *AmE* 'suːdoʊ/ *combining form* (in nouns, adjectives and adverbs) not genuine; false or pretended: *pseudo-intellectual* ◇ *pseudo-science*

pseudo·nym /'suːdənɪm; *BrE* also 'sjuː-/ *noun* a name used by sb, especially a writer, instead of their real name: *She writes* **under a pseudonym.**—compare PEN-NAME ▶ **pseud·onym·ous** /suːˈdɒnɪməs; sjuː-; *AmE* suːˈdɑːn-/ *adj.* [only before noun]

psor·ia·sis /səˈraɪəsɪs/ *noun* [U] (*medical*) a skin disease that causes rough red areas where the skin comes off in small pieces

psst /pst/ *exclamation* the way of writing the sound people say when they want to attract sb's attention quietly: *Psst! Let's get out now before they see us!*

psych /saɪk/ *verb* [PHRV] **ˌpsych sb↔'out (of sth)** (*informal*) to make an opponent feel less confident by saying or doing things that make you seem better, stronger, etc. than them **ˌpsych sb/yourself 'up (for sth)** (*informal*) to prepare sb/yourself mentally for sth difficult or unpleasant: *I'd got myself all psyched up for the interview and then it was called off at the last minute.*—see also PSYCHED

psy·che /'saɪki/ *noun* (*formal*) the mind; your deepest feelings and attitudes: *the human/feminine/national psyche*

psyched /saɪkt/ *adj.* [not before noun] (*informal, especially AmE*) excited, especially about sth that is going to happen: *The kids are really psyched about the vacation.*

psy·che·delia /ˌsaɪkəˈdiːliə/ *noun* [U] music, art, fashion, etc. that is created as a result of the effects of psychedelic drugs

psy·che·del·ic /ˌsaɪkəˈdelɪk/ *adj.* [usually before noun] **1** (of drugs) causing the user to see and hear things that are not there or that do not exist (= to HALLUCINATE) **2** (of

æ	ɑː	e	ɜː	ə	ɪ	iː	i	ɒ	ɔː	ʌ	ʊ	u	uː
cat	father	ten	bird	about	sit	see	many	got	saw	cup	put	actual	too

(BrE)

P

art, music, clothes, etc.) having bright colours, strange sounds, etc. like those that are experienced when taking psychedelic drugs

psy·chi·at·ric /ˌsaɪkiˈætrɪk/ *adj.* relating to PSYCHIATRY or to mental illness: *a psychiatric hospital/nurse* ◊ *psychiatric treatment* ◊ *psychiatric disorders*—compare MENTAL

psych·iatrist /saɪˈkaɪətrɪst/ *noun* a doctor who studies and treats mental illnesses

psych·iatry /saɪˈkaɪətri/ *noun* [U] the study and treatment of mental illness

psy·chic /ˈsaɪkɪk/ *adj., noun*
■ *adj.* **1** (also *less frequent* **psych·ical** /ˈsaɪkɪkl/) connected with strange powers of the mind and not able to be explained by natural laws: *psychic energy/forces/phenomena* ◊ *psychic powers* ◊ *psychic healing* **2** (of a person) seeming to have strange mental powers and to be able to do things that are not possible according to natural laws: *She claims to be psychic and helps people to contact the dead.* ◊ *How am I supposed to know—I'm not psychic!* **3** (also *less frequent* **psych·ical**) (*formal*) connected with the mind rather than the body ▶ **psych·ic·al·ly** /-kli/ *adv.*
■ *noun* a person who claims to have strange mental powers so that they can do things that are not possible according to natural laws, such as predicting the future and speaking to dead people

psy·cho /ˈsaɪkəʊ; *AmE* -koʊ/ *noun* (*pl.* **-os**) (*informal*) a person who is mentally ill and who behaves in a very strange violent way ▶ **psy·cho** *adj.*

psycho- /ˈsaɪkəʊ; *AmE* -koʊ/ (also **psych-**) *combining form* in nouns, adjectives and adverbs) connected with the mind: *psychology* ◊ *psychiatric*

psy·cho·ana·lyse (*BrE*) (*AmE* **-yze**) /ˌsaɪkəʊˈænəlaɪz; *AmE* -koʊ-/ (also **ana·lyse**, **ana·lyze**) *verb* [VN] to treat or study sb using psychoanalysis

psy·cho·analy·sis /ˌsaɪkəʊəˈnæləsɪs; *AmE* -koʊə-/ (also **an·aly·sis**) *noun* [U] a method of treating sb who is mentally ill by asking them to talk about past experiences and feelings in order to try to find explanations for their present problems ▶ **psy·cho·ana·lyt·ic** /ˌsaɪkəʊˌænəˈlɪtɪk; *AmE* -koʊ-/ *adj.* [only before noun]: *a psychoanalytic approach* **psy·cho·ana·lyt·ic·al·ly** /-ɪkli/ *adv.*

psy·cho·ana·lyst /ˌsaɪkəʊˈænəlɪst; *AmE* -koʊ-/ (also **ana·lyst**) *noun* a person who treats patients using psychoanalysis

psy·cho·bab·ble /ˈsaɪkəʊbæbl; *AmE* -koʊ-/ *noun* [U] (*informal, disapproving*) the language that people use when they talk about feelings and emotional problems, that sounds very scientific, but really has little meaning

psy·cho·drama /ˈsaɪkəʊdrɑːmə; *AmE* -koʊ-/ *noun* **1** a way of treating people who are mentally ill by encouraging them to act events from their past to help them understand their feelings **2** a play or film/movie that makes the minds and feelings of the characters more important than the events

psy·cho·logic·al /ˌsaɪkəˈlɒdʒɪkl; *AmE* -ˈlɑːdʒ-/ *adj.* **1** [usually before noun] connected with a person's mind and the way in which it works: *the psychological development of children* ◊ *Abuse can lead to both psychological and emotional problems.* ◊ *Her symptoms are more psychological than physical* (= imaginary rather than real). ◊ *Victory in the last game gave them a psychological advantage over their opponents.* ◊ *a psychological novel* (= one that examines the minds of the characters) **2** [only before noun] connected with the study of PSYCHOLOGY: *psychological research* ▶ **psy·cho·logic·al·ly** /-kli/ *adv.*: *psychologically harmful* ◊ *Psychologically, the defeat was devastating.* **IDM** the **psychological** **moment** the best time to do sth in order for it to be successful

psychological **warfare** *noun* [U] things that are said and done in order to make an opponent believe that they cannot win a war, a competition, etc.

psych·olo·gist /saɪˈkɒlədʒɪst; *AmE* -ˈkɑːl-/ *noun* a scientist who studies and is trained in psychology: *an educational psychologist* ◊ *a clinical psychologist* (= one who treats people with mental disorders or problems)

psych·ology /saɪˈkɒlədʒi; *AmE* -ˈkɑːl-/ *noun* **1** [U] the scientific study of the mind and how it influences behaviour: *social/educational/child psychology* **2** [sing.] the kind of mind that sb has that makes them think or behave in a particular way: *the psychology of small boys* **3** [sing.] how the mind influences behaviour in a particular area of life: *the psychology of interpersonal relationships*

psy·cho·met·ric /ˌsaɪkəˈmetrɪk/ *adj.* [only before noun] (*technical*) used for measuring mental abilities and processes: *psychometric testing*

psy·cho·path /ˈsaɪkəpæθ/ *noun* a person suffering from a serious mental illness that causes them to behave in a violent way towards other people ▶ **psy·cho·path·ic** /ˌsaɪkəˈpæθɪk/ *adj.*: *a psychopathic disorder/killer*

psy·cho·path·ology /ˌsaɪkəʊpəˈθɒlədʒi; *AmE* -koʊpəˈθɑːl-/ *noun* [U] **1** the scientific study of mental disorders **2** a disorder that affects sb's mind or their behaviour

psych·osis /saɪˈkəʊsɪs; *AmE* -ˈkoʊ-/ *noun* [C, U] (*pl.* **psych·oses** /-siːz/) a serious mental illness that affects the whole personality—see also PSYCHOTIC

psy·cho·somat·ic /ˌsaɪkəʊsəˈmætɪk; *AmE* -koʊ-/ *adj.* **1** (of an illness) caused by mental problems, such as stress and worry, rather than physical problems: *Tests showed that her problems were more than merely psychosomatic.* **2** (*technical*) connected with the relationship between the mind and the body

psy·cho·ther·apy /ˌsaɪkəʊˈθerəpi; *AmE* -koʊ-/ (also **ther·apy**) *noun* [U] the treatment of mental illness by discussing sb's problems with them rather than by giving them drugs ▶ **psy·cho·ther·ap·ist** /-pɪst/ (also **ther·ap·ist**) *noun*

psych·ot·ic /saɪˈkɒtɪk; *AmE* -ˈkɑːt-/ *noun* (*medical*) a person suffering from severe mental illness ▶ **psych·ot·ic** *adj.*: *a psychotic disorder/illness* ◊ *a psychotic individual/patient*—see also PSYCHOSIS

PT /ˌpiː ˈtiː/ *abbr.* **1** (*BrE*) the abbreviation for 'physical training' (sport and physical exercise that is taught in schools, in the army, etc.) **2** (also **P/T**) (in writing) PART-TIME: *The course is 1 year FT, 2 years PT.*

pt (also **pt.** especially in *AmE*) *abbr.* **1** part: *Shakespeare's Henry IV Pt 2* **2** pint **3** point: *The winner scored 10 pts.* **4** (**Pt.**) (especially on a map) port: *Pt. Moresby*

PTA /ˌpiː tiː ˈeɪ/ *noun* the abbreviation for 'parent-teacher association' (a group run by parents and teachers in a school that organizes social events and helps the school in different ways)

Pte *abbr.* (*BrE*) (in writing) PRIVATE: *Pte Jim Hill*

ptero·dac·tyl /ˌterəˈdæktɪl/ *noun* a flying reptile that lived millions of years ago

PTO /ˌpiː tiː ˈəʊ; *AmE* ˈoʊ/ *abbr.* (*BrE*) please turn over (written at the bottom of a page to show that there is more on the other side)

pub /pʌb/ (also *formal* **public** **house**) (both *BrE*) *noun* a building where people go to drink and meet their friends. Pubs serve alcoholic and other drinks, and often also food: *They've gone down the pub for a drink.* ◊ *a pub lunch* ◊ *the landlord of the local pub*

pub crawl *noun* (*BrE, informal*) a visit to several pubs, going straight from one to the next, drinking at each of them

pu·berty /ˈpjuːbəti; *AmE* -bərti/ *noun* [U] the period of a person's life during which their sexual organs develop and they become capable of having children: *to reach puberty*—see also ADOLESCENCE

pu·bes·cent /pjuːˈbesnt/ *adj.* [usually before noun] (*formal*) in the period of a person's life when they are changing physically from a child to an adult: *pubescent boys/girls*

pubic /ˈpjuːbɪk/ *adj.* [only before noun] connected with the part of a person's body near their sexual organs: *pubic hair* ◊ *the pubic bone*

pub·lic /ˈpʌblɪk/ *adj., noun*
■ *adj.*
OF ORDINARY PEOPLE **1** [only before noun] connected with

aɪ	aʊ	eɪ	əʊ	oʊ	ɔɪ	ɪə	eə	ʊə	j	w
my	now	say	go	go	boy	near	hair	pure	yes	wet
			(BrE)	(AmE)						

ordinary people in society in general: *The campaign is designed to increase public awareness of the issues.* ◊ *Levels of waste from the factory may be a danger to public health.* ◊ *Why would the closure of hospitals be in the public interest* (= useful to ordinary people)*?* ◊ *The media has a powerful influence on public opinion.* ◊ *The government had to bow to public pressure.*

FOR EVERYONE | **2** [only before noun] provided, especially by the government, for the use of people in general: *a public education system* ◊ *a public library/telephone* ◊ *public transport/transportation* OPP PRIVATE

OF GOVERNMENT | **3** [only before noun] connected with the government and the services it provides: *public money/spending/funding/expenditure* ◊ *He spent much of his career in public office* (= working in the government). ◊ *(BrE) the public purse* (= the money that the government can spend) ◊ *The rail industry is no longer in public ownership* (= controlled by the government). OPP PRIVATE

SEEN/HEARD BY PEOPLE | **4** known to people in general: *a public figure* (= a person who is well known because they are often on the television, radio, etc.) ◊ *Details of the government report have not yet been made public.* ◊ *She entered public life* (= started a job in which she became known to the public) *at the age of 25.* OPP PRIVATE **5** open to people in general; intended to be seen or heard by people in general: *a public apology/inquiry/investigation* ◊ *The painting will be put on public display next week.* ◊ *This may be the band's last public appearance together.*

PLACE | **6** where there are a lot of people who can see and hear you: *Let's go somewhere a little less public.* OPP PRIVATE

▶ **pub·lic·ly** /-kli/ *adv.*: *a publicly owned company* ◊ *He later publicly apologized for his comments.* ◊ *This information is not publicly available.*

IDM **go 'public 1** to tell people about sth that is a secret **2** (of a company) to start selling shares on the STOCK EXCHANGE **in the public 'eye** well known to many people through newspapers and television: *She doesn't want her children growing up in the public eye.*—more at KNOWLEDGE

■ *noun* [sing.+ sing./pl. *v.*]

ORDINARY PEOPLE | **1** (**the public**) ordinary people in society in general: *The palace is now open to the public.* ◊ *There have been many complaints from members of the public.* ◊ *The public has/have a right to know what is contained in the report.*—see also THE GENERAL PUBLIC

GROUP OF PEOPLE | **2** a group of people who share a particular interest or who are involved in the same activity: *the theatre-going public* ◊ *She knows how to keep her public* (= for example, the people who buy her books) *satisfied.*

IDM **in 'public** when other people, especially people you do not know, are present: *She doesn't like to be seen in public without her make-up on.*—compare IN PRIVATE—more at WASH *v.*

,public 'access *noun* [U] **1** the right of people in general to go into particular buildings or areas of land or to obtain particular information: *public access to the countryside* **2** (in the US and some other countries) the right of people in general to use television or radio channels to present their own programmes: *a public access channel*

,public ad'dress system *noun* (*abbr.* **PA system**) an electronic system that uses MICROPHONES and LOUDSPEAKERS to make music, voices, etc. louder so that they can be heard by everyone in a particular place or building

,public af'fairs *noun* [pl.] issues and questions about social, economic, political or business activities, etc. that affect ordinary people in general: *the director of public affairs for the space centre* ◊ *a public affairs department*

pub·lican /ˈpʌblɪkən/ *noun* (*BrE, formal*) a person who owns or manages a pub

pub·li·ca·tion /ˌpʌblɪˈkeɪʃn/ *noun* **1** [U, C] the act of printing a book, a magazine, etc. and making it available to the public; a book, a magazine, etc. that has been published: *the publication date* ◊ *the publication of his first novel* ◊ *specialist publications* **2** [U] the act of printing sth in a newspaper, report, etc. so that the public knows about it: *a delay in the publication of the exam results* ◊

The newspaper continues to defend its publication of the photographs.

,public 'bar *noun* (in Britain) a bar in a pub with simple or less comfortable furniture than the other bars—compare LOUNGE BAR

,public 'company (also **,public ,limited 'company**) (both *BrE*) (*AmE* **,public corpo'ration**) *noun* (*abbr.* **plc, PLC**) a company that sells shares in itself to the public

,public con'venience *noun* (*BrE, formal*) a public building containing toilets that are provided for anyone to use

,public corpo'ration *noun* **1** (*AmE*) = PUBLIC COMPANY **2** (*BrE*) an organization that is owned by the government and that provides a national service

,public de'fender *noun* (*law*) (in the US) a lawyer who is paid by the government to defend people in court if they cannot pay for a lawyer themselves

,public 'domain *noun* [sing.] something that is in the public domain is available for everyone to use or to discuss and is not secret: *The information has been placed in the public domain.* ◊ *public domain software*

,public 'holiday *noun* a day on which most of the shops/stores, businesses and schools in a country are closed, often to celebrate a particular event—compare BANK HOLIDAY

,public 'house *noun* (*BrE, formal*) = PUB

,public 'housing *noun* [U] (in the US) houses and flats/apartments that are built by the government for people who do not have enough money to pay for private accommodation

pub·li·cist /ˈpʌblɪsɪst/ *noun* a person whose job is to make sth known to the public, for example a new product, actor, etc.

pub·li·city /pʌbˈlɪsəti/ *noun* [U] **1** the attention that is given to sb/sth by newspapers, television, etc: *good/bad/adverse publicity* ◊ *There has been a great deal of publicity surrounding his disappearance.* ◊ *The trial took place amid a blaze of* (= a lot of) *publicity.* **2** the business of attracting the attention of the public to sth/sb; the things that are done to attract attention: *She works in publicity.* ◊ *There has been a lot of advance publicity for her new film.* ◊ *publicity material* ◊ *a publicity campaign* ◊ *The band dressed up as the Beatles as a publicity stunt.*

pub·li·cize (*BrE* also **-ise**) /ˈpʌblɪsaɪz/ *verb* [VN] to make sth known to the public; to advertise sth: *They flew to Europe to publicize the plight of the refugees.* ◊ *a much/highly/widely publicized speech* (= that has received a lot of attention on television, in newspapers, etc.) ◊ *He was in London publicizing his new biography of Kennedy.*

,public ,limited 'company *noun* (*BrE*) (*abbr.* **plc**) = PUBLIC COMPANY

,public 'nuisance *noun* **1** [sing., U] (*law*) an illegal act that causes harm to people in general: *He was charged with committing (a) public nuisance.* **2** [C, usually sing.] (*informal*) a person or a thing that annoys a lot of people

,public 'property *noun* [U] **1** (especially *law*) land, buildings, etc. that are owned by the government and can be used by everyone **2** a person or a thing that everyone has a right to know about: *Sophie became public property when she married into the royal family.*

,public 'prosecutor *noun* (*BrE*) a lawyer who works for the government and tries to prove people guilty in a court of law—see also DISTRICT ATTORNEY

,public re'lations *noun* **1** [U] (*abbr.* **PR**) the business of giving the public information about a particular organization or person in order to create a good impression: *She works in public relations.* ◊ *a public relations exercise* **2** [pl.] the state of the relationship between an organization and the public: *Sponsoring the local team is good for public relations.*

,public 'school *noun* [C, U] **1** (in Britain, especially in England) a private school for young people between the ages of 13 and 18, whose parents pay for their education. The students often live at the school while they are studying: *He was educated at (a) public school.*—compare

b	d	f	g	h	k	l	m	n	p	r
bad	did	fall	get	hat	cat	leg	man	now	pen	red

PREPARATORY SCHOOL, PRIVATE SCHOOL **2** (**'public school**) (in the US, Australia, Scotland and other countries) a free local school paid for by the government—compare STATE SCHOOL

the ˌpublic 'sector *noun* [sing.] (*economics*) the part of the economy of a country that is owned or controlled by the government—compare THE PRIVATE SECTOR

ˌpublic 'service *noun* **1** [C] a service such as transport or health care that a government or an official organization provides for people in general in a particular society: *to improve public services in the area* ◊ *a public service broadcast* **2** [C, U] something that is done to help people rather than to make a profit: *to do/perform a public service* **3** [U] the government and government departments: *to work in public service* ◊ *public service workers*

ˌpublic-'spirited *adj.* willing to do things that will help other people in society: *a public-spirited man/act* ◊ *That was very public-spirited of you.* ▶ **ˌpublic 'spirit** *noun* [U]

ˌpublic u'tility *noun* (*formal*) a private company that must obey government rules, that supplies essential services such as gas, water and electricity to the public

ˌpublic 'works *noun* [pl.] building work, such as that of hospitals, schools and roads, that is paid for by the government

pub·lish /ˈpʌblɪʃ/ *verb* **1** [VN] to produce a book, magazine, CD-ROM, etc. and sell it to the public: *The first edition was published in 1998.* ◊ *He works for a company that publishes reference books.* ◊ *Most of our titles are also published on CD-ROM.* **2** [VN] to print a letter, an article, etc. in a newspaper or magazine: *Pictures of the suspect were published in all the daily papers.* **3** [VN] to make sth available to the public on the Internet: *The report will be published on the Internet.* **4** (of an author) to have your work printed and sold to the public: [VN] *She hasn't published anything for years.* ◊ [V] *University teachers are under pressure to publish.* **5** [VN] (*formal*) to make official information known to the public SYN RELEASE: *The findings of the committee will be published on Friday.*

pub·lish·er /ˈpʌblɪʃə(r)/ *noun* a person or company that prepares and prints books, magazines, newspapers or electronic products and makes them available to the public

pub·lish·ing /ˈpʌblɪʃɪŋ/ *noun* [U] the profession or business of preparing and printing books, magazines, CD-ROMs, etc. and selling or making them available to the public: *a publishing house* (= company)—see also DESKTOP PUBLISHING

puce /pjuːs/ *adj.* reddish-purple in colour: *His face was puce with rage.* ▶ **puce** *noun* [U]

puck /pʌk/ *noun* a hard flat rubber disc that is used as a ball in ice hockey—picture at HOCKEY

puck·er /ˈpʌkə(r)/ *verb* ~ (sth) (up) to form or to make sth form small folds or lines: [V] *His face puckered, and he was ready to cry.* ◊ [VN] *She puckered her lips.* ◊ *puckered fabric*

puck·ish /ˈpʌkɪʃ/ *adj.* [usually before noun] (*literary*) enjoying playing tricks on other people SYN MISCHIEVOUS

pud /pʊd/ *noun* (*BrE, informal*) = PUDDING

pud·ding /ˈpʊdɪŋ/ (also *informal* **pud**) (both *BrE*) *noun* [U, C] **1** a sweet dish eaten at the end of a meal: *What's for pudding?* ◊ *I haven't made a pudding today.* SYN AFTERS, DESSERT, SWEET—picture on page A1 **2** (*BrE*) a hot sweet dish, often like a cake, made from flour, fat and eggs with fruit, jam, etc. in or on it: *treacle pudding* ◊ *bread and butter pudding* (= made with bread, butter and milk)—see also CHRISTMAS PUDDING, RICE PUDDING, SPONGE PUDDING, SUMMER PUDDING **3** (*BrE*) a hot dish like a pie with soft pastry made from flour, fat and eggs and usually filled with meat: *a steak and kidney pudding* **4** (*AmE*) a cold DESSERT (= a sweet dish) like cream flavoured with fruit, chocolate, etc.: *chocolate pudding*—see also BLACK PUDDING, YORKSHIRE PUDDING IDM see OVER-EGG, PROOF

'pudding basin *noun* (*BrE*) a deep round bowl that is used for mixing food or for cooking puddings in

pud·dle /ˈpʌdl/ *noun* a small amount of water or other liquid, especially rain, that has collected in one place on the ground

pu·denda /pjuːˈdendə/ *noun* [pl.] (*old-fashioned, formal*) the sexual organs that are outside the body, especially those of a woman

pudgy /ˈpʌdʒi/ *adj.* = PODGY

pu·er·ile /ˈpjʊəraɪl; *AmE* ˈpjʊrəl/ *adj.* (*disapproving*) silly; suitable for a child rather than an adult SYN CHILDISH: *puerile behaviour/excuses*

puff /pʌf/ *verb, noun*

■ *verb* **1** ~ (at/on sth) to smoke a cigarette, pipe, etc: [V] *He puffed (away) on his pipe.* ◊ [VN] *I sat puffing my cigar.* **2** ~ (sth) (out) to make smoke or steam blow out in clouds; to blow out in clouds: [VN] *Chimneys were puffing out clouds of smoke.* ◊ [V] *Steam puffed out.* **3** (*informal*) to breathe loudly and quickly, especially after you have been running: [V] *I was starting to puff a little from the climb.* [also V speech] —see also PUFFED, PUFFED OUT **4** [V+adv./prep.] to move in a particular direction, sending out small clouds of smoke or steam: *The train puffed into the station.* IDM **be puffed up with 'pride, etc.** to be too full of pride, etc: *He felt grown-up, puffed up with self-importance.* **ˌpuff and 'pant** (also **ˌpuff and 'blow**, *informal*) to breathe quickly and loudly through your mouth after physical effort: *Eventually, puffing and panting, he arrived at the gate.*—more at HUFF *v.* PHRV **ˌpuff sth↔'out** to make sth bigger and rounder, especially by filling it with air: *She puffed out her cheeks.* **ˌpuff 'up| ˌpuff sth↔'up** to swell or to make sth swell: *Her cheeks puffed up.* ◊ *The frog puffed itself up.*

■ *noun* **1** [C] an act of breathing in sth such as smoke from a cigarette, or drugs: *He had a few puffs at the cigar.* ◊ *Take two puffs from the inhaler every four hours.* **2** [C] a small amount of air, smoke, etc. that is blown from somewhere: *a puff of wind* ◊ *Puffs of white smoke came from the chimney.* ◊ *Any chance of success seemed to vanish in a puff of smoke* (= to disappear quickly). **3** [C] a hollow piece of light pastry that is filled with cream, jam, etc.—see also CREAM PUFF **4** (*AmE* also **'puff piece**) [C] (*informal, usually disapproving*) a piece of writing or speech that praises sb/sth too much **5** [U] (*informal, especially BrE*) breath: *The hill was very steep and I soon ran out of puff.*—see also POWDER PUFF

puff·ball /ˈpʌfbɔːl/ *noun* a FUNGUS with a round brown head, that bursts when it is ripe to release its seeds

puffed /pʌft/ (also **ˌpuffed 'out**) *adj.* [not before noun] (*BrE, informal*) breathing quickly and with difficulty because you have been having a lot of physical exercise

puff·er /ˈpʌfə(r)/ *noun* (*informal*) = INHALER

puf·fin /ˈpʌfɪn/ *noun* a black and white seabird with a large, brightly coloured beak, common in the N Atlantic—picture on page A6

ˌpuff 'pastry *noun* [U] a type of light pastry that forms many thin layers when baked, used for making pies, cakes, etc.

'puff piece *noun* (*AmE*) = PUFF

ˌpuff 'sleeve (also **ˌpuffed 'sleeve**) *noun* a type of sleeve on a piece of clothing that fits close to the body at the shoulder and the lower edge and is wider in the middle, forming a round shape

puffy /ˈpʌfi/ *adj.* (**puff·ier, puffi·est**) **1** (of eyes, faces, etc.) looking swollen (= larger, rounder, etc. than usual): *Her eyes were puffy from crying.* **2** (of clouds, etc.) looking soft, round and white ▶ **puf·fi·ness** *noun* [U]

pug /pʌg/ *noun* a small dog with short hair and a wide flat face with deep folds of skin

pu·gil·ist /ˈpjuːdʒɪlɪst/ *noun* (*old-fashioned*) a boxer ▶ **pu·gil·ism** /-lɪzəm/ *noun* [U] **pu·gil·is·tic** /ˌpjuːdʒɪˈlɪstɪk/ *adj.*

pug·na·cious /pʌɡˈneɪʃəs/ *adj.* (*formal*) having a strong desire to argue or fight with other people: *a pugnacious man/attitude* ▶ **pug·na·cious·ly** *adv.* **pug·na·city** /pʌɡˈnæsəti/ *noun* [U]

puke /pjuːk/ *verb* ~ (sth) (up) (*informal*) to VOMIT: [V] *The baby puked all over me this morning.* ◊ *That guy makes me puke!* (= makes me angry) ◊ [VN] *I puked up my dinner.* ▶ **puke** *noun* [U]: *to be covered in puke*

pukka /ˈpʌkə/ *adj.* (*BrE*) **1** (*old-fashioned*) genuine; not a copy; appropriate in a particular social situation: *pukka riding boots* **2** (*informal*) of very good quality

pull /pʊl/ *verb, noun*

■ *verb*

MOVE/REMOVE STH | **1** to hold sth firmly and use force in order to move it or try to move it towards yourself: [V] *You push and I'll pull.* ◊ *Don't pull so hard or the handle will come off.* ◊ *I pulled on the rope to see if it was secure.* ◊ [VN] *Stop pulling her hair!* ◊ *She pulled him gently towards her.* ◊ [VN-ADJ] *Pull the door shut.* **2** [VN] [*usually +adv. / prep.*] to remove sth from a place by pulling: *Pull the plug out.* ◊ *She pulled off her boots.* ◊ *He pulled a gun on me* (= took out a gun and aimed it at me). **3** [VN+*adv. / prep.*] to move sb/sth in a particular direction by pulling: *Pull your chair nearer the table.* ◊ *He pulled his sweater on / pulled on his sweater.* ◊ *She took his arm and pulled him along.* **4** [VN] to hold or be attached to sth and move it along behind you: *In this area oxen are used to pull carts.*

BODY | **5** [+*adv. / prep.*] to move your body or a part of your body in a particular direction, especially using force: [V] *He tried to kiss her but she pulled away.* ◊ [VN] *The dog snapped at her and she quickly pulled back her hand.* ◊ [VN-ADJ] *John **pulled** himself **free** and ran off.*

CURTAINS | **6** [VN] to open or close curtains, etc: *Pull the curtains—it's dark outside.*

MUSCLE | **7** [VN] to damage a muscle, etc. by using too much force: *to pull a muscle / ligament / tendon*

SWITCH | **8** [VN] to move a switch, etc. towards yourself or down in order to operate a machine or piece of equipment: *Pull the lever to start the motor.* ◊ *Don't pull the trigger!*

VEHICLE/ENGINE | **9** ~ (sth) to the right/the left/one side to move or make a vehicle move sideways: [V] *The wheel is pulling to the left.* ◊ [VN] *She pulled the car to the right to avoid the dog.* **10** [V] (of an engine) to work hard and use a lot of power: *The old car pulled hard as we drove slowly up the hill.*

BOAT | **11** [*usually +adv. / prep.*] to use OARS to move a boat along: [V] *They pulled towards the shore.* [also VN]

CROWD/SUPPORT | **12** [VN] ~ sb/sth (in) to attract the interest or support of sb/sth: *They pulled in huge crowds on their latest tour.*

ATTRACT SEXUALLY | **13** (*BrE, informal*) to attract sb sexually: [VN] *He can still pull the girls.* ◊ [V] *She's hoping to pull tonight.*

TRICK/CRIME | **14** [VN] (*informal*) to succeed in playing a trick on sb, committing a crime, etc: *He's pulling some sort of trick on you.*

CANCEL | **15** [VN] (*informal*) to cancel an event; to stop showing an advertisement, etc: *The gig was pulled at the last moment.*

IDM **pull a 'fast one (on sb)** (*slang*) to trick sb **pull sb's 'leg** (*informal*) to play a joke on sb, usually by making them believe sth that is not true **pull the 'other one (—it's got 'bells on)** (*BrE, spoken*) used to show that you do not believe what sb has just said **pull out all the 'stops** (*informal*) to make the greatest effort possible to achieve sth **pull the 'plug on sb/sth** (*informal*) to put an end to sb's project, a plan, etc. **pull your 'punches** (*informal*) (usually used in negative sentences) to express sth less strongly than you are able to, for example to avoid upsetting or shocking sb: *Her articles certainly don't pull any punches.* **pull sth/a ,rabbit out of the 'hat** (*informal*) to suddenly produce sth as a solution to a problem **pull 'rank (on sb)** to make use of your place or status in society or at work to make sb do what you want **pull the rug (out) from under sb's 'feet** (*informal*) to take help or support away from sb suddenly **pull your 'socks up** (*BrE, informal*) to try to improve your performance, work, behaviour, etc: *You're going to have to pull your socks up.* **pull 'strings (for sb)** (*AmE also* **pull 'wires**) (*informal*) to use your influence in order to get an advantage for sb **pull the 'strings** to control events or the actions of other people **pull your 'weight** to work as hard as everyone else in a job, an activity, etc. **pull the 'wool over sb's 'eyes** (*informal*) to try to deceive sb; to hide your real actions or intentions from sb—more at BOOTSTRAP, FACE *n.*, HORN, PIECE *n.*, SHRED *n.*

PHRV **,pull a'head (of sb/sth)** to move in front of sb/sth: *The cyclists were together until the bend, when Tyler pulled ahead.* **,pull sb/sth a'part** to separate people or animals that are fighting **,pull sth a'part** to separate sth into pieces by pulling different parts of it in different directions **'pull at sth** = PULL ON STH **,pull a'way (from sth)** (of a vehicle) to start moving: *They waved as the bus pulled away.* **,pull 'back 1** (of an army) to move back from a place **SYN** WITHDRAW **2** to decide not to do sth that you were intending to do, because of possible problems **SYN** WITHDRAW: *Their sponsors pulled back at the last minute.* **,pull sb↔'back** to make an army move back from a place **,pull 'back|,pull sth↔'back** (*sport*) to improve a team's position in a game: *Rangers pulled back to 4–3.* ◊ *They pulled back a goal just before half-time.* **,pull sb↔'down** (*especially AmE*) to make sb less happy, healthy or successful **,pull sth↔'down 1** to destroy a building completely **SYN** DEMOLISH **2** = PULL STH IN **,pull sb↔'in** (*informal*) to bring sb to a police station in order to ask them questions about a crime **,pull sth↔'in/'down** (*informal*) to earn the large amount of money mentioned: *I reckon she's pulling in over $100000.* **,pull 'in (to sth) 1** (of a train) to enter a station and stop **2** (*BrE*) (of a vehicle or its driver) to move to the side of the road or to the place mentioned and stop: *The police car signalled to us to pull in.* **,pull 'off|,pull 'off sth** (of a vehicle or its driver) to leave the road in order to stop for a short time **,pull sth↔'off** (*informal*) to succeed in doing sth difficult: *We pulled off the deal.* ◊ *I never thought you'd pull it off.* **'pull on/at sth** to take long deep breaths from a cigarette, etc. **,pull 'out** (of a vehicle or its driver) to move away from the side of the road, etc: *A car suddenly pulled out in front of me.* **,pull 'out (of sth) 1** (of a train) to leave a station **2** to move away from sth or stop being involved in it **SYN** WITHDRAW: *The project became so expensive that we had to pull out.* **,pull sb/sth 'out (of sth)** to make sb/sth move away from sth or stop being involved in it **SYN** WITHDRAW: *They are pulling their troops out of the war zone.*—related noun PULL-OUT **,pull 'over** (of a vehicle or its driver) to move to the side of the road in order to stop or let sth pass **,pull sb/sth↔'over** (of the police) to make a driver or vehicle move to the side of the road **,pull 'through|,pull 'through sth 1** to get better after a serious illness, operation, etc: *The doctors think she will pull through.* **2** to succeed in doing sth very difficult: *It's going to be tough but we'll pull through it together.* **,pull sb 'through|,pull sb 'through sth 1** to help sb get better after a serious illness, operation, etc. **2** to help sb succeed in doing sth very difficult: *I relied on my instincts to pull me through.* **,pull to'gether** to act, work, etc. together with other people in an organized way and without fighting **,pull yourself to'gether** to take control of your feelings and behave in a calm way: *Stop crying and pull yourself together!* **,pull 'up** (of a vehicle or its driver) to stop: *He pulled up at the traffic lights.* **,pull sb 'up** (*BrE, informal*) to criticize sb for sth that they have done wrong

■ *noun*

TRYING TO MOVE STH | **1** [C] an act of trying to make sth move by holding it firmly and bringing it towards you: *I gave the door a sharp pull and it opened.* ◊ *One last pull on the rope should do it.*

PHYSICAL FORCE | **2** [sing.] **the ~ (of sth)** a strong physical force that makes sth move in a particular direction: *the earth's gravitational pull*

ATTRACTION | **3** [C, usually sing.] **the ~ (of sth)** the fact of sth attracting you or having a strong effect on you: *The magnetic pull of the city was hard to resist.*

INFLUENCE | **4** [U] (*informal*) power and influence over other people: *people who have a lot of pull with the media*

ON CIGARETTE/DRINK | **5** [C] ~ (at/on sth) an act of taking a deep breath of smoke from a cigarette, etc. or a deep drink of something: *She took a long pull on her cigarette.*

WALK UP HILL | **6** [C, usually sing.] (*BrE*) a difficult walk up a steep hill: *It's a long pull up to the summit.*

æ	ɑː	e	ɜː	ə	ɪ	iː	i	ɒ	ɔː	ʌ	ʊ	u	uː
cat	father	ten	bird	about	sit	see	many	got	saw	cup	put	actual	too
								(BrE)					

MUSCLE INJURY | **7** [C] an injury to a muscle caused by using too much force

HANDLE/ROPE | **8** [C] (especially in compounds) something such as a handle or rope that you use to pull sth: *a bell/ door pull*—see also RING PULL

IDM **on the ˈpull** (*BrE, slang*) (of a person) trying to find a sexual partner

ˈpull date *noun* (*AmE*) = SELL-BY DATE

ˈpull-down *adj.* **1** designed to be used by being pulled down: *a pull-down bed* **2 ~ menu** (*computing*) a list of possible choices that appears on a computer screen below a MENU title—picture on page 251

pul·let /ˈpʊlɪt/ *noun* a young chicken, especially one that is less than one year old

pul·ley /ˈpʊli/ *noun* a wheel or set of wheels over which a rope or chain is pulled in order to lift or lower heavy objects: *a system of ropes and pulleys*

ˈpulling power (*BrE*) (*AmE* **ˈdrawing power**) *noun* [U] the ability of sb/sth to attract people

Pull·man /ˈpʊlmən/ *noun* (*pl.* **Pull·mans**) a type of very comfortable railway carriage

ˈpull-out *noun* **1** a part of a magazine, newspaper, etc. that can be taken out easily and kept separately: *an eight-page pull-out on health* ◊ *a pull-out guide* **2** an act of taking an army away from a particular place; an act of taking an organization out of a system

pull·over /ˈpʊləʊvə(r)/ *AmE* -oʊ-/ *noun* (*especially BrE*) a knitted woollen or cotton piece of clothing for the upper part of the body, with long sleeves and no buttons

ˈpull-tab *noun* (*AmE*) = RING PULL

ˈpull-up (*also* **ˈchin-up** especially in *AmE*) *noun* [usually pl.] an exercise in which you hold onto a high bar above your head and pull yourself up towards it—picture at SIT-UP

pul·mon·ary /ˈpʌlmənəri; *AmE* -neri/ *adj.* [only before noun] (*medical*) connected with the lungs

pulp /pʌlp/ *noun, verb, adj.*
▪ *noun* **1** [sing., U] a soft wet substance that is made especially by crushing sth: *Cook the fruit gently until it forms a pulp.* ◊ *His face had been* **beaten to a pulp** (= very badly beaten). **2** [U] a soft substance that is made by crushing wood, fabric or other material and then used to make paper: *paper/wood pulp* **3** [U] the soft part inside some fruit and vegetables **SYN** FLESH ▶ **pulpy** *adj.*: *Cook the fruit slowly until soft and pulpy.*
▪ *verb* [VN] to crush or beat sth so that it becomes soft and wet: *Unsold copies of the novel had to be pulped.* ◊ *pulped fruit*
▪ *adj.* [only before noun] (of books, magazines, etc.) badly written and often intended to shock people: *pulp fiction/ horror*

pul·pit /ˈpʊlpɪt/ *noun* a small platform in a church that is like a box and is high above the ground, where a priest, etc. stands to speak to the people: (*figurative*) *The policy has been widely condemned from the pulpit* (= by priests and other church leaders).

pul·sar /ˈpʌlsɑː(r)/ *noun* (*astronomy*) a star that cannot be seen but that sends out regular rapid radio signals—compare QUASAR

pul·sate /pʌlˈseɪt; *AmE* ˈpʌlseɪt/ *verb* [V] **1** to make strong regular movements or sounds: *pulsating rhythms* ◊ *a pulsating headache* ◊ *Lights were pulsating in the sky.* **2 ~** (**with sth**) to be full of excitement or energy: *a pulsating game* ◊ *The streets were pulsating with life.* ▶ **pul·sa·tion** /pʌlˈseɪʃn/ *noun* [C, U]

pulse /pʌls/ *noun, verb*
▪ *noun* **1** [usually sing.] the regular beat of blood as it is pumped around the body, that can be felt in different places, especially on the inside part of the wrist; the number of times the blood beats in a minute: *a strong/ weak pulse* ◊ *an abnormally high pulse rate* ◊ *The doctor* **took/felt my pulse.** ◊ *Fear sent her* **pulse racing** (= made it beat very quickly). **2** a strong regular beat in music **SYN** TEMPO: *the throbbing pulse of the drums* **3** a single short increase in the amount of light, sound or electricity produced by a machine, etc.: *pulse waves* ◊ *sound pulses*

4 (**pulses**) [pl.] the seeds of some plants that are eaten as food, such as peas and LENTILS **IDM** see FINGER *n.*
▪ *verb* [V] **1** to move, beat or flow with strong regular movements or sounds **SYN** THROB: *A vein pulsed in his temple.* ◊ *the pulsing rhythm of the music* ◊ (*figurative*) *A rush of joy pulsed through his body.* **2 ~** (**with sth**) (*written*) to be full of a feeling such as excitement or energy: *The auditorium pulsed with excitement.*

pul·ver·ize (*BrE* also **-ise**) /ˈpʌlvəraɪz/ *verb* [VN] **1** (*formal*) to crush sth into a fine powder: *pulverized bones* **2** (*informal, especially BrE*) to defeat or destroy sb/sth completely: *We pulverized the opposition.*

puma /ˈpjuːmə; *AmE* ˈpuːmə/ (*especially BrE*) (*AmE* usually **couˈgar**) (*AmE* also **ˈmountain lion, ˈpanˈther**) *noun* a large American wild animal of the cat family, with yellowish-brown or greyish fur

pum·ice /ˈpʌmɪs/ (also **ˈpumice stone**) *noun* [U] a type of grey stone that comes from VOLCANOES and is very light in weight. It is used in powder form for cleaning and polishing, and in pieces for rubbing on the skin to soften it.

pum·mel /ˈpʌml/ *verb* (**-ll-**, *AmE* **-l-**) to keep hitting sb/ sth hard, especially with your FISTS (= tightly closed hands): [VN] *He pummelled the pillow with his fists.* ◊ (*figurative*) *She pummelled* (= strongly criticized) *her opponents.* ◊ [V] *Her fists pummelled at his chest.*

pump /pʌmp/ *noun, verb*
▪ *noun* **1** a machine that is used to force liquid, gas or air into or out of sth: *She washed her face at the pump in front of the inn.* ◊ (*BrE*) *a petrol pump* ◊ (*AmE*) *a gas pump* ◊ *a foot/hand pump* (= that you work by using your foot or hand) ◊ *a bicycle pump*—see also STOMACH PUMP—picture at BICYCLE **2** (*BrE*) = PLIMSOLL **3** (*especially AmE*) = COURT SHOE **4** (*BrE*) a light soft shoe that you wear for dancing or exercise: *ballet pumps* **IDM** see PRIME *v.*
▪ *verb* **1** to make water, air, gas, etc. flow in a particular direction by using a pump or sth that works like a pump: [VN] *The engine is used for pumping water out of the mine.* ◊ *The heart pumps blood around the body.* ◊ *The lake had been pumped dry.* [also V] **2** [V+*adv./prep.*] (of a liquid) to flow in a particular direction as if it is being forced by a pump: *Blood was pumping out of his wound.* **3** [VN] to move sth quickly up and down or in and out: *He kept pumping my hand up and down.* ◊ *I pumped the handle like crazy.* **4** [V] to move quickly up and down or in and out: *She sprinted for the line, legs pumping.* ◊ *My heart was pumping with excitement.* **5** [VN] **~ sb** (**for sth**) (*informal*) to try to get information from sb by asking them a lot of questions: *See if you can pump him for more details.* **IDM** **pump ˈbullets, ˈshots, etc. into sb** to fire a lot of bullets into sb **pump sb full of sth** to fill sb with sth, especially drugs: *They pumped her full of painkillers.* **pump ˈiron** (*informal*) to do exercises in which you lift heavy weights in order to strengthen your muscles **pump sb's ˈstomach** to remove the contents of sb's stomach using a pump, because they have swallowed sth harmful **PHRV** **ˌpump sth ˈinto sth** | **ˌpump sth ˈin** to put a lot of money into sth: *He pumped all his savings into the business.* **ˌpump sth ˈinto sb** to force a lot of sth into sb: *It's difficult to pump facts and figures into tired students.* **ˌpump sth↔ˈout** (*informal*) to produce sth in large amounts: *loudspeakers pumping out rock music* ◊ *Our cars pump out thousands of tons of poisonous fumes every year.* **ˌpump sb↔ˈup** [usually passive] to make sb feel more excited or determined **ˌpump sth↔ˈup 1** to fill a tyre, etc. with air using a pump **2** (*informal*) to increase the amount, value or volume of sth: *Interest rates were pumped up last week.*

pump·kin /ˈpʌmpkɪn/ *noun* [U, C] a large round vegetable with thick orange skin. The seeds can be dried and eaten and the soft flesh can be cooked as a vegetable or in sweet pies: *Pumpkin pie is a traditional American dish served on Thanksgiving.*—picture on page A3

ˈpump-priming *noun* [U] the act of investing money to encourage growth in an industry or a business, especially by a government

pun /pʌn/ *noun, verb*

aɪ	aʊ	eɪ	əʊ	oʊ	ɔɪ	ɪə	eə	ʊə	j	w
my	now	say	go (BrE)	go (AmE)	boy	near	hair	pure	yes	wet

■ *noun* ~ (**on sth**) the clever or humorous use of a word that has more than one meaning, or of words that have different meanings but sound the same: *We're banking on them lending us the money—no pun intended!*—compare WORDPLAY

■ *verb* (**-nn-**) [V] to make a pun

Punch /pʌntʃ/ *noun* IDM
see PLEASED

punch /pʌntʃ/ *verb, noun*

■ *verb* [VN] **1** ~ **sb/sth** (**in/on sth**) to hit sb/sth hard with your FIST (= closed hand): *He was kicked and punched as he lay on the ground.* ◊ *She punched him on the nose.* ◊ *He was punching the air in triumph.* **2** ~ **sth (in/through sth)** to make a hole in sth with a punch or some other sharp object: *to punch a time card* ◊ *The machine punches a row of holes in the metal sheet.* **3** [VN] to press buttons or keys on a computer, telephone, etc. in order to operate it: *I punched the button to summon the elevator.* ▶ **punch·er** *noun*: *He's one of boxing's strongest punchers.* PHRV **punch 'in/'out** (*AmE*) to record the time you arrive at/leave work by putting a card into a special machine—see also CLOCK IN/ON, CLOCK OUT/OFF **punch sth↔'in | punch sth 'into sth** to put information into a computer by pressing the keys: *He punched in the security code.* **punch sb 'out** (*AmE, informal*) to hit sb so hard that they fall down **punch sth↔'out 1** to press a combination of buttons or keys on a computer, telephone, etc: *He picked up the telephone and punched out his friend's number.* **2** to make a hole in sth or knock sth out by hitting it very hard: *I felt as if all my teeth had been punched out.* **3** to cut sth from paper, wood, metal, etc. with a special tool

She punched the air in triumph.

■ *noun* **1** [C] a hard hit made with the FIST (= closed hand): *a punch in the face* ◊ *Hill threw a punch at the police officer.* ◊ *a knockout punch* ◊ *He shot out his right arm and landed a punch on Lorrimer's nose.* **2** [U] the power to interest people: *It's a well-constructed crime story, told with speed and punch.* **3** [C] a tool or machine for cutting holes in paper, leather or metal: *a hole punch*—picture at STATIONERY **4** [U] a hot or cold drink made by mixing water, fruit juice, spices, and usually wine or another alcoholic drink: *rum punch* IDM see BEAT *v.*, PACK *v.*, PULL *v.*, ROLL *v.*

Punch and Judy show /ˌpʌntʃ ən ˈdʒuːdi ʃəʊ; *AmE* ʃoʊ/ *noun* (in Britain) a traditional type of entertainment for children in which PUPPETS are used to tell stories about Punch who is always fighting with his wife Judy

punch·bag /ˈpʌntʃbæg/ (*BrE*) (*AmE* ˈpunching bag) *noun* a heavy leather bag, hung on a rope, which is PUNCHED, especially by boxers as part of training, or as a form of exercise

punch·ball /ˈpʌntʃbɔːl/ *noun* a heavy leather ball, fixed on a spring, which is PUNCHED, especially by boxers as a part of training, or as a form of exercise

punch·bowl /ˈpʌntʃbəʊl; *AmE* -boʊl/ *noun* a bowl in which punch (= the drink) is served

punch·card /ˈpʌntʃkɑːd; *AmE* -kɑːrd/ (also ˌpunched ˈcard) *noun* a card on which, in the past, information was recorded as lines of holes and used for giving instructions, etc. to computers and other machines

ˈ**punch-drunk** (also ˌslap-ˈhappy especially in *AmE*) *adj.* **1** (of a boxer) confused as a result of being PUNCHED on the head many times **2** unable to think clearly; in a confused state

ˈ**punching bag** *noun* (*AmE*) = PUNCHBAG

punch·line /ˈpʌntʃlaɪn/ (also *AmE informal* ˈtag line) *noun* the last few words of a joke that make it funny

ˈ**punch-up** *noun* (*BrE, informal*) a physical fight

punchy /ˈpʌntʃi/ *adj.* (of a speech, song, etc.) having a strong effect because it expresses sth clearly in only a few words: *a bright, punchy style of writing*

punc·tili·ous /pʌŋkˈtɪliəs/ *adj.* (*formal*) very careful to behave correctly or to carry out your duties exactly as you should: *a punctilious host* ▶ **punc·tili·ous·ly** *adv.* **punc·tili·ous·ness** *noun* [U]

punc·tual /ˈpʌŋktʃuəl/ *adj.* happening or doing sth at the arranged or correct time; not late: *She has been reliable and punctual.* ◊ *a punctual start at 9 o'clock* ▶ **punc·tu·al·ity** /ˌpʌŋktʃuˈæləti/ *noun* [U] **punc·tu·al·ly** /ˈpʌŋktʃuəli/ *adv.*: *They always pay punctually.*

punc·tu·ate /ˈpʌŋktʃueɪt/ *verb* **1** [VN] [often passive] ~ **sth (with sth)** to interrupt sth at intervals: *Her speech was punctuated by bursts of applause.* **2** [V, VN] to divide writing into sentences and phrases by using special marks, for example COMMAS, question marks, etc.

punc·tu·ation /ˌpʌŋktʃuˈeɪʃn/ *noun* [U] the marks used in writing that divide sentences and phrases; the system of using these marks ⇨ Appendix 4

ˌ**punctu'ation mark** *noun* a sign or mark used in writing to divide sentences and phrases

punc·ture /ˈpʌŋktʃə(r)/ *noun, verb*

■ *noun* **1** (*BrE*) a small hole in a tyre made by a sharp point: *I had a puncture on the way and arrived late.*—see also FLAT *n.* (6) **2** a small hole, especially in the skin, made by a sharp point

■ *verb* **1** to make a small hole in sth; to get a small hole: [VN] *to puncture a tyre/balloon* ◊ *She was taken to the hospital with broken ribs and a punctured lung.* ◊ [V] *One of the front tyres had punctured.* **2** [VN] (*written*) to suddenly make sb feel less confident, proud, etc: *to puncture sb's confidence/complacency/illusions*

pun·dit /ˈpʌndɪt/ *noun* a person who knows a lot about a particular subject and who often talks about it in public; an expert

pun·gent /ˈpʌndʒənt/ *adj.* **1** having a strong taste or smell: *the pungent smell of burning rubber* **2** direct and having a strong effect: *pungent remarks/criticism* ▶ **pun·gency** /-nsi/ *noun* [U] **pung·ent·ly** *adv.*

pun·ish /ˈpʌnɪʃ/ *verb* [VN] **1** ~ **sb** (**for sth/for doing sth**) to make sb suffer because they have broken the law or done sth wrong: *Those responsible for this crime will be severely punished.* ◊ *He was punished for refusing to answer their questions.* ◊ *My parents used to punish me by not letting me watch TV.* **2** ~ **sth** (**by/with sth**) to set the punishment for a particular crime: *In those days murder was always punished with the death penalty.* **3** ~ **yourself** (**for sth**) to blame yourself for sth that has happened

pun·ish·able /ˈpʌnɪʃəbl/ *adj.* ~ (**by/with sth**) (of a crime) that can be punished, especially by law: *a crime punishable by/with imprisonment* ◊ *Giving false information to the police is a punishable offence.*

pun·ish·ing /ˈpʌnɪʃɪŋ/ *adj.* [usually before noun] long and difficult and making you work hard so you become very tired: *The President has a punishing schedule for the next six months.*

pun·ish·ment /ˈpʌnɪʃmənt/ *noun* **1** [U, C] ~ (**for sth**) an act or a way of punishing sb: *to inflict/impose/mete out punishment* ◊ *What is the punishment for murder?* ◊ *There is little evidence that harsher punishments deter any better than more lenient ones.* ◊ *The punishment should fit the crime.* ◊ *He was sent to his room as a punishment.*—see also CAPITAL PUNISHMENT, CORPORAL PUNISHMENT **2** [U] rough treatment: *The carpet by the door takes the most punishment.*

pu·ni·tive /ˈpjuːnətɪv/ *adj.* [usually before noun] (*formal*) **1** intended as punishment: *There are calls for more punitive measures against people who drink and drive.* ◊ (*AmE*) *He was awarded punitive damages* (= in a court of law). **2** very severe and that people find very difficult to pay: *punitive taxes* ▶ **pu·ni·tive·ly** *adv.*

Pun·jabi /pʊnˈdʒɑːbi/ *noun* **1** [C] a person from the Punjab area in NW India and Pakistan **2** [U] the language of people from the Punjab ▶ **Pun·jabi** *adj.*

punk /pʌŋk/ *noun* **1** (also ˌpunk ˈrock) [U] a type of loud and aggressive ROCK music popular in the late 1970s and early 1980s: *a punk band* **2** (also ˌpunk ˈrocker) [C] a person who likes punk music and dresses like a punk musician, for example by wearing metal chains, leather clothes and having brightly coloured hair: *a punk haircut*

3 [C] (*informal disapproving, especially AmE*) a young man or boy who behaves in a rude or violent way

pun·net /ˈpʌnɪt/ *noun* (*BrE*) a small box or basket that soft fruit is often sold in

punt¹ /pʌnt/ *noun, verb*—see also PUNT²

■ *noun* **1** a long shallow boat with a flat bottom and square ends which is moved by pushing the end of a long pole against the bottom of a river—picture at BOAT **2** (*BrE, informal*) a bet: *The investment is little more than a punt.* **3** (in rugby or American football) a long kick made after dropping the ball from your hands

▶ *verb* **1** to travel in a punt, especially for pleasure: [V] *We spent the day punting on the river.* ◇ *to go punting* [also VN] **2** [VN] to kick a ball hard so that it goes a long way, sometimes after it has dropped from your hands and before it reaches the ground

punt² /pʊnt/ *noun* the unit of money in the Republic of Ireland (to be replaced by the euro)—see also PUNT¹

punt·er /ˈpʌntə(r)/ *noun* (*BrE, informal*) **1** a person who buys or uses a particular product or service; a customer: *It's important to keep the punters happy.* **2** a person who gambles on the result of a horse race

puny /ˈpjuːni/ *adj.* (*disapproving*) **1** small and weak: *The lamb was a puny little thing.* **2** not very impressive: *They laughed at my puny efforts.*

pup /pʌp/ *noun* **1** = PUPPY **2** a young animal of various SPECIES (= types): *a seal pup* **IDM** **sell sb/buy a pup** (*old-fashioned, BrE, informal*) to sell sb or be sold sth that has no value or is worth much less than the price paid for it

pupa /ˈpjuːpə/ *noun* (*pl.* **pupae** /ˈpjuːpiː/) an insect in the stage of development between a LARVA and an adult insect—compare CHRYSALIS

pu·pate /pjuːˈpeɪt; AmE ˈpjuːpeɪt/ *verb* [V] (*biology*) to develop into a pupa

pupil /ˈpjuːpl/ *noun* **1** (*especially BrE*, becoming *old-fashioned*) a person who is being taught, especially a child in a school: *How many pupils does the school have?* ◇ *She now teaches only private pupils.* ⇨ note at STUDENT **2** a person who is taught artistic, musical, etc. skills by an expert: *The painting is by a pupil of Rembrandt.* **3** the small round black area at the centre of the eye: *Her pupils were dilated.*—compare IRIS—picture at BODY

pup·pet /ˈpʌpɪt/ *noun* **1** a model of a person or an animal that can be made to move, for example by pulling strings attached to parts of its body or by putting your hand inside it. A puppet with strings is also called a MARIONETTE: *a wooden/hand puppet* ◇ *a puppet show*—see also GLOVE PUPPET **2** (*usually disapproving*) a person or group whose actions are controlled by another: *The occupying forces set up a* **puppet government**.

pup·pet·eer /ˌpʌpɪˈtɪə(r); AmE -ˈtɪr/ *noun* a person who performs with puppets

pup·pet·ry /ˈpʌpɪtri/ *noun* [U] the art and skill of making and using puppets

puppy /ˈpʌpi/ *noun* (*pl.* **-ies**) (also **pup**) **1** a young dog: *a litter of puppies* ◇ *a Labrador puppy* **2** (*old-fashioned, informal, disapproving*) a proud or rude young man

'puppy fat (*BrE*) (*AmE* **'baby fat**) *noun* [U] fat on a child's body that disappears as the child grows older

'puppy love *noun* [U] feelings of love that a young person has for sb else and that adults do not think is very serious

pur·chase /ˈpɜːtʃəs; AmE ˈpɜːrtʃəs/ *noun, verb*

■ *noun* (*formal* or *written*) **1** [U, C] the act or process or buying sth: *to make a purchase* (= buy sth) ◇ *Keep your receipt as proof of purchase.* ◇ *The company has just announced its £27 million purchase of Park Hotel.*—see also HIRE PURCHASE **2** [C] something that you have bought: *major purchases, such as a new car* ◇ *If you are not satisfied with your purchase we will give you a full refund.* **3** [U, sing.] (*technical*) a firm hold on sth with the hands or feet, for example when you are climbing: *She tried to get a purchase on the slippery rock.*

■ *verb* [VN] ~ **sth** (**from sb**) (*formal* or *written*) to buy sth: *The equipment can be purchased from your local supplier.* ◇ *They purchased the land for $1 million.* ◇ *Please ensure*

that you purchase your ticket in advance. ◇ (*figurative*) *Victory was purchased* (= achieved) *at too great a price.*

'purchase price *noun* [usually sing.] (*formal*) the price that is paid for sth you buy: *the purchase price of the house*

pur·chaser /ˈpɜːtʃəsə(r); AmE ˈpɜːrtʃ-/ *noun* (*formal*) a person who buys sth—compare BUYER

pur·chas·ing /ˈpɜːtʃəsɪŋ; AmE ˈpɜːrtʃ-/ *noun* [U] (*business*) the activity of buying things, especially for a company: *the company's purchasing manager*

'purchasing power *noun* [U] **1** money that people have available to buy goods with **2** the amount that a unit of money can buy: *the peso's purchasing power*

pur·dah /ˈpɜːdə; AmE ˈpɜːrdə/ *noun* [U] the system in some Muslim and Hindu societies by which women live in a separate part of a house or cover their faces so that men do not see them: *to be in purdah* ◇ *He kept his daughters in virtual purdah.*

pure /pjʊə(r); AmE pjʊr/ *adj.* (**purer** /ˈpjʊərə(r); AmE ˈpjʊr-/, **purest** /ˈpjʊərɪst; AmE ˈpjʊr-/)

NOT MIXED **1** [usually before noun] not mixed with anything else; with nothing added: *pure gold/silk* ◇ *These shirts are 100% pure cotton.* ◇ *Classical dance in its purest form requires symmetry and balance.* ◇ *One movie is classified as pure art, the other as entertainment.*

CLEAN **2** clean and not containing any harmful substances: *a bottle of pure water* ◇ *The air was sweet and pure.* OPP IMPURE

COMPLETE **3** [only before noun] complete and total: *They met by pure chance.* ◇ *She laughed with pure joy.*

MORALLY GOOD **4** without evil thoughts or actions, especially sexual ones; morally good: *to lead a pure life* ◇ *His motives were pure.* ◇ (*literary*) *to be pure in body and mind* OPP IMPURE

COLOUR/SOUND/LIGHT **5** very clear; perfect: *beaches of pure white sand* ◇ *a pure note/tone/voice*

SUBJECT YOU STUDY **6** [only before noun] concerned with increasing knowledge of the subject rather than with using knowledge in practical ways: *pure mathematics* ◇ *technology as opposed to pure science subjects*—compare APPLIED

BREED/RACE **7** not mixed with any other breed or race, etc: *These cattle are one of the purest breeds in Britain.*—see also PURE-BRED

—see also PURIFY, PURITY

IDM **,pure and 'simple** used after the noun that it refers to in order to emphasize that there is nothing but the thing you have just mentioned involved in sth: *It's laziness, pure and simple.*

'pure-bred *adj.* (of an animal) born from parents of the same breed, not from a mix of two or more breeds

purée /ˈpjʊəreɪ; AmE pjʊˈreɪ/ *noun, verb*

■ *noun* [U, C] food in the form of a thick liquid made by crushing fruit or cooked vegetables in a small amount of water: *apple purée*

■ *verb* (**pur·éed, pur·éed**) [VN] to make food into a purée: *puréed apples*

pure·ly /ˈpjʊəli; AmE ˈpjʊrli/ *adv.* only; completely: *I saw the letter purely by chance.* ◇ *The charity is run on a purely voluntary basis.* ◇ *She took the job purely and simply for the money.*

pur·ga·tive /ˈpɜːɡətɪv; AmE ˈpɜːrɡ-/ *noun* a substance, especially a medicine, that causes your bowels to empty ▶ **pur·ga·tive** *adj.*

pur·ga·tory /ˈpɜːɡətri; AmE ˈpɜːrɡətɔːri/ *noun* [U] **1** (*usually* **Purgatory**) (in Roman Catholic teaching) a place or state in which the souls of dead people suffer for the bad things they did when they were living, so that they can become pure enough to go to heaven **2** (*spoken, humorous*) any place or state of suffering: *Getting up at four o'clock every morning is sheer purgatory.*

purge /pɜːdʒ; AmE pɜːrdʒ/ *verb, noun*

■ *verb* [VN] **1** ~ **sth** (**of sb**) | ~ **sb** (**from sth**) to remove people from an organization, often violently, because their opinions or activities are unacceptable to the people in power: *His first act as leader was to purge the party of*

s	t	v	z	ʃ	ʒ	tʃ	dʒ	θ	ð	ŋ
see	tea	van	zoo	shoe	vision	chain	jam	thin	this	sing

extremists. ◊ *He purged extremists from the party.* **2 ~ yourself/sb/sth (of sth)| ~ sth (from sth)** *(written)* to make yourself/sb/sth pure, healthy or clean by getting rid of bad thoughts or feelings: *We need to purge our sport of racism.* ◊ *Nothing could purge the guilt from her mind.*
■ *noun* the act of removing people, often violently, from an organization because their views are unacceptable to the people who have power

pur·ify /ˈpjʊərɪfaɪ; *AmE* ˈpjʊr-/ *verb* (**puri·fies, puri·fy·ing, puri·fied, puri·fied**) [VN] **1** to make sth pure by removing substances that are dirty, harmful or not wanted: *One tablet will purify a litre of water in 10 minutes.* **2** to make sb pure by removing evil from their souls: *Hindus purify themselves by bathing in the river Ganges.* **3 ~ sth (from sth)** *(technical)* to take a pure form of a substance out of another substance that contains it ▶ **puri·fi·ca·tion** /ˌpjʊərɪfɪˈkeɪʃn; *AmE* ˌpjʊr-/ *noun* [U]: *a water purification plant*

pur·ist /ˈpjʊərɪst; *AmE* ˈpjʊr-/ *noun* a person who thinks things should be done in the traditional way and who has strong opinions on what is correct in language, art, etc. ▶ **pur·ism** /ˈpjʊərɪzəm; *AmE* ˈpjʊr-/ *noun* [U]

pur·itan /ˈpjʊərɪtən; *AmE* ˈpjʊr-/ *noun, adj.*
■ *noun* **1** (usually *disapproving*) a person who has very strict moral attitudes and who thinks that pleasure is bad **2** (**Puritan**) a member of a Protestant group of Christians in England in the 16th and 17th centuries who wanted to worship God in a simple way
■ *adj.* **1** (**Puritan**) connected with the Puritans and their beliefs **2** = PURITANICAL

pur·it·an·ical /ˌpjʊərɪˈtænɪkl; *AmE* ˌpjʊr-/ (also **pur·itan**) *adj.* (usually *disapproving*) having very strict moral attitudes: *Their parents had a puritanical streak and didn't approve of dancing.*

pur·itan·ism /ˈpjʊərɪtənɪzəm; *AmE* ˈpjʊr-/ *noun* [U] **1** (**Puritanism**) the beliefs and practices of the Puritans **2** very strict moral attitudes

pur·ity /ˈpjʊərəti; *AmE* ˈpjʊr-/ *noun* [U] the state or quality of being pure: *The purity of the water is tested regularly.* ◊ *moral/spiritual purity* OPP IMPURITY

purl /pɜːl; *AmE* pɜːrl/ *noun* [U] a stitch used in KNITTING ▶ **purl** *verb* [V]

pur·loin /pɜːˈlɔɪn; ˈpɜːlɔɪn; *AmE* pɜːrˈl-; ˈpɜːrl-/ *verb* [VN] **~ sth (from sb/sth)** *(formal or humorous)* to steal sth or use it without permission: *We purloined a couple of old computers from work.*

pur·ple /ˈpɜːpl; *AmE* ˈpɜːrpl/ *adj.* **1** having the colour of blue and red mixed together: *a purple flower/bruise* ◊ *His face was purple with rage.* **2 ~ prose/passage** writing or a piece of writing that is too grand in style ▶ **pur·ple** *noun* [U, C]: *She was dressed in purple.*

Purple ˈHeart *noun* a medal given to a member of the armed forces of the US who has been wounded in battle

ˈpurple patch *noun* (*BrE*) a period of success or good luck: *He was enjoying a purple patch and scored 11 goals in 14 games.*

purp·lish /ˈpɜːplɪʃ; *AmE* ˈpɜːrp-/ *adj.* fairly purple in colour: *purplish lips/skin*

pur·port *verb, noun*
■ *verb* /pəˈpɔːt; *AmE* pərˈpɔːrt/ [V to inf] *(formal)* to claim to be sth or to have done sth, when this may not be true: *The book does not purport to be a complete history of the period.*
■ *noun* /ˈpɜːpɔːt; *AmE* ˈpɜːrpɔːrt/ [sing.] **the ~ of sth** *(formal)* the general meaning of sth

pur·ported /pəˈpɔːtɪd; *AmE* pərˈpɔːrt-/ *adj.* [only before noun] *(formal)* that has been stated to have happened or to be true, when this might not be the case: *the scene of the purported crime* ▶ **pur·port·ed·ly** *adv.*: *a letter purportedly written by Mozart*

pur·pose /ˈpɜːpəs; *AmE* ˈpɜːrpəs/ *noun* **1** [C] the intention, aim or function of sth; the thing that sth is supposed to achieve: *Our campaign's main purpose is to raise money.* ◊ *The purpose of the book is to provide a complete guide to the university.* ◊ *A meeting was called for the purpose of appointing a new treasurer.* ◊ *The experiments serve no useful purpose* (= are not useful). ◊ *The build-*

ing is used for religious purposes. ⇨ note at CAUSE **2** (**purposes**) [pl.] what is needed in a particular situation: *These gifts count as income for tax purposes.* ◊ *For the purposes of this study, the three groups have been combined.* **3** [C, U] meaning that is important and valuable to you: *Volunteer work gives her life* (*a sense of*) *purpose.* **4** [U] the ability to plan sth and work successfully to achieve it SYN DETERMINATION: *He was enormous confidence and strength of purpose.*—see also CROSS PURPOSES IDM **on ˈpurpose** not by accident; deliberately: *He did it on purpose, knowing it would annoy her.* **to little/no ˈpurpose** *(formal)* with little/no useful effect or result—more at INTENT *n.*, PRACTICAL *adj.*

ˌpurpose-ˈbuilt *adj.* (*BrE*) designed and built for a particular purpose

pur·pose·ful /ˈpɜːpəsfl; *AmE* ˈpɜːrp-/ *adj.* having a useful purpose; acting with a clear aim and with determination: *Purposeful work is an important part of the regime for young offenders.* ◊ *She looked purposeful and determined.* ▶ **pur·pose·ful·ly** /-fəli/ *adv.* **pur·pose·ful·ness** *noun* [U]

pur·pose·less /ˈpɜːpələs; *AmE* ˈpɜːrp-/ *adj.* having no meaning, use or clear aim: *purposeless destruction*

pur·pose·ly /ˈpɜːpəsli; *AmE* ˈpɜːrp-/ *adv.* on purpose; deliberately: *He sat down, purposely avoiding her gaze.*

pur·pos·ive /ˈpɜːpəsɪv; *AmE* ˈpɜːrp-/ *adj.* (*formal*) having a clear and definite purpose

purr /pɜː(r)/ *verb* **1** [V] when a cat **purrs**, it makes a low continuous sound in the throat, especially when it is happy or comfortable **2** [V] (of a machine or vehicle) to make a low continuous sound; to move making such a sound: *a purring engine* ◊ *The car purred away.* **3** to speak in a low and gentle voice, for example to show you are happy or satisfied, or because you want to attract sb or get them to do sth: [V] *He was purring with satisfaction.* [also V speech] ▶ **purr** (also **pur·ring**) *noun* [sing.]: *the purr of a contented cat/a car engine*

purse /pɜːs; *AmE* pɜːrs/ *noun, verb*
■ *noun* **1** [C] (*especially BrE*) a small bag made of leather, plastic, etc. for carrying coins and often also paper money, cards, etc., used especially by women: *I took a coin out of my purse and gave it to the child.*—compare CHANGE PURSE, WALLET—picture at MONEY **2** [C] (*AmE*) = HANDBAG **3** [sing.] the amount of money that is available to a person, an organization or a government to spend: *We have holidays to suit every purse.* ◊ *Should spending on the arts be met out of the **public purse*** (= from government money)? **4** [C] (*sport*) a sum of money given as a prize in a boxing match IDM see SILK
■ *verb* [VN] **~ your lips** to form your lips into a small tight round shape, for example to show disapproval

---

BRITISH / AMERICAN
purse / handbag / wallet

A **purse** (*BrE*) / a **ᴄhange purse** or **coin purse** (*AmE*) is a small bag for carrying money, including coins.

A **handbag** (also **purse** in *AmE*) is a bag that women especially carry with them to hold their money, keys, etc.

A **wallet** (also **billfold** in *AmE*) is a small leather or plastic case used for keeping bank notes, cards, etc. in.

---

pur·ser /ˈpɜːsə(r); *AmE* ˈpɜːrs-/ *noun* an officer on a ship who is responsible for taking care of the passengers, and for the accounts

the ˈpurse strings *noun* [pl.] a way of referring to money and how it is controlled or spent: *Who holds the purse strings in your house?* ◊ *The government will have to tighten the purse strings* (= spend less).

pur·su·ance /pəˈsjuːəns; *AmE* pərˈsuː-/ *noun* IDM **in pursuance of sth** (*formal or law*) in order to do sth; in the process of doing sth: *They may need to borrow money in pursuance of their legal action.*

pur·su·ant /pəˈsjuːənt; *AmE* pərˈsuː-/ *adj.* **~ to sth** (*formal or law*) according to or following sth, especially a rule or law

---

(BrE)

pur·sue /pə'sjuː; *AmE* pər'suː/ *verb* (*formal*) **1** [VN] to do sth or try to achieve sth over a period of time: *to pursue a goal/an aim/an objective* ◊ *We intend to pursue this policy with determination.* ◊ *She wishes to pursue a medical career.* **2** to continue to discuss, find out about or be involved in sth: [VN] *to pursue legal action* ◊ *We have decided not to pursue the matter.* [also V speech] **3** [VN] to follow or chase sb/sth, especially in order to catch them: *She left the theatre, hotly pursued by the press.* ◊ *Police pursued the car at high speed.*

pur·suer /pə'sjuːə(r); *AmE* pər'suː-/ *noun* (*written*) a person who is following or chasing sb

pur·suit /pə'sjuːt; *AmE* pər'suːt/ *noun* **1** [U] ~ **of sth** the act of looking for or trying to find sth: *the pursuit of happiness/knowledge/profit* ◊ *She travelled the world in pursuit of her dreams.* **2** [U] the act of following or chasing sb: *We drove away with two police cars in pursuit* (= following). ◊ *I galloped off on my horse with Rosie in hot pursuit* (= following quickly behind). **3** [C, usually pl.] something that you give your time and energy to, that you do as a hobby: *outdoor/leisure/intellectual/artistic pursuits*

puru·lent /'pjʊərələnt; *AmE* 'pjʊr-/ *adj.* (*medical*) containing or producing PUS: *a purulent discharge from the wound*

pur·vey /pə'veɪ; *AmE* pər've ɪ/ *verb* [VN] (*formal*) to supply food, services or information to people

pur·vey·or /pə'veɪə(r); *AmE* pər'v-/ *noun* (*formal*) a person or company that supplies sth

pur·view /'pɜːvjuː; *AmE* 'pɜːrv-/ *noun* [U] IDM **within/outside the purview of sth** (*formal*) within the limits of what a person, an organization, etc. is responsible for; dealt with by a document, law, etc.

pus /pʌs/ *noun* [U] a thick yellowish or greenish liquid that is produced in an infected wound

push /pʊʃ/ *verb, noun*

■ *verb*

USING HANDS/ARMS/BODY | **1** [often +*adv./prep.*] to use your hands, arms or body in order to make sb/sth move forward or away from you; to move part of your body into a particular position: [V] *We pushed and pushed but the piano wouldn't move.* ◊ *Push hard when I tell you to.* ◊ *She pushed at the door but it wouldn't budge.* ◊ *You push and I'll pull.* ◊ [VN] *He walked slowly up the hill pushing his bike.* ◊ *She pushed the cup towards me.* ◊ *He pushed his chair back and stood up.* ◊ *He tried to kiss her but she pushed him away.* ◊ *She pushed her face towards him.* ◊ [VN-ADJ] *I pushed the door open.* **2** [+*adv./prep.*] to use force to move past sb/sth using your hands, arms, etc: [V] *The fans pushed against the barrier.* ◊ *People were pushing and shoving to get to the front.* ◊ [VN] *Try and push your way through the crowd.*

AFFECT STH | **3** [VN+*adv./prep.*] to affect sth so that it reaches a particular level or state: *This development could push the country into recession.* ◊ *The rise in interest rates will push prices up.*

SWITCH/BUTTON | **4** [VN] to press a switch, button, etc., for example in order to make a machine start working: *I went into the elevator and pushed the button for the top floor.*

PERSUADE | **5** ~ **sb** (**into sth/into doing sth**)| ~ **sb** (**to do sth**) to persuade or encourage sb to do sth that they may not want to do: [VN] *My teacher pushed me into entering the competition.* ◊ [VN to inf] *No one pushed you to take the job, did they?*

WORK HARD | **6** [VN] to make sb work hard: *The music teacher really pushes her pupils.* ◊ *Lucy should push herself a little harder.*

PUT PRESSURE ON SB | **7** [VN] (*informal*) to put pressure on sb and make them angry or upset: *Her parents are very tolerant, but sometimes she pushes them too far.*

NEW IDEA/PRODUCT | **8** [VN] (*informal*) to try hard to persuade people to accept or agree with a new idea, buy a new product, etc: *The interview gave him a chance to push his latest movie.* ◊ *She didn't want to push the point any further at that moment.*

SELL DRUGS | **9** [VN] (*informal*) to sell illegal drugs

OF ARMY | **10** [V+*adv./prep.*] to move forward quickly through an area: *The army pushed (on) towards the Nile.*

IDM **be ˌpushing '40, '50, etc.** (*informal*) to be nearly 40, 50, etc. years old **be ˌpushing up (the) 'daisies** (*old-fashioned, humorous*) to be dead and in a grave **push the 'boat out** (*BrE, informal*) to spend a lot of money on enjoying yourself or celebrating sth **push your 'luck | ˌpush it/things** to take a risk because you have successfully avoided problems in the past: *You didn't get caught last time, but don't push your luck!* **push sth to the back of your 'mind** to try to forget about sth unpleasant: *I tried to push the thought to the back of my mind.*—more at PANIC BUTTON

PHR V **ˌpush sb a'bout/a'round** to give orders to sb in a rude or unpleasant way **ˌpush a'head/'forward (with sth)** to continue with a plan in a determined way: *The government is pushing ahead with its electoral reforms.* **ˌpush sth↔'aside** to avoid thinking about sth: *He pushed aside the feelings of fear.* **ˌpush sth 'back** to make the time or date of a meeting, etc. later than originally planned: *The start of the game was pushed back from 2 p.m. to 4 p.m.* **'push for sth | 'push sb for sth** to repeatedly ask for sth or try to make sth happen because you think it is very important: *The pressure group is pushing for a ban on GM foods.* ◊ *I'm going to have to push you for an answer.* **ˌpush 'forward** to continue moving or travelling somewhere, especially when it is a long distance or difficult **ˌpush yourself/sb 'forward** to make other people think about and notice you or sb else: *She had to push herself forward to get a promotion.* **ˌpush 'in** (*BrE*) (*AmE* ˌcut 'in) to go in front of other people who are waiting **ˌpush 'off 1** (*BrE, spoken*) used to tell sb rudely to go away: *Hey, what are you doing? Push off!* **2** to move away from the shore in a boat, or from the side of a swimming pool, etc. **ˌpush 'on** to continue with a journey or an activity: *We rested for a while then pushed on to the next camp.* **ˌpush sb↔'out** to make sb leave a place or an organization **ˌpush sb/sth↔'out** to make sth less important than it was; to replace sth **ˌpush sth↔'out** to produce sth in large quantities: *factories pushing out cheap cotton shirts* **ˌpush sb/sth 'over** to make sb/sth fall to the ground by pushing them: *Sam pushed me over in the playground.*—see also PUSHOVER **ˌpush sth↔'through** to get a new law or plan officially accepted: *The government is pushing the changes through before the election.*

■ *noun*

USING HANDS/ARMS/BODY | **1** an act of pushing sth/sb: *She gave him a gentle push.* ◊ *The car won't start. Can you give it a push?* ◊ **At the push of a button** (= very easily) he could get a whole list of names.

OF ARMY | **2** a large and determined military attack: *a final push against the enemy* ◊ (*figurative*) *The firm has begun a major push into the European market.*

EFFORT | **3** ~ **for sth** a determined effort to achieve sth: *The push for reform started in 1989.*

IDM **at a 'push** (*BrE, informal*) used to say that sth is possible, but only with difficulty: *We can provide accommodation for six people at a push.* **give sb/get the 'push** (*BrE, informal*) to dismiss sb/to be dismissed from your job: *They gave him the push after only six weeks.* **when ˌpush comes to 'shove** (*informal*) when there is no other choice; when everything else has failed

push·bike /'pʊʃbaɪk/ *noun* (*old-fashioned, BrE*) a bicycle

'push-button *adj.* [only before noun] operated by pressing buttons with your fingers: *a push-button phone*
► **'push-button** *noun*

hood (*BrE*)/
canopy (*AmE*)

carrycot (*BrE*)

pram (*BrE*)/
baby carriage (*AmE*)

pushchair (*BrE*)/
stroller (*AmE*)

baby carrier

push·chair /'pʊʃtʃeə(r)/ *AmE* -tʃer/ (*BrE*) (*AmE* **stroll-er**) *noun* a small folding seat on wheels in which a small child sits and is pushed along—compare BUGGY

pushed /pʊʃt/ *adj.* [not before noun] (*informal*) **1** ~ (to do sth) having difficulty doing sth: *You'll be hard pushed to finish this today.* **2** ~ for sth not having enough of sth: *to be pushed for money/time* **3** busy: *I know you're pushed, but can you make tomorrow's meeting?*

push·er /'pʊʃə(r)/ *noun* (*informal*) a person who sells illegal drugs: *drug pushers*—see also PEN-PUSHER

push·over /'pʊʃəʊvə(r)/ *AmE* -oʊ-/ *noun* (*informal*) **1** a thing that is easy to do or win: *The game will be a pushover.* **2** a person who is easy to persuade or influence: *I don't think she'll agree—she's no pushover.*

push·pin /'pʊʃpɪn/ *noun* (*AmE*) a type of DRAWING PIN with a coloured plastic head that is not flat—picture at STATIONERY

'push-start *verb* [VN] (*especially BrE*) to push a vehicle in order to make the engine start ▶ **'push-start** *noun*—see also KICK-START

'push-up *noun* (*especially AmE*) = PRESS-UP

pushy /'pʊʃi/ *adj.* (*informal, disapproving*) trying hard to get what you want, especially in a way that seems rude: *a pushy salesman* ▶ **pushi·ness** *noun* [U]

pu·sil·lan·im·ous /ˌpjuːsɪ'lænɪməs/ *adj.* (*formal*) frightened to take risks SYN COWARDLY

puss /pʊs/ *noun* (*especially BrE*) used when you are calling or talking to a cat

pussy /'pʊsi/ *noun* (*pl.* -ies) **1** (also **'pussy cat**) a child's word for a cat **2** (⚠, *slang*) the female sexual organs, especially the VULVA

pussy·foot /'pʊsifʊt/ *verb* [V] ~ (about/around) (*informal*, usually *disapproving*) to be careful or anxious about expressing your opinion in case you upset sb

'pussy willow *noun* a small tree with flowers in spring that are like soft fur

pus·tule /'pʌstjuːl; *AmE* -tʃuːl/ *noun* (*formal* or *medical*) a spot on the skin containing PUS

put /pʊt/ *verb* (**put·ting, put, put**)

IN PLACE/POSITION | **1** [VN+*adv./prep.*] to move sth into a particular place or position: *Put the cases down there, please.* ◊ *Did you put sugar in my coffee?* ◊ *Put your hand up if you need more paper.* **2** [VN+*adv./prep.*] to move sth into a particular place or position using force: *He put his fist through a glass door.* **3** [VN+*adv./prep.*] to cause sb/sth to go to a particular place: *Her family put her into a nursing home.* ◊ *It was the year the Americans put a man on the moon.*

ATTACH | **4** [VN+*adv./prep.*] to attach or fix sth to sth else: *We had to put new locks on all the doors.*

WRITE | **5** [VN] [usually +*adv./prep.*] to write sth or make a mark on sth: *Put your name here.* ◊ *Friday at 11? I'll put it in my diary.* ◊ *I couldn't read what she had put.*

INTO STATE/CONDITION | **6** [VN+*adv./prep.*] to bring sb/sth into the state or condition mentioned: *I was put in charge of the office.* ◊ *The incident put her in a bad mood.* ◊ *Put yourself in my position. What would you have done?* ◊ *I tried to put the matter into perspective.* ◊ *Don't go putting yourself at risk.* ◊ *It was time to put their suggestion into practice.* ◊ *This new injury will put him out of action for several weeks.*

AFFECT SB/STH | **7** [VN+*adv./prep.*] ~ sth on/onto/to sth to make sb/sth feel sth or be affected by sth: *Her new job has put a great strain on her.* ◊ *They put pressure on her to resign.* ◊ *It's time you put a stop to this childish behaviour.*

GIVE VALUE/RANK | **8** [VN] ~ sth on sth to give or attach a particular level of importance, trust, value, etc. to sth: *Our company puts the emphasis on quality.* ◊ *He put a limit on the amount we could spend.* **9** [VN+*adv./prep.*] to consider sb/sth to belong to the class or level mentioned: *I'd put her in the top rank of modern novelists.*

EXPRESS | **10** [VN+*adv./prep.*] to express or state sth in a particular way: *She put it very tactfully.* ◊ *Put simply, we accept their offer or go bankrupt.* ◊ *I was, to put it mildly, annoyed* (= I was extremely angry). ◊ *He was too trust-*

ing—or, *to put it another way*, he had no head for business. ◊ *The meat was—how shall I put it?—a little overdone.* ◊ *As T.S. Eliot puts it …* ◊ *She had never tried to put this feeling into words.* ◊ *Can you help me put this letter into good English, please?*

IN SPORT | **11** [VN] to throw the SHOT

IDM Most idioms containing **put** are at the entries for the nouns and adjectives in the idioms, for example **put your foot in it** is at foot. **put it a'bout** (*BrE, informal*) to have many sexual partners **I wouldn't put it 'past sb (to do sth)** (*informal*) used to say that you think sb is capable of doing sth wrong, illegal, etc. **put it to sb that …** to suggest sth to sb so see if they can argue against it: *I put it to you that you are the only person who had a motive for the crime.* **put one 'over on sb** (*spoken*) to persuade sb to believe sth that is not true: *Don't try to put one over on me!* **put sb 'through it** (*informal, especially BrE*) to force sb to experience sth difficult or unpleasant: *They really put me through it* (= asked me difficult questions) *at the interview.* **put to'gether** used when comparing or contrasting sb/sth with a group of other people or things to mean 'combined' or 'in total': *Your department spent more last year than all the others put together.*

PHRV **put sth↔a'bout** (*BrE, informal*) to tell a lot of people news, information, etc. that may be false: [+that] *Someone's been putting it about that you plan to resign.*

put sth above sth = PUT STH BEFORE STH

put yourself/sth↔a'cross/'over (to sb) to communicate your ideas, feelings, etc. successfully to sb: *She's not very good at putting her views across.*

put sth↔a'side 1 to ignore or forget sth, usually a feeling or difference of opinion SYN DISREGARD: *They decided to put aside their differences.* **2** (also **put sth↔'by** especially in *BrE*) to save money for a particular purpose

put sth at sth to calculate sb/sth to be a particular age, weight, amount, etc: *The damage to the building is put at over $1 million.*

put sb↔a'way [often passive] (*informal*) to send sb to prison, to a mental hospital, etc. **put sth↔a'way 1** to put sth in the place where it is kept because you have finished using it: *I'm just going to put the car away* (= in the garage). **2** to save money to spend later: *She has a few thousand dollars put away for her retirement.* **3** (*informal*) to eat or drink large quantities of sth: *He must have put away a bottle of whisky last night.*

put sth↔'back 1 to return sth to its usual place or to the place where it was before it was moved: *If you use something, put it back!* **2** to move sth to a later time or date SYN POSTPONE: *The meeting has been put back to next week.* ◊ *The meeting will be delayed:* **3** to cause sth to be delayed: *Poor trading figures put back our plans for expansion.* **4** to move the hands of a clock so that they show the correct earlier time: *Remember to put your clocks back tonight* (= because the time has officially changed).

put sth before/above sth to treat sth as more important than sth else

put sth be'hind you to try to forget about an unpleasant experience and think about the future

put sth↔'by = PUT STH ASIDE

put 'down (of an aircraft or its pilot) to land: *He put down in a field.* **put sb↔'down** (*informal*) to make sb look or feel stupid, especially in front of other people—related noun PUT-DOWN **put sth↔'down 1** to stop holding sth and place it on a table, shelf, etc: *Put that knife down before you hurt somebody!* ◊ *It's a great book. I couldn't put it down.* ◊ (*BrE*) *She put the phone down on me* (= put the receiver down before I had finished speaking). **2** to write sth; to make a note of sth: *The meeting's on the 22nd. Put it down in your diary.* **3** to pay part of the cost of sth: *We put a 5% deposit down on the house.* **4** to stop sb by force SYN CRUSH: *to put down a rebellion* ◊ *The military government is determined to put down all opposition.* **5** [often passive] to kill an animal, usually by giving it a drug, because it is old or sick: *We had to have our cat put down.* **6** (*BrE*) to put a baby to bed: *Can you be quiet—I've just put the baby down.* **7** to present sth formally for discussion by a parliament or committee SYN TABLE: *to put down a motion/an amendment* **‚put sb 'down as sth** to consider or judge sb to be a particular type of person: *I'd put them both down as retired teachers.* **‚put sb 'down for sth** to put sb's name on a list, etc. for sth: *Put me down for three tickets for Saturday.* ◇ *They've put their son down for the local school.* **'put sth down to sth** to consider that sth is caused by sth: *What do you put her success down to?*

‚put sth↔'forth (*formal*) = PUT STH OUT

‚put yourself/sb/sth↔'forward to suggest yourself/sb as a candidate for a job or position: *Can I put you/your name forward for club secretary?* **‚put sth↔'forward 1** to move sth to an earlier time or date: *We've put the wedding forward by one week.* **2** to move the hands of a clock to the correct later time: *Remember to put your clocks forward tonight* (= because the time has officially changed). **3** to suggest sth for discussion: *to put forward an argument/a plan/a suggestion*

‚put sb↔'in to elect a political party to govern a country: *Who will the voters put in this time?* **‚put sth↔'in 1** to fix equipment or furniture into position so that it can be used SYN INSTALL: *We're having a new shower put in.* **2** to include sth in a letter, story, etc. **3** to interrupt another speaker in order to say sth: *Could I put a word in?* ◇[+speech] *'But what about us?' he put in.* **4** to officially make a claim, request, etc: *The company has put in a claim for damages.* **5** (also **'put sth into sth**) to spend a lot of time or make a lot of effort doing sth: *She often puts in twelve hours' work a day.* ◇[+-ing] *He's putting a lot of work into improving his French.*—related noun INPUT **6** (also **'put sth into sth**) to use or give money: [+-ing] *He's put all his savings into buying that house.* **‚put 'in (at ...)|'put into ...** (of a boat or its sailors) to enter a port: *They put in at Lagos for repairs.* OPP PUT OUT (TO .../ FROM ...) **‚put 'in for sth** (*especially BrE*) to officially ask for sth: *Are you going to put in for that job?* **‚put yourself/ sb/sth 'in for sth** to enter yourself/sb/sth for a competition

‚put sth 'into sth 1 to add a quality to sth: *He put as much feeling into his voice as he could.* **2** = PUT STH IN (5, 6)

‚put sb↔'off 1 to cancel a meeting or an arrangement that you have made with sb: *It's too late to put them off now.* **2** to make sb dislike sb/sth or not trust them/it: *She's very clever but her manner does tend to put people off.* ◇ *Don't put her off by how it looks—it tastes delicious.*—see also OFF-PUTTING **3** (also **‚put sb 'off sth**) to disturb sb who is trying to give all their attention to sth that they are doing: *Don't put me off when I'm trying to concentrate.* ◇ *The sudden noise put her off her game.* **4** (*BrE*) (of a vehicle or its driver) to stop in order to allow sb to leave: *I asked the bus driver to put me off at the station.* **‚put sb 'off sth/sb** to make sb lose interest in or enthusiasm for sth/sb: *He was put off science by bad teaching.* ◇[+-ing] *The accident put her off driving for life.* **‚put sth↔'off** to change sth to a later time or date SYN DELAY: *We've had to put off our wedding until September.* ◇[+-ing] *He keeps putting off going to the dentist.*

put sb on to give sb the telephone so that they can talk to the person at the other end: *Hi, Dad—can you put Nicky on?* **'put sth↔'on 1** to dress yourself in sth: *Hurry up! Put your coat on!* OPP TAKE OFF **2** to apply sth to your skin, face, etc: *She's just putting on her make-up.* **3** to switch on a piece of equipment: *I'll put the kettle on for tea.* ◇ *She put on the brakes suddenly.* **4** to make a tape, CD, etc. begin to play: *Do you mind if I put some music on?* **5** to become heavier, especially by the amount mentioned SYN GAIN: *She looks like she's put on weight.* ◇ *He must have put on several kilos.* **6** to provide sth specially: *The city is putting on extra buses during the summer.* **7** to produce or present a play, a show, etc: *The local drama club is putting on 'Macbeth' at the Playhouse.* **8** to pretend to have a particular feeling, quality, way of speaking, etc: *He put on an American accent.* ◇ *I don't think she was hurt. She was just putting it on.* **‚put sth 'on sth 1** to add an amount of money or a tax to the cost of sth: *The government has put ten pence on the price of twenty cigar-*

ettes. **2** to bet money on sth: *I've never put money on a horse.* ◇ *I put £5 on him to win.*

‚put sb 'onto sb/sth 1 to tell the police, etc. about where a criminal is or about a crime: *What first put the police onto the scam?* **2** to tell sb about sb/sth that they may like or find useful: *Who put you onto this restaurant—it's great!*

‚put 'out (*AmE, slang*) to agree to have sex with sb **‚put yourself 'out (for sb)** (*informal*) to make a special effort to do sth for sb: *Please don't put yourself out on my account.* **‚put sb 'out 1** to cause sb trouble, extra work, etc: *I hope our arriving late didn't put them out.* **2** (**be put out**) to be upset or offended: *He looked really put out.* **3** to make sb unconscious: *These pills should put him out for a few hours.* **‚put sth↔'out 1** to take sth out of your house and leave it, for example for sb to collect: (*BrE*) *to put the rubbish out* ◇ (*AmE*) *to put the garbage/trash out* ◇ *Have you put the cat out?* **2** to place sth where it will be noticed and used: *Have you put out clean towels for the guests?* **3** to stop sth from burning or shining: *to put out a candle/ cigarette/light* ◇ *Firefighters soon put the fire out.* **4** to produce sth, especially for sale: *The plant puts out 500 new cars a week.*—related noun OUTPUT **5** to publish or broadcast sth: *Police have put out a description of the man they wish to question.* **6** to give a job or task to a worker who is not your employee or to a company that is not part of your own group or organization: *A lot of the work is put out to freelancers.* **7** to make a figure, result, etc. wrong: *The rise in interest rates put our estimates out by several thousands.* **8** to push a bone out of its normal position SYN DISLOCATE: *She fell off her horse and put her shoulder out.* **9** (also *formal* **‚put sth↔'forth**) to develop or produce new leaves, SHOOTS, etc. **‚put 'out (to .../ from ...)** (of a boat or its sailors) to leave a port: *to put out to sea* ◇ *We put out from Liverpool.* OPP PUT IN (AT ...)

‚put yourself/sth 'over (to sb) = PUT YOURSELF/ STH ACROSS (TO SB)

‚put sth↔'through to continue with and complete a plan, programme, etc: *We managed to put the deal through.* **‚put sb 'through sth 1** to make sb experience sth very difficult or unpleasant: *You have put your family through a lot recently.* **2** to arrange or pay for sb to attend a school, college, etc: *He put all his children through college.* **‚put sb/sth 'through (to sb/...)** to connect sb by telephone: *Could you put me through to the manager, please?*

'put sb to sth to cause sb trouble, difficulty, etc: *I hope we're not putting you to too much trouble.* **'put sth to sb 1** to offer a suggestion to sb so that they can accept or reject it: *Your proposal will be put to the board of directors.* **2** to ask sb a question: *The audience is now invited to put questions to the speaker.*

‚put sth↔to'gether to make or prepare sth by fitting or collecting parts together: *to put together a model plane/ an essay/a meal* ◇ *I think we can put together a very strong case for the defence.*

'put sth towards sth to give money to pay part of the cost of sth: *Here's $100 to put towards your ski trip.*

‚put 'up sth 1 to show a particular level of skill, determination, etc. in a fight or contest: *They surrendered without putting up much of a fight.* ◇ *The team put up a great performance* (= played very well). **2** to suggest an idea, etc. for other people to discuss: *to put up an argument/a case/a proposal* **‚put sb↔'up 1** to let sb stay at your home: *We can put you up for the night.* **2** to suggest or present sb as a candidate for a job or position: *The Green Party hopes to put up more candidates in the next election.* **‚put sth↔'up 1** to raise sth or put it in a higher position: *to put up a flag* ◇ *She's put her hair up.* **2** to build sth or place sth somewhere: *to put up a building/ fence/memorial/tent* **3** to fix sth in a place where it will be seen SYN DISPLAY: *to put up a notice/a poster* **4** to raise or increase sth: *They've put up the rent by £20 a month.* **5** to provide or lend money: *A local businessman has put up the £500000 needed to save the club.* **‚put 'up (at ...)** (*especially BrE*) to stay somewhere for the night: *We put up at a motel.* **‚put 'up for sth|‚put yourself 'up for sth** to offer yourself as a candidate for a job or position: *She is putting up for election to the committee.* **put sb 'up to sth** (*informal*) to encourage or persuade sb to to do sth wrong or stupid: *Some of the older boys must have put him up to it.* **put 'up with sb/sth** to accept sb/sth that is annoying, unpleasant, etc. without complaining SYN TOLERATE: *I don't know how she puts up with him.* ◊ *I'm not going to put up with their smoking any longer.*

pu·ta·tive /ˈpjuːtətɪv/ *adj.* [only before noun] (*formal* or *law*) believed to be the person or thing mentioned: *the putative father of this child*

'put-down *noun* (*informal*) a remark or criticism that is intended to make sb look or feel stupid: *She couldn't think of a good put-down quickly enough.*

'put-on *noun* [usually sing.] (*AmE*) something that is done to trick or deceive people

pu·tre·fac·tion /ˌpjuːtrɪˈfækʃn/ *noun* [U] (*formal*) the process of decaying, especially that of a dead body

pu·trefy /ˈpjuːtrɪfaɪ/ *verb* (**pu·tre·fies, pu·tre·fy·ing, pu·tre·fied, pu·tre·fied**) [V] (*formal*) to decay and smell very bad SYN ROT

pu·trid /ˈpjuːtrɪd/ *adj.* **1** (of dead animals or plants) decaying and therefore smelling very bad: *the putrid smell of rotten meat* **2** (*informal*) very unpleasant: *a putrid pink colour*

putsch /pʊtʃ/ *noun* (from *German*) a sudden attempt to remove a government by force

putt /pʌt/ *verb* [V, VN] (in golf) to hit the ball gently when it is on the short grass near the hole, so that it rolls across the ground a short distance into or towards the hole ▶ **putt** *noun*

putt·er /ˈpʌtə(r)/ *verb, noun*
■ *verb* [V] **1** (*BrE*) (of a boat or vehicle) to make a repeated low sound as it moves slowly: *the puttering of the engine as it reduced speed* **2** (*AmE*) = POTTER: *I spent the morning puttering around the house.*
■ *noun* (in the game of golf) the type of CLUB that is used for putting (= hitting the ball short distances)

'putting green *noun* a small GOLF COURSE on an area of smooth short grass where people can practise PUTTING

putty /ˈpʌti/ *noun* [U] a soft sticky substance that becomes hard when it is dry and that is used for fixing glass into window frames IDM **(like) putty in sb's 'hands** easily controlled or influenced by another person: *She'll persuade him. He's like putty in her hands.*

put-up 'job *noun* [usually sing.] (*BrE, informal*) a plan or an event that has been arranged secretly in order to trick or deceive sb

'put-upon *adj.* treated in an unfair way by sb because they take advantage of your kindness or willingness to do things: *his much put-upon wife*

puz·zle /ˈpʌzl/ *noun, verb*
■ *noun* **1** a game, etc. that you have to think about carefully in order to answer it or do it: *a crossword puzzle* ◊ *a book of puzzles for children* **2** (*especially AmE*) = JIGSAW **3** [usually sing.] something that is difficult to understand or explain SYN MYSTERY: *The deeper meaning of the poem remains a puzzle.*
■ *verb* [VN] to make sb feel confused because they do not understand sth: *What puzzles me is why he left the country without telling anyone.* ▶ **puz·zling** /ˈpʌzlɪŋ/ *adj.*: *one of the most puzzling aspects of the crime* PHRV **'puzzle over/about sth** to think hard about sth in order to understand or explain it: *Karen puzzled over the question all evening.* **puzzle sth↔'out** to find the answer to a difficult or confusing problem by thinking carefully: [+wh-] *He was trying to puzzle out why he had been brought to the house.*

puz·zled /ˈpʌzld/ *adj.* unable to understand sth or the reason for sth: *She had a **puzzled** look on her face.* ◊ *Scientists are puzzled as to why the whale had swum to the shore.* ◊ *He looked puzzled so I repeated the question.*

puzzle·ment /ˈpʌzlmənt/ *noun* [U] (*formal*) a feeling of being confused because you do not understand sth: *She frowned in puzzlement.*

puz·zler /ˈpʌzlə(r)/ *noun* (*informal*) something that makes you feel confused

PVC /ˌpiː viː ˈsiː/ *noun* [U] a strong plastic material used for a wide variety of products, such as clothing, pipes, floor coverings, etc.

p.w. *abbr.* (*BrE*) per week: *Rent is £100 p.w.*

pygmy (also **pigmy**) /ˈpɪɡmi/ *noun, adj.*
■ *noun* (*pl.* **-ies**) **1** (**Pygmy**) a member of a race of very short people living in parts of Africa and SE Asia **2** (*disapproving*) a very small person or thing or one that is weak in some way: *He regarded them as intellectual pygmies.*
■ *adj.* [only before noun] used to describe a plant or SPECIES (= type) of animal that is much smaller than other similar kinds: *a pygmy shrew*

py·ja·mas (*BrE*) (*AmE* **pa·ja·mas**) /pəˈdʒɑːməz; *AmE* -ˈdʒæm-/ *noun* [pl.] **1** a loose jacket and trousers/pants worn in bed: *a pair of pyjamas*—picture on page A5 **2** loose trousers/pants tied around the waist, worn by Muslims of both sexes in some Asian countries ▶ **py·jama** (*BrE*) (*AmE* **pa·jama**) *adj.* [only before noun]: *pyjama bottoms* IDM see CAT

pylon /ˈpaɪlən; *AmE* also -lɑːn/ *noun* a tall metal structure that is used for carrying electricity wires high above the ground

pyra·mid /ˈpɪrəmɪd/ *noun* **1** a large building with a square or TRIANGULAR base and sloping sides that meet in a point at the top. The ancient Egyptians built stone pyramids as places to bury their kings and queens. **2** (*geometry*) a solid shape with a square or TRIANGULAR base and sloping sides that meet in a point at the top—picture at SOLID **3** an object or a pile of things that has the shape of a pyramid: *a pyramid of cans in a shop window* **4** an organization or a system in which there are fewer people at each level as you get near the top: *a management pyramid* ▶ **pyr·am·idal** /ˈpɪrəmɪdl/ *adj.*

pyramid 'selling *noun* [U] a way of selling things in which sb buys the right to sell a company's goods and then sells the goods to other people. These other people sell the goods again to others.

pyre /ˈpaɪə(r)/ *noun* a large pile of wood on which a dead body is placed and burned in a funeral ceremony

Pyrex™ /ˈpaɪreks/ *noun* [U] a type of hard glass that does not break at high temperatures, and is often used to make dishes for cooking food in

pyr·ites /paɪˈraɪtiːz; *AmE* pəˈr-/ *noun* [U] a shiny yellow mineral that is a natural compound of SULPHUR and a metal such as iron: *iron/copper pyrites*

pyro·mania /ˌpaɪrəʊˈmeɪniə; *AmE* ˌpaɪroʊ-/ *noun* [U] (*technical*) a mental illness that causes a strong desire to set fire to things

pyro·maniac /ˌpaɪrəʊˈmeɪniæk; *AmE* ˌpaɪroʊ-/ *noun* **1** (*technical*) a person who suffers from pyromania **2** (*informal, humorous*) a person who enjoys making or watching fires

pyro·tech·nics /ˌpaɪrəˈtekn ɪks/ *noun* **1** [U+sing./pl. *v.*] (*technical*) FIREWORKS or a display of FIREWORKS **2** [pl.] (*formal*) a clever and complicated display of skill, for example by a musician, writer or speaker: *guitar pyrotechnics* ▶ **pyro·tech·nic** *adj.* [usually before noun]

Pyr·rhic vic·tory /ˌpɪrɪk ˈvɪktəri/ *noun* a victory that is not worth winning because the winner has suffered or lost so much in winning it ORIGIN From **Pyrrhus**, the king of Epirus who defeated the Romans in 279BC but lost many of his own men.

py·thon /ˈpaɪθən; *AmE* -θɑːn/ *noun* a large tropical snake that kills animals for food by winding its long body around them and crushing them

æ   ɑː   e   ɜː   ə   ɪ   iː   i   ɒ   ɔː   ʌ   ʊ   u   uː
cat father ten bird about sit see many got saw cup put actual too
                                              (BrE)

Qq

Q *noun* /kjuː/ *abbr.*
- *noun* (also **q**) [C, U] (*pl.* **Q's, q's** /kjuːz/) the 17th letter of the English alphabet: *'Queen' begins with (a) Q/'Q'.*—see also Q-TIP
- *abbr.* question

QC /ˌkjuː ˈsiː/ *noun* (in Britain) the highest level of BARRISTER, who can speak for the government in a court of law. QC is an abbreviation for 'Queen's Counsel' and is used when there is a queen in Britain.—compare KC

QED (*BrE*) (also **Q.E.D.** *AmE, BrE*) /ˌkjuː iː ˈdiː/ *abbr.* that is what I wanted to prove and I have proved it (from Latin 'quod erat demonstrandum')

qt *abbr.* (in writing) QUART

ˈQ-tip™ *noun* (*AmE*) = COTTON BUD

qua /kweɪ; kwɑː/ *prep.* (from *Latin, formal*) as sth; in the role of sth: *The soldier acted qua soldier, not as a human being.*—see also SINE QUA NON

quack /kwæk/ *noun, verb*
- *noun* **1** the sound that a duck makes **2** (*informal, disapproving*) a person who dishonestly claims to have medical knowledge or skills: *quack doctors ◊ I've got a check-up with the quack* (= the doctor) *next week.*
- *verb* [V] when a duck **quacks** it makes the noise that is typical of ducks

quack·ery /ˈkwækəri/ *noun* [U] the methods or behaviour of sb who pretends to have medical knowledge

quad /kwɒd; *AmE* kwɑːd/ *noun* **1** = QUADRANGLE **2** = QUAD-RUPLET

quad·ran·gle /ˈkwɒdræŋgl; *AmE* ˈkwɑːd-/ (also **quad**) *noun* an open square area that has buildings all around it, especially in a school or college

quad·rant /ˈkwɒdrənt; *AmE* ˈkwɑːd-/ *noun* **1** (*geometry*) a quarter of a circle or of its CIRCUMFERENCE (= the distance around it)—picture at CIRCLE **2** an instrument for measuring angles, especially to check your position at sea or to look at stars

quadra·phon·ic (also **quadro·phon·ic**) /ˌkwɒdrə'fɒnɪk; *AmE* ˌkwɑːdrə'fɑːn-/ *adj.* (of a system of recording or broadcasting sound) coming from four different SPEAKERS at the same time—compare MONO, STEREO

quad·rat·ic /kwɒ'drætɪk; *AmE* kwɑː'd-/ *adj.* (*mathematics*) involving an unknown quantity that is multiplied by itself once only: *a quadratic equation*

quadri- /ˈkwɒdrɪ-; *AmE* ˈkwɑːd-/ (also **quadr-**) *combining form* (in nouns, adjectives and adverbs) four; having four: *quadrilateral ◊ quadruplet*

quad·ri·lat·eral /ˌkwɒdrɪ'lætərəl; *AmE* ˌkwɑːd-/ *noun* (*geometry*) a flat shape with four straight sides ▶ **quad·ri·lat·eral** *adj.*

quad·rille /kwə'drɪl/ *noun* a dance for four or more couples in a square, popular in the past

quadri·ple·gic /ˌkwɒdrɪ'pliːdʒɪk; *AmE* ˌkwɑːd-/ *noun* a person who is permanently unable to use their arms and legs ▶ **quadri·ple·gic** *adj.*

quadro·phon·ic *adj.* = QUADRAPHONIC

quad·ru·ped /ˈkwɒdruped; *AmE* ˈkwɑːd-/ *noun* (*technical*) any creature with four feet—compare BIPED

quad·ru·ple *verb, adj., det.*
- *verb* /kwɒ'druːpl; *AmE* kwɑː'd-/ to become four times bigger; to make sth four times bigger: [V] *Sales have quadrupled in the last five years.* [also VN]
- *adj.* [only before noun] *det.* /ˈkwɒdrupl; *AmE* kwɑː'druːpl/ **1** consisting of four parts, people or groups: *a quadruple alliance* **2** being four times as much or as many: *a quadruple whisky ◊ This year we produced quadruple the amount produced in 1998.*

quad·ru·plet /ˈkwɒdruplət; kwɒ'druːplət; *AmE* kwɑː-/ (also **quad**) *noun* one of four children born at the same time to the same mother

quaff /kwɒf; *AmE* kwæf; kwɑːf/ *verb* [VN] (*old-fashioned* or *literary*) to drink a large amount of sth quickly

quag·mire /ˈkwægmaɪə(r); *BrE* also ˈkwɒg-/ *noun* **1** an area of soft wet ground **2** a difficult or dangerous situation

quail /kweɪl/ *noun, verb*
- *noun* [C, U] (*pl.* **quails** or **quail**) a small brown bird, whose meat and eggs are used for food; the meat of this bird
- *verb* [V] ~ (at/before sb/sth) (*literary*) to feel frightened or to show that you are frightened

quaint /kweɪnt/ *adj.* attractive in an unusual or old-fashioned way: *quaint old customs ◊ a quaint and charming seaside village* ▶ **quaint·ly** *adv.* **quaint·ness** *noun* [U]

quake /kweɪk/ *verb, noun*
- *verb* [V] **1** ~ (with sth) (of a person) to shake because you are very frightened or nervous [SYN] TREMBLE: *Quaking with fear, Polly slowly opened the door.* **2** (of the earth or a building) to move or shake violently: *The ground quaked as the bomb exploded.*
- *noun* (*informal*) = EARTHQUAKE

Quaker /ˈkweɪkə(r)/ *noun* a member of the Society of Friends, a Christian religious group that meets without any formal ceremony and is strongly opposed to violence and war ▶ **Quaker** *adj.*: *a Quaker school*

quali·fi·ca·tion /ˌkwɒlɪfɪ'keɪʃn; *AmE* ˌkwɑːl-/ *noun* **1** [C, usually pl.] an exam that you have passed or a course of study that you have successfully completed: *academic/educational/professional/vocational qualifications ◊ a nursing/teaching qualification ◊ He left school with no formal qualifications. ◊ In this job, experience counts for more than paper qualifications.* **2** [C] a skill or type of experience that you need for a particular job or activity: *Previous teaching experience is a necessary qualification for this job.* **3** [C, U] information that you add to a statement to limit the effect that it has or the way it is applied: *I accept his theories, but not without certain qualifications. ◊ The plan was approved without qualification.* **4** [U] the fact of passing an exam, completing a course of training or reaching the standard necessary to do a job or take part in a competition: *Nurses in training should be given a guarantee of employment following qualification. ◊ A victory in this game will earn them qualification for the World Cup.*

quali·fied /ˈkwɒlɪfaɪd; *AmE* ˈkwɑːl-/ *adj.* **1** ~ (for sth) having passed the exams or completed the training that are necessary in order to do a particular job; having the experience to do a particular job: *a qualified accountant/teacher ◊ to be highly/suitably/fully qualified ◊ She's extremely well qualified for the job.* **2** [not before noun] ~ (to do sth) having the practical knowledge or skills to do sth: *I don't know much about it, so I don't feel qualified to comment.* **3** [usually before noun] (of approval, support, etc.) limited in some way: *The plan was given only qualified support. ◊ The project was only a qualified success.*

quali·fier /ˈkwɒlɪfaɪə(r); *AmE* ˈkwɑːl-/ *noun* **1** a person or team that has defeated others in order to enter a particular competition **2** a game or match that a person or team has to win in order to enter a particular competition: *a World Cup qualifier* **3** (*grammar*) a word, especially an adjective or adverb, that describes another word in a particular way: *In 'the open door', 'open' is a qualifier, describing the door.*

quali·fy /'kwɒlɪfaɪ; *AmE* 'kwɑːl-/ *verb* (**quali·fies, quali·fy·ing, quali·fied, quali·fied**)

FOR JOB | **1** [V] ~ (**as sth**) to reach the standard of ability or knowledge needed to do a particular job, for example by completing a course of study or passing exams: *How long does it take to qualify?* ◊ *He qualified as a doctor last year.*

GIVE SKILLS/KNOWLEDGE | **2** ~ **sb** (**for sth**) to give sb the skills and knowledge they need to do sth: [VN] *This training course will qualify you for a better job.* ◊ [VN to inf] *The test qualifies you to drive heavy vehicles.*

HAVE/GIVE RIGHT | **3** ~ (**sb**) (**for sth**) to have or give sb the right to do sth: [V] *If you live in the area, you qualify for a parking permit.* ◊ *To qualify, you must have lived in this country for at least three years.* ◊ [VN] *Paying a fee doesn't automatically qualify you for membership.*

FOR COMPETITION | **4** [V] ~ (**for sth**) to be of a high enough standard to enter a competition; to defeat another person or team in order to enter or continue in a competition: *He failed to qualify.* ◊ *They qualified for the World Cup.*

FIT DESCRIPTION | **5** ~ (**sth**) (**as sth**) to have the right qualities to be described as a particular thing: [V] *Do you think this dress qualifies as evening wear?* ◊ [VN] *It's an old building, but that doesn't qualify it as an ancient monument!*

STATEMENT | **6** [VN] to add sth to a previous statement to make the meaning less strong or less general: *I want to qualify what I said earlier—I didn't mean he couldn't do the job, only that he would need supervision.*

GRAMMAR | **7** [VN] (of a word) to describe another word in a particular way: *In 'the open door', 'open' is an adjective qualifying 'door'.*

quali·ta·tive /'kwɒlɪtətɪv; *AmE* 'kwɑːləteɪt-/ *adj.* [usually before noun] connected with how good sth is, rather than with how much of it there is: *qualitative analysis/research* ◊ *There are qualitative differences between the two products.*—compare QUANTITATIVE ▶ **quali·ta·tive·ly** *adv.*: *qualitatively different*

qual·ity /'kwɒləti; *AmE* 'kwɑːl-/ *noun, adj.*

■ *noun* (*pl.* **-ies**) **1** [U, C] the standard of sth when it is compared to other things like it; how good or bad sth is: *to be of good/poor/top quality* ◊ *goods of a high quality* ◊ *high-quality goods* ◊ *a decline in water/air quality* ◊ *When costs are cut product quality suffers.* ◊ *Their quality of life improved dramatically when they moved to France.* **2** [U] a high standard: *contemporary writers of quality* ◊ *We aim to provide quality at reasonable prices.* **3** [C] a thing that is part of a person's character, especially sth good: *personal qualities such as honesty and generosity* ◊ *to lack/possess leadership qualities* **4** [C, U] a feature of sth, especially one that makes it different from sth else: *the special quality of light and shade in her paintings* **5** [C] (*BrE*) = QUALITY NEWSPAPER

■ *adj.* **1** [only before noun] used especially by people trying to sell goods or services to say that sth is of a high quality: *We specialize in quality furniture.* ◊ *quality service at a competitive price* **2** (*BrE, slang*) very good: *'What was the film like?' 'Quality!'*

'quality assurance *noun* [U] the practice of managing the way goods are produced or services are provided to make sure they are kept at a high standard

'quality control *noun* [U] the practice of checking goods as they are being produced, to make sure that they are of a high standard

quality 'newspaper (also *less frequent* **qual·ity**) *noun* (*BrE*) a newspaper that is intended for people who are intelligent and educated—compare TABLOID

'quality time *noun* [U] time spent giving your full attention to sb, especially to your children after work

qualm /kwɑːm; kwɔːm/ *noun* [usually pl.] ~ (**about sth**) a feeling of doubt or worry about whether what you are doing is right: *He had been working very hard so he had no qualms about taking a few days off.*

quan·dary /'kwɒndəri; *AmE* 'kwɑːn-/ *noun* [usually sing.] (*pl.* **-ies**) the state of not being able to decide what to do in a difficult situation: *George was in a quandary—should he go or shouldn't he?*

quango /'kwæŋgəʊ; *AmE* -goʊ/ *noun* (*pl.* **-os**) (often *dis-*

approving) (in Britain) an organization dealing with public matters, started by the government, but working independently and with its own legal powers

quanta *pl.* of QUANTUM

quan·tify /'kwɒntɪfaɪ; *AmE* 'kwɑːn-/ *verb* (**quan·ti·fies, quan·ti·fy·ing, quan·ti·fied, quan·ti·fied**) [VN] to describe or express sth as an amount or a number: *The risks to health are impossible to quantify.* ▶ **quan·ti·fi·able** *adj.*: *quantifiable data* **quan·ti·fi·ca·tion** /ˌkwɒntɪfɪ'keɪʃn; *AmE* ˌkwɑːn-/ *noun* [U]

quan·ti·ta·tive /'kwɒntɪtətɪv; *AmE* 'kwɑːntəteɪt-/ *adj.* connected with the amount or number of sth rather than with how good it is: *quantitative analysis/research* ◊ *There is no difference between the two in quantitative terms.*—compare QUALITATIVE

quan·tity /'kwɒntəti; *AmE* 'kwɑːn-/ *noun* (*pl.* **-ies**) **1** [C, U] an amount or a number of sth: *a large/small quantity of sth* ◊ *enormous/vast/huge quantities of food* ◊ *a product that is cheap to produce in large quantities* ◊ *Is it available in sufficient quantity?* **2** [U] the measurement of sth by saying how much of it there is: *The data is limited in terms of both quality and quantity.* **3** [C, U] a large amount or number of sth: *The police found a quantity of drugs at his home.* ◊ *It's cheaper to buy goods in quantity.* ◊ *I was overwhelmed by the sheer quantity of information available.* IDM see UNKNOWN

'quantity surveyor *noun* (*BrE*) a person whose job is to calculate the quantity of materials needed for building sth, how much it will cost and how long it will take

quan·tum /'kwɒntəm; *AmE* 'kwɑːn-/ *noun* (*pl.* **quanta** /-tə/) (*physics*) a very small quantity of ELECTROMAGNETIC energy

quantum 'leap (also *less frequent* ˌ**quantum 'jump**) *noun* a sudden, great and important change, improvement or development: *This discovery marks a quantum leap forward in the fight against cancer.*

quantum me'chanics *noun* [U] (*physics*) the branch of MECHANICS that deals with movement and force in pieces of matter smaller than atoms

'quantum theory *noun* [U] (*physics*) a theory based on the idea that energy exists in units that cannot be divided

quar·an·tine /'kwɒrəntiːn; *AmE* 'kwɔːr-; 'kwɑːr-/ *noun, verb*

■ *noun* [U] a period of time when an animal or a person that has or may have a disease is kept away from others in order to prevent the disease from spreading: *The dog was kept in quarantine for six months.* ◊ *quarantine regulations*

■ *verb* [VN] to put an animal or a person into quarantine

quark /kwɑːk; *AmE* kwɑːrk/ *noun* (*physics*) a very small part of MATTER (= a substance). There are several types of quark and it is thought that PROTONS, NEUTRONS, etc. are formed from them.

quar·rel /'kwɒrəl; *AmE* 'kwɔːr-; 'kwɑːr-/ *noun, verb*

■ *noun* **1** [C] ~ (**with sb/between A and B**) (**about/over sth**) an angry argument or disagreement between people, often about a personal matter: *a family quarrel* ◊ *He did not mention the quarrel with his wife.* ◊ *They had a quarrel about money.* ◊ *Were you at any time aware of a quarrel between the two of them?* **2** [U] ~ (**with sb/sth**) (especially in negative sentences) a reason for complaining about sb/sth or for disagreeing with sb/sth: *We have no quarrel with his methods.* IDM see PICK v.

■ *verb* (**-ll-**, *AmE* **-l-**) [V] ~ (**with sb**) (**about/over sth**) to have an angry argument or disagreement: *My sister and I used to quarrel all the time.* ◊ *She quarrelled with her brother over their father's will.* PHRV **'quarrel with sb/sth** to disagree with sb/sth: *Nobody could quarrel with your conclusions.*

quar·rel·some /'kwɒrəlsəm; *AmE* 'kwɔːr-; 'kwɑːr-/ *adj.* (of a person) liking to argue with other people

quarry /'kwɒri; *AmE* 'kwɔːri; 'kwɑːri/ *noun, verb*

■ *noun* (*pl.* **-ies**) **1** [C] a place where large amounts of stone, etc. are dug out of the ground: *a chalk/slate quarry* ◊ *the site of a disused quarry*—compare MINE *n.* (1) **2** [sing.] an animal or a person that is being hunted or followed: *The* *hunters lost sight of their quarry in the forest.* ◊ *The photographers pursued their quarry through the streets.*

■ *verb* (quar·ries, quarry·ing, quar·ried, quar·ried) **~ (for)** **sth** | **~ sth (from/out of sth)** to take stone, etc. out of a quarry: [VN] *The local rock is quarried from the hillside.* ◊ *The area is being quarried for limestone.* [also V]
▶ **quarry·ing** *noun* [U]: *There has been quarrying in the area for centuries.*

quart /kwɔːt; *AmE* kwɔːrt/ *noun* (*abbr.* qt) a unit for measuring liquids, equal to 2 PINTS or about 1.14 litres in the UK and 0.94 of a litre in the US **IDM** **put a quart into a pint 'pot** (*BrE*) to put sth into a space that is too small for it

quar·ter /ˈkwɔːtə(r); *AmE* ˈkwɔːrt-/ *noun, verb*
■ *noun*
1 OF 4 PARTS | **1** (also **fourth** especially in *AmE*) [C] one of four equal parts of sth: *a quarter of a mile* ◊ *The programme lasted an hour and a quarter.* ◊ *Cut the apple into quarters.* ◊ *The theatre was about three quarters full.* ⇨ note at HALF
15 MINUTES | **2** [C] a period of 15 minutes either before or after every hour: *It's (a) quarter to four now—I'll meet you at quarter past.* ◊ (*AmE* also *It's (a) quarter of four now—I'll meet you at a quarter after.*
3 MONTHS | **3** [C] a period of three months, used especially as a period for which bills are paid or a company's income is calculated
PART OF TOWN | **4** [C, usually sing.] a district or part of a town: *the Latin quarter* ◊ *the historic quarter of the city*
PERSON/GROUP | **5** [C] a person or group of people, especially as a source of help, information or a reaction: *Support for the plan came from an unexpected quarter.* ◊ *The news was greeted with dismay in some quarters.*
25 CENTS | **6** [C] a coin of the US and Canada worth 25 cents
ROOMS TO LIVE IN | **7** (quarters) [pl.] rooms that are provided for soldiers, servants, etc. to live in: *We were moved to more comfortable living quarters.* ◊ *married quarters*
OF MOON | **8** [C] the period of time twice a month when we can see a quarter of the moon: *The moon is in its first quarter.*
IN SPORT | **9** [C] one of the four periods of time into which a game of American football is divided
WEIGHT | **10** [C] a unit for measuring weight, 28 pounds in the UK or 25 pounds in the US; a quarter of a HUNDRED-WEIGHT
PITY | **11** [U] (*old-fashioned* or *literary*) pity or MERCY that sb shows towards an enemy or opponent who is in their power: *His rivals knew that they could expect no quarter from such a ruthless adversary.*
IDM see CLOSE² *adj.*
■ *verb* [VN]
DIVIDE INTO 4 | **1** to cut or divide sth into four parts: *She peeled and quartered an apple.*
PROVIDE ROOMS | **2** (*formal*) to provide sb with a place to eat and sleep: *Three hundred soldiers were quartered in the town.*

quar·ter·back /ˈkwɔːtəbæk; *AmE* ˈkwɔːrtərbæk/ *noun, verb*
■ *noun* (in American football) the player who directs the team's attacking play and passes the ball to other players at the start of each attack
■ *verb* **1** [V] (in American football) to play as a quarterback **2** [VN] to direct or organize sth

'quarter day *noun* (*BrE, technical*) the first day of a QUARTER (= a period of three months) on which payments must be made, for example at the STOCK EXCHANGE

quar·ter·deck /ˈkwɔːtədek; *AmE* ˈkwɔːrtərdek/ *noun* a part of the upper level of a ship, at the back, that is used mainly by officers

,quarter-'final *noun* (in sports or competitions) one of the four games or matches to decide the players or teams for the SEMI-FINALS of a competition

quar·ter·ly /ˈkwɔːtəli; *AmE* ˈkwɔːrtərli/ *adj., adv., noun*
■ *adj.* produced or happening every three months: *a quarterly meeting of the board* ▶ **quar·ter·ly** *adv.*: *to pay the rent quarterly*

■ *noun* (*pl.* **-ies**) a magazine, etc. published four times a year

quar·ter·mas·ter /ˈkwɔːtəmɑːstə(r); *AmE* ˈkwɔːrtərmæs-/ *noun* an officer in the army who is in charge of providing food, uniforms and accommodation

'quarter note *noun* (*AmE, music*) = CROTCHET

'quarter sessions *noun* [pl.] (in England, in the past) a court of law with limited powers that was held every three months

quar·tet /kwɔːˈtet; *AmE* kwɔːrˈtet/ *noun* **1** [C+sing./pl. *v.*] a group of four musicians or singers who play or sing together: *the Amadeus Quartet* **2** [C] a piece of music for four musicians or singers: *a Beethoven string quartet* **3** [C+sing./pl. *v.*] a set of four people or things: *the last in a quartet of novels*

quarto /ˈkwɔːtəʊ; *AmE* ˈkwɔːrtoʊ/ *noun* (*pl.* **-os**) (*technical*) **1** [U] a size of page made by folding a standard sheet of paper twice to make eight pages **2** [C] a book with pages in quarto size

quartz /kwɔːts; *AmE* kwɔːrts/ *noun* [U] a hard mineral, often in CRYSTAL form, that is used to make very accurate clocks and watches

qua·sar /ˈkweɪzɑː(r)/ *noun* (*astronomy*) a large object like a star, that is far away and that shines very brightly and occasionally sends out strong radio signals—compare PULSAR

quash /kwɒʃ; *AmE* kwɑːʃ/ *verb* [VN] **1** (*law*) to officially say that a decision in a court of law is no longer valid or correct **SYN** OVERTURN: *His conviction was later quashed by the Court of Appeal.* **2** (*written*) to take action to stop sth from continuing: *The rumours were quickly quashed.*

quasi- /ˈkweɪzaɪ; -saɪ/ *combining form* (in adjectives and nouns) **1** that appears to be sth but is not really so: *a quasi-scientific explanation* **2** partly; almost: *a quasi-official body*

quat·rain /ˈkwɒtreɪn; *AmE* ˈkwɑːt-/ *noun* (*technical*) a poem or verse of a poem that has four lines

qua·ver /ˈkweɪvə(r)/ *verb, noun*
■ *verb* if sb's voice **quavers**, it is unsteady, usually because the person is nervous or afraid: [V] *'I'm not safe here, am I?' she asked in a quavering voice.* [also V speech] ▶ **qua·very** /ˈkweɪvəri/ *adj.*: *a quavery voice*
■ *noun* **1** (*BrE*) (*AmE* **'eighth note**) (*music*) a note that lasts half as long as a CROTCHET/QUARTER NOTE—picture at MUSIC **2** [usually sing.] a shaking sound in sb's voice

quay /kiː/ *noun* a platform in a harbour where boats come in to load, etc: *A crowd was waiting on the quay.*

quay·side /ˈkiːsaɪd/ *noun* [usually sing.] a quay and the area near it: *crowds waiting on/at the quayside to welcome them*

queasy /ˈkwiːzi/ *adj.* **1** feeling sick; wanting to VOMIT: *Travelling by boat makes me queasy.* **2** slightly nervous or worried about sth: *Now she'd arrived she felt queasy inside.* ▶ **queas·ily** *adv.* **queasi·ness** *noun* [U]

queen /kwiːn/ *noun*
FEMALE RULER | **1** the female ruler of an independent state that has a royal family: *to become/be crowned queen* ◊ *kings and queens* ◊ *the Queen of Norway* ◊ *Queen Victoria* **2** (also ,queen 'consort) the wife of a king
BEST IN GROUP | **3 ~ (of sth)** a woman, place or thing that is thought to be one of the best in a particular group or area: *the queen of fashion* ◊ *a movie queen* ◊ *Venice, queen of the Adriatic*
AT FESTIVAL | **4** a woman or girl chosen to perform official duties at a festival or celebration: *a carnival queen* ◊ *May queen* (= at a festival to celebrate the coming of spring) ◊ *a homecoming queen*—see also BEAUTY QUEEN
IN CHESS | **5** the most powerful piece used in the game of CHESS that can move any number of squares in any direction—picture on page A8
IN CARDS | **6** a playing card with the picture of a queen on it—picture on page A8
INSECT | **7** a large female insect that lays eggs for the whole group: *a queen bee*
HOMOSEXUAL | **8** (*informal*, ⚠) an offensive word for a male

s	t	v	z	ʃ	ʒ	tʃ	dʒ	θ	ð	ŋ
see	tea	van	zoo	shoe	vision	chain	jam	thin	this	sing

HOMOSEXUAL who behaves more like a woman than a man: *a drag queen* (= a man dressed in women's clothes)

IDM see ENGLISH, EVIDENCE, UNCROWNED

queen 'bee *noun* **1** a female bee that produces eggs for the whole group of bees in a HIVE—compare DRONE, WORKER **2** a woman who behaves as if she is the most important person in a particular place or group

queen·ly /'kwiːnli/ *adj.* of, like or suitable for a queen: *She gave a queenly wave.*

queen 'mother *noun* a title given to the wife of a king who has died and who is the mother of the new king or queen: *Queen Elizabeth, the Queen Mother*

Queen's 'Counsel *noun* = QC

queen-size *adj.* (*AmE*) (of beds, sheets, etc.) larger than a standard size but not as big as KING-SIZE

queer /kwɪə(r); *AmE* kwɪr/ *adj., noun, verb*

■ *adj.* (**queer·er, queer·est**) **1** (*old-fashioned*) strange or unusual: *His face was a queer pink colour.* **2** (⚠, *slang*) an offensive way of describing a HOMOSEXUAL, especially a man, which is, however, also used by some homosexuals about themselves **IDM** see FISH *n.*

■ *noun* (⚠, *slang*) an offensive word for a HOMOSEXUAL, especially a man, which is, however, also used by some homosexuals about themselves

■ *verb* **IDM** **queer sb's 'pitch | queer the 'pitch (for sb)** (*BrE, informal*) to spoil sb's plans or their chances of getting sth

queer·ly /'kwɪəli; *AmE* 'kwɪrli/ *adv.* in a strange or unusual way: *He looked at me queerly.*

quell /kwel/ *verb* [VN] **1** to stop sth such as violent behaviour or protests: *Extra police were called in to quell the disturbances.* ◊ (*figurative*) *She started to giggle, but Bob quelled her with a look.* **2** to stop or reduce strong or unpleasant feelings: *to quell your fears/doubt/excitement*

quench /kwentʃ/ *verb* [VN] **1 ~ your thirst** to drink so that you no longer feel thirsty **SYN** SLAKE **2** (*written*) to stop a fire from burning: *Firemen tried to quench the flames raging through the building.*

queru·lous /'kwerələs; -rjə-/ *adj.* (*formal, disapproving*) complaining; showing that you are annoyed: *He complained in a querulous voice about having been woken up.* ▶ **queru·lous·ly** *adv.*

query /'kwɪəri; *AmE* 'kwɪri/ *noun, verb*

■ *noun* (*pl.* **-ies**) **1** a question, especially one asking for information or expressing a doubt about sth: *Our assistants will be happy to answer your queries.* ◊ *If you have a query about your insurance policy, contact our helpline.* **2** a question mark to show that sth has not been finished or decided: *Put a query against Jack's name—I'm not sure if he's coming.*

■ *verb* (**quer·ies, query·ing, quer·ied, quer·ied**) **1** to express doubt about whether sth is correct or not: [VN] *We queried the bill as it seemed far too high.* ◊ *I'm not in a position to query their decision.* [also V **wh-**] **2** [V speech] (*written*) to ask a question: *'Who will be leading the team?' queried Simon.*

quest /kwest/ *noun, verb*

■ *noun* (*formal* or *literary*) **~ (for sth)** a long search for sth, especially for some quality such as happiness: *the quest for happiness/knowledge/truth* ◊ *He set off in quest of adventure.*

■ *verb* [V] **~ (for sth)** (*formal* or *literary*) to search for sth that is difficult to find

ques·tion /'kwestʃən/ *noun, verb*

■ *noun* **1** [C] a sentence, phrase or word that asks for information: *to ask/answer a question* ◊ *Question 3 was very difficult.* ◊ *In the exam there's sure to be a question on energy.* ◊ *The question is, how much are they going to pay you?* ◊ (*formal*) *The question arises as to whether or not he knew of the situation.* ◊ *The key question of what caused the leak remains unanswered.* ◊ (*formal*) *He put a question to the minister about the recent reforms.* ◊ *I hope the police don't ask any awkward questions.* ◊ *In an interview try to ask open questions that don't just need 'Yes' or 'No' as an answer.* **2** [C] **~ (of sth)** a matter or topic that needs to be discussed or dealt with: *Let's look at the question of security.* ◊ *The question which needs to be addressed is one of funding.* ◊ *Which route is better remains an open question* (= it is not decided). **3** [U] doubt or uncertainty about sth: *Her honesty is beyond question.* ◊ *His suitability for the job is open to question.* ◊ *Her version of events was accepted without question.* **IDM** **bring/throw sth into 'question** to cause sth to become a matter for doubt and discussion: *This case brings into question the whole purpose of the law.* **come into 'question** to become a matter for doubt and discussion **good 'question!** (*spoken*) used to show that you do not know the answer to a question: *'How much is all this going to cost?' 'Good question!'* **in 'question 1** that is being discussed: *On the day in question we were in Cardiff.* **2** in doubt; uncertain: *The future of public transport is not in question.* **just/merely/only a question of (sth/doing sth)** used to say that sth is not difficult to predict, explain, do, etc: *It's merely a question of time before the business collapses.* ◊ *It's just a question of deciding what you really want.* **out of the 'question** impossible or not allowed and therefore not worth discussing: *Another trip abroad this year is out of the question.* **there is/was no question of (sth happening/sb doing sth)** there is/was no possibility of sth: *There was no question of him cancelling the trip so near the departure date.*—more at BEG, CALL *v.*, MOOT *adj.*, POP *v.*

■ *verb* **1** [VN] **~ sb (about/on sth)** to ask sb questions about sth, especially officially: *She was arrested and questioned about the fire.* ◊ *The students were questioned on the books they had been studying.* ◊ *Over half of those questioned said they rarely took any exercise.* [also V **speech**] **2** to have or express doubts or suspicions about sth: [VN] *I just accepted what he told me. I never thought to question it.* ◊ *No one has ever questioned her judgement.* ◊ [V **wh-**] *He questioned whether the accident was solely the truck driver's fault.*

ques·tion·able /'kwestʃənəbl/ *adj.* **1** that you have doubts about because you think it is not accurate or correct: *The conclusions that they come to are highly questionable.* ◊ *It is questionable whether this is a good way of solving the problem.* **2** likely to be dishonest or morally wrong: *Her motives for helping are questionable.* ▶ **ques·tion·ably** /-əbli/ *adv.*

ques·tion·er /'kwestʃənə(r)/ *noun* a person who asks questions, especially in a broadcast programme or a public debate

ques·tion·ing /'kwestʃənɪŋ/ *noun, adj.*

■ *noun* [U] the activity of asking sb questions: *He was taken to the police station for questioning.* ◊ *They faced some hostile questioning over the cost of the project.*

■ *adj.* showing that you need information, or that you have doubts: *a questioning look* ◊ *She raised a questioning eyebrow.* ▶ **ques·tion·ing·ly** *adv.*

'question mark *noun* the mark (?) used in writing after a question ⇨ Appendix 4 **IDM** **a 'question mark over/against sth** used to say that sth is not certain: *There's still a big question mark hanging over his future with the team.*

'question master (also **quiz·master**) (both *BrE*) *noun* a person who asks the questions in a QUIZ, especially on television or the radio

ques·tion·naire /ˌkwestʃə'neə(r); *AmE* -'ner/ *noun* **~ (on/about sth)** a written list of questions that are answered by a number of people so that information can be collected from the answers: *to complete a questionnaire* ◊ (*BrE*) *to fill in a questionnaire* ◊ (*especially AmE*) *to fill out a questionnaire*

'question tag (also **'tag question**) *noun* (*grammar*) a phrase such as *isn't it?* or *don't you?* that you add to the end of a statement in order to turn it into a question or check that the statement is correct, as in *You like mushrooms, don't you?*

queue /kjuː/ *noun, verb*

■ *noun* **1** (*BrE*) (*AmE* **line**) a line of people, cars, etc. waiting for sth or to do sth: *the bus queue* ◊ *I had to join a queue for the toilets.* ◊ *How long were you in the queue?* ◊ *There was a queue of traffic waiting to turn right.* **2** (*com-*

æ	ɑː	e	ɜː	ə	ɪ	iː	i	ɒ	ɔː	ʌ	ʊ	u	uː
cat	father	ten	bird	about	sit	see	many	got	saw	cup	put	actual	too

(BrE)

puting) a list of items of data stored in a particular order IDM see JUMP *v.*

■ *verb* (**queu·ing** or **queue·ing**) **1** [V] (*BrE*) ~ (**up**) (**for sth**) to wait in a line of people, vehicles, etc. in order to do sth, get sth or go somewhere: *We had to queue up for an hour for the tickets.* ◇ *Queue here for taxis.* **2** (*computing*) to add tasks to other tasks so that they are ready to be done in order; to come together to be done in order: [VN] *The system queues the jobs before they are processed.* [also V] PHR V **be ˌqueuing ˈup (for sth/to do sth)** if people are said to be **queuing up** for sth or to do sth, a lot of them want to have it or do it: *Italian football clubs are queuing up to sign the young star.*

quib·ble /ˈkwɪbl/ *verb, noun*
■ *verb* [V] ~ (**about/over sth**) to argue or complain about a small matter or an unimportant detail: *It isn't worth quibbling over such a small amount.*
■ *noun* a small complaint or criticism, especially one that is not important: *minor quibbles*

quiche /kiːʃ/ *noun* [C, U] an open pie filled with a mixture of eggs and milk with meat, vegetables, cheese, etc: *a mushroom quiche*—compare FLAN, TART

quick /kwɪk/ *adj., adv., noun*
■ *adj.* (**quick·er, quick·est**) **1** done with speed; taking or lasting a short time: *She gave him a quick glance.* ◇ *These cakes are very quick and easy to make.* ◇ *Would you like a quick drink?* ◇ *The doctor said she'd make a quick recovery.* ◇ *It's quicker by train.* ◇ *Are you sure this is the quickest way?* ◇ *Have you finished already? That was quick!* ◇ *His quick thinking saved her life.* ◇ *He fired three shots in quick succession.*—see also DOUBLE QUICK **2** ~ (**to do sth**) moving or doing sth fast: *a quick learner/worker* ◇ *The kids were quick to learn.* ◇ *She was quick* (= too quick) *to point out the mistakes I'd made.* ◇ *Her quick hands suddenly stopped moving.* ◇ *Try to be quick! We're late already.* ◇ *Once again, his quick wits* (= quick thinking) *got him out of an awkward situation.* ◇ *(AmE, informal) He's a quick study* (= he learns quickly). **3** [only before noun] happening very soon or without delay: *We need to make a quick decision.* ◇ *The company wants quick results.* ⇨ note at FAST IDM **to have a quick ˈtemper** to become angry easily—more at BUCK *n.*, DRAW *n.*, MARK *n.*, UPTAKE
■ *adv.* (**quick·er, quick·est**) **1** quickly; fast: *Come as quick as you can!* ◇ *Let's see who can get there quickest.* ◇ *It's another of his schemes to get rich quick.* **2** (**quick-**) (in adjectives) doing the thing mentioned quickly: *quick-thinking* ◇ *quick-growing* IDM (**as) quick as a ˈflash** very quickly: *Quick as a flash she was at his side.*
■ *noun* (**the quick**) [sing.] the soft, sensitive flesh that is under the fingernails: *She has bitten her nails down to the quick.* IDM **cut sb to the ˈquick** to upset sb very much by doing or saying sth unkind

---

WHICH WORD?

quick / quickly / fast

Quickly is the usual adverb from **quick**: *I quickly realized that I was on the wrong train.* ◇ *My heart started to beat more quickly.*

Quick is sometimes used as an adverb in very informal language, especially as an exclamation: *Come on! Quick! They'll see us!* **Quicker** is used more often: *My heart started to beat much quicker.* ◇ *The quicker I get you away from here, the better.*

Fast is more often used when you are talking about the speed that somebody or something moves at: *How fast can a cheetah run?* ◇ *Can't you drive any faster?* ◇ ~~You're driving too quickly.~~ There is no word **fastly**.

⇨ note at SOON

---

quick·en /ˈkwɪkən/ *verb* (*written*) **1** to become quicker or make sth quicker: [V] *She felt her heartbeat quicken as he approached.* ◇ [VN] *He quickened his pace to catch up with them.* **2** to become more active; to make sth more active: [V] *His interest quickened as he heard more about the plan.* [also VN]

ˌquick-ˈfire *adj.* [only before noun] (of a series of things) done or said very fast, one after the other: *a series of quick-fire questions*

quickie /ˈkwɪki/ *noun* (*informal*) **1** a thing that only takes a short time: *I've got a question—it's just a quickie.* ◇ *a quickie divorce* **2** a sexual act that takes a very short time

quick·lime /ˈkwɪklaɪm/ *noun* [U] = LIME (1)

quick·ly /ˈkwɪkli/ *adv.* **1** fast: *She walked quickly away.* ◇ *We'll repair it as quickly as possible.* **2** soon; after a short time: *He replied to my letter very quickly.* ◇ *It quickly became clear that she was dying.* ⇨ note at QUICK, SOON

quick·ness /ˈkwɪknəs/ *noun* [U] the quality of being fast, especially at thinking, etc: *She was known for the quickness of her wit.* ◇ *He amazes me with his quickness and eagerness to learn.*

ˈquick one *noun* (*BrE, informal*) a drink, usually an alcoholic one, taken quickly

quick·sand /ˈkwɪksænd/ *noun* [U] (also **quick·sands** [pl.]) **1** deep wet sand that you sink into if you walk on it **2** a situation that is dangerous or difficult to escape from

quick·sil·ver /ˈkwɪksɪlvə(r)/ *noun, adj.*
■ *noun* [U] (*old use*) = MERCURY
■ *adj.* [only before noun] (*literary*) changing or moving very quickly: *his quicksilver temperament*

quick·step /ˈkwɪkstep/ *noun* a dance for two people together, with a lot of fast steps; a piece of music for this dance

ˌquick-ˈtempered *adj.* likely to become angry very quickly: *a quick-tempered woman*

ˌquick-ˈwitted *adj.* able to think quickly; intelligent: *a quick-witted student/response* OPP SLOW-WITTED

quid /kwɪd/ *noun* (*pl.* **quid**) (*BrE, informal*) one pound in money: *Can you lend me five quid?* IDM **quids in** in a position of having made a profit, especially a good profit

quid pro quo /ˌkwɪd prəʊ ˈkwəʊ; *AmE* proʊ ˈkwoʊ/ *noun* [sing.] (*from Latin*) a thing given in return for sth else

qui·es·cent /kwiˈesnt/ *adj.* **1** (*formal*) quiet; not active **2** (*medical*) (of a disease, etc.) not developing, especially when this is probably only a temporary state ▶ **qui·es·cence** /-sns/ *noun* [U]

quiet /ˈkwaɪət/ *adj., noun, verb*
■ *adj.* (**quiet·er, quiet·est**) **1** making very little noise: *her quiet voice/footsteps* ◇ *a more efficient engine* ◇ *Could you keep the kids quiet while I'm on the phone?* ◇ *She went very quiet* (= did not say much) *so I knew she was upset.* ◇ *'Be quiet,' said the teacher.* ◇ *She crept downstairs* (*as) quiet as a mouse.* **2** without many people or much noise or activity: *a quiet house/street/town* ◇ *They lead a quiet life.* ◇ *Business is usually quieter at this time of year.* ◇ *They had a quiet wedding.* **3** not disturbed; peaceful: *to have a quiet drink* ◇ *I was looking forward to a quiet evening at home.* **4** (of a person) tending not to talk very much: *She was quiet and shy.* **5** (of a feeling or an attitude) definite but not expressed in an obvious way: *He had an air of quiet authority.* ▶ **quiet·ly** *adv.*: *to speak/ move quietly* ◇ *I spent a few hours quietly relaxing.* ◇ *He is quietly confident that they can succeed.* ◇ *a quietly-spoken woman* **quiet·ness** *noun* [U]: *the quietness of the countryside* ◇ *His quietness worried her.* IDM **keep quiet about sth | keep sth quiet** to say nothing about sth; to keep sth secret: *I've decided to resign but I'd rather you kept quiet about it.*
■ *noun* [U] the state of being calm and without much noise: *the quiet of his own room* ◇ *the quiet of the early morning* ◇ *I go to the library for a little peace and quiet.* IDM **on the ˈquiet** without telling anyone SYN SECRETLY
■ *verb* ~ (**sb/sth**) (**down**) (*especially AmE*) to become calmer or less noisy; to make sb/sth calmer or less noisy: [V] *The demonstrators quieted down when the police arrived.* ◇ [VN] *He's very good at quieting the kids.*

quiet·en /ˈkwaɪətn/ *verb* ~ (**sb/sth**) (**down**) (*BrE*) to become calmer or less noisy; to make sb/sth calmer or less noisy: [V] *The chatter of voices gradually quietened.* ◇ *Things seem to have quietened down a bit this afternoon* (= we are not so busy, etc.). [also VN]

quiet·ude /ˈkwaɪətjuːd; *AmE* -tuːd/ *noun* [U] (*literary*) the

---

aɪ	aʊ	eɪ	əʊ	oʊ	ɔɪ	ɪə	eə	ʊə	j	w
my	now	say	go (BrE)	go (AmE)	boy	near	hair	pure	yes	wet

state of being still and quiet [SYN] CALM: *a moment of quietude*

quiff /kwɪf/ *noun* a piece of hair at the front of the head that is brushed upwards and backwards

quill /kwɪl/ *noun* **1** (also **'quill feather**) a large feather from the wing or tail of a bird **2** (also **,quill 'pen**) a pen made from a quill feather **3** one of the long sharp stiff SPINES on a PORCUPINE

quilt /kwɪlt/ *noun* **1** a decorative cover for a bed, made of two layers with soft material between them: *a patchwork quilt*—picture at BED **2** (*BrE*) = DUVET—compare COMFORTER

quilt·ed /'kwɪltɪd/ *adj.* (of clothes, etc.) made of two layers of fabric with soft material between them, held in place by lines of stitches: *a quilted jacket/bedcover*

quilt·ing /'kwɪltɪŋ/ *noun* [U] the work of making a QUILT; fabric that is used for this

quin /kwɪn/ *noun* (*BrE, informal*) = QUINTUPLET

quince /kwɪns/ *noun* a hard bitter yellow fruit used for making jam, etc. It grows on a tree, also called a **quince**: *quince jelly* ◊ *a flowering quince*

quin·ine /kwɪ'niːn; 'kwɪniːn; *AmE* also 'kwaɪnaɪn/ *noun* [U] a drug made from the bark of a S American tree, used in the past to treat MALARIA

quint /kwɪnt/ *noun* (*AmE, informal*) = QUINTUPLET

quint·es·sence /kwɪn'tesns/ *noun* [sing.] **the ~ of sth** (*formal*) **1** the perfect example of sth: *It was the quintessence of an English manor house.* **2** the most important features of sth: *a painting that captures the quintessence of Viennese elegance* ▶ **quint·es·sen·tial** /ˌkwɪntɪ'senʃl/ *adj.*: *He was the quintessential tough guy.* **quint·es·sen·tial·ly** /-ʃəli/ *adv.*: *a sense of humour that is quintessentially British*

quin·tet /kwɪn'tet/ *noun* **1** [C+sing./pl. *v.*] a group of five musicians or singers who play or sing together: *the Miles Davis Quintet* **2** [C] a piece of music for five musicians or singers: *a string quintet*

quin·tu·plet /'kwɪntjʊplət; kwɪn'tjuːplət; -'tʌpl-/ (also *BrE informal* **quin**) (also *AmE informal* **quint**) *noun* one of five children born at the same time to the same mother

quip /kwɪp/ *noun, verb*
■ *noun* a quick and clever remark: *to make a quip*
■ *verb* (**-pp-**) [V speech] to make a quick and clever remark

quirk /kwɜːk; *AmE* kwɜːrk/ *noun* **1** an aspect of sb's personality or behaviour that is a little strange **2** a strange thing that happens, especially accidentally: *By a strange quirk of fate they had booked into the same hotel.* ▶ **quirky** *adj.*: *a quirky sense of humour*

quis·ling /'kwɪzlɪŋ/ *noun* (*disapproving*) a person who helps an enemy that has taken control of his or her country

quit /kwɪt/ *verb* (**quit·ting, quit, quit**) (*BrE also* **quit·ting, quit·ted, quit·ted**) **1 ~ (as sth)** (*informal*) to leave your job, school, etc: [V] *If I don't get more money I'll quit.* ◊ *He has decided to quit as manager of the team.* ◊ [VN] *He quit the show last year because of bad health.* **2** (*informal, especially AmE*) to stop doing sth: [VN-ing] *I've quit smoking.* ◊ [VN] *Just quit it!* ◊ [V] *We only just started. We're not going to quit now.* **3** to leave the place where you live: [VN] *We decided it was time to quit the city.* ◊ [V] *The landlord gave them all notice to quit.*

quite /kwaɪt/ *adv.* **1** (*BrE*) (not used with a negative) to some degree [SYN] FAIRLY, PRETTY: *quite big/good/cold/warm/interesting* ◊ *He plays quite well.* ◊ *I quite like opera.* [HELP] When **quite** is used with an adjective before a noun, it comes before *a* or *an*. You can say: *It's quite a small house.* or *Their house is quite small.* but not ~~It's a quite small house.~~ **2** (*BrE*) to the greatest possible degree [SYN] COMPLETELY, ABSOLUTELY, ENTIRELY: *quite delicious/amazing/empty/perfect* ◊ *This is quite a different problem.* ◊ *I'm **quite happy** to wait for you here.* ◊ *Flying is **quite the best** way to travel.* ◊ *It wasn't quite as simple as I thought it would be.* ◊ **Quite frankly,** *I don't blame you.* ◊ *I've had **quite enough** of your tantrums.* ◊ *Are you **quite sure**?* ◊ *I **quite agree**.* ◊ *I don't quite know what to do next.*

◊ **Quite apart from** *all the work, he had financial problems.* ◊ *The theatre was **not quite** (= was almost) full.* ◊ *It's like being in the Alps, but not quite.* ◊ (*spoken*) '*I almost think she prefers animals to people.*' '**Quite right too,**' *said Bill.* ◊ '*I'm sorry to be so difficult.*' '**That's quite all right.**' **3** to a great degree; very; really: *You'll be quite comfortable here.* ◊ *I can see it quite clearly.* ◊ (*AmE*) '*You've no intention of coming back?*' '*I'm quite sorry, but no, I have not.*' **4** (also *formal* **quite so**) (*BrE*) used to agree with sb or show that you understand them: '*He's bound to feel shaken after his accident.*' '*Quite.*' [IDM] **'quite a/the sth** (also *informal* **'quite some sth**) used to show that a person or thing is particularly impressive or unusual in some way: *She's quite a beauty.* ◊ *We found it quite a change when we moved to London.* ◊ *He's quite the little gentleman, isn't he?* ◊ *It must be quite some car.* **quite a 'lot (of sth)** (also *BrE informal* **quite a 'bit**) a large number or amount of sth: *We drank quite a lot of wine.* **'quite some sth 1** a large amount of sth: *She hasn't been seen for quite some time.* **2** (*informal*) = QUITE A/THE STH—more at CONTRARY, FEW *pron.*

WHICH WORD?
quite / fairly / rather / pretty

Look at these examples:
The exam was fairly difficult.
The exam was quite difficult.
The exam was rather difficult.

Quite is a little stronger than **fairly** and **rather** is a little stronger than **quite**. **Rather** is not very common in *AmE*; **pretty** has the same meaning and this is used in informal *BrE* too: *The exam was pretty difficult.*

In *BrE* **quite** has two meanings: *I feel quite tired today* (=fairly tired). With adjectives that describe an extreme state ('non-gradable' adjectives) it means 'completely' or 'absolutely': *I feel quite exhausted.* With some adjectives, both meanings are possible. The speaker's stress and intonation will show you which is meant: *Your essay is 'quite good* (= fairly good – it could be better); *Your essay is quite 'good* (= very good, especially when this is unexpected).

In *AmE* **quite** usually means something like 'very', not 'fairly' or 'rather'. **Pretty** is used instead for this sense.

quits /kwɪts/ *adj.* [IDM] **be quits (with sb)** (*informal*) when two people **are quits**, they do not owe each other anything, especially money: *I'll give you £5 and then we're quits.* [IDM] see CALL *v.*, DOUBLE *n.*

quit·ter /'kwɪtə(r)/ *noun* (often *disapproving*) a person who gives up easily and does not finish a task they have started

quiver /'kwɪvə(r)/ *verb, noun*
■ *verb* [V] to shake slightly; to make a slight movement [SYN] TREMBLE: *Her lip quivered and then she started to cry.* ◊ *The memory of that day made him quiver with anger.*
■ *noun* **1** an emotion that has an effect on your body; a slight movement in part of your body: *He felt a quiver of excitement run through him.* ◊ *Jane couldn't help the quiver in her voice.* **2** a case for carrying arrows

quix·ot·ic /kwɪk'sɒtɪk; *AmE* -'sɑːtɪk/ *adj.* (*formal*) having or involving imaginative ideas or plans that are usually not practical

quiz /kwɪz/ *noun, verb*
■ *noun* (*pl.* **quiz·zes**) **1** a competition or game in which people try to answer questions to test their knowledge: *a general knowledge quiz* ◊ *a television quiz show* **2** (*especially AmE*) an informal test given to students: *a reading comprehension quiz*—see also POP QUIZ ⇨ note at EXAM
■ *verb* (**-zz-**) [VN] **1 ~ sb (about sb/sth)** | **~ sb (on/over sth)** to ask sb a lot of questions about sth in order to get information from them: *Four men are being quizzed by police about the murder.* ◊ *We were quizzed on our views about education.* **2** (*AmE*) to give students an informal test: *You will be quizzed on chapter 6 tomorrow.*

quiz·master /'kwɪzmɑːstə(r); *AmE* -mæs-/ *noun* = QUESTION MASTER

Q

quiz·zical /ˈkwɪzɪkl/ *adj.* (of an expression) showing that you are slightly surprised or amused: *a quizzical expression/smile/face* ◊ *He gave me a quizzical look when I ordered champagne.* ▶ **quiz·zi·cal·ly** /-kli/ *adv.*: *She looked at him quizzically.*

quoit /kɔɪt; kwɔɪt/ *noun* **1** [C] a ring that is thrown onto a small post in the game of quoits **2** (**quoits**) [U] a game in which rings are thrown onto a small post

Quonset hut™ /ˈkwɒnset hʌt; *AmE* ˈkwɑːn-/ *noun* (*AmE*) = NISSEN HUT

Quorn™ /kwɔːn; *AmE* kwɔːrn/ *noun* [U] (*BrE*) a substance made from a type of MUSHROOM, used in cooking instead of meat

quorum /ˈkwɔːrəm/ *noun* [sing.] the smallest number of people who must be at a meeting before it can begin or decisions can be made

quota /ˈkwəʊtə; *AmE* ˈkwoʊtə/ *noun* **1** [C] the limited number or amount of people or things that is officially allowed: *to introduce a strict import quota on grain* ◊ *a quota system for accepting refugees* **2** [C] an amount of sth that sb expects or needs to have or achieve: *I'm going home now—I've done my quota of work for the day.* ◊ *to get your full quota of sleep* **3** [sing.] (*politics*) a fixed number of votes that a candidate needs in order to be elected: *He was 76 votes short of the quota.*

quot·able /ˈkwəʊtəbl; *AmE* ˈkwoʊ-/ *adj.* (of a statement) interesting or amusing and worth repeating

quota·tion /kwəʊˈteɪʃn; *AmE* kwoʊ-/ *noun* **1** (also *informal* **quote**) [C] a group of words or a short piece of writing taken from a book, play, speech, etc. and repeated because it is interesting or useful: *The book began with a quotation from Goethe.* ◊ *a dictionary of quotations*—see also MISQUOTATION **2** [U] the act of repeating sth interesting or useful that another person has written or said: *The writer illustrates his point by quotation from a number of sources.* **3** (also *informal* **quote**) a statement of how much money a particular piece of work will cost: *You need to get a written quotation before they start work.* **4** [C] (*finance*) a statement of the current value of goods or STOCKS: *the latest quotations from the Stock Exchange*

quoˈtation marks (also **quotes**, **ˈspeech marks**) (*BrE* also **inˈvert·ed commas**) *noun* [pl.] a pair of marks (' ') or (" ") placed around a word, sentence, etc. to show that it is what sb said or wrote, that it is a title or that you are using it in an unusual way ⇨ Appendix 4

quote /kwəʊt; *AmE* kwoʊt/ *verb, noun*
■ *verb*
REPEAT EXACT WORDS | **1** ~ (sth) (from sb/sth)| ~ (sb) (as doing sth) to repeat the exact words that another person

has said or written: [VN] *He quoted a passage from the minister's speech.* ◊ *to quote Shakespeare* ◊ *The figures quoted in this article refer only to Britain.* ◊ *The President was quoted in the press as saying* that he disagreed with the decision. ◊ *'It will all be gone tomorrow.' '* **Can I quote you on that?** *'* ◊ **Don't quote me on this** (= this is not an official statement), *but I think he is going to resign.* ◊ *Quote this reference number in all correspondence.* ◊ [V] *She said, and I quote, 'Life is meaningless without love.'* ◊ [Vspeech] *'The man who is tired of London is tired of life,' he quoted.*—see also MISQUOTE
GIVE EXAMPLE | **2** to mention an example of sth to support what you are saying: [VNN] *Can you quote me an instance of when this happened?* [also VN]
GIVE PRICE | **3** ~ (sb) (sth) (for sth/for doing sth) to tell a customer how much money you will charge them for a job, service or product: [VNN] *They quoted us £300 for installing a shower unit.* [also VN, V] **4** [VN] ~ sth (at sth) (*finance*) to give a market price for shares, gold or foreign money: *Yesterday the pound was quoted at $1.8285, unchanged from Monday.* **5** [VN] (*finance*) to give the prices for a business company's shares on a STOCK EXCHANGE: *Several football clubs are now quoted on the Stock Exchange.*
IDM **ˈquote (…ˈunquote)** (*spoken*) used to show the beginning (and end) of a word, phrase, etc. that has been said or written by sb else: *It was quote, 'the hardest decision of my life', unquote, and one that he lived to regret.*
■ *noun* (*informal*)
EXACT WORDS | **1** = QUOTATION
PUNCTUATION | **2** (**quotes**) [pl.] = QUOTATION MARKS: *If you take text from other sources, place it **in quotes**.*

quoth /kwəʊθ; *AmE* kwoʊθ/ *verb* [Vspeech] (*old use* or *humorous*) used meaning 'said' before 'I' 'he' or 'she'

quo·tid·ian /kwɒˈtɪdiən; kwəʊˈt-; *AmE* kwoʊ-/ *adj.* (*formal*) ordinary; typical of what happens every day: *their quotidian existence*

quo·tient /ˈkwəʊʃnt; *AmE* ˈkwoʊ-/ *noun* (*mathematics*) a number which is the result when one number is divided by another—see also INTELLIGENCE QUOTIENT

Qur'an *noun* = KORAN

q.v. /ˌkjuː ˈviː/ *abbr.* used in books to tell a reader that there is more information in another part of the book (from Latin 'quod vide')

qwerty (also **QWERTY**) /ˈkwɜːti; *AmE* ˈkwɜːrti/ *adj.* [usually before noun] (of a keyboard on a computer or TYPE-WRITER) with the keys arranged in the usual way with Q, W, E, R, T and Y on the left of the top row of letters

Rr

R /ɑː(r)/ *noun, abbr.*

■ *noun* (also **r**) [C, U] (*pl.* **R's, r's** /ɑːz/) the 18th letter of the English alphabet: *'Rose' begins with (an) R/'R'.* **IDM** see THREE

■ *abbr.* **1** (*BrE*) Queen; King (from Latin 'Regina; Rex'): *Elizabeth R.* **2** (**R.**) (especially on maps) River: *R. Trent* **3** (also **R.** especially in *AmE*) (in politics in the US) REPUBLICAN **4** (*BrE*) (in abbreviations) Royal: *the RAC* (= Royal Automobile Club) **5** (*AmE*) a label for a film/movie that is not suitable for people under the age of 17 to see without an adult present (abbreviation for 'restricted')— see also R & B, R. & D.

rabbi /'ræbaɪ/ *noun* a Jewish religious leader or a teacher of Jewish law: *the Chief Rabbi* (= the leader of Jewish communities in a particular country) ◊ *Rabbi Hugo Grin*

rab·bin·ical /rə'bɪnɪkl/ (also **rab·bin·ic**) *adj.* connected with rabbis or Jewish law or teaching

rab·bit /'ræbɪt/ *noun, verb*

■ *noun* **1** [C] a small animal with soft fur, long ears and a short tail. Rabbits live in holes in the ground or are kept as pets or for food: *a rabbit hole/warren/hutch*—compare HARE **2** [U] meat from a rabbit **IDM** see PULL *v.*

■ *verb* [V] (**go rabbiting**) to hunt or shoot rabbits **PHRV** ,**rabbit 'on (about sb/sth)** (*BrE, informal, disapproving*) to talk continuously about things that are not important or interesting

'**rabbit warren** (also **war·ren**) *noun* **1** a system of holes and underground tunnels where wild rabbits live **2** (*disapproving*) a building or part of a city with many narrow passages or streets

rab·ble /'ræbl/ *noun* [sing.+ sing./pl. *v.*] (*disapproving*) **1** a large amount of noisy people who are or may become violent: *a disorganized/drunken rabble* **2** (**the rabble**) ordinary people or people who are considered to have a low social position: *a speech that appealed to the rabble*

'**rabble-rouser** *noun* a person who makes speeches to crowds of people intending to make them angry or excited, especially for political aims ▶ '**rabble-rousing** *adj.* '**rabble-rousing** *noun* [U]

rabid /'ræbɪd; 'reɪb-/ *adj.* **1** [usually before noun] (*disapproving*) (of a type of person) having very strong feelings about sth and acting in an unacceptable way: *rabid right-wing fanatics* ◊ *the rabid tabloid press* **2** [usually before noun] (*disapproving*) (of feelings or opinions) violent or extreme: *rabid speculation* **3** suffering from rabies: *a rabid dog* ▶ **rabid·ly** *adv.*

ra·bies /'reɪbiːz/ *noun* [U] a disease of dogs and other animals that causes MADNESS and death. Infected animals can pass the disease to humans by biting them.

RAC /,ɑːr eɪ 'siː/ *abbr.* Royal Automobile Club. The RAC is a British organization which provides services for car owners.

rac·coon (also **ra·coon**) /rə'kuːn; *AmE* ræ-/ *noun* **1** a small N American animal with greyish-brown fur, black marks on its face and a thick tail **2** [U] the fur of the raccoon

race /reɪs/ *noun, verb*

■ *noun*
COMPETITION | **1** [C] ~ (**between A and B**) | ~ (**against sb**) a competition between people, animals, vehicles, etc. to see which one is the faster or fastest: *I bet I'd win a race between us two!* ◊ *He's already in training for the big race against Bailey.* ◊ *Their horse came third in the race last year.* ◊ *a boat/horse/road race* ◊ *a five-kilometre race* ◊ *Shall we have a race to the end of the beach?* **2** [sing.] ~ (**for sth/to do sth**) a situation in which a number of

people, groups, organizations, etc. are competing, especially for political power or to achieve sth first: *the race for the presidency* ◊ *The race is on* (= has begun) *to find a cure for this disease.*—see also RAT RACE

FOR HORSES | **3** (**the races**) [pl.] a series of horse races that happen at one place on a particular day: *to go to the races* PEOPLE | **4** [C, U] one of the main groups that humans can be divided into according to their physical differences, for example the colour of their skin: *the Caucasian/Mongolian race* ◊ *people of mixed race* ◊ *This custom is found in people of all races throughout the world.* ◊ *legislation against discrimination on the grounds of race or sex* **5** [C] a group of people who share the same language, history, culture, etc: *the Nordic races* ◊ *He admired Canadians as a hardy and determined race.*—see also HUMAN RACE

ANIMALS/PLANTS | **6** [C] a breed or type of animal or plant: *a race of cattle*

IDM a ,**race against 'time/the 'clock** a situation in which you have to do sth or finish sth very fast before it is too late—more at HORSE *n.*

■ *verb*
COMPETE | **1** ~ (**against**) sb/sth to compete against sb/sth to see who can go faster or the fastest, do sth first, etc.; to take part in a race or races: [V] *Who will he be racing against in the next round?* ◊ *They raced to a thrilling victory in the relay.* ◊ *She'll be racing for the senior team next year.* ◊ [VN] *We raced each other back to the car.* ◊ [Vtoinf] *Television companies are racing to be the first to screen his life story.* **2** [VN] to make an animal or a vehicle compete in a race: *to race dogs/horses/pigeons* ◊ *to race motorbikes*

MOVE FAST | **3** [+adv./prep.] to move very fast; to move sb/sth very fast: [V] *He raced up the stairs.* ◊ *The days seemed to race past.* ◊ [VN] *The injured man was raced to the hospital.* ◊ *She raced her car through the narrow streets of the town.*

OF HEART/MIND/THOUGHTS | **4** [V] to function very quickly because you are afraid, excited, etc: *My mind raced as I tried to work out what was happening.* ◊ *She took a deep breath to calm her racing pulse.*

OF ENGINE | **5** [V] to run too fast: *The truck came to rest against a tree, its engine racing.*

'**race car** *noun* (*AmE*) = RACING CAR

'**race·course** /'reɪskɔːs; *AmE* -kɔːrs/ (*BrE*) (*AmE* **race-track**) *noun* a track where horses race and the buildings, etc. that are connected with it

'**race·goer** /'reɪsɡəʊə(r); *AmE* -ɡoʊ-/ *noun* (*BrE*) a person who goes to horse races

'**race·horse** /'reɪshɔːs; *AmE* -hɔːrs/ *noun* a horse that is bred and trained to run in races

'**race meeting** *noun* (*BrE*) a series of races, especially for horses, held at one course over one day or several days

racer /'reɪsə(r)/ *noun* **1** a person or an animal that competes in races: *Italy's champion downhill racer* **2** a car, boat, etc. designed for racing: *an ocean racer*

,**race re'lations** *noun* [pl.] the relationships between people of different races who live in the same community

'**race riot** *noun* violent behaviour between people of different races living in the same community

race·track /'reɪstræk/ *noun* **1** a track for races between runners, cars, bicycles, etc: *You can't cross the road—it's like a racetrack.* **2** (*AmE*) = RACECOURSE

ra·cial /'reɪʃl/ *adj.* **1** [only before noun] happening or existing between people of different races: *racial hatred/*

æ	ɑː	e	ɜː	ə	ɪ	iː	i	ɒ	ɔː	ʌ	ʊ	u	uː
cat	father	ten	bird	about	sit	see	many	got	saw	cup	put	actual	too
								(BrE)					

prejudice/tension/violence ◊ *racial equality* ◊ *They have pledged to end **racial discrimination** in areas such as employment*. **2** [usually before noun] connected with a person's race: *racial groups/minorities* ◊ *a person's racial origin* ▶ **ra·cial·ly** /-ʃəli/ *adv.*: *The attacks were not racially motivated.* ◊ *racially mixed schools*

ra·cial·ism /'reɪʃəlɪzəm/ *noun* [U] (*old-fashioned, BrE*) = RACISM

ra·cial·ist /'reɪʃəlɪst/ *noun, adj.* (*old-fashioned, BrE*) = RACIST

ra·cing /'reɪsɪŋ/ *noun* [U] **1** the sport of racing horses: *a racing stable*—see also FLAT RACING, HORSE RACING **2** (usually in compounds) any sport that involves competing in races: *motor/yacht/greyhound racing* ◊ *a racing driver*

'racing car (*BrE*) (*AmE* **'race car**) *noun* a car that has been specially designed for motor racing

ra·cism /'reɪsɪzəm/ *noun* [U] (*disapproving*) **1** the unfair treatment of people who belong to a different race; violent behaviour towards them: *a victim of racism* ◊ *ugly outbreaks of racism* **2** the belief that some races of people are better than others: *irrational racism* ▶ **ra·cist** /'reɪsɪst/ *noun*: *He's a racist.* **ra·cist** *adj.*: *racist groups/thugs* ◊ *racist attitudes/attacks/remarks*

rack /ræk/ *noun, verb*

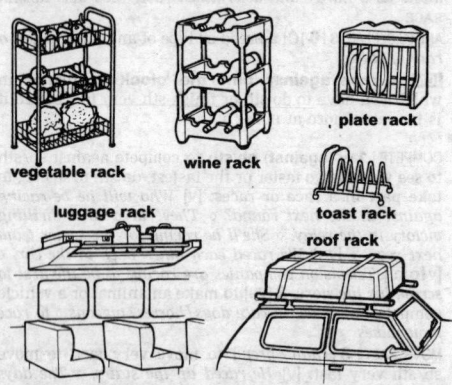

vegetable rack   wine rack   plate rack

luggage rack   toast rack

roof rack

■ *noun* **1** (often in compounds) a piece of equipment, usually made of metal or wooden bars, that is used for holding things or for hanging things on: *a vegetable/wine/plate/toast rack* ◊ *I looked through a rack of clothes at the back of the shop.*—see also LUGGAGE RACK, ROOF RACK **2** (usually **the rack**) an instrument of TORTURE, used in the past for punishing and hurting people. Their arms and legs were tied to the wooden frame and then pulled in opposite directions, stretching the body: *to put sb on the rack* **3** ~ **of lamb/pork** a particular piece of meat that includes the front RIBS and is cooked in the oven: *a rack of lamb* **IDM** **go to ,rack and 'ruin** to get into a bad condition: *They let the house go to rack and ruin.* **off the 'rack** (*AmE*) = OFF THE PEG at PEG *n*. **on the 'rack** feeling extreme pressure, anxiety or pain

■ *verb* (also *less frequent* **wrack**) [VN] [often passive] to make sb suffer great physical or mental pain: *to be racked with/by guilt* ◊ *Her face was racked with pain.* ◊ *Violent sobs racked her whole body.* **IDM** **rack your 'brain(s)** (also *less frequent* **wrack your 'brain(s)**) to think very hard or for a long time about sth: *She racked her brains, trying to remember exactly what she had said.* **PHRV** **,rack 'up sth** (*especially AmE*) to collect sth, such as profits or losses in a business, or points in a competition: *The company racked up $200 million in losses in two years.* ◊ *In ten years of boxing he racked up a record 176 wins.*

racket /'rækɪt/ *noun* **1** [sing.] (*informal*) a loud unpleasant noise: *Stop making that terrible racket!* **2** [C] (*informal*) a dishonest or illegal way of getting money: *a protection/extortion/drugs racket* **3** (also **rac·quet**) [C] a piece of sports equipment used for hitting the ball, etc. in the games of tennis, SQUASH or BADMINTON. It has an OVAL frame, with strings stretched across and down it.

—compare BAT **4** (**rackets, racquets**) [U] a game for two or four people played with rackets and a small hard ball in a court with four walls—compare SQUASH

rack·et·eer /ˌrækə'tɪə(r); *AmE* -'tɪr/ *noun* (*disapproving*) a person who makes money through dishonest or illegal activities ▶ **rack·et·eer·ing** *noun* [U]

ra·con·teur /ˌrækɒn'tɜː(r); *AmE* -kɑːn-/ *noun* a person who is good at telling stories in an interesting and amusing way

ra·coon *noun* = RACCOON

rac·quet = RACKET

rac·quet·ball /'rækɪtbɔːl/ *noun* [U] a game played especially in the US by two or four players on a court with four walls, using RACKETS and a small hollow rubber ball

racy /'reɪsi/ *adj.* (**raci·er, raci·est**) having a style that is exciting and amusing, sometimes in a way that is connected with sex: *a racy novel*

radar /'reɪdɑː(r)/ *noun* [U] a system that uses radio waves to find the position and movement of objects, for example planes and ships, when they cannot be seen: *They located the ship by radar.* ◊ *a radar screen/operator*—compare SONAR

'radar trap *noun* (*BrE*) = SPEED TRAP

rad·dled /'rædld/ *adj.* (*BrE*) (of a person, their face, etc.) looking very tired **SYN** WORN

ra·dial /'reɪdiəl/ *adj., noun*
■ *adj.* having a pattern of lines, etc. that go out from a central point towards the edge of a circle: *the radial pattern of public transport facilities* ▶ **ra·di·al·ly** /-iəli/ *adv.*
■ *noun* (*BrE* also **,radial 'tyre**) (*AmE* also **,radial 'tire**) a car tyre with strong threads inside that point away from the outside part and make the tyre stronger and safer

ra·di·ance /'reɪdiəns/ *noun* [U] **1** a special bright quality that shows in sb's face, for example because they are very happy or healthy: *the youthful radiance of her beauty* **2** warm light shining from sth: *the radiance of the sunset*

ra·di·ant /'reɪdiənt/ *adj.* **1** ~ **(with sth)** showing great happiness, love or health: *a radiant smile* ◊ *The bride looked radiant.* ◊ *She was radiant with health.* **2** giving a warm bright light: *The sun was radiant in a clear blue sky.* **3** [only before noun] (*technical*) sent out in rays from a central point: *the radiant heat/energy of the sun* ◊ *a radiant heater* (= one that sends out heat in rays) ▶ **ra·di·ant·ly** *adv.*: *He smiled radiantly.*

ra·di·ate /'reɪdieɪt/ *verb* **1** if a person **radiates** a particular quality or emotion, or if it **radiates** from them, people can see it very clearly: [VN] *He radiated self-confidence and optimism.* [also V] **2** if sth **radiates** heat, light or energy or heat, etc. **radiates** from it, the heat is sent out in all directions: [V] *Heat radiates from the stove.* [also VN] **3** [V+*adv./prep.*] (of lines, etc.) to spread out in all directions from a central point: *Five roads radiate from the square.* ◊ *The pain started in my stomach and radiated all over my body.*

ra·di·ation /ˌreɪdi'eɪʃn/ *noun* **1** [U, C] powerful and very dangerous rays that are sent out from RADIOACTIVE substances: *high levels/doses of radiation that damage cells* ◊ *the link between exposure to radiation and childhood cancer* ◊ *a radiation leak from a nuclear power station* ◊ *the radiations emitted by radium* **2** [U] heat, energy, etc. that is sent out in the form of rays: *ultraviolet radiation* ◊ *electromagnetic radiation from power lines* **3** (also **,radi·'ation therapy**) [U] the treatment of CANCER and other diseases using radiation—compare CHEMOTHERAPY, RADIOTHERAPY

ra·di·ator /'reɪdieɪtə(r)/ *noun* **1** a hollow metal device for heating rooms. Radiators are usually connected by pipes through which hot water is pumped: *a central heating system with a radiator in each room* **2** a device for cooling the engine of a vehicle or an aircraft

rad·ical /'rædɪkl/ *adj., noun*
■ *adj.* [usually before noun] **1** concerning the most basic and important parts of sth; thorough and complete: *the need for radical changes in education* ◊ *demands for radical reform of the law* ◊ *radical differences between the sexes* **2** new, different and likely to have a great effect: *radical ideas* ◊ *a radical solution to the problem* ◊ *radical*

proposals/measures **3** in favour of thorough and complete political or social change: *the radical wing of the party* ◊ *radical politicians/students/writers* **4** (*AmE*, *slang*) very good ▶ **rad·ic·al·ly** /-kli/ *adv.*: *The new methods are radically different from the old.* ◊ *Attitudes have changed radically.*

■ *noun* a person with radical opinions: *political/religious radicals*

rad·ic·al·ism /'rædɪkəlɪzəm/ *noun* [U] belief in RADICAL ideas and principles: *political/social radicalism*

rad·ic·al·ize (*BrE* also **-ise**) /'rædɪklaɪz/ *verb* [VN] to make people more willing to consider new and different policies, ideas, etc.; to make people more politically RADICAL: *Recent events have radicalized opinion on educational matters.*

radii *pl.* of RADIUS

radio /'reɪdiəʊ; *AmE* -oʊ/ *noun, verb*

■ *noun* **1** (often **the radio**) [U, sing.] the activity of broadcasting programmes for people to listen to; the programmes that are broadcast: *The interview was broadcast on radio and television.* ◊ *The play was written specially for radio.* ◊ *I listen to the radio on the way to work.* ◊ *Did you hear the interview with him on the radio?* ◊ *local/national radio* ◊ *a radio programme/reporter/station* **2** [C] a piece of equipment used for listening to programmes that are broadcast to the public: *to turn the radio on/off* ◊ *a car radio* ◊ *a radio cassette player*—see also CLOCK RADIO **3** [U] the process of sending and receiving messages through the air using ELECTROMAGNETIC waves: *He was unable to contact Blake by radio.* ◊ *to keep in radio contact* ◊ *radio signals/waves* **4** [C] a piece of equipment, for example on ships or planes, for sending and receiving radio signals: *to hear a gale warning on/over the ship's radio*

■ *verb* (**ra·dio·ing, ra·dioed, ra·dioed**) to send a message to sb by radio: [V] *The police officer radioed for help.* ◊ [VN] *The warning was radioed to headquarters.* [also V that, VN that, VN to inf]

radio- /'reɪdiəʊ; *AmE* -oʊ/ *combining form* (in nouns, adjectives and adverbs) **1** connected with radio waves or broadcasting: *radio-controlled* **2** connected with RADIO-ACTIVITY: *radiotherapy*

radio·active /ˌreɪdiəʊ'æktɪv; *AmE* -oʊ'æk-/ *adj.* sending out harmful RADIATION caused when the NUCLEI (= central parts) of atoms are broken up ▶ **radio·activ·ity** /ˌreɪdiəʊæk'tɪvəti; *AmE* -oʊæk-/ *noun* [U]: *the study of radioactivity* ◊ *a rise in the level of radioactivity*

radio·car·bon /ˌreɪdiəʊ'kɑːbən; *AmE* -oʊ'kɑːrb-/ *noun* [U] a RADIOACTIVE form of CARBON that is present in the materials of which living things are formed, used in CARBON DATING: *radiocarbon analysis*

radiocarbon 'dating *noun* [U] (*formal*) = CARBON DATING

radio-con'trolled *adj.* controlled from a distance by radio signals

radi·og·raph·er /ˌreɪdi'ɒgrəfə(r); *AmE* -'ɑːg-/ *noun* a person working in a hospital whose job is to take X-RAY photographs or to use X-RAYS to treat some illnesses, such as CANCER

radi·og·raphy /ˌreɪdi'ɒgrəfi; *AmE* -'ɑːg-/ *noun* [U] the process or job of taking X-RAY photographs

radi·olo·gist /ˌreɪdi'ɒlədʒɪst; *AmE* -'ɑːlə-/ *noun* a doctor who is trained in radiology

radi·ology /ˌreɪdi'ɒlədʒi; *AmE* -'ɑːlə-/ *noun* [U] the study and different types of RADIATION in medicine, for example to treat diseases

radio-'telephone *noun* a telephone that works by sending and receiving radio signals, used especially in cars, boats, etc.

radio 'telescope *noun* a piece of equipment that receives radio waves from space and is used for finding stars and the position of spacecraft, etc.

radio·ther·apy /ˌreɪdiəʊ'θerəpi; *AmE* -oʊ'θe-/ *noun* [U] the treatment of disease by RADIATION: *a course of radiotherapy*—compare CHEMOTHERAPY ▶ **radio·thera·pist** *noun*

rad·ish /'rædɪʃ/ *noun* [C, U] a small crisp red or white

root vegetable with a strong taste, eaten raw in salads: *a bunch of radishes*—picture on page A3

ra·dium /'reɪdiəm/ *noun* [U] (*symb* Ra) a chemical element. Radium is a white RADIOACTIVE metal used in the treatment of diseases such as CANCER.

ra·dius /'reɪdiəs/ *noun* (*pl.* **-dii** /-diaɪ/) **1** a straight line between the centre of a circle and any point on its outer edge; the length of this line—compare DIAMETER—picture at CIRCLE **2** a circular area that covers the distance mentioned from a central point: *They deliver to within a 5-mile radius of the store.* **3** (*anatomy*) the shorter bone of the two bones in the lower part of the arm between the elbow and the wrist, on the same side as the thumb—see also ULNA—picture at BODY

radon /'reɪdɒn; *AmE* -dɑːn/ *noun* [U] (*symb* Rn) a chemical element. Radon is a colourless RADIOACTIVE gas used in the treatment of diseases such as CANCER.

RAF /ˌɑːr eɪ 'ef; or, in informal use, ræf/ *abbr.* Royal Air Force (the British air force): *He was an RAF pilot.*

raf·fia /'ræfiə/ *noun* [U] soft material that looks like string and is made from the leaves of a type of PALM tree, used for weaving baskets, MATS, etc. or for tying things

raff·ish /'ræfɪʃ/ *adj.* (of sb's behaviour, clothes, etc.) not very acceptable according to some social standards, but interesting and attractive: *He had a cosmopolitan, slightly raffish air.*

raf·fle /'ræfl/ *noun, verb*

■ *noun* a way of making money for a particular project or organization. People buy tickets with numbers on them and some of these numbers are later chosen to win prizes.—compare LOTTERY

■ *verb* [VN] to give sth as a prize in a raffle

raft /rɑːft; *AmE* ræft/ *noun* **1** a flat structure made of pieces of wood tied together and used as a boat or floating platform **2** a small boat made of rubber or plastic that is filled with air: *an inflatable raft*—picture at BOAT **3** [usually sing.] **~ of sth** (*informal*) a large number or amount of sth: *a whole raft of new proposals*

raft·er /'rɑːftə(r); *AmE* 'ræf-/ *noun* [C, usually pl.] one of the sloping pieces of wood that support a roof

raft·ing /'rɑːftɪŋ; *AmE* 'ræft-/ *noun* [U] the sport or activity of travelling down a river on a RAFT: *We went white-water rafting on the Colorado River.*

rag /ræg/ *noun, verb*

■ *noun* **1** [C, U] a piece of old, often torn, cloth used especially for cleaning things—see also GLAD RAGS **2** [C] (*informal*, usually *disapproving*) a newspaper that you believe to be of low quality: *the local rag* **3** a piece of RAGTIME music **4** (*BrE*) [U, C] an event or a series of events organized by students each year to raise money for charity: *rag week* IDM **in 'rags** wearing very old torn clothes: *The children were dressed in rags.* **(from) ˌrags to 'riches** from being extremely poor to being very rich: *a rags-to-riches story* ◊ *Hers was a classic tale of rags to riches.* **lose your 'rag** (*BrE, informal*) to get angry—more at RED *adj.*

■ *verb* (**-gg-**) [VN] **~ sb (about sth)** (*old-fashioned, BrE*) to laugh at and/or play tricks on sb SYN TEASE

raga /'rɑːgə/ *noun* a traditional pattern of notes used in Indian music; a piece of music based on one of these patterns

raga·muf·fin /'rægəmʌfɪn/ *noun* (*old-fashioned*) a person, especially a child, in dirty torn clothes

rag·bag /'rægbæg/ *noun* [sing.] a collection of things that appear to have little connection with each other: *a ragbag of ideas/memories/stories*

ˌrag 'doll *noun* a soft DOLL made from pieces of fabric

rage /reɪdʒ/ *noun, verb*

■ *noun* [U, C] a feeling of violent anger that is difficult to control: *His face was dark with rage.* ◊ *to be shaking/trembling/speechless with rage* ◊ *Sue stormed out of the room in a rage.* ◊ *He flies into a rage if you even mention the subject.* IDM **be all the 'rage** (*informal*) to be very popular and fashionable

■ *verb* **1 ~ (at/against/about sb/sth)** to show that you are very angry about sth or with sb, especially by shouting: [V] *He raged against the injustice of it all.* ◊ [V speech] *'That's unfair!' she raged.* **2** [V] **~ (on)** (of a storm, battle, argument, etc.) to continue in a violent way: *The riots raged for three days.* ◊ *The blizzard was still raging outside.* **3** [V, usually +*adv.*/*prep.*] (of an illness, a fire, etc.) to spread very quickly: *Forest fires were raging out of control.* ◊ *A flu epidemic raged through Europe.*

rag·ga /'rægə/ *noun* [U] a type of pop music from the West Indies that contains features of REGGAE and HIP HOP

rag·ged /'rægɪd/ *adj.* **1** (of clothes) old and torn: *a ragged jacket*—picture at JAGGED **2** (of people) wearing old or torn clothes: *ragged children* **3** having an outline, edge or surface that is not straight or even: *ragged clouds* ◊ *a ragged coastline* ◊ *I could hear the sound of his ragged breathing.* ◊ *Their performance was still very ragged.* **5** (*informal*) very tired, especially after physical effort ▶ **rag·ged·ly** *adv.*: *raggedly dressed* ◊ *She was breathing raggedly.* **rag·ged·ness** *noun* [U] **IDM** ,**run sb** '**ragged** (*informal*) to make sb do a lot of work or make a big effort so that they become tired

ra·ging /'reɪdʒɪŋ/ *adj.* [only before noun] **1** (of feelings or emotions) very strong: *a raging appetite/thirst* ◊ *raging lust/jealousy* **2** (of natural forces) very powerful: *a raging storm/tempest* ◊ *The stream had become a raging torrent.* ◊ *The building was now a raging inferno.* **3** (of a pain or an illness) very strong or painful: *I've got a raging headache.* **4** very serious and causing strong feelings: *His speech has provoked a raging debate.*

rag·lan /'ræglən/ *adj.* [only before noun] **1** (of a sleeve) sewn to the front and back of a coat, sweater, etc. in a line that slopes down from the neck to under the arm **2** (of a coat, sweater, etc.) having raglan sleeves: *a raglan cardigan*

ra·gout /ræ'guː; 'ræguː/ *noun* [C, U] (from *French*) a hot dish of meat and vegetables boiled together with various spices

rag·tag /'rægtæg/ *adj.* [usually before noun] (*informal*) (of a group of people or an organization) not well organized; giving a bad impression: *a ragtag band of rebels*

rag·time /'rægtaɪm/ *noun* [U] an early form of jazz, especially for the piano, first played by African American musicians in the early 1900s

the '**rag trade** *noun* [sing.] (*old-fashioned, informal*) the business of designing, making and selling clothes

rag·wort /'rægwɜːt; *AmE* -wɜːrt/ *noun* [U] a wild plant with yellow flowers, poisonous to cows and horses

raid /reɪd/ *noun, verb*
- *noun* ~ (**on sth**) **1** a short surprise attack on an enemy by soldiers, ships or aircraft: *They carried out a bombing raid on enemy bases.*—see also AIR RAID **2** a surprise visit by the police looking for criminals or for illegal goods or drugs: *They were arrested during a dawn raid.* **3** an attack on a building, etc. in order to commit a crime: *an armed bank raid*—see also RAM-RAIDING
- *verb* [VN] **1** (of police) to visit a person or place without warning to look for criminals, illegal goods, drugs, etc: *The house was raided in the early hours.* **2** (of soldiers, fighting planes, etc.) to attack a place without warning: *Villages along the border are regularly raided.* ◊ *a raiding party* (= a group of soldiers, etc. that attack a place) **3** to enter a place, usually using force, and steal from it: *Many treasures were lost when the tombs were raided in the last century.* ◊ (*humorous*) *I caught him raiding the fridge again* (= taking food from it).

raid·er /'reɪdə(r)/ *noun* a person who makes a criminal raid on a place: *armed/masked raiders*

rail /reɪl/ *noun, verb*
- *noun* **1** [C] a wooden or metal bar placed around sth as a barrier or to provide support: *She leaned on the ship's rail and gazed out to sea.*—see also GUARD RAIL, HANDRAIL **2** [C] a bar fixed to the wall for hanging things on: *a picture/curtain/towel rail* **3** [C, usually pl.] each of the two metal bars that form the track that trains run on **4** [U] (often before another noun) railways/railroads as a means of transport: *to travel/send sth by rail* ◊ *rail travel/services/fares* ◊ *a rail link/network* **IDM** **go off the** '**rails** (*BrE, informal*) **1** to start behaving in a strange or unacceptable manner, for example, drinking a lot or taking drugs **2** to lose control and stop functioning cor-

rectly: *The company has gone badly off the rails in recent years.* **get back on the** '**rails** (*informal*) to become successful again after a period of failure, or to begin functioning normally again—more at JUMP *v.*
- *verb* ~ (**at/against sth/sb**) (*formal*) to complain about sth/sb in a very angry way: [V] *She railed against the injustice of it all.* [also V speech] **PHRV** ,**rail sth** '**in**/'**off** to separate an area or object from others by placing rails around it: *The machine was railed off as a safety precaution.*

rail·card /'reɪlkɑːd; *AmE* -kɑːrd/ *noun* (*BrE*) a card that allows sb to travel by train at a reduced price

rail·head /'reɪlhed/ *noun* (*technical*) the point at which a railway/railroad ends

rail·ing /'reɪlɪŋ/ *noun* [C, usually pl.] a fence made of upright metal bars; one of these bars: *iron railings* ◊ *I chained my bike to the park railings.* ◊ *She leaned out over the railing.*

rail·man /'reɪlmən/ *noun* (*BrE*) (*pl.* -**men** /-men/) = RAIL-WAYMAN

rail·road /'reɪlrəʊd; *AmE* -roʊd/ *noun, verb*
- *noun* (*AmE*) = RAILWAY
- *verb* [VN] **1** ~ **sb** (**into sth**/**into doing sth**) to force sb to do sth before they have had enough time to decide whether or not they want to do it **2** ~ **sth** (**through**/**through sth**) to make a group of people accept a decision, law, etc. quickly by putting pressure on them: *The bill was railroaded through the House.* **3** (*AmE*) to decide that sb is guilty of a crime, without giving them a fair trial

'**railroad crossing** *noun* (*AmE*) = LEVEL CROSSING

rail·road·er /'reɪlrəʊdə(r); *AmE* -roʊd-/ *noun* (*AmE*) = RAILWAYMAN

rail·way /'reɪlweɪ/ (*BrE*) (*AmE* **rail·road**) *noun* **1** (*BrE* also '**railway line**) a track with rails on which trains run: *The railway is still under construction.* ◊ *a disused railway* **2** a system of tracks, together with the trains that run on them, and the organization and people needed to operate them: *Her father worked on the railways.* ◊ *a railway station/worker/company* ◊ *the Midland Railway* ◊ *a model railway*

rail·way·man /'reɪlweɪmən/ *noun* (*pl.* -**men** /-mən/) (also **rail·man**) (both *BrE*) (*AmE* **rail·road·er**) a person who works for a rail company

rai·ment /'reɪmənt/ *noun* [U] (*old use*) clothing

rain /reɪn/ *noun, verb*
- *noun* **1** [U, sing.] water that falls from the clouds in separate drops: *There will be rain in all parts tomorrow.* ◊ *Rain is forecast for the weekend.* ◊ *Don't go out in the rain.* ◊ *It's pouring with rain* (= raining very hard). ◊ *heavy/torrential/driving rain* ◊ *The rain poured down.* ◊ *It looks like rain* (= as if it is going to rain). ◊ *A light rain began to fall.* ◊ *I think I felt a drop of rain.*—see also ACID RAIN, RAINY ⇨ note at WEATHER **2** (**the rains**) [pl.] the season of heavy continuous rain in tropical countries: *The rains come in September.* **3** [sing.] ~ **of sth** a large number of things falling from the sky at the same time: *a rain of arrows/stones* **IDM** **come** ,**rain, come** '**shine** | (**come**) ,**rain or** '**shine** whether there is rain or sun; whatever happens: *He goes jogging every morning, rain or shine.*—more at RIGHT *adj.*
- *verb* **1** [V] when **it rains**, water falls from the sky in drops: *Is it raining?* ◊ *It had been raining hard all night.* ◊ *It hardly rained at all last summer.* ◊ *It started to rain.* **2** ~ (**sth**) (**down**) (**on sb/sth**) to fall or to make sth fall on sb/sth in large quantities: [V] *Bombs rained (down) on the city's streets.* ◊ *Falling debris rained on us from above.* ◊ *He covered his face as the blows rained down on him* (= he was hit repeatedly). ◊ [VN] *The volcano erupted, raining hot ash over a wide area.* **IDM** **be raining cats and** '**dogs** (*informal*) to be raining heavily **it never rains but it** '**pours** (*BrE*) (*AmE* **when it rains, it** '**pours**) (*saying*) used to say that when one bad thing happens to you, other bad things happen soon after ,**rain on sb's** '**parade** (*AmE*) to spoil sth for sb **PHRV** be ,**rained** '**off** (*BrE*) (*AmE* be ,**rained** '**out**) (of an event) to be cancelled or to have to stop because it is raining: *The game has been rained off again.*

rain·bow /ˈreɪnbəʊ; AmE -boʊ/ noun an arch of different colours that appears in the sky when the sun shines through rain: *all the colours of the rainbow*

'rain check noun (*especially AmE*) a ticket that can be used later if a game, show, etc. is cancelled because of rain **IDM** **take a rain check (on sth)** (*informal, especially AmE*) to refuse an offer or invitation but say that you might accept it later: *'Are you coming for a drink?' 'Can I take a rain check?—I must get this finished tonight.'*

rain·coat /ˈreɪnkəʊt; AmE -koʊt/ noun a long light coat that keeps you dry in the rain—picture on page A5

rain·drop /ˈreɪndrɒp; AmE -drɑːp/ noun a single drop of rain

rain·fall /ˈreɪnfɔːl/ noun [U, sing.] the total amount of rain that falls in a particular area in a particular amount of time; an occasion when rain falls: *There has been below average rainfall this month.* ◊ *an average annual rainfall of 10 cm*

rain·for·est /ˈreɪnfɒrɪst; AmE -fɔːr-; -fɑːr-/ noun a thick forest in tropical parts of the world that have a lot of rain: *the Amazon rainforest*

rain·proof /ˈreɪnpruːf/ adj. that can keep rain out: *a rainproof jacket*

rain·storm /ˈreɪnstɔːm; AmE -stɔːrm/ noun a heavy fall of rain

rain·water /ˈreɪnwɔːtə(r)/ noun [U] water that has fallen as rain: *a barrel for collecting rainwater*

rainy /ˈreɪni/ adj. (**rain·ier**, **rain·iest**) having or bringing a lot of rain: *a rainy day* ◊ *the rainy season* ◊ *the rainiest place in Britain* **IDM** **save, keep, etc. sth for a ˌrainy 'day** to save sth, especially money, for a time when you will really need it

raise /reɪz/ verb, noun

■ *verb*

<u>MOVE UPWARDS</u> | **1** [VN] to lift or move sth to a higher level: *She raised the gun and fired.* ◊ *He raised a hand in greeting.* ◊ *She raised her eyes from her work.* **OPP** LOWER ⇨ note at RISE **2** [VN] to move sth/sb/yourself to an upright position: *Somehow we managed to raise her to her feet.* ◊ *He raised himself up on one elbow.* **OPP** LOWER

<u>INCREASE</u> | **3** [VN] **~ sth (to sth)** to increase the amount or level of sth: *to raise salaries/prices/taxes* ◊ *They raised their offer to $500.* ◊ *We need to raise public awareness of the issue.* ◊ *How can we raise standards in schools? Don't tell her about the job until you know for sure—we don't want to **raise her hopes** (= make her hope too much).* ◊ *I've never heard him even **raise his voice** (= speak louder because he was angry).*

<u>COLLECT MONEY/PEOPLE</u> | **4** [VN] to bring or collect money or people together; to manage to get or form sth: *to raise funds/a loan* ◊ *We are **raising money** for charity.* ◊ *He set about **raising an army.***—see also FUND-RAISER

<u>MENTION SUBJECT</u> | **5** [VN] to mention sth for people to discuss or sb to deal with: *The book **raises** many important questions.* ◊ *I'm glad you raised the subject of money.*

<u>CAUSE</u> | **6** to cause or produce sth; to make sth appear: *to raise doubts/fears/suspicions in people's minds* ◊ *The plans for the new development have raised angry protests from local residents.* ◊ *It wasn't an easy audience but he raised a few laughs with his jokes.* ◊ *It had been a difficult day but she managed to raise a smile.* ◊ *The horses' hooves raised a cloud of dust.*—see also CURTAIN-RAISER

<u>CHILD/ANIMAL</u> | **7** (*especially AmE*) to care for a child or young animal until it is able to take care of itself: [VN] *They were both raised in the South.* ◊ *kids raised on a diet of hamburgers* ◊ [VN-N] *They raised her (as) a Catholic.* ◊ *I was **born and raised** a city boy.*—compare BRING UP

<u>FARM ANIMALS/CROPS</u> | **8** [VN] to breed particular farm animals; to grow particular crops: *to raise cattle/corn*

<u>END STH</u> | **9** [VN] to end a restriction on sb/sth: *to raise a blockade/a ban/an embargo/a siege*

<u>ON RADIO/PHONE</u> | **10** [VN] to contact sb and speak to them by radio or telephone: *We managed to raise him on his mobile phone.*

<u>DEAD PERSON</u> | **11** [VN] **~ sb (from sth)** to make sb who has

died come to life again: *Christians believe that God raised Jesus from the dead.*

IDM **raise a/your ˈhand against/to sb** to hit or threaten to hit sb **raise your 'eyebrows (at sth)** [often passive] to show that you disapprove of or are surprised by sth: *Eyebrows were raised when he arrived without his wife.* **raise your 'glass (to sb)** to hold up your glass and wish sb happiness, good luck, etc. before you drink **raise 'hell** (*informal*) to protest angrily, especially in a way that causes trouble for sb **raise the 'roof** to produce or make sb produce a lot of noise in a building, for example by shouting or CHEERING: *Their cheers raised the roof.* **raise sb's 'spirits** to make sb feel more cheerful or brave: *The sunny weather raised my spirits a little.*—more at ANTE, HACKLES, SIGHT n., TEMPERATURE

PHRV **ˈraise sth to sb/sth** to build or place a statue, etc. somewhere in honour or memory of sb/sth: *The town raised a memorial to those killed in the war.*

■ *noun* (*AmE*) = RISE

raised /reɪzd/ adj. higher than the area around: *a raised platform*

rai·sin /ˈreɪzn/ noun a dried grape, used in cakes, etc.

rais·ing /ˈreɪzɪŋ/ noun [U, sing.] the act of raising sth: *consciousness raising* ◊ *a raising of standards in schools*—see also FUND-RAISING

rai·son d'être /ˌreɪzɒ ˈdetrə; AmE ˌreɪzoʊn/ noun [sing.] (from *French*) the most important reason for sb's/sth's existence: *Work seems to be her sole raison d'être.*

the Raj /rɑːdʒ/ noun [sing.] British rule in India before 1947

raja (also **rajah**) /ˈrɑːdʒə/ noun an Indian king or prince who ruled over a state in the past

rake /reɪk/ noun, verb

■ *noun* **1** [C] a garden tool with a long handle and a row of metal points at the end, used for gathering fallen leaves and making soil smooth—picture at GARDEN **2** [C] (*old-fashioned*) a man, especially a rich and fashionable one, who is thought to have low moral standards, for example because he drinks or gambles a lot or has sex with a lot of women **3** [sing.] (*technical*) the amount by which sth, especially the stage in a theatre, slopes

■ *verb* **1** to pull a rake over a surface in order to make it level or to remove sth: [VN] *The leaves had been raked into a pile.* ◊ (*figurative*) *She raked a comb through her hair.* ◊ [VN-ADJ] *First rake the soil smooth.* [also V] **2** [VN] to point a camera, light, gun, etc. at sb/sth and move it slowly from one side to the other: *They raked the streets with machine-gun fire.* ◊ *Searchlights raked the grounds.* **3** [V+adv./prep.] to search a place carefully for sth: *She raked around in her bag for her keys.* **4** [VN, V] to scratch the surface of sth with a sharp object, especially your nails **IDM** **rake sb over the 'coals** (*AmE*) = HAUL SB OVER THE COALS at HAUL **PHRV** **ˌrake 'in sth** (*informal*) to earn a lot of money, especially when it is done easily: *The movie raked in more than $300 million.* ◊ *She's been **raking it in** since she started her new job.* **ˌrake 'over sth** (*informal, disapproving*) to examine sth that happened in the past in great detail and keep talking about it, when it should be forgotten: *She had no desire to rake over the past.* **ˌrake sth↔'up** (*informal, disapproving*) to mention sth unpleasant that happened in the past and that other people would like to forget: *Raking up the past will only make things worse.*

raked /reɪkt/ adj. (*technical*) placed on a slope: *raked seating*

'rake-off noun (*informal*) a share of profits, especially from dishonest or illegal activity

rak·ish /ˈreɪkɪʃ/ adj. **1** (of a man) acting like a RAKE (=in an immoral, etc. way): *He plays the novel's rakish hero.* **2** (of a hat) worn at an angle, and making the person wearing it look relaxed and confident: *He was wearing his hat at a rakish angle.* ▶ **rak·ish·ly** adv.

rally /ˈræli/ noun, verb

■ *noun* **1** [C] a large public meeting, especially one held to support a particular idea or political party: *to attend/hold a rally* ◊ *a peace/protest rally* ◊ *a mass rally in support of the strike*—see also PEP RALLY **2** [C] (*BrE*) a race

R

æ	ɑː	e	ɜː	ə	ɪ	iː	i	ɒ	ɔː	ʌ	ʊ	u	uː
cat	father	ten	bird	about	sit	see	many	got	saw	cup	put	actual	too

(BrE)

for motor vehicles over public roads: *the Monte Carlo rally* ◇ *rally driving* **3** [C] (in tennis and similar sports) a series of hits of the ball before a point is scored **4** [sing.] (in sport or on the Stock Exchange) an act of returning to a strong position after a period of difficulty or weakness: *After a furious late rally, they finally scored.* ◇ *a rally in shares on the stock market*

■ *verb* (ral·lies, rally·ing, ral·lied, ral·lied) **1 ~** (sb/sth) (around/behind/to sb/sth) to come together or bring people together in order to help or support sb/sth: [V] *The cabinet rallied behind the Prime Minister.* ◇ *Many national newspapers rallied to his support.* ◇ [VN] *They have rallied a great deal of support for their campaign.* **2** [V] to become healthier, stronger, etc. after a period of illness, weakness, etc: *He never really rallied after the operation.* ◇ *The champion rallied to win the second set 6–3.* **3** [V] (*finance*) (especially of share prices or a country's money) to increase in value after falling in value: *The company's shares had rallied slightly by the close of trading.* ◇ *The pound rallied against the dollar.* PHRV ,**rally 'round/ a'round| ,rally 'round/a'round sb** (of a group of people) to work together in order to help sb who is in a difficult or unpleasant situation: *The whole family rallied round when Mum was ill.*

'**rallying cry** *noun* a phrase or an idea that is used to encourage people to support sb/sth

'**rallying point** *noun* a person, a group, an event, etc. that makes people come together in support of sth

RAM /ræm/ *noun* [U] the abbreviation for 'random access memory' (computer memory in which data can be changed or removed and can be looked at in any order): *32 megabytes of RAM*

ram /ræm/ *verb, noun*

■ *verb* (-mm-) **1** [VN] (of a vehicle, a ship, etc.) to drive into or hit another vehicle, ship, etc. with force, sometimes deliberately: *Two passengers were injured when their taxi was rammed from behind by a bus.* **2** [VN+adv./prep.] to push sth somewhere with force: *She rammed the key into the lock.* ◇ (*figurative*) *The spending cuts had been rammed through Congress.* IDM ,**ram sth** ↩ '**home** (especially BrE) to emphasize an idea, argument, etc. very strongly to make sure people listen to it—more at THROAT PHRV ,**ram 'into sth| ,ram sth 'into sth** to hit against sth or to make sth hit against sth with force: *He rammed his truck into the back of the one in front.*

■ *noun* **1** a male sheep—compare EWE **2** a part in a machine that is used for hitting sth very hard or for lifting or moving things: *hydraulic rams*—see also BATTERING RAM

Ram·adan /ˈræmədæn; ˌræməˈdæn/ *noun* [U] the 9th month of the Muslim year, when Muslims do not eat or drink between SUNRISE and SUNSET.

ram·ble /ˈræmbl/ *verb, noun*

■ *verb* [V] **1** [+adv./prep.] (BrE) to walk for pleasure, especially in the countryside: *We spent the summer rambling in Ireland.* **2** (BrE) ~ (on) (about sb/sth) to talk about sb/sth in a confused way, especially for a long time: *He had lost track of what he was saying and began to ramble.* ◇ *What is she rambling on about now?* **3** (of plants) to grow in many different directions, especially over other plants or objects: *Climbing plants rambled over the front of the house.*—see also RAMBLING

■ *noun* a long walk for pleasure: *to go for/on a ramble in the country*

ram·bler /ˈræmblə(r)/ *noun* **1** (especially BrE) a person who walks in the countryside for pleasure, especially as part of an organized group **2** a plant, especially a rose, that grows up walls, fences, etc.

ram·bling /ˈræmblɪŋ/ *adj., noun*

■ *adj.* **1** (of a building) spreading in various directions with no particular pattern: *They live in a rambling old house in the country.* **2** (of speech or writing) very long and confused: *a rambling speech/letter* **3** (of a plant) growing or climbing in all directions, for example up a wall: *a rambling rose*

■ *noun* **1** [U] (especially BrE) the activity of walking for pleasure in the countryside: *a rambling club* **2** (ramblings) [pl.] speech or writing that continues for a long

time without saying much and seems very confused: *the ramblings of a madman*

ram·bunc·tious /ræmˈbʌŋkʃəs/ *adj.* (*informal, especially AmE*) = RUMBUSTIOUS

ram·ekin /ˈræmɪkɪn/ *noun* a small dish for baking and serving food for one person

ram·ifi·ca·tion /ˌræmɪfɪˈkeɪʃn/ *noun* [usually pl.] one of the large number of complicated and unexpected results that follow an action or a decision: *These changes are bound to have widespread social ramifications.*

ramp /ræmp/ *noun* **1** a slope that joins two parts of a road, path, building, etc. when one is higher than the other: *Ramps should be provided for wheelchair users.* **2** (AmE) = SLIP ROAD: *a freeway exit ramp* **3** a slope or set of steps that can be moved, used for loading a vehicle or getting on or off a plane: *a loading ramp*

ram·page /ˈræmpeɪdʒ; ˈræmpeɪdʒ/ *noun, verb*

■ *noun* [usually sing.] a sudden period of wild and violent behaviour, often causing damage and destruction: *Gangs of youths went on the rampage in the city yesterday.*

■ *verb* [V+adv./prep.] (of people or animals) to move through a place in a group, usually breaking things and causing damage: *Several thousand demonstrators rampaged through the centre of the city.* ◇ *a herd of rampaging elephants*

ram·pant /ˈræmpənt/ *adj.* **1** (of sth bad) existing or spreading everywhere in a way that cannot be controlled: *rampant corruption/inflation* ◇ *Unemployment is now rampant in most of Europe.* **2** (of plants) growing thickly and very fast in a way that cannot be controlled ▶ **ram·pant·ly** *adv.*

ram·part /ˈræmpɑːt; AmE -pɑːrt/ *noun* [usually pl.] a high wide wall of stone or earth with a path on top, built around a castle, town, etc. to defend it

'**ram-raiding** *noun* [U] (BrE) the crime of driving a vehicle into a shop/store window in order to steal goods ▶ '**ram-raid** *noun* '**ram-raid** [VN] '**ram-raider** *noun*

ram·rod /ˈræmrɒd; AmE -rɑːd/ *noun* an iron rod used in the past to push explosive material into a gun IDM ,**ramrod 'straight | (as) straight as a 'ramrod** (of a person) with a very straight back and looking serious and formal

ram·shackle /ˈræmʃækl/ *adj.* **1** (of buildings, vehicles, furniture, etc.) in a very bad condition and needing repair: *a ramshackle house* **2** (of an organization or a system) badly organized or designed and not likely to last very long

ran *pt* of RUN

ranch /rɑːntʃ; AmE ræntʃ/ *noun* a large farm, especially in N America or Australia, where cows, horses, sheep, etc. are bred: *a cattle/sheep ranch* ◇ *ranch hands* (= the people who work on a ranch)—see also DUDE RANCH

ranch·er /ˈrɑːntʃə(r); AmE ˈræntʃər/ *noun* a person who owns, manages or works on a ranch: *a cattle rancher*

'**ranch house** *noun* **1** a house on a ranch **2** (AmE) a house built all on one level, that is very wide but not very deep from front to back and has a roof that is not very steep—compare BUNGALOW

ranch·ing /ˈrɑːntʃɪŋ; AmE ˈræntʃɪŋ/ *noun* [U] the activity of running a RANCH: *cattle/sheep ranching*

ran·cid /ˈrænsɪd/ *adj.* if food containing fat is **rancid**, it tastes or smells unpleasant because it is no longer fresh: *rancid butter*

ran·cour (BrE) (AmE **ran·cor**) /ˈræŋkə(r)/ *noun* [U] (*formal*) feelings of hatred and a desire to hurt other people, especially because you think that sb has done sth wrong: *She learned to accept criticism without rancour.* ▶ **ran·cor·ous** /ˈræŋkərəs/ *adj.*: *a rancorous legal battle*

rand /rænd; *in South Africa, commonly* rɑːnt/ *noun* (pl. **rand**) the unit of money in the Republic of South Africa

R & B /ˌɑːr ən ˈbiː/ *abbr.* RHYTHM AND BLUES

R & D /ˌɑːr ən ˈdiː/ *abbr.* RESEARCH AND DEVELOPMENT

ran·dom /ˈrændəm/ *adj., noun*

■ *adj.* [usually before noun] done, chosen, etc. without sb thinking or deciding in advance what is going to happen: *the random killing of innocent people* ◇ *a random sample/*

aɪ	aʊ	eɪ	əʊ	oʊ	ɔɪ	ɪə	eə	ʊə	j	w
my	now	say	go	go	boy	near	hair	pure	yes	wet
			(BrE)	(AmE)						

selection (= in which each thing has an equal chance of being chosen) ◊ *The information is processed in a random order.* ▶ **ran·dom·ly** *adv.*: *The winning numbers are randomly selected by computer.* **ran·dom·ness** *noun* [U]: *It introduced an element of randomness to the situation.*

■ *noun* IDM **at 'random** without thinking or deciding in advance what is going to happen: *She opened the book at random* (= not at any particular page) *and started reading.* ◊ *The terrorists fired into the crowd at random.* ◊ *Names were chosen at random from a list.*

,random 'access *noun* [U] (*computing*) the ability in a computer to go straight to data items without having to read through items stored previously

,random-,access 'memory *noun* [U] (*computing*) = RAM

ran·dom·ize (*BrE* also **-ise**) /'rændəmaɪz/ *verb* [VN] (*technical*) to use a method in an experiment, a piece of research, etc. that gives every item an equal chance of being considered; to put things in a RANDOM order

randy /'rændi/ *adj.* (**ran·dier, ran·di·est**) (*BrE, informal*) sexually excited: *to feel/get randy*

rang *pt of* RING

range /reɪndʒ/ *noun, verb*
■ *noun*
VARIETY | **1** [C, usually sing.] **~ (of sth)** a variety of things of a particular type: *The hotel offers **a wide range of** facilities and services.* ◊ *There is **a full range of** activities for children.*

LIMITS | **2** [C, usually sing.] the limits between which sth varies: *Most of the students are in the 17-20 age range.* ◊ *There will be an increase **in the range of** 0 to 3 per cent.* ◊ *It's difficult to find a house in our price range* (= that we can afford). ◊ *This was **outside the range of his** experience.*

OF PRODUCTS | **3** [C] a set of products of a particular type: *our new range of hair products*—see also MID-RANGE, TOP-OF-THE-RANGE

DISTANCE | **4** [C, U] the distance over which sth can be seen or heard: *The child was now out of her range of vision* (= not near enough for her to see). **5** [C, U] the distance over which a gun or other weapon can hit things: *These missiles have a range of 300 miles.*—see also CLOSE-RANGE, LONG-RANGE, SHORT-RANGE **6** [C] the distance that a vehicle will travel before it needs more fuel

OF MOUNTAINS | **7** [C] a line or group of mountains or hills: *the great mountain range of the Alps*

FOR SHOOTING | **8** [C] an area of land where people can practise shooting or where bombs, etc. can be tested: *a shooting range*—see also RIFLE RANGE

OVEN | **9** [C] a large piece of equipment that can burn various fuels and is kept hot all the time, used for cooking, especially in the past **10** (*AmE*) = COOKER

FOR COWS | **11** (**the range**) [sing.] (*AmE*) a large open area for keeping cows, etc.

—see also FREE-RANGE
IDM **in/within 'range (of sth)** near enough to be reached, seen or heard: *He shouted angrily at anyone within range.* **out of 'range (of sth)** too far away to be reached, seen or heard: *The cat stayed well out of range of the children.*

■ *verb*
VARY | **1** [V] **~ from A to B** | **~ between A and B** to vary between two particular amounts, sizes, etc., including others between them: *to range in size/length/price from A to B* ◊ *Estimates of the damage range between $1 million and $5 million.* ◊ *Accommodation ranges from tourist class to luxury hotels.* **2** [V+adv./prep.] **~ (from A to B)** to include a variety of different things in addition to those mentioned: *She has had a number of different jobs, ranging from chef to swimming instructor.* ◊ *The conversation ranged widely* (= covered a lot of different topics).—see also WIDE-RANGING

ARRANGE | **3** [VN+adv./prep.] [usually passive] (*formal*) to arrange people or things in a particular position or order: *The delegates ranged themselves around the table.* ◊ *Spectators were ranged along the whole route of the procession.*

MOVE AROUND | **4** to move around an area: [V+adv./prep.]

He ranges far and wide in search of inspiration for his paintings. ◊ [VN] *Her eyes ranged the room.*

PHRV ,range yourself/sb a'gainst/'with sb/sth [usually passive] to join with other people to oppose sb/sth: *The whole family seemed ranged against him.* 'range over sth to include a variety of different subjects: *His lecture ranged over a number of topics.*

ran·ger /'reɪndʒə(r)/ *noun* **1** a person whose job is to take care of a park, a forest or an area of countryside **2** '**Ranger (Guide)** a girl who belongs to the part of the Guide Association in Britain for girls between the ages of 14 and 19

rangy /'reɪndʒi/ *adj.* (*written*) (of a person or an animal) having long thin arms and/or legs

rank /ræŋk/ *noun, verb, adj.*
■ *noun*
POSITION IN ORGANIZATION/ARMY, etc. | **1** [U, C] the position, especially a high position, that sb has in a particular organization, society, etc: *She was not used to mixing with people of high social rank.* ◊ *He rose through the ranks to become managing director.* ◊ *Within months she was elevated to ministerial rank.*—see also RANKING **2** [C, U] the position that sb has in the army, navy, police, etc: *He was soon promoted to the rank of captain.* ◊ *officers of junior/senior rank* ◊ *a campaign to attract more women into the military ranks* ◊ *officers, and other ranks* (= people who are not officers) ◊ *The colonel was stripped of his rank* (= lost his position as colonel). **3** (**the ranks**) [pl.] the position of ordinary soldiers rather than officers: *He served in the ranks for most of the war.* ◊ *He rose from the ranks* (= from being an ordinary soldier) *to become a warrant officer.*

QUALITY | **4** [sing.] the degree to which sb/sth is of high quality: *a painter of the first rank* ◊ *Britain is no longer in the front rank of world powers.* ◊ *The findings are arranged in rank order according to performance.*

MEMBERS OF GROUP | **5** (**the ranks**) [pl.] the members of a particular group or organization: *We have a number of international players in our ranks.* ◊ *At 50, he was forced to join the ranks of the unemployed.* ◊ *There were serious divisions within the party's own ranks.*

LINE/ROW | **6** [C] a line or row of soldiers, police, etc. standing next to each other: *They watched as ranks of marching infantry passed the window.* **7** [C] a line or row of people or things: *massed ranks of spectators* ◊ *The trees grew in serried ranks* (= very closely together).—see also TAXI RANK

IDM break 'ranks **1** (of soldiers, police, etc.) to fail to remain in line **2** (of the members of a group) to refuse to support a group or an organization of which they are members: *Large numbers of MPs felt compelled to break ranks over the issue.*—more at CLOSE¹ *v.*, PULL *v.*

■ *verb* (not used in the progressive tenses)
GIVE POSITION | **1 ~ (sb) (as sth)** to give sb/sth a particular position on a scale according to quality, importance, success, etc.; to have a position of this kind: [VN] *The tasks have been ranked in order of difficulty.* ◊ *She is currently the highest ranked player in the world.* ◊ *top-ranked players* ◊ [VN-ADJ] *Last year, he was ranked second in his age group.* ◊ [V-ADJ] *At the height of her career she ranked second in the world.* ◊ [VN-N] *The university is ranked number one in the country for engineering.* ◊ [V, often+adv./prep.] *The restaurant ranks among the finest in town.* ◊ *It certainly doesn't rank as his greatest win.* ◊ *This must rank with* (= be as good as) *one of the greatest movies ever made.* ◊ [V] (*AmE*) *You just don't rank* (= you're not good enough).

PUT IN LINE/ROW | **2** [VN] [usually passive] to arrange objects in a line or row

■ *adj.* **1** having a strong unpleasant smell: *The house was full of the rank smell of urine.* **2** [only before noun] used to emphasize a particular quality, state, etc: *an example of rank stupidity* ◊ *The winning horse was a rank outsider.* **3** (of plants, etc.) growing too thickly: *an area overgrown with rank grass and nettles*

the ,rank and 'file *noun* [sing.+ sing./pl. *v.*] **1** the ordinary soldiers who are not officers **2** the ordinary

	b	d	f	g	h	k	l	m	n	p	r
	bad	did	fall	get	hat	cat	leg	man	now	pen	red

members of an organization: *the rank and file of the workforce ◊ rank-and-file members*

rank·ing /ˈræŋkɪŋ/ *noun, adj.*

■ *noun* **1** the position of sb/sth on a scale that shows how good or important they are in relation to other similar people or things, especially in sport: *He has improved his ranking this season from 67th to 30th. ◊ She has retained her No.1 world ranking.* **2 (the rankings)** [pl.] an official list showing the best players of a particular sport in order of how successful they are

■ *adj.* **1** (*especially AmE*) having a high or the highest rank in an organization, etc: *a ranking diplomat ◊ He was the ranking officer* (= the most senior officer present at a particular time). **2** (in compounds) having the particular rank mentioned: *high-ranking/low-ranking police officers ◊ a top-ranking player*

ran·kle /ˈræŋkl/ *verb* ~ (**with sb**) if sth such as an event or a remark **rankles**, it makes you feel angry or upset for a long time: [V] *Her comments still rankled. ◊ His decision to sell the land still rankled with her.* [also VN]

ran·sack /ˈrænsæk/ *verb* [VN] ~ **sth** (**for sth**) to search a place, making it untidy and causing damage, usually because you are looking for sth: *The house had been ransacked by burglars.*

ran·som /ˈrænsəm/ *noun, verb*

■ *noun* [C, U] money that is paid to sb so that they will set free a person who is being kept as a prisoner by them: *The kidnappers demanded a ransom of £50000 from his family. ◊ a ransom demand/note ◊ ransom money ◊ They are refusing to pay ransom for her release.* **IDM** **hold sb to 'ransom** **1** to keep sb as a prisoner and demand that other people pay you an amount of money before you set them free **2** (*disapproving*) to take action that puts sb in a very difficult situation in order to force them to do what you want—more at KING

■ *verb* [VN] to pay money to sb so that they will set free the person that they are keeping as a prisoner: *The kidnapped children were all ransomed and returned home unharmed.*

rant /rænt/ *verb* [V, V speech] ~ (**on**) (**about sth**)| ~ (**at sb**) (*disapproving*) to speak or complain about sth in a loud and/or angry way ▶ **rant** *noun* **IDM** ,**rant and 'rave** (*disapproving*) to show that you are angry by shouting or complaining loudly for a long time

rant·ings /ˈræntɪŋz/ *noun* [pl.] loud or angry comments or speeches that continue for a long time

rap /ræp/ *noun, verb*

■ *noun* **1** [C] a quick sharp hit or knock: *There was a sharp rap on the door.* **2** [U] a type of modern music with a fast strong rhythm and words which are spoken fast, not sung: *a rap song/artist* **3** [C] a rap song **4** [C] (*AmE, informal*) a criminal CONVICTION (= the fact of being found guilty of a crime): *a police rap sheet* (= a record of the crimes sb has committed) **5** [sing.] (*AmE, informal*) an unfair judgement on sth or sb: *He denounced the criticisms as 'just one bum rap after another.' ◊ Wolves get a bad rap, says a woman who owns three.* **IDM** (**give sb/ get**) **a rap on/over/across the 'knuckles** (*informal*) (to give sb/receive) strong criticism for sth: *We got a rap over the knuckles for being late.* **take the 'rap** (**for sb/sth**) (*informal*) to be blamed or punished, especially for sth you have not done: *She was prepared to take the rap for the shoplifting, though it had been her sister's idea.*—more at BEAT *v.*

■ *verb* (**-pp-**) **1** to hit a hard object or surface several times quickly, making a noise: [V] *She rapped angrily on the door. ◊* [VN] *He rapped the table with his pen.* **2** ~ **sth** (**out**) to say sth suddenly and quickly in a loud, angry way: [VN] *He walked through the store, rapping out orders to his staff.* [also V speech] **3** [VN] ~ **sb/sth** (**for sth/for doing sth**) (used mainly in newspapers) to criticize sb severely, usually publicly: *Some of the teachers were rapped for poor performance.* **4** [V, VN] (*music*) to say the words of a rap—see also RAPPER **IDM** ,**rap sb on/over the 'knuckles** | **rap sb's 'knuckles** to criticize sb for sth: *The company was rapped over the knuckles for broadcasting the interview.*

ra·pa·cious /rəˈpeɪʃəs/ *adj.* (*formal, disapproving*) wanting more money or goods than you need or have a right to ▶ **ra·pa·cious·ly** *adv.* **rap·acity** /rəˈpæsəti/ *noun* [U]: *the rapacity of landowners seeking greater profit*

rape /reɪp/ *verb, noun*

■ *verb* [VN] to force sb to have sex with you when they do not want to by threatening them or using violence—see also RAPIST

■ *noun* **1** [U, C] the crime of forcing sb to have sex with you, especially using violence: *He was charged with rape. ◊ a rape victim ◊ an increase in the number of reported rapes*—see also DATE RAPE, RAPIST **2** [sing.] ~ (**of sth**) (*literary*) the act of destroying or spoiling an area in a way that seems unnecessary **3** (also ,**oilseed 'rape**) [U] a plant with bright yellow flowers, grown as food for farm animals and for its seeds that are used to make oil: *a field of rape ◊ refined rape oil*

rapid /ˈræpɪd/ *adj.* **1** [usually before noun] happening in a short period of time: *rapid change/expansion/growth ◊ a rapid rise/decline in sales ◊ The patient made a rapid recovery.* **2** done or happening very quickly: *a rapid pulse/heartbeat ◊ The guard fired four shots in rapid succession. ◊ The disease is spreading at a rapid rate.* ⇨ note at FAST ▶ **rap·id·ity** /rəˈpɪdəti/ *noun* [U]: *the rapidity of economic growth ◊ The disease is spreading with alarming rapidity.* **rap·id·ly** *adv.*: *a rapidly growing economy ◊ Crime figures are rising rapidly.*

'**rapid-fire** *adj.* [only before noun] **1** (of questions, comments, etc.) spoken very quickly, one after the other **2** (of a gun) able to shoot bullets very quickly, one after the other

rapids /ˈræpɪdz/ *noun* [pl.] part of a river where the water flows very fast, usually over rocks: *to shoot the rapids* (= to travel quickly when in a boat)

,**rapid 'transit** *noun* [U] (*especially AmE*) the system of fast public transport in cities, especially the SUBWAY

ra·pier /ˈreɪpiə(r)/ *noun* a long thin light SWORD that has two sharp edges: (*figurative*) *rapier wit* (= very quick sharp wit)

rap·ist /ˈreɪpɪst/ *noun* a person who forces sb to have sex when they do not want to (= RAPES them)

rap·pel /ræˈpel/ *verb* [V] (*AmE*) = ABSEIL ▶ **rap·pel** *noun*

rap·per /ˈræpə(r)/ *noun* a person who speaks the words of a RAP song

rap·port /ræˈpɔː(r)/ *noun* [sing., U] ~ (**with sb**)| ~ (**between A and B**) a friendly relationship in which people understand each other very well: *She understood the importance of establishing a close rapport with clients. ◊ Honesty is essential if there is to be good rapport between patient and therapist.*

rap·por·teur /ˌræpɔːˈtɜː(r); AmE -pɔːrˈt-/ *noun* (from French, *technical*) a person officially chosen by an organization to investigate a problem and report on it: *the UN special rapporteur on human rights*

rap·proche·ment /ræˈprɒʃmɒ̃; ræˈprəʊʃmɒ̃; AmE ˌræprəʊʃˈmɑːn; -prɑː-/ *noun* [sing., U] ~ (**with sb**)| ~ (**between A and B**) (from French, *formal*) a situation in which the relationship between two countries or groups of people becomes more friendly after a period during which they were enemies: *policies aimed at bringing about a rapprochement with China ◊ There now seems little chance of rapprochement between the warring factions.*

rapt /ræpt/ *adj.* (*written*) so interested in one particular thing that you are not aware of anything else: *a rapt audience ◊ She listened to the speaker with rapt attention.*

rap·tor /ˈræptə(r)/ *noun* (*technical*) any BIRD OF PREY (= a bird that kills other creatures for food)

rap·ture /ˈræptʃə(r)/ *noun* [U] (*formal*) a feeling of extreme pleasure and happiness: *Charles listened with rapture to her singing. ◊ The children gazed at her in rapture.* **IDM** **be in, go into, etc. 'raptures (about/over sb/sth)** to feel or express extreme pleasure or enthusiasm for sb/sth: *The critics went into raptures about her performance. ◊ The last minute goal sent the fans into raptures.*

rap·tur·ous /ˈræptʃərəs/ *adj.* [usually before noun]

expressing extreme pleasure or enthusiasm for sb/sth: *rapturous applause* ◊ *The Olympic team was given a rapturous welcome.* ▶ **rap·tur·ous·ly** *adv.*

rare /reə(r); *AmE* rer/ *adj.* (**rarer, rar·est**) **1 ~ (for sb/sth to do sth)| ~ (to do sth)** not done, seen, happening, etc. very often: *a rare disease/occurrence/sight* ◊ *It's extremely rare for it to be this hot in April.* ◊ *It is rare to find such loyalty these days.* ◊ *On the rare occasions when they met he hardly even dared speak to her.* ◊ *It was a rare (= very great) honour to be made a fellow of the college.* **2** existing only in small numbers and therefore valuable or interesting: *a rare book/coin/stamp* ◊ *a rare breed/plant* ◊ *This species is extremely rare.* **3** (of meat) cooked for only a short time so that the inside is still red—compare WELL DONE—see also RARITY

rare·bit /ˈreəbɪt; *AmE* ˈrerbɪt/ *noun* = WELSH RAREBIT

rar·efied /ˈreərɪfaɪd; *AmE* ˈrerə-/ *adj.* [usually before noun] **1** (often *disapproving*) understood or experienced by only a very small group of people who share a particular area of knowledge or activity: *the rarefied atmosphere of academic life* **2** (of air) containing less OXYGEN than usual

rare·ly /ˈreəli; *AmE* ˈrerli/ *adv.* not very often: *She is rarely seen in public nowadays.* ◊ *We rarely agree on what to do.* ◊ *a rarely-performed play* ◊ (*formal*) *Rarely has a debate attracted so much media attention.*

rar·ing /ˈreərɪŋ; *AmE* ˈrer-/ *adj.* **~ to do sth** (*informal*) very enthusiastic about starting to do sth: *The new recruits arrived early, all dressed up and raring to go* (= to start). ◊ *She is raring to get back to work after her operation.*

rar·ity /ˈreərəti; *AmE* ˈrer-/ *noun* (*pl.* **-ies**) **1** [C] a person or thing that is unusual and is therefore often valuable or interesting: *Women are still something of a rarity in senior positions in business.* ◊ *His collection of plants contains many rarities.* **2** (also *less frequent* **rare·ness**) [U] the quality of being rare: *The value of antiques will depend on their condition and rarity.*

ras·cal /ˈrɑːskl; *AmE* ˈræskl/ *noun* **1** (*humorous*) a person, especially a child or man, who shows a lack of respect for other people and enjoys playing tricks on them: *Come here, you little rascal!* **2** (*old-fashioned*) a dishonest man ▶ **ras·cal·ly** *adj.* (*old-fashioned*)

rash /ræʃ/ *noun, adj.*
■ *noun* **1** [C, usually sing.] an area of red spots on a person's skin, caused by an illness or a reaction to sth: *I woke up covered in a rash.* ◊ *I come out in a rash* (= a rash appears on my skin) *if I eat chocolate.* ◊ *The sun brought her out in* (= caused) *an itchy rash.* ◊ *a heat rash* (= caused by heat)—compare SPOT **2** [sing.] **~ (of sth)** a lot of sth; a series of unpleasant things that happen over a short period of time [SYN] SPATE: *a rash of movies about life in prison* ◊ *There has been a rash of burglaries in the area over the last month.*
■ *adj.* **~ (to do sth)** (of people or their actions) doing sth that may not be sensible without first thinking about the possible results; done in this way: *a rash young man* ◊ *It would be rash to assume that everyone will agree with you on this.* ◊ *Think twice before doing anything rash.* ◊ *This is what happens when you make rash decisions.* ▶ **rash·ly** *adv.*: *She had rashly promised to lend him the money.* ◊ *I see now that I may have acted rashly.* **rash·ness** *noun* [U]: *He bitterly regretted his rashness.*

rash·er /ˈræʃə(r)/ *noun* (*especially BrE*) a thin slice of BACON (= meat from the back or sides of a pig): *a fried egg and two rashers of bacon*

rasp /rɑːsp; *AmE* ræsp/ *noun, verb*
■ *noun* **1** [sing.] an unpleasant harsh sound **2** [C] a metal tool with a long blade covered with rows of sharp points, used for making rough surfaces smooth
■ *verb* **1 ~ (sth) (out)** to say sth in an unpleasant harsh voice: [V speech] *'Where have you been?' she rasped.* ◊ [VN] *He rasped out some instructions.* [also V] **2** [V] to make an unpleasant harsh sound: *a rasping cough/voice* **3** [VN] to rub a surface with a rasp or with sth rough that works or feels like a rasp: *The wind rasped his face.*

rasp·berry /ˈrɑːzbəri; *AmE* ˈræzberi/ *noun* (*pl.* **-ies**) **1** a small dark red soft fruit that grows on bushes: *raspberry jam*—picture on page A2 **2** (*AmE* also **Bronx ˈcheer**) (*informal*) a rude sound made by sticking out the tongue and blowing: *to blow a raspberry at sb*

raspy /ˈrɑːspi; *AmE* ˈræspi/ *adj.* (of sb's voice) having a rough sound, as if the person has a sore throat

Ras·ta·far·ian /ˌræstəˈfeəriən; *AmE* -ˈfer-/ (also *informal* **Rasta**) *noun* a member of a Jamaican religious group which worships the former Emperor of Ethiopia, Haile Selassie, and which believes that black people will one day return to Africa. Rastafarians often wear DREADLOCKS and have other distinguishing patterns of behaviour and dress. ▶ **Ras·ta·far·ian** (also *informal* **Rasta**) *adj.* **Ras·ta·far·ian·ism** *noun* [U]

rat /ræt/ *noun, verb*
■ *noun* **1** a small animal with a long tail, that looks like a large mouse, usually considered a PEST (= an animal which is disliked because it destroys food or spreads disease): *rat poison* **2** (*informal, disapproving*) an unpleasant person, especially one who is not loyal or tricks sb: *You mean he just walked out on her after fifteen years? What a rat!* [IDM] see SINK v., SMELL v.
■ *verb* (**-tt-**) [PHR V] **ˈrat on sb** (*informal*) to tell sb in authority about sth wrong that sb else has done: *Where I come from, you don't rat on your friends.* **ˈrat on sth** (*BrE, informal*) to not do sth that you have agreed or promised to do: *The government is accused of ratting on its promises to the unemployed.*

rata ⇨ PRO RATA

ˈrat-arsed *adj.* (*BrE, slang*) extremely drunk

ˌrat-a-tat-ˈtat *noun* [sing.] = RAT-TAT

rat·bag /ˈrætbæg/ *noun* (*BrE, slang*) an unpleasant or disgusting person

ratchet /ˈrætʃɪt/ *noun* a wheel or bar with teeth along the edge and a metal piece that fits between the teeth, allowing movement in one direction only

rate /reɪt/ *noun, verb*
■ *noun* **1** [C] a measurement of the speed at which sth happens: *Most people walk at an average rate of 5 kilometres an hour.* ◊ *The number of reported crimes is increasing at an alarming rate.* ◊ *Figures published today show another fall in the rate of inflation.* ◊ *At the rate you work, you'll never finish!* **2** [C] a measurement of the number of times sth happens or exists during a particular period: *Local businesses are closing at a/the rate of three a year.* ◊ *a high/low/rising rate of unemployment* ◊ *the annual crime/divorce rate* ◊ *His pulse rate dropped suddenly.* ◊ *a high success/failure rate*—see also BIRTH RATE, DEATH RATE **3** [C] a fixed amount of money that is charged or paid for sth: *advertising/insurance/postal rates* ◊ *a low/high hourly rate of pay* ◊ *We offer special reduced rates for students.* ◊ *a fixed-rate mortgage* (= one in which the amount of money repaid each month is fixed for a particular period) ◊ *the basic rate of tax* (= the lowest amount that is paid by everyone) ◊ *exchange/interest rates* ◊ *rates of exchange/interest*—see also BASE RATE **4** (**rates**) [pl.] (in Britain) a tax paid by businesses to a local authority for land and buildings that they use and in the past also paid by anyone who owned a house: *business rates*—see also FIRST-RATE, SECOND-RATE, THIRD-RATE [IDM] **at ˈany rate** (*spoken*) **1** used to say that a particular fact is true in spite of what has happened in the past or what may happen in the future: *Well, that's one good piece of news at any rate.* ◊ *I may be away on business next week but at any rate I'll be back by Friday.* **2** used to show that you are being more accurate about sth that you have just said: *He said he'll be coming tomorrow. At any rate, I think that's what he said.* **3** used to show that what you have just said is not as important as what you are going to say: *There were maybe 60 or 70 people there. At any rate, the room was packed.* **at a rate of ˈknots** (*BrE, informal*) very quickly at **ˈthis/ˈthat rate** (*spoken*) used to say what will happen if a particular situation continues to develop in the same way: *At this rate, we'll soon be bankrupt.*—more at GOING *adj.*
■ *verb* (not used in the progressive tenses) **1 ~ sb/sth (as) sth| ~ as sth** to have or think that sb/sth has a particular

æ	ɑː	e	ɜː	ə	ɪ	iː	i	ɒ	ɔː	ʌ	ʊ	uː
cat	father	ten	bird	about	sit	see	many	got	saw	cup	put	actual	too

(BrE)

level of quality, value, etc: [VN] *The university is* **highly rated** *for its research.* ◊ *They rated him highly as a colleague.* ◊ [VN-ADJ] *Voters continue to rate education high on their list of priorities.* ◊ [VN-N] *The show was rated (as) a success by critics and audiences.* ◊ [V] *The match rated as one of their worst defeats.* ◊ [V-ADJ] *I'm afraid our needs do not rate very high with this administration.* **2** [VN] (*informal*) to think that sb/sth is good: *What did you think of the movie? I didn't rate it myself.* **3** [usually passive] to place sb/sth in a particular position on a scale in relation to similar people or things [SYN] RANK: [VN] *The schools were rated according to their exam results.* ◊ *a top-rated programme* ◊ [VN-N] *She is currently rated number two in the world.* **4** [VN] to be good, important, etc. enough to be treated in a particular way [SYN] MERIT: *The incident didn't even* **rate a mention** *in the press.* **5** [VN] [usually passive] to state that a film/movie or video is suitable for a particular audience—see also X-RATED, ZERO-RATED

'rate cap *noun* (in the US) a limit placed on the amount of interest banks, etc. may charge

rate·pay·er /ˈreɪtpeɪə(r)/ *noun* (in Britain in the past) a person who paid taxes to the local authority on the buildings and land they owned

ra·ther /ˈrɑːðə(r)/; *AmE* ˈræðər/ *adv.*, *exclamation*
■ *adv.* **1** used to mean 'fairly' or 'to some degree', often when you are expressing slight criticism, disappointment or surprise: *The instructions were rather complicated.* ◊ *She fell and hurt her leg rather badly.* ◊ *I didn't fail the exam; in fact I did rather well!* ◊ *It was a rather difficult question.* ◊ *It was* **rather a** *difficult question.* ◊ *He looks rather like his father.* ◊ *The patient has responded to the treatment rather better than expected.* ◊ *He was conscious that he was talking* **rather too** *much.* ⇨ note at QUITE **2** used with a verb to make a statement sound less strong: *I rather suspect we're making a mistake.* ◊ *We were rather hoping you'd be able to do it by Friday.* **3** used to correct sth you have said, or to give more accurate information: *She worked as a secretary, or rather, a personal assistant.* ◊ *In the end he had to walk—or rather run—to the office.* **4** used to introduce an idea that is different or opposite to the idea that you have stated previously: *The walls were not white, but rather a sort of dirty grey.* [IDM] **rather you, him, etc. than 'me** (*informal*) used for saying that you would not like to do sth that another person is going to do: *'I'm going climbing tomorrow.' 'Rather you than me!'* **rather than** instead of sb/sth: *I think I'll have a cold drink rather than coffee.* ◊ *Why didn't you ask for help, rather than trying to do it on your own?* **would rather…(than)** (usually shortened to *'d rather*) would prefer to: *She'd rather die than give a speech.* ◊ *'Do you want to come with us?' 'No, I'd rather not.'* ◊ *Would you rather walk or take the bus?* ◊ *'Do you mind if I smoke?' 'Well, I'd rather you didn't.'*
■ *exclamation* / also ˌrɑːˈðɜː(r)/ (*old-fashioned, BrE*) used to agree with sb's suggestion: *'How about a trip to the beach?' 'Rather!'*

rat·ify /ˈrætɪfaɪ/ *verb* (**rati·fies**, **rati·fy·ing**, **rati·fied**, **rati·fied**) [VN] to make an agreement officially valid by voting for or signing it: *The treaty was ratified by all the member states.* ▶ **rati·fi·ca·tion** /ˌrætɪfɪˈkeɪʃn/ *noun* [U]

rat·ing /ˈreɪtɪŋ/ *noun* **1** [C] a measurement of how good, popular, important, etc. sb/sth is, especially in relation to other people or things: *The poll gave a popular approval rating of 39% for the President.* ◊ *Education has been given a high-priority rating by the new administration.* ◊ *The 'Cosby Show' was the highest-rated network show with a rating of 26.*—see also CREDIT RATING **2** (**the ratings**) [pl.] a set of figures that show how many people watch or listen to a particular television or radio programme, used to show how popular a programme is: *The show has gone up in the ratings.* **3** [C] a number or letter that shows which groups of people a particular film/movie is suitable for: *The film was given a 15 rating by British censors.* ◊ *The movie carries an R rating.* **4** [C] (*BrE*) a sailor in the navy who is not an officer

ratio /ˈreɪʃiəʊ; *AmE* -oʊ/ *noun* (*pl.* **-os**) ~ **(of A to B)** the relationship between two groups of people or things that is represented by two numbers showing how much larger one group is than the other: *What is the ratio of men to women in the department?* ◊ *The school has a very high teacher-student ratio.* ◊ *The ratio of applications to available places currently stands at 100:1.*

rati·ocin·ation /ˌrætiˌɒsɪˈneɪʃn; *AmE* ˌreɪʃioʊ-/ *noun* [U] (*formal*) the process of thinking or arguing about sth in a logical way

ra·tion /ˈræʃn/ *noun*, *verb*
■ *noun* **1** [C] a fixed amount of food, fuel, etc. that you are officially allowed to have when there is not enough for everyone to have as much as they want, for example during a war: *the weekly butter ration* **2** (**rations**) [pl.] a fixed amount of food given regularly to a soldier or to sb who is in a place where there is not much food available: *We're* **on short rations** (= allowed less than usual) *until fresh supplies arrive.* ◊ *Once these latest rations run out, the country will again face hunger and starvation.* **3** [sing.] ~ **(of sth)** an amount of sth that is thought to be normal or fair: *As part of the diet, allow yourself a small daily ration of sugar.* ◊ *I've had my ration of problems for one day—you deal with it!*
■ *verb* [VN] [often passive] ~ **sb/sth (to sth)** to limit the amount of sth that sb is allowed to have, especially because there is not enough of it available: *Eggs were rationed during the war.* ◊ *The villagers are rationed to two litres of water a day.*

ra·tion·al /ˈræʃnəl/ *adj.* **1** (of behaviour, ideas, etc.) based on reason rather than emotions: *a rational argument/choice/decision* ◊ *rational analysis/thought* ◊ *There is no rational explanation for his actions.* **2** (of a person) able to think clearly and make decisions based on reason rather than emotions: *No rational person would ever behave like that.* [OPP] IRRATIONAL ▶ **ra·tion·al·ity** /ˌræʃəˈnæləti/ *noun* [U]: *the rationality of his argument* **ra·tion·al·ly** /ˈræʃnəli/ *adv.*: *to act/behave/think rationally* ◊ *She argued her case calmly and rationally.*

ra·tion·ale /ˌræʃəˈnɑːl; *AmE* -ˈnæl/ *noun* ~ **(behind/for/of sth)** (*formal*) the principles or reasons which explain a particular decision, course of action, belief, etc: *What is the rationale behind these new exams?*

ra·tion·al·ism /ˈræʃnəlɪzəm/ *noun* [U] (*philosophy*) the belief that all behaviour, opinions, etc. should be based on reason rather than on emotions or religious beliefs

ra·tion·al·ist /ˈræʃnəlɪst/ *noun* a person who believes in rationalism ▶ **ra·tion·al·ist** (also **ra·tion·al·is·tic** /ˌræʃnəˈlɪstɪk/) *adj.* [usually before noun]: *a rationalistic approach/position*

ra·tion·al·ize (*BrE* also **-ise**) /ˈræʃnəlaɪz/ *verb* **1** to find or try to find a logical reason to explain why sb thinks, behaves, etc. in a way that is difficult to understand: [VN] *an attempt to rationalize his violent behaviour* [also V] **2** (*BrE*) to make changes to a business, system, etc. in order to make it more efficient, especially by spending less money: [VN] *Twenty workers lost their jobs when the department was rationalized.* [also V] ▶ **ra·tion·al·iza·tion, -isa·tion** /ˌræʃnəlaɪˈzeɪʃn; *AmE* -ləˈz-/ *noun* [U, C]: *No amount of rationalization could justify his actions.* ◊ *a need for rationalization of the industry*

ra·tion·ing /ˈræʃnɪŋ/ *noun* [U] the policy of limiting the amount of food, fuel, etc. that people are allowed to have when there is not enough for everyone to have as much as they want

the 'rat race *noun* [sing.] (*disapproving*) the way of life of people living and working in a large city where everyone competes in an aggressive way with each other in order to be more successful, earn more money, etc.

rat·tan /ræˈtæn/ *noun* [U] a SE Asian climbing plant with long thin strong stems used especially for making furniture: *a rattan chair*

rat-'tat (also **rat-a-tat-'tat**) *noun* [sing.] the sound of knocking, especially on a door

rat·tle /ˈrætl/ *verb*, *noun*
■ *verb* (*informal*) **1** to make a series of short loud sounds when hitting against sth hard; to make sth do this: [V] *Every time a bus went past, the windows rattled.* [also VN] **2** [V+*adv.*/*prep.*] (of a vehicle) to make a series of short loud sounds as it moves somewhere: *A convoy of trucks rattled by.* **3** [VN] to make sb nervous or frightened [SYN]

UNNERVE: *He was clearly rattled by the question.*—see also SABRE-RATTLING **IDM** **,rattle sb's 'cage** (*spoken*) to annoy sb: *Who's rattled his cage?* **PHR V** **,rattle a'round|,rattle a'round sth** (*informal*) to be living, working, etc. in a room or building that is too big: *She spent the last few years alone, rattling around the old family home.* **,rattle sth↔'off** to say sth aloud from memory without having to think too hard: *She can rattle off the names of all the presidents of the US.* **,rattle 'on (about sth)** (*informal*) to talk continuously about sth that is not important or interesting, especially in an annoying way
- *noun* **1** (also **rat·tling**) [usually sing.] a series of short loud sounds made when hard objects hit against each other: *the rattle of gunfire* ◇ *From the kitchen came a rattling of cups and saucers.*—see also DEATH RATTLE **2** a baby's toy that makes a series of short loud sounds when it is shaken (*BrE*) a wooden object that is held in one hand and makes a series of short loud sounds when you spin it round, used, for example, by people watching a football match

rattle·snake /ˈrætlsneɪk/ (also *informal* **rat·tler** /ˈrætlə(r)/) *noun* a poisonous American snake that makes a noise like a rattle with its tail when it is angry or afraid

rat·tling /ˈrætlɪŋ/ *adv.* **~ good** (*old-fashioned, BrE*) very good: *This book is a rattling good read.*

ratty /ˈræti/ *adj.* **1** (*BrE, informal*) becoming angry very easily **SYN** GRUMPY, IRRITABLE: *He gets ratty if he doesn't get enough sleep.* **2** (*AmE, informal*) in bad condition **SYN** SHABBY: *long ratty hair* ◇ *a ratty old pair of jeans* **3** looking like a rat

rau·cous /ˈrɔːkəs/ *adj.* sounding loud and harsh: *raucous laughter/shouting* ◇ *a raucous voice* ◇ *a group of raucous young men* ▶ **rau·cous·ly** *adv.* **rau·cous·ness** *noun* [U]

raunchy /ˈrɔːntʃi/ *adj.* (*informal*) **1** intended to be sexually exciting **SYN** SEXY: *a raunchy magazine/movie* ◇ *Their stage act is a little too raunchy for television.* **2** (*AmE*) looking dirty and untidy: *a raunchy old man*

rav·age /ˈrævɪdʒ/ *verb* [VN] [usually passive] to badly damage sth: *a country ravaged by civil war* ◇ *a recession that has ravaged the textile industry*

rav·ages /ˈrævɪdʒɪz/ *noun* [pl.] **the ~ of sth** (*written*) the destruction caused by sth: *the ravages of inflation/poverty/war* ◇ *Her looks had not survived **the ravages of** time.*

rave /reɪv/ *verb, noun*
- *verb* **1** **~ (about sb/sth)** to talk or write about sth in a very enthusiastic way: [V] *The critics raved about his performance in 'Hamlet'.* [also V speech] **2** **~ (at sb)** to shout in a loud and emotional way at sb because you are angry with them: [V] *She was shouting and raving at them.* [also V speech] **3** **~ (at sb)** to talk or shout in a way that is not logical or sensible: [V] *He wandered the streets raving at passers-by.* [also V speech] **IDM** see RANT
- *noun* (*BrE*) **1** (in Britain) a large party, held outside or in an empty building, at which people dance to fast electronic music and often take illegal drugs: *an all-night rave* **2** (*AmE*) = RAVE REVIEW

raven /ˈreɪvn/ *noun, adj.*
- *noun* a large bird of the CROW family, with shiny black feathers and a harsh cry
- *adj.* [only before noun] (*literary*) (of hair) shiny and black: *raven-haired*

raven·ing /ˈrævənɪŋ/ *adj.* (*literary*) (especially of animals) fierce and hungry: *He says the media are ravening wolves.*

rav·en·ous /ˈrævənəs/ *adj.* **1** (of a person or an animal) extremely hungry **SYN** STARVING: *What's for lunch? I'm absolutely ravenous.* **2** [only before noun] (of hunger) very great: *a ravenous appetite* ▶ **rav·en·ous·ly** *adv.*

raver /ˈreɪvə(r)/ *noun* (*BrE, informal*) **1** (often *humorous*) a person who likes going out and who has an exciting social life **2** a person who goes to RAVES

,rave re'view (*AmE* also **rave**) *noun* an article in a newspaper or magazine that is very enthusiastic about a particular film/movie, book, etc: *Her performance won rave reviews from the critics.*

rav·ine /rəˈviːn/ *noun* a deep, very narrow valley with steep sides—picture at MOUNTAIN

rav·ing /ˈreɪvɪŋ/ *adj., adv.*
- *adj.* [only before noun] **1** (of a person) talking or behaving in a way that shows they are crazy: *The man's a raving lunatic.* **2** used to emphasize a particular state or quality: *She's no raving beauty.* ◇ *His latest novel is already a raving success.*
- *adv.* **IDM** **(stark) raving 'mad/'bonkers** (*informal*) completely crazy

rav·ings /ˈreɪvɪŋz/ *noun* [pl.] words that have no meaning, spoken by sb who is crazy: *He dismissed her words as the ravings of a hysterical woman.*

ravi·oli /ˌræviˈəʊli; *AmE* -ˈoʊli/ *noun* [U] PASTA in the shape of small squares filled with meat, cheese, etc., usually served with a sauce

rav·ish /ˈrævɪʃ/ *verb* [VN] (*literary*) **1** (of a man) to force a woman to have sex **SYN** RAPE **2** [usually passive] to give sb great pleasure

rav·ish·ing /ˈrævɪʃɪŋ/ *adj.* extremely beautiful **SYN** GORGEOUS: *a ravishing blonde/dress/smile* ▶ **rav·ish·ing·ly** *adv.*: *ravishingly beautiful*

raw /rɔː/ *adj., noun*
- *adj.*
FOOD | **1** not cooked: *raw meat* ◇ *These fish are often eaten raw.*
MATERIALS | **2** [usually before noun] in its natural state; not yet changed or made into sth else: *the supply of raw materials to factories* ◇ *raw cotton/sugar/wool* ◇ (*figurative*) *Her childhood provided the raw material for her first novel.*
INFORMATION | **3** [usually before noun] not yet organized into a form in which it can be easily used or understood: *This information is only raw data and will need further analysis.*
EMOTIONS/QUALITIES | **4** [usually before noun] powerful and natural; not controlled or trained: *songs full of raw emotion* ◇ *He started with nothing but raw talent and determination.*
PART OF BODY | **5** red and painful because the skin has been damaged: *There were raw patches on her feet where the shoes had rubbed.*
PERSON | **6** [usually before noun] new to a job or an activity and therefore without experience or skill: *a raw beginner* ◇ *raw recruits* (= for example, in the army)
WEATHER | **7** very cold: *a raw north wind* ◇ *It had been a wet raw winter.*
DESCRIPTION | **8** honest, direct and sometimes shocking: *a raw portrayal of working-class life* ◇ (*AmE*) *raw language* (= containing many sexual details)
▶ **raw·ness** *noun* [U]
IDM **a raw 'deal** the fact of sb being treated unfairly: *Older workers often get a raw deal.*
- *noun*
IDM **catch/touch sb on the 'raw** (*BrE*) to upset sb by reminding them of sth they are particularly sensitive about **in the 'raw** in a way that does not hide the unpleasant aspects of sth: *He spent a couple of months on the streets to experience life in the raw.*—more at NERVE *n.*

raw·hide /ˈrɔːhaɪd/ *noun* [U] natural leather that has not had any special treatment

ray /reɪ/ *noun* **1** a narrow beam of light, heat or other energy: *the sun's rays* ◇ *ultraviolet rays* ◇ *The windows were shining in the reflected rays of the setting sun.*—see also COSMIC RAYS, GAMMA RAYS, X-RAY **2** **~ of sth** a small amount of sth good or of sth that you are hoping for: *There was just one small ray of hope.* **3** a sea fish with a large broad flat body and a long tail, that is used for food **4** (also **re**) (*music*) the second note of a MAJOR scale **IDM** **a ,ray of 'sunshine** (*informal*) a person or thing that makes life brighter or more cheerful

rayon /ˈreɪɒn; *AmE* -ɑːn/ *noun* [U] a smooth fabric made from CELLULOSE, used for making clothes

raze /reɪz/ *verb* [VN] [usually passive] to completely destroy a building, town, etc. so that nothing is left: *The village was **razed to the ground.***

b	d	f	g	h	k	l	m	n	p	r
bad	did	fall	get	hat	cat	leg	man	now	pen	red

razor /ˈreɪzə(r)/ *noun* an instrument that is used for shaving: *an electric razor* ◊ *a cut-throat/safety/disposable razor*—compare SHAVER **IDM** **be on the 'razor's edge | be on a 'razor edge** to be in a difficult situation where any mistake may be very dangerous: *Social workers operate on the razor's edge.*

'razor blade *noun* a thin sharp piece of metal that is used in a razor, especially one that can be thrown away when it is no longer sharp

razor-'sharp *adj.* **1** extremely sharp: *razor-sharp teeth* **2** showing that sb is extremely intelligent: *a razor-sharp mind*

'razor-thin *adj.* [only before noun] (*AmE*) (of a victory in an election, etc.) won by a very small number of votes

'razor wire *noun* [U] strong wire with sharp blades sticking out, placed on top of walls and around areas of land to keep people out

raz·zle /ˈræzl/ *noun* **IDM** **be/go (out) on the razzle** (*BrE, informal*) to go out drinking, dancing and enjoying yourself

razz·ma·tazz /ˌræzməˈtæz/ (also **raz·za·ma·tazz** /ˌræzəməˈtæz/) *noun* [U] (*informal*) a lot of noisy exciting activity that is intended to attract people's attention

RC /ˌɑː ˈsiː, *AmE* ˌɑːr/ *abbr.* ROMAN CATHOLIC: *St Mary's RC Church*

Rd (also **Rd.** especially in *AmE*) *abbr.* (used in written addresses) Road: *12 Ashton Rd*

RE /ˌɑːr ˈiː/ *noun* [U] the abbreviation for 'religious education' (taught as a subject in schools): *an RE teacher*

re¹ /reɪ/ = RAY

re² /riː/ *prep.* (*written*) used at the beginning of a business letter, etc. to introduce the subject that it is about: *Re your letter of 1 September ...* ◊ *Re: travel expenses*

re- /riː/ *prefix* (in verbs and related nouns, adjectives and adverbs) again: *reapply* ◊ *reincarnation* ◊ *reassuring*

reach /riːtʃ/ *verb, noun*
∎ *verb*
ARRIVE | **1** [VN] to arrive at the place that you have been travelling to: *They didn't reach the border until after dark.* ◊ *I hope this letter reaches you.* **2** [VN] to come to sb's attention: *The rumours eventually reached the President.*
LEVEL/SPEED/STAGE | **3** [VN] to increase to a particular level, speed, etc. over a period of time: *The conflict has now reached a new level of intensity.* ◊ *Daytime temperatures can reach 40°C.* **4** [VN] to arrive at a particular point or stage of sth after a period of time: *He first reached the finals in 1998.* ◊ *The negotiations have reached deadlock.*
ACHIEVE AIM | **5** [VN] to achieve a particular aim **SYN** ARRIVE AT: *to reach a conclusion/decision/verdict/compromise* ◊ *Politicians again failed to reach an agreement.*—see also FAR-REACHING
WITH HAND/ARM | **6** [+adv./prep.] to stretch your hand towards sth in order to touch it, pick it up, etc: [V] *She reached inside her bag for a pen.* ◊ [VN] *He reached out his hand to touch her.* **7** to be able to stretch your hand far enough in order to touch sth, pick sth up, etc: [V] *'Grab the end of the rope.' 'I can't reach that far!'* ◊ [VN] *Can you reach the light switch from where you're sitting?* **8** ~ **sth (down) for sb | ~ sb (down) sth** to stretch your hand out or up in order to get sth for sb: [VN, VNN] *Can you reach that box down for me?* ◊ *Can you reach me down that box?*
BE LONG ENOUGH | **9** to be big enough, long enough, etc. to arrive at a particular point: [V+adv./prep.] *The carpet only reached halfway across the room.* ◊ [VN] *Is the cable long enough to reach the socket?*
CONTACT SB | **10** [VN] to communicate with sb, especially by telephone: *Do you know where I can reach him?*
BE SEEN/HEARD BY SB | **11** [VN] to be seen or heard by sb: *Through television and radio we are able to reach a wider audience.*
IDM **reach for the 'stars** to try to be successful at sth that is difficult—more at EAR
PHRV **reach 'out to sb** to show sb that you are interested in them and/or want to help them: *The church needs to find new ways of reaching out to young people.*

∎ *noun*
OF ARMS | **1** [sing., U] the distance over which you can stretch your arms to touch sth; the distance over which a particular object can be used to touch sth else: *As a boxer, his long reach gives him a significant advantage.* ◊ *The shot was well beyond the reach of the goalkeeper.* ◊ *Cleaning fluids should be kept out of the reach of children.* ◊ *He lashed out angrily, hitting anyone within his reach.* ◊ *Use shears with a long reach for cutting high hedges.*
OF POWER/INFLUENCE | **2** [sing., U] the limit to which sb/sth has the power or influence to do sth: *Such matters are beyond the reach of the law.* ◊ *Victory is now out of her reach.* ◊ *The basic model is priced well within the reach of most people.* ◊ *The company has now overtaken IBM in terms of size and reach.*
OF RIVER | **3** [C, usually pl.] a straight section of water between two bends on a river: *the upper/lower reaches of the Nile* (= the part that is furthest from/nearest to the sea)
PLACE FAR FROM CENTRE | **4** (**reaches**) [pl.] **the outer, further, etc. ~ of sth** the parts of an area or a place that are a long way from the centre: *the outer reaches of space* ◊ *the eastern reaches of the continent* ◊ (*figurative*) *an exploration of the deepest reaches of the human mind*
SECTIONS OF ORGANIZATION | **5** (**reaches**) [pl.] **the higher, lower, etc. ~ of sth** the higher, etc. sections of an organization, a system, etc: *There are still few women in the upper reaches of the civil service.* ◊ *Many clubs in the lower reaches of the league are in financial difficulty.*
IDM **within (easy) 'reach (of sth)** close to sth: *The house is within easy reach of schools and sports facilities.*

reach·able /ˈriːtʃəbl/ *adj.* [not before noun] that is possible to reach: *The farm is only reachable by car.*

react /riˈækt/ *verb* [V] **1** ~ **(to sth) (by doing sth)** to change or behave in a particular way as a result of or in response to sth: *Local residents have reacted angrily to the news.* ◊ *I nudged her but she didn't react.* ◊ *You never know how he is going to react.* ◊ *The market reacted by falling a further two points.* **2** to become ill/sick after eating, breathing, etc. a particular substance: *People can react badly to certain food additives.* **3** ~ **(with sth)| ~ (together)** (*chemistry*) (of substances) to experience a chemical or physical change when coming into contact with another substance: *Iron reacts with water and air to produce rust.* **PHRV** **re·act a'gainst sb/sth** to show dislike or opposition in response to sth, especially by deliberately doing the opposite of what sb wants you to do: *He reacted strongly against the artistic conventions of his time.*

react·ant /riˈæktənt/ *noun* (*chemistry*) a substance that takes part in and is changed by a chemical reaction

re·ac·tion /riˈækʃn/ *noun*
TO EVENT/SITUATION | **1** [C, U] ~ **(to sb/sth)** what you do, say or think as a result of sth that has happened: *What was his reaction to the news?* ◊ *My immediate reaction was one of shock.* ◊ *A spokesman said the changes were not in reaction to the company's recent losses.* ◊ *There has been a mixed reaction to her appointment as director.* ◊ *The decision provoked an angry reaction from local residents.* ◊ *I tried shaking him but there was no reaction.*
CHANGE IN ATTITUDES | **2** [C usually sing, U] ~ **(against sth)** a change in people's attitudes or behaviour caused by disapproval of the attitudes, etc. of the past: *The return to traditional family values is a reaction against the permissiveness of recent decades.*
TO DRUGS | **3** [C, U] a response by the body, usually a bad one, to a drug, chemical substance, etc: *to suffer/have an allergic reaction to a drug*
TO DANGER | **4** (**reactions**) [pl.] the ability to move quickly in response to sth, especially if in danger: *a skilled driver with quick reactions*
AGAINST PROGRESS | **5** [U] opposition to social or political progress or change: *The forces of reaction made change difficult.*
SCIENCE | **6** [C, U] (*technical*) a chemical change produced by two or more substances acting on each other: *a chemical/nuclear reaction*—see also CHAIN REACTION **7** [U, C] a

	s	t	v	z	ʃ	ʒ	tʃ	dʒ	θ	ð	ŋ
	see	tea	van	zoo	shoe	vision	chain	jam	thin	this	sing

force shown by sth in response to another force, which is of equal strength and acts in the opposite direction

re·ac·tion·ary /riˈækʃənri; *AmE* -neri/ *noun* (*pl.* **-ies**) (*disapproving*) a person who is opposed to political or social change ▶ **re·ac·tion·ary** *adj.*: *a reactionary attitude/government*

re·acti·vate /riˈæktɪveɪt/ *verb* [VN] (*written*) to make sth start working or happening again after a period of time

re·act·ive /riˈæktɪv/ *adj.* **1** (*formal*) showing a reaction or response: *The police presented a reactive rather than preventive strategy against crime.*—compare PROACTIVE **2** (*chemistry*) tending to show chemical change when mixed with another substance: *highly reactive substances*

re·act·or /riˈæktə(r)/ (also **,nuclear reˈactor**) *noun* a large structure used for the controlled production of nuclear energy

read *verb* /riːd/ *noun* /riːd/ *adj.* /red/

■ *verb* /riːd/ (**read, read** /red/)

WORDS/SYMBOLS **1** (not used in the progressive tenses) to look at and understand the meaning of written or printed words or symbols: [V] *She's still learning to read.* ◊ *Some children can read and write before they go to school.* ◊ [VN] *I can't read your writing.* ◊ *Can you read music?* ◊ *I'm trying to read the map.* **2 ~** (**sth**) (**to sb/yourself**) to go through written or printed words, etc. in silence or aloud to others: [V] *I'm going to go to bed and read.* ◊ *He liked reading to his grandchildren.* ◊ [VN] *to read a book/a magazine/the newspaper* ◊ *Have you read any Steinbeck* (= novels by him)? ◊ *He read the poem aloud.* ◊ [VN, VNN] *Go on—read it to us.* ◊ *She read us a story.*—see also PROOF-READ

DISCOVER BY READING **3 ~** (**about/of sth**) (not used in the progressive tenses) to discover or find out about sb/sth by reading: [V] *I read about the accident in the local paper.* ◊ [Vthat] *I read that he had resigned.* ◊ [VN] *Don't believe everything you read in the papers.*

SB'S MIND/THOUGHTS **4** [VN] **~ sb's mind/thoughts** to guess what sb else is thinking

SB'S LIPS **5** [VN] **~ sb's lips** to look at the movements of sb's lips to learn what they are saying—see also LIP-READ

UNDERSTAND **6** [VN] **~ sth** (**as sth**) to understand sth in a particular way [SYN] INTERPRET: *How do you read the present situation?* ◊ *Silence must not always be read as consent.*

OF A PIECE OF WRITING **7** [Vspeech] to have sth written on it; to be written in a particular way: *The sign read 'No admittance'.* ◊ *I've changed the last paragraph. It now reads as follows ...* **8** [V] to give a particular impression when read: *Generally, the article reads very well.* ◊ *The poem reads like* (= sounds as if it is) *a translation.*

MEASURING INSTRUMENT **9** [VN] (of measuring instruments) to show a particular weight, pressure, etc: *What does the thermometer read?* **10** [VN] to get information from a measuring instrument: *A man came to read the gas meter.*

HEAR **11** [VN] to hear and understand sb speaking on a radio set: *'Do you read me?' 'I'm reading you loud and clear.'*

REPLACE WORD **12** [VN] **~ A for B** | **~ B as A** to replace one word, etc. with another when correcting a text: *For 'madam' in line 3 read 'madman'.*

SUBJECT AT UNIVERSITY **13 ~** (**for**) **sth** (*BrE*, rather *old-fashioned*) to study a subject, especially at a university: [VN] *I read English at Oxford.* ◊ [V] *She's reading for a law degree.*

COMPUTING **14** [VN] **~ sth** (**into sth**) (of a computer or the person using it) to take information from a disk: *My computer can't read the disk you sent.* ◊ *to read a file into a computer*

[IDM] **,read between the 'lines** to look for or discover a meaning in sth that is not openly stated: *Reading between the lines, I think Clare needs money.* **,read sb like a 'book** to understand easily what sb is thinking or feeling **,read my 'lips** (*spoken*) used to tell sb to listen carefully to what you are saying: *Read my lips: no new taxes* (= I promise there will be no new taxes). **,read (sb) the 'Riot Act** (*BrE*) to tell sb forcefully that they must not do sth

[ORIGIN] From an Act of Parliament passed in 1715 to prevent riots. It made it illegal for a group of twelve or more people to refuse to split up if they were ordered to do so and part of the Act was read to them. **,take it/sth as 'read** (*BrE*) to accept sth without discussing it: *Can we take it as read that you want the job?*

[PHRV] **,read sth↔'back** to read a message, etc. aloud in order to check that it is correct **,read sth 'into sth** to think that sth means more than it really does: *Don't read too much into what she says.* **,read 'on** to continue reading: *That's the story so far. Now read on ...* **,read sth↔'out** to read sth aloud, especially to other people **,read sth↔'over/'through** to read sth carefully from beginning to end to look for mistakes or check details **,read sth↔'up** | **,read 'up on sb/sth** to read a lot about a subject: *I'll need to read up on the case before the meeting.*

■ *noun* /riːd/ [sing.] (*informal*) **1** (*especially BrE*) an act or period of reading sth: *I was having a quiet read when the phone rang.* **2 a good, interesting, etc. ~** a book, article, etc. that is good, etc: *His thrillers are always a gripping read.*

■ *adj.* /red/ (used after an adverb) (of a person) having knowledge that has been gained from reading books, etc: *She's very widely read in law.*—see also WELL READ

read·able /ˈriːdəbl/ *adj.* **1** (of a book, article, etc.) that is easy, interesting and enjoyable to read **2** (of written or printed words) clear and easy to read [SYN] LEGIBLE—see also MACHINE-READABLE ▶ **read·abil·ity** /ˌriːdəˈbɪləti/ *noun* [U]

read·er /ˈriːdə(r)/ *noun* **1** a person who reads, especially one who reads a lot or in a particular way: *an avid reader of science fiction* ◊ *a fast/slow reader* ◊ *The reader is left to draw his or her own conclusions.* **2** a person who reads a particular newspaper, magazine, etc: *readers' letters* ◊ *Are you a 'Times' reader?* **3** an easy book that is intended to help people learn to read their own or a foreign language: *a series of graded English readers* **4** (usually **Reader**) a senior teacher at a British university just below the rank of a PROFESSOR: *She is Reader in Music at Edinburgh.* **5** (*computing*) an electronic device that reads data stored in one form and changes it into another form so that a computer can perform operations on it **6** (*technical*) a machine that produces on a screen a large image of a text stored on a MICROFICHE or MICROFILM—see also MIND-READER, NEWSREADER

read·er·ship /ˈriːdəʃɪp; *AmE* -dərʃ-/ *noun* **1** [usually sing.] the number or type of people who read a particular newspaper, magazine, etc: *a readership of around 10000* ◊ *In its new format, the magazine hopes to attract a much wider readership.* **2** (usually **Readership**) **~** (**in sth**) (*BrE*) the position of a Reader at a university

read·ily /ˈredɪli/ *adv.* **1** quickly and without difficulty: *All ingredients are readily available from your local store.* **2** in a way that shows you do not object to sth: *Most people readily accept the need for laws.*

readi·ness /ˈredinəs/ *noun* **1** [U] **~** (**for sth**) the state of being ready or prepared for sth: *Everyone has doubts about their readiness for parenthood.* **2** [U, sing.] **~** (**of sb**) (**to do sth**) the state of being willing to do sth: *Over half the people interviewed expressed their readiness to die for their country.*

read·ing /ˈriːdɪŋ/ *noun*

ACTIVITY **1** [U] the activity of sb who reads: *My hobbies include reading and painting.* ◊ *He needs more help with his reading.* ◊ *Are you any good at map reading?* ◊ *reading glasses* (= worn when reading) ◊ *a reading lamp/light* (= one that can be moved to shine light onto sth that you are reading) **2** [sing.] an act of reading sth: *A closer* (= more detailed) *reading of the text reveals just how desperate he was feeling.* ◊ *We are all expected to attend the reading of her will.*

BOOKS/ARTICLES **3** [U] books, articles, etc. that are intended to be read: *reading matter/material* ◊ *a series of reading books for children* ◊ *a reading list* (= a list of books, etc. that students are expected to read for a particular subject) ◊ *further reading* (= at the end of a book, a list of other books that give more information about the same subject) ◊ *The report makes for interesting reading*

R

æ	ɑː	e	ɜː	ə	ɪ	iː	i	ɒ	ɔː	ʌ	ʊ	u	uː
cat	father	ten	bird	about	sit	see	many	got	saw	cup	put	actual	too
								(BrE)					

(= it is interesting to read) ◊ *The article is not exactly light reading* (= it is not easy to read).

WAY OF UNDERSTANDING | **4** [C] ~ (**of sth**) the particular way in which you understand a book, situation, etc. SYN INTERPRETATION: *a literal reading of the text* ◊ *My own reading of events is less optimistic.*

MEASUREMENT | **5** [C] the amount or number shown on an instrument used for measuring sth: *Meter readings are taken every three months.*

EVENT | **6** [C] an event at which sth is read to an audience for entertainment; a piece of literature that is read at such an event: *a poetry reading* ◊ *The evening ended with a reading from her latest novel.*

FROM BIBLE | **7** [C] a short section from the Bible that is read aloud as part of a religious service: *The reading today is from the Book of Daniel.*

IN PARLIAMENT | **8** [C] one of the stages during which a BILL (= a proposal for a new law) must be discussed and accepted by a parliament before it can become law

R

'**reading age** *noun* a person's ability to read, measured by comparing it with the average ability of children of a particular age: *a 30-year-old man with a reading age of eight*

'**reading room** *noun* a room in a library, club, etc. where people can read or study

re·ad·just /ˌriːəˈdʒʌst/ *verb* **1** [V] ~ (**to sth**) to get used to a changed or new situation: *Children are highly adaptable—they just need time to readjust.* ◊ *Once again he had to readjust to living alone.* **2** to change or move sth slightly: *She got out of the car and readjusted her dress.* ▶ **re·ad·just·ment** *noun* [C, U]: *He has made a number of readjustments to his technique.* ◊ *a painful period of readjustment*

re·ad·mit /ˌriːədˈmɪt/ *verb* (**-tt-**) [VN] [often passive] ~ **sb** (**to sth**) **1** to allow sb to join a group, an organization or an institution again **2** to take sb into a hospital again after they had been allowed to leave: *He was readmitted only a week after being discharged.* ▶ **re·ad·mis·sion** /ˌriːədˈmɪʃn/ *noun* [U, C] ~ (**to sth**)

'**read-only 'memory** *noun* [U] (*computing*) = ROM

'**read-out** (*computing*) a display of information on a computer screen—compare PRINTOUT

ready /ˈredi/ *adj., adv., verb, noun*
■ *adj.* (**read·ier, readi·est**)

PREPARED/AVAILABLE | **1** [not before noun] ~ (**for sth**) | ~ (**to do sth**) fully prepared for what you are going to do: *Are you nearly ready?* ◊ *I'm just getting the kids ready for school.* ◊ *Right, we're ready to go.* ◊ *'Shall we go?' 'I'm ready when you are!'* ◊ *Volunteers were ready and waiting to pack the food in boxes.* ◊ *I was twenty years old and ready for anything.* **2** [not before noun] ~ (**for sth**) | ~ (**to do sth**) completed and available to be used: *Come on, dinner's ready!* ◊ *The new building should be ready by 2002.* ◊ *Can you help me get everything ready for the party?* ◊ *The contract will be ready to sign in two weeks.* **3** available to be used easily and immediately: *All the relevant records are easily available ready to hand.* ◊ (*BrE*) *a ready meal* (= one that you buy already prepared and that you only have to heat up) ◊ *a ready supply of wood* ◊ *a ready source of income*—see also READILY, READINESS, ROUGH-AND-READY

WILLING | **4** [not before noun] ~ (**for/with sth**) | ~ (**to do sth**) willing and quick to do or give sth: *I was very angry and ready for a fight.* ◊ *She's always ready with advice.* ◊ *He's always ready to help his friends.* ◊ *Don't be so ready to believe the worst about people.*

LIKELY TO DO STH | **5** ~ **to do sth** likely to do sth very soon: *She looked ready to collapse at any minute.*

NEEDING STH | **6** ~ **for sth** needing sth as soon as possible: *Right, I'm ready for bed.* ◊ *After the long walk, we were all ready for a drink.*

QUICK/CLEVER | **7** [only before noun] quick and clever: *She has great charm and a ready wit.*

IDM **make 'ready (for sth)** (*formal*) to prepare: *to make ready for the President's visit* **ready, steady, 'go!** (*BrE*) (also (**get) ready, (get) set, 'go** *AmE, BrE*) what you say

to tell people to start a race ˌ**ready to 'roll** (*informal*) ready to start: *The show is just about ready to roll.*
■ *verb* (**read·ies, ready·ing, read·ied, read·ied**) ~ **sb/your-self/sth (for sth)** (*formal*) to prepare sb/yourself/sth for sth: [VN] *Western companies were readying themselves for the challenge from Eastern markets.* [also V to inf, VN to inf]
■ *adv.* (used before a past participle, especially in compounds) already done: *ready-cooked meals* ◊ *The concrete was ready mixed.*
■ *noun* (**the ready**) [sing.] (also **read·ies** [pl.]) (*BrE, informal*) money that you can use immediately
IDM **at the 'ready** available to be used immediately: *We all had our cameras at the ready.*

ˌ**ready-'made** *adj.* **1** prepared in advance so that you can eat or use it immediately: *ready-made pastry/pizzas* **2** (*old-fashioned*) (especially of clothes) made in standard sizes, not to the measurements of a particular customer: *a ready-made suit* **3** already provided for you so you do not need to produce or think about it yourself: *When he married her he also took on a ready-made family.*

ˌ**ready 'money** (also ˌ**ready 'cash**) *noun* [U] (*informal*) money in the form of coins and notes that you can spend immediately

ˌ**ready-to-'wear** *adj.* (of clothes) made in standard sizes, not to the measurements of a particular customer: *this winter's ready-to-wear collections from top designers*

re·affirm /ˌriːəˈfɜːm; *AmE* -ˈfɜːrm/ *verb* [VN] (*written*) to state sth again in order to emphasize that it is still true: *The President reaffirmed his commitment to democratic elections.* ▶ **re·affirm·ation** /ˌriːˌæfəˈmeɪʃn; *AmE* -fərˈm-/ *noun* [C, U]

re·affor·esta·tion /ˌriːəˌfɒrɪˈsteɪʃn; *AmE* -ˌfɔːr-; -ˌfɑːr-/ *noun* [U] (*BrE, technical*) = REFORESTATION

re·agent /riˈeɪdʒənt/ *noun* (*chemistry*) a substance used to cause a chemical reaction, especially in order to find out if another substance is present

real /ˈriːəl; *BrE* usually rɪəl/ *adj., adv.*
■ *adj.*

NOT IMAGINED | **1** actually existing or happening and not imagined or pretended: *It wasn't a ghost; it was a real person.* ◊ *pictures of animals, both real and mythological* ◊ *In the movies guns kill people instantly, but it's not like that in real life.* ◊ *Politicians seem to be out of touch with the real world.*

PROBLEM/DANGER | **2** a **real** problem, danger, etc. is one that actually exists, is serious, and should not be ignored: *The growth of violent crime is a very real problem.* ◊ *There's no real possibility of them changing their minds.* ◊ *We have a real chance of success.*

TRUE | **3** [only before noun] actual or true, rather than what appears to be true: *Tell me the real reason.* ◊ *Bono's real name is Paul Hewson.* ◊ *See the real Africa on one of our walking safaris.*

GENUINE | **4** [only before noun] having all the important qualities that it should have to deserve to be called what it is called: *She never had any real friends at school.* ◊ *his first real kiss* **5** genuine and not false or artificial: *Are those real flowers?* ◊ *real gold/silk/leather*

FEELINGS/QUALITIES | **6** strong and sincere: *I had no real interest in politics.* ◊ *He was making a real effort to be nice to her.* ◊ *She has not shown any real regret for what she did.*

FOR EMPHASIS | **7** [only before noun] used to emphasize a state or quality: *He looks a real idiot.* ◊ *This accident could have produced a real tragedy.* ◊ *Her next play was a real contrast.*

MONEY/INCOMES | **8** [only before noun] when the effect of such things as price rises on the power of money to buy things is included in the sums: *Real wage costs have risen by 10% in the past year.* ◊ *This represents a reduction of 5% in real terms.*

IDM **for 'real** genuine or serious: *This is not a fire drill—it's for real.* ◊ (*AmE*) *He managed to convince voters that he was for real.* **get 'real** (*informal*) used to tell sb that they are behaving in a stupid or unreasonable way **the ˌreal 'thing** (*informal*) the genuine thing: *Are you sure it's the*

aɪ	aʊ	eɪ	əʊ	oʊ	ɔɪ	ɪə	eə	ʊə	j	w
my	now	say	go	go	boy	near	hair	pure	yes	wet
			(BrE)	(AmE)						

real thing (= love), *not just infatuation?*—more at McCoy, POWER *n*.

■ *adv.* (*AmE, ScotE, informal*) very: *That tastes real good.* ◊ *He's a real nice guy.* ◊ *I'm real sorry.*

WHICH WORD?
real / true   (?)

There is a difference between **real** and **true** in their main meanings. Something that is **real** actually exists or happens and is not imagined: *Was it real or was it a dream?* Something is **true** if it agrees with the known facts and is not invented: *Is the news true?* ◊ *a movie based on a true story.*

In some other meanings, both words can be used. For example, you can use either **real** or **true** to talk about what is actually the case when this is different from what appears to be the case: *Tell me the real reason why he resigned.* ◊ *He seems quiet but reveals his true character on the football field.* You can also use either word to talk about an example of something that has all the important qualities it should have: *She was his first real girlfriend.* ◊ *This job will be a true test of the new system.*

,**real ¹ale** *noun* [U, C] (*BrE*) a type of beer that is made and stored in the traditional way

¹**real estate** *noun* [U] (*especially AmE*) **1** (also **realty**) property in the form of land or buildings: *My father sold real estate.* **2** the business of selling houses or land for building: *to work in real estate*

¹**real estate agent** *noun* = ESTATE AGENT

re·align /ˌriːəˈlaɪn/ *verb* [VN] (*written*) **1** to change the position or direction of sth slightly: *The road was realigned to improve visibility.* **2** to make changes to sth in order to adapt it to a new situation: *The company has been forced to realign its operations in the area.* **3** ~ **yourself** (**with sb/sth**) to change your opinions, policies, etc. so that they are the same as those of another person, group, etc: *The rebel MPs have realigned themselves with the opposition party.* ▶ **re·align·ment** *noun* [U, C] ~ (**of sth**): *the realignment of personal goals* ◊ *political realignments*

real·ism /ˈriːəlɪzəm; *BrE* also ˈrɪəl-/ *noun* [U] **1** a way of seeing, accepting and dealing with situations as they really are without being influenced by your emotions or false hopes: *There was a new mood of realism among the leaders at the peace talks.* **2** (of novels, paintings, films/movies, etc.) the quality of being very like real life: *the gritty realism of the new drama serial* **3** (also **Real-ism**) a style in art or literature that shows things and people as they are in real life—compare ROMANTICISM, IDEALISM

real·ist /ˈriːəlɪst; *BrE* also ˈrɪə-/ *noun* **1** a person who accepts and deals with a situation as it really is and does not try to pretend that it is different: *I'm a realist—I know you can't change people overnight.* **2** a writer, painter, etc. whose work represents things as they are in real life

real·is·tic /ˌriːəˈlɪstɪk; *BrE* also ˌrɪə-/ *adj.* ~ (**to do sth**) **1** accepting in a sensible way what it is actually possible to do or achieve in a particular situation: *a realistic assessment/view* ◊ *We have to be realistic about our chances of winning.* ◊ *It is not realistic to expect people to spend so much money.* **2** sensible and appropriate; possible to achieve: *We must set realistic goals.* ◊ *a realistic target/deadline* ◊ *to pay a realistic price/salary* **3** representing things as they are in real life: *a realistic drawing* ◊ *We try to make these training courses as realistic as possible.* OPP UNREALISTIC

real·is·tic·al·ly /ˌriːəˈlɪstɪkli; *BrE* also ˌrɪə-/ *adv.* **1** used to say what you think can actually be achieved in a particular situation: *Realistically, there is little prospect of a ceasefire.* **2** in a way that shows sb accepts in a sensible way what it is actually possible to do or achieve: *How many can you realistically hope to sell?* ◊ *Kate spoke realistically about the task ahead.* **3** in a way that represents things as they are in real life: *a fireplace with realistically glowing coals*

real·ity /riˈæləti/ *noun* (*pl.* **-ies**) **1** [U] the true situation and the problems that actually exist in life, in contrast to how you would like life to be: *She refuses to face reality.* ◊ *You're out of touch with reality.* ◊ *The reality is that there is not enough money to pay for this project.* **2** [C] a thing that is actually experienced or seen, in contrast to what people might imagine: *the harsh realities of life* ◊ *This decision reflects the realities of the political situation.* ◊ *Will time travel ever become a reality?* **IDM in re'ality** used to say that a situation is different from what has just been said or from what people believe: *Outwardly she seemed confident but in reality she felt extremely nervous.*—see also VIRTUAL REALITY

real·iz·able (*BrE* also **-is·able**) /ˈriːəlaɪzəbl; *BrE* also ˈrɪə-/ *adj.* **1** possible to achieve or make happen: *realizable objectives/goals* **2** that can be sold and turned into money: *realizable assets*

real·iza·tion (*BrE* also **-isa·tion**) /ˌriːəlaɪˈzeɪʃn; ˌrɪəl-; *AmE* ˌriːələˈz-/ *noun* **1** [U, sing.] ~ (**that ...**) | ~ (**of sth**) the process of becoming aware of sth: *the sudden realization of what she had done* ◊ *There is a growing realization that changes must be made.* **2** [U] ~ (**of sth**) the process of achieving a particular aim, etc: *It was the realization of his greatest ambition.* ◊ *the realization of political goals* **3** [U] ~ **of your assets** (*formal*) the act of selling sth that you own, such as property, in order to get the money that you need for sth **4** [U, C] ~ (**of sth**) (*formal*) the act of producing a sound, play, design, etc.; or the thing that is produced

real·ize (*BrE* also **-ise**) /ˈriːəlaɪz; *BrE* also ˈrɪəl-/ *verb*
BE/BECOME AWARE | **1** (not used in the progressive tenses) to understand or become aware of a particular fact or situation: [V(**that**)] *I didn't realize (that) you were so unhappy.* ◊ *The moment I saw her, I realized something was wrong.* ◊ [Vwh-] *I don't think you realize how important this is to her.* ◊ [V] *The situation was more complicated than they had at first realized.* ◊ *They managed to leave without any of us realizing.* ◊ [VN] *I hope you realize the seriousness of this crime.* ◊ *Only later did she realize her mistake.* ◊ [VNthat] *There was a cheer when it was realized that everyone was safely back.*
ACHIEVE STH | **2** [VN] to achieve sth important that you very much want to do: *She never realized her ambition of becoming a professional singer.* ◊ *We try to help all students realize their full potential* (= be as successful as they are able to be).
HAPPEN | **3** [VN] [usually passive] if sb's fears are realized, the things that they are afraid will happen, do happen: *His worst fears were realized when he saw that the door had been forced open.*
SELL | **4** [VN] ~ **your assets** (*formal*) to sell things that you own, for example property, in order to get the money that you need for sth **5** [VN] (*formal*) (of goods, etc.) to be sold for a particular amount of money: *The paintings realized $2 million at auction.*
MAKE STH REAL | **6** [VN] (*formal*) to produce sth that can be seen or heard, based on written information or instructions: *The stage designs have been beautifully realized.*

,**real-'life** *adj.* [only before noun] actually happening or existing in life, not in books, stories or films/movies: *a novel based on real-life events* ◊ *a real-life Romeo and Juliet* OPP FICTIONAL

re·allo·cate /ˌriːˈæləkeɪt/ *verb* [VN] ~ **sth** (**to sb/sth**) to change the way money or materials are shared between different people, groups, projects, etc. SYN REDISTRIBUTE: *Government funds were reallocated to the new local authorities.* ▶ **re·allo·ca·tion** /ˌriːˌæləˈkeɪʃn/ *noun* [U]

real·ly /ˈriːəli; *BrE* also ˈrɪəli/ *adv.* **1** used to say what is actually the fact or the truth about sth: *What do you really think about it?* ◊ *Tell me what really happened.* ◊ *They are not really my aunt and uncle.* ◊ *I can't believe I am really going to meet the princess.* **2** (usually *spoken*) used to emphasize sth you are saying or an opinion you are giving: *I want to help, I really do.* ◊ *Now I really must go.* ◊ *I really don't mind.* ◊ *He really likes you.* ◊ *I really and truly am in love this time.* **3** used to emphasize an adjective or adverb: *a really hot fire* ◊ *I'm really sorry.*

---

b	d	f	g	h	k	l	m	n	p	r
bad	did	fall	get	hat	cat	leg	man	now	pen	red

4 (usually *spoken*) used, often in negative sentences, to reduce the force of sth you are saying: *I don't really agree with that.* ◊ *It doesn't really matter.* ◊ *'Did you enjoy the book?' ' Not really '* (= 'no' or 'not very much'). **HELP** The position of **really** can change the meaning of the sentence. **I don't really know** means that you are not sure about something; **I really don't know** emphasizes that you do not know. (Look at sense 2.) **5** (usually *spoken*) used in questions and negative sentences when you want sb to say 'no': *Do you really expect me to believe that?* ◊ *I don't really need to go, do I?* **6** (*spoken*) used to express interest in or surprise at what sb is saying: *'We're going to Japan next month.' 'Oh, really?'* ◊ *'She's resigned.' 'Really? Are you sure?'* **7** (*spoken*) used to show that you disapprove of sth sb has done: *Really, you could have told us before.*

realm /relm/ *noun* **1** an area of activity, interest, or knowledge: *in the realm of literature / science* ◊ *At the end of the speech he seemed to be moving* **into the realms of** *fantasy.* **2** (*formal*) a country ruled by a king or queen: *the defence of the realm* **IDM beyond / within the realms of possibility** not possible / possible: *A successful outcome is not beyond the realms of possibility.*

real·po·li·tik /reɪˈɑːlpɒlitiːk; *AmE* -pɑːl-/ *noun* [U] (from *German*) a system of politics that is based on the actual situation and needs of a country or political party rather than on moral principles

,real 'time *noun* [U] (*computing*) the fact that there is only a very short time between a computer system receiving information and dealing with it: *To make the training realistic the simulation operates* **in real time.** ◊ *real-time missile guidance systems*

Real·tor™ /ˈriːəltə(r)/ *noun* (*AmE*) = ESTATE AGENT

realty /ˈriːəlti/ *noun* [U] (*especially AmE*) = REAL ESTATE

ream /riːm/ *noun* **1** (**reams**) [pl.] (*informal*) a large quantity of writing: *She wrote reams in the exam.* **2** [C] (*technical*) 500 sheets of paper

re·ani·mate /riːˈænimeɪt/ *verb* [VN] (*formal*) to give sb / sth new life or energy

reap /riːp/ *verb* **1** [VN] to obtain sth, especially sth good, as a direct result of sth that you have done: *They are now reaping the rewards of all their hard work.* **2** [V, VN] to cut and collect a crop, especially corn, from a field **IDM reap a / the 'harvest** (*BrE*) to benefit or suffer as a direct result of sth that you have done **you ,reap what you 'sow** (*saying*) you have to deal with the bad effects or results of sth that you originally started

reap·er /ˈriːpə(r)/ *noun* a person or a machine that cuts and collects crops on a farm—see also THE GRIM REAPER

re·appear /ˌriːəˈpɪə(r); *AmE* -ˈpɪr/ *verb* [V] to appear again after not being heard of or seen for a period of time: *She went upstairs and did not reappear until morning.* ◊ *The moon reappeared from behind a cloud.* ▶ **re·appear·ance** /-rəns/ *noun* [U, sing.]

re·apply /ˌriːəˈplaɪ/ *verb* (**re·applies, re·apply·ing, re·applied, re·applied**) **1** [VN] to put another layer of a substance on a surface: *Sunblock should be reapplied every hour.* **2** [V] **~ (for sth)** to make another formal request for sth: *Previous applicants for the post need not reapply.* **3** [VN] to use sth again, especially in a different situation: *Students are taught a number of skills that can be reapplied throughout their studies.*

re·appoint /ˌriːəˈpɔɪnt/ *verb* **~ sb (as) sth | ~ sb (to sth)** to give sb the job that they used to have in the past: [VN, VN-N] *After the trial he was reappointed (as) treasurer.* ▶ **re·appoint·ment** *noun* [U]

re·appraisal /ˌriːəˈpreɪzl/ *noun* [C usually sing, U] the act of examining sth again to see if it needs to be changed: *a reappraisal of the country's defence needs*

re·appraise /ˌriːəˈpreɪz/ *verb* [VN] (*formal*) to think again about the value or nature of sth to see if your opinion about it should be changed **SYN** REASSESS: *The system needs to be continually reappraised.*

rear /rɪə(r); *AmE* rɪr/ *noun, adj, verb*

■ *noun* **1** (usually **the rear**) [sing.] the back part of sth: *A trailer was attached to the rear of the truck.* ◊ *There are toilets at both front and rear of the plane.* ◊ *A high gate*

blocks the only entrance **to the rear.** ⇨ note at BACK **2** (also **,rear 'end**) [C, usually sing.] (*informal*) the part of the body that you sit on **SYN** BOTTOM: *a kick in the rear* **IDM ,bring up the 'rear** to be at the back of a line of people, or last in a race

■ *adj.* [only before noun] at or near the back of sth: *front and rear windows* ◊ *the rear entrance of the building*

■ *verb* **1** [VN] [often passive] **~ sb / sth (on sth)** to care for young children or animals until they are fully grown **SYN** BRING SB UP, RAISE: *She reared a family of five on her own.* **2** [VN] to breed or keep animals or birds, for example on a farm: *to rear poultry / cattle* **3** [V] **~ (up)** (of an animal, especially a horse) to raise itself on its back legs, with the front legs in the air: *The horse reared, throwing its rider.* **4** [V] (of sth large) to seem to lean over you, especially in a threatening way: *The great bulk of the building reared up against the night sky.* **IDM sth rears its (ugly) 'head** if sth unpleasant **rears its head** or **rears its ugly head**, it appears or happens **PHRV 'rear sb / sth on sth** [usually passive] to give a person or an animal a particular type of food, entertainment, etc. while they are young: *I was the son of sailors and reared on stories of the sea.*

,rear 'admiral *noun* an officer of very high rank in the navy: *Rear Admiral Baines*

'rear-end *verb* [VN] (*informal, especially AmE*) (of a vehicle or driver) to drive into the back of another vehicle: *There was a loud crash as someone rear-ended me.*

rear·guard /ˈrɪəɡɑːd; *AmE* ˈrɪrɡɑːrd/ *noun* (usually **the rearguard**) [sing.+ sing. / pl. *v*.] a group of soldiers that protect the back part of an army especially when the army is RETREATING after it has been defeated **OPP** VAN-GUARD

,rearguard 'action *noun* [usually sing.] a struggle to change or stop sth even when it is not likely that you will succeed: *They have been fighting a rearguard action for two years to stop their house being demolished.*

rear·ing /ˈrɪərɪŋ; *AmE* ˈrɪrɪŋ/ *noun* [U] **1** the process of caring for children as they grow up, teaching them how to behave as members of society **2** the process of breeding animals or birds and caring for them as they grow: *livestock rearing*

rearm /riːˈɑːm; *AmE* -ˈɑːrm/ *verb* to obtain, or supply sb with, new or better weapons, armies, etc: [V] *The country was forbidden to rearm under the terms of the treaty.* ◊ [VN] *Rebel troops were being rearmed.* ▶ **re·arma·ment** /riːˈɑːməmənt; *AmE* -ˈɑːrm-/ *noun* [U]

rear·most /ˈrɪəməʊst; *AmE* ˈrɪrmoʊst/ *adj.* (*formal*) furthest back: *the rearmost section of the aircraft*

re·arrange /ˌriːəˈreɪndʒ/ *verb* [VN] **1** to change the position or order of things; to change your position: *We've rearranged the furniture in the bedroom.* ◊ *She rearranged herself in another pose.* **2** to change the time, date or place of an event **SYN** RESCHEDULE: *Can we rearrange the meeting for next Tuesday at 2?* ▶ **re·arrange·ment** *noun* [C, U]

,rear-view 'mirror *noun* a mirror in which a driver can see the traffic behind—picture at CAR

rear·ward /ˈrɪəwəd; *AmE* ˈrɪrwərd/ *adj.* (*formal*) at or near the back of sth: *rearward seats / wheels*

rea·son /ˈriːzn/ *noun, verb*

■ *noun* **1** [C] **~ (why ...) | ~ (that ...) | ~ (for sth / for doing sth)** a cause or an explanation for sth that has happened or that sb has done: *I'd like to know the reason why you're so late.* ◊ *We aren't going for the* **simple reason** *that we can't afford it.* ◊ *She gave no reasons for her decision.* ◊ *I have no particular reason for doubting him.* ◊ *He said no but he didn't* **give a reason.** ◊ *For* **some reason** (= one that I don't know or don't understand) *we all have to come in early tomorrow.* ◊ *She resigned for* **personal reasons.** ◊ *For reasons of security the door is always kept locked.* ◊ *He wants to keep them all in his office* **for reasons best known to himself.** ◊ *people who, for whatever reason, are unable to support themselves* ◊ *'Why did she do that?' 'She must* **have her reasons** (= secret reasons which she does not want to tell).* ◊ *(formal) He was excused* **by reason of** (= because of) *his age.* ⇨ note at CAUSE **2** [U] **~ (to do sth) | ~ (why ...) | ~ (for sth / for doing sth)** a fact that makes it right or fair to do sth: *They have reason to believe that he is lying.* ◇ *We have every reason* (= have very good reasons) *to feel optimistic.* ◇ *This result gives us all the more reason for optimism.* ◇ *She complained, with reason* (= rightly), *that she had been underpaid.* **3** [U] the power of the mind to think in a logical way, to understand and have opinions, etc: *Only human beings are capable of reason* (= of thinking in a logical way, etc.). ◇ *to lose your reason* (= become mentally ill) **4** [U] what is possible, practical or right: *I can't get her to* **listen to reason.** ◇ *Why can't they see reason?* ◇ *to be open. to reason* (= to be willing to accept sensible advice) ◇ *He's looking for a job and he's willing to do anything within reason.* IDM **it ,stands to 'reason** (*informal*) it must be clear to any sensible person who thinks about it: *It stands to reason that they'll go if you don't pay them enough.*—more at RHYME *n.*

■ *verb* **1** to form a judgement about a situation by considering the facts and using your power to think in a logical way: [V that] *She reasoned that she must have left her bag on the train.* ◇ [V] *They couldn't fire him, he reasoned. He was the only one who knew how the system worked.* [also V speech] **2** [V] to use your power to think and understand: *the human ability to reason* PHRV **,reason sth 'out** to try and find the answer to a problem by using your power to think in a logical way: *Reason it out for yourself!* **'reason with sb** to talk to sb in order to persuade them to be more sensible: *I tried to reason with him, but he wouldn't listen.*

WHICH WORD?

reason / explanation / excuse / pretext / grounds (?)

A **reason** is the cause of something or something that explains why a particular thing has happened: *His reason for resigning was that he was under stress.* ◇ *She didn't give a reason for her decision.* ◇ *Police cannot name the man for legal reasons.*

If you describe something as an **explanation** rather than a **reason**, you may simply be repeating what someone has said: *His explanation for resigning was that he was under stress* (= that is what he said and it may or may not be true).

An **excuse** may be true or invented and is a reason that you give to explain or defend your behaviour. If you call something an **excuse** you may not believe that it is true or you may think that it is not a good enough reason: *What's your excuse for being late this time?*

A **pretext** is a false reason that someone gives for doing something in order to hide the real reason: *He got into the house on the pretext of checking the gas* (= but he really wanted to steal something).

The **grounds** for something are the reasons for doing, saying or believing it, especially in a formal or legal situation: *I left my job on medical grounds.* ◇ *She had good grounds for divorce.*

---

rea·son·able /ˈriːznəbl/ *adj.* **1 ~ (to do sth)** fair, practical and sensible: *It is reasonable to assume that he knew beforehand that this would happen.* ◇ *Be reasonable! We can't work late every night.* ◇ *Any reasonable person would have done exactly as you did.* ◇ *The prosecution has to prove beyond reasonable doubt that he is guilty of murder.* OPP UNREASONABLE **2** acceptable and appropriate in a particular situation: *He made us a reasonable offer for the car.* ◇ *You must submit your claim within a reasonable time.* **3** (of prices) not too expensive SYN FAIR: *We sell good quality food at reasonable prices.* **4** [usually before noun] fairly good, but not very good SYN AVERAGE: *a reasonable standard of living* ◇ *The hotel was reasonable, I suppose* (= but not excellent). ▶ **rea·son·able·ness** *noun* [U]

rea·son·ably /ˈriːznəbli/ *adv.* **1** to a degree that is fairly good but not very good: *The instructions are reasonably straightforward.* ◇ *She seems reasonably happy in her new*

job. **2** in a logical and sensible way: *We tried to discuss the matter calmly and reasonably.* **3** in a fair way: *He couldn't reasonably be expected to pay back the loan all at once.* ◇ *The apartments are reasonably priced* (= not too expensive).

rea·soned /ˈriːzənd/ *adj.* [only before noun] (of an argument, opinion, etc.) presented in a logical way that shows careful thought

rea·son·ing /ˈriːzənɪŋ/ *noun* [U] the process of forming about things in a logical way; opinions and ideas that are based on logical thinking: *What is the reasoning behind this decision?* ◇ *This line of reasoning is faulty.*

re·assem·ble /ˌriːəˈsembl/ *verb* **1** [VN] to fit the parts of sth together again after it has been taken apart: *We had to take the table apart and reassemble it upstairs.* **2** [V] to meet together again as a group after a break: *The class reassembled after lunch.*

re·assert /ˌriːəˈsɜːt; *AmE* -ˈsɜːrt/ *verb* **1** [VN] to make other people recognize again your right or authority to do sth, after a period when this has been in doubt: *She found it necessary to reassert her position.* **2** [VN] **~ itself** to start to have an effect again, after a period of not having any effect: *He thought about giving up his job, but then common sense reasserted itself.* **3** to state again, clearly and firmly, that sth is true: [V that] *He reasserted that all parties should be involved in the talks.* ◇ [VN] *Traditional values have been reasserted.* ▶ **re·asser·tion** *noun* [sing., U]

re·assess /ˌriːəˈses/ *verb* [VN] to think again about sth to decide if you need to change your opinion of it SYN REAPPRAISE: *After reassessing the situation, she decided to do nothing.* ▶ **re·assess·ment** *noun* [U, C]

re·assign /ˌriːəˈsaɪn/ *verb* [VN] [often passive] **~ sb (to sth)** to give sb a duty, position, or responsibility again: *After his election defeat he was reassigned to the diplomatic service.*

re·assur·ance /ˌriːəˈʃʊərəns; -ˈʃɔːr-; *AmE* -ˈʃʊr-/ *noun* **~ (that …)** **1** [U] the fact of giving advice or help that takes away a person's fears or doubts: *to give/provide/offer reassurance* **2** [C] something that is said or done to take away a person's fears or doubts: *We have been given reassurances that the water is safe to drink.*

re·assure /ˌriːəˈʃʊə(r); -ˈʃɔː(r); *AmE* -ˈʃʊr/ *verb* [V] **~ sb (about sth)** to say or do sth that makes sb less frightened or worried: [VN] *They tried to reassure her, but she still felt anxious.* ◇ [VN that] *The doctor reassured him that there was nothing seriously wrong.*

re·assur·ing /ˌriːəˈʃʊərɪŋ; -ˈʃɔːr-; *AmE* -ˈʃʊr-/ *adj.* making you feel less worried or uncertain about sth: *a reassuring smile* ◇ *It's reassuring (to know) that we've got the money if necessary.* ▶ **re·assur·ing·ly** *adv.*: *She smiled reassuringly.*

re·awaken /ˌriːəˈweɪkən/ *verb* [VN] (*written*) to make you feel a particular emotion again or to make you remember sth again SYN REKINDLE: *The place reawakened childhood memories.*

re·bate /ˈriːbeɪt/ *noun* **1** an amount of money that is paid back to you because you have paid too much: *a tax rebate* **2** an amount of money that is taken away from the cost of sth, before you pay for it: *Buyers are offered a cash rebate.*

rebel *noun, verb*
■ *noun* /ˈrebl/ **1** a person who fights against the government of their country: *rebel forces* ◇ *Armed rebels advanced towards the capital.* **2** a person who opposes sb in authority over them within an organization, a political party, etc. **3** a person who does not like to obey rules or who does not accept normal standards of behaviour, dress, etc: *I've always been the rebel of the family.*
■ *verb* /rɪˈbel/ [V] (**-ll-**) **~ (against sb/sth)** to fight against or refuse to obey an authority, for example a government, a system, your parents, etc: *He later rebelled against his strict religious upbringing.* ◇ *Most teenagers find something to rebel against.*

re·bel·lion /rɪˈbeljən/ *noun* **~ (against sb/sth)** **1** [U, C] an attempt by some of the people in a country to change their government, using violence: *The north of the country rose in rebellion against the government.* ◇ *The army*

æ	ɑː	e	ɜː	ə	ɪ	iː	i	ɒ	ɔː	ʌ	ʊ	u	uː
cat	father	ten	bird	about	sit	see	many	got	saw	cup	put	actual	too
								(BrE)					

put down the *rebellion*. **2** [U, C] opposition to authority within an organization, a political party, etc: *(a) back-bench rebellion* **3** [U] opposition to authority; being unwilling to obey rules or accept normal standards of behaviour, dress, etc: *Teenage rebellion often starts in the home.*

re·bel·li·ous /rɪˈbeljəs/ *adj.* **1** unwilling to obey rules or accept normal standards of behaviour, dress, etc: *rebellious teenagers ◇ He has always had a rebellious streak.* **2** opposed to the government of a country; opposed to those in authority within an organization: *rebellious cities/factions* ▶ **re·bel·li·ous·ly** *adv.*: *'I don't care!' she said rebelliously.* **re·bel·li·ous·ness** *noun* [U]

re·birth /ˌriːˈbɜːθ; *AmE* -ˈbɜːrθ/ *noun* [U, sing.] **1** a period of new life, growth or activity: *the seasonal cycle of death and rebirth* **2** a spiritual change when a person's faith becomes stronger or they CONVERT to another religion

re·boot /ˌriːˈbuːt/ *verb* [VN, V] (*computing*) if you **reboot** a computer or it **reboots**, you switch it off and then start it again immediately

re·born /ˌriːˈbɔːn; *AmE* -ˈbɔːrn/ *verb, adj.*
■ *verb* [VN] (**be reborn**) (used only in the passive without *by*) **1** to become active or popular again: *With the coming of television, old legends such as those of Robin Hood and King Arthur were reborn.* **2** to be born again: *If you were reborn as an animal, which animal would you be?*
■ *adj.* **1** having become active again: *a reborn version of social democracy* **2** having experienced a complete spiritual change: *reborn evangelical Christians*—see also BORN-AGAIN

re·bound *verb, noun*
■ *verb* /rɪˈbaʊnd/ [V] **1 ~ (from/off sth)** to bounce back after hitting sth: *The ball rebounded from the goalpost and Owen headed it in.* **2 ~ (on sb)** (*formal*) if sth that you do **rebounds** on you, it has an unpleasant effect on you, especially when the effect was intended for sb else [SYN] BACKFIRE **3** (*business*) (of prices, etc.) to rise again after they have fallen: *Share prices rebounded after Friday's losses.*
■ *noun* /ˈriːbaʊnd/ **1** (*sport*) a ball that hits sth and bounces back **2** (in basketball) the act of catching the ball after a player has thrown it at the BASKET and has not scored a point **3** (especially *business*) a positive reaction that happens after sth negative: *There are signs of an economic rebound.* [IDM] **on the ˈrebound** while you are sad and confused, especially after a relationship has ended

re·buff /rɪˈbʌf/ *noun* (*formal*) an unkind refusal of a friendly offer, request or suggestion: *Her offer of help was met with a sharp rebuff.* ▶ **re·buff** *verb*: [VN] *They rebuffed her request for help.*

re·build /ˌriːˈbɪld/ *verb* (**re·built**, **re·built** /ˌriːˈbɪlt/) [VN] **1** to build or put sth together again: *After the earthquake, the people set about rebuilding their homes. ◇ He rebuilt the engine using parts from cars that had been scrapped.* **2** to make sth/sb complete and strong again: *When she lost her job, she had to rebuild her life completely. ◇ attempts to rebuild the shattered post-war economy*

re·build·ing /ˌriːˈbɪldɪŋ/ *noun* [U, sing.] the process of building sth again: *the rebuilding of London's churches after the Great Fire of 1666*

re·buke /rɪˈbjuːk/ *verb* [VN] [often passive] **~ sb (for sth/ for doing sth)** (*formal*) to speak severely to sb because they have done sth wrong [SYN] REPRIMAND: *The company was publicly rebuked for having neglected safety procedures.* ▶ **re·buke** *noun* [C, U]: *He was silenced by her stinging rebuke.*

rebut /rɪˈbʌt/ *verb* (**-tt-**) [VN] (*formal*) to say or prove that a statement or criticism is false [SYN] REFUTE: *an attempt to publicly rebut rumours of a divorce* ▶ **re·but·tal** /-tl/ *noun* [C, U]: *The accusations met with a firm rebuttal.*

re·cal·ci·trant /rɪˈkælsɪtrənt/ *adj.* (*formal*) unwilling to obey rules or follow instructions; difficult to control: *a recalcitrant child/attitude* ▶ **re·cal·ci·trance** /-əns/ *noun* [U]

re·call *verb, noun*
■ *verb* /rɪˈkɔːl/ **1** (*formal*) (not used in the progressive tenses) to remember sth: [VN] *She could not recall his*

name. ◇ [V] *If I recall correctly, he lives in Luton.* ◇ [V-ing] *I can't recall meeting her before.* ◇ [Vthat] *He recalled that she always came home late on Wednesdays.* ◇ [Vwh-] *Can you recall exactly what happened?* [also VN-ing, V speech] **2** (not used in the progressive tenses) to make sb think of sth: *The poem recalls Eliot's 'The Waste Land'.* **3** [VN] to order sb to return: *Both countries recalled their ambassadors. ◇ He was recalled to military duty. ◇ They have both been recalled to the Welsh squad* (= selected as members of the team after a time when they were not selected). **4** [VN] to ask for sth to be returned, often because there is sth wrong with it: *The company has recalled all the faulty hairdryers.*
■ *noun* /rɪˈkɔːl, ˈriːkɔːl/ **1** [U] the ability to remember sth that you have learned or sth that has happened in the past: *She has amazing powers of recall. ◇ to have instant recall* (= to be able to remember sth immediately) ◇ *to have total recall* (= to be able to remember all the details of sth) **2** [sing.] an official order or request for sb/sth to return, or for sth to be given back: *Thomas's recall to the Welsh team* [IDM] **beyond reˈcall** impossible to bring back to the original state; impossible to remember

re·cant /rɪˈkænt/ *verb* [VN, V] (*formal*) to say, often publicly, that you no longer have the same belief or opinion that you had before ▶ **re·can·ta·tion** /ˌriːkænˈteɪʃn/ *noun* [C, U]

recap /ˈriːkæp/ *verb, noun*
■ *verb* (**-pp-**) **~ (on sth)** | **~ sth** = RECAPITULATE: [V] *Let me just recap on what we've decided so far.* [also VN, Vwh-]
■ *noun* = RECAPITULATION

re·cap·itu·late /ˌriːkəˈpɪtʃuleɪt/ *verb* (*formal*) (also **recap**) **~ (on sth)** | **~ sth** to repeat or give a summary of what has already been said, decided, etc: [V] *To recapitulate briefly, the three main points are these ...* [also VN, Vwh-] ▶ **re·cap·itu·la·tion** /ˌriːkəpɪtʃuˈleɪʃn/ *noun* [C, U] (*formal*) (also **recap**)

re·cap·ture /ˌriːˈkæptʃə(r)/ *verb* [VN] **1** to win back a place, position, etc. that was previously taken from you by an enemy or a competitor: *Government troops soon recaptured the island.* **2** to catch a person or an animal that has escaped **3** to bring back a feeling or repeat an experience that you had in the past: *He was trying to recapture the happiness of his youth.* ▶ **re·cap·ture** *noun* [U]: *the recapture of towns occupied by the rebels*

re·cast /ˌriːˈkɑːst; *AmE* -ˈkæst/ *verb* (**re·cast**, **re·cast**) [VN] **1 ~ sth (as/in sth)** to change sth by organizing or presenting it in a different way: *She recast her lecture as a radio talk.* **2 ~ sb (as sth)** to change the actors or the role of a particular actor in a play, etc.

recce /ˈreki/ *noun* (*BrE, informal*) = RECONNAISSANCE: *to do a quick recce of an area*

re·cede /rɪˈsiːd/ *verb* [V] **1** (*written*) to move gradually away from sb or away from a previous position: *The sound of the truck receded into the distance. ◇ She watched his receding figure.* **2** (*written*) (especially of a problem, feeling or quality) to become gradually weaker or smaller: *The prospect of bankruptcy has now receded* (= it is less likely). ◇ *The pain was receding slightly.* **3** (of hair) to stop growing at the front of the head: *a middle-aged man with receding hair/a receding hairline* **4 a ~ chin** a chin that slopes backwards towards the neck

re·ceipt /rɪˈsiːt/ *noun* **1** (*AmE* also **ˈsales slip**) [C] **~ (for sth)** a piece of paper that shows that goods or services have been paid for: *Can I have a receipt, please? ◇ to make out* (= write) *a receipt* **2** (*formal*) **~ (of sth)** [U] the act of receiving sth: *to acknowledge receipt of a letter ◇ The goods will be dispatched on receipt of an order form. ◇ Are you in receipt of any state benefits?* **3** (**receipts**) [pl.] (*business*) money that a business, bank or government receives: *net/gross receipts*

re·ceiv·able /rɪˈsiːvəbl/ *adj.* (*business*) (usually following a noun) (of bills, accounts, etc.) for which money has not yet been received: *accounts receivable*

re·ceiv·ables /rɪˈsiːvəblz/ *noun* [pl.] (*business*) money that is owed to a business

re·ceive /rɪˈsiːv/ *verb*
GET/ACCEPT **1** [VN] **~ sth (from sb/sth)** (rather *formal*) to

get or accept sth that is sent or given to you: *to receive a letter/present/phone call* ◊ *to receive information/payment/thanks* ◊ *He received an award for bravery from the police service.*

TREATMENT/INJURY | **2** [VN] **~ sth (from sb)** to experience or be given a particular type of treatment or an injury: *We received a warm welcome from our hosts.* ◊ *Emergency cases will receive professional attention immediately.* ◊ *to receive severe injuries*

REACT TO STH | **3** [VN] [usually passive] **~ sth (with sth)** to react to sth new, in a particular way: *The play was well received by the critics.* ◊ *The statistics were received with concern.*

GUESTS | **4** [VN] [often passive] **~ sb (with sth) | ~ sb (as sth)** (*formal*) to welcome or entertain a guest, especially formally: *He was received as an honoured guest at the White House.*

AS MEMBER OF STH | **5** [VN] **~ sb (into sth)** to officially recognize and accept sb as a member of a group: *Three young people were received into the Church at Easter.*

TV/RADIO | **6** [VN] to change broadcast signals into sounds or pictures on a television, radio, etc: *to receive programmes via satellite* **7** [VN] to be able to hear a radio message that is being sent by sb: *I'm receiving you loud and clear.*

STOLEN GOODS | **8** [VN, V] (*especially BrE*) to buy or accept goods that you know have been stolen

IN SPORT | **9** (in tennis, etc.) to be the player that the SERVER hits the ball to: [V] *Hingis won the toss and chose to receive.* [also VN] —picture on page 1250

IDM be at/on the re'ceiving end (of sth) (*informal*) to be the person that an action, etc. is directed at, especially an unpleasant one: *She found herself on the receiving end of a great deal of criticism.*

re·ceived /rɪ'siːvd/ *adj.* [only before noun] (*formal*) accepted by most people as being correct: *The received wisdom is that they cannot win.*

re·ceived pronunci·'ation *noun* [U] = RP

re·ceiver /rɪ'siːvə(r)/ *noun* **1** the part of a telephone that you hold close to your mouth and ear: *to pick up/lift/put down/replace the receiver*—compare HANDSET **2** a piece of radio or television equipment that changes broadcast signals into sound or pictures: *a satellite receiver*—compare TRANSMITTER **3** (also **of,ficial re'ceiver**) (*law*) a person who is chosen by a court of law to be in charge of a company that is BANKRUPT: *to call in the receivers* **4** a person who receives sth: *Molly's more of a giver than a receiver.* **5** a person who buys or accepts stolen goods, knowing that they have been stolen **6** (in American football) a player who plays in a position in which the ball can be caught when it is being passed forward

re·ceiv·er·ship /rɪ'siːvəʃɪp; *AmE* -vərʃ-/ *noun* [U] (*law*) the state of a business being controlled by an official receiver because it has no money

re·cent /'riːsnt/ *adj.* [usually before noun] that happened or began only a short time ago: *a recent development/discovery/event* ◊ *his most recent visit to Poland* ◊ *There have been many changes in recent years.*

re·cent·ly /'riːsntli/ *adv.* not long ago: *We received a letter from him recently.* ◊ *Until recently they were living in York.* ◊ *I haven't seen them recently* (= it is some time since I saw them). ◊ *Have you used it recently* (= in the recent past)?

re·cep·tacle /rɪ'septəkl/ *noun* **1 ~ (for sth)** (*formal*) a container for putting sth in: (*figurative*) *The seas have been used as a receptacle for a range of industrial toxins.* **2** (*AmE*) = SOCKET (1)

re·cep·tion /rɪ'sepʃn/ *noun* **1** [U] (*especially BrE*) the area inside the entrance of a hotel, an office building, etc. where guests or visitors go first when they arrive: *the reception area* ◊ *We arranged to meet in reception at 6.30.* ◊ *You can leave a message with reception.* ◊ (*AmE, BrE*) *the reception desk* **2** [C] a formal social occasion to welcome sb or celebrate sth: *a wedding reception* **3** [sing.] the type of welcome that is given to sb/sth: *Her latest album has met with a mixed reception from fans.* ◊ *Delegates gave him a warm reception as he called for more spend-*

ing on education. **4** [U] the quality of radio and television signals that are broadcast: *good/bad reception* **5** [U] the act of receiving or welcoming sb: *the reception of refugees from the war zone* ◊ (*BrE*) *a reception class* (= the first class at school for children aged 4 or 5) ◊ (*BrE*) *a reception centre for refugees* (= a place where people can receive temporary help and accommodation)

re·cep·tion·ist /rɪ'sepʃənɪst/ *noun* a person whose job is to deal with people arriving at or telephoning a hotel, an office building, a doctor's SURGERY, etc.

re'ception room *noun* (*BrE*) (used especially when advertising houses for sale) a room in a house where people can sit, for example a living room or DINING ROOM

re·cep·tive /rɪ'septɪv/ *adj.* **~ (to sth)** willing to listen to or to accept new ideas or suggestions: *She was always receptive to new ideas.* ◊ *He gave an impressive speech to a receptive audience.* ▶ **re·cep·tive·ness, re·cep·tiv·ity** /,riːsep'tɪvəti/ *noun* [U]: *receptivity to change*

re·cep·tor /rɪ'septə(r)/ *noun* (*biology*) a nerve ending in the body that reacts to changes such as heat or cold and makes the body react in a particular way

re·cess *noun, verb*

■ *noun* /rɪ'ses; 'riːses/ **1** [C, U] a period of time during the year when the members of a parliament, committee, etc. do not meet **2** [C] a short break in a trial in a court of law: *The judge called a short recess.* **3** [U] (*AmE*) = BREAK ➪ note at BREAK **4** [C] a part of a wall that is set further back than the rest of the wall, forming a space [SYN] ALCOVE: *a recess for books* **5** [C, usually pl.] the part of a place that is furthest from the light and hard to see or get to: *He stared into the dark recesses of the room.* ◊ (*figurative*) *The doubt was still there, in the deep recesses of her mind.*

■ *verb* /rɪ'ses/ [often passive] **1** (*AmE*) to take or to order a recess: [VN] *The hearing was recessed for the weekend.* [also V] **2** [VN] **~ sth (in/into sth)** to put sth in a position that is set back into a wall, etc: *The lights should be recessed into the ceiling.* ◊ *recessed shelves*

re·ces·sion /rɪ'seʃn/ *noun* **1** [C, U] a difficult time for the economy of a country, when there is less trade and industrial activity than usual and more people are unemployed: *the impact of the current recession on manufacturing* ◊ *The economy is in deep recession.* ◊ *active policies to pull the country out of recession* **2** [U] (*formal*) the movement backwards of sth from a previous position: *the gradual recession of the flood water*

re·ces·sion·ary /rɪ'seʃnri; *AmE* -neri/ *adj.* [only before noun] connected with a recession or likely to cause one: *recessionary conditions*

re·ces·sive /rɪ'sesɪv/ *adj.* (*biology*) a **recessive** physical characteristic only appears in a child if it has two GENES for this characteristic, one from each parent. It does not appear if a DOMINANT characteristic is also present.

re·charge /,riː'tʃɑːdʒ; *AmE* -'tʃɑːrdʒ/ *verb* **1** to fill a battery with electrical power; to be filled with electrical power: [VN] *He plugged his razor in to recharge it.* ◊ [V] *The drill takes about three hours to recharge.* **2** [V] (*informal*) to get back your strength and energy by resting for a time: *We needed the break in order to recharge.* ▶ **re·charge·able** *adj.*: *rechargeable batteries* [IDM] **recharge your 'batteries** to get back your strength and energy by resting for a while

re·cher·ché /rə'ʃeʃeɪ; *AmE* ,rəʃer'ʃeɪ/ *adj.* (from French, *formal*, usually *disapproving*) unusual and not easy to understand, chosen in order to impress people

re·cid·iv·ist /rɪ'sɪdɪvɪst/ *noun* (*formal*) a person who continues to commit crimes, and seems unable to stop, even after being punished ▶ **re·cid·iv·ism** /-ɪzəm/ *noun* [U]

re·cipe /'resəpi/ *noun* **1 ~ (for sth)** a set of instructions that tells you how to cook sth and the items of food you need for it: *a recipe for chicken soup* ◊ *vegetarian recipes* ◊ *a recipe book* **2 ~ for sth** a method or an idea that seems likely to have a particular result: *His plans are a recipe for disaster.* ◊ *What's her recipe for success?*

re·cipi·ent /rɪ'sɪpiənt/ *noun* (*formal*) a person who receives sth: *recipients of awards/services/funds*

R

b	d	f	g	h	k	l	m	n	p	r
bad	did	fall	get	hat	cat	leg	man	now	pen	red

re·cip·ro·cal /rɪˈsɪprəkl/ *adj.* involving two people or groups who agree to help each other or behave in the same way to each other: *The two colleges have a reciprocal arrangement whereby students from one college can attend classes at the other.* ▶ **re·cip·ro·cal·ly** /-kli/ *adv.*

re·cip·ro·cate /rɪˈsɪprəkeɪt/ *verb* **1 ~ (sth) (with sth)** to behave or feel towards sb in the same way as they behave or feel towards you: [VN] *Her passion for him was not reciprocated.* ◊ *They wanted to reciprocate the kindness that had been shown to them.* ◊ *He smiled but his smile was not reciprocated.* ◊ *I wasn't sure whether to laugh or to reciprocate with a remark of my own.* **2** [V] *(technical)* to move backwards and forwards in a straight line: *a reciprocating action/movement* ▶ **re·cip·ro·ca·tion** /rɪˌsɪprəˈkeɪʃn/ *noun* [U]

reci·procity /ˌresɪˈprɒsəti; *AmE* -ˈprɑːs-/ *noun* [U] *(formal)* a situation in which two people, countries, etc. provide the same help or advantages to each other

re·cital /rɪˈsaɪtl/ *noun* **1** a public performance of music or poetry, usually given by one person or a small group: *to give a piano recital* **2** a spoken description of a series of events, etc. that is often long and boring

reci·ta·tion /ˌresɪˈteɪʃn/ *noun* **1** [C, U] an act of saying aloud a piece of poetry or literature that you have learned **2** [U] an act of talking or writing about a series of things: *She continued her recitation of the week's events.*

reci·ta·tive /ˌresɪtəˈtiːv/ *noun* [C, U] *(music)* a passage in an opera or ORATORIO that is sung in the rhythm of ordinary speech with many words on the same note

re·cite /rɪˈsaɪt/ *verb* **1 ~ (sth) (to sb)** to say aloud a poem, piece of literature, etc. that you have learned, especially to an audience: [VN] *Each child had to recite a poem to the class.* [also V, V wh-, V speech] **2 ~ sth (to sb)** to say aloud a list or series of things: [VN] *They recited all their grievances to me.* ◊ *She could recite a list of all the kings and queens.* [also V wh-, V speech]

reck·less /ˈrekləs/ *adj.* showing a lack of care about danger and the possible results of your actions: *He showed a reckless disregard for his own safety.* ◊ *She was a good rider, but reckless.* ◊ *He had always been reckless with money.* ◊ *(BrE)* *to cause death by reckless driving* ▶ **reck·less·ly** *adv.*: *He admitted driving recklessly.* **reck·less·ness** *noun* [U]

reckon /ˈrekən/ *verb* **1** *(informal)* to think sth or have an opinion about sth: [V (that)] *I reckon (that) I'm going to get that job.* ◊ *(spoken)* *He'll be famous one day. What do you reckon* (= do you agree)? ◊ [V] *It's worth a lot of money, I reckon.* ◊ *(spoken)* '*They'll never find out.*' '*You reckon?*' (= I think you may be wrong about that) **2 (be reckoned)** (not used in the progressive tenses) to be generally considered to be sth: [VN to inf] *Children are reckoned to be more sophisticated nowadays.* ◊ [VN-N] *It was generally reckoned a success.* [also VN-ADJ] **3** [V to inf] *(informal)* to expect to do sth: *We reckon to finish by ten.* **4 ~ sth (at sth)** to calculate an amount, a number, etc: [VN] *The age of the earth is reckoned at about 4600 million years.* ◊ [V (that)] *They reckon (that) their profits are down by at least 20%.* ◊ [VN to inf] *The journey was reckoned to take about two hours.* **HELP** This pattern is usually used in the passive. [also VN that] **PHRV** **ˈreckon on sth** to expect sth to happen or to rely on sth happening: *They hadn't reckoned on a rebellion.* ◊ [+ -ing] *We'd reckoned on having good weather.* **ˌreckon sth↔ˈup** *(especially BrE)* to calculate the total amount or number of sth: *He reckoned up the cost of everything in his mind.* **ˈreckon with sb/sth 1** [usually passive] to consider or treat sb/sth as a serious opponent, problem, etc: *They were already a political force to be reckoned with.* **2** (usually used in negative sentences) to consider sth as a possible problem that you should be prepared for: [+ -ing] *I didn't reckon with getting caught up in so much traffic.* **ˈreckon without sb/sth** *(especially BrE)* to not consider sb/sth as a possible problem that you should be prepared for: *They had reckoned without the determination of the opposition.*

reck·on·ing /ˈrekənɪŋ/ *noun* **1** [U, C] the act of calculating sth, especially in a way that is not very exact: *By my reckoning you still owe me £5.* **2** [C usually sing, U] a time

when sb's actions will be judged to be right or wrong and they may be punished: *In the final reckoning truth is rewarded.* ◊ *Officials concerned with environmental policy predict that a day of reckoning will come.* **IDM** **in/into/out of the ˈreckoning** *(especially BrE)* (especially in sport) among/not among those who are likely to win or be successful: *Phelan is fit again and could come into the reckoning.*

re·claim /rɪˈkleɪm/ *verb* [VN] **1 ~ sth (from sb/sth)** to get sth back or to ask to have it back after it has been lost, taken away, etc: *You'll have to go to the police station to reclaim your wallet.* ◊ *The team reclaimed the title from their rivals.*—see also BAGGAGE RECLAIM **2 ~ sth (from sth)** to make land that is naturally too wet or too dry suitable to be built on, farmed, etc: *The site for the airport will be reclaimed from the swamp.* ◊ *reclaimed marshland* **3** [usually passive] if a piece of land **is reclaimed by** desert, forest, etc., it turns back into desert, etc. after being used for farming or building **4 ~ sth (from sth)** to obtain materials from waste products so that they can be used again—see also RECYCLE **5 ~ sb (from sth)** to rescue sb from a bad or criminal way of life ▶ **rec·lam·ation** /ˌrekləˈmeɪʃn/ *noun* [U]: *land reclamation*

re·cline /rɪˈklaɪn/ *verb* **1** [V] **~ (against/in/on sth)** *(formal)* to sit or lie in a relaxed way, with your body leaning backwards: *She was reclining on a sofa.* ◊ *a reclining figure* (for example in a painting) **2** when a seat **reclines** or when you **recline** a seat, the back of it moves into a comfortable sloping position: [V] *a reclining chair/seat* [also VN]

re·cliner /rɪˈklaɪnə(r)/ (also **reˈcliner chair**) *noun* (*especially AmE*) a soft comfortable chair with a back that can be pushed back at an angle so that you can lean back in it—picture at CHAIR

re·cluse /rɪˈkluːs/ *noun* a person who lives alone and likes to avoid other people: *to lead the life of a recluse* ▶ **re·clu·sive** /rɪˈkluːsɪv/ *adj.*: *a reclusive millionaire/lifestyle*

rec·og·ni·tion /ˌrekəɡˈnɪʃn/ *noun* **1** [U] the act of remembering who sb is when you see them, or of identifying what sth is: *He glanced briefly towards her but there was no sign of recognition.* ◊ *the automatic recognition of handwriting and printed text by computer* **2** [sing., U] **~ (that ...)** the act of accepting that sth exists, is true or is official: *a growing recognition that older people have potential too* ◊ *There is a general recognition of the urgent need for reform.* ◊ *to seek international/official/formal recognition as a sovereign state* **3** [U] **~ (for sth)** public praise and reward for sb's work or actions: *She gained only minimal recognition for her work.* ◊ *He received the award in recognition of his success over the past year.* **IDM** **to change, alter, etc. beyond/out of (all) recogˈnition** to change so much that you can hardly recognize it: *The town has changed beyond recognition since I was last here.*

rec·og·niz·able (*BrE* also **-is·able**) /ˈrekəɡnaɪzəbl; ˌrekəɡˈnaɪzəbl/ *adj.* **~ (as sth/sb)** easy to know or identify: *The building was easily recognizable as a prison.* ◊ *After so many years she was still instantly recognizable.* **OPP** UNRECOGNIZABLE ▶ **rec·og·niz·ably, -is·ably** /-əbli/ *adv.*

rec·og·niz·ance (*BrE* also **-sance**) /rɪˈkɒɡnɪzəns; *AmE* -ˈkɑːɡ-/ *noun* [U] *(law)* a promise by sb who is accused of a crime to appear in a court of law on a particular date; a sum of money paid as a GUARANTEE of this promise

rec·og·nize (*BrE* also **-ise**) /ˈrekəɡnaɪz/ *verb* (not used in the progressive tenses) **1** [VN] **~ sb/sth (by/from sth)** to know who sb is or what sth is when you see or hear them, because you have seen or heard them or it before: *I recognized him as soon as he came in the room.* ◊ *Do you recognize this tune?* ◊ *I recognized her by her red hair.* **2 ~ sth (as sth)** to admit or to be aware that sth exists or is true: [VN] *They recognized the need to take the problem seriously.* ◊ *Drugs were not recognized as a problem then.* ◊ [V wh-] *Nobody recognized how urgent the situation was.* ◊ [V that] *We recognized that the task was not straight-*

forward. ◊ [VN **that**] *It was recognized that this solution could only be temporary.* [also VN **to** inf] **3** ~ **sb/sth (as sth)** to accept and approve of sb/sth officially: [VN] *recognized schools/qualifications* ◊ *The UK has refused to recognize the new regime.* ◊ [VN **to** inf] *He is recognized to be their natural leader.* **HELP** This pattern is usually used in the passive. **4** [VN] **(be recognized (as sth))** to be thought of as very good or important by people in general: *The book is now recognized as a classic.* ◊ *She's a recognized authority on the subject.* **5** [VN] to give sb official thanks for sth that they have done or achieved: *His services to the state were recognized with the award of a knighthood.*

re·coil *verb, noun*
■ *verb* /rɪˈkɔɪl/ [V] **1** ~ **(from sb/sth)** | ~ **(at sth)** (*written*) to move your body quickly away from sb/sth because you find them or it frightening or unpleasant: *She recoiled from his touch.* ◊ *He recoiled in horror at the sight of the corpse.* **2** ~ **(from sth/from doing sth)** | ~ **(at sth)** (*written*) to react to an idea or a situation with strong dislike or fear: *She recoiled from the idea of betraying her own brother.* **3** (of a gun) to move suddenly backwards when you fire it
■ *noun* /ˈriːkɔɪl/ [U, sing.] a sudden movement backwards, especially of a gun when it is fired

rec·ol·lect /ˌrekəˈlekt/ *verb* (not used in the progressive tenses) (rather *formal*) to remember sth, especially by making an effort to remember it: [VN] *She could no longer recollect the details of the letter.* ◊ [V **wh-**] *I don't recollect what he said.* ◊ [VN -**ing**] *I recollect him/his saying that it was dangerous.* ◊ [V] *As far as I can recollect, she wasn't there on that occasion.* [also V **speech**, V **that**, V -**ing**]

rec·ol·lec·tion /ˌrekəˈlekʃn/ *noun* (*formal*) **1** [U] ~ **(of sth/of doing sth)** the ability to remember sth; the act of remembering sth **SYN** MEMORY: *I have no recollection of meeting her before.* ◊ *My recollection of events differs from his.* ◊ *To the best of my recollection* (= if I remember correctly) *I was not present at that meeting.* **2** [C] a thing that you remember from the past **SYN** MEMORY: *to have a clear/vivid/dim/vague recollection of sth*

re·com·mence /ˌriːkəˈmens/ *verb* (*formal*) to begin again; to start doing sth again: [V] *Work on the bridge will recommence next month.* ◊ [VN] *The two countries agreed to recommence talks the following week.* [also V -**ing**]

rec·om·mend /ˌrekəˈmend/ *verb* **1** [VN] ~ **sb/sth (to sb) (for/as sth)** to tell sb that sth is good or useful, or that sb would be suitable for a particular job, etc: *Can you recommend a good hotel?* ◊ *I recommend the book to all my students.* ◊ *She was recommended for the post by a colleague.* ◊ *The hotel's new restaurant comes highly recommended* (= a lot of people have praised it). **2** to advise a particular course of action; to advise sb to do sth: [VN] *The report recommended a 10% pay increase.* ◊ *It is dangerous to exceed the recommended dose.* ◊ *a recommended price of $50* ◊ [V **(that)**] *I recommend (that) he see a lawyer.* ◊ (*BrE also*) *I recommend (that) he should see a lawyer.* ◊ [VN **(that)**] *It is strongly recommended that the machines should be checked every year.* ◊ [VN **to** inf] *We'd recommend you to book your flight early.* ◊ [V -**ing**] *He recommended reading the book before seeing the movie.* [also VN -**ing**, V **wh-**] **3** [VN] ~ **sb/sth (to sb)** to make sb/sth seem attractive or good: *This system has much to recommend it.*

rec·om·men·da·tion /ˌrekəmenˈdeɪʃn/ *noun* **1** [C] ~ **(to sb) (for/on/about sth)** an official suggestion about the best thing to do: *to accept/reject a recommendation* ◊ *The committee made recommendations to the board on teachers' pay and conditions.* ◊ *I had the operation on the recommendation of my doctor.* **2** [U] the act of telling sb that sth is good or useful or that sb would be suitable for a particular job, etc: *We chose the hotel on their recommendation* (= because they recommended it). ◊ *It's best to find a builder through personal recommendation.* **3** [C] (*especially AmE*) a formal letter or statement that sb would be suitable for a particular job, etc: *The company gave her a glowing recommendation.*

rec·om·pense /ˈrekəmpens/ *noun, verb*
■ *noun* [U] ~ **(for sth/sb)** (*formal*) something, usually money, that you are given because you have suffered in some way, or as a payment for sth: *There must be* adequate recompense for workers who lose their jobs. ◊ *I received $1000 in recompense for loss of earnings.*
■ *verb* [VN] ~ **sb (for sth)** (*formal*) to do sth for sb or give them a payment for sth that they have suffered **SYN** COMPENSATE: *There was no attempt to recompense the miners for the loss of their jobs.*

recon /ˈriːkɒn; *AmE* rɪˈkɑːn/ *noun* [C, U] (*AmE, informal*) = RECONNAISSANCE

rec·on·cile /ˈrekənsaɪl/ *verb* [VN] **1** ~ **sth (with sth)** to find a satisfactory way of dealing with two or more ideas, needs, etc. that seem to be opposed to each other: *an attempt to reconcile the need for industrial development with concern for the environment* ◊ *It was hard to reconcile his career ambitions with the needs of his children.* **2** [usually passive] ~ **sb (with sb)** to make people become friends again after an argument or a disagreement: *The pair were reconciled after Jackson made a public apology.* ◊ *He has recently been reconciled with his wife.* **3** ~ **sb/ yourself (to sth)** to make sb/yourself accept an unpleasant situation because it is not possible to change it: *He could not reconcile himself to the prospect of losing her.* ▶ **rec·on·cil·able** /ˌrekənˈsaɪləbl/ *adj.*

rec·on·cili·ation /ˌrekənsɪliˈeɪʃn/ *noun* **1** [sing.] ~ **(between A and B)** | ~ **(with sb)** an end to a disagreement and the start of a good relationship again: *Their change of policy brought about a reconciliation with Britain.* **2** [U] ~ **(between A and B)** | ~ **(with sth)** the process of making it possible for two different ideas, facts, etc. to exist together without being opposed to each other: *the reconciliation between environment and development* ◊ *the reconciliation of rights and duties within a democracy*

rec·on·dite /ˈrekəndaɪt/ *adj.* (*formal*) not known about or understood by many people

re·con·di·tion /ˌriːkənˈdɪʃn/ *verb* [VN] [often passive] to repair sth so that it is in good condition and works well: *a reconditioned engine*

re·con·nais·sance /rɪˈkɒnɪsns; *AmE* -ˈkɑːn-/ (also *BrE informal* **recce**) (also *AmE informal* **recon**) *noun* [C, U] the activity of getting information about an area for military purposes, using soldiers, planes, etc: *to make an aerial reconnaissance of the island* ◊ *Time spent on reconnaissance is seldom wasted.* ◊ *a reconnaissance aircraft/ mission/satellite*

rec·on·noitre (*BrE*) (*AmE* -**ter**) /ˌrekəˈnɔɪtə(r)/ *verb* to get information about an area, especially for military purposes, by using soldiers, planes, etc: [VN] *A naval patrol was sent to reconnoitre the approaches to the bay.* [also V]

re·con·sider /ˌriːkənˈsɪdə(r)/ *verb* to think about sth again, especially because you might want to change a previous decision or opinion: [VN] *to reconsider your decision/position* ◊ *The company was forced to reconsider its plans for expansion.* ◊ [V] *Recent information may persuade the board to reconsider.* [also V **wh-**] ▶ **re·con·sid·er·ation** /ˌriːkənsɪdəˈreɪʃn/ *noun* [U, sing.]

re·con·sti·tute /ˌriːˈkɒnstɪtjuːt; *AmE* -ˈkɑːnstətuːt/ *verb* [VN] **1** ~ **sth/itself (as sth)** (*formal*) to form an organization or a group again in a different way: *The group reconstituted itself as a political party.* **2** [usually passive] to bring dried food, etc. back to its original form by adding water: *reconstituted orange juice/eggs* ▶ **re·con·sti·tu·tion** /ˌriːkɒnstɪˈtjuːʃn; *AmE* -ˌkɑːnstəˈtuːʃn/ *noun* [U]

re·con·struct /ˌriːkənˈstrʌkt/ *verb* [VN] **1** ~ **sth (from sth)** to build or make sth again that has been damaged or that no longer exists: *They have tried to reconstruct the settlement as it would have been in Iron Age times.* **2** to be able to describe or show exactly how a past event happened, using the information you have gathered: *Investigators are trying to reconstruct the circumstances of the crash.*

re·con·struc·tion /ˌriːkənˈstrʌkʃn/ *noun* **1** [U] the process of changing or improving the condition of sth or the way it works; the process of putting sth back into the state it was in before: *the reconstruction of the educational system* ◊ *the post-war reconstruction of Germany* ◊ *a reconstruction period* **2** [U] the activity of building again sth

æ	ɑː	e	ɜː	ə	ɪ	iː	i	ɒ	ɔː	ʌ	ʊ	u	uː
cat	father	ten	bird	about	sit	see	many	got	saw	cup	put	actual	too
								(BrE)					

R

that has been damaged or destroyed: *the reconstruction of the sea walls* **3** [C] a copy of sth that no longer exists: *The doorway is a 19th century reconstruction of Norman work.* **4** [C] a short film showing events that are known to have happened in order to try and get more information or better understanding, especially about a crime: *Last night police staged a reconstruction of the incident.*

re·con·struct·ive /ˌriːkənˈstrʌktɪv/ *adj.* [only before noun] (of medical treatment) that involves RECONSTRUCT-ING part of a person's body because it has been badly damaged or because the person wants to change its shape: *reconstructive surgery*

re·con·vene /ˌriːkənˈviːn/ *verb* [V, VN] if a meeting, parliament, etc. **reconvenes** or if sb **reconvenes** it, it meets again after a break

re·cord *noun, verb*
■ *noun* /ˈrekɔːd; AmE ˈrekərd/
WRITTEN ACCOUNT | **1** [C] ~ **(of sth)** a written account of sth that is kept so that it can be looked at and used in the future: *You should keep a record of your expenses.* ◊ *medical/dental records* ◊ *Last summer was the wettest on record.*
MUSIC | **2** [C] a thin round piece of plastic on which music, etc. is recorded: *to play a record* ◊ *a record collection* ◊ *a record company* (= one which produces and sells records)
HIGHEST/BEST | **3** [C] the best result or the highest or lowest level that has ever been reached, especially in sport: *She holds the world record for the 100 metres.* ◊ *to break the record* (= to achieve a better result than there has ever been before) ◊ *to set a new record* ◊ *There was a record number of candidates for the post.* ◊ *I got to work in record time.* ◊ *record profits/sales* ◊ *Unemployment has reached a record high* (= the highest level ever).
OF SB/STH'S PAST | **4** [sing.] ~ **(on sth)** the facts that are known about sb/sth's past behaviour, character, achievements, etc: *The report criticizes the government's record on housing.* ◊ *The airline has a good safety record.* ◊ *He has an impressive record of achievement.*—see also TRACK RECORD
OF CRIMES | **5** (also ˌcriminal ˈrecord) [C] the fact of having committed crimes in the past: *Does he have a record?*
IDM **(just) for the ˈrecord 1** used to show that you want what you are saying to be officially written down and remembered **2** used to emphasize a point that you are making, so that the person you are speaking to takes notice: *And, for the record, he would be the last person I'd ask.* ˌoff the ˈrecord if you tell sb sth **off the record**, it is not yet official and you do not want them to repeat it publicly **put/place sth on (the) ˈrecord | be/go on (the) ˈrecord (as saying …)** to say sth publicly or officially so that it may be written down and repeated: *He didn't want to go on the record as either praising or criticizing the proposal.* ◊ *I should like to place on record my sincere thanks to all those who have given support.* **put/set the ˈrecord straight** to give people the correct information about sth in order to make it clear that what they previously believed was in fact wrong—more at MATTER *n.*
■ *verb* /rɪˈkɔːd; AmE rɪˈkɔːrd/
KEEP ACCOUNT | **1** to keep a permanent account of facts or events by writing them down, filming them, storing them in a computer, etc: [VN] *Her childhood is recorded in the diaries of those years.* ◊ *You should record all your expenses during your trip.* ◊ [Vwh-] *His job is to record how politicians vote on major issues.* [also Vthat, VN that]
MAKE COPY | **2** to make a copy of music, a film/movie, etc. by storing it on tape or a disc so that you can listen to or watch it again: [VN] *Did you remember to record 'Friends' for me?* ◊ *a recorded programme/concert* ◊ [VN-ing] *He recorded the class rehearsing before the performance.* ◊ [V] *Tell me when the tape starts recording.*
MUSIC | **3** to perform music so that it can be copied onto and kept on tape: [VN] *The band is back in the US record-ing their new album.* [also V]
MAKE OFFICIAL STATEMENT | **4** to make an official or legal statement about sth: [VN] *The coroner recorded a verdict of accidental death.* [also Vthat]

OF MEASURING INSTRUMENT | **5** to show a particular measure-ment or amount: [VN] *The thermometer recorded a tem-perature of 40°C.* [also Vwh-]

ˈrecord-breaker *noun* a person or thing that achieves a better result or higher level than has ever been achieved before ► **ˈrecord-breaking** *adj.* [only before noun]: *a record-breaking jump*

reˌcorded deˈlivery (BrE) (AmE ˌcertified ˈmail) *noun* [U] a method of sending a letter or parcel/package in which the person sending it gets an official note to say it has been posted and the person receiving it must sign a form when it is delivered: *I'd like to send this (by) recorded delivery.*—compare REGISTERED MAIL

re·cord·er /rɪˈkɔːdə(r); AmE -ˈkɔːrd-/ *noun* **1** (in com-pounds) a machine for recording sound or pictures or both: *a tape/cassette recorder* ◊ *a video recorder*—see also FLIGHT RECORDER **2** a musical instrument in the shape of a pipe that you blow into, with holes that you cover with your fingers **3** a judge in a court of law in some parts of Britain and the US **4** a person who keeps a record of events or facts

ˈrecord holder *noun* a person who has achieved the best result that has ever been achieved in a sport

re·cord·ing /rɪˈkɔːdɪŋ; AmE -ˈkɔːrd-/ *noun* **1** [C] sound or pictures that have been recorded on tape, video, etc: *a cassette/tape/video recording* ◊ *a hit recording on cassette and CD* **2** [U] the process of making a record, tape, film/movie, etc: *during the recording of the show* ◊ *recording equipment/techniques* ◊ *a recording session/studio* **3** [U] the process or act of writing down and storing informa-tion for official purposes: *the recording of financial trans-actions*

ˈrecord player *noun* a piece of equipment for playing records in order to listen to the music, etc. on them

re·count¹ /rɪˈkaʊnt/ *verb* ~ **sth (to sb)** (*formal*) to tell sb about sth, especially sth that you have experienced: [VN] *She was asked to recount the details of the conversation to the court.* ◊ [Vwh-] *They recounted what had happened during those years.* [also Vspeech]

re·count² /ˌriːˈkaʊnt/ *verb* [VN] to count sth again, espe-cially votes ► **re·count** /ˈriːkaʊnt/ *noun*: *The defeated candidate demanded a recount.*

re·coup /rɪˈkuːp/ *verb* [VN] to get back an amount of money that you have spent or lost SYN RECOVER: *We hope to recoup our initial investment in the first year.*

re·course /rɪˈkɔːs; AmE ˈriːkɔːrs/ *noun* [U] (*formal*) the fact of having to, or being able to, use sth that can provide help in a difficult situation: *Your only recourse is legal action.* ◊ *She made a complete recovery without recourse to surgery.* ◊ *The government, when necessary has recourse to the armed forces.*

re·cover /rɪˈkʌvə(r)/ *verb*
FROM ILLNESS | **1** [V] ~ **(from sth)** to get well again after being ill/sick, hurt, etc: *He's still recovering from his operation.*
FROM STH UNPLEASANT | **2** [V] ~ **(from sth)** to return to a normal state after an unpleasant or unusual experience or a period of difficulty: *It can take many years to recover from the death of a loved one.* ◊ *The economy is at last beginning to recover.*
MONEY | **3** [VN] ~ **sth (from sb/sth)** to get back the same amount of money that you have spent or that is owed to you SYN RECOUP: *He is unlikely to ever recover his legal costs.*
STH LOST/STOLEN | **4** [VN] ~ **sth (from sb/sth)** to get back or find sth that was lost, stolen or missing: *The police eventu-ally recovered the stolen paintings.* ◊ *Six bodies were recovered from the wreckage.*
POSITION/STATUS | **5** [VN] to win back a position, level, sta-tus, etc. that has been lost SYN REGAIN: *The team recovered its lead in the second half.*
SENSES/EMOTIONS | **6** [VN] to get back the use of your senses, control of your emotions, etc. SYN REGAIN: *It took her a few minutes to recover consciousness.* ◊ *to recover your*

aɪ	aʊ	eɪ	əʊ	oʊ	ɔɪ	ɪə	eə	ʊə	j	w
my	now	say	go	go	boy	near	hair	pure	yes	wet
			(BrE)	(AmE)						

sight/hearing ◊ *She seemed upset but quickly recovered herself.*

▶ **re·covered** *adj.* [not before noun]: *She is now fully recovered from her injuries.*

re-cover /ˌriːˈkʌvə(r)/ *verb* [VN] to put a new cover on sth

re·cov·er·able /rɪˈkʌvərəbl/ *adj.* **1** that you can get back after it has been spent or lost: *Travel expenses will be recoverable from the company.* ◊ *recoverable costs/damages* **2** that can be obtained from the ground: *recoverable oil reserves*

re·cov·ery /rɪˈkʌvəri/ *noun* (*pl.* **-ies**) **1** [U, C, usually sing.] ~ **(from sth)** the process of becoming well again after an illness or injury: *My father has made a full recovery from the operation.* ◊ *to make a remarkable/quick/speedy/slow recovery* ◊ *She is on the road to* (= making progress towards) *recovery.* **2** [U, C, usually sing.] ~ **(in sth)** the process of improving or becoming stronger again: *The government is forecasting an economic recovery.* ◊ *a recovery in consumer spending* ◊ *The economy is showing signs of recovery.* **3** [U] ~ **(of sth)** the action or process of getting sth back that has been lost or stolen: *There is a reward for information leading to the recovery of the missing diamonds.* **4** [U] (also re**'covery room** [C]) the room in a hospital where patients are kept immediately after an operation: *Your mother is now in recovery.*

re-create /ˌriːkriˈeɪt/ *verb* [VN] to make sth that existed in the past exist or seem to exist again: *The movie recreates the glamour of 1940s Hollywood.* ▶ **re·cre·ation** /-ˈeɪʃn/ *noun* [C, U]: *The writer attempts a recreation of the sights and sounds of his childhood.*

rec·re·ation /ˌrekriˈeɪʃn/ *noun* **1** [U] the fact of people doing things for enjoyment, when they are not working: *the need to improve facilities for leisure and recreation* ◊ *the increasing use of land for recreation* **2** [C] (*BrE*) a particular activity that sb does when they are not working: *His recreations include golf, football and shooting.*

rec·re·ation·al /ˌrekriˈeɪʃənl/ *adj.* connected with activities that people do for enjoyment when they are not working: *recreational activities/facilities* ◊ *These areas are set aside for public recreational use.*

recre'ational vehicle *noun* (*AmE*) (*abbr.* **RV**) = CAMPER (2)

recre'ation ground *noun* (*BrE*) an area of land used by the public for sports and games

recre'ation room (also *AmE informal* **'rec room**) *noun* **1** a room in a school, a hospital, an office building, etc. in which people can relax, play games, etc. **2** (*AmE*) a room in a private house used for games, entertainment, etc.

re·crim·in·ation /rɪˌkrɪmɪˈneɪʃn/ *noun* [C, usually pl., U] an angry statement that sb makes accusing sb else of sth, especially in response to a similar statement from them: *bitter recriminations* ◊ *We spent the rest of the evening in mutual recrimination.* ▶ **re·crim·in·atory** /rɪˈkrɪmɪnətri; *AmE* -tɔːri/ *adj.*

rec room /ˈrek ruːm; *AmE* rʊm/ *noun* (*AmE, informal*) = RECREATION ROOM

re-cruit /rɪˈkruːt/ *verb, noun*
- *verb* **1** to find new people to join a company, an organization, the armed forces, etc: [VN] *The police are trying to recruit more officers from ethnic minorities.* ◊ *They recruited several new members to the club.* ◊ [V] *He's responsible for recruiting at all levels.* [also VN to inf] **2** [VN to inf] to persuade sb to do sth, especially to help you: *We were recruited to help peel the vegetables.* **3** [VN] to form a new army, team, etc. by persuading new people to join it: *to recruit a task force* ▶ **re·cruit·er** *noun* **re·cruit·ment** *noun* [U]: *the recruitment of new members* ◊ *a recruitment drive*
- *noun* **1** a person who has recently joined the armed forces or the police: *the training of new recruits* ◊ *He spoke of us scornfully as raw recruits* (= people without training or experience) **2** a person who joins an organization, a company, etc: *attempts to attract new recruits to the nursing profession*

rec·tal /ˈrektəl/ *adj.* (*anatomy*) relating to the RECTUM: *rectal cancer*

rect·angle /ˈrektæŋgl/ *noun* a flat shape with four straight sides, two of which are longer than the other two, and four angles of 90°—picture at PARALLELOGRAM ▶ **rect·angu·lar** /rekˈtæŋgjələ(r)/ *adj.*

rect·ify /ˈrektɪfaɪ/ *verb* (**rec·ti·fies, rec·ti·fy·ing, rec·ti·fied, rec·ti·fied**) [VN] (*formal*) to put right sth that is wrong SYN CORRECT: *to rectify a fault/mistake* ◊ *We must take steps to rectify the situation.* ▶ **rec·ti·fi·ca·tion** /ˌrektɪfɪˈkeɪʃn/ *noun* [U]

rec·ti·lin·ear /ˌrektɪˈlɪniə(r)/ *adj.* (*technical*) **1** in a straight line: *rectilinear motion* **2** having straight lines: *rectilinear forms*

rec·ti·tude /ˈrektɪtjuːd; *AmE* -tuːd/ *noun* [U] (*formal*) the quality of thinking or behaving in a correct and honest way: *to have a sense of moral rectitude*

recto /ˈrektəʊ; *AmE* -toʊ/ *noun* (*pl.* **-os**) (*technical*) the page on the right side of an open book OPP VERSO

rec·tor /ˈrektə(r)/ *noun* **1** an Anglican priest who is in charge of a particular area, (called a PARISH). In the past a rector received an income directly from this area.—compare VICAR **2** (in Britain) a person who is in charge of a university, college or school

rec·tory /ˈrektəri/ *noun* (*pl.* **-ies**) *noun* a house where the rector of a church lives, or lived in the past

rec·tum /ˈrektəm/ *noun* (*pl.* **rec·tums** or **recta** /ˈrektə/) (*anatomy*) the end section of the tube through which solid waste leaves the body at the ANUS—picture at BODY

re·cum·bent /rɪˈkʌmbənt/ *adj.* [usually before noun] (*formal*) (of a person's body or position) lying down: *her recumbent body/form* ◊ *in a recumbent posture*

re·cu·per·ate /rɪˈkuːpəreɪt/ *verb* (*formal*) **1** [V] ~ **(from sth)** to get back your health, strength or energy after being ill/sick, tired, injured, etc. SYN RECOVER: *He's still recuperating from his operation.* ◊ *After an exhausting few weeks I needed some time to recuperate.* **2** [VN] to get back money that you have spent or lost SYN RECOVER, RECOUP: *He hoped to recuperate at least some of his losses.* ▶ **re·cu·per·ation** /rɪˌkuːpəˈreɪʃn/ *noun* [U]: *It was a period of rest and recuperation.*

re·cu·pera·tive /rɪˈkuːpərətɪv/ *adj.* (*formal*) helping you to get better after you have been ill/sick, very tired, etc: *the recuperative powers of a good night's sleep*

recur /rɪˈkɜː(r)/ *verb* (**-rr-**) [V] to happen again or a number of times: *This theme recurs several times throughout the book.* ◊ *a recurring illness/problem/nightmare*

re·cur·rence /rɪˈkʌrəns; *AmE* -ˈkɜːr-/ *noun* [C, usually sing, U] if there is **a recurrence of** sth, it happens again: *attempts to prevent a recurrence of the illness/problem*

re·cur·rent /rɪˈkʌrənt; *AmE* -ˈkɜːr-/ *adj.* that happens again and again: *recurrent bleeding/infections* ◊ *recurrent costs/expenditure*

re,curring 'decimal *noun* (*mathematics*) a DECIMAL FRACTION in which the same figure or group of figures is repeated for ever, for example 3.999…: *The recurring decimal 3.999…is also described as 3.9 recurring.*

re·cycle /ˌriːˈsaɪkl/ *verb* [VN] **1** to treat things that have already been used so that they can be used again: *Denmark recycles nearly 85% of its paper.* ◊ *This envelope is made from recycled paper.* **2** to use the same ideas, methods, jokes, etc. again: *He recycled all his old jokes.* ▶ **re·cyc·lable** /ˌriːˈsaɪkləbl/ *adj.*: *recyclable plastic* **re·cyc·ling** *noun* [U]: *the recycling of glass* ◊ *a recycling plant*

red /red/ *adj., noun*
- *adj.* (**red·der, red·dest**) (*informal*) **1** having the colour of blood or fire: *a red car/sunset* ◊ *The lights* (= traffic lights) *changed to red before I could get across.* **2** (of the eyes) BLOODSHOT (= with thin lines of blood in them) or surrounded by red or very pink skin: *Her eyes were red from crying.* **3** (of the face) bright red or pink, especially because you are angry, embarrassed or ashamed: *He stammered something and went very red in the face.* **4** (of hair or an animal's fur) reddish-brown in colour: *a red-haired girl* ◊ *red deer/squirrels*—see also REDHEAD

b	d	f	g	h	k	l	m	n	p	r
bad	**did**	**fall**	**get**	**hat**	**cat**	**leg**	**man**	**now**	**pen**	**red**

5 (*informal*) (sometimes *disapproving*, *politics*) having very LEFT-WING political opinions—compare PINK ▶ **red-ness** *noun* [U, sing.]: *You may notice redness and swelling after the injection.* **IDM** **red in ˌtooth and ˈclaw** involving opposition or competition that is violent and without pity: *nature, red in tooth and claw* **a red rag to a ˈbull** something that is likely to make sb very angry—more at PAINT *v.*

■ *noun* **1** [C, U] the colour of blood or fire: *She often wears red.* ◇ *the reds and browns of the woods in the fall* (= of the leaves) ◇ *I've marked the corrections in red* (= in red ink). ◇ *The traffic lights were on red.* **2** [U, C] red wine: *Would you prefer red or white?* ◇ *an Italian red* **3** [C] (*informal*) (*disapproving*, *politics*) a person with very LEFT-WING political opinions—compare PINKO **IDM** **be in the ˈred** (*informal*) to owe money to your bank because you have spent more than you have in your account: *The company has plunged $37 million into the red.*—compare BE IN THE BLACK **see ˈred** (*informal*) to become very angry

ˌred aˈlert *noun* [U, sing.] a situation in which you are prepared for sth dangerous to happen; a warning of this: *Following the bomb blast, local hospitals have been put on red alert.*

ˌred-ˈblooded *adj.* [usually before noun] (*informal*) full of strength and energy, often sexual energy: *red-blooded young males*

ˈred-brick *adj.* [usually before noun] **1** (of buildings, walls, etc.) built with bricks of a reddish-brown colour: *red-brick cottages* **2** (becoming *old-fashioned*) (of universities in Britain) built in the late 19th or early 20th century, in contrast to older universities, such as Oxford and Cambridge—compare OXBRIDGE

ˌred ˈcard *noun* (in football) a card shown by the REFEREE to a player who has broken the rules of the game and is not allowed to play for the rest of the game—compare YELLOW CARD

ˌred ˈcarpet (usually **the red carpet**) *noun* [sing.] a strip of red carpet laid on the ground for an important visitor to walk on when he or she arrives: *I didn't expect to be given the red carpet treatment!*

ˌred ˈcent *noun* [sing.] (*AmE*) (especially after a negative) a very small amount of money: *I didn't get a red cent for all my work.*

the ˌRed ˈCrescent *noun* [sing.] the name used by national branches in Muslim countries of the International Movement of the Red Cross and the Red Crescent, an organization that takes care of people suffering because of war or natural disasters

the ˌRed ˈCross *noun* [sing.] an international organization that takes care of people suffering because of war or natural disasters. Its full name is the International Movement of the Red Cross and the Red Crescent.

red-cur-rant /ˌredˈkʌrənt; *AmE* -ˈkɜːr-/ *noun* a very small red berry that grows in bunches on a bush and can be eaten: *redcurrant jelly* ◇ *a redcurrant bush*

red-den /ˈredn/ *verb* to become red; to make sth red: [V] *The sky was reddening.* ◇ *He could feel his face reddening with embarrassment.* ◇ *He stared at her and she reddened.* [also VN]

red-dish /ˈredɪʃ/ *adj.* fairly red in colour: *reddish hair/ fur*

re-dec-or-ate /ˌriːˈdekəreɪt/ *verb* to put new paint and/or paper on the walls of a room or house: [V] *We've just redecorated.* ◇ [VN] *The house has been fully redecorated.* ▶ **re-dec-or-ation** /ˌriːˌdekəˈreɪʃn/ *noun* [U]

re-deem /rɪˈdiːm/ *verb* [VN] **1** to make sb/sth seem less bad [SYN] COMPENSATE FOR: *The excellent acting wasn't enough to redeem a weak plot.* ◇ *The only redeeming feature of the job* (= good thing about it) *is the salary.* **2** ~ **yourself** to do sth to improve the opinion that people have of you, especially after you have done sth bad: *He has a chance to redeem himself after last week's mistakes.* **3** (in Christianity) to save sb from the power of evil: *Jesus Christ came to redeem us from sin.* **4** to pay the full sum of money that you owe sb; to pay a debt: *to redeem a loan/mortgage* **5** to exchange sth such as shares or VOUCHERS for money or goods: *This voucher can be*

redeemed at any of our branches. **6** to get back a valuable object from sb by paying them back the money you borrowed from them in exchange for the object: *He was able to redeem his watch from the pawnshop.* **7** (*formal*) ~ **a pledge/promise** to do what you have promised to do

re-deem-able /rɪˈdiːməbl/ *adj.* ~ (**against sth**) that can be exchanged for money or goods: *These vouchers are redeemable against any future purchase.*

Re-deem-er /rɪˈdiːmə(r)/ *noun* (**the Redeemer**) [sing.] (*literary*) Jesus Christ

re-define /ˌriːdɪˈfaɪn/ *verb* to change the nature or limits of sth; to make people consider sth in a new way: [VN] *The new constitution redefined the powers of the president.* ◇ [Vwh-] *We need to redefine what we mean by democracy.* ▶ **re-def-in-ition** /ˌriːdefɪˈnɪʃn/ *noun* [U, C]

re-demp-tion /rɪˈdempʃn/ *noun* [U] **1** (*formal*) the act of saving or state of being saved from the power of evil; the act of REDEEMING: *the redemption of the world from sin* **2** (*finance*) the act of exchanging shares for money (= of REDEEMING them) **IDM** **beyond/past reˈdemption** too bad to be saved or improved

re-demp-tive /rɪˈdemptɪv/ *adj.* (*formal*) that saves you from the power of evil: *the redemptive power of love*

re-deploy /ˌriːdɪˈplɔɪ/ *verb* [VN] ~ **sb/sth** (**to sth**) to move sb/sth to a new position or job: *Our troops are to be redeployed elsewhere.* ◇ *Most of the employees will be redeployed to other parts of the company.* ▶ **re-deploy-ment** *noun* [U]: *the redeployment of staff/resources*

re-design /ˌriːdɪˈzaɪn/ *verb* [VN] to design sth again, in a different way ▶ **re-design** *noun* [U, C]

re-develop /ˌriːdɪˈveləp/ *verb* to change an area by building new roads, houses, factories, etc: [VN] *The city has plans to redevelop the site.* [also V] ▶ **re-devel-op-ment** *noun* [U]: *inner-city redevelopment*

ˈred-eye *noun* **1** (also **ˌred-eye ˈflight**) [C] (*informal*, especially *AmE*) a flight in a plane at night, on which you cannot get enough sleep: *We took the red-eye to Boston.* **2** [U] the appearance of having red eyes that people sometimes have in photographs taken using FLASH

ˌred-ˈfaced *adj.* with a red face, especially because you are embarrassed or angry

ˌred ˈflag *noun* **1** a flag used to warn people of danger **2** a red flag as a symbol of revolution or COMMUNISM

ˌred ˈgiant *noun* (*astronomy*) a large star towards the end of its life that is relatively cool and gives out a reddish light

ˌred-ˈhanded *adj.* **IDM** see CATCH *v.*

red-head /ˈredhed/ *noun* a person who has red hair ▶ **ˌred-ˈheaded** *adj.*: *a red-headed girl*

ˌred ˈherring *noun* an unimportant fact, idea, event, etc. that takes people's attention away from the important ones **ORIGIN** From the custom of using the scent of a smoked, dried herring (which was red) to train dogs to hunt.

ˌred-ˈhot *adj.* **1** (of metal or sth burning) so hot that it looks red: *Red-hot coals glowed in the fire.* **2** showing strong feeling: *her red-hot anger* **3** (*informal*) new, exciting and of great interest to people: *a red-hot issue* **4** used to describe the person, animal or team that is considered almost certain to win a race, etc: *The race was won by the red-hot favourite.*

ˌRed ˈIndian (also **red-skin**) *noun* (*old-fashioned*, ⚠) a very offensive word for a Native American

re-dir-ect /ˌriːdəˈrekt; -dɪ-; -daɪ-/ *verb* [VN] ~ **sth** (**to sth**) **1** to use sth, for example money, in a different way or for a different purpose: *Resources are being redirected to this important new project.* **2** to send sth to a different address or in a different direction: *Inquiries on this matter are being redirected to the press office.* ◇ (*BrE*) *Make sure you get your mail redirected to your new address.* ▶ **re-dir-ection** *noun* [sing., U]: *a sudden redirection of economic policy* ◇ (*BrE*) *the redirection of mail*

re-dis-cover /ˌriːdɪˈskʌvə(r)/ *verb* [VN] to find again sth that had been forgotten or lost ▶ **re-dis-cov-ery** /ˌriːdɪˈskʌvəri/ *noun* [U, C] (*pl.* **-ies**)

re-dis-trib-ute /ˌriːdɪˈstrɪbjuːt; ˌriːˈdɪs-/ *verb* [VN] to share sth out among people in a different way: *Wealth needs to be redistributed from the rich to the poor.* ▶ **re·dis·tri·bu·tion** /ˌriːdɪstrɪˈbjuːʃn/ *noun* [U, sing.]: *the redistribution of wealth*

,**red-'letter day** *noun* an important day, or a day that you will remember, because of sth good that happened then

,**red 'light** *noun* a signal telling the driver of a vehicle to stop: *to go through a red light* (= not to stop at one)—picture at FILTER

,**red-'light district** *noun* a part of a town where there are many prostitutes

,**red 'meat** *noun* [U] meat that is dark brown in colour when it has been cooked, such as beef and LAMB—compare WHITE MEAT

red·neck /ˈrednek/ *noun* (*informal, disapproving*) (sometimes *offensive*) a man who lives in a country area of the US, has little education and has strong CONSERVATIVE political opinions

redo /ˌriːˈduː/ *verb* (**re·does** /-ˈdʌz/ **redid** /-ˈdɪd/ **re·done** /-ˈdʌn/) [VN] to do sth again or differently: *A whole day's work had to be redone.* ◇ *We've just redone the bathroom* (= decorated it again).

redo·lent /ˈredələnt/ *adj.* [not before noun] ~ **of/with** sth (*literary*) **1** making you think of the thing mentioned: *an atmosphere redolent of the sea and ships* **2** smelling strongly of the thing mentioned: *a kitchen redolent with the smell of baking* ▶ **redo·lence** /-əns/ *noun* [U]

re·double /ˌriːˈdʌbl/ *verb* [VN] (*written*) to increase sth or make it stronger: *The leading banks are expected to redouble their efforts to keep the value of the dollar down.* ◇ *redoubled strength/enthusiasm*

re·doubt /rɪˈdaʊt/ *noun* **1** (*literary*) a place or situation in which sb/sth is protected when they are being attacked or threatened **2** a small building from which soldiers can fight and defend themselves

re·doubt·able /rɪˈdaʊtəbl/ *adj.* (*formal*) if a person is redoubtable, they have very strong qualities that make you respect them and perhaps feel afraid of them: *a redoubtable leader*

re·dound /rɪˈdaʊnd/ *verb* PHRV **re'dound to sth** (*rare, formal*) to improve the impression that people have of you: *Their defeat redounds to the glory of those whom they attacked.*

,**red 'panda** *noun* = PANDA (2)

,**red 'pepper** *noun* **1** [C, U] a hollow red fruit that is eaten, raw or cooked, as a vegetable **2** [U] (*especially AmE*) = CAYENNE

re·draft /ˌriːˈdrɑːft; *AmE* -ˈdræft/ *verb* [VN] to write an article, a letter, etc. again in order to improve it or make changes ▶ **'re·draft** *noun*

re·draw /ˌriːˈdrɔː/ *verb* (**re·drew** /-ˈdruː/ **re·drawn** /-ˈdrɔːn/) [VN] to make changes to sth such as the borders of a country or region, a plan, an arrangement, etc: *After the war the map of Europe was redrawn.* ◇ *to redraw the boundaries between male and female roles in the home*

re·dress *verb, noun*
■ *verb* /rɪˈdres/ [VN] (*formal*) to correct sth that is unfair or wrong: *to redress an injustice/a grievance* IDM **redress the 'balance** to make a situation equal or fair again
■ *noun* /rɪˈdres; ˈriːdres/ [U] ~ (**for/against sth**) (*formal*) payment, etc. that you should get for sth wrong that has happened to you or harm that you have suffered SYN COMPENSATION: *to seek legal redress for unfair dismissal* ◇ *to have little/no prospect of redress*

red·skin /ˈredskɪn/ *noun* (*old-fashioned*, ⚠, *offensive*) = RED INDIAN

,**red 'tape** *noun* [U] (*disapproving*) official rules that seem more complicated than necessary and prevent things from being done quickly ORIGIN From the custom of tying up official documents with red or pink tape.

re·duce /rɪˈdjuːs; *AmE* -ˈduːs/ *verb* **1** [VN] ~ **sth (from sth) (to sth)** | ~ **sth (by sth)** to make sth less or smaller in size, quantity, price, etc: *Reduce speed now* (= on a sign). ◇ *Costs have been reduced by 20% over the past year.* ◇ *Giving up smoking reduces the risk of heart disease.* ◇ *The*

number of employees was reduced from 40 to 25. **2** [VN, V] if you reduce a liquid or a liquid reduces, you boil it so that it becomes less in quantity **3** [V] (*AmE, informal*) to lose weight by limiting the amount and type of food that you eat: *a reducing plan* IDM **re,duced 'circumstances** the state of being poorer than you were before. People say 'living in reduced circumstances' to avoid saying 'poor'. PHRV **re'duce sb/sth (from sth) to sth/to doing sth** [usually passive] to force sb/sth into a particular state or condition, usually a worse one: *a beautiful building reduced to rubble* ◇ *She was reduced to tears by their criticisms.* ◇ *They were reduced to begging in the streets.* **re'duce sth to sth** to change sth to a more general or more simple form: *We can reduce the problem to two main issues.*

re·du·cible /rɪˈdjuːsəbl; *AmE* -ˈduːs-/ *adj.* ~ **to sth** (*formal*) that can be described or considered simply as sth: *The problem is not reducible to one of money.*

re·duc·tion /rɪˈdʌkʃn/ *noun* **1** [C, U] ~ **(in sth)** an act of making sth less or smaller; the state of being made less or smaller: *a 33% reduction in the number of hospital beds available* ◇ *There has been some reduction in unemployment.* ◇ *a significant/substantial/drastic reduction in costs* **2** [C] an amount of money by which sth is made cheaper: *There are reductions for children sharing a room with two adults.* **3** [C] a copy of a photograph, map, picture, etc. that is made smaller than the original one OPP ENLARGEMENT

re·duc·tion·ism /rɪˈdʌkʃənɪzəm/ *noun* [U] (*technical*) (often *disapproving*) the belief that complicated things can be explained by considering them as a combination of simple parts ▶ **re·duc·tion·ist** /-ɪst/ *adj., noun*

re·duc·tive /rɪˈdʌktɪv/ *adj.* (*formal*, often *disapproving*) that tries to explain sth complicated by considering it as a combination of simple parts

re·dun·dancy /rɪˈdʌndənsi/ *noun* (*pl.* -ies) **1** [U, C, usually pl.] (*BrE*) the situation when sb has to leave their job because there is no more work available for them: *Thousands of factory workers are facing redundancy in the New Year.* ◇ *to accept/take voluntary redundancy* (= to offer to leave your job) ◇ *the threat of compulsory redundancies* ◇ *redundancy payments*—see also LAY-OFF **2** [U] (*formal* or *technical*) the state of not being necessary or useful: *Natural language is characterized by redundancy* (= words are used that are not really necessary for sb to understand the meaning).

re·dun·dant /rɪˈdʌndənt/ *adj.* **1** (*BrE*) (of a person) without a job because there is no more work available for you in a company: *to be made redundant from your job* ◇ *redundant employees/workers* **2** not needed or useful: *The picture has too much redundant detail.* ▶ **re·dun·dant·ly** *adv.*

,**red 'wine** *noun* **1** [U, C] wine that gets its red colour from the skins of the grapes **2** [C] a glass of red wine—compare ROSÉ, WHITE WINE

red·wood /ˈredwʊd/ *noun* **1** [C] a very tall tree that grows especially in California: *giant redwoods* **2** [U] the reddish wood of the redwood tree

reed /riːd/ *noun* **1** a tall plant like grass with a hollow stem that grows in or near water: *reed beds* (= where they grow) ◇ *The edge of the lake was fringed with reeds.* **2** a small thin piece of CANE, metal or plastic in some musical instruments such as the OBOE or the CLARINET that moves very quickly when air is blown over it, producing a sound—picture on page 840

,**re-'educate** *verb* [VN] to teach sb to think or behave in a new or different way ▶ **re-edu'cation** *noun* [U]

reedy /ˈriːdi/ *adj.* [usually before noun] **1** (of a voice or sound) high and not very pleasant **2** full of reeds: *reedy river banks*

reef /riːf/ *noun, verb*
■ *noun* **1** a long line of rocks or sand near the surface of the sea: *a coral reef*—picture at COAST **2** a part of a sail that can be tied or rolled up to make the sail smaller in a strong wind
■ *verb* [VN] (*technical*) to make a sail smaller by tying or rolling up part of it

R

æ	ɑː	e	ɜː	ə	ɪ	iː	i	ɒ	ɔː	ʌ	ʊ	u	uː
cat	father	ten	bird	about	sit	see	many	got	saw	cup	put	actual	too
								(BrE)					

reef·er /ˈriːfə(r)/ *noun* **1** (also **ˈreefer jacket**) a short thick woollen jacket, usually dark blue, with two rows of buttons **2** (*old-fashioned*, *slang*) a cigarette containing MARIJUANA

ˈreef knot (*especially BrE*) (*AmE usually* **ˈsquare knot**) *noun* a type of double knot that will not become undone easily

reek /riːk/ *verb, noun*
■ *verb* [V] ~ (**of sth**) **1** to smell very strongly of sth unpleasant: *His breath reeked of tobacco.* **2** (*disapproving*) to suggest very strongly that sth unpleasant or suspicious is involved in a situation: *Her denials reeked of hypocrisy.*
■ *noun* [sing.] a strong unpleasant smell: *the reek of cigarettes and beer*

reel /riːl/ *noun, verb*

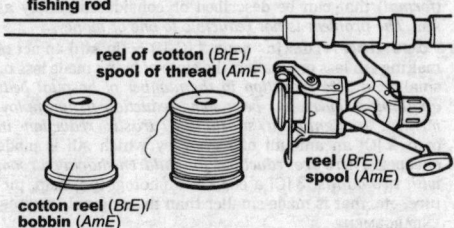

fishing rod

reel of cotton (*BrE*)/
spool of thread (*AmE*)

reel (*BrE*)/
spool (*AmE*)

cotton reel (*BrE*)/
bobbin (*AmE*)

■ *noun* **1** (*especially BrE*) (*AmE usually* **spool**) a round object around which you wind such things as cotton thread, wire or film; the film, wire, thread, etc. that is wound around a reel: *a cotton reel* ◊ *a reel on a fishing rod* ◊ *reels of magnetic tape* ◊ *a new reel of film* ◊ *The hero was killed in the final reel* (= in the final part of the film/movie).—picture at GARDEN **2** a fast Scottish, Irish or American dance, usually for two or four couples; a piece of music for this dance
■ *verb* [V] **1** [usually+*adv. / prep.*] to move in a very unsteady way, for example because you are drunk or have been hit: *I punched him on the chin, sending him reeling backwards.* ◊ *She was reeling after several glasses of wine.* **2** ~ (**at/from/with sth**) to feel very shocked or upset about sth: *I was still reeling from the shock.* **3** to seem to be spinning around and around: *When he opened his eyes, the room was reeling.* PHRV ˌreel sth↔ˈin/ˈout to wind sth on/off a reel: *I slowly reeled the fish in.* ˌreel sth↔ˈoff to say or repeat sth quickly without having to stop or think about it: *She immediately reeled off several names.*

ˌre-eˈlect *verb* ~ sb (**to sth**)| ~ sb (**as**) sth to elect sb again: [VN] *She was re-elected to parliament.* ◊ [VN-N] *The committee voted to re-elect him (as) chairman.* ▶ ˌre-eˈlection *noun* [U]: (*BrE*) *to stand for re-election* ◊ (*AmE*) *to run for re-election*

ˌre-eˈnact *verb* [VN] to repeat the actions of a past event: *Members of the English Civil War Society will re-enact the battle.* ▶ ˌre-eˈnactment *noun*

ˌre-ˈenter *verb* [VN, V] to return to a place or to an area of activity that you used to be in

ˌre-ˈentry *noun* [U] ~ (**into sth**) **1** the act of returning to a place or an area of activity that you used to be in: *She feared she would not be granted re-entry into Britain.* ◊ *a re-entry programme for nurses* (= for nurses returning to work after a long time doing sth else) **2** the return of a spacecraft into the earth's atmosphere: *The capsule gets very hot on re-entry.*

ˌre-eˈxamine *verb* [VN] to examine or think about sth again, especially because you may need to change your opinion SYN REASSESS: *All the evidence needs to be re-examined.* ▶ ˌre-eˈxamination *noun* [U, sing.]

ref /ref/ *noun* (*informal*) = REFEREE (1): *The game's not over till the ref blows the whistle.*

ref. /ref/ *abbr.* reference (used especially in business as a way of identifying sth such as a document): *our ref.: 3498*

re·fec·tory /rɪˈfektri/ *noun* (*pl.* **-ies**) a large room in which meals are served, especially in a religious institution and in some schools and colleges in Britain: *a refectory table*

refer /rɪˈfɜː(r)/ *verb* (**-rr-**) PHRV **reˈfer to sb/sth** (**as sth**) to mention or speak about sb/sth: *The victims were not referred to by name.* ◊ *Her mother never referred to him again.* ◊ *You know who I'm referring to.* ◊ *She always referred to Ben as 'that nice man'.* ◊ *I promised not to refer to the matter again.* **reˈfer to sb/sth 1** to describe or be connected to sb/sth: *The star refers to items which are intended for the advanced learner.* ◊ *The term 'Arts' usually refers to humanities and social sciences.* ◊ *This paragraph refers to the events of last year.* **2** to look at sth or ask a person for information CONSULT: *You may refer to your notes if you want.* ◊ *to refer to a dictionary/an expert* **reˈfer sb/sth to sb/sth** to send sb/sth to sb/sth for help, advice or a decision: *My doctor referred me to a specialist.* ◊ *The case was referred to the Court of Appeal.* ◊ (*formal*) *May I refer you to my letter of 14 May?*

re·fer·able /rɪˈfɜːrəbl; ˈrefrəbl/ *adj.* ~ **to sth** (*formal*) that can be related to sth else: *These symptoms may be referable to virus infection rather than parasites.*

ref·er·ee /ˌrefəˈriː/ *noun, verb*
■ *noun* **1** (also *informal* **ref**) the official who controls the game in some sports, such as football, basketball and boxing: *He was sent off for arguing with the referee.*—compare UMPIRE **2** (*BrE*) a person who gives information about your character and ability, usually in a letter, for example when you are applying for a job **3** a person who is asked to settle a disagreement: *to act as a referee between the parties involved* **4** a person who reads and checks the quality of a technical article before it is published
■ *verb* **1** to act as the referee in a game: [V] *a refereeing decision* ◊ [VN] *Who refereed the final?* **2** [VN] to read and check the quality of a technical article before it is published

ref·er·ence /ˈrefrəns/ *noun, verb*
■ *noun*
MENTIONING SB/STH | **1** [C, U] ~ (**to sb/sth**) a thing you say or write that mentions sb/sth else; the act of mentioning sb/sth: *The book is full of references to growing up in India.* ◊ *She made no reference to her illness but only to her future plans.* ◊ *the President's passing reference to* (= brief mention of) *the end of the war*
LOOKING FOR INFORMATION | **2** [U] the act of looking at sth for information: *Keep the list of numbers near the phone for easy reference.* ◊ *I wrote down the name of the hotel for future reference* (= because it might be useful in the future). ◊ *The library contains many popular works of reference* (= reference books).
ASKING FOR ADVICE | **3** [U] (*formal*) ~ (**to sb/sth**) the act of asking sb for help or advice: *The emergency nurse can treat minor injuries without reference to a doctor.*
NUMBER/WORD/SYMBOL | **4** [C] (*abbr.* **ref.**) a number, word or symbol that shows where sth is on a map, or where you can find a piece of information: *The map reference is Y4.* ◊ *Please quote your reference number when making an enquiry.*
FOR NEW JOB | **5** [C] a letter written by sb who knows you, giving information about your character and abilities, especially to a new employer: *We will take up references after the interview.* **6** [C] a person who agrees to write a reference, for you, for example when you are applying for a job SYN REFEREE: *My previous boss will act as a reference for me.*
IN BOOK | **7** [C] a note in a book that tells you where a particular piece of information comes from: *There is a list of references at the end of each chapter.*
—see also CROSS-REFERENCE, FRAME OF REFERENCE, TERMS OF REFERENCE
IDM **in/with reference to** (*formal* or *written*) used to say what you are talking or writing about: *With reference to your letter of July 22…*
■ *verb* [VN] (*written*) to refer to sth; to provide a book, etc. with references: *Each chapter is referenced, citing literature up to 1999.*

'reference book *noun* a book that contains facts and information, that you look at when you need to find out sth particular

'reference library *noun* a library containing books that can be read in the library but cannot be borrowed—compare LENDING LIBRARY

'reference point *noun* a standard by which sth can be judged or compared

ref·er·en·dum /ˌrefəˈrendəm/ *noun* (*pl.* **ref·er·en·dums** or **ref·er·en·da**) [C, U] ~ (**on sth**) an occasion when all the people of a country can vote on an important issue: *Ireland decided to hold a referendum on divorce.* ◊ *The changes were approved by referendum.*

re·fer·ral /rɪˈfɜːrəl/ *noun* [U, C] ~ (**to sb/sth**) the act of sending sb who needs professional help to a person or place that can provide it: *illnesses requiring referral to hospitals* ◊ *to make a referral*

re·fill *verb, noun*
■ *verb* /ˌriːˈfɪl/ [VN] to fill sth again: *He refilled her glass.* ► **re·fill·able** /ˌriːˈfɪləbl/ *adj.*: *a refillable gas cylinder*
■ *noun* /ˈriːfɪl/ **1** another drink of the same type: *Would you like a refill?* **2** an amount of sth, sold in a cheap container, that you use to fill up a more expensive container that is now empty

re·fi·nance /ˌriːˈfaɪnæns/ *verb* [VN, V] (*finance*) to borrow money in order to pay a debt

re·fine /rɪˈfaɪn/ *verb* [VN] **1** to make a substance pure by taking other substances out of it: *the process of refining oil/sugar* **2** to improve sth by making small changes to it: *She has refined her playing technique over the years.*

re·fined /rɪˈfaɪnd/ *adj.* **1** [usually before noun] (of a substance) made pure by having other substances taken out of it: *refined sugar* **2** (of a person) polite, well educated and able to judge the quality of things; having the sort of manners that are considered typical of a high social class: *She was a lady of very refined tastes.* OPP UNREFINED

re·fine·ment /rɪˈfaɪnmənt/ *noun* **1** [C] a small change to sth that improves it: *This particular model has a further refinement.* **2** [C] ~ **of sth** a thing that is an improvement on an earlier, similar thing: *The new plan is a refinement of the one before.* **3** [U] the process of improving sth or of making sth pure: *the refinement of industrial techniques* ◊ *the refinement of uranium* **4** [U] the quality of being polite and well educated and able to judge the quality of things; the state of having the sort of manners that are considered typical of a high social class: *a person of considerable refinement* ◊ *an atmosphere of refinement*

re·finer /rɪˈfaɪnə(r)/ *noun* a person or company that refines substances such as sugar or oil: *oil refiners*

re·finery /rɪˈfaɪnəri/ *noun* (*pl.* **-ies**) a factory where a substance such as oil is REFINED (= made pure): *an oil refinery* ◊ *a sugar refinery*

refit /ˌriːˈfɪt/ *verb* [VN] (**-tt-**) to repair or fit new parts, equipment, etc. to sth: *He spent £70000 refitting his yacht.* ► **refit** /ˈriːfɪt/ *noun*: *The ship has undergone a complete refit.*

re·flate /ˌriːˈfleɪt/ *verb* [VN, V] (*economics*) to increase the amount of money that is used in a country, usually in order to increase the demand for goods—compare DEFLATE, INFLATE ► **re·fla·tion** /ˌriːˈfleɪʃn/ *noun* [U] **re·fla·tion·ary** /ˌriːˈfleɪʃnri; *AmE* -neri/ *adj.*: *reflationary policies/measures*

re·flect /rɪˈflekt/ *verb* **1** [VN] [usually passive] ~ **sb/sth** (**in sth**) to show the image of sb/sth on the surface of sth such as a mirror, water or glass: *His face was reflected in the mirror.* ◊ *She could see herself reflected in his eyes.* **2** [VN] to throw back light, heat, sound, etc. from a surface: *The windows reflected the bright afternoon sunlight.* ◊ *When the sun's rays hit the earth, a lot of the heat is reflected back into space.* ◊ *This material absorbs the sound, and doesn't reflect it.* **3** [VN] to show or be a sign of the nature of sth or of sb's attitude or feeling: *Our newspaper aims to reflect the views of the local community.* ◊ *His music reflects his interest in African culture.* **4** ~ (**on/upon sth**) to think carefully and deeply about sth: [V] *Before I decide, I need time to reflect.* ◊ *She was left to reflect on the implications of her decision.* ◊ [V that] *On the*

way home he reflected that the interview had gone well. [also V wh-, V speech] **IDM** **reflect well, badly, etc. on sb/sth** to make sb/sth appear to be good, bad, etc. to other people: *This incident reflects badly on everyone involved.*

re·flected 'glory *noun* [U] (*disapproving*) admiration or praise that is given to sb, not because of sth that they have done, but because of sth that sb connected with them has done: *She basked in the reflected glory of her daughter's success.*

re·flec·tion (*BrE* also *less frequent* **re·flex·ion**) /rɪˈflekʃn/ *noun* **1** [C] an image in a mirror, on a shiny surface, on water, etc: *He admired his reflection in the mirror.* **2** [U] the action or process of sending back light, heat, sound, etc. from a surface **3** [C] a sign that shows the state or nature of sth: *Your clothes are often a reflection of your personality.* ◊ *The increase in crime is a sad reflection on* (= shows sth bad about) *our society today.* **4** [U] careful thought about sth, sometimes over a long period of time: *She decided on reflection to accept his offer after all.* ◊ *A week off would give him time for reflection.* **5** [C, usually pl.] your written or spoken thoughts about a particular subject or topic: *a book of her reflections on childhood* **6** [C] an account or a description of sth: *The article is an accurate reflection of events that day.* **IDM** see MATURE *adj.*

re·flect·ive /rɪˈflektɪv/ *adj.* **1** (*written*) thinking deeply about things: *a quiet and reflective man* **2** **reflective** surfaces send back light or heat: *reflective car number plates* ◊ *On dark nights children should wear reflective clothing.* **3** ~ **of sth** (*written*) typical of a particular situation or thing; showing the state or nature of sth: *His abilities are not reflective of the team as a whole.* ◊ *Everything you do or say is reflective of your personality.* ► **re·flect·ive·ly** *adv.*: *She sipped her wine reflectively.*

re·flect·or /rɪˈflektə(r)/ *noun* **1** a surface that reflects light **2** a small piece of special glass or plastic that is put on a bicycle, or on clothing, so that it can be seen at night when light shines on it—picture at BICYCLE

re·flex /ˈriːfleks/ *noun* an action or a movement of your body that happens naturally in response to sth and that you cannot control; sth that you do without thinking: *The doctor tested her reflexes.* ◊ *to have quick/slow reflexes* ◊ *a reflex response/reaction* ◊ *Only the goalkeeper's reflexes* (= his ability to react quickly) *stopped the ball from going in.* ◊ *Almost as a reflex action, I grab my pen as the phone rings.*

reflex 'angle *noun* an angle of more than 180°—compare ACUTE ANGLE, OBTUSE ANGLE, RIGHT ANGLE

re·flex·ion (*BrE*) = REFLECTION

re·flex·ive /rɪˈfleksɪv/ *adj.* a **reflexive** word or form of a word shows that the action of the verb affects the person who performs the action: *In 'He cut himself', 'cut' is a reflexive verb and 'himself' is a reflexive pronoun.*

re·float /ˌriːˈfləʊt; *AmE* -ˈfloʊt/ *verb* [VN] to make a boat or ship float again, for example after it has become stuck on the bottom in shallow water

re·for·est·ation /ˌriːfɒrɪˈsteɪʃn; *AmE* -fɔːr-; -fɑːr-/ (*BrE* also **re·affor·est·ation**) *noun* (*technical*) the act of planting new trees in an area where there used to be a forest—compare DEFORESTATION

re·form /rɪˈfɔːm; *AmE* rɪˈfɔːrm/ *verb, noun*
■ *verb* **1** [VN] to improve a system, an organization, a law, etc. by making changes to it: *proposals to reform the social security system* ◊ *The law needs to be reformed.* **2** to improve your behaviour; to make sb do this: [VN] *She thought she could reform him.* ◊ [V] *He has promised to reform.* ► **re·formed** *adj.*: *a reformed character/alcoholic* ◊ *a Reformed Jew* (= one who practises a form of Judaism that has changed some aspects of worship in order to adapt to modern society)
■ *noun* [U, C] change that is made to a social system, an organization, etc. in order to improve or correct it: *a government committed to reform* ◊ *economic/electoral/constitutional reform* ◊ *the reform of the educational system* ◊ *reforms in education* ◊ *far-reaching/major/sweeping reforms*

b	d	f	g	h	k	l	m	n	p	r
bad	did	fall	get	hat	cat	leg	man	now	pen	red

re-'form *verb* to form again or form sth again, especially into a different group or pattern: [V] *The band is re-forming after 23 years.* ◊ [VN] *The party has recently been re-formed.*

ref·or·ma·tion /ˌrefəˈmeɪʃn; *AmE* -fərˈm-/ *noun* **1** [U] (*formal*) the act of improving or changing sb/sth **2** (**the Reformation**) [sing.] new ideas in religion in 16th century Europe that led to attempts to reform the Roman Catholic Church and to the forming of the Protestant Churches; the period of time when these changes were taking place

re·forma·tory /rɪˈfɔːmətri; *AmE* rɪˈfɔːrmətɔːri/ (*pl.* -ies) (also **re'form school**) *noun* (*AmE*) (*old-fashioned* in British English) a type of school that young criminals are sent to instead of prison

re·form·er /rɪˈfɔːmə(r); *AmE* -ˈfɔːrm-/ *noun* a person who works to achieve political or social change: *social/political/religious reformers*

re·form·ist /rɪˈfɔːmɪst; *AmE* -ˈfɔːrm-/ *adj.* wanting or trying to change political or social situations: *a reformist leader/party* ◊ *a reformist programme/movement* ▶ **re·form·ist** *noun*

re·fract /rɪˈfrækt/ *verb* [VN] (*physics*) (of water, air, glass, etc.) to make a ray of light change direction when it goes through at an angle: *Light is refracted when passed through a prism.* ▶ **re·frac·tion** /rɪˈfrækʃn/ *noun* [U]

re·frac·tory /rɪˈfræktəri/ *adj.* **1** (*formal*) (of a person) difficult to control; behaving badly **2** (*medical*) (of a disease or medical condition) difficult to treat or cure

re·frain /rɪˈfreɪn/ *verb, noun*
▪ *verb* [V] ~ (**from sth/from doing sth**) (*formal*) to stop yourself from doing sth, especially sth that you want to do: *Please refrain from smoking.* ◊ *They appealed to the protesters to refrain from violence.* ◊ *He has refrained from criticizing the government in public.*
▪ *noun* **1** a comment or complaint that is often repeated: *Complaints about poor food in schools have become a familiar refrain.* **2** the part of a song that is repeated after each verse [SYN] CHORUS

re·fresh /rɪˈfreʃ/ *verb* [VN] **1** to make sb feel less tired or less hot: *The long sleep had refreshed her.* ◊ *He refreshed himself with a cool shower.* **2** (*informal, especially AmE*) to fill sb's glass or cup again: *Let me refresh your glass.* **3** ~ **your/sb's memory** to remind yourself/sb of sth, especially with the help of sth that can be seen or heard: *He had to refresh his memory by looking at his notes.*

re'fresher course (also **re·fresh·er** especially in *AmE*) *noun* a short period of training to improve your skills or to teach you about new ideas and developments in your job

re·fresh·ing /rɪˈfreʃɪŋ/ *adj.* **1** pleasantly new or different: *It made a refreshing change to be taken seriously for once.* ◊ *It's refreshing to meet someone who is so dedicated to their work.* **2** making you feel less tired or hot: *a refreshing drink/shower* ◊ *The breeze was cool and refreshing.* ▶ **re·fresh·ing·ly** *adv.*: *refreshingly different/honest/simple* ◊ *The house was refreshingly cool inside.*

re·fresh·ment /rɪˈfreʃmənt/ *noun* **1** (**refreshments**) [pl.] drinks and small amounts of food that are provided or sold to people in a public place or at a public event: *Light refreshments will be served during the break.* ◊ *Tickets include the price of refreshments.* **2** [U] (*formal*) food and drink: *In York we had a short stop for refreshment.* ◊ *Can we offer you some refreshment?* ◊ *a refreshment room/kiosk/tent* ◊ (*humorous*) *liquid refreshment* (= alcoholic drink) **3** [U] (*formal*) the fact of making sb feel stronger or less tired or hot: *a place to rest and find refreshment for mind and body*

re·friger·ate /rɪˈfrɪdʒəreɪt/ *verb* [VN] to make food, etc. cold in order to keep it fresh or preserve it: *Once opened, this product should be kept refrigerated.* ◊ *a refrigerated lorry/truck* ▶ **re·friger·ation** /rɪˌfrɪdʒəˈreɪʃn/ *noun* [U]: *Keep all meat products under refrigeration.*

re·friger·ator /rɪˈfrɪdʒəreɪtə(r)/ *noun* (*formal or AmE*) = FRIDGE

re·fuel /ˌriːˈfjuːəl/ *verb* (-ll-, *AmE* -l-) to fill sth, especially a plane, with fuel in order to continue a journey; to be filled with fuel: [VN] *to refuel a plane* ◊ [V] *The planes needed to refuel before the next mission.* ◊ *a refuelling stop*

ref·uge /ˈrefjuːdʒ/ *noun* **1** [U] ~ (**from sb/sth**) shelter or protection from danger, trouble, etc: *A further 300 people have taken refuge in the US embassy.* ◊ *They were forced to seek refuge from the fighting.* ◊ *a place of refuge* ◊ *As the situation at home got worse she increasingly took refuge in her work.* **2** [C] ~ (**from sb/sth**) a place, person or thing that provides shelter or protection for sb/sth: *He regarded the room as a refuge from the outside world.* ◊ *a wetland refuge for birds, waders and wild fowl* **3** [C] a building that provides a temporary home for people in need of shelter or protection from sb/sth: *a women's refuge* ◊ *a refuge for the homeless* **4** (*BrE*) = TRAFFIC ISLAND

refu·gee /ˌrefjuˈdʒiː/ *noun* a person who has been forced to leave their country or home, because there is a war or for political, religious or social reasons: *a steady flow of refugees from the war zone* ◊ *political/economic refugees* ◊ *a refugee camp*

re·fund *noun, verb*
▪ *noun* /ˈriːfʌnd/ a sum of money that is paid back to you, especially because you paid too much or because you returned goods to a shop/store: *a tax refund* ◊ *to claim/demand/receive a refund* ◊ *If there is a delay of 12 hours or more, you will receive a full refund of the price of your trip.*
▪ *verb* /rɪˈfʌnd/ ~ **sth** (**to sb**)| ~ **sb sth** to give sb their money back, especially because they have paid too much or because they are not satisfied with sth they bought: [VN] *Tickets cannot be exchanged or money refunded.* ◊ [VN, VNN] *We will refund your money to you in full if you are not entirely satisfied.* ◊ *We will refund you your money in full.* ▶ **re·fund·able** *adj.*: *a refundable deposit* ◊ *Tickets are not refundable.*

re·fur·bish /ˌriːˈfɜːbɪʃ; *AmE* -ˈfɜːrb-/ *verb* [VN] to clean and decorate a room, building, etc. in order to make it more attractive, more useful, etc: *The theatre has been extensively refurbished.* ▶ **re·fur·bish·ment** *noun* [U, C]: *The hotel is closed for refurbishment.*

re·fusal /rɪˈfjuːzl/ *noun* [U, C] ~ (**of sth**)| ~ (**to do sth**) an act of saying or showing that you will not do, give or accept sth: *the refusal of a request/an invitation/an offer* ◊ *a blunt/flat/curt refusal* ◊ *His refusal to discuss the matter is very annoying.—see also* FIRST REFUSAL

re·fuse¹ /rɪˈfjuːz/ *verb* **1** to say that you will not do sth that sb has asked you to do: [V] *Go on, ask her; she can hardly refuse.* ◊ [V to inf] *He flatly refused to discuss the matter.* ◊ *She refused to accept that there was a problem.* **2** [VN] to say that you do not want sth that has been offered to you [SYN] TURN DOWN: *I politely refused their invitation.* ◊ *The job offer was simply too good to refuse.* **3** [VNN] to say that you will not give sb sth that they want or need: *They refused him a visa.* ◊ *She would never refuse her kids anything.*

re·fuse² /ˈrefjuːs/ *noun* [U] (*written*) waste material that has been thrown away [SYN] RUBBISH/GARBAGE: *domestic/household refuse* ◊ *the city refuse dump* ◊ *refuse collection/disposal* ⇨ *note at* RUBBISH

'refuse collector (*BrE*) (*AmE* **'garbage collector**) *noun* (*formal*) = DUSTMAN

re·fute /rɪˈfjuːt/ *verb* [VN] (*formal*) **1** to prove that sth is wrong [SYN] REBUT: *to refute an argument/a theory* **2** to say that sth is not true or fair [SYN] DENY: *She refutes any suggestion that she behaved unprofessionally.* ▶ **re·fut·able** /-əbl/ *adj.* **refu·ta·tion** /ˌrefjuˈteɪʃn/ *noun* [C, U]: *a refutation of previously held views*

reg /redʒ/ *abbr.* (*BrE, informal*) REGISTRATION: *a V reg car* (= a car with 'V' in its registration number, showing the year that it was registered)

re·gain /rɪˈɡeɪn/ *verb* **1** to get back sth you no longer have, especially an ability or a quality: [VN] *I struggled to regain some dignity.* ◊ *The party has regained control of the region.* ◊ *She paused on the edge, trying to regain her balance.* ◊ *He did not regain consciousness* (= wake up after being unconscious) *for several days.* **2** (*literary*) to get back to a place that you have left: *They finally managed to regain the beach.*

regal /ˈriːɡl/ *adj.* typical of a king or queen, and therefore

impressive: *regal power* ◊ *the regal splendour of the palace* ◊ *She dismissed him with a regal gesture.*—compare ROYAL
► **re·gal·ly** /-ɡəli/ *adv.*

re·gale /rɪˈɡeɪl/ *verb* PHRV **reˈgale sb with sth** to amuse or entertain sb with stories, jokes, etc: *He regaled us with tales of his days as a jazz pianist.*

re·galia /rɪˈɡeɪliə/ *noun* [U] the special clothes that are worn or objects that are carried at official ceremonies: *a portrait of the queen in full regalia*

re·gard /rɪˈɡɑːd; *AmE* rɪˈɡɑːrd/ *verb, noun*

■ *verb* [VN] **1** ~ **sb/sth (with sth)** | ~ **sb/sth as sth** to think about sb/sth in a particular way: *Her work is very highly regarded.* ◊ *Capital punishment was regarded as inhuman and immoral.* ◊ *He regards himself as a patriot.* ◊ *She is widely regarded as the current leader's natural successor.* **2** (*formal*) to look at sb/sth, especially in a particular way: *He regarded us suspiciously.* IDM **as regards sb/sth** (*formal*) concerning or in connection with sb/sth: *I have little information as regards his fitness for the post.* ◊ *As regards the first point in your letter ...*

■ *noun* **1** [U] ~ **to/for sb/sth** (*formal*) attention to or thought and care for sb/sth: *to do sth with scant/little/no regard for sb/sth* ◊ *to have/pay/show little regard for other people's property* ◊ *He was driving without regard to speed limits.* ◊ *Social services should pay proper regard to the needs of inner-city areas.* **2** [U] ~ **(for sb/sth)** (*formal*) respect or admiration for sb: *He held her in high regard* (= had a good opinion of her). ◊ *I had great regard for his abilities.* ◊ *Children no longer have proper regard for their parents and teachers.* **3** (**regards**) [pl.] used to send greetings at the end of a letter, or when asking sb to give your greetings to another person who is not present: *With kind regards, Yours ...* ◊ *Give your brother my regards when you see him.* IDM **have reˈgard to sth** (*law*) to remember and think carefully about sth: *It is always necessary to have regard to the terms of the contract.* **in this/that reˈgard** (*formal*) concerning what has just been mentioned: *I have nothing further to say in this regard.* **in/with regard to sb/sth** (*formal*) concerning sb/sth; about sb/sth: *a country's laws in regard to human rights* ◊ *The company's position with regard to overtime is made clear in their contracts.*—more at AS *conj.*

re·gard·ing /rɪˈɡɑːdɪŋ; *AmE* -ˈɡɑːrd-/ *prep.* concerning sb/sth; about sb/sth: *She has said nothing regarding your request.* ◊ *Call me if you have any problems regarding your work.*

re·gard·less /rɪˈɡɑːdləs; *AmE* -ˈɡɑːrd-/ *adv.* paying no attention, even if the situation is bad or there are difficulties: *The weather was terrible but we carried on regardless.*

reˈgardless of *prep.* paying no attention to sth/sb; treating sth/sb as not being important: *The club welcomes all new members regardless of age.* ◊ *He went ahead and did it, regardless of the consequences.* ◊ *The amount will be paid to everyone regardless of whether they have children or not.*

re·gatta /rɪˈɡætə/ *noun* a sporting event in which races between rowing boats or sailing boats are held

Re·gency /ˈriːdʒənsi/ *adj.* [usually before noun] of or in the style of the period 1811–20 in Britain, when George, Prince of Wales, was REGENT (= ruled the country in place of the king, his father): *Regency architecture/furniture*

re·gency /ˈriːdʒənsi/ *noun* (*pl.* **-ies**) a period of government by a REGENT (= a person who rules a country in place of the king or queen)

re·gen·er·ate /rɪˈdʒenəreɪt/ *verb* **1** [VN] to make an area, institution, etc. develop and grow strong again: *The money will be used to regenerate the commercial heart of the town.* **2** (*biology*) to grow again; to make sth grow again: [V] *Once destroyed, brain cells do not regenerate.* ◊ [VN] *If the woodland is left alone, it will regenerate itself in a few years.* ► **re·gen·er·ation** /rɪˌdʒenəˈreɪʃn/ *noun* [U]: *economic/environmental regeneration* ◊ *the regeneration of cells in the body* **re·gen·era·tive** /rɪˈdʒenərətɪv/ *adj.*: *the regenerative powers of nature*

re·gent (also **Re·gent**) /ˈriːdʒənt/ *noun* a person who rules a country because the king or queen is too young,

old, ill, etc: *to act as regent* ► **re·gent** (also **Re·gent**) *adj.* [after noun]: *the Prince Regent*

reg·gae /ˈreɡeɪ/ *noun* [U] a type of West Indian popular music with strong rhythms

regi·cide /ˈredʒɪsaɪd/ *noun* [U, C] (*formal*) the crime of killing a king or queen; a person who is guilty of this crime

re·gime /reɪˈʒiːm/ *noun* **1** a method or system of government, especially one that has not been elected in a fair way: *a fascist/totalitarian/military regime* ◊ *an oppressive/brutal regime* **2** a method or system of organizing or managing sth: *Our tax regime is one of the most favourable in Europe.* **3** = REGIMEN: *a·dietary/fitness regime*

regi·men /ˈredʒɪmən/ (also **re·gime**) *noun* (*medical* or *formal*) a set of rules about food and exercise or medical treatment that you follow in order to stay healthy or to improve your health: *a strict regimen* ◊ *a daily regimen of exercise*

regi·ment /ˈredʒɪmənt/ *noun* [C+sing./pl. *v.*] **1** a large group of soldiers that is commanded by a COLONEL **2** (*written*) a large number of people or things

regi·men·tal /ˌredʒɪˈmentl/ *adj.* [only before noun] connected with a particular regiment of soldiers: *a regimental flag/band/parade* ◊ *regimental headquarters*

regi·men·ted /ˈredʒɪmentɪd/ *adj.* (*disapproving*) **1** involving strict discipline and/or organization: *The school imposes a very regimented lifestyle on its students.* **2** arranged in strict groups, patterns, etc: *regimented lines of trees* ► **regi·men·ta·tion** /ˌredʒɪmenˈteɪʃn/ *noun* [U]: *She rebelled against the regimentation of school life.*

re·gion /ˈriːdʒən/ *noun* **1** [C] a large area of land, usually without exact limits or borders: *the Arctic/tropical/desert regions* ◊ *one of the most densely populated regions of North America* **2** [C] one of the areas that a country is divided into, that has its own customs and/or its own government: *the Basque region of Spain* **3** (**the regions**) [pl.] (*BrE*) all of a country except the capital city: *People in the regions should not have to travel to London to fly to the United States.* **4** [C] a part of the body, usually one that has a particular character or problem: *pains in the abdominal region* IDM **in the region of** used when you are giving a number, price, etc. to show that it is not exact: *He earns somewhere in the region of £20000.*

re·gion·al /ˈriːdʒənl/ *adj.* [usually before noun] of or relating to a region: *regional variations in pronunciation* ◊ *the conflict between regional and national interests* ◊ *regional councils/elections/newspapers* ► **re·gion·al·ly** /-nəli/ *adv.*: *regionally based television companies*

regis·ter /ˈredʒɪstə(r)/ *verb, noun*

■ *verb*

PUT NAME ON LIST **1** ~ **(at/for/with sth)** | ~ **sth (in sth)** | ~ **(sb) as sth** to record your/sb's/sth's name on an official list: [VN] *to register a birth/marriage/death* ◊ *to register a company/trademark* ◊ *The ship was registered in Panama.* ◊ [VN-ADJ] *She is officially registered (as) disabled.* ◊ [V] *to register with a doctor/dentist* ◊ *to register at a hotel*

GIVE OPINION PUBLICLY **2** [VN] (*formal*) to make your opinion known officially or publicly: *China has registered a protest over foreign intervention.*

ON MEASURING INSTRUMENT **3** if a measuring instrument **registers** an amount or sth **registers** an amount on a measuring instrument, the instrument shows or records that amount: [V-N] *The thermometer registered 32°C.* ◊ *The earthquake registered 3 on the Richter scale.* ◊ *The stock exchange has registered huge losses this week.* [also V]

SHOW FEELING **4** [no passive] (*formal*) to show or express a feeling: [VN] *Her face registered disapproval.* ◊ [V] *Shock registered on everyone's face.*

NOTICE STH **5** [no passive] (often used in negative sentences) to notice sth and remember it; to be noticed: [VN] *He barely registered our presence.* ◊ [V] *I told her my name, but it obviously didn't register.*

LETTER/PACKAGE **6** [VN] [usually passive] to send sth by mail, paying extra money to protect it against loss or damage: *Can I register this, please?* ◊ *a registered letter*

■ *noun*

LIST OF NAMES **1** [C] an official list or record of names, items, etc.; a book that contains such a list: *a parish register* (= of births, marriages and deaths) ◊ *to be on the electoral register/register of voters* ◊ *Could you sign the hotel register please, sir?* ◊ (*BrE*) *The teacher called the register* (= checked who was present at school).

OF VOICE/INSTRUMENT | **2** [C] the range, or part of a range, of a human voice or a musical instrument: *in the upper/middle register* ◊ *the lower register of a clarinet/piano*

OF WRITING/SPEECH | **3** [C, U] (*linguistics*) the level and style of a piece of writing or speech, that is usually appropriate to the situation that it is used in: *The essay suddenly switches from a formal to an informal register.*

FOR HOT/COLD AIR | **4** [C] (*AmE*) an opening, with a cover that you can have open or shut, that allows hot or cold air from a heating or cooling system into a room—compare VENT

MACHINE | **5** [C] (*AmE*) = CASH REGISTER

registered 'mail (*BrE* also **registered 'post**) *noun* [U] a method of sending a letter or package in which the person sending it can claim money in COMPENSATION if it arrives late or is lost or damaged—compare RECORDED DELIVERY

registered 'nurse *noun* (*abbr.* RN) **1** (*AmE*) a nurse who has a degree in NURSING and who has passed an exam to be allowed to work in a particular state **2** (*BrE*) a nurse who has an official qualification

registered 'trademark *noun* (*symb* ®) the sign or name of a product, etc. that is officially recorded and protected so that nobody else can use it

register office *noun* the official way of referring to a REGISTRY OFFICE

regis·trar /ˌredʒɪ'strɑː(r); 'redʒɪstrɑː(r)/ *noun* **1** a person whose job is to keep official records, especially of births, marriages and deaths **2** the senior administrative officer in a college or university **3** a doctor working in a British hospital who is training to become a specialist in a particular area of medicine: *a surgical/paediatric registrar*—compare CONSULTANT, RESIDENT

regis·tra·tion /ˌredʒɪ'streɪʃn/ *noun* [U, C] **1** the act of making an official record of sth/sb: *the registration of letters/parcels* ◊ *the registration of students for a course* ◊ *registration fees* ◊ *vehicle/birth/death registrations* **2** a document showing that an official record has been made of sth—compare LOGBOOK **3** (*BrE*) = REGISTRATION NUMBER

regi'stration number (also **regis·tra·tion**) (both *BrE*) (*AmE* **license (plate) number**) *noun* the series of letters and numbers that are shown on a NUMBER PLATE at the front and back of a vehicle to identify it—picture at CAR

regis·try /'redʒɪstri/ *noun* (*pl.* -ies) a place where REGISTERS (= official lists) are kept

'registry office (also **'register office**) *noun* (in Britain) a place where CIVIL marriages (= that do not involve a religious ceremony) are performed and where records of births, marriages and deaths are made: *to get married in/at a registry office*

re·gress /rɪ'gres/ *verb* [V] ~ (**to sth**) (*formal*, usually *disapproving*) to return to an earlier or less advanced form or way of behaving

re·gres·sion /rɪ'greʃn/ *noun* [U, C] ~ (**to sth**) the process of going back to an earlier or less advanced form or state

re·gres·sive /rɪ'gresɪv/ *adj.* **1** becoming or making sth less advanced: *The policy has been condemned as a regressive step.* **2** (*technical*) (of taxes) having less effect on the rich than on the poor

re·gret /rɪ'gret/ *verb, noun*
■ *verb* (-tt-) **1** to feel sorry about sth you have done or about sth that you have not been able to do: [VN] *If you don't do it now, you'll only regret it.* ◊ *The decision could be one he lives to regret.* ◊ *'I've had a wonderful life,' she said, 'I don't regret a thing.'* ◊ [V-ing] *He bitterly regretted ever having mentioned it.* ◊ [Vwh-] *I deeply regret what I said.* [also Vthat] **2** (*formal*) used to say in a polite or formal way that you are sorry or sad about a situation: [VN] *The airline regrets any inconvenience.* ◊ [Vthat] *I regret that I*

am unable to accept your kind invitation. ◊ [Vtoinf] *We regret to inform you that your application has not been successful.* ◊ [VNthat] *It is to be regretted that so many young people leave school without qualifications.*
■ *noun* [U, C] a feeling of sadness or disappointment that you have because of sth that has happened or sth that you have done or not done: *It is with great regret that I accept your resignation.* ◊ *She expressed her regret at the decision.* ◊ *a pang/twinge of regret* ◊ *I have no regrets about leaving Newcastle* (= I do not feel sorry about it). ◊ *What is your greatest regret* (= the thing that you are most sorry about doing or not doing)? ◊ *He gave up teaching in 1997, much to the regret of his students.*

re·gret·ful /rɪ'gretfl/ *adj.* feeling or showing sadness or disappointment because of sth that has happened or sth that you have done or not done: *a regretful look/smile*

re·gret·ful·ly /rɪ'gretfəli/ *adv.* **1** in a way that shows you are sad or disappointed about sth: *'I'm afraid not,' he said regretfully.* ◊ *Emma shook her head regretfully.* **2** used to show that you are sorry that sth is the case and you wish the situation were different SYN REGRETTABLY: *Regretfully, mounting costs have forced the museum to close.*

WHICH WORD?

regretfully / regretfully (?)

Regretfully and **regretfully** can both be used as sentence adverbs to show that you are sorry about something and wish the situation were different: *Regretfully, some jobs will be lost.* ◊ *Regrettably, some jobs will be lost.*

Regretfully can also be used to mean 'in a way that shows you are sad or disappointed about something': *He sighed regretfully.*

---

re·gret·table /rɪ'gretəbl/ *adj.* ~ (**that...**) that you are sorry about and wish had not happened: *It is regrettable that the police were not informed sooner.* ◊ *The loss of jobs is highly regrettable.* ► **re·gret·tably** /-əbli/ *adv.*: *Regrettably, crime has been increasing in this area.*

re·group /ˌriː'gruːp/ *verb* ~ (**sth**) (**for sth**) to arrange differently the way people or soldiers work together, especially in order to continue fighting or attacking sb: [VN] *They regrouped their forces and renewed the attack.* ◊ [V] *After its election defeat, the party needs to regroup.*

regu·lar /'regjələ(r)/ *adj., noun*
■ *adj.*
FOLLOWING PATTERN | **1** following a pattern, especially with the same time and space in between each thing and the next: *regular breathing* ◊ *a regular pulse/heartbeat* ◊ *A light flashed at regular intervals.* ◊ *There is a regular bus service to the airport.* ◊ *regular meetings/visits* ◊ *The equipment is checked on a regular basis.* OPP IRREGULAR
FREQUENT | **2** done or happening often: *Do you take regular exercise?* ◊ *Domestic violence is a regular occurrence in some families.* OPP IRREGULAR **3** [only before noun] (of people) doing the same thing or going to the same place often: *our regular customers/readers/viewers* ◊ *regular offenders* (= against the law) ◊ *He was a regular visitor to her house.*
USUAL | **4** [only before noun] usual: *I couldn't see my regular doctor today.* ◊ *On Monday he would have to return to his regular duties.* ◊ *It's important to follow the regular procedure.*
EVENLY SHAPED | **5** evenly shaped: *a face with regular features* ◊ *a regular geometric pattern* OPP IRREGULAR
PERMANENT | **6** lasting or happening over a long period: *a regular job/income* ◊ *She couldn't find any regular employment.*
STANDARD SIZE | **7** (*especially AmE*) of a standard size: *Regular or large fries?*
ORDINARY | **8** [only before noun] (*especially AmE*) ordinary; without any special or extra features: *Do you want regular or diet cola?* ◊ (*approving*) *He's just a regular guy who loves his dog.*
SOLDIER | **9** [only before noun] belonging to or connected

---

aɪ	aʊ	eɪ	əʊ	oʊ	ɔɪ	ɪə	eə	ʊə	j	w
my	now	say	go	go	boy	near	hair	pure	yes	wet
			(BrE)	(AmE)						

with the permanent armed forces or police force of a country: *a regular army/soldier* OPP IRREGULAR

GRAMMAR | **10** (especially of verbs or nouns) changing their form in the same way as most other verbs and nouns: *The past participle of regular verbs ends in '-ed'.* OPP IRREGULAR

FOR EMPHASIS | **11** (*informal*) used for emphasis to show that sb/sth is an exact or clear example of the thing mentioned: *The whole thing was a regular disaster.*

■ *noun*

CUSTOMER | **1** a customer who often goes to a particular shop/store, pub, restaurant, etc: *He's one of our regulars.*

MEMBER OF TEAM | **2** a person who often plays in a particular team, takes part in a particular television show, etc: *We are missing six first-team regulars because of injury.*

SOLDIER | **3** a professional soldier who belongs to a country's permanent army

reg·u·lar·ity /ˌreɡjuˈlærəti/ *noun* [U] **1** [U] the fact that the same thing happens again and again, and usually with the same length of time between each time it happens: *Aircraft passed overhead* **with monotonous regularity**. ◊ *None of the lights seemed to work with any regularity.* **2** [U] the fact that sth is arranged evenly or in an organized pattern: *the striking regularity of her features* **3** [C] a thing that has a pattern to it: *to observe regularities in the behaviour of the animals*—compare IRREGULARITY

reg·u·lar·ize (*BrE* also **-ise**) /ˈreɡjələraɪz/ *verb* [VN] to make a situation that already exists legal or official: *Illegal immigrants were given the opportunity to regularize their position.*

reg·u·lar·ly /ˈreɡjələli; *AmE* -lərli/ *adv.* **1** at regular intervals or times: *to go to church regularly* ◊ *We meet regularly to discuss the progress of the project.* **2** often: *I go there quite regularly.* **3** in an even or balanced way: *The plants were spaced regularly, about 50 cm apart.*

reg·u·late /ˈreɡjuleɪt/ *verb* **1** to control sth by means of rules: [VN] *The activities of credit companies are regulated by law.* ◊ *It is up to the regulating authority to put the measures into effect.* **2** [VN] to control the speed, pressure, temperature, etc. in a machine or system: *This valve regulates the flow of water.*

reg·u·la·tion /ˌreɡjuˈleɪʃn/ *noun, adj.*

■ *noun* **1** [C, usually pl.] an official rule made by a government or some other authority: *too many* **rules and regulations** ◊ *fire/safety/building regulations* ◊ *to comply with the regulations* ◊ **Under the new regulations** *spending on office equipment will be strictly controlled.* ◊ *the strict regulations governing the sale of weapons* **2** [U] controlling sth by means of rules: *the voluntary regulation of the press*

■ *adj.* [only before noun] that must be worn or used according to the official rules: *in regulation uniform*

reg·u·la·tor /ˈreɡjuleɪtə(r)/ *noun* **1** a person or an organization that officially controls an area of business or industry and makes sure that it is operating fairly **2** a device that automatically controls sth such as speed, temperature or pressure

reg·u·la·tory /ˈreɡjələtəri; *AmE* -tɔːri/ *adj.* [usually before noun] having the power to control an area of business or industry and make sure that it is operating fairly: *regulatory bodies/authorities/agencies* ◊ *regulatory procedures*

re·gur·gi·tate /rɪˈɡɜːdʒɪteɪt; *AmE* -ˈɡɜːrdʒ-/ *verb* [VN] **1** (*formal*) to bring food that has been swallowed back up into the mouth again: *The bird regurgitates half-digested fish to feed its young.* **2** (*disapproving*) to repeat sth you have heard or read without really thinking about it or understanding it ▶ **re·gur·gi·ta·tion** /rɪˌɡɜːdʒɪˈteɪʃn; *AmE* -ˌɡɜːrdʒ-/ *noun* [U]

rehab /ˈriːhæb/ *noun* [U] (*especially AmE*) the process of helping to cure sb who has a problem with drugs or alcohol: *to go into rehab* ◊ *a rehab clinic*

re·habili·tate /ˌriːəˈbɪlɪteɪt/ *verb* [VN] **1** to help sb to have a normal, useful life again after they have been very ill/sick or in prison for a long time: *a unit for rehabilitating drug addicts* **2** to begin to consider that sb is good or

acceptable after a long period during which they were considered bad or unacceptable: *He played a major role in rehabilitating Magritte as an artist.* **3** to return a building to its previous good condition: *Billions of pounds are being spent on rehabilitating inner-city areas.* ▶ **re·habili·ta·tion** /ˌriːəˌbɪlɪˈteɪʃn/ *noun* [U]: *a drug rehabilitation centre* ◊ *the rehabilitation of the steel industry*

re·hash /ˌriːˈhæʃ/ *verb* [VN] (*disapproving*) to arrange ideas, pieces of writing or pieces of film into a new form but without any great change or improvement: *He just rehashes songs from the 60s.* ▶ **re·hash** /ˈriːhæʃ/ *noun* [sing.] (*disapproving*): *The movie is just a rehash of the best TV episodes.*

re·hear·ing /ˌriːˈhɪərɪŋ; *AmE* -ˈhɪr-/ *noun* (*law*) an opportunity for a case to be heard or considered again in a court of law

re·hearsal /rɪˈhɜːsl; *AmE* rɪˈhɜːrsl/ *noun* **1** [C, U] time that is spent practising a play or piece of music in preparation for a public performance: *to have/hold a rehearsal* ◊ *We only had six days of rehearsal.* ◊ *Our new production of 'Hamlet' is currently* **in rehearsal**. ◊ *a rehearsal room*—see also DRESS REHEARSAL **2** [C, usually sing.] ~ **(for sth)** an experience or event that helps to prepare you for sth that is going to happen in the future: *These training exercises are designed to be a rehearsal for the invasion.* **3** [C, usually sing.] ~ **of sth** (*formal*) the act of repeating sth that has been said before: *We listened to his lengthy rehearsal of the arguments.*

re·hearse /rɪˈhɜːs; *AmE* rɪˈhɜːrs/ *verb* **1** ~ **(for sth)** to practise or make people practise a play, piece of music, etc. in preparation for a public performance: [V] *We were given only two weeks to rehearse.* ◊ [VN] *Today, we'll just be rehearsing the final scene.* ◊ *The actors were poorly rehearsed.* **2** [VN] to prepare in your mind or practise privately what you are going to do or say to sb: *She walked along rehearsing her excuse for being late.* **3** [VN] (*formal*, usually *disapproving*) to repeat ideas or opinions that have often been expressed before

re·heat /ˌriːˈhiːt/ *verb* [VN] to heat cooked food again after it has been left to go cold

re·house /ˌriːˈhaʊz/ *verb* [VN] to provide sb with a different home to live in, especially a better one: *Thousands of earthquake victims are still waiting to be rehoused.*

reign /reɪn/ *noun, verb*

■ *noun* **1** the period during which a king, queen, EMPEROR, etc. rules: *in/during the reign of Charles II* **2** the period during which sb is in charge of an organization, a team, etc.

■ *verb* [V] **1** ~ **(over sb/sth)** to rule as king, queen, EMPEROR, etc: *the reigning monarch* ◊ *Queen Victoria reigned from 1837 to 1901.* ◊ *Herod reigned over Palestine at that time.* **2** ~ **(over sb/sth)** to be the best or most important in a particular situation or area of skill: *the reigning champion* ◊ *In the field of classical music, he still* **reigns supreme**. **3** (*literary*) (of an idea, a feeling or an atmosphere) to be the most obvious feature of a place or moment: *At last* **silence reigned** (= there was complete silence).

ˌreign of ˈterror *noun* (*pl.* **reigns of terror**) a period during which there is a lot of violence and many people are killed by the ruler or people in power

re·im·burse /ˌriːɪmˈbɜːs; *AmE* -ˈbɜːrs/ *verb* [VN] ~ **sb (for sth)** (*formal*) to pay back money to sb which they have spent or lost: *We will reimburse any expenses incurred.* ◊ *You will be reimbursed for any loss or damage caused by our company.* ▶ **re·im·burse·ment** *noun* [U]

rein /reɪn/ *noun, verb*

■ *noun* **1** [C, usually pl.] a long, narrow, leather band that is fastened around a horse's neck and is held by the rider in order to control the horse: *She pulled gently on the reins.* **2** (**reins**) [pl.] (*BrE*) straps worn by a small child and held by an adult in order to stop the child from walking off and getting lost **3** (**the reins**) [pl.] the state of being in control or the leader of sth: *It was time to* **hand over the reins** *of power* (= to give control to sb else). ◊ *The vice-president was forced to* **take up the reins** *of office.* IDM **give/allow sb/sth free/full ˈrein** | **give/allow free/**

---

full '**rein** sth to give sb complete freedom of action; to allow a feeling to be expressed freely: *The designer was given free rein.* ◇ *The script allows full rein to her larger-than-life acting style.*—more at TIGHT

■ *verb* PHRV ,**rein** sth↔'**in** | ,**rein** sth↔'**back 1** to start to control sb/sth more strictly SYN CHECK: *We need to rein back public spending.* ◇ *She kept her emotions tightly reined in.* **2** to stop a horse or make it go more slowly by pulling back the reins

re·in·car·nate /ˌriːɪn'kɑːneɪt; *AmE* -'kɑːrn-/ *verb* [often passive] ~ sb/sth (**in/as** sb/sth) to be born again in another body after you have died; to make sb be born again in this way: [VN] *They believe humans are reincarnated in animal form.* [also V]

re·in·car·na·tion /ˌriːɪnkɑː'neɪʃn; *AmE* -kɑːr'n-/ *noun* **1** [U] the belief that after sb's death their soul lives again in a new body **2** [C, usually sing.] a person or an animal whose body contains the soul of a dead person: *He thinks he's the reincarnation of Attila the Hun.*

rein·deer /'reɪndɪə(r); *AmE* -dɪr/ *noun* (*pl.* **rein·deer**) a large deer with long ANTLERS (= horns shaped like branches), that lives in cold northern regions: *herds of reindeer*

re·in·force /ˌriːɪn'fɔːs; *AmE* -'fɔːrs/ *verb* [VN] **1** to make a feeling, an idea, etc. stronger: *The experience reinforced my sense of loss.* ◇ *Such jokes tend to reinforce racial stereotypes.* ◇ *The climate of political confusion has only reinforced the country's economic decline.* ◇ *Success in the talks will reinforce his reputation as an international statesman.* **2** to make a structure or material stronger, especially by adding another material to it: *All buildings are now reinforced to withstand earthquakes.* ◇ *reinforced plastic/steel* **3** to send more people or equipment in order to make an army, etc. stronger: *The UN has undertaken to reinforce its military presence along the borders.*

,**reinforced** '**concrete** *noun* [U] CONCRETE with metal bars or wires inside to make it stronger

re·in·force·ment /ˌriːɪn'fɔːsmənt; *AmE* -'fɔːrs-/ *noun* **1** (**reinforcements**) [pl.] extra soldiers or police officers who are sent to a place because more are needed: *to send in reinforcements* **2** [U, sing.] the act of making sth stronger, especially a feeling or an idea: *the reinforcement of existing prejudices by the media*

re·in·state /ˌriːɪn'steɪt/ *verb* [VN] ~ sb/sth (**in/as** sth) **1** to give back a job or position that had been taken away from sb: *He was reinstated in his post.* **2** to return sth to its previous position or status: *There have been repeated calls to reinstate the death penalty.* ◇ *Tennis has now been reinstated as an Olympic sport.* ► **re·in·state·ment** *noun* [U]

re·in·sur·ance /ˌriːɪn'ʃʊərəns; -'ʃɔːr-; *AmE* -'ʃʊr-/ *noun* [U] (*finance*) the practice of one insurance company buying insurance from another company against any losses that result from claims that are made against it

re·in·ter·pret /ˌriːɪn'tɜːprɪt; *AmE* -'tɜːrp-/ *verb* [VN] to INTERPRET (= understand and present) sth in a new or different way: *This new production radically reinterprets the play.* ► **re·in·ter·pret·ation** /ˌriːɪnˌtɜːprɪ'teɪʃn; *AmE* -ˌtɜːrp-/ *noun* [C, U]

re·in·tro·duce /ˌriːɪntrə'djuːs; *AmE* -'duːs/ *verb* [VN] **1** to start to use sth again SYN BRING BACK: *to reintroduce the death penalty* ◇ *plans to reintroduce trams to the city* **2** to put a type of animal, bird or plant back into a region where it once lived ► **re·in·tro·duc·tion** *noun* [U, C]

re·in·vent /ˌriːɪn'vent/ *verb* [VN] ~ **sth/yourself** (**as** sth) to present yourself/sth in a new form or with a new image: *The former wild man of rock has reinvented himself as a respectable family man.* IDM **reinvent the wheel** to waste time creating sth that already exists and works well: *There's no point in us reinventing the wheel.*

re·in·vest /ˌriːɪn'vest/ *verb* [VN, V] to put profits that have been made on an INVESTMENT back into the same investment or into a new one

re·issue /ˌriː'ɪʃuː/ *verb, noun*
■ *verb* [VN] ~ **sth** (**as** sth) to publish or produce again a book, record, etc. that has not been available for some

time: *old jazz recordings reissued on CD* ◇ *The novel was reissued in paperback.*
■ *noun* an old book or record that has been published or produced again after not being available for some time

re·iter·ate /ri'ɪtəreɪt/ *verb* (*formal*) to repeat sth that you have already said, especially to emphasize it: [VN] *to reiterate an argument/a demand/an offer* ◇ [V that] *Let me reiterate that we are fully committed to this policy.* [also V speech] ► **re·iter·ation** /riˌɪtə'reɪʃn/ *noun* [sing.]: *a reiteration of her previous statement*

re·ject *verb, noun*
■ *verb* /rɪ'dʒekt/ [VN]
ARGUMENT/IDEA/PLAN | **1** to refuse to accept or consider sth: *to reject an argument/a claim/a decision/an offer/a suggestion* ◇ *The prime minister rejected any idea of reforming the system.* ◇ *The proposal was firmly rejected.*
SB FOR JOB | **2** to refuse to accept sb for a job, position, etc: *Please reject the following candidates ...* ◇ *I've been rejected by all the universities I applied to.*
NOT USE/PUBLISH | **3** to decide not to use, sell, publish, etc. sth because its quality is not good enough: *Imperfect articles are rejected by our quality control.*
NEW ORGAN | **4** (of the body) to not accept a new organ after a TRANSPLANT operation, by producing substances that attack the organ: *Her body has already rejected two kidneys.*
NOT LOVE | **5** to fail to give a person or an animal enough care or affection: *The lioness rejected the smallest cub, which died.* ◇ *When her husband left home she felt rejected and useless.*
► **re·jec·tion** /rɪ'dʒekʃn/ *noun* [U, C]: *Her proposal met with unanimous rejection.* ◇ *a rejection letter* (= a letter in which you are told, for example, that you have not been accepted for a job) ◇ *painful feelings of rejection*
■ *noun* /'riːdʒekt/
STH THAT CANNOT BE USED | **1** something that cannot be used or sold because there is sth wrong with it
PERSON | **2** a person who has not been accepted as a member of a team, society, etc: *one of society's rejects*

rejig /ˌriː'dʒɪg/ *verb* (**-gg-**) (*BrE*) (*AmE* **rejig·ger** /ˌriː'dʒɪgə(r)/) [VN] (*informal*) to make changes to sth; to arrange sth differently

re·joice /rɪ'dʒɔɪs/ *verb* ~ (**at/in/over** sth) (*formal*) to express great happiness about sth SYN CELEBRATE: [V] *When the war ended, people finally had cause to rejoice.* ◇ *The motor industry is rejoicing at the cut in car tax.* ◇ [V to inf] *They rejoiced to see their son well again.* [also V that] IDM **rejoice in the name of ...** (*BrE, humorous*) to have a name that sounds funny: *He rejoiced in the name of Owen Owen.*

re·joi·cing /rɪ'dʒɔɪsɪŋ/ *noun* [U] (also **re·joi·cings** [pl.]) the happy celebration of sth: *a time of great rejoicing*

re·join[1] /ˌriː'dʒɔɪn/ *verb* to join sb/sth again after leaving them: [V] *to rejoin a club/company* ◇ *She hung up the phone and rejoined them at the table.* ◇ *The path goes through a wood before rejoining the main road.* [also V]

re·join[2] /rɪ'dʒɔɪn/ *verb* (*formal*) to say sth as an answer, especially sth quick, critical or amusing: [V speech] *'You're wrong!' she rejoined.* [also V that]

re·join·der /rɪ'dʒɔɪndə(r)/ *noun* [usually sing.] (*formal*) a reply, especially a quick, critical or amusing one: *'No!' was his curt rejoinder.*

re·ju·ven·ate /rɪ'dʒuːvəneɪt/ *verb* [VN] to make sb/sth look or feel younger or more lively: *His new job seemed to rejuvenate him.* ◇ *special creams to rejuvenate the skin* ► **re·ju·ven·ation** /rɪˌdʒuːvə'neɪʃn/ *noun* [U, sing.]

re·kin·dle /ˌriː'kɪndl/ *verb* [VN] (*written*) to make sth become active again SYN REAWAKEN: *to rekindle feelings/hopes/interest/memories* ◇ *The sight of her after so many years rekindled his passion.*

re·laid *pt, pp* of RELAY

re·lapse *noun, verb*
■ *noun* /rɪ'læps; 'riːlæps/ [C, U] the fact of becoming ill/sick again after making an improvement: *to have/suffer a relapse* ◇ *a risk of relapse*
■ *verb* /rɪ'læps/ [V] ~ (**into** sth) to go back into a previous condition or into a worse state after making an improve-

ment: *They relapsed into silence.* ◊ *He relapsed into his old bad habits.* ◊ *Two days after leaving the hospital she relapsed into a coma.*

re·late /rɪˈleɪt/ *verb* **1** [VN] **~ A (to B)** show or make a connection between two or more things: *I found it difficult to relate the two ideas in my mind.* ◊ *In the future, pay increases will be related to productivity.* **2 ~ sth (to sb)** (*formal*) to give a spoken or written report of sth; to tell a story: [VN] *She relates her childhood experiences in the first chapters.* ◊ *He related the facts of the case to journalists.* [V wh-] *She related how he had run away from home as a boy.* [also V that] **PHRV** **reˈlate to sth/sb 1** to be connected with sth/sb; to refer to sth/sb: *We shall discuss the problem as it relates to our specific case.* ◊ *The second paragraph relates to the situation in Scotland.* **2** to be able to understand and have sympathy with sb/sth: *Many adults can't relate to children.* ◊ *Our product needs an image that people can relate to.*

re·lated /rɪˈleɪtɪd/ *adj.* **~ (to sth/sb) 1** connected with sth/sb in some way: *Much of the crime in this area is related to drug abuse.* ◊ *These problems are closely related.* ◊ *a related issue/question* ◊ *a stress-related illness* **2** in the same family: *Are you related to Margaret?* ◊ *We're distantly related.* **3** belonging to the same group: *related species/languages* ◊ *The llama is related to the camel.* **OPP** UNRELATED ▶ **re·lated·ness** *noun* [U]

re·la·tion /rɪˈleɪʃn/ *noun* **1** (**relations**) [pl.] **~ (between A and B)** | **~ (with sb/sth)** the way in which two people, groups or countries behave towards each other or deal with each other: *diplomatic/international/foreign relations* ◊ *US-Chinese relations* ◊ *Relations with neighbouring countries are under strain at present.* ◊ *We seek to improve relations between our two countries.* ◊ *teacher-pupil relations* ◊ (*formal*) *to have sexual relations* (= to have sex)— see also INDUSTRIAL RELATIONS, PUBLIC RELATIONS, RACE RELATIONS **2** [U, C] **~ (between A and B)** | **~ (to sth)** the way in which two or more things are connected: *the relation between rainfall and crop yields* ◊ *the relation of the farmer to the land* ◊ *The fee they are offering bears no relation to the amount of work involved.* ◊ (*formal*) *I have some comments to make in relation to* (= concerning) *this matter.* ◊ *Its brain is small in relation to* (= compared with) *its body.* **3** [C] a person who is in the same family as sb else **SYN** RELATIVE: *a close/near/distant relation of mine* ◊ *a relation by marriage* ◊ *a party for friends and relations* ◊ *He's called Brady too, but we're no relation* (= not related). ◊ *Is he any relation to you?*—see also BLOOD RELATION, POOR RELATION

re·la·tion·al /rɪˈleɪʃənl/ *adj.* (*formal* or *technical*) existing or considered in relation to sth else: *a relational database* (= one that can recognize the connection between stored items of information)

re·la·tion·ship /rɪˈleɪʃnʃɪp/ *noun* **1** [C] **~ (between A and B)** | **~ (with sb)** the way in which two people, groups or countries behave towards each other or deal with each other: *The relationship between the police and the local community has improved.* ◊ *She has a very close relationship with her sister.* ◊ *I have established a good working relationship with my boss.* ◊ *a master-servant relationship*—see also LOVE-HATE RELATIONSHIP **2** [C] **~ (between A and B)** | **~ (with sb)** a loving and/or sexual friendship between two people: *Their affair did not develop into a lasting relationship.* ◊ *She's had a series of miserable relationships.* **3** [C, U] **~ (between A and B)** | **~ (to sth)** the way in which two or more things are connected: *the relationship between mental and physical health* ◊ *This comment bore no relationship to the subject of our conversation.* ◊ *People alter their voices in relationship to background noise.* **4** [C, U] **~ (between A and B)** the way in which a person is related to sb else in a family: *a father-son relationship* ◊ *I'm not sure of the exact relationship between them—I think they're cousins.*

rela·tive /ˈrelətɪv/ *adj., noun*
■ *adj.* (*formal*) **1** considered and judged by being compared with sth else: *the relative merits of the two plans* **2 ~ (to sth)** considered according to its position or connection with sth else: *the position of the sun relative to the earth* **3** [only before noun] that exists or that has a particular

quality only when compared with sth else: *They now live in relative comfort* (= compared with how they lived before). ◊ *Given the failure of the previous plan, this turned out to be a relative success.* ◊ (*spoken*) *It's all relative though, isn't it? We never had any money when I was a kid and $500 was a fortune to us.*—compare ABSOLUTE **4 ~ to sth** (*formal*) having a connection with sth; referring to sth: *the facts relative to the case* **5** (*grammar*) referring to an earlier noun, sentence or part of a sentence: *In 'the man who came', 'who' is a relative pronoun and 'who came' is a relative clause.*
■ *noun* **1** a person who is in the same family as sb else **SYN** RELATION: *a close/distant relative* ◊ *her friends and relatives* **2** a thing that belongs to the same group as sth else: *The ibex is a distant relative of the mountain goat.*

rela·tive·ly /ˈrelətɪvli/ *adv.* to a fairly large degree, especially in comparison to others: *I found the test relatively easy.* ◊ *We had relatively few applications for the job.* ◊ *Lack of exercise is also a risk factor for heart disease but it's relatively small when compared with the others.* **IDM** **ˈrelatively speaking** used when you are comparing sth with all similar things: *Relatively speaking, these jobs provide good salaries.*

rela·tiv·ism /ˈrelətɪvɪzəm/ *noun* [U] (*formal*) the belief that truth is not always and generally valid, but can be judged only in relation to other things, such as your personal situation: *moral/cultural relativism* ▶ **rela·tiv·ist** *adj.*: *a relativist view/position* **rela·tiv·ist** *noun*

rela·tiv·ity /ˌreləˈtɪvəti/ *noun* [U] **1** (*physics*) Einstein's theory of the universe based on the principle that all movement is relative and that time is a fourth DIMENSION related to space **2** (*formal*) the state of being relative and only able to be judged when compared with sth else

re·launch /ˌriːˈlɔːntʃ/ *verb* [VN] to start or present sth again in a new or different way, especially a product for sale ▶ **re·launch** /ˈriːlɔːntʃ/ *noun*: *a party to mark the relaunch of the magazine*

relax /rɪˈlæks/ *verb* **1** [V] **~ (with sth)** to rest while you are doing sth enjoyable, especially after work or effort: *When I get home from work I like to relax with a glass of wine.* ◊ *Just relax and enjoy the movie.* ◊ *I'm going to spend the weekend just relaxing.* **2** to become or make sb become calmer and less worried: [V] *I'll only relax when I know you're safe.* ◊ *Relax! Everything will be OK.* [also VN] **3** to become or make sth become less tight or stiff: [V] *Allow your muscles to relax completely.* ◊ [VN] *The massage relaxed my tense back muscles.* ◊ *He relaxed his grip on her arm.* ◊ (*figurative*) *The dictator refuses to relax his grip on power.* **4** [VN] to allow rules, laws, etc. to become less strict: *The council has relaxed the ban on dogs in city parks.* **5** [VN] to allow your attention or effort to become weaker: *You cannot afford to relax your concentration for a moment.*

re·lax·ation /ˌriːlækˈseɪʃn/ *noun* **1** [U] ways of resting and enjoying yourself; time spent resting and enjoying yourself: *I go hill-walking for relaxation.* ◊ *a few days of relaxation* ◊ *relaxation techniques* **2** [C] something pleasant you do in order to rest, especially after you have been working: *Fishing is his favourite relaxation.* **3** [U, C, usually sing.] the act of making a rule or some form of control less strict or severe: *the relaxation of foreign currency controls* ◊ *a relaxation of travel restrictions*

re·laxed /rɪˈlækst/ *adj.* **1 ~ (about sth)** (of a person) calm and not anxious or worried: *He appeared relaxed and confident before the match.* ◊ *She had a very relaxed manner.* **2** (of a place) calm and informal: *a family-run hotel with a relaxed atmosphere* **3 ~ (about sth)** not caring too much about discipline or making people follow rules: *I take a fairly relaxed attitude towards what the kids wear to school.*

re·lax·ing /rɪˈlæksɪŋ/ *adj.* helping you to rest and become less anxious: *a relaxing drink/walk/evening*

relay *verb, noun*
■ *verb* /ˈriːleɪ; rɪˈleɪ/ [VN] **1** to receive and send on information, news, etc. to sb: *He relayed the message to his boss.* ◊ *Instructions were relayed to him by phone.* **2** to broadcast

R

æ	ɑː	e	ɜː	ə	ɪ	iː	i	ɒ	ɔː	ʌ	ʊ	u	uː
cat	father	ten	bird	about	sit	see	many	got	saw	cup	put	actual	too

(BrE)

television or radio signals: *The game was relayed by satellite to audiences all over the world.*

■ *noun* /ˈriːleɪ/ **1** (also **ˈrelay race**) a race between teams in which each member of the team runs or swims one section of the race: *the 4 × 100m relay* ◊ *a relay team/squad* ◊ *the sprint relay*—picture on page 1251 **2** a fresh set of people or animals that take the place of others that are tired or have finished a period of work: *Rescuers worked in relays to save the trapped miners.* **3** an electronic device that receives radio or television signals and sends them on again with greater strength: *a relay station/satellite*

re·lease /rɪˈliːs/ *verb, noun*
■ *verb* [VN]
SET SB/STH FREE | **1** ~ sb/sth (from sth) to let sb/sth come out of a place where they have been kept or trapped: *to release a prisoner/hostage* ◊ *Firefighters took two hours to release the driver from the wreckage.*
STOP HOLDING STH | **2** to stop holding sth or stop it from being held so that it can move, fly, fall, etc. freely: *He refused to release her arm.* ◊ *10000 balloons were released at the ceremony.* ◊ *Intense heat is released in the reaction.*
FEELINGS | **3** to express feelings such as anger or worry in order to get rid of them: *She burst into tears, releasing all her pent-up emotions.*
FREE SB FROM DUTY | **4** ~ sb (from sth) to free sb from a duty, responsibility, contract, etc: *The club is releasing some of its older players.* ◊ *The new law released employers from their obligation to recognize unions.*
PART OF MACHINE | **5** to remove sth from a fixed position, allowing sth else to move or function: *to release the clutch/handbrake/switch*
MAKE LESS TIGHT | **6** to make sth less tight: *You need to release the tension in these shoulder muscles.*
MAKE AVAILABLE | **7** to make sth available to the public: *Police have released no further details about the accident.* ◊ *to release a movie/book/CD* ◊ *new products released onto the market* **8** to make sth available that had previously been restricted: *The new building programme will go ahead as soon as the government releases the funds.*
■ *noun*
SETTING SB/STH FREE | **1** [U, sing.] ~ (of sb) (from sth) the act of setting a person or an animal free; the state of being set free: *The government has been working to secure the release of the hostages.* ◊ *She can expect an early release from prison.*
MAKING STH AVAILABLE | **2** [U, sing.] the act of making sth available to the public: *The new software is planned for release in April.* ◊ *The movie goes on general release (= will be widely shown in cinemas/movie theaters) next week.* **3** [C] a thing that is made available to the public, especially a new CD or film/movie: *the latest new releases*
OF GAS/CHEMICAL | **4** [U, C] the act of letting a gas, chemical, etc. come out of the container where it has been safely held: *the release of carbon dioxide into the atmosphere* ◊ *to monitor radiation releases*
FROM UNPLEASANT FEELING | **5** [U, sing.] the feeling that you are free from pain, anxiety or some other unpleasant feeling: *a sense of release after the exam* ◊ *I think her death was a merciful release.*
—see also PRESS RELEASE

rele·gate /ˈrelɪgeɪt/ *verb* [VN] **1** ~ sb/sth (to sth) to give sb a lower or less important position, rank, etc. than before: *She was then relegated to the role of assistant.* ◊ *He relegated the incident to the back of his mind.* **2** [usually passive] (*especially BrE*) to move a sports team, especially a football team, to a lower position within an official LEAGUE [OPP] PROMOTE ▶ **rele·ga·tion** /ˌrelɪˈgeɪʃn/ *noun* [U]: *teams threatened with relegation*

re·lent /rɪˈlent/ *verb* [V] **1** to finally agree to sth after refusing: *'Well, just for a little while then,' she said, finally relenting.* **2** to become less determined, strong, etc: *After two days the rain relented slightly and we were able to leave the hotel.* ◊ *The police will not relent in their fight against crime.*

re·lent·less /rɪˈlentləs/ *adj.* **1** not stopping or getting less strong: *her relentless pursuit of perfection* ◊ *The sun* was relentless. **2** refusing to give up or be less strict or severe: *a relentless enemy* ◊ *You have to be as single-minded and relentless as your rivals if you want to get to the top.* ▶ **re·lent·less·ly** *adv.*: *He went on relentlessly with his questions.*

rele·vant /ˈreləvənt/ *adj.* ~ (to sth/sb) **1** closely connected with the subject you are discussing or the situation you are thinking about: *a relevant suggestion/question/point* ◊ *These comments are not directly relevant to this enquiry.* ◊ *Do you have the relevant experience?* [OPP] IRRELEVANT **2** having ideas that are valuable and useful to people in their lives and work: *Her novel is still relevant today.* ▶ **rele·vance** /-əns/ *noun* [U]: *I don't see the relevance of your question.* ◊ *What he said has no direct relevance to the matter in hand.* ◊ *a classic play of contemporary relevance* **rele·vant·ly** *adv.*: *The applicant has experience in teaching and, more relevantly, in industry.*

re·li·able /rɪˈlaɪəbl/ *adj.* **1** that can be trusted to do sth well; that you can rely on [SYN] DEPENDABLE: *We are looking for someone who is reliable and hard-working.* ◊ *a reliable friend/supplier/supporter* ◊ *My car's not as reliable as it used to be.* **2** that is likely to be correct or true: *Our information comes from a reliable source.* ◊ *a reliable witness* [OPP] UNRELIABLE ▶ **re·li·abil·ity** /rɪˌlaɪəˈbɪləti/ *noun* [U]: *The incident cast doubt on her motives and reliability.* ◊ *The reliability of these results has been questioned.* **re·li·ably** /-əbli/ *adv.*: *I am reliably informed (= told by sb who knows the facts) that the company is being sold.*

re·li·ance /rɪˈlaɪəns/ *noun* [U, sing.] ~ (on/upon sb/sth) the state of needing sb/sth in order to survive, be successful, etc.; the fact of being able to rely on sb/sth [SYN] DEPENDENCE: *Heavy reliance on one client is not without risk when building up a business.* ◊ *Such learning methods encourage too great a reliance upon the teacher.* ◊ *The study programme concentrates more on group work and places less reliance on (= depends less on) lectures.* ◊ *I wouldn't place too much reliance on (= trust) these figures.*

re·li·ant /rɪˈlaɪənt/ *adj.* ~ on/upon sb/sth needing sb/sth in order to survive, be successful, etc. [SYN] DEPENDENT: *The hostel is heavily reliant upon charity.*—see also SELF-RELIANT

relic /ˈrelɪk/ *noun* **1** ~ (of/from sth) an object, a tradition, etc. that has survived from a period of time that no longer exists: *The building stands as the last remaining relic of the town's cotton industry.* **2** a part of the body or clothing of a holy person, or sth that they owned, that is kept after their death and respected as a religious object: *holy/sacred relics*

re·lief /rɪˈliːf/ *noun*
REMOVAL OF ANXIETY/PAIN | **1** [U, sing.] the feeling of happiness that you have when sth unpleasant stops or does not happen: *a sense of relief* ◊ *We all breathed a sigh of relief when he left.* ◊ *She sighed with relief.* ◊ *Much to my relief the car was not damaged.* ◊ *News of their safety came as a great relief.* ◊ *It was a relief to be able to talk to someone about it.* ◊ *What a relief!* **2** [U] ~ (from/of sth) the act of removing or reducing pain, anxiety, etc: *modern methods of pain relief* ◊ *the relief of misery/poverty/suffering*
HELP | **3** [U] food, money, medicine, etc. that is given to help people in places where there has been a war or natural disaster: *famine relief* ◊ *a relief agency/organization/worker* **4** [U] (*especially AmE*) financial help given by the government to people who need it
ON TAX | **5** [U] = TAX RELIEF: *relief on mortgage interest payments*
STH DIFFERENT | **6** [U, sing.] ~ (from sth) something that is interesting or enjoyable that replaces sth boring, difficult or unpleasant for a short period of time: *a few moments of light relief in an otherwise dull performance* ◊ *There was little comic relief in his speech.* ◊ *The calm of the countryside came as a welcome relief from the hustle and bustle of city life.*
WORKERS | **7** [C+sing./pl. v.] (often used as an adjective) a person or group of people that replaces another when they have finished working for the day or when they are

sick: *The next crew relief comes on duty at 9 o'clock.* ◊ *relief drivers*

FROM ENEMY | **8** [sing.] **~ of ...** the act of freeing a town, etc. from an enemy army that has surrounded it

IN ART | **9** [U, C] a way of decorating wood, stone, etc. by cutting designs into the surface of it so that some parts stick out more than others; a design that is made in this way: *The column was decorated in high relief* (= with designs that stick out a lot) *with scenes from Greek mythology.* ◊ *The bronze doors are covered with sculpted reliefs.*

MAKING STH NOTICEABLE | **10** [U] the effect of colours, light, etc. that makes an object more noticeable than others around it: *The snow-capped mountain stood out in sharp relief against the blue sky.* **11** [U] the quality of a particular situation, problem, etc. that makes it more noticeable than before: *Their differences have been thrown into sharp relief by the present crisis.*

re·lief map *noun* a map that uses various colours, etc. to show the different heights of hills, valleys, etc.

re·lief road *noun* (*BrE*) a road that vehicles can use to avoid an area of heavy traffic, especially a road built for this purpose

re·lieve /rɪˈliːv/ *verb* [VN] **1** to remove or reduce an unpleasant feeling or pain: *to relieve the symptoms of a cold* ◊ *to relieve anxiety/guilt/stress* ◊ *Being able to tell the truth at last seemed to relieve her.* **2** to make a problem less serious: *efforts to relieve famine in Africa* ◊ *to relieve traffic congestion/unemployment* **3** to make sth less boring, especially by introducing sth different: *We played cards to relieve the boredom of the long wait.* ◊ *The black and white pattern is relieved by tiny coloured flowers.* **4** to replace sb who is on duty: *to relieve a driver/sentry* ◊ *You'll be relieved at six o'clock.* **5** to free a town, etc. from an enemy army that has surrounded it **6 ~ yourself** a polite way of referring to going to the toilet: *I had to relieve myself behind a bush.* PHRV **re'lieve sb of sth 1** to help sb by taking sth heavy or difficult from them: *Let me relieve you of some of your bags.* ◊ *The new secretary will relieve us of some of the paperwork.* **2** (*informal, ironic*) to steal sth from sb: *A boy with a knife relieved him of his wallet.* **3** to dismiss sb from a job, position, etc: *General Beale was relieved of his command.*

re·lieved /rɪˈliːvd/ *adj.* **~ (to see, hear, find, etc. sth)** | **~ (that ...)** feeling happy because sth unpleasant has stopped or has not happened; showing this: *She sounded relieved.* ◊ *You'll be relieved to know your jobs are safe.* ◊ *I'm just relieved that nobody was hurt.* ◊ *They exchanged relieved glances.*

re·li·gion /rɪˈlɪdʒən/ *noun* **1** [U] the belief in the existence of a god or gods, and the activities that are connected with the worship of them: *Is there always a conflict between science and religion?* **2** [C] one of the systems of faith that are based on the belief in the existence of a particular god or gods: *the Jewish religion* ◊ *Christianity, Islam and other world religions* ◊ *The law states that everyone has the right to practise their own religion.* **3** [sing.] a particular interest or influence that is very important in your life: *For him, football is an absolute religion.* IDM **get re'ligion** (*informal, disapproving*) to suddenly become interested in religion

re·ligi·os·ity /rɪˌlɪdʒiˈɒsəti; *AmE* -ˈɑːsəti/ *noun* [U] (sometimes *disapproving*) the state of being religious or too religious

re·li·gious /rɪˈlɪdʒəs/ *adj.* **1** [only before noun] connected with religion or with a particular religion: *religious beliefs/faith* ◊ *religious education* (= education about religion) ◊ *religious instruction* (= instruction in a particular religion) ◊ *religious groups/leaders* ◊ *objects which have a religious significance* **2** (of a person) believing strongly in the existence of a god or gods SYN DEVOUT: *His wife is very religious.* ▶ **re·li·gious·ness** *noun* [U]

re·li·gious·ly /rɪˈlɪdʒəsli/ *adv.* **1** very carefully or regularly: *She followed the instructions religiously.* ◊ *They go to Greece religiously every year.* **2** in a way that is connected with religion: *Were you brought up religiously?*

re·lin·quish /rɪˈlɪŋkwɪʃ/ *verb* [VN] **~ sth (to sb)** (*formal*) to stop having sth, especially when this happens unwill-

ingly: *He was forced to relinquish control of the company.* ◊ *They had relinquished all hope that she was alive.* ◊ *She relinquished possession of the house to her sister.*

reli·quary /ˈrelɪkwəri; *AmE* -kweri/ *noun* (*pl.* **-ies**) a container in which a RELIC of a holy person is kept

rel·ish /ˈrelɪʃ/ *verb, noun*
■ *verb* to get great pleasure from sth; to want very much to do or have sth: [VN] *to relish a fight/challenge/debate* ◊ *to relish the idea/thought of sth* ◊ *I don't relish the prospect of getting up early tomorrow.* ◊ [V-**ing**] *Nobody relishes cleaning the oven.* [also VN-**ing**]
■ *noun* **1** [U] (*written*) great enjoyment or pleasure: *She savoured the moment with obvious relish.* **2** [U, C] a cold thick spicy sauce made from fruit and vegetables that have been boiled, served with meat, cheese, etc.

re·live /ˌriːˈlɪv/ *verb* [VN] to experience sth again, especially in your imagination: *He relives the horror of the crash every night in his dreams.*

re·load /ˌriːˈləʊd; *AmE* -ˈloʊd/ *verb* **1** [V, VN] to put more bullets into a gun, more film into a camera, etc. **2** [VN] to put data or a program into the memory of a computer again **3** [VN] to fill a container, vehicle, machine, etc. again

re·locate /ˌriːləʊˈkeɪt; *AmE* ˌriːˈloʊkeɪt/ *verb* (especially of a company or workers) to move or to move sb/sth to a new place to work or operate: [V] *The firm may be forced to relocate from New York to Stanford.* ◊ *Some were unwilling to relocate.* ◊ [VN] *The company relocated its head office to Stanford.* ▶ **re·loca·tion** /ˌriːləʊˈkeɪʃn; *AmE* ˌriːloʊ-/ *noun* [U]: *relocation costs/expenses*

re·luc·tant /rɪˈlʌktənt/ *adj.* **~ (to do sth)** hesitating before doing sth because you do not want to do it or because you are not sure that it is the right thing to do: *reluctant agreement/support* ◊ *She was reluctant to admit she was wrong.* ◊ *He finally gave a reluctant smile.* ◊ *a reluctant hero* (= a person who does not want to be called a hero) ▶ **re·luc·tance** /-əns/ *noun* [U, sing.] **~ (to do sth)**: *There is still some reluctance on the part of employers to become involved in this project.* ◊ *They finally agreed to our terms with a certain reluctance.* **re·luc·tant·ly** *adv.*: *We reluctantly agreed to go with her.*

rely /rɪˈlaɪ/ *verb* (**re·lies, rely·ing, re·lied, re·lied**) PHRV **re'ly on/upon sb/ sth 1** to need or be dependent on sb/sth: *As babies, we rely entirely on others for food.* ◊ [+ **to** inf] *These days we rely heavily on computers to organize our work.* ◊ [+-**ing**] *The industry relies on the price of raw materials remaining low.* **2** to trust or have faith in sb/sth: *You should rely on your own judgement.* ◊ [+ **to** inf] *You can rely on me to keep your secret.* ◊ *He can't be relied on to tell the truth.*

WORD FAMILY
rely *v.*
reliable *adj.* (≠ unreliable)
reliability *n.* (≠ unreliability)
reliance *n.*

REM /ˌɑːr iː ˈem/ *abbr.* rapid eye movement (describes a period of sleep during which you dream and your eyes make many small movements)

re·main /rɪˈmeɪn/ *verb* (*formal*) (not usually in the progressive tenses) **1** *linking verb* to continue to be sth; to be still in the same state or condition: [V-ADJ] *to remain silent/standing/seated/motionless* ◊ *Train fares are likely to remain unchanged.* ◊ *It remains true that sport is about competing well, not winning.* ◊ [V-N] *In spite of their quarrel, they remain the best of friends.* ◊ *He will remain (as) manager of the club until the end of his contract.* **2** [V] to still be present after the other parts have been removed, used, etc.; to continue to exist: *Very little of the house remained after the fire.* ◊ *Only about half of the original workforce remains.* ◊ *There were only ten minutes remaining.* **3** to still need to be done, said, or dealt with: [V to inf] *Much remains to be done.* ◊ *It remains to be seen* (= it will only be known later) *whether you are right.* ◊ [V] *There remained one significant problem.* ◊ *Questions remain about the president's honesty.* ◊ [V(that)] *I feel sorry for her, but the fact remains (that) she lied to us.* **4** [V] [usually +adv./prep.] to stay in the same place; to not leave: *They remained in Mexico until June.* ◊ *The*

R

plane remained on the ground. ◇ *She left, but I remained behind.* **IDM** see ALOOF

re·main·der /rɪˈmeɪndə(r)/ *noun, verb*
- *noun* **1** (usually **the remainder**) [sing.+ sing./pl. *v.*] (*written*) the remaining people, things or time **SYN** THE REST: *I kept some of his books and gave away the remainder.* **HELP** When **the remainder** refers to a plural noun, the verb is plural: *Most of our employees work in New York; the remainder are in London.* **2** [C, usually sing.] (*mathematics*) the numbers left after one number has been SUBTRACTED from another, or one number has been divided into another: *Divide 2 into 7, and the answer is 3, remainder 1.* **3** [C] a book that has been remaindered
- *verb* [V, VN] (usually passive) to sell books at a reduced price

re·mains /rɪˈmeɪnz/ *noun* [pl.] **1** ~ (**of sth**) the parts of sth that are left after the other parts have been used, eaten, removed, etc: *She fed the remains of her lunch to the dog.* **2** the parts of ancient objects and buildings that have survived and are discovered in the present day: *prehistoric remains* ◇ *the remains of a Roman fort* **3** (*formal*) the body of a dead person or animal: *human remains*

re·make *noun, verb*
- *noun* /ˈriːmeɪk/ a new or different version of an old film/movie or song
- *verb* /ˌriːˈmeɪk/ (**re·made, re·made** /-ˈmeɪd/) [VN] to make a new or different version of sth such as an old film/movie or song; to make sth again: *'The Seven Samurai' was remade in Hollywood as 'The Magnificent Seven'.*

re·mand /rɪˈmɑːnd; *AmE* -ˈmænd/ *verb, noun*
- *verb* [VN] [usually+*adv./prep.*] [usually passive] to send sb away from a court of law to wait for their trial which will take place at a later date: [VN] *The two men were charged with burglary and remanded in custody* (= sent to prison until their trial). ◇ *She was remanded on bail* (= allowed to go free until the trial after leaving a sum of money with the court).
- *noun* [U, C, pl.] the process of keeping sb in prison while they are waiting for their trial: *He is currently being held on remand.* ◇ *a remand prisoner*

re'mand centre *noun* (*BrE*) a place where young people are sent when they are accused of a crime and are waiting for their trial

re·mark /rɪˈmɑːk; *AmE* -ˈmɑːrk/ *noun, verb*
- *noun* **1** [C] something that you say or write which expresses an opinion, thought, etc. about sb/sth **SYN** COMMENT: *a cutting/pointed/racist remark* ◇ *He made a number of rude remarks about the food.* ◇ *What exactly did you mean by that last remark?* **2** [U] (*old-fashioned* or *formal*) the quality of being important or interesting enough to be noticed: *The exhibition contains nothing that is worthy of remark.*
- *verb* ~ (**on/upon sth/sb**)| ~ (**how ...**) to say or write a comment about sth/sb:[V] *The judges remarked on the high standard of entries for the competition.* ◇ *She remarked how tired I was looking.*[V speech] *'It's much colder than yesterday,' he remarked casually.* ◇ [V that] *Critics remarked that the play was not original.* ◇ [VN] *The similarities between the two have often been remarked on.* **HELP** This pattern is only used in the passive and **on** must be included.

re·mark·able /rɪˈmɑːkəbl; *AmE* -ˈmɑːrk-/ *adj.* ~ (**for sth**)| ~ (**that ...**) unusual or surprising in a way that causes people to take notice: *a remarkable achievement/career/talent* ◇ *She was a truly remarkable woman.* ◇ *The area is remarkable for its scenery.* ◇ *It is remarkable that nobody noticed sooner.* **OPP** UNREMARKABLE ▶ **re·mark·ably** /-əbli/ *adv.*: *The car is in remarkably good condition for its age.* ◇ *Remarkably, nobody was killed.*

re·marry /ˌriːˈmæri/ *verb* (**re·mar·ries, re·marry·ing, re·mar·ried, re·mar·ried**) [V] to marry again after being divorced or after your husband or wife has died ▶ **re·mar·riage** /ˌriːˈmærɪdʒ/ *noun* [U, C]

re·mas·ter /ˌriːˈmɑːstə(r); *AmE* -ˈmæs-/ *verb* [VN] to make a new MASTER copy of a recording in order to improve the

sound quality: *All the tracks have been digitally remastered from the original tapes.*

re·match /ˈriːmætʃ/ *noun* [usually sing.] a match or game played again between the same people or teams, especially because neither side won the first match or game

re·medi·able /rɪˈmiːdiəbl/ *adj.* (*formal*) that can be solved or cured: *remediable problems/diseases*

re·med·ial /rɪˈmiːdiəl/ *adj.* [only before noun] **1** aimed at solving a problem, especially when this involves correcting or improving sth that has been done wrong: *remedial treatment/surgery* (= for a medical problem) ◇ *Remedial action must be taken now.* **2** connected with school students who are slower at learning than others: *remedial education* ◇ *a remedial class*

rem·edy /ˈremədi/ *noun, verb*
- *noun* (*pl.* **-ies**) ~ (**for/to sth**) **1** a way of dealing with or improving an unpleasant or difficult situation: *There is no simple remedy for unemployment.* ◇ *There are a number of possible remedies to this problem.* **2** a treatment or medicine to cure a disease or reduce pain that is not very serious: *a natural/herbal remedy* ◇ *an excellent home remedy for sore throats* **3** ~ (**against sth**) (*law*) a way of dealing with a problem, using the processes of the law: *Holding copyright provides the only legal remedy against unauthorized copying.* ◇ *What's my remedy in law in this case?*
- *verb* (**rem·ed·ies, rem·edy·ing, rem·ed·ied, rem·ed·ied**) [VN] to correct or improve sth: *to remedy a deficiency/problem/mistake* ◇ *This situation is easily remedied.*

re·mem·ber /rɪˈmembə(r)/ *verb* (not usually used in the progressive tenses)
SB/STH FROM THE PAST **1** to have or keep an image in your memory of an event, a person, a place, etc. from the past: [VN] *This is Carla. Do you remember her?* ◇ *I don't remember my first day at school.* ◇ *He still remembered her as the lively teenager he'd known years before.* ◇ [V] *As far as I can remember, this is the third time we've met.* ◇ [V-ing] *Do you remember switching the lights off before we came out?* ◇ *I vaguely remember hearing him come in.* ◇ [VN-ing] *I can still vividly remember my grandfather teaching me to play cards.* ◇ (*formal*) *I can't remember his taking a single day off work.* ◇ [V (that)] *I remember (that) we used to go and see them most weekends.*
FACT/INFORMATION **2** to bring back to your mind a fact, piece of information, etc. that you knew: [VN] *I'm sorry—I can't remember your name.* ◇ [V wh-] *Can you remember how much money we spent?* ◇ [V] *You were going to help me with this. Remember?* ◇ [V (that)] *Remember that we're going out tonight.* **3** [V (that)] to keep an important fact in your mind: *Remember (that) you may feel sleepy after taking the pills.* ◇ [VN (that)] *It should be remembered that the majority of accidents happen in the home.*
STH YOU HAVE TO DO **4** to not forget to do sth; to actually do what you have to do: [V to inf] *Remember to call me when you arrive!* ◇ [VN] *Did you remember your homework* (= to bring it)*?* **HELP** Notice the difference between **remember doing sth** and **remember to do sth**: *I remember posting the letter* means 'I have an image in my memory of doing it'; *I remembered to post the letter* means 'I didn't forget to do it.'
IN PRAYERS **5** [VN] to think about sb with respect, especially when saying a prayer: *a church service to remember the war dead*
GIVE PRESENT **6** [VN] to give money, a present, etc. to sb/sth: *My aunt always remembers my birthday* (= by sending a card or present). ◇ *His grandfather remembered him* (= left him money) *in his will.*
IDM **be re'membered for sth** | **be re'membered as sth** to be famous or known for a particular thing that you have done in the past: *He is best remembered as the man who brought jazz to England.* **PHRV** **re'member me to sb** (*especially BrE*) used to ask sb to give your greetings to sb else: *Remember me to your parents.*

re·mem·brance /rɪˈmembrəns/ *noun* **1** [U] the act or process of remembering an event in the past or a person

R

who is dead: *A service was held in remembrance of local soldiers killed in the war.* ◊ *a remembrance service* ◊ (*formal*) *He smiled at the remembrance of their first kiss.* **2** [C] (*formal*) an object that causes you to remember sb/sth; a memory of sb/sth: *The cenotaph stands as a remembrance of those killed during the war.*

Re·membrance 'Sunday (also **Re'membrance Day**) *noun* the Sunday nearest to the 11 November on which those killed in war, especially the wars of 1914–18 and 1939–45, are remembered in ceremonies and church services in Britain—see also MEMORIAL DAY, VETERANS DAY

re·mind /rɪ'maɪnd/ *verb* ~ **sb** (**about/of sth**) to help sb remember sth important that they must do: [VN] *I'm sorry, I've forgotten your name. Can you remind me?* ◊ *That* (= what you have just said, done, etc.) *reminds me, I must get some cash.* ◊ *'Don't forget the camera.' 'Remind me about it nearer the time.'* ◊ [VN to inf] *Remind me to phone Alan before I go out.* ◊ [VN (**that**)] *Passengers are reminded (that) no smoking is allowed on this train.* ◊ [VN wh-] *Can someone remind me what I should do next?* ◊ [VN speech] *'You had an accident,' he reminded her.* PHRV **re'mind sb of sb/sth** if sb/sth **reminds** you of sb/sth else, they make you remember or think about the other person, place, thing, etc. because they are similar in some way: *You remind me of your father when you say that.* ◊ *That smell reminds me of France.*

re·mind·er /rɪ'maɪndə(r)/ *noun* **1** ~ (**of sb/sth**)| ~ (**that…**) something that makes you think about or remember sb/sth, that you have forgotten or would like to forget: *The sheer size of the cathedral is a constant reminder to the tourist of the power of religion.* ◊ *The incident served as a timely reminder of just how dangerous mountaineering can be.* **2** a letter or note informing sb that they have not done sth

rem·in·isce /ˌremɪ'nɪs/ *verb* [V] ~ (**about sth/sb**) to think, talk or write about a happy time in your past: *We spent a happy evening reminiscing about the past.*

rem·in·is·cence /ˌremɪ'nɪsns/ *noun* **1** [C, usually pl.] a spoken or written description of sth that sb remembers about their past life SYN MEMORY: *The book is a collection of his reminiscences about the actress.* ◊ *reminiscences of a wartime childhood* **2** [U] the act of remembering things that happened in the past **3** [C, usually pl.] something that reminds you of sth similar: *Her music is full of reminiscences of African rhythms.*

rem·in·is·cent /ˌremɪ'nɪsnt/ *adj.* **1** ~ **of sb/sth** reminding you of sb/sth: *The way he laughed was strongly reminiscent of his father.* **2** [only before noun] (*formal*) showing that you are thinking about the past, especially in a way that causes you pleasure: *a reminiscent smile*

re·miss /rɪ'mɪs/ *adj.* [not before noun] ~ (**of sb**) (**to do sth**)| ~ (**in sth/in doing sth**) (*formal*) not giving sth enough care and attention SYN NEGLIGENT: *It was remiss of them not to inform us of these changes sooner.* ◊ *She had clearly been remiss in her duty.*

re·mis·sion /rɪ'mɪʃn/ *noun* [U, C] **1** a period during which a serious illness improves for a time and the patient seems to get better: *The patient has been in remission for the past six months.* ◊ *The symptoms reappeared after only a short remission.* **2** (*BrE*) a reduction in the amount of time sb spends in prison, especially because they have behaved well: *With remission for good behaviour, he could be out by the end of the year.* **3** (*formal*) an act of reducing or cancelling the amount of money that sb has to pay: *New businesses may qualify for tax remission.* ◊ *There is a partial remission of fees for overseas students.*

remit *noun, verb*
■ *noun* /'ri:mɪt; rɪ'mɪt/ [usually sing.] ~ (**of sb/sth**)| ~ (**to do sth**) (*BrE*) the area of activity over which a particular person or group has authority, control or influence: *Such decisions are outside the remit of this committee.* ◊ *In future, staff recruitment will fall within the remit of the division manager.* ◊ *a remit to report on medical services*
■ *verb* /rɪ'mɪt/ (-**tt**-) [VN] (*formal*) **1** ~ **sth** (**to sb**) to send money, etc. to a person or place: *to remit fees/funds* ◊ *Payment will be remitted to you in full.* **2** to cancel or free

sb from a debt, duty, punishment, etc: *to remit a tax/a fine/fees* ◊ *to remit a prison sentence*—see also UNREMITTING PHRV **re'mit sth to sb** [usually passive] (*law*) to send a matter to an authority so that a decision can be made: *The case was remitted to the Court of Appeal.*

re·mit·tance /rɪ'mɪtns/ *noun* **1** [C] (*formal*) a sum of money that is sent to sb in order to pay for sth: *Please return the completed form with your remittance.* **2** [U] the act of sending money to sb in order to pay for sth: *Remittance can be made by cheque or credit card.*

remix /ˌriː'mɪks/ *verb* [VN] to make a new version of a recorded piece of music by using a machine to arrange the separate parts of the recording differently, add new parts, etc. ▶ **remix** /'riːmɪks/ (also **mix**) *noun* **re·mixer** *noun*: *the skills of remixer Tom Moulton*

rem·nant /'remnənt/ *noun* **1** [usually pl.] a part of sth that is left after the other parts have been used, removed, destroyed, etc: *The woods are remnants of a huge forest which once covered the whole area.* **2** a small piece of fabric that is left when the rest has been sold

re·model /ˌriː'mɒdl; *AmE* -'mɑːdl/ *verb* (-**ll**-, *AmE* -**l**-) [VN] to change the structure or shape of sth: *The interior of the building has been completely remodelled.*

rem·on·strance /rɪ'mɒnstrəns; *AmE* -'mɑːn-/ *noun* [C, U] (*formal*) a protest or complaint

rem·on·strate /'remənstreɪt; *AmE* rɪ'mɑːnstreɪt/ *verb* ~ (**with sb**) (**about sth**) (*formal*) to protest or complain about sth/sb: [V] *They remonstrated with the official about the decision.* [also V speech]

re·morse /rɪ'mɔːs; *AmE* rɪ'mɔːrs/ *noun* [U] ~ (**for sth/for doing sth**) the feeling of being extremely sorry for sth wrong or bad that you have done SYN REGRET: *I felt guilty and full of remorse.* ◊ *He was filled with remorse for not believing her.* ▶ **re·morse·ful** /-fl/ *adj.* **re·morse·ful·ly** /-fəli/ *adv.*

re·morse·less /rɪ'mɔːsləs; *AmE* -'mɔːrs-/ *adj.* (*written*) **1** (especially of an unpleasant situation) seeming to continue or become worse in a way that cannot be stopped SYN RELENTLESS: *the remorseless increase in crime* **2** cruel and having or showing no pity for other people SYN MERCILESS: *a remorseless killer* ▶ **re·morse·less·ly** *adv.*

re·mort·gage /ˌriː'mɔːgɪdʒ; *AmE* -'mɔːrg-/ *verb* [V, VN] to arrange a second MORTGAGE on your house or apartment, or to increase or change your first one ▶ **re·mort·gage** *noun*

re·mote /rɪ'məʊt; *AmE* rɪ'moʊt/ *adj., noun*
■ *adj.* (**re·moter, re·mot·est**)
PLACE | **1** ~ (**from sth**) far away from places where other people live SYN ISOLATED: *a remote beach* ◊ *one of the remotest areas of the world* ◊ *The farmhouse is remote from any other buildings.*
TIME | **2** [only before noun] far away in time SYN DISTANT: *in the remote past/future* ◊ *a remote ancestor* (= who lived a long time ago) ◊ *a remote dream/goal*
RELATIVES | **3** [only before noun] (of people) not closely related SYN DISTANT: *a remote cousin*
COMPUTER/SYSTEM | **4** that you can connect to from far away, using an electronic link: *a remote terminal/database*
DIFFERENT | **5** ~ (**from sth**) very different from sth: *His theories are somewhat remote from reality.*
NOT FRIENDLY | **6** (of people or their behaviour) not very friendly or interested in other people SYN DISTANT
VERY SMALL | **7** not very great: *There is still a remote chance that they will find her alive.* ◊ *I don't have the remotest idea what you're talking about.*
▶ **re·mote·ness** *noun* [U]: *the geographical remoteness of the island* ◊ *His remoteness made her feel unloved.*
■ *noun* (*informal*) = REMOTE CONTROL

re·mote 'access *noun* [U] the use of a computer system, etc. that is in another place, that you can connect to when you are far away, using an electronic link

re·mote con'trol *noun* **1** [U] the ability to operate a machine from a distance using radio or electrical signals: *It works by remote control.* ◊ *a remote-control camera* **2** (also *informal* **re·mote, zap·per**) [C] a device that

æ	ɑː	e	ɜː	ə	ɪ	iː	i	ɒ	ɔː	ʌ	ʊ	u	uː
cat	father	ten	bird	about	sit	see	many	got	saw	cup	put	actual	too

(BrE)

allows you to operate a television, etc. from a distance: *I can't find the remote control.* ▶ **re**‧**mote-con'trolled** *adj.*: *remote-controlled equipment*

re‧**mote**‧**ly** /rɪ'məʊtli; *AmE* -'moʊt-/ *adv.* **1** (usually in negative sentences) to a very slight degree: *It wasn't even remotely funny* (= it wasn't at all funny). ◇ *The two incidents were only remotely connected.* ◇ *I suppose it's remotely possible.* **2** from a distance: *remotely operated* **3** far away from places where other people live: *The church is remotely situated on the north coast of the island.*

re‧**mote 'sensing** *noun* [U] the use of SATELLITES to search for and collect information about the earth

re‧**mould** /ˌriː'məʊld; *AmE* -'moʊld/ *verb* [VN] (*BrE, formal*) to change sth such as an idea, a system, etc: *attempts to remould policy to make it more acceptable*

re‧**mount** /ˌriː'maʊnt/ *verb* **1** [V, VN] to get on a horse, bicycle, etc. again after getting off it or falling off it **2** [VN] to organize and begin sth a second time

re‧**mov**‧**able** /rɪ'muːvəbl/ *adj.* [usually before noun] that can be taken off or out of sth [SYN] DETACHABLE: *The dryer has a removable filter.*

re‧**moval** /rɪ'muːvl/ *noun* **1** [U] ~ (of sb/sth) the act of taking sb/sth away from a particular place: *Clearance of the site required the removal of a number of trees.* ◇ *the removal of a tumour* **2** [U] ~ (of sth) the act of getting rid of sth: *stain removal* ◇ *the removal of trade barriers* **3** [U] ~ (of sb) the act of dismissing sb from their job: *events leading to the removal of the president from office* **4** [C] (*BrE*) an act of taking furniture, etc. from one house to another: *house removals* ◇ *a removal company/firm* ◇ *When are the removal men coming?*

re'moval van (also **'furniture van**) (both *BrE*) (*AmE* **'moving van**) *noun* a large van used for moving furniture from one house to another

re‧**move** /rɪ'muːv/ *verb, noun*

■ *verb* [VN] **1** ~ sth/sb (from sth/sb) (*written*) to take sth/sb away from a place: *He removed his hand from her shoulder.* ◇ *Illegally parked vehicles will be removed.* ◇ *Three children were removed from the school for persistent bad behaviour.* **2** (*written*) to take off clothing, etc. from the body: *She removed her glasses and rubbed her eyes.* **3** ~ sth (from sb/sth) to get rid of sth unpleasant, dirty, etc.; to make sth disappear: *She has had the tumour removed.* ◇ *to remove problems/obstacles/objections* ◇ *The news removed any doubts about the company's future.* ◇ *It was impossible to remove the stain from the tablecloth.* **4** to dismiss sb from their position or job: *The elections removed the government from power.* [IDM] **once, twice, etc. re'moved** (of a COUSIN) belonging to a different GENERATION: *He's my cousin's son so he's my first cousin once removed.* **be far/further/furthest removed from sth** to be very different from sth; to not be connected with sth: *Many of these books are far removed from the reality of the children's lives.*

■ *noun* [C, U] (*formal*) an amount by which two things are separated: *Charlotte seemed to be living at one remove from reality.*

re‧**mover** /rɪ'muːvə(r)/ *noun* **1** [U, C] (usually in compounds) a substance used for getting rid of marks, paint, etc: *nail varnish remover* ◇ *stain remover* **2** [usually pl.] (*BrE*) a person or company whose job is to take furniture, etc. from one house to another: *a firm of removers*

re‧**mu**‧**ner**‧**ate** /rɪ'mjuːnəreɪt/ *verb* [VN] [usually passive] ~ sb (for sth) (*formal*) to pay sb for work that they have done

re‧**mu**‧**ner**‧**ation** /rɪˌmjuːnə'reɪʃn/ *noun* [U, C] (*formal*) an amount of money that is paid to sb for the work they have done

re‧**mu**‧**nera**‧**tive** /rɪ'mjuːnərətɪv/ *adj.* [usually before noun] (*formal*) paying a lot of money: *remunerative work*

REN /ˌɑːr iː 'en/ *abbr.* registered enrolled nurse

re‧**nais**‧**sance** /rɪ'neɪsns; *AmE* 'renəsɑːns/ *noun* [sing.] **1** (**the Renaissance**) the period in Europe during the 14th, 15th and 16th centuries when people became interested in the ideas and culture of ancient Greece and Rome and used these influences in their own art, literature, etc: *Renaissance art* **2** a situation when there is new

interest in a particular subject, form of art, etc. after a period when it was not very popular [SYN] REVIVAL

renal /'riːnl/ *adj.* [usually before noun] (*medical*) relating to or involving the KIDNEYS: *renal failure*

re‧**name** /ˌriː'neɪm/ *verb* to give sb/sth a new name: [VN] *to rename a street* ◇ [VN-N] *Leningrad was renamed St Petersburg.*

rend /rend/ *verb* (**rent, rent** /rent/) [VN] (*old use* or *literary*) to tear sth apart with force or violence: *They rent their clothes in grief.* ◇ (*figurative*) *a country rent in two by civil war* ◇ (*figurative*) *Loud screams rent the air.*—see also HEART-RENDING

ren‧**der** /'rendə(r)/ *verb*

CAUSE SB/STH TO BE STH ▸ **1** [VN-ADJ] (*formal*) to cause sb/sth to be in a particular state or condition: *to render sth harmless/useless/ineffective* ◇ *Hundreds of people were rendered homeless by the earthquake.*

GIVE HELP ▸ **2** ~ sth (to sb/sth) | ~ (sb) sth (*formal*) to give sb sth, especially in return for sth or because it is expected: [VN, VNN] *to render a service to sb* ◇ *to render sb a service* ◇ [VN] *They rendered assistance to the disaster victims.* ◇ *It was payment for services rendered.*

PRESENT STH ▸ **3** [VN] (*formal*) to present sth, especially when it is done officially: *The committee was asked to render a report on the housing situation.*

EXPRESS/PERFORM ▸ **4** [VN] (*formal*) to express or perform sth: *He stood up and rendered a beautiful version of 'Summertime'.* ◇ *The artist has rendered the stormy sea in dark greens and browns.*

TRANSLATE ▸ **5** [VN] ~ sth (as sth) | ~ sth (into sth) to express sth in a different language; to translate: *The Italian phrase can be rendered as 'I did my best'.* ◇ *It's a concept that is difficult to render into English.*

WALL ▸ **6** [VN] (*BrE, technical*) to cover a wall with a layer of PLASTER or CEMENT: *a rendered building/wall*

MELT ▸ **7** [VN] ~ sth (down) to make fat liquid by heating it; to melt sth

ren‧**der**‧**ing** /'rendərɪŋ/ *noun* **1** [C] the performance of a piece of music, a role in a play, etc.; the particular way in which sth is performed: *her dramatic rendering of Lady Macbeth* **2** [C] a piece of writing that has been translated into a different language; the particular way in which it has been translated: *a faithful rendering of the original text* **3** [U, C] (*technical*) a layer of PLASTER or CEMENT that is put on a brick or stone wall in order to make it smooth

ren‧**dez**‧**vous** /'rɒndɪvuː; -deɪ-; *AmE* 'rɑːn-/ *noun, verb*

■ *noun* (*pl.* **ren**‧**dez**‧**vous** /-vuːz/) (*from French*) **1** ~ (with sb) an arrangement to meet sb at a particular time and place **2** a place where people have arranged to meet: *He didn't recognize the address of the rendezvous.* **3** a cafe, bar, etc. that is a popular place for people to meet: *a lively Paris rendezvous*

■ *verb* (**ren**‧**dez**‧**voused** /-vuːd/, **ren**‧**dez**‧**voused**) [V] ~ (with sb) (*from French*) to meet at a time and place that have been arranged in advance

ren‧**di**‧**tion** /ren'dɪʃn/ *noun* the performance of sth, especially a song or piece of music; the particular way in which it is performed: *The band gave a live rendition of their latest single.*

rene‧**gade** /'renɪɡeɪd/ *noun* (*formal, disapproving*) **1** (often used as an adjective) a person who leaves one political, religious, etc. group to join another that has very different views **2** a person who opposes and lives outside a group or society that they used to belong to: *teenage renegades*

re‧**nege** /rɪ'niːɡ; rɪ'neɪɡ/ *verb* [V] ~ (on sth) (*formal*) to break a promise, an agreement, etc: *to renege on a deal/debt/contract*

renew /rɪ'njuː; *AmE* -'nuː/ *verb* [VN] **1** to begin sth again after a pause or an interruption [SYN] RESUME: *The army renewed its assault on the capital.* ◇ *We have to renew our efforts to attract young players.* ◇ *The annual dinner is a chance to renew acquaintance with old friends.* **2** to make sth valid for a further period of time: *to renew a licence/lease/subscription/contract* ◇ *How do I go about renewing my passport?* ◇ *I'd like to renew these library books* (= arrange to borrow them for a further period of time). **3** to

aɪ	aʊ	eɪ	əʊ	oʊ	ɔɪ	ɪə	eə	ʊə	j	w
my	now	say	go	go	boy	near	hair	pure	yes	wet
			(BrE)	(AmE)						

R

emphasize sth by saying or stating it again: *to renew an appeal/a request/a complaint* ◇ *Community leaders have renewed calls for a peaceful settlement.* ◇ *The project is to go ahead following renewed promises of aid from the UN.* **4** to change sth that is old or damaged and replace it with sth new of the same kind: *The wiring in your house should be renewed every ten to fifteen years.*

re·new·able /rɪˈnjuːəbl; *AmE* -ˈnuː-/ *adj.* **1** [usually before noun] (of energy and natural RESOURCES) that is replaced naturally or controlled carefully and can therefore be used without the risk of finishing it all: *renewable sources of energy such as wind and solar power* **2** (of a contract, ticket, etc.) that can be made valid for a further period of time after it has finished: *a renewable lease* ◇ *The work permit is not renewable.* OPP NON-RENEWABLE

re·newal /rɪˈnjuːəl; *AmE* -ˈnuːəl/ *noun* [U, C] **1 ~ (of sth)** a situation in which sth begins again after a pause or an interruption: *a renewal of interest in traditional teaching methods* **2** the act of making a contract, etc. valid for a further period of time after it has finished: *The lease comes up for renewal at the end of the month.* ◇ *the renewal date/fee* **3** a situation in which sth is replaced, improved or made more successful: *economic renewal* ◇ *urban renewal* (= the act of improving the buildings, etc. in a particular area)

re·newed /rɪˈnjuːd; *AmE* rɪˈnuːd/ *adj.* [usually before noun] happening again with increased interest or strength: *Renewed fighting has been reported on the border.* ◇ *renewed determination/enthusiasm*

ren·net /ˈrenɪt/ *noun* [U] a substance that makes milk thick and sour and is used in making cheese

re·nounce /rɪˈnaʊns/ *verb* [VN] (*formal*) **1** to state officially that you are no longer going to keep a title, position, etc. SYN GIVE UP: *to renounce a claim/title/privilege/right* ◇ *to renounce your citizenship* **2** to state publicly that you no longer have a particular belief or that you will no longer behave in a particular way: *to renounce ideals/principles/beliefs* ◇ *to renounce terrorism/war* ◇ *a joint declaration renouncing the use of violence* **3** to state publicly that you no longer wish to have a connection with sb/sth because you disapprove of them: *He had renounced his former associates.*—see also RENUNCIATION

reno·vate /ˈrenəveɪt/ *verb* [VN] to repair and paint an old building, a piece of furniture, etc. so that it is in good condition again ▶ **reno·va·tion** /ˌrenəˈveɪʃn/ *noun* [U, C, usually pl.]: *buildings in need of renovation* ◇ *There will be extensive renovations to the hospital.*

re·nown /rɪˈnaʊn/ *noun* [U] (*formal*) fame and respect because of sth you have done that people admire: *He won renown as a fair judge.* ◇ *a pianist of some/international/great renown*

re·nowned /rɪˈnaʊnd/ *adj.* **~ (as/for sth)** famous and respected: *a renowned author* ◇ *It is renowned as one of the region's best restaurants.* ◇ *She is renowned for her patience.*

rent /rent/ *noun, verb*—see also REND *v.*
▪ *noun* **1** [U, C] an amount of money that you regularly pay so that you can use a house, etc: *How much rent do you pay for this place?* ◇ *The landlord has put the rent up again.* ◇ *a month's rent in advance* ◇ *a high/low/fair rent* ◇ (*BrE*) *a rent book* (= used to record payments of rent)—compare HIRE *n.* **2** [U, C] (*especially AmE*) = RENTAL (1) **3** [C] a torn place in a piece of material or clothing IDM **for rent** (*especially AmE*) (especially on printed signs) available to rent
▪ *verb* **1 ~ sth (from sb)** to regularly pay money to sb so that you can use sth that they own, such as a house, some land, a machine, etc: [VN] *to live in rented accommodation/housing/property* ◇ *Who do you rent the land from?* [also V] **2 ~ sth (out) (to sb)** to allow sb to use sth that you own such as a house or some land in exchange for regular payments: [VN] *He rents rooms in his house to students.* ◇ *The land is rented out to other farmers.* ◇ *She agreed to rent the room to me.* ◇ [VNN] *She agreed to rent me the room.* **3** [VN] (*especially AmE*) to pay money to sb so that you can use sth for a short period of time: *We rented*

a car for the week and explored the area. ◇ *Shall we rent a movie this evening?* ◇ *We rented a villa in Spain last summer.*—compare HIRE *v.* (1) **4** [V] (*AmE*) to be available for sb to use if they pay a particular amount of money: *The apartment rents for $500 a month.*

rent-a- *combining form* (*informal*, often *humorous*) (in nouns and adjectives) showing that the thing mentioned can be hired/rented: *rent-a-car* ◇ *rent-a-crowd*

ren·tal /ˈrentl/ *noun* **1** (also **rent** especially in *AmE*) [U, C, usually sing.] the amount of money that you pay to use sth for a particular period of time: *Telephone charges include line rental.* **2** [U] the act of renting sth or an arrangement to rent sth: *the world's largest car rental company* ◇ *video rental* ◇ (especially *AmE*) *a rental car* ◇ *a minimum rental period of three months*—compare HIRE **3** [C] (*especially AmE*) a house, car, or piece of equipment that you can rent: *'Is this your own car?' 'No, it's a rental.'*

rent boy *noun* (*BrE*) a young male prostitute

rent·ed /ˈrentɪd/ *adj.* that you pay rent for: *a rented studio*

rent·er /ˈrentə(r)/ *noun* **1** a person who rents sth: *house buyers and renters* **2** (*AmE*) a person or an organization that provides sth for people to rent: *the nation's biggest automobile renter*

rent-'free *adj.* for which no rent is paid: *rent-free housing* ▶ **rent-'free** *adv.*

re·nun·ci·ation /rɪˌnʌnsiˈeɪʃn/ *noun* [U] (*formal*) **1** [U, C] an act of stating publicly that you no longer believe sth or that you are giving sth up: *a/the renunciation of violence* **2** [U] the act of rejecting physical pleasures, especially for religious reasons—see also RENOUNCE

re·open /ˌriːˈəʊpən; *AmE* -ˈoʊ-/ *verb* **1** to open a shop/store, theatre, etc. again, or to be opened again, after being closed for a period of time: [VN] *The school was reopened just two weeks after the fire.* ◇ [V] *The store will reopen at 9 a.m. on 2 January.* **2** to deal with or begin sth again after a period of time; to start again after a period of time: [VN] *to reopen an argument/a discussion/a debate* ◇ *The police have decided to reopen the case.* ◇ *Management have agreed to reopen talks with the union.* ◇ [V] *The trial reopened on 6 March.* ▶ **re·open·ing** /ˌriːˈəʊpənɪŋ; *AmE* -ˈoʊ-/ *noun* [U, sing.] IDM **re,open old 'wounds** to remind sb of sth unpleasant that happened or existed in the past

re·order /ˌriːˈɔːdə(r); *AmE* -ˈɔːrd-/ *verb* **1** to ask sb to supply you with more of a product: *Please quote this reference number when reordering stock.* [also V] **2** [VN] to change the order in which sth is arranged

re·organ·ize (*BrE* also **-ise**) /riˈɔːɡənaɪz; *AmE* -ˈɔːrɡ-/

verb [VN, V] to change the way in which sth is organized or done ▶ **re·organ·iza·tion, -isa·tion** /ˌriːˌɔːgənaɪˈzeɪʃn; *AmE* -ˌɔːrgənəˈz-/ *noun* [U, C]: *the reorganization of the school system*

Rep. *abbr.* (in American politics) **1** REPRESENTATIVE **2** REPUBLICAN

rep /rep/ *noun* (*informal*) **1** [C] = SALES REPRESENTATIVE, REPRESENTATIVE **2** [C] a person who speaks officially for a group of people, especially at work (abbreviation for 'representative'): *a union rep* **3** [U] (*informal*) the abbreviation for REPERTORY

re·paid *pt, pp* of REPAY

re·pair /rɪˈpeə(r); *AmE* -ˈper/ *verb, noun*
- *verb* [VN] **1** to mend sth that is broken, damaged or torn: *to repair a car/roof/road/television* ◇ *It's almost 15 years old. It isn't worth **having it repaired**.* **2** to say or do sth in order to improve a bad or unpleasant situation: *It was too late to repair the damage done to their relationship.* **PHRV** **re'pair to ...** (*formal* or *humorous*) to go to a particular place
- *noun* [C, U] an act of repairing sth: *They agreed to pay the costs of any repairs.* ◇ *I took my bike in **for repair**.* ◇ *The building was **in need of repair**.* ◇ *a TV repair shop* ◇ *The car was damaged **beyond repair** (= it was too badly damaged to be repaired).* ◇ *The hotel is currently **under repair** (= being repaired).* ◇ *The bridge will remain closed until essential repair work has been carried out.* **IDM** **in good, bad, etc. re'pair | in a good, bad, etc. state of re'pair** (*formal*) in good, etc. condition

re·pair·able /rɪˈpeərəbl; *AmE* -ˈper-/ *adj.* [not usually before noun] that can be repaired **OPP** IRREPARABLE

re·pair·man /rɪˈpeəmæn; *AmE* -ˈperm-/ *noun* (*pl.* -men /-men/) (also **re·pair·er** especially in *BrE*) a person whose job is to repair things: *a TV repairman*

rep·ar·ation /ˌrepəˈreɪʃn/ *noun* (*formal*) **1** (**reparations**) [pl.] money that is paid by a country that has lost a war, for the damage, injuries, etc. that it has caused **2** [U] the act of giving sth to sb or doing sth for them in order to show that you are sorry for suffering that you have caused: *Offenders should be forced to **make reparation to** the community.*

rep·ar·tee /ˌrepɑːˈtiː; *AmE* -ɑːrˈtiː/ *noun* [U] clever and amusing comments and replies that are made quickly

re·past /rɪˈpɑːst; *AmE* -ˈpæst/ *noun* (*old-fashioned* or *formal*) a meal

re·pat·ri·ate /ˌriːˈpætrieɪt; *AmE* -ˈpeɪt-/ *verb* [VN] **1** to send or bring sb back to their own country: *The refugees were forcibly repatriated.* **2** (*business*) to send money or profits back to your own country: *An agreement between the countries enables companies to repatriate their profits freely.* ▶ **re·pat·ri·ation** /ˌriːˌpætriˈeɪʃn; *AmE* -ˌpeɪt-/ *noun* [U, C]: *the repatriation of immigrants/profits* ◇ *a voluntary repatriation programme*

repay /rɪˈpeɪ/ *verb* (**re·paid, re·paid** /rɪˈpeɪd/) **1** ~ sth (to sb)| ~ (sb) sth to pay back the money that you have borrowed from sb: [VN] *to repay a debt/loan/mortgage* ◇ *When are you going to repay them?* ◇ *I'll repay the money I owe them next week.* ◇ [VNN] *I fully intend to repay them the money that they lent me.* **2** [VN] ~ sb (for sth)| ~ sth (with sth) to give sth to sb or do sth for them in return for sth that they have done for you: *How can I ever repay you for your generosity?* ◇ *Their trust was repaid with fierce loyalty.* **3** [VN] (*BrE, formal*) if sth **repays** your attention, interest, study, etc., it is worth spending time to look at it, etc: *The report repays careful reading.*

re·pay·able /rɪˈpeɪəbl/ *adj.* that can or must be paid back: *The loan is repayable in monthly instalments.*

re·pay·ment /rɪˈpeɪmənt/ *noun* **1** [U] the act of paying back money that you have borrowed from a bank, etc: *The loan is due for repayment by the end of the year.* **2** [C, usually pl.] a sum of money that you pay regularly to a bank, etc. until you have returned all the money that you owe: *We were unable to meet (= pay) the repayments on the loan.* ◇ *mortgage repayments*

re'payment mortgage *noun* (*BrE*) a type of MORT-GAGE in which you pay regular sums of money to the

bank, etc. until you have returned all the money and interest that you owe—compare ENDOWMENT MORTGAGE

re·peal /rɪˈpiːl/ *verb* [VN] if a government or other group or person with authority **repeals** a law, that law is no longer valid ▶ **re·peal** *noun* [U]

re·peat /rɪˈpiːt/ *verb, noun*
- *verb*

WORD FAMILY
repeat *v., n.*
repeatable *adj.* (≠ unrepeatable)
repeated *adj.*
repetition *n.*
repetitive *adj.*
repetitious *adj.*

SAY/WRITE AGAIN **1** ~ (**sth/ yourself**) to say or write sth again or more than once: [VN] *to repeat a question/warning* ◇ *I'm sorry—could you repeat that?* ◇ *She kept repeating his name softly over and over again.* ◇ *The opposition have been repeating their calls for the president's resignation.* ◇ *Do say if I'm **repeating myself** (= if I have already said this).* ◇ [Vthat] *He's fond of repeating that the company's success is all down to him.*

DO AGAIN **2** [VN] to do or produce sth again or more than once: *to repeat a mistake/a process/an exercise* ◇ *The treatment should be repeated every two to three hours.* ◇ *They are hoping to repeat last year's victory.* ◇ *These offers are unlikely to be repeated.* ◇ *The programmes will be repeated next year.* ◇ *to repeat the class/year/grade* (= in a school, to take the class/year/grade again) ◇ [V] *Lift and lower the right leg 20 times. Repeat with the left leg.*

HAPPEN AGAIN **3** ~ (**itself**) to happen more than once in the same way: [VN] *History has a strange way of repeating itself.* ◇ [V] *a repeating pattern/design*

WHAT SB ELSE SAID **4** [VN] ~ sth (to sb) to tell sb sth that you have heard or been told by sb else: *I don't want you to repeat a word of this to anyone.* ◇ *The rumour has been widely repeated in the press.* **5** ~ (sth) (after sb) to say aloud sth that sb else has said, especially in order to learn it: [VN] *Listen and repeat each sentence after me.* ◇ *Can you repeat what I've just said word for word?* ◇ [Vspeech] *'Are you really sure?' she repeated.*

OF FOOD **6** [V] ~ (on sb) (*BrE, informal*) if food **repeats**, you can taste it for some time after you have eaten it: *Do you find that onions repeat on you?*

FOR EMPHASIS **7** used to emphasize sth that you have already said: [V] *The claims are, I repeat, totally unfounded.* ◇ [VN] *I am not, repeat not, travelling in the same car as him!*

- *noun* **1** a television or radio programme that has been broadcast before: *'Is it a new series?' 'No, a repeat'.* **2** an event that is very similar to sth that happened before: *A repeat of the 1906 earthquake could kill up to 11000 people.* ◇ *She didn't want a **repeat performance** of what had happened the night before.* ◇ (*business*) *a repeat order* (= for a further supply of the same goods) **3** (*music*) a passage that is repeated

re·peat·able /rɪˈpiːtəbl/ *adj.* [not usually before noun] **1** (of a comment, etc.) (usually in negative sentences) polite and not offensive: *His reply was not repeatable.* **2** that can be repeated **OPP** UNREPEATABLE

re·peated /rɪˈpiːtɪd/ *adj.* [only before noun] happening, said or done many times: *repeated absences from work* ▶ **re·peat·ed·ly** *adv.*: *The victim had been stabbed repeatedly in the chest.*

re·peat·er /rɪˈpiːtə(r)/ *noun* (*technical*) a gun that you can fire several times without having to load it again

repel /rɪˈpel/ *verb* (-ll-) **1** [VN] (*formal*) to successfully fight sb who is attacking you, your country, etc. and drive them away: *to repel an attack/invasion/invader* ◇ *Troops repelled an attempt to infiltrate the south of the island.* ◇ (*figurative*) *The reptile's prickly skin repels nearly all of its predators.* **2** [VN] to drive, push or keep sth away: *a cream that repels insects* ◇ *The fabric has been treated to repel water.* **3** [VN] (not used in the progressive tenses) to make sb feel horror or disgust: *I was repelled by the smell.* **4** (*technical*) if one thing **repels** another, or if two things **repel** each other, an electrical or MAGNETIC force pushes them apart: [VN] *Like poles repel each other.* [alsoV] **OPP** ATTRACT—see also REPULSION, REPULSIVE

re·pel·lent /rɪˈpelənt/ adj., noun
■ adj. **1** ~ (to sb) (formal) very unpleasant; causing strong dislike: *I found the pictures repellent.* ◇ *Their political ideas are repellent to most people.* **2** (in compounds) not letting a particular substance, especially water, pass through it: *water-repellent fabric*
■ noun [U, C] **1** a substance that is used for keeping insects away from you: *(an) insect repellent* **2** a substance that is used on fabric, stone, etc. to prevent water from passing through it: *(a) water repellent*

re·pent /rɪˈpent/ verb ~ (of sth) (formal) to feel and show that you are sorry for sth bad or wrong that you have done: [V] *God welcomes the sinner who repents.* ◇ *She had repented of what she had done.* ◇ [VN] *He came to repent his hasty decision* (= wished he had not taken it).

re·pent·ance /rɪˈpentəns/ noun [U] ~ (for sth) the fact of showing that you are sorry for sth wrong that you have done: *He shows no sign of repentance.*

re·pent·ant /rɪˈpentənt/ adj. feeling or showing that you are sorry for sth wrong that you have done: *She was not in the least repentant.* [OPP] UNREPENTANT

re·per·cus·sion /ˌriːpəˈkʌʃn; AmE -pərˈk-/ noun [usually pl.] (written) an indirect and usually bad result of an action or event that may happen some time afterwards [SYN] CONSEQUENCE: *The collapse of the company will have repercussions for the whole industry.*

rep·er·toire /ˈrepətwɑː(r); AmE -pərt-/ noun **1** (also formal **rep·er·tory**) all the plays, songs, pieces of music, etc. that a performer knows and can perform: *to add to/extend your repertoire* ◇ *a pianist with a wide repertoire* **2** all the things that a person is able to do: *a young child's growing verbal repertoire*

rep·er·tory /ˈrepətri; AmE ˈrepərtɔːri/ noun **1** (also informal **rep**) [U] the type of work of a theatre company in which different plays are performed for short periods of time: *an actor in repertory* ◇ *a repertory actor/theatre/company* **2** [C] (formal) = REPERTOIRE

repe·ti·tion /ˌrepəˈtɪʃn/ noun **1** [U, C] the fact of doing or saying the same thing many times: *learning by repetition* **2** [C] a thing that has been done or said before: *We do not want to see a repetition of last year's tragic events.*

repe·ti·tious /ˌrepəˈtɪʃəs/ adj. (often disapproving) involving sth that is often repeated: *a long and repetitious speech* ▶ **repe·ti·tious·ly** adv. **repe·ti·tious·ness** noun

re·peti·tive /rɪˈpetətɪv/ adj. **1** saying or doing the same thing many times, so that it becomes boring: *Machines can now perform many repetitive tasks in the home.* **2** repeated many times: *a repetitive pattern of behaviour* ▶ **re·peti·tive·ly** adv. **re·peti·tive·ness** noun [U]

re·phrase /ˌriːˈfreɪz/ verb [VN] to say or write sth using different words in order to make the meaning clearer

re·place /rɪˈpleɪs/ verb [VN] **1** to be used instead of sth/sb else; to do sth instead of sb/sth else: *The new design will eventually replace all existing models.* ◇ *Teachers will never be replaced by computers in the classroom.* ◇ *She replaced her husband as the local doctor.* **2** ~ sb/sth (with/by sb/sth) to remove sb/sth and put another person or thing in their place: *He will be difficult to replace when he leaves.* ◇ *It is not a good idea to miss meals and replace them with snacks.* **3** to change sth that is old, damaged, etc. for a similar thing that is newer or better: *All the old carpets need replacing.* ◇ *You'll be expected to replace any broken glasses.* **4** to put sth back in the place where it was before: *I replaced the cup carefully in the saucer.* ◇ *to replace the handset* (= after using the telephone).

re·place·able /rɪˈpleɪsəbl/ adj. that can be replaced [OPP] IRREPLACEABLE

re·place·ment /rɪˈpleɪsmənt/ noun **1** [U] the act of replacing one thing with another, especially sth that is newer or better: *the replacement of worn car parts* ◇ *replacement windows* **2** [C] a thing that replaces sth, especially because the first thing is old, broken, etc: *a hip replacement* **3** [C] ~ (for sb) a person who replaces another person in an organization, especially in their job: *We need to find a replacement for Sue.*

re·play noun, verb
■ noun /ˈriːpleɪ/ **1** (BrE, sport) a game that is played again because neither side won in the previous game **2** the playing again of a short section of a film/movie, tape, etc. especially to look at or listen to sth more carefully: *We watched a replay of the wedding on video.*—see also ACTION REPLAY **3** (informal) something that is repeated or happens in exactly the same way as it did before: *This election will not be a replay of the last one.*
■ verb /ˌriːˈpleɪ/ [VN] **1** [usually passive] to play a football game, etc. again because neither team won the first game **2** to play again sth that has been recorded on tape, film, etc: *The police replayed footage of the accident over and over again.* ◇ *(figurative) He replayed the scene in his mind* (= he thought about it many times).

re·plen·ish /rɪˈplenɪʃ/ verb [VN] ~ sth (with sth) (formal) to make sth full again by replacing what has been used: *to replenish food and water supplies* ◇ *Allow me to replenish your glass.* ▶ **re·plen·ish·ment** noun [U]

re·plete /rɪˈpliːt/ adj. **1** [not before noun] ~ (with sth) (formal) filled with sth; with a full supply of sth: *literature replete with drama and excitement* **2** (old-fashioned or formal) very full of food

rep·lica /ˈreplɪkə/ noun a very good or exact copy of sth: *a replica of the Eiffel tower* ◇ *The weapon used in the raid was a replica.* ◇ *replica guns* ◇ *Amy was a younger replica of her mother.*

rep·li·cate /ˈreplɪkeɪt/ verb **1** [VN] (formal) to copy sth exactly [SYN] DUPLICATE: *Subsequent experiments failed to replicate these findings.* **2** ~ (itself) (technical) (of a VIRUS or a MOLECULE) to produce exact copies of itself: *The drug prevents the virus from replicating itself.* [also V] ▶ **rep·li·ca·tion** /ˌreplɪˈkeɪʃn/ noun [U, C]

reply /rɪˈplaɪ/ verb, noun
■ verb (re·plies, re·ply·ing, re·plied, re·plied) ~ (to sb/sth) (with sth) **1** to say or write sth as an answer to sb/sth: [V] *to reply to a question/advertisement* ◇ *He never replied to any of my letters.* ◇ *She only replied with a smile.* ◇ [V speech] *'I won't let you down,' he replied confidently.* ◇ [V that] *The senator replied that he was not in a position to comment.* ⇨ note at ANSWER **2** [V] ~ (to sth) (with sth) to do sth as a reaction to sth that sb has said or done: *Italy took an early lead but Brazil replied with two goals in the last five minutes.* ◇ *The terrorists replied to the government's statement with more violence.*
■ noun [C, U] an act of replying to sth/sb in speech, writing or by some action: *We had over 100 replies to our advertisement.* ◇ *I asked her what her name was but she made no reply.* ◇ *(formal) I am writing in reply to your letter of 16 March.* ◇ *(BrE) a reply-paid envelope* (= on which you do not have to put a stamp because it has already been paid for) ⇨ note at ANSWER

re·port /rɪˈpɔːt; AmE rɪˈpɔːrt/ verb, noun
■ verb
GIVE INFORMATION | **1** ~ (on sth) (to sb)| ~ sth (to sb)| ~ sb/sth (as sth/as doing sth) to give people information about sth that you have heard, seen, done, etc: [VN] *The crash happened seconds after the pilot reported engine trouble.* ◇ *Call me urgently if you have anything to report.* ◇ *The company is expected to report record profits this year.* ◇ *The house was reported as being in excellent condition.* ◇ [V] *The committee will report on its research next month.* ◇ [V-ing] *The neighbours reported seeing him leave the building around noon.* ◇ [VN-ADJ] *The doctor reported the patient fully recovered.* ◇ *The house was reported to be in excellent condition.* ◇ *She was reported by the hospital spokesman to be making excellent progress.* [HELP] This pattern is only used in the passive. [also V speech, V (that), V wh-, VN-ing]
NEWS/STORY | **2** ~ (on) sth to present a written or spoken account of an event in a newspaper, on television, etc: [VN] *The stabbing was reported in the local press.* ◇ [VN that] *It was reported that several people had been arrested.* ◇ [V] *She reports on royal stories for the BBC.* ◇ *(BrE) Reporting restrictions on the trial have been lifted* (= it can now legally be reported). [also V that] **3** (be reported) used to show that sth has been stated, and you do not know if it is true or not: [VN to inf] *She is reported to earn over $10 million a year.* ◇ [VN] *The President is*

æ   ɑː   e   ɜː   ə   ɪ   iː   i   ɒ   ɔː   ʌ   ʊ   u   uː
cat   father   ten   bird   about   sit   see   many   got   saw   cup   put   actual   too
(BrE)

reported as saying that he needs a break. ◊ [VN **that**] *It was reported that changes were being considered.*

CRIME/ACCIDENT, etc. | **4 ~ sth (to sb)** | **~ sb (to sb) (for sth/ for doing sth)** to tell a person in authority about a crime, an accident, an illness, etc. or about sth bad that sb has done: [VN] *Have you reported the accident to the police yet?* ◊ *He's already been reported twice for arriving late.* ◊ *a decrease in the number of reported cases of Aids* ◊ [VN-ADJ] *She has reported her daughter missing.*

ARRIVE | **5** [V] **~ (to sb/sth) (for sth)** to tell sb that you have arrived, for example for work or for a meeting with sb: *You should report for duty at 9.30 a.m.* ◊ *All visitors must report to the reception desk on arrival.*

[PHRV] **re,port 'back** to return to a place, especially in order to work again: *Take an hour for lunch and report back at 2.* **re,port 'back (on sth) (to sb)** to give sb information about sth that they have asked you to find out about: *Find out as much as you can about him and report back to me.* ◊ *One person in the group should be prepared to report back to the class on your discussion.* ◊ [+that] *They reported back that no laws had actually been broken.* **re'port to sb** (not used in the progressive tenses) (*business*) if you **report to** a particular manager in an organization that you work for, they are officially responsible for your work and tell you what to do

■ *noun*

OF NEWS | **1 ~ (on/of sth)** a written or spoken account of an event, especially one that is published or broadcast: *Are these newspaper reports true?* ◊ *a weather report*

INFORMATION | **2 ~ (on sth)** a spoken or written description of sth containing information that sb needs to have: *a police/medical report* ◊ *Can you give us a progress report?*

OFFICIAL STUDY | **3 ~ (on sth)** an official document written by a group of people who have examined a particular situation or problem: *The committee will publish their report on the health service in a few weeks.*

STORY | **4** a story or piece of information that may or may not be true: *I don't believe these reports of UFO sightings.* ◊ *There are unconfirmed reports of a shooting in the capital.*

ON STUDENT'S WORK | **5** (*BrE*) (*AmE* **re'port card**) a written statement about a student's work at school, college, etc: *a school report* ◊ *to get a good/bad report*

OF GUN | **6** (*written*) the sound of an explosion or of a gun being fired: *a loud report*

[IDM] **of bad/good re'port** (*formal*) talked about by people in a bad/good way

re·por·tage /ˌrɪˈpɔːtɪdʒ; ˌrepɔːˈtɑːʒ; *AmE* rɪˈpɔːrt-; ˌrepɔːrˈt-/ *noun* [U] (*formal*) the reporting of news or the typical style in which this is done in newspapers, or on TV and radio

re·port·ed·ly /rɪˈpɔːtɪdli; *AmE* -ˈpɔːrt-/ *adv.* according to what some people say: *The band have reportedly decided to split up.*

re,ported 'question *noun* (*grammar*) = INDIRECT QUESTION

re,ported 'speech (also ,indirect 'speech) *noun* [U] (*grammar*) a report of what sb has said that does not use their exact words: *In reported speech, 'I'll come later' becomes 'He said he'd come later'.*

re·port·er /rɪˈpɔːtə(r); *AmE* -ˈpɔːrt-/ *noun* a person who collects and reports news for newspapers, radio or television: *a reporter from the New York Times* ◊ *a crime reporter*—compare JOURNALIST—see also CUB REPORTER

re·port·ing /rɪˈpɔːtɪŋ; *AmE* -ˈpɔːrt-/ *noun* [U] the presenting and writing about news on television and radio, and in newspapers: *accurate/balanced/objective reporting*

re·pose /rɪˈpəʊz; *AmE* rɪˈpoʊz/ *noun, verb*

■ *noun* [U] (*literary*) a state of rest, sleep or feeling calm: *She went outside seeking a few moments of repose.* ◊ *In repose, his face was sad.*

■ *verb* [V+adv./prep.] (*literary*) **1** (of an object) to be or be kept in a particular place **2** (of a person) to lie or rest in a particular place

re·posi·tory /rɪˈpɒzətri; *AmE* rɪˈpɑːzətɔːri/ *noun* (*pl.* **-ies**) **1** (*written*) a place where a large number of things can be kept or stored: *an underground repository for radioactive*

waste **2** (*formal*) a person or book that is full of information: *My father is a repository of family history.*

re·pos·sess /ˌriːpəˈzes/ *verb* [VN] [usually passive] to take back property or goods from sb who has arranged to buy them but who still owes money for them or cannot pay

re·pos·ses·sion /ˌriːpəˈzeʃn/ *noun* **1** [U, C] the act of repossessing property, goods, etc: *families threatened with repossession* ◊ *a repossession order* ◊ *Early action could prevent a large number of repossessions.* **2** [C] a house, car, etc. that has been repossessed: *Auctions are the best place for buying repossessions.*

rep·re·hen·sible /ˌreprɪˈhensəbl/ *adj.* (*formal*) morally wrong and deserving criticism: *His conduct was thoroughly reprehensible.*

rep·re·sent /ˌreprɪˈzent/ *verb*

ACT/SPEAK FOR SB | **1** [VN] [often passive] to be a member of a group of people and act or speak on their behalf at an event, a meeting, etc: *The competition attracted over 500 contestants representing 8 different countries.* ◊ *Local businesses are well represented on the committee* (= there are a lot of people from them on the committee). ◊ *The President was represented at the ceremony by the Vice-President.* **2** [VN] to act or speak officially for sb and defend their interests: *The union represents over 200000 teachers.* ◊ *The association was formed to* **represent the interests of** *women artists.* ◊ *Ms Dale is representing the defendant* (= is his/her lawyer) *in the case.*

BE EQUAL TO | **3** *linking verb* [V-N] (not used in the progressive tenses) to be sth [SYN] CONSTITUTE: *This contract represents 20% of the company's annual revenue.* ◊ *This decision represents a significant departure from previous policy.*

BE EXAMPLE OF | **4** [VN] [no passive] to be an example or expression of sth: *a project representing all that is good in the community* ◊ *Those comments do not represent the views of us all.*

BE SYMBOL | **5** [VN] (not used in the progressive tenses) to be a symbol of sth [SYN] SYMBOLIZE: *Each colour on the chart represents a different department.* ◊ *Wind direction is represented by arrows.*

IN PICTURE | **6 ~ sb/sth (as sb/sth)** to show sb/sth, especially in a picture [SYN] DEPICT: [VN] *The carvings represent a hunting scene.* ◊ *The results are represented in fig.3 below.* [also VN -ing]

DESCRIBE | **7** [VN] **~ sb (as sth)** (*formal*) to present or describe sb/sth in a particular way, especially when this may not be fair: *The king is represented as a villain in the play.* ◊ *The risks were represented as negligible.*

MAKE FORMAL STATEMENT | **8 ~ sth (to sb)** (*formal*) to make a formal statement to sb in authority to make your opinions known or to protest: [VN] *They represented their concerns to the authorities.* [also V that]

re-present /ˌriː prɪˈzent/ *verb* [VN] to give, show or send sth again, especially a cheque, bill, etc. that has not been paid

rep·re·sen·ta·tion /ˌreprɪzenˈteɪʃn/ *noun* **1** [U, C] the act of presenting sb/sth in a particular way; something that shows or describes sth: *the negative representation of single mothers in the media* ◊ *The snake swallowing its tail is a representation of infinity.* **2** [U] the fact of having representatives who will speak or vote for you or on your behalf: *The green movement lacks effective representation in Parliament.* ◊ *The accused was not allowed legal representation.*—see also PROPORTIONAL REPRESENTATION **3** (**representations**) [pl.] (*formal, especially BrE*) formal statements made to sb in authority, especially in order to make your opinions known or to protest: *We have made* **representations** *to the prime minister, but without success.*

rep·re·sen·ta·tion·al /ˌreprɪzenˈteɪʃnl/ *adj.* **1** (*technical*) (especially of a style of art or painting) trying to show things as they really are—compare ABSTRACT **2** involving the act of representing sb/sth: *local representational democracy*

rep·re·sen·ta·tive /ˌreprɪˈzentətɪv/ *noun, adj.*

■ *noun* ~ **(of sb/sth) 1** a person who has been chosen to speak or vote for sb else or on behalf of a group: *a representative of the UN* ◊ *our elected representatives in government* ◊ *a student/union representative* ◊ *The committee includes representatives from industry.* **2** (also *informal* **rep**) a person who works for a company and travels around selling its products: *a sales representative* ◊ *She's our representative in France.* **3** a person chosen to take the place of sb else: *He was the Queen's representative at the ceremony.* **4** a person who is typical of a particular group: *The singer is regarded as a representative of the youth of her generation.* **5** (**Representative**) (*abbr.* **Rep.**) (in the US) a member of the House of Representatives, the Lower House of Congress; a member of the House of Representatives in the lower house of a state parliament
■ *adj.* **1** ~ **(of sb/sth)** typical of a particular group of people: *Is a questionnaire answered by 500 people truly representative of the population as a whole?* **2** [usually before noun] containing or including examples of all the different types of people or things in a large group: *a representative sample of teachers* ~ **(of sth)** able to be used as a typical example of sth: *The painting is not representative of his work of the period.* **4** (of a system of government, etc.) consisting of people who have been chosen to speak or vote on behalf of the rest of a group: *a representative democracy* [OPP] UNREPRESENTATIVE

re·press /rɪˈpres/ *verb* [VN] **1** to try not to have or show an emotion, a feeling, etc: *to repress a shudder/sigh/smile* ◊ *He burst in, making no effort to repress his fury.* **2** [often passive] to use political and/or military force to control a group of people and restrict their freedom

re·pressed /rɪˈprest/ *adj.* **1** (of a person) having emotions or desires that are not allowed to be expressed **2** (of emotions) not expressed openly: *repressed anger*

re·pres·sion /rɪˈpreʃn/ *noun* [U] **1** the act of using force to control a group of people and restrict their freedom: *government repression* **2** the act of controlling strong emotions and desires and not allowing them to be expressed so that they no longer seem to exist: *sexual repression*

re·pres·sive /rɪˈpresɪv/ *adj.* **1** (of a system of government) controlling people by force and restricting their freedom: *a repressive regime/measure/law* **2** controlling emotions and desires and not allowing them to be expressed ▶ **re·pres·sive·ly** *adv.* **re·pres·sive·ness** *noun* [U]

re·prieve /rɪˈpriːv/ *verb, noun*
■ *verb* [VN] [usually passive] (not usually used in the progressive tenses) **1** to officially cancel or delay a punishment for a prisoner who is CONDEMNED to death: *a reprieved murderer* **2** to officially cancel or delay plans to close sth or end sth: *70 jobs have been reprieved until next April.*
■ *noun* [usually sing.] **1** an official order stopping a punishment, especially for a prisoner who is CONDEMNED to death **2** a delay before sth bad happens: *Campaigners have won a reprieve for the hospital threatened with closure.*

rep·ri·mand /ˈreprɪmɑːnd; *AmE* -mænd/ *verb* ~ **sb (for sth)** to tell sb officially that you do not approve of them or their actions: [VN] *The officers were severely reprimanded for their unprofessional behaviour.* [also V speech] ▶ **rep·ri·mand** *noun* [C, U]: *He received a severe reprimand for his behaviour.*

re·print *verb, noun*
■ *verb* /ˌriːˈprɪnt/ [VN] [usually passive] to print more copies of a book, article, etc. with few or no changes
■ *noun* /ˈriːprɪnt/ **1** an act of printing more copies of a book because all the others have been sold **2** a book that has been reprinted

re·prisal /rɪˈpraɪzl/ *noun* [C, U] (*written*) a violent or aggressive act towards sb because of sth bad that they have done towards you: *They did not want to give evidence for fear of reprisals.* ◊ *They shot ten hostages in reprisal for the assassination of their leader.*

re·prise /rɪˈpriːz/ *noun* [usually sing.] a repeated part of sth, especially a piece of music

re·proach /rɪˈprəʊtʃ; *AmE* -ˈproʊtʃ/ *noun, verb*

■ *noun* (*formal*) **1** [U] blame or criticism for sth you have done: *His voice was full of reproach.* ◊ *The captain's behaviour is above/beyond reproach* (= you cannot criticize it). **2** [C] a word or remark expressing blame or criticism: *He listened to his wife's bitter reproaches.* **3** [U] a state of shame or loss of honour: *Her actions brought reproach upon herself.* **4** [sing.] ~ **(to sb/sth)** a person or thing that brings shame on sb/sth: *Such living conditions are a reproach to our society.*
■ *verb* (*formal*) **1** ~ **sb (for sth/for doing sth)** | ~ **sb (with sth/with doing sth)** to blame or criticize sb for sth that they have done or not done, because you are disappointed in them: [VN] *She was reproached by colleagues for leaking the story to the press.* [also V speech, VN speech] **2** [VN] ~ **yourself (for sth/for doing sth)** | ~ **yourself (with sth)** to feel guilty about sth that you think you should have done differently: *He reproached himself for not telling her the truth.*

re·proach·ful /rɪˈprəʊtʃfl; *AmE* -ˈproʊtʃ-/ *adj.* expressing blame or criticism: *a reproachful look* ▶ **re·proach·ful·ly** /-fəli/ *adv.*

rep·ro·bate /ˈreprəbeɪt/ *noun* (*formal* or *humorous*) a person who behaves in a way that society thinks is immoral ▶ **rep·ro·bate** *adj.* [only before noun]: *reprobate behaviour*

re·pro·duce /ˌriːprəˈdjuːs; *AmE* -ˈduːs/ *verb* **1** [VN] to make a copy of a picture, piece of text, etc: *It is illegal to reproduce these worksheets without permission from the publisher.* ◊ *The photocopier reproduces colours very well.* **2** [VN] to produce sth again; to make sth happen again in the same way: *The computer program reproduces the effects of earthquakes on buildings.* ◊ *The atmosphere of the novel is successfully reproduced in the movie.* **3** if people, plants, animals, etc. **reproduce** or **reproduce themselves**, they produce young: [V] *Most reptiles reproduce by laying eggs on land.* ◊ [VN] *cells reproducing themselves* (= making new ones) ▶ **re·pro·du·cible** /-əbl/ *adj.*

re·pro·duc·tion /ˌriːprəˈdʌkʃn/ *noun* **1** [U] the act or process of producing babies, young animals or plants: *sexual reproduction* ◊ *They are studying reproduction in shellfish.* **2** [U] the act or process of producing copies of a document, book, picture, etc: *Use a black pen on white paper to ensure good reproduction.* **3** [U] the process of recording sounds onto tapes, records, videos, etc: *Digital recording gives excellent sound reproduction.* **4** [C] a thing that has been reproduced, especially a copy of a work of art: *a catalogue with colour reproductions of the paintings for sale* ◊ *reproduction furniture* (= furniture made as a copy of an earlier style)

re·pro·duc·tive /ˌriːprəˈdʌktɪv/ *adj.* [only before noun] connected with reproducing babies, young animals or plants: *reproductive organs/patterns/systems*

re·proof /rɪˈpruːf/ *noun* (*formal*) **1** [U] blame or disapproval: *His words were a mixture of pity and reproof.* **2** [C] a remark that expresses blame or disapproval: *She received a mild reproof from the teacher.*

re·prove /rɪˈpruːv/ *verb* ~ **sb (for sth/for doing sth)** (*formal*) to tell sb that you do not approve of sth that they have done: [VN] *Charles reproved her for rushing away.* [also V speech, VN speech] ▶ **re·prov·ing** *adj.* [usually before noun]: *a reproving glance* **re·prov·ing·ly** *adv.*

rep·tile /ˈreptaɪl; *AmE* also -tl/ *noun* any animal that has cold blood and skin covered in scales, and that lays eggs. Snakes, CROCODILES and TORTOISES are all reptiles.—compare AMPHIBIAN—picture on page A7 ▶ **rep·til·ian** /repˈtɪliən/ *adj.*: *our reptilian ancestors* ◊ (*figurative*) *He licked his lips in an unpleasantly reptilian way.*

re·pub·lic /rɪˈpʌblɪk/ *noun* a country that is governed by a president and politicians elected by the people and where there is no king or queen: *newly independent republics* ◊ *the Republic of Ireland*—compare MONARCHY

re·pub·lic·an /rɪˈpʌblɪkən/ *noun, adj.*
■ *noun* **1** a person who supports a form of government with a president and politicians elected by the people with no king or queen—compare ROYALIST **2** (**Republican**) (*abbr.* **R, Rep.**) a member or supporter of the Republican

b	d	f	g	h	k	l	m	n	p	r
bad	did	fall	get	hat	cat	leg	man	now	pen	red

R

Party—compare DEMOCRAT **3** (**Republican**) a person from Northern Ireland who believes that Northern Ireland should be part of the Republic of Ireland and not part of the United Kingdom—compare LOYALIST
■ *adj.* **1** connected with or like a republic; supporting the principles of a republic: *a republican government/movement* **2** (also **Republican**) (*abbr.* **R, Rep.**) connected with the Republican Party **3** (also **Republican**) connected with or supporting the Republicans in Northern Ireland ▶ **re·pub·lic·an·ism** (also **Re·pub·lic·an·ism**) *noun* [U]: *a strong commitment to Republicanism*

the Re'publican Party *noun* [sing.] one of the two main political parties in the US, usually considered to support CONSERVATIVE views, and to want to limit the power of central government—compare THE DEMOCRATIC PARTY

re·pu·di·ate /rɪ'pjuːdieɪt/ *verb* [VN] (*formal*) **1** to refuse to accept sth [SYN] REJECT: *to repudiate a proposal/suggestion* ◇ *The West has chosen to repudiate all responsibility for these refugees.* **2** to say officially and/or publicly that sth is not true [SYN] DENY: *to repudiate an article/a report/a claim* **3** to refuse to do sth, especially sth that you are legally required to do: *to repudiate a contract/an agreement* **4** (*old-fashioned*) to refuse to be connected with sb any longer [SYN] DISOWN: *He repudiated his first wife and married her sister.* ▶ **re·pu·di·ation** /rɪˌpjuːdi'eɪʃn/ *noun* [U]

re·pug·nance /rɪ'pʌgnəns/ *noun* [U] (*formal*) a strong feeling of dislike or disgust about sth: *She was trying to overcome her physical repugnance for him.*

re·pug·nant /rɪ'pʌgnənt/ *adj.* [not usually before noun] **~ (to sb)** (*formal*) making you feel strong dislike or disgust: *We found his suggestion absolutely repugnant.* ◇ *The idea of eating meat was repugnant to her.*

re·pulse /rɪ'pʌls/ *verb* [VN] (*formal*) **1** [usually passive] to make sb feel disgust or strong dislike [SYN] REPEL: *I was repulsed by the horrible smell.* **2** to fight sb who is attacking you and drive them away [SYN] REPEL: *to repulse an attack/invasion/offensive* **3** to refuse to accept sb's help, attempts to be friendly, etc: *Each time I tried to help I was repulsed.* ◇ *She repulsed his advances.*

re·pul·sion /rɪ'pʌlʃn/ *noun* [U] **1** a feeling of very strong dislike of sth that you find extremely unpleasant **2** (*physics*) the force by which objects tend to push each other away: *the forces of attraction and repulsion*—see also REPEL—compare ATTRACTION

re·pul·sive /rɪ'pʌlsɪv/ *adj.* **1** causing a feeling of strong dislike; very unpleasant: *a repulsive sight/smell/habit* ◇ *What a repulsive man!* **2** (*physics*) causing repulsion (= a force that pushes away): *repulsive forces* ▶ **re·pul·sive·ly** *adv.*: *repulsively ugly*

rep·ut·able /'repjətəbl/ *adj.* that people consider to be honest and to provide a good service: *a reputable dealer/company/supplier*—compare DISREPUTABLE

repu·ta·tion /ˌrepju'teɪʃn/ *noun* [C, U] **~ (as sth)** | **~ (for sth/for doing sth)** the opinion that people have about what sb/sth is like, based on what has happened in the past: *to earn/establish/build a reputation* ◇ *to have a good/bad reputation* ◇ *She soon acquired a reputation as a first-class cook.* ◇ *I'm aware of Mark's reputation for being late.* ◇ *to damage/ruin sb's reputation* ◇ *The weather in England is living up to its reputation* (= is exactly as expected).

re·pute /rɪ'pjuːt/ *noun* [U] (*formal*) the opinion that people have of sb/sth [SYN] REPUTATION: *I know him only by repute.* ◇ *She is a writer of international repute.* ◇ *My parents were artists of (some) repute* (= having a very good reputation).

re·puted /rɪ'pjuːtɪd/ *adj.* [not usually before noun] **~ (to be sth/to have done sth)** generally thought to be sth or to have done sth, although this is not certain: *He is reputed to be the best heart surgeon in the country.* ◇ *The house is wrongly reputed to have been the poet's birthplace.* ◇ *She sold her share of the company for a reputed £7 million.* ▶ **re·puted·ly** *adv.*

re·quest /rɪ'kwest/ *noun, verb*

■ *noun* **~ (for sth)** | **~ (that …)** **1** the action of asking for sth formally and politely: *They made a request for further aid.* ◇ *He was there at the request of his manager/at his manager's request* (= because his manager had asked him to go). ◇ *The writer's name was withheld by request* (= because the writer asked for this to be done). ◇ *Catalogues are available on request.* **2** a thing that you formally ask for: *My request was granted.* ◇ *a radio request programme* (= a programme of music, songs, etc. that listeners have asked for)
■ *verb* **~ sth (from sb)** (*formal*) to ask for sth or ask sb to do sth in a polite or formal way: [VN] *She requested permission to film at the White House.* ◇ *You can request a free copy of the leaflet.* ◇ [VNtoinf] *We were requested to assemble in the lobby.* ◇ *You are requested not to smoke in the restaurant.* ◇ [Vthat] *She requested that no one be told of her decision until the next meeting.* ◇ (*BrE* also) *She requested that no one should be told of her decision.* [alsoVspeech]

re·quiem /'rekwiəm, -iem/ (also ˌrequiem 'mass) *noun* **1** a Christian ceremony for a person who has recently died, at which people say prayers for his or her soul **2** a piece of music for this ceremony

re·quire /rɪ'kwaɪə(r)/ *verb* (not usually used in the progressive tenses) (*formal*) **1** to need sth; to depend on sb/sth: [VN] *These pets require a lot of care and attention.* ◇ *This condition requires urgent treatment.* ◇ *Do you require anything else?* (= in a shop/store, for example) ◇ [VNtoinf] *True marriage requires us to show trust and loyalty.* ◇ [Vthat] *The situation required that he be present.* ◇ (*BrE* also) *The situation required that he should be present.* ◇ [V-ing] *Lentils do not require soaking before cooking.* **2** [often passive] **~ sth (of sb)** to make sb do or have sth, especially because it is necessary according to a particular law or set of rules: [VN] *What exactly is required of a receptionist* (= what are they expected to do)? ◇ *The wearing of seat belts is required by law.* ◇ *'Hamlet' is required reading* (= must be read) *for this course.* ◇ *Several students failed to reach the required standard.* ◇ [VNtoinf] *All candidates will be required to take a short test.* [alsoVthat]

re·quire·ment /rɪ'kwaɪəmənt/ *AmE* -'kwaɪərm-/ *noun* (*formal*) **1** (usually **requirements**) [pl.] something that you need or want: *the basic requirements of life* ◇ *a software package to meet your requirements* ◇ *Our immediate requirement is extra staff.* ◇ *These goods are surplus to requirements* (= more than we need). **2** something that you must have in order to do sth else: *to meet/fulfil/satisfy the requirements* ◇ *What is the minimum entrance requirement for this course?*

requis·ite /'rekwɪzɪt/ *adj., noun*
■ *adj.* [only before noun] (*formal*) necessary for a particular purpose: *She lacks the requisite experience for the job.* ◇ *They were not able to start the meeting until the requisite number of members were present.*
■ *noun* **~ (for/of sth)** (*formal*) something that you need for a particular purpose: *toilet requisites* (= soap, TOOTHPASTE, etc.) ◇ *A university degree has become a requisite for entry into most professions.*—compare PREREQUISITE

requi·si·tion /ˌrekwɪ'zɪʃn/ *noun, verb*
■ *noun* [C, U] a formal, official written request or demand for sth: *the requisition of ships by the government* ◇ *a requisition form/order*
■ *verb* [VN] to officially demand the use of a building, vehicle, etc., especially during a war or an emergency: *The school was requisitioned as a military hospital.*

re·quite /rɪ'kwaɪt/ *verb* [VN] (*formal*) to give sth such as love, kindness, a favour, etc. in return for what sb has given you: *requited love*—compare UNREQUITED

re·route *verb* [VN] to change the route that a road, vehicle, etc. normally follows

rerun *noun, verb*
■ *noun* /'riːrʌn/ **1** a television programme that is shown again: *reruns of old TV shows* **2** an event, such as a race or competition, that is held again: *Officials have ordered a rerun of the last race.* **3** something that is done in the same way as sth in the past: *We wanted to avoid a rerun of last year's disastrous trip.*

s	t	v	z	ʃ	ʒ	tʃ	dʒ	θ	ð	ŋ
see	tea	van	zoo	shoe	vision	chain	jam	thin	this	sing

■ *verb* /ˌriːˈrʌn/ (**re·run·ning, reran** /ˌriːˈræn/ **rerun**) [VN]
1 to show a film/movie, television programme, etc. again
2 to do sth again in a similar way: *to rerun an experiment*
3 to run a race again

re·sale /ˈriːseɪl; ˌriːˈseɪl/ *noun* [U] the sale to another
person of sth that you have bought: *the resale value of a
car*

re·sched·ule /ˌriːˈʃedjuːl; AmE ˌriːˈskedʒuːl/ *verb* **1 ~
sth (for/to sth)** to change the time at which sth has been
arranged to happen, especially so that it takes place later:
[VN] *The meeting has been rescheduled for next week.*
[also VN to inf] **2** [VN] (*finance*) to arrange for sb to pay back
money that they have borrowed at a later date than was
originally agreed: *to reschedule a loan* ▶ **re·sched·ul·ing**
noun [U, sing.]

re·scind /rɪˈsɪnd/ *verb* [VN] (*formal*) to officially state
that a law, contract, decision, etc. is no longer valid

res·cue /ˈreskjuː/ *verb, noun*
■ *verb* **~ sb/sth (from sth/sb)** to save sb/sth from a dangerous or harmful situation: [VN] *He rescued a child from
drowning.* ◊ *They were eventually rescued by helicopter.* ◊
The house was rescued from demolition. ◊ *You rescued me
from an embarrassing situation.* ◊ [VN-ADJ] *She had despaired of ever being rescued alive.* ▶ **res·cuer** *noun*
■ *noun* **1** [U] the act of saving sb/sth from a dangerous or
difficult situation; the fact of being saved: *We had given
up hope of rescue.* ◊ *A wealthy benefactor **came to their
rescue** with a generous donation.* ◊ *a rescue attempt/
operation* ◊ *a mountain rescue team* ◊ *rescue workers/
boats/helicopters* **2** [C] an occasion when sb/sth is saved
from a dangerous or difficult situation: *Ten fishermen
were saved in a daring sea rescue.*

re·search *noun, verb*
■ *noun* /rɪˈsɜːtʃ; ˈriːsɜːtʃ; AmE -sɜːrtʃ/ [U] (also **re·searches**
[pl.] especially in *BrE*) **~ (into/on sth/sb)** a careful study
of a subject, especially in order to discover new facts or
information about it: *medical/economic/historical/scien-
tific research* ◊ *to do/conduct/undertake research* ◊ *He has
carried out extensive research into renewable energy
sources.* ◊ *Recent research on deaf children has produced
some interesting findings about their speech.* ◊ *What have
their researches shown?* ◊ *a research project/grant/stu-
dent*—see also MARKET RESEARCH, OPERATIONAL RESEARCH
■ *verb* /rɪˈsɜːtʃ; AmE -ˈsɜːrtʃ/ **~ (into/in/on sth)** to study sth
carefully and try to discover new facts about it: [V]
They're researching into ways of improving people's diet. ◊
[VN] *to research a problem/topic/market* ◊ *He spent 20
years researching Nazi Germany.* ◊ *She's in New York
researching her new book* (= finding facts and information
to put in it). [also V wh-] ▶ **re·search·er** *noun*

re·search and de·velopment *noun* [U] (*abbr.* **R &
D**) (in industry, etc.) work that tries to find new products
and processes or to improve existing ones

re·sell /ˌriːˈsel/ *verb* (**re·sold, re·sold** /ˌriːˈsəʊld; AmE
-ˈsoʊld/) [VN] to sell sth that you have bought: *He resells
the goods at a profit.*

re·sem·blance /rɪˈzembləns/ *noun* [C, U] **~ (to sb/sth)** |
~ (between A and B) the fact of being or looking similar
to sb/sth: *a striking/close/strong resemblance* ◊ *family
resemblances* ◊ *She bears an uncanny **resemblance** to
Barbra Streisand.* ◊ *The resemblance between the two
signatures was remarkable.* ◊ *The movie **bears little
resemblance** to the original novel.*

re·sem·ble /rɪˈzembl/ *verb* [VN] [no passive] (not used in
the progressive tenses) to look like or be similar to
another person or thing: *She closely resembles her sister.* ◊
So many hotels resemble each other. ◊ *The plant resembles
grass in appearance.*

re·sent /rɪˈzent/ *verb* to feel bitter or angry about sth,
especially because you feel it is unfair: [VN] *I deeply
resented her criticism.* ◊ [V-ing] *He bitterly resents being
treated like a child.* ◊ [VN-ing] *She resented him making all
the decisions.* ◊ (*formal*) *She resented his making all the
decisions.*

re·sent·ful /rɪˈzentfl/ *adj.* **~ (of/at/about sth)** feeling
bitter or angry about sth that you think is unfair: *a
resentful look/expression/voice* ◊ *They seemed to be resent-*

ful of our presence there. ◊ *She was resentful at having
been left out of the team.* ▶ **re·sent·ful·ly** /-fəli/ *adv.*

re·sent·ment /rɪˈzentmənt/ *noun* [U, sing.] a feeling of
anger or unhappiness about sth that you think is unfair:
to feel/harbour/bear resentment towards/against sb ◊
*She could not conceal the deep resentment she felt at the
way she had been treated.*

re·ser·va·tion /ˌrezəˈveɪʃn; AmE -zərˈv-/ *noun* **1** [C] an
arrangement for a seat on a plane or train, a room in a
hotel, etc. to be kept for you: *I'll call the restaurant and
make a reservation.* ◊ *We have reservations in the name
of Grant.*—compare BOOKING **2** [C, U] a feeling of doubt
about a plan or an idea: *I have serious reservations about
his ability to do the job.* ◊ *They support the measures
without reservation (= completely).* **3** (also **re·serve**) [C]
an area of land in the US that is kept separate for Native
Americans to live in—see also CENTRAL RESERVATION

re·serve /rɪˈzɜːv; AmE rɪˈzɜːrv/ *verb, noun*
■ *verb* [VN] **1 ~ sth (for sb/sth)** to ask for a seat, table,
room, etc. to be available for you or sb else at a future
time: *I'd like to reserve a table for three for eight o'clock.* ◊
I've reserved a room in the name of Jones.—compare BOOK
2 ~ sth (for sb/sth) to keep sth for sb/sth, so that it
cannot be used by any other person or for any other
reason: *These seats are reserved for special guests.* ◊ *I'd
prefer to reserve* (*my*) *judgement* (= not make a decision)
until I know all the facts. **3** to have or keep a particular
power: *The management **reserves the right** to refuse
admission.* ◊ (*law*) *All rights reserved* (= nobody else can
publish or copy this).
■ *noun*
  SUPPLY | **1** [C, usually pl.] a supply of sth that is available
to be used in the future or when it is needed: *large oil and
gas reserves* ◊ *He discovered unexpected reserves of
strength.* ◊ *reserve assets/funds*
  PROTECTED LAND | **2** (*AmE* also **pre·serve**) [C] a piece of
land that is a protected area for animals, plants, etc: *a
wildlife reserve*—see also GAME RESERVE, NATURE RESERVE
3 [C] = RESERVATION
  QUALITY/FEELING | **4** [U] the quality that sb has when they
do not talk easily to other people about their ideas,
feelings, etc: *She found it difficult to make friends because
of her natural reserve.* **5** [U] (*formal*) a feeling that you do
not want to accept or agree to sth, etc. until you are quite
sure that it is all right to do so: *Any contract should be
treated **with reserve** until it has been checked.* ◊ *She
trusted him **without reserve** (= completely).*
  IN SPORT | **6** [C] an extra player who plays in a team when
one of the other players is injured or not available to play
7 (**the reserves**) [pl.] a team that plays when the usual
one is not available
  MILITARY FORCE | **8** (**the reserve**) [sing.] (also **the reserves**
[pl.]) an extra military force, etc. that is not part of a
country's regular forces, but is available to be used when
needed: *the army reserve(s)* ◊ *the reserve police*
  PRICE | **9** (also **re·serve price**) [C] (*BrE*) the lowest price
that sb will accept for sth, especially sth that is sold at an
AUCTION: *The painting failed to reach its reserve and
was withdrawn from the sale.*
  IDM **in re·serve** available to be used in the future or
when needed: *The money was being **kept in reserve** for
their retirement.* ◊ *200 police officers were **held in reserve**.*

re·served /rɪˈzɜːvd; AmE rɪˈzɜːrvd/ *adj.* (of a person or
their character) slow or unwilling to show feelings or
express opinions: *a reserved man/manner*—compare
UNRESERVED

re·serv·ist /rɪˈzɜːvɪst; AmE -ˈzɜːrv-/ *noun* a soldier, etc.
who is a member of the reserves (= a military force that
can be used in an emergency)

res·er·voir /ˈrezəvwɑː(r); AmE ˈrezərv-/ *noun* **1** a natural
or artificial lake where water is stored before it is taken
by pipes to houses, etc. **2** (*written*) a large amount of sth
that is available to be used **3** (*technical*) a place in an
engine or a machine where a liquid is kept before it is
used: *an oil reservoir*

reset /ˌriːˈset/ *verb* (**re·set·ting, reset, reset**) [VN] **1** to
change a machine, an instrument or a control so that it

R

æ	ɑː	e	ɜː	ə	ɪ	iː	i	ɒ	ɔː	ʌ	ʊ	u	uː
cat	father	ten	bird	about	sit	see	many	got	saw	cup	put	actual	too

(BrE)

R

gives a different time or number or is ready to use again: *You need to reset your watch to local time.* ◇ *I've reset the heating to stay on all day.* **2** [often passive] to place sth in the correct position again: *to reset a broken bone*

re·set·tle /ˌriːˈsetl/ *verb* **1** to help people go and live in a new country or area; to go and live in a new country or area: [VN] *Many of the refugees were resettled in Britain and Canada.* [also V] **2** [VN] to start to use an area again as a place to live: *The region was only resettled 200 years later.* **3** to make yourself comfortable in a new position: [V] *The birds flew around and then resettled on the pond.* [also VN] ▶ **re·set·tle·ment** *noun* [U]: *the resettlement of refugees* ◇ *a resettlement agency/area/programme*

re·shape /ˌriːˈʃeɪp/ *verb* [VN] to change the shape or structure of sth

re·shuf·fle /ˌriːˈʃʌfl/ (also *less frequent* **shuf·fle**) *verb* to change around the jobs that a group of people do, for example in the British Government: [VN] *The Prime Minister eventually decided against reshuffling the Cabinet.* [also V] ▶ **re·shuf·fle** /ˈriːʃʌfl/ *noun: a Cabinet reshuffle*

res·ide /rɪˈzaɪd/ *verb* [V+*adv./prep.*] (*formal*) to live in a particular place: *He returned to Britain in 1939, having resided abroad for many years.* ◇ *Do you still reside at Elm Road?* **PHRV** **re'side in sb/sth** to be in sb/sth; to be caused by sth: *The poem's main interest resides in the use of dialect.* ◇ *The source of the problem resides in the fact that the currency is too strong.* **re'side in/with sb/sth** (of a power, a right, etc.) to belong to sb/sth: *The ultimate authority resides with the board of directors.*

resi·dence /ˈrezɪdəns/ *noun* (*formal*) **1** [C] a house, especially a large or impressive one: *a desirable family residence for sale* (= for example, in an advertisement) ◇ *10 Downing Street is the British Prime Minister's official residence.* **2** [U] the state of living in a particular place: *a hall of residence* (= for university or college students) ◇ (*formal*) *They were not able to* **take up residence** *in their new home until the spring.* ◇ *Please state your occupation and place of residence.* ◇ *The flag flies when the Queen is* **in residence**. **3** (also **resi·dency**) [U] permission to live in a country that is not your own: *They have been denied residence in this country.* ◇ *a residence permit* **IDM** **in 'residence** having an official position in a particular place such as a college or university: *a writer/an artist/a musician in residence*

resi·dency /ˈrezɪdənsi/ *noun* (*pl.* **-ies**) (*formal*) **1** [U, C] = RESIDENCE: *She has been granted permanent residency in Britain.* **2** [U, C] the period of time that an artist, a writer or a musician spends working for a particular institution **3** [U] the state of living in a particular place: *a residency requirement for students* **4** [U, C] (*especially AmE*) the period of time when a doctor working in a hospital receives special advanced training **5** (also **resi·dence**) [C] the official house of sb such as an AMBASSADOR

resi·dent /ˈrezɪdənt/ *noun, adj.*
■ *noun* **1** a person who lives in a particular place or who has their home there: *a resident of the United States* ◇ *There were confrontations between local residents and the police.* **2** a person who is staying in a hotel: *The hotel restaurant is open to non-residents.* **3** a doctor working in a hospital in the US who is receiving special advanced training—compare REGISTRAR
■ *adj.* living in a particular place: *the town's resident population* (= not tourists or visitors) ◇ *to be resident abroad/ in the US* ◇ *Tom's our resident expert* (= our own expert) *on foreign movies.*

resi·den·tial /ˌrezɪˈdenʃl/ *adj.* [usually before noun] **1** (of an area of a town) suitable for living in; consisting of houses rather than factories or offices: *a quiet residential area* **2** (of a job, a course, etc.) requiring a person to live at a particular place; offering living accommodation: *a residential language course* ◇ *a residential home for the elderly* ◇ *residential care for children*

'residents' association *noun* a group of people who live in a particular area and join together to discuss the problems of that area

re·sidual /rɪˈzɪdjuəl; *AmE* -dʒu-/ *adj.* [only before noun]

(*formal*) remaining at the end of a process: *There are still a few residual problems with the computer program.*

re·sidu·ary /rɪˈzɪdjuəri; *AmE* -dʒueri/ *adj.* **1** (*law*) remaining from the money and property left by a person who has died after all debts, gifts, etc. have been paid: *a residuary bequest* **2** (*technical*) remaining at the end of a process

resi·due /ˈrezɪdjuː; *AmE* -duː/ *noun* **1** (*technical*) a small amount of sth that remains at the end of a process: *pesticide residues in fruit and vegetables* **2** (*law*) the part of the money, property, etc. of a person who has died that remains after all the debts, gifts, etc. have been paid: *The residue of the estate was divided equally among his children.*

re·sign /rɪˈzaɪn/ *verb* ~ **(from sth)** | ~ **(as sth)** to officially tell sb that you are leaving your job, an organization, etc: [V] *He resigned as manager after eight years.* ◇ *Two members resigned from the board in protest.* ◇ [VN] *My father resigned his directorship last year.* **PHRV** **re'sign yourself to sth** to accept sth unpleasant that cannot be changed or avoided: *She resigned herself to her fate.* ◇ [+-ing] *We had to resign ourselves to making a loss on the sale.*

res·ig·na·tion /ˌrezɪɡˈneɪʃn/ *noun* **1** [U, C] the act of giving up your job or position; the occasion when you do this: *a letter of resignation* ◇ *There were calls for her resignation from the board of directors.* ◇ *Further resignations are expected.* **2** [C] a letter, for example to your employers, to say that you are giving up your job or position: *to offer/hand in/tender your resignation* ◇ *We haven't received his resignation yet.* **3** [U] patient willingness to accept a difficult or unpleasant situation that you cannot change: *They accepted their defeat with resignation.*

re·signed /rɪˈzaɪnd/ *adj.* ~ **(to sth/doing sth)** being willing to calmly accept sth unpleasant or difficult that you cannot change: *a resigned sigh/smile/voice* ◇ *He was resigned to never seeing his birthplace again.* ▶ **re·sign·ed·ly** /-nɪdli/ *adv.*: *'I suppose you're right,' she said resignedly.*

re·sili·ence /rɪˈzɪliəns/ (also *less frequent* **re·sili·ency** /-nsi/) *noun* [U] **1** the ability of people or things to feel better quickly after sth unpleasant, such as shock, injury, etc: *He showed great courage and resilience in fighting back from a losing position to win the game.* **2** the ability of a substance to return to its original shape after it has been bent, stretched or pressed: *the natural beauty and resilience of wool*

re·sili·ent /rɪˈzɪliənt/ *adj.* **1** able to feel better quickly after sth unpleasant such as shock, injury, etc: *He'll get over it—young people are amazingly resilient.* **2** (of a substance) returning to its original shape after being bent, stretched, or pressed ▶ **re·sili·ent·ly** *adv.*

resin /ˈrezɪn; *AmE* ˈrezn/ *noun* [C, U] **1** a sticky substance that is produced by some trees and is used in making VARNISH, medicine, etc. **2** an artificial substance similar to resin, used in making plastics ▶ **res·in·ous** /ˈrezɪnəs; *AmE* ˈrezənəs/ *adj.*: *the resinous scent of pine trees*

re·sist /rɪˈzɪst/ *verb* **1** to refuse to accept sth and try to stop it from happening: [VN] *to resist change* ◇ *They are determined to resist pressure to change the law.* ◇ [V-ing] *The bank strongly resisted cutting interest rates.* [also V] **2** to fight back when attacked; to use force to stop sth from happening: [V] *He tried to pin me down, but I resisted.* ◇ [VN] *She was charged with resisting arrest.* **3** (usually in negative sentences) to stop yourself from having sth you like or doing sth you very much want to do: [VN] *I finished the cake. I* **couldn't resist it**. ◇ *I found the temptation to miss the class too hard to resist.* ◇ [V-ing] *He couldn't resist showing off his new car.* [also V] **4** [VN] to not be harmed or damaged by sth: *A healthy diet should help your body resist infection.* ◇ *This new paint is designed to resist heat.*

re·sist·ance /rɪˈzɪstəns/ *noun* **1** [U, sing.] ~ **(to sb/sth)** dislike of or opposition to a plan, an idea, etc.; refusal to obey: *As with all new ideas it met with resistance.* ◇ *There has been a lot of resistance to this new law.* ◇ *Resistance to change has nearly destroyed the industry.* **2** [U, sing.] ~ **(to**

aɪ	aʊ	eɪ	əʊ	oʊ	ɔɪ	ɪə	eə	ʊə	j	w
my	now	say	go	go	boy	near	hair	pure	yes	wet
			(BrE)	(AmE)						

sb/sth) the act of using force to oppose sb/sth: *armed resistance* ◇ *The defenders put up a strong resistance.* ◇ *The demonstrators offered little or no resistance to the police.* **3** [U, sing.] **~ (to sth)** the power not to be affected by sth: *Aids lowers the body's resistance to infection.* **4** [U, sing.] **~ (to sth)** a force that stops sth moving or makes it move more slowly: *low/high wind resistance* (= in the design of planes or cars) **5** [U, C] (*physics*) (*symb* **R**) the fact of not CONDUCTING heat or electricity; a measurement of this **6** (often **the Resistance**) [sing.+ sing./pl. *v.*] a secret organization that resists the authorities, especially in a country that an enemy has control of: *resistance fighters/forces* **IDM** see LINE *n.*

re·sist·ant /rɪˈzɪstənt/ *adj.* **~ (to sth)** **1** not affected by sth; able to resist sth: *plants that are resistant to disease* **2** opposing sth and trying to stop it happening: *Elderly people are not always resistant to change.* **3** (**-resistant**) (in adjectives) not damaged by the thing mentioned: *disease-resistant plants* ◇ *fire-resistant materials*—see also HEAT-RESISTANT, WATER-RESISTANT

re·sist·er /rɪˈzɪstə(r)/ *noun* a person who resists sb/sth

re·sist·ible /rɪˈzɪstəbl/ *adj.* (*rare*) that can be resisted **OPP** IRRESISTIBLE

re·sis·tor /rɪˈzɪstə(r)/ *noun* (*technical*) a device that has RESISTANCE to an electric current in a CIRCUIT

resit /ˌriːˈsɪt/ *verb* (**re·sit·ting, resat, resat** /ˌriːˈsæt/) (also **re·take**) [VN, V] (*BrE*) to take an exam or a test again, usually after failing it the first time ▶ **resit** /ˈriːsɪt/ (also **re·take**) *noun*: *Students are only allowed one resit.*

reso·lute /ˈrezəluːt/ *adj.* having or showing great determination: *resolute action/leadership* ◇ *He became even more resolute in his opposition to the plan.* **OPP** IRRESOLUTE ▶ **reso·lute·ly** *adv.*: *They remain resolutely opposed to the idea.* **reso·lute·ness** *noun* [U]

reso·lution /ˌrezəˈluːʃn/ *noun* **1** [C] a formal statement of an opinion agreed on by a committee or a council, especially by means of a vote: *to pass/adopt/carry a resolution* **2** [U, sing.] the act of solving or settling a problem, dispute, etc: *the resolution of the dispute* ◇ *The government is pressing for an early resolution of the hostage crisis.* **3** [U] the quality of being resolute or determined **SYN** RESOLVE: *The reforms owe a great deal to the resolution of one man.* **4** [C] **~ (to do sth)** a firm decision to do or not to do sth: *She made a resolution to visit her relatives more often.* ◇ *Have you made any New Year's resolutions* (= for example, to give up smoking from 1 January)? **5** [U, sing.] the power of a computer screen, printer, etc. to give a clear image, depending on the size of the dots that make up the image: *high-resolution graphics*

re·solve /rɪˈzɒlv/ *AmE* rɪˈzɑːlv/ *verb, noun*
■ *verb* (*written*) **1** [VN] to find a satisfactory solution to a problem or difficulty: *to resolve an issue/a dispute/a conflict/a crisis* ◇ *Attempts are being made to resolve the problem of security in schools.* ◇ *Both sides met in order to try to resolve their differences.* **2** **~ (on sth/on doing sth)** to make a firm decision to do sth: [V to inf] *He resolved not to tell her the truth.* ◇ [V (that)] *She resolved (that) she would never see him again.* ◇ [V] *We had resolved on making an early start.* **3** (of a committee, meeting, etc.) to reach a decision by means of a formal vote: [V that] *It was resolved that the matter be referred to a higher authority.* ◇ [V to inf] *The Supreme Council resolved to resume control over the national press.* **PHRV** **reˈsolve into sth | reˈsolve sth into sth** **1** to separate or to be separated into its parts: *to resolve a complex argument into its basic elements* **2** (of sth seen or heard at a distance) to gradually turn into a different form when it is seen or heard more clearly: *The orange light resolved itself into four lanterns.* **3** to gradually become or be understood as sth: *The discussion eventually resolved itself into two main issues.*
■ *noun* [U] **~ (to do sth)** (*formal*) strong determination to achieve sth **SYN** RESOLUTION: *The difficulties in her way merely strengthened her resolve.* ◇ *The government reiterated its resolve to uncover the truth.*

re·solved /rɪˈzɒlvd/ *AmE* rɪˈzɑːlvd/ *adj.* [not before noun]

~ (to do sth) (*formal*) determined: *I was resolved not to see him.*

res·on·ance /ˈrezənəns/ *noun* **1** [U] (*formal*) (of sound) the quality of being resonant: *Her voice had a strange and thrilling resonance.* **2** [C, U] (*technical*) the sound or other VIBRATION produced in an object by sound or VIBRATIONS of a similar FREQUENCY from another object **3** [U, C] (*formal*) (in a piece of writing, music, etc.) the power to bring images, feelings, etc. into the mind of the person reading or listening; the images, etc. produced in this way

res·on·ant /ˈrezənənt/ *adj.* **1** (*formal*) (of sound) deep, clear and continuing for a long time: *a deep resonant voice* **2** (*technical*) causing sounds to continue for a long time: *resonant frequencies* **3** (*literary*) having the power to bring images, feelings, memories, etc. into your mind: *a poem filled with resonant imagery* ▶ **res·on·ant·ly** *adv.*

res·on·ate /ˈrezəneɪt/ *verb* [V] (*formal*) **1** (of a voice, an instrument, etc.) to make a deep, clear sound that continues for a long time: *Her voice resonated through the theatre.* **2** **~ (with sth)** (of a place) to be filled with sound; to make a sound continue longer: *a resonating chamber* ◇ *The room resonated with the chatter of 100 people.* **3** **~ (with sb/sth)** to remind sb of sth; to be similar to what sb thinks or believes: *These issues resonated with the voters.* **PHRV** **ˈresonate with sth** (*literary*) to be full of a particular quality or feeling: *She makes a simple story resonate with complex themes and emotions.*

res·on·ator /ˈrezəneɪtə(r)/ *noun* (*technical*) a device for making sound louder and stronger, especially in a musical instrument

re·sort /rɪˈzɔːt; *AmE* rɪˈzɔːrt/ *noun, verb*
■ *noun* **1** [C] a place where a lot of people go on holiday/vacation: *seaside/ski/mountain resorts* ◇ (*BrE*) *a popular holiday resort* ◇ *the resort town of Byron Bay* **2** [U] **~ to sth** the act of using sth, especially sth bad or unpleasant, because nothing else is possible: *There are hopes that the conflict can be resolved without resort to violence.* **3** **the first/last/final ~** the first or last course of action that you should or can take in a particular situation: *Strike action should be regarded as a last resort, when all attempts to negotiate have failed.* ◇ *In the last resort* (= at the most basic level) *what really moves us is our personal convictions.*
■ *verb* **PHRV** **reˈsort to sth** to make use of sth, especially sth bad, as a means of achieving sth, often because there is no other possible solution: *They felt obliged to resort to violence.* ◇ [+ -ing] *We may have to resort to using untrained staff.*

re·sound /rɪˈzaʊnd/ *verb* [V] (*written*) **1** **~ (through sth)** (of a sound, voice, etc.) to fill a place with sound: *Laughter resounded through the house.* ◇ (*figurative*) *The tragedy resounded around the world.* **2** **~ (with/to sth)** (of a place) to be filled with sound: *The street resounded to the thud of marching feet.* ◇ *The room resounded with screams and shouts.*

re·sound·ing /rɪˈzaʊndɪŋ/ *adj.* [only before noun] **1** very great: *a resounding victory/win/defeat* ◇ *The evening was a resounding success.* **2** (of a sound) very loud and continuing for a long time ▶ **re·sound·ing·ly** *adv.*

re·source /rɪˈsɔːs; -ˈzɔːs; *AmE* ˈriːsɔːrs; rɪˈsɔːrs/ *noun, verb*
■ *noun* **1** [C, usually pl.] a supply of sth that a country, an organization or a person has and can use, especially to increase their wealth: *the exploitation of minerals and other natural resources* ◇ *We do not have the resources* (= money) *to update our computer software.* ◇ *We must make the most efficient use of the available financial resources.* ◇ *We agreed to pool our resources* (= so that everyone gives sth).—see also HUMAN RESOURCES **2** [C] something that can be used to help achieve an aim, especially a book, equipment, etc. that provides information for teachers and students: *The database could be used as a teaching resource in colleges.* ◇ *Time is your most valuable resource, especially in examinations.* ◇ *resource books for teachers* **3** (**resources**) [pl.] personal qualities such as courage and imagination that help you deal with difficult

R

situations: *He has no inner resources and hates being alone.*

■ *verb* [VN] to provide sth with the money or equipment that is needed: *Schools in the area are still inadequately resourced.*

re·source·ful /rɪ'sɔːsfl; -'zɔːs-; AmE -'sɔːrs-/ *adj.* (*approving*) good at finding ways of doing things and solving problems, etc. ▶ **re·source·ful·ly** /-fəli/ *adv.* **re·source·ful·ness** *noun* [U]

re·spect /rɪ'spekt/ *noun, verb*

■ *noun* **1** [U, sing.] ~ (for sb/sth) a feeling of admiration for sb/sth because of their good qualities or achievements: *I have the greatest respect for your brother.* ◊ *A two-minute silence was held as a **mark of respect.*** ◊ *A deep mutual respect and understanding developed between them.*—see also SELF-RESPECT OPP DISRESPECT **2** [U, sing.] ~ (for sb/sth) polite behaviour towards or care for sb/sth that you think is important: *to show a lack of respect for authority* ◊ *He has no respect for her feelings.* ◊ *Everyone has a right to be **treated with respect.*** OPP DISRESPECT **3** [C] a particular aspect or detail of sth: *In this respect we are very fortunate.* ◊ *There was one respect, however, in which they differed.* ◊ *in all/some/many respects* IDM **in respect of sth** (*formal or business*) **1** concerning: *A writ was served on the firm in respect of their unpaid bill.* **2** in payment for sth: *money received in respect of overtime worked* **with re'spect | with all due re'spect** (*formal*) used before disagreeing with sb in order to seem polite: *With respect, sir, I cannot agree.* **with respect to sth** (*formal or business*) concerning: *The two groups were similar with respect to income and status.*—more at DUE *adj.*, PAY *v.*

■ *verb* [VN] **1** (not usually used in the progressive tenses) ~ sb/sth (for sth) to have a very good opinion of sb/sth; to admire sb/sth: *I respect Jack's opinion on most subjects.* ◊ *She had always been honest with me, and I respect her for that.* ◊ *a much loved and highly respected teacher* **2** to be careful about sth; to make sure you do not do sth that sb would consider to be wrong: *to respect other people's property* ◊ *She promised to respect our wishes.* ◊ *He doesn't respect other people's right to privacy.* **3** to agree not to break a law, principle, etc: *The new leader has promised to respect the constitution.*

re·spect·abil·ity /rɪ,spektə'bɪləti/ *noun* [U] the fact of being considered socially acceptable: *middle-class notions of respectability*

re·spect·able /rɪ'spektəbl/ *adj.* **1** considered by society to be acceptable, good or correct: *a highly respectable neighbourhood* ◊ *a respectable married man* ◊ *Go and make yourself look respectable.* OPP DISREPUTABLE **2** fairly good; that there is not reason to be ashamed of: *a perfectly respectable result* ▶ **re·spect·ably** *adv.*: *respectably dressed*

re·spect·er /rɪ'spektə(r)/ *noun* IDM **be no respecter of 'persons** to treat everyone in the same way, without being influenced by their importance, wealth, etc.

re·spect·ful /rɪ'spektfl/ *adj.* showing or feeling RESPECT: *The onlookers stood at a respectful distance.* ◊ *We were brought up to be respectful of authority.* OPP DISRESPECTFUL ▶ **re·spect·ful·ly** /-fəli/ *adv.*: *He listened respectfully.*

re·spect·ing /rɪ'spektɪŋ/ *prep.* (*formal*) concerning: *information respecting the child's whereabouts*

re·spect·ive /rɪ'spektɪv/ *adj.* [only before noun] belonging or relating separately to each of the people or things already mentioned: *They are each recognized specialists in their respective fields.* ◊ *the respective roles of men and women in society*—compare IRRESPECTIVE

re·spect·ive·ly /rɪ'spektɪvli/ *adv.* in the same order as the people or things already mentioned: *Julie Wilson and Mark Thomas, aged 17 and 19 respectively*

res·pir·ation /,respə'reɪʃn/ *noun* [U] (*formal*) the act of breathing: *Blood pressure and respiration are also recorded.*—see also ARTIFICIAL RESPIRATION

res·pir·ator /'respəreɪtə(r)/ *noun* **1** a piece of equipment that makes it possible for sb to breathe over a long period when they are unable to do so naturally: *She was put on a respirator.* **2** a device worn over the nose and mouth to

allow sb to breathe in a place where there is a lot of smoke, gas, etc.

re·spira·tory /rə'spɪrətri; 'respərətri; AmE 'respərətɔːri/ *adj.* connected with breathing: *the respiratory tract/system* ◊ *respiratory diseases*

re·spire /rɪ'spaɪə(r)/ *verb* [V] (*technical*) to breathe

res·pite /'respaɪt; AmE 'respɪt/ *noun* [sing., U] **1** ~ (from sth) a short break or escape from sth difficult or unpleasant: *The drug brought a brief respite from the pain.* ◊ *There was no respite from the suffocating heat.* ◊ *She continued to work without respite.* ◊ ***respite care*** (= temporary care arranged for old, mentally ill, etc. people so that the people who usually care for them can have a rest) **2** a short delay allowed before sth difficult or unpleasant must be done: *His creditors agreed to give him a temporary respite.*

re·splen·dent /rɪ'splendənt/ *adj.* (*formal or literary*) ~ (in sth) bright and colourful in an impressive way: *He glimpsed Sonia, resplendent in a red silk dress.* ▶ **re·splen·dent·ly** *adv.*

re·spond /rɪ'spɒnd; AmE rɪ'spaːnd/ *verb* **1** ~ (to sb/sth) (with sth) (rather *formal*) to give a spoken or written answer to sb/sth SYN REPLY: [V] *I asked him his name, but he didn't respond.* ◊ *She never responded to my letter.* ◊ [V speech] '*I'm not sure,' she responded.* ◊ [V that] *When asked about the company's future, the director responded that he remained optimistic.* ⇨ note at ANSWER **2** [V] ~ (to sth) (with sth/by doing sth) to do sth as a reaction to sth that sb has said or done SYN REACT: *How did they respond to the news?* ◊ *The government responded by banning all future demonstrations.* **3** [V] ~ (to sth/sb) to react quickly or in the correct way to sth/sb: *The car responds very well to the controls.* ◊ *You can rely on him to respond to a challenge.* **4** [V] ~ (to sth) to improve as a result of a particular kind of treatment: *The infection did not respond to the drugs.*

re·spond·ent /rɪ'spɒndənt; AmE -'spaːnd-/ *noun* **1** a person who answers questions, especially in a SURVEY: *60% of the respondents agreed with the suggestion* **2** (*law*) a person who is accused of sth

re·sponse /rɪ'spɒns; AmE rɪ'spaːns/ *noun* ~ (to sb/sth) **1** [C, U] a spoken or written answer: *She made no response.* ◊ *In response to your inquiry ...* ◊ *I received an encouraging response to my advertisement.* **2** [C, U] a reaction to sth that has happened or been said: *The news provoked an angry response.* ◊ *a positive response* ◊ *I knocked on the door but there was no response.* ◊ *The product was developed in response to customer demand.* ◊ *We sent out over 1000 letters but the **response rate** has been low* (= few people replied). **3** [C, usually pl.] a part of a church service that the people sing or speak as an answer to the part that the priest sings or speaks

re·spon·si·bil·ity /rɪ,spɒnsə'bɪləti; AmE -,spaːn-/ *noun* (*pl.* -ies) **1** [U, C] ~ (for sth/for doing sth) | ~ (to do sth) a duty to deal with or take care of sb/sth, so that you may be blamed if sth goes wrong: *We are recruiting a sales manager with responsibility for the European market.* ◊ *They have responsibility for ensuring that the rules are enforced.* ◊ *It is their responsibility to ensure that the rules are enforced.* ◊ *to take/assume overall responsibility for personnel* ◊ *parental rights and responsibilities* ◊ *I don't feel ready to take on new responsibilities.* ◊ *to be in a position of responsibility* ◊ *I did it on my own responsibility* (= without being told to and being willing to take the blame if it had gone wrong). **2** [U] ~ (for sth) blame for sth bad that has happened: *The bank refuses to accept responsibility for the mistake.* ◊ *Nobody has claimed responsibility for the bombing.*—see also DIMINISHED RESPONSIBILITY **3** [U, C] ~ (to/towards sb) | ~ (to do sth) a duty to help or take care of sb because of your job, position, etc: *She feels a strong sense of responsibility towards her employees.* ◊ *I think we have a moral responsibility to help these countries.*

re·spon·sible /rɪ'spɒnsəbl; AmE -'spaːn-/ *adj.* HAVING JOB/DUTY | **1** ~ (for sb/sth) | ~ (for doing sth) having the job or duty of doing sth or taking care of sb/sth, so that you may be blamed if sth goes wrong: *Mike is* responsible for designing the entire project. ◊ *Even where parents no longer live together, they each continue to be responsible for their children.*

CAUSING STH | **2 ~ (for sth)** being able to be blamed for sth: *Who's responsible for this mess?* ◊ *Everything will be done to bring those responsible to justice.* ◊ *He is mentally ill and cannot* **be held responsible** *for his actions.* **3 ~ (for sth)** being the cause of sth: *Cigarette smoking is responsible for about 90% of deaths from lung cancer.*

TO SB IN AUTHORITY | **4 ~ to sb/sth** to have to report to sb/sth with authority or in a higher position and explain to them what you have done: *The Council of Ministers is responsible to the Assembly.*

RELIABLE | **5** (of people or their actions or behaviour) that you can trust and rely on: *Clare has a mature and responsible attitude to work.* OPP IRRESPONSIBLE

JOB | **6** [usually before noun] needing sb who can be trusted and relied on; involving important duties: *a responsible job/position*

re·spon·sibly /rɪ'spɒnsəbli/ *AmE* -'spɑːn-/ *adv.* in a sensible way that shows you can be trusted: *to act/behave responsibly* OPP IRRESPONSIBLY

re·spon·sive /rɪ'spɒnsɪv/ *AmE* -'spɑːn-/ *adj.* **~ (to sb/sth)** **1** [not usually before noun] reacting quickly and in a positive way: *Firms have to be responsive to consumer demand.* ◊ *a flu virus that is not responsive to treatment* **2** reacting with interest or enthusiasm: *The club is responsive to suggestions or new ideas.* ◊ *a responsive and enthusiastic audience* OPP UNRESPONSIVE ► **re·spon·sive·ly** *adv.* **re·spon·sive·ness** *noun* [U]: *a lack of responsiveness to client needs*

re·spray /ˌriː'spreɪ/ *verb* [VN] to change the colour of sth, especially a car, by painting it with a spray ► **re·spray** /'riːspreɪ/ *noun* [usually sing.]

rest /rest/ *noun, verb*

■ *noun*

REMAINING PART/PEOPLE/THINGS | **1** [sing.] **the ~ (of sth)** the remaining part of sth: *the rest of the world/my life/her money* ◊ *How would you like to spend the rest of the day?* ◊ *Take what you want and throw the rest away.* **2** [pl.] **the ~ (of sth)** the remaining people or things; the others: *Don't blame Alex. He's human, like the rest of us.* ◊ *The first question was difficult, but the rest were pretty easy.*

PERIOD OF RELAXING | **3** [C, U] **~ (from sth)** a period of relaxing, sleeping or doing nothing after a period of activity: *I had a good night's rest.* ◊ *We stopped for a well-earned rest.* ◊ *to have/take a rest from all your hard work* ◊ *Try to get some rest—you have a busy day tomorrow.* ◊ *There are no matches tomorrow, which is a* **rest day**, *but the tournament resumes on Monday.*

SUPPORT | **4** [C] (often in compounds) an object that is used to support or hold sth: *an armrest* (= for example on a seat or chair) ◊ *a headrest/footrest*

IN MUSIC | **5** [C, U] a period of silence between notes; a sign that shows a rest between notes—picture at MUSIC

IDM **and (all) the 'rest (of it)** (*spoken*) used at the end of a list to mean everything else that you might expect to be on the list: *She believes in God and heaven and hell and the rest.* **and the 'rest** (*spoken*) used to say that the actual amount or number of sth is much higher than sb has stated: *'We've run up a cost of 250 quid …' 'And the rest, and the rest!'* **at 'rest 1** (*technical*) not moving: *At rest the insect looks like a dead leaf.* **2** dead and therefore free from trouble or anxiety. People say 'at rest' to avoid saying 'dead': *She now* **lies at rest** *in the churchyard.* **come to 'rest** to stop moving: *The car crashed through the barrier and came to rest in a field.* ◊ *His eyes came to rest on Clara's face.* **for the 'rest** (*BrE, formal*) apart from that; as far as other matters are concerned **give it a 'rest** (*BrE, spoken*) used to tell sb to stop talking about sth because they are annoying you **give sth a 'rest** (*informal*) to stop doing sth for a while **lay sb to 'rest** to bury sb. People say 'to lay sb to rest' to avoid saying 'to bury' sb: *George was laid to rest beside his parents.* **lay/put sth to 'rest** to stop sth by showing it is not true: *The announcement finally laid all the speculation about their future to rest.* **the rest is 'history** used when you are

telling a story to say that you do not need to tell the end of it, because everyone knows it already—more at MIND *n.*, WICKED *n.*

■ *verb*

RELAX | **1** to relax, sleep or do nothing after a period of activity or illness; to not use a part of your body for some time: [V] *The doctor told me to rest.* ◊ *I can* **rest easy** (= stop worrying) *knowing that she's safely home.* ◊ *(figurative) He won't rest* (= will never be satisfied) *until he finds her.* ◊ [VN] *Rest your eyes every half an hour.* ◊ *I awoke feeling rested and refreshed.*

SUPPORT | **2** [VN+*adv./prep.*] to support sth by putting it on or against sth; to be supported in this way: [V, VN] *His chin rested on his hands.* ◊ *He rested his chin in his hands.* ◊ [VN] *Rest your head on my shoulder.* ◊ [V] *Their bikes were resting against the wall.*

BE LEFT | **3** if you let a matter **rest**, you stop discussing it or dealing with it: *The matter cannot rest there—I intend to sue.*

BE BURIED | **4** [V+*adv./prep.*] to be buried. People say 'rest' to avoid saying 'be buried': *She rests beside her husband in the local cemetery.* ◊ *May he* **rest in peace.**—see also RIP

IDM **I ˌrest my 'case** (*spoken, law* or *humorous*) to have no more to say about sth, especially because you think you have proved your point **rest as'sured (that …)** (*formal*) used to emphasize that what you say is true or will definitely happen: *You may rest assured that we will do all we can to find him.*—more at GOD, LAUREL

PHRV **'rest on/upon sb/sth 1** to depend or rely on sb/sth: *All our hopes now rest on you.* **2** to look at sb/sth: *Her eyes rested on the piece of paper in my hand.* **'rest on sth** to be based on sth: *The whole argument rests on a false assumption.* **'rest with sb (to do sth)** (*formal*) if it rests with sb to do sth, it is their responsibility to do it: *It rests with management to justify their actions.* ◊ *The final decision rests with the doctors.*

'rest area, **'rest stop** *noun* (*AmE*) an area beside an important road where people can stop their cars to rest, eat food, etc.—compare LAY-BY

re·start /ˌriː'stɑːt; *AmE* -'stɑːrt/ *verb* to start again, or to make sth start again, after it has stopped: [VN] *to restart a game/car/meeting* ◊ *The doctors struggled to restart his heart.* [also V] ► **re·start** /'riːstɑːt; *AmE* -stɑːrt/ *noun*

re·state /ˌriː'steɪt/ *verb* [VN] (*formal*) to say sth again or in a different way, especially so that it is more clearly or strongly expressed ► **re·state·ment** *noun* [U]

res·taur·ant /'restrɒnt; *AmE* -trɑːnt; -tərɑːnt/ *noun* a place where you can buy and eat a meal: *an Italian restaurant* ◊ *We had a meal in a restaurant.* ◊ *We went out to a restaurant to celebrate.* ◊ *a restaurant owner* ◊ *a self-service restaurant*—compare CAFE

'restaurant car *noun* (*BrE*) = DINING CAR

res·taura·teur /ˌrestərə'tɜː(r)/ *noun* (*formal*) a person who owns and manages a restaurant

rest·ful /'restfl/ *adj.* that makes you feel relaxed and peaceful: *a hotel with a restful atmosphere*

'rest home *noun* a place where old or sick people are cared for

'resting place *noun* **1** a grave. People say 'resting place' to avoid saying 'grave': *her final/last resting place* **2** a place where you can rest

res·ti·tu·tion /ˌrestɪ'tjuːʃn; *AmE* -'tuː-/ *noun* [U] **~ (of sth) (to sb/sth) 1** (*formal*) the act of giving back sth that was lost or stolen to its owner: *the restitution of property seized under Communist rule* **2** (*law*) payment, usually money, for some harm or wrong that sb has suffered

rest·ive /'restɪv/ *adj.* (*formal*) unable to stay still, or unwilling to be controlled, especially because you feel bored or not satisfied ► **rest·ive·ness** *noun* [U]

rest·less /'restləs/ *adj.* **1** unable to stay still or be happy where you are, because you are bored or need a change: *The audience was becoming restless.* ◊ *After five years in the job, he was beginning to feel restless.* **2** without real rest or sleep: *a restless night* ► **rest·less·ly** *adv.*: *He moved restlessly from one foot to another.* **rest·less·ness** *noun* [U]: *the restlessness of youth*

re·stock /ˌriː'stɒk; *AmE* -'stɑːk/ *verb* [VN, V] **~ sth (with**

R

æ	ɑː	e	ɜː	ə	ɪ	iː	i	ɒ	ɔː	ʌ	ʊ	uː
cat	father	ten	bird	about	sit	see	many	got	saw	cup	put	actual	too
								(BrE)				

sth) to fill sth with new or different things to replace those that have been used, sold, etc.; to get a new supply of sth

res·tor·ation /ˌrestəˈreɪʃn/ *noun* **1** [U, C] the work of repairing and cleaning an old building, a painting, etc. so that its condition is as good as it originally was: *The palace is closed for restoration.* ◊ *restoration work* **2** [U, C] **~ of sth** the act of bringing back a system, a law, etc. that existed previously: *the restoration of diplomatic relations between the two countries* ◊ *the restoration of democracy/the monarchy* **3** [U] **~ (of sth)** the act of returning sth to its correct place, condition or owner: *the restoration of the Elgin marbles to Greece* **4 (the Restor-ation)** [sing.] the time in Britain in 1660 when, following a period with no king or queen, Charles II became king: *Restoration comedy/poetry* (= written during and after this time)

re·stora·tive /rɪˈstɔːrətɪv/ *adj., noun*
- *adj.* **1** (*formal*) making you feel strong and healthy again: *the restorative power of fresh air* **2** (*medical*) connected with treatment that repairs the body or a part of it: *restorative dentistry/surgery*
- *noun* (*old-fashioned*) a thing that makes you feel better, stronger, etc: *Sleep is the best restorative there is.*

re·store /rɪˈstɔː(r)/ *verb* [VN] **1 ~ sth (to sb)** to bring back a situation or feeling that existed before: *The measures are intended to restore public confidence in the economy.* ◊ *Order was quickly restored after the riots.* ◊ *Such kindness restores your faith in human nature* (= makes you believe most people are kind). ◊ *The most recent operation restored his sight* (= made him able to see again). **2 ~ sb/sth to sth** to bring sb/sth back to a former condition, place or position: *He is now fully restored to health.* ◊ *We hope to restore the garden to its former glory* (= make it as beautiful as it used to be). **3 ~ sth (to sth)** to repair a building, work of art, piece of furniture, etc. so that it looks as good as it did originally: *Her job is restoring old paintings.* ◊ *The house has been lovingly restored to the way it looked in 1900 when it was built.* **4** to bring a law, tradition, way of working, etc. back into use: *to restore ancient rights/traditions* ◊ *The death penalty was restored in 1982.* **5 ~ sth (to sb/sth)** (*formal*) to give sth that was lost or stolen back to sb: *The police have now restored the painting to its rightful owner.*

re·storer /rɪˈstɔːrə(r)/ *noun* a person whose job is to repair old buildings, works of art, etc. so that they look as they did when new

re·strain /rɪˈstreɪn/ *verb* [VN] **1 ~ sb/sth (from sth/from doing sth)** to stop sb/sth from doing sth, especially by using physical force: *The prisoner had to be restrained by the police.* ◊ *I had to restrain her from hitting out at passers-by.* ◊ *They have obtained an injunction restraining the company from selling the product.* ◊ *Morse placed a restraining hand on Lewis's arm.* **2 ~ yourself (from sth/from doing sth)** to stop yourself from feeling an emotion or doing sth that you would wish to do: *John managed to restrain his anger.* ◊ *She had to restrain herself from crying out in pain.* **3** to stop sth that is growing or increasing from becoming too large: *The government is taking steps to restrain inflation.*

re·strained /rɪˈstreɪnd/ *adj.* **1** showing calm control rather than emotion: *her restrained smile* **2** not too colourful or brightly decorated: *The costumes and lighting in the play were restrained.*

re·straining order *noun* **~ (against sb)** (*especially AmE*) an official order given by a judge which demands that sth must or must not be done. A restraining order does not require a trial in a court of law but only lasts for a limited period of time.—compare INJUNCTION

re·straint /rɪˈstreɪnt/ *noun* **1** [C, usually pl.] **~ (on sb/sth)** a rule, a law, an idea, etc. that limits or controls what people can do: *The government has imposed export restraints on some products.* ◊ *social restraints on drinking alcohol* **2** [U] the act of controlling or limiting sth because it is necessary or sensible to do so: *wage restraint* **3** [U] the quality of behaving calmly and with control: *The police appealed to the crowd for restraint.* ◊ *He exercised*

considerable **restraint** *in ignoring the insults.* **4** [U] (*formal*) the use of physical force to control sb who is behaving in a violent way: *the physical restraint of prisoners* **5** [C] (*formal*) a type of SEAT BELT or safety device: *Children must use an approved child restraint or adult seat belt.*

re·strict /rɪˈstrɪkt/ *verb* [VN] **1 ~ sth (to sth)** to limit the size, amount or range of sth: *In Britain speed is restricted to 30 m.p.h. in towns.* ◊ *We restrict the number of students per class to 10.* ◊ *Fog severely restricted visibility.* **2** to stop sb/sth from moving or acting freely: *The long skirt restricted her movements.* ◊ *Having small children tends to restrict your freedom.* **3 ~ sth (to sb)** to control sth with rules or laws: *Access to the club is restricted to members only.* **4 ~ yourself/sb (to sth/to doing sth)** to allow yourself or sb to have only a limited amount of sth or to do only a particular kind of activity: *I restrict myself to one cup of coffee a day.*

re·stricted /rɪˈstrɪktɪd/ *adj.* **1** limited or small in size or amount: *a restricted space* ◊ *a restricted range of foods* **2** limited in what you are able to do: *In those days women led fairly restricted lives.* ◊ *Her vision is restricted in one eye.* **3** controlled by rules or laws: *to allow children only restricted access to the Internet* ◊ (*BrE*) *a restricted area* (= controlled by laws about speed or PARKING) ◊ *The tournament is restricted to players under the age of 23.* **4** [usually before noun] (of a place) only open to people with special permission, especially because it is secret or dangerous: *to enter a restricted zone* **5** (*BrE*) officially secret and only available to people with special permission [SYN] CLASSIFIED: *a restricted document* [OPP] UNRESTRICTED

re·stric·tion /rɪˈstrɪkʃn/ *noun* **1** [C] **~ (on sth)** a rule or law that limits what you can do or what can happen: *import/speed/travel restrictions* ◊ *to impose/place a restriction on sth* ◊ *The government has agreed to lift restrictions on press freedom.* **2** [U] the act of limiting or controlling sb/sth: *sports clothes that prevent any restriction of movement* **3** [C] a thing that limits the amount of freedom you have: *the restrictions of a prison*

re·strict·ive /rɪˈstrɪktɪv/ *adj.* preventing people from doing what they want: *restrictive laws/policies*

re·strictive 'practices *noun* [pl.] (*BrE*, often *disap-proving*) agreements or ways of working that limit the freedom of workers or employers in order to prevent competition or to protect people's jobs

rest·room /ˈrestruːm; -rʊm/ *noun* (*AmE*) a room with a toilet in a public place, such as a theatre or restaurant

re·struc·ture /ˌriːˈstrʌktʃə(r)/ *verb* [VN, V] to organize sth such as a system or a company in a new and different way ▶ **re·struc·tur·ing** *noun* [U, C, usually sing.]: *restructuring charges/costs*

re·sult /rɪˈzʌlt/ *noun, verb*
- *noun*
CAUSED BY STH | **1** [C, U] **~ (of sth)** a thing that is caused or produced because of sth else: *She died **as a result of** her injuries.* ◊ *The failure of the company was a direct result of bad management.* ◊ *He made one big mistake, and, as a result, lost his job.* ◊ *The farm was flooded, with the **result that** most of the harvest was lost.* ◊ *The **end result** (= the final one) of her hard work was a place at medical school.* ◊ *This book is the result of 25 years of research.*
OF GAME/ELECTION | **2** [C] **~ (of sth)** the final score or the name of the winner in a sports event, competition, election, etc: *They will announce the result of the vote tonight.* ◊ *the election results* ◊ *the football results* **3** [C, usually sing.] (*BrE, informal*) a victory, especially in a game of football: *We badly need to get a result from this match.*
OF EXAM | **4** [C, usually pl.] (*BrE*) the mark/grade you get in an exam or in a number of exams: *Have you had your results yet?*
OF TEST/RESEARCH | **5** [C] **~ (of sth)** the information that you get from a scientific test or piece of research: *the result of an X-ray/an experiment*
SUCCESS | **6** (**results**) [pl.] things that are achieved success-fully: *The project is beginning to show results.* ◊ *a coach who knows how to get results from his players*

aɪ	aʊ	eɪ	əʊ	oʊ	ɔɪ	ɪə	eə	ʊə	j	w
my	now	say	go (BrE)	go (AmE)	boy	near	hair	pure	yes	wet

■ *verb* [V] ~ **(from sth)** to happen because of sth else that happened first: *job losses resulting from changes in production* ◊ *When water levels rise, flooding results.* ◊ *It was a large explosion and the resulting damage was extensive.* PHRV **re'sult in sth** to make sth happen: *The cyclone has resulted in many thousands of deaths.* ◊ [+ -ing] *These policies resulted in many elderly and disabled people suffering hardship.*

re·sult·ant /rɪˈzʌltənt/ *adj.* [only before noun] (*formal*) caused by the thing that has just been mentioned: *the growing economic crisis and resultant unemployment*

re·sume /rɪˈzuːm; *BrE* also -ˈzjuː-/ *verb* (*formal*) **1** if you **resume** an activity, or if it **resumes**, it begins again or continues after an interruption: [VN] *to resume talks/ negotiations* ◊ *She resumed her career after an interval of six years.* ◊ [V] *The noise resumed, louder than before.* ◊ *There is no sign of the peace talks resuming.* ◊ [V -ing] *He got back in the car and resumed driving.* **2** [VN] ~ **your seat/place/position** to go back to the seat or place that you had before

re·sumé /ˈrezjumeɪ; *AmE* ˈrezəmeɪ/ *noun* **1** ~ **(of sth)** a short summary or account of sth: *a brief resumé of events so far* **2** (*AmE*) = CURRICULUM VITAE (1) ⇨ Study page B15

re·sump·tion /rɪˈzʌmpʃn/ *noun* [sing., U] ~ **(of sth)** (*formal*) the act of beginning sth again after it has stopped: *We are hoping for an early resumption of peace talks.*

re·sur·face /ˌriːˈsɜːfɪs; *AmE* -ˈsɜːrf-/ *verb* **1** [V] to come to the surface again after being under water or under the ground: *The submarine resurfaced.* ◊ (*figurative*) *All the old hostilities resurfaced when they met again.* **2** [VN] to put a new surface on a road, path, etc.

re·sur·gence /rɪˈsɜːdʒəns; *AmE* -ˈsɜːrdʒ-/ *noun* [sing., U] the return and growth of an activity that had stopped: *a resurgence of interest in the artist's work*

re·sur·gent /rɪˈsɜːdʒənt; *AmE* -ˈsɜːrdʒ-/ *adj.* [usually before noun] (*formal*) becoming stronger or more popular again: *a resurgent economy* ◊ *resurgent nationalism*

res·ur·rect /ˌrezəˈrekt/ *verb* [VN] **1** to bring back into use sth, such as a belief, a practice, etc., that had disappeared or been forgotten: *The campaign for spelling reform has been resurrected.* ◊ *He has succeeded in resurrecting his career in television.* **2** to bring a dead person back to life

res·ur·rec·tion /ˌrezəˈrekʃn/ *noun* **1 (the Resurrection)** [sing.] (in the Christian religion) the time when Jesus Christ returned to life again after his death; the time when all dead people will become alive again, when the world ends **2** [U, sing.] a new beginning for sth which is old or which had disappeared or become weak: *the resurrection of the British motor industry*

re·sus·ci·tate /rɪˈsʌsɪteɪt/ *verb* [VN] to make sb start breathing again or become conscious again after they have almost died: *He had a heart attack and all attempts to resuscitate him failed.* ◊ (*figurative*) *efforts to resuscitate the Japanese economy* ► **re·sus·ci·ta·tion** /rɪˌsʌsɪˈteɪʃn/ *noun* [U]: *frantic attempts at resuscitation*—see also MOUTH-TO-MOUTH RESUSCITATION

re·tail¹ /ˈriːteɪl/ *noun, adv., verb*—see also RETAIL² *verb*
■ *noun* [U] the selling of goods to the public, usually through shops/stores: *The recommended retail price is £9.99.* ◊ *department stores and other retail outlets* ◊ *the retail trade*—compare WHOLESALE ► **re·tail** *adv.*: *to buy/ sell retail* (= in a shop/store)
■ *verb* **1** [VN] to sell goods to the public, usually through shops/stores: *The firm manufactures and retails its own range of sportswear.* **2** [V] ~ **at/for sth** (*business*) to be sold at a particular price: *The book retails at £14.95.*

re·tail² /rɪˈteɪl/ *verb* [VN] ~ **sth (to sb)** (*formal*) to tell people about sth, especially about a person's behaviour or private life: *She retailed the neighbours' activities with relish.*—see also RETAIL¹

re·tail·er /ˈriːteɪlə(r)/ *noun* (*written*) a person or business that sells goods to the public

re·tail·ing /ˈriːteɪlɪŋ/ *noun* [U] the business of selling goods to the public, usually through shops/stores: *career opportunities in retailing*—compare WHOLESALING

ˌretail 'price index (also **'price index**) *noun* [sing.] (*abbr.* **RPI**) (in Britain) a list of the prices of some ordinary goods and services which shows how much these prices change each month—see also CONSUMER PRICE INDEX

re·tain /rɪˈteɪn/ *verb* [VN] (rather *formal*) **1** to keep sth; to continue to have sth: *to retain your freedom/independence* ◊ *He struggled to retain control of the situation.* ◊ *The house retains much of its original charm.* ◊ *She retained her tennis title for the third year.* **2** to continue to hold or contain sth: *a soil that retains moisture* ◊ *This information is no longer retained within the computer's main memory.* ◊ (*figurative*) *She has a good memory and finds it easy to retain facts.* **3** (*law*) if a member of the public **retains** sb such as a lawyer, he or she pays money regularly or in advance so the lawyer, etc. will do work for him or her: *a retaining fee* ◊ *to retain the services of a lawyer*—see also RETENTION, RETENTIVE

re·tain·er /rɪˈteɪnə(r)/ *noun* **1** a sum of money that is paid to sb to make sure they will be available to do work when they are needed: *The agency will pay you a monthly retainer.* **2** (*BrE*) a small amount of rent that you pay for a room, etc. when you are not there in order to keep it available for your use **3** (*AmE*) a device that keeps a person's teeth straight after they have had ORTHODONTIC treatment with a BRACE **4** (*old-fashioned*) a servant, especially one who has been with a family for a long time

re·tain·ing /rɪˈteɪnɪŋ/ *adj.* [only before noun] (*technical*) intended to keep sth in the correct position: *a retaining screw/strap*

re·take *verb, noun*
■ *verb* /ˌriːˈteɪk/ (**re·took** /-ˈtʊk/, **re·taken** /-ˈteɪkən/) [VN] **1** (especially of an army) to take control of sth such as a town again: *Government forces moved in to retake the city.* ◊ (*figurative*) *Moore fought back to retake the lead later in the race.* **2** = RESIT
■ *noun* /ˈriːteɪk/ **1** the act of filming a scene in a film/movie again, because it was not right before **2** = RESIT

re·tali·ate /rɪˈtælieɪt/ *verb* [V] ~ **(against sb/sth)** | ~ **(by doing sth/with sth)** to do sth harmful to sb because they have harmed you first: *to retaliate against an attack/ injustice* ◊ *The boy hit his sister, who retaliated by kicking him.* ► **re·tali·atory** /rɪˈtæliətri; *AmE* -tɔːri/ *adj.*: *retaliatory action*

re·tali·ation /rɪˌtæliˈeɪʃn/ *noun* [U] ~ **(against sb/sth)** **(for sth)** action that a person takes against sb who has harmed them in some way: *retaliation against UN workers* ◊ *The shooting may have been **in retaliation for** the arrest of the terrorist suspects.*

re·tard *verb, noun*
■ *verb* /rɪˈtɑːd; *AmE* rɪˈtɑːrd/ [VN] (*formal*) to make the development or progress of sth slower: *The progression of the disease can be retarded by early surgery.* ► **re·tard·ation** /ˌriːtɑːˈdeɪʃn; *AmE* ˌriːtɑːrˈd-/ *noun* [U]: *Many factors can lead to growth retardation in unborn babies.*
■ *noun* /ˈriːtɑːd; *AmE* ˈriːtɑːrd/ (*slang*) an offensive way of describing sb who is not intelligent or who has not developed normally

re·tard·ed /rɪˈtɑːdɪd; *AmE* -ˈtɑːrd-/ *adj.* (*old-fashioned, offensive*) less developed mentally than is normal for a particular age

retch /retʃ/ *verb* [V] to make sounds and movements as if you are VOMITING although you do not actually do so: *The smell made her retch.*

re·tell /ˌriːˈtel/ *verb* (**re·told, re·told** /-ˈtəʊld; *AmE* -ˈtoʊld/) [VN] to tell a story again, often in a different way

re·ten·tion /rɪˈtenʃn/ *noun* [U] (*formal*) **1** the action of keeping sth rather than losing it or stopping it: *The company needs to improve its training and retention of staff.* **2** the action of keeping liquid, heat, etc. inside sth rather than letting it escape: *Eating too much salt can cause fluid retention.* **3** the ability to remember things: *Visual material aids the retention of information.*—see also RETAIN

re·ten·tive /rɪˈtentɪv/ *adj.* (of the memory) able to store facts and remember things easily—see also RETAIN

re·think /ˌriːˈθɪŋk/ *verb* (**re·thought, re·thought** /-ˈθɔːt/)

R

to think again about an idea, a course of action, etc., especially in order to change it: [VN] *to rethink a plan/an approach/an attitude* [also V] ▶ **re·think** /ˌriːˈθɪŋk/ (also **re·think·ing**) *noun* [sing.]: *a major/radical rethink of company policy*

reti·cent /ˈretɪsnt/ *adj.* ~ **(about sth)** unwilling to tell people about things: *She was shy and reticent.* ◇ *He was extremely reticent about his personal life.* ▶ **reti·cence** /-sns/ *noun* [U] (*formal*)

ret·ina /ˈretɪnə; *AmE* ˈretənə/ *noun* (*pl.* **ret·inas** or **ret·inae** /-niː/) a layer of tissue at the back of the eye that is sensitive to light and sends signals to the brain about what is seen—picture at BODY

ret·inue /ˈretɪnjuː; *AmE* ˈretənuː/ *noun* [sing.+ sing./pl. *v.*] a group of people who travel with an important person to provide help and support

re·tire /rɪˈtaɪə(r)/ *verb*

FROM JOB | **1** ~ **(from sth)** | ~ **(as sth)** to stop doing your job, especially because you have reached a particular age or because you are ill/sick; to tell sb they must stop doing their job: [V] *She was forced to retire early from teaching because of ill health.* ◇ *My dream is to retire to a villa in France.* ◇ *He has no plans to retire as editor of the magazine.* ◇ *The company's official retiring age is 65.* ◇ [VN] *She was retired on medical grounds.*

IN SPORT | **2** ~ **(from sth)** to stop competing during a game, race, etc., usually because you are injured: [V] *She fell badly, spraining her ankle, and had to retire.* ◇ [V-ADJ] *He retired hurt in the first five minutes of the game.*

FROM/TO A PLACE | **3** (*formal*) to leave a place, especially to go somewhere quieter or more private: *The jury retired to consider the evidence.* ◇ *After dinner he likes to retire to his study.*

OF ARMY | **4** [V] (*formal*) to move back from a battle in order to organize your soldiers in a different way

GO TO BED | **5** [V] (*literary*) to go to bed: *I retired late, for as always the morning would arrive too soon.*

re·tired /rɪˈtaɪəd; *AmE* rɪˈtaɪərd/ *adj.* having retired from work: *a retired doctor* ◇ *Dad is retired now.*

re·tir·ee /ˌrɪtaɪəˈriː/ *noun* (*AmE*) a person who has stopped working because of their age

re·tire·ment /rɪˈtaɪəmənt; *AmE* -ˈtaɪərm-/ *noun* **1** [U, C] the fact of stopping work because you have reached a particular age; the time when you do this: *At 60, he was now approaching retirement.* ◇ *Susan is going to take early retirement* (= retire before the usual age). ◇ *retirement age* ◇ *a retirement pension/plan* **2** [U, sing.] the period of your life after you have stopped work at a particular age: *to provide for retirement* ◇ *We all wish you a long and happy retirement.* ◇ *Up to a third of one's life is now being spent in retirement.* **3** [U] ~ **(from sth)** the act of stopping a particular type of work, especially in sport, politics, etc: *He announced his retirement from football.* ◇ *She came out of retirement to win two gold medals at the championships.*

re'tirement home *noun* = OLD PEOPLE'S HOME

re·tir·ing /rɪˈtaɪərɪŋ/ *adj.* preferring not to spend time with other people; shy: *a quiet, retiring man*

re·tool /ˌriːˈtuːl/ *verb* **1** [VN, V] to replace or change the machines or equipment in a factory so that it can produce new or better goods **2** [VN] (*AmE, informal*) to organize sth in a new or different way: *The senator retooled his style and his campaign manager.*

re·tort /rɪˈtɔːt; *AmE* rɪˈtɔːrt/ *verb, noun*
- *verb* to reply quickly to a comment, in an angry, offended or humorous way: [V speech] '*Don't be ridiculous!*' *Pat retorted angrily.* ◇ [V that] *Sam retorted that it was my fault as much as his.*
- *noun* **1** a quick, angry or humorous reply: *She bit back* (= stopped herself from making) *a sharp retort.* **2** a closed bottle with a long narrow bent SPOUT that is used in a LABORATORY for heating chemicals—picture at LABORATORY

re·touch /ˌriːˈtʌtʃ/ *verb* [VN] to make small changes to a picture or photograph so that it looks better

re·trace /rɪˈtreɪs/ *verb* [VN] **1** to go back along exactly the same path or route that you have come along: *She turned around and began to retrace her steps towards the house.* **2** to make the same trip that sb else has made in the past: *They are hoping to retrace the epic voyage of Christopher Columbus.* **3** to find out what sb has done or where they have been: *Detectives are trying to retrace her movements on the night she disappeared.*

re·tract /rɪˈtrækt/ *verb* **1** (*formal*) to say that sth you have said earlier is not true or correct or that you did not mean it: [VN] *He made a false confession which he later retracted.* ◇ *They tried to persuade me to retract my words.* **2** [VN] (*formal*) to refuse to keep an agreement, a promise, etc: *to retract a bid/an offer* **3** (*technical*) to move back into the main part of sth; to pull sth back into the main part of sth: [V] *The animal retracted into its shell.* ◇ [VN] *The undercarriage was fully retracted.*

re·tract·able /rɪˈtræktəbl/ *adj.* that can be moved or pulled back into the main part of sth: *a knife with a retractable blade*

re·trac·tion /rɪˈtrækʃn/ *noun* (*formal*) **1** [C] a statement saying that sth you previously said or wrote is not true: *He demanded a full retraction of the allegations against him.* **2** [U] (*technical*) the act of pulling sth back (= retracting it): *the retraction of a cat's claws*

re·train /ˌriːˈtreɪn/ *verb* ~ **(sb)** **(as sth)** to learn, or to teach sb, a new type of work, a new skill, etc: [V] *nurses retraining for work in the community* ◇ *She retrained as a teacher.* ◇ [VN to inf] *Staff have been retrained to use the new technology.* [also VN] ▶ **re·train·ing** *noun* [U]

re·tread /ˈriːtred/ *noun* **1** a tyre made by putting a new rubber surface on an old tyre **2** (*AmE, disapproving*) a book, film/movie, song, etc. that contains ideas that have been used before

re·treat /rɪˈtriːt/ *verb, noun*
- *verb*
FROM DANGER/DEFEAT | **1** [V] to move away from a place or an enemy because you are in danger or because you have been defeated: *The army was forced to retreat after suffering heavy losses.* ◇ *We retreated back down the mountain.*—compare ADVANCE

MOVE AWAY/BACK | **2** [V] to move away or back: *He watched her retreating figure.* ◇ *The flood waters slowly retreated.*

CHANGE DECISION | **3** [V +adv./prep.] to change your mind about sth because of criticism or because a situation has become too difficult [SYN] BACK OFF: *The government had retreated from its pledge to reduce class sizes.*

TO QUIET PLACE | **4** [V] [usually +adv./prep.] to escape to a place that is quieter or safer: *Bored with the conversation, she retreated to her bedroom.* ◇ (*figurative*) *He retreated into a world of fantasy.*

FINANCE | **5** [VN] to lose value: *Share prices retreated 45p to 538p.*
- *noun*
FROM DANGER/DEFEAT | **1** [C usually sing, U] a movement away from a place or an enemy because of danger or defeat: *Hitler's retreat from Russia* ◇ *The army was in full retreat* (= retreating very quickly). ◇ *to sound the retreat* (= to give a loud signal for an army to move away)

ESCAPE | **2** [C usually sing, U] ~ **(from/into sth)** an act of trying to escape from a particular situation to one that you think is safer or more pleasant: *Is watching television a retreat from reality?*

CHANGE OF DECISION | **3** [C, usually sing.] an act of changing a decision because of criticism or because a situation has become too difficult: *The Senator made an embarrassing retreat from his earlier position.*

QUIET PLACE | **4** [C] a quiet, private place that you go to in order to get away from your usual life: *a country retreat* **5** [U, C] a period of time when sb stops their usual activities and goes to a quiet place for prayer and thought; an organized event when people can do this: *He went into retreat and tried to resolve the conflicts within himself.* ◇ *to go on a Buddhist retreat*

[IDM] see BEAT *v.*

re·trench /rɪˈtrentʃ/ *verb* [V] (*formal*) (of a business, government, etc.) to spend less money; to reduce costs ▶ **re·trench·ment** *noun* [U, C]: *a period of retrenchment*

	s	t	v	z	ʃ	ʒ	tʃ	dʒ	θ	ð	ŋ
	see	tea	van	zoo	shoe	vision	chain	jam	thin	this	sing

re·trial /ˌriːˈtraɪəl/ *noun* [usually sing.] a new trial of a person whose criminal offence has already been judged once in a court of law

ret·ri·bu·tion /ˌretrɪˈbjuːʃn/ *noun* [U] ~ (**for sth**) (*formal*) severe punishment for sth seriously wrong that sb has done: *People are seeking retribution for the latest terrorist outrages.* ◊ *fear of divine retribution* (= punishment from God) ▶ **re·tribu·tive** *adj.* [usually before noun]: *retributive justice*

re·trieval /rɪˈtriːvl/ *noun* [U] **1** (*formal*) the process of getting sth back, especially from a place where it should not be: *The ship was buried, beyond retrieval, at the bottom of the sea.* ◊ (*figurative*) *By then the situation was beyond retrieval* (= impossible to put right). **2** (*computing*) the process of getting back information that is stored on a computer: *methods of information retrieval* ◊ *retrieval programs/skills/systems*

re·trieve /rɪˈtriːv/ *verb* [VN] **1** ~ **sth** (**from sb/sth**) (*formal*) to bring or get sth back, especially from a place where it should not be: *She bent to retrieve her comb from the floor.* ◊ *The police have managed to retrieve some of the stolen money.* **2** (*computing*) to find and get back data or information that has been stored in the memory of a computer: *to retrieve information from the database* ◊ *The program allows you to retrieve items quickly by searching under a keyword.* **3** to make a bad situation better; to get back sth that was lost: *You can only retrieve the situation by apologizing.* ◊ *Employers are anxious to retrieve the investment they have made in training their employees.* ▶ **re·triev·able** /rɪˈtriːvəbl/ *adj.* OPP IRRETRIEVABLE

re·triever /rɪˈtriːvə(r)/ *noun* a large dog used in hunting to bring back birds that have been shot—see also GOLDEN RETRIEVER

retro /ˈretrəʊ; *AmE* -troʊ/ *adj.* using styles or fashions from the recent past: *the current Seventies retro trend*

retro- /ˈretrəʊ; *AmE* -troʊ/ *prefix* (in nouns, adjectives and adverbs) back or backwards: *retrograde* ◊ *retrospectively*

retro·active /ˌretrəʊˈæktɪv; *AmE* -troʊ-/ *adj.* (*formal*) = RETROSPECTIVE ▶ **retro·active·ly** *adv.*: *The ruling should be applied retroactively.*

retro·fit /ˈretrəʊfɪt; *AmE* -troʊ-/ *verb* (-**tt**-) [VN] to put a new piece of equipment into a machine that did not have it when it was built; to provide a machine with a new part, etc: *Voice recorders were retrofitted into planes already in service.* ◊ *They retrofitted the plane with improved seating.* ▶ **retro·fit** *noun*

retro·grade /ˈretrəgreɪd/ *adj.* (*formal, disapproving*) (of an action) making a situation worse or returning to how things were in the past: *The closure of the factory is a retrograde step.*

retro·gres·sive /ˌretrəˈɡresɪv/ *adj.* (*formal, disapproving*) returning to old-fashioned ideas or methods instead of making progress: *a retrogressive change* OPP PROGRESSIVE

retro·spect /ˈretrəspekt/ *noun* IDM **in retrospect** thinking about a past event or situation, often with a different opinion of it from the one you had at the time: *In retrospect, I think that I was wrong.* ◊ *The decision seems extremely odd, in retrospect.*

retro·spec·tion /ˌretrəˈspekʃn/ *noun* [U] (*formal*) thinking about past events or situations: *to indulge in idle retrospection*

retro·spect·ive /ˌretrəˈspektɪv/ *adj., noun*
▪ *adj.* **1** thinking about or connected with sth that happened in the past: *She felt a pang of retrospective sympathy for Mel.* **2** (also *less frequent, formal* **retro·active**) (of a new law or decision) intended to take effect from a particular date in the past rather than from the present date: *retrospective legislation* ◊ *retrospective pay awards* ▶ **retro·spect·ive·ly** *adv.*: *She wrote retrospectively about her childhood.* ◊ *The new rule will be applied retrospectively.*
▪ *noun* a public EXHIBITION of the work that an artist has done in the past, showing how his or her work has developed

retry /ˌriːˈtraɪ/ *verb* (**re·tries, re·try·ing, re·tried, re·tried**)
1 [VN] to examine a person or case again in a court of law:

He was retried and executed. ◊ *They have decided to retry the case.* **2** [V] to make another attempt to do sth, especially on a computer

ret·sina /retˈsiːnə/ *noun* [U, C] a type of red or white wine from Greece that is given a special flavour with RESIN(1)

re·turn /rɪˈtɜːn; *AmE* rɪˈtɜːrn/ *verb, noun*
▪ *verb*
COME/GO BACK | **1** [V] ~ (**to…**) (**from…**) to come or go back from one place to another: *I waited a long time for him to return.* ◊ *She's returning to Australia tomorrow after six months in Europe.* ◊ *I returned from work to find the house empty.* ◊ *When did she return home from the trip?* ◊ *I had to return to the store to look for my purse.*
BRING/GIVE BACK | **2** ~ **sb/sth** (**to sb/sth**) to bring, give, put or send sth back to sb/sth: *We had to return the hairdryer to the store because it was faulty.* ◊ *I must return some books to the library.* ◊ *Don't forget to return my pen!* ◊ [VN-ADJ] *I returned the letter unopened.*
OF FEELING/QUALITY | **3** [V] to come back again: *The following day the pain returned.* ◊ *Her suspicions returned when things started going missing again.*
TO PREVIOUS SUBJECT/ACTIVITY | **4** [V] ~ (**to sth**) to start discussing a subject you were discussing earlier, or doing an activity you were doing earlier: *He returns to this topic later in the report.* ◊ *She looked up briefly then returned to her sewing.* ◊ *The doctor may allow her to return to work next week.*
TO PREVIOUS STATE | **5** [V] ~ **to sth** to go back to a previous state: *Train services have returned to normal after the strike.*
DO/GIVE THE SAME | **6** [VN] to do or give sth to sb because they have done or given the same to you first; to have the same feeling about sb that they have about you: *to return a favour/greeting/stare* ◊ *She phoned him several times but he was too busy to return her call.* ◊ *It's time we returned their invitation* (= invite them to sth as they invited us to sth first). ◊ *He did not return her love.*
IN TENNIS | **7** [VN] to hit the ball back to your opponent during a game: *to return a service/shot*
A VERDICT | **8** [VN] ~ **a verdict** to give a decision about sth in a court of law: *The jury returned a verdict of not guilty.*
ELECT POLITICIAN | **9** [VN] [usually passive] ~ **sb** (**to sth**) | ~ **sb** (**as sth**) (*BrE*) to elect sb to a political position
PROFIT/LOSS | **10** [VN] (*business*) to give or produce a particular amount of money as a profit or loss: *to return a high rate of interest* ◊ *Last year the company returned a loss of £157 million.*
▪ *noun*
COMING BACK | **1** [sing.] ~ (**to…**) (**from…**) the action of arriving in or coming back to a place that you were in before: *He was met by his brother on his return from Italy.* ◊ *I saw the play on its return to Broadway.* ◊ *on the return flight/journey/trip*
GIVING/SENDING BACK | **2** [U, sing.] the action of giving, putting or sending sth/sb back: *We would appreciate the prompt return of books to the library.* ◊ *The judge ordered the return of the child to his mother.* ◊ *Write your return address* (= the address that a reply should be sent to) *on the back of the envelope.*
OF FEELING/STATE | **3** [sing.] ~ (**of sth**) the situation when a feeling or state that has not been experienced for some time starts again: *the return of spring* ◊ *a return of my doubts/suspicions/symptoms*
TO PREVIOUS SITUATION/ACTIVITY | **4** [sing.] ~ **to sth** the action of going back to an activity or a situation that you used to do or be in: *his return to power/public life* ◊ *They appealed for a return to work* (= after a strike).
PROFIT | **5** [U, C] the amount of profit that you get from sth: *a high rate of return on capital* ◊ *farmers seeking to improve returns from their crops*
OFFICIAL REPORT | **6** [C] an official report or statement that gives particular information to the government or another body: *census returns* ◊ *election returns* (= the number of votes for each candidate in an election)—see also TAX RETURN

R

æ	ɑː	e	ɜː	ə	ɪ	iː	i	ɒ	ɔː	ʌ	ʊ	u	uː
cat	father	ten	bird	about	sit	see	many	got	saw	cup	put	actual	too

(BrE)

TICKET | **7** [C] (*BrE*) = RETURN TICKET: '*Brighton, please.*' '*Single or return?*' ◇ *A return is cheaper than two singles.* ◇ *the return fare to London*—see also DAY RETURN **8** [C] a ticket for the theatre or a sports game that was bought by sb but is given back to be sold again

ON COMPUTER | **9** [U] (also **re'turn key** [C]) the button that you press on a computer when you reach the end of an instruction, or to begin a new line: *To exit this option, press return.*

IN TENNIS | **10** [C] (in tennis and some other sports) the action of hitting the ball, etc. back to your opponent: *a powerful return of serve*

IDM **by re'turn (of 'post)** (*BrE*) using the next available post; as soon as possible: *Please reply by return of post.* **in re'turn (for sth)** **1** as a way of thanking sb or paying them for sth they have done: *Can I buy you lunch in return for your help?* **2** as a response or reaction to sth: *I asked her opinion, but she just asked me a question in return.*—more at HAPPY, POINT *n.*, SALE *n.*

re·turn·able /rɪˈtɜːnəbl; *AmE* -ˈtɜːrn-/ *adj.* **1** (*formal*) that can or must be given back after a period of time: *A returnable deposit is payable on arrival.* ◇ *The application form is returnable not later than 7th June.* **2** (of bottles and containers) that can be taken back to a shop/store in order to be used again: *returnable bottles* **OPP** NON-RETURNABLE

re·turn·ee /rɪˌtɜːˈniː; *AmE* rɪˌtɜːrˈniː/ *noun* [usually pl.] (*especially AmE*) a person who returns to their own country, after living in another country

re·turn·er /rɪˈtɜːnə(r); *AmE* -ˈtɜːrn-/ *noun* (*BrE*) a person who goes back to work after not working for a long time: *women returners* ◇ *courses for adult returners*

re'turning officer *noun* (*BrE*) an official in a particular area who is responsible for arranging an election and announcing the result

re,turn 'match (also **re,turn 'game**) *noun* (*especially BrE*) a second match or game between the same two players or teams

re,turn 'ticket (also **re·turn**) (both *BrE*) (*AmE* ,round-trip 'ticket) *noun* a ticket for a journey to a place and back again

re,turn 'visit *noun* a trip to a place that you have been to once before, or a trip to see sb who has already come to see you: *This hotel is worth a return visit.* ◇ *The US president is making a return visit to Moscow.*

re·unify /ˌriːˈjuːnɪfaɪ/ *verb* (**re·uni·fies**, **re·uni·fy·ing**, **re·uni·fied**, **re·uni·fied**) [VN] [often passive] to join together two or more regions or parts of a country so that they form a single political unit again ▶ **re·uni·fi·ca·tion** /ˌriːˌjuːnɪfɪˈkeɪʃn/ *noun* [U]: *the reunification of Germany*

re·union /ˌriːˈjuːnɪən/ *noun* **1** [C] a social occasion or party attended by a group of people who have not seen each other for a long time: *a family reunion* ◇ *the school's annual reunion* ◇ *a reunion of the class of '85* **2** [C, U] ~ (with sb) | ~ (between A and B) the act of people coming together after they have been apart for some time: *an emotional reunion between mother and son* ◇ *Christmas is a time of reunion.* **3** [U] the action of becoming a single group or organization again: *the reunion of the Church of England with the Church of Rome*

re·unite /ˌriːjuːˈnaɪt/ *verb* **1** ~ A with B | ~ A and B [usually passive] to bring two or more people together again after they have been separated for a long time; to come together again: [VN] *Last night she was reunited with her children.* ◇ *The family was reunited after the war.* ◇ [V] *There have been rumours that the band will reunite for a world tour.* **2** to join together again separate areas or separate groups within an organization, a political party, etc.; to come together again: [VN] *As leader, his main aim is to reunite the party.* [also V]

re·us·able /ˌriːˈjuːzəbl/ *adj.* that can be used again: *reusable plastic bottles*

reuse /ˌriːˈjuːz/ *verb* [VN] to use sth again: *Please reuse your envelopes.* ▶ **reuse** /ˌriːˈjuːs/ *noun* [U]: *the reuse of materials*

Rev. (*BrE* also **Revd**) *abbr.* (used before a name) REVEREND: *Rev. Jesse Jackson*

rev /rev/ *verb, noun*
■ *verb* (**-vv-**) ~ (**sth**) (**up**) when you **rev** an engine or it **revs**, it runs quickly: [VN] *The taxi driver revved up his engine.* ◇ [V] *I could hear the car revving outside.*
■ *noun* (*informal*) a complete turn of an engine, used when talking about an engine's speed **SYN** REVOLUTION: *4 000 revs per minute* ◇ *The needle on the rev counter soared.*

re·value /ˌriːˈvæljuː/ *verb* **1** [VN] to estimate the value of sth again, especially giving it a higher value **2** to increase the value of the money of a country when it is exchanged for the money of another country: [VN] *The yen is to be revalued.* [also V] DEVALUE ◇ **OPP** ▶ **re·valu·ation** /ˌriːˌd væljuˈeɪʃn/ *noun* [U, C, usually sing.]: *the revaluation of the pound*

re·vamp /ˌriːˈvæmp/ *verb* [VN] to make changes to the form of sth, usually to improve its appearance ▶ **re·vamp** *noun* [sing.]: *Could your kitchen do with a revamp?*

re·veal /rɪˈviːl/ *verb* **1** ~ sth (to sb) to make sth known to sb: [VN] *to reveal a secret* ◇ *Details of the murder were revealed by the local paper.* ◇ [V (that)] *The report reveals (that) the company made a loss of £20 million last year.* ◇ [VN (that)] *It was revealed that important evidence had been suppressed.* ◇ [V wh-] *Officers could not reveal how he died.* [also VN to inf] **2** [VN] to show sth that previously could not be seen: *He laughed, revealing a line of white teeth.* ◇ *The door opened to reveal a cosy little room.* ◇ *She crouched in the dark, too frightened to reveal herself.*— see also REVELATION, REVELATORY

re·veal·ing /rɪˈviːlɪŋ/ *adj.* **1** giving you interesting information that you did not know before: *The document provided a revealing insight into the government's priorities.* ◇ *The answers the children gave were extremely revealing.* **2** (of clothes) allowing more of sb's body to be seen than usual: *a revealing blouse/dress* ▶ **re·veal·ing·ly** *adv.*: *He spoke revealingly about his problems.*

re·veille /rɪˈvæli; *AmE* ˈrevəli/ *noun* [U] a tune that is played to wake soldiers in the morning; the time when it is played: *Reveille sounded at first light.*

revel /ˈrevl/ *verb, noun*
■ *verb* (**-ll-**, *AmE* **-l-**) [V] to spend time enjoying yourself in a noisy, enthusiastic way **PHRV** **'revel in sth** to enjoy sth very much: *She was clearly revelling in all the attention.* ◇ [+ -ing] *Some people seem to revel in annoying others.*
■ *noun* [usually pl.] (*literary*) noisy celebrations

reve·la·tion /ˌrevəˈleɪʃn/ *noun* **1** [C] ~ (about/concerning sth) | ~ (that …) a fact that people are made aware of, especially one that has been secret and is surprising: *startling/sensational revelations about her private life* **2** [U] ~ (of sth) the act of making people aware of sth that has been secret: *The company's financial problems followed the revelation of a major fraud scandal.* **3** [C, U] something that is considered to be a sign or message from God—see also REVEAL **IDM** **come as/be a revelation (to sb)** to be a completely new or surprising experience; to be different from what was expected: *His performance in the race today was a revelation to everyone.* ◇ *My trip to Texas was a revelation.*

rev·ela·tory /ˌrevəˈleɪtəri; *AmE* ˈrevələtɔːri/ *adj.* (*formal*) making people aware of sth that they did not know before: *a revelatory experience/insight*—see also REVEAL

rev·el·ler (*BrE*) (*AmE* **rev·el·er**) /ˈrevələ(r)/ *noun* a person who is having fun in a noisy way, usually with a group of other people and often after drinking alcohol

rev·el·ry /ˈrevlri/ *noun* [U] (also **rev·el·ries** [pl.]) noisy fun, usually involving a lot of eating and drinking: *We could hear sounds of revelry from next door.* ◇ *New Year revelries*

re·venge /rɪˈvendʒ/ *noun, verb*
■ *noun* [U] **1** something that you do in order to make sb suffer because they have made you suffer: *He swore to take (his) revenge on his political enemies.* ◇ *She is seeking revenge for the murder of her husband.* ◇ *The bombing was in revenge for the assassination.* ◇ *an act of revenge* ◇ *revenge attacks/killings* **2** (*sport*) the defeat of a person or team that defeated you in a previous game: *The*

aɪ	aʊ	eɪ	əʊ	oʊ	ɔɪ	ɪə	eə	ʊə	j	w
my	now	say	go	go	boy	near	hair	pure	yes	wet
			(BrE)	(AmE)						

team wanted to get revenge for their defeat earlier in the season.

■ *verb* PHRV re'venge yourself on sb| be re'venged on sb (*literary*) to punish or hurt sb because they have made you suffer: *She vowed to be revenged on them all.* ⇨ note at AVENGE

rev·enue /ˈrevənjuː; *AmE* -nuː/ *noun* [U] (also rev·enues [pl.]) the money that a government receives from taxes or that an organization, etc. receives from its business: *a shortfall in tax revenue* ◊ *Advertising revenue finances the commercial television channels.* ◊ *a slump in oil revenues* ◊ *The company's annual revenues rose by 30%.*—see also THE INLAND REVENUE

re·ver·ber·ate /rɪˈvɜːbəreɪt; *AmE* -ˈvɜːrb-/ *verb* [V] **1** (of a sound) to be repeated several times as it bounces off different surfaces SYN ECHO: *Her voice reverberated around the hall.* **2 ~ (with/to sth)** (of a place) to seem to shake because of a loud noise: *The hall reverberated with the sound of music and dancing.* **3** (*formal*) to have a strong effect on people for a long time or over a large area: *Repercussions of the case continue to reverberate through the financial world.*

re·ver·ber·ation /rɪˌvɜːbəˈreɪʃn; *AmE* -ˌvɜːrb-/ *noun* **1** [C, usually pl., U] a loud noise that continues for some time after it has been produced because of the surfaces around it SYN ECHO **2** (reverberations) [pl.] the effects of sth that happens, especially unpleasant ones that spread among a large number of people SYN REPERCUSSION

re·vere /rɪˈvɪə(r); *AmE* rɪˈvɪr/ *verb* [VN] [usually passive] **~ sb (as sth)** (*formal*) to feel great respect or admiration for sb/sth: *a trumpeter revered by fellow musicians*

rev·er·ence /ˈrevərəns/ *noun* [U] **~ (for sb/sth)** (*formal*) a feeling of great respect or admiration for sb/sth: *The poem conveys his deep reverence for nature.* ◊ *The crowd knelt in reverence and worship.*

rev·er·end /ˈrevərənd/ *adj.* [only before noun] (*abbr.* Rev.) the title of a member of the clergy that is also sometimes used to talk to or about one: *the Reverend Charles Dodgson* ◊ *Good morning, Reverend.*—see also RIGHT REVEREND

Reverend 'Mother *noun* a title of respect used when talking to or about a MOTHER SUPERIOR (= the head of a female religious community)

rev·er·ent /ˈrevərənt/ *adj.* (*formal*) showing great respect and admiration ▶ rev·er·ent·ly *adv.*

rev·er·en·tial /ˌrevəˈrenʃl/ *adj.* (*formal*) full of respect or admiration: *His name was always mentioned in almost reverential tones.* ▶ rev·er·en·tial·ly /-ʃəli/ *adv.*: *She lowered her voice reverentially.*

rev·erie /ˈrevəri/ *noun* [C, U] (*formal*) a state of thinking about pleasant things, almost as though you are dreaming: *She was jolted out of her reverie as the door opened.*

re·ver·sal /rɪˈvɜːsl; *AmE* rɪˈvɜːrsl/ *noun* **1** [C, U] **~ (of sth)** a change of sth so that it is the opposite of what it was: *a complete/dramatic/sudden reversal of policy* ◊ *the reversal of a decision/position/trend* ◊ *The government suffered a total reversal of fortunes last week.* **2** [C] a change from being successful to having problems or being defeated: *the team's recent reversal* ◊ *The company's financial problems were only a temporary reversal.* **3** [C, U] an exchange of positions or functions between two or more people: *It's a complete role reversal/reversal of roles* (= for example when a husband cares for the house and children while the wife works).

re·verse /rɪˈvɜːs; *AmE* rɪˈvɜːrs/ *verb, noun, adj.*
■ *verb*
CHANGE TO OPPOSITE | **1** [VN] to change sth completely so that it is the opposite of what it was before: *to reverse a procedure/process/trend* ◊ *The government has failed to reverse the economic decline.* ◊ *It is sometimes possible to arrest or reverse the disease.* **2** [VN] to change a previous decision, law, etc. to the opposite one: *The Court of Appeal reversed the decision.* ◊ *The policy is likely to be reversed if there is a change of government.* **3** [VN] to turn sth the opposite way around or change the order of sth around: *Writing is reversed in a mirror.* ◊ *You should reverse the order of these pages.*

EXCHANGE TWO THINGS | **4** [VN] to exchange the positions or functions of two things: *It felt as if we had reversed our roles of parent and child.* ◊ *She used to work for me, but our situations are now reversed.*

YOURSELF | **5** [VN] **~ yourself (on sth)** (*AmE*) to admit you were wrong or to stop having a particular position in an argument: *He has reversed himself on a dozen issues.*

VEHICLE | **6** (*especially BrE*) when a vehicle or its driver reverses or the driver reverses a vehicle, the vehicle goes backwards: [VN] *Now reverse the car.* ◊ [V] *He reversed around the corner.* ◊ *She reversed into a parking space.* ◊ *Caution! This truck is reversing.*—compare BACK v.

TELEPHONE CALL | **7** [VN] **~ (the) charges** (*BrE*) to make a telephone call that will be paid for by the person you are calling, not by you: *a reverse charges call*—see also COLLECT *adj.*

■ *noun*
OPPOSITE | **1** (the reverse) [sing.] the opposite of what has just been mentioned: *This problem is the reverse of the previous one.* ◊ *Although I expected to enjoy living in the country, in fact the reverse is true.* ◊ *In the south, the reverse applies.* ◊ *It wasn't easy to persuade her to come—quite the reverse.*

BACK | **2** (the reverse) [sing.] the back of a coin, piece of material, piece of paper, etc.

IN VEHICLE | **3** (also re,verse 'gear) [U] the mechanism used to make a vehicle move backwards: *Put the car in/into reverse.*

LOSS/DEFEAT | **4** [C] (*formal*) a loss or defeat; a change from success to failure: *Property values have suffered another reverse.* ◊ *a damaging political reverse*

IDM in re'verse in the opposite order or way SYN BACKWARDS: *The secret number is my phone number in reverse.* ◊ *We did a similar trip to you, but in reverse.* go/put sth into re'verse to start to happen or to make sth happen in the opposite way: *In the 1980s economic growth went into reverse.*

■ *adj.* [only before noun]
OPPOSITE | **1** opposite to what has been mentioned: *to travel in the reverse direction* ◊ *The winners were announced in reverse order* (= the person in the lowest place was announced first). ◊ *The experiment had the reverse effect to what was intended.*

BACK | **2** opposite to the front: *Iron the garment on the reverse side.*

re·vers·ible /rɪˈvɜːsəbl; *AmE* -ˈvɜːrs-/ *adj.* **1** (of clothes, materials, etc.) that can be turned inside out and worn or used with either side showing: *a reversible jacket* **2** (of a process, an action or a disease) that can be changed so that sth returns to its original state or situation: *Is the trend towards privatization reversible?* ◊ *reversible kidney failure* OPP IRREVERSIBLE ▶ re·vers·ibil·ity /rɪˌvɜːsəˈbɪləti; *AmE* -ˌvɜːrs-/ *noun* [U] (*formal*): *Reversibility depends on the severity of the damage to the brain.*

re'versing light (*BrE*) (*AmE* 'backup light) *noun* a white light at the back of a vehicle that comes on when the vehicle moves backwards

re·ver·sion /rɪˈvɜːʃn; *AmE* rɪˈvɜːrʒn/ *noun* **1** [U, sing.] **~ (to sth)** (*formal*) the act or process of returning to a former state or condition: *a reversion to traditional farming methods* **2** [U, C] (*law*) the return of land or property to sb: *the reversion of Hong Kong to China* **3** (*AmE, law*) = LEASEBACK

re·vert /rɪˈvɜːt; *AmE* rɪˈvɜːrt/ *verb* PHRV re'vert to sb/sth (*law*) (of property, rights, etc.) to return to the original owner again—see also REVERSION re'vert to sth (*formal*) **1** to return to a former state; to start doing sth again that you used to do in the past: *After her divorce she reverted to her maiden name.* ◊ *His manner seems to have reverted to normal.* ◊ *Try not to revert to your old eating habits.* **2** to return to an earlier topic or subject: *So, to revert to your earlier question ...* ◊ *The conversation kept reverting to the events of March 6th.*

re·view /rɪˈvjuː/ *noun, verb*
■ *noun* **1** [U, C] an examination of sth, with the intention of changing it if necessary: *the government's review of its education policy* ◊ *The case is subject to judicial review.* ◊

	b	d	f	g	h	k	l	m	n	p	r
	bad	did	fall	get	hat	cat	leg	man	now	pen	red

R

*His parole application is **up for review** next week.* ◇ *The terms of the contract are **under review.*** ◇ *a pay/salary review* ◇ *a review body/date/panel* **2** [C, U] a report in a newspaper or magazine in which sb gives their opinion of a book, play, film/movie, etc.; the act of writing this kind of report: *a book review* ◇ *the reviews (page) in the papers* ◇ *enthusiastic/good/mixed/rave reviews in the national press* ◇ *He submitted his latest novel for review.* **3** [C] a report on a subject or on a series of events: *a review of customer complaints* ◇ *to publish a review of recent cancer research* **4** [C] (*formal*) a ceremony that involves an official INSPECTION of soldiers, etc. by an important visitor: *to hold a review of the fleet*
■ *verb* [VN] **1** to carefully examine or consider sth again, especially so that you can decide if it is necessary to make changes: *to review the evidence* ◇ *The government will review the situation later in the year.* ◇ *Staff performance is reviewed annually.* **2** to think about past events, for example to try to understand why they happened: *to review your failures and triumphs* ◇ *She had been reviewing the previous week on her way home.* **3** to write a report of a book, play, film/movie, etc. in which you give your opinion of it: *The play was reviewed in the national newspapers.* **4** to make an official INSPECTION of a group of soldiers, etc. in a military ceremony: *The Commander-in-Chief reviewed the troops.* **5** (*especially AmE*) to look again at sth you have read or studied

re·view·er /rɪˈvjuːə(r)/ *noun* **1** a person who writes reviews of books, films/movies or plays: *a book reviewer for 'The Guardian'* **2** a person who examines or considers sth carefully, for example to see if any changes need to be made: (*BrE*) *a rent reviewer*

re·vile /rɪˈvaɪl/ *verb* [VN] [usually passive] ~ **sb (for sth/ for doing sth)** (*formal*) to criticize sb/sth in a way that shows how much you dislike them

re·vise /rɪˈvaɪz/ *verb* **1** [VN] to change your opinions or plans, for example because of sth you have learned: *I can see I will have to revise my opinions of his abilities now.* ◇ *The government may need to revise its policy in the light of this report.* **2** [VN] to change sth, such as a book or an estimate, in order to correct or improve it: *a revised edition of a textbook* ◇ *I'll prepare a revised estimate for you.* ◇ *We may have to revise this figure upwards.* **3** (*BrE*) to prepare for an exam by looking again at work that you have done: [V] *I spent the weekend revising for my exam.* ◇ *I can't come out tonight. I have to revise.* ◇ [VN] *I'm revising Geography today.*

re·vi·sion /rɪˈvɪʒn/ *noun* **1** [C] a change or set of changes to sth: *He made some minor revisions to the report before printing it out.* **2** [U, C] the act of changing sth, or of examining sth with the intention of changing it: *a system in need of revision* ◇ *a revision of trading standards* **3** [U] (*BrE*) the process of learning work for an exam: *Have you started your revision yet?*

re·vi·sion·ism /rɪˈvɪʒənɪzəm/ *noun* [U] (often *disapproving, politics*) ideas that are different from, and want to change, the main ideas or practices of a political system, especially Marxism ► **re·vi·sion·ist** /-ʒənɪst/ *noun: bourgeois revisionists* **re·vi·sion·ist** /-ʒənɪst/ *adj.: revisionist history/historians*

re·visit /ˌriːˈvɪzɪt/ *verb* [VN] (*written*) **1** to visit a place again, especially after a long period of time **2** to return to an idea or a subject and discuss it again: *It's an idea that may be worth revisiting at a later date.*

re·vit·al·ize (*BrE* also **-ise**) /ˌriːˈvaɪtəlaɪz/ *verb* [VN] to make sth stronger, more active or more healthy: *measures to revitalize the inner cities* ◇ *The local economy has been revitalized.* ► **re·vit·al·iza·tion, -isa·tion** /ˌriːˌvaɪt-əlaɪˈzeɪʃn; AmE -lə'z-/ *noun* [U]: *the revitalization of the steel industry*

re·vival /rɪˈvaɪvl/ *noun* **1** [U, C] an improvement in the condition or strength of sth: *the revival of trade* ◇ *an economic revival* ◇ *a revival of interest in folk music* **2** [C, U] the process of sth becoming or being made popular or fashionable again: *a religious revival* ◇ *Jazz is enjoying a revival.* **3** [C] a new production of a play that

has not been performed for some time: *a revival of Peter Shaffer's 'Equus'*

re·vival·ism /rɪˈvaɪvəlɪzəm/ *noun* [U] **1** the process of creating interest in sth again, especially religion: *Christian revivalism* **2** the practice of using ideas, designs, etc. from the past: *revivalism in architecture*

re·vival·ist /rɪˈvaɪvəlɪst/ *noun* a person who tries to make sth popular again: *Christian revivalists* ► **re·vival·ist** *adj.: revivalist ideas/movements/styles* ◇ *a revivalist preacher*

re·vive /rɪˈvaɪv/ *verb* **1** to become, or to make sb/sth become, conscious or healthy and strong again: [V] *The flowers soon revived in water.* ◇ *The economy is beginning to revive.* ◇ [VN] *The paramedics couldn't revive her.* ◇ *This movie is intended to revive her flagging career.* **2** [VN] to make sth start being used or done again: *This quaint custom should be revived.* ◇ *She has been trying to revive the debate over equal pay.* **3** [VN] to produce again a play, etc. that has not been performed for some time: *This 1930s musical is being revived at the National Theatre.*—see also REVIVAL

re·viv·ify /riːˈvɪvɪfaɪ/ *verb* (**re·vivi·fies, re·vivi·fy·ing, re·vivi·fied, re·vivi·fied**) [VN] (*rare, formal*) to give new life or health to sth

revo·ca·tion /ˌrevəˈkeɪʃn/ *noun* [U, C] (*formal*) the act of cancelling a law, etc: *the revocation of planning permission*

re·voke /rɪˈvəʊk; AmE -ˈvoʊk/ *verb* [VN] (*formal*) to officially cancel sth so that it is no longer valid

re·volt /rɪˈvəʊlt; AmE -ˈvoʊlt/ *noun, verb*
■ *noun* [C, U] a protest against authority, especially that of a government, often involving violence; the action of protesting against authority: *the Peasants' Revolt of 1381* ◇ *to lead/stage a revolt* ◇ *The army quickly crushed the revolt.* ◇ *the biggest back-bench revolt this government has ever seen* ◇ *Attempts to negotiate peace ended in armed revolt.* ◇ (*formal*) *The people rose in revolt.*
■ *verb* **1** [V] ~ **(against sb/sth)** to take violent action against the people in power: *Finally the people revolted against the military dictatorship.* ◇ *The peasants threatened to revolt.*—see also REVOLUTION **2** [V] ~ **(against sth)** to behave in a way that is the opposite of what sb expects of you, especially in protest: *Teenagers often revolt against parental discipline.* **3** [VN] to make you feel horror or disgust: *All the violence in the movie revolted me.* ◇ *The way he ate his food revolted me.*—see also REVULSION

re·volt·ing /rɪˈvəʊltɪŋ; AmE -ˈvoʊlt-/ *adj.* extremely unpleasant SYN DISGUSTING: *a revolting smell* ◇ *a revolting little man* ► **re·volt·ing·ly** *adv.: She's revoltingly overweight.*

revo·lu·tion /ˌrevəˈluːʃn/ *noun* **1** [C, U] an attempt, by a large number of people, to change the government of a country, especially by violent action: *a bourgeois/socialist revolution* ◇ *the outbreak of the French Revolution in 1789* ◇ *to cause/start a revolution* ◇ *a country on the brink of revolution*—see also COUNTER-REVOLUTION, REVOLT **2** [C] ~ **(in sth)** a great change in conditions, ways of working, beliefs, etc. that affects large numbers of people: *a cultural/social/scientific revolution* ◇ *A revolution in information technology is taking place.*—see also INDUSTRIAL REVOLUTION **3** [C, U] ~ **(around/on sth)** a complete circular movement around a point, especially of one planet around another: *the revolution of the earth around the sun*—see also REVOLVE **4** (also *informal* **rev**) [C] a circular movement made by sth fixed to a central point, for example in a car engine: *rotating at 300 revolutions per minute*

revo·lu·tion·ary /ˌrevəˈluːʃənəri; AmE -neri/ *adj., noun*
■ *adj.* **1** [usually before noun] connected with political revolution: *a revolutionary leader/movement* ◇ *revolutionary uprisings* **2** involving a great or complete change: *a revolutionary idea* ◇ *a time of rapid and revolutionary change*
■ *noun* (*pl.* **-ies**) a person who starts or supports a revolution, especially a political one: *socialist/student revolutionaries*

revo·lu·tion·ize (*BrE* also **-ise**) /ˌrevəˈluːʃənaɪz/ *verb*

[VN] to completely change the way that sth is done: *Aerial photography has revolutionized the study of archaeology.*

re·volve /rɪˈvɒlv; *AmE* rɪˈvɑːlv/ *verb* [V] to go in a circle around a central point: *The fan revolved slowly.* ◊ *The earth revolves on its axis.* **PHRV re'volve around/round sth** to move around sth in a circle: *The earth revolves around the sun.* **re'volve around/round sb/sth** to have sb/sth as the main interest or subject: *His whole life revolves around surfing.* ◊ *She thinks that the world revolves around her.* ◊ *The discussion revolved around the question of changing the club's name.*

re·volver /rɪˈvɒlvə(r); *AmE* -ˈvɑːl-/ *noun* a small gun that has a container for bullets that turns around so that shots can be fired quickly without having to stop to put more bullets in

re·volv·ing /rɪˈvɒlvɪŋ; *AmE* -ˈvɑːl-/ *adj.* [usually before noun] able to turn in a circle: *a revolving chair* ◊ *The theatre has a revolving stage.*

revolving 'door *noun* a type of door in an entrance to a large building that turns around in a circle as people go through it

revue /rɪˈvjuː/ *noun* [C, U] a show in a theatre, with songs, dances, jokes, short plays, etc., often about recent events: *a musical/comedy/satirical revue*

re·vul·sion /rɪˈvʌlʃn/ *noun* [U, sing.] ~ (at/against/from sth) (*formal*) a strong feeling of disgust or horror: *a feeling/look of revulsion* ◊ *She felt a deep sense of revulsion at the violence.* ◊ *I started to feel a revulsion against their decadent lifestyle.* ◊ *Most people viewed the bombings with revulsion.*—see also REVOLT

re·ward /rɪˈwɔːd; *AmE* rɪˈwɔːrd/ *noun, verb*
■ *noun* ~ (for sth/for doing sth) **1** [C, U] a thing that you are given because you have done sth good, worked hard, etc: *a cash/financial reward* ◊ *a reward for good behaviour* ◊ *The company is now reaping the rewards of their investments.* ◊ *You deserve a reward for being so helpful.* ◊ *Winning the match was just reward for the effort the team had made.* **2** [C] an amount of money that is offered to sb for helping the police to find a criminal or for finding sth that is lost: *A £100 reward has been offered for the return of the necklace.*
■ *verb* [VN] [often passive] ~ sb (for sth/for doing sth) to give sth to sb because they have done sth good, worked hard, etc: *She was rewarded for her efforts with a cash bonus.* ◊ *He rewarded us handsomely* (= with a lot of money) *for helping him.* ◊ *She started singing to the baby and was rewarded with a smile.* ◊ *Our patience was finally rewarded.*

re·ward·ing /rɪˈwɔːdɪŋ; *AmE* -ˈwɔːrd-/ *adj.* (of an activity, etc.) worth doing; that makes you happy because you think it is useful or important [SYN] SATISFYING: *a rewarding experience/job* ◊ *Teaching is not very financially rewarding* (= is not very well paid). [OPP] UNREWARDING

re·wind /ˌriːˈwaɪnd/ *verb* (**re·wound**, **re·wound** /-ˈwaʊnd/) [VN, V] to make a tape in a cassette player, etc. go backwards

re·wire /ˌriːˈwaɪə(r)/ *verb* [VN] to put new electrical wires into a building or piece of equipment

re·word /ˌriːˈwɜːd; *AmE* -ˈwɜːrd/ *verb* [VN] (*written*) to write sth again using different words in order to make it clearer or more acceptable ▶ **re·word·ing** *noun* [C, U]

re·work /ˌriːˈwɜːk; *AmE* -ˈwɜːrk/ *verb* [VN] to make changes to sth in order to improve it or make it more suitable ▶ **re·work·ing** *noun*: [C, U] *The movie is a reworking of the Frankenstein story.*

re·write /ˌriːˈraɪt; *AmE* -ˈraʊt; *AmE* -ˈroʊt/, **re·writ·ten** /-ˈrɪtn/) [VN] to write sth again in a different way, usually in order to improve it or because there is some new information: *I intend to rewrite the story for younger children.* ◊ *This essay will have to be completely rewritten.* ◊ *an attempt to rewrite history* (= to present historical events in a way that shows or proves what you want them to) ▶ **re·write** /ˈriːraɪt/ *noun*

RGN /ˌɑː dʒiː ˈen; *AmE* ˌɑːr dʒiː ˈen/ *abbr.* registered general nurse

rhap·sod·ize (*BrE* also **-ise**) /ˈræpsədaɪz/ *verb*

[V, V speech] ~ (about/over sth) (*rare, formal*) to talk or write with great enthusiasm about sth

rhap·sody /ˈræpsədi/ *noun* (*pl.* **-ies**) **1** (often in titles) a piece of music that is full of feeling and is not regular in form: *Liszt's Hungarian Rhapsodies* **2** (*written*) the expression of great enthusiasm or happiness in speech or writing ▶ **rhap·sodic** /ræpˈsɒdɪk; *AmE* -ˈsɑːdɪk/ *adj.*

rhe·sus factor /ˈriːsəs fæktə(r)/ *noun* [sing.] (*medical*) a substance present in the red blood cells of around 85% of humans. Its presence (**rhesus positive**) or ABSENCE (**rhesus negative**) can be dangerous for babies when they are born and for people having BLOOD TRANSFUSIONS.

rhe·sus monkey /ˈriːsəs mʌŋki/ *noun* a small N Indian monkey, often used in scientific experiments

rhet·oric /ˈretərɪk/ *noun* [U] **1** (*formal*, often *disapproving*) speech or writing that is intended to influence people, but that is not completely honest or sincere: *the rhetoric of political slogans* ◊ *empty rhetoric* **2** (*formal*) the skill of using language in speech or writing in a special way that influences or entertains people

rhet·oric·al /rɪˈtɒrɪkl; *AmE* -ˈtɔːr-; -ˈtɑːr-/ *adj.* **1** (of a question) asked only to make a statement or to produce an effect rather than to get an answer: *'Don't you care what I do?' he asked, but it was a rhetorical question.* **2** (*formal*, often *disapproving*) (of a speech or piece of writing) intended to influence people, but not completely honest or sincere **3** (*formal*) connected with the art of RHETORIC: *the use of rhetorical devices such as metaphor and irony* ▶ **rhet·oric·al·ly** /-kli/ *adv.*: *'Do you think I'm stupid?' she asked rhetorically.* ◊ *a rhetorically structured essay*

rheu,matic 'fever *noun* [U] a serious disease that causes fever with swelling and pain in the joints

rheuma·tism /ˈruːmətɪzəm/ *noun* [U] a disease that makes the muscles and joints painful, stiff and swollen ▶ **rheum·at·ic** /ruˈmætɪk/ *adj.*: *rheumatic complaints/pains*

rheuma·toid arth·ritis /ˌruːmətɔɪd ɑːˈθraɪtɪs; *AmE* ɑːrˈθ-/ *noun* [U] (*medical*) a disease that gets worse over a period of time and causes painful swelling and permanent damage in the joints of the body, especially the fingers, wrists, feet and ankles

rhine·stone /ˈraɪnstəʊn; *AmE* -stoʊn/ *noun* a clear colourless stone that is intended to look like a diamond, used in cheap jewellery

rhino /ˈraɪnəʊ; *AmE* -noʊ/ *noun* (*pl.* **-os**) (*informal*) = RHINOCEROS: *a black/white rhino* ◊ *rhino horn*

rhi·noceros /raɪˈnɒsərəs; *AmE* -ˈnɑːs-/ *noun* (*pl.* **rhi·noceros** or **rhi·nocer·oses**) (also *informal* **rhino**) a large heavy animal with very thick skin and either one or two horns on its nose, that lives in Africa and S Asia—picture on page A6

rhi·zome /ˈraɪzəʊm; *AmE* -zoʊm/ *noun* (*technical*) the thick stem of some plants, such as IRIS and MINT, that grows along or under the ground and has roots and stems growing from it

rhodo·den·dron /ˌrəʊdəˈdendrən; *AmE* ˌroʊ-/ *noun* a bush with large red, purple, pink or white flowers

rhom·boid /ˈrɒmbɔɪd; *AmE* ˈrɑːm-/ *noun* (*geometry*) a flat shape with four straight sides, with only the opposite sides and angles equal to each other—picture at PARALLELOGRAM

rhom·bus /ˈrɒmbəs; *AmE* ˈrɑːm-/ *noun* (*geometry*) a flat shape with four equal sides and four angles which are not 90°—picture at PARALLELOGRAM

rhu·barb /ˈruːbɑːb; *AmE* -bɑːrb/ *noun* [U] **1** the thick red stems of a garden plant, also called **rhubarb**, that are cooked and eaten as a fruit: *rhubarb pie* **2** a word that a group of actors repeat on stage to give the impression of a lot of people talking at the same time

rhumba = RUMBA

rhyme /raɪm/ *noun, verb*
■ *noun* **1** [C] a word that has the same sound or ends with the same sound as another word: *Can you think of a rhyme for 'beauty'?* **2** [C] a short poem in which the last word in the line has the same sound as the last word in

æ	ɑː	e	ɜː	ə	ɪ	iː	i	ɒ	ɔː	ʌ	ʊ	u	uː
cat	father	ten	bird	about	sit	see	many	got	saw	cup	put	actual	too
								(BrE)					

R

R

another line, especially the next one: *children's rhymes and stories*—see also NURSERY RHYME **3** [U] the use of words in a poem or song that have the same sound, especially at the ends of lines: *a poem written in rhyme* ◇ *the poet's use of rhyme* **IDM** **there's no ,rhyme or 'reason to/for sth | without ,rhyme or 'reason** if there is no **rhyme or reason to sth** or it happens **without rhyme or reason**, it happens in a way that cannot be easily explained or understood

■ *verb* **1** [V] ~ **(with sth)** if two words, syllables, etc. **rhyme**, or if one **rhymes** with the other, they have or end with the same sound: *'Though' rhymes with 'low'.* ◇ *'Tough' and 'through' don't rhyme.* ◇ *rhyming couplets* **2** [VN] ~ **sth (with sth)** to put words that sound the same together, for example when you are writing poetry: *You can rhyme 'girl' with 'curl'.* **3** [V] (of a poem) to have lines that end with the same sound: *I prefer poems that rhyme.*

'rhyming slang *noun* [U] a way of talking in which you use words or phrases that rhyme with the word you mean, instead of using that word. For example in COCKNEY rhyming slang 'apples and pears' means 'stairs'.

rhythm /'rɪðəm/ *noun* [U, C] **1** a strong regular repeated pattern of sounds or movements: *to the rhythm of the music* ◇ *music with a fast/slow/steady rhythm* ◇ *jazz rhythms* ◇ *He can't seem to play in rhythm.* ◇ *The boat rocked up and down in rhythm with the sea.* ◇ *the rhythm of her breathing* ◇ *a dancer with a natural sense of rhythm* (= the ability to move in time to a fixed beat) **2** a regular pattern of changes or events: *the rhythm of the seasons/tides* ◇ *biological/body rhythms*

,rhythm and 'blues *noun* [U] (*abbr.* **R & B**) a type of music that is a mixture of BLUES and jazz and has a strong rhythm

rhyth·mic /'rɪðmɪk/ (also *less frequent* **rhyth·mic·al** /'rɪðmɪkl/) *adj.* having a regular pattern of sounds, movements or events: *music with a fast, rhythmic beat* ◇ *Do the exercises with slow, rhythmic movements.* ◇ *the rhythmic ticking of the clock* ▶ **rhyth·mic·al·ly** /-kli/ *adv.*

'rhythm section *noun* the part of a band that supplies the rhythm, usually consisting of drums, BASS, and sometimes piano

rib /rɪb/ *noun, verb*

■ *noun* **1** [C] any of the curved bones that are connected to the SPINE and surround the chest: *a broken/bruised/cracked rib* ◇ *Stop poking me in the ribs!*—see also RIBCAGE—picture at BODY **2** [U, C] a piece of meat with one or more bones from the ribs of an animal—see also SPARE RIB **3** [C] a curved piece of wood, metal or plastic that forms the frame of a boat, roof, etc. and makes it stronger **4** [U, C] a way of knitting that produces a pattern of vertical lines in which some are higher than others: *a rib cotton sweater* **IDM** see DIG *v.*

■ *verb* (**-bb-**) [VN] ~ **sb (about/over sth)** (*old-fashioned, informal*) to laugh at sb and make jokes about them, but in a friendly way

rib·ald /'rɪbld; 'raɪbɔːld/ *adj.* (*written*) (of language or behaviour) referring to sex in a rude but humorous way

rib·ald·ry /'rɪbldri; 'raɪb-/ *noun* (*written*) language or behaviour that refers to sex in a rude but humorous way

ribbed /rɪbd/ *adj.* (especially of fabrics for clothes) having raised lines: *a ribbed sweater*

rib·bing /'rɪbɪŋ/ *noun* [U] **1** a pattern of raised lines in knitting or on a surface **2** (*old-fashioned, informal*) the act of making fun of sb in a friendly way **SYN** TEASING

rib·bon /'rɪbən/ *noun* **1** [U, C] a narrow strip of material, used to tie things or for decoration: *a present tied with yellow ribbon* ◇ *lengths/pieces of velvet ribbon* ◇ *She was wearing two blue silk ribbons in her hair.*—picture at ROPE **2** [C] something that is long and narrow in shape: *The road was a ribbon of moonlight.* ◇ (*BrE*) *Ribbon developments* (= lines of buildings) *extended along the main road.* **3** [C] a ribbon in special colours, or tied in a special way, that is given to sb as a prize or as a military honour, or that is worn by sb to show that they belong to a particular political party—compare ROSETTE **4** [C] a long strip of material containing ink that you put into

TYPEWRITERS and some computer printers **IDM** **cut/tear, etc. sth to 'ribbons** to cut/tear, etc. sth very badly

rib·cage /'rɪbkeɪdʒ/ *noun* the structure of curved bones, (called RIBS), that surrounds and protects the chest

rice /raɪs/ *noun* [U] short, narrow white or brown grain grown on wet land in hot countries as food; the plant that produces this grain: *a grain of rice* ◇ *boiled/steamed/fried rice* ◇ *long-/short-grain rice* ◇ *brown rice* (= without its outer covering removed) ◇ *rice paddies* (= rice fields)—picture at CEREAL

,rice 'pudding *noun* [U, C] a hot DESSERT (= a sweet dish) made from rice cooked with milk and sugar

rich /rɪtʃ/ *adj.* (**rich·er, rich·est**)

WITH A LOT OF MONEY | **1** having a lot of money or property: *one of the richest women in the world* ◇ *Nobody gets rich from writing nowadays.* ◇ (*slang*) *to be filthy/stinking* (= extremely) *rich* **OPP** POOR **2** (**the rich**) *noun* [pl.] people who have a lot of money or property: *It's a favourite resort for the rich and famous.* **OPP** THE POOR **3** (of a country) producing a lot of wealth so that many of its people can live at a high standard: *the richest countries/economies/nations* **OPP** POOR

FULL OF VARIETY | **4** very interesting and full of variety: *the region's rich history and culture* ◇ *She leads a rich and varied life.*

CONTAINING/PROVIDING STH | **5** ~ **(in sth)** (often in compounds) containing or providing a large supply of sth: *Oranges are rich in vitamin C.* ◇ *The area is rich in wildlife.* ◇ *His novels are a rich source of material for the movie industry.* ◇ *iron-rich rocks* **OPP** POOR

FOOD | **6** containing a lot of fat, butter, eggs, etc. and making you feel full quickly: *a rich creamy sauce* ◇ *a rich chocolate cake*

SOIL | **7** containing the substances that make it good for growing plants in: *a rich well-drained soil* **OPP** POOR

COLOURS/SOUNDS | **8** (of colours, sounds, smells and tastes) strong or deep; very beautiful or pleasing: *rich dark reds*

EXPENSIVE | **9** (*literary*) expensive and beautiful: *The rooms were decorated with rich fabrics.*

CRITICISM | **10** (*spoken, especially BrE*) used to say that a criticism sb makes is surprising and not reasonable, because they have the same fault: *Me? Lazy? That's rich, coming from you!*—compare RICHNESS

IDM see STRIKE *v.*

riches /'rɪtʃɪz/ *noun* [pl.] (especially *written*) large amounts of money and valuable or beautiful possessions: *a career that brought him fame and riches* ◇ *material/spiritual riches* **IDM** see EMBARRASSMENT, RAG *n.*

rich·ly /'rɪtʃli/ *adv.* **1** in a beautiful and expensive manner: *a richly decorated/furnished room* **2** used to express the fact that sth has a pleasant strong colour, taste or smell: *a richly-flavoured sauce* ◇ *The polished floor glowed richly.* **3** in a generous way: *She was richly rewarded for all her hard work.* **4** in a way that people think is right and good: *richly deserved success* ◇ *richly earned respect* **5** used to express the fact that the quality or thing mentioned is present in large amounts: *richly varied countryside* ◇ *a richly atmospheric novel*

rich·ness /'rɪtʃnəs/ *noun* [U] the state of being rich in sth, such as colour, minerals or interesting qualities: *The richness and variety of marine life.*—compare WEALTH

Rich·ter scale /'rɪktə skeɪl; *AmE* 'rɪktər/ *noun* (**the Richter scale**) [sing.] a system for measuring how strong an earthquake is: *an earthquake measuring 7·3 on the Richter scale*

rick /rɪk/ *noun, verb*

■ *noun* a large pile of HAY or STRAW that is built in a regular shape and covered to protect it from rain

■ *verb* [VN] (*BrE*) to injure a part of your body by twisting it suddenly

rick·ets /'rɪkɪts/ *noun* [U] a disease of children caused by a lack of good food that makes the bones become soft and badly formed, especially in the legs

rick·ety /'rɪkəti/ *adj.* not strong or well made; likely to break: *a rickety chair/staircase*

rick·shaw /'rɪkʃɔː/ *noun* a small light vehicle with two

aɪ	aʊ	eɪ	əʊ	oʊ	ɔɪ	ɪə	eə	ʊə	j	w
my	now	say	go	go	boy	near	hair	pure	yes	wet
			(BrE)	(AmE)						

wheels used in some Asian countries to carry passengers. The rickshaw is pulled by sb walking or riding a bicycle.

rico·chet /'rɪkəʃeɪ/ *verb, noun*

■ *verb* (**rico·chet·ing** /'rɪkəʃeɪɪŋ/ **rico·cheted, rico·cheted** /'rɪkəʃeɪd/, *BrE* also **rico·chet·ting** /'rɪkəʃetɪŋ/ **rico·chet·ted** /'rɪkəʃetɪd/) [V+*adv./prep.*] (of a moving object) to hit a surface and come off it fast at a different angle: *The bullet ricocheted off a nearby wall.*

The ball ricocheted off the goalpost.

■ *noun* **1** [C] a ball, bullet or stone that ricochets: *A woman protester was killed by a ricochet (bullet).* **2** [U] the action of ricocheting: *the ricochet of bricks and bottles off police riot shields*

rid /rɪd/ *verb* (**rid·ding, rid, rid**) **IDM** **be ˈrid of sb/sth** (*formal*) to be free of sb/sth that has been annoying you or that you do not want: *She wanted to be rid of her parents and their authority.* ◊ *I was glad to be rid of the car when I finally sold it.* ◊ (*BrE*) *He was a nuisance and we're all **well rid of** him* (= we'll be much better without him). **get ˈrid of sb/sth** to make yourself free of sb/sth that is annoying you or that you do not want; to throw sth away: *Try and get rid of your visitors before I get there.* ◊ *The problem is getting rid of nuclear waste.* ◊ *I can't get rid of this headache.* ◊ *We got rid of all the old furniture.*—more at WANT *v.* **PHR V** **ˈrid sb/sth of sb/sth** (*written*) to remove sth that is causing a problem from a place, group, etc: *Further measures will be taken to rid our streets of crime.* **ˈrid yourself of sb/sth** (*formal*) to make yourself free from sb/sth that is annoying you or causing you a problem: *to rid yourself of fear/guilt/pain* ◊ *He wanted to rid himself of the burden of the secret.*

rid·dance /'rɪdns/ *noun* [U] **IDM** **good ˈriddance (to sb/sth)** an unkind way of saying that you are pleased that sb/sth has gone: *'Goodbye and good riddance!' she said to him angrily as he left.*

rid·den /'rɪdn/ *adj.*—see also RIDE *v.* (usually in compounds) full of a particular unpleasant thing: *a disease-ridden slum* ◊ *a class-ridden society* ◊ *She was guilt-ridden at the way she had treated him.* ◊ *She was ridden with guilt.*

rid·dle /'rɪdl/ *noun, verb*

■ *noun* **1** a question that is difficult to understand, and that has a surprising answer, that you ask sb as a game: *Stop talking in riddles* (= asking questions that are confusing)—*say what you mean.* ◊ *to solve the riddle of the Sphinx* **2** a mysterious event or situation that you cannot explain: *the riddle of how the baby died*

■ *verb* [VN] [usually passive] to make a lot of holes in sb/sth: *The car was riddled with bullets.* **IDM** **be ˈriddled with sth** to be full of sth, especially sth bad or unpleasant: *His body was riddled with cancer.* ◊ *Her typing was slow and riddled with mistakes.*

ride /raɪd/ *verb, noun*

■ *verb* (**rode** /rəʊd/; *AmE* roʊd/ **rid·den** /'rɪdn/)

HORSE | **1** [often +*adv./prep.*] to sit on a horse, etc. and control it as it moves: [V] *I learnt to ride as a child.* ◊ *They rode along narrow country lanes.* ◊ *He was riding on a large black horse.* ◊ [VN] *She had never ridden a horse before.* ◊ *He's ridden six winners so far this year* (= in horse racing). **2** [V] (**go riding**) (*BrE*) (*AmE* **go ˈhorseback riding**) to spend time riding a horse for pleasure: *How often do you go riding?*

BICYCLE/MOTORCYCLE | **3** [often +*adv./prep.*] to sit on and control a bicycle, motorcycle, etc: [VN] *The boys were riding their bikes around the streets.* ◊ *He rode a Harley Davidson.* ◊ [V] *The ground there is too rough to ride over.*

IN VEHICLE | **4** [usually +*adv./prep.*] to travel in a vehicle, especially as a passenger: [V] *I walked back while the others rode in the car.* ◊ (*AmE*) [VN] *to ride the subway/an elevator* ◊ *She rode the bus to school every day.*

ON WATER/AIR | **5** [usually +*adv./prep.*] to float or be supported on water or air: [V] *We watched the balloon riding high above the fields.* ◊ [VN] *surfers riding the waves*

GO THROUGH AREA | **6** [VN] to go through or over an area on a horse, bicycle, etc: *We rode the mountain trails.*

IDM **be riding for a ˈfall** to be doing sth that involves risks and that may end in disaster **be riding ˈhigh** to be successful or very confident: *The company is riding high this year.* **let sth ˈride** to decide to do nothing about a problem that you know you may have to deal with later: *He was rude to me but I let it ride this time.* **ride the crest of sth** to enjoy great success or support because of a particular situation or event: *The band is riding the crest of its last tour.* **ride ˈherd on sb/sth** (*AmE, informal*) to keep watch or control over sb/sth: *police riding herd on crowds of youths on the streets* **ride ˈshotgun** (*AmE, informal*) to ride in the front passenger seat of a car or truck **ride a/the wave of sth** to enjoy or be supported by the particular situation or quality mentioned: *Schools are riding a wave of renewed public interest.* **PHR V** **ˈride on sth** (usually used in the progressive tenses) to depend on sth: *My whole future is riding on this interview.* **ride sth↔ˈout** to manage to survive a difficult situation or time without having to make great changes **ride ˈup** (of clothing) to move gradually upwards, out of position: *Short skirts tend to ride up when you sit down.*

■ *noun*

IN VEHICLE | **1** a short journey in a vehicle, on a bicycle, etc: *a train ride through beautiful countryside* ◊ *It's a ten-minute bus ride from here to town.* ◊ *Steve gave me a ride on his motorbike.* ◊ *We went for a ride on our bikes.* ◊ *a bike ride* **2** (*AmE*) = LIFT: *She hitched a ride to the station.* ◊ *We managed to get a ride into town when we missed the bus.* **3** the kind of journey you make in a car, etc: *a smooth/comfortable ride* ◊ (*figurative*) *The new legislation faces a bumpy ride* (= will meet with opposition and difficulties).

ON HORSE | **4** a short journey on a horse, etc: *a pony ride* ◊ *The kids had a ride on an elephant at the zoo.* ◊ *He goes for a ride most mornings.*

AT FUNFAIR | **5** a large machine at a FUNFAIR or amusement park that you ride on for amusement or excitement; an occasion when you go on one of these: *The rides are free.* ◊ *a roller coaster ride*

IDM **come/go along for the ˈride** (*informal*) to join in an activity for pleasure but without being seriously interested in it **have a rough/an easy ˈride | give sb a rough/an easy ˈride** (*informal*) to experience/not experience difficulties when you are doing sth; to make things difficult/easy for sb: *He will be given a rough ride at the party conference.* **take sb for a ˈride** (*informal*) to cheat or trick sb: *It's not a pleasant feeling to discover you've been taken for a ride by someone you trusted.*—more at FREE *adj.*

rider /'raɪdə(r)/ *noun* **1** a person who rides a horse, bicycle or motorcycle: *Three riders* (= people riding horses) *were approaching.* ◊ *horses and their riders* ◊ *She's an experienced rider.* ◊ *a motorcycle dispatch rider* **2** ~ (**to sth**) an extra piece of information that is added to an official document

ridge /rɪdʒ/ *noun, verb*

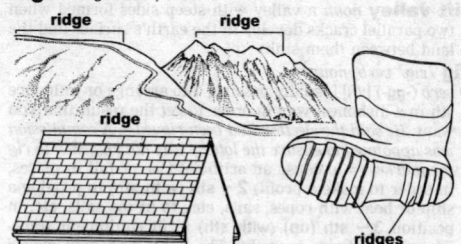
ridge   ridge   ridge   ridges

■ *noun* **1** a narrow area of high land along the top of a line of hills; a high pointed area near the top of a mountain: *walking along the ridge* ◊ *the north-east ridge of Mount*

b	d	f	g	h	k	l	m	n	p	r
bad	**did**	**fall**	**get**	**hat**	**cat**	**leg**	**man**	**now**	**pen**	**red**

Everest—picture at MOUNTAIN **2** a raised line on the surface of sth; the point where two sloping surfaces join: *The ridges on the soles of my boots stopped me from slipping.* ◊ *the ridge of the roof* **3** [C] ~ **(of high pressure)** (*technical*) a long narrow area of high pressure in the atmosphere—compare TROUGH
- *verb* [VN] [usually passive] to make narrow raised lines or areas on the surface of sth

ridged /rɪdʒd/ *adj.* (of an object or area) with raised lines on the surface

ridi·cule /ˈrɪdɪkjuːl/ *noun, verb*
- *noun* [U] unkind comments that make fun of sb or make them look silly: *She is an object of ridicule in the tabloid newspapers.* ◊ *to hold sb up to ridicule* (= make fun of sb publicly)
- *verb* [VN] to make sb/sth look silly by laughing at them or it in an unkind way

ri·dicu·lous /rɪˈdɪkjələs/ *adj.* very silly or unreasonable: *I look ridiculous in this hat.* ◊ *Don't be ridiculous! You can't pay £50 for a T-shirt!* ▶ **ri·dicu·lous·ly** *adv.*: *The meal was ridiculously expensive.* **ri·dicu·lous·ness** *noun* [U] **IDM** see SUBLIME *n.*

rid·ing /ˈraɪdɪŋ/ (*BrE* also **ˈhorse riding**) (*AmE* also **ˈhorseback riding**) *noun* [U] the sport or activity of riding horses: *I'm taking riding lessons.* ◊ *riding boots* ◊ (*BrE*) *to go riding* ◊ (*AmE*) *to go horseback riding*

rife /raɪf/ *adj.* [not before noun] **1** if sth bad or unpleasant is rife in a place, it is very common there: *It is a country where corruption is rife.* ◊ *Rumours are rife that he is going to resign.* **2** ~ **(with sth)** full of sth bad or unpleasant: *Los Angeles is rife with gossip about the stars' private lives.*

riff /rɪf/ *noun* a short repeated pattern of notes in popular music or jazz

rif·fle /ˈrɪfl/ *verb* ~ **(through)** sth to turn over papers or the pages of a book quickly and without reading them all: [V] *He was riffling through the papers on his desk.* ◊ [VN] *to riffle the pages of a book*

riff-raff /ˈrɪf ræf/ *noun* [U+sing./pl. v.] (*disapproving*) an insulting way of referring to people of low social class or people who are not considered socially acceptable

rifle /ˈraɪfl/ *noun, verb*
- *noun* a gun with a long BARREL which you hold to your shoulder to fire
- *verb* **1** ~ **(through)** sth to search quickly through sth in order to find or steal sth: [V] *She rifled through her clothes for something suitable to wear.* [also VN] **2** [VN] to steal sth from somewhere: *His wallet had been rifled.* **3** [VN+adv./prep.] to kick a ball very hard and straight in a game of football

rifle·man /ˈraɪflmən/ *noun* (*pl.* **-men** /-mən/) a soldier who carries a rifle

ˈrifle range *noun* **1** [C] a place where people practise shooting with rifles **2** [U] the distance that a bullet from a rifle will travel

rift /rɪft/ *noun* **1** a serious disagreement between people that stops their relationship from continuing: *The rift within the party deepens.* ◊ *a serious marriage rift* ◊ *Efforts to heal the rift between the two countries have failed.* **2** a large crack or opening in the ground, rocks or clouds

ˈrift valley *noun* a valley with steep sides formed when two parallel cracks develop in the earth's surface and the land between them sinks

rig /rɪg/ *verb, noun*
- *verb* (**-gg-**) [VN] [usually passive] **1** to arrange or influence sth in a dishonest way in order to get the result that you want: *He said the election had been rigged.* ◊ *A commission was appointed to ensure the lottery was not rigged.* ◊ *to rig the market* (= to cause an artificial rise or fall in prices, in order to make a profit) **2** ~ **sth (with sth)** to provide a ship or boat with ropes, sails, etc.; to fit the sails, etc. in position **3** ~ **sth (up) (with sth)** to fit equipment somewhere, sometimes secretly: *The lights had been rigged (up) but not yet tested.* ◊ *The car had been rigged with about 300 lbs of explosive.* **PHRV** ˌ**rig sb/yourself**↔**ˈout (in/with sth)** [often passive] (*old-fashioned*) to provide

sb/sth with a particular kind of clothes or equipment: *I was accepted for the job and rigged out in a uniform.* ˌ**rig sth**↔**ˈup** to make or to build sth quickly, using whatever materials are available: *We managed to rig up a shelter for the night.*
- *noun* **1** (especially in compounds) a large piece of equipment that is used for taking oil or gas from the ground or the bottom of the sea: *an oil rig* **2** the way that the MASTS and sails on a boat, etc. are arranged **3** (*AmE, informal*) a large lorry/truck **4** equipment that is used for a special purpose: *a CB radio rig*

rig·ging /ˈrɪgɪŋ/ *noun* [U] **1** the ropes that support the MASTS and sails of a boat or ship **2** the act of influencing sth in a dishonest way in order to get the result that you want: *vote rigging*

right /raɪt/ *adj., adv., noun, verb, exclamation*
- *adj.*
MORALLY GOOD | **1** [not usually before noun] ~ **(to do sth)** morally good or acceptable; what is correct according to law or a person's duty: *You were quite right to criticize him.* ◊ *Is it ever right to kill?* ◊ *It seems only right to warn you of the risk.* ◊ *I hope we're doing the right thing.* OPP WRONG

TRUE/CORRECT | **2** true or correct as a fact: *Did you get the answer right?* ◊ *'What's the right time?' '10.37.'* ◊ *'David, isn't it?' 'Yes, that's right.'* ◊ (*spoken*) *It was Monday you went to see Angie, right?* ◊ (*spoken*) *Let me get this right* (= understand correctly)—*you want us to do an extra ten hours' work for no extra pay?* ◊ *'I'll have to do it again.' 'Too right you will* (= there is no doubt about it).*'* OPP WRONG **3** correct for a particular situation or thing, or for a particular person: *Have you got the right money* (= the exact amount) *for the bus fare?* ◊ *Is this the right way to the beach?* ◊ *You're not holding it the right way up.* ◊ *Are you sure you've got that on the right way round?* ◊ *Next time we'll get it right.* ◊ *He's the right man for the job.* ◊ *I'm glad you split up. She wasn't right for you.* ◊ *I was waiting for the right moment to ask him.* ◊ *She knows all the right people* (= important people, for example those who can help her career). ◊ *His success was down to being in the right place at the right time* (= being able to take opportunities when they came). OPP WRONG **4** [not before noun] ~ **(about sth)** | ~ **(to do sth)** | ~ **(in doing sth)** correct in your opinion or judgement: *She was right about Tom having no money.* ◊ *You're right to be cautious.* ◊ *'It's not easy.' 'Yeah, you're right.'* ◊ *Am I right in thinking we've met before?* OPP WRONG

NORMAL | **5** [not before noun] in a normal or satisfactory condition: *I don't feel quite right today* (= I feel ill/sick). ◊ *That sausage doesn't smell right.* ◊ *Things aren't right between her parents.* ◊ *If only I could have helped put matters right.* ◊ *He's not quite right in the head* (= not mentally normal). OPP WRONG

NOT LEFT | **6** [only before noun] of, on or towards the side of the body that is towards the east when a person faces north: *my right eye/shoe* ◊ *Keep on the right side of the road.* ◊ *Take a right turn at the intersection.*—see also RIGHT-WING OPP LEFT

COMPLETE | **7** [only before noun] (*BrE, informal*, especially *disapproving*) used to emphasize sth bad: *You made a right mess of that!* ◊ *I felt a right idiot.*

—see also ALL RIGHT ▶ **right·ness** *noun* [U]: *the rightness* (= justice) *of their cause* ◊ *the rightness of his decision*
IDM ˌ**give your right ˈarm for sth/to do sth** (*informal*) used to say that sb is willing to give up a lot in order to have or do sth that they really want: *I'd have given my right arm to have been there with them.* **(not) in your right ˈmind** (not) mentally normal **(as) right as ˈrain** (*informal*) in excellent health or condition **right eˈnough** (*spoken*) certainly; in a way that cannot be DENIED: *You heard me right enough* (= so don't pretend that you did not). **right ˈon** (*spoken*) used to express strong approval or encouragement—see also RIGHT-ON ˌ**right side ˈup** (*AmE*) with the top part turned to the top; in the correct, normal position: *I dropped my toast, but luckily it fell right side up.* OPP UPSIDE DOWN—more at ALL RIGHT *adj.*, FOOT *n.*, HEAD *n.*, HEART, IDEA, MR, NOTE *n.*, SIDE *n.*, TRACK *n.*

■ *adv.*

<u>EXACTLY</u> | **1** exactly; directly: *Lee was standing right behind her.* ◇ *The wind was right in our faces.* ◇ *I'm right behind you on this one* (= I am supporting you). ◇ *The bus came right on time.*

<u>COMPLETELY</u> | **2** all the way; completely: *The car spun right off the track.* ◇ *I'm right out of ideas.* ◇ *She kept right on swimming until she reached the other side.*

<u>IMMEDIATELY</u> | **3** (*informal*) immediately; without delay: *I'll be right back.* ◇ *I'll be right with you* (= I am coming very soon).

<u>CORRECTLY</u> | **4** correctly: *You guessed right.* OPP WRONG

<u>SATISFACTORILY</u> | **5** in a satisfactory way: *Nothing's going right for me today.* OPP WRONG

<u>NOT LEFT</u> | **6** on or to the right side: *Turn right at the end of the street.* OPP WRONG

IDM ˌright and ˈleft everywhere: *She owes money right and left.* **right aˈway/ˈoff** immediately; without delay: *I want it sent right away.* ◇ *I told him right off what I thought of him.* ˌ**right, left and ˈcentre** = LEFT, RIGHT AND CENTRE at LEFT *adv.* **right ˈnow 1** at this moment: *He's not in the office right now.* **2** immediately: *Do it right now!* **see sb ˈright** (*AmE* also **do sb ˈright**) (*informal*) to make sure that sb has all they need or want: *You needn't worry about money—I'll see you right.*—more at ALLEY, SERVE *v.*

■ *noun*

<u>STH MORALLY GOOD</u> | **1** [U, C] what is morally good or correct: *She doesn't understand the difference between right and wrong.* ◇ *You did right to tell me about it.* ◇ *They both had some right on their side.* ◇ *He wouldn't apologize. He knew he was* **in the right** (= had justice on his side). ◇ *It was difficult to establish* **the rights and wrongs** (= the true facts) *of the matter.* OPP WRONG

<u>MORAL/LEGAL CLAIM</u> | **2** [C, U] **~ (to sth/to do sth)** a moral or legal claim to have or get sth or to behave in a particular way: *Everyone has a right to a fair trial.* ◇ **You have no right** *to stop me from going in there.* ◇ **What gives you the right** *to do that?* ◇ *She* **had every right** *to be angry.* ◇ *You're quite* **within your rights** *to ask for your money back.* ◇ **By rights** (= if justice were done) *half the money should be mine.* ◇ *There is no right of appeal against the decision.* ◇ *Education is provided by the state* **as of right** (= everyone has a right to it). ◇ *The property belongs to her* **by right.** ◇ *They had fought hard for* **equal rights.** ◇ *animal rights campaigners*—see also CIVIL RIGHTS, HUMAN RIGHT

<u>FOR BOOK/MOVIE, etc.</u> | **3** (**rights**) [pl.] the authority to perform, publish, film, etc. a particular work, event, etc: *He sold the rights for $2 million.* ◇ *all rights reserved* (= protected or kept for the owners of the book, film/movie, etc.)

<u>NOT LEFT SIDE</u> | **4** (**the/sb's right**) [sing.] the right side or direction: *Take the first street on the right.* ◇ *She seated me on her right.* OPP LEFT **5** [sing.] **the first, second, etc. ~** the first, second, etc. road on the right side: *Take the first right, then the second left.* OPP LEFT **6** (**a right**) [sing.] a turn to the right: *to make a right* ◇ (*AmE, informal*) *to hang a right* OPP LEFT

<u>POLITICS</u> | **7** (**the right, the Right**) [sing.+ sing./pl. *v.*] political groups that most strongly support the CAPITALIST system—compare RIGHT WING: *The Right in British politics is represented by the Conservative Party.* OPP LEFT **8** (**the right**) [sing.+ sing./pl. *v.*] the part of a political party whose members are least in favour of social change: *He's on the right of the Labour Party.* OPP LEFT

<u>IN BOXING</u> | **9** a blow that is made with your right hand OPP LEFT

IDM **bang to ˈrights** (*BrE*) (*AmE* **dead to ˈrights**) (*informal*) in the act of committing a crime, so that you cannot claim to be innocent: *We've got you bang to rights handling stolen property.* **do ˈright by sb** (*old-fashioned*) to treat sb fairly **in your own ˈright** because of your personal qualifications or efforts, not because of your connection with sb else: *She sings with a rock band, but she's also a jazz musician in her own right.* **put/set sb/sth to ˈrights** to correct sb/sth; to put things in their right places or right order: *It took me ages to put things to*

rights after the workmen had left.—more at, WORLD, WRONG *n.*

■ *verb* [VN]

<u>RETURN TO POSITION</u> | **1** to return sb/sth/yourself to the normal, upright position: *They learnt to right a capsized canoe.* ◇ *At last the plane* **righted itself** *and flew on.*

<u>CORRECT</u> | **2** to correct sth that is wrong or not in its normal state: *Righting the economy will demand major cuts in expenditure.*

IDM **right a ˈwrong** to do sth to correct an unfair situation or sth bad that you have done

■ *exclamation* (*BrE, informal*) **1** used to show that you accept a statement or an order: *'You may find it hurts a little at first.' 'Right.'* ◇ *'Barry's here.' 'Oh, right.'* ◇ *'I'll have a whisky and soda.' 'Right you are, sir.'* **2** used to get sb's attention to say that you are ready to do sth, or to tell them to do sth: *Right! Let's get going.* **3** used to check that sb agrees with you or has understood you: *So that's twenty of each sort, right?* ◇ *And I didn't think any more of it, right, but Mum says I should see a doctor.*

WHICH WORD?

right / rightly

Right and **rightly** can both be used as adverbs. In the sense 'correctly' or 'in the right way', **right** is the usual adverb. It is only used after verbs: *He did it right.* ◇ *Did I spell your name right?* **Rightly** cannot be used like this. In formal language **correctly** is used: *Is your name spelled correctly?*

The usual meaning of **rightly** is 'for a good reason' and it comes before an adjective: *They are rightly proud of their children.* It can be used to mean 'correctly' before a verb or in particular phrases: *As you rightly say, we have a serious problem.* In *AmE* **rightly** is not at all common.

ˈ**right angle** *noun* an angle of 90°: *Place the table at right angles/at a right angle to the wall*—compare ACUTE ANGLE, OBTUSE ANGLE, REFLEX ANGLE—picture at TRIANGLE

ˈ**right-angled** *adj.* having or consisting of a right angle: (*BrE*) *a right-angled triangle*—picture at TRIANGLE

right·eous /ˈraɪtʃəs/ *adj.* (*formal*) **1** morally right and good: *a righteous God* **2** that you think is acceptable or fair from a moral point of view: *righteous anger/indignation/rage*—see also SELF-RIGHTEOUS ▶ **right·eous·ly** *adv.* **right·eous·ness** *noun* [U]

right·ful /ˈraɪtfl/ *adj.* [only before noun] (*formal*) that is correct, right or legal: *The stolen car was returned to its* **rightful owner.** ▶ **right·ful·ly** /-fəli/ *adv.*: *She was only claiming what was rightfully hers.*

ˌ**right-hand** *adj.* [only before noun] **1** on the right side of sth: *on the right-hand side of the road* ◇ *the top right-hand corner of the screen* **2** intended for use by your right hand: *a right-hand glove* OPP LEFT-HAND

ˌ**right-hand ˈdrive** *adj.* (of a vehicle) with the driver's seat and STEERING WHEEL on the right side OPP LEFT-HAND DRIVE

ˌ**right-ˈhanded** *adj.* **1** a person who is **right-handed** uses their right hand for writing, using tools, etc. **2** a **right-handed** tool is designed to be used with the right hand ▶ ˌ**right-ˈhanded** *adv.*

ˌ**right-ˈhander** *noun* **1** a person who uses their right hand for writing, using tools, etc. **2** a hit with the right hand OPP LEFT-HANDER

ˌ**right-hand ˈman** *noun* [sing.] a person who helps sb a lot and who they rely on, especially in an important job: *the President's right-hand man*

ˌ**Right ˈHonourable** *adj.* [only before noun] (*abbr.* **Rt Hon**) **1** (**the Right Honourable …**) a title of respect used when talking to or about a person of high social rank, especially a LORD **2** (**the/my Right Honourable …**) the title of respect used by Members of Parliament in Britain when talking to or about a senior Member of Parliament during a debate: *my Right Honourable friend, the Secretary of State for the Environment*—compare HONOURABLE

right·ist /ˈraɪtɪst/ *noun* a person who supports RIGHT-

æ	ɑː	e	ɜː	ə	ɪ	iː	i	ɒ	ɔː	ʌ	ʊ	u	uː
cat	father	ten	bird	about	sit	see	many	got	saw	cup	put	actual	too

(BrE)

WING political parties and their ideas [SYN] RIGHT-WINGER [OPP] LEFTIST ▶ **right·ist** adj.

right·ly /ˈraɪtli/ adv. **1** for a good reason [SYN] JUSTIFI-ABLY: *The school was rightly proud of the excellent exam results.* ◊ *He was proud of his beautiful house, and rightly so.* ◊ *Quite rightly, the environment is of great concern.* **2** in a correct or accurate way: *Rightly or wrongly, many older people are afraid of violence in the streets.* ◊ *As she rightly pointed out the illness can affect adults as well as children.* ◊ (spoken) *I can't rightly say what happened.* ◊ (spoken) *I don't rightly know where he's gone.* ◊ (spoken) *If I remember rightly, there's a train at six o'clock.* ⇨ note at RIGHT

right-'minded adj. (of a person) having beliefs and opinions that most people approve of: *Any right-minded person would be offended by this book.*

righto /ˈraɪtəʊ; AmE -oʊ/ exclamation (old-fashioned, BrE, informal) = RIGHT

right of a'bode noun [U] official permission that allows a person to live in a particular country

right of 'way noun (pl. **rights of 'way**) **1** [U] (especially BrE) legal permission to go onto or through another person's land: *Private property—no right of way.* **2** [C] (especially BrE) a public path that goes through private land: *a public right of way for walkers* **3** [U] the right to drive across or into a road before another vehicle: *I had right of way at the junction.* ◊ *Whose right of way is it?*

right-'on adj. (informal, sometimes disapproving) having political opinions or being aware of social issues that are fashionable and LEFT-WING: *right-on middle-class intellectuals*

Right 'Reverend adj. [only before noun] (abbr. **Rt Revd**) a title of respect used when talking about a BISHOP (= a senior priest): *the Right Reverend Anthony Hunter, Bishop of Huddersfield*

'rights issue noun (business) an offer to buy shares in a company at a cheaper price to people who already own some shares in it

right·ward /ˈraɪtwəd; AmE -wərd/ (also **right·wards** /ˈraɪtwədz; AmE -wərdz/ especially in BrE) adj. **1** on or to the right: *a rightward movement* **2** towards more RIGHT-WING political ideas: *a rightward shift in voting patterns* ▶ **right·ward** (also **right·wards**) adv.

the right 'wing noun **1** [sing.+ sing./pl. v.] the part of a political party whose members are least in favour of social change: *He is on the right wing of the party.* **2** [C, U] an attacking player or a position on the right side of the field in a game of football, etc.

right-'wing adj. strongly supporting the CAPITALIST system: *right-wing opinions/policies/views*

right-'winger noun **1** a person on the right wing of a political party: *She is a prominent Tory right-winger.* **2** a person who plays on the right side of the field in a game of football, etc. [OPP] LEFT-WINGER

righty-ho /ˌraɪtiˈhəʊ; AmE -ˈhoʊ/ exclamation (old-fashioned, BrE, informal) = RIGHT

rigid /ˈrɪdʒɪd/ adj. **1** (often disapproving) (of rules, methods, etc.) very strict and difficult to change: *The curriculum was too narrow and too rigid.* ◊ *His rigid adherence to the rules made him unpopular.* **2** (of a person) not willing to change their ideas or behaviour: *rigid attitudes* **3** (of an object or substance) stiff and difficult to move or bend: *a rigid support for the tent* ◊ *She sat upright, her body rigid with fear.* ◊ (figurative) *I was bored rigid* (= extremely bored). ▶ **ri·gid·ity** /rɪˈdʒɪdəti/ noun [U, C]: *the rigidity of the law on this issue* ◊ *the rigidity of the metal bar* **ri·gid·ly** adv.: *The speed limit must be rigidly enforced.* ◊ *She stared rigidly ahead.*

rig·mar·ole /ˈrɪgmərəʊl; AmE -roʊl/ noun **1** [U] a long and complicated process that is annoying and seems unnecessary: *I couldn't face the whole rigmarole of getting a work permit again.* **2** [U, sing.] a long and complicated story

rigor mor·tis /ˌrɪgə ˈmɔːtɪs; AmE ˌrɪgər ˈmɔːrtɪs/ noun [U] the process by which the body becomes stiff after death: *Rigor mortis had already set in.*

rig·or·ous /ˈrɪgərəs/ adj. **1** done carefully and with a lot

of attention to detail [SYN] THOROUGH: *a rigorous analysis/investigation* **2** demanding that particular rules, processes, etc. are strictly followed [SYN] STRICT: *The work failed to meet their rigorous standards.* ▶ **rig·or·ous·ly** adv.: *The country's press is rigorously controlled.*

rig·our (BrE) (AmE **rigor**) /ˈrɪgə(r)/ noun **1** [U] the fact of being careful and paying great attention to detail: *academic/intellectual/scientific rigour* **2** [U] (formal) the fact of being strict or severe [SYN] SEVERITY: *This crime must be treated with the full rigour of the law.* **3** (**the rigours of sth**) [pl.] the difficulties and unpleasant conditions of sth: *The plants were unable to withstand the rigours of a harsh winter.*

rile /raɪl/ verb to annoy sb or make them angry: [VN] *Nothing ever seemed to rile him.* [also VN that] [IDM] **be/get (all) riled 'up** (informal, especially AmE) to be or get very annoyed

rim /rɪm/ noun, verb
■ noun **1** the edge of sth that is circular: *He looked at them over the rim of his glass.* ◊ *The rims of her eyes were red with crying.* ◊ *spectacles with gold rims*—picture at EDGE **2** the metal edge of a wheel onto which the tyre is fixed—picture at BICYCLE **3** (**-rimmed**) adj. having a particular type of rim: *gold-rimmed spectacles* ◊ *red-rimmed eyes* (= for example, from crying)—see also HORN-RIMMED
■ verb (**-mm-**) [VN] [often passive] (formal) to form an edge around sth

rime /raɪm/ noun [U] (literary) FROST

rim·less /ˈrɪmləs/ adj. [only before noun] (of glasses) having LENSES (= the transparent parts that you look through) that are not surrounded by frames

rind /raɪnd/ noun **1** [U] the thick outer skin of some types of fruit: *lemon rind*—compare PEEL, SKIN, ZEST **2** [U, C] the thick outer skin of some foods such as BACON and some types of cheese

ring[1] /rɪŋ/ noun, verb—see also RING[2]

ring / onion ring / smoke ring / boxing ring

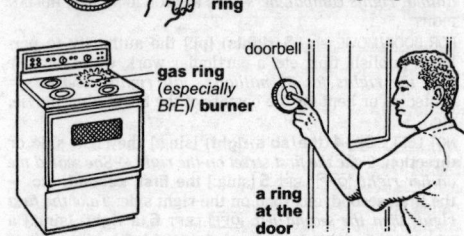

gas ring (especially BrE)/ burner / doorbell / a ring at the door

■ noun
JEWELLERY | **1** [C] a piece of jewellery that you wear on your finger, consisting of a circular band of gold, silver, etc., sometimes decorated with precious stones: *a gold ring* ◊ *A large diamond glittered on her ring finger* (= the finger next to the little finger, especially on the left hand).—see also ENGAGEMENT RING, SIGNET RING, WEDDING RING—picture at JEWELLERY

CIRCLE | **2** [C] an object in the shape of a circle with a large hole in the middle: *a key ring* ◊ *curtain rings* ◊ *onion rings* **3** [C] a circular mark or shape: *She had dark rings around her eyes from lack of sleep.* ◊ *The children sat on the floor in a ring.*

FOR PERFORMANCE/COMPETITION | **4** [C] an enclosed area in which animals or people perform or compete, with seats around the outside for the audience: *a boxing ring* ◊ *a circus ring* ◊ *The next competitor rode into the ring.*—see also BULLRING

FOR COOKING | **5** [C] (especially BrE) a small flat plate on a cooker/stove that is heated by gas or electricity and is used for cooking on **SYN** BURNER: *to turn off the gas ring*—picture on page 274

GROUP OF PEOPLE | **6** [C] a group of people who are working together, especially in secret or illegally: *a spy ring* ◊ *a drugs ring*

IDM **run 'rings around/round sb** (*informal*) to be much better at doing sth than sb else—more at HAT

■ *verb* (**ringed, ringed**) [VN]

SURROUND | **1** [often passive] **~ sb/sth (with sth)** to surround sb/sth: *Thousands of demonstrators ringed the building.*

BIRD'S LEG | **2** to put a metal ring around a bird's leg so that it can be easily identified in the future

DRAW CIRCLE | **3** (*especially BrE*) to draw a circle around sth **SYN** CIRCLE: *Ring the correct answer in pencil.*

ring² /rɪŋ/ *verb, noun*—see also RING¹

■ *verb* (**rang** /ræŋ/ **rung** /rʌŋ/)

TELEPHONE | **1** (*BrE*) (also **call** *AmE, BrE*) **~ sb/stn (up)** to telephone sb/sth: [VN] *I'll ring you up later.* ◊ *He rang up the police station.* ◊ *When is the best time to ring New York?* ◊ [V] *David rang up while you were out.* ◊ *He said he was ringing from London.* ◊ *I'm ringing about your advertisement in the paper.* ◊ *Could you ring for a cab?* ◊ *She rang to say she'd be late.* ⇨ note at PHONE **2** [V] (of a telephone) to make a sound because sb is trying to telephone you: *Will you answer the telephone if it rings?*

BELL | **3** if you **ring** a bell or if a bell **rings**, it produces a sound: [VN] *Someone was ringing the doorbell.* ◊ [V] *The church bells rang.* ◊ *Just ring for the nurse* (= attract the nurse's attention by ringing a bell) *if you need her.*

WITH SOUND | **4** [V] **~ (with sth)** (*literary*) to be full of a sound; to be filled with sound: *The house rang with children's laughter.* ◊ *Applause rang through the hall.*

WITH QUALITY | **5** [V] to be full of a particular quality: *His words rang with pride.*

OF EARS | **6** [V] to be uncomfortable and be unable to hear clearly, usually because you have heard a loud noise, etc: *The music was so loud it made my ears ring.*

IDM **ring a 'bell** (*informal*) to sound familiar to you, as though you have heard it before: *His name rings a bell but I can't think where we met.* **ring the 'changes (with sth)** (*BrE*) to make changes to sth in order to have greater variety: *Ring the changes with a new colour.* **,ring in your 'ears/'head** to make you feel that you can still hear sth: *His warning was still ringing in my ears.* **,ring off the 'hook** (usually used in the progressive tenses) (*AmE*) (of a telephone) to ring many times: *The phone has been ringing off the hook with offers of help.* **ring 'true/ 'hollow/'false** to give the impression of being sincere/ true or not sincere/true: *It may seem a strange story but it rings true to me.*—more at ALARM *n.* **PHRV** **,ring 'back | ,ring sb↔'back** (*BrE*) to telephone sb again, for example because they were not there when you called earlier, or to return a call they made to you: *He isn't here now—could you ring back later?* ◊ *I'll ask Simon to ring you back when he gets in.* **,ring 'in** (*BrE*) to telephone a television or radio show, or the place where you work **,ring 'in sth** to ring bells to celebrate sth, especially the new year **,ring 'off** (*BrE*) to put down the telephone because you have finished speaking: *He rang off before I could explain.* **,ring 'out** to be heard loudly and clearly: *A number of shots rang out.* **,ring 'round | ,ring 'round sb/sth** (*BrE*) to telephone a number of people in order to organize sth or to get some information, etc. **,ring 'through (to sb)** (*BrE*) to make a telephone call to sb, especially within the same building: *Reception just rang through to say my visitor has arrived.* **,ring sth↔'up** to enter the cost of goods being bought in a shop/store on a CASH REGISTER by pressing the buttons; to make sales of a particular value: *She rang up all the items on the till.* ◊ *The company rang up sales of $166 million last year.*

■ *noun*

OF BELL | **1** [C] the sound that a bell makes; the act of ringing a bell: *There was a ring at the door.* ◊ *He gave a couple of loud rings on the doorbell.*

SOUND | **2** [sing.] a loud clear sound: *the ring of horse's hooves on the cobblestones*

QUALITY | **3** [sing.] **~ (of sth)** a particular quality that words, sounds, etc. have: *His explanation has a ring of truth about it.* ◊ *Her protestation of innocence had a hollow ring to it* (= did not sound sincere). ◊ *The story had a familiar ring to it* (= as if I had heard it before).

IDM **give sb a 'ring** (*BrE, informal*) to make a telephone call to sb: *I'll give you a ring tomorrow.* ⇨ note at PHONE

'ring binder *noun* (*BrE*) a file for holding papers, in which metal rings go through the edges of the pages, holding them in place—picture at STATIONERY

ringed /rɪŋd/ *adj.* [only before noun] **1** having a ring or rings on: *a ringed hand/finger* **2** (especially of an animal or bird) having a mark or marks like a ring on it: *a ringed plover*

ringer /'rɪŋə(r)/ *noun* **1** = BELL-RINGER **2** (*AmE*) a horse or person that takes part in a race illegally, for example by using a false name **IDM** see DEAD *adj.*

'ring-fence *verb* [VN] (*BrE, technical*) to protect a particular sum of money by putting restrictions on it so that it can only be used for a particular purpose

'ring finger *noun* the finger next to the smallest one, especially on the left hand, on which a wedding ring is traditionally worn—picture at BODY

ringing /'rɪŋɪŋ/ *adj., noun*
■ *adj.* [only before noun] **1** (of a sound) loud and clear: *a ringing voice* **2** (of a statement, etc.) powerful and made with a lot of force: *a ringing endorsement of her leadership*
■ *noun* [sing., U] an act or a sound of ringing: *There was an unpleasant ringing in my ears.*

ring-lead·er /'rɪŋliːdə(r)/ *noun* (*disapproving*) a person who leads others in crime or in causing trouble

ring·let /'rɪŋlət/ *noun* [usually pl.] a long curl of hair hanging down from sb's head

ring·mas·ter /'rɪŋmɑːstə(r); *AmE* -mæs-/ *noun* a person in charge of a CIRCUS performance

'ring pull (*BrE*) (*AmE* **'pull-tab, tab**) *noun* a small piece of metal with a ring attached which is pulled to open cans of food, drink, etc.—picture at PACKAGING

'ring road (*BrE*) (*AmE* **'outer belt**) *noun* a road that is built around a city or town to reduce traffic in the centre

ring·side /'rɪŋsaɪd/ *noun* [U] the area closest to the enclosed space in which a boxing match or CIRCUS takes place: *According to law, a doctor must be present at the ringside.* ◊ *a ringside seat*

ring·toss /'rɪŋtɒs; *AmE* -tɔːs/ *noun* [U] (*AmE*) = HOOPLA (2)

ring·worm /'rɪŋwɜːm; *AmE* -wɜːrm/ *noun* [U] an infectious skin disease that produces round red areas, especially on the head or the feet

rink /rɪŋk/ *noun* **1** = ICE RINK **2** = SKATING RINK

rinse /rɪns/ *verb, noun*
■ *verb* [VN] **1** to wash sth with clean water only, not using soap: *Rinse the cooked pasta with boiling water.* **2** to remove the soap from sth with clean water after washing it **3** [+*adv./prep.*] to remove dirt, etc. from sth by washing it with clean water: *She rinsed the mud from her hands.* ◊ *I wanted to rinse the taste out of my mouth.* **PHRV** **,rinse sth↔'out** to make sth clean, especially a container, by washing it with water: *Rinse the cup out before use.*
■ *noun* **1** [C] an act of rinsing sth: *I gave the glass a rinse.* ◊ *Fabric conditioner is added during the final rinse.* **2** [C, U] a liquid that you put on your hair when it is wet in order to change its colour: *a blue rinse* **3** [C, U] a liquid used for cleaning the mouth and teeth

riot /'raɪət/ *noun, verb*
■ *noun* **1** [C] a situation in which a group of people behave in a violent way in a public place, often as a protest: *One prison guard was killed when a riot broke out in the jail.* ◊ *food/race riots* **2** [sing.] **~ of sth** (*written*) a collection of a lot of different types of the same thing: *The garden was a riot of colour.* **3** (**a riot**) [sing.] (*old-fashioned, informal*) a person or an event that is very amusing and enjoyable

R

b	d	f	g	h	k	l	m	n	p	r
bad	did	fall	get	hat	cat	leg	**man**	now	pen	red

R

IDM run **'riot 1** (of people) to behave in a way that is violent and/or not under control: *They let their kids run riot.* **2** if your imagination, a feeling, etc. **runs riot**, you allow it to develop and continue without trying to control it: *An artist must learn to let his imagination run riot.* **3** (of plants) to grow and spread quickly—more at READ *v.*
- *verb* [V] (of a crowd of people) to behave in a violent way in a public place, often as a protest ▶ **riot·er** *noun*: *Rioters set fire to parked cars.* **riot·ing** *noun* [U]: *Serious rioting broke out in the capital.*

'riot gear *noun* [U] the clothes and equipment used by the police when they are dealing with riots

riot·ous /'raɪətəs/ *adj.* [usually before noun] **1** (*formal or law*) noisy and/or violent, especially in a public place: *riotous behaviour/crowds/demonstrations* ◊ *The organizers of the march were charged with assault and riotous assembly.* **2** noisy, exciting and enjoyable in an uncontrolled way: *a riotous evening/party* ◊ *riotous laughter*

riot·ous·ly /'raɪətəsli/ *adv.* extremely: *riotously enjoyable/funny*

'riot police *noun* [pl.] police who are trained to deal with people RIOTING

'riot shield (also **shield**) *noun* a piece of equipment made from strong plastic, used by the police to protect themselves from angry crowds

RIP (*BrE*) (also **R.I.P.** *AmE, BrE*) /ˌɑːr aɪ 'piː/ *abbr.* rest in peace (often written on graves)

rip /rɪp/ *verb, noun*
- *verb* (-pp-) **1** to tear sth or to become torn, often suddenly or violently: [VN] *I ripped my jeans on the fence.* ◊ *The flags had been ripped in two.* ◊ [VN-ADJ] *She ripped the letter open.* ◊ [V] *I heard the tent rip.* **2** [VN+adv./prep.] to remove sth quickly or violently, often by pulling it: *He ripped off his tie.* ◊ *The carpet had been ripped from the stairs.* **IDM** let **'rip (at sb)** (*informal*) to speak or do sth with great force, enthusiasm, etc. and without control: *When she gets angry with her boyfriend, she really lets rip at him.* ◊ *The group let rip with a single from their new album.* **let 'rip | let sth 'rip** (*informal*) **1** to go or allow sth such as a car to go as fast as possible: *Once on the open road, he let rip.* ◊ *Come on Steve—let her rip.* **2** to do sth or to allow sth to happen as fast as possible: *This would cause inflation to let rip again.* **rip sb/sth a'part/to 'shreds/to 'bits, etc.** to destroy sth; to criticize sb very strongly—more at HEART, LIMB **PHRV 'rip at sth** to attack sth violently, usually by tearing or cutting it ,**rip 'into sb (for/with sth)** to criticize sb and tell them that you are very angry with them ,**rip 'into/'through sb/sth** to go very quickly and violently into or through sb/sth: *A bullet ripped into his shoulder.* ,**rip sb↔'off** [usually passive] (*informal*) to cheat sb, by making them pay too much, by selling them sth of poor quality, etc: *Tourists complain of being ripped off by local cab drivers.*—related noun RIP-OFF ,**rip 'off sth** (*slang*) to steal sth: *Thieves broke in and ripped off five computers.* ,**rip sth↔'up** to tear sth into small pieces: *He ripped up the letter and threw it in the fire.*
- *noun* [usually sing.] a long tear in fabric, paper, etc.

rip·cord /'rɪpkɔːd; *AmE* -kɔːrd/ *noun* the string that you pull to open a PARACHUTE

ripe /raɪp/ *adj.* (**riper, rip·est**) **1** (of fruit or crops) fully grown and ready to be eaten: *Pick the tomatoes before they get too ripe.* **OPP** UNRIPE **2** (of cheese or wine) having a flavour that has fully developed **SYN** MATURE **3** (of a smell) strong and unpleasant **4** ~ **(for sth)** ready or suitable for sth to happen: *This land is ripe for development.* ◊ *The conditions were ripe for social change.* ◊ *Reforms were promised when the time was ripe.* ▶ **ripe·ness** *noun* [U] **IDM a/the ripe old age (of ...)** an age that is considered to be very old: *He lived to the ripe old age of 91.*

ripen /'raɪpən/ *verb* [V, VN] to become ripe; to make sth ripe

'rip-off *noun* (*informal*) **1** [usually sing.] something that is not worth what you pay for it: *$70 for a T-shirt! What a rip-off!* **2** ~ **(of sth)** a copy of sth, especially one that is less expensive or not as good as the original thing: *The single is a rip-off of a 70s hit.*

ri·poste /rɪ'pɒst; *AmE* rɪ'poʊst/ *noun* (*formal*) **1** a quick and clever reply, especially to criticism: *a witty riposte* **2** a course of action that takes place in response to sth that has happened: *The US delivered an early riposte to the air attack.* ▶ **ri·poste** *verb* [V **speech**]

rip·ple /'rɪpl/ *noun, verb*
- *noun* **1** a small wave on the surface of a liquid, especially water in a lake, etc: *The air was so still that there was hardly a ripple on the pond's surface.* **2** a thing that looks or moves like a small wave **3** [usually sing.] ~ **of sth** a sound that gradually becomes louder and then quieter again: *a ripple of applause/laughter* **4** [usually sing.] ~ **of sth** a feeling that gradually spreads through a person or group of people: *A ripple of fear passed through him.* ◊ *The announcement sent a ripple of excitement through the crowd.*
- *verb* **1** to move or to make sth move in very small waves: [V] *The sea rippled and sparkled.* ◊ *rippling muscles* ◊ [VN] *The wind rippled the wheat in the fields.* **2** [V+adv./prep.] (of a feeling, etc.) to spread through a person or a group of people like a wave: *A gasp rippled through the crowd.*

'ripple effect *noun* a situation in which an event or action has an effect on sth, which then has an effect on sth else: *His resignation will have a ripple effect on the whole department.*

'rip-roaring *adj.* [only before noun] (*informal*) **1** noisy, exciting and/or full of activity: *a rip-roaring celebration* **2** ~ **drunk** extremely drunk **3** ~ **success** a great success

rise /raɪz/ *noun, verb*
- *noun*
  - INCREASE | **1** [C] ~ **(in sth)** an increase in an amount, a number or a level: *The industry is feeling the effects of recent price rises.* ◊ *There has been a **sharp rise** in the number of people out of work.* **2** [C] (*BrE*) (*AmE* **raise**) an increase in the money you are paid for the work you do: *I'm going to ask for a rise.* ◊ *He criticized the huge pay rises awarded to industry bosses.*
  - IN POWER/IMPORTANCE | **3** [sing.] ~ **(of sb/sth)** the act of becoming more important, successful, powerful, etc: *the rise of fascism in Europe* ◊ *the **rise and fall** of the British Empire* ◊ *her meteoric **rise to power***
  - UPWARD MOVEMENT | **4** [sing.] an upward movement: *She watched the gentle rise and fall of his chest as he slept.*
  - SLOPING LAND | **5** [C] an area of land that slopes upwards: *The church was built at the top of a small rise.*—see also HIGH-RISE
  - **IDM get a rise out of sb** to make sb react in an angry way by saying sth that you know will annoy them, especially as a joke **give 'rise to sth** (*formal*) to cause sth to happen or exist: *The novel's success gave rise to a number of sequels.*
- *verb* (**rose** /rəʊz; *AmE* roʊz/ **risen** /'rɪzn/) [V]
  - MOVE UPWARDS | **1** to come or go upwards; to reach a higher level or position: *Smoke was rising from the chimney.* ◊ *The river has risen (by) several metres.*
  - GET UP | **2** (*written*) to get up from a lying, sitting or kneeling position: *He was accustomed to rising (= getting out of bed) early.* ◊ *They rose from the table.* ◊ *She rose to her feet.*
  - OF SUN/MOON | **3** when the sun, moon, etc. **rises**, it appears above the HORIZON: *The sun rises in the east.* **OPP** SET
  - END MEETING | **4** (*formal*) (of a group of people) to end a meeting **SYN** ADJOURN: *The House (= members of the House of Commons) rose at 10 p.m.*
  - INCREASE | **5** to increase in amount or number: *rising fuel bills/divorce rates* ◊ *The price of gas rose.* ◊ *Gas rose in price.* ◊ *Unemployment rose (by) 3%.* ◊ *Air pollution has risen above an acceptable level.*
  - BECOME POWERFUL/IMPORTANT | **6** to become more successful, important, powerful, etc: *a rising young politician* ◊ *She rose to power in the 70s.* ◊ *He rose to the rank of general.* ◊ *She rose through the ranks to become managing director.*
  - OF SOUND | **7** (*written*) if a sound **rises**, it become louder and higher: *Her voice rose angrily.*
  - OF WIND | **8** if the wind **rises**, it begins to blow more strongly **SYN** GET UP

s	t	v	z	ʃ	ʒ	tʃ	dʒ	θ	ð	ŋ
see	tea	van	zoo	shoe	vision	chain	jam	thin	this	sing

OF FEELING | **9** (*written*) if a feeling **rises** inside you, it begins and gets stronger: *He felt anger rising inside him.* ◊ *Her spirits rose* (= she felt happier) *at the news.*

OF YOUR COLOUR | **10** (*written*) if your colour **rises**, your face becomes pink or red with embarrassment

OF HAIR | **11** if hair **rises**, it becomes upright instead of lying flat: *The hair on the back of my neck rose when I heard the scream.*

FIGHT | **12** ~ (**up**) (**against sb/sth**) (*formal*) to begin to fight against your ruler or government or against a foreign army SYN REBEL: *The peasants rose in revolt.* ◊ *He called on the people to rise up against the invaders.*—related noun UPRISING

BECOME VISIBLE | **13** (*written*) to be or become visible above the surroundings: *Mountains rose in the distance.*

OF LAND | **14** if land **rises**, it slopes upwards: *The ground rose steeply all around.*

OF BEGINNING OF RIVER | **15** a river **rises** where it begins to flow: *The Thames rises in the Cotswold hills.*

OF BREAD/CAKES | **16** when bread, cakes, etc. **rise**, they swell because of the action of YEAST or BAKING POWDER

OF DEAD PERSON | **17** ~ (**from sth**) to come to life again: *to rise from the dead* ◊ (*figurative*) *Can a new party rise from the ashes of the old one?*

IDM ,rise and 'shine (*old-fashioned*) usually used in orders to tell sb to get out of bed and be active—more at HEIGHT, HACKLES

PHR V ,rise a'bove sth (*written*) **1** to not be affected or limited by problems, insults, etc: *She had the courage and determination to rise above her physical disability.* **2** to be wise enough or morally good enough not to do sth wrong or not to think the same as other people: *I try to rise above prejudice.* **3** to be of a higher standard than other things of a similar kind: *His work rarely rises above the mediocre.* 'rise to sth **1** to show that you are able to deal with an unexpected situation, problem, etc: *Luckily, my mother rose to the occasion.* ◊ *He was determined to rise to the challenge.* **2** to react when sb is deliberately trying to make you angry or get you interested in sth: *I refuse to rise to that sort of comment.* ◊ *As soon as I mentioned money he rose to the bait.*

WHICH WORD?   (**?**)
rise / raise

Verbs

Raise is a verb that must have an object and rise is used without an object. When you **raise** something, you lift it to a higher position or increase it: *He raised his head from the pillow.* ◊ *We were forced to raise the price.* When people or things **rise**, they move from a lower to a higher position: *She rose from the chair.* ◊ *The helicopter rose into the air.* Rise can also mean 'to increase in number or quantity': *Costs are always rising.*

Nouns

The noun **rise** means a movement upwards or an increase in an amount or quantity: *a rise in interest rates.* In BrE it can also be used to mean an increase in pay: *Should I ask my boss for a rise?* In AmE this is a **raise**: *a three per cent pay raise.* Rise can also mean the process of becoming more powerful or important: *his dramatic rise to power.*

---

riser /'raɪzə(r)/ *noun* **1** early/late ~ a person who usually gets out of bed early/late in the morning **2** (*technical*) the upright part between two steps in a set of stairs—compare TREAD

ris·ible /'rɪzəbl/ *adj.* (*formal, disapproving*) deserving to be laughed at rather than taken seriously SYN LUDICROUS, RIDICULOUS

ris·ing /'raɪzɪŋ/ *noun* a situation in which a group of people protest against, and try to get rid of, a government, a leader, etc. SYN REVOLT, UPRISING: *The rising was crushed by government troops.*

,rising 'damp *noun* (*BrE*) [U] a condition in which water comes up from the ground into the walls of a building, causing damage

risk /rɪsk/ *noun, verb*

■ *noun* **1** [C, U] ~ (**of sth**) | ~ (**that …**) | ~ (**to sb/sth**) the possibility of sth bad happening at some time in the future; a situation that could be dangerous or have a bad result: *Smoking can increase the risk of developing heart disease.* ◊ *Patients should be made aware of the risks involved with this treatment.* ◊ *There is still a risk that the whole deal will fall through.* ◊ *The chemicals* **pose little risk** (= are not dangerous) *to human health.* ◊ *a* **calculated risk** (= one that you think is small compared with the possible benefits) ◊ *Any business venture contains an* **element of risk**. ◊ *We could probably trust her with the information but it's just not worth the risk.* **2** [C] ~ (**to sth**) a person or thing that is likely to cause problems or danger at some time in the future: *The group was considered to be a risk to national security.* ◊ *a major* **health/fire risk** **3** [C] **a good/bad/poor** ~ a person or business that a bank or an insurance company is willing/unwilling to lend money or sell insurance to because they are likely/unlikely to pay back the money etc: *With five previous claims, he's now a bad insurance risk.* IDM **at** 'risk (**from/of sth**) in danger of sth unpleasant or harmful happening: *As with all diseases, certain groups will be more at risk than others.* ◊ *If we go to war, innocent lives will be* **put at risk**. at the 'risk of doing sth used to introduce sth that may sound stupid or may offend sb: *At the risk of showing my ignorance, how exactly does the Internet work?* at risk to yourself/sb/sth with the possibility of harming yourself/sb/sth: *He dived in to save the dog at considerable risk to his own life.* do sth at your ,own 'risk to do sth even though you have been warned about the possible dangers and will have to take responsibility for anything bad that happens: *Persons swimming beyond this point do so at their own risk* (= on a notice). ◊ *Valuables are left at their owner's risk* (= on a notice). run the 'risk (of doing sth) | run 'risks to be or put yourself in a situation in which sth bad could happen to you: *We don't want to run the risk of losing their business.* ◊ *Investment is all about running risks.* take a 'risk | take 'risks to do sth even though you know that sth bad could happen as a result: *That's a risk I'm not prepared to take.* ◊ *You have no right to take risks with other people's lives.*

■ *verb* **1** [VN] to put sth valuable or important in a dangerous situation, in which it could be lost or damaged: *He risked his life to save her.* ◊ *She was risking her own and her children's health.* ◊ *He risked all his money on a game of cards.* **2** to do sth that may mean that you get into a situation which is unpleasant for you: [VN] *There was no choice. If they stayed there, they risked death.* ◊ [V-ing] *They knew they risked being arrested.* [also VN -ing] **3** to do sth that you know is not really a good idea or may not succeed: [VN] *He risked a glance at her furious face.* ◊ *It was a difficult decision but we decided to risk it.* ◊ [V-ing] *We've been advised not to risk travelling in these conditions.* IDM risk ,life and 'limb | risk your 'neck to risk being killed or injured in order to do sth

'risk-taking *noun* [U] the practice of doing things that involve risks in order to achieve sth

risky /'rɪski/ *adj.* (**risk·ier, risk·iest** HELP You can also use **more risky** and **most risky**.) involving the possibility of sth bad happening: *Life as an aid worker can be a* **risky business** (= very dangerous). ◊ *a risky investment* ◊ *It's far too risky to generalize from one set of results.* ▶ **risk·ily** /-ɪli/ *adv.* **risk·iness** /-inəs/ *noun* [U]

ris·otto /rɪ'zɒtəʊ; *AmE* rɪ'sɔːtoʊ; -'zɔː-/ *noun* (*pl.* **-os**) [C, U] an Italian dish of rice cooked with vegetables, meat, etc.

ris·qué /'rɪskeɪ; *AmE* rɪ'skeɪ/ *adj.* a risqué performance, comment, joke, etc. is a little shocking, usually because it is about sex

ris·sole /'rɪsəʊl; *AmE* -soʊl/ *noun* (*BrE*) a small flat mass or ball of chopped meat (sometimes covered with BREADCRUMBS) that is fried

rite /raɪt/ *noun* a ceremony performed by a particular group of people, often for religious purposes: *fertility/*

æ	ɑː	e	ɜː	ə	ɪ	iː	i	ɒ	ɔː	ʌ	ʊ	u	uː
cat	father	ten	bird	about	sit	see	many	got	saw	cup	put	actual	too
								(BrE)					

funeral rites ◊ initiation rites (= performed when a new member joins a secret society)—see also THE LAST RITES

rite of passage noun a ceremony or an event that marks an important stage in sb's life

rit·ual /ˈrɪtʃuəl/ noun, adj.

■ noun [C, U] **1** a series of actions that are always carried out in the same way, especially as part of a religious ceremony: religious/pagan rituals ◊ She objects to the ritual of organized religion. **2** something that is done regularly and always in the same way: Sunday lunch with the in-laws has become something of a ritual.
■ adj. [only before noun] **1** done as part of a ritual or ceremony: ritual chanting/practices **2** always done or said in the same way, especially when this is not sincere: ritual expressions of sympathy ▶ **ritu·al·ly** adv.: The goat was ritually slaughtered.

ritu·al·is·tic /ˌrɪtʃuəˈlɪstɪk/ adj. [usually before noun] **1** connected with the rituals performed as part of a ceremony: a ritualistic act of worship **2** always done or said in the same way, especially when this is not sincere

ritu·al·ize (BrE also **-ise**) /ˈrɪtʃuəlaɪz/ verb [VN] [usually passive] (written) to do sth in the same way or pattern every time: ritualized expressions of grief

ritzy /ˈrɪtsi/ adj. (informal) expensive and fashionable: a ritzy nightclub

rival /ˈraɪvl/ noun, adj., verb

■ noun ~ (to sb/sth) (for sth) a person, company, or thing that competes with another in sport, business, etc: The two teams have always been rivals. ◊ The Japanese are our biggest economic rivals. ◊ This latest design has no rivals (= it is easily the best design available). ▶ **rival** adj. [only before noun]: a rival bid/claim/offer ◊ fighting between rival groups ◊ He was shot by a member of a rival gang.
■ verb (-ll-, AmE also -l-) [VN] ~ sb/sth (for/in sth) to be as good, impressive, etc. as sb/sth else: You will find scenery to rival anything you can see in the Alps.—see also UNRIVALLED

ri·val·ry /ˈraɪvlri/ noun [C, U] (pl. -ries) ~ (with sb/sth) (for sth) | ~ (between A and B) (for sth) a state in which two people, companies, etc. are competing for the same thing: a fierce rivalry for world supremacy ◊ There is a certain amount of friendly rivalry between the teams. ◊ political rivalries ◊ sibling rivalry (= between brothers and sisters)

riven /ˈrɪvn/ adj. [not before noun] ~ (by/with sth) (formal) **1** (of a group of people) divided because of disagreements, especially in a violent way: a party riven by internal disputes **2** (of an object) divided into two or more pieces

river /ˈrɪvə(r)/ noun **1** (abbr. R.) a natural flow of water that continues in a long line across land to the sea/ocean: the River Thames ◊ the Hudson River ◊ the river bank (= the ground at the side of a river) ◊ to travel up/down river (= in the opposite direction to/in the same direction as the way in which the river is flowing) ◊ the mouth of the river (= where it enters the sea/ocean) ◊ a houseboat on the river ◊ They have a house on the river (= beside it). **2** ~ (of sth) a large amount of liquid that is flowing in a particular direction: Rivers of molten lava flowed down the mountain. IDM see SELL v.

river bed noun the area of ground over which a river usually flows: a dried-up river bed

river·front /ˈrɪvəfrʌnt; AmE -vərf-/ noun [sing.] (especially AmE) an area of land next to a river with buildings, shops/stores, restaurants, etc. on it

river·side /ˈrɪvəsaɪd; AmE -vərs-/ noun [sing.] the ground along either side of a river: a riverside path/restaurant ◊ a walk by the riverside

rivet /ˈrɪvɪt/ noun, verb

■ noun a metal pin that is used to fasten two pieces of leather, metal, etc. together
■ verb [VN] [usually passive] **1** to hold sb's interest or attention so completely that they cannot look away or think of anything else: I was absolutely riveted by her story. ◊ My eyes were riveted on the figure lying in the road. **2** to fasten sth with rivets: The steel plates were riveted

together. IDM **be riveted to the spot/ground** to be so shocked or frightened that you cannot move

rivet·ing /ˈrɪvɪtɪŋ/ adj. (approving) so interesting or exciting that it holds your attention completely

rivi·era /ˌrɪviˈeərə; AmE -ˈerə/ noun (often **Riviera**) an area by the sea that is warm and popular for holidays, especially the Mediterranean coast of France: the French Riviera

rivu·let /ˈrɪvjələt/ noun (formal or written) a very small river; a small stream of water or other liquid: Rivulets of sweat ran down her back.

RM /ˌɑːr ˈem/ abbr. (in Britain) Royal Marine—see also MARINE

RN /ˌɑːr ˈen/ abbr. **1** registered nurse **2** (in Britain) Royal Navy

RNA /ˌɑːr en ˈeɪ/ noun [U] (chemistry) a chemical present in all living cells; like DNA it is a type of NUCLEIC ACID

roach /rəʊtʃ; AmE roʊtʃ/ noun **1** (AmE, informal) = COCKROACH: The apartments were infested with rats and roaches. **2** (pl. **roach**) a small European FRESHWATER fish **3** (slang) the end part of a cigarette containing MARIJUANA

road /rəʊd; AmE roʊd/ noun **1** a hard surface built for vehicles to travel on: a main/major/minor road ◊ a country/mountain road ◊ They live just along/up/down the road (= further on the same road). ◊ The house is on a very busy road. ◊ He was walking along the road when he was attacked. ◊ It takes about four hours by road (= driving). ◊ It would be better to transport the goods by rail rather than by road. ◊ Take the first road on the left and then follow the signs. ◊ We parked on a side road. ◊ road accidents/safety/users ◊ a road map ⇨ note on page 1107 **2** (**Road**) (abbr. **Rd**) used in names of roads, especially in towns: 35 York Road **3** the way to achieving sth: to be on the road to success/recovery ◊ We have discussed privatization, but we would prefer not to go down that particular road. IDM **any road** (NorthE) = ANYWAY **one for the road** (spoken) a last alcoholic drink before you leave a party, etc. **on the road 1** travelling, especially for long distances or periods of time: The band has been on the road for six months. **2** (of a car) in good condition so that it can be legally driven: It will cost about £500 to get the car back on the road. **3** moving from place to place, and having no permanent home: Life on the road can be very hard.—more at END n., FURTHER adv., HIT v., SHOW n.

road·block /ˈrəʊdblɒk; AmE ˈroʊdblɑːk/ noun **1** a barrier put across the road by the police or army so that they can stop and search vehicles **2** (AmE) something that stops a plan from going ahead: The project faces legal roadblocks.

road hog noun (informal, disapproving) a person who drives in a dangerous way without thinking about the safety of other road users

road·house /ˈrəʊdhaʊs; AmE ˈroʊd-/ noun (old-fashioned, AmE) a restaurant or bar on a main road in the country

roadie /ˈrəʊdi; AmE ˈroʊdi/ noun (informal) a person who works with musicians, especially pop bands, when they are on tour, and helps move and set up their equipment

road rage noun [U] a situation in which a driver becomes extremely angry or violent with the driver of another car because of the way they are driving

road·run·ner /ˈrəʊdrʌnə(r); AmE ˈroʊd-/ noun a N American bird of the CUCKOO family, that lives in desert areas and can run very fast

road sense noun [U] the ability to behave in a safe way when driving, walking, etc. on roads

road·show /ˈrəʊdʃəʊ; AmE ˈroʊdʃoʊ/ noun a travelling show arranged by a radio or television programme, or by a magazine, company or political party

road·side /ˈrəʊdsaɪd; AmE ˈroʊd-/ noun the edge of the road: We parked by the roadside. ◊ a roadside cafe

road sign noun a sign near a road giving information or instructions to drivers

road tax noun [U] (in Britain) a tax that sb who owns a car must pay to drive on the roads

road test noun a test to see how a car functions or what condition it is in ▶ **road-test** verb [VN]

R

MORE ABOUT
roads

Roads and streets

In a town or city, **street** is the most general word for a road with houses and buildings on one or both sides: *a street map of London.* **Street** is not used for roads between towns, but streets in towns are often called **Road**: *Oxford Street ◊ Edgware Road.* A **road map** of France would show you the major routes between, around and through towns and cities.

Other words used in the names of streets include: **Circle, Court, Crescent, Drive, Hill** and **Way. Avenue** suggests a wide street lined with trees. A **lane** is a narrow street between buildings or, in *BrE*, a narrow country road.

The high street

High street is used in *BrE*, especially as a name, for the main street of a town, where most shops, banks, etc. are: *the record store in the High Street ◊ high street shops.* In *AmE* **Main Street** is often used as a name for this street.

Larger roads

British and American English use different words for the roads that connect towns and cities. **Motorways**, (for example, the M57) in *BrE*, **freeways, highways** or **interstates**, (for example State Route 347, Interstate 94, the Long Island Expressway) in *AmE*, are large divided roads built for long-distance traffic to avoid towns.

A **ring road** (*BrE*) / an **outer belt** (*AmE*) is built around a city or town to reduce traffic in the centre. This can also be called a **beltway** in *AmE*, although this usually refers to the road around Washington D.C. A **bypass** passes around a town or city rather than through the centre.

---

road·way /'rəʊdweɪ; *AmE* 'roʊd-/ *noun* [C, U] a road or the part of a road used by vehicles

road·works /'rəʊdwɜːks; *AmE* 'roʊdwɜːrks/ *noun* [pl.] (*BrE*) repairs that are being done to the road; an area where these repairs are being done

road·worthy /'rəʊdwɜːði; *AmE* 'roʊdwɜːrði/ *adj.* (of a vehicle) in a safe condition to drive ▶ **road·worthi·ness** *noun* [U]

roam /rəʊm; *AmE* roʊm/ *verb* **1** to walk or travel around an area without any definite aim or direction [SYN] WAN-DER: [V, often +*adv.* / *prep.*] *The sheep are allowed to roam freely on this land.* ◊ [VN] *to roam the countryside / the streets* **2** ~ (**over**) *sth/sb* (of the eyes or hands) to move slowly over every part of sb/sth: [V] *His gaze roamed over her.* ◊ [VN] *Her eyes roamed the room.*

roan /rəʊn; *AmE* roʊn/ *noun* an animal, especially a horse, that has hair of two colours mixed together: *a strawberry roan* (= with a mixture of brown and grey hair that looks pink) ▶ **roan** *adj.* [only before noun]: *a roan mare*

roar /rɔː(r)/ *verb, noun*
■ *verb* **1** [V] to make a very loud, deep sound: *We heard a lion roar.* ◊ *The gun roared deafeningly.* ◊ *The engine* **roared to life** (= started noisily). ◊ *The wind was roaring in my ears.* **2** ~ (**sth**) (**out**) to shout sth very loudly: [V] *The crowd roared.* ◊ [VN] *The fans roared (out) their approval.* ◊ [V speech] *'Stand back,' he roared.* **3** [V] ~ (**with laughter**) to laugh very loudly: *He looked so funny, we all roared.* ◊ *It made them roar with laughter.* **4** [V +*adv.* / *prep.*] (of a vehicle or its rider / driver) to move very fast, making a lot of noise: *She put her foot down and the car roared away.* **5** [V] (of a fire) to burn brightly with a lot of flames, heat and noise: *A log fire was roaring in the hearth.*
■ *noun* **1** a loud deep sound made by an animal, especially a lion, or by sb's voice: *His speech was greeted by a roar of applause.* ◊ *roars of laughter* **2** a loud continuous noise

made by the wind or sea, or by a machine: *I could barely hear above the roar of traffic.*

roar·ing /'rɔːrɪŋ/ *adj.* [only before noun] **1** making a continuous loud deep noise: *All we could hear was the sound of roaring water.* **2** (of a fire) burning with a lot of flames and heat [IDM] **do a 'roaring trade (in sth)** (*informal*) to sell a lot of sth very quickly **,roaring 'drunk** extremely drunk and noisy **a ,roaring suc'cess** (*informal*) a very great success

roast /rəʊst; *AmE* roʊst/ *verb, noun, adj.*
■ *verb* **1** to cook food, especially meat, without liquid in an oven or over a fire; to be cooked in this way: [VN] *to roast a chicken* ◊ [V] *the smell of roasting meat* ⇨ vocabulary notes on page 275 **2** [VN] to cook nuts, beans, etc. in order to dry them and turn them brown: *roasted chestnuts / coffee beans / peanuts* **3** [VN] (*informal* or *humorous*) to be very angry with sb; to criticize sb strongly **4** (*informal*) to become or to make sth become very hot in the sun or by a fire: [V] *She could feel her skin beginning to roast.* [also VN]
■ *noun* **1** (*BrE* also **joint**) a large piece of meat that is cooked whole in the oven: *the Sunday roast* **2** (*AmE*) (often in compounds) a party that takes place in sb's garden/yard at which food is cooked over an open fire: *a hot dog roast* **3** (*AmE*) an event, especially a meal, at which people celebrate sb's life by telling funny stories, insulting jokes, etc. about them
■ *adj.* [only before noun] cooked in an oven or over a fire: *roast chicken / beef / chestnuts*

roast·ing /'rəʊstɪŋ; *AmE* 'roʊ-/ *adj., noun*
■ *adj.* **1** [only before noun] used for roasting meat, vegetables, etc: *a roasting dish* **2** (also **,roasting 'hot**) so hot that you feel uncomfortable: *I'm roasting in this sweater.* ◊ *a roasting hot day*
■ *noun* [sing.] (*informal*) [IDM] **give sb/get a 'roasting** to criticize sb or be criticized in an angry way

rob /rɒb; *AmE* rɑːb/ *verb* (**-bb-**) [VN] ~ *sb/sth* (**of sth**) to steal money or property from a person or place: *to rob a bank* ◊ *The tomb had been robbed of its treasures.* ⇨ note at STEAL [IDM] **,rob sb 'blind** (*informal*) to cheat or deceive sb so that they lose a lot of money **rob ,Peter to pay 'Paul** (*saying*) to borrow money from one person to pay back what you owe to another person; to take money from one thing to use for sth else [PHR V] **'rob sb/sth of sth** [often passive] to prevent sb having sth that they need or deserve: *A last-minute goal robbed the team of victory.* ◊ *He had been robbed of his dignity.*

rob·ber /'rɒbə(r); *AmE* 'rɑːb-/ *noun* a person who steals from a person or place, especially using violence or threats: *a bank robber* ⇨ note at STEAL

rob·bery /'rɒbəri; *AmE* 'rɑːb-/ *noun* [U, C] (*pl.* **-ies**) the crime of stealing money or goods from a bank, shop/store, person, etc., especially using violence or threats: *armed robbery* (= using a gun, knife, etc.) ◊ *There has been a spate of robberies in the area recently.*—compare BURGLARY, THEFT [IDM] see DAYLIGHT

robe /rəʊb; *AmE* roʊb/ *noun, verb*
■ *noun* **1** a long loose outer piece of clothing, especially one worn as a sign of rank or office at a special ceremony: *coronation robes* ◊ *cardinals in scarlet robes* **2** = BATHROBE
■ *verb* [VN] [usually passive] (*formal*) to dress sb/yourself in long loose clothes or in the way mentioned: *a robed choir* ◊ *The priests were robed in black.*

robin /'rɒbɪn; *AmE* 'rɑːb-/ *noun* **1** a small brown European bird with a red breast **2** a grey American bird with a red breast, larger than a European robin—see also ROUND ROBIN

robot /'rəʊbɒt; *AmE* 'roʊbɑːt/ *noun* a machine that can do some tasks that a human can do and that works automatically or is controlled by a computer: *These cars are built by robots.*

ro·bot·ic /rəʊ'bɒtɪk; *AmE* roʊ'bɑːtɪk/ *adj.* **1** connected with robots: *a robotic arm* **2** like a robot, making stiff movements, speaking without feeling or expression, etc: *robotic movements*

ro·bot·ics /rəʊ'bɒtɪks; *AmE* roʊ'bɑː-/ *noun* [U] the science of designing and operating ROBOTS

ro·bust /rəʊ'bʌst; *AmE* roʊ-/ *adj.* **1** strong and healthy:

---

b	d	f	g	h	k	l	m	n	p	r
bad	did	fall	get	hat	cat	leg	man	now	pen	red

She was almost 90, but still very robust. **2** strong; able to survive being used a lot and not likely to break SYN STURDY: *a robust piece of equipment* **3** (of a system or an organization) strong and not likely to fail or become weak: *robust economic growth* **4** strong and full of determination; showing that you are sure about what you are doing or saying: *It was a typically robust performance by the Foreign Secretary.* ▶ **ro·bust·ly** *adv.*: *The furniture was robustly constructed.* ◇ *They defended their policies robustly.* **ro·bust·ness** *noun* [U]

rock /rɒk; *AmE* rɑːk/ *noun, verb*

■ *noun*
HARD MATERIAL | **1** [U, C] the hard solid material that forms part of the surface of the earth and some other planets: *They drilled through several layers of rock to reach the oil.* ◇ *a collapsed sea cave with striking **rock formations** (= shapes made naturally from rock)* ◇ *The tunnel was blasted out of solid rock.* ◇ *volcanic/igneous/sedimentary rocks* **2** [C] a mass of rock standing above the earth's surface or in the sea/ocean: *the Rock of Gibraltar* ◇ *The ship crashed into the infamous Sker Point rocks and broke into three pieces.* **3** [C] a large single piece of rock: *They clambered over the rocks at the foot of the cliff.* ◇ *The sign said 'Danger: falling rocks'.*
STONE | **4** [C] (*AmE*) a small stone: *Protesters pelted the soldiers with rocks.*
MUSIC | **5** (also **'rock music**) [U] a type of loud modern music with a strong beat played on electric guitars and drums: *hard/punk rock* ◇ *a rock band/star*
SWEET/CANDY | **6** (*BrE*) (*AmE* **,rock 'candy**) [U] a type of hard sweet/candy made in long sticks, often sold at holiday/vacation RESORTS (= towns) by the sea/ocean: *a stick of Brighton rock*
JEWEL | **7** [C, usually pl.] (*AmE, informal*) a jewel, especially a diamond
IDM **(caught/stuck) between a ,rock and a 'hard place** in a situation where you have to choose between two things, both of which are unpleasant **on the 'rocks 1** a relationship or business that is on the rocks is having difficulties and is likely to fail soon: *Sue's marriage is on the rocks.* **2** (of drinks) served with pieces of ice but no water: *Scotch on the rocks*—more at STEADY *adj.*

■ *verb*
MOVE GENTLY | **1** [usually +*adv./prep.*] to move gently backwards and forwards or from side to side; to make sb/sth move in this way: [V] *The boat rocked from side to side in the waves.* ◇ *She was rocking backwards and forwards in her seat.* ◇ [VN] *He rocked the baby gently in his arms.*
SHOCK | **2** [VN] [often passive] (*written*) to shock sb/sth very much or make them afraid: *The country was rocked by a series of political scandals.* ◇ *The news rocked the world.*
SHAKE | **3** to shake or to make sth shake violently: [V] *The whole house rocked when the bomb exploded.* ◇ [VN] *The town was rocked by an earthquake.* ◇ (*figurative*) *The scandal rocked the government (= made the situation difficult for it).*
DANCE | **4** [V] to dance to ROCK MUSIC
IDM **rock the 'boat** (*informal*) to do sth that upsets a situation and causes problems: *She was told to keep her mouth shut and not rock the boat.*—more at FOUNDATION

rocka·billy /'rɒkəbɪli; *AmE* 'rɑːk-/ *noun* [U] a type of American music that combines ROCK AND ROLL and country music

,rock and 'roll (also **,rock 'n' 'roll**) *noun* [U] a type of music popular in the 1950s with a strong beat and simple tunes

,rock 'bottom *noun* [U] (*informal*) the lowest point or level that is possible: *Prices hit rock bottom.* ◇ *The marriage had reached rock bottom.* ▶ **,rock-'bottom** *adj.*: *rock-bottom prices*

,rock 'candy *noun* [U] (*AmE*) = ROCK (6)

'rock climbing *noun* [U] the sport or activity of climbing steep rock surfaces: *to go rock climbing*

rock·er /'rɒkə(r); *AmE* 'rɑːk-/ *noun* **1** one of the two curved pieces of wood on the bottom of a ROCKING CHAIR

2 (*especially AmE*) = ROCKING CHAIR **3** (**Rocker**) (*BrE*) a member of a group of young people in Britain, especially in the 1960s, who liked to wear leather jackets, ride motorcycles and listen to ROCK MUSIC—compare MOD **4** a person who performs, dances to or enjoys ROCK MUSIC IDM **be ,off your 'rocker** (*informal, spoken*) to be crazy

rock·ery /'rɒkəri; *AmE* 'rɑːk-/ *noun* (*pl.* **-ies**) (also **'rock garden**) a garden or part of a garden consisting of an arrangement of large stones with plants growing among them

rocket /'rɒkɪt; *AmE* 'rɑːkɪt/ *noun, verb*

■ *noun* **1** [C] a spacecraft in the shape of a tube that is driven by a stream of gases let out behind it when fuel is burned inside: *a space rocket* ◇ *The rocket was launched in March 1980.* ◇ *The idea took off like a rocket (= it immediately became popular).* **2** [C] a MISSILE (= a weapon that travels through the air) that carries a bomb and is driven by a stream of burning gases: *a rocket attack* ◇ *A rocket smashed into the side of the building.* **3** [C] a FIREWORK that goes high into the air and then explodes with coloured lights **4** [U] (*BrE*) (*AmE* **aru·gula**) a plant with long green leaves that have a strong flavour and are eaten raw in salads IDM **to give sb a 'rocket | to get a 'rocket** (*BrE, informal*) to speak angrily to sb because they have done sth wrong; to be spoken to angrily for this reason

■ *verb* **1** [V] to increase very quickly and suddenly: *rocketing crime/prices* ◇ *Unemployment has rocketed up again.* ◇ *The total has rocketed from 376 to 532.* **2** [V+*adv./prep.*] to move very fast: *The car rocketed out of a side street.* **3** to achieve or to make sb/sth achieve a successful position very quickly: [V] *The band rocketed to stardom with their first single.* [also VN] **4** [VN] to attack a place with rockets

'rock face *noun* [sing.] a vertical surface of rock, especially on a mountain

rock·fall /'rɒkfɔːl; *AmE* 'rɑːk-/ *noun* the fact of rocks falling down; a pile of rocks that have fallen

'rock garden *noun* = ROCKERY

,rock-'hard *adj.* extremely hard or strong: *The ground is still rock-hard.*

'rocking chair (also **rock·er** especially in *AmE*) *noun* a chair with two curved pieces of wood under it that make it move backwards and forwards—picture at CHAIR

'rocking horse *noun* a wooden horse for children that can be made to ROCK backwards and forwards

'rock music *noun* = ROCK

rock 'n' roll *noun* = ROCK AND ROLL

'rock pool (*BrE*) (*AmE* **'tide pool**) *noun* a small amount of water that collects between the rocks by the sea/ocean

,rock 'solid *adj.* **1** that you can trust not to change or to disappear: *The support for the party was rock solid.* **2** extremely hard and not likely to break

rocky /'rɒki; *AmE* 'rɑːki/ *adj.* (**rock·ier, rocki·est**) **1** made of rock; full of rocks: *a rocky coastline* ◇ *rocky soil* **2** difficult and not certain to continue or to be successful: *a rocky marriage*

ro·coco (also **Ro·coco**) /rə'kəʊkəʊ; *AmE* rə'koʊkoʊ/ *adj.* used to describe a style of architecture, furniture, etc. that has a lot of decoration, especially in the shape of curls; used to describe a style of literature or music that has a lot of detail and decoration. The rococo style was popular in the 18th century: *a rococo palace/garden/mirror* ▶ **ro·coco** (also **Ro·coco**) *noun* [U]: *She had a passion for Italian rococo.*

rod /rɒd; *AmE* rɑːd/ *noun* **1** (often used in compounds) a long straight piece of wood, metal or glass—see also LIGHTNING ROD—picture at LABORATORY **2** = FISHING ROD: *fishing with rod and line* **3** (also **the rod**) (*old-fashioned*) a stick that is used for hitting people as a punishment: *There used to be a saying: 'Spare the rod and spoil the child.'* **4** (*AmE, slang*) a small gun IDM **make a rod for your own 'back** to do sth that will cause problems for you in the future—more at BEAT *v.*, RULE *v.*

rode *pt* of RIDE

ro·dent /'rəʊdnt; *AmE* 'roʊ-/ *noun* any small animal that belongs to a group of animals with strong sharp front teeth. Mice, rats and rabbits are all rodents.—picture on page A6

rodeo /ˈrəʊdiəʊ; rəʊˈdeɪəʊ; AmE ˈroʊdioʊ; roʊˈdeɪoʊ/ noun (pl. -os) a public competition, especially in the US, in which COWBOYS show their skill at riding wild horses and catching CATTLE with ropes

roe /rəʊ; AmE roʊ/ noun **1** [U, C] the mass of eggs inside a female fish (**hard roe**) or the SPERM of a male fish (**soft roe**), used as food: *Taramasalata is made from cod's roe, olive oil and garlic.* **2** = ROE DEER

'roe deer noun (pl. roe deer) (also **roe**) a small European and Asian deer

roger /ˈrɒdʒə(r); AmE ˈrɑːdʒ-/ exclamation, verb
■ exclamation people say **Roger!** in communication by radio to show that they have understood a message
■ verb [VN] (BrE, ⚠, slang) (of a man) to have sex with sb

rogue /rəʊg; AmE roʊg/ noun, adj.
■ noun **1** (humorous) a person who behaves badly, but in a harmless way: *He's a bit of a rogue, but very charming.* **2** (old-fashioned) a man who is dishonest and immoral: *a rogues' gallery* (= a collection of pictures of criminals)
■ adj. [only before noun] **1** (of an animal) living apart from the main group, and possibly dangerous **2** behaving differently from other similar people or things, often causing damage: *a rogue gene* ◇ *a rogue police officer*

roguish /ˈrəʊgɪʃ; AmE ˈroʊ-/ adj. (usually approving) (of a person) pleasant and amusing but looking as if they might do sth wrong: *a roguish smile* ▶ **roguish·ly** adv.

rois·ter·ing /ˈrɔɪstərɪŋ/ adj. (old-fashioned) having fun in a cheerful, noisy way

role /rəʊl; AmE roʊl/ noun **1** the function or position that sb has or is expected to have in an organization, in society or in a relationship: *the role of the teacher in the classroom* ◇ *She refused to take on the traditional woman's role.* ◇ *In many marriages there has been a complete role reversal* (= change of roles) *with the man staying at home and the woman going out to work.* **2** an actor's part in a play, film/movie, etc: *It is one of the greatest roles she has played.* ◇ *Who is in the leading role* (= the most important one)? **3** the degree to which sb/sth is involved in a situation or an activity and the effect that they have on it: *the role of diet in preventing disease* ◇ *The media play a major role in influencing people's opinions.* ◇ *a key/vital role*

'role model noun a person that you admire and try to copy

'role-play noun a learning activity in which you behave in the way sb else would behave in a particular situation: *Role-play allows students to practise language in a safe situation.* ▶ **'role-play** verb [V, VN]

roll /rəʊl; AmE roʊl/ noun, verb
■ noun
OF PAPER/FABRIC, etc. | **1** [C] ~ (of sth) a long piece of paper, fabric, film, etc. that has been wrapped around itself or a tube several times so that it forms the shape of a tube: *a roll of carpet/film* ◇ *Wallpaper is sold in rolls.*—see also TOILET ROLL
OF SWEETS/CANDY | **2** (AmE) a paper tube wrapped around sweets/candy, etc: *a roll of mints*—picture at PACKAGING
BREAD | **3** (also **'bread 'roll**) [C] a small LOAF of bread for one person: *Soup and a roll: £1.50* ◇ *(especially BrE) a chicken/ham roll* (= filled with chicken/ham)—compare BUN—see also SAUSAGE ROLL, SPRING ROLL, SWISS ROLL—picture on page A1
OF BODY | **4** [sing.] an act of rolling the body over and over: *The kittens were enjoying a roll in the sunshine.* **5** [C] a physical exercise in which you roll your body on the ground, moving your back and legs over your head: *a forward/backward roll*
OF SHIP/PLANE | **6** [U] the act of moving from side to side so that one side is higher than the other—compare PITCH n. (8)
OF FAT | **7** [C] an area of too much fat on your body, especially around your waist: *Rolls of fat hung over his belt.*
LIST OF NAMES | **8** [C] an official list of names: *the electoral*

roll (= a list of all the people who can vote in an election) ◇ *The chairman called/took the roll* (= called out the names on a list to check that everyone was present).—see also PAYROLL
SOUND | **9** [C] ~ (of sth) a deep continuous sound: *the distant roll of thunder* ◇ *a drum roll*
OF DICE | **10** [C] an act of rolling a DICE: *The order of play is decided by the roll of a dice.*
—see also ROCK AND ROLL
IDM **be on a 'roll** (informal) to be experiencing a period of success at what you are doing: *Don't stop me now—I'm on a roll!* **a ,roll in the 'hay** (informal) an act of having sex with sb
■ verb
TURN OVER | **1** [+adv./prep.] to turn over and over and move in a particular direction; to make a round object do this: [V] *The ball rolled down the hill.* ◇ *We watched the waves rolling onto the beach.* ◇ [VN] *Delivery men were rolling barrels across the yard.* **2** [usually +adv./prep.] to turn over and over or round and round while remaining in the same place; to make sb do this: [V] *a dog rolling in the mud* ◇ [VN] *He was rolling a pencil between his fingers.* ◇ [V, VN] *Her eyes rolled.* ◇ *She rolled her eyes upwards* (= to show surprise or disapproval). **3** ~ (sb/sth) over (onto sth)| ~ (sb/sth) (over) onto sth to turn over to face a different direction; to make sb/sth do this: [V] *She rolled over to let the sun brown her back.* ◇ *He rolled onto his back.* ◇ [VN] *I rolled the baby over onto its stomach.* ◇ (AmE) *She rolled her car in a 100 mph crash.* ◇ *to roll a dice/die* (= in a game)
MOVE ON WHEELS | **4** [usually +adv./prep.] to move smoothly (on wheels or as if on wheels); to make sth do this: [V] *The car began to roll back down the hill.* ◇ *The traffic rolled slowly forwards.* ◇ *Mist was rolling in from the sea.* ◇ [VN] *He rolled the trolley across the room.*
MAKE BALL/TUBE | **5** ~ (sth) (up) (into sth) to make sth/ yourself into the shape of a ball or tube: [VN] *I rolled the string into a ball.* ◇ *We rolled up the carpet.* ◇ *a rolled-up newspaper* ◇ *I always roll my own* (= make my own cigarettes). ◇ [V] *The hedgehog rolled up into a ball.*—compare UNROLL
FOLD CLOTHING | **6** [VN +adv./prep.] ~ (sth) (up) to fold the edge of a piece of clothing, etc. over and over on itself to make it shorter: *Roll up your sleeves.* ◇ *She rolled her jeans to her knees.*
MAKE STH FLAT | **7** [VN] to make sth flat by pushing sth heavy over it: *Roll the pastry on a floured surface.*
WRAP UP | **8** [VN] ~ sb/sth/yourself (up) in sth to wrap or cover sb/sth/yourself in sth: *Roll the meat in the breadcrumbs.* ◇ *He rolled himself up in the blanket.*
OF SHIP/PLANE/WALK | **9** to move or make sth move from side to side: [V] *He walked with a rolling gait.* ◇ *The ship was rolling heavily to and fro.* [also VN] —compare PITCH v. (6)
MAKE SOUND | **10** to make a long continuous sound: [V] *rolling drums* ◇ *Thunder rolled.* ◇ [VN] *to roll your r's* (= by letting your tongue VIBRATE with each 'r' sound)
MACHINE | **11** when a machine **rolls** or sb **rolls** it, it operates: [V] *They had to repeat the scene because the cameras weren't rolling.* ◇ [VN] *Roll the cameras!*
IDM **be 'rolling in money/it** (informal) to have a lot of money **rolled into 'one** combined in one person or thing: *Banks are several businesses rolled into one.* **,rolling in the 'aisles** laughing a lot: *She soon had us rolling in the aisles.* **'roll on ...!** (spoken, BrE) used to say that you want sth to happen or arrive soon: *Roll on Friday!* **roll up your 'sleeves** to prepare to work or fight **roll with the 'punches** to adapt yourself to a difficult situation—more at BALL n., GRAVE¹ n., HEAD n., READY adj., TONGUE n.
PHRV **,roll a'round** (BrE also **,roll a'bout**) to be laughing so much that you can hardly control yourself **,roll sth↔'back 1** to turn or force sth back or further away: *to roll back the frontiers of space* **2** to reduce prices, etc: *to roll back inflation* **,roll sth↔'down 1** to open sth by turning a handle: *He rolled down his car window and started shouting at them.* **2** to make a rolled piece of clothing, etc. hang or lie flat: *to roll down a*

æ	ɑː	e	ɜː	ə	ɪ	iː	i	ɒ	ɔː	ʌ	ʊ	u	uː
cat	father	ten	bird	about	sit	see	many	got	saw	cup	put	actual	too

(BrE)

blind/your sleeves **roll 'in** (*informal*) **1** to arrive in great numbers or amounts: *Offers of help are still rolling in.* **2** to arrive late at a place, without seeming worried or sorry: *Steve rolled in around lunchtime.* **roll sth↔'out 1** to make sth flat by pushing sth over it: *Roll out the pastry.* **2** to officially make a new product available or start a new political CAMPAIGN [SYN] LAUNCH: *The new model is to be rolled out in July.*—related noun ROLL-OUT **roll 'up** (*informal*) to arrive: *Bill finally rolled up two hours late.* ◊ *Roll up! Roll up!* (= used to invite people who are passing to form an audience) **roll sth↔'up** to close sth by turning a handle: *She rolled up all the windows.*

roll·back /'rəʊlbæk; *AmE* 'roʊl-/ *noun* [sing., U] (*especially AmE*) **1** a reduction in a price or in pay, to a past level **2** the act of changing a situation, law, etc. back to what it was before

'roll-call *noun* [U, sing.] the reading aloud of a list of names to check who is there: *Roll-call will be at 7 a.m.* ◊ *The guest list reads like a roll-call of the nation's heroes.*

roll·er /'rəʊlə(r); *AmE* 'roʊ-/ *noun* **1** a piece of wood, metal or plastic, shaped like a tube, that rolls over and over and is used in machines, for example to make sth flat, or to move sth: *the heavy steel rollers under the conveyor belt* ◊ *a roller blind* (= a blind for a window that is wound on a roller) ◊ *a roller towel* (= a long piece of towel on a roller, usually used in a public place)—picture at BLIND **2** (often in compounds) a machine or piece of equipment with a part shaped like a tube so that it rolls backwards and forwards. It may be used for making sth flat, crushing or spreading sth: *Flatten the surface of the grass with a roller.* ◊ *a paint roller*—see also STEAMROLLER **3** a piece of wood or metal, shaped like a tube, that is used for moving heavy objects: *We'll need to move the piano on rollers.* **4** a long, powerful wave in the sea/ocean: *Huge Atlantic rollers crashed onto the rocks.* **5** a small plastic tube that hair is rolled around to give it curls [SYN] CURLER: *heated rollers* ◊ *Her hair was in rollers.*—see also HIGH ROLLER

Roll·er·blade™ (*BrE*) (*AmE* **Roller Blade**™) /'rəʊləbleɪd; *AmE* 'roʊlərb-/ (also **in-line 'skate**) *noun* a type of boot with a line of small wheels attached to the bottom ▶ **Roll·er·blade** *verb* [V] —picture on page A8

'roller coaster *noun* **1** a track at a FAIRGROUND that goes up and down very steep slopes and that people ride on in a small train for fun and excitement: *a roller-coaster ride* **2** a situation that keeps changing very quickly: *The last few weeks have been a real roller coaster.*

'roller skate (also **skate**) *noun, verb*
■ *noun* a type of boot with two pairs of small wheels attached to the bottom: *a pair of roller skates*
■ *verb* [V] to move over a hard surface wearing roller skates ▶ **'roller skating** (also **skat·ing**) *noun* [U]

rol·licking /'rɒlɪkɪŋ; *AmE* 'rɑːl-/ *adj., noun*
■ *adj.* [only before noun] cheerful and often noisy: *a rollicking comedy*
■ *noun* (*informal, BrE*) angry criticism for sth bad sb has done: *He gave us both a rollicking.*

roll·ing /'rəʊlɪŋ; *AmE* 'roʊ-/ *adj.* [only before noun] **1** (of hills or countryside) having gentle slopes **2** done in regular stages or at regular intervals over a period of time: *a rolling programme of reform*

'rolling mill *noun* a machine or factory that produces flat sheets of metal

'rolling pin *noun* a wooden or glass kitchen UTENSIL (= a tool) in the shape of a tube, used for rolling pastry flat—picture at KITCHEN

'rolling stock *noun* [U] the engines, trains, etc. that are used on a railway/railroad

roll of 'honour (*BrE*) (*AmE* **'honor roll**) *noun* [usually sing.] a list of people who are being praised officially for sth they have done

'roll-on *adj.* [only before noun] spread or put on the body using a ball that moves around in the top of a bottle or container: *a roll-on deodorant* ▶ **'roll-on** *noun*

roll-on roll-'off *adj.* [usually before noun] (*abbr.* **'ro-ro**) (*BrE*) (of a ship) designed so that cars can be driven straight on and off: *a roll-on roll-off car ferry*

'roll-out *noun* an occasion when a company introduces a new product, especially an aircraft, to the public

roll·over /'rəʊləʊvə(r); *AmE* 'roʊloʊvər/ *noun* **1** [U] (*technical*) the act of allowing money that is owed to be paid at a later date **2** [U, C] (*BrE*) a prize of money in a competition or LOTTERY in a particular week, that is added to the prize given in the following week if nobody wins it: *a rollover jackpot* **3** [U] (*especially AmE*) the turning over of a vehicle during an accident

'roll-up *noun* (*BrE, informal*) a cigarette that you make yourself with tobacco and special paper

roly-poly /ˌrəʊli 'pəʊli; *AmE* ˌroʊli 'poʊli/ *adj., noun*
■ *adj.* [only before noun] (*informal*) (of people) short, round and fat
■ *noun* (*pl.* **-ies**) (also **roly-poly 'pudding**) [U, C] (*BrE*) a hot DESSERT (= a sweet dish) made from SUET pastry spread with jam and rolled up

ROM /rɒm; *AmE* rɑːm/ *noun* [U] the abbreviation for 'read-only memory' (computer memory that contains instructions or data that cannot be changed or removed): *ROM chips*—compare CD-ROM

ro·maine /rəʊ'meɪn; *AmE* roʊ-/ *noun* [C, U] (*AmE*) = COS LETTUCE

Roman /'rəʊmən; *AmE* 'roʊ-/ *adj., noun*
■ *adj.* **1** of or connected with ancient Rome or the Roman Empire: *a Roman road/temple/villa* ◊ *Roman Britain* **2** of or connected with the modern city of Rome **3** of or connected with the Roman Catholic Church: *the Roman rite* **4 roman** type is ordinary upright printing type: *Definitions in this dictionary are printed in roman type.*—compare ITALIC
■ *noun* **1** [C] a member of the ancient Roman republic or empire: *after the Romans invaded Britain* **2** [C] a person from the modern city of Rome **3** (**roman**) [U] the ordinary style of printing that uses small upright letters, like these words—compare ITALICS [IDM] see ROME

the ˌRoman 'alphabet *noun* [sing.] the alphabet that is used in English and in most Western European languages

ˌRoman 'Catholic (also **Cath·olic**) *noun* (*abbr.* **RC**) a member of the part of the Christian Church that has the POPE as its leader ▶ **ˌRoman 'Catholic** (also **Cath·olic**) *adj.* **ˌRoman Ca'tholicism** (also **Cath·oli·cism**) *noun* [U]

Ro·mance /rəʊ'mæns; *AmE* roʊ-/ *adj.* [only before noun] Romance languages, such as French, Italian and Spanish, are languages that developed from Latin

ro·mance /rəʊ'mæns; *AmE* roʊ-/ *noun, verb*
■ *noun* **1** [C] an exciting, usually short, relationship between two people who are in love with each other: *a teenage/holiday romance* ◊ *They had a whirlwind romance.* **2** [U] love or the feeling of being in love: *Spring is here and romance is in the air.* ◊ *How can you put the romance back into your marriage?* **3** [U] a feeling of excitement and adventure, especially connected to a particular place or activity: *the romance of travel* **4** [C] a story about a love affair: *She's a compulsive reader of romances.* **5** [C] a story of excitement and adventure, often set in the past: *medieval romances*
■ *verb* (*written*) **1** [V] to tell stories that are not true or to describe sth in a way that makes it seem more exciting or interesting than it really is **2** [VN] to have or to try to have a romantic relationship with sb

Ro·man·esque /ˌrəʊmə'nesk; *AmE* ˌroʊ-/ *adj.* used to describe a style of architecture that was popular in Western Europe from the 10th to the 12th centuries and that had round arches, thick walls and tall PILLARS—see also NORMAN

ˌRoman 'nose *noun* a nose that curves out at the top

ˌRoman 'numeral *noun* one of the letters used by the ancient Romans to represent numbers and still used today, in some situations. In this system I = 1, V = 5, X = 10, L = 50, C = 100, D = 500, M = 1000 and these letters are used in combinations to form other numbers: *Henry VIII* ◊ *Copyright BBC MCMXCVII (1997)*—compare ARABIC NUMERAL

ro·man·tic /rəʊ'mæntɪk; *AmE* roʊ-/ *adj., noun*

aɪ	aʊ	eɪ	əʊ	oʊ	ɔɪ	ɪə	eə	ʊə	j	w
my	now	say	go	go	boy	near	hair	pure	yes	wet
			(BrE)	(AmE)						

■ *adj.* **1** connected or concerned with love or a sexual relationship: *a romantic candlelit dinner* ◊ *romantic stories/fiction/comedy* ◊ *I'm not interested in a romantic relationship.* **2** (of people) showing feelings of love: *Why don't you ever give me flowers? I wish you'd be more romantic.* **3** beautiful in a way that makes you think of love or feel strong emotions: *romantic music* ◊ *romantic mountain scenery* **4** very imaginative and emotional; not looking at situations in a realistic way: *a romantic view of life* ◊ *When I was younger, I had romantic ideas of becoming a writer.* **5** (**Ro·man·tic**) [usually before noun] used to describe literature, music or art, especially of the 19th century, that is concerned with strong feelings, imagination and a return to nature, rather than reason, order and INTELLECTUAL ideas: *the Romantic movement* ◊ *poets/composers of the Romantic period* ◊ *Keats is one of the greatest Romantic poets.* ▶ **ro·man·tic·al·ly** /-kli/ *adv.*: *to be romantically involved with sb* ◊ *Their names have been linked romantically.* ◊ *He talked romantically of the past and his youth.*

■ *noun* **1** a person who is very imaginative and emotional, and who has ideas and hopes that may not be realistic: *an incurable romantic* ◊ *He was a romantic at heart and longed for adventure.* **2** (**Ro·man·tic**) a writer, a musician or an artist who writes, etc. in the style of Romanticism

ro·man·ti·cism /rəʊˈmæntɪsɪzəm; *AmE* roʊ-/ *noun* [U] **1** (also **Ro·man·ti·cism**) a style and movement in art, music and literature in the late 18th and early 19th century, in which strong feelings, imagination and a return to nature were more important than reason, order and intellectual ideas—compare REALISM **2** the quality of seeing people, events and situations as more exciting and interesting than they really are **3** strong feelings of love; the fact of showing emotion, affection, etc.

ro·man·ti·cize (*BrE* also **-ise**) /rəʊˈmæntɪsaɪz; *AmE* roʊ-/ *verb* to make sth seem more attractive or interesting than it really is: [VN] *romanticizing the past* ◊ *a romanticized picture of parenthood* [also V]

Rom·any /ˈrɒməni; ˈrəʊm-; *AmE* ˈrɑːm-; ˈroʊm-/ *noun* (*pl.* **-ies**) **1** [C] a member of a race of people, originally from Asia, who travel around and traditionally live in CARAVANS SYN GYPSY **2** [U] the language of Romany people ▶ **Rom·any** *adj.* [usually before noun]

Rome /rəʊm; *AmE* roʊm/ *noun* IDM **Rome wasn't built in a 'day** (*saying*) used to say that a complicated task will take a long time and needs patience **when in 'Rome (do as the 'Romans do)** (*saying*) used to say that when you are in a foreign country, or a situation you are not familiar with, you should behave in the way that the people around you behave

romp /rɒmp; *AmE* rɑːmp; rɔːmp/ *verb, noun*

■ *verb* [V, usually +*adv./prep.*] to play in a happy and noisy way: *kids romping around in the snow* ◊ *Two fox cubs romped playfully on the river bank.* IDM **romp home/to victory** to easily win a race or competition: *Their horse romped home in the 2 o'clock race.* ◊ *The Dutch team romped to a 5–1 victory over Napoli.* PHRV **romp a'way/a'head** (*BrE, informal*) to increase, make progress or win quickly and easily **romp 'through (sth)** (*BrE, informal*) to do sth easily and quickly: *She romped through the exam questions.*

■ *noun* (often used in newspapers) (*informal*) **1** [C] an enjoyable sexual experience that is not serious: *politicians involved in sex romps with call-girls* **2** [C] an amusing book, play or film/movie that is full of action or adventure: *His latest film is an enjoyable romp.* **3** [sing.] an easy victory in a sports competition: *They won in a 5–1 romp.*

romp·ers /ˈrɒmpəz; *AmE* ˈrɑːmpərz; ˈrɔːm-/ *noun* [pl.] (also **'romper suit** [C]) (*old-fashioned*) a piece of clothing worn by a baby, that covers the body and legs

rondo /ˈrɒndəʊ; *AmE* ˈrɑːndoʊ/ *noun* (*pl.* **-os**) a piece of music in which the main tune is repeated several times, sometimes forming part of a longer piece

rood screen /ˈruːd skriːn/ *noun* (*technical*) a wooden or stone structure in some churches that divides the part near the ALTAR from the rest of the church

roof /ruːf/ *noun, verb*

■ *noun* (*pl.* **roofs**) **1** the structure that covers or forms the top of a building or vehicle: *a flat/sloping roof* ◊ *a thatched/slate roof* ◊ *The corner of the classroom was damp where the roof had leaked.* ◊ *Tim climbed on to the garage roof.* ◊ *The roof of the car was not damaged in the accident.*—see also SUNROOF—picture at HOUSE **2** (-roofed) (in *adjectives*) having the type of roof mentioned: *flat-roofed buildings* **3** the top of an underground space such as a tunnel or CAVE **4** ~ **of your mouth** the top of the inside of your mouth IDM **go through the 'roof 1** (of prices, etc.) to rise or increase very quickly: *House prices here have gone through the roof.* **2** (also **hit the 'roof**) (*informal*) to become very angry **have a 'roof over your head** to have somewhere to live: *Thanks to Bob's generosity, I still have a roof over my head.* **under one 'roof | under the same 'roof** in the same building or house: *There are various stores and restaurants all under one roof.* ◊ *I don't think I can live under the same roof as you any longer.* **under your 'roof** in your home: *I don't want her under my roof again.*—more at HIT *v.*, RAISE *v.*

■ *verb* ~ **sth (in/over) | ~ sth (with/in sth)** [VN] [often passive] to cover sth with a roof; to put a roof on a building: *The shopping centre is not roofed over.* ◊ *Their cottage was roofed with green slate.*

'roof garden *noun* a garden on the flat roof of a building

roof·ing /ˈruːfɪŋ/ *noun* [U] **1** material used for making or covering roofs: *timber roofing* ◊ *roofing felt/slates/tiles* **2** the process of building roofs: *a roofing contractor*

'roof rack *noun* a metal frame fixed to the roof of a car and used for carrying bags, cases and other large objects—picture at RACK, CAR

roof·top /ˈruːftɒp; *AmE* -tɑːp/ *noun* the outside part of the roof of a building: *From the hill we looked out over the rooftops of Athens.* ◊ *The prisoners staged a rooftop protest.* IDM **,shout, etc. sth from the 'rooftops** to talk about sth in a very public way: *He was in love and wanted to shout it from the rooftops.*

rook /rʊk/ *noun* **1** a large black bird of the CROW family. Rooks build their nests in groups at the tops of trees. **2** = CASTLE

rookie /ˈrʊki/ *noun* (*informal*) **1** (*especially AmE*) a person who has just started a job or an activity and has very little experience: *a rookie police officer* **2** (*AmE*) a member of a sports team in his or her first full year of playing that sport

room /ruːm; rʊm/ *noun, verb*

■ *noun*

  IN BUILDING | **1** [C] a part of a building that has its own walls, floor and ceiling and is usually used for a particular purpose: *He walked out of the room and slammed the door.* ◊ *They were in the next room and we could hear every word they said.* ◊ *a dining/living/sitting room* ◊ *They had to sit in the waiting room for an hour.* ◊ *I think Simon is in his room* (= bedroom). ◊ (*spoken*) *I don't want to watch television. I'll be in the other room* (= a different room). HELP There are many compounds ending in **room**. You will find them at their place in the alphabet.

  -ROOMED/-ROOM | **2** (in *adjectives*) having the number of rooms mentioned: *a three-roomed/three-room apartment*

  IN HOTEL | **3** [C] a bedroom in a hotel, etc: *a double/single room* ◊ *I'd like to book a room with a view of the lake.* ◊ *She lets out rooms to students.*

  PLACE TO LIVE | **4** (**rooms**) [pl.] (*old-fashioned, BrE*) a set of two or more rooms that you rent to live in SYN LODGINGS: *They lived in rooms in Kensington.*

  SPACE | **5** [U] ~ **(for sb/sth) | ~ (to do sth)** empty space that can be used for a particular purpose: *Is there enough room for me in the car?* ◊ *There's room for one more at the table.* ◊ *Do you have room for a computer on your desk?* ◊ *Yes, there's plenty of room.* ◊ *I'll move the table—it takes up too much room.* ◊ *How can we make room for all the furniture?* ◊ *Make sure you have plenty of room to sit comfortably.*—see also ELBOW ROOM, HEADROOM, HOUSEROOM, LEGROOM, STANDING ROOM ⟹ note at PLACE

  POSSIBILITY | **6** ~ **for sth** the possibility of sth existing or

R

happening; the opportunity to do sth: *He had to be certain. There could be **no room for doubt**.* ◊ *There's some room for improvement in your work* (= it is not as good as it could be). ◊ *It is important to give children room to think for themselves.*

PEOPLE | **7** [sing.] all the people in a room: *The whole room burst into applause.*

IDM **no room to swing a ˈcat** (*informal*) when sb says **there's no room to swing a cat**, they mean that a room is very small and that there is not enough space—more at MANOEUVRE *n.*, SMOKE *n.*

■ *verb* [V] (*AmE*) ~ **(with sb)** | ~ **(together)** to rent a room somewhere; to share a rented room or flat/apartment with sb: *She and Nancy roomed together at college.*

room·ful /ˈruːmfʊl; ˈrʊm-/ *noun* [sing.] a large number of people or things that are in a room: *He announced his resignation to a roomful of reporters.* ◊ *a roomful of old books*

ˈrooming house *noun* (*AmE*) a building where rooms with furniture can be rented for living in

ˈroom-mate *noun* **1** a person that you share a room with, especially at a college or university **2** (*AmE*) = FLATMATE

ˈroom service *noun* [U] a service provided in a hotel, by which guests can order food and drink to be brought to their rooms: *He ordered coffee from room service.*

roomy /ˈruːmi; ˈrʊmi/ *adj.* (**room·ier, roomi·est**) (*approving*) having a lot of space inside: *a surprisingly roomy house/car* ▶ **roomi·ness** *noun* [U] (*rare*)

roost /ruːst/ *noun, verb*

■ *noun* a place where birds sleep **IDM** see RULE *v.*

■ *verb* [V] (of birds) to rest or go to sleep somewhere **IDM** see HOME *adv.*

roost·er /ˈruːstə(r)/ *noun* (*especially AmE*) = COCK

root /ruːt/ *noun, verb*

■ *noun*

OF PLANT | **1** [C] the part of a plant that grows under the ground and absorbs water and minerals that it sends to the rest of the plant: *deep spreading roots* ◊ *I pulled the plant up by* (= including) **the roots**. ◊ *Tree roots can cause damage to buildings.* ◊ *root crops/vegetables* (= plants whose roots you can eat, such as carrots)—see also GRASS ROOTS, TAPROOT—picture at PLANT

OF HAIR/TOOTH/NAIL | **2** [C] the part of a hair, tooth, nail or tongue that attaches it to the rest of the body: *hair that is blonde at the ends and dark at the roots*

MAIN CAUSE OF PROBLEM | **3** [C, usually sing.] the main cause of sth, such as a problem or difficult situation: *Money, or love of money, is said to be the root of all evil.* ◊ *We have to get to the root of the problem.* ◊ *What lies at the root of his troubles is a sense of insecurity.* ◊ *What would you say was the root cause of the problem?*

ORIGIN | **4** [C, usually pl.] the origin or basis of sth: *Flamenco has its roots in Arabic music.*

CONNECTION WITH PLACE | **5** (**roots**) [pl.] the feelings or connections that you have with a place because you have lived there or your family came from there: *I'm proud of my Italian roots.* ◊ *After 20 years in America, I still feel my roots are in England.*

OF WORD | **6** [C] (*linguistics*) the part of a word that has the main meaning and that its other forms are based on; a word that other words are formed from: *'Walk' is the root of 'walks', 'walked', 'walking' and 'walker'.*

MATHEMATICS | **7** [C] a quantity which, when multiplied by itself a particular number of times, produces another quantity—see also CUBE ROOT, SQUARE ROOT

IDM **put down ˈroots 1** (of a plant) to develop roots **2** to settle and live in one place: *After ten years travelling the world, she felt it was time to put down roots somewhere.* **ˌroot and ˈbranch** thoroughly and completely: *The government set out to destroy the organization root and branch.* ◊ *root-and-branch reforms* **take ˈroot 1** (of a plant) to develop roots **2** (of an idea) to become accepted widely: *Fortunately, militarism failed to take root in Europe as a whole.*

■ *verb*

OF PLANTS | **1** [V, VN] to grow roots; to make or encourage a plant to grow roots

SEARCH | **2** [V+*adv./prep.*] ~ **(about/around) for sth** | ~ **(through sth) (for sth)** to search for sth by moving things or turning things over: *pigs rooting for food* ◊ *'It must be here somewhere,' she said, rooting through the suitcase.* ◊ *Who's been rooting around in my desk?*

PHRV **ˈroot for sb/sth** [no passive] (usually used in the progressive tenses) (*informal*) to support or encourage sb in a sports competition or when they are in a difficult situation: *We're rooting for the Bulls.* ◊ *Good luck—I'm rooting for you!* **ˌroot sth/sb↔ˈout 1** to find the person or thing that is causing a problem and remove or get rid of them **2** to find sb/sth after searching for a long time: *I'll root out the photo for you.* **ˌroot sb to ˈsth** to make sb unable to move because of fear, shock, etc: *Embarrassment rooted her to the spot.* **ˌroot sth↔ˈup** to dig or pull up a plant with its roots

ˈroot beer *noun* **1** [U] a sweet FIZZY drink (= with bubbles), that does not contain alcohol, made from GINGER and the roots of other plants. It is drunk especially in the US. **2** [C] a bottle, can or glass of root beer: *Two root beers.*

root·ed /ˈruːtɪd/ *adj.* **1** ~ **in sth** developing from or being strongly influenced by sth: *His problems are deeply rooted in his childhood experiences.* **2** fixed in one place; not moving or changing: *She was rooted to her chair.* ◊ *Their life is rooted in Chicago now.* ◊ *Life in the countryside remained firmly rooted in the past.* ◊ *Racism is still deeply rooted in our society.*—see also DEEP-ROOTED **IDM** **rooted to the ˈspot** so frightened or shocked that you cannot move

root·less /ˈruːtləs/ *adj.* having nowhere that you really think of as home, or as the place where you belong: *She had had a rootless childhood moving from town to town.* ▶ **root·less·ness** *noun* [U]

rope /rəʊp; *AmE* roʊp/ *noun, verb*

■ *noun* **1** [C, U] very strong thick string made by twisting thinner strings, wires, etc. together: *The rope broke and she fell 50 metres onto the rocks.* ◊ *We tied his hands together with rope.* ◊ *The anchor was attached to a length of rope.* ◊ *Coils of rope lay on the quayside.*—picture on page 1113—see also JUMP ROPE, SKIPPING ROPE, TOW ROPE **2** (**the ropes**) [pl.] the fence made of rope that is around the edge of the area where a boxing or WRESTLING match takes place **3** [C] a number of similar things attached together by a string or thread: *a rope of pearls/beads* **IDM** **give sb enough ˈrope** to allow sb freedom to do what they want, especially in the hope that they will make a mistake or look silly: *The question was vague, giving the interviewee enough rope to hang herself.* **on the ˈropes** (*informal*) very close to being defeated **show sb/know/learn the ˈropes** (*informal*) to show sb/know/learn how a particular job should be done—more at END *n.*, MONEY

■ *verb* [VN] **1** [+*adv./prep.*] ~ **A and B together** | ~ **A to B** to tie one person or thing to another with a rope: *Thieves had roped the guard's feet together.* ◊ *I roped the goat to a post.* **2** to tie sth with a rope so that it is held tightly and safely: *I closed and roped the trunk.* **3** (*especially AmE*) to catch an animal by throwing a circle of rope around it **PHRV** **ˌrope sb↔ˈin** | **ˌrope sb ˈinto sth** [usually passive] (*informal*) to persuade sb to join in an activity or to help to do sth, even when they do not want to: [+ to inf] *Everyone was roped in to help with the show.* ◊ [+ -ing] *Ben was roped in to making the coffee for the whole team.* **ˌrope sth↔ˈoff** to separate an area from another one, using ropes, to stop people from entering it: *Police roped off the street to investigate the accident.*

ˌrope ˈladder *noun* a ladder made of two long ropes connected by short pieces of wood or metal at regular intervals

ropy (also **ropey**) /ˈrəʊpi; *AmE* ˈroʊpi/ *adj.* (*BrE, informal*) **1** not in good condition; of bad quality: *We spent the night in a ropy old tent.* **2** feeling slightly ill/sick: *I felt a bit ropy earlier this week, but I'm better now.*

ro-ro /ˈrəʊrəʊ; *AmE* ˈroʊroʊ/ *abbr.* (*BrE*) ROLL-ON ROLL-OFF

ros·ary /ˈrəʊzəri; *AmE* ˈroʊ-/ *noun* (*pl.* **-ies**) **1** [C] a string of BEADS that are used by some Roman Catholics for counting prayers as they say them **2** (**the Rosary**) [sing.]

s	t	v	z	ʃ	ʒ	tʃ	dʒ	θ	ð	ŋ
see	tea	van	zoo	shoe	vision	chain	jam	thin	this	sing

R

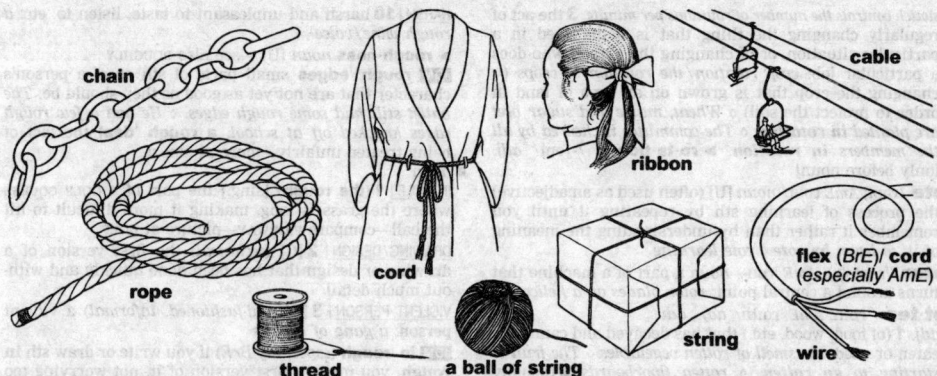

chain

cable

ribbon

rope

cord

flex (BrE)/ cord
(especially AmE)

thread

a ball of string

string

wire

the set of prayers said by Roman Catholics while counting rosary BEADS

rose /rəʊz; AmE roʊz/ noun, adj.—see also RISE v.
- noun **1** [C] a flower with a sweet smell that grows on a bush with THORNS (= sharp pointed growths) on its stems. There are many different types of rose: *a bunch of red roses* ◇ *a rose bush/garden* ◇ *a climbing/rambling rose* **2** (also ,rose 'pink) [U] a pink colour **3** [C] a piece of metal or plastic with small holes in it that is attached to the end of a pipe or WATERING CAN so that the water comes out in a fine spray when you are watering plants—picture at GARDEN **4** = CEILING ROSE **IDM** **be coming up 'roses** (*informal*) (of a situation) to be developing in a successful way: *Everything's coming up roses!* **put 'roses in sb's cheeks** (*BrE, informal*) to make sb look healthy—more at BED n., SMELL v.
- adj. (also ,rose 'pink) pink in colour: *The walls were rose pink.*

rosé /'rəʊzeɪ; AmE roʊ'zeɪ/ noun [U, C] (from *French*) a light pink wine: *a bottle of rosé* ◇ *an excellent rosé*—compare RED WINE, WHITE WINE

ros·eate /'rəʊziət; AmE 'roʊ-/ adj. [usually before noun] (*literary* or *technical*) pink in colour: *the roseate glow of dawn*

rose·bud /'rəʊzbʌd; AmE 'roʊz-/ noun the flower of a rose before it is open

'rose-coloured (*BrE*) (*AmE* **'rose-colored**) adj. **1** pink in colour **2** (also **'rose-tinted**) used to describe an idea or a way of looking at a situation as being better or more positive than it really is: *a rose-tinted vision of the world* ◇ *He tends to view the world through rose-coloured spectacles.*

'rose hip noun = HIP

rose·mary /'rəʊzməri; AmE 'roʊzmeri/ noun [U] a bush with small narrow leaves that smell sweet and are used in cooking as a herb

ros·ette /rəʊ'zet; AmE roʊ-/ noun **1** a circular decoration made of RIBBON that is worn by supporters of a political party or sports team, or to show that sb has won a prize **2** a thing that has the shape of a rose: *The leaves formed a dark green rosette.*

'rose water noun [U] a liquid with a sweet smell made from roses, used as a PERFUME or in cooking

,rose 'window noun a decorative circular window in a church, often with coloured glass (= STAINED GLASS) in it

rose·wood /'rəʊzwʊd; AmE 'roʊz-/ noun [U] the hard reddish-brown wood of a tropical tree, that has a pleasant smell and is used for making expensive furniture

Rosh Hash·ana (also **Rosh Hash·anah**) /ˌrɒʃ hə'ʃɑːnə; AmE ˌrɑː ʃ/ noun [U] the Jewish New Year festival, held in September

rosin /'rɒzɪn; AmE 'rɑːzn/ noun [U] a substance that is used on the BOW of a musical instrument such as a violin so that it moves across the STRINGS more easily ► **rosin** verb [VN]

ros·ter /'rɒstə(r); AmE 'rɑːs-/ noun, verb
- noun **1** a list of people's names and the jobs that they have to do at a particular time **SYN** ROTA: *a duty roster* **2** a list of the names of people who are available to do a job, play in a team, etc.
- verb (*BrE*) to put sb's name on a roster: [VN] *The driver was rostered for Sunday.* [also VN to inf]

ros·trum /'rɒstrəm; AmE 'rɑːs-/ noun (pl. **ros·trums** or **ros·tra** /-trə/) a small raised platform that a person stands on to make a speech, CONDUCT music, receive a prize, etc: *He climbed on to the winner's rostrum.*

rosy /'rəʊzi; AmE 'roʊzi/ adj. (**rosi·er**, **rosi·est**) **1** pink and pleasant in appearance: *She had rosy cheeks.* ◇ *The sky was turning rosy over the harbour.* **2** likely to be good or successful: *The future is looking very rosy for our company.* ◇ *She **painted a rosy picture** of their life together in Italy* (= made it appear to be very good and perhaps better than it really was). **IDM** see GARDEN n.

rot /rɒt; AmE rɑːt/ verb, noun
- verb (**-tt-**) to decay, or make sth decay, naturally and gradually **SYN** DECOMPOSE: [V] *rotting leaves/fruit* ◇ *The window frame had **rotted away** completely.* ◇ (*figurative*) *prisoners thrown in jail and **left to rot*** ◇ [VN] *Too much sugar will rot your teeth.*—see also ROTTEN
- noun [U] **1** the process or state of decaying and falling apart: *The wood must not get damp as rot can quickly result.*—see also DRY ROT **2** (**the rot**) used to describe the fact that a situation is getting worse: *The rot set in last year when they reorganized the department.* ◇ *The team should manage to **stop the rot** if they play well this week.* **3** (*old-fashioned, BrE*) nonsense; silly things that sb says **SYN** RUBBISH: *Don't talk such rot!*

rota /'rəʊtə; AmE 'roʊtə/ noun (pl. **rotas**) (*BrE*) a list of jobs that need to be done and the people who will do them in turn **SYN** ROSTER: *Dave organized a cleaning rota.* ◇ *We share out the babysitting on a rota basis.*

ro·tary /'rəʊtəri; AmE 'roʊ-/ adj., noun
- adj. [only before noun] **1** (of a movement) moving in a circle around a central fixed point: *rotary motion* **2** (of a machine or piece of equipment) having parts that move in this way: *a rotary engine*
- noun (pl. **-ies**) (*AmE*) = ROUNDABOUT

ro·tate /rəʊ'teɪt; AmE 'roʊteɪt/ verb **1** ~ (**about/around** sth) to move or turn around a central fixed point; to make sth do this: [V] *Stay well away from the helicopter when its blades start to rotate.* ◇ *winds rotating around the eye of a hurricane* ◇ [VN] *Rotate the wheel through 180 degrees.* **2** if a job **rotates**, or if people **rotate** a job, they regularly change the job or regularly change who does the job: [V] *The EU presidency rotates among the members.* ◇ *When I joined the company, I rotated around the different sections.* ◇ [VN] *We rotate the night shift so no one has to do it all the time.* ► **ro·tat·ing** adj. [only before noun]: *rotating parts* ◇ *a rotating presidency*

ro·ta·tion /rəʊ'teɪʃn; AmE roʊ-/ noun **1** [U] the action of an object moving in a circle around a central fixed point: *the daily rotation of the earth on its axis* **2** [C] one complete movement in a circle around a fixed point: *This*

æ	ɑː	e	ɜː	ə	ɪ	iː	i	ɒ	ɔː	ʌ	ʊ	u	uː
cat	father	ten	bird	about	sit	see	many	got	saw	cup	put	actual	too

(BrE)

switch controls the number of rotations per minute. **3** the act of regularly changing the thing that is being used in a particular situation, or of changing the person who does a particular job: *crop rotation/the rotation of crops* (= changing the crop that is grown on an area of land in order to protect the soil) ◇ *Wheat, maize and sugar beet are planted in rotation.* ◇ *The committee is chaired by all the members in rotation.* ▶ **ro·ta·tion·al** /-ʃənl/ *adj.* [only before noun]

rote /rəʊt; *AmE* roʊt/ *noun* [U] (often used as an adjective) the process of learning sth by repeating it until you remember it rather than by understanding the meaning of it: *to learn by rote* ◇ *rote learning*

rotor /'rəʊtə(r); *AmE* 'roʊ-/ *noun* a part of a machine that turns around a central point: *rotor blades on a helicopter*

rot·ten /'rɒtn; *AmE* 'rɑːtn/ *adj., adv.*
■ *adj.* **1** (of food, wood, etc.) that has decayed and cannot be eaten or used: *the smell of rotten vegetables* ◇ *The fruit is starting to go rotten.* ◇ *rotten floorboards* **2** [usually before noun] (*informal*) very bad **SYN** TERRIBLE: *I've had a rotten day!* ◇ *What rotten luck!* ◇ *She's a rotten singer.* **3** [usually before noun] (*informal*) dishonest: *The organization is rotten to the core.* **4** [not before noun] (*informal*) looking or feeling ill/sick: *She felt rotten.* **5** [not before noun] (*informal*) feeling guilty about sth you have done: *I feel rotten about leaving them behind.* **6** [only before noun] (*informal*) used to emphasize that you are angry or upset about sth: *You can keep your rotten money!* ▶ **rot·ten·ness** *noun* [U] **IDM** **a rotten 'apple** one bad person who has a bad effect on others in a group
■ *adv.* (*informal*) to a large degree; very much: *She spoils the children rotten.* ◇ (*BrE*) *He fancies you (something) rotten.*

rot·ter /'rɒtə(r); *AmE* 'rɑːt-/ *noun* (*old-fashioned, BrE, informal*) a person who behaves badly towards other people

Rott·weiler /'rɒtwaɪlə(r); -vaɪ-; *AmE* 'rɑːtwaɪ-/ *noun* a large dog that can be very fierce

ro·tund /rəʊ'tʌnd; *AmE* roʊ-/ *adj.* (*formal or humorous*) having a fat round body: *the rotund figure of Mr Stevens* ▶ **ro·tund·ity** *noun* [U]

ro·tunda /rəʊ'tʌndə; *AmE* roʊ-/ *noun* a round building or hall, especially one with a curved roof (= a DOME)

rou·ble (*especially BrE*) (*AmE* usually **ruble**) /'ruːbl/ *noun* the unit of money in Russia

rouge /ruːʒ/ *noun* [U] (*old-fashioned*) a red powder used by women for giving colour to their cheeks ▶ **rouge** *verb* [VN]

rough /rʌf/ *adj., noun, verb, adv.*
■ *adj.* (**rough·er, rough·est**)
NOT SMOOTH | **1** having a surface that is not even or regular: *rough ground* ◇ *The skin on her hands was hard and rough.* ◇ *Trim rough edges with a sharp knife.* OPP SMOOTH
NOT EXACT | **2** (*written*) not exact; not including all details **SYN** APPROXIMATE: *a rough calculation/estimate of the cost* ◇ *I've got a rough idea of where I want to go.* ◇ *There were about 20 people there,* **at a rough guess.** ◇ *a rough draft of a speech* ◇ *a rough drawing/sketch*
VIOLENT | **3** not gentle or careful; violent: *This watch is not designed for rough treatment.* ◇ *They complained of rough handling by the guards.* ◇ *rough kids* ◇ *Don't try any* **rough stuff** *with me!* **4** where there is a lot of violence or crime: *the roughest neighbourhood in the city*
SEA | **5** having large and dangerous waves: *It was too rough to sail that night.*
WEATHER | **6** wild and with storms
UNPLEASANT | **7** difficult and unpleasant **SYN** TOUGH: *He's had a really* **rough time** *recently* (= he's had a lot of problems). ◇ *We'll get someone in to do the rough work* (= the hard physical work).
NOT WELL | **8** not feeling well: *You look rough—are you OK?* ◇ *I had a rough night* (= I didn't sleep well).
PLAIN/BASIC | **9** simply made and not finished in every detail; plain or basic: *rough wooden tables* ◇ *a rough road/track* ◇ (*BrE*) *rough paper for making notes on*

HARSH | **10** harsh and unpleasant to taste, listen to, etc: *a rough wine/voice*
▶ **rough·ness** *noun* [U] —see also ROUGHLY
IDM **rough 'edges** small parts of sth or of a person's character that are not yet as good as they should be: *The ballet still had some rough edges.* ◇ *He had a few rough edges knocked off at school.* **a rough 'deal** the fact of being treated unfairly—more at RIDE *n.*
■ *noun*
IN GOLF | **1 (the rough)** [sing.] the part of a GOLF COURSE where the grass is long, making it more difficult to hit the ball—compare FAIRWAY—picture at GOLF
DRAWING/DESIGN | **2** [C] (*technical*) the first version of a drawing or design that has been done quickly and without much detail
VIOLENT PERSON | **3** [C] (*old-fashioned, informal*) a violent person: *a gang of roughs*
IDM **in 'rough** (*especially BrE*) if you write or draw sth **in rough**, you make a first version of it, not worrying too much about mistakes or details **take the rough with the 'smooth** to accept the unpleasant or difficult things that happen in life as well as the good things—more at BIT
■ *verb*
IDM **'rough it** (*informal*) to live in a way that is not very comfortable for a short time: *We can sleep on the beach. I don't mind roughing it for a night or two.*
PHRV **rough sth↔'out** to draw or write sth without including all the details: *I've roughed out a few ideas.* **rough sb↔'up** (*informal*) to hurt sb by hitting or kicking them: *He claimed that guards had roughed him up in prison.*
■ *adv.* using force or violence: *Do they always play this rough?*
IDM **live/sleep 'rough** (*BrE*) to live or sleep outdoors, usually because you have no home and no money: *young people sleeping rough on the streets*

rough·age /'rʌfɪdʒ/ *noun* [U] the part of food that helps to keep a person healthy by keeping the bowels working and moving other food quickly through the body **SYN** FIBRE

rough-and-'ready *adj.* [usually before noun] **1** simple and prepared quickly but good enough for a particular situation: *a rough-and-ready guide to the education system* **2** (of a person) not very polite, educated or fashionable

rough and 'tumble *noun* [U, sing.] **1** **~ (of sth)** a situation in which people compete with each other and are aggressive in order to get what they want: *the rough and tumble of politics* **2** noisy and slightly violent behaviour when children or animals are playing together

rough·cast /'rʌfkɑːst; *AmE* -kæst/ *noun* [U] a type of PLASTER containing small stones that is used for covering the outside walls of buildings ▶ **rough·cast** *adj.*

rough 'diamond (*BrE*) (*AmE* **diamond in the 'rough**) *noun* a person who has many good qualities even though they do not seem to be very polite, educated, etc.

rough·en /'rʌfn/ *verb* to become rough; to make sth rough: [V] *His voice roughened with every word.* ◇ [VN] *Cold weather roughens your skin.*

rough-'hewn *adj.* [only before noun] **1** (of stone, wood, etc.) cut in a way that leaves it with a rough surface: *rough-hewn walls* ◇ (*figurative*) *the rough-hewn features of his face* **2** (*written*) (of a person or their behaviour) not very polite or educated

rough 'justice *noun* [U] **1** punishment that does not seem fair: *It was rough justice that they lost in the closing seconds of the game.* **2** treatment that is fair but not official or expected: *There was a certain amount of rough justice in his downfall.*

rough·ly /'rʌfli/ *adv.* **1** approximately but not exactly: *Sales are up by roughly 10%.* ◇ *We live roughly halfway between here and the coast.* ◇ *They all left at roughly the same time.* ◇ **Roughly speaking,** *we receive about fifty letters a week on the subject.* **2** using force or not being careful and gentle: *He pushed her roughly out of the way.* ◇ *'What do you want?' she demanded roughly.* **3** in a way that does not leave a smooth surface: *roughly plastered walls*

rough·neck /'rʌfnek/ *noun* (*informal*) **1** (*especially AmE*) a man who is noisy, rude and aggressive **2** a man who works on an OIL RIG

rough·shod /'rʌfʃɒd; *AmE* -ʃɑːd/ *adv.* **IDM** **ride, etc. 'roughshod over sb** (*especially BrE*) (*AmE* usually **run 'roughshod over sb**) to treat sb badly and not worry about their feelings

roul·ette /ruː'let/ *noun* [U] a gambling game in which a ball is dropped onto a moving wheel that has holes with numbers on it. Players bet on which hole the ball will be in when the wheel stops.—see also RUSSIAN ROULETTE

round /raʊnd/ *adj., adv., prep., noun, verb*

■ *adj.* (**round·er, round·est**) **1** shaped like a circle or a ball: *a round table/plate* ◇ *These glasses suit people with round faces.* ◇ *The fruit are small and round.* ◇ *Rugby isn't played with a round ball.* ◇ *the discovery that the world is round* ◇ *The child was watching it all with big round eyes* (= showing interest). ◇ *a T-shirt with a round neck*—see also ROUND-EYED, ROUND-TABLE **2** having a curved shape: *the round green hills of Donegal* ◇ *round brackets* (= in punctuation) ◇ *She had a small mouth and round pink cheeks.* **3** [only before noun] a **round** figure or amount is one that is given as a whole number, usually one ending in 0 or 5: *Make it a round figure—say forty dollars.* ◇ *Two thousand is a nice round number—put that down.* ◇ *Well, in round figures* (= not giving the exact figures) *we've spent twenty thousand so far.* ▸ **round·ness** *noun* [U] (*written*): *His face had lost its boyish roundness.*

■ *adv.* (*especially BrE*) (*AmE* usually **around**) For the special uses of **round** in phrasal verbs, look at the verb entries. For example, the meaning of **come round to sth** is given in the phrasal verb section of the entry for **come**. **1** moving in a circle: *Everybody joins hands and dances round.* ◇ *How do you make the wheels go round?* ◇ *The children were spinning round and round.* ◇ (*figurative*) *The thought kept going round and round in her head.* **2** measuring or marking the edge or outside of sth: *a young tree measuring only 18 inches round* ◇ *They've built a high fence all round to keep intruders out.* **3** on all sides of sb/sth: *A large crowd had gathered round to watch.* **4** at various places in an area: *People stood round waiting for something to happen.* **5** in a circle or curve to face another way or the opposite way: *He turned the car round and drove back again.* ◇ *She looked round at the sound of his voice.* **6** to the other side of sth: *We walked round to the back of the house.* ◇ *The road's blocked—you'll have to drive the long way round.* **7** from one place, person, etc. to another: *They've moved all the furniture round.* ◇ *He went round interviewing people about local traditions.* ◇ *Pass the biscuits round.* ◇ *Have we enough cups to go round?* **8** (*informal*) to or at a particular place, especially where sb lives: *I'll be round in an hour.* ◇ *We've invited the Frasers round this evening.* ⇨ note at AROUND **IDM** **,round a'bout 1** in the area near a place: *in Oxford and the villages round about* **2** approximately: *We're leaving round about ten.* ◇ *A new roof will cost round about £3000.* —more at TIME

■ *prep.* (*especially BrE*) (*AmE* usually **around**) **1** in a circle: *the first woman to sail round the world* ◇ *The earth moves round the sun.* **2** on, to or from the other side of sth: *Our house is round the next bend.* ◇ *There she is, coming round the corner.* ◇ *There must be a way round the problem.* **3** on all sides of sb/sth; surrounding sb/sth: *She put her arms round him.* ◇ *He had a scarf round his neck.* ◇ *They were all sitting round the table.* **4** in or to many parts of sth: *She looked all round the room.* **5** to fit in with particular people, ideas, etc: *He has to organize his life round the kids.* ⇨ note at AROUND **IDM** **,round 'here** near where you are now or where you live: *There are no decent schools round here.*

■ *noun*
STAGE IN PROCESS | **1** a set of events which form part of a longer process: *the next round of peace talks* ◇ *a new round of pay bargaining* ◇ *the final round of voting in the election*
IN SPORT | **2** a stage in a sports competition: *the qualifying rounds of the National Championships* ◇ *Rafter was*

knocked *out of the tournament in the third round.* **3** a stage in a boxing or WRESTLING match: *The fight only lasted five rounds.* **4** a complete game of golf; a complete way around the COURSE in some other sports, such as SHOWJUMPING: *We played a round of golf.* ◇ *the first horse to jump a clear round*
REGULAR ACTIVITIES/ROUTE | **5** a regular series of activities: *the daily round of school life* ◇ *Her life is one long round of parties and fun.* **6** a regular route that sb takes when delivering or collecting sth; a regular series of visits that sb makes: *Dr Green was on her daily ward rounds.* ◇ (*BrE*) *a postman on his delivery round*—see also MILK ROUND, PAPER ROUND
DRINKS | **7** a number of drinks bought by one person for all the others in a group: *a round of drinks* ◇ *It's my round* (= it is my turn to pay for the next set of drinks).
BREAD | **8** (*BrE*) a whole slice of bread; sandwiches made from two whole slices of bread: *Who's for another round of toast?* ◇ *two rounds of beef sandwiches*
CIRCULAR OBJECT | **9** a circular object or piece of sth: *Cut the pastry into rounds.*
OF APPLAUSE/CHEERS | **10** ~ **of applause/cheers** a short period during which people show their approval of sb/sth by CLAPPING, etc: *There was a great round of applause when the dance ended.*
SHOT | **11** a single shot from a gun; a bullet for one shot: *They fired several rounds at the crowd.* ◇ *We only have three rounds of ammunition left.*
SONG | **12** (*music*) a song for two or more voices in which each sings the same tune but starts at a different time
IDM **do/go the 'rounds (of sth) 1** (*BrE*) (*AmE* **make the 'rounds**) if news or a joke **does the rounds**, it is passed on quickly from one person to another **2** (*also* **make the 'rounds** *AmE, BrE*) to go around from place to place, especially when looking for work or support for a political CAMPAIGN, etc: *He's doing the rounds of insurance firms.* **in the 'round 1** (of a work of art) made so that it can be seen from all sides: *an opportunity to see Canova's work in the round* **2** (of a theatre or play) with the people watching all around a central stage

■ *verb* **1** [VN] to go around a corner of a building, a bend in the road, etc: *The boat rounded the tip of the island.* ◇ *We rounded the bend at high speed.* **2** to make sth into a round shape; to form into a round shape: [VN] *She rounded her lips and whistled.* ◇ [V] *His eyes rounded with horror.* **3** [VN] ~ **sth (up/down) (to sth)** to increase or decrease a number to the next highest or lowest whole number
PHRV **,round sth↔'off (with sth) 1** (*AmE* also **,round sth↔'out**) to finish an activity or complete sth in a good or suitable way: *She rounded off the tour with a concert at Carnegie Hall.* **2** to take the sharp or rough edges off sth: *You can round off the corners with sandpaper.* **'round on sb** to suddenly speak angrily to sb and criticize or attack them: *He rounded on journalists, calling them 'a pack of vultures'.* **,round sb/sth↔'up 1** to find and gather together people, animals or things: *I rounded up a few friends for a party.* ◇ *The cattle are rounded up in the evenings.* **2** if police or soldiers **round up** a group of people, they find them and arrest or capture them: *A number of suspects were rounded up and questioned.*—related noun ROUND-UP

round·about /'raʊndəbaʊt/ *noun, adj.*
■ *noun* (*BrE*) **1** (*AmE* **'traffic circle, ro·tary**) a place where two or more roads meet, forming a circle that all traffic must go around in the same direction: *At the roundabout, take the second exit.* **2** (*AmE* **'merry-go-round**) a circular platform for children to play on in a park, etc. that is pushed round while the children are sitting on it **3** (*BrE*) = MERRY-GO-ROUND (1) **IDM** see SWING *n.*
■ *adj.* [usually before noun] not done or said using the shortest, simplest or most direct way possible: *It was a difficult and roundabout trip.* ◇ *He told us, in a very roundabout way, that he was thinking of leaving.*

'round bracket *noun* (*BrE*) = BRACKET

round·ed /'raʊndɪd/ *adj.* [usually before noun] **1** having a round shape: *a surface with rounded edges* ◇ *rounded*

R

shoulders **2** having a wide variety of qualities that combine to produce sth pleasant, complete and balanced: *a smooth rounded taste/sound* ◊ *a fully rounded education—*see also WELL ROUNDED

roundel /ˈraʊndl/ *noun* (*technical*) a circular design that is used as a decoration or to identify an aircraft

round·ers /ˈraʊndəz; *AmE* -ərz/ *noun* [U] a British game played especially in schools by two teams using a bat and ball. Each player tries to hit the ball and then run around the four sides of a square before the other team can return the ball.—compare BASEBALL

round-eyed *adj.* with eyes that are fully open because of surprise, fear, etc.

round·ly /ˈraʊndli/ *adv.* strongly or by a large number of people: *The report has been roundly criticized.* ◊ *They were roundly defeated* (= they lost by a large number of points).

round 'robin *noun* **1** a letter that has been signed by a large number of people who wish to express their opinions about sth **2** (*sport*) a competition in which every player or team plays every other player or team

round-'shouldered *adj.* with shoulders that are bent forward or sloping downwards

'round-table *adj.* [only before noun] (of discussions, meetings, etc.) at which everyone is equal and has the same rights: *round-table talks/negotiations*

round-the-'clock (also **a,round-the-'clock**) *adj.* [only before noun] lasting or happening all day and night: *round-the-clock nursing care—*see also CLOCK

round 'trip *noun* [C,U] a journey to a place and back again: *a 30-mile round trip to work* ◊ (*AmE*) *It's 30 miles round trip to work.* ▶ **round-'trip** *adj.* (*AmE*): *a round-trip ticket—*see also RETURN TICKET

'round-up *noun* [usually sing.] **1** a summary of the most important points of a particular subject, especially the news: *We'll be back after the break with a round-up of today's other stories.* **2** an act of bringing people or animals together in one place for a particular purpose: *the round-up of sheep for shearing*

round·worm /ˈraʊndwɜːm; *AmE* -wɜːrm/ *noun* a small worm that lives in the INTESTINES of pigs, humans and some other animals

rouse /raʊz/ *verb* **1** [VN] ~ **sb** (**from sleep/bed**) (*formal*) to wake sb up, especially when they are sleeping deeply: *The telephone roused me from my sleep at 6 a.m.* ◊ *Nicky roused her with a gentle nudge.* **2** ~ **sb/yourself** (**to sth**) to make sb want to start doing sth when they were not active or interested in doing it: [VN] *A lot of people were roused to action by the appeal.* ◊ [VN to inf] *Richard couldn't rouse himself to say anything in reply.* **3** [VN] (*formal*) to make sb feel a particular emotion: *to rouse sb's anger/fear/curiosity* ◊ *What roused your suspicions* (= what made you suspicious)? **4** [VN] [usually passive] to make sb angry, excited or full of emotion: *Chris is not easily roused.—*see also AROUSE

rous·ing /ˈraʊzɪŋ/ *adj.* [usually before noun] **1** full of energy and enthusiasm: *a rousing cheer* ◊ *The team was given a rousing reception by the fans.* **2** intended to make other people feel enthusiastic about sth: *a rousing speech*

roust /raʊst/ *verb* [VN] (*AmE*) ~ **sb** (**from sth**) to disturb sb or make them move from a place

roust·about /ˈraʊstəbaʊt/ *noun* (*especially AmE*) a man with no special skills who does temporary work, for example on an OIL RIG or in a CIRCUS

rout /raʊt/ *noun, verb*
■ *noun* [sing.] a situation in which sb is defeated easily and completely in a battle or competition: *Only the skill of the goalkeeper prevented the match from turning into a rout.* IDM **put sb to 'rout** (*literary*) to defeat sb easily and completely
■ *verb* [VN] to defeat sb completely in a competition, a battle, etc: *The Buffalo Bills routed the Atlanta Falcons 41–14.*

route /ruːt; *AmE* also raʊt/ *noun, verb*
■ *noun* **1** ~ (**from A to B**) a way that you follow to get from one place to another: *Which is the best route to take?* ◊

Motorists are advised to find an alternative route. ◊ *a scenic/coastal route* ◊ *the quickest route from Florence to Rome* ◊ *an escape route—*see also EN ROUTE **2** a fixed way along which a bus, train, etc. regularly travels or goods are regularly sent: *The house is not on a bus route.* ◊ *shipping routes* ◊ *a cycle route* (= a path that is only for cyclists) **3** ~ (**to sth**) a particular way of achieving sth: *the route to fame/power/success* **4** used before the number of a main road in the US: *Route 66*
■ *verb* (**rout·ing** or **route·ing**, **rout·ed**, **rout·ed**) [VN] [usually +adv./prep.] to send sb/sth by a particular route: *Satellites route data all over the globe.*

rou·tine /ruːˈtiːn/ *noun, adj.*
■ *noun* **1** [C,U] the normal order and way in which you regularly do things: *We are trying to get the baby into a routine for feeding and sleeping.* ◊ *Make exercise a part of your daily routine.* ◊ *We clean and repair the machines as a matter of routine.* **2** [U] (*disapproving*) a situation in which life is boring because things are always done in the same way: *She needed a break from routine.* **3** [C] a series of movements, jokes, etc. that are part of a performance: *a dance routine* **4** [C] (*computing*) a list of instructions that enable a computer to perform a particular task
■ *adj.* [usually before noun] **1** done or happening as a normal part of a particular job, situation or process: *routine enquiries/questions/tests* ◊ *The fault was discovered during a routine check.* **2** not unusual or different in any way: *He died of a heart attack during a routine operation.* **3** (*disapproving*) ordinary and boring SYN DULL: *a routine job/task/life* ◊ *This type of work rapidly becomes routine.* ▶ **rou·tine·ly** *adv.*: *Visitors are routinely checked as they enter the building.*

rove /rəʊv; *AmE* roʊv/ *verb* **1** (*written*) to travel from one place to another, often with no particular purpose [V +adv./prep.] *A quarter of a million refugees roved around the country.* ◊ [VN] *bands of thieves who roved the countryside.* **2** [V, usually +adv./prep.] if sb's eyes rove, the person keeps looking in different directions: *Ali's eyes roved over the map.*

rover /ˈrəʊvə(r); *AmE* ˈroʊ-/ *noun* (*literary*) a person who likes to travel a lot rather than live in one place

rov·ing /ˈrəʊvɪŋ; *AmE* ˈroʊ-/ *adj.* [usually before noun] travelling from one place to another and not staying anywhere permanently: *a roving reporter for ABC news* ◊ *Patrick's roving lifestyle takes him between London and Los Angeles.* IDM **have a roving 'eye** (*old-fashioned*) to always be looking for the chance to have a new sexual relationship

row¹ /rəʊ; *AmE* roʊ/ *noun, verb—*see also ROW²
■ *noun* **1** ~ (**of sb/sth**) a number of people standing or sitting next to each other in a line; a number of objects arranged in a line: *a row of children/shops/trees* ◊ *We sat in a row at the back of the room.* ◊ *The vegetables were planted in neat rows.* **2** a line of seats in a cinema/movie theater, etc: *Let's sit in the back row.* ◊ *Our seats are five rows from the front.* **3** a complete line of stitches in knitting or CROCHET—picture at SEW **4** (**Row**) used in the name of some roads: *Manor Row* **5** [usually sing.] an act of rowing a boat; the period of time spent doing this: *We went for a row on the lake.—*see also DEATH ROW, SKID ROW IDM **in a 'row 1** if sth happens several times in a row, it happens in exactly the same way each time, and nothing different happens in the time between: *This is her third win in a row.* **2** if sth happens for several days, etc. in a row, it happens on each of those days: *Inflation has fallen for the third month in a row.*
■ *verb* **1** to move a boat through water using OARS (= long wooden poles with flat ends): [V] *We rowed around the island.* ◊ [VN] *Grace rowed the boat out to sea again.* **2** [VN] to take sb somewhere in a boat with OARS: *The fisherman rowed us back to the shore.*

row² /raʊ/ *noun, verb—*see also ROW¹
■ *noun* (*informal, especially BrE*) **1** [C] ~ (**over sth**) a serious disagreement between people, organizations, etc. about sth: *A row has broken out over education.* **2** [C] a noisy argument between two or more people SYN QUARREL: *She left him after a blazing row.* ◊ *family rows* ◊ *He*

had a row with his son. **3** [sing.] a loud unpleasant noise [SYN] DIN, RACKET: *Who's making that row?*

■ *verb* [V] **~ (with sb)** (*BrE, informal*) to have a noisy argument: *Mike and Sue are always rowing.* ◊ *She had rowed with her parents about her boyfriend.*

rowan /'rəʊən; 'raʊən; *AmE* 'roʊən; 'raʊən/ (also **rowan tree**, ˌmountain 'ash**) *noun* a small tree that has red berries in the autumn/fall

row·boat /'rəʊbəʊt; *AmE* 'roʊboʊt/ *noun* (*AmE*) = ROWING BOAT

rowdy /'raʊdi/ *adj.* (**row·dier, row·di·est**) (of people) making a lot of noise or likely to cause trouble: *a rowdy crowd at the pub* ► **row·dily** *adv.* **row·di·ness** *noun* [U] **rowdy** *noun* (*pl.* **-ies**): *rowdies and troublemakers*

rowdy·ism /'raʊdiɪzəm/ *noun* [U] behaviour that is noisy and causes trouble

rower /'rəʊə(r); *AmE* 'roʊ-/ *noun* a person who rows a boat

row house /'rəʊ haʊs; *AmE* 'roʊ/ *noun* (*AmE*) = TERRACED HOUSE

row·ing /'rəʊɪŋ; *AmE* 'roʊɪŋ/ *noun* [U] the sport or activity of travelling in a boat using OARS: *to go rowing*

'**rowing boat** (*BrE*) (*AmE* **row·boat**) *noun* a small open boat that you row with OARS—picture at BOAT

'**rowing machine** *noun* a piece of sports equipment on which you make the same movements as sb who is rowing a boat

row·lock /'rɒlək; 'rəʊlɒk; *AmE* 'rɑːl-; 'roʊlɑːk/ (*BrE*) (*AmE* **oar·lock**) *noun* a device fixed to the side of a boat for holding an OAR

royal /'rɔɪəl/ *adj., noun*

■ *adj.* [only before noun] **1** connected with or belonging to the king or queen of a country: *the royal family* ◊ *the royal household*—compare REGAL **2** (*abbr.* **R**) used in the names of organizations that serve or are supported by a king or queen: *the Royal Navy* ◊ *the Royal Society for the Protection of Birds* **3** impressive; suitable for a king or queen: *We were given a royal welcome.* [IDM] **the royal 'we'** the use of 'we' to mean 'I', used traditionally by a king or queen

■ *noun* [usually pl.] (*informal*) a member of a royal family

ˌroyal 'blue *adj.* deep bright blue ► ˌroyal 'blue *noun* [U]

ˌRoyal Com'mission *noun* **~ (on/into sth)|** **~ (to do sth)** (in Britain) a group of people who are officially chosen to examine a particular law or subject and suggest any changes or new laws that should be introduced

ˌRoyal 'Highness *noun* (**His/Her/Your Royal Highness**) a title of respect used when talking to or about a member of the royal family: *Their Royal Highnesses, the Duke and Duchess of Kent*

roy·al·ist /'rɔɪəlɪst/ *noun* a person who believes that a country should have a king or queen [SYN] MONARCHIST—compare REPUBLICAN ► **roy·al·ist** *adj.*

roy·al·ly /'rɔɪəli/ *adv.* (*old-fashioned*) very well; in a very impressive way or to a great degree

roy·alty /'rɔɪəlti/ *noun* (*pl.* **-ies**) **1** [U] one or more members of a royal family: *The gala evening was attended by royalty and politicians.* ◊ *We were treated like royalty.* **2** [C, usually pl.] a sum of money that is paid to sb who has written a book, piece of music, etc. each time that it is sold or performed: *All royalties from the record will go to Aids charities.* ◊ *She received £2000 in royalties.* **3** [C, usually pl.] a sum of money that is paid by an oil or MINING company to the owner of the land that they are working on

RP /ˌɑː 'piː; *AmE* ˌɑːr/ *noun* [U] the abbreviation for 'received pronunciation' (the standard form of British pronunciation, based on educated speech in Southern England): *RP is the accent most commonly taught in language schools.*

RPI /ˌɑː piː 'aɪ; *AmE* ˌɑːr/ *abbr.* RETAIL PRICE INDEX

rpm /ˌɑː piː 'em; *AmE* ˌɑːr/ *abbr.* revolutions per minute (a measurement of the speed of an engine or a record when it is playing)

RRP /ˌɑː(r) ɑː 'piː; *AmE* ˌɑːr ɑːr/ *abbr.* recommended retail price

RSA /ˌɑːr es 'eɪ/ *abbr.* (*BrE*) Royal Society of Arts

RSI /ˌɑːr es 'aɪ/ *noun* [U] the abbreviation for 'repetitive strain injury' (pain and swelling, especially in the arms and hands, caused by performing the same movement many times in a job or an activity): *The spread of computers in offices has led to a rise in cases of RSI.*

RSVP (*BrE*) (also **R.S.V.P.** *AmE, BrE*) /ˌɑːr es viː 'piː/ *abbr.* (written on invitations) please reply (from French 'répondez s'il vous plaît')

Rt Hon *abbr.* (*BrE*) (in writing) RIGHT HONOURABLE

Rt Revd (also **Rt. Rev.**) *abbr.* (*BrE*) (in writing) RIGHT REVEREND

rub /rʌb/ *verb, noun*

■ *verb* (**-bb-**) **1 ~ sth (with sth)** to move your hand, or sth such as a cloth, backwards and forwards over a surface while pressing firmly: [VN] *She rubbed her chin thoughtfully.* ◊ *Rub the surface with sandpaper before painting.* ◊ *The cat rubbed itself against my legs.* ◊ [V] *I rubbed at the stain on the cloth.* ◊ *Animals had been rubbing against the trees.* ◊ [VN-ADJ] *Rub the surface smooth.* **2 ~ (sth) (together)** to press two surfaces against each other and move them backwards and forwards; to be pressed together and move in this way: [VN] *She rubbed her hands in delight.* ◊ [V] *It sounded like two pieces of wood rubbing together.* **3 ~ (on/against sth)** (of a surface) to move backwards and forwards many times against sth while pressing it, especially causing pain or damage: [V] *The back of my shoe is rubbing.* ◊ *The wheel is rubbing on the mudguard.* ◊ [VN-ADJ] *The horse's neck was rubbed raw* (= until the skin came off) *where the rope had been.* [also VN] **4** [VN+*adv./prep.*] to spread a liquid or other substance over a surface while pressing firmly: *She rubbed the lotion into her skin.* [IDM] **rub sb's 'nose in it** (*informal*) to keep reminding sb in an unkind way of their past mistakes **rub 'salt into the wound | rub 'salt into sb's wounds** to make a difficult experience even more difficult for sb **rub 'shoulders with sb** (*AmE* also **rub 'elbows with sb**) to meet and spend time with a famous person, socially or as part of your job **rub sb up the wrong 'way** (*BrE*) (*AmE* **rub sb the wrong 'way**) (*informal*) to make sb annoyed or angry, often without intending to, by doing or saying sth that offends them—more at TWO [PHRV] ˌrub a'long (with sb/together) (*BrE, informal*) (of two people) to live or work together in a satisfactory way ˌrub sb/oneself/sth↔'down to rub the skin of a person, horse, etc. hard with sth to make it clean and dry: *I came out of the water and rubbed myself down with a towel.* ˌrub sth↔'down to make sth smooth by rubbing it with a special material ˌrub it 'in|ˌrub sth 'in [no passive] to keep reminding sb of sth they feel embarrassed about and want to forget: *I know I was stupid; you don't have to rub it in.* ˌrub 'off (on/onto sb) (of personal qualities, behaviour, opinions, etc.) to become part of a person's character as a result of that person spending time with sb who has those qualities, etc: *Her sense of fun has rubbed off on her children.* ˌrub sth↔'off (sth)|ˌrub 'off to remove sth or to be removed by rubbing: *She rubbed off the dead skin.* ◊ *The gold colouring had begun to rub off.* ◊ (*BrE*) *If you write on the blackboard, rub it off at the end of the lesson.* ˌrub sb↔'out (*AmE, slang*) to murder sb ˌrub sth↔'out (*BrE*) (also **erase** *AmE, BrE*) to remove the marks made by a pencil, etc., using a RUBBER: *to rub out a mistake/word/drawing*

■ *noun* **1** [C, usually sing.] an act of rubbing a surface: *She gave her knee a quick rub.* **2 (the rub)** [sing.] (*formal or humorous*) a problem or difficulty: *The hotel is in the middle of nowhere and there lies the rub. We don't have a car.*

rub·ber /'rʌbə(r)/ *noun* **1** [U] a strong substance that can be stretched and does not allow liquids to pass through it, used for making tyres, boots, etc. It is made from the juice of a tropical plant or is produced using chemicals: *a ball made of rubber* ◊ *a rubber tree*—see also FOAM RUBBER **2** [C] (*BrE*) (also **eraser** *AmE, BrE*) a small piece of rubber or a similar substance, used for removing pencil marks from paper; a piece of soft material used for removing chalk marks from a BLACKBOARD **3** [C]

æ	ɑː	e	ɜː	ə	ɪ	iː	i	ɒ	ɔː	ʌ	ʊ	u	uː
cat	father	ten	bird	about	sit	see	many	got	saw	cup	put	actual	too
								(BrE)					

R

(*old-fashioned, informal, especially AmE*) = CONDOM **4** [C] (in some card games or sports) a competition consisting of a series of games or matches between the same teams or players ▶ **rub·ber** *adj.* [usually before noun]: *a rubber ball ◊ rubber gloves*

,rubber **'band** (*BrE* also e,lastic **'band**) *noun* a thin circular piece of rubber used for holding things together—picture at STATIONERY

,rubber **'boot** *noun* (*AmE*) = WELLINGTON

,rubber **'bullet** *noun* a bullet made of rubber intended to injure but not to kill people, used by the army or police to control violent crowds

,rubber **'dinghy** (also **dinghy**) (*AmE* also ,rubber **'raft**) *noun* a small boat made of rubber that is filled with air, used especially for rescuing people from ships and planes—picture at BOAT

rub·ber·ized (*BrE* also **-ised**) /ˈrʌbəraɪzd/ *adj.* [only before noun] covered with rubber: *rubberized cloth*

rub·ber·neck /ˈrʌbənek; *AmE* -bərn-/ *verb* [V] (*informal, especially AmE*) to turn to look at sth while you are driving past it

'rubber **plant** *noun* a plant with thick shiny green leaves, often grown indoors

,rubber **'stamp** *noun* **1** a small tool that you hold in your hand and use for printing the date, the name of an organization, etc. on a document—picture at STATIONERY **2** (*disapproving*) a person or group that automatically gives approval to the actions or decisions of others: *Parliament is seen as a rubber stamp for decisions made elsewhere.*

,rubber-'stamp *verb* [VN] (often *disapproving*) to give official approval to a law, plan, decision, etc., especially without considering it carefully

rub·bery /ˈrʌbəri/ *adj.* **1** looking or feeling like rubber: *The eggs were overcooked and rubbery. ◊ He had large rubbery lips.* **2** (of legs or knees) feeling weak and unable to support your weight: *They leaned against each other on rubbery legs.*

rub·bing /ˈrʌbɪŋ/ *noun* a copy of writing or a design on a piece of stone or metal that is made by placing a piece of paper over it and rubbing with chalk, a pencil, etc.—see also BRASS RUBBING

'rubbing **alcohol** *noun* [U] (*AmE*) = SURGICAL SPIRIT

rub·bish /ˈrʌbɪʃ/ *noun, verb*
- *noun* [U] **1** (*especially BrE*) things that you throw away because you no longer want or need them: *a rubbish bag/bin ◊ a rubbish dump/heap/tip ◊ The streets were littered with rubbish. ◊ garden/household rubbish*—see also GARBAGE, TRASH **2** (*BrE, informal*) (also used as an adjective) something that you think is of poor quality: *I thought the play was rubbish! ◊ Do we have to listen to this rubbish music? ◊ (BrE, informal) comments, ideas, etc. that you think are stupid or wrong* SYN NONSENSE: *Rubbish! You're not fat! ◊ You're talking a load of rubbish! ◊ It's not rubbish—it's true!*
- *verb* (*AmE* **trash**) [VN] (*BrE, informal*) to criticize sb/sth severely or treat them as though they are of no value

---

BRITISH / AMERICAN
rubbish / garbage / trash / refuse

Rubbish is the usual word in *BrE* for the things that you throw away because you no longer want or need them. **Garbage** and **trash** are both used in *AmE*. Inside the home, **garbage** tends to mean waste food and other wet material, while **trash** is paper, cardboard and dry material.

In *BrE*, you put your **rubbish** in a **dustbin** in the street to be collected by the **dustmen**. In *AmE*, your **garbage** and **trash** goes in a **garbage / trash can** in the street and is collected by **garbage men / collectors**.

Refuse is a formal word and is used in both *BrE* and *AmE*. **Refuse collector** is the formal word for a dustman or garbage collector.

---

rub·bishy /ˈrʌbɪʃi/ *adj.* (*BrE, informal*) of very poor quality: *rubbishy old films*

rub·ble /ˈrʌbl/ *noun* [U] broken stones or bricks from a building or wall that has been destroyed or damaged: *The bomb reduced the houses to rubble.*

Rube Goldberg /ˌruːb ˈɡəʊldbɜːɡ; *AmE* ˈɡoʊldbɜːrɡ/ (*AmE*) *adj.* [only before noun] (*humorous*) = HEATH ROBINSON

ru·bella /ruːˈbelə/ *noun* [U] (especially *medical*) = GERMAN MEASLES

Ru·bi·con /ˈruːbɪkən; *AmE* -kɑːn/ (**the Rubicon**) *noun* [sing.] the point at which a decision has been taken which can no longer be changed: *Today we cross the Rubicon. There is no going back* ORIGIN From the **Rubicon**, a stream which formed the border between Italy and Gaul. When Julius Caesar broke the law by crossing it with his army in 49BC, it led inevitably to war.

ru·bi·cund /ˈruːbɪkənd/ *adj.* (*literary*) (of a person's face) having a healthy red colour

ruble *noun* (especially *AmE*) = ROUBLE

ru·bric /ˈruːbrɪk/ *noun* (*formal*) a title or set of instructions written in a book, an exam paper, etc.

ruby /ˈruːbi/ *noun* (*pl.* **-ies**) **1** [C] a dark red precious stone: *a ruby ring* **2** [U] a dark red colour ▶ **ruby** *adj.*: *ruby lips*

,ruby **'wedding** (*BrE*) (*AmE* ,ruby anni'versary) (also ,ruby **'wedding anniversary** *AmE, BrE*) *noun* the 40th anniversary of a wedding—compare DIAMOND WEDDING, GOLDEN WEDDING, SILVER WEDDING

RUC /ˌɑː juː ˈsiː; *AmE* ˌɑːr/ *abbr.* Royal Ulster Constabulary (the police force in Northern Ireland)

ruched /ruːʃt/ *adj.* (of fabric, clothes, etc.) sewn together so that they hang in folds: *ruched curtains*

ruck /rʌk/ *noun, verb*
- *noun* **1** [C] (in rugby) a group of players who gather round the ball when it is lying on the ground and push each other in order to get the ball **2** [sing.] a group of people standing closely together or fighting **3** (**the ruck**) [sing.] (*disapproving*) ordinary people or events: *She saw marriage to him as a way out of the ruck.*
- *verb* [V] (in rugby) to do or take part in a ruck (1) PHRV ,ruck **'up**|,ruck sth↔'up (of fabric) to form untidy folds; to make sth do this: *Your dress is rucked up at the back.*

ruck·sack /ˈrʌksæk/ (*BrE*) (also **back·pack** *AmE, BrE*) *noun* a large bag, often supported on a light metal frame, carried on the back and used especially by people who go climbing or walking—picture at BAG

ruckus /ˈrʌkəs/ *noun* [sing.] (*informal, especially AmE*) a situation in which there is a lot of noisy activity, confusion or argument

ruc·tions /ˈrʌkʃnz/ *noun* [pl.] (*especially BrE*) angry protests or arguments: *There'll be ructions if her father ever finds out.*

rud·der /ˈrʌdə(r)/ *noun* a piece of wood or metal at the back of a boat or an aircraft that is used for controlling its direction—picture at YACHT, PLANE

rud·der·less /ˈrʌdələs; *AmE* -dərl-/ *adj.* (*formal*) with nobody in control; not knowing what to do: *At no time should a government be rudderless, without a leader.*

ruddy /ˈrʌdi/ *adj., adv.*
- *adj.* **1** (of a person's face) looking red and healthy: *ruddy cheeks ◊ a ruddy complexion* **2** (*literary*) red in colour: *a ruddy sky* **3** [only before noun] (*BrE, informal*) a mild swear word that some people use to show that they are annoyed: *I can't get the ruddy car to start!*
- *adv.* (*BrE, informal*) a mild swear word used by some people to emphasize what they are saying, especially when they are annoyed: *There was a ruddy great hole in the ceiling.*

rude /ruːd/ *adj.* (**ruder**, **rud·est**) **1** ~ (**to sb**) (**about sb/sth**)|~ (**to do sth**) having or showing a lack of respect for other people and their feelings SYN IMPOLITE: *a rude comment/remark ◊ The man was downright rude to us. ◊ She was very rude about my driving. ◊ Why are you so rude to your mother? ◊ It's rude to speak when you're eating.* **2** (*especially BrE*) (*AmE* usually **crude**) connected

---

aɪ	aʊ	eɪ	əʊ	oʊ	ɔɪ	ɪə	eə	ʊə	j	w
my	now	say	go	go	boy	near	hair	pure	yes	wet
			(BrE)	(AmE)						

with sex or the body in a way that people find offensive or embarrassing: *a rude gesture/suggestion* ◊ *Someone made a rude noise.* ◊ *The joke is too rude to repeat.* **3** [only before noun] (*written*) sudden, unpleasant and unexpected: *Those expecting good news will get a rude shock.* ◊ *If the players think they can win this match easily, they are in for* **a rude awakening.** **4** (*literary*) made in a simple, basic way SYN PRIMITIVE: *rude shacks* ▶ **rude·ness** *noun* [U]: *She was critical to the point of rudeness.* IDM **in rude 'health** (*old-fashioned, BrE*) looking or feeling very healthy

rude·ly /ˈruːdli/ *adv.* **1** in a way that shows a lack of respect for other people and their feelings: *They brushed rudely past us.* ◊ *'What do you want?' she asked rudely.* **2** in a way that is sudden, unpleasant and unexpected: *I was rudely awakened by the phone ringing.* ◊ *As I was saying before I was so rudely interrupted …*

ru·di·men·tary /ˌruːdɪˈmentri/ *adj.* **1** (*formal*) dealing with only the most basic matters or ideas SYN BASIC: *They were given only rudimentary training in the job.* **2** (*formal or technical*) not highly or fully developed SYN BASIC: *rudimentary housing/weapons* ◊ *Health care in the village is still quite rudimentary.* ◊ *Some dinosaurs had only rudimentary teeth.*

ru·di·ments /ˈruːdɪmənts/ *noun* [pl.] **the ~ (of sth)** (*formal*) the most basic or essential facts of a particular subject, skill, etc.

rue /ruː/ *verb* (**rue·ing** or **ruing, rued, rued**) [VN] (*old-fashioned or formal*) to feel bad about sth that happened or sth that you did because it had bad results SYN REGRET: *He rued the day they had bought such a large house.*

rue·ful /ˈruːfl/ *adj.* (*written*) feeling or showing that you are sad or sorry: *a rueful expression/laugh* ◊ *Jenny gave a rueful smile.* ▶ **rue·ful·ly** /ˈruːfəli/ *adv.*: *He laughed ruefully.* ◊ *'So this is goodbye,' she said ruefully.*

ruff /rʌf/ *noun* **1** a ring of coloured or marked feathers or fur around the neck of a bird or an animal **2** a wide stiff white collar with many folds in it, worn especially in the 16th and 17th centuries

ruf·fian /ˈrʌfiən/ *noun* (*old-fashioned*) a violent man, especially one who commits crimes

ruf·fle /ˈrʌfl/ *verb, noun*
■ *verb* [VN] **1 ~ sth (up)** to disturb the smooth surface of sth, so that it is not even: *She ruffled his hair affectionately.* ◊ *The bird ruffled up its feathers.* **2** [often passive] to make sb annoyed, worried or upset: *Nothing ever seems to ruffle Susan.* ◊ *She was obviously ruffled by his question.* ◊ *He never gets ruffled, even under pressure.* IDM **ruffle sb's/a few 'feathers** (*informal*) to annoy or upset sb or a group of people: *The senator's speech ruffled a few feathers in the business world.*—more at SMOOTH *v.*
■ *noun* [usually pl.] a strip of fabric that is sewn in folds and is used to decorate a piece of clothing at the neck or wrists SYN FRILL—picture at FRILL

ruf·fled /ˈrʌfld/ *adj.* decorated with ruffles SYN FRILLED: *a ruffled blouse*

rug /rʌɡ/ *noun* **1** a piece of thick material like a small carpet that is used for covering or decorating part of a floor: *a hearth rug* (= in front of a fireplace) **2** (*BrE*) a piece of thick warm material, like a BLANKET, that is used for wrapping around your legs to keep warm IDM see PULL *v.*, SWEEP *v.*

rugby /ˈrʌɡbi/ (*sometimes* **Rugby**) (*also* **rugby 'football**) *noun* [U] a game played by two teams of 13 or 15 players, using an OVAL ball which may be kicked or carried. Teams try to put the ball over the other team's line: *a rugby ball/club/match/game* ORIGIN Named after Rugby school, where the game was first played.

Rugby 'League *noun* [U] a form of rugby, with 13 players in a team

Rugby 'Union (*also informal* **rug·ger** *especially in BrE*) *noun* [U] a form of rugby, with 15 players in a team

rug·ged /ˈrʌɡɪd/ *adj.* **1** (of the landscape) not level or smooth and having rocks rather than plants or trees: *rugged cliffs* ◊ *The countryside around here is very rugged.* ◊ *They admired the rugged beauty of the coastline.* ◊ *He*

loves the rugged outdoor life (= the lack of comfort connected with being outside). **2** [usually before noun] (*approving*) (of a man's face) having strong, attractive features **3** [usually before noun] (of a person) determined to succeed in a difficult situation, even if this means using force or upsetting other people: *a rugged individualist* **4** (of equipment, clothing, etc.) strong and designed to be used in difficult conditions: *A less rugged vehicle would never have made the trip.* ◊ *rugged outdoor clothing* ▶ **rug·ged·ly** *adv.*: *ruggedly handsome* **rug·ged·ness** *noun* [U]

rug·ger /ˈrʌɡə(r)/ *noun* [U] (*informal, especially BrE*) = RUGBY UNION

ruin /ˈruːɪn/ *verb, noun*
■ *verb* [VN] **1** to damage sth so badly that it loses all its value, pleasure, etc.; to spoil sth: *The bad weather ruined our trip.* ◊ *That one mistake ruined his chances of getting the job.* ◊ *My new shoes got ruined in the mud.* ◊ *The crops were ruined by the late frost.* **2** to make sb/sth lose all their money, their position, etc: *If she loses the court case it will ruin her.* ◊ *The country was ruined by the war.*
■ *noun* **1** [U] the state or process of being destroyed or severely damaged: *A large number of churches fell into ruin after the revolution.* **2** [U] the fact of having no money, of having lost your job, position, etc: *The divorce ultimately led to his ruin.* ◊ *The bank stepped in to save the company from financial ruin.* **3** [sing.] something that causes a person, company, etc. to lose all their money, job, position, etc: *Gambling was his ruin.* **4** [C] (*also* **ruins** [pl.]) the parts of a building that remain after it has been destroyed or severely damaged: *The old mill is now little more than a ruin.* ◊ *We visited the ruins of a Norman castle.* ◊ (*figurative*) *He was determined to build a new life out of the ruins of his career.* IDM **in 'ruins** destroyed or severely damaged: *Years of fighting have left the area in ruins.* ◊ *The scandal left his reputation in ruins.*—more at RACK *n.*

ruin·ation /ˌruːɪˈneɪʃn/ *noun* [U] (*formal*) the process of destroying sth/sb or being destroyed: *Urban development has led to the ruination of vast areas of countryside.*

ruined /ˈruːɪnd/ *adj.* [only before noun] (of a building, town, etc.) destroyed or severely damaged so that only parts remain: *a ruined castle*

ruin·ous /ˈruːɪnəs/ *adj.* (*written*) **1** costing a lot of money and more than you can AFFORD: *ruinous legal fees* **2** causing serious problems or damage: *The decision was to prove ruinous.* **3** (*formal*) (of a town, building, etc.) destroyed or severely damaged: *a ruinous chapel* ◊ *The buildings were in a ruinous state.* ▶ **ruin·ous·ly** *adv.*: *ruinously expensive*

rule /ruːl/ *noun, verb*
■ *noun*
OF ACTIVITY/GAME **1** [C] a statement of what may, must or must not be done in a particular situation or when playing a game: *to follow/obey/observe the rules* ◊ *It's against all rules and regulations.* ◊ *to break a rule* (= not follow it) ◊ *This explains the rules under which the library operates.* ◊ *Without unwritten rules civilized life would be impossible.*—see also GROUND RULE

ADVICE **2** [C] a statement of what you are advised to do in a particular situation: *There are no hard and fast rules for planning healthy meals.* ◊ *The first rule is to make eye contact with your interviewer.*—see also GOLDEN RULE

HABIT/NORMALLY TRUE **3** [C, usually sing.] a habit; the normal state of things; what is true in most cases: *He makes it a rule never to borrow money.* ◊ *I go to bed early as a rule.* ◊ *Cold winters here are the exception rather than the rule* (= are rare). ◊ *As a general rule vegetable oils are better for you than animal fats.*

OF SYSTEM **4** [C] a statement of what is possible according to a particular system, for example the grammar of a language: *the rules of grammar*

GOVERNMENT/CONTROL **5** [U] the government of a country or control of a group of people by a particular person, group or system: *under Communist/colonial British/civilian/military rule* ◊ *majority rule* (= government by the political party that most people have voted for) ◊ *The 1972* *act imposed **direct rule** from Westminster.*—see also HOME RULE

MEASURING TOOL | **6** [C] a measuring instrument with a straight edge—see also SLIDE RULE

IDM **bend/stretch the 'rules** to change the rules to suit a particular person or situation **play by sb's (own) 'rules** if sb **plays by their own rules** or makes other people **play by their rules**, they set the conditions for doing business or having a relationship **play by the 'rules** to deal fairly and honestly with people **the rules of the 'game** the standards of behaviour that most people accept or that actually operate in a particular area of life or business **the rule of 'law** the condition in which all members of society, including its rulers, accept the authority of the law **a rule of 'thumb** a practical method of doing or measuring sth, usually based on past experience rather than on exact measurement **work to 'rule** to follow the rules of your job in a very strict way in order to cause delay, as a form of protest against your employer or your working conditions—see also WORK-TO-RULE—more at EXCEPTION

■ *verb*

GOVERN/CONTROL | **1** ~ **(over sb/sth)** to control and have authority over a country, a group of people, etc: [VN] *At that time John ruled England.* ◊ (*figurative*) *Eighty million years ago, dinosaurs ruled the earth.* ◊ *Charles I ruled for eleven years.* ◊ *She once ruled over a vast empire.* ◊ (*figurative*) *After the revolution, anarchy ruled.* **2** [VN] (*often passive*) (*often disapproving*) to be the main thing that influences and controls sb/sth: *The pursuit of money ruled his life.* ◊ *We live in a society where we are ruled by the clock.*

GIVE OFFICIAL DECISION | **3** ~ **(on sth)** to give an official decision about sth: [V] *The court will rule on the legality of the action.* ◊ *The judge ruled against/in favour of the plaintiff.* ◊ [VN-ADJ] *The deal may be ruled illegal.* ◊ [V that] *The court ruled that the women were unfairly dismissed.* [also VN to inf, VN that]

DRAW STRAIGHT LINE | **4** to draw a straight line using sth that has a firm straight edge: *Rule a line at the end of every piece of work.*

IDM **rule the 'roost** (*informal*) to be the most powerful member of a group **rule (sb/sth) with a rod of 'iron** to control a person or a group of people very severely—more at COURT *n.*, DIVIDE *v.*, HEART

PHRV **,rule 'off| ,rule sth↔'off** to separate sth from the next section of writing by drawing a line underneath it **,rule sb/sth↔'out 1** ~ **(as sth)** to state that sth is not possible or that sb/sth is not suitable **SYN** EXCLUDE: *Police have not ruled out the possibility that the man was murdered.* ◊ *The proposed solution was ruled out as too expensive.* **2** to prevent sb from doing sth; to prevent sth from happening: *His age effectively ruled him out as a possible candidate.* **,rule sb 'out of sth** [usually passive] (*in sport*) to state that a player or competitor will not be able to take part in a sporting event; to prevent a player from taking part: *Owen has been ruled out of tonight's match with a knee injury.*

'rule book (usually **the rule book**) *noun* the set of rules that must be followed in a particular job, organization or game

ruled /ruːld/ *adj.* ruled paper has lines printed across it

ruler /'ruːlə(r)/ *noun* **1** a person who rules or governs **2** a straight strip of wood, plastic or metal, marked in CENTIMETRES or INCHES, used for measuring or for drawing straight lines

rul·ing /'ruːlɪŋ/ *noun, adj.*
■ *noun* ~ **(on sth)** an official decision made by sb in a position of authority, especially a judge: *The court will make its ruling on the case next week.*
■ *adj.* [only before noun] having control over a particular group, country, etc: *the ruling party*

rum /rʌm/ *noun, adj.*
■ *noun* **1** [U, C] a strong alcoholic drink made from the juice of SUGAR CANE **2** [C] a glass of rum
■ *adj.* [usually before noun] (*old-fashioned, BrE, informal*) strange **SYN** ODD, PECULIAR

rumba (also **rhumba**) /'rʌmbə/ *noun* a fast dance originally from Cuba; a piece of music for this dance

rum·ble /'rʌmbl/ *verb, noun*
■ *verb* **1** [V] to make a long deep sound or series of sounds: *The machine rumbled as it started up.* ◊ *thunder rumbling in the distance* ◊ *I'm so hungry my stomach's rumbling.* **2** [V+adv./prep.] to move slowly and heavily, making a rumbling sound: *tanks rumbling through the streets* **3** [VN] (*BrE, informal*) to discover the truth about sb or what they are trying to hide: *They knew they had been rumbled.* **4** (*AmE, informal*) (of a GANG of young people) to fight against another GANG **PHRV** **,rumble 'on** (*written, especially BrE*) (of an argument, a dispute, etc.) to continue slowly and steadily for a long time: *Discussions rumble on over the siting of the new airport.*
■ *noun* **1** [U, C] ~ **(of sth)** a long deep sound or series of sounds: *the rumble of laughter/thunder/gunfire* ◊ *Inside, the noise of the traffic was reduced to a distant rumble.* ◊ (*figurative*) *Although an agreement has been reached, rumbles of resentment can still be heard.* **2** [C] (*AmE, informal*) a fight in the street between two or more GANGS (= groups of young people)

'rumble strip *noun* (*informal*) a series of raised strips across a road or along its edge that make a loud noise when a vehicle drives over them in order to warn the driver to slow down or that he or she is too close to the edge of the road

rum·bling /'rʌmblɪŋ/ *noun* **1** (also used as an adjective) a long deep sound or series of sounds: *the rumblings of thunder* ◊ *a rumbling noise* ◊ (*figurative*) *the rumblings of discontent* **2** [usually pl.] things that people are saying that may not be true **SYN** RUMOUR: *There are rumblings that the election may have to be postponed.*

rum·bus·tious /rʌm'bʌstʃəs/ (*especially BrE*) (*AmE usually* **ram·bunc·tious**) *adj.* [usually before noun] (*informal*) full of energy in a cheerful and noisy way **SYN** BOISTEROUS

ru·min·ant /'ruːmɪnənt/ *noun* (*technical*) any animal that brings back food from its stomach and chews it again. Cows and sheep are both ruminants. ▶ **ru·min·ant** *adj.*: *ruminant animals*

ru·min·ate /'ruːmɪneɪt/ *verb* [V, V speech] (*formal*) ~ **(on/over/about sth)** to think deeply about sth ▶ **ru·min·ation** /,ruːmɪ'neɪʃn/ *noun* [C, U]

ru·mina·tive /'ruːmɪnətɪv; *AmE* -neɪtɪv/ *adj.* (*formal*) tending to think deeply and carefully about things **SYN** PENSIVE, THOUGHTFUL: *in a ruminative mood* ▶ **ru·mina·tive·ly** *adv.*

rum·mage /'rʌmɪdʒ/ *verb, noun*
■ *verb* [V+adv./prep.] to move things around carelessly while searching for sth: *She was rummaging around in her bag for her keys.* ◊ *I rummaged through the contents of the box until I found the book I wanted.*
■ *noun* [sing.] the act of looking for sth among a group of other objects in a way that makes them untidy: *Have a rummage around in the drawer and see if you can find a pen.*

'rummage sale *noun* (*especially AmE*) = JUMBLE SALE

rummy /'rʌmi/ *noun* [U] a simple card game in which players try to collect particular combinations of cards

ru·mour (*BrE*) (*AmE* **rumor**) /'ruːmə(r)/ *noun, verb*
■ *noun* [C, U] ~ **(of/about sth)| ~ (that...)** a piece of information, or a story, that people talk about, but that may not be true: *to start/spread a rumour* ◊ *There are widespread rumours of job losses.* ◊ *Some malicious rumours are circulating about his past.* ◊ *I heard a rumour that they are getting married.* ◊ *Many of the stories are based on rumour.* ◊ ***Rumour has it*** (= people say) *that he was murdered.*
■ *verb* **(be rumoured)** to be reported as a rumour and possibly not true: [VN (that)] *It's widely rumoured that she's getting promoted.* ◊ [VN to inf] *He was rumoured to be involved in the crime.* ▶ **ru·moured** *adj.* [only before noun]: *He denied his father's rumoured love affair.*

rumour-monger (*BrE*) (*AmE* **ru·mor·mon·ger**) /'ruːmə mʌŋgə(r); *AmE* 'ruːmər/ *noun* a person who spreads rumours

s	t	v	z	ʃ	ʒ	tʃ	dʒ	θ	ð	ŋ
see	tea	van	zoo	shoe	vision	chain	jam	thin	this	sing

rump /rʌmp/ *noun* **1** [C] the round area of flesh at the top of the back legs of an animal that has four legs: *He slapped the horse on the rump.* **2** [U] (also **,rump 'steak** [C, U]) a piece of good quality meat cut from the rump of a cow **3** [C, usually sing.] (*humorous*) the part of the body that you sit on SYN BACKSIDE **4** [sing.] (*BrE*) the small or unimportant part of a group or an organization that remains when most of its members have left: *The election reduced the party to a rump.*

rum·ple /'rʌmpl/ *verb* [VN] to make sth untidy or not smooth and neat: *She rumpled his hair playfully.* ◇ *The bed was rumpled where he had slept.* ◇ *a rumpled linen suit*

rum·pus /'rʌmpəs/ *noun* [usually sing.] (*informal*) a lot of noise that is made especially by people who are complaining about sth SYN COMMOTION: *to cause a rumpus*

run /rʌn/ *verb, noun*

■ *verb* (**running, ran** /ræn/ **run**)

MOVE FAST ON FOOT | **1** [V] to move using your legs, going faster than when you walk: *Can you run as fast as Mike?* ◇ *They turned and ran when they saw us coming.* ◇ *She* **came running** *to meet us.* ◇ *The dogs ran off as soon as we appeared.* HELP In spoken English **run** can be used with **and** plus another verb, instead of with **to** and the infinitive, especially to tell somebody to hurry and do something: *Run and get your swimsuits, kids.* ◇ *I ran and knocked on the nearest door.* **2** [VN] to travel over a particular distance by running: *Who was the first person to run a mile in under four minutes?*—see also MILE **3** [V] (sometimes **go running**) to run as a sport: *She used to run when she was at college.* ◇ *I often go running before work.*

RACE | **4** ~ **(in sth)** to take part in a race: [V] *Gail Devers will be running in the 100 metres tonight.* ◇ *There are only five horses running in the first race.* ◇ *to run the marathon* ◇ *Johnson ran a fine race to take the gold medal.*—see also RUNNER (1) **5** [VN] [often passive] to make a race take place: *The Derby will be run in spite of the bad weather.*

HURRY | **6** [V+*adv. / prep.*] to hurry from one place to another: *I've spent the whole day running around after the kids.*

MANAGE | **7** [VN] to be in charge of a business, etc: *to run a hotel / store / language school* ◇ *He has no idea how to run a business.* ◇ *Stop trying to* **run my life** (= organize it) *for me.* ◇ *The shareholders want more say in how the company is run.* ◇ *a badly-run company* ◇ *state-run industries*—see also RUNNING *n.* (2)

PROVIDE | **8** [VN] to make a service, course of study, etc. available to people SYN ORGANIZE: *The college runs summer courses for foreign students.*

VEHICLE / MACHINE | **9** [VN] to own and use a vehicle or machine: *I can't afford to run a car on my salary.* **10** ~ **(on sth)** to operate or function; to make sth do this: [V] *Stan had the chainsaw running.* ◇ *Our van runs on* (= uses) *diesel.* ◇ (*figurative*) *Her life had always run smoothly before.* ◇ [VN] *Could you run the engine for a moment?*

BUSES / TRAINS | **11** [V, usually+*adv. / prep.*] to travel on a particular route: *Buses to Oxford run every half-hour.* ◇ *All the trains* **are running late** (= are leaving later than planned). **12** [VN, usually+*adv. / prep.*] to make buses, trains, etc. travel on a particular route: *They run extra trains during the rush hour.*

DRIVE SB | **13** [VN+*adv. / prep.*] (*informal*) to drive sb to a place in a car: *Shall I run you home?*

MOVE SOMEWHERE | **14** [V+*adv. / prep.*] to move, especially quickly, in a particular direction: *The car ran off the road into a ditch.* ◇ *A shiver ran down my spine.* ◇ *The sledge ran smoothly over the frozen snow.* ◇ *The old tramlines are still there but now no trams run on them.* **15** [VN+*adv. / prep.*] to move sth in a particular direction: *She ran her fingers nervously through her hair.* ◇ *I* **ran my eyes over** *the page.*

LEAD / STRETCH | **16** [+*adv. / prep.*] to lead or stretch from one place to another; to make sth do this: [V] *He had a scar running down his left cheek.* ◇ *The road runs parallel*

to the river. ◇ [VN] *We ran a cable from the lights to the stage.*

CONTINUE FOR TIME | **17** [V] ~ **(for sth)** to continue for a particular period of time without stopping: *Her last musical ran for six months on Broadway.* ◇ *This debate will* **run and run!** **18** [V] ~ **(for sth)** to operate or be valid for a particular period of time: *The permit runs for three months.* ◇ *The lease on my house only has a year left to run.*

HAPPEN | **19** [V+*adv. / prep.*] (usually used in the progressive tenses) to happen at the time mentioned: *Programmes are* **running** *a few minutes* **behind schedule** *this evening.* ◇ *The murderer was given three life sentences, to run concurrently.*

GUNS, DRUGS, etc. | **20** [VN, usually+*adv. / prep.*] to bring or take sth into a country illegally and secretly SYN SMUGGLE: *He used to run guns across the border.*—see also RUNNER

OF STORY / ARGUMENT | **21** to have particular words, contents, etc: [V] *Their argument ran something like this ...* ◇ [V speech] *'Ten shot dead by gunmen,' ran the newspaper headline.*

LIQUID | **22** [V+*adv. / prep.*] to flow: *The tears ran down her cheeks.* ◇ *Water was running all over the bathroom floor.* **23** ~ **sth (for sb)** | ~ **(sb) sth** to make liquid flow: [VN] *She ran hot water into the bucket.* ◇ *to* **run the hot tap** (= to turn it so that water flows from it) ◇ [VN, VNN] *I'll run a* **bath** *for you.* ◇ *I'll run you a bath.* **24** [V] to send out a liquid: *Who left the tap running?* ◇ *Your nose is running* (= MUCUS *is flowing from it).* ◇ *The smoke makes my eyes run.* **25** [V] ~ **with sth** (usually used in the progressive tenses) to be covered with a liquid: *His face was running with sweat.* ◇ *The bathroom floor was running with water.*

OF COLOUR | **26** [V] if the colour **runs** in a piece of clothing when it gets wet, it dissolves and may come out of the clothing into other things

MELT | **27** [V] (of a solid substance) to melt: *The wax began to run.*—see also RUNNY

BE / BECOME | **28** [V-ADJ] to become different in a particular way, especially a bad way: *The river* **ran dry** (= stopped flowing) *during the drought.* ◇ *Supplies are running low.* ◇ *We've* **run short** *of milk.* ◇ *You've got your rivals* **running scared.** **29** [V] ~ **at sth** to be at or near a particular level: *Inflation was running at 26%.*

OF NEWSPAPER / MAGAZINE | **30** [VN] to print and publish an item or a story: *On advice from their lawyers they decided not to run the story.*

A TEST / CHECK | **31** [VN] ~ **a test / check (on sth)** to do a test/check on sth: *The doctors decided to run some more tests on the blood samples.*

IN ELECTION | **32** [V] ~ **(for sb/sth)** | ~ **(in sth)** to be a candidate in an election for a political position, especially in the US: *Clinton ran a second time in 1996.* ◇ *to run for president* ◇ *to run in the election*—compare STAND *v.* (16)

OF TIGHTS / STOCKINGS | **33** [V] (*AmE*) if TIGHTS or STOCKINGS **run**, a long thin hole appears in them SYN LADDER

IDM Most idioms containing **run** are at the entries for the nouns and adjectives in the idioms, for example **run riot** is at **riot**. **come 'running** to be pleased to do what sb wants: *She knew she had only to call and he would come running.* **'run for it** (often used in orders) to run in order to escape from sb/sth **,up and 'running** working fully and correctly: *It will be a lot easier when we have the database up and running.*

PHRV **'run across sb/sth** to meet sb or find sth by chance

,run 'after sb (*informal*) to try to have a romantic or sexual relationship with sb: *He's always running after younger women.* **,run 'after sb/sth** to run to try to catch sb/sth

,run a'long (*old-fashioned, informal*) used in orders to tell sb, especially a child, to go away

,run a'round with sb (*AmE* also **'run with sb**) (usually *disapproving*) to spend a lot of time with sb: *She's always running around with older men.*

'run at sb [no passive] to run towards sb to attack or as if to attack them: *He ran at me with a knife.*

æ	ɑː	e	ɜː	ə	ɪ	iː	i	ɒ	ɔː	ʌ	ʊ	u	uː
cat	father	ten	bird	about	sit	see	many	got	saw	cup	put	actual	too
								(BrE)					

,run a'way (from sb/...) to leave sb/a place suddenly; to escape from sb/a place: *He ran away from home at the age of thirteen.* ◊ *Looking at all the accusing faces, she felt a sudden urge to run away.*—related noun RUNAWAY ,run a'way from sth to try to avoid sth because you are shy, lack confidence, etc: *You can't just run away from the situation.* ,run a'way with you if a feeling runs away with you, it gets out of your control: *Her imagination tends to run away with her.* ,run a'way/'off with sb|,run a'way/'off (together) to leave home, your husband, wife, etc. in order to have a relationship with another person: *She ran away with her boss.* ◊ *She and her boss ran away together.* ,run a'way with sth 1 to win sth clearly or easily 2 (*spoken*) to believe sth that is not true: *I don't want you to run away with the impression that all I do is sign cheques all day.*

,run back 'over sth to discuss or consider sth again [SYN] REVIEW: *I'll run back over the procedure once again.* ,run sth 'by/'past sb (*informal*) to show sb sth or tell sb about an idea in order to see their reaction to it

,run 'down 1 to lose power or stop working: *The battery has run down.* 2 to stop functioning gradually or become smaller in size or number: *British manufacturing industry has been running down for years.*—related noun RUN-DOWN ,run sth 'down 1 to make sth lose power or stop working: *If you leave your headlights on you'll soon run down the battery.* 2 to make sth stop functioning gradually or become smaller in size or number: *The company is running down its sales force.*—related noun RUNDOWN ,run sb/sth↔'down 1 (of a vehicle or its driver) to hit sb/sth and knock them/it to the ground 2 to criticize sb/sth in an unkind way: *He's always running her down in front of other people.* 3 to find sb/sth after a search: *She finally ran the professor down in the library.*

,run sb↔'in (*old-fashioned, informal*) to arrest sb and take them to a police station ,run sth↔'in (*BrE*) (in the past) to prepare the engine of a new car for normal use by driving slowly and carefully: (*figurative*) *Whatever system you choose, it must be run in properly.*

,run 'into sb to meet sb by chance: *Guess who I ran into today!* 'run into sth 1 to enter an area of bad weather while travelling: *We ran into thick fog on the way home.* 2 to experience difficulties, etc: *Be careful not to run into debt.* ◊ *to run into danger/trouble/difficulties* 3 to reach a particular level or amount: *Her income runs into six figures* (= is more than £100000, $100000, etc.). 'run into sb/sth to crash into sb/sth: *The bus went out of control and ran into a line of people.* 'run sth into sb/sth to make a vehicle crash into sb/sth: *He ran his car into a tree.*

,run 'off (*BrE*) (of a liquid) to flow out of a container ,run sth↔'off 1 to copy sth on a machine: *Could you run off twenty copies of the agenda?* 2 to cause a race to be run: *The heats of the 200 metres will be run off tomorrow.* 3 to make a liquid flow out of a container ,run 'off with sb|,run 'off (together) = RUN AWAY WITH SB ,run 'off with sth to steal sth and take it away: *The treasurer had run off with the club's funds.*

,run 'on to continue without stopping; to continue longer than is necessary or expected: *The meeting will finish promptly—I don't want it to run on.* 'run on sth [no passive] if your thoughts, a discussion, etc. run on a subject, you think or talk a lot about that subject

,run 'out 1 if a supply of sth runs out, it is used up or finished: *Time is running out for the trapped miners.* 2 if an agreement or a document runs out, it becomes no longer valid [SYN] EXPIRE ,run 'out (of sth) to use up or finish a supply of sth: *We ran out of fuel.* ◊ *Could I have a cigarette? I seem to have run out.* ,run 'out on sb (*informal*) to leave sb that you live with, especially when they need your help ,run sb↔'out [often passive] (in cricket) to make a player stop BATTING by hitting the WICKET with the ball before the player has completed his or her run ,run 'over if a container or its contents run over, the contents come over the edge of the container [SYN] OVERFLOW ,run sb/sth↔'over (of a vehicle or its driver) to knock a person or an animal down and drive over their body or a part of it: *Two children were run over and killed.* ,run 'over sth to read through or practise sth

quickly: *She ran over her notes before giving the lecture.* ,run sth 'past sb = RUN STH BY/PAST SB: *Run that past me again.*

,run sb↔'through (*literary*) to kill sb by sticking a knife, SWORD, etc. through them ,run 'through sth (*written*) 1 [no passive] to pass quickly through sth: *An angry murmur ran through the crowd.* ◊ *Thoughts of revenge kept running through his mind.* 2 [no passive] to be present in every part of sth: *A deep melancholy runs through her poetry.* 3 to discuss, repeat or read sth quickly: *He ran through the names on the list.* ◊ *Could we run through your proposals once again?* 4 to perform, act or practise sth: *Can we run through Scene 3 again, please?*—related noun RUN-THROUGH 5 to use up or spend money carelessly: *She ran through the entire amount within two years.*

'run to sth 1 to be of a particular size or amount: *The book runs to nearly 800 pages.* 2 (*especially BrE*) if you or your money will not run to sth, you do not have enough money for sth: *Our funds won't run to a trip abroad this year.*

,run sth↔'up 1 to allow a bill, debt, etc. to reach a large total: *How had he managed to run up so many debts?* 2 to make a piece of clothing quickly, especially by sewing: *to run up a blouse* 3 to raise sth, especially a flag ,run 'up against sth to experience a difficulty: *The government is running up against considerable opposition to its tax reforms.*

■ noun

ON FOOT | 1 [C] an act of running; a period of time spent running or the distance that sb runs: *I go for a run every morning.* ◊ *a five-mile run* ◊ *Catching sight of her he broke into a run* (= started running). ◊ *I decided to make a run for it* (= to escape by running). ◊ *She took the stairs at a run.*—see also FUN RUN

TRIP | 2 [C] a trip by car, plane, boat, etc., especially a short one or one that is made regularly: *They took the car out for a run.* ◊ *an enemy aircraft on a bombing run*

OF SUCCESS/FAILURE | 3 [C] a period of sth good or bad happening; a series of successes or failures: *a run of good/bad luck* ◊ *Liverpool lost to Leeds, ending an unbeaten run of 18 games.*

OF PLAY/MOVIE | 4 [C] a series of performances of a play or film/movie: *The show had a record-breaking run in the London theatre.*

OF PRODUCT | 5 [C] the amount of a product that a company decides to make at one time: *The first print run of 6000 copies sold out.*

SUDDEN DEMAND | 6 [C, usually sing.] ~ on sth a sudden demand for sth by a lot of people: *a run on the pound/dollar* ◊ *When the new currency measures were announced there was a run on the bank* (= a lot of people suddenly took their money out of the bank).

WAY THINGS HAPPEN | 7 [sing.] the ~ of sth the way things usually happen; the way things seem to be happening on a particular occasion: *In the normal run of things the only exercise he gets is climbing in and out of taxis.* ◊ (*BrE*) *Wise scored in the 15th minute against the run of play* (= although the other team had seemed more likely to score).

IN SPORTS | 8 [C] a sloping track used in skiing and some other sports: *a ski/toboggan run* 9 [C] a point scored in the game of cricket or baseball: *Our team won by four runs.*—see also HOME RUN

IN ELECTION | 10 [sing.] (*AmE*) an act of trying to get elected to public office: *He made an unsuccessful run for governor in 1998.*

FOR ANIMALS/BIRDS | 11 [C] (often in compounds) an enclosed area in which animals or birds are kept as pets or on a farm: *a chicken run*

IN MUSIC | 12 [C] a series of notes sung or played quickly up or down the SCALE

IN CARD GAMES | 13 [C] a series of cards held by one player

IN TIGHTS/STOCKINGS | 14 [C] (*AmE*) = LADDER

ILLNESS | 15 (the runs) [pl.] (*informal*) = DIARRHOEA
—see also DRY RUN, DUMMY RUN, TRIAL RUN

IDM **the common, general, ordinary, usual run (of sth)** the average type of sth: *He was very different from the general run of American movie stars.* **give sb/get/ have the 'run of sth** to give sb/get/have permission to make full use of sth: *Her dogs have the run of the house.* **give sb a (good) run for their 'money** to make sb try very hard, using all their skill and effort, in order to beat you in a game or competition **on the 'run 1** trying to avoid being captured: *He's on the run from the police.* **2** (*informal*) continuously active and moving around: *I've been on the run all day and I'm exhausted.*—more at LONG *adj.*, SHORT *adj.*

run·about /ˈrʌnəbaʊt/ *noun* (*BrE, informal*) a small car, especially one used for short journeys

run·around /ˈrʌnəraʊnd/ *noun* **IDM** **give sb the 'run-around** (*informal*) to treat sb badly by not telling them the truth, or by not giving them the help or the information they need, and sending them somewhere else

run·away /ˈrʌnəweɪ/ *adj., noun*
■ *adj.* [only before noun] **1** (of a person) having left without telling anyone: *a hostel for runaway children* **2** (of an animal or a vehicle) not under the control of its owner, rider or driver: *a runaway horse/car* **3** happening very easily or quickly, and not able to be controlled: *a runaway winner/victory* ◊ *the runaway success of her first play* ◊ *runaway inflation*
■ *noun* a person who has suddenly left or escaped from sb/sth, especially a child who has left home without telling anyone: *teenage runaways living on the streets*

run-'down *adj.* **1** (of a building or place) in very bad condition; that has not been looked after **SYN** NEGLECTED: *run-down inner-city areas* **2** (of a business, etc.) not as busy or as active as it used to be: *run-down transport services* **3** [not before noun] (of a person) tired or slightly ill/sick, especially from working hard: *to be/feel/get run-down*

run·down /ˈrʌndaʊn/ *noun* [usually sing.] **1** ~ **(in/of sth)** (*BrE*) a reduction in the amount, size or activity of sth, especially a business: *a rundown of rural transport services* **2** ~ **(on/of sth)** an explanation or a description of sth: *I can give you a brief rundown on each of the job applicants.*

rune /ruːn/ *noun* **1** one of the letters in an alphabet that people in Northern Europe used in ancient times and carved on wood or stone **2** a symbol that has a mysterious or magic meaning ▶ **runic** *adj.*: *runic inscriptions*

rung /rʌŋ/ *noun* one of the bars that forms a step in a ladder: *He put his foot on the bottom rung to keep the ladder steady.* ◊ (*figurative*) *to get a foot on the bottom rung of the career ladder* ◊ *She was a few rungs above him on the social ladder.*—see also RING *v.*

'run-in *noun* **1** ~ **(with sb)** (*informal*) an argument or a fight: *The fiery player has had numerous run-ins with referees.* **2** ~ **(to sth)** (*BrE*) = RUN-UP

run·nel /ˈrʌnl/ *noun* (*formal or literary*) a small stream or channel

run·ner /ˈrʌnə(r)/ *noun* **1** a person or an animal that runs, especially one taking part in a race: *a long-distance/cross-country/marathon runner* ◊ *a list of runners* (= horses in a race) *and riders*—see also FORERUNNER, FRONT RUNNER, ROADRUNNER **2** (especially in compounds) a person who takes goods illegally into or out of a place: *a drug runner*—see also GUNRUNNER **3** a strip of metal, plastic or wood that sth slides on or can move along on: *the runners of a sledge* **4** a plant stem that grows along the ground and puts down roots to form a new plant **5** a long narrow piece of fabric or carpet on a piece of furniture or on the floor **6** a person in a company or an organization whose job is to take messages, documents, etc. from one place to another **IDM** **do a 'runner** (*BrE, informal*) to leave or run away from somewhere in a hurry, especially to avoid paying a bill or receiving a punishment

runner 'bean (also **string 'bean**) *noun* (both *BrE*) a type of bean which is a long flat green POD growing on a climbing plant also called a **runner bean**. The PODS are cut up, cooked and eaten as a vegetable.

runner-'up *noun* (*pl.* **runners-up**) a person or team that finishes second in a race or competition; a person or team that has not finished first but that wins a prize: *Winner: Kay Hall. Runner-up: Chris Platts.* ◊ *They finished runners-up behind Sweden.* ◊ *The runners-up will all receive a £50 prize.*

run·ning /ˈrʌnɪŋ/ *noun, adj.*
■ *noun* [U] **1** the action or sport of running: *to go/take up running* ◊ *running shoes* **2** the activity of managing or operating sth: *the day-to-day running of a business* ◊ *the running costs of a car* (for example of fuel, repairs, insurance) **3** (-running) (in compounds) the activity of bringing sth such as drugs, guns, etc. into a country secretly and illegally: *drug-running* ◊ *gunrunning* **IDM** **in/ out of the 'running (for sth)** (*informal*) having some/no chance of succeeding or achieving sth **make the 'running** (*BrE, informal*) to set the speed at which sth is done; to take the lead in doing sth
■ *adj.* **1** used after a number and a noun such as 'year' 'day' or 'time', to say that sth has happened in the same way several times, without a change: *She's won the championship three years running.* ◊ *It was the third day running that the train had been late.* ◊ *No party has won an election four times running.* **2 running water** is water that is flowing somewhere or water that is supplied to a building and available to be used through taps/faucets: *I can hear the sound of running water.* ◊ *a remote cottage without electricity or running water* **3** [only before noun] lasting a long time; continuous **SYN** ONGOING: *For years he had fought a running battle with the authorities over the land.* ◊ *a running argument* ◊ *His old raincoat became a running joke* (= people kept laughing at it).—see also LONG-RUNNING **4** (-running) (in compounds) running or flowing in the way mentioned: *a fast-running river* **IDM** **(go and) take a running 'jump** (*old-fashioned, spoken*) used to tell sb in a rude way to go away—more at ORDER *n.*

running 'commentary *noun* a continuous description of an event, especially a sporting event, that sb gives as it happens: *to give a running commentary on the game* ◊ *My small son kept up a running commentary for the whole trip.*

'running mate *noun* [usually sing.] (*politics*) (in the US) a person who is chosen by the candidate in an election, especially that for president, to support them and to have the next highest political position if they win: *The presidential nominee was advised to choose a woman as a running mate.*

'running order *noun* [sing.] the order of the items in a television programme or a show; the order that members of a team will play in

running re'pairs *noun* [pl.] (*BrE*) small things that you do to a piece of clothing, a vehicle, a machine, etc. to mend it or to keep it working

running 'sore *noun* a small area on the body that is infected and has liquid (called PUS) coming out of it

'running time *noun* the amount of time that a film/ movie, a journey, etc. lasts

running 'total *noun* the total number or amount of things, money, etc. that changes as you add each new item

runny /ˈrʌni/ *adj.* (**run·nier**, **run·ni·est**) **1** (of your nose or eyes) producing a lot of liquid, for example when you have a cold **2** having more liquid than is usual; not solid: *runny honey* ◊ *Omelettes should be runny in the middle.*

'run-off *noun* **1** [C] a second vote or competition that is held to find a winner because two competitors in the first competition got the same result **2** [U, C] rain, water or other liquid that runs off land into streams and rivers

run-of-the-'mill *adj.* (often *disapproving*) ordinary, with no special or interesting features: *a run-of-the-mill job*

runt /rʌnt/ *noun* **1** the smallest, weakest animal of the young that are born from the same mother at the same time: *the runt of the litter* **2** (*slang, disapproving*) a rude way of referring to a small, weak or unimportant person

'run-through *noun* a practice for a performance of a play, show, etc. SYN REHEARSAL

'run-up *noun* (*BrE*) **1** (also *less frequent* **'run in**) ~ **(to sth)** a period of time leading up to an important event; the preparation for this: *an increase in spending in the run-up to Christmas* ◊ *during the run-up to the election* **2** the act of running or the distance you run, to gain speed before you jump a long distance, throw a ball, etc.

run·way /'rʌnweɪ/ *noun* **1** a long narrow strip of ground with a hard surface that an aircraft takes off from and lands on **2** (*AmE*) = CATWALK

rupee /ruː'piː/ *noun* the unit of money in India, Pakistan and some other countries

rup·ture /'rʌptʃə(r)/ *noun, verb*
■ *noun* [C, U] **1** (*medical*) an injury in which sth inside the body breaks apart or bursts: *the rupture of a blood vessel* **2** a situation when sth breaks or bursts: *ruptures of oil and water pipelines* **3** (*informal*) a HERNIA of the ABDOMEN: *I nearly gave myself a rupture lifting that pile of books.* **4** (*formal*) the ending of agreement or of good relations between people, countries, etc: *a rupture in relations between the two countries* ◊ *Nothing could heal the rupture with his father.*
■ *verb* **1** (*medical*) to burst or break apart sth inside the body; to be broken or burst apart: [VN] *a ruptured appendix/spleen/artery* ◊ *He ruptured himself* (= got a HERNIA) *trying to lift the piano.* [also V] **2** to make sth such as a container or a pipe break or burst; to be broken or burst: [VN] *The impact ruptured both fuel tanks.* ◊ [V] *A pipe ruptured, leaking water all over the house.* **3** [VN] (*written*) to make an agreement or good relations between people or countries end: *the risk of rupturing North-South relations*

rural /'rʊərəl; *AmE* 'rʊrəl/ *adj.* [usually before noun] connected with or like the countryside: *rural areas/communities* ◊ *a rural economy/society* ◊ *rural America* ◊ *a rural way of life*—compare URBAN

ˌrural 'dean *noun* = DEAN

ruse /ruːz/ *noun* (*written*) a way of doing sth or of getting sth by deceiving sb SYN TRICK

rush /rʌʃ/ *verb, noun*
■ *verb*
MOVE FAST ▶ **1** to move or to do sth with great speed, often too fast: [V, usually +*adv./prep.*] *We've got plenty of time; there's no need to rush.* ◊ *the sound of rushing water* ◊ *Don't rush off, I haven't finished.* ◊ *I've been rushing around all day trying to get everything done.* ◊ *People rushed to buy shares in the company.* ◊ [VN] *We had to rush our meal.*
TAKE/SEND QUICKLY ▶ **2** to transport or send sb/sth somewhere with great speed: [VN+*adv./prep.*] *Ambulances rushed the injured to the hospital.* ◊ *Relief supplies were rushed in.* [also VNN]
DO STH TOO QUICKLY ▶ **3** ~ **(sb) (into sth/into doing sth)** to do sth or to make sb do sth without thinking about it carefully: [V] *We don't want to rush into having a baby.* ◊ [VN] *Don't rush me. I need time to think about it.* ◊ *I'm not going to be rushed into anything.*
ATTACK ▶ **4** [VN] to try to attack or capture sb/sth suddenly: *A group of prisoners rushed an officer and managed to break out.* ◊ *Fans rushed the stage after the concert.*
IN AMERICAN FOOTBALL ▶ **5** [VN] (*AmE*) to run into sb who has the ball **6** [V] (*AmE*) to move forward and gain ground by carrying the ball and not passing it
IN AMERICAN COLLEGES ▶ **7** [VN] (*AmE*) to give a lot of attention to sb, especially to a student because you want them to join your FRATERNITY or SORORITY: *He is being rushed by Sigma Nu and Phi Delta.*
IDM see FOOT *n.*
PHRV ˌrush sth↔'out to produce sth very quickly: *The editors rushed out an item on the crash for the late news.* ˌrush sth↔'through| ˌrush sth 'through sth to deal with official business very quickly by making the usual process shorter than usual: *to rush a bill through Parliament*
■ *noun*
FAST MOVEMENT ▶ **1** [sing.] a sudden movement forward made by a lot of people or things: *Shoppers made a rush*

for the exits. ◊ *She was trampled in the rush to get out.* ◊ *They listened to the rush of the sea below.*
HURRY ▶ **2** [sing., U] a situation in which you are in a hurry and need to do things quickly: *I can't stop—I'm in a rush.* ◊ *What's the rush?* ◊ *'I'll let you have the book back tomorrow.' 'There's no rush.'* ◊ *The words came out in a rush.* ◊ *a rush job* (= one that has been done quickly)
BUSY SITUATION ▶ **3** [sing.] a situation in which people are very busy and there is a lot of activity: *The evening rush was just starting.* ◊ *the Christmas rush*
OF FEELING ▶ **4** [sing.] ~ **(of sth)** a sudden increase in the amount of sth SYN SURGE: *She felt a rush of blood to her cheeks.* ◊ *a rush of adrenalin* **5** [sing.] ~ **(of sth)** a sudden strong feeling or emotion: *a sudden rush of excitement/fear/anger*
SUDDEN DEMAND ▶ **6** [sing.] ~ **(on/for sth)** a sudden large demand for goods, etc: *There's been a rush on umbrellas this week.*—see also GOLD RUSH
PLANT ▶ **7** [C, usually pl.] a tall plant like grass that grows near water. Its long thin stems can be dried and used for making baskets, the seats of chairs, etc: *rush matting*
OF FILM/MOVIE ▶ **8** (**rushes**) [pl.] (*technical*) the first prints of a film/movie before they have been EDITED
IN AMERICAN COLLEGES ▶ **9** [sing.] (*AmE*) the time when parties are held for students who want to join a FRATERNITY or SORORITY: *rush week* ◊ *a rush party*

'rush hour *noun* [C usually sing, U] the time, usually twice a day, when the roads are full of traffic and trains are crowded because people are travelling to or from work: *the morning/evening rush hour* ◊ *Don't travel at rush hour.* ◊ *rush-hour traffic*

rusk /rʌsk/ *noun* (*especially BrE*) a hard crisp biscuit for babies to eat

rus·set /'rʌsɪt/ *adj.* reddish-brown in colour ▶ **rus·set** *noun* [U]: *leaves of russet and gold*

ˌRussian rou'lette *noun* [U] a dangerous game in which a person shoots at their own head with a gun that contains a bullet in only one of its CHAMBERS, so that the person does not know if the gun will fire or not

rust /rʌst/ *noun, verb*
■ *noun* [U] **1** a reddish-brown substance that is formed on some metals by the action of water and air: *pipes covered with rust* ◊ *rust spots* ◊ *a rust-coloured dress*—see also RUSTY **2** a plant disease that causes reddish-brown spots; the FUNGUS that causes this disease
■ *verb* if metal **rusts** or sth **rusts** it, it becomes covered with rust: [V] *old rusting farming implements* ◊ *Brass doesn't rust.* ◊ [VN] *Water had got in and rusted the engine.* ▶ **rust·ed** *adj.*: *rusted iron*—see also RUSTY PHRV ˌrust a'way to be gradually destroyed by rust

'rust belt *noun* (*especially AmE*) a region that used to have a lot of industry, but that has now decreased in importance and wealth

rus·tic /'rʌstɪk/ *adj., noun*
■ *adj.* **1** (*approving*) typical of the country or of country people; simple: *an old cottage full of rustic charm* **2** made very simply of rough wood: *a rustic garden seat* ◊ *a rustic fence* ▶ **rus·ti·city** /rʌ'stɪsəti/ *noun* [U]
■ *noun* (*disapproving* or *humorous*) a person who lives in or comes from the country

rus·tle /'rʌsl/ *verb, noun*
■ *verb* **1** if sth dry and light **rustles** or you **rustle** it, it makes a sound like paper, leaves, etc. moving or rubbing together: [V] *The sound of the trees rustling in the breeze* [also VN] **2** [VN] to steal farm animals PHRV ˌrustle sth↔'up (for sb) (*informal*) to make or find sth quickly for sb and without planning: *I'm sure I can rustle you up a sandwich.* ◊ *They have been busy rustling up new business.*
■ *noun* [sing.] a light dry sound like leaves or pieces of paper moving or rubbing against each other: *There was a rustle of paper as people turned the pages.* ◊ *I heard a faint rustle in the bushes.*

rust·ler /'rʌslə(r)/ *noun* a person who steals farm animals

rust·ling /'rʌslɪŋ/ *noun* **1** [U, C] the sound of light, dry things moving together: *the soft rustling of leaves* **2** [U] the act of stealing farm animals

s	t	v	z	ʃ	ʒ	tʃ	dʒ	θ	ð	ŋ
see	tea	van	zoo	shoe	vision	chain	jam	thin	this	sing

R

rust·proof /'rʌstpruːf/ *adj.* **rustproof** metal has had a substance put on it so that it will not RUST

rusty /'rʌsti/ *adj.* **1** covered with RUST: *rusty metal* ◊ *a rusty old car/nail* **2** [not usually before noun] (*informal*) (of a sport, skill, etc.) not as good as it used to be, because you have not been practising: *My tennis is very rusty these days.* ▶ **rusti·ness** *noun* [U]

rut /rʌt/ *noun* **1** [C] a deep track that a wheel makes in soft ground **2** [C] a boring way of life that does not change: *I gave up my job because I felt I was stuck in a rut.* ◊ *If you don't go out and meet new people, it's easy to get into a rut.* **3** [U] (also **the rut**) [sing.] the time of year when male animals, especially deer, become sexually active—see also RUTTED, RUTTING

ru·ta·baga /ˌruːtəˈbeɪgə/ *noun* [C, U] (*AmE*) = SWEDE

ruth·less /'ruːθləs/ *adj.* (*disapproving*) (of people or their behaviour) hard and cruel; determined to get what you want and not caring if you hurt other people: *a ruthless dictator* ◊ *The way she behaved towards him was utterly*

ruthless. ◊ *He has a ruthless determination to succeed.* ◊ *We'll have to be ruthless if we want to make this company more efficient.* ▶ **ruth·less·ly** *adv.* **ruth·less·ness** *noun* [U]

rut·ted /'rʌtɪd/ *adj.* (of a road or path) with deep tracks that have been made by wheels—see also RUT (1)

rut·ting /'rʌtɪŋ/ *adj.* (of male animals, especially deer) in a time of sexual activity: *rutting deer* ◊ *the rutting season*—see also RUT (3)

RV /ˌɑː 'viː; *AmE* ˌɑːr/ *noun* (*AmE*) = CAMPER (the abbreviation for 'recreational vehicle')

Rx /ˌɑːr 'eks/ *noun* (*AmE*) **1** the written abbreviation for a doctor's PRESCRIPTION **2** a solution to a problem: *There's no Rx for unemployment.*

-ry ⇨ -ERY

rye /raɪ/ *noun* [U] a plant that looks like BARLEY but that produces larger grain, grown as food for animals and for making flour and whisky; the grain of this plant: *rye bread* ◊ *rye whisky*—picture at CEREAL

R

æ	ɑː	e	ɜː	ə	ɪ	iː	i	ɒ	ɔː	ʌ	ʊ	u	uː
cat	father	ten	bird	about	sit	see	many	got	saw	cup	put	actual	too

(BrE)

Ss

S /es/ *noun, abbr.*

- *noun* (also **s**) [C, U] (*pl.* **S's, s's** /ˈesɪz/) the 19th letter of the English alphabet: *'Snow' begins with (an) S/'S'.*—see also S-BEND
- *abbr.* **1** (*pl.* **SS**) Saint **2** (especially for sizes of clothes) small **3** (*AmE* also **So.**) south; southern: *S Yorkshire*—see also S AND H

-'s /s/ *suffix, short form*

- *suffix* (added to nouns) **1** belonging to: *the woman's hat ◇ Peter's desk ◇ children's clothes* **2** used to refer to sb's home or, in British English, a particular shop: *Shall we go to David's?* (= David's house) *tonight? ◇* (*BrE*) *I'll call in at the chemist's on my way home*
- *short form* (*informal*) **1** used after *he, she* or *it* and *where, what, who* or *how* to mean 'is' or 'has': *She's still in the bath. ◇ What's he doing now? ◇ It's time to go now. ◇ Who's taken my pen? ◇ Where's he gone? ◇ It's gone wrong again.* **2** (used after *let* when making a suggestion that includes yourself and others) us: *Let's go out for lunch.*

-s' *suffix* (forming the end of plural nouns) belonging to: *the cats' tails ◇ their wives' jobs*

SA *abbr.* South Africa

sab·bath /ˈsæbəθ/ (**the Sabbath**) *noun* [sing.] (in Judaism and Christianity) the holy day of the week that is used for resting and worshipping God. For Jews this day is Saturday and for Christians it is Sunday: *to keep/break the Sabbath* (= to obey/disobey the religious rules for this day)

sab·bat·ic·al /səˈbætɪkl/ *noun* [C, U] a period of time when sb, especially a teacher at a university, is allowed to stop their normal work in order to study or travel: *to take a year's sabbatical ◇ a sabbatical term/year ◇ He's on sabbatical.*

saber (*AmE*) = SABRE

sable /ˈseɪbl/ *noun* **1** [C] a small animal from northern Asia with dark yellowish-brown fur **2** [U] the skin and fur of the sable, used for making expensive coats and artists' brushes

sabo·tage /ˈsæbətɑːʒ/ *noun, verb*

- *noun* [U] the act of doing deliberate damage to equipment, transport, machines, etc. to prevent an enemy from using them or to protest about sth: *an act of economic/military/industrial sabotage ◇ Police investigating the train derailment have not ruled out sabotage.*
- *verb* [VN] **1** to damage, destroy or spoil sth deliberately to prevent an enemy from using it or to protest about sth: *The main electricity supply had been sabotaged by the rebels. ◇ Protesters failed to sabotage the peace talks.* **2** to make sth no longer possible or successful: *The rise in interest rates sabotaged any chance of the firm's recovery.*

sabo·teur /ˌsæbəˈtɜː(r)/ *noun* a person who does deliberate damage to sth to prevent an enemy from using it, or to protest about sth: *Saboteurs blew up a small section of the track. ◇* (*BrE*) **hunt saboteurs** (= people who try to stop people from hunting foxes, etc.)

sabre (*AmE* **saber**) /ˈseɪbə(r)/ *noun* **1** a heavy SWORD with a curved blade **2** a light SWORD with a thin blade used in the sport of FENCING

'sabre-rattling (*BrE*) (*AmE* **'saber rattling**) *noun* [U] the act of trying to frighten sb by threatening to use force

sac /sæk/ *noun* a part inside the body of a person, an animal or a plant, that is shaped like a bag, has thin skin around it, and contains liquid or air

sac·charin /ˈsækərɪn/ *noun* [U] a sweet chemical substance used instead of sugar, especially by people who are trying to lose weight

sac·char·ine (also *less frequent* **sac·char·in**)

/ˈsækəriːn; ˌrɪn/ *adj.* (*disapproving*) (of people or things) too emotional in a way that seems exaggerated: *a saccharine smile ◇ saccharine songs*

sa·chet /ˈsæʃeɪ; *AmE* sæˈʃeɪ/ *noun* **1** (*BrE*) (*AmE* **packet**) a closed plastic or paper packet that contains a very small amount of liquid or a powder: *a sachet of sauce/sugar/shampoo*—picture at PACKAGING **2** a small bag containing dried herbs or flowers that you put with your clothes to make them smell pleasant

sack /sæk/ *noun, verb*

- *noun* **1** [C] a large bag with no handles, made of strong rough material or strong paper or plastic, used for storing and carrying, for example flour, coal, etc. **2** [C] the contents of a sack: *They got through a sack of potatoes. ◇* (*AmE*) *two sacks of groceries* **3** (**the sack**) [sing.] (*informal, especially AmE*) a bed: *He caught them in the sack together.* **4** (usually **the sack**) [sing.] (*formal*) the act of stealing or destroying property in a captured town: *the sack of Rome* IDM **get the 'sack | give sb the 'sack** (*informal*) if you **get the sack** or sb **gives you the sack**, you are told that you can no longer work for a company, etc., usually because of sth that you have done wrong—more at HIT *v.*
- *verb* [VN] **1** (*informal, especially BrE*) to dismiss sb from a job SYN FIRE: *She was sacked for refusing to work on Sundays.* **2** (of an army, etc., especially in the past) to destroy things and steal property in a town or building: *Rome was sacked by the Goths in 410.* **3** [VN] (in American football) to knock down the QUARTERBACK PHRV **,sack 'out** (*AmE, informal*) to go to sleep or to bed: *We watched a video and sacked out on the couch.*

sack·cloth /ˈsækklɒθ; *AmE* ˈklɔːθ/ (also **sack·ing**) *noun* [U] a rough fabric made from JUTE, etc., used for making sacks IDM **wear, put on, etc. ,sackcloth and 'ashes** to behave in a way that shows that you are sorry for sth that you have done

sack·ful /ˈsækfʊl/ *noun* the amount contained in a SACK: *two sackfuls of flour*

sack·ing /ˈsækɪŋ/ *noun* **1** [C] an act of SACKING sb (= dismissing them from their job) **2** [U] = SACKCLOTH

sac·ra·ment /ˈsækrəmənt/ *noun* (in Christianity) **1** [C] an important religious ceremony such as marriage, BAPTISM or COMMUNION **2** (**the sacrament**) [sing.] the bread and wine that are eaten and drunk during the service of COMMUNION: *to receive the sacrament* ▶ **sac·ra·men·tal** /ˌsækrəˈmentl/ *adj.* [usually before noun]: *sacramental wine*

sac·red /ˈseɪkrɪd/ *adj.* **1** connected with God or a god; considered to be holy: *a sacred image/shrine/temple ◇ sacred music ◇ Cows are sacred to Hindus.* **2** very important and treated with great respect: *Human life must always be sacred. ◇ For journalists nothing is sacred* (= they can write about anything). *◇ Some companies offer five-year plans but there is nothing sacred about this length of time* (= it can be changed). ▶ **sac·red·ness** *noun* [U]—see also SANCTITY

,sacred 'cow *noun* (*disapproving*) a custom, system, etc. that has existed for a long time and that many people think should not be questioned or criticized

sac·ri·fice /ˈsækrɪfaɪs/ *noun, verb*

- *noun* [C, U] the fact of giving up sth important or valuable to you in order to get or do sth that seems more important; sth that you give up in this way: *The makers of the product assured us that there had been no sacrifice of quality. ◇ Her parents made sacrifices so that she could have a good education. ◇ to make the final/supreme sacrifice* (= to die for your country, to save a friend, etc.)

aɪ	aʊ	eɪ	əʊ	oʊ	ɔɪ	ɪə	eə	ʊə	j	w
my	now	say	go (BrE)	go (AmE)	boy	near	hair	pure	yes	wet

2 ~ (to sb) [C, U] the act of offering sth to a god, especially an animal that has been killed in a special way; an animal, etc. that is offered in this way: *They offered sacrifices to the gods.* ◊ *a human sacrifice* (= a person killed as a sacrifice)
■ *verb* **1** [VN] **~ sth (for sb/sth)** to give up sth that is important or valuable to you in order to get or do sth that seems more important for yourself or for another person: *She sacrificed everything for her children.* ◊ *The designers have sacrificed speed for fuel economy.* ◊ *Would you sacrifice a football game to go out with a girl?* **2** [VN, V] to kill an animal or a person and offer it or them to a god, in order to please the god

sac·ri·fi·cial /ˌsækrɪˈfɪʃl/ *adj.* [usually before noun] offered as a sacrifice: *a sacrificial lamb*

sac·ri·lege /ˈsækrəlɪdʒ/ *noun* [U, sing.] an act of treating a holy thing or place without respect: *(figurative)* *It would be sacrilege to alter the composer's original markings.* ▶ **sac·ri·le·gious** /ˌsækrəˈlɪdʒəs/ *adj.*

sac·ris·tan /ˈsækrɪstən/ *noun* a person whose job is to look after the holy objects in a Christian church and to prepare the ALTAR for services

sac·risty /ˈsækrɪsti/ *noun* (*pl.* **-ies**) a room in a church where a priest prepares for a service by putting on special clothes and where various objects used in worship are kept **SYN** VESTRY

sacro·sanct /ˈsækrəʊsæŋkt; *AmE* -kroʊ-/ *adj.* that is considered to be too important to change or question: *I'll work till late in the evening, but my weekends are sacrosanct.*

sad /sæd/ *adj.* (**sad·der, sad·dest**)
UNHAPPY | **1 ~ (to do sth)| ~ (that...)** unhappy or showing unhappiness: *We are very sad to hear that you are leaving.* ◊ *I was sad that she had to go.* ◊ *She looked sad and tired.* ◊ *I felt terribly sad about it.* ◊ *He gave a slight, sad smile.* ◊ *The divorce left him sadder and wiser* (= having learned from the unpleasant experience). **2 ~ (to do sth)| ~ (that ...)** that makes you feel unhappy: *a sad story/poem/song* ◊ *It was sad to see them go.* ◊ *It is sad that so many of his paintings have been lost.* ◊ *We had some sad news yesterday.* ◊ *He's a sad case—his wife died last year and he can't seem to manage without her.* ◊ *Sad to say* (= unfortunately) *the house has now been demolished.*
UNACCEPTABLE | **3** unacceptable; deserving blame or criticism: *a sad state of affairs* ◊ *It's a sad fact that many of those killed were children.*
BORING | **4** (*spoken, slang*) boring or not fashionable: *You sad old man.*
IN POOR CONDITION | **5** in poor condition: *The salad consisted of a few leaves of sad-looking lettuce.*
—see also SADLY, SADNESS

sad·den /ˈsædn/ *verb* [often passive] (*formal*) to make sb sad: [VN] *We were deeply saddened by the news of her death.* ◊ [VN to inf] *Fans were saddened to see the former champion play so badly.* ◊ [VN that] *It saddened her that people could be so cruel.*

sad·dle /ˈsædl/ *noun, verb*
■ *noun* **1** a leather seat for a rider on a horse: *She swung herself into the saddle.* **2** a seat on a bicycle or motorcycle—picture at BICYCLE **3** a piece of meat from the back of an animal **IDM** **in the 'saddle 1** in a position of authority and control **2** riding a horse: *Three weeks after the accident he was back in the saddle.*
■ *verb* [VN] to put a saddle on a horse: *Their horses were saddled and waiting.* **PHRV** **ˌsaddle 'up| ˌsaddle sth↔'up** to put a saddle on a horse: *He saddled up and rode off.* **'saddle sb/yourself with sth** [often passive] to give sb/yourself an unpleasant responsibility, task, debt, etc: *I've been saddled with organizing the conference.* ◊ *The company was saddled with debts of £12 million.*

saddle·bag /ˈsædlbæg/ *noun* **1** one of a pair of bags put over the back of a horse **2** a bag attached to the back of a bicycle or motorcycle saddle

sad·dler /ˈsædlə(r)/ *noun* a person whose job is making, repairing and selling SADDLES and other leather goods

sad·dlery /ˈsædləri/ *noun* [U] SADDLES and leather goods for horses; the art of making these

'saddle-sore *adj.* feeling sore and stiff after riding a horse

sadhu /ˈsɑːduː/ *noun* (*pl.* **-us**) a Hindu holy man, especially one who lives apart from people and society

sad·ism /ˈseɪdɪzəm/ *noun* [U] **1** enjoyment from watching or making sb suffer: *There's a streak of sadism in his nature.* **2** a need to hurt sb in order to get sexual pleasure—compare MASOCHISM

sad·ist /ˈseɪdɪst/ *noun* a person who gets pleasure, especially sexual pleasure, from hurting other people ▶ **sad·is·tic** /səˈdɪstɪk/ *adj.*: *He took sadistic pleasure in taunting the boy.* **sad·is·tic·al·ly** *adv.*

sadly /ˈsædli/ *adv.* **1** unfortunately: *Sadly, after eight years of marriage they had grown apart.* **2** in a sad way: *She shook her head sadly.* **3** very much and in a way that makes you sad: *She will be sadly missed.* ◊ *They had hoped to win and were sadly disappointed.* ◊ *If you think I'm going to help you again, you're sadly* (= completely) *mistaken.*

sad·ness /ˈsædnəs/ *noun* **1** [U, sing.] the feeling of being sad: *memories tinged with sadness* ◊ *I felt a deep sadness.* **2** [C, usually pl.] something which makes you sad: *our joys and sadnesses*

sado·maso·chism /ˌseɪdəʊˈmæsəkɪzəm; *AmE* -doʊ-/ *noun* [U] enjoyment from hurting sb and being hurt, especially during sexual activity ▶ **sado·maso·chist** /ˌseɪdəʊˈmæsəkɪst; *AmE* -doʊ-/ *noun* **sado·maso·chis·tic** /ˌseɪdəʊˌmæsəˈkɪstɪk; *AmE* -doʊ-/ *adj.*

sae /ˌes eɪ ˈiː/ *noun* (*BrE*) an envelope on which you have written your name and address and usually put a stamp so that sb else can use it to send sth to you (abbreviation for 'stamped addressed envelope' or 'self-addressed envelope'): *Please enclose an sae for your test results.*—compare SASE

sa·fari /səˈfɑːri/ *noun* [U, C] a trip to see or hunt wild animals, especially in E Africa: *to be/go on safari*

sa'fari park *noun* a park in which wild animals move around freely and are watched by visitors from their cars

safe /seɪf/ *adj., noun*
■ *adj.* (**safer, saf·est**)
PROTECTED | **1** [not before noun] **~ (from sb/sth)** protected from any danger or harm: *The children are quite safe here.* ◊ *She didn't feel safe on her own.* ◊ *Will the car be safe parked in the road?* ◊ *They aimed to make the country safe from terrorist attacks.* ◊ *Your secret is safe with me* (= I will not tell anyone else). **OPP** UNSAFE
WITHOUT PHYSICAL DANGER | **2 ~ (to do sth)| ~ (for sb)** not likely to lead to any physical harm or danger: *a safe and effective remedy for coughs and colds* ◊ *Is the water here safe to drink?* ◊ *The street is not safe for children to play in.* ◊ *It is one of the safest cars in the world.* ◊ *We watched the explosion from a safe distance.* ◊ *Builders were called in to make the building safe.* **OPP** UNSAFE
NOT HARMED/LOST | **3** [not before noun] not harmed, damaged, lost, etc: *We were glad she let us know she was safe.* ◊ *The missing child was found safe and well.* ◊ *They turned up safe and sound.* ◊ *A reward was offered for the animal's safe return.*
PLACE | **4** where sb/sth is not likely to be in danger or to be lost: *We all want to live in safer cities.* ◊ *Keep your passport in a safe place.* **OPP** UNSAFE
WITHOUT RISK | **5 ~ (to do sth)** not involving much or any risk; not likely to be wrong or to upset sb: *a safe investment* ◊ *a safe subject for discussion* ◊ *It's safe to assume (that)* there will always be a demand for new software. ◊ *It would be safer to take more money with you in case of emergency.* ◊ *(disapproving)* *The show was well performed, but so safe and predictable.*
PERSON | **6** [usually before noun] doing an activity in a careful way: *a safe driver/worker*
LAW | **7** based on good evidence: *a safe verdict* **OPP** UNSAFE
—see also FAIL-SAFE
IDM **ˌbetter ˌsafe than 'sorry** (*saying*) used to say that it is wiser to be too careful than to act too quickly and do sth you may later wish you had not **in safe 'hands | in the safe hands of sb** being taken care of well by sb: *I've*

S

left the kids in *safe hands*—*with my parents.* ◊ *Their problem was in the safe hands of the experts.* **on the 'safe side** being especially careful; taking no risks: *I took some extra cash just to be on the safe side.* **play (it) 'safe** to be careful; to avoid risks **(as)** ˌsafe as 'houses (*BrE*) very safe **safe in the knowledge that** confident because you know that sth is true or will happen: *She went out safe in the knowledge that she looked fabulous.* **a safe pair of 'hands** (*especially BrE*) a person that you can trust to do a job well—more at BET *n.*

■ *noun* a strong metal box or cupboard with a complicated lock, used for storing valuable things in, for example, money or jewels

ˌsafe 'conduct (also ˌsafe 'passage) *noun* [U, C] official protection from being attacked, arrested, etc. when passing through an area; a document that promises this: *The guerillas were promised safe conduct out of the country.*

'safe deposit box (also 'safety deposit box) *noun* a metal box for storing valuable things, usually kept in a special room at a bank

safe·guard /'seɪfgɑːd; *AmE* -gɑːrd/ *verb, noun*

■ *verb* ~ sth (against/from sth) | ~ against sth (*formal*) to protect sth from loss, harm or damage; to keep sth safe: [VN] *to safeguard sb's interests/rights/privacy* ◊ *to safeguard jobs/the environment* ◊ *The new card will safeguard the company against fraud.* ◊ [V] *The leaflet explains how to safeguard against dangers in the home.*

■ *noun* ~ (against sth) something that is designed to protect people from harm, risk or danger: *Stronger legal safeguards are needed to protect the consumer.*

ˌsafe 'haven *noun* a place where sb can go to be safe from danger or attack

'safe house *noun* a house used by people who are hiding, for example by criminals hiding from the police, or by people who are being protected by the police from other people who may wish to harm them

ˌsafe 'keeping *noun* [U] **1** the fact of sth being in a safe place where it will not be lost or damaged: *She had put her watch in her pocket for safe keeping.* **2** the fact of sb/sth being taken care of by sb who can be trusted: *The documents are in the safe keeping of our lawyers.*

safe·ly /'seɪfli/ *adv.* **1** without being harmed, damaged or lost: *The plane landed safely.* **2** in a way that does not cause harm or that protects sb/sth from harm: *The bomb has been safely disposed of.* ◊ *The money is safely locked in a drawer.* **3** without much possibility of being wrong: *We can safely say that he will accept the job.* **4** without any possibility of the situation changing: *I thought the kids were safely tucked up in bed.* **5** without any problems being caused; with no risk: *These recommendations can safely be ignored.*

ˌsafe 'passage *noun* [U, C] = SAFE CONDUCT

the 'safe period *noun* [sing.] the time just before and during a woman's PERIOD when she is unlikely to become pregnant

ˌsafe 'seat *noun* (*BrE*) a CONSTITUENCY where a particular political party has a lot of support and is unlikely to be defeated in an election

ˌsafe 'sex *noun* [U] sexual activity in which people try to protect themselves from AIDS and other sexual diseases, for example by using a CONDOM

safety /'seɪfti/ *noun* (*pl.* **-ies**) **1** [U] the state of being safe and protected from danger or harm: *a place where children can play in safety* ◊ *The police are concerned for the safety of the 12-year-old boy who has been missing for three days.* ◊ *He was kept in custody for his own safety.* **2** [U] the state of not being dangerous: *I'm worried about the safety of the treatment.* ◊ *safety standards/measures/precautions* ◊ *a local campaign to improve road safety* ◊ *The airline has an excellent safety record.* **3** [U] a place where you are safe: *I managed to swim to safety.* ◊ *We watched the lions from the safety of the car.* ◊ *They reached safety seconds before the building was engulfed in flames.* **4** [C] (*AmE*) = SAFETY CATCH ▪IDM▪ ˌsafety 'first (*saying*) safety is the most important thing **there's** ˌsafety in 'numbers (*saying*) being in a group makes you safer and makes you feel more confident

'safety belt *noun* = SEAT BELT

'safety catch (*especially BrE*) (*AmE* usually **safety**) *noun* a device that stops a gun from being fired or a machine from working by accident

'safety deposit box *noun* = SAFE DEPOSIT BOX

'safety glass *noun* [U] strong glass that does not break into sharp pieces

'safety island *noun* (*AmE*) = TRAFFIC ISLAND

'safety net *noun* **1** an arrangement that helps to prevent disaster if sth goes wrong: *a financial safety net* ◊ *people who have fallen through the safety net and ended up homeless on the streets* **2** a net placed underneath ACROBATS, etc. to catch them if they fall

'safety pin *noun* a pin with a point bent back towards the head, that is covered when closed so that it cannot hurt you—picture at FASTENER

'safety razor *noun* a RAZOR with a cover over the blade to stop it from cutting the skin—compare CUT-THROAT RAZOR

'safety valve *noun* **1** a device that lets out steam or pressure in a machine when it becomes too great **2** a harmless way of letting out feelings of anger, excitement, etc: *Exercise is a good safety valve for the tension that builds up at work.*

saf·fron /'sæfrən/ *noun* [U] **1** a bright yellow powder made from CROCUS flowers, used in cooking to give colour to food **2** a bright orange-yellow colour ▶ **saf·fron** *adj.*: *Buddhist monks in saffron robes*

sag /sæg/ *verb* (**-gg-**) [V] **1** to hang or bend down in the middle, especially of weight or pressure: *a sagging roof* ◊ *The tent began to sag under the weight of the rain.* ◊ *Your skin starts to sag as you get older.* **2** to become weaker or fewer: *Their share of the vote sagged badly at the last election.* ▶ **sag** *noun* [U, C, usually sing.]: *Weight has caused the sag.* ▪IDM▪ see JAW *n.*

saga /'sɑːgə/ *noun* **1** a long traditional story about adventures and brave acts, especially one from Norway or Iceland **2** a long story about events over a period of many years: *She has written a huge and compelling family saga.* **3** a long series of events or adventures and/or a report about them: *The front page is devoted to the continuing saga of the hijack.* ◊ (*humorous*) *the saga of how I missed the plane*

sa·ga·cious /sə'geɪʃəs/ *adj.* (*formal*) showing good judgement and understanding ▪SYN▪ WISE ▶ **sa·ga·city** /sə'gæsəti/ *noun* [U]

sage /seɪdʒ/ *noun, adj.*

■ *noun* **1** [U] a plant with flat, light green leaves that have a strong smell and are used in cooking as a herb: *duck with sage and onion stuffing* **2** [C] (*formal*) a very wise person: *ancient Indian sages* ◊ *political/economic sages*

■ *adj.* (*literary*) wise, especially because you have a lot of experience ▶ **sage·ly** *adv.*: *She nodded sagely.*

sage·brush /'seɪdʒbrʌʃ/ *noun* [U] a plant with leaves that smell sweet that grows in dry regions in the western US; an area of ground covered with sagebrush

saggy /'sægi/ *adj.* (*informal*) no longer firm; hanging or sinking down in way that is not attractive: *a saggy mattress*

Sa·git·tar·ius /ˌsædʒɪ'teəriəs; *AmE* -'ter-/ *noun* **1** [U] the 9th sign of the ZODIAC, the ARCHER **2** [sing.] a person born under the influence of this sign, that is between 22 November and 20 December, approximately ▶ **Sa·git·tar·ian** *noun, adj.*

sago /'seɪgəʊ; *AmE* -goʊ/ *noun* [U] hard white grains made from the soft inside of a type of PALM tree, often cooked with milk to make a DESSERT: *sago pudding*

sahib /sɑːb; 'sɑːɪb/ *noun* used in India, especially in the past, to address a European man, especially one with some social or official status

said /sed/ **1** *pt, pp* of SAY **2** *adj.* [only before noun] (*formal* or *law*) = AFOREMENTIONED: *the said company*

sail /seɪl/ *verb, noun*

■ *verb* **1** (of a boat or ship or the people on it) to travel on water using sails or an engine: [V, usually +*adv./prep.*] *to sail up the coast/into harbour* ◊ *The dinghy sailed*

s	t	v	z	ʃ	ʒ	tʃ	dʒ	θ	ð	ŋ
see	tea	van	zoo	shoe	vision	chain	jam	thin	this	sing

smoothly across the lake. ◊ *The ferry sails from Newhaven to Dieppe.* ◊ *one of the first people to sail around the world* ◊ [VN] *to sail the Atlantic* **2** (also **go sailing**) to control or travel on a boat with a sail, especially as a sport: [V] *We spent the weekend sailing off the south coast.* ◊ *Do you go* **sailing** *often?* ◊ [VN] *She sails her own yacht.* **3** [V] (of a boat or ship or the people in it) to begin a journey on water: *We sail at 2 p.m. tomorrow.* ◊ *He sailed for the West Indies from Portsmouth.* **4** [V+*adv.*/*prep.*] to move quickly and smoothly in a particular direction; (of people) to move in a confident manner: *clouds sailing across the sky* ◊ *The ball sailed over the goalie's head.* ◊ *She sailed past me, ignoring me completely.* **IDM** **sail close to the 'wind** to take a risk by doing sth that is dangerous or that may be illegal **PHR V** ,**sail 'through (sth)** to pass an exam, a test, etc. without any difficulty

■ *noun* **1** [C, U] a sheet of strong fabric which the wind blows against to make a boat or ship travel through the water: *As the boat moved down the river the wind began to fill the sails.* ◊ *a ship* **under sail** (= using sails) ◊ *in the days of sail* (= when ships all used sails) ◊ *Mrs Healy moved away like a ship in full sail* (= with all its sails spread out). **2** [sing.] a trip in a boat or ship: *We went for a sail.* ◊ *a two-hour sail across the bay* **3** [C] a set of boards attached to the arm of a WINDMILL **IDM** **set 'sail (from/ for ...)** (*formal*) to begin a trip by sea: *a liner setting sail from New York* ◊ *We set sail (for France) at high tide.*—more at TRIM *v.*, WIND¹*n.*

sail·board /'seɪlbɔːd; *AmE* -bɔːrd/ (also **board**) *noun* = WINDSURFER

sail·boat /'seɪlbəʊt; *AmE* -boʊt/ *noun* (*AmE*) = SAILING BOAT, YACHT

sail·ing /'seɪlɪŋ/ *noun* **1** [U] the sport or activity of travelling in a boat with sails: *to go sailing* ◊ *a sailing club* **2** [C] one of the regular times that a ship leaves a port: *There are six sailings a day from Dover to Ostend.* ◊ *What time is the next sailing?* **IDM** see CLEAR *adj.*, PLAIN *adj.*

'**sailing boat** (*BrE*) (*AmE* **sail·boat**) *noun* a boat with sails

'**sailing ship** *noun* a ship with sails

sail·or /'seɪlə(r)/ *noun* **1** a person who works on a ship as a member of the CREW **2** a person who sails a boat **IDM** **a good/bad 'sailor** a person who rarely/always becomes sick at sea

'**sailor suit** *noun* a suit for a child made in the style of an old-fashioned sailor's uniform

saint /seɪnt; *or, in British use before names,* snt/ *noun* **1** (*abbr.* **S, St**) a person that the Christian Church recognizes as being very holy, because of the way they have lived or died: *St John* ◊ *St Valentine's Day* ◊ *The children were all named after saints.*—see also PATRON SAINT St Bernard **2** a very good, kind or patient person: *She's a saint to go on living with that man.* ◊ *His behaviour would try the patience of a saint.* ▶ **saint·hood** *noun* [U]

saint·ed /'seɪntɪd/ *adj.* [usually before noun] (*old-fashioned* or *humorous*) considered or officially stated to be a saint: *And how is my sainted sister?*

saint·ly /'seɪntli/ *adj.* like a saint; very holy and good: *to lead a saintly life* ▶ **saint·li·ness** *noun* [U]

'**saint's day** *noun* (in the Christian Church) a day of the year when a particular saint is remembered and on which, in some countries, people who are named after that saint have celebrations

saith /seθ/ (*old use*) says

sake¹ /seɪk/ *noun*—see also SAKE² **IDM** **for Christ's, God's, goodness', heaven's, pity's, etc.** '**sake** used to emphasize that it is important to do sth or when you are annoyed about sth: *Do be careful, for goodness' sake.* ◊ *Oh, for heaven's sake!* ◊ *For pity's sake, help me!* **HELP** Some people find the use of **Christ, God** or **heaven** here offensive. **for sth's 'own sake** because of the interest or value sth has, not because of the advantages it may bring: *I believe in education for its own sake.* ◊ *art for art's sake* **for the sake of sb/sth** | **for sb's/sth's sake** in order to help sb/sth or because you like sb/sth: *They stayed together for the sake of the children.* ◊ *You can do it. Please, for my sake.* ◊ *I hope you're right, for all our sakes* (= because this

is important for all of us). **for the sake of sth/of doing sth** in order to get or keep sth: *The translation sacrifices naturalness for the sake of accuracy.* ◊ *She gave up smoking for the sake of her health.* ◊ *Don't get married just for the sake of it.* ◊ *Let's suppose, for the sake of argument* (= in order to have a discussion), *that interest rates went up by 2%.*—more at OLD

sake² (also **saki**) /'sɑːki/ *noun* [U] a Japanese alcoholic drink made from rice—see also SAKE¹

sa·laam /sə'lɑːm/ *verb* [V, VN] (in some Eastern countries) to greet sb in a formal way by bending forward from the waist and putting your right hand on your forehead ▶ **sa·laam** *noun*

sal·acious /sə'leɪʃəs/ *adj.* (*formal*) (of stories, pictures, etc.) encouraging sexual desire or containing too much sexual detail: *salacious gossip* ▶ **sal·acious·ness** *noun* [U]

salad /'sæləd/ *noun* **1** [U, C] a mixture of raw vegetables such as LETTUCE, tomato and CUCUMBER, usually served with other food as part of a meal: *All main courses come with salad or vegetables.* ◊ *Is cold meat and salad OK for lunch?* ◊ *a side salad* (= a small bowl of salad served with the main course of a meal) ◊ *a salad bowl* (= a large bowl for serving salad in)—see also GREEN SALAD **2** [C, U] (in compounds) meat, fish, cheese, etc. served with salad: *a chicken/beef salad* **3** [U, C] (in compounds) raw or cooked vegetables, etc. that are cut into small pieces, often mixed with MAYONNAISE and served cold with other food: *bean/ carrot/potato salad* ◊ *a pasta/rice salad*—see also FRUIT SALAD **4** [U] any green vegetable, especially LETTUCE, that is eaten raw in a salad: *salad leaves/plants* **IDM** **your** '**salad days** (*old-fashioned*) the time when you are young and do not have much experience of life

'**salad cream** *noun* [U] (*BrE*) a pale yellow sauce, similar to MAYONNAISE, sold in bottles and eaten on salads, in sandwiches, etc.

'**salad dressing** *noun* [U, C] = DRESSING

sala·man·der /'sæləmændə(r)/ *noun* an animal like a LIZARD, with short legs and a long tail, that lives both on land and in water (= is an AMPHIBIAN)—picture on page A7

sa·lami /sə'lɑːmi/ *noun* [U, C] (*pl.* **sa·lamis**) a type of large spicy sausage served cold in thin slices

sal·ar·ied /'sælərid/ *adj.* **1** (of a person) receiving a salary: *a salaried employee* **2** (of a job) for which a salary is paid: *a salaried position*

sal·ary /'sæləri/ *noun* (*pl.* **-ies**) money that employees receive for doing their job, especially professional employees or people working in an office, usually paid every month: *an annual salary of $40000* ◊ *a 9% salary increase* ◊ *She's on a salary of $24000.* ◊ *He gets a basic salary plus commission.*—compare WAGE

sale /seɪl/ *noun* **1** [U, C] an act or the process of selling sth: *the sale of cars/clothes/goods* ◊ *regulations governing the sale of alcoholic beverages* ◊ *I haven't made a sale all week.* ◊ *She gets 10% commission on each sale.* **2** (**sales**) [pl.] the number of items sold: *Retail sales fell in November by 10%.* ◊ *Export sales were up by 32% last year.* ◊ *The company reported booming sales figures.* ◊ *a sales drive/ campaign* (= a special effort to sell more) **3** (**sales**) [U] (also '**sales department** [C]) the part of a company that deals with selling its products: *a sales and marketing director* ◊ *She works in sales/the sales department.* ◊ *The Weldon Group has a 6000 strong sales force.* **4** [C] an occasion when a shop/store sells its goods at a lower price than usual: *The sale starts on December 28th.* ◊ *the January sales* ◊ *I bought a coat in the sales.* ◊ *sale prices/ goods* **5** [C] an occasion when goods are sold, especially an AUCTION: *a contemporary art sale*—see also CAR BOOT SALE, GARAGE SALE, JUMBLE SALE **IDM** **for 'sale** available to be bought, especially from the owner: *I'm sorry, it's not for sale.* ◊ *They've* **put their house up for sale.** ◊ *an increase in the number of stolen vehicles being offered for sale* ◊ *a 'for sale' sign* **on 'sale 1** available to be bought, especially in a shop/store: *Tickets are on sale from the booking office.* ◊ *The new model goes on sale next month.* **2** (*especially AmE*) being offered at a reduced price: *All*

S

æ	ɑː	e	ɜː	ə	ɪ	iː	i	ɒ	ɔː	ʌ	ʊ	u	uː
cat	father	ten	bird	about	sit	see	many	got	saw	cup	put	actual	too

(BrE)

video equipment is on sale today and tomorrow. **(on) ,sale or re'turn** (*BrE*) (of goods) supplied with the agreement that any item that is not sold can be sent back without having to be paid for

sale·able /'seɪləbl/ *adj.* good enough to be sold; that sb will want to buy: *a saleable commodity/product* ◊ *not in saleable condition* **OPP** UNSALEABLE

sale·room /'seɪlruːm; -rʊm/ (*BrE*) (*AmE* **sales·room**) *noun* a room where goods are sold at an AUCTION

'sales clerk *noun* (*AmE*) = SHOP ASSISTANT

sales·man /'seɪlzmən/, **sales·woman** /'seɪlzwʊmən/ *noun* (*pl.* **-men** /-mən/) (**-women** /-wɪmɪn/) a man or woman whose job is to sell goods, for example, in a shop/store: *a car salesman* ⇨ note at GENDER

sales·man·ship /'seɪlzmənʃɪp/ *noun* [U] skill in persuading people to buy things

sales·per·son /'seɪlzpɜːsn; *AmE* -pɜːrsn/ *noun* (*pl.* **-people**) a person whose job is to sell goods, for example, in a shop/store

'sales representative (also *informal* **'sales rep, rep**) *noun* an employee of a company who travels around a particular area selling the company's goods to shops/stores, etc.

sales·room /'seɪlzruːm; -rʊm/ *noun* (*AmE*) = SALEROOM

'sales slip *noun* (*AmE*) = RECEIPT

'sales talk *noun* [U] talk that tries to persuade sb to buy sth

'sales tax *noun* [U, C] (in some countries) the part of the price you pay when you buy sth that goes to the government as tax

sa·li·ent /'seɪliənt/ *adj.* [only before noun] most important or noticeable: *She pointed out the salient features of the new design.* ◊ *He summarized the salient points.*

sa·line /'seɪlaɪn; *AmE* -liːn/ *adj., noun*
■ *adj.* [usually before noun] (*technical*) containing salt: *Wash the lenses in saline solution.* ▶ **sal·in·ity** /sə'lɪnəti/ *noun* [U]: *to measure the salinity of the water*
■ *noun* [U] (*technical*) a mixture of salt in water

sal·iva /sə'laɪvə/ *noun* [U] the liquid that is produced in your mouth that helps you to swallow food

sal·iv·ary /sə'laɪvəri; 'sælɪvəri; *AmE* 'sæləveri/ *adj.* (*technical*) of or producing saliva

sali·vate /'sælɪveɪt/ *verb* [V] (*formal*) to produce more SALIVA in your mouth than usual, especially when you see or smell food: (*figurative*) *He was salivating over the thought of the million dollars.* ▶ **sali·va·tion** /ˌsælɪ'veɪʃn/ *noun* [U]

sal·low /'sæləʊ; *AmE* -loʊ/ *adj., noun*
■ *adj.* (of a person's skin or face) having a slightly yellow colour that does not look healthy
■ *noun* a type of WILLOW tree that does not grow very tall

sally /'sæli/ *noun, verb*
■ *noun* (*pl.* **sal·lies**) **1** a remark that is intended to entertain or amuse sb: *Everyone waited for his next sally.* **2** a sudden attack by an enemy
■ *verb* (**sal·lies, sally·ing, sal·lied, sal·lied**) **PHRV** **,sally 'forth/'out** (*old-fashioned* or *literary*) to leave a place in a determined or enthusiastic way

sal·mon /'sæmən/ *noun* [C, U] (*pl.* **sal·mon**) a large fish with silver skin and pink flesh that is used for food. Salmon live in the sea but swim up rivers to lay their eggs: *a whole salmon* ◊ *smoked salmon* ◊ *wild and farmed salmon*

sal·mon·ella /ˌsælmə'nelə/ *noun* [U] a type of bacteria that makes people sick if they eat infected food; an illness caused by this bacteria: *cases of salmonella poisoning* ◊ *an outbreak of salmonella*

,salmon 'pink *adj.* orange-pink in colour, like the flesh of a salmon ▶ **,salmon 'pink** *noun* [U]

salon /'sælɒn; *AmE* sə'lɑːn/ *noun* **1** a shop/store that gives customers hair or beauty treatment or that sells expensive clothes: *a beauty salon* ◊ *a hairdressing salon* **2** (*old-fashioned*) a room in a large house used for entertaining guests **3** (in the past) a regular meeting of writers, artists and other guests at the house of a famous or important person: *a literary salon*

sal·oon /sə'luːn/ *noun* **1** (also **sa'loon car**) (both *BrE*) (*AmE* **sedan**) a car with four doors and a BOOT (= space at the back for carrying things) which is separated from the part where the driver and passengers sit: *a five-seater family saloon*—picture at CAR **2** (also **sa'loon bar**) (both *BrE*) = LOUNGE BAR **3** a bar where alcoholic drinks were sold in the western US in the past **4** a large comfortable room on a ship, used by the passengers to sit and relax in

salsa /'sælsə; *AmE* 'sɑːlsə/ *noun* [U] **1** a type of Latin American dance music **2** a sauce eaten with Mexican food

sal·sify /'sælsəfi/ *noun* [U] (*BrE*) a plant with a long root that is cooked and eaten as a vegetable

salt /sɔːlt; *BrE* also sɒlt/ *noun, verb, adj.*
■ *noun* **1** [U] a white substance that is added to food to give it a better flavour or to preserve it. Salt is obtained from mines and is also found in sea water. It is sometimes called **common salt** to distinguish it from other chemical salts. **SYN** SODIUM CHLORIDE: *Pass the salt, please.* ◊ *a pinch of salt* (= a small amount of it) ◊ *Season with salt and pepper.* ◊ *sea salt*—see also ROCK SALT **2** [C] (*chemistry*) a chemical compound of a metal and an acid: *mineral salts*—see also EPSOM SALTS **3** (**salts**) [pl.] a substance that looks or tastes like salt: *bath salts* (= used to give a pleasant smell to bath water)—see also SMELLING SALTS **IDM** **the salt of the 'earth** a very good and honest person that you can always depend on—more at DOSE *n.*, PINCH *n.*, RUB *v.*, WORTH *adj.*
■ *verb* [VN] **1** [usually passive] to put salt on or in food: *salted peanuts* ◊ *a pan of boiling salted water* **2** ~ **sth (down)** to preserve food with salt: *salted fish* **3** to put salt on roads to melt ice or snow **PHRV** **,salt sth↔a'way** to save sth for the future, secretly and usually dishonestly: *She salted away the profits in foreign bank accounts.*
■ *adj.* [only before noun] containing, tasting of or preserved with salt: *salt water* ◊ *salt beef*

salt·box /'sɔːltbɒks; *AmE* -bɑːks *BrE* also 'sɒlt-/ *noun* (*AmE*) a house that has two floors at the front and one floor at the back, with a roof that slopes down between the two floors

'salt cellar 1 (*BrE*) (*AmE* **'salt shaker**) *noun* a small container for salt, usually with one hole in the top, that is used at the table **2** (*AmE*) a small open dish containing salt

salt·petre (*BrE*) (*AmE* **salt·peter**) /ˌsɔːlt'piːtə(r)/ *BrE* also ˌsɒlt-/ *noun* [U] a white powder used for preserving food and making matches and GUNPOWDER

'salt truck *noun* (*AmE*) = GRITTER

'salt water *noun* [U] sea water; water containing salt ▶ **'salt·water** *adj.* [only before noun]: *saltwater fish*—compare FRESHWATER

salty /'sɔːlti; *BrE* also 'sɒlti/ *adj.* (*comparative* **salt·ier**, no *superlative*) **1** containing or tasting of salt: *salty food* ◊ *salty sea air*—compare SWEET **2** (*old-fashioned*) (of language or humour) amusing and sometimes slightly rude ▶ **salti·ness** *noun* [U]: *She could taste the saltiness of her tears.*

sa·lu·bri·ous /sə'luːbriəs/ *adj.* (*formal*) (of a place) pleasant to live in; clean and healthy: *We had to move to a house in a less salubrious area.*

salu·tary /'sæljətri; *AmE* -teri/ *adj.* (of an experience) having a good effect on sb/sth, though often seeming unpleasant: *a salutary lesson/experience/warning* ◊ *The accident was a salutary reminder of the dangers of climbing.*

sa·lu·ta·tion /ˌsæljuː'teɪʃn/ *noun* (*formal*) **1** [C, U] a greeting or the action of greeting sb **2** [C] (*technical*) the words that are used in a letter to address the person you are writing to, for example 'Dear Sir'

sa·lute /sə'luːt/ *verb, noun*
■ *verb* **1** to touch the side of your head with the fingers of your right hand to show respect, especially in the armed forces: [V] *The sergeant stood to attention and saluted.* ◊ [VN] *to salute the flag/an officer* **2** [VN] (*formal*) to express respect and admiration for sb/sth: *The players saluted the fans before leaving the field.* ◊ *The president saluted the*

aɪ	aʊ	eɪ	əʊ	oʊ	ɔɪ	ɪə	eə	ʊə	j	w
my	now	say	go	go	boy	near	hair	pure	yes	wet
			(BrE)	(AmE)						

S

courage and self-sacrifice of those who fought for their country.
- *noun* **1** [C] the action of raising your right hand to the side of your head as a sign of respect, especially between soldiers and officers **2** [C, U] a thing that you say or do to show your admiration or respect for sb/sth or to welcome sb: *He raised his hat as a friendly salute.* ◊ *His first words were a salute to the people of South Africa.* ◊ *They all raised their glasses in salute.* **3** [C] an official occasion when guns are fired into the air to show respect for an important person: *a 21-gun salute*

sal·vage /ˈsælvɪdʒ/ *noun, verb*
- *noun* [U] **1** the act of saving things that have been, or are likely to be, damaged or lost, especially in a disaster or an accident: *the salvage of the wrecked tanker* ◊ *a salvage company/operation/team* **2** the things that are saved from a disaster or an accident: *an exhibition of the salvage from the wreck*
- *verb* [VN] **1** ~ **sth (from sth)** to save a badly damaged ship, etc. from being lost completely; to save parts or property from a damaged ship or from a fire, etc: *The wreck was salvaged by a team from the RAF.* ◊ *We only managed to salvage two paintings from the fire.* ◊ *The house was built using salvaged materials.* **2** to manage to rescue sth from a difficult situation; to stop a bad situation from being a complete failure: *What can I do to salvage my reputation?* (= get a good reputation again) ◊ *He wondered what he could do to salvage the situation.* ◊ *United lost 5–2, salvaging a little pride with two late goals.*

sal·va·tion /sælˈveɪʃn/ *noun* [U] **1** (in Christianity) the state of being saved from the power of evil: *to pray for the salvation of the world* **2** a way of protecting sb from danger, disaster, loss, etc: *Group therapy classes have been his salvation.*

the Sal·vation Army *noun* [sing.] a Christian organization whose members wear military uniforms and work to help poor people

salve *noun, verb*
- *noun* /sælv; AmE also sæv/ [U, C] a substance that you put on a wound or sore skin to help it heal or to protect it: *lip salve*
- *verb* /sælv/ [VN] ~ **your conscience** (*formal*) to do sth that makes you feel less guilty: *He took them presents to salve his conscience.*

sal·ver /ˈsælvə(r)/ *noun* a large plate, usually made of metal, on which drinks or food are served at a formal event

salvo /ˈsælvəʊ; AmE -voʊ/ *noun* (*pl.* **-os** or **-oes**) the act of firing several guns or dropping several bombs, etc. at the same time; a sudden attack: *The first salvo exploded a short distance away.* ◊ (*figurative*) *The newspaper article was the opening salvo in what proved to be a long battle.* ◊ *This statement provoked a salvo of accusations.*

Sa·mar·itan /səˈmærɪtən/ *noun* **IDM a good Sa·mar·itan** a person who gives help and sympathy to people who need it

samba /ˈsæmbə/ *noun* a fast dance originally from Brazil; a piece of music for this dance

same /seɪm/ *adj., pron., adv.*
- *adj.* **1** exactly the one or ones referred to or mentioned; not different: *We have lived in the same house for twenty years.* ◊ *She's still the same fun-loving person that I knew at college.* ◊ *This one works in exactly the same way as the other.* ◊ *They both said much the same thing.* ◊ *He used the very same* (= exactly the same) *words.* ◊ *I resigned last Friday and left that same day.* **2** exactly like the one or ones referred to or mentioned: *I bought the same car as yours* (= another car of that type). ◊ *She was wearing the same dress that I had on.* ◊ *The same thing happened to me last week.* **IDM** Idioms containing **same** are at the entries for the nouns and verbs in the idioms, for example **be in the same boat** is at **boat**.
- *pron.* **1 the ~ (as ...)** the same thing or things: *I would do the same again.* ◊ *I think the same as you do about this.* ◊ *Just do the same as me* (= as I do). ◊ *His latest movie is just more of the same—exotic locations, car chases and a final shoot-out.* ◊ (*spoken*) *'I'll have coffee.' 'Same for me, please*

(= I will have one too).' **2 the ~ (as ...)** having the same number, colour, size, quality, etc: *There are several brands and they're not all the same.* ◊ *I'd like one the same as yours.* **3** (**the same**) (*BrE*) the same person: *'Was that George on the phone?' 'The same* (= yes, it was George).' **IDM ,all/ ,just the 'same** in spite of this **SYN** NEVERTHELESS: *He's not very reliable, but I like him just the same.* ◊ *'Will you stay for lunch?' 'No, but thanks all the same.'* ◊ *All the same, there's some truth in what she says.* **be all the 'same to sb** to not be important to sb: *It's all the same to me whether we eat now or later.* **,one and the 'same** the same person or thing: *It turns out that her aunt and my cousin are one and the same.* **(the) ,same a'gain** (*spoken*) used to ask sb to serve you the same drink as before: *Same again, please!* **,same 'here** (*spoken*) used to say that sth is also true of you: *'I can't wait to see it.' 'Same here.'* **(the) ,same to 'you** (*spoken*) used to answer a greeting, an insult, etc: *'Happy Christmas!' 'And the same to you!'* ◊ *'Get lost!' 'Same to you!'*
- *adv.* (usually **the same**) in the same way; SIMILARLY: *Babies all look the same to me.* ◊ *We treat boys exactly the same as girls.* ◊ (*informal*) *He gave me five dollars, same as usual.*

same·ness /ˈseɪmnəs/ *noun* [U] the quality of being the same; a lack of variety: *She grew tired of the sameness of the food.*

samey /ˈseɪmi/ *adj.* (*BrE, informal, disapproving*) not changing or different and therefore boring

sa·mosa /səˈməʊsə; AmE -ˈmoʊ-/ *noun* a type of hot spicy Indian food consisting of a triangle of thin crisp pastry filled with meat or vegetables and fried

samo·var /ˈsæməvɑː(r)/ *noun* a large container for heating water, used especially in Russia for making tea

sam·pan /ˈsæmpæn/ *noun* a small boat with a flat bottom used along the coast and rivers of China

sam·ple /ˈsɑːmpl; AmE ˈsæmpl/ *noun, verb*
- *noun* **1** a number of people or things taken from a larger group and used in tests to provide information about the group: *The interviews were given to a random sample of students.* ◊ *The survey covers a representative sample of schools.* ◊ *a sample survey* **2** a small amount of a substance taken from a larger amount and tested in order to obtain information about the substance: *a blood sample* ◊ *Samples of the water contained pesticide.* **3** a small amount or example of sth that can be looked at or tried to see what it is like: *'I'd like to see a sample of your work,' said the manager.* ◊ *a free sample of shampoo* ◊ *sample exam papers*
- *verb* [VN] **1** to try a small amount of a particular food to see what it is like; to experience sth for a short time to see what it is like: *I sampled the delights of Greek cooking for the first time.* **2** (*technical*) to test, question, etc., part of sth or of a group of people in order to find out what the rest is like: *12% of the children sampled said they prefer cats to dogs.* **3** (*technical*) to record part of a piece of music, or a sound, in order to use it in a new piece of music

sam·pler /ˈsɑːmplə(r); AmE ˈsæm-/ *noun* **1** a piece of fabric decorated with different stitches that people made in the past to show a person's skill at sewing **2** a collection that shows typical examples of sth, especially pieces of music

sam·pling /ˈsɑːmplɪŋ; AmE ˈsæm-/ *noun* [U] **1** the process of taking a SAMPLE: *statistical sampling* **2** the process of copying and recording parts of a piece of music in an electronic form so that they can be used in a different piece of music

sam·urai /ˈsæmʊraɪ/ *noun* (*pl.* **sam·urai**) (in the past) a member of a powerful military class in Japan

sana·tor·ium /ˌsænəˈtɔːriəm/ (*AmE* also **sani·tar·ium**, **sana·tar·ium** /ˌsænəˈteəriəm; AmE -ˈter-/) *noun* (*pl.* **-riums** or **-ria** /-riə/) a place like a hospital where patients who have a lasting illness or who are getting better after an illness are treated

sanc·tify /ˈsæŋktɪfaɪ/ *verb* (**sanc·ti·fies**, **sanc·ti·fy·ing**, **sanc·ti·fied**, **sanc·ti·fied**) [VN] [usually passive] (*formal*) **1** to make sth holy **2** to make sth seem right or legal; to

S

give official approval to sth: *This was a practice sanctified by tradition.* ▶ **sanc·ti·fi·ca·tion** /ˌsæŋktɪfɪˈkeɪʃn/ *noun* [U]

sanc·ti·mo·ni·ous /ˌsæŋktɪˈməʊniəs; *AmE* -ˈmoʊ-/ *adj.* (*disapproving*) giving the impression that you feel you are better and more moral than other people: *the sanctimonious middle class* ▶ **sanc·ti·mo·ni·ous·ly** *adv.* **sanc·ti·mo·ni·ous·ness** *noun* [U]

sanc·tion /ˈsæŋkʃn/ *noun, verb*
■ *noun* **1** [C, usually pl.] ~ (**against sb**) an official order that limits trade, contact, etc. with a particular country, in order to make it do sth, such as obeying international law: *Trade sanctions were imposed against any country that refused to sign the agreement.* ◇ *The economic sanctions have been lifted.* **2** [U] (*formal*) official permission or approval for an action or a change: *These changes will require the sanction of the court.* **3** [C] ~ (**against sth**) a course of action that can be used, if necessary, to make people obey a law or behave in a particular way: *The ultimate sanction will be the closure of the restaurant.*
■ *verb* [VN] **1** (*formal*) to give permission for sth to take place: *The government refused to sanction a further cut in interest rates.* **2** (*technical*) to punish sb/sth; to IMPOSE a sanction (1) on sth

sanc·tity /ˈsæŋktəti/ *noun* [U] **1** ~ (**of sth**) the state of being very important and worth protecting and preserving: *the sanctity of marriage* **2** the state of being holy: *a life of sanctity, like that of St Francis*

sanc·tu·ary /ˈsæŋktʃuəri; *AmE* -ueri/ *noun* (*pl.* **-ies**) **1** [C] an area where wild birds or animals are protected and encouraged to breed: *a bird/wildlife sanctuary* **2** [U] safety and protection, especially for people who are being chased or attacked: *to take sanctuary in a place* ◇ *The government offered sanctuary to 4000 refugees.* ◇ *She longed for the sanctuary of her own home.* **3** [C, usually sing.] a safe place, especially one where people who are being chased or attacked can stay and be protected: *The church became a sanctuary for the refugees.* **4** [C] a holy building or the part of it that is considered the most holy

sanc·tum /ˈsæŋktəm/ *noun* [usually sing.] (*formal*) **1** a private room where sb can go and not be disturbed: *She once allowed me into her **inner sanctum.*** **2** a holy place

sand /sænd/ *noun, verb*
■ *noun* **1** [U] a substance that consists of very small fine grains of rock. Sand is found on beaches, in deserts, etc: *a grain of sand* ◇ *Concrete is a mixture of sand and cement.* ◇ *His hair was the colour of sand.* ◇ *The children were playing in the sand* (= for example, in a SANDPIT). **2** [U, C, usually pl.] a large area of sand on a beach: *We went for a walk along the sand.* ◇ *children playing on the sand* ◇ *miles of golden sands*—see also SANDY [IDM] see HEAD *n.*, SHIFT *v.*
■ *verb* [VN] ~ **sth** (**down**) = SANDPAPER

san·dal /ˈsændl/ *noun* a type of light open shoe that is worn in warm weather. The top part consists of leather bands that attach the sole to your foot: *open-toed sandals*—picture at SHOE

san·dalled (*BrE*) (*AmE* **san·daled**) /ˈsændld/ *adj.* [only before noun] wearing sandals: *sandalled feet*

san·dal·wood /ˈsændlwʊd/ *noun* [U] a type of oil with a sweet smell that is obtained from a hard tropical wood, also called **sandalwood**, and is used to make PERFUME

sand·bag /ˈsændbæɡ/ *noun, verb*
■ *noun* a bag filled with sand used to build a wall as a protection against floods or explosions
■ *verb* (**-gg-**) [VN] **1** to put sandbags in or around sth as protection against floods or explosions **2** (*informal, especially AmE*) to attack sb by criticizing them strongly; to treat sb badly

sand·bank /ˈsændbæŋk/ *noun* a bank or raised area of sand in a river or the sea—picture at COAST

sand·bar /ˈsændbɑː(r)/ *noun* a long mass of sand at the point where a river meets the sea that is formed by the movement of the water

sand·blast /ˈsændblɑːst; *AmE* -blæst/ *verb* [VN] [often passive] to clean, polish, decorate, etc. a surface by firing sand at it from a special machine

sand·box /ˈsændbɒks; *AmE* -bɑːks/ *noun* (*AmE*) = SANDPIT

sand·cas·tle /ˈsændkɑːsl; *AmE* -kæsl/ *noun* a pile of sand made to look like a castle, usually by a child on a beach

ˈsand dune *noun* = DUNE

sand·er /ˈsændə(r)/ *noun* an electric tool with a rough surface used for making wood smooth

s and h (also **s & h**) *abbr.* (*AmE*) shipping and handling—compare P. AND P.

sand·man /ˈsændmæn/ *noun* (**the sandman**) [sing.] an imaginary man who is said to make children fall asleep

sand·paper /ˈsændpeɪpə(r)/ *noun, verb*
■ *noun* [U] strong paper with a rough surface covered with sand or a similar substance, used for rubbing surfaces in order to make them smooth
■ *verb* [VN] (also **sand**) ~ **sth** (**down**) to make sth smooth by rubbing it with sandpaper

sand·piper /ˈsændpaɪpə(r)/ *noun* a small bird with long legs and a long beak that lives near rivers and lakes

sand·pit /ˈsændpɪt/ (*BrE*) (*AmE* **sand·box**) *noun* an area in the ground or a shallow container, filled with sand for children to play in

sand·stone /ˈsændstəʊn; *AmE* -stoʊn/ *noun* [U] a type of stone that is formed of grains of sand tightly pressed together, used in building

sand·storm /ˈsændstɔːm; *AmE* -stɔːrm/ *noun* a storm in a desert in which sand is blown into the air by strong winds

ˈsand trap (also **trap**) *noun* (both *AmE*) = BUNKER

sand·wich /ˈsænwɪtʃ; -wɪdʒ/ *noun, verb*
■ *noun* **1** (also *BrE informal* **sar·nie**) two slices of bread, often spread with butter, with a layer of meat, cheese, etc. between them: *a ham/chicken sandwich* ◇ *a sandwich bar* (= a place that sells sandwiches)—see also CLUB SANDWICH—picture on page A1 **2** (*BrE*) (in compounds) a SPONGE CAKE consisting of two layers with jam and/or cream between them: *a chocolate sponge sandwich* ◇ *a sandwich tin* (= for baking such a cake in)
■ *verb* [PHRV] **ˈsandwich sb/sth between sb/sth** [usually passive] to fit sth/sb into a very small space between two other things or people, or between two times: *I was sandwiched between two fat men on the bus.* **ˌsandwich A and B toˈgether** (**with sth**) to put sth between two things to join them: *Sandwich the cakes together with cream.*

ˈsandwich board *noun* a pair of boards with advertisements on them that sb wears at the front and back of their body as they walk around in public

ˈsandwich course *noun* (*BrE*) a course of study which includes periods of study and periods of working in business or industry

sandy /ˈsændi/ *adj.* **1** covered with or containing sand: *a sandy beach* ◇ *sandy soil* **2** (of hair) having a light colour, between yellow and red

sane /seɪn/ *adj.* (**saner**, **san·est**) **1** having a normal healthy mind; not mentally ill: *No sane person would do that.* ◇ *Being able to get out of the city at the weekend **keeps me sane.*** **2** sensible and reasonable: *a sane idea/argument/policy* [OPP] INSANE—see also SANITY

sang *pt* of SING

sang·froid /ˌsɒŋˈfrwɑː; *AmE* sɑːŋ-/ *noun* [U] (from *French*) the ability to remain calm in a difficult or dangerous situation

san·gria /ˈsæŋɡriə; sænˈɡriːə/ *noun* [U] (from *Spanish*) an alcoholic drink made of red wine mixed with fruit, and sometimes with water, fruit juice, LEMONADE or BRANDY added

san·guine /ˈsæŋɡwɪn/ *adj.* ~ (**about sth**) (*formal*) cheerful and confident about the future [SYN] OPTIMISTIC: *They are less sanguine about the company's long-term prospects.* ◇ *He tends to **take a sanguine view** of the problems involved.*

sani·tar·ium (*AmE*) = SANATORIUM

sani·tary /ˈsænətri; *AmE* -teri/ *adj.* **1** [only before noun] connected with keeping places clean and healthy to live in, especially by removing human waste: *Overcrowding*

s	t	v	z	ʃ	ʒ	tʃ	dʒ	θ	ð	ŋ
see	tea	van	zoo	shoe	vision	chain	jam	thin	this	sing

and poor sanitary conditions led to disease in the refugee camps. ◊ *The hut had no cooking or sanitary facilities.* **2** clean; not likely to cause health problems SYN HYGIENIC: *The new houses were more sanitary than the old ones had been.* OPP INSANITARY

'sanitary towel (*BrE*) (*AmE* **'sanitary napkin**) *noun* a thick piece of soft material that women wear outside their body to absorb the blood during their PERIOD—compare TAMPON

sani·ta·tion /ˌsænɪˈteɪʃn/ *noun* [U] the equipment and systems that keep places clean, especially by removing human waste: *disease resulting from poor sanitation*

sani·tize (*BrE* also **-ise**) /ˈsænɪtaɪz/ *verb* [VN] (*formal*) **1** (*disapproving*) to remove the parts of sth that could be considered unpleasant: *This sanitized account of his life does not mention his time in prison.* **2** to clean sth thoroughly using chemicals to remove bacteria

san·ity /ˈsænəti/ *noun* [U] **1** the state of having a normal healthy mind: *His behaviour was so strange that I began to doubt his sanity.* ◊ *to hang on to/keep/preserve your sanity* **2** the state of being sensible and reasonable: *After a series of road accidents the police pleaded for sanity among drivers.* OPP INSANITY—see also SANE

sank *pt* of SINK

sans serif (also **san·serif**) /ˌsæn ˈserɪf/ *noun* [U] (*technical*) (in printing) a TYPEFACE in which the letters have no SERIF

Santa Claus /ˈsæntə klɔːz/ (also *informal* **Santa**) = FATHER CHRISTMAS

sap /sæp/ *noun, verb*
■ *noun* **1** [U] the liquid in a plant or tree that carries food to all its parts: *Maple syrup is made from sap extracted from the sugar maple tree.* **2** [C] (*informal, especially AmE*) a stupid person that you can easily trick or treat unfairly
■ *verb* (**-pp-**) [VN] **~ sth| ~ sb (of sth)** to make sth/sb weaker; to destroy sth gradually: *The hot sun sapped our energy.* ◊ *Years of failure have sapped him of his confidence.*

sap·ling /ˈsæplɪŋ/ *noun* a young tree

sap·per /ˈsæpə(r)/ *noun* (*BrE*) a soldier whose job is to build or repair roads, bridges, etc.

sap·phire /ˈsæfaɪə(r)/ *noun* **1** [C, U] a clear, bright blue precious stone **2** [U] a bright blue colour ▶ **sap·phire** *adj.*: *sapphire eyes*

sappy /ˈsæpi/ *adj.* **1** (*AmE, informal*) = SOPPY **2** (of plants) full of SAP (= liquid)

sar·casm /ˈsɑːkæzəm; *AmE* ˈsɑːrk-/ *noun* [U] a way of using words that are the opposite of what you mean in order to be unpleasant to sb or to make fun of them: *'That will be useful,' she snapped with heavy sarcasm* (= she really thought it would not be useful at all). ◊ *a hint/touch/trace of sarcasm in his voice*

sar·cas·tic /sɑːˈkæstɪk; *AmE* sɑːrˈk-/ (also *BrE informal* **sarky**) *adj.* showing or expressing sarcasm: *sarcastic comments/remarks* ◊ *a sarcastic manner/smile/tone* ◊ *'There's no need to be sarcastic,' she said.* ▶ **sar·cas·tic·al·ly** /-kli/ *adv.*

sar·copha·gus /sɑːˈkɒfəgəs; *AmE* sɑːrˈkɑːf-/ *noun* (*pl.* **sar·coph·agi** /sɑːˈkɒfəgaɪ; *AmE* sɑːrˈkɑːf-/) a stone COFFIN (= box that a dead person is buried in), especially one that is decorated, used in ancient times

sar·dine /sɑːˈdiːn; *AmE* ˌsɑːrˈd-/ *noun* a small young sea fish (for example, a young PILCHARD) that is either eaten fresh or preserved in tins/cans IDM **(packed, crammed, etc.) like sar'dines** (*informal*) pressed tightly together in a way that is uncomfortable or unpleasant

sar·don·ic /sɑːˈdɒnɪk; *AmE* sɑːrˈdɑːnɪk/ *adj.* (*written, disapproving*) showing that you think that you are better than other people and do not take them seriously SYN MOCKING: *a sardonic comment/smile/tone* ▶ **sar·don·ic·al·ly** /-kli/ *adv.*

sarge /sɑːdʒ; *AmE* sɑːrdʒ/ *noun* (*informal*) used to talk to or about a SERGEANT

sari /ˈsɑːri/ *noun* a long piece of fabric that is wrapped around the body and worn as the main piece of clothing, especially by Indian women

sarky /ˈsɑːki; *AmE* ˈsɑːrki/ *adj.* (*BrE, informal*) = SARCASTIC

sar·nie /ˈsɑːni; *AmE* ˈsɑːrni/ *noun* (*BrE, informal*) = SANDWICH

sar·ong /səˈrɒŋ; *AmE* -ˈrɔːŋ; -ˈrɑːŋ/ *noun* a long piece of fabric wrapped around the body from the waist or the chest, worn by Malaysian and Indonesian men and women

sar·tor·ial /sɑːˈtɔːriəl; *AmE* sɑːrˈt-/ *adj.* [only before noun] (*formal*) relating to clothes, especially men's clothes, and the way they are made or worn ▶ **sar·tor·ial·ly** /-riəli/ *adv.*

SAS /ˌes eɪ ˈes/ *abbr.* Special Air Service (a group of highly trained soldiers in Britain who are used on very secret or difficult military operations)

SASE *noun* (*AmE*) an envelope on which you have written your name and address and put a stamp so that sb else can use it to send sth to you (abbreviation used in writing for 'self-addressed stamped envelope')—compare SAE

sash /sæʃ/ *noun* **1** a long strip of fabric worn around the waist or over one shoulder, especially as part of a uniform **2** either of a pair of windows, one above the other, that are opened and closed by sliding them up and down inside the frame

sashay /ˈsæʃeɪ; *AmE* sæˈʃeɪ/ *verb* [V+adv./prep.] to walk in a very confident but relaxed way, especially in order to be noticed

ˌsash 'window *noun* a window that consists of two separate parts, one above the other that you open by sliding one of the parts up or down—picture at HOUSE

sass /sæs/ *noun, verb*
■ *noun* [U] (*informal, especially AmE*) behaviour or talk that is rude and lacking respect: *Don't give me any of your sass!*
■ *verb* [VN] (*AmE, informal*) to speak to sb in a rude way, without respect: *Don't sass your mother!*

Sas·sen·ach /ˈsæsənæk; -næx/ *noun* (*ScotE, disapproving or humorous*) an English person ▶ **Sas·sen·ach** *adj.*

sassy /ˈsæsi/ *adj.* (*informal, especially AmE*) **1** (*disapproving*) rude; showing a lack of respect **2** (*approving*) fashionable and confident: *his sassy, streetwise daughter* ◊ *a sassy black linen dress*

SAT /sæt/ *noun* **1** (SAT™) (in the US) a test taken by high school students who want to go to a college or university (the abbreviation for 'scholastic aptitude test'): *to take the SAT* ◊ *I scored 1050 on the SAT.* ◊ *a SAT score* **2** (in Britain) the abbreviation for 'Standard Assessment Task'

sat *pt, pp* of SIT

Satan /ˈseɪtn/ *noun* the Devil

sa·tan·ic /səˈtænɪk/ *adj.* **1** (often **Sa·tan·ic**) connected with the worship of the Devil: *satanic cults/rites/rituals* **2** (*written*) extremely wicked and evil

sa·tan·ism /ˈseɪtənɪzəm/ *noun* [U] the worship of Satan ▶ **sa·tan·ist** /ˈseɪtənɪst/ *noun*

satchel /ˈsætʃəl/ *noun* a leather bag that you hang over your shoulder or wear on your back, that children used to use for carrying their books to school

sated /ˈseɪtɪd/ *adj.* [not usually before noun] **~ (with sth)** (*formal*) having had so much of sth that you do not need any more: *sated with food/pleasure*

sat·el·lite /ˈsætəlaɪt/ *noun* **1** an electronic device that is sent into space and moves around the earth or another planet. It is used for communicating by radio, television, etc. and for providing information: *a weather/communications satellite* ◊ *The interview came live by satellite from Hollywood.* ◊ *satellite television/TV* (= broadcast using a satellite) ◊ *a satellite broadcast/channel/picture* **2** a natural object that moves around a larger natural object in space: *The moon is a satellite of earth.* **3** a town, a country or an organization that is controlled by and dependent on another larger or more powerful one: *satellite states*

'satellite dish *noun* a piece of equipment that receives signals from a satellite, used to enable people to watch satellite television

æ	ɑː	e	ɜː	ə	ɪ	iː	i	ɒ	ɔː	ʌ	ʊ	u	uː
cat	father	ten	bird	about	sit	see	many	got	saw	cup	put	actual	too
								(BrE)					

'satellite station *noun* **1** a company that broadcasts television programmes using a satellite **2** a place where special equipment is used to follow the movements of satellites and receive information from them

sa·ti·ate /ˈseɪʃieɪt/ *verb* [VN] [usually passive] (*formal*) to give sb so much of sth so that they do not feel they want any more ▶ **sa·ti·ation** /ˌseɪʃiˈeɪʃn/ *noun* [U]

satin /ˈsætɪn; *AmE* ˈsætn/ *noun, adj.*
■ *noun* [U] a woven fabric with a smooth shiny surface: *a white satin dress/ribbon*
■ *adj.* [only before noun] having the smooth shiny appearance of satin: *The paint has a satin finish.*

sat·ire /ˈsætaɪə(r)/ *noun* [U,C] a way of criticizing a person, an idea or an institution in which you use humour to show their faults or weaknesses; a piece of writing that uses this type of criticism: *political/social satire* ◇ *a work full of savage/biting satire* ◇ *The novel is a stinging satire on American politics.*

sa·tir·ic·al /səˈtɪrɪkl/ (also *less frequent* **sa·tir·ic** /səˈtɪrɪk/) *adj.* using satire to criticize sb/sth: *a satirical cartoon/magazine/poem* ▶ **sa·tir·ic·al·ly** /-kli/ *adv.*

sat·ir·ist /ˈsætərɪst/ *noun* a person who writes or uses SATIRE

sat·ir·ize (*BrE* also **-ise**) /ˈsætəraɪz/ *verb* [VN] to use SATIRE to show the faults in a person, an organization, a system, etc.

sat·is·fac·tion /ˌsætɪsˈfækʃn/ *noun* **1** [U,C] the good feeling that you have when you have achieved sth or when sth that you wanted to happen does happen; sth that gives you this feeling: *to gain/get/derive satisfaction from sth* ◇ *a look/smile of satisfaction* ◇ *She looked back on her career with great satisfaction.* ◇ *He had the satisfaction of seeing his book become a best-seller.* ◇ *She didn't want to give him the satisfaction of seeing her cry.* ◇ *The company is trying to improve customer satisfaction.* ◇ *He was enjoying all the satisfactions of being a parent.*—see also DISSATISFACTION **2** [U] the act of FULFILLING a need or desire: *the satisfaction of sexual desires* ◇ *the satisfaction of your goals/ambitions* **3** (*formal*) an acceptable way of dealing with a complaint, a debt, an injury, etc: *I complained to the manager but I didn't get any satisfaction.* **IDM** **to sb's satis'faction 1** they are pleased with it: *The affair was settled to the complete satisfaction of the client.* **2** if you prove sth **to sb's satisfaction**, they believe or accept it: *Can you demonstrate to our satisfaction that your story is true?*

sat·is·fac·tory /ˌsætɪsˈfæktəri/ *adj.* good enough for a particular purpose; acceptable: *a satisfactory explanation/answer/solution/conclusion* ◇ *The work is satisfactory but not outstanding.* ◇ *The existing law is not wholly satisfactory.* **OPP** UNSATISFACTORY ⇨ note at ENOUGH ▶ **sat·is·fac·tor·ily** /-tərəli/ *adv.*: *Her disappearance has never been satisfactorily explained.* ◇ *Our complaint was dealt with satisfactorily.*

sat·is·fied /ˈsætɪsfaɪd/ *adj.* ~ **(with sb/sth) 1** pleased because you have achieved sth or because sth that you wanted to happen has happened: *a satisfied smile* ◇ *Keep all letters from satisfied customers.* ◇ *She's never satisfied with what she's got.* **OPP** DISSATISFIED **2** ~ **(that ...)** believing or accepting that sth is true **SYN** CONVINCED: *I'm satisfied that they are telling the truth.*—compare UNSATISFIED

sat·isfy /ˈsætɪsfaɪ/ *verb* (**sat·is·fies, sat·is·fy·ing, sat·is·fied, sat·is·fied**) **1** [VN] (not used in the progressive tenses) to make sb pleased by doing or giving them what they want: *Nothing satisfies him—he's always complaining.* ◇ *The proposed plan will not satisfy everyone.* **2** [VN] to provide what is wanted, needed or asked for: *to satisfy sb's hunger/curiosity* ◇ *The education system must satisfy the needs of all children.* ◇ *We cannot satisfy demand for the product.* ◇ *She failed to satisfy all the requirements for entry to the college.* **3** (not used in the progressive tenses) ~ **sb (of sth)** to show or prove to sb that sth is true or has been done: [VN] *Her explanation did not satisfy the teacher.* ◇ *People need to be satisfied of the need for a new system.* ◇

[VN (that)] *Once I had satisfied myself (that) it was the right decision, we went ahead.*

sat·is·fy·ing /ˈsætɪsfaɪɪŋ/ *adj.* giving pleasure because it provides sth you need or want: *a satisfying meal* ◇ *a satisfying experience* ◇ *It's satisfying to play a game really well.* ▶ **sat·is·fy·ing·ly** *adv.*

sat·suma /sætˈsuːmə/ *noun* a type of small orange without seeds and with loose skin that comes off easily

sat·ur·ate /ˈsætʃəreɪt/ *verb* [VN] **1** (*technical*) to make sth completely wet **SYN** SOAK: *The continuous rain had saturated the soil.* **2** [often passive] ~ **sth/sb (with/in sth)** to fill sth/sb completely with sth so that it is impossible or useless to add any more: *The company claimed to have saturated the market for personal organizers* (= so that no new buyers could be found).

sat·ur·ated /ˈsætʃəreɪtɪd/ *adj.* **1** [not usually before noun] completely wet **SYN** SOAKED **2** [usually before noun] (*chemistry*) **saturated** fats are not easily processed by the body when eaten because of the way their chemical structure is arranged: *dairy products high in saturated fats*—see also POLYUNSATURATED—compare UNSATURATED **3** [usually before noun] (*chemistry*) if a chemical SOLUTION (= a liquid with sth dissolved in it) is **saturated**, it contains the greatest possible amount of the substance that has been dissolved in it: *a saturated solution of sodium chloride* **4** [usually before noun] (*written*) (of colours) very strong: *bold contrasts of saturated reds and greens*

sat·ur·ation /ˌsætʃəˈreɪʃn/ *noun* [U] **1** (often *figurative*) the state or process that happens when no more of sth can be be accepted or added because there is already too much of it or too many of them: *a business beset by price wars and market saturation* (= the fact that no new customers can be found) ◇ *saturation bombing of the city* (= covering the whole city) ◇ *There was saturation coverage* (= so much that it was impossible to avoid it or add to it) *of the event by the media.* **2** (*chemistry*) the degree to which sth is absorbed in sth else, expressed as a PERCENTAGE of the greatest possible

satu'ration point *noun* [U, sing.] **1** the stage at which no more of sth can be accepted or added because there is already too much of it or too many of them: *The market for computer games has reached saturation point.* **2** (*chemistry*) the stage at which no more of a substance can be absorbed into a liquid or VAPOUR

Sat·ur·day /ˈsætədeɪ; -di; *AmE* ˈsætərd-/ *noun* [C, U] (*abbr.* **Sat.**) the day of the week after Friday and before Sunday **HELP** To see how **Saturday** is used, look at the examples at **Monday**. **ORIGIN** From the Old English for 'day of Saturn', translated from Latin *Saturni dies*.

Sat·urn /ˈsætɜːn; -tən; *AmE* ˈtɜːrn/ *noun* a large planet in the SOLAR SYSTEM that has rings around it and is 6th in order of distance from the sun

sat·ur·nine /ˈsætənaɪn; *AmE* ˈtərn-/ *adj.* (*literary*) (of a person or their face) looking serious and threatening

satyr /ˈsætə(r)/ *noun* (in ancient Greek stories) a god of the woods, with a man's face and body and a goat's legs and horns

sauce /sɔːs/ *noun* **1** [C, U] a thick liquid that is eaten with food to add flavour to it: *tomato/cranberry/chilli sauce* ◇ *chicken in a white wine sauce* ◇ *ice cream with a hot fudge sauce*—see also SOY SAUCE, TARTARE SAUCE, WHITE SAUCE **2** [U] (*old-fashioned, BrE, informal*) talk or behaviour that is annoying or lacking in respect **SYN** CHEEK **IDM** **what's ˌsauce for the 'goose is ˌsauce for the 'gander** (*old-fashioned, saying*) what one person is allowed to do, another person must be allowed to do in a similar situation

'sauce boat *noun* a long low JUG used for serving or pouring sauce at a meal

sauce·pan /ˈsɔːspən; *AmE* -pæn/ (*especially BrE*) (*AmE* usually **pot**) *noun* a deep round metal pot with a lid and one long handle or two short handles, used for cooking things over heat—picture at PAN

sau·cer /ˈsɔːsə(r)/ *noun* a small shallow round dish that a cup stands on; an object that is shaped like this: *cups and saucers*—see also FLYING SAUCER—picture at CUP

S

aɪ	aʊ	eɪ	əʊ	oʊ	ɔɪ	ɪə	eə	ʊə	j	w
my	now	say	go	go	boy	near	hair	pure	yes	wet
			(BrE)	(AmE)						

saucy /ˈsɔːsi/ adj. rude or referring to sex in a way that is amusing but not offensive SYN CHEEKY: *saucy comments/jokes* ◊ *a saucy smile* ▶ **sau·cily** /-ɪli/ adv.

sauer·kraut /ˈsaʊəkraʊt; AmE ˈsaʊərk-/ noun [U] (from German) CABBAGE (= a type of green vegetable) that is preserved in salt water and then cooked

sauna /ˈsɔːnə; ˈsaʊnə/ noun a type of bath in which you sit or lie in a small room (also called a **sauna**) which has been heated to a very high temperature by burning coal or wood. Some saunas involve the use of steam which is produced by pouring water over the hot coal or wood: *to have a sauna* ◊ *a hotel with a swimming pool and sauna* ◊ *to have/take a sauna*

saun·ter /ˈsɔːntə(r)/ verb [V+adv./prep.] to walk in a slow relaxed way: *He sauntered by, looking as if he had all the time in the world.* ▶ **saun·ter** noun [sing.]: *This part of the route should be an easy saunter.*

saus·age /ˈsɒsɪdʒ; AmE ˈsɔːs-/ noun [C, U] a mixture of finely chopped meat, fat, bread, etc. in a long tube of skin, cooked and eaten whole or served cold in thin slices: *beef/pork sausages* ◊ *200g of garlic sausage* IDM **not a ˈsausage** (old-fashioned, informal) nothing at all

ˈsausage dog noun (BrE, informal) = DACHSHUND

ˈsausage meat noun [U] the mixture of finely chopped meat, fat, bread, etc. used for making sausages

ˌsausage ˈroll noun (BrE) a small tube of pastry filled with sausage meat and cooked

sauté /ˈsəʊteɪ; AmE soʊˈteɪ/ verb (**sauté·ing, sautéed, sautéed** or **sauté·ing, sautéd, sautéd**) [VN] to fry food quickly in a little hot fat ▶ **sauté** adj. [only before noun]: *sauté potatoes*

sav·age /ˈsævɪdʒ/ adj., noun, verb
■ adj. **1** fierce and violent; causing great harm: *savage dogs* ◊ *She had been badly hurt in what police described as 'a savage attack'.* ◊ *savage public spending cuts* **2** involving very strong criticism: *The article was a savage attack on the government's record.* **3** [only before noun] (old-fashioned, ⚠) an offensive way of referring to groups of people or customs that are considered to be simple and not highly developed SYN PRIMITIVE: *a savage tribe* ▶ **sav·age·ly** adv.: *savagely attacked/criticized* ◊ *'No!' he snarled savagely.*
■ noun (old-fashioned, ⚠) an offensive word for a person who belongs to a tribe that is simple and not developed: *the development of the human race from primitive savages* ◊ *He described the terrorist attack as the work of savages* (= cruel and violent people).
■ verb [VN] **1** [usually passive] (of an animal) to attack sb violently, causing serious injury: *She was savaged to death by a bear.* **2** (written) to criticize sb/sth severely: *Her latest novel has been savaged by the critics.*

sav·agery /ˈsævɪdʒri/ noun [U] behaviour that is very cruel and violent: *The police were shocked by the savagery of the attacks.* ◊ *She replied with a savagery that took him by surprise.*

sa·van·nah (also **sa·vanna**) /səˈvænə/ noun [C, U] a wide flat open area of land, especially in Africa, that is covered with grass but has few trees—compare VELD

sav·ant /ˈsævənt; AmE sæˈvɑːnt/ noun (formal) **1** a person with great knowledge and ability **2** a person who is less intelligent than others but who has particular unusual abilities that other people do not have

save /seɪv/ verb, noun, prep., conj.
■ verb
KEEP SAFE | **1** [VN] ~ sb/sth (from sth/from doing sth) to keep sb/sth safe from death, harm, loss, etc: *to save sb's life* ◊ *to save a rare species (from extinction)* ◊ *Doctors were unable to save her.* ◊ *She saved a little girl from falling into the water.* ◊ *He's trying to save their marriage.* ◊ *She needs to win the next two games to save the match.* ◊ *Thanks for doing that. You saved my life* (= helped me a lot).
MONEY | **2** ~ (sth) (up) (for sth) to keep money instead of spending it, especially in order to buy a particular thing: [V] *I'm not very good at saving.* ◊ *I'm saving for a new bike.* ◊ *We've been saving up to go to Australia.* ◊ [VN] *You*

should save a little each week. ◊ *I've saved almost £100 so far.*
COLLECT STH | **3** [VN] to collect sth because you like it or for a special purpose: *I've been saving theatre programmes for years.* ◊ *If you save ten tokens you can get a T-shirt.*
KEEP FOR FUTURE | **4** ~ sth (for sth/sb) to keep sth to use or enjoy in the future: [VN, VNN] *Save some food for me.* ◊ *Save me some food.* ◊ [VN] *He's saving his strength for the last part of the race.* ◊ *We'll eat some now and save some for tomorrow.*
NOT WASTE | **5** ~ (sth) on sth | ~ sth (on sth) to avoid wasting sth or using more than necessary: [VN] *We'll take a cab to save time.* ◊ *Book early and save £50!* ◊ *We should try to save water and electricity.* ◊ *The government is trying to save £1 million on defence.* ◊ [VNN] *If we go this way it will save us two hours on the trip.* ◊ [V] *I save on fares by walking to work.*
AVOID STH BAD | **6** to avoid doing sth difficult or unpleasant; to make sb able to avoid doing sth difficult or unpleasant: [VN] *The prize money saved her from having to find a job.* ◊ *She did it herself to save argument.* ◊ [VNN] *Thanks for sending that letter for me—it saved me a trip.* ◊ [V-ing] *He's grown a beard to save shaving.* ◊ [VN-ing] *If you phone for an appointment, it'll save you waiting.*
IN SPORT | **7** (in football, hockey, etc.) to prevent an opponent's shot from going in the goal: [V] *The goalie saved brilliantly from Johnson's long-range shot.* ◊ [VN] *to save a penalty*—picture on page 1250
COMPUTING | **8** to make a computer keep work, for example by putting it on a disk: [VN] *Save data frequently.* [also V]
IDM **not be able to do sth to ˌsave your ˈlife** (informal) to be completely unable to do sth: *He can't interview people to save his life.* **save sb's ˈbacon/ˈneck** to rescue sb from a very difficult situation **save the ˈday/situˈation** to prevent failure or defeat, when this seems certain to happen: *Owen's late goal saved the day for Liverpool.* **save (sb's) ˈface** to avoid or help sb avoid embarrassment: *She was fired, but she saved face by telling everyone she'd resigned.* **save your ˈbreath** (spoken) used to tell sb that it is not worth wasting time and effort saying sth because it will not change anything: *Save your breath—you'll never persuade her.* **save your (own) ˈskin/ˈhide/ˈneck** to try to avoid death, punishment, etc., especially by leaving others in an extremely difficult situation: *To save his own skin, he lied and blamed the accident on his friend.*
■ noun (in football, etc.) an action by the GOALKEEPER that stops a goal being scored: *He made a spectacular save.*
■ prep. (also **save for**) (old use or formal) except sth: *They knew nothing about her save her name.*
■ conj. (old use or formal) except: *They found out nothing more save that she had borne a child.*

saver /ˈseɪvə(r)/ noun **1** a person who saves money and puts it in a bank, etc. for future use: *The increase in interest rates is good news for savers.* **2** (often in compounds) something that helps you spend less money or use less of the thing mentioned: *a money/time saver* ◊ *Their new model of dishwasher is a great water and energy saver.*—see also LIFESAVER

sav·ing /ˈseɪvɪŋ/ noun **1** [C] an amount of sth such as time or money that you do not need to use or spend: *Buy three and make a saving of 55p.* ◊ *With the new boiler you can make big savings on fuel bills.* **2** (**savings**) [pl.] money that you have saved, especially in a bank, etc: *He put all his savings into buying a boat.* **3** (-**saving**) (in adjectives) that prevents the waste of the thing mentioned or stops it from being necessary: *energy-saving modifications* ◊ *labour-saving devices* ◊ *space-saving fitted furniture*—see also FACE-SAVING

ˌsaving ˈgrace noun [usually sing.] the one good quality that a person or thing has that prevents them or it from being completely bad: *Her sense of humour is her saving grace.*

ˌsavings and ˈloan association noun (AmE) = BUILDING SOCIETY

sa·viour (BrE) (AmE **sa·vior**) /ˈseɪvjə(r)/ noun **1** a person who rescues sb/sth from a dangerous or difficult situation: *The new manager has been hailed as the saviour of the club.* **2** (**the Saviour**) used in the Christian religion as another name for Jesus Christ

savoir faire /ˌsævwɑː ˈfeə(r); *AmE* ˌsævwɑːr ˈfer/ *noun* [U] (from *French, approving*) the ability to behave in the appropriate way in social situations

sa·vory (*AmE*) = SAVOURY

sa·vour (*BrE*) (*AmE* **savor**) /ˈseɪvə(r)/ *verb, noun*
■ *verb* [VN] **1** to enjoy the full taste or flavour of sth, especially by eating or drinking it slowly: *He ate his meal slowly, savouring every mouthful.* **2** to enjoy a feeling or an experience thoroughly [SYN] RELISH: *I wanted to savour every moment.* PHRV **ˈsavour of sth** [no passive] (*formal*) to seem to have an amount of sth, especially sth bad: *His recent comments savour of hypocrisy.*
■ *noun* [usually sing.] (*formal* or *literary*) a taste or smell, especially a pleasant one: (*figurative*) *For Emma, life had lost its savour.*

sa·voury (*BrE*) (*AmE* **sa·vory**) /ˈseɪvəri/ *adj., noun*
■ *adj.* **1** having a taste that is salty not sweet: *savoury dishes/snacks* **2** having a pleasant taste or smell: *a savoury smell from the kitchen*—see also UNSAVOURY
■ *noun* [usually pl.] (*pl.* **-ies**) a small amount of a food with a salty taste, not a sweet one, often served at a party, etc.

savvy /ˈsævi/ *noun, adj.*
■ *noun* [U] (*informal*) practical knowledge or understanding of sth: *business/political savvy*
■ *adj.* (*informal, especially AmE*) having practical knowledge and understanding of sth; having COMMON SENSE: *savvy shoppers/travellers*

saw /sɔː/ *noun, verb*—see also SEE *v.*
■ *noun* **1** (often in compounds) a tool that has a long blade with sharp points (called TEETH) along one of its edges. A saw is moved backwards and forwards by hand or driven by electricity and is used for cutting wood or metal.—see also CHAINSAW, CIRCULAR SAW, HACKSAW, HANDSAW, JIGSAW **2** (*old-fashioned*) a short phrase or sentence that states a general truth about life or gives advice
■ *verb* (**sawed, sawn** /sɔːn/) (*AmE also* **sawed, sawed**) **1** to use a saw to cut sth: [V] *The workmen sawed and hammered all day.* ◊ *He accidentally sawed through a cable.* ◊ [VN] *She sawed the plank in half.* **2** ~ (**away**) (**at sth**) to move sth backwards and forwards on sth as if using a saw: [V] *She sawed away at her violin.* ◊ *He was sawing energetically at a loaf of bread.* [also VN] PHRV **ˌsaw sth↔ˈdown** to cut sth and bring it to the ground using a saw: *The tree had to be sawn down.* **ˌsaw sth↔ˈoff**, **ˌsaw sth ˈoff sth** to remove sth by cutting it with a saw: *We sawed the dead branches off the tree.* **ˌsaw sth↔ˈup (into sth)** to cut sth into pieces with a saw: *We sawed the wood up into logs.*

saw·dust /ˈsɔːdʌst/ *noun* [U] very small pieces of wood that fall as powder when wood is cut with a SAW

saw·mill /ˈsɔːmɪl/ *noun* a factory in which wood is cut into boards using machinery

sax /sæks/ *noun* (*informal*) = SAXOPHONE

Saxon /ˈsæksn/ *noun* a member of a race of people once living in NW Germany, some of whom settled in Britain in the 5th and 6th centuries—see also ANGLO-SAXON
▶ **Saxon** *adj.*: *Saxon churches/kings*

saxo·phone /ˈsæksəfəʊn; *AmE* -foʊn/ (*also informal* **sax**) *noun* a metal musical instrument that you blow into, used especially in jazz—picture on page 841

sax·opho·nist /sækˈsɒfənɪst; *AmE* ˈsæksəfoʊnɪst/ *noun* a person who plays the saxophone

say /seɪ/ *verb, noun, exclamation*
■ *verb* (**says** /sez/ **said, said** /sed/)
SPEAK | **1** ~ sth (**to sb**) to speak or tell sb sth, using words: [V speech] *'Hello!' she said.* ◊ *'That was marvellous,' said Daniel.* HELP In stories the subject often comes after **said**, **says** or **say** when it follows the actual words spoken, unless it is a pronoun: [VN] *Be quiet, I have something to say.* ◊ *She said nothing to me about it.* ◊ *Having said that* (= despite what I have just said), *I agree with your other point.* ◊ *He knew that if he wasn't back by midnight, his parents would have something to say about it* (= be

angry). ◊ *That's a terrible thing to say.* ◊ *I didn't believe a word she said.* ◊ [V(that)] *He said (that) his name was Sam.* ◊ [VNthat] *It is said that she lived to be over 100.* ◊[Vwh-] *She finds it hard to say what she feels.* ◊ [V] *I said to myself* (= thought), *'That can't be right!'* ◊ *'That's impossible!'* ' *So you say* (= but I think you may be wrong).' ◊ *'Why can't I go out now?' 'Because I say so.'* ◊ *'What do you want it for?'* ***I'd rather not say.'*** ◊ [Vtoinf] *He said to meet him here.* ◊ [VNtoinf] *He is said to have been a brilliant scholar.* HELP This pattern is only used in the passive.
REPEAT WORDS | **2** [VN] to repeat words, phrases, etc: *to say a prayer* ◊ *Try to say that line with more conviction.*
EXPRESS OPINION | **3** to express an opinion on sth: [VN] *Say what you like* (= although you disagree) *about her, she's a fine singer.* ◊ *I'll say this for them, they're a very efficient company.* ◊ *Anna thinks I'm lazy—what do you say* (= what is your opinion)? ◊ [V(that)] *I can't say I blame her for resigning* (= I think she was right). ◊ *I say* (= suggest) *we go without them.* ◊ *I wouldn't say they were rich* (= in my opinion they are not rich). ◊ *That's not to say it's a bad movie* (= it is good but it is not without faults). ◊ [Vwh-] *It's hard to say what caused the accident.* ◊ [V] *'When will it be finished?' 'I couldn't say* (= I don't know).'
GIVE EXAMPLE | **4** [no passive] to suggest or give sth as an example or a possibility: [VN] *You could learn the basics in, let's say, three months.* ◊ *Let's take any writer, say* (= for example) *Dickens …* ◊ [V(that)] *Say you lose your job: what would you do then?*
SHOW THOUGHTS/FEELINGS | **5** [VN] ~ sth (**to sb**) to make thoughts, feelings, etc. clear to sb by using words, looks, movements, etc: *His angry glance said it all.* ◊ *That says it all really, doesn't it?* (= it shows clearly what is true) ◊ *Just what is the artist trying to say in her work?*
GIVE WRITTEN INFORMATION | **6** [no passive] (of sth that is written or can be seen) to give particular information or instructions: [V speech] *The notice said 'Keep Out'.* ◊ [VN] *The clock said three o'clock.* ◊ [V(that)] *The instructions say (that) we should leave it to set for four hours.* ◊ [Vwh-] *The book doesn't say where he was born.* ◊ [Vtoinf] *The guidebook says to turn left.*
IDM **before you can say Jack ˈRobinson** (*old-fashioned*) very quickly; in a very short time **ˌgo without ˈsaying** to be very obvious or easy to predict: *Of course I'll help you. That goes without saying.* **have something, nothing, etc. to ˈsay for yourself** to be ready, unwilling, etc. to talk or give your views on sth: *She doesn't have much to say for herself* (= doesn't take part in conversation). ◊ *He had plenty to say for himself* (= he had a lot of opinions and was willing to talk). ◊ *Late again— what have you got to say for yourself* (= what is your excuse)? **ˈI'll say!** (*old-fashioned, spoken*) used to say 'yes' in a very forceful way: *'Does she see him often?' 'I'll say! Nearly every day.'* **I ˈmust say** (*spoken*) used to emphasize an opinion: *Well, I must say, that's the funniest thing I've heard all week.* **ˌI ˈsay** (*old-fashioned, BrE, spoken*) **1** used to express surprise, shock, etc: *I say! What a huge cake!* **2** used to attract sb's attention or introduce a new subject of conversation: *I say, can you lend me five pounds?* **it says a ˈlot, very ˈlittle, etc. for sb/sth** (*informal*) it shows a good/bad quality that sb/sth has: *It says a lot for her that she never lost her temper.* ◊ *It didn't say much for their efficiency that the order arrived a week late.* **I ˌwouldn't ˈsay ˈno (to sth)** (*spoken*) used to say that you would like sth or to accept sth that is offered: *I wouldn't say no to a pizza.* ◊ *'Tea, Brian?' 'I wouldn't say no.'* **least ˈsaid ˌsoonest ˈmended** (*BrE, saying*) a bad situation will pass or be forgotten most quickly if nothing more is said about it **the less/least said the ˈbetter** the best thing to do is say as little as possible about sth **never say ˈdie** (*saying*) do not stop hoping **ˈnot to say** used to introduce a stronger way of describing sth: *a difficult, not to say impossible, task* **say ˈcheese** used to ask sb to smile before you take their photograph **say ˈno (to sth)** to refuse an offer, a suggestion, etc: *If you don't invest in this, you're saying no to a potential fortune.* **ˌsay no ˈmore** (*spoken*) used to say that you understand exactly what sb

S

means or is trying to say, so it is unnecessary to say anything more: *'They went to Paris together.' 'Say no more!'* **,say your 'piece** to say exactly what you feel or think **say 'what?** (*AmE, spoken*) used to express surprise at what sb has just said: *'He's getting married.' 'Say what?'* **say 'when** used to ask sb to tell you when you should stop pouring a drink or serving food for them because they have enough **'that is to say** in other words: *three days from now, that is to say on Friday* **that's not 'saying much** used to say that sth is not very unusual or special: *She's a better player than me, but that's not saying much* (= because I am a very bad player). **there's no 'saying** used to say that it is impossible to predict what might happen: *There's no saying how he'll react.* **there's something, not much, etc. to be said for sth/doing sth** there are/are not good reasons for doing sth, believing sth or agreeing with sth **to ,say the 'least** without exaggerating at all: *I was surprised, to say the least.* **to say 'nothing of sth** used to introduce a further fact or thing in addition to those already mentioned SYN NOT TO MENTION: *It was too expensive, to say nothing of the time it wasted.* **well 'said!** (*spoken*) I agree completely: *'We must stand up for ourselves.' 'Well said, John.'* **,what do/would you 'say (to sth/doing sth)** (*spoken*) would you like sth/to do sth?: *What do you say to eating out tonight?* ◊ *Let's go away for a weekend. What do you say?* **what/ whatever sb says, 'goes** (*informal*, often *humorous*) a particular person must be obeyed: *Sarah wanted the kitchen painted green, and what she says, goes.* **whatever you 'say** (*spoken*) used to agree to sb's suggestion because you do not want to argue **when ,all is said and 'done** when everything is considered: *I know you're upset, but when all's said and done it isn't exactly a disaster.* **who can 'say (…)?** (*spoken*) used to say that nobody knows the answer to a question: *Who can say what will happen next year?* **who 'says (…)?** (*spoken*) used to disagree with a statement or an opinion: *Who says I can't do it?* **who's to say (…)?** (*spoken*) used to say that sth might happen or might have happened in a particular way, because nobody really knows: *Who's to say we would not have succeeded if we'd had more time?* **you can say 'that again** (*spoken*) I agree with you completely: *'He's in a bad mood today.' 'You can say that again!'* **you can't say 'fairer (than 'that)** (*BrE, spoken*) used to say that you think the offer you are making is reasonable or generous: *Look, I'll give you £100 for it. I can't say fairer than that.* **you don't 'say!** (*spoken*, often *ironic*) used to express surprise: *'They left without us.' 'You don't say!'* (= I'm not surprised) **you 'said it!** (*spoken*) **1** (*BrE*) used to agree with sb when they say sth about themselves that you would not have been rude enough to say yourself: *'I know I'm not the world's greatest cook.' 'You said it!'* **2** (*AmE*) used to agree with sb's suggestion—more at DARE *v*., EASY *adj*., ENOUGH *pron*., GLAD, LET *v*., MEAN *v*., NEEDLESS, RECORD *n*., SOON, SORRY *adj*., SUFFICE, WORD *n*.

■ *noun* [sing., U] **~ (in sth)** the right to influence sth by giving your opinion before a decision is made: *We had no say in the decision to sell the company.* ◊ *People want a greater say in local government.* ◊ *The judge has the final say on the sentence.*

IDM **have your 'say** (*informal*) to have the opportunity to express yourself fully about sth: *She won't be happy until she's had her say.*—see also SAY YOUR PIECE

■ *exclamation* (*AmE, informal*) **1** used for showing surprise or pleasure: *Say, that's a nice haircut!* **2** used for attracting sb's attention or for making a suggestion or comment: *Say, how about going to a movie tonight?*

say·ing /ˈseɪɪŋ/ *noun* a well-known phrase or statement that expresses sth about life that most people believe is wise and true: *'Accidents will happen', as the saying goes.*

'say-so *noun* [sing.] (*informal*) permission that sb gives to do sth: *Nothing could be done without her say-so.* ◊ *He has the final say-so on these matters* (= the right to make decisions). IDM **on sb's 'say-so** based on a statement that sb makes without giving any proof: *He hired and fired people on his partner's say-so.*

'S-bend *noun* a bend in a road or pipe that is shaped like an S

scab /skæb/ *noun* **1** [C] a hard dry covering that forms over a wound as it heals **2** [U] a skin disease of animals **3** [U] a disease of plants, especially apples and potatoes, that causes a rough surface **4** [C] (*informal, disapproving*) a worker who refuses to join a strike or takes the place of sb on strike SYN BLACKLEG

scab·bard /ˈskæbəd; *AmE* -bərd/ *noun* a cover for a SWORD that is made of leather or metal SYN SHEATH

sca·bies /ˈskeɪbiːz/ *noun* [U] a skin disease that causes ITCHING and small red raised spots

scab·rous /ˈskeɪbrəs; ˈskæb-/ *adj.* **1** (*formal*) offensive or shocking in a sexual way **2** (*technical*) having a rough surface: *scabrous skin*

scads /skædz/ *noun* [pl.] **~ (of sth)** (*informal, especially AmE*) large numbers or amounts of sth: *scads of $20 bills*

scaf·fold /ˈskæfəʊld; *AmE* -foʊld/ *noun* **1** a platform used when EXECUTING criminals by cutting off their heads or hanging them from a rope **2** a structure made of scaffolding, for workers to stand on when they are working on a building

scaf·fold·ing /ˈskæfəldɪŋ/ *noun* [U] metal poles and wooden boards that are joined together to make a structure for workers to stand on when they are working high up on the outside wall of a building

sca·lar /ˈskeɪlə(r)/ *adj.* (*mathematics*) (of a quantity) having size but no direction—compare VECTOR ▶ **sca·lar** *noun*

scala·wag /ˈskæləwæg/ *noun* (*AmE, informal*) = SCALLY-WAG

scald /skɔːld/ *verb, noun*
■ *verb* [VN] to burn yourself or part of your body with very hot liquid or steam: *Be careful not to scald yourself with the steam.* ◊ (*figurative*) *Tears scalded her eyes.*
■ *noun* an injury to the skin from very hot liquid or steam

scald·ing /ˈskɔːldɪŋ/ *adj.* hot enough to SCALD: *scalding water* ◊ (*figurative*) *Scalding tears poured down her face.* ▶ **scald·ing** *adv.*: *scalding hot*

scale /skeɪl/ *noun, verb*
■ *noun*
SIZE **1** [sing., U] **~ (of sth)** the size or extent of sth, especially when compared with sth else: *They entertain on a large scale* (= they hold expensive parties with a lot of guests). ◊ *Here was corruption on a grand scale.* ◊ *On a global scale, 77% of energy is created from fossil fuels.* ◊ *to achieve economies of scale in production* (= to produce many items so the cost of producing each one is reduced) ◊ *It was impossible to comprehend the full scale of the disaster.* ◊ *It was not until morning that the sheer scale of*

æ	ɑː	e	ɜː	ə	ɪ	iː	i	ɒ	ɔː	ʌ	ʊ	u	uː
cat	father	ten	bird	about	sit	see	many	got	saw	cup	put	actual	too

(BrE)

scale

scales (*AmE also* scale)   scale

the scale of C   fish scales

the damage could be seen (= how great it was).—see also FULL-SCALE, LARGE-SCALE, SMALL-SCALE

RANGE OF LEVELS | **2** [C] a range of levels or numbers used for measuring sth: *a five-point pay scale ◇ to evaluate performance on a scale from 1 to 10*—see also RICHTER SCALE, SLIDING SCALE, TIMESCALE **3** [C, usually sing.] the set of all the different levels of sth, from the lowest to the highest: *At the other end of the scale, life is a constant struggle to get enough to eat. ◇ the social scale*

MARKS FOR MEASURING | **4** [C] a series of marks at regular intervals on an instrument that is used for measuring: *How much does it read on the scale?*

WEIGHING INSTRUMENT | **5** (scales) [pl.] (*AmE also* scale) an instrument for weighing people or things: *bathroom/kitchen/weighing scales ◇ (figurative) the scales of justice* (= represented as the two pans on a BALANCE (5))

OF MAP/DIAGRAM/MODEL | **6** [C] the relation between the actual size of sth and its size on a map, diagram or model that represents it: *a scale of 1:25000 ◇ a scale model/drawing ◇ Both plans are drawn to the same scale. ◇ Is this diagram to scale* (= are all its parts the same size and shape in relation to each other as they are in the thing represented)*?*

IN MUSIC | **7** [C] a series of musical notes moving upwards or downwards, with fixed intervals between each note, especially a series of eight starting on a particular note: *the scale of C major ◇ to practise scales on the piano*—compare KEY *n.* (4), OCTAVE

OF FISH/REPTILE | **8** [C] any of the thin plates of hard material that cover the skin of many fish and reptiles—picture on page A7

IN WATER PIPES, etc. | **9** (*BrE also* fur) [U] a hard greyish-white substance that is sometimes left inside water pipes and containers for heating water—see also LIMESCALE

ON TEETH | **10** [U] a hard substance that forms on teeth, especially when they are not cleaned regularly—compare PLAQUE

IDM see TIP *v.*

■ *verb* [VN]

CLIMB | **1** (*written*) to climb to the top of sth very high and steep: *the first woman to scale Mount Everest ◇ (figurative) He has scaled the heights in his profession.*

FISH | **2** to remove the small flat hard pieces of skin from a fish

TEETH | **3** to remove TARTAR from the teeth by SCRAPING: *The dentist scaled and polished my teeth.*

CHANGE SIZE | **4** (*technical*) to change the size of sth: *Text can be scaled from 4 points to 108 points without any loss of quality.*

PHR V ,scale sth↔'down (*AmE also* ,scale sth↔'back) to reduce the number, size or extent of sth: *We are thinking of scaling down our training programmes next year. ◇ The IMF has scaled back its growth forecasts for*

the next decade. ,scale sth↔'up to increase the size or number of sth

scal·lion /'skæliən/ *noun* (*AmE*) = SPRING ONION

scal·lop *noun, verb*
■ *noun* /'skɒləp; *AmE* 'skæləp/ **1** a shellfish that can be eaten, with two flat round shells that fit together: *a scallop shell* **2** any one of a series of small curves cut on the edge of fabric, pastry, etc. for decoration
■ *verb* [VN] [usually passive] to decorate the edge of sth with small curves: *a scalloped edge*

scally·wag /'skæliwæg/ (*BrE*) (*AmE* scala·wag) *noun* (*informal*) a person, especially a child, who behaves badly, but not in a serious way

scalp /skælp/ *noun, verb*
■ *noun* **1** the skin that covers the part of the head where the hair grows: *A dry scalp can lead to dandruff.* **2** (in the past) the skin and hair that was removed from the head of a dead enemy by some Native American tribes as a sign of victory **3** (*informal*) a symbol of the fact that sb has been defeated or punished: *They have claimed some impressive scalps in their bid for the championship.*
■ *verb* [VN] **1** to remove the skin and hair from the top of an enemy's head as a sign of victory: *(figurative, informal) If he finds me here, he'll scalp me!* **2** (*AmE*) = TOUT

scal·pel /'skælpəl/ *noun* a small sharp knife used by doctors in medical operations

scalp·er /'skælpə(r)/ *noun* (*AmE*) = TOUT: *ticket scalpers*

scaly /'skeɪli/ *adj.* (of skin) covered with SCALES

scam /skæm/ *noun* (*informal*) a clever and dishonest plan for making money

scamp /skæmp/ *noun* (*old-fashioned*) a child who enjoys playing tricks and causing trouble

scam·per /'skæmpə(r)/ *verb* [V+*adv. / prep.*] (especially of children or small animals) to move quickly with short light steps

scampi /'skæmpi/ *noun* [U+sing./ pl. *v.*] (*BrE*) large PRAWNS (= a type of sea creature) covered with BREAD-CRUMBS or BATTER and fried: *scampi and chips*

scan /skæn/ *verb, noun*
■ *verb* (-nn-) **1** [VN] ~ sth (for sth) to look at every part of sth carefully, especially because you are looking for a particular thing or person: *He scanned the horizon for any sign of land. ◇ She scanned his face anxiously.* **2** ~ (through) sth (for sth) to look quickly but not very carefully at a document, etc: [VN] *I scanned the list quickly for my name. ◇* [V] *She scanned through the newspaper over breakfast.* **3** [VN] to get an image of an object, a part of sb's body, etc. on a computer by passing a beam of X-RAYS, ULTRASOUND waves or ELECTROMAGNETIC waves over it in a special machine: *Their brains are scanned so that researchers can monitor the progress of the disease.* **4** [VN] (of a light, RADAR, etc.) to pass across an area: *Concealed video cameras scan every part of the compound.* **5** [V] (of poetry) to have a regular rhythm according to fixed rules: *This line doesn't scan.* **PHR V** ,scan sth 'into sth | ,scan sth 'in (*computing*) to pass an electronic beam over sth in order to put it in the memory of a computer: *Text and pictures can be scanned into the computer.*
■ *noun* **1** [C] a medical test in which a machine produces a picture of the inside of a person's body on a computer screen after taking X-RAYS: *to do/have a brain scan* **2** [C] a medical test for pregnant women in which a machine uses ULTRASOUND to produce a picture of a baby inside its mother's body: *to have a scan* **3** [sing.] the act of looking quickly through sth written or printed, usually in order to find sth

scan·dal /'skændl/ *noun* **1** [C, U] behaviour or an event that people think is morally or legally wrong and causes public feelings of shock or anger: *a series of sex scandals ◇ to cause/create a scandal ◇ The scandal broke* (= became known to the public) *in 1998. ◇ There has been no hint of scandal during his time in office.* **2** [U] talk or reports about the shocking or immoral things that people have done or are thought to have done: *to spread scandal ◇ newspapers full of scandal* **3** [sing.] ~ (that...) an action, attitude, etc. that you think is shocking and not at all

aɪ	aʊ	eɪ	əʊ	oʊ	ɔɪ	ɪə	eə	ʊə	j	w
my	now	say	go	go	boy	near	hair	pure	yes	wet
			(BrE)	(AmE)						

S

acceptable: *It is a scandal that such a large town has no orchestra.*

scan·dal·ize (*BrE* also **-ise**) /ˈskændəlaɪz/ *verb* [VN] to do sth that people find very shocking: *She scandalized her family with her extravagant lifestyle.*

scan·dal·mon·ger /ˈskændlmʌŋgə(r)/ *noun* (*disapproving*) a person who spreads stories about the shocking or immoral things that other people have done

scan·dal·ous /ˈskændələs/ *adj.* **1** ~ (**that...**) shocking and unacceptable: *a scandalous waste of money* ◊ *It is scandalous that he has not been punished.* **2** [only before noun] containing talk about the shocking or immoral things that people have done or are thought to have done: *scandalous stories* ▶ **scan·dal·ous·ly** *adv.*: *scandalously low pay*

Scan·di·navian /ˌskændɪˈneɪviən/ *adj.* of or connected with the countries of Scandinavia, especially Norway, Sweden and Denmark

scan·ner /ˈskænə(r)/ *noun* **1** a device for examining sth or recording sth using beams of light sound or X-RAYS: *The identity cards are examined by an electronic scanner.* ◊ *a document scanner* (= that stores the contents of a document on a computer) **2** a machine used by doctors to produce a picture of the inside of a person's body on a computer screen: *a body scanner* ◊ *an ultrasound/X-ray scanner* **3** a piece of equipment for receiving and sending RADAR signals

scant /skænt/ *adj.* [only before noun] hardly any; not very much and not as much as there should be: *I paid scant attention to what she was saying.* ◊ *The firefighters went back into the house with scant regard for their own safety.*

scanty /ˈskænti/ *adj.* too little in size or amount for what is needed: *Details of his life are scanty.* ◊ *scanty evidence* ◊ *a scanty bikini* ▶ **scant·ily** *adv.*: *scantily dressed models*

-scape *combining form* (in nouns) a view or scene of: *landscape* ◊ *seascape* ◊ *moonscape*

scape·goat /ˈskeɪpgəʊt; *AmE* -goʊt/ *noun* a person who is blamed for sth bad that sb else has done or for some failure [SYN] FALL GUY: *She felt she had been made a scapegoat for her boss's incompetence.* ▶ **scape·goat** *verb* [VN]

scap·ula /ˈskæpjʊlə/ *noun* (*pl.* **scapu·lae** /-liː/ or **scapu·las**) (*anatomy*) the SHOULDER BLADE

scar /skɑː(r)/ *noun, verb*
■ *noun* **1** a mark that is left on the skin after a wound has healed: *a scar on his cheek* ◊ *Will the operation leave a scar?* ◊ *scar tissue* **2** a permanent feeling of great sadness or mental pain that a person is left with after an unpleasant experience: *His years in prison have left deep scars.* **3** something unpleasant or ugly that spoils the appearance or public image of sth: *The town still bears the scars of war.* ◊ *Racism has been a scar on the game.* **4** an area of a hill or cliff where there is bare rock and no grass
■ *verb* [VN] [often passive] **1** (of a wound, etc.) to leave a mark on the skin after it has healed: *His face was badly scarred.* **2** (of an unpleasant experience) to leave sb with a feeling of sadness or mental pain: *The experience left her scarred for life.* **3** to spoil the appearance of sth: *The hills are scarred by quarries.* ◊ *battle-scarred buildings*

scarab /ˈskærəb/ (also **'scarab beetle**) *noun* a large black BEETLE (= an insect with a hard shell); a design showing a scarab beetle

scarce /skeəs; *AmE* skers/ *adj., adv.*
■ *adj.* (**scar·cer, scar·cest**) if sth is scarce, there is not enough of it and it is only available in small quantities: *scarce resources* ◊ *Details of the accident are scarce.* ◊ *Food was becoming scarce.* [IDM] **,make oneself 'scarce** (*informal*) to leave somewhere and stay away for a time in order to avoid an unpleasant situation
■ *adv.* (*literary*) only just; almost not: *I can scarce remember him.*

scarce·ly /ˈskeəsli; *AmE* ˈskers-/ *adv.* **1** only just; almost not: *I can scarcely believe it.* ◊ *We scarcely ever meet.* ◊ *Scarcely a week goes by without some new scandal in the papers.* **2** used to say that sth happens immediately after sth else happens: *He had scarcely put the phone down*

when the doorbell rang. ◊ *Scarcely had the game started when it began to rain.* **3** used to suggest that sth is not at all reasonable or likely: *It was scarcely an occasion for laughter.* ◊ *She could scarcely complain, could she?* ⇨ note at HARDLY

scar·city /ˈskeəsəti; *AmE* ˈskers-/ *noun* [U, C] (*pl.* **-ies**) it there is a **scarcity of** sth, there is not enough of it and it is difficult to obtain it [SYN] SHORTAGE: *a time of scarcity* ◊ *a scarcity of food/resources/data*

scare /skeə(r); *AmE* sker/ *verb, noun*
■ *verb* **1** to frighten sb: [VN] *You scared me.* ◊ [VN to inf] *It scared me to think I was alone in the building.* ◊ [V] to become frightened: *He doesn't scare easily.*—see also SCARY [IDM] **scare the 'shit out of sb | scare sb 'shitless** (🛆, *slang*) to frighten sb very much—more at DAYLIGHTS, DEATH, LIFE [PHRV] **,scare sb↔a'way/'off** to make sb go away by frightening them: *They managed to scare the bears away.* **'scare sb into doing sth** to frighten sb in order to make them do sth: *Local businesses were scared into paying protection money.* **,scare sb↔'off** to accidentally make sb afraid of or nervous about doing sth that they were going to do: *Rising prices are scaring customers off.* **,scare 'up sth** (*AmE, informal*) to find or make sth by using whatever is available: *I'll see if I can scare up enough chairs for us all.*
■ *noun* **1** [C] (used especially in newspapers) a situation in which a lot of people are anxious or frightened about sth: *a bomb/health scare* ◊ *recent scares about pesticides in food* ◊ *a scare story* (= a news report that spreads more anxiety or fear about sth than is necessary) ◊ *to cause a major scare* ◊ *scare tactics* (= ways of persuading people to do sth by frightening them) **2** [sing.] a sudden feeling of fear: *You gave me a scare!* ◊ *We've had quite a scare.*—see also SCARY

scare·crow /ˈskeəkrəʊ; *AmE* ˈskerkroʊ/ *noun* a figure made to look like a person, that is dressed in old clothes and put in a field to frighten birds away

scared /skeəd; *AmE* skerd/ *adj.* ~ (of sb/sth)| ~ (of doing sth)| ~ (to do sth)| ~ (that...) frightened of sth or afraid that sth bad might happen: *She is scared of going out alone.* ◊ *He's scared of heights.* ◊ *People are scared to use the buses late at night.* ◊ *I'm scared (that) I'm going to fall.* ◊ *The thieves got scared and ran away.* ◊ *a scared face/look* ◊ *I was scared to death* (= very frightened). ◊ *We were scared stiff* (= very frightened). ⇨ note at AFRAID [IDM] see SHADOW *n.*, WIT, WITLESS

scare·mon·ger /ˈskeəmʌŋgə(r); *AmE* ˈskerm-/ *noun* (*disapproving*) a person who spreads stories deliberately to make people frightened or nervous ▶ **scare·monger·ing** *noun* [U]

scarf /skɑːf; *AmE* skɑːrf/ *noun, verb*
■ *noun* (*pl.* **scarves** /skɑːvz; *AmE* skɑːrvz/ or *less frequent* **scarfs**) a piece of fabric worn for warmth or decoration around the neck or, by women, over the shoulders or hair: *a woollen/silk scarf*
■ *verb* [V, VN] (*AmE, informal*) = SCOFF

scar·ify /ˈskærɪfaɪ; ˈskeə-; *AmE* ˈsker-/ *verb* (**scari·fies, scari·fy·ing, scari·fied, scari·fied**) [VN] (*technical*) **1** to break up an area of grass, etc. and remove pieces of material from it that are not wanted **2** to make cuts in the surface of sth, especially skin

scar·let /ˈskɑːlət; *AmE* ˈskɑːrlət/ *adj.* bright red in colour: *scarlet berries/flowers* ◊ *She went scarlet with embarrassment.* ▶ **scar·let** *noun* [U]

,scarlet 'fever *noun* [U] a serious infectious disease that causes fever and red marks on the skin

,scarlet 'woman *noun* (*old-fashioned*) a woman who has sexual relationships with many different people

scarp /skɑːp; *AmE* skɑːrp/ *noun* (*technical*) a very steep slope

scar·per /ˈskɑːpə(r); *AmE* ˈskɑːrp-/ *verb* [V] (*BrE, informal*) to run away; to leave: *The police arrived, so we scarpered.*

scarves *pl.* of SCARF

scary /ˈskeəri; *AmE* ˈskeri/ *adj.* (**scari·er, scari·est**) (*informal*) frightening: *It was a really scary moment.* ◊ *a scary movie*—see also SCARE *v.*

S

scath·ing /ˈskeɪðɪŋ/ adj. ~ (about sb/sth) criticizing sb or sth very severely: *a scathing attack on the new management* ◊ *He was scathing about the government's performance.* ▶ **scath·ing·ly** adv.: *'Oh, she's just a kid,' he said scathingly.*

scato·logic·al /ˌskætəˈlɒdʒɪkl; AmE -ˈlɑːdʒ-/ adj. (formal) connected with human waste from the body in an unpleasant way: *scatological humour*

scat·ter /ˈskætə(r)/ verb, noun
■ verb **1** [VN] ~ sth (on/over/around sth) | ~ sth (with sth) to throw or drop things in different directions so that they cover an area of ground: *Scatter the grass seed over the lawn.* ◊ *Scatter the lawn with grass seed.* ◊ *They scattered his ashes at sea.* **2** to move or to make people or animals move very quickly in different directions: [V] *At the first gunshot, the crowd scattered.* ◊ [VN] *The explosion scattered a flock of birds roosting in the trees.*
■ noun [usually sing.] (also **scat·ter·ing** /ˈskætərɪŋ/ [sing.]) a small amount or number of things spread over an area: *a scatter/scattering of houses*

scat·ter·brain /ˈskætəbreɪn; AmE -tərb-/ noun (informal) a person who is always losing or forgetting things and cannot think in an organized way ▶ **scat·ter·brained** adj.

scat·tered /ˈskætəd; AmE -tərd/ adj. spread far apart over a wide area or over a long period of time: *a few scattered settlements* ◊ *sunshine with scattered showers* ◊ *Her family are scattered around the world.*

scatty /ˈskæti/ adj. (BrE, informal) tending to forget things and behave in a slightly silly way

scav·enge /ˈskævɪndʒ/ verb **1** ~ (for sth) (of a person, an animal or a bird) to search through waste for things that can be used or eaten: [VN] *Much of their furniture was scavenged from other people's garbage.* ◊ [V] *Dogs and foxes scavenged through the trash cans for something to eat.* **2** (of animals or birds) to eat dead animals that have been killed by another animal, by a car, etc: [VN] *Crows scavenge carrion left on the roads.* ◊ [V] *Some fish scavenge on dead fish in the wild.*

scav·en·ger /ˈskævɪndʒə(r)/ noun an animal, a bird or a person that scavenges

SCE /ˌes siː ˈiː/ abbr. Scottish Certificate of Education (exams taken by Scottish school students at two different levels at the ages of 16 and 17)—see also HIGHER, STANDARD GRADE

scen·ario /səˈnɑːriəʊ; AmE səˈnærioʊ/ noun (pl. -os) **1** a description of how things might happen in the future: *Let me suggest a possible scenario.* ◊ *The worst-case scenario* (= the worst possible thing that could happen) *would be for the factory to be closed down.* ◊ *a nightmare scenario* **2** a written outline of what happens in a film/movie or play

scene /siːn/ noun
PLACE | **1** [C, usually sing.] ~ (of sth) the place where sth happens, especially sth unpleasant: *the scene of the accident/attack/crime* ◊ *Firefighters were on the scene immediately.* ◊ *Italy was the scene of many demonstrations at that time.*
EVENT | **2** [C] ~ (of sth) an event or a situation that you see, especially one of a particular type: *a scene of panic/terror/violence* ◊ *The team's victory produced scenes of joy all over the country.* ◊ *She witnessed some very distressing scenes.*
IN MOVIE/PLAY, etc. | **3** [C] a part of a film/movie, play or book in which the action happens in one place or is of one particular type: *The movie opens with a scene in a New York apartment.* ◊ *love/sex scenes* ◊ *I got very nervous before my big scene* (= the one where I have a very important part). **4** [C] one of the small sections that a play or an opera is divided into: *Act I, Scene 2 of 'Macbeth'*
AREA OF ACTIVITY | **5** (the scene, the … scene) [sing.] (informal) a particular area of activity or way of life and the people who are part of it: *After years at the top, she just vanished from the scene.* ◊ *the club/dance/music scene* ◊ *A newcomer has appeared on the fashion scene.*
VIEW | **6** [C] a view that you see: *a delightful rural scene* ◊ *They went abroad for a change of scene* (= to see and experience new surroundings).
PAINTING/PHOTOGRAPH | **7** [C] a painting, drawing, or photograph of a place and the things that are happening there: *an exhibition of Parisian street scenes*
ARGUMENT | **8** [C, usually sing.] a loud, angry argument, especially one that happens in public and is embarrassing: *She had made a scene in the middle of the party.* ◊ *'Please leave,' he said. 'I don't want a scene.'*
IDM **behind the 'scenes 1** in the part of a theatre, etc. that the public does not usually see: *The students were able to go behind the scenes to see how programmes are made.* **2** in a way that people in general are not aware of: *A lot of negotiating has been going on behind the scenes.* ◊ *behind-the-scenes work* **not sb's 'scene** (informal) not the type of thing that sb likes or enjoys doing **set the 'scene (for sth) 1** to create a situation in which sth can easily happen or develop: *His arrival set the scene for another argument.* **2** to give sb the information and details they need in order to understand what comes next: *The first part of the programme was just setting the scene.*

scen·ery /ˈsiːnəri/ noun [U] **1** the natural features of an area, such as mountains, valleys, rivers and forests, when you are thinking about them being attractive to look at: *The scenery is magnificent.* ◊ *to enjoy the scenery* ⇨ note at LANDSCAPE **2** the painted background that is used to represent natural features or buildings on a theatre stage

scenic /ˈsiːnɪk/ adj. **1** [usually before noun] having beautiful natural scenery: *an area of scenic beauty* ◊ *They took the scenic route back to the hotel.* ◊ *a scenic drive* **2** [only before noun] connected with scenery in a theatre: *scenic designs* ▶ **scen·ic·al·ly** /-kli/ adv.: *scenically attractive areas*

scent /sent/ noun, verb
■ noun **1** [U, C] the pleasant smell that sth has: *The air was filled with the scent of wild flowers.* ◊ *These flowers have no scent.* **2** [U, C, usually sing.] the smell that a person or an animal leaves behind and that other animals such as dogs can follow: *The dogs must have lost her scent.* **3** [U] (especially BrE) a liquid with a pleasant smell that you wear on your skin to make it smell nice: *a bottle of scent* **4** ~ of sth [sing.] the feeling that sth is present or is going to happen very soon: *The scent of victory was in the air.*
IDM **put/throw sb off the 'scent** to do sth to stop sb from finding you or discovering sth **on the 'scent (of sth)** close to discovering sth
■ verb [VN] **1** to find sth by using the sense of smell: *The dog scented a rabbit.* **2** (written) to begin to feel that sth exists or is about to happen: *The press could scent a scandal.* ◊ *By then, the team was scenting victory.* **3** ~ sth (with sth) [often passive] to give sth a particular, pleasant smell: *Roses scented the night air.* ◊ *Scent the room with your favourite aromas.*

scent·ed /ˈsentɪd/ adj. having a strong pleasant smell: *scented pine woods*

scep·ter (AmE) = SCEPTRE

scep·tic (BrE) (AmE **skep·tic**) /ˈskeptɪk/ noun a person who usually doubts that claims or statements are true, especially those that other people believe in: *I am a born sceptic.* ◊ *He was unable to convince the sceptics in the audience.*

scep·tical (AmE **skep·tical**) /ˈskeptɪkl/ adj. ~ (about/of sth) having doubts that a claim or statement is true or that sth will happen: *I am sceptical about his chances of winning.* ◊ *The public remain sceptical of these claims.* ◊ *She looked highly sceptical.* ▶ **scep·tic·al·ly** (AmE **skep·tic·al·ly**) /-kli/ adv.

scep·ti·cism (AmE **skep·ti·cism**) /ˈskeptɪsɪzəm/ noun [U, sing.] an attitude of doubting that claims or statements are true or that sth will happen: *Such claims should be regarded with a certain amount of scepticism.*

sceptre (BrE) (AmE **scep·ter**) /ˈseptə(r)/ noun a decorated rod carried by a king or queen at ceremonies as a symbol of their power—compare MACE, ORB

Schad·en·freude /ˈʃɑːdnfrɔɪdə/ noun [U] (from Ger-

man) a feeling of pleasure at the bad things that happen to other people

sched·ule /ˈʃedjuːl; *AmE* ˈskedʒuːl/ *noun, verb*

■ *noun* **1** [C, U] a plan that lists all the work that you have to do and when you must do each thing: *I have a hectic schedule for the next few days.* ◊ *We're working to a tight schedule* (= we have a lot of things to do in a short time). ◊ *Filming began on schedule* (= at the planned time). ◊ *The new bridge has been finished two years ahead of schedule.* ◊ *The tunnel project has already fallen behind schedule.* **2** [C] (*AmE*) = TIMETABLE: *a train schedule* **3** [C] a list of the television and radio programmes that are on a particular channel and the times that they start: *The channel's schedules are filled with old films and repeats.* **4** [C] a written list of things, for example prices, rates or conditions: *tax schedules* ⇨ note at AGENDA

■ *verb* **1** ~ **sth (for sth)** [usually passive] to arrange for sth to happen at a particular time: [VN] *The meeting is scheduled for Friday afternoon.* ◊ *One of the scheduled events is a talk on alternative medicine.* ◊ *We'll be stopping here for longer than scheduled.* ◊ [VN to inf] *I'm scheduled to arrive in LA at 5 o'clock.* **2** [VN] ~ **sth (as sth)** (*formal*) to include sth in an official list of things: *The substance has been scheduled as a poison.* ▶ **sched·uler** *noun*: *The President's schedulers allowed 90 minutes for TV interviews.*

ˈscheduled flight *noun* a plane service that leaves at a regular time each day or week—compare CHARTER FLIGHT

schema /ˈskiːmə/ *noun* (*pl.* **sche·mas** or **sche·mata** /-mətə; skiːˈmɑːtə/) (*technical*) an outline of a plan or theory

sche·mat·ic /skiːˈmætɪk/ *adj.* **1** in the form of a diagram that shows the main features or relationships but not the details: *a schematic diagram* **2** according to a fixed plan or pattern: *The play has a very schematic plot.* ▶ **sche·mat·ic·al·ly** /-kli/ *adv.*: *The process is shown schematically in figure 3.*

sche·ma·tize (*BrE* also **-ise**) /ˈskiːmətaɪz/ *verb* [VN] (*technical*) to organize sth in a system: *schematized data*

scheme /skiːm/ *noun, verb*

■ *noun* ~ **(for doing sth)** | ~ **(to do sth) 1** (*BrE*) a plan or system for doing or organizing sth: *a training/insurance scheme* ◊ *a local scheme for recycling newspapers* ◊ *to introduce/operate a scheme to improve links between schools and industry* ◊ *Under the new scheme only successful schools will be given extra funding.*—see also COLOUR SCHEME, PENSION SCHEME **2** a plan for getting money or some other advantage for yourself, especially one that involves deceiving other people: *an elaborate scheme to avoid taxes* **IDM** **the/sb's ˈscheme of things** the way things seem to be organized; the way sb wants everything to be organized: *My personal problems are not really important in the overall scheme of things.* ◊ *I don't think marriage figures in his scheme of things.*

■ *verb* (*disapproving*) to make secret plans to do sth that will help yourself and possibly harm others: [V] *She seemed to feel that we were all scheming against her.* ◊ [V to inf] *His colleagues, meanwhile, were busily scheming to get rid of him.* ◊ [VN] *Her enemies were scheming her downfall.*

schemer /ˈskiːmə(r)/ *noun* (*disapproving*) a person who plans secretly to do sth for their own advantage

schem·ing /ˈskiːmɪŋ/ *adj.* (*formal*) often planning secretly to do sth for your own advantage, especially by deceiving other people

scherzo /ˈskeətsəʊ; *AmE* ˈskertsoʊ/ *noun* (*pl.* **-os**) a short, lively piece of music, that is often part of a longer piece

schism /ˈskɪzəm; ˈsɪzəm/ *noun* [C, U] (*formal*) strong disagreement within an organization, especially a religious one, that makes its members divide into separate groups: *the threat of a schism within the Church* ▶ **schis·mat·ic** /skɪzˈmætɪk; sɪzˈmætɪk/ *adj.*

schist /ʃɪst/ *noun* [U] a type of rock formed of layers of different minerals, that breaks naturally into thin flat pieces

schiz·oid /ˈskɪtsɔɪd/ *adj.* (*technical*) similar to or suffering from schizophrenia: *schizoid tendencies*

schizo·phre·nia /ˌskɪtsəˈfriːniə/ *noun* [U] a mental illness in which a person becomes unable to link thought, emotion and behaviour, leading to WITHDRAWAL from reality and personal relationships

schizo·phren·ic /ˌskɪtsəˈfrenɪk/ *noun* a person who suffers from schizophrenia ▶ **schizo·phren·ic** *adj.*

schlep (also **schlepp**) /ʃlep/ *verb* (**-pp-**) (*informal, especially AmE*) **1** [V+adv./prep.] to go somewhere, especially if it is a slow, difficult journey, or you do not want to go: *The restaurant's supposed to be great but I don't feel like schlepping all the way out there.* **2** [VN] to carry or pull sth heavy: *I'm not schlepping these suitcases all over town.* **ORIGIN** From Yiddish *shlepn*, 'to drag'. ▶ **schlep** (also **schlepp**) *noun* [sing.]

schlock /ʃlɒk; *AmE* ʃlɑːk/ *noun* [U] (*AmE, informal*) things that are cheap and of poor quality: *stores full of schlock*

schmaltz /ʃmɔːlts/ *noun* [U] (*informal, disapproving*) the quality of being too SENTIMENTAL ▶ **schmaltzy** *adj.*

schmo (also **schmoe**) /ʃməʊ; *AmE* ʃmoʊ/ *noun* (*pl.* **-oes**) (*AmE, informal, disapproving*) a person who is stupid or foolish in an annoying way

schmooze /ʃmuːz/ *verb* [V] ~ **(with sb)** (*informal, especially AmE*) to talk in an informal and friendly way about things that are not important **SYN** CHAT ▶ **schmooz·er** *noun*

schmuck /ʃmʌk/ *noun* (*informal disapproving, especially AmE*) a stupid person: *He's such a schmuck!*

schnapps /ʃnæps/ *noun* [U] (from *German*) a strong alcoholic drink made from grain

schnook /ʃnʊk/ *noun* (*AmE, informal, disapproving*) a stupid or unimportant person

scholar /ˈskɒlə(r); *AmE* ˈskɑːl-/ *noun* **1** a person who knows a lot about a particular subject because they have studied it in detail: *a biblical/classical scholar* ◊ *He was the most distinguished scholar in his field.* **2** a student who has been given a scholarship to study at a school, college or university: *a Rhodes scholar* **3** (*BrE, informal*) a clever person who works hard at school: *I was never much of a scholar.*

schol·ar·ly /ˈskɒləli; *AmE* ˈskɑːlərli/ *adj.* **1** (of a person) spending a lot of time studying and having a lot of knowledge about an academic subject: *He was a very scholarly young man.* **2** connected with academic study: *a scholarly journal* ◊ *There was an explosion of scholarly interest in her poetry.*

schol·ar·ship /ˈskɒləʃɪp; *AmE* ˈskɑːlərʃɪp/ *noun* **1** [C] an amount of money given to sb by an organization to help pay for their education: *She won a scholarship to study at Stanford.* ◊ *He went to drama school on a scholarship.* **2** [U] the serious study of an academic subject and the knowledge and methods involved: *a magnificent work of scholarship*

scho·las·tic /skəˈlæstɪk/ *adj.* [only before noun] (*formal*) **1** connected with schools and education: *scholastic achievements* **2** connected with scholasticism

scho·las·ti·cism /skəˈlæstɪsɪzəm/ *noun* [U] a system of philosophy, based on religious principles and writing, that was taught in universities in the Middle Ages

school /skuːl/ *noun, verb*

■ *noun*

WHERE CHILDREN LEARN **1** [C] a place where children go to be educated: *My brother and I went to the same school.* ◊ (*formal*) *Which school do they attend?* ◊ *I'm going to the school today to talk to Kim's teacher.* ◊ *We need more money for roads, hospitals and schools.* ◊ *school buildings/rules/buses* **2** [U] (used without *the* or *a*) the process of learning in a school; the time during your life when you go to a school: (*BrE*) *to start/leave school* ◊ (*AmE*) *to start/quit school* ◊ *Where did you go to school?* ◊ (*BrE*) *All my kids are still at school.* ◊ (*AmE*) *All my kids are still in school.* ◊ (*AmE*) *to teach school* (= teach in a school) ◊ *The transition from school to work can be difficult.* **3** [U] (used without *the* or *a*) the time during the day when children are working in a school: *Shall I meet you after school today?* ◊ *School begins at 9.* ◊ *The kids are at/in school until 3.30.* ◊ *after-school activities/clubs*

æ	ɑː	e	ɜː	ə	ɪ	iː	i	ɒ	ɔː	ʌ	ʊ	u	uː
cat	father	ten	bird	about	sit	see	many	got	saw	cup	put	actual	too

(BrE)

S

S

In *BrE* someone who is attending school is **at school**: *I was at school with her sister*. In *AmE* **in school** is used: *I have a ten-year-old in school*. **In school** in *AmE* can also mean 'attending a university'.

STUDENTS AND TEACHERS | **4** (**the school**) [sing.] all the children or students and the teachers in a school: *I had to stand up in front of the whole school*.

FOR PARTICULAR SKILL | **5** [C] (often in compounds) a place where people go to learn a particular subject or skill: *a drama/language/riding school* ◊ *the London Business School*

COLLEGE/UNIVERSITY | **6** [C, U] (*AmE, informal*) a college or university; the time that you spend there: *famous schools like Yale and Harvard* ◊ *I've known her since law school*. ◊ *Where did you go to school?*—see also GRADUATE SCHOOL **7** [C] a department of a college or university that teaches a particular subject: *the university medical/law school* ◊ *the School of Dentistry/Languages*

OF WRITERS/ARTISTS | **8** [C] a group of writers, artists, etc. whose style of work or opinions have been influenced by the same person or ideas: *the Dutch school of painting*

OF FISH | **9** [C] a large number of fish or other sea animals, swimming together: *a school of dolphins/sharks/whales*—compare SHOAL

HELP There are many compounds ending in **school**. You will find them at their place in the alphabet.

IDM **school(s) of 'thought** a way of thinking that a number of people share: *There are two schools of thought about how this illness should be treated.*—more at OLD

GRAMMAR POINT
school

When a **school** is being referred to as an institution, you do not need to use *the*: *When do the children finish school?* When you are talking about a particular building, *the* is used: *I'll meet you outside the school.* **Prison**, **jail**, **court**, and **church** work in the same way: *Her husband spent three years in prison.*

⇨ note at COLLEGE, HOSPITAL

■ *verb*
YOURSELF/ANIMAL | **1** ~ **sb/yourself** (**in sth**) (*formal*) to train sb/yourself/an animal to do sth: [VN] *to school a horse* ◊ *She had schooled herself in patience.* ◊ [VN to inf] *I have schooled myself to remain calm under pressure.*
CHILD | **2** [VN] (*formal*) to educate a child: *She should be schooled with her peers.*

'school age *noun* [U] the age or period when a child normally attends school: *children of school age* ◊ *school-age children*

school·boy /'sku:lbɔɪ/ *noun* a boy who attends school

school·child /'sku:ltʃaɪld/ *noun* (*pl.* **school·chil·dren** /-tʃɪldrən/) (also *informal* **school·kid**) a child who attends school

school·days /'sku:ldeɪz/ *noun* [pl.] the period in your life when you go to school: *She hadn't seen Laura since her schooldays.*

'school district *noun* (in the US) an area that contains several schools that are governed together

'school friend (also *less frequent* **school·mate**) *noun* (*especially BrE*) a friend who attends or attended the same school as you: *She met up with some of her old* (= former) *school friends.*

school·girl /'sku:lgɜ:l; *AmE* -gɜ:rl/ *noun* a girl who attends school

school·house /'sku:lhaʊs/ *noun* **1** a school building, especially a small one in a village in the past **2** a house for a teacher next to a small school

school·ing /'sku:lɪŋ/ *noun* [U] the education you receive at school: *secondary schooling* ◊ *He had very little schooling.*

school·kid /'sku:lkɪd/ *noun* (*informal*) = SCHOOLCHILD

school-'leaver *noun* (*BrE*) a person who has just left school, especially when they are looking for a job: *the problem of rising unemployment among school-leavers*

school-marm /'sku:l mɑ:m; *AmE* mɑ:rm/ *noun* (*disapproving, especially AmE*) a woman who teaches in a school, especially one who is old-fashioned and strict ▶ **school-marm·ish** *adj.*

school·mas·ter /'sku:lmɑ:stə(r); *AmE* -mæs-/, **school·mis·tress** /'sku:lmɪstrəs/ *noun* (*old-fashioned, especially BrE*) a teacher in a school, especially a private school—compare MASTER

school·mate /'sku:lmeɪt/ *noun* (*especially BrE*) = SCHOOL FRIEND

school 'run *noun* [sing.] (*BrE*) the journey that parents make to take their children to school or to bring them home again

school·teach·er /'sku:lti:tʃə(r)/ *noun* a person whose job is teaching in a school

schooner /'sku:nə(r)/ *noun* **1** a sailing ship with two or more MASTS (= posts that support the sails) **2** a tall glass for SHERRY or beer

schtick *noun* = SHTICK

schwa /ʃwɑ:/ *noun* (*phonetics*) a vowel sound in parts of words that are not stressed, for example the 'a' in *about* or the 'e' in *moment*; the PHONETIC symbol for this, /ə/

sci·at·ic /saɪˈætɪk/ *adj.* [only before noun] (*anatomy*) of the hip or of the nerve which goes from the PELVIS to the THIGH (= the **sciatic nerve**)

sci·at·ica /saɪˈætɪkə/ *noun* [U] pain in the back, hip and outer side of the leg, caused by pressure on the sciatic nerve

sci·ence /'saɪəns/ *noun* **1** [U] knowledge about the structure and behaviour of the natural and physical world, based on facts that you can prove, for example by experiments: *new developments in science and technology* ◊ *the advance of modern science* ◊ *the laws of science* **2** [U] the study of science: *science students/teachers/courses* **3** [U, C] a particular branch of science: *to study one of the sciences*—compare ART (6), HUMANITIES **4** [sing.] a system for organizing the knowledge about a particular subject, especially one concerned with aspects of human behaviour or society: *Is there an adequate basis for a science of international politics?*—see also DOMESTIC SCIENCE, EARTH SCIENCE, LIFE SCIENCES, NATURAL SCIENCE, POLITICAL SCIENCE, SOCIAL SCIENCE **IDM** see BLIND *v.*

science 'fiction (also *informal* **'sci-fi**) *noun* [U] a type of book, film/movie, etc. that is based on imagined scientific discoveries of the future, and often deals with space travel and life on other planets

'science park *noun* an area where there are a lot of companies or organizations involved in scientific research and development

sci·en·tif·ic /ˌsaɪənˈtɪfɪk/ *adj.* [usually before noun] **1** involving science; connected with science: *a scientific discovery/study/adviser* ◊ *scientific knowledge/research/instruments* ◊ *sites of scientific interest* **2** (of a way of doing sth or thinking) careful and logical: *He took a very scientific approach to management.* ◊ *We need to be more scientific about this problem.* **OPP** UNSCIENTIFIC—compare NON-SCIENTIFIC ▶ **sci·en·tif·ic·al·ly** /-kli/ *adv.*

sci·en·tist /'saɪəntɪst/ *noun* a person who studies one or more of the NATURAL SCIENCES (= for example, physics, chemistry and biology): *a research scientist* ◊ *nuclear scientists* ◊ *scientists and engineers* ◊ *the cartoon figure of the mad scientist working in his laboratory*—see also COMPUTER SCIENTIST, POLITICAL SCIENTIST, SOCIAL SCIENTIST

Sci·en·tol·ogy™ /ˌsaɪənˈtɒlədʒi; *AmE* -ˈtɑ:l-/ *noun* [U] a religious system based on getting knowledge of yourself and spiritual FULFILMENT through courses of study and training ▶ **Sci·en·tolo·gist** *noun*

sci-fi /'saɪ faɪ/ *noun* [U] (*informal*) = SCIENCE FICTION

scimi·tar /'sɪmɪtə(r)/ *noun* a short curved SWORD with one sharp edge, used especially in eastern countries

scin·tilla /sɪnˈtɪlə/ *noun* [sing.] ~ (**of sth**) (*formal*)

aɪ	aʊ	eɪ	əʊ	oʊ	ɔɪ	ɪə	eə	ʊə	j	w
my	now	say	go	go	boy	near	hair	pure	yes	wet
			(BrE)	(AmE)						

(usually in negative sentences) a very small amount of sth: *There is not a scintilla of truth in what she says.*

scin·til·lat·ing /ˈsɪntɪleɪtɪŋ/ *adj.* very clever, amusing and interesting: *a scintillating performance/conversation* ◊ *Statistics on unemployment levels hardly make for scintillating reading.*

scion /ˈsaɪən/ *noun* **1** (*formal or literary*) a young member of a family, especially a famous or important one **2** (*technical*) a piece of a plant, especially one cut to make a new plant

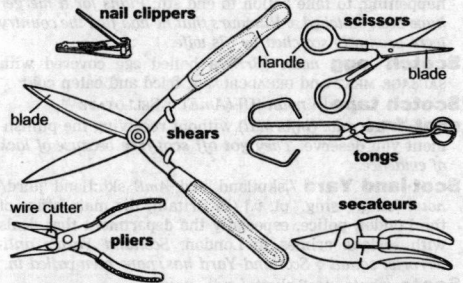

scis·sors /ˈsɪzəz; *AmE* ˈsɪzərz/ *noun* [pl.] a tool for cutting paper or fabric, that has two sharp blades with handles, joined together in the middle: *a pair of scissors*—see also NAIL SCISSORS ▶ **scis·sor** *adj.* [only before noun]: *The legs move in a scissor action.*

scler·osis /skləˈrəʊsɪs; *AmE* -ˈroʊ-/ *noun* [U] (*medical*) a condition in which soft tissue in the body becomes hard, in a way that is not normal—see also MULTIPLE SCLEROSIS ▶ **scler·otic** /skləˈrɒtɪk; *AmE* -ˈrɑːt-/ *adj.*

scoff /skɒf; *AmE* skɔːf; skɑːf/ *verb* **1** ~ (at sb/sth) to talk about sb/sth in a way that makes it clear that you think they are stupid or ridiculous: [V] *He scoffed at our amateurish attempts.* ◊ *Don't scoff—she's absolutely right.* [also V speech] **2** [VN] (*BrE*) (*AmE* scarf) (*informal*) to eat a lot of sth quickly: *Who scoffed all the grapes?*

scold /skəʊld; *AmE* skoʊld/ *verb* ~ sb (for sth/for doing sth) (*formal*) to speak angrily to sb, especially a child, because they have done sth wrong SYN TELL OFF: [VN] *He scolded them for arriving late.* [also V speech, V] ▶ **scold·ing** *noun* [usually sing.]: *I got a scolding from my mother.*

scone /skɒn; skəʊn; *AmE* skɑːn; skoʊn/ *noun* (*BrE*) a small round cake, sometimes with dried fruit in it and often eaten with butter, jam and cream spread on it—picture on page A1

scoop /skuːp/ *noun, verb*
▪ *noun* **1** a tool like a large spoon with a deep bowl, used for picking up substances in powder form like flour, or for serving food like ice cream **2** the amount picked up by a scoop: *two scoops of mashed potato* **3** a piece of important or exciting news that is printed in one newspaper before other newspapers know about it
▪ *verb* [VN] **1** [usually +adv./prep.] ~ sth (up) to move or lift sth with a scoop or sth like a scoop: *She scooped ice cream into their bowls.* ◊ *He quickly scooped the money up from the desk.* ◊ *First, scoop a hole in the soil.* ◊ *Scoop out the melon flesh.* **2** [+adv./prep.] ~ sb/sth (up) to move or lift sb/sth with a quick continuous movement: *She scooped the child up in her arms.* ◊ *He quickly scooped his clothes from the chair.* **3** to publish a story before all the other newspapers, television companies, etc: *The paper had inside information and scooped all its rivals.* **4** (*informal*) to win sth, especially a large sum of money or a prize: *He scooped £10000 on the lottery.*

scoot /skuːt/ *verb* [V, usually +adv./prep.] (*informal*) to go or leave somewhere in a hurry: *I'd better scoot or I'll be late.* ◊ *They scooted off to Dublin for the weekend.*

scoot·er /ˈskuːtə(r)/ *noun* **1** (*BrE*) (also **ˈmotor scooter** *AmE, BrE*) a light motorcycle, usually with small wheels and a curved metal cover at the front to protect the rider's legs—picture at MOTORCYCLE **2** a child's vehicle with two small wheels attached to a narrow board with

an upright handle. The rider holds the handle, puts one foot on the board and pushes against the ground with the other.

scope /skəʊp; *AmE* skoʊp/ *noun* [U] **1** ~ (for sth) | ~ (for sb) (to do sth) the opportunity or ability to do or achieve sth SYN POTENTIAL: *There's still plenty of scope for improvement.* ◊ *The extra money will give us the scope to improve our facilities.* ◊ *Her job offers very little scope for promotion.* ◊ *First try to do something that is within your scope.* **2** the range of things that a subject, an organization, an activity, etc. deals with: *Our powers are limited in scope.* ◊ *This subject lies beyond the scope of our investigation.* ◊ *These issues were outside the scope of the article.* **3** (**-scope**) (in nouns) an instrument for looking through or watching sth with: *microscope* ◊ *telescope*

scorch /skɔːtʃ; *AmE* skɔːrtʃ/ *verb* **1** to burn and slightly damage a surface by making it too hot; to be slightly burned by heat: [VN] *I scorched my dress when I was ironing it.* ◊ [V] *Don't stand so near the fire—your coat is scorching!* [also VN-ADJ] **2** to become or to make sth become dry and brown, especially from the heat of the sun or from chemicals: [VN] *scorched grass* ◊ [V] *The leaves will scorch if you water them in the sun.* **3** [V+adv./prep.] (*BrE, informal*) to move very fast: *The car scorched off down the road.*

scorched ˈearth policy *noun* (in a war) a policy of destroying anything in a particular area that may be useful to the enemy

scorch·er /ˈskɔːtʃə(r); *AmE* ˈskɔːrtʃ-/ *noun* (*informal*) **1** a very hot day **2** (*BrE*) (used mainly in newspapers) a very good stroke, shot, etc. in a sport: *a scorcher of a free kick*

scorch·ing /ˈskɔːtʃɪŋ; *AmE* ˈskɔːrtʃ-/ *adj.* (*informal*) **1** very hot: *a scorching hot day* **2** (*especially BrE*) used to emphasize how strong, powerful, etc. sth is: *a scorching critique of the government's economic policy* ◊ *a scorching 6–1 victory*

ˈscorch mark *noun* a mark made on a surface by burning

score /skɔː(r)/ *noun, verb*
▪ *noun*
POINTS/GOALS, etc. | **1** [C] the number of points, goals, etc. scored by each player or team in a game or competition: *a high/low score* ◊ *What's the score now?* ◊ *The final score was 4–3.* ◊ *I'll keep (the) score.* **2** [C] (*especially AmE*) the number of points sb gets for correct answers in a test: *college entrance test scores* ◊ *an IQ score of 120* ◊ *a perfect score*

MUSIC | **3** [C] a written or printed version of a piece of music showing what each instrument is to play or what each voice is to sing: *an orchestral score* ◊ *the score of Verdi's 'Requiem'* **4** [C] the music written for a film/movie or play: *The film picked up awards for best director and best original score.*

TWENTY | **5** [C] (*pl.* **score**) a set or group of 20 or approximately 20: *Several cabs and a score of cars were parked outside.* ◊ *Doyle's success brought imitators by the score* (= very many). ◊ *the biblical age of three score years and ten* (= 70)

MANY | **6** (**scores**) [pl.] very many: *There were scores of boxes and crates, all waiting to be checked and loaded.*

CUT | **7** [C] a cut in a surface, made with a sharp tool

FACTS ABOUT SITUATION | **8** (**the score**) [sing.] (*informal*) the real facts about the present situation: *What's the score?* ◊ *You don't have to lie to me. I know the score.*

IDM **on ˈthat/ˈthis score** as far as that/this is concerned: *You don't have to worry on that score.*—more at EVEN *v.*, SETTLE *v.*
▪ *verb*
GIVE/GET POINTS/GOALS | **1** to win points, goals, etc. in a game or competition: [V] *Fraser scored again in the second half.* ◊ [VN] *to score a goal/try/touchdown/victory* **2** [V] to keep a record of the points, goals, etc. won in a game or competition: *Who's going to score?* **3** to gain marks in a test or an exam: [VN] *She scored 98% in the French test.* ◊ [V] *Girls usually score highly in language exams.* **4** [VN] to give sth/sb a particular number of points: *The tests are*

b	d	f	g	h	k	l	m	n	p	r
bad	did	fall	get	hat	cat	leg	man	now	pen	red

scored by psychologists. ◊ *Score each criterion on a scale of 1 to 5.* ◊ *a scoring system* **5** [VN] to be worth a particular number of points: *Each correct answer will score two points.*

SUCCEED | **6** to succeed; to have an advantage: [VN] *The army continued to score successes in the south.* ◊ [V] *She's scored again with her latest blockbuster.*

ARRANGE/WRITE MUSIC | **7** [VN] [usually passive] ~ **sth (for sth)** to arrange a piece of music for one or more musical instruments or for voices: *The piece is scored for violin, viola and cello.* ◊ *The director invited him to score the movie* (= write the music for it).

CUT | **8** [VN] to make a cut or mark on a surface: *Score the card first with a knife.*

HAVE SEX | **9** [V] ~ **(with sb)** *(slang)* (especially of a man) to have sex with a new partner: *Did you score last night?*

BUY DRUGS | **10** [VN, V] *(slang)* to buy or get illegal drugs

IDM **,score a 'point/'points (off/against/over sb)** = SCORE OFF SB

PHRV **'score off sb** [no passive] *(especially BrE)* to show that you are better than sb, especially by making clever remarks, for example in an argument: *He was always trying to score off his teachers.* **,score sth↔'out/ 'through** to draw a line or lines through sth: *Her name had been scored out on the list.*

score·board /'skɔːbɔːd; *AmE* 'skɔːrbɔːrd/ *noun* a large board on which the score in a game or competition is shown

score·card /'skɔːkɑːd; *AmE* 'skɔːrkɑːrd/ *noun* a card or piece of paper that people watching a game can use to write the score on, or on which the score can be officially recorded

'score draw *noun (BrE)* the result of a football match in which both teams score the same number of goals

score·less /'skɔːləs; *AmE* 'skɔːrləs/ *adj.* (of a game) without either team getting any points, goals, etc: *a scoreless draw*

score·line /'skɔːlaɪn; *AmE* 'skɔːrl-/ *noun (BrE)* (used mainly in newspapers) the final score or result in a game, competition, etc: *a 2–1 scoreline* ◊ *The team did not play as badly as the scoreline suggests.*

scor·er /'skɔːrə(r)/ *noun* **1** (in sports) a player who scores points, goals, etc: *United's top scorer* **2** a person who keeps a record of the points, goals, etc. scored in a game or competition **3 a high/low** ~ a person who gets a high/low number of points in a test or exam

'score sheet *noun (BrE)* a piece of paper on which the score of a game can be officially recorded **IDM** **get your name on the 'score sheet** *(informal)* (used in newspapers) to score a goal, etc.

scorn /skɔːn; *AmE* skɔːrn/ *noun, verb*
▪ *noun* [U] ~ **(for sb/sth)** a strong feeling that sb/sth is stupid or not good enough, usually shown by the way you speak **SYN** CONTEMPT: *Her fellow teachers greeted her proposal with scorn.* ◊ *They had nothing but scorn for his political views.* ◊ *She was unable to hide the scorn in her voice.* **IDM** **pour/heap 'scorn on sb/sth** to speak about sb/sth in a way that shows that you do not respect them or have a good opinion of them
▪ *verb* **1** [VN] to feel or show that you think sb/sth is stupid and you do not respect them or it: *She scorned their views as old-fashioned.* **2** *(formal)* to refuse to have or do sth because you are too proud: [VN] *to scorn an invitation/ offer* ◊ [Vtoinf] *She would have scorned to stoop to such tactics.* **IDM** see HELL

scorn·ful /'skɔːnfl; *AmE* 'skɔːrnfl/ *adj.* ~ **(of sth)** showing or feeling scorn: *a scornful laugh* ◊ *He was scornful of such 'female' activities as cooking.* ▶ **scorn·ful·ly** /-fəli/ *adv.*: *She laughed scornfully.*

Scor·pio /'skɔːpiəʊ; *AmE* 'skɔːrpioʊ/ *noun* **1** [U] the 8th sign of the ZODIAC, the SCORPION **2** [C] *(pl. -os)* a person born under the influence of this sign, that is between 23 October and 21 November, approximately

scor·pion /'skɔːpiən; *AmE* 'skɔːrp-/ *noun* a small creature like an insect with six legs, two front CLAWS (= curved and pointed limbs) and a long tail that curves

over its back and can give a poisonous sting. Scorpions live in hot countries.—picture on page A7

Scot /skɒt; *AmE* skɑːt/ *noun* **1** a person from Scotland **2 (the Scots)** (also *less frequent* **the Scottish**) [pl.] the people of Scotland ⇨ note at SCOTTISH

Scotch /skɒtʃ; *AmE* skɑːtʃ/ *noun, adj.*
▪ *noun* **1** [U] the type of whisky made in Scotland: *a bottle of Scotch* **2** [C] a glass of Scotch: *Do you want a Scotch?*
▪ *adj.* of or connected with Scotland ⇨ note at SCOTTISH

scotch /skɒtʃ; *AmE* skɑːtʃ/ *verb* [VN] to stop sth from happening; to take action to end sth: *Plans for a merger have been scotched.* ◊ *Rumours that he had fled the country were promptly scotched by his wife.*

,Scotch 'egg *noun (BrE)* a boiled egg covered with SAUSAGE MEAT and BREADCRUMBS, fried and eaten cold

'Scotch tape™ *noun* [U] *(AmE)* = SELLOTAPE™

,scot-'free *adv.* *(informal)* without receiving the punishment you deserve: *They got off scot-free because of lack of evidence.*

Scot·land Yard /,skɒtlənd 'jɑːd; *AmE* ,skɑːtlənd 'jɑːrd/ *noun* [sing.+ sing./ pl. *v.*] (in Britain) the main office of the London police, especially the department that deals with serious crimes in London: *Scotland Yard's anti-terrorist squad* ◊ *Scotland Yard has/have been called in.*

Scots /skɒts; *AmE* skɑːts/ *adj., noun*
▪ *adj.* of or connected with Scotland, and especially with the English language as spoken in Scotland or the Scots language: *He spoke with a Scots accent.* ◊ *She comes from an old Scots family.*
▪ *noun* [U] a language spoken in Scotland, closely related to English but with many differences—compare GAELIC ⇨ note at SCOTTISH

Scot·tish /'skɒtɪʃ; *AmE* 'skɑːtɪʃ/ *adj.* **1** of or connected with Scotland or its people: *the Scottish Highlands* ◊ *Scottish dancing* **2 (the Scottish)** *noun* [pl.] *(rare)* = THE SCOTS

WHICH WORD?
Scottish / Scots / Scotch / Scot

The adjective **Scottish** is the most general word used to describe the people and things of Scotland, while **Scots** is only used to describe its people, its law and especially its language: *Scottish dancing* ◊ *the new Scottish parliament* ◊ *a well-known Scots poet* ◊ *a slight Scots accent.*

The adjective **Scotch** is now mainly used in fixed expressions such as *Scotch whisky* and *Scotch broth* and sounds old-fashioned or insulting if it is used in any other way.

The noun **Scotch** means whisky, and the noun **Scots** refers to a language spoken in Scotland, closely related to English. A person who comes from Scotland is a **Scot**: *The Scots won their match against England.*

⇨ note at BRITISH

scoun·drel /'skaʊndrəl/ *noun (old-fashioned)* a man who treats other people badly, especially by being dishonest or immoral

scour /'skaʊə(r)/ *verb* [VN] **1** ~ **sth (for sb/sth)** to search a place or thing thoroughly in order to find sb/sth: *We scoured the area for somewhere to pitch our tent.* **2** ~ **sth (out)** to clean sth by rubbing its surface hard with rough material: *I had to scour out the pans.* **3** ~ **sth (away/out)| ~ sth (from/out of sth)** to make a passage, hole, or mark in the ground, rocks, etc. as the result of movement, especially over a long period: *The water had raced down the slope and scoured out the bed of a stream.*

scour·er /'skaʊərə(r)/ (also **'scouring pad**) *noun* a small ball of wire or stiff plastic used for cleaning pans

scourge /skɜːdʒ; *AmE* skɜːrdʒ/ *noun, verb*
▪ *noun* **1** [usually sing.] ~ **(of sb/sth)** *(written)* a person or thing that causes trouble or suffering: *the scourge of war/ disease/poverty* ◊ *Pirates are once again the scourge of the China Sea.* ◊ *Inflation was the scourge of the 1970s.* **2** a WHIP used to punish people in the past

■ *verb* [VN] **1** [usually passive] (*literary*) to cause trouble or suffering to sb: *He lay awake, scourged by his conscience.* **2** (*old use*) to hit sb with a scourge

Scouse /skaʊs/ *noun* (*BrE, informal*) **1** (also **Scouser** /'skaʊsə(r)/) [C] a person from Liverpool in NW England **2** [U] a way of speaking, used by people from Liverpool ▶ **Scouse** *adj.*: *a Scouse accent*

scout /skaʊt/ *noun, verb*
■ *noun* **1** (**the Scouts**) [pl.] an organization (officially called the **Scout Association**) originally for boys, which trains young people in practical skills and does a lot of activities with them, for example camping: *to join the Scouts* **2** (*BrE*) a boy or girl who is a member of the Scouts: *Both my brothers were scouts.* ◊ *a scout troop*—see also BOY SCOUT, GUIDE—compare BROWNIE **3** a person, an aircraft, etc. sent ahead to get information about the enemy's position, strength, etc. **4** = TALENT SCOUT
■ *verb* **1** ~ (**around**) (**for sb/sth**) to search an area or various areas in order to find or discover sth: [VN] *They scouted the area for somewhere to stay the night.* ◊ [V] *The kids were scouting around for wood for the fire.* ◊ *a military scouting party* **2** to look for sports players, actors, musicians, etc. who have special ability, so you can offer them work: [V] *He scouts for Manchester United.* [also VN] **PHRV** ,scout sth↔'out to find out what an area is like or where sth is, by searching: *We went ahead to scout out the lie of the land.*

scout·er /'skaʊtə(r)/ *noun* a person who is the leader of a group of scouts

scout·ing /'skaʊtɪŋ/ *noun* [U] the activities that boy and girl SCOUTS take part in; the Scout organization

scowl /skaʊl/ *verb, noun*
■ *verb* [V] ~ (**at sb/sth**) to look at sb/sth in an angry or annoyed way |SYN| GLOWER: *The receptionist scowled at me.*
■ *noun* an angry look or expression: *He looked up at me with a scowl.*

Scrab·ble™ /'skræbl/ *noun* [U] a board game in which players try to make words from letters printed on small plastic blocks and connect them to words that have already been placed on the board

scrab·ble /'skræbl/ *verb* [V] [usually+*adv.*/*prep.*] ~ (**around/about**) (**for sth**) (*especially BrE*) to try to find or to do sth in a hurry or with difficulty, often by moving your hands or feet about quickly, with much control: *She scrabbled around in her bag for her glasses.* ◊ *He was scrabbling for a foothold on the steep slope.* ◊ *a sound like rats scrabbling on the other side of the wall*

scrag·gly /'skrægli/ *adj.* (*AmE, informal*) thin and growing in a way that is not even: *a scraggly beard*

scraggy /'skrægi/ *adj.* (*disapproving*) (of people or animals) very thin and not looking healthy: *women with scraggy necks* ◊ *a scraggy old cat*

scram /skræm/ *verb* (**-mm-**) [V] (*old-fashioned, slang*) (usually used in orders) to go away quickly: *Scram! I don't want you here.*

scram·ble /'skræmbl/ *verb, noun*
■ *verb*
WALK/CLIMB | **1** [V+*adv.*/*prep.*] to move quickly, especially with difficulty, using your hands to help you: *She managed to scramble over the wall.* ◊ *He scrambled to his feet as we came in.* ◊ *They finally scrambled ashore.*
PUSH/FIGHT | **2** ~ (**for sth**) to push, fight or compete with others in order to get or to reach sth: [V] *The audience scrambled for the exits.* ◊ [V to inf] *Shoppers were scrambling to get the best bargains.*
ACHIEVE STH WITH DIFFICULTY | **3** [VN] to manage to achieve sth with difficulty, or in a hurry, without much control: *Cork scrambled a 1–0 win over Monaghan.* ◊ *Owen managed to scramble the ball into the net.*
EGGS | **4** [VN] [usually passive] to cook an egg by mixing the white and yellow parts together and heating them, sometimes with milk and butter: *scrambled eggs*
TELEPHONE/RADIO | **5** [VN] [often passive] to change the way that a telephone or radio message sounds so that only people with special equipment can understand it: *scrambled satellite signals*

CONFUSE THOUGHTS | **6** [VN] to confuse sb's thoughts, ideas, etc. so that they have no order: *Alcohol seemed to have scrambled his brain.*
AIRCRAFT | **7** [usually passive] to order that planes, etc. should take off immediately in an emergency; to take off immediately in an emergency: [VN] *A helicopter was scrambled to help rescue three young climbers.* ◊ [V] *They scrambled as soon as the call came through.*
■ *noun*
DIFFICULT WALK/CLIMB | **1** [sing.] a difficult walk or climb over rough ground, especially one in which you have to use your hands
PUSH/FIGHT | **2** [sing.] ~ (**for sth**) a situation in which people push, fight or compete with each other in order to get or do sth: *There was a mad scramble for the best seats.*
MOTORCYCLE RACE | **3** [C] a race for motorcycles over rough ground

scram·bler /'skræmblə(r)/ *noun* a device that changes radio or telephone signals or messages so that they cannot be understood by other people

scram·bling /'skræmblɪŋ/ *noun* [U] (*BrE*) = MOTOCROSS

scrap /skræp/ *noun, verb*
■ *noun* **1** [C] a small piece of sth, especially paper, fabric, etc: *She scribbled his phone number on a scrap of paper.* ◊ (*figurative*) *scraps of news/information* ◊ (*figurative*) *She was just a scrap of a thing* (= small and thin). **2** [sing.] (usually with a negative) a small amount of sth: *It won't make a scrap of difference.* ◊ *There's not a scrap of evidence to support his claim.* ◊ *a barren landscape without a scrap of vegetation* **3** (**scraps**) [pl.] food left after a meal: *Give the scraps to the dog.* **4** [U] things that are not wanted or cannot be used for their original purpose, but which have some value for the material they are made of: *We sold the car for scrap* (= so that any good parts can be used again). ◊ *scrap metal/iron* ◊ *a scrap merchant/dealer* (= a person who buys and sells scrap) **5** (*informal*) a short fight or quarrel: *He was always getting into scraps at school.*—see also SCRAPPY
■ *verb* (**-pp-**) **1** [VN] [often passive] to cancel or get rid of sth that is no longer practical or useful: *They had been forced to scrap plans for a new school building.* ◊ *The oldest of the aircraft were scrapped.* **2** [V] (*informal*) to fight with sb: *The bigger boys started scrapping.*

scrap·book /'skræpbʊk/ *noun* a book with empty pages where you can stick pictures, newspaper articles, etc.

scrape /skreɪp/ *verb, noun*
■ *verb*
REMOVE | **1** to remove sth from a surface by moving sth sharp and hard like a knife across it: [VN, usually+*adv.*/*prep.*] *She scraped the mud off her boots.* ◊ [VN-ADJ] *The kids had scraped their plates clean.*
DAMAGE | **2** [VN] [usually+*adv.*/*prep.*] to rub sth accidentally so that it gets damaged or hurt: *I scraped the side of my car on the wall.* ◊ *Sorry, I've scraped some paint off the car.* ◊ *She fell and scraped her knee.* ◊ *The wire had scraped the skin from her fingers.*
MAKE SOUND | **3** [usually+*adv.*/*prep.*] to make an unpleasant noise by rubbing against a hard surface; to make sth do this: [V] *I could hear his pen scraping across the paper.* ◊ (*disapproving*) *We could hear her scraping away at the violin.* ◊ [VN] *Don't scrape your chairs on the floor.*
WIN WITH DIFFICULTY | **4** to manage to win or to get sth with difficulty: [VN] *The team scraped a narrow victory last year.* ◊ (*BrE*) *I just scraped a pass in the exam.* ◊ *They scraped a living by playing music on the streets.* ◊ [V] *The government scraped home* (= just won) *by three votes.*
MAKE HOLE IN GROUND | **5** [VN] ~ **sth** (**out**) to make a hole or hollow place in the ground: *He found a suitable place, scraped a hole and buried the bag in it.*
PULL HAIR BACK | **6** [VN] ~ **your hair back** to pull your hair tightly back, away from your face: *Her hair was scraped back from her face in a ponytail.*
IDM **scrape (the bottom of) the 'barrel** (*disapproving*) to have to use whatever things or people you can get, because there is not much choice available—more at BOW¹ *v.*
PHRV ,scrape 'by (on sth) to manage to live on the money you have, but with difficulty: *I can just scrape by*

S

on what my parents give me. ˌscrape ˈin⏐ ˌscrape ˈinto sth to manage to get a job, a position, a place at college, etc., but with difficulty: *He scraped in with 180 votes.* ◇ *Our team just scraped into the semi-finals.* ˌscrape sth‹·›ˈout to remove sth from inside sth else, using sth sharp or hard like a knife: *Scrape out the flesh of the melon with a spoon.* ˌscrape ˈthrough⏐ ˌscrape ˈthrough sth to succeed in doing sth with difficulty, especially in passing an exam: *I might scrape through the exam if I'm lucky.* ˌscrape sth‹·›toˈgether/ˈup to obtain or collect together sth, but with difficulty: *We managed to scrape together eight volunteers.*

■ *noun*

ACTION/SOUND⏐ **1** [sing.] the action or unpleasant sound of one thing rubbing roughly against another: *the scrape of iron on stone*

DAMAGE⏐ **2** [C] an injury or a mark caused by rubbing against sth rough: *She emerged from the overturned car with only a few scrapes and bruises.*

DIFFICULT SITUATION⏐ **3** [C] (*old-fashioned*) a difficult situation that you have caused yourself: *He was always getting into scrapes as a boy.*

scraper /ˈskreɪpə(r)/ *noun* a tool used for scraping, for example for scraping mud from shoes or ice from a car

ˈscrap heap *noun* a pile of things, especially of metal, that are no longer wanted or useful **IDM** **on the ˈscrap heap** (*informal*) no longer wanted or considered useful

scra·pie /ˈskreɪpi/ *noun* [U] a brain disease of sheep that causes death

scrap·ing /ˈskreɪpɪŋ/ *noun* [usually pl.] a small amount of sth produced by scratching a surface

ˈscrap paper *noun* [U] loose pieces of paper used for writing notes on

scrappy /ˈskræpi/ *adj.* (**scrap·pier**, **scrap·pi·est**) **1** consisting of individual sections, events, etc. that are not organized into a whole: *a scrappy essay* ◇ *The concert was rather a scrappy affair.* **2** (*especially BrE*) not tidy and often of poor quality: *The note was written on a scrappy bit of paper.*—see also SCRAP IN.

scrap·yard /ˈskræpjɑːd; *AmE* -jɑːrd/ (*BrE*) (also **junk·yard** *AmE, BrE*) *noun* a place where old cars, machines, etc. are collected, so that parts of them, or the metal they are made of, can be sold to be used again

scratch /skrætʃ/ *verb, noun, adj.*

■ *verb*

RUB WITH YOUR NAILS⏐ **1** ~ (**at sth**) to rub your skin with your nails, usually because it is ITCHING: [VN] *John yawned and scratched his chin.* ◇ *The dog scratched itself behind the ear.* ◇ [V] *Try not to scratch.* ◇ *She scratched at the insect bites on her arm.*

CUT SKIN⏐ **2** ~ (**sb/sth/yourself**) (**on sth**) to cut or damage your skin slightly with sth sharp: [VN] *I'd scratched my leg and it was bleeding.* ◇ *She scratched herself on a nail.* ◇ [V] *Does the cat scratch?*

DAMAGE SURFACE⏐ **3** [VN] to damage the surface of sth, especially accidentally, by making thin shallow marks on it: *Be careful not to scratch the furniture.* ◇ *The car's paintwork is badly scratched.*

MAKE/REMOVE MARK⏐ **4** [VN+*adv./prep.*] to make or remove a mark, etc. on sth deliberately, by rubbing it with sth hard or sharp: *They scratched lines in the dirt to mark out a pitch.* ◇ *Some graffiti had been scratched on the back of the door.* ◇ *We scratched some of the dirt away.* ◇ (*figurative*) *You can scratch my name off the list.*

MAKE SOUND⏐ **5** [V] [usually+*adv./prep.*] to make an irritating noise by rubbing sth with sth sharp: *The dog kept scratching at the door to go out.* ◇ *His pen scratched away on the paper.*

A LIVING⏐ **6** [VN] ~ **a living** to make enough money to live on, but with difficulty

CANCEL⏐ **7** ~ (**sb/sth**) (**from sth**) to decide that sth cannot happen or sb/sth cannot take part in sth, before it starts: [VN] *to scratch a rocket launch* ◇ *The horse was scratched from the race because of injury.* ◇ [V] *She had scratched because of a knee injury.*

IDM **scratch your ˈhead (over sth)** to think hard in order to find an answer to sth **scratch the ˈsurface (of**

sth) to deal with, understand, or find out about only a small part of a subject or problem ˌyou scratch ˈmy back and ˌI'll scratch ˈyours (*saying*) used to say that if sb helps you, you will help them, even if this is unfair to others

PHRV ˌscratch aˈbout/aˈround (**for sth**) to search for sth, especially with difficulty ˌscratch sth‹·›ˈout to remove a word, especially a name, from sth written, usually by putting a line through it

■ *noun*

MARK/CUT⏐ **1** [C] a mark, a cut or an injury made by scratching sb's skin or the surface of sth: *Her hands were covered in scratches from the brambles.* ◇ *a scratch on the paintwork* ◇ *It's only a scratch* (= a very slight injury). ◇ *He escaped without a scratch* (= was not hurt at all).

SOUND⏐ **2** [sing.] the unpleasant sound of sth sharp or rough being rubbed against a surface

WITH YOUR NAILS⏐ **3** [sing.] the act of scratching a part of your body when it ITCHES: *Go on, have a good scratch!*

IDM **from ˈscratch** without any previous preparation or knowledge: *I learned German from scratch in six months.* ◇ *They decided to dismantle the machine and start again from scratch.* (**be/come**) **up to ˈscratch⏐ (bring sb/sth**) **up to ˈscratch** as good as sth/sb should be; satisfactory: *His work simply isn't up to scratch.* ◇ *It'll take months to bring the band up to scratch.*

■ *adj.* (*BrE*) **1** put together in a hurry using whatever people or materials are available: *a scratch team* **2** (especially in golf) with no HANDICAP: *a scratch player*

scratch·card /ˈskrætʃkɑːd; *AmE* -kɑːrd/ *noun* a card that you buy that has an area that you scratch off to find out if you have won some money or a prize

ˈscratch pad *noun* (*AmE*) a small book of cheap paper for writing notes on

scratchy /ˈskrætʃi/ *adj.* **1** (of clothes or fabric) rough and unpleasant to the touch: *This sweater is too scratchy.* ◇ *a scratchy blanket* **2** (of a record, voice, etc.) making a rough, unpleasant sound like sth being scratched across a surface: *a scratchy recording of Mario Lanza* ◇ *a scratchy pen* **3** (of writing or drawings) done without care

scrawl /skrɔːl/ *verb, noun*

■ *verb* ~ (**sth**) (**across/in/on sth**) to write sth in a careless untidy way, making it difficult to read **SYN** SCRIBBLE: [VN] *I tried to read his directions, scrawled on a piece of paper.* ◇ [V] *Someone had scrawled all over my notes.*

■ *noun* a careless untidy way of writing; sth written in this way: *Her signature was an illegible scrawl.* ◇ *I can't be expected to read this scrawl!* ◇ *The paper was covered in scrawls.*

scrawny /ˈskrɔːni/ *adj.* (*disapproving*) (of people or animals) very thin in a way that is not attractive: *He had long scrawny fingers.*

scream /skriːm/ *verb, noun*

■ *verb* **1** ~ (**out**) (**in/with sth**) to give a loud, high cry, because you are hurt, frightened, excited, etc. **SYN** SHRIEK: [V] *He covered his mouth to stop her from screaming.* ◇ *The kids were screaming with excitement.* ◇ *People ran for the exits, screaming out in terror.* ◇ [VN-ADJ] *The baby was screaming itself hoarse.* **2** ~ (**sth**) (**out**) (**at sb**) ~ (**out**) (**for sth/sb**) to shout sth in a loud, high voice because of fear, anger, etc. **SYN** YELL: [V speech] *'Help!' she screamed.* ◇ [V] *Someone was screaming for help.* ◇ *He screamed at me to stop.* ◇ [VN] *She screamed abuse at him.* ◇ [V that] *His sister screamed out that he was crazy.* **3** [V] [usually+*adv./prep.*] to make a loud, high noise; to move fast, making this noise **SYN** SCREECH: *Lights flashed and sirens screamed.* ◇ *The powerboat screamed out to sea.* ⇨ note at SHOUT **IDM** **scream blue ˈmurder** (*BrE*) (*AmE* **scream bloody ˈmurder**) to scream loudly and for a long time, especially in order to protest about sth **PHRV** ˌscream ˈout (**for sth**) to be in need of attention in a very noticeable way: *These books scream out to be included in a list of favourites.*

■ *noun* **1** [C] a loud high cry made by sb who is hurt, frightened, excited, etc.; a loud high noise: *She let out a scream of pain.* ◇ *They ignored the baby's screams.* ◇ *He drove off with a scream of tyres.* **2** [sing.] (*old-fashioned*,

aɪ	aʊ	eɪ	əʊ	oʊ	ɔɪ	ɪə	eə	ʊə	j	w
my	now	say	go (BrE)	go (AmE)	boy	near	hair	pure	yes	wet

informal) a person or thing that causes you to laugh: *He's a scream.*

scream·ing·ly /ˈskriːmɪŋli/ *adv.* extremely: *It was screamingly obvious what we should do next.*

scree /skriː/ *noun* [U, C] an area of small loose stones, especially on a mountain, which may slide when you walk on them

screech /skriːtʃ/ *verb, noun*
- *verb* **1** to make a loud high unpleasant sound; to say sth using this sound: [V] *Monkeys were screeching in the trees.* ◊ *The wind screeched in his ears.* ◊ *screeching brakes* ◊ *He screeched with pain.* ◊ [V **speech**] *'No, don't!' she screeched.* ◊ [VN] *He screeched something at me.* **2** [V] (usually+*adv. / prep.*) (of a vehicle) to make a loud high unpleasant noise as it moves: *The car screeched to a halt outside the hospital.* ◊ *A police car screeched out of a side street.*
- *noun* a loud high unpleasant cry or noise: *a screech of brakes/tyres* ◊ *She suddenly let out a screech.*

screed /skriːd/ *noun* a long piece of writing, especially one that is not very interesting

screen /skriːn/ *noun, verb*
- *noun*
  OF TV/COMPUTER | **1** [C] the flat surface at the front of a television or computer, on which you see pictures or information: *a computer/radar screen* ◊ *a monitor with a 21 inch screen* ◊ *They were staring at the television screen.* ◊ *Move your cursor to the top of the screen.* ◊ *the screen display/image* ◊ *Can you do a printout of this screen for me* (= of all the information on it)?—see also ON-SCREEN
  FILMS/MOVIES/TV | **2** [C] the large flat surface that films/movies or pictures are shown on: *a cinema/movie screen* ◊ *an eight-screen cinema* ◊ *The movie will be coming to your screens shortly.* **3** (often **the screen**) [sing., U] films/movies or television in general: *He has adapted the play for the screen.* ◊ *Some actors never watch themselves on screen.* ◊ *She was a star of stage and screen* (= plays and films/movies). ◊ *a screen actor/debut*—see also OFF-SCREEN, SILVER SCREEN, SMALL SCREEN
  PIECE OF FURNITURE | **4** [C] an upright piece of furniture or equipment that is fixed or that can be moved to divide a room or to keep one area hidden or separate: *The nurse put a screen around the bed.* ◊ *A wooden screen hid one corner of the room.*—see also FIRE SCREEN
  FOR HIDING/PROTECTING STH/SB | **5** [C] ~ (of sth) something that prevents sb from seeing or being aware of sth, or that protects sb/sth: *We planted a screen of tall trees.* ◊ *A screen of bodyguards protected the President.* ◊ (*figurative*) *All the research was conducted behind a screen of secrecy.*—see also SMOKESCREEN, SUNSCREEN, WINDSCREEN
  ON WINDOW/DOOR | **6** [C] (*especially AmE*) a wire or plastic net that is held in a frame and fastened on a window, or a door, to let in air but keep out insects: *Do you have screens on your windows?* ◊ *screen windows/doors*—picture at HOUSE
  IN CHURCH | **7** [C] a wood or stone structure in a church, that partly separates the main area from the ALTAR or CHOIR
- *verb* [VN]
  HIDE STH/SB | **1** ~ sth/sb (from sth/sb) to hide or protect sth/sb by placing sth in front of or around them: *Dark glasses screened his eyes from the sun.*
  PROTECT SB | **2** ~ sb from sth to protect sb from sth dangerous or unpleasant, especially to protect sb who has done sth illegal or dishonest
  FOR DISEASE | **3** [often passive] ~ (sb) (for sth) to examine people in order to find out if they have a particular disease or illness: *Men over 55 should be regularly screened for prostate cancer.*
  EMPLOYEES | **4** (of a company, an organization, etc.) to find out information about people who work or who want to work for you in order to make sure that they can be trusted: *Government employees may be screened by the security services.*
  SHOW FILM/MOVIE/PROGRAMME | **5** [usually passive] to show a

film/movie, etc. in a cinema/movie theater or on television: *a list of films to be screened as part of the festival*
PHRV ˌscreen sth↔'off [often passive] to separate part of a room, etc. from the rest of it by putting a screen around it: *Beds can be screened off to give patients more privacy.* ˌscreen sb↔'out to decide not to allow sb to join an organization, enter a country, etc. because you think they may cause trouble ˌscreen sth↔'out to prevent sth harmful from entering or going through sth: *The ozone layer screens out dangerous ultraviolet rays from the sun.*

screen·ing /ˈskriːnɪŋ/ *noun* **1** [C] the act of showing a film/movie or television programme: *This will be the movie's first screening in this country.* **2** [U, C] the testing or examining of a large number of people or things for disease, faults, etc: *breast cancer screening*

screen·play /ˈskriːnpleɪ/ *noun* the words that are written for a film/movie (= the SCRIPT), together with instructions for how it is to be acted and filmed

ˈ**screen saver** *noun* a computer program that replaces a screen display on a computer with another, moving, display after a particular length of time, to stop the screen from being damaged

ˈ**screen test** *noun* a test to see if sb is suitable to appear in a film/movie

screen·writer /ˈskriːnraɪtə(r)/ *noun* a person who writes SCREENPLAYS—compare PLAYWRIGHT, SCRIPTWRITER

screw /skruː/ *noun, verb*
- *noun* **1** [C] a thin pointed piece of metal like a nail with a raised SPIRAL line (called a THREAD) along it and a line or cross cut into its head. Screws are turned and pressed into wood, metal, etc. with a SCREWDRIVER in order to fasten two things together: *One of the screws is loose.* ◊ *Now tighten all the screws.*—see also CORKSCREW—picture at TOOL **2** [C] an act of turning a screw **3** [sing.] (△, *slang*) an act of having sex: *He hadn't had a screw for weeks.* **4** [sing.] (△, *slang*) a partner in sex: *a good screw* **5** [C] ~ a PROPELLER on a ship, a motor boat or an aircraft: *a twin-screw cruiser* **6** [C] (*BrE, slang*) a prison officer **IDM have a 'screw loose** to be slightly strange in your behaviour **put the 'screws on (sb)** to force sb to do sth by frightening and threatening them—more at TURN *n.*
- *verb* **1** [VN+*adv. / prep.*] to fasten one thing to another or make sth tight with a screw or screws: *The bookcase is screwed to the wall.* ◊ *You need to screw all the parts together.* ◊ *Now screw down the lid.* **2** to twist sth around in order to fasten it in place: [VN+*adv. / prep.*] *She screwed the cap back on the jar.* ◊ [VN-ADJ] *Screw the bolt tight.* **3** [V] to be attached by screwing: *The bulb should just screw into the socket.* ◊ *The lid simply screws on.* **4** [VN] ~ sth up (into sth)| ~ sth (up) into sth to squeeze sth, especially a piece of paper, into a tight ball: *I screwed up the letter and threw it into the fire.* ◊ *Screw the foil into a little ball.*—see also SCREWED-UP **5** [VN] ~ sb (for sth) (*slang*) to cheat sb, especially by making them pay too much money for sth: *We've been screwed.* ◊ *How much did they screw you for* (= how much did you have to pay)? **6** (△, *slang*) to have sex with sb: [V] *a couple screwing in the back of a car* ◊ [VN] *He accused me of screwing his wife.* **IDM screw 'him, 'you, 'that, etc.** (△, *slang*) an offensive way of showing that you are annoyed or do not care about sb/sth **screw up your 'courage** to force yourself to be brave enough to do sth: *I finally screwed up my courage and went to the dentist.*—more at HEAD *n.* **PHRV** ˌscrew a'round (△, *slang*) to have sex with a lot of different people ˌscrew sth 'from/'out of sb to force sb to give you sth: *They screwed the money out of her by threats.* ˌscrew 'up (*slang, especially AmE*) to do sth badly or spoil sth: *You really screwed up there!*—related noun SCREW-UP ˌscrew sb↔'up (*slang*) to upset or confuse sb so much that they are not able to deal with problems in their life: *Her father's death really screwed her up.*—see also SCREWED-UP ˌscrew sth↔'up **1** to fasten sth with screws: *to screw up a crate* **2** to fasten sth by turning it: *I screwed up the jar and put it back on the shelf.* **OPP** UNSCREW **3** (*slang*) to do sth badly or spoil sth: *Don't screw it up this time.* ˌscrew your 'eyes/'face↔'up to tighten the muscles of your eyes or face because the light is too

strong, you are in pain, etc: *He took a sip of the medicine and screwed up his face.*

screw·ball /'skruːbɔːl/ *noun* (*informal, especially AmE*) a strange or crazy person: *That guy's a complete screwball.*

screw·driver /'skruːdraɪvə(r)/ *noun* a tool with a narrow blade that is specially shaped at the end, used for turning screws—picture at TOOL

screwed-'up *adj.* **1** (*informal*) upset and anxious, especially because of sth bad that has happened to you in the past: *an extremely screwed-up kid* **2** (*especially BrE*) twisted into a ball: *a screwed-up tissue* **3** if your face or eyes are **screwed-up**, the muscles are tight, because you are worried, in pain, etc., or because the light is too bright

screw-top (also **screw-topped**) *adj.* [only before noun] (of a container) having a top or lid that SCREWS onto it

screwy /'skruːi/ *adj.* (*informal*) strange or crazy: *What a screwy idea!*

scrib·ble /'skrɪbl/ *verb, noun*
■ *verb* **1** ~ (sth) (down) to write sth quickly and carelessly, especially because you do not have much time SYN SCRAWL: [VN] *He scribbled a note to his sister before leaving.* ◇ *She scribbled down her phone number and pushed it into his hand.* ◇ [V] *Throughout the interview the journalists scribbled away furiously.* **2** [V] [usually+adv./prep.] to draw marks that do not mean anything: *Someone had scribbled all over the table in crayon.*
■ *noun* **1** [U, sing.] careless and untidy writing SYN SCRAWL: *How do you expect me to read this scribble?* **2** [C, usually pl.] marks or pictures that seem to have no meaning SYN SCRAWL: *The page was covered with a mass of scribbles.*

scrib·bler /'skrɪblə(r)/ *noun* (*disapproving* or *humorous*) a journalist, author or other writer

scribe /skraɪb/ *noun* a person who made copies of written documents before printing was invented

scrim·mage /'skrɪmɪdʒ/ *noun* **1** a confused struggle or fight **2** (in American football) a period of play that begins with the ball being placed on the ground **3** (*AmE*) a practice game of American football, basketball, etc.

scrimp /skrɪmp/ *verb* [V] to spend very little money on the things that you need to live, especially so that you can save it to spend on sth else: *They scrimped and saved to give the children a good education.*

scrip /skrɪp/ *noun* (*business*) an extra share in a business, given out instead of a DIVIDEND

script /skrɪpt/ *noun, verb*
■ *noun* **1** [C] a written text of a play, film/movie, broadcast, talk, etc: *That line isn't in the original script.* **2** [U] writing done by hand: *She admired his neat script.*—see also MANUSCRIPT **3** [U, C] a set of letters in which a language is written SYN ALPHABET: *a document in Cyrillic script* **4** [C] (*BrE*) a candidate's written answer or answers in an exam
■ *verb* [VN] [often passive] to write the script for a film/movie, play, etc.

script·ed /'skrɪptɪd/ *adj.* read from a script: *a scripted talk* OPP UNSCRIPTED

scrip·ture /'skrɪptʃə(r)/ *noun* **1** (**Scripture**) [U] (also **the Scriptures** [pl.]) the Bible **2** (**scriptures**) [pl.] the holy books of a particular religion: *Hindu scriptures* ▶ **scrip·tural** /'skrɪptʃərəl/ *adj.*: *scriptural references*

script·writer /'skrɪptraɪtə(r)/ *noun* a person who writes the words for films/movies, television and radio plays—compare PLAYWRIGHT, SCREENWRITER

scroll /skrəʊl; *AmE* skroʊl/ *noun, verb*
■ *noun* **1** a long roll of paper for writing on **2** a decoration cut in stone or wood with a curved shape like a roll of paper
■ *verb* (*computing*) to move text on a computer screen up or down so that you can read different parts of it: [V+adv./prep.] *Use the arrow keys to scroll through the list of files.* ◇ *Scroll down to the bottom of the document.* ◇ [VN] *Use the arrow keys to scroll the list of files.*

'scroll bar *noun* (*computing*) a strip at the edge of a computer screen that you use to scroll through a file with, using a mouse—picture on page 251

Scrooge /skruːdʒ/ *noun* [usually sing.] (*informal, disapproving*) a person who is very unwilling to spend money than by paying for it SYN SPONGE: [VN] *He's always ORIGIN* From **Ebenezer Scrooge**, a character in Charles Dickens' *A Christmas Carol* who is extremely mean.

scro·tum /'skrəʊtəm; *AmE* 'skroʊ-/ *noun* (*pl.* **scro·tums** or **scrota** /'skrəʊtə; *AmE* 'skroʊ-/) the bag of skin that contains the TESTICLES in men and most male animals

scrounge /skraʊndʒ/ *verb, noun*
■ *verb* ~ (sth) (off/from sb)| ~ (for sth) (*informal, disapproving*) to get sth from sb by asking them for it rather than by paying for it SYN SPONGE: [VN] *He's always scrounging free meals off us.* ◇ [V] *What is she scrounging for this time?* ▶ **scroun·ger** *noun*: *a campaign against welfare scroungers*
■ *noun* IDM **on the 'scrounge** (*BrE, informal, disapproving*) trying to get sth by persuading sb to give it to you: *That brother of yours is always on the scrounge.*

scrub /skrʌb/ *verb, noun*
■ *verb* (-bb-) **1** ~ sth (down)| ~ (at sth) to clean sth by rubbing it hard, perhaps with a brush and usually with soap and water: [VN] *I found him in the kitchen, scrubbing the floor.* ◇ *She scrubbed the counters down with bleach.* ◇ [V] *The woman scrubbed at her face with a tissue.* ◇ [VN-ADJ] *Scrub the vegetables clean.* **2** [VN] (*informal*) to cancel sth that you have arranged to do PHRV **,scrub sth↔'off|** **scrub sth off sth** to remove sth from the surface of an object by rubbing it hard with a brush, etc: *This treatment involves scrubbing off the top layer of dead skin.* **,scrub sth↔'out** to clean the inside of sth by rubbing it hard with a brush and usually with soap and water: *He scrubbed out the pans and left them to drain.* **,scrub 'up** (of a doctor, nurse, etc.) to wash your hands and arms before performing a medical operation
■ *noun* **1** [sing.] an act of scrubbing sth: *I've given the floor a good scrub.* **2** [U] small bushes and trees: *The bird disappeared into the scrub.* **3** (also **scrub·land** /'skrʌblənd/) [U] an area of land covered with small bushes and trees

scrub·ber /'skrʌbə(r)/ *noun* **1** (*BrE, informal*) an offensive word for a prostitute or for a woman who has sex with a lot of men **2** a brush or other object that you use for cleaning things, for example pans

'scrubbing brush (*AmE* **'scrub brush**) *noun* a stiff brush for cleaning floors and other surfaces

scrubby /'skrʌbi/ *adj.* **1** covered with small bushes and trees: *a scrubby hillside* **2** (of trees) small and not fully developed: *scrubby vegetation/bushes*

scruff /skrʌf/ *noun* (*BrE, informal*) a dirty or untidy person IDM **by the scruff of the/sb's 'neck** roughly holding the back of an animal's or person's neck: *She grabbed him by the scruff of the neck and threw him out.*

scruffy /'skrʌfi/ *adj.* (**scruff·ier**, **scruffi·est**) (*informal*) dirty or untidy: *He looked a little scruffy.* ◇ *She was wearing a scruffy pair of jeans.* ▶ **scruff·ily** *adv.* **scruffi·ness** *noun* [U]

scrum /skrʌm/ *noun* **1** (also *formal* **scrum·mage**) a part of a rugby game when players from both sides link themselves together in a group, with their heads down, and push against the other side. The ball is then thrown between them and each side tries to get it **2** the group of players who link themselves together in a scrum **3** a crowd of people who are pushing each other: *There was a real scrum when the bus arrived.*

,scrum 'half *noun* (in rugby) a player who puts the ball into the scrum

scrum·mage /'skrʌmɪdʒ/ *noun, verb*
■ *noun* (*formal*) = SCRUM
■ *verb* (also **,scrum 'down**) [V] (*sport*) to form a SCRUM during a game of rugby

scrump·tious /'skrʌmpʃəs/ *adj.* (*informal*) tasting very good SYN DELICIOUS: *scrumptious desserts*

scrumpy /'skrʌmpi/ *noun* [U] (*BrE*) a type of strong CIDER (= an alcoholic drink made from apples), made especially in the west of England

s	t	v	z	ʃ	ʒ	tʃ	dʒ	θ	ð	ŋ
see	tea	van	zoo	shoe	vision	chain	jam	thin	this	sing

scrunch /skrʌntʃ/ *verb* **1** [V] to make a loud sound like the one that is made when you walk on small stones (= GRAVEL): *The snow scrunched underfoot.* **2** [VN] ~ **sth (up)** to squeeze sth into a small round shape in your hands: *He scrunched up the note and threw it on the fire.* **3** [VN] ~ **sth (up)** to make sth become smaller: *The hedgehog scrunched itself up into a ball.* ▶ **scrunch** *noun* [sing.]: *the scrunch of tyres on the gravel*

scru·ple /'skru:pl/ *noun, verb*
■ *noun* [C, usually pl., U] a feeling that prevents you from doing sth that you think may be morally wrong: *I overcame my moral scruples.* ◊ *He had no scruples about spying on her.* ◊ *She is totally without scruple.*
■ *verb* [V to inf] **(not scruple to do sth)** (*formal*) to be willing to do sth even if it might be wrong or immoral

scru·pu·lous /'skru:pjələs/ *adj.* **1** careful about paying attention to every detail SYN METICULOUS: *You must be scrupulous about hygiene when you're preparing a baby's feed.* ◊ *scrupulous attention to detail* **2** ~ **(in sth/in doing sth)** careful to be honest and do what is right: *She had a reputation for scrupulous honesty.* ◊ *He was scrupulous in all his business dealings.* OPP UNSCRUPULOUS ▶ **scru·pu·lous·ly** *adv.*: *Her house is scrupulously clean.* ◊ *to be scrupulously fair / honest*

scru·tin·eer /ˌskru:tə'nɪə(r)/; *AmE* -'nɪr/ *noun* (*BrE*) a person who checks that an election or other vote is organized correctly and fairly

scru·tin·ize (*BrE* also **-ise**) /'skru:tənaɪz/ *verb* [VN] (*written*) to look at or examine sb/sth carefully: *She leaned forward to scrutinize their faces.* ◊ *The statement was carefully scrutinized before publication.*

scru·tiny /'skru:təni/ *noun* [U] (*formal*) careful and thorough examination: *Her argument doesn't really stand up to scrutiny.* ◊ *Foreign policy has come under close scrutiny recently.* ◊ *The documents should be available for public scrutiny.*

scuba-diving /'sku:bə daɪvɪŋ/ (also **scuba**) *noun* [U] the sport or activity of swimming underwater using special breathing equipment. This consists of a container of air which you carry on your back and a tube through which you breathe the air: *to go scuba-diving*—picture at SNORKELLING

scud /skʌd/ *verb* (-dd-) [V+*adv.* / *prep.*] (*literary*) (of clouds) to move quickly across the sky

scuff /skʌf/ *verb* [VN] **1** ~ **sth (on sth)** to make a mark on the smooth surface of sth when you rub it against sth rough: *I scuffed the heel of my shoe on the stonework.* **2** ~ **your feet, heels, etc.** to drag your feet along the ground as you walk ▶ **scuffed** *adj.*: *After only one day, his shoes were already scuffed and dirty.* **scuff** (also **'scuff mark**) *noun*

scuf·fle /'skʌfl/ *noun, verb*
■ *noun* ~ **(with sb)** a short and not very violent fight or struggle: *Scuffles broke out between police and demonstrators.* ◊ *He was involved in a scuffle with a photographer.*
■ *verb* [V] **1** ~ **(with sb)** (of two or more people) to fight or struggle with each other for a short time, in a way that is not very serious: *She scuffled with photographers as she left her hotel.* **2** [+*adv.* / *prep.*] to move quickly making a quiet rubbing noise: *Some animal was scuffling in the bushes.*

scuf·fling /'skʌflɪŋ/ *noun* [U] a low noise made by sth moving around: *He could hear whispering and scuffling on the other side of the door.*

scull /skʌl/ *noun, verb*
■ *noun* **1** [C, usually pl.] one of a pair of small OARS used by a single person rowing a boat, one in each hand **2** (**sculls**) [pl.] a race between small light boats with pairs of sculls: *single / double sculls* (= with one / two people in each boat) **3** [C] a small light boat used in sculls races
■ *verb* [V] to ROW a boat using sculls

scull·er /'skʌlə(r)/ *noun* a person who rows with sculls

scull·ery /'skʌləri/ *noun* (*pl.* **-ies**) a small room next to the kitchen in an old house, originally used for washing dishes, etc.

sculling /'skʌlɪŋ/ *noun* [U] the sport of racing with SCULLS

sculpt /skʌlpt/ *verb* [VN] [usually passive] **1** ~ **sth (in / from / out of sth)** to make figures or objects by carving or shaping wood, stone, clay, metal, etc: *a display of animals sculpted in ice* ◊ *The figures were sculpted from single blocks of marble.* **2** (*written*) to give sth a particular shape: *a coastline sculpted by the wind and sea* ◊ (*figurative*) *a firmly sculpted mouth*

sculp·tor /'skʌlptə(r)/ *noun* a person who makes SCULPTURES

sculp·tress /'skʌlptrəs/ *noun* a woman who makes SCULPTURES

sculp·ture /'skʌlptʃə(r)/ *noun* **1** [C, U] a work of art that is a solid figure or object made by carving or shaping wood, stone, clay, metal, etc: *a marble sculpture of Venus* ◊ *He collects modern sculpture.* **2** [U] the art of making sculptures: *the techniques of sculpture in stone* ▶ **sculptural** /'skʌlptʃərəl/ *adj.*: *sculptural decoration*

sculp·tured /'skʌlptʃəd; *AmE* -tʃərd/ *adj.* [usually before noun] **1** (of figures or objects) carved or shaped from wood, stone, clay, metal, etc. **2** (*approving*) (of part of the body) having a clear and pleasing shape: *sculptured cheekbones*

scum /skʌm/ *noun* **1** [U, sing.] a layer of bubbles or an unpleasant substance that forms on the surface of a liquid: *Skim off any scum.* ◊ *stinking water covered by a thick green scum* **2** (*informal*) [pl.] an insulting word for people that you strongly disapprove of: *Don't waste your sympathy on scum like that.* ◊ *Drug dealers are the scum of the earth* (= the worst people there are). ▶ **scummy** /'skʌmi/ *adj.*: *scummy water* ◊ *scummy people dropping litter*

scum·bag /'skʌmbæg/ *noun* (*slang, offensive*) an unpleasant person

scup·per /'skʌpə(r)/ *verb* [VN] (*BrE, informal*) to cause sb/sth to fail SYN FOIL: *The residents' protests scuppered their plans for developing the land.*

scur·ril·ous /'skʌrələs; *AmE* 'skɜːr-/ *adj.* (*formal*) very rude and insulting, and intended to damage sb's reputation: *scurrilous gossip / rumours / attacks* ▶ **scur·ril·ous·ly** *adv.*

scurry /'skʌri; *AmE* 'skɜːri/ *verb* (**scur·ries, scurry·ing, scur·ried, scur·ried**) [V+*adv.* / *prep.*] to run with quick short steps SYN SCUTTLE: *She said goodbye and scurried back to work.* ◊ *Ants scurried around the pile of rotting food.* ▶ **scurry** *noun* [sing.]

scurvy /'skɜːvi; *AmE* 'skɜːrvi/ *noun* [U] a disease caused by a lack of VITAMIN C from not eating enough fruit and vegetables

scut·tle /'skʌtl/ *verb, noun*
■ *verb* **1** [V+*adv.* / *prep.*] to run with quick short steps SYN SCURRY: *She scuttled off when she heard the sound of his voice.* ◊ *He held his breath as a rat scuttled past.* **2** [VN] to deliberately cause sth to fail SYN FOIL: *Shareholders successfully scuttled the deal.* **3** [VN] to sink a ship deliberately by making holes in the side or bottom of it
■ *noun* = COAL SCUTTLE

scuttle-butt /'skʌtlbʌt/ *noun* [U] (*AmE, slang*) stories about other people's private lives, that may be unkind or not true SYN GOSSIP

scuzzy /'skʌzi/ *adj.* (*informal, especially AmE*) dirty and unpleasant

scythe /saɪð/ *noun, verb*
■ *noun* a tool with a long handle and a slightly curved blade, used for cutting long grass and corn
■ *verb* to cut grass, corn, etc. with a scythe: [VN] *the scent of newly scythed grass* ◊ [V] (*figurative*) *The plane scythed through buildings in the city's suburbs.*

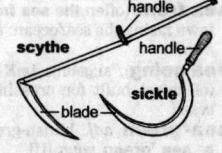

SDLP /ˌes di: el 'pi:/ *abbr.* (in N Ireland) Social and Democratic Labour Party

SE *abbr.* south-east; south-eastern: *SE Asia*

æ	ɑː	e	ɜː	ə	ɪ	iː	i	ɒ	ɔː	ʌ	ʊ	u	uː
cat	father	ten	bird	about	sit	see	many	got	saw	cup	put	actual	too

(BrE)

S

sea /siː/ *noun* **1** (often **the sea**) [U] (also *literary* **seas** [pl.]) (*especially BrE*) the salt water that covers most of the earth's surface and surrounds its continents and islands: *to travel by sea* ◊ *a cottage by the sea* ◊ *The waste was dumped in the sea.* ◊ *Now the wreck is lying at the bottom of the sea.* ◊ *We left port and headed for the open sea* (= far away from land). ◊ *the cold seas of the Antarctic* ◊ *a sea voyage* ◊ *a hotel room with sea view*—see also THE HIGH SEAS, OCEAN—picture at COAST **2** [C] (often **Sea**, especially as part of a name) a large area of salt water that is part of an ocean or surrounded by land: *the North Sea* ◊ *the Caspian Sea* **3** [C] (also **seas** [pl.]) the movement of the waves of the sea: *It was a calm sea.* ◊ *The sea was very rough.* **4** [sing.] **~ of sth** a large amount of sth that stretches over a wide area: *He looked down at the sea of smiling faces before him.* IDM **at ˈsea 1** on the sea, especially in a ship, or in the sea: *It happened on the second night at sea.* ◊ *They were lost at sea.* **2** confused and not knowing what to do: *I'm all at sea with these new regulations.* **go to ˈsea** to become a sailor **out to ˈsea** far away from land where the sea is deepest: *She fell overboard and was swept out to sea.* **put (out) to ˈsea** to leave a port or harbour by ship or boat—more at DEVIL, FISH *n.*

BRITISH / AMERICAN
sea / ocean

In *BrE*, the usual word for the mass of salt water that covers most of the earth's surface is the **sea**. In *AmE*, the usual word is the **ocean**: *A swimmer drowned in the sea / ocean this morning.*

The names of particular areas of seas, however, are fixed: *the Mediterranean Sea* ◊ *the Atlantic Ocean.*

Sea / ocean are also used if you go to the coast on holiday / vacation: *We're spending a week at the sea / ocean in June.* In *AmE* it is also common to say: *We're going to the beach on vacation.*

⇨ note at COAST

ˌsea ˈair *noun* [U] air near the sea/ocean, thought to be good for the health: *a breath of sea air*

ˈsea anemone *noun* a simple, brightly-coloured sea creature that sticks onto rocks and looks like a flower

the ˈsea bed *noun* [sing.] the floor of the sea/ocean

sea·bird /ˈsiːbɜːd; *AmE* -bɜːrd/ *noun* a bird that lives close to the sea, for example on cliffs or islands, and gets its food from it—picture on page A6

sea·board /ˈsiːbɔːd; *AmE* -bɔːrd/ *noun* the part of a country that is along its coast: *Australia's eastern seaboard*

sea·borne /ˈsiːbɔːn; *AmE* -bɔːrn/ *adj.* [only before noun] carried in ships: *a seaborne invasion*

ˌsea ˈbreeze *noun* a wind blowing from the sea/ocean towards the land

ˈsea change *noun* [usually sing.] (*written*) a strong and noticeable change in a situation

sea·far·er /ˈsiːfeərə(r); *AmE* -fer-/ *noun* (*old-fashioned* or *formal*) a sailor

sea·far·ing /ˈsiːfeərɪŋ; *AmE* -fer-/ *adj.* [only before noun] connected with work or travel on the sea/ocean: *a seafaring nation* ▶ **sea·far·ing** *noun* [U]

ˈsea fish *noun* (*pl.* **sea fish**) a fish that lives in the sea, rather than in rivers or lakes

sea·food /ˈsiːfuːd/ *noun* [U] fish and sea creatures that can be eaten, especially shellfish: *a seafood restaurant* ◊ *a seafood cocktail*

ˈsea front (often **the sea front**) *noun* [sing.] the part of a town facing the sea/ocean: *the grand houses along the sea front*

sea·going /ˈsiːɡəʊɪŋ; *AmE* -ɡoʊ-/ *adj.* [only before noun] (of ships) built for crossing the sea/ocean: *a seagoing vessel*

ˌsea-ˈgreen *adj.* bluish-green in colour, like the sea ▶ ˌsea ˈgreen *noun* [U]

sea·gull /ˈsiːɡʌl/ *noun* = GULL: *a flock of seagulls*

ˈsea horse *noun* a small sea fish that swims upright and has a head that looks like the head of a horse

seal /siːl/ *noun, verb*

■ *noun*
SEA ANIMAL **1** [C] a sea animal that eats fish and lives around coasts. There are many types of seal, some of which are hunted for their fur: *a colony of seals* ◊ *grey seals basking on the rocks*
OFFICIAL MARK **2** [C] an official design or mark, stamped on a document to show that it is genuine and carries the authority of a particular person or organization: *The letter bore the president's seal.*
MAKING STH DEFINITE **3** [sing.] a thing that makes sth definite: *The project has been given the government's seal of approval* (= official approval). ◊ *I looked upon the gift as a seal on our friendship.*
ON CONTAINERS **4** [C] a substance, strip of material, etc. used to fill a crack so that air, liquid, etc. cannot get in or out: *a jar with a rubber seal in the lid* ◊ *Only drink bottled water and check the seal isn't broken.*
ON LETTERS/BOXES **5** [C] a piece of WAX (= a soft substance produced by bees), soft metal or paper that is placed across the opening of sth such as a letter or box and which has to be broken before the letter or box can be opened: *He broke the wax seal and unrolled the paper.* **6** a piece of metal, a ring, etc. with a design on it, used for stamping a WAX or metal seal
IDM **set the ˈseal on sth** (*formal*) to make sth definite or complete: *Her election to the premiership set the seal on a remarkable political career.* **under ˈseal** (*formal*) (of a document) in a sealed envelope that cannot be opened before a particular time
■ *verb* [VN]
CLOSE ENVELOPE **1** **~ sth (up/down)** to close an envelope, etc. by sticking the edges of the opening together: *Make sure you've signed the cheque before sealing the envelope.* ◊ *a sealed bid* (= one that is kept in a sealed envelope and therefore remains secret until all other bids have been received)
CLOSE CONTAINER **2** [often passive] **~ sth (up) (with sth)** to close a container tightly or fill a crack, etc., especially so that air, liquid, etc. cannot get in or out: *The organs are kept in sealed plastic bags.*
COVER SURFACE **3** [often passive] **~ sth (with sth)** to cover the surface of sth with a substance in order to protect it: *The floors had been stripped and sealed with varnish.*
MAKE STH DEFINITE **4** (*written*) to make sth definite, so that it cannot be changed or argued about: *to seal a contract/ deal* ◊ *They drank a glass of wine to seal their new friendship.* ◊ *The discovery of new evidence sealed his fate* (= nothing could prevent what was going to happen to him).
CLOSE BORDERS/EXITS **5** (of the police, army, etc.) to prevent people from passing through a place: *Troops have sealed the borders between the countries.*
IDM see LIP, SIGN *v.*
PHRV ˌseal sth↔ˈin to prevent sth that is contained in sth else from escaping ˈseal sth in sth to put sth in an envelope, container, etc. and seal it: *The body was sealed in a lead coffin.* ˌseal sth↔ˈoff (of the police, army) to prevent people from entering a particular area

seal·ant /ˈsiːlənt/ (also **seal·er**) *noun* [U, C] a substance that is put onto a surface to stop air, water, etc. from entering or escaping from it

ˈsea legs *noun* [pl.] the ability to walk easily on a moving ship and not to feel sick at sea: *It won't take you long to find your sea legs.*

seal·er /ˈsiːlə(r)/ *noun* **1** = SEALANT **2** a person who hunts SEALS

ˈsea level *noun* [U] the average height of the sea/ocean, used as the basis for measuring the height of all places on land: *50 metres above sea level*

seal·ing /ˈsiːlɪŋ/ *noun* [U] the activity of hunting SEALS

ˈsealing wax *noun* [U] a type of WAX that melts quickly when it is heated and becomes hard quickly when it cools, used in the past for SEALING letters, etc.

ˈsea lion *noun* a large SEAL (= a sea animal with thick fur, that eats fish and lives around the coast) that lives by the Pacific Ocean

---

seam /siːm/ *noun* **1** a line along which two edges of fabric, etc. are joined or sewn together: *a shoulder seam*—picture at SEW **2** a thin layer of coal or other material, between layers of rock under the ground: *They struck a rich seam of iron ore.* ◊ *(figurative) The book is a rich seam of information.* **3** a line where two edges meet, for example the edges of wooden boards: *Light was spilling in through the seams of the door.* **IDM** **be bursting/bulging at the ˈseams** (*informal*) to be very full, especially of people **be falling/coming apart at the ˈseams** (*informal*) to be going very badly wrong and likely to stop functioning completely: *She was falling apart at the seams, spending most of her time in tears.*—more at FRAY *v.*

sea·man /ˈsiːmən/ *noun* (*pl.* **-men** /-mən/) a member of the navy or a sailor on a ship below the rank of an officer: *Seaman Bates* ◊ *a merchant seaman*—see also ABLE SEA-MAN, ORDINARY SEAMAN

sea·man·ship /ˈsiːmənʃɪp/ *noun* [U] skill in sailing a boat or ship

seamed /siːmd/ *adj.* **1** having a seam or seams: *seamed stockings* **2** (*written*) covered with deep lines: *an old man with a brown seamed face*

ˈsea mile *noun* = NAUTICAL MILE

seam·less /ˈsiːmləs/ *adj.* **1** without a SEAM: *a seamless garment* **2** with no spaces or pauses between one part and the next: *a seamless flow of talk* ▶ **seam·less·ly** *adv.*

seam·stress /ˈsiːmstrəs; ˈsem-/ *noun* (*old-fashioned*) a woman who can sew and make clothes or whose job is sewing and making clothes

seamy /ˈsiːmi/ *adj.* (**seam·ier**, **seami·est**) unpleasant and immoral [SYN] SORDID: *a seamy sex scandal* ◊ *the seamier side of life*

se·ance /ˈseɪɒns; *AmE* ˈseɪɑːns/ *noun* a meeting at which people try to make contact with and talk to the spirits of dead people

sea·plane /ˈsiːpleɪn/ (*AmE* also **hydro·plane**) *noun* a plane that can take off from and land on water

sea·port /ˈsiːpɔːt; *AmE* -pɔːrt/ *noun* a town with a harbour used by large ships: *the Baltic seaports*

ˈsea power *noun* **1** [U] the ability to control the seas with a strong navy **2** [C] a country with a strong navy

sear /sɪə(r); *AmE* sɪr/ *verb* **1** [VN] to burn the surface of sth in a way that is sudden and powerful: *The heat of the sun seared their faces.* ◊ *spicy food that sears the mouth* ◊ *Sear the meat first* (= cook the outside of it quickly at a high temperature) *to retain its juices.* **2** (*written*) to cause sb to feel sudden and great pain: [V+adv./prep.] *The pain seared along her arm.* ◊ [VN] *Feelings of guilt seared him.*—see also SEARING

search /sɜːtʃ; *AmE* sɜːrtʃ/ *noun, verb*
■ *noun* **1** ~ (for sb/sth) an attempt to find sb/sth, especially by looking carefully for them/it: *After a long search for the murder weapon, the police found a knife.* ◊ *Detectives carried out a thorough search of the building.* ◊ *She went into the kitchen* **in search of** (= looking for) *a drink.* ◊ *The search for a cure goes on.* ◊ **The search is on** (= has begun) *for someone to fill the post.* ◊ *Eventually the search was called off.* ◊ *a mountain* **search and rescue** *team* **2** (*computing*) an act of looking for information in a computer DATABASE or NETWORK: *to do a search on the Internet* ◊ *a* **search engine** (= a program that does searches)
■ *verb* **1** ~ (sth) (for sth/sb) to look carefully for sth/sb; to examine a particular place when looking for sb/sth: [V+adv./prep.] *She searched in vain for her passport.* ◊ *The customs officers searched through our bags.* ◊ *I've searched high and low for those files but I can't find them anywhere.* ◊ [VN] *His house had clearly been searched and the book was missing.* ◊ *Firefighters searched the buildings for survivors.* ◊ *searching the Web for interesting sites* ◊ [V, VN] *Police searched for clues in the area.* ◊ *Police searched the area for clues.* **2** [VN] ~ **sb (for sth)** (especially of the police) to examine sb's clothes, their pockets, etc. in order to find sth that they may be hiding: *Visitors are regularly searched as they enter the building.* ◊ *The youths were arrested and searched for anything that would incriminate them.*—see also STRIP-SEARCH **3** [V] ~ (for sth)

to think carefully about sth, especially in order to find the answer to a problem: *He searched desperately for something to say.*—see also SOUL-SEARCHING **IDM** **ˌsearch ˈme** (*spoken*) used to emphasize that you do not know the answer to sb's question: *'Why didn't she say anything?' 'Search me!'* **PHRV** **ˌsearch sth/sb↔ˈout** to look for sth/sb until you find them: *Fighter pilots searched out and attacked enemy aircraft.*

search·er /ˈsɜːtʃə(r); *AmE* ˈsɜːrtʃ-/ *noun* **1** a person who is trying to find sth/sb **2** (*computing*) a program that helps you find information in a computer DATABASE or NETWORK; a search engine

search·ing /ˈsɜːtʃɪŋ; *AmE* ˈsɜːrtʃ-/ *adj.* [usually before noun] (of a look, a question, etc.) trying to find out the truth about sth; thorough and serious ▶ **search·ing·ly** *adv.*

search·light /ˈsɜːtʃlaɪt; *AmE* ˈsɜːrtʃ-/ *noun* a powerful lamp that can be turned in any direction, used, for example, for finding people or vehicles at night

ˈsearch party *noun* [C+sing./pl. *v.*] an organized group of people who are looking for a person or thing that is missing or lost

ˈsearch warrant *noun* an official document that allows the police to search a building, for example to look for stolen property

sear·ing /ˈsɪərɪŋ; *AmE* ˈsɪrɪŋ/ *adj.* [usually before noun] (*written*) **1** so strong that it seems to burn you: *the searing heat of a tropical summer* ◊ *He felt a searing pain in his neck.* **2** (of words or speech) powerful and critical: *The article was a searing attack on the government.* ▶ **sear·ing·ly** *adv.*—see also SEAR

sea·scape /ˈsiːskeɪp/ *noun* a picture or view of the sea—compare TOWNSCAPE

ˈsea shanty *noun* (*BrE*) = SHANTY

sea·shell /ˈsiːʃel/ *noun* the shell of a small creature that lives in the sea, often found empty when the creature has died

sea·shore /ˈsiːʃɔː(r)/ (usually **the seashore**) *noun* [usually sing.] the land along the edge of the sea or ocean, usually where there is sand and rocks

sea·sick /ˈsiːsɪk/ *adj.* [not usually before noun] feeling ill/sick or wanting to VOMIT when you are travelling on a boat or ship: *to be/feel/get seasick* ▶ **sea·sick·ness** *noun* [U]

sea·side /ˈsiːsaɪd/ (often **the seaside**) *noun* [sing.] (*especially BrE*) an area that is by the sea, especially one where people go for a day or a holiday/vacation: *a trip to the seaside* ◊ *a day at/by the seaside* ▶ **sea·side** *adj.* [only before noun]: *a seaside resort* ◊ *a seaside vacation home* ⇨ note at COAST

sea·son /ˈsiːzn/ *noun, verb*
■ *noun* **1** any of the four main periods of the year: spring, summer, autumn/fall and winter: *the changing seasons* **2** **the dry/rainy/wet ~** a period of the year in tropical countries when it is either very dry or it rains a lot **3** a period of time during a year when a particular activity happens or is done: *the cricket/hunting/shooting season* ◊ *He scored his first goal of the season on Saturday.* ◊ *The female changes colour during the* **breeding season.** ◊ *The hotels are always full during the* **peak season** (= when most people are on holiday/vacation). ◊ *(BrE) the holiday season* ◊ *(AmE) the tourist season* ◊ *(AmE) the holiday season* (= the time of Thanksgiving, Hanukkah, Christmas and New Year) ◊ *(BrE) the festive season* (= Christmas)—see also CLOSE SEASON, HIGH SEASON, LOW SEASON, OFF SEASON, THE SILLY SEASON **4** a period of time in which a play is shown in one place; a series of plays, films/movies or television programmes: *The play opens for a second season in London next week.* ◊ *a season of films by Alfred Hitchcock* **5** a period of time during one year when a particular style of clothes, hair, etc. is popular and fashionable: *This season's look is soft and romantic.* **IDM** **in ˈseason 1** (of fruit or vegetables) easily available and ready to eat because it is the right time of year for them: *Strawberries are now in season.* **2** (of a female animal) ready to MATE **out of ˈseason 1** (of fruit or vegetables) not easily available because it is not the right time of

S

year for them **2** at the times of year when few people go on holiday/vacation: *Hotels are cheaper out of season.* **season's 'greetings** (*written*) used as a greeting at Christmas
■ *verb* **~ sth (with sth)** to add salt, pepper, etc. to food in order to give it more flavour: [VN] *Season the lamb with garlic and rosemary.* ◊ [V] *Add the mushrooms and onions, and season to taste* (= add as much salt, pepper, etc. as you think is necessary).

sea·son·able /ˈsiːznəbl/ *adj.* usual or suitable for the time of year: *seasonable temperatures* OPP UNSEASONABLE

sea·son·al /ˈsiːzənl/ *adj.* **1** happening or needed during a particular season; varying with the seasons: *seasonal workers brought in to cope with the Christmas period* ◊ *seasonal variations in unemployment figures* **2** typical of or suitable for the time of year, especially Christmas: *seasonal decorations* OPP UNSEASONAL ▶ **sea·son·al·ly** /-nəli/ *adv.*: *seasonally adjusted unemployment figures* (= not including the changes that always happen in different seasons)

sea·son·al·ity /ˌsiːzəˈnæləti/ *noun* [U, sing.] (*technical*) the fact of varying with the seasons: *a high degree of climatic seasonality*

sea·soned /ˈsiːznd/ *adj.* **1** [usually before noun] (of a person) having a lot of experience of a particular activity: *a seasoned campaigner/performer/traveller* **2** (of food) with salt, pepper, etc. added to it **3** (of wood) made suitable for use by being left outside: *seasoned oak/timber*

sea·son·ing /ˈsiːzənɪŋ/ *noun* [U, C] a substance used to add flavour to food, especially salt and pepper

'season ticket *noun* a ticket that you can use many times within a particular period, for example on a regular train or bus journey, or for a series of games, sports, etc., and that costs less than paying separately each time: *an annual/a monthly season ticket* ◊ *a season ticket holder*

seat /siːt/ *noun, verb*
■ *noun*
PLACE TO SIT | **1** a place where you can sit, for example a chair: *She sat back in her seat.* ◊ *He put his shopping on the seat behind him.* ◊ *Please take a seat* (= sit down). ◊ *a window/corner seat* (= one near a window/in a corner) ◊ *a child seat* (= for a child in a car) ◊ *We used the branch of an old tree as a seat.* ◊ *We all filed back to our seats in silence.*—see also BACK SEAT, BUCKET SEAT, HOT SEAT, LOVE SEAT
-SEATER | **2** (in nouns and adjectives) with the number of seats mentioned: (*BrE*) *a ten-seater minibus* ◊ *an all-seater stadium* (= in which nobody is allowed to stand)
PART OF CHAIR | **3** the part of a chair, etc. on which you actually sit: *a steel chair with a plastic seat*
IN PLANE/TRAIN/THEATRE | **4** a place where you pay to sit in a plane, train, theatre, etc: *to book/reserve a seat* (= for a concert, etc.) ◊ *There are no seats left on that flight.*
OFFICIAL POSITION | **5** an official position as a member of a parliament, council, committee, etc: *a seat on the city council/in Parliament/in Congress* ◊ *to win/lose a seat* (= in an election) ◊ (*BrE*) *to take your seat* (= to begin your duties, especially in Parliament) ◊ *The majority of seats on the board will be held by business representatives.*—see also SAFE SEAT
TOWN/CITY | **6** ~ **of sth** (*formal*) a place where people are involved in a particular activity, especially a city that has a university or the offices of a government: *Washington is the seat of government of the US.* ◊ *a university town renowned as a seat of learning*
COUNTRY HOUSE | **7** (also ,country 'seat) (both *BrE*) a large house in the country, that belongs to a member of the upper class: *the family seat in Norfolk*
PART OF BODY | **8** (especially *formal*) the part of the body on which a person sits SYN BUTTOCKS
PART OF TROUSERS/PANTS | **9** the part of a pair of trousers/pants that covers a person's seat
IDM **(fly) by the seat of your 'pants** to act without careful thought and without a plan that you have made in advance, hoping that you will be lucky and be successful **be in the 'driving seat** (*BrE*) (*AmE* **be in the 'driver's**

seat**)** to be the person in control of a situation—more at BACK SEAT, BUM *n.*, EDGE *n.*
■ *verb* [VN]
SIT DOWN | **1 ~ (yourself)** (*formal*) to give sb a place to sit; to sit down in a place: *Please wait to be seated* (= in a restaurant, etc.). ◊ *Please be seated* (= sit down). ◊ *He seated himself behind the desk.* ◊ *Please remain seated until the aircraft has come to a halt.* ◊ *The bus can carry 42 seated passengers.*
OF BUILDING/VEHICLE | **2** to have enough seats for a particular number of people: *The aircraft seats 200 passengers.*

'seat belt (also **'safety belt**) *noun* a belt that is attached to the seat in a car or a plane and that you fasten around yourself so that you are not thrown out of the seat if there is an accident: *Fasten your seat belts.*—picture at CAR

seat·ing /ˈsiːtɪŋ/ *noun* [U] places to sit; seats: *The theatre has seating for about 500 people.* ◊ *The room had a seating capacity of over 200.* ◊ *the seating arrangements for the conference*

'sea turtle *noun* (*AmE*) = TURTLE

'sea urchin (also **ur·chin**) *noun* a small sea creature with a round prickly shell

,sea 'wall *noun* a large strong wall built to stop the sea from flowing onto the land

sea·ward /ˈsiːwəd; *AmE* -wərd/ *adj.* towards the sea; in the direction of the sea: *the seaward side of the coastal road* ▶ **sea·ward** (also **sea·wards** /-wədz; *AmE* -wərdz/) *adv.*: *Her gaze was fixed seawards.*

'sea water *noun* [U] water from the sea or ocean, that is salty

sea·way /ˈsiːweɪ/ *noun* a passage from the sea through the land along which large ships can travel

sea·weed /ˈsiːwiːd/ *noun* [U, C] a plant that grows in the sea or ocean, or on rocks at the edge of the sea or ocean. There are many different types of seaweed, some of which are eaten as food.

sea·worthy /ˈsiːwɜːði; *AmE* -wɜːrði/ *adj.* (of a ship) in a suitable condition to sail ▶ **sea·worthi·ness** *noun* [U]

se·ba·ceous /sɪˈbeɪʃəs/ *adj.* [usually before noun] (*biology*) producing a substance like oil in the body: *the sebaceous glands in the skin*

Sec. (*AmE* also **Secy.**) *abbr.* secretary

sec /sek/ *noun* **(a sec)** [sing.] (*informal*) a very short time; a second: *Stay there. I'll be back in a sec.* ◊ *Hang on* (= wait) *a sec.*

sec. *abbr.* second(s)

seca·teurs /ˌsekəˈtɜːz; *AmE* -ˈtɜːrz/ *noun* [pl.] (*BrE*) a garden tool like a pair of strong scissors, used for cutting plant stems and small branches: *a pair of secateurs*—picture at SCISSORS

se·cede /sɪˈsiːd/ *verb* [V] **~ (from sth)** (*formal*) (of a state, country, etc.) to officially leave an organization of states, countries, etc. and become independent: *The Republic of Panama seceded from Colombia in 1903.*

se·ces·sion /sɪˈseʃn/ *noun* [U, C] **~ (from sth)** the fact of an area or group becoming independent from the country or larger group that it belongs to

se·ces·sion·ist /sɪˈseʃənɪst/ *adj.* [only before noun] supporting or connected with secession: *secessionist groups* ▶ **se·ces·sion·ist** *noun*: *a military campaign against the secessionists*

se·cluded /sɪˈkluːdɪd/ *adj.* **1** (of a place) quiet and private; not used or disturbed by other people: *a secluded garden/beach/spot* **2** without much contact with other people: *to lead a secluded life*

se·clu·sion /sɪˈkluːʒn/ *noun* [U] the state of being private or of having little contact with other people: *the seclusion and peace of the island*

sec·ond¹ /ˈsekənd/ *det., ordinal number, adv., noun, verb*—see also SECOND²
■ *det., ordinal number* **1** happening or coming next after the first in a series of similar things or people; 2nd: *This is the second time it's happened.* ◊ *Italy scored a second goal just after half-time.* ◊ *the second of June/June 2nd* ◊ *He was the second to arrive.* ◊ *We have one child and are*

s	t	v	z	ʃ	ʒ	tʃ	dʒ	θ	ð	ŋ
see	tea	van	zoo	shoe	vision	chain	jam	thin	this	sing

expecting our second in July. **2** next in order of import-ance, size, quality, etc. to one other person or thing: *Osaka is Japan's **second-largest** city / Japan's **second** city.* ◊ *The spreadsheet application is **second** only to word processing in terms of popularity.* ◊ *As a dancer, he is **second to none** (= nobody is a better dancer than he is).* **3** [only before noun] another; in addition to one that you already own or use: *They have a **second home** in Tuscany.* ◊ *teachers of English as a **second language** (= to people who already speak one or more other languages)*

■ *adv.* **1** after one other person or thing in order or import-ance: *She **came second** in the marathon.* ◊ *I agreed to speak second.* ◊ *He is a writer first and a scientist second.* **2** used to introduce the second of a list of points you want to make in a speech or piece of writing [SYN] SECONDLY: *She did it first because she wanted to, and second because I asked her to.*

■ *noun* **1** [C] (*symb* *"*) (*abbr.* **sec.**) a unit for measuring time. There are 60 seconds in one minute: *She can run 100 metres in just over 11 seconds.* ◊ *For several seconds he did not reply.* ◊ *The light flashes **every** 5 seconds.* ◊ *The water flows at about 1.5 metres **per** second.* **2** [C] (also *informal* **sec**) a very short time [SYN] MOMENT: *I'll be with you in a second.* ◊ *I'll phone home **in / within** seconds.*—see also SPLIT SECOND **3** [C] (*symb* *"*) a unit for measuring angles. There are 60 seconds in one minute: *1° 6′ 10″* (= one degree, six minutes and ten seconds) **4** (**seconds**) [pl.] (*spoken*) a second amount of the same food that you have just eaten: *Seconds, anybody?* **5** [C, usually pl.] an item that is sold at a lower price than usual because it is not perfect **6** (also **,second 'gear**) [U] one of four or five positions of the GEARS in a vehicle: *When it's icy, move off **in second**.* **7** [C] a level of univer-sity degree at British universities. An **upper second** is a good degree and a **lower second** is average.—compare FIRST *n.* (4), THIRD *n.* (2) **8** [C] a person whose role is to help and support sb else, for example in a boxing match or in a formal DUEL in the past [IDM] see JUST *adv.*, WAIT *v.*

■ *verb* [VN] to state officially at a meeting that you support another person's idea, suggestion, etc. so that it can be discussed and/or voted on: *Any proposal must be seconded by two other members of the committee.* ◊ (*spoken*) *'Thank God that's finished.' 'I'll second that!'* (= I agree)' —compare PROPOSE

se·cond² /sɪ'kɒnd; *AmE* -'kɑːnd/ *verb* [VN] [usually pas-sive] ~ **sb** (**from sth**) (**to sth**) (*especially BrE*) to send an employee to another department, office, etc. in order to do a different job for a short period of time: *Each year two teachers are seconded to industry for six months.*—see also SECOND¹ ► **se·cond·ment** (*BrE*) *noun* [U, C]: *They met while she was on **secondment** from the Foreign Office.*

sec·ond·ary /'sekəndri; *AmE* -deri/ *adj.* **1** ~ (**to sth**) less important than sth else: *a secondary consideration / issue / role* ◊ *Experience is what matters—age is of secondary importance.* ◊ *Raising animals was only secondary to other forms of farming.* **2** happening as a result of sth else: *a secondary infection / tumour* ◊ *a secondary effect* ◊ *a second-ary colour* (= made from mixing two primary colours) **3** [only before noun] connected with teaching children of 11-18 years: *secondary teachers* ◊ *the secondary curricu-lum*—compare ELEMENTARY, PRIMARY, TERTIARY ► **sec-ond·ar·ily** /'sekəndrəli; *AmE* ˌsekən'derəli/ *adv.*: *Poverty is primarily a cause of illness and only secondarily its effect.*

,secondary edu'cation *noun* [U] (*especially BrE*) edu-cation for children between the ages of 11 and 18: *primary and secondary education*

,secondary 'modern *noun* (in Britain until the 1970s) a school for young people between the ages of 11 and 16 who did not go to a GRAMMAR SCHOOL

'secondary school *noun* a school for young people between the ages of 11 and 16 or 18—compare PRIMARY SCHOOL, HIGH SCHOOL

'secondary source *noun* a book or other source of information where the writer has taken the information from some other source and not collected it himself or herself—compare PRIMARY SOURCE

,secondary 'stress *noun* [U, C] (*phonetics*) the second strongest stress that is put on a syllable in a word or a phrase when it is spoken—compare PRIMARY STRESS

,second 'best *adj.* **1** not as good as the best: *The two teams seemed evenly matched but Arsenal **came off second best** (= did not win).* ◊ *my second-best suit* **2** not exactly what you want; not perfect: *a second-best choice / option / solution* ► **,second 'best** *noun* [U]: *Sometimes you have to **settle for** (= be content with) second best.*

,second 'chamber *noun* (*especially BrE*) = UPPER HOUSE

,second 'class *noun* [U] **1** a way of travelling on a train or ship that costs less and is less comfortable than FIRST CLASS. In Britain this is now usually called **standard class**. **2** (in Britain) the class of mail that costs less and takes longer to arrive than FIRST CLASS **3** (in the US) the system of sending newspapers and magazines by mail **4** [U, sing.] the second highest standard of degree given by a British university, often divided into upper second class and lower second class

,second-'class *adj.* **1** (*disapproving*) (of a person) less important than other people: *Older people should not be treated as second-class citizens.* **2** of a lower standard or quality than the best: *a second-class education* **3** [only before noun] connected with the less expensive way of travelling on a train, ship, etc: *second-class carriages / compartments / passengers* **4** [only before noun] (in Brit-ain) connected with letters, parcels/packages, etc. that you pay less to send and that are delivered less quickly: *second-class letters / stamps* **5** (in the US) connected with the system of sending newspapers and magazines by mail **6** [only before noun] used to describe a British university degree which is good but not of the highest class: *Appli-cants should have at least a second-class honours degree.* ► **,second-'class** *adv.*: *to send a letter second-class* ◊ *to travel second-class*

the ,Second 'Coming *noun* [sing.] a day in the future when Christians believe Jesus Christ will come back to earth

,second 'cousin *noun* a child of a COUSIN of your mother or father

,second-de'gree *adj.* [only before noun] **1** ~ **murder, assault, burglary, etc.** (*especially AmE*) murder, etc. that is less serious than FIRST-DEGREE crimes **2** ~ **burns** burns of the second most serious of three kinds, causing BLIS-TERS but no permanent marks—compare FIRST-DEGREE, THIRD-DEGREE

sec·ond·er /'sekəndə(r)/ *noun* a person who SECONDS a proposal, etc. (= supports it so that it can be discussed)— compare PROPOSER

,second-'guess *verb* **1** [VN] to guess what sb will do before they do it: *It was impossible to second-guess the decision of the jury.* **2** (*especially AmE*) to criticize sb after a decision has been made; to criticize sth after it has happened: [VN] *There's no point in second-guessing the issue now.* [also V]

'second hand *noun* the hand on some watches and clocks that shows seconds

,second-'hand *adj.* **1** not new; owned by sb else before: *second-hand cars* ◊ *a second-hand bookshop* (= for selling second-hand books) **2** (*often disapproving*) (of news, infor-mation, etc.) learned from other people, not from your own experience: *second-hand knowledge / opinions* ► **,second-'hand** *adv.*: *I bought the camera second-hand.* ◊ *I only heard about it second-hand.*—compare FIRST-HAND

,second 'home *noun* **1** [C] a house or flat/apartment that sb owns as well as their main home and uses, for example, for holidays/vacations **2** [sing.] a place where sb lives and which they know as well as, and like as much as, their home

,second in com'mand *noun* a person who has the second highest rank in a group and takes charge when the leader is not there

,second 'language *noun* a language that sb learns to speak well and that they use for work or at school, but that is not the language they learned first: *ESL or English as a Second Language*

S

æ	ɑː	e	ɜː	ə	ɪ	iː	i	ɒ	ɔː	ʌ	ʊ	u	uː
cat	father	ten	bird	about	sit	see	many	got	saw	cup	put	actual	too
								(BrE)					

,second lieu'tenant *noun* an officer of lower rank in the army or the US air force just below the rank of a LIEUTENANT

sec·ond·ly /'sekəndli/ *adv.* used to introduce the second of a list of points you want to make in a speech or piece of writing: *Firstly, it's expensive, and secondly, it's too slow.*

'second name *noun* (*especially BrE*) **1** a family name or SURNAME **2** a second personal name: *His second name is Willem, after his grandfather.*

,second 'nature *noun* [U] ~ (to sb) (to do sth) something that you do very easily and naturally, because it is part of your character or you have done it so many times

the ,second 'person *noun* [sing.] (*grammar*) the form of a pronoun or verb used when addressing sb: *In the phrase 'you are', the verb 'are' is in the second person and the word 'you' is a second-person pronoun.*—compare THE FIRST PERSON, THE THIRD PERSON

,second-'rate *adj.* not very good or impressive: *a second-rate player*

,second 'sight *noun* [U] the ability that some people seem to have to know or see what will happen in the future or what is happening in a different place

,second-'string *adj.* [only before noun] (*especially AmE*) (usually of a player in a sports team) only used occasionally where sb/sth else is not available: *a second-string quarterback* ▶ **,second 'string** *noun*: *Wilson was a second string for New Zealand in last week's match.*

,second 'wind *noun* [sing.] (*informal*) new energy that makes you able to continue with sth that had made you tired

se·crecy /'si:krəsi/ *noun* [U] the fact of making sure that nothing is known about sth; the state of being secret: *the need for absolute secrecy in this matter* ◊ *Everyone involved was sworn to secrecy.* ◊ *The whole affair is still shrouded in secrecy.*

se·cret /'si:krət/ *adj., noun*
■ *adj.* **1** ~ (from sb) known about by only a few people; kept hidden from others: *secret information/meetings/talks* ◊ *He tried to keep it secret from his family.* ◊ *Details of the proposals remain secret.* ◊ *a secret passage leading to the beach*—see also TOP SECRET **2** [only before noun] used to describe actions and behaviour that you do not tell other people about: *He's a secret drinker.* ◊ *I didn't know you were a secret football fan.* ◊ *her secret hopes/fears* ◊ *a secret room* **3** [not usually before noun] ~ (about sth) (of a person or their behaviour) liking to have secrets that other people do not know about; showing this SYN SECRETIVE: *They were so secret about everything.* ◊ *Jessica caught a secret smile flitting between the two of them.* ▶ **se·cret·ly** *adv.*: *The police had secretly filmed the conversations.* ◊ *She was secretly pleased to see him.*
■ *noun* **1** [C] something that is known about by only a few people and not told to others: *Can you keep a secret?* ◊ *The location of the ship is a closely-guarded secret.* ◊ *Shall we let him in on* (= tell him) *the secret?* ◊ *He made no secret of his ambition* (= he didn't try to hide it). ◊ *She was dismissed for revealing trade secrets.* ◊ *official/State secrets* **2** (usually **the secret**) [sing.] the best or only way to achieve sth; the way a particular person achieves sth: *Careful planning is the secret of success.* ◊ *She still looks so young. What's her secret?* **3** [C, usually pl.] a thing that is not yet fully understood or that is difficult to understand: *the secrets of life/the universe* IDM **in 'secret** without other people knowing about it: *The meeting was held in secret.*—more at OPEN *adj.*

,secret 'agent (also **agent**) *noun* a person who is used by a government to find out secret information about other countries or governments SYN SPY

sec·re·tar·ial /,sekrə'teəriəl; *AmE* -'ter-/ *adj.* involving or connected with the work of a secretary: *secretarial work/qualifications*

sec·re·tar·iat /,sekrə'teəriət; -iæt; *AmE* -'ter-/ *noun* the administrative department of a large international or political organization, especially the office of a SECRETARY GENERAL

sec·re·tary /'sekrətri; *AmE* -teri/ *noun* (*pl.* **-ies**) (*abbr.* **Sec.**) **1** a person who works in an office, working for

another person, dealing with letters and telephone calls, typing, keeping records, arranging meetings with people, etc: *a legal/medical secretary* ◊ *Please contact my secretary to make an appointment.*—see also PRIVATE SECRETARY **2** an official of a club, society, etc. who deals with writing letters, keeping records, and making business arrangements: *the membership secretary* **3** (**Secretary**) = SECRETARY OF STATE—see also HOME SECRETARY, PERMANENT UNDERSECRETARY **4** (*AmE*) the head of a government department, chosen by the President: *Secretary of the Treasury* **5** (in Britain) an assistant of a government minister, an AMBASSADOR, etc.—see also UNDERSECRETARY

,Secretary 'General *noun* the person who is in charge of the administrative department of a large international or political organization: *the former Secretary General of NATO*

,Secretary of 'State *noun* **1** (also **Sec·re·tary**) (in Britain) the head of an important government department: *the Secretary of State for Education and Employment* ◊ *the Education Secretary* ◊ *the Foreign Secretary* **2** (in the US) the head of the government department that deals with foreign affairs

se·crete /sɪ'kri:t/ *verb* [VN] **1** (of part of the body or a plant) to produce a liquid substance: *Insulin is secreted by the pancreas.* **2** ~ sth (in sth) (*formal*) to hide sth, especially sth small: *The drugs were secreted in the lining of his case.*

se·cre·tion /sɪ'kri:ʃn/ *noun* (*technical*) **1** [U] the process by which liquid substances are produced by parts of the body or plants: *the secretion of bile by the liver* **2** [C, usually pl.] a liquid substance produced by parts of the body or plants: *bodily secretions*

se·cret·ive /'si:krətɪv/ *adj.* ~ (about sth) tending or liking to hide your thoughts, feelings, ideas, etc. from other people: *He's very secretive about his work.* ◊ *The child became secretive and withdrawn.* ▶ **se·cret·ive·ly** *adv.* **se·cret·ive·ness** *noun* [U]

,secret po'lice *noun* [sing.+ sing./pl. *v.*] a police force that works secretly to make sure that citizens behave as their government wants

,secret 'service *noun* [usually sing.] a government department that is responsible for protecting its government's military and political secrets and for finding out the secrets of other governments

sect /sekt/ *noun* a small group of people who belong to a particular religion but who have some beliefs or practices which separate them from the rest of the group

sect·ar·ian /sek'teəriən; *AmE* -'ter-/ *adj.* [usually before noun] (often *disapproving*) connected with the differences that exist between groups of people who have different religious views: *sectarian attacks/violence* ◊ *attempts to break down the sectarian divide in Northern Ireland*

sect·ar·ian·ism /sek'teəriənɪzəm; *AmE* -'ter-/ *noun* [U] (often *disapproving*) strong support for one particular religious or political group, especially when this leads to violence between different groups

sec·tion /'sekʃn/ *noun, verb*
■ *noun*
PART/PIECE **1** [C] any of the parts into which sth is divided: *That section of the road is still closed.* ◊ *The library has a large biology section.* ◊ *the tail section of the plane* **2** [C] a separate part of a structure from which the whole can be put together: *The shed comes in sections that you assemble yourself.*
OF DOCUMENT/BOOK **3** [C] a separate part of a document, book, etc: *These issues will be discussed more fully in the next section.* ◊ *the sports section of the newspaper*
GROUP OF PEOPLE **4** [C] a separate group within a larger group of people: *an issue that will affect large sections of the population* ◊ *the brass section of an orchestra*—see also RHYTHM SECTION
OF ORGANIZATION **5** [C] a department in an organization, institution, etc: *He's the director of the finance section.*
DIAGRAM **6** [C] a drawing or diagram of sth as it would look if it were cut from top to bottom or from one side to the other: *The illustration shows a section through a leaf.*

aɪ	aʊ	eɪ	əʊ	oʊ	ɔɪ	ɪə	eə	ʊə	j	w
my	now	say	go (BrE)	go (AmE)	boy	near	hair	pure	yes	wet

◊ *The architect drew the house in section.*—see also CROSS SECTION

MEDICAL | **7** [C, U] (*medical*) the act of cutting or separating sth in an operation: *The surgeon performed a section* (= made a cut) *on the vein.*—see also CAESAREAN **8** [C] (*medical, biology*) a very thin flat piece cut from body tissue to be looked at under a MICROSCOPE: *to examine a section from the kidney*

■ *verb* [VN]

MEDICAL/BIOLOGY | **1** (*medical*) to divide body tissue by cutting **2** (*biology*) to cut animal or plant tissue into thin slices in order to look at it under a MICROSCOPE

MENTAL PATIENT | **3** [often passive] (*BrE*) to officially send sb with a mental illness to a PSYCHIATRIC hospital

PHRV ˌsection sth↔'off to separate an area from a larger one: *Parts of the town had been sectioned off.*

sec·tion·al /'sekʃənl/ *adj.* [usually before noun] **1** connected with one particular group within a community or an organization: *the sectional interests of managers and workers* **2** made of separate sections: *a sectional building* **3** connected with a CROSS SECTION of sth (= a surface or an image formed by cutting through sth from top to bottom): *a sectional drawing*

sec·tor /'sektə(r)/ *noun* **1** a part of an area of activity, especially of a country's economy: *the manufacturing sector* ◊ *service-sector jobs* (= in hotels, restaurants, etc.)— see also THE PRIVATE SECTOR, THE PUBLIC SECTOR **2** a part of a particular area, especially an area under military control: *each sector of the search/war zone* **3** (*geometry*) a part of a circle lying between two straight lines drawn from the centre to the edge—picture at CIRCLE

secu·lar /'sekjələ(r)/ *adj.* **1** not connected with spiritual or religious matters: *secular art/education/music* **2** (of priests) living among ordinary people rather than in a religious community

secu·lar·ism /'sekjələrɪzəm/ *noun* [U] (*technical*) the belief that religion should not be involved in the organization of society, education, etc. ▶ **secu·lar·ist** /-lərɪst/ *adj.* [usually before noun]

secu·lar·iza·tion (*BrE* also **-isa·tion**) /ˌsekjələraɪˈzeɪʃn; *AmE* -rəˈz-/ *noun* [U] the act or process of removing the influence or power that religion has over sth: *the secularization of society/education*

secu·lar·ize (*BrE* also **-ise**) /'sekjələraɪz/ *verb* [VN] [often passive] to make sth SECULAR ; to remove sth from the control or influence of religion: *a secularized society*

se·cure /sɪˈkjʊə(r); *AmE* səˈkjʊr/ *adj.*, *verb*

■ *adj.*

HAPPY/CONFIDENT | **1** feeling happy and confident about yourself or a particular situation: *At last they were able to feel secure about the future.* ◊ *She finished the match, secure in the knowledge that she was through to the next round.* **OPP** INSECURE

CERTAIN/SAFE | **2** likely to continue or be successful for a long time **SYN** SAFE: *a secure job/income* ◊ *It's not a very secure way to make a living.* ◊ *The future of the company looks secure.* **OPP** INSECURE **3** ~ (**against/from sth**) that cannot be affected or harmed by sth: *Information must be stored so that it is secure from accidental deletion.*

BUILDING/DOOR/ROOM | **4** guarded and/or made stronger so that it is difficult for people to enter or leave: *Check that all windows and doors have been made as secure as possible.* ◊ *a secure unit for child offenders* **OPP** INSECURE

FIRM | **5** not likely to move, fall down, etc: *The aerial doesn't look very secure to me.* ◊ *It was difficult to maintain a secure foothold on the ice.* ◊ (*figurative*) *Our relationship was now on a more secure footing.* **OPP** INSECURE

▶ **se·cure·ly** *adv.*: *She locked the door securely behind her.* ◊ *Make sure the ropes are securely fastened.* ◊ *Democracy is becoming more securely established in Eastern Europe.*

■ *verb*

GET STH | **1** ~ **sth** (**for sb/sth**) | ~ **sb sth** (*formal*) to obtain or achieve sth, especially when this means using a lot of effort: [VN] *to secure a contract/deal* ◊ *The team managed to secure a place in the finals.* ◊ *She secured 2000 votes.* ◊

[VN, VNN] *He secured a place for himself at law school.* ◊ *He secured himself a place at law school.*

FASTEN FIRMLY | **2** [VN] ~ **sth** (**to sth**) to attach or fasten sth firmly: *She secured the rope firmly to the back of the car.* ◊ *The tables on board were secured firmly to the floor.*

PROTECT FROM HARM | **3** [VN] ~ **sth** (**against sth**) to protect sth so that it is safe and difficult to attack or damage: *to secure a property against intruders* ◊ *The windows were secured with locks and bars.* ◊ (*figurative*) *a savings plan that will secure your child's future*

A LOAN | **4** [VN] to legally agree to give sb property or goods that are worth the same amount as the money that you have borrowed from them, if you are unable to pay the money back: *a short-term loan secured on the house*

se·cur·ity /sɪˈkjʊərəti; *AmE* səˈkjʊr-/ *noun* (*pl.* **-ies**)

PROTECTION | **1** [U] the activities involved in protecting a country, building or person against attack, danger, etc: *national security* (= the defence of a country) ◊ *airport/hotel security* ◊ *The visit took place amidst tight security* (= the use of many police officers). ◊ *the security forces/services* (= the police, army, etc.) ◊ *a high/maximum security prison* (= for dangerous criminals)—see also HIGH-SECURITY **2** [U+sing./pl. *v.*] the department of a large company or organization that deals with the protection of its buildings, equipment and staff: *Security was/were called to the incident.* **3** [U] protection against sth bad that might happen in the future: *financial security* ◊ *Job security* (= the guarantee that you will keep your job) *is a thing of the past.*

FEELING HAPPY/SAFE | **4** [U] the state of feeling happy and safe from danger or worry: *the security of a loving family life* ◊ *She'd allowed herself to be lulled into a false sense of security* (= a feeling that she was safe when in fact she was in danger).

FOR A LOAN | **5** [U, C] a valuable item, such as a house, that you agree to give to sb if you are unable to pay back the money that you have borrowed from them: *His home and business are being held as security for the loan.*

SHARES IN COMPANY | **6** (**securities**) [pl.] (*finance*) documents proving that sb is the owner of shares, etc. in a particular company

—see also SOCIAL SECURITY

se'curity guard *noun* a person whose job is to guard money, valuables, a building, etc.

se'curity risk *noun* a person who cannot be given secret information because they are a danger to a particular country, organization, etc., especially because of their political beliefs

Se'curity Service *noun* a government organization that protects a country and its secrets from enemies

Secy. *abbr.* (*AmE*) = SEC.

sedan /sɪˈdæn/ *noun* (*AmE*) = SALOON (1)

se,dan 'chair *noun* a box containing a seat for one person, carried on poles by two people, used in the 17th and 18th centuries

sed·ate /sɪˈdeɪt/ *adj.*, *verb*

■ *adj.* [usually before noun] **1** slow, calm and relaxed **SYN** UNHURRIED: *a sedate game of golf* ◊ *We followed the youngsters at a more sedate pace.* **2** quiet, especially in a way that lacks excitement: *a sedate country town* **3** (of a person) quiet and serious in a way that seems formal: *a sedate, sober man* ▶ **sed·ate·ly** *adv.*

■ *verb* [VN] [often passive] to give sb drugs in order to make them calm and or to make them sleep: *Most of the patients are heavily sedated.*

sed·ation /sɪˈdeɪʃn/ *noun* [U] the act of giving sb drugs in order to make them calm or to make them sleep; the state that results from this: *The victim's wife was last night being kept under sedation in the local hospital.*

seda·tive /'sedətɪv/ *noun* a drug that makes sb go to sleep or makes them feel calm and relaxed ▶ **seda·tive** *adj.* [usually before noun]: *sedative drugs/effects*

sed·en·tary /'sedntri; *AmE* -teri/ *adj.* **1** (of work, activities, etc.) in which you spend a lot of time sitting down: *a sedentary job/occupation* ◊ *a sedentary lifestyle* **2** (of people) spending a lot of time sitting down and not moving: *He became increasingly sedentary in later life.* **3** (*technical*) (of people or animals) that stay and live in the same place or area: *Rhinos are largely sedentary animals.* ◊ *a sedentary population*

Seder /ˈseɪdə(r)/ *noun* a Jewish CEREMONIAL service and dinner on the first night or first two nights of Passover

sedge /sedʒ/ *noun* [U] a plant like grass that grows in wet ground or near water

sedi·ment /ˈsedɪmənt/ *noun* [U] **1** the solid material that settles at the bottom of a liquid **2** (*geology*) sand, stones, mud, etc. carried by water or wind and left, for example, on the bottom of a lake, river, etc.

sedi·ment·ary /ˌsedɪˈmentri/ *adj.* (*geology*) connected with or formed from the sand, stones, mud, etc. that settle at the bottom of lakes, etc: *sedimentary layers/rocks/deposits*

sedi·men·ta·tion /ˌsedɪmenˈteɪʃn/ *noun* [U] (*geology*) the process of DEPOSITING (= leaving) sediment

se·di·tion /sɪˈdɪʃn/ *noun* [U] (*formal*) the use of words or actions that are intended to encourage people to oppose a government: *to be charged with sedition* ▶ **se·di·tious** /sɪˈdɪʃəs/ *adj.*: *seditious activity*

se·duce /sɪˈdjuːs; *AmE* -ˈduːs/ *verb* [VN] **1** to persuade sb to have sex with you, especially sb who is younger or who has less experience than you **2** ~ **sb** (**into sth/into doing sth**) to persuade sb to do sth that they would not usually agree to do by making it seem very attractive: *The promise of huge profits seduced him into parting with his money.*

se·du·cer /sɪˈdjuːsə(r); *AmE* sɪˈduːsə(r)/ *noun* a person who persuades sb to have sex with them

se·duc·tion /sɪˈdʌkʃn/ *noun* **1** [U, C] the act of persuading sb to have sex with you: *Cleopatra's seduction of Caesar* **2** [C, usually pl., U] ~ (**of sth**) the qualities or features of sth that make it seem attractive: *Who could resist the seductions of the tropical island?*

se·duc·tive /sɪˈdʌktɪv/ *adj.* **1** sexually attractive: *a seductive woman/voice* **2** attractive in a way that makes you want to have or do sth: *The idea of retiring to the south of France is highly seductive.* ▶ **se·duc·tive·ly** *adv.* **se·duc·tive·ness** *noun* [U]

se·duc·tress /sɪˈdʌktrəs/ *noun* a woman who persuades sb to have sex with her

see /siː/ *verb, noun*

■ *verb* (**saw** /sɔː/ **seen** /siːn/)

USE EYES | **1** (not used in the progressive tenses) to become aware of sb/sth by using your eyes: [VN] *She looked for him but couldn't see him in the crowd.* ◊ [V(that)] *He could see (that) she had been crying.* ◊ [Vwh-] *Did you see what happened?* ◊ [VN-ADJ] *I hate to see you unhappy.* ◊ [V, VN] *The opera was the place to **see and be seen** (= by other important or fashionable people).* ◊ [VN-ing] *She was seen running away from the scene of the crime.* ◊ [VNinf] *I saw you put the key in your pocket.* ◊ [VNtoinf] *He was seen to enter the building about the time the crime was committed.* **HELP** This pattern is only used in the passive. **2** (not usually used in the progressive tenses) to have or use the power of sight: [V] *She will never see again (= she has become blind).* ◊ *On a clear day you **can see** for miles from here.* ◊ [Vtoinf] *It was getting dark and I **couldn't see** to read.*

WATCH | **3** [VN] (not usually used in the progressive tenses) to watch a game, television programme, performance, etc: *Did you see that programme on Brazil last night?* ◊ *In the evening we went to see a movie.* ◊ *Fifty thousand people saw the match.*

LOOK UP INFORMATION | **4** [VN] (used in orders) to look at sth in order to find information: *See page 158.*

MEET BY CHANCE | **5** [VN] (not usually used in the progressive tenses) to be near and recognize sb; to meet sb by chance: *Guess who I saw at the party last night!*

VISIT | **6** [VN] to visit sb: *Come and see us again soon.*

HAVE MEETING | **7** [VN] ~ **sb** (**about sth**) to have a meeting with sb: *You ought to **see** a doctor **about** that cough.* ◊ *What is it you want to see me about?* ◊ *I can only see you for five minutes.*

SPEND TIME | **8** [VN] (often used in the progressive tenses) to spend time with sb: *Are you seeing anyone (= having a romantic relationship with anyone)?* ◊ *They've been **seeing a lot of each other** (= spending a lot of time together) recently.*

UNDERSTAND | **9** (not usually used in the progressive tenses) to understand sth: [V] *'It opens like this.' 'Oh, I see.'* ◊ [VN] *He didn't see the joke.* ◊ *I don't think she saw **the point** of the story.* ◊ *I can see both sides of the argument.* ◊ *Make Lydia **see reason** (= be sensible), will you?* ◊ [V(that)] *Can't you see (that) he's taking advantage of you?* ◊ *I don't see that it matters what Josh thinks.* ◊ [Vwh-] *'It's broken.' 'Oh yes, I see what you mean.'* ◊ *'Can we go swimming?' ' I don't see why not (= yes, you can).'* ◊ [VNtoinf] *The government not only has to do something, it must be seen to be doing something (= people must be aware that it is doing sth).* **HELP** This pattern is only used with see in the passive.

HAVE OPINION | **10** [VN+adv./prep.] (not usually used in the progressive tenses) to have an opinion of sth: *I see things differently now.* ◊ *Try to see things from her point of view.* ◊ *Lack of money is the main problem, **as I see it** (= in my opinion).* ◊ ***The way I see it**, you have three main problems.*

IMAGINE | **11** ~ **sb/sth** (**as sth**) (not used in the progressive tenses) to consider sth as a future possibility; to imagine sb/sth as sth: [VN-ing] *I can't see her changing her mind.* ◊ [VN] *His colleagues see him as a future director.*

FIND OUT | **12** (not usually used in the progressive tenses) to find out sth by looking, asking or waiting: [V] *'Has the mail come yet?' 'I'll just go and see.'* ◊ *'Is he going to get better?' 'I don't know, we'll just have to **wait and see**.'* ◊ [Vwh-] *Go and see what the kids are doing, will you?* ◊ *We'll have to **see how it goes**.* ◊ [V(that)] *I see (that) interest rates are going up again.* ◊ [VNthat] *It can be seen that certain groups are more at risk than others.* **13** (not usually used in the progressive tenses) to find out or decide sth by thinking or considering: [V] *'Will you be able to help us?' 'I don't know, I'll have to see.'* ◊ *'Can I go to the party?' ' We'll see (= I'll decide later).* ◊ [Vwh-] *I'll see what I can do to help.*

MAKE SURE | **14** [Vthat] (not usually used in the progressive tenses) to make sure that you do sth or that sth is done: *See that all the doors are locked before you leave.*

EXPERIENCE | **15** [VN] (not used in the progressive tenses) to experience or suffer sth: *He has seen a great deal in his long life.* ◊ *I hope I never live to **see the day** when computers finally replace books.* ◊ *It didn't surprise her—she **had seen it all before**.*

WITNESS EVENT | **16** [VN] (not used in the progressive tenses) to be the time when an event happens: *Next year sees the centenary of Verdi's death.* **17** [VN] (not used in the progressive tenses) to be the place where an event happens [SYN] WITNESS: *This stadium has seen many thrilling football games.*

HELP | **18** [VN+adv./prep.] to go with sb to help or protect them: *I saw the old lady across (= helped her cross) the road.* ◊ *May I **see you home** (= go with you as far as your house)?* ◊ *My secretary will **see you out** (= show you the way out of the building).*

IDM Most idioms containing **see** are at the entries for the nouns and adjectives in the idioms, for example **not see the wood for the trees** is at **wood**. **for all (the world) to ˈsee** clearly visible; in a way that is clearly visible **see sth ˈcoming** to realize that there is going to be a problem before it happens: *We should have seen it coming. There was no way he could keep going under all that pressure.* **ˌsee for yourˈself** to find out or look at sth yourself in order to be sure that what sb is saying is true: *If you don't believe me, go and see for yourself!* **see sb/sth for what they ˈare/it ˈis** to realize that sb/sth is not as good, pleasant, etc. as they/it seem **seeing that …** (also *informal* **seeing as (how)** …) because of the fact that …: *Seeing that he's been off sick all week he's unlikely to come.* **ˈsee you (aˈround)** | (**I'll**) **be ˈseeing you** | **ˌsee you ˈlater** (*spoken*) goodbye: *I'd better be going now. See you!*

you 'see (*spoken*) used when you are explaining sth: *You see, the thing is, we won't be finished before Friday.* PHRV **'see about sth** to deal with sth: *I must see about* (= prepare) *lunch.* ◊ *He says he won't help, does he? Well, we'll soon see about that* (= I will demand that he does help).* ◊*[+ -ing]* *I'll have to see about getting that roof repaired.* **'see sth in sb/sth** to find sb/sth attractive or interesting: *I don't know what she sees in him.* ,**see sb↔'off 1** to go to a station, an airport, etc. to say goodbye to sb who is starting a journey **2** (*BrE*) to force sb to leave a place, for example by chasing them: *The dogs saw them off in no time.* **3** (*BrE*) to defeat sb in a game, fight, etc: *The home team saw off the challengers by 68 points to 47.* ,**see sth↔'out** (not used in the progressive tenses) to last until the end of sth: *They had enough fuel to see the winter out.* ,**see 'over sth** (*BrE*) to visit and look at a place carefully: *We need to see over the house before we can make you an offer.* ,**see 'through sb/sth** (not used in the progressive tenses) to realize the truth about sb/sth so that you are not deceived: *We saw through him from the start.* ◊ *I can see through your little game* (= I am aware of the trick you are trying to play on me). ,**see sth 'through** (not usually used in the progressive tenses) to not give up doing a task, project, etc. until it is finished: *She's determined to see the job through.* ,**see sb 'through| see sb through sth** (not used in the progressive tenses) to give help or support to sb for a particular period of time: *Her courage and good humour saw her through.* ◊ *I only have $20 to see me through the week.* **'see to sth** to deal with sth: *Will you see to the arrangements for the next meeting?* ◊ *Don't worry—I'll see to it.* ◊ *We'll have to get that door seen to* (= repaired). **'see to it that ...** to make sure that ...: *Can you see to it that the fax goes this afternoon?*
■ *noun* (*formal*) the district or office of a BISHOP or an ARCHBISHOP: *the Holy See* (= the office of the POPE)

VOCABULARY BUILDING
different words for **seeing**

notice	*I noticed that she was wearing a wedding ring.* ◊ *She climbed over the gate without being noticed.*
spot	*We tried to spot her in the crowd.*
glimpse	*I glimpsed him through the window as the car sped past.*
catch a glimpse of	*I just caught a glimpse of the bird before it flew off.*
catch sight of	*If you're lucky you may catch sight of a herd of wild goats.*
make sth out	*Can you make out what that sign says?*
observe	(*formal*) *Police observed him entering the building at 3.30.*
witness	*Did anyone witness the accident?*
sight	(*written*) *After a week at sea they sighted land.*

⇨ note at LOOK

---

seed /si:d/ *noun, verb*
■ *noun*
OF PLANTS/FRUIT | **1** [C, U] the small hard part produced by a plant, from which a new plant can grow: *a packet of wild flower seeds* ◊ *sunflower / sesame seeds* ◊ *Sow the seeds outdoors in spring.* ◊ *These vegetables can be grown from seed.* ◊ *seed potatoes* (= used for planting) **2** [C] (*AmE*) = PIP (2)
BEGINNING | **3** [C, usually pl.] ~ **(of sth)** the beginning of a feeling or a development which continues to grow: *the seeds of conflict / rebellion* ◊ *This planted the seeds of doubt in my mind.*
IN TENNIS | **4** [C] (especially in tennis) one of the best players in a competition. The seeds are given a position in a list to try and make sure that they do not play each other in the early parts of the competition: *The top seed won comfortably.* ◊ *the number one seed*
OF A MAN | **5** [U] (*old-fashioned* or *humorous*) SEMEN **6** [U] (*literary*) all the people who are descended from one man
IDM **go/run to 'seed 1** (especially of a vegetable plant) to produce flowers and seeds as well as leaves: *The lettuces*

had all *run to seed.* **2** to become much less attractive or good because of lack of attention: *After his divorce, he let himself go to seed.*—more at SOW *v.*
■ *verb*
OF A PLANT | **1** [V] to produce seeds **2** [VN] ~ **itself** to produce other plants using its own seeds
AREA OF GROUND | **3** [VN] [usually passive] ~ **sth (with sth)** to plant seeds in an area of ground: *a newly seeded lawn*
IN TENNIS | **4** [VN] [usually passive] to make sb a seed in a competition: *He has been seeded 14th at Wimbledon next week.*

seed·bed /'si:dbed/ *noun* **1** an area of soil which has been specially prepared for planting seeds in **2** [usually sing.] ~ **(of/for sth)** a place or situation in which sth can develop

'seed corn *noun* [U] **1** the grain that is kept for planting the next year's crops **2** people or things that will be successful or useful in the future

seed·ed /'si:dɪd/ *adj.* [usually before noun] **1** (especially of a tennis player) given a number showing that they are one of the best players in a particular competition: *a seeded player* **2** (of fruit) with the seeds removed: *seeded tomatoes*

seed·less /'si:dləs/ *adj.* [usually before noun] (of fruit) having no seeds: *seedless grapes / raisins*

seed·ling /'si:dlɪŋ/ *noun* a young plant that has grown from a seed

'seed money (also **'seed capital**) *noun* [U] money to start a new business, project, etc.

'seed pearl *noun* a small PEARL

seeds·man /'si:dzmən/ *noun* (*pl.* -**men** /-mən/) a person who grows and sells seeds

seedy /'si:di/ *adj.* (**seed·ier, seedi·est**) (*disapproving*) dirty and unpleasant, possibly connected with immoral or illegal activities: *a seedy bar* ◊ *the seedy world of prostitution* ◊ *a seedy-looking man* ▶ **seedi·ness** *noun* [U]

,**Seeing 'Eye dog**™ *noun* (*AmE*) = GUIDE DOG

seek /si:k/ *verb* (**sought, sought** /sɔ:t/) (*formal*) **1** ~ **(for) sth/sb** to look for sth/sb: [VN] *Drivers are advised to seek alternative routes.* ◊ [V] (*BrE*) *They sought in vain for somewhere to shelter.* **2** to try to obtain or achieve sth: [VN] *to seek compensation / funding* ◊ *Highly qualified secretary seeks employment.* (= in an advertisement) ◊ *We are currently seeking new ways of expanding our membership.* [also V] **3** [VN] ~ **sth (from sb)** to ask sb for sth: *I think it's time we sought legal advice.* ◊ *She managed to calm him down and seek help from a neighbour.* **4** [V to inf] to try to do sth: *They quickly sought to distance themselves from the protesters.* **5** **(-seeking)** (in adjectives and nouns) looking for or trying to get the thing mentioned; the activity of doing this: *attention-seeking behaviour* ◊ *Voluntary work can provide a framework for job-seeking.*—see also HEAT-SEEKING, SELF-SEEKING—see also HIDE-AND-SEEK IDM **seek your 'fortune** (*literary*) to try to find a way to become rich, especially by going to another place PHRV ,**seek sb/sth 'out** to look for and find sb/sth, especially when this means using a lot of effort

seek·er /'si:kə(r)/ *noun* (often in compounds) a person who is trying to find or get the thing mentioned: *an attention-/a publicity seeker* ◊ *seekers of/after the truth*—see also ASYLUM SEEKER, JOB SEEKER

seem /si:m/ *linking verb* **1** ~ **(to sb) (to be) sth| ~ like sth** (not used in the progressive tenses) to give the impression of being or doing sth; to appear: [V-ADJ] *You seem happy.* ◊ *Do whatever seems best to you.* ◊ [V-N] *He seems a nice man.* ◊ [V] *It seemed like a good idea at the time.* ◊ *'He'll be there, then?' ' So it seems* (= people say so).' ◊ *It always seemed as though they would get married.* ◊ [V that] *It seems that they know what they're doing.* ◊ [V to inf] *They seem to know what they're doing.* **2** [V to inf] used to make what you say about your thoughts, feelings or actions less forceful: *I seem to have left my book at home.* ◊ *I can't seem to* (= I've tried, but I can't) *get started today.* **3** **(it seems, it would seem)** used to suggest that sth is true when you are not certain or when you want to be polite: [V (that)] *It would seem that we all agree.* ◊

æ	ɑ:	e	ɜ:	ə	ɪ	i:	i	ɒ	ɔ:	ʌ	ʊ	u	u:
cat	father	ten	bird	about	sit	see	many	got	saw	cup	put	actual	too

(BrE)

[V-ADJ] *It seems only reasonable to ask students to buy a dictionary.*

seem·ing /'si:mɪŋ/ *adj.* [only before noun] (*formal*) appearing to be sth that may not be true SYN APPARENT: *a seeming contradiction/impossibility* ◊ *She handled the matter with seeming indifference.*

seem·ing·ly /'si:mɪŋli/ *adv.* **1** in a way that appears to be true but may in fact not be: *a seemingly stupid question* ◊ *a seemingly endless journey* **2** according to what you have read or heard SYN APPARENTLY: *Seemingly, he borrowed the money from the bank.*

seem·ly /'si:mli/ *adv.* (*old-fashioned* or *formal*) appropriate for a particular social situation OPP UNSEEMLY

seen *pp of* SEE

seep /si:p/ *verb* [V+adv./prep.] (especially of liquids) to flow slowly and in small quantities through sth or into sth: *Blood was beginning to seep through the bandages.* ◊ *Water seeped from a crack in the pipe.* ◊ (*figurative*) *Gradually the pain seeped away.*

seep·age /'si:pɪdʒ/ *noun* [U, C, usually pl.] the process by which a liquid flows slowly and in small quantities through sth; the result of this process: *Water gradually escapes through by seepage through the ground.* ◊ *oil seepages*

seer /sɪə(r); *AmE* sɪr/ *noun* (in the past) a person who claimed that they could see what was going to happen in the future

seer·sucker /'sɪəsʌkə(r); *AmE* 'sɪrs-/ *noun* [U] a light cotton fabric with a pattern of raised lines and squares on its surface

'see-saw *noun, verb*
■ *noun* **1** (*AmE* also **'teeter-totter**) [C] a piece of equipment for children to play on consisting of a long flat piece of wood that is supported in the middle. A child sits at each end and makes the see-saw move up and down. **2** [sing.] a situation in which things keep changing from one state to another and back again
■ *verb* [V] to keep changing from one situation, opinion, emotion, etc. to another and back again: *Her emotions see-sawed from anger to fear.* ◊ *Share prices see-sawed all day.*

seethe /si:ð/ *verb* [V] **1** ~ (**with sth**)| ~ (**at sth**) to be extremely angry about sth but try not to show other people how angry you are SYN FUME: *She seethed silently in the corner.* ◊ *He marched off, seething with frustration.* **2** ~ (**with sth**) (*written*) (of a place) to be full of a lot of people or animals, especially when they are all moving around: *The resort is seething with tourists all year round.* ◊ *He became caught up in a seething mass of arms and legs.* **3** (*written*) (of liquids) to move around quickly and violently: *The grey ocean seethed beneath them.*

'see-through *adj.* (of fabric) very thin so that you can see through it: *a see-through blouse*

seg·ment *noun, verb*
■ *noun* /'segmənt/ **1** a part of sth that is separate from the other parts or can be considered separately: *She cleaned a small segment of the painting.* ◊ *Lines divide the area into segments.* **2** one of the sections of an orange, a lemon, etc.—picture on page A2 **3** (*geometry*) a part of a circle separated from the rest by a single line—picture at CIRCLE
■ *verb* /seg'ment/ [VN] [often passive] (*technical*) to divide sth into different parts: *Market researchers often segment the population on the basis of age and social class.* ◊ *The worm has a segmented body* (= with different sections joined together).

seg·men·ta·tion /ˌsegmen'teɪʃn/ *noun* [U, C, usually pl.] (*technical*) the act of dividing sth into different parts; one of these parts: *the segmentation of social classes*

seg·re·gate /'segrɪgeɪt/ *verb* [VN] **1** ~ **sb** (**from sb**) to separate people of different races, religions or sexes and treat them differently: *a culture in which women are segregated from men* ◊ *a racially segregated community* ◊ *a segregated school* (= one for students of one race or religion only) OPP INTEGRATE **2** ~ **sth** (**from sth**) to keep one thing separate from another: *In all our restaurants, smoking and non-smoking areas are segregated from each other.*

seg·re·ga·tion /ˌsegrɪ'geɪʃn/ *noun* [U] **1** the act or pol-

icy of separating people of different races, religions or sexes and treating them differently: *racial/religious/sex segregation* ◊ *segregation by age and sex* **2** (*formal*) the act of separating people or things from a larger group: *the segregation of smokers and non-smokers in restaurants*

seg·re·ga·tion·ist /ˌsegrɪ'geɪʃənɪst/ *adj.* supporting the separation of people according to their sex, race or religion: *segregationist policies* ▸ **seg·re·ga·tion·ist** *noun*

segue /'segweɪ/ *verb* [V+adv./prep.] to move smoothly from one song, subject, place, etc. to another: *a spiritual that segued into a singalong chorus* ◊ *He then segued into a discussion of atheism.* ▸ **segue** *noun*

seis·mic /'saɪzmɪk/ *adj.* [only before noun] connected with or caused by earthquakes: *seismic data/waves*

seis·mo·graph /'saɪzməgrɑːf; *AmE* -græf/ *noun* an instrument that measures and records information about earthquakes

seis·mol·ogy /saɪz'mɒlədʒi; *AmE* -'mɑːl-/ *noun* [U] the scientific study of earthquakes ▸ **seis·mo·logical** /ˌsaɪzmə'lɒdʒɪkl; *AmE* -'lɑːdʒ-/ *adj.*: *the National Seismological Institute* **seis·mo·gist** /-dʒɪst/ *noun*

seize /si:z/ *verb* [VN] **1** ~ **sth** (**from sb**) to take sb/sth in your hand suddenly and using force SYN GRAB: *She tried to seize the gun from him.* ◊ *He seized her by the arm.* ◊ *She seized hold of my hand.* **2** ~ **sth** (**from sb**) to take control of a place or situation, often suddenly and violently: *They seized the airport in a surprise attack.* ◊ *The army has seized control of the country.* ◊ *He seized power in a military coup.* **3** to arrest or capture sb: *The men were seized as they left the building.* **4** to take illegal or stolen goods away from sb: *A large quantity of drugs was seized during the raid.* **5** ~ **a chance, an opportunity, the initiative, etc.** to be quick to make use of a chance, an opportunity, etc. SYN GRAB: *The party seized the initiative with both hands* (= quickly and with enthusiasm). **6** (of an emotion) to affect sb suddenly and deeply: *Panic seized her.* ◊ *He was seized by curiosity.* PHRV **'seize on/upon sth** to suddenly show a lot of interest in sth, especially because you can use it to your advantage SYN POUNCE ON/UPON: *The rumours were eagerly seized upon by the local press.* ˌ**seize 'up 1** (of the parts of a machine) to stop moving or working correctly: *The engine suddenly seized up.* **2** if a part of your body **seizes up**, you are unable to move it easily and it is often painful

seiz·ure /'si:ʒə(r)/ *noun* **1** [U, C] ~ (**of sth**) the use of legal authority to take sth from sb; an amount of sth that is taken in this way: *The court ordered the seizure of his assets.* ◊ *the largest ever seizure of cocaine at a British port* **2** [U] ~ (**of sth**) the act of using force to take control of a country, town, etc: *the army's seizure of power* ◊ *the seizure of Burma by Japan in 1942* **3** (*old-fashioned*) [C] a sudden attack of an illness, especially one that affects the brain

sel·dom /'seldəm/ *adv.* not often SYN RARELY: *He had seldom seen a child with so much talent.* ◊ *She seldom, if ever, goes to the theatre.* ◊ *They seldom watch television these days.* ◊ (*literary*) *Seldom had he seen such beauty.*

se·lect /sɪ'lekt/ *verb, adj.*
■ *verb* ~ **sb/sth** (**as/for sth**)| ~ **sb/sth** (**from sth**) to choose sb/sth, usually carefully, from a group of people or things: [VN] *He hasn't been selected for the team.* ◊ *All our hotels have been carefully selected for the excellent value they provide.* ◊ *She was selected as the parliamentary candidate for Bath.* ◊ *a randomly selected sample of 23 schools* ◊ *selected poems of T.S. Eliot* ◊ *This model is available at selected stores only.* ◊ *Select 'New Mail' from the 'Send' menu.* ◊ [VN to inf] *Six theatre companies have been selected to take part in this year's festival.* [also ∨ wh-]
■ *adj.* **1** [only before noun] carefully chosen as the best out of a larger group of people or things: *a select wine list* ◊ *Only a select few* (= a small number of people) *have been invited to the wedding.* **2** (of a society, club, place, etc.) used by people who have a lot of money or a high social position SYN EXCLUSIVE: *They live in a very select area.* ◊ *a select club/restaurant*

se·lect com'mittee *noun* (*BrE*) a small group of politicians or experts that have been chosen to examine a particular subject or problem

se·lec·tion /sɪ'lekʃn/ *noun* **1** [U] the process of choosing sb/sth carefully from a group of people or things: *The final team selection will be made tomorrow.* ◊ *the random selection of numbers* ◊ *selection criteria* ◊ *the selection process* **2** [C] a number of people or things that have been chosen from a larger group: *A selection of reader's comments are published below.* **3** [C] a collection of things from which sth can be chosen SYN CHOICE, RANGE: *The showroom has a* **wide selection** *of kitchens.*—see also NATURAL SELECTION

se·lect·ive /sɪ'lektɪv/ *adj.* **1** [usually before noun] affecting or concerned with only a small number of people or things from a larger group: *the selective breeding of cattle* ◊ *selective strike action* **2 ~ (about/in sth)** tending to be careful about what or who you choose: *You will have to be selective about which information to include in the report.* ◊ *Their admissions policy is very selective.* ◊ *a selective school* (= one that chooses which children to admit, especially according to ability) ▶ **se·lect·ive·ly** *adv.*: *The product will be selectively marketed in Europe and the US.* **se·lect·iv·ity** /sɪˌlek'tɪvəti/ *noun* [U]: *Schools are tending towards greater selectivity.*

se·lect·or /sɪ'lektə(r)/ *noun* **1** (*BrE*) a person who chooses the members of a particular sports team **2** a device in an engine, a piece of machinery, etc. that allows you to choose a particular function: *a gear selector* ◊ *a selector lever/switch*

self /self/ *noun* (*pl.* **selves** /selvz/) **1** [C, usually sing.] the type of person you are, especially the way you normally behave, look or feel: *You'll soon be feeling your old self again* (= feeling well or happy again). ◊ *He's not his usual happy self this morning.* ◊ *Only with a few people could she be her real self* (= show what she was really like rather than what she pretended to be). ◊ *his private/ professional self* (= how he behaves at home/work) **2** [U] (also **the self** [sing.]) (*formal*) a person's personality or character that makes them different from other people: *Many people living in institutions have lost their sense of self* (= the feeling that they are individual people). ◊ *the inner self* (= a person's emotional and spiritual character) ◊ *a lack of confidence in the self* **3** [U] (*formal*) your own advantage or pleasure rather than that of other people: *She didn't do it for any reason of self.* **4** [C] used to refer to a person: *Jon gave his whole self to his job.* ◊ *You didn't hurt your little self, did you?* ◊ *We look forward to seeing Mrs Brown and* **your good self** *this evening.* IDM see FORMER

self- /self/ *combining form* (in nouns and adjectives) of, to or by yourself or itself: *self-control* ◊ *self-addressed* ◊ *self-taught*

self-ab'sorbed *adj.* only concerned about or interested in yourself ▶ **self-ab'sorp·tion** *noun* [U]

self-'access *noun* [U] a method of learning in which students choose their materials and use them to study on their own: *a self-access centre/library*

self-ad'hesive *adj.* [usually before noun] covered on one side with a sticky substance so that it can be stuck to sth without the use of glue, etc: *self-adhesive tape*

self-ap'point·ed *adj.* [usually before noun] (usually *disapproving*) giving yourself a particular title, job, etc., especially without the agreement of other people

self-ap'prais·al *noun* [U, C] an act or the process of judging your own work or achievements: *Students are given the opportunity for self-appraisal.*

self-as'sembly *adj.* (of furniture) bought in several parts that you have to put together yourself: *cheap self-assembly kitchen units* ▶ **self-as'sembly** *noun* [U]: *kitchen units for self-assembly*

self-as'sert·ive *adj.* very confident and not afraid to express your opinions ▶ **self-as'sertion**, **self-as'sert·ive·ness** *noun* [U]

self-as'sess·ment *noun* [U] **1** the process of judging your own progress, achievements, etc. **2** (*BrE*) a system of paying tax in which you calculate yourself how much you should pay

self-as'sured *adj.* having a lot of confidence in yourself and your abilities SYN CONFIDENT ▶ **self-as'surance** *noun* [U]

self-a'wareness *noun* [U] knowledge and understanding of your own character ▶ **self-a'ware** *adj.*

self-'catering *adj.* [usually before noun] (*BrE*) a self-catering holiday is one which provides you with accommodation and the equipment that is necessary to cook your own meals: *self-catering accommodation* ▶ **self-'catering** *noun* [U] (*BrE*): *All prices are based on a week's self-catering in shared accommodation.*

self-'centred (*BrE*) (*AmE* **self-'centered**) *adj.* (*disapproving*) tending to think only about yourself and not thinking about the needs or feelings of other people ▶ **self-'centred·ness** (*BrE*) (*AmE* **self-'centered·ness**) *noun* [U]

self-con'fessed *adj.* [only before noun] admitting that you are a particular type of person or have a particular problem, especially a bad one: *a self-confessed criminal/ cynic*

self-'confident *adj.* having confidence in yourself and your abilities SYN SELF-ASSURED, CONFIDENT: *a self-confident child* ◊ *a self-confident manner* ▶ **self-'confidence** *noun* [U]: *He has no self-confidence.*

self-congratu·'la·tion *noun* [U] (usually *disapproving*) a way of behaving that shows that you think you have done sth very well and are pleased with yourself ▶ **self-con'gratu·la·tory** *adj.*: *The winners gave themselves a self-congratulatory round of applause.*

self-'conscious *adj.* **1 ~ (about sth)** nervous or embarrassed about your appearance or what other people think of you: *He's always been self-conscious about being so short.* ◊ *She was a shy, self-conscious girl.* **2** (often *disapproving*) done in a way that shows you are aware of the effect that is being produced: *The humour of the play is self-conscious and contrived.* OPP UNSELFCONSCIOUS ▶ **self-'consciously** *adv.*: *She was self-consciously aware of his stare.* **self-'conscious·ness** *noun* [U]

self-con'tained *adj.* **1** not needing or depending on other people: *Her father was a quiet self-contained man.* ◊ *a self-contained life* **2** able to operate or exist without outside help or influence SYN INDEPENDENT: *a self-contained community* ◊ *Each chapter is self-contained and can be studied in isolation.* **3** [usually before noun] (*BrE*) (of a flat/apartment) having its own kitchen, bathroom and entrance: *self-contained accommodation*

self-contra'dict·ory *adj.* containing two ideas or statements that cannot both be true ▶ **self-contra'diction** *noun* [U]

self-con'trol *noun* [U] the ability to remain calm and not show your emotions even though you are feeling angry, excited, etc: *to lose/regain your self-control* ◊ *It took all his self-control not to shout at them.* ▶ **self-con'trolled** *adj.*

self-'criticism *noun* [U] the process of looking at and judging your own faults or weaknesses ▶ **self-'critical** *adj.*: *Don't be too self-critical.*

self-de'ception *noun* [U] the act of making yourself believe sth that you know is not true

self-de'feat·ing *adj.* causing more problems and difficulties instead of solving them; not achieving what you wanted to achieve but having an opposite effect: *Paying children too much attention when they misbehave can be self-defeating.*

self-de'fence (*BrE*) (*AmE* **self-de'fense**) *noun* [U] **1** something you say or do in order to protect yourself when you are being attacked, criticized, etc: *The man later told police that he was acting* **in self-defence**. **2** the skill of being able to protect yourself from physical attack without using weapons: *I'm taking classes in self-defence.*

self-de'nial *noun* [U] the act of not having or doing the things you like, either because you do not have enough money, or for moral or religious reasons: *a life of self-denial and sacrifice* ◊ *an act of self-denial*

	b	d	f	g	h	k	l	m	n	p	r
	bad	did	fall	get	hat	cat	leg	man	now	pen	red

,self-'deprecat·ing adj. (written) done in a way that makes your own achievements or abilities seem unimportant: *He gave a self-deprecating shrug.* ► **,self-depre'ca·tion** noun [U]

,self-de'struct verb [V] (especially of an explosive device, a machine, etc.) to destroy itself, usually by exploding: *This tape will self-destruct in 30 seconds.* ◊ (figurative) *In the last half-hour of the movie the plot rapidly self-destructs.*

,self-de'struc·tion noun [U] the act of doing things to deliberately harm yourself: *He wanted Jill to give up her life of alcohol and self-destruction.* ► **,self-de'structive**

,self-de,termi'n·ation noun [U] **1** the right of a country and its people to be independent and to choose their own government and political system SYN INDEPENDENCE **2** the right or ability of a person to control their own fate

,self-'discip·line noun [U] the ability to make yourself do sth, especially sth difficult or unpleasant: *It takes a lot of self-discipline to go jogging in winter.*

,self-'doubt noun [U, C] the feeling that you are not good enough: *His life was plagued by fear and self-doubt.*

,self-'drive adj. [only before noun] (BrE) **1** a self-drive car is one that you hire and drive yourself **2** a self-drive holiday is one on which you use your own car to travel to the holiday area

,self-'educated adj. having learned things by reading books, etc. rather than at school or college

,self-ef'facing adj. not wanting to attract attention to yourself or your abilities SYN MODEST: *In spite of her success, she remains self-effacing and reserved.* ◊ *a shy, self-effacing man* ► **,self-ef'face·ment** noun [U]

,self-em'ployed adj. working for yourself and not employed by a company, etc: *a self-employed musician* ◊ *I decided to become self-employed.* ◊ *retirement plans for the self-employed* (= people who are self-employed) ► **,self-em'ploy·ment** noun [U]

,self-e'steem noun [U] a feeling of being happy with your own character and abilities: *to have **high/low** self-esteem* ◊ *You need to build your self-esteem.*

,self-'evident adj. obvious and needing no further proof or explanation: *The dangers of such action are self-evident.* ◊ *a self-evident truth* ► **,self-'evident·ly** adv.

,self-ex,ami'n·ation noun [U] **1** the study of your own behaviour and beliefs to find out if they are right or wrong: *spiritual self-examination* **2** the act of checking your body for any signs of illness

,self-ex'plana·tory adj. easy to understand and not needing any more explanation: *I think the title is self-explanatory.*

,self-ex'pres·sion noun [U] the expression of your thoughts or feelings, especially through activities such as writing, painting, dancing, etc: *You should encourage your child's attempts at self-expression.*

,self-ful'fil·ling adj. [usually before noun] a self-fulfilling PROPHECY is one that becomes true because people expect it to be true and behave in a way that will make it happen: *If you expect to fail, you will fail. It's a self-fulfilling prophecy.*

,self-ful'fil·ment (BrE) (also **,self-ful'fill·ment** AmE, BrE) noun [U] the feeling of being happy and satisfied that you have everything you want or need

,self-'govern·ment noun [U] the government or control of a country or an organization by its own people or members, not by others ► **,self-'govern·ing** adj.

,self-'help noun [U] the act of relying on your own efforts and abilities in order to solve your problems, rather than depending on other people for help ► **,self-'help** adj. [only before noun]: *a self-help discussion group for people suffering from depression* (= whose members help each other)

,self-'image noun the opinion or idea you have of yourself, especially of your appearance or abilities: *to have a positive/poor self-image*

,self-im'port·ant adj. (disapproving) thinking that you are more important than other people ► **,self-im'port·ance** noun [U] **,self-im'port·ant·ly** adv.

,self-im'posed adj. [usually before noun] a self-imposed task, duty, etc. is one that you force yourself to do rather than one that sb else forces you to do: *a self-imposed deadline*

,self-in'duced adj. (of illness, problems, etc.) caused by yourself: *self-induced vomiting*

,self-in'dulgent adj. (disapproving) allowing yourself to have or do things that you like, especially when you do this too much or too often: *a self-indulgent lifestyle* ◊ *She writes a tedious and self-indulgent column for a Sunday paper.* ► **,self-in'dulgence** noun [U]

,self-in'flict·ed adj. a self-inflicted injury, problem, etc. is one that you cause for yourself: *a self-inflicted wound* ◊ *Most of Ian's problems are self-inflicted.*

,self-'interest noun [U] (disapproving) the fact of sb only considering their own interests and of not caring about things that would help other people: *Not all of them were acting out of self-interest.* ► **,self-'interest·ed** adj.

self·ish /'selfɪʃ/ adj. caring only about yourself rather than about other people: *selfish behaviour/demands* ◊ *Do you think I'm being selfish by not letting her go?* ◊ *What a selfish thing to do!* ◊ *It was selfish of him to leave all the work to you.* OPP UNSELFISH, SELFLESS ► **self·ly** adv.: *She looked forward, a little selfishly, to a weekend away from her family.* **self·ish·ness** noun [U]: *He was the victim of his own greed and selfishness.*

self·less /'selfləs/ adj. thinking more about the needs, happiness, etc. of other people than about your own: *a life of selfless service to the community* OPP SELFISH ► **self·less·ly** adv. **self·less·ness** noun [U]

,self-'made adj. [usually before noun] having become rich and successful through your own hard work rather than having had money given to you: *He was proud of the fact that he was a self-made man.*

,self-muti'la·tion noun [U] the act of wounding yourself, especially when this is a sign of mental illness

,self-o'pinion·ated adj. (disapproving) believing that your own opinions are always right and refusing to listen to those of other people SYN OPINIONATED

,self-'pity noun [U] (often disapproving) a feeling of pity for yourself, especially because of sth unpleasant or unfair that has happened to you: *She's not someone who likes to **wallow in self-pity**.* ◊ *tears of self-pity* ◊ *A wave of self-pity came over him.* ► **,self-'pitying** adj.

,self-'portrait noun a painting that you do of yourself: *a Rembrandt self-portrait*

,self-pos'sessed adj. able to remain calm and confident in a difficult situation: *She always seems so calm and self-possessed.* ► **,self-pos'ses·sion** noun [U]: *He soon recovered his usual self-possession.*

,self-preser'va·tion noun [U] the fact of protecting yourself in a dangerous or difficult situation: *She was held back by some sense of self-preservation.*

,self-pro'claimed adj. (often disapproving) giving yourself a particular title, job, etc. without the agreement or permission of other people

,self-raising 'flour (BrE) (AmE **'baking flour**, **,self-rising 'flour**) noun [U] flour that contains BAKING POWDER—compare PLAIN FLOUR

,self-re'liant adj. able to do or decide things by yourself, rather than depending on other people for help SYN INDEPENDENT ► **,self-re'liance** noun [U]

,self-re'spect noun [U] a feeling of pride in yourself that what you do, say, etc. is right and good: *Despite poverty and appalling conditions, these people still manage to keep their dignity and self-respect.*

,self-re'spect·ing adj. [only before noun] (especially in negative sentences) having pride in yourself because you believe that what you do is right and good: *No self-respecting journalist would ever work for that newspaper.*

,self-re'straint noun [U] the ability to stop yourself doing or saying sth that you want to because you know it is better not to: *She exercised all her self-restraint and kept quiet.*

,self-'righteous adj. (disapproving) feeling or behaving as if what you say or do is always morally right, and

	s	t	v	z	ʃ	ʒ	tʃ	dʒ	θ	ð	ŋ
	see	tea	van	zoo	shoe	vision	chain	jam	thin	this	sing

other people are wrong ▶ ˌself-'righteous·ly adv. ˌself-'righteous·ness noun [U]

ˌself-rising 'flour noun [U] (AmE) = SELF-RAISING FLOUR

ˌself-'rule noun [U] the governing of a country or an area by its own people

ˌself-'sacrifice noun [U] (approving) the act of not allowing yourself to have or do sth in order to help other people: the courage and self-sacrifice of those who fought in the war ◊ an act of heroic self-sacrifice ▶ ˌself-'sacrificing adj.: self-sacrificing behaviour/love

self-'same /'selfseɪm/ adj. [only before noun] (written) (the, this, etc. selfsame …) used to emphasize that two people or things are the same: Jane had been wondering that selfsame thing.

ˌself-'satisfied adj. (disapproving) too pleased with yourself or your own achievements SYN SMUG: He had a self-satisfied smirk on his face. ▶ ˌself-satis'fac·tion noun [U]: a look of self-satisfaction

ˌself-'seeking adj. (disapproving) interested only in your own needs and interests rather than thinking about the needs of other people ▶ ˌself-'seeking noun [U]: They were accused of self-seeking and corruption.

ˌself-'service adj. [usually before noun] a self-service shop/store, restaurant, etc. is one in which customers serve themselves and then pay for the goods ▶ ˌself-'service noun [U]: The cafe provides quick self-service at low prices.

ˌself-'serving adj. (disapproving) interested only in gaining an advantage for yourself: He was a ruthless, self-serving politician.

ˌself-'starter noun (approving) a person who is able to work on their own and make their own decisions without needing anyone to tell them what to do

ˌself-'styled adj. [only before noun] (disapproving) using a name or title that you have given yourself, especially when you do not have the right to do it: the self-styled king of fashion

ˌself-su'fficient adj. ~ (in sth) able to do or produce everything that you need without the help of other people: The country is totally self-sufficient in food production. ◊ policies to encourage people to become more self-sufficient and less dependent on welfare ▶ ˌself-su'fficiency noun [U]

ˌself-sup'port·ing adj. having enough money to be able to operate without financial help from other people

ˌself-'taught adj. having learned sth by reading books, etc., rather than by sb teaching you: a self-taught artist

ˌself-'willed adj. (disapproving) determined to do what you want without caring about other people: Even at four years old, Carol was stubborn and self-willed.

ˌself-'worth noun [U] a feeling of confidence in yourself that you are a good and useful person: Praise your child to increase her sense of self-worth.

sell /sel/ verb, noun
■ verb (sold, sold /səʊld; AmE soʊld/)
EXCHANGE FOR MONEY | 1 ~ sth (to sb) (at/for sth)|~ sb sth (at/for sth) to give sth to sb in exchange for money: [VN, VNN] I sold my car to James for £800. ◊ I sold James my car for £800. ◊ [VN] They sold the business at a profit/loss (= they gained/lost money when they sold it). ◊ [V] We offered them a good price but they wouldn't sell.
OFFER FOR SALE | 2 [VN] to offer sth for people to buy: Most supermarkets sell a range of organic products. ◊ Do you sell stamps? ◊ to sell insurance/advertising space
BE BOUGHT | 3 to be bought by people in the way or in the numbers mentioned; to be offered at the price mentioned: [VN] The magazine sells 300000 copies a week. ◊ [V] The book sold well and was reprinted many times. ◊ The new design just didn't sell (= nobody bought it). ◊ The pens sell for just 50p each.
PERSUADE | 4 to make people want to buy sth: [V] You may not like it but advertising sells. ◊ [VN] It is quality not price that sells our products. 5 [VN] ~ sth/yourself (to sb) to persuade sb that sth is a good idea, service, product, etc.; to persuade sb that you are the right person for a job, position, etc: Now we have to try and sell the idea to

management. ◊ You really have to sell yourself at a job interview.
TAKE MONEY/REWARD | 6 [VN] ~ yourself (to sb) (disapproving) to accept money or a reward from sb for doing sth that is against your principles SYN PROSTITUTE
—see also SALE
IDM be 'sold on sth (informal) to be very enthusiastic about sth: We were really sold on the idea. sell your 'body to have sex with sb in exchange for money sell sb down the 'river (informal) to betray sb you have promised to help ORIGIN From the custom of buying and selling slaves on the plantations on the Mississippi river in America. Slaves who caused trouble for their masters could be sold to plantation owners lower down the river, where conditions would be worse. sell sb/yourself 'short to not value sb/yourself highly enough and show this by the way you treat or present them/yourself sell your 'soul (to the devil) to do anything, even sth bad or dishonest, in return for money, success or power—more at HOT adj., PUP
PHRV ˌsell sth↔'off 1 to sell things cheaply because you want to get rid of them or because you need the money 2 to sell all or part of an industry, a company or land: The Church sold off the land for housing.—related noun SELL-OFF ˌsell 'out| be ˌsold 'out (of tickets for a concert, football game, etc.) to be all sold: The tickets sold out within hours. ◊ This week's performances are completely sold out. ˌsell 'out (of sth)| be ˌsold 'out (of sth) to have sold all the available items, tickets, etc: I'm sorry, we've sold out of bread. ◊ We are already sold out for what should be a fantastic game. ˌsell 'out (to sb/sth) 1 (disapproving) to change or give up your beliefs or principles: He's a talented screenwriter who has sold out to TV soap operas. 2 to sell your business or a part of your business: The company eventually sold out to a multinational media group.—related noun SELL-OUT ˌsell 'up| ˌsell sth↔'up (especially BrE) to sell your home, possessions, business, etc., usually because you are leaving the country or RETIRING
■ noun [sing.] (BrE, informal) something that is not as good as it seemed to be: The band only played for about half an hour—it was a real sell.—see also HARD SELL

'sell-by date (BrE) (AmE 'pull date) noun the date printed on food packages, etc. after which the food must not be sold: This milk is past its sell-by date. ◊ (figurative) These policies are way past their sell-by date.

sell·er /'selə(r)/ noun 1 a person who sells sth: a flower seller ◊ The law is intended to protect both the buyer and the seller.—see also BOOKSELLER—compare VENDOR 2 a good, poor, etc. ~ a product that has been sold in the amounts or way mentioned: This particular model is one of our biggest sellers.—see also BEST-SELLER IDM a ˌseller's 'market a situation in which people selling sth have an advantage, because there is not a lot of a particular item for sale, and prices can be kept high

'selling point noun a feature of sth that makes people want to buy or use it: The price is obviously one of the main selling points. ◊ Sales departments try to identify a product's USP or 'unique selling point'.

'selling price noun the price at which sth is sold—compare ASKING PRICE, COST PRICE

'sell-off noun 1 (BrE) the sale by the government of an industry or a service to individual people or private companies 2 (AmE, business) the sale of a large number of STOCKS and SHARES, after which their value usually falls

Sel·lo·tape™ /'seləteɪp/ noun (also 'sticky tape) (both BrE) (AmE 'Scotch tape™) [U] clear plastic tape that is sticky on one side, used for sticking things together: a roll of Sellotape ◊ The envelope was stuck down with Sellotape.—picture at STATIONERY

sel·lo·tape /'seləteɪp/ verb [VN] ~ sth (to sth) (BrE) to join or stick things together with Sellotape: We found a note sellotaped to the front door.

'sell-out noun [usually sing.] 1 a play, concert, etc. for which all the tickets have been sold: Next week's final looks like being a sell-out. ◊ a sell-out tour 2 a situation in

æ	ɑː	e	ɜː	ə	ɪ	iː	i	ɒ	ɒ	ɔː	ʌ	ʊ	u	uː
cat	father	ten	bird	about	sit	see	many	got		saw	cup	put	actual	too

(BrE)

S

which sb betrays a person or group who trusted them, by not doing sth that they promised to do, or by doing sth that they promised not to do: *The workers see the deal as a union sell-out to management.*

selt·zer /'seltzə(r)/ *noun* [U, C] FIZZY water (= with bubbles), usually containing minerals, used as a drink

selves *pl.* of SELF

se·man·tic /sɪ'mæntɪk/ *adj.* [usually before noun] (*linguistics*) connected with the meaning of words and sentences: *semantic theory/analysis* ▶ **se·man·tic·al·ly** *adv.*: *semantically related words*

se·man·tics /sɪ'mæntɪks/ *noun* [U] (*linguistics*) **1** the study of the meanings of words and phrases **2** the meaning of words, phrases or systems: *the semantics of the language*

sema·phore /'seməfɔː(r)/ *noun, verb*
■ *noun* [U] a system for sending signals in which you hold your arms or two flags in particular positions to represent different letters of the alphabet
■ *verb* [V, VN, V**that**] to send a message to sb by semaphore or a similar system of signals

semb·lance /'sembləns/ *noun* [sing., U] **~ of sth** (*written*) a situation in which sth seems to exist although this may not, in fact, be the case: *The ceasefire brought about a semblance of peace.* ◇ *Life at last returned to some semblance of normality.*

semen /'siːmen/ *noun* [U] the whitish liquid containing SPERM that is produced by the sex organs of men and male animals

se·mes·ter /sɪ'mestə(r)/ *noun* (especially in the US) one of the two periods that the school or college year is divided into: *the spring/fall semester*—compare TRIMESTER

semi /'semi/ *noun* (*pl.* **semis**) (*BrE, informal*) a SEMIDETACHED house (= one that is joined to another house by one shared wall): *suburban semis*

semi- /'semi/ *prefix* (in adjectives and nouns) half; partly: *semicircular* ◇ *semi-final*

semi·auto·mat·ic *adj.* (of a gun) able to load bullets automatically, and therefore very quickly, but not firing automatically ▶ **semi-auto·mat·ic** *noun*

semi·breve /'semibriːv/ (*BrE*) (*AmE* **'whole note**) *noun* (*music*) a note that lasts as long as four CROTCHETS/QUARTER NOTES—picture at MUSIC

semi·circle /'semisɜːkl; *AmE* -sɜːrkl/ *noun* **1** (*geometry*) one half of a circle—picture at CIRCLE **2** the line that encloses a semicircle **3** a thing, or a group of people or things, shaped like a semicircle: *a semicircle of chairs* ◇ *We sat in a semicircle round the fire.* ▶ **semi·cir·cu·lar** /,semi'sɜːkjələ(r); *AmE* -'sɜːrk-/ *adj.*: *a semicircular driveway*

semi·colon /,semi'kəʊlən; *AmE* 'semikoʊ-/ *noun* the mark (;) used to separate the parts of a complicated sentence or items in a detailed list, showing a pause that is longer than a COMMA but shorter than a FULL STOP—compare COLON ⇨ Appendix 4

semi·con·duct·or /,semikən'dʌktə(r)/ *noun* (*technical*) **1** a solid substance that CONDUCTS electricity in particular conditions, better than INSULATORS but not as well as CONDUCTORS **2** a device containing a semiconductor used in ELECTRONICS

semi·de·tached *adj.* (*BrE*) (of a house) joined to another house by a wall on one side that is shared ▶ **semi-de·tached** *noun*—compare DETACHED—see also SEMI, TERRACED

semi·final *noun* one of the two games or parts of a sports competition that are held to decide who will compete in the last part of the FINAL): *He's through to the semi-final of the men's singles.* ▶ **semi-finalist** *noun*: *They are semi-finalists for the fourth year in succession.*

sem·inal /'semɪnl/ *adj.* **1** (*formal*) very important and having a strong influence on later developments: *a seminal work/article/study* **2** [usually before noun] (*technical*) of or containing SEMEN: *seminal fluid*

sem·inar /'semɪnɑː(r)/ *noun* **1** a class at a university or college when a small group of students and a teacher discuss or study a particular topic: *Teaching is by lectures and seminars.* ◇ *a graduate seminar* ◇ *a seminar room/group* **2** a meeting for discussion or training: *a one-day management seminar*

sem·in·ar·ian /,semɪ'neəriən; *AmE* -'ner-/ *noun* a student in a seminary

sem·in·ary /'semɪnəri; *AmE* -neri/ *noun* (*pl.* **-ies**) a college where priests, ministers or RABBIS are trained

semi·ot·ics /,semi'ɒtɪks; *AmE* -'ɑːtɪks/ *noun* [U] the study of signs and symbols and of their meaning and use ▶ **semi·ot·ic** *adj.*: *semiotic analysis*

semi-precious *adj.* [usually before noun] (of a jewel) less valuable than the most valuable types of jewels: *semi-precious stones*

semi·pro·fes·sion·al *adj.* semi-professional musicians or sports players are paid for what they do, but do not do it as their main job ▶ **semi-pro·fes·sion·al** *noun*

semi·quaver /'semikweɪvə(r)/ (*BrE*) (*AmE* **six'teenth note**) *noun* (*music*) a note that lasts half as long as a QUAVER/EIGHTH NOTE—picture at MUSIC

semi-skilled *adj.* [usually before noun] (of workers) having some special training or qualifications, but less than skilled people: *a semi-skilled machine operator* ◇ *semi-skilled jobs* (= for people who have some special training)

semi-skimmed *adj.* (*BrE*) (of milk) that has had a lot of the fat removed

Sem·it·ic /sə'mɪtɪk/ *adj.* **1** of or connected with a family of languages that includes Hebrew and Arabic **2** of or connected with the people who speak Semitic languages, especially Hebrew and Arabic

semi·tone /'semitəʊn; *AmE* -toʊn/ (*BrE*) (*AmE* **'half step**, **'half-tone**) *noun* (*music*) half a TONE on a musical scale, for example the INTERVAL between C and C♯ or between E and F—compare STEP *n.* (10)

semi-tropic·al *adj.* = SUBTROPICAL

semi·vowel /'semivaʊəl/ *noun* (*phonetics*) a speech sound that sounds like a vowel but functions as a consonant, for example /w, j/

semo·lina /,semə'liːnə/ *noun* [U] **1** large hard grains of wheat used for making PASTA and sweet dishes **2** a sweet dish made from semolina and milk, eaten for DESSERT in Britain and for breakfast in the US

sem·tex /'semteks/ *noun* [U] a powerful explosive substance that is used for making bombs, often illegally

Sen. *abbr.* SENATOR: *Sen. John K Nordqvist*

sen·ate /'senət/ *noun* (usually **the Senate**) **1** [sing.] one of the two groups of elected politicians who make laws in some countries, for example in the US, France and Australia. The Senate is smaller than the other group but higher in rank. Many state parliaments in the US also have a Senate: *a member of the Senate* ◇ *a Senate committee*—compare CONGRESS, THE HOUSE OF REPRESENTATIVES **2** [C usually sing, U] (in some countries) the group of people who control a university: *the senate of London University* **3** [sing.] (in ancient Rome) the most important council of the government; the building where the council met

sen·ator /'senətə(r)/ *noun* (often **Senator**) (*abbr.* **Sen.**) a member of a senate: *Senator McCarthy* ◇ *He has served as a Democratic senator for Texas since 1994.* ▶ **sen·at·or·ial** /,senə'tɔːriəl/ *adj.* [only before noun]: *a senatorial candidate/committee*

send /send/ *verb* (**sent, sent** /sent/)
BY MAIL/RADIO **1 ~ sth (to sb)**|**~ sb sth** to make sth go or be taken to a place, especially by post/mail, radio, etc: [VN] *to send a letter/package/cheque/fax/e-mail* ◇ *She sent the letter by airmail.* ◇ (*BrE*) *to send sth by post* ◇ (*AmE*) *to send sth by mail* ◇ *A radio signal was sent to the spacecraft.* ◇ *The CD player was faulty so we sent it back to the manufacturers.* ◇ [VN, VNN] *Have you sent a postcard to your mother yet?* ◇ *Have you sent your mother a postcard yet?*
MESSAGE **2** to tell sb sth by sending them a message: [VN] *My parents send their love.* ◇ *What sort of message is that sending to young people?* ◇ [VNN] *He sent me word to come.*

◊ [VN(that)] *She sent word (that) she could not come.* ◊ [Vtoinf] *(formal) She sent to say that she was coming home.*

SB SOMEWHERE | **3** to tell sb to go somewhere or to do sth; to arrange for sb to go somewhere: [VN, usually +adv. / prep.] *Ed couldn't make it so they sent me instead.* ◊ *She sent the kids to bed early.* ◊ *to send sb to prison / boarding school* ◊ [VNtoinf] *I've sent Tom to buy some milk.*

MAKE STH MOVE QUICKLY | **4** to make sth/sb move quickly or suddenly: [VN-ING] *Every step he took sent the pain shooting up his leg.* ◊ *The punch sent him flying.* ◊ [VN+adv. / prep.] *The report sent share prices down a further 8p.*

MAKE SB REACT | **5 ~ sb (to/into sth)** to make sb behave or react in a particular way: [VN] *Her music always sends me to sleep.* ◊ *Her account of the visit sent us into fits of laughter.* ◊ [VN-ADJ] *All the publicity nearly sent him crazy.*

IDM **send sb 'packing** *(informal)* to tell sb firmly or rudely to go away—more at COVENTRY, LOVE *n.*

PHRV **,send a'way (to sb) (for sth)** = SEND OFF (FOR STH) **,send sb↔'down** *(BrE)* **1** *(informal)* to send sb to prison **2** *(old-fashioned)* to order a student to leave a university because of bad behaviour **'send for sb** to ask or tell sb to come to you, especially in order to help you: *Send for a doctor, quickly!* **'send for sth** to ask sb to bring or deliver sth to you: *His son found him and sent for help.* ◊ *She sent for the latest sales figures.* **,send sb 'forth** *(old-fashioned or literary)* to send sb away from you to another place **,send 'forth sth** *(formal)* to produce a sound, signal, etc. so that other people can hear it, receive it, etc: *He opened his mouth and sent forth a stream of noise.* **,send sb↔'in** to order sb to go to a place to deal with a difficult situation: *Troops were sent in to restore order.* **,send sth↔'in** to send sth by post/mail to a place where it will be dealt with: *Have you sent in your application yet?* **,send 'off (for sth) | ,send a'way (to sb) (for sth)** to write to sb and ask them to send you sth by post/mail: *I've sent off for some books for my course.* **,send sb↔'off** *(BrE)* (in a sports game) to order sb to leave the field because they have broken the rules of the game: *Beckham was sent off for a foul in the second half.*—related noun SENDING-OFF **,send sth↔'off** to send sth to a place by post/mail: *I'm sending the files off to my boss tomorrow.* **,send sth↔'on 1** to send sth to a place so that it arrives before you get there: *We sent our furniture on by ship.* **2** to send a letter that has been sent to sb's old address to their new address [SYN] FORWARD **3** to send sth from one place/person to another: *They arranged for the information to be sent on to us.* **,send 'out for sth** to ask a restaurant or shop/store to deliver food to you at home or at work: *Let's send out for a pizza.* **,send sth↔'out 1** to send sth to a lot of different people or places: *Have the invitations been sent out yet?* **2** to produce sth, such as light, a signal, sound, etc. [SYN] EMIT **,send sb/sth↔'up** *(BrE, informal)* to make people laugh at sb/sth by copying them/it in a funny way: *a TV programme that sends up politicians*—related noun SEND-UP

send·er /'sendə(r)/ *noun* a person who sends sth: *If undelivered, please return to sender.*

,sending-'off *noun* (*pl.* sendings-off) *(BrE)* (in football) a situation when a REFEREE tells a player to leave the field because they have broken the rules in a serious way

'send-off *noun* *(informal)* an occasion when people come together to say goodbye to sb who is leaving

'send-up *noun* *(informal)* an act of making sb/sth look silly by copying them in a funny way

sen·es·cence /sɪ'nesns/ *noun* [U] *(formal or technical)* the process of becoming old and showing the effects of old age ▶ **sen·es·cent** *adj.*

se·nile /'siːnaɪl/ *adj.* behaving in a confused or strange way, and unable to remember things, because of old age: *I think she's going senile.* ▶ **sen·il·ity** /sə'nɪləti/ *noun* [U]: *an old man on the verge of senility*

,senile de'mentia *noun* [U] a serious mental disorder in old people that causes loss of memory, loss of control of the body, etc.

se·nior /'siːniə(r)/ *adj., noun*

■ *adj.*

OF HIGH RANK | **1 ~ (to sb)** high in rank or status; higher in rank or status than others: *a senior officer / manager / lecturer* ◊ *a senior partner in a law firm* ◊ *a senior post / position* ◊ *I have ten years' experience at senior management level.* ◊ *(BrE) Junior nurses usually work alongside more senior nurses.* ◊ *He is senior to me.* ◊ *The meeting should be chaired by the most senior person present.*

IN SPORT | **2** [only before noun] for adults or people at a more advanced level: *to take part in senior competitions* ◊ *He won the senior men's 400 metres.*

FATHER | **3 (Senior)** *(abbr.* **Snr., Sr)** used after the name of a man who has the same name as his son, to avoid confusion

SCHOOL/COLLEGE | **4** [only before noun] *(BrE)* (of a school or part of a school) for children over the age of 11 or 13 **5** [only before noun] *(AmE)* connected with the last year in high school or college: *the senior prom*

■ *noun*

OLDER PERSON | **1** a person who is older than sb else: *She was ten years his senior.* ◊ *My brother is my senior by two years.*—compare JUNIOR **2** *(especially AmE)* = SENIOR CITIZEN

HIGHER RANK | **3** a person who is higher in rank or status: *She felt unappreciated both by her colleagues and her seniors.*

IN SPORT | **4** adults or people who have reached an advanced level: *tennis coaching for juniors and seniors*

IN SCHOOL/COLLEGE | **5** *(BrE)* a child at a senior school; an older child in a school **6** (in the US and some other countries) a student in the last year at a high school or college: *high school seniors*—compare SOPHOMORE

,senior 'citizen (also **se·nior** especially in *AmE*) *noun* an older person, especially sb who has RETIRED from work. People often call sb a 'senior citizen' to avoid saying that they are old or using the word 'old-age pensioner'.

,senior 'high school (also **,senior 'high**) *noun* (in the US) a school for young people between the ages of 14 and 18—compare JUNIOR HIGH SCHOOL

sen·i·or·ity /ˌsiːni'ɒrəti; *AmE* -'ɔːr-; -'ɑːr-/ *noun* [U] **1** the fact of being older or of a higher rank than others: *a position of seniority* **2** the rank that you have in a company because of the length of time you have worked there: *a lawyer with five years' seniority* ◊ *Should promotion be based on merit or seniority?*

sen·sa·tion /sen'seɪʃn/ *noun* **1** [C] a feeling that you get when sth affects your body: *a tingling / burning / pleasant sensation* ◊ *I had a sensation of falling, as if in a dream.* **2** [U] the ability to feel through your sense of touch [SYN] FEELING: *She seemed to have lost all sensation in her arms.* **3** [C, usually sing.] a general feeling or impression that is difficult to explain; an experience or a memory: *He had the eerie sensation of being watched.* ◊ *When I arrived, I had the sensation that she had been expecting me.* **4** [C usually sing, U] very great surprise, excitement, or interest among a lot of people; the person or the thing that causes this surprise: *News of his arrest caused a sensation.* ◊ *The band became a sensation overnight.*

sen·sa·tion·al /sen'seɪʃənl/ *adj.* **1** causing great surprise, excitement, or interest: *The result was a sensational 4–1 victory.* **2** *(disapproving)* (of a newspaper, etc.) trying to get your interest by presenting facts or events as worse or more shocking than they really are: *sensational news stories* **3** *(informal)* extremely good; wonderful: *You look sensational in that dress!* ▶ **sen·sa·tion·al·ly** /-ʃənəli/: *They won sensationally against the top team.* ◊ *The incident was sensationally reported in the press.* ◊ *He's sensationally good-looking!*

sen·sa·tion·al·ism /sen'seɪʃənəlɪzəm/ *noun* [U] *(disapproving)* a way of getting people's interest by using shocking words or by presenting facts and events as worse or more shocking than they really are ▶ **sen·sa·tion·al·ist** /-ʃənəlɪst/ *adj.*: *sensationalist headlines/newspapers*

sen·sa·tion·al·ize (*BrE* also **-ise**) /sen'seɪʃənəlaɪz/ *verb* [VN] *(disapproving)* to exaggerate a story so that it seems more exciting or shocking than it really is

sense /sens/ *noun, verb*

■ *noun*

SIGHT/HEARING, etc. 1 [C] one of the five powers (sight, hearing, smell, taste and touch) that your body uses to get information about the world around you: *the five senses* ◊ *Dogs have a keen (= strong) sense of smell.* ◊ *the sense organs (= eyes, ears, nose, etc.)* ◊ *I could hardly believe the evidence of my own senses (= what I could see, hear, etc.).* ◊ *The mixture of sights, smells and sounds around her made her senses reel.*—see also SIXTH SENSE

FEELING 2 [C] a feeling about sth important: *He felt an overwhelming sense of loss.* ◊ *a strong sense of purpose/ identity/duty* ◊ *Doesn't she have any sense of guilt about what she did?* ◊ *Helmets can give cyclists a false sense of security.* ◊ *I had the sense that he was worried about something.*

UNDERSTANDING/JUDGEMENT 3 [sing.] an understanding about sth; an ability to judge sth: *One of the most important things in a partner is a sense of humour (= the ability to find things funny or make people laugh).* ◊ *He has a very good sense of direction (= finds the way to a place easily).* ◊ *She has lost all sense of direction in her life.* ◊ *Always try to keep a sense of proportion (= of the relative importance of different things).* ◊ *a sense of rhythm/timing* ◊ *Alex doesn't have any dress sense (= does not know which clothes look attractive).*—see also ROAD SENSE 4 [U] good understanding and judgement; knowledge of what is sensible or practical behaviour: *You should have the sense to take advice when it is offered.* ◊ *There's no sense in (= it is not sensible) worrying about it now.* ◊ *Can't you talk sense (= say sth sensible)?* ◊ *There's a lot of sense in what Mary says.*—see also COMMON SENSE, GOOD SENSE

NORMAL STATE OF MIND 5 (senses) [pl.] a normal state of mind; the ability to think clearly: *If she threatens to leave, it should bring him to his senses.* ◊ *He waited for Dora to come to her senses and return.* ◊ *(old-fashioned) Are you out of your senses? You'll be killed!* ◊ *(old-fashioned) Why does she want to marry him? She must have taken leave of her senses.*

MEANING 6 [C] the meaning that a word or phrase has; a way of understanding sth: *The word 'love' is used in different senses by different people.* ◊ *education in its broadest sense* ◊ *He was a true friend, in every sense of the word (= in every possible way).* ◊ *In a sense (= in one way) it doesn't matter any more.* ◊ *In some senses (= in one or more ways) the criticisms were justified.* ◊ *(formal) In no sense can the issue be said to be resolved.* ◊ *There is a sense in which we are all to blame for the tragedy.* ⇨ note at SENSIBLE

IDM **knock/talk some 'sense into sb** to try and persuade sb to stop behaving in a stupid way, sometimes using rough or violent methods: *Try and talk some sense into her before she makes the wrong decision.* **make 'sense 1** to have a meaning that you can easily understand: *This sentence doesn't make sense.* **2** to be a sensible thing to do: *It makes sense to buy the most up-to-date version.* **3** to be easy to understand or explain: *John wasn't making much sense on the phone.* ◊ *Who would send me all these flowers? It makes no sense.* **make 'sense of sth** to understand sth that is difficult or has no clear meaning: *I can't make sense of that painting.* **see 'sense** to start to be sensible or reasonable **a sense of oc'casion** a feeling or understanding that an event is important or special: *Candles on the table gave the evening a sense of occasion.*

■ *verb* (not used in the progressive tenses)

BECOME AWARE 1 to become aware of sth even though you cannot see it, hear it, etc: [VN] *Sensing danger, they started to run.* ◊ [V] *Thomas, she sensed, could convince anyone of anything.* [also VN -ing, VN inf, V wh-] ◊ [V (that)] *Lisa sensed that he did not believe her.*

OF MACHINE 2 [VN] to discover and record sth: *equipment that senses the presence of toxic gases*

sense·less /'senslas/ *adj.* **1** *(disapproving)* having no meaning or purpose **SYN** POINTLESS: *senseless destruction/violence* ◊ *His death was a senseless waste of life.* ◊ *It's senseless to continue any further.* **2** [not before noun]

unconscious: *He was beaten senseless.* ◊ *She drank herself senseless.* **3** not using good judgement: *The police blamed senseless drivers who went too fast.* ▶ **sense·less·ly** *adv.*

sens·ibil·ity /ˌsensə'bɪləti/ *noun* (*pl.* **-ies**) **1** [U, C] the ability to experience and understand deep feelings, especially in art and literature: *a man of impeccable manners, charm and sensibility* ◊ *musical/artistic sensibility* **2** (sensibilities) [pl.] a person's feelings, especially when the person is easily offended or influenced by sth: *The article offended her religious sensibilities.* ◊ *The play gave no thought to the sensibilities of the audience.*

sens·ible /'sensəbl/ *adj.* **1** (of people and their behaviour) able to make good judgements based on reason and experience rather than emotion; practical: *a sensible person/decision/precaution* ◊ *I think that's a very sensible idea.* ◊ *Say something sensible.* ◊ *I think the sensible thing would be to take a taxi home.* **2** (of clothes, etc.) useful rather than fashionable: *sensible shoes* **3** *(formal or literary)* aware of sth: *I am sensible of the fact that mathematics is not a popular subject.* **OPP** for sense 3 INSENSIBLE **HELP** Use **silly** (sense 1) or **impractical** (senses 1 and 2) as the opposite for the other senses. ▶ **sens·ibly** /-əbli/ *adv.*: *to eat/behave/drive/talk sensibly* ◊ *He decided, very sensibly, not to drive when he was so tired.* ◊ *She's always very sensibly dressed.*

> **WHICH WORD?**
> **sensible / sensitive**
>
> **Sensible** and **sensitive** are connected with 2 different meanings of sense.
> **Sensible** refers to your ability to make good judgements: *She gave me some very sensible advice.* ◊ *It wasn't very sensible to go out on your own so late at night.*
> **Sensitive** refers to how easily you react to things and how much you are aware of things or other people: *a soap for sensitive skin* ◊ *This movie may upset a sensitive child.*

sen·si·tive /'sensətɪv/ *adj.*

TO PEOPLE'S FEELINGS 1 ~ (to sth) aware of and able to understand other people and their feelings: *a sensitive and caring man* ◊ *She is very sensitive to other people's feelings.* **OPP** INSENSITIVE

TO ART/MUSIC/LITERATURE 2 able to understand art, music and literature and to express yourself through them: *an actor's sensitive reading of the poem* ◊ *a sensitive musician/poet* ◊ *a sensitive portrait*

EASILY UPSET 3 ~ (about/to sth) easily offended or upset: *You're far too sensitive.* ◊ *He's very sensitive about his weight.* ◊ *She's very sensitive to criticism.* **OPP** INSENSITIVE

INFORMATION/SUBJECT 4 that you have to treat with great care because it may offend people or make them angry: *Health care is a politically sensitive issue.* ◊ *That's a sensitive area.*

TO COLD/LIGHT/FOOD, etc. 5 ~ (to sth) reacting quickly or more than usual to sth: *sensitive areas of the body* ◊ *My teeth are very sensitive to cold food.* **OPP** INSENSITIVE

TO SMALL CHANGES 6 ~ (to sth) able to measure very small changes: *a sensitive barometer/instrument* ◊ *The eyes can be a sensitive indicator of health.* ◊ *(figurative) The Stock Exchange is very sensitive to political change.* **OPP** INSENSITIVE

▶ **sen·si·tive·ly** *adv.*: *She handled the matter sensitively and effectively.* ◊ *He writes sensitively.* **IDM** see NERVE *n.*

sen·si·tiv·ity /ˌsensə'tɪvəti/ *noun* (*pl.* **-ies**)

TO PEOPLE'S FEELINGS 1 [U] ~ (to sth) the ability to understand other people's feelings: *sensitivity to the needs of children* ◊ *She pointed out with tact and sensitivity exactly where he had gone wrong.* **OPP** INSENSITIVITY

TO ART/MUSIC/LITERATURE 2 [U] the ability to understand art, music and literature and to express yourself through them: *She played with great sensitivity.*

BEING EASILY UPSET 3 [U, C, usually pl.] a tendency to be easily offended or upset by sth: *He's a mixture of anger and sensitivity.* ◊ *She was blind to the feelings and sensitivities of other people.* **OPP** INSENSITIVITY

s	t	v	z	ʃ	ʒ	tʃ	dʒ	θ	ð	ŋ
see	tea	van	zoo	shoe	vision	chain	jam	thin	this	sing

OF INFORMATION/SUBJECT | **4** [U] the fact of needing to be treated very carefully because it may offend or upset people: *Confidentiality is important because of the sensitivity of the information.*

TO FOOD/COLD/LIGHT, etc. | **5** [U, C, usually pl.] *(technical)* the quality of reacting quickly or more than usual to sth: *food sensitivity ◇ allergies and sensitivities ◇ Some children develop a sensitivity to cow's milk. ◇ The eyes of some fish have a greater sensitivity to light than ours do.*

TO SMALL CHANGES | **6** [U] the ability to measure very small changes: *the sensitivity of the test* OPP INSENSITIVITY

sen·si·tize (*BrE* also **-ise**) /ˈsensətaɪz/ *verb* [VN] [usually passive] **1 ~ sb/sth (to sth)** to make sb/sth more aware of sth, especially a problem or sth bad: *People are becoming more sensitized to the dangers threatening the environment.* **2** *(technical)* to treat a material or piece of equipment so that it will be sensitive to physical or chemical changes ▶ **sen·si·tiza·tion, -isa·tion** /ˌsensətaɪzˈeɪʃn/ *noun* [U]

sen·sor /ˈsensə(r)/ *noun* a device that can react to light, heat, pressure, etc. in order to make a machine, etc. do sth or show sth: *security lights with an infrared sensor* (= that come on when a person is near them)

sens·ory /ˈsensəri/ *adj.* [usually before noun] *(technical)* connected with your physical senses: *sensory organs ◇ sensory deprivation*

sens·ual /ˈsenʃuəl/ *adj.* **1** connected with your physical feelings; giving pleasure to your physical senses, especially sexual pleasure: *sensual pleasure/delight ◇ Food is a great sensual experience.* **2** suggesting an interest in physical pleasure, especially sexual pleasure: *sensual lips/eyes ◇ He was darkly sensual and mysterious.* ▶ **sen·su·al·ity** /ˌsenʃuˈæləti/ *noun* [U]: *the sensuality of his poetry* **sen·su·al·ly** /-ʃuəli/ *adv.*

WHICH WORD?
sensual / sensuous / sensory   (?)

These adjectives are frequently used with the following nouns:

sensual ~	sensuous ~	sensory ~
pleasure	mouth	perception
mouth	lips	stimulation
desire	pleasure	experience
woman	colour	deprivation
voice	music	

Sensual and **sensuous** are very similar and refer to things that give pleasure to your senses, especially sexual pleasure, or that suggest an interest in sexual pleasure.

Sensuous also describes the pleasure that art and music can give to your senses.

Sensory is used in technical contexts and means 'connected with the senses'.

---

sen·su·ous /ˈsenʃuəs/ *adj.* **1** giving pleasure to your senses: *sensuous pleasure/music ◇ I'm drawn to the poetic, sensuous qualities of her paintings.* **2** suggesting an interest in sexual pleasure: *his full sensuous lips* ▶ **sen·su·ous·ly** *adv.* **sen·su·ous·ness** *noun* [U]

sent *pt, pp* of SEND

sen·tence /ˈsentəns/ *noun, verb*
■ *noun* **1** [C] *(grammar)* a set of words expressing a statement, a question or an order, usually containing a subject and a verb. In written English sentences begin with a capital letter and end with a full stop (.), a question mark (?) or an EXCLAMATION mark (!). **2** [C, U] the punishment given by a court of law: *a jail/prison sentence ◇ a light/heavy sentence ◇ to be under sentence of death ◇ The judge passed sentence* (= said what the punishment would be). *◇ The prisoner has served* (= completed) *his sentence and will be released tomorrow.*—see also DEATH SENTENCE, LIFE SENTENCE
■ *verb* [often passive] **~ sb (to sth)** to say officially in a court of law that sb is to receive a particular punish-

ment: [VN] *to be sentenced to death/life imprisonment/three years in prison* [also VN to inf]

sen·ten·tious /senˈtenʃəs/ *adj. (formal, disapproving)* trying to sound important or intelligent, especially by expressing moral judgements: *sententious remarks* ▶ **sen·ten·tious·ly** *adv.*

sen·tient /ˈsentiənt; ˈsenʃnt/ *adj.* [usually before noun] *(formal)* able to see or feel things through the senses: *Man is a sentient being.*

sen·ti·ment /ˈsentɪmənt/ *noun* **1** [C, U] *(formal)* a feeling or an opinion, especially one based on emotions SYN VIEW: *the spread of nationalist sentiments ◇ This is a sentiment I wholeheartedly agree with. ◇ Public sentiment is against any change to the law.* **2** [U] (sometimes *disapproving*) feelings of pity, romantic love, sadness, etc. which may be too strong or not appropriate: *There was no fatherly affection, no display of sentiment. ◇ There is no room for sentiment in business.*

sen·ti·men·tal /ˌsentɪˈmentl/ *adj.* **1** connected with your emotions, rather than reason: *He has a strong sentimental attachment to the place. ◇ She kept the letters for sentimental reasons. ◇ The ring wasn't worth very much but it had great sentimental value.* **2** (often *disapproving*) producing emotions such as pity, romantic love or sadness, which may be too strong or not appropriate; feeling these emotions too much: *a slushy, sentimental love story ◇ Her book is honest without being sentimental. ◇ He's not the sort of man who gets sentimental about old friendships.* OPP UNSENTIMENTAL ▶ **sen·ti·men·tal·ly** /-təli/ *adv.*

sen·ti·men·tal·ist /ˌsentɪˈmentəlɪst/ *noun* (sometimes *disapproving*) a person who is sentimental about things

sen·ti·men·tal·ity /ˌsentɪmenˈtæləti/ *noun* [U] (*disapproving*) the quality of being too sentimental

sen·ti·men·tal·ize (*BrE* also **-ise**) /ˌsentɪˈmentəlaɪz/ *verb* (*disapproving*) to present sth in an emotional way, emphasizing its good aspects and not mentioning its bad aspects: [VN] *Jackie was careful not to sentimentalize country life.* [also V]

sen·ti·nel /ˈsentɪnl/ *noun* (*literary*) a soldier whose job is to guard sth SYN SENTRY: *(figurative) a tall round tower standing sentinel over the river*

sen·try /ˈsentri/ *noun* (*pl.* **-ies**) a soldier whose job is to guard sth: *to be on sentry duty*

ˈsentry box *noun* a small shelter for a sentry to stand in

sepal /ˈsepl/ *noun* (*technical*) a part of a flower, like a leaf, that lies under and supports the PETALS (= the delicate coloured parts that make up the head of the flower). Each flower has a ring of sepals called a CALYX.

sep·ar·able /ˈsepərəbl/ *adj.* **~ (from sth)** that can be separated from sth, or considered separately: *The moral question is not entirely separable from the financial one.* OPP INSEPARABLE ▶ **sep·ar·abil·ity** /ˌseprəˈbɪləti/ *noun* [U]

sep·ar·ate *adj., verb*
■ *adj.* /ˈseprət/ **1 ~ (from sth/sb)** forming a unit by itself; not joined to sth else: *separate bedrooms/offices ◇ Raw meat must be kept separate from cooked meat. ◇ The school is housed in two separate buildings.* **2** [usually before noun] different; not connected: *It happened on three separate occasions. ◇ For the past three years they have been leading totally separate lives.* ▶ **sep·ar·ate·ness** *noun* [U, sing.]: *Japan's long-standing sense of separateness and uniqueness* IDM **go your separate ways 1** to end a relationship with sb **2** to go in a different direction from sb you have been travelling with—more at COVER *n.*
■ *verb* /ˈsepəreɪt/ **1 ~ (sth) (from/and sth)** to divide into different parts or groups; to divide things into different parts or groups: [V] *Stir the sauce constantly so that it does not separate.* [VN] *It is impossible to separate belief from emotion. ◇ Separate the eggs* (= separate the YOLK from the white). *◇ Make a list of points and separate them into 'desirable' and 'essential'.* **2 ~ sb/sth (from/and sb/sth)** to move apart; to make people or things move apart: [V] *We separated into several different search parties. ◇ South America separated from Africa 200 million years ago. ◇ South America and Africa separated 200 million years ago.*

S

æ	ɑː	e	ɜː	ə	ɪ	iː	i	ɒ	ɔː	ʌ	ʊ	u	uː
cat	father	ten	bird	about	sit	see	many	got	saw	cup	put	actual	too

(BrE)

◊ [VN] *Police tried to separate the two men who were fighting.* ◊ *The war separated many families.* ◊ *Those suffering from infectious diseases were separated from the other patients.* **3** [VN] **~ sb (from/and sb)** to be between two people, areas, countries, etc. so that they are not touching or connected: *A thousand kilometres separates the two cities.* ◊ *A high wall separated our back yard from the playing field.* **4** [V] **~ (from sb)** to stop living together as a couple with your husband, wife or partner: *He separated from his wife after 20 years of marriage.* ◊ *They separated last year.* **5** [VN] **~ sb/sth (from sb/sth)** to make sb/sth different in some way from sb/sth else: *Politics is the only thing that separates us* (= that we disagree about). ◊ *Her lack of religious faith separated her from the rest of her family.* ◊ *The judges found it impossible to separate the two contestants* (= they gave them equal scores). ◊ *Only four points separate the top three teams.* **IDM** see MAN *n.*, SHEEP, WHEAT **PHRV** **,separate 'out | ,separate sth ↔ 'out** to divide into different parts; to divide sth into different parts: *to separate out different meanings*

sep·ar·ated /ˈsepəreɪtɪd/ *adj.* **~ (from sb)** no longer living with your husband, wife or partner: *Her parents are separated but not divorced.* ◊ *He's been separated from his wife for a year.*

sep·ar·ate·ly /ˈseprətli/ *adv.* **~ (from sb/sth)** as a separate person or thing; not together: *They were photographed separately and then as a group.* ◊ *Last year's figures are shown separately.*

sep·ar·ates /ˈseprəts/ *noun* [pl.] individual pieces of clothing, for example skirts, jackets, and trousers/pants, that are designed to be worn together in different combinations

sep·ar·ation /ˌsepəˈreɪʃn/ *noun* **1** [U, sing.] **~ (from sb/sth) | ~ (between A and B)** the act of separating people or things; the state of being separate: *the state's eventual separation from the federation* ◊ *the need for a clear separation between Church and State* **2** [C] a period of time that people spend apart from each other: *They were reunited after a separation of more than 20 years.* **3** [C] a decision that a husband and wife make to live apart while they are still legally married: *a legal separation*—compare DIVORCE

sep·ar·at·ist /ˈseprətɪst/ *noun* a member of a group of people within a country who want to separate from the rest of the country and form their own government: *Basque separatists* ▶ **sep·ar·at·ism** /ˈseprətɪzəm/ *noun* [U]: *There has been an alarming rise in separatism and inter-ethnic violence in the country.* **sep·ar·at·ist** *adj.*: *a separatist movement*

sep·ar·ator /ˈsepəreɪtə(r)/ *noun* a machine for separating things

sepia /ˈsiːpiə/ *noun* [U] **1** a brown substance used in inks and paints and used in the past for printing photographs **2** a reddish-brown colour ▶ **sepia** *adj.* [usually before noun]: *sepia ink/prints/photographs*

sep·sis /ˈsepsɪs/ *noun* [U] (*medical*) an infection of part of the body in which PUS is produced

Sep·tem·ber /sepˈtembə(r)/ *noun* [U, C] (*abbr.* **Sept.**) the 9th month of the year, between August and October **HELP** To see how **September** is used, look at the examples at **April**.

sep·tet /sepˈtet/ *noun* **1** [C+sing./pl. *v.*] a group of seven musicians or singers **2** [C] a piece of music for seven musicians or singers

sep·tic /ˈseptɪk/ *adj.* (of a wound or part of the body) infected with harmful bacteria: *a septic finger* ◊ *A dirty cut may go septic.* **OPP** ASEPTIC

septi·cae·mia (*BrE*) (*AmE* **septi·ce·mia**) /ˌseptɪˈsiːmiə/ *noun* [U] (*medical*) infection of the blood by harmful bacteria **SYN** BLOOD POISONING

,septic 'tank *noun* a large container, usually underground, that holds human waste from toilets until the action of bacteria makes it liquid enough to soak into the ground

sep·tua·gen·ar·ian /ˌseptjuədʒəˈneəriən; *AmE* -tʃuədʒə-ˈner-/ *noun* (*formal*) a person between 70 and 79 years old

se·pul·chral /səˈpʌlkrəl/ *adj.* **1** (*literary*) looking or

sounding sad and serious; making you think of death: *He spoke in sepulchral tones.* **2** (*technical*) connected with burying dead people, or graves or sepulchres: *a sepulchral monument*

sep·ul·chre (*BrE*) (*AmE* **sep·ul·cher**) /ˈseplkə(r)/ *noun* (*old use*) a place for a dead body, either cut in rock or built of stone

se·quel /ˈsiːkwəl/ *noun* **~ (to sth)** **1** a book, film/movie, play, etc. that continues the story of an earlier one: *a sequel to the hit movie 'Sister Act'*—compare PREQUEL **2** [usually sing.] something that happens after an earlier event or as a result of an earlier event: *There was an interesting sequel to these events later in the year.*

se·quence /ˈsiːkwəns/ *noun, verb*
■ *noun* **1** [C] a set of events, actions, numbers, etc. which have a particular order and which lead to a particular result: *He described the sequence of events leading up to the robbery.* **2** [C, U] the order that events, actions, etc. happen in or should happen in: *The tasks had to be performed in a particular sequence.* ◊ *Number the pages in sequence.* ◊ *These pages are out of sequence.* **3** [C] a part of a film/movie that deals with one subject or topic or consists of one scene: *the dream sequence in the middle of the movie*
■ *verb* [VN] (*technical*) to arrange things into a sequence ▶ **se·quen·cing** *noun* [U]

the ,sequence of 'tenses *noun* [sing.] (*grammar*) the rules according to which the tense of a SUBORDINATE CLAUSE depends on the tense of a main CLAUSE, so that, for example, 'I think *that you* are *wrong*' becomes 'I thought *that you* were *wrong*' in the past tense

se·quen·tial /sɪˈkwenʃl/ *adj.* (*formal*) following in order of time or place: *sequential data processing* ▶ **se·quen·tial·ly** /-ʃəli/ *adv.*: *data stored sequentially on a computer*

se·ques·ter /sɪˈkwestə(r)/ *verb* [VN] (*law*) **1** = SEQUESTRATE **2** to keep a JURY together in a place, in order to prevent them from talking to other people about a case in a court of law, or learning about it in the newspapers, on television, etc.

se·ques·tered /sɪˈkwestəd; *AmE* -tərd/ *adj.* [usually before noun] (*literary*) (of a place) quiet and far away from people

se·ques·trate /ˈsiːkwəstreɪt/ (also **se·ques·ter**) *verb* [VN] (*law*) to take control of sb's property or ASSETS until a debt has been paid ▶ **se·ques·tra·tion** /ˌsiːkwəˈstreɪʃn/ *noun* [U, C]

se·quin /ˈsiːkwɪn/ *noun* a small circular shiny disc sewn onto clothing as decoration ▶ **se·quinned** /ˈsiːkwɪnd/ *adj.* [usually before noun]

se·quoia /sɪˈkwɔɪə/ *noun* a very tall N American tree that can live a very long time

sera *pl.* of SERUM

ser·aph /ˈserəf/ *noun* (*pl.* **ser·aph·im** /-fɪm/ or **ser·aphs**) an ANGEL of the highest rank—compare CHERUB

ser·aph·ic /səˈræfɪk/ *adj.* (*literary*) **1** as beautiful, pure, etc. as an angel: *a seraphic child/nature* **2** extremely happy: *a seraphic smile*

ser·en·ade /ˌserəˈneɪd/ *noun, verb*
■ *noun* **1** a song or tune played or sung at night by a lover outside the window of the woman he loves **2** a gentle piece of music in several parts, usually for a small group of instruments
■ *verb* [VN] to sing or play music to sb (as done in the past by a man singing under her window to the woman he loved)

ser·en·dip·ity /ˌserənˈdɪpəti/ *noun* [U] (*written*) the fact of sth interesting or pleasant happening by chance ▶ **ser·en·dip·it·ous** /-ˈdɪpətəs/ *adj.*: *serendipitous discoveries*

se·rene /səˈriːn/ *adj.* calm and peaceful: *The child's face was serene and beautiful.* ◊ *a lake, still and serene in the sunlight* ▶ **se·rene·ly** *adv.*: *serenely beautiful* ◊ *She smiled serenely.* **se·ren·ity** /səˈrenəti/ *noun* [U, sing.]: *The hotel offers a haven of peace and serenity away from the bustle of the city.*

serf /sɜːf; *AmE* sɜːrf/ *noun* (in the past) a person who was forced to live and work on land that belonged to a LANDOWNER whom they had to obey

aɪ	aʊ	eɪ	əʊ	oʊ	ɔɪ	ɪə	eə	ʊə	j	w
my	now	say	go (BrE)	go (AmE)	boy	near	hair	pure	yes	wet

serf·dom /'sɜːfdəm; AmE 'sɜːrf-/ noun [U] the system under which crops were grown by serfs; the state of being a serf: *the abolition of serfdom in Russia in 1861*

serge /sɜːdʒ; AmE sɜːrdʒ/ noun [U] a strong woollen fabric used for making clothes: *a blue serge suit*

ser·geant /'sɑːdʒənt; AmE 'sɑːrdʒ-/ noun (abbr. **Sergt, Sgt**) **1** a member of one of the middle ranks in the army and the air force, below an officer: *Sergeant Salter*—see also FLIGHT SERGEANT, STAFF SERGEANT **2** (in Britain) a police officer just below the rank of an INSPECTOR **3** (in the US) a police officer just below the rank of a LIEUTEN-ANT or CAPTAIN—see also SARGE

,sergeant 'major noun (often used as a title) **1** a soldier of middle rank in the British army who is responsible for helping the administrative officer of a particular REGI-MENT (= a large group of soldiers) **2** a soldier in the US army of the highest rank of NON-COMMISSIONED officers

ser·ial /'sɪəriəl; AmE 'sɪr-/ noun, adj.

■ noun a story on television or the radio, or in a magazine, that is broadcast or published in several separate parts: *a classic drama serial*

■ adj. **1** [usually before noun] (*technical*) arranged in a series: *tasks carried out in the same serial order* **2** [only before noun] doing the same thing in the same way several times: *a serial rapist* **3** [only before noun] (of a story, etc.) broadcast or published in several separate parts: *a novel in serial form* ► **seri·al·ly** /-iəli/ adv.

seri·al·ize (*BrE* also **-ise**) /'sɪəriəlaɪz; AmE 'sɪr-/ verb [VN] to publish or broadcast sth in parts as a serial: *The novel was serialized on TV in six parts.* ► **seri·al·iza-tion, -isa·tion** /,sɪəriəlaɪ'zeɪʃn; AmE ,sɪriələ'z-/ noun [C, U]: *a newspaper serialization of the book*

,serial 'killer noun a person who murders several people one after the other in a similar way

'serial number noun a number put on a product, such as a camera, television, etc. in order to identify it

ser·ies /'sɪəriːz; AmE 'sɪr-/ noun (pl. **ser·ies**) **1** [C, usually sing.] **~ of sth** several events or things of a similar kind that happen one after the other: *The incident sparked off a whole series of events that nobody had foreseen.* ◊ *the first / latest in a series of articles on the nature of modern society* **2** [C] a set of radio or television programmes that deal with the same subject or that have the same characters **3** [C] (*sport*) a set of sports games played between the same two teams: *England have lost the Test series* (= of cricket matches) *against India.* ◊ *the World Series* (= in baseball) **4** [U, C] (*technical*) an electrical CIRCUIT in which the current passes through all the parts in the correct order

serif /'serɪf/ noun a short line at the top or bottom of some styles of printed letters: *a serif typeface*—compare SANS SERIF

ser·ious /'sɪəriəs; AmE 'sɪr-/ adj.

BAD | **1** bad or dangerous: *a serious illness / problem / offence* ◊ *to cause serious injury / damage* ◊ *They pose a serious threat to security.* ◊ *The consequences could be serious.*

NEEDING THOUGHT | **2** needing to be thought about carefully; not only for pleasure: *a serious article* ◊ *a serious news-paper* ◊ *It's time to give serious consideration to this matter.*

IMPORTANT | **3** that must be treated as important: *We need to get down to the serious business of working out costs.* ◊ *The team is a serious contender for the title this year.*

NOT SILLY | **4** thinking about things in a careful and sens-ible way; not silly: *Be serious for a moment; this is import-ant.* ◊ *I'm afraid I'm not a very serious person.*

NOT JOKING | **5 ~ (about sb/sth)** | **~ (about doing sth)** sin-cere about sth; not joking or meant as a joke: *Believe me, I'm deadly* (= extremely) *serious.* ◊ *Don't laugh, it's a serious suggestion.* ◊ *Is she serious about wanting to sell the house?* ◊ *He's really serious about Penny and wants to get engaged.*

LARGE AMOUNT | **6** (*informal*) used to emphasize that there is a large amount of sth: *You can earn serious money doing that.* ◊ *I'm ready to do some serious eating* (= I am very hungry).

ser·ious·ly /'sɪəriəsli; AmE 'sɪr-/ adv. **1** in a serious way: *to be seriously ill / injured* ◊ *You're not seriously expecting me to believe that?* ◊ *They are seriously concerned about security.* ◊ *Smoking can seriously damage your health.* **2** (*spoken*) used at the beginning of a sentence to show a change from joking to being more serious: *Seriously though, it could be really dangerous.* **3** (*informal*) very; extremely: *They're seriously rich.* **IDM** **take sb/sth 'ser-iously** to think that sb/sth is important and deserves your attention and respect: *We take threats of this kind very seriously.* ◊ *Why can't you ever take anything ser-iously?*

ser·ious·ness /'sɪəriəsnəs; AmE 'sɪr-/ noun [U, sing.] the state of being serious: *He spoke with a seriousness that was unusual in him.* **IDM** **in all 'seriousness** very ser-iously; not as a joke

ser·mon /'sɜːmən; AmE 'sɜːrmən/ noun **1** a talk on a moral or religious subject, usually given by a religious leader during a service **2** (*informal*, usually *disapprov-ing*) moral advice that a person tries to give you in a long talk

ser·mon·ize (*BrE* also **-ise**) /'sɜːmənaɪz; AmE 'sɜːrm-/ verb [V] (*disapproving*) to give moral advice, especially when it is boring or not wanted

ser·pent /'sɜːpənt; AmE 'sɜːrp-/ noun (*literary*) a snake, especially a large one

ser·pen·tine /'sɜːpəntaɪn; AmE 'sɜːrpənti:n/ adj. (*liter-ary*) bending and twisting like a snake: *the serpentine course of the river*

ser·rated /sə'reɪtɪd/ adj. having a series of sharp points on the edge like a SAW: *a knife with a serrated edge*—picture at CUTLERY

ser·ried /'serid/ adj. [usually before noun] (*literary*) standing or arranged closely together in rows or lines: *serried ranks of soldiers*

serum /'sɪərəm; AmE 'sɪrəm/ noun (pl. **sera** /-rə/ or **ser-ums**) **1** [U] (*biology*) the thin liquid that remains from blood when the rest has CLOTTED **2** [U, C] (*medical*) serum taken from the blood of an animal and given to people to protect them from disease, poison, etc: *snakebite serum* **3** [U] any liquid like water in body TISSUE

ser·vant /'sɜːvənt; AmE 'sɜːrv-/ noun **1** a person who works in another person's house, and cooks, cleans, etc. for them: *a domestic servant* ◊ *They treat their mother like a servant.* **2** a person who works for a company or an organization: *a public servant*—see also CIVIL SERVANT **3** a person or thing that is controlled by sth: *He was willing to make himself a servant of his art.* **IDM** see OBEDIENT

serve /sɜːv; AmE sɜːrv/ verb, noun

■ verb

FOOD/DRINK | **1 ~ sth (with sth)** | **~ sth (to sb)** | **~ sb sth** to give sb food or drink, for example at a restaurant or during a meal: [VN] *Breakfast is served between 7 and 10 a.m.* ◊ *Serve the lamb with new potatoes and green beans.* ◊ *They served a wonderful meal to more than fifty delegates.* ◊ *The delegates were served with a wonderful meal.* ◊ *Pour the sauce over the pasta and serve immediately.* ◊ [VNN] *She served us a delicious lunch.* ◊ [V] *Shall I serve?* ◊ [VN-ADJ] *The quiche can be served hot or cold.* **2** [VN] (of an amount of food) to be enough for sb/sth: *This dish will serve four hungry people.*

CUSTOMERS | **3** (*especially BrE*) to help a customer or sell them sth in a shop/store: [VN] *Are you being served?* [also V]

BE USEFUL | **4** [VN] to be useful to sb in achieving or satisfy-ing sth: *These experiments serve no useful purpose.* ◊ *Most of their economic policies serve the interests of big business.* ◊ *How can we best serve the needs of future generations?* ◊ *His linguistic ability served him well in his chosen profession.*

PROVIDE STH | **5** [VN] **~ sb (with sth)** to provide an area or a group of people with a product or service: *The town is well served with buses and major road links.* ◊ *The centre will serve the whole community.*

BE SUITABLE | **6** [V] **~ (as sth)** to be suitable for a particular use, especially when nothing else is available: *The sofa will serve as a bed for a night or two.*

S

HAVE PARTICULAR RESULT | **7 ~ (as sth)** to have a particular effect or result: [V] *The judge said the punishment would serve as a warning to others.* ◊ [Vtoinf] *The attack was unsuccessful and served only to alert the enemy.*

WORK | **8 ~ (sb) (as sth)| ~ (in/on/with sth)| ~ (under/ with sb)** to work or perform duties for a person, an organization, a country, etc: [V] *He served as a captain in the army.* ◊ *She served in the medical corps.* ◊ *He served under Edward Heath in the 1970s.* ◊ [VN] *I wanted to work somewhere where I could serve the community.* ◊ *He served the family faithfully for many years* (= as a servant). **9 ~ (as sth)** to spend a period of time in a particular job or training for a job: [VN] *He served a one-year apprentice-ship.* ◊ [V] *She was elected to serve for another year as secretary of the local party.*

TIME IN PRISON | **10** [VN] to spend a period of time in prison: *prisoners serving life sentences* ◊ *She is serving two years for theft.* ◊ *He has **served time** (= been to prison) before.*

OFFICIAL DOCUMENT | **11** [VN] **~ sth (on sb)| ~ sb with sth** (*law*) to give or send sb an official document, especially one that orders them to appear in a court of law: *to serve a writ/summons on sb* ◊ *to serve sb with a writ/summons*

IN SPORT | **12** (in tennis, etc.) to start playing by throwing the ball into the air and hitting it: [V] *Who's serving?* ◊ [VN] *She served an ace.*—picture on page 1250

IDM **it serves sb 'right (for doing sth)** used to say that sth that has happened to sb is their own fault and they deserve it: *Left you, did she? It serves you right for being so selfish.* **serve your/its 'turn** (*BrE*) to be useful for a particular purpose or period of time **serve two 'masters** (usually used in negative sentences) to support two opposing parties, principles, etc. at the same time—more at FIRST *adv.*, MEMORY

PHRV **,serve sth↔'out 1** to continue doing sth, especially working or staying in prison, for a fixed period of time that has been set: *He has three more years in prison before he's served out his sentence.* ◊ (*BrE*) *They didn't want me to serve out my notice.* **2** (*BrE*) = SERVE STH UP **,serve sth↔'up** (*BrE* also **,serve sth↔'out**) **1** to put food onto plates and give it to people: *He served up a delicious meal.* **2** to give or offer sth: *She served up the usual excuse.*

■ *noun* (in tennis, etc.) the action of serving the ball to your opponent

ser·ver /ˈsɜːvə(r); *AmE* ˈsɜːrv-/ *noun* **1** (*computing*) a computer program that controls or supplies information to several computers connected in a NETWORK; the main computer on which this program is run: *a file/print server* **2** (*sport*) a player who is serving, for example in tennis **3** [usually pl.] a kitchen UTENSIL (= tool) used for putting food onto sb's plate: *salad servers*—picture at CUTLERY **4** (*AmE*) a person who serves food in a restaurant; a WAITER or WAITRESS **5** a person who helps a priest during a church service

serv·ery /ˈsɜːvəri; *AmE* ˈsɜːrv-/ *noun* (*pl.* **-ies**) (*BrE*) part of a restaurant where you collect your food to take back to your table

ser·vice /ˈsɜːvɪs; *AmE* ˈsɜːrv-/ *noun, verb*

■ *noun*

PROVIDING STH | **1** [C] a system that provides sth that the public needs, organized by the government or a private company: *the ambulance/bus/telephone service* ◊ *The government aims to improve **public** services, especially education.* ◊ *Essential services* (= the supply of water, gas, electricity) *will be maintained.*—see also EMERGENCY SERVICES, POSTAL SERVICE **2** (also **Service**) [C] an organization or a company that provides sth for the public or does sth for the government: *the prison service* ◊ *BBC World Service*—see also CIVIL SERVICE, DIPLOMATIC SERVICE, FIRE SERVICE, HEALTH SERVICE, INTERNAL REVENUE SERVICE, NATIONAL HEALTH SERVICE, SECRET SERVICE, SECURITY SERVICE, SOCIAL SERVICES **3** [C, U] a business whose work involves doing sth for customers but not producing goods; the work that such a business does: *financial/banking/insurance services* ◊ *the development of new goods and services* ◊ *Smith's Catering Services* (= a company) *offers the best value.* ◊ *We guarantee (an) excellent*

service. ◊ *the service sector* (= the part of the economy involved in this type of business) ◊ *a service industry*

IN HOTEL/SHOP/RESTAURANT | **4** [U] the serving of customers in hotels, restaurants, and shops/stores: *The food was good but the service was very slow.* ◊ *10% will be added to your bill for service.* ◊ *Our main concern is to provide quality **customer service**.*—see also ROOM SERVICE, SELF-SERVICE

WORK FOR ORGANIZATION | **5** [U] **~ (to sth)** the work that sb does for an organization, etc., especially when it continues for a long time or is admired very much: *She has just celebrated 25 years' service with the company.* ◊ *The employees have good conditions of service.* ◊ *After retiring, she became involved in voluntary service in the local community.*—see also JURY SERVICE

OF VEHICLE/MACHINE | **6** [U] the use that you can get from a vehicle or machine; the state of being used: *That computer gave us very good service.* ◊ *The ship will be taken out of service within two years.* **7** [C] an examination of a vehicle or machine followed by any work that is necessary to keep it operating well: *I had taken the car in for a service.* ◊ *We offer excellent **after sales service** on all our goods.* ◊ *a service engineer*

SKILLS/HELP | **8** [usually pl.] **~ (of sb)| ~ (as sb/sth)** the particular skills or help that a person is able to offer: *You need the services of a good lawyer.* ◊ *He offered his services as a driver.*

ARMY/NAVY/AIR FORCE | **9** [C, usually pl., U] the army, the navy and the air force; the work done by people in them: *Most of the boys went straight into the services.* ◊ *He saw service in North Africa.* ◊ *a service family*—see also ACTIVE SERVICE, MILITARY SERVICE, NATIONAL SERVICE

RELIGIOUS CEREMONY | **10** [C] a religious ceremony: *to attend morning/evening service* ◊ *a funeral/marriage/memorial service*

BUS/TRAIN | **11** [C, usually sing.] a bus, train, etc. that goes regularly to a particular place at a particular time: *the cancellation of the 10.15 service to Glasgow*

ON MOTORWAY | **12** (**services**) [sing.+ sing./pl. *v.*] (*BrE*) a place beside a motorway where you can stop for petrol, a meal, the toilets, etc: *motorway services* ◊ *It's five miles to the next services.*—see also SERVICE AREA, SERVICE STATION

IN TENNIS | **13** [C] an act of hitting the ball in order to start playing; the way that you hit it [SYN] SERVE: *It's your service* (= your turn to start playing). ◊ *Her service has improved.*

SET OF PLATES | **14** [C] a complete set of plates, dishes, etc. that match each other: *a tea service* (= cups, SAUCERS, a TEAPOT and plates, for serving tea)—see also DINNER SERVICE

BEING SERVANT | **15** [U] (*old-fashioned*) the state or position of being a servant: *to be in/go into service* (= to be/become a servant)

OF OFFICIAL DOCUMENT | **16** [U] (*law*) the formal giving of an official document, etc. to sb: *the service of a demand for payment*

IDM **at the 'service of sb/sth | at sb's 'service** completely available for sb to use or to help sb: *Health care must be at the service of all who need it.* (*formal or humorous*) *If you need anything, I am at your service.* **be of 'service (to sb)** (*formal*) to be useful or helpful: *Can I be of service to anyone?* **do sb a/no 'service** (*formal*) to do sth that is helpful/not helpful to sb: *She was doing herself no service by remaining silent.*—more at PRESS *v.*

■ *verb* [VN]

VEHICLE/MACHINE | **1** [usually passive] to examine a vehicle or machine and repair it if necessary so that it continues to work correctly: *We need to have the car serviced.*

PROVIDE STH | **2** (*written*) to provide people with sth they need, such as shops/stores, or a transport system [SYN] SERVE: *Botley is well serviced by a regular bus route into Oxford.* ◊ *This department services the international sales force* (= provides services for it).

PAY INTEREST | **3** (*technical*) to pay interest on money that has been borrowed: *The company can no longer service its debts.*

ser·vice·able /ˈsɜːvɪsəbl; *AmE* ˈsɜːrv-/ *adj.* suitable to be

used: *The carpet is worn but still serviceable.* OPP UNSER-
VICEABLE

'service area *noun* (*BrE*) a place on a motorway where
you can stop and buy food, petrol, have a meal, go to the
toilet, etc.

'service charge *noun* **1** an amount of money that is
added to a bill, as an extra charge for a service: *That will
be $50, plus a service charge of $2.50.* **2** (*BrE*) an amount of
money that is added to a bill in a restaurant, for example
10% of the total, that goes to pay for the work of the staff
3 an amount of money that is paid to the owner of an
apartment building for services such as putting out rub-
bish/garbage, cleaning the stairs, etc.

ser·vice·man /'sɜːvɪsmən; *AmE* 'sɜːrv-/, **ser·vice·**
woman /'sɜːvɪswʊmən; *AmE* 'sɜːrv-/ *noun* (*pl.* **-men**
/-mən/, **-women** /-wɪmɪn/) a man or woman who is a
member of the armed forces

'service road (*AmE* also **'frontage road**) *noun* a side
road that runs parallel to a main road, that you use to
reach houses, shops/stores, etc.

'service station *noun* **1** = PETROL STATION **2** (*BrE*) an
area and building beside a motorway where you can buy
food and petrol, go to the toilet, etc: *a motorway service
station*

ser·vic·ing /'sɜːvɪsɪŋ; *AmE* 'sɜːrv-/ *noun* [U] **1** the act of
checking and repairing a vehicle, machine, etc. to keep it
in good condition: *Like any other type of equipment it
requires regular servicing.* **2** (*finance*) the act of paying
interest on money that has been borrowed: *debt servicing*

ser·vi·ette /ˌsɜːvi'et; *AmE* ˌsɜːrv-/ *noun* (*BrE*) a piece of
fabric or paper used at meals for protecting your clothes
and cleaning your lips and fingers SYN NAPKIN

ser·vile /'sɜːvaɪl; *AmE* 'sɜːrvl; -vaɪl/ *adj.* (*disapproving*)
wanting too much to please sb and obey them: *Parents
have no right to demand servile obedience from their children.* ▶ **ser·vil·ity** /sɜː'vɪləti; *AmE* sɜːr'v-/ *noun* [U]

serv·ing /'sɜːvɪŋ; *AmE* 'sɜːrvɪŋ/ *noun* an amount of food
for one person: *This recipe will be enough for four serv-
ings.*

ser·vi·tude /'sɜːvɪtjuːd; *AmE* 'sɜːrvətuːd/ *noun* [U]
(*formal*) the condition of being a slave or being forced to
obey another person

servo /'sɜːvəʊ; *AmE* 'sɜːrvoʊ/ *noun* (*pl.* **-os**) (*technical*) a
mechanism that controls a larger mechanism

ses·ame /'sesəmi/ *noun* [U] a tropical plant grown for
its seeds and their oil that are used in cooking: *sesame
seeds*—picture on page A1—see also OPEN SESAME

ses·sion /'seʃn/ *noun* **1** a period of time that is spent
doing a particular activity: *a photo/recording/training
session* ◊ *The course is made up of 12 two-hour sessions.*—
see also JAM SESSION **2** a formal meeting or series of
meetings of a court of law, a parliament, etc.; a period of
time when such meetings are held: *a session of the UN
General Assembly* ◊ *The court is now in session.* ◊ *The
committee met in closed session* (= with nobody else
present).—see also QUARTER SESSIONS **3** (*ScotE*) a school or
university year

set /set/ *verb, noun, adj.*
■ *verb* (**set·ting**, **set**, **set**)

‣ PUT/START | **1** [VN+*adv./prep.*] to put sth/sb in a particular
place or position: *She set a tray down on the table.* ◊ *They
ate everything that was set in front of them.* ◊ *The house is
set* (= situated) *in fifty acres of parkland.* **2** to cause sb/sth
to be in a particular state; to start sth happening: [VN,
+*adv./prep.*] *Her manner immediately set everyone at their
ease.* ◊ *He pulled the lever and set the machine in motion.* ◊
[VN-ADJ] *The hijackers set the hostages free.* ◊ [VN-ing] *Her
remarks set me thinking.*

‣ PLAY/BOOK/MOVIE | **3** [VN] [usually passive] to place the
action of a play, novel or film/movie in a particular
place, time, etc: *The novel is set in London in the 1960s.*

‣ CLOCK/MACHINE | **4** [VN] to prepare or arrange sth so that it
is ready for use or in position: *She set the camera on
automatic.* ◊ *I set my watch by* (= make it show the same
time as) *the TV.* ◊ *Set the alarm for 7 o'clock.*

‣ TABLE | **5** [VN] ~ a/the table to arrange knives, forks, etc.

on a table for a meal: *Could you set the table for dinner?* ◊
The table was set for six guests.

‣ JEWELLERY | **6** [VN] [usually passive] ~ A in B | ~ B with A
to put a precious stone into a piece of jewellery: *She had
the sapphire set in a gold ring.* ◊ *Her bracelet was set with
emeralds.*

‣ ARRANGE | **7** [VN] to arrange or fix sth; to decide on sth:
They haven't set a date for their wedding yet. ◊ *The
government has set strict limits on public spending this
year.*

‣ EXAMPLE/STANDARD, etc. | **8** [VN] to fix sth so that others copy
it or try to achieve it: *This could set a new fashion.* ◊
They set high standards of customer service. ◊ *I am
unwilling to set a precedent.* ◊ *She set a new world
record for the high jump.* ◊ *I rely on you to set a good
example.*

‣ WORK/TASK | **9** ~ sth (for sb) | ~ sb (to do sth) to give sb a
piece of work, a task, etc: [VN] *Who will be setting* (=
writing the questions for) *the French exam?* ◊ *What books
have been set* (= are to be studied) *for the English course?* ◊
[VNN, VN] *She's set herself a difficult task.* ◊ *She's set a
difficult task for herself.* ◊ [VN to inf] *I've set myself to finish
the job by the end of the month.*—see also SET BOOK

‣ BECOME FIRM | **10** to become firm or hard: [V] *Leave the
concrete to set for a few hours.* ◊ [V-ADJ] *The glue had set
hard.*

‣ FACE | **11** [VN] [usually passive] to fix your face into a firm
expression: *Her jaw was set in a determined manner.*

‣ HAIR | **12** [VN] to arrange sb's hair while it is wet so that it
dries in a particular style: *She had her hair washed and
set.*

‣ BONE | **13** [VN] to put a broken bone into a fixed position
and hold it there, so that it will heal; to heal in this way:
The surgeon set her broken arm. [also V]

‣ FOR PRINTING | **14** [VN] (*technical*) to prepare a book, etc. for
printing: *Books were previously set by hand but much of
the work is now done by computer.*—see also TYPESETTER

‣ WORDS TO MUSIC | **15** [VN] ~ sth (to sth) to write music to go
with words: *Schubert set many poems to music.*

‣ OF SUN/MOON | **16** [V] to go down below the HORIZON: *We sat
and watched the sun setting.*—see also SUNSET OPP RISE

IDM Idioms containing **set** are at the entries for the
nouns and adjectives in the idioms, for example **set the
pace** is at **pace** *n.*

PHR V **'set about sb** (*BrE, old-fashioned, informal*) to
attack sb **'set about sth** [no passive] to start doing sth:
She set about the business of cleaning the house. ◊ [+-ing]
We need to set about finding a solution.

,set sb a'gainst sb to make sb oppose a friend, relative,
etc: *She accused her husband of setting the children
against her.* **set sth (off) against sth 1** to judge sb/sth
by comparing good or positive qualities with bad or
negative ones: *Set against the benefits of the new technology, there is also a strong possibility that jobs will be lost.*
2 (*finance*) to record sth as a business cost as a way of
reducing the amount of tax you must pay: *to set capital
costs off against tax*

,set sb/sth a'part (from sb/sth) to make sb/sth different
from or better than others: *Her clear and elegant writing
sets her apart from other journalists.* **,set sth ↔ a'part**
(for sth) [usually passive] to keep sth for a special use or
purpose: *Two rooms were set apart for use as libraries.*

,set sth ↔ a'side 1 to move sth to one side until you need
it **2** to save or keep money or time for a particular
purpose: *She tries to set aside some money every month.*
3 to not consider sth, because other things are more
important: *Let's set aside my personal feelings for now.*
4 (*law*) to state that a decision made by a court of law is
not legally valid: *The verdict was set aside by the Appeal
Court.*—related noun SET-ASIDE

,set sth/sb ↔ 'back to delay the progress of sth/sb by a
particular time: *The bad weather set back the building
programme by several weeks.*—related noun SETBACK **,set
sb 'back sth** [no passive] (*informal*) to cost sb a particular amount of money: *The repairs could set you back over
£200.* **,set sth 'back (from sth)** [usually passive] to place

---

æ	ɑː	e	ɜː	ə	ɪ	iː	i	ɒ	ɔː	ʌ	ʊ	u	uː
cat	father	ten	bird	about	sit	see	many	got	saw	cup	put	actual	too

(BrE)

sth, especially a building, at a distance from sth: *The house is set well back from the road.*

,set sb↔'down (*BrE*) (of a bus or train, or its driver) to stop and allow sb to get off: *Passengers may be set down and picked up only at the official stops.* **,set sth↔'down 1** to write sth down on paper in order to record it **2** to give sth as a rule, principle, etc: *The standards were set down by the governing body.*

,set 'forth (*literary*) to start a journey **,set sth↔'forth** (*formal*) to present sth or make it known: *The President set forth his views in a television broadcast.*

,set 'in (of rain, bad weather, infection, etc.) to begin and seem likely to continue: *The rain seemed to have set in for the day.* **,set sth 'in/'into sth** [usually passive] to fasten sth into a flat surface so that it does not stick out from it: *a plaque set into the wall*

,set 'off to begin a journey: *We set off for London just after ten.* **,set sth↔'off 1** to make a bomb, etc. explode: *A gang of boys were setting off fireworks in the street.* **2** to make an ALARM start ringing: *Opening this door will set off the alarm.* **3** to start a process or series of events: *Panic on the stock market set off a wave of selling.* **4** to make sth more noticeable or attractive by being placed near it: *That blouse sets off the blue of her eyes.* **,set sb 'off (doing sth)** to make sb start doing sth such as laughing, crying or talking

'set on/upon sb [usually passive] to attack sb suddenly: *I opened the gate, and was immediately set on by a large dog.* **'set sb/sth on sb** to make a person or an animal attack sb suddenly: *The farmer threatened to set his dogs on us.*

,set 'out 1 to leave a place and begin a journey: *They set out on the last stage of their journey.* **2** to begin a job, task, etc. with a particular aim or goal: *She set out to break the world record.* ◊ *They succeeded in what they set out to do.* **,set sth↔'out 1** to arrange or display things: *We'll need to set out some chairs for the meeting.* ◊ *Her work is always very well set out.* **2** to present ideas, facts, etc. in an organized way, in speech or writing: *He set out his objections to the plan.* ◊ *She set out the reasons for her resignation in a long letter.*

,set 'to (*old-fashioned, informal*) to begin doing sth in a busy or determined way

,set sb↔'up 1 to provide sb with the money that they need in order to do sth: *A bank loan helped to set him up in business.* **2** (*informal*) to make sb healthier, stronger, more lively, etc: *The break from work really set me up for the new year.* **3** (*informal*) to trick sb, especially by making them appear guilty of sth: *He denied the charges, saying the police had set him up.*—related noun SET-UP **,set sth↔'up 1** to build sth or put sth somewhere: *The police set up roadblocks on routes out of the city.* **2** to make a piece of equipment or a machine ready for use: *She set up her stereo in her bedroom.* **3** to arrange for sth to happen: *I've set up a meeting for Friday.* **4** to create sth or start it: *to set up a business* ◊ *A fund will be set up for the dead men's families.* **5** to start a process or a series of events: *The slump on Wall Street set up a chain reaction in stock markets around the world.*—related noun SET-UP **,set (yourself) 'up (as sb)** to start running a business: *She took out a bank loan and set up on her own.* ◊ *After leaving college, he set himself up as a freelance photographer.*

■ *noun*

GROUP | **1** [C] **~ (of sth)** a group of similar things that belong together in some way: *a set of six chairs* ◊ *a complete set of her novels* ◊ *a set of false teeth* ◊ *a new set of rules to learn* ◊ *You can borrow my keys—I have a spare set.*—see also TEA SET **2** [C] a group of objects used together, for example for playing a game: *a chess set* **3** [C+sing./pl. *v.*] (sometimes *disapproving*) a group of people who have similar interests and spend a lot of time together socially: *the smart set* (= rich, fashionable people) ◊ *Dublin's literary set*—see also THE JET SET

TV/RADIO | **4** [C] a piece of equipment for receiving television or radio signals

FOR PLAY/MOVIE | **5** (*AmE* also **set-ting**) [C] the scenery used for a play, film/movie, etc: *We need volunteers to help build and paint the set.* **6** [C, U] a place where a play

is performed or part of a film/movie is filmed: *The cast must all be on (the) set by 7 a.m.*

IN SPORT | **7** [C] one section of a match in games such as tennis or VOLLEYBALL: *She won in straight sets* (= without losing a set).

MATHEMATICS | **8** [C] a group of things that have a shared quality: *set function/theory*

POP MUSIC | **9** [C] a series of songs or pieces of music that a musician or group performs at a concert: *a stunning solo set of ten songs*

CLASS | **10** [C] (*BrE*) a group of school students with a similar ability in a particular subject: *She's in the top set for French.*

OF FACE/BODY | **11** [sing.] **~ of sth** the way in which sb's face or body is fixed in a particular expression, especially one showing determination: *She admired the firm set of his jaw.*

HAIR | **12** [sing.] an act of arranging hair in a particular style while it is wet: *A shampoo and set costs £15.*

BECOMING FIRM | **13** [sing.] the state of becoming firm or solid

ANIMAL'S HOME | **14** [C] = SETT

PLANT | **15** [C] a young plant, SHOOT etc. for planting: *onion sets*

■ *adj.*

IN POSITION | **1** in a particular position: *a house set in 40 acres of parkland* ◊ *He had close-set eyes.*

PLANNED | **2** [usually before noun] planned or fixed: *Each person was given set jobs to do.* ◊ *The school funds a set number of free places.* ◊ *Mornings in our house always follow a set pattern.*—see also SET BOOK

OPINIONS/IDEAS | **3** not likely to change: *set ideas/opinions/views on how to teach* ◊ *As people get older, they get set in their ways.*

MEAL | **4** [only before noun] (of a meal in a restaurant) having a fixed price and a limited choice of dishes: *a set dinner/lunch/meal* ◊ *Shall we have the set menu?*

LIKELY/READY | **5** **~ for sth/ ~ to do sth** likely to do sth; ready for sth or to do sth: *Interest rates look set to rise again.* ◊ *The team looks set for victory.* ◊ *Be set to leave by 10 o'clock*

FACE | **6** [usually before noun] (of a person's expression) fixed; not natural: *a set smile* ◊ *His face took on a set expression.*

IDM **be (dead) set against sth/against doing sth** to be strongly opposed to sth: *Why are you so dead set against the idea?* **be 'set on sth/on doing sth** to want to do or have sth very much; to be determined to do sth—more at MARK *n.*

'set-aside *noun* [U] a system in which the government pays farmers not to use some of their land for growing crops; the land that the farmers are paid not to use

set·back /'setbæk/ *noun* a difficulty or problem that delays or prevents sth, or makes a situation worse: *The team suffered a major setback when their best player was injured.* ◊ *The breakdown in talks represents a temporary setback in the peace process.*

,set 'book (also **,set 'text**) *noun* (both *BrE*) a book that students must study for a particular exam

,set 'piece *noun* **1** a part of a play, film/movie, piece of music, etc. that has a well-known pattern or style, and is used to create a particular effect **2** (*BrE*) a move in a game, especially football, that is well planned and practised

'set square (*BrE*) (*AmE* **tri·angle**) *noun* an instrument for drawing straight lines and angles, made from a flat piece of plastic or metal in the shape of a triangle with one angle of 90°

sett (also **set**) /set/ *noun* a hole in the ground where a BADGER lives

set·tee /se'ti:/ *noun* (*BrE*) a long comfortable seat with a back and arms, for two or more people to sit on **SYN** SOFA, COUCH

set·ter /'setə(r)/ *noun* **1** a large dog with long hair, sometimes used in hunting. There are several types of setter:

aɪ	aʊ	eɪ	əʊ	oʊ	ɔɪ	ɪə	eə	ʊə	j	w
my	now	say	go (BrE)	go (AmE)	boy	near	hair	pure	yes	wet

an Irish setter ◊ *a red setter* **2** (often in compounds) a person who sets sth: *a quiz setter*—see also JET-SETTER, PACESETTER, TRENDSETTER

set·ting /'setɪŋ/ *noun* **1** a set of surroundings; the place at which sth happens: *a rural/an ideal/a beautiful/an idyllic setting* ◊ *It was the perfect setting for a wonderful Christmas.* ◊ *People tend to behave differently in different social settings.* **2** the place and time at which the action of a play, novel, etc. takes place: *short stories with a contemporary setting* **3** (*AmE*) = SET (5) **4** a position at which the controls on a machine can be set, to set the speed, height, temperature, etc: *The performance of the engine was tested at different settings.* **5** (*music*) music written to go with a poem, etc: *Schubert's setting of a poem by Goethe* **6** a piece of metal in which a precious stone is fixed to form a piece of jewellery: *a ruby in a heavy gold setting* **7** a complete set of equipment for eating with (knife, fork, spoon, glass, etc.) for one person, arranged on a table: *a place setting*

set·tle /'setl/ *verb, noun*
■ *verb*
UNDERLINE END ARGUMENT | **1** to put an end to an argument or a disagreement: [VN] *to settle a dispute/an argument/a matter* ◊ *It's time you settled your differences with your father.* ◊ [V] *There is pressure on the unions to settle.* ◊ *The company has agreed to settle out of court* (= come to an agreement without going to court).

DECIDE/ARRANGE | **2** to decide or arrange sth finally: [VN] [often passive] *It's all settled—we're leaving on the nine o'clock plane.* ◊ (spoken) *Bob will be there? That settles it. I'm not coming.* ◊ *He had to settle his affairs* (= arrange all his personal business) *in Paris before he could return home.* [also VN that]

CHOOSE PERMANENT HOME | **3** [V +adv./prep.] to make a place your permanent home: *She settled in Vienna after her father's death.* **4** (of a group of people) to make your permanent home in a country or an area as COLONISTS: [VN] [usually passive] *This region was settled by the Dutch in the nineteenth century.* [also V]

INTO COMFORTABLE POSITION/STATE | **5** ~ (**back**) to make yourself or sb else comfortable in a new position: [V] *Ellie settled back in her seat.* ◊ [VN] *He settled himself comfortably in his usual chair.* ◊ *I settled her on the sofa and put a blanket over her.* **6** [VN +adv./prep.] to put sth carefully in a position so that it does not move: *She settled the blanket around her knees.* **7** to become or make sb/sth become calm or relaxed: [V] *The baby wouldn't settle.* ◊ [VN] *I took a pill to help settle my nerves.* ◊ *This should settle your stomach.*

COME TO REST | **8** [V] ~ (**on/over sth**) to fall from above and come to rest on sth; to stay for some time on sth: *Dust had settled on everything.* ◊ *Two birds settled on the fence.* ◊ *I don't think the snow will settle* (= remain on the ground without melting). ◊ *His gaze settled on her face.*

SINK DOWN | **9** to sink slowly down; to make sth do this: [V] *The contents of the package may have settled in transit.* [also VN]

PAY MONEY | **10** ~ **sth** | ~ (**up**) (**with sb**) to pay the money that you owe: [VN] *Please settle your bill before leaving the hotel.* ◊ *The insurance company is refusing to settle her claim.* ◊ [V] *Let me settle with you for the meal.* ◊ *I'll pay now—we can settle up later.*

IDM **settle a 'score/an ac'count** (**with sb**) | **settle an old 'score** to hurt or punish sb who has harmed or cheated you in the past: *'Who would do such a thing?' 'Maybe someone with an old score to settle.'*—more at DUST *n.*

PHRV ,**settle 'down 1** to get into a comfortable position, either sitting or lying: *I settled down with a book.* **2** to start to have a quieter way of life, living in one place: *When are you going to get married and settle down?* ,**settle 'down** | ,**settle sb↔'down** to become or make sb become calm, less excited, etc: *It always takes the class a while to settle down at the start of the lesson.* **settle** (**down**) **to sth** to begin to give your attention to sth: *They finally settled down to a discussion of the main issues.* ◊ *He found it hard to settle to his work.* '**settle for sth** to accept sth that is not completely satisfactory but is the best that

is available: *In the end they had to settle for a draw.* ◊ *I couldn't afford the house I really wanted, so I had to settle for second best.* ,**settle 'in** | ,**settle 'into sth** to move into a new home, job, etc. and start to feel comfortable there: *How are the kids settling into their new school?* '**settle on sth** to choose or make a decision about sth after thinking about it: *Have you settled on a name for the baby yet?* '**settle sth on sb** (*law*) to formally arrange to give money or property to sb, especially in a WILL

■ *noun* an old-fashioned piece of furniture with a long wooden seat and a high back and arms, often also with a box for storing things under the seat

set·tled /'setld/ *adj.* **1** not likely to change or move: *dry and settled weather* ◊ *a settled way of life* **2** comfortable and happy with your home, job, way of life, etc: *You'll feel more settled when you've been here a few weeks.* OPP UNSETTLED

settle·ment /'setlmənt/ *noun* **1** [C] an official agreement that ends an argument between two people or groups: *to negotiate a peace settlement* ◊ *The management and unions have reached a settlement over new working conditions.* ◊ *an out-of-court settlement* (= money that is paid to sb or an agreement that is made to stop sb going to court) **2** [U] the action of reaching an agreement: *the settlement of a claim/dispute* **3** [C] (*law*) the conditions, or a document stating the conditions, on which money or property is given to sb: *a divorce/marriage/property settlement* **4** [U] the action of paying back money that you owe: *the settlement of a debt* ◊ *a cheque in settlement of a bill* **5** [C] a place where people have come to live and make their homes, especially where few or no people lived before: *signs of an Iron Age settlement* **6** [U] the process of people making their homes in a place: *the settlement of the American West*

set·tler /'setlə(r)/ *noun* a person who goes to live in a new country or region: *white settlers in Africa*

,**set-'to** *noun* [sing.] (*informal, especially BrE*) a small fight or an argument

,**set-,top 'box** *noun* a device that changes a DIGITAL television signal into a form which can be seen on an ordinary television

'**set-up** *noun* [usually sing.] (*informal*) **1** a way of organizing sth; a system: *I've only been here a couple of weeks and I don't really know the set-up.* **2** a situation in which sb tricks you or makes it seem as if you have done sth wrong: *He didn't steal the goods. It was a set-up.*

seven /'sevn/ *number* 7 HELP There are examples of how to use numbers at the entry for **five**. IDM see SIX

seven·teen /,sevn'ti:n/ *number* 17 ▶ **seven·teenth** /,sevn'ti:nθ/ *ordinal number*

sev·enth /'sevnθ/ *ordinal number, noun*
■ *ordinal number* 7th HELP There are examples of how to use ordinal numbers at the entry for **fifth**. IDM **in seventh 'heaven** extremely happy: *Now that he's been promoted he's in seventh heaven.*
■ *noun* each of seven equal parts of sth

sev·enty /'sevnti/ *number* **1** 70 **2** (**the seventies**) [pl.] numbers, years or temperatures from 70 to 79 ▶ **seven·ti·eth** /'sevntiəθ/ *ordinal number*: *his seventieth birthday* IDM **in your 'seventies** between the ages of 70 and 79

sever /'sevə(r)/ *verb* [VN] (*formal*) **1** ~ **sth** (**from sth**) to cut sth into two pieces; to cut sth off sth: *to sever a rope* ◊ *a severed artery* ◊ *His hand was severed from his arm.* **2** to completely end a relationship or all communication with sb: *The two countries have severed all diplomatic links.* ◊ *to sever relations/ties/connections*

sev·eral /'sevrəl/ *det., pron., adj.*
■ *det., pron.* more than two but not very many: *Several letters arrived this morning.* ◊ *He's written several books about India.* ◊ *Several more people than usual came to the meeting.* ◊ *If you're looking for a photo of Alice you'll find several in here.* ◊ *Several of the paintings were destroyed in the fire.*
■ *adj.* (*formal*) separate: *They said goodbye and went their several ways.*

sev·er·al·ly /'sevrəli/ *adv.* (*formal or law*) separately:

b	d	f	g	h	k	l	m	n	p	r
bad	did	fall	get	hat	cat	leg	man	now	pen	red

*Tenants are **jointly and severally** liable for payment of the rent.*

sev·er·ance /ˈsevərəns/ *noun* [sing., U] (*formal*) **1** the act of ending a connection or relationship: *the severance of diplomatic relations* ◇ *the severance of Church and State* **2** the act of ending sb's contract of employment: *employees given notice of severance* ◇ *severance pay/terms*

se·vere /sɪˈvɪə(r); *AmE* -ˈvɪr/ *adj.* (**se·ver·er, se·ver·est**)
<u>VERY BAD</u> **1** extremely bad or serious: *a severe handicap* ◇ *His injuries are severe.* ◇ *severe weather conditions* ◇ *a severe winter* (= one during which the weather conditions are extremely bad) ◇ *The party suffered severe losses during the last election.* ◇ *a severe shortage of qualified staff*
<u>PUNISHMENT</u> **2 ~ (on/with sb)** punishing sb in an extreme way when they break a particular set of rules [SYN] HARSH: *The courts are becoming more severe on young offenders.* ◇ *a severe punishment/sentence*
<u>NOT KIND</u> **3** not kind or sympathetic and showing disapproval of sb/sth: *a severe look/expression* ◇ *She was a severe woman who seldom smiled.*
<u>VERY DIFFICULT</u> **4** extremely difficult and requiring a lot of skill or ability [SYN] STIFF: *The marathon is a severe test of stamina.*
<u>STYLE/APPEARANCE/CLOTHING</u> **5** (*disapproving*) extremely plain and lacking any decoration: *Modern furniture is a little too severe for my taste.* ◇ *Her hair was short and severe.*

▶ **se·vere·ly** *adv.*: *severely disabled* ◇ *areas severely affected by unemployment* ◇ *Anyone breaking the law will be severely punished.* ◇ *a severely critical report* ◇ *Her hair was tied severely in a bun.* **se·ver·ity** /sɪˈverəti/ *noun* [U]: *A prison sentence should match the severity of the crime.* ◇ *The chances of a full recovery will depend on the severity of her injuries.* ◇ *the severity of the problem* ◇ *He frowned with mock severity.* ◇ *The elaborate facade contrasts strongly with the severity of the interior.*

sew /səʊ; *AmE* soʊ/ *verb* (**sewed, sewn** /səʊn; *AmE* soʊn/ or **sewed**) **1** to use a needle and thread to make stitches in fabric: [V] *My mother taught me how to sew.* ◇ *to sew by hand/machine* ◇ [VN] *to sew a seam/hem* **2** [VN] **~ sth (on)** to make, repair or attach sth using a needle and thread: *She sews all her own clothes.* ◇ *Can you sew a button on for me?* [PHRV] **ˌsew sth↔ˈup 1** to join or repair sth by sewing: *to sew up a seam* **2** [often passive] (*informal*) to arrange sth in a satisfactory way: *It didn't take me long to sew up the deal.* ◇ *They think they **have** the election **sewn up*** (= they think they are definitely going to win).

sew·age /ˈsuːɪdʒ; *BrE* also ˈsjuː-/ *noun* [U] used water and waste substances that are produced by human bodies, that are carried away from houses and factories through special pipes (= SEWERS): *a ban on the dumping of raw sewage* (= that has not been treated with chemicals) *at sea* ◇ *sewage pipes/disposal*

ˈsewage farm *noun* (*BrE*) = SEWAGE WORKS

ˈsewage plant (also **sewage ˈtreatment plant**) *noun* (*especially AmE*) = SEWAGE WORKS

ˈsewage works (also **sewage ˈtreatment works, sewage disˈposal works**) *noun* [C+sing./pl. *v.*] (*pl.* **ˈsewage works**) (*BrE*) a place where chemicals are used to clean sewage so that it can then be allowed to go into rivers, etc. or used to make MANURE

sewer /ˈsuːə(r); *BrE* also ˈsjuː-/ *noun* an underground pipe that is used to carry sewage away from houses, factories, etc.

sew·er·age /ˈsuːərɪdʒ/ *noun* [U] the system by which sewage is carried away from houses, factories, etc. and is cleaned and made safe by adding chemicals to it: *an increase in water and sewerage charges*

ˈsewer grate *noun* (*AmE*) = DRAIN—picture at HOUSE

sew·ing /ˈsəʊɪŋ; *AmE* ˈsoʊ-/ *noun* [U] **1** the activity of making, repairing or decorating things made of fabric using a needle and thread: *knitting and sewing* **2** something that is being sewn: *a pile of sewing*

ˈsewing machine *noun* a machine that is used for sewing things that are made of fabric

sewn *pp of* SEW

sex /seks/ *noun, verb*
■ *noun* **1** [U, C] the state of being male or female [SYN] GENDER: *How can you tell what sex a fish is?* ◇ *a process that allows couples to choose the sex of their baby* ◇ *Please indicate your sex and date of birth below.* ◇ *sex discrimination* (= the act of treating men and women differently in an unfair way) **2** [C] either of the two groups that people, animals and plants are divided into according to their function of producing young: *a member of **the opposite sex*** ◇ *single sex schools/education*—see also FAIR SEX **3** [U] physical activity between two people in which they touch each other's sexual organs, and which may include SEXUAL INTERCOURSE: *It is illegal to **have sex** with a person under the age of 16.* ◇ *gay sex* ◇ *the sex act* ◇ *a sex attack/crime* ◇ *a sex shop* (= one selling magazines, objects, etc. that are connected with sex) ◇ *sex education in schools* ◇ *These drugs may affect your sex drive* (= your interest in sex and the ability to have it).—see also SAFE SEX, SEXUAL INTERCOURSE **4** (**-sexed**) (in adjectives) having the amount

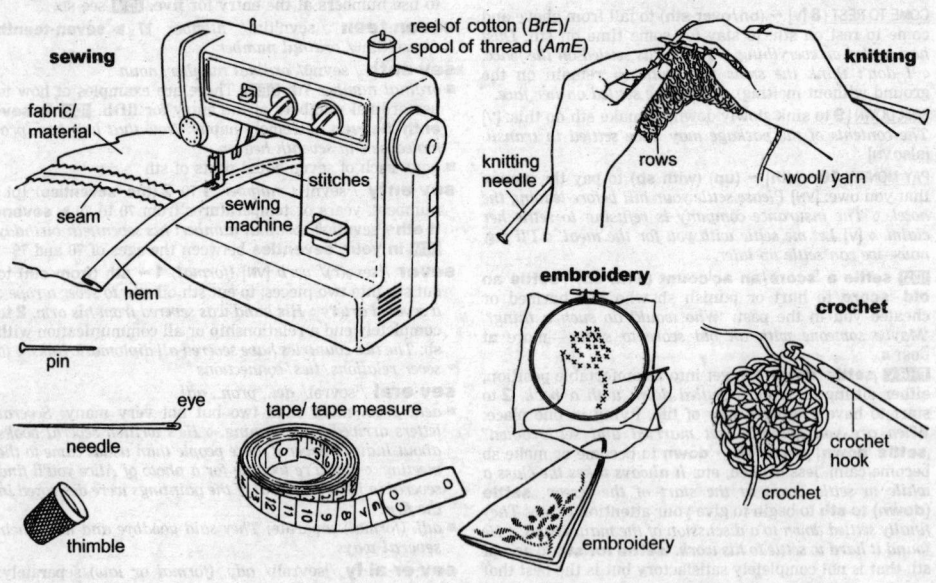

sewing
reel of cotton (*BrE*)
spool of thread (*AmE*)
fabric/material
stitches
seam
sewing machine
hem
pin
eye
needle
tape/tape measure
thimble

knitting
knitting needle
rows
wool/yarn

embroidery

crochet
crochet hook
crochet

embroidery

of sexual activity or desire mentioned: *a highly-sexed woman*

■ *verb* [VN] (*technical*) to examine an animal in order to find out whether it is male or female

'sex appeal *noun* [U] the quality of being attractive in a sexual way: *He exudes sex appeal.*

'sex change *noun* [usually sing.] a medical operation in which parts of a person's body are changed so that they become like a person of the opposite sex

'sex chromosome *noun* (*biology*) a CHROMOSOME that decides the sex of an animal or a plant—see also X CHROMOSOME, Y CHROMOSOME

sex·ism /ˈseksɪzəm/ *noun* [U] the unfair treatment of people, especially women, because of their sex; the attitude that causes this: *legislation designed to combat sexism in the work place* ◊ *a study of sexism in language*

sex·ist /ˈseksɪst/ *noun* (*disapproving*) a person who treats other people, especially women, unfairly because of their sex or who makes offensive remarks about them ▶ **sex·ist** *adj.*: *a sexist attitude/remark* ◊ *sexist language*

sex·less /ˈsekslǝs/ *adj.* **1** that is neither male nor female, or does not seem to be either male or female: *a sexless child/figure* **2** in which there is no sexual desire or activity

'sex life *noun* a person's sexual activities: *ways to improve your sex life*

'sex maniac *noun* a person who wants to have sex all the time

'sex object *noun* a person considered only for their sexual attraction and not for their character or their intelligence

'sex offender *noun* a person who has been found guilty of illegal sexual acts

sex·ology /sekˈsɒlǝdʒi; *AmE* -ˈsɑːl-/ *noun* [U] the scientific study of human sexual behaviour ▶ **sex·olo·gist** /-dʒɪst/ *noun*

'sex symbol *noun* a famous person who is thought by many people to be sexually attractive

sex·tant /ˈsekstǝnt/ *noun* an instrument for measuring angles and distances, used to calculate the exact position of a ship or an aircraft

sex·tet /seksˈtet/ *noun* **1** [C+sing./pl. *v.*] a group of six musicians or singers who play or sing together **2** [C] a piece of music for six musicians or singers

sex·ton /ˈsekstǝn/ *noun* a person whose job is to take care of a church and its surroundings, ring the church bell, etc.

sex·tu·plet /ˈsekstjuplǝt; sekˈstju:plǝt; -ˈstʌp-/ *noun* one of six children born at the same time to the same mother

sex·ual /ˈsekʃuǝl/ *adj.* **1** [usually before noun] connected with the physical activity of sex: *sexual activity/behaviour/desire* ◊ *They were not having a sexual relationship at the time.* ◊ *Her interest in him is purely sexual.* ◊ *sexual orientation* (= whether you are heterosexual or homosexual) **2** [only before noun] connected with the process of producing young: *the sexual organs* (= the penis, vagina, etc.) ◊ *sexual reproduction* **3** [usually before noun] connected with the state of being male or female: *sexual characteristics/differences* ▶ **sex·ual·ly** /ˈsekʃǝli/ *adv.*: *sexually abused children* ◊ *She finds him sexually attractive.* ◊ *sexually explicit* ◊ *Girls become sexually mature earlier than boys.*

,sexual ha'rassment *noun* [U] comments about sex, physical contact, etc. usually happening at work, that a person finds annoying and offensive

,sexual 'intercourse (also **inter·course**) (also *formal* **co·itus**) *noun* [U] (*formal*) the physical activity of sex, usually describing the act of a man putting his PENIS inside a woman's VAGINA

sexu·al·ity /ˌsekʃuˈælǝti/ *noun* [U] the feelings and activities connected with a person's sexual desires: *male/female sexuality* ◊ *He was confused about his sexuality.*

,sexually trans,mitted di'sease *noun* [C, U] (*abbr.* **STD**) any disease that is spread through sexual intercourse, such as SYPHILIS

sexy /ˈseksi/ *adj.* (**sex·ier**, **sexi·est**) **1** (of a person) sexu-

---

ally attractive: *the sexy lead singer* ◊ *She looked incredibly sexy in a black evening gown.* **2** sexually exciting: *sexy clothes/underwear* ◊ *a sexy look/smile* **3** (of a person) sexually excited: *The music and wine began to make him feel sexy.* **4** exciting and interesting: *a sexy new range of software* ◊ *Accountancy just isn't sexy.* ▶ **sex·ily** *adv.* **sexi·ness** *noun* [U]

Sgt (especially *BrE*) (also **Sgt.** *AmE*, *BrE*) *abbr.* SERGEANT: *Sgt Williams*

sh (also **shh**) /ʃ/ *exclamation* the way of writing the sound people make when they are telling sb to be quiet: *Sh! Keep your voice down!*

shabby /ˈʃæbi/ *adj.* (**shab·bier**, **shab·bi·est**) **1** (of buildings, clothes, objects, etc.) in poor condition because they have been used a lot: *The outside of the house was beginning to look shabby.* ◊ *She wore shabby old jeans and a T-shirt.* **2** (of a person) badly dressed in clothes that have been worn a lot: *The old man was shabby and unkempt.* **3** (of behaviour) unfair or unreasonable: *She tried to make up for her shabby treatment of him.* ▶ **shab·bily** /ˈʃæbɪli/ *adv.*: *shabbily dressed* ◊ *I think you were very shabbily treated.* **shab·bi·ness** *noun* [U]

shack /ʃæk/ *noun*, *verb*
■ *noun* a small building, usually made of wood or metal, that has not been built well
■ *verb* PHRV **,shack 'up with sb** | **be ,shacked 'up with sb** (*slang*) to start/be living with sb that you have a sexual relationship with, but that you are not married to: *I hear he's shacked up with some woman.*

shackle /ˈʃækl/ *verb* [VN] **1** to put shackles on sb: *The hostage had been shackled to a radiator.* ◊ *The prisoners were kept shackled during the trial.* **2** [usually passive] to prevent sb from behaving or speaking as they want: *She is opposed to shackling the press with privacy laws.*

shackles /ˈʃæklz/ *noun* [pl.] **1** two metal rings joined together by a chain and placed around a prisoner's wrists or ankles to prevent them from escaping or moving easily **2** ~ (of sth) (*formal*) a particular state, set of conditions or circumstances, etc. that prevent you from saying or doing what you want: *a country struggling to free itself from the shackles of colonialism*

shade /ʃeɪd/ *noun*, *verb*
■ *noun*
OUT OF SUN | **1** [U] ~ (of sth) an area that is dark and cool under or behind sth, for example a tree or building, because the sun's light does not get to it: *We sat down in the shade of the wall.* ◊ *The temperature can reach 40°C in the shade.* ◊ *The trees provide shade for the animals in the summer.*—see also SHADY

shadow   shade

ON LAMP | **2** [C] a thing that you use to prevent light from coming through or to make it less bright: *I bought a new shade for the lamp.* ◊ *an eyeshade*—see also LAMPSHADE, SUNSHADE

ON WINDOW | **3** [C] (also **'window shade**) (both *AmE*) = BLIND

OF COLOUR | **4** [C] ~ (of sth) a particular form of a colour, that is, how dark or light it is: *a delicate/pale/rich/soft shade of red* ◊ *Cool pastel shades are just right for summer.*

IN PICTURE | **5** [U] the dark areas in a picture, especially the use of these to produce variety: *The painting needs more light and shade.*

OF OPINION/FEELING | **6** [C, usually pl.] ~ of sth a different kind or level of opinion, feeling, etc: *politicians of all shades of opinion* ◊ *The word can have many shades of meaning.*

SLIGHTLY | **7** (**a shade**) [sing.] (*written*) a little; slightly: *He was feeling a shade disappointed.* ◊ *Her skirt was a shade too short.*

FOR EYES | **8** (**shades**) [pl.] (*informal*) = SUNGLASSES

STH THAT REMINDS YOU | **9** (**shades**) [pl.] ~ of sb/sth (*informal*) used when you are referring to things that remind

æ	ɑː	e	ɜː	ə	ɪ	iː	i	ɒ	ɔː	ʌ	ʊ	u	uː
cat	father	ten	bird	about	sit	see	many	got	saw	cup	put	actual	too

(BrE)

S

you of a particular person, thing or time: *short skirts and long boots—shades of the 1960s*

GHOST | **10** [C] (*literary*) the spirit of a dead person; a ghost

IDM **put sb/sth in the 'shade** to be much better or more impressive than sb/sth: *I tried hard but her work put mine in the shade.*

■ *verb* [VN]

FROM DIRECT LIGHT | **1** ~ sb/sth (from/against sth) to prevent direct light from reaching sth: *The courtyard was shaded by high trees.* ◊ *She shaded her eyes against the sun.*

LAMP | **2** [usually passive] to provide a screen for a lamp, light, etc. to make it less bright: *a shaded lamp*

PART OF PICTURE | **3** ~ sth (in) to make a part of a drawing, etc. darker, for example with an area of colour or with pencil lines: *What do the shaded areas on the map represent?* ◊ *I'm going to shade this part in.*

JUST WIN | **4** (*BrE, informal*) to just win a contest

PHRV ,shade 'into sth to change gradually into sth else, so that you cannot tell where one thing ends and the other thing begins: *The scarlet of the wings shades into pink at the tips.* ◊ *Distrust of foreigners can shade into racism.*

WHICH WORD?
shade / shadow (?)

Shade [U] is an area or a part of a place that is protected from the heat of the sun and so is darker and cooler: *Let's sit in the shade for a while.*

A **shadow** [C] is the dark shape made when a light shines on a person or an object: *As the sun went down we cast long shadows on the lawn.*

Shadow [U] is an area of darkness in which it is difficult to distinguish things easily: *Her face was in deep shadow.*

---

shad·ing /ˈʃeɪdɪŋ/ *noun* **1** [U] the use of colour, pencil lines, etc. to give an impression of light and shade in a picture or to emphasize areas of a map, diagram, etc. **2 (shadings)** [pl.] slight differences that exist between different aspects of the same thing: *the shadings of opinion found among church leaders*

shadow /ˈʃædəʊ; *AmE* -doʊ/ *noun, verb, adj.*

■ *noun*

DARK SHAPE | **1** [C] the dark shape that sb/sth's form makes on a surface, for example on the ground, when they are between the light and the surface: *The children were having fun, chasing each other's shadows.* ◊ *The ship's sail cast a shadow on the water.* ◊ *The shadows lengthened as the sun went down.* ◊ (*figurative*) *He didn't want to cast a shadow on* (= spoil) *their happiness.*—picture at SHADE ⇨ note at SHADE

DARKNESS | **2** [U] (also **shadows** [pl.]) darkness in a place or on sth, especially so that you cannot easily see who or what is there: *His face was deep in shadow, turned away from her.* ◊ *I thought I saw a figure standing in the shadows.* ⇨ note at SHADE

SMALL AMOUNT | **3** [sing.] ~ of sth a very small amount of sth: *A shadow of a smile touched his mouth.* ◊ *She knew beyond a shadow of a doubt* (= with no doubt at all) *that he was lying.*

INFLUENCE | **4** [sing.] ~ of sb/sth the strong (usually bad) influence of sb/sth: *The new leader wants to escape from the shadow of his predecessor.* ◊ *These people have been living for years under the shadow of fear.*

UNDER EYES | **5** (**shadows**) [pl.] dark areas under sb's eyes, because they are tired, etc: *She looked pale, with deep shadows under her eyes.*

SB THAT FOLLOWS SB | **6** [C] a person or an animal that follows sb else all the time

STH NOT REAL | **7** [C] a thing that is not real or possible to obtain: *You can't spend all your life chasing shadows.*

—see also EYESHADOW, FIVE O'CLOCK SHADOW

IDM **be frightened/nervous/scared of your own 'shadow** to be very easily frightened; to be very nervous

in/under the 'shadow of 1 very close to: *The new market is in the shadow of the City Hall.* **2** when you say that sb is **in/under the shadow of** another person, you mean that they do not receive as much attention as that person—more at FORMER

■ *verb* [VN]

FOLLOW AND WATCH | **1** to follow and watch sb closely and often secretly: *He was shadowed for a week by the secret police.* **2** to be with sb who is doing a particular job, so that you can learn about it: *It is often helpful for teachers to shadow managers in industry.*

COVER WITH SHADOW | **3** to cover sth with a shadow: *A wide-brimmed hat shadowed her face.* ◊ *The bay was shadowed by magnificent cliffs.*

—see also OVERSHADOW

■ *adj.* [only before noun] (*BrE, politics*) used to refer to senior politicians of the main opposition party who would become government ministers if their party won the next election: *the shadow Chancellor* ◊ *the shadow Cabinet*

'shadow-box *verb* [V] to BOX with an imaginary opponent, especially for physical exercise or in order to train ▶ **'shadow-boxing** *noun* [U]

shad·owy /ˈʃædəʊi; *AmE* -doʊi/ *adj.* **1** dark and full of shadows: *Someone was waiting in the shadowy doorway.* **2** [usually before noun] difficult to see because there is not much light: *Shadowy figures approached them out of the fog.* **3** [usually before noun] that not much is known about **SYN** MYSTERIOUS: *the shadowy world of terrorism*

shady /ˈʃeɪdi/ *adj.* (**shadi·er, shadi·est**) **1** protected from direct sunlight by trees, buildings, etc: *a shady garden/forest* ◊ *We went to find somewhere cool and shady to have a drink.* **2** (of a tree, etc.) providing shade from the sunlight **3** [usually before noun] (*informal*) seeming to be dishonest or illegal: *a shady businessman/deal* ◊ *a shady character*

shaft /ʃɑːft; *AmE* ʃæft/ *noun, verb*

■ *noun* **1** (often in compounds) a long, narrow, usually vertical passage in a building or underground, used especially for a lift/elevator or as a way of allowing air in or out: *a lift/elevator shaft* ◊ *a mineshaft* ◊ *a ventilation shaft* **2** the long narrow part of an arrow, hammer, GOLF CLUB, etc. **3** (often in compounds) a metal bar that joins parts of a machine or an engine together, enabling power and movement to be passed from one part to another—see also CAMSHAFT, CRANKSHAFT **4** [usually pl.] either of the two poles at the front of a carriage or CART between which a horse is fastened in order to pull it **5** ~ of light, sunlight, etc. (*literary*) a narrow beam of light: *A shaft of moonlight fell on the lake.* ◊ (*figurative*) *a shaft of inspiration* **6** ~ of pain, fear, etc. (*literary*) a sudden strong feeling of pain, etc. that travels through your body: *Shafts of fear ran through her as she heard footsteps behind her.* **7** ~ of sth (*formal*) a clever remark that is intended to upset or annoy sb: *a shaft of wit/criticism* **IDM** **give sb the 'shaft** (*AmE, informal*) to treat sb unfairly

■ *verb* [VN] (*informal*) to treat sb unfairly or cheat them

shag /ʃæg/ *noun, verb, adj.*

■ *noun* **1** [U] a strong type of tobacco cut into long thin pieces **2** [C] a large black sea bird with a long neck **3** [C, usually sing.] (*BrE, △, slang*) an act of sex with sb: *Fancy a shag?*

■ *verb* (**-gg-**) [V, VN] (*BrE, △, slang*) to have sex with sb

■ *adj.* [only before noun] used to describe a carpet, etc. that has long woollen threads

shagged /ʃæɡd/ (also **,shagged 'out**) *adj.* [not before noun] (*BrE, △, slang*) very tired

shaggy /ˈʃæɡi/ *adj.* **1** (of hair, fur, etc.) long and untidy: *a shaggy mane of hair* **2** having long untidy hair, fur, etc: *a huge shaggy white dog*

,shaggy-'dog story *noun* a very long joke with a silly or disappointing ending

shah /ʃɑː/ *noun* the title of the kings of Iran in the past

shaikh = SHEIKH

shake /ʃeɪk/ *verb, noun*

■ *verb* (**shook** /ʃʊk/ **shaken** /ˈʃeɪkən/)

OBJECT/BUILDING/PERSON | **1** to move or make sb/sth move

---

with short quick movements from side to side or up and down: [V] *The whole house shakes when a train goes past.* ◊ [VN] *Shake the bottle well before use.* ◊ *He shook her violently by the shoulders.* ◊ [VN-ADJ] *She shook her hair loose.* **2** [VN+*adv.*/*prep.*] to move sth in a particular direction by shaking: *She bent down to shake a pebble out of her shoe.*

YOUR HEAD | **3** [VN] ~ **your head** to turn your head from side to side as a way of saying 'no' or to show sadness, disapproval, doubt, etc: *She shook her head in disbelief.*

HANDS | **4** [VN]~ **sb's hand** | ~ **hands (with sb) (on sth)** | ~ **sb by the hand** to take sb's hand and move it up and down as a greeting or to show that you agree about sth: *Do people in Italy shake hands when they meet?* ◊ *They shook hands on the deal* (= to show that they had reached an agreement). ◊ *Our host shook each of us warmly by the hand.*

YOUR FIST | **5** [VN]~ **your fist (at sb)** to show that you are angry with sb; to threaten sb by shaking your FIST (= closed hand)

OF BODY | **6** [V] ~ **(with sth)** to make short quick movements that you cannot control, for example because you are cold or afraid [SYN] TREMBLE: *He was shaking with fear.* ◊ *I was **shaking like a leaf**.* ◊ *Her hands had started to shake.*

OF VOICE | **7** [V] ~ **(with sth)** (of sb's voice) to sound unsteady, usually because you are nervous, upset or angry

SHOCK SB | **8** [VN] ~ **sb (up)** (not used in the progressive tenses) to shock or upset sb very much: *He was badly shaken by the news of her death.* ◊ *The accident really shook her up.*

BELIEF/IDEA | **9** [VN] to make a belief or an idea less certain: *to shake somebody's faith/belief* ◊ *This announcement is bound to shake the confidence of the industry.*

GET RID OF | **10** [VN] ~ **sth (off)** to get rid of sth: *I can't seem to shake off this cold.* ◊ *He couldn't shake the feeling that there was something wrong.*

[IDM] **shake in your 'shoes** (*informal*) to be very frightened or nervous **shake a 'leg** (*old-fashioned, informal*) used to tell sb to start to do sth or to hurry—more at FOUNDATION

[PHR V] ,**shake 'down** (*informal*) to become familiar with a new situation and begin to work well in it ,**shake sb/ sth‹›'down** (*AmE, informal*) **1** to search a person or place in a very thorough way—related noun SHAKEDOWN **2** to threaten sb in order to get money from them ,**shake sb‹›'off** to get away from sb who is chasing or following you '**shake on sth** to shake hands in order to show that sth has been agreed: *They shook on the deal.* ◊ *Let's shake on it.* ,**shake sth‹›'out** to open or spread sth by shaking, especially so that bits of dirt, dust, etc. come off it: *to shake out a duster* ,**shake sb‹›'up** to surprise sb and make them think about sth in a different way, become more active, etc: *Shaken up by the early goal against them, the team began to fight back.* ,**shake sth‹›'up** to make important changes in an organization, a profession, etc. in order to make it more efficient: *The whole industry needs shaking up.*—related noun SHAKE-UP

■ **noun**

MOVEMENT | **1** [C, usually sing.] an act of shaking sth/sb: *Give the bottle a good shake before opening.* ◊ *He dismissed the idea with a firm shake of his head* (= turning it from side to side to mean 'no'). ◊ *She gave him a shake to wake him.*—see also HANDSHAKE

OF BODY | **2** (**the shakes**) [pl.] (*informal*) a physical condition in which you cannot stop your body from shaking because of fear, illness, or because you have drunk too much alcohol: *I always **get the shakes** before exams.*

DRINK | **3** [C] = MILKSHAKE: *a strawberry shake*

[IDM] **in two 'shakes** | **in a couple of 'shakes** (*informal*) very soon—more at FAIR *adj.*, GREAT *adj.*

shake·down /'ʃeɪkdaʊn/ *noun* (*AmE, informal*) **1** a situation in which sb tries to force sb else to give them money using violence, threats, etc. **2** a thorough search of sb/sth: *a police shakedown of the area* **3** a test of a

vehicle to see if there are any problems before it is used generally

shaken /'ʃeɪkən/ (also **shaken 'up**) *adj.* [not usually before noun] shocked, upset or frightened by sth

'**shake-out** *noun* [usually sing.] **1** a situation in which people lose their jobs and less successful companies are forced to close because of competition and difficult economic conditions **2** = SHAKE-UP

shaker /'ʃeɪkə(r)/ *noun* **1** (often in compounds) a container that is used for shaking things: *a salt shaker* ◊ *a cocktail shaker* **2** (**Shaker**) a member of a religious group in the US who live simply in a community and do not marry or have partners [IDM] see MOVER

'**shake-up** (also '**shake-out**) *noun* ~ **(in/of sth)** a situation in which a lot of changes are made to a company, an organization, etc. in order to improve the way in which it works: *a management shake-up*

shak·ing /'ʃeɪkɪŋ/ *noun* [sing., U] the act of shaking sth/sb or the fact of being shaken

shaky /'ʃeɪki/ *adj.* (**shaki·er**, **shaki·est**) **1** shaking and feeling weak because of illness, emotion or old age: *Her voice sounded shaky on the phone.* ◊ *The old man was very shaky on his feet.* **2** not firm or safe; not certain: *That ladder looks a little shaky.* ◊ (*figurative*) *Her memories of the accident are a little shaky.* ◊ (*figurative*) *The protesters are **on shaky ground*** (= it is not certain that their claims are valid). **3** not seeming very successful; likely to fail: *Business is looking shaky at the moment.* ◊ *After a shaky start, they fought back to win 3–2.* ▶ **shaki·ly** /-ɪli/ *adv.*: *'Get the doctor,' he whispered shakily.*

shale /ʃeɪl/ *noun* [U] a type of soft stone that splits easily into thin flat layers ▶ **shaly** *adj.*

shall /ʃəl; *strong form* ʃæl/ *modal verb* (*negative* **shall not** *short form* **shan't** /ʃɑːnt/ *pt* **should** /ʃʊd/ *negative* **should not** *short form* **shouldn't** /'ʃʊdnt/) (*especially BrE*) **1** (*becoming old-fashioned*) used with *I* and *we* for talking about or predicting the future: *This time next week I shall be in Scotland.* ◊ *We shan't be gone long.* ◊ *I said that I should be pleased to help.* **2** used in questions with *I* and *we* for making offers or suggestions or asking advice: *Shall I send you the book?* ◊ *What shall we do this weekend?* ◊ *Let's look at it again, shall we?* **3** (*old-fashioned or formal*) used to show that you are determined, or to give an order or instruction: *He is determined that you shall succeed.* ◊ *Candidates shall remain in their seats until all the papers have been collected.* ➪ note at MODAL

GRAMMAR POINT

shall / will

In modern English the traditional difference between **shall** and **will** has almost disappeared, and **shall** is not used very much at all, especially in *AmE*. **Shall** is now only used with *I* and *we*, and often sounds formal and old-fashioned. People are more likely to say: *I'll* (= I will) *be late* and *'You'll* (= you will) *apologize immediately.' 'No I won't!'.*

In *BrE* **shall** is still used with *I* and *we* in questions or when you want to make a suggestion or an offer: *What shall I wear to the party?* ◊ *Shall we order some coffee?* ◊ *I'll drive, shall I?*

➪ note at SHOULD

---

shal·lot /ʃə'lɒt; *AmE* -'lɑːt/ *noun* a vegetable like a small onion with a very strong taste—picture on page A3

shal·low /'ʃæləʊ; *AmE* -loʊ/ *adj.* (**shal·low·er**, **shal·lowest**) **1** not having much distance between the top or surface and the bottom: *a shallow dish* ◊ *They were playing in the shallow end* (= of the swimming pool). ◊ *These fish are found in shallow waters around the coast.* [OPP] DEEP **2** (*disapproving*) (of a person, an idea, a comment, etc.) not showing serious thought, feelings, etc. about sth **3 shallow breathing** involves taking in only a small amount of air each time ▶ **shal·low·ly** *adv.*: *He was breathing shallowly.* **shal·low·ness** *noun* [U]

shal·lows /'ʃæləʊz; *AmE* -loʊz/ (**the shallows**) *noun* [pl.] a shallow place in a river or the sea

S

sha·lom /ʃəˈlɒm; AmE ʃəˈlɔːm/ exclamation a Hebrew word for 'hello' or 'goodbye' that means 'peace'

shalt /ʃælt/ verb (**thou shalt**) (old use) used to mean 'you shall', when talking to one person

sham /ʃæm/ noun, adj., verb

■ noun (disapproving) **1** [sing.] a situation, feeling, system, etc. that is not as good or true as it seems to be: The latest crime figures are a complete sham. **2** [C, usually sing.] a person who pretends to be sth that they are not **3** [U] behaviour, feelings, words, etc. that are intended to make sb/sth seem to be better than they really are: Their promises turned out to be full of sham and hypocrisy.
■ adj. [only before noun] (usually disapproving) not genuine but intended to seem real SYN FALSE: a sham marriage
■ verb (-mm-) to pretend sth: [V] Is he really sick or is he just shamming? [also V-ADJ, VN]

shaman /ˈʃeɪmən; ˈʃɑːmən; ˈʃæmən/ noun a person in some religions and societies who is believed to be able to contact good and evil spirits and cure people of illnesses

sham·ble /ˈʃæmbl/ verb [V, usually +adv./prep.] to walk in an awkward or lazy way, dragging your feet along the ground: The old porter shambled along behind her. ◊ a shambling gait/figure

sham·bles /ˈʃæmblz/ (**a shambles**) noun [sing.] (informal) **1** a situation in which there is a lot of confusion or disorder SYN MESS: The press conference was a complete shambles. ◊ What a shambles! ◊ The government is **in a shambles** over Europe. **2** a place which is dirty or untidy SYN MESS: The house was a shambles.

sham·bol·ic /ʃæmˈbɒlɪk; AmE -ˈbɑːl-/ adj. (BrE, informal) lacking order or organization SYN DISORGANIZED: a shambolic campaign

shame /ʃeɪm/ noun, verb

■ noun **1** [U] the feelings of guilt, sadness and embarrassment that you have when you know that sth you have done is wrong or stupid: His face burned with shame. ◊ She hung her head in shame. ◊ He could not live with the shame of other people knowing the truth. ◊ **To my shame** (= I feel shame that) I refused to listen to her side of the story. **2** [U] (formal) (only used in questions and negative sentences) the ability to feel shame at sth you have done: Have you no shame? **3** (**a shame**) [sing.] used to say that sth is a cause for feeling sad or disappointed: **What a shame** they couldn't come. ◊ **It's a shame about** Tim, isn't it? ◊ **It's a shame that** she wasn't here to see it. ◊ It would be **a crying shame** (= a great shame) not to take them up on the offer. **4** [U] the loss of respect that is caused when you do sth wrong or stupid: There is **no shame in** wanting to be successful. ◊ (formal) She felt that her failure would **bring shame on** her family. IDM **put sb/sth to ˈshame** to be much better than sb/sth: Their presentation put ours to shame. **ˈshame on you, him, etc.** (spoken) used to say that sb should feel ashamed for sth they have said or done
■ verb [VN] **1** (written) to make sb feel ashamed: His generosity shamed them all. **2** (formal) to make sb feel that they have lost honour or respect: You have shamed your family. PHRV **ˈshame sb into doing sth** to persuade sb to do sth by making them feel ashamed not to do it: She shamed her father into promising more help.

shame·faced /ˌʃeɪmˈfeɪst/ adj. feeling or looking ashamed because you have done sth bad or stupid: a shamefaced smile ▶ **shame·faced·ly** /ˌʃeɪmˈfeɪstli; -ˈfeɪsɪdli/ adv.

shame·ful /ˈʃeɪmfl/ adj. that should make you feel ashamed: shameful behaviour ◊ a shameful secret/thought ◊ It was shameful the way she was treated. ▶ **shame·ful·ly** /-fəli/ adv.

shame·less /ˈʃeɪmləs/ adj. (disapproving) not feeling ashamed of sth you have done, although other people think you should: a shameless display of greed ▶ **shame·less·ly** adv.: He shamelessly admits his part in the crime. **shame·less·ness** noun [U]

sham·ing /ˈʃeɪmɪŋ/ adj. causing sb to feel ashamed: a shaming defeat by a less experienced team

sham·poo /ʃæmˈpuː/ noun, verb

■ noun (pl. -os) **1** [C, U] a liquid soap that is used for washing your hair; a similar liquid used for cleaning carpets, furniture covers or a car: a shampoo for greasy hair ◊ carpet shampoo **2** [C, usually sing.] an act of washing your hair using shampoo: Rinse the hair thoroughly after each shampoo. ◊ a shampoo and set (= an act of washing and styling sb's hair)
■ verb (**sham·pooed, sham·pooed**) [VN] to wash or clean hair, carpets, etc. with shampoo

sham·rock /ˈʃæmrɒk; AmE -rɑːk/ noun a small plant with three leaves on each stem. The shamrock is the national symbol of Ireland.

shandy /ˈʃændi/ noun (pl. -ies) (BrE) **1** [U] a drink made by mixing beer with LEMONADE **2** [C] a glass or can of shandy: Two shandies, please.

shang·hai /ʃæŋˈhaɪ/ verb (**shang·hai·ing** /-ˈhaɪɪŋ/, **shang·haied, shang·haied** /-ˈhaɪd/) [VN] ~ **sb (into doing sth)** (old-fashioned, informal) to trick or force sb into doing sth that they do not really want to do

shank /ʃæŋk/ noun **1** the straight narrow part between the two ends of a tool or an object **2** the part of an animal's or a person's leg between the knee and ankle IDM **(on) Shanks's ˈpony** (BrE, informal) walking, rather than travelling by car, bus, etc. SYN ON FOOT

shan't short form of SHALL NOT

shanty /ˈʃænti/ noun (pl. -ies) **1** a small house, built of pieces of wood, metal and cardboard, where very poor people live, especially on the edge of a big city **2** (also **ˈsea shanty**) (both BrE) (AmE **chanty, chantey**) a song that sailors traditionally used to sing while pulling ropes, etc.

ˈshanty town noun an area in or near a town where poor people live in shanties

shape /ʃeɪp/ noun, verb

■ noun **1** [C, U] the form of the outer edges or surfaces of sth; an example of sth that has a particular form: a rectangular shape ◊ The pool was **in the shape of** a heart. ◊ The island was originally circular **in shape**. ◊ Squares, circles and triangles are types of shape. ◊ Candles come in **all shapes and sizes**. ◊ You can recognize the fish by the shape of their fins. ◊ This old T-shirt has completely lost its shape. ◊ (figurative) The government provides money **in the shape of** (= consisting of) grants and student loans. **2** [C] a person or thing that is difficult to see clearly SYN FIGURE: Ghostly shapes moved around in the dark. **3** [U] the physical condition of sb/sth: What sort of shape was the car in after the accident? ◊ He's **in good shape** for a man of his age. ◊ I like to **keep in shape** (= keep fit). **4** [U] the particular qualities or characteristics of sth: Will new technology change the shape of broadcasting? IDM **get (yourself) into ˈshape** to take exercise, eat healthy food, etc. in order to become physically fit **get/knock/lick sb into ˈshape** to train sb so that they do a particular job, task, etc. well **get/knock/lick sth into ˈshape** to make sth more acceptable, organized or successful: I've got all the information together but it still needs knocking into shape. **give ˈshape to sth** (formal) to express or explain a particular idea, plan, etc. **in ˈany (way,) shape or form** (informal) of any type: I don't approve of violence in any shape or form. **out of ˈshape 1** not having the normal shape: The wheel had been twisted out of shape. **2** (of a person) not in good physical condition **the ˌshape of ˌthings to ˈcome** the way things are likely to develop in the future **take ˈshape** to develop and become more complete or organized: The garden is beginning to take shape.
■ verb **1** [VN] ~ **A (into B)** to make sth into a particular shape: Shape the dough into a ball. ◊ This tool is used for shaping wood. **2** [VN] to have an important influence on the way that sb/sth develops: His ideas had been shaped by his experiences during the war. ◊ She had a leading role in shaping party policy. **3** [V to inf] to prepare to do sth, especially hit or kick sth: She was shaping to hit her second shot. IDM **ˈshape up or ship ˈout** (AmE, informal) used to tell sb that if they do not improve, work harder, etc. they will have to leave their job, position, etc: He finally faced up to his drug problem when his band told

s	t	v	z	ʃ	ʒ	tʃ	dʒ	θ	ð	ŋ
see	tea	van	zoo	shoe	vision	chain	jam	thin	this	sing

him to shape up or ship out. **PHR V** ,shape ˈup **1** to develop in a particular way, especially in a satisfactory way: *Our plans are shaping up nicely* (= showing signs that they will be successful). **2** (*informal*) to improve your behaviour, work harder, etc: *If he doesn't shape up, he'll soon be out of a job.*

shaped /ʃeɪpt/ *adj.* having the type of shape mentioned: *a huge balloon shaped like a giant cow* ◊ *almond-shaped eyes* ◊ *an L-shaped room*—see also PEAR-SHAPED

shape·less /ˈʃeɪpləs/ *adj.* [usually before noun] (often *disapproving*) **1** not having any definite shape: *a shapeless sweater* **2** lacking clear organization: *a shapeless and incoherent story* ▶ **shape·less·ly** *adv.* **shape·less·ness** *noun* [U]

shape·ly /ˈʃeɪpli/ *adj.* (especially of a woman's body) having an attractive curved shape: *a shapely young woman* ◊ *a shapely figure/leg*

shard /ʃɑːd/ *noun* /ʃɑːrd/ (also **sherd**) *noun* (*written*) a piece of broken glass, metal, etc: *shards of glass/pottery*

share /ʃeə(r)/; *AmE* /ʃer/ *verb, noun*

■ *verb*

USE AT SAME TIME | **1** ~ (**sth**) (**with sb**) to have or use sth at the same time as sb else: [VN] *Sue shares a house with three other students.* ◊ [V] *There isn't an empty table. Would you mind sharing?*—see also JOB-SHARING

DIVIDE BETWEEN PEOPLE | **2** [VN] ~ **sth** (**out**) (**among/between sb**) to divide sth between two or more people: *We shared the pizza between the four of us.* ◊ *Rita shared her money out among her six grandchildren.*—see also POWER-SHARING

GIVE SOME OF YOURS | **3** ~ (**sth**) (**with sb**) to give some of what you have to sb else; to let sb use sth that is yours: [VN] *Eli shared his chocolate with the other kids.* ◊ *The conference is a good place to share information and exchange ideas.* ◊ [V] *John had no brothers or sisters and wasn't used to sharing.*

FEELINGS/IDEAS/PROBLEMS | **4** ~ (**in**) **sth** | ~ **sth** (**with sb**) to have the same feelings, ideas, experiences, etc. as sb else: [VN] *They shared a common interest in botany.* ◊ *People often share their political views with their parents.* ◊ *a view that is widely shared* ◊ *shared values* ◊ [V] *I didn't really share in her love of animals.* **5** ~ **sth** (**with sb**) to tell other people about your ideas, experiences and feelings: [VN] *Men often don't like to share their problems.* ◊ *The two friends shared everything—they had no secrets.* ◊ *Would you like to share your experience with the rest of the group?* ◊ [V] *The group listens while one person shares* (= tells other people about their experiences, feelings, etc.).

BLAME/RESPONSIBILITY | **6** ~ (**in**) **sth** | ~ **sth** (**with sb**) to be equally involved in sth or responsible for sth: [V] *I try to get the kids to share in the housework.* ◊ [VN] *Both drivers shared the blame for the accident.*

IDM **share and share aˈlike** (*saying*) used to say that everyone should share things equally and in a fair way

■ *noun*

PART/AMOUNT OF STH | **1** [C, usually sing.] ~ (**of/in sth**) one part of sth that is divided between two or more people: *How much was your share of the winnings?* ◊ *Next year we hope to have a bigger share of the market.* ◊ (*BrE*) *I'm looking for a flat share* (= a flat that is shared by two or more people who are not related).—see also MARKET SHARE, TIMESHARE **2** [sing.] ~ (**of sth**) the part that sb has in a particular activity that involves several people: *We all did our share.* ◊ *Everyone must accept their share of the blame.* **3** [sing.] ~ (**of sth**) an amount of sth that is thought to be normal or acceptable for one person: *I've had my share of luck in the past.* ◊ *I've done my share of worrying for one day!*

IN BUSINESS | **4** [C] ~ (**in sth**) any of the units of equal value into which a company is divided and sold to raise money. People who own shares receive part of the company's profits: *shares in British Telecom* ◊ *a fall/increase in share prices*—compare STOCK *n.* (4)—see also ORDINARY SHARE

FARM EQUIPMENT | **5** [C] (*AmE*) = PLOUGHSHARE

IDM see CAKE *n.*, FAIR *adj.*, LION, PIE

share-crop·per /ˈʃeəkrɒpə(r)/; *AmE* /ˈʃerkrɑːpər/ *noun*

(especially *AmE*) a farmer who gives part of his or her crop as rent to the owner of the land

share·hold·er /ˈʃeəhəʊldə(r)/; *AmE* /ˈʃerhoʊ-/ *noun* an owner of shares in a company or business

share·hold·ing /ˈʃeəhəʊldɪŋ/; *AmE* /ˈʃerhoʊ-/ *noun* the amount of a company or business that sb owns in the form of shares: *They have a 51 per cent shareholding in the business.*

ˈ**share index** *noun* [usually sing.] a list that shows the current value of shares on the STOCK MARKET, based on the prices of shares of particular companies

ˈ**share-out** *noun* [usually sing.] (*BrE*) an act of dividing sth between two or more people; the amount of sth that one person receives when it is divided

share·ware /ˈʃeəweə(r)/; *AmE* /ˈʃerwer/ *noun* [U] (*computing*) computer SOFTWARE (= programs, etc.) that is available free for a user to test, after which they must pay if they wish to continue using it—compare FREEWARE

sha·ria /ʃəˈriːə/ (also **sha·riah**) *noun* [U] the system of religious laws that Muslims follow

shark /ʃɑːk/; *AmE* /ʃɑːrk/ *noun* **1** a large sea fish with very sharp teeth and a pointed FIN on its back. There are several types of shark, some of which can attack people swimming: *a Great White Shark* ◊ *a fatal shark attack* **2** (*informal, disapproving*) a person who is dishonest in business, especially sb who gives bad advice and gets people to pay too much for sth—see also LOAN SHARK

sharp /ʃɑːp/; *AmE* /ʃɑːrp/ *adj., adv., noun*

■ *adj.* (**sharp·er**, **sharp·est**)

EDGE/POINT | **1** having a fine edge or point, especially of sth that can cut or make a hole in sth: *a sharp knife/pencil* ◊ *sharp teeth/claws* **OPP** BLUNT

RISE/DROP/CHANGE | **2** [usually before noun] sudden and rapid, especially of a change in sth: *a sharp drop in prices* ◊ *a sharp rise in crime* ◊ *a sharp fall/decline/increase/reduction in sth* ◊ *He heard a sharp intake of breath.* ◊ *We need to give young criminals a short, sharp shock* (= a punishment that is very unpleasant for a short time).

CLEAR/DEFINITE | **3** [usually before noun] clear and definite: *a sharp outline* ◊ *The photograph is not very sharp* (= there are no clear contrasts between areas of light and shade). ◊ *She drew a sharp distinction between domestic and international politics.* ◊ *In sharp contrast to her mood, the clouds were breaking up to reveal a blue sky.* ◊ *The issue must be brought into sharper focus.*

MIND/EYES | **4** (of people or their minds, eyes, etc.) quick to notice or understand things or to react: *to have sharp eyes/ears/reflexes* ◊ *a girl of sharp intelligence* ◊ *a sharp sense of humour* ◊ *He kept a sharp lookout for any strangers.* ◊ *It was very sharp of you to see that!*

CRITICAL | **5** ~ (**with sb**) (of a person or what they say) critical or harsh: *sharp criticism/words* ◊ *Emma has a sharp tongue* (= she often speaks in a harsh or unkind way). ◊ *He was very sharp with me when I was late.*

SOUNDS | **6** [usually before noun] loud, sudden and often high in tone: *She read out the list in sharp, clipped tones.* ◊ *There was a sharp knock on the door.*

FEELING | **7** (of a physical feeling or an emotion) very strong and sudden, often like being cut or wounded: *He winced as a sharp pain shot through his leg.* ◊ *Polly felt a sharp pang of jealousy.*

CURVES | **8** changing direction suddenly: *a sharp bend in the road* ◊ *a sharp turn to the left*

FLAVOUR/SMELL | **9** strong and slightly bitter: *The cheese has a distinctively sharp taste.*

FROST/WIND | **10** used to describe a very cold or very severe FROST or wind—see also RAZOR-SHARP

CLEVER AND DISHONEST | **11** (*disapproving*) (of a person or their way of doing business) clever but possibly dishonest: *His lawyer's a sharp operator.* ◊ *The firm had to face some sharp practice from competing companies.*

CLOTHES | **12** [usually before noun] (of clothes or the way sb dresses) fashionable and new: (*BrE, disapproving*) *The consultants were a group of men in sharp suits.* ◊ (*AmE, approving*) *Todd is a really sharp dresser!*

S

æ	ɑː	e	ɜː	ə	ɪ	iː	i	ɒ	ɔː	ʌ	ʊ	u	uː
cat	father	ten	bird	about	sit	see	many	got	saw	cup	put	actual	too
								(BrE)					

FACE/FEATURES | **13** not full or round in shape: *a man with a thin face and sharp features* (= a pointed nose and chin)

IN MUSIC | **14** used after the name of a note to mean a note a SEMITONE/HALF TONE higher: *the Piano Sonata in C sharp minor* OPP FLAT—compare NATURAL—picture at MUSIC **15** above the correct PITCH (= how high or low a note sounds): *That note sounded sharp.* OPP FLAT

IDM **look 'sharp** (*BrE*) used in orders to tell sb to be quick or to hurry: *You'd better look sharp or you'll be late.* **the 'sharp end (of sth)** (*BrE, informal*) the place or position of greatest difficulty or responsibility: *He started work at the sharp end of the business, as a salesman.*

■ *adv.*

EXACTLY | **1** used after an expression for a time of day to mean 'exactly': *Please be here at seven o'clock sharp.*

LEFT/RIGHT | **2** (*BrE*) ~ **left/right** turning suddenly to the left or right

MUSIC | **3** (*comparative* **sharp·er**, no *superlative*) above the correct PITCH (= how high or low a note sounds) OPP FLAT

■ *noun* (*music*) a note played a SEMITONE/HALF TONE higher than the note that is named. The written symbol is (♯): *It's a difficult piece to play, full of sharps and flats.* OPP FLAT—compare NATURAL

sharp·en /ˈʃɑːpən; *AmE* ˈʃɑːrpən/ *verb* **1** to make sth sharper; to become sharper: [VN] *This knife needs sharpening.* ◊ [V] *The outline of the trees sharpened as it grew lighter.* **2** if a sense or feeling **sharpens** or sth **sharpens** it, it becomes stronger and/or clearer: [VN] *The sea air sharpened our appetites.* [also V] **3** [VN] to make a disagreement between people, or an issue on which people disagree, clearer and more likely to produce a result: *There is a need to sharpen the focus of the discussion.* **4** ~ **(sth) (up)** to become or make sth better, more skilful, more effective, etc. than before SYN IMPROVE: [V] *He needs to sharpen up before the Olympic trials.* ◊ [VN] *She's doing a course to sharpen her business skills.* **5** [V, VN] if your voice **sharpens** or sth **sharpens** it, it becomes high and loud in an unpleasant way

sharp·en·er /ˈʃɑːpnə(r); *AmE* ˈʃɑːrp-/ *noun* (usually in compounds) a tool or machine that makes things sharp: *a pencil sharpener* ◊ *a knife sharpener*

sharp-'eyed *adj.* able to see very well and quick to notice things

sharp·ish /ˈʃɑːpɪʃ; *AmE* ˈʃɑːrpɪʃ/ *adv.* (*BrE, informal*) quickly; in a short time

sharp·ly /ˈʃɑːpli; *AmE* ˈʃɑːrpli/ *adv.* **1** in a critical, harsh or severe way: *The report was sharply critical of the police.* ◊ *'Is there a problem?' he asked sharply.* **2** suddenly and by a large amount SYN DRAMATICALLY: *Profits fell sharply following the takeover.* ◊ *The road fell sharply to the sea.* **3** in a way that clearly shows the differences between two things: *Their experiences contrast sharply with those of other children.* **4** quickly and suddenly or loudly: *She moved sharply across the room to block his exit.* ◊ *He rapped sharply on the window.* **5** used to emphasize that sth has a sharp point or edge: *sharply pointed*

sharp·shoot·er /ˈʃɑːpʃuːtə(r); *AmE* ˈʃɑːrp-/ *noun* a person who is skilled at shooting a gun

sharp *pt, pp* of SHIT

shat·ter /ˈʃætə(r)/ *verb* **1** ~ **(sth) (into sth)** to suddenly break into small pieces; to make sth suddenly break into small pieces: [V] *He dropped the vase and it shattered into pieces on the floor.* ◊ [VN] *The explosion shattered all the windows in the building.* ◊ *the sound of shattering glass* **2** ~ **(sth) (into sth)** to destroy sth completely, especially sb's feelings, hopes or beliefs; to be destroyed in this way: [VN] *Anna's self-confidence had been completely shattered.* ◊ *Her experience of divorce shattered her illusions about love.* ◊ [V] *My whole world shattered into a million pieces.* **3** [VN] to make sb feel extremely shocked and upset: *The unexpected death of their son shattered them.*

shat·tered /ˈʃætəd; *AmE* -tərd/ *adj.* **1** very shocked and upset: *The experience left her feeling absolutely shattered.* **2** (*BrE, informal*) very tired SYN EXHAUSTED

shat·ter·ing /ˈʃætərɪŋ/ *adj.* **1** very shocking and upsetting: *a shattering experience* ◊ *The news of his death came*

as a shattering blow. **2** very loud SYN DEAFENING: *a shattering crash of thunder* ▶ **shat·ter·ing·ly** *adv.*

'shatter-proof *adj.* designed not to SHATTER: *shatter-proof glass*

shave /ʃeɪv/ *verb, noun*
■ *verb* **1** to cut hair from the skin, especially the face, using a RAZOR: [V] *Mike cut himself shaving.* ◊ [VN] *The nurse washed and shaved him.* ◊ *a shaved head*—see also SHAVEN—picture at HAIR **2** [VN] to cut a small amount off a price, etc: *The firm had shaved profit margins.* PHRV **shave sth↔'off** | **shave sth off sth 1** to remove a BEARD or MOUSTACHE by shaving: *Charles decided to shave off his beard.* **2** to cut very thin pieces from the surface of wood, etc: *I had to shave a few millimetres off the door to make it shut.* **3** to reduce a number by a very small amount: *Keith shaved a tenth of a second off his best time in the 200 metres.*
■ *noun* an act of shaving: *I need a shave.* ◊ *to have a shave* IDM see CLOSE²*adj.*

shaven /ˈʃeɪvn/ *adj.* with all the hair shaved off: *a shaven head*—see also CLEAN-SHAVEN—compare UNSHAVEN

shaver /ˈʃeɪvə(r)/ (also e,lectric 'razor) *noun* an electric tool for shaving—compare RAZOR

'shaving cream, 'shaving foam *noun* [U] special cream or FOAM for spreading over the face with a **shaving brush** before shaving

shav·ings /ˈʃeɪvɪŋz/ *noun* [pl.] thin pieces cut from a piece of wood, etc. using a sharp tool, especially a PLANE: *wood shavings*

shawl /ʃɔːl/ *noun* a large piece of fabric worn by a woman around the shoulders or head, or wrapped around a baby

she /ʃi; *strong form* ʃiː/ *pron., noun*
■ *pron.* (used as the subject of a verb) a female person or animal that has already been mentioned or is easily identified: *'What does your sister do?' 'She's a dentist.'* ◊ *Doesn't she* (= the woman we are looking at) *look like Sue?*—compare HER
■ *noun* **1** [sing.] (*informal*) a female: *What a sweet little dog. Is it a he or a she?* **2** (**she-**) (in compound nouns) a female animal: *a she-wolf*

sheaf /ʃiːf/ *noun* (*pl.* **sheaves** /ʃiːvz/) **1** a number of pieces of paper tied or held together: *He waved a sheaf of documents at me.* **2** a bunch of corn or wheat tied together after being cut

shear /ʃɪə(r); *AmE* ʃɪr/ *verb* (**sheared, shorn** /ʃɔːn; *AmE* ʃɔːrn/ or **sheared**) **1** [VN] to cut the wool off a sheep: *It was time for the sheep to be shorn.* ◊ *sheep shearing* **2** [VN] (*formal*) to cut off sb's hair: *shorn hair* **3** ~ **(sth) (off)** (*technical*) (especially of metal) to break under pressure; to cut through sth and make it break: [V] *The bolts holding the wheel in place sheared off.* [also VN] PHRV **be 'shorn of sth** (*literary*) to have sth important taken away from you: *Shorn of his power, the deposed king went into exile.*

shears /ʃɪəz; *AmE* ʃɪrz/ *noun* [pl.] a garden tool like a very large pair of scissors, used for cutting bushes and HEDGES: *a pair of garden shears*—see also PINKING SHEARS—picture at SCISSORS

sheath /ʃiːθ/ *noun* (*pl.* **sheaths** /ʃiːðz/) **1** a cover that fits closely over the blade of a knife or other sharp weapon or tool: *He put the dagger back in its sheath.* **2** any protective covering that fits closely over sth: *the sheath around an electric cable* **3** (*BrE*) = CONDOM **4** a woman's dress that fits the body closely: *a simple black silk sheath*

sheathe /ʃiːð/ *verb* [VN] **1** (*literary*) to put a knife or SWORD into a sheath **2** [usually passive] ~ **sth (in/with sth)** to cover sth in a material, especially in order to protect it

sheaves *pl.* of SHEAF

she·bang /ʃɪˈbæŋ/ *noun* IDM **the whole she'bang** (*informal*) the whole thing; everything

she·been /ʃɪˈbiːn/ *noun* (*informal, especially IrishE*) a place where alcoholic drinks are sold illegally

shed /ʃed/ *noun, verb*
■ *noun* (often in compounds) **1** a small simple building, usually built of wood or metal, used for keeping things

aɪ	aʊ	eɪ	əʊ	oʊ	ɔɪ	ɪə	eə	ʊə	j	w
my	now	say	go	go	boy	near	hair	pure	yes	wet
			(BrE)	(AmE)						

in: *a bicycle/tool shed* ◊ *(BrE) a garden shed* **2** *(BrE)* a large industrial building, used for working in or keeping equipment: *an engine shed*—see also COWSHED, POTTING SHED, WOODSHED

■ *verb* (**shed·ding, shed, shed**) [VN]
GET RID OF | **1** (often used in newspapers) to get rid of sth that is no longer wanted: *The factory is shedding a large number of jobs.* ◊ *a quick way to shed unwanted pounds* (= extra weight or fat on your body) ◊ *Museums have been trying hard to shed their stuffy image.*
DROP | **2** *(formal)* to let sth fall; to drop sth: *Luke shed his clothes onto the floor.* ◊ *A duck's feathers shed water immediately.* **3** *(BrE)* (of a vehicle) to lose or drop what it is carrying: *The traffic jam was caused by a lorry shedding its load.*
SKIN/LEAVES | **4** if an animal **sheds** its skin, or a plant **sheds** leaves, it loses them naturally: *How often does a snake shed its skin?* ◊ *trees that shed their leaves in autumn*
LIGHT | **5** ~ sth (on/over sb/sth) to send light over sth; to let light fall somewhere: *The candles shed a soft glow on her face.*
TEARS | **6** *(formal or literary)* if you **shed** tears, you cry: *She shed no tears when she heard he was dead.*
BLOOD | **7** *(formal)* if you **shed** blood, you kill or injure people, especially in a war: *How much blood will be shed before the fighting ends?*—see also BLOODSHED
IDM see LIGHT *n.*

she'd /ʃiːd/ *short form* **1** she had **2** she would

sheen /ʃiːn/ *noun* [sing., U] a soft smooth shiny quality: *hair with a healthy sheen*

sheep /ʃiːp/ *noun* (*pl.* **sheep**) an animal with a thick coat, kept on farms for its meat (called MUTTON or LAMB) or its wool: *a flock of sheep* ◊ *Sheep were grazing in the fields.*—compare EWE, LAMB, RAM—see also BLACK SHEEP
IDM **like 'sheep** *(disapproving)* if people behave like sheep, they all do what the others are doing, without thinking for themselves **sort out/separate the ˌsheep from the 'goats** to distinguish good people from bad people—more at COUNT *v.*, WOLF *n.*

'sheep dip *noun* [U, C] a liquid which is used to kill insects, etc. in a sheep's coat; the container in which sheep are put to treat them with this

sheep·dog /ˈʃiːpdɒɡ; *AmE* -dɔːɡ/ *noun* **1** a dog that is trained to help control sheep on a farm **2** *(BrE)* a dog of a breed that is often used for controlling sheep, especially a COLLIE—see also OLD ENGLISH SHEEPDOG

sheep·herd·er /ˈʃiːphɜːdə(r); *AmE* -hɜːrd-/ *noun* *(AmE)* = SHEPHERD

sheep·ish /ˈʃiːpɪʃ/ *adj.* looking or feeling embarrassed because you have done sth silly or wrong: *Mary gave her a sheepish grin.* ▶ **sheep·ish·ly** *adv.*

sheep·skin /ˈʃiːpskɪn/ *noun* [U, C] the skin of a sheep with the wool still on it: *a sheepskin coat/rug*

sheer /ʃɪə(r); *AmE* ʃɪr/ *adj., adv., verb*
■ *adj.* **1** [only before noun] used to emphasize the size, degree or amount of sth: *The area is under threat from the sheer number of tourists using it.* ◊ *We were impressed by the sheer size of the cathedral.* **2** [only before noun] complete and not mixed with anything else: *The concert was sheer delight.* ◊ *I only agreed out of sheer desperation.* **3** very steep: *sheer cliffs/slopes* ◊ *Outside there was a sheer drop down to the sea below.* **4** (of fabrics, etc.) thin, light and almost transparent: *sheer nylon*
■ *adv.* straight up or down: *The cliffs rise sheer from the beach.* ◊ *The ground dropped sheer away at our feet.*
■ *verb* PHRV **ˌsheer a'way/'off (from sth)** to change direction suddenly, especially in order to avoid hitting sth: *(figurative) Her mind sheered away from images she did not wish to dwell on.*

sheet /ʃiːt/ *noun*
ON BED | **1** a large piece of thin fabric used on a bed to lie on or lie under: *Have you changed the sheets* (= put clean sheets on the bed)? ◊ *He slid between the sheets and closed his eyes.*—picture at BED
OF PAPER | **2** a piece of paper for writing or printing on,

etc. usually in a standard size: *a clean/blank sheet of paper* (= with no writing on it) ◊ *Start each answer on a fresh sheet.* ◊ *Pick up one of our free information sheets at reception.*
FLAT THIN PIECE | **3** a flat thin piece of any material, normally square or RECTANGULAR: *a sheet of glass/steel* ◊ *sheet metal* (= metal that has been made into thin sheets) ◊ *Place the dough on a baking sheet* (= for cooking sth in an oven).
WIDE FLAT AREA | **4** a wide flat area of sth, covering the surface of sth else: *The road was covered with a sheet of ice.*
OF FIRE/WATER | **5** a large moving mass of fire or water: *a sheet of flame* ◊ *The rain was coming down in sheets* (= very heavily).
ON SAIL | **6** *(technical)* a rope or chain fastened to the lower corner of a sail to hold it and to control the angle of the sail
HELP There are other compounds ending **sheet**. You will find them at their place in the alphabet. IDM see CLEAN *adj.*

sheet·ing /ˈʃiːtɪŋ/ *noun* [U] **1** metal, plastic, etc. made into flat thin pieces: *metal/plastic/polythene/metal sheeting* **2** fabric used for making sheets for beds

ˌsheet 'lightning *noun* [U] LIGHTNING that appears as a broad area of light in the sky—compare FORKED LIGHTNING

'sheet music *noun* [U] printed music as opposed to recorded music; printed music published on separate sheets of paper that are not fastened together to form a book

sheikh /ʃeɪk; ʃiːk/ (also **shaikh** /ʃeɪk/) *noun* **1** an Arab prince or leader; the head of an Arab village, tribe, etc. **2** a leader in a Muslim community or organization

sheikh·dom /ˈʃeɪkdəm; ˈʃiːk-/ *noun* an area of land ruled by a sheikh

sheila /ˈʃiːlə/ *noun* (*AustralE, NZE, slang*) a girl or young woman

shekel /ˈʃekl/ *noun* **1** the unit of money in Israel **2** an ancient silver coin used by the Jews

shelf /ʃelf/ *noun* (*pl.* **shelves** /ʃelvz/) **1** a flat board, made of wood, metal, glass, etc., fixed to the wall or forming part of a cupboard/closet, BOOKCASE, etc., for things to be placed on: *I helped him put up some shelves in his bedroom.* ◊ *The book I wanted was on the top shelf.* ◊ *supermarket/library shelves* ◊ *empty shelves* **2** *(geology)* a thing shaped like a shelf, especially a piece of rock sticking out from a cliff or from the edge of a mass of land under the sea: *the continental shelf*—see also SHELVE IDM **on the 'shelf** *(informal)* **1** not wanted by anyone; not used **2** *(old-fashioned)* (especially of women) considered to be too old to get married **off the 'shelf** that can be bought immediately and does not have to be specially designed or ordered: *I bought this package off the shelf.* ◊ *off-the-shelf software packages*—compare OFF THE PEG at PEG *n.*

'shelf life *noun* [usually sing.] the length of time that food, etc. can be kept before it is too old to be sold

shell /ʃel/ *noun, verb*
■ *noun* **1** [C, U] the hard outer part of eggs, nuts, some seeds and some animals: *We collected shells on the beach.* ◊ *snail/mussel/walnut shells* ◊ *earrings made out of coconut shell*—see also EGGSHELL, NUTSHELL, SEASHELL, TORTOISESHELL—picture on pages A2 and A7 **2** [C] any object that looks like the shell of a SNAIL or sea creature: *pasta shells* **3** [C] a metal case filled with explosive, to be fired from a large gun **4** *(AmE)* = CARTRIDGE **5** [C] the walls or outer structure of sth, for example, an empty building or ship after a fire or a bomb attack: *The house was now a shell gutted by flames.* ◊ *(figurative) My life has been an empty shell since he died.* **6** [C] any structure that forms a hard outer frame: *the body shell of a car* **7** [sing.] the outer layer of sb's personality; how they seem to be or feel: *She had developed a shell of indifference.* IDM **come out of your 'shell** to become less shy and more confident when talking to other people **to go/retreat etc. into your 'shell** to become shyer and avoid talking to other people:

S

Whenever my friends are here, she just withdraws into her shell.

■ *verb* **1** to fire shells at sth: [VN] *They shelled the city all night.* ◊ [V] *Just as they were leaving the rebels started shelling.* **2** [VN] to remove the shell or covering from nuts, peas, etc. PHRV ,shell 'out (for sth)| ,shell sth↔'out (for sth) (*informal*) to pay a lot of money for sth SYN FORK OUT: *The band shelled out $100000 for a mobile recording studio.*

she'll /ʃiːl/ *short form* she will

shel·lac /ʃəˈlæk; ˈʃelæk/ *noun* [U] a natural substance used in making varnish to protect surfaces and make them hard

shell·fire /ˈʃelfaɪə(r)/ *noun* [U] attacks or explosions caused by SHELLS being fired from large guns

shell·fish /ˈʃelfɪʃ/ *noun* (*pl.* **shell·fish**) a creature with a shell, that lives in water, especially one of the types that can be eaten. OYSTERS and CRABS are all shellfish.—compare CRUSTACEAN, MOLLUSC

shell·ing /ˈʃelɪŋ/ *noun* [U] the firing of SHELLS from large guns: *We suffered weeks of heavy shelling.*

'shell shock *noun* [U] a mental illness that can affect soldiers who have been in battle for a long time

'shell-shocked *adj.* **1** shocked, confused or anxious because of a difficult situation, and unable to think or act normally: *I felt completely shell-shocked after I heard the news.* **2** suffering from shell shock

'shell suit *noun* (*BrE*) a loose pair of trousers/pants and matching jacket worn as informal clothes. Shell suits are made of a light, slightly shiny, material and are often brightly coloured.—compare TRACKSUIT

shel·ter /ˈʃeltə(r)/ *noun, verb*
■ *noun* **1** [U] the fact of having a place to live or stay, considered as a basic human need: *Human beings need food, clothing and shelter.* ◊ *They were anxious to find shelter for the night.* **2** [U] ~ (from sth) protection from rain, danger or attack: *to take shelter from the rain/ wind/weather* ◊ *The fox was running for the shelter of the trees.* ◊ *People were desperately seeking shelter from the gunfire.* **3** [C] (often in compounds) a structure built to give protection, especially from the weather or from attack: *They built a rough shelter from old pieces of wood and cardboard.* ◊ *an air-raid shelter*—see also BUS SHELTER **4** [C] a building, usually owned by a charity, that provides a place to stay for people without a home, or protection for people or animals who have been badly treated: *a night shelter for the homeless* ◊ *an animal shelter*—see also HOSTEL
■ *verb* **1** [VN] ~ sb/sth (from sb/sth) to give sb/sth a place where they are protected from the weather or from danger; to protect sb/sth: *Trees shelter the house from the wind.* ◊ *helping the poor and sheltering the homeless* ◊ *Perhaps I sheltered my daughter too much* (= protected her too much from unpleasant or difficult experiences). **2** [V] ~ (from sth) to stay in a place that protects you from the weather or from danger: *We sheltered from the rain in a doorway.*

shel·tered /ˈʃeltəd; *AmE* -tərd/ *adj.* **1** (of a place) protected from bad weather: *a sheltered bay/beach* **2** (sometimes *disapproving*) protected from the more unpleasant aspects or difficulties of life: *She had a very sheltered childhood.* ◊ *They both lead very sheltered lives.* **3** [only before noun] (*BrE*) (of houses, flats/apartments, etc.) designed for people, especially old people, who can still live fairly independent lives, but with staff available to help them if necessary: *sheltered accommodation/housing* ◊ *a sheltered workshop for the blind*

shelve /ʃelv/ *verb* **1** [VN] to decide not to continue with a plan, either for a short time or permanently: *The government has shelved the idea until at least next year.* **2** [VN] to put books, etc. on a shelf **3** [V] [usually+adv./prep.] (of land) to slope downwards: *The beach shelved gently down to the water.*

shelves *pl.* of SHELF

shelv·ing /ˈʃelvɪŋ/ *noun* [U] shelves; material for making shelves: *wooden shelving*

she·nani·gans /ʃɪˈnænɪɡənz/ *noun* [pl.] (*informal*) secret or dishonest activities that people find interesting or amusing: *political/financial/sexual shenanigans*

shep·herd /ˈʃepəd; *AmE* -ərd/ *noun, verb*
■ *noun* (*AmE* **sheep·herd·er**) a person whose job is to take care of sheep
■ *verb* [VN+*adv./prep.*] to guide sb or a group of people somewhere, making sure they go where you want them to go: *He shepherded her towards a line of taxis.*

shep·herd·ess /ˌʃepəˈdes; ˈʃepədəs; *AmE* ˌʃepərˈdes; ˈʃepərdəs/ *noun* (*old-fashioned*) a woman who takes care of sheep

,shepherd's 'pie (also ,cottage 'pie) *noun* [C, U] (*BrE*) a dish of MINCED (= finely chopped) meat covered with a layer of MASHED potato

sher·bet /ˈʃɜːbət; *AmE* ˈʃɜːrbət/ *noun* **1** [U] (*BrE*) a powder that tastes of fruit and FIZZES when you put it in your mouth, eaten as a sweet/candy **2** [C, U] (*AmE*, becoming *old-fashioned*) = SORBET

sherd /ʃɜːd; *AmE* ʃɜːrd/ *noun* = SHARD

sher·iff /ˈʃerɪf/ *noun* **1** (in the US) an elected officer responsible for keeping law and order in a county or town **2** (often **High Sheriff**) (in England and Wales) an officer representing the king or queen in counties, and some cities, who performs some legal duties and attends ceremonies **3** (in Scotland) a judge

'sheriff court *noun* a lower court of law in Scotland

Sherpa /ˈʃɜːpə; *AmE* ˈʃɜːrpə/ *noun* a member of a Himalayan people, who often guide people in the mountains, sometimes carrying their bags, etc.

sherry /ˈʃeri/ *noun* (*pl.* **-ies**) **1** [U, C] a strong yellow or brown wine, originally from southern Spain. It is often drunk before meals: *sweet/dry sherry* ◊ *cream sherry* (= a type of very sweet sherry) ◊ *fine quality sherries* ◊ *a sherry glass* (= a type of small narrow wine glass) **2** [C] a glass of sherry: *I'll have a sherry.*

she's *short form* **1** /ʃiːz; ʃiz/ she is **2** /ʃiːz/ she has

,Shetland 'pony *noun* a very small, strong horse with a rough coat

shh = SH

Shia (also **Shi'a**) /ˈʃiə/ *noun* (*pl.* **Shia** or **Shias**) **1** [U] one of the two main branches of the Islamic religion—compare SUNNI **2** [C] (also **Shi·ite**, **Shi'ite**) a member of the Shia branch of Islam

shib·bo·leth /ˈʃɪbəleθ/ *noun* (*formal*) **1** an old idea, principle or phrase that is no longer accepted by many people as important or appropriate to modern life **2** a custom, word, etc. that distinguishes one group of people from another ORIGIN From a Hebrew word meaning 'ear of corn'. In the Bible story, Jephthah, the leader of the Gileadites, was able to use it as a test to tell which were his own men, because foreigners found the 'sh' sound difficult to pronounce.

shied *pt*, *pp* of SHY

shield /ʃiːld/ *noun, verb*
■ *noun* **1** a large piece of metal or leather carried by soldiers in the past to protect the body when fighting **2** = RIOT SHIELD **3** a person or thing used to protect sb/sth, especially by forming a barrier: *The gunman used the hostages as a human shield.* ◊ *Water is not an effective shield against the sun's more harmful rays.* ◊ *She hid her true feelings behind a shield of cold indifference.* **4** a plate or screen that protects a machine or the person using it from damage or injury **5** an object in the shape of a shield, given as a prize in a sports competition, etc. **6** a drawing or model of a shield showing a COAT OF ARMS **7** (*AmE*) a police officer's BADGE
■ *verb* [VN] **1** ~ sb/sth (from sb/sth) to protect sb/sth from danger, harm or sth unpleasant: *I shielded my eyes against the glare.* ◊ *The ozone layer shields the earth from the sun's ultraviolet rays.* ◊ *Police believe that somebody is shielding the killer.* ◊ *You can't shield her from the truth forever.* **2** to put a shield around a piece of machinery, etc. in order to protect the person using it

shift /ʃɪft/ *verb, noun*

s	t	v	z	ʃ	ʒ	tʃ	dʒ	θ	ð	ŋ
see	tea	van	zoo	shoe	vision	chain	jam	thin	this	sing

■ *verb*

MOVE | **1** ~ (sth) (from ...) (to ...) to move, or move sth, from one position or place to another: [V] *The action of the novel shifts from Paris to London.* ◊ *Lydia shifted uncomfortably in her chair.* ◊ [VN] *He shifted his gaze from the child to her.* ◊ *Could you help me shift some furniture?* ◊ *She shifted her weight from one foot to the other.* **2** [V, VN] ~ (yourself) (*BrE, informal*) to move quickly SYN HURRY

SITUATION/OPINION/POLICY | **3** [V] ~ (from ...) (to/towards/toward ...) (of a situation, an opinion, a policy etc.) to change from one state, position, etc. to another: *Public attitudes towards marriage have shifted over the past 50 years.* ◊ *The balance of power shifted away from workers towards employers.* **4** [VN] ~ sth (from ...) (to/towards/toward ...) to change your opinion of or attitude towards sth, or change the way that you do sth: *We need to shift the focus of this debate.* ◊ *The new policy shifted the emphasis away from fighting inflation.*

RESPONSIBILITY | **5** [VN] ~ responsibility/blame (for sth) (onto sb) to make sb else responsible for sth you should do or sth bad that you have done: *He tried to shift the blame for his mistakes onto his colleagues.*

REMOVE MARK | **6** [VN] to remove sth such as a dirty mark: *a detergent that shifts even the most stubborn stains*

SELL GOODS | **7** [VN] to sell goods, especially goods that are difficult to sell: *They cut prices drastically to try and shift stock.*

IN VEHICLE | **8** [V] (*AmE*) to change the GEARS when you are driving a vehicle: *to shift into second gear*

IDM **shift your 'ground** (usually *disapproving*) to change your opinion about a subject, especially during a discussion **(the) ,shifting 'sands (of sth)** used to describe a situation that changes so often that it is difficult to understand or deal with it

PHRV **,shift for your'self** (*BrE*) to do things without help from other people: *You're going to have to shift for yourself from now on.*

■ *noun*

CHANGE | **1** [C] ~ (in sth) a change in position or direction: *a gradual shift in the population away from the countryside to the towns* ◊ *a dramatic shift in public opinion* ◊ *a shift of emphasis*

PERIOD OF WORK | **2** [C] a period of time worked by a group of workers who start work as another group finishes: *to be on the day/night shift at the factory* ◊ *to work an eight-hour shift* ◊ *working in shifts* ◊ *shift workers/work* **3** [C+sing./pl. *v.*] the workers who work a particular shift: *The night shift has/have just come off duty.*

ON COMPUTER | **4** [U] the mechanism on a TYPEWRITER or computer keyboard that allows capital letters or a different set of characters to be typed: *a shift key*

CLOTHING | **5** [C] a woman's simple straight dress **6** [C] a simple straight piece of clothing worn by women in the past as underwear

shift·less /'ʃɪftləs/ *adj.* (*disapproving*) lazy and having no AMBITION to succeed in life

shifty /'ʃɪfti/ *adj.* (*informal*) seeming to be dishonest; looking guilty about sth: *shifty eyes* ◊ *to look shifty* ▶ **shift·ily** /-ɪli/ *adv.*

Shi·ite (also **Shi'ite**) /'ʃiːaɪt/ *noun* a member of one of the main branches of Islam (called Shia)—compare SUNNI ▶ **Shi·ite** (also **Shi'ite**) *adj.* [usually before noun]

shil·ling /'ʃɪlɪŋ/ *noun* **1** a British coin in use until 1971, worth 12 old pence. There were 20 shillings in one pound. **2** the unit of money in Kenya, Uganda, Tanzania and Somalia

shilly-shally /'ʃɪli ˌʃæli/ *verb* (**shilly-shallies, shilly-shally·ing, shilly-shallied, shilly-shallied**) [V] (*informal, disapproving*) to take a long time to do sth, especially to make a decision SYN DITHER: *Stop shilly-shallying and make up your mind.*

shim·mer /'ʃɪmə(r)/ *verb, noun*
■ *verb* [V] (*written*) to shine with a soft light that seems to move slightly: *The sea was shimmering in the sunlight.*
■ *noun* [U, sing.] (*written*) a shining light that seems to move slightly: *the shimmer of silk* ◊ *a shimmer of moonlight in the dark sky*

shimmy /'ʃɪmi/ *verb* (**shim·mies, shimmy·ing, shim-**

mied, shim·mied) [V+*adv./prep.*] to dance or move in a way that involves shaking your hips and shoulders: *She shimmied onto the dance floor.*

shin /ʃɪn/ *noun, verb*
■ *noun* the front part of the leg below the knee—picture at BODY
■ *verb* (-nn-) (*BrE*) (*AmE* **shinny**) PHRV **'shin/'shinny up/down sth** (*informal*) to climb up or down sth quickly, using your hands and legs: *He shinned down the drainpipe and ran off.*

'shin bone *noun* the front and larger bone of the two bones in the lower part of the leg between the knee and the ankle SYN TIBIA—picture at BODY

shin·dig /'ʃɪndɪɡ/ *noun* (*informal*) a big noisy party

shine /ʃaɪn/ *verb, noun*
■ *verb* (**shone, shone** /ʃɒn; *AmE* ʃoʊn/) HELP In sense 3 **shined** is used for the past tense and past participle. **1** [V] to produce or reflect light; to be bright: *The sun shone brightly in a cloudless sky.* ◊ *The dark polished wood shone like glass.* ◊ (*figurative*) *Her eyes were shining with excitement.* ◊ *Excitement was shining in her eyes.* **2** [VN] to aim or point the light of a lamp, etc. in a particular direction: *He shone the flashlight around the cellar.* ◊ (*figurative*) *Campaigners are shining a spotlight on the world's diminishing natural resources.* **3** (**shined, shined**) [VN] to polish sth; to make sth smooth and bright: *He shined shoes and sold newspapers to make money.* **4** [V] to be very good at sth: *He failed to shine academically but he was very good at sports.* ◊ *She has set a shining example of loyal service over four decades.*—see also SHINY IDM see HAY, KNIGHT *n.*, RISE *v.* PHRV **,shine 'through (sth)** (of a quality) to be easy to see or notice: *Her old professional skills shone through.*
■ *noun* [sing.] the bright quality that sth has when light is reflected on it: *a shampoo that gives your hair body and shine* IDM **take a 'shine to sb/sth** (*informal*) to begin to like sb very much as soon as you see or meet them **take the 'shine off sth** (*informal*) to make sth seem much less good than it did at first—more at RAIN *n.*

shingle /'ʃɪŋɡl/ *noun* **1** [U] a mass of small smooth stones on a beach or at the side of a river: *a shingle beach/bank* **2** [C, U] a small flat piece of wood that is used to cover a wall or roof of a building **3** [C] (*AmE*) a board with a sign on it, in front of a doctor's or lawyer's office: *He hung out his own shingle* (= started a business as a doctor or lawyer).

shin·gled /'ʃɪŋɡld/ *adj.* (of a roof, building, etc.) covered with shingles

shin·gles /'ʃɪŋɡlz/ *noun* [U] a disease that affects the nerves and produces a band of painful spots on the skin

'shin guard (*BrE* also **'shin pad**) *noun* a piece of thick material that is used to protect the lower front part of the leg when playing football, etc.

shinny /'ʃɪni/ *verb* (**shin·nies, shinny·ing, shin·nied, shin·nied**) (*AmE*) = SHIN

shiny /'ʃaɪni/ *adj.* (**shini·er, shini·est**) smooth and bright; reflecting the light: *shiny black hair/shoes* ◊ *His face was red and shiny.*

ship /ʃɪp/ *noun, verb*
■ *noun* a large boat that carries people or goods by sea: *There are two restaurants on board ship.* ◊ *a sailing/cargo/cruise ship* ◊ *a ship's captain/crew/company/cook* ◊ *Raw materials and labour come by ship, rail or road.*—see also AIRSHIP, FLAGSHIP, LIGHTSHIP IDM see JUMP *v.*, SINK *v.*, TIGHT
■ *verb* (-pp-) **1** [VN] to send or transport sb/sth by ship or by another means of transport: *The company ships its goods all over the world.* ◊ *He was arrested and shipped back to the UK for trial.* **2** (*computing*) to be available to be bought; to make sth available to be bought: [V] *The software is due to ship next month.* ◊ [VN] *The company continues to ship more computer systems than its rivals.* **3** [VN] ~ water (of a boat, etc.) to have water coming in over the sides IDM see SHAPE *v.* PHRV **,ship sb↔'off** (*disapproving*) to send sb to a place where they will stay: *The children were shipped off to a boarding school at an early age.*

S

æ	ɑː	e	ɜː	ə	ɪ	iː	i	ɒ	ɔː	ʌ	ʊ	u	uː
cat	father	ten	bird	about	sit	see	many	got	saw	cup	put	actual	too

(BrE)

-ship *suffix* (in nouns) **1** the state or quality of: *ownership* ◊ *friendship* **2** the status or office of: *citizenship* ◊ *professorship* **3** skill or ability as: *musicianship* **4** the group of: *membership*

ship·board /'ʃɪpbɔːd; *AmE* -bɔːrd/ *adj.* [only before noun] happening on a ship: *shipboard romances*

ship·build·er /'ʃɪpbɪldə(r)/ *noun* a person or company that builds ships ► **ship·build·ing** *noun* [U]: *the shipbuilding industry*

ship·load /'ʃɪpləʊd; *AmE* -loʊd/ *noun* as many goods or passengers as a ship can carry: *a shipload of food and medical supplies*

ship·mate /'ʃɪpmeɪt/ *noun* sailors who are **shipmates** are sailing on the same ship as each other

ship·ment /'ʃɪpmənt/ *noun* **1** [U] the process of sending goods from one place to another: *The goods are ready for shipment.* ◊ *the illegal shipment of arms* ◊ *shipment costs/dates* **2** [C] a load of goods that are sent from one place to another: *arms shipments* ◊ *a shipment of arms*

ship·owner /'ʃɪpəʊnə(r); *AmE* -oʊn-/ *noun* a person who owns a ship or ships

ship·per /'ʃɪpə(r)/ *noun* a person or company that arranges for goods to be sent from one place to another, especially by ship

ship·ping /'ʃɪpɪŋ/ *noun* [U] **1** ships in general or considered as a group: *The canal is open to shipping.* ◊ *the shipping forecast* (= a report for ships on the weather conditions at sea) ◊ *international shipping lanes* (= routes for ships) **2** the activity of carrying people or goods from one place to another by ship: *a shipping company/group/line*

'ship's chandler *noun* = CHANDLER

ship·shape /'ʃɪpʃeɪp/ *adj.* [not usually before noun] clean and neat; in good condition and ready to use

'ship-to-shore *adj.* [only before noun] providing communication between people on a ship and people on land: *a ship-to-shore radio*

ship·wreck /'ʃɪprek/ *noun, verb*
- *noun* **1** [U, C] the loss or destruction of a ship at sea because of a storm or because it hits rocks, etc: *They narrowly escaped shipwreck in a storm in the North Sea.* **2** [C] a ship that has been lost or destroyed at sea: *The contents of shipwrecks belong to the state.*
- *verb* [VN] (**be shipwrecked**) to be left somewhere after the ship that you have been sailing in has been lost or destroyed at sea: *They were shipwrecked off the coast of Africa.* ► **ship·wrecked** *adj.*: *a shipwrecked sailor*

ship·yard /'ʃɪpjɑːd; *AmE* -jɑːrd/ *noun* a place where ships are built or repaired: *shipyard workers*

shire /'ʃaɪə(r); or, in compounds, -ʃə(r)/ *noun* (*BrE*) **1** [C] (*old use*) a county (now used in the names of some counties in Britain, for example *Hampshire, Yorkshire*) **2** (**the Shires**) (also **the Shire Counties**) [pl.] counties in central England that are in country areas

'shire horse *noun* a large powerful horse, used for pulling loads

shirk /ʃɜːk; *AmE* ʃɜːrk/ *verb* ~ (**from**) (**sth/doing sth**) to avoid doing sth you should do, especially because you are too lazy: [V] *Discipline in the company was strict and no one shirked.* ◊ *A determined burglar will not shirk from breaking a window to gain entry.* ◊ [VN] *She never shirked her responsibilities.* [also V-ing] ► **shirk·er** *noun*

shirt /ʃɜːt; *AmE* ʃɜːrt/ *noun* a piece of clothing worn on the upper part of the body, especially by men, made of light fabric, with sleeves, a collar and buttons down the front: *to wear a shirt and tie* ◊ *a short-sleeved shirt*—picture on page A4—see also NIGHTSHIRT, STUFFED SHIRT, SWEATSHIRT, T-SHIRT **IDM** **keep your 'shirt on** (*informal*) used to tell sb not to get angry: *Keep your shirt on! It was only a joke.* **put your 'shirt on sb/sth** (*BrE, informal*) to bet all your money on sb/sth **the ,shirt off sb's 'back** anything that sb has, including the things they really need themselves, that sb else takes from them or they are willing to give

'shirt front *noun* the front part of a shirt, especially the stiff front part of a formal white shirt

shirt·sleeve /'ʃɜːtsliːv; *AmE* 'ʃɜːrt-/ *noun* [usually pl.] a sleeve of a shirt **IDM** **in (your) 'shirtsleeves** wearing a shirt without a jacket, etc. on top of it

'shirt tail *noun* the part of a shirt that is below the waist and is usually inside your trousers/pants

shirty /'ʃɜːti; *AmE* 'ʃɜːrti/ *adj.* ~ (**with sb**) (*BrE, informal*) angry or annoyed with sb about sth, and acting in a rude way

shish kebab /'ʃɪʃ kɪbæb/ *noun* (*especially AmE*) = KEBAB

shit /ʃɪt/ *exclamation, noun, verb, adj.*
- *exclamation* (⚠, *slang*) a swear word that many people find offensive, used to show that you are angry or annoyed: *Shit! I've lost my keys!* **HELP** Less offensive exclamations to use are **blast**, **darn** it (especially *AmE*), **damn** or (*BrE*) **bother**.
- *noun* (⚠, *slang*) **1** [U] solid waste matter from the bowels **SYN** EXCREMENT: *a pile of dog shit on the path* **HELP** A more polite way to express this example would be 'a pile of dog dirt'. **2** [sing.] an act of emptying solid waste matter from the bowels: *to have/need a shit* **3** [U] stupid remarks or writing; nonsense: *You're talking shit!* ◊ *She's so full of shit.*—see also BULLSHIT **4** [C] (*disapproving*) an unpleasant person who treats other people badly: *He's an arrogant little shit.* **5** [U] criticism or unfair treatment: *I'm not going to take any shit from them.* **IDM** **beat, kick, etc. the 'shit out of sb** to attack sb violently so that you injure them **in the 'shit** | **in ,deep 'shit** in trouble: *I'll be in the shit if I don't get this work finished today.* ◊ *You're in deep shit now.* **like 'shit** really bad, ill/sick etc.; really badly: *I woke up feeling like shit.* ◊ *We get treated like shit in this job.* **No 'shit!** (often *ironic*) used to show that you are surprised, impressed, etc. or that you are pretending to be **not give a 'shit (about sb/sth)** to not care at all about sb/sth: *He doesn't give a shit about anybody else.* **when the ,shit hits the 'fan** when sb in authority finds out about sth bad or wrong that sb has done: *When the shit hits the fan, I don't want to be here.*—more at CROCK, SCARE *v.*
- *verb* (**shit·ting, shit, shit**) (⚠, *slang*) **HELP** **shat** /ʃæt/ and, in *BrE*, **shit·ted** are also used for the past tense and past participle. **1** [V, VN] to empty solid waste matter from the bowels **HELP** A more polite way of expressing this is 'to go to the toilet/lavatory' (*BrE*), 'to go to the bathroom' (*AmE*) or 'to go'. A more formal expression is 'to empty the bowels'. **2** [VN] (~ **yourself**) to empty solid waste matter from the bowels accidentally **3** [VN] (~ **yourself**) to be very frightened
- *adj.* (⚠ *slang, especially BrE*) very bad: *You're shit and you know you are!* ◊ *They're a shit team.*

shite /ʃaɪt/ *exclamation, noun* [U] (*BrE*, ⚠, *slang*) another word for SHIT

shit·less /'ʃɪtləs/ *adj.* (⚠, *slang*) **IDM** see SCARE *v.*

,shit 'scared *adj.* [not before noun] (⚠, *slang*) very frightened

shitty /'ʃɪti/ *adj.* (⚠, *slang*) **1** unpleasant; very bad: *I'm not going to eat this shitty food.* ◊ *a shitty week at work* **2** unfair or unkind: *What a shitty way to treat a friend!*

shiver /'ʃɪvə(r)/ *verb, noun*
- *verb* [V] ~ (**with sth**) (of a person) to shake slightly because you are cold, frightened, excited, etc: *to shiver with cold/tiredness/excitement/pleasure* ◊ *Don't stand outside shivering—come inside and get warm!* ◊ *He shivered at the thought of the cold, dark sea.*
- *noun* **1** [C] a sudden shaking movement of your body because you are cold, frightened, excited, etc: *The sound of his voice sent shivers down her spine.* ◊ *He felt a cold shiver of fear run through him.* **2** (**the shivers**) [pl.] shaking movements of your body because of fear or a high temperature: *I don't like him. He gives me the shivers.* ◊ *Symptoms include headaches, vomiting and the shivers.*

shiv·ery /'ʃɪvəri/ *adj.* shaking with cold, fear, illness, etc.

shoal /ʃəʊl; *AmE* ʃoʊl/ *noun* **1** a large number of fish swimming together as a group—compare SCHOOL (9) **2** a small hill of sand just below the surface of the sea: *The boat ran aground on a shoal.*

shock /ʃɒk; *AmE* ʃɑːk/ *noun, verb*

■ *noun*

UNPLEASANT SURPRISE | **1** [C usually sing, U] an unpleasant feeling as a result of sth bad happening; the event that causes this feeling: *The news of his death* **came as a shock** *to us all.* ◊ *He's still in* **a state of shock.** ◊ *I got a terrible shock the other day.* ◊ *She still hadn't got over the shock of seeing him again.* ◊ (*informal*) *If you think the job will be easy, you're* **in for a shock.** ◊ *Losing in the first round was* **a shock to the system** (= it was a more of a shock because it was not expected). ◊ *The team suffered a shock defeat in the first round.*—see also CULTURE SHOCK

MEDICAL | **2** [U] a serious medical condition, usually the result of injury in which a person has lost a lot of blood and they are extremely weak: *She was taken to hospital* **suffering from shock.** ◊ *He isn't seriously injured but he is in* (**a state of**) **shock.**—see also SHELL SHOCK, TOXIC SHOCK SYNDROME

VIOLENT SHAKING | **3** [C, U] a violent shaking movement that is caused by an explosion, earthquake, etc: *The shock of the explosion could be felt up to six miles away.* ◊ *The bumper absorbs shock on impact.*

FROM ELECTRICITY | **4** [C] = ELECTRIC SHOCK: *Don't touch that wire or you'll get a shock.*

OF HAIR | **5** a thick mass of hair on a person's head

IDM ,**shock** '**horror** (*BrE, informal*, often *humorous*) used when you pretend to be shocked by sth that is not really very serious or surprising

■ *verb*

SURPRISE AND UPSET | **1** to surprise and upset sb: [VN] *It shocks you when something like that happens.* ◊ *We were all shocked at the news of his death.* ◊ [VN that] *Neighbours were shocked that such an attack could happen in their area.* ◊ [VN to inf] *I was shocked to hear that he had resigned.*

OFFEND/DISGUST | **2** (of bad language, immoral behaviour, etc.) to make sb feel offended or disgusted: [V] *These movies deliberately set out to shock.* ◊ [VN] *She enjoys shocking people by saying outrageous things.* [also VN to inf]

▶ **shocked** *adj.*: *For a few minutes we stood in shocked silence.*

'**shock absorber** *noun* a device that is fitted to each wheel of a vehicle in order to reduce the effects of travelling over rough ground, so that passengers can be more comfortable

shock·er /'ʃɒkə(r); *AmE* 'ʃɑːk-/ *noun* (*informal*) (often used in newspapers) a film/movie, piece of news or person that shocks you

shock·ing /'ʃɒkɪŋ; *AmE* 'ʃɑːk-/ *adj.* **1** that offends or upsets people; that is morally wrong: *shocking behaviour* ◊ *shocking news* ◊ *It is shocking that they involved children in the crime.* ◊ *a shocking waste of money* **2** (*informal, especially BrE*) very bad: *The house was left in a shocking state.* ▶ **shock·ing·ly** *adv.*: *a shockingly high mortality rate* ◊ *She looked shockingly ill.*

,**shocking** '**pink** *adj.* very bright pink in colour ▶ ,**shocking** '**pink** *noun* [U]

'**shock tactics** *noun* [pl.] actions that are done to deliberately shock people in order to persuade them to do sth or to react in a particular way

'**shock therapy** (also '**shock treatment**) *noun* [U] a way of treating mental illness by giving ELECTRIC SHOCKS or a drug that has a similar effect

'**shock troops** *noun* [pl.] soldiers who are specially trained to make sudden attacks on the enemy

'**shock wave** *noun* **1** a movement of very high air pressure that is caused by an explosion, earthquake, etc. **2** (**shock waves**) [pl.] feelings of shock that people experience when sth bad happens suddenly: *The murder sent shock waves through the whole community.*

shod /ʃɒd; *AmE* ʃɑːd/ *adj.* (*literary*) wearing shoes of the type mentioned: *She turned on her elegantly shod heel.*—see also SHOE, SHOEING, SHOD, SHOD *v.*

shoddy /'ʃɒdi; *AmE* 'ʃɑːdi/ *adj.* (**shod·dier, shod·di·est**) **1** (of goods, work, etc.) made or done badly and with not enough care: *I always complain about bad service or shoddy goods.* ◊ *He was accused of shoddy workmanship.* **2** dishonest or unfair: *shoddy treatment* ▶ **shod·dily** *adv.* **shod·di·ness** *noun* [U]

shoe /ʃuː/ *noun, verb*

■ *noun* **1** one of a pair of outer coverings for your feet, usually made of leather or plastic: *a pair of shoes* ◊ *He took his shoes and socks off.* ◊ *What's your shoe size?* ◊ *a shoe brush* ◊ *shoe polish*—see also SNOWSHOE **2** = HORSESHOE **IDM** **be in sb's shoes** | **put yourself in sb's shoes** to be in, or imagine that you are in, another person's situation, especially when it is an unpleasant or difficult one: *I wouldn't like to be in your shoes when they find out about it.* **if** ,**I were in** '**your shoes** used to introduce a piece of advice you are giving to sb: *If I were in your shoes, I'd resign immediately.* **if the shoe fits** (*AmE*) = IF THE CAP FITS at CAP **the shoe is on the other** '**foot** (*AmE*) = THE BOOT IS ON THE OTHER FOOT at BOOT—more at FILL *v.*, SHAKE *v.*, STEP *v.*

■ *verb* (**shoe·ing, shod, shod** /ʃɒd; *AmE* ʃɑːd/) [VN] to put one or more HORSESHOES on a horse: *The horses were sent to the blacksmith to be shod.*

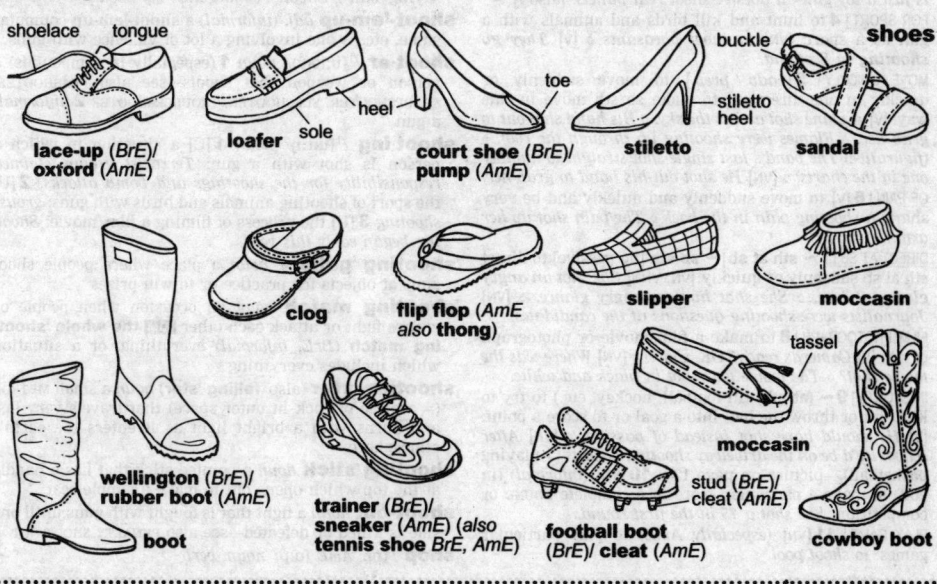

shoes

shoelace   tongue

lace-up (*BrE*)/ **oxford** (*AmE*)

loafer   sole   heel

court shoe (*BrE*)/ **pump** (*AmE*)   toe

stiletto   stiletto heel

buckle   **sandal**

clog   **flip flop** (*AmE* also **thong**)   **slipper**   **moccasin**

wellington (*BrE*)/ **rubber boot** (*AmE*)   **boot**

trainer (*BrE*)/ **sneaker** (*AmE*) (also **tennis shoe** *BrE, AmE*)

football boot (*BrE*)/ **cleat** (*AmE*)   **stud** (*BrE*)/ cleat (*AmE*)

moccasin   tassel

cowboy boot

shoe·horn /'ʃuːhɔːn; *AmE* -hɔːrn/ *noun, verb*
- *noun* a curved piece of plastic or metal, used to help your heel slide into a shoe
- *verb* [VN+*adv./prep.*] to succeed in putting sth into a small space or a place where it does not fit very easily: *They managed to shoehorn the material onto just one CD.*

shoe·lace /'ʃuːleɪs/ (also **lace**) *noun* a long thin piece of material like string that goes through the holes on a shoe and is used to fasten it: *a pair of shoelaces* ◊ *to tie/untie your shoelaces* ◊ *Your shoelace is undone.*

shoe·maker /'ʃuːmeɪkə(r)/ *noun* a person whose job is making shoes and boots—compare COBBLER ▶ **shoe·mak·ing** *noun* [U]

shoe·shine /'ʃuːʃaɪn/ *noun* (*especially AmE*) the activity of cleaning people's shoes for money: *a shoeshine boy/man* ◊ *a shoeshine stand on West 32nd Street*

shoe·string /'ʃuːstrɪŋ/ *noun, adj.*
- *noun* IDM **on a 'shoestring** (*informal*) using very little money: *In the early years, the business was run on a shoestring.*
- *adj.* [only before noun] (*informal*) that uses very little money: *The club exists on a shoestring budget.*

sho·gun /'ʃəʊɡən; *AmE* 'ʃoʊ-/ *noun* (in the past) a Japanese military leader

shone *pt, pp* of SHINE

shoo /ʃuː/ *verb, exclamation*
- *verb* (**shoo·ing, shooed, shooed**) [VN] to make sb/sth go away or to another place, especially by saying 'shoo'! and waving your arms and hands: *He shooed the dog out of the kitchen.*
- *exclamation* used to tell a child or an animal to go away

'shoo-in *noun* ~ (**for sth**)|~ (**to do sth**) (*AmE, informal*) a person or team that will win easily

shook *pt, pp* of SHAKE

shoot /ʃuːt/ *verb, noun, exclamation*
- *verb* (**shot, shot** /ʃɒt; *AmE* ʃɑːt/)
  WEAPON | **1** ~ (**sth**) (**at sb/sth**)|~ **sth** (**from sth**) to fire a gun or other weapon; to fire sth from a weapon: [V] *Don't shoot—I surrender.* ◊ *troops shooting at the enemy* ◊ *a serious shooting incident* ◊ *The police rarely* **shoot to kill** (= try to kill the people they shoot at). ◊ [VN] *He shot an arrow from his bow.* ◊ *They shot the lock off* (= removed it by shooting). **2** to kill or wound a person or an animal with a bullet, etc: [VN] *A man was shot in the leg.* ◊ *He shot himself during a fit of depression.* ◊ *The guards were ordered to* **shoot on sight** *anyone trying to escape.* ◊ [VN-ADJ] *Three people were* **shot dead** *during the robbery.* **3** (of a gun or other weapon) to fire bullets, etc: [VN] *This is just a toy gun—it doesn't shoot real bullets.* [also V]
  FOR SPORT | **4** to hunt and kill birds and animals with a gun as a sport: [VN] *to shoot pheasants* ◊ [V] *They go* **shooting** *in Scotland.*
  MOVE QUICKLY | **5** [+*adv./prep.*] to move suddenly or quickly in one direction; to move sb/sth move in this way: [V] *A plane shot across the sky.* ◊ *His hand shot out to grab her.* ◊ *Flames were shooting up through the roof.* ◊ (*figurative*) *The band's last single shot straight to number one in the charts.* ◊ [VN] *He shot out his hand to grab her.*
  OF PAIN | **6** [V] to move suddenly and quickly and be very sharp: *a shooting pain in the back* ◊ *The pain shot up her arm.*
  DIRECT AT SB | **7** ~ **sth at sb**|~ **sb sth** [no passive] to direct sth at sb suddenly or quickly: [VN, VNN] *She shot an angry glance at him.* ◊ *She shot him an angry glance.* ◊ [VN] *Journalists were shooting questions at the candidates.*
  FILM/PHOTOGRAPH | **8** to make a film/movie or photograph of sth: [V] *Cameras ready? OK, shoot!* ◊ [VN] *Where was the movie shot?* ◊ *The movie was shot in black and white.*
  IN SPORTS | **9** ~ (**at sth**) (in football, hockey, etc.) to try to kick, hit or throw the ball into a goal or to score a point: [V] *He should have shot instead of passing.* ◊ [VN] *After school we'd be on the driveway shooting baskets* (= playing basketball).—picture on page 1250 **10** [VN] (*informal*) (in golf) to make a particular score in a complete ROUND or competition: *She shot a 75 in the first round.*
  PLAY GAME | **11** [VN] (*especially AmE*) to play particular games: *to shoot pool*

  SPEAK | **12** (**shoot!**) [V] (*spoken, especially AmE*) used to tell sb to say what they want to say: *You want to tell me something? OK, shoot!*
  IDM **be/get 'shot of sth/sb** (*BrE, informal*) to no longer have sth; to get rid of sth: *I'll be glad to get shot of this car.* **have shot your 'bolt** (*informal*) to have used all your power, money or supplies **shoot the 'breeze/'bull** (*AmE, informal*) to have a conversation in an informal way: *We sat around in the bar, shooting the breeze.* **shoot from the 'hip** to react quickly without thinking carefully first **shoot yourself in the 'foot** (*informal*) to do or say sth that will cause you a lot of trouble or harm, especially when you are trying to get an advantage for yourself **shoot it 'out (with sb)** (*informal*) to fight against sb with guns, especially until one side is killed or defeated: *The gang decided to shoot it out with the police.*—related noun SHOOT-OUT **shoot your 'mouth off (about sth)** (*informal*) **1** to talk with too much pride about sth **2** to talk about sth that is private or secret **shoot the 'rapids** to go in a boat over part of a river where the water flows very fast **PHRV** **shoot sb/sth ↔ 'down 1** to make sb/sth fall to the ground by shooting them/it: *Several planes were shot down by enemy fire.* **2** to be very critical of sb's ideas, opinions, etc: *His latest theory has been shot down in flames.* **'shoot for sth** (*AmE, informal*) to try to achieve or get sth, especially sth difficult: *We've been shooting for a pay raise for months.* **shoot 'off** (*informal*) to leave very quickly: *I had to shoot off at the end of the meeting.* **shoot 'through** (*AustralE, NZE, informal*) to leave, especially in order to avoid sb/sth: *I was only five when my Dad shot through.* **shoot 'up 1** to grow very quickly: *Their kids have shot up since I last saw them.* **2** to rise suddenly by a large amount: *Ticket prices shot up last year.* **shoot sth ↔ 'up 1** to cause great damage to sth by shooting **2** [no passive] (*slang*) to INJECT an illegal drug directly into your blood
- *noun*
  PLANT | **1** the part that grows up from the ground when a plant starts to grow; a new part that grows on plants or trees: *new green shoots* ◊ *bamboo shoots*—picture at PLANT
  FILM/PHOTOGRAPHS | **2** an occasion when sb takes professional photographs for a particular purpose or makes a film/movie: *a fashion shoot*
  FOR SPORT | **3** (*especially BrE*) an occasion when a group of people hunt and shoot animals or birds for sport; the land where this happens
- *exclamation* (*AmE*) used to show that you are annoyed when you do sth stupid or when sth goes wrong (to avoid saying 'shit'): *Shoot! I've forgotten my book!*

'shoot-'em-up *adj.* (*informal*) a **shoot-'em-up** computer game, etc. is one involving a lot of violence with guns

shoot·er /'ʃuːtə(r)/ *noun* **1** (especially in compounds) a person or weapon that shoots—see also PEASHOOTER, SHARPSHOOTER, SIX-SHOOTER, TROUBLESHOOTER **2** (*informal*) a gun

shoot·ing /'ʃuːtɪŋ/ *noun* **1** [C] a situation in which a person is shot with a gun: *Terrorist groups claimed responsibility for the shootings and bomb attacks.* **2** [U] the sport of shooting animals and birds with guns: *grouse shooting* **3** [U] the process of filming a film/movie: *Shooting began early this year.*

'shooting gallery *noun* a place where people shoot guns at objects for practice or to win prizes

'shooting match *noun* an occasion when people or groups fight or attack each other IDM **the whole 'shooting match** (*BrE, informal*) everything, or a situation which includes everything

'shooting 'star (also **'falling 'star**) *noun* a small METEOR (= a piece of rock in outer space) that travels very fast and burns with a bright light as it enters the earth's atmosphere

'shooting stick *noun* a pointed stick that has a handle at the top which opens out to make a simple seat

'shoot-out *noun* a fight that is fought with guns until one side is killed or defeated—see also PENALTY SHOOT-OUT

shop /ʃɒp; *AmE* ʃɑːp/ *noun, verb*

s	t	v	z	ʃ	ʒ	tʃ	dʒ	θ	ð	ŋ
see	tea	van	zoo	shoe	vision	chain	jam	thin	this	sing

S

■ *noun*

WHERE YOU BUY STH | **1** [C] (*especially BrE*) a building or part of a building where you can buy goods or services: *a pet/shoe shop* ◊ *There's a little gift shop around the corner.* ◊ (*BrE*) *a butcher's shop* ◊ (*AmE*) *a butcher shop* ◊ (*BrE*) *I'm just going down to the shops. Can I get you anything?*—see also BUCKET SHOP, COFFEE SHOP, CORNER SHOP

FOR MAKING/REPAIRING THINGS | **2** (also **work·shop**) [C] (especially in compounds) a place where things are made or repaired, especially part of a factory where a particular type of work is done: *a repair shop* ◊ *a paint shop* (= where cars are painted)—see also BODY SHOP

SHOPPING | **3** [sing.] (*BrE, informal*) an act of going shopping, especially for food and other items needed in the house: *I do my weekly shop at the supermarket.*

SCHOOL SUBJECT | **4** (also **'shop class**) [U] (both *AmE*) = INDUSTRIAL ARTS

ROOM FOR TOOLS | **5** (also **work·shop**) [C] (*AmE*) a room in a house where tools are kept for making repairs to the house, building things out of wood, etc.

IDM **all 'over the shop** (*BrE, informal*) = ALL OVER THE PLACE at PLACE *n.* **,set up 'shop** to start a business: *American Technologies set up shop in Warsaw in 1990.*—more at BULL, HIT *v.*, MIND *v.*, SHUT *v.*, TALK *v.*

■ *verb* (**-pp-**)

BUY | **1** [V] ~ (**for sth**) to buy things in shops/stores: *to shop for food/clothes/presents* ◊ *He likes to shop at the local market.* **2** (**go shopping**) [V] to spend time going to shops/stores and looking for things to buy: *There should be plenty of time to go shopping before we leave New York.* ◊ *'Where's Mum?' 'She went shopping.'*

TELL POLICE ABOUT SB | **3** [VN] ~ **sb** (**to sb**) (*BrE, informal*) to give information to sb, especially to the police, about sb who has committed a crime: *He didn't expect his own mother to shop him to the police.*

PHRV **,shop a'round** (**for sth**) to compare the quality or prices of goods or services that are offered by different shops/stores, companies, etc. so that you can choose the best: *Shop around for the best deal.*

'shop assistant (also **as·sis·tant**) (both *BrE*) (*AmE* **'sales clerk**, **clerk**) *noun* a person whose job is to serve customers in a shop/store

'shop-bought (*BrE*) (*AmE* **store-bought**) *adj.* [only before noun] bought from a shop/store and not made at home: *shop-bought cakes*

shop·fit·ting /'ʃɒpfɪtɪŋ; *AmE* 'ʃɑːp-/ *noun* [U] the business of putting equipment and furniture into shops/stores ▶ **shop·fit·ter** *noun*

,shop 'floor *noun* [sing.] (*BrE*) **1** the area in a factory where the goods are made by the workers: *to work on the shop floor* **2** the workers in a factory, not the managers

shop·front /'ʃɒpfrʌnt; *AmE* 'ʃɑːp-/ (*BrE*) (*AmE* **store-front**) *noun* the outside of a shop/store that faces the street

shop·keep·er /'ʃɒpkiːpə(r); *AmE* 'ʃɑːp-/ (also **store-keep·er** especially in *AmE*) *noun* a person who owns or manages a shop/store, usually a small one

shop·lift·ing /'ʃɒplɪftɪŋ; *AmE* 'ʃɑːp-/ *noun* [U] the crime of stealing goods from a shop/store by deliberately leaving without paying for them ▶ **shop·lift** *verb* [V] **shop·lift·er** *noun*: *Shoplifters will be prosecuted.*

shop·per /'ʃɒpə(r); *AmE* 'ʃɑːp-/ *noun* a person who buys goods from shops/stores: *The streets were full of Christmas shoppers.*

shop·ping /'ʃɒpɪŋ; *AmE* 'ʃɑːp-/ *noun* [U] **1** the activity of going to shops/stores and buying things: (*BrE*) *When shall I do the shopping?* ◊ (*BrE*) *We do our shopping on Saturdays.* ◊ *a shopping bag/basket* ◊ *a shopping trolley* ◊ (*AmE*) *a shopping cart*—see also WINDOW-SHOPPING **2** (*especially BrE*) the things that you have bought from shops/stores: *to put the shopping in the car*

'shopping arcade *noun* = ARCADE

'shopping centre (*BrE*) (*AmE* **'shopping center**) *noun* a group of shops/stores built together, sometimes under one roof

'shopping list *noun* a list that you make of all the things that you need to buy when you go shopping: (*figurative*)

The union presented a shopping list of demands to the management.

'shopping mall (also **mall**) (both *especially AmE*) (*BrE* also **ar·cade**, **'shopping arcade**) *noun* a large group of shops/stores built together under one roof and closed to traffic

'shop-soiled (*BrE*) (*AmE* **shop·worn**) *adj.* (of goods) dirty or not in perfect condition because they have been in a shop/store for a long time: *a sale of shop-soiled goods at half price*

,shop 'steward *noun* (*especially BrE*) a person who is elected by members of a trade union in a factory or company to represent them in meetings with managers

shop·worn /'ʃɒpwɔːn; *AmE* 'ʃɑːpwɔːrn/ *adj.* (*AmE*) = SHOP-SOILED: (*figurative*) *a shopworn argument* (= that is no longer new or useful)

shore /ʃɔː(r)/ *noun, verb*

■ *noun* **1** [C, U] the land along the edge of the sea or ocean, a lake or another large area of water: *a rocky/sandy shore* ◊ *to swim from the boat to the shore* ◊ *a house on the shores of the lake* ◊ *The ship was anchored off shore.* ⇨ note at COAST **2** (**shores**) [pl.] (*especially literary*) a country, especially one with a coast: *foreign/distant shores*

■ *verb* PHRV **,shore sth↔'up 1** to support part of a building or other large structure by placing large pieces of wood or metal against or under it so that it does not fall down: *Timbers were used to shore up the tunnel.* **2** to help to support sth that is weak or going to fail: *The measures were aimed at shoring up the economy.*

shore·line /'ʃɔːlaɪn; *AmE* 'ʃɔːrl-/ *noun* [usually sing.] the edge of the sea, the ocean or a lake: *a rocky shoreline* ◊ *The road follows the shoreline for a few miles.*

shorn *pp of* SHEAR

short /ʃɔːt; *AmE* ʃɔːrt/ *adj., adv., noun, verb*

■ *adj.* (**short·er**, **short·est**)

LENGTH/DISTANCE | **1** measuring or covering a small length or distance, or a smaller length or distance than usual: *He had short curly hair.* ◊ *a short walk/drive/flight* ◊ *a short skirt* OPP LONG

HEIGHT | **2** (of a person) small in height: *She was short and dumpy.* OPP TALL

TIME | **3** lasting or taking a small amount of time or less time than usual: *I'm going to France for a short break.* ◊ *Which is the shortest day of the year?* ◊ *a short book/list* (= taking a short time to read/deal with) ◊ *She has a very short memory* (= remembers only things that have happened recently) ◊ (*spoken*) *Life's too short to sit around moping.* ◊ *It was all over in a relatively short space of time.* OPP LONG **4** [only before noun] (of a period of time) seeming to have passed very quickly: *Just two short years ago he was the best player in the country.* OPP LONG

NOT ENOUGH | **5** [not before noun] ~ (**of sth**) not having enough of sth; lacking sth: *I'm afraid I'm a little short* (= of money) *this month.* ◊ *She is not short of excuses when things go wrong.* **6** ~ **on sth** (*informal*) lacking or not having enough of a particular quality: *He was a big strapping guy but short on brains.* **7** [not before noun] not easily available; not supplying as much as you need: *Money was short at that time.* **8** [not before noun] ~ (**of sth**) less than the number, amount or distance mentioned or needed: *Her last throw was only three centimetres short of the world record.* ◊ *The team was five players short.* ◊ *She was just short of her 90th birthday when she died.*

OF BREATH | **9** ~ **of breath** having difficulty breathing, for example because of illness: *a fat man, always short of breath*

NAME/WORD | **10** ~ **for sth** being a shorter form of a name or word: *Call me Jo—it's short for Joanna.* ◊ *file transfer protocol or FTP for short*

RUDE | **11** [not before noun] ~ (**with sb**) (of a person) speaking to sb using few words in a way that seems rude: *I'm sorry I was short with you earlier—I had other things on my mind.*

VOWEL | **12** (*phonetics*) a **short** vowel is pronounced for a shorter time than other vowels: *Compare the short vowel in 'full' and the long vowel in 'fool'.* OPP LONG

—see also SHORTLY ▶ **short·ness** *noun* [U]: *She suffered from shortness of breath.*

IDM a ˌbrick short of a ˈload, two ˌsandwiches short of a ˈpicnic, etc. (*informal*) (of a person) stupid; not very intelligent **get the short end of the ˈstick** (*AmE*) = DRAW THE SHORT STRAW at DRAW *v.* **give sb/sth/get short ˈshrift** to give sb/sth little attention or sympathy **have/ be on a short ˈfuse** to have a tendency to get angry quickly and easily: *You may find your temper on a short fuse when confronting your teenager.* **in ˌshort ˈorder** quickly and without trouble **in the ˈshort run** concerning the immediate future: *In the short run, unemployment may fall.* **in ˌshort supˈply** not existing in large enough quantities to satisfy demand: *Basic foodstuffs were in short supply.* ◊ *Sunshine will be in short supply for the west coast.* **little/nothing short of ˈsth** used when you are saying that sth is almost true, or is equal to sth: *Last year's figures were little short of disastrous.* ◊ *The transformation has been nothing short of a miracle.* **make short ˈwork of sth/sb** to defeat, deal with sth/sb quickly: *Liverpool made short work of the opposition* (= in a football game). ◊ *He made short work of his lunch* (= ate it quickly). **ˌshort and ˈsweet** (*informal*) pleasant but not lasting a long time: *We haven't much time so I'll keep it short and sweet.*—more at DRAW *v.*, LONG *adj.*, MEASURE *n.*, NOTICE *n.*, TERM *n.*, THICK *adj.*

■ *adv.* (**short·er, short·est**) **1** if you go short of or run short of sth, you do not have enough of it: *I'd never let you go short of anything.* ◊ *Mothers regularly go short of food to ensure their children have enough.* ◊ *They had run short of* (= used most of their supply of) *fuel.* **2** not as far as you need or expect: *All too often you pitch the ball short.* **3** before the time expected or arranged; before the natural time: *a career tragically cut short by illness* ◊ *I'm afraid I'm going to have to stop you short there, as time is running out.*

IDM **be caught ˈshort** (*BrE* also **be taken ˈshort**) **1** (*BrE, informal*) to suddenly feel an urgent need to go to the toilet **2** to be put at a disadvantage **fall ˈshort of sth** to fail to reach the standard that you expected or need: *The hotel fell far short of their expectations.* **short of (doing) sth** without sth; without doing sth; unless sth happens: *Short of a miracle, we're certain to lose.* ◊ *Short of asking her to leave* (= and we don't want to do that) *there's not a lot we can do about the situation.* **pull, bring, etc. sb up ˈshort** to make sb suddenly stop what they are doing: *I was brought up short by a terrible thought.*—more at SELL *v.*, STOP *v.*

■ *noun* (*informal*)—see also SHORTS **1** (*BrE*) a small strong alcoholic drink, for example of whisky **2** a short film/ movie, especially one that is shown before the main film **3** = SHORT CIRCUIT

IDM **in ˈshort** in a few words: *His novels belong to a great but vanished age. They are, in short, old-fashioned.*—more at LONG *adj.*

■ *verb* ~ (**sth**) (**out**) (*informal*) = SHORT-CIRCUIT: [V] *Lightning crackled overhead as cables shorted out.* [also VN]

short·age /ˈʃɔːtɪdʒ; *AmE* ˈʃɔːrt-/ *noun* [C, U] a situation when there is not enough of the people or things that are needed: *food/housing/water shortages* ◊ *a shortage of funds/space* ◊ *There is no shortage of* (= there are plenty of) *things to do in the town.*

ˌshort ˌback and ˈsides *noun* [sing.] (*old-fashioned*) a way of cutting a man's hair so that the hair is very short at the sides and the back of the head

short·bread /ˈʃɔːtbred; *AmE* ˈʃɔːrt-/ (*BrE* also **short·cake**) *noun* [U] a rich crisp biscuit/cookie made with flour, sugar and a lot of butter

short·cake /ˈʃɔːtkeɪk; *AmE* ˈʃɔːrt-/ *noun* [U] **1** (*BrE*) = SHORTBREAD **2** a cake with a pastry base and cream and fruit on top: *strawberry shortcake*

ˌshort-ˈchange *verb* [VN] [often passive] **1** to give back less than the correct amount of money to sb who has paid for sth with more than the exact price: *I think I've been short-changed at the bar.* **2** to treat sb unfairly by not giving them what they have earned or deserve: *America*

is short-changing half its young adults by treating those who don't attend college as failures.

ˌshort ˈcircuit (also *informal* **short**) *noun* a failure in an electrical CIRCUIT, when electricity travels along the wrong route because of damaged wires or a fault in the connections between the wires

ˌshort-ˈcircuit (also *informal* **short**) *verb* **1** to have a short circuit; to make sth have a short circuit: [V] *The wires had short-circuited and burnt out.* [also VN] **2** [VN] to succeed in doing sth more quickly than usual, without going through all the normal processes, which would take longer

short·com·ing /ˈʃɔːtkʌmɪŋ; *AmE* ˈʃɔːrt-/ *noun* [usually pl.] a fault in sb's character, a plan, a system, etc. SYN DEFECT: *She made me aware of my own shortcomings.*

short·crust pastry /ˌʃɔːtkrʌst ˈpeɪstri; *AmE* ˌʃɔːrt-/ *noun* [U] a type of pastry that CRUMBLES easily, used for making pies, etc.

ˌshort ˈcut (also **short cut**) *noun* **1** a quicker or shorter way of getting to a place: *You can take a short cut across the field.* **2** a way of doing sth that is quicker than the usual way: *There are no short cuts to economic recovery.*

short·en /ˈʃɔːtn; *AmE* ˈʃɔːrtn/ *verb* ~ (**sth to sth**) to make sth shorter; to become shorter: [VN] *Injury problems could shorten his career.* ◊ *a shortened version of the game* ◊ *Her name's Katherine, generally shortened to Kay.* ◊ [V] *In November the temperatures drop and the days shorten.* OPP LENGTHEN

short·en·ing /ˈʃɔːtnɪŋ; *AmE* ˈʃɔːrt-/ *noun* [U] fat that is used for making pastry

short·fall /ˈʃɔːtfɔːl; *AmE* ˈʃɔːrt-/ *noun* ~ (**in sth**) if there is a **shortfall** in sth, there is less of it than you need or expect: *a shortfall of over 500000 tonnes in the grain supply*

short·hand /ˈʃɔːthænd; *AmE* ˈʃɔːrt-/ *noun* **1** (*AmE* also **sten·og·raphy**) [U] a quick way of writing using special signs or abbreviations, used especially to record what sb is saying: *typing and shorthand* ◊ *to take sth down in shorthand* ◊ *a shorthand typist* **2** [U, C] ~ (**for sth**) a shorter way of saying or referring to sth, which may not be as accurate as the more complicated way of saying it

ˌshort-ˈhanded *adj.* [not usually before noun] not having as many workers or people who can help as you need SYN SHORT-STAFFED

ˈshort-haul *adj.* [only before noun] that involves transporting people or goods over short distances, especially by plane OPP LONG-HAUL

short·list /ˈʃɔːtlɪst; *AmE* ˈʃɔːrt-/ *noun, verb*
■ *noun* [usually sing.] a small number of candidates for a job, etc., who have been chosen from all the people who applied: *to draw up a shortlist* ◊ *a shortlist for a literary prize* ◊ *She is one of the four people on my shortlist of great singers.*
■ *verb* [VN] [usually passive] ~ **sb/sth** (**for sth**) (*BrE*) to put sb/sth on a shortlist for a job, prize, etc: *Candidates who are shortlisted for interview will be contacted by the end of the week.*

ˌshort-ˈlived *adj.* lasting only for a short time

short·ly /ˈʃɔːtli; *AmE* ˈʃɔːrt-/ *adv.* **1** a short time; not long: *She arrived shortly after us.* ◊ *I saw him shortly before he died.* **2** soon: *I'll be ready shortly.* **3** in an angry and impatient way SYN SHARPLY

ˌshort-order ˈcook *noun* a person who works in a restaurant cooking food that can be prepared quickly

ˌshort-ˈrange *adj.* [usually before noun] **1** (of weapons) designed to travel only over short distances: *short-range missiles* **2** (of plans, etc.) connected with a short period of time in the future: *a short-range weather forecast*—compare LONG-RANGE

shorts /ʃɔːts; *AmE* ʃɔːrts/ *noun* [pl.] **1** short trousers/ pants that end above or at the knee, worn when playing sports, in hot weather or by children: *a pair of tennis shorts* ◊ *He was wearing a T-shirt and shorts.* **2** (*AmE*) = BOXER SHORTS

ˌshort-ˈsighted *adj.* **1** (*especially BrE*) (*AmE* usually ˌnear-ˈsighted) able to see things clearly only if they are very close to you OPP LONG-SIGHTED **2** not thinking carefully about the possible effects of sth or what might happen in the future: *a short-sighted policy* ▶ **,short 'sight** *noun* [U]: *She suffered from short sight.* **,short-'sighted·ly** *adv.* **,short-'sighted·ness** *noun* [U]: *an eye test to detect short-sightedness* ◊ *Many people accused the government of short-sightedness.*

,short-'staffed *adj.* [not usually before noun] having fewer members of staff than you need or usually have SYN SHORT-HANDED—see also UNDERSTAFFED

,short-'stay *adj.* [only before noun] (*BrE*) (of a place) where you only stay for a short time: *a short-stay car park*

,short 'story *noun* a story, usually about imaginary characters and events, that is short enough to be read from beginning to end without stopping

,short 'temper *noun* [sing.] a tendency to become angry very quickly and easily ▶ **,short-'tempered** *adj.*

,short-'term *adj.* [usually before noun] lasting a short time; designed only for a short period of time in the future: *a short-term loan* ◊ *to find work on a short-term contract* ◊ *short-term aims/plans/forecasts* ◊ *a short-term solution to the problem* ◊ *His short-term memory* (= the ability to remember things that happened a short time ago) *is failing.*—compare LONG-TERM

,short-'termism *noun* [U] a way of thinking or planning that is concerned with the advantages or profits you could have now, rather than the effects in the future

,short 'time *noun* [U] (*BrE*) if workers are put on **short time**, they work for fewer hours than usual, because there is not enough work to do or not enough money to pay them

,short 'wave *noun* [C, U] (*abbr.* **SW**) a radio wave that has a FREQUENCY greater than 3 MEGAHERTZ: *a short-wave radio/broadcast*—compare LONG WAVE, MEDIUM WAVE

shot /ʃɒt; *AmE* ʃɑːt/ *noun, adj.*—see also SHOOT, SHOT, SHOT *v.*

■ *noun*

WITH GUN **1** [C] **~** **(at sb/sth)** the act of firing a gun; the sound this makes: *The man fired several shots from his pistol.* ◊ *Someone took a shot at the car.* ◊ *We heard some shots in the distance.*—see also GUNSHOT, POTSHOT **2** [C] **a good, bad, etc. ~** a person who shoots a gun in a particular way (well, badly, etc.)

BULLETS **3** (also **,lead 'shot**) [U] a large number of small metal balls that you fire together from a SHOTGUN—see also BUCKSHOT **4** [C] (*pl.* **shot**) a large stone or metal ball that was shot from a CANNON or large gun in the past

REMARK/ACTION **5** [C] a remark or an action that is usually one of a series, and is aimed against sb/sth that you are arguing or competing with: *This statement was the opening shot in the argument.* ◊ *The supermarket fired the first shot in a price war today.*

ATTEMPT **6** [C, usually sing.] **~** **(at sth/at doing sth)** (*informal*) the act of trying to do or achieve sth: *The team are looking good for a shot at the title.* ◊ *I've never produced a play before but I'll have a shot at it.* ◊ *I'm willing to give it a shot.* ◊ *Just give it your best shot* (= try as hard as you can) *and you'll be fine.*

IN SPORT **7** [C] the action of hitting, kicking or throwing the ball in order to score a point or goal in a game: *Taylor scored with a low shot into the corner of the net.* ◊ *Good shot!* **8** (often **the shot**) [sing.] the heavy ball that is used in the sports competition called THE SHOT-PUT

PHOTOGRAPH **9** [C] a photograph: *I got some good shots of people at the party.*—see also MUG SHOT, SNAPSHOT

SCENE IN FILM/MOVIE **10** [C] a scene in a film/movie that is filmed continuously by one camera: *the opening shot of a character walking across a desert*

DRUG **11** [C] (*informal, especially AmE*) a small amount of a drug that is put into your body using a SYRINGE SYN INJECTION: *a flu shot* (= to protect you against flu) ◊ *a shot of morphine*

DRINK **12** [C] (*informal*) a small amount of a drink, especially a strong alcoholic one: *a shot of whisky*

OF SPACECRAFT **13** [C] an occasion when a spacecraft is

sent into space: *The space shot was shown live on television.*

HORSE/DOG IN RACE **14** [sing.] (used with numbers) a horse, dog, etc. that has the particular chance of winning a race that is mentioned: *The horse is a 10-1 shot.*

HELP You will find other compounds ending in **shot** at their place in the alphabet.

IDM **like a 'shot** (*informal*) very quickly and without hesitating: *If I had the chance to go there, I'd go like a shot.* **a shot across the/sb's 'bows** something that you say or do as a warning to sb about what might happen if they do not change, etc. **a shot in the 'arm** something that gives sb/sth the help or encouragement they need—more at BIG *adj.*, CALL *v.*, DARK *n.*, LONG *adj.*, PARTING *adj.*

■ *adj.* **1 ~** **(with sth)** (of fabric, hair, etc.) having another colour showing through or mixed with the main colour: *shot silk* **2** [not before noun] (*informal*) in a very bad condition; destroyed: *The brakes on this car are shot.* ◊ *I'm shot—I'm too old for this job.* ◊ *After the accident his nerves were shot to pieces.*

IDM **be/get 'shot of sb/sth** (*BrE, informal*) to get rid of sb/sth so you no longer have the problems they cause **shot through with sth** containing a lot of a particular colour, quality or feature: *a voice shot through with emotion*

shot·gun /'ʃɒtɡʌn; *AmE* 'ʃɑːt-/ *noun* a long gun that fires a lot of small metal bullets, (called SHOT), and is used especially for shooting birds or animals: *The raiders were armed with sawn-off shotguns.* ◊ (*AmE*) **sawed-off shotguns** IDM see RIDE *v.*

,shotgun 'wedding (also **,shotgun 'marriage**) *noun* (*old-fashioned, informal*) a wedding that has to take place quickly, for example because the woman is pregnant

the 'shot-put *noun* [sing.] (also **'shot-putting**, **,putting the 'shot**) the event or sport of throwing a heavy metal ball (called a SHOT) as far as possible—picture on page 1251

> **GRAMMAR POINT**
> **should / ought / had better**
>
> **Should** and **ought to** are both used to say that something is the best thing or the right thing to do, but **should** is much more common: *You should take the baby to the doctor's.* ◊ *I ought to give up smoking.* In questions, **should** is usually instead of **ought to**: *Should we call the doctor?*
>
> **Had better** can also be used to say what is the best thing to do in a situation that is happening now: *We'd better hurry or we'll miss the train.*
>
> You form the past by using **should have** or **ought to have**: *She should have asked for some help.* ◊ *You ought to have been more careful.*
>
> The forms **should not** or **shouldn't** (and **ought not to** or **oughtn't to**, which are rare in *AmE* and formal in *BrE*) are used to say that something is a bad idea or the wrong thing to do: *You shouldn't drive so fast.*
>
> The forms **should not have** or **shouldn't have** and, much less frequently, **ought not to have** or **oughtn't to have** are used to talk about the past: *I'm sorry, I shouldn't have lost my temper.*

should /ʃəd; *strong form* ʃʊd/ *modal verb* (*negative* **should not**, *short form* **shouldn't** /'ʃʊdnt/) **1** used to show what is right, appropriate, etc., especially when criticizing sb's actions: *You shouldn't drink and drive.* ◊ *He should have been more careful.* **2** used for giving or asking for advice: *You should stop worrying about it* ◊ *Should I call him and apologize?* ◊ *I should wait a little longer, if I were you.* ◊ (*ironic*) *'She doesn't think she'll get a job.' 'She should worry, with all her qualifications* (= she does not need to worry).' **3** used to say that you expect sth is true or will happen: *We should arrive before dark.* ◊ *I should have finished the book by Friday.* ◊ *The roads should be less crowded today.* **4** used to say that sth that was expected has not happened: *It should be snowing now, according to the weather forecast.* ◊ *The bus should have arrived ten minutes ago.* **5** (*BrE, formal*) used after *I* or *we* instead of

b	d	f	g	h	k	l	m	n	p	r
bad	did	fall	get	hat	cat	leg	man	now	pen	red

S

would for describing what you would do if sth else happened first: *If I were asked to work on Sundays, I should resign.* **6** (*formal*) used to refer to a possible event or situation: *If you should change your mind, do let me know.* ◊ *In case you should need any help, here's my number.* ◊ *Should anyone call* (= if anyone calls), *please tell them I'm busy.* **7** used as the past form of *shall* when reporting what sb has said: *He asked me what time he should come.* (= His words were: 'What time shall I come?') ◊ (*BrE, formal*) *I said (that) I should be glad to help.* **8** (*BrE*) used after *that* when sth is suggested or arranged: *She recommended that I should take some time off.* ◊ *In order that training should be effective it must be planned systematically.* **HELP** In both *AmE* and *BrE* this idea can be expressed without 'should': *She recommended that I take some time off.* ◊ *In order that training be effective ...* **9** used after *that* after many adjectives that describe feelings: *I'm anxious that we should allow plenty of time.* ◊ *I find it astonishing that he should be so rude to you.* **10** (*BrE, formal*) used with *I* and *we* in polite requests: *I should like to call my lawyer.* ◊ *We should be grateful for your help.* **11** used with *I* and *we* to give opinions that you are not certain about: *I should imagine it will take about three hours.* ◊ *'Is this enough food for everyone?' 'I should think so.'* ◊ *'Will it matter?' 'I shouldn't think so.'* **12** used for expressing strong agreement: *'I know it's expensive but it will last for years.' 'I should hope so too!'* ◊ *'Nobody will oppose it.' 'I should think not!'* **13** *why, how, who, what ~ sb/sth do* used to refuse sth or to show that you are annoyed at a request; used to express surprise about an event or a situation: *Why should I help him? He's never done anything for me.* ◊ *How should I know where you've left your bag?* ◊ *I got on the bus and who should be sitting in front of me but Tony!* **14** used to tell sb that sth would amuse or surprise them if they saw or experienced it: *You should have seen her face when she found out!* ⇨ note at MODAL

GRAMMAR POINT
should / would

In modern English, the traditional difference between **should** and **would** in reported sentences, conditions, requests, etc. has disappeared and **should** is not used very much at all. In spoken English the short form **'d** is usually used: *I said I'd (I would) be late.* ◊ *He'd (he would) have liked to have been an actor.* ◊ *I'd (I would) really prefer tea.*

The main use of **should** now is to tell somebody what they ought to do, to give advice, or to add emphasis: *We should really go and visit them soon.* ◊ *You should have seen it!*

---

shoul·der /ˈʃəʊldə(r); *AmE* ˈʃoʊ-/ *noun, verb*
■ *noun*

PART OF BODY | **1** [C] either of the two parts of the body between the top of each arm and the neck: *He slung the bag over his shoulder.* ◊ *She tapped him on the shoulder.* ◊ *He looked back over his shoulder.* ◊ *She **shrugged her shoulders*** (= showing that she didn't know or care). ◊ *an off-the-shoulder dress* ◊ *He carried the child on his shoulders.*—picture at BODY

-SHOULDERED | **2** (in adjectives) having the type of shoulders mentioned: *broad-shouldered*—see also ROUND-SHOULDERED

CLOTHING | **3** [C] the part of a piece of clothing that covers the shoulder: *a jacket with padded shoulders*

MEAT | **4** [U, C] *~ (of sth)* meat from the top part of one of the front legs of an animal that has four legs

OF MOUNTAIN/BOTTLE, etc. | **5** [C] *~ (of sth)* a part of sth, such as a bottle or mountain, that is shaped like a shoulder: *The village lay just around the shoulder of the hill.*

SIDE OF ROAD | **6** [C] (*AmE*) an area of ground at the side of a road where vehicles can stop in an emergency: *No shoulder for next 5 miles.*—see also HARD SHOULDER, SOFT SHOULDER

IDM **be looking over your 'shoulder** to be anxious and have the feeling that sb is going to do sth unpleasant or harmful to you **on sb's shoulders** if blame, guilt, etc. is **on sb's shoulders,** they must take responsibility for it **put your shoulder to the 'wheel** to start working very hard at a particular task **a shoulder to 'cry on** (used to describe a person who listens to your problems and gives you sympathy) **shoulder to 'shoulder (with sb) 1** physically close to sb **2** as one group that has the same aims, opinions, etc.—more at CHIP *n.,* COLD *adj.,* HEAD *n.,* OLD, RUB *v.,* STRAIGHT *adv.*
■ *verb*

ACCEPT RESPONSIBILITY | **1** [VN] to accept the responsibility for sth: *to shoulder the responsibility/blame for sth* ◊ *women who shoulder the double burden of childcare and full-time work*

PUSH WITH SHOULDER | **2** [+adv./prep.] to push forward with your shoulder in order to get somewhere: [VN] *He shouldered his way through the crowd and went after her.* ◊ [V] *She shouldered past a woman with a screaming baby.* **3** [VN+adv./prep.] to push sb/sth out of your way with your shoulder: *He shouldered the man aside.*

CARRY ON SHOULDER | **4** [VN] to carry sth on your shoulder: *She shouldered her bag and set off home.*

'shoulder bag *noun* a bag, especially a handbag, that has a long strap and is carried over the shoulder

'shoulder blade *noun* either of the two large flat bones at the top of the back SYN SCAPULA—picture at BODY

,shoulder-'high *adj.* as high as a person's shoulders: *a shoulder-high wall* ► **,shoulder-'high** *adv.*: *They carried him shoulder-high through the crowd.*

'shoulder-length *adj.* (especially of hair) long enough to reach your shoulders

'shoulder pad *noun* [usually pl.] a small piece of thick fabric that is sewn into the shoulders of a dress, jacket, etc. to make a person's shoulders look bigger

'shoulder strap *noun* **1** a strip of fabric on a dress or other piece of clothing that goes over your shoulder from the front to the back **2** a long strip of fabric, leather, etc. that is attached to a bag so that you can carry it over your shoulder

shout /ʃaʊt/ *verb, noun*
■ *verb* **1** *~ (sth) (at/to sb)|~ (at sb to do sth)* to say sth in a loud voice; to speak loudly/angrily to sb: [V] *Stop shouting and listen!* ◊ *I shouted for help but nobody came.* ◊ *She shouted at him to shut the gate.* ◊ *Then he started shouting and swearing at her.* ◊ [VN] *to shout abuse/encouragement/orders* ◊ [V that] *He shouted that he couldn't swim.* ◊ [VN-ADJ] *She shouted herself hoarse, cheering on the team.* ◊ [V speech] *'Run!' he shouted.* **2** [V] *~ (out)* to make a loud noise: *She shouted out in pain when she tried to move her leg.* **PHRV** **,shout sb↔'down** to shout so that sb who is speaking cannot be heard: *The speaker was shouted down by a group of protesters.* **,shout sth↔'out** to say sth in a loud voice so that it can be clearly heard: *Don't shout out all the answers.* ◊ [+ speech] *'I'm over here!' I shouted out.*—note on page 1189
■ *noun* **1** a loud cry of anger, fear, excitement, etc: *loud/angry/distant shouts* ◊ *a shout of anger/pain/joy* ◊ *I heard her warning shout too late.* **2** (*AustralE, BrE, informal*) a person's turn to buy drinks: *What are you drinking? It's my shout.* **IDM** **be ,in with a 'shout (of sth/of doing sth)** (*informal*) to have a good chance of winning sth or of achieving sth **give sb a 'shout** (*spoken*) to tell sb sth: *Give me a shout when you're ready.*

shout·ing /ˈʃaʊtɪŋ/ *noun* [U] loud cries from a number of people: *Didn't you hear all the shouting?* **IDM** **be all over bar the 'shouting** (*BrE*) (of an activity or a competition) to be almost finished or decided, so that there is no doubt about the final result **within 'shouting distance** (*especially AmE*) = WITHIN SPITTING DISTANCE at SPIT *v.*

'shouting match *noun* an argument or a quarrel when people shout loudly at each other

shove /ʃʌv/ *verb, noun*
■ *verb* **1** to push sb/sth in a rough way: [V] *The crowd was pushing and shoving to get a better view.* ◊ *The door wouldn't open no matter how hard she shoved.* ◊ [VN] [usually+adv./prep.] *He shoved her down the stairs.* **2** [VN] [usually+adv./prep.] (*informal*) to put sth some-

S

WHICH WORD?
shout/cry/scream

These verbs describe the different kinds of loud noise
people make when they are angry, frightened or
upset. People **shout** when they are angry or want to
get somebody's attention: *He always seems to be
shouting at the kids these days.* ◇ *I can hear you —
there's no need to shout.* **Yell** can also be used,
especially in spoken English. **Cry** with this meaning
now sounds old-fashioned. When people **scream**
they make a very loud, high noise because they are
in great pain or are very frightened or excited: *There
was broken glass everywhere and people were screaming.* You can also use these words with 'out': *She
shouted out in pain as they tried to move her.*

where roughly or carelessly: *She shoved the book into her
bag and hurried off.* ◇ *He came over and shoved a piece of
paper into my hand.* ◇ *Shove your suitcase under the bed.*
IDM **'shove it** (*informal, especially AmE*) used to say
rudely that you will not accept or do sth: *'The boss wants
that report now.' 'Yeah? Tell him he can shove it.'* **PHR V**
,shove 'off (*BrE, spoken*) used to tell sb rudely to go away
,shove 'up (*BrE, spoken*) to move in order to make a
space for sb to sit down beside you: *Shove up! Jan wants
to sit down.*
- *noun* [usually sing.] a strong push: *to give sb/sth a shove*
IDM see PUSH *n.*

shovel /'ʃʌvl/ *noun, verb*
- *noun* **1** a tool with a long handle and a broad blade with
curved edges, used for moving earth, snow, sand, etc:
workmen with picks and shovels—compare SPADE—picture at GARDEN **2** the part of a large machine or vehicle
that digs or moves earth
- *verb* (**-ll-**, *AmE* **-l-**) [VN] to lift and move earth, stones, coal,
etc. with a shovel: *A gang of workmen were shovelling
rubble onto a truck.* ◇ *They went out in freezing conditions
to shovel snow.* ◇ (*AmE*) *to shovel the sidewalk/driveway*
(= to remove snow) ◇ (*figurative*) *He sat at the table,
shovelling food into his mouth.*

shovel·ful /'ʃʌvlfʊl/ *noun* the amount that a shovel can
hold

show /ʃəʊ; *AmE* ʃoʊ/ *verb, noun*
- *verb* (**showed**, **shown** /ʃəʊn/; *AmE* ʃoʊn/ or, rarely,
showed)
MAKE CLEAR | **1** to make sth clear; to prove sth: [V(that)]
The figures clearly show that her claims are false. ◇
[VN**that**] *Market research has shown us that people want
quality, not just low prices.* ◇ [VN] *a report showing the
company's current situation* ◇ [VN**to inf**] *His new book
shows him to be a first-rate storyteller.* ◇ [V**wh-**] *This shows
how people are influenced by TV advertisements.*
[also VN **wh-**]
LET SB SEE STH | **2 ~ sth (to sb)| ~ (sb) sth** to let sb see sth:
[VN] *If there's a letter from France please show it to me.* ◇
You have to show your ticket as you go in. ◇ [VN, VNN] *Have
you shown your work to anyone?* ◇ *Have you shown anyone
your work?*
TEACH | **3 ~ sth to sb| ~ sb sth** to help sb to do sth by
letting them watch you do it or by explaining it: [VN, VNN]
She showed the technique to her students. ◇ *She showed her
students the technique.* ◇ [VN**wh-**] *Can you show me how to
do it?*
POINT | **4** to point to sth so that sb can see where or what it
is: [VNN] *He showed me our location on the map.* ◇ [VN**wh-**]
Show me which picture you drew.
GUIDE | **5** to lead or guide sb to a place: [VN, +*adv. / prep.*]
The attendant showed us to our seats. ◇ *We were shown
into the waiting room.* ◇ [VNN] *I'll go first and show you
the way.*
QUALITY/BEHAVIOUR/FEELING | **6** to make it clear that you
have a particular quality: [VN] *to show great courage/
determination* ◇ [VN-ADJ] *She had shown herself unable to
deal with money.* ◇ [VN**to inf**] *He has shown himself to be
ready to make compromises.* [also V**that**] **7 ~ sth (for/to
sb)| ~ (sb) sth** to behave in a particular way towards

sb: [VN, VNN] *They showed no respect for their parents.* ◇
They showed their parents no respect. **8** if a feeling or
quality **shows**, or if you **show** it, people can see it: [V]
Fear showed in his eyes. ◇ *She tried not to let her disappointment show.* ◇ [VN] *Her expression showed her disappointment.* ◇ *James began to* **show signs of** *impatience.* ◇
[V**wh-**] *She tried not to show how disappointed she was.*
BE VISIBLE | **9** if sth **shows**, people can see it. If sth **shows**
a mark, dirt, etc., the mark can be seen: [V] *She had a warm
woollen hat on that left only her eyes and nose showing.* ◇
[VN] *Their new white carpet showed every mark.*
INFORMATION | **10** [VN] (not usually used in the progressive
tenses) to give particular information, or a time or measurement: *The map shows the principal towns and rivers.* ◇
The clock showed midnight. ◇ *The end-of-year accounts
show a loss.*
OF PICTURE/PHOTOGRAPH | **11 ~ sth| ~ sb (as sth)** to be of
sb/sth; to represent sb/sth: [VN] *She had objected to a
photo showing her in a bikini.* [also VN-**ing**]
FOR PUBLIC TO SEE | **12** to be or make sth available for the
public to see: [V] *The movie is now showing at all major
movie theaters.* ◇ [VN] *The movie is being shown now.* ◇ *She
plans to show her paintings early next year.*
PROVE | **13** [no passive] (*informal*) to prove that you can do
sth or are sth: [VN] *They think I can't do it, but I'll show
them!* ◇ [VN**to inf**] *He has shown himself to be a caring
father.* [also VNN]
ARRIVE | **14** [V] (*informal, especially AmE*) to arrive where
you have arranged to meet sb or do sth: *I waited an hour
but he didn't show.*—see also SHOW UP
ANIMAL | **15** [VN] to enter an animal in a competition
IDM **it goes to 'show** used to say that sth proves sth: *It
just goes to show what you can do when you really try.*
show sb the 'door to ask sb to leave, because they are
no longer welcome **show your 'face** to appear among
your friends or in public: *She stayed at home, afraid to
show her face.* **show your 'hand/'cards** (*BrE*) (*AmE* **tip
your 'hand**) to make your plans or intentions known
show sb who's 'boss to make it clear to sb that you
have more power and authority than they have **show the
'way** to do sth first so that other people can follow **show
'willing** (*BrE*) to show that you are ready to help, work
hard, etc. if necessary **(have) something, nothing, etc.
to 'show for sth** (to have) something, nothing, etc. as a
result of sth: *All those years of hard work, and nothing to
show for it!*—more at FLAG *n.*, PACE *n.*, ROPE *n.*
PHR V **,show sb a'round/'round (sth)** to be a guide for
sb when they visit a place for the first time to show them
what is interesting: *We were shown around the school by
one of the students.* ◇ *Has anyone shown you round yet?*
,show 'off (*informal, disapproving*) to try to impress
others by talking about your abilities, possessions, etc:
He's just showing off because that girl he likes is here.—
related noun SHOW-OFF **,show sb/sth↔'off 1** to show
people sb/sth that you are proud of: *She wanted to show
off her new husband at the party.* ◇ [+**wh-**] *He likes to show
off how well he speaks French.* **2** (of clothing) to make sb
look attractive, by showing their best features: *a dress
that shows off her figure* **,show 'through| ,show 'through
sth** to be able to be seen behind or under sth else: *The
writing on the other side of the page shows through.* ◇
(*figurative*) *When he spoke, his bitterness showed through.*
◇ *Veins showed through her pale skin.* **,show 'up** (*informal*) to arrive where you have arranged to meet sb or do
sth: *It was getting late when she finally showed up.* **,show
'up| ,show sth↔'up** to become visible; to make sth
become visible: *a broken bone showed up on the X-ray* ◇
The harsh light showed up the lines on her face. **,show
sb↔'up 1** (*BrE, informal*) to make sb feel embarrassed
by behaving badly: *He showed me up by snoring during
the concert.* **2** to make sb feel embarrassed by doing sth
better than them: *Don't worry about being shown up by
the kids—they've always used computers.*
- *noun*
ENTERTAINMENT | **1** [C] a theatre performance, especially
one that includes singing and dancing: *to see/watch/go to
a show* ◇ *a one-woman/-man show* ◇ *to put on/stage a
show* ◇ *She's the* **star of the show***!*—see also FLOOR SHOW,

æ	ɑː	e	ɜː	ə	ɪ	iː	i	ɒ	ɔː	ʌ	ʊ	u	uː
cat	father	ten	bird	about	sit	see	many	got	saw	cup	put	actual	too
								(BrE)					

S

ROADSHOW **2** [C] a programme on television or the radio: *to host a TV/radio show* ◇ *a comedy/quiz show*—see also CHAT SHOW, GAME SHOW, ROADSHOW, TALK SHOW

OF COLLECTION OF THINGS | **3** [C, U] an occasion when a collection of things are brought together for people to look at [SYN] EXHIBITION: *an agricultural show* ◇ *the Paris fashion shows* ◇ *The latest computers will be on show at the exhibition.*—see also PEEP SHOW

OF FEELING | **4** [C] an action or a way of behaving that shows how you feel [SYN] DISPLAY: *a show of emotion/gratitude/temper* ◇ *a show of support/unity* ◇ *A show of force by 4000 soldiers led to an agreement being reached quickly.*

INSINCERE ACT | **5** [U, sing.] something that is done only to give a good impression, but is not sincere: *He may seem charming, but it's all show!* ◇ *She pretends to be interested in opera, but it's only for show.* ◇ *He made a great show of affection, but I knew he didn't mean it.*

COLOURFUL SIGHT | **6** [C, U] a colourful or pleasing sight [SYN] DISPLAY: *a lovely show of spring flowers*

EVENT/SITUATION | **7** [sing.] (*informal*) an event, a business or a situation where sth is being done or organized: *She runs the whole show.* ◇ *I won't interfere—it's your show.*

GOOD/POOR SHOW | **8** [C, usually sing.] (*informal, especially BrE*) something that is done in a particular way: *The team put on a good show in the competition.* ◇ *It's a poor show if he forgets your birthday.*

IDM **for 'show** intended to be seen but not used: *These items are just for show—they're not for sale.* **get the ˌshow on the 'road** (*spoken*) to start an activity or a journey: *Let's get this show on the road!* **(jolly) good 'show!** (*old-fashioned, BrE, informal*) used to show you like sth or to say that sb has done sth well **a show of 'hands** a group of people each raising a hand to vote for or against sth—more at STEAL

'show business (also *informal* **show·biz** /'ʃəʊbɪz; AmE 'ʃoʊ-/) *noun* [U] the business of providing public entertainment, for example in the theatre, in films/movies or in television: *to be/work in show business* ◇ *show-business people/stars* ◇ *That's showbiz!*

show·case /'ʃəʊkeɪs; AmE 'ʃoʊ-/ *noun* **1** [usually sing.] **~ (for sb/sth)** an event that presents sb's abilities or the good qualities of sth in an attractive way: *The festival was a showcase for young British musicians.* **2** a box with a glass top or sides that is used for showing objects in a shop/store, museum, etc. ▸ **show·case** *verb*: [VN] *Jack was looking for a film role that would showcase all his talents.*

show·down /'ʃəʊdaʊn; AmE 'ʃoʊ-/ *noun* [usually sing.] an argument, a fight or a test that will settle a disagreement that has lasted for a long time: *Management are facing a showdown with union members today.* ◇ *Fans gathered outside the stadium for the final showdown* (= the game that will decide the winner of the competition).

shower /'ʃaʊə(r)/ *noun, verb*
■ *noun* **1** a piece of equipment producing a spray of water that you stand under to wash yourself; the small room or part of a room that contains a shower: *a hotel room with bath and shower* ◇ *He's in the shower.* ◇ *a shower cubicle* **2** the act of washing yourself with a shower: (*especially BrE*) *to have a shower* ◇ (*especially AmE*) *to take a shower* ◇ *shower gel* **3** a short period of rain or snow: *wintry/scattered snow showers* ◇ *April showers* ◇ *We were caught in a heavy shower.* **4** a large number of things that arrive or fall together: *a shower of glass/leaves* ◇ *a shower of sparks from the fire* ◇ *a shower of kisses/insults* **5** (*AmE*) a party at which you give presents to a woman who is getting married or having a baby: *a bridal/baby shower*
■ *verb* **1** [V] to wash yourself under a shower: *She showered and dressed and went downstairs.* **2** [V] **~ (down) on sb/sth** | **~ down** to fall onto sb/sth, especially in a lot of small pieces: *Volcanic ash showered down on the town after the eruption.* **3** [VN] **~ sb with sth** to drop a lot of small things onto sb: *The bride and groom were showered with rice as they left the church.* ◇ *The roof collapsed, showering us with dust and debris.* **4** [VN] **~ sb with sth** | **~ sth on sb** to give sb a lot of sth: *He showered her with gifts.* ◇ *He showered gifts on her.*

show·ery /'ʃaʊəri/ *adj.* (of the weather) with frequent showers of rain: *a showery day*

show·girl /'ʃəʊɡɜːl; AmE 'ʃoʊɡɜːrl/ *noun* a female performer who sings and dances in a musical show

show·ground /'ʃəʊɡraʊnd; AmE 'ʃoʊ-/ *noun* a large outdoor area where FAIRS, farm shows, etc. take place

'show house (also **'show home**) (both *BrE*) (*AmE* **'model home**) *noun* a house in a group of new houses that has been painted and filled with furniture, so that people who might want to buy one of the houses can see what they will be like

show·ing /'ʃəʊɪŋ; AmE 'ʃoʊ-/ *noun* **1** an act of showing a film/movie: *There are three showings a day.* **2** [usually sing.] evidence of how well or how badly sb/sth is performing: *the strong/poor showing of the Green Party in the election* ◇ *On* (= judging by) *last week's showing, the team is unlikely to win today.*

show·jump·ing /'ʃəʊdʒʌmpɪŋ; AmE 'ʃoʊ-/ *noun* [U] the sport of riding a horse and jumping over a set of fences as quickly as possible

show·man /'ʃəʊmən; AmE 'ʃoʊ-/ *noun* (pl. **-men** /-mən/) **1** a person who does things in an entertaining way and is good at getting people's attention **2** a person who organizes public entertainments, especially at FAIRGROUNDS: *travelling showmen*

show·man·ship /'ʃəʊmənʃɪp; AmE 'ʃoʊ-/ *noun* [U] skill in doing things in an entertaining way and getting a lot of attention

shown *pp of* SHOW

'show-off *noun* (*informal, disapproving*) a person who tries to impress other people by showing how good he or she is at doing sth

show·piece /'ʃəʊpiːs; AmE 'ʃoʊ-/ *noun* an excellent example of sth that people are meant to see and admire

show·place /'ʃəʊpleɪs; AmE 'ʃoʊ-/ *noun* a place of great beauty, historical interest, etc. that is open to the public

show·room /'ʃəʊruːm; -rʊm; AmE 'ʃoʊ-/ *noun* a large shop/store in which goods for sale, especially cars and electrical goods, are displayed: *a car showroom*

'show-stopper *noun* (*informal*) a performance that is very impressive and receives a lot of APPLAUSE from the audience ▸ **'show-stopping** *adj.* [only before noun]: *a show-stopping performance*

show·time /'ʃəʊtaɪm; AmE 'ʃoʊ-/ *noun* [U] the time that a theatre performance will begin: *It's five minutes to showtime and the theatre is packed.* ◇ (*figurative, AmE*) *Everybody ready? It's showtime!*

'show trial *noun* an unfair trial of sb in a court of law, organized by a government for political reasons, not in order to find out the truth

showy /'ʃəʊi; AmE 'ʃoʊi/ *adj.* (often *disapproving*) so bright, colourful, large or exaggerated that it attracts a lot of attention: *showy flowers* ▸ **show·ily** /-ɪli/ *adv.* **showi·ness** *noun* [U]

shrank *pt of* SHRINK

shrap·nel /'ʃræpnəl/ *noun* [U] small pieces of metal that are thrown outwards from an exploding bomb

shred /ʃred/ *verb, noun*
■ *verb* (-dd-) [VN] to cut or tear sth into small pieces: *Serve the fish on a bed of shredded lettuce.* ◇ *He was accused of shredding documents relating to the case* (= putting them in a SHREDDER).
■ *noun* **1** [usually pl.] a small thin piece that has been torn or cut from sth: *shreds of fabric/paper* ◇ *His jacket had been torn to shreds by the barbed wire.* **2** [usually sing.] **~ of sth** (used especially in negative sentences) a very small amount of sth: *There is not a shred of evidence to support his claim.* IDM **in 'shreds 1** very badly damaged: *Her nerves were in shreds.* ◇ *The country's economy is in shreds.* **2** torn in many places: *The document was in shreds on the floor.* **pick/pull/tear sb/sth to 'pieces/ 'shreds** (*informal*) to criticize sb, or their work or ideas, very severely

shred·der /'ʃredə(r)/ *noun* a machine that tears sth into small pieces, especially paper, so that nobody can read what was printed on it

shrew /ʃruː/ *noun* **1** a small animal like a mouse with a long nose **2** (*old-fashioned*) a bad-tempered unpleasant woman

shrewd /ʃruːd/ *adj.* (**shrewd·er, shrewd·est**) **1** clever at understanding and making judgements about a situation SYN ASTUTE: *a shrewd businessman* ◊ *She is a shrewd judge of character.* **2** showing good judgement and likely to be right: *a shrewd guess/move* ◊ *I have a shrewd idea who the mystery caller was.* ▶ **shrewd·ly** *adv.* **shrewd·ness** *noun* [U]

shrew·ish /ˈʃruːɪʃ/ *adj.* (*old-fashioned*) (of women) bad-tempered and always arguing

shriek /ʃriːk/ *verb, noun*
■ *verb* **1** [V] ~ (**with sth**) | ~ (**at sb**) to give a loud high shout, for example when you are excited, frightened or in pain SYN SCREAM: *She shrieked in fright.* ◊ *The audience was shrieking with laughter.* ◊ (*figurative*) *The answer shrieked at her* (= was very obvious). **2** ~ (**sth**) (**at sb**) to say sth in a loud, high voice SYN SCREAM: [VN] *She was shrieking abuse at them as they carried her off.* ◊ [V speech] *'Look out!' he shrieked.*
■ *noun* a loud high shout, for example one that you make when you are excited, frightened or in pain: *She let out a piercing shriek.* ◊ *a shriek of pain/delight/surprise*

shrift /ʃrɪft/ *noun* IDM see SHORT *adj.*

shrike /ʃraɪk/ *noun* a bird with a strong beak, that catches small birds and insects and sticks them on thorn bushes

shrill /ʃrɪl/ *adj., verb*
■ *adj.* (**shrill·er, shrill·est**) **1** (of sounds or voices) very high and loud, in an unpleasant way: *a shrill voice/whistle/laugh* **2** loud and determined but often unreasonable: *shrill demands/protests/threats* ▶ **shrilly** /ˈʃrɪli/ *adv.* **shrill·ness** *noun* [U]
■ *verb* (*written*) **1** [V] to make an unpleasant high loud sound: *Behind him, the telephone shrilled.* **2** [V speech] to say sth in a loud, high voice: *'Wait for me!' she shrilled.*

shrimp /ʃrɪmp/ *noun* (*pl.* **shrimps** or **shrimp**) **1** a small shellfish that can be eaten, like a PRAWN but smaller. Shrimps turn pink when cooked. **2** (*AmE*) = PRAWN: *grilled shrimp*—picture on page A7

shrimp·ing /ˈʃrɪmpɪŋ/ *noun* [U] the activity of catching shrimps: *a shrimping net* ▶ **shrimp·er** *noun* (*especially AmE*): *shrimpers and fishermen in the gulf of Mexico*

shrine /ʃraɪn/ *noun* **1** ~ (**to sb/sth**) | ~ (**of sb/sth**) a place where people come to worship because it is connected with a holy person or event: *a shrine to the Virgin Mary* ◊ *to visit the shrine of Mecca* **2** ~ (**to sb/sth**) | ~ (**for sb**) a place that people visit because it is connected with sb/sth that is important to them: *Wimbledon is a shrine for all lovers of tennis.*

shrink /ʃrɪŋk/ *verb, noun*
■ *verb* (**shrank** /ʃræŋk/, **shrunk** /ʃrʌŋk/) or (**shrunk, shrunk**) **1** to become smaller, especially when washed in water that is too hot; to make clothes, fabric, etc. smaller in this way: [V] *My sweater shrank in the wash.* [also VN] **2** to become or to make sth smaller in size or amount: [V] *The tumour had shrunk to the size of a pea.* ◊ *The market for their products is shrinking.* ◊ *There was a movie called 'Honey I shrunk the kids!'.* ◊ [VN] *Television in a sense has shrunk the world.*—see also SHRUNKEN **3** [V + adv. / prep.] to move back or away from sth because you are frightened or shocked: *He shrank back against the wall as he heard them approaching.* IDM a ,shrinking 'violet (*humorous*) a way of describing a very shy person PHRV 'shrink from sth (*written*) to be unwilling to do sth that is difficult or unpleasant: *We made it clear to them that we would not shrink from confrontation.* ◊ [+ -ing] *They did not shrink from doing what was right.*
■ *noun* (*slang, humorous*) a PSYCHIATRIST or PSYCHOLOGIST

shrink·age /ˈʃrɪŋkɪdʒ/ *noun* [U] the process of becoming smaller in size; the amount by which sth becomes smaller: *the shrinkage of heavy industry* ◊ *She bought a slightly larger size to allow for shrinkage.*

shrink-wrapped *adj.* wrapped tightly in a thin plastic covering

shrivel /ˈʃrɪvl/ *verb* (**-ll-**, *AmE* **-l-**) ~ (**sth**) (**up**) to become

or make sth dry and WRINKLED from heat, cold or old age: [V] *The leaves on the plant had shrivelled up from lack of water.* ◊ [VN] *The prolonged hot weather had shrivelled the grapes in every vineyard.* ▶ **shriv·elled** *adj.*: *He had become a shrivelled old man.*

shroud /ʃraʊd/ *noun, verb*
■ *noun* **1** a piece of fabric that a dead person's body is wrapped in before it is buried **2** ~ **of sth** (*written*) a thing that covers, surrounds or hides sth: *The organization is cloaked in a shroud of secrecy.* ◊ *a shroud of smoke*
■ *verb* [VN] [*usually passive*] ~ **sth in sth 1** (of darkness, clouds, fabric, etc.) to cover or hide sth: *The city was shrouded in mist.* ◊ *furniture shrouded in dust sheets* **2** to hide information or keep it secret and mysterious: *His family background is shrouded in mystery.*

Shrove Tuesday /ˌʃrəʊv ˈtjuːzdeɪ, -di; *AmE* ˌʃrəʊv ˈtuːz-/ *noun* [U, C] (in the Christian Church) the day before the beginning of Lent —compare MARDI GRAS, PANCAKE DAY—see also ASH WEDNESDAY

shrub /ʃrʌb/ *noun* a large plant that is smaller than a tree and that has several stems of wood coming from the ground: *evergreen shrubs* ◊ *shrub roses*

shrub·bery /ˈʃrʌbəri/ *noun* [C, U] (*pl.* **-ies**) an area planted with shrubs

shrug /ʃrʌg/ *verb* (**-gg-**) [no passive] to raise your shoulders and then lower them to show that you do not know or care about sth: [V] *Sam shrugged and said nothing.* ◊ [VN] *'I don't know,' Anna replied, shrugging her shoulders.* ▶ **shrug** *noun* [*usually sing.*]: *Andy gave a shrug. 'It doesn't matter.'* PHRV ,shrug sth 'off/a'side to treat sth as if it is not important SYN DISMISS: *Shrugging off her injury, she played on.* ◊ *He shrugged aside suggestions that he resign.* ,shrug sb/sth 'off/a'way to push sb/sth back or away with your shoulders: *Kevin shrugged off his jacket* ◊ *She shrugged him away angrily.*

'How should I know?' he shrugged.

shrunk *pt, pp* of SHRINK

shrunk·en /ˈʃrʌŋkən/ *adj.* [*usually before noun*] that has become smaller (and less attractive): *a shrunken old woman*

shtick (also **schtick**) /ʃtɪk/ *noun* [U, sing.] (*especially AmE*) **1** a style of humour that is typical of a particular performer **2** a particular ability that sb has: *That's not my shtick.*

shuck /ʃʌk/ *noun, verb*
■ *noun* (*AmE*) the outer covering of a nut, plant, etc. or an OYSTER or a CLAM
■ *verb* [VN] (*AmE*) to remove the shell or covering of nuts, shellfish, etc.

shucks /ʃʌks/ *exclamation* (*old-fashioned, AmE, informal*) used to express embarrassment or disappointment

shud·der /ˈʃʌdə(r)/ *verb, noun*
■ *verb* **1** ~ (**with sth**) | ~ (**at sth**) to shake because you are cold or frightened, or because of a strong feeling: [V] *Just thinking about the accident makes me shudder.* ◊ *Alone in the car, she shuddered with fear.* ◊ *I shuddered at the thought of all the trouble I'd caused.* ◊ [V to inf] *I shudder to think how much this is all going to cost* (= I don't want to think about it because it is too unpleasant). **2** [V] (of a vehicle, machine, etc.) to shake very hard: *The bus shuddered to a halt.*
■ *noun* [*usually sing.*] **1** a shaking movement you make because you are cold, frightened or disgusted: *a shudder of fear* ◊ *She gave an involuntary shudder.* ◊ *A cold shudder ran through him.* **2** a strong shaking movement: *The elevator rose with a shudder.*

shuf·fle /ˈʃʌfl/ *verb, noun*
■ *verb* **1** [V + adv. / prep.] to walk slowly without lifting your feet completely off the ground: *He shuffled across the room*

S

to the window. ◇ *The line shuffled forward a little.* **2** to move from one foot to another; to move your feet in an awkward or embarrassed way: [VN] *Jenny shuffled her feet and blushed with shame.* [also V] **3** to mix cards up in a pack/deck of playing cards before playing a game: [VN] *Shuffle the cards and deal out seven to each player.* [also V] **4** [VN] to move paper or things into different positions or a different order: *I shuffled the documents on my desk.*
■ *noun* [usually sing.] **1** a slow walk in which you take small steps and do not lift your feet completely off the ground: *The old man walked with a shuffle.* ◇ *There was a shuffle of feet as the room emptied.* **2** the act of mixing cards before a card game: *Give the cards a good shuffle.* **3** (*rare*) = RESHUFFLE

shun /ʃʌn/ *verb* (-nn-) [VN] (*written*) to avoid sb/sth: *She was shunned by her family when she remarried.* ◇ *an actor who shuns publicity*

shunt /ʃʌnt/ *verb* [VN] **1** to move a train or a railway carriage/train car from one track to another **2** [+adv./prep.] (usually *disapproving*) to move sb/sth to a different place, especially a less important one: *John was shunted sideways to a job in sales.*

shush /ʃʊʃ/ *exclamation, verb*
■ *exclamation* used to tell sb to be quiet
■ *verb* [VN] to tell sb to be quiet, especially by saying 'shush', or by putting your finger against your lips: *Lyn shushed the children.*

shut /ʃʌt/ *verb, adj.*
■ *verb* (**shut·ting, shut, shut**) **1** to make sth close; to become closed: [VN] *Philip went into his room and shut the door behind him.* ◇ *I can't shut my suitcase—it's too full.* ◇ *She shut her eyes and fell asleep immediately.* ◇ *He shut his book and looked up.* ◇ [V] *The window won't shut* ◇ *The doors open and shut automatically.* **2** (*BrE*) when a shop/store, restaurant, etc. **shuts** or when sb **shuts** it, it stops being open for business and you cannot go into it: [V] *The bank shuts at 4.* [also VN] ⇨ note at CLOSE¹ **IDM shut your 'mouth! / 'face!** (*slang*) a rude way of telling sb to be quiet or stop talking **shut up 'shop** (*BrE, informal*) to close a business permanently or to stop working for the day—more at DOOR, EAR, EYE *n.*, MOUTH *n.* **PHRV ˌshut sb/ sth↔a'way** to put sb/sth in a place where other people cannot see or find them **ˌshut yourself a'way** to go somewhere where you will be completely alone: *Mary always shuts herself away in her room while she's working.* **ˌshut 'down** (of a factory, shop/store, etc. or a machine) to stop opening for business; to stop working: *The theatre shut down after more than half a century.*—related noun SHUTDOWN **ˌshut sth↔'down** to stop a factory, shop/store, etc. from opening for business; to stop a machine from working: *The computer system will be shut down over the weekend.*—related noun SHUTDOWN **ˌshut sb/yourself 'in (sth)** to put sb in a room and keep them there; to go to a room and stay there: *She shut the dog in the shed while she prepared the barbecue.* **'shut sth in sth** to trap sth by closing a door, lid, etc. on it: *Sam shut his finger in the car door.* **ˌshut 'off** (of a machine, tool, etc.) to stop working: *The engines shut off automatically in an emergency.* **ˌshut sth↔'off 1** to stop a machine, tool, etc. from working: *I wish someone would shut off that car alarm.* **2** to stop a supply of gas, water, etc. from flowing or reaching a place: *A valve immediately shuts off the gas when the lid is closed.* **ˌshut yourself 'off (from sth)** to avoid seeing people or having contact with anyone: *Martin shut himself off from the world to write his book.* **ˌshut sb/sth 'off from sth** to separate sb/sth from sth: *Bosnia is shut off from the Adriatic by the mountains.* **ˌshut sb/sth↔'out (of sth) 1** to prevent sb/sth from entering a place: *Mum, Ben keeps shutting me out of the bedroom!* ◇ *sunglasses that shut out 99% of the sun's harmful rays* **2** to not allow a person to share or be part of your thoughts; to stop yourself from having particular feelings: *I wanted to shut John out of my life for ever.* ◇ *She learned to shut out her angry feelings.* ◇ *If you shut me out, how can I help you?* **ˌshut 'up** (*informal*) to stop talking (often used as an order as a rude way of telling sb to stop talking): *Just shut up and listen!* ◇ *Will you tell Mike to shut up?* ◇ *When they'd finally shut up, I started again.* **ˌshut sb 'up to**

make sb stop talking: *She kicked Anne under the table to shut her up.* **ˌshut sth↔'up** to close a room, house, etc: *The summer house was shut up for another year and we went back to the city.* **ˌshut sb/sth 'up (in sth)** to keep sb/sth in a place and prevent them from going anywhere: *He shuts himself up with that computer for hours.*
■ *adj.* [not before noun] **1** not open SYN CLOSED: *The door was shut.* ◇ *She slammed the door shut.* ◇ *Keep your eyes shut.* **2** (*BrE*) not open for business SYN CLOSED: *Unfortunately the bank is shut now.*

shut·down /'ʃʌtdaʊn/ *noun* the act of closing a factory or business or stopping a large machine from working, either temporarily or permanently: *factory shutdowns* ◇ *the nuclear reactor's emergency shutdown procedures*

'shut-eye *noun* [U] (*informal*) sleep

'shut-in *noun* (*AmE*) a person who cannot leave their home very easily because they are ill/sick or DISABLED

'shut-out *noun* (*AmE*) a game in which one team prevents the other from scoring

shut·ter /'ʃʌtə(r)/ *noun* **1** [usually pl.] one of a pair of wooden or metal covers that can be closed over the outside of a window to keep out light or protect the windows from damage: *to open/close the shutters* ◇ (*BrE, figurative*) *More than 70000 shopkeepers have been forced to put up the shutters* (= close down their businesses) *in the past year.*—picture at BLIND, HOUSE **2** the part of a camera that opens to allow light to pass through the LENS when you take a photograph **IDM bring/put down the 'shutters** to stop letting sb know what your thoughts or feelings are; to stop letting yourself think about sth

shut·tered /'ʃʌtəd; *AmE* -tərd/ *adj.* with the shutters closed; with shutters fitted

shut·tle /'ʃʌtl/ *noun, verb*
■ *noun* **1** a plane, bus or train that travels regularly between two places: *a shuttle service between London and Edinburgh* **2** = SPACE SHUTTLE **3** a pointed tool used in weaving to pull a thread backwards and forwards over the other threads that pass along the length of the fabric
■ *verb* [+adv./prep.] **1** [V] ~ (**between A and B**) to travel between two places frequently: *Her childhood was spent shuttling between her mother and father.* **2** [VN] to carry people between two places that are close, making regular journeys between the two places: *A bus shuttles passengers back and forth from the station to the terminal.*

shuttle·cock /'ʃʌtlkɒk; *AmE* -kɑːk/ (*AmE* also **bird·ie**) *noun* the object that players hit backwards and forwards in the game of BADMINTON

ˌshuttle di'plomacy *noun* [U] international talks carried out by sb who travels between two or more countries to talk to the different governments involved

shy /ʃaɪ/ *adj., verb*
■ *adj.* (**shyer, shy·est**) **1** (of people) nervous or embarrassed about meeting and speaking to other people: *a quiet, shy man* ◇ *Don't be shy—come and say hello.* ◇ *She was too shy to ask anyone for help.* ◇ *As a teenager I was painfully shy.* ◇ *She's very shy with adults.* **2** showing that sb is nervous or embarrassed about meeting and speaking to other people: *a shy smile/glance* **3** (of animals) easily frightened and not willing to come near people: *The panda is a shy creature.* **4** [not before noun] ~ of/about (doing) sth afraid of doing sth or being involved in sth: *The band has never been shy of publicity.* ◇ *He disliked her and had never been shy of saying so.* **5** [not before noun] ~ (of sth) (*informal, especially AmE*) lacking the amount that is needed: *He died before Christmas, only a month shy of his 90th birthday.* ◇ *We are still two players shy (of a full team).* **6** (-shy) (in compounds) avoiding or not liking the thing mentioned: *camera-shy* ◇ *He's always been work-shy.* ► **shyly** *adv.* **shy·ness** *noun* [U] **IDM** see FIGHT *v.*, ONCE *adv.*
■ *verb* (**shies, shy·ing, shied, shied** /ʃaɪd/) [V] ~ (**at sth**) (especially of a horse) to turn away suddenly because of fear or surprise: *My horse shied at the unfamiliar noise.*—see also COCONUT SHY **PHRV ˌshy a'way (from sth)** to avoid doing sth because you are nervous or frightened: *Hugh never shied away from his responsibilities.* ◇ *The newspapers have shied away from investigating the story.*

s	t	v	z	ʃ	ʒ	tʃ	dʒ	θ	ð	ŋ
see	tea	van	zoo	shoe	vision	chain	jam	thin	this	sing

shy·ster /ˈʃaɪstə(r)/ *noun* (*informal, especially AmE*) a dishonest person, especially a lawyer

SI /ˌes ˈaɪ/ *abbr.* International System (used to describe units of measurement; from French 'Système International'): *SI units*

Siamese cat /ˌsaɪəmiːz ˈkæt/ (also **Siam·ese**) *noun* a cat with short pale fur and a brown face, ears, tail and feet

Siamese ˈtwin (also *technical* **conˌjoined ˈtwin**) *noun* one of two people who are born with their bodies joined together in some way, sometimes sharing the same organs

sibi·lant /ˈsɪbɪlənt/ *adj., noun*
- *adj.* (*formal or literary*) making an 's' or 'sh' sound: *the sibilant sound of whispering*
- *noun* (*phonetics*) a sibilant sound made in speech, such as /s, z, ʃ/ or /ʒ/

sib·ling /ˈsɪblɪŋ/ *noun* (*formal or technical*) a brother or sister: *squabbles between siblings* ◊ **sibling rivalry** (= competition between brothers and sisters)

sic /sɪk; siːk/ *adv., verb*
- *adv.* (from *Latin*) written after a word that you have copied from somewhere, to show that you know that the word is wrongly spelled or wrong in some other way: *In the letter to parents it said: 'The school is proud of it's [sic] record of excellence'.*
- *verb* (**-cc-**) [VN] (*AmE, informal*) to attack sb: *Sic him, Duke!* (= said to a dog) **PHRV** **ˈsic sth on sb** (*informal*) to tell a dog to attack sb

sick /sɪk/ *adj., noun, verb*
- *adj.*
  ILL | **1** physically or mentally ill: *a sick child/relative/bird* ◊ *Her mother's very sick.* ◊ *Peter has* **been off sick** (= away from work because he is ill) *for two weeks.* ◊ *Emma has just* **called in sick** (= telephoned to say she will not be coming to work because she is ill). ◊ *Britain's workers* **went sick** (= did not go to work because they were ill) *for a record number of days last year.* ◊ (*AmE*) *I can't afford to* **get sick** (= become ill). ⇨ vocabulary notes on page 599
  WANTING TO VOMIT | **2** [not usually before noun] (*especially BrE*) feeling that you want to VOMIT: *If you eat any more cake you'll* **make yourself sick.** ◊ *a sick feeling in your stomach*
  -SICK | **3** (in compounds) feeling sick as a result of travelling on a ship, plane, etc: *seasick* ◊ *airsick* ◊ *carsick* ◊ *travel-sick*
  BORED | **4** **~ of sb/sth** | **~ of doing sth** (*informal*) bored with or annoyed about sth that has been happening for a long time, and wanting it to stop: *I'm sick of the way you've treated me.* ◊ *We're sick of waiting around like this.* ◊ *I'm* **sick and tired** *of your moaning.* ◊ *I'm* **sick to death** *of all of you!*
  CRUEL/STRANGE | **5** (*informal*) (especially of humour) dealing with suffering, disease or death in a cruel way that some people think is offensive: *a sick joke* ◊ *That's really sick.* **6** (*informal*) getting enjoyment from doing strange or cruel things: *a sick mind* ◊ *People think I'm sick for having a rat as a pet.* ◊ *We live in a sick society.*—see also HOMESICK, LOVESICK
  IDM **be ˈsick** (*BrE*) to bring food from your stomach back out through your mouth **SYN** VOMIT: *I was sick three times in the night.* ◊ *She had been violently sick.* **be worried ˈsick; be ˈsick with worry** to be extremely worried: *Where have you been? I've been worried sick about you.* **fall ˈsick** (also *old-fashioned* **take ˈsick**) (*formal*) to become ill **make sb ˈsick** to make sb angry or disgusted: *His hypocrisy makes me sick.* **(as) sick as a ˈdog** (*informal*) feeling very ill; VOMITING a lot **(as) sick as a ˈparrot** (*BrE, humorous*) very disappointed **sick at ˈheart** (*formal*) very unhappy or disappointed **sick to your ˈstomach 1** feeling very angry or worried: *Nora turned sick to her stomach on hearing this news.* **2** (*AmE*) = SICK (2)
- *noun*
  VOMIT | **1** [U] (*BrE, informal*) food that you bring back up from your stomach through your mouth **SYN** VOMIT
  ILL PEOPLE | **2** (**the sick**) [pl.] people who are ill

- *verb*
  PHRV **ˌsick sth↔ˈup** (*BrE, informal*) to bring sth up from the stomach back out through your mouth **SYN** VOMIT: *She'd sicked up her milk.*

sick·bay /ˈsɪkbeɪ/ *noun* a room or rooms, for example on a ship or in a school, with beds for people who are ill/sick

sick·bed /ˈsɪkbed/ *noun* [sing.] the bed on which a person who is ill/sick is lying: *The President left his sickbed to attend the ceremony.*

sick·en /ˈsɪkən/ *verb* (*BrE*) **1** [VN] to make sb feel very shocked and angry **SYN** DISGUST: *The public is becoming sickened by these pictures of violence and death.* **2** [V] to become ill: (*old-fashioned*) *The baby sickened and died before his first birthday.* ◊ (*BrE*) *Faye hasn't eaten all day—she must* **be sickening for something.**

sick·en·ing /ˈsɪkənɪŋ/ *adj.* **1** making you feel disgusted or shocked: *She was the victim of a sickening attack.* ◊ *the sickening stench of burnt flesh* **2** making you afraid that sb has been badly hurt or that sth has been broken: *Her head hit the ground with a sickening thud.* **3** (*informal, spoken*) making you feel jealous or annoyed: *'She's off to the Bahamas for a month.' 'How sickening!'* ▶ **sick·en·ing·ly** *adv.*

sickie /ˈsɪki/ *noun* (*BrE, informal*) a day when you say that you are ill/sick and cannot go to work when it is not really true

sickle /ˈsɪkl/ *noun* a tool with a curved blade and a short handle, used for cutting grass or corn—see also HAMMER AND SICKLE—picture at SCYTHE

ˈsick leave *noun* [U] permission to be away from work because of illness; the period of time spent away from work: *to be on sick leave*

sick·ly /ˈsɪkli/ *adj.* **1** often ill/sick: *He was a sickly child.* **2** not looking healthy and strong: *She looked pale and sickly.* ◊ *sickly plants* **3** that makes you feel sick, especially because it is too sweet or full of false emotion: *a sickly sweet smell* ◊ *She gave me a sickly smile.* **4** (of colours) unpleasant to look at: *The walls were painted a sickly green colour.*

sick·ness /ˈsɪknəs/ *noun* **1** [U] illness; bad health: *She's been off work because of sickness.* ◊ *insurance against sickness and unemployment* **2** [U, C, usually sing.] a particular type of illness or disease: *altitude/travel/radiation sickness*—see also SLEEPING SICKNESS **3** [U] (*especially BrE*) the feeling that you are likely to VOMIT (= bring food back up from the stomach to the mouth); the fact of VOMITING: *symptoms include sickness and diarrhoea* ◊ *The sickness passed off after a while.*—see also MORNING SICKNESS **4** [sing.] a feeling of great sadness, disappointment or disgust: *He felt a sickness rise in him at the thought of leaving.*

ˈsickness benefit *noun* [U] (*BrE*) money paid by the government to people who are away from work because of illness—compare SICK PAY

sicko /ˈsɪkəʊ; *AmE* -koʊ/ *noun* (pl. **-os**) (*informal, especially AmE*) a person who gets enjoyment from doing strange and cruel things: *child molesters and other sickos*

sick·out /ˈsɪkaʊt/ *noun* (*AmE*) a strike in which all the workers at a company say they are sick and stay at home

ˈsick pay *noun* [U] pay given to an employee who is away from work because of illness—compare SICKNESS BENEFIT

sick·room /ˈsɪkruːm; -rʊm/ *noun* a room in which a person who is ill/sick is lying in bed

side /saɪd/ *noun, verb*
- *noun*
  LEFT/RIGHT | **1** [C, usually sing.] either of the two halves of a surface, an object or an area that is divided by an imaginary central line: *We drive on the left-hand side of the road in this country.* ◊ *the right side of the brain* ◊ *satellite links to the other side of the world* ◊ *She was on the far side of the room.* ◊ *They crossed from one side of London to the other.* ◊ *Keep on your side of the bed!* **2** [C, usually sing.] a position or an area to the left or right of sth: *There is a large window on either side of the front door.* ◊ *He crossed the bridge to the other side of the*

æ	ɑː	e	ɜː	ə	ɪ	iː	i	ɒ	ɔː	ʌ	ʊ	u	uː
cat	father	ten	bird	about	sit	see	many	got	saw	cup	put	actual	too
								(BrE)					

river. ◊ *people on both sides of the Atlantic* ◊ *She tilted her head to one side.*

NOT TOP OR BOTTOM | **3** [C] one of the flat surfaces of sth that is not the top or bottom, front or back: *Write your name on the side of the box.* ◊ *There's a scratch on the side of my car.* ◊ *The kitchen door is at the side of the house.* ◊ *a side door/entrance/window* ◊ *Now lay the jar on its side.* **4** [C] the upright or sloping surface around sth, but not the top or bottom of it: *A path went up the side of the hill.* ◊ *Brush the sides of the tin with butter.*—see also HILLSIDE, MOUN-TAINSIDE

EDGE | **5** [C] a part or an area of sth near the edge and away from the middle: *She sat on the side of the bed.* ◊ *A van was parked at the side of the road.* ◊ *the south side of the lake*—see also BEDSIDE, FIRESIDE, RINGSIDE, RIVERSIDE, ROADSIDE, SEASIDE

OF BODY | **6** [C, usually sing.] either the right or left part of a person's body, from the ARMPIT (= where the arm joins the body) to the hip: *She has a pain down her right side.* ◊ *He was lying on his side.*

NEAR TO SB/STH | **7** [sing.] a place or position very near to sb/sth: *Keep close to my side.* ◊ *Her husband stood at her side.*

OF STH FLAT AND THIN | **8** [C] either of two surfaces of sth flat and thin, such as paper or fabric: *Write on one side of the paper only.* ◊ *Fry the steaks for two minutes on each side.* ◊ *Let's listen to side A of the tape.*

PAGE | **9** [C] the amount of writing needed to fill one side of a sheet of paper: *He told us not to write more than three sides.*

MATHEMATICS | **10** [C] any of the flat surfaces of a solid object: *A cube has six sides.* **11** [C] any of the lines that form a flat shape such as a square or triangle: *a shape with five sides* ◊ *The farm buildings form three sides of a square.*

-SIDED | **12** used in adjectives to state the number or type of sides: *a six-sided object* ◊ *a glass-sided container*

IN WAR/ARGUMENT | **13** [C] one of the two or more people or groups taking part in a dispute, war, etc: *Each side is capable of destroying the other in a nuclear war.* ◊ *We have finally reached an agreement acceptable to all sides.* ◊ *At some point during the war he seems to have **changed sides**.* **14** [C] one of the opinions, attitudes or positions held by sb in an argument, a business arrangement, etc: *We heard both sides of the argument.* ◊ *I just want you to hear my side of the story first.* ◊ *There are, of course, arguments on both sides.* ◊ *Will you keep your side of the bargain?*

ASPECT | **15** [C] a particular aspect of sth, especially a situation or a person's character: *These poems reveal her gentle side.* ◊ *This is a side of Alan that I never knew existed.* ◊ *It's good you can see the funny side of the situation.* ◊ *I'll take care of that side of things.* **16** [U] (*BrE, informal*) a part of sb's character that makes them think they are better than other people: *There was **no side to** him at all.*

SPORTS TEAM | **17** [C] (*BrE*) a sports team: *As captain, Pryce is confident of leading his side to victory.* ◊ *The French have a very strong side.* ◊ *five-a-side football*

OF FAMILY | **18** [C] the part of your family that people belong to who are related either to your mother or to your father: *a cousin on my father's side* (= a child of my father's brother or sister)

MEAT | **19** [C] **a ~ of beef/bacon, etc.** one of the two halves of an animal that has been killed for meat

TV CHANNEL | **20** [C] (*old-fashioned, BrE, informal*) a television channel: *What's on the other side?*

IDM **come down on 'one side of the fence or the 'other** to choose between two possible choices **from ,side to 'side** moving to the left and then to the right: *He shook his head slowly from side to side.* ◊ *The ship rolled from side to side.* **get on the right/wrong 'side of sb** to make sb pleased with you/annoyed with you **have sth on your 'side** to have sth as an advantage that will make it more likely that you will achieve sth: *She may not win this year, but she does have youth on her side.* **let the 'side down** (*especially BrE*) to fail to give your friends, family,

etc. the help and support they expect, or to behave in a way that makes them disappointed: *You can always rely on Maggie—she'd never let the side down.* **not leave sb's 'side** to stay with sb, especially in order to take care of them **on/from all 'sides | on/from every 'side** in or from all directions; everywhere: *We realized we were surrounded on all sides.* ◊ *Disaster threatens on every side.* **on the 'big, 'small, 'high, etc. side** (*informal*) slightly too big, small, high, etc: *These shoes are a little on the tight side.* **on the other side of the 'fence** in a situation that is different from the one that you are in **on the ,right/,wrong side of '40, '50, etc.** (*informal*) younger or older than 40, 50, etc. years of age **on the 'side** (*informal*) **1** in addition to your main job: *a mechanic who buys and sells cars on the side* **2** secretly or illegally: *He's married but he has a girlfriend on the side.* **3** (*especially AmE*) (of food in a restaurant) served at the same time as the main part of the meal, but on a separate plate **on/to one 'side 1** out of your way: *I left my bags on one side.* **2** to be dealt with later: *I put his complaint to one side until I had more time.* ◊ *Leaving that to one side for a moment, are there any other questions?* **be on sb's 'side** to support and agree with sb: *I'm definitely on your side in this.* ◊ *Whose side are you on anyway?* **the other side of the 'coin** the aspect of a situation that is the opposite of or contrasts with the one you have been talking about **,side by 'side 1** close together and facing in the same direction: *There were two children ahead, walking side by side.* ◊ *They sat on the desk, side by side.* **2** together, without any difficulties: *We have been using both systems, side by side, for two years.* ◊ *The two communities exist happily side by side.* **take 'sides** to express support for sb in a dispute: *She didn't think it was wise to take sides in their argument.* **take/draw sb to one 'side** to speak to sb in private, especially in order to warn or tell them about sth **this side of ...** before a particular time, event, age, etc: *They aren't likely to arrive this side of mid-night.*—more at BED *n.*, BIT, BRIGHT *adj.*, CREDIT *n.*, DISTAFF, ERR, GRASS *n.*, KNOW *v.*, LAUGH *v.*, RIGHT *adj.*, SAFE *adj.*, SPLIT *v.*, THORN, TIME *n.*, TWO, WRONG *adj.*

▪ verb
PHRV **'side with sb (against sb/sth)** to support one person or group in an argument against sb else: *The kids always sided with their mother against me.*

side-board /'saɪdbɔːd; *AmE* -bɔːrd/ *noun* **1** (*AmE* also **buf·fet**) a piece of furniture in a DINING ROOM for putting food on before it is served, with drawers for storing knives, forks, etc. **2** (**side-boards**) (also **side·burns** /'saɪdbɜːnz; *AmE* -bɜːrnz/) [pl.] hair that grows down the sides of a man's face in front of his ears—picture at HAIR

side-car /'saɪdkɑː(r)/ *noun* a small vehicle attached to the side of a motorcycle in which a passenger can ride

'side dish *noun* a small amount of food, for example a salad, served with the main course of a meal

'side effect *noun* [usually pl.] **1** an extra and usually bad effect that a drug has on you, as well as curing illness or pain **2** an unexpected result of a situation or course of action that happens as well as the result you were aiming for

'side issue *noun* an issue that is less important than the main issue, and may take attention away from it

side-kick /'saɪdkɪk/ *noun* (*informal*) a person who helps another more important or more intelligent person: *Batman and his young sidekick Robin*

side-light /'saɪdlaɪt/ *noun* **1 ~ (on sb/sth)** a piece of information, usually given accidentally or in connection with another subject, that helps you to understand sb/sth **2** (*BrE*) either of a pair of small lights at the front of a vehicle

side-line /'saɪdlaɪn/ *noun, verb*
▪ noun **1** [C] an activity that you do as well as your main job in order to earn extra money **2** (**sidelines**) [pl.] the lines along the two long sides of a sports field, tennis court, etc. that mark the outer edges; the area just outside these: *The coach stood on the sidelines yelling instructions to the players.* **IDM** **on/from the 'sidelines** watching sth but not actually involved in it: *He was*

aɪ	aʊ	eɪ	əʊ	oʊ	ɔɪ	ɪə	eə	ʊə	j	w
my	now	say	go (BrE)	go (AmE)	boy	near	hair	pure	yes	wet

content to watch from the sidelines as his wife built up a successful business empire.

■ *verb* [VN] [usually passive] **1** to prevent sb from playing in a team, especially because of an injury: *The player has been sidelined by a knee injury.* **2** to prevent sb from having an important part in sth that other people are doing: *The vice-president is increasingly being sidelined.*

side·long /ˈsaɪdlɒŋ; *AmE* -lɔːŋ/ *adj.* [only before noun] (of a look) out of the corner of your eye, especially in a way that is secret or disapproving: *She cast a sidelong glance at Eric to see if he had noticed her blunder.* ▶ **side·long** *adv.*: *She looked sidelong at him.*

ˌside-ˈon *adv.* (*BrE*) coming from the side rather than from the front or back: *The car hit us side-on.*

ˈside order *noun* a small amount of food ordered in a restaurant to go with the main dish, but served separately: *a side order of fries*

ˈside road *noun* a smaller and less important road leading off a main road

ˈside-saddle *adv.* if you ride a horse **side-saddle**, you ride with both your legs on the same side of the horse

side·show /ˈsaɪdʃəʊ; *AmE* -ʃoʊ/ *noun* **1** a separate small show or attraction at a FAIR or CIRCUS where you pay to see a performance or take part in a game **2** an activity or event that is much less important than the main activity or event

side·step /ˈsaɪdstep/ *verb* (-pp-) **1** [VN] to avoid answering a question or dealing with a problem: *Did you notice how she neatly sidestepped the question?* **2** to avoid sth, for example being hit, by stepping to one side: [VN] *He cleverly sidestepped the tackle.* [also V]

ˈside street *noun* a less important street leading off a road in a town

side·swipe /ˈsaɪdswaɪp/ *noun* **1** (*AmE*) a hit from the side: *a sideswipe by a truck* **2** ~ (**at sb/sth**) (*informal*) a critical comment made about sb/sth while you are talking about sb/sth completely different: *It was a good speech, but he couldn't resist taking a sideswipe at his opponent.* ▶ **side·swipe** *verb*: [VN] (*AmE*) *The bus sideswiped two parked cars.*

side·track /ˈsaɪdtræk/ *verb* [VN] [usually passive] to make sb start to talk about or do sth that is different from the main thing that they are supposed to be talking about or doing: *I was supposed to be writing a letter but I'm afraid I got sidetracked.*

side·walk /ˈsaɪdwɔːk/ *noun* (*AmE*) = PAVEMENT

side·ways /ˈsaɪdweɪz/ *adv.* **1** to, towards or from the side: *He looked sideways at her.* ◊ *The truck skidded sideways across the road.* ◊ *He has been moved sideways* (= moved to another job at the same level as before, not higher or lower). **2** with one side facing forwards: *She sat sideways on the chair.* ▶ **side·ways** *adj.*: *She slid him a sideways glance.* ◊ *a sideways move* IDM see KNOCK *v.*

sid·ing /ˈsaɪdɪŋ/ *noun* **1** a short track beside a main railway/railroad line, where trains can stand when they are not being used **2** (*AmE*) protective material used to cover the outside walls of buildings—picture at HOUSE

sidle /ˈsaɪdl/ *verb* [V+*adv.*/*prep.*] to walk somewhere in a shy or uncertain way as if you do not want to be noticed: *She sidled up to me and whispered something in my ear.*

SIDS /ˌes aɪ diː ˈes/ *abbr.* [U] the abbreviation for 'sudden infant death syndrome' (the sudden death while sleeping of a baby which appears to be healthy) SYN COT DEATH

siege /siːdʒ/ *noun* **1** a military operation in which an army tries to capture a town by surrounding it and stopping the supply of food, etc. to the people inside: *the siege of Troy* ◊ *The siege was finally lifted* (= ended) *after six months.* ◊ *The police placed the city centre under a virtual state of siege* (= it was hard to get in or out). **2** a situation in which the police surround a building where people are living or hiding, in order to make them come out—see also BESIEGE IDM **under ˈsiege 1** surrounded by an army or the police in a siege **2** being criticized all the time or put under pressure by problems, questions, etc. **lay ˈsiege to sth 1** to begin a siege of a town, building, etc. **2** to surround a building, especially in order to speak

to or question the person or people living or working there

ˈsiege mentality *noun* [sing., U] a feeling that you are surrounded by enemies and must protect yourself

si·enna /siˈenə/ *noun* [U] a type of dark yellow or red clay used for giving colour to paints, etc.

si·erra /siˈerə/ *noun* (especially in place names) a long range of steep mountains with sharp points, especially in Spain and America: *the Sierra Nevada*

si·esta /siˈestə/ *noun* a rest or sleep taken in the early afternoon, especially in hot countries: *to have/take a siesta*—compare NAP

sieve /sɪv/ *noun, verb*

■ *noun* a tool for separating solids from liquids or larger solids from smaller solids, made of a wire or plastic net attached to a ring. The liquid or small pieces pass through the net but the larger pieces do not.—picture at KITCHEN IDM **have a memory/mind like a ˈsieve** (*informal*) to have a very bad memory; to forget things easily

■ *verb* [VN] to put sth through a sieve

sift /sɪft/ *verb* **1** [VN] to put flour or some other fine substance through a SIEVE/SIFTER: *Sift the flour into a bowl.* **2** ~ (**through**) **sth** to examine sth very carefully in order to decide what is important or useful or to find sth important: [VN] *We will sift every scrap of evidence.* ◊ [V] *Crash investigators have been sifting through the wreckage of the aircraft.* **3** [VN] ~ **sth** (**out**) **from sth** to separate sth from a group of things: *He sifted the relevant data from the rest.* ◊ *She looked quickly through the papers, sifting out from the pile anything that looked interesting.* PHRV **ˌsift sth↔ˈout 1** to remove sth that you do not want from a substance by putting it through a SIEVE: *Put the flour through a sieve to sift out the lumps.* **2** to separate sth, usually sth you do not want, from a group of things: *We need to sift out the applications that have no chance of succeeding.*

sift·er /ˈsɪftə(r)/ *noun* **1** (*AmE*) a small SIEVE used for sifting flour—picture at KITCHEN **2** a container with a lot of small holes in the top, used for shaking flour or sugar onto things: *a sugar sifter*

sigh /saɪ/ *verb, noun*

■ *verb* **1** [V] ~ (**with sth**) to take and then let out a long deep breath that can be heard, to show that you are disappointed, sad, tired, etc: *He sighed deeply at the thought.* ◊ *She sighed with relief that it was all over.* **2** [V speech] to say sth with a sigh: *'Oh well, better luck next time,' she sighed.* **3** [V] (*literary*) (especially of the wind) to make a long sound like a sigh

■ *noun* an act or the sound of sighing: *to give/heave/let out a sigh* ◊ *a deep/long sigh* ◊ *'I'll wait,' he said with a sigh.* ◊ *We all breathed a sigh of relief when it was over.*

WHICH WORD?
sight / eyesight

Sight is a general word for the ability that people have to see: *to lose your sight* ◊ *She only has a little sight in one eye.*

You use **eyesight** to talk about how well somebody is able to see: *I've always had poor eyesight.* Sight can also be used like this: *a sight/an eyesight test* ◊ *My grandmother's sight/eyesight is still good.*

---

sight /saɪt/ *noun, verb*

■ *noun*

ABILITY TO SEE ‖ **1** [U] the ability to see: *to lose your sight* (= to become blind) ◊ *She has very good sight.* ◊ *The disease has affected her sight.* ◊ *He has very little sight in his right eye.*—see also EYESIGHT

ACT OF SEEING ‖ **2** [U] ~ **of sb/sth** the act of seeing sb/sth: *After ten days at sea, we had our first sight of land.* ◊ *I have been known to faint at the sight of blood.* ◊ *The soldiers were given orders to shoot on sight* (= as soon as they saw sb). ◊ *She caught sight of a car in the distance.*

HOW FAR YOU CAN SEE ‖ **3** [U] the area or distance within which sb can see or sth can be seen: *There was no one in sight.* ◊ *At last we came in sight of a few houses.* ◊ *A bicycle came into sight on the main road.* ◊ *The end is in* sight (= will happen soon). ◊ *Leave any valuables in your car **out of sight**.* ◊ *Keep **out of sight*** (= stay where you cannot be seen). ◊ *She never lets her daughter **out of her sight*** (= always keeps her where she can see her). ◊ *Get out of my **sight**!* (= Go away!) ◊ *The boat disappeared **from sight**.* ◊ *The house was **hidden from sight** behind some trees.* ◊ *He had placed himself directly in my **line of sight**.*

<u>WHAT YOU CAN SEE</u> | **4** [C] a thing that you see or can see: *It's a spectacular sight as the flamingos lift into the air.* ◊ *The museum attempts to recreate **the sights and sounds of** wartime Britain.* ◊ *He was a **sorry sight**, soaked to the skin and shivering.* ◊ *The bird is now a rare sight in this country.*

<u>INTERESTING PLACES</u> | **5** (**sights**) [pl.] the interesting places, especially in a town or city, that are often visited by tourists: *We're going to Paris for the weekend to **see the sights**.*

<u>RIDICULOUS/UNTIDY PERSON</u> | **6** (**a sight**) [sing.] (*informal, especially BrE*) a person or thing that looks ridiculous, untidy, unpleasant, etc: *She looks a sight in that hat!*

<u>ON GUN/TELESCOPE</u> | **7** [C, usually pl.] a device that you look through to aim a gun, etc. or to look at sth through a TELESCOPE, etc: *He had the deer **in his sights** now.* ◊ (*figurative*) *Even as a young actress, she always had Hollywood firmly **in her sights*** (= as her final goal).

IDM **at first 'sight 1** when you first begin to consider sth: *At first sight, it may look like a generous offer, but always read the small print.* **2** when you see sb/sth for the first time: *It was **love at first sight*** (= we fell in love the first time we saw each other). **hate, be sick of, etc. the 'sight of sb/sth** (*informal*) to hate, etc. sb/sth very much: *I can't stand the sight of him!* **in the sight of sb/in sb's sight** (*formal*) in sb's opinion: *We are all equal in the sight of God.* **lose 'sight of sb/sth 1** to become no longer able to see sb/sth: *They finally lost sight of land.* **2** to stop considering sth; to forget sth: *We must not lose sight of our original aim.* **,out of 'sight, ,out of 'mind** (*saying*) used to say sb will quickly be forgotten when they are no longer with you **raise/lower your 'sights** to expect more/less from a situation **set your sights on sth/on doing sth** to decide that you want sth and to try very hard to get it: *She's set her sights on getting into Harvard.* **a (damn, etc.) sight better, etc. | a (damn, etc.) sight too good, etc.** (*informal*) very much better; much too good, etc: *She's done a darn sight better than I have.* ◊ *It's worth a damn sight more than I thought.* **a ,sight for sore 'eyes** (*spoken*) a person or thing that you are pleased to see; something that is very pleasant to look at **sight un'seen** if you buy sth **sight unseen**, you do not have an opportunity to see it before you buy it—more at HEAVE *v.*, KNOW *v.*, NOWHERE, PRETTY *adj.*

■ *verb* [VN] (*written*) to suddenly see sth, especially sth you have been looking for: *After twelve days at sea, they sighted land.*

> **WHICH WORD?**   **(?)**
> **sight / view**
>
> Both **sight** and **view** can be used when you are saying whether you can see something: *There was no one in sight/view.*
>
> **Sight** can be used to talk about the act of seeing: *I had my first sight of the city from the river.* You can also use **sight** to mean something that you can see: *Sunset over the lake is a beautiful sight.*
>
> **View** describes the whole area you can see from a particular place: *From the top of the tower I had a wonderful view of the city.*

---

sight·ed /'saɪtɪd/ *adj.* **1** able to see; not blind: *the blind parents of sighted children* **2** (**-sighted**) (in compounds) able to see in the way mentioned: *partially sighted* ◊ *short-sighted* ◊ *long-sighted*

sight·ing /'saɪtɪŋ/ *noun* an occasion when sb sees sth/sth, especially sth unusual or sth that lasts for only a short time: *a reported sighting of the Loch Ness monster*

---

sight·less /'saɪtləs/ *adj.* (*literary*) unable to see **SYN** BLIND: *The statue stared down at them with sightless eyes.*

'sight-read *verb* [V, VN] to play or sing written music when you see it for the first time, without practising it first ► **'sight-reader** *noun*: *He's an excellent sight-reader.* **'sight-reading** *noun* [U]

sight·see·ing /'saɪtsiːɪŋ/ *noun* [U] the activity of visiting interesting buildings and places as a tourist: *to go sightseeing* ◊ *Did you have a chance to **do any sightseeing?*** ◊ *a sightseeing tour of the city* ► **sight·see** *verb* [V] (only used in the progressive tenses) **sight·seer** *noun*: *Oxford attracts large numbers of visitors and sightseers.*

sign /saɪn/ *noun, verb*
■ *noun*

<u>SHOWING STH</u> | **1** [C, U] **~ (of sth)** | **~ (that...)** an event, an action, a fact, etc. that shows that sth exists, is happening or may happen in the future **SYN** INDICATION: *Headaches may be a sign of stress.* ◊ *There is no sign of John anywhere.* ◊ *Call the police at the first sign of trouble.* ◊ *The gloomy weather **shows no sign of** improving.* ◊ *Her work is **showing some signs of** improvement.* ◊ *The fact that he didn't say 'no' immediately is a **good sign**.* ◊ *If an interview is too easy, it's a **sure sign that** you haven't got the job.* ◊ *There was no **sign of life** in the house* (= there seemed to be nobody there).

<u>FOR INFORMATION/WARNING</u> | **2** [C] a piece of paper, wood or metal that has writing or a picture on it that gives you information, instructions, a warning, etc: *a road/traffic sign* ◊ *a shop/pub sign* ◊ *The sign on the wall said 'Now wash your hands'.* ◊ *Follow the signs for the city centre.*

<u>MOVEMENT/SOUND</u> | **3** [C] a movement or sound that you make to tell sb sth: *He gave us a thumbs-up sign.* ◊ *She nodded as a sign for us to sit down.*—see also V-SIGN

<u>SYMBOL</u> | **4** [C] a mark used to represent sth, especially in mathematics: *a plus/minus sign* (+/−) ◊ *a pound/dollar sign* (£/$)

<u>STAR SIGN</u> | **5** [C] (*informal*) = STAR SIGN: *What sign are you?*

IDM **a ,sign of the 'times** something that you feel shows what things are like now, especially how bad they are

■ *verb*

<u>YOUR NAME</u> | **1** to write your name on a document, letter, etc. to show that you have written it, that you agree with what it says, or that it is genuine: [V, VN] *Sign here, please.* ◊ *Sign your name here, please.* ◊ [VN] *You haven't signed the letter.* ◊ *to sign a deal/contract/cheque* ◊ *The treaty was signed on 24 March.* ◊ *The player was signing autographs for a group of fans.* ◊ [VN-N] *He signed himself 'Jimmy'.*

<u>CONTRACT</u> | **2** to arrange for sb, for example a sports player or musician, to sign a contract agreeing to work for your company; to sign a contract agreeing to work for a company: [VN] *United have just signed a new goalie.* ◊ [V] *He signed for United yesterday.* ◊ *The band signed with Virgin Records.*

<u>MAKE MOVEMENT/SOUND</u> | **3 ~ (to sb) (to do sth)** to make a request or tell sb to do sth by using a sign, especially a hand movement: [V**to**inf] *The hotel manager signed to the porter to pick up my case.* [also V**that**]

<u>FOR DEAF PERSON</u> | **4** to use sign language to communicate with sb: [V] *She learnt to sign to help her deaf child.* ◊ [VN] *An increasing number of plays are now being signed.*

► **sign·er** *noun*: *the signers of the petition* ◊ *signers communicating information to deaf people*

IDM **,signed and 'sealed | ,signed, ,sealed and de'livered** definite, because all the legal documents have been signed **sign on the dotted 'line** (*informal*) to sign a document to show that you have agreed to buy sth or do sth: *Just sign on the dotted line and the car is yours.*—more at PLEDGE *n.*

PHR V **,sign sth↔a'way** to lose your rights or property by signing a document **'sign for sth** to sign a document to show that you have received sth: *Someone must sign for the package when we deliver it.* **,sign 'in/'out | ,sign sb↔'in/'out** to write your/sb's name when you arrive at or leave an office, a club, etc: *All visitors must sign in on arrival.* ◊ *You must sign guests out when they leave the club.* **,sign 'off 1** (*BrE*) to end a letter: *She signed off with*

'Yours, Janet'. **2** to end a broadcast by saying goodbye or playing a piece of music ,sign sth↔'off to give your formal approval to sth, by signing your name ,sign 'off on sth *(AmE, informal)* to express your approval of sth formally and definitely: *The President hasn't signed off on this report.* ,sign 'on *(BrE, informal)* to sign a form stating that you are an unemployed person so that you can receive payment from the government ,sign 'on/'up| ,sign sb↔'on/'up to sign a form or contract which says that you agree to do a job or become a soldier; to persuade sb to sign a form or contract like this: *He signed on for five years in the army.* ◊ *The company has signed up three top models for the fashion show.* ,sign sth↔'over (to sb) to give your rights or property to sb else by signing a document: *She has signed the house over to her daughter.* ,sign 'up (for sth) to arrange to do a course of study by adding your name to the list of people doing it

---

WHICH WORD?
sign / signal

Sign and **signal** can be used with very similar meanings. Both words can mean a movement or sound made to tell someone something: *Don't move until I give the sign/signal.*

They can also both mean something that indicates that something exists or may happen, but a **sign** is usually something that you can find or see, while **signal** is used for something that is done intentionally or that suggests you should take some action: *early signs of the disease* ◊ *the first signs of spring* ◊ *danger/warning signals* ◊ *Local people regarded the President's visit as a clear signal of his support.*

With other meanings, only one of these words can be used: *a road sign* ◊ *a dollar sign* ◊ *a faint radio signal* ◊ *The train waited while the signals were on red.*

---

sig·nal /'sɪgnəl/ *noun, verb, adj.*

■ *noun* **1** a movement or sound that you make to give sb information, instructions, a warning, etc. [SYN] SIGN: *a danger/warning/distress signal* ◊ *At an agreed signal they left the room.* ◊ *The siren was a signal for everyone to leave the building.* ◊ *When I give the signal, run!* ◊ *(AmE) All I get is a busy signal when I dial his number* (= his phone is being used).—see also TURN SIGNAL **2** an event, an action, a fact, etc. that shows that sth exists or is likely to happen [SYN] SIGN, INDICATION: *The rise in inflation is a clear signal that the government's policies are not working.* ◊ *Chest pains can be a warning signal of heart problems.* **3** a piece of equipment that uses different coloured lights to tell drivers to slow down, stop, etc., used especially on railways/railroads and roads: *traffic signals* ◊ *a stop signal* **4** a series of electrical waves that carry sounds, pictures or messages, for example to a radio or television: *TV signals* ◊ *a high frequency signal* ◊ *a sound/radio/radar signal* ◊ *to detect/pick up signals* ◊ *to emit a signal*

■ *verb* (-ll-, *AmE* -l-) **1** ~ (to sb) to make a movement or sound to give sb a message, an order, etc: [V] *Don't fire until I signal.* ◊ *Did you signal before you turned right?* ◊ *He signalled to the waiter for the bill.* ◊ [VN] *The referee signalled a foul.* ◊ [V(that)] *She signalled (that) it was time to leave.* ◊ [Vtoinf] *He signalled to us to join him.* ◊ [VNtoinf] *She signalled him to follow.* ◊ [Vwh-] *You must signal which way you are going to turn.* **2** [VN] to be a sign that sth exists or is likely to happen: *This announcement signalled a clear change of policy.* ◊ *The scandal surely signals the end of his political career.* **3** to do sth to make your feelings or opinions known: [VN] *She signalled his discontent by refusing to vote.* ◊ [V(that)] *She has signalled (that) she is willing to stand as a candidate.*

■ *adj.* [only before noun] *(formal)* important: *a signal success/honour* ▶ **sig·nal·ly** /-nəli/ *adv.:* *They have signally failed to keep their election promises.*

'signal box *noun (BrE)* a building beside a railway/railroad from which rail signals are operated

sig·nal·ler *(AmE also* **sig·nal·er**) /'sɪgnələ(r)/ *noun* = SIGNALMAN

sig·nal·man /'sɪgnəlmən/ *noun (pl.* **-men** /-mən/) *(also* **sig·nal·ler**) *(BrE)* **1** a person whose job is operating signals on a railway **2** a person trained to give and receive signals in the army or navy

sig·na·tory /'sɪgnətri; *AmE* -tɔːri/ *noun (pl.* **-ies**) ~ **(to/of sth)** *(formal)* a person, a country or an organization that has signed an official agreement: *a signatory of the Declaration of Independence* ◊ *Many countries are signatories to/of the Berne Convention.*

sig·na·ture /'sɪgnətʃə(r)/ *noun* **1** [C] your name as you usually write it, for example at the end of a letter: *Someone had forged her signature on the cheque.* ◊ *They collected 10000 signatures for their petition.* ◊ *He was attacked for having put his signature to the deal.* **2** [U] *(formal)* the act of signing sth: *Two copies of the contract will be sent to you for signature.* **3** [C, usually sing.] a particular quality that makes sth different from other similar things and makes it easy to recognize: *Bright colours are his signature.*—see also KEY SIGNATURE, TIME SIGNATURE

'signature tune *noun (BrE)* a short tune played at the beginning and end of a particular television or radio programme, or one that is connected with a particular performer—compare THEME MUSIC

sign·board /'saɪnbɔːd; *AmE* -bɔːrd/ *noun* a piece of wood that has some information on it, such as a name, and is displayed outside a shop/store, hotel, etc.

'sig·net ring /'sɪgnət rɪŋ/ *noun* a ring with a design cut into it, that you wear on your finger—picture at JEWELLERY

sig·nifi·cance /sɪg'nɪfɪkəns/ *noun* [U, C] **1** the importance of sth, especially when this has an effect on what happens in the future: *a decision of major political significance* ◊ *The new drug has great significance for the treatment of the disease.* ◊ *We should be fully aware of the significance of television in shaping our ideas.* [OPP] INSIGNIFICANCE **2** the meaning of sth: *She couldn't grasp the full significance of what he had said.* ◊ *Do these symbols have any particular significance?*

sig·nifi·cant /sɪg'nɪfɪkənt/ *adj.* **1** large or important enough to have an effect or to be noticed: *a highly significant discovery* ◊ *The results of the experiment are not statistically significant.* ◊ *There are no significant differences between the two groups of students.* ◊ *Your work has shown a significant improvement.* [OPP] INSIGNIFICANT **2** having a particular meaning: *It is significant that he changed his will only days before his death.* **3** [usually before noun] having a special or secret meaning that is not understood by everyone [SYN] MEANINGFUL: *a significant look/smile*

sig·nifi·cant·ly /sɪg'nɪfɪkəntli/ *adv.* **1** in a way that is large or important enough to have an effect on sth or to be noticed: *The two sets of figures are not significantly different from each other.* ◊ *Profits have increased significantly over the past few years.* **2** in a way that has a particular meaning: *Significantly, he did not deny that there might be an election.* **3** in a way that has a special or secret meaning: *She paused significantly before she answered.*

sig,nificant 'other *noun (often humorous)* your husband, wife, partner or sb that you have a special relationship with

sig·ni·fi·ca·tion /ˌsɪgnɪfɪ'keɪʃn/ *noun (formal or linguistics)* [U, C] the exact meaning of sth, especially a word or phrase

sig·nify /'sɪgnɪfaɪ/ *verb* (**sig·ni·fies, sig·ni·fy·ing, sig·ni·fied, sig·ni·fied**) *(formal)* **1** to be a sign of sth; to mean sth: [VN] *The church bell used to be rung to signify disaster.* ◊ *This decision signified a radical change in their policies.* ◊ [Vthat] *This mark signifies that the products conform to an approved standard.* ◊ *The white belt signifies that he's an absolute beginner.* **2** to do sth to make your feelings, intentions, etc. known: [VN] *She signified her approval with a smile.* ◊ [Vthat] *He nodded to signify that he agreed.* **3** [V] (usually used in questions or negative sentences) to be important or to matter: *His presence no longer signified.*

sign·ing /'saɪnɪŋ/ *noun* **1** [U] the act of writing your

æ	ɑː	e	ɜː	ə	ɪ	iː	i	ɒ	ɔː	ʌ	ʊ	u	uː
cat	father	ten	bird	about	sit	see	many	got	saw	cup	put	actual	too
								(BrE)					

name at the end of an official document to show that you accept it: *the signing of the Treaty of Rome* **2** [C] (*BrE*) a person who has just signed a contract to join a particular sports team or record or film company **3** [U] the act of making an official contract that arranges for sb to join a sports team or a record or film company **4** [U] the act of using sign language: *the use of signing in classrooms*

ˈsign language *noun* [U, C] a system of communicating with people who cannot hear, by using hand movements rather than spoken words

sign·post /ˈsaɪnpəʊst; *AmE* -poʊst/ *noun, verb*
■ *noun* a sign at the side of a road giving information about the direction and distance of places: *Follow the signposts to the superstore.* ◇ (*figurative*) *The chapter headings are useful signposts to the content of the book.*
■ *verb* [VN] (*BrE*) **1** [usually passive] to mark a road, place, etc. with signposts: *The route is well signposted.* ◇ *The lane is signposted 'To the beach'.* **2** to show clearly the way that an argument, a speech, etc. will develop: *You need to signpost for the reader the various points you are going to make.* ▶ **sign·post·ing** *noun* [U]

Sikh /siːk/ *noun* a member of a religion (called **Sikhism**) that developed from Hinduism in Punjab in the late 15th century and is based on a belief that there is only one God ▶ **Sikh** *adj.*

sil·age /ˈsaɪlɪdʒ/ *noun* [U] grass or other green crops that are stored without being dried and are used to feed farm animals in winter

si·lence /ˈsaɪləns/ *noun, verb, exclamation*
■ *noun* **1** [U] a complete lack of noise or sound: *Their footsteps echoed in the silence.* ◇ *A scream broke the silence of the night.* **2** [C, U] a situation when nobody is speaking: *an embarrassed/awkward silence* ◇ *a moment's stunned silence* ◇ *I got used to his long silences.* ◇ *They finished their meal* **in total silence**. ◇ *She lapsed into silence again.* ◇ *There was a deafening silence* (= one that is very noticeable). ◇ *a two-minute silence in honour of those who had died* **3** [U, sing.] ~ (**on sth**) a situation in which sb refuses to talk about sth or to answer questions: *She broke her public silence in a TV interview.* ◇ *The company's silence on the subject has been taken as an admission of guilt.* ◇ *the right to silence* (= the legal right not to say anything when you are arrested) ◇ *There is* **a conspiracy of silence** *about what is happening* (= everyone has agreed not to discuss it). **4** [U] a situation in which people do not communicate with each other by letter or telephone: *The phone call came after months of silence.* IDM **ˌsilence is ˈgolden** (*saying*) it is often best not to say anything—more at PREGNANT
■ *verb* [VN] (*written*) **1** to make sb/sth stop speaking or making a noise: *She silenced him with a glare.* ◇ *Our bombs silenced the enemy's guns* (= they destroyed them). **2** to make sb stop expressing opinions that are opposed to yours: *All protest had been silenced.* ◇ *Her recent achievements have silenced her critics.* IDM see HEAVY *adj.*
■ *exclamation* (*formal*) used to tell people to be quiet: *Silence in court!*

si·len·cer /ˈsaɪlənsə(r)/ *noun* **1** (*BrE*) (*AmE* **muf·fler**) a device that is fixed to the EXHAUST of a vehicle in order to reduce the amount of noise that the engine makes **2** a device that is fixed to the end of a gun in order to reduce the amount of noise that it makes when it is fired

si·lent /ˈsaɪlənt/ *adj.* **1** (of a person) not speaking: *to remain/stay/keep silent* ◇ *They huddled together in silent groups.* ◇ *As the curtain rose, the audience* **fell silent**. **2** [only before noun] (especially of a man) not talking very much [SYN] QUIET: *He's the strong, silent type.* **3** where there is little or no sound; making little or no sound [SYN] QUIET: *At last the traffic fell silent.* ◇ *The streets were silent and deserted.* **4** [only before noun] not expressed with words or sound: *a silent prayer/protest* ◇ *They nodded in silent agreement.* **5** ~ (**on/about sth**) not giving information about sth; refusing to speak about sth: *The report is strangely silent on this issue.* ◇ *the right to* **remain silent** (= the legal right not to say anything when you are arrested) **6** [only before noun] (of old films/movies) with pictures but no sound: *a silent film/movie* ◇

stars of the silent screen **7** (of a letter in a word) written but not pronounced: *The 'b' in 'lamb' is silent.*

si·lent·ly /ˈsaɪləntli/ *adv.* **1** without speaking: *They marched silently through the streets.* **2** without making any or much sound: *She crept silently out of the room.* **3** without using words or sounds to express sth: *She prayed silently.* ◇ *He silently agreed with much of what she had said.* IDM **sit/stand ˌsilently ˈby** to do or say nothing to help sb or deal with a difficult situation

the ˌsilent maˈjority *noun* [usually sing.] the large number of people in a country who think the same as each other, but do not express their views publicly

ˌsilent ˈpartner *noun* (*AmE*) = SLEEPING PARTNER

sil·hou·ette /ˌsɪluˈet/ *noun, verb*
■ *noun* **1** [C, U] the dark outline or shape of a person or an object that you see against a light background: *the silhouette of chimneys and towers* ◇ *The mountains stood out* **in silhouette**. **2** [C] the shape of a person's body or of an object: *The dress is fitted to give you a flattering silhouette.* **3** [C] a picture that shows sb/sth as a black shape against a light background, especially one that shows the side view of a person's face
■ *verb* [VN] [usually passive] ~ **sb/sth** (**against sth**) to make sth appear as a silhouette: *A figure stood in the doorway, silhouetted against the light.*

sil·ica /ˈsɪlɪkə/ *noun* [U] (*symb* SiO₂) a chemical compound of silicon found in sand and in rocks such as QUARTZ, used in making glass and CEMENT

sili·cate /ˈsɪlɪkeɪt/ *noun* [C, U] **1** (*chemistry*) a compound containing SILICON, OXYGEN and one or more metals: *aluminium silicate* **2** a mineral that contains silica. There are many different silicates and they form a large part of the earth's CRUST.

sil·icon /ˈsɪlɪkən/ *noun* [U] (*symb* Si) a chemical element. Silicon exists as a grey solid or as a brown powder and is found in rocks and sand. It is used in making glass and TRANSISTORS.

ˌsilicon ˈchip *noun* a very small piece of silicon used to carry a complicated electronic CIRCUIT

sili·cone /ˈsɪlɪkəʊn; *AmE* -koʊn/ *noun* [U] a chemical compound of silicon. There are several different types of silicone, used to make paint, artificial rubber, VARNISH, etc: *a silicone breast implant*

silk /sɪlk/ *noun* **1** [U] fine soft thread produced by SILKWORMS **2** [U] a fine smooth fabric made from silk thread: *a silk blouse* ◇ *silk stockings* ◇ *made of pure silk* ◇ *Her skin was* **as smooth as silk**. **3** [U] silk thread used for sewing **4** (**silks**) [pl.] clothes made of silk, especially the coloured shirts worn by people riding horses in a race (= JOCKEYS) **5** [C] (*BrE, law*) a type of lawyer who represents the government (= a KING'S/QUEEN'S COUNSEL): *to take silk* (= to become this type of lawyer) IDM **make a silk ˌpurse out of a sow's ˈear** to succeed in making sth good out of material that does not seem very good at all

silk·en /ˈsɪlkən/ *adj.* (*literary*) **1** [usually before noun] soft, smooth and shiny like silk: *silken hair/skin* **2** [usually before noun] smooth and gentle: *her silken voice/touch* **3** [only before noun] made of silk: *silken ribbons*

ˈsilk-screen *adj.* [only before noun] involving a method of printing in which ink is forced through a design cut in a piece of fine fabric: *silk-screen printing/prints* ▶ **ˈsilk-screen** *noun*: *Warhol's silk-screen of Marilyn Monroe* **ˈsilk-screen** *verb* [VN]

silk·worm /ˈsɪlkwɜːm; *AmE* -wɜːrm/ *noun* a CATERPILLAR (= a small creature like a worm with legs) that produces silk thread

silky /ˈsɪlki/ *adj.* **1** soft, smooth and shiny like silk: *soft, silky hair/fur* **2** [usually before noun] smooth and gentle: *He spoke in a silky tone.* **3** made of silk or a fabric that looks like silk: *a silky dress* ▶ **silk·ily** *adv.*: *'How have I changed?' he asked silkily.* **silki·ness** *noun* [U] **silky** *adv.*: *The leaves are grey and silky smooth.*

sill /sɪl/ *noun* **1** = WINDOW SILL **2** a piece of metal that forms part of the frame of a vehicle below the doors

silly /ˈsɪli/ *adj., noun*
■ *adj.* (**sil·lier, sil·li·est**) **1** showing a lack of thought, understanding or judgement [SYN] FOOLISH: *a silly idea/question*

aɪ	aʊ	eɪ	əʊ	oʊ	ɔɪ	ɪə	eə	ʊə	j	w
my	now	say	go	go	boy	near	hair	pure	yes	wet
			(BrE)	(AmE)						

◊ *That was a silly thing to do!* ◊ *Her work is full of silly mistakes.* ◊ *'I can walk home.' 'Don't be silly—it's much too far!'* ◊ *You silly boy!* **2** stupid or embarrassing, especially in a way that is more typical of a child than an adult SYN RIDICULOUS: *a silly sense of humour* ◊ *a silly game/joke* ◊ *I feel silly in these clothes.* ◊ *She had a silly grin on her face.* ◊ *(especially BrE) I got it for a silly price* (= very cheap). ▶ **sil·li·ness** *noun* [U] IDM **,drink, ,laugh, ,shout, etc. yourself 'silly** (*informal*) to drink, laugh, shout, etc. so much that you cannot behave in a sensible way **play 'silly buggers** (*BrE, informal*) to behave in a stupid and annoying way—more at GAME *n.*

■ *noun* (also *less frequent* **,silly 'billy**) [sing.] (*spoken*) often used when speaking to children to say that they are not behaving in a sensible way: *No, silly, those aren't your shoes!*

the 'silly season *noun* [sing.] (*BrE*) the time, usually in the summer, when newspapers are full of unimportant stories because there is little serious news

silo /'saɪləʊ; *AmE* -loʊ/ *noun* (*pl.* **-os**) **1** a tall tower on a farm used for storing grain, etc. **2** an underground place where nuclear weapons or dangerous substances are kept **3** an underground place where SILAGE is made and stored

silt /sɪlt/ *noun, verb*
■ *noun* [U] sand, mud, etc. that is carried by flowing water and is left at the mouth of a river or in a harbour ▶ **silty** *adj.*: *silty soils*
■ *verb* PHRV **,silt sth↔'up | ,silt 'up** to block sth with silt; to become blocked with silt: *Sand has silted up the river delta.* ◊ *The harbour has now silted up.*

sil·ver /'sɪlvə(r)/ *noun, adj., verb*
■ *noun* **1** [U] (*symb* Ag) a chemical element. Silver is a greyish-white precious metal used for making coins, jewellery, ornaments, etc: *a silver candlestick/chain/coin* ◊ *made of solid silver* ◊ *a silver mine* **2** [U] coins that are made of silver or a metal that looks like silver: *I need £2 in silver for the parking meter.* **3** [U] dishes, ornaments, etc. that are made of silver: *They've had to sell the family silver to pay the bills.* **4** [U] a shiny greyish-white colour—see also SILVERY **5** [U, C] = SILVER MEDAL: *She won silver in last year's championships.* ◊ *The team won two silvers and a bronze.* IDM **(hand sb sth) on a silver 'platter** to give sth to sb without expecting them to do or give anything in return—more at BORN, CLOUD *n.*, CROSS *v.*
■ *adj.* shiny greyish-white in colour: *a silver car/dress* ◊ *silver hair*—see also SILVERY
■ *verb* [VN] **1** [usually passive] to cover the surface of sth with a thin layer of silver or sth that looks like silver **2** (*especially literary*) to make sth become bright like silver: *Moonlight was silvering the countryside.*

,silver anni'versary *noun* (*especially AmE*) **1** = SILVER WEDDING **2** = SILVER JUBILEE

,silver 'birch *noun* [C, U] a tree with smooth, very pale grey or white bark and thin branches, that grows in northern countries

sil·ver·fish /'sɪlvəfɪʃ; *AmE* -vərf-/ *noun* (*pl.* **sil·ver·fish**) a small insect without wings that is silver in colour and that lives in houses

,silver 'foil *noun* [U] (*BrE*) = FOIL

,silver 'jubilee (*BrE*) (*AmE* **,silver anni'versary**) *noun* [usually sing.] the 25th anniversary of an important event; a celebration of sth that began 25 years ago: *the silver jubilee of the Queen's coronation* ◊ *The college celebrated its silver jubilee last year.*—compare DIAMOND JUBILEE, GOLDEN JUBILEE

,silver 'medal *noun* [C] (also **sil·ver** [U, C]) a medal that is given to the person or the team that wins the second prize in a race or competition: *an Olympic silver medal winner*—compare BRONZE MEDAL, GOLD MEDAL ▶ **,silver 'medallist** (*BrE*) (*AmE* **,silver 'medalist**) *noun*: *He's an Olympic silver medallist.*

,silver 'paper *noun* [U] (*BrE*) very thin, shiny sheets of ALUMINIUM that are used for wrapping chocolate, etc.

,silver 'plate *noun* [U] metal that is covered with a thin layer of silver; objects that are made of this metal ▶ **,silver-'plated** *adj.*

the ,silver 'screen *noun* [sing.] (*old-fashioned*) the film/movie industry

sil·ver·smith /'sɪlvəsmɪθ; *AmE* -vərs-/ *noun* a person who makes, repairs or sells articles made of silver

sil·ver·ware /'sɪlvəweə(r); *AmE* -vərwer/ *noun* [U] **1** objects that are made of or covered with silver, especially knives, forks, dishes, etc. that are used for eating and serving food: *a piece of silverware* **2** (*AmE*) = CUTLERY **3** (*BrE, informal*) a silver cup that you win in a sports competition SYN TROPHY

,silver 'wedding (*BrE*) (*AmE* **,silver anni'versary**) (also **,silver 'wedding anniversary** *AmE, BrE*) *noun* the 25th anniversary of a wedding: *They celebrated their silver wedding in May.*—compare DIAMOND WEDDING, GOLDEN WEDDING, RUBY WEDDING

sil·very /'sɪlvəri/ *adj.* [usually before noun] **1** shiny like silver; having the colour of silver: *silvery water/light/ fish* ◊ *a silvery grey/blue colour* **2** (*literary*) (especially of a voice) having a pleasant musical sound

sim·ian /'sɪmiən/ *adj.* (*technical*) like a monkey, especially an APE; connected with monkeys or APES

simi·lar /'sɪmələ(r)/ *adj.* **~ (to sb/sth)| ~ (in sth)** like sb/sth but not exactly the same: *We have very similar interests.* ◊ *My teaching style is similar to that of most other teachers.* ◊ *The two houses are similar in size.* ◊ *The brothers look very similar.* ◊ *All our patients have broadly similar problems.* OPP DIFFERENT, DISSIMILAR

simi·lar·ity /,sɪmə'lærəti/ *noun* (*pl.* **-ies**) **1** [U, sing.] **~ (between A and B)| ~ (to sb/sth)| ~ (in sth)** the state of being like sb/sth but not exactly the same: *The report highlights the similarity between the two groups.* ◊ *She bears a **striking similarity** to her mother.* ◊ *There is some similarity in the way they sing.* ◊ *They are both doctors but that is where the similarity ends.* **2** [C] **~ (in/of sth)| ~ (to/ with sb/sth)** a feature that things or people have that makes them like each other: *a study of the similarities and differences between the two countries* ◊ *similarities in/ of style* ◊ *The karate bout has many similarities to a boxing match.* OPP DIFFERENCE, DISSIMILARITY

simi·lar·ly /'sɪmələli; *AmE* -lərli/ *adv.* **1** in almost the same way: *Husband and wife were similarly successful in their chosen careers.* **2** used to say that two facts, actions, statements, etc. are like each other: *The United States won most of the track and field events. Similarly, in swimming, the top three places went to Americans.*

sim·ile /'sɪməli/ *noun* [C, U] (*technical*) a word or phrase that compares sth to sth else, using the words *like* or *as*, for example *a face like a mask* or *as white as snow*; the use of such words and phrases—compare METAPHOR

sim·mer /'sɪmə(r)/ *verb, noun*
■ *verb* **1** to cook sth by keeping it almost at boiling point; to be cooked in this way: [VN] *Simmer the sauce gently for 10 minutes.* ◊ [V] *Leave the soup to simmer.* **2** [V] **~ (with sth)** to be filled with a strong feeling, especially anger, which you have difficulty controlling: *She was still simmering with resentment.* ◊ *Anger simmered inside him.* **3** [V] (of an argument, a dispute, etc.) to develop for a period of time without any real anger or' violence being shown: *This argument has been simmering for months.* ◊ *The simmering dispute finally erupted.* PHRV **,simmer 'down** (*informal*) to become calm after a period of anger or excitement: *I left him alone until he simmered down.* ◊ *Things have simmered down since the riots last week.*
■ *noun* [sing.] the state when sth is almost boiling: *Bring the sauce to a simmer and cook for 5 minutes.*

sim·per /'sɪmpə(r)/ *verb* (*written*) to smile in a silly and annoying way: *a silly simpering girl* ◊ *He just simpered at me.* ◊ [V speech] *'You're such a darling,' she simpered.* ▶ **sim·per** *noun* [sing.] **sim·per·ing·ly** /'sɪmpərɪŋli/ *adv.*

sim·ple /'sɪmpl/ *adj.* (**sim·pler, sim·plest**) HELP You can also use **more simple** and **most simple**.
EASY **1** not complicated; easy to understand or do: *a simple method/solution/task* ◊ *The answer is really quite simple.* ◊ *This machine is very simple to use.* ◊ (*especially spoken*) *We lost because we played badly. It's **as simple as that**.* ◊ *Give the necessary information but **keep it simple**.*
BASIC/PLAIN **2** basic or plain without anything extra or

b	d	f	g	h	k	l	m	n	p	r
bad	did	fall	get	hat	cat	leg	man	now	pen	red

unnecessary: *simple but elegant clothes* ◊ *We had a simple meal of soup and bread.* ◊ *The accommodation is simple but spacious.* OPP FANCY

FOR EMPHASIS | **3** used before a noun to emphasize that it is exactly that and nothing else: *Nobody wanted to believe the simple truth.* ◊ *It was a matter of simple survival.* ◊ *It's nothing to worry about—just a simple headache.* ◊ *I had to do it **for the simple reason that** (= because) I couldn't trust anyone else.*

WITH FEW PARTS | **4** [usually before noun] consisting of only a few parts; not complicated in structure: *simple forms of life, for example amoebas* ◊ *a simple design/machine/plan* ◊ *(grammar) a simple sentence* (= one with only one verb)

ORDINARY | **5** [only before noun] (of a person) ordinary; not special: *I'm a simple country girl.*

NOT INTELLIGENT | **6** [not usually before noun] (of a person) not very intelligent; not mentally normal: *He's not mad—just a bit simple.*

GRAMMAR | **7** used to describe the present or past tense of a verb that is formed without using an AUXILIARY verb, as in *She loves him* or *He arrived late.*: *the simple present/past tense*
—see also SIMPLY IDM SEE PURE

S ¦simple ˈfracture *noun* an injury when a bone in your body is broken but does not come through the skin—compare COMPOUND FRACTURE

¦simple ˈinterest *noun* [U] (*finance*) interest that is paid only on the original amount of money that you invested, and not on any interest that it has earned—compare COMPOUND INTEREST

¦simple-ˈminded *adj.* (*disapproving*) not intelligent; not able to understand how complicated things are: *a simple-minded person* ◊ *a simple-minded view/approach*

simple·ton /ˈsɪmpltən/ *noun* (*old-fashioned*) a person who is not very intelligent and can be tricked easily

sim·pli·city /sɪmˈplɪsəti/ *noun* (*pl.* **-ies**) **1** [U] the quality of being easy to understand or use: *the relative simplicity of the new PC* ◊ *For the sake of simplicity, let's divide the discussion into two parts.* **2** [U] (*approving*) the quality of being natural and plain: *the simplicity of the architecture* ◊ *the simplicity of country living* **3** [C, usually pl.] an aspect of sth that is easy, natural or plain: *the simplicities of our old way of life* IDM **be sim,plicity it'self** to be very easy or plain: *Programming the video is simplicity itself.*

sim·pli·fi·ca·tion /ˌsɪmplɪfɪˈkeɪʃn/ *noun* **1** [U, sing.] the process of making sth easier to do or understand: *Complaints have led to (a) simplification of the rules.* **2** [C] the thing that results when you make a problem, statement, system, etc. easier to understand or do: *A number of simplifications have been made to the taxation system.*—compare OVERSIMPLIFICATION at OVERSIMPLIFY

sim·plify /ˈsɪmplɪfaɪ/ *verb* (**sim·pli·fies, sim·pli·fy·ing, sim·pli·fied, sim·pli·fied**) [VN] to make sth easier to do or understand: *The application forms have now been simplified.* ◊ *I hope his appointment will **simplify matters**.* ◊ *a simplified version of the story for young children*

sim·plis·tic /sɪmˈplɪstɪk/ *adj.* (*disapproving*) making a problem, situation, etc. seem less difficult or complicated than it really is: *a simplistic approach/view/solution* ▶ **sim·plis·tic·al·ly** /-kli/ *adv.*

simp·ly /ˈsɪmpli/ *adv.* **1** used to emphasize how easy or basic sth is SYN JUST: *Simply add hot water and stir.* ◊ *The runway is simply a strip of grass.* ◊ *Fame is often simply a matter of being in the right place at the right time.* ◊ *You can enjoy all the water sports, or simply lie on the beach.* **2** used to emphasize a statement SYN ABSOLUTELY: *You simply must see the play.* ◊ *The view is simply wonderful!* ◊ *That is simply not true!* ◊ *I haven't seen her for simply ages.* **3** in a way that is easy to understand: *The book explains grammar simply and clearly.* ◊ *Anyway, **to put it simply**, we still owe them £2000.* **4** in a way that is natural and plain: *The rooms are simply furnished.* ◊ *They live simply* (= they do not spend much money). **5** used to introduce a summary or an explanation of sth that you have just said or done: *I don't want to be rude, **it's simply that** we have to be careful who we give this information to.*

simu·lac·rum /ˌsɪmjuˈleɪkrəm/ *noun* (*pl.* **simu·lacra**

/-krə/) (*formal*) something that looks like sb/sth else or that is made to look like sb/sth else SYN COPY

simu·late /ˈsɪmjuleɪt/ *verb* [VN] **1** to pretend that you have a particular feeling: *I tried to simulate surprise at the news.* **2** to create particular conditions that exist in real life using computers, models, etc., usually for study or training purposes: *Computer software can be used to simulate conditions on the sea bed.* ◊ *Role-playing is a useful way of simulating real-life situations.* **3** to be made to look like sth else: *a gas heater that simulates a coal fire*

simu·lated /ˈsɪmjuleɪtɪd/ *adj.* [only before noun] not real, but made to look, feel, etc. like the real thing SYN ARTIFICIAL: *simulated fur/leather* ◊ *'How wonderful!' she said with simulated enthusiasm.*

simu·la·tion /ˌsɪmjuˈleɪʃn/ *noun* **1** [C, U] a situation in which a particular set of conditions is created artificially in order to study or experience sth that could exist in reality: *a computer simulation of how the planet functions* ◊ *a simulation model* **2** [U] the act of pretending that sth is real when it is not: *the simulation of genuine concern*

simu·la·tor /ˈsɪmjuleɪtə(r)/ *noun* a piece of equipment that artificially creates a particular set of conditions in order to train sb to deal with a situation that they may experience in reality: *a flight simulator*

sim·ul·cast /ˈsɪmlkɑːst; *AmE* also ˈsaɪm-/ *verb* (**sim·ul·cast, sim·ul·cast**) [VN] (*especially AmE*) to broadcast sth on radio and television at the same time or on both AM and FM radio ▶ **sim·ul·cast** *noun*

sim·ul·tan·eous /ˌsɪmlˈteɪniəs; *AmE* ˌsaɪml-/ *adj.* happening or done at the same time as sth else: *There were several simultaneous attacks by the rebels.* ◊ *Any ceasefire would be simultaneous with the withdrawal of US forces.* ◊ *simultaneous translation/interpreting* ▶ **sim·ul·tan·eity** /ˌsɪmltəˈneɪəti; *AmE* ˌsaɪmltəˈniːəti/ *noun* [U] **sim·ul·tan·eous·ly** *adv.*: *The game will be broadcast simultaneously on TV and radio.*

sin /sɪn/ *noun, verb, abbr.*
- *noun* **1** [C] an offence against God or against a religious or moral law: *to commit a sin* ◊ *Confess your sins to God and he will forgive you.* ◊ *The Bible says that stealing is a sin.*—see also MORTAL SIN, ORIGINAL SIN **2** [U] the act of breaking a religious or moral law: *a life of sin* **3** [C, usually sing.] (*informal*) an action that people strongly disapprove of: *It's a sin to waste taxpayers' money like that.*—see also SINFUL, SINNER IDM **be/do sth for your sins** (*spoken humorous, especially BrE*) used to say that sth that sb does is like a punishment: *She works with us in Accounts, for her sins!* **(as) miserable/ugly as ˈsin** (*spoken*) used to emphasize that sb is very unhappy or ugly—more at MULTITUDE, LIVE[1]
- *verb* (**-nn-**) [V] to break a religious or moral law: *Forgive me, Lord, for I have sinned.* ◊ *He was **more sinned against than sinning** (= although he did wrong, other people treated him even worse).*
- *abbr.* (*mathematics*) SINE

ˈsin bin *noun* (*slang*) (in some sports, for example ice hockey) a place away from the playing area where the REFEREE sends a player who has broken the rules

since /sɪns/ *prep., conj., adv.*
- *prep.* **1** (used with the present, perfect or past perfect tense) from a time in the past until a later past time, or until now: *She's been off work since Tuesday.* ◊ *We've lived here since 1994.* ◊ *I haven't eaten since breakfast.* ◊ *He's been working in a bank since leaving school.* ◊ *Since the party she had only spoken to him once.* ◊ *'They've split up.' ' Since when? '* ◊ *That was years ago. I've changed jobs since then.* HELP Use not **since**, with a period of time: *I've been learning English for five years.* ◊ ~~I've been learning English since five years.~~ **2** ~ **when?** used when you are showing that you are angry about sth: *Since when did he ever listen to me?*
- *conj.* **1** (used with the present perfect, past perfect or simple present tense in the main clause) from an event in the past until a later past event, or until now: *Cath hasn't phoned since she went to Berlin.* ◊ *It was the first time I'd had visitors since I'd moved to London.* ◊ *It's twenty years since I've seen her.* ◊ *How long is it since we last went to the*

	s	t	v	z	ʃ	ʒ	tʃ	dʒ	θ	ð	ŋ
	see	tea	van	zoo	shoe	vision	chain	jam	thin	this	sing

theatre? ◊ *She had been worrying **ever since** the letter arrived.* **2** because; as: *We thought that, since we were in the area, we'd stop by and see them.*

■ *adv.* (used with the present, perfect or past perfect tense) **1** from a time in the past until a later past time, or until now: *He left home two weeks ago and we haven't heard from him since.* ◊ *The original building **has long since** (= long before now) been demolished.* **2** at a time after a particular time in the past: *We were divorced two years ago and she has since remarried.*

sin·cere /sɪnˈsɪə(r); *AmE* -ˈsɪr/ *adj.* (*superlative* **sin·cer·est**, no *comparative*) **1** (of feelings, beliefs or behaviour) showing what you really think or feel SYN GENUINE: *a sincere attempt to resolve the problem* ◊ *sincere concern/gratitude/regret* ◊ *Please accept our sincere thanks.* ◊ *a sincere apology* **2** ~ **(in sth)** (of a person) saying only what you really think or feel SYN HONEST: *He seemed sincere enough when he said he wanted to help.* ◊ *She is never completely sincere in what she says about people.* OPP INSINCERE ▶ **sin·cer·ity** /sɪnˈserəti/ *noun* [U]: *The sincerity of his beliefs is unquestionable.* ◊ *She spoke with total sincerity.* ◊ *I can say **in all sincerity** that I knew nothing of these plans.*

sin·cere·ly /sɪnˈsɪəli; *AmE* -ˈsɪrli/ *adv.* in a way that shows what you really feel or think about sb/sth: *I sincerely believe that this is the right decision.* ◊ *'I won't let you down.' 'I sincerely hope not.'* IDM **Yours sincerely** (*BrE*) (*AmE* **Sincerely (yours)**) (*formal*, *written*) used at the end of a formal letter before you sign your name, when you have addressed sb by their name ⇨ Study page B14

sine /saɪn/ *noun* (*abbr.* **sin**) (*mathematics*) the RATIO of the length of the side opposite one of the angles in a RIGHT-ANGLED triangle that are less than 90° to the length of the longest side—compare COSINE, TANGENT

sine·cure /ˈsaɪnɪkjʊə(r); ˈsaɪn-; *AmE* -kjʊr/ *noun* (*formal*) a job that you are paid for even though it involves little or no work

sine qua non /ˌsaɪni kwɑː ˈnəʊn; *AmE* ˈnoʊn/ *noun* [sing.] ~ **(of/for sth)** (from *Latin*, *formal*) something that is essential before you can achieve sth else

sinew /ˈsɪnjuː/ *noun* **1** [C, U] a strong band of tissue in the body that joins a muscle to a bone **2** [usually pl.] (*literary*) a source of strength or power: *the sinews of economic life* IDM see STRAIN *v.*

sinewy /ˈsɪnjuːi/ *adj.* (of a person or an animal) having a thin body and strong muscles

sin·ful /ˈsɪnfl/ *adj.* morally wrong or wicked: *sinful acts/thoughts* ◊ *It is sinful to lie.* ◊ (*informal*) *It's sinful to waste good food!* ▶ **sin·ful·ly** /-fəli/ *adv.* **sin·ful·ness** *noun* [U]

sing /sɪŋ/ *verb* (**sang** /sæŋ/, **sung** /sʌŋ/) **1** to make musical sounds with your voice in the form of a song or tune: [V] *She usually sings in the shower.* ◊ *I just can't sing in tune!* ◊ *He was singing softly to the baby.* ◊ [VN, VNN] *Will you sing a song to us?* ◊ *Will you sing us a song?* ◊ [VN] *Now I'd like to sing a song by the Beatles.* ◊ *She sang the baby to sleep* (= sang until the baby went to sleep). **2** [V] (of birds) to make high musical sounds: *The birds were singing outside my window.* **3** [V] to make a high ringing sound like a whistle: *Bullets sang past my ears.* ▶ **sing** *noun* [sing.]: *Let's have a sing.* IDM **sing a different 'tune** to change your opinion about sb/sth or your attitude towards sb/sth PHRV **sing a'long (with sb/sth)** | **sing a'long (to sth)** to sing together with sb who is already singing or while a record, radio, or musical instrument is playing: *Do sing along if you know the words.* ◊ *She loves singing along to the radio.*—related noun SINGALONG **'sing of sth** (*old-fashioned* or *formal*) to mention sth in a song or a poem, especially to praise it: *Poets used to sing of such heroic deeds.* **,sing 'out** to sing or say sth clearly and loudly: *A voice suddenly sang out above the rest.* **,sing 'up** (*BrE*) (*AmE* **,sing 'out**) to sing more loudly: *Sing up, let's hear you.*

sing·along /ˈsɪŋəlɒŋ; *AmE* -lɔːŋ/ (*BrE* also **'sing-song**) *noun* an informal occasion at which people sing songs together: *a singalong in the local bar*

singe /sɪndʒ/ *verb* (**singe·ing**, **singed**, **singed**) to burn

the surface of sth slightly, usually by mistake; to be burnt in this way: [VN] *He singed his hair as he tried to light his cigarette.* ◊ [V] *the smell of singeing fur*

sing·er /ˈsɪŋə(r)/ *noun* a person who sings, or whose job is singing, especially in public: *She's a wonderful singer.* ◊ *an opera singer*

sing·ing /ˈsɪŋɪŋ/ *noun* [U] the activity of making musical sounds with your voice: *the beautiful singing of birds* ◊ *choral/folk singing* ◊ *There was singing and dancing all night.* ◊ *a singing career/teacher* ◊ *She has a beautiful singing voice.*

sin·gle /ˈsɪŋgl/ *adj.*, *noun*, *verb*
■ *adj.*
ONE | **1** [only before noun] only one: *He sent her a single red rose.* ◊ *a single-sex school* (= for boys only or for girls only) ◊ *All these jobs can now be done by one single machine.* ◊ *I couldn't understand a single word she said!* ◊ *the European single currency, the euro*
FOR EMPHASIS | **2** [only before noun] used to emphasize that you are referring to one particular person or thing on its own: *Unemployment is the single most important factor in the growing crime rates.* ◊ *We eat rice **every single day!***
NOT MARRIED | **3** (of a person) not married or having a romantic relationship with sb: *The apartments are ideal for single people living alone.* ◊ *Are you still single?*—see also SINGLE PARENT
FOR ONE PERSON | **4** [only before noun] intended to be used by only one person: *a single bed/room*—compare DOUBLE *adj.* (3)
TICKET | **5** [only before noun] (*BrE*) (also **one-way** *AmE*, *BrE*) a single ticket, etc. can be used for travelling to a place but not back again: *a single ticket* ◊ *How much is the single fare to Glasgow?*—compare RETURN *n.* (7)
IDM see FILE *n.*, GLANCE *n.*
■ *noun*
TICKET | **1** [C] (*BrE*) a ticket that allows you to travel to a place but not back again: *How much is a single to York?*—compare RETURN *n.* (7)
TAPE/CD | **2** [C] a tape, CD, etc. with only one song on each side; the main song on this tape or CD: *The group releases its new single next week.*—compare ALBUM
ROOM | **3** [C] a room in a hotel, etc. for one person: *Singles are available from £50 per night.*—compare DOUBLE *n.* (5)
UNMARRIED PEOPLE | **4** (**singles**) [pl.] people who are not married and do not have a romantic relationship with sb else: *They organize parties for singles.* ◊ *a singles bar/club*
IN SPORT | **5** (**singles**) [U] (especially in tennis) a game when only one player plays against one other; a series of two or more of these games: *the women's singles champion* ◊ *the first round of the men's singles* ◊ *a singles match* ◊ *She's won three singles titles this year.*—compare DOUBLES *n.* (6) **6** [C] (in cricket) a hit from which a player scores one RUN (= point) **7** (in baseball) a hit that only allows the player to run to FIRST BASE
■ *verb*
PHRV **,single sb/sth↔'out (for sth/as sb/sth)** to choose sb/sth from a group for special attention: *She was singled out for criticism.* ◊ *He was singled out as the outstanding performer of the games.*

,single-'breasted *adj.* (of a jacket or coat) having only one row of buttons that fasten in the middle—compare DOUBLE-BREASTED—picture on page A4

,single 'combat *noun* [U] fighting between two people, usually with weapons

,single-'decker *noun* a bus with only one level—compare DOUBLE-DECKER—picture at BUS

,single 'figures *noun* [pl.] a number that is less than ten: *Inflation is down to single figures.* ◊ *The number of people who fail each year is now in single figures.*

,single-'handed *adv.* on your own with nobody helping you: *to sail around the world single-handed* ▶ **,single-'handed** *adj.*: *a single-handed voyage/yachtsman* **,single-'handed·ly** *adv.*

,single 'market *noun* [usually sing.] (*economics*) a group of countries that have few or no restrictions on the movement of goods, money and people between the members of the group

S

æ	ɑː	e	ɜː	ə	ɪ	iː	i	ɒ	ɔː	ʌ	ʊ	uː
cat	father	ten	bird	about	sit	see	many	got	saw	cup	put	actual	too

(BrE)

single-'minded *adj.* only thinking about one particular aim or goal because you are determined to achieve sth: *the single-minded pursuit of power* ◇ *She is very single-minded about her career.* ▶ **,single-'minded·ly** *adv.* **,single-'minded·ness** *noun* [U]

single·ness /'sɪŋglnəs/ *noun* [U] **1 ~ of purpose** the ability to think about one particular aim or goal because you are determined to succeed **2** the state of not being married or having a partner

,single 'parent *noun* a person who looks after their child or children without a husband, wife or partner: *a single-parent family*

sing·let /'sɪŋglət/ *noun* (*BrE*) a piece of clothing without sleeves, worn under or instead of a shirt; a similar piece of clothing worn by runners, etc.—compare VEST

sin·gly /'sɪŋgli/ *adv.* alone; one at a time SYN INDIVIDU-ALLY: *The stamps are available singly or in books of ten.* ◇ *Guests arrived singly or in groups.*

'sing-song *noun, adj.*

■ *noun* **1** [C] (*BrE*) = SINGALONG **2** [sing.] a way of speaking in which a person's voice keeps rising and falling: *She spoke to the child in her soft Irish singsong.*

■ *adj.* [only before noun] a **sing-song** voice keeps rising and falling

sin·gu·lar /'sɪŋgjələ(r)/ *noun, adj.*

■ *noun* (*grammar*) a form of a noun or verb that refers to one person or thing: *The singular of 'bacteria' is 'bacterium'.* ◇ *The verb should be in the singular.*—compare PLURAL

■ *adj.* **1** (*grammar*) connected with or having the singular form: *a singular noun/verb/ending* **2** (*formal*) very great or obvious: *landscape of singular beauty* ◇ *He shows a singular lack of concern for other people's feelings.* **3** (*literary*) unusual; strange: *a singular style of dress/writing*

sin·gu·lar·ity /,sɪŋgju'lærəti/ *noun* (*pl.* **-ies**) [U] (*formal*) the quality of sth that makes it unusual or strange

sin·gu·lar·ly /'sɪŋgjələli/ *AmE* -lərli/ *adv.* (*formal*) very; in an unusual way: *singularly beautiful/foolish* ◇ *He chose a singularly inappropriate moment to make his request.*

Sin·hal·ese /,sɪnhə'liːz/ ,sɪnə-/ *noun* (*pl.* **Sin·hal·ese**) **1** [C] a member of a race of people originally from northern India and now living in Sri Lanka **2** [U] the language of the Sinhalese ▶ **Sin·hal·ese** *adj.*

sin·is·ter /'sɪnɪstə(r)/ *adj.* seeming evil or dangerous; making you think sth bad will happen: *There was something cold and sinister about him.* ◇ *There is another, more sinister, possibility.*

sink /sɪŋk/ *verb, noun*

■ *verb* (**sank** /sæŋk/ **sunk** /sʌŋk/) or (*less frequent* **sunk, sunk**)

<u>IN WATER/MUD, etc.</u> | **1** [V] to go down below the surface or towards the bottom of a liquid or soft substance: *The ship sank to the bottom of the sea.* ◇ *We're sinking!* ◇ *The wheels started to sink into the mud.*

<u>BOAT</u> | **2** [VN] to damage a boat or ship so that it goes below the surface of the sea, etc: *a battleship sunk by a torpedo*

<u>FALL/SIT DOWN</u> | **3** [V+*adv./prep.*] (of a person) to move downwards, especially by falling or sitting down: *I sank into an armchair.* ◇ *She sank back into her seat, exhausted.* ◇ *The old man had sunk to his knees.*

<u>MOVE DOWNWARDS</u> | **4** [V] (of an object) to move slowly downwards: *The sun was sinking in the west.* ◇ *The foundations of the building are starting to sink.*

<u>DECREASE</u> | **5** [V] to decrease in amount, volume, strength, etc: *The pound has sunk to its lowest recorded level against the dollar.* ◇ *He is clearly sinking fast* (= getting weaker quickly and will soon die).

<u>OF VOICE</u> | **6** [V] (*written*) to become quieter: *Her voice sank to a whisper.*

<u>DIG IN GROUND</u> | **7** [VN] to make a deep hole in the ground: *to sink a well/shaft/mine* **8** [VN] to place sth in the ground by digging: *to sink a post into the ground*—see also SUNKEN

<u>PREVENT SUCCESS</u> | **9** [VN] (*informal*) to prevent sb or sb's plans from succeeding: *I think I've just sunk my chances of getting the job.* ◇ *If the car breaks down, we'll be sunk* (= have serious problems).

<u>BALL</u> | **10** [VN] to hit a ball into a hole in golf or SNOOKER: *He sank a 12-foot putt to win the match.*

<u>ALCOHOL</u> | **11** [VN] (*BrE, informal*) to drink sth quickly, especially a large amount of alcohol: *We sank three pints each in 10 minutes.*

IDM **be 'sunk in sth** to be in a state of unhappiness or deep thought: *She just sat there, sunk in thought.* **(like rats) deserting/leaving a sinking 'ship** (*humorous, disapproving*) used to talk about people who leave an organization, a company, etc. that is having difficulties, without caring about the people who are left: *I might have known he'd be the first rat to desert this sinking ship!* **sink your 'differences** to agree to forget about your disagreements: *We need to sink our differences and present a united opposition to the plan.* **a/that 'sinking feeling** (*informal*) an unpleasant feeling that you get when you realize that sth bad has happened or is going to happen **,sink or 'swim** to be in a situation where you will either succeed by your own efforts or fail completely: *The new students were just left to sink or swim.* **,sink so 'low** | **sink to sth** to have such low moral standards that you do sth very bad: *Stealing from your friends? How could you sink so low?* ◇ *I can't believe that anyone would sink to such depths.*—more at HEART

PHRV **,sink 'in** | **,sink 'into sth 1** (of words, an event, etc.) to be fully understood or realized: *He paused to allow his words to sink in.* ◇ *The full scale of the disaster has yet to sink in.* **2** (of liquids) to go down into another substance through the surface: *The rain sank into the dry ground.* **'sink into sth** to go gradually into a less active, happy or pleasant state: *She sank into a deep sleep.* ◇ *He sank deeper into depression.* **,sink 'into sth** | **sink sth into sth** to go, or to make sth sharp go, deep into sth solid: *The dog sank its teeth into my leg* (= bit it). ◇ *I felt her nails sink into my wrist.* **,sink sth 'into sth** to spend a lot of money on a business or an activity, for example in order to make money from it in the future: *We sank all our savings into the venture.*

■ *noun* **1** a large open container in a kitchen that has taps/faucets to supply water and that you use for washing dishes in: *Don't just leave your dirty plates in the sink!* ◇ *I felt chained to the kitchen sink* (= I had to spend all my time doing jobs in the house).—picture at PLUG **2** (*especially AmE*) = WASHBASIN IDM see KITCHEN

sink·er /'sɪŋkə(r)/ *noun* a weight that is attached to a FISHING LINE or net to keep it under the water IDM see HOOK *n.*

sin·ner /'sɪnə(r)/ *noun* (*formal*) a person who has committed a SIN or SINS (= broken God's law)

Sino- /'saɪnəʊ; *AmE* -noʊ/ *combining form* (in nouns and adjectives) Chinese: *Sino-Japanese relations*

sinu·ous /'sɪnjuəs/ *adj.* (*literary*) turning while moving, in a graceful way; having many curves: *a sinuous movement* ◇ *the sinuous grace of a cat* ◇ *the sinuous course of the river* ▶ **sinu·ous·ly** *adv.*

si·nus /'saɪnəs/ *noun* any of the hollow spaces in the bones of the head that are connected to the inside of the nose: *blocked sinuses*

si·nus·itis /,saɪnə'saɪtɪs/ *noun* [U] the painful swelling of the sinuses

-sion ➪ -ION

sip /sɪp/ *verb, noun*

■ *verb* (**-pp-**) **~ (sth)** | **~ (at sth)** to drink sth, taking a very small amount each time: [V] *She sat there, sipping at her tea.* ◇ [VN] *He slowly sipped his wine.*

■ *noun* a very small amount of a drink that you take into your mouth: *to have/take a sip of water*

si·phon (also **sy·phon**) /'saɪfn/ *noun, verb*

■ *noun* a tube that is used for moving liquid from one container to another, using pressure from the atmosphere

■ *verb* [VN] [usually +*adv./prep.*] **1** to move a liquid from one container to another, using a siphon: *I siphoned the gasoline out of the car into a can.* ◇ *The waste liquid needs to be siphoned off.* **2** (*informal*) to remove money from one place and move it to another, especially dishonestly or illegally SYN DIVERT: *She has been accused of siphoning* *off thousands of pounds from the company into her own bank account.*

sir /sɜː(r)/ /sə(r)/ *noun* **1** used as a polite way of addressing a man whose name you do not know, for example in a shop/store or restaurant, or to show respect: *Good morning, sir. Can I help you?* ◊ *Are you ready to order, sir?* ◊ *'Report to me tomorrow, corporal!' 'Yes, sir!'* ◊ *'Thank you very much.' 'You're welcome, sir. Have a nice day.'*—compare MA'AM—see also MADAM **2** (**Dear Sir/Sirs**) used at the beginning of a formal business letter when you do not know the name of the man or people that you are dealing with: *Dear Sir/Sirs* ◊ *Dear Sir or Madam* ⇨ Study page B14 **3** (**Sir**) /sɜː(r); sə(r)/ a title that is used before the first name of a man who has received one of the highest British honours (= a KNIGHT), or before the first name of a BARONET: *Sir Paul McCartney* ◊ *Thank you, Sir Paul.*—compare LADY **4** (*BrE*) used as a form of address by children in school to a male teacher: *Please, sir, can I open a window?*—compare MISS IDM **,no 'sir! | ,no sir'ree!** /səˈriː/ (*spoken, especially AmE*) certainly not: *We will never allow that to happen! No sir!* **,yes 'sir! | ,yes sir'ree!** used to emphasize that sth is true: *That's a fine car you have. Yes sir!*

sire /ˈsaɪə(r)/ *noun, verb*
- *noun* **1** (*technical*) the male parent of an animal, especially a horse—compare DAM **2** (*old use*) a word that people used when they addressed a king
- *verb* [VN] **1** to be the male parent of an animal, especially a horse **2** (*old-fashioned* or *humorous*) to become the father of a child

siren /ˈsaɪrən/ *noun* **1** a device that makes a long loud sound as a signal or warning: *an air-raid siren* ◊ *A police car raced past with its siren wailing.* **2** (in ancient Greek stories) any of a group of sea creatures that were part woman, part bird, whose beautiful singing made sailors sail towards them into rocks or dangerous waters **3** a woman who is very attractive or beautiful but also dangerous **4 ~ voices/song/call** (*literary*) the TEMPTATION to do sth that seems very attractive but that will have bad results: *The government must resist the siren voices calling for tax cuts.*

sir·loin /ˈsɜːlɔɪn; *AmE* ˈsɜːrl-/ (also **,sirloin 'steak**) *noun* [U, C] good quality beef that is cut from a cow's back

sisal /ˈsaɪsl/ *noun* [U] strong FIBRES made from the leaves of a tropical plant also called **sisal**, used for making rope, floor coverings, etc.

sissy (*BrE* also **cissy**) /ˈsɪsi/ *noun* (*pl.* **-ies**) (*informal, disapproving*) a boy that other men or boys laugh at because they think he is weak or frightened, or only interested in the sort of things girls like ▶ **sissy** *adj.*

sis·ter /ˈsɪstə(r)/ *noun* **1** a girl or woman who has the same mother and father as another person: *She's my sister.* ◊ *an older/younger sister* ◊ (*informal*) *a big/little/kid sister* ◊ *We're sisters.* ◊ *Do you have any brothers or sisters?* ◊ *My best friend has been like a sister to me (= very close).*—see also HALF-SISTER, STEPSISTER **2** used for talking to or about other members of a women's organization or other women who have the same ideas, purpose, etc. as yourself: *They supported their sisters in the dispute.* **3** (**Sister**) (*BrE*) a senior female nurse who is in charge of a hospital WARD—see also CHARGE NURSE **4** (**Sister**) a female member of a religious group, especially a NUN: *Sister Mary* ◊ *the Sisters of Charity* **5** (in the US) a member of a SORORITY (= a club for a group of female students at a college or university) **6** (*AmE, informal*) used by black people as a form of address for a black woman **7** (usually used as an adjective) a thing that belongs to the same type or group as sth else: *our sister company in Italy* ◊ *a sister ship*

sis·ter·hood /ˈsɪstəhʊd; *AmE* -tərh-/ *noun* **1** [U] the close loyal relationship between women who share ideas and aims **2** [C+sing./pl. *v.*] a group of women who live in a community together, especially a religious one: *a sisterhood of nuns*

'sister-in-law *noun* (*pl.* **sisters-in-law**) the sister of your husband or wife; your brother's wife; the wife of your husband or wife's brother—compare BROTHER-IN-LAW

sis·ter·ly /ˈsɪstəli; *AmE* -tərli/ *adj.* typical of or like a sister: *She gave him a sisterly kiss.*

sit /sɪt/ *verb* (**sit·ting, sat, sat** /sæt/)
ON CHAIR, etc. | **1** to rest your weight on your bottom with your back upright, for example on/in a chair: [V, usually +*adv./prep.*] *She sat and stared at the letter in front of her.* ◊ *May I sit here?* ◊ *Just sit still!* ◊ *He went and sat beside her.* ◊ *She was sitting at her desk.* ◊ [V-ing] *We sat talking for hours.*—see also SIT DOWN **2** [VN+*adv./prep.*] to put sb in a sitting position: *He lifted the child and sat her on the wall.*
OF THINGS | **3** to be in a particular place: [V, +*adv./prep.*] *A large bus was sitting outside.* ◊ *The pot was sitting in a pool of water.* ◊ *The jacket sat beautifully on her shoulders* (= fitted well). ◊ [V-ADJ] *The box sat unopened on the shelf.*
HAVE OFFICIAL POSITION | **4** [V] **~ in/on/for sth|~ as sth** to have an official position as sth or as a member of sth: *He was sitting as a temporary judge.* ◊ *She sat on a number of committees.* ◊ *For years he sat for Henley* (= was the MP for that constituency). ◊ *They both sat as MPs in the House of Commons.*
OF PARLIAMENT, etc. | **5** [V] (of a parliament, committee, court of law, etc.) to meet in order to do official business: *Parliament sits for less than six months of the year.*
EXAM | **6 ~ (for) sth** (*BrE*, rather *formal*) to do an exam: [VN] *Candidates will sit the examinations in June.* ◊ *Most of the students sit at least 5 GCSEs.* ◊ [V] *He was about to sit for his entrance exam.*
OF BIRD | **7** [V] [usually +*adv./prep.*] to rest on a branch, etc. or to stay on a nest to keep the eggs warm
OF DOG | **8** [V] to sit on its bottom with its front legs straight: *Rover! Sit!*
TAKE CARE OF CHILDREN | **9** [V] **~ (for sb)** = BABYSIT: *Who's sitting for you?*—see also HOUSE-SIT

IDM **be ,sitting 'pretty** (*informal*) to be in a good situation, especially when others are not **sit at sb's 'feet** to admire sb very much, especially a teacher or sb from whom you try to learn **sit comfortably/easily/well, etc. (with sth)** (*written*) to seem right, natural, suitable, etc. in a particular place or situation: *His views did not sit comfortably with the management line.* **sit in 'judgement (on/over/upon sb)** to decide whether sb's behaviour is right or wrong, especially when you have no right to do this: *How dare you sit in judgement on me?* **sit on the 'fence** to avoid becoming involved in deciding or influencing sth: *He tends to sit on the fence at meetings.* **,sit 'tight 1** to stay where you are rather than moving away or changing position: *We sat tight and waited to be rescued.* **2** to stay in the same situation, without changing your mind or taking any action: *Shareholders are being advised to sit tight until the crisis passes.*—more at BOLT *adv.*, LAUREL, SILENTLY

PHRV **,sit a'bout/a'round** (often *disapproving*) to spend time doing nothing very useful: *I'm far too busy to sit around here.* ◊ [+-ing] *He just sits around watching videos.* **,sit 'back 1** to sit on sth, usually a chair, in a relaxed position: *He sat back in his chair and started to read.* **2** to relax, especially by not getting too involved in or anxious about sth: *She's not the kind of person who can sit back and let others do all the work.* **,sit 'by** to take no action to stop sth bad or wrong from happening: *We cannot just sit by and watch this tragedy happen.* **,sit 'down | ,sit yourself 'down** to move from a standing position to a sitting position: *Please sit down.* ◊ *He sat down on the bed.* ◊ *They sat down to consider the problem.* ◊ *Come in and sit yourselves down.* **sit down and do sth** to give sth time and attention in order to try to solve a problem or achieve sth: *This is something that we should sit down and discuss as a team.* **'sit for sb/sth** [no passive] to be a model for an artist or a photographer: *to sit for your portrait* ◊ *She sat for Augustus John.* **,sit 'in for sb** to do sb's job or perform their duties while they are away, ill, etc. SYN STAND IN FOR **,sit 'in on sth** to attend a meeting, class, etc. in order to listen to or learn from it rather than to take an active part: *I was allowed to sit in on an executive meeting.* **'sit on sth** (*informal*) to have received

S

a letter, report, etc. from sb and then not replied or taken any action concerning it: *They have been sitting on my application for a month now.* ˌsit sth↔'out 1 to stay in a place and wait for sth unpleasant or boring to finish: *We sat out the storm in a cafe.* 2 to not take part in a dance, game or other activity 'sit through sth to stay until the end of a performance, speech, meeting, etc. that you think is boring or too long: *We had to sit through nearly two hours of speeches.* ˌsit 'up 1 to be or move yourself into a sitting position, rather than lying down or leaning back: *Do you feel well enough to sit up yet?* ◇ *Sit up straight—don't slouch.* 2 to not go to bed until later than usual: *We sat up half the night, talking.* ˌsit 'up (and do sth) (*informal*) to start to pay careful attention to what is happening, being said, etc: *The proposal had made his clients sit up and take notice.* ˌsit sb 'up to move sb into a sitting position after they have been lying down

> **GRAMMAR POINT**
> **sit**
>
> You can use *on*, *in* and *at* with **sit**. You **sit on** a chair, a step, the edge of the table, etc. You **sit in** an armchair. If you are **sitting at** a table, desk, etc. you are sitting in a chair close to it, usually so that you can eat a meal, do some work, etc.

sitar /sɪ'tɑː(r); 'sɪtɑː(r)/ *noun* a musical instrument from India like a guitar, with a long neck and two sets of metal strings

sit·com /'sɪtkɒm; *AmE* -kɑːm/ (also *formal* ˌsituation 'comedy) *noun* [C, U] a regular programme on television that shows the same characters in different amusing situations

'sit-down *noun* 1 [C] a strike or protest in which people sit down to block a road or the entrance to a building until people listen to their demands 2 [sing.] (*BrE, informal*) a rest while sitting in a chair: *I need a cup of tea and a sit-down.* ▶ **'sit-down** *adj.* [only before noun]: *a sit-down protest* ◇ *a sit-down meal for 50 wedding guests* (= served to people sitting at tables)

site /saɪt/ *noun, verb*
■ *noun* 1 a place where a building, town, etc. was, is or will be situated: *the site of a sixteenth century abbey* ◇ *to work on a building/construction site* ◇ *A site has been chosen for the new school.* ◇ *All the materials are on site so that work can start immediately.* 2 a place where sth has happened or that is used for sth: *the site of the battle* ◇ *an archaeological site* ◇ *a camping/caravan site* 3 (*computing*) a place on the Internet where a company, an organization, a university, etc. puts information: *a website*
■ *verb* [VN+*adv./prep.*] [often passive] to build or place sth in a particular position: *There was a meeting to discuss the siting of the new school.* ◇ *The castle is magnificently sited high up on a cliff.*

'sit-in *noun* a protest in which a group of workers, students, etc. refuse to leave their factory, college, etc. until people listen to their demands: *to hold/stage a sit-in*

sit·ter /'sɪtə(r)/ *noun* 1 a person who sits or stands somewhere so that sb can paint a picture of them or photograph them 2 (*especially AmE*) = BABYSITTER 3 (*BrE, informal*) (in football) an easy chance to score a goal

sit·ting /'sɪtɪŋ/ *noun* 1 a period of time during which a court of law or a parliament deals with its business 2 a time when a meal is served in a hotel, etc. to a number of people at the same time: *A hundred people can be served at one sitting* (= at the same time). 3 a period of time that a person spends sitting and doing an activity: *I read the book in one sitting.* 4 a period of time when sb sits or stands to have their picture painted or be photographed

ˌsitting 'duck *noun* a person or thing that is easy to attack

'sitting room *noun* (*BrE*) = LIVING ROOM

ˌsitting 'tenant *noun* (*BrE*) a person who is living in a rented house or flat and who has the legal right to stay there

situ ⇨ IN SITU

situ·ate /'sɪtʃueɪt/ *verb* [VN+*adv./prep.*] (*formal*) 1 to build or place sth in a particular position 2 to consider how an idea, event, etc. is related to other things that influence your view of it: *Let me try and situate the events in their historical context.*

situ·ated /'sɪtʃueɪtɪd/ *adj.* [not before noun] 1 in a particular place or position: *My bedroom was situated on the top floor of the house.* ◇ *The hotel is beautifully situated in a quiet spot near the river.* ◇ *All the best theatres and restaurants are situated within a few minutes' walk of each other.* 2 (*formal*) (of a person, an organization, etc.) in a particular situation or in particular circumstances: *Small businesses are well situated to benefit from the single market.*

situ·ation /ˌsɪtʃu'eɪʃn/ *noun* 1 all the circumstances and things that are happening at a particular time and in a particular place: *to be in a difficult situation* ◇ *You could get into a situation where you have to decide immediately.* ◇ *We have all been in similar embarrassing situations.* ◇ *the present economic/financial/political situation* ◇ *He could see no way out of the situation.* ◇ *In your situation, I would look for another job.* ◇ *What we have here is a crisis situation.* ◇ *I'm in a no-win situation* (= whatever I do will be bad for me). 2 (*written*) the kind of area or surroundings that a building or town has: *The town is in a delightful situation in a wide green valley.* 3 (*old-fashioned* or *written*) a job: *Situations Vacant* (= the title of the section in a newspaper where jobs are advertised)

ˌsituation 'comedy *noun* [C, U] (*formal*) = SITCOM

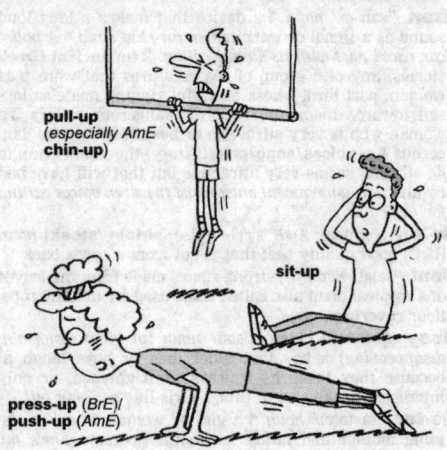

pull-up
(especially AmE
chin-up)

sit-up

press-up (*BrE*)/
push-up (*AmE*)

'sit-up *noun* an exercise for making your stomach muscles strong, in which you lie on your back on the floor and raise the top part of your body to a sitting position

six /sɪks/ *number* 6 HELP There are examples of how to use numbers at the entry for five. IDM at ˌsixes and 'sevens (*informal*) in confusion; not well organized: *I haven't had time to clear up, so I'm all at sixes and sevens.* hit/knock sb for 'six (*BrE*) to affect sb very deeply: *The business over the lawsuit had really knocked her for six.* it's six of ˌone and half a dozen of the 'other used to say that there is not much real difference between two possible choices

'six-figure *adj.* [only before noun] used to describe a number that is 100000 or more: *a six-figure salary*

six·fold /'sɪksfəʊld; *AmE* -foʊld/ *adj., adv.* ⇨ -FOLD

'six-gun *noun* = SIX-SHOOTER

'six-pack *noun* 1 a set of six bottles or cans sold together, especially of beer 2 (*informal*) stomach muscles that are very strong and that you can see clearly across sb's stomach

six·pence /'sɪkspəns/ *noun* a British coin in use until 1971, worth six old pence

s	t	v	z	ʃ	ʒ	tʃ	dʒ	θ	ð	ŋ
see	tea	van	zoo	shoe	vision	chain	jam	thin	this	sing

'six-shooter (also **'six-gun**) *noun* (*especially AmE*) a small gun that holds six bullets

six·teen /ˌsɪksˈtiːn/ *number* 16 ▶ **six·teenth** /ˌsɪksˈtiːnθ/ *ordinal number*

ˌsix'teenth note *noun* (*AmE, music*) = SEMIQUAVER

sixth /sɪksθ/ *ordinal number, noun*
■ *ordinal number* 6th **HELP** There are examples of how to use ordinal numbers at the entry for **fifth**.
■ *noun* each of six equal parts of sth

'sixth form *noun* [usually sing.] (*BrE*) the two final years at school for students between the ages of 16 and 18 who are preparing to take A-LEVELS (= advanced level exams): *Sue is in the sixth form now.*

'sixth-form college *noun* (in Britain) a school for students over the age of 16

'sixth-former *noun* (*BrE*) a student who is in the sixth form at school

ˌsixth 'sense *noun* [sing.] a special ability to know sth without using any of the five senses that include sight, touch, etc: *My sixth sense told me to stay here and wait.*

sixty /ˈsɪksti/ *number* 1 60 **(the sixties)** [pl.] numbers, years or temperatures from 60 to 69 ▶ **six·ti·eth** /ˈsɪkstiəθ/ *ordinal number* **IDM in your 'sixties** between the ages of 60 and 69

size /saɪz/ *noun, verb*
■ *noun*
　HOW LARGE/SMALL | **1** [U, C] how large or small a person or thing is: *an area the size of* (= the same size as) *Wales ◇ They complained about the size of their gas bill. ◇ Dogs come in all shapes and sizes. ◇ The facilities are excellent for a town that size. ◇ The kitchen is a good size* (= not small). *◇ It's similar in size to a tomato.* **2** [U] the large amount or extent of sth: *You should have seen the size of their house! ◇ We were shocked at the size of his debts.*
　OF CLOTHES/SHOES/GOODS | **3** [C] one of a number of standard measurements in which clothes, shoes and other goods are made and sold: *The jacket was the wrong size. It's not my size. ◇ They didn't have the jacket in my size. ◇ She's a size 12 in clothes. ◇ The hats are made in three sizes: small, medium and large. ◇ I need a bigger/smaller size. ◇ What size do you take? ◇ She takes a size 5 in shoes. ◇ Try this one for size* (= to see if it is the correct size). *◇ The glass can be cut to size* (= cut to the exact measurements) *for you.* **HELP** To ask about the size of something, you usually say *How big?* You use *What size?* to ask about something that is produced in fixed measurements.
　-SIZED/-SIZE | **4** (in adjectives) having the size mentioned: *a medium-sized house ◇ Cut it into bite-size pieces.*—see also KING-SIZE, MAN-SIZED, PINT-SIZED, QUEEN-SIZE
　STICKY SUBSTANCE | **5** [U] a sticky substance that is used for making material stiff or for preparing walls for WALL-PAPER
　IDM cut sb down to 'size to show sb that they are not as important as they think they are **that's about the 'size of it** (*spoken*) that's how the situation seems to be: *'So they won't pay up?' 'That's about the size of it.'*
■ *verb* [VN]
　GIVE SIZE | **1** [usually passive] to mark the size of sth; to give a size to sth: *The screws are sized in millimetres.*
　CHANGE SIZE | **2** [usually passive] to change the size of sth: *The fonts can be sized according to what effect you want.*
　MAKE STICKY | **3** to cover sth with a sticky substance called SIZE
　PHRV ˌsize sb/sth ↔ 'up (*informal*) to form a judgement or an opinion about sb/sth **SYN** SUM UP: *She knew that he was looking at her, sizing her up. ◇ He sized up the situation very quickly.*

size·able (also **siz·able**) /ˈsaɪzəbl/ *adj.* fairly large: *The town has a sizeable Sikh population.*

siz·zle /ˈsɪzl/ *verb* [V] to make the sound of food frying in hot oil: *sizzling sausages/fat* ▶ **siz·zle** *noun* [sing.]

siz·zling /ˈsɪzlɪŋ/ *adj.* **1** very hot: *sizzling summer temperatures* **2** very exciting: *a sizzling love affair*

ska /skɑː/ *noun* [U] a type of West Indian pop music with a strong beat

skate /skeɪt/ *verb, noun*

■ *verb* **1** to move on skates (usually referring to ICE SKAT-ING, if no other information is given): [V] *Can you skate? ◇ It was so cold that we were able to go skating on the lake. ◇* [VN] *He skated an exciting programme at the American Championships.* **2** [V] to ride on a SKATEBOARD **IDM** see THIN *adj.* **PHRV ˌskate 'over sth** to avoid talking about or considering a difficult subject: *He politely skated over the issue.*
■ *noun* **1** = ICE SKATE, ROLLER SKATE: *a pair of skates* **2** (*pl.* **skate** or **skates**) a large flat sea fish that can be eaten **IDM get/put your 'skates on** (*BrE, informal*) used to tell sb to hurry: *Get your skates on or you'll miss the bus.*

skate·board /ˈskeɪtbɔːd; *AmE* -bɔːrd/ *noun* a short narrow board with small wheels at each end, which you stand on and ride as a sport ▶ **skate·board** *verb* [V] **skate·board·ing** *noun* [U]—picture on page A8

skater /ˈskeɪtə(r)/ *noun* a person who skates for pleasure or as a sport: *a figure/speed skater ◇ ice skaters*

skat·ing /ˈskeɪtɪŋ/ *noun* [U] **1** (also **'ice skating**) the sport or activity of moving on ice on SKATES: *to go skating*—see also FIGURE-SKATING, SPEED SKATING **2** = ROLLER SKATING **IDM** see THIN *adj.*

'skating rink (also **rink**) *noun* **1** = ICE RINK **2** an area or a building where you can ROLLER SKATE

ske·dad·dle /skɪˈdædl/ *verb* [V] (*spoken, humorous*) to move away or leave a place quickly, especially in order to avoid sb

skeet shooting /ˈskiːt ʃuːtɪŋ/ *noun* (*AmE*) = CLAY PIGEON SHOOTING

skein /skeɪn/ *noun* a long piece of wool, thread, or YARN that is loosely tied together

skel·etal /ˈskelətl/ *adj.* **1** (*technical*) connected with the skeleton of a person or an animal **2** looking like a skeleton: *skeletal figures dressed in rags* **3** that exists only in a basic form, as an outline: *He has written only a skeletal plot for the book so far.*

skel·eton /ˈskelɪtn/ *noun* **1** the structure of bones that supports the body of a person or an animal; a model of this structure: *The human skeleton consists of 206 bones. ◇ a dinosaur skeleton*—picture at BODY **2** (*informal*) a very thin person or animal: *The disease has reduced her to a skeleton.* **3** [C, usually sing.] the main structure that supports a building, etc: *Only the concrete skeleton of the factory remained.* **4** [C, usually sing.] the basic outline of a plan, piece of writing, etc. to which more details can be added later: *Examples were used to flesh out the skeleton of the argument.* **5** ~ **staff, crew, etc.** the smallest number of people, etc. that you need to do sth: *There will only be a skeleton staff on duty over the holiday. ◇ We managed to operate a skeleton bus service during the strike.* **IDM a skeleton in the 'cupboard** (*BrE*) (also **a skeleton in the 'closet** *AmE, BrE*) (*informal*) something shocking, embarrassing, etc. that has happened to you or your family in the past that you want to keep secret

'skeleton key *noun* a key that will open several different locks

skep·tic, skep·tical, skep·ti·cism (*AmE*) = SCEP-TIC, SCEPTICAL, SCEPTICISM

sketch /sketʃ/ *noun, verb*
■ *noun* **1** a simple picture that is drawn quickly and does not have many details: *The artist is making sketches for his next painting. ◇ She drew a sketch map of the area to show us the way.* **2** a short funny scene on television, in the theatre, etc: *The drama group did a sketch about a couple buying a new car.* **3** a short report or story that gives only basic details about sth: *a biographical sketch of the Prime Minister*
■ *verb* **1** to make a quick drawing of sb/sth: [VN] *He quickly sketched the view from the window.* [also V] **2** [VN] ~ **sth (out)** to give a general description of sth, giving only the basic facts **SYN** OUTLINE: *She sketched out her plan for tackling the problem.* **3** [VN] (*literary*) to do sth in a quick and careless way, as if you do not really mean it: *He sketched a smile.* **PHRV ˌsketch sth ↔ 'in** to give more information or details about sth: *You need to sketch in his character a little more.*

S

æ	ɑː	e	ɜː	ə	ɪ	iː	i	ɒ	ɔː	ʌ	ʊ	u	uː
cat	father	ten	bird	about	sit	see	many	got	saw	cup	put	actual	too

(BrE)

sketch·book /'sketʃbʊk/ (also **'sketch pad**) *noun* a book of sheets of paper for drawing on

sketchy /'sketʃi/ *adj.* (**sketch·ier, sketch·iest**) not complete or detailed and therefore not very useful: *He gave us only a very sketchy account of his visit.* ◊ *sketchy notes* ▸ **sketch·ily** *adv.* **sketchi·ness** *noun* [U]

skew /skjuː/ *verb* **1** [VN] to change or influence sth with the result that it is not accurate, fair, normal, etc: *to skew the statistics* **2** [V+adv. / prep.] (*BrE*) to move or lie at an angle, especially in a position that is not normal: *The ball skewed off at a right angle.*

skewed /skjuːd/ *adj.* **1** (of information) not accurate or correct SYN DISTORTED: *skewed statistics* **2** ~ (**towards sb/sth**) directed towards a particular group, place, etc. in a way that may not be accurate or fair: *The book is heavily skewed towards American readers.* **3** not straight or level SYN CROOKED: *The car had ended up skewed across the road.*—see also ASKEW

skew·er /'skjuːə(r)/ *noun, verb*
- *noun* a long thin pointed piece of metal or wood that is pushed through pieces of meat, vegetables, etc. to hold them together while they are cooking, or used to test whether sth is completely cooked
- *verb* [VN] to push a skewer or other thin pointed object through sth

skew-'whiff *adj.* (*BrE, informal*) not straight

ski /skiː/ *noun, adj., verb*
- *noun* (*pl.* **skis**) **1** one of a pair of long narrow pieces of wood, metal or plastic that you attach to boots so that you can move smoothly over snow: *a pair of skis*—picture at SKIING **2** = WATERSKI
- *adj.* [only before noun] connected with the sport of skiing: *ski boots* ◊ *the ski slopes*
- *verb* (**ski·ing, skied, skied**) [V] **1** [usually+adv. / prep.] to move over snow on skis, especially as a sport: *How well do you ski?* ◊ *We skied down the slope one by one.* **2** (go skiing) to spend time skiing for pleasure: *We went skiing in France in March.*—see also SKIING, WATERSKI

skid /skɪd/ *verb, noun*
- *verb* (**-dd-**) [V] **1** (usually of a vehicle) to slide sideways or forwards in an uncontrolled way: *The car skidded on the ice and went straight into the wall.* ◊ *She could feel they were skidding.* ◊ *The taxi skidded to a halt just in time.* ◊ *Her foot skidded on the wet floor and she fell heavily.*
- *noun* **1** the movement of a vehicle when it suddenly slides sideways in an uncontrolled way: *The motorbike went into a skid.* ◊ *The skid marks on the road showed how fast the car had been travelling.* **2** a part that is underneath some aircraft, beside the wheels, and is used for landing: *the skids of a helicopter* IDM **put the 'skids under sb/sth** (*informal*) to stop sb/sth from being successful or making progress **be on the 'skids** (*informal*) to be in a bad situation that will get worse

skid·pan /'skɪdpæn/ *noun* an area with a surface that is especially prepared so that drivers can practise controlling skids

skid 'row *noun* [U] (*informal, especially AmE*) used to describe the poorest part of a town, the sort of place where people who have no home or job and who drink too much live: *to be on skid row*

skier /'skiːə(r)/ *noun* a person who skis

skies *pl.* of SKY

skiff /skɪf/ *noun* a small light boat for rowing or sailing, usually for one person

skif·fle /'skɪfl/ *noun* a type of music popular in the 1950s, that was a mixture of jazz and FOLK MUSIC

ski·ing /'skiːɪŋ/ *noun* [U] the sport or activity of moving over snow on skis: *to go downhill/cross-country skiing* ◊ *a skiing holiday/instructor/lesson/vacation*

'ski jump *noun* a very steep artificial slope that ends suddenly and that is covered with snow. People ski down the slope, jump off the end and see how far they can travel through the air before landing. ▸ **'ski-jumper** *noun* **'ski-jumping** *noun* [U]: *Is ski-jumping an Olympic sport?* ◊ *the Swiss ski-jumping team*

skil·ful (*BrE*) (*AmE* **skill·ful**) /'skɪlfl/ *adj.* **1** (of a person) good at doing sth, especially sth that needs a particular

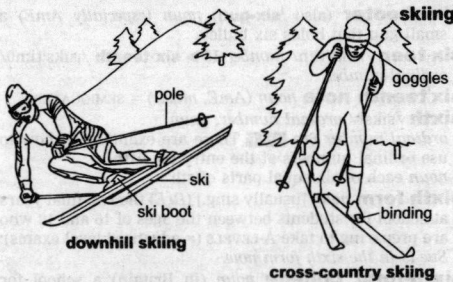

skiing / goggles / pole / ski / ski boot / binding
downhill skiing **cross-country skiing**

ability or special training: *a skilful player/performer/teacher* **2** made or done very well: *Thanks to her skilful handling of the affair, the problem was averted.* ▸ **skil·ful·ly** /-fəli/ *adv.*

'ski lift *noun* a machine for taking SKIERS up a slope so that they can then ski down

skill /skɪl/ *noun* **1** [U] ~ (**in/at sth**)| ~ (**in/at doing sth**) the ability to do sth well: *The job requires skill and an eye for detail.* ◊ *What made him remarkable as a photographer was his skill in capturing the moment.* **2** [C] a particular ability or type of ability: *We need people with practical skills like carpentry.* ◊ *management skills*

skilled /skɪld/ *adj.* **1** ~ (**in/at sth**)| ~ (**in/at doing sth**) having enough ability, experience and knowledge to be able to do sth well: *a skilled engineer/negotiator/craftsman* ◊ *She is highly skilled at dealing with difficult customers.* ◊ *a shortage of skilled labour* (= people who have had training in a skill) **2** (of a job) needing special abilities or training: *Furniture-making is very skilled work.* OPP UNSKILLED

skil·let /'skɪlɪt/ *noun* (*AmE*) = FRYING PAN

skill·ful (*AmE*) = SKILFUL

skim /skɪm/ *verb* (**-mm-**) **1** [VN] ~ (**sth off/from**) sth to remove fat, cream, etc. from the surface of a liquid: *Skim the scum off the jam and let it cool.* ◊ *Skim the jam and let it cool.* **2** [no passive] ~ (**along/over, etc.**) sth to move quickly and lightly over a surface, not touching it or only touching it occasionally; to make sth do this: [V] *We watched the birds skimming over the lake.* ◊ [VN] *The speedboat took off, skimming the waves.* ◊ (*figurative*) *This report has barely skimmed the surface of the subject.* ◊ (*BrE*) *Small boys were skimming stones across the water.*—see also SKIP **3** ~ (**through/over**) sth to read sth quickly in order to find a particular point or the main points: [V] *He skimmed through the article trying to find his name.* ◊ [VN] *I always skim the financial section of the newspaper.* PHRV **,skim sth/sb↔'off** to take for yourself the best part of sth, often in an unfair way: *Private companies should not be allowed to skim off profitable sectors of the postal service.*

,skimmed 'milk (*BrE*) (also **,skim 'milk** *AmE, BrE*) *noun* [U] milk that contains less fat than normal because the cream has been removed from it

skimp /skɪmp/ *verb* [V] ~ (**on sth**) to try to spend less time, money, etc. on sth than is really needed: *Older people should not skimp on food or heating.*

skimpy /'skɪmpi/ *adj.* (**skimp·ier, skimpi·est**) **1** (of clothes) very small and not covering much of your body: *a skimpy dress* **2** (*disapproving*) not large enough in amount or size: *a skimpy meal* ◊ *They provided only skimpy details.*

skin /skɪn/ *noun, verb*
- *noun*
ON BODY | **1** [U, C] the layer of tissue that covers the body: *to have dark/fair/olive skin* ◊ *The snake sheds its skin once a year.* ◊ *cosmetics for sensitive skins* ◊ *skin cancer*—see also FORESKIN, REDSKIN
-SKINNED | **2** (in adjectives) having the type of skin mentioned: *dark-skinned* ◊ *fair-skinned*—see also THICK-SKINNED, THIN-SKINNED
OF DEAD ANIMAL | **3** [C, U] (often in compounds) the skin of a dead animal with or without its fur, used for making

aɪ	aʊ	eɪ	əʊ	oʊ	ɔɪ	ɪə	eə	ʊə	j	w
my	now	say	go	go	boy	near	hair	pure	yes	wet
			(BrE)	(AmE)						

S

leather, etc: *The skins are removed and laid out to dry.* ◊ *a tiger skin rug*

OF FRUIT/VEGETABLES | **4** [C, U] the outer layer of some fruit and vegetables: *Remove the skins by soaking the tomatoes in hot water.*—see also BANANA SKIN—compare PEEL, RIND, ZEST—picture on page A2

OF SAUSAGE | **5** [C, U] the thin outer layer of a sausage: *Prick the skins before grilling.*

ON LIQUIDS | **6** [C, U] the thin layer that forms on the surface of some liquids, especially when they become cold: *A skin had formed on the top of the milk.*

OUTSIDE LAYER | **7** [C] a layer that covers the outside of sth: *the outer skin of the earth* ◊ *the metal skin of the aircraft* —see also OILSKIN

IDM **by the ˌskin of your ˈteeth** (*informal*) if you do sth by the skin of your teeth, you only just manage to do it **get under sb's ˈskin** (*informal*) *Don't let him get under your skin.* **have got sb under your ˈskin** (*informal*) to be extremely attracted to sb **it's no skin off ˈmy, ˈyour, ˈhis, etc. nose** (*informal*) used to say that sb is not upset or annoyed about sth because it does not affect them in a bad way **make your ˈskin crawl** to make you feel afraid or full of disgust **(nothing but/all/only) skin and ˈbone** (*informal*) extremely thin in a way that is not attractive or healthy—more at JUMP *v.*, SAVE *v.*, THICK *adj.*, THIN *adj.*

■ *verb* (-nn-) [VN]

ANIMAL/FRUIT/VEGETABLE | **1** to take the skin off an animal, a fruit or a vegetable: *You'll need four ripe tomatoes, skinned and chopped.*

PART OF BODY | **2** to accidentally rub the skin off part of your body: *He skinned his knees climbing down the tree.*

IDM see EYE *n.*

ˌskin-ˈdeep *adj.* [not usually before noun] (of a feeling or an attitude) not as important or strongly felt as it appears to be [SYN] SUPERFICIAL **IDM** see BEAUTY

ˈskin diving *noun* [U] the sport or activity of swimming underwater with simple breathing equipment but without a special protective suit: *to go skin diving* ▶ **ˈskin-diver** *noun*

skin-flint /ˈskɪnflɪnt/ *noun* (*informal, disapproving*) a person who does not like spending money [SYN] MISER

skin-ful /ˈskɪnfʊl/ *noun* [usually sing.] (*BrE, slang*) a large quantity of alcohol to drink, enough to make you very drunk

ˈskin graft *noun* a medical operation in which healthy skin is taken from one part of sb's body and placed over another part to replace skin that has been burned or damaged; a piece of skin that is moved in this way

skin-head /ˈskɪnhed/ *noun* a young person with very short hair, especially one who is violent, aggressive and RACIST

skinny /ˈskɪni/ *adj.* (**skin-nier, skin-ni-est**) **1** (*informal, usually disapproving*) very thin, especially in a way that you find unpleasant or ugly: *skinny arms/legs* **2** (of clothes) designed to fit closely to the body: *a skinny sweater*

ˈskinny-dipping *noun* [U] (*informal*) swimming naked

skint /skɪnt/ *adj.* [not usually before noun] (*BrE, informal*) having no money: *I can't go out tonight—I'm skint.*

skin-tight /skɪnˈtaɪt/ *adj.* (of clothes) fitting very closely to the body: *a skintight dress*

skip /skɪp/ *verb, noun*

■ *verb* (-pp-)

MOVE WITH JUMPS | **1** [V] [usually+*adv./prep.*] to move forwards lightly and quickly making a little jump with each step: *She skipped happily along beside me.*

JUMP OVER ROPE | **2** [V] (*BrE*) (*AmE* **jump ˈrope, ˌskip ˈrope**) to jump over a rope which is held at both ends by yourself or by two other people and is passed again and again over your head and under your feet: *He skips for about 20 minutes a day.* ◊ *The girls were skipping in the playground.*—picture on page A8

NOT DO STH | **3** [VN] to not do sth that you usually do or should do: *I often skip breakfast altogether.* ◊ *She decided to skip the afternoon's class.* **4** to leave out sth that would

normally be the next thing that you would do, read, etc: [VN] *You can skip the next chapter if you have covered the topic in class.* ◊ [V] *I skipped over the last part of the book.* ◊ *I suggest we skip to the last item on the agenda.*

CHANGE QUICKLY | **5** [V+*adv./prep.*] to move from one place to another or from one subject to another very quickly: *She kept skipping from one topic of conversation to another.*

LEAVE SECRETLY | **6** [VN] to leave a place secretly or suddenly: [VN] *The bombers skipped the country shortly after the blast.*

STONES | **7** [VN] (*BrE* also **skim**) to make a flat stone jump across the surface of water: *The boys were skipping stones across the pond.*

IDM **ˈskip it** (*spoken, informal*) used to tell sb rudely that you do not want to talk about sth or repeat what you have said: *'What were you saying?' 'Oh, skip it!'*

PHRV **ˌskip ˈoff/ˈout** to leave secretly or suddenly **ˌskip ˈout on sb** (*AmE*) to leave sb, especially when they need you: *One day he just skipped out on his wife, leaving her with four kids to take care of.*

■ *noun*

MOVEMENT | **1** a skipping movement: *She gave a skip and a jump and was off down the street.*

CONTAINER FOR WASTE | **2** (*BrE*) (*AmE* **Dumpster**™) a large open container for putting old bricks, rubbish/garbage, etc. in. The skip is then loaded on a lorry/truck and taken away.

skip-per /ˈskɪpə(r)/ *noun, verb*

■ *noun* **1** the captain of a small ship or fishing boat **2** (*informal, especially BrE*) the captain of a sports team

■ *verb* [VN] to be the captain of a boat, sports team, etc: *to skipper a yacht* ◊ (*especially BrE*) *He skippered the team to victory.*

ˈskipping rope (*BrE*) (*AmE* **ˈjump rope**) *noun* a piece of rope, usually with a handle at each end, that you hold, turn over your head and then jump over, for fun or to keep fit—picture on page A8

skir-mish /ˈskɜːmɪʃ; *AmE* ˈskɜːrmɪʃ/ *noun, verb*

■ *noun* **1** a short fight between small groups of soldiers, etc., especially one that is not planned: *Several people were killed in skirmishes during the night.* **2** a short argument, especially between political opponents

■ *verb* [V] to take part in a short fight or argument ▶ **skir-mish-er** *noun* **skir-mish-ing** *noun* [U]: *There are reports of skirmishing along the border.*

skirt /skɜːt; *AmE* skɜːrt/ *noun, verb*

■ *noun* **1** [C] a piece of clothing for a woman or girl that hangs from the waist: *a long/short/straight/pleated skirt* **2** [C] (also **skirts**) [pl.] the part of a dress, coat, etc. that hangs below the waist **3** [C] an outer covering or protective part for the base of a vehicle or machine: *the rubber skirt around the bottom of a hovercraft*—picture at BOAT

■ *verb* **1** to be or go around the edge of sth: [VN] *They followed the road that skirted the lake.* ◊ [V] *I skirted around the field and crossed the bridge.* **2** **~ (around/round sth)** to avoid talking about a subject, especially because it is difficult or embarrassing: [VN] *He carefully skirted the issue of where they would live.* ◊ [V] *She tactfully skirted around the subject of money.*

ˈskirting board (also **skirt-ing**) (both *BrE*) (*AmE* **base-board**) *noun* [C, U] a narrow piece of wood that is fixed along the bottom of the walls in a house—picture at ALCOVE

ˈski run (also **run**) *noun* a track that is marked on a slope that you ski down

skit /skɪt/ *noun* **~ (on sth)** a short piece of humorous writing or a performance that makes fun of sb/sth by copying them: *a skit on daytime TV programmes*

skit-ter /ˈskɪtə(r)/ *verb* [V+*adv./prep.*] to run or move very quickly and lightly

skit-tish /ˈskɪtɪʃ/ *adj.* **1** (of horses) easily excited or frightened and therefore difficult to control **2** (of people) not very serious and with ideas and feelings that keep changing **3** (*especially AmE, business*) likely to change suddenly: *skittish financial markets* ▶ **skit-tish-ly** *adv.* **skit-tish-ness** *noun* [U]

S

b	d	f	g	h	k	l	m	n	p	r
bad	**did**	**fall**	**get**	**hat**	**cat**	**leg**	**man**	**now**	**pen**	**red**

skit·tle /ˈskɪtl/ *noun* **1** [C] a wooden or plastic object used in the game of skittles **2 (skittles)** [U] a game in which players try to knock over as many skittles as possible by rolling a ball at them

skive /skaɪv/ *verb* ~ **(off)** (*BrE, informal*) to avoid work or school by staying away or leaving early SYN BUNK OFF: [V] *'Where's Tom?' 'Skiving as usual.'* ◇ *She always skives off early on Fridays.* ◇ [VN] *I skived the last lecture.*

skivvy /ˈskɪvi/ *noun, verb*
■ *noun* (*pl.* **-ies**) (*BrE, informal*) a servant, usually female, who does all the dirty or boring jobs in a house: *He treats his wife like a skivvy.*
■ *verb* (**skiv·vies, skivvy·ing, skiv·vied, skiv·vied**) [V] (*BrE, informal*) to do dirty or boring jobs: *Her aunt kept her skivvying day and night.*

skua /ˈskjuːə/ *noun* a large brownish seabird that eats fish, which it sometimes steals from other birds

skul·dug·gery (also **skull·dug·gery**) /skʌlˈdʌgəri/ *noun* [U] (*old-fashioned* or *humorous*) dishonest behaviour or activities

skulk /skʌlk/ *verb* [V+adv./prep.] (*disapproving*) to hide or move around secretly, especially when you are planning sth bad: *There was someone skulking behind the bushes.*

skull /skʌl/ *noun* **1** the bone structure that forms the head and surrounds and protects the brain SYN CRANIUM: *a fractured skull*—picture at BODY **2** (*informal*) the head or the brain: *Her skull was crammed with too many thoughts.* ◇ (*informal*) *When will he get it into his thick skull that I never want to see him again!*

skull and ˈcrossbones *noun* [sing.] a picture of a human skull above two crossed bones, used in the past on the flags of PIRATE ships, and now used as a warning on containers with dangerous substances inside

skull·cap /ˈskʌlkæp/ *noun* a small round cap worn on top of the head, especially by Jewish men and Catholic BISHOPS—see also YARMULKE

skunk /skʌŋk/ (*AmE* also **pole·cat**) *noun* a small black and white N American animal that can produce a strong unpleasant smell to defend itself when it is attacked IDM see DRUNK *adj.*

sky /skaɪ/ *noun* [C, U] (*pl.* **skies**) the space above the earth that you can see when you look up, where clouds and the sun, moon and stars appear HELP You usually say **the sky**. When **sky** is used with an adjective or adjectival phrase, use **a...sky**. You can also use the plural form **skies**, especially when you are thinking about the great extent of the sky: *What's that in the sky?* ◇ *The sky suddenly went dark and it started to rain.* ◇ *the night sky* ◇ *a cloudless sky* ◇ *cloudless skies* ◇ *a land of blue skies and sunshine* ◇ *The skies above London were ablaze with a spectacular firework display.* IDM **the sky's the ˈlimit** (*informal, spoken*) there is no limit to what sb can achieve, earn, do, etc: *With a talent like his, the sky's the limit.*—more at GREAT *adj.*, PIE, PRAISE *v.*

sky-ˈblue *adj.* bright blue in colour, like the sky on a clear day ▶ **sky ˈblue** *noun* [U]

sky·cap /ˈskaɪkæp/ *noun* (*AmE*) a person whose job is to carry people's bags at an airport

sky·div·ing /ˈskaɪdaɪvɪŋ/ *noun* [U] a sport in which you jump from a plane and fall for as long as you safely can before opening your PARACHUTE: *to go skydiving* ▶ **sky·diver** *noun*

sky-ˈhigh *adj.* very high; too high: *His confidence is still sky-high.* ◇ *sky-high interest rates* ▶ **sky-ˈhigh** *adv.*: *After the election, prices went sky-high.*

sky·lark /ˈskaɪlɑːk; *AmE* -lɑːrk/ *noun* a small bird that sings while it flies high up in the sky

sky·light /ˈskaɪlaɪt/ *noun* a small window in a roof—picture at HOUSE

sky·line /ˈskaɪlaɪn/ *noun* the outline of buildings, trees, hills, etc. seen against the sky: *the New York skyline*

sky·rocket /ˈskaɪrɒkɪt; *AmE* -rɑːk-/ *verb* [V] (of prices, etc.) to rise quickly to a very high level

sky·scraper /ˈskaɪskreɪpə(r)/ *noun* a very tall building in a city

sky·wards /ˈskaɪwədz; *AmE* -wərdz/ (also **sky·ward**) *adv.* towards the sky; up into the sky: *She pointed skywards.* ◇ *The rocket soared skywards.*

slab /slæb/ *noun* **1** a thick flat piece of stone, wood or other hard material: *a slab of marble/concrete* ◇ *The road was paved with smooth stone slabs.* ◇ *paving slabs* ◇ *a dead body on the slab* (= on a table in a MORTUARY) **2** a thick, flat slice or piece of sth: *a slab of chocolate* ◇ *slabs of meat*

slack /slæk/ *adj., noun, verb*
■ *adj.* (**slack·er, slack·est**) **1** not stretched tight: *She was staring into space, her mouth slack.* ◇ *The rope suddenly went slack.* ◇ *slack muscles* **2** (of business) not having many customers or sales; not busy: *a slack period* ◇ *slack demand for beef* **3** (*disapproving*) (of a person) not putting enough care, attention or energy into sth and so not doing it well enough: *He's been very slack in his work lately.* ◇ *Discipline in the classroom is very slack.* ▶ **slack·ly** *adv.*: *Her arms hung slackly by her sides.* **slack·ness** *noun* [U]
■ *noun* **1** [U]—see also SLACKS **1** the part of a rope, etc. that is hanging loosely: *There's too much slack in the tow rope.* **2** people, money or space that is not being used fully in an organization: *There's very little slack in the budget.* **3** very small pieces of coal IDM **take up the ˈslack 1** to improve the way money or people are used in an organization **2** to pull on a rope, etc. until it is tight
■ *verb* [V] to work less hard than you usually do or should do PHRV **ˌslack ˈoff (on sth)** to do sth more slowly or with less energy than before: *He's gone from success to success in his movie career, and there's no sign of him slacking off.*

slack·en /ˈslækən/ *verb* **1** ~ **sth** to gradually become, or to make sth become, slower, less active, etc: [V] *We've been really busy, but things are starting to slacken off now.* ◇ [VN] *She slackened her pace a little* (= walked a little more slowly). **2** to become or to make sth become less tight: [V] *His grip slackened and she pulled away from him.* ◇ [VN] *He slackened the ropes slightly.*

slack·er /ˈslækə(r)/ *noun* (*informal, disapproving*) a person who is lazy and avoids work

slacks /slæks/ *noun* [pl.] (*old-fashioned* or *AmE, formal*) trousers/pants for men or women, that are not part of a suit: *a pair of slacks*

slag /slæg/ *noun, verb*
■ *noun* **1** [U] the waste material that remains after metal has been removed from rock **2** [C] (*BrE, slang*) an offensive word for a woman, used to suggest that she has a lot of sexual partners
■ *verb* (**-gg-**) PHRV **ˌslag sb↔ˈoff** (*BrE, slang*) to say cruel or critical things about sb: *I hate the way he's always slagging off his colleagues.*

ˈslag heap *noun* (*BrE*) a large pile of slag from a mine

slain *pp* of SLAY

slake /sleɪk/ *verb* [VN] (*literary*) **1** ~ **your thirst** to drink so that you no longer feel thirsty SYN QUENCH **2** to satisfy a desire

sla·lom /ˈslɑːləm/ *noun* a race for people on skis or in CANOES along a winding course marked by poles

slam /slæm/ *verb, noun*
■ *verb* (**-mm-**) **1** to shut, or to make sth shut, with a lot of force, making a loud noise: [V] *I heard the door slam behind him.* ◇ *A window slammed shut in the wind.* ◇ [VN] *He stormed out of the house, slamming the door as he left.* ◇ [VN-ADJ] *She slammed the lid shut.* **2** [VN+adv./prep.] to put, push or throw sth into a particular place or position with a lot of force: *She slammed down the phone angrily.* ◇ *He slammed on the brakes* (= stopped the car very suddenly). **3** (used especially in newspapers) to criticize sb/sth very strongly: *The government has been slammed for failing to take firm action against drinking and driving.* IDM see DOOR PHRV **slam into/against sb/sth | slam sth into/against sb/sth** to crash into sth with a lot of force; to make sth crash into sth with a lot of force: *The car skidded and slammed into a tree.* ◇ *The force of the explosion slammed me against the wall.*

■ *noun* [usually sing.] an act of slamming sth; the noise of sth being slammed: *She gave the door a good hard slam.*—see also GRAND SLAM

'slam-dunk *verb* [VN] (in basketball) to jump up and put the ball through the net with a lot of force ▶ **'slam dunk** *noun*

slam·mer /'slæmə(r)/ *noun* (**the slammer**) [sing.] (*slang*) prison

slan·der /'slɑːndə(r); *AmE* 'slæn-/ *noun, verb*
■ *noun* [C, U] a false spoken statement intended to damage the good opinion people have of sb; the legal offence of making this kind of statement: *a vicious slander on the company's good name* ◊ *He's suing them for slander.*—compare LIBEL ▶ **slan·der·ous** /-dərəs/ *adj.*: *a slanderous attack/remark/statement*
■ *verb* [VN] to make a false spoken statement about sb that is intended to damage the good opinion that people have of them: *He angrily accused the investigators of slandering both him and his family.*—compare LIBEL

slang /slæŋ/ *noun* [U] very informal words and expressions that are more common in spoken language, especially used by a particular group of people, for example, children, criminals, soldiers, etc: *army/teenage slang* ◊ *a slang word/expression/term*—see also RHYMING SLANG

'slanging match *noun* (*BrE, informal*) an angry argument in which people insult each other

slant /slɑːnt; *AmE* slænt/ *verb, noun*
■ *verb* **1** [+adv. / prep.] to slope or to make sth slope in a particular direction or at a particular angle: [V] (*literary*) *The sun slanted through the window.* ◊ [VN] *Slant your skis a little more to the left.* **2** [VN] (sometimes *disapproving*) to present information from a particular point of view, especially in an unfair way: *The findings of the report had been slanted in favour of the manufacturers.*
■ *noun* **1** a sloping position: *The sofa faced the fire at a slant.* ◊ *Cut the flower stems on the slant.* **2** ~ (**on sth/sb**) a way of thinking about sth, especially one that shows support for a particular point of view: *She put a new slant on the play.*

slant·ed /'slɑːntɪd; *AmE* 'slæntɪd/ *adj.* **1** sloping in one direction: *She had slanted brown eyes.* **2** ~ (**towards sb/sth**) tending to be in favour of one person or thing in a way that may be unfair to others: *a biased and slanted view of events*

slant·ing /'slɑːntɪŋ; *AmE* 'slæntɪŋ/ *adj.* not straight or level; sloping: *slanting eyes/handwriting/rain*

slap /slæp/ *verb, noun, adv.*
■ *verb* (**-pp-**) [VN] **1** to hit sb/sth with the flat part of your hand: *She slapped his face hard.* ◊ *She slapped him hard across the face.* ◊ *'Congratulations!' he said, slapping me on the back.* **2** [VN+adv. / prep.] to put sth on a surface in a quick, careless and often noisy way, especially because you are angry: *He slapped the newspaper down on the desk.* ◊ *She slapped a $10 bill into my hand.* **3** [V+adv. / prep.] to hit against sth with the noise of sb being slapped: *The water slapped against the side of the boat.* PHRV **,slap sb a'bout/a'round** (*informal*) to hit sb regularly or often: *Her ex-husband used to slap her around.* **,slap sb/sth↔'down** (*informal*) to criticize sb in an unfair way, often in public, so that they feel embarrassed or less confident **'slap sth on sb/sth** (*informal*) to order, especially in a sudden or an unfair way, that sth must happen or sb must do sth: *The company slapped a no-smoking ban on the premises.* **,slap sth 'on sth** (*informal*) to increase the price of sth suddenly: *They've slapped 50p on the price of a pack of cigarettes.* **,slap sth↔'on**, **,slap sth↔'on** to spread sth on a surface in a quick, careless way: *Just slap some paint on the walls and it'll look fine.* ◊ *I'd better slap some make-up on before I go out.*
■ *noun* **1** the action of hitting sb/sth with the flat part of your hand: *She gave him a slap across the face.* ◊ *He gave me a hearty slap on the back.* **2** the noise made by hitting sb/sth with the flat part of your hand; a similar noise made by sth else: *the gentle slap of water against the shore* IDM **slap and 'tickle** (*old-fashioned, BrE, informal*) enthusiastic kissing and CUDDLING between lovers **a slap in the 'face** an action that seems to be intended as a

deliberate insult to sb **a slap on the 'wrist** (*informal*) a warning or mild punishment
■ *adv.* (also **,slap 'bang**) (*informal*) **1** straight, and with great force: *Storming out of her room, she went slap into Luke.* **2** exactly: *Their apartment is slap bang in the middle of town.*

slap·dash /'slæpdæʃ/ *adj.* done, or doing sth, too quickly and carelessly: *She has a very slapdash approach to keeping accounts.* ◊ *a slapdash piece of writing*

,slap-'happy *adj.* (*informal*) **1** cheerful, but careless about things that should be taken seriously: *a slap-happy approach to life* **2** (*especially AmE*) = PUNCH-DRUNK

slap·per /'slæpə(r)/ *noun* (*BrE, slang*) an offensive word for a woman, used to suggest that she has a lot of sexual partners

slap·stick /'slæpstɪk/ *noun* [U] the type of humour that is based on simple actions, for example people hitting each other, falling down, etc.

'slap-up *adj.* [only before noun] (*BrE, informal*) (of a meal) large and very good

slash /slæʃ/ *verb, noun*
■ *verb* [VN] **1** to make a long cut with a sharp object, especially in a violent way: *Someone had slashed the tyres on my car.* ◊ *She tried to kill herself by slashing her wrists.* ◊ *We had to slash our way through the undergrowth with sticks.* **2** [often passive] (often used in newspapers) to reduce sth by a large amount: *to slash costs/prices/fares* ◊ *The workforce has been slashed by half.* PHRV **'slash at sb/sth (with sth)** to attack sb violently with a knife, etc.
■ *noun* **1** [C] a sharp movement made with a knife, etc. in order to cut sb/sth **2** [C] a long narrow wound or cut: *a slash across his right cheek* ◊ (*figurative*) *Her mouth was a slash of red lipstick.* **3** [C] (*BrE also* **ob·lique**) the symbol (/) used to show ALTERNATIVES, as in *lunch and/or dinner* and *4/5 people* and to write FRACTIONS, as in *3/4*—see also BACKSLASH ⇨ Appendix 4 **4 a slash** [sing.] (*BrE, slang*) an act of URINATING: *He's just nipped out to have a slash.*

slat /slæt/ *noun* one of a series of thin flat pieces of wood, metal or plastic, used in furniture, fences, etc.—picture at BLIND

slate /sleɪt/ *noun, verb*
■ *noun* **1** [U] a type of dark grey stone that splits easily into thin flat layers: *a slate quarry* ◊ *The walls were mostly slate.* ◊ *The sea was the colour of slate.* **2** [C] a small thin piece of slate, used for covering roofs: *A loose slate had fallen from the roof.*—picture at HOUSE **3** [C] (*AmE*) a list of the candidates in an election: *a slate of candidates* ◊ *the Democratic slate* **4** [C] a small sheet of slate in a wooden frame, used in the past in schools for children to write on IDM see CLEAN *adj.*, WIPE *v.*
■ *verb* **1** [VN] ~ **sb/sth (for sth)** (*BrE, written*) to criticize sb/sth, especially in a newspaper: *to slate a book/play/writer* ◊ *The critics slated his latest production.* **2** ~ **sth (for sth)** [usually passive] to plan that sth will happen at a particular time in the future: [VN] *The next conference is slated for July.* ◊ *The houses were first slated for demolition five years ago.* ◊ [VN to inf] *The new store is slated to open in spring.* **3** [usually passive] ~ **sb (for sth)** (*informal, especially AmE*) to suggest or choose sb for a job, position, etc: [VN] *I was told that I was being slated for promotion.* ◊ [VN to inf] *He is slated to play the lead in Spielberg's next movie.*

slated /'sleɪtɪd/ *adj.* covered with pieces of SLATE: *a slated roof*

,slate-'grey *adj.* bluish-grey in colour, like slate

slather /'slæðə(r)/ *verb* PHRV **'slather sth on sth**, **'slather with/in sth**, **,slather sth↔'on** to cover sth with a thick layer of a substance: *hot dogs slathered with mustard*

slat·ted /'slætɪd/ *adj.* [usually before noun] made of slats: *slatted blinds/chairs/shelves*

slat·tern /'slætən; *AmE* -tərn/ *noun* (*old-fashioned*) a dirty untidy woman ▶ **slat·tern·ly** *adj.*: *a slatternly girl*

slaugh·ter /'slɔːtə(r)/ *noun, verb*
■ *noun* [U] **1** the killing of animals for their meat: *cows taken for slaughter* **2** the cruel killing of large numbers of

æ	ɑː	e	ɜː	ə	ɪ	iː	i	ɒ	ɔː	ʌ	ʊ	u	uː
cat	father	ten	bird	about	sit	see	many	got	saw	cup	put	actual	too
								(BrE)					

people at one time, especially in a war SYN MASSACRE: *the wholesale slaughter of innocent people* IDM see LAMB *n.*

■ *verb* [VN] **1** to kill an animal, usually for its meat: *The lambs are taken to the local abattoir to be slaughtered.* **2** to kill a large number of people or animals violently: *Men, women and children were slaughtered and villages destroyed.* **3** (*informal*) to defeat sb/sth by a large number of points in a sports game, competition, etc: *We were slaughtered 10–1 by the home team.*

slaugh·ter·house /ˈslɔːtəhaʊs; *AmE* -tərh-/ *noun* (*BrE* also **ab·at·toir**) a building where animals are killed for food

Slav /slɑːv/ *noun* a member of any of the races of people of central and eastern Europe who speak Slavic languages

slave /sleɪv/ *noun, verb*
■ *noun* **1** a person who is legally owned by another person and is forced to work for them: *She treated her daughter like a slave.* **2** ~ **of/to sth** a person who is so strongly influenced by sth that they cannot live without it, or cannot make their own decisions: *We are slaves of the motor car.* ◊ *Sue's a slave to fashion.*
■ *verb* [V] [usually +*adv./prep.*] ~ **(away) (at sth)** to work very hard: *I've been slaving away all day trying to get this work finished.* ◊ *I haven't got time to spend hours slaving over a hot stove* (= doing a lot of cooking).

ˈslave-driver *noun* (*disapproving*) a person who makes people work extremely hard

ˌslave ˈlabour (*BrE*) (*AmE* **ˌslave ˈlabor**) *noun* [U] **1** work that is done by slaves; the slaves who do the work: *Huge palaces were built by slave labour.* **2** (*informal*) work that is very hard and very badly paid: *I left because the job was just slave labour.*

slaver¹ /ˈslævə(r)/ *verb* [V] (usually of an animal) to let SALIVA (= the liquid produced in the mouth) run out of the mouth, especially because of hunger or excitement: *slavering dogs*

slaver² /ˈsleɪvə(r)/ *noun* **1** (in the past) a person who bought and sold slaves **2** a ship that was used in the past for carrying slaves

slav·ery /ˈsleɪvəri/ *noun* [U] **1** the state of being a slave: *to be sold/born into slavery* **2** the practice of having slaves: *the abolition of slavery*

ˈslave trade *noun* [sing.] the buying and selling of people as slaves, especially in the 17th–19th centuries

Slav·ic /ˈslɑːvɪk/ (also **Slav·on·ic**) *adj.* of or connected with Slavs or their languages, which include Russian, Polish and Czech

slav·ish /ˈsleɪvɪʃ/ *adj.* (*disapproving*) following or copying sb/sth exactly without having any original thought at all ▶ **slav·ish·ly** *adv.*

Sla·von·ic /sləˈvɒnɪk; *AmE* -ˈvɑːn-/ *adj.* = SLAVIC

slay /sleɪ/ *verb* (**slew** /sluː/ **slain** /sleɪn/) [VN] **1** (*old-fashioned* or *literary*) to kill sb/sth in a war or a fight: *St George slew the dragon.* **2** (*especially AmE*) (used especially in newspapers) to murder sb: *Two passengers were slain by the hijackers.* **3** (*old-fashioned informal, especially AmE*) to have a strong effect on sb: *Those old movies still slay me!* ▶ **slay·ing** *noun* (*especially AmE*): *the drug-related slayings of five people*

sleaze /sliːz/ *noun* **1** [U] (*BrE*) dishonest, immoral or illegal behaviour, especially by politicians: *allegations of sleaze* ◊ *The candidate was seriously damaged by the sleaze factor.* **2** [U] behaviour or conditions that are immoral, unpleasant and not socially acceptable: *the sleaze of a town that was once a naval base* **3** [C] (also **sleaze·bag** /ˈsliːzbæɡ/ **sleaze·ball** /ˈsliːzbɔːl/, especially in *AmE*) a dishonest or immoral person

sleazy /ˈsliːzi/ *adj.* (**sleaz·ier, sleazi·est**) (*informal*) **1** (of a place) dirty, unpleasant and not socially acceptable: *a sleazy bar* ◊ *a sleazy neighbourhood* **2** (of people) immoral and unpleasant: *a sleazy reporter/lawyer* ▶ **sleazi·ness** *noun* [U]

sled /sled/ *noun, verb* (**-dd-**) (*especially AmE*) = SLEDGE

sledge /sledʒ/ (*BrE*) (also **sled** *AmE, BrE*) *noun, verb*
■ *noun* a vehicle for travelling over snow and ice, with long narrow strips of wood or metal instead of wheels. Larger sledges are pulled by horses or dogs and smaller ones are

used for going down hills as a sport or for pleasure.—compare SLEIGH, TOBOGGAN
■ *verb* [V] to ride on a sledge/ sled: *We were hoping we could go sledging.*

sledge·ham·mer /ˈsledʒhæmə(r)/ *noun* a large heavy hammer with a long handle IDM **use a ˌsledgehammer to crack a ˈnut** to use more force than is necessary

sleek /sliːk/ *adj.* (**sleek·er, sleek·est**) **1** (*approving*) smooth and shiny: *sleek black hair/fur* ◊ *the sleek dark head of a seal* **2** (*approving*) having an elegant smooth shape: *a sleek yacht* ◊ *the sleek lines of the new car* **3** (often *disapproving*) (of a person) looking rich, and dressed in elegant and expensive clothes: *a sleek and ambitious politician* ◊ *sleek businessmen/lawyers* ▶ **sleek·ly** *adv.* **sleek·ness** *noun* [U]

sleep /sliːp/ *verb, noun*
■ *verb* (**slept, slept** /slept/) **1** [V] [often +*adv./prep.*] to rest with your eyes closed and your mind and body not active: *to sleep well/deeply/soundly/badly* ◊ *I couldn't sleep because of the noise.* ◊ *I had to sleep on the sofa.* ◊ *He slept solidly for ten hours.* ◊ *I slept at my sister's house last night* (= stayed the night there). ◊ *We both slept right through* (= were not woken up by) *the storm.* ◊ *She only sleeps for four hours a night.* ◊ *We sometimes sleep late at the weekends* (= until late in the morning). ◊ *I put the sleeping baby down gently.* ◊ *What are our sleeping arrangements here* (= where shall we sleep)? HELP It is more common to say that somebody **is asleep** than to say that somebody **is sleeping.** Sleep can only be used in the passive with a preposition such as **in** or **on**: *It was clear her bed hadn't been slept in.* **2** [VN] [no passive] to have enough beds for a particular number of people: *The apartment sleeps six.* ◊ *The hotel sleeps 120 guests.* IDM **let sleeping dogs ˈlie** (*saying*) to avoid mentioning a subject or sth that happened in the past, in order to avoid any problems or arguments **sleep like a ˈlog/ˈbaby** (*informal*) to sleep very well **sleep ˈtight** (*informal, spoken*) used especially to children before they go to bed to say that you hope they sleep well: *Good night, sleep tight!*—more at ROUGH *adv.*, WINK *n.* PHRV **ˌsleep aˈround** (*informal, disapproving*) to have sex with a lot of different people **ˌsleep ˈin** to sleep until after the time you usually get up in the morning **ˌsleep sth↔ˈoff** to get better after sth, especially drinking too much alcohol, by sleeping: *Let's leave him to sleep it off.* **ˈsleep on sth** (*informal*) to delay making a decision about sth until the next day, so that you have time to think about it: *Could I sleep on it and let you know tomorrow?* **ˌsleep ˈover** to stay the night at sb else's home: *It's very late now—why don't you sleep over?* ◊ *Can I sleep over at my friend's house?*—related noun SLEEPOVER **ˈsleep together|ˈsleep with sb** (*informal*) to have sex with sb, especially sb you are not married to: *I know he's going out with her, but I don't think they're sleeping together.* ◊ *Everyone knows she sleeps with the boss.*
■ *noun* **1** [U] the natural state of rest in which your eyes are closed, your body is not active, and your mind is not conscious: *I need to get some sleep.* ◊ *I didn't get much sleep last night.* ◊ *Can you give me something to help me get to sleep* (= start sleeping)? ◊ *Go to sleep—it's late.* ◊ *He cried out in his sleep.* ◊ *Anxiety can be caused by lack of sleep.* ◊ *His talk nearly sent me to sleep* (= it was boring). ◊ *Try to go back to sleep.* **2** [sing.] a period of sleep: *Did you have a good sleep?* ◊ *Ros fell into a deep sleep.* ◊ *I'll feel better after a good night's sleep* (= a night when I sleep well). **3** [U] (*informal*) the substance that sometimes forms in the corners of your eyes after you have been sleeping IDM **be able to do sth in your ˈsleep** (*informal*) to be able to do sth very easily because you have done it many times before **ˌgo to ˈsleep** (*informal*) if part of your body **goes to sleep**, you lose the sense of feeling in it, usually because it has been in the same position for too long **not lose ˈsleep/lose no ˈsleep over sth** to not worry much about sth: *It's not worth losing sleep over.* **put sb to ˈsleep** (*informal*) to make sb unconscious before an operation by using drugs, (called an ANAESTHETIC) **put sth to ˈsleep** to kill a sick or injured animal by giving it drugs so that it dies without

aɪ	aʊ	eɪ	əʊ	oʊ	ɔɪ	ɪə	eə	ʊə	j	w
my	now	say	go (BrE)	go (AmE)	boy	near	hair	pure	yes	wet

pain. People say 'put to sleep' to avoid saying 'kill'.— more at WINK n.

sleep·er /'sli:pə(r)/ noun **1** (used with an adjective) a person who sleeps in a particular way: *a heavy/light/ sound sleeper* **2** a person who is asleep: *Only the snores of the sleepers broke the silence of the house.* **3** a night train with beds for passengers on it: *the London–Edinburgh sleeper* **4** = SLEEPING CAR **5** (BrE) (AmE **tie**) one of the heavy beams of wood or CONCRETE on which the rails on a railway/railroad track are laid **6** (*informal, especially AmE*) a film/movie, play or book that for a long time is not very successful and then is suddenly a success

'sleeping bag noun a thick warm bag that you use for sleeping in, for example when you are camping—picture at BED

'sleeping car (also **sleep·er**) noun a railway/railroad carriage with beds for people to sleep in

,sleeping 'partner (BrE) (AmE **,silent 'partner**) noun a person who has put money into a business company but who is not actually involved in running it

'sleeping pill (BrE also **'sleeping tablet**) noun a PILL containing a drug that helps you to sleep

,sleeping po'liceman noun (BrE, informal) = SPEED HUMP

'sleeping sickness noun [U] a tropical disease carried by the TSETSE FLY that causes a feeling of wanting to go to sleep and usually causes death

sleep·less /'sli:pləs/ adj. **1** [only before noun] without sleep: *I've had a few sleepless nights recently.* **2** [not before noun] not able to sleep: *She lay sleepless until dawn.* ► **sleep·less·ly** adv. **sleep·less·ness** noun [U]: *to suffer from sleeplessness*—see also INSOMNIA

sleep·over /'sli:pəʊvə(r); AmE -oʊ-/ (AmE also **'slumber party**) noun a party for children or young people when a group of them spend the night at one house

sleep·walk /'sli:pwɔːk/ verb [V] to walk around while you are asleep ► **sleep·walk·er** (also formal **som·nam·bu·list**) noun

sleepy /'sli:pi/ adj. (**sleep·ier, sleepi·est**) **1** needing sleep; ready to go to sleep: *a sleepy child* ◊ *He had begun to feel sleepy.* ◊ *The heat and the wine made her sleepy.* **2** (of places) quiet and where nothing much happens: *a sleepy little town* ► **sleep·ily** /-ɪli/ adv.: *She yawned sleepily.*

sleet /sli:t/ noun, verb
■ noun [U] a mixture of rain and snow
■ verb [V] when it sleets, a mixture of rain and snow falls from the sky: *It's sleeting!*

sleeve /sli:v/ noun **1** a part of a piece of clothing that covers all or part of your arm: *a dress with short/long sleeves* ◊ *Dan rolled up his sleeves and washed his hands.*— see also SHIRTSLEEVE—picture on page A4 **2** (**-sleeved**) (in adjectives) having sleeves of the type mentioned: *a short-sleeved shirt* **3** (also **jacket** especially in AmE) a stiff paper or cardboard envelope for a record: *a colourful sleeve design* ◊ *sleeve notes* (= information about the music or the performers on the record) **4** a tube that covers a part of a machine to protect it ► **sleeve·less** adj.: *a sleeveless dress* IDM **have/keep sth up your 'sleeve** to keep a plan or an idea secret until you need to use it—more at ACE n., CARD n., LAUGH v., ROLL v., TRICK n., WEAR v.

sleigh /sleɪ/ noun a SLEDGE (= a vehicle that slides over snow), especially one pulled by horses: *a sleigh ride*

sleight /slaɪt/ noun IDM **,sleight of 'hand 1** skilful movements of your hand that other people cannot see: *The trick is done simply by sleight of hand.* **2** an act of deceiving people in a clever way

slen·der /'slendə(r)/ adj. (**slen·derer, slen·derest**) HELP You can also use **more slender** and **most slender**. **1** (*approving*) (of people or their bodies) thin in an attractive or graceful way SYN SLIM: *her slender figure* ◊ *long, slender fingers* ◊ *a slender young woman* **2** thin or narrow: *a glass with a slender stem* **3** small in amount or size and hardly enough: *to win by a slender margin/ majority* ◊ *people of slender means* (= with little money) ◊ *Australia held a slender 1–0 lead at half-time.* ► **slen·der·ness** noun [U]

slept pt, pp of SLEEP

sleuth /slu:θ/ noun (*old-fashioned* or *humorous*) a person who investigates crimes SYN DETECTIVE: *an amateur sleuth*

sleuth·ing /'slu:θɪŋ/ noun [U] the act of investigating a crime or mysterious event: *to do some private sleuthing*

slew /slu:/ verb, noun—see also SLAY v.
■ verb [+adv./prep.] (especially of a vehicle) to turn or slide suddenly in another direction; to make a vehicle do this: [V] *The car skidded and slewed sideways.* ◊ [VN] *He slewed the motorbike over as they hit the freeway.*
■ noun [sing.] **~ of sth** (*informal, especially AmE*) a large number or amount of sth: *This year has seen a whole slew of novels set in Hong Kong.*

slice /slaɪs/ noun, verb
■ noun **1** a thin flat piece of food that has been cut off a larger piece: *a slice of bread/ham* ◊ *Cut the meat into thin slices.*—picture on page A1 **2** (*informal*) a part or share of sth: *Our firm is well placed to grab a large slice of the market.* ◊ *The rent for my room was a large slice out of my budget.* **3** a kitchen UTENSIL (= tool) that you use to lift and serve pieces of food: *a fish slice* **4** (*sport*) (in golf, tennis, etc.) a stroke that makes the ball spin to one side rather than going straight ahead IDM **a ,slice of 'life** a film/movie, play or book that gives a very realistic view of ordinary life—more at PIE, ACTION, CAKE n.
■ verb **1** [VN] **~ sth (up)** to cut sth into slices: *to slice (up) onions/mushrooms/meat* ◊ *Slice the cucumber thinly.* ◊ *a sliced loaf* ◊ *a loaf of sliced bread* **2** [usually +adv./prep.] to cut sth easily with or as if with a sharp blade: [V] *He accidentally sliced through his finger.* ◊ *A piece of glass sliced into his shoulder.* ◊ (*figurative*) *Her speech sliced through all the confusion surrounding the situation.* ◊ [VN] *The knife sliced his jacket.* ◊ (*figurative*) *The ship sliced the water.* [also VN-ADJ] **3** [VN] (*sport*) to hit a ball so that it spins and does not move in the expected direction: *He managed to slice a shot over the net.* **4** [VN] (in golf) to hit the ball so that it flies away in a curve, usually without meaning to **5** [VN] (AmE, informal) to reduce sth by a large amount: *The new tax has sliced annual bonuses by 30 percent.* IDM see THING, WAY n. PHRV **,slice sth↔'off/ a'way | ,slice sth 'off sth** to cut sth from a larger piece: *Slice a piece off.* ◊ (*figurative*) *He sliced two seconds off the world record.*

slick /slɪk/ adj., noun, verb
■ adj. (**slick·er, slick·est**) **1** (*sometimes disapproving*) done or made in a way that is clever and efficient but often does not seem to be sincere or lacks important ideas: *a slick advertising campaign* ◊ *a slick performance* ◊ *You had to admire the slick presentation of last night's awards ceremony.* **2** (*sometimes disapproving*) speaking very easily and smoothly but in a way that does not seem sincere SYN GLIB: *slick TV presenters* ◊ *a slick salesman* ◊ *Her reply was too fast, too slick.* **3** done quickly and smoothly: *The crowd enjoyed the team's slick passing.* ◊ *a slick gear change* **4** smooth and difficult to hold or move on: *The roads were slick with rain.* ► **slick·ly** adv.: *The magazine is slickly produced.* **slick·ness** noun [U]
■ noun **1** (also **'oil slick**) an area of oil that is floating on the surface of the sea **2** a small area of sth wet and shiny: *a slick of sweat*
■ verb [VN+adv./prep.] [usually passive] to make hair very flat and smooth by putting oil, water, etc. on it: *His hair was slicked back/down with gel.*

slick·er /'slɪkə(r)/ noun (AmE) a long loose coat that keeps you dry in the rain—see also CITY SLICKER

slide /slaɪd/ verb, noun
■ verb (**slid, slid** /slɪd/)
MOVE SMOOTHLY/QUIETLY **1** [usually +adv./prep.] to move easily over a smooth or wet surface; to make sth move in this way: *We slid down the grassy slope.* ◊ *The drawers slide in and out easily.* ◊ [VN] *She slid her hand along the rail.* ◊ [V-ADJ] *The automatic doors slid open.* [also VN-ADJ] **2** [+adv./prep.] to move quickly and quietly, for example in order not to be noticed; to make sth move in this way: [V] *He slid into bed.* ◊ *She slid out while no one was*

looking. ◊ [VN] *The man slid the money quickly into his pocket.*

BECOME LOWER/WORSE | **3** [V] ~ **(from …) (to …)** to become gradually lower or of less value: *Shares slid to a 10-year low.* **4** [V] ~ **(down/into/towards sth)** to move gradually into a worse situation: *The industry has slid into decline.* ◊ *They were sliding towards bankruptcy.* ◊ *He got depressed and began to let things slide* (= failed to give things the attention they needed).

■ *noun*

BECOMING LOWER/WORSE | **1** [C, usually sing.] a change to a lower or worse condition: *a downward slide in the price of oil* ◊ *the team's slide down the table* ◊ *talks to prevent a slide into civil war* ◊ *The economy is on the slide* (= getting worse).

ON ICE | **2** [sing.] a long, smooth movement on ice or a smooth surface: *Her car went into a slide.*

FOR CHILDREN | **3** [C] a structure with a steep slope that children use for sliding down: *to go down the slide*

FALL OF ROCK | **4** [C] a sudden fall of a large amount of rock or earth down a hill: *I was afraid of starting a slide of loose stones.*—see also LANDSLIDE

PHOTOGRAPH | **5** [C] a small piece of film held in a frame that can be shown on a screen when you shine a light through it [SYN] TRANSPARENCY: *a talk with colour slides* ◊ *a slide show/projector*

FOR MICROSCOPE | **6** [C] a small piece of glass that sth is placed on so that it can be 'looked at under a MICROSCOPE—picture at LABORATORY

PART OF MUSICAL INSTRUMENT | **7** [C] a part of a musical instrument or other device that slides backwards and forwards

FOR HAIR | **8** [C] (*BrE*) = HAIRSLIDE

'slide rule *noun* a long narrow instrument like a ruler, with a middle part that slides backwards and forwards, used for calculating numbers

,sliding 'door *noun* a door that slides across an opening rather than swinging away from it

,sliding 'scale *noun* a system in which the rate at which sth is paid varies according to particular conditions: *Fees are calculated on a sliding scale according to income* (= richer people pay more).

slight /slaɪt/ *adj., noun, verb*

■ *adj.* (**slight·er, slight·est**) **1** very small in degree: *a slight increase / change / delay / difference* ◊ *I woke up with a slight headache.* ◊ *The damage was slight.* ◊ *She takes offence at the slightest thing* (= is very easily offended). ◊ *There was not the slightest hint of trouble.* ◊ *He is, without the slightest doubt, the greatest living novelist.* **2** small and thin in size: *a slight figure/man* **3** (*formal*) not deserving serious attention: *This is a very slight novel.* [IDM] **not in the 'slightest** not at all: *He didn't seem to mind in the slightest.*

■ *noun* ~ **(on sb/sth)** an act or a remark that criticizes sth or offends sb: *Nick took her comment as a slight on his abilities as a manager.*

■ *verb* [VN] [usually passive] to treat sb rudely or without respect; to insult sb: *She felt slighted because she hadn't been invited.* ▶ **slight·ing** *adj.* [only before noun]: *slighting remarks/references*

slight·ly /'slaɪtli/ *adv.* **1** a little: *a slightly different version* ◊ *We took a slightly more direct route.* ◊ *I knew her slightly.* ◊ *'Are you worried?' 'Only slightly.'* **2** a **slightly built** person is small and thin

slim /slɪm/ *adj., verb*

■ *adj.* (**slim·mer, slim·mest**) **1** (*approving*) (of a person) thin, in a way that is attractive: *a slim figure / body / waist* ◊ *She was tall and slim.* ◊ *How do you manage to stay so slim?* ◊ (*figurative*) *Many companies are a lot slimmer than they used to be* (= have fewer workers). **2** thinner than usual: *a slim volume of poetry* **3** not as big as you would like or expect; small: *a slim chance of success* ◊ *The party was returned to power with a slim majority.*—see also SLIMMER, SLIMMING ▶ **slim·ness** *noun* [U]

■ *verb* (**-mm-**) [V] (*BrE*) (usually used in the progressive tenses) to try to become thinner, for example by eating less: *You can still eat breakfast when you are slimming.*

[PHRV] **,slim 'down** to become thinner, for example as a result of eating less: *She slimmed down to 60 kilos before her wedding.* **,slim 'down | ,slim sth↔'down** to make a company or an organization smaller, by reducing the number of jobs in it; to be made smaller in this way: *They're restructuring and slimming down the workforce.* ◊ *The industry may have to slim down even further.* ◊ *the new, slimmed-down company*—see also SLIMMING

slime /slaɪm/ *noun* [U] any unpleasant thick liquid substance: *The pond was full of mud and green slime.*—see also SLIMY

slim·line /'slɪmlaɪn/ *adj.* [only before noun] **1** smaller or thinner in design than usual: *a slimline phone* **2** (*BrE*) (of a drink) containing very little sugar: *slimline tonic water*

slim·mer /'slɪmə(r)/ *noun* (*BrE*) a person who is trying to lose weight: *a calorie-controlled diet for slimmers*—see also SLIM

slim·ming /'slɪmɪŋ/ *noun* [U] (*BrE*) the practice of trying to lose weight: *a slimming club*—see also SLIM

slimy /'slaɪmi/ *adj.* (**slimi·er, slimi·est**) **1** like or covered with SLIME: *thick slimy mud* ◊ *The walls were black, cold and slimy.* **2** (*informal, disapproving*) (of a person or their manner) polite and extremely friendly in a way that is not sincere or honest

sling /slɪŋ/ *verb, noun*

sling | sling

■ *verb* (**slung, slung** /slʌŋ/) [usually +*adv.* / *prep.*] **1** (*informal, especially BrE*) to throw sth somewhere in a careless way: [VN] *Don't just sling your clothes on the floor.* ◊ [VNN] *Sling me an apple, will you?*—see also MUD-SLINGING **2** [VN] [often passive] to put sth somewhere where it hangs loosely: *Her bag was slung over her shoulder.* ◊ *We slung a hammock between two trees.* **3** [VN] [often passive] (*informal*) to put sb somewhere by force; to make sb leave somewhere: *They were slung out of the club for fighting.* [IDM] **sling your 'hook** (*BrE, informal*) (used especially in orders) to go away

■ *noun* **1** a band of fabric that is tied around a person's neck and used to support a broken or injured arm: *He had his arm in a sling.* **2** a device consisting of a band, ropes, etc. for holding and lifting heavy objects: *The engine was lifted in a sling of steel rope.* **3** a device like a bag for carrying a baby on your back or in front of you **4** (in the past) a simple weapon made from a band of leather, etc., used for throwing stones

sling·back /'slɪŋbæk/ *noun* a woman's shoe that is open at the back with a strap around the heel

sling·shot /'slɪŋʃɒt; *AmE* -ʃɑːt/ *noun* (*AmE*) = CATAPULT

slink /slɪŋk/ *verb* (**slunk, slunk** /slʌŋk/) [V +*adv.* / *prep.*] to move somewhere very quietly and slowly, especially because you are ashamed or do not want to be seen: *John was trying to slink into the house by the back door.* ◊ *The dog howled and slunk away.*

slinky /'slɪŋki/ *adj.* **1** (of a woman's clothes) fitting closely to the body in a sexually attractive way: *a slinky black dress* **2** (of movement or sound) smooth and slow, often in a way that is sexually attractive: *a slinky voice*

slip /slɪp/ *verb, noun*

■ *verb* (**-pp-**)

SLIDE/FALL | **1** [V] ~ **(over)** to slide a short distance accidentally so that you fall or nearly fall: *She slipped over on the ice and broke her leg.* ◊ *As I ran up the stairs, my foot slipped and I fell.*

OUT OF POSITION | **2** [V] [usually +*adv.* / *prep.*] to slide out of position or out of your hand: *His hat had slipped over one eye.* ◊ *The fish slipped out of my hand.* ◊ *The child slipped from his grasp and ran off.* ◊ (*figurative*) *She was careful not to let her control slip.*

GO/PUT QUICKLY | **3** [V +*adv.* / *prep.*] to go somewhere quickly and quietly, especially without being noticed: *She slipped out of the house before the others were awake.* ◊ *The ship slipped into the harbour at night.* ◊ (*figurative*) *She knew that time was slipping away.* **4** to put sth somewhere quickly, quietly or secretly: [VN +*adv.* / *prep.*] *Anna* *slipped her hand into his.* ◊ *He slipped the letter back into its envelope.* ◊ *I managed to slip a few jokes into my speech.* ◊ *I managed to* **slip in** *a few jokes.* ◊ [VNN, VN] *They'd slipped the guards some money.* ◊ *They'd slipped some money to the guards.*

BECOME WORSE | **5** [V] to fall to a lower level; to become worse: *His popularity has slipped recently.* ◊ *The director never lets the tension slip.* ◊ *That's three times she's beaten me—I must be slipping!*

INTO DIFFICULT SITUATION | **6** [V+*adv./prep.*] to pass into a particular state or situation, especially a difficult or unpleasant one: *He began to* **slip into** *debt.* ◊ *The patient had* **slipped into** *a coma.* ◊ *We seem to have slipped behind schedule.*

CLOTHES ON/OFF | **7** [+*adv./prep.*] to put clothes on or to take them off quickly and easily: [V] *to slip into/out of a dress* ◊ [VN] *to slip your shoes on/off* ◊ *He slipped a coat over his sweatshirt.*

GET FREE | **8** to get free; to make sth/sb/yourself free from sth: [VN] *The ship had slipped its moorings in the night.* ◊ [V-ADJ] *The animal had* **slipped free** *and escaped.* [also VN-ADJ]

IDM **let** '**slip sth** to give sb information that is supposed to be secret: *I happened to* **let it slip** *that he had given me £1 000 for the car.* ◊ *She tried not to let slip what she knew.* **let sth** '**slip (through your fingers)** to miss or fail to use an opportunity: *Don't let the chance to work abroad slip through your fingers.* **slip your** '**mind** if sth **slips your mind**, you forget it or forget to do it: *I'm sorry I didn't tell you. It completely slipped my mind.* ,**slip one** '**over on sb** (*informal*) to trick sb **slip through the** '**net** when sb/sth **slips through the net**, an organization or a system fails to find them and deal with them: *We tried to contact all former students, but one or two slipped through the net.*—more at GEAR *n.*, TONGUE *n.*

PHRV ,**slip a**'**way** to stop existing; to disappear or die: *Their support gradually slipped away.* ,**slip** '**out** when sth **slips out**, you say it without really intending to: *I'm sorry I said that. It just slipped out.* ,**slip** '**up** (*informal*) to make a careless mistake: *We can't afford to slip up.*—related noun SLIP-UP

■ *noun*

SMALL MISTAKE | **1** a small mistake, usually made by being careless or not paying attention: *He recited the whole poem without making a single slip.*—see also FREUDIAN SLIP

PIECE OF PAPER | **2** a small piece of paper, especially one for writing on or with sth printed on it: *I wrote it down on a slip of paper.* ◊ *a betting slip*—see also PAYSLIP

ACT OF SLIPPING | **3** an act of slipping: *One slip and you could fall to your death.*

CLOTHING | **4** a piece of women's underwear like a thin dress or skirt, worn under a dress

IN CRICKET | **5** a player who stands behind and to one side of the BATSMAN and tries to catch the ball; the position on the field where this player stands

IDM **give sb the** '**slip** (*informal*) to escape or get away from sb who is following or chasing you **a** '**slip of a boy, girl, etc.** (*old-fashioned*) a small or thin, usually young, person **a slip of the** '**pen/**'**tongue** a small mistake in sth that you write or say: *Did I call you Richard? Sorry, Robert, just a slip of the tongue.*

'**slip cover** *noun* (*AmE*) = LOOSE COVER

'**slip-on** *noun* a shoe that you can slide your feet into without having to tie LACES: *a pair of slip-ons/slip-on shoes*

slip·page /'slɪpɪdʒ/ *noun* [U, C, usually sing.] (*written*) **1** failure to achieve an aim or complete a task by a particular date **2** a slight or gradual fall in the amount, value, etc. of sth

,**slipped** '**disc** *noun* a painful condition caused when one of the DISCS between the bones of the SPINE in a person's back moves out of place

slip·per /'slɪpə(r)/ *noun* a loose soft shoe that you wear in the house: *a pair of slippers*—see also CARPET SLIPPER—picture at SHOE

slip·pery /'slɪpəri/ *adj.* **1** (also *informal* **slippy**) difficult to hold or to stand or move on, because it is smooth, wet or polished: *slippery like a fish* ◊ *In places the path can be wet and slippery.* ◊ *His hand was slippery with sweat.* **2** (*informal*) (of a person) that you cannot trust: *Don't believe what he says—he's a slippery customer.* **3** (*informal*) (of a situation, subject, problem, etc.) difficult to deal with and that you have to think about carefully: *Freedom is a slippery concept* (= because its meaning changes according to your point of view). **IDM** **the/a slippery** '**slope** a course of action that is difficult to stop once it has begun, and can lead to serious problems or disaster

'**slip road** (*BrE*) (*AmE* **ramp**) *noun* a road used for driving onto or off a motorway/freeway—compare ACCESS ROAD

slip·shod /'slɪpʃɒd; *AmE* -ʃɑːd/ *adj.* done without care; doing things without care **SYN** CARELESS: *The work was done in a slipshod manner.*

slip·stream /'slɪpstriːm/ *noun* [sing.] the stream of air behind a vehicle that is moving very fast

'**slip-up** *noun* (*informal*) a careless mistake: *We cannot afford another slip-up like this one.*

slip·way /'slɪpweɪ/ *noun* a sloping track leading down to water, on which ships are built or pulled up out of the water for repairs, or from which they are LAUNCHED (= put into the water)

slit /slɪt/ *noun, verb*
■ *noun* a long narrow cut or opening: *a long skirt with a slit up the side* ◊ *His eyes narrowed into slits.*
■ *verb* (**slit·ting, slit, slit**) to make a long narrow cut or opening in sth: [VN] *Slit the roll with a sharp knife.* ◊ *The child's throat had been slit.* ◊ *Her skirt was slit at both sides* (= designed with an opening at the bottom on each side). ◊ [VN-ADJ] *He slit open the envelope and took out the letter.*

slither /'slɪðə(r)/ *verb* [V+*adv./prep.*] **1** to move somewhere in a smooth, controlled way, often close to the ground: *The snake slithered away as we approached.* **2** to move somewhere without much control, for example because the ground is steep or wet: *We slithered down the slope to the road.* ◊ *They were slithering around on the ice.*

sliver /'slɪvə(r)/ *noun* a small or thin piece of sth that is cut or broken off from a larger piece: *slivers of glass/wood* ◊ (*figurative*) *A sliver of light showed under the door.*

Sloane /sləʊn; *AmE* sloʊn/ *noun* (*BrE, informal, often disapproving*) a young person, especially a woman, from a rich upper-class background, especially one who lives in a fashionable area of London

slob /slɒb; *AmE* slɑːb/ *noun, verb*
■ *noun* (*informal, disapproving*) a person who is lazy and dirty or untidy: *Get out of bed, you fat slob!*
■ *verb* (**-bb-**) **PHRV** ,**slob a**'**round/**'**out** (*BrE, slang*) to spend time being lazy and doing nothing

slob·ber /'slɒbə(r); *AmE* 'slɑːb-/ *verb* [V] to let SALIVA come out of your mouth: *The baby was slobbering all over her bib.* **PHRV** '**slobber over sb/sth** (*informal, disapproving*) to show how much you like or want sb/sth without any pride or control

sloe /sləʊ; *AmE* sloʊ/ *noun* a bitter wild fruit like a small PLUM that grows on a bush called a BLACKTHORN

slog /slɒg; *AmE* slɑːg/ *verb, noun*
■ *verb* (**-gg-**) (*informal*) **1** ~ (**through sth**)|~ (**away**) (**at sth**) to work hard and steadily at sth, especially sth that takes a long time and is boring or difficult: [V] *He's been slogging away at that piece of music for weeks.* ◊ [VN] *She slogged her way through four piles of ironing.* **2** [V+*adv./prep.*] to walk or travel somewhere steadily, with great effort or difficulty: *He started to slog his way through the undergrowth.* ◊ *I've been slogging around the streets of London all day.* **3** [VN, V] [usually +*adv./prep.*] to hit a ball very hard but often without skill **IDM** ,**slog it** '**out** (*BrE, informal*) to fight or compete in order to prove who is the strongest, the best, etc.—more at GUT *n.*
■ *noun* [U, C, usually sing.] a period of hard work or effort: *Writing the book took ten months of hard slog.* ◊ *It was a long slog to the top of the mountain.*

slo·gan /'sləʊgən; *AmE* 'sloʊ-/ (also *AmE informal* '**tag**

æ	ɑː	e	ɜː	ə	ɪ	iː	i	ɒ	ɔː	ʌ	ʊ	u	uː
cat	father	ten	bird	about	sit	see	many	got	saw	cup	put	actual	too
								(BrE)					

line) *noun* a word or phrase that is easy to remember, used for example by a political party or in advertising to attract people's attention or to suggest an idea quickly: *an advertising / a campaign slogan* ◊ *The crowd began chanting anti-government slogans.*

slo·gan·eer·ing /ˌsləʊgəˈnɪərɪŋ; *AmE* ˌsloʊgəˈnɪrɪŋ/ *noun* [U] (*disapproving*) the use of slogans in advertisements, by politicians, etc.

sloop /sluːp/ *noun* a small sailing ship with one MAST (= a post to support the sails)

slop /slɒp; *AmE* slɑːp/ *verb, noun*

■ *verb* (**-pp-**) **1** [V +*adv. / prep.*] (of a liquid) to move around in a container, often so that some liquid comes out over the edge: *Water was slopping around in the bottom of the boat.* ◊ *As he put the glass down the beer slopped over onto the table.* **2** [VN] [usually +*adv. / prep.*] to make liquid or food come out of a container in an untidy way: *He got out of the bath, slopping water over the sides.* ◊ *She slopped some beans onto a plate.* **PHRV** ˌslop aˈbout / aˈround (*BrE, informal*) **1** to spend time relaxing or being lazy: *He used to slop around all day in his pyjamas.* **2** to move around in water, mud. etc: *She was enjoying slopping about in the water.* ˌslop ˈout (*BrE*) when prisoners **slop out**, they empty the containers that they use as toilets

■ *noun* [U] (also **slops** [pl.]) **1** waste food, sometimes fed to animals **2** liquid or partly liquid waste, for example URINE or dirty water from baths: *a slop bucket*

slope /sləʊp; *AmE* sloʊp/ *noun, verb*

■ *noun* **1** [C] a surface or piece of land that slopes (= higher at one end than the other): *a grassy / wooded slope* ◊ *The town is built on a slope.* **2** [C, usually pl.] an area of land that is part of a mountain or hill: *the eastern slopes of the Andes* ◊ *ski slopes* ◊ *He spends all winter on the slopes* (= skiing).—picture at MOUNTAIN **3** [sing., U] the amount by which sth slopes: *a gentle / steep slope* ◊ *a slope of 45 degrees* ◊ *the angle of slope* **IDM** see SLIPPERY

■ *verb* [V] **1** [usually +*adv. / prep.*] (of a horizontal surface) to be at an angle so that it is higher at one end than the other: *The garden slopes away towards the river.* ◊ *The path sloped gently down.* ◊ *sloping shoulders* **2** [usually +*adv. / prep.*] (of sth vertical) to be at an angle rather than being straight or upright: *His handwriting slopes backwards.* ◊ *It was a very old house with sloping walls.* **3** [V +*adv. / prep.*] (*BrE, informal*) to go somewhere quietly, especially in order to avoid sth / sb: *They got bored waiting for him and sloped off.*

sloppy /ˈslɒpi; *AmE* ˈslɑːpi/ *adj.* (**slop·pier, slop·pi·est**) **1** that shows a lack of care, thought or effort: *sloppy thinking / speech* ◊ *Your work is sloppy.* ◊ *a sloppy writer / worker / dresser* **2** (of clothes) loose and without much shape: *a sloppy T-shirt* **3** (*informal, especially BrE*) romantic in a silly or embarrassing way: *a sloppy, sentimental love story* **4** containing too much liquid: *Don't make the mixture too sloppy.* ◊ (*informal*) *She gave him a big sloppy kiss.* ▶ **slop·pily** /-ɪli/ *adv.*: *a sloppily run department* **slop·pi·ness** *noun* [U]: *There is no excuse for sloppiness in your work.*

sloppy joe /ˌslɒpi ˈdʒəʊ; *AmE* ˌslɑːpi ˈdʒoʊ/ *noun* (*AmE*) finely chopped meat served in a spicy tomato sauce inside a BUN (= bread roll)

slosh /slɒʃ; *AmE* slɑːʃ/ *verb* [+*adv. / prep.*] (*informal*) **1** [V] (of liquid) to move around making a lot of noise or coming out over the edge of sth: *The water was sloshing around under our feet.* ◊ *Some of the paint sloshed out of the can.* **2** [VN] to make liquid move in a noisy way; to use liquid carelessly: *The children were sloshing water everywhere.* ◊ *She sloshed coffee into the mugs.* **3** [V] to walk noisily in water or mud: *We all sloshed around in the puddles.* **PHRV** ˌslosh aˈbout / aˈround (*BrE, informal*) (especially of money) to be available or present in large quantities: *There's a lot of money sloshing around in professional tennis.*

sloshed /slɒʃt; *AmE* slɑːʃt/ *adj.* (*slang*) drunk

slot /slɒt; *AmE* slɑːt/ *noun, verb*

■ *noun* **1** a long narrow opening, into which you put or fit sth: *to put some coins in the slot* **2** a position, a time or an opportunity for sb / sth, for example in a list, a pro-

gramme of events or a series of broadcasts: *He has a regular slot on the late-night programme.* ◊ *Their album has occupied the Number One slot for the past six weeks.* ◊ *the airport's take-off and landing slots*

■ *verb* (**-tt-**) [+*adv. / prep.*] to put sth into a space that is available or designed for it; to fit into such a space: [VN] *He slotted a cassette into the VCR.* ◊ *The bed comes in sections which can be quickly slotted together.* ◊ [V] *The dishwasher slots neatly between the cupboards.* **IDM** see PLACE *n.* **PHRV** ˌslot sb/sth↔ˈin to manage to find a position, a time or an opportunity for sb / sth: *I can slot you in between 3 and 4.* ◊ *We slotted in some extra lessons before the exam.*

sloth /sləʊθ; *AmE* sloʊθ/ *noun* **1** [C] a S American animal that lives in trees and moves very slowly **2** [U] (*formal*) the bad habit of being lazy and unwilling to work

sloth·ful /ˈsləʊθfl; *AmE* ˈsloʊθfl/ *adj.* (*formal*) lazy

'slot machine *noun* **1** (*BrE*) a machine with an opening for coins, used for selling things such as cigarettes and bars of chocolate **2** (*especially AmE*) = FRUIT MACHINE

slot·ted /ˈslɒtɪd; *AmE* ˈslɑːt-/ *adj.* [usually before noun] (especially *technical*) having a SLOT or SLOTS in it: *a screw with a slotted head*

ˌslotted ˈspoon *noun* a large spoon with holes in it

slouch /slaʊtʃ/ *verb, noun*

■ *verb* [V] [usually +*adv. / prep.*] to stand, sit or move in a lazy way, often with your shoulders and head bent forward: *Several students were slouching against the wall.* ◊ *Sit up straight. Don't slouch.*

■ *noun* [usually sing.] a way of standing or sitting in which your shoulders are not straight, so that you look tired or lazy **IDM** be no ˈslouch (*informal*) to be very good at sth or quick to do sth: *She's no slouch on the guitar.*

slough¹ /slʌf/ *verb* [VN] ~ sth (off) to lose a layer of dead skin, etc: *a snake sloughing its skin* ◊ *Slough off dead skin cells by using a facial scrub.* **PHRV** ˌslough sth↔ˈoff (*formal*) to get rid of sth that you no longer want: *Responsibilities are not sloughed off so easily.*

slough² /slaʊ; *AmE* sluː/ *noun* (*literary*) **1** [sing.] ~ of misery, despair, etc. a state of sadness with no hope **2** [C] a very soft wet area of land

slov·en·ly /ˈslʌvnli/ *adj.* careless, untidy or dirty in appearance or habits: *He grew lazy and slovenly in his habits.* ◊ *a slovenly attitude / appearance* ▶ **slov·en·li·ness** *noun* [U]

slow /sləʊ; *AmE* sloʊ/ *adj., adv., verb*

■ *adj.* (**slow·er, slow·est**)

<u>NOT FAST</u> **1** not moving, acting or done quickly; taking a long time; not fast: *a slow driver / walker / reader* ◊ *Progress was slower than expected.* ◊ *The country is experiencing slow but steady economic growth.* ◊ *Collecting data is a painfully slow process.* ◊ *a slow, lingering death* ◊ *Oh you're so slow; come on, hurry up!* ◊ *The slow movement opens with a cello solo.* ◊ *She gave a slow smile.* **2** not going or allowing you to go at a fast speed: *I missed the fast train and had to get the slow one* (= the one that stops at all the stations). ◊ *We drove in the slow lane.*

<u>WITH DELAY</u> **3** ~ to do sth / ~ (in) doing sth hesitating to do sth or not doing sth immediately: *She wasn't slow to realize what was going on.* ◊ *His poetry was slow in achieving recognition.* ◊ *They were very slow paying me.*

<u>NOT CLEVER</u> **4** not quick to learn; finding things hard to understand: *He's the slowest in the class.*

<u>NOT BUSY</u> **5** not very busy; containing little action: *Sales are slow* (= not many goods are being sold).

<u>WATCH / CLOCK</u> **6** [not before noun] showing a time earlier than the correct time: *My watch is five minutes slow* (= it shows 1.45 when it is 1.50).

<u>IN PHOTOGRAPHY</u> **7** slow film is not very sensitive to light

▶ **slow·ness** *noun* [U]: *There was impatience over the slowness of reform.*

IDM do a slow ˈburn (*AmE, informal*) to slowly get angry—more at MARK *n.*, UPTAKE

■ *adv.* (**slow·er, slow·est**) (used especially in the comparative and superlative forms, or in compounds) at a slow

aɪ	aʊ	eɪ	əʊ	oʊ	ɔɪ	ɪə	eə	ʊə	j	w
my	now	say	go	go	boy	near	hair	pure	yes	wet
			(BrE)	(AmE)						

speed SYN SLOWLY: *Could you go a little slower?* ◊ *slow-drying paint* ◊ *slow-moving traffic* ◊ (*AmE*) *Drive slow!* IDM **go ˈslow (on sth)** to show less enthusiasm for achieving sth: *The government is going slow on tax reforms.*—see also GO-SLOW

■ *verb* **~ (sth/sb) (down/up)** to go or to make sth/sb go at a slower speed or be less active: [V] *The car slowed down as it approached the junction.* ◊ *The bus slowed to a halt.* ◊ *Economic growth has slowed a little.* ◊ *The game slowed up a little in the second half.* ◊ *You must slow down a little* (= work less hard) *or you'll make yourself ill.* ◊ [VN] *The ice on the roads was slowing us down.* ◊ *We hope to slow the spread of the disease.*—see also SLOWDOWN

WHICH WORD?
slow / slowly

Slowly is the usual adverb from the adjective **slow**. **Slow** is sometimes used as an adverb in informal language, on road signs, etc. It can also be used to form compounds: *Slow. Major road ahead.* ◊ *a slow-acting drug* ◊ ~~*They walk very slow.*~~ In the comparative both **slower** and **more slowly** are used: *Can you speak slower/more slowly?*

---

slow·coach /ˈsləʊkəʊtʃ; *AmE* ˈsloʊkoʊtʃ/ (*BrE*) (*AmE* **ˈslow·poke**) *noun* (*informal*) a person who moves, acts or works too slowly

slow·down /ˈsləʊdaʊn; *AmE* ˈsloʊ-/ *noun* **1** a reduction in speed or activity: *a slowdown in economic growth* **2** (*AmE*) = GO-SLOW

ˈslow lane *noun* [sing.] the part of a main road such as a motorway where vehicles drive slowest IDM **in the ˈslow lane** not making progress as fast as other people, countries, companies, etc.

slow·ly /ˈsləʊli; *AmE* ˈsloʊli/ *adv.* at a slow speed; not quickly: *to move/walk/turn slowly* ◊ *Please could you speak more slowly?* ◊ *The boat chugged slowly along.* ◊ *He found that life moved slowly in the countryside.* ◊ *Don't rush into a decision.* **Take it slowly.** ◊ *Slowly things began to improve.* ➪ note at SLOW IDM **ˌslowly but ˈsurely** making slow but definite progress: *We'll get there slowly but surely.*

ˌslow ˈmotion *noun* [U] (in a film/movie or on television) the method of showing action at a much slower speed than it happened in real life: *Some scenes were filmed in slow motion.* ◊ *a slow-motion replay*

slow·poke /ˈsləʊpəʊk; *AmE* ˈsloʊpoʊk/ *noun* (*AmE*, *informal*) = SLOWCOACH

ˈslow-witted *adj.* not able to think quickly; slow to learn or understand things OPP QUICK-WITTED

ˈslow-worm *noun* a small European reptile with no legs, like a snake

SLR /ˌes el ˈɑː(r)/ *abbr.* single-lens reflex (= used to describe a camera in which there is one LENS which is used both for the film, and for the photographer to look through)

sludge /slʌdʒ/ *noun* [U] **1** thick, soft, wet mud or a substance that looks like it: *There was some sludge at the bottom of the tank.* **2** industrial or human waste that has been treated: *industrial/chemical sludge* ◊ *the use of sewage sludge as a fertilizer on farm land*

slug /slʌg/ *noun, verb*
■ *noun* **1** a small soft creature, like a SNAIL without a shell, that moves very slowly and often eats garden plants—picture on page A7 **2** (*informal*) a small amount of a strong alcoholic drink: *He took another slug of whisky.* **3** (*informal*, *especially AmE*) a bullet **4** (*AmE*, *informal*) a piece of metal shaped like a coin used to get things from machines, etc., sometimes illegally
■ *verb* (-**gg**-) [VN] **1** (*informal*) to hit sb hard, especially with your closed hand **2** (in baseball) to hit the ball hard IDM **ˌslug it ˈout** to fight or compete until it is clear who has won

slug·gish /ˈslʌgɪʃ/ *adj.* moving, reacting or working more slowly than normal and in a way that seems lazy: *sluggish traffic* ◊ *a sluggish economy* ◊ *the sluggish black*

waters of the canal ◊ *He felt very heavy and sluggish after the meal.* ▶ **slug·gish·ly** *adv.* **slug·gish·ness** *noun* [U]

sluice /sluːs/ *noun, verb*
■ *noun* (also **ˈsluice gate**) a sliding gate or other device for controlling the flow of water out of or into a canal, etc.
■ *verb* **1** [VN] **~ sth (down/out)** | **~ sth (with sth)** to wash sth with a stream of water: *The ship's crew was sluicing down the deck.* ◊ *I quickly sluiced my face with cold water.* **2** [V+adv./prep.] (of water) to flow somewhere in large quantities: *Rain was sluicing down.*

slum /slʌm/ *noun, verb*
■ *noun* an area of a city that is very poor and where the houses are dirty and in bad condition: *a slum area/district* ◊ *city/urban slums* ◊ *She was brought up in the slums of London.*
■ *verb* (-**mm**-) [V] (usually **be slumming**) (*informal*) to spend time in places or conditions that are much worse than those you are used to: *There are plenty of ways you can cut costs on your trip without slumming.* IDM **ˈslum it** to accept conditions that are worse than those you are used to: *Several businessmen had to slum it in economy class.*

slum·ber /ˈslʌmbə(r)/ *noun, verb*
■ *noun* [U, C, usually pl.] (*literary*) sleep; a time when sb is asleep: *She fell into deep slumber.*
■ *verb* [V] (*literary*) to sleep

ˈslumber party *noun* (*AmE*) = SLEEPOVER

slump /slʌmp/ *noun, verb*
■ *verb* [V] **1** **~ (by sth)** | **~ (from sth) (to sth)** to fall in price, value, number, etc., suddenly and by a large amount: *Sales have slumped this year.* ◊ *Profits slumped by over 50%.* ◊ *The paper's circulation has slumped to 90000.* **2** [+adv./prep.] to sit or fall down heavily: *The old man slumped down in his chair.* ◊ *She slumped to her knees.*
■ *noun* **1** **~ (in sth)** a sudden fall in sales, prices, the value of sth, etc: *a slump in sales/profits* **2** a period when a country's economy or a business is doing very badly: *the slump of the 1930s* ◊ *Housing sales are finally coming out of a three-month slump.* ◊ *The toy industry is in a slump.*—compare BOOM *n.* (1)

slumped /slʌmpt/ *adj.* [not usually before noun] **~ (against/over sth)** sitting with your body leaning forward, for example because you are asleep or unconscious: *The driver was slumped exhausted over the wheel.* ◊ *There was a slumped figure in the chair.*

slung *pt, pp* of SLING

slunk *pt, pp* of SLINK

slur /slɜː(r)/ *verb, noun*
■ *verb* (-**rr**-) **1** to pronounce words in a way that is not clear so that they run into each other, usually because you are drunk or tired: [VN] *She had drunk too much and her speech was slurred.* [also V **speech**] **2** (*music*) to play or sing a group of two or more musical notes so that each one runs smoothly into the next **3** [VN] to harm sb's reputation by making unfair or false statements about them: *She accused the programme of slurring the company's name.*
■ *noun* **1** **~ (on sb/sth)** an unfair remark about sb/sth that may damage other people's opinion of them: *She had dared to cast a slur on his character.* ◊ (*especially AmE*) *The crowd started throwing bottles and shouting racial slurs.* **2** (*music*) a curved sign used to show that two or more notes are to be played smoothly and without a break

slurp /slɜːp; *AmE* slɜːrp/ *verb* (*informal*) **1** to make a loud noise while you are drinking sth: [VN] *He was slurping his tea.* ◊ [V] *She slurped noisily from her cup.* **2** [V] to make a noise like this: *The water slurped in the tank.* ▶ **slurp** *noun* [usually sing.]: *She took a slurp from her mug.*

slurry /ˈslʌri; *AmE* ˈslɜːri/ *noun* [U] a thick liquid consisting of water mixed with animal waste, clay, coal dust or CEMENT

slush /slʌʃ/ *noun* [U] **1** partly melted snow that is usually dirty: *In the city the clean white snow had turned to grey slush.* **2** (*informal, disapproving*) stories, films/movies or feelings that are considered to be silly and without value because they are too emotional and romantic ▶ **slushy** *adj.*: *slushy pavements* ◊ *slushy romantic fiction*

---

b	d	f	g	h	k	l	m	n	p	r
bad	did	fall	get	hat	cat	leg	man	now	pen	red

S

'slush fund *noun* (*disapproving*) a sum of money kept for illegal purposes, especially in politics

slut /slʌt/ *noun* (*disapproving*, *offensive*) **1** a woman who has many sexual partners **2** a woman who is very untidy or lazy ▶ **slut·tish** *adj*.

sly /slaɪ/ *adj*. **1** (*disapproving*) acting or done in a secret or dishonest way, often intending to trick people SYN CUNNING: *a sly political move* ◊ (*humorous*) *You sly old devil! How long have you known?* **2** [usually before noun] suggesting that you know sth secret that other people do not know SYN KNOWING: *a sly smile/grin/look/glance* ▶ **slyly** *adv*.: *He glanced at her slyly.* **sly·ness** *noun* [U] IDM **on the 'sly** secretly; not wanting other people to discover what you are doing: *He has to visit them on the sly.*

smack /smæk/ *verb*, *noun*, *adv*.
■ *verb* **1** [VN] (*especially BrE*) to hit sb with your open hand, especially as a punishment: *I think it's wrong to smack children.*—compare SPANK **2** [VN+*adv./prep.*] to put sth somewhere with a lot of force so that it makes a loud noise: *She smacked her hand down on to the table.* ◊ *He smacked a fist into the palm of his hand.* **3** [V+*adv./prep.*] to hit against sth with a lot of force: *Two players accidentally smacked into each other.* IDM see LIP PHRV **smack of sth** to seem to contain or involve a particular unpleasant quality: *Her behaviour smacks of hypocrisy.* ◊ *Today's announcement smacks of a government cover-up.*
■ *noun* **1** [C] (*especially BrE*) a sharp hit given with your open hand, especially to a child as a punishment: *You'll get a smack on your backside if you're not careful.* **2** [C] (*informal*) a hard hit given with a closed hand: *a smack on the jaw* **3** [C, usually sing.] a short loud sound: *She closed the ledger with a smack.* **4** [C] (*informal*) a loud kiss: *a smack on the lips/cheek* **5** [U] (*slang*) the drug HEROIN: *smack addicts/dealers* **6** [C] (*BrE*) a small fishing boat
■ *adv.* (*informal*) **1** (*AmE* also **'smack-dab**) exactly or directly in a place: *It landed **smack in the middle** of the carpet.* **2** with sudden, violent force, often making a loud noise: *The car drove smack into a brick wall.* ◊ *He hit me smack in the mouth.*

smack·er /'smækə(r)/ *noun* **1** (*informal*) a loud kiss **2** (*slang*) a British pound or US dollar

smack·ing /'smækɪŋ/ *noun* [sing., U] (*especially BrE*) an act of hitting sb, especially a child, several times with your open hand, as a punishment: *He gave both of the children a good smacking.* ◊ *We don't approve of smacking.*

small /smɔːl/ *adj.*, *adv.*, *noun*
■ *adj.* (**small·er**, **small·est**)
NOT LARGE **1** not large in size, number, degree, amount, etc: *a small house/town/car/man* ◊ *A much smaller number of students passed than I had expected.* ◊ *They're having a relatively small wedding.* ◊ *a small claims court* (= for legal claims for small amounts of money) ◊ *That dress is too small for you.* ◊ *'I don't agree,' he said in a small* (= quiet) *voice.* **2** (*abbr.* **S**) used to describe one size in a range of sizes of clothes, food, products used in the house, etc: *small, medium, large* ◊ *This is too big—have you got a small one?* **3** not as big as sth else of the same kind: *the small intestine*
YOUNG **4** young: *They have three small children.* ◊ *We travelled around a lot when I was small.* ◊ *As a small boy he had spent most of his time with his grandparents.*
NOT IMPORTANT **5** slight; not important: *I made only a few small changes to the report.* ◊ *She noticed several small errors in his work.* ◊ *Everything had been planned down to the smallest detail.* ◊ *It was **no small** achievement getting her to agree to the deal.*
BUSINESS **6** [usually before noun] not doing business on a very large scale: *a small farmer/shopkeeper* ◊ *The government is planning to give more help to small businesses.*
LETTERS **7** [usually before noun] not written or printed as CAPITALS: *Should I write 'god' with a small 'g' or a capital?* ◊ *She's a socialist with a small 's'* (= she believes in socialist ideas but is not a member of a socialist party).
NOT MUCH **8** [only before noun] (used with uncountable

nouns) little; not much: *The government has small cause for optimism.*
▶ **small·ness** *noun* [U]
IDM **be grateful/thankful for small 'mercies** to be happy that a situation that is bad is not as bad as it could have been: *Well, at least you weren't hurt. I suppose we should be grateful for small mercies.* **it's a ˌsmall 'world** (*saying*) used to express your surprise when you meet sb you know in an unexpected place, or when you are talking to sb and find out that you both know the same person **look/feel 'small** to look or feel stupid, weak, ashamed, etc.—more at BIG *adj.*, GREAT *adj.*, HOUR, SWEAT *v.*, WAY *n.*, WONDER *n.*
■ *adv.* (**small·er**, **small·est**) **1** into small pieces: *Chop the cabbage up small.* **2** in a small size: *You can fit it all in if you write very small.*
■ *noun* **1 the ~ of the/sb's back** [sing.] the lower part of the back where it curves in: *He felt a sharp pain in the small of his back.* **2** (**smalls**) [pl.] (*old-fashioned*, *BrE*, *informal*) small items of clothing, especially underwear

> **WHICH WORD?**
> **small / little**
>
> These adjectives are frequently used with the following nouns:
>
> | **small ~** | **little ~** |
> |---|---|
> | number | girl |
> | group | smile |
> | children | man |
> | business | things |
> | house | boys |
>
> **Small** is the most usual opposite of **big** or **large**. It can be used in the comparative and superlative and with adverbs such as *rather, quite, fairly* and *pretty*: *Our house is smaller than yours but I think the kitchen is bigger.* ◊ *The town is pretty small.*
>
> **Little** is usually used to show how you feel about a person or a thing, and especially after other adjectives such as *ugly, nice, cute*, etc: *a cute little baby* ◊ *You poor little thing!* It can also show that you think a person or thing is not important: *You'll just feel a little sting — it won't hurt.* ◊ *a dreadful little man* (*BrE*). Note that it is usually only used before a noun and that it is rarely used in the comparative and superlative.
>
> **Little** is also used with proper names: *Little Italy is an area of New York where many Italians live.*

'small ads *noun* [pl.] (*BrE*, *informal*) = CLASSIFIED ADVERTISEMENTS

'small arms *noun* [pl.] small light weapons that you can carry in your hands

small 'beer (*BrE*) (*AmE* ˌsmall po'tatoes) *noun* [U] (*informal*) a person or thing that has no great importance or value, especially when compared with sb/sth else

small 'change *noun* [U] **1 ~ (in sth)** coins of low value: *Have you got any small change for the phone?* **2** something that is of little value when compared with sth else

ˌsmall 'fortune *noun* [usually sing.] (*informal*) a lot of money: *That holiday cost me a small fortune.*

'small fry *noun* [U+sing./pl. *v.*] (*informal*) people or things that are considered unimportant compared to sb/sth else: *That's small fry to her.* ◊ *People like us are small fry to such a large business.*

small·hold·er /'smɔːlhəʊldə(r)/; *AmE* -hoʊ-/ *noun* (*BrE*) a person who owns or rents a small piece of land for farming

small·hold·ing /'smɔːlhəʊldɪŋ/; *AmE* -hoʊ-/ *noun* a small piece of land used for farming

small·ish /'smɔːlɪʃ/ *adj.* fairly small: *a smallish town/child*

small-'minded *adj.* (*disapproving*) having fixed opinions and ways of doing things and not willing to change them or consider other people's opinions or feelings; interested in small problems and details and not in

S

things which are really important ▶ **,small-'minded-ness** *noun* [U]

,small po'tatoes *noun* [U] (*AmE*) = SMALL BEER

small·pox /'smɔːlpɒks; *AmE* -pɑːks/ *noun* [U] a serious infectious disease (now extremely rare) that causes fever, leaves permanent marks on the skin and often causes death

the ,small 'print (*BrE*) (*AmE* **the ,fine 'print**) *noun* [U] the important details of an agreement or a legal document that are usually printed in small type and are therefore easy to miss: *Read all the small print before signing.*

,small-'scale *adj.* **1** (of an organization, activity, etc.) not large in size or extent; limited in what it does: *small-scale farming* ◊ *a small-scale study of couples in second marriages* **2** (of maps, drawings, etc.) drawn to a small SCALE so that not many details are shown OPP LARGE-SCALE

the ,small 'screen *noun* [sing.] television (when contrasted with cinema): *This will be the film's first showing on the small screen.* ◊ *his first small-screen role*

'small talk *noun* [U] polite conversation about ordinary or unimportant subjects, especially at social occasions

'small-time *adj.* [only before noun] (*informal, disapproving*) (often of criminals) not very important or successful SYN PETTY: *a small-time crook*—compare BIG TIME

'small-town *adj.* [only before noun] **1** (*disapproving*) not showing much interest in new ideas or what is happening outside your own environment SYN NARROW-MINDED: *small-town values/views* **2** connected with a small town: *small-town America* (= people who live in small towns in America)

smarmy /'smɑːmi; *AmE* 'smɑːrmi/ *adj.* (*BrE, informal, disapproving*) too polite in a way that is not sincere: *a smarmy salesman/comment*

smart /smɑːt; *AmE* smɑːrt/ *adj., verb*
■ *adj.* (**smart·er**, **smart·est**)
CLEAN/NEAT | **1** (*especially BrE*) (of people) looking clean and neat; well dressed in fashionable and/or formal clothes: *You look very smart in that suit.* **2** (*especially BrE*) (of clothes, etc.) clean, neat and looking new and attractive: *They were wearing their smartest clothes.* ◊ *a smart car*
INTELLIGENT | **3** (*especially AmE*) intelligent: *She's smarter than her brother.* ◊ *That was a smart career move.* ◊ *OK, I admit it was not the smartest thing I ever did* (= it was a stupid thing to do). ◊ *The smart money is on Liam Neeson for best actor* (= smart people are betting on him).
FASHIONABLE | **4** (*especially BrE*) connected with fashionable rich people: *smart hotels/restaurants* ◊ *She mixes with the smart set.*
QUICK | **5** (of a movement, etc.) quick and usually done with force: *He was struck with a smart crack on the head.* ◊ *We set off at a smart pace.*
WEAPON/BOMB | **6** a very accurate weapon/bomb that is controlled by computers
▶ **smart·ly** *adv.* (*especially BrE*): *smartly dressed* ◊ *He ran off pretty smartly* (= quickly and suddenly). **smart·ness** *noun* [U]
■ *verb* [V] **1** ~ (from sth) to feel a sharp stinging pain in a part of your body: *His eyes were smarting from the smoke.* **2** ~ (from/over sth) to feel upset about a criticism, failure, etc: *They are still smarting from the 4–0 defeat last week.*

smart alec (*BrE*) (*AmE* **smart aleck**) /'smɑːt ælɪk; *AmE* 'smɑːrt/ (also **'smarty-pants**) (*BrE* also **'smart-arse**) (*AmE* also **'smart-ass**) *noun* (*informal, disapproving*) somebody who thinks they are very clever and likes to show people this in an annoying way

'smart card *noun* a small plastic card on which information is stored in electronic form

smart·en /'smɑːtn; *AmE* 'smɑːrtn/ *verb* PHRV **,smarten sb/sth↔'up|,smarten (yourself) 'up** (*especially BrE*) to make yourself, another person or a place look neater or more attractive: *The hotel has been smartened up by the new owners.*

smarts /smɑːts; *AmE* smɑːrts/ *noun* [U] (*AmE, informal*) intelligence: *She made it to the top on her smarts and hard work.*

'smarty-pants *noun* = SMART ALEC

smash /smæʃ/ *verb, noun*
■ *verb*
BREAK | **1** to break sth, or to be broken, violently and noisily into many pieces: [VN] *Several windows had been smashed.* ◊ *He smashed the radio to pieces.* ◊ [V] *The glass bowl smashed into a thousand pieces.*
HIT VERY HARD | **2** to move with a lot of force against sth solid; to make sth do this: [V, +adv./prep.] *the sound of waves smashing against the rocks* ◊ *The car smashed into a tree.* ◊ [VN] *Mark smashed his fist down on the desk.* **3** [+adv./prep.] to hit sth very hard and break it, in order to get through it: [VN] *They had to smash holes in the ice.* ◊ *The elephant smashed its way through the trees.* ◊ [VN-ADJ] *We had to smash the door open.* ◊ [V] *They had smashed through a glass door to get in.* **4** [VN] to hit sth/sb very hard: *He smashed the ball into the goal.*
DESTROY/DEFEAT | **5** [VN] to destroy, defeat or put an end to sth/sb: *Police say they have smashed a major drugs ring.* ◊ *She has smashed the world record* (= broken it by a large amount).
CRASH VEHICLE | **6** [VN] **~ sth (up)** to crash a vehicle: *He's smashed (up) his new car.*
IN TENNIS, etc. | **7** [VN] to hit a high ball downwards and very hard over the net
PHRV **,smash sth↔'down** to make sth fall down by hitting it hard and breaking it: *The police had to smash the door down.* **,smash sth↔'in** to make a hole in sth by hitting it with a lot of force: *Vandals had smashed the door in.* ◊ (*informal*) *I wanted to smash his face in* (= hit him hard in the face). **,smash sth↔'up** to destroy sth deliberately: *Youths had broken into the bar and smashed the place up.*
■ *noun*
ACT OF BREAKING | **1** [sing.] an act of breaking sth noisily into pieces; the sound this makes: *The cup hit the floor with a smash.*
VEHICLE CRASH | **2** [C] (*BrE*) an accident in which a vehicle hits another vehicle: *a car smash*
IN TENNIS, etc. | **3** [C] a way of hitting the ball downwards and very hard
SONG/MOVIE/PLAY | **4** (also **,smash 'hit**) [C] a song, film/movie or play that is very popular: *her latest chart smash*

,smash-and-'grab *adj.* [only before noun] (*BrE*) relating to the act of stealing from a shop/store by breaking a window and taking the goods you can see or reach easily: *a smash-and-grab raid*

smashed /smæʃt/ *adj.* [not before noun] (*slang*) very drunk

smash·er /'smæʃə(r)/ *noun* (*old-fashioned, BrE, informal*) a very good or attractive person or thing

smash·ing /'smæʃɪŋ/ *adj.* (*old-fashioned, BrE, informal*) very good or enjoyable: *We had a smashing time.* ◊ *You look smashing!*

smat·ter·ing /'smætərɪŋ/ *noun* [sing.] **~ (of sth)** a small amount of sth, especially knowledge of a language: *He only has a smattering of French.*

smear /smɪə(r); *AmE* smɪr/ *verb, noun*
■ *verb* **1** [VN] **~ sth on/over sth|~ sth with sth** to spread an OILY or soft substance over a surface in a rough or careless way: *The children had smeared mud on the walls.* ◊ *The children had smeared the walls with mud.* ◊ *His face was smeared with blood.* **2** [VN] to make sth dirty or GREASY: *His glasses were smeared.* ◊ *smeared windows* **3** [VN] to damage sb's reputation by saying unpleasant things about them that are not true: *The story was an attempt to smear the party leader.* **4** to rub writing, a drawing, etc. so that it is no longer clear; to become not clear in this way SYN SMUDGE: [VN] *The last few words of the letter were smeared.* [also V]
■ *noun* **1** an OILY or dirty mark: *a smear of jam/paint* **2** an untrue story about sb that is intended to damage their reputation, especially in politics: *He was a victim of a smear campaign.* **3** (*BrE*) = SMEAR TEST

æ	ɑː	e	ɜː	ə	ɪ	iː	i	ɒ	ɔː	ʌ	ʊ	u	uː
cat	father	ten	bird	about	sit	see	many	got	saw	cup	put	actual	too
											(BrE)		

'smear test (also **smear**, ˌcervical **'smear**) (all *BrE*) (*AmE* **'Pap smear**) *noun* a medical test in which a very small amount of tissue from a woman's CERVIX is removed and examined for CANCER cells

smell /smel/ *verb, noun*
▪ *verb* (**smelled, smelled**) (*BrE* also **smelt, smelt** /smelt/)
1 ~ (of sth) to have a particular smell: [V-ADJ] *The room smelt damp.* ◇ *Dinner smells good.* ◇ *a bunch of sweet-smelling flowers* ◇ [V] *His breath smelt of garlic.* ◇ *What does the perfume smell like?* **2** [no passive] (not used in the progressive tenses; often with **can** or **could**) to notice or recognize a particular smell: [VN] *He said he could smell gas when he entered the room.* ◇ *The dog had smelt a rabbit.* ◇ *I could smell alcohol on his breath.* ◇ [VN-ing] *Can you smell something burning?* [also V(that)] **3** [VN] (not usually used in the passive) to put your nose near sth and breathe in so that you can discover or identify its smell: *Smell this and tell me what you think it is.* ◇ *I bent down to smell the flowers.* **4** [V] (not used in the progressive tenses) to have an unpleasant smell: *The drains smell.* ◇ *It smells in here.* ◇ *He hadn't washed for days and was beginning to smell.* **5** [V] (not used in the progressive tenses) to be able to smell: *Can birds smell?* **6** [VN] [no passive] (*written*) to feel that sth exists or is going to happen: *He smelt danger.* ◇ *I can smell trouble.* **IDM** **come up/out of sth smelling of 'roses** (*informal*) to still have a good reputation, even though you have been involved in sth that might have given people a bad opinion of you: *Nobody ever knew the details and he came out of the deal smelling of roses.* ˌsmell a **'rat** (*informal*) to suspect that sth is wrong about a situation **PHRV** ˌsmell sb/sth ↔ 'out **1** to be aware of fear, danger, trouble, etc. in a situation: *He could always smell out fear.* **2** to find sth by smelling: *dogs trained to smell out drugs*
▪ *noun* **1** [C, U] the quality of sth that people and animals sense through their noses: *a faint/strong smell of garlic* ◇ *a sweet/fresh/musty smell* ◇ *There was a smell of burning in the air.* ◇ *The smells from the kitchen filled the room.* **2** [sing.] an unpleasant smell: *What's that smell?* ◇ *Yuk! What a smell!* **3** [U] the ability to sense things with the nose: *Dogs have a very good sense of smell.* ◇ *Taste and smell are closely connected.* **4** [C] the act of smelling sth: *He took one smell of the liquid and his eyes began to water.* **IDM** see SWEET *adj.*

VOCABULARY BUILDING
smells

Describing smells

These adjectives describe pleasant smells:
scented candles
aromatic oils
fragrant perfume
sweet-smelling flowers

To describe unpleasant smells you can use:
smelly cheese
stinking fish
musty old books
acrid smoke

Types of smell:

Pleasant smells:
the rich **aroma** of fresh coffee
a herb with a delicate **fragrance**
a rose's sweet **perfume**
the **scent** of wild flowers

Unpleasant smells:
nasty household **odours**
the **stench** of rotting meat
the **stink** of stale sweat
the **reek** of beer and tobacco

'smelling salts *noun* [pl.] a chemical with a very strong smell, kept in a small bottle, used especially in the past for putting under the nose of a person who has lost consciousness

smelly /'smeli/ *adj.* (**smell·ier, smelli·est**) (*informal*) having an unpleasant smell: *smelly feet/cheese*

smelt /smelt/ *verb* [VN] to heat and melt ORE (= rock that contains metal) in order to obtain the metal it contains: *a method of smelting iron*—see also SMELL *v.*

smelt·er /'smeltə(r)/ *noun* a piece of equipment for smelting metal

smidgen (also **smidg·eon, smid·gin**) /'smɪdʒən/ *noun* [sing.] ~ (of sth) (*informal*) a small piece or amount of sth: *'Sugar?' 'Just a smidgen.'*

smile /smaɪl/ *verb, noun*
▪ *verb* **1** [V] ~ (at sb/sth) to make a smile appear on your face: *to smile sweetly/faintly/broadly* ◇ *She smiled at him and he smiled back.* ◇ *He smiled with relief.* ◇ *He never seems to smile.* ◇ *I had to smile at* (= was amused by) *his optimism.* **2** to say or express sth with a smile: [VN] *She smiled her thanks.* ◇ [V speech] *'Perfect,' he smiled.* **3** [VN] [no passive] (*written*) to give a smile of a particular type: *to smile a slow/small/grim/knowing smile* ◇ *She smiled a smile of dry amusement.* **IDM** see EAR **PHRV** ˌsmile on **sb/sth** (*formal*) if luck, etc. **smiles on** you, you are lucky or successful
▪ *noun* the expression that you have on your face when you are happy, amused, etc. in which the corners of your mouth turn upwards: *'Oh, hello,' he said, with a smile.* ◇ *She gave a wry smile.* ◇ *He had a big smile on his face.* ◇ *I'm going to **wipe that smile off your face** (= make you stop thinking this is funny).* **IDM** **all 'smiles** looking very happy, especially soon after you have been looking worried or sad: *Twelve hours later she was all smiles again.*

smil·ing·ly /'smaɪlɪŋli/ *adv.* with a smile or smiles

smirk /smɜːk; *AmE* smɜːrk/ *verb* [V] to smile in a silly or unpleasant way that shows that you are pleased with yourself, know sth that other people do not know, etc: *It was hard not to smirk.* ◇ *He smirked unpleasantly when we told him the bad news.* ▶ **smirk** *noun*: *She had a self-satisfied smirk on her face.*

smite /smaɪt/ *verb* (**smote** /sməʊt; *AmE* smoʊt/, **smit·ten** /'smɪtn/) [VN] (*old use* or *literary*) **1** to hit sb/sth hard; to attack or punish sb **2** to have a great effect on sb, especially an unpleasant or serious one: *Suddenly my conscience smote me.*—see also SMITTEN

smith /smɪθ/ *noun* = BLACKSMITH—see also GOLDSMITH, GUNSMITH, LOCKSMITH, SILVERSMITH

smith·er·eens /ˌsmɪðə'riːnz/ *noun* [pl.] **IDM** **smash, blow, etc. sth to smithe'reens** (*informal*) to destroy sth completely by breaking it into small pieces: *The bomb blew the car to smithereens.*

smithy /'smɪði/ *noun* (*pl.* **-ies**) a place where a BLACKSMITH works

smit·ten /'smɪtn/ *adj.* [only before noun] **1** ~ (with/by sb/sth) (*especially humorous*) suddenly feeling that you are in love with sb: *From the moment they met, he was completely smitten by her.* **2** ~ with/by sth severely affected by a feeling, disease, etc: *She was suddenly smitten with remorse.*—see also SMITE

smock /smɒk; *AmE* smɑːk/ *noun* **1** a loose comfortable piece of clothing like a long shirt, worn especially by women: *a shapeless cotton smock* **2** a long loose piece of clothing worn over other clothes to protect them from dirt, etc: *The artist's smock was covered in paint.*

smog /smɒg; *AmE* smɑːg; smɔːg/ *noun* [U, C] a form of air POLLUTION that is or looks like a mixture of smoke and FOG, especially in cities: *attempts to reduce smog caused by traffic fumes*

smoke /sməʊk; *AmE* smoʊk/ *noun, verb*
▪ *noun* **1** [U] the grey, white or black gas that is produced by sth burning: *cigarette smoke* ◇ *Clouds of thick black smoke billowed from the car's exhaust.* ◇ *a smoke alarm/detector* (= a device that makes a noise if smoke is in the air to warn you of a fire) **2** [C, usually sing.] an act of smoking a cigarette: *Are you coming outside for a smoke?* **IDM** **go up in 'smoke 1** to be completely burnt: *The whole house went up in smoke.* **2** if your plans, hopes, etc. **go up in smoke**, they fail completely **(there is) no smoke without 'fire** (*BrE*) (*AmE* **where there's smoke, there's 'fire**) (*saying*) if sth bad is being said about

aɪ	aʊ	eɪ	əʊ	oʊ	ɔɪ	ɪə	eə	ʊə	j	w
my	now	say	go	go	boy	near	hair	pure	yes	wet
			(BrE)	(AmE)						

sb/sth, it usually has some truth in it **a smoke-filled 'room** (*disapproving*) a decision that people describe as being made in **a smoke-filled room** is made by a small group of people at a private meeting, rather than in an open and DEMOCRATIC way

■ *verb* **1** to suck smoke from a cigarette, pipe, etc. into your mouth and let it out again: [VN] *He was smoking a large cigar.* ◊ *How many cigarettes do you smoke a day?* ◊ [V] *Do you mind if I smoke?* **2** [V] to use cigarettes, etc. in this way as a habit: *Do you smoke?* ◊ *She smokes heavily.* **3** [V] to produce smoke: *smoking factory chimneys* ◊ *the smoking remains of burnt-out cars* ◊ *This fireplace smokes badly* (= sends smoke into the room instead of up the chimney). **4** [VN] [usually passive] to preserve meat or fish by hanging it in smoke from wood fires to give it a special taste: *smoked salmon/mackerel/cheese* PHRV **,smoke sb/sth↔'out 1** to force sb/sth to come out of a place by filling it with smoke: *to smoke out wasps from a nest* **2** to take action to discover where sb is hiding or to make a secret publicly known: *The police are determined to smoke out the leaders of the gang.*

'smoke bomb *noun* a bomb that produces clouds of smoke when it explodes

'smoke-free *adj.* free from cigarette smoke; where smoking is not allowed: *a smoke-free working environment*

smoke·less /'sməʊkləs; AmE 'smoʊk-/ *adj.* [usually before noun] **1** able to burn without producing smoke: *smokeless fuels* **2** free from smoke: *a smokeless zone* (= where smoke from factories or houses is not allowed)

smoker /'sməʊkə(r); AmE 'smoʊk-/ *noun* a person who smokes tobacco regularly: *a heavy smoker* (= sb who smokes a lot) ◊ *a smoker's cough* ◊ *a cigarette/cigar/pipe smoker* OPP NON-SMOKER

smoke·screen /'sməʊkskri:n; AmE 'smoʊk-/ *noun* **1** something that you do or say in order to hide what you are really doing or intending **2** a cloud of smoke used to hide soldiers, ships, etc. during a battle

smoke·stack /'sməʊkstæk; AmE 'smoʊk-/ *noun* (*especially AmE*) **1** a tall chimney that takes away smoke from factories **2** = FUNNEL

smok·ing /'sməʊkɪŋ; AmE 'smoʊk-/ *noun* the activity or habit of smoking cigarettes, etc: *No Smoking* (for example, on a notice) ◊ *He's trying to give up smoking.*

'smoking jacket *noun* a man's comfortable jacket worn in the past, often made of VELVET

smoky /'sməʊki; AmE 'smoʊki/ *adj.* (**smoki·er, smoki·est**) **1** full of smoke: *a smoky atmosphere* ◊ *a smoky pub/restaurant* **2** producing a lot of smoke: *smoky chimneys/fires* **3** tasting or smelling like smoke: *This wine has a slightly smoky flavour.* **4** having the colour or appearance of smoke: *smoky blue glass*

smol·der (*AmE*) = SMOULDER

smooch /smu:tʃ/ *verb* [V] (*informal*) to kiss and hold sb closely, especially when you are dancing slowly

smooth /smu:ð/ *adj., verb*

■ *adj.* (**smooth·er, smooth·est**)
  FLAT/EVEN | **1** completely flat and even, without any lumps, holes or rough areas: *a lotion to make your skin feel soft and smooth* ◊ *The water was as smooth as glass.* ◊ *a paint that gives a smooth, silky finish* ◊ *Over the years, the stone steps had worn smooth.* OPP ROUGH
  WITHOUT LUMPS | **2** (of a liquid mixture) without any lumps: *Mix the flour with the milk to form a smooth paste.*
  WITHOUT PROBLEMS | **3** happening or continuing without any problems: *They are introducing new measures to ensure the smooth running of the business.* ◊ *They could not ensure the smooth transfer of political power.*
  MOVEMENT | **4** even and regular, without sudden stops and starts: *The car's improved suspension gives you a smoother ride.* ◊ *The plane made a smooth landing.* ◊ *She swung herself over the gate in one smooth movement.*
  MAN | **5** (often *disapproving*) (of people, especially men, and their behaviour) very polite and pleasant, but in a way that is often not very sincere: *I don't like him. He's far too smooth for me.* ◊ *He's something of a smooth operator.*

DRINK/TASTE | **6** pleasant and not bitter: *This coffee has a smooth, rich taste.*

VOICE/MUSIC | **7** pleasant to hear, and without any harsh sounds: *a smooth flowing melody*

▶ **smooth·ness** *noun* [U]: *the smoothness of her skin* ◊ *They admired the smoothness and efficiency with which the business was run.* IDM see ROUGH *n.*

■ *verb* **1** ~ sth (**back/down/out**) to make sth smooth: [VN] *rocks smoothed by the sea* ◊ *He smoothed his hair back.* ◊ *She was smoothing out the creases in her skirt.* ◊ [VN-ADJ] *He took the letter and smoothed it flat on the table.* **2** ~ sth **on/into/over sth** to put a layer of a soft substance over a surface: *Smooth the icing over the top of the cake.* IDM **smooth the 'path/'way** to make it easier for sb/sth to develop or make progress: *These negotiations are intended to smooth the path to a peace treaty.* **smooth (sb's) ruffled 'feathers** to make sb feel less angry or offended PHRV **,smooth sth↔a'way/'out** to make problems or difficulties disappear: *Any differences between the groups were soon smoothed away.* **,smooth sth↔'over** to make problems or difficulties seem less important or serious, especially by talking to people: *She spoke to both sides in the dispute in an attempt to smooth things over.*

smoothie /'smu:ði/ *noun* **1** (*informal*) a man who dresses well and talks very politely and confidently but who is often not honest or sincere **2** (*AmE, AustralE*) a drink made of fruit or fruit juice mixed with milk or ice cream

smooth·ly /'smu:ðli/ *adv.* **1** in an even way, without suddenly stopping and starting again: *Traffic is now flowing smoothly again.* ◊ *The engine was running smoothly.* **2** without problems or difficulties: *The interview went smoothly.* **3** in a calm or confident way: *'Would you like to come this way?' he said smoothly.* **4** in a way that produces a smooth surface or mixture: *a smoothly polished table* ◊ *The colours blend smoothly together.*

,smooth-'talking *adj.* (usually *disapproving*) talking very politely and confidently, especially to persuade sb to do sth, but in a way that may not be honest or sincere: *a smooth-talking lawyer*

smor·gas·bord /'smɔːɡəsbɔːd; AmE 'smɔːrɡəsbɔːrd/ *noun* [U, sing.] (from *Swedish*) a meal at which you serve yourself from a large range of hot and cold dishes

smote *pt* of SMITE

smother /'smʌðə(r)/ *verb* [VN] **1** ~ sb (**with sth**) to kill sb by covering their face so that they cannot breathe: *He smothered the baby with a pillow.* **2** ~ sth/sb **with/in sth** to cover sth/sb thickly or with too much of sth: *a rich dessert smothered in cream* ◊ *She smothered him with kisses.* **3** to prevent sth from developing or being expressed SYN STIFLE: *to smother a yawn/giggle/grin* ◊ *The voices of the opposition were effectively smothered.* **4** to give sb too much love or protection so that they feel restricted: *Her husband was very loving, but she felt smothered.* **5** to make a fire stop burning by covering it with sth: *He tried to smother the flames with a blanket.*

smoul·der (*BrE*) (*AmE* **smol·der**) /'sməʊldə(r); AmE 'smoʊ-/ *verb* [V] **1** to burn slowly without a flame: *The bonfire was still smouldering the next day.* ◊ *a smouldering cigarette* ◊ (*figurative*) *The feud smouldered on for years.* **2** (*written*) to be filled with a strong emotion that you do not fully express: *His eyes smouldered with anger.* ◊ *Anger smouldered in his eyes.*

smudge /smʌdʒ/ *noun, verb*

■ *noun* a dirty mark with no clear shape: *a smudge of lipstick on a cup*

■ *verb* **1** to touch or rub sth, especially wet ink or paint, so that it is no longer clear; to become not clear in this way: [VN] *He had smudged his signature with his sleeve.* ◊ *Tears had smudged her mascara.* ◊ [V] *Her lipstick had smudged.* **2** [VN] to make a dirty mark on a surface: *The mirror was smudged with fingerprints.*

smudgy /'smʌdʒi/ *adj.* **1** with dirty marks on **2** (of a picture, writing, etc.) with edges that are not clear SYN BLURRED

smug /smʌɡ/ *adj.* (*disapproving*) looking or feeling too

b	d	f	g	h	k	l	m	n	p	r
bad	did	fall	get	hat	cat	leg	man	now	pen	red

pleased about sth you have done or achieved: *a smug expression/smile/face* ◊ *What are you looking so smug about?* ▶ **smug·ly** *adv.* **smug·ness** *noun* [U]

smug·gle /ˈsmʌgl/ *verb* [VN] [usually+*adv./prep.*] to take, send or bring goods or people secretly and illegally into or out of a country, etc: *They were caught smuggling diamonds into the country.* ◊ *He managed to smuggle a gun into the prison.* ◊ *smuggled drugs*

smug·gler /ˈsmʌglə(r)/ *noun* a person who takes goods into or out of a country illegally

smug·gling /ˈsmʌglɪŋ/ *noun* [U] the crime of taking, sending or bringing goods secretly and illegally into or out of a country: *drug smuggling*

smut /smʌt/ *noun* **1** [U] (*informal*) stories, pictures or comments about sex that deal with it in a way that some people find offensive **2** [C, U] dirt, ash, etc. that causes a black mark on sth; a black mark made by this

smutty /ˈsmʌti/ *adj.* [usually before noun] (*informal*) (of stories, pictures and comments) dealing with sex in a way that some people find offensive: *smutty jokes*

snack /snæk/ *noun, verb*
■ *noun* (*informal*) a small meal or amount of food, usually eaten in a hurry: *a mid-morning snack* ◊ *I only have time for a snack at lunchtime.* ◊ *Do you serve bar snacks?* ◊ *a snack lunch*
■ *verb* [V] **~ on sth** to eat snacks between or instead of main meals: *It's healthier to snack on fruit rather than chocolate.*

'snack bar *noun* a place where you can buy a small quick meal, such as a sandwich

snaf·fle /ˈsnæfl/ *verb* [VN] (*BrE, informal*) to take sth quickly for yourself, especially before anyone else has had the time or opportunity

snafu /snæˈfuː/ *noun* [sing.] (*AmE, informal*) a situation in which nothing happens as planned: *It was another bureaucratic snafu.*

snag /snæg/ *noun, verb*
■ *noun* **1** a problem or difficulty, especially one that is small, hidden or unexpected: *There is just one small snag—where is the money coming from?* ◊ *Let me know if you run into any snags.* **2** an object or a part of an object that is rough or sharp and may cut sth
■ *verb* (-gg-) **1 ~ (sth) (on/in sth)** to catch or tear sth on sth rough or sharp; to become caught or torn in this way: [VN] *I snagged my sweater on the wire fence.* ◊ *The fence snagged my sweater.* ◊ [V] *The nets snagged on some rocks.* **2** (*AmE, informal*) to succeed in getting sth quickly, often before other people: *I snagged a ride from Joe.*

snail /sneɪl/ *noun* a small soft creature with a hard round shell on its back, that moves very slowly and often eats garden plants. Some types of snail can be eaten.—picture on page A7 **IDM at a 'snail's pace** very slowly

'snail mail *noun* [U] (*informal, humorous*) used especially by people who use e-mail on computers to describe the system of sending letters by ordinary mail

snake /sneɪk/ *noun, verb*
■ *noun* a reptile with a very long thin body and no legs. There are many types of snake, some of which are poisonous: *a snake coiled up in the grass* ◊ *Venomous snakes spit and hiss when they are cornered.* **IDM a ,snake (in the 'grass)** (*disapproving*) a person who pretends to be your friend but who cannot be trusted
■ *verb* [+*adv./prep.*] (*written*) to move like a snake, in long twisting curves; to go in a particular direction in long twisting curves: [V] *The road snaked away into the distance.* ◊ [VN] *The procession snaked its way through narrow streets.*

snake·bite /ˈsneɪkbaɪt/ *noun* [C, U] a wound that you get when a poisonous snake bites you

'snake charmer *noun* an entertainer who seems to be able to control snakes and make them move by playing music to them

,snakes and 'ladders (*BrE*) (*AmE* ,Chutes and 'Ladders*) ™ *noun* [U] a children's game played on a special board with pictures of snakes and ladders on it. Players move their pieces up the ladders to go forward and down the snakes to go back.

snake·skin /ˈsneɪkskɪn/ *noun* [U] the skin of a snake, used for making expensive shoes, bags, etc.

snap /snæp/ *verb, noun, adj., exclamation*
■ *verb* (-pp-)
BREAK | **1 ~ (sth) (off)** to break sth suddenly with a sharp noise; to be broken in this way: [VN] *The wind had snapped the tree in two.* ◊ *He snapped a twig off a bush.* ◊ [V] *Suddenly, the rope snapped.* ◊ *The branch she was standing on must have snapped off.*
OPEN/CLOSE/MOVE INTO POSITION | **2** [usually+*adv./prep.*] to move, or to move sth, into a particular position quickly, especially with a sudden sharp noise: [V-ADJ] *The lid snapped shut.* ◊ *His eyes snapped open.* ◊ [V] *He snapped to attention and saluted.* ◊ [VN-ADJ] *She snapped the bag shut.*
SPEAK IMPATIENTLY | **3 ~ (at sb)** to speak or say sth in an impatient, usually angry, voice: [V speech] *'Don't just stand there,' she snapped.* ◊ [V] *I was tempted to snap back angrily at him.* ◊ [VN] *He snapped a reply.*
OF ANIMAL | **4** [V] **~ (at sb/sth)** to try to bite sb/sth: *The dogs snarled and snapped at our heels.*
TAKE PHOTOGRAPH | **5** (*informal*) to take a photograph: [VN] *A passing tourist snapped the incident.* ◊ [V] *She seemed oblivious to the crowds of photographers snapping away.*
LOSE CONTROL | **6** [V] to suddenly be unable to control your feelings any longer because the situation has become too difficult: *My patience finally snapped.* ◊ *When he said that, something snapped inside her.* ◊ *And that did it. I snapped.*
FASTEN CLOTHING | **7** [V, VN] (*AmE*) to fasten a piece of clothing with a snap
IDM snap your 'fingers to make a sharp noise by moving your second or third finger quickly against your thumb, to attract sb's attention, or to mark the beat of music, for example: *He snapped his fingers for the waiter to bring more wine.* **,snap 'out of it/sth | ,snap sb 'out of it/sth** [no passive] (*informal*) to make an effort to stop feeling unhappy or depressed; to help sb to stop feeling unhappy: *You've been depressed for weeks. It's time you snapped out of it.* **,snap 'to it** (*informal*) used, especially in orders, to tell sb to start working harder or more quickly—more at HEAD *n.*
PHRV ,snap sth↔'out to say sth in a sharp unpleasant way: *The sergeant snapped out an order.* **,snap sth↔'up** to buy or obtain sth quickly because it is cheap or you want it very much: *All the best bargains were snapped up within hours.* ◊ (*figurative*) *She's been snapped up by Hollywood to star in two major movies.*
■ *noun*
SHARP NOISE | **1** [C] a sudden sharp noise, especially one made by sth closing or breaking: *She closed her purse with a snap.* ◊ *the snap of a twig*
PHOTOGRAPH | **2** (also **snap·shot**) [C] a photograph, especially one taken quickly: *She showed us her holiday snaps.*
CARD GAME | **3** (**Snap**) [U] a card game in which players take turns to put cards down and try to be the first to call out 'snap' when two similar cards are put down together
FASTENER | **4** (*AmE*) = PRESS STUD
—see also BRANDY SNAP, COLD SNAP
IDM be a 'snap (*AmE, informal*) to be very easy to do: *This job's a snap.*
■ *adj.* [only before noun] made or done quickly and without careful thought or preparation: *a snap decision/election*
■ *exclamation* **1** you say **snap!** in the card game called 'Snap' when two cards that are the same are put down **2** (*BrE, spoken*) people say **snap!** to show that they are surprised when two things are the same: *Snap! I've just bought that CD too!*

snap·dragon /ˈsnæpdrægən/ *noun* a small garden plant with red, white, yellow or pink flowers that open and shut like a mouth when squeezed

snap·per /ˈsnæpə(r)/ *noun* **1** [C, U] a fish that lives in warm seas and is used for food **2** [C] (*informal*) a photographer, especially one who takes pictures of famous people for newspapers and magazines

snappy /ˈsnæpi/ *adj.* (**snap·pier**, **snap·pi·est**) **1** (of a remark, title, etc.) clever or amusing and short: *a snappy headline/title/slogan* ◊ *a snappy answer/remark* **2** [usu-

s	t	v	z	ʃ	ʒ	tʃ	dʒ	θ	ð	ŋ
see	tea	van	zoo	shoe	vision	chain	jam	thin	this	sing

ally before noun] (*informal*) attractive and fashionable: *a snappy outfit* ◊ *She's a snappy dresser.* **3** (of people or their behaviour) tending to speak to people in a bad-tempered, impatient way: *Interruptions make her snappy and nervous.* **4** lively; quick: *a snappy tune* ◊ *a snappy tennis player* ▸ **snap·pily** *adv.*: *He summarized the speech snappily.* ◊ *snappily dressed* ◊ *'What?' she asked snappily.* **snap·pi·ness** *noun* [U] **IDM** ,**make it 'snappy** (*informal*) used to tell sb to do sth quickly or to hurry

snap·shot /'snæpʃɒt; *AmE* -ʃɑːt/ *noun* **1** = SNAP: *snapshots of the children* **2** [usually sing.] a short description or a small amount of information that gives you an idea of what sth is like

snare /sneə(r); *AmE* sner/ *noun, verb*
■ *noun* **1** a device used for catching small animals and birds, especially one that holds their leg so that they cannot escape **2** (*formal*) a situation which seems attractive but is unpleasant and difficult to escape from: *City life can be full of snares for young people.*
■ *verb* [VN] to catch sth, especially an animal, in a snare: *to snare a rabbit* ◊ (*figurative*) *Her one thought was to snare a rich husband.* ◊ (*figurative*) *He found himself snared in a web of intrigue.*

'**snare drum** *noun* a small drum with metal strings across one side that make a continuous sound when the drum is hit—picture on page 841

snarl /snɑːl; *AmE* snɑːrl/ *verb, noun*
■ *verb* **1** [V] **~ (at sb/sth)** (of dogs, etc.) to show the teeth and make a deep angry noise in the throat: *The dog snarled at us.* **2 ~ (sth) (at sb)** to speak in an angry or bad tempered way: [Vspeech] *'Get out of here!' he snarled.* ◊ [VN] *She snarled abuse at anyone who happened to walk past.* **PHRV** ,**snarl 'up**| ,**snarl sth⟷'up** to involve sb/sth in a situation that stops their movement or progress; to become involved in a situation like this: *The sheets kept getting snarled up.* ◊ *The accident snarled up the traffic all day.*—related noun SNARL-UP
■ *noun* **1** [usually sing.] a deep sound that an animal makes when it is angry and shows its teeth: *The dog bared its teeth in a snarl.* **2** [usually sing.] an act of speaking in an angry or bad-tempered way; the sound you make when you are angry, in pain, etc: *a snarl of pain/hate* ◊ *She answered with an angry snarl.* **3** = SNARL-UP: *rush-hour traffic snarls* **4** (*informal*) something that has become twisted in an untidy way: *She used conditioner to remove the snarls from her hair.*

'**snarl-up** (also **snarl**) *noun* (*BrE, informal*) a situation in which traffic is unable to move

snatch /snætʃ/ *verb, noun*
■ *verb* **1** [usually +adv. / prep.] to take sth quickly and often rudely or roughly: [VN] *She managed to snatch the gun from his hand.* ◊ *Gordon snatched up his jacket and left the room.* ◊ [V] *Hey, you kids! Don't all snatch!* **2** [VN] to take sb/sth away from a person or place, especially by force; to steal sth: *The raiders snatched $100 from the cash register.* ◊ *The baby was snatched from its parents' car.* **3** [VN] to take or get sth quickly, especially because you do not have much time: *I managed to snatch an hour's sleep.* ◊ *The team snatched a dramatic victory in the last minute of the game.* **PHRV** '**snatch at sth 1** to try to take hold of sth with your hands: *He snatched at the steering wheel but I pushed him away.* ◊ (*figurative*) *The wind snatched at our clothes.* **2** to take an opportunity to do sth: *We snatched at every moment we could be together.*
■ *noun* **1** a very small part of a conversation or some music that you hear **SYN** SNIPPET: *a snatch of music* ◊ *I only caught snatches of the conversation.* **2** an act of moving your hand very quickly to take or steal sth: *a bag/cash snatch* ◊ *to make a snatch at sth* **IDM** **in** '**snatches** for short periods rather than continuously: *Sleep came to him in brief snatches.*

snatch·er /'snætʃə(r)/ *noun* (often in compounds) a person who takes sth quickly with their hand and steals it: *a handbag/purse snatcher*

snazzy /'snæzi/ *adj.* (**snaz·zier, snaz·zi·est**) (*informal*) (of clothes, cars, etc.) fashionable, bright and modern, and attracting your attention: *a snazzy suit/car*

sneak /sniːk/ *verb, noun, adj.*
■ *verb* **HELP** The usual past form is **sneaked**, but **snuck** is now very common in informal speech in *AmE* and some people use it in *BrE* too. However, many people consider it incorrect and it should not be used in formal writing. **1** [V+adv. / prep.] to go somewhere secretly, trying to avoid being seen: *What are you doing sneaking around out there?* **2** to do sth or take sb/sth somewhere secretly, often without permission: [VN] *We sneaked a look at her private diary.* ◊ *I was caught sneaking my kitten into the school.* ◊ [VN, VNN] *I managed to sneak a note to him.* ◊ *I managed to sneak him a note.* **3** [VN] (*informal*) to secretly take sth small or unimportant: *I sneaked a cake when they were out of the room.* **4** [V] **~ (on sb) (to sb)** (*old-fashioned, BrE, disapproving*) to tell an adult that another child has done sth wrong, especially in order to cause trouble **SYN** SNITCH: *Did you sneak on me to the teacher?* **PHRV** ,**sneak 'up (on sb/sth)** to move towards sb very quietly so that they do not see or hear you until you reach them: *He sneaked up on his sister and shouted 'Boo!'.*
■ *noun* (*old-fashioned, BrE, disapproving*) a person, especially a child, who tells sb about sth wrong that another person has done **SYN** SNITCH
■ *adj.* [only before noun] done without any warning: *a sneak attack/raid*

sneak·er /'sniːkə(r)/ *noun* (*AmE*) = TRAINER: *He wore old jeans and a pair of sneakers.*

sneak·ing /'sniːkɪŋ/ *adj.* [only before noun] if you have a **sneaking** feeling for sb or about sth, you do not want to admit it to other people, because you feel embarrassed, or you are not sure that this feeling is right: *She had always had a sneaking affection for him.* ◊ *I have a sneaking suspicion that she knows more than she's telling us.*

,**sneak 'preview** *noun* an opportunity to see sth before it is officially shown to the public

'**sneak thief** *noun* a person who steals things without using force or breaking doors or windows

sneaky /'sniːki/ *adj.* (*informal*) behaving in a secret and sometimes dishonest or unpleasant way: *I took a sneaky glance at my watch.* ◊ *That was a sneaky trick to play!* ▸ **sneak·ily** /'sniːkɪli/ *adv.*

sneer /snɪə(r); *AmE* snɪr/ *verb, noun*
■ *verb* **~ (at sb/sth)** to show that you have no respect for sb by the expression on your face or by the way you speak: [V] *He sneered at people who liked pop music.* ◊ *a sneering comment/smile/laugh* ◊ *'You? A writer?' she sneered.* ▸ **sneer·ing·ly** /'snɪərɪŋli; *AmE* 'snɪr-/ *adv.*
■ *noun* [usually sing.] an unpleasant look, smile or comment that shows you do not respect sb/sth

sneeze /sniːz/ *verb, noun*
■ *verb* [V] to have air come suddenly and noisily out through your nose and mouth in a way that you cannot control, for example because you have a cold: *I've been sneezing all morning.*—picture on page 599 **IDM** **not to be 'sneezed at** (*informal*) good enough to be accepted or considered seriously: *In those days, $20 was not a sum to be sneezed at.*
■ *noun* the act of sneezing or the noise you make when you sneeze: *coughs and sneezes* ◊ *She gave a violent sneeze.*

snicker /'snɪkə(r)/ *verb* [V] (*especially AmE*) = SNIGGER ▸ **snicker** *noun*

snide /snaɪd/ *adj.* (*informal*) criticizing sb/sth in an unkind and indirect way: *snide comments/remarks*

sniff /snɪf/ *verb, noun*
■ *verb* **1** [V] to breathe air in through your nose in a way that makes a sound, especially when you are crying, have a cold, etc: *We all had colds and couldn't stop sniffing and sneezing.* **2 ~ (at) (sth)** to breathe air in through the nose in order to discover or enjoy the smell of sth: [VN] *sniffing the fresh morning air* ◊ *to sniff glue* ◊ [V] *The dog sniffed at my shoes.*—see also GLUE-SNIFFING **3** to say sth in a complaining or disapproving way: [Vspeech] *'It's hardly what I'd call elegant,' she sniffed.* [alsoV, VN] **IDM** **not to be 'sniffed at** (*informal*) good enough to be accepted or considered seriously: *In those days, $20 was not a sum to be sniffed at.* **PHRV** ,**sniff a'round/'round** (*informal*) to try to find out information about sb/sth, especially secret

S

æ	ɑː	e	ɜː	ə	ɪ	iː	i	ɒ	ɔː	ʌ	ʊ	u	uː
cat	father	ten	bird	about	sit	see	many	got	saw	cup	put	actual	too

(BrE)

information: *We don't want journalists sniffing around.* '**sniff around/round sb** [no passive] (*especially BrE*) to try to get sb as a lover, employee, etc: *Hollywood agents have been sniffing around him.* '**sniff at sth** to show no interest in or respect for sth: *He sniffed at my efforts at writing.* ,**sniff sb/sth↔'out 1** to discover or find sb/sth by using your sense of smell: *The dogs are trained to ˌsniff out drugs.* **2** (*informal*) to discover or find sb/sth by looking: *Journalists are good at sniffing out a scandal.*
- *noun* **1** [C] an act or the sound of sniffing: *She took a deep sniff of the perfume.* ◊ *My mother gave a sniff of disapproval.* ◊ *His sobs soon turned to sniffs.* **2** [sing.] **~ of** an idea of what sth is like or that sth is going to happen: *The sniff of power went to his head.* ◊ *They make threats but back down at the first sniff of trouble.* **3** [sing.] **~ of** sth a small chance of sth: *She didn't get even a sniff at a medal.* **IDM** **have a (good) ˌsniff aˈround** to examine a place carefully

'**sniffer dog** *noun* (*informal, especially BrE*) a dog that is trained to find drugs or explosives by smell

snif·fle /'snɪfl/ *verb, noun*
- *verb* [V, Vspeech] to sniff or keep sniffing, especially because you are crying or have a cold
- *noun* an act or the sound of sniffling: *After a while, her sniffles died away.* **IDM** **get, have, etc. the ˈsniffles** (*informal*) to get, have, etc. a slight cold

sniffy /'snɪfi/ *adj.* **~ (about sth)** (*informal*) not approving of sth/sb because you think they are not good enough for you

snif·ter /'snɪftə(r)/ *noun* **1** (*especially AmE*) a large glass used for drinking BRANDY **2** (*old-fashioned, BrE, informal*) a small amount of a strong alcoholic drink

snig·ger /'snɪgə(r)/ *verb, noun*
- *verb* (*BrE*) (also **snicker** *AmE, BrE*) **~ (at sb/sth)** to laugh in a quiet unpleasant way, especially at sth rude or at sb's problems or mistakes: [V] *What are you sniggering at?* [also V speech]
- *noun* (*BrE*) (also **snicker** *AmE, BrE*) a quiet unpleasant laugh, especially at sth rude or at sb's problems or mistakes

snip /snɪp/ *verb, noun*
- *verb* (-pp-) **~ (at/through) sth** to cut sth with scissors using short quick strokes: [VN] *Snip a tiny hole in the paper.* ◊ [V] *She snipped at the loose threads hanging down.* **PHRV** ,**snip sth↔'off** to remove sth by cutting it with scissors in short quick strokes: *Snip off the end of the tube.*
- *noun* **1** [C] an act of cutting sth with scissors; the sound that this makes: *Make a series of small snips along the edge of the fabric.* ◊ *Snip, snip, went the scissors.* **2** (**snips**) [pl.] a tool like large scissors, used for cutting metal **3** (**a snip**) [sing.] (*BrE, informal*) a thing that is cheap and good value: *It's a snip at only £25.*

snipe /snaɪp/ *verb, noun*
- *verb* [V] **~ (at sb/sth) 1** to shoot at sb from a hiding place, usually from a distance: *Gunmen continued to snipe at people leaving their homes to find food.* **2** to criticize sb in an unpleasant way ▶ **snip·ing** *noun* [U]: *Aid workers remain in the area despite continuous sniping.*
- *noun* (*pl.* **snipe**) a bird with a long straight beak that lives on wet ground

sniper /'snaɪpə(r)/ *noun* a person who shoots at sb from a hidden position

snip·pet /'snɪpɪt/ *noun* **1** a small piece of information or news: *Have you got any interesting snippets for me?* ◊ *a snippet of information/gossip* **2** a short piece of a conversation, piece of music, etc. **SYN** SNATCH, EXTRACT

snippy /'snɪpi/ *adj.* (*AmE, informal*) rude; not showing respect

snitch /snɪtʃ/ *verb* [V] **~ (on sb) (to sb)** (*informal, disapproving*) to tell a parent, teacher, etc. about sth wrong that another child has done **SYN** SNEAK: *Johnnie snitched on me to his mom.* ▶ **snitch** *noun*: *You little snitch! I'll never tell you anything again!*

snivel /'snɪvl/ *verb* (-ll-, *AmE* -l-) [V] to cry and complain in a way that people think is annoying

sniv·el·ling (*BrE*) (*AmE* **sniv·el·ing**) /'snɪvlɪŋ/ *adj.* [only before noun] (*disapproving*) tending to cry or complain a lot in a way that annoys people: *a snivelling little brat*

snob /snɒb; *AmE* snɑːb/ *noun* (*disapproving*) **1** a person who admires people in the higher social classes too much and has no respect for people in the lower social classes: *She's such a snob!* **2** a person who thinks they are much better than other people because they are intelligent or like things that many people do not like: *an intellectual snob* ◊ *a food/wine snob* ◊ *There is a* **snob value** *in driving the latest model.*

snob·bery /'snɒbəri; *AmE* 'snɑːb-/ *noun* [U] (*disapproving*) the attitudes and behaviour of people who are snobs: *cultural/intellectual snobbery*—see also INVERTED SNOBBERY

snob·bish /'snɒbɪʃ; *AmE* 'snɑːb-/ (also *informal* **snobby** /'snɒbi; *AmE* 'snɑːbi/) *adj.* (*disapproving*) thinking that having a high social class is very important; feeling that you are better than other people because you are more intelligent or like things that many people do not like ▶ **snob·bish·ness** *noun* [U]

snog /snɒg; *AmE* snɑːg; snɔːg/ *verb* (-gg-) (*BrE, informal*) (of two people) to kiss each other, especially for a long time: [V] *They were snogging on the sofa.* ◊ [VN] *I caught him snogging my friend.* ▶ **snog** *noun* [sing.]

snook /snuːk/ *noun* **IDM** see COCK *v.*

snook·er /'snuːkə(r)/ *noun, verb*
- *noun* **1** [U] a game for two people played on a long table covered with green fabric. Players use CUES (= long sticks) to hit a white ball against other balls (15 red and 6 of other colours) in order to get the coloured balls into pockets at the edge of the table, in a particular set order: *a snooker player/table*—compare BILLIARDS, POOL **2** [C] a position in snooker in which one player has made it very difficult for the opponent to play a shot within the rules
- *verb* [VN] [usually passive] **1** (in the game of snooker) to have your opponent in a snooker(2) **2** (*BrE, informal*) to make it impossible for sb to do sth, especially sth they want to do: *Any plans I'd had for the weekend were by now well and truly snookered.* **3** (*AmE, informal*) to deceive or trick sb

snoop /snuːp/ *verb, noun*
- *verb* [V] **~ (around/round sth)| ~ (on sb)** (*informal, disapproving*) to find out private things about sb, especially by looking secretly around a place: *Someone's been snooping around my apartment.* ◊ *journalists snooping on politicians* ▶ **snoop·er** *noun* = SNOOP
- *noun* **1** (also **snoop·er**) a person who looks around a place secretly to find out private things about sb **2** [sing.] a secret look around a place: *He had a snoop around her office.*

snooty /'snuːti/ (also *informal* **snotty**) *adj.* (*disapproving*) treating people as if they are not as good or as important as you ▶ **snooti·ness** *noun* [U]

snooze /snuːz/ *verb* [V] (*informal*) to have a short light sleep, especially during the day and usually not in bed: *My brother was snoozing on the sofa.* ▶ **snooze** *noun* [sing.]: *I often have a snooze after lunch.*

snore /snɔː(r)/ *verb, noun*
- *verb* [V] to breathe noisily through your nose and mouth while you are asleep: *I could hear Paul snoring in the next room.* ▶ **snorer** *noun* **snor·ing** *noun* [U]: *heavy/loud/gentle snoring*
- *noun* noisy breathing while you are asleep: *She lay awake listening to his snores.*

snor·kel /'snɔːkl; *AmE* 'snɔːrkl/ *noun* a tube that you can breathe air through when you are swimming under the surface of the water ▶ **snor·kel** *verb* [V]

snor·kel·ling (*BrE*) (*AmE* **snor·kel·ing**) /'snɔːkəlɪŋ; *AmE* 'snɔːrk-/ *noun* [U] the sport or activity of swimming underwater with a snorkel: *to go snorkelling*

snort /snɔːt; *AmE* snɔːrt/ *verb, noun*
- *verb* **1** to make a loud sound by breathing air out noisily through your nose, especially to show that you are angry or amused: [V] *to snort with laughter/annoyance* ◊ *She snorted in disgust.* ◊ *The horse snorted and tossed its head.* ◊ [V speech] *'You!' he snorted contemptuously.* **2** [VN]

aɪ	aʊ	eɪ	əʊ	oʊ	ɔɪ	ɪə	eə	ʊə	j	w
my	now	say	go	go	boy	near	hair	pure	yes	wet
			(BrE)	(AmE)						

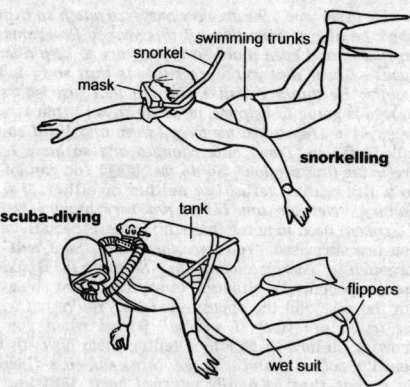

snorkel

swimming trunks

mask

snorkelling

scuba-diving

tank

flippers

wet suit

snowboarder

snowboard

(*slang*) to take drugs by breathing them in through the nose: *to snort cocaine*

■ *noun* **1** a loud sound that you make by breathing air out noisily through your nose, especially to show that you are angry or amused: *to give a snort of disgust / laughter / derision* ◊ *I could hear the snort and stamp of a horse.* **2** (*slang*) a small amount of a drug that is breathed in through the nose; an act of taking a drug in this way: *to take a snort of cocaine*

snot /snɒt; *AmE* snɑːt/ *noun* [U] (*informal*) a word that some people find offensive, used to describe the liquid substance (= MUCUS) that is produced in the nose

snotty /ˈsnɒti; *AmE* ˈsnɑːti/ (also ˌsnotty-ˈnosed) *adj.* (*informal*) **1** = SNOOTY **2** full of or covered in snot: *a snotty nose* ◊ *snotty kids*

snout /snaʊt/ *noun* **1** the long nose and area around the mouth of some types of animal, such as a pig—compare MUZZLE—picture on page A6 **2** (*informal, humorous*) a person's nose **3** a part of sth that sticks out at the front: *the snout of a pistol*

snow /snəʊ; *AmE* snoʊ/ *noun, verb*
■ *noun* **1** [U] small soft white pieces, (called FLAKES), of frozen water that fall from the sky in cold weather; this substance when it is lying on the ground: *Snow was falling heavily.* ◊ *We had snow in May this year.* ◊ *The snow was beginning to melt.* ◊ *Children were playing in the snow.* ◊ *20 cm of snow was / were expected today.* ◊ *The snow didn't settle* (= stay on the ground). ◊ *Her skin was as white as snow.* **2** (snows) [pl.] (*literary*) an amount of snow that falls in one particular place or at one particular time: *the first snows of winter* ◊ *the snows of Everest* **IDM** **as clean, pure, etc. as the driven 'snow** extremely clean, pure, etc.
■ *verb* **1** [V] when **it snows**, snow falls from the sky: *It's been snowing heavily all day.* ◊ *It snowed for three days without stopping.* **2** [VN] (*AmE, informal*) to impress sb a lot by the things you say, especially if these are not true or not sincere: *He really snowed me with all his talk of buying a Porsche.* **IDM** **be snowed 'in / 'up** to be unable to leave a place because of heavy snow **be snowed 'under (with sth)** to have more things, especially work, than you feel able to deal with: *I'd love to come but I'm completely snowed under at the moment.* **be snowed 'up** (especially of a road) to be blocked with snow

snow-ball /ˈsnəʊbɔːl; *AmE* ˈsnoʊ-/ *noun, verb*
■ *noun* **1** [C] a ball that you make out of snow to throw at sb/sth in a game: *a snowball fight* **2** [sing.] (often used as an adjective) a situation that develops more and more quickly as it continues: *All this publicity has had a snowball effect on the sales of their latest album.* **IDM** **not have a ˌsnowball's chance in 'hell (of doing sth)** (*informal*) to have no chance at all of doing sth
■ *verb* [V] if a problem, a plan, an activity, etc. **snowballs**, it quickly becomes much bigger, more serious, more important, etc: *Opposition to the proposals has snowballed.*

snow-blow-er /ˈsnəʊbləʊə(r); *AmE* ˈsnoʊbloʊər/ *noun* a

machine that removes snow from roads or paths by blowing it to one side

snow-board-ing /ˈsnəʊbɔːdɪŋ; *AmE* ˈsnoʊbɔːrd-/ *noun* [U] the sport of moving over snow on a long wide board called a **snowboard**: *to go snow-boarding* ◊ *Snowboarding is now an Olympic sport.*
▶ **snow-board-er** *noun*

snow-bound /ˈsnəʊbaʊnd; *AmE* ˈsnoʊ-/ *adj.* **1** (of a person or vehicle) trapped in a particular place and unable to move because a lot of snow has fallen **2** (of a road or building) that you cannot use or reach because a lot of snow has fallen

'snow-capped *adj.* (*literary*) (of mountains and hills) covered with snow on top

'snow chains *noun* [pl.] chains that are put on the wheels of a car so that it can drive over snow

'snow-covered (also *literary* **'snow-clad**) *adj.* [usually before noun] covered with snow: *snow-covered fields / mountains*

snow-drift /ˈsnəʊdrɪft; *AmE* ˈsnoʊ-/ *noun* a deep pile of snow that has been blown together by the wind

snow-drop /ˈsnəʊdrɒp; *AmE* ˈsnoʊdrɑːp/ *noun* a small white flower that appears in early spring

snow-fall /ˈsnəʊfɔːl; *AmE* ˈsnoʊ-/ *noun* [C, U] an occasion when snow falls; the amount of snow that falls in a particular place in a period of time: *a heavy / light snow-fall* ◊ *an area of low snowfall* ◊ *What is the average annual snowfall for this state?*

snow-field /ˈsnəʊfiːld; *AmE* ˈsnoʊ-/ *noun* a large area that is always covered with snow, for example in the mountains

snow-flake /ˈsnəʊfleɪk; *AmE* ˈsnoʊ-/ *noun* a small soft piece of frozen water that falls from the sky as snow

'snow job *noun* (*AmE, informal*) an attempt to deceive sb or to persuade them to support sth by telling them things that are not true, or by praising them too much

snow-line /ˈsnəʊlaɪn; *AmE* ˈsnoʊ-/ (**the snowline**) *noun* [sing.] the level on mountains above which snow never melts completely

snow-man /ˈsnəʊmæn; *AmE* ˈsnoʊ-/ *noun* (*pl.* **-men** /-men/) a figure like a man that people, especially children, make out of snow for fun

snow-mobile /ˈsnəʊməbiːl; *AmE* ˈsnoʊmoʊ-/ *noun* a motor vehicle that can move over snow and ice easily

'snow pea *noun* [usually pl.] (*AmE*) = MANGETOUT

snow-plough (*BrE*) (*AmE* **snow-plow**) /ˈsnəʊplaʊ; *AmE* ˈsnoʊ-/ *noun, verb*
■ *noun* a vehicle or machine for cleaning snow from roads or railways
■ *verb* [V] to bring the two points of your skis together, in order to slow down or stop

snow-shoe /ˈsnəʊʃuː; *AmE* ˈsnoʊ-/ *noun* one of a pair of flat frames that you attach to the bottom of your shoes so that you can walk on deep snow without sinking in

snow-storm /ˈsnəʊstɔːm; *AmE* ˈsnoʊstɔːrm/ *noun* a very heavy fall of snow, usually with a strong wind

ˌsnow-'white *adj.* (*written*) pure white in colour: *snow-white sheets*

snowy /ˈsnəʊi; *AmE* ˈsnoʊi/ *adj.* **1** [usually before noun] covered with snow: *snowy fields / peaks* **2** (of a period of time) when a lot of snow falls: *a snowy weekend* **3** (*literary*) very white, like new snow: *snowy hair*

SNP /ˌes en ˈpiː/ *abbr.* Scottish National Party (a Scottish political party which believes that Scotland should be independent)

snub /snʌb/ *verb, noun*
■ *verb* (**-bb-**) [VN] **1** to insult sb, especially by ignoring them when you meet: *I tried to be friendly, but she snubbed me*

completely. **2** to refuse to attend or accept sth, for example as a protest: *All the country's leading players snubbed the tournament.*

■ *noun* ~ **(to sb)** an action or a comment that is deliberately rude in order to show sb that you do not like or respect them: *Her refusal to attend the dinner is being seen as a deliberate snub to the President.*

■ *adj.* [only before noun] (of a nose) short, flat and turned up at the end ▶ **,snub-'nosed** *adj.: a snub-nosed child* ◇ *a snub-nosed revolver* (= with a short barrel)

snuck *pt, pp* of SNEAK

snuff /snʌf/ *verb, noun*

■ *verb* [VN] **1** ~ **sth** (**out**) to stop a small flame from burning, especially by pressing it between your fingers or covering it with sth **2** (of an animal) to smell sth by breathing in noisily through the nose: [V] *The dogs were snuffing gently at my feet.* [also VN] **IDM** **'snuff it** (*BrE, humorous, slang*) to die **PHRV** **,snuff sth↔'out** (*written*) to stop or destroy sth completely: *An innocent child's life has been snuffed out by this senseless shooting.*

■ *noun* [U] tobacco in the form of a powder that people take by breathing it into their noses

snuff-box /'snʌfbɒks; *AmE* -baːks/ *noun* a small, usually decorated, box for holding snuff

snuf·fle /'snʌfl/ *verb, noun*

■ *verb* **1** to breathe noisily because you have a cold or you are crying [SYN] SNIFF: [V] *I could hear the child snuffling in her sleep.* [also V speech] **2** [V] ~ **(about/around)** if an animal **snuffles**, it breathes noisily through its nose, especially while it is smelling sth: *The dog was snuffling around in the bushes.*

■ *noun* (also *less frequent* **snuf·fling**) an act or the sound of snuffling: *The silence was broken only by the snuffles of the dogs.* ◇ *His breath came in snuffles.* **IDM** **get, have, etc. the 'snuffles** (*informal*) to get/have a cold

snug /snʌg/ *adj., noun*

■ *adj.* **1** warm, comfortable and protected, especially from the cold [SYN] COSY: *a snug little house* ◇ *I spent the afternoon snug and warm in bed.* **2** fitting sb/sth closely: *The elastic at the waist gives a nice snug fit.* ◇ *These jeans are a bit snug* (= too tight). ▶ **snug·ly** *adv.: I left the children tucked up snugly in bed.* ◇ *The lid should fit snugly.* **snug·ness** *noun* [U]

■ *noun* (*BrE*) a small comfortable room in a pub, with seats for only a few people

snug·gle /'snʌgl/ *verb* ~ **(up to sb/sth)** [+adv. / prep.] to get into, or to put sb/sth into, a warm comfortable position, especially close to sb: [V] *The child snuggled up to her mother.* ◇ *He snuggled down under the bedclothes.* ◇ *She snuggled closer.* ◇ [VN] *He snuggled his head onto her shoulder.*

So. *abbr.* (*AmE*) south; southern

so /səʊ; *AmE* soʊ/ *adv., conj., noun*

■ *adv.* **1** ~ **...(that) ...| ~ ...as to do sth** to such a great degree: *Don't look so angry.* ◇ *There's no need to worry so.* ◇ *She spoke so quietly (that) I could hardly hear her.* ◇ *I'm not so stupid as to believe that.* ◇ (*formal, especially BrE*) *Would you be so kind as to lock the door when you leave?* **2** (*especially spoken*) very; extremely: *The girls looked so pretty in their summer dresses.* ◇ *I'm so glad to see you.* ◇ *We have so much to do.* ◇ *Their attitude is so very English.* ◇ *The article was just so much* (= nothing but) *nonsense.* (*BrE*) *He sat there ever so quietly.* ◇ (*BrE*) *I do love it so.* **3** not ~ ...(**as** ...) (used in comparisons) not to the same degree: *I haven't enjoyed myself so much for a long time.* *It wasn't so good as last time.* ◇ *It's not so easy as you'd think.* ◇ *He was not so quick a learner as his brother.* ◇ *It's not so much a hobby as a career* (= more like a career than a hobby). ◇ (*disapproving*) *Off she went without so much as* (= without even) *a 'goodbye'.* **4** (*spoken*) used to show the size, amount or number of sth: *The fish was about so big* (= said when using your hands to show the size). ◇ *There are only so many* (= only a limited number of) *hours in a day.* **5** used to refer back to sth that has already been mentioned: *'Is he coming?' 'I hope so.'* ◇ *'Did they mind?' 'I don't think so.'* ◇ *If she notices, she never says so.* ◇ *I might be away next week. If so, I won't*

be able to see you. ◇ *We are very busy—so much so that we won't be able to take time off this year.* ◇ *Programs are expensive, and even more so if you have to keep altering them.* ◇ *I hear that you're a writer—is that so* (= is that true)? ◇ *He thinks I dislike him but that just isn't so.* ◇ *George is going to help me, or so he says* (= that is what he says). ◇ *They asked me to call them and I did so* (= I called). **6** also: *Times have changed and so have I.* ◇ *'I prefer the first version.' 'So do we.'* **HELP** You cannot use **so** with negative verbs. Use **neither** or **either**: *'I'm not hungry.' 'Neither am I/I'm not very hungry either.'* **7** (*spoken*) used to agree that sth is true, especially when you are surprised: *'You were there, too.' 'So I was—I'd forgotten.'* ◇ *'There's another one.' 'So there is.'* **8** (*spoken*) used, especially by children, to say that what sb says is not the case and the opposite is true: *'You're not telling the truth, are you?' 'I am, so!'* **9** used when you are showing sb how to do sth or telling them how sth happened: (*spoken*) *Stand with you arms out, so.* ◇ (*literary*) *So it was that he finally returned home.* **IDM** **and 'so forth | and 'so on (and 'so forth)** used at the end of a list to show that it continues in the same way: *We discussed everything—when to go, what to see and so on.* **...or so** used after a number, an amount, etc. to show that it is not exact: *There were twenty or so* (= about twenty) *people there.* ◇ *We stayed for an hour or so.* **so as to do sth** with the intention of doing sth: *We went early so as to get good seats.* **so 'be it** (*formal*) used to show that you accept sth and will not try to change it or cannot change it: *If he doesn't want to be involved, then so be it.* **,so much for 'sth 1** used to show that you have finished talking about sth: *So much for the situation in Germany. Now we turn our attention to France.* **2** (*informal*) used to suggest that sth has not been successful or useful: *So much for that idea!* **so ...that** (*formal*) in such a way that: *The programme has been so organized that none of the talks overlap.*

■ *conj.* **1** used to show the reason for sth: *It was still painful so I went to see a doctor.* **2** ~ **(that ...)** used to show the result of sth: *Nothing more was heard from him so that we began to wonder if he was dead.* **3** ~ **(that ...)** used to show the purpose of sth: *But I gave you a map so you wouldn't get lost!* ◇ *She worked hard so that everything would be ready in time.* **4** used to introduce the next part of a story: *So after shouting and screaming for an hour she walked out in tears.* **5** (*spoken*) used to show that you think sth is not important, especially after sb has criticized you for it: *So I had a couple of drinks on the way home. What's wrong with that?* ◇ *'You've been smoking again.' 'So?'* **6** (*spoken*) used to introduce a comment or a question: *So, let's see. What do we need to take?* ◇ *So, what have you been doing today?* **7** (*spoken*) used when you are making a final statement: *So, that's it for today.* **8** (*spoken*) used in questions to refer to sth that has just been said: *So there's nothing we can do about it?* ◇ *'I've just got back from a trip to Rome.' 'So, how was it?'* **9** used when stating that two events, situations, etc. are similar: *Just as large companies are having to cut back, so small businesses are being forced to close.* **IDM** **so 'what?** (*spoken*) used to show that you think sth is not important, especially after sb has criticized you for it: *'He's fifteen years younger than you!' 'So what?'* ◇ *So what if nobody else agrees with me?*

■ *noun* = SOH

soak /səʊk; *AmE* soʊk/ *verb, noun*

■ *verb* **1** ~ **(sth) (in sth)** to put sth in liquid for a time so that it becomes completely wet; to become completely wet in this way: [VN] *I usually soak the beans overnight.* ◇ *If you soak the tablecloth before you wash it, the stains should come out.* ◇ [V] *Leave the apricots to soak for 20 minutes.* ◇ *I'm going to go and soak in the bath.* **2** [VN] to make sb/sth completely wet: *A sudden shower of rain soaked the spectators.* **3** [VN] (*informal*) to obtain a lot of money from sb by making them pay very high taxes or prices: *He was accused of soaking his clients.* **PHRV** **'soak into/through sth| soak 'in** (of a liquid) to enter or pass through sth: *Blood had soaked through the bandage.* **,soak sth↔'off/'out** to remove sth by leaving it in water

s	t	v	z	ʃ	ʒ	tʃ	dʒ	θ	ð	ŋ
see	tea	van	zoo	shoe	vision	chain	jam	thin	this	sing

,soak sth ↔ 'up 1 to take in or absorb liquid: *Use a cloth to soak up some of the excess water.* **2** to absorb sth into your senses, your body or your mind: *We were just sitting soaking up the atmosphere.*
- *noun* (also **soak·ing**) [sing.] **1** an act of leaving sth in a liquid for a period of time; an act of making sb/sth wet: *Give the shirt a good soak before you wash it.* **2** (*informal*) a period of time spent in a bath

soaked /səʊkt; *AmE* soʊkt/ *adj.* **1** [not usually before noun] **~ (with sth)** very wet SYN DRENCHED: *He woke up soaked with sweat.* ◊ *You're soaked through!* (= completely wet) ◊ *They were soaked to the skin.* ◊ *You'll get soaked if you go out in this rain.* ◊ *Your clothes are soaked!* **2** (**-soaked**) used with nouns to form adjectives describing sth that is made completely wet with the thing mentioned: *a blood-soaked cloth* ◊ *rain-soaked clothing*

soak·ing /'səʊkɪŋ; *AmE* 'soʊ-/ (also **,soaking 'wet**) *adj.* completely wet: *That coat is soaking—take it off.* ◊ *We arrived home soaking wet.*

so-and-so /'səʊ ən səʊ; *AmE* 'soʊ ən soʊ/ *noun* (*pl.* **so-and-sos**) (*informal*) **1** [usually sing.] used to refer to a person, thing, etc. when you do not know their name or when you are talking in a general way: *Let's imagine Mrs So-and-so walks in. What would you say to her?* ◊ *What would you say to Mrs So-and-so who has called to complain about a noisy neighbour?* **2** an annoying or unpleasant person. People sometimes say **so-and-so** to avoid using an offensive word: *He's an ungrateful so-and-so.*

soap /səʊp; *AmE* soʊp/ *noun, verb*
- *noun* **1** [U, C] a substance that you use with water for washing your body: *soap and water* ◊ *a bar/piece of soap* ◊ *soap bubbles* **2** [C] (*informal*) = SOAP OPERA
- *verb* [VN] to rub yourself/sb/sth with soap—see also SOFT-SOAP

soap·box /'səʊpbɒks; *AmE* 'soʊpbɑːks/ *noun* a small temporary platform that sb stands on to make a speech in a public place, usually outdoors IDM **get/be on your 'soapbox** (*informal*) to express the strong opinions that you have about a particular subject

'soap flakes *noun* [pl.] very small thin pieces of soap that you buy in packets and use for washing your clothes by hand

'soap opera (also *informal* **soap**) *noun* [C, U] a story about the lives and problems of a group of people which is broadcast every day or several times a week on television or radio

'soap powder *noun* [U, C] (*BrE*) a powder made from soap and other substances that you use for washing your clothes, especially in a machine

soap·stone /'səʊpstəʊn; *AmE* 'soʊpstoʊn/ *noun* [U] a type of soft stone that feels like soap, used in making ornaments

soap·suds /'səʊpsʌdz; *AmE* 'soʊp-/ *noun* [pl.] = SUDS

soapy /'səʊpi; *AmE* 'soʊpi/ *adj.* [usually before noun] **1** full of soap; covered with soap **2** tasting or feeling like soap

soar /sɔː(r)/ *verb* [V] (*written*) **1** if the value, amount or level of sth **soars**, it rises very quickly: *soaring costs/prices/temperatures* ◊ *Air pollution will soon soar above safety levels.* ◊ *Unemployment has soared to 18%.* **2 ~ (up) (into sth)** to rise quickly and smoothly up into the air: *The rocket soared (up) into the air.* ◊ (*figurative*) *Her spirits soared* (= she became very happy and excited). **3** to fly very high in the air or remain high in the air: *an eagle soaring high above the cliffs* **4** to be very high or tall: *soaring hills/mountains* ◊ *The building soared above us.* **5** when music **soars**, it becomes higher or louder: *soaring strings*

SOB /,es əʊ 'biː; *AmE* ,es oʊ 'biː/ *noun* (*slang, especially AmE*) = SON OF A BITCH

sob /sɒb; *AmE* sɑːb/ *verb, noun*
- *verb* (**-bb-**) **1** [V] to cry noisily, taking sudden, sharp breaths: *I heard a child sobbing loudly.* ◊ *He started to sob uncontrollably.* **2 ~ sth (out)** to say sth while you are crying: [V speech] *'I hate him,' she sobbed.* ◊ [VN] *He sobbed out his troubles.* IDM **sob your 'heart out** to cry noisily for a long time because you are very sad

- *noun* an act or the sound of sobbing: *He gave a deep sob.* ◊ *Her body was racked* (= shaken) *with sobs.*

sober /'səʊbə(r); *AmE* 'soʊ-/ *adj., verb*
- *adj.* **1** [not usually before noun] not drunk (= not affected by alcohol): *I promised him that I'd stay sober tonight.* ◊ *He was **as sober as a judge*** (= completely sober). **2** (of people and their behaviour) serious and sensible: *a sober assessment of the situation* ◊ *He is honest, sober and hardworking.* ◊ **On sober reflection** (= after some serious thought), *I don't think I really need a car after all.* **3** (of colours or clothes) plain and not bright: *a sober grey suit* ▶ **sober·ly** *adv.* IDM SEE STONE COLD
- *verb* to make sb behave or think in a more serious and sensible way; to become more serious and sensible: [VN] *The bad news sobered us for a while.* ◊ [V] *He suddenly sobered.* PHRV **,sober 'up, ,sober sb 'up** to become or to make sb no longer drunk: *Stay here with us until you've sobered up.*

sober·ing /'səʊbərɪŋ; *AmE* 'soʊ-/ *adj.* making you feel serious and think carefully: *a sobering effect/experience/thought* ◊ *It is sobering to realize that this is not a new problem.*

so·bri·ety /sə'braɪəti/ *noun* [U] (*formal*) **1** the state of being sober (= not being drunk) **2** the fact of being sensible and serious

so·bri·quet /'səʊbrɪkeɪ; *AmE* 'soʊ-/ (also **sou·bri·quet**) *noun* (*written*) an informal name or title that you give sb/sth SYN NICKNAME

'sob story *noun* (*informal, disapproving*) a story that sb tells you just to make you feel sorry for them, especially one that does not have that effect or is not true

Soc. *abbr.* (in writing) SOCIETY: *Royal Geographical Soc.*

,so-'called *adj.* **1** [only before noun] used to show that you do not think that the word or phrase that is being used to describe sb/sth is appropriate: *the opinion of a so-called 'expert'* ◊ *How have these so-called improvements helped the local community?* **2** [usually before noun] used to introduce the word that people usually use to describe sth: *artists from the so-called 'School of London'*

soc·cer /'sɒkə(r); *AmE* 'sɑːk-/ *noun* [U] = FOOTBALL (1): *soccer players/fans* ◊ *a soccer pitch/team/match*—picture on page 1250

so·ci·able /'səʊʃəbl; *AmE* 'soʊ-/ (also *less frequent* **social**) *adj.* (of people) enjoying spending time with other people: *She's a sociable child who'll talk to anyone.* ◊ *I'm not feeling very sociable this evening.* ◊ *We had a very sociable weekend* (= we did a lot of things with other people).—compare ANTISOCIAL OPP UNSOCIABLE ▶ **so·ci·abil·ity** /,səʊʃə'bɪləti; *AmE* ,soʊ-/ *noun* [U]

so·cial /'səʊʃl; *AmE* 'soʊʃl/ *adj., noun*
- *adj.*
  CONNECTED WITH SOCIETY | **1** [only before noun] connected with society and the way it is organized: *social issues/problems/reforms* ◊ *a call for social and economic change* **2** [only before noun] connected with your position in society: *social class/background* ◊ *social advancement* (= improving your position in society)
  ACTIVITIES WITH OTHERS | **3** [only before noun] connected with activities in which people meet each other for pleasure: *a busy/hectic social life* ◊ *Team sports help to develop a child's social skills* (= the ability to talk easily to other people and do things in a group). ◊ *Social events and training days are arranged for all the staff.* ◊ *Join a social club to make new friends.*
  ANIMALS | **4** [only before noun] (*technical*) living naturally in groups, rather than alone
  FRIENDLY | **5** = SOCIABLE
  ▶ **so·cial·ly** /-ʃəli/ *adv.*: *The reforms will bring benefits, socially and politically.* ◊ *This type of behaviour is no longer socially acceptable.* ◊ *a socially disadvantaged family* (= one that is poor and from a low social class) ◊ *We meet at work, but never socially.* ◊ *Carnivores are usually socially complex mammals.*
- *noun* **1** [C] (*old-fashioned*) a party that is organized by a group or club: *a youth club social* **2** (**the social**) [U] (*BrE, spoken*) = SOCIAL SECURITY: *We're living on the social now.*

æ	ɑː	e	ɜː	ə	ɪ	iː	i	ɒ	ɔː	ʌ	ʊ	u	uː
cat	father	ten	bird	about	sit	see	many	got	saw	cup	put	actual	too

(BrE)

S

,social 'climber *noun* (*disapproving*) a person who tries to improve their position in society by becoming friendly with people who belong to a higher social class

,social 'conscience *noun* [sing., U] the state of being aware of the problems that affect a lot of people in society, such as being poor or having no home, and wanting to do sth to help these people

,social de'mocracy *noun* [U, C] a political system that combines the principles of SOCIALISM with the greater personal freedom of DEMOCRACY; a country that has this political system of government ▶ ,social 'democrat *noun* ,social demo'cratic *adj.* [only before noun]

,social engi'neering *noun* [U] the attempt to change society and to deal with social problems according to particular political beliefs, for example by changing the law

'social fund *noun* [usually sing.] a sum of money that can be used to help people who have financial, family or other social problems

,social 'housing *noun* [U] (in Britain) houses or flats/ apartments that are provided by a local council or another organization for people to buy or rent at a low price

so·cial·ism /ˈsəʊʃəlɪzəm; AmE ˈsoʊ-/ *noun* [U] a set of political and economic theories based on the belief that everyone has an equal right to a share of a country's wealth and that the government should own and control the main industries—compare CAPITALISM, COMMUNISM, SOCIAL DEMOCRACY

so·cial·ist /ˈsəʊʃəlɪst; AmE ˈsoʊ-/ *noun* a person who believes in or supports socialism; a member of a political party that believes in socialism ▶ so·cial·ist *adj.* [usually before noun]: *a socialist country/government/polit-ician* ◇ *socialist beliefs/ideals/traditions* ◇ *the ruling Socialist Party*

so·cial·is·tic /ˌsəʊʃəˈlɪstɪk; AmE ˌsoʊ-/ *adj.* [usually before noun] (often *disapproving*) having some of the features of socialism

so·cial·ite /ˈsəʊʃəlaɪt; AmE ˈsoʊ-/ *noun* (sometimes *disapproving*) a person who goes to a lot of fashionable parties and is often written about in the newspapers, etc.

so·cial·iza·tion (*BrE* also -isa·tion) /ˌsəʊʃəlaɪˈzeɪʃn; AmE ˌsoʊʃələˈz-/ *noun* [U] (*formal*) the process by which sb, especially a child, learns to behave in a way that is acceptable in their society

so·cial·ize (*BrE* also -ise) /ˈsəʊʃəlaɪz; AmE ˈsoʊ-/ *verb* **1** [V] ~ (**with sb**) to meet and spend time with people in a friendly way, in order to enjoy yourself: *I enjoy socializ-ing with the other students.* ◇ *Maybe you should socialize more.* **2** [VN] [often passive] (*formal*) to teach people to behave in ways that are acceptable to their society: *The family has the important function of socializing children.* [also VN to inf] **3** [VN] [usually passive] to organize sth according to the principles of SOCIALISM

,social 'science *noun* **1** (also ,social 'studies) [U] the study of people in society **2** [C] a particular subject con-nected with the study of people in society, for example geography, ECONOMICS or SOCIOLOGY

,social 'scientist *noun* a person who studies social science

,social se'curity *noun* [U] **1** (*BrE*) (also wel·fare *AmE, BrE*) money that the government pays regularly to people who are poor, unemployed, sick, etc: *to live on social security* ◇ *social security payments* ◇ *the Department of Social Security* **2** (Social Security) (*AmE*) a system in which people pay money regularly to the government when they are working and receive payments from the government when they are unable to work, especially when they are sick or too old to work—compare NATIONAL INSURANCE

,social 'services *noun* [pl.] a system that is organized by the local government to help people who have finan-cial or family problems; the department or the people who provide this help: *a leaflet on the range of social services available* ◇ *the local social services department*

'social work *noun* [U] paid work that involves giving help and advice to people living in the community who have financial or family problems

'social worker *noun* a person whose job is social work

so·ci·etal /səˈsaɪətl/ *adj.* [only before noun] (*technical*) connected with society and the way it is organized: *socie-tal values/structure*

so·ci·ety /səˈsaɪəti/ *noun* (*pl.* -ies) **1** [U] people in gen-eral, living together in communities: *policies that will benefit society as a whole* ◇ *Racism exists at all levels of society.* ◇ *They carried out research into the roles of men and women in today's society.* **2** [C, U] a particular com-munity of people who share the same customs, laws, etc: *modern industrial societies* ◇ *demand created by a con-sumer society* ◇ *Can Britain ever be a classless society?* ◇ *They were discussing the problems of Western society.* **3** [C] (*abbr.* Soc.) (especially in names) a group of people who join together for a particular purpose SYN ASSOCIATION: *a member of the drama society* ◇ *the American Society of Newspaper Editors*—see also BUILDING SOCIETY **4** [U] the group of people in a country who are fashionable, rich and powerful: *Their daughter married into high society.* ◇ *a society wedding* **5** [U] (*formal*) the state of being with other people SYN COMPANY: *He was a solitary man who avoided the society of others.*

socio- /ˈsəʊsiəʊ; AmE ˈsoʊsioʊ/ *combining form* (in nouns, adjectives and adverbs) connected with society or the study of society: *socio-economic* ◇ *sociolinguistics*

soci·olo·gist /ˌsəʊsiˈɒlədʒɪst; AmE ˌsoʊsiˈɑːl-/ *noun* a person who studies sociology

soci·ology /ˌsəʊsiˈɒlədʒi; AmE ˌsoʊsiˈɑːl-/ *noun* [U] the scientific study of the nature and development of society and social behaviour ▶ socio·logic·al /ˌsəʊsiəˈlɒdʒɪkl; AmE ˌsoʊsiəˈlɑːdʒ-/ *adj.*: *sociological research/theories* socio·logic·al·ly /-kli/ *adv.*

socio·path /ˈsəʊsiəʊpæθ; AmE ˈsoʊsioʊ-/ *noun* a person who has a mental illness and who behaves in an aggres-sive or dangerous way towards other people

sock /sɒk; AmE sɑːk/ *noun, verb*
■ *noun* **1** a piece of clothing that is worn over the foot, ankle and lower part of the leg, especially inside a shoe: *a pair of socks* **2** (*informal*) a strong blow, especially with the FIST: *to give sb a sock on the jaw* IDM blow/knock sb's 'socks off (*informal*) to surprise or impress sb very much put a 'sock in it (*old-fashioned, BrE, informal*) used to tell sb to stop talking or making a noise—more at PULL *v.*
■ *verb* [VN] (*informal*) to hit sb hard: *She got angry and socked him in the mouth.* ◇ (*figurative*) *The banks are socking customers with higher charges.* IDM 'sock it to sb (*informal* or *humorous*) to do sth or tell sb sth in a strong and effective way: *Go in there and sock it to 'em!* PHR V ,sock sth↔a'way (*AmE*) to save money

socket /ˈsɒkɪt; AmE ˈsɑːkɪt/ *noun* **1** (also 'power point) (both *BrE*) (*AmE* out·let, re·cep·tacle) a device in a wall that you put a PLUG into in order to connect electrical equipment to the power supply of a building: *a mains/ wall socket*—picture at PLUG **2** a device on a piece of electrical equipment that you can fix a PLUG, a light BULB, etc. into: *an aerial socket on the television* **3** a curved hollow space in the surface of sth that another part fits into or moves around in: *His eyes bulged in their sockets.*

sod /sɒd; AmE sɑːd/ *noun, verb*
■ *noun* **1** (*BrE*, △, *slang*) used to refer to a person, espe-cially a man, that you are annoyed with or think is unpleasant: *You stupid sod!* **2** (*BrE*, △, *slang*) used with an adjective to refer to a person, especially a man: *The poor old sod got the sack yesterday.* ◇ *You lucky sod!* HELP You can use words like man, boy, devil or thing instead. **3** (*BrE*, △, *slang*) a thing that is difficult or causes prob-lems: *It was a real sod of a job.* **4** [sing.] (*formal* or *literary*) a layer of earth with grass growing on it; a piece of this that has been removed: *under the sod* (= in your grave)
■ *verb* (-dd-) [VN] (*BrE*, △, *slang*) (only used in orders) a swear word that many people find offensive, used when sb is annoyed about sth or to show that they do not care about sth: *Sod this car! It's always breaking down.* ◇ *Oh,*

sod it! I'm not doing any more. **IDM** see LARK *n*. **PHRV** ,sod
'off (*BrE*, △, *slang*) (usually used in orders) to go away:
Sod off, the pair of you!

soda /'səʊdə; *AmE* 'soʊdə/ *noun* **1** [U, C] = SODA WATER:
Add some soda to the whisky, please. ◊ *A Scotch and soda*
2 (also *old-fashioned* 'soda pop) (both *AmE*) [U, C] a
sweet FIZZY drink (= a drink with bubbles) made with
soda water, fruit flavour and sometimes ice cream: *Do
you have any diet soda?* ◊ *He had an ice-cream soda.* **3** [U] a
chemical substance in common use that is a compound of
SODIUM: *baking/washing soda*—see also CAUSTIC SODA,
SODIUM BICARBONATE, SODIUM CARBONATE

'soda fountain *noun* (*old-fashioned, AmE*) a type of cafe
where you can buy sodas to drink, ice creams, etc.

,sod 'all *noun* [U] (*BrE*, △, *slang*) a phrase that some
people find offensive, used to mean 'none at all' or 'nothing at all'

'soda water (also soda) *noun* **1** [U] FIZZY water (= water
with bubbles) used as a drink on its own or to mix with
alcoholic drinks or fruit juice **2** [C] a glass of soda water

sod·den /'sɒdn; *AmE* 'sɑːdn/ *adj*. **1** extremely wet **SYN**
SOAKED: *sodden clothing/grass* ◊ *We arrived home completely sodden.* **2** (**-sodden**) extremely wet with the thing
mentioned: *a rain-sodden jacket*

sod·ding /'sɒdɪŋ; *AmE* 'sɑːd-/ *adj*. [only before noun]
(*BrE*, △, *slang*) a swear word that many people find
offensive, used to emphasize a comment or an angry
statement: *I couldn't understand a sodding thing!*

so·dium /'səʊdiəm; *AmE* 'soʊ-/ *noun* [U] (*symb* **Na**) a
chemical element. Sodium is a soft silver-white metal
that is found naturally only in compounds, such as salt.

,sodium bi'carbonate (also bi,carbonate of 'soda,
'baking soda) (also *informal* **bi-carb**) *noun* [U] (*symb*
NaHCO₃) a chemical compound in the form of a white
powder that dissolves and is used in baking to make
cakes, etc. rise and become light, and in making FIZZY
drinks and some medicines

sodium carbonate /ˌsəʊdiəm 'kɑːbənət; *AmE* ˌsoʊ-;
'kɑːrb-/ (also 'washing soda) *noun* [U] (*symb* **Na₂CO₃**) a
chemical compound in the form of white CRYSTALS or
powder that dissolves and is used in making glass, soap
and paper, and for softening water

,sodium 'chloride *noun* [U] (*symb* **NaCl**) common salt
(a chemical compound of SODIUM and CHLORINE)

sod·om·ite /'sɒdəmaɪt; *AmE* 'sɑːd-/ *noun* (*old-fashioned,
formal*) a person who practises sodomy

sod·om·ize (*BrE* also **-ise**) /'sɒdəmaɪz; *AmE* 'sɑːd-/ *verb*
[VN] (*disapproving*) to have ANAL sex with sb

sod·omy /'sɒdəmi; *AmE* 'sɑːd-/ *noun* [U] a sexual act in
which a man puts his PENIS in sb's, especially another
man's, ANUS

,Sod's 'Law *noun* [U] (*BrE, humorous*) the tendency for
things to happen in just the way that you do not want,
and in a way that is not useful: *We always play better
when we are not being recorded—but that's Sod's Law,
isn't it?* ◊ *It was Sod's Law—the only day he could manage
was the day I couldn't miss work.*

sofa /'səʊfə; *AmE* 'soʊfə/ *noun* a long comfortable seat
with a back and arms, for two or more people to sit on
SYN SETTEE, COUCH—picture at CHAIR

'sofa bed *noun* a sofa that can be folded out to form a
bed—picture at BED

soft /sɒft; *AmE* sɔːft/ *adj*. (**soft·er, soft·est**)
‣ NOT HARD | **1** changing shape easily when pressed; not stiff
or firm: *soft margarine* ◊ *soft feather pillows* ◊ *The grass
was soft and springy.* **2** less hard than average: *soft rocks
such as limestone* ◊ *soft cheeses* **OPP** HARD
‣ NOT ROUGH | **3** smooth and pleasant to touch: *soft skin/
hair/fur* ◊ *a dress made from the finest, softest silk* **OPP**
ROUGH
‣ WITHOUT ANGLES/EDGES | **4** not having sharp angles or hard
edges: *This season's fashions focus on warm tones and soft
lines.* ◊ *The moon's pale light cast soft shadows.*
‣ LIGHT/COLOURS | **5** [usually before noun] not too bright, in a
way that is pleasant and relaxing to the eyes: *a soft pink* ◊
the soft glow of candlelight **OPP** HARSH

‣ RAIN/WIND | **6** not strong or violent: *A soft breeze rustled the
trees.*
‣ SOUNDS | **7** not loud, and usually pleasant and gentle: *soft
background music* ◊ *a soft voice*
‣ SYMPATHETIC | **8** kind and sympathetic; easily affected by
other people's suffering: *Julia's soft heart was touched by
his grief.* **OPP** HARD
‣ NOT STRICT | **9** ~ (on sb/sth)| ~ (with sb) (usually *disap-
proving*) not strict or severe; not strict or severe enough:
The government is not becoming soft on crime. ◊ *If you're
too soft with these kids they'll never respect you.* **OPP**
TOUGH
‣ CRAZY | **10** (*informal, disapproving*) stupid or crazy: *He
must be going soft in the head.*
‣ NOT BRAVE/TOUGH ENOUGH | **11** (*informal, disapproving*) not
brave enough; wanting to be safe and comfortable: *Stay
in a hotel? Don't be so soft. I want to camp out under the
stars.*
‣ TOO EASY | **12** (*disapproving*) not involving much work; too
easy and comfortable: *They had got too used to the soft life
at home.* **OPP** HARD
‣ WATER | **13** not containing mineral salts and therefore
good for washing: *You won't need much soap—the water
here is very soft.* **OPP** HARD
‣ CONSONANTS | **14** (*phonetics*) not sounding hard, for
example 'c' in 'city' and 'g' in 'general' **OPP** HARD
‣ **soft·ness** *noun* [U, sing.]: *the softness of her skin/voice*
◊ *the softness of the water*—see also SOFTLY
IDM have a soft 'spot for sb/sth (*informal*) to like
sb/sth: *She's always had a soft spot for you.*—more at
OPTION, TOUCH *n*.

soft·ball /'sɒftbɔːl; *AmE* 'sɔːft-/ *noun* **1** [U] a game similar
to baseball but played on a smaller field with a larger
softer ball **2** [C] the ball used in softball

,soft-'boiled *adj*. (of eggs) boiled for a short time so that
the YOLK is still soft or liquid—compare HARD-BOILED

,soft 'drink *noun* a cold drink that does not contain
alcohol—compare HARD *adj*. (11)

,soft 'drug *noun* an illegal drug, such as CANNABIS, that
some people take for pleasure, that is not considered very
harmful or likely to cause ADDICTION—compare HARD
DRUG

soft·en /'sɒfn; *AmE* 'sɔːfn/ *verb* **1** to become, or to make
sth softer: [V] *Fry the onions until they soften.* ◊ [VN] *a
lotion to soften the skin* ◊ *Linseed oil will soften stiff
leather.* **2** to become or to make sth less bright or harsh:
[VN] *Trees soften the outline of the house.* [also V] **3** to
become or to make sb/sth more sympathetic and less
severe or critical: [V] *She felt herself softening towards
him.* ◊ *His face softened as he looked at his son.* ◊ [VN] *She
softened her tone a little.* **4** [VN] to reduce the force or the
unpleasant effects of sth: *Air bags are designed to soften
the impact of a car crash.* **IDM** see BLOW *n*. **PHRV** ,soften
sb↔'up (*informal*) **1** to try to persuade sb to do sth for
you by being very nice to them before you ask them:
*Potential customers are softened up with free gifts before
the sales talk.* **2** to make an enemy weaker and easier to
attack

soft·en·er /'sɒfnə(r); *AmE* 'sɔːf-/ *noun* **1** [C] a device that
is used with chemicals to make hard water soft: *a water
softener* **2** [U, C] a substance that you add when washing
clothes to make them feel soft

,soft 'focus *noun* [U] a method of producing a photograph so that the edges of the image are not clear, in
order to make it look more romantic and attractive

,soft 'fruit *noun* [C, U] small fruits without stones/pits or
hard skin, such as STRAWBERRIES or CURRANTS

,soft 'furnishings *noun* [pl.] (*BrE*) cushions, curtains
and other things made from fabric in a house

,soft-'hearted *adj*. kind, sympathetic and emotional—
compare HARD-HEARTED

softie (also **softy**) /'sɒfti; *AmE* 'sɔːfti/ *noun* (*pl*. **-ies**)
(*informal*) a kind, sympathetic or emotional person:
There's no need to be afraid of him—he's a big softie.

soft·ly /'sɒftli; *AmE* 'sɔːftli/ *adv*. in a soft way: *She closed
the door softly behind her.* ◊ *'I missed you,' he said softly.* ◊

She stroked his hand softly. ◊ The room was softly lit by a lamp. ◊ a softly tailored suit

,softly-'softly adj. (BrE, informal) (of a way of doing sth) careful and patient, with no sudden actions: The police used a softly-softly approach with him.

,softly-'spoken adj. = SOFT-SPOKEN

,soft-'pedal verb ~ (on) sth (informal) to treat sth as less serious or important than it really is: [VN] Television has been accused of soft-pedalling bad news. [also V]

,soft 'porn noun [U] films/movies, books, pictures, etc. that show or describe sexual activity in a way that is sexually exciting but not in a very detailed or violent way—compare HARD PORN

,soft 'sell noun [U] a method of selling that involves persuading sb to buy sth rather than using pressure or aggressive methods—compare HARD SELL

,soft 'shoulder noun (AmE) = VERGE

,soft-'soap verb [VN] (informal) to say nice things to sb in order to persuade them to do sth ▶ **,soft 'soap** noun [U]

,soft-'spoken (also less frequent **,softly-'spoken**) adj. having a gentle and quiet voice

'soft-top noun a type of car that has a soft roof that can be folded down or removed; the roof of such a car—see also CONVERTIBLE

,soft 'toy (BrE) (also **,stuffed 'animal** AmE, BrE) noun a toy in the shape of an animal, made of fabric and filled with a soft substance—picture on page A8

soft·ware /'sɒftweə(r); AmE 'sɔːftwer/ noun [U] the programs, etc. used to operate a computer: applications/ system software—compare HARDWARE

'software engineer noun a person who writes computer PROGRAMS

'software package noun (computing) = PACKAGE (4)

soft·wood /'sɒftwʊd; AmE 'sɔːft-/ noun [U, C] wood from trees such as PINE, that is cheap to produce and can be cut easily—compare HARDWOOD

softy noun = SOFTIE

soggy /'sɒgi; AmE 'sɑːgi/ adj. (sog·gier, sog·gi·est) wet and soft, usually in a way that is unpleasant: We squelched over the soggy ground. ◊ soggy bread/cornflakes

soh (also **so**) /səʊ; AmE soʊ/ (also **sol**) noun (music) the fifth note of a MAJOR scale

soi·gnée /'swɑːnjeɪ; AmE swɑːˈnjeɪ/ adj. (from French, formal) (used of women) elegant; carefully and neatly dressed

soil /sɔɪl/ noun, verb
■ noun [U, C] **1** the top layer of the earth in which plants, trees, etc. grow: poor/dry/acid/sandy soil ◊ the study of rocks and soils ◊ soil erosion ⇨ note at EARTH **2** (literary) a country; an area of land: It was the first time I had set foot on African soil.
■ verb [VN] [often passive] (formal) to make sth dirty: soiled bedding/linen ◊ (figurative) I don't want you soiling your hands with this sort of work (= doing sth unpleasant or wrong).—see also SHOP-SOILED

soirée /'swɑːreɪ; AmE swɑːˈreɪ/ noun (from French, formal) a formal party in the evening, especially at sb's home

so·journ /'sɒdʒən; AmE soʊdʒɜːrn/ noun (literary) a temporary stay in a place away from your home ▶ **so·journ** verb [V+adv./prep.]

sol /sɒl; AmE soʊl/ noun = SOH

sol·ace /'sɒləs; AmE 'sɑːləs/ noun [U, sing.] (formal) a feeling of emotional comfort when you are sad or disappointed; a person or thing that makes you feel better or happier when you are sad or disappointed: He sought solace in the whisky bottle. ◊ She turned to Rob for solace. ◊ His grandchildren were a solace in his old age. ▶ **so·lace** verb: [VN] (literary) She smiled, as though solaced by the memory.

solar /'səʊlə(r); AmE 'soʊ-/ adj. [only before noun] **1** of or connected with the sun: solar radiation ◊ the solar cycle **2** using the sun's energy: solar power/heating

,solar 'cell noun a device that changes energy from sunlight and heat into electricity

sol·ar·ium /sə'leəriəm; AmE -'ler-/ noun a room enclosed mainly by glass or having special lamps, where people go to get a SUNTAN (= make their skin go brown) in real or artificial sunlight

,solar 'panel noun a piece of equipment on a roof that collects energy from sunlight in order to heat water and produce electricity

solar plexus /,səʊlə 'pleksəs; AmE ,soʊlər/ noun [sing.] **1** (anatomy) a system of nerves behind the stomach **2** (informal) the part of the body at the top of the stomach, below the RIBS: a painful punch in the solar plexus

'solar system noun **1** (the solar system) [sing.] the sun and all the planets that move around it **2** [C] any group of planets that all move around the same star

,solar 'year noun the time it takes the earth to go around the sun once, approximately 365¼ days

sold pt, pp of SELL

sol·der /'səʊldə(r); 'sɒldə(r); AmE 'sɑːdər/ noun, verb
■ noun [U] a mixture of metals that is heated and melted and then used to join metals, wires, etc. together
■ verb [VN] ~ sth (to/onto sth) | ~ (A and B together) to join pieces of metal or wire with solder

'soldering iron noun a tool that is heated and used for joining metals and wires by soldering them

sol·dier /'səʊldʒə(r); AmE 'soʊl-/ noun, verb
■ noun a member of an army, especially one who is not an officer: soldiers in uniform ◊ soldiers on duty/leave
■ verb PHRV **,soldier 'on** to continue with what you are doing or trying to achieve, especially when this is difficult or unpleasant

sol·dier·ing /'səʊldʒərɪŋ; AmE 'soʊl-/ noun [U] the life or activity of being a soldier

sol·dier·ly /'səʊldʒəli; AmE 'soʊldʒərli/ adj. typical of a good soldier

,soldier of 'fortune noun a person who fights for any country or person who will pay them SYN MERCENARY

sol·diery /'səʊldʒəri; AmE 'soʊl-/ noun [U+sing./pl. v.] (old-fashioned) a group of soldiers, especially of a particular kind

,sold 'out adj. **1** if a concert, match, etc. is sold out, there are no more tickets available for it **2** if a shop/store is sold out of a product, it has no more of it left to sell

sole /səʊl; AmE soʊl/ adj., noun, verb
■ adj. [only before noun] **1** only; single: the sole surviving member of the family ◊ My sole reason for coming here was to see you. ◊ This is the sole means of access to the building. **2** belonging to one person or group; not shared: She has sole responsibility for the project. ◊ the sole owner
■ noun **1** [C] the bottom surface of the foot: The hot sand burned the soles of their feet. **2** [C] the bottom part of a shoe or sock, not including the heel: leather/rubber soles—compare HEEL n. (3)—picture at SHOE **3** (-soled) (in adjectives) having the type of soles mentioned: rubber-soled shoes **4** [U, C] (pl. sole) a flat sea fish that is used for food
■ verb [VN] [usually passive] to repair a shoe by replacing the sole

sol·ecism /'sɒlɪsɪzəm; AmE 'sɑːl-/ noun (formal) **1** a mistake in the use of language in speech or writing **2** an example of bad manners or unacceptable behaviour

sole·ly /'səʊlli; AmE 'soʊlli/ adv. only; not involving sb/ sth else: She was motivated solely by self-interest. ◊ Selection is based solely on merit. ◊ He became solely responsible for the firm.

sol·emn /'sɒləm; AmE 'sɑːləm/ adj. **1** (of a person) not happy or smiling; looking very serious: Her face grew solemn. ◊ a solemn expression **2** done, said, etc. in a very serious and sincere way: a solemn oath/undertaking/vow **3** (of a religious ceremony or formal occasion) performed in a serious way: a solemn festival/ceremony/ritual ▶ **sol·emn·ly** adv.: He nodded solemnly. ◊ She solemnly promised not to say a word to anyone about it. ◊ The choir walked solemnly past.

so·lem·nity /sə'lemnəti/ noun **1** [U] the quality of being solemn: He was smiling, but his eyes retained a look of solemnity. ◊ She handed him the envelope with mock solemnity. ◊ He was buried with great pomp and solemnity.

s	t	v	z	ʃ	ʒ	tʃ	dʒ	θ	ð	ŋ
see	tea	van	zoo	shoe	vision	chain	jam	thin	this	sing

2 (**solemnities**) [pl.] (*formal*) formal things that people do at a serious event or occasion: *to observe the solemnities of the occasion*

sol·em·nize (*BrE* also **-ise**) /ˈsɒləmnaɪz; *AmE* ˈsɑːl-/ *verb* [VN] (*formal*) to perform a religious ceremony, especially a marriage

so·licit /səˈlɪsɪt/ *verb* **1 ~ sth (from sb)** | **~ (sb) (for sth)** (*formal*) to ask sb for sth, such as support, money, or information; to try to get sth or persuade sb to do sth: [VN] *They were planning to solicit funds from a number of organizations.* ◊ *They send representatives abroad to solicit business.* ◊ *Historians and critics are solicited for their opinions.* ◊ [V] *to solicit for money* [also VN to inf] **2** (of a prostitute) to offer to have sex with people in return for money: [V] *Prostitutes solicited openly in the streets.* ◊ *the crime of soliciting* [also VN] ▶ **so·lici·ta·tion** /səˌlɪsɪˈteɪʃn/ *noun* [U, C] (*especially AmE*): *the solicitation of money for election funds*

so·lici·tor /səˈlɪsɪtə(r)/ *noun* (*BrE*) a lawyer who prepares legal documents, for example for the sale of land or buildings, advises people on legal matters, and can speak for them in some courts of law ⇨ note at LAWYER

So,licitor 'General *noun* (*pl.* **Solicitors General**) a senior legal officer in Britain or the US, next in rank below the ATTORNEY-GENERAL

so·lici·tous /səˈlɪsɪtəs/ *adj.* (*formal*) being very concerned for sb and wanting to make sure that they are comfortable, well or happy ▶ **so·lici·tous·ly** *adv.* (*formal*)

so·lici·tude /səˈlɪsɪtjuːd; *AmE* -tuːd/ *noun* [U] **~ (for sb/ sth)** (*formal*) anxious care for sb's comfort, health or happiness: *I was touched by his solicitude for the boy.*

solid /ˈsɒlɪd; *AmE* ˈsɑːl-/ *adj., noun*

■ *adj.*

NOT LIQUID/GAS | **1** hard or firm; not in the form of a liquid or gas: *The planet Jupiter may have no solid surface at all.* ◊ *The boat bumped against a solid object.* ◊ *She had refused all solid food.* ◊ *It was so cold that the stream had frozen solid.* ◊ *The boiler uses solid fuel.*

WITHOUT HOLES OR SPACES | **2** having no holes or spaces inside; not hollow: *They were drilling through solid rock.* ◊ *The stores are packed solid* (= very full and crowded) *at this time of year.*

STRONG | **3** strong and made well: *These chains seem fairly solid.*

RELIABLE | **4** that you can rely on; having a strong basis: *As yet, they have no solid evidence.* ◊ *His advice was always solid and practical.* ◊ *This provided a solid foundation for their marriage.* ◊ *The Irish team were solid as a rock in defence.*

GOOD BUT NOT SPECIAL | **5** definitely good and steady but perhaps not excellent or special: *1999 was a year of solid achievement.* ◊ *He's a solid player.*

MATERIAL | **6** [only before noun] made completely of the material mentioned (that is, the material is not only on the surface): *a solid gold bracelet*

PERIOD OF TIME | **7** (*informal*) without a pause; continuous: *The essay represents a solid week's work.* ◊ *It rained for two hours solid this afternoon.*

COLOUR | **8** of the colour mentioned and no other colour: *One cat is black and white, the other solid black.*

SHAPE | **9** (*geometry*) a shape that is **solid** has length, width and height and is not flat: *A cube is a solid figure.*

IN AGREEMENT | **10** in complete agreement; agreed on by everyone: *The department was solid against the changes.* ◊ *The strike was solid, supported by all the members.*

—see also ROCK SOLID

■ *noun*

NOT LIQUID/GAS | **1** a substance or an object that is solid, not a liquid or a gas: *liquids and solids* ◊ *The baby is not yet on solids* (= eating solid food).

SHAPE | **2** (*geometry*) a shape which has length, width and height, such as a CUBE

soli·dar·ity /ˌsɒlɪˈdærəti; *AmE* ˌsɑːl-/ *noun* [U] **~ (with sb)** support by one person or group of people for another because they share feelings, opinions, aims, etc: *family/ community/social solidarity* ◊ *to express/show solidarity*

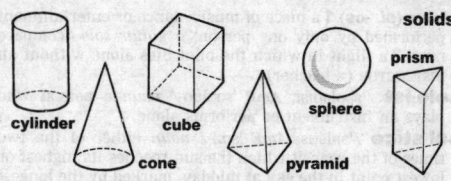

solids

cylinder   cube   sphere   prism

cone   pyramid

with sb ◊ *Demonstrations were held as a gesture of solidarity with the hunger strikers.*

so·lid·ify /səˈlɪdɪfaɪ/ *verb* (**so·lidi·fies, so·lidi·fy·ing, so·lidi·fied, so·lidi·fied**) **~ (into sth)** **1** to become solid; to make sth solid: [V] *The mixture will solidify into toffee.* ◊ [VN] *solidified lava* **2** (*written*) (of ideas, etc.) to become or to make sth become more definite and less likely to change: [V] *Vague objections to the system solidified into firm opposition.* ◊ [VN] *They solidified their position as Britain's top band.* ▶ **so·lidi·fi·ca·tion** /səˌlɪdɪfɪˈkeɪʃn/ *noun* [U]

so·lid·ity /səˈlɪdəti/ *noun* [U] the quality or state of being solid: *the strength and solidity of Romanesque architecture* ◊ *Her writings have extraordinary depth and solidity.* ◊ *the solidity of his support for his staff*

sol·id·ly /ˈsɒlɪdli; *AmE* ˈsɑːl-/ *adv.* **1** in a firm and strong way: *a large, solidly-built house* ◊ *He stood solidly in my path.* **2** continuously; without stopping: *It rained solidly for three hours.* **3** agreeing with or supporting sb/sth completely: *Her colleagues were solidly behind her.* ◊ *The state is solidly Republican.*

so·lilo·quy /səˈlɪləkwi/ *noun* [C, U] (*pl.* **-ies**) a speech in a play in which a character, who is alone on the stage, speaks his or her thoughts aloud; the act of speaking thoughts aloud in this way: *Hamlet's famous soliloquy, 'To be or not to be ...'* ◊ *the playwright's use of soliloquy—* compare MONOLOGUE ▶ **so·lilo·quize, -ise** /səˈlɪləkwaɪz/ *verb* [V]

sol·ip·sism /ˈsɒlɪpsɪzəm; *AmE* ˈsoʊl-; ˈsɑːl-/ *noun* [U] (*philosophy*) the theory that only the self exists or can be known ▶ **sol·ip·sis·tic** /ˌsɒlɪpˈsɪstɪk; *AmE* ˌsɑːl-; ˌsoʊl-/ *adj.*

soli·taire /ˌsɒlɪˈteə(r); *AmE* ˈsɑːləter/ *noun* **1** [U] (*BrE*) a game for one person in which you remove pieces from their places on a special board after moving other pieces over them. The aim is to finish with only one piece left on the board. **2** [U] (*AmE*) = PATIENCE (3) **3** [C] a single jewel; a piece of jewellery with a single jewel in it: *a solitaire ring*

soli·tary /ˈsɒlətri; *AmE* ˈsɑːləteri/ *adj., noun*

■ *adj.* **1** [usually before noun] done alone; without other people: *She enjoys long solitary walks.* ◊ *He led a solitary life.* **2** (of a person or an animal) enjoying being alone; frequently spending time alone: *He was a solitary child.* ◊ *Tigers are solitary animals.* **3** (of a person, thing or place) alone, with no other people or things around: *a solitary farm* ◊ *A solitary light burned dimly in the hall.* **4** [usually before noun] (especially in negative sentences and questions) only one; single: *There was not a solitary shred of evidence* (= none at all). ▶ **soli·tari·ness** *noun* [U]

■ *noun* (*pl.* **-ies**) **1** [U] (*informal*) = SOLITARY CONFINEMENT **2** [C] (*formal*) a person who chooses to live alone

,solitary con'finement (also *informal* **soli·tary**) *noun* [U] a punishment in which a prisoner is kept alone in a separate cell: *to be in solitary confinement*

soli·tude /ˈsɒlɪtjuːd; *AmE* ˈsɒlətuːd/ *noun* [U] the state of being alone, especially when you find this pleasant: *She longed for peace and solitude.* ◊ *I returned to the solitude of my room.*

solo /ˈsəʊləʊ; *AmE* ˈsoʊloʊ/ *adj., noun*

■ *adj.* [only before noun] **1** done by one person alone, without anyone helping them: *his first solo flight* ◊ *a solo effort* **2** connected with or played as a musical solo: *a solo artist* (= for example a singer who sings on their own, not as part of group) ◊ *a piece for solo violin* ▶ **solo** *adv.*: *She wanted to fly solo across the Atlantic.* ◊ *After three years with the band he decided to go solo.*

æ	ɑː	e	ɜː	ə	ɪ	iː	i	ɒ	ɔː	ʌ	ʊ	u	uː
cat	father	ten	bird	about	sit	see	many	got (BrE)	saw	cup	put	actual	too

S

■ *noun* (*pl.* **-os**) **1** a piece of music, dance or entertainment performed by only one person: *a guitar solo*—compare DUET **2** a flight in which the pilot flies alone without an INSTRUCTOR (= teacher)

solo·ist /ˈsəʊləʊɪst; *AmE* ˈsoʊloʊ-/ *noun* a person who plays an instrument or performs alone

sol·stice /ˈsɒlstɪs; *AmE* ˈsɑːl-/ *noun* either of the two times of the year at which the sun reaches its highest or lowest point in the sky at midday, marked by the longest and shortest days: *the summer/winter solstice*

sol·uble /ˈsɒljəbl; *AmE* ˈsɑːl-/ *adj.* **1** ~ (**in sth**) that can be dissolved in a liquid: *soluble aspirin* ◊ *Glucose is soluble in water.* **2** (*formal*) (of a problem) that can be solved OPP INSOLUBLE ▶ **solu·bil·ity** /ˌsɒljuˈbɪləti; *AmE* ˌsɑːl-/ *noun* [U]

so·lu·tion /səˈluːʃn/ *noun* **1** [C] ~ (**to sth**) a way of solving a problem or dealing with a difficult situation: *Attempts to find a solution have failed.* ◊ *There's no simple solution to this problem.* ◊ *Do you have a better solution?* **2** [C] ~ (**to sth**) an answer to a PUZZLE: *The solution to last week's quiz is on page 81.* **3** [C, U] a liquid in which sth is dissolved: *an alkaline solution* ◊ *saline solution* **4** [U] the process of dissolving a solid or gas in a liquid: *the solution of glucose in water*

solve /sɒlv; *AmE* sɑːlv/ *verb* [VN] **1** to find a way of dealing with a problem or difficult situation: *Attempts are being made to solve the problem of waste disposal.* **2** to find the correct answer or explanation for sth: *to solve an equation/puzzle/riddle* ◊ *to solve a crime/mystery*

solv·ency /ˈsɒlvənsi; *AmE* ˈsɑːl-/ *noun* [U] (*written*) the state of not being in debt (= not owing money)

solv·ent /ˈsɒlvənt; *AmE* ˈsɑːl-/ *noun, adj.*
■ *noun* [U, C] a substance, especially a liquid, that can dissolve another substance
■ *adj.* **1** [not usually before noun] having enough money to pay your debts; not in debt OPP INSOLVENT **2** (*technical*) able to dissolve another substance, or be dissolved in another substance: *Lead is more solvent in acidic water.*

ˈsolvent abuse *noun* [U] the practice of breathing in gases from glue or similar substances in order to produce a state of excitement—see also GLUE-SNIFFING

solv·er /ˈsɒlvə(r); *AmE* ˈsɑːl-/ *noun* a person who finds an answer to a problem or a difficult situation: *She's a good problem solver.*

sombre (*BrE*) (*AmE* **som·ber**) /ˈsɒmbə(r); *AmE* ˈsɑːm-/ *adj.* **1** dark in colour; dull: *dressed in sombre shades of grey and black* **2** sad and serious: *Paul was in a quiet and sombre mood.* ◊ *The year had ended on a sombre note.* ▶ **sombre·ly** (*BrE*) (*AmE* **som·ber·ly**) *adv.* **sombre·ness** (*BrE*) (*AmE* **som·ber·ness**) *noun* [U]

som·brero /sɒmˈbreərəʊ; *AmE* sɑːmˈbreroʊ/ *noun* (*pl.* **-os**) a Mexican hat for men that is tall with a very wide BRIM, turned up at the edges

some *det., pron., adv.*
■ *det.* /səm; *strong form* sʌm/ **1** used with uncountable nouns or plural countable nouns to mean 'an amount of or 'a number of', when the amount or number is not given: *There's still some wine in the bottle.* ◊ *Have some more vegetables.* HELP In negative sentences and questions **any** is usually used instead of 'some': *I don't want any more vegetables.* ◊ *Is there any wine left?* However, **some** is used in questions that expect a positive reply: *Would you like some milk in your coffee?* ◊ *Didn't you borrow some books of mine?* **2** /sʌm/ used to refer to certain members of a group or certain types of a thing, but not all of them: *Some people find this more difficult than others.* ◊ *Some people never seem to put on weight while others are always on a diet.* ◊ *I like some modern music* (= but not all of it). **3** /sʌm/ a large number or amount of sth: *It was with some surprise that I heard the news.* ◊ *We've known each other for some years now.* ◊ *We're going to be working together for some time* (= a long time). **4** /sʌm/ a small amount or number of sth: *There is some hope that things will improve.* **5** used with singular countable nouns to refer to a person, place, thing or time that is not known or not identified: *There must be some mistake.* ◊ *He's in some kind of trouble.* ◊ *She won a*

competition in *some newspaper or other.* ◊ *I'll see you again some time, I'm sure.* **6** /sʌm/ (*informal, sometimes ironic*) used to express a positive or negative opinion about sb/sth: *That was some party!* ◊ *Some expert you are! You know even less than me.*
■ *pron.* /sʌm/ ~ (**of sb/sth**) **1** used to refer to an amount of sth or a number of people or things when the amount or number is not given: *Some disapprove of the idea.* ◊ *You'll find some in the drawer.* ◊ *Here are some of our suggestions.* HELP In negative sentences and questions **any** is usually used instead of 'some': *I don't want any.* ◊ *Do you have any of the larger ones?* However, **some** is used in questions that expect a positive reply: *Would you like some?* ◊ *Weren't you looking for some of those?* **2** a part of the whole number or amount being considered: *All these students are good, but some work harder than others.* ◊ *Some of the music was weird.* IDM **...and ˈthen some** (*informal*) and a lot more than that: *We got our money's worth and then some.*
■ *adv.* /sʌm/ **1** used before numbers to mean 'approximately': *Some thirty people attended the funeral.* **2** (*AmE, informal*) to some degree: *He needs feeding up some.* ◊ *'Are you finding the work any easier?' 'Some.'*

-some *suffix* **1** (in adjectives) producing; likely to: *fearsome* ◊ *quarrelsome* **2** (in nouns) a group of the number mentioned: *a foursome*

some·body /ˈsʌmbədi/ *pron.* = SOMEONE: *Somebody should have told me.* ◊ *She thinks she's really somebody in that car.* OPP NOBODY

ˈsome day (also **some·day**) *adv.* at some time in the future: *Some day he'll be famous.*

some·how /ˈsʌmhaʊ/ *adv.* **1** (also *AmE informal* **some·way, some·ways**) in a way that is not known or certain: *We must stop him from seeing her somehow.* ◊ *Somehow or other I must get a new job.* **2** for a reason that you do not know or understand: *Somehow, I don't feel I can trust him.* ◊ *She looked different somehow.*

some·one /ˈsʌmwʌn/ (also **some·body**) *pron.* **1** a person who is not known or mentioned by name: *There's someone at the door.* ◊ *Someone's left their bag behind.* ◊ *It's time for someone new* (= a new person) *to take over.* ◊ *It couldn't have been me—it must have been someone else* (= a different person). ◊ *Should we call a doctor or someone?* HELP The difference between **someone** and **anyone** is the same as the difference between **some** and **any**. Look at the notes there. **2** an important person: *He was a small-time lawyer keen to be someone*—compare NOBODY

some·place /ˈsʌmpleɪs/ *adv., pron.* (*AmE*) = SOMEWHERE: *It has to go someplace.* ◊ *Can't you do that someplace else?* ◊ *We need to find someplace to live.*

som·er·sault /ˈsʌməsɔːlt; *AmE* -mərs-/ *noun, verb*
■ *noun* a movement in which sb turns over completely, with their feet over their head, on the ground or in the air: *to do/turn a somersault* ◊ *He turned back somersaults.* ◊ (*figurative*) *Her heart did a complete somersault when she saw him.*
■ *verb* [V] [usually +*adv./prep.*] to turn over completely in the air: *The car hit the kerb and somersaulted into the air.*

some·thing /ˈsʌmθɪŋ/ *pron., adv.*
■ *pron.* **1** a thing that is not known or mentioned by name: *We stopped for something to eat.* ◊ *Give me something to do.* ◊ *There's something wrong with the TV.* ◊ *There's something about this place that frightens me.* ◊ *Don't just stand there. Do something!* ◊ *His name is Alan something* (= I don't know his other name). ◊ *She's a professor of something or other* (= I'm not sure what) *at Leeds.* ◊ *He's something in* (= has a job connected with) *television.* ◊ *The car hit a tree or something.* ◊ *I could just eat a little something.* HELP The difference between **something** and **anything** is the same as the difference between **some** and **any**. Look at the notes there. **2** (*informal*) a thing that is thought to be important or worth taking notice of: *There's something in* (= some truth or some fact or opinion worth considering in) *what he says.* ◊ *It's quite something* (= a thing that you should feel happy about) *to have a job at all these days.* ◊ *'We should finish by tomorrow.' 'That's something'* (= a good thing), *anyway.'*

3 (*informal*) used to show that a description or an amount, etc. is not exact: *She called at* **something** *after ten o'clock.* ◊ *a new comedy aimed at* **thirty-somethings** (= people between thirty and forty years old) ◊ *It tastes* **something like** *melon.* ◊ *They pay six pounds an hour.* **Something like that.** ◊ *She found herself* **something of a** (= to some degree a) *celebrity.* ◊ *The programme's* **something to do with** (= in some way about) *the environment.* ◊ *He gave her a wry look,* **something between** *amusement and regret.* **IDM something 'else 1** a different thing; another thing: *He said something else that I thought was interesting.* **2** (*informal*) a person, a thing or an event that is much better than others of a similar type: *I've seen some fine players, but she's something else.*
■ *adv.* (*non-standard*) used with an adjective to emphasize a statement: *She was swearing something terrible.*

some·time /ˈsʌmtaɪm/ *adv., adj.*
■ *adv.* (also **'some time**) at a time that you do not know exactly or has not yet been decided: *I saw him sometime last summer.* ◊ *We must get together sometime.*
■ *adj.* [only before noun] (*formal*) **1** used to refer to what sb used to be: *Thomas Atkins, sometime vicar of this parish* **2** (*AmE*) used to refer to what sb does occasionally: *a sometime contributor to this magazine*

some·times /ˈsʌmtaɪmz/ *adv.* occasionally rather than all of the time: *Sometimes I go by car.* ◊ *He sometimes writes to me.* ◊ *I like to be on my own sometimes.*

some·way /ˈsʌmweɪ/ (also **some·ways**) *adv.* (*AmE, informal*) = SOMEHOW

some·what /ˈsʌmwɒt; *AmE* -wʌt/ *adv.* to some degree; rather: *I was somewhat surprised to see him.* ◊ *The situation has changed somewhat since we last met.* ◊ *What happened to them remains somewhat of a mystery.*

some·where /ˈsʌmweə(r); *AmE* -wer/ (*AmE* also **some·place**) *adv.* in, at or to some place that you do not know or do not mention by name: *I've seen him somewhere before.* ◊ *Can we go somewhere warm?* ◊ *I've already looked there—it must be* **somewhere else.** ◊ *He went to school in York or somewhere* (= I'm not sure where). ◊ *They live* **somewhere or other** *in France.* **HELP** The difference between **somewhere** and **anywhere** is the same as the difference between **some** and **any**. Look at the notes there. ▶ **some·where** (*AmE* also **some·place**) *pron.*: *We need to find* **somewhere to** (= a place to) *live.* ◊ *I know somewhere we can go.* **IDM 'get somewhere** (*informal*) to make progress in what you are doing **somewhere around, between, etc. sth** approximately the number or amount mentioned: *It cost somewhere around two thousand dollars.*

som·nam·bu·list /sɒmˈnæmbjəlɪst; *AmE* saːm-/ *noun* (*formal*) = SLEEPWALKER ▶ **som·nam·bu·lism** /-lɪzəm/ *noun* [U]

som·no·lent /ˈsɒmnələnt; *AmE* ˈsaːm-/ *adj.* (*written*) **1** almost asleep: *a somnolent cat* ◊ (*figurative*) *a somnolent town* **2** making you feel tired: *a somnolent Sunday afternoon* ▶ **som·no·lence** *noun* [U]

son /sʌn/ *noun* **1** [C] a person's male child: *We have two sons and a daughter.* ◊ *They have three grown-up sons.* ◊ *He's the son of an Oxford professor.* ◊ *Maine & Sons, Grocers* (= the name of a company on a sign) **2** [sing.] (*spoken, informal*) a friendly form of address that is used by an older man to a young man or boy: *Well, son, how can I help you?* **3** [C] (*literary*) a man who belongs to a particular place or country, etc: *one of France's most famous sons* **4** (**my son**) (*spoken, formal*) used by a priest to address a boy or man **5** (**the Son**) [sing.] Jesus Christ as the second member of the TRINITY: *the Father, the Son and the Holy Spirit* **IDM** see FATHER *n.,* FAVOURITE *adj.,* PRODIGAL

sonar /ˈsəʊnɑː(r); *AmE* ˈsoʊ-/ *noun* [U] equipment or a system for finding objects underwater using sound waves—compare RADAR

son·ata /səˈnɑːtə/ *noun* a piece of music for one instrument or for one instrument and piano, usually divided into three or four parts: *Beethoven's piano sonatas* ◊ *a violin sonata*

son et lu·mi·ère /ˌsɒn eɪ ˈluːmjeə(r); *AmE* ˌsaːn eɪ

lu·mi·ère/ *noun* [U] (from *French*) a performance held at night at a famous place that tells its history with special lights and sound

song /sɒŋ; *AmE* sɔːŋ/ *noun* **1** [C] a short piece of music with words that you sing: *a folk/love/pop song* ◊ *We sang a song together.*—see also SWANSONG **2** [U] songs in general; music for singing: *The story is told through song and dance.* ◊ *Suddenly he* **burst into song** (= started to sing) —see also PLAINSONG **3** [U, C] the musical sounds that birds make: *the song of the blackbird* **IDM for a 'song** (*informal*) very cheaply; at a low price **a song and 'dance (about sth) 1** (*BrE, informal, disapproving*) if you make a **song and dance** about sth, you complain or talk about it too much when this is not necessary **2** [C] (*AmE, informal*) a long explanation about sth, or excuse for sth **on 'song** (*informal*) working or performing well: *The whole team was on song.*

song·bird /ˈsɒŋbɜːd; *AmE* ˈsɔːŋbɜːrd/ *noun* a bird that has a musical call, for example a BLACKBIRD or THRUSH

song·book /ˈsɒŋbʊk; *AmE* ˈsɔːŋ-/ *noun* a book containing the music and words of different songs

song·ster /ˈsɒŋstə(r); *AmE* ˈsɔːŋ-/ *noun* (*old-fashioned*) **1** a word sometimes used in newspapers to mean 'singer' **2** a SONGBIRD

song·stress /ˈsɒŋstrəs; *AmE* ˈsɔːŋ-/ *noun* a word sometimes used in newspapers to mean 'a woman singer'

song·writer /ˈsɒŋraɪtə(r); *AmE* ˈsɔːŋ-/ *noun* a person who writes the words and usually also the music for songs

song·writ·ing /ˈsɒŋraɪtɪŋ; *AmE* ˈsɔːŋ-/ *noun* [U] the process of writing songs

sonic /ˈsɒnɪk; *AmE* ˈsaːnɪk/ *adj.* (*technical*) connected with sound or the speed of sound: *sonic waves*

sonic 'boom *noun* the explosive sound that is made when an aircraft travels faster than the speed of sound

son-in-law *noun* (*pl.* **sons-in-law**) the husband of your daughter—compare DAUGHTER-IN-LAW

son·net /ˈsɒnɪt; *AmE* ˈsaːnɪt/ *noun* a poem that has 14 lines, each containing 10 syllables, and a fixed pattern of rhyme: *Shakespeare's sonnets*

sonny /ˈsʌni/ *noun* [sing.] (*old-fashioned*) a word used by an older person to address a young man or boy

son of a 'bitch *noun* (*pl.* **sons of bitches**) (also **SOB** especially in *AmE*) (△, *slang*) an offensive word for a person that you think is bad or very unpleasant: *I'll kill that son of a bitch when I get my hands on him!*

son of a 'gun *noun* (*AmE, informal, spoken*) **1** a person or thing that you are annoyed with: *My car's at the shop—the son of a gun broke down again.* **2** used to express the fact that you are surprised or annoyed: *Well, son of a gun—and I thought the old guy couldn't dance!* **3** (*old-fashioned*) used by a man to address or talk about a male friend that he admires and likes: *Frank, you old son of a gun—I haven't seen you for months.*

son·or·ous /ˈsɒnərəs; *AmE* ˈsaːn-; səˈnɔːrəs/ *adj.* (*formal*) having a pleasant full deep sound: *a sonorous voice* ▶ **son·or·ity** /səˈnɒrəti; *AmE* -ˈnɔːr-; -ˈnɑːr-/ *noun* [U, C]: *the rich sonority of the bass* **son·or·ous·ly** *adv.*

soon /suːn/ *adv.* (**soon·er, soon·est**) **1** in a short time from now; a short time after sth else has happened: *We'll be home soon.* / *We'll soon be home.* ◊ *She sold the house* **soon after** *her husband died.* ◊ *I soon realized the mistake.* ◊ *It soon became clear that the programme was a failure.* ◊ (*spoken*) *See you soon!* **2** early; quickly: *How soon can you get here?* ◊ *We'll deliver the goods* **as soon as** *we can.* ◊ *Please send it* **as soon as possible.** ◊ *Next Monday is the soonest we can deliver.* ◊ *They arrived home sooner than expected.* ◊ *The sooner we set off, the sooner we will arrive.* ◊ *The note said, 'Call Bill soonest'* (= as soon as possible). ◊ (*written*) *All too soon the party was over.*—see also ASAP **IDM no sooner said than 'done** used to say that sth will be done immediately **no sooner...than...** (*written*) used to say that sth happens immediately after sth else: *No sooner had she said it than she burst into tears.* ⇨ note at HARDLY **the ˌsooner the 'better** very soon; as soon as possible: *'When shall I tell him?' 'The sooner the better.'* **ˌsooner or 'later** at some time in the

b	d	f	g	h	k	l	m	n	p	r
bad	did	fall	get	hat	cat	leg	man	now	pen	red

future, even if you are not sure exactly when: *Sooner or later you will have to make a decision.* **ˌsooner rather than ˈlater** after a short time rather than after a long time: *We urged them to sort out the problem sooner rather than later.* **I, etc. would sooner do sth (than sth else)** to prefer to do sth (than do sth else): *She'd sooner share a house with other students than live at home with her parents.*—more at ANY TIME, JUST *adv.*, SAY *v.*

WHICH WORD?

soon / early / quickly

Soon usually means 'a short time from now' or 'after then': *I'll see you soon.* ◊ *She soon regretted what she'd done.* In the comparative or superlative or in expressions such as *as soon as possible*, **soon** emphasizes that something is done without delay: *Please reply as soon as possible.* ◊ *The sooner you start, the sooner you'll finish.*

Early means 'near the beginning of a period of time': *I've got to get up very early tomorrow.* ◊ *I'll see you early next week.* It can also mean 'before the usual or expected time': *A few guests arrived early.* **Early** does not mean 'a short time from now'.

Quickly is usually used to talk about the speed with which something is done, but can also be used like **soon** to mean 'after a short time' or 'without delay': *The journey passed very quickly.* ◊ *Please phone back as quickly/soon as possible.*

⇨ note at QUICK

---

soot /sʊt/ *noun* [U] black powder that is produced when wood, coal, etc. is burnt—see also SOOTY

soothe /suːð/ *verb* [VN] **1** to make sb who is anxious, upset, etc. feel calmer: *The music soothed her for a while.* **2** to make a tense or painful part of your body feel more comfortable: *This should soothe the pain.* ◊ *Take a warm bath to soothe tense, tired muscles.* ▶ **sooth·ing** *adj.*: *a soothing voice/lotion* **sooth·ing·ly** *adv.*: '*There's no need to worry,' he said soothingly.* PHR V **ˈsoothe sth↔away** to remove a pain or an unpleasant feeling: *The pain can be soothed away with massage.* ◊ *She quickly soothed away his fears.*

sooth·say·er /ˈsuːθseɪə(r)/ *noun* (*old use*) a person who is believed to be able to tell what will happen in the future

sooty /ˈsʊti/ *adj.* **1** covered with SOOT **2** of the colour of SOOT

sop /sɒp; AmE sɑːp/ *noun* [usually sing.] **~ (to sb/sth)** a small, not very important, thing that is offered to sb who is angry or disappointed in order to make them feel better

so·phis·ti·cate /səˈfɪstɪkeɪt/ *noun* (*formal*) a sophisticated person

so·phis·ti·cated /səˈfɪstɪkeɪtɪd/ *adj.* **1** having a lot of experience of the world and knowing about fashion, culture and other things that people think are socially important: *the sophisticated pleasures of city life* ◊ *Mark is a smart and sophisticated young man.*—compare NAIVE **2** (of a machine, system, etc.) clever and complicated in the way that it works or is presented: *highly sophisticated computer systems* ◊ *Medical techniques are becoming more sophisticated all the time.* **3** (of a person) able to understand difficult or complicated ideas: *a sophisticated audience* OPP UNSOPHISTICATED

so·phis·ti·ca·tion /səˌfɪstɪˈkeɪʃn/ *noun* [U] the quality of being sophisticated

soph·is·try /ˈsɒfɪstri; AmE ˈsɑːf-/ *noun* (*pl.* **-ies**) (*formal*) **1** [U] the use of clever arguments to persuade people that sth is true when it is really false **2** [C] a reason or an explanation that tries to show that sth is true when it is really false

sopho·more /ˈsɒfəmɔː(r); AmE ˈsɑːf-/ *noun* (*AmE*) **1** a student in the second year of a course of study at a college or university **2** a high school student in the 10th GRADE—compare FRESHMAN, JUNIOR, SENIOR

---

sop·or·if·ic /ˌsɒpəˈrɪfɪk; AmE ˌsɑːp-/ *adj.* (*formal*) making you feel like going to sleep: *the soporific effect of the sun*

sop·ping /ˈsɒpɪŋ; AmE ˈsɑːp-/ (also ˌsopping ˈwet) *adj.* (*informal*) very wet

soppy /ˈsɒpi; AmE ˈsɑːpi/ (*especially BrE*) (*AmE usually* **sappy**) *adj.* (*informal*) silly and SENTIMENTAL; full of unnecessary emotion: *soppy love songs* ◊ *She is soppy about cats.*

sop·rano /səˈprɑːnəʊ; AmE səˈprɑːnoʊ; -ˈpræn-/ *noun, adj.*
■ *noun* (*pl.* **-os** /-nəʊz/) a singing voice with the highest range for a woman or boy; a singer with a soprano voice—compare ALTO, MEZZO-SOPRANO, TREBLE
■ *adj.* [only before noun] (of a musical instrument) with the highest range of notes in its group: *a soprano saxophone*—compare ALTO, BASS, TENOR

sor·bet /ˈsɔːbeɪ; AmE ˈsɔːrbət/ (*BrE also* ˈwater ice) *noun* [C, U] a sweet frozen food made from sugar, water and fruit juice, often eaten as a DESSERT

sor·cer·er /ˈsɔːsərə(r); AmE ˈsɔːrs-/ *noun* (in stories) a man with magic powers, who is helped by evil spirits

sor·cer·ess /ˈsɔːsərəs; AmE ˈsɔːrs-/ *noun* (in stories) a woman with magic powers, who is helped by evil spirits

sor·cery /ˈsɔːsəri; AmE ˈsɔːrs-/ *noun* [U] magic that uses evil spirits

sor·did /ˈsɔːdɪd; AmE ˈsɔːrdɪd/ *adj.* **1** immoral or dishonest: *It was a shock to discover the truth about his sordid past.* ◊ *I didn't want to hear the sordid details of their relationship.* **2** very dirty and unpleasant: *people living in sordid conditions*

sore /sɔː(r)/ *adj., noun*
■ *adj.* **1** if a part of your body is **sore**, it is painful, and often red, especially because of infection or because a muscle has been used too much: *to have a sore throat* ◊ *His feet were sore after the walk.* ◊ *My stomach is still sore* (= painful) *after the operation.* **2** [not before noun] **~ (at sb/about sth)** (*informal, especially AmE*) upset and angry especially because you have been treated unfairly ▶ **sore·ness** *noun* [U]: *an ointment to reduce soreness and swelling* IDM **a ˌsore ˈpoint** a subject that makes you feel angry or upset when it is mentioned: *It's a sore point with Sue's parents that the children have not been baptized yet.* **stand/stick out like a sore ˈthumb** to be very noticeable in an unpleasant way—more at BEAR *n.*, SIGHT *n.*
■ *noun* a painful, often red, place on your body where there is a wound or an infection: *open sores*—see also BEDSORE, CANKER SORE, COLD SORE

sore·ly /ˈsɔːli; AmE ˈsɔːrli/ *adv.* seriously; very much: *I was sorely tempted to complain, but I didn't.* ◊ *If you don't come to the reunion you'll be sorely missed.*

sor·ghum /ˈsɔːgəm; AmE ˈsɔːrgəm/ *noun* [U] very small grain grown as food in tropical countries; the plant that produces this grain

sor·or·ity /səˈrɒrəti; AmE -ˈrɔːr-; -ˈrɑːr-/ *noun* (*pl.* **-ies**) (*AmE*) a club for a group of women students at an American college or university—compare FRATERNITY

sor·rel /ˈsɒrəl; AmE ˈsɔːr-; ˈsɑːr-/ *noun* [U] a plant with leaves that taste bitter and are used in cooking as a herb

sor·row /ˈsɒrəʊ; AmE ˈsɑːroʊ/ *noun, verb*
■ *noun* **1** [U] **~ (at/for/over sth)** a feeling of great sadness because sth very bad has happened SYN GRIEF: *He expressed his sorrow at the news of her death.* ◊ *They said that the decision was made more in sorrow than in anger.* **2** [C] a very sad event or situation: *the joys and sorrows of childhood*
■ *verb* [V] **~ (over sth)** (*literary*) to feel or express great sadness: *the sorrowing relatives* ◊ *They had sorrowed over his death.*

sor·row·ful /ˈsɒrəfl; AmE ˈsɑːroʊ-; ˈsɔː-/ *adj.* (*literary*) very sad: *her sorrowful eyes* ▶ **sor·row·ful·ly** /-fəli/ *adv.*

sorry /ˈsɒri; AmE ˈsɑːri; ˈsɔːri/ *adj., exclamation*
■ *adj.* (**sor·rier**, **sor·ri·est**) HELP You can also use **more sorry** and **most sorry**. **1** [not before noun] **~ (that ...)** | **~ (to see, hear, etc.)** feeling sad and sympathetic: *I'm sorry that your husband lost his job.* ◊ *We're sorry to hear that your father's in hospital again.* ◊ *No one is sorrier than I am about what happened.* **2** [not before noun] **~ (for/**

---

s	t	v	z	ʃ	ʒ	tʃ	dʒ	θ	ð	ŋ
see	tea	van	zoo	shoe	vision	chain	jam	thin	this	sing

about sth) feeling sad and ashamed about sth that has been done: *We're very sorry about the damage to your car.* ◇ *She was sorry that she'd lost her temper.* ◇ *If you say you're sorry we'll forgive you.* ◇ *He says he's really sorry for taking the car without asking.* **3** [not before noun] **~ (that ...) | ~ (to do sth)** feeling disappointed about sth and wishing you had done sth different or had not done sth: *She was sorry that she'd lost contact with Mary.* ◇ *You'll be sorry if I catch you!* ◇ *I was genuinely sorry to be leaving college.* **4** [only before noun] very sad or bad, especially making you feel pity or disapproval: *The business is in a sorry state.* ◇ *They were a sorry sight when they eventually got off the boat.* **IDM** **be/feel sorry for sb** to feel pity or sympathy for sb: *He decided to help Jan as he felt sorry for her.* **feel sorry for yourself** (*informal, disapproving*) to feel unhappy; to pity yourself: *Stop feeling sorry for yourself and think about other people for a change.* **I'm 'sorry to say** used for saying that sth is disappointing: *He didn't accept the job, I'm sorry to say.* **I'm sorry** (*spoken*) **1** used when you are APOLOGIZING for sth: *I'm sorry, I forgot.* ◇ *Oh, I'm sorry. Have I taken the one you wanted?* ◇ *I'm sorry. I can't make it tomorrow.* **2** used for disagreeing with sb or politely saying 'no': *I'm sorry, I don't agree.* ◇ *I'm sorry, I'd rather you didn't go.* **3** used for introducing bad news: *I'm sorry to have to tell you you've failed.*—more at SAFE *adj.*

■ *exclamation* **1** used when you are APOLOGIZING for sth: *Sorry I'm late!* ◇ *Did I stand on your foot? Sorry!* ◇ *Sorry to bother you, but could I speak to you for a moment?* ◇ *Sorry, we don't allow dogs in the house.* ◇ *He didn't even say sorry.* **2** (*especially BrE*) used for asking sb to repeat sth that you have not heard clearly: *Sorry? Could you repeat the question?* **3** used for correcting yourself when you have said sth wrong: *Take the first turning, sorry, the third turning on the right.*

sort /sɔːt; *AmE* sɔːrt/ *noun, verb*

■ *noun* **1** [C] a group or type of people or things that are similar in a particular way: *'What sort of music do you like?' 'Oh, all sorts.'* ◇ *This sort of problem is quite common.* / *These sorts of problems are quite common.* ◇ *He's the sort of person who only cares about money.* ◇ *There are all sorts of jobs you could do.* ◇ *For dessert there's a fruit pie of some sort* (= you are not sure what kind). ◇ (*spoken*) *Most people went on training courses of one sort or another* (= of various types) *last year.* ◇ (*spoken*) *There were snacks—peanuts, olives, that sort of thing.* ◇ (*spoken*) *There are all sorts of activities* (= many different ones) *for kids at the camp site.* ◇ (*spoken*) *What sort of price did you want to pay?* (= approximately how much) ◇ (*spoken*) *What sort of time do you call this?* (= I'm very angry that you have come so late). ⇨ note at KIND **2** [C, usually sing.] (*informal, especially BrE*) a particular type of person: *My brother would never cheat on his wife; he's not that sort.* **3** (*computing*) [sing.] the process of putting data in a particular order: *to do a sort* **IDM** **it takes all sorts (to make a world)** used to say that you think sb's behaviour is very strange or unusual but that everyone is different and likes different things **of 'sorts** (*informal*) used when you are saying that sth is not a good example of a particular type of thing: *He offered us an apology of sorts and we accepted it.* **out of 'sorts** (*especially BrE*) ill/sick or upset: *She was tired and out of sorts by the time she arrived home.* ◇ *Are you feeling all right? You look a bit out of sorts.* **sort of** (*informal*) **1** to some extent but in a way that you cannot easily describe: *She sort of pretends that she doesn't really care.* ◇ *'Do you understand?' 'Sort of.'* **2** (also **sort of like**) (*BrE, spoken*) used when you cannot think of a good word to use to describe sth, or what to say next: *We're sort of like doing it the wrong way.* **a sort of sth** (*informal*) used for describing sth in a not very exact way: *I had a sort of feeling that he wouldn't come.* ◇ *They're a sort of greenish-blue colour.*—more at KIND *n.*

■ *verb* [VN] **1 ~ sth (into sth)** to arrange things in groups or in a particular order according to their type, etc.; to separate things of one type from others: *sorting the mail* ◇ *The computer sorts the words into alphabetical order.* ◇ *Rubbish can easily be separated and sorted into plastics,*

glass and paper.—see also SORT OUT **2** [often passive] (*informal, especially BrE*) to deal with a problem or organize sth/sb in a satisfactory way: *Don't worry. We'll soon have this sorted.* ◇ *It's our problem. We'll get it sorted.* ◇ *It's all sorted.* ◇ *It's time you got yourself sorted.* **IDM** see MAN *n.*, SHEEP, WHEAT **PHRV** **,sort itself 'out** (of a problem) to stop being a problem without anyone having to take action: *It will all sort itself out in the end.* **,sort sth ↔ 'out 1** (*informal*) to organize the contents of sth; to tidy sth: *The cupboards need sorting out.* **2** to organize sth in a satisfactory way: *If you're going to the bus station, can you sort out the tickets for tomorrow?* **,sort sth ↔ 'out (from sth)** to separate sth from a larger group: *Could you sort out the toys that can be thrown away?* ◇ *It was difficult to sort out the lies from the truth.*—related noun SORT-OUT **,sort sth/sb/yourself 'out** (*especially BrE*) to deal with sb's/your own problems in a satisfactory way: *If you can wait a moment, I'll sort it all out for you.* ◇ *You load up the car and I'll sort the kids out.* **,sort sb ↔ 'out** (*informal*) to deal with sb who is causing trouble, etc. especially by punishing or attacking them: *Wait till I get my hands on him—I'll soon sort him out!* **'sort through sth (for sth)** to look through a number of things, either in order to find sth or to put them in order: *I sorted through my paperwork.* ◇ *She sorted through her suitcase for something to wear.*

sor·tie /'sɔːti; *AmE* 'sɔːrti/ *noun* **1** a flight that is made by an aircraft during military operations; an attack made by soldiers **SYN** RAID **2** a short trip away from your home or the place where you are **SYN** FORAY: *I went on a shopping sortie with my mother.* **3 ~ into sth** an effort that you make to do or join sth new **SYN** FORAY: *His first sortie into politics was unsuccessful.*

'sort-out *noun* (*BrE, informal*) an act of arranging or organizing the contents of sth in a tidy or neat way and removing things you do not want

SOS /ˌes əʊ 'es; *AmE* oʊ/ *noun* [sing.] **1** a signal or message that a ship or plane sends when it needs urgent help: *to send an SOS* ◇ *an SOS message* **2** an urgent request for help: *We've received an SOS from the area asking for food parcels.*—see also MAYDAY

,so-'so *adj.* (*informal*) not particularly good or bad; average: *'How are you feeling today?' 'So-so.'* ▶ **,so-'so** *adv.*: *I only did so-so in the exam.*

sotto voce /ˌsɒtəʊ 'vəʊtʃi; *AmE* ˌsɑːtoʊ 'voʊ-/ *adv.* (from *Italian, written*) in a quiet voice so that not everyone can hear ▶ **sotto voce** *adj.*

sou·bri·quet /'suːbrɪkeɪ/ *noun* = SOBRIQUET

souf·flé /'suːfleɪ; *AmE* suː'fleɪ/ *noun* [C, U] a dish made from egg whites, milk and flour mixed together to make it light, flavoured with cheese, fruit, etc. and baked until it rises: *a chocolate/cheese soufflé*

sought *pt, pp* of SEEK

'sought after *adj.* wanted by many people, because it is of very good quality or difficult to get or to find: *This design is the most sought after.* ◇ *a much sought-after actress*

soul /səʊl; *AmE* soʊl/ *noun*

SPIRIT OF PERSON | **1** [C] the spiritual part of a person, believed to exist after death: *He believed his immortal soul was in peril.* ◇ *The howling wind sounded like the wailing of lost souls* (= the spirits of dead people who are not in heaven).

INNER CHARACTER | **2** [C] a person's inner character, containing their true thoughts and feelings: *There was a feeling of restlessness deep in her soul.*

SPIRITUAL/MORAL/ARTISTIC QUALITIES | **3** [sing.] the spiritual and moral qualities of humans in general: *the dark side of the human soul* **4** [U, C] strong and good human feeling, especially that gives a work of art its quality or enables sb to recognize and enjoy that quality: *It was a very polished performance, but it lacked soul.* **5** [sing.] **the ~ of sth** a perfect example of a good quality: *He is the soul of discretion.*

PERSON | **6** [C] (*becoming old-fashioned*) a person of a particular type: *She's lost all her money, poor soul.* ◇ *You're a*

æ	ɑː	e	ɜː	ə	ɪ	iː	i	ɒ	ɔː	ʌ	ʊ	u	uː
cat	father	ten	bird	about	sit	see	many	got	saw	cup	put	actual	too

(BrE)

brave *soul*. **7** [C] (especially in negative sentences) a person: *There wasn't a soul in sight* (= nobody was in sight). ◇ *Don't tell a soul* (= do not tell anyone). ◇ (*literary*) *a village of 300 souls* (= with 300 people living there)

MUSIC | **8** (also **'soul music**) [U] a type of music that expresses strong emotions, made popular by African American musicians: *a soul singer*

IDM **good for the 'soul** (*humorous*) good for you, even if it seems unpleasant: *'Want a ride?' 'No thanks. Walking is good for the soul.'*—more at BARE *v.*, BODY, GOD, HEART, LIFE, SELL *v.*

'soul-destroying *adj.* (of a job or task) very dull and boring, because it has to be repeated many times or because there will never be any improvement

'soul food *noun* [U] the type of food that was traditionally eaten by black people in the southern US

soul·ful /'səʊlfl; *AmE* 'soʊl-/ *adj.* expressing deep feelings, especially feelings of sadness or love: *soulful eyes* ◇ *a soulful melody* ▶ **soul·ful·ly** /-fəli/ *adv.* **soul·ful·ness** *noun* [U]

soul·less /'səʊlləs; *AmE* 'soʊl-/ *adj.* **1** (of things and places) lacking any attractive or interesting qualities that make people feel happy [SYN] DEPRESSING: *They live in soulless concrete blocks.* **2** (of a person) lacking the ability to feel emotions

'soul mate *noun* a person that you have a special friendship with because you understand each other's feelings and interests

'soul music *noun* [U] = SOUL

'soul-searching *noun* [U] the careful examination of your thoughts and feelings, for example in order to reach the correct decision or solution to sth

sound /saʊnd/ *noun, verb, adj., adv.*

■ *noun*

STH YOU HEAR | **1** [C] something that you can hear: *a high/low sound* ◇ *a clicking/buzzing/scratching sound* ◇ *the different sounds and smells of the forest* ◇ *She heard the sound of footsteps outside.* ◇ *He crept into the house trying not to make a sound.* **2** [U] continuous rapid movements, (called VIBRATIONS) that travel through air or water and can be heard when they reach a person's or an animal's ear: *Sound travels more slowly than light.* ⇨ note at NOISE

FROM TELEVISION/RADIO | **3** [U] what you can hear coming from a television, radio, etc., or as part of a film/movie: *Could you turn the sound down?* ◇ *The sound quality of the tapes was excellent.* ◇ *a sound engineer*

OF MUSICIANS | **4** [C, U] the effect that is produced by the music of a particular singer or group of musicians: *I like their sound.*

IMPRESSION | **5** [sing.] **the ~ of** sth the idea or impression that you get of sb/sth from what sb says or what you read: *They had a wonderful time by the sound of it.* ◇ *From the sound of things you were lucky to find him.* ◇ *They're consulting a lawyer? I don't like the sound of that.*

WATER | **6** [C] (often in place names) a narrow passage of water that joins two larger areas of water [SYN] STRAIT

IDM **like, etc. the sound of your own 'voice** (*disapproving*) to like talking a lot or too much, usually without wanting to listen to other people **within (the) sound of** **sth** (*BrE*) near enough to be able to hear sth: *a house within sound of the sea*

■ *verb* (not usually used in the progressive tenses)

GIVE IMPRESSION | **1** *linking verb* to give a particular impression when heard or read about: [V-ADJ] *His voice sounded strange on the phone.* ◇ *She didn't sound surprised when I told her the news.* ◇ *His explanation sounds reasonable to me.* ◇ *Leo made it sound so easy. But it wasn't.* ◇ [V-N] *She sounds just the person we need for the job.* ◇ [V] *You sounded just like your father when you said that.* ◇ *I hope I don't sound as if/as though I'm criticizing you.* **HELP** In spoken English people often use **like** instead of **as if** or **as though**, especially in *AmE*, but this is considered incorrect in written *BrE*.

-SOUNDING | **2** (in adjectives) giving the impression of having a particular sound: *an Italian-sounding name* ◇ *fine-sounding words*

PRODUCE SOUND | **3** to produce a sound; to make sth such as a musical instrument produce a sound: [V] *The bell sounded for the end of the class.* ◇ [VN] *Passing motorists sounded their horns in support.*

GIVE WARNING/SIGNAL | **4** [VN] to give a signal such as a warning by making a sound: *When I saw the smoke, I tried to sound the alarm.* ◇ (*figurative*) *Scientists have sounded a note of caution on the technique.* ◇ *Leaving him out of the team may* **sound the death knell** *for our chances of winning* (= signal the end of our chances).

PRONOUNCE | **5** [VN] (*technical*) to pronounce sth: *You don't sound the 'b' in the word comb.*

MEASURE DEPTH | **6** [VN, V] (*technical*) to measure the depth of the sea or a lake by using a line with a weight attached, or an electronic instrument

IDM see NOTE *n.*, SUSPICIOUSLY

PHR V **,sound 'off (about sth)** (*informal, disapproving*) to express your opinions loudly or in an aggressive way **,sound sb↔'out (about/on sth)|** **,sound sth↔'out** to try to find out from sb what they think about sth, often in an indirect way: *I wanted to sound him out about a job.* ◇ *They decided to sound out her interest in the project.*

■ *adj.* (**sound·er, sound·est**)

RELIABLE | **1** sensible; that you can rely on and that will probably give good results: *a person of sound judgement* ◇ *to reach a sound conclusion* ◇ *He gave me some very sound advice.* ◇ *This gives the design team a sound basis for their work.* **OPP** UNSOUND

THOROUGH | **2** [only before noun] good and thorough: *a sound knowledge/understanding of sth* ◇ *He has* **a sound grasp** *of the issues.*

NOT DAMAGED/HURT | **3** in good condition; not damaged, hurt, etc: *We arrived home safe and sound.* ◇ *to be of sound mind* (= not mentally ill) ◇ *The house needs attention but the roof is sound.* **OPP** UNSOUND

SLEEP | **4** [usually before noun] deep and peaceful: *to have a sound night's sleep* ◇ *to be a sound sleeper*

GOOD, BUT NOT EXCELLENT | **5** good and accurate, but not excellent: *a sound piece of writing* ◇ *a sound tennis player*

PHYSICAL PUNISHMENT | **6** severe: *to give sb a sound beating*

▶ **sound·ness** *noun* [U]: *soundness of judgement* ◇ *financial soundness* ◇ *the soundness of the building's foundations*—see also SOUNDLY

IDM **(as) sound as a 'bell** (*informal*) in perfect condition
■ *adv.* **~ asleep** very deeply asleep

the 'sound barrier *noun* [sing.] the point at which an aircraft's speed is the same as the speed of sound, causing reduced control, a very loud noise (called a SONIC BOOM) and various other effects: *to break the sound barrier* (= to travel faster than the speed of sound)

'sound bite *noun* a very short part of a speech, usually one made by a politician, that is broadcast on a news programme on television or the radio

'sound card *noun* (*computing*) a device that can be put into a computer to allow the use of sound with MULTIMEDIA SOFTWARE

'sound check *noun* a process of checking that the equipment used for recording music, or for playing music at a concert, is working correctly and producing sound of a good quality

'sound effect *noun* [usually pl.] a sound that is made artificially, for example the sound of the wind or a battle, and used in a film/movie, play, computer game, etc. to make it more realistic

'sound engineer *noun* a person who works in a recording or broadcasting STUDIO and whose job is to control the levels and balance of sound

'sounding board *noun* (*written*) a person or group of people that you discuss your ideas with before you make them known or reach a decision

sound·ings /'saʊndɪŋz/ *noun* [pl.] **1** careful questions that are asked in order to find out people's opinions about sth: *They will take soundings among party members.* ◇ *What do your soundings show?* **2** measurements that are made to find out how deep water is: *They took soundings along the canal.*

aɪ	aʊ	eɪ	əʊ	oʊ	ɔɪ	ɪə	eə	ʊə	j	w
my	now	say	go (BrE)	go (AmE)	boy	near	hair	pure	yes	wet

sound·less /'saʊndləs/ *adj.* (*written*) without making any sound; silent: *Her lips parted in a soundless scream.* ▶ **sound·less·ly** *adv.*

sound·ly /'saʊndli/ *adv.* **1** if you sleep **soundly**, you sleep very well and very deeply **2** in a way that is sensible or can be relied on: *Your information is soundly based.* ◊ *a soundly-based conclusion* **3** completely and thoroughly: *The team was soundly defeated.* **4** strongly; firmly: *These houses are soundly built.* **5** very well, but not in an excellent way: *He played soundly.* **6** (of physical punishment) severely: *He was soundly beaten by his mother.*

sound·proof /'saʊndpruːf/ (also **sound·proofed**) *adj.* made so that sound cannot pass through it or into it: *a soundproof room* ▶ **sound·proof** *verb* [VN]

'sound system *noun* equipment for playing recorded or live music and for making it louder

sound·track /'saʊndtræk/ *noun* **1** all the music, speech and sounds that are recorded for a film/movie: *The soundtrack of 'Casablanca' took weeks to edit.* **2** some of the music, and sometimes some speech, from a film/movie or musical play that is recorded on tape or disc for people to buy: *I've just bought the soundtrack of the latest Tarantino movie.*

'sound wave *noun* a VIBRATION in the air, in water, etc. that we hear as sound

soup /suːp/ *noun, verb*
■ *noun* [U, C] a liquid food made by boiling meat, vegetables, etc. in water, often eaten as the first course of a meal: *a bowl of tomato/chicken soup* ◊ (*BrE*) *tinned/packet soups* ◊ (*AmE*) *canned/packaged soups* ◊ *a soup spoon/plate*—picture at CUTLERY
■ *verb* PHRV **,soup sth↔'up** (*informal*) to make changes to sth such as a car or computer, so that it is more powerful or exciting than before

soup·çon /'suːpsɒn; *AmE* '-sɑːn/ *noun* [sing.] (from French, sometimes *humorous*) a very small amount

'soup kitchen *noun* a place where people who have no money can get soup and other food free

sour /'saʊə(r)/ *adj., verb*
■ *adj.* **1** having a bitter taste like the taste of a lemon or of fruit that is not ripe: *sour apples* ◊ *a sour flavour* OPP SWEET—see also SWEET-AND-SOUR **2** (especially of milk) having an unpleasant taste or smell because it is not fresh: *to turn/go sour* **3** (of people) not cheerful; bad-tempered and unpleasant: *a sour and disillusioned woman* ◊ *a sour face/smile* ◊ *The meeting ended on a sour note with several people walking out.* ▶ **sour·ly** *adv.*: *'Who asked you?' he said sourly.* **sour·ness** *noun* [U]: *the sourness of the fruit* ◊ *his increasing sourness* IDM **go/turn 'sour** to stop being pleasant or satisfactory: *Their relationship soon went sour.* **sour 'grapes** (*saying*) used to show that you think sb is jealous and is pretending that sth is not important: *He said he didn't want the job anyway, but that's just sour grapes.*
■ *verb* **1** (of relationships, attitudes, people, etc.) to change so that they become less pleasant or friendly than before; to make sth do this: [V] *The atmosphere at the house soured.* ◊ [VN] *The disagreement over trade tariffs has soured relations between the two countries.* **2** [V, VN] if milk **sours** or if sth **sours** it, it becomes sour and has an unpleasant taste or smell

source /sɔːs; *AmE* sɔːrs/ *noun, verb*
■ *noun* **1** a place, person or thing that you get sth from: *renewable energy sources* ◊ *Your local library will be a useful source of information.* ◊ *What is their main source of income?* **2** [usually pl.] a person, book or document that provides information, especially for study, a piece of written work or news: *He refused to name his sources.* ◊ *Government sources indicated yesterday that cuts may have to be made.* ◊ *source material* ◊ *Historians use a wide range of primary and secondary sources for their research.* **3** a person or thing that causes sth, especially a problem: *a source of pollution/violence* ◊ *a source of anxiety/confusion* **4** the place where a river or stream starts: *the source of the Nile* IDM **at 'source** at the place or the point that

sth comes from or begins from: *Is your salary taxed at source* (= by your employer)?
■ *verb* [VN] [often passive] **~ sth (from ...)** (*business*) to get sth from a particular place: *We source all the meat sold in our stores from British farms.*—see also OUTSOURCE

'source code *noun* [U] (*computing*) a computer program written in text form that must be translated into MACHINE CODE before it can run on a computer

,sour 'cream (*BrE* also **,soured 'cream**) *noun* [U] cream that has been made sour by adding bacteria to it, used in cooking

sour·dough /'saʊədəʊ; *AmE* 'saʊərdoʊ/ *noun* [U] DOUGH (= a mixture of flour, fat and water) that is left to FERMENT so that it has a sour taste, used for making bread; bread made with this DOUGH

sour·puss /'saʊəpʊs; *AmE* 'saʊərpʊs/ *noun* (*informal*) a person who is not cheerful or pleasant

souse /saʊs/ *verb* [VN] [usually passive] to soak sth/sb completely in a liquid

soused /saʊst/ *adj.* **1** [only before noun] (of fish) preserved in salt water and VINEGAR: *soused herring* **2** (*old-fashioned, informal*) drunk

south /saʊθ/ *noun, adj., adv.*
■ *noun* [U, sing.] (*abbr.* S) **1** (usually **the south**) the direction that is on your right when you watch the sun rise; one of the four main points of the COMPASS: *Which way is south?* ◊ *warmer weather coming from the south* ◊ *He lives to the south of* (= further south than) *the city.*—compare EAST, NORTH, WEST—picture at COMPASS **2** (**the south, the South**) the southern part of a country, a region or the world: *birds flying to the south for the winter* ◊ *They bought a villa in the South of France* ◊ *Houses are less expensive in the North than in the South* (= of England). **3** (**the South**) the southern states of the US—see also THE DEEP SOUTH **4** (**the South**) the poorer countries in the southern half of the world
■ *adj.* (*abbr.* S, So.) [only before noun] **1** in or towards the south: *South Wales* ◊ *They live on the south coast.* **2** a **south wind** blows from the south—compare SOUTHERLY
■ *adv.* towards the south: *This room faces south.* IDM **down 'south** (*informal*) to or in the south, especially of England: *They've gone to live down south.*

south·bound /'saʊθbaʊnd/ *adj.* travelling or leading towards the south: *southbound traffic* ◊ *the southbound carriageway of the motorway*

,south-'east *noun* (usually **the south-east**) [sing.] (*abbr.* SE) the direction or region halfway between south and east—picture at COMPASS ▶ **,south-'east** *adv., adj.*

,south-'easter·ly *adj.* **1** [only before noun] in or towards the south-east **2** [usually before noun] (of winds) blowing from the south-east

,south-'eastern *adj.* [only before noun] (*abbr.* SE) connected with the south-east

,south-'eastwards (also **,south-'eastward**) *adv.* towards the south-east ▶ **,south-'eastward** *adj.*

south·er·ly /'sʌðəli; *AmE* -ərli/ *adj., noun*
■ *adj.* **1** [only before noun] in or towards the south: *travelling in a southerly direction* **2** [usually before noun] (of winds) blowing from the south: *a warm southerly breeze*—compare SOUTH
■ *noun* (*pl.* -**ies**) a wind that blows from the south: *warm southerlies*

south·ern /'sʌðən; *AmE* -ərn/ (also **Southern**) *adj.* (*abbr.* S) [usually before noun] situated in the south or facing south; connected with or typical of the south part of the world or a region: *the northern slopes of the mountains* ◊ *southern Spain* ◊ *a southern accent/climate*

south·ern·er /'sʌðənə(r); *AmE* -ərn-/ *noun* a person who comes from or lives in the southern part of a country

south·ern·most /'sʌðənməʊst; *AmE* -ərnmoʊst/ *adj.* [usually before noun] furthest south: *the southernmost part of the island*

south·paw /'saʊθpɔː/ *noun* (*informal, especially AmE*) a person who prefers to use their left hand rather than their right, especially in a sport such as boxing

the ,South 'Pole *noun* [sing.] the point of the earth that is furthest south

S

S

south·wards /ˈsaʊθwədz; *AmE* -wərdz/ (also **south-ward**) *adv.* towards the south: *to go/look/turn south-wards* ▸ **south·ward** *adj.*: *in a southward direction*

south-'west *noun* (usually **the south-west**) [sing.] (*abbr.* **SW**) the direction or region halfway between south and west—picture at COMPASS ◇ **south-'west** *adv., adj.*

south-'wester·ly *adj.* **1** [only before noun] in or towards the south-west **2** [usually before noun] (of winds) blowing from the south-west

south-'western *adj.* [only before noun] (*abbr.* **SW**) connected with the south-west

south-'westwards (also **south-'westward**) *adv.* towards the south-west ▸ **south-'westward** *adj.*

sou·venir /ˌsuːvəˈnɪə(r); *AmE* -ˈnɪr; ˈsuːvənɪr/ *noun* a thing that you buy and/or keep to remind yourself of a place, an occasion, or a holiday/vacation; something that you bring back for other people when you have been on holiday/vacation: *I bought the ring as a souvenir of Greece.*

sou'·wester /ˌsaʊˈwestə(r)/ *noun* **1** a hat made of shiny material that keeps out the rain, with a long wide piece at the back to protect the neck **2** a strong wind or storm coming from the south-west

sov·er·eign /ˈsɒvrɪn; *AmE* ˈsɑːvrən/ *noun, adj.*
■ *noun* **1** (*formal*) a king or queen **2** an old British gold coin worth one pound
■ *adj.* (*formal*) **1** [only before noun] (of a country or state) free to govern itself; completely independent **2** having complete power or the greatest power in the country: *a sovereign ruler* ◇ *Parliament must always remain sovereign.*

sov·er·eign·ty /ˈsɒvrənti; *AmE* ˈsɑːv-/ *noun* [U] (*formal*) **1** ~ (over sth) complete power to govern a country: *The country claimed sovereignty over the island.* ◇ *the sovereignty of Parliament* ◇ (*figurative*) *the idea of consumer sovereignty* **2** the state of being a country with freedom to govern itself: *The declaration proclaimed the full sovereignty of the republic.*

So·viet /ˈsəʊviət; ˈsɒv-; *AmE* ˈsoʊviet; ˈsɑːv-/ *adj.* [usually before noun] connected with the former USSR: *Soviet Russia* ◇ *Soviet troops*

so·viet /ˈsəʊviət; ˈsɒv-; *AmE* ˈsoʊviet; ˈsɑːv-/ *noun* **1** [C] an elected local, district or national council in the former USSR **2** (**the Soviets**) [pl.] (*especially AmE*) the people of the former USSR

sow¹ /saʊ; *AmE* soʊ/ *verb*—see also SOW² (**sowed, sown** /səʊn; *AmE* soʊn/ or (**sowed, sowed**) **1** ~ sth (in/on sth) | ~ sth (with sth) to plant or spread seeds in or on the ground: [VN] *Sow the seeds in rows.* ◇ *The fields around had been sown with wheat.* ◇ [V] *Water well after sowing.* **2** [VN] ~ sth (in sth) to introduce or spread feelings or ideas, especially ones that cause trouble: *to sow doubt in sb's mind* ◇ *to sow confusion/dissension* **IDM** **sow the seeds of sth** to start the process that leads to a particular situation or result: *In this way he sowed the seeds of his own success.* **sow (your) wild 'oats** (of young men) to go through a period of wild behaviour while young, especially having a lot of romantic or sexual relationships—more at REAP

sow² /saʊ/ *noun* a female pig—compare BOAR, HOG—see also SOW¹ **IDM** see SILK

sower /ˈsəʊə(r); *AmE* ˈsoʊ-/ *noun* a person or machine that puts seeds in the ground

soya /ˈsɔɪə/ (*BrE*) (*AmE* **soy**) *noun* [U] the plant on which soya beans grow; the food obtained from soya beans: *a soya crop* ◇ *soya flour/milk/oil*

'soya bean (*BrE*) (*AmE* **soy·bean**) /ˈsɔɪ biːn/ *noun* a type of bean, originally from SE Asia, that is used instead of meat or animal PROTEIN in some types of food: *a soya bean casserole*

soy sauce /ˌsɔɪ ˈsɔːs/ (also **soya 'sauce**) *noun* [U] a thin dark brown sauce that is made from SOYA BEANS and has a salty taste, used in Chinese and Japanese cooking

soz·zled /ˈsɒzld; *AmE* ˈsɑːzld/ *adj.* (*BrE, slang*) very drunk

spa /spɑː/ *noun* **1** a place where water with minerals in

it, that is considered to be good for your health, comes up naturally out of the ground; the name given to a town that has such a place and where there are, or were, places where people could drink the water: *Leamington Spa* ◇ *a spa town/resort* ◇ *spa waters* **2** (*especially AmE*) a place where people can relax and improve their health, with, for example, a swimming pool: *a superb health spa which includes sauna, Turkish bath and fitness rooms* **3** (*especially AmE*) = JACUZZI

space /speɪs/ *noun, verb*
■ *noun*
EMPTY AREA | **1** [U] an amount of an area or of a place that is empty or that is available for use **SYN** ROOM: *disk/floor/office/shelf space* ◇ *We must make good use of the available space.* ◇ *That desk takes up too much space.* ◇ *There is very little storage space in the department.* ◇ *Can we make space for an extra chair?* ▷ note at PLACE **2** [C] an area or a place that is empty: *a large/small/narrow/wide space* ◇ *a space two metres by three metres* ◇ *a parking space* ◇ *crowded together in a confined space* ◇ *I'll clear a space for your books.* ◇ *Put it in the space between the table and the wall.* **3** [U] the quality of being large and empty, allowing you to move freely **SYN** SPACIOUSNESS: *The room has been furnished and decorated to give a feeling of space.* **4** [C, U] a large area of land that has no buildings on it: *the wide open spaces of the Canadian prairies* ◇ *It's a city with fine buildings and plenty of open space.*
OUTSIDE EARTH'S ATMOSPHERE | **5** (also **outer 'space**) [U] the area outside the earth's atmosphere where all the other planets and stars are: *the first woman in space* ◇ *the possibility of visitors from outer space* ◇ *a space flight/mission*
PERIOD OF TIME | **6** [C, usually sing.] a period of time: *Forty-four people died in the space of five days.* ◇ *They had achieved a lot in a short space of time.* ◇ *Leave a space of two weeks between appointments.*
IN WRITING/PRINTING | **7** [U, C] the part of a line, page or document that is empty and is available for use: *Don't waste space by leaving a wide margin.* ◇ *There was not enough space to print all the letters we received.* ◇ *Leave a space after the comma.*
FREEDOM | **8** [U] the freedom and the time to think or do what you want to: *She was upset and needed space.* ◇ *You have to give teenagers plenty of space.*—see also BREATHING SPACE
WHERE THINGS EXIST/MOVE | **9** [U] the whole area in which all things exist and move: *It is quite possible that space and time are finite.*
IDM **look/stare/gaze into 'space** to look straight in front of you without looking at a particular thing, usually because you are thinking about sth—more at WASTE *n.*, WATCH *v.*
■ *verb* [VN] [usually +*adv./prep.*] [often passive] to arrange things so that they have regular spaces between them: *evenly/widely spaced plants* ◇ *a row of closely spaced dots* ◇ *Space the posts about a metre apart.*
PHR V **space 'out** (*informal, especially AmE*) to take no notice of what is happening around you, especially as a result of taking drugs—see also SPACED OUT **,space sth ↔ 'out** to arrange things with a wide space between them: *The houses are spaced out in this area of town.*

'space-age *adj.* [usually before noun] (*informal*) (especially of design or technology) very modern and advanced: *a space-age kitchen*

'space bar *noun* a bar on the keyboard of a computer or TYPEWRITER that you press to make spaces between words

space·craft /ˈspeɪskrɑːft; *AmE* -kræft/ *noun* (*pl.* **space-craft**) a vehicle that travels in space

,spaced 'out (also **spacey**) *adj.* (*informal*) not completely conscious of what is happening around you, often because of taking drugs

'space heater *noun* (*AmE*) an electric device for heating a room

space·man /ˈspeɪsmæn/ *noun* (*pl.* **-men** /-men/) **1** (*informal*) a man who travels into space; an ASTRONAUT **2** (in stories) a being that visits the earth from another planet **SYN** ALIEN—see also SPACEWOMAN

s	t	v	z	ʃ	ʒ	tʃ	dʒ	θ	ð	ŋ
see	tea	van	zoo	shoe	vision	chain	jam	thin	this	sing

'space probe *noun* = PROBE

space·ship /'speɪsʃɪp/ *noun* a vehicle that travels in space, carrying people

'space shuttle (also **shuttle**) *noun* a spacecraft designed to be used, for example, for travelling between the earth and a space station

'space station *noun* a large structure that is sent into space and remains above the earth as a base for people working and travelling in space

space·suit /'speɪssuːt; *BrE* also -sjuːt/ *noun* a special suit that covers the whole body and has a supply of air, allowing sb to survive and move around in space

'space-time *noun* [U] (*physics*) the universe considered as a CONTINUUM with four measurements—length, width, depth and time—inside which any event or physical object is LOCATED

space·woman /'speɪswʊmən/ *noun* (*pl.* **-women** /-wɪmɪn/) a woman who travels into space

spacey /'speɪsi/ *adj.* = SPACED OUT

spa·cial *adj.* = SPATIAL

spa·cing /'speɪsɪŋ/ *noun* [U] **1** the amount of space that is left between things, especially between the words or lines printed on a page: *single/double spacing* (= with one or two lines left between lines of type) **2** the amount of time that is left between things happening: *In music, the spacing of intervals is vital.*

spa·cious /'speɪʃəs/ *adj.* (*approving*) (of a room or building) large and with plenty of space for people to move around in ▶ **spa·cious·ly** *adv.* **spa·cious·ness** *noun* [U]: *White walls can give a feeling of spaciousness.*

spade /speɪd/ *noun* **1** [C] a garden tool with a broad metal blade and a long handle, used for digging: *Turn the soil over with a spade.* ◊ *The children took their buckets and spades to the beach.*—compare SHOVEL—picture at GARDEN **2** (**spades**) [pl., U] one of the four sets of cards (called SUITS) in a pack/deck of cards. The cards have a black design shaped like pointed leaves with short stems: *the five/queen/ace of spades*—picture on page A8 **3** [C] a card from the set of spades: *You must play a spade if you have one.* IDM **in 'spades** (*informal*) in large amounts or to a great degree: *He'd got his revenge now, and in spades.*—more at CALL *v.*

spade·work /'speɪdwɜːk; *AmE* -wɜːrk/ *noun* [U] the hard work that has to be done in order to prepare for sth

spa·ghetti /spə'geti/ *noun* [U] PASTA in the shape of long thin sticks that look like string when they are cooked

spaghetti bolognese /spəˌgeti ˌbɒlə'neɪz; *AmE* ˌbɑːlə-/ *noun* [U, C] a dish of spaghetti with a sauce of meat, tomatoes, etc.

spake /speɪk/ (*old use*) *pt* of SPEAK

spam /spæm/ *noun* [U] **1** (**Spam**™) finely chopped cooked meat that has been pressed together in a container, usually sold in cans and served cold in slices **2** (*informal*) advertising material sent by e-mail to people who have not asked for it—compare JUNK MAIL

spam·ming /'spæmɪŋ/ *noun* [U] (*informal*) the practice of sending mail, especially advertising material, through the Internet to a large number of people, who have not asked for it

span /spæn/ *noun, verb, adj.*
■ *noun* **1** the length of time that sth lasts or is able to continue: *I worked with him over a span of six years.* ◊ *The project must be completed within a specific time span.* ◊ *Small children have a short attention span.*—see also LIFESPAN **2** ~ (**of sth**) a range or variety of sth: *Managers have a wide span of control.* ◊ *These forests cover a broad span of latitudes.* **3** the part of a bridge or an arch between one vertical support and another: *The bridge crosses the river in a single span.* **4** the width of sth from one side to the other: *The kite has a span of 1.5 metres.*—see also WINGSPAN
■ *verb* (**-nn-**) [VN] **1** to last all through a period of time or to cover the whole of it: *His acting career spanned 55 years.* ◊ *Family photos spanning five generations were stolen.* **2** to include a large area or a lot of things: *The operation, which spanned nine countries, resulted in 200 arrests.* **3** to

stretch right across sth, from one side to the other: *a series of bridges spanning the river*
■ *adj.* IDM see SPICK

Span·dex™ /'spændeks/ *noun* = LYCRA

span·gle /'spæŋgl/ *verb, noun*
■ *verb* [VN] [usually passive] ~ **sth** (**with sth**) to cover or to decorate sth with small pieces of sth shiny—see also STAR-SPANGLED BANNER
■ *noun* a small piece of shiny metal or plastic used to decorate clothes [SYN] SEQUIN: *a dress covered with red spangles*

span·iel /'spænjəl/ *noun* a dog with large soft ears that hang down. There are several types of spaniel: *a cocker spaniel* ◊ *a springer spaniel*

Spanish moss /ˌspænɪʃ 'mɒs; *AmE* 'mɔːs/ *noun* [U] a tropical American plant that has long thin grey leaves and that grows over other trees

spank /spæŋk/ *verb* [VN] to hit sb, especially a child, several times on their bottom as a punishment—compare SMACK ▶ **spank** *noun*

spank·ing /'spæŋkɪŋ/ *noun, adv., adj.*
■ *noun* [C, U] a series of hits on the bottom, given to sb, especially a child, as a punishment: *to give sb a spanking* ◊ *I don't agree with spanking.*
■ *adv.* (*informal*) when you say that sth is **spanking** new, etc. you are emphasizing that it is very new, etc.
■ *adj.* [only before noun] (*informal*) very fast, good or impressive: *The horse set off at a spanking pace.*

span·ner /'spænə(r)/ (*BrE*) (also **wrench** *AmE, BrE*) *noun* a metal tool with a specially shaped end for holding and turning NUTS and BOLTS (= small metal rings and pins that hold things together): *I'll need a spanner to change the back wheel.*—compare ADJUSTABLE SPANNER—picture at TOOL IDM (**throw**) **a 'spanner in the works** (*BrE*) (*AmE* (**throw**) **a** (**'monkey**) **'wrench in the works**) (to cause) a delay or problem with sth that sb is planning or doing

spar /spɑː(r)/ *verb, noun*
■ *verb* (**-rr-**) [V] ~ (**with sb**) **1** to make the movements used in boxing, either in training or to test the speed of your opponent's reaction **2** to argue with sb, usually in a friendly way
■ *noun* **1** a strong pole used to support the sails, etc. on a ship **2** a structure that supports the wing of an aircraft

spare /speə(r); *AmE* sper/ *adj., verb, noun*
■ *adj.*
NOT USED/NEEDED | **1** [usually before noun] that is not being used or is not needed at the present time: *We've got a spare bedroom, if you'd like to stay.* ◊ *I'm afraid I haven't got any spare cash.* ◊ *Are there any tickets going spare* (= are there any available, not being used by sb else)?
EXTRA | **2** [only before noun] kept in case you need to replace the one you usually use; extra: *a spare key/tyre* ◊ *Take some spare clothes in case you get wet.*
TIME | **3** available to do what you want with rather than work: *He's studying music in his spare time.* ◊ *I haven't had a spare moment this morning.*
PERSON | **4** (*written*) thin, and usually quite tall
IDM **go 'spare** (*BrE, informal*) to become very angry or upset
■ *verb*
TIME/MONEY/ROOM/THOUGHT, etc. | **1** ~ **sth/sb** (**for sb/sth**) | ~ (**sb**) **sth** to make sth such as time or money available to sb or for sth, especially when it requires an effort for you to do this: [VN] *I'd love to have a break, but I can't spare the time just now.* ◊ *We can only spare one room for you.* ◊ *Could you spare one of your staff to help us out?* ◊ *You should spare a thought for* (= think about) *the person who cleans up after you.* ◊ [VNN] *Surely you can spare me a few minutes?*
SAVE SB PAIN/TROUBLE | **2** ~ **sb/yourself** (**from**) **sth** to save sb/yourself from having to go through an unpleasant experience: [VNN] *He wanted to spare his mother any anxiety.* ◊ *Please spare me* (= do not tell me) *the gruesome details.* ◊ *You could have spared yourself an unnecessary trip by phoning in advance.* ◊ [VN] *She was spared from the ordeal of appearing in court.*

S

æ	ɑː	e	ɜː	ə	ɪ	iː	i	ɒ	ɔː	ʌ	ʊ	u	uː
cat	father	ten	bird	about	sit	see	many	got	saw	cup	put	actual	too
								(BrE)					

NOT HARM/DAMAGE | 3 [usually passive] ~ **sb/sth (from sth)** (*literary*) to allow sb/sth to escape harm, damage or death, especially when others do not escape it: [VN] *They killed the men but spared the children.* ◇ *During the bombing only one house was spared* (= was not hit by a bomb). [also VNN]

NO EFFORT/EXPENSE, etc. | 4 [VN] to do everything possible to achieve sth or to do sth well without trying to limit the time or money involved: *He spared no effort to make her happy again.* ◇ *No expense was spared in furnishing the new office.*

WORK HARD | 5 [VN] **not ~ yourself** to work as hard as possible

IDM **spare sb's 'blushes** (*BrE*) to save sb from an embarrassing situation: *A last minute goal spared their blushes.* **spare sb's 'feelings** to be careful not to do or say anything that might upset sb **to 'spare** if you have time, money, etc. **to spare,** you have more than you need: *I've got absolutely no money to spare this month.* ◇ *We arrived at the airport with five minutes to spare.*

■ *noun* **1** an extra thing that you keep in case you need to replace the one you usually use (used especially about a tyre of a car): *to get the spare out of the boot/trunk* ◇ *I've lost my key and I haven't got a spare.* **2** (**spares**) [pl.] (*especially BrE*) = SPARE PARTS: *It can be difficult to get spares for some older makes of car.*

,**spare 'part** *noun* [usually pl.] a new part that you buy to replace an old or broken part of car, machine, etc.

,**spare 'rib** *noun* a RIB of PORK (= meat from a pig) with most of the meat cut off: *barbecued spare ribs*

,**spare 'tyre** (*BrE*) (*AmE* ,**spare 'tire**) *noun* **1** an extra wheel for a car **2** (*BrE*) a large roll of fat around sb's waist

spar·ing /ˈspeərɪŋ; *AmE* ˈsper-/ *adj.* ~ **(with sth)** careful to use or give only a little of sth: *Doctors now advise only sparing use of such creams.* ◇ *He was always sparing with his praise.* ▶ **spar·ing·ly** *adv.:* *Use the cream very sparingly.*

spark /spɑːk; *AmE* spɑːrk/ *noun, verb*
■ *noun* **1** [C] a very small burning piece of material that is produced by sth that is burning or by hitting two hard substances together: *A shower of sparks flew up the chimney.* **2** [C] a small flash of light produced by an electric current: *sparks from a faulty light switch* ◇ *A spark ignites the fuel in a car engine.* **3** [C, usually sing.] ~ **of sth** a small amount of a particular quality or feeling: *For a moment, she felt a spark of hope.* **4** [U, sing.] a special quality of energy, intelligence or enthusiasm that makes sb very imaginative, amusing, etc: *As a writer he seemed to lack creative spark.* **5** [C] an action or event that causes sth important to develop, especially trouble or violence: *These were the sparks of revolution.* **6** [C, usually pl.] feelings of anger or excitement between people: *Sparks flew at the meeting* (= there was a lot of argument). **IDM** see BRIGHT *adj.*
■ *verb* **1** [VN] ~ **sth (off)** to cause sth to start or develop, especially suddenly: *The proposal would spark a storm of protest around the country.* ◇ *The riots were sparked off by the arrest of a local leader.* ◇ *Winds brought down power lines, sparking a fire.* **2** [V] to produce small flashes of fire or electricity: *a sparking, crackling fire* ◇ (*figurative*) *The game suddenly sparked to life.*

spar·kle /ˈspɑːkl; *AmE* ˈspɑːrkl/ *verb, noun*
■ *verb* [V] ~ **(with sth)** **1** to shine brightly with small flashes of light: *sparkling eyes* ◇ *Her jewellery sparkled in the candlelight.* ◇ *The sky sparkled with brilliant stars.* **2** to be full of life, enthusiasm or humour: *He always sparkles at parties.*
■ *noun* [C, U] **1** a series of flashes of light produced by light hitting a shiny surface: *the sparkle of glass/crystal* ◇ *the sparkles of light on water* ◇ (*figurative*) *There was a sparkle of excitement in her eyes.* **2** the quality of being lively and original: *The performance lacked sparkle.*

spark·ler /ˈspɑːklə(r); *AmE* ˈspɑːrk-/ *noun* a type of small FIREWORK that you hold in your hand and light. It burns with many bright sparks.

spark·ling /ˈspɑːklɪŋ; *AmE* ˈspɑːrk-/ *adj.* (also *less frequent, informal* **sparkly** /ˈspɑːkli; *AmE* ˈspɑːrkli/) **1** shining and flashing with light: *the calm and sparkling waters of the lake* ◇ *sparkling blue eyes* **2** (of drinks) containing bubbles of gas: *a sparkling wine* ◇ *sparkling mineral water* **3** interesting and amusing: *a sparkling conversation/personality* **4** excellent; of very good quality **SYN** BRILLIANT: *The champion was in sparkling form.*

'**spark plug** (also **plug**) (*BrE* also '**sparking plug**) *noun* a part in a car engine that produces a SPARK (= flash of electricity) which makes the fuel burn and starts the engine

sparky /ˈspɑːki; *AmE* ˈspɑːrki/ *adj.* (*BrE, informal*) full of life; interesting and amusing: *a sparky personality/kid*

'**sparring partner** *noun* **1** a person that you regularly have friendly arguments or discussions with **2** (in boxing) a person that a boxer regularly practises with during training

spar·row /ˈspærəʊ; *AmE* -roʊ/ *noun* a small brown and grey bird, common in many parts of the world

spar·row·hawk /ˈspærəʊhɔːk; *AmE* -roʊ-/ *noun* a small BIRD OF PREY (= a bird that kills other creatures for food) of the HAWK family

sparse /spɑːs; *AmE* spɑːrs/ *adj.* (*comparative* **sparser**, no *superlative*) only present in small amounts or numbers and often spread over a large area: *the sparse population of the islands* ◇ *Vegetation becomes sparse higher up the mountains.* ◇ *The information available on the subject is sparse.* ▶ **sparse·ly** *adv.:* *a sparsely populated area* **sparse·ness** *noun* [U]

spar·tan /ˈspɑːtn; *AmE* ˈspɑːrtn/ *adj.* (of conditions) simple or harsh; lacking anything that makes life easier or more pleasant **ORIGIN** From **Sparta**, a powerful city in ancient Greece, where the people were not interested in comfort or luxury. **OPP** LUXURIOUS

spasm /ˈspæzəm/ *noun* **1** [C, U] a sudden and often painful tightening of a muscle, which you cannot control: *She felt a muscle spasm in her back.* ◇ *The injection sent his leg into spasm.* **2** [C] ~ **(of sth)** a sudden strong feeling or reaction that lasts for a short time: *a spasm of anxiety/anger/coughing/pain*

spas·mod·ic /spæzˈmɒdɪk; *AmE* -ˈmɑːd-/ *adj.* **1** happening suddenly for short periods of time; not regular or continuous: *a spasmodic interest in politics* ◇ *There was spasmodic fighting in the area yesterday.* **2** (*technical*) caused by your muscles becoming tight in a way that you cannot control: *spasmodic movements* ▶ **spas·mod·ic·al·ly** /-kli/ *adv.*

spas·tic /ˈspæstɪk/ *adj.* **1** (*medical or old-fashioned*) having or caused by CEREBRAL PALSY, an illness which makes it difficult for sb to control their muscles and movements. Using this word is now often considered offensive: *spastic children* ◇ *spastic reactions* **2** (*informal*) an offensive word, sometimes used by children to mean 'stupid' ▶ **spas·tic** *noun*

spat /spæt/ *noun* **1** (*informal*) a short argument or disagreement about sth unimportant **2** [usually pl.] a fabric covering for the ankle that was worn in the past by men over the shoe and fastened with buttons at the side—see also SPIT, SPITTING, SPAT, SPAT *v.*

spate /speɪt/ *noun* [usually sing.] ~ **of sth** a large number of things, which are usually unpleasant, that happen suddenly within a short period of time: *The bombing was the latest in a spate of terrorist attacks.* **IDM** **in (full) 'spate** (*especially BrE*) (of a river) containing more water and flowing more strongly than usual: *After heavy rain, the river was in spate.* ◇ (*figurative*) *Celia was in full spate* (= completely involved in talking and not likely to stop or able to be interrupted).

spa·tial (also **spa·cial**) /ˈspeɪʃl/ *adj.* (*formal or technical*) relating to space and the position, size, shape, etc. of things in it: *changes taking place in the spatial distribution of the population* ◇ *the development of a child's spatial awareness* (= the ability to judge the positions and sizes of objects) ▶ **spa·tial·ly** /-ʃəli/ *adv.*

spat·ter /ˈspætə(r)/ *verb, noun*
■ *verb* **1** ~ **sb/sth (with sth)** | ~ **sth (on/over sb/sth)** to cover sb/sth with drops of liquid, dirt, etc., especially

aɪ	aʊ	eɪ	əʊ	oʊ	ɔɪ	ɪə	eə	ʊə	j	w
my	now	say	go	go	boy	near	hair	pure	yes	wet
			(BrE)	(AmE)						

accidentally: [VN] *blood-spattered walls* ◊ *As the bus passed, it spattered us with mud.* ◊ *Oil was spattered on the floor.* [also V] **2** [V+*adv./prep.*] (of liquid) to fall on a surface in drops, often noisily: *We heard the rain spattering on the roof.*

■ *noun* (also **spat·ter·ing**) [sing.] ~ **(of sth)** a number of drops of a liquid or small amounts of sth that hit a surface; the noise this makes: *a spatter of rain against the window* ◊ *a spattering of blood* ◊ (*figurative*) *a spatter of applause*

spat·ula /'spætʃələ/ *noun* **1** a tool with a broad flat blade used for mixing and spreading things, especially in cooking and painting—picture at LABORATORY **2** (*especially AmE*) = FISH SLICE **3** (*BrE*) (*AmE* **'tongue depressor**) a thin flat instrument that doctors use for pressing the tongue down when they are examining sb's throat

spawn /spɔːn/ *verb, noun*
■ *verb* **1** [V, VN] (of fish, FROGS, etc.) to lay eggs **2** [VN] (often *disapproving*) to cause sth to develop or be produced: *The band's album spawned a string of hit singles.*
■ *noun* [U] a soft substance containing the eggs of fish, FROGS etc.—see also FROGSPAWN

spay /speɪ/ *verb* [VN] (*technical*) to remove the OVARIES of a female animal, to prevent it from breeding: *Have you had your cat spayed?*

speak /spiːk/ *verb* (**spoke** /spəʊk; *AmE* spoʊk/ **spoken** /'spəʊkən; *AmE* 'spoʊ-/)

HAVE CONVERSATION | **1** [V] ~ **(to sb) (about sth/sb)** | ~ **(with sb) (about sth/sb)** to talk to sb about sth; to have a conversation with sb: *I've spoken to the manager about it.* ◊ *The President refused to speak to the waiting journalists.* ◊ (*especially AmE*) *Can I speak with you for a minute?* ◊ *'Can I speak to Susan?' 'Speaking.'* (= at the beginning of a telephone conversation) ◊ *'Do you know him?' 'Not to speak to.'* (= only by sight) ◊ *I saw her in the street but we didn't speak.*

USE VOICE | **2** [V] to use your voice to say sth: *He can't speak because of a throat infection.* ◊ *Please speak more slowly.* ◊ *Without speaking, she stood up and went out.* ◊ *He speaks with a strange accent.* ◊ *She has a beautiful speaking voice.*

MENTION/DESCRIBE | **3** [V] ~ **of/about sth/sb** to mention or describe sth/sb: *She still speaks about him with great affection.* ◊ *Witnesses spoke of a great ball of flame.* ◊ *Speaking of travelling,* (= referring back to a subject just mentioned) *are you going anywhere exciting this year?*

A LANGUAGE | **4** [VN] (not used in the progressive tenses) to be able to use a particular language: *to speak several languages/a little Urdu/an unusual dialect* ◊ *Do you speak English?* **5** to use a particular language to express yourself: [VN] *What language is it they're speaking?* ◊ [V] *Would you prefer it if we spoke in German?*

-SPEAKING | **6** (in adjectives) speaking the language mentioned: *French-speaking Canada* ◊ *non-English-speaking students*

-SPEAK | **7** (in nouns) (*informal*, often *disapproving*) the language or JARGON of a particular group, organization or subject: *computerspeak* ◊ *eurospeak*

MAKE SPEECH | **8** [V] [usually +*adv./prep.*] to make a speech to an audience: *to speak in public/on the radio/at a conference/to Congress* ◊ *Professor Wilson was invited to speak about the results of his research.* ◊ *She spoke in favour of the new tax.*

SAY/STATE | **9** [VN] to say or state sth: *She was clearly speaking the truth.* ◊ *He spoke the final words of the play.*—see also SPOKEN

IDM **be on 'speaking terms (with sb)** | **be 'speaking (to sb)** to be willing to be polite or friendly towards sb, especially after an argument: *She's not been on speaking terms with her uncle for years.* ◊ *Are they speaking to each other again yet?* **no sth/nothing to 'speak of** | **not to 'speak of** such a small amount of sth that is not worth mentioning: *She's saved a little money but nothing to speak of.* ◊ *They've got no friends to speak of.* **generally, 'broadly, 'roughly, 'relatively, etc. speaking** used to show that what you are saying is true in a general, etc. way: *Generally speaking, the more you pay, the more you get.* ◊ *There are, broadly speaking, two ways of doing this.*

◊ *Personally speaking, I've always preferred Italian food.* **,so to 'speak** used to emphasize that you are expressing sth in an unusual or amusing way: *They were all very similar. All cut from the same cloth, so to speak.* **speak for it'self/them'selves** to be so easy to see and understand that you do not need to say anything else about it/them: *Her success speaks for itself.* **speak for my'self/her'self/ him'self, etc.** to express what you think or want yourself, rather than sb else doing it for you: *I'm quite capable of speaking for myself, thank you!* **speak for your'self** (*spoken, informal*) used to tell sb that a general statement they have just made is not true of you: *'We didn't play very well.' 'Speak for yourself!'* (= I think that I played well) **speaking as sth** used to say that you are the type of person mentioned and are expressing your opinion from that point of view: *Speaking as a parent, I'm very concerned about standards in education.* **speak your 'mind** to say exactly what you think, in a very direct way **,speak out of 'turn** to say sth when you should not, for example because it is not the right time or you are not the right person to say it **speak 'volumes (about/for sth/sb)** to tell you a lot about sth/sb, without the need for words **speak 'well/'ill of sb** (*formal*) to say good or bad things about sb—more at ACTION *n.*, DEVIL, FACT, ILL *n.*, LANGUAGE, MANNER, STRICTLY, TURN *n.*

PHRV **'speak for sb** to state the views or wishes of a person or a group; to act as a representative for sb **'speak of sth** (*formal*) to be evidence that sth exists or is present: *Everything here speaks of perfect good taste.* **,speak 'out (against sth)** to state your opinions publicly, especially in opposition to sth and in a way that takes courage: *He was the only one to speak out against the decision.*—see also OUTSPOKEN **'speak to sb (about sth)** (*informal*) to talk to sb in a serious way about sth wrong they have done, to try and stop them doing it again **,speak 'up** usually used in orders to tell sb to speak more loudly: *Please speak up—we can't hear you at the back.* **,speak 'up (for sb/sth)** to say what you think clearly and freely, especially in order to support or defend sb/sth

---

WHICH WORD? (?)
speak / talk

Speak and **talk** have similar meanings.
Talk is more common in spoken English and usually suggests that two or more people are having a conversation or discussing something: *We talked on the phone for nearly an hour.* ◊ *John and I have been talking about our families.* ◊ *Could I talk to you about the travel arrangements?* **Talk with** is more formal than **talk to** in *BrE*, but it is very general in *AmE*: *He refused to talk with/to reporters.*
Speak is a little more formal and suggests that someone is using their voice or that one person is saying something to a group: *I was so shocked I couldn't speak.* ◊ *Could you speak louder?* ◊ *A doctor spoke to the class about/on stress.* **Speak to / with** is often used in polite requests, for example when you are making a phone call. **Speak with** is a little more formal in *BrE*: *Hello, could I speak to Michael?* ◊ *I'd like to speak to/with the manager, please.*
When a noun follows **speak**, it must be a language: *He speaks Italian.* **Talk** can be followed by nouns such as *business* or *sense.*

---

speak·easy /'spiːkiːzi/ *noun* (*pl.* **-ies**) a place in the US where people could buy alcohol illegally, at the time in the 1920s and 1930s when it was illegal to make or sell alcohol

speak·er /'spiːkə(r)/ *noun* **1** a person who gives a talk or makes a speech: *Sir David Bellamy was a guest speaker at the conference.* ◊ *She was a brilliant public speaker.* **2** a person who is or was speaking: *I looked around to see who the speaker was.* **3** a person who speaks a particular language: *French speakers* ◊ *native speakers of English* **4** (**the**) **Speaker** the title of the person whose job is to control the discussions in a parliament: *the Speaker of the House of Commons/Representatives* **5** the part of a radio

S

---

b	d	f	g	h	k	l	m	n	p	r
bad	**did**	**fall**	**get**	**hat**	**cat**	**leg**	**man**	**now**	**pen**	**red**

or piece of musical or computing equipment that the sound comes out of: *a CD player and radio with two ultra-slim speakers*—picture on page 250—see also LOUDSPEAKER

speak·er·phone /'spi:kəfəʊn; *AmE* -ərfoʊn/ *noun* (*AmE*) a telephone that can be used without being held, because it contains a MICROPHONE and a LOUDSPEAKER

spear /spɪə(r); *AmE* spɪr/ *noun, verb*
- *noun* **1** a weapon with a long wooden handle and a sharp metal point used for fighting, hunting and fishing in the past **2** the long pointed stem of some plants—picture on page A3
- *verb* [VN] to push or throw a spear or other pointed object through sth/sb: *They were standing in the river spearing fish.* ◊ *She speared an olive with her fork.*

spear·head /'spɪəhed; *AmE* 'spɪrhed/ *noun, verb*
- *noun* [usually sing.] (*written*) a person or group that begins an activity or leads an attack against sb/sth
- *verb* [VN] (*written*) to begin an activity or lead an attack against sb/sth: *He is spearheading a campaign for a new stadium in the town.*

spear·mint /'spɪəmɪnt; *AmE* 'spɪrm-/ *noun* [U] a type of MINT used especially in making sweets/candy and TOOTHPASTE: *spearmint chewing gum*—compare PEPPERMINT

spec /spek/ *noun* (*BrE*) (*AmE* **specs**) a detailed description of sth, especially the design and materials needed to produce sth: *We want the machine manufactured to our own spec.*—see also SPECIFICATION, SPECS **IDM** **on 'spec** (*BrE, informal*) when you do sth **on spec**, you are trying to achieve sth without organizing it in advance, but hoping you will be lucky: *I went to the concert on spec—I hadn't reserved a seat.*

spe·cial /'speʃl/ *adj., noun*
- *adj.* **1** [usually before noun] not ordinary or usual; different from what is normal: *The school will only allow this in special circumstances.* ◊ *Some of the officials have special privileges.* ◊ *There is something special about this place.* **2** more important than others; deserving or getting more attention than usual: *What are your special interests?* ◊ *She's a very special friend.* ◊ *Our special guest on next week's show will be…* ◊ *Don't lose it—it's special.* **3** organized or intended for a particular purpose: *a special event/occasion* ◊ *These teachers need special training.* **4** used by or intended for one particular person or group of people: *She has a special way of smiling.* ◊ *He sent a special message to the men.* **5** [only before noun] better or more than usual: *As an only child she got special attention.* ◊ *Please take special care of it.*—compare ESPECIAL
- *noun* **1** something that is not usually available but is provided for a particular purpose or on one occasion: *an election-night special on television* ◊ *The menu changes regularly and there are daily specials to choose from.* **2** (*informal, especially AmE*) a price for a particular product in a shop/store or restaurant that is lower than usual: *There's a special on coffee this week.*

'special agent *noun* a DETECTIVE who works for the FEDERAL government in the US, for example for the FBI

'Special Branch *noun* [sing.+ sing./pl. *v.*] the department of the British police force that deals with the defence of the country against political crimes and TERRORISM

‚special 'constable *noun* (in Britain) a person who is not a professional police officer but who is trained to help the police force, especially during an emergency

‚special de'livery *noun* [U] a service that delivers a letter, etc. faster than normal

‚special edu'cation *noun* [U] the education of children who have physical or learning problems

‚special ef'fects *noun* [pl.] unusual or exciting pieces of action in films/movies or television programmes, that are created by computers or clever photography to show things that do not normally exist or happen

spe·cial·ism /'speʃəlɪzəm/ *noun* **1** [C] an area of study or work that sb SPECIALIZES in: *a business degree with a specialism in computing* ◊ *Dr Crane's specialism is tropical diseases.* **2** [U] the fact of SPECIALIZING in a particular subject

spe·cial·ist /'speʃəlɪst/ *noun* **1** a person who is an expert in a particular area of work or study: *a specialist in Japanese history* **2** a doctor who has SPECIALIZED in a particular area of medicine: *a cancer specialist*—compare GENERALIST ▶ **spe·cial·ist** *adj.* [only before noun]: *specialist magazines/shops* ◊ *You need some specialist advice.*

spe·ci·al·ity /ˌspeʃi'æləti/ (*BrE*) (also **spe·cial·ty** *AmE, BrE*) *noun* (pl. **-ies**) **1** a type of food or product that a restaurant or place is famous for because it is so good: *Seafood is a speciality on the island.* ◊ *local specialities* **2** an area of work or study that sb gives most of their attention to and knows a lot about; sth that sb is good at: *My speciality is international tax law.*

spe·cial·ize (*BrE* also **-ise**) /'speʃəlaɪz/ *verb* [V] **~ (in sth)** to become an expert in a particular area of work, study or business; to spend more time on one area of work, etc. than on others: *He specialized in criminal law.* ◊ *Many students prefer not to specialize too soon.* ◊ *The shop specializes in hand-made chocolates.* ▶ **spe·cial·iza·tion, -isa·tion** /ˌspeʃəlaɪˈzeɪʃn; *AmE* -lə'z-/ *noun* [U]

spe·cial·ized (*BrE* also **-ised**) /'speʃəlaɪzd/ *adj.* designed or developed for a particular purpose or area of knowledge: *specialized equipment* ◊ *specialized skills*

‚special 'licence *noun* (*BrE*) a LICENCE allowing two people to get married at a time or place that is not usually allowed

spe·cial·ly /'speʃəli/ *adv.* **1** for a particular purpose, person, etc: *The ring was specially made for her.* ◊ *a specially designed diet plan* ◊ *We came specially to see you.* **2** (*informal*) more than usual or more than other things: *It will be hard to work today—specially when it's so warm and sunny outside.* ◊ *I hate homework. Specially history.* ⇨ note at ESPECIALLY

‚special 'needs *noun* [pl.] (*especially BrE*) needs that a person has because of mental or physical problems: *She teaches children with special needs.*

‚special 'offer *noun* [C, U] a product that is sold at less than its usual price, especially in order to persuade people to buy it; the act of offering goods in this way: *Shop around for special offers.* ◊ *a special offer on perfume* ◊ *French wine is on special offer this week.*

‚special 'pleading *noun* [U] trying to persuade sb about sth by mentioning only the arguments that support your point of view and ignoring the arguments that do not support it

‚special 'school *noun* a school for children who have physical or learning problems

spe·cialty /'speʃəlti/ *noun* (*especially AmE*) = SPECIALITY: *regional specialties* ◊ *specialty foods/stores* ◊ *Her specialty is taxation law.*

spe·cies /'spi:ʃi:z/ *noun* (pl. **spe·cies**) a group into which animals, plants, etc. that are able to breed with each other are divided, smaller than a GENUS and identified by a Latin name: *a rare species of beetle* ◊ *There are many species of dog(s).* ◊ *a conservation area for endangered species*

spe·cif·ic /spə'sɪfɪk/ *adj.* **1** detailed and exact **SYN** PRECISE: *I gave you specific instructions.* ◊ *'I'd like your help tomorrow.' 'Can you be more specific* (= tell me exactly what you want)*?'* **2** [usually before noun] connected with one particular thing only **SYN** PARTICULAR: *children's television programmes aimed at a specific age group* ◊ *The money was collected for a specific purpose.* ◊ *children with specific learning difficulties* (= in one area only) **3** **~ to sth** (*formal*) existing only in one place or limited to one thing **SYN** PECULIAR: *a belief that is specific to this part of Africa*

spe·cif·ic·al·ly /spə'sɪfɪkli/ *adv.* **1** in a detailed and exact way: *I specifically told you not to go near the water!* **2** connected with or intended for one particular thing only: *liquid vitamins specifically designed for children* ◊ *a magazine aimed specifically at working women* **3** used when you want to add more detailed and exact information: *The newspaper, or more specifically, the editor, was taken to court for publishing the photographs.*

speci·fi·ca·tion /ˌspesɪfɪ'keɪʃn/ *noun* [C, U] a detailed description of how sth is, or should be, designed or made: *the technical specifications of the new model* (= of car) ◊

The house has been built exactly to our specifications. ◊ *The office was furnished to a high specification.*

speci·fi·city /ˌspesɪˈfɪsəti/ *noun* [U] (*formal*) the quality of being specific

spe·cif·ics /spəˈsɪfɪks/ *noun* [pl.] the details of a subject that you need to think about or discuss: *Okay, that's the broad plan—let's get down to the specifics.*

spe·cify /ˈspesɪfaɪ/ *verb* (**speci·fies, speci·fy·ing, speci·fied, speci·fied**) to state sth, especially by giving an exact measurement, time, exact instructions, etc: [VN] *Remember to specify your size when ordering clothes.* ◊ *Forms must be returned by the specified date.* ◊ [V wh-] *The contract clearly specifies who can operate the machinery.* ◊ [V that] *The regulations specify that calculators may not be used in the examination.*

speci·men /ˈspesɪmən/ *noun* **1** a small amount of sth that shows what the rest of it is like: *Astronauts have brought back specimens of rock from the moon.* **2** an example of sth, especially an animal or a plant: *The aquarium has some interesting specimens of unusual tropical fish.* ◊ *Redwood trees can live for a long time; one specimen is 4000 years old.* ◊ (*humorous*) *They were fine specimens of British youth!* **3** a small quantity of blood, URINE, etc. that is taken from sb and tested by a doctor: *to provide/take a specimen*

spe·cious /ˈspiːʃəs/ *adj.* (*formal*) seeming right or true but actually wrong or false: *a specious argument*

speck /spek/ *noun* a very small spot; a small piece of dirt, etc: *The ship was now just a speck in the distance.* ◊ *specks of dust/dirt*

speckle /ˈspekl/ *noun* [usually pl.] a small coloured mark or spot on a background of a different colour

speck·led /ˈspekld/ *adj.* covered with small marks or spots

specs /speks/ *noun* [pl.] **1** (*informal, especially BrE*) = GLASSES: *I need a new pair of specs.* **2** (*AmE*) = SPEC

spec·tacle /ˈspektəkl/ *noun* **1** (**spectacles**) [pl.] (*formal*) = GLASSES: *a pair of spectacles* ◊ *a spectacle case* (= to put your glasses in) **2** [C, U] a performance or an event that is very impressive and exciting to look at: *The carnival parade was a magnificent spectacle.* **3** [C] a sight or view that is very impressive to look at: *The sunset was a stunning spectacle.* **4** [sing.] an unusual or surprising sight or situation that attracts a lot of attention: *I remember the sad spectacle of her standing in her wedding dress, covered in mud.* **IDM** **make a ˈspectacle of yourself** to draw attention to yourself by behaving or dressing in a ridiculous way in public

spec·tacu·lar /spekˈtækjələ(r)/ *adj., noun*
■ *adj.* very impressive: *spectacular scenery/views* ◊ *Giggs scored a spectacular goal.* ◊ *It was a spectacular achievement on their part.* ▶ **spec·tacu·lar·ly** *adv.*: *It has been a spectacularly successful year.*
■ *noun* an impressive show or performance: *a Christmas TV spectacular*

spec·tate /spekˈteɪt/ *verb* [V] to watch sth, especially a sports event

spec·ta·tor /spekˈteɪtə(r); AmE ˈspekteɪtər/ *noun* a person who is watching an event, especially a sports event

specˈtator sport *noun* a sport that many people watch; a sport that is interesting to watch

spec·tra *pl.* of SPECTRUM

spec·tral /ˈspektrəl/ *adj.* **1** (*literary*) like a ghost; connected with a ghost **2** (*technical*) connected with a SPECTRUM: *spectral bands*

spectre (*BrE*) (*AmE* **spec·ter**) /ˈspektə(r)/ *noun* **1** ~ (of sth) something unpleasant that people are afraid might happen in the future: *The country is haunted by the spectre of civil war.* **2** (*literary*) a ghost: *Was he a spectre returning to haunt her?*

spec·trom·eter /spekˈtrɒmɪtə(r); AmE -ˈtrɑːm-/ *noun* (*technical*) a piece of equipment for measuring the WAVELENGTHS of SPECTRA

spec·tro·scope /ˈspektrəskəʊp; AmE -skoʊp/ *noun* (*technical*) a piece of equipment for forming and looking at SPECTRA ▶ **spec·tro·scop·ic** /ˌspektrəˈskɒpɪk; AmE -ˈskɑːp-/ *adj.*: *spectroscopic analysis*

spec·tros·copy /spekˈtrɒskəpi; AmE -ˈtrɑːs-/ *noun* [U] the study of forming and looking at SPECTRA using SPECTROMETERS, SPECTROSCOPES, etc.

spec·trum /ˈspektrəm/ *noun* (*pl.* **spec·tra** /ˈspektrə/) **1** a band of coloured lights in order of their WAVELENGTHS, as seen in a RAINBOW and into which a ray of light may be separated: *A spectrum is formed by a ray of light passing through a prism.* ◊ *Red and violet are at opposite ends of the spectrum.* **2** a range of sound waves or several other types of wave: *the electromagnetic/radio/sound spectrum* **3** [usually sing.] (*written*) a complete or wide range of related qualities, ideas, etc: *a broad spectrum of interests* ◊ *We shall hear views from across the political spectrum.*

specu·late /ˈspekjuleɪt/ *verb* **1** ~ (about/on sth) to form an opinion about sth without knowing all the details or facts: [V] *We all speculated about the reasons for her resignation.* ◊ {V wh-] *It is useless to speculate why he did it.* ◊ [V that] *We can speculate that the stone circles were used in some sort of pagan ceremony.* **2** [V] ~ (in/on sth) to buy goods, property, shares, etc., hoping to make a profit when you sell them, but with the risk of losing money: *He likes to speculate on the stock market.*

specu·la·tion /ˌspekjuˈleɪʃn/ *noun* **1** [U, C] ~ (that …)| ~ (about/over sth) the act of forming opinions about what has happened or what might happen without knowing all the facts: *There was widespread speculation that she was going to resign.* ◊ *His private life is the subject of much speculation.* ◊ *Today's announcement ends months of speculation about the company's future.* ◊ *She dismissed the newspaper reports as pure speculation.* ◊ *Our speculations proved right.* **2** [U, C] ~ (in sth) the activity of buying and selling goods or shares in a company in the hope of making a profit, but with the risk of losing money: *speculation in oil*

specu·la·tive /ˈspekjulətɪv; AmE also ˈspekjəleɪtɪv/ *adj.* (*especially written*) **1** based on guessing or on opinions that have been formed without knowing all the facts: *The report is highly speculative and should be ignored.* **2** showing that you are trying to guess sth: *She cast a speculative look at Kate.* **3** (of business activity) done in the hope of making a profit but involving the risk of losing money: *speculative investment*

specu·la·tor /ˈspekjuleɪtə(r)/ *noun* a person who buys and sells goods or shares in a company in the hope of making a profit: *property/currency speculators*

sped *pt, pp* of SPEED

speech /spiːtʃ/ *noun* **1** [C] ~ (on/about sth) a formal talk that a person gives to an audience: *to give/make/deliver a speech on human rights* ◊ *He made the announcement in a speech on television.* ◊ *Several people made speeches at the wedding.* **2** [U] the ability to speak: *I seemed to have lost the power of speech.* ◊ *a speech defect* ◊ *freedom of speech* (= the right to say openly what you think) **3** [U] the way in which a particular person speaks: *Her speech was slurred—she was clearly drunk.* **4** [U] the language used when speaking: *This expression is used mainly in speech, not in writing.* ◊ *speech sounds* **5** [C] a group of lines that an actor speaks in a play in the theatre: *She has the longest speech in the play.*—see also FIGURE OF SPEECH

ˈspeech bubble *noun* a circle around the words that sb says in a CARTOON

ˈspeech day *noun* an event held once a year in some British schools at which there are speeches and prizes

speechi·fy·ing /ˈspiːtʃɪfaɪɪŋ/ *noun* [U] (*informal, disapproving*) the act of making speeches in a very formal way, trying to sound important ▶ **speech·ify** /ˈspiːtʃɪfaɪ/ *verb* (**speechi·fies, speechi·fy·ing, speechi·fied, speechi·fied**) [V]

speech·less /ˈspiːtʃləs/ *adj.* not able to speak, especially because you are extremely angry or surprised: *Laura was speechless with rage.* ◊ *His words left her speechless.* ▶ **speech·less·ly** *adv.* **speech·less·ness** *noun* [U]

ˈspeech marks *noun* [pl.] = QUOTATION MARKS

ˌspeech ˈtherapy *noun* [U] special treatment to help people who have problems in speaking clearly, for

æ	ɑː	e	ɜː	ə	ɪ	iː	i	ɒ	ɔː	ʌ	ʊ	u	uː
cat	father	ten	bird	about	sit	see	many	got	saw	cup	put	actual	too

(BrE)

example in pronouncing particular sounds ▶ ˌspeech 'therapist *noun*

speed /spiːd/ *noun, verb*
■ *noun*
RATE OF MOVEMENT/ACTION | **1** [C, U] the rate at which sb/sth moves or travels: *He reduced speed and turned sharp left.* ◇ *The train began to pick up speed* (= go faster). ◇ *The car was gathering speed.* ◇ *a speed of 50 mph / 80 kph* ◇ *at high / low / full / top speed* ◇ *at breakneck speed* (= dangerously fast) ◇ *travelling at the speed of light / sound* **2** [C, U] the rate at which sth happens or is done: *the processing speed of the computer* ◇ *This course is designed so that students can progress at their own speed.* ◇ *We aim to increase the speed of delivery* (= how quickly goods are sent). **3** [U] the quality of being quick or rapid: *The accident was due to excessive speed.* ◇ *Speed is his greatest asset as a tennis player.* ◇ *She was overtaken by the speed of events* (= things happened more quickly than she expected). ◇ (*formal*) *A car flashed past them at speed* (= fast).
IN PHOTOGRAPHY | **4** [C] a measurement of how sensitive photographic film is to light **5** [C] the time taken by a camera SHUTTER to open and close: *Higher shutter speeds are best used only in good light.*
ON BICYCLE/CAR | **6** [C] (especially in compounds) a GEAR on a bicycle, in a car, etc: *a four-speed gearbox* ◇ *a ten-speed mountain bike*
DRUG | **7** [U] (*informal*) an illegal AMPHETAMINE drug that is taken to give feelings of excitement and energy
IDM **be up to ˈspeed (on sth) 1** (of a person, company, etc.) performing at an expected rate or level: *the cost of bringing the chosen schools up to speed* **2** (of a person) having the most recent and accurate information or knowledge: *I'll bring you up to speed on the latest developments.* **full speed / steam aˈhead** with as much speed or energy as possible—more at HASTE, TURN *n.*
■ *verb* (**speed·ed, speed·ed** HELP In senses 1 and 2 **sped** is also used for the past tense and past participle.)
MOVE/HAPPEN QUICKLY | **1** [V+*adv. / prep.*] (*written*) to move along quickly: *The car sped along the road towards the village.* ◇ *He sped away on his bike.* **2** [VN+*adv. / prep.*] (*written*) to take sb/sth somewhere very quickly, especially in a vehicle: *The cab speeded them into the centre of the city.* **3** [VN] (*written*) to make sth happen more quickly: *The drugs will speed her recovery.*
DRIVE TOO FAST | **4** [V] (usually used in the progressive tenses) to drive faster than the speed that is legally allowed: *The police caught him speeding.*
PHRV ˌspeed ˈup, ˌspeed sth↔ˈup to move or happen faster; to make sth move or happen faster: *The train soon speeded up.* ◇ *Can you try and speed things up a bit?*

speed·boat /ˈspiːdbəʊt; *AmE* -boʊt/ *noun* a motor boat that can travel very fast

ˈspeed hump (*especially BrE*) (*AmE usually* **ˈspeed bump**) (also *BrE informal* ˌsleeping poˈliceman) *noun* a raised area across a road that is put there to make traffic go slower

speed·ing /ˈspiːdɪŋ/ *noun* [U] the traffic offence of driving faster than the legal limit: *Max was fined £300 for speeding.*

ˈspeed limit *noun* the highest speed at which you can legally drive on a particular road: *You should always keep to the speed limit.* ◇ *to break / exceed the speed limit* ◇ *The road has a 30 mph speed limit.*

speed·om·eter /spiːˈdɒmɪtə(r); *AmE* -ˈdɑːm-/ *noun* an instrument in a vehicle which shows how fast the vehicle is going—picture at CAR

ˈspeed skating *noun* [U] the sport of SKATING on ice as fast as possible—compare FIGURE-SKATING

ˈspeed trap (*BrE* also **ˈradar trap**) *noun* a place on a road where police use special equipment to catch drivers who are going too fast

speed·way /ˈspiːdweɪ/ *noun* **1** [U] (*BrE*) the sport of racing motorcycles on a special track **2** [C] (*AmE*) a special track for racing cars or motorcycles on

speedy /ˈspiːdi/ *adj.* (**speed·ier, speedi·est**) **1** happening or done quickly or without delay: *We wish you a speedy*

recovery (= from an illness or injury). ◇ *a speedy reply / response* **2** moving or working very quickly: *speedy computers* ⇨ note at FAST ▶ **speed·ily** *adv.*: *All enquiries will be dealt with as speedily as possible.*

spele·olo·gist /ˌspiːliˈɒlədʒɪst; *AmE* -ˈɑːlə-/ *noun* a scientist who studies CAVES or a person who goes into caves as a sport—compare CAVER, POTHOLER, SPELUNKER ▶ **spele·ology** /ˌspiːliˈɒlədʒi; *AmE* -ˈɑːlə-/ *noun* [U]

spell /spel/ *verb, noun*
■ *verb* (**spelt, spelt** /spelt/) or (**spelled, spelled**) **1** [VN] to say or write the letters of a word in the correct order: *How do you spell your surname?* ◇ *I thought her name was Catherine, but it's Kathryn spelt with a 'K'.* **2** to form words correctly from individual letters: [V] *I've never been able to spell.* ◇ [VN-ADJ] *You've spelt my name wrong.*—see also MISSPELL **3** [VN] (of letters of a word) to form words when they are put together in a particular order: *C—A—T spells 'cat'.* **4** [VN] **~ sth (for sb/sth)** to have sth, usually sth bad, as a result; to mean sth, usually sth bad: *The crop failure spelt disaster for many farmers.* PHRV ˌspell sth↔ˈout **1** to explain sth in a simple, clear way: *You know what I mean—I'm sure I don't need to spell it out.* ◇ [+wh-] *Let me spell out why we need more money.* **2** to say or write the letters of a word in the right order: *Could you spell that name out again?*
■ *noun* **1** [C] a short period of time during which sth lasts: *a spell of warm weather* ◇ *a cold / hot / wet / bright spell* ◇ *There will be rain at first, with sunny spells later.* ◇ *She went to the doctor complaining of dizzy spells.* **2** [C] a period of time doing sth or working somewhere: *She had a spell as a singer before becoming an actress.* ◇ *I spent a brief spell on the Washington Post.* **3** [C] words that are thought to have magic power or to make a piece of magic work; a piece of magic that happens when sb says these magic words: *a book of spells* ◇ *The wizard recited a spell.* ◇ *to cast / put a spell on sb* ◇ *to be under a spell* (= affected by magic) **4** [sing.] a quality that a person or thing has that makes them so attractive or interesting that they have a strong influence on you: *I completely fell under her spell.* ◇ *It was a magic night until the spell was broken.* IDM see CAST *v.*, WEAVE *v.*

spell·bind·ing /ˈspelbaɪndɪŋ/ *adj.* holding your attention completely: *a spellbinding performance*

spell·bound /ˈspelbaʊnd/ *adj.* [not usually before noun] with your attention completely held by what you are listening to or watching: *a storyteller who can hold audiences spellbound*

ˈspell check *verb* [VN] to use a computer program to check your writing to see if your spelling is correct ▶ **ˈspell check** *noun* = SPELLCHECKER

spell·checker /ˈspeltʃekə(r)/ *noun* a computer program that checks your writing to see if your spelling is correct

spell·er /ˈspelə(r)/ *noun* if sb is a **good/bad speller**, they find it easy/difficult to spell words correctly

spell·ing /ˈspelɪŋ/ *noun* **1** [U] the act of forming words correctly from individual letters; the ability to do this: *a spelling mistake / test* ◇ *the differences between British and American spelling* ◇ *My spelling is terrible.* **2** [C] the way that a word is spelt: *a list of difficult spellings*

spelt *pt, pp* of SPELL

spe·lunk·ing /spɪˈlʌŋkɪŋ/ *noun* [U] (*AmE*) = CAVING ▶ **spe·lunk·er** *noun* (*AmE*) = CAVER—compare SPELEOLOGIST

spend /spend/ *verb, noun*
■ *verb* (**spent, spent** /spent/) **1 ~ sth (on sth/on doing sth)** to give money to pay for goods, services, etc: [VN] *I've spent all my money already.* ◇ *She spent £100 on a new dress.* ◇ [VN-ing] *The company has spent thousands of pounds updating their computer systems.* [also V] **2 ~ sth (on sth) / ~ sth (doing sth/in doing sth)** to use time for a particular purpose; to pass time: [VN] *We spent the weekend in Paris.* ◇ *How long did you spend on your homework?* ◇ *How do you spend your spare time?* ◇ *Most of her life was spent in caring for others.* ◇ [VN-ing] *I spend too much time watching television.* **3** [VN] [often passive] to use energy, effort, etc., especially until it has all been used: *She*

S

spends too much effort on things that don't matter.—see also SPENT **IDM** **spend the 'night with sb 1** to stay with sb for a night: *My daughter's spending the night with a friend.* **2** (also **spend the 'night together**) to stay with sb for a night and have sex with them **spend a 'penny** (*old-fashioned, BrE, informal*) people say 'spend a penny' to avoid saying 'use the toilet'

■ *noun* [sing.] (*informal*) the amount of money spent for a particular purpose or over a particular length of time: *The average spend at the cafe is £10 a head.*

spend·er /'spendə(r)/ *noun* a person who spends money in the particular way mentioned: *a big spender* (= who spends a lot of money)

spend·ing /'spendɪŋ/ *noun* [U] the amount of money that is spent by a government or an organization: *to increase/reduce public spending*

'spending money *noun* [U] money that you can spend on personal things for pleasure or entertainment: *You'll need to take money for food and some spending money.*— compare POCKET MONEY

spend·thrift /'spendθrɪft/ *noun* (*disapproving*) a person who spends too much money or who wastes money ▶ **spend·thrift** *adj.* [usually before noun]: *spendthrift governments/institutions*

spent /spent/ *adj.* **1** [usually before noun] that has been used, so that it cannot be used again: *spent bullets/ matches* ◊ *spent blooms* (= flowers that have died) **2** (*written*) very tired: *After the gruelling test, he felt totally spent.* **IDM** **a ,spent 'force** a person or group that no longer has any power or influence—see also SPEND, SPENT, SPENT *v.*

sperm /spɜːm; *AmE* spɜːrm/ *noun* (*pl.* **sperm** or **sperms**) **1** [C] a cell that is produced by the sex organs of a male and that can combine with a female egg to produce young: *He has a low sperm count* (= very few live male cells). **2** [U] the liquid that is produced by the male sex organs that contains these cells **SYN** SEMEN

sperm·ato·zoon /ˌspɜːmətəˈzəʊən; *AmE* ˌspɜːrmətəˈzoʊən/ *noun* (*pl.* **sperm·ato·zoa** /-ˈzəʊə; *AmE* -ˈzoʊə/) (*biology*) a sperm

'sperm bank *noun* a place where sperm is kept and then used to help women become pregnant artificially

spermi·cide /'spɜːmɪsaɪd; *AmE* 'spɜːrm-/ *noun* [U, C] a substance that kills SPERM, used during sex to prevent the woman from becoming pregnant ▶ **spermi·cidal** /ˌspɜːmɪˈsaɪdl; *AmE* ˌspɜːrm-/ *adj.* [only before noun]

'sperm whale *noun* a large WHALE that is hunted for its oil and fat—picture on page A6

spew /spjuː/ *verb* **1** [+*adv./prep.*] to flow out quickly, or to make sth flow out quickly, in large amounts: [V] *Flames spewed from the aircraft's engine.* ◊ [VN] *Massive chimneys were spewing out smoke and flames.* **2 ~ (sth) (up)** (*BrE, informal*) to VOMIT: [V] *He spewed up on the pavement.* ◊ [VN] *She spewed up the entire meal.*

sphag·num /'sfægnəm/ (also **'Sphagnum moss**) *noun* [U] a type of MOSS that grows in wet areas, used especially for planting plants in pots, making FERTILIZER, etc.

sphere /sfɪə(r); *AmE* sfɪr/ *noun* **1** (*geometry*) a solid figure that is completely round, with every point on its surface at an equal distance from the centre—picture on page at SOLID **2** any object that is completely round, for example a ball **3** an area of activity, influence or interest; a particular section of society: *the political/economic sphere* ◊ *This area was formerly within the sphere of influence of the US.* ◊ *He and I moved in totally different social spheres.* **4 (-sphere)** (in nouns) a region that surrounds a planet, especially the earth: *ionosphere* ◊ *atmosphere*

spher·ic·al /'sferɪkl/ *adj.* shaped like a sphere

spher·oid /'sfɪərɔɪd; *AmE* 'sfɪr-/ *noun* (*technical*) a solid object that is approximately the same shape as a SPHERE

sphinc·ter /'sfɪŋktə(r)/ *noun* (*anatomy*) a ring of muscle that surrounds an opening in the body and can tighten to close it: *the anal sphincter*

sphinx /sfɪŋks/ *noun* (often **the Sphinx**) an ancient Egyptian stone statue of a creature with a human head and the body of a lion lying down. In ancient Greek stories the Sphinx spoke in RIDDLES.

spic /spɪk/ *noun* (⚠ *slang, especially AmE*) a very offensive word for a person from a country where Spanish is spoken, for example a Mexican or Puerto Rican **IDM** **,spic and 'span** = SPICK AND SPAN at SPICK

spice /spaɪs/ *noun, verb*

■ *noun* **1** [C, U] one of the various types of powder or seed that come from plants and are used in cooking. Spices have a strong taste and smell: *common spices such as ginger and cinnamon* ◊ *a spice jar/rack* **2** [U] extra interest or excitement: *We need an exciting trip to add some spice to our lives.* **IDM** see VARIETY

■ *verb* [VN] **~ sth (up) (with sth) 1** to add spice to food in order to give it more flavour: *highly spiced dishes* **2** to add interest or excitement to sth: *He exaggerated the details to spice up the story.* ◊ *Her conversation is always spiced with humour.*

spick /spɪk/ *adj.* **IDM** **,spick and 'span** (also **,spic and 'span**) [not usually before noun] neat and clean: *Their house is always spick and span.*

spicy /'spaɪsi/ *adj.* (**spici·er, spici·est**) **1** (of food) having a strong taste because spices have been used to flavour it: *spicy chicken wings* **2** (*informal*) (of a story, piece of news, etc.) exciting and slightly shocking ▶ **spici·ness** *noun* [U]

spider /'spaɪdə(r)/ *noun* a small creature with eight thin legs. Many spiders spin WEBS (= nets of thin threads) to catch insects for food: *She stared in horror at the hairy black spider.*—picture on page A7

'spider monkey *noun* a S American monkey with very long limbs and a long PREHENSILE tail—picture on page A6

'spider's web (*especially BrE*) (also **'spider web** especially in *AmE*) (also **web**) *noun* a fine net of threads made by a spider to catch insects: (*figurative*) *a spider's web of overhead wires and cables* ◊ (*figurative*) *to be caught in a spider's web of confusion*—see also COBWEB

spi·dery /'spaɪdəri/ *adj.* long and thin, like the legs of a spider: *spidery fingers* ◊ *spidery writing* (= consisting of thin lines that are not very clear)

spied *pt, pp* of SPY

spiel /ʃpiːl; spiːl/ *noun* (*informal, usually disapproving*) a long speech that sb has used many times, that is intended to persuade you to believe sth or buy sth

spiff /spɪf/ *verb* **PHR V** **,spiff 'up**, **,spiff sb/sth↔'up** (*AmE, informal*) to make yourself/sb/sth look neat and attractive: *He got all spiffed up.* ◊ *She spiffed up her old shoes.*

spiffy /'spɪfi/ *adj.* (*AmE, informal*) attractive and fashionable

spigot /'spɪgət/ *noun* **1** (*technical*) a device in a tap/ faucet that controls the flow of liquid from a container **2** (*AmE*) any tap/faucet, especially one outdoors

spike /spaɪk/ *noun, verb*

■ *noun* **1** [C] a thin object with a sharp point, especially a pointed piece of metal, wood, etc: *a row of iron spikes on a wall* ◊ *Her hair stood up in spikes.*—see also SPIKE HEEL **2** [C, usually pl.] a metal point attached to the sole of a sports shoe to prevent you from slipping while running— compare CLEAT **3 (spikes)** [pl.] shoes fitted with these metal spikes, used for running: *a pair of spikes* **4** [C] a long pointed group of flowers that grow together on a single stem

■ *verb* [VN] **1** to push a sharp piece of metal, wood, etc. into sb/sth; to injure sth on a sharp point **2 ~ sth (with sth)** to add alcohol, poison or a drug to sb's drink or food without them knowing: *He gave her a drink spiked with tranquillizers* ◊ (*figurative*) *Her words were spiked with malice.* **3** to reject sth that a person has written or said; to prevent sth from happening or being made public: *The article was spiked for fear of legal action against the newspaper.* **IDM** **spike sb's 'guns** (*BrE*) to spoil the plans of an opponent

spiked /spaɪkt/ *adj.* with one or more spikes: *spiked running shoes* ◊ *short spiked hair*

,spike 'heel *noun* (*especially AmE*) a very thin high heel on a woman's shoe; a shoe with such a heel **SYN** STILETTO

b	d	f	g	h	k	l	m	n	p	r
bad	did	fall	get	hat	cat	leg	man	now	pen	red

spiky /'spaɪki/ *adj.* **1** having sharp points: *spiky leaves/plants* **2** (of hair) sticking straight up from the head **3** (*BrE*) (of people) easily annoyed or offended ▶ **spiki·ness** *noun* [U]

spiky hair

spill /spɪl/ *verb, noun*

■ *verb* (**spilled, spilled**) (*BrE* also **spilt, spilt** /spɪlt/) **1** (especially of liquid) to accidentally flow over the edge of a container; to make liquid do this: [V] *Water had spilled out of the bucket onto the floor.* ◇ [VN] *He startled her and made her spill her drink.* ◇ *Thousands of gallons of crude oil were spilled into the ocean.* **2** [V+adv./prep.] (of people) to come out of a place in large numbers and spread out: *The doors opened and people spilled into the street.* ◇ (*figurative*) *Light spilled from the windows.* **IDM** **spill the 'beans** (*informal*) to tell sb sth that should be kept secret or private **spill (sb's) 'blood** (*formal or literary*) to kill or wound people: *Nothing can justify spilling innocent blood.* **spill your 'guts (to sb)** (*AmE, informal*) to tell sb everything you know or feel about sth, because you are upset—more at CRY *v.* **PHRV** **spill 'out | spill 'out** to tell sb all about a problem etc. very quickly; to come out quickly: *Has she been spilling out her troubles to you again?* ◇ *When he started to speak, the words just spilled out.* **spill 'over (into sth)** **1** to fill a container and go over the edge: *She filled the glass so full that the water spilled over.* ◇ (*figurative*) *Her emotions suddenly spilled over.* **2** to start in one area and then affect other areas: *Unrest has spilt over into areas outside the city.* ◇ *The effects of stress at work can spill over into home life.*—related noun OVERSPILL, SPILLOVER

■ *noun* **1** (also *formal* **spill·age**) [C, U] an act of letting a liquid come or fall out of a container; the amount of liquid that comes or falls out: *Many seabirds died as a result of the oil spill.* ◇ *I wiped up the coffee spills on the table.* **2** [C] a long match, or a thin piece of twisted paper, used for lighting fires, oil lamps, etc. **3** [C, usually sing.] a fall, especially from a bicycle or a boat: *to take a spill* **IDM** see THRILL *n.*

spill·age /'spɪlɪdʒ/ *noun* [U, C] (*formal*) = SPILL: *Put the bottle in a plastic bag in case of spillage.*

spill·over /'spɪləʊvə(r); *AmE* -oʊ-/ *noun* [C, U] **1** something that is too large or too much for the place where it starts, and spreads to other places: *A second room was needed for the spillover of staff and reporters.* **2** the results or the effects of sth that have spread to other situations or places

spin /spɪn/ *verb, noun*

■ *verb* (**spin·ning, spun, spun** /spʌn/)

TURN ROUND QUICKLY | **1** ~ (sth) (round/around) to turn round and round quickly; to make sth do this: [V] *The plane was spinning out of control.* ◇ *a spinning ice skater* ◇ *My head is spinning* (= I feel as if my head is going around and I can't balance). ◇ [VN] *to spin a ball/coin/wheel* **2** ~ (round/around) to turn round quickly once; to make sb do this: [V] *He spun around to face her.* [also VN]

MAKE THREAD | **3** ~ (A into B) | ~ (B from A) to make thread from wool, cotton, silk, etc. by twisting it: [V] *She sat by the window spinning.* ◇ [VN] *to spin and knit wool* ◇ *spinning silk into thread*

OF SPIDER/SILKWORM | **4** [VN] to produce thread from its body to make a WEB or COCOON: *a spider spinning a web*

DRIVE/TRAVEL QUICKLY | **5** [V+adv./prep.] to drive or travel quickly: *They went spinning along the roads on their bikes.*

DRY CLOTHES | **6** [VN] to remove the water from clothes that have just been washed, in a SPIN DRYER

PRESENT INFORMATION | **7** [VN] to present information or a situation in a particular way, especially one that makes you or your ideas seem good: *An aide was already spinning the senator's defeat as 'almost as good as an outright win'.*

IDM **spin (sb) a 'yarn, 'tale, etc.** to tell sb a long story that is not true, usually in order to deceive them—more at HEEL *n.* **PHRV** **spin 'off (from sth) | spin sth↔'off (from sth)** to happen or to produce sth as a new or unexpected result of sth that already exists: *products spinning off from favourite books* ◇ *toys spun off from the popular children's TV programme*—related noun SPIN-OFF, **spin sth↔'off** (*business*) (especially *AmE*) to form a new company from parts of an existing one: *The transportction operation will be spun off into a separate company.* **spin sth↔'out** to make sth last as long as possible

■ *noun*

FAST TURNING MOVEMENT | **1** [C, U] a very fast turning movement: *the earth's spin* ◇ *the spin of a wheel* ◇ *The dance was full of twists and spins.* ◇ *Give the washing a short spin.* **2** [C, usually sing.] if an aircraft goes into a **spin**, it falls and turns round rapidly

IN CAR | **3** [C] (*informal*, becoming *old-fashioned*) a short ride in a car for pleasure

IN TENNIS/CRICKET | **4** [U] the way you make a ball turn very fast when you throw it or hit it: *a spin bowler* (= in cricket, a bowler who uses spin)—see also TOPSPIN

ON INFORMATION | **5** [sing., U] (*informal*) a way of presenting information or a situation in a particular way, especially one that makes you or your ideas seem good: *Politicians put their own spin on the economic situation.*

IDM **in a (flat) 'spin** very confused, worried or excited: *Her resignation put her colleagues in a spin.*

spina bif·ida /ˌspaɪnə 'bɪfɪdə/ *noun* [U] a medical condition in which some bones in the SPINE have not developed normally at birth, often causing PARALYSIS (= loss of control or feeling) in the legs

spin·ach /'spɪnɪtʃ; -ɪdʒ/ *noun* [U] a vegetable with large dark green leaves that are usually eaten cooked

spinal /'spaɪnl/ *adj.* [usually before noun] (*technical*) connected with the SPINE (= the long bone in the back): *spinal injuries*

spinal 'column *noun* the SPINE

spinal 'cord *noun* the mass of nerves inside the SPINE that connects all parts of the body to the brain—picture at BODY

spinal tap *noun* (*AmE*) = LUMBAR PUNCTURE

spin·dle /'spɪndl/ *noun* **1** a rod that turns in a machine, or that another part of the machine turns around **2** a thin pointed rod used for spinning wool into thread by hand

spindly /'spɪndli/ *adj.* (*informal*, often *disapproving*) very long and thin and not strong: *spindly legs*

spin doctor *noun* (*informal*) a person whose job is to present information to the public about a politician, an organization, etc. in the way that seems most positive

spin 'dryer (also **spin 'drier**) *noun* (*BrE*) a machine that partly dries clothes that you have washed by turning them round and round very fast to remove the water—compare TUMBLE-DRYER ▶ **spin-'dry** *verb* [VN]

spine /spaɪn/ *noun* **1** the row of small bones that are connected together down the middle of the back **SYN** BACKBONE—picture at BODY **2** any of the sharp pointed parts like needles on some plants and animals: *Porcupines use their spines to protect themselves.*—see also SPINY **3** the narrow part of the cover of a book that the pages are joined to

spine-chilling *adj.* frightening in an exciting way: *a spine-chilling horror story*

spine·less /'spaɪnləs/ *adj.* **1** (*disapproving*) (of people) weak and easily frightened **2** (of animals) having no SPINE (= the long bone in the back)

spi·net /spɪ'net; *AmE* 'spɪnət/ *noun* **1** a kind of HARPSICHORD (= an early type of musical instrument), played like a piano **2** ~ **piano/organ** (*AmE*) a small upright piano/electronic ORGAN

spine-tingling *adj.* (of an event, a piece of music, etc.) enjoyable because it is very exciting or frightening

spin·naker /'spɪnəkə(r)/ *noun* a large extra sail on a

	s	t	v	z	ʃ	ʒ	tʃ	dʒ	θ	ð	ŋ
	see	tea	van	zoo	shoe	vision	chain	jam	thin	this	sing

racing YACHT that you use when the wind is coming from behind—picture at YACHT

spin·ner /'spɪnə(r)/ *noun* **1** (in cricket) a BOWLER who uses SPIN when throwing the ball; a SPIN BOWLER **2** a person who spins thread **3** a device that spins around, used on a fishing line to attract fish

spin·ney /'spɪni/ *noun* (*BrE*) a small area of trees SYN COPSE

spin·ning /'spɪnɪŋ/ *noun* [U] the art or the process of twisting wool, etc. to make thread

'spinning wheel *noun* a simple machine that people used in their homes in the past for twisting wool, etc. It has a large wheel operated with the foot.

'spin-off *noun* ~ (**from/of sth**) **1** an unexpected but useful result of an activity that is designed to produce sth else: *commercial spin-offs from medical research* **2** a book, a film/movie, a television programme, or an object that is based on a book, film/movie or television series that has been very successful: *The TV comedy series is a spin-off of the original movie.* ◇ *spin-off merchandise from the latest Disney movie*

spin·ster /'spɪnstə(r)/ *noun* (*old-fashioned*, often *disapproving*) a woman who is not married, especially an older woman who is not likely to marry HELP This word should not now be used to mean simply a woman who is not married.—compare BACHELOR ▶ **spin·ster·hood** /-hʊd/ *noun* [U]: *For most women, marriage used to bring a higher status than spinsterhood.*

spiny /'spaɪni/ *adj.* (of animals or plants) having sharp points like needles: *spiny sea urchins* ◇ *spiny leaves*—see also SPINE

spiral /'spaɪrəl/ *noun, adj., verb*

■ *noun* **1** a shape or design, consisting of a continuous curved line that winds around a central point, with each curve further away from the centre: *The birds circled in a slow spiral above the house.* **2** a continuous harmful increase or decrease in sth, that gradually gets faster and faster: *the destructive spiral of violence in the inner cities* ◇ *measures to control the inflationary spiral* ◇ *the upward/downward spiral of sales*

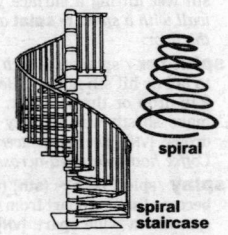

spiral

spiral staircase

■ *adj.* moving in a continuous curve that winds around a central point: *a spiral staircase* ◇ *A snail's shell is spiral in form.* ▶ **spir·al·ly** *adv.*

■ *verb* (**-ll-**, *AmE* usually **-l-**) [V, usually +*adv./prep.*] **1** to move in continuous circles, going upwards or downwards: *Smoke spiralled into the sky.* ◇ *The plane spiralled down to the ground.* **2** to increase rapidly: *the spiralling cost of health care* ◇ *Prices are spiralling out of control.* PHRV ,spiral 'down/'downward to decrease rapidly

spire /'spaɪə(r)/ *noun* a tall pointed structure on the top of a building, especially a church: *a magnificent view of the spires of the city*—picture at STEEPLE

spirit /'spɪrɪt/ *noun, verb*

■ *noun*

MIND/FEELINGS/CHARACTER | **1** [U, C] the part of a person that includes their mind, feelings and character rather than their body: *the power of the human spirit to overcome difficulties* **2** (**spirits**) [pl.] a person's feelings or state of mind: *to be in high/low spirits* ◇ *You must try and keep your spirits up* (= stay cheerful). *My spirits sank at the prospect of starting all over again.* **3** [C] (always with an adjective) a person of the type mentioned: *a brave/generous/mean/proud spirit* (= people who like the same things as you) ◇ *She was one of the leading spirits of the reform movement.*—see also FREE SPIRIT

COURAGE/DETERMINATION | **4** [U] courage, determination or energy: *Show a little fighting spirit.* ◇ *Although the team lost, they played with tremendous spirit.* ◇ *They took away his freedom and broke his spirit.*

LOYAL FEELINGS | **5** [U, sing.] loyal feelings towards a group, team or society: *There's not much community spirit around here.*—see also TEAM SPIRIT

ATTITUDE | **6** [sing.] a state of mind or mood; an attitude: *We approached the situation in the wrong spirit.* ◇ *'OK, I'll try'. 'That's the spirit* (= the right attitude).' ◇ *The party went well because everyone entered into the spirit of things.*—see also PARTY SPIRIT

TYPICAL QUALITY | **7** [sing.] the typical or most important quality or mood of sth: *the spirit of the times* ◇ *the pioneer spirit*

REAL MEANING | **8** [U] the real or intended meaning or purpose of sth: *Obey the spirit, not the letter* (= the narrow meaning of the words) *of the law.*

SOUL | **9** [C] the soul thought of as separate from the body and believed to live on after death; a GHOST: *He is dead, but his spirit lives on.* ◇ *It was believed that people could be possessed by evil spirits.*—see also THE HOLY SPIRIT

IMAGINARY CREATURE | **10** [C] (*old-fashioned*) an imaginary creature with magic powers, for example, a FAIRY or an ELF

ALCOHOL | **11** [C, usually pl.] (*especially BrE*) a strong alcoholic drink: *I don't drink whisky or brandy or any other spirits.* **12** [U] a special type of alcohol used in industry or medicine—see also METHYLATED SPIRIT, SURGICAL SPIRIT, WHITE SPIRIT

IDM in 'spirit in your thoughts: *I shall be with you in spirit* (= thinking about you though not with you physically). **the ,spirit is 'willing (but the ,flesh is 'weak)** (*humorous, saying*) you intend to do good things but you are too lazy, weak or busy to actually do them **as/when/if the ,spirit 'moves you** as/when/if you feel like it: *I'll go for a run this evening, if the spirit moves me.*—more at FIGHT *v.*, RAISE *v.*

■ *verb* [VN+*adv./prep.*] to take sb/sth away in a quick, secret or mysterious way: *After the concert, the band was spirited away before their fans could get near them.*

spir·it·ed /'spɪrɪtɪd/ *adj.* [usually before noun] full of energy, determination or courage: *a spirited young woman* ◇ *a spirited horse* ◇ *a spirited discussion/conversation* ◇ *She put up a spirited defence in the final game.*—compare DISPIRITED—see also HIGH-SPIRITED, PUBLIC-SPIRITED ▶ **spir·it·ed·ly** *adv.*

spir·it·less /'spɪrɪtləs/ *adj.* (*formal*) without energy, enthusiasm or determination: *a pale, spiritless child* ◇ *a spiritless argument*

'spirit level (also **level**) *noun* a glass tube partly filled with liquid, with a bubble of air inside. Spirit levels are used to test whether a surface is level, by the position of the bubble.

spir·it·ual /'spɪrɪtʃuəl/ *adj., noun*

■ *adj.* [usually before noun] **1** connected with the human spirit, rather than the body or physical things: *a spiritual experience* ◇ *spiritual development/growth/needs* ◇ *a lack of spiritual values in the modern world* ◇ *We're concerned about your spiritual welfare.* OPP MATERIAL **2** connected with religion: *a spiritual leader*—compare TEMPORAL ▶ **spir·itu·al·ly** /-tʃuəli/ *adv.*: *a spiritually uplifting book* IDM **your ,spiritual 'home** the place where you are happiest, especially a country where you feel you belong more than in your own country because you share the ideas and attitudes of the people who live there

■ *noun* (also **Negro 'spiritual**) a religious song of the type originally sung by black slaves in America

spir·itu·al·ism /'spɪrɪtʃuəlɪzəm/ *noun* [U] the belief that people who have died can send messages to living people, usually through a MEDIUM (= a person who has special powers)

spir·itu·al·ist /'spɪrɪtʃuəlɪst/ *noun* a person who believes that people who have died can send messages to living people

spir·itu·al·ity /ˌspɪrɪtʃu'æləti/ *noun* [U] the quality of being concerned with religion or the human spirit

spit /spɪt/ *verb, noun*

■ *verb* (**spit·ting, spat, spat** /spæt/ HELP spit is also sometimes used for the past tense and past participle, especially in *AmE*.)

æ	ɑː	e	ɜː	ə	ɪ	iː	i	ɒ	ɔː	ʌ	ʊ	u	uː
cat	father	ten	bird	about	sit	see	many	got	saw	cup	put	actual	too

(BrE)

S

FROM MOUTH | **1** [VN] **~ sth (out)** to force liquid, food, etc. out of your mouth: *She took a mouthful of food and then suddenly spat it out.* ◊ *He was spitting blood from a badly cut lip.* **2** [V] **~ (at/on sb/sth)** to force SALIVA (= the liquid that is produced in the mouth) out of your mouth, often as a sign of anger or lack of respect: *He coughed and spat.* ◊ *The prisoners were spat on by their guards.* ◊ *She spat in his face and went out.*

SAY STH ANGRILY | **3** to say sth in an angry or forceful way: [V speech] *'You liar!' she spat.* ◊ [VN] *He was dragged out of the court, spitting abuse at the judge and jury.*

OF AN ANIMAL | **4** [V] to make a short angry sound: *Snakes spit and hiss when they are cornered.*

OF STH COOKING/BURNING | **5** [V] to make a noise and throw out fat, SPARKS, etc: *sausages spitting in the frying pan* ◊ *The logs on the fire crackled and spat.*

RAIN | **6** [V] (*informal*) (only used in the progressive tenses) when **it is spitting**, it is raining lightly

IDM **spit it 'out** (*spoken*) usually used in orders to tell sb to say sth when they seem frightened or unwilling to speak: *If you've got something to say, spit it out!* **spit 'venom/'blood** to show that you are very angry; to speak in an angry way **within 'spitting distance (of sth)** (*BrE*) (also **within 'shouting distance** *AmE, BrE*) (*spoken, informal*) very close—more at IMAGE **PHRV** **spit 'up** (*AmE, informal*) (especially of a baby) to VOMIT

■ *noun*

IN/FROM MOUTH | **1** [U] the liquid that is produced in your mouth **SYN** SALIVA **2** [C, usually sing.] the act of spitting liquid or food out of your mouth

PIECE OF LAND | **3** [C] a long thin piece of land that sticks out into the sea/ocean, a lake, etc.—picture at COAST

FOR COOKING MEAT | **4** [C] a long thin metal rod that you put through meat to hold and turn it while you cook it over a fire

IDM **spit and 'polish** (*informal*) thorough cleaning and polishing of sth

spite /spaɪt/ *noun, verb*

■ *noun* [U] a feeling of wanting to hurt or upset sb **SYN** MALICE: *I'm sure he only said it out of spite.* **IDM** **in 'spite of sth** if you say that sb did sth **in spite of** a fact, you mean it is surprising that that fact did not prevent them from doing it **SYN** DESPITE: *In spite of his age, he still leads an active life.* ◊ *They went swimming in spite of all the danger signs.* ◊ *English became the official language for business in spite of the fact that the population was largely Chinese.* **in 'spite of yourself** if you do sth **in spite of yourself**, you do it although you did not intend or expect to: *He fell asleep, in spite of himself.*

■ *verb* [VN] (only used in the infinitive with *to*) to deliberately annoy or upset sb: *They're playing the music so loud just to spite us.* **IDM** see NOSE *n*.

spite·ful /'spaɪtfl/ *adj.* behaving in an unkind way in order to hurt or upset sb **SYN** MALICIOUS ▶ **spite·ful·ly** /-fəli/ *adv.* *'I don't need you,' she said spitefully.* **spite·ful·ness** *noun* [U]

spit·tle /'spɪtl/ *noun* [U] (*old-fashioned*) the liquid that forms in the mouth **SYN** SPIT, SALIVA

spit·toon /spɪ'tuːn/ *noun* a container, used especially in the past, for people to SPIT into

spiv /spɪv/ *noun* (*BrE, slang, disapproving*) a man who makes his money by being dishonest in business, especially one who dresses in a way that makes people believe he is rich and successful

splash /splæʃ/ *verb, noun*

■ *verb* **1** [V] (of liquid) to fall noisily onto a surface: *Water splashed onto the floor.* ◊ *Rain splashed against the windows.* **2** [VN] **~ sth (on/onto/over sb/sth)** | **~ sb/sth (with sth)** to make sb/sth wet by making water, mud, etc. fall on them/it: *He splashed cold water on his face.* ◊ *He splashed his face with cold water.* ◊ *My clothes were splashed with mud.* ◊ *Stop splashing me!* **3** [V] to move through water making drops fly everywhere: *The kids were splashing through the puddles.* ◊ *People were having fun in the pool, swimming or just splashing around.* **4** [VN] **~ sth with sth** [usually passive] to decorate sth with areas of bright colour, not in a regular pattern: *The walls were splashed with patches of blue and purple.* **PHRV** **'splash sth across/over sth** to put a photograph, news story, etc. in a place where it will be easily noticed **splash 'down** (of a spacecraft) to land in the sea or ocean—related noun SPLASHDOWN **splash 'out (on sth)** | **splash sth↔'out (on/for sth)** (*BrE, informal*) to spend a lot of money on sth: *We're going to splash out and buy a new car.* ◊ *He splashed out hundreds of pounds on designer clothes.*

■ *noun* **1** [C] the sound of sth hitting liquid or of liquid hitting sth: *We heard the splash when she fell into the pool.* **2** [C] a small amount of liquid that falls onto sth; the mark that this makes: *splashes of water on the floor* ◊ *dark splashes of mud on her skirt* ◊ *Any splashes on the skin should be removed immediately.* **3** [C] a small area of bright colour or light that contrasts with the colours around it: *These flowers will give a splash of colour throughout the summer.* **4** [sing.] (*BrE, informal*) a small amount of liquid that you add to a drink—compare DASH **5** [sing.] an article in a newspaper, etc. that is intended to attract a lot of attention **IDM** **make/cause, etc. a 'splash** (*informal*) to do sth in a way that attracts a lot of attention, or causes a lot of excitement

splash·down /'splæʃdaʊn/ *noun* [C, U] a landing of a spacecraft in the sea/ocean: *Splashdown is scheduled for 0500 hours.*

splashy /'splæʃi/ *adj.* (**splash·ier**, **splashi·est**) (*especially AmE*) bright and very easy to notice: *a splashy advertising campaign*

splat /splæt/ *noun* [sing.] (*informal*) the sound made by sth wet hitting a surface, etc: *The tomato hit the wall with a splat.* ▶ **splat** *adv.*: *The omelette fell splat onto the floor.*

splat·ter /'splætə(r)/ *verb* **1** [V] (of large drops of liquid) to fall or hit sth noisily: *Heavy rain splattered on the roof.* **2** to drop or throw water, paint, mud, etc. on sb/sth; to make sb/sth wet or dirty by landing on them in large drops: [VN] *The walls were splattered with blood.* ◊ [V] *Coffee had splattered across the front of his shirt.*

splay /spleɪ/ *verb* **~ (sth) (out)** to make fingers, legs, etc. become further apart from each other or spread out; to be spread out wide apart: [VN] *She lay on the bed, her arms and legs splayed out.* ◊ [V] *His long fingers splayed across her back.*

spleen /spliːn/ *noun* **1** [C] a small organ near the stomach that controls the quality of the blood: *a ruptured spleen*—picture at BODY **2** [U] (*literary*) anger: *He vented his spleen* (= shouted in an angry way) *on the assembled crowd.*

splen·did /'splendɪd/ *adj., exclamation*

■ *adj.* (*especially BrE*) **1** (*old-fashioned*) excellent; very good: *What a splendid idea!* ◊ *We've all had a splendid time.* **2** very impressive; very beautiful: *a splendid house/castle* ◊ *The hotel stands in splendid isolation, surrounded by moorland.* ▶ **splen·did·ly** *adv.*: *You all played splendidly.*

■ *exclamation* (*old-fashioned, especially BrE*) used to express approval or pleasure

splen·dour (*BrE*) (*AmE* **splen·dor**) /'splendə(r)/ *noun* **1** [U] grand and impressive beauty: *a view of Rheims Cathedral, in all its splendour* ◊ *The palace has been restored to its former splendour.* **2** (**splendours**) [pl.] the beautiful and impressive features or qualities of sth, especially a place: *the splendours of Rome* (= its fine buildings, etc.)

splice /splaɪs/ *verb, noun*

■ *verb* **~ sth (together)** **1** to join the ends of two pieces of rope by weaving them together **2** to join the ends of two pieces of film, tape, etc. by sticking them together **IDM** **get 'spliced** (*old-fashioned, BrE, informal*) to get married

■ *noun* the place where two pieces of film, tape, rope, etc. have been joined

spli·cer /'splaɪsə(r)/ *noun* a person or machine that joins pieces of tape, cable, etc. together

spliff /splɪf/ *noun* (*BrE, slang*) a cigarette containing CANNABIS

splint /splɪnt/ *noun* a long piece of wood or metal that is tied to a broken arm or leg to keep it still and in the right position

splin·ter /ˈsplɪntə(r)/ *noun, verb*

■ *noun* a small thin sharp piece of wood, metal, glass, etc. that has broken off a larger piece: *splinters of glass* ◊ *to remove a splinter from your finger*

■ *verb* **1** (of wood, glass, stone, etc.) to break, or to make sth break, into small, thin sharp pieces: [V] *The mirror cracked but did not splinter.* ◊ [VN] *The impact splintered the wood.* **2** [V] (of a group of people) to divide into smaller groups that are no longer connected; to separate from a larger group: *The party began to splinter.* ◊ *Several firms have splintered off from the original company.*

ˈsplinter group *noun* a small group of people that has separated from a larger one, especially in politics

split /splɪt/ *verb, noun*

■ *verb* (**split·ting, split, split**)

DIVIDE | **1** to divide, or to make a group of people divide, into smaller groups that have very different opinions: [VN] *a debate that has split the country **down the middle*** ◊ [V] *The committee split over government subsidies.* **2 ~ (sth) (into sth)** to divide, or to make sth divide, into two or more parts: [VN] *She split the class into groups of four.* ◊ [V] *The results split neatly into two groups.*—see also SPLIT UP **3** [VN] **~ sth (between sb/sth)| ~ sth (with sb)** to divide sth into two or more parts and share it between different people, activities, etc: *She split the money she won with her brother.* ◊ *We share a house and split all the bills.* ◊ *His time is split between the London and Paris offices.*—see also SPLIT UP

TEAR | **4 ~ (sth)** to tear, or to make sth tear, along a straight line: [V] *Her dress had split along the seam.* ◊ [V-ADJ] *The cushion split open and sent feathers everywhere.* ◊ [VN] *Don't tell me you've split another pair of pants!* [also VN-ADJ]

CUT | **5 ~ sth (open)** to cut sb's skin and make it bleed: [VN-ADJ] *She split her head open on the cupboard door.* ◊ [VN] *How did you split your lip?*

END RELATIONSHIP | **6** [V] **~ (from/with sb)** to leave sb and stop having a relationship with them: *The singer split with his wife last June.* ◊ *She intends to split from the band at the end of the tour.*—see also SPLIT UP

LEAVE | **7** [V] (*old-fashioned, informal*) to leave a place quickly: *Let's split!*

IDM **split the ˈdifference** (when discussing a price, etc.) to agree on an amount that is exactly halfway between the two amounts that have been suggested **split ˈhairs** to pay too much attention to an argument to differences that are very small and not important **split an inˈfinitive** to place an adverb between 'to' and the INFINITIVE of a verb, for example, to say 'to strongly deny a rumour'. Some people consider this to be bad English style. **split your ˈsides (laughing/with laughter)** to laugh a lot at sb/sth **split the ˈticket** (*AmE, politics*) to vote for candidates from more than one party—more at MIDDLE *n.*

PHR V **ˌsplit aˈway/ˈoff (from sth)| ˌsplit sth↔aˈway/ ˈoff (from sth)** to separate from, or to separate sth from, a larger object or group: *A rebel faction has split away from the main group.* ◊ *The storm split a branch off from the main trunk.* **ˈsplit on sb (to sb)** (*BrE, informal*) to tell sb in authority about sth wrong, dishonest etc. that sb else has done: *Don't worry—he won't split on us.* **ˌsplit ˈup (with sb)** to stop having a relationship with sb: *My parents split up last year.* ◊ *She's split up with her boyfriend.* **ˌsplit sb ˈup** to make two people stop having a relationship with each other: *My friend is doing her best to split us up.* **ˌsplit sb ˈup| ˌsplit ˈup** to divide a group of people into smaller parts; to become divided up in this way: *We were split up into groups to discuss the question.* ◊ *Let's split up now and meet again at lunchtime.* **ˌsplit sth↔ˈup** to divide sth into smaller parts: *The day was split up into 6 one-hour sessions.*

■ *noun*

DISAGREEMENT | **1** [C] **~ (between A and B)| ~ (with sb/sth)** a disagreement that divides a group of people or makes sb separate from sb else: *a damaging split within the party leadership* ◊ *the years following his bitter split with his wife*

DIVISION | **2** [sing.] a division between two or more things; one of the parts that sth is divided into: *He demanded a 50–50 split in the profits.*

TEAR/HOLE | **3** [C] a long crack or hole made when sth tears: *There's a big split in the tent.*

BANANA DISH | **4** [C] a sweet dish made from fruit, especially a BANANA cut in two along its length, with cream, ice cream, etc. on top: *a banana split*

BODY POSITION | **5** (**the splits**) [pl.] (*AmE also* **split** [sing.]) a position in which you stretch your legs flat across the floor in opposite directions with the rest of your body upright: *a gymnast **doing the splits***

ˌsplit ˈends *noun* [pl.] if you have **split ends**, some of your hairs have divided into parts at the ends because they are dry or in poor condition

ˌsplit inˈfinitive *noun* (*grammar*) the form of the verb with *to*, with an adverb placed between *to* and the verb, as in *She seems to really like it.* Some people consider this to be bad English style.

ˌsplit-ˈlevel *adj.* (of a room, floor, etc.) having parts at different levels

ˌsplit ˈscreen *noun* a way of displaying two or more pictures or pieces of information at the same time on a television, cinema or computer screen ▶ **ˌsplit-ˈscreen** *adj.* [only before noun]: *a movie with several split-screen sequences*

ˌsplit ˈsecond *noun* a very short moment of time: *Their eyes met for a split second.*

ˈsplit-second *adj.* [only before noun] done very quickly or very accurately: *She had to make a split-second decision.* ◊ *The success of the raid depended on split-second timing.*

ˌsplit ˈticket *noun* (in elections in the US) a vote in which sb votes for candidates from two different parties ▶ **ˌsplit-ˈticket** *adj.*: *a split-ticket vote*

split·ting /ˈsplɪtɪŋ/ *adj.* [only before noun] if you have a **splitting headache**, you have a very bad pain in your head

splodge /splɒdʒ; *AmE* splɑːdʒ/ (*also* **splotch** /splɒtʃ; *AmE* splɑːtʃ/, *AmE, BrE*) *noun* a large mark or spot of ink, paint, mud, etc.; a small area of colour or light: *He had a splodge of oil on his cheek.*

splurge /splɜːdʒ; *AmE* splɜːrdʒ/ *noun, verb*

■ *noun* [usually sing.] (*informal*) an act of spending a lot of money on sth that you do not really need

■ *verb* [VN, V] **~ (sth) (on sth)** (*informal*) to spend a lot of money on sth that you do not really need

splut·ter /ˈsplʌtə(r)/ *verb, noun*

■ *verb* **1 ~ sth (out)| ~ (with sth)** to speak quickly and with difficulty, making short SPITTING sounds, because you are angry or embarrassed [SYN] SPUTTER: [V speech] *'But, but ...you can't!' she spluttered.* ◊ [VN] *Her father spluttered indignation.* [also V] **2** [V] to make a series of short explosive sounds [SYN] SPUTTER: *The firework spluttered and went out.* ◊ *She fled from the blaze, **coughing and spluttering**.*

■ *noun* a short explosive sound: *The car started with a splutter.*

spoil /spɔɪl/ *verb, noun*

■ *verb* (**spoiled, spoiled** /spɔɪld/) (*BrE also* **spoilt, spoilt** /spɔɪlt/) **1** [VN] to change sth good into sth bad, unpleasant, useless, etc. [SYN] RUIN: *Our camping trip was spoilt by bad weather.* ◊ *Don't let him spoil your evening.* ◊ *The tall buildings have spoiled the view.* ◊ *Don't eat too many nuts—you'll spoil your appetite* (= will no longer be hungry at mealtime). ◊ (*BrE*) *spoiled ballot papers* (= not valid because not correctly marked) **2** [VN] to give a child everything that they ask for and not enough discipline in a way that has a bad effect on their character and behaviour: *She spoils those kids of hers.* **3** [VN] **~ sb/ yourself** to make sb/yourself happy by doing sth special: *Why not spoil yourself with a weekend in a top hotel?* ◊ *He*

really spoiled me on my birthday. **4** [V] (of food) to become bad so that it can no longer be eaten **IDM** be ˈspoiling for a fight to want to fight with sb very much—more at COOK *n.*
- *noun* **1** (the spoils) [pl.] (*formal* or *literary*) goods stolen from a place by thieves or by an army that has won a battle or war: *the spoils of war/conquest* ◇ *The robbers divided up the spoils.* **2** (spoils) [pl.] the profits or advantages that sb gets from being successful: *the spoils of high office* ◇ *The two teams shared the spoils with a 1–1 result.* **3** [U] (*technical*) waste material that is brought up when a hole is dug, etc.

spoil·age /ˈspɔɪlɪdʒ/ *noun* [U] (*technical*) the decay of food which means that it can no longer be used

spoil·er /ˈspɔɪlə(r)/ *noun* **1** a part of an aircraft's wing that can be raised in order to interrupt the flow of air over it and so slow the aircraft's speed—picture at PLANE **2** a raised part on a fast car that prevents it from being lifted off the road when travelling very fast: *rear/front spoilers* **3** (*especially AmE*) a candidate for a political office who is unlikely to win but who may get enough votes to prevent one of the main candidates from winning **4** a person or thing that spoils sth

spoil·sport /ˈspɔɪlspɔːt; *AmE* -spɔːrt/ *noun* (*informal*) a person who spoils other people's enjoyment, for example by not taking part in an activity or by trying to stop other people from doing it: *Don't be such a spoilsport!*

spoilt /spɔɪlt/ (*BrE*) (also **spoiled** /spɔɪld/, *AmE, BrE*) *adj.* (of a child) rude and badly behaved because they are given everything they ask for and not enough discipline: *a spoiled brat* ◇ *He's spoilt rotten* (= a lot). **IDM** be spoilt for ˈchoice (*BrE*) to have such a lot of things to choose from that it is very difficult to make a decision

spoke /spəʊk; *AmE* spoʊk/ *noun* one of the thin bars or rods that connect the centre of a wheel to its outer edge, for example on a bicycle—picture at BICYCLE **IDM** put a ˈspoke in sb's wheel (*BrE*) to prevent sb from carrying out their plans—see also SPEAK, SPOKE, SPOKEN *v.*

spoken /ˈspəʊkən; *AmE* ˈspoʊ-/ **1** *pp* of SPEAK **2** (-spoken) (in adjectives) speaking in the way mentioned: *a quietly spoken man*—see also OUTSPOKEN

ˈspoken for *adj.* [not before noun] already claimed or being kept for sb: *I'm afraid you can't sit there—those seats are spoken for.* ◇ *Liza is already spoken for* (= she is already married or has a boyfriend).

the ˌspoken ˈword *noun* [sing.] language expressed in speech, rather than being written or sung

spokes·man /ˈspəʊksmən; *AmE* ˈspoʊ-/, **spokes·woman** /ˈspəʊkswʊmən; *AmE* ˈspoʊ-/ *noun* (*pl.* **-men** /-mən/, **-women** /-wɪmɪn/) ~ (for sb/sth) a person who speaks on behalf of a group or an organization: *a police spokesman* ◇ *A spokeswoman for the government denied the rumours.* ⇨ note at GENDER

spokes·per·son /ˈspəʊkspɜːsn; *AmE* ˈspoʊkspɜːrsn/ *noun* (*pl.* **-persons** or **-people**) ~ (for sb/sth) a person who speaks on behalf of a group or an organization

sponge /spʌndʒ/ *noun, verb*
- *noun* **1** [C] a piece of artificial or natural material that is soft and light and full of holes and can hold water easily, used for washing or cleaning: *a bath sponge* (= to wash your body with in the bath) ◇ (*figurative*) *His mind was like a sponge, ready to absorb anything.* **2** [U] artificial sponge used for filling furniture, cushions, etc. **3** [C] a simple sea creature with a light body full of holes, from which natural sponge is obtained **4** [C, U] (*BrE*) = SPONGE CAKE: *a chocolate sponge*—picture on page A1
- *verb* **1** [VN] ~ sb/yourself/sth (down) to wash sb/yourself/sth with a wet cloth or SPONGE: *She sponged his hot face.* ◇ *Take your jacket off and I'll sponge it down with water.* **2** [VN+*adv.*/*prep.*] to remove sth using a wet cloth or SPONGE: *We tried to sponge the blood off my shirt.* **3** [V] ~ (off/on sb) (*informal, disapproving*) to get money, food, etc. regularly from other people without doing anything for them or offering to pay: *He spent his whole life sponging off his relatives.*

ˈsponge bag (also ˈtoilet bag, ˈwash·bag) *noun* (all *BrE*) a small bag for holding your soap, TOOTHBRUSH, etc., especially when you are travelling

ˈsponge cake (also **sponge**) *noun* [C, U] (*BrE*) a light cake made from eggs, sugar and flour, with or without fat—picture on page A1

ˌsponge ˈpudding *noun* [U, C] (*BrE*) a hot DESSERT (= a sweet dish) like a sponge cake that usually has jam or fruit on top: *sponge pudding and custard*

spon·ger /ˈspʌndʒə(r)/ *noun* (*disapproving*) a person who gets money, food, etc. from other people without doing anything for them or offering to pay

spongi·form /ˈspʌndʒɪfɔːm; *AmE* -fɔːrm/ *adj.* (*medical*) having or relating to a structure with holes in it like a SPONGE—see also BSE

spongy /ˈspʌndʒi/ *adj.* soft and able to absorb water easily like a SPONGE: *spongy moss* ◇ *The ground was soft and spongy.* ◇ *The bread had a spongy texture.* ▶ **spon·gi·ness** *noun* [U]

spon·sor /ˈspɒnsə(r); *AmE* ˈspɑːn-/ *noun, verb*
- *noun* **1** a person or company that pays for a radio or television programme, or for a concert or sporting event, usually in return for advertising: *The race organizers are trying to attract sponsors.* **2** a person who agrees to give sb money for a charity if that person succeeds in completing a particular activity: *I'm collecting sponsors for next week's charity run.* **3** a person or company that supports sb by paying for their training or education: *Unless he can find a sponsor he'll be forced to retire from athletics.* **4** a person who introduces and supports a proposal for a new law, etc: *the sponsor of the new immigration bill* **5** a person who agrees to be officially responsible for another person **6** a person who presents a child for Christian BAPTISM or CONFIRMATION **SYN** GODPARENT
- *verb* **1** [VN] (of a company, etc.) to pay the costs of a particular event, programme, etc. as a way of advertising: *sports events sponsored by the tobacco industry* **2** [VN] to arrange for sth official to take place: *The US is sponsoring negotiations between the two sides.* **3** to agree to give sb money for a charity if they complete a particular task: [VN] *Will you sponsor me for a charity walk I'm doing?* ◇ *a sponsored walk/swim* [also VN to inf] **4** [VN] to support sb by paying for their training or education: *She found a company to sponsor her through college.* **5** [VN] (*technical*) to introduce a proposal for a new law, etc: *The bill was sponsored by a Labour MP.*

spon·sor·ship /ˈspɒnsəʃɪp; *AmE* ˈspɑːnsərʃɪp/ *noun* [U] **1** financial support from a sponsor: *a $50 million sponsorship deal* ◇ *The project needs to raise £8 million in sponsorship.* ◇ *We need to find sponsorship for the expedition.* **2** the act of sponsoring sb/sth or being sponsored: *the senator's sponsorship of the job training legislation*

spon·tan·eity /ˌspɒntəˈneɪəti; *AmE* ˌspɑːn-/ *noun* [U] the quality of being spontaneous

spon·tan·eous /spɒnˈteɪniəs; *AmE* spɑːn-/ *adj.* **1** not planned but done because you suddenly want to do it: *a spontaneous offer of help* ◇ *The audience burst into spontaneous applause.* **2** (of a person) often doing things without planning to, because they suddenly want to do them **3** (*technical*) happening naturally, without being made to happen: *spontaneous remission of the disease* ◇ *a spontaneous abortion* (= a MISCARRIAGE) **4** done naturally, without being forced or practised: *a tape recording of spontaneous speech* ◇ *a wonderfully spontaneous performance of the piece* ▶ **spon·tan·eous·ly** *adv.*: *We spontaneously started to dance.* ◇ *The bleeding often stops spontaneously.*

spon,taneous com'bustion *noun* [U] the burning of a mineral or vegetable substance caused by chemical changes inside it and not by fire or heat from outside

spoof /spuːf/ *noun* (*informal*) a humorous copy of a film/movie, television programme, etc. that exaggerates its main features: *It's a spoof on horror movies.* ◇ *a spoof game show/a game show spoof* ▶ **spoof** *verb* [V, VN]

spook /spuːk/ *noun, verb*
- *noun* (*informal*) **1** a ghost: *a castle haunted by spooks* **2** (*especially AmE*) a spy: *a CIA spook*
- *verb* (*informal, especially AmE*) to frighten a person or an animal; to become frightened: [VN] [usually passive] *We were spooked by the strange noises and lights.* ◇ [V] *The horse spooked at the siren.*

s	t	v	z	ʃ	ʒ	tʃ	dʒ	θ	ð	ŋ
see	tea	van	zoo	shoe	vision	chain	jam	thin	this	sing

spooky /'spuːki/ *adj.* (**spook·ier**, **spooki·est**) **HELP** You can also use **more spooky** and **most spooky**. (*informal*) strange and frightening: *a spooky old house* ◊ *a spooky atmosphere/feeling* ◊ *I was just thinking about her when she phoned. Spooky!*

spool /spuːl/ *noun, verb*
■ *noun* (*especially AmE*) = REEL (1): *a spool of thread*
■ *verb* [VN+adv. / prep.] **1** to wind sth onto or off a spool **2** [VN, V] (*computing*) to move data and store it for a short time, for example on a disk, especially before it is printed

spoon /spuːn/ *noun, verb*
■ *noun* **1** a tool that has a handle with a shallow bowl at the end, used for stirring, serving and eating food: *a soup spoon* ◊ *a wooden spoon*—see also DESSERTSPOON, GREASY SPOON, TABLESPOON, TEASPOON—picture at CUTLERY **2** = SPOONFUL **IDM** see BORN
■ *verb* [VN+adv. / prep.] to lift and move food with a spoon: *She spooned the sauce over the chicken pieces.*

spoon·er·ism /'spuːnərɪzəm/ *noun* a mistake in which you accidentally change around the first sounds of two words when saying them, often with a humorous result, for example *well-boiled icicle* for *well-oiled bicycle* **ORIGIN** Named after **W.A. Spooner**, (1844–1930), the head of New College, Oxford, who was said to make many mistakes like this when he spoke.

spoon-feed *verb* [VN] **1 ~ sb (with sth)** | **~ sth to sb** (*disapproving*) to teach people sth in a way that gives them too much help and does not make them think for themselves: *The students here do not expect to be spoon-fed.* ◊ *They had information spoon-fed to them.* **2** to feed sb, especially a baby, with a spoon

spoon·ful /'spuːnfʊl/ (also **spoon**) *noun* the amount that a spoon can hold: *two spoonfuls of sugar*

spoor /spʊə(r); *AmE* spʊr/ *noun* [sing.] a track or smell that a wild animal leaves as it travels

spor·ad·ic /spə'rædɪk/ *adj.* (*written*) happening only occasionally or at intervals that are not regular: *sporadic fighting/gunfire/violence* ◊ *sporadic outbreaks of the disease* ▶ **spor·ad·ic·al·ly** /-kli/ *adv.*

spore /spɔː(r)/ *noun* (*biology*) one of the very small cells like seeds that are produced by some plants and that develop into new plants: *Ferns, mosses and fungi produce spores.*

spor·ran /'spɒrən; *AmE* 'spɔːrən; 'spɑː-/ *noun* a flat bag, usually made of leather or fur, that is worn by men in front of the KILT as part of the Scottish national dress

sport /spɔːt; *AmE* spɔːrt/ *noun, verb*
■ *noun* **1** [U] (*BrE*) (*AmE* **sports** [pl.]) activity that you do for pleasure and that needs physical effort or skill, usually done in a special area and according to fixed rules: *There are excellent facilities for sport and recreation.* ◊ *I'm not interested in sport.* ◊ *the use of drugs in sport* ⇨ vocabulary notes and pictures on pages 1250–1 **2** [C] a particular form of sport: *What's your favourite sport?* ◊ *team / water sports* ◊ *a sports club*—see also BLOOD SPORT, FIELD SPORTS, SPECTATOR SPORT, WINTER SPORTS **3** [C] (*informal*, especially *AustralE*) used as a friendly way of greeting sb, especially a man **4** [U] (*formal*) amusement or fun: *The comments were only made in sport.* ◊ *to make sport of* (= to joke about) *sb/sth* **5** [C] (*technical*) a plant or an animal that is different in a noticeable way from its usual type **IDM** **be a (good)** '**sport** (*informal*) to be generous, cheerful and pleasant, especially in a difficult situation: *She's a good sport.* ◊ *Go on, be a sport* (= used when asking sb to help you).
■ *verb* **1** [VN] to have or wear sth in a proud way so that everyone can see: *to sport a beard / a diamond ring / a flower in your buttonhole* **2** [V+adv. / prep.] (*literary*) to play in a happy and lively way

sport·ing /'spɔːtɪŋ; *AmE* 'spɔːrtɪŋ/ *adj.* **1** [only before noun] connected with sports: *a major sporting event* ◊ *a range of sporting activities* ◊ *His main sporting interests are golf and tennis.* ◊ (*AmE*) *a store selling sporting goods* **2** (*especially BrE*) fair and generous in your treatment of other people, especially in a game or sport **OPP** for sense 2 UNSPORTING ▶ **sport·ing·ly** *adv.*: *He sportingly agreed to*

play the point again. **IDM** **a** ,**sporting** '**chance** a reasonable chance of success

'**sports car** (*AmE* also '**sport car**) *noun* a low fast car, often with a roof that can be folded back

'**sports·cast** /'spɔːtskɑːst; *AmE* 'spɔːrtskæst/ *noun* (*AmE*) a television or radio broadcast of sports news or a sports event

'**sports·cast·er** /'spɔːtskɑːstə(r); *AmE* 'spɔːrtskæstər/ *noun* (*AmE*) a person who introduces and presents a sportscast

'**sports centre** *noun* (*BrE*) a building where the public can go to play many different kinds of sports, swim, etc.

'**sports day** (*BrE*) (*AmE* '**field day**) *noun* a special day at school when there are no classes and children compete in sports events

'**sports jacket** (*AmE* also '**sport jacket**) *noun* a man's jacket for informal occasions, sometimes made of TWEED

sports·man /'spɔːtsmən; *AmE* 'spɔːrts-/, **sports·woman** /'spɔːtswʊmən; *AmE* 'spɔːrts-/ *noun* (*pl.* **-men** /-mən/, **-women** /-wɪmɪn/) (*especially BrE*) a person who takes part in sport, especially sb who is very good at it **SYN** ATHLETE: *a keen sportswoman* ◊ *He is one of this country's top professional sportsmen.*

sports·man·like /'spɔːtsmənlaɪk; *AmE* 'spɔːrts-/ *adj.* behaving in a fair, generous and polite way, especially when playing a sport or game: *a sportsmanlike attitude*

sports·man·ship /'spɔːtsmənʃɪp; *AmE* 'spɔːrts-/ *noun* [U] fair, generous and polite behaviour, especially when playing a sport or game: *He has a reputation for fair play and good sportsmanship.*

sports·per·son /'spɔːtspɜːsn; *AmE* 'spɔːrtspɜːrsn/ *noun* (*pl.* **-persons** or **-people**) (*especially BrE*) a person who takes part in sport, especially sb who is very good at it **SYN** ATHLETE

'**sports shirt** (*AmE* also '**sport shirt**) *noun* a man's shirt for informal occasions

sports·wear /'spɔːtsweə(r); *AmE* 'spɔːrtswer/ *noun* [U] **1** (*especially BrE*) clothes that are worn for playing sports, or in informal situations **2** (*especially AmE*) clothes that are worn in informal situations

sporty /'spɔːti; *AmE* 'spɔːrti/ *adj.* (**sport·ier**, **sporti·est**) (*informal*) **1** (*especially BrE*) liking or good at sport: *I'm not very sporty.* **2** (of clothes) bright, attractive and informal; looking suitable for wearing for sports: *a sporty cotton top* **3** (of cars) fast and elegant: *a sporty Mercedes*

spot /spɒt; *AmE* spɑːt/ *noun, verb*
■ *noun*
SMALL MARK | **1** a small round area that has a different colour or feels different from the surface it is on: *Which has spots, the leopard or the tiger?* ◊ *The male bird has a red spot on its beak.* ◊ (*BrE*) *She was wearing a black skirt with white spots.*—see also BEAUTY SPOT, SUNSPOT **2** a small dirty mark on sth: *His jacket was covered with spots of mud.* ◊ *grease / rust spots* **3** [usually pl.] a small mark or lump on a person's skin, sometimes with a yellow head to it: *The baby's whole body was covered in small red spots.* ◊ (*BrE*) *teenagers worried about their spots*—compare PIMPLE, RASH, ZIT

PLACE | **4** a particular area or place: *a quiet / secluded / lonely spot* ◊ *He showed me the exact spot where he had asked her to marry him.* ◊ *She stood rooted to the spot with fear* (= unable to move). ◊ *a picnic / tourist spot*—see also BLACK SPOT, BLIND SPOT, HOT SPOT, NIGHTSPOT, TROUBLE SPOT

SMALL AMOUNT | **5** [usually sing.] **~ of sth** (*BrE*, *informal*) a small amount of sth: *He's in a spot of trouble.* ◊ *Would you like a spot of lunch?* **6** [usually pl.] **~ (of sth)** a small amount of a liquid: *I felt a few spots of rain.*

PART OF SHOW | **7** a part of a television, radio, club or theatre show that is given to a particular entertainer or type of entertainment: *a guest / solo spot*

IN COMPETITION | **8** a position in a competition or an event: *two teams battling for top spot*

LIGHT | **9** (*informal*) = SPOTLIGHT

BUSINESS | **10** [sing.] (used before nouns to make compound nouns) connected with a system of trading where

æ	ɑː	e	ɜː	ə	ɪ	iː	i	ɒ	ɔː	ʌ	ʊ	u	uː
cat	father	ten	bird	about	sit	see	many	got	saw	cup	put	actual	too

(BrE)

 Sport

Talking about a particular sport

You can **play** particular sports:

- *Do you play tennis?*
- *I usually play football on Saturdays.*

This is used particularly for competitive sports in which one team or person **plays** or **plays against** another:

- *We played them in last year's final.*
- *Who are you playing against this afternoon?*

Members of a sports team **play for** their team:

- *He used to play for the Dallas Cowboys.*

If the name of a sport or an activity ends in **-ing** we often use it with the verb **to go**:

- *I go swimming twice a week.*
- *Have you ever been rock climbing?*

Typical sports and activities with this pattern include **go skiing**, **go sailing**, **go riding** (*BrE*) or **go horseback riding** (*AmE*) and **go dancing**.

Check at the entry for each sport to see if it can be used in this way.

> **GRAMMAR POINT**
>
> Names of American sports teams always start with 'the'; names of British sports teams almost never do. Names of sports teams may look either singular or plural but always take a plural verb:
>
> - *The Jazz are playing the Chicago Bulls.*
> - *Aston Villa have started the season well.*
>
> Teams are often referred to just by the name of the place they come from. In American English this means a singular verb is used, but in British English the verb is still plural.
>
> - *Cincinnati is having a great season.*
> - *Norwich were disappointed with the score.*

Other sports and activities can take the verbs **to do** or **to go to**:

- *I do aerobics once or twice a week.*
- *I go to judo (= to my judo class) on Mondays.*

football (*BrE*)/soccer

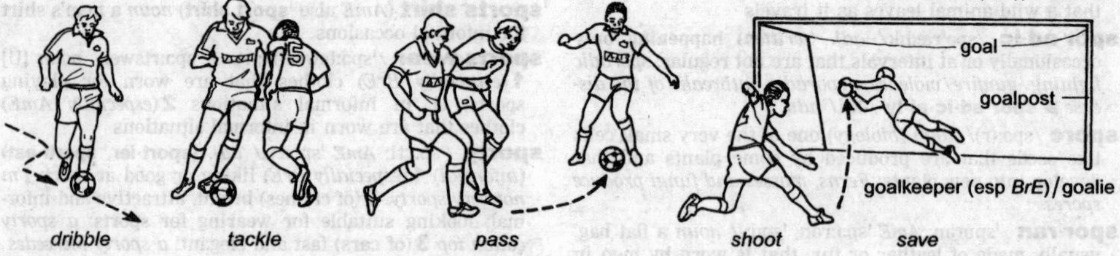

dribble · tackle · pass · shoot · save

goal · goalpost · goalkeeper (esp *BrE*)/goalie

tennis

receive · net · serve · court

basketball

backboard · hoop · basket · dribble · pass · dunk

cricket

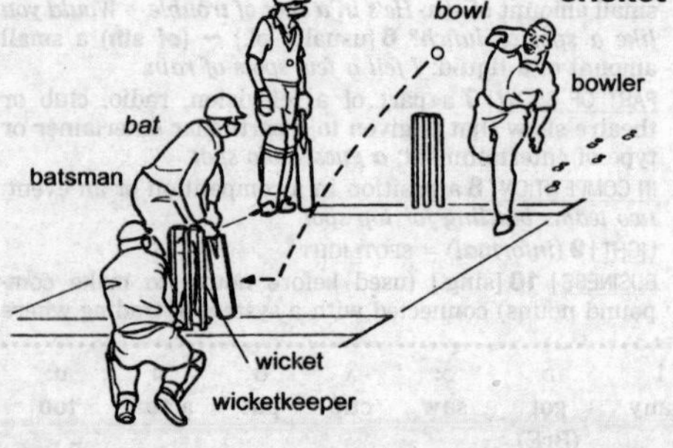

bowl · bowler · bat · batsman · wicket · wicketkeeper

baseball

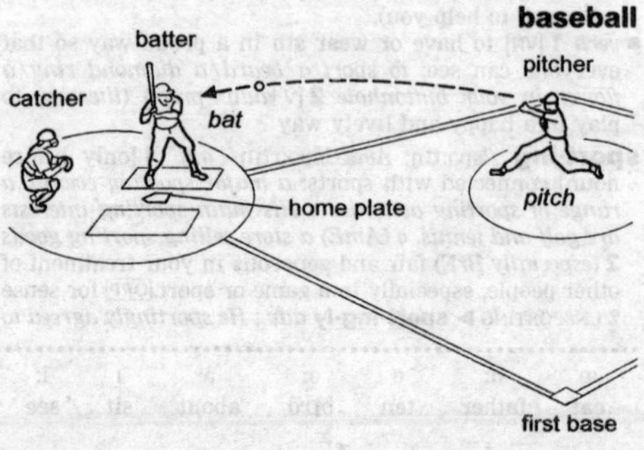

batter · catcher · bat · home plate · pitcher · pitch · first base

Talking about sports in general

You can **do sport** (*BrE*) …
- *Do you do a lot of sport?*

… or you can **play sports** (esp *AmE*):
- *We played sports together when we were kids.*

But these verbs are not used very often. It is more usual to talk about **liking** sport/sports or **being good at** sport/sports:
- *Are you good at sport?* (*BrE*) or
  Are you good at sports? (*AmE*)
- *What sports do you like best?*

Do **not** say that you 'practise' sport or a sport if you just mean that you do or play it. Say:
- *I love sport.* (*BrE*) or *I love sports.* (*AmE*)
  (No other verb is necessary.)
- **not** *I love practising sport.*

Say which sports you play:
- *Every Sunday I play volleyball or badminton with my friends.*
- **not** *Every Sunday I practise sport with my friends.*

However, you can use the verb 'practise', especially in American English (where it is spelt 'practice') if it means 'to train':
- *The team is practicing for its big game.* (*AmE*)
- *The team are in training for their big match.* (*BrE*)

GRAMMAR POINT

The names of sports can be used like adjectives before other nouns:
- *a tennis match*
- *cycling shorts*
- *a football team*

The words **sports** and **sporting** (but **not** 'sport') can be used in the same way:
- *a sports club*
- *sports shoes*
- *a sporting event*
- *sporting goods*

People who take part in sports

A person who **plays** a particular sport is usually called a football/tennis/basketball **player**:
- *Welsh rugby players could get £2000 each from a new sponsorship deal.*

Some sports have a special name for the players or people who do them. Some of these names end in **-er** but others do not follow a particular pattern. Check near the entry for each sport to find the correct word.
- *talented young footballers* (*BrE* only)
- *an Olympic boxer*

- *top athletes from around the world*
- *cyclists competing in the Tour de France*

> More illustrations of sports at
> GOLF, HOCKEY, SKIING and SWIMMING.

athletics (*BrE*)/
track and field (*AmE*)

track events
run the 100 metres, the relay

baton

starting block   **the 100 metres**

the relay   **the hurdles**   lane

the pole vault

field events
do the long jump, the high jump, the pole vault
throw the javelin, the discus, the hammer
put the shot

the long jump

the high jump

the javelin   **the discus**   **the hammer**   **the shot put**

S

goods are delivered and paid for immediately after sale: *spot prices* ◊ *spot goods*

IDM **in a (tight) 'spot** (*informal*) in a difficult situation **on the 'spot 1** immediately: *He answered the question on the spot.* ◊ *an on-the-spot parking fine* **2** at the actual place where sth is happening: *An ambulance was on the spot within minutes.* ◊ *an on-the-spot report* **3** in one exact place, without moving in any direction: *Running on the spot is good exercise.* **put sb on the 'spot** to make sb feel awkward or embarrassed by asking them a difficult question: *The interviewer's questions really put him on the spot.*—more at BRIGHT *adj.*, GLUE *v.*, HIT *v.*, KNOCK *v.*, LEOPARD, RIVET *v.*, SOFT

▪ *verb* (**-tt-**) **1** (not used in the progressive tenses) to see or notice a person or thing, especially suddenly or when it is not easy to do so: [VN] *I finally spotted my friend in the crowd.* ◊ *I've just spotted a mistake on the front cover.* ◊ *Can you spot the difference between these two pictures?* ◊ [VN-ing] *Neighbours spotted smoke coming out of the house.* ◊ [V that] *No one spotted that the gun was a fake.* ◊ [V wh-] *I soon spotted what the mistake was.*—see also SPOTTER **2** [VN] (*AmE, sport*) to give your opponent or the other team an advantage: *We spotted the opposing team two goals.*

IDM **be spotted with sth** to be covered with small round marks of sth: *His shirt was spotted with oil.*

spot 'check *noun* a check that is made suddenly and without warning on a few things or people chosen from a group to see that everything is satisfactory: *to carry out random spot checks on vehicles*

spot·less /'spɒtləs; *AmE* 'spɑːt-/ *adj.* perfectly clean: *a spotless white shirt* ◊ *She keeps the house spotless.* ◊ (*figurative*) *He has a spotless record so far.* ▸ **spot·less·ly** *adv.*: *spotlessly clean*

spot·light /'spɒtlaɪt; *AmE* 'spɑːt-/ *noun, verb*

▪ *noun* **1** (also *informal* **spot**) [C] a light with a single, very bright beam that can be directed at a particular place or person; the area of light from this: *The room was lit by spotlights.* ◊ *She stood alone on stage in the spotlight.* **2** (**the spotlight**) [sing.] attention from newspapers, television and the public: *Unemployment is once again in the spotlight.* ◊ *The issue will come under the spotlight when parliament reassembles.* ◊ *The report has turned the spotlight on the startling rise in street crime.* ◊ *She was happy to share the spotlight with her sister.*

▪ *verb* (**spot·lit, spot·lit** /-lɪt/ **HELP** Especially in sense 2, **spot·light·ed** is also used for the past tense and past participle.) [VN] **1** to shine a spotlight on sb/sth: *a spotlit stage* **2** to give special attention to a problem, situation, etc. so that people notice it **SYN** HIGHLIGHT: *The programme spotlights serious financial problems in the health service.*

spot 'on *adj.* [not before noun] (*BrE, informal*) exactly right: *His assessment of the situation was spot on.*

spot·ted /'spɒtɪd; *AmE* 'spɑːt-/ *adj.* **1** (of fabric, etc.) having a regular pattern of round dots on it: *a black and white spotted dress* **2** having dark marks on it, sometimes in a pattern: *a leopard's spotted coat*

spotted 'dick *noun* [U] (*BrE*) a hot DESSERT (= a sweet dish) like a SPONGE CAKE with dried fruit in it

spot·ter /'spɒtə(r); *AmE* 'spɑːt-/ *noun* **1** (especially in compounds) a person who looks for a particular type of thing or person, as a hobby or job: *a talent spotter* (= sb who visits clubs and theatres looking for new performers)—see also TRAINSPOTTER **2** (also '**spotter plane**) a plane used for finding out what an enemy is doing

spotty /'spɒti; *AmE* 'spɑːti/ *adj.* **1** (*BrE*, usually *disapproving*) (of a person) having a lot of spots on the skin: *a spotty adolescent* ◊ *a spotty face/skin* **2** (*AmE*) = PATCHY (2)

spouse /spaʊs; spaʊz/ *noun* (*formal* or *law*) a husband or wife: *Fill in your spouse's name here.* ▸ **spou·sal** /'spaʊzl; 'spaʊsl/ *adj.* [only before noun] (*AmE, formal*): *spousal consent/support* ◊ *spousal abuse*

spout /spaʊt/ *noun, verb*

▪ *noun* **1** [C] a pipe or tube on a container, that you can pour liquid out through: *the spout of a teapot* **2** a stream of liquid coming out of somewhere with great force **IDM**

be/go up the 'spout (*BrE, slang*) to be/go wrong; to be spoilt or not working: *Well, that's my holiday plans gone up the spout!*

▪ *verb* **1** to send out sth, especially a liquid, in a stream with great force; to come out of sth in this way: [VN] *The wound was still spouting blood.* ◊ [V+adv./prep.] *Clear water spouted from the fountains.* **2** [V] (of a WHALE) to send out a stream of water from a hole in its head **3 ~ (off/on) (about sth)** (*informal, disapproving*) to speak a lot about sth; to repeat sth in a boring or annoying way: [V] *He's always spouting off about being a vegetarian.* ◊ *What are you spouting on about now?* ◊ [VN] *He could spout poetry for hours.* ◊ *She could do nothing but spout insults.* ◊ *The article was full of the usual clichés spouted by fashion editors.*

sprain /spreɪn/ *verb* [VN] to injure a joint in your body, especially your wrist or ankle, by suddenly twisting it: *I stumbled and sprained my ankle.* ▸ **sprain** *noun*: *a bad ankle sprain*

sprang *pt* of SPRING

sprat /spræt/ *noun* a very small European sea fish that is used for food

sprawl /sprɔːl/ *verb, noun*

▪ *verb* [V+adv./prep.] **1** to sit or lie with your arms and legs spread out in a relaxed or awkward way: *He was sprawling in an armchair in front of the TV.* ◊ *Something hit her and* **sent her sprawling** *to the ground.* ◊ *I tripped and* **went sprawling.** **2** to spread in an untidy way; to cover a large area: *The town sprawled along the side of the lake.*

▪ *noun* **1** [C usually sing, U] a large area covered with buildings that spreads from the city into the countryside in an ugly way: *attempts to control the fast-growing* **urban sprawl** **2** [C, usually sing.] an act of spreading to cover a large area in an untidy way; sth that spreads like this

sprawled /sprɔːld/ *adj.* sitting or lying with your arms and legs spread out in a lazy or awkward way: *He was lying sprawled in an armchair, watching TV.*

sprawl·ing /'sprɔːlɪŋ/ *adj.* [only before noun] spreading in an untidy way: *a modern sprawling town* ◊ *sprawling handwriting*

spray /spreɪ/ *noun, verb*

▪ *noun* **1** [U, C] very small drops of a liquid that are sent through the air, for example by the wind: *sea spray* ◊ *A cloud of fine spray came up from the waterfall.* ◊ (*figurative*) *a spray of machine-gun bullets* **2** [U, C] (especially in compounds) a substance that is forced out of a container such as an AEROSOL, in very small drops: *a can of insect spray* (= used to kill insects) ◊ *body spray*—see also HAIRSPRAY—picture at PACKAGING **3** [C] a device or container, for example, an AEROSOL, that you use to apply liquid in fine drops: *I need a new throat spray.* ◊ *It's better to buy a non-aerosol spray.* **4** [C] an act of applying liquid to sth in very small drops: *I'll just give the plants a quick spray.* **5** [C] a small branch of a tree or plant, with its leaves and flowers or berries, that you use for decoration **6** [C] an attractive arrangement of flowers or jewels, that you wear: *a spray of orchids*

▪ *verb* **1 ~ sth (on/onto/over sb/sth)** | **~ sb/sth (with sth)** to cover sb/sth with very small drops of a liquid that are forced out of a container or sent through the air: [VN] *Spray the conditioner onto your wet hair.* ◊ *The crops are regularly sprayed with pesticide.* ◊ [VN-ADJ] *She's had the car sprayed blue.* ◊ [V] *Champagne sprayed everywhere.* **2 ~ sb/sth (with sth)** to cover sb/sth with a lot of small things with a lot of force: [VN] *The gunman sprayed the building with bullets.* ◊ [V] *Pieces of glass sprayed all over the room.* **3** [V] (especially of a male cat) to leave small amounts of URINE to mark its own area

spray can *noun* a small metal container that has paint in it under pressure and that you use to spray paint onto sth

spray·er /'spreɪə(r)/ *noun* a piece of equipment used for spraying liquid, especially paint or a substance used to kill insects that damage crops: *a paint/crop sprayer*

spray gun *noun* a device for spraying paint onto a surface, that works by air pressure

s	t	v	z	ʃ	ʒ	tʃ	dʒ	θ	ð	ŋ
see	tea	van	zoo	shoe	vision	chain	jam	thin	this	sing

'spray-on *adj.* [only before noun] (especially *BrE*) that you can spray onto sth/sb from a special container: *a spray-on water repellent for shoes*

'spray paint *noun* [U] paint that is kept in a container under pressure and that you can spray onto sth ▶ **'spray-paint** *verb* [VN]

spread /spred/ *verb, noun*
■ *verb* (**spread, spread**)

OPEN/ARRANGE | **1** [VN] ~ **sth** (**out**) (**on/over sth**) to open sth that has been folded so that it covers a larger area than before: *to spread a cloth on a table* ◊ *Sue spread the map out on the floor.* ◊ *The bird spread its wings.* **2** [VN] ~ **sth** (**out**) (**on/over sth**) to arrange objects so that they cover a large area and can be seen easily: *Papers had been spread out on the desk.*

ARMS/LEGS | **3** [VN] ~ **sth** (**out**) to move your arms, legs, fingers, etc. far apart from each other: *She spread her arms and the child ran towards her.*

AMONG PEOPLE | **4** to affect or make sth affect, be known by, or used by more and more people: [V, usually +*adv./prep.*] *The disease spreads easily.* ◊ *Within weeks, his confidence had spread throughout the team.* ◊ *Use of computers spread rapidly during that period.* ◊ [VN] *to spread rumours/lies about sb* ◊ *The disease is spread by mosquitoes.*

COVER LARGE AREA | **5** [usually +*adv./prep.*] to cover, or to make sth cover, a larger and larger area: [V] *The fire rapidly spread to adjoining buildings.* ◊ *Water began to spread across the floor.* ◊ *A smile spread slowly across her face.* ◊ [VN] *Using too much water could spread the stain.* **6** [VN] to cause sb/sth to be in a number of different places: *Seeds and pollen are spread by the wind.* ◊ *We have 10000 members spread all over the country.* **7** [V+*adv./prep.*] ~ (**out**) to cover a large area: *The valley spread out beneath us.*

SOFT LAYER | **8** ~ (**A on/over B**) | ~ (**B with A**) to put a layer of a substance onto the surface of sth; to be able to be put onto a surface: [VN] *to spread butter on pieces of toast* ◊ *pieces of toast spread with butter* ◊ [V] *If the paint is too thick, it will not spread evenly.*

DIVIDE/SHARE | **9** [VN] ~ **sth** (**out**) (**over sth**) to separate sth into parts and divide them between different times or different people: *A series of five interviews will be spread over two days.* ◊ *Why not pay monthly and spread the cost of your car insurance?* ◊ *We attempted to spread the work-load between the departments.*

▶ **spread·er** *noun*: *a spreader of gossip* ◊ *a glue spreader*
IDM **spread like 'wildfire** (of news, etc.) to become known by more and more people very quickly **spread your 'net** to consider a wide range of possibilities or cover a large area, especially to try to find sb/sth: *They have spread their net far and wide in the search for a new team coach.* **spread your 'wings** to become more independent and confident and try new activities, etc: *Going to college gave her the chance to spread her wings.* **spread the 'word** to tell people about sth
PHRV **,spread 'out** | **,spread yourself 'out 1** to stretch your body or arrange your things over a large area: *There's more room to spread out in first class.* ◊ *Do you have to spread yourself out all over the sofa?* **2** to separate from other people in a group, to cover a larger area: *The searchers spread out to cover the area faster.*

■ *noun*
INCREASE | **1** [U] an increase in the amount or number of sth that there is, or in the area that is affected by sth: *to prevent the spread of disease/infection* ◊ *to encourage the spread of information/knowledge* ◊ *Shut doors to delay the spread of fire.* ◊ *the spread of a city into the surrounding areas*—see also MIDDLE-AGE SPREAD

RANGE/VARIETY | **2** [C, usually sing.] a range or variety of people or things: *a broad spread of investments/opinions*

ON BREAD | **3** [C, U] a soft food that you put on bread: *Use a low-fat spread instead of butter.* ◊ *cheese spread*

AREA COVERED | **4** [usually sing.] ~ (**of sth**) the area that sth exists in or happens in: *The company has a good geographical spread of hotels in this country.* **5** [usually sing.] ~ (**of sth**) how wide sth is or the area that sth covers: *The bird's wings have a spread of nearly a metre.*

IN NEWSPAPER/MAGAZINE | **6** [C] an article or advertisement in a newspaper or magazine, especially one that covers two opposite pages: *The story continued with a double-page spread on the inside pages.*—see also CENTRE SPREAD

MEAL | **7** [C] (*informal*) a large meal, especially one that is prepared for a special occasion: *They had laid on a huge spread for the party.*

OF LAND/WATER | **8** [usually sing.] ~ (**of sth**) (*AmE*) an area of land or water: *a vast spread of water* ◊ (*AmE*) *They have a huge spread in California* (= a large farm or ranch).

FINANCE | **9** [U] the difference between two rates or prices

ON BED | **10** [C] (*AmE*) = BEDSPREAD

spread-eagled /ˌspredˈiːgld/ (*BrE*) (*AmE* **spread-eagle**) *adj.* [not usually before noun] in a position with your arms and legs spread out: *He lay spreadeagled on the floor.* ▶ **spread·eagle** *verb* [VN]

spread·sheet /ˈspredʃiːt/ *noun* a computer program that is used, for example, when doing financial or project planning. You enter data in rows and columns and the program calculates costs, etc. from it.

spree /spriː/ *noun* **1** a short period of time that you spend doing one particular activity that you enjoy, but often too much of it: *a shopping/spending spree* ◊ *He's out on a spree.* **2** (used especially in newspapers) a period of activity, especially criminal activity: *to go on a killing/wrecking spree*

sprig /sprɪg/ *noun* a small stem with leaves on it from a plant or bush, used in cooking or as a decoration: *a sprig of parsley/holly/heather*

sprigged /sprɪgd/ *adj.* (especially of fabric or paper) decorated with patterns of stems with leaves or flowers on

spright·ly /ˈspraɪtli/ (also *less frequent* **spry**) *adj.* (especially of older people) full of life and energy: *a sprightly 80-year-old* ▶ **spright·li·ness** *noun* [U]

spring /sprɪŋ/ *noun, verb*

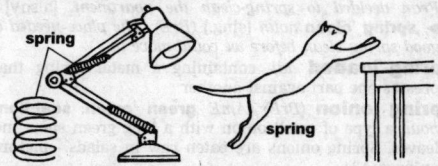

spring   spring

■ *noun*
SEASON | **1** [U, C] the season between winter and summer when plants begin to grow: *flowers that bloom in spring/in the spring* ◊ *He was born in the spring of 1944.* ◊ *There's a feeling of spring in the air today.* ◊ *spring flowers/weather*

TWISTED WIRE | **2** [C] a twisted piece of metal that can be pushed, pressed or pulled but which always returns to its original shape or position afterwards: *bed springs* **3** [U] the ability of a spring to return to its original position: *The mattress has lost its spring.*

WATER | **4** [C] a place where water comes naturally to the surface from under the ground: *a mountain spring* ◊ *spring water*

CHEERFUL QUALITY | **5** [U, sing.] a cheerful, lively quality: *She walked along with a spring in her step.*

SUDDEN JUMP | **6** [C] a quick sudden jump upwards or forwards: *With a spring, the cat leapt on to the table.*

IDM see JOY
■ *verb* (**sprang** /spræŋ/ **sprung** /sprʌŋ/) (*AmE* also **sprung, sprung**)
JUMP/MOVE SUDDENLY | **1** [V] [usually +*adv./prep.*] (of a person or an animal) to move suddenly and with one quick movement in a particular direction: *He turned off the alarm and sprang out of bed.* ◊ *Everyone sprang to their feet* (= stood up suddenly) *when the principal walked in.* ◊ *The cat crouched ready to spring.* ◊ (*figurative*) *to spring to sb's defence/assistance* (= to quickly defend or help sb) **2** (of an object) to move suddenly and violently: [V, +*adv./prep.*] *The branch sprang back and hit him in the face.* ◊ [V-ADJ] *She turned the key and the lid sprang open.*

æ	ɑː	e	ɜː	ə	ɪ	iː	i	ɒ	ɔː	ʌ	ʊ	u	uː
cat	father	ten	bird	about	sit	see	many	got	saw	cup	put	actual	too
								(BrE)					

SURPRISE | **3** [VN] **~ sth (on sb)** to do sth, ask sth or say sth that sb is not expecting: *She sprang a surprise by winning the tournament.* ◊ *I'm sorry to spring it on you, but I've been offered another job.*

APPEAR SUDDENLY | **4** [V+*adv. / prep.*] to appear or come somewhere suddenly: *Tears sprang to her eyes.*

FREE PRISONER | **5** [VN] (*informal*) to help a prisoner to escape: *Plans to spring the hostages have failed.*

IDM ,spring into 'action | ,spring into/to 'life (of a person, machine, etc.) to suddenly start working or doing sth: *'Let's go!' he said, springing into action.* ◊ *The town springs into life* (= becomes busy) *during the carnival.* **spring a 'leak** (of a boat or container) to develop a hole through which water or another liquid can pass **spring a 'trap 1** to make a trap for catching animals close suddenly **2** to try to trick sb into doing or saying sth; to succeed in this—more at MIND *n.*

PHRV 'spring from sth (*written*) to be caused by sth; to start from sth: *The idea for the novel sprang from a trip to India.* 'spring from ... (*spoken, informal*) to appear suddenly and unexpectedly from a particular place: *Where on earth did you spring from?* ,spring 'up to appear or develop quickly and/or suddenly: *Play areas for children are springing up all over the place.*

spring·board /ˈsprɪŋbɔːd; *AmE* -bɔːrd/ *noun* **1** a strong board that you jump on and use to help you jump high in DIVING and GYMNASTICS **2 ~ (for/to sth)** something that helps you start an activity, especially by giving you ideas: *The document provided a springboard for a lot of useful discussion.*

spring·bok /ˈsprɪŋbɒk; *AmE* -bɑːk/ *noun* a small S African ANTELOPE (= an African animal like a deer) that can jump high into the air

,spring 'chicken *noun* **IDM** be no ,spring 'chicken (*humorous*) to be no longer young

,spring-'clean *verb* to clean a house, room, etc. thoroughly, including the parts you do not usually clean: [VN] *Fran decided to spring-clean the apartment.* [also V] ▶ ,spring 'clean *noun* [sing.] (*BrE*): *The place needed a good spring clean before we could move in.*

,spring-'loaded *adj.* containing a metal spring that presses one part against another

,spring 'onion (*BrE*) (*AmE* ,green 'onion, scal·lion) *noun* a type of small onion with a long green stem and leaves. Spring onions are eaten raw in salads.—picture on page A3

,spring 'roll (*especially BrE*) *noun* a type of Chinese food consisting of a tube of thin pastry, filled with vegetables and/or meat and fried until it is crisp—see also EGG ROLL

,spring 'tide *noun* a TIDE in which there is a very great rise and fall of the sea, and which happens near the new moon and the full moon each month

spring·time /ˈsprɪŋtaɪm/ *noun* [U] (*especially written*) the season of spring: *a visit to Holland in springtime/in the springtime*

springy /ˈsprɪŋi/ (**spring·ier, springi·est**) *adj.* **1** returning quickly to the original shape after being pushed, pulled, stretched, etc: *We walked across the springy grass.* **2** full of energy and confidence: *She's 73, but hasn't lost that youthful, springy step.*

sprin·kle /ˈsprɪŋkl/ *verb, noun*
■ *verb* **1** [VN] **~ A on/onto/over B | ~ B with A** to throw small pieces of sth or drops of a liquid on sth: *She sprinkled sugar over the strawberries.* ◊ *She sprinkled the strawberries with sugar.* ◊ *Sprinkle chocolate on top of the cake.* **2** [VN] [usually passive] **~ sth with sth** to include a few of sth in sth else: *His poems are sprinkled with quotations from ancient Greek.* **3** [V] (*AmE*) if it **sprinkles**, it rains lightly: *It's only sprinkling. We can still go out.*
■ *noun* [sing.] **1** = SPRINKLING: *Add a sprinkle of cheese and serve.* **2** (*especially AmE*) light rain: *We've only had a few sprinkles (of rain) recently.*

sprink·ler /ˈsprɪŋklə(r)/ *noun* **1** a device with holes in that is used to spray water in drops on plants, soil or grass **2** a device inside a building which automatically sprays out water if there is a rise in temperature because of a fire

sprink·ling /ˈsprɪŋklɪŋ/ (also **sprin·kle**) *noun* a small amount or number of sth that is dropped, spread or included somewhere: *Add a sprinkling of pepper.* ◊ *There was a sprinkling of freckles on her cheeks.* ◊ *Most were men, but there was also a sprinkling of young women.*

sprint /sprɪnt/ *verb, noun*
■ *verb* to run a short distance very fast: [V, usually +*adv./ prep.*] *He sprinted for the line.* ◊ *Three runners sprinted past.* ◊ *She jumped out of the car and sprinted for the front door.* ◊ [VN] *I sprinted the last few metres.*
■ *noun* **1** a race in which the competitors run, swim, etc. very fast over a short distance: *a 100-metre sprint* ◊ *the world sprint champion* **2** [usually sing.] a short period of running, swimming, etc. very fast: *a sprint for the line* ◊ *a sprint for the bus* ◊ *She won in a sprint finish.* ▶ **sprint·er** *noun*

sprite /spraɪt/ *noun* (in stories) a small creature with magic powers, especially one that is graceful or likes playing tricks

spritz /sprɪts/ *verb* [VN] (*especially AmE*) to spray very small drops of liquid on sth quickly: *Lightly spritz your hair with water.* ▶ **spritz** *noun*

spritz·er /ˈsprɪtsə(r)/ *noun* a drink made with wine mixed with SODA WATER: *a white wine spritzer*

sprocket /ˈsprɒkɪt; *AmE* ˈsprɑːkɪt/ *noun* **1** (also ˈsprocket wheel) a wheel with a row of teeth around the edge that connect with the holes of a bicycle chain or with holes in a film, etc. in order to turn it—picture at BICYCLE **2** one of the teeth on such a wheel

sprog /sprɒg; *AmE* sprɑːg/ *noun* (*BrE, informal, humorous*) a child or baby

sprout /spraʊt/ *verb, noun*
■ *verb* **1** [V] (of plants, vegetables, etc.) to produce new leaves or BUDS: *The seeds will sprout in a few days.* ◊ *new leaves sprouting from the trees* **2** to appear; to develop sth, especially in large numbers: [V] *Hundreds of mushrooms had sprouted up overnight.* ◊ [VN] *The town has sprouted shopping malls, discos and nightclubs in recent years.* **3** to start to grow sth; to start to grow on sb/sth: [VN] *Tim has sprouted a beard since we last saw him.* ◊ [V] *Hair sprouted from his chest.*
■ *noun* **1** = BRUSSELS SPROUT **2** a new part growing on a plant

spruce /spruːs/ *noun, verb, adj.*
■ *noun* **1** [C, U] an EVERGREEN forest tree with leaves like needles **2** [U] the soft wood of the spruce, used, for example, in making paper
■ *verb* **PHRV** ,spruce 'up, ,spruce sb/sth/yourself‹ › 'up to make sb/sth/yourself clean and neat: *She spruced up for the interview.* ◊ *The city is sprucing up its museums and galleries.* ◊ *I spruced myself up before I went out.*
■ *adj.* (of people or places) neat and clean in appearance

sprung /sprʌŋ/ *adj.* fitted with metal springs: *a sprung mattress*—see also SPRING, SPRANG, SPRUNG *v.*

spry /spraɪ/ *adj.* = SPRIGHTLY

spud /spʌd/ *noun* (*BrE, informal*) a potato

spume /spjuːm/ *noun* [U] (*literary*) the mass of white bubbles that forms in waves when the sea is rough **SYN** FOAM

spun *pp of* SPIN

spunk /spʌŋk/ *noun* **1** [U] (*informal*) courage; determination **2** [U] (*BrE*, △, *slang*) = SEMEN **3** [C] (*informal*, especially *AustralE*) a sexually attractive man

spunky /ˈspʌŋki/ *adj.* (*informal*) brave and determined; full of enthusiasm: *She is bright, tough and spunky.*

spur /spɜː(r)/ *noun, verb*
■ *noun* **1** a sharp pointed object that riders sometimes wear on the heels of their boots and use to encourage their horse to go faster **2** [usually sing.] **~ (to sth)** a fact or an event that makes you want to do sth better or more quickly: *His speech was a powerful spur to action.* **3** an area of high ground that sticks out from a mountain or hill—picture at MOUNTAIN **4** a road or a railway/railroad track that leads from the main road or line **IDM** on the ,spur of the 'moment suddenly, without planning in advance: *I phoned him up on the spur of the moment.* ◊ *a*

aɪ	aʊ	eɪ	əʊ	oʊ	ɔɪ	ɪə	eə	ʊə	j	w
my	now	say	go	go	boy	near	hair	pure	yes	wet
			(BrE)	(AmE)						

spur-of-the-moment decision **win/ earn your 'spurs** (*formal*) to achieve fame or success

■ *verb* (**-rr-**) [VN] **1** ~ sb/sth (on) (to sth/ to do sth) to encourage sb to do sth or to encourage them to try harder to achieve sth: *Her difficult childhood spurred her on to succeed.* ◊ *I was spurred into action by the letter.* ◊ *The band has been spurred on by the success of their last single.* **2** to make sth happen faster or sooner: *The agreement is essential to spurring economic growth around the world.* **3** to encourage a horse to go faster, especially by pushing the spurs on your boots into its side

spuri·ous /'spjʊəriəs; *AmE* 'spjʊr-/ *adj.* **1** false, although seeming to be genuine: *He had managed to create the entirely spurious impression that the company was thriving.* **2** based on false ideas or ways of thinking: *a spurious argument* ▶ **spuri·ous·ly** *adv.*

spurn /spɜːn; *AmE* spɜːrn/ *verb* [VN] (*written*) to reject or refuse sb/sth, especially in a proud way: *Eve spurned Mark's invitation.* ◊ *a spurned lover*

spurt /spɜːt; *AmE* spɜːrt/ *verb, noun*
■ *verb* **1** ~ (out) (from sth) (of liquid or flames) to burst or pour out suddenly in a fast stream; to produce a sudden fast stream of liquid or flames: [V] *Blood was spurting from her nose.* ◊ *Red and yellow flames spurted out of the fire.* ◊ [VN] *Her nose was spurting blood.* ◊ *The volcano spurted clouds of steam and ash high into the air.* **2** [V+*adv./prep.*] to increase your speed for a short time to get somewhere faster: *She spurted past me to get to the line first.*
■ *noun* **1** an amount of liquid or flames that comes out of somewhere with great force: *a great spurt of blood* ◊ *The water came out of the tap in spurts.* **2** a sudden increase in speed, effort, activity or emotion for a short period of time: *You'd better put on a spurt* (= hurry up) *if you want to finish that work today.* ◊ *Babies get very hungry during growth spurts.* ◊ *a sudden spurt of anger/laughter/interest*

sput·ter /'spʌtə(r)/ *verb* **1** [V] if an engine, a lamp or a fire **sputters**, it makes a series of short explosive sounds [SYN] SPLUTTER: *Suddenly the car sputtered and stopped.* ◊ *sputtering fireworks* **2** to speak quickly and with difficulty, making soft SPITTING sounds, because you are angry or shocked [SYN] SPLUTTER: [V speech] '*W-What?*' *sputtered Anna.* [also VN]

spu·tum /'spjuːtəm/ *noun* [U] (*medical*) liquid from the throat or lungs, especially when it is coughed up because of disease: *blood in the sputum*

spy /spaɪ/ *noun, verb*
■ *noun* (*pl.* **-ies**) a person who tries to get secret information about another country, organization, or person, especially sb who is employed by a government or the police: *a government/police spy* ◊ *He worked as a British spy in Russia.* ◊ *a spy plane/satellite* (= used to watch the activities of the enemy) ◊ *a spy ring* ◊ *Video spy cameras are being used in public places.*
■ *verb* (**spies, spy·ing, spied, spied**) **1** [V] to collect secret information about another country, organization or person: *He spied for his government for more than ten years.* **2** [VN] (*literary* or *formal*) to suddenly see or notice sth/sth: *In the distance we spied the Pacific for the first time.* [IDM] **,spy out the 'land** to collect information before deciding what to do [PHRV] **'spy on sb/sth** to watch sb/sth secretly: *Have you been spying on me?* **,spy sth↔'out** to get information about sth

Sq. *abbr.* (used in written addresses) SQUARE: *6 Hanover Sq.*

sq (also **sq.** especially in *AmE*) *abbr.* (in measurements) square: *10 sq cm*

squab·ble /'skwɒbl; *AmE* 'skwɑːbl/ *verb* [V] ~ (with sb) (about/over sth) to quarrel noisily about sth that is not very important: *My sisters were squabbling over what to watch on TV.* ▶ **squab·ble** *noun*: *family squabbles* ◊ *There were endless squabbles over who should sit where.*

squad /skwɒd; *AmE* skwɑːd/ *noun* [C+sing./pl. *v.*] **1** a section of a police force that deals with a particular type of crime: *the drugs/fraud squad* ◊ *an anti-terrorist squad*—see also FLYING SQUAD **2** (in sport) a group of

players or competitors from which a team is chosen for a particular game or match: *the Olympic/national squad* **3** a small group of soldiers working or being trained together—see also FIRING SQUAD **4** a group of people who kill their opponents, usually for political reasons: *a death/hit/assassination squad*

'squad car *noun* a police car

squad·die /'skwɒdi; *AmE* 'skwɑːdi/ *noun* (*BrE, slang*) a new soldier; a soldier of low rank

squad·ron /'skwɒdrən; *AmE* 'skwɑːd-/ *noun* [C+sing./pl. *v.*] a group of military aircraft or ships forming a section of a military force: *a bomber/fighter squadron*

'squadron leader *noun* an officer of high rank in the British air force

squalid /'skwɒlɪd; *AmE* 'skwɑːlɪd/ *adj.* (*disapproving*) **1** (of places and living conditions) very dirty and unpleasant: *squalid housing* ◊ *squalid, overcrowded refugee camps* **2** (of situations or activities) involving low moral standards or dishonest behaviour [SYN] SORDID: *It was a squalid affair involving prostitutes and drugs.*

squall /skwɔːl/ *noun, verb*
■ *noun* a sudden strong and violent wind, often during rain or snow storms
■ *verb* [V] (usually used in the progressive tenses) (*disapproving*) to cry very loudly and noisily: *squalling kids*

squally /'skwɔːli/ *adj.* (of weather) involving sudden, violent and strong winds: *squally showers/winds*

squalor /'skwɒlə(r); *AmE* 'skwɑːl-/ *noun* [U] dirty and unpleasant conditions: *the poverty and squalor of the slums* ◊ *He had lost his job and was living in squalor.*

squan·der /'skwɒndə(r); *AmE* 'skwɑːn-/ *verb* [VN] ~ sth (on sb/sth) to waste money, time, etc. in a stupid or careless way: *My uncle squandered all his money on gambling.* ◊ *She squandered her chances of winning.*

square /skweə(r); *AmE* skwer/ *adj., noun, verb, adv.*
■ *adj.*
▸ SHAPE | **1** (*geometry*) having four straight equal sides and four angles of 90°: *a square room/table*—picture at PARALLELOGRAM **2** forming an angle of 90° exactly or approximately: *The book had rounded, not square, corners.* ◊ *square shoulders* ◊ *He had a firm, square jaw.*
▸ MEASUREMENT | **3** used after a unit of measurement to say that sth measures the same amount on each of four sides: *a carpet four metres square* **4** (*abbr.* **sq**) used after a number to give a measurement of area: *an area of 36 square metres*
▸ BROAD/SOLID | **5** used to describe sth that is broad or that looks solid in shape: *a man/woman of square build*—see also FOUR-SQUARE
▸ LEVEL/PARALLEL | **6** [not before noun] ~ (with sth) level with or parallel to sth: *tables arranged square with the wall*
▸ WITH MONEY | **7** (*informal*) if two people are square, neither of them owes money to the other: *Here's the £10 I owe you—now we're square.*
▸ IN SPORT | **8** ~ (with sb) if two teams are square, they have the same number of points: *The teams were all square at half-time.*
▸ FAIR/HONEST | **9** fair or honest, especially in business matters: *a square deal* ◊ *Are you being square with me?*
▸ IN AGREEMENT | **10** ~ with sth in agreement with sth: *That isn't quite square with what you said yesterday.*
▸ BORING | **11** (*informal, disapproving*) (of a person) considered to be boring, for example, because they are old-fashioned or work too hard at school
[IDM] **a square 'meal** a good, satisfying meal: *He looks as though he hasn't had a square meal for weeks.* **a square 'peg (in a round 'hole)** (*BrE, informal*) a person who does not feel happy or comfortable in a particular situation, or who is not suitable for it
■ *noun*
▸ SHAPE | **1** [C] a shape with four straight sides of equal length and four angles of 90°; a piece of sth that has this shape: *First break the chocolate into squares.* ◊ *The floor was tiled in squares of grey and white marble.*
▸ IN TOWN | **2** [C] an open area in a town, usually with four sides, surrounded by buildings: *The hotel is just off the*

main square. ◊ *the market/town/village square* **3 (Square)** [sing.] (*abbr.* **Sq.**) (used in addresses): *They live at 95 Russell Square.*

MATHEMATICS | **4** [C] the number obtained when you multiply a number by itself: *The square of 7 is 49.*
—see also SET SQUARE, T-SQUARE

BORING PERSON | **5** [C] (*informal, disapproving*) a person who is considered to be boring, for example because they are old-fashioned or because they work too hard at school **IDM** **back to square 'one** a return to the situation you were in at the beginning of a project, task, etc., because you have made no real progress: *If this suggestion isn't accepted, we'll be back to square one.*

■ *verb* [VN]
SHAPE | **1** ~ **sth** (**off**) to make sth have straight edges and corners: *It was like trying to **square a circle**. That is, it was impossible.* ◊ *The boat is rounded at the front but squared off at the back.*

MATHEMATICS | **2** [usually passive] to multiply a number by itself: *Three squared is written 3². ◊ Four squared equals 16.*

SHOULDERS | **3** if you **square** yourself, or **square** your shoulders, you make your back and shoulders straight to show you are ready or determined to do sth: *Bruno squared himself to face the waiting journalists.*

IN SPORT | **4** (*especially BrE*) to make the number of points you have scored in a game or competition equal to those of your opponents: *His goal squared the game 1–1.*

PAY MONEY | **5** (*informal*) to pay money to sb in order to get their help: *They must have squared the mayor before they got their plan underway.*

PHRV **,square sth↔a'way** [usually passive] (*AmE*) to put sth in order; to finish sth completely **,square 'off (against sb)** (*AmE*) to fight or prepare to fight sb **,square up (to sb/sth) 1** to face a difficult situation and deal with it in a determined way **2** to face sb as if you are going to fight them: *Diane squared up to him defiantly.* **,square 'up (with sb)** to pay money that you owe: *Can I leave you to square up with the waiter?* **'square sth with sth | 'square with sth** to make two ideas, facts or situations agree or combine well with each other; to agree or be CONSISTENT with another idea, fact or situation: *The interests of farmers need to be squared with those of consumers.* ◊ *How can you **square this with your conscience?*** ◊ *Your theory does not square with the facts.* **'square sth with sb** to ask permission or check with sb that they approve of what you want to do: *I think I'll be able to come, but I'll square it with my parents first.*

■ *adv.* (only used *after* the verb) directly; not at an angle **SYN** SQUARELY: *I looked her square in the face.* **IDM** see FAIR *adv.*

,square 'bracket (*BrE*) (*AmE* **bracket**) *noun* [usually pl.] either of a pair of marks, [ ], placed at the beginning and end of extra information in a text, especially comments made by an EDITOR ⇨ Appendix 4

squared /skweəd; *AmE* skwerd/ *adj.* marked with squares; divided into squares: *squared paper*

'square dance *noun* **1** a traditional dance from the US in which groups of four couples dance together, starting the dance by facing each other in a square **2** a social event at which people dance square dances

'square knot *noun* (*AmE*) = REEF KNOT

square·ly /'skweəli; *AmE* 'skwerli/ *adv.* (usually used *after* the verb) **1** directly; not at an angle or to one side: *She looked at me squarely in the eye.* ◊ *He stood squarely in front of them, blocking the entrance.* ◊ (*figurative*) *We must meet the challenge squarely* (= not try to avoid it). **2** directly or exactly; without any uncertainty: *The responsibility for the crisis rests squarely on the government.* ◊ *The show is aimed squarely at people under the age of 25.* **IDM** see FAIRLY

,square 'root *noun* (*mathematics*) a number which when multiplied by itself produces a particular number: *The square root of 64 (√ 64) is 8 (8×8=64).*—compare CUBE ROOT

squar·ish /'skweərɪʃ; *AmE* 'skwer-/ *adj.* almost square in shape

squash /skwɒʃ; *AmE* skwɑːʃ; skwɔːʃ/ *verb, noun*

■ *verb* **1** ~ **sth** (**against sth**) to press sth so that it becomes soft, damaged or flat, or changes shape: [VN] *The tomatoes at the bottom of the bag had been squashed.* ◊ *He squashed his nose against the window.* ◊ [VN-ADJ] *Squash your cans flat before recycling.* **2** [+*adv./prep.*] to push sb/sth or yourself into a space that is too small: [V] *We all squashed into the back of the car.* ◊ [VN] *How many people are they going to try and squash into this bus?* ◊ *She was squashed between the door and the table.* **3** [VN] to stop sth from continuing; to destroy sth because it is a problem for you: *to squash a plan/an idea/a revolt* ◊ *If parents don't answer children's questions, their natural curiosity will be squashed.* ◊ *The statement was an attempt to squash the rumours.* **PHRV** **,squash 'up (against sb/sth) | ,squash sb/sth↔'up (against sb/sth)** to move so close to sb/sth else that it is uncomfortable: *We squashed up to make room for Sue.* ◊ *I was squashed up against the wall.*

■ *noun* **1** (also *formal* **'squash rackets**) [U] a game for two players, played in a court enclosed by four walls, using RACKETS and a small rubber ball: *a squash court* ◊ *to play squash* **2** [U, C] (*BrE*) a drink made with fruit juice, sugar and water: *a glass of orange/lemon squash* ◊ *Two orange squashes, please.* **3** [C, U] (*pl.* **squash**, *BrE* also **squashes**) a type of vegetable that grows on the ground. **Winter squash** have hard skin and orange flesh. **Summer squash** have soft yellow or green skin and white flesh.—picture on page A3 **4** [sing.] (*informal*) if sth is a **squash**, there is hardly enough room for everything or everyone to fit into a small space: *It's a real squash with six of us in the car.*

squashy /'skwɒʃi; *AmE* 'skwɑːʃi; 'skwɔːʃi/ *adj.* soft and easy to crush or squeeze

squat /skwɒt; *AmE* skwɑːt/ *verb, noun, adj.*

■ *verb* (-tt-) **1** [V] ~ (**down**) to sit on your heels with your knees bent up close to your body: *Children were squatting on the floor.*—picture at KNEEL **2** to live in a building or on land which is not yours, without the owner's permission: [V] *They ended up squatting in the empty houses on Oxford Road.* [also VN]

■ *noun* **1** a building that people are living in without permission and without paying rent: *to live in a squat* **2** a squatting position of the body

■ *adj.* short and wide or fat, in a way that is not attractive: *a squat tower* ◊ *a squat muscular man with a shaven head*

squat·ter /'skwɒtə(r); *AmE* 'skwɑːt-/ *noun* a person who is living in a building or on land without permission and without paying rent

squaw /skwɔː/ *noun* (*old use*) a word for a Native American woman that is now often considered offensive

squawk /skwɔːk/ *verb* **1** [V] (of birds) to make a loud sharp sound: *The parrot squawked and flew away.* **2** to speak or make a noise in a loud, sharp voice because you are angry, surprised, etc: [V speech] '*You did what?!*' *she squawked.* [also V] ▶ **squawk** *noun*: *The bird gave a startled squawk.* ◊ *a squawk of protest*

squeak /skwiːk/ *verb, noun*

■ *verb* **1** [V] to make a short high sound that is not very loud: *My new shoes squeak.* ◊ *The mouse ran away, squeaking with fear.* ◊ *One wheel makes a horrible squeaking noise.* **2** to speak in a very high voice, especially when you are nervous or excited: [V speech] '*Let go of me!*' *he squeaked nervously.* [also V] **3** [V+*adv./prep.*] to only just manage to win sth, pass a test, etc: *We squeaked into the final with a goal in the last minute.*

■ *noun* a short, high cry or sound, that is not usually very loud: *the squeak of a mouse* ◊ *Shirley gave a little squeak of surprise.*

squeaky /'skwiːki/ *adj.* making a short, high sound; squeaking: *squeaky floorboards* ◊ *a high squeaky voice*

,squeaky 'clean *adj.* (*informal*) **1** completely clean, and therefore attractive: *squeaky clean hair* **2** morally correct in every way; that cannot be criticized: *an all-American boy with a squeaky clean image.*

squeal /skwiːl/ *verb, noun*

■ *verb* **1** [V] to make a long, high sound: *The pigs were squealing.* ◊ *The car squealed to a halt.* ◊ *Children were running around squealing with excitement.* **2** to speak in a

s	t	v	z	ʃ	ʒ	tʃ	dʒ	θ	ð	ŋ
see	tea	van	zoo	shoe	vision	chain	jam	thin	this	sing

S

very high voice, especially when you are excited or nervous: [V**speech**] *'Don't!' she squealed.* [alsoV] **3** [V] **~ (on sb)** (*informal, disapproving*) to give information, especially to the police, about sth illegal that sb has done: *Someone must have squealed on him.*

■ *noun* a long high cry or sound: *a squeal of pain* ◊ *a squeal of delight* ◊ *He stopped with a squeal of brakes.*

squeam·ish /ˈskwiːmɪʃ/ *adj.* **1** easily upset, or made to feel sick by unpleasant sights or situations, especially when the sight of blood is involved **2** not wanting to do sth that might be considered dishonest or immoral **3** (**the squeamish**) *noun* [pl.] people who are squeamish: *This movie is not for the squeamish.*

squee·gee /ˈskwiːdʒiː/ *noun* **1** a tool with a rubber edge and a handle, used for removing water from smooth surfaces such as windows **2** a tool for washing floors, that has a long handle with two thick pieces of soft material at the end, which may be squeezed together using a mechanism attached to the handle

squeeze /skwiːz/ *verb, noun*

■ *verb*

PRESS WITH FINGERS | **1** to press sth firmly, especially with your fingers: [VN] *to squeeze a tube of toothpaste* ◊ *to squeeze the trigger of a gun* (= to fire it) ◊ *He squeezed her hand and smiled at her.* ◊ [V] *Just take hold of the tube and squeeze.*

GET LIQUID OUT | **2 ~ sth (out of/from sth)** | **~ sth (out)** to get liquid out of sth by pressing or twisting it hard: [VN] *to squeeze the juice from a lemon* ◊ *He took off his wet clothes and squeezed the water out.* ◊ *freshly squeezed orange juice* ◊ (*figurative*) *She felt as if every drop of emotion had been squeezed from her.* [alsoVN-ADJ]

INTO/THROUGH SMALL SPACE | **3 ~ (sb/sth) into, through, etc. sth** | **~ through, in, past, etc.** to force sb/sth/yourself into or through a small space: [VN] *We managed to squeeze six people into the car.* ◊ (*figurative*) *We managed to squeeze a lot into a week* (= we did a lot of different things). ◊ [V] *to squeeze into a tight dress / a parking space* ◊ *to squeeze through a gap in the hedge / a crowd* ◊ *If you move forward a little, I can squeeze past.*

THREATEN | **4** [VN] **~ sb (for sth)** (*informal*) to get sth by putting pressure on sb, threatening them, etc: *He's squeezing me for £500.*

LIMIT MONEY | **5** [VN] to strictly limit or reduce the amount of money that sb/sth had or can use: *High interest rates have squeezed the industry hard.* ◊ *The banks have had their profits squeezed this year.*

IDM ˌsqueeze sb ˈdry to get as much money, information, etc. out of sb as you can

PHRV ˌsqueeze sb/sth↔ˈin to give time to sb/sth, although you are very busy: *If you come this afternoon the doctor will try to squeeze you in.* ˌsqueeze sb/sth↔ˈout (of sth) to prevent sb/sth from continuing to do sth or be in business: *Supermarkets are squeezing out small shops.* ˌsqueeze sth ˈout of/ˈfrom sb to get sth by putting pressure on sb, threatening them, etc: *to squeeze a confession from a suspect* ˌsqueeze ˈup (against sb/sth) | ˌsqueeze sb↔ˈup (against sb/sth) to move close to sb/sth so that you are pressed against them/it: *There'll be enough room if we all squeeze up a little.* ◊ *I had to sit squeezed up against the wall.*

■ *noun*

PRESSING WITH FINGERS | **1** [C, usually sing.] an act of pressing sth, usually with your hands: *He gave my hand a little squeeze.* ◊ *Give the tube another squeeze.*

OF LIQUID | **2** [C] a small amount of liquid that is produced by pressing sth: *a squeeze of lemon juice*

IN SMALL SPACE | **3** [sing.] a situation where it is almost impossible for a number of people or things to fit into a small or restricted space: *It was a tight squeeze but we finally got everything into the case.* ◊ *Seven people in the car was a bit of a squeeze.*

REDUCTION IN MONEY | **4** [C, usually sing.] a reduction in the amount of money, jobs, etc. available; a difficult situation caused by this: *a squeeze on jobs / profits / benefits* ◊ *We're really feeling the squeeze since I lost my job.*

BOYFRIEND/GIRLFRIEND | **5** [sing.] (*informal, especially AmE*) a boyfriend or girlfriend: *Who's his main squeeze?*

IDM put the ˈsqueeze on sb (to do sth) (*informal*) to put pressure on sb to act in a particular way; to make a situation difficult for sb

squelch /skweltʃ/ *verb* **1** [V] (*often +adv. / prep.*] to make a wet sucking sound: *The mud squelched as I walked through it.* ◊ *Her wet shoes squelched at every step.* ◊ *We squelched across the muddy field.* **2** [VN] (*AmE*) to stop sth from growing, increasing or developing **SYN** SQUASH: *to squelch a rumour / strike / fire* ▶ **squelch** *noun* [usually sing.]: *He pulled his foot out of the mud with a squelch.* **squelchy** *adj.*: *squelchy ground / tomatoes*

squib /skwɪb/ *noun* a small FIREWORK **IDM** see DAMP *adj.*

squid /skwɪd/ *noun* [C, U] (*pl.* **squid** or **squids**) a sea creature that has a long soft body and ten short arms around its mouth, and that is sometimes used for food

squidgy /ˈskwɪdʒi/ *adj.* (*informal, especially BrE*) soft and wet, and easily SQUASHED

squiffy /ˈskwɪfi/ *adj.* (*BrE, informal*) slightly drunk

squig·gle /ˈskwɪɡl/ *noun* a line, for example in sb's HANDWRITING that is drawn or written in a careless way with twists and curls in it: *Are these dots and squiggles supposed to be your signature?* ▶ **squig·gly** /ˈskwɪɡli/ *adj.*

squint /skwɪnt/ *verb, noun*

■ *verb* **1** to look at sth with your eyes partly shut in order to keep out bright light or to see better: [V] *to squint into / against the sun* ◊ *She was squinting through the keyhole.* ◊ [VN] *When he squinted his eyes, he could just make out a house in the distance.* **2** [V] (*BrE*) (of an eye) to look in a different direction from the other eye: *His left eye squints a little.* **3** [V] to have eyes that look in different directions: *Does she squint?*

■ *noun* **1** [C, usually sing.] a disorder of the eye muscles which causes each eye to look in a different direction: *He was born with a squint.* **2** [sing.] (*BrE, informal*) a short look: *Have a squint at this.*

squire /ˈskwaɪə(r)/ *noun* **1** (also **Squire**) (in the past in England) a man of high social status who owned most of the land in a particular country area **2** (**Squire**) (*BrE, informal or humorous*) used by a man as a friendly way of addressing another man: *What can I get you, Squire?* **3** (in the past) a young man who was an assistant to a KNIGHT before becoming a KNIGHT himself

squirm /skwɜːm; *AmE* skwɜːrm/ *verb* **1** to move around a lot making small twisting movements, because you are nervous, uncomfortable, etc: [V, usually +adv. / prep.] *The children were squirming restlessly in their seats.* ◊ [V-ADJ] *Someone grabbed him but he managed to squirm free.* **2** [V] to feel great embarrassment or shame: *It made him squirm to think how badly he'd messed up the interview.*

squir·rel /ˈskwɪrəl; *AmE* ˈskwɜːrəl/ *noun, verb*

■ *noun* a small animal with a long thick tail and red, grey or black fur. Squirrels eat nuts and live in trees.—picture on page A6—see also GROUND SQUIRREL

■ *verb* (-ll-, *AmE* -l-) **PHRV** ˌsquirrel sth↔aˈway to hide or store sth so that it can be used later: *She had money squirrelled away in various bank accounts.*

squirt /skwɜːt; *AmE* skwɜːrt/ *verb, noun*

■ *verb* **1** [usually +adv. / prep.] to force liquid, gas, etc. in a thin fast stream through a narrow opening; to be forced out of a narrow opening in this way: [VN] *The snake can squirt poison from a distance of a metre.* ◊ *I desperately squirted water on the flames.* ◊ [V] *When I cut the lemon, juice squirted in my eye.* **2** [VN] **~ sb/sth (with sth)** to hit sb/sth with a stream of water, gas, etc: *The children were squirting each other with water from the hose.* ◊ *He squirted a water pistol at me* (= made the water come out of it).

■ *noun* **1** a thin, fast stream of a liquid that comes out of a small opening: *a squirt of perfume* **2** (*informal, disapproving*) a word used to refer to a short, young or unimportant person that you do not like or that you find annoying

squish /skwɪʃ/ *verb* (*informal*) **1** [V, VN] if sth soft **squishes** or **is squished**, it is crushed out of shape when it is pressed **2** [V] to make a soft wet sucking sound

æ	ɑː	e	ɜː	ə	ɪ	iː	i	ɒ	ɔː	ʌ	ʊ	u	uː
cat	father	ten	bird	about	sit	see	many	got	saw	cup	put	actual	too
								(BrE)					

squishy /ˈskwɪʃi/ *adj.* (*informal*) soft and wet

Sr (also **Sr.** especially in *AmE*) *abbr.* SENIOR—compare JR

SS *abbr.* **1** Saints: *SS Philip and James* **2** /ˌes ˈes/ STEAM-SHIP: *the SS Titanic*

St *abbr.* **1** (also **st**) (both *BrE*) (also **St.**, **st.** *AmE*, *BrE*) (used in written addresses) Street: *Fleet St* **2** (St.) (*AmE*) State **3** (also **St.** especially in *AmE*) Saint

st (*BrE*) (also **st.** *AmE*, *BrE*) *abbr.* STONE (a British measurement of weight): *9st 2lb*

stab /stæb/ *verb, noun*

■ *verb* (**-bb-**) **1** [VN] to push a sharp, pointed object, especially a knife, into sb, killing or injuring them: *He was stabbed to death in a racist attack.* ◇ *She stabbed him in the arm with a screwdriver.* **2** ~ (**sth**) (**at sb**) | ~ **sb/sth** (**with sth**) | ~ (**sth**) (**at/into/through sth**) to make a short, forceful movement with a finger or pointed object: [VN] *He stabbed his finger angrily at my chest.* ◇ *She stabbed the air with her fork.* ◇ [V] (*figurative*) *The pain stabbed at his chest.* **IDM** **stab sb in the ˈback** to do or say sth that harms sb who trusts you **SYN** BETRAY

■ *noun* **1** an act of stabbing or trying to stab sb/sth; a wound caused by stabbing: *He received several stabs in the chest.* ◇ *She died of a single stab wound to the heart.* **2** a sudden sharp pain or unpleasant feeling: *She felt a sudden stab of pain in the chest.* ◇ *a stab of guilt/fear/pity/jealousy* **3** [usually sing.] ~ (**at sth/at doing sth**) (*informal*) an attempt to do sth: *He found the test difficult but nevertheless made a good stab at it.* ◇ *Countless people have had a stab at solving the riddle.* **IDM** **a ˌstab in the ˈback** (*informal*) an act that harms sb, done by a person they thought was a friend—more at DARK *n.*

stab·bing /ˈstæbɪŋ/ *noun, adj.*
■ *noun* an occasion when a person is stabbed with a knife or other pointed object: *a fatal stabbing*
■ *adj.* [usually before noun] (of pain) very sharp, sudden and strong

sta·bil·ity /stəˈbɪləti/ *noun* [U] the quality or state of being steady and not changing or being disturbed in any way (= the quality of being STABLE): *political/economic/ social stability* ◇ *the stability of the dollar on the world's money markets* **OPP** INSTABILITY

sta·bil·ize (*BrE* also **-ise**) /ˈsteɪbəlaɪz/ *verb* to become or to make sth become firm, steady and unlikely to change; to make sth STABLE: [V] *The patient's condition stabilized.* ◇ [VN] *government measures to stabilize prices* ◇ *Doctors stabilized the patient's condition.*—compare DESTABILIZE ▶ **sta·bil·iza·tion, -isa·tion** /ˌsteɪbəlaɪˈzeɪʃn; *AmE* -ləˈz-/ [U]: *economic stabilization*

sta·bil·izer (*BrE* also **-iser**) /ˈsteɪbəlaɪzə(r)/ *noun* **1** a device that keeps sth steady, especially one that stops an aircraft or a ship from rolling to one side **2** (**stabilizers**) [pl.] (*BrE*) (*AmE* **ˈtraining wheels**) small wheels that are fitted at each side of the back wheel on a child's bicycle to keep it upright

stable /ˈsteɪbl/ *adj., noun, verb*
■ *adj.* **1** firmly fixed; not likely to move, change or fail **SYN** STEADY: *stable prices/employment* ◇ *a stable relationship* ◇ *This ladder doesn't seem very stable.* ◇ *The patient's condition is stable* (= it is not getting worse). **2** (of a person) calm and reasonable; not easily upset **SYN** BALANCED: *Mentally, she is not very stable.* **3** (*technical*) (of a substance) staying in the same chemical or ATOMIC state: *chemically stable* **OPP** UNSTABLE ▶ **sta·bly** /ˈsteɪbli/ *adv.*
■ *noun* **1** [C] a building in which horses are kept: *The horse was led back to its stable.* **2** (*BrE* also **stables**) [C+sing./ pl. *v.*] an organization that keeps horses for a particular purpose: (*BrE*) *a riding/racing stables* ◇ *His stables are near Oxford.* **3** [C] a group of RACEHORSES owned or trained by the same person: *There have been just three winners from his stable this season.* **4** [sing.] a group of people who work or trained in the same place; a group of products made by the same company: *actors from the*

WORD FAMILY
stable *adj.* (≠ unstable)
stability *n.* (≠ instability)
stabilize *v.*

same stable ◇ *the latest printer from the Epson stable* **IDM** **close, lock, etc. the stable door after the horse has ˈbolted** (*BrE*) (*AmE* **close, etc. the barn door after the horse has eˈscaped**) to try to prevent or avoid loss or damage when it is already too late to do so
■ *verb* [VN] to put or keep a horse in a stable: *Where do you stable your pony?*

ˈstable boy, **ˈstable girl** (*BrE* also **ˈstable lad**) *noun* a person who works in a stable

stable·man /ˈsteɪblmən/ *noun* (**-men** /-mən/) a person who works in a stable

stab·ling /ˈsteɪblɪŋ/ *noun* [U] buildings or space where horses can be kept

stac·cato /stəˈkɑːtəʊ; *AmE* -toʊ/ *adj.* **1** (*music*) with each note played separately in order to produce short, sharp sounds: *staccato sounds* **OPP** LEGATO **2** with short, sharp sounds: *a peculiar staccato voice* ◇ *staccato bursts of gun-fire* ▶ **stac·cato** *adv.*

stack /stæk/ *noun, verb*
■ *noun* **1** [C] a pile of sth, usually neatly arranged: *a stack of plates/books* ◇ *a stack hi-fi system* (= where radio, CD player, etc. are arranged on top of each other)—see also HAYSTACK **2** [C] ~ (**of sth**) (*informal, especially BrE*) a large number or amount of sth; a lot of sth: *stacks of money* ◇ *There's a stack of unopened mail waiting for you at the house.* ◇ *I've got stacks of work to do.* **3** [C] a tall chimney, especially on a factory—see also CHIMNEY STACK, SMOKESTACK **4** (**the stacks**) [pl.] the part of a library, sometimes not open to the public, where books that are not often needed are stored: *The books you need will have to be brought up from the stacks.* **5** [C] (*computing*) a way of storing information in a computer in which the most recently stored item is the first to be RETRIEVED (= found or got back) **IDM** see BLOW *v.*
■ *verb* **1** ~ (**sth**) (**up**) to arrange objects neatly in a pile; to be arranged in this way: [VN] *to stack plates/boxes* ◇ *Logs stacked up against a wall.* ◇ [V] *Do these chairs stack?* ◇ *stacking chairs* **2** [VN] ~ **sth** (**with sth**) to fill sth with piles of things: *They were busy stacking the shelves with goods.* **3** [V, VN] ~ (**sth**) (**up**) if aircraft **stack** (**up**) or **are stacked** (**up**) over an airport, there are several flying around waiting for their turn to land **PHR V** **ˌstack ˈup 1** to keep increasing in quantity until there is a large pile, a long line, etc: *Cars quickly stacked up behind the bus.* ◇ *During the strike, refuse has been stacking up in the streets.* **2** ~ (**against sb/sth**) (*informal*) to compare to sb/sth else: *Let's try him in the team and see how he stacks up.* ◇ *This year's figures didn't stack up to those of 1999* (= they were not as good).

stacked /stækt/ *adj.* [not usually before noun] if a surface is **stacked with** objects, there are large numbers or piles of them on it: *a table stacked with glasses* ◇ *shelves stacked with files* **IDM** **the cards/odds are stacked aˈgainst you** you are unlikely to succeed because the conditions are not good for you **the cards/odds are stacked in your ˈfavour** you are likely to succeed because the conditions are good and you have an advantage

sta·dium /ˈsteɪdiəm/ *noun* (*pl.* **sta·diums** or **-dia** /-diə/) a large sports ground surrounded by rows of seats and usually other buildings: *a football/sports stadium*

staff /stɑːf; *AmE* stæf/ *noun, verb*
■ *noun* **1** [C, usually sing.] all the workers employed in an organization considered as a group: *medical/library staff* ◇ (*BrE*) *teaching staff* ◇ (*BrE*) *We have 20 part-time members of staff.* ◇ (*AmE*) *staff members* ◇ *staff development/ training* ◇ *a staff restaurant/meeting* ◇ (*especially BrE*) *a lawyer on the staff of the Worldwide Fund for Nature*—see also GROUND STAFF **2** [sing.] (*AmE*) the people who work at a school, college or university, but who do not teach students: *students, faculty and staff* **3** [C+sing./pl. *v.*] a group of senior army officers who help a commanding officer: *a staff officer*—see also CHIEF OF STAFF, GENERAL STAFF **4** (*old-fashioned* or *formal*) a long stick used as a support when walking or climbing, as a weapon, or as a symbol of authority **5** [C] (*music,*

especially AmE = STAVE **IDM** the ˌstaff of ˈlife (*literary*) a basic food, especially bread

▪ *verb* [VN] [usually passive] to work in an institution, a company, etc.; to provide people to work there: *The advice centre is staffed entirely by volunteers.* ◇ *The charity provided money to staff and equip two hospitals.* ◇ *a fully staffed department*—see also OVERSTAFFED, SHORT-STAFFED, UNDERSTAFFED ▶ **staf·fing** *noun* [U]: *staffing levels*

> **GRAMMAR POINT**
> **staff**
>
>
>
> In *BrE* **staff** (sense 1) can be singular: *a staff of ten* (= a group of ten people) or plural: *I have ten staff working for me.* If it is the subject of a verb this verb is plural: *The staff in this shop are very helpful.*
> In *AmE* **staff** (senses 1 and 2) can only be singular: *a staff of ten* (but not *ten staff.*) ◇ *The staff in this store is very helpful.*
> The plural form **staffs** is less frequent but is used in both *BrE* and *AmE* to refer to more than one group of people: *the senator and his staff* (singular) ◇ *senators and their staffs* (plural).

ˈstaff nurse *noun* (in Britain) a qualified hospital nurse

ˈstaff officer *noun* a military officer who helps an officer of very high rank or who works at a military HEADQUARTERS or a government department

ˈstaff sergeant *noun* a member of the army or the US air force just above the rank of a SERGEANT: *Staff Sergeant Bob Woods*

stag /stæg/ *noun* a male deer—compare BUCK, DOE, HART

stage /steɪdʒ/ *noun, verb*

▪ *noun*

PERIOD/STATE | **1** [C] a period or state that sth/sb passes through while developing or making progress: *This technology is still in its early stages.* ◇ *The children are at different stages of development.* ◇ *The product is at the design stage.* ◇ *People tend to work hard at this stage of life.* ◇ *At one stage it looked as though they would win.*

PART OF PROCESS | **2** [C] a separate part that a process, etc. is divided into: *We did the first stage of the trip by train.* ◇ *The police are building up a picture of the incident stage by stage.* ◇ *The pay increase will be introduced in stages* (= not all at once). ◇ *We can take the argument one stage further.*

THEATRE | **3** [C] a raised area, usually in a theatre, etc. where actors, dancers, etc. perform: *The audience threw flowers onto the stage.* ◇ *There were more than 50 people on stage in one scene.* ◇ *They marched off stage to the sound of trumpets.*—see also BACKSTAGE, OFFSTAGE, ONSTAGE **4** (often **the stage**) [sing.] the theatre and the world of acting as a form of entertainment: *His parents didn't want him to go on the stage* (= to be an actor). ◇ *She was a popular star of stage and screen* (= theatre and cinema / movies).

IN POLITICS | **5** [sing.] an area of activity where important things happen, especially in politics: *She was forced to the centre of the political stage.* ◇ *Germany is playing a leading role on the international stage.*—see also CENTRE STAGE

CARRIAGE | **6** [C] (*old-fashioned, informal*) = STAGECOACH

—see also LANDING STAGE

IDM set the ˈstage for sth to make it possible for sth to happen; to make sth likely to happen

▪ *verb* [VN] **1** to organize and present a play or an event for people to see: *to stage a ceremony / an event / an exhibition* ◇ *The local theatre group is staging a production of 'Hamlet'.* ◇ *Birmingham has bid to stage the next national athletics championships.* **2** to organize and take part in action that needs careful planning, especially as a public protest: *to stage a strike / demonstration / march / protest* **3** to make sth happen: *The dollar staged a recovery earlier today.* ◇ *After five years in retirement, he staged a comeback to international tennis.*

stage·coach /ˈsteɪdʒkəʊtʃ; *AmE* -koʊtʃ/ *noun* a large carriage pulled by horses, that was used in the past to carry passengers, and often mail, along a regular route

ˈstage direction *noun* a note in the text of a play telling actors when to come on to or leave the stage, what actions to perform, etc.

ˌstage ˈdoor *noun* the entrance at the back of a theatre used by actors, staff, etc.

ˈstage fright *noun* [U] nervous feelings felt by performers before they appear in front of an audience

stage·hand /ˈsteɪdʒhænd/ *noun* a person whose job is to help move scenery, etc. in a theatre, to prepare the stage for the next play or the next part of a play

ˌstage ˈleft *adv.* on the left side of a stage in a theatre, as seen by an actor facing the audience

ˌstage-ˈmanage *verb* [VN] **1** to act as stage manager for a performance in a theatre **2** to arrange and carefully plan an event that the public will see, especially in order to give a particular impression

ˌstage ˈmanager *noun* the person who is responsible for the stage, lights, scenery, etc. during the performance of a play in a theatre

ˈstage name *noun* a name that an actor uses instead of his or her real name

ˌstage ˈright *adv.* on the right side of a stage in a theatre, as seen by an actor facing the audience

ˈstage-struck *adj.* enjoying the theatre a lot and wishing very much to become an actor

ˌstage ˈwhisper *noun* **1** words that are spoken quietly by an actor to the audience and that the other people on stage are not supposed to hear **2** words that are spoken quietly by sb but that they in fact want everyone to hear: *'I knew this would happen,' she said in a stage whisper.*

stagey = STAGY

stag·fla·tion /stæɡˈfleɪʃn/ *noun* [U] an economic situation where there is such high INFLATION (= prices rising continuously) but no increase in employment and business activity

stag·ger /ˈstæɡə(r)/ *verb* **1** to walk with weak unsteady steps, as if you are about to fall: [V, usually +*adv. / prep.*] *The injured woman staggered to her feet.* ◇ *He staggered home, drunk.* ◇ *We seem to stagger from one crisis to the next.* ◇ (*figurative*) *The company is staggering under the weight of a £10m debt* ◇ [VN] *I managed to stagger the last few steps.* **2** to shock or surprise sb very much: [VN] *Her remarks staggered me.* ◇ [Vthat] *It staggers me that the government is doing nothing about it.* **3** [VN] to arrange for events that would normally happen at the same time to start or happen at different times: *There were so many runners, that they had to stagger the start.* ▶ **stag·ger** *noun*: *to walk with a stagger*

stag·gered /ˈstæɡəd; *AmE* -ɡərd/ *adj.* **1** [not before noun] ~ (at/by sth) | ~ (to hear, learn, see, etc.) very surprised and shocked at sth you are told or at sth that happens: *I was staggered at the amount of money the ring cost.* **2** arranged in such a way that not everything happens at the same time: *staggered working hours* (= people start and finish at different times)

stag·ger·ing /ˈstæɡərɪŋ/ *adj.* so large, shocking or surprising that it is difficult to believe **SYN** ASTOUNDING: *They paid a staggering £1 million for the house.* ▶ **stag·ger·ing·ly** *adv.*: *staggeringly beautiful / expensive*

sta·ging /ˈsteɪdʒɪŋ/ *noun* **1** [C, U] the way in which a play is produced and presented on stage: *a modern staging of 'King Lear'* **2** [U] a temporary platform used for standing or working on

ˈstaging post *noun* a place where people, planes, ships, etc. regularly stop during a long journey

stag·nant /ˈstæɡnənt/ *adj.* **1** stagnant water or air is not moving and therefore smells unpleasant: *a stagnant pond / pool* **2** not developing, growing or changing: *Major new investments are aimed at reviving the stagnant economy.*

stag·nate /stæɡˈneɪt; *AmE* ˈstæɡneɪt/ *verb* [V] **1** to stop developing or making progress: *Profits have stagnated.* ◇ *I feel I'm stagnating in this job.* **2** to be or become stagnant: *The water in the pond was stagnating.* ▶ **stag·na·tion** /stæɡˈneɪʃn/ *noun* [U]: *a period of economic stagnation*

ˈstag night *noun* [usually sing.] **1** (*BrE*) the night before a man's wedding, often spent with his male friends

S

2 (also **'stag party**) (both *BrE*) (*AmE* **'bachelor party**) a party that a man has with his male friends just before he gets married, often the night before—compare HEN PARTY

stagy (also **stagey**) /'steɪdʒi/ *adj.* not natural, as if it is being acted by sb in a play: *He fell to the ground writhing in stagy agony.*

staid /steɪd/ *adj.* (**staid·er, staid·est**) not amusing or interesting; boring and old-fashioned: *The museum is trying to get rid of its staid image.*

stain /steɪn/ *verb, noun*
■ *verb* **1 ~ (sth) (with sth)** to leave marks that are difficult to remove on sth; to be marked in this way: [VN] *I hope it doesn't stain the carpet.* ◊ [V] *This carpet stains easily.* ◊ [VN-ADJ] *The juice from the berries stained their fingers red.* **2** to change the colour of sth using a coloured liquid: [VN] *to stain wood* ◊ *Stain the specimen before looking at it under the microscope.* ◊ [VN-ADJ] *They stained the floors dark brown.* **3** [VN] (*written*) to damage the opinion that people have of sth: *The events had stained the city's reputation unfairly.*
■ *noun* **1** [C] a dirty mark on sth, that is difficult to remove: *a blood/a coffee/an ink stain* ◊ **stubborn stains** (= that are very difficult to remove) ◊ *How can I get this stain out?* **2** [U, C] a liquid used for changing the colour of wood or fabric **3** [sing.] **a ~ on sth** (*written*) something that damages a person's reputation, so that people think badly of them: *He left the court without a stain on his character.*

stained /steɪnd/ *adj.* (often in compounds) covered with stains or marked with a stain: *My dress was stained.* ◊ *paint-stained jeans*

stained 'glass *noun* [U] pieces of coloured glass that are put together to make windows, especially in churches

stain·less steel /ˌsteɪnləs 'stiːl/ *noun* [U] a type of steel that does not RUST (= change colour)

stair /steə(r); *AmE* ster/ *noun* **1** (**stairs**) [pl.] a set of steps built between two floors inside a building: *We had to carry the piano up three flights of stairs.* ◊ *The children ran up/down the stairs.* ◊ *at the bottom/top of the stairs* ◊ *He remembered passing her on the stairs.*—see also DOWNSTAIRS, UPSTAIRS **2** [C] one of the steps in a set of stairs: *How many stairs are there up to the second floor?* **3** [sing.] (*literary*) = STAIRCASE: *The house had a panelled hall and a fine oak stair.* ▶ **stair** *adj.* [only before noun]: *the stair carpet* IDM **below 'stairs** (*old-fashioned, BrE*) in the part of a house where the servants lived in the past

stair·case /'steəkeɪs; *AmE* 'sterk-/ *noun* a set of stairs inside a building including the posts and rails (= BANISTERS) that are fixed at the side: *a marble/stone/wooden staircase* ◊ *a spiral staircase* (= a set of stairs that curve upwards around a central post)

stair·way /'steəweɪ; *AmE* 'sterweɪ/ *noun* a staircase or set of stairs, inside or outside a building

stair·well /'steəwel; *AmE* 'sterwel/ *noun* [usually sing.] the space in a building in which the stairs are built

stake /steɪk/ *noun, verb*
■ *noun* **1** [C] a wooden or metal post that is pointed at one end and pushed into the ground in order to support sth, mark a particular place, etc. **2** (**the stake**) [sing.] a wooden post that sb could be tied to in former times before being burnt to death (= killed by fire) as a punishment: *Joan of Arc was burnt at the stake.* **3** [C] money that sb invests in a company: *a 20% stake in the business* **4** [sing.] **~ in sth** an important part or share in a business, plan, etc. that is important to you and that you want to be successful: *She has a personal stake in the success of the play.* ◊ *Many young people no longer feel they have a stake in society.* **5** [C, usually pl.] something that you risk losing, especially money, when you try to predict the result of a race, game, etc., or when you are involved in an activity that can succeed or fail: *They were playing cards for high stakes* (= a lot of money). **6** (**stakes**) [pl.] the money that is paid to the winners in horse racing IDM **at 'stake** that can be won or lost, depending on the success of a particular action: *We cannot afford to take risks when peoples' lives are at stake.* ◊ *The prize at stake*

is a place in the final. **go to the 'stake over/for sth** to be prepared to do anything in order to defend your opinions or beliefs **in the ... stakes** used to say how much of a particular quality a person has, as if they were in a competition in which some people are more successful than others: *John doesn't do too well in the personality stakes.*
■ *verb* [VN] **1 ~ sth (on sth)** to risk money or sth important on the result of sth: *He staked £25 on the favourite* (= for example, in horse racing). ◊ *She staked her political career on tax reform, and lost.* ◊ *That's him over there—I'd stake my life on it* (= I am completely confident). **2 ~ sth (up)** to support sth with a stake: *to stake newly planted trees* IDM **stake (out) a/your 'claim (to/for/on sth)** to say or show publicly that you think sth should be yours: *Adams staked his claim for a place in the Olympic team with his easy win yesterday.* PHRV **stake sth↔'out 1** to clearly mark the limits of sth that you claim is yours **2** to state your opinion, position, etc. on sth very clearly: *The President staked out his position on the issue.* **3** to watch a place secretly, especially for signs of illegal activity: *Detectives had been staking out the house for several weeks.*—related noun STAKE-OUT

stake·hold·er /'steɪkhəʊldə(r); *AmE* -hoʊ-/ *noun* **1** a person or company that is involved in a particular organization, project, system, etc., especially because they have invested money in it: *The government has said it wants to create a **stakeholder economy** in which all members of society feel that they have an interest in its success.* **2** a person who holds all the bets placed on a game or race and who pays the money to the winner

'stake-out *noun* a situation in which police watch a building secretly to find evidence of illegal activities

stal·ac·tite /'stæləktaɪt; *AmE* stə'læktaɪt/ *noun* a long pointed piece of rock hanging down from the roof of a CAVE (= a hollow place underground), formed over a long period of time as water containing LIME runs off the roof

stal·ag·mite /'stæləgmaɪt; *AmE* stə'læg-/ *noun* a piece of rock pointing upwards from the floor of a CAVE (= a hollow place underground), that is formed over a long period of time from drops of water containing LIME that fall from the roof

stale /steɪl/ *adj.* **1** (of food, especially bread and cake) no longer fresh and therefore unpleasant to eat **2** (of air, smoke, etc.) no longer fresh; smelling unpleasant: *stale cigarette smoke* ◊ *stale sweat* **3** something that is stale has been said or done too many times before and is no longer interesting or exciting: *stale jokes/news* ◊ *Their marriage had gone stale.* **4** a person who is stale has done the same thing for too long and so is unable to do it well, feel enthusiastic about it or produce any new ideas: *After ten years in the job, she felt stale and needed a change.* ◊ *The cast is changed regularly to stop the actors from getting stale.* ▶ **stale·ness** *noun* [U]

stale·mate /'steɪlmeɪt/ *noun* **1** [U, C, usually sing.] a situation in a dispute or competition in which neither side is able to win or make any progress: *The talks ended in (a) stalemate.* **2** [U, sing.] (in CHESS) a situation in which a player cannot successfully move any of their pieces and the game ends without a winner—compare CHECKMATE

stalk /stɔːk/ *noun, verb*
■ *noun* **1** a thin stem that supports a leaf, flower or fruit and joins it to another part of the plant or tree; the main stem of a plant: *flowers on long stalks* ◊ *celery stalks* ◊ *He ate the apple, stalk and all.*—picture at PLANT **2** a long thin structure that supports sth, especially an organ in some animals, and joins it on to another part: *Crabs and lobsters have eyes on stalks.*
■ *verb* **1** to move slowly and quietly towards an animal or a person, in order to kill, catch or harm it or them: [VN] *The lion was stalking a zebra.* ◊ *He stalked his victim as she walked home, before attacking and robbing her.* [also V] **2** [VN] to illegally follow and watch sb over a long period of time, in a way that is annoying or frightening: *She claimed that he had been stalking her over a period of*

three years. **3** [V+adv./prep.] to walk in an angry or proud way: *He stalked off without a word.* **4** (*written*) to move through a place in an unpleasant or threatening way: [VN] *The gunmen stalked the building, looking for victims.* ◊ (*figurative*) *Fear stalks the streets of the city at night.* [also V]

stalk·er /ˈstɔːkə(r)/ *noun* **1** a person who follows and watches another person over a long period of time in a way that is annoying or frightening **2** a person who follows an animal quietly and slowly, especially in order to kill or capture it

stalk·ing /ˈstɔːkɪŋ/ *noun* [U] the crime of following and watching sb over a long period of time in a way that is annoying or frightening

ˈstalking horse *noun* [sing.] **1** a person or thing that is used to hide the real purpose of a particular course of action **2** a politician who competes against the leader of their party in order to see how much support the leader has; a stronger candidate can then compete against the leader more seriously

stall /stɔːl/ *noun, verb*
■ *noun* **1** [C] a table or small shop with an open front that people sell things from, especially at a market [SYN] STAND: *a market stall*—see also BOOKSTALL **2** [C] a section inside a farm building that is large enough for one animal to be kept in **3** [C] (*especially AmE*) a small enclosed area of a room that contains a shower or toilet **4** (**the stalls**) [pl.] (*BrE*) (*AmE* **the orchestra** [sing.]) the seats that are nearest to the stage in a theatre: *the front row of the stalls* **5** [C, usually pl.] the seats at the front of a church where the CHOIR (= singers) and priests sit **6** [C, usually sing.] a situation in which a vehicle's engine suddenly stops because it is not getting enough power **7** [C, usually sing.] a situation in which an aircraft loses speed and goes steeply downwards
■ *verb* **1** (of a vehicle or an engine) to stop suddenly because of a lack of power or speed; to make a vehicle or engine do this: [V] *The car stalled and refused to start again.* ◊ [VN] *I stalled the car three times during my driving test.* **2** [V] ~ (**on/over sth**) to try to avoid doing sth or answering a question so that you have more time: *They are still stalling on the deal.* ◊ *'What do you mean?' she asked, stalling for time.* **3** [VN] to make sb wait so that you have more time to do sth: *See if you can stall her while I finish searching her office.* **4** to stop sth from happening until a later date; to stop making progress: [VN] *attempts to revive the stalled peace plan* ◊ [V] *Discussions have once again stalled.*

stall·hold·er /ˈstɔːlhəʊldə(r); *AmE* -hoʊ-/ *noun* (*BrE*) a person who sells things from a stall in a market, etc.

stal·lion /ˈstæliən/ *noun* a fully grown male horse, especially one that is used for breeding—compare COLT, GELDING, MARE

stal·wart /ˈstɔːlwət; *AmE* -wərt/ *noun, adj.*
■ *noun* ~ (**of sth**) a loyal supporter who does a lot of work for an organization, especially a political party
■ *adj.* [usually before noun] **1** that is loyal and you can rely on, even in a difficult situation: *stalwart supporters* **2** (*formal*) physically strong

sta·men /ˈsteɪmən/ *noun* (*technical*) a small thin male part in the middle of a flower that produces POLLEN and is made up of a STALK supporting an ANTHER. The centre of each flower usually has several stamens.

stam·ina /ˈstæmɪnə/ *noun* [U] the physical or mental strength that enables you to do sth difficult for long periods of time: *It takes a lot of stamina to run a marathon.*

stam·mer /ˈstæmə(r)/ *verb, noun*
■ *verb* to speak with difficulty, repeating sounds or words and often stopping, before saying things correctly [SYN] STUTTER: [V] *Many children stammer but grow out of it.* ◊ [V speech] *'W-w-what?' he stammered.* ◊ [VN] *She was barely able to stammer out a description of her attacker.* ▶ **stam·mer·er** *noun*
■ *noun* [sing.] a problem that sb has in speaking in which they repeat sounds or words or often pause before saying things correctly

stamp /stæmp/ *noun, verb*
■ *noun*
ON LETTER/PACKAGE | **1** (also *formal* **ˈpostage stamp**) [C] a small piece of paper with a design on it that you buy and stick on an envelope or a parcel/package before you post it: *a 28p stamp* ◊ *Could I have three first-class stamps, please?* ◊ *He has been collecting stamps since he was eight.* ◊ *a stamp album*

She stamped her foot.

PRINTING TOOL | **2** [C] a tool for printing the date or a design or mark onto a surface: *a date stamp*—see also RUBBER STAMP
PRINTED DESIGN/WORDS | **3** [C] a design or words made by stamping sth onto a surface: *The passports, with the visa stamps, were waiting at the embassy.* ◊ (*figurative*) *The project has the government's stamp of approval.*
PROOF OF PAYMENT | **4** [C] a small piece of paper with a design on it, stuck on a document to show that a particular amount of money has been paid: *a TV licence stamp*
CHARACTER/QUALITY | **5** ~ (**of sth**) (*formal*) the mark or sign of a particular quality or person: *All his work bears the stamp of authority.* **6** [sing.] (*formal*) a kind or class, especially of people: *men of a different stamp*
OF FOOT | **7** an act or sound of stamping the foot: *The stamp of hoofs alerted Isabel.*
■ *verb*
FOOT | **1** to put your foot down heavily and noisily on the ground: [VN] *I tried stamping my feet to keep warm.* ◊ *Sam stamped his foot in anger.* ◊ [V] *The audience were stamping and cheering.*
WALK | **2** [V+adv./prep.] to walk with loud heavy steps [SYN] STAMP: *She turned and stamped out of the room.*
PRINT DESIGN/WORDS | **3** [VN] [often passive] ~ **A on B** | ~ **B** (**with A**) to print letters, words, a design, etc. onto sth using a special tool: *I'll stamp the company name on your cheque.* ◊ *Wait here to have your passport stamped.* ◊ *The maker's name was stamped in gold on the box.* ◊ *The box was stamped with the maker's name.*—see also RUBBER-STAMP, STAMP STH ON STH
SHOW FEELING/QUALITY | **4** [VN] [usually passive] to make a feeling show clearly on sb's face, in their actions, etc: *Their faces were stamped with hostility.* ◊ *The crime had revenge stamped all over it.* **5** [VN] ~ **sb as sth** to show that sb has a particular quality: *Her success has stamped her as one of the country's top riders.*
ON LETTER/PACKAGE | **6** [VN] [usually passive] to stick a stamp on a letter or parcel/package
CUT OUT OBJECT | **7** [VN] ~ **sth** (**out**) (**of/from sth**) to cut and shape an object from a piece of metal or plastic using a special machine or tool—see also STAMP STH OUT
[PHRV] **ˈstamp on sth 1** to put your foot down with force on sth: *The child stamped on the spider.* **2** to stop sth from happening or stop sb from doing sth, especially by using force or authority: *All attempts at modernization were stamped on by senior officials.* **ˈstamp sth on sth** to make sth have an important effect or influence on sth: *She stamped her own interpretation on the role.* ◊ *The date is forever stamped on her memory.* ˌ**stamp sth**⟷**ˈout 1** to get rid of sth that is bad, unpleasant or dangerous, especially by using force or a lot of effort: *to stamp out racism/drug abuse/rebellion* **2** to put out a fire by bringing your foot down heavily on it

ˈstamp collecting *noun* [U] the hobby of collecting stamps ▶ **ˈstamp collector** *noun*

ˈstamp duty *noun* [U] a tax in Britain on some legal documents

ˌ**stamped addressed ˈenvelope** *noun* (*abbr.* SAE) (*BrE*) an envelope in which you have written your name and address and put a stamp so that sb else can use it to send sth to you: *Please enclose a stamped addressed envelope to get your test results.*

stam·pede /stæmˈpiːd/ *noun, verb*

æ	ɑː	e	ɜː	ə	ɪ	iː	i	ɒ	ɔː	ʌ	ʊ	u	uː
cat	father	ten	bird	about	sit	see	many	got	saw	cup	put	actual	too

(BrE)

■ *noun* [C, usually sing.] **1** a situation in which a group of people or large animals such as horses suddenly start running in the same direction, especially because they are frightened or excited: *A stampede broke out when the doors opened.* **2** a situation in which a lot of people are trying to do or achieve the same thing at the same time: *Falling interest rates has led to a stampede to buy property.*

■ *verb* **1** (of large animals or people) to run in a stampede; to make animals do this: [V] *a herd of stampeding elephants* ◊ *A huge bunch of kids came stampeding down the corridor.* [also VN] **2** [VN] [usually passive] ~ **sb (into sth/ into doing sth)** to make sb rush into doing sth without giving them time to think about it: *I refuse to be stampeded into making any hasty decisions.*

'stamping ground (*AmE* also **'stomping ground**) *noun* (*informal*) a place that sb likes and where they often go [SYN] HAUNT

stance /stɑːns; *BrE* also stɑːns/ *noun* **1** ~ **(on sth)** the opinions that sb has about sth and expresses publicly [SYN] POSITION: *What is the newspaper's stance on the war?* ◊ *He is known for his anti-abortion stance.* **2** the way in which sb stands, especially when playing a sport

stanch /stɔːntʃ; stæntʃ/ *verb* [VN] (*especially AmE*) = STAUNCH

stan·chion /'stæntʃən; 'stɑːn-/ *noun* (*formal*) a vertical pole used to support sth

stand /stænd/ *verb, noun*

■ *verb* (**stood, stood** /stʊd/)

ON FEET/BE UPRIGHT | **1** [V] to be on your feet; to be upright: *She was too weak to stand.* ◊ *a bird standing on one leg* ◊ *Don't just stand there—do something!* ◊ *I was standing only a few feet away.* ◊ **Stand still** while I take your photo. ◊ *We all stood around in the corridor waiting.* ◊ *to stand on your head / hands* (= to be upside down, balancing on your head / hands). ◊ *After the earthquake, only a few houses were left standing.* **2** [V] ~ **(up)** to get up onto your feet from another position: *Everyone stood when the President came in.* ◊ *I stood up in order to get a better view.*

PUT UPRIGHT | **3** [VN+*adv./prep.*] to put sth/sb in an upright position somewhere: *Stand the ladder up against the wall.* ◊ *I stood the little girl on a chair so that she could see.*

BE IN PLACE/CONDITION | **4** [v+*adv./prep.*] (*written*) to be in a particular place: *The castle stands on the site of an ancient battlefield.* ◊ *An old oak tree once stood here.* **5** [V-ADJ] to be in a particular condition or situation: *The house stood empty for a long time.* ◊ *'You're wrong about the date—it was 1988.' 'I stand corrected* (= accept that I was wrong).*'* ◊ [V] *You never know where you stand with her—one minute she's friendly, the next she'll hardly speak to you.* ◊ *As things stand, there is little chance of a quick settlement of the dispute.*

BE AT HEIGHT/LEVEL | **6** [V-N] (not used in the progressive tenses) to be a particular height: *The tower stands 30 metres high.* **7** [V] ~ **at sth** to be at a particular level, amount, height, etc: *Interest rates stand at 3%.* ◊ *The world record then stood at 6.59 metres.*

OF CAR/TRAIN, etc. | **8** [V+*adv./prep.*] to be in a particular place, especially while waiting to go somewhere: *The train standing at platform 3 is for London, Victoria.*

OF LIQUID/MIXTURE | **9** [V] to remain still, without moving or being moved: *Mix the batter and let it stand for twenty minutes.* ◊ *standing pools of rainwater*

OFFER/DECISION | **10** [V] if an offer, a decision, etc. made earlier **stands**, it is still valid: *My offer still stands.* ◊ *The world record stood for 20 years.*

BE LIKELY TO DO STH | **11** [V to inf] to be in a situation where you are likely to do sth: *You stand to make a lot from this deal.*

HAVE OPINION | **12** [V] ~ **(on sth)** to have a particular attitude or opinion about sth or towards sb: *Where do you stand on private education?*

DISLIKE | **13** [no passive] (not used in the progressive tenses) used especially in negative sentences and questions to emphasize that you do not like sb/sth: [VN] *I can't stand his brother.* ◊ *I can't stand the sight of blood.* ◊ *I can't stand it when you do that.* ◊ [V-ing] *She couldn't*

stand being kept waiting. ◊ [VN-ing] *I can't stand people interrupting all the time.* ◊ *How do you stand him being here all the time?*

SURVIVE TREATMENT | **14** [VN] used especially with *can/could* to say that sb/sth can survive sth or can TOLERATE sth without being hurt or damaged: *His heart won't stand the strain much longer.* ◊ *Modern plastics can stand very high and very low temperatures.*

BUY DRINK/MEAL | **15** [no passive] to buy a drink or meal for sb: [VN] *He stood drinks all round.* ◊ [VNN] *She was kind enough to stand us a meal.*

IN ELECTION | **16** (*especially BrE*) (*AmE* usually **run**) [V] ~ **(for/as sth)** to be a candidate in an election: *He stood for parliament* (= tried to get elected as an MP). ◊ *She stood unsuccessfully as a candidate in the local elections.*

[IDM] Idioms containing **stand** are at the entries for the nouns and adjectives in the idioms, for example **stand on ceremony** is at **ceremony**.

[PHRV] **,stand a'side 1** to move to one side: *She stood aside to let us pass.* **2** to not get involved in sth: *Don't stand aside and let others do all the work.* **3** to stop doing a job so sb else can do it

,stand 'back (from sth) 1 to move back from a place: *The police ordered the crowd to stand back.* **2** to be situated away from sth: *The house stands back from the road.* **3** to think about a situation as if you are not involved in it: *It's time to stand back and look at your career so far.*

,stand 'by 1 to be present while sth bad is happening but not do anything to stop it: *How can you stand by and see him accused of something he didn't do?*—related noun BYSTANDER **2** to be ready for action: *The troops are standing by.*—related noun STANDBY, **'stand by sb** to help sb or be friends with them, even in difficult situations: *her famous song, 'Stand by your man'* **'stand by sth** to still believe or agree with sth you said, decided or agreed earlier: *She still stands by every word she said.*

,stand 'down 1 ~ **(as sth)** to leave a job or position: *He stood down to make way for someone younger.* **2** (of a witness) to leave the STAND in a court of law after giving evidence

'stand for sth [no passive] **1** (not used in the progressive tenses) to be an abbreviation or symbol of sth: *'The bomb's by T.C. Smith.' 'What does the 'T.C.' stand for?'* **2** to support sth: *I hated the organization and all it stood for* (= the ideas that it supported). **3** (**not stand for sth**) to not let sb do sth or sth happen: *I'm not standing for it any longer.*

,stand 'in (for sb) to take sb's place [SYN] DEPUTIZE: *My assistant will stand in for me while I'm away.*—related noun STAND-IN

,stand 'out (as sth) to be much better or more important than sb/sth: *Four points stand out as being more important than the rest.*—see also OUTSTANDING **,stand 'out (from/against sth)** to be easily seen; to be noticeable: *The lettering stood out well against the dark background.* ◊ *She's the sort of person who stands out in a crowd.*

,stand 'over sb be near sb and watch them: *I don't like you standing over me while I am cooking.*

,stand 'up to be on your feet: *There were no seats left so I had to stand up.* ◊ *You'll look taller if you stand up straight.* **,stand sb 'up** (*informal*) to deliberately not meet sb you have arranged to meet, especially sb you are having a romantic relationship with: *I've been stood up!* **,stand 'up for sb/sth** to support or defend sb/sth: *Always stand up for your friends.* ◊ *You must stand up for your rights.* ◊ *She had learnt to stand up for herself.* **,stand 'up (to sth)** to remain valid even when tested, examined closely, etc: *His argument simply doesn't stand up to close scrutiny.* ◊ *I'm afraid this document will never stand up in a court of law.* **,stand 'up to sb** to resist sb; to not accept bad treatment from sb without complaining: *It was brave of her to stand up to those bullies.* **,stand 'up to sth** (of materials, products, etc.) to remain in good condition in spite of rough treatment [SYN] WITHSTAND: *The carpet is designed to stand up to a lot of wear and tear.*

■ *noun*

OPINION | **1** [usually sing.] an attitude towards sth or an opinion that you make clear to people: *to take a firm/*

aɪ	aʊ	eɪ	əʊ	oʊ	ɔɪ	ɪə	eə	ʊə	j	w
my	now	say	go	go	boy	near	hair	pure	yes	wet
			(BrE)	(AmE)						

strong stand on sth ◊ *He was criticized for his tough stand on immigration.*

DEFENCE | **2** [usually sing.] a strong effort to defend yourself or your opinion about sth: *We must **make a stand against** further job losses.* ◊ *the rebels' desperate last stand*

FOR SHOWING/HOLDING STH | **3** a table or an upright structure that goods are sold from, especially in the street or at a market [SYN] STALL: *a hamburger/ice cream/newspaper stand*—see also NEWS-STAND **4** (*especially BrE*) a table or an upright structure where things are displayed or advertised, for example at an EXHIBITION: *a display/exhibition/trade stand* **5** (often in compounds) a piece of equipment or furniture that you use for holding a particular type of thing: *a bicycle/microphone/cake stand*—see also MUSIC STAND, NIGHTSTAND, WASHSTAND

AT SPORTS GROUND | **6** a large sloping structure at a STADIUM with rows where people sit or stand to watch the game: *We had seats in the east stand.*—see also GRAND-STAND

IN COURT OF LAW | **7** [usually sing.] = WITNESS BOX: *He took the stand as the first witness.*

IN CRICKET | **8** [usually sing.] the period of time in which two people who are BATTING (= hitting the ball) play together and score points: *Clinch and Harris shared an opening stand of 69.*

FOR BAND/ORCHESTRA, etc. | **9** a raised platform for a band, an orchestra, a speaker, etc.—see also BANDSTAND

FOR TAXIS/BUSES, etc. | **10** a place where taxis, buses, etc. park while they are waiting for passengers—compare TAXI RANK

OF PLANTS/TREES | **11** ~ (of sth) (*technical*) a group of plants or trees of one kind: *a stand of pines*

—see also HANDSTAND, ONE-NIGHT STAND [IDM] see FIRM *adj.*

'stand-alone *adj.* [usually before noun] (especially of a computer) able to be operated on its own without being connected to a larger system

stand·ard /ˈstændəd; *AmE* -dərd/ *noun, adj.*

■ *noun*

LEVEL OF QUALITY | **1** [C, U] ~ (of sth) a level of quality, especially one that people think is acceptable: *a fall in academic standards* ◊ *We aim to maintain **high standards** of customer care.* ◊ *The standard of this year's applications is very low.* ◊ *He failed to **reach the required standard**, and did not qualify for the race.* ◊ *Her work is not **up to standard** (= of a good enough standard).* ◊ *Who **sets the standard** for water quality?* ◊ *A number of Britain's beaches fail to **meet European standards** on cleanliness.* ◊ *In the shanty towns there are very poor **living standards**.*—see also STANDARD OF LIVING **2** [C, usually pl.] a level of quality that is normal or acceptable for a particular person or in a particular situation: *You'd better **lower your standards** if you want to find somewhere cheap to live.* ◊ *It was a simple meal **by** Eddie's **standards**.* ◊ *The equipment is slow and heavy **by modern standards**.*

LEVEL OF BEHAVIOUR | **3** (**standards**) [pl.] a level of behaviour that sb considers to be morally acceptable: *a man of high moral standards* ◊ *Standards aren't what they used to be.*—see also DOUBLE STANDARD

UNIT OF MEASUREMENT | **4** [C] a unit of measurement that is officially used; an official rule used when producing sth: *a reduction in the weight standard of silver coins* ◊ *industry standards*—see also GOLD STANDARD

FLAG | **5** [C] a flag that is used during official ceremonies, especially one connected with a particular military group

SONG | **6** [C] a song that has been recorded by many different singers

■ *adj.*

AVERAGE/NORMAL | **1** average or normal rather than having special or unusual features: *A standard letter was sent to all candidates.* ◊ *Televisions are a standard feature in most hotel rooms.* ◊ *the standard rate of tax* (= paid by everyone) ◊ *It is standard practice to search visitors as they enter the building.* ◊ *All vehicles come with a catalytic converter **as standard**.*

SIZE/MEASUREMENT | **2** [usually before noun] following a

particular standard set, for example, by an industry: *standard sizes of clothes* ◊ *Washing machines have standard measurements to fit under kitchen units.*

BOOK/WRITER | **3** [only before noun] read by most people who are studying a particular subject

LANGUAGE | **4** [usually before noun] (of spelling, pronunciation, grammar. etc.) believed to be correct and used by most people: *Standard English*—compare NON-STANDARD, SUB-STANDARD

'standard-bearer *noun* (*written*) a leader in a political group or CAMPAIGN: *a standard-bearer of the left/right of the party*

'standard de'duction *noun* [usually sing.] (*AmE*) a fixed amount of money that you can earn free of tax

'standard devi'ation *noun* (*mathematics*) the amount by which measurements in a set vary from the average for the set

'Standard Grade *noun* (in Scotland) an exam in a particular subject at a lower level than HIGHERS. Standard Grades are usually taken in a number of different subjects at the age of 16.

stand·ard·ize (*BrE* also **-ise**) /ˈstændədaɪz; *AmE* -dərd-/ *verb* [VN] to make objects or activities of the same type have the same features or qualities; to make sth standard: *attempts to standardize legislation on the matter* ▶ **stand·ard·iza·tion**, **-isa·tion** /ˌstændədaɪˈzeɪʃn; *AmE* -dərdə'z-/ *noun* [U]: *the standardization of components*

'standard lamp (*BrE*) (*AmE* **'floor lamp**) *noun* a tall lamp that stands on the floor

'standard of 'living *noun* (*pl.* **,standards of 'living**) the amount of money and level of comfort that a particular person or group has

'standard time *noun* [U] the official time of a country or an area

stand·by /ˈstændbaɪ/ *noun, adj.*

■ *noun* (*pl.* **stand·bys**) *noun* a person or thing that can always be used if needed, for example if sb/sth else is not available or if there is an emergency: *I always keep a pizza in the freezer as a standby* ◊ *a standby electricity generator* [IDM] **on 'standby 1** ready to do sth immediately if needed or asked: *The emergency services were put on standby after a bomb warning.* **2** ready to travel or go somewhere if a ticket or sth that is needed suddenly becomes available: *He was put on standby for the flight to New York.*

■ *adj.* [only before noun] a **standby** ticket for a flight, theatre, etc. cannot be bought in advance and is only available a very short time before the plane leaves or the performance starts: *a standby ticket/passenger*

'stand-in *noun* **1** a person who does sb's job for a short time when they are not available: *I acted as Tom's stand-in when he was away.* ◊ *the stand-in captain* **2** a person who replaces an actor in some scenes in a film/movie, especially dangerous ones

stand·ing /ˈstændɪŋ/ *adj., noun*

■ *adj.* [only before noun] **1** existing or arranged permanently, not formed or made for a particular situation: *a standing army* ◊ (*BrE*) *a **standing charge** (= an amount of money that you pay in order to use a service, such as gas or water)* ◊ *a **standing committee*** ◊ *It's a **standing joke** (= something that a group of people regularly laugh at).* ◊ *We have a **standing invitation** to visit them anytime.* **2** done from a position in which you are standing rather than sitting or running: *a standing jump/start*—see also FREE-STANDING

■ *noun* [U] **1** the position or reputation of sb/sth within a group of people or in an organization [SYN] STATUS: *the high/low standing of politicians with the public* ◊ *The contract has no legal standing.* **2** [U] the period of time that sth has existed: *a friendship of many years' standing*—see also LONG-STANDING **3** (**standings**) [pl.] a list of people, teams, etc. showing their positions in a sports competition

'standing 'order *noun* [C, U] an instruction that you give to your bank to pay sb a fixed amount of money from

S

your account on the same day each week/month, etc.—compare BANKER'S ORDER, DIRECT DEBIT

'standing room noun [U] space for people to stand in, especially in a theatre, sports ground, etc: *standing room for 12000 supporters* ◊ *It was **standing room only** at the concert* (= all the seats were sold).

'stand-off noun ~ **(between A and B)** a situation in a dispute in which no agreement can be reached SYN DEADLOCK

stand-off-ish /ˌstænd'ɒfɪʃ; *AmE* -'ɔːf-; -'ɑːf-/ adj. (*informal*) not friendly towards other people SYN ALOOF

stand-out /'stændaʊt/ noun (*AmE, informal*) a person or thing that is very noticeable because they are better, more impressive, etc. than others in a group

stand-pipe /'stændpaɪp/ noun a pipe that is connected to a public water supply and used to provide water outside a building

stand-point /'stændpɔɪnt/ noun [usually sing.] a point of view or way of thinking about ideas or situations SYN PERSPECTIVE: *a modern/political/theoretical standpoint* ◊ *He is writing from the standpoint of someone who knows what life is like in prison.*

stand-still /'stændstɪl/ noun [sing.] a situation in which all activity or movement has stopped: *The security alert **brought** the airport **to a standstill**.* ◊ *Traffic in the northbound lane is **at a complete standstill**.*

'stand-up adj. [only before noun] **1** stand-up COMEDY consists of one person standing in front of an audience and telling jokes **2** (*especially BrE*) a **stand-up** argument, fight, etc. is one in which people shout loudly at each other or are violent towards each other **3** worn, used, etc. in an upright position: *a stand-up collar*

stank pt of STINK

Stan-ley knife /'stænli naɪf/ noun (*BrE*) a very sharp knife with a blade in the shape of a triangle that can be replaced

stanza /'stænzə/ noun (*technical*) a group of lines in a repeated pattern that form a unit in some types of poem SYN VERSE

staple /'steɪpl/ adj., noun, verb
■ adj. [only before noun] forming a basic, large or important part of sth: *The staple crop is rice.* ◊ *Jeans are a staple part of everyone's wardrobe.*
■ noun **1** a small piece of wire that is used in a device called a STAPLER and is pushed through pieces of paper and bent over at the ends in order to fasten the pieces of paper together—picture at STATIONERY **2** a small piece of metal in the shape of a U that is hit into wooden surfaces using a hammer, used especially for holding electrical wires in place **3** a basic type of food that is used a lot: *Aid workers helped distribute corn, milk and other staples.* **4** something that is produced by a country and is important for its economy: *Rubber became the staple of the Malayan economy.* **5** ~ **(of sth)** a large or important part of sth: *Royal gossip is a staple of the tabloid press.*
■ verb [VN+adv./prep.] to attach one thing to another using a staple or staples: *Staple the invoice to the receipt.* ◊ *Staple the invoice and the receipt together.*

ˌstaple 'diet noun [U, C] ~ **(of sth)** **1** the food that a person or an animal normally eats: *a staple diet of meat and potatoes* ◊ *Bamboo is the panda's staple diet.* **2** something that is used a lot: *Sex and violence seem to be the staple diet of television drama.*

stapler /'steɪplə(r)/ noun a small device used for putting staples into paper, etc.—picture at STATIONERY

star /stɑː(r)/ noun, verb
■ noun
IN SKY | **1** [C] a large ball of burning gas in space that we see as a point of light in the sky at night: *There was a big moon and hundreds of stars were shining overhead.* ◊ *Sirius is the brightest star in the sky.* ◊ *We camped out **under the stars**.*—see also FALLING STAR, LODESTAR, POLE STAR, SHOOTING STAR, STARRY
SHAPE | **2** [C] an object, a decoration, a mark, etc., usually with five or six points, whose shape represents a star: *a horse with a white star on its forehead* ◊ *a sheriff's star*

◊ *I've put a star by the names of the girls in the class.* ◊ *a four-star general*
MARK OF QUALITY | **3** [C, usually sing.] a mark that represents a star and tells you how good sth is, especially a hotel or restaurant: *three-/four-/five-star hotels* ◊ *What star rating does this restaurant have?*
PERFORMER | **4** [C] a famous and excellent singer, performer, sports player, etc: *pop/rock/Hollywood stars* ◊ *a football/tennis star* ◊ *He's so good—I'm sure he'll be a big star.* ◊ *She acts well but she hasn't got **star quality**.* ◊ *The best models receive **star treatment**.*—see also ALL-STAR, FILM STAR, MEGASTAR, MOVIE STAR, SUPERSTAR **5** [C] a person who has the main part, or one of the main parts, in a film/movie, play, etc: *She was the star of many popular television series.* ◊ *The **star of the show** was a young Italian singer.* ◊ *the **star role/part**—*see also STAR TURN
BEST OF GROUP | **6** [C] (*often used before another noun*) a person or thing that is the best of a group: *a star student* ◊ *He was the star performer at the championships.* ◊ *The star prize is a weekend for two in Paris.* ◊ *The monkey was the **star attraction** (*= the best or most popular act) *at the show.*
HELPFUL PERSON | **7** [C, usually sing.] (*spoken, informal*) used to show that you feel very grateful for sth that sb has done or that you think they are wonderful: *Thanks! You're a star!*
INFLUENCE ON SB'S FUTURE | **8** (**stars**) [pl.] a description of what is going to happen to sb in the future, based on the position of the stars and planets when they were born SYN HOROSCOPE: *Do you read your stars in the paper?* **9** [C] a planet or force that some people believe to influence a person's life: *You must have been born under a lucky star!*—see also ILL-STARRED
IDM **see 'stars** (*informal*) to see flashes of light in front of your eyes, usually because you have been hit on the head—more at REACH v., THANK
■ verb (**-rr-**)
PERFORM IN MOVIE/PLAY | **1** [V] ~ **(with/opposite sb)** **(in sth)** to have one of the main parts in a film/movie, play, etc: *She starred opposite Jack Nicholson in 'As Good as it Gets'.* ◊ *No one has yet been chosen for the **starring role** (*= the main part). **2** [VN] [no passive] if a film/movie, play, etc. stars sb, that person has one of the main parts: *a movie starring Tom Cruise and Demi Moore* ◊ *The studio wants to star her in a sequel to last year's hit.*—see also CO-STAR
MARK WITH SYMBOL | **3** [VN] [usually passive] to put a symbol shaped like a star (called an ASTERISK) next to a word, etc. in order to make people notice it: *Treat all the sections that have been starred as priority.*

star-board /'stɑːbəd; *AmE* 'stɑːrbərd/ noun [U] the side of a ship or an aircraft that is on the right when you are facing forward—compare PORT

starch /stɑːtʃ; *AmE* stɑːrtʃ/ noun, verb
■ noun **1** [U, C] a white CARBOHYDRATE food substance found in potatoes, flour, rice, etc.; food containing this: *rice/potato starch* ◊ *You need to cut down on starch.* **2** [U] starch prepared in powder form or as a spray and used for making clothes, sheets, etc. stiff: *Spray starch on the shirt collars before ironing them.*
■ verb [VN] [usually passive] to make clothes, sheets, etc. stiff using starch: *a starched white shirt*

starchy /'stɑːtʃi; *AmE* 'stɑːrtʃi/ adj. (of food) containing a lot of starch

'star-crossed adj. (*literary*) not able to be happy because of bad luck or fate: *Shakespeare's star-crossed lovers, Romeo and Juliet*

star-dom /'stɑːdəm; *AmE* 'stɑːrdəm/ noun [U] the state of being famous as an actor, a singer, etc: *The group is being **tipped for stardom** (*= people say they will be famous). ◊ *She **shot to stardom** in a Broadway musical.*

stare /steə(r); *AmE* ster/ verb, noun
■ verb [V] ~ **(at sb/sth)** to look at sb/sth for a long time: *I screamed and everyone stared.* ◊ *I stared blankly at the paper in front of me.* ◊ *He sat **staring into space** (*= looking at nothing). ◊ *She looked at them with dark staring eyes.* IDM **be staring sb in the 'face 1** to be obvious

or easy to see: *The answer was staring us in the face.* **2** to be certain to happen: *Defeat was staring them in the face.* **be staring sth in the 'face** to be unable to avoid sth: *They were staring defeat in the face.* PHRV ,**stare sb 'out** (*BrE*) (also ,**stare sb 'down** especially in *AmE*) to look into sb's eyes for a long time until they feel embarrassed and are forced to look away

■ *noun* an act of looking at sb/sth for a long time, especially in a way that is unfriendly or that shows surprise: *She gave him a blank stare.*

star·fish /'stɑːfɪʃ; *AmE* 'stɑːrfɪʃ/ *noun* (*pl.* **star·fish**) a flat sea creature in the shape of a star with five arms

star·fruit /'stɑːfruːt; *AmE* 'stɑːrf-/ *noun* (*pl.* **star·fruit**) a green or yellow tropical fruit with a shape like a star—picture on page A2

star·gazer /'stɑːɡeɪzə(r); *AmE* 'stɑːrɡ-/ *noun* (*informal*) a person who studies ASTROLOGY or ASTRONOMY ▶ **star·gaz·ing** *noun* [U]

stark /stɑːk; *AmE* stɑːrk/ *adj., adv.*

■ *adj.* (**stark·er, stark·est**) **1** (often *disapproving*) looking severe and without any colour or decoration: *I think white would be too stark for the bedroom.* ◊ *The hills stood stark against the winter sky.* **2** unpleasant; real, and impossible to avoid: *The author paints a stark picture of life in a prison camp.* ◊ *a stark choice/warning* ◊ *The remains of the building stand as a stark reminder of the fire.* ◊ *He now faces the **stark reality** of life in prison.* **3** very different to sth in a way that is easy to see: *stark alternatives/differences* ◊ *Social divisions in the city are stark.* ◊ *The good weather was **in stark contrast to** the storms of previous weeks.* **4** [only before noun] complete and total: *The children watched in stark terror.* ▶ **stark·ly** *adv.*: *The interior is starkly simple.* ◊ *The lighthouse stood out starkly against the dark sky.* ◊ *We are starkly aware of the risks.* **stark·ness** *noun* [U]

■ *adv.* **~ naked** completely naked IDM see RAVING

stark·ers /'stɑːkəz; *AmE* 'stɑːrkərz/ *adj.* [not before noun] (*BrE, informal*) not wearing any clothes SYN NAKED

star·less /'stɑːləs; *AmE* 'stɑːrləs/ *adj.* with no stars in the sky: *a starless night*

star·let /'stɑːlət; *AmE* 'stɑːrlət/ *noun* a young woman actor who plays small parts and hopes to become famous

star·light /'stɑːlaɪt; *AmE* 'stɑːrl-/ *noun* [U] light from the stars: *We walked home by starlight.*

star·ling /'stɑːlɪŋ; *AmE* 'stɑːrlɪŋ/ *noun* a common bird with dark shiny feathers and a noisy call: *a flock of starlings*

star·lit /'stɑːlɪt; *AmE* 'stɑːrlɪt/ *adj.* (*written*) with light from the stars: *a starlit night*

Star of 'David *noun* (*pl.* **Stars of David**) a star with six points that is used as a symbol of Judaism and the state of Israel

starry /'stɑːri/ *noun* [usually before noun] **1** (of the sky) full of stars: *a beautiful starry night* **2** looking like a star: *starry flowers* **3** (of eyes) shining like stars

,**starry-'eyed** *adj.* (*informal*) full of emotion, hopes or dreams about sb/sth in a way that is not realistic

the ,Stars and 'Stripes *noun* [sing.] the national flag of the US

'**star sign** (also *informal* **sign**) *noun* one of the twelve signs of the ZODIAC: *'What's your star sign?' 'Aquarius.'*

the ,Star-Spangled 'Banner *noun* [sing.] the national ANTHEM (= song) of the US

'**star-studded** *adj.* (*written*) including many famous performers: *a star-studded cast*

start /stɑːt; *AmE* stɑːrt/ *verb, noun*

■ *verb*

DOING STH | **1** to begin doing sth: [VN] *I start work at nine.* ◊ *He's just started a new job.* ◊ *I only started* (= began to read) *this book yesterday.* ◊ *We need to start* (= begin using) *a new jar of coffee.* ◊ *The kids start school next week.* ◊ [V to inf] *It started to rain.* ◊ *Mistakes were starting to creep in.* ◊ [V-ing] *She started laughing.* ◊ [V] *It's a long story. Where shall I start?* ◊ *It's time you started on your homework.* ◊ *Let's start by reviewing what we did last*

week. ◊ *Can you start* (= a new job) *on Monday?* ◊ [V-ADJ] *The best professional musicians start young.*

HAPPENING | **2** to start happening; to make sth start happening: [V] *When does the class start?* ◊ *Have you any idea where the rumour started?* ◊ [VN] *Who started the fire?* ◊ *Do you start the day with a good breakfast?* ◊ *You're always trying to start an argument.* ◊ [VN-ing] *The news started me thinking.*

MACHINE/VEHICLE | **3** when you **start** a machine or a vehicle or it **starts**, it begins to operate: [VN] *Start the engines!* ◊ *I can't get the car started.* ◊ [V] *The car won't start.*

EXISTING | **4** ~ (sth) (up) to begin to exist; to make sth begin to exist: [V] *There are a lot of small businesses starting up in that area.* ◊ [VN] *They decided to start a catering business.* ◊ *She started a yoga class at work.*

JOURNEY | **5** [V] ~ (out) to begin a journey; to leave: *What time are we starting tomorrow?*

GOING/WALKING | **6** [V+*adv. / prep.*] to begin to move in a particular direction: *I started after her* (= began to follow her) *to tell her the news.* ◊ *He started for the door, but I blocked his way.*

IN PARTICULAR WAY/FROM PLACE/LEVEL | **7** ~ (out/off) (sth) (as sth) to begin, or to begin sth such as a career, in a particular way that changed later: [V] *She started as a secretary but ended up running the department.* ◊ *The company started out with 30 employees.* ◊ [VN] *He started life as a teacher before turning to journalism.* **8** [V+*adv. / prep.*] to begin from a particular place, amount or situation: *The trail starts just outside the town.* ◊ *Hotel prices start at £65 a night for a double room.* ◊ *The evening started badly when the speaker failed to turn up.*

MOVE SUDDENLY | **9** [V] to move suddenly and quickly because you are surprised or afraid SYN JUMP: *The sudden noise made her start.*

⇨ note at BEGIN

IDM ,**don't (you) 'start** (*spoken, informal*) used to tell sb not to complain or be critical: *Don't start! I told you I'd be late.* **you, he, she, etc. 'started it** (*spoken, informal*) you, he, she, etc. began a fight or an argument: *'Stop fighting, you two!' 'He started it!'* '**start something** (*informal*) to cause trouble **to 'start with 1** used when you are giving the first and most important reason for sth: *To start with it's much too expensive …* **2** at the beginning: *The club had only six members to start with.* ◊ *I'll have melon to start with.* ◊ *She wasn't keen on the idea to start with.*—more at ALARM *n.*, BALL *n.*, FOOT *n.*

PHRV ,**start 'back** to begin to return somewhere: *Isn't it time we started back?* ,**start 'off 1** to begin to move: *The horse started off at a steady trot.* **2** to begin happening; to begin doing sth: *The discussion started off mildly enough.* **3** to begin by doing or being sth: *Let's start off with some gentle exercises.* ◊ *We started off by introducing ourselves.* ◊[+ADJ] *The leaves start off green but turn red later.* ◊[+-ing] *I started off working quite hard, but it didn't last.* ,**start sb 'off (on sth) 1** [no passive] to make sb begin doing sth: *What started her off on that crazy idea?* ◊ *Don't say anything to her—you'll start her off again* (= make her get angry). ◊[+-ing] *Kevin started us all off laughing.* **2** to help sb begin doing sth: *My mother started me off on the piano when I was three.* ◊[+-ing] *His father started him off farming.* '**start on sb** [no passive] to attack sb physically or with words ,**start 'on at sb (about sth)** | ,**start 'on (at sb) about sth** (*informal*) to begin to complain about sth or criticize sb: *She started on at me again about getting some new clothes.* ◊ *Don't start on about him not having a job.* ,**start 'out 1** to begin to do sth, especially in business or work: *to start out in business* ◊ *She started out on her legal career in 1963.* **2** to have a particular intention when you begin sth: [+ to inf] *I started out to write a short story, but it soon developed into a novel.* ,**start 'over** (*especially AmE*) to begin again: *She wasn't happy with our work and made us start over.* ,**start 'up** | ,**start sth ↔ 'up** to begin working, happening, etc.; to make sth do this: *I heard his car start up.* ◊ *Start up the engines!*—see also START-UP

■ *noun*

BEGINNING | **1** [C, usually sing.] the point at which sth begins: *a perfect start to the day* ◊ *Things didn't look too*

æ	ɑː	e	ɜː	ə	ɪ	iː	i	ɒ	ɔː	ʌ	ʊ	u	uː
cat	father	ten	bird	about	sit	see	many	got	saw	cup	put	actual	too
								(BrE)					

S

hopeful at the start of the year. ◊ If we don't hurry, we'll miss the start of the game. ◊ The meeting **got off to a good/bad start** (= started well/badly). ◊ The trip was a disaster **from start to finish**. ◊ We've had problems **(right) from the start**. ◊ (informal) This could be the start of something big. **2** [sing.] the act or process of beginning sth: I'll paint the ceiling if you **make a start on** the walls. ◊ I want to make an early start in the morning. ◊ She's moving abroad to make a **fresh start** (= to begin a new life).—see also FALSE START, KICK-START

OPPORTUNITY | **3** [C, usually sing.] the opportunity that you are given to begin sth in a successful way: They worked hard to give their children a good **start in life**. ◊ The job gave him his start in journalism.

IN RACE | **4** (the start) [sing.] the place where a race begins: The runners/riders lined up at the start. **5** [C, usually sing.] an amount of time or distance that sb has as an advantage over other people at the beginning of a race: She went into the second round with a five-minute start on the rest of the cyclists. ◊ I gave the younger children a start.—see also HEAD START **6** [C, usually pl.] (sport) a race or competition that sb has taken part in: She has been beaten only once in six starts.

SUDDEN MOVEMENT | **7** [C, usually sing.] an act of moving your body quickly and suddenly because you are surprised, afraid, etc: She woke from the dream **with a start**. ◊ You gave me quite a start!

IDM **for a ˈstart** (spoken) used to emphasize the first of a list of reasons, opinions, etc: I'm not working there—for a start, it's too far to travel.—more at FIT n., FLYING START

start·er /ˈstɑːtə(r); AmE ˈstɑːrt-/ noun **1** (especially BrE) (AmE usually **ap·pe·tiz·er**) a small amount of food that is served before the main course of a meal: This dish serves 4–6 people as a starter.—compare HORS D'OEUVRE **2** a person, horse, car, etc. that is in a race at the beginning: Only 8 of the 28 starters completed the course.—compare NON-STARTER **3** a person who gives the signal for a race to start **4** a device used for starting the engine of a vehicle **5** a person who begins doing a particular activity in the way mentioned: He was a late starter in the theatre (= older than most people when they start). ◊ a slow starter—see also SELF-STARTER **6** (often used as an adjective) something that is intended to be used by sb who is starting to do sth: a starter home (= a small home for sb who is buying property for the first time) ◊ a starter kit/pack **IDM** **for ˈstarters** (spoken) used to emphasize the first of a list of reasons, opinions, etc., or to say what happens first **under ˌstarters ˈorders** (of a runner, rider, etc.) waiting for a signal to start the race

ˈstarting blocks (also **the blocks**) noun [pl.] the two blocks on the ground that runners push their feet against at the beginning of a race—picture on page 1251

ˈstarting gate noun a barrier that is raised to let horses or dogs start running in a race

ˈstarting point noun **1** ~ (for sth) a thing, an idea or a set of facts that can be used to begin a discussion or process: The TV documentary served as a useful starting point for our discussion. **2** the place where you begin a journey

ˈstarting price noun the final ODDS that are given for a horse or dog just before a race begins

star·tle /ˈstɑːtl; AmE ˈstɑːrtl/ verb to surprise sb suddenly in a way that slightly shocks or frightens them: [VN] I didn't mean to startle you. ◊ The explosion startled the horse. ◊ I was startled by her question. ◊ [VN to inf] It startled me to find her sitting in my office. ▶ **star·tled** /ˈstɑːtld; AmE ˈstɑːrtld/ adj.: She looked at him with startled eyes. ◊ He looked startled. ◊ She jumped back like a startled rabbit.

start·ling /ˈstɑːtlɪŋ; AmE ˈstɑːrt-/ adj. **1** extremely unusual and surprising: a startling contrast/discovery ◊ startling revelations in the Sunday papers **2** (of a colour) extremely bright: startling blue eyes ▶ **star·tling·ly** adv.

ˈstart-up adj. [only before noun] connected with starting a new business or project: start-up costs/problems

ˌstar ˈturn noun [usually sing.] the main performer or entertainer in a show

star·va·tion /stɑːˈveɪʃn; AmE stɑːrˈv-/ noun [U] the state of suffering and death caused by having no food: to die of/from starvation ◊ Millions will face starvation next year as a result of the drought. ◊ a **starvation diet** (= one in which you do not have much to eat) ◊ They were on **starvation wages** (= extremely low wages).

starve /stɑːv; AmE stɑːrv/ verb **1** to suffer or die because you do not have enough food to eat; to make sb suffer or die in this way: [V] The animals were left to starve to death. ◊ pictures of starving children ◊ The new job doesn't pay as much but we won't starve! ◊ [VN] She's starving herself to try to lose weight. **2** (-starved) (in adjectives) not having sth that you need: supply-starved rebels—see also CASH-STARVED **IDM** **be ˈstarving (for sth)** (also **be ˈstarved** especially in AmE) (informal) to feel very hungry: When's food? I'm starving! **PHRV** **starve sb into sth/into doing sth** to force sb to do sth by not allowing them to get any food or money: The blockade was aimed at starving the country into submission. **starve sb/sth of sth** (AmE also **starve sb/sth for sth**) [usually passive] to not give sth that is needed: I felt starved of intelligent conversation. ◊ The department has been starved of resources. **ˌstarve sb↔ˈout (of sth)** to force sb to leave a particular building or area by not allowing them to get any food

stash /stæʃ/ verb, noun
■ verb [VN +adv./prep.] (informal) to store sth in a safe or secret place: She has a fortune **stashed away** in various bank accounts.
■ noun [usually sing.] (informal) an amount of sth that is kept secretly: a stash of money

sta·sis /ˈsteɪsɪs/ noun [U, C] (pl. **sta·ses** /-siːz/) (formal) a situation in which there is no change or development

state /steɪt/ noun, adj., verb
■ noun
CONDITION OF SB/STH | **1** [C] the mental, emotional or physical condition that a person or thing is in: a confused **state of mind** ◊ He was in a state of permanent depression. ◊ A report condemned the state of prisoners' cells. ◊ anxieties about the state of the country's economy ◊ The building is in a bad **state of repair** (= needs to be repaired). ◊ She was in a **state of shock**. ◊ (BrE, informal) Look at the state of you! You can't go out looking like that. ◊ You're **not in a fit state** to drive. ⇨ note at CONDITION

COUNTRY | **2** (also **State**) [C] a country considered as an organized political community controlled by one government: the Baltic States ◊ the State of Israel ◊ European Union member states—see also CITY STATE, NATION STATE, POLICE STATE, WELFARE STATE ⇨ note at COUNTRY

PART OF COUNTRY | **3** (also **State**) [C] (abbr. **St.**) an organized political community forming part of a country: the states of Victoria and Western Australia ◊ the southern States of the US

GOVERNMENT | **4** (also **the State**) [U, sing.] the government of a country: matters/affairs of state ◊ people who are financially dependent on the state ◊ a state-owned company ◊ They wish to limit the power of the State.

OFFICIAL CEREMONY | **5** [U] the formal ceremonies connected with high levels of government or with kings and queens: The president was driven **in state** through the streets.

THE US | **6** (the States) [pl.] (informal) the United States of America: I've never been to the States.

IDM **be in/get into a ˈstate** (informal, especially BrE) **1** to be/become excited or anxious: She was in a real state about her exams. **2** to be dirty or untidy: What a state this place is in! **in a state of ˈgrace** (in the Roman Catholic Church) having been forgiven by God for the wrong or evil things you have done: He died in a state of grace. **a state of afˈfairs** a situation: This state of affairs can no longer be ignored. **the state of ˈplay 1** the stage that has been reached in a dispute, process, etc. which has not yet been completed: What is the current state of play in the peace talks? **2** (especially BrE) the score in a sports match, especially in cricket **turn State's ˈevidence** (AmE) = TURN KING'S/QUEEN'S EVIDENCE at EVIDENCE—more at LIE v., NANNY

■ adj. (also **State**) [only before noun]

aɪ	aʊ	eɪ	əʊ	oʊ	ɔɪ	ɪə	eə	ʊə	j	w
my	now	say	go (BrE)	go (AmE)	boy	near	hair	pure	yes	wet

<u>GOVERNMENT</u> | **1** provided or controlled by the government of a country: *state education* ◇ *families dependent on state benefits* (= in Britain, money given by the government to people who are poor) ◇ *state secrets* (= information that could be harmful to a country if it were discovered by an enemy)

<u>OFFICIAL</u> | **2** connected with the leader of a country attending an official ceremony: *The Queen is on a state visit to Moscow.* ◇ *the state opening of Parliament* ◇ *the state apartments/rooms* (= used for official ceremonies)

<u>PART OF COUNTRY</u> | **3** connected with a particular state of a country, especially in the US: *a state prison/hospital/ university* ◇ *state police/troopers* ◇ *a state holiday/tax*

■ *verb* **1** to formally write or say sth, especially in a careful and clear way: [VN] *He has already stated his intention to run for election.* ◇ *The facts are clearly stated in the report.* ◇ *There is no need to state the obvious* (= to say sth that everyone already knows). ◇ [V wh-] *State clearly how many tickets you require.* ◇ [V that] *He stated categorically that he knew nothing about the deal.* ◇ [VN that] *It was stated that standards at the hospital were dropping.* ◇ [VN to inf] *The contract was stated to be invalid.* **HELP** This pattern is usually used in the passive. **2** [VN] [usually passive] to fix or announce the details of sth, especially on a written document: *This is not one of their stated aims.* ◇ *You must arrive at the time stated.* ◇ *Do not exceed the stated dose* (= of medicine).

the 'State Department *noun* the US government department of foreign affairs

state·hood /'steɪthʊd/ *noun* [U] (*written*) **1** the fact of being an independent country and of having the rights and powers of a country **2** the condition of being one of the states within a country such as the US or Australia: *West Virginia was granted statehood in 1863.*

'state house *noun* [usually sing.] (in the US) a building in which a state LEGISLATURE (= parliament) meets

state·less /'steɪtləs/ *adj.* not officially a citizen of any country ▶ **state·less·ness** *noun* [U]

,state 'line *noun* the line between two states in the US: *the Nevada-California state line*

state·ly /'steɪtli/ *adj.* **1** impressive in size, appearance or manner: *an avenue of stately chestnut trees* ◇ *a tall, stately woman* **2** slow, formal and graceful: *a stately dance* ◇ *The procession made its stately progress through the streets of the city.* ▶ **state·li·ness** *noun* [U]

,stately 'home *noun* (*BrE*) a large, impressive house of historical interest, especially one that the public may visit

state·ment /'steɪtmənt/ *noun, verb*

■ *noun* **1** [C] something that you say or write that gives information or an opinion: *Are the following statements true or false?* ◇ *Your statement is misleading.* ◇ *Is that a statement or a question?* ◇ *The play makes a strong political statement.* **2** [C] ~ (**on/about sth**) a formal or official account of facts or opinions: *a public/a written/an official statement* ◇ *A government spokesperson made a statement to the press.* ◇ *The prime minister is expected to issue a statement on the policy change this afternoon.* ◇ *The police asked me to make a statement* (= a written account of facts concerning a crime, used in court if legal action follows). **3** [C] a printed record of money paid, received, etc: *The directors are responsible for preparing the company's financial statements.* ◇ *My bank sends me monthly statements.*—see also BANK STATEMENT **4** [C] (in Britain) an official report on a child's special needs made by a local education authority: *a statement of special educational needs* **5** [U] (*formal*) the act of stating or expressing sth in words: *When writing instructions, clarity of statement is the most important thing.*

■ *verb* [VN] [often passive] (in Britain) to officially decide and report that a child has special needs for his or her education: *statemented children*

,state of 'siege *noun* a situation in which the government limits people's freedom to enter or leave a city, town or building

,state of the 'art *adj.* using the most modern or advanced techniques or methods; as good as it can be at the present time: *The system was state of the art.* ◇ *a state-of-the-art system*

state·room /'steɪtruːm; -rʊm/ *noun* **1** a private room on a large ship **2** a room used by important government members, members of a royal family, etc. on formal occasions

'state school (*BrE*) (*AmE* **'public school**) *noun* a school that is paid for by the government and provides free education—compare PRIVATE SCHOOL, PUBLIC SCHOOL

state·side /'steɪtsaɪd/ *adj., adv.* (*AmE, informal*) connected with the US; in or towards the US (used when the person speaking is not in the US): *When are you next planning a trip stateside?*

states·man /'steɪtsmən/ *noun* (*pl.* **-men** /-mən/) a wise, experienced and respected political leader: *the party's elder statesman*

states·man·like /'steɪtsmənlaɪk/ *adj.* having or showing the qualities and abilities of a statesman: *He was commended for his statesmanlike handling of the crisis.*

states·man·ship /'steɪtsmənʃɪp/ *noun* [U] skill in managing state affairs

state·wide /'steɪtwaɪd/ *adj., adv.* happening or existing in all parts of a state of the US: *a statewide election/poll* ◇ *She won 10% of the vote statewide.*

static /'stætɪk/ *adj., noun*

■ *adj.* **1** not moving, changing or developing: *The balance sheet provides a static picture of the financial position at a point in time.* ◇ *Prices on the stock market, which have been static, are now rising again.* ◇ *a static population level* **2** (*physics*) (of a force) acting as a weight but not producing movement: *static pressure* **OPP** DYNAMIC

■ *noun* [U] **1** noise or other effects that disturb radio or television signals and are caused by particular conditions in the atmosphere **2** (also **,static elec'tricity**) electricity that gathers on or in an object which cannot CONDUCT a current: *My hair gets full of static when I brush it.* **3** (*statics*) the science that deals with the forces that balance each other to keep objects in a state of rest—compare DYNAMICS

sta·tion /'steɪʃn/ *noun, verb*

■ *noun*

<u>FOR TRAINS/BUSES</u> | **1** a place where trains stop so that passengers can get on and off; the buildings connected with this: (*BrE*) *a railway station* ◇ (*especially AmE*) *a train station* ◇ (*BrE*) *a tube/an underground station* ◇ (*AmE*) *a subway station* ◇ *I get off at the next station* ◇ *We met in front of the main station.* **2** (usually in compounds) a place where buses and COACHES stop; the buildings connected with this: *a bus/coach station*

<u>FOR WORK/SERVICE</u> | **3** (usually in compounds) a place or building where a service is organized and provided or a special type of work is done: *a police/fire station* ◇ (*BrE*) *a petrol station* ◇ (*AmE*) *a gas station* ◇ *an agricultural research station* ◇ *a pollution monitoring station*—compare SPACE STATION

<u>RADIO/TV COMPANY</u> | **4** (often in compounds) a radio or television company and the programmes it broadcasts: *a local radio/TV station* ◇ *He tuned to another station.*

<u>SOCIAL POSITION</u> | **5** (*old-fashioned* or *formal*) your social position: *She was definitely getting ideas above her station.*

<u>POSITION</u> | **6** a place where sb has to wait and watch or be ready to do work if needed: *You are not to leave your station without permission.*

<u>LARGE FARM</u> | **7** (usually in compounds) a large sheep or CATTLE farm in Australia or New Zealand

<u>FOR ARMY/NAVY</u> | **8** a small base for the army or navy; the people living in it: *a naval station*—see also ACTION STATIONS **IDM** see PANIC *n.*

■ *verb* [VN+*adv./prep.*]

<u>ARMED FORCES</u> | **1** [often passive] to send sb, especially from one of the armed forces, to work in a place for a period of time: *troops stationed abroad*

<u>GO TO POSITION</u> | **2** ~ **sb/yourself** ... (*formal*) to go somewhere and stand or sit there, especially to wait for sth; to send sb somewhere to do this: *She stationed herself at the window to await his return.*

b	d	f	g	h	k	l	m	n	p	r
bad	did	fall	get	hat	cat	leg	man	now	pen	red

stationery and office supplies

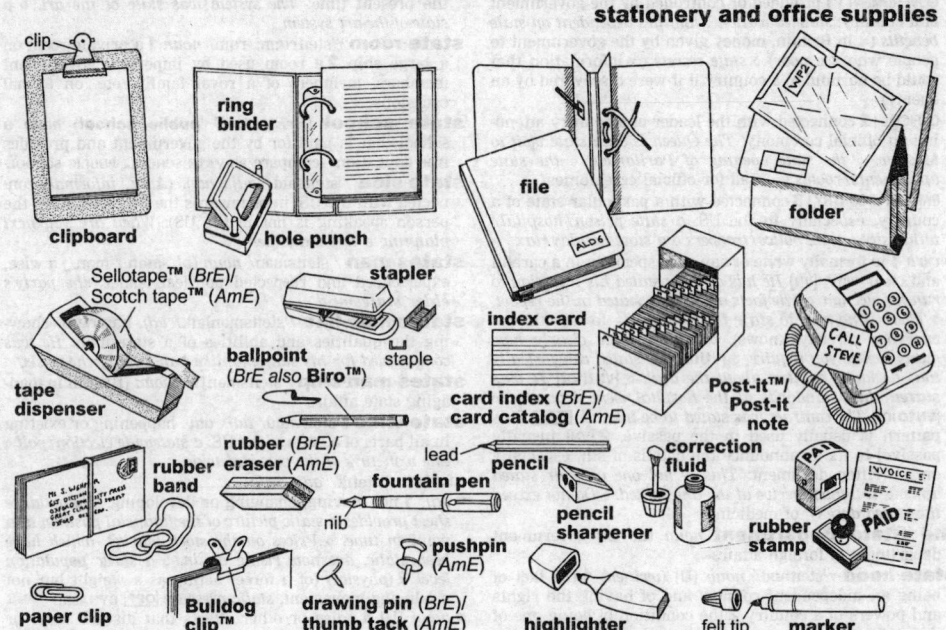

clip

ring binder

file

folder

clipboard

hole punch

Sellotape™ (BrE)/
Scotch tape™ (AmE)

stapler

staple

tape dispenser

ballpoint
(BrE also **Biro™**)

index card

card index (BrE)/
card catalog (AmE)

Post-it™/
Post-it note

CALL STEVE

rubber band

rubber (BrE)/
eraser (AmE)

lead   pencil

correction fluid

fountain pen

nib

pushpin
(AmE)

pencil sharpener

rubber stamp

INVOICE

PAID

paper clip

Bulldog
clip™

drawing pin (BrE)/
thumb tack (AmE)

highlighter

felt tip   **marker**

ˈstation agent noun (AmE) = STATIONMASTER

sta·tion·ary /ˈsteɪʃənri; AmE -neri/ adj. **1** not moving; not intended to be moved: I remained stationary. ◊ The car collided with a stationary vehicle. ◊ a stationary exercise bike OPP MOBILE **2** not changing in condition or quantity: a stationary population

sta·tion·er /ˈsteɪʃənə(r)/ noun (especially BrE) **1** a person who owns or manages a shop selling stationery **2** (**stationer's**) (pl. **stationers**) a shop that sells stationery: Is there a stationer's near here?

sta·tion·ery /ˈsteɪʃənri; AmE -neri/ noun [U] **1** materials for writing and for using in an office, for example paper, pens and envelopes **2** special paper for writing letters on

ˈstation house noun (AmE) = POLICE STATION

sta·tion·mas·ter /ˈsteɪʃnmɑːstə(r); AmE -mæs-/ (BrE) (AmE **ˈstation agent**) noun a person in charge of a train station

ˈstation wagon noun (AmE) = ESTATE CAR

stat·is·tic /stəˈtɪstɪk/ noun **1** (**statistics**) (also informal **stats**) [pl.] a collection of information shown in numbers: crime/unemployment statistics ◊ According to official statistics the disease killed over 500 people. ◊ **Statistics show** that far more people are able to ride a bicycle than can drive a car. ◊ These statistics are misleading.—see also VITAL STATISTICS **2** (**statistics**) (also informal **stats**) [U] the science of collecting and analysing statistics: There is a compulsory course in statistics. **3** [C] a piece of information shown in numbers: An important statistic is that 94 per cent of crime relates to property. ◊ I felt I was no longer being treated as a person but as a statistic. ▶ **stat·is·tic·al** /stəˈtɪstɪkl/ adj.: statistical analysis/methods/data **stat·is·tic·al·ly** /-kli/ adv.: The difference between the two samples was not statistically significant.

stat·is·ti·cian /ˌstætɪˈstɪʃn/ noun a person who studies or works with statistics

stats /stæts/ noun (informal) = STATISTICS

statu·ary /ˈstætʃuəri; AmE -eri/ noun [U] (formal) statues: a collection of marble statuary

statue /ˈstætʃuː/ noun a figure of a person or an animal in stone, metal, etc., usually the same size as in real life or larger

statu·esque /ˌstætʃuˈesk/ adj. (written) (usually used about a woman) tall and beautiful in an impressive way; like a statue

statu·ette /ˌstætʃuˈet/ noun a small statue

stat·ure /ˈstætʃə(r)/ noun [U] (written) **1** the importance and respect that a person has because of their ability and achievements: an actress of considerable stature ◊ The orchestra has grown in stature. **2** a person's height: a woman of short stature ◊ He is small in stature.

sta·tus /ˈsteɪtəs/ noun [U, C, usually sing.] **1** the. legal position of a person, group or country: They were granted refugee status. ◊ The party was denied legal status. **2** [U, C, usually sing.] the social or professional position of sb/sth in relation to others: low status jobs ◊ to have a high social status ◊ Women are only asking to be given equal status with men. ◊ She achieved celebrity status overnight. **3** [U] high rank or social position: The job brings with it status and a high income. **4** [U, C, usually sing.] the level of importance that is given to sth: the high status accorded to science in our culture **5** [U] the situation at a particular time during a process: What is the current status of our application for funds?

sta·tus quo /ˌsteɪtəs ˈkwəʊ; AmE ˈkwoʊ/ noun [sing.] (from Latin) the situation as it is now, or as it was before a recent change: to defend/restore the status quo ◊ conservatives who want to maintain the status quo.

ˈstatus symbol noun a possession that people think shows their high social status and wealth: Exotic pets are the latest status symbol.

stat·ute /ˈstætʃuːt/ noun **1** a law that is passed by a parliament, council, etc. and formally written down: Penalties are laid down in the statute. ◊ Corporal punishment was banned **by statute** in 1987. **2** a formal rule of an organization or institution: Under the statutes of the university they had no power to dismiss him.

ˈstatute book noun a collection of all the laws made by a government: It's not yet **on the statute book** (= it has not yet become law).

ˈstatute law noun [U] all the written laws of a parliament, etc. as a group—compare CASE LAW, COMMON LAW

ˌstatute of limiˈtations noun (law) the legal limit on the period of time within which action can be taken on a crime or other legal question

statu·tory /ˈstætʃətri; AmE -tɔːri/ adj. [usually before noun] fixed by law; that must be done by law: *The authority failed to carry out its statutory duties.* ◊ *When you buy foods you have certain statutory rights.* ▶ **statu·tor·ily** *adv.*

statutory 'offence *noun* (*law*) a crime that is described by law and can be punished by a court

statutory 'rape *noun* [U] (*AmE, law*) the crime of having sex with sb who is not legally old enough

staunch /stɔːntʃ/ *adj., verb*

■ *adj.* (*superlative* **staunch·est**, no *comparative*) strong and loyal in your opinions and attitude: *a staunch supporter of the monarchy* ◊ *one of the president's staunchest allies* ◊ *a staunch Catholic* ▶ **staunch·ly** *adv.*: *She staunchly defended the new policy.* ◊ *The family was staunchly Protestant.* **staunch·ness** *noun* [U]

■ *verb* (also **stanch** /stɔːntʃ; stæntʃ/ especially in *AmE*) [VN] (*formal*) to stop the flow of sth, especially blood

stave /steɪv/ *noun, verb*

■ *noun* **1** a strong stick or pole: *fence staves* **2** (*BrE*) (also **staff** *AmE, BrE*) (*music*) a set of five lines on which music is written—picture at MUSIC

■ *verb* (**staved, staved**) *or* (**stove, stove** /stəʊv; *AmE* stoʊv/) PHRV **stave sth↔'in** to break or damage sth by making part of it fall inwards: *The side of the boat was staved in when it hit the rocks.* **stave sth↔'off** (**staved, staved**) to prevent sth bad from affecting you for a period of time; to delay sb/sth: *to stave off hunger/illness/inflation/bankruptcy* ◊ *The company managed to stave off bankruptcy for another few months.*

stay /steɪ/ *verb, noun*

■ *verb* **1** to continue to be in a particular place for a period of time without moving away: [V] *to stay in bed/in the house/in your room* '*Do you want a drink?*' '*No, thanks, I can't stay.*' ◊ *Stay there and don't move!* ◊ *We ended up staying for lunch.* ◊ *She stayed at home* (= did not go out to work) *while the children were young.* ◊ *I'm **staying late** at the office tonight.* ◊ *My hat won't stay on!* ◊ *Can you **stay behind** after the others have gone and help me clear up?* ◊ *I can stay a few minutes longer.* ◊ *We stayed to see what would happen.* ◊ [V-ing] *They stayed talking until well into the night.* HELP In spoken English **stay** can be used with **and** plus another verb, instead of with **to** and the infinitive, to show purpose or to tell somebody what to do: *I'll stay and help you.* ◊ *Can you stay and keep an eye on the baby?* **2** to continue to be in a particular state or situation: [V-ADJ] *He never stays angry for long.* ◊ *I can't stay awake any longer.* ◊ *The store stays open until late on Thursdays.* ◊ [V+adv./prep.] *I don't know why they stay together* (= remain married or in a relationship). ◊ *Inflation stayed below 4% last month.* ◊ [V-N] *We promised to stay friends for ever.* **3** [V] to live in a place temporarily as a guest or visitor: *We found out we were staying in the same hotel.* ◊ *My sister's coming to stay next week.* ◊ *He's staying with friends this weekend.* ◊ *I stayed three nights at my cousin's house.* HELP In Scottish English, **stay** can mean 'to live in a place permanently': *Where do you stay* (= where do you live)? IDM **be here to 'stay | have come to 'stay** to be accepted or used by most people and therefore a permanent part of our lives: *It looks like televised trials are here to stay.* **stay!** (*spoken*) used to tell a dog not to move **stay the 'course** to continue doing sth until it has finished or been completed, even though it is difficult: *Very few of the trainees have stayed the course.* **stay your 'hand** (*old-fashioned* or *literary*) to stop yourself from doing sth; to prevent you from doing sth **stay the 'night** (*especially BrE*) to sleep at sb's house for one night: *You can always stay the night at our house.* **stay 'put** (*informal*) if sb/sth **stays put**, they continue to be in the place where they are or where they have been put— more at CLEAR *adv.*, LOOSE *adj.* PHRV **stay a'round** (*informal*) to not leave somewhere: *I'll stay around in case you need me.* ◊ *They didn't stay around to be caught.* **stay a'way (from sb/sth)** to not go near a particular person or place: *I want you to stay away from my daughter.* **stay 'in** to not go out or to remain indoors: *I feel like staying in tonight.* **stay 'on** to continue studying, working, etc. somewhere for longer than expected or after other people have left: *She's staying on at university to do research.*

stay 'out 1 to continue to be outdoors or away from your house at night: *I don't like you staying out so late.* **2** (of workers) to continue to be on strike **stay 'out of sth 1** to not become involved in sth that does not concern you: *I wish you'd stay out of my business!* **2** to avoid sth: *to stay out of trouble/sight* **stay 'over** to sleep at sb's house for one night: *We have a spare bed if you want to stay over.* **stay 'up** to go to bed later than usual: *You've got school tomorrow. I don't want you **staying up late**.*

■ *noun* **1** a period of staying; a visit: *I enjoyed my stay in Prague.* ◊ *an overnight stay* **2** a rope or wire that supports a ship's MAST, a pole, etc.—see also MAINSTAY IDM **a 'stay of exe'cution** (*especially law*) a delay in carrying out the order of a court: *to grant a stay of execution*

'stay-at-home *noun* (*informal*, often *disapproving*) a person who rarely goes out or does anything exciting

stay·er /'steɪə(r)/ *noun* (*BrE*) a person or an animal, especially a horse, with the ability to keep going in a tiring race or competition

'staying power *noun* [U] the ability to continue doing sth difficult or tiring until it is finished SYN STAMINA

St Bernard /ˌsnt 'bɜːnəd; *AmE* ˌseɪnt bɜːr'nɑːrd/ *noun* a large strong dog, originally from Switzerland, where it was trained to help find people who were lost in the snow

STD /ˌes tiː 'diː/ *noun* **1** a disease that is passed from one person to another during sexual activity (abbreviation for 'sexually transmitted disease') **2** (*BrE*) a system of making direct telephone calls over long distances (abbreviation for 'subscriber trunk dialling')

stead /sted/ *noun* IDM **in sb's/sth's 'stead** (*formal*) instead of sb/sth: *Foxton was dismissed and John Smith was appointed in his stead.* **stand sb in good 'stead** to be useful or helpful to sb when needed: *Your languages will stand you in good stead when it comes to finding a job.*

stead·fast /'stedfɑːst; *AmE* -fæst/ *adj.* **~ (in sth)** (*literary, approving*) not changing in your attitudes or aims: *steadfast loyalty* ◊ *He remained steadfast in his determination to bring the killers to justice.* ▶ **stead·fast·ly** *adv.* **stead·fast·ness** *noun* [U]

steady /'stedi/ *adj., verb, adv., exclamation*

■ *adj.* (**stead·ier, steadi·est**) **1** developing, growing, etc. gradually and in an even and regular way: *a steady increase/decline in numbers* ◊ *five years of steady economic growth* ◊ *We are making slow but steady progress.* ◊ *The castle receives a **steady stream** of visitors.* **2** not changing and not interrupted SYN REGULAR: *His breathing was steady.* ◊ *a steady job/income* ◊ *She drove at a steady 50 mph* ◊ *They set off at a steady pace.* ◊ *a steady boyfriend/ girlfriend* (= with whom you have a serious relationship or one that has lasted a long time) ◊ *to have a steady relationship* **3** firmly fixed, supported or balanced; not shaking or likely to fall down: *He held the boat steady as she got in.* ◊ *I met his steady gaze.* ◊ *Such fine work requires a steady eye and a **steady hand**.* ◊ *She's not very steady on her feet these days.* OPP UNSTEADY **4** (of a person) sensible; who can be relied on ▶ **stead·ily**: *The company's exports have been increasing steadily.* ◊ *The situation got steadily worse.* ◊ *He looked at her steadily.* ◊ *The rain fell steadily.* **steadi·ness** *noun* [U] IDM **(as) steady as a 'rock** extremely steady and calm; that you can rely on—more at READY *adj.*

■ *verb* (**stead·ies, steady·ing, stead·ied, stead·ied**) **1 ~ (yourself/sb/sth)** to stop yourself/sb/sth from moving, shaking or falling; to stop moving, shaking or falling: [VN] *She steadied herself against the wall.* ◊ [V] *The lift rocked slightly, steadied, and the doors opened.* **2** [V] to stop changing and become regular again: *Her heartbeat steadied.* ◊ *The pound steadied against the dollar.* **3** [VN] to make sb/sth calm: *He took a few deep breaths to steady his nerves.*

■ *adv.* in a way that is steady and does not change or shake: *In trading today the dollar held steady against the yen.* IDM **go 'steady (with sb)** (*old-fashioned, informal*) to have a romantic or sexual relationship with sb, in which you see the other person regularly

■ *exclamation* (*informal*) **1 ~ on** (becoming *old-fashioned*) used to tell sb to be careful about what they are saying or

æ	ɑː	e	ɜː	ə	ɪ	iː	i	ɒ	ɔː	ʌ	ʊ	u	uː
cat	father	ten	bird	about	sit	see	many	got	saw	cup	put	actual	too
								(BrE)					

doing, for example because it is extreme or not appropriate: *Steady on! You can't say things like that about somebody you've never met.* **2** used to tell sb to be careful: *Steady! You're going to fall off that wall if you're not careful.*

steak /steɪk/ *noun* **1** (also *less frequent* **beef-steak**) [U, C] a thick slice of good quality beef: *fillet/rump/sirloin steak* ◊ *How would you like your steak done?* ◊ *a steak knife* (= one with a special blade for eating steak with)— picture at CUTLERY **2** [U, C] a thick slice of any type of meat: *pork steak* ◊ *a gammon steak* **3** [U] (often in compounds) beef that is not of the best quality, often sold in small pieces and used in pies, STEWS, etc: *braising/stewing steak* ◊ *a steak and kidney pie* **4** [C] a large thick piece of fish: *a cod/salmon steak*

steal /stiːl/ *verb, noun*
■ *verb* (**stole** /stəʊl; *AmE* stoʊl/ **stolen** /ˈstəʊlən; *AmE* ˈstoʊ-/) **1** ~ (**sth**) (**from sb/sth**) to take sth from a person, shop/store, etc. without permission and without intending to return it or pay for it: [V] *We found out he'd been stealing from us for years.* ◊ *I'll report you to the police if I catch you stealing again.* ◊ [VN] *My wallet was stolen.* ◊ *I had my wallet stolen.* ◊ *Thieves stole jewellery worth over £10000.* ◊ *It's a crime to handle stolen goods.* ◊ (*figurative*) *to steal sb's ideas* [V+adv./prep.] **2** to move secretly and quietly so that other people do not notice you: *She stole out of the room so as not to wake the baby.* ◊ (*figurative*) *A chill stole over her body.* **3** [VN] (in baseball) to run to the next BASE before another player from your team hits the ball, so that you are closer to scoring: *He tried to steal second base but was out.* **IDM** **steal a ˈglance/ˈlook (at sb/sth)** (*written*) to look at sb/sth quickly so that nobody sees you doing it **steal sb's ˈheart** (*literary*) to make sb fall in love with you **steal a ˈkiss (from sb)** (*literary*) to kiss sb suddenly or secretly **steal a ˈmarch (on sb)** [no passive] (*written*) to gain an advantage over sb by doing sth before them: *The company is looking at ways to steal a march on its European competitors.* **steal the ˈshow** [no passive] to attract more attention and praise than other people in a particular situation: *As always, the children stole the show.* **steal sb's ˈthunder** to get the attention, success, etc. that sb else was expecting, usually by saying or doing what they had intended to say or do
■ *noun* (*AmE*) (in baseball) the act of running to another BASE while the PITCHER is throwing the ball **IDM** **be a ˈsteal** (*especially AmE*) to be for sale at an unexpectedly low price: *This suit is a steal at $80.*

stealth /stelθ/ *noun, adj.*
■ *noun* [U] the fact of doing sth in a quiet or secret way: *The government was accused of trying to introduce the tax by stealth.* ◊ *Lions rely on stealth when hunting.*
■ *adj.* [only before noun] (of an aircraft) designed in a way that makes it difficult to be discovered by RADAR: *a stealth bomber*

stealthy /ˈstelθi/ *adj.* doing things quietly or secretly; done quietly or secretly: *a stealthy animal* ◊ *a stealthy movement* ▶ **stealth-ily** /-ɪli/ *adv.*

steam /stiːm/ *noun, verb*
■ *noun* [U] **1** the hot gas that water changes into when it boils: *Steam rose from the boiling kettle.* **2** the power that is produced from steam under pressure, used to operate engines, machines, etc: *the introduction of steam in the 18th century* ◊ *steam power* ◊ *the steam age* ◊ *a steam train/engine* **3** very small drops of water that form in the air or on cold surfaces when warm air suddenly cools: *She wiped the steam from her glasses.* **IDM** **full speed/steam aˈhead** with as much speed or energy as possible **ˌget up/ˌpick up ˈsteam 1** (*informal*) to become gradually more powerful, active, etc: *His election campaign is beginning to get up steam.* **2** (of a vehicle) to increase speed gradually **ˌlet off ˈsteam** (*informal*) to get rid of your energy, anger or strong emotions by doing sth active or noisy: *I went for a long walk to let off steam.* **ˌrun out of ˈsteam** (*informal*) to lose energy and enthusiasm and stop doing sth, or do it less well **get, etc. somewhere under your own ˈsteam** (*BrE, informal*) to go somewhere without help from other people: *I'll get to the party under my own steam.*

■ *verb* **1** [V] to send out steam: *Our damp clothes steamed in the heat.* ◊ *a mug of steaming hot coffee* **2** to place food over boiling water so that it cooks in the steam; to be cooked in this way: [VN] *steamed fish/vegetables* [also V] ⇨ vocabulary notes on page 274 **3** [V+adv./prep.] (of a boat, ship, etc.) to move using the power produced by steam: *The boat steamed across the lake.* **4** [V+adv./prep.] (especially of a person) to go somewhere very quickly: *He spotted her steaming down the corridor towards him.* ◊ (*figurative*) *The company is steaming ahead with its investment programme.* **IDM** **be/get (all) steamed ˈup (about/over sth)** (*BrE*) (*AmE* **be ˈsteamed (about sth)**) (*informal*) to be/become very angry or excited about sth: *You're getting all steamed up about nothing!* **PHR V** **ˌsteam sth↔ˈoff | ˌsteam sth ˈoff sth** to remove one piece of paper from another using steam to soften the glue that is holding them together **ˌsteam sth↔ˈopen** to open an envelope using steam to soften the glue **ˌsteam ˈup | ˌsteam sth↔ˈup** to become, or to make sth become, covered with steam: *As he walked in, his glasses steamed up.*

steam-boat /ˈstiːmbəʊt; *AmE* -boʊt/ *noun* a boat driven by steam, used especially in the past on rivers and along coasts

steam-er /ˈstiːmə(r)/ *noun* **1** a boat or ship driven by steam—see also PADDLE STEAMER **2** a metal container with small holes in it, that is placed over a pan of boiling water in order to cook food in the steam—picture at PAN

steam-roll-er /ˈstiːmrəʊlə(r); *AmE* -roʊ-/ *noun, verb*
■ *noun* a large slow vehicle with a ROLLER used for making roads flat
■ *verb* (*AmE usually* **ˈsteam roll**) to defeat sb or force them to do sth, using your power or authority: [VN] *The team steamrollered their way to victory.* ◊ *She knew that she'd let herself be steamrollered.* [also V]

aɪ	aʊ	eɪ	əʊ	oʊ	ɔɪ	ɪə	eə	ʊə	j	w
my	now	say	go (BrE)	go (AmE)	boy	near	hair	pure	yes	wet

steam·ship /ˈstiːmʃɪp/ *noun* (*abbr.* **SS**) a ship driven by steam

steamy /ˈstiːmi/ *adj.* **1** full of steam; covered with steam: *a steamy bathroom* ◊ *steamy windows* ◊ *the steamy heat of Tokyo* **2** (*informal*) sexually exciting [SYN] EROTIC: *a steamy love scene*

steed /stiːd/ *noun* (*literary* or *humorous*) a horse to ride on

steel /stiːl/ *noun, verb*
■ *noun* [U] **1** a strong hard metal that is made of a mixture of iron and CARBON: *the iron and steel industry* ◊ *The frame is made of steel.* ◊ *The bridge is reinforced with huge steel girders.*—see also STAINLESS STEEL **2** the industry that produces steel: *Steel used to be important in South Wales.* ◊ *steel workers* ◊ *a steel town* **3** (*old use* or *literary*) weapons that are used for fighting: *the clash of steel* [IDM] **of 'steel** having a quality like steel, especially a strong, cold or hard quality: *She felt a hand of steel* (= a strong, firm hand) *on her arm.* ◊ *You need a cool head and **nerves of steel*** (= great courage). ◊ *There was a hint of steel in his voice* (= he sounded cold and firm).
■ *verb* ~ **yourself** (**for/against sth**) to prepare yourself to deal with sth unpleasant: [VN] *As she waited, she steeled herself for disappointment.* ◊ [VN to inf] *He steeled himself to tell them the truth.*

steel 'band *noun* a group of musicians who play music on drums that are made from empty metal oil containers. Steel bands originally came from the West Indies.

steel 'wool (*BrE* also **wire 'wool**) *noun* [U] a mass of fine steel threads that you use for cleaning pots and pans, making surfaces smooth, etc.

steel·work·er /ˈstiːlwɜːkə(r); *AmE* -wɜːrk-/ *noun* a person who works in a place where steel is made

steel·works /ˈstiːlwɜːks; *AmE* -wɜːrks/ *noun* (*pl.* **steel-works**) [C+sing./pl. *v.*] a factory where steel is made

steely /ˈstiːli/ *adj.* **1** (of a person's character or behaviour) strong, hard and unfriendly: *a cold, steely voice* ◊ *a look of steely determination* **2** like steel in colour: *steely blue eyes* ◊ *The sky was cold and steely.* ► **steeli·ness** *noun* [U]

steep /stiːp/ *adj., verb*
■ *adj.* (**steep·er, steep·est**) **1** (of a slope, hill, etc.) rising or falling quickly, not gradually: *a steep hill/slope/bank* ◊ *a steep climb/descent/drop* ◊ *a steep flight of stairs* ◊ *The path grew steeper as we climbed higher.* **2** [usually before noun] (of a rise or fall in an amount) sudden and very big: *a steep decline in the birth rate* ◊ *a steep rise in unemployment* **3** (*informal*) (of a price or demand) too much; unreasonable: *£2 for a cup of coffee seems a little steep to me.* ► **steep·ly** *adv.*: *a steeply sloping roof* ◊ *The path climbed steeply upwards.* ◊ *Prices rose steeply.* **steep·ness** *noun* [U]
■ *verb* [IDM] **be 'steeped in sth** (*written*) to have a lot of a particular quality: *a city steeped in history* [PHRV] **'steep sth in sth** to put food in a liquid and leave it for some time so that it becomes soft and flavoured by the liquid **'steep yourself in sth** (*written*) to spend a lot of time thinking or learning about sth: *They spent a month steeping themselves in Chinese culture.*

steep·en /ˈstiːpən/ *verb* to become or to make sth become steeper: [V] *After a couple of miles, the slope steepened considerably.* [also VN]

steeple /ˈstiːpl/ *noun* a tall pointed tower on the roof of a church, often with a SPIRE on it

steeple·chase /ˈstiːpltʃeɪs/ (also **chase**) *noun* **1** a long race in

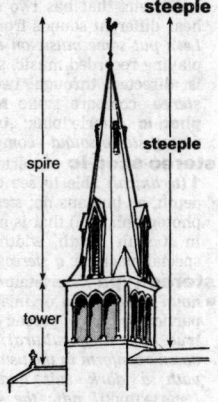

which horses have to jump over fences, water, etc.—compare FLAT RACING **2** a long race in which people run and jump over gates and water, etc. around a track

steeple·chaser /ˈstiːpltʃeɪsə(r)/ *noun* a horse or a person that takes part in steeplechases

steeple·jack /ˈstiːpldʒæk/ *noun* a person whose job is painting or repairing towers, tall chimneys, etc.

steer /stɪə(r); *AmE* stɪr/ *verb, noun*
■ *verb* **1** to control the direction in which a boat, car, etc. moves: [VN] *He steered the boat into the harbour.* ◊ (*figurative*) *He took her arm and steered her towards the door.* ◊ [V] *You row and I'll steer.* **2** (of a boat, car, etc.) to move in a particular direction: [VN] *The ship steered a course between the islands.* ◊ [V] *The ship steered into port.* **3** [VN+adv./prep.] to take control of a situation and influence the way in which it develops: *He managed to steer the conversation away from his divorce.* ◊ *She steered the team to victory.* ◊ *The skill is in steering a middle course between the two extremes.* [IDM] see CLEAR *adv.*
■ *noun* a BULL (= a male cow) that has been CASTRATED (= had part of its sex organs removed), kept for its meat—compare BULLOCK, OX

steer·age /ˈstɪərɪdʒ; *AmE* ˈstɪr-/ *noun* [U] (in the past) the part of a ship where passengers with the cheapest tickets used to travel: *steerage passengers*

steer·ing /ˈstɪərɪŋ; *AmE* ˈstɪr-/ *noun* [U] the mechanism of a vehicle that you use to control the direction it goes in—see also POWER STEERING

'steering column *noun* the part of a car or other vehicle that the STEERING WHEEL is fitted on

'steering committee, 'steering group *noun* a group of people that a government or an organization chooses to direct an activity and to decide how it will be done

'steering wheel *noun* the wheel that the driver turns to control the direction that a vehicle goes in—picture at CAR

stel·lar /ˈstelə(r)/ *adj.* [usually before noun] **1** (*technical*) connected with the stars—compare INTERSTELLAR **2** (*informal*) excellent: *a stellar performance/career*

stem /stem/ *noun, verb*
■ *noun* **1** the main long thin part of a plant above the ground from which the leaves or flowers grow; a smaller part that grows from this and supports flowers or leaves: *long, trailing stems of ivy* ◊ *a tall plant with branching stems*—picture at PLANT **2** the long thin part of a wine glass between the bowl and the base—picture at GLASS **3** the thin tube of a tobacco pipe **4** (**-stemmed**) (in adjectives) having one or more stems of the type mentioned: *a long-stemmed rose* ◊ *slender-stemmed wine glasses* **5** (*grammar*) the main part of a word that stays the same when endings are added to it: *'Writ' is the stem of the forms 'writes', 'writing' and 'written'.* [IDM] **from ˌstem to 'stern** all the way from the front of a ship to the back
■ *verb* (**-mm-**) [VN] to stop sth that is flowing from spreading or increasing: *The cut was bandaged to stem the bleeding.* ◊ *They discussed ways of stemming the flow of smuggled drugs.* ◊ *The government had failed to stem the tide of factory closures.* [PHRV] **'stem from sth** (not used in the progressive tenses) to be the result of sth: *Most people's insecurities stem from something that happened in their childhood.*

stench /stentʃ/ *noun* [sing.] a strong, very unpleasant smell: *an overpowering stench of rotting fish* ◊ (*figurative*) *The stench of treachery hung in the air.*

sten·cil /ˈstensl/ *noun, verb*
■ *noun* a thin piece of metal, plastic or card with a design cut out of it, that you put onto a surface and paint over so that the design is left on the surface; the pattern or design that is produced in this way—picture at FRIEZE
■ *verb* (**-ll-**, *AmE* also **-l-**) [VN, V] to make letters or a design on sth using a stencil

steno /ˈstenəʊ; *AmE* -noʊ/ *noun* (*pl.* **-os**) (*AmE, informal*) **1** [C] = STENOGRAPHER **2** [U] = STENOGRAPHY

sten·og·raph·er /stəˈnɒɡrəfə(r); *AmE* -ˈnɑːɡ-/ (also *informal* **steno**) *noun* (*especially AmE*) a person whose

Figure labels (on illustration): steeple, steeple, spire, tower

S

job is to write down what sb else says, using a quick system of signs or abbreviations

sten·og·ra·phy /stəˈnɒgrəfi; *AmE* -ˈnɑːg-/ (also *informal* **steno**) *noun* [U] (*AmE*) = SHORTHAND

sten·tor·ian /stenˈtɔːriən/ *adj.* (*formal*) (of a voice) loud and powerful

step /step/ *noun, verb*

■ *noun*

MOVEMENT/SOUND | **1** [C] the act of lifting your foot and putting it down in order to walk or move somewhere; the sound this makes: *a baby's first steps* ◇ *He took a step towards the door.* ◇ *We heard steps outside.*—see also FOOTSTEP, GOOSE-STEP

WAY OF WALKING | **2** [C, usually sing.] the way that sb walks: *He walked with a quick light step.*

DISTANCE | **3** [C] the distance that you cover when you take a step: *It's only a few steps further.* ◇ *He turned around and retraced his steps* (= went back the way he had come). ◇ *She moved a step closer to me.* ◇ *The hotel is only a short step from the beach.*

IN SERIES/PROCESS | **4** [C] one of a series of things that you do in order to achieve sth: *This was a first step towards a united Europe.* ◇ *We are taking steps to prevent pollution.* ◇ *This won't solve the problem but it's a step in the right direction.* ◇ *The new drug is a major step forward in the treatment of the disease.* **5** [C] one of a series of things that sb does or that happen, which forms part of a process SYN STAGE: *Having completed the first stage, you can move on to step 2.* ◇ *I'd like to take this idea a step further.* ◇ *This was a big step up* (= to a better position) *in his career.* ◇ *I'll explain it to you step by step.* ◇ *a step-by-step guide to building your own home*

STAIR | **6** [C] a surface that you put your foot on in order to walk to a higher or lower level, especially one of a series: *She was sitting on the bottom step of the staircase.* ◇ *We walked down some stone steps to the beach.* ◇ *A short flight of steps led up to the door.*—see also DOORSTEP

IN DANCE | **7** [C, usually pl.] a series of movements that you make with your feet and which form a dance: *Do you know the steps of this dance?*—see also QUICKSTEP

EXERCISE | **8** [U] (often in compounds) a type of exercise that you do by stepping on and off a raised piece of equipment: *step aerobics* ◇ *a step class*

LADDER | **9** (**steps**) [pl.] (*BrE*) = STEPLADDER: *a pair of steps* ◇ *We need the steps to get into the attic.*

IN MUSIC | **10** [C] (*AmE*) the interval between two notes that are next to each other in a scale—compare TONE (7), SEMITONE

IDM **break 'step** to change the way you are walking so that you do not walk in the same rhythm as the people you are walking or marching with **fall into 'step (beside/with sb)** (*written*) to change the way you are walking so that you start walking in the same rhythm as the person you are walking with: *He caught her up and fell into step beside her.* **in/out of 'step (with sb/sth)** **1** putting your feet on the ground in the right/wrong way, according to the rhythm of the music or the people you are moving with: *I found myself marching in step with the music.* **2** having ideas that are the same as or different from other people's: *She was out of step with her colleagues.* **mind/watch your 'step 1** to walk carefully **2** to behave in a careful and sensible way: *You'd better watch your step with him if you don't want trouble.* **a/one step a'head (of sb/sth)** when you are one step ahead of sb/sth, you manage to avoid them or to achieve sth more quickly than they do

■ *verb* (**-pp-**) [V+adv./prep.] to lift your foot and move it in a particular direction or put it on or in sth; to move a short distance: *to step onto/off a bus* ◇ *I stepped forward when my name was called out.* ◇ *She stepped aside to let them pass.* ◇ *We stepped carefully over the broken glass.* ◇ *I turned around quickly and stepped on his toes.* ◇ *She opened the door and stepped out into the sunshine.* ◇ (*figurative*) *Going into the hotel is like stepping back in time.*

IDM **step into the 'breach** to do sb's job or work when they are suddenly or unexpectedly unable to do it **step into sb's 'shoes** to continue a job or the work that sb

else has started **'step on it** (*spoken*) used especially in orders to tell sb to drive faster **step on sb's 'toes** (*AmE*) = TREAD ON SB'S TOES at TOE *n.* **step out of 'line | be/get out of 'line** to behave badly or break the rules

PHR V **step 'back (from sth)** to think about a situation calmly, as if you are not involved in it yourself: *We are learning to step back from ourselves and identify our strengths and weaknesses.* **step a'side/'down** to leave an important job or position and let sb else take your place **step 'forward** to offer to help sb or give information **step 'in** to help sb in a dispute or difficult situation: *A local businessman stepped in with a large donation for the school.* ◇ *The team coach was forced to step in to stop the two athletes from coming to blows.* **step 'out** (*especially AmE*) to go out: *I'm just going to step out for a few minutes.* **step 'up** to come forward: *She stepped up to receive her prize.* **step sth ⟷ 'up** to increase the amount, speed, etc. of sth: *He has stepped up his training to prepare for the race.*

step- /step-/ *combining form* (in nouns) related as a result of one parent marrying again: *stepmother*

step·brother /ˈstepbrʌðə(r)/ *noun* the son from an earlier marriage of your STEPMOTHER or STEPFATHER—compare HALF-BROTHER

step·child /ˈsteptʃaɪld/ *noun* (*pl.* **step·chil·dren** /-tʃɪldrən/) a child of your husband or wife by an earlier marriage

step·daugh·ter /ˈstepdɔːtə(r)/ *noun* a daughter that your husband or wife has from an earlier marriage to another person

step·father /ˈstepfɑːðə(r)/ *noun* the man who is married to your mother but who is not your real father

step·lad·der /ˈsteplædə(r)/ *noun* a short ladder that is made of two parts, one with steps, that are joined together at the top, so that it can stand on its own or be folded flat for carrying or storing

step·mother /ˈstepmʌðə(r)/ *noun* the woman who is married to your father but who is not your real mother

'step-parent *noun* a stepmother or stepfather

steppe /step/ *noun* [C, usually pl., U] a large area of land with grass but few trees, especially in SE Europe and Siberia: *the vast Russian steppes*

'stepping stone *noun* **1** one of a line of flat stones that you step on in order to cross a stream or river **2** something that allows you to make progress or begin to achieve sth: *a stepping stone to a more lucrative career*

step·sis·ter /ˈstepsɪstə(r)/ *noun* the daughter from an earlier marriage of your STEPMOTHER or STEPFATHER—compare HALF-SISTER

step·son /ˈstepsʌn/ *noun* a son that your husband or wife has from an earlier marriage to another person

-ster *suffix* (in nouns) a person who is connected with or has the quality of: *gangster* ◇ *youngster*

stereo /ˈsteriəʊ; *AmE* -oʊ/ *noun* (*pl.* **-os**) **1** (also **'stereo system**) [C] a machine that plays CDs or cassettes, or a radio, etc. that has two separate SPEAKERS so that you hear different sounds from each: *a car/personal stereo* ◇ *Let's put some music on the stereo.* **2** [U] the system for playing recorded music, speech, etc. in which the sound is directed through two channels: *to broadcast in stereo*—compare MONO ▶ **stereo** (also *formal* **stereo·phon·ic** /ˌsteriəˈfɒnɪk; *AmE* -ˈfɑːnɪk/) *adj.* [only before noun]: *stereo sound*—compare QUADRAPHONIC

stereo·scop·ic /ˌsteriəˈskɒpɪk; *AmE* -ˈskɑːpɪk/ *adj.* **1** (*technical*) able to see objects with length, width and depth, as humans do: *stereoscopic vision* **2** (of a picture, photograph, etc.) that is made so that you see the objects in it with length, width, and depth when you use a special machine: *a stereoscopic image/photograph*

stereo·type /ˈsteriətaɪp/ *noun, verb*

■ *noun* a fixed idea or image that many people have of a particular type of person or thing, but which is often not true in reality: *cultural/gender/racial stereotypes* ◇ *He doesn't conform to the usual stereotype of the businessman with a dark suit and briefcase.* ▶ **stereo·typ·ical** /ˌsteriəˈtɪpɪkl/ *adj.*: *the stereotypical image of feminine behaviour*

s	t	v	z	ʃ	ʒ	tʃ	dʒ	θ	ð	ŋ
see	tea	van	zoo	shoe	vision	chain	jam	thin	this	sing

■ *verb* [VN] [often passive] ~ *sb* (**as sth**) to form a fixed idea about a person or thing which may not really be true: *Children from certain backgrounds tend to be stereotyped by their teachers.* ◇ *Why are professors stereotyped as absent-minded?* ▶ **stereo·type** *adj.*: *a play full of stereotyped characters* **stereo·typ·ing** *noun* [U]: *sexual stereotyping*

ster·ile /'steraɪl; *AmE* 'sterəl/ *adj.* **1** (of humans or animals) not able to produce children or young animals [SYN] INFERTILE—compare FERTILE **2** completely clean and free from bacteria: *sterile bandages/equipment* ◇ *sterile water* **3** (of a discussion, an argument, etc.) not producing any useful result: *a sterile debate* **4** lacking individual personality, imagination or new ideas: *The room felt cold and sterile.* ◇ *He felt creatively and emotionally sterile.* **5** (of land) not good enough to produce crops ▶ **ster·il·ity** /stə'rɪləti/ *noun* [U]: *The disease can cause sterility in men and women.* ◇ *the meaningless sterility of statistics*

ster·il·ize (*BrE* also **-ise**) /'sterəlaɪz/ *verb* [VN] **1** [often passive] to kill the bacteria in sth: *to sterilize surgical instruments* ◇ *sterilized milk/water* **2** [usually passive] to make a person or an animal unable to have babies, especially by removing or blocking their sex organs ▶ **ster·il·iza·tion**, **-isa·tion** /ˌsterəlaɪ'zeɪʃn; *AmE* -lə'z-/ *noun* [U, C] **ster·il·iz·ing**, **-is·ing** *adj.* [only before noun]: *sterilizing fluid/tablets*

ster·il·izer (*BrE* also **-iser**) /'sterəlaɪzə(r)/ *noun* a machine or piece of equipment that you use to make objects or substances completely clean and free from bacteria

ster·ling /'stɜːlɪŋ; *AmE* 'stɜːrlɪŋ/ *noun, adj.*
■ *noun* [U] the money system of Britain, based on the pound: *the value of sterling* ◇ *You can be paid in pounds sterling or American dollars.*
■ *adj.* [usually before noun] (*formal*) of excellent quality: *He has done **sterling work** on the finance committee.*

ˌsterling 'silver *noun* [U] silver of a particular standard of PURITY

stern /stɜːn; *AmE* stɜːrn/ *adj., noun*
■ *adj.* (**stern·er**, **stern·est**) **1** serious and often disapproving; expecting sb to obey you: *a stern face/expression/look* ◇ *a stern warning* ◇ *Her voice was stern.* ◇ *The police are planning sterner measures to combat crime.* **2** serious and difficult: *a stern test of nerves* ◇ *We face stern opposition.* ▶ **stern·ly** *adv.* **stern·ness** *noun* [U] [IDM] **be made of sterner 'stuff** to have a stronger character and to be more determined in dealing with problems than other people
■ *noun* the back end of a ship or boat: *to stand in/on/at the stern*—compare BOW¹ *n.*, POOP—picture at BOAT, YACHT [IDM] see STEM *n.*

ster·num /'stɜːnəm; *AmE* 'stɜːrnəm/ *noun* (*pl.* **ster·nums** or **sterna** /-nə/) (*anatomy*) the BREASTBONE

ster·oid /'steroɪd; *BrE* also 'stɪər-; *AmE* also 'stɪr-/ *noun* a chemical substance produced naturally in the body. There are several different steroids and they can be used to treat various diseases and are also sometimes used illegally by people playing sports to improve their performance.

stetho·scope /'steθəskəʊp; *AmE* -skoʊp/ *noun* an instrument that a doctor uses to listen to sb's heart and breathing

stet·son (*BrE*) (*AmE* **Stetson**™) /'stetsn/ *noun* a tall hat with a wide BRIM, worn especially by American COWBOYS

steve·dore /'stiːvədɔː(r)/ *noun* a person whose job is moving goods on and off ships—see also DOCKER

stew /stjuː; *AmE* stuː/ *noun, verb*
■ *noun* [U, C] a dish of meat and vegetables cooked slowly in liquid in a container that has a lid: *beef stew and dumplings* ◇ *I'm making a stew for lunch.* [IDM] **get (yourself)/be in a 'stew (about/over sth)** (*informal*) to become/feel very anxious or upset about sth: *There's no point getting in a stew about it.*
■ *verb* **1** to cook sth slowly, or allow sth to cook slowly, in liquid in a closed dish: [VN] *stewed apples* ◇ [V] *The meat needs to stew for two hours.*—see also STEWED **2** [V] (usually +*adv./prep.*) to think or worry about sth: *I've been*

stewing over the problem for a while. ◇ *Leave him to stew.* [IDM] **let sb stew in their own 'juice** (*informal*) to leave sb to worry and suffer the unpleasant effects of their own actions

stew·ard /'stjuːəd; *AmE* 'stuːərd/ *noun* **1** a man whose job is to take care of passengers on a ship, an aircraft or a train and who brings them meals, etc: *a ship's steward* **2** a person employed to manage another person's property, especially a large house or land **3** (*BrE*) a person who helps to organize a large public event, for example, a race, public meeting, etc. **4** (*BrE*) a person whose job is to arrange for the supply of food to a college, club, etc.—see also SHOP STEWARD

stew·ard·ess /ˌstjuːə'des; 'stjuːə-; *AmE* 'stuːərdəs/ *noun* **1** = AIR HOSTESS **2** a woman whose job is to take care of the passengers on a ship or train

stew·ard·ship /'stjuːədʃɪp; *AmE* 'stuːərdʃɪp/ *noun* [U] (*formal*) the act of taking care of or managing sth, for example, property, an organization, money or valuable objects: *The organization certainly prospered under his stewardship.*

stewed /stjuːd; *AmE* stuːd/ *adj.* (of tea) tasting too strong and bitter because it has been left in the pot too long

stick /stɪk/ *verb, noun*
■ *verb* (**stuck, stuck** /stʌk/)
PUSH STH IN | **1** [+*adv./prep.*] to push sth, usually a sharp object, into sth; to be pushed into sth: [VN] *The nurse stuck the needle into my arm.* ◇ *Don't stick your fingers through the bars of the cage.* ◇ [V] *I found a nail sticking in the tyre.*
ATTACH | **2** [+*adv./prep.*] to fix sth to sth else, usually with a sticky substance; to become fixed to sth in this way: [VN] *He stuck a stamp on the envelope.* ◇ *We used glue to stick the broken pieces together.* ◇ *I stuck the photos into an album.* ◇ [V] *Her wet clothes were sticking to her body.* ◇ *The glue's useless—the pieces just won't stick.*
PUT | **3** [VN+*adv./prep.*] (*informal*) to put sth in a place, especially quickly or carelessly: *Stick your bags down there.* ◇ *He stuck his hands in his pockets and strolled off.* ◇ *Can you stick this on the noticeboard?* ◇ *Peter stuck his head around the door and said, 'Coffee, anyone?'* ◇ (*spoken*) *Stick 'em up!* (= put your hands above your head—I have a gun)
BECOME FIXED | **4** [V] ~ (**in sth**) to become fixed in one position and impossible to move: *The key has stuck in the lock.* ◇ *This drawer keeps sticking.*
DIFFICULT SITUATION | **5** (*BrE, informal*) (usually used in negative sentences and questions) to accept a difficult or unpleasant situation or person: [VN] *I don't know how you stick that job.* ◇ *They're always arguing—I can't stick it any longer.* ◇ *The problem is, my mother can't stick my boyfriend.* ◇ [V-*ing*] *John can't stick living with his parents.*
BECOME ACCEPTED | **6** [V] to become accepted: *The police couldn't **make the charges stick** (= show them to be true).* ◇ *His friends called him Bart and **the name has stuck** (= has become the name that everyone calls him).*
IN CARD GAMES | **7** [V] to not take any more cards—see also STUCK
[IDM] **stick in your 'mind** (of a memory, an image, etc.) to be remembered for a long time: *One of his paintings in particular sticks in my mind.* **stick in your 'throat/'craw** (*informal*) **1** (of words) to be difficult or impossible to say **2** (of a situation) to be difficult or impossible to accept; to make you angry **stick your 'neck out** (*informal*) to do or say sth when there is a risk that you may be wrong **stick to your 'guns** (*informal*) to refuse to change your mind about sth even when other people are trying to persuade you that you are wrong—more at BOOT *n.*, FINGER *n.*, KNIFE *n.*, MILE, NOSE *n.*, OAR, SORE *adj.*, TELL
[PHR V] ˌstick a'round (*informal*) to stay in a place, waiting for sth to happen or for sb to arrive: *Stick around; we'll need you to help us later.* 'stick at sth to work in a serious and determined way to achieve sth: *If you want to play an instrument well, you've got to stick at it.* 'stick by sb [no passive] to be loyal to a person and support them, especially in a difficult situation: *Her husband was*

æ	ɑː	e	ɜː	ə	ɪ	iː	i	ɒ	ɔː	ʌ	ʊ	u	uː
cat	father	ten	bird	about	sit	see	many	got	saw	cup	put	actual	too
								(BrE)					

S

charged with fraud but she stuck by him. **'stick by sth** [no passive] to do what you promised or planned to do: *They stuck by their decision.* **,stick sth↔'down** (*informal*) to write sth somewhere: *I think I'll stick my name down on the list.* **,stick 'out** to be noticeable or easily seen: *They wrote the notice in big red letters so that it would stick out.* **,stick 'out (of sth)| ,stick sth↔'out (of sth)** to be further out than sth else or come through a hole; to push sth further out than sth else or through a hole: *His ears stick out.* ◊ *She stuck her tongue out at me.* ◊ *Don't stick your arm out of the car window.* **,stick it/sth 'out** (*informal*) to continue doing sth to the end, even when it is difficult or boring: *She didn't like the course but she stuck it out to get the certificate.* **,stick 'out for sth** (*informal*) to refuse to give up until you get what you need or want: *They are sticking out for a higher pay rise.* **'stick to sth 1** to continue doing sth in spite of difficulties: *She finds it impossible to stick to a diet.* **2** to continue doing or using sth and not want to change it: *He promised to help us and he stuck to his word* (= he did as he had promised). ◊ *'Shall we meet on Friday this week?' 'No, let's stick to Saturday.'* ◊ *She stuck to her story.* **,stick to'gether** (*informal*) (of people) to stay together and support each other **,stick 'up** to point upwards or be above a surface: *The branch was sticking up out of the water.* **,stick 'up for sb/yourself/sth** [no passive] to support or defend sb/yourself/sth: *Stick up for what you believe.* ◊ *She taught her children to stick up for themselves at school.* ◊ *Don't worry—I'll stick up for you.* **'stick with sb/sth** [no passive] (*informal*) **1** to stay close to sb so that they can help you **2** to continue with sth or continue doing sth: *They decided to stick with their original plan.*

■ *noun*

FROM TREE | **1** [C] a thin piece of wood that has fallen or been broken from a tree: *We collected dry sticks to start a fire.* ◊ *The boys were throwing sticks and stones at the dog.* ◊ *Her arms and legs were like sticks* (= very thin).

FOR WALKING | **2** [C] (*especially BrE*) = WALKING STICK: *The old lady leant on her stick as she talked.*—see also SHOOTING STICK

IN SPORT | **3** [C] a long thin object that is used in some sports to hit or control the ball: *a hockey stick*

LONG THIN PIECE | **4** [C] (often in compounds) a long thin piece of sth: *a stick of dynamite* ◊ *carrot sticks* ◊ (*AmE*) *a stick of butter*—picture at PACKAGING—see also FRENCH STICK **5** [C] (often in compounds) a thin piece of wood or plastic that you use for a particular purpose: *pieces of pineapple on sticks* ◊ *The men were carrying spades and measuring sticks.*—see also CHOPSTICK, COCKTAIL STICK, DRUMSTICK, MATCHSTICK, YARDSTICK

OF GLUE, etc. | **6** [C] a quantity of a substance, such as solid glue, that is sold in a small container with round ends and straight sides, and can be pushed further out of the container as it is used—see also LIPSTICK

IN PLANE/VEHICLE | **7** [C] (*informal, especially AmE*) the control stick of a plane—see also JOYSTICK **8** [C] (*informal, especially AmE*) a handle used to change the GEARS of a vehicle—see also GEAR LEVER, STICK SHIFT

FOR ORCHESTRA | **9** [C] a BATON, used by the person who CONDUCTS an orchestra

CRITICISM | **10** [U] (*BrE, informal*) criticism or harsh words: *The referee got a lot of stick from the home fans.*

COUNTRY AREAS | **11** (**the sticks**) [pl.] (*informal*) country areas, a long way from cities: *We live out in the sticks.*

PERSON | **12** [C] (*old-fashioned, BrE, informal*) a person: *He's not such a bad old stick.*

HELP There are many other compounds ending in **stick**. You will find them at their place in the alphabet. **IDM** see BEAT *v.*, BIG *adj.*, CARROT, CLEFT *adj.*, SHORT *n.*, UP *v.*, WRONG *adj.*

stick·er /'stɪkə(r)/ *noun* a sticky label with a picture or message on it, that you stick on to sth: *window/car/bumper stickers*

'stick figure *noun* (*AmE*) = MATCHSTICK FIGURE

'sticking plaster *noun* (*BrE*) = PLASTER

'sticking point *noun* something that people do not agree on and that prevents progress in a discussion: *This was one of the major sticking points in the negotiations.*

'stick insect *noun* a large insect with a long thin body that looks like a stick

'stick-in-the-mud *noun* (*informal, disapproving*) a person who refuses to try anything new or exciting

stickle·back /'stɪklbæk/ *noun* a small FRESHWATER fish with sharp points on its back

stick·ler /'stɪklə(r)/ *noun* ~ (**for sth**) a person who thinks that a particular quality or type of behaviour is very important and expects other people to think and behave in the same way: *a stickler for punctuality*

'stick-on *adj.* [only before noun] (of an object) with glue on one side so that it sticks to sth: *stick-on badges/labels*

stick·pin /'stɪkpɪn/ *noun* (*AmE*) a decorative pin that is worn on a tie to keep it in place, or as a piece of jewellery

'stick shift *noun* (*AmE*) **1** = GEAR LEVER **2** a vehicle that has a stick shift—compare AUTOMATIC *n.*

sticky /'stɪki/ *adj.* (**stick·ier, sticki·est**) **1** made of or covered in a substance that sticks to things that touch it: *sticky fingers covered in jam* ◊ *Stir in the milk to make a soft but not sticky dough.* **2** (of paper, labels, etc.) with

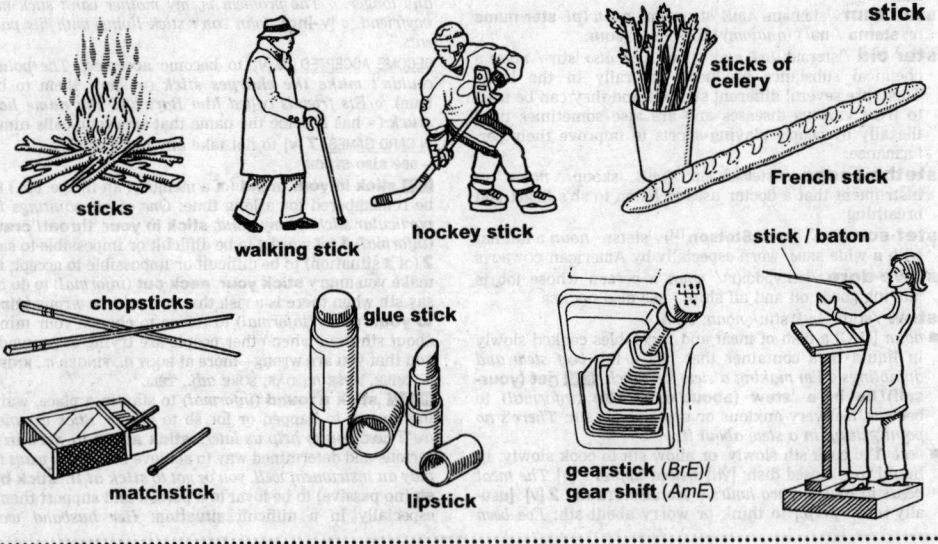

stick

sticks of celery

sticks

walking stick

hockey stick

French stick

chopsticks

glue stick

stick / baton

matchstick

lipstick

gearstick (*BrE*)/
gear shift (*AmE*)

glue on one side so that you can stick it to a surface **3** (*informal*) (of the weather) hot and damp: *a sticky, humid afternoon* **4** (*informal*) (of a person) feeling hot and uncomfortable SYN SWEATY **5** (*informal*) difficult or unpleasant: *a sticky problem/situation* ▶ **-ili/** *adv.* **sticki·ness** *noun* [U] IDM **have sticky 'fingers** (*informal*) to be likely to steal sth **a ,sticky 'wicket** (*BrE, informal*) a difficult situation—more at END *n.*

'sticky tape *noun* [U] (*BrE*) = SELLOTAPE™

stiff /stɪf/ *adj., adv., noun, verb*
■ *adj.* (**stiff·er, stiff·est**)
<u>DIFFICULT TO BEND/MOVE</u> **1** firm and difficult to bend or move: *stiff cardboard ◊ a stiff brush ◊ The windows were stiff and she couldn't get them open. ◊ I've got a stiff neck.*
<u>MUSCLES</u> **2** when a person is **stiff**, their muscles hurt when they move them: *I'm really stiff after that bike ride yesterday.*
<u>MIXTURE</u> **3** thick and almost solid; difficult to stir: *Whisk the egg whites until stiff.*
<u>DIFFICULT/SEVERE</u> **4** more difficult or severe than usual: *It was a stiff climb to the top of the hill. ◊ The company faces stiff competition from its rivals. ◊ The new proposals have met with stiff opposition. ◊ There are stiff fines for breaking the rules. ◊ a stiff breeze/wind* (= one that blows strongly)
<u>NOT FRIENDLY</u> **5** (of a person or their behaviour) not friendly or relaxed: *The speech he made to welcome them was stiff and formal.*
<u>PRICE</u> **6** (*informal*) costing a lot or too much: *There's a stiff £6 entrance fee to the exhibition.*
<u>ALCOHOLIC DRINK</u> **7** [only before noun] strong; containing a lot of alcohol: *a stiff whisky*
▶ **stiff·ly** *adv.* **stiff·ness** *noun* [U]: *pain and stiffness in her legs*
IDM **(keep) a stiff upper 'lip** to keep calm and hide your feelings when you are in pain or in a difficult situation
■ *adv.* **1** (*informal*) very much; to an extreme degree: *be bored/scared/worried stiff* **2 frozen ~** (of wet material) very cold and hard because the water has become ice: *The clothes on the washing line were frozen stiff. ◊ I came home from the game frozen stiff* (= very cold).
■ *noun* (*slang*) the body of a dead person
■ *verb* [VN] (*AmE, informal*) to cheat sb or not pay them what you owe them, especially by not leaving any money as a TIP

stiff·en /'stɪfn/ *verb* **1 ~** (**sth**) (**with sth**) to make yourself or part of your body firm, straight and still, especially because you are angry or frightened: [V] *She stiffened with fear. ◊* [VN] *I stiffened my back and faced him.* **2 ~** (**up**)|**~ sth** (of part of the body) to become, or to make sth become, difficult to bend or move: [V] *My muscles had stiffened up after the climb. ◊* [VN] *stiffened legs/muscles* **3** to make an attitude or idea stronger or more powerful; to become stronger: [VN] *The threat of punishment has only stiffened their resolve* (= made them even more determined to do sth). [also V] **4** [VN] **~ sth** (**with sth**) to make sth, such as fabric, firm and unable to bend: *a starch to stiffen fabrics*

,stiff-'necked *adj.* proud and refusing to change

stifle /'staɪfl/ *verb* **1** [VN] to prevent sth from happening; to prevent a feeling from being expressed: *She managed to stifle a yawn. ◊ to stifle a cry/giggle ◊ They hope the new rules will not stifle creativity. ◊ The government failed to stifle the unrest.* **2** to feel unable to breathe, or to make sb unable to breathe, because it is too hot and/or there is no fresh air: [V] *I felt I was stifling in the airless room. ◊* [VN] *Most of the victims were stifled by the fumes.* ▶ **stif·ling** /'staɪflɪŋ/ *adj.*: *a stifling smell/room ◊ 'It's stifling in here—can we open a window?'* **stif·ling·ly** *adv.*: *The room was stiflingly hot.*

stigma /'stɪɡmə/ *noun* [U, C, usually sing.] feelings of disapproval that people have about particular illnesses or ways of behaving: *the social stigma of alcoholism ◊ There is no longer any stigma attached to being divorced.*

stig·mata /'stɪɡmətə; stɪɡ'mɑːtə/ *noun* [pl.] marks that look like the wounds made by nails on the body of Jesus Christ, believed by some Christians to have appeared as holy marks on the bodies of some saints

stig·ma·tize (*BrE* also **-ise**) /'stɪɡmətaɪz/ *verb* [VN] [usually passive] (*written*) to treat sb in a way that makes them feel that they are very bad or unimportant ▶ **stig·ma·tiza·tion, -isa·tion** /,stɪɡmətaɪ'zeɪʃn; *AmE* -tə'z-/ *noun* [U]

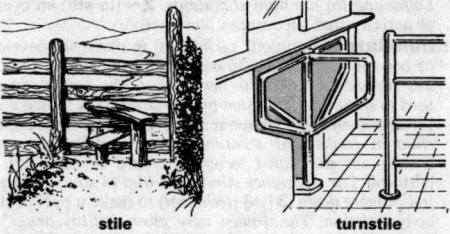

stile   turnstile

stile /staɪl/ *noun* a set of steps that help people climb over a fence or gate, in a field, etc.

stil·etto /stɪ'letəʊ; *AmE* -toʊ/ *noun* (*pl.* **-os** or **-oes**) **1** (also **,stiletto 'heel**) (*especially BrE*) a woman's shoe with a very high narrow heel; the heel on such a shoe SYN SPIKE HEEL—picture at SHOE **2** a small knife with a narrow pointed blade

still /stɪl/ *adv., adj., noun, verb*
■ *adv.* **1** continuing until a particular point in time and not finishing: *I wrote to them last month and I'm still waiting for a reply. ◊ Mum, I'm still hungry! ◊ Do you still live at the same address? ◊ There's still time to change your mind. ◊ It was, and still is, my favourite movie.* **2** in spite of what has just been said: *Although he promised faithfully to come, I still didn't think he would. ◊ We searched everywhere but we still couldn't find it. ◊ The weather was cold and wet. Still, we had a great time.* **3** used for making a comparison stronger: *The next day was warmer still. ◊ If you can manage to get two tickets that's better still.* **4 ~ more/another** even more: *There was still more bad news to come.* IDM see LESS *adv.*
■ *adj.* **1** not moving; calm and quiet: *still water ◊ Keep still while I brush your hair. ◊ The kids found it hard to stay still. ◊ Can't you sit still? ◊ We stayed in a village where time has stood still* (= life has not changed for many years). **2** with no wind: *a still summer's day ◊ the still night air* **3** (*BrE*) (of a drink) not containing bubbles of gas; not FIZZY: *still mineral water* IDM **the still of the 'night** (*literary*) the time during the night when it is silent and calm **still waters run 'deep** (*saying*) a person who seems to be quiet or shy may surprise you by knowing a lot or having deep feelings
■ *noun* **1** a photograph of a scene from a film/movie or video: *a publicity still from his new movie ◊ The police studied the stills from the security video.* **2** a piece of equipment that is used for making strong alcoholic drinks: *a whisky still*—see also DISTIL
■ *verb* (*literary*) to become calm and quiet; to make sth calm and quiet: [V] *The wind stilled. ◊* [VN] *She spoke quietly to still the frightened child. ◊* (*figurative*) *to still sb's doubts/fears*

still·birth /'stɪlbɜːθ; *AmE* -bɜːrθ/ *noun* [C, U] a birth in which the baby is born dead

still·born /'stɪlbɔːn; *AmE* -bɔːrn/ *adj.* **1** born dead: *a stillborn baby* **2** not successful; not developing

,still 'life *noun* [U, C] (*pl.* **,still 'lifes**) the art of painting or drawing arrangements of objects such as flowers, fruit, etc.; a painting, etc. like this

still·ness /'stɪlnəs/ *noun* [U] the quality of being quiet and not moving: *Sound of footsteps on the path broke the stillness.*

stilt /stɪlt/ *noun* [usually pl.] **1** one of a set of posts that support a building so that it is high above the ground or water **2** one of two long pieces of wood that have a step on the side that you can stand on, so that you can walk above the ground: *a circus performer on stilts*

stilt·ed /'stɪltɪd/ *adj.* (*disapproving*) (of a way of speaking

b	d	f	g	h	k	l	m	n	p	r
bad	**did**	**fall**	**get**	**hat**	**cat**	**leg**	**man**	**now**	**pen**	**red**

or writing) not natural or relaxed; too formal: *We made stilted conversation for a few moments.* ▶ **stilt·ed·ly** *adv.*

Stil·ton™ /'stɪltən/ *noun* [U, C] a type of English cheese with blue lines of MOULD running through it and a strong flavour

stimu·lant /'stɪmjələnt/ *noun* **1** a drug or substance that makes you feel more awake and gives you more energy: *Coffee and tea are mild stimulants.* **2 ~ (to sth)** an event or activity that encourages more activity

stimu·late /'stɪmjuleɪt/ *verb* **1** [VN] to make sth develop or become more active; to encourage sth: *The exhibition has stimulated interest in her work.* ◊ *The article can be used to stimulate discussion among students.* **2** to make sb interested and excited about sth: [VN] *Parents should give children books that stimulate them.* ◊ *Both men and women are stimulated by erotic photos (= sexually).* [VN to inf] *The conference stimulated him to study the subject in more depth.* **3** [VN] (*technical*) to make a part of the body function: *The women were given fertility drugs to stimulate the ovaries.* ▶ **stimu·la·tion** /ˌstɪmju'leɪʃn/ *noun* [U]: *sensory / intellectual / sexual / visual / physical stimulation*

stimu·lat·ing /'stɪmjuleɪtɪŋ/ *adj.* **1** full of interesting or exciting ideas; making people feel enthusiastic: *a stimulating book / discussion* ◊ *a stimulating teacher* **2** making you feel more active and healthy

stimu·lus /'stɪmjələs/ *noun* (*pl.* **stim·uli** /-laɪ/) **~ (to / for sth)| ~ (to do sth)** **1** [usually sing.] something that helps sb/sth to develop better or more quickly: *Books provide children with ideas and a stimulus for play.* ◊ *The new tax laws should act as a stimulus to exports.* **2** something that produces a reaction in a human being, an animal or a plant: *sensory / verbal / visual stimuli* ◊ *The animals were conditioned to respond to auditory stimuli (= sounds).*

sting /stɪŋ/ *verb, noun*
■ *verb* (**stung, stung** /stʌŋ/) **1** (of an insect or plant) to touch your skin or make a very small hole in it so that you feel a sharp pain: [VN] *I was stung on the arm by a wasp.* ◊ [V] *Be careful of the nettles—they sting!* **2** to feel, or to make sb feel, a sharp pain in a part of their body: [V] *I put some antiseptic on the cut and it stung for a moment.* ◊ *My eyes were stinging from the smoke.* ◊ [VN] *Tears stung her eyes.* **3** [VN] **~ sb (to / into sth)| ~ sb (into doing sth)** to make sb feel angry or upset: *He was stung by their criticism.* ◊ *Their cruel remarks stung her into action.* ◊ *They launched a stinging attack on the government.* **4** [VN] [often passive] **~ sb (for sth)** (*informal*) to charge sb more money than they expected; to charge sb who did not expect to pay: *I got stung for a £100 meal.* PHRV '**sting sb for sth** (*BrE, informal*) to borrow money from sb
■ *noun* **1** (*AmE also* **sting·er**) [C] the sharp pointed part of an insect or creature that can go into the skin leaving a small, painful and sometimes poisonous wound: *the sting of a bee* ◊ *The scorpion has a sting in its tail.*—picture on page A7 **2** [C] a wound that is made when an insect, a creature or a plant stings you: *A wasp or bee sting is painful but not necessarily serious.* **3** [C, U] any sharp pain in your body or mind: *the sting of salt in a wound* ◊ *There was a sting of sarcasm in his voice.* ◊ *He smiled at her, trying to **take the sting out** of his words (= trying to make the situation less painful or difficult).* **4** [C] (*AmE*) a clever secret plan by the police to catch criminals: *a sting operation to catch heroin dealers in Detroit* **5** [C] (*especially AmE*) a clever plan by criminals to cheat people out of a lot of money IDM **a ˌsting in the 'tail** (*informal*) an unpleasant feature that comes at the end of a story, an event, etc. and spoils it

'**stinging nettle** *noun* = NETTLE

sting·ray /'stɪŋreɪ/ *noun* a large wide flat sea fish that has a long tail with a sharp sting in it that can cause serious wounds

stingy /'stɪndʒi/ *adj.* (*informal*) not given or giving willingly; not generous, especially with money: *You're stingy! (= not willing to spend money)* ◊ *Don't be so stingy with the cream!* ▶ **stingi·ness** *noun* [U]

stink /stɪŋk/ *verb, noun*

■ *verb* (**stank** /stæŋk/, **stunk** /stʌŋk/) or (**stunk, stunk**) [V] **~ (of sth)** (*informal*) **1** to have a strong, unpleasant smell: *Her breath stank of garlic.* ◊ *It stinks of smoke in here.* **2** to seem very bad, unpleasant or dishonest: *The whole business stank of corruption.* ◊ *'What do you think of the idea?' 'I think it stinks.'* PHRV ˌ**stink sth↔'out** to fill a place with a strong, unpleasant smell: *She stinks out the whole house with her incense and candles.*
■ *noun* (*informal*) **1** [C, usually sing.] a very unpleasant smell: *the stink of sweat and urine* **2** [sing.] a lot of trouble and anger about sth: *The whole business caused quite a stink.* ◊ *We'll kick up a stink (= complain a lot and cause trouble) if they try to close the school down.*

'**stink bomb** *noun* a container that produces a very bad smell when it is broken. Stink bombs are used for playing tricks on people.

stink·er /'stɪŋkə(r)/ *noun* (*informal*) a person or thing that is very unpleasant or difficult: *It's been a real stinker of a day.*

stink·ing /'stɪŋkɪŋ/ *adj., adv.*
■ *adj.* **1** having a very strong, unpleasant smell: *I was pushed into a filthy, stinking room.* **2** [only before noun] (*informal, especially BrE*) very bad or unpleasant: *I've got a stinking cold.* **3** [only before noun] (*BrE, informal*) showing a lot of anger: *I wrote them a stinking letter to complain.*
■ *adv.* (*informal, usually disapproving*) extremely: *They must be stinking rich.*

stint /stɪnt/ *noun, verb*
■ *noun* **~ (as sth)** a period of time that you spend working somewhere or doing a particular activity: *He did a stint abroad early in his career.* ◊ *a two-year stint in the Navy* ◊ *I've done my stint in the kitchen for today.*
■ *verb* **~ (on sth)| ~ (yourself)** (usually used in negative sentences) to provide or use only a small amount of sth: [V] *She never stints on the food at her parties.* ◊ [VN] *We don't need to stint ourselves—have some more!*—see also UNSTINTING

sti·pend /'staɪpend/ *noun* (*formal*) an amount of money that is paid regularly to sb, especially a priest, as wages or money to live on: *an annual / monthly stipend* ◊ (*especially AmE*) *a summer internship with a small stipend*

sti·pen·diary /staɪ'pendiəri; *AmE* -dieri/ *noun* (*pl.* **-ies**) (*also* **sti,pendiary 'magistrate**) (in Britain) a MAGISTRATE who is paid for his or her work

stip·ple /'stɪpl/ *verb* [VN] [often passive] (*technical*) to paint or draw sth using small dots or marks: *a stippled effect* ▶ **stip·pling** /'stɪplɪŋ/ *noun* [U]

stipu·late /'stɪpjuleɪt/ *verb* (*formal*) to state clearly and firmly that sth must be done, or how it must be done: [VN] *A delivery date is stipulated in the contract.* ◊ [V that] *The job advertisement stipulates that the applicant must have three years' experience.* [also V wh-] ▶ **stipu·la·tion** /ˌstɪpju'leɪʃn/ *noun* [C, U]: *The only stipulation is that the topic you choose must be related to your studies.*

stir /stɜː(r)/ *verb, noun*
■ *verb* (**-rr-**)
MIX | **1** [VN] **~ sth (into sth)| ~ sth (in)** to move a liquid or substance around, using a spoon or sth similar, in order to mix it thoroughly: *She stirred her tea.* ◊ *Stir the paint before you use it.* ◊ *The vegetables are stirred into the rice while it is hot.* ◊ *Stir in the milk until the sauce thickens.*
MOVE | **2** to move, or to make sth move, slightly: [V] *She heard the baby stir in the next room.* ◊ [VN] *A slight breeze was stirring the branches.* ◊ *A noise stirred me from sleep.* **3** to move, or to make sb move, in order to do sth: [V] *You haven't stirred from that chair all evening!* ◊ [VN] *Come on, stir yourself. You're late!* ◊ *Their complaints have finally stirred him into action.*
FEELINGS | **4** [VN] **~ sb (to sth)** to make sb excited or make them feel sth strongly: *a book that really stirs the imagination* ◊ *She was stirred by his sad story.* **5** [V] (of a feeling or a mood) to begin to be felt: *A feeling of guilt began to stir in her.* ◊ *New optimism was stirring throughout the country.*
CAUSE TROUBLE | **6** (*BrE, informal, disapproving*) to try to

cause trouble: [VN] *You're just stirring it!* [also V] —see also STIRRER

IDM **stir your 'stumps** (*old-fashioned, BrE, informal*) to begin to move; to hurry

PHRV **,stir sb↔'up** to encourage sb to do sth; to make sb feel they must do sth ,**stir sth↔'up 1** to make people feel strong emotions: *to stir up anger/discontent/hatred* **2** to try to cause arguments or problems: *to stir up a debate* ◊ *Whenever he's around, he always manages to stir up trouble.* ◊ *We've got enough problems without you trying to stir things up.* **3** to make sth move around in water or air: *The wind stirred up a lot of dust.*

■ *noun* **1** [sing.] excitement, anger or shock that is felt by a number of people: *Her resignation caused quite a stir.* **2** [C, usually sing.] the action of stirring sth: *Could you give the rice a stir?*

'stir-crazy *adj.* (*informal, especially AmE*) showing signs of mental illness because of being kept in prison

'stir-fry *verb, noun*
■ *verb* [VN] to cook thin strips of vegetables or meat quickly by stirring them in very hot oil: *stir-fried chicken*—picture on page 275
■ *noun* hot dish made by stir-frying small pieces of meat, fish and/or vegetables

stir·rer /'stɜːrə(r)/ *noun* (*BrE, informal, disapproving*) a person who likes causing trouble, especially between other people by spreading secrets

stir·ring /'stɜːrɪŋ/ *noun, adj.*
■ *noun* ~ (**of sth**) the beginning of a feeling, an idea or a development: *She felt a stirring of anger.* ◊ *the first stirrings of spring in the air*
■ *adj.* [usually before noun] causing strong feelings; exciting: *a stirring performance/song* ◊ *stirring memories*

stir·rup /'stɪrəp/ *noun* one of the metal rings that hang down on each side of a horse's SADDLE, used to support the rider's foot

stitch /stɪtʃ/ *noun, verb*
■ *noun* **1** [C] one of the small lines of thread that you can see on a piece of fabric after it has been sewn; the action that produces this: *Try to keep the stitches small and straight.*—picture at SEW **2** [C] one of the small circles of wool that you make around the needle when you are knitting: *to drop a stitch* (= to lose one that you have made) **3** [C, U] (especially in compounds) a particular style of sewing or knitting that you use to make the pattern you want **4** [C] a short piece of thread, etc. that doctors use to sew the edges of a wound together: *The cut needed eight stitches.* ◊ *I had six stitches in my foot after the accident.* **5** [C, usually sing.] a sudden pain in the side of your body, usually caused by running or laughing: *Can we slow down? I've got a stitch.* **IDM** in 'stitches (*informal*) laughing a lot: *The play had us in stitches.* not have a stitch 'on | not be wearing a 'stitch (*informal*) to be naked a stitch in 'time (saves 'nine) (*saying*) it is better to deal with sth immediately because if you wait it may become worse or more difficult and cause extra work
■ *verb* [VN] to sew sth; to use a needle and thread to mend, join, or decorate pieces of fabric: *Her wedding dress was stitched by hand.* ◊ (*figurative*) *An agreement was hastily stitched together* (= made very quickly). **PHRV** ,**stitch sb↔'up** (*BrE, informal*) to cheat sb or put them in a position where they seem guilty of sth they have not done ,**stitch sth↔'up 1** to use a needle and thread to join things together: *to stitch up a wound/cut/tear* **2** (*BrE, informal*) to arrange or complete sth: *to stitch up a deal* ◊ *They think they have the US market stitched up.*

stitch·ing /'stɪtʃɪŋ/ *noun* [U] a row of stitches: *The stitching has come undone.*

stoat /stəʊt; *AmE* stoʊt/ *noun* a small wild animal with a long body and brown fur that, in northern areas, turns white in winter. The white fur is called ERMINE.

stock /stɒk; *AmE* stɑːk/ *noun, verb, adj.*
■ *noun*
SUPPLY | **1** [U, C] a supply of goods that is available for sale in a shop/store: *We have a fast turnover of stock.* ◊ *That*

particular model is not currently **in stock**. ◊ *I'm afraid we're temporarily **out of stock**. ◊ *We don't carry a large stock of pine furniture.* **2** [C, U] ~ (**of sth**) a supply of sth that is available for use: *She's built up a good stock of teaching materials over the years.* ◊ *Food stocks are running low.* ◊ *a country's housing stock* (= all the houses available for living in)

FINANCE | **3** [U] the value of the shares in a company that have been sold **4** [C, usually pl.] a share that sb has bought in a company or business: *stock prices* ◊ *stocks and shares*—compare SHARE *n.* (4) **5** [U, C] (*BrE*) money that is lent to a government at a fixed rate of interest; an official document that gives details of this: *government stock*

FARM ANIMALS | **6** [U] farm animals, such as cows and sheep, that are kept for their meat, wool, etc: *breeding stock*—see also LIVESTOCK

FAMILY/ANCESTORS | **7** [U] **of farming, noble, French, etc.** ~ having the type of family or ancestors mentioned

FOOD | **8** [U, C] a liquid made by cooking bones, meat, etc. in water, used for making soups and sauces: *fish/vegetable stock*

FOR PUNISHMENT | **9** (**stocks**) [pl.] a wooden structure with holes for the feet, used in the past to lock criminals in as a form of punishment, especially in a public place—compare PILLORY

RESPECT | **10** [U] (*formal*) the degree to which sb is respected or liked by other people: *Their stock is high/low.*

OF GUN | **11** [C] the part of a gun that you hold against your shoulder when firing it

PLANT | **12** [U, C] a garden plant with brightly coloured flowers with a sweet smell **13** [C] (*technical*) a plant from which a stem is taken to be added to another plant so that the two grow together; the plant onto which this stem is added

THEATRE | **14** [C] (*AmE*) = STOCK COMPANY
—see also LAUGHING STOCK, ROLLING STOCK **IDM** on the 'stocks in the process of being made, built or prepared: *Our new model is already on the stocks and will be available in the spring.* take 'stock (of sth) to stop and think carefully about the way in which a particular situation is developing in order to decide what to do next—more at LOCK *n.*—see also STOCKTAKING
■ *verb* [VN] **1** (of a shop/store) to keep a supply of a particular type of goods to sell: *Do you stock green tea?* ◊ *We stock a wide range of camping equipment.* **2** [often passive] ~ sth (with sth) to fill sth with food, books, etc: *The pond was well stocked with fish.* ◊ *a well-stocked library* **PHRV** ,**stock sth↔'up** to fill sth with goods, food, etc: *We need to stock up the freezer.* ,**stock 'up (on/with sth)** to buy a lot of sth so that you can use it later: *We ought to stock up on film before our trip.*
■ *adj.* [only before noun] **1** (*disapproving*) a stock excuse, answer, etc. is one that is often used because it is easy and convenient, but that is not very original: *'No comment,' was the actor's stock response.* **2** usually available for sale in a shop/store: *stock sizes*

stock·ade /stɒˈkeɪd; *AmE* stɑːˈk-/ *noun* a line or wall of strong wooden posts built to defend a place

stock·broker /'stɒkbrəʊkə(r); *AmE* 'stɑːkbroʊ-/ (also **broker**) *noun* a person or an organization that buys and sells STOCKS and shares for other people

stock·brok·ing /'stɒkbrəʊkɪŋ; *AmE* 'stɑːkbroʊ-/ *noun* [U] the work of a stockbroker

'stock car *noun* an ordinary car that has been strengthened for use in stock-car racing

'stock-car racing *noun* [U] (*BrE*) (*AmE* ,**demolition 'derby** [C]) a type of race in which the competing cars are allowed to hit each other

'stock company *noun* (*AmE*) **1** a company owned by people who have shares in it **2** (also **stock**) a theatre company that does several different plays in a season; a REPERTORY company

'stock cube *noun* a solid CUBE made from the dried juices of meat or vegetables, sold in packets and used for making soups, sauces, etc.

æ	ɑː	e	ɜː	ə	ɪ	iː	i	ɒ	ɔː	ʌ	ʊ	u	uː
cat	father	ten	bird	about	sit	see	many	got	saw	cup	put	actual	too

(BrE)

'stock exchange *noun* [usually sing.] a place where shares in companies are bought and sold; all of the business activity involved in doing this: *the London Stock Exchange* ◊ *to lose money on the stock exchange*

stock·hold·er /ˈstɒkhəʊldə(r); *AmE* ˈstɑːkhoʊ-/ *noun* (*especially AmE*) a person who owns STOCKS and shares in a business

stock·ing /ˈstɒkɪŋ; *AmE* ˈstɑːk-/ *noun* **1** either of a pair of thin pieces of clothing that fit closely over a woman's legs and feet: *a pair of silk stockings*—compare TIGHTS—see also BODY STOCKING **2** = CHRISTMAS STOCKING [IDM] **in your ˌstocking(ed) 'feet** wearing socks or stockings but not shoes

'stocking filler (*BrE*) (*AmE* **'stocking stuffer**) *noun* a small present that is put in a CHRISTMAS STOCKING

ˌstock-in-'trade *noun* [U] a person's stock-in-trade is sth that they do, say or use very often or too often: *Famous people and their private lives are the stock-in-trade of the popular newspapers.*

stock·ist /ˈstɒkɪst; *AmE* ˈstɑːk-/ *noun* (*BrE*) a shop/store or company that sells a particular product or type of goods: *The paints are available from stockists throughout the UK.*

stock·man /ˈstɒkmən; *AmE* ˈstɑːk-/ *noun* (*pl.* **-men** /-mən/) **1** (*especially AustralE*) a man whose job is to take care of farm animals **2** (*AmE*) a man who owns farm animals **3** (*AmE*) a man who is in charge of the goods in a WAREHOUSE, etc.

'stock market (also **mar·ket**) *noun* the business of buying and selling shares in companies and the place where this happens; a STOCK EXCHANGE: *to make money on the stock market* ◊ *a stock market crash* (= when prices of shares fall suddenly and people lose money)

stock·pile /ˈstɒkpaɪl; *AmE* ˈstɑːk-/ *noun, verb*
■ *noun* a large supply of sth that is kept to be used in the future if necessary: *the world's stockpile of nuclear weapons*
■ *verb* [VN] to collect and keep a large supply of sth: *to stockpile food/fuel*

stock·room /ˈstɒkruːm; -rʊm; *AmE* ˈstɑːk-/ *noun* a room for storing things in a shop/store, an office, etc.

ˌstock-'still *adv.* without moving at all: *We stood stock-still watching the animals.*

stock·tak·ing /ˈstɒkteɪkɪŋ; *AmE* ˈstɑːk-/ *noun* [U] **1** (*especially BrE*) the process of making a list of all the goods in a shop/store or business—compare INVENTORY **2** the process of thinking carefully about your own situation or position: *She had some mental stocktaking to do.*

stocky /ˈstɒki; *AmE* ˈstɑːki/ *adj.* (**stock·ier, stocki·est**) (of a person) short, with a strong, solid body: *a stocky figure/build* ▶ **stock·ily** *adv.*

stock·yard /ˈstɒkjɑːd; *AmE* ˈstɑːkjɑːrd/ *noun* a place where farm animals are kept for a short time before they are sold at a market

stodge /stɒdʒ; *AmE* stɑːdʒ/ *noun* [U] (*BrE, informal*, usually *disapproving*) heavy food that makes you feel very full

stodgy /ˈstɒdʒi; *AmE* ˈstɑːdʒi/ *adj.* (*informal disapproving, especially BrE*) **1** (of food) heavy and making you feel very full: *stodgy puddings* **2** serious and boring; not exciting

stoic /ˈstəʊɪk; *AmE* ˈstoʊɪk/ *noun* (*formal*) a person who is able to suffer pain or trouble without complaining or showing what they are feeling ▶ **stoic** (also **sto·ic·al** /-kl/) *adj.*: *her stoic endurance* ◊ *his stoical acceptance of death* **sto·ic·al·ly** /-kli/ *adv.* [ORIGIN] From the Stoics, a group of ancient Greek philosophers, who believed that wise people should not allow themselves to be affected by painful or pleasant experiences.

sto·icism /ˈstəʊɪsɪzəm; *AmE* ˈstoʊ-/ *noun* [U] (*formal*) the fact of not complaining or showing what you are feeling when you are suffering: *She endured her long illness with stoicism.*

stoke /stəʊk; *AmE* stoʊk/ *verb* [VN] **1** ~ sth (up) (with sth) to add fuel to a fire, etc: *to stoke up a fire with more coal* ◊ *to stoke a furnace* **2** ~ sth (up) to make people feel sth more strongly: *to stoke up anger/envy* ◊ *The publicity was intended to stoke up interest in her music.* [PHR V] **ˌstoke 'up (on/with sth)** (*informal*) to eat or drink a lot of sth, especially so that you do not feel hungry later: *Stoke up for the day on a good breakfast.*

stoker /ˈstəʊkə(r); *AmE* ˈstoʊ-/ *noun* a person whose job is to add coal or other fuel to a fire, etc., especially on a ship or a steam train

stole /stəʊl; *AmE* stoʊl/ *noun* a piece of clothing consisting of a wide band of fabric or fur, worn by a woman around the shoulders; a similar piece of clothing worn by a priest—see also STEAL, STOLE, STOLEN *v.*

stolid /ˈstɒlɪd; *AmE* ˈstɑːl-/ *adj.* (usually *disapproving*) not showing much emotion or interest; remaining always the same and not reacting or changing: *Mark sat stolid and silent.* ▶ **stol·id·ly** *adv.* **stol·id·ity** /stəˈlɪdəti/ *noun* [U]

stom·ach /ˈstʌmək/ *noun, verb*
■ *noun* the organ inside the body where food goes when you swallow it; the front part of the body below the chest: *stomach pains* ◊ *an upset stomach* ◊ (*BrE* also) *a stomach upset* ◊ *It's not a good idea to drink* (= alcohol) *on an empty stomach* (= without having eaten anything). ◊ *You shouldn't exercise on a full stomach.* ◊ *The attacker kicked him in the stomach.* ◊ *Lie on your stomach with your arms by your side.*—see also TUMMY—picture at BODY [IDM] **have no 'stomach for sth** to not want to eat sth: *She had no stomach for the leftover stew.* **2** to not have the desire or courage to do sth: *They had no stomach for a fight.* **turn your 'stomach** to make you feel upset, sick or disgusted: *Pictures of the burnt corpses turned my stomach.*—more at BUTTERFLY, EYE *n.*, FEEL *v.*, PIT *n.*, PUMP *v.*, STRONG
■ *verb* [VN] (*especially in negative sentences or questions*) **1** to approve of sth and be able to enjoy it; to enjoy being with a person: *I can't stomach violent films.* ◊ *I find him very hard to stomach.* **2** to be able to eat sth without feeling ill/sick: *She couldn't stomach any breakfast.*

'stomach ache *noun* [C, U] pain in or near your stomach

'stomach pump *noun* a machine with a tube that doctors use to remove poisonous substances from sb's stomach through their mouth

stomp /stɒmp; *AmE* stɑːmp/ *verb* [V+*adv./prep.*] (*informal*) to walk, dance, or move with heavy steps: *She stomped angrily out of the office.* ◊ *The children were stomping around noisily.*

'stomping ground *noun* (*AmE, informal*) = STAMPING GROUND

stone /stəʊn; *AmE* stoʊn/ *noun, verb*
■ *noun*
HARD SUBSTANCE **1** [U] (often used before nouns or in compounds) a hard solid mineral substance that is found in the ground, often used for building: *Most of the houses are built of stone.* ◊ *stone walls* ◊ *a stone bridge/floor/carving* ◊ *a flight of stone steps*—see also DRYSTONE WALL, LIMESTONE, SANDSTONE, SOAPSTONE **2** [C] (*especially BrE*) a small piece of rock of any shape: *a pile of stones* ◊ *Some children were throwing stones into the lake.*—see also HAILSTONE **3** [C] (usually in compounds) a piece of stone shaped for a particular purpose: *These words are carved on the stone beside his grave.*—see also CORNERSTONE, FOUNDATION STONE, GRAVESTONE, HEADSTONE, LODESTONE, MILLSTONE, PAVING STONE, STEPPING STONE, TOMBSTONE
JEWEL **4** [C] = PRECIOUS STONE
IN FRUIT **5** [C] (*especially BrE*) (*AmE usually* **pit**) a hard shell containing the nut or seed in the middle of some types of fruit: *cherry/peach stones*—picture on page A2
IN BODY **6** [C] (often in compounds) a small piece of hard material that can form in the BLADDER or KIDNEY and cause pain: *kidney stones*—see also GALLSTONE
MEASUREMENT OF WEIGHT **7** [C] (*pl.* **stone**) (*abbr.* **st**) (in Britain) a unit for measuring weight, equal to 6.35 kg or 14 pounds: *He weighs over 15 stone.* ◊ *She's trying to lose a stone.*
[IDM] **leave no stone un'turned** to try every possible course of action in order to find or achieve sth **a 'stone's throw** a very short distance away: *We live just a stone's*

aɪ	aʊ	eɪ	əʊ	oʊ	ɔɪ	ɪə	eə	ʊə	j	w
my	now	say	go	go	boy	near	hair	pure	yes	wet
			(BrE)	(AmE)						

throw from here. ◊ *The hotel is within a stone's throw of the beach.*—more at BLOOD *n.*, CARVE, HEART, KILL *v.*, PEOPLE *n.*

■ *verb* [VN]

THROW STONES | **1** [usually passive] to throw stones at sb/sth: *Shops were looted and vehicles stoned.* ◊ *to be stoned to death* (= as a punishment)

FRUIT | **2** (*BrE*) (also **pit** *AmE*, *BrE*) to remove the hard seed (= the stone/pit) from the inside of a fruit: *stoned black olives*

IDM **,stone the 'crows | ,stone 'me** (*old-fashioned*, *BrE*) used to express surprise, shock, anger, etc.

the 'Stone Age *noun* [sing.] the very early period of human history when tools and weapons were made of stone

,stone 'cold *adj.* completely cold, when it should be warm or hot: *The soup was stone cold.* IDM **,stone-cold 'sober** having drunk no alcohol at all

stoned /stəʊnd; *AmE* stoʊnd/ *adj.* [not usually before noun] (*slang*) not behaving or thinking normally because of the effects of a drug such as MARIJUANA or alcohol

,stone 'dead *adj.* (*BrE*) completely dead or completely destroyed

,stone 'deaf *adj.* completely unable to hear

stone·ground /'stəʊngraʊnd; *AmE* 'stoʊn-/ *adj.* (of flour for bread, etc.) made by being crushed between heavy stones

stone·mason /'stəʊnmeɪsn; *AmE* 'stoʊn-/ *noun* a person whose job is cutting and preparing stone for buildings

stone·wall /ˌstəʊn'wɔːl; *AmE* 'stoʊn-/ *verb* [VN, V] (especially in politics) to delay a discussion or decision by refusing to answer questions or by talking a lot

stone·ware /'stəʊnweə(r); *AmE* 'stoʊnwer/ *noun* [U] pots, dishes, etc. made from clay that contains a small amount of the hard stone called FLINT

stone·washed /'stəʊnwɒʃt; *AmE* 'stoʊnwɑːʃt; -wɔːʃt/ *adj.* (of jeans, etc.) washed in a special way so that the fabric loses some colour and looks older

stone·work /'stəʊnwɜːk; *AmE* 'stoʊnwɜːrk/ *noun* [U] the parts of a building that are made of stone

stoni·ly /'stəʊnɪli; *AmE* 'stoʊn-/ *adv.* in a way that shows a lack of feeling or sympathy: *She stared stonily at him for a minute.*

stony /'stəʊni; *AmE* 'stoʊni/ *adj.* (**stoni·er**, **stoni·est**) **1** having a lot of stones on it or in it: *a stony beach* ◊ *stony ground/soil* **2** showing a lack of feeling or sympathy: *They listened to him in stony silence.* IDM **fall on stony 'ground** to fail to produce the result or the effect that you hope for; to have little success **stony 'broke** = FLAT BROKE at FLAT *adv.*

,stony-'faced *adj.* not showing any friendly feelings

stood *pt, pp* of STAND

stooge /stuːdʒ/ *noun* **1** (*informal*, usually *disapproving*) a person who is used by sb to do things that are unpleasant or dishonest **2** a performer in a show whose role is to appear silly so that the other performers can make jokes about him or her

stool /stuːl/ *noun* **1** (often in compounds) a seat with legs but with nothing to support your back or arms: *a bar stool* ◊ *a piano stool*—picture at BAR, CHAIR **2** (*medical*) a piece of solid waste from your body IDM see TWO

'stool pigeon *noun* (*informal*) a person, especially a criminal, who helps the police to catch another criminal, for example by spending time with them and getting secret information SYN INFORMER

stoop /stuːp/ *verb, noun*

■ *verb* [V] **1** ~ (**down**) to bend your body forwards and downwards: *She stooped down to pick up the child.* ◊ *The doorway was so low that he had to stoop.* **2** to stand or walk with your head and shoulders bent forwards: *He tends to stoop because he's so tall.* IDM **stoop so 'low (as to do sth)** (*written*) to lower your moral standards far enough to do sth bad or unpleasant: *She was unwilling to believe anyone would stoop so low as to steal a ring from a dead woman's finger.* PHR V **'stoop to sth** to lower your moral standards to do sth bad or unpleasant: *You surely*

don't think I'd stoop to that! ◊ [+ -ing] *I didn't think he'd stoop to cheating.*

■ *noun* **1** [sing.] if sb has a **stoop**, their shoulders are always bent forward **2** [C] (*AmE*) a raised area outside the door of a house with steps leading up to it: *the front stoop*

stop /stɒp; *AmE* stɑːp/ *verb, noun*

■ *verb* (**-pp-**)

NOT MOVE | **1** to no longer move; to make sb/sth no longer move: [V] *The car stopped at the traffic lights.* ◊ *We stopped for the night in Port Augusta.* ◊ [VN] *He was stopped by the police for speeding.*

NOT CONTINUE | **2** to no longer continue to do sth; to make sb/sth no longer do sth: [V -ing] *That phone never stops ringing!* ◊ *Please stop crying and tell me what's wrong.* ◊ [V] *She criticizes everyone and the trouble is, she doesn't know when to stop.* ◊ (*spoken*) *Can't you just stop?* ◊ [VN] *Stop me* (= make me stop talking) *if I'm boring you.* ◊ (*spoken*) *Stop it! You're hurting me.* ◊ [V wh-] *Mike immediately stopped what he was doing.* HELP Notice the difference between **stop doing sth** and **stop to do sth**: *We stopped taking pictures.* means 'We were no longer taking pictures.'; *We stopped to take pictures.* means 'We stopped what we were doing so that we could start taking pictures.'

END | **3** to end or finish; to make sth end or finish: [V] *When is this fighting going to stop?* ◊ *The bus service stops at midnight.* ◊ [V -ing] *Has it stopped raining yet?* ◊ [VN] *Doctors couldn't stop the bleeding.* ◊ *The referee was forced to stop the game because of heavy snow.*

PREVENT | **4** ~ **sb/sth (from doing sth)** | *BrE* also ~ **sb/sth (doing sth)** to prevent sb from doing sth; to prevent sth from happening: [VN] *I want to go and you can't stop me.* ◊ *We need more laws to stop pollution.* ◊ *There's nothing to stop you from accepting the offer.* ◊ *There's no stopping us now* (= nothing can prevent us from achieving what we want to achieve). ◊ *You can't stop people from saying what they think.* ◊ (*BrE* also) [VN -ing] *You can't stop people saying what they think.*

FOR SHORT TIME | **5** [V] ~ (**for sth**) | ~ (**to do sth**) to end an activity for a short time in order to do sth: *I'm hungry. Let's stop for lunch.* ◊ *We stopped to admire the scenery.* ◊ *People just don't stop to think about the consequences.* HELP In spoken English, **stop** can be used with **and** plus another verb, instead of with **to** and the infinitive, to show purpose: *He stopped and bought some flowers.* ◊ *Let's stop and look at the map.*

NOT FUNCTION | **6** to no longer work or function; to make sth no longer work or function: [V] *Why has the engine stopped?* ◊ *I felt as if my heart had stopped.* ◊ [VN] *I stopped the tape and pressed rewind.*

STAY | **7** [V] ~ (**for sth**) (*BrE*, *informal*) to stay somewhere for a short time, especially at sb's house: *I'm not stopping. I just came to give you this message.* ◊ *Can you stop for tea?*

MONEY | **8** [VN] ~ **sth (from sth)** to prevent money from being paid: *to stop a cheque* (= tell the bank not to pay it) ◊ (*BrE*) *Dad threatened to stop £1 a week from our pocket money if we didn't clean our rooms.*

CLOSE HOLE | **9** [VN] ~ **sth (up) (with sth)** to block, fill or close a hole, an opening, etc: *Stop up the other end of the hose, will you?* ◊ *I stopped my ears but still heard her cry out.*

IDM **stop at 'nothing** to be willing to do anything to get what you want, even if it is dishonest or wrong **,stop the 'clock** to stop measuring time in a game or an activity that has a time limit **,stop 'short | ,stop sb 'short** to suddenly stop, or make sb suddenly stop, doing sth: *He stopped short when he heard his name.* **stop short of sth/ of doing sth** to be unwilling to do sth because it may involve a risk, but to nearly do it: *She stopped short of calling the president a liar.*—more at BUCK *n.*, TRACK *n.* PHR V **,stop 'by (sth)** to make a short visit somewhere: *I'll stop by this evening for a chat.* ◊ *Could you stop by the store on the way home for some bread?* **,stop 'in** (*BrE*, *informal*) to stay at home rather than go out **,stop 'off (at/in ...)** to make a short visit somewhere during a trip in order to do sth: *We stopped off at a hotel for the night.*

,stop 'out (*BrE, informal*) to stay out late at night ,stop 'over (at/in ...) to stay somewhere for a short time during a long journey: *I wanted to stop over in India on the way to Australia.*—related noun STOPOVER ,stop 'up (*BrE, informal*) to stay up late

■ noun

ACT OF STOPPING | **1** an act of stopping or stopping sth; the state of being stopped: *The trip included an overnight stop in Brussels.* ◊ *She brought the car to a stop.* ◊ *Work has temporarily come to a stop while the funding is reviewed.* ◊ *It is time to put a stop to the violence.* ◊ *Babies do not grow at a steady rate but in stops and starts.*—see also NON-STOP, WHISTLE-STOP

OF BUS/TRAIN | **2** a place where a bus or train stops regularly for passengers to get on or off: *I get off at the next stop.* ◊ *Is this your stop?*—see also BUS STOP, PIT STOP, REQUEST STOP

PUNCTUATION | **3** (*BrE*) = FULL STOP

MUSIC | **4** a row of pipes on an ORGAN that produce the different sounds **5** a handle on an ORGAN that the player pushes in or pulls out to control the sound produced by the pipes

PHONETICS | **6** a speech sound made by stopping the flow of air coming out of the mouth and then suddenly releasing it, for example /p, k, t/ SYN PLOSIVE—see also GLOTTAL STOP

IDM see FULL STOP, PULL *v.*

stop·cock /'stɒpkɒk; *AmE* 'stɑːpkɑːk/ (also **cock**) noun a tap that controls the flow of liquid or gas through a pipe

stop·gap /'stɒpgæp; *AmE* 'stɑːp-/ noun something that you use or do for a short time while you are looking for sth better: *The arrangement was only intended as a stopgap.* ◊ *a stopgap measure*

,stop-'go *adj.* [usually before noun] (*BrE, disapproving*) used to describe the policy of first restricting and then encouraging economic activity and growth: *the damaging stop-go economic cycle*

'stop light noun [C] **1** (*BrE*) a red TRAFFIC LIGHT **2** (also **stop·lights** [pl.]) (*AmE*) = TRAFFIC LIGHT **3** (*AmE*) = BRAKE LIGHT

stop·over /'stɒpəʊvə(r); *AmE* 'stɑːpoʊ-/ (*AmE* also **lay·over**) noun a short stay somewhere between two parts of a journey: *We had a two-day stopover in Fiji on the way to Australia.*

stop·page /'stɒpɪdʒ; *AmE* 'stɑːp-/ noun **1** [C] a situation in which people stop working as part of a protest or strike **2** [C] (*sport*) an interruption in the game for a particular reason: *Play resumed quickly after the stoppage.* ◊ *stoppage time* (= added on at the end of the game if there have been stoppages) **3** [C] a situation in which sth does not move forward or is blocked: *a stoppage of blood to the heart* **4** (**stoppages**) [pl.] (*old-fashioned, BrE, formal*) an amount of money that an employer takes from people's wages for tax and other payments

stop·per /'stɒpə(r); *AmE* 'stɑːp-/ (*AmE* also **plug**) noun an object that fits into the top of a bottle to close it: *a glass/plastic stopper* ◊ *a bottle stopper*—picture at LABORATORY ▶ **stop·per** verb [VN]

'stopping train noun (*BrE*) a train that stops at a lot of stations between main stations

,stop 'press noun [U] late news that is added to a newspaper after printing has begun

stop·watch /'stɒpwɒtʃ; *AmE* 'stɑːpwɑːtʃ/ noun a watch that you can stop and start by pressing buttons, in order to time a race, etc. accurately

stor·age /'stɔːrɪdʒ/ noun [U] **1** the process of keeping sth in a particular place until it is needed; the space where things can be kept: *tables that fold flat for storage* ◊ *There's a lot of storage space in the loft.* ◊ *food storage facilities* ◊ *We need more storage now.*—see also COLD STORAGE **2** (*computing*) the process of keeping information, etc. on a computer; the way it is kept: *the storage and retrieval of information* ◊ *data storage* **3** the process of paying to keep furniture, etc. in a special building until you want it: *When we moved we had to put our furniture in storage for a while.*

'**storage heater** noun (*BrE*) an electric HEATER that stores heat when electricity is cheaper, for example at night

store /stɔː(r)/ noun, verb

■ noun **1** [C] a large shop that sells many different types of goods: *a big department store*—see also CHAIN STORE, VARIETY STORE **2** [C] (*AmE*) a shop, large or small: *a health food store* ◊ *a liquor store*—see also CONSIGNMENT STORE, CONVENIENCE STORE, GENERAL STORE **3** [C] a quantity or supply of sth that you have and use: *her secret store of chocolate* ◊ *There is a vast store of knowledge in the world on every conceivable subject.* **4** (**stores**) [pl.] goods of a particular kind or for a particular purpose: *medical/military stores* **5** [C] (often **stores**) [pl.] a place where goods of a particular kind are kept: *a grain store* ◊ *weapons stores* IDM **in store (for sb)** waiting to happen to sb: *We don't know what life holds in store for us.* ◊ *If she had known what lay in store for her, she would never have agreed to go.* ◊ *They think it'll be easy but they have a surprise in store.* **set/put (great, etc.) 'store by sth** to believe in sth; to consider sth to be important: *She sets great store by her appearance.* ◊ *It is unwise to put too much store by these statistics.*—more at HIT *v.*, MIND *v.*

■ verb [VN] **1** ~ **sth (away/up)** to put sth somewhere and keep it there to use later: *animals storing up food for the winter* ◊ *You can store coffee beans in the freezer to keep them fresh.* ◊ *He hoped the electronic equipment was safely stored away.* **2** to keep information or facts in a computer or in your brain: *Thousands of pieces of data are stored in a computer's memory.* PHR V ,store sth↔'up to not express strong feelings or deal with problems when you have them, especially when this causes problems later: *She had stored up all her anger and eventually snapped.* ◊ *By ignoring your feelings you are only storing up trouble for yourself.*

'**store-bought** *adj.* (*AmE*) = SHOP-BOUGHT: *store-bought cookies*

'**store-brand** *adj.* (*AmE*) = OWN-BRAND

'**store card** noun a card that a particular shop/store provides for regular customers so that they can use it to buy goods that they will pay for later—compare CREDIT CARD

'**store detective** noun a person employed by a large shop/store to watch customers and make sure they do not steal goods

store·front /'stɔːfrʌnt; *AmE* 'stɔːrf-/ noun (*AmE*) **1** = SHOPFRONT **2** a room at the front of a shop/store: *They run their business from a small storefront.* ◊ *a storefront office*

store·house /'stɔːhaʊs; *AmE* 'stɔːrh-/ noun **1** a building where things are stored SYN WAREHOUSE **2** ~ **of information, knowledge, etc.** a place or thing that has or contains a lot of information: *This book is a storehouse of useful information.*

store·keep·er /'stɔːkiːpə(r); *AmE* 'stɔːrk-/ noun (*especially AmE*) = SHOPKEEPER

store·room /'stɔːruːm; -rʊm/ noun a room used for storing things

storey (*especially BrE*) (*AmE usually* **story**) /'stɔːri/ noun (*pl.* **stor·eys**, *AmE* **stor·ies**) **1** a level of a building; a floor: *the upper/lower storey of the house* ◊ *a single-storey/two-storey/three-storey building*—see also MULTI-STOREY **2** (**-storeyed**) (*AmE* **-storied**) (in adjectives) (of a building) having the number of levels mentioned: *a four-storeyed building*

┌───┐
│ **WHICH WORD?**   (?) │
│ **storey / floor**   │
├───┤
│ You use **storey** (*BrE*)/**story** (*AmE*) mainly when you │
│ are talking about the number of levels a building has: │
│ *a five-storey house* ◊ *The office building is five storeys │
│ high.*   │
│   │
│ **Floor** is used mainly to talk about which particular level │
│ in the building someone lives on, goes to, etc.: *His │
│ office is on the fifth floor.*   │
│ ➪ note at FLOOR   │
└───┘

stor·ied /ˈstɔːrid/ *adj.* (*AmE*) **1** [only before noun] mentioned in stories; famous; well known: *the rock star's storied career* **2** (*-storied*) = -STOREYED at STOREY

stork /stɔːk; *AmE* stɔːrk/ *noun* a large black and white bird with a long beak and neck and long legs, that lives near water but often builds its nest on the top of a high building

storm /stɔːm; *AmE* stɔːrm/ *noun, verb*
■ *noun* **1** very bad weather with strong winds and rain, and often THUNDER and LIGHTNING: *fierce/heavy/violent storms* ◇ *A few minutes later the storm broke* (= began). ◇ *I think we're in for a storm* (= going to have one). ◇ *storm damage* ⇨ note at WEATHER **2** (in compounds) very bad weather of the type mentioned: *a thunderstorm/snowstorm/sandstorm*—see also ELECTRIC STORM, RAINSTORM **3 ~** (**of sth**) a situation in which a lot of people suddenly express very strong feelings about sth: *a storm of protest/controversy* **4 ~ of sth** a sudden loud noise that is caused by emotion or excitement SYN ROAR: *a storm of applause/weeping*—see also BRAINSTORM IDM **a storm in a ˈteacup** (*BrE*) (*AmE* **a tempest in a ˈteapot**) a lot of anger or worry about sth that is not important **take sth/sb by ˈstorm 1** to be extremely successful very quickly in a particular place or among particular people: *The play took London by storm.* **2** to attack a place suddenly and capture it—more at CALM *n.*, PORT
■ *verb* **1** to suddenly attack a place: [VN] *Police stormed the building and captured the gunman.* ◇ [V] *Soldiers stormed into the city at dawn.* **2** [V+adv./prep.] to go somewhere quickly and in an angry, noisy way: *She stormed into my office waving a newspaper.* ◇ *He burst into tears and stormed off.* **3** [Vspeech] (*written*) to say sth in a loud angry way: *'Don't you know who I am?' she stormed.*

ˈstorm cloud *noun* [usually pl.] a dark cloud that you see when bad weather is coming: (*figurative*) *The storm clouds of revolution were gathering.*

ˈstorm door *noun* an extra door that is fitted to the outside door of a house, etc. to give protection from bad weather or the winter

ˈstorm-tossed *adj.* [only before noun] (*literary*) affected or damaged by storms

ˈstorm trooper *noun* a soldier who is specially trained for violent attacks, especially one in Nazi Germany in the 1930s and 1940s

stormy /ˈstɔːmi; *AmE* ˈstɔːrmi/ *adj.* (**storm·ier, stormi·est**) **1** with strong winds and heavy rain or snow: *a dark and stormy night* ◇ *stormy weather/seas* **2** full of strong feelings and angry arguments: *a stormy debate/meeting/relationship*

story /ˈstɔːri/ *noun* (*pl.* **-ies**) **1 ~** (**about/of sth/sb**) a description of events and people that the writer or speaker has invented in order to entertain people: *adventure/detective/love stories* ◇ *a book of short stories* ◇ *a story about time travel* ◇ *Shall I tell you a story?* ◇ *He read the children a story.* ◇ *a bedtime story*—see also FAIRY STORY, GHOST STORY, SHORT STORY **2 ~** (**about/of sth/sb**) an account, often spoken, of what happened to sb or of how sth happened: *It was many years before the full story was made public.* ◇ *The police didn't believe her story.* ◇ *We must stick to our story about the accident.* ◇ *I can't decide until I've heard both sides of the story.* ◇ *It's a story of courage.* ◇ *Many years later I returned to Africa but that's another story* (= I am not going to talk about it now).—see also COCK AND BULL STORY, HARD-LUCK STORY, LIFE STORY, SHAGGY-DOG STORY, SOB STORY, SUCCESS STORY, TALL STORY **3** an account of past events or of how sth has developed: *He told us the story of his life.* ◇ *the story of the Beatles* ◇ *the story of the building of the bridge* **4** a report in a newspaper, magazine or news broadcast: *a front-page story* ◇ *Now for a summary of tonight's main news stories.*—see also COVER STORY, LEAD STORY **5** (also **story-line**) the series of events in a book, film/movie, play, etc. SYN PLOT: *Her novels always have the same basic story.* **6** (*informal*) something that sb says which is not true: *She knew the child had been telling stories again.* **7** (*AmE*) = STOREY IDM **the story goes (that)** ... | **so the story goes** used to describe sth that people are saying

although it may not be correct: *She never saw him again—or so the story goes.* **that's the ˌstory of my ˈlife** (*informal*) when you say **that's the story of my life** about an unfortunate experience you have had, you mean you have had many similar experiences—more at LIKELY *adj.*, LONG *adj.*, OLD, PITCH *v.*, TELL

story·board /ˈstɔːribɔːd; *AmE* -bɔːrd/ *noun* a series of drawings or pictures that show the outline of the story of a film/movie, etc.

story·book /ˈstɔːribʊk/ *noun* a book of stories for children: *a picture in a storybook* ◇ *storybook characters* ◇ *storybook adventures* (= like the ones in stories for children)

story·tell·er /ˈstɔːritelə(r)/ *noun* a person who tells or writes stories ▶ **story·tell·ing** *noun* [U]

stoup /stuːp/ *noun* (*technical*) a stone container for holy water in a church

stout /staʊt/ *adj., noun*
■ *adj.* (**stout·er, stout·est**) **1** (of a person) rather fat **2** [usually before noun] strong and thick: *a stout pair of shoes* **3** [usually before noun] (*formal*) brave and determined: *He put up a stout defence in court.* ◇ *This requires a stout heart.* ▶ **stout·ly** *adv.*: *He was tall and stoutly built.* ◇ *'I disagree,' said Polly stoutly.* **stout·ness** *noun* [U]
■ *noun* [U, C] strong dark beer made with MALT or BARLEY

stove /stəʊv; *AmE* stoʊv/ *noun* **1** a piece of equipment that can burn various fuels and is used for heating rooms: *a gas/wood-burning stove* **2** (*especially AmE*) = COOKER: *She put a pan of water on the stove.* ◇ (*AmE, BrE*) *Most people don't want to spend hours slaving over a hot stove* (= cooking).—see also STAVE, STOVE, STOVE *v.*

stow /stəʊ; *AmE* stoʊ/ *verb* [VN] **~ sth (away) (in sth)** to put sth in a safe place: *She found a seat, stowed her backpack and sat down.* ◇ *His passport was stowed away in the desk.* PHRV **ˌstow aˈway** to hide in a ship, plane, etc. in order to travel secretly: *At the age of 13 he had stowed away on a ship bound for Rio.*—related noun STOWAWAY

stow·age /ˈstəʊɪdʒ; *AmE* ˈstoʊ-/ *noun* [U] space provided for stowing things away, in a boat or a plane

stow·away /ˈstəʊəweɪ; *AmE* ˈstoʊ-/ *noun* a person who hides in a ship or plane before it leaves, in order to travel without paying or being seen

strad·dle /ˈstrædl/ *verb* [VN] **1** to sit or stand with one of your legs on either side of sb/sth: *He swung his leg over the motorcycle, straddling it easily.* **2** to cross, or exist on both sides of, a river, a road or an area of land: *The mountains straddle the French-Swiss border.* **3** to exist within, or include, different periods of time, activities or groups of people: *a writer who straddles two cultures*

strafe /strɑːf; *AmE* streɪf/ *verb* [VN] to attack a place with bullets or bombs from an aircraft flying low

strag·gle /ˈstrægl/ *verb* [V] [usually+adv./prep.] **1** to grow, spread or move in an untidy way in different directions: *Her hair was straggling over her eyes.* ◇ *The town straggled to an end and the fields began.* **2** to move slowly behind a group of people that you are with so that you become separated from them: *On the way the kids straggled behind us.*

strag·gler /ˈstræglə(r)/ *noun* [usually pl.] a person or an animal that is among the last or the slowest in a group to do sth, for example, to finish a race or leave a place

strag·gly /ˈstrægli/ *adj.* growing or hanging in a way that does not look tidy or attractive: *a thin woman with grey, straggly hair*

straight /streɪt/ *adv., adj., noun*
■ *adv.* (**straight·er, straight·est**)
NOT IN CURVE | **1** not in a curve or at an angle; in a straight line: *Keep straight on for two miles.* ◇ *Can you stretch your arms out straighter?* ◇ *He was too tired to walk straight.* ◇ *I can't shoot straight* (= accurately). ◇ *She looked me straight in the eye.*
IMMEDIATELY | **2** by a direct route; immediately: *Come straight home after school.* ◇ *I was so tired I went straight to bed.* ◇ *She went straight from college to a top job.* ◇ *I'm going to the library straight after the class.* ◇ *I'll come straight to the point—your work isn't good enough.*

æ	ɑː	e	ɜː	ə	ɪ	iː	i	ɒ	ɔː	ʌ	ʊ	u	uː
cat	father	ten	bird	about	sit	see	many	got	saw	cup	put	actual	too

(BrE)

IN LEVEL/CORRECT POSITION | **3** in or into a level or upright position; in or into the correct position: *Sit up straight!* ◊ *She pulled her hat straight.*

HONESTLY | **4** honestly and directly: *I told him straight that I didn't like him.* ◊ *Are you playing straight with me?*

WITHOUT INTERRUPTION | **5** continuously without interruption: *They had been working for 16 hours straight.*

IDM go 'straight (*informal*) to stop being a criminal and live an honest life **play it 'straight** to be honest and not try to deceive sb **,straight a'way** immediately; without delay: *I'll do it straight away.* **,straight from the 'shoulder** if you say sth **straight from the shoulder**, you are being very honest and direct, even if what you are saying is critical **,straight 'off/'out** (*informal*) without hesitating: *She asked him straight off what he thought about it all.* **,straight 'up** (*BrE, spoken, informal*) used to ask if what sb has said is true or to emphasize that what you have said is true: *I saw it—straight up!*—more at THINK *v.*

■ *adj.* (**straight·er, straight·est**)

WITHOUT CURVES | **1** without a bend or curve; going in one direction only: *a straight line/road* ◊ *long straight hair* (= without curls) ◊ *a boat sailing* **in a straight line** ◊ *straight-backed chairs*

CLOTHING | **2** not fitting close to the body and not curving away from the body: *a straight skirt*

AIM/BLOW | **3** going directly to the correct place: *a straight punch to the face*

IN LEVEL/CORRECT POSITION | **4** positioned in the correct way; level, upright or parallel to sth: *Is my tie straight?*

CLEAN/NEAT | **5** [not usually before noun] clean and neat, with everything in the correct place: *It took hours to get the house straight.*

HONEST | **6** honest and direct: *a straight answer to a straight question* ◊ *I don't think you're being straight with me.* ◊ *It's time for some* **straight talking**.

CHOICE | **7** [only before noun] simple; involving only two clear choices: *It was a* **straight choice** *between taking the job and staying out of work.* ◊ (*BrE*) *The election was a* **straight fight** *between the two main parties.*

ACTOR/PLAY | **8** [only before noun] (of an actor or a play) not connected with COMEDY or musical theatre, but with serious theatre

WITHOUT INTERRUPTION | **9** [only before noun] one after another in a series, without interruption: *The team has had five straight wins.*

ALCOHOLIC DRINK | **10** (*AmE*) (*BrE* **neat**) not mixed with water or anything else

NORMAL/BORING | **11** (*informal*) you can use **straight** to describe a person who is normal and ordinary, but who you consider dull and boring

SEX | **12** (*informal*) HETEROSEXUAL **OPP** GAY

▶ **straight·ness** *noun* [U]

IDM (earn/get) straight 'A's (*especially AmE*) (to get) the best marks/grades in all your classes: *a straight A student* **get sth 'straight** to make a situation clear; to make sure that you or sb else understands the situation: *Let's get this straight—you really had no idea where he was?* **a straight 'face** if you say you keep a **straight face**, you do not laugh or smile, although you find sth funny—see also STRAIGHT-FACED **put/set sb 'straight (about/on sth)** to correct sb's mistake; to make sure that sb knows the correct facts when they have had the wrong idea or impression **the ,straight and 'narrow** (*informal*) the honest and morally acceptable way of living: *His wife is trying to keep him on the straight and narrow.*—more at RAMROD, RECORD *n.*

■ *noun*

SEX | **1** (*informal*) a person who has sexual relationships with people of the opposite sex, rather than the same sex: *gays and straights*

OF ROAD/TRACK | **2** (*AmE* also **straight·away**) a straight part of a RACETRACK or road—see also THE HOME STRAIGHT

,straight 'arrow *noun* (*AmE, informal*) a person who is very honest or who never does anything new, exciting or different

straight·away /ˌstreɪtəˈweɪ/ *adv., noun*

■ *adv.* immediately; at once: *You'd better call the doctor straightaway.*

■ *noun* (*AmE*) = STRAIGHT (2)

'straight edge *noun* a strip of wood, metal or plastic with a straight edge used for drawing accurate straight lines, or checking them

straight·en /ˈstreɪtn/ *verb* **1** ~ (sth) (out) to become straight; to make sth straight: [VN] *I straightened my tie and walked in.* ◊ [V] *The road bends here then straightens out.* **2** ~ (sth) (up) to make your body straight and upright: [VN] *He stood up and straightened his shoulders.* ◊ *I straightened myself up to answer the question.* ◊ [V] *Straighten up slowly, then repeat the exercise ten times.* **PHRV ,straighten sb↔'out** to help sb to deal with problems or understand a confused situation **,straighten sth↔'out** to deal with a confused situation by organizing things that are causing problems: *I need time to straighten out my finances.* **,straighten sth↔'up** to make sth neat and tidy

,straight-'faced *adj.* without laughing or smiling, even though you may be amused

straight·for·ward /ˌstreɪtˈfɔːwəd; *AmE* -ˈfɔːrwərd/ *adj.* **1** easy to do or to understand; not complicated: *a straightforward process/operation/solution* ◊ *It's quite straightforward to get here.* **2** (of a person or their behaviour) honest and open; not trying to deceive sb or hide sth ▶ **straight·for·ward·ly** *adv.*: *Let me put it more straightforwardly.* ◊ *a straightforwardly pleasant man* **straight·for·ward·ness** *noun* [U]

straight·jacket *noun* = STRAITJACKET

,straight-'laced *adj.* = STRAIT-LACED

'straight man *noun* a person in a show whose role is to provide the main entertainer with opportunities to make jokes

strain /streɪn/ *noun, verb*

■ *noun*

WORRY/ANXIETY | **1** [U, C] pressure on sb/sth because they have too much to do or manage, or sth very difficult to deal with; the problems, worry or anxiety that this produces: *Their marriage is* **under great strain** *at the moment.* ◊ *These repayments are* **putting a strain on** *our finances.* ◊ *Relax, and let us* **take the strain** (= do things for you). ◊ *The transport service cannot cope with the strain of so many additional passengers.* ◊ *You will learn to cope with the* **stresses and strains** *of public life.* ◊ *I found it a strain having to concentrate for so long.* ◊ *There are strains in the relationship between the two countries.*

PHYSICAL PRESSURE | **2** [U, C] the pressure that is put on sth when a physical force stretches, pushes, or pulls it: *The rope broke* **under the strain**. ◊ *You should try not to place too much strain on muscles and joints.* ◊ *The ground here cannot* **take the strain** *of a large building.* ◊ *The cable has a 140kg* **breaking strain** (= it will break when it is stretched or pulled by a force greater than this).

INJURY | **3** [C, U] an injury to a part of your body, such as a muscle, that is caused by using it too much or by twisting it: *a calf/groin/leg strain* ◊ *muscle strain*

TYPE OF PLANT/ANIMAL/DISEASE | **4** [C] a particular type of plant or animal, or of a disease caused by bacteria, etc: *a new strain of mosquitoes resistant to the poison* ◊ *This is only one of the many strains of the disease.*

IN SB'S CHARACTER | **5** [C, usually sing.] a particular tendency in the character of a person or group, or a quality in their manner **SYN** STREAK: *He had a definite strain of snobbery in him.*

OF MUSIC | **6** [C, usually pl.] (*formal*) the sound of music being played or sung: *She could hear the strains of Mozart through the window.*

■ *verb*

INJURE | **1** [VN] to injure yourself or part of your body by making it work too hard: *to strain a muscle* ◊ *You'll strain your back carrying those heavy suitcases.*

MAKE EFFORT | **2** ~ (sth) (for sth) | ~ (sth) (to do sth) to make an effort to do sth, using all your mental or physical strength: [VN to inf] *I strained my ears* (= listened very hard) *to catch what they were saying.* ◊ [VN] *Necks were strained for a glimpse of the stranger.* ◊ [V to inf] *People*

aɪ	aʊ	eɪ	əʊ	oʊ	ɔɪ	ɪə	eə	ʊə	j	w
my	now	say	go (BrE)	go (AmE)	boy	near	hair	pure	yes	wet

were straining to see what was going on. ◊ [V] *He burst to the surface, straining for air.* ◊ *Bend gently to the left without straining.*

<u>STRETCH TO LIMIT</u> **3** [VN] to try to make sth do more than it is able to do: *The sudden influx of visitors is straining hotels in the town to the limit.* ◊ *His constant complaints were straining our patience.* ◊ *The dispute has strained relations between the two countries* (= made them difficult).

<u>PUSH/PULL HARD</u> **4** [V+*adv.* / *prep.*] to push hard against sth; to pull hard on sth: *She strained against the ropes that held her.* ◊ *The dogs were straining at the leash, eager to get to the park.*

<u>SEPARATE SOLID FROM LIQUID</u> **5** [VN] ~ **sth** (**off**) to pour food, etc. through sth with very small holes in it, for example a SIEVE, in order to separate the solid part from the liquid part: *Use a colander to strain the vegetables.* ◊ *Strain off any excess liquid.*

IDM **strain at the ˈleash** (*informal*) to want to do sth very much: *Like all youngsters, he's straining at the leash to leave home.* **strain every ˈnerve/ˈsinew (to do sth)** (*written*) to try as hard as you can to do sth—more at CREAK *v.*

strained /streɪnd/ *adj.* **1** showing the effects of worry or pressure SYN TENSE: *Her face looked strained and weary.* ◊ *He spoke in a low, strained voice.* **2** (of a situation) not relaxed or friendly SYN TENSE: *There was a strained atmosphere throughout the meeting.* ◊ *Relations between the two families are strained.* **3** not natural; produced by a deliberate effort SYN FORCED: *She gave a strained laugh.*

strain·er /ˈstreɪnə(r)/ *noun* a kitchen UTENSIL (= a tool) with a lot of small holes in it, used for separating solids from liquids: *a tea-strainer*

strait /streɪt/ *noun* **1** (also **straits**) [pl.] (especially in the names of places) a narrow passage of water that connects two seas or large areas of water: *the Strait(s) of Gibraltar* **2** (**straits**) [pl.] a very difficult situation especially because of lack of money: *The factory is in dire straits.* ◊ *She found herself in desperate financial straits.*

strait·ened /ˈstreɪtnd/ *adj.* [only before noun] (*formal*) without enough money or as much money as there was before: *The family of eight was living in straitened circumstances.*

strait·jacket (also **straight·jacket**) /ˈstreɪtdʒækɪt/ *noun* **1** a piece of clothing like a jacket with long arms which are tied to prevent the person wearing it from behaving violently. Straitjackets are sometimes used to control people who are mentally ill. **2** (*disapproving*) a thing that stops sth from growing or developing: *the straitjacket of taxation*

strait-laced (also **straight-laced**) /ˌstreɪt ˈleɪst/ *adj.* (*disapproving*) having strict or old-fashioned ideas about people's moral behaviour

strand /strænd/ *noun, verb*
■ *noun* **1** a single thin piece of thread, wire, hair, etc: *a strand of wool* ◊ *a few strands of dark hair* ◊ *She wore a single strand of pearls around her neck.* **2** one of the different parts of an idea, a plan, a story, etc: *We heard every strand of political opinion.* ◊ *The author draws the different strands of the plot together in the final chapter.* **3** (*literary* or *IrishE*) the shore of the sea or ocean, or of a lake or river
■ *verb* [VN] (usually passive) **1** to leave sb in a place from which they have no way of leaving: *The strike left hundreds of tourists stranded at the airport.* **2** to make a boat, fish, WHALE, etc. be left on the shore and unable to return to the water: *The ship was stranded on a sandbank.*

strange /streɪndʒ/ *adj.* (**stran·ger**, **stran·gest**) **1** ~ (that/how ...) unusual or surprising, especially in a way that is difficult to understand: *A strange thing happened this morning.* ◊ *She was looking at me in a very strange way.* ◊ *It's strange (that) we haven't heard from him.* ◊ *It's strange how childhood impressions linger.* ◊ *That's strange—the front door's open.* ◊ *I'm looking forward to the exam, strange as it may seem.* ◊ *There was something strange about her eyes.* ◊ *Strange to say, I don't really enjoy television.* **2** ~ (**to sb**) not familiar because you have not

been there before or met the person before: *a strange country/city/neighbourhood* ◊ *to wake up in a strange bed* ◊ *Never accept lifts from strange men.* ◊ *At first the place was strange to me.* ▶ **strange·ness** *noun* [U] IDM **feel ˈstrange** to not feel comfortable in a situation; to have an unpleasant physical feeling: *She felt strange sitting at her father's desk.* ◊ *It was terribly hot and I started to feel strange.*—more at TRUTH

strange·ly /ˈstreɪndʒli/ *adv.* in an unusual or surprising way: *She's been acting very strangely lately.* ◊ *The house was strangely quiet.* ◊ *strangely shaped rocks* ◊ **Strangely enough**, *I don't feel at all nervous.*

strang·er /ˈstreɪndʒə(r)/ *noun* **1** ~ (**to sb**) a person that you do not know: *There was a complete stranger sitting at my desk.* ◊ *They got on well together although they were total strangers.* ◊ *We've told our daughter not to speak to strangers.* ◊ *She remained a stranger to me.* **2** ~ (**to ...**) a person who is in a place that they have not been in before: *Sorry, I don't know where the bank is. I'm a stranger here myself.* ◊ *He must have been a stranger to the town.* IDM **be no/a ˈstranger to sth** (*formal*) to be familiar/not familiar with sth because you have/have not experienced it many times before: *He is no stranger to controversy.*

stran·gle /ˈstræŋɡl/ *verb* [VN] **1** to kill sb by squeezing or pressing on their throat and neck: *to strangle sb to death* ◊ *He strangled her with her own scarf.* **2** (*written*) to prevent sth from growing or developing: *The current monetary policy is strangling the economy.*

stran·gled /ˈstræŋɡld/ *adj.* (of a cry, sb's voice, etc.) a cry or other sound that is not clear because it stops before it has completely finished: *There was a strangled cry from the other room.* ◊ *a strangled gasp/voice/whisper*

strangle·hold /ˈstræŋɡlhəʊld; *AmE* -hoʊld/ *noun* [sing.] **1** a strong hold around sb's neck that makes it difficult for them to breathe **2** ~ (**on sth**) complete control over sth that makes it impossible for it to grow or develop well: *The company now had a stranglehold on the market.*

stran·gler /ˈstræŋɡlə(r)/ *noun* a person who kills sb by squeezing their throat tightly

stran·gu·lated /ˈstræŋɡjuleɪtɪd/ *adj.* **1** (*medical*) (of a part of the body) squeezed so tightly that blood etc. cannot pass through it **2** (*written*) (of a voice) sounding as though the throat is tightly squeezed, usually because of fear or worry: *He gave a strangulated squawk.*

stran·gu·la·tion /ˌstræŋɡjuˈleɪʃn/ *noun* [U] **1** the act of killing sb by squeezing their throat tightly; the state of being killed in this way: *to die of slow strangulation* **2** (*disapproving*) the act of preventing sth from growing or developing: *the strangulation of the human spirit*

strap /stræp/ *noun, verb*
■ *noun* a strip of leather, fabric or other material that is used to fasten sth, keep sth in place, carry sth or hold onto sth: *the shoulder straps of her dress* ◊ *a watch with a leather strap*—picture at BAG
■ *verb* (**-pp-**) [VN] **1** [+*adv.* / *prep.*] to fasten sb/sth in place using a strap or straps: *He strapped the knife to his leg.* ◊ *Everything had to be strapped down to stop it from sliding around.* ◊ *Are you strapped in* (= wearing a seat belt in a car, plane, etc.)? **2** ~ (**up**) **sth** to wrap strips of material around a wound or an injured part of the body: *I have to keep my leg strapped up for six weeks.*

strap·less /ˈstræpləs/ *adj.* (especially of a dress or BRA) without straps

strapped /stræpt/ *adj.* ~ (**for cash, funds, etc.**) (*informal*) having little or not enough money: *I'm strapped for cash at the moment—can I pay you later?*

strap·ping /ˈstræpɪŋ/ *adj.* [only before noun] (*informal*) (of people) big, tall and strong: *a strapping lad*

strata *pl.* of STRATUM

strata·gem /ˈstrætədʒəm/ *noun* (*formal*) a trick or plan that you use to gain an advantage or to deceive an opponent: *to adopt a cunning stratagem*

stra·tegic /strəˈtiːdʒɪk/ (also *less frequent* **stra·tegic·al** /-dʒɪkl/) *adj.* [usually before noun] **1** done as part of a plan that is meant to achieve a particular purpose or to

S

b	d	f	g	h	k	l	m	n	p	r
bad	did	fall	get	hat	cat	leg	man	now	pen	red

gain an advantage: *strategic planning* ◊ *a strategic decision to sell off part of the business* ◊ *Cameras were set up at strategic points* (= in places where they would be most effective) *along the route.* **2** connected with getting an advantage in a war or other military situation: *Malta was of vital strategic importance during the war.* **3** (of weapons, especially nuclear weapons) intended to be fired at an enemy's country rather than used in a battle: *strategic missiles*—compare TACTICAL (3) ▶ **stra·tegic·al·ly** /-kli/ *adv.*: *a strategically placed microphone* ◊ *a strategically important target*

strat·egist /ˈstrætədʒɪst/ *noun* a person who is skilled at planning things, especially military activities

strat·egy /ˈstrætədʒi/ *noun* (*pl.* **-ies**) **1** [C] ~ (**for doing sth**)| ~ (**to do sth**) a plan that is intended to achieve a particular purpose: *to develop a strategy for dealing with unemployment* ◊ *It's all part of an overall strategy to gain promotion.* ◊ *the government's economic strategy* **2** [U] the process of planning sth or carrying out a plan in a skilful way: *marketing strategy* **3** [U, C] the skill of planning the movements of armies in a battle or war; an example of doing this: *military strategy* ◊ *defence strategies*—compare TACTIC

strati·fi·ca·tion /ˌstrætɪfɪˈkeɪʃn/ *noun* [U] (*technical*) the division of sth into different layers or groups: *social stratification*

strat·ify /ˈstrætɪfaɪ/ *verb* (**strati·fies, strati·fy·ing, strati·fied, strati·fied**) [VN] [usually passive] (*formal* or *technical*) to arrange sth in layers or STRATA: *a highly stratified society* ◊ *stratified rock*

strato·sphere /ˈstrætəsfɪə(r); *AmE* -sfɪr/ *noun* (**the stratosphere**) [sing.] the layer of the earth's atmosphere between about 10 and 50 kilometres above the surface of the earth—compare IONOSPHERE ▶ **strato·spher·ic** /ˌstrætəˈsferɪk/ *adj.*: *stratospheric clouds/ozone*

stra·tum /ˈstrɑːtəm; *AmE* ˈstreɪtəm/ *noun* (*pl.* **strata** /-tə/) **1** (*geology*) a layer or set of layers of rock, earth, etc. **2** (*written*) a class in a society: *people from all social strata*

straw /strɔː/ *noun* **1** [U] stems of wheat or other grain plants that have been cut and dried. Straw is used for making MATS, hats, etc., for packing things to protect them, and as food for animals or for them to sleep on: *a mattress filled with straw* ◊ *a straw hat*—compare HAY **2** [C] a single stem or piece of straw: *He was leaning over the gate chewing on a straw.* **3** (also **ˈdrinking straw**) a thin tube of plastic or paper that you suck a drink through ⟦IDM⟧ **clutch/grasp at ˈstraws** to try all possible means to find a solution or some hope in a difficult or unpleasant situation, even though this seems very unlikely **the last/final ˈstraw | the ˌstraw that breaks the camel's ˈback** the last in a series of bad events, etc. that makes it impossible for you to accept a situation any longer **a straw in the ˈwind** (*BrE*) a small sign of what might happen in the future—more at BRICK *n.*, DRAW *v.*

straw·berry /ˈstrɔːbəri; *AmE* -beri/ *noun* (*pl.* **-ies**) a soft red fruit with very small yellow seeds on the surface, that grows on a low plant: *strawberries and cream* ◊ *strawberry plants*—picture on page A2

ˌstraw ˈpoll (*AmE* also **ˌstraw ˈvote**) *noun* an occasion when a number of people are asked in an informal way to give their opinion about sth or to say how they are likely to vote in an election

stray /streɪ/ *verb, adj., noun*
- *verb* [V] **1** [usually+*adv./prep.*] to move away from the place where you should be, without intending to: *He strayed into the path of an oncoming car.* ◊ *Her eyes kept straying over to the clock on the wall.* ◊ *Her parents fear that, living in this neighbourhood, she might stray into the wrong company.* **2** [usually+*adv./prep.*] to begin to think about or discuss a different subject from the one you should be thinking about or discussing: *My mind kept straying back to our last talk together.* ◊ *We seem to be straying from the main theme of the debate.* **3** (of a person who is married or in a relationship) to have a sexual relationship with sb who is not your usual partner: *It had*

never occurred to her that her husband might stray while he was away on business.
- *adj.* [only before noun] **1** (of animals normally kept as pets) lost from home; having no home: *stray dogs/cats* **2** separated from other things or people of the same kind: *A civilian was killed by a stray bullet.* ◊ *a few stray hairs*
- *noun* **1** an animal that has got lost or separated from its owner or that has no owner—see also WAIF **2** a person or thing that is not in the right place or is separated from others of the same kind

streak /striːk/ *noun, verb*
- *noun* **1** a long thin mark or line that is a different colour from the surface it is on: *There was a streak of blood on his face.* ◊ *streaks of grey in her hair* ◊ *dirty streaks on the window* **2** a part of a person's character, especially an unpleasant part: *a ruthless/vicious/mean streak* ◊ *a streak of cruelty* **3** a series of successes or failures, especially in a sport or in gambling: *a streak of good luck* ◊ *to hit* (= have) *a winning streak* ◊ *to be on a losing streak* ◊ *a lucky/unlucky streak*
- *verb* **1** [VN] ~ **sth** (**with sth**) to mark or cover sth with streaks: *Tears streaked her face.* ◊ *His face was streaked with mud.* ◊ *She's had her hair streaked* (= had special chemicals put on her hair so that it has attractive coloured lines in it). **2** [V+*adv./prep.*] to move very fast in a particular direction: *A car pulled out and streaked off down the road.* **3** [V, usually+*adv./prep.*] (*informal*) to run through a public place with no clothes on as a way of getting attention

streak·er /ˈstriːkə(r)/ *noun* a person who runs through a public place with no clothes on as a way of getting attention

streaky /ˈstriːki/ *adj.* marked with lines of a different colour: *streaky blonde hair* ◊ *The wallpaper was streaky with grease.* ◊ (*BrE*) *streaky bacon* (= with layers of fat in it)

stream /striːm/ *noun, verb*
- *noun* **1** a small narrow river: *mountain/underground streams*—see also DOWNSTREAM, UPSTREAM, THE GULF STREAM **2** ~ (**of sth**) a continuous flow of liquid or gas: *A stream of blood flowed from the wound.*—see also BLOODSTREAM **3** ~ (**of sth/sb**) a continuous flow of people or vehicles: *I've had a steady stream of visitors.* ◊ *Cars filed past in an endless stream.* **4** ~ **of sth** a large number of things that happen one after the other: *a constant stream of enquiries/complaints* ◊ *The agency provided me with a steady stream of work.* **5** (*especially BrE*) a group in which students of the same age and level of ability are placed in some schools: *She was put into the fast stream.* ⟦IDM⟧ **be/come on ˈstream** to be in operation or available: *The new computer system comes on stream next month.*
- *verb* **1** ~ (**from sth**)| ~ (**with sth**) (of liquid or gas) to move or pour out in a continuous flow; to produce a continuous flow of liquid or gas: [V] *Tears streamed down his face.* ◊ *a streaming cold* (= with a lot of liquid coming from the nose) ◊ *Blood was streaming from her head.* ◊ *Her head was streaming with blood.* ◊ [V, VN] *Black smoke streamed from the exhaust.* ◊ *The exhaust streamed black smoke.* **2** (of people or things) [V+*adv./prep.*] to move somewhere in large numbers, one after the other: *People streamed across the bridge.* **3** [V] to move freely, especially in the wind or water: *Her scarf streamed behind her.* **4** [VN] [usually passive] (*especially BrE*) (*AmE* usually **track**) (in schools) to put school students into groups according to their ability: *Pupils are streamed for French and Maths.*

stream·er /ˈstriːmə(r)/ *noun* **1** a long narrow piece of coloured paper, used to decorate a place for a party or other celebration **2** a long narrow piece of fabric or other material

stream·ing /ˈstriːmɪŋ/ *noun* [U] (*especially BrE*) the policy of dividing school students into groups of the same level of ability

stream·line /ˈstriːmlaɪn/ *verb* [VN] [usually passive] **1** to give sth a smooth even shape so that it can move quickly and easily through air or water: *The cars all have a new streamlined design.* **2** to make a system, an organization, etc. work better, especially in a way that saves money: *The production process is to be streamlined.*

s	t	v	z	ʃ	ʒ	tʃ	dʒ	θ	ð	ŋ
see	tea	van	zoo	shoe	vision	chain	jam	thin	this	sing

,stream of 'consciousness *noun* [U] a continuous flow of ideas, thoughts, and feelings, as they are experienced by a person; a style of writing that expresses this without using the usual methods of description and conversation

street /striːt/ *noun* (*abbr.* **St, st**) a public road in a city or town that has houses and buildings on one side or both sides: *The bank is just across the street.* ◊ *to walk along/down/up the street* ◊ *the town's narrow cobbled streets* ◊ *92nd Street* ◊ *10 Downing Street* ◊ *He is used to being recognized* **in the street**. ◊ *a street map/plan of York* ◊ *street theatre/musicians* ◊ *My office is* **at street level** (= on the ground floor). ◊ *It's not safe to* **walk the streets** *at night.*—see also BACKSTREET, HIGH STREET, SIDE STREET ⇨ note at ROAD **IDM** **(out) on the 'streets/'street** (*informal*) without a home; outside, not in a house or other building: *the problems of young people living on the streets* ◊ *If it had been right to me I would have put him out on the street long ago.* **on/walking the 'streets** working as a prostitute **'streets ahead (of sb/sth)** (*BrE, informal*) much better or more advanced than sb/sth else: *a country that is streets ahead in the control of environmental pollution* ◊ *Beth is streets ahead of all the other students in her year.* **the streets are ,paved with 'gold** (*saying*) used to say that it seems easy to make money in a place **(right) up your 'street** (*especially BrE*) (*AmE usually* **(right) up your 'alley**) (*informal*) very suitable for you because it is sth that you know a lot about or are very interested in: *This job seems right up your street.*—more at EASY *adj.*, HIT *v.*, MAN *n.*

street-car /'striːtkɑː(r)/ *noun* (*AmE*) = TRAM

'street cred (also **cred**) (*informal*) (also *less frequent* **'street credibility**) *noun* [U] a way of behaving and dressing that is acceptable to young people, especially those who live in cities and have experienced the problems of real life: *Those clothes do nothing for your street cred.*

,street 'furniture *noun* [U] (*technical*) equipment such as road signs, street lights, etc. placed at the side of a road

'street light (*BrE also* **'street lamp**) *noun* a light at the top of a tall post in the street—compare LAMP POST

'street people *noun* (*especially AmE*) people who have no home and who live outside in a town SYN THE HOMELESS

street-smart /'striːtsmɑːt; *AmE* -smɑːrt/ *adj.* (*AmE*) = STREETWISE

'street value *noun* [usually sing.] a price for which sth that is illegal or has been obtained illegally can be sold: *drugs with a street value of over £1 million*

street-walk-er /'striːtwɔːkə(r)/ *noun* (*old-fashioned*) a prostitute who looks for customers on the streets

street-wise /'striːtwaɪz/ (*AmE also* **street-smart**) *adj.* (*informal*) having the knowledge and experience that is needed to deal with the difficulties and dangers of life in a big city: *Kids seem much more streetwise these days.*

strength /streŋθ/ *noun*
BEING PHYSICALLY STRONG | **1** [U, sing.] **~ to do sth** the quality of being physically strong: *He pushed against the rock with all his strength.* ◊ *It may take a few weeks for you to build up your strength again.* ◊ *She didn't have the strength to walk any further.* ◊ *He had a physical strength that matched his outward appearance.* **2** [U] the ability that sth has to resist force or hold heavy weights without breaking or being damaged: *the strength of a rope/box*
BEING BRAVE | **3** [U, sing.] the quality of being brave and determined in a difficult situation: *During this ordeal he was able to draw strength from his faith.* ◊ *She has a remarkable* **inner strength**. ◊ *You have shown great* **strength of character**.
POWER/INFLUENCE | **4** [U] the power and influence that sb/sth has: *Political power depends upon economic strength.* ◊ *Their superior military strength gives them a huge advantage.* ◊ *to negotiate from* **a position of strength** ◊ *The rally was intended to be a show of strength by the socialists.*
OF OPINION/FEELING | **5** [U] how strong or deeply felt an opinion or a feeling is: *the strength of public opinion* ◊ *This view has recently gathered strength* (= become stronger or more widely held). ◊ *I was surprised by the strength of her feelings.*
ADVANTAGE | **6** [C] a quality or an ability that a person or thing has that gives them an advantage: *The ability to keep calm is one of her many strengths.* ◊ *the strengths and weaknesses of an argument*
OF NATURAL FORCE | **7** [U] how strong a natural force is: *the strength of the sun* ◊ *wind strength* ◊ *the strength and direction of the tide*
OF FLAVOUR | **8** [U, C] how strong a particular flavour or substance is: *Add more curry powder depending on the strength required.* ◊ *a range of beers with different strengths* (= with different amounts of alcohol in them)
OF CURRENCY | **9** [U] how strong a country's CURRENCY (= unit of money) is in relation to other countries' CURRENCIES: *the strength of the dollar*
NUMBER IN GROUP | **10** [U] the number of people in a group, a team or an organization: *The strength of the workforce is about to be doubled from 3000 to 6000.* ◊ *The team will be* **back at full strength** (= with all the best players) *for the next match.* ◊ *The protesters turned out* **in strength** (= in large numbers). ◊ *These cuts have left the local police force* **under strength** (= with fewer members than it needs).
IDM **go from ,strength to 'strength** to become more and more successful: *Since her appointment the department has gone from strength to strength.* **on the strength of sth** because sb has been influenced or persuaded by sth: *I got the job on the strength of your recommendation.*—more at TOWER *n.*

strength-en /'streŋθn/ *verb* to become stronger; to make sb/sth stronger: [V] *Her position in the party has strengthened in recent weeks.* ◊ *Yesterday the pound strengthened against the dollar.* ◊ *The wind had strengthened overnight.* ◊ [VN] *Repairs are necessary to strengthen the bridge.* ◊ *The exercises are designed to strengthen your stomach muscles.* ◊ *The move is clearly intended to strengthen the President's position as head of state.* ◊ *The new manager has strengthened the side by bringing in several younger players.* ◊ *Their attitude only strengthened his resolve to fight on.* ◊ *The new evidence will strengthen their case.* **OPP** WEAKEN

strenu-ous /'strenjuəs/ *adj.* **1** needing great effort and energy: *a strenuous climb/walk* ◊ *Avoid strenuous exercise immediately after a meal.* ◊ *How about a stroll in the park? Nothing too strenuous.* **2** showing great energy and determination: *The ship went down although strenuous efforts were made to save it.* ▶ **strenu-ous-ly** *adv.*: *He still works out strenuously every morning.* ◊ *The government strenuously denies the allegations.*

strep throat /,strep 'θrəʊt/ *noun* (*AmE, informal*) an infection of the throat

S

æ	ɑː	e	ɜː	ə	ɪ	iː	i	ɒ	ɔː	ʌ	ʊ	u	uː
cat	father	ten	bird	about	sit	see	many	got	saw	cup	put	actual	too
								(BrE)					

strepto·coc·cus /ˌstreptəˈkɒkəs; AmE -ˈkɑːkəs/ noun (pl. -cocci /-ˈkɒkaɪ; AmE -ˈkɑːkaɪ/) (medical) a type of bacteria, some types of which can cause serious infections and illnesses

stress /stres/ noun, verb

■ noun

MENTAL PRESSURE | **1** [U, C] pressure or worry caused by the problems in sb's life: *Things can easily go wrong when people are* **under stress**. ◊ *to suffer from stress* ◊ *coping with stress* ◊ *She failed to withstand the* **stresses and strains** *of public life.* ◊ *stress-related illnesses* ◊ *emotional/ mental stress* ◊ *Stress is often a factor in the development of long-term sickness.* ◊ *stress* **management** (= dealing with stress)

PHYSICAL PRESSURE | **2** [U, C] ~ **(on sth)** pressure put on sth that can damage it or make it lose its shape: *When you have an injury you start putting stress on other parts of your body.* ◊ *a stress fracture of the foot* (= one caused by such pressure)

EMPHASIS | **3** [U] ~ **(on sth)** special importance given to sth: *She* **lays** great *stress* **on** *punctuation.* ◊ *I think the company places too much stress on cost and not enough on quality.*

ON WORD/SYLLABLE | **4** [U, C] (phonetics) an extra force used when pronouncing a particular word or syllable: *We worked on pronunciation, stress and intonation.* ◊ *primary/secondary stress* ◊ *In 'strategic' the stress falls on the second syllable*—compare INTONATION

IN MUSIC | **5** [U, C] extra force used when making a particular sound in music

ILLNESS | **6** [U] illness caused by difficult physical conditions: *Those most vulnerable to heat stress are the elderly.*

■ verb

EMPHASIZE | **1** to emphasize a fact, an idea, etc: [VN] *He stressed the importance of a good education.* ◊ [V that] *I must stress that everything I've told you is strictly confidential.* ◊ [V speech] *'There is,' Johnson stressed, 'no real alternative.'* ◊ [VN that] *It must be stressed that this disease is very rare.* [also V wh-]

WORD/SYLLABLE | **2** [VN] to give extra force to a word or syllable when saying it: *You stress the first syllable in 'happiness'.*

stressed /strest/ adj. **1** (also informal ˌstressed ˈout) [not before noun] too anxious and tired to be able to relax: *He was feeling very stressed and tired.* **2** (of a syllable) pronounced with emphasis OPP UNSTRESSED **3** [only before noun] (technical) that has had a lot of physical pressure put on it: *stressed metal*

stress·ful /ˈstresfl/ adj. causing a lot of anxiety and worry: *a stressful job/situation/lifestyle* ◊ *It was a very stressful time for all of us.*

ˈstress mark noun a mark used to show where the stress is placed on a particular word or syllable—see also PRIMARY STRESS, SECONDARY STRESS

stretch /stretʃ/ verb, noun

■ verb

MAKE BIGGER/LOOSER | **1** to make sth longer, wider or looser, for example, by pulling it; to become longer, etc. in this way: [VN] *Is there any way of stretching shoes?* ◊ [V] *This sweater has stretched.* **2** [V] (of fabric) to become bigger or longer when you pull it and return to its original shape when you stop: *The jeans stretch to provide a perfect fit.*

PULL TIGHT | **3** to pull sth so that it is smooth and tight: [VN] *Stretch the fabric tightly over the frame.* ◊ [VN-ADJ] *Make sure that the rope is stretched tight.*

YOUR BODY | **4** to put your arms or legs out straight and tighten your muscles: [V] *He stretched and yawned lazily.* ◊ [VN] *The exercises are designed to stretch and tone your leg muscles.*

REACH WITH ARM | **5** [+adv./prep.] to put out an arm or a leg in order to reach sth: [V] *She stretched across the table for the butter.* ◊ [VN] *I stretched out a hand and picked up the book.*

OVER AREA | **6** [V+adv./prep.] to spread over an area of land: *Fields and hills stretched out as far as we could see.*

OVER TIME | **7** [V+adv./prep.] to continue over a period of time: *The town's history stretches back to before 1500.* ◊ *Endless summer days stretched out before us.* ◊ *The talks look set to stretch into a second week.*

MONEY/SUPPLIES | **8** [V] ~ **(to sth)** (used in negative sentences and questions about an amount of money) to be enough to buy or pay for sth: *I need a new car, but my savings won't stretch to it.* **9** [VN] to make use of all your money, supplies, etc: *The influx of refugees has* **stretched** *the country's resources* **to the limit**.

SB'S SKILL/INTELLIGENCE | **10** [VN] to make use of all sb's skill, intelligence, etc: *I need a job that will stretch me.* ◊ *We can't take on any more work—we're fully stretched as it is.*

TRUTH/BELIEF | **11** [VN] to use sth in a way that would not normally be considered fair, acceptable, etc: *He admitted that he had maybe* **stretched** *the truth* (= not been completely honest) *a little.* ◊ *The play's plot* **stretches** *credulity* **to the limit**.

IDM **stretch your 'legs** (informal) to go for a short walk after sitting for some time: *It was good to get out of the car and stretch our legs.* **stretch a 'point** to allow or do sth that is not usually acceptable, especially because of a particular situation—more at RULE n.

PHRV ˌstretch ˈout| ˌstretch yourself ˈout to lie down, usually in order to relax or sleep: *He stretched himself out on the sofa and fell asleep.*

■ noun

AREA OF LAND/WATER | **1** [C] ~ **(of sth)** an area of land or water, especially a long one: *an unspoilt stretch of coastline* ◊ *a particularly dangerous stretch of road* ◊ *You rarely see boats on this stretch of the river.*

PERIOD OF TIME | **2** [C] a continuous period of time SYN SPELL: *They worked in four-hour stretches.* ◊ *She used to read for hours* **at a stretch** (= without stopping). **3** [C, usually sing.] (informal) a period of time that sb spends in prison: *He did a ten-year stretch for fraud.*

OF BODY | **4** [C, U] an act of stretching out your limbs or your body and tightening the muscles; the state of being stretched: *We got out of the car and had a good stretch.* ◊ *Only do these more difficult stretches when you are warmed up.* ◊ *Stay in this position and feel the stretch in your legs.*

OF FABRIC | **5** [U] the ability to be made longer or wider without breaking or tearing: *You need a material with plenty of stretch in it.* ◊ *stretch jeans*

ON RACE TRACK | **6** [C, usually sing.] a straight part at the end of a racing track SYN STRAIGHT: *the finishing/home stretch* ◊ (figurative) *The campaign has entered its final stretch.*

IDM **at full 'stretch** using as much energy as possible, or the greatest possible amount of supplies: *Fire crews have been operating at full stretch.* **not by any stretch of the imagination | by no stretch of the imagination** used to say strongly that sth is not true, even if you try to imagine or believe it: *She could not, by any stretch of the imagination, be called beautiful.*

stretch·er /ˈstretʃə(r)/ noun, verb

■ noun a long piece of strong fabric with a pole on each side, used for carrying sb who is sick or injured and who cannot walk: *He was carried off on a stretcher.* ◊ *stretcher cases* (= people too badly injured to be able to walk)

■ verb [VN+adv./prep.] [usually passive] to carry sb somewhere on a stretcher: *He was stretchered off the pitch with a broken leg.*

ˈstretcher-bearer noun a person who helps to carry a stretcher, especially in a war or when there is a very serious accident

ˈstretch limo noun (pl. stretch limos) (also formal ˌstretch limouˈsine) a very large car that has been made longer so that it can have extra seats

ˈstretch marks noun [pl.] the marks that are left on a person's skin after it has been stretched, particularly after a woman has been pregnant

stretchy /ˈstretʃi/ adj. that can easily be made longer or wider without tearing or breaking: *stretchy fabric* ◊ *a stretchy skirt*

strew /struː/ verb (strewed, strewed or strewn /struːn/)

aɪ	aʊ	eɪ	ɔʊ	oʊ	ɔɪ	ɪə	eə	ʊə	j	w
my	now	say	go	go	boy	near	hair	pure	yes	wet
			(BrE)	(AmE)						

1 [VN] [usually passive] **~ A on, over, across, etc. B | ~ B with A** to cover a surface with things: *Clothes were strewn across the floor.* ◇ *The floor was strewn with clothes.* ◇ (*figurative*) *The way ahead is strewn with difficulties.* **2** [VN] to be spread or lying over a surface: *Leaves strewed the path.*

strewth /struːθ/ *exclamation* (*old-fashioned, BrE, slang*) used to express surprise, anger, etc.

stricken /ˈstrɪkən/ *adj.* (*formal*) **1 ~ (with sth)** seriously affected by an unpleasant feeling or disease or by a difficult situation: *She raised her stricken face and begged for help.* ◇ *Whole villages were stricken with the disease.* ◇ *We went to the aid of the stricken boat.* **2** (in compounds) seriously affected by the thing mentioned: *poverty-stricken families*—see also PANIC-STRICKEN, GRIEF-STRICKEN, HORROR-STRICKEN, STRIKE *v.*

strict /strɪkt/ *adj.* (**strict·er, strict·est**) **1** that must be obeyed exactly: *strict rules/regulations/discipline* ◇ *She left strict instructions that she was not to be disturbed.* ◇ *He told me **in the strictest confidence** (= on the understanding that I would tell nobody else).* ◇ *She's on a very strict diet.* **2** demanding that rules, especially rules about behaviour, should be obeyed: *a strict teacher/parent/disciplinarian* ◇ *She's very strict about things like homework.* ◇ *They were always very strict with their children.* **3** obeying the rules of a particular religion, belief, etc. exactly: *a strict Muslim/Catholic/vegetarian* **4** [usually before noun] very exact and clearly defined: *It wasn't illegal in the strict sense (of the word).* ▶ **strict·ness** *noun* [U]

strict·ly /ˈstrɪktli/ *adv.* **1** with a lot of control and rules that must be obeyed: *She was brought up very strictly.* ◇ *The industry is strictly regulated.* **2** used to emphasize that sth happens or must happen in all circumstances [SYN] ABSOLUTELY: *Smoking is strictly forbidden.* ◇ *My letter is, of course, strictly private and confidential.* **3** in all details; exactly: *This is not strictly true.* **4** used to emphasize that sth only applies to one particular person, thing or situation [SYN] PURELY: *We'll look at the problem from a strictly legal point of view.* ◇ *I know we're friends, but this is strictly business.* [IDM] **'strictly speaking** if you are using words or rules in their exact or correct sense: *Strictly speaking, the book is not a novel, but a short story.* ◇ *Using the word in that context is not, strictly speaking, correct.*

stric·ture /ˈstrɪktʃə(r)/ *noun* (*formal*) **1** [usually pl.] **~ (on sb/sth)** a severe criticism, especially of sb's behaviour **2 ~ (against/on sth)** a rule or situation that restricts your behaviour [SYN] RESTRICTION: *social/economic strictures* ◇ *strictures against civil servants expressing political opinions*

stride /straɪd/ *noun, verb*
- *verb* (*pt* **strode** /strəʊd/ *AmE* stroʊd/) (not used in the perfect tenses) [V+*adv./prep.*] to walk with long steps in a particular direction: *We strode across the snowy fields.* ◇ *She came striding along to meet me.*
- *noun* **1** one long step; the distance covered by a step: *He crossed the room in two strides.* ◇ *I was gaining on the other runners with every stride.* **2** your way of walking or running: *his familiar purposeful stride* ◇ *She did not slow her stride until she was face to face with us.* **3** an improvement in the way sth is developing: *We're making great strides in the search for a cure.* [IDM] **get into your 'stride** (*BrE*) (*AmE* **hit (your) 'stride**) to begin to do sth with confidence and at a good speed after a slow, uncertain start: *After a nervous start, he finally got into his stride in the second set.* **put sb off their 'stride** to make sb take their attention off what they are doing and stop doing it so well (**match sb**) **,stride for 'stride** to keep doing sth as well as sb else, even though they keep making it harder for you: *We've managed to match our closest competitors stride for stride as regards prices.* **take sth in your 'stride** (*BrE*) (*AmE* **take sth in 'stride**) to accept and deal with sth difficult without letting it worry you too much **without breaking 'stride** (*especially AmE*) without stopping what you are doing

stri·dent /ˈstraɪdnt/ *adj.* **1** having a loud harsh and unpleasant sound: *a strident voice/tone* ◇ *strident music* **2** aggressive and determined: *He is a strident advocate of*

nuclear power. ◇ *The plan has provided strident criticism from local residents.* ▶ **stri·dency** /ˈstraɪdənsi/ *noun* [U] **stri·dent·ly** *adv.*

strife /straɪf/ *noun* [U] (*formal* or *literary*) angry or violent disagreement between two people or groups of people [SYN] CONFLICT: *civil/industrial/political strife* ◇ *The country was torn apart by strife.*

strike /straɪk/ *verb, noun*
- *verb* (**struck, struck** /strʌk/) (*AmE also* **struck, strick·en** /ˈstrɪkən/)

HIT SB/STH | **1** [VN] (*formal*) to hit sb/sth hard or with force: *The ship struck a rock.* ◇ *The child ran into the road and was struck by a car.* ◇ *The tree was struck by lightning.* ◇ *He fell, striking his head on the edge of the table.* ◇ *The stone struck her on the forehead.* **2** (*formal*) to hit sb/sth with your hand or a weapon: [VN] *She struck him in the face.* ◇ *He struck the table with his fist.* ◇ *Who struck the first blow (= started the fight)?* [also VNN]

KICK/HIT BALL | **3** [VN] (*formal*) to hit or kick a ball, etc: *He walked up to the penalty spot and struck the ball firmly into the back of the net.*

ATTACK | **4** [V] to attack sb/sth, especially suddenly: *The lion crouched ready to strike.* ◇ *Police fear that the killer may strike again.*

OF DISASTER/DISEASE | **5** (*written*) to happen suddenly and have a harmful or damaging effect on sb/sth: [V] *Two days later tragedy struck.* ◇ [VN] *The area was struck by an outbreak of cholera.*

THOUGHT/IDEA/IMPRESSION | **6** (not used in the progressive tenses) (of a thought or an idea) to come into sb's mind suddenly: [VN] *An awful thought has just struck me.* ◇ *I was struck by her resemblance to my aunt.* ◇ [VN wh-] *It suddenly struck me how we could improve the situation.* **7 ~ sb (as sth)** to give sb a particular impression: [VN] *His reaction struck me as odd.* ◇ *How does the idea strike you?* ◇ *She strikes me as a very efficient person.* ◇ [VN (that)] *It strikes me that nobody is really in favour of the changes.*

OF LIGHT | **8** [VN] to fall on a surface: *The windows sparkled as the sun struck the glass.*

DUMB/DEAF/BLIND | **9** [VN-ADJ] [usually passive] to put sb suddenly into a particular state: *to be struck dumb/deaf/blind*

OF WORKERS | **10** [V] to refuse to work as a protest: *The union has voted to strike for a pay increase of 6%.* ◇ *Striking workers picketed the factory.*

MATCH | **11** to rub sth such as a match against a surface so that it produces a flame; to produce a flame when rubbed against a rough surface: [VN] *to strike a match on a wall* ◇ *The sword struck sparks off the stone floor.* ◇ [V] *The matches were damp and he couldn't make them strike.*

OF CLOCK | **12** to show the time by making a ringing noise, etc: [V] *Did you hear the clock strike?* ◇ [VN] *The clock has just struck three.*

MAKE SOUND | **13** [VN] to produce a musical note, sound, etc. by pressing a key or hitting sth: *to strike a chord on the piano*

GOLD/OIL, etc. | **14** [VN] to discover gold, oil, etc. by digging or DRILLING: *They had struck oil!*

GO WITH PURPOSE | **15** [V+*adv./prep.*] **~ (off/out)** to go somewhere with great energy or purpose: *We left the road and struck off across the fields.*

[IDM] **be 'struck by/on/with sb/sth** (*informal*) to be impressed or interested by sb/sth; to like sb/sth very much: *I was struck by her youth and enthusiasm.* ◇ *We're not very struck on that new restaurant.* **strike a 'balance (between A and B)** to manage to find a way of being fair to two opposing things; to find a COMPROMISE between two things **strike a 'bargain/'deal** to make an agreement with sb in which both sides have an advantage **strike a blow for/against/at sth** to do sth in support of/against a belief, principle, etc: *He felt that they had struck a blow for democracy.* **strike fear, etc. into sb/sb's heart** (*formal*) to make sb be afraid, etc. **strike 'gold** to find or do sth that brings you a lot of success or money: *He has struck gold with his latest novel.* **strike it 'rich** (*informal*) to get a lot of money, especially suddenly or unexpectedly

b	d	f	g	h	k	l	m	n	p	r
bad	did	fall	get	hat	cat	leg	man	now	pen	red

strike (it) ˈlucky (*informal*) to have good luck: *We certainly struck it lucky with the weather.* **strike a** ˈpose/an ˈattitude to hold your body in a particular way to create a particular impression: *to strike a dramatic/heroic pose* **strike while the iron is** ˈhot (*saying*) to make use of an opportunity immediately **within** ˈstriking distance (of sth) near enough to be reached or attacked easily; near enough to reach or attack sth easily: *The beach is within striking distance.* ◊ *The cat was now within striking distance of the duck.*—more at CHORD, HARD *adj.*, HOME *adv.*, LIGHTNING *n.*, NOTE *n.*, PAY DIRT

PHRV ˈstrike at sb/sth 1 to try to hit sb/sth, especially with a weapon: *He struck at me repeatedly with a stick.* 2 to cause damage or have a serious effect on sb/sth: *to strike at the root of the problem* ◊ *criticisms that strike at the heart of the party's policies* ˌstrike ˈback (at/against sb) to try to harm sb in return for an attack or injury you have received ˌstrike sb ˈdown [usually passive] 1 (of a disease, etc.) to make sb unable to lead an active life; to make sb seriously ill; to kill sb: *He was struck down by cancer at the age of thirty.* 2 to hit sb very hard, so that they fall to the ground ˌstrike sth↔ˈoff to remove sth with a sharp blow; to cut sth off: *He struck off the rotten branches with an axe.* ˌstrike sb/sth ˈoff (sth) to remove sb/sth's name from sth, such as the list of members of a professional group: *Strike her name off the list.* ◊ *The doctor was struck off* (= not allowed to continue to work as a doctor) *for incompetence.* ˌstrike ˈout 1 to start being independent: *I knew it was time I struck out on my own.* 2 (*AmE, informal*) to fail or be unsuccessful: *The movie struck out and didn't win a single Oscar.* ˌstrike ˈout (at sb/sth) 1 to aim a sudden violent blow at sb/sth: *He lost his temper and struck out wildly.* 2 to criticize sb/sth, especially in a public speech or in a book or newspaper: *In a recent article she strikes out at her critics.* ˌstrike sth↔ˈout/ˈthrough to remove sth by drawing a line through it [SYN] CROSS OUT: *The editor struck out the whole paragraph.* ˌstrike ˈout (for/towards sth) to move in a determined way (towards sth): *He struck out* (= started swimming) *towards the shore.* ˌstrike ˈup (with sth)| ˌstrike ˈup sth (of a band, an orchestra, etc.) to begin to play a piece of music: *The orchestra struck up and the curtain rose.* ◊ *The band struck up a waltz.* ˌstrike ˈup sth (with sb) to begin a friendship, a relationship, a conversation, etc: *He would often strike up conversations with complete strangers.*

■ *noun*

OF WORKERS | 1 a period of time when an organized group of employees of a company stops working because of a disagreement over pay or conditions: *the train drivers' strike* ◊ *a strike by teachers* ◊ *a general/unofficial/one-day strike* ◊ *Air traffic controllers are threatening to come out on/go on strike.* ◊ *Half the workforce are now (out) on strike.* ◊ *The train drivers have voted to take strike action.* ◊ *The student union has called for a rent strike* (= a refusal to pay rent as a protest).—see also HUNGER STRIKE

ATTACK | 2 a military attack, especially by aircraft dropping bombs: *an air strike* ◊ *a lightning strike* (= a very quick, sudden attack) ◊ *They decided to launch a pre-emptive strike.*

HITTING/KICKING | 3 [usually sing.] an act of hitting or kicking sth/sb: *His spectacular strike in the second half made the score 2–0.*

IN BASEBALL | 4 an unsuccessful attempt to hit the ball

IN BOWLING | 5 a situation in TENPIN BOWLING when a player knocks down all the PINS with the first ball

DISCOVERY OF OIL | 6 [usually sing.] a sudden discovery of sth valuable, especially oil

ˈstrike-bound *adj.* unable to operate because employees have stopped working as a protest: *a strike-bound airport*

ˈstrike-breaker *noun* a person who continues to work while other employees are on strike; a person who is employed to replace people who are on strike—compare BLACKLEG ▶ ˈstrike-breaking *noun* [U]

ˈstrike force *noun* [C+sing./pl. *v.*] a military or police force that is ready to act quickly when necessary

strike·out /ˈstraɪkaʊt/ *noun* (in baseball) a situation in which the player who is supposed to be hitting the ball is out and has to stop because he or she has tried to hit the ball three times and failed

striker /ˈstraɪkə(r)/ *noun* 1 a worker who has stopped working because of a disagreement over pay or conditions 2 (in football) a player whose main job is to attack and try to score goals

ˈstrike rate *noun* [usually sing.] (*sport*) the number of times a player is successful in relation to the number of times they try to score or win

strik·ing /ˈstraɪkɪŋ/ *adj.* 1 interesting and unusual enough to attract attention [SYN] MARKED: *a striking feature/example* ◊ *She bears a striking resemblance to her older sister.* ◊ **In striking contrast** to their brothers, the girls were both intelligent and charming. 2 very attractive, often in an unusual way [SYN] STUNNING: *striking good looks* ◊ *She was undoubtedly a very striking young woman.* ▶ **strik·ing·ly** *adv.*: *The two polls produced strikingly different results.* ◊ *She is strikingly beautiful.*

Strim·mer™ /ˈstrɪmə(r)/ *noun* (*BrE*) an electric garden tool held in the hands and used for cutting grass that is difficult to cut with a larger machine

string /strɪŋ/ *noun, verb, adj.*

■ *noun*

FOR TYING/FASTENING | 1 [U, C] material made of several threads twisted together, used for tying things together; a piece of string used to fasten or pull sth or keep sth in place: *a piece/length of string* ◊ *He wrapped the package in brown paper and tied it with string.* ◊ *The key is hanging on a string by the door.*—see also DRAWSTRING, THE PURSE STRINGS—picture at ROPE

THINGS JOINED | 2 [C] a set or series of things that are joined together, for example on a string: *a string of pearls* ◊ *The molecules join together to form long strings.*

SERIES | 3 [C] a series of things or people that come closely one after another: *a string of hits/successes* ◊ *He owns a string of racing stables.*

COMPUTING | 4 [C] a series of CHARACTERS (= letters, numbers, etc.)

MUSICAL INSTRUMENTS | 5 [C] a tightly stretched piece of wire, NYLON, or CATGUT on a musical instrument, that produces a musical note when the instrument is played—picture at PIANO 6 (the strings) [pl.] the group of musical instruments in an orchestra that have strings, for example violins, the people who play them: *The opening theme is taken up by the strings.*—compare BRASS, PERCUSSION, WOODWIND—picture on page 840

ON TENNIS RACKET | 7 [C] any of the tightly stretched pieces of NYLON, etc. in a RACKET, used for hitting balls in tennis and some other games—see also G-STRING

IDM have another string/more strings to your bow (*BrE*) to have more than one skill or plan that you can used if you need to (with) no ˈstrings (attached) with no special conditions or restrictions: *It's a business proposition, pure and simple. No strings attached.*—more at APRON, LONG *adj.*, PULL *v.*

■ *verb* (strung, strung /strʌŋ/) [VN]

HANG DECORATION | 1 [+*adv.*/*prep.*] ~ A on, along, in, etc. B| ~ B with A to hang or tie sth in place, especially as decoration: *We strung paper lanterns up in the trees.* ◊ *Flags were strung out along the route.* ◊ *The route was strung with flags.*

JOIN THINGS | 2 [+*adv.*/*prep.*] to put a series of small objects on string, etc.; to join things together with string, etc: *She had strung the shells on a silver chain.* ◊ (*figurative*) *carbon atoms strung together to form giant molecules*

RACKET/MUSICAL INSTRUMENT | 3 to put a string or strings on a RACKET or musical instrument

—see also HIGHLY STRUNG

PHRV ˌstring sb aˈlong (*informal*) to allow sb to believe sth that is not true, for example that you love them, intend to help them, etc: *She has no intention of giving you a divorce; she's just stringing you along.* ˌstring aˈlong (with sb) (*BrE, informal*) to go somewhere with sb, especially because you have nothing else to do ˌstring sth↔ˈout to make sth last longer than expected or neces-

s	t	v	z	ʃ	ʒ	tʃ	dʒ	θ	ð	ŋ
see	tea	van	zoo	shoe	vision	chain	jam	thin	this	sing

sary: *They seem determined to string the talks out for an indefinite period.*—see also STRUNG OUT ,**string sth↔to'gether** to combine words or phrases to form sentences: *I can barely string two words together in Japanese.* ,**string sb↔'up** (*informal*) to kill sb by hanging them, especially illegally: *If I ever find out who did this, I'll string them up.*

■ *adj.* [only before noun]

MUSICAL INSTRUMENT | **1** consisting of musical instruments that have strings; connected with these musical instruments: *a string quartet* ◊ *a string player*

MADE OF STRING | **2** made of string or sth like string: *a string bag/vest*

,**string 'bean** *noun* **1** (*BrE*) = RUNNER BEAN **2** (*AmE*) = GREEN BEAN

,**stringed 'instrument** *noun* any musical instrument with strings that you play with your fingers or with a BOW

strin·gent /'strɪndʒənt/ *adj.* (*formal*) **1** (of a law, rule, regulation, etc.) very strict and that must be obeyed: *stringent air quality regulations* ◊ *Licences are only granted under the most stringent conditions.* **2** (of financial conditions) difficult and very strictly controlled because there is not much money: *the government's stringent economic policies* ▶ **strin·gency** /-nsi/ *noun* [U]: *a period of financial stringency* **strin·gent·ly** *adv.*: *The rules are stringently enforced.*

string·er /'strɪŋə(r)/ *noun* a journalist who is not on the regular staff of a newspaper, but who often supplies stories for it

stringy /'strɪŋi/ *adj.* (*disapproving*) **1** (of hair) long and thin and looking as if it has not been washed **2** (of food) containing long thin pieces like string and difficult to chew: *tough, stringy meat* **3** (of a person or part of their body) thin so that you can see the muscles: *a stringy neck*

strip /strɪp/ *verb, noun*

■ *verb* (**-pp-**)

TAKE OFF CLOTHES | **1** ~ **sth (off)** | ~ **(down to sth)** | ~ **sb (to sth)** to take off all or most of your clothes: [V] *I stripped and washed myself all over.* ◊ *We stripped off and ran down to the water.* ◊ *She stripped down to her underwear.* ◊ [VN] *He stood there **stripped to the waist** (= the upper part of his body was bare).* ◊ [VN-ADJ] *He was **stripped naked** and left in a cell.*

REMOVE LAYER | **2** [VN] ~ **sth (off)** | ~ **A (off/from B)** / ~ **B (of A)** to remove a layer from sth, especially so that it is completely bare: *Strip off all the existing paint.* ◊ *Deer had stripped the tree of its bark.* ◊ *Deer had stripped all the bark off the tree.* ◊ *After the guests had gone, I stripped all the beds* (= removed all the sheets in order to wash them).

REMOVE EVERYTHING | **3** ~ **sth (out)** to remove all the things from a place and leave it empty: [VN] *We had to strip out all the old wiring and start again.* ◊ [VN-ADJ] *Thieves had stripped the house bare.*

MACHINE | **4** [VN] ~ **sth (down)** to separate a machine, etc. into parts so that they can be cleaned or repaired SYN DISMANTLE: *He strips and cleans his rifle every morning.* ◊ *They taught us how to strip down a car engine and put it back together again.*

PUNISHMENT | **5** [VN] ~ **sb of sth** to take away property or honours from sb, as a punishment: *He was disgraced and stripped of his title.*

PHRV ,**strip sth↔a'way 1** to remove a layer from sth: *First, you need to strip away all the old plaster.* **2** to remove anything that is not true or necessary: *The movie aims to strip away the lies surrounding Kennedy's life and death.*

■ *noun*

LONG, NARROW PIECE | **1** a long narrow piece of paper, metal, fabric, etc: *a strip of material* ◊ *Cut the meat into strips.*—see also RUMBLE STRIP **2** a long narrow area of land, sea, etc: *the Gaza Strip* ◊ *a tiny strip of garden* ◊ *The islands are separated by a narrow strip of water.*—see also AIRSTRIP, LANDING STRIP

OF SPORTS TEAM | **3** [usually sing.] (*BrE*) the uniform that is worn by the member of a sports team when they are playing: *Juventus in their famous black and white strip* ◊

*the team's **away strip** (= that they use when playing games away from home)*

TAKING CLOTHES OFF | **4** [usually sing.] an act of taking your clothes off, especially in a sexually exciting way and in front of an audience: *to do a strip* ◊ *a strip show*—see also STRIPTEASE

STREET | **5** (*AmE*) a street that has many shops, stores, restaurants, etc. along it: *Sunset Strip*

PICTURE STORY | **6** (*AmE*) = COMIC STRIP

IDM see TEAR¹*v.*

,**strip car'toon** (also **car·toon**) *noun* (*BrE*) = COMIC STRIP

'**strip club** (also '**strip joint** especially in *AmE*) *noun* a club where people go to watch performers take their clothes off in a sexually exciting way

stripe /straɪp/ *noun* **1** a long narrow line of colour, that is a different colour from the areas next to it: *a zebra's black and white stripes* ◊ *a white tablecloth with red stripes*—see also PINSTRIPE, THE STARS AND STRIPES **2** a narrow piece of fabric, often in the shape of a V, that is worn on the uniform of a soldier or police officer to show their rank: *a uniform with a sergeant's stripes on the sleeve*

striped /straɪpt/ (also *BrE informal* **stripy**) *adj.* marked with a pattern of stripes: *a striped shirt* ◊ *a blue and white striped jacket*—picture on page A4

'**strip light** *noun* a light consisting of a long glass tube that is used especially in offices, kitchens, etc. ▶ '**strip lighting** *noun* [U]

strip·ling /'strɪplɪŋ/ *noun* (*old-fashioned* or *humorous*) a young man who is older than a boy but who does not seem to be a real man yet

'**strip mining** *noun* [U] (*AmE*) a type of mining in which coal is taken out of the ground near the surface—see also OPENCAST

strip·per /'strɪpə(r)/ *noun* **1** [C] a performer who takes his or her clothes off in a sexually exciting way in front of an audience: *a male stripper* **2** [U, C] (especially in compounds) a substance or tool that is used for removing paint, etc. from sth: *The vandals threw paint stripper on the car.*

'**strip search** *noun* an act of searching a person for illegal drugs, weapons, etc., for example at an airport or in a prison, after they have been made to take off all their clothes ▶ '**strip-search** *verb* [VN]

strip·tease /'strɪptiːz/ *noun* [C, U] a form of entertainment, for example in a bar or club, when a performer removes his or her clothes in a sexually exciting way, usually to music, in front of an audience

stripy (also **stripey**) /'straɪpi/ *adj.* (*BrE, informal*) = STRIPED: *a stripy jumper/cat*

strive /straɪv/ *verb* (**strove** /strəʊv/; *AmE* strouv/ **striven** /'strɪvn/ or *less frequent* **strived, strived**) ~ (**for/against sth**) (*formal*) to try very hard to achieve sth or to defeat sth: [V] *We encourage all members to strive for the highest standards.* ◊ *striving against corruption* ◊ [V to inf] *Newspaper editors all strive to be first with a story.* ▶ **striv·ing** *noun* [U, sing.]: *our striving for perfection*

strobe /'strəʊb; *AmE* 'stroʊb/ (also '**strobe light**) *noun* a bright light that flashes rapidly on and off, used especially at DISCOS

strode *pt* of STRIDE

stroke /strəʊk; *AmE* stroʊk/ *noun, verb*

■ *noun*

HITTING MOVEMENT | **1** an act of hitting a ball, for example with a bat or RACKET: *What a beautiful stroke!* ◊ *He won by two strokes* (= in golf, by taking two fewer strokes than his opponent). **2** a single movement of the arm when hitting sb/sth: *His punishment was six strokes of the cane.*

IN SWIMMING/ROWING | **3** any of a series of repeated movements in swimming or rowing: *She took a few more strokes to reach the bank.*—picture at SWIMMING **4** (often in compounds) a style of swimming: *Butterfly is the only stroke I can't do.*—see also BACKSTROKE, BREASTSTROKE **5** the person who sets the speed at which everyone in a boat rows

GENTLE TOUCH | **6** [usually sing.] (*especially BrE*) an act of

æ	ɑː	e	ɜː	ə	ɪ	iː	i	ɒ	ɔː	ʌ	ʊ	u	uː
cat	father	ten	bird	about	sit	see	many	got	saw	cup	put	actual	too
								(BrE)					

S

moving your hand gently over a surface, usually several times: *He gave the cat a stroke.*

OF PEN/BRUSH | **7** a mark made by moving a pen, brush, etc. once across a surface: *to paint with fine brush strokes* ◊ *At the stroke of a pen* (= by signing sth) *they removed thousands of people from the welfare system.*

ACTION | **8** ~ **(of sth)** a single successful action or event: *Your idea was a **stroke of genius**.* ◊ *It was a **stroke of luck** that I found you here.* ◊ *It was a **bold stroke** to reveal the identity of the murderer on the first page.* ◊ *She **never does a stroke (of work)*** (= never does any work).—see also MASTER STROKE

OF CLOCK | **9** each of the sounds made by a clock or bell giving the hours: *At the first stroke it will be 9 o'clock exactly.* ◊ *on the stroke of three* (= at 3 o'clock exactly)

ILLNESS | **10** a sudden serious illness when a blood VESSEL (= tube) in the brain bursts or is blocked, which can cause death or the loss of the ability to move or to speak clearly: *to have/suffer a stroke* ◊ *The stroke left him partly paralysed.*

IDM **at a (single) 'stroke | at one 'stroke** with a single immediate action: *They threatened to cancel the whole project at a stroke.* **put sb off their 'stroke** (*BrE*) to make sb make a mistake or hesitate in what they are doing
■ *verb* [VN]

TOUCH GENTLY | **1** (*especially BrE*) to move your hand gently and slowly over an animal's fur or hair: *He's a beautiful dog. Can I stroke him?*—see also PET **2** to move your hand gently over a surface, sb's hair, etc: *He stroked her hair affectionately.*

MOVE STH GENTLY | **3** [+*adv./prep.*] to move sth somewhere with a gentle movement: *She stroked away his tears.* ◊ *He stroked the ball between the posts.*

BE NICE TO SB | **4** (*informal, especially AmE*) to be very nice to sb, especially to get them to do what you want

stroll /strəʊl; *AmE* stroʊl/ *verb, noun*
■ *verb* [V] [usually +*adv./prep.*] to walk somewhere in a slow relaxed way: *People were strolling along the beach.*
■ *noun* a slow relaxed walk: *We went for a stroll in the park.*

stroll·er /'strəʊlə(r); *AmE* 'stroʊl-/ *noun* **1** a person who is enjoying a slow relaxed walk: *The street was crowded with evening strollers.* **2** (*AmE*) = BUGGY, PUSHCHAIR

strong /strɒŋ; *AmE* strɔːŋ/ *adj.* (**strong·er** /-gə(r)/, **strong·est** /-gɪst/)

HAVING PHYSICAL POWER | **1** (of people, animals, etc.) having a lot of physical power so that you can lift heavy weights, do hard physical work, etc: *strong muscles/arms* ◊ *She wasn't a strong swimmer* (= she could not swim well). ◊ *He's strong enough to lift a car!* **2** (of a natural or physical force) having great power: *Stay indoors in the middle of the day, when the sun is strongest.* ◊ *a strong wind/current* ◊ *a strong magnet* **3** having a powerful effect on the body or mind: *a strong drug*

HAVING POWER OVER PEOPLE | **4** having a lot of power or influence: *a strong leader/government* **5 (the strong)** [pl.] people who are rich or powerful

HARD TO RESIST/DEFEAT/ATTACK | **6** very powerful and difficult for people to fight against or defeat: *a strong army/team* ◊ (*figurative*) *The temptation to tell her everything was very strong.* **7** (of an argument, evidence, etc.) difficult to attack or criticize: *There is strong evidence of a link between exercise and a healthy heart.* ◊ *You have a strong case for getting your job back.*

OPINION/BELIEF/FEELING | **8** [only before noun] (of a person) holding an opinion or a belief very firmly and seriously: *a strong supporter/opponent of the government* **9** (of an opinion, a belief or a feeling) very powerful: *strong support for/opposition to the government* ◊ *People have strong feelings about this issue.*

NOT EASILY BROKEN | **10** (of objects) not easily broken or damaged; made well: *a strong stick/rope/chair*

NOT EASILY UPSET | **11** not easily upset or frightened; not easily influenced by other people: *You need strong nerves to ride a bike in London.* ◊ *It's difficult, I know. But be strong!* ◊ *a strong character/personality* ◊ *She's had a strong will since she was a baby.*—see also HEADSTRONG, STRONG-MINDED, STRONG-WILLED

LIKELY TO SUCCEED | **12** likely to succeed or happen: *a strong candidate for the job* ◊ *You're in a strong position to negotiate a deal.* ◊ *There's a strong possibility that we'll lose the game.*

GOOD AT STH | **13** good at sth: *The play has a very strong cast.* ◊ *Mathematics was never my strong point* (= I was never very good at it).

NUMBER | **14** great in number: *There was a strong police presence at the demonstration.* **15** used after numbers to show the size of a group: *a 5000-strong crowd* ◊ *The crowd was 5000 strong.*

HEALTHY | **16** (of a person) not easily affected by disease; healthy: *Are you feeling stronger now after your rest?*

FIRMLY ESTABLISHED | **17** firmly established; difficult to destroy: *a strong marriage* ◊ *The college has strong links with local industry.*

BUSINESS | **18** (of prices, an economy, etc.) having a value that is high or increasing: *strong share prices* ◊ *The euro is getting stronger against the dollar.* **19** (of a business or an industry) in a safe financial position: *Their catering business remained strong despite the recession.*

EASY TO SEE/HEAR/FEEL/SMELL | **20** easy to see, hear, feel or smell; very great or INTENSE: *a strong smell* ◊ *a strong feeling of nausea* ◊ *a strong voice* (= loud) ◊ *strong colours* ◊ *a face with strong features* (= large and noticeable) ◊ *She spoke with a strong Australian accent.* ◊ *He was under strong pressure to resign.*

FOOD | **21** having a lot of flavour: *strong cheese/mustard*

DRINKS | **22** containing a lot of a substance: *strong black coffee*

WORDS | **23** (of words or language) very forceful, often causing offence to people: *The movie has been edited for strong language* (= swearing).

GRAMMAR | **24** [usually before noun] (of a verb) forming the past tense by changing a vowel, not by adding a regular ending, for example *sing, sang*

PHONETICS | **25** [usually before noun] used to describe the way some words are pronounced when they have stress. For example, the strong form of *and* is /ænd/.

—see also STRENGTH **OPP** WEAK ▶ **strong·ly** *adv.*: *a strongly-built boat* ◊ *a light shining strongly* ◊ *a strongly-worded protest* ◊ *He was strongly opposed to the idea.* ◊ *This is an issue I feel strongly about* (= I have firm opinions about). ◊ *The room smelt strongly of polish.*

IDM **be a bit 'strong** (*BrE, informal*) used to say that you think what sb has said is unfair or too critical **be 'strong on sth 1** to be good at sth: *I'm not very strong on dates* (= I can't remember the dates of important events). **2** to have a lot of sth: *The report was strong on criticism, but short on practical suggestions.* **be sb's 'strong suit** to be a subject that sb knows a lot about: *I'm afraid geography is not my strong suit.* **come on 'strong** (*informal*) to make your feelings clear in an aggressive way, especially your sexual feelings towards sb **going 'strong** (*informal*) to continue to be healthy, active or successful: *My grandmother is 90 and still going strong.* **have a strong 'stomach** to be able to see or do unpleasant things without feeling sick or upset—more at CARD *n.*

'strong-arm *adj.* [only before noun] (*disapproving*) using threats or violence in order to make people do what you want: *to use strong-arm tactics/methods against your political opponents*

strong·box /'strɒŋbɒks; *AmE* 'strɔːŋbɑːks/ *noun* a strong, usually metal, box for keeping valuable things in

strong·hold /'strɒŋhəʊld; *AmE* 'strɔːŋhoʊld/ *noun* **1** an area in which there is a lot of support for a particular belief or group of people, especially a political party: *a Republican stronghold/a stronghold of Republicanism* **2** a castle or a place that is strongly built and difficult to attack **3** an area where there are a large number of a particular type of animal: *This valley is one of the last strongholds of the Siberian tiger.*

strong·man /'strɒŋmæn; *AmE* 'strɔːŋ-/ *noun* (pl. **-men** /-men/) **1** a leader who uses threats or violence to rule a country: *The country has been under the control of military strongmen for a long time.* **2** a physically very strong man, especially sb who performs in a CIRCUS

aɪ	aʊ	eɪ	əʊ	oʊ	ɔɪ	ɪə	eə	ʊə	j	w
my	now	say	go	go	boy	near	hair	pure	yes	wet
			(BrE)	(AmE)						

,**strong-'minded** *adj.* having strong opinions that are not easily influenced by what other people think or say [SYN] DETERMINED

strong·room /ˈstrɒnruːm; -rʊm; *AmE* ˈstrɔːŋ-/ *noun* a room, for example in a bank, with thick walls and a strong solid door, where valuable items are kept

,**strong-'willed** *adj.* determined to do what you want to do, even if other people advise you not to

stron·tium /ˈstrɒntiəm; ˈstrɒnʃ-; *AmE* ˈstrɑːnʃ-; ˈstrɑːnt-/ *noun* [U] (*symb* **Sr**) a chemical element. Strontium is a soft silver-white metal.

strop /strɒp; *AmE* strɑːp/ *noun* [sing.] (*BrE, informal*) a very bad mood when you are annoyed about sth: *Don't get in a strop—I'm only a few minutes late.*

stroppy /ˈstrɒpi; *AmE* ˈstrɑːpi/ *adj.* (*BrE, informal*) (of a person) easily annoyed and difficult to deal with: *Don't get stroppy with me—it isn't my fault!*

strove *pt* of STRIVE

struck *pt, pp* of STRIKE

struc·tural /ˈstrʌktʃərəl/ *adj.* [usually before noun] connected with the way in which sth is built or organized: *Storms have caused structural damage to hundreds of homes.* ◇ *There have been some fundamental structural changes in society.* ◇ *a structural engineer* (= a person who is qualified to design large buildings, bridges, etc.) ▶ **struc·tur·al·ly** /-ərəli/ *adv.*: *The building is structurally sound.* ◇ *The languages are structurally different.*

struc·tur·al·ism /ˈstrʌktʃərəlɪzəm/ *noun* [U] (in literature, language and social science) a theory that considers any text as a structure whose various parts only have meaning when they are considered in relation to each other—compare DECONSTRUCTION ▶ **struc·tur·al·ist** /-rəlɪst/ *noun, adj.*: *a structuralist critic/approach*

struc·ture /ˈstrʌktʃə(r)/ *noun, verb*
■ *noun* **1** [U, C] the way in which the parts of sth are connected together, arranged or organized; a particular arrangement of parts: *the structure of the building/ human body* ◇ *changes in the social and economic structure of society* ◇ *the grammatical structures of a language* ◇ *a career/salary/tax structure* **2** [C] a thing that is made of several parts, especially a building: *a stone/brick/ wooden structure* **3** [U, C] the state of being well organized or planned with all the parts linked together; a careful plan: *Your essay needs* (a) *structure.*
■ *verb* [VN] [usually passive] **~ sth** (**around sth**) to arrange or organize sth into a system or pattern: *How well does the teacher structure the lessons?* ◇ *The exhibition is structured around the themes of work and leisure.* ◇ *Make use of the toys in structured group activities.*

stru·del /ˈstruːdl/ *noun* [U, C] (from *German*) a cake made from pieces of fruit, especially apple, rolled in thin pastry and baked

strug·gle /ˈstrʌɡl/ *verb, noun*
■ *verb* **1 ~** (**for sth**) to try very hard to do sth when it is difficult or when there are a lot of problems: [V] *a country struggling for independence* ◇ *Shona* **struggled for breath.** ◇ *life as a struggling artist* (= one who is very poor) ◇ [Vtoinf] *They struggled just to pay their bills.* **2** [V+adv./prep.] to move somewhere or do sth with difficulty: *I struggled up the hill with the heavy bags.* ◇ *Paul struggled out of his wheelchair.* **3** [V] **~** (**against/with sb/sth**) to fight against sb/sth in order to prevent a bad situation or result: *He struggled against cancer for two years.* ◇ *Lisa struggled with her conscience before talking to the police.* **4** [V] **~** (**with sb**) to fight sb or try to get away from them: *Ben and Jack struggled together on the grass.* ◇ *I struggled and screamed for help.* ◇ *James was hit in the mouth as he struggled with the raiders.* ◇ *How did she manage to* **struggle free?** **5** [V] **~** (**with sb**) (**for sth**) to compete or argue with sb, especially in order to get sth: *rival leaders struggling for power* [PHRV] ,**struggle a'long/'on** to continue in spite of problems: *The business struggled along for some time.* ◇ *Life is hard but we all have to struggle on.*
■ *noun* **1** [C] **~** (**with sb**) (**for/against sth**)| **~** (**with sb**) (**to do sth**)| **~** (**between A and B**) a hard fight in which people try to obtain or achieve sth, especially sth that sb

else does not want them to have: *a power/leadership struggle* ◇ *a struggle for freedom/independence* ◇ *the struggle between good and evil* ◇ *He is engaged in a bitter struggle with his rival to get control of the company.* ◇ *She will not give up her children without a struggle.* **2** [C] a physical fight between two people or groups of people, especially when one of them is trying to escape, or to get sth from the other: *There were no signs of a struggle at the murder scene.* ◇ *After a short struggle, I managed to get the knife away from him.* **3** [sing.] **~** (**to do sth**) something that is difficult for you to do or achieve: *It was a real struggle to be ready on time.*

strum /strʌm/ *verb* (**-mm-**) **~** (**on**) **sth** to play a guitar or similar instrument by moving your fingers up and down across the strings: [V] *As she sang she strummed on a guitar.* [also VN]

strung *pt, pp* of STRING

,**strung 'out** *adj.* [not before noun] **1** spread out in a line: *a group of riders strung out along the beach* **2 ~** (**on sth**) (*slang*) strongly affected by an illegal drug such as HEROIN

,**strung 'up** *adj.* [not before noun] (*BrE, informal*) very nervous, worried or excited

strut /strʌt/ *verb, noun*
■ *verb* (**-tt-**) [V] to walk proudly with your head up and chest out to show that you think you are important: *The players strutted and posed for the cameras.* [IDM] ,**strut your 'stuff** (*informal*) to proudly show your ability, especially at dancing or performing: *strutting your stuff to the latest chart hits*
■ *noun* **1** a long thin piece of wood or metal used to support or strengthen part of a vehicle or building **2** [sing.] (*disapproving*) an act of walking in a proud and confident way

strych·nine /ˈstrɪkniːn/ *noun* [U] a poisonous substance used in very small amounts as a medicine

stub /stʌb/ *noun, verb*
■ *noun* **1** a short piece of a cigarette, pencil, etc. that is left when the rest of it has been used **2** the small part of a ticket, cheque, etc. that you keep as a record when you have given the main part to sb
■ *verb* (**-bb-**) [VN] **~ your toe** (**against/on sth**) to hurt your toe by accidentally hitting it against sth hard [PHRV] ,**stub sth↔'out** to stop a cigarette, etc. from burning by pressing the end against sth hard

stub·ble /ˈstʌbl/ *noun* [U] **1** the lower short stiff part of the stems of crops such as wheat, etc. that are left in the ground after the top part has been cut and collected **2** the short stiff hairs that grow on a man's face when he has not shaved recently—picture at HAIR ▶ **stub·bly** /ˈstʌbli/ *adj.*

stub·born /ˈstʌbən; *AmE* -bərn/ *adj.* **1** (often *disapproving*) determined not to change your opinion or attitude [SYN] OBSTINATE: *He was too stubborn to admit that he was wrong.* ◇ *She can be* **as stubborn as a mule.** ◇ *stubborn pride* ◇ *a stubborn resistance to change* ◇ *a stubborn refusal to listen* **2** difficult to get rid of or deal with: *a stubborn cough/stain* ◇ *a stubborn problem* ▶ **stubborn·ly** *adv.*: *She stubbornly refused to pay.* ◇ *Unemployment remains stubbornly high.* **stub·born·ness** *noun* [U]

stubby /ˈstʌbi/ *adj.* [usually before noun] short and thick: *stubby fingers*

stucco /ˈstʌkəʊ; *AmE* -koʊ/ *noun* [U] a type of PLASTER that is used for covering ceilings and the outside walls of buildings ▶ **stuc·coed** *adj.*: *a stuccoed house/wall*

stuck /stʌk/ *adj.* [not before noun]—see also STICK *v.* **1** unable to move or to be moved: *The wheels were stuck in the mud.* ◇ *This drawer keeps* **getting stuck.** ◇ *She got the key stuck in the lock.* ◇ *I can't get out—I'm stuck.* **2** in an unpleasant situation or place that you cannot escape from: *We were stuck in traffic for over an hour.* ◇ *I hate being stuck at home all day.* **3 ~** (**on sth**) unable to answer or understand sth: *I got stuck on the first question.* ◇ *I'll help you if you're stuck.* **4 ~** (**for sth**) not knowing what to do in a particular situation: *If you're stuck for something to do tonight, come out with us.* ◇ *I've never known him to be stuck for words before.* **5 ~ with sb/sth** (*informal*) unable to get rid of sb/sth that you do not want: *I was*

	b		d		f		g		h		k		l		m		n		p		r
	bad		did		fall		get		hat		cat		leg		man		now		pen		red

S

stuck with him for the whole journey. IDM ₁**get stuck ʹin** | ₁**get stuck ʹinto sth** (*BrE, informal*) to start doing sth in an enthusiastic way, especially to start eating—more at GROOVE, ROCK *n.*, TIME WARP

₁**stuck-ʹup** *adj.* (*informal, disapproving*) thinking that you are more important than other people and behaving in an unfriendly way towards them SYN SNOBBISH

stud /stʌd/ *noun* **1** [C] a small piece of jewellery with a rod that is pushed through a hole in your ear, nose, etc: *diamond studs*—picture at JEWELLERY **2** [C] a small round piece of metal that is attached to the surface of sth, especially for decoration: *a leather jacket with studs on the back* **3** [C, usually pl.] (*BrE*) one of several small metal or plastic objects that are fixed to the bottom part of a FOOTBALL BOOT or running shoe—compare CLEAT—picture at SHOE **4** [C] a small metal object used in the past for fastening a collar onto a shirt—see also PRESS STUD **5** [C, U] an animal, especially a horse, that is kept for breeding; the place where animals, especially horses, are kept for breeding: *a stud farm* ◊ *The horse was retired from racing and put out to stud* (= kept for breeding). **6** [C] (*informal*) a man who has many sexual partners and who is thought to be sexually attractive

stud·ded /stʌdɪd/ *adj.* **1** decorated with small raised pieces of metal: *a studded leather belt* **2** ~ **with sth** (*written*) having a lot of sth on or in it: *The sky was clear and studded with stars.* ◊ *an essay studded with quotations*—see also STAR-STUDDED ► **stud** *verb* (**-dd-**): [VN] *Stars studded the sky.*

stu·dent /ʹstjuːdnt; *AmE* ʹstuː-/ *noun* **1** a person who is studying at a university or college: *a medical/science student* ◊ *a graduate/postgraduate/research student* ◊ *an overseas student* ◊ *a student teacher/nurse* ◊ *a student grant/loan* (= money that is given/lent to students to pay for their studies) ◊ *She's a student at Sussex University.*—see also MATURE STUDENT **2** (*especially AmE*) a person who is studying at a school, especially a secondary school: *a 15-year-old high school student*—compare PUPIL **3** ~ **of sth** a person who is very interested in a particular subject: *a keen student of human nature*

WHICH WORD?

student / pupil / undergraduate / graduate / postgraduate

A **student** is a person who is studying at a school, college, university, etc. In *BrE* until recently **pupil** was used for children at school, but this is becoming old-fashioned and **student** is used instead, except for young children.

An **undergraduate** is a student who is studying for their first degree at a university or college.

In *BrE*, a **graduate** is a person who has completed a first degree at a university or college. In *AmE* **graduate** is usually used with another noun and can also apply to a person who has finished high school: *a high school graduate* ◊ *a graduate student.*

A **postgraduate** is a person who has finished a first degree and is doing advanced study or research. This is the usual term in *BrE*, but it is formal in *AmE* and **graduate student** is usually used instead.

stu·dent·ship /ʹstjuːdəntʃɪp; *AmE* ʹstuː-/ *noun* (*BrE*) one of a small number of places that a university gives to students who wish to continue studying or to do research after they have finished their degree; an amount of money that is given to a student who wins one of these places

₁**studentsʹ ʹunion** (also ₁**student ʹunion**) *noun* **1** a building where students at a university or college can go to meet socially **2** (*BrE*) an association of students at a particular university or college, concerned with students' rights and WELFARE

stud·ied /ʹstʌdɪd/ *adj.* [only before noun] (*written*) deliberate and carefully planned: *She introduced herself with studied casualness.*

stu·dio /ʹstjuːdiəʊ; *AmE* ʹstuːdioʊ/ *noun* (*pl.* **-os**) **1** a room

where radio or television programmes are recorded and broadcast from, or where music is recorded: *a television studio* ◊ *a studio audience* (= one in a studio, that can be seen or heard as a programme is broadcast) ◊ *a recording studio* **2** a place where films/movies are made or produced **3** a company that makes films/movies: *She works for a major Hollywood studio.* ◊ *a studio executive* **4** a room where an artist works: *a sculptor's/photographer's studio* **5** a place where dancing is taught or where dancers practise: *a dance studio* **6** (*BrE* also ʹ**studio flat**) (*AmE* also ʹ**studio apartment**) a small flat/apartment with one main room for living and sleeping in and usually a kitchen and BATHROOM

stu·di·ous /ʹstjuːdiəs; *AmE* ʹstuː-/ *adj.* spending a lot of time studying or reading: *a studious young man*

stu·di·ous·ly /ʹstjuːdiəsli; *AmE* ʹstuː-/ *adv.* in a way that is carefully planned and deliberate: *He studiously avoided answering the question.*

study /ʹstʌdi/ *noun, verb*

■ *noun* (*pl.* **-ies**)

▶ ACTIVITY OF LEARNING ◀ **1** [U] the activity of learning or gaining knowledge, either from books or by examining things in the world: *a room set aside for private study* ◊ *academic/literary/scientific study* ◊ *It is important to develop good study skills.* ◊ *Physiology is the study of how living things work.* **2** (**studies**) [pl.] (*formal*) a particular person's learning activities, for example at a college or university: *to continue/pursue your studies*

▶ ACADEMIC SUBJECT ◀ **3** (**studies**) [U+sing./pl. *v.*] (used in the names of some academic subjects): *business/media/American studies*

▶ DETAILED EXAMINATION ◀ **4** [U] the act of considering or examining sth in detail: *These proposals deserve careful study.* **5** [C] a piece of research that examines a subject or question in detail: *to make/carry out/conduct a study* ◊ *This study shows/confirms/suggests that …* ◊ *a detailed study of how animals adapt to their environment* ◊ *scientific studies of fishing grounds and methods of fishing*—see also CASE STUDY

▶ ROOM ◀ **6** [C] a room, especially in sb's home, used for reading and writing

▶ ART ◀ **7** [C] a drawing or painting of sth, especially one done for practice or before doing a larger picture: *a study of Chartres Cathedral* ◊ *a nude study*

▶ MUSIC ◀ **8** (*BrE*) (also **étude** *AmE, BrE*) [C] a piece of music designed to give a player practice in technical skills

▶ PERFECT EXAMPLE ◀ **9** [sing.] ~ (**in sth**) (*written*) a perfect example of sth: *His face was a study in concentration.*

■ *verb* (**stud·ies**, **study·ing**, **stud·ied**, **stud·ied**)

▶ LEARN ◀ **1** ~ (**sth**) (**at …**) | ~ (**for sth**) to spend time learning about a subject by reading, going to college, etc: [VN] *How long have you been studying English?* ◊ [V] *Don't disturb Jane, she's studying for her exams.* ◊ *My brother studied at the Royal College of Art.* ◊ *a composer who studied under Nadia Boulanger* (= Nadia Boulanger taught the composer) ◊ [V to inf] *Nina is studying to be an architect.*

▶ EXAMINE CAREFULLY ◀ **2** [VN] to watch, or look at sb/sth carefully in order to find out sth: *Scientists are studying photographs of the planet for signs of life.* ◊ *He studied her face thoughtfully.* ◊ *Fran was studying the menu.* **3** to examine sth carefully in order to understand it: [VN] *We will study the report carefully before making a decision.* ◊ [V wh-] *The group will study how the region coped with the loss of thousands of jobs.*

ʹ**study hall** *noun* [U] (*AmE*) a period of time during the school day when students study quietly on their own, usually with a teacher present

stuff /stʌf/ *noun, verb*

■ *noun* [U] **1** (*informal, sometimes disapproving*) used to refer to a substance, material, group of objects, etc. when you do not know the name, when the name is not important or when it is obvious what you are talking about: *What's all that sticky stuff on the carpet?* ◊ *The chairs were covered in some sort of plastic stuff.* ◊ *This wine is good stuff.* ◊ (*disapproving*) *I don't know how you can eat that stuff!* ◊ *They sell stationery and stuff (like that).* ◊ *Where's all my stuff* (= my possessions)? ◊ (*disapproving*)

Could you move all that stuff off the table?—see also FOODSTUFF **2** (*informal*) used to refer in a general way to things that people do, say, think, etc: *I've got loads of stuff to do today.* ◊ *I like reading* **and stuff.** ◊ *The band did some* **great stuff** *on their first album.* ◊ *This is all* **good stuff.** *Well done!* ◊ *What's all this 'Mrs Smith' stuff? Call me Anna.* ◊ *I don't believe in* **all that stuff** *about ghosts.* **3** ~ **(of sth)** (*formal or literary*) the most important feature of sth; something that sth else is based on or is made from: *The trip was magical; the stuff of which dreams are made.* ◊ *Parades and marches were the* **very stuff** *of politics in the region.* ◊ *Let's see what stuff you're made of* (= what sort of person you are).—see also HOT STUFF **IDM** **do your 'stuff** (*informal*) to do what you are good at or what you have been trained to do: *Some members of the team are just not doing their stuff* (= doing as well as they should). ◊ (*figurative*) *The medicine has clearly done its stuff.* **not give a 'stuff** (*BrE, slang*) to not care at all about sth—more at KID *n.,* KNOW *v.,* STERN *adj.,* STRUT *v.,* SWEAT *v.*

■ *verb* **1** ~ **A (with B)** | ~ **B (in, into, under, etc. A)** to fill a space or container tightly with sth: [VN] *She had 500 envelopes to stuff with leaflets.* ◊ *She had 500 leaflets to stuff into envelopes.* ◊ *The fridge is stuffed to bursting.* ◊ *My nose is* **stuffed up** (= blocked because of illness). ◊ [VN-ADJ] *All the drawers* **were stuffed full** *of letters and papers.* **2** [VN+adv. / prep.] to push sth quickly and carelessly into a small space: *She stuffed the money under a cushion.* ◊ *His hands were stuffed in his pockets.* **3** [VN] to fill a vegetable, chicken, etc. with another type of food: *Are you going to stuff the turkey?* ◊ *stuffed peppers* **4** [VN] ~ **sb/yourself (with sth)** | ~ **your face** (*informal*) to eat a lot of food or too much food; to give sb a lot or too much to eat: *He sat at the table stuffing himself.* ◊ *Don't stuff the kids with chocolate before their dinner.* ◊ *We stuffed our faces at the party.* **5** [VN] [usually passive] to fill the dead body of an animal with material and preserve it, so that it keeps its original shape and appearance: *They had had their pet dog stuffed.* **IDM** **get 'stuffed** (*BrE, spoken*) used to tell sb in a rude and angry way to go away, or that you do not want sth: *If they don't offer you more money, tell them to get stuffed.* **'stuff it** (*spoken, informal*) used to show that you have changed your mind about sth or do not care about sth: *I didn't want a part in the play, then I thought*—*stuff it*—*why not?* **you, etc. can stuff sth** (*spoken, informal*) used to tell sb in a rude and angry way that you do not want sth: *I told them they could stuff their job.*

stuffed /stʌft/ *adj.* [not before noun] (*informal*) having eaten so much that you cannot eat anything else **SYN** FULL

stuffed 'animal *noun* **1** (*especially AmE*) = SOFT TOY—picture on page A8 **2** a dead animal that has been STUFFED: *stuffed animals in glass cases*

stuffed 'shirt *noun* (*informal, disapproving*) a person who is very serious, formal or old-fashioned

stuff·ing /'stʌfɪŋ/ *noun* [U] **1** (*AmE* also **dress·ing**) a mixture of finely chopped food, such as bread, onions and herbs, placed inside a chicken, etc. before it is cooked to give it flavour **2** soft material used to fill cushions, toys, etc. **IDM** more at KNOCK *v.*

stuffy /'stʌfi/ *adj.* (**stuff·ier, stuffi·est**) **1** (of a building, room, etc.) warm in an unpleasant way and without enough fresh air: *a stuffy room/atmosphere* ◊ *It gets very hot and stuffy in here in summer.* **2** (*informal, disapproving*) very serious, formal, boring or old-fashioned: *a stuffy, formal family* ◊ *plain, stuffy clothes* ▶ **stuffi·ness** *noun* [U]

stul·ti·fy·ing /'stʌltɪfaɪɪŋ/ *adj.* (*formal*) making you feel very bored and unable to think of new ideas: *the stultifying effects of work that never varies* ▶ **stul·tify** *verb* (**stul·ti·fies, stul·ti·fy·ing, stul·ti·fied, stul·ti·fied**) [VN] **stul·ti·fy·ing·ly** *adv.*

stum·ble /'stʌmbl/ *verb* [V] **1** ~ **(over/on sth)** to hit your foot against sth while you are walking or running and almost fall: *The child stumbled and fell.* ◊ *I stumbled over a rock.* **2** [+adv. / prep.] to walk or move in an unsteady way: *Max stumbled out of bed sleepily.* ◊ *We were stum-*

bling around in the dark looking for a candle. **3** ~ **(over/ through sth)** to make a mistake or mistakes and stop while you are speaking, reading to sb or playing music: *In her nervousness she stumbled over her words.* ◊ *I stumbled through the piano piece with difficulty.* ▶ **stum·ble** *noun* **PHRV** **'stumble across/on/upon sth/sb** to discover sth/sb unexpectedly: *Police have stumbled across a huge drugs ring.* **'stumble into sth** to become involved in sth by chance: *I stumbled into acting when I left college.*

'stumbling block *noun* ~ **(to sth)** | ~ **(to doing sth)** something that causes problems and prevents you from achieving your aim

stump /stʌmp/ *noun, verb*
■ *noun* **1** [C] the bottom part of a tree left in the ground after the rest has fallen or been cut down **2** [C] the end of sth or the part that is left after the main part has been cut, broken off or worn away: *the stump of a pencil/tooth* **3** [C] the short part of sb's leg or arm that is left after the rest has been cut off **4** [C, usually pl.] (in cricket) one of the set of three upright wooden sticks (called **the stumps**) that form the WICKET **5** (**the stump**) [sing.] (*informal, especially AmE*) the fact of a politician before an election going to different places and trying to get people's support by making speeches: *The senator gave his standard stump speech.* ◊ *politicians* **on the stump**
■ *verb* **1** [VN] [usually passive] (*informal*) to ask sb a question that is too difficult for them to answer or give them a problem that they cannot solve: *I'm stumped. I don't know how they got here before us.* ◊ *Kate was* **stumped for words** (= unable to answer). **2** [V+adv. / prep.] to walk in a noisy, heavy way, especially because you are angry or upset **SYN** STOMP: *He stumped off, muttering under his breath.* **3** (*AmE*) to travel around making political speeches, especially before an election: [V+adv. / prep.] *He stumped around the country trying to build up support.* [also VN] **4** [VN] (in cricket) to put a BATSMAN out of the game by touching the stumps with the ball when he or she is out of the area in which the ball can be hit **PHRV** **,stump 'up (for sth)** | **,stump 'up sth (for sth)** (*BrE, informal*) to pay money for sth **SYN** COUGH UP: *We were asked to stump up for the repairs.* ◊ *Who is going to stump up the extra money?*

stumpy /'stʌmpi/ *adj.* (*disapproving*) short and thick **SYN** STUBBY: *stumpy fingers* ◊ *a stumpy tail*

stun /stʌn/ *verb* (**-nn-**) [VN] **1** to make a person or an animal unconscious for a short time, especially by hitting them on the head: *The fall stunned me for a moment.* ◊ *The animals are stunned before slaughter.* **2** to surprise or shock sb so much that they cannot think clearly or speak: *Her words stunned me*—*I had no idea she felt that way.* **3** to impress sb very much: *They were stunned by the view from the summit.* ▶ **stunned** *adj.*: *She was too stunned to speak.* ◊ *There was a* **stunned silence** *when I told them the news.*

stung *pt, pp* of STING

'stun gun *noun* a weapon that makes a person or an animal unconscious or unable to move for a short time, usually by giving them a small electric shock

stunk *pp* of STINK

stun·ner /'stʌnə(r)/ *noun* (*informal*) **1** a person (especially a woman) or a thing that is very attractive or exciting to look at: *His daughter is a real stunner.* ◊ *The movie is visually a stunner.* **2** something, such as a piece of news, that is very surprising or shocking

stun·ning /'stʌnɪŋ/ *adj.* **1** extremely attractive or impressive **SYN** BEAUTIFUL: *a stunning woman* ◊ *You look absolutely stunning!* ◊ *a stunning view of the lake* ◊ *His performance was simply stunning.* **2** extremely surprising or shocking: *He suffered a stunning defeat in the election.* ▶ **stun·ning·ly** *adv.*: *stunningly beautiful* ◊ *a stunningly simple idea*

stunt /stʌnt/ *noun, verb*
■ *noun* **1** a dangerous and difficult action that sb does to entertain people, especially as part of a film/movie: *He did all his own stunts.* ◊ *a stunt pilot/rider* **2** (*sometimes disapproving*) something that is done in order to attract people's attention: *a publicity stunt* **3** (*informal*) a stupid

æ	ɑː	e	ɜː	ə	ɪ	iː	i	ɒ	ɔː	ʌ	ʊ	u	uː
cat	father	ten	bird	about	sit	see	many	got	saw	cup	put	actual	too
							(BrE)						

S

or dangerous act: *I've had enough of her childish stunts.* ◊ *Don't you ever pull a stunt like that again!*

■ *verb* [VN] to prevent sb/sth from growing or developing as much as they/it should: *The constant winds had stunted the growth of plants and bushes.* ◊ *His illness had not stunted his creativity.*

stunt·ed /ˈstʌntɪd/ *adj.* that has not been able to grow or develop as much as it should: *stunted trees* ◊ *the stunted lives of children deprived of education*

stunt·man /ˈstʌntmæn/, **stunt·woman** /ˈstʌnt-wʊmən/ *noun* (*pl.* **-men** /-men/ **-women** /-wɪmɪn/) a person whose job is to do dangerous things in place of an actor in a film/movie, etc.; a person who does dangerous things in order to entertain people

stu·pefy /ˈstjuːpɪfaɪ; *AmE* ˈstuː-/ *verb* (**stu·pe·fies, stu·pe·fy·ing, stu·pe·fied, stu·pe·fied**) [VN] [often passive] to surprise or shock sb; to make sb unable to think clearly: *He was stupefied by the amount they had spent.* ◊ *She was stupefied with cold.* ▶ **stu·pe·fac·tion** /ˌstjuːpɪˈfækʃn; *AmE* ˌstuː-/ *noun* [U]

stu·pe·fy·ing /ˈstjuːpɪfaɪɪŋ; *AmE* ˈstuː-/ *adj.* **1** making you unable to think clearly: *stupefying boredom* **2** very surprising or shocking: *His next action was utterly stupefying.* ▶ **stu·pe·fy·ing·ly** *adv.*: *The party was stupefyingly dull.*

stu·pen·dous /stjuːˈpendəs; *AmE* stuː-/ *adj.* extremely large or impressive, especially greater or better than you expect [SYN] STAGGERING: *stupendous efforts/achievements* ◊ *stupendous views over the sea* ◊ *stupendous costs* ▶ **stu·pen·dous·ly** *adv.*

stu·pid /ˈstjuːpɪd; *AmE* ˈstuː-/ *adj., noun*

■ *adj.* (**stu·pider, stu·pidest**) [HELP] **more stupid** and **most stupid** are also common. **1** showing a lack of thought or good judgement [SYN] FOOLISH, SILLY: *a stupid mistake/question/idea/joke* ◊ *It was a pretty stupid thing to do.* ◊ *I was stupid enough to believe him.* ◊ *It was stupid of you to get involved.* **2** (*disapproving*) (of a person) slow to learn or understand things; not clever or intelligent: *He'll manage—he isn't stupid.* ◊ *She always makes me feel really stupid.* **3** [only before noun] (*spoken*) used to emphasize that you are annoyed with sb/sth: *I can't get the stupid thing open!* ◊ *Get your stupid feet off the chair!* ▶ **stu·pid·ly** *adv.*: *I stupidly agreed to lend him the money.* ◊ *Todd stared stupidly at the screen.*

■ *noun* [sing.] (*informal*) if you call sb **stupid**, you are telling them, usually in a joking way, that you think they are not being very intelligent: *Yes, stupid, it's you I'm talking to!*

stu·pid·ity /stjuːˈpɪdəti; *AmE* stuː-/ *noun* (*pl.* **-ies**) **1** [U, C, usually pl.] behaviour that shows a lack of thought or good judgement: *I couldn't believe my own stupidity.* ◊ *the errors and stupidities of youth* **2** [U] the state or quality of being slow to learn and not clever or intelligent

stu·por /ˈstjuːpə(r); *AmE* ˈstuː-/ *noun* [sing., U] (*written*) a state in which you are unable to think, hear, etc. clearly, especially because you have drunk too much alcohol, taken drugs or had a shock: *He drank himself into a stupor.* ◊ *a drunken stupor* ◊ *She was led away in a state of stupor.*

sturdy /ˈstɜːdi; *AmE* ˈstɜːrdi/ *adj.* (**stur·dier, stur·di·est**) **1** (of an object) strong and not easily damaged [SYN] ROBUST: *a sturdy pair of boots* ◊ *a sturdy table* **2** (of people and animals, or their bodies) physically strong and healthy: *a man of sturdy build* ◊ *sturdy legs* ◊ *a sturdy breed of cattle* **3** not easily influenced or changed by other people [SYN] FIRM, DETERMINED: *The village has always maintained a sturdy independence.* ◊ *a sturdy defence of the government's position* ▶ **stur·dily** /-ɪli/ *adv.*: *The boat was sturdily made.* ◊ *a sturdily built young man* ◊ *a sturdily independent community* **stur·di·ness** *noun* [U]

stur·geon /ˈstɜːdʒən; *AmE* ˈstɜːrdʒən/ *noun* [C, U] (*pl.* **stur·geon** or **stur·geons**) a large sea and FRESHWATER fish that lives in northern regions. Sturgeon are used for food and the eggs (called CAVIAR) are also eaten.

stut·ter /ˈstʌtə(r)/ *verb, noun*

■ *verb* **1** to have difficulty speaking because you cannot stop yourself from repeating the first sound of some words several times [SYN] STAMMER: [V **speech**] *'W-w-what?' he stuttered.* ◊ [VN] *I managed to stutter a reply.* [also V] **2** [V] (of a vehicle or an engine) to move or start with difficulty, making short sharp noises or movements: *The car stuttered along in first gear.*

■ *noun* [sing.] a speech problem in which a person finds it difficult to say the first sound of a word and repeats it several times: *He had a terrible stutter.*

sty /staɪ/ *noun* **1** (*pl.* **sties**) = PIGSTY **2** (also **stye**) (*pl.* **sties** or **styes**) an infection of the EYELID (= the skin above or below the eye) which makes it red and sore

Sty·gian /ˈstɪdʒiən/ *adj.* [usually before noun] (*literary*) very dark: *Stygian darkness/gloom* [ORIGIN] From the Styx, the river in the underworld which the souls of the dead had to cross in Greek myth.

style /staɪl/ *noun, verb*

■ *noun*

WAY STH IS DONE **1** [C, U] ~ (of sth) the particular way in which sth is done: *a style of leadership/management* ◊ *furniture to suit your style of living* ◊ *a study of different learning/teaching styles* ◊ *I like your style* (= I like the way you do things). ◊ *Caution was not her style* (= not the way she usually behaved).—see also LIFESTYLE

DESIGN OF CLOTHES/HAIR **2** [C] a particular design of sth, especially clothes: *We stock a wide variety of styles and sizes.* ◊ *Have you thought about having your hair in a shorter style?*—see also HAIRSTYLE **3** [U] the quality of being fashionable in the clothes that you wear: *Hot tips for style-conscious teenagers.* ◊ *Short skirts are back in style* (=fashionable).

BEING ELEGANT **4** [U] the quality of being elegant and made to a high standard: *The hotel has been redecorated but it's lost a lot of its style.* ◊ *She does everything with style and grace.*

OF BOOK/PAINTING/BUILDING **5** [C, U] the features of a book, painting, building, etc. that make it typical of a particular author, artist, historical period, etc: *a style of architecture* ◊ *a fine example of Gothic style* ◊ *a parody written in the style of Molière*

USE OF LANGUAGE **6** [U, C] the correct use of language: *It's not considered good style to start a sentence with 'but'.* ◊ *Please follow house style* (= the rules of spelling, etc. used by a particular publishing company).

-STYLE **7** (in adjectives) having the type of style mentioned: *Italian-style gardens* ◊ *a buffet-style breakfast*—see also OLD-STYLE

[IDM] **be more sb's ˈstyle** to be what sb prefers or what suits sb: *I'm surprised he rides a motorbike—I'd have thought big cars were more his style.* **in (great, grand, etc.) style** in an impressive way: *She always celebrates her birthday in style.* ◊ *He won the championship in fine/great style.*—more at CRAMP *v.*

■ *verb*

CLOTHES/HAIR, etc. **1** [VN] to design, make or shape sth in a particular way: *an elegantly styled jacket* ◊ *He'd had his hair styled at an expensive salon.*

GIVE NAME/TITLE **2** [VN-N] (*formal*) to give sb/sth/yourself a particular name or title: *He styled himself Major Carter.*

[PHRV] **ˈstyle sth/yourself on sth/sb** to copy the style, manner or appearance of sb/sth [SYN] MODEL: *a coffee bar styled on a Parisian cafe* ◊ *He styled himself on Elvis Presley.*

styl·ing /ˈstaɪlɪŋ/ *noun* [U] **1** the act of cutting and/or shaping hair in a particular style: *styling gel/mousse* **2** the way in which sth is designed: *The car has been criticized for its outdated body styling.*

styl·ish /ˈstaɪlɪʃ/ *adj.* (*approving*) fashionable; elegant and attractive: *his stylish wife* ◊ *a stylish restaurant* ◊ *It was a stylish performance by both artists.* ▶ **styl·ish·ly** *adv.* **styl·ish·ness** *noun* [U]

styl·ist /ˈstaɪlɪst/ *noun* **1** a person whose job is cutting and shaping people's hair: *She was the salon's top stylist.* **2** a person, for example a writer, who takes great care to write or say sth in an elegant or unusual way **3** a person whose job is to create or design a particular style or image for a product, an advertisement, etc.

styl·is·tic /staɪˈlɪstɪk/ *adj.* [only before noun] connected

aɪ	aʊ	eɪ	əʊ	oʊ	ɔɪ	ɪə	eə	ʊə	j	w
my	now	say	go	go	boy	near	hair	pure	yes	wet
			(BrE)	(AmE)						

with the style an artist uses in a particular piece of art, writing or music: *stylistic analysis / features / devices* ▶ **styl·is·tic·al·ly** /-kli/ *adv.*

styl·is·tics /staɪˈlɪstɪks/ *noun* [U] the study of style and the methods used in written language

styl·ized (*BrE* also **-ised**) /ˈstaɪlaɪzd/ *adj.* drawn, written, etc. in a way that is not natural or realistic: *a stylized drawing of a house* ◇ *the highly stylized form of acting in Japanese theatre* ▶ **styl·iza·tion, -isa·tion** /ˌstaɪlaɪˈzeɪʃn; *AmE* -ləˈz-/ *noun* [U]

sty·lus /ˈstaɪləs/ *noun* (*pl.* **sty·luses**) a device on a RECORD PLAYER that looks like a small needle and is placed on the record in order to play it

sty·mie /ˈstaɪmi/ *verb* (**sty·mie·ing** or **sty·mying, stymied, sty·mied**) [VN] (*informal*) to prevent sb from doing sth that they have planned or want to do; to prevent sth from happening SYN FOIL

Styro·foam™ /ˈstaɪrəfəʊm; *AmE* -foʊm/ *noun* [U] (*especially AmE*) = POLYSTYRENE: *Styrofoam cups*

suave /swɑːv/ *adj.* (especially of a man) confident, elegant and polite, sometimes in a way that does not seem sincere ▶ **suave·ly** *adv.*

sub /sʌb/ *noun* (*informal*) **1** = SUBMARINE **2** a SUBSTITUTE (= a player who replaces another player in a team): *He came on as sub.* **3** (*BrE*) a SUBSCRIPTION (= money that you pay regularly when you are a member of a club, etc.) **4** (*BrE*) a SUBEDITOR

sub- /sʌb/ *prefix* **1** (in nouns and adjectives) below; less than: *sub-zero temperatures* ◇ *a subtropical* (= almost tropical) *climate* ◇ *sub-standard* ◇ *a sub lieutenant* **2** (in nouns and adjectives) under: *subway* ◇ *submarine* **3** (in verbs and nouns) a smaller part of sth: *subdivide* ◇ *subset*

sub·al·tern /ˈsʌbltən; *AmE* səˈbɔːltərn/ *noun* any officer in the British army who is lower in rank than a captain

sub-aqua /ˌsʌb ˈækwə/ *adj.* [only before noun] done or used underwater: *sub-aqua diving / equipment*

sub·atom·ic /ˌsʌbəˈtɒmɪk; *AmE* -ˈtɑːm-/ *adj.* [usually before noun] (*technical*) smaller than, or found in, an atom: *subatomic particles*

sub·com·mit·tee /ˈsʌbkəmɪti/ *noun* [C+sing./pl. *v.*] a smaller committee formed from a main committee in order to study a particular subject in more detail

sub·com·pact /ˈsʌbkəmpækt/ *noun* (*AmE*) a small car, smaller than a COMPACT

sub·con·scious /ˌsʌbˈkɒnʃəs; *AmE* -ˈkɑːn-/ *adj., noun*
■ *adj.* [usually before noun] connected with feelings that influence your behaviour even though you are not aware of them: *subconscious desires / fears* ◇ *the subconscious mind*—compare CONSCIOUS, UNCONSCIOUS ▶ **sub·con·scious·ly** *adv.*: *Subconsciously, she was looking for the father she had never known.*
■ *noun* (**the / your subconscious**) [sing.] the part of your mind that contains feelings that you are not aware of—compare THE UNCONSCIOUS

sub·con·tin·ent /ˌsʌbˈkɒntɪnənt; *AmE* -ˈkɑːn-/ *noun* [usually sing.] a large land mass that forms part of a continent, especially the part of Asia that includes India, Pakistan and Bangladesh: *the Indian subcontinent*

sub·con·tract *verb, noun*
■ *verb* /ˌsʌbkənˈtrækt; *AmE* ˌsʌbˈkɑːntrækt/ ~ **sth** (**to sb**) to pay a person or company to do some of the work that you have been given a contract to do: [VN, VN to inf] *We subcontracted the work to a small engineering firm.* ◇ *We subcontracted a small engineering firm to do the work.* ▶ **sub·con·tract·ing** *noun* [U]
■ *noun* /ˌsʌbˈkɒntrækt; *AmE* -kɑːn-/ a contract to do part of the work that has been given to another person or company

sub·con·tract·or /ˌsʌbkənˈtræktə(r); *AmE* sʌbˈkɑːn·træk-/ *noun* a person or company that does part of the work given to another person or company

sub·cul·ture /ˈsʌbkʌltʃə(r)/ *noun* (sometimes *disapproving*) the behaviour and beliefs of a particular group of people in society that are different from those of most people: *the criminal / drug / youth subculture*

sub·cuta·ne·ous /ˌsʌbkjuˈteɪniəs/ *adj.* [usually before noun] (*technical*) under the skin: *a subcutaneous injection* ▶ **sub·cuta·ne·ous·ly** *adv.*

sub·div·ide /ˈsʌbdɪvaɪd; ˌsʌbdɪˈvaɪd/ *verb* [VN, V] [often passive] ~ (**sth**) (**into sth**) to divide sth into smaller parts; to be divided into smaller parts

sub·div·ision *noun* **1** /ˌsʌbdɪˈvɪʒn/ [U] the act of dividing a part of sth into smaller parts **2** /ˈsʌbdɪvɪʒn/ [C] one of the smaller parts into which a part of sth has been divided: *a police subdivision* (= the area covered by one particular police force) ◇ *subdivisions within the Hindu caste system* **3** /ˈsʌbdɪvɪʒn/ [C] (*AmE*) one of the parts of an area of land that has been divided up for building houses on

sub·due /səbˈdjuː; *AmE* -ˈduː/ *verb* [VN] (rather *formal*) **1** to bring sb/sth under control, especially by using force SYN DEFEAT: *Troops were called in to subdue the rebels.* ◇ *government efforts to subdue inflation* **2** to calm or control your feelings: *Julia had to subdue an urge to stroke his hair.*

sub·dued /səbˈdjuːd; *AmE* -ˈduːd/ *adj.* **1** (of a person) unusually quiet, and possibly unhappy: *He seemed a bit subdued to me.* ◇ *She was in a subdued mood.* ◇ *The reception was a subdued affair.* **2** (of light or colours) not very bright: *subdued lighting* **3** (of sounds) not very loud: *a subdued conversation* ◇ *the sound of subdued laughter* **4** (of business activity) not very busy; with not much activity: *a subdued housing market* ◇ *a period of subdued trading*

sub·edi·tor /ˌsʌbˈedɪtə(r)/ (also *informal* **sub**) *noun* (*BrE*) a person whose job is to check and make changes to the text of a newspaper or magazine before it is printed

sub·group /ˈsʌbgruːp/ *noun* a smaller group made up of members of a larger group: *population subgroups*

'sub-head·ing *noun* a title given to any of the sections into which a longer piece of writing has been divided

sub·human /ˌsʌbˈhjuːmən/ *adj.* (*disapproving*) not working or behaving like a normal human being; not fit for human beings: *subhuman behaviour* ◇ *They were living in subhuman conditions.*—compare INHUMAN, SUPERHUMAN

sub·ject *noun, adj., verb*
■ *noun* /ˈsʌbdʒɪkt; -dʒekt/
OF CONVERSATION / BOOK | **1** [C] a thing or person that is being discussed, described or dealt with: *an unpleasant subject of conversation* ◇ *books on many different subjects* ◇ *a magazine article on the subject of space travel* ◇ *I have nothing more to say on the subject.* ◇ *I wish you'd change the subject* (= talk about sth else). ◇ *How did we get onto the subject of marriage?* ◇ *We seem to have got off the subject we're meant to be discussing.* ◇ *Nelson Mandela is the subject of a new biography.* ◇ *Climate change is still very much a subject for debate.*

AT SCHOOL / COLLEGE | **2** [C] an area of knowledge studied in a school, college, etc: *Biology and English are my favourite subjects.*

OF PICTURE / PHOTOGRAPH | **3** a person or thing that is the main feature of a picture or photograph, or that a work of art is based on: *Focus the camera on the subject.* ◇ *Classical landscapes were a popular subject with many 18th-century painters.*

OF EXPERIMENT | **4** [C] a person or thing being used to study sth, especially in an experiment: *We need male subjects between the ages of 18 and 25 for the experiment.*

GRAMMAR | **5** [C] a noun, noun phrase or pronoun representing the person or thing that performs the action of the verb (*I* in *I sat down.*), about which sth is stated (*the house* in *The house is very old.*) or, in a PASSIVE sentence, that is affected by the action of the verb (*the tree* in *The tree was blown down in the storm.*)—compare OBJECT *n.* (4), PREDICATE

OF COUNTRY | **6** a person who has the right to belong to a particular country, especially one with a king or queen: *a British / French subject* ▷ note at CITIZEN

■ *adj.* /ˈsʌbdʒekt; -dʒɪkt/ **1** ~ **to sth** likely to be affected by sth, especially sth bad: *Flights are subject to delay because of the fog.* ◇ *Smokers are more subject to heart attacks than non-smokers.* **2** ~ **to sth** depending on sth in order to be

completed or agreed: *The article is ready to publish, subject to your approval.* ◊ *All the holidays on offer are subject to availability.* **3 ~ to sth/sb** under the authority of sth/sb: *All nuclear installations are subject to international safeguards.* ◊ *As a diplomat, he is not subject to local laws.* **4** [only before noun] (*formal*) controlled by the government of another country: *subject peoples*
■ *verb* /səbˈdʒekt/ [VN] **~ sth** (**to sth**) (*formal*) to bring a country or group of people under your control, especially by using force: *The Roman Empire subjected most of Europe to its rule.* ▶ **sub·jec·tion** /səbˈdʒekʃn/ *noun* [U]
PHRV **subˈject sb/sth to sth** [often passive] (*written*) to make sb/sth experience, suffer or be affected by sth, usually sth unpleasant: *to be subjected to abuse/ridicule/harassment/criticism* ◊ *The city was subjected to heavy bombing.*

sub·ject·ive /səbˈdʒektɪv/ *adj.* **1** based on your own ideas or opinions rather than facts and therefore sometimes unfair: *a highly subjective point of view* ◊ *Everyone's opinion is bound to be subjective.* **2** (of ideas, feelings or experiences) existing in sb's mind rather than in the real world **OPP** OBJECTIVE ▶ **sub·ject·ive·ly** *adv.*: *People who are less subjectively involved are better judges.* ◊ *subjectively perceived changes* **sub·ject·iv·ity** /ˌsʌbdʒekˈtɪvəti/ *noun* [U]: *There is an element of subjectivity in her criticism.*

sub·ject·iv·ism /səbˈdʒektɪvɪzəm/ *noun* [U] (*philosophy*) the theory that all knowledge and moral values are subjective rather than based on truth that actually exists in the real world

ˈsubject matter *noun* [U] the ideas or information contained in a book, speech, painting, etc: *The artist was revolutionary in both subject matter and technique.* ◊ *She's searching for subject matter for her new book.*

sub ju·dice /ˌsʌb ˈdʒuːdəsi; -seɪ/ *adj.* [not usually before noun] (*from Latin, law*) if a legal case is **sub judice**, it is still being discussed in a court of law and it is therefore illegal for anyone to talk about it on the television, in newspapers, etc.

sub·ju·gate /ˈsʌbdʒugeɪt/ *verb* [VN] [usually passive] (*formal*) to defeat sb/sth; to gain control over sb/sth: *a subjugated race* ◊ *Her personal ambitions had been subjugated to* (= considered less important than) *the needs of her family.* ▶ **sub·ju·ga·tion** /ˌsʌbdʒuˈgeɪʃn/ *noun* [U] (*formal*): *the subjugation of women/Ireland*

sub·junct·ive /səbˈdʒʌŋktɪv/ *noun* (*grammar*) the form (or MOOD) of a verb that expresses wishes, possibility or uncertainty; a verb in this form: *The verb is in the subjunctive.* ◊ *In 'I wish I were taller', 'were' is a subjunctive.* ▶ **sub·junct·ive** *adj.*: *the subjunctive mood*

sub·let /ˌsʌbˈlet/ *verb* (**sub·let·ting, sub·let, sub·let**) [VN, V] **~ (sth) (to sb)** to rent to sb else all or part of a property that you rent from the owner

ˌsub lieuˈtenant *noun* an officer in the British navy just below the rank of LIEUTENANT

sub·lim·ate /ˈsʌblɪmeɪt/ *verb* [VN] (*psychology*) to direct your energy, especially sexual energy, to socially acceptable activities such as work, exercise, art, etc. ▶ **sub·lim·ation** /ˌsʌblɪˈmeɪʃn/ *noun* [U]

sub·lime /səˈblaɪm/ *adj., noun*
■ *adj.* **1** (*written*) of very high quality and causing great admiration: *sublime beauty* ◊ *a sublime combination of flavours* ◊ *The location of the hotel is sublime.* **2** (*formal, often disapproving*) (of a person's behaviour or attitudes) extreme, especially in a way that shows they are not aware of what they are doing or are not concerned about what happens because of it: *the sublime confidence of youth* ◊ *He battled on, in the sublime conviction that he was in the right.* ▶ **sub·lime·ly** *adv.*: *sublimely beautiful* ◊ *She was sublimely unaware of the trouble she had caused.* **sub·lim·ity** /səˈblɪməti/ *noun* [U]
■ *noun* (**the sublime**) [sing.] (*written*) something that is sublime: *He transforms the most ordinary subject into the sublime.* **IDM** **from the sublime to the riˈdiculous** used to describe a situation in which sth serious, important or of high quality is followed by sth silly, unimportant or of poor quality

sub·lim·inal /ˌsʌbˈlɪmɪnl/ *adj.* affecting your mind even though you are not aware of it: *subliminal advertising* ▶ **sub·lim·in·al·ly** *adv.*

ˌsub-maˈchine gun *noun* a light MACHINE GUN that you can hold in your hands to fire

sub·mar·ine /ˌsʌbməˈriːn; ˈsʌbməriːn/ *noun, adj.*
■ *noun* (also *informal* **sub**) **1** a ship that can travel underwater: *a nuclear submarine* ◊ *a submarine base* **2** (also **ˌsubmarine ˈsandwich, hero**) (all *AmE*) a long bread roll split open along its length and filled with various types of food—picture on page A1
■ *adj.* [only before noun] (*technical*) existing or situated under the sea: *submarine plant life* ◊ *submarine cables*

sub·mar·iner /sʌbˈmærɪnə(r); *AmE* also ˈsʌbməriːnər/ *noun* a sailor who works on a submarine

sub·merge /səbˈmɜːdʒ; *AmE* -ˈmɜːrdʒ/ *verb* **1** to go under the surface of water or liquid; to put sth or make sth go under the surface of water or liquid: [V] *The submarine had had time to submerge before the warship could approach.* ◊ [VN] *The fields had been submerged by flood water.* **2** [VN] (*written*) to hide ideas, feelings, opinions, etc. completely: *Doubts that had been submerged in her mind suddenly resurfaced.* ▶ **sub·merged** *adj.*: *Her submerged car was discovered in the river by police divers.* **sub·mer·sion** /səbˈmɜːʃn; *AmE* -ˈmɜːrʒn/ *noun* [U]

sub·mers·ible /səbˈmɜːsəbl; *AmE* -ˈmɜːrs-/ *adj., noun*
■ *adj.* (*AmE* also **sub·merg·ible** /səbˈmɜːdʒəbl; *AmE* -ˈmɜːrdʒ-/) that can be used under water: *a submersible camera*
■ *noun* a SUBMARINE (= a ship that can travel underwater) that goes underwater for short periods

sub·mis·sion /səbˈmɪʃn/ *noun* **1** [U] the act of accepting that sb has defeated you and that you must obey them: *a gesture of submission* ◊ *to beat/force/starve sb into submission* **2** [U, C] the act of giving a document, proposal, etc. to sb in authority so that they can study or consider it; the document, etc. that you give: *When is the final date for the submission of proposals?* ◊ *They prepared a report for submission to the council.* ◊ *The deadline is 1 October and late submissions will not be marked.* ◊ *All parties will have the opportunity to* **make submissions** *relating to this case.* **3** [C] (*law*) a statement that is made to a judge in a court of law

sub·mis·sive /səbˈmɪsɪv/ *adj.* willing to obey sb whatever they want you to do: *She followed him like a submissive child.* **OPP** ASSERTIVE ▶ **sub·mis·sive·ly** *adv.*: *'You're right and I was wrong,' he said submissively.* **sub·mis·sive·ness** *noun* [U]

sub·mit /səbˈmɪt/ *verb* (**-tt-**) **1** [VN] **~ sth (to sb/sth)** to give a document, proposal, etc. to sb in authority so that they can study or consider it: *to submit an application/a claim/a complaint* ◊ *Completed projects must be submitted by 10 March.* **2 ~ (yourself) (to sb/sth)** to accept the authority, control or greater strength of sb/sth; to agree to sth because of this **SYN** YIELD, GIVE IN TO SB/STH: *She refused to submit to threats.* ◊ *He submitted himself to a search by the guards.* **3** [Vthat] (*law* or *formal*) to say or suggest sth: *Counsel for the defence submitted that the evidence was inadmissible.*

sub·nor·mal /ˌsʌbˈnɔːml; *AmE* -ˈnɔːrml/ *adj.* **1** (*technical*) lower than normal: *subnormal temperatures* **2** (sometimes *offensive*) having less than the normal level of intelligence: *educationally subnormal children*

sub·or·din·ate *adj., noun, verb*
■ *adj.* /səˈbɔːdɪnət; *AmE* -ˈbɔːrd-/ **1 ~ (to sb)** having less power or authority than sb else in a group or an organization: *In many societies women are subordinate to men.* ◊ *a subordinate minister/officer* **2 ~ (to sth)** less important than sth else: *All other issues are subordinate to this one.*
■ *noun* /səˈbɔːdɪnət; *AmE* -ˈbɔːrd-/ a person who has a position with less authority and power than sb else in an organization: *the relationship between subordinates and superiors*
■ *verb* /səˈbɔːdɪneɪt; *AmE* -ˈbɔːrd-/ [VN] **~ sb/sth (to sb/sth)** to treat sb/sth as less important than sb/sth else: *Safety considerations were subordinated to commercial interests.*

s	t	v	z	ʃ	ʒ	tʃ	dʒ	θ	ð	ŋ
see	tea	van	zoo	shoe	vision	chain	jam	thin	this	sing

S

▶ **sub·or·din·ation** /səˌbɔːdɪˈneɪʃn; *AmE* -ˌbɔːrd-/ *noun* [U]

su,bordinate 'clause (also **de,pendent 'clause**) *noun* (*grammar*) a group of words that is not a sentence but adds information to the main part of a sentence, for example *when it rang* in *She answered the phone when it rang.*—compare COORDINATE CLAUSE, MAIN CLAUSE

sub·orn /səˈbɔːn; *AmE* səˈbɔːrn/ *verb* [VN] (*law*) to pay or persuade sb to do sth illegal, especially to tell lies in a court of law: *to suborn a witness*

'sub·plot *noun* a series of events in a play, novel, etc. that is separate from but linked to the main story

sub·poena /səˈpiːnə/ *noun, verb*
■ *noun* (*law*) a written order to attend a court of law as a WITNESS to give evidence
■ *verb* (*law*) to order sb to attend a court of law and give evidence as a WITNESS: [VN to inf] *The court subpoenaed her to appear as a witness.* [also VN]

sub·scribe /səbˈskraɪb/ *verb* **1** [V] ~ (**to sth**) to pay money, normally once a year, to receive regular copies of a newspaper, magazine, etc: *Which journals does the library subscribe to?* **2** [V] ~ (**to sth**) to pay money regularly to be a member of an organization or to support a charity: *He subscribes regularly to Amnesty International.* **3** [V] ~ (**for sth**) (*finance*) to apply to buy shares in a company—see also OVERSUBSCRIBED **4** [VN] [usually passive] to apply to take part in an activity, use a service, etc: *The tour of Edinburgh is fully subscribed.* **PHRV** **sub'scribe to sth** (*formal*) to agree with or support an opinion, a theory, etc: *The authorities no longer subscribe to the view that disabled people are unsuitable as teachers.*

sub·scriber /səbˈskraɪbə(r)/ *noun* **1** a person who pays money, usually once a year, to receive regular copies of a magazine or newspaper: *subscribers to 'New Scientist'* **2** (*BrE*) a person who gives money regularly to help the work of an organization such as a charity **3** a person who pays to receive a service: *subscribers to cable television*

sub·scrip·tion /səbˈskrɪpʃn/ *noun* [C, U] **1** ~ (**to/for sth**) an amount of money you pay, usually once a year, to receive regular copies of a newspaper or magazine, etc.; the act of paying this money: *to take out an annual subscription to 'Newsweek'* ◇ *to cancel/renew your subscription* ◇ *Copies are available by subscription.* **2** (*BrE, informal*) a sum of money that you pay regularly to be a member of a club or to receive a service; the act of paying this money: *money raised through subscription and advertising* **3** a sum of money given regularly to a charity; the act of paying this money: *A statue in his memory was erected by public subscription.*

sub·sec·tion /ˈsʌbsekʃn/ *noun* a part of a section, especially of a legal document: *The case is described in subsection six below.*

sub·se·quent /ˈsʌbsɪkwənt/ *adj.* (*formal*) happening after sth else: *subsequent years/generations* ◇ *Subsequent events confirmed our doubts.*

sub·se·quent·ly /ˈsʌbsɪkwəntli/ *adv.* (*formal*) afterwards; later; after sth else has happened: *The original interview notes were subsequently lost.* ◇ *Subsequently, new guidelines were issued to all employees.*

'subsequent to *prep.* (*formal*) after; following: *There have been further developments subsequent to our meeting.*

sub·ser·vi·ent /səbˈsɜːviənt; *AmE* -ˈsɜːrv-/ *adj.* **1** ~ (**to sb/sth**) (*disapproving*) too willing to obey other people: *The press was accused of being subservient to the government.* ◇ *She did not wish to leave him, but she could not accept her subservient role.* **2** ~ (**to sth**) (*formal*) less important than sth else: *The needs of individuals were subservient to those of the group as a whole.* ▶ **sub·ser·vi·ence** /-əns/ *noun* [U]

sub·set /ˈsʌbset/ *noun* (*technical*) a smaller group of people or things formed from the members of a larger group: *a subset of the people who took part in the survey*

sub·side /səbˈsaɪd/ *verb* [V] **1** to become calmer or quieter: *She waited nervously for his anger to subside.* ◇ *When the rain had subsided we continued our walk.* ◇ *I took an aspirin and the pain gradually subsided.* **2** (of water) to go back to a normal level: *The flood waters*

gradually subsided. **3** (of land or a building) to sink to a lower level; to sink lower into the ground: *Weak foundations caused the house to subside.*

sub·sid·ence /səbˈsaɪdns; ˈsʌbsɪdns/ *noun* [U] the process by which an area of land sinks to a lower level than normal, or by which a building sinks into the ground

sub·sid·iary /səbˈsɪdiəri; *AmE* -dieri/ *adj., noun*
■ *adj.* **1** ~ (**to sth**) connected with sth but less important than it: *a subsidiary matter/subject* ◇ *subsidiary information* **2** (of a business company) owned or controlled by another company
■ *noun* (*pl.* **-ies**) a business company that is owned or controlled by another larger company: *She's working for an overseas subsidiary of the company.*

sub·sid·ize (*BrE* also **-ise**) /ˈsʌbsɪdaɪz/ *verb* [VN] to give money to sb or an organization to help pay for sth; to give a subsidy: *The housing projects are subsidized by the government.* ◇ *She's not prepared to subsidize his gambling any longer.* ▶ **sub·sid·iza·tion, -isa·tion** /ˌsʌbsɪdaɪˈzeɪʃn; *AmE* -dəˈz-/ *noun* [U]

sub·sidy /ˈsʌbsədi/ *noun* (*pl.* **-ies**) [C, U] money that is paid by a government or an organization to reduce the costs of services or of producing goods so that their prices can be kept low: *agricultural/state/housing subsidies* ◇ *to increase/reduce the level of subsidy*

sub·sist /səbˈsɪst/ *verb* [V] **1** ~ (**on sth**) to manage to stay alive, especially with limited food or money: *Old people often subsist on very small incomes.* **2** (*formal*) to exist; to be valid: *The terms of the contract subsist.*

sub·sist·ence /səbˈsɪstəns/ *noun* [U] the state of having just enough money or food to stay alive: *Many families are living below the level of subsistence.* ◇ *to live at/above/below (the) subsistence level* ◇ *They had no visible means of subsistence.* ◇ *subsistence agriculture/farming* (= growing enough only to live on, not to sell) ◇ *subsistence crops* ◇ *He worked a 16-hour day for a subsistence wage* (= enough money to buy only basic necessities).

sub·soil /ˈsʌbsɔɪl/ *noun* [U] the layer of soil between the surface of the ground and the hard rock underneath it—compare TOPSOIL

sub·son·ic /ˌsʌbˈsɒnɪk; *AmE* -ˈsɑːn-/ *adj.* less than the speed of sound; flying at less than the speed of sound—compare SUPERSONIC

sub·stance /ˈsʌbstəns/ *noun* **1** [C] a type of solid, liquid or gas that has particular qualities: *a chemical/radio-active substance* ◇ *banned/illegal substances* (= drugs) ◇ *a sticky/rich/fatty substance* **2** [U] (*written*) the quality of being based on facts or the truth: *It was malicious gossip, completely **without substance**.* ◇ *The commission's report **gives substance to** these allegations.* ◇ *There is some substance in what he says.* **3** [U] the most important or main part of sth: *Love and guilt form **the substance of** his new book.* ◇ *I agree with what she said **in substance**, though not with every detail.* **4** [U] (*formal*) importance **SYN** SIGNIFICANCE: *matters of substance* ◇ *Nothing of any substance was achieved in the meeting.* **IDM** **a man/woman of 'substance** (*formal*) a rich and powerful man or woman

sub-'standard *adj.* not as good as normal; not acceptable: *sub-standard goods*

sub·stan·tial /səbˈstænʃl/ *adj.* **1** large in amount or value; important **SYN** CONSIDERABLE: *substantial sums of money* ◇ *a substantial change/improvement* ◇ *Substantial numbers of people support the reforms.* ◇ *He ate a substantial breakfast.* **2** [usually before noun] (*formal*) large and solid; strongly built: *a substantial house*

sub·stan·tial·ly /səbˈstænʃəli/ *adv.* **1** very much; a lot **SYN** CONSIDERABLY: *The costs have increased substantially.* ◇ *The plane was substantially damaged in the crash.* **2** (*formal*) mainly; in most details, even if not completely: *What she says is substantially true.*

sub·stan·ti·ate /səbˈstænʃieɪt/ *verb* [VN] (*formal*) to provide information or evidence to prove that sth is true: *The results of the tests substantiated his claims.* ▶ **sub·stan·ti·ation** /səbˌstænʃiˈeɪʃn/ *noun* [U]

sub·stan·tive /səbˈstæntɪv; ˈsʌbstəntɪv/ *adj., noun*

S

æ	ɑː	e	ɜː	ə	ɪ	iː	i	ɒ	ɔː	ʌ	ʊ	u	uː
cat	father	ten	bird	about	sit	see	many	got	saw	cup	put	actual	too
								(BrE)					

■ *adj.* (*formal*) dealing with real, important or serious matters: *substantive issues/matters* ◇ *The report concluded that no substantive changes were necessary.*

■ *noun* (*old-fashioned, grammar*) a noun

sub·sta·tion /ˈsʌbsteɪʃn/ *noun* a place where the strength of electric power from a POWER STATION is reduced before it is passed on to homes and businesses

sub·sti·tute /ˈsʌbstɪtjuːt; *AmE* -tuːt/ *noun, verb*

■ *noun* **1** ~ (**for sb/sth**) a person or thing that you use or have instead of the one you normally use or have: *a meat/milk substitute* ◇ *Paul's father only saw him as a substitute for his dead brother.* ◇ *A substitute family* ◇ *The course teaches you the theory but there's no substitute for practical experience.* ◇ *The local bus service was a poor substitute for their car.* **2** (also *informal* **sub**) a player who replaces another player in a sports game: *He was brought on as (a) substitute after half-time.*

■ *verb* ~ **A** (**for B**)/~ **B** (**with/by A**)/~ **for sb/sth** to take the place of sth else; to use sb/sth instead of sb/sth else: [V] *Nothing can substitute for the advice your doctor is able to give you.* [VN] *Margarine can be substituted for butter in this recipe.* ◇ *Butter can be substituted with margarine in this recipe.* ◇ *Beckham was substituted in the second half after a knee injury* (= somebody else played instead of Beckham in the second half). **HELP** With **for**, with or by are not used, as in the last example, it can be difficult to tell whether the person or thing mentioned is being used, or has been replaced by somebody or something else. The context will usually make this clear. ▶ **sub·sti·tu·tion** /ˌsʌbstɪˈtjuːʃn; *AmE* -ˈtuː-/ *noun* [U, C]: *the substitution of low-fat spreads for butter* ◇ *Two substitutions were made during the game.*

ˌsubstitute 'teacher *noun* (*AmE*) = SUPPLY TEACHER

sub·stra·tum /ˈsʌbstrɑːtəm; *AmE* ˈsʌbstreɪtəm/ *noun* (*pl.* **sub·strata** /-strɑːtə; *AmE* ˈsʌbstreɪtə/) (*technical*) a layer of sth, especially rock or soil, that is below another layer: *a substratum of clay* ◇ *the substrata of society*

sub·struc·ture /ˈsʌbstrʌktʃə(r)/ *noun* a base or structure that is below another structure and that supports it: *a substructure of timber piles* ◇ (*figurative*) *the substructure of national culture*—compare SUPERSTRUCTURE

sub·sume /səbˈsjuːm; *AmE* -ˈsuːm/ *verb* [VN+*adv.*/*prep.*] [usually passive] (*formal*) to include sth in a particular group and not consider it separately: *All these different phenomena can be subsumed under just two broad categories.*

sub·tend /səbˈtend/ *verb* [VN] (*geometry*) (of a line or CHORD) to be opposite to an ARC or angle

sub·ter·fuge /ˈsʌbtəfjuːdʒ; *AmE* -tərf-/ *noun* [U, C] (*formal*) a secret, usually dishonest, way of behaving or doing sth: *Journalists often use subterfuge to obtain material for stories.* ◇ *a political subterfuge*

sub·ter·ra·nean /ˌsʌbtəˈreɪniən/ *adj.* [usually before noun] (*formal*) under the ground: *a subterranean cave/tunnel/passage*

sub·text /ˈsʌbtekst/ *noun* a hidden meaning or reason for doing sth

sub·title /ˈsʌbtaɪtl/ *noun, verb*

■ *noun* **1** [usually pl.] words that translate what is said in a film/movie into a different language and appear on the screen at the bottom. Subtitles are also used, especially on television, to help DEAF people (= people who cannot hear well): *a Polish film with English subtitles* ◇ *Is the film dubbed or are there subtitles?* **2** a second title of a book that appears after the main title and gives more information

■ *verb* [usually passive] to give a subtitle or subtitles to a book, film/movie, etc: [VN] *a Spanish film subtitled in English* ◇ [VN-N] *The book is subtitled 'New language for new times'.*—compare DUB

sub·tle /ˈsʌtl/ *adj.* (**sub·tler, sub·tlest**) **HELP** more subtle is also common. **1** (often *approving*) not very noticeable or obvious: *subtle colours/flavours* ◇ *subtle changes/differences/distinctions* ◇ *The fragrance is a subtle blend of jasmine and sandalwood.* ◇ *She's been dropping subtle hints about what she'd like as a present.* **2** (of a person or their behaviour) behaving in a clever way, and using

indirect methods, in order to achieve sth: *There was nothing subtle or sophisticated about him.* ◇ *I decided to try a more subtle approach.* **3** organized in a clever way: *a subtle strategy/plan/technique* ◇ *a subtle use of lighting in the play* **4** good at noticing and understanding things: *The job required a subtle mind.* ▶ **subtly** /ˈsʌtli/ *adv.*: *Her version of events is subtly different from what actually happened.* ◇ *Not very subtly, he raised the subject of money.*

subtle·ty /ˈsʌtlti/ *noun* (*pl.* **-ies**) **1** [U] the quality of being subtle: *It's a thrilling movie even though it lacks subtlety.* **2** [C, usually pl.] the small but important details or aspects of sth: *the subtleties of language* ◇ *the subtleties of the British constitution*

sub·total /ˈsʌbtəʊtl; *AmE* -toʊtl/ *noun* the total of a set of numbers which is then added to other totals to give a final number

sub·tract /səbˈtrækt/ *verb* [VN] ~ **sth** (**from sth**) to take a number or an amount away from another number or amount: *6 subtracted from 9 is 3* (9 − 6 = 3) **OPP** ADD ▶ **sub·trac·tion** /səbˈtrækʃn/—compare ADDITION *noun* [U, C]

sub·trop·ic·al /ˌsʌbˈtrɒpɪkl; *AmE* -ˈtrɑːp-/ (also **ˌsemi-ˈtropical**) *adj.* in or connected with regions that are near tropical parts of the world

sub·urb /ˈsʌbɜːb; *AmE* -ɜːrb/ *noun* (also *AmE informal* **the burbs** [pl.]) an area where people live that is outside the centre of a city: *a suburb of London* ◇ *a London suburb* ◇ *They live in the SUBURBS.*

sub·ur·ban /səˈbɜːbən; *AmE* -ˈbɜːrb-/ *adj.* **1** in or connected with a suburb: *suburban areas/streets/houses/life* ◇ *life in suburban London* **2** (*disapproving*) boring and ordinary: *a suburban lifestyle*

sub·ur·ban·ite /səˈbɜːbənaɪt; *AmE* -ˈbɜːrb-/ *noun* (often *disapproving*) a person who lives in the SUBURBS of a city: *middle-class suburbanites*

sub·ur·bia /səˈbɜːbiə; *AmE* -ˈbɜːrb-/ *noun* [U] (often *disapproving*) the SUBURBS and the way of life, attitudes, etc. of the people who live there

sub·ven·tion /səbˈvenʃn/ *noun* (*formal*) an amount of money that is given by a government, etc. to help an organization

sub·ver·sive /səbˈvɜːsɪv; *AmE* -ˈvɜːrs-/ *adj.* trying or likely to destroy or damage a government or political system by attacking it secretly or indirectly: *subversive literature/activities* ▶ **sub·ver·sive** *noun*: *He was a known political subversive.* **sub·ver·sive·ly** *adv.* **sub·ver·sive·ness** *noun* [U]

sub·vert /səbˈvɜːt; *AmE* -ˈvɜːrt/ *verb* (*formal*) **1** [VN, V] to try to destroy the authority of a political, religious, etc. system by attacking it secretly or indirectly **SYN** UNDERMINE **2** [VN] to try to destroy a person's beliefs or loyalties **SYN** UNDERMINE ▶ **sub·ver·sion** /səbˈvɜːʃn; *AmE* -ˈvɜːrʒn/ *noun* [U]

sub·way /ˈsʌbweɪ/ *noun* **1** (*BrE*) a path that goes under a road, etc. which people can use to cross to the other side **SYN** UNDERPASS **2** (*AmE*) an underground railway/railroad system in a city: *the New York subway* ◇ *a subway station/train* ◇ *a downtown subway stop* ◇ *to ride/take the subway* ⇨ note at UNDERGROUND

ˌsub-'zero *adj.* [usually before noun] (of temperatures) below zero

suc·ceed /səkˈsiːd/ *verb* **1** [V] ~ (**in doing sth**) to achieve sth that you have been trying to do or get; to have the result or effect that was intended: *Our plan succeeded.* ◇ *He succeeded in getting a place at art school.* ◇ *I tried to discuss it with her but only succeeded in making her angry* (= I failed and did the opposite of what I intended).—see also SUCCESS **2** [V] ~ (**in sth**) | ~ (**as sth**) to be successful in your job, earning money, power, respect, etc: *You will have to work hard if you are to succeed.* ◇ *She doesn't have the ruthlessness required to succeed in business.* ◇ *He had hoped to succeed as a violinist.*—see also SUCCESS **3** [VN] to come next after sb/sth and take their/its place or position: *Who succeeded Kennedy as President?* ◇ *Their early success was succeeded by a period of miserable failure.* ◇ *Strands of DNA are reproduced through succeeding generations.*—see also SUCCESSION **4** [V] ~ (**to sth**) to gain the right to a title, property, etc. when sb

aɪ	aʊ	eɪ	əʊ	oʊ	ɔɪ	ɪə	eə	ʊə	j	w
my	now	say	go	go	boy	near	hair	pure	yes	wet
			(BrE)	(AmE)						

dies: *She succeeded to the throne* (= became queen) *in 1558.*—see also SUCCESSION **IDM** **nothing succeeds like suc'cess** (*saying*) when you are successful in one area of your life, it often leads to success in other areas

suc·cess /sək'ses/ *noun* **1** [U] ~ (**in sth/in doing sth**) the fact that you have achieved sth that you want and have been trying to do or get; the fact of becoming rich or famous or of getting a high social position: *What's the secret of your success?* ◊ *I didn't* **have much success** *in finding a job.* ◊ *Confidence is* **the key to success.** ◊ *commercial/economic/electoral success* ◊ *Their plan will probably* **meet with little success.** ◊ *She was surprised by the book's success* (= that it had sold a lot of copies). ◊ *They didn't have much success in life.* **2** [C] a person or thing that has achieved a good result and been successful: *The party was a big success.* ◊ *He's proud of his daughter's successes.* ◊ *She wasn't a success as a teacher.* ◊ *He was determined to* **make a success** *of the business.* **OPP** FAILURE **IDM** see ROARING, SUCCEED, SWEET *adj.*

suc·cess·ful /sək'sesfl/ *adj.* **1** ~ (**in sth/in doing sth**)|~ (**at sth/at doing sth**) achieving your aims or what was intended: *They were successful in winning the contract.* ◊ *I wasn't very successful at keeping the news secret.* ◊ *We congratulated them on the successful completion of the project.* **2** having become popular and/or made a lot of money: *The play was very successful on Broadway.* ◊ *a successful career/actor* ◊ *The company has had another successful year.* **OPP** UNSUCCESSFUL ▶ **suc·cess·ful·ly** /-fəli/ *adv.*

suc·ces·sion /sək'seʃn/ *noun* **1** [C, usually sing.] a number of people or things that follow each other in time or order; a series: *a succession of events/problems/visitors* ◊ *He's been hit by a succession of injuries since he joined the team.* ◊ *She has won the award for the third year in succession.* ◊ *They had three children in quick succession.* ◊ *The gunman fired three times in rapid succession.* **2** [U] the regular pattern of one thing following another thing: *the succession of the seasons* **3** [U] the act of taking over an official position or title; the right to take over an official position or title, especially to become the king or queen of a country: *He became chairman* **in succession to** *Bernard Allen.* ◊ *She's third* **in order of succession** *to the throne.*—see also SUCCEED

suc·ces·sive /sək'sesɪv/ *adj.* [only before noun] following immediately one after the other: *This was their fourth successive win.* ◊ *Successive governments have tried to tackle the problem.* ◊ *There has been low rainfall for two successive years.* ▶ **suc·ces·sively** *adv.*: *This concept has been applied successively to painting, architecture and sculpture.*

suc·ces·sor /sək'sesə(r)/ *noun* ~ (**to sb/sth**) a person or thing that comes after sb/sth else and takes their/its place: *Who's the likely successor to Blair as party leader?* ◊ *This car is the successor to the popular Ford Mondeo.*—compare PREDECESSOR

suc'cess story *noun* a person or thing that is very successful

suc·cinct /sək'sɪŋkt/ *adj.* (*approving*) expressed clearly and in a few words: *Keep your answers as succinct as possible.* ▶ **suc·cinct·ly** *adv.*: *You put that very succinctly.* **suc·cinct·ness** *noun* [U]

suc·cour (*AmE* **suc·cor**) /'sʌkə(r)/ *noun, verb*
■ *noun* [U] (*literary*) help that you give to sb who is suffering or having problems: *to give/bring succour to the sick and wounded*
■ *verb* [VN] (*literary*) to help sb who is suffering or having problems

suc·cu·bus /'sʌkjʊbəs/ *noun* (*pl.* **suc·cu·bi** /-baɪ/) (*literary*) a female evil spirit, supposed to have sex with a sleeping man—compare INCUBUS

suc·cu·lent /'sʌkjələnt/ *adj., noun*
■ *adj.* **1** (*approving*) (of fruit, vegetables and meat) containing a lot of juice and tasting good: *a succulent pear/steak* **2** (*technical*) (of plants) having leaves and stems that are thick and contain a lot of water ▶ **suc·cu·lence** /-əns/ *noun* [U]
■ *noun* (*technical*) any plant with leaves and stems that are thick and contain a lot of water, for example a CACTUS

suc·cumb /sə'kʌm/ *verb* [V] ~ (**to sth**) to fail to resist an attack, an illness, a TEMPTATION, etc: *The town succumbed after a short siege.* ◊ *His career was cut short when he succumbed to cancer.* ◊ *He finally succumbed to Lucy's charms and agreed to her request.*

such /sʌtʃ/ *det., pron.* **1** of the type already mentioned: *They had been invited to a Hindu wedding and were not sure what happened on such occasions.* ◊ *He said he didn't have time or made* **some such** *excuse.* ◊ *She longed to find somebody who understood her problems, and in him she thought she had found such a person.* ◊ *We were second-class citizens and they treated us* **as such.** ◊ *Accountants were boring. Such* (= that) *was her opinion before meeting Ian!* **2** of the type that you are just going to mention: **There is no such thing** *as a free lunch.* ◊ *Such advice as he was given* (= he was given very little advice) *has proved almost worthless.* ◊ *The knot was fastened* **in such a way** *that it was impossible to undo.* ◊ *The damage was such that it would cost thousands to repair.* **3** ~ (**is, was, etc.**) **sth that …** used to emphasize the great degree of sth: *This issue was of such importance that we could not afford to ignore it.* ◊ *Why are you in such a hurry?* ◊ (*informal*) *It's such a beautiful day!* ◊ (*formal*) *Such is the elegance of this typeface that it is still a favourite of designers.* **IDM** **…and such** and similar things or people: *The centre offers activities like canoeing and sailing and such.* **as 'such** as the word is usually understood; in the exact sense of the word: *The new job is not a promotion as such but it has good prospects.* ◊ *'Well, did they offer it to you?' 'No, not as such, but they said I had a good chance.'* **such as 1** for example: *Wild flowers such as orchids and primroses are becoming rare.* ◊ *'There are loads of things to do.' 'Such as?'* (= give me an example) **2** of a kind that; like: *Opportunities such as this did not come every day.* ,**such as it 'is/they 'are** used to say that there is not much of sth or that it is of poor quality: *The food, such as it was, was served at nine o'clock.*

'**such-and-such** *pron., det.* (*spoken*) used for referring to sth without saying exactly what it is: *Always say at the start of an application that you're applying for such-and-such a job because …*

such·like /'sʌtʃlaɪk/ *pron.* things of the type mentioned: *You can buy brushes, paint, varnish and suchlike there.* ▶ **such·like** *det.*: *food, drink, clothing and suchlike provisions*

suck /sʌk/ *verb, noun*
■ *verb* **1** [VN] [usually +adv./prep.] to take liquid, air, etc. into your mouth by using the muscles of your lips: *to suck the juice from an orange* ◊ *She was noisily sucking up milk through a straw.* **2** ~ (**at, on**) **sth** to keep sth in your mouth and pull on it with your lips and tongue: [V, VN] *She sucked on a mint.* ◊ *She sucked a mint.* ◊ [VN] *Stop sucking your thumb!* ◊ [V] *The baby sucked at its mother's breast.* **3** to take liquid, air, etc. out of sth: [VN+adv./prep.] *The pump sucks air out through the valve.* ◊ [VN-ADJ] *Greenfly can literally suck a plant dry.* **4** [VN+adv./prep.] to pull sb/sth with great force in a particular direction: *The canoe was sucked down into the whirlpool.* **5** (**sth sucks**) [V] (*slang*) used to say that sth is very bad: *Their new CD sucks.* **IDM** ,**suck it and 'see** (*BrE, informal*) used to say that the only way to know if sth is suitable is to try it ,**suck it 'up** (*AmE, informal*) to accept sth bad and deal with it well, controlling your emotions—more at DRY *adj.*, TEACH **PHRV** ,**suck sb 'in**| ,**suck sb 'into sth** [usually passive] to involve sb in an activity or a situation, especially one they do not want to be involved in ,**suck 'up (to sb)** (*informal, disapproving*) to try to please sb in authority by praising them too much, helping them, etc., in order to gain some advantage for yourself
■ *noun* [usually sing.] an act of sucking

suck·er /'sʌkə(r)/ *noun* **1** (*informal*) a person who is easily tricked or persuaded to do sth **2** ~ **for sb/sth** (*informal*) a person who cannot resist sb/sth or likes sb/sth very much: *I've always been a sucker for men with green eyes.* **3** a special organ on the body of some animals that enables them to stick to a surface **4** a disc shaped

b	d	f	g	h	k	l	m	n	p	r
bad	**did**	**fall**	**get**	**hat**	**cat**	**leg**	**man**	**now**	**pen**	**red**

like a cup, usually made of rubber or plastic, that sticks to a surface when you press it against it **5** a part of a tree or bush that grows from the roots rather than from the main stem or the branches and can form a new tree or bush **6** (*AmE, slang*) used to refer in a general way to a person or thing, especially for emphasis: *The pilot said, 'I don't know how I got the sucker down safely.'* **7** (*AmE, informal*) = LOLLIPOP

suck·le /'sʌkl/ *verb* **1** [VN] (of a woman or female animal) to feed a baby or young animal with milk from the breast or UDDER: *a cow suckling her calves* ◊ (*old-fashioned*) *a mother suckling a baby* **2** [V] (of a baby or young animal) to drink milk from its mother's breast or UDDER

suck·ling /'sʌklɪŋ/ *noun* (*old-fashioned*) a baby or young animal that is still drinking milk from its mother **IDM** see MOUTH *n.*

su·crose /'su:krəʊz; -krəʊs; *AmE* -kroʊs; -kroʊz/ *noun* [U] (*chemistry*) the form of sugar that is obtained from SUGAR CANE and SUGAR BEET

suc·tion /'sʌkʃn/ *noun* [U] the process of removing air or liquid from a space or container so that sth else can be sucked into it or so that two surfaces can stick together: *Vacuum cleaners work by suction.* ◊ *a suction pump/pad* ▶ **suc·tion** *verb* [VN] (*technical*)

sud·den /'sʌdn/ *adj.* happening or done quickly and unexpectedly: *a sudden change/decision* ◊ *Don't make any sudden movements.* ◊ *His death was very sudden.* ▶ **sud·den·ness** *noun* [U] **IDM** **all of a 'sudden** quickly and unexpectedly: *All of a sudden someone grabbed me around the neck.*

ˌsudden 'death *noun* [U] a way of deciding the winner of a game when the scores are equal at the end. The players or teams continue playing and the game ends as soon as one of them gains the lead: *a sudden-death play-off in golf*

sud·den·ly /'sʌdənli/ *adv.* quickly and unexpectedly: *'Listen!' said Doyle suddenly.* ◊ *I suddenly realized what I had to do.* ◊ *It all happened so suddenly.*

suds /sʌdz/ (also **soap·suds**) *noun* **1** [pl.] a mass of very small bubbles that forms on top of water that has soap in it: *She was up to her elbows in suds.* **2** [U] (*old-fashioned, AmE, informal*) beer

sue /su:; *BrE* also sju:/ *verb* **1** ~ (**sb**) (**for sth**) to make a claim against sb in a court of law about sth that they have said or done to harm you: [VN] *to sue sb for breach of contract* ◊ *to sue sb for damages/$10 million* (= in order to get money from sb) ◊ [V] *They threatened to sue if the work was not completed.* **2** [V] ~ **for sth** (*formal*) to formally ask for sth, especially in a court of law: *to sue for divorce* ◊ *The rebels were forced to sue for peace.*

suede /sweɪd/ *noun* [U] soft leather with a surface like VELVET on one side, used especially for making clothes and shoes: *a suede jacket*

suet /'su:ɪt; *BrE* also 'sju:ɪt/ *noun* [U] hard fat from around the KIDNEYS of cows, sheep, etc., used in cooking: *suet pudding* (= one made using suet)

suf·fer /'sʌfə(r)/ *verb* **1** [V] ~ (**from sth**) | ~ (**for sth**) to be badly affected by a disease, pain, sadness, a lack of sth, etc: *I hate to see animals suffering.* ◊ *He suffers from asthma.* ◊ *road accident victims suffering from shock* ◊ *Many companies are suffering from a shortage of skilled staff.* ◊ *He made a rash decision and now he is suffering for it.* **2** [VN] to experience sth unpleasant, such as injury, defeat or loss: *He suffered a massive heart attack.* ◊ *The party suffered a humiliating defeat in the general election.* ◊ *The company suffered huge losses in the last financial year.* **3** [V] to become worse: *His school work is suffering because of family problems.* **IDM** **not suffer fools 'gladly** to have very little patience with people that you think are stupid: *She was a forceful personality who didn't suffer fools gladly.*

suf·fer·ance /'sʌfərəns/ *noun* [U] **IDM** **on 'sufferance** if you do sth **on sufferance**, sb allows you to do it although they do not really want you to: *He's only staying here on sufferance.*

suf·fer·er /'sʌfərə(r)/ *noun* a person who suffers, espe-

cially sb who is suffering from a disease: *cancer sufferers* ◊ *She received many letters of support from fellow sufferers.*

suf·fer·ing /'sʌfərɪŋ/ *noun* **1** [U] physical or mental pain: *Death finally brought an end to her suffering.* ◊ *This war has caused widespread human suffering.* **2** (**sufferings**) [pl.] feelings of pain and unhappiness: *The hospice aims to ease the sufferings of the dying.*

suf·fice /sə'faɪs/ *verb* (*formal*) (not used in the progressive tenses) to be enough for sb/sth: [V] *Generally a brief note or a phone call will suffice.* ◊ [V to inf] *One example will suffice to illustrate the point.* **IDM** **suffice (it) to say (that)** ... used to suggest that although you could say more, what you do say will be enough to explain what you mean

suf·fi·ciency /sə'fɪʃnsi/ *noun* [sing.] ~ (**of sth**) (*formal*) an amount that is enough for a particular purpose

suf·fi·cient /sə'fɪʃnt/ *adj.* ~ (**to do sth**) | ~ (**for sth/sb**) enough for a particular purpose; as much as you need: *Allow sufficient time to get there.* ◊ *These reasons are not sufficient to justify the ban.* ◊ *Is £100 sufficient for your expenses?* **OPP** INSUFFICIENT—see also SELF-SUFFICIENT ⇨ note at ENOUGH ▶ **suf·fi·cient·ly** *adv.*: *The following day she felt sufficiently well to go to work.*

suf·fix /'sʌfɪks/ *noun* (*grammar*) a letter or group of letters added to the end of a word to make another word, such as *-ly* in *quickly* or *-ness* in *sadness*—compare AFFIX, PREFIX

suf·fo·cate /'sʌfəkeɪt/ *verb* **1** to die because there is no air to breathe; to kill sb by not letting them breathe air: [V] *Many dogs have suffocated in hot cars.* ◊ [VN] *The couple were suffocated by fumes from a faulty gas fire.* ◊ *He put the pillow over her face and suffocated her.* ◊ (*figurative*) *She felt suffocated by all the rules and regulations.* **2** [V] (**be suffocating**) if **it is suffocating**, it is very hot and there is little fresh air: *Can I open a window? It's suffocating in here!* ▶ **suf·fo·ca·tion** /ˌsʌfə'keɪʃn/ *noun* [U]: *to die from/of suffocation*

suf·fo·cat·ing /'sʌfəkeɪtɪŋ/ *adj.* **1** making it difficult to breathe normally: *The afternoon heat was suffocating.* **2** restricting what sb/sth can do: *Some marriages can sometimes feel suffocating.*

suf·fra·gan /'sʌfrəgən/ (also **suffragan 'bishop**) *noun* a BISHOP who is an assistant to a bishop of a particular DIOCESE

suf·frage /'sʌfrɪdʒ/ *noun* [U] the right to vote in political elections: *universal suffrage* (= the right of all adults to vote) ◊ *women's suffrage*

suf·fra·gette /ˌsʌfrə'dʒet/ *noun* a member of a group of women who, in Britain and the US in the early part of the 20th century, worked to get the right for women to vote in political elections

suf·fuse /sə'fju:z/ *verb* [VN] [often passive] ~ **sb/sth** (**with sth**) (*literary*) (especially of a colour, light or feeling) to spread all over or through sb/sth: *Her face was suffused with colour.* ◊ *Colour suffused her face.*

Sufi /'su:fi/ *noun* a member of a Muslim group who try to become united with God through prayer and MEDITATION and by living a very simple, strict life ▶ **Suf·ism** *noun* [U]

sugar /'ʃʊgə(r)/ *noun, verb, exclamation*
■ *noun* **1** [U] a sweet substance, often in the form of white or brown CRYSTALS, made from the juices of various plants, used in cooking or to make tea, coffee, etc. sweeter: *a sugar plantation/refinery/bowl* ◊ *This juice contains no added sugar.* ◊ *Do you take sugar* (= have it in your tea, coffee, etc.)?—see also BROWN SUGAR, CANE SUGAR, CASTER SUGAR, GRANULATED SUGAR, ICING SUGAR **2** [C] the amount of sugar that a small spoon can hold or that is contained in a small CUBE, added to tea, coffee, etc: *How many sugars do you take in coffee?* **3** [C, usually pl.] (*technical*) any of various sweet substances that are found naturally in plants, fruit, etc: *fruit sugars* ◊ *a person's blood sugar level* (= the amount of GLUCOSE in their blood) **4** [U] (*spoken, especially AmE*) a way of addressing sb that you like or love: *See you later, sugar.*
■ *verb* [VN] to add sugar to sth; to cover sth in sugar **IDM** see PILL

s	t	v	z	ʃ	ʒ	tʃ	dʒ	θ	ð	ŋ
see	tea	van	zoo	shoe	vision	chain	jam	thin	this	sing

■ *exclamation* used to show that you are annoyed when you do sth stupid or when sth goes wrong (to avoid saying 'shit'): *Oh sugar! I've forgotten my book!*

'sugar beet *noun* [U] a plant with a large round root, from which sugar is made

'sugar cane *noun* [U] a tall tropical plant with thick stems from which sugar is made

'sugar-coat *verb* [VN] to do sth that makes an unpleasant situation seem less unpleasant

ˌsugar-'coated *adj.* **1** covered with sugar **2** (*disapproving*) made to seem attractive, in a way that deceives people: *a sugar-coated promise*

'sugar cube *noun* (*especially AmE*) = SUGAR LUMP

'sugar daddy *noun* (*informal*) a rich older man who gives presents and money to a much younger woman, usually in return for sex

'sugar lump (also **lump**) (both *BrE*) (also **'sugar cube** *AmE, BrE*) *noun* a small CUBE of sugar, used in cups of tea or coffee

sug·ary /ˈʃʊgəri/ *adj.* **1** containing sugar; tasting of sugar: *sugary snacks/drinks* **2** (*disapproving*) seeming too full of emotion in a way that is not sincere [SYN] SENTIMENTAL: *a sugary smile* ◇ *sugary pop music*

sug·gest /səˈdʒest; *AmE* also səɡˈdʒ-/ *verb* **1** ~ sth (to sb) to put forward an idea or a plan for other people to think about [SYN] PROPOSE: [VN] *May I suggest a white wine with this dish, Sir?* ◇ *A solution immediately suggested itself to me* (= I immediately thought of a solution). ◇ [V(that)] *I suggest (that) we go out to eat.* ◇ [V-ing] *I suggested going in my car.* ◇ [VNthat] *It has been suggested that bright children take their exams early.* ◇ (*BrE* also) *It has been suggested that bright children should take their exams early.* **2** ~ sb/sth (for sth)| ~ sb/sth (as sth) to tell sb about a suitable person, thing, method, etc. for a particular job or purpose [SYN] RECOMMEND: [VN] *Who would you suggest for the job?* ◇ *She suggested Paris as a good place for the conference.* ◇ *Can you suggest a good dictionary?* [HELP] You cannot 'suggest somebody something': ~~Can you suggest me a good dictionary?~~ [VWH-] *Can you suggest how I might contact him?* **3** ~ sth (to sb) to put an idea into sb's mind; to make sb think that sth is true: [V(that)] *All the evidence suggests (that) he stole the money.* ◇ [VN] *The symptoms suggest a minor heart attack.* ◇ *What do these results suggest to you?* **4** to state sth indirectly [SYN] IMPLY: [V(that)] *Are you suggesting (that) I'm lazy?* ◇ [VN] *I would never suggest such a thing.*

sug·gest·ible /səˈdʒestəbl; *AmE* also səɡˈdʒ-/ *adj.* easily influenced by other people: *He was young and highly suggestible.*

sug·ges·tion /səˈdʒestʃən; *AmE* also səɡˈdʒ-/ *noun* **1** [C] ~ (for/about/on sth)| ~ (that...) an idea or a plan that you mention for sb else to think about: *Can I make a suggestion?* ◇ *Do you have any suggestions?* ◇ *I'd like to hear your suggestions for ways of raising money.* ◇ *Are there any suggestions about how best to tackle the problem?* ◇ *We welcome any comments and suggestions on these proposals.* ◇ *He agreed with my suggestion that we should change the date.* ◇ *We are open to suggestions* (= willing to listen to ideas from other people). ◇ *We need to get it there by four. Any suggestions?* **2** [U, C, usually sing.] ~ of/that a reason to think that sth, especially sth bad, is true: *A spokesman dismissed any suggestion of a boardroom rift.* ◇ *There was no suggestion that he was doing anything illegal.* **3** [C, usually sing.] a slight amount or sign of sth: *She looked at me with just a suggestion of a smile.* **4** [U] (*written*) putting an idea into people's minds by connecting it with other ideas: *Most advertisements work through suggestion.* ◇ *the power of suggestion* [IDM] **at/on sb's sug'gestion** because sb suggested it: *At his suggestion, I bought the more expensive printer.*

sug·gest·ive /səˈdʒestɪv; *AmE* also səɡˈdʒ-/ *adj.* **1** ~ (of sth) reminding you of sth or making you think about sth: *music that is suggestive of warm summer days* **2** making people think about sex: *suggestive jokes* ◇ *to make suggestive remarks* ▶ **sug·gest·ive·ly** *adv.*: *He leered suggestively.*

sui·cidal /ˌsuːɪˈsaɪdl; *BrE* also ˌsjuːɪ-/ *adj.* **1** people who

are **suicidal** feel that they want to kill themselves: *On bad days I even felt suicidal.* ◇ *suicidal tendencies* **2** very dangerous and likely to lead to death; likely to cause very serious problems or disaster: *a suicidal leap into the swollen river* ◇ *It would be suicidal to risk going out in this weather.* ◇ *The new economic policies could prove suicidal for the party.* ▶ **sui·cid·al·ly** /-dəli/ *adv.*: *suicidally depressed*

sui·cide /ˈsuːɪsaɪd; *BrE* also ˈsjuː-/ *noun* **1** [U, C] the act of killing yourself deliberately: *to commit suicide* ◇ *an attempted suicide* (= one in which the person survives) ◇ *a suicide letter/note* (= written before sb tries to commit suicide) ◇ *a suicide bomber* (= who expects to die while trying to kill other people with a bomb) **2** [U] a course of action that is likely to ruin your career, position in society, etc: *It would have been political suicide for him to challenge the allegations in court.* **3** [C] (*formal*) a person who commits suicide

'suicide pact *noun* an agreement between two or more people to kill themselves at the same time

sui generis /ˌsuːiː ˈdʒenərɪs/ *adj.* (from *Latin, formal*) different from all other people or things [SYN] UNIQUE

suit /suːt; *BrE* also sjuːt/ *noun, verb*

■ *noun* **1** a set of clothes made of the same fabric, including a jacket and trousers/pants or a skirt: *a business suit* ◇ *a pinstripe suit* ◇ *a two-/three-piece suit* (= of two/three pieces of clothing)—see also JUMPSUIT, LOUNGE SUIT, SAILOR SUIT, SHELL SUIT, SWEATSUIT, TRACKSUIT, TROUSER SUIT **2** a set of clothing worn for a particular activity: *a diving suit* ◇ *a suit of armour*—see also BOILER SUIT, SPACESUIT, SWIMSUIT, WET SUIT **3** any of the four sets that form a pack/deck of cards: *The suits are called hearts, clubs, diamonds and spades.*—picture on page A8 **4** = LAWSUIT: *to file/bring a suit against* sb ◇ *a divorce suit*—see also PATERNITY SUIT [IDM] see BIRTHDAY, FOLLOW, STRONG

■ *verb* [no passive] (not used in the progressive tenses) **1** to be convenient or useful for sb: [VN] *Choose a computer to suit your particular needs.* ◇ *If we met at 2, would that suit you?* ◇ *If you want to go by bus, that suits me fine.* ◇ *He can be very helpful, but only when it suits him.* ◇ [VNto inf] *It suits me to start work at a later time.* **2** [VN] (*especially of clothes, colours, etc.*) to make you look attractive: *Blue suits you. You should wear it more often.* ◇ *I don't think this coat really suits me.* **3** (*especially BrE*) [VN] (usually used in negative sentences) to be right or good for sb/sth: *This hot weather doesn't suit me.* [IDM] **suit your/sb's book** (*BrE, informal*) to be convenient or useful for you/sb: *Well, if you're honest and hard-working, that suits our book.* **suit sb ˌdown to the 'ground** (*BrE, informal*) to be very convenient or acceptable for sb: *This job suits me down to the ground.* **ˌsuit your'self** (*informal*) **1** to do exactly what you would like: *I choose my assignments to suit myself.* **2** usually used in orders to tell sb to do what they want, even though it annoys you: *'I think I'll stay in this evening.' 'Suit yourself!'* [PHRV] **'suit sth to sth/sb** to make sth appropriate for sth/sb: *He can suit his conversation to whoever he's with.*

suit·able /ˈsuːtəbl; *BrE* also ˈsjuː-/ *adj.* ~ (for sth/sb)| ~ (to do sth) right or appropriate for a particular purpose or occasion: *a suitable candidate* ◇ *This programme is not suitable for children.* ◇ *a suitable place for a picnic* ◇ *I don't have anything suitable to wear for the party.* ◇ *Would now be a suitable moment to discuss my report?* [OPP] UNSUITABLE ▶ **suit·abil·ity** /ˌsuːtəˈbɪləti; ˌsjuː-/ *noun* [U]: *There is no doubt about her suitability for the job.*

suit·ably /ˈsuːtəbli; *BrE* also ˈsjuː-/ *adv.* **1** in a way that is right or appropriate for a particular purpose or occasion: *I am not really suitably dressed for a party.* ◇ *suitably qualified candidates* **2** showing the feelings, etc. that you would expect in a particular situation: *He was suitably impressed when I told him I'd won.*

suit·case /ˈsuːtkeɪs; *BrE* also ˈsjuː-/ (also **case**) *noun* a case with flat sides and a handle, used for carrying clothes, etc. when you are travelling: *to pack/unpack a suitcase*—picture at BAG

suite /swiːt/ *noun* **1** a set of rooms, especially in a hotel:

S

æ	ɑː	e	ɜː	ə	ɪ	iː	i	ɒ	ɔː	ʌ	ʊ	u	uː
cat	father	ten	bird	about	sit	see	many	got	saw	cup	put	actual	too
								(BrE)					

a hotel/private/honeymoon suite ◇ *a suite of rooms/ offices*—see also EN SUITE **2** a set of matching pieces of furniture: *a bathroom/bedroom suite* ◇ (*BrE*) *a three-piece suite with two armchairs and a sofa* **3** a piece of music made up of three or more related parts, for example pieces from an opera: *Stravinsky's Firebird Suite* **4** (*computing*) a set of related computer programs: *a suite of software development tools*

suit·ed /ˈsuːtɪd; *BrE also* ˈsjuː-/ *adj.* [not before noun] **1** ~ **(to/for sb/sth)** right or appropriate for sb/sth: *She was ideally suited to the part of Eva Peron.* ◇ *He is not really suited for a teaching career.* ◇ *This diet is suited to anyone who wants to lose weight fast.* [OPP] UNSUITED **2** if two people are **suited** or **well suited**, they are likely to make a good couple: *Jo and I are very well suited.* ◇ *They were not suited to one another.* [OPP] UNSUITED **3** (**-suited**) (in compounds) wearing a suit of the type mentioned: *sober-suited city businessmen*

suit·or /ˈsuːtə(r); *BrE also* ˈsjuː-/ *noun* **1** (*old-fashioned*) a man who wants to marry a particular woman **2** (*business*) a company that wants to buy another company: *a hostile/ friendly suitor* ◇ *a merger proposal from an unwanted suitor*

sul·fate, sul·fide, sul·fur, sul·fur·ic acid (*AmE*) = SULPHATE, SULPHIDE, SULPHUR, SULPHURIC ACID

sulk /sʌlk/ *verb, noun*
■ *verb* [V] (*disapproving*) to look angry and refuse to speak or smile because you want people to know that you are upset about sth: *He went off to sulk in his room.*
■ *noun* (*BrE also* **the sulks** [pl.]) a period of being silent and bad-tempered because you are angry about sth: *Jo was in a sulk upstairs.* ◇ *to have the sulks*

sulky /ˈsʌlki/ *adj.* (*disapproving*) silent or bad-tempered because you are angry about sth: *Sarah had looked sulky all morning.* ◇ *a sulky child* ▶ **sulk·ily** /-ɪli/ *adv.* **sulki·ness** *noun* [U]

sul·len /ˈsʌlən/ *adj.* (*disapproving*) **1** silent and bad-tempered, either on a particular occasion or because it is part of your character: *Bob looked pale and sullen.* ◇ *She gave him a sullen glare.* ◇ *sullen teenagers* **2** (*literary*) (of the sky or weather) dark and unpleasant: *a sullen grey sky* ▶ **sul·len·ly** *adv.* **sul·len·ness** *noun* [U]

sully /ˈsʌli/ *verb* (**sul·lies, sully·ing, sul·lied, sul·lied**) [VN] (*formal or literary*) **1** to spoil or lower the value of sth: *By cheating they have sullied the good name of their country.* **2** to make sth dirty: *She wondered if she dared risk sullying the gleaming sink.*

sul·phate (*BrE*) (*AmE* **sul·fate**) /ˈsʌlfeɪt/ *noun* [C, U] (*chemistry*) a compound of SULPHURIC ACID and a chemical element: *copper sulphate*

sul·phide (*BrE*) (*AmE* **sul·fide**) /ˈsʌlfaɪd/ *noun* [C, U] (*chemistry*) a compound of sulphur and another chemical element

sul·phur (*BrE*) (*AmE* **sul·fur**) /ˈsʌlfə(r)/ *noun* [U] (*symb* **S**) a chemical element. Sulphur is a pale yellow substance that produces a strong unpleasant smell when it burns and is used in medicine and industry. ▶ **sul·phur·ous** (*BrE*) (*AmE* **sul·fur·ous**) /ˈsʌlfərəs/ *adj.*: *sulphurous fumes*

sulphur di·oxide (*BrE*) (*AmE* **sulfur di·oxide**) *noun* [U] (*symb* SO_2) a poisonous gas with a strong smell, that is used in industry and causes air POLLUTION

sul·phur·ic acid (*BrE*) (*AmE* **sul·fur·ic acid**) /sʌl-ˌfjʊərɪk ˈæsɪd; *AmE* -ˌfjʊr-/ *noun* [U] (*chemistry*) (*symb* H_2SO_4) a strong colourless acid

sul·tan /ˈsʌltən/ *noun* the title given to Muslim rulers in some countries: *the Sultan of Brunei*

sul·tana /sʌlˈtɑːnə; *AmE* -ˈtænə/ (*BrE*) (*AmE* **golden rai·sin**) *noun* a small dried grape without seeds, used in cakes, etc.

sul·tan·ate /ˈsʌltəneɪt/ *noun* **1** the rank or position of a sultan **2** an area of land that is ruled over by a SULTAN: *the Sultanate of Oman* **3** the period of time during which sb is a SULTAN

sul·try /ˈsʌltri/ *adj.* **1** (of the weather or air) very hot and uncomfortable: *a sultry summer afternoon* ◇ *The weather was still very heavy and sultry.* **2** (*written*) (of a woman or

her appearance) sexually attractive; seeming to have strong sexual feelings: *a sultry smile/voice* ◇ *a sultry singer* ▶ **sul·tri·ness** *noun* [U]

sum /sʌm/ *noun, verb*
■ *noun* **1** [C] ~ **(of sth)** an amount of money: *You will be fined the sum of £200.* ◇ *a large sum of money* ◇ *a six-figure sum*—see also LUMP SUM **2** [C, usually sing.] ~ **(of sth)** the number you get when you add two or more numbers together: *The sum of 7 and 12 is 19.* **3** (*also* **sum 'total**) [sing.] **the ~ of sth** all of sth, especially when you think that it is not very much: *This is the sum of my achievements so far.* **4** [C] a simple problem that involves calculating numbers: *to do a sum in your head* ◇ *I was good at sums at school.* ◇ *If I've got my sums right, I should be able to afford the rent.* [IDM] **be greater/more than the ,sum of its 'parts** to be better or more effective as a group than you would think just by looking at the individual members of the group **in 'sum** (*formal*) used to introduce a short statement of the main points of a discussion, speech, etc.
■ *verb* (**-mm-**) [PHRV] **,sum 'up**|**,sum sth↔'up 1** to state the main points of sth in a short and clear form [SYN] SUMMARIZE: *To sum up, there are three main ways of tackling the problem …* ◇ [+wh-] *Can I just sum up what we've agreed so far?* **2** (of a judge) to give a summary of the main facts and arguments in a legal case, near the end of a trial—related noun SUMMING-UP **,sum sb/sth↔'up 1** to describe or show the most typical characteristics of sb/ sth, especially in a few words: *Totally lazy—that just about sums him up.* **2** to form or express an opinion of sb/sth [SYN] SIZE UP: *She quickly summed up the situation and took control.*—related noun SUMMING-UP

summa cum laude /ˌsʊmə kʊm ˈlɔːdi; ˈlaʊdeɪ/ *adv., adj.* (*from Latin*) (in the US) at the highest level of achievement that students can reach when they finish their studies at college: *He graduated summa cum laude from Harvard.*—compare CUM LAUDE, MAGNA CUM LAUDE

sum·mar·ize (*BrE also* **-ise**) /ˈsʌməraɪz/ *verb* to give a summary of sth: [VN] *The results of the research are summarized at the end of the chapter.* [also V]

sum·mary /ˈsʌməri/ *noun, adj.*
■ *noun* (*pl.* **-ies**) a short statement that gives only the main points of sth, not the details: *The following is a summary of our conclusions.* ◇ *a news summary* ◇ *a two-page summary of a government report* ◇ *In summary, this was a disappointing performance.*
■ *adj.* [only before noun] **1** (*formal*) giving only the main points of sth, not the details: *a summary financial statement* ◇ *I made a summary report for the records.* **2** (*sometimes disapproving*) done immediately, without paying attention to the normal process that should be followed: *summary justice/execution* ◇ *a summary judgement* ▶ **sum·mar·ily** /ˈsʌmərəli; *AmE* səˈmerəli/ *adv.*: *to be summarily dismissed/executed*

sum·mat /ˈsʌmət; ˈsəmət/ *noun* (*NorthE, non-standard*) a way of writing the spoken form of 'something'

sum·ma·tion /sʌˈmeɪʃn/ *noun* (*rare, formal*) **1** [usually sing.] a summary of what has been done or said: *What he said was a fair summation of the discussion.* **2** a collection of different parts that forms a complete account or impression of sb/sth: *The exhibition presents a summation of the artist's career.*

sum·mer /ˈsʌmə(r)/ *noun* [U, C] the warmest season of the year, coming between spring and autumn/fall: *We're going away in the summer.* ◇ *It's very hot here in summer.* ◇ *in the summer of 1999* ◇ *late/early summer* ◇ *this/ next/last summer* ◇ *a cool/hot/wet summer* ◇ *It is now high summer* (= the hottest part of summer). ◇ *a summer's day* ◇ *a summer dress* ◇ *the summer holidays/vacation* ◇ *two summers ago*—see also INDIAN SUMMER

'summer camp *noun* [C, U] (in the US) a place where children go during the summer and take part in sports and other activities

'summer house *noun* a small building in a garden/ yard for sitting in in good weather

aɪ	aʊ	eɪ	əʊ	oʊ	ɔɪ	ɪə	eə	ʊə	j	w
my	now	say	go (BrE)	go (AmE)	boy	near	hair	pure	yes	wet

,summer 'pudding noun [C, U] (BrE) a cold DESSERT (= a sweet dish) made from berries surrounded by slices of bread that have been soaked in their juice

'summer school noun [C, U] courses that are held in the summer at a university or college or, in the US, at a school

'summer time (BrE) (AmE **'daylight saving time**) noun the period between March and October during which in some countries the clocks are put forward one hour, so that it is light for an extra hour in the evening

sum·mer·time /ˈsʌmətaɪm; AmE -mərt-/ noun [U] the season of summer: *It's beautiful here in (the) summertime.*

sum·mery /ˈsʌməri/ adj. typical of or suitable for the summer: *summery weather ◊ a light summery dress*

,summing-'up noun (pl. **summings-up**) **1** a speech that the judge makes near the end of a trial in a court of law, in which he or she reminds the JURY about the evidence and the most important points in the case before the JURY makes its decision **2** an occasion when sb states the main points of an argument, etc.

sum·mit /ˈsʌmɪt/ noun **1** the highest point of sth, especially the top of a mountain: *We reached the summit at noon. ◊ This path leads to the summit. ◊ (figurative) the summit of his career*—picture at MOUNTAIN **2** an official meeting or series of meetings between the leaders of two or more governments at which they discuss important matters: *a summit in Moscow ◊ a summit conference*

sum·mon /ˈsʌmən/ verb **1** (formal) to order sb to appear in a court of law SYN SUMMONS: [VN to inf] *He was summoned to appear before the magistrates.* [also VN] **2 ~ sb (to sth)** (formal) to order sb to come to you: [VN] *In May 1688 he was urgently summoned to London. ◊ She summoned the waiter.* [also VN to inf] **3** [VN] (formal) to arrange an official meeting SYN CONVENE: *to summon a conference/meeting* **4** [VN] (formal) to call for or try to obtain sth: *to summon assistance/help/reinforcements* **5** [VN] **~ sth (up)** to make an effort to produce a particular quality in yourself, especially when you find it difficult SYN MUSTER: *She was trying to summon up the courage to leave him. ◊ I couldn't even summon the energy to get out of bed.* PHRV **,summon sth↔'up** to make a feeling, an idea, a memory, etc. come into your mind SYN EVOKE: *The book summoned up memories of my childhood*

sum·mons /ˈsʌmənz/ noun, verb
■ noun (pl. **sum·monses** /-zɪz/) **1** (AmE also **cit·ation**) an order to appear in a court of law: *to issue a summons against sb ◊ The police have been unable to serve a summons on him. ◊ She received a summons to appear in court the following week.* **2** an order to come and see sb: *to obey a royal summons*
■ verb **~ sb (for sth)** to order sb to appear in a court of law SYN SUMMON: [VN] *She was summonsed for speeding. ◊* [VN to inf] *He was summonsed to appear in court.*

sumo /ˈsuːməʊ; AmE -moʊ/ (also **,sumo 'wrestling**) noun [U] a Japanese style of WRESTLING, in which the competitors are extremely large: *a sumo wrestler*

sump /sʌmp/ noun **1** a hole or hollow area in which liquid waste collects **2** (AmE also **'oil pan**) the place under an engine that holds the engine oil

sump·tu·ous /ˈsʌmptʃuəs/ adj. (written) very expensive and looking very impressive: *a sumptuous meal/room ◊ We dined in sumptuous surroundings.* ▶ **sump·tu·ous·ly** adv. **sump·tu·ous·ness** noun [U]

,sum 'total noun [sing.] (sometimes disapproving) the whole of sth; everything SYN SUM: *A photo, a book of poems and a gold ring—this was the sum total of his possessions.*

sun /sʌn/ noun, verb
■ noun **1** (the sun, the Sun) [sing.] the star that shines in the sky during the day and gives the earth heat and light: *the sun's rays ◊ the rising/setting sun ◊ The sun was shining and birds were singing. ◊ The sun was just setting. ◊ The sun gets the sun in the mornings. ◊ We sat in the sun. ◊ The sun was blazing hot. ◊ Too much sun ages the skin. ◊ We did our best to keep out of the sun. ◊ They've booked a* **2** (usually the sun) [sing., U] the light and heat from the sun SYN SUNSHINE: *the warmth of the afternoon sun ◊ This room gets the sun in the mornings.*

holiday in the sun (= in a place that is warm and sunny). ◊ *Her face had obviously caught the sun* (= become red or brown) *on holiday.*—see also SUNNY **3** [C] any star around which planets move IDM **under the 'sun** used to emphasize that you are talking about a very large number of things: *We talked about everything under the sun. ◊ I've been called all the names under the sun!* **with the 'sun** when the sun rises or sets: *I get up with the sun.*—more at HAY, PLACE n.
■ verb (-nn-) [VN] **~ yourself** to sit or lie in a place where the sun is shining on you: *We lay sunning ourselves on the deck.*

'sun-baked adj. **1** made hard and dry by the heat of the sun: *sun-baked earth* **2** receiving a lot of light and heat from the sun: *sun-baked beaches*

sun·bathe /ˈsʌnbeɪð/ verb [V] to sit or lie in the sun, especially in order to go brown and get a SUNTAN ⇨ note at BATH

sun·beam /ˈsʌnbiːm/ noun a ray of sunlight

sun·bed /ˈsʌnbed/ noun **1** a bed for lying on under a SUNLAMP **2** = SUNLOUNGER

Sun·belt /ˈsʌnbelt/ (the Sunbelt) noun [sing.] the southern and south-western parts of the US

sun·block /ˈsʌnblɒk; AmE -blɑːk/ noun [U, C] a cream that you put on your skin to protect it completely from the harmful effects of the sun

sun·burn /ˈsʌnbɜːn; AmE -bɜːrn/ noun [U] the condition of having painful red skin because you have spent too much time in the sun—compare SUNTAN

sun·burned /ˈsʌnbɜːnd; AmE -bɜːrnd/ (also **sun·burnt** /ˈsʌnbɜːnt; AmE -bɜːrnt/) adj. **1** suffering from sunburn: *Her shoulders were badly sunburned.* **2** (BrE) (of a person or of skin) having an attractive brown colour from being in the sun: *She looked fit and sunburnt.*

sun·dae /ˈsʌndeɪ; -di/ noun a cold DESSERT (= a sweet dish) of ice cream covered with a sweet sauce, nuts, pieces of fruit, etc., usually served in a tall glass: *a hot chocolate fudge sundae*

Sun·day /ˈsʌndeɪ; -di/ noun (abbr. Sun.) **1** [C, U] the day of the week after Saturday and before Monday HELP To see how Sunday is used, look at the examples at Monday. ORIGIN From the Old English for 'day of the sun', translated from Latin dies solis. **2** [C, usually pl.] (BrE, informal) a newspaper published on a Sunday IDM **your ,Sunday 'best** (informal, humorous) your best clothes: *I put on my Sunday best for the occasion.*—more at MONTH

'Sunday school noun [C, U] a class that is organized by a church or SYNAGOGUE where children can go for a short time on Sundays to learn about the Christian or Jewish religion

sun·der /ˈsʌndə(r)/ verb [VN] **~ sth/sb (from sth/sb)** (formal or literary) to split or break sth/sb apart, especially by force—see also ASUNDER

sun·dial /ˈsʌndaɪəl/ noun
a device used outdoors, especially in the past, for telling the time when the sun is shining. A pointed piece of metal throws a shadow on a flat surface that is marked with the hours like a clock, and the shadow moves around as the sun moves across the sky.

sundial

sun·down /ˈsʌndaʊn/ noun [U] (especially AmE) the time when the sun goes down and night begins SYN SUNSET: *The celebration begins at sundown.*

'sun-drenched adj. [only before noun] (approving) having a lot of hot sun: *sun-drenched Mediterranean beaches*

sun·dress /ˈsʌndres/ noun a dress that does not cover the arms, neck or shoulders, worn in hot weather

'sun-dried adj. [only before noun] (especially of food) dried naturally by the heat of the sun: *sun-dried tomatoes*

sun·dries /ˈsʌndriz/ noun [pl.] (written) various items, especially small ones, that are not important enough to be named separately: *You can claim up to £10 a day for sundries.*

sun·dry /ˈsʌndri/ *adj.* [only before noun] (*formal*) various; not important enough to be named separately: *a watch, a notebook, a diary and sundry other items* **IDM** ˌ**all and** ˈ**sundry** (*informal*) everyone, not just a few special people: *She was known to all and sundry as Bella.* ◊ *The club is open to all and sundry.*

sun·flower /ˈsʌnflaʊə(r)/ *noun* a very tall plant with large yellow flowers, grown in gardens or for its seeds and their oil that are used in cooking: *sunflower oil*

sung *pp of* SING

sun·glasses /ˈsʌnɡlɑːsɪz; *AmE* -ɡlæs-/ (also *informal* **shades**) *noun* [pl.] a pair of glasses with dark glass in them that you wear to protect your eyes from bright sunlight: *a pair of sunglasses*—see also DARK GLASSES

sun·hat /ˈsʌnhæt/ *noun* a hat worn to protect the head and neck from the sun—picture at HAT

sunk *pp of* SINK

sunk·en /ˈsʌŋkən/ *adj.* **1** [only before noun] that has fallen to the bottom of the sea, or the ocean, or of a lake or river: *a sunken ship* ◊ *sunken treasure* **2** (of eyes or cheeks) hollow and falling inwards as a result of disease, hunger or age: *His eyes were dark and sunken.* **3** [only before noun] at a lower level than the area around: *a sunken bath/garden*

sun·lamp /ˈsʌnlæmp/ *noun* a lamp that produces ULTRAVIOLET light that has the same effect as the sun and can turn the skin brown

sun·less /ˈsʌnləs/ *adj.* without any sun; receiving no light from the sun: *a sunless day* ◊ *the sunless side of the house*

sun·light /ˈsʌnlaɪt/ *noun* [U] the light from the sun: *a ray/pool of sunlight* ◊ *shafts of bright sunlight* ◊ *The morning sunlight flooded into the room.*

sun·lit /ˈsʌnlɪt/ *adj.* [usually before noun] (*written*) receiving light from the sun: *sunlit water/streets/rooms*

ˈ**sun lounge** (*BrE*) (also **sun·room** *AmE, BrE*) *noun* a room with large windows, and often a glass roof, that lets in a lot of sunlight

sun·loun·ger /ˈsʌnlaʊndʒə(r)/ (also **loun·ger, sun·bed**) *noun* (*BrE*) a chair with a long seat that supports your legs, used for sitting or lying on in the sun—picture at CHAIR

Sunni /ˈsʊni; ˈsʌni/ *noun* (*pl.* **Sunni** or **Sun·nis**) **1** [U] one of the two main branches of the Islamic religion—compare SHIA **2** [C] a member of the Sunni branch of Islam—compare SHIITE ▶ **Sun·nite** /ˈsʊnaɪt; ˈsʌn-/ *adj.* [usually before noun]

sunny /ˈsʌni/ *adj.* (**sun·nier, sun·ni·est**) **1** with a lot of bright light from the sun: *a sunny day/afternoon* ◊ *sunny weather* ◊ *The outlook for the weekend is hot and sunny.* ◊ *a sunny garden* ◊ *Italy was at its sunniest.* **2** cheerful and happy: *a sunny disposition/smile*

ˈ**sunny side** *noun* the side of sth that receives most light from the sun: (*figurative*) *the sunny side of life* (= the more cheerful aspects of life) **IDM** ˌ**sunny-side** ˈ**up** (*AmE*) (of an egg) fried on one side only

sun·rise /ˈsʌnraɪz/ *noun* **1** [U] the time when the sun first appears in the sky in the morning **SYN** DAWN: *We got up at sunrise.* **2** [C, usually sing.] the colours in the part of the sky where the sun first appears in the morning: *the pinks and yellows of the sunrise*

ˈ**sunrise industry** *noun* a new industry, especially one connected with electronics or computers, that is successful and growing

sun·roof /ˈsʌnruːf/ *noun* (*pl.* **-roofs**) a part of the roof of a car that you can open to let air and light in—picture at CAR

sun·room /ˈsʌnruːm; -rʊm/ *noun* (*especially AmE*) = SUN LOUNGE

sun·screen /ˈsʌnskriːn/ *noun* [C, U] a cream or liquid that you put on your skin to protect it from the harmful effects of the sun: *a high factor* (= strong) *sunscreen*

sun·set /ˈsʌnset/ *noun* **1** [U] the time when the sun goes down and night begins: *Every evening at sunset the flag*

was lowered. **2** [C] the colours in the part of the sky where the sun slowly goes down in the evening: *a spectacular sunset*

sun·shade /ˈsʌnʃeɪd/ *noun* **1** (*BrE*) an object, sometimes shaped like an umbrella, that is used to protect people from hot sun—picture at HOUSE **2** a type of light umbrella that people use to protect themselves or babies from the sun: *a child's buggy fitted with a sunshade*—compare PARASOL **3** (**sunshades**) [pl.] a pair of dark glasses that you wear to protect your eyes from bright sunlight, especially ones that fix on to your ordinary glasses

sun·shine /ˈsʌnʃaɪn/ *noun* [U] **1** the light and heat of the sun: *the warm spring sunshine* **2** (*informal*) happiness: *She brought sunshine into our dull lives.* **3** (*BrE, informal*) used for addressing sb in a friendly, or sometimes a rude way: *Hello, sunshine!* ◊ *Look, sunshine, who do you think you're talking to?* **IDM** see RAY

sun·spot /ˈsʌnspɒt; *AmE* -spɑːt/ *noun* a dark area that sometimes appears on the sun's surface

sun·stroke /ˈsʌnstrəʊk; *AmE* -stroʊk/ *noun* [U] an illness with fever, weakness, HEADACHE, etc. caused by too much direct sunlight, especially on the head

sun·tan /ˈsʌntæn/ *noun* [usually sing.] = TAN: *Where have you been to get that suntan?*—compare SUNBURN ▶ **sun·tan** *adj.* [only before noun]: *suntan oil* **sun·tanned** *adj.* = TANNED: *a suntanned face*

sun·trap /ˈsʌntræp/ *noun* a place that is sheltered from the wind and gets a lot of sun

ˈ**sun-up** *noun* [U] (*especially AmE*) the time when the sun rises and day begins

ˈ**sun-worshipper** *noun* (*informal*) a person who enjoys lying in the sun very much

sup /sʌp/ *verb* (**-pp-**) [V, VN] (*NorthE* or *old-fashioned*) to drink sth, especially in small amounts ▶ **sup** *noun*

super /ˈsuːpə(r); *BrE also* ˈsjuː-/ *adj., adv., noun*

■ *adj.* (*informal*, *becoming old-fashioned*) extremely good: *a super meal/place* ◊ *We had a super time in Italy.* ◊ *'The pilot did a super job,' a passenger said afterwards.* ◊ *She was super* (= very kind) *when I was having problems.*

■ *adv.* (*informal*) especially; particularly: *He's been super understanding.*

■ *noun* **1** (*BrE, informal*) a SUPERINTENDENT in the police **2** (*AmE*) a SUPERINTENDENT of a building

super- /ˈsuːpə(r); *BrE also* ˈsjuː-/ *combining form* **1** (in adjectives, adverbs and nouns) extremely; more or better than normal: *super-rich* ◊ *superhuman* ◊ *superglue* **2** (in nouns and verbs) above; over: *superstructure* ◊ *superimpose*

super·abun·dance /ˌsuːpərəˈbʌndəns; *BrE also* ˌsjuː-/ *noun* [sing., U] (*formal*) much more than enough of sth: *a superabundance of energy* ▶ **super·abun·dant** *adj.*

super·annu·ated /ˌsuːpərˈænjueɪtɪd; *BrE also* ˌsjuː-/ *adj.* [usually before noun] (*formal* or *humorous*) (of people or things) too old for work or to be used for their original purpose: *superannuated rock stars*

super·annu·ation /ˌsuːpərˌænjuˈeɪʃn; *BrE also* ˌsjuː-/ *noun* [U] (*especially BrE*) a PENSION that you get, usually from your employer, when you stop working when you are old and that you pay for while you are working; the money that you pay for this

su·perb /suːˈpɜːb; sjuː-; *AmE* suːˈpɜːrb/ *adj.* excellent; of very good quality: *a superb player/meal/goal* ◊ *The car's in superb condition.* ◊ *His performance was absolutely superb.* ◊ *You look superb.* ▶ **su·perb·ly** *adv.*: *a superbly illustrated book* ◊ *She plays superbly.*

super·charged /ˈsuːpətʃɑːdʒd; ˈsjuː-; *AmE* ˈsuːpərtʃɑːrdʒd/ *adj.* **1** (of an engine) powerful because it is supplied with air or fuel at a pressure that is higher than normal **2** (*informal*) stronger, more powerful or more effective than usual: *supercharged words, like 'terrorism' or 'fascism'* ▶ **super·charg·er** *noun*: *VW's supercharger for its 16-valve engine*

super·cili·ous /ˌsuːpəˈsɪliəs; ˈsjuː-; *AmE* ˌsuːpərˈs-/ *adj.* (*disapproving*) behaving towards other people as if you think you are better than they are **SYN** SUPERIOR: *The dress shop assistant was very supercilious.* ◊ *She gave a*

S

s	t	v	z	ʃ	ʒ	tʃ	dʒ	θ	ð	ŋ
see	tea	van	zoo	shoe	vision	chain	jam	thin	this	sing

supercilious smile. ▶ **super·cili·ous·ly** *adv.* **super·cili·ous·ness** *noun* [U]

super·com·put·er /ˈsuːpəkəmpjuːtə(r); ˈsjuː-; *AmE* ˈsuːpərk-/ *noun* a powerful computer with a large amount of memory and a very fast CENTRAL PROCESSING UNIT

super·con·duct·iv·ity /ˌsuːpəˌkɒndʌkˈtɪvəti; ˌsjuː-; *AmE* ˌsuːpərˌkɑːn-/ *noun* [U] (*physics*) the PROPERTY (= characteristic) of some substances at very low temperatures to let electricity flow with no RESISTANCE

super·con·duct·or /ˈsuːpəkəndʌktə(r); ˈsjuː-; *AmE* ˈsuːpərk-/ *noun* (*physics*) a substance that has SUPERCONDUCTIVITY

super·ego /ˌsuːpərˈiːɡəʊ; ˌsjuː-; *AmE* ˌsuːpərˈiːɡoʊ/ *noun* [usually sing.] (*pl.* **-os**) (*psychology*) the part of the mind that makes you aware of right and wrong and makes you feel guilty if you do wrong—compare EGO, ID

super·fi·cial /ˌsuːpəˈfɪʃl; ˌsjuː-; *AmE* ˌsuːpərˈf-/ *adj.* **1** (often *disapproving*) not studying or looking at sth thoroughly; seeing only what is obvious: *a superficial analysis/approach/examination/view* ◇ *The book shows a somewhat superficial understanding of the historical context.* **2** appearing to be true, real or important until you look at it more carefully: *superficial differences/similarities* ◇ *When you first meet her, she gives a superficial impression of warmth and friendliness.* **3** (of a wound or damage) only affecting the surface and therefore not serious: *a superficial scratch/cut/injury* ◇ *superficial burns* **4** (*disapproving*) not concerned with anything serious or important and lacking any depth of understanding or feeling SYN SHALLOW: *a superficial mind/person/friendship* ◇ *The guests engaged in superficial chatter.* **5** (*technical*) of or on the surface of sth: *superficial veins* ◇ *a superficial deposit of acidic soils* ▶ **super·fici·al·ity** /ˌsuːpəˌfɪʃiˈæləti; ˌsjuː-; *AmE* ˌsuːpərˌf-/ *noun* [U] **super·fi·cial·ly** /-ˈfəli/ *adv.*

su·per·flu·ous /suːˈpɜːfluəs; sjuː-; *AmE* suːˈpɜːrf-/ *adj.* more than you need or want SYN UNNECESSARY: *She gave him a look that made words superfluous.* ▶ **su·per·flu·ity** /ˌsuːpəˈfluːəti; ˌsjuː-; *AmE* ˌsuːpərˈf-/ *noun* [U, sing.] (*formal*) **su·per·flu·ous·ly** *adv.*

super·glue /ˈsuːpəɡluː; ˈsjuː-; *AmE* ˈsuːpərɡ-/ *noun* [U] a very strong glue that sticks very quickly and is used in small quantities for repairing things in the home

super·grass /ˈsuːpəɡrɑːs; ˈsjuː-; *AmE* ˈsuːpərɡræs/ *noun* (*BrE, informal*) a criminal who informs the police about the activities of a large number of other criminals, usually in order to get a less severe punishment—compare GRASS *n.* (5)

super·hero /ˈsuːpəhɪərəʊ; ˈsjuː-; *AmE* ˈsuːpərhɪroʊ; -hiːroʊ/ *noun* (*pl.* **-oes**) a character in a story, film/movie, etc. who has unusual strength or power and uses it to help people; a real person who has done sth unusually brave to help sb

super·high·way /ˈsuːpəhaɪweɪ; ˈsjuː-; *AmE* ˈsuːpərh-/ *noun* a way of quickly sending information such as video, sound and pictures through a computer NETWORK, especially the Internet—see also INFORMATION SUPERHIGHWAY

super·human /ˌsuːpəˈhjuːmən; ˌsjuː-; *AmE* ˌsuːpərˈh-/ *adj.* having much greater power, knowledge, etc. than is normal: *superhuman courage/strength* ◇ *It took an almost superhuman effort to contain his anger.*—compare SUBHUMAN

super·im·pose /ˌsuːpərɪmˈpəʊz; *AmE* -ˈpoʊz; *BrE* also ˌsjuː-/ *verb* [VN] **~ sth (on/onto sth)** **1** to put one image on top of another so that the two can be seen combined: *A diagram of the new road layout was superimposed on a map of the city.* **2** to make a system or pattern combine with an existing system or pattern that contrasts with it ▶ **super·im·pos·it·ion** /ˌsuːpərˌɪmpəˈzɪʃn; *BrE* also ˌsjuː-/ *noun* [U]

super·in·tend /ˌsuːpərɪnˈtend; *BrE* also ˌsjuː-/ *verb* [VN] (*formal*) to be in charge of sth and make sure that everything is working, being done, etc. as it should be SYN SUPERVISE: *He superintended the building work.* ▶ **super·in·tend·ence** /-əns/ *noun* [U]

super·in·tend·ent /ˌsuːpərɪnˈtendənt; *BrE* also ˌsjuː-/ *noun* **1** a person who has a lot of authority and manages and controls an activity, a place, a group of workers, etc: *a park superintendent* ◇ *the superintendent of schools in Dallas* **2** (*abbr.* Supt) (in Britain) ≥ police officer just above the rank of CHIEF INSPECTOR: *Superintendent Livesey* **3** (*abbr.* Supt.) (in the US) the head of a police department **4** (*AmE*) a person whose job is to be in charge of a building and make small repairs, etc. to it

su·per·ior /suːˈpɪəriə(r); sjuː-; *AmE* suːˈpɪr-/ *adj., noun*
■ *adj.* **1** ~ **(to sb/sth)** better in quality than sb/sth else; greater than sb/sth else: *vastly superior* ◇ *superior intelligence/strength/knowledge* ◇ *This model is technically superior to its competitors.* ◇ *Liverpool were clearly the superior team.* ◇ *The enemy won because of their superior numbers.* OPP INFERIOR **2** ~ **(to sb)** higher in rank, importance or position: *my superior officer* ◇ *to have superior status* ◇ *a superior court of law* OPP INFERIOR **3** (*disapproving*) showing by your behaviour that you think you are better than others: *a superior air/manner/smile* ◇ *He always looks so superior.* **4** (used especially in advertisements) of very good quality; better than other similar things: *superior apartments/wines*
■ *noun* **1** a person of higher rank, status or position: *your social superiors* ◇ *He's my immediate superior* (= the person directly above me). ◇ *I'm going to complain to your superiors.* OPP INFERIOR **2** used in titles for the head of a religious community: *Mother Superior*

su·per·ior·ity /suːˌpɪəriˈɒrəti; sjuː-; *AmE* suːˌpɪriˈɔːr-; -ˈɑːr-/ *noun* [U] **1** ~ **(in sth)** ~ **(to/over sth/sb)** the state or quality of being better, more skilful, more powerful, greater, etc. than others: *the superiority of this operating system* ◇ *to have naval/air superiority* (= more ships/planes than the enemy) **2** behaviour that shows that you think you are better than other people: *an air/a sense of superiority* OPP INFERIORITY

su·per·la·tive /suːˈpɜːlətɪv; sjuː-; *AmE* suːˈpɜːrl-/ *adj., noun*
■ *adj.* **1** excellent: *a superlative achievement/performance* **2** (*grammar*) relating to adjectives or adverbs that express the highest degree of sth, for example *best, worst, slowest* and *most difficult*—compare COMPARATIVE ▶ **su·per·la·tive·ly** *adv.*
■ *noun* (*grammar*) the form of an adjective or adverb that expresses the highest degree of sth: *It's hard to find enough superlatives to describe this book.*—compare COMPARATIVE

super·man /ˈsuːpəmæn; ˈsjuː-; *AmE* ˈsuːpərm-/ *noun* (*pl.* **-men** /-men/) a man who is unusually strong or intelligent or who can do sth extremely well—compare SUPERWOMAN

super·mar·ket /ˈsuːpəmɑːkɪt; ˈsjuː-; *AmE* ˈsuːpərmɑːrkət/ (*AmE* also **ˈgrocery store**) *noun* a large shop/store that sells food, drinks and goods used in the home. People choose what they want from the shelves and pay for it as they leave.

super·model /ˈsuːpəmɒdl; ˈsjuː-; *AmE* ˈsuːpərmɑːdl/ *noun* a very successful, famous and highly paid fashion model

super·nat·ural /ˌsuːpəˈnætʃrəl; ˌsjuː-; *AmE* ˌsuːpərˈn-/ *adj.* **1** that cannot be explained by the laws of science and that seems to involve gods or magic: *supernatural forces/powers* ◇ *supernatural strength*—compare NATURAL **2** (the supernatural) *noun* [sing.] events, forces or powers that cannot be explained by the laws of science and that seem to involve gods or magic: *a belief in/a fear of the supernatural* ▶ **super·nat·ur·al·ly** /-ˈnætʃrəli/ *adv.*

super·nova /ˌsuːpəˈnəʊvə; ˌsjuː-; *AmE* ˌsuːpərˈnoʊvə/ *noun* (*pl.* **super·novae** /-viː/ or **super·novas**) (*astronomy*) a star that suddenly becomes much brighter because it is exploding—compare NOVA

super·numer·ary /ˌsuːpəˈnjuːmərəri; ˌsjuː-; *AmE* ˌsuːpərˈnuːməreri/ *adj.* (*rare, formal*) more than you normally need; extra: *supernumerary posts for trainees*

super·power /ˈsuːpəpaʊə(r); ˈsjuː-; *AmE* ˈsuːpərp-/ *noun* one of the countries in the world that has very great military or economic power and a lot of influence, for example the US

super·script /ˈsuːpəskrɪpt; ˈsjuː-; *AmE* ˈsuːpərs-/ *adj.*

S

(*technical*) written or printed above the normal line of writing or printing ▶ **super·script** *noun* [U]

super·sede /ˌsuːpəˈsiːd; ˌsjuː-; *AmE* ˌsuːpərˈs-/ *verb* [VN] [often passive] to take the place of sth/sb that is considered to be old-fashioned or no longer the best available: *The theory has been superseded by more recent research.*

super·sonic /ˌsuːpəˈsɒnɪk; ˌsjuː-; *AmE* ˌsuːpərˈsɑːnɪk/ *adj.* faster than the speed of sound: *a supersonic aircraft ◇ supersonic flight*—compare SUBSONIC

super·star /ˈsuːpəstɑː(r); ˈsjuː-; *AmE* ˈsuːpərs-/ *noun* a very famous performer, for example an actor, a singer or a sports player

super·state /ˈsuːpəsteɪt; ˈsjuː-; *AmE* ˈsuːpərs-/ *noun* a very powerful state, especially one that is formed by several nations joining or working together: *the European superstate*

super·sti·tion /ˌsuːpəˈstɪʃn; ˌsjuː-; *AmE* ˌsuːpərˈs-/ *noun* [U, C] (often *disapproving*) the belief that particular events happen in a way that cannot be explained by reason or science; the belief that particular events bring good or bad luck: *According to superstition, breaking a mirror brings bad luck. ◇ Most cultures have their superstitions.*

super·sti·tious /ˌsuːpəˈstɪʃəs; ˌsjuː-; *AmE* ˌsuːpərˈs-/ *adj.* believing in superstitions: *superstitious beliefs/fears/practices ◇ I'm superstitious about the number 13.* ▶ **super·sti·tious·ly** *adv.*

super·store /ˈsuːpəstɔː(r); ˈsjuː-; *AmE* ˈsuːpərs-/ *noun* a very large supermarket or a large shop/store that sells a wide variety of one type of goods: *a computer superstore*

super·struc·ture /ˈsuːpəstrʌktʃə(r); ˈsjuː-; *AmE* ˈsuːpərs-/ *noun* **1** a structure that is built on top of sth, for example the upper parts of a ship or the part of a building above the ground—compare SUBSTRUCTURE **2** (*formal*) the systems and beliefs in a society that have developed from more simple ones: *the relationship between the economic base of society and the political superstructure of power*

super·tank·er /ˈsuːpətæŋkə(r); ˈsjuː-; *AmE* ˈsuːpərt-/ *noun* a very large ship for carrying oil, etc.

super·vene /ˌsuːpəˈviːn; ˌsjuː-; *AmE* ˌsuːpərˈv-/ *verb* [V] (*formal*) to happen, especially unexpectedly, and have a powerful effect on the existing situation

super·vise /ˈsuːpəvaɪz; ˈsjuː-; *AmE* ˈsuːpərv-/ *verb* to be in charge of sb/sth and make sure that everything is done correctly, safely, etc: [VN] *to supervise building work ◇* [VN-**ing**] *She supervised the children playing near the pool.* [also V] ▶ **super·vi·sion** /ˌsuːpəˈvɪʒn; ˌsjuː-; *AmE* ˌsuːpərˈv-/ *noun* [U, C]: *Very young children should not be left to play without supervision. ◇ The drug should only be used under medical supervision. ◇ I have weekly supervisions* (= meetings with a TUTOR or supervisor).

super·visor /ˈsuːpəvaɪzə(r); ˈsjuː-; *AmE* ˈsuːpərv-/ *noun* a person who supervises sb/sth: *I have a meeting with my supervisor about my research topic.* ▶ **super·vis·ory** /ˌsuːpəˈvaɪzəri; ˌsjuː-; *AmE* ˌsuːpərˈv-/ *adj.*: *She has a supervisory role on the project.*

super·woman /ˈsuːpəwʊmən; ˈsjuː-; *AmE* ˈsuːpərw-/ *noun* (*pl.* -**women** /-wɪmɪn/) a woman who is unusually strong or intelligent or who can do sth extremely well, especially a woman who has a successful career and also looks after her home and family well—compare SUPERMAN

su·pine /ˈsuːpaɪn; *BrE* also ˈsjuː-/ *adj.* (*formal*) **1** lying flat on your back: *a supine position*—compare PRONE **2** (*disapproving*) not willing to act or disagree with sb because you are lazy or morally weak: *the supine attitude of some of our politicians* ▶ **su·pine·ly** *adv.*

sup·per /ˈsʌpə(r)/ *noun* [U, C] the last meal of the day, either a main meal, usually smaller and less formal than dinner, or a SNACK eaten before you go to bed: *I'll do my homework after supper. ◇ What's for supper? ◇ We'll have an early supper tonight.*—compare TEA (6) ⇨ note at MEAL

sup·plant /səˈplɑːnt; *AmE* -ˈplænt/ *verb* [VN] (*written*) to take the place of sb/sth (especially sb/sth older or less modern) SYN REPLACE: *Their work has been largely sup-*

planted by the use of a computer program that fulfils the same function.

sup·ple /ˈsʌpl/ *adj.* **1** able to bend and move parts of your body easily into different positions: *her slim, supple body ◇ These exercises will help to keep you supple.* **2** soft and able to bend easily without cracking: *Moisturizing cream helps to keep your skin soft and supple.* ▶ **supple·ness** *noun* [U]

sup·ple·ment *noun, verb*
■ *noun* /ˈsʌplɪmənt/ **1** ~ (**to sth**) a thing that is added to sth else to improve or complete it: *vitamin/dietary supplements* (= vitamins and other foods eaten in addition to what you usually eat) *◇ Industrial sponsorship is a supplement to government funding.* **2** an extra separate section, often in the form of a magazine, that is sold with a newspaper: *the Sunday colour supplements* **3** ~ (**to sth**) a book or a section at the end of a book that gives extra information or deals with a special subject: *the supplement to the Oxford English Dictionary* **4** an amount of money that you pay for an extra service or item, especially in addition to the basic cost of a holiday/vacation: *There is a £10 supplement for a single room. ◇ Safety deposit boxes are available at a supplement.*
■ *verb* /ˈsʌplɪment/ [VN] ~ **sth** (**with sth**) to add sth to sth in order to improve it or make it more complete: *a diet supplemented with vitamin pills ◇ He supplements his income by giving private lessons.*

sup·ple·men·tary /ˌsʌplɪˈmentri/ (*especially BrE*) (*AmE* usually **sup·ple·men·tal** /ˌsʌplɪˈmentl/) *adj.* provided in addition to sth else in order to improve or complete it: *supplementary information/income*

sup·pli·cant /ˈsʌplɪkənt/ (also **sup·pli·ant** /ˈsʌpliənt/) *noun* (*formal*) a person who asks for sth in a HUMBLE way, especially from God or a powerful person

sup·pli·ca·tion /ˌsʌplɪˈkeɪʃn/ *noun* [U, C] (*formal*) the act of asking for sth with a very HUMBLE request or prayer: *She knelt in supplication.*

sup·plier /səˈplaɪə(r)/ *noun* a person or company that supplies goods: *a leading supplier of computers in the UK*

sup·ply /səˈplaɪ/ *noun, verb*
■ *noun* **1** [C] an amount of sth that is provided or available to be used: *The water supply is unsafe. ◇ Supplies of food are almost exhausted. ◇ We cannot guarantee adequate supplies of raw materials.* **2** (**supplies**) [pl.] the things such as food, medicines, fuel, etc. that are needed by a group of people, for example an army or EXPEDITION: *Our supplies were running out. ◇ a transport plane carrying food and medical supplies for refugees* **3** [U] the act of supplying sth: *The UN has agreed to allow the supply of emergency aid. ◇ A stroke can disrupt the supply of oxygen to the brain. ◇ The electricity supply* (= the system supplying electricity) *had been cut off.* IDM see SHORT *adj.*
■ *verb* (**sup·plies**, **sup·ply·ing**, **sup·plied**, **sup·plied**) [VN] ~ **sb/sth** (**with sth**) | ~ **sth** (**to sb/sth**) to provide sb/sth with sth that they need or want, especially in large quantities: *Foreign governments supplied arms to the rebels. ◇ Foreign governments supplied the rebels with arms. ◇ Local schools supply many of the volunteers. ◇ foods supplying our daily vitamin needs*

sup·ply and de·mand *noun* [U] (*economics*) the relationship between the amount of goods or services that are available and the amount that people want to buy, especially when this controls prices

sup·ply line *noun* a route along which food, equipment, etc. is transported to an army during a war

sup·ply-side *adj.* [only before noun] (*economics*) connected with the policy of reducing taxes in order to encourage economic growth: *supply-side economics/policies*

sup·ply teacher (*BrE*) (*AmE* **'substitute teacher**) *noun* a teacher employed to do the work of another teacher who is away because of illness, etc.

sup·port /səˈpɔːt; *AmE* səˈpɔːrt/ *verb, noun*
■ *verb* [VN]
ENCOURAGE/GIVE HELP ▶ **1** ~ **sb/sth** (**in sth**) to help or encourage sb/sth by saying or showing that you agree with them/it SYN BACK: *to support a proposal/ban/*

aɪ	aʊ	eɪ	əʊ	oʊ	ɔɪ	ɪə	eə	ʊə	j	w
my	now	say	go	go	boy	near	hair	pure	yes	wet
			(BrE)	(AmE)						

reform ◊ *The government supported the unions in their demand for a minimum wage.* ◊ *These measures are* **strongly supported** *by environmental groups.* ◊ *If you raise it at the meeting, I'll support you.* **2** to give or be ready to give help to sb if they need it: *an organization that supports people with Aids* ◊ *The company will support customers in Europe* (= solve their problems with the product).

PROVIDE MONEY, etc. | **3** to help or encourage sth to be successful by giving it money: *Several major companies are supporting the project.* **4** to provide everything necessary, especially money, so that sb/sth can live or exist: *Mark has two children to support from his first marriage.* ◊ *He turned to crime to support his drug habit.* ◊ *The atmosphere of Mars could not support life.*

HOLD IN POSITION | **5** to hold sb/sth in position; to prevent sb/sth from falling: *a platform supported by concrete pillars* ◊ *Support the baby's head when you hold it.*

HELP PROVE STH | **6** to help to show that sth is true: *The witness's story was not supported by the evidence.*

SPORTS TEAM | **7** (*BrE*) to like a particular sports team, watch their games, etc: *Which team do you support?*

■ **noun**

ENCOURAGEMENT/MONEY | **1** [U] ~ **(for sth)** encouragement and help that you give to sb/sth because you approve of them and want them to be successful: *There is strong public support for the change.* ◊ *Can I rely on your support* (= will you vote for me) *in the election?* ◊ *Only a few people spoke* **in support of** *the proposal.* ◊ *Local businesses have provided* **financial support.** ◊ *She has no visible means of support* (= no work, income etc.).

HELP | **2** [U] sympathy and help that you give to sb who is in a difficult or unhappy situation: *Her family and friends have given her lots of support.*—see also MORAL SUPPORT

HOLDING IN POSITION | **3** [C] a thing that holds sth and prevents it from falling: *The supports under the bridge were starting to bend.* ◊ (*figurative*) *When my father died, Jim was a real support.* **4** [U] the act of holding sth firmly in position or preventing it from falling: *I wrapped a bandage around my ankle to give it some support.* ◊ *She held on to his arm for support.* **5** [C] something you wear to hold an injured or weak part of your body firmly in position: *a knee/back support*

PROOF | **6** [U] evidence that helps to show that sth is true or correct: *The statistics offer further support for our theory.*

sup·port·er /səˈpɔːtə(r); *AmE* -ˈpɔːrt-/ *noun* **1** a person who supports a political party, an idea, etc: *a strong/ loyal/staunch supporter* ◊ *Labour supporters* **2** (*BrE*) a person who supports a particular sports team SYN FAN: *I'm an Arsenal supporter.*

sup·port group *noun* a group of people who meet to help each other with a particular problem: *a support group for single parents*

sup·port·ing /səˈpɔːtɪŋ; *AmE* -ˈpɔːrt-/ *adj.* [only before noun] **1** a **supporting** actor in a play or film/movie has an important part but not the leading one: *The movie featured Robert Lindsay in a supporting role.* **2** (*written*) helping to show that sth is true: *There was a wealth of supporting evidence.* **3** carrying the weight of sth: *a supporting wall*

sup·port·ive /səˈpɔːtɪv; *AmE* -ˈpɔːrt-/ *adj.* giving help, encouragement or sympathy to sb: *a supportive family* ◊ *She was very supportive during my father's illness.*

sup·pose /səˈpəʊz; *AmE* səˈpoʊz/ *verb* **1** to think or believe that sth is true or possible (based on the knowledge that you have): [V] *Getting a visa isn't as simple as you might suppose.* ◊ *Prices will go up, I suppose.* ◊ [VN to inf] (*formal*) *This combination of qualities is generally supposed to be extremely rare.* ◊ [VN to inf, VN-ADJ] (*formal*) *She had supposed him (to be) very rich.* ◊ [VN-N] (*formal*) *I had supposed his wife a younger woman.* ◊ [V (that)] *I don't suppose for a minute that he'll agree* (= I'm sure that he won't). ◊ *Why do you suppose he resigned?* ◊ *There is no reason to suppose she's lying.* ◊ *I suppose you think that's funny, do you?* (= showing anger). HELP 'That' is nearly always left out, especially in speech.

2 to pretend that sth is true; to imagine what would happen if sth were true: [V (that)] *Suppose flights are fully booked on that day—which other day could we go?* ◊ *Let us suppose, for example, that you are married with two children.* ◊ [VN] (*formal*) *The theory supposes the existence of life on other planets.* ◊ [VN-ADJ] (*formal*) *Suppose him dead—what then?* [also VN-N, VN to inf] **3** used to make a statement, request or suggestion less direct or less strong: [V] *I could take you in the car, I suppose* (= but I don't really want to). ◊ *'Can I borrow the car?' 'I suppose so'* (= Yes, but I'm not happy about it). ◊ [V (that)] *I don't suppose (that) I could have a look at your newspaper, could I?* ◊ *Suppose we take a later train?* IDM **be supposed to do/be sth 1** to be expected or required to do/be sth according to a rule, a custom, an arrangement, etc: *You're supposed to buy a ticket, but not many people do.* ◊ *I thought we were supposed to be paid today.* ◊ *The engine doesn't sound like it's supposed to.* ◊ *You were supposed to be here an hour ago!* ◊ *How was I supposed to know you were waiting for me?* ◊ *'Yes and no.' 'What is that supposed to mean?'* (= showing that you are annoyed) **2** to be generally believed or expected to be/do sth: *I haven't seen it myself, but it's supposed to be a great movie.* **not be supposed to do sth:** to not be allowed to do sth: *You're not supposed to walk on the grass.*

sup·posed /səˈpəʊzd; *AmE* səˈpoʊzd/ *adj.* [only before noun] used to show that you think that a claim, statement or way of describing sb/sth is not true or correct, although it is generally believed to be SYN ALLEGED: *This is the opinion of the supposed experts.* ◊ *When did this supposed accident happen?*

sup·posed·ly /səˈpəʊzɪdli; *AmE* -ˈpoʊ-/ *adv.* according to what is generally thought or believed but not known for certain SYN ALLEGEDLY: *The novel is supposedly based on a true story.*

sup·pos·ing /səˈpəʊzɪŋ; *AmE* -ˈpoʊ-/ *conj.* ~ **(that)** used to ask sb to pretend that sth is true or to imagine that sth will happen: *Supposing (that) you are wrong, what will you do then?* ◊ *But supposing he sees us?*

sup·pos·ition /ˌsʌpəˈzɪʃn/ *noun* (*formal*) **1** [C] ~ **(that…)** an idea that you think is true although you may not be able to prove it SYN ASSUMPTION: *The police are working on the supposition that he was murdered.* **2** [U] the act of believing or claiming that sth is true even though it cannot be proved: *The report is based entirely on supposition.*

sup·posi·tory /səˈpɒzətri; *AmE* səˈpɑːzətɔːri/ *noun* (*pl.* -ies) a small piece of solid medicine that is placed in the RECTUM or VAGINA and left to dissolve gradually

sup·press /səˈpres/ *verb* [VN] **1** (usually *disapproving*) (of a government, ruler, etc.) to put an end, often by force, to a group or an activity that is believed to threaten authority: *The rebellion was brutally suppressed.* **2** (usually *disapproving*) to prevent sth from being published or made known: *The police were accused of suppressing vital evidence.* **3** to prevent yourself from having or expressing a feeling or an emotion: *to suppress a smile/yawn/shiver* ◊ *She was unable to suppress her anger.* **4** to prevent sth from growing, developing or continuing: *drugs that suppress the appetite*

sup·pres·sant /səˈpresnt/ *noun* a drug that is used to prevent one of the body's functions from working normally: *an appetite suppressant*

sup·pres·sion /səˈpreʃn/ *noun* [U] the act of SUPPRESSING sth: *the suppression of a rebellion/free speech/the truth* ◊ *the suppression of emotion/feelings*

sup·pres·sor /səˈpresə(r)/ *noun* a thing or person that SUPPRESSES sb/sth: *the body's pain suppressors*

sup·pur·ate /ˈsʌpjureɪt/ *verb* [V] (*formal*) (of a cut, wound, etc.) to produce a thick yellow liquid (called PUS) because of infection ▶ **sup·pur·ation** /ˌsʌpjuˈreɪʃn/ *noun* [U]

supra·nation·al /ˌsuːprəˈnæʃnəl; *BrE also* ˌsjuː-/ *adj.* (*formal*) involving more than one country: *a supranational authority*

su·prema·cist /suːˈpreməsɪst; *BrE also* sjuː-/ *noun* a person who believes that their own race is better than others and should be in power: *a white supremacist*

su·prem·acy /suːˈpreməsi; *BrE also* sjuː-/ *noun* [U] ~ **(over sb/sth)** (*written*) a position in which you have more power, authority or status than anyone else: *the battle for supremacy in the region* ◊ *the dangerous notion of white supremacy* (= that white races are better than others and should control them) ◊ *The company has established total supremacy over its rivals.*

su·preme /suːˈpriːm; *BrE also* sjuː-/ *adj.* [usually before noun] **1** highest in rank or position: *the Supreme Commander of the armed forces* ◊ *the supreme champion* ◊ *It is an event in which she **reigns supreme**.* **2** very great or the greatest in degree: *to make the **supreme sacrifice*** (= die for what you believe in) ◊ *a supreme effort / achievement* ◊ *She smiled with supreme confidence.*

the ˌSupreme ˈBeing *noun* [sing.] (*formal*) God

the Suˌpreme ˈCourt (also ˌHigh ˈCourt) *noun* [sing.] the highest court of law in a country or state

su·preme·ly /suːˈpriːmli; *BrE also* sjuː-/ *adv.* (*written*) extremely: *supremely happy / confident* ◊ *They managed it all supremely well.*

su·premo /suːˈpriːməʊ; sjuː-; *AmE* suːˈpriːmoʊ/ *noun* (*pl.* -os) (*BrE, informal*) a person who has the most power or authority in a particular business or activity: *the Microsoft supremo, Bill Gates*

Supt (also **Supt.** especially in *AmE*) *abbr.* (in the police force) SUPERINTENDENT: *Chief Supt Pauline Clark*

sur·charge /ˈsɜːtʃɑːdʒ; *AmE* ˈsɜːrtʃɑːrdʒ/ *noun, verb*
■ *noun* ~ **(on sth)** an extra amount of money that you must pay in addition to the usual price
■ *verb* to make sb pay a surcharge: [VNN] *We were surcharged £50 for travelling on a Friday.* [also VN]

sure /ʃʊə(r); ʃɔː(r); *AmE* ʃʊr/ *adj., adv.*
■ *adj.* (**surer, sur·est**) **HELP** You can also use **more sure** and **most sure**, especially in sense 1. **1** [not before noun] ~ **(of/about sth)** | ~ **(that ...)** confident that you know sth or that you are right **SYN** CERTAIN: *'Is that John over there?' ' **I'm not sure** '.* ◊ *You don't sound very sure.* ◊ *I'm pretty sure (that) he'll agree.* ◊ *Are you sure you don't mind?* ◊ *I hope you are sure of your facts.* ◊ *Are you sure about that?* ◊ *Ask me if you're **not sure how** to do it.* ◊ *I'm **not sure whether** I should tell you this.* ◊ **OPP** UNSURE **2** [not before noun] ~ **of sth/of doing sth** certain that you will receive sth or that sth will happen: *You're always sure of a warm welcome there.* ◊ *England must win this game to be sure of qualifying for the World Cup.* **3** ~ **to do sth** certain to do sth or to happen: *The exhibition is sure to be popular.* ◊ *It's sure to rain.* **4** [usually before noun] that can be trusted or relied on: *It's a **sure sign** of economic recovery.* ◊ *There's only one sure way to do it.* ◊ *Bush is a **sure bet** for the presidential nominations* (= certain to succeed). **5** [usually before noun] steady and confident: *We admired her sure touch at the keyboard.* **IDM** **be sure to do sth** used to tell sb to do sth: *Be sure to give your family my regards.* **HELP** In spoken English and plus another verb can be used instead of to and the infinitive: *Be sure and call me tomorrow.* **for sure** (*informal*) without doubt: *No one knows for sure what happened.* ◊ *I think he'll be back on Monday, but I can't say for sure.* ◊ **One thing is for sure**—*it's not going to be easy.* ◊ (*AmE*) *'Will you be there?' 'For sure.'* **make ˈsure (of sth/that ...) 1** to do sth in order to be certain that sth else happens: *Make sure (that) no one finds out about this.* ◊ *They scored another goal and made sure of victory.* ◊ *Our staff will do their best to make sure you enjoy your visit.* **2** to check that sth is true or has been done: *She looked around to make sure that she was alone.* ◊ *I think the door's locked, but I'll just go and make sure.* **ˈsure of yourself** (sometimes *disapproving*) very confident: *She seems very sure of herself.* **ˌsure ˈthing** (*spoken, especially AmE*) used to say 'yes' to a suggestion or request: *'Are you coming?' 'Sure thing.'* **to be ˈsure** (*formal*) used to admit that sth is true: *He is intelligent, to be sure, but he's also very lazy.*
■ *adv.* (*informal, especially AmE*) **1** used to say 'yes' to sb: *'Will you open the wine?' 'Sure, where is it?'* ◊ *Did it hurt? Sure it hurt.* **2** used to emphasize sth that you are saying:

Boy, it sure is hot. ◊ *'Amazing view'. 'Sure is.'* ◊ *That song sure as hell sounds familiar.* ◊ *He sure looked unhappy.* **3** used to reply to sb who has just thanked you for sth: *'Thanks for the ride.' 'Sure—anytime.'* **IDM (as) sure as eggs is ˈeggs** (*old-fashioned, BrE, informal*) used to say that sth is definitely true **ˌsure eˈnough** used to say that sth happened as expected: *I said he'd forget, and sure enough he did.*

ˈsure-fire *adj.* [only before noun] (*informal*) certain to be successful or to happen as you expect: *a sure-fire success* ◊ *Bad behaviour is a sure-fire way of getting people's attention.*

ˌsure-ˈfooted *adj.* **1** not likely to fall when walking or climbing on rough ground **2** confident and unlikely to make mistakes, especially in difficult situations

sure·ly /ˈʃʊəli; ˈʃɔːli; *AmE* ˈʃʊrli/ *adv.* **1** used to show that you are almost certain of what you are saying and want other people to agree with you: *Surely we should do something about it?* ◊ *It's surely only a matter of time before he is found, isn't it?* **2** used with a negative to show that sth surprises you and you do not want to believe it: *Surely you don't think I was responsible for this?* ◊ *'They're getting married.' ' Surely not! '* ◊ *They won't go, surely.* **3** (*formal*) without doubt; certainly: *He knew that if help did not arrive soon they would surely die.* **4** (*old-fashioned, AmE, spoken*) used to say 'yes' to sb or to agree to sth **IDM** see SLOWLY

sure·ness /ˈʃʊənəs; ˈʃɔː-; *AmE* ˈʃʊrnəs/ *noun* [U] the quality of being confident and steady; not hesitating or doubting: *an artist's sureness of touch* ◊ *her sureness that she had done the right thing*

surety /ˈʃʊərəti; ˈʃɔː-; *AmE* ˈʃʊr-/ *noun* [C, U] (*pl.* -ies)

S

(law) **1** money given as a promise that you will pay a debt, appear in a court of law, etc: *She was granted bail with a surety of $500.* **2** a person who accepts responsibility if sb else does not pay a debt, appear in a court of law, etc: *to act as surety for sb*

surf /sɜːf; *AmE* sɜːrf/ *noun, verb*
- *noun* [U] large waves in the sea or ocean, and the white FOAM that they produce as they fall on the shore or on rocks: *the sound of surf breaking on the beach* ◊ *Sydney, surf capital of the world* (= where the sport of surfing is very popular)
- *verb* **1** [V, VN] (often **go surfing**) to take part in the sport of riding on waves on a SURFBOARD **2** [VN] **~ the net/ Internet** to use the Internet: *I was surfing the net looking for information on Indian music.*

sur·face /'sɜːfɪs; *AmE* 'sɜːrfɪs/ *noun, verb*
- *noun* **1** [C] the outside or top layer of sth: *an uneven surface* ◊ *We'll need a flat surface to play the game on.* ◊ *Teeth have a hard surface layer called enamel.* ◊ *a broad leaf with a large surface area* **2** [C, usually sing.] the top layer of an area of water or land: *the earth's surface* ◊ *These plants float on the surface of the water.* **3** [C] the flat upper part of a piece of furniture, that is used for working on: *a work surface* ◊ *She's cleaned all the kitchen surfaces.* **4** [sing.] the outer appearance of a person, thing or situation; the qualities that you see or notice, that are not hidden: *Rage bubbled just below the surface of his mind.* **IDM** **on the 'surface** when not thought about deeply or thoroughly; when not looked at carefully: *It seems like a good idea on the surface but there are sure to be problems.* ◊ *On the surface, he appeared unchanged.*—more at SCRATCH *v.*
- *verb* **1** [V] to come up to the surface of water: *The ducks dived and surfaced again several metres away.* **2** [V] to suddenly appear or become obvious after having been hidden for a while: *Doubts began to surface.* ◊ *She surfaced again years later in London.* **3** [V] (*informal*) to wake up or get up after being asleep: *He finally surfaced around noon.* **4** [VN] to put a surface on a road, path, etc.

'surface mail *noun* [U] letters, etc. carried by road, rail or sea, not by air

,surface 'tension *noun* [U] (*technical*) the PROPERTY (= characteristic) of liquids by which they form a layer at their surface, and which makes sure that this surface covers as small an area as possible

,surface-to-'air *adj.* [only before noun] (especially of MISSILES) fired from the ground or from ships and aimed at aircraft

,surface-to-'surface *adj.* [only before noun] (especially of MISSILES) fired from the ground or from ships and aimed at another point on the ground or a ship

surf·board /'sɜːfbɔːd; *AmE* 'sɜːrfbɔːrd/ (also **board**) *noun* a long narrow board used for SURFING

sur·feit /'sɜːfɪt; *AmE* 'sɜːrfɪt/ *noun* [usually sing.] **~ (of sth)** (*formal*) an amount that is too large

surf·er /'sɜːfə(r); *AmE* 'sɜːrfər/ *noun* **1** a person who goes SURFING **2** (also **'net surfer**) (*informal*) a person who spends a lot of time using the Internet

surf·ing /'sɜːfɪŋ; *AmE* 'sɜːrf-/ *noun* [U] **1** the sport of riding on waves while standing on a narrow board called a SURFBOARD: *to go surfing* **2** the activity of looking at different things on the Internet in order to find sth interesting, or of changing between TV channels in order to find an interesting programme

surge /sɜːdʒ; *AmE* sɜːrdʒ/ *verb, noun*
- *verb* [V] **1** [+adv. /prep.] to move quickly and forcefully in a particular direction: *The gates opened and the crowd surged forward.* ◊ *Flood waters surged into their homes.* **2** [usually +adv. /prep.] to fill sb with a strong feeling: *Relief surged through her.* **3** (of prices, profits, etc.) to suddenly increase in value: *Share prices surged.*—related noun UPSURGE
- *noun* **1 ~ (of sth)** a sudden increase of a strong feeling: *She felt a sudden surge of anger.* ◊ *a surge of excitement/ panic/relief*—see also UPSURGE **2 ~ (in/of sth)** a sudden increase in the amount or number of sth; a large amount of sth: *a surge in consumer spending* ◊ *We are having*

trouble keeping up with the recent surge in demand.—see also UPSURGE **3 ~ (of sth)** a sudden, strong forward or upward movement: *a tidal surge*

sur·geon /'sɜːdʒən; *AmE* 'sɜːrdʒən/ *noun* a doctor who is trained to perform medical operations in a hospital: *a brain/heart surgeon*—compare PHYSICIAN

,Surgeon 'General *noun* (*pl.* **Surgeons General**) (in the US) the head of a public health service or of a medical service in the armed forces: *Surgeon General's warning: cigarette smoking causes cancer*

sur·gery /'sɜːdʒəri; *AmE* 'sɜːrdʒ-/ *noun* (*pl.* **-ies**) **1** [U] medical treatment of injuries or diseases that involves cutting open the body and often removing or replacing some parts; the branch of medicine connected with this treatment: *major/minor surgery* ◊ *to undergo heart surgery* ◊ *He will require surgery on his left knee.*—see also OPEN-HEART SURGERY, PLASTIC SURGERY **2** [U, C] (*BrE*) the time during which a doctor, dentist or VET is available to see patients: *morning/afternoon/evening surgery* ◊ *surgery hours* ◊ *Is there a surgery this evening?* **3** [C] (*BrE*) (*AmE* **office**) a place where a doctor, dentist or VET sees patients: *a doctor's/dentist's surgery* **4** [C] (*BrE*) a time when people can meet their Member of Parliament to ask questions and get help: *a constituency surgery*

sur·gi·cal /'sɜːdʒɪkl; *AmE* 'sɜːrdʒ-/ *adj.* [only before noun] used in or connected with surgery: *surgical intervention/ procedures/gloves* ◊ *a surgical ward* (= for patients having operations) ▶ **sur·gi·cal·ly** /-kli/ *adv.*: *The lumps will need to be surgically removed.*

,surgical 'spirit (*BrE*) (*AmE* **'rubbing alcohol**) *noun* [U] a clear liquid, consisting mainly of alcohol, used for cleaning wounds, etc.

surly /'sɜːli; *AmE* 'sɜːrli/ *adj.* (**sur·lier**, **sur·li·est**) bad-tempered and rude: *a surly face/manner/youth* ▶ **sur·li·ness** *noun* [U]

sur·mise *verb, noun*
- *verb* /sə'maɪz; *AmE* sər'm-/ (*formal*) to guess or suppose sth using the evidence you have, without definitely knowing [SYN] CONJECTURE: [V(that)] *From the looks on their faces, I surmised that they had had an argument.* [also V, V speech, VN, V wh-]
- *noun* /'sɜːmaɪz; *AmE* 'sɜːrm-/ [U, C, usually sing.] (*formal*) a guess based on some facts that you know already: *This is pure surmise on my part.*

sur·mount /sə'maʊnt; *AmE* sər'm-/ *verb* [VN] (*formal*) **1** to deal successfully with a difficulty [SYN] OVERCOME: *She was well aware of the difficulties that had to be surmounted.* **2** [usually passive] to be placed on top of sth: *a high column surmounted by a statue*

sur·name /'sɜːneɪm; *AmE* 'sɜːrn-/ *noun* a name shared by all the members of a family (written last in English names)—compare FAMILY NAME, LAST NAME

sur·pass /sə'pɑːs; *AmE* sər'pæs/ *verb* (*formal*) to do or be better than sb/sth: [VN] *He hopes one day to surpass the world record.* ◊ *Its success has surpassed all expectations.* ◊ *Her cooking was always good, but this time she had surpassed herself* (= done better than her own high standards). ◊ [V] *scenery of surpassing beauty*

sur·plice /'sɜːpləs; *AmE* 'sɜːrp-/ *noun* a loose white piece of clothing with wide sleeves worn by priests and singers in the CHOIR during church services

sur·plus /'sɜːpləs; *AmE* 'sɜːrp-/ *noun, adj.*
- *noun* [C, U] **1** an amount that is extra or more than you need: *agricultural/food surpluses* ◊ *Wheat was in surplus that year.* **2** the amount by which the amount of money received is greater than the amount of money spent: *a trade surplus of £400 million* ◊ *The balance of payments was in surplus last year* (= the value of exports was greater than the value of imports).—compare DEFICIT
- *adj.* **~ (to sth)** more than is needed or used: *surplus cash/ funds* ◊ *Surplus grain is being sold for export.* ◊ *These items are surplus to requirements* (= not needed).

sur·prise /sə'praɪz; *AmE* sər'p-/ *noun, verb*
- *noun* **1** [C] an event, a piece of news, etc. that is unexpected or that happens suddenly: *What a nice surprise!* ◊ *a surprise attack/announcement/visit* ◊ *There are few surprises in this year's budget.* ◊ *I have a surprise for you!* ◊ *It*

æ	ɑː	e	ɜː	ə	ɪ	iː	i	ɒ	ɔː	ʌ	ʊ	u	uː
cat	father	ten	bird	about	sit	see	many	got	saw	cup	put	actual	too
								(BrE)					

comes as no surprise to learn that they broke their promises. ◇ Her letter came as a complete surprise. ◇ There are lots of surprises in store for visitors to the gallery. ◇ Visitors to the gallery are in for a few surprises. 2 [U, C] ~ (at sth) | ~ (at seeing, hearing, etc.) a feeling caused by sth happening suddenly or unexpectedly: a look of surprise ◇ She looked up in surprise. ◇ He gasped with surprise at her strength. ◇ They couldn't conceal their surprise at seeing us together. ◇ I got a surprise when I saw the bill. ◇ Much to my surprise, I passed. ◇ To everyone's surprise, the plan succeeded. ◇ Imagine our surprise when he walked into the room! 3 [U] the use of methods that cause feelings of surprise: A successful campaign should have an element of surprise. **IDM** sur‚prise, sur'prise (spoken) 1 (ironic, often disapproving) used to show that sth is not a surprise to you, as you could easily have predicted that it would happen or be true: One of the candidates was the manager's niece, and surprise, surprise, she got the job. 2 used when giving sb a surprise: Surprise, surprise! Look who's here! take sb/sth by sur'prise to attack or capture sb/sth unexpectedly or without warning: The police took the burglars by surprise. take sb by sur'prise to happen unexpectedly so that sb is slightly shocked; to surprise sb: His frankness took her by surprise.
■ verb [VN] 1 to make sb feel surprised: [VN] It wouldn't surprise me if they got married soon. ◇ [VN wh-] It's always surprised me how popular he is. ◇ [VN that] It surprises me that you've never sung professionally. ◇ [VN to inf] Would it surprise you to know that I'm thinking of leaving? 2 [VN] to attack, discover, etc. sb suddenly and unexpectedly: The army attacked at night to surprise the rebels. ◇ We arrived home early and surprised a burglar trying to break in.

sur·prised /sə'praɪzd; AmE sər'p-/ adj. ~ (at/by sb/sth) | ~ (that ...) | ~ (to see, hear, etc.) feeling or showing surprise: a surprised look/expression ◇ She looked surprised when I told her. ◇ I was surprised at how quickly she agreed. ◇ I'm surprised at you, behaving like that in front of the kids. ◇ They were surprised to find that he'd already left. ◇ You shouldn't be surprised (that) he didn't come. ◇ Don't be surprised if I pretend not to recognise you. ◇ 'Will she cancel the party?' ' I wouldn't be surprised.'—compare UNSURPRISED

sur·pris·ing /sə'praɪzɪŋ; AmE sər'p-/ adj. causing surprise: It's not surprising (that) they lost. ◇ We had a surprising amount in common. ◇ It's surprising what people will do for money. ► **sur·pris·ing·ly** adv.: She looked surprisingly well. ◇ Surprisingly, he agreed straight away. ◇ Not surprisingly on such a hot afternoon, the river was very busy.

sur·real /sə'riːəl/ (also less frequent **sur·real·is·tic**) adj. very strange; more like a dream than reality, with ideas and images mixed together in a strange way

sur·real·ism /sə'riːəlɪzəm/ noun [U] a 20th century style and movement in art and literature in which images and events that are not connected are put together in a strange or impossible way, like a dream, to try to express what is happening deep in the mind ► **sur·real·ist** adj. [usually before noun]: a surrealist painter/painting **sur·real·ist** noun: the surrealist Salvador Dali

sur·real·is·tic /sə‚riːə'lɪstɪk/ adj. 1 = SURREAL 2 connected with surrealism: a surrealistic painting

sur·ren·der /sə'rendə(r)/ verb, noun
■ verb 1 ~ (yourself) (to sb) to admit that you have been defeated and want to stop fighting; to allow yourself to be caught, taken prisoner, etc: [V] The rebel soldiers were forced to surrender. ◇ [VN] The hijackers eventually surrendered themselves to the police. 2 [VN] ~ sth/sb (to sb) (formal) to give up sth/sb when you are forced to SYN RELINQUISH: He agreed to surrender all claims to the property. ◇ They surrendered their guns to the police. ◇ The defendant was released to await trial but had to surrender her passport. **PHRV** sur'render to sth | sur'render yourself to sth (formal) to stop trying to prevent yourself from having a feeling, habit, etc. and allow it to control what you do: He finally surrendered to his craving for drugs. ◇ She surrendered herself to sleep.

■ noun [U, sing.] 1 ~ (to sb/sth) an act of admitting that you have been defeated and want to stop fighting: They demanded (an) unconditional surrender. 2 the fact of allowing yourself to be controlled by sth: They accused the government of a surrender to business interests. 3 ~ of sth (to sb) an act of giving sth to sb else even though you do not want to, especially after a battle, etc: They insisted on the immediate surrender of all weapons.

sur·rep·ti·tious /‚sʌrəp'tɪʃəs; AmE ‚sɜːr-/ adj. (written) done secretly or quickly, in the hope that other people will not notice: She sneaked a surreptitious glance at her watch. ► **sur·rep·ti·tious·ly** adv.

sur·ro·gacy /'sʌrəgəsi; AmE 'sɜːr-/ noun [U] the practice of giving birth to a baby for another woman who is unable to have babies herself

sur·ro·gate /'sʌrəgət; AmE 'sɜːr-/ adj. (formal) used to describe a person or thing that takes the place of, or is used instead of, sb/sth else: She saw him as a sort of surrogate father. ► **sur·ro·gate** noun

‚surrogate 'mother noun a woman who gives birth to a baby for another woman who is unable to have babies herself

sur·round /sə'raʊnd/ verb, noun
■ verb [VN] ~ sth/sb (with sth) 1 to be all around sth/sb: Tall trees surround the lake. ◇ The lake is surrounded with/by trees. ◇ the membranes surrounding the brain ◇ As a child I was surrounded by love and kindness. 2 ~ sb/sth (with sb/sth) to move into position all around sb/sth, especially so as to prevent them from escaping; to move sb/sth into position in this way: Police surrounded the building. ◇ They've surrounded the building with police. 3 to be closely connected with sth/sb: publicity surrounding the divorce 4 ~ yourself with sb/sth to choose to have particular people or things near you all the time: I like to surround myself with beautiful things.
■ noun a border or an area around the edge of sth, especially one that is decorated

sur·round·ing /sə'raʊndɪŋ/ adj. [only before noun] that is near or around sth: Oxford and the surrounding area

sur·round·ings /sə'raʊndɪŋz/ noun [pl.] everything that is around or near sb/sth SYN ENVIRONMENT: to work in pleasant surroundings ◇ The buildings have been designed to blend in with their surroundings.

sur·tax /'sɜːtæks; AmE 'sɜːrt-/ noun [U] a tax charged at a higher rate than the normal rate, on income above a particular level

sur·veil·lance /sɜː'veɪləns; AmE sɜːr'v-/ noun [U] (written) the act of carefully watching a person suspected of a crime or a place where a crime may be committed: The police are keeping the suspects under constant surveillance. ◇ surveillance cameras/equipment

sur·vey noun, verb
■ noun /'sɜːveɪ; AmE 'sɜːrveɪ/ 1 an investigation of the opinions, behaviour, etc. of a particular group of people, which is usually done by asking them questions: A recent survey showed 75% of those questioned were in favour of the plan. ◇ The survey found/revealed that ... ◇ to conduct/carry out a survey 2 the act of examining and recording the measurements, features, etc. of an area of land in order to make a map or plan of it: an aerial survey (= made by taking photographs from an aircraft) ◇ a geological survey 3 (BrE) an examination of the condition of a house, etc., usually done for sb who is thinking of buying it 4 a general study, view or description or sth: a comprehensive survey of modern music
■ verb /sə'veɪ; AmE sər'veɪ/ [VN] 1 to look carefully at the whole of sth, especially in order to get a general impression of it: The next morning we surveyed the damage caused by the fire. ◇ He surveyed himself in the mirror before going out. 2 to study and give a general description of sth: This chapter briefly surveys the current state of European politics. 3 to measure and record the features of an area of land, for example in order to make a map or in preparation for building 4 (BrE) to examine a building to make sure it is in good condition 5 to investigate the opinions or behaviour of a group of people by asking

aɪ	aʊ	eɪ	əʊ	oʊ	ɔɪ	ɪə	eə	ʊə	j	w
my	now	say	go	go	boy	near	hair	pure	yes	wet
			(BrE)	(AmE)						

them a series of questions: *We surveyed 500 smokers and found that over three quarters would like to give up.*

sur·vey·or /səˈveɪə(r); *AmE* sərˈv-/ *noun* **1** a person whose job is to examine a building to make sure its structure is in good condition or to examine and record the details of a piece of land **2** (*BrE*) an official whose job is to check that sth is accurate, of good quality, etc: *the surveyor of public works*—see also QUANTITY SURVEYOR

sur·vival /səˈvaɪvl; *AmE* sərˈv-/ *noun* **1** [U] the state of continuing to live or exist, often in spite of difficulty or danger: *the struggle/battle/fight for survival* ◇ *His only chance of survival was a heart transplant.* ◇ *Exporting is necessary for our economic survival.* ◇ *Continued trade in these products is a threat to the survival of the species.* **2** [C] ~ (**from sth**) something that has continued to exist from an earlier time SYN RELIC: *The ceremony is a survival from pre-Christian times.* IDM **the surˌvival of the ˈfittest** the principle that only the people or things that are best adapted to their surroundings will continue to exist

sur·vive /səˈvaɪv; *AmE* sərˈv-/ *verb* **1** [V] ~ (**from sth**)| ~ (**on sth**)| ~ (**as sth**) to continue to live or exist: *She was the last surviving member of the family.* ◇ *Of the six people injured in the crash, only two survived.* ◇ *Some strange customs have survived from earlier times.* ◇ *I can't survive on £40 a week* (= it is not enough for my basic needs). ◇ *He survived as party leader until his second election defeat.* ◇ (*humorous*) *'How are you these days?' 'Oh, surviving.'* **2** to continue to live or exist in spite of a dangerous event or time: [VN] *The company managed to survive the crisis.* ◇ *Many birds didn't survive the severe winter.* ◇ [VN-ADJ] *Few buildings survived the war intact.* **3** [VN] to live or exist longer than sb/sth SYN OUTLIVE: *She survived her husband by ten years.*

sur·vivor /səˈvaɪvə(r); *AmE* sərˈv-/ *noun* a person who continues to live, especially in spite of being nearly killed or experiencing great danger or difficulty: *the sole/only survivor of the massacre* ◇ *The plane crashed in an area of dense jungle. There were no survivors.* ◇ *There are only a few survivors from the original team* (= members who remain in it while others have been replaced). ◇ *She'll cope. She's one of life's great survivors* (= sb who deals very well with difficult situations).

sus·cep·ti·bil·ity /səˌseptəˈbɪləti/ *noun* (*pl.* **-ies**) (*written*) **1** [U, sing.] ~ (**to sth**) the state of being very likely to be influenced, harmed or affected by sth: *susceptibility to disease/infection* **2** (**susceptibilities**) [pl.] a person's feelings which are likely to be easily hurt SYN SENSIBILITIES

sus·cep·tible /səˈseptəbl/ *adj.* **1** [not usually before noun] ~ (**to sb/sth**) very likely to be influenced, harmed or affected by sb/sth: *He's highly susceptible to flattery.* ◇ *Some of these plants are more susceptible to frost damage than others.* ◇ *Salt intake may lead to raised blood pressure in susceptible adults.* **2** easily influenced by feelings and emotions SYN IMPRESSIONABLE: *She was both charming and susceptible.* **3** ~ (**of sth**) (*formal*) allowing sth; capable of sth: *Is this situation not susceptible of improvement by legislation?*

sushi /ˈsuːʃi/ *noun* [U] a Japanese dish of small cakes of cold cooked rice, flavoured with VINEGAR and served with raw fish, etc. on top: *a sushi bar*

sus·pect *verb, noun, adj.*
- *verb* /səˈspekt/ (not used in the progressive tenses) **1** to have an idea that sth is probably true or likely to happen, especially sth bad, but without having definite proof: [VN] *If you suspect a gas leak, do not strike a match or even turn on an electric light.* ◇ *Suspecting nothing, he walked right into the trap.* ◇ [V(that)] *I began to suspect (that) they were trying to get rid of me.* ◇ [V] *As I had suspected all along, he was not a real policeman.* [also VN to inf, VN that] **2** [VN] to be suspicious about sth; to not trust sb: *I suspected her motives in offering to help.* **3** [VN] ~ **sb** (**of sth/of doing sth**) to have an idea that sb is guilty of sth, without having definite proof: *He resigned after being suspected of theft.* ◇ *The drug is suspected of causing over 200 deaths.* ◇ *Whom do the police suspect?*—see also SUSPI-

CION, SUSPICIOUS ► **sus·pected** *adj.*: *a suspected broken arm* ◇ *suspected tax evasion* ◇ *suspected terrorists*
- *noun* /ˈsʌspekt/ a person who is suspected of a crime or of having done sth wrong: *a murder suspect* ◇ *He is the* **prime suspect** *in the case.*
- *adj.* /ˈsʌspekt/ **1** that may be false and that cannot be relied on: *Some of the evidence they produced was highly suspect.* **2** that you suspect to be dangerous or illegal: *a suspect package* (= one that may contain drugs, a bomb, etc.)

sus·pend /səˈspend/ *verb* [VN] **1** [usually +*adv./prep.*] ~ **sth/sb** (**from sth**) (**by/on sth**) to hang sth from sth else: *A lamp was suspended from the ceiling.* ◇ *Her body was found suspended by a rope.* **2** to officially stop sth for a time; to prevent sth from being active, used, etc. for a time: *Production has been suspended while safety checks are carried out.* ◇ *The constitution was suspended as the fighting grew worse.* ◇ *In the theatre we willingly* **suspend disbelief** (= temporarily believe that the characters, etc. are real). **3** to officially delay sth; to arrange for sth to happen later than planned: *The introduction of the new system has been suspended until next year.* ◇ *to suspend judgement* (= delay forming or expressing an opinion) **4** [usually passive] ~ **sb** (**from sth**) to officially prevent sb from doing their job, going to school, etc. for a time: *The police officer was suspended while the complaint was investigated.* ◇ *She was suspended from school for a week.* **5** (**be suspended in sth**) (*technical*) to float in liquid or air without moving: *Small droplets are held suspended in the atmosphere.*—see also SUSPENSION

susˌpended aniˈmation *noun* [U] **1** the state of being alive but not conscious or active **2** a feeling that you cannot do anything because you are waiting for sth to happen

susˌpended ˈsentence *noun* a punishment given to a criminal in a court of law which means that they will only go to prison if they commit another crime within a particular period of time

sus·pend·er /səˈspendə(r)/ *noun* **1** [C, usually pl.] (*BrE*) (*AmE* **gar·ter**) a short elastic fastening for holding up a sock or STOCKING **2** (**suspenders**) [pl.] (*AmE*) = BRACES at BRACE—picture on page A4

suˈspender belt *noun* (*BrE*) (*AmE* **ˈgarter belt**) a piece of women's underwear like a belt, worn around the waist, with fastenings for holding STOCKINGS up

sus·pense /səˈspens/ *noun* [U] a feeling of worry or excitement that you have when you feel that sth is going to happen, sb is going to tell you some news, etc: *a tale of mystery and suspense* ◇ *Don't* **keep us in suspense**. *Tell us what happened!* ◇ *I couldn't bear the suspense a moment longer.*

sus·pen·sion /səˈspenʃn/ *noun* **1** [U, C] the act of officially removing sb from their job, school, team, etc. for a period of time, usually as a punishment: *suspension from school* ◇ *The two players are appealing against their suspensions.* **2** [U, sing.] the act of delaying sth for a period of time, until a decision has been taken: *These events have led to the suspension of talks.* **3** [U, C] the system by which a vehicle is supported on its wheels and which makes it more comfortable to ride in when the road surface is not even: *the front/rear suspension*—picture at BICYCLE **4** [C, U] (*technical*) a liquid with very small pieces of solid matter floating in it; the state of such a liquid—see also SUSPEND

suˈspension bridge *noun* a bridge that hangs from steel cables that are supported by towers at each end

sus·pi·cion /səˈspɪʃn/ *noun* **1** [U, C] ~ (**that …**) a feeling that sb has done sth wrong, illegal or dishonest, even though you have no proof: *They drove away slowly to avoid arousing suspicion.* ◇ *He was arrested* **on suspicion** *of murder.* ◇ *I have a* **sneaking suspicion** *that she's not telling the truth.* ◇ *My suspicions were confirmed when police raided the property.*—see also SUSPECT **2** [C] ~ (**that …**) a feeling or belief that sth is true, even though you have no proof: *I have a horrible suspicion that we've come to the wrong station.* **3** [U, C] the feeling that you cannot trust sb/sth: *Their offer was greeted with some*

S

suspicion. **4** [sing.] **~ of sth** (*formal*) a small amount of sth SYN HINT: *His mouth quivered in the suspicion of a smile.* IDM **above/beyond su'spicion** too good, honest, etc. to have done sth wrong, illegal or dishonest: *Nobody who was near the scene of the crime is above suspicion.* **under su'spicion (of sth)** suspected of doing sth wrong, illegal or dishonest: *The whole family is currently under suspicion of her murder.* ◊ *A number of surgeons came **under suspicion** of unethical behaviour.*—more at FINGER *n.*

sus·pi·cious /sə'spɪʃəs/ *adj.* **1 ~ (of/about sb/sth)** feeling that sb has done sth wrong, illegal or dishonest, without having any proof: *They became suspicious of his behaviour and contacted the police.* ◊ *a suspicious glance/ look* ◊ *You have a very suspicious mind* (= you always think that people are behaving in an illegal or suspicious way). **2** making you feel that sth is wrong, illegal or dishonest: *Didn't you notice anything suspicious in his behaviour?* ◊ *She died in* **suspicious circumstances.** ◊ *It was all very suspicious.* **3 ~ (of sb/sth)** not willing or able to trust sb/sth: *I was suspicious of his motives.* ◊ *Many were suspicious of reform.*—see also SUSPECT

sus·pi·cious·ly /sə'spɪʃəsli/ *adv.* **1** in a way that shows you think sb has done sth wrong, illegal or dishonest: *The man looked at her suspiciously.* **2** in a way that makes people think sth wrong, illegal or dishonest is happening: *Let me know if you see anyone acting suspiciously.* **3** in a way that shows you think there may be sth wrong with sth: *She eyed the fish on her plate suspiciously.* IDM **look/ sound suspiciously like sth** (often *humorous*) to be very similar to sth: *Their latest single sounds suspiciously like the last one.*

suss (also **sus**) /sʌs/ *verb* **~ (sb/sth) (out)** (*BrE, informal*) to realize sth; to understand the important things about sb/sth: [VN] *I think I've* **got him sussed** (= now I understand him). ◊ *If you want to succeed in business you have to suss out the competition.* ◊ [V] *He cheated on her for years, but she never sussed.* [also V**that**, V**wh-**]

sus·tain /sə'steɪn/ *verb* [VN] **1** to provide enough of what sb/sth needs in order to live or exist: *Few planets can sustain life.* ◊ *I only had a little chocolate to sustain me on my walk.* ◊ *The love and support of his family sustained him during his time in prison.* **2** to make sth continue for some time without becoming less SYN MAINTAIN: *a period of sustained economic growth* ◊ *a sustained attack/effort* ◊ *She managed to sustain everyone's interest until the end of her speech.* **3** (*formal*) to experience sth bad SYN SUFFER: *to sustain damage/an injury/a defeat* ◊ *The company sustained losses of millions of dollars.* **4** to provide evidence to support an opinion, a theory, etc: *The evidence is not detailed enough to sustain his argument.* **5** (*formal*) to support a weight without breaking or falling: *The ice will not sustain your weight.* **6** (*law*) to decide that a claim, etc. is valid: *The court sustained his claim that the contract was illegal.* ◊ *Objection sustained!* (= said by a judge when a lawyer makes an objection in court)

sus·tain·able /sə'steɪnəbl/ *adj.* **1** involving the use of natural products and energy in a way that does not harm the environment: *sustainable forest management* ◊ *an environmentally sustainable society* ◊ *that can continue or be continued for a long time: sustainable economic growth/recovery* OPP UNSUSTAINABLE ▶ **sus·tain·abil·ity** /sə,steɪnə'bɪləti/ *noun* [U]

sus·ten·ance /'sʌstənəns/ *noun* [U] (*formal*) **1** the food and drink that people, animals and plants need to live and stay healthy: *Rice was the basis of daily sustenance.* ◊ *There's not much sustenance in a bowl of soup.* ◊ (*figurative*) *Arguing would only give further sustenance to his allegations.* **2 ~ (of sth)** the process of making sth continue to exist: *Elections are essential for the sustenance of parliamentary democracy.*

su·ture /'suːtʃə(r)/ *noun, verb*
■ *noun* (*medical*) a stitch or stitches made when sewing up a wound, especially after an operation
■ *verb* [VN] (*medical*) to sew up a wound

su·zer·ainty /'suːzəreɪnti; -rənti/ *noun* [U] (*formal*) the right of a country to rule over another country

svelte /svelt; sfelt/ *adj.* (*approving*) (of a person, especially a woman) thin in a graceful and attractive way

SW *abbr.* **1** (*especially BrE*) SHORT WAVE: *SW and LW radio* **2** south-west; south-western: *SW Australia*

swab /swɒb; *AmE* swɑːb/ *noun, verb*
■ *noun* **1** a piece of soft material used by a doctor, nurse, etc. for cleaning wounds or taking a SAMPLE from sb's body for testing **2** an act of taking a SAMPLE from sb's body, with a swab: *to take a throat swab*
■ *verb* [VN] **1** to clean or remove liquid from a wound, etc., using a swab **2 ~ sth (down)** to clean or wash a floor, surface, etc. using water and a cloth, etc.

swad·dle /'swɒdl; *AmE* 'swɑːdl/ *verb* [VN] (*old-fashioned*) to wrap sb/sth, especially a baby, tightly in clothes or a piece of fabric

'swaddling clothes *noun* [pl.] strips of fabric used in the past for swaddling a baby

swag /swæg/ *noun* **1** [U] (*old-fashioned, informal*) goods that have been stolen SYN LOOT **2** [C, usually pl.] fabric that is hung in large curved folds as decoration, especially above a window

swag·ger /'swægə(r)/ *verb, noun*
■ *verb* [V] [usually+*adv./prep.*] (usually *disapproving*) to walk in an extremely proud and confident way: *He swaggered into the room looking very pleased with himself.*
■ *noun* [sing.] (*disapproving*) a way of walking or behaving that seems too confident: *She walked to the front of the class with a swagger.*

Swa·hili /swɑː'hiːli; swə'h-/ *noun* [U] a language widely used in E Africa, especially between people who speak different first languages

swain /sweɪn/ *noun* (*old use* or *humorous*) a young man who is in love

swal·low /'swɒləʊ; *AmE* 'swɑːloʊ/ *verb, noun*
■ *verb*
FOOD/DRINK | **1** to make food, drink, etc. go down your throat into your stomach: [VN] *Always chew food well before swallowing it.* ◊ [VN-ADJ] *The pills should be swallowed whole.* ◊ [V] *I had a sore throat and it hurt to swallow.*
MOVE THROAT MUSCLES | **2** [V] to move the muscles of your throat as if you were swallowing sth, especially because you are nervous: *She swallowed hard and told him the bad news.*
COMPLETELY COVER | **3** [VN] [often passive] **~ sb/sth (up)** to take sb/sth in or completely cover it so that they cannot be seen or no longer exist separately: *I watched her walk down the road until she was swallowed by the darkness.* ◊ *Large areas of countryside have been swallowed up by towns.*
USE UP MONEY | **4** [VN] **~ sb/sth (up)** to use up sth completely, especially an amount of money: *Most of my salary gets swallowed (up) by the rent and bills.*
BELIEVE | **5** to accept that sth is true; to believe sth: [VN] *I found her excuse very hard to swallow.* ◊ [VN-ADJ] *He told her a pack of lies, but she swallowed it whole.*
FEELINGS | **6** [VN] to hide your feelings: *to swallow your doubts/anger* ◊ *You're going to have to swallow your pride and ask for your job back.*
ACCEPT INSULTS | **7** [VN] to accept insults, criticisms, etc. without complaining or protesting: *I was surprised that he just sat there and swallowed all their remarks.*
IDM see BITTER *adj.*
■ *noun*
BIRD | **1** a small bird with long pointed wings and a tail with two points, that spends the winter in Africa but flies to northern countries for the summer
OF FOOD/DRINK | **2** an act of swallowing; an amount of food or drink that is swallowed at one time: *She took a swallow of coffee.*

swam *pt* of SWIM

swami /'swɑːmi/ *noun* (also used as a title) a Hindu religious teacher: *Swami Vivekanand*

swamp /swɒmp; *AmE* swɑːmp/ *noun, verb*

- **noun** [C, U] an area of ground that is very wet or covered with water and in which plants, trees, etc. are growing: *tropical swamps* ▶ **swampy** *adj.*: *swampy forests/ground*
- **verb** [VN] [often passive] **1** ~ **sb/sth (with sth)** to make sb have more of sth than they can deal with SYN INUNDATE: *The department was swamped with job applications.* ◇ *In summer visitors swamp the island.* **2** to fill or cover sth with a lot of water: *The little boat was swamped by the waves.*

swan /swɒn; *AmE* swɑːn/ *noun, verb*
- **noun** a large graceful bird that is usually white and has a long thin neck. Swans live on or near water.
- **verb** (**-nn-**) [V+*adv.*/*prep.*] (*BrE, informal, disapproving*) to go around enjoying yourself in a way that annoys other people or makes them jealous: *They've gone swanning off to Paris for the weekend.*

swank /swæŋk/ *verb* [V] (*old-fashioned, BrE, informal, disapproving*) to behave in way that is too proud or confident

swanky /'swæŋki/ (**swank·ier, swanki·est**) (*especially BrE*) (also **swank** especially in *AmE*) *adj.* (*informal, disapproving*) fashionable and expensive in a way that is intended to impress people SYN POSH: *a swanky hotel/car*

swan·song /'swɒnsɒŋ; *AmE* 'swɑːnsɔːŋ/ *noun* [sing.] the last piece of work produced by an artist, a musician, etc. or the last performance by an actor, ATHLETE, etc.

swap (also **swop**) /swɒp; *AmE* swɑːp/ *verb, noun*
- **verb** (**-pp-**) **1** ~ **(sth) (with sb)** ~ **sth for sth** to give sth to sb and receive sth in exchange: [V] *I've finished this magazine. Can I swap with you?* ◇ [VN] *I swapped my red scarf for her blue one.* ◇ *Can we* **swap places***? I can't see the screen.* ◇ *We spent the evening in the pub* **swapping stories** (= telling each other stories) *about our travels.* ◇ [VNN] *I swapped him my CD for his cassette.* **2** [V] ~ **(over)** to start doing sb else's job, etc. while they do yours: *I'll drive there and then we'll swap over on the way back.* **3** [VN] ~ **sb/sth (for sb/sth)** ~ **sb/sth (over)** (*especially BrE*) to replace sth with sth else: *I think I'll swap this sweater for one in another colour.* ◇ *I'm going to swap you over. Mike will go first and Jon will go second.* IDM see PLACE *n.*
- **noun 1** [usually sing.] an act of exchanging one thing or person for another: *Let's* **do a swap***. You work Friday night and I'll do Saturday.* **2** a thing or person that has been exchanged for another: *Most of my football stickers are swaps.*

sward /swɔːd; *AmE* swɔːrd/ *noun* [C, U] (*literary*) an area of grass

swarm /swɔːm; *AmE* swɔːrm/ *noun, verb*
- **noun** ~ **(of sth) 1** a large group of insects, especially bees, moving together in the same direction: *a swarm of bees/locusts/flies* **2** a large group of people, especially when they are all moving quickly in the same direction
- **verb** [V] **1** [+*adv.*/*prep.*] (often *disapproving*) (of people, animals, etc.) to move around in a large group: *Tourists were swarming all over the island.* **2** (of bees and other flying insects) to move around together in a large group, looking for a place to live PHRV **swarm with sb/sth** to be full of people or things: *The capital city is swarming with police.*

swar·thy /'swɔːði; *AmE* 'swɔːrði/ *adj.* (especially of a person or their face) having dark skin: *a swarthy complexion/face/man*

swash·buck·ling /'swɒʃbʌklɪŋ; *AmE* 'swɑː-ʃ-; 'swɔː-ʃ-/ *adj.* [only before noun] (especially of films/movies) set in the past and full of action, adventure, fighting with SWORDS, etc.: *a swashbuckling tale of adventure on the high seas* ◇ *the swashbuckling hero of Hollywood epics*

swas·tika /'swɒstɪkə; *AmE* 'swɑːs-/ *noun* an ancient symbol in the form of a cross with its ends bent at an angle of 90°, used in the 20th century as the symbol of the German Nazi party

swat /swɒt; *AmE* swɑːt/ *verb* (**-tt-**) [VN] to hit sth, especially an insect, using your hand or a flat object ▶ **swat** *noun*

swatch /swɒtʃ; *AmE* swɑːtʃ/ *noun* a small piece of fabric used to show people what a larger piece would look or feel like

swathe /sweɪð/ *noun, verb*
- **noun** (also **swath** /swɒθ; *AmE* swɑːθ/) (*written*) **1** a long strip of land, especially one on which the plants or crops have been cut: *The combine had cut a swathe around the edge of the field.* ◇ *Development has affected vast swathes of our countryside.* **2** a large strip or area of sth: *a swathe of hair/fabric/sunlight* IDM **cut a 'swathe through sth** (of a person, fire, etc.) to pass through a particular area destroying a large part of it
- **verb** [VN] [usually passive] ~ **sb/sth (in sth)** (*written*) to wrap or cover sb/sth in sth: *He was lying on the hospital bed, swathed in bandages.*

'SWAT team *noun* (*especially AmE*) a group of police officers who are especially trained to deal with violent situations. SWAT stands for 'Special Weapons and Tactics'.

sway /sweɪ/ *verb, noun*
- **verb 1** [usually +*adv.*/*prep.*] to move slowly from side to side; to move sth in this way: [V] *The branches were swaying in the wind.* ◇ *Vicky swayed and fell.* ◇ [VN] *They danced rhythmically, swaying their hips to the music.* **2** [VN] [often passive] to persuade sb to believe sth or do sth SYN INFLUENCE: *He's easily swayed.* ◇ *She wasn't swayed by his good looks or his clever talk.*
- **noun** [U] **1** a movement from side to side: *The sway of the yacht was making her feel sick.* **2** (*literary*) power or influence over sb: *Rebel forces held sway over much of the island.* ◇ *She was brought up under the sway of Communism.* ◇ *He was quick to exploit those who fell* **under his sway***.*

swear /sweə(r); *AmE* swer/ *verb* (**swore** /swɔː(r)/ **sworn** /swɔːn; *AmE* swɔːrn/) **1** [V] ~ **(at sb/sth)** to use rude or offensive language, usually because you are angry: *She fell over and swore loudly.* ◇ *I don't like to hear children swearing.* ◇ *Why did you let him swear at you like that?* **2** [no passive] to make a serious promise to do sth: [VN] *He swore revenge on the man who had killed his father.* ◇ [V(**that**)] *I swear (that) I'll never leave you.* HELP 'That' is usually left out, especially in speech. [Vto inf] *She made him swear not to tell anyone.* **3** ~ **(to sb)** | ~ **(on sth)** to promise that you are telling the truth: [V(**that**)] *She swore (that) she'd never seen him before.* ◇ *I could have sworn* (= I am sure) *I heard the phone ring.* ◇ [V] *I* **swear to God** *I had nothing to do with it.* **4** ~ **(on sth)** to make a public or official promise, especially in a court of law: [V] *Witnesses were required to swear on the Bible.* ◇ [Vthat] *Are you willing to stand up in court and swear that you don't recognize him?* ◇ [Vto inf] *Remember, you have sworn to tell the truth.* ◇ [VN] *Barons had to swear an oath of allegiance to the king.* **5** [VN] ~ **sb to secrecy/silence** to make sb promise not to tell sth to anyone: *Everyone was sworn to secrecy about what had happened.*—see also SWORN IDM **swear 'blind** (*informal*) to say that sth is definitely true **swear like a 'trooper** (*old-fashioned, BrE*) to often use very rude or offensive language PHRV **'swear by sb/sth 1** to name sb/sth to show that you are making a serious promise: *I swear by almighty God that I will tell the truth.* **2** (not used in progressive tenses) to be certain that sth is good or useful: *She swears by meditation as a way of relieving stress.* **,swear sb↔'in** | **swear sb into sth** [often passive] to make sb promise to do a job correctly, to be loyal to an organization, a country, etc: *He was sworn in as president.* ◇ *The new prime minister was sworn into office.*—related noun SWEARING-IN **'swear to sth** (*informal*) to say that sth is definitely true: *I think I put the keys back in the drawer, but I couldn't swear to it* (= I'm not completely sure).

swear·ing /'sweərɪŋ; *AmE* 'swerɪŋ/ *noun* [U] rude or offensive language used especially when angry: *Giles was shocked at the swearing.*

,swearing-'in *noun* [U, sing.] the act of publicly asking sb to promise to be loyal and perform their duties well when they start a new job, etc: *the swearing-in of the new President*

'swear word *noun* a rude or offensive word, used especially to express anger

S

æ	ɑː	e	ɜː	ə	ɪ	iː	i	ɒ	ɔː	ʌ	ʊ	u	uː
cat	father	ten	bird	about	sit	see	many	got	saw	cup	put	actual	too
								(BrE)					

sweat /swet/ *noun, verb*

■ *noun*

LIQUID ON SKIN | **1** [U] drops of liquid that appear on the surface of your skin when you are hot, ill/sick or afraid [SYN] PERSPIRATION: *beads of sweat* ◊ *She wiped the sweat from her face.* ◊ *By the end of the match, the sweat was pouring off him.*—see also SWEATY **2** [usually sing.] the state of being covered with sweat: *I woke up in a sweat.* ◊ *She completed the routine without even* **working up a sweat.** ◊ *He* **breaks out in a sweat** *just at the thought of flying.* ◊ *He started having night sweats.*—see also COLD SWEAT

HARD WORK | **3** [U] hard work or effort: (*informal*) *Growing your own vegetables sounds like a lot of sweat.* ◊ (*literary*) *She achieved success by* **the sweat of her brow** (= by working very hard).

CLOTHES | **4** (**sweats**) [pl.] (*informal, especially AmE*) a SWEATSUIT or SWEATPANTS: *I hung around the house all day in my sweats.*—picture on page A5

[IDM] **be/get in a 'sweat** (**about sth**) to be/become anxious or frightened about sth **no 'sweat** (*spoken*) used to tell sb that sth is not difficult or a problem when they thank you or ask you to do sth: *'Thanks for everything.' 'Hey, no sweat!'*—more at BLOOD *n.*

■ *verb*

PRODUCE LIQUID ON SKIN/SURFACE | **1** when you **sweat**, drops of liquid appear on the surface of your skin, for example when you are hot, ill/sick or afraid [SYN] PERSPIRE: [V] *to sweat heavily* ◊ [VN] *He was* **sweating buckets** (= a lot). **2** [V] if sth **sweats**, the liquid that is contained in it appears on its surface: *The cheese was beginning to sweat.*

WORK HARD | **3** [V] **~** (**over sth**) to work hard at sth: *Are you still sweating over that report?*

WORRY | **4** [V] (*informal*) to worry or feel anxious about sth: *They really made me sweat during the interview.*

HEAT FOOD | **5** [VN, V] (*BrE*) if you **sweat** meat or vegetables or let them **sweat**, you heat them slowly with a little fat in a pan that is covered with a lid

[IDM] **sweat 'blood** (*informal*) to work very hard **don't 'sweat it** (*AmE, spoken*) used to tell sb to stop worrying about sth **don't sweat the 'small stuff** (*AmE, spoken*) used to tell sb not to worry about small details or unimportant things—more at GUT *n.*

[PHRV] **,sweat sth↔'off** to lose weight by doing a lot of hard exercise to make yourself sweat **,sweat it 'out** (*informal*) to be waiting for sth difficult or unpleasant to end, and be feeling anxious about it

sweat·band /'swetbænd/ *noun* a band of fabric worn around the head or wrist, for absorbing sweat

,sweated 'labour *noun* [U] (*BrE*) hard work that is done for low wages in poor conditions; the people who do this work

sweat·er /'swetə(r)/ *noun* a knitted woollen or cotton piece of clothing for the upper part of the body, with long sleeves. In British English the word is used to describe a piece of clothing with no buttons. In American English a sweater can have buttons and be like a jacket.—picture on page A5

sweat·pants /'swetpænts/ *noun* [pl.] loose warm trousers/pants, usually made of thick cotton and worn for relaxing or playing sports in—picture on page A5

sweat·shirt /'swetʃɜːt; *AmE* -ʃɜːrt/ *noun* a piece of clothing for the upper part of the body, with long sleeves, usually made of thick cotton and often worn for sports—picture on page A5

sweat·shop /'swetʃɒp; *AmE* -ʃɑːp/ *noun* (*disapproving*) a place where people work for low wages in poor conditions

sweat·suit /'swetsuːt; *BrE* also -sjuːt/ *noun* (also *informal* **sweats** [pl.]) (both *AmE*) a sweatshirt and SWEATPANTS worn together, for relaxing or playing sports in

sweaty /'sweti/ *adj.* **1** covered or damp with sweat: *sweaty feet/socks* ◊ *He felt all hot and sweaty.* **2** [only before noun] making you become hot and covered with sweat: *It was sweaty work, under the hot sun.*

swede /swiːd/ (*BrE*) (*AmE* **ru·ta·baga**) (*ScotE* **tur·nip**) *noun* [C, U] a large round yellow root vegetable—picture on page A3

sweep /swiːp/ *verb, noun*

■ *verb* (**swept, swept** /swept/)

WITH BRUSH | **1** to clean a room, surface, etc. using a BROOM (= a type of brush on a long handle): [VN] *to sweep the floor/street/stairs* ◊ [VN-ADJ] *The showroom had been emptied and swept clean.* [also V] **2** [VN+adv./prep.] to remove sth from a surface using a brush, your hand, etc: *She swept the crumbs into the wastebasket.* ◊ *He swept the leaves up into a pile.*

MOVE QUICKLY/WITH FORCE | **3** [VN+adv./prep.] to move or push sb/sth suddenly and with a lot of force: *The little boat was swept out to sea.* ◊ *She let herself be swept along by the crowd.* **4** (of weather, fire, etc.) to move suddenly and/or with force over an area or in a particular direction: [V+adv./prep.] *Rain swept in through the broken windows.* ◊ [VN] *Strong winds regularly sweep the islands.*

OF A PERSON | **5** [V+adv./prep.] to move quickly and/or smoothly, especially in a way that impresses or is intended to impress other people: *Without another word she swept out of the room.* ◊ (*figurative*) *He swept into the lead with an almost perfect performance.* **6** [VN+adv./prep.] to move sth, especially your hand or arm, quickly and smoothly in a particular direction: *He rushed to greet her, sweeping his arms wide.*

OF FEELINGS | **7** [V+adv./prep.] to suddenly affect sb strongly: *A wave of tiredness swept over her.* ◊ *Memories came sweeping back.*

OF IDEAS/FASHIONS | **8** to spread quickly: [V+adv./prep.] *Rumours of his resignation swept through the company.* ◊ [VN] *the latest craze sweeping America*

LOOK/MOVE OVER AREA | **9** to move over an area, especially in order to look for sth: [V+adv./prep.] *His eyes swept around the room.* ◊ [VN] *Searchlights swept the sky.*

TOUCH SURFACE | **10** [VN] to move, or move sth, over a surface, touching it lightly: *Her dress swept the ground as she walked.*

HAIR | **11** [VN+adv./prep.] to brush, comb, etc. your hair in a particular direction: *Her hair was swept back from her face.*

OF LANDSCAPE | **12** [V+adv./prep.] to form a long smooth curve: *The hotel gardens sweep down to the beach.*

[IDM] **sweep the 'board** to win all the prizes, etc. in a competition **,sweep sb off their 'feet** to make sb fall suddenly and deeply in love with you **sweep (sb) to 'power** to win an election by a large number of votes; to make sb win an election with a large number of votes **sweep sth under the 'carpet** (*AmE* also **sweep sth under the 'rug**) to try to stop people from finding out about sth wrong, illegal, embarrassing, etc. that has happened or that you have done

[PHRV] **,sweep sb a'long/a'way** [usually passive] to make sb very interested or involved in sth, especially in a way that makes them forget everything else: *They were swept along by the force of their emotions.* **,sweep sth↔'side** to ignore sth completely: *All their advice was swept aside.* **,sweep sth↔a'way** to get rid of sth completely: *Any doubts had long since been swept away.* **,sweep sth↔'out** to remove all the dust, dirt, etc. from a room or building using a brush **,sweep sb↔'up** to lift sb up with a sudden smooth movement: *He swept her up into his arms.*

■ *noun*

WITH BRUSH | **1** [C, usually sing.] an act of cleaning a room, surface, etc. using a BROOM: *Give the room a good sweep.*

CURVING MOVEMENT | **2** [C] a smooth curving movement: *He indicated the door with a sweep of his arm.*

LANDSCAPE | **3** [C, usually sing.] a long, often curved, piece of road, river, coast, etc: *the broad sweep of white cliffs around the bay*

RANGE | **4** [U] the range of an idea, a piece of writing, etc. that considers many different things: *Her book covers the long sweep of the country's history.*

MOVEMENT/SEARCH OVER AREA | **5** [C] a movement over an

aɪ	aʊ	eɪ	əʊ	oʊ	ɔɪ	ɪə	eə	ʊə	j	w
my	now	say	go (BrE)	go (AmE)	boy	near	hair	pure	yes	wet

area, for example in order to search for sth or attack sth: *The rescue helicopter made another sweep over the bay.* CHIMNEY | **6** [C] = CHIMNEY SWEEP **IDM** see CLEAN *adj.*

sweep·er /'swiːpə(r)/ *noun* **1** a person whose job is to sweep sth: *a road sweeper* **2** a thing that sweeps sth: *a carpet sweeper*—see also MINESWEEPER **3** (*BrE*) (in football) a player who plays behind the other defending players in order to try and stop anyone who passes them

sweep·ing /'swiːpɪŋ/ *adj.* **1** [usually before noun] having an important effect on a large part of sth: *sweeping reforms / changes* ◊ *Security forces were given sweeping powers to search homes.* **2** [usually before noun] (*disapproving*) too general and failing to think about or understand particular examples: *a sweeping generalization / statement* **3** ~ *victory* a victory by a large number of votes, etc. **4** [only before noun] forming a curved shape: *a sweeping gesture* (= with your hand or arm) ◊ *a sweeping staircase*

sweep·stake /'swiːpsteɪk/ (*AmE* also **sweep·stakes** [pl.]) *noun* a type of betting in which the winner gets all the money bet by everyone else

sweet /swiːt/ *adj., noun*
■ *adj.* (**sweet·er, sweet·est**)
FOOD/DRINK | **1** containing, or tasting as if it contains, a lot of sugar: *a cup of hot sweet tea* ◊ *Too much sweet food is bad for your teeth.* ◊ *I had a craving for something sweet.* ◊ *This wine is too sweet for me.*—compare BITTER, SALTY **OPP** SOUR
SMELL | **2** having a pleasant smell: *a sweet-smelling rose* ◊ *The air was sweet with incense.*
SOUND | **3** having a pleasant sound: *a sweet voice*
PURE | **4** pleasant and not containing any harmful substances: *the sweet air of a mountain village*
SATISFYING | **5** making you feel happy and/or satisfied: *Good night. Sweet dreams.* ◊ *I can't tell you how sweet this victory is.*
ATTRACTIVE | **6** (*especially BrE*) (especially of children or small things) attractive **SYN** CUTE: *His sister's a sweet young thing.* ◊ *You look sweet in this photograph.* ◊ *We stayed in a sweet little hotel on the seafront.*
KIND | **7** having or showing a kind character: *a sweet old lady* ◊ *She gave him her sweetest smile.* ◊ *It was sweet of them to offer to help.*
GOOD | **8** (**Sweet!**) (*AmE, informal*) used to show that you approve of sth: *Free tickets? Sweet!*
—see also BITTER-SWEET
IDM be **'sweet on sb** (*old-fashioned, informal*) to like sb very much in a romantic way **have a sweet 'tooth** (*informal*) to like food that contains a lot of sugar **in your ˌown sweet 'time/'way** how and when you want to, even though this might annoy other people: *He always does the work, but in his own sweet time.* **keep sb 'sweet** (*informal*) to say or do pleasant things in order to keep sb in a good mood so that they will agree to do sth for you **sweet F'A | sweet Fanny 'Adams** (*BrE, informal*) nothing at all. People say 'sweet FA' to avoid saying 'FUCK ALL'. **sweet 'nothings** romantic words: *to whisper sweet nothings in sb's ear* **the sweet smell of suc'cess** (*informal*) the pleasant feeling of being successful—more at HOME *n.*, SHORT *adj.*
■ *noun*
FOOD | **1** [C] (*BrE*) a small piece of sweet food, usually made with sugar and/or chocolate and eaten between meals **SYN** CANDY: *a packet of boiled sweets* ◊ *a sweet shop* **2** [C, U] (*BrE*) a sweet dish eaten at the end of a meal: *I haven't made a sweet today.* ◊ *Would you like some more sweet?* **SYN** AFTERS, DESSERT, PUDDING
PERSON | **3** [U] (*spoken, old-fashioned*) a way of addressing sb that you like or love: *Don't you worry, my sweet.*

sweet-and-'sour *adj.* [only before noun] (of food) cooked in a sauce that contains sugar and VINEGAR or lemon: *Chinese sweet-and-sour pork*

sweet·bread /'swiːtbred/ *noun* [usually pl.] the PANCREAS of a young cow or sheep, eaten as food

sweet·corn /'swiːtkɔːn; *AmE* -kɔːrn/ (*BrE* **corn**)

noun [U] the yellow seeds of a type of MAIZE plant, also called **sweetcorn**, which grow on thick stems and are cooked and eaten as a vegetable: *tinned sweetcorn*—see also CORN ON THE COB—picture on page A3

sweet·en /'swiːtn/ *verb* [VN] **1** to make food or drinks taste sweeter by adding sugar, etc. **2** ~ **sb** (**up**) (*informal*) to try to make sb more willing to help you, agree to sth, etc. by giving them money, praising them, etc. **3** to make sth more pleasant or acceptable: *The fall in inflation did little to sweeten news of massive job losses.* **IDM** see PILL

sweet·en·er /'swiːtnə(r)/ *noun* **1** [U, C] a substance used to make food or drink taste sweeter, used instead of sugar: *artificial sweetener(s)* **2** [C] (*informal*) something that is given to sb in order to persuade them to do sth, especially when this is done in a secret or dishonest way

sweet·heart /'swiːthɑːt; *AmE* -hɑːrt/ *noun* **1** [sing.] used to address sb in a way that shows affection: *Do you want a drink, sweetheart?* **2** [C] (becoming *old-fashioned*) a person with whom sb is having a romantic relationship: *They were childhood sweethearts.*

sweetie /'swiːti/ *noun* (*informal*) **1** [C] (*BrE*) a child's word for a sweet/a piece of candy **2** [C] a person who is kind and easy to like: *He's a real sweetie.* **3** [sing.] used to address sb in a way that shows affection

sweet·ish /'swiːtɪʃ/ *adj.* fairly sweet

sweet·ly /'swiːtli/ *adv.* **1** in a pleasant way: *She smiled sweetly at him.* **2** in a way that smells sweet: *a sweetly scented flower* **3** in a way that is without difficulties or problems: *Everything went sweetly and according to plan.* ◊ *He headed the ball sweetly into the back of the net.*

sweet·meat /'swiːtmiːt/ *noun* (*old use*) a sweet/candy; any food preserved in sugar

sweet·ness /'swiːtnəs/ *noun* [U] **1** the quality of being pleasant: *a smile of great sweetness* **2** the quality of tasting or smelling sweet: *The air was filled with the sweetness of mimosa.* **IDM** be **(all) ˌsweetness and 'light 1** (of a person) to be pleasant, friendly and polite **2** (of a situation) to be enjoyable and easy to deal with: *It's not all sweetness and light being an actor.*

ˌsweet 'pea *noun* a climbing garden plant with pale flowers that have a sweet smell

ˌsweet po'tato *noun* [C, U] a root vegetable that looks like a red potato, but that is yellow inside and tastes sweet—picture on page A3

'sweet-talk *verb* [VN] ~ **sb** (**into sth/into doing sth**) (*disapproving*) to try to persuade sb to do sth by praising them and telling them things they like to hear: *I can't believe you let him sweet-talk you into working for him!* ▶ **'sweet talk** *noun* [U]

swell /swel/ *verb, noun, adj.*
■ *verb* (**swelled** /sweld/, **swol·len** /'swəʊlən/; *AmE* 'swoʊ-) or (**swelled, swelled**) **1** [V] ~ (**up**) to become bigger or rounder: *Her arm was beginning to swell up where the bee had stung her.* ◊ *Cook the lentils for 20 minutes until they swell and soften.* **2** ~ (**sth**) (**out**) to curve or make sth curve outwards: [V] *The sails swelled (out) in the wind.* ◊ [VN] *The wind swelled (out) the sails.* **3** ~ (**sth**) (**to sth**) to increase or make sth increase in number or size: [VN] *Last year's profits were swelled by a fall in production costs.* ◊ *We are looking for more volunteers to swell the ranks* (= increase the number) *of those already helping.* ◊ [V] *Membership has swelled to over 20000.* **4** [V] (of a sound) to become louder: *The cheering swelled through the hall.* **5** [V] ~ (**with sth**) to be filled with a strong emotion: *to swell with pride/joy*—see also SWOLLEN
■ *noun* **1** [C, usually sing.] the movement of the sea when it rises and falls without the waves breaking: *The boat was caught in a heavy* (= strong) *swell.* **2** [sing.] (*written*) the curved shape of sth, especially a part of the body: *the firm swell of her breasts* **3** [sing.] a situation in which sth increases in size, number, strength, etc: *a growing swell of support* ◊ *a swell of panic/pride*—see also GROUNDSWELL **4** [sing.] (of music or noise) a gradual increase in the volume of sth **SYN** CRESCENDO **5** (*old-fashioned, informal*) an important or fashionable person
■ *adj.* (*old-fashioned, AmE, informal*) very good, enjoyable, etc: *We had a swell time.*

b	d	f	g	h	k	l	m	n	p	r
bad	did	fall	get	hat	cat	leg	man	now	pen	red

swell·ing /ˈswelɪŋ/ noun **1** [U] the condition of being larger or rounder than normal (= of being SWOLLEN): *Use ice to reduce the swelling.* **2** [C] a place on your body that has become larger or rounder than normal as the result of an illness or injury: *The fall left her with a painful swelling above her eye.*

swel·ter /ˈsweltə(r)/ verb [V] to be very hot in a way that makes you feel uncomfortable: *Passengers sweltered in temperatures of over 90°F.* ▶ **swel·ter·ing** adj.: *sweltering heat*

swept pt, pp of SWEEP

swerve /swɜːv; AmE swɜːrv/ verb [V] (especially of a vehicle) to change direction suddenly, especially in order to avoid hitting sb/sth: *She swerved sharply to avoid a cyclist.* ◊ *The bus suddenly swerved into his path.* ◊ *The ball swerved into the net.* ▶ **swerve** noun

swift /swɪft/ adj., noun
■ adj. (**swift·er**, **swift·est**) (written) **1** ~ (to do sth) happening or done quickly and immediately; doing sth quickly: *swift action/progress* ◊ *a swift decision/glance* ◊ *He rose to his feet in one swift movement.* ◊ *The White House was swift to deny the rumours.* **2** moving very quickly; able to move very quickly: *a swift current/runner* ➾ note at FAST ▶ **swift·ly** adv. **swift·ness** noun [U, sing.]
■ noun a small bird with long narrow wings, similar to a SWALLOW

swig /swɪg/ verb (**-gg-**) [VN] (informal) to take a quick drink of sth, especially alcohol: *They sat around swigging beer from bottles.* ▶ **swig** noun: *She took a swig of wine and lit a cigarette.*

swill /swɪl/ verb, noun
■ verb **1** [VN] ~ sth (out/down) (especially BrE) to clean sth by pouring large amounts of water in, on or through it: *She swilled the glasses with clean water.* **2** [VN] ~ sth (down) (informal) to drink sth quickly and/or in large quantities **3** [+adv./prep.] to move, or to make a liquid move, in a particular direction or around a particular place: [VN] *He swilled the juice around in his glass.* ◊ [V] *Water swilled around in the bottom of the boat.*
■ noun [U] **1** (also **pig·swill**) a mixture of waste food and water that is given to pigs to eat **2** (AmE) any liquid waste or dirt

swim /swɪm/ verb, noun
■ verb (**swim·ming**, **swam** /swæm/ **swum** /swʌm/) **1** (of a person) to move through water in a horizontal position using the arms and legs: [V] *I can't swim.* ◊ *The boys swam across the lake.* ◊ *They spent the day swimming and sunbathing.* ◊ [VN] *Can you swim backstroke yet?* ◊ *How long will it take her to swim the Channel?* ➾ note at BATH **2** [V] (**go swimming**) to spend time swimming for pleasure: *I go swimming twice a week.* **3** [V] [usually +adv./prep.] (of a fish, etc.) to move through or across water: *A shoal of fish swam past.* ◊ *Ducks were swimming around on the river.* **4** [V] (usually **be swimming**) ~ (in/with sth) to be covered with a lot of liquid: *The main course was swimming in oil.* ◊ *Her eyes were swimming with tears.* **5** [V] (of objects, etc.) to seem to be moving around, especially when you are ill/sick or drunk: *The pages swam before her eyes.* **6** [V] to feel confused and/or as if everything is spinning around: *His head swam and he swayed dizzily.* **IDM** see SINK v.
■ noun [sing.] a period of time during which you swim: *Let's go for a swim.* **IDM** in the **'swim (of things)** (informal) involved in things that are happening in society or in a particular situation

swim·mer /ˈswɪmə(r)/ noun a person who can swim; a person who is swimming: *a good/keen/strong swimmer* ◊ *They watched the swimmers splashing through the water.* ◊ *a shallow pool for non-swimmers*

swim·ming /ˈswɪmɪŋ/ noun [U] the sport or activity of swimming: *Swimming is good exercise.*

'swimming bath noun [usually pl.] (old-fashioned, BrE) a public swimming pool inside a building: *to go to the local swimming baths*

'swimming cap (also **'swimming hat**) (both BrE) (also **'bathing cap** AmE, BrE) noun a soft rubber or plastic

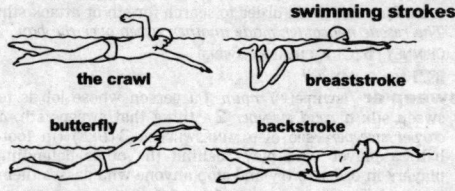

swimming strokes
the crawl
breaststroke
butterfly
backstroke

cap that fits closely over your head to keep your hair dry while you are swimming

'swimming costume noun (BrE) (also **swim·suit** BrE, AmE) (also **'bathing suit** AmE or old-fashioned) a piece of clothing worn for swimming, especially the type worn by women and girls

swim·ming·ly /ˈswɪmɪŋli/ adv. (informal) without any problems or difficulties: *We hope everything will go swimmingly.*

'swimming pool (also **pool**) noun **1** an area of water that has been created for people to swim in: *an indoor/outdoor swimming pool* ◊ *a heated swimming pool* ◊ *an open-air swimming pool* **2** the building that contains a public swimming pool: *She trained five times a week at her local swimming pool.*

'swimming trunks (also **trunks**) noun [pl.] a piece of clothing covering the lower part of the body and sometimes the top part of the legs, worn by men and boys for swimming: *a pair of swimming trunks*—picture at SNORKELLING

swim·suit /ˈswɪmsuːt; BrE also -sjuːt/ noun = SWIMMING COSTUME

swim·wear /ˈswɪmweə(r); AmE -wer/ noun [U] (written) clothing that you wear for swimming in

swin·dle /ˈswɪndl/ verb, noun
■ verb [VN] ~ sb (out of sth) | ~ sth (out of sb) to cheat sb in order to get sth, especially money, from them: *They swindled him out of hundreds of dollars.* ◊ *They swindled hundreds of dollars out of him.* ▶ **swind·ler** /ˈswɪndlə(r)/ noun
■ noun [usually sing.] a situation in which sb uses dishonest or illegal methods in order to get money from a company, another person, etc: *an insurance swindle*

swine /swaɪn/ noun (pl. **swines** or **swine**) **1** [C] (informal) an unpleasant person: *He's an arrogant little swine!* ◊ (figurative) *The car can be a swine to start.* **2** (**swine**) [pl.] (old use or technical) pigs: *a herd of swine* ◊ *swine fever* (= a disease of pigs) **IDM** see PEARL

swing /swɪŋ/ verb, noun
■ verb (**swung**, **swung** /swʌŋ/)
HANG AND MOVE | **1** to move backwards or forwards or from side to side while hanging from a fixed point; to make sth do this: [V] *His arms swung as he walked.* ◊ *A set of keys swung from her belt.* ◊ *As he pushed her, she swung higher and higher* (= while sitting on a swing). ◊ [VN] *He sat on the stool, swinging his legs.* **2** [+adv./prep.] to move from one place to another by holding sth that is fixed and pulling yourself along, up, etc: [VN] *He swung himself out of the car.* ◊ [V] *The gunshot sent monkeys swinging away through the trees.*
MOVE IN CURVE | **3** [+adv./prep.] to move or make sth move with a wide curved movement: [V] *A line of cars swung out of the palace gates.* ◊ [VN] *He swung his legs over the side of the bed.* ◊ [V-ADJ, VN-ADJ] *The door swung open.* ◊ *She swung the door open.*
TURN QUICKLY | **4** [+adv./prep.] to turn or change direction suddenly; to make sth do this: [V] *The bus swung sharply to the left.* ◊ [VN] *He swung the camera around to face the opposite direction.*
TRY TO HIT | **5** ~ (at sb/sth) to try to hit sb/sth: [V] *She swung at me with the iron bar.* ◊ [VN] *He swung another punch in my direction.*
CHANGE OPINION/MOOD | **6** ~ (from A) (to B) | ~ (between A and B) to change or make sb/sth change from one opinion, mood, etc. to another: [V] *The state has swung from Republican to Democrat.* ◊ *His emotions swung between fear and curiosity.* ◊ *The game could swing either*

S

way (= either side could win it). ◊ [VN] *I managed to swing them round to my point of view.*

DO/GET STH | **7** (*informal*) to succeed in getting or achieving sth, sometimes in a slightly dishonest way: [VN] *We're trying to swing it so that we can travel on the same flight.* ◊ [VNN] *Is there any chance of you swinging us a couple of tickets?*

OF MUSIC | **8** [V] to have a strong rhythm

OF PARTY | **9** [V] (*informal*) if a party, etc. **is swinging**, there are a lot of people there having a good time

IDM **swing the ˈbalance** = TIP THE BALANCE/SCALE at TIP *v.* **swing both ˈways** (*informal*) to be BISEXUAL (= sexually attracted to both men and women) **ˌswing into ˈaction** to start doing sth quickly and with a lot of energy—more at ROOM *n.*

PHRV **ˌswing ˈby| ˈswing by sth** (*AmE, informal*) to visit a place or person for a short time DROP BY: *I'll swing by your house on the way home from work.*

■ *noun*

MOVEMENT | **1** [C] a swinging movement or rhythm: *He took a wild swing at the ball.* ◊ *the swing of her hips*

OF OPINION/MOOD | **2** [C] a change from one opinion or situation to another; the amount by which sth changes: *He is liable to abrupt mood swings/swings of mood* (= for example from being very happy to being very sad). ◊ *Voting showed a 10% swing to Labour.*

HANGING SEAT | **3** [C] a seat for swinging on, hung from above on ropes or chains: *The kids were playing on the swings.*—picture at HOUSE

IN GOLF | **4** [sing.] the swinging movement you make with your arms and body when you hit the ball in the game of golf: *I need to work on my swing.*

MUSIC | **5** [U] a type of jazz with a smooth rhythm, played especially by big dance bands in the 1930s

IDM **get in/into the ˈswing (of sth)** (*informal*) to get used to an activity or a situation and become fully involved in it: *I've only been here a week so I haven't got into the swing of things yet.* **go with a ˈswing** (*BrE*) **1** (of a party or an activity) to be lively and enjoyable: *She made the whole party go with a swing.* **2** (of music) to have a strong rhythm **in full ˈswing** having reached a very lively level: *When we arrived the party was already in full swing.* **ˌswings and ˈroundabouts** (*BrE, informal*) used to say that there are advantages and disadvantages whatever decision you make: *If you earn more, you pay more in tax, so it's all swings and roundabouts.*

ˌswing ˈbridge *noun* (*BrE*) a bridge that can be moved to one side to allow tall ships to pass

ˌswing ˈdoor (*AmE* **ˌswinging ˈdoor**) *noun* a door that you can open in either direction and that closes itself when you stop holding it open

swinge·ing /ˈswɪndʒɪn/ *adj.* [usually before noun] (*BrE, written*) **1** large and likely to cause people problems, especially financial problems: *swingeing cuts/fines/increases* **2** extremely critical of sb/sth: *a swingeing attack on government policy*

swing·er /ˈswɪnə(r)/ *noun* (*old-fashioned, informal*) **1** a person who is fashionable and has an active social life **2** a person who has sex with many different people

swing·ing /ˈswɪnɪn/ *adj.* [usually before noun] (*old-fashioned, informal*) lively and fashionable

ˌswinging ˈdoor *noun* (*AmE*) = SWING DOOR

swipe /swaɪp/ *verb, noun*

■ *verb* **1** ~ (at) sb/sth to hit or try to hit sb/sth with your hand or an object by swinging your arm: [V] *He swiped at the ball and missed.* [also VN] **2** [VN] (*informal*) to steal **SYN** PINCH: *They're always swiping other kids' sweets.* **3** [VN] to pass a plastic card, such as a CREDIT CARD, through a special machine that is able to read the information that is stored on it: *The cash register only opens once the card has been swiped.*

■ *noun* ~ (at sb/sth) (*informal*) **1** an act of hitting or trying to hit sb/sth by swinging your arm or sth that you are holding: *She took a swipe at him with her umbrella.* **2** an act of criticizing sb/sth: *He used the interview to take a swipe at his critics.*

ˈswipe card *noun* a special plastic card with information recorded on it which can be read by an electronic device: *Access to the building is by swipe card only.*

swirl /swɜːl; *AmE* swɜːrl/ *verb, noun*

■ *verb* [usually +*adv./prep.*] to move around quickly with a circular movement; to make sth do this: [V] *The water swirled down the drain.* ◊ *A long skirt swirled around her ankles.* ◊ *swirling mists* ◊ [VN] *He took a mouthful of water and swirled it around his mouth.*

■ *noun* **1** the movement of sth that twists and turns in different directions and at different speeds **2** a pattern or an object that twists in a circular shape

swish /swɪʃ/ *verb, noun, adj.*

■ *verb* to move quickly through the air in a way that makes a soft sound; to make sth do this: [V] *A large car swished past them and turned into the embassy gates.* ◊ [VN] *She swished her racket aggressively through the air.* ◊ [V,VN] *The pony's tail swished.* ◊ *The pony swished its tail.*

■ *noun* [sing.] the movement or soft sound made by sth moving quickly, especially through the air: *She turned away with a swish of her skirt.*

■ *adj.* (*BrE, informal*) looking expensive and fashionable **SYN** SMART: *a swish restaurant*

Swiss chard /ˌswɪs ˈtʃɑːd/ *noun* [U] = CHARD

ˌSwiss ˈcheese *noun* [U, C] any hard cheese with holes in it

ˌSwiss ˈroll (*BrE*) (*AmE* **ˈjelly roll**) *noun* a thin flat cake that is spread with jam, etc. and rolled up—picture on page A1

switch /swɪtʃ/ *noun, verb*

■ *noun* **1** a small device that you press or move up and down in order to turn a light or piece of electrical equipment on and off: *a light switch* ◊ *an on-off switch* ◊ *That was in the days before electricity was available* **at the flick of a switch.** ◊ *Which switch do I press to turn it off?* ◊ *to throw a switch* (= to move a large switch) **2** ~ (in/of sth)| ~ (from A to B) a change from one thing to another, especially when this is sudden and complete: *a switch of priorities* ◊ *She made the switch from full-time to part-time work when her first child was born.* ◊ *a policy switch* **3** (*AmE*) the POINTS on a railway/railroad line **4** a thin stick that bends easily: *a riding switch*

■ *verb* **1** ~ (sth) (over) (from sth) (to sth)| ~ (between A and B) to change or make sth change from one thing to another: [V] *We're in the process of switching over to a new system of invoicing.* ◊ *Press these two keys to switch between documents on screen.* ◊ [VN] *When did you switch jobs?* **2** [VN] ~ sth (with sth)| ~ sth (over/around/round) to exchange one thing for another **SYN** SWAP: *The dates of the last two exams have been switched.* ◊ *I see you've switched the furniture around* (= changed its position). ◊ *Do you think she'll notice if I switch my glass with hers?* **3** ~ (sth) (with sth)| ~ sth (over/around/round) to do sb else's job for a short time or work during different hours so that they can do your job or work during your usual hours **SYN** SWAP: [V] *I can't work next weekend—will you switch with me?* ◊ [VN] *Have you been able to switch your shift with anyone?* **PHRV** **ˌswitch ˈoff** (*informal*) to stop thinking about sth or paying attention to sb/sth: *When I hear the word 'football' I switch off* (= because I am not interested in it). ◊ *The only time he really switches off* (= stops thinking about work, etc.) *is when we're on vacation.* **ˌswitch ˈoff/ˈon| ˌswitch sth↔ˈoff/ˈon** to turn a light, machine, etc. off/on by pressing a button or switch: *Please switch the lights off as you leave.* ◊ *How do you switch this thing on?* ◊ *We only switched on halfway through the programme.* **ˌswitch ˈover| ˌswitch sth↔ˈover** (*BrE*) to change stations on a radio or television

switch·back /ˈswɪtʃbæk/ *noun* **1** a road or railway/railroad track that has many sharp bends as it goes up a steep hill, or one that rises and falls steeply many times **2** (*AmE*) a sharp bend in a road that is going up a steep hill **3** (*old-fashioned, BrE*) = ROLLER COASTER

switch·blade /ˈswɪtʃbleɪd/ *noun* (*especially AmE*) = FLICK KNIFE

switch·board /ˈswɪtʃbɔːd; *AmE* -bɔːrd/ *noun* the central

æ	ɑː	e	ɜː	ə	ɪ	iː	i	ɒ	ɔː	ʌ	ʊ	u	uː
cat	father	ten	bird	about	sit	see	many	got	saw	cup	put	actual	too
								(BrE)					

part of a telephone system used by a company, etc., where telephone calls are answered and PUT THROUGH (= connected) to the appropriate person or department; the people who work this equipment: *a switchboard operator* ◇ *Call the switchboard and ask for extension 410.* ◇ *Hundreds of fans jammed the switchboard for over an hour.*

swivel /ˈswɪvl/ *noun, verb*
- *noun* (often used as an adjective) a device used to connect two parts of an object together, allowing one part to turn around without moving the other: *a swivel chair* (= one on which the seat turns around without moving the base)—picture at CHAIR
- *verb* (-ll-, *AmE* -l-) [usually +*adv./prep.*] **1** to turn or make sth turn around a fixed central point: [VN] *She swivelled the chair around to face them.* [also V] **2** to turn or move your body, eyes or head around quickly to face another direction: [V] *He swivelled around to look at her.* [also VN]

swizz (also **swiz**) /swɪz/ *noun* [usually sing.] (*informal*) something unfair or disappointing: *What a swizz!*

swol·len /ˈswəʊlən/ *adj.* **1** (of a part of the body) larger than normal, especially as a result of a disease or an injury: *swollen joints/glands/feet* ◇ *Her eyes were red and swollen from crying.* **2** (of a river) containing more water than normal—see also SWELL *v.*

swoon /swuːn/ *verb* [V] **1** ~ (**over sb**) to feel very excited, emotional, etc. about sb that you think is sexually attractive, so that you almost lose consciousness: *He's used to having women swooning over him.* **2** (*old-fashioned*) to lose consciousness [SYN] FAINT ▶ **swoon** *noun* [sing.] (*old-fashioned*): *to fall/go into a swoon*

swoop /swuːp/ *verb, noun*
- *verb* [V] **1** [usually +*adv./prep.*] (of a bird or plane) to fly quickly and suddenly downwards, especially in order to attack sb/sth: *The aircraft swooped down over the buildings.* **2** ~ (**on sb/sth**) (especially of police or soldiers) to visit or attack sb/sth suddenly and without warning: *Officers swooped on the vehicles as they left the ferry.*
- *noun* **1** an act of moving suddenly and quickly through the air in a downward direction, as a bird does **2** ~ (**on sth/sb**) an act of arriving somewhere or attacking sth/sb in a way that is sudden and unexpected: *Large quantities of drugs were found during a police swoop on the star's New York home.* [IDM] see FELL *adj.*

swop /swɒp/ = SWAP

sword /sɔːd; *AmE* sɔːrd/ *noun* a weapon with a long metal blade and a handle: *to draw/sheathe a sword* (= to take it out/put it into its cover) [IDM] **put sb to the 'sword** (*old-fashioned* or *literary*) to kill sb with a sword **a/the sword of 'Damocles** (*literary*) a bad or unpleasant thing that might happen to you at any time and that makes you feel worried or frightened [ORIGIN] From the legend in which **Damocles** had to sit at a meal at the court of Dionysius with a sword hanging by a single hair above his head. He had praised Dionysius' happiness, and Dionysius wanted him to understand how quickly happiness can be lost. **turn swords into 'ploughshares** (*literary*) to stop fighting and return to peaceful activities—more at CROSS *v.*, DOUBLE-EDGED

'sword dance *noun* a Scottish dance in which people dance between and over SWORDS that are placed on the ground

sword·fish /ˈsɔːdfɪʃ; *AmE* ˈsɔːrd-/ *noun* [C, U] (*pl.* **swordfish**) a large sea fish with a very long thin pointed upper jaw: *swordfish steaks*

swords·man /ˈsɔːdzmən; *AmE* ˈsɔːrdz-/ *noun* (*pl.* **-men** /-mən/) (usually used with an adjective) a person who fights with a SWORD: *a fine swordsman*

swore *pt* of SWEAR

sworn /swɔːn; *AmE* swɔːrn/ *adj.* [only before noun] **1** made after you have promised to tell the truth, especially in a court of law: *a sworn statement* **2** ~ **enemies** people, countries, etc. that have a strong hatred for each other—see also SWEAR *v.*

swot /swɒt; *AmE* swɑːt/ *noun, verb*
- *noun* (*BrE*) (*AmE* **grind**) (*informal, disapproving*) a person who spends too much time studying

- *verb* [V] ~ (**for sth**) (*BrE, informal*) to study very hard, especially in order to prepare for an exam [PHRV] **,swot sth↔'up** | **,swot 'up on sth** (*BrE, informal*) to study a particular subject very hard, especially in order to prepare for an exam: *Make sure you swot up on the company before the interview.*

swum *pp* of SWIM

swung *pt, pp* of SWING

syb·ar·it·ic /ˌsɪbəˈrɪtɪk/ *adj.* [usually before noun] (*rare, formal*) connected with a desire for pleasure: *his sybaritic lifestyle*

syca·more /ˈsɪkəmɔː(r)/ *noun* **1** [C, U] (*especially BrE*) a European tree of the MAPLE family, with leaves that have five points and seeds shaped like a pair of wings **2** [C] (*especially AmE*) an American PLANE TREE **3** [U] the valuable hard wood of the European sycamore

syco·phant /ˈsɪkəfænt/ *noun* (*formal, disapproving*) a person who praises important or powerful people too much and in a way that is not sincere, especially in order to get sth from them ▶ **syco·phancy** /ˈsɪkəfənsi/ *noun* [U] **syco·phan·tic** /ˌsɪkəˈfæntɪk/ *adj.*: *a sycophantic admirer/letter/review*

syl·lab·ic /sɪˈlæbɪk/ *adj.* [phonetics] **1** based on syllables: *syllabic stress* **2** (of a consonant) forming a whole syllable, for example /l/ in 'bottle' /ˈbɒtl/; *AmE* ˈbɑːtl/

syl·lable /ˈsɪləbl/ *noun* any of the units into which a word is divided, containing a vowel sound and usually one or more consonants: *a word with two syllables* ◇ *a two-syllable word* ◇ *'Potato' is stressed on the second syllable.* [IDM] see WORD *n.*

syl·la·bub /ˈsɪləbʌb/ *noun* [C, U] (*BrE*) a cold DESSERT (= a sweet dish) made from cream that has been mixed very quickly with sugar, wine, fruit juice, etc. to make it thick

syl·la·bus /ˈsɪləbəs/ *noun* (*pl.* **syl·la·buses** or *less frequent* **syl·labi** /ˈsɪləbaɪ/) a list of the topics, books, etc. that students should study in a particular subject at school or college—compare CURRICULUM

syl·lo·gism /ˈsɪlədʒɪzəm/ *noun* (*technical*) a way of arguing in which two statements are used to prove that a third statement is true, for example: 'All humans must die; I am a human; therefore I must die.' ▶ **syl·lo·gist·ic** /ˌsɪləˈdʒɪstɪk/ *adj.* [only before noun]

syl·van /ˈsɪlvən/ *adj.* (*literary*) connected with woods and trees: *sylvan surroundings*

sym·bi·osis /ˌsɪmbaɪˈəʊsɪs; *AmE* -ˈoʊsɪs/ *noun* [U, C] (*pl.* **sym·bi·oses** /-ˈəʊsiːz; *AmE* -ˈoʊsiːz/) **1** (*biology*) the relationship between two different living creatures that live close together and depend on each other in particular ways, each getting particular benefits from the other **2** a relationship between people, companies, etc. that is to the advantage of both ▶ **sym·bi·ot·ic** /-ˈɒtɪk; *AmE* -ˈɑːtɪk/ *adj.*: *a symbiotic relationship* **sym·bi·ot·ic·al·ly** /ˌsɪmbaɪˈɒtɪkli; *AmE* -ˈɑːtɪk-/ *adv.*

sym·bol /ˈsɪmbl/ *noun* **1** ~ (**of sth**) a person, an object, an event, etc. that represents a more general quality or situation: *White has always been a symbol of purity in Western cultures.* ◇ *Mandela became a symbol of the anti-apartheid struggle.* **2** ~ (**for sth**) a sign, number, letter, etc. that has a fixed meaning, especially in science, mathematics and music: *What is the chemical symbol for copper?* ◇ *A list of symbols used on the map is given in the index.*—see also SEX SYMBOL, STATUS SYMBOL

sym·bol·ic /sɪmˈbɒlɪk; *AmE* -ˈbɑːlɪk/ *adj.* ~ (**of sth**) containing symbols, or being used as a symbol: *The dove is symbolic of peace.* ◇ *He shook his fist in a symbolic gesture of defiance.* ◇ *The Channel Tunnel has enormous symbolic significance for a united Europe.* ◇ *The new regulations are largely symbolic* (= they will not have any real effect). ▶ **sym·bol·ic·al·ly** /sɪmˈbɒlɪkli; *AmE* -ˈbɑːlɪk-/ *adv.*: *a symbolically significant gesture*

sym·bol·ism /ˈsɪmbəlɪzəm/ *noun* [U] the use of symbols to represent ideas, especially in art and literature: *poetry full of religious symbolism* ▶ **sym·bol·ist** /ˈsɪmbəlɪst/ *adj., noun*: *the symbolist poet Rimbaud*

sym·bol·ize (*BrE* also **-ise**) /ˈsɪmbəlaɪz/ *verb* [VN] to be a symbol of sth [SYN] REPRESENT: *The use of light and dark*

aɪ	aʊ	eɪ	əʊ	oʊ	ɔɪ	ɪə	eə	ʊə	j	w
my	now	say	go	go	boy	near	hair	pure	yes	wet
			(BrE)	(AmE)						

symbolizes good and evil. ◊ *He came to symbolize his country's struggle for independence.*

sym·met·rical /sɪˈmetrɪkl/ (also **sym·met·ric** /sɪˈmetrɪk/) *adj.* (of a body, a design, an object, etc.) having two halves, parts or sides that are the same in size and shape: *a symmetrical pattern/shape* ◊ *People's bodies are never quite symmetrical.* [OPP] ASYMMETRIC ▶ **sym·met·ric·al·ly** /-kli/ *adv.*

sym·metry /ˈsɪmətri/ *noun* [U] **1** the exact match in size and shape between two halves, parts or sides of sth: *the perfect symmetry of the garden design*—picture at AXIS **2** the quality of being very similar or equal: *the increasing symmetry between men's and women's jobs*

sym·pa·thet·ic /ˌsɪmpəˈθetɪk/ *adj.* **1** ~ (**to/towards sb**) kind to sb who is hurt or sad; showing that you understand and care about their problems: *a sympathetic friend/listener/employer* ◊ *I did not feel at all sympathetic towards Kate.* ◊ *I'm here if you need a **sympathetic ear** (= sb to talk to about your problems).* **2** ~ (**to/towards sb/sth**) showing that you approve of sb/sth or that you share their views and are willing to support them: *to be sympathetic to aims/causes/ideas* ◊ *Russian newspapers are largely sympathetic to the president.* **3** (of a person) easy to like: *a sympathetic character in a novel* ◊ *I don't find her a very sympathetic person.* [HELP] This meaning is not very common and you should use **likeable** or **pleasant** instead. [OPP] UNSYMPATHETIC ▶ **sym·pa·thet·ic·al·ly** *adv.*: *to nod/look/smile at sb sympathetically* ◊ *We hope this application will be treated sympathetically (= it will be approved).*

sym·pa·thize (*BrE* also **-ise**) /ˈsɪmpəθaɪz/ *verb* **1** ~ (**with sb/sth**) to feel sorry for sb; to show that you understand and feel sorry about sb's problems: [V] *I find it very hard to sympathize with him.* [also V speech] **2** [V] ~ **with sb/sth** to support sb/sth: *He has never really sympathized with the aims of Animal Rights activists.*

sym·pa·thizer (*BrE* also **-iser**) /ˈsɪmpəθaɪzə(r)/ *noun* a person who supports or approves of sb/sth, especially a political cause or party: *communist sympathizers*

sym·pathy /ˈsɪmpəθi/ *noun* (*pl.* **-ies**) **1** [U, C, usually pl.] the feeling of being sorry for sb; showing that you understand and care about sb's problems: *to express/feel/have sympathy for sb* ◊ *I have no sympathy for Jan, it's all her own fault.* ◊ *I wish he'd show me a little more sympathy.* ◊ *Our heartfelt sympathy goes out to the victims of the war.* ◊ (*formal*) *May we offer our deepest sympathies on the death of your wife.* **2** [U, C, usually pl.] the act of showing support for or approval of an idea, a cause, an organization, etc: *The seamen went on strike **in sympathy with** (= to show their support for) the dockers.* ◊ *Her sympathies lie with the anti-abortion lobby.* **3** [U] friendship and understanding between people who have similar opinions or interests: *There was no personal sympathy between them.* [IDM] **in ˈsympathy with sth** (*written*) happening because sth else has happened: *Share prices slipped in sympathy with the German market.* **out of ˈsympathy with sb/sth** (*written*) not agreeing with or not wanting to support sb/sth

sym·phony /ˈsɪmfəni/ *noun* (*pl.* **-ies**) a long complicated piece of music for a large orchestra, in three or four main parts (called MOVEMENTS): *Beethoven's Fifth Symphony* ◊ *a symphony orchestra* ▶ **sym·phon·ic** /sɪmˈfɒnɪk; *AmE* -ˈfɑːn-/ *adj.*: *Mozart's symphonic works*

sym·po·sium /sɪmˈpəʊziəm; *AmE* -ˈpoʊ-/ *noun* (*pl.* **sym·po·sia** /-ziə/ *or* **sym·po·siums**) ~ (**on sth**) a meeting at which experts have discussions about a particular subject; a small CONFERENCE

symp·tom /ˈsɪmptəm/ *noun* **1** a change in your body or mind that shows that you are not healthy: *cold/flu symptoms* ◊ *Look out for symptoms of depression.* **2** a sign that sth exists, especially sth bad: *The rise in inflation was just one symptom of the poor state of the economy.*

symp·tom·at·ic /ˌsɪmptəˈmætɪk/ *adj.* ~ (**of sth**) (*written*) being a sign of an illness or a problem: *a symptomatic infection* ◊ *These disagreements are symptomatic of the tensions within the party.*

symp·tom·ize /ˈsɪmptəmaɪz/ *verb* [VN] (*AmE*) to be a sign or SYMPTOM of sth

syna·gogue /ˈsɪnəgɒg; *AmE* -gɑːg/ *noun* a building where Jews meet for religious worship and teaching

syn·apse /ˈsaɪnæps; ˈsɪn-/ *noun* (*biology*) a connection between two nerve cells ▶ **syn·ap·tic** /saɪˈnæptɪk; sɪn-/ *adj.*: *the synaptic membranes*

sync (also **synch**) /sɪŋk/ *noun* [U] (*informal*) [IDM] **in ˈsync** moving or working at exactly the same time and speed as sb/sth else: *The soundtrack is **not in sync** with the picture.* **out of ˈsync** not moving or working at exactly the same time and speed as sb/sth else—see also LYP-SYNC, SYNCHRONIZATION

syn·chron·ize (*BrE* also **-ise**) /ˈsɪŋkrənaɪz/ *verb* ~ (**sth**) (**with sth**) to happen at the same time or to move at the same speed as sth; to make sth do this: [V] *The sound track did not synchronize with the action.* ◊ [VN] *Let's synchronize our watches (= make them show exactly the same time).* ▶ **syn·chron·iza·tion, -isa·tion** /ˌsɪŋkrənaɪˈzeɪʃn; *AmE* -nəˈz-/ (also *informal* **sync**) *noun* [U]

ˌsynchronized ˈswimming (*BrE* also **-ised**) *noun* [U] a sport in which groups of SWIMMERS move in patterns in the water to music

syn·chron·ous /ˈsɪŋkrənəs/ *adj.* (*technical*) happening or existing at the same time: *synchronous experiences/development*

syn·co·pated /ˈsɪŋkəpeɪtɪd/ *adj.* (*music*) in syncopated rhythm the strong beats are made weak and the weak beats are made strong ▶ **syn·co·pa·tion** /ˌsɪŋkəˈpeɪʃn/ *noun* [U]

syn·dic·al·ism /ˈsɪndɪkəlɪzəm/ *noun* [U] the belief that factories, businesses, etc. should be owned and managed by all the people who work in them

syn·dic·al·ist /ˈsɪndɪkəlɪst/ *noun* a person who believes in syndicalism ▶ **syn·dic·al·ist** *adj.*

syn·di·cate *noun, verb*
■ *noun* /ˈsɪndɪkət/ a group of people or companies who work together and help each other in order to achieve a particular aim
■ *verb* /ˈsɪndɪkeɪt/ [VN] [usually passive] to sell an article, a photograph, a television programme, etc. to several different newspapers, etc: *His column is syndicated throughout the world.* ▶ **syn·di·ca·tion** /ˌsɪndɪˈkeɪʃn/ *noun* [U]

syn·drome /ˈsɪndrəʊm; *AmE* -droʊm/ *noun* **1** a set of physical conditions that show you have a particular disease or medical problem: *PMS or premenstrual syndrome* ◊ *This syndrome is associated with frequent coughing.*—see also AIDS, DOWN'S SYNDROME **2** a set of opinions or a way of behaving that is typical of a particular type of person, attitude or social problem: *With teenagers, be prepared for the 'Me, me, me!' syndrome (= they think of themselves first).*

syn·ergy /ˈsɪnədʒi; *AmE* -ərdʒi/ *noun* [U, C] (*pl.* **-ies**) (*technical*) the extra energy, power, success, etc. that is achieved by two or more people or companies working together, instead of on their own

synod /ˈsɪnəd; *BrE* also -nɒd/ *noun* an official meeting of Church members to discuss religious matters and make important decisions

syno·nym /ˈsɪnənɪm/ *noun* a word or expression that has the same or nearly the same meaning as another in the same language: *'Big' and 'large' are synonyms.*—compare ANTONYM

syn·onym·ous /sɪˈnɒnɪməs; *AmE* -ˈnɑːn-/ *adj.* **1** (of words or expressions) having the same, or nearly the same, meaning **2** ~ (**with sth**) so closely connected with sth that the two things appear to be the same: *Wealth is not necessarily synonymous with happiness.*

syn·op·sis /sɪˈnɒpsɪs; *AmE* -ˈnɑːp-/ *noun* (*pl.* **syn·op·ses** /-siːz/) a summary of a piece of writing, a play, etc. ▶ **syn·op·tic** /sɪˈnɒptɪk; *AmE* -ˈnɑːp-/ *adj.* (*formal*)

syn·tac·tic /sɪnˈtæktɪk/ *adj.* (*linguistics*) connected with SYNTAX: *syntactic rules/structures* ▶ **syn·tac·tic·al·ly** /sɪnˈtæktɪkli/ *adv.*: *to be syntactically correct/incorrect*

syn·tax /ˈsɪntæks/ *noun* [U] **1** (*linguistics*) the way that words and phrases are put together to form sentences in

S

b	d	f	g	h	k	l	m	n	p	r
bad	**did**	**fall**	**get**	**hat**	**cat**	**leg**	**man**	**now**	**pen**	**red**

a language; the rules of grammar for this—compare MORPHOLOGY **2** (*computing*) the rules that state how words and phrases must be used in a computer language: *The instructions were not carried out because of a syntax error.*

syn·the·sis /ˈsɪnθəsɪs/ *noun* (*pl.* **syn·the·ses** /-siːz/) **1** [U, C] ~ (**of sth**) the act of combining separate ideas, beliefs, styles, etc.; a mixture or combination of ideas, beliefs, styles, etc: *the synthesis of art with everyday life ◊ a synthesis between/of traditional and modern values* **2** [U] (*technical*) the natural chemical production of a substance in animals and plants: *protein synthesis* **3** [U] (*technical*) the artificial production of a substance that is present naturally in animals and plants: *the synthesis of penicillin* **4** [U] the production of sounds, music or speech by electronic means: *digital/sound/speech synthesis*

syn·the·size (*BrE* also **-ise**) /ˈsɪnθəsaɪz/ *verb* [VN] **1** (*technical*) to produce a substance by means of chemical or BIOLOGICAL processes **2** to produce sounds, music or speech using electronic equipment **3** to combine separate ideas, beliefs, styles, etc.

syn·the·sizer (*BrE* also **-iser**) /ˈsɪnθəsaɪzə(r)/ *noun* an electronic machine for producing different sounds. Synthesizers are used as musical instruments, especially for copying the sounds of other instruments, and for copying speech sounds: *a voice/speech synthesizer*—compare KEY-BOARD (3)

syn·thet·ic /sɪnˈθetɪk/ *adj., noun*
■ *adj.* artificial; made by combining chemical substances rather than being produced naturally by plants or animals [SYN] MAN-MADE: *synthetic drugs/fabrics* ▶ **syn·thet·ic·al·ly** /-kli/ *adv.*
■ *noun* an artificial substance or material: *cotton fabrics and synthetics*

syph·il·is /ˈsɪfɪlɪs/ *noun* [U] a disease that gets worse over a period of time, spreading from the sexual organs to the skin, bones, muscles and brain. It is caught by having sex with an infected person. ▶ **syph·il·it·ic** /ˌsɪfɪˈlɪtɪk/ *adj.*

sy·phon = SIPHON

syr·inge /sɪˈrɪndʒ/ *noun, verb*
■ *noun* **1** (also **hypo·der·mic**, ˌhypodermic **sy'ringe**) a plastic or glass tube with a long hollow needle that is used for putting drugs, etc. into a person's body or for taking a small amount of blood from a person—picture on page 599 **2** a plastic or glass tube with a rubber part at the end, used for sucking up liquid and then pushing it out—picture at LABORATORY
■ *verb* [VN] (*BrE*) to clean sth with a SYRINGE: *to have your ears syringed*

syrup /ˈsɪrəp/ *noun* [U] **1** a sweet liquid made from sugar and water, often used in cans of fruit: *pears in syrup* **2** any thick sweet liquid made with sugar, used especially

as a sauce: (*BrE*) *syrup sponge and custard*—see also CORN SYRUP, GOLDEN SYRUP, MAPLE SYRUP

syr·upy /ˈsɪrəpi/ *adj.* **1** thick and sticky like syrup; containing syrup **2** (*disapproving*) extremely emotional and romantic and therefore unpleasant; too SENTIMENTAL: *a syrupy romantic novel*

sys·tem /ˈsɪstəm/ *noun* **1** [C] ~ (**of/for sth**) an organized set of ideas or theories or a particular way of doing sth: *the British educational system ◊ a new system for assessing personal tax bills ◊ a system of government*—see also BINARY, METRIC SYSTEM **2** [C] a group of things, pieces of equipment, etc. that are connected or work together: *a transport system ◊ heating systems ◊ a computer/stereo system ◊ a security system*—see also ECOSYSTEM, EXPERT SYSTEM, OPERATING SYSTEM, PUBLIC ADDRESS SYSTEM, SOLAR SYSTEM **3** [C] a human or an animal body, or a part of it, when it is being thought of as the organs and processes that make it function: *You have to wait until the drugs have passed out of your system. ◊ the male reproductive system*—see also CENTRAL NERVOUS SYSTEM, DIGESTIVE SYSTEM, IMMUNE SYSTEM **4** (**the system**) [sing.] (*informal*, usually *disapproving*) the rules or people that control a country or an organization, especially when they seem to be unfair because you cannot change them: *You can't beat the system* (= you must accept it). *◊ young people rebelling against the system* [IDM] **get sth out of your 'system** (*informal*) to do sth so that you no longer feel a very strong emotion or have a strong desire: *I was very angry with him, but now I feel I've got it out of my system.*

sys·tem·at·ic /ˌsɪstəˈmætɪk/ *adj.* done according to a system or plan, in a thorough, efficient or determined way: *a systematic approach to solving the problem ◊ a systematic attempt to destroy the organization ◊ The prisoner was subjected to systematic torture.* [OPP] UNSYSTEMATIC ▶ **sys·tem·at·ic·al·ly** /-kli/ *adv.*: *The search was carried out systematically.*

sys·tem·atize (*BrE* also **-ise**) /ˈsɪstəmətaɪz/ *verb* [VN] (*formal*) to arrange sth according to a system ▶ **sys·tem·atiza·tion**, **-isa·tion** /ˌsɪstəmətaɪˈzeɪʃn; *AmE* -təˈz-/ *noun* [U]

sys·tem·ic /sɪˈstemɪk; sɪˈstiːmɪk/ *adj.* (*technical*) **1** affecting or connected with the whole of sth, especially the human body **2** **systemic** chemicals or drugs that are used to treat diseases in plants or animals enter the body of the plant or animal and spread to all parts of it: *systemic weedkillers* ▶ **sys·tem·ic·al·ly** *adv.*

'systems analyst *noun* a person whose job is to analyse the needs of a business company or an organization and then design a way of carrying out processes and working efficiently using computer programs ▶ **'systems analysis** *noun* [U]

Tt

T (also **t**) /tiː/ *noun* [C, U] (*pl.* **T's, t's** /tiːz/) the 20th letter of the English alphabet: *'Tin' begins with (a) T/'T'.*—see also T-BONE STEAK, T-JUNCTION, T-SHIRT, T-SQUARE **IDM** **to a 'T/'tee** (*informal*) used to say that sth is exactly right for sb, succeeds in doing sth in exactly the right way, etc: *Her new job suits her to a T.* ◊ *The novel captures the feeling of the pre-war period to a T.*—more at DOT *v.*

TA /ˌtiː 'eɪ/ *abbr.* **1** (*BrE*) TERRITORIAL ARMY **2** (*AmE*) TEACHING ASSISTANT

ta /tɑː/ *exclamation* (*BrE, slang*) thank you

tab /tæb/ *noun* **1** a small piece of paper, fabric, metal, etc. that sticks out from the edge of sth, and that is used to give information about it, or to hold it, fasten it, etc: *Insert tab A into slot 1* (= for example to make a model, box, etc.). **2** = TAB STOP **3** (*AmE*) = RING PULL **4** a bill for goods you receive but pay for later, especially for food or drinks in a restaurant or bar; the price or cost of sth: *a bar tab* ◊ *Can I put it on my tab?* ◊ *The tab for the meeting could be $3000.* **5** (*informal*) a small solid piece of an illegal drug: *a tab of Ecstasy* **IDM** **keep (close) tabs on sb/sth** (*informal*) to watch sb/sth carefully in order to know what is happening so that you can control a particular situation: *It's not always possible to keep tabs on everyone's movements.*—more at PICK *v.*

Tab·asco™ /tə'bæskəʊ; *AmE* -koʊ/ *noun* [U] a red spicy sauce made from PEPPERS

tabby /'tæbi/ *noun* (*pl.* **-ies**) (also **'tabby cat**) a cat with brown or grey fur marked with dark lines or spots

tab·er·nacle /'tæbənækl; *AmE* -bərn-/ *noun* **1** [C] a place of worship for some groups of Christians: *a Baptist/ Mormon tabernacle* **2 (the tabernacle)** [sing.] a small place of worship that could be moved, used by the Jews in ancient times when they were travelling in the desert

table /'teɪbl/ *noun, verb*

■ *noun*

FURNITURE | **1** a piece of furniture that consists of a flat top supported by legs: *a kitchen table* ◊ *A table for two, please* (= in a restaurant). ◊ *I'd like to book a table for tonight.* ◊ *to set the table* (= to put the plates, knives, etc. on it for a meal) ◊ (*BrE* also) *to lay the table* ◊ *to clear the table* (= take away the dirty plates, etc. at the end of a meal) ◊ *He questioned her next morning over the breakfast table* (= during breakfast). ◊ (*BrE, formal*) *Children must learn to behave at table.* ◊ *a table lamp* (= one that stands on a table) ◊ *a billiard/snooker/pool table* **HELP** There are many compounds ending in **table**. You will find them at their place in the alphabet.

PEOPLE | **2** the people sitting at a table for a meal or to play cards, etc: *He kept the whole table entertained with his jokes.*—see also ROUND-TABLE

LIST OF FACTS/NUMBERS | **3** a list of facts or numbers arranged in a special order, usually in rows and columns: *a table of contents* (= a list of the main points or information in a book, usually at the front of the book) ◊ *Table 2 shows how prices and earnings have increased over the past 20 years.*—see also THE PERIODIC TABLE

IN SPORT | **4** a list of sports teams, countries, schools, etc. that shows their position in a competition, etc: *If Arsenal win this game they'll go to the top of the table.* ◊ *school performance league tables*

MATHEMATICS | **5** = MULTIPLICATION TABLE: *Do you know your six times table?*

—see also TURNTABLE, WATER TABLE

IDM **on the 'table 1** (*BrE*) (of a plan, suggestion, etc.) offered to people so that they can consider or discuss it: *Management have put several new proposals on the table.* **2** (*especially AmE*) (of a plan, suggestion, etc.) not going to be discussed or considered until a future date **turn the**

'tables (on sb) to change a situation so that you are now in a stronger position than the person who used to be in a stronger position than you—more at CARD *n.*, DRINK *v.*, WAIT *v.*

■ *verb* [VN] **1** (*BrE*) to present sth formally for discussion: *to table a question in Parliament* ◊ *They have tabled a motion for debate at the next Party Conference.* **2** (*AmE*) to leave an idea, a proposal, etc. to be discussed at a later date: *They voted to table the proposal until the following meeting.*

tab·leau /'tæbləʊ; *AmE* -loʊ/ *noun* (*pl.* **tab·leaux** /-ləʊ; -ləʊz; *AmE* -loʊ; -loʊz/) **1** a scene showing, for example, events and people from history, that is presented by a group of actors who do not move or speak: *The procession included a tableau of the Battle of Hastings.* ◊ (*figurative*) *She stood at the door observing the peaceful domestic tableau around the fire.* **2** a work of art, especially one carved out of stone, showing a group of people, animals, etc.

table·cloth /'teɪblklɒθ; *AmE* -klɔːθ/ *noun* a cloth that you use for covering a table, especially when you have a meal

table d'hôte /ˌtɑːbl 'dəʊt; *AmE* 'doʊt/ *adj.* a **table d'hôte** meal in a restaurant costs a fixed price and there are only a limited number of dishes to choose from: *the table d'hôte menu* ▶ **table d'hôte** *noun* [U]: *The restaurant offers both table d'hôte and à la carte.*

'table linen *noun* [U] the cloths that you use during a meal, for example TABLECLOTHS and NAPKINS

'table manners *noun* [pl.] the behaviour that is considered correct while you are having a meal at a table with other people

'table mat (*BrE*) *noun* a small piece of wood or fabric that you put under a hot dish or plate to protect the surface of the table

'table napkin *noun* = NAPKIN

table·spoon /'teɪblspuːn/ *noun* **1** a large spoon, used especially for serving food—picture at CUTLERY **2** (also **table·spoon·ful** /-fʊl/) (*abbr.* **tbsp**) the amount a tablespoon can hold: *Add two tablespoons of water.*

tab·let /'tæblət/ *noun* **1** (*especially BrE*) a small round solid piece of medicine that you swallow [SYN] PILL: *vitamin tablets* ◊ *Take two tablets with water before meals.*—picture on page 599 **2** an amount of another substance in a small round solid piece: *water purification tablets* **3** a flat piece of stone that has words written on it, especially one that has been fixed to a wall in memory of an important person or event: *The school has a memorial tablet engraved with the name of the founder.* ◊ (*figurative*) *We can be very flexible—our entry requirements are not set in tablets of stone* (= they can be changed). **4 ~ of soap** (*old-fashioned, formal*) a piece of soap

'table tennis (also *informal* **'ping-pong**) *noun* [U] a game played like tennis with bats and a small plastic ball on a table with a net across it

'table top *noun* the top or the surface of a table ▶ **'table-top** *adj.* [only before noun]: *a table-top machine* (= that can be used on a table) ◊ *a table-top sale* (= where goods for sale are displayed on tables)

table·ware /'teɪblweə(r); *AmE* -wer/ *noun* [U] the word used in shops/stores, etc. for items that you use for meals, such as plates, glasses, knives and forks

tab·loid /'tæblɔɪd/ *noun* (sometimes *disapproving*) a newspaper with small pages (usually half the size of those in larger papers). Tabloids usually have short articles and a lot of pictures and stories about famous people, and are thought of as less serious than other newspapers: *The story made the front page in all the*

æ	ɑː	e	ɜː	ə	ɪ	iː	i	ɒ	ɔː	ʌ	ʊ	u	uː
cat	father	ten	bird	about	sit	see	many	got	saw	cup	put	actual	too
								(BrE)					

tabloids.—compare BROADSHEET, QUALITY NEWSPAPER
▶ **tab·loid** *adj.* [only before noun]: *tabloid journalists* ◊ *a tabloid newspaper* ◊ *the tabloid press*

taboo /təˈbuː/ *noun* (*pl.* **ta·boos**) ~ **(against/on sth) 1** a cultural or religious custom that does not allow people to do, use or talk about a particular thing as people find it offensive or embarrassing: *an incest taboo* ◊ *a taboo on working on a Sunday* ◊ *to break/violate a taboo* ◊ *Death is one of the great taboos in our culture.* **2** a general agreement not to do sth or talk about sth: *The subject is still a taboo in our family.* ▶ **taboo** *adj.*: *in the days when sex was a taboo subject*

ta·boo words *noun* [pl.] words that many people consider offensive or shocking, for example because they refer to sex, the body or people's race

'tab stop (also **tab**) *noun* a fixed position in a line of a document that you are typing that shows where a piece of text or a column of figures, etc. will begin

tabu·lar /ˈtæbjələ(r)/ *adj.* [usually before noun] (*written*) presented or arranged in a TABLE (= in rows and columns): *tabular data* ◊ *The results are presented* **in** *tabular form.*

tabu·late /ˈtæbjuleɪt/ *verb* [VN] to arrange facts or figures in columns or lists so that they can be read easily ▶ **tabu·la·tion** /ˌtæbjuˈleɪʃn/ *noun* [U, C]

tacho·graph /ˈtækəɡrɑːf; *AmE* -ɡræf/ *noun* a device that is used in vehicles such as large lorries/trucks and some types of buses to measure their speed, how far they have travelled and when the driver has stopped to rest

tacit /ˈtæsɪt/ *adj.* [usually before noun] (*written*) that is suggested indirectly or understood, rather than said in words: *tacit approval/support/knowledge* ◊ *By* **tacit agreement**, *the subject was never mentioned again.* ▶ **tacit·ly** *adv.*

taci·turn /ˈtæsɪtɜːn; *AmE* -tɜːrn/ *adj.* tending not to say very much, in a way that seems unfriendly: *a taciturn and serious young man* ▶ **taci·turn·ity** /ˌtæsɪˈtɜːnəti; *AmE* -ˈtɜːrn-/ *noun* [U]

tack /tæk/ *noun, verb*
■ *noun* **1** [U, sing.] the way in which you deal with a particular situation; the direction of your words or thoughts: *a complete/sudden change of tack* ◊ *It was a brave decision to* **change tack** *in the middle of the project.* ◊ *When threats failed, she decided to* **try/take a different tack.** ◊ *His thoughts wandered off on another tack.* **2** [C, U] (*technical*) the direction that a boat with sails takes as it sails at an angle to the wind in order to fill its sails: *They were sailing on (a) port/starboard tack* (= with the wind coming from the left/right side). **3** [C] a small nail with a sharp point and a flat head, used especially for fixing a carpet to the floor: *a carpet tack*—compare NAIL *n.* (2) **4** [C] (*AmE*) = DRAWING PIN—see also BLU-TACK **5** [C] a long loose stitch used for holding pieces of fabric together temporarily, before you sew them finally **6** [U] (*technical*) the equipment that you need for riding a horse, such as a SADDLE and BRIDLE **IDM** see BRASS
■ *verb* **1** [VN+*adv./prep.*] to fasten sth in place with a tack or tacks: *The carpet was tacked to the floor.* **2** [VN] to fasten pieces of fabric together temporarily with long, loose stitches before sewing it finally: *She tacked the sleeve of the blouse into the armhole.* **3** [V] (*technical*) to change the direction of a sailing boat so that the wind blows onto the sails from the opposite side; to do this several times in order to travel in the direction that the wind is coming from **PHRV** **tack sth↔'on**, **tack sth 'onto sth** (*informal*) to add sth to sth that already exists, especially in a careless way: *The poems were tacked on at the end of the book.*

tackle /ˈtækl/ *verb, noun*
■ *verb* **1** [VN] to make a determined effort to deal with a difficult problem or situation: *The government is determined to tackle inflation.* ◊ *I think I'll tackle the repairs next weekend.* **2** [VN] ~ **sb (about sth)** to speak to sb about a problem or difficult situation **SYN** CONFRONT: *I tackled him about the money he owed me.* **3** (in football, hockey, etc.) to try and take the ball from an opponent: [VN] *He was tackled just outside the penalty area.* [also V] —picture

on page 1250 **4** [V, VN] (in rugby or American football) to make an opponent fall to the ground in order to stop them running **5** [VN] to deal with sb who is violent or threatening you: *He tackled a masked intruder at his home.*
■ *noun* **1** [C] an act of trying to take the ball from an opponent in football, etc.; an act of knocking an opponent to the ground in rugby or American football **2** [C] (*AmE*) (in American football) a player whose job is to stop opponents by knocking them to the ground **3** [U] the equipment used to do a particular sport or activity, especially fishing **4** [U] (*BrE*, *slang*) a man's sexual organs—see also BLOCK AND TACKLE

tack·ler /ˈtæklə(r)/ *noun* (*BrE*) a player who tries to take the ball from an opponent in football, etc.

tacky /ˈtæki/ *adj.* **1** (*informal*) cheap, badly made and/or lacking in taste: *tacky souvenirs* ◊ *The movie had a really tacky ending.* **2** (of paint, glue, etc.) not dry and therefore slightly sticky ▶ **tacki·ness** *noun* [U]

taco /ˈtækəʊ; *AmE* ˈtɑːkoʊ/ *noun* (*pl.* **-os**) (from *Spanish*) a type of Mexican food consisting of a crisp fried PANCAKE that is folded over and filled with meat, beans, etc.

tact /tækt/ *noun* [U] the ability to deal with difficult or embarrassing situations carefully and without doing or saying anything that will annoy or upset other people: *Settling the dispute required great tact and diplomacy.* ◊ *She is not exactly known for her tact.*

tact·ful /ˈtæktfl/ *adj.* careful not to say or do anything that will annoy or upset other people: *That wasn't a very tactful thing to say!* ◊ *I tried to find a tactful way of telling her the truth.* **OPP** TACTLESS ▶ **tact·ful·ly** /-fəli/ *adv.*: *a tactfully worded reply* ◊ *I tactfully suggested he should see a doctor.*

tac·tic /ˈtæktɪk/ *noun* **1** [C, usually pl.] the particular method you use to achieve sth: *They tried all kinds of tactics to get us to go.* ◊ *This was just the latest in a series of* **delaying tactics.** ◊ *The manager discussed tactics with his team.* ◊ *Confrontation is not always the best tactic.* ◊ *It's time to try a change of tactic.* **2** (**tactics**) [pl.] the art of moving soldiers and military equipment around during a battle or war in order to use them in the most effective way—compare STRATEGY

tac·tic·al /ˈtæktɪkl/ *adj.* **1** [usually before noun] connected with the particular method you use to achieve sth: *tactical discussions/planning* ◊ *to have a tactical advantage* ◊ *Telling your boss you were looking for a new job was a tactical error* (= it was the wrong thing to do at that time). **2** [usually before noun] carefully planned in order to achieve a particular aim: *a tactical decision/retreat*—see also TACTICAL VOTING **3** [only before noun] (especially of weapons) used or having an effect over short distances or for a short time: *tactical aircraft/missiles* ◊ *tactical nuclear weapons*—compare STRATEGIC (3) **4** [only before noun] connected with military tactics: *He was given tactical command of the operation.* ▶ **tac·tic·al·ly** /-kli/ *adv.*: *At the time, it was tactically the right thing to do.* ◊ *The enemy was tactically superior.*

tactical 'voting *noun* [U] (*BrE*) the act of voting for a particular person or political party, not because you support them, but in order to prevent sb else from being elected

tac·ti·cian /tækˈtɪʃn/ *noun* a person who is very clever at planning the best way to achieve sth: *a fine political tactician*

tact·ile /ˈtæktaɪl; *AmE* -tl/ *adj.* [usually before noun] (*formal*) connected with the sense of touch; using your sense of touch: *tactile sensations/stimuli* ◊ *visual and tactile communication* ◊ *tactile fabric* (= pleasant to touch) ◊ *tactile displays/maps* (= that you can touch and feel) ◊ *He's a very tactile man* (= he enjoys touching people).

tact·less /ˈtæktləs/ *adj.* saying or doing things that are likely to annoy or to upset other people: *a tactless question/remark* ◊ *It was tactless of you to comment on his hair!* **OPP** TACTFUL ▶ **tact·less·ly** *adv.* **tact·less·ness** *noun* [U]

tad /tæd/ *noun* (**a tad**) [sing.] (*informal*) a very small amount: *Could you turn the sound down just a tad?* ▶ **a tad** *adv.*: *It's a tad too expensive for me.*

tad·pole /'tædpəʊl; *AmE* -poʊl/ *noun* a small creature with a large head and a small tail, that lives in water and is the young form of a FROG or TOAD—picture on page A7

tae kwon do /ˌtaɪ ˌkwɒn 'dəʊ/ *noun* [U] a Korean system of fighting without weapons, similar to KARATE

taf·feta /'tæfɪtə/ *noun* [U] a stiff shiny fabric made from silk or a similar material, used especially for making dresses

Taffy /'tæfi/ *noun* (*pl.* **-ies**) (also **Taff** /tæf/) (*BrE, informal, often offensive*) a person from Wales

taffy /'tæfi/ *noun* [U] (*AmE*) a type of soft sweet/candy made of brown sugar boiled until it is very thick and given different shapes and colours

tag /tæg/ *noun, verb*
■ *noun* **1** [C] (often in compounds) a small piece of paper, fabric, plastic, etc. attached to sth to identify it or give information about it: *He put name tags on all his shirts.* ◇ *a gift tag* (= tied to a present) ◇ *The police use electronic tags to monitor the whereabouts of young offenders on probation.*—see also PRICE TAG **2** [C, usually sing.] a name or phrase that is used to describe a person or thing in some way: *They are finally ready to drop the tag 'the new Beatles'.* ◇ *The 'lucky' tag stuck for years.* **3** [C] (*linguistics*) a word or phrase that is added to a sentence for emphasis, for example *I do* in *Yes, I do*—see also QUESTION TAG **4** [C] a short QUOTATION or saying in a foreign language: *the Latin tag 'Si vis pacem, para bellum'* (= if you want peace, prepare for war) **5** (*BrE* also **tig**) [U] a children's game in which one child chases the others and tries to touch one of them
■ *verb* (**-gg-**) **1** [VN] to fasten a tag onto sth/sb: *Each animal was tagged with a number for identification.*—see also ELECTRONIC TAGGING **2** [VN] **~ sb/sth as sth** to give sb/sth a name that describes what they are or do [SYN] LABEL: *The country no longer wanted to be tagged as a Third World nation.* [PHRV] **ˌtag aˈlong (behind/with sb)** to go somewhere with sb, especially when you have not been asked or invited: *Do you mind if I tag along with you tonight?* **ˌtag sth↔ˈon**, **ˌtag sth ˈonto sth** to add sth to the end of sth that already exists, especially in a careless way: *An apology was tagged onto the end of the letter.*

ˈtag line *noun* (*AmE, informal*) **1** = PUNCHLINE **2** = SLOGAN

ˈtag question *noun* (*grammar*) = QUESTION TAG

t'ai chi ch'uan /ˌtaɪ tʃiː 'tʃwɑːn/ (also **t'ai chi**) *noun* [U] a Chinese system of exercises consisting of sets of very slow controlled movements

tail /teɪl/ *noun, verb*
■ *noun*
OF BIRD/ANIMAL/FISH | **1** [C] the part that sticks out and can be moved at the back of the body of a bird, an animal or a fish: *The dog ran up, wagging its tail.* ◇ *The male has beautiful tail feathers.*—picture on pages A6 and A7
-TAILED | **2** (in adjectives) having the type of tail mentioned: *a white-tailed eagle*
OF PLANE/SPACECRAFT | **3** [C] the back part of a plane, spacecraft, etc.: *the tail wing*—picture at PLANE
BACK/END OF STH | **4** [C] **~ (of sth)** a part of sth that sticks out at the back like a tail: *the tail of a kite/comet* **5** [C] **~ (of sth)** the last part of sth that is moving away from you: *the tail of the storm/procession*—see also TAIL END
JACKET | **6** (**tails**) [pl.] (also **tail·coat** [C]) a long jacket divided at the back below the waist into two pieces that become narrower at the bottom, worn by men at very formal events: *The men all wore top hat and tails.*—see also COAT-TAILS, SHIRT TAIL—compare DINNER JACKET, MORNING COAT
SIDE OF COIN | **7** (**tails**) [U] the side of a coin that does not have a picture of the head of a person on it, used as one choice when a coin is TOSSED to decide sth—compare HEADS *n.* (5)
PERSON WHO FOLLOWS SB | **8** [C] (*informal*) a person who is sent to follow sb secretly and find out information about

where that person goes, what they do, etc: *The police have put a tail on him.*
—see also PONYTAIL ▶ **tail·less** *adj.*: *Manx cats are tailless.*
[IDM] **on sb's ˈtail** (*informal*) following behind sb very closely, especially in a car **the tail (is) wagging the ˈdog** used to describe a situation in which the most important aspect is being influenced and controlled by sb/sth that is not as important **turn ˈtail** to run away from a fight or dangerous situation: *When they heard the sirens, they turned tail and ran.* **with your tail between your ˈlegs** (*informal*) feeling ashamed, embarrassed or unhappy because you have been defeated or punished—more at BRIGHT-EYED, HEAD *n.*, NOSE *n.*, STING *n.*
■ *verb* [VN] to follow sb closely, especially in order to watch where they go and what they do [SYN] SHADOW: *A private detective had been tailing them for several weeks.* [IDM] see TOP *v.*
[PHRV] **ˌtail aˈway/ˈoff** (*especially BrE*) to become smaller or weaker: *The number of tourists tails off in October.* ◇ *'But why...?' Her voice tailed away.* **ˌtail ˈback** (of traffic) to form a tailback

tail·back /'teɪlbæk/ *noun* (*BrE*) a long line of traffic that is moving slowly or not moving at all, because sth is blocking the road

tail·board /'teɪlbɔːd; *AmE* -bɔːrd/ *noun* = TAILGATE

tail·bone /'teɪlbəʊn; *AmE* -boʊn/ *noun* the small bone at the bottom of the SPINE [SYN] COCCYX

tail·coat /'teɪlkəʊt; *AmE* -koʊt/ *noun* a long jacket divided at the back below the waist into two pieces that become narrower at the bottom, worn by men at formal events [SYN] TAILS

ˌtail ˈend *noun* [sing.] the very last part of sth: *the tail end of the queue* ◇ *I only caught the tail end of the conversation.*

tail·gate /'teɪlgeɪt/ *noun, verb*
■ *noun* **1** (also **tail·board**) a door at the back of a lorry/truck that opens downwards and that you can lower or remove when you are loading or unloading the vehicle **2** the door that opens upwards at the back of a car that has three or five doors (called a HATCHBACK)
■ *verb* **1** [V, VN] (*informal, especially AmE*) to drive too closely behind another vehicle **2** [V] (*AmE*) to eat food and drinks outdoors, served from the tailgate of a car

ˈtail light *noun* a red light at the back of a car, bicycle or train

tailor /'teɪlə(r)/ *noun, verb*
■ *noun* a person whose job is to make men's clothes, especially sb who makes suits, jackets, etc. for individual customers
■ *verb* **~ sth to/for sb/sth** to make or adapt sth for a particular purpose, a particular person, etc: [VN] *Special programmes of study are tailored to the needs of specific groups.* ◇ [VN to inf] *Most travel agents are prepared to tailor travel arrangements to meet individual requirements.*

tailored /'teɪləd; *AmE* -lərd/ *adj.* **1** (of clothes) made to fit well or closely: *a tailored jacket* **2** made for a particular person or purpose [SYN] TAILOR-MADE: *a tailored programme* ◇ *tailored benefits*

tailor·ing /'teɪlərɪŋ/ *noun* [U] **1** the style or the way in which a suit, jacket, etc. is made: *Clever tailoring can flatter your figure.* **2** the job of making men's clothes: *a tailoring business*

ˌtailor-ˈmade *adj.* **1 ~ (for sb/sth)** | **~ (to sth/to do sth)** made for a particular person or purpose, and therefore very suitable: *a tailor-made course of study* ◇ *a trip tailor-made just for you* ◇ (*figurative*) *She seems tailor-made for the job* (= perfectly suited for it). **2** (of clothes) made by a TAILOR for a particular person: *a tailor-made suit*

tail·piece /'teɪlpiːs/ *noun* **1 ~ (to sth)** a part that you add to the end of a piece of writing to make it longer or complete **2** (*music*) a piece of wood that the lower ends of the strings of some musical instruments are attached to

tail·pipe /'teɪlpaɪp/ *noun* (*especially AmE*) = EXHAUST (2)

tail·spin /'teɪlspɪn/ *noun* [sing.] **1** a situation in which a pilot loses control of an aircraft and it spins as it falls quickly towards the ground, with the back making larger

b	d	f	g	h	k	l	m	n	p	r
bad	did	fall	get	hat	cat	leg	man	now	pen	red

circles than the front **2** a situation that suddenly becomes much worse and is not under control: *Following the announcement, share prices went into a tailspin.*

tail·wind /ˈteɪlwɪnd/ *noun* a wind that blows from behind a moving vehicle, a runner, etc.—compare HEAD-WIND

taint /teɪnt/ *verb, noun*

■ *verb* [VN] [often passive] **~ sth (with sth)** (*formal*) to damage or spoil the quality of sth or the opinion that people have of sb/sth: *The administration was tainted with scandal.* ▶ **taint·ed** *adj.*: *tainted drinking water*

■ *noun* [usually sing.] the effect of sth bad or unpleasant that spoils the quality of sb/sth: *to be free from the taint of corruption*

take /teɪk/ *verb, noun*

■ *verb* (**took** /tʊk/ **taken** /ˈteɪkən/)

CARRY/LEAD | **1 ~ sth (with you)** | **~ sth (to sb)** | **~ (sb) sth** to carry or move sth from one place to another: [VN] *I forgot to take my bag with me when I got off the bus.* ◊ *Take this to the bank for me, would you?* ◊ [VN, VNN] *Shall I take a gift to my host family?* ◊ *Shall I take my host family a gift?* **2** to go with sb from one place to another, especially to guide or lead them: [VN] *It's too far to walk—I'll take you by car.* ◊ *A boy took us to our room.* ◊ [VN-ing] *I'm taking the kids swimming later.* ◊ [VNtoinf] *The boys were taken to see their grandparents most week-ends.* **3** [VN+adv./prep.] to make sb/sth go from one level, situation, etc. to another: *Her energy and talent took her to the top of her profession.* ◊ *The new loan takes the total debt to $100000.* ◊ *I'd like to take my argument a stage further.*

REACH AND HOLD | **4** [VN] to put your hands or arms around sb/sth and hold them/it; to reach for sb/sth and hold them/it: *I passed him the rope and he took it.* ◊ *Free newspapers: please take one.* ◊ *Can you take* (= hold) *the baby for a moment?* ◊ *He took her hand / took her by the hand* (= held her hand, for example to lead her some-where). ◊ *She took the child in her arms and kissed him.*

REMOVE | **5** [VN+adv./prep.] to remove sth/sb from a place or a person: *Will you take your books off the table?* ◊ *The sign must be taken down.* ◊ *He took some keys out of his pocket.* ◊ *My name had been taken off the list.* ◊ *She was playing with a knife, so I took it away from her.* ◊ (*infor-mal*) *She was playing with a knife, so I took it off her.* ◊ (*figurative*) *The new sports centre will **take the pressure off** the old one.* **6** [VN] to remove sth without permission or by mistake: *Someone has taken my scarf.* ◊ *Did the burglars take anything valuable?* ◊ (*figurative*) *The storms **took the lives** of 50 people.* **7** [VN] **~ sth from sth/out of sth** to get sth from a particular source: *The scientists are taking water samples from the river.* ◊ *Part of her article is taken straight* (= copied) *out of my book.* ◊ *The machine takes its name from its inventor.*

CAPTURE | **8 ~ sth (from sb)** to capture a place or person; to get control of sth: [VN] *The rebels succeeded in taking the town.* ◊ *The state has **taken control** of the company.* ◊ [VN-N] *The rebels took him prisoner.* ◊ *He was taken pris-oner by the rebels.*

CHOOSE/BUY | **9** [VN] to choose, buy or rent sth: *I'll take the grey jacket.* ◊ *We took a room at the hotel for two nights.* **10** [VN] (*formal*) to buy a newspaper or magazine regu-larly: *We take the 'Express'.*

EAT/DRINK | **11** [VN] to eat, drink, etc. sth: *Do you take sugar in your coffee?* ◊ *The doctor has given me some medicine to take for my cough.* ◊ *He started taking drugs* (= illegal drugs) *at college.*

MATHEMATICS | **12** [VN] **~ A (away) from B** | **~ A away** (not used in the progressive tenses) to reduce one number by the value of another SYN SUBTRACT: *Take 5 from 12 and you're left with 7.* ◊ (*spoken, informal*) *80 take away 5 is 75.*

WRITE DOWN | **13** [VN] to find out and record sth; to write sth down: *The police officer took my name and address.* ◊ *Did you take notes in the class?*

PHOTOGRAPH | **14** [VN] to photograph sb/sth: *to take a photo-graph / picture / snapshot of sb/sth* ◊ *to have your picture / photo taken*

MEASUREMENT | **15** [VN] to test or measure sth: *to take sb's*

pulse / temperature ◊ *I need to have my blood pressure taken.*

SEAT | **16** [VN] to sit down in or use a chair, etc: *Are these seats taken?* ◊ *Come in; take a seat.*

GIVE EXAMPLE | **17** [VN] used to introduce sb/sth as an example: *Lots of couples have problems in the first year of marriage. Take Ann and Paul.*

ACCEPT/RECEIVE | **18** [VN] (not usually used in the progres-sive tenses or in the passive) to accept or receive sth: *If they offer me the job, I'll take it.* ◊ *She was accused of taking bribes.* ◊ *Does the hotel take credit cards?* ◊ *I'll take the call in my office.* ◊ *Why should I **take the blame** for somebody else's mistakes?* ◊ *If you **take my advice** you'll have nothing more to do with him.* ◊ *Will you take $10 for the book* (= will you sell it for $10)? ◊ *The store took* (= sold goods worth) *$100000 last week.* **19** [VN] (not usually used in the progressive tenses) to accept sb as a customer, patient, etc: *The school doesn't take boys* (= only has girls). ◊ *The dentist can't take any new patients.* **20** [VN] (not usually used in the progressive tenses) to experience or be affected by sth: *The school took the full force of the explosion.* ◊ *Can the ropes **take the strain*** (= not break)? ◊ *The team took a terrible beating.* **21** [VN] [no passive] (not usually used in the progressive tenses) to be able to bear sth: *She can't take criticism.* ◊ *I don't think I can take much more of this heat.* ◊ *I find his attitude a little hard to take.* **22** [VN+adv./prep.] to react to sth/sb in a particular way: *He took the criticism surprisingly well.* ◊ *These threats are not to be taken lightly.* ◊ *I wish you'd take me seriously.* ◊ *She took it in the spirit in which it was intended.*

CONSIDER | **23 ~ sth (as sth)** (not used in the progressive tenses) to understand or consider sth in a particular way: [VN] *She took what he said as a compliment.* ◊ *How am I supposed to take that remark?* ◊ *Taken overall, the project was a success.* ◊ [VNtoinf] *What did you take his comments to mean?* **24 ~ sb/sth for sb/sth/to be sb/sth** (not used in the progressive tenses) to consider sb/sth to be sb/sth, especially when you are wrong: [VN] *Even the experts took the painting for a genuine Van Gogh.* ◊ (*spoken*) *Of course I didn't do it! What do you take me for* (= what sort of person do you think I am)? ◊ [VNtoinf] *I took the man with him to be his father.*

HAVE FEELING/OPINION | **25** [VN] (not usually used in the progressive tenses) to have a particular feeling, opinion or attitude: *My parents always took an interest in my hobbies.* ◊ *Don't **take offence*** (= be offended) *at what I said.* ◊ *I took an instant dislike to him.* ◊ *He takes the view that children are responsible for their own actions.*

ACTION | **26** [VN] to use a particular course of action in order to deal with or achieve sth: *The government is taking action to combat drug abuse.* ◊ *We need to take a different approach to the problem.* **27** [VN] used with nouns to say that sb is doing sth, performing an action, etc: *to take a step / walk / stroll* ◊ *to take a bath / shower / wash* ◊ *to take a look / glance* ◊ *to take a bite / drink / sip* ◊ *to take a deep breath* ◊ *to take a break / rest* ◊ *No decision will be taken on the matter until next week.*

FORM/POSITION | **28** [VN] to have a particular form, position or state: *Our next class will take the form of a debate.* ◊ *The new President takes office in January.*

TIME | **29** [no passive] to need or require a particular amount of time: [VN] *The journey to the airport takes about half an hour.* ◊ *It takes about half an hour to get to the airport.* ◊ [VNN] *It took her three hours to repair her bike.* ◊ [VNtoinf] *That cut is taking a long time to heal.* ◊ [VNN, VN] *It'll take her time to recover from the illness.* ◊ *It'll take time* (= take a long time) *for her to recover from the illness.* ◊ [V] *I need a shower—I won't take long.* ⇨ note at LAST[1]

NEED | **30** [no passive] to need or require sth in order to happen or be done: [VNtoinf] *It only takes one careless driver to cause an accident.* ◊ *It doesn't take much to make her angry.* ◊ [VN] (*informal*) *He didn't take much persuad-ing* (= he was easily persuaded). **31** [VN] [no passive] (not used in the progressive tenses) (of machines, etc.) to use sth in order to work: *All new cars take unleaded petrol.*

SIZE OF SHOES/CLOTHES | **32** [VN] [no passive] (not used in

s	t	v	z	ʃ	ʒ	tʃ	dʒ	θ	ð	ŋ
see	tea	van	zoo	shoe	vision	chain	jam	thin	this	sing

the progressive tenses) to wear a particular size in shoes or clothes: *What size shoes do you take?*

HOLD/CONTAIN | **33** [VN] [no passive] (not used in the progressive tenses) to have enough space for sth/sb; to be able to hold or contain a particular quantity: *The bus can take 60 passengers.* ◊ *The tank takes 50 litres.*

TEACH/LEAD | **34** [VN] ~ **sb (for sth)** | ~ **sth** to be the teacher or leader in a class or a religious service: *The head teacher usually takes us for French.*

STUDY | **35** [VN] to study a subject at school, college, etc: *She is planning to take a computer course.* ◊ *How many subjects are you taking this year?*

EXAM | **36** [VN] to do an exam or a test: *When did you take your driving test?*

TRANSPORT/ROAD | **37** [VN] to use a form of transport, a road, a path, etc. to go to a place: *to take the bus/plane/train* ◊ *to take a cab* ◊ *Take the second road on the right.* ◊ *It's more interesting to take the coast road.*

GO OVER/AROUND | **38** [VN] to go over or around sth: *The horse took the first fence well.* ◊ *He takes bends much too fast.*

IN FOOTBALL | **39** [VN] (of a person playing football, etc.) to kick or throw the ball from a fixed or agreed position: *to take a penalty/free kick/corner*

VOTE/SURVEY | **40** [VN] to use a particular method to find out people's opinions: *to take a vote/poll/survey*

BE SUCCESSFUL | **41** [V] to be successful; to work: *The skin graft failed to take.*

GRAMMAR | **42** [VN] (not used in the progressive tenses) of verbs, nouns, etc.) to have or require sth when used in a sentence or other structure: *The verb 'rely' takes the preposition 'on'.*

IDM Most idioms containing **take** are at the entries for the nouns and adjectives in the idioms, for example **take the biscuit** is at biscuit.   **I/you, etc. can't take sb 'anywhere** (*informal*, often *humorous*) used to say that you cannot trust sb to behave well in public: *You haven't spilled your coffee again! I can't take you anywhere!* **have (got) what it 'takes** (*informal*) to have the qualities, ability, etc. needed to be successful **take sth as it 'comes** | **take sb as they 'come** to accept sth/sb without wishing it/them to be different or without thinking about it/them very much in advance: *She takes life as it comes.* **'take it (that...)** to suppose; to ASSUME: *I take it you won't be coming to the party?* **take it from 'me (that...)** (*informal*) used to emphasize that what you are going to say is the truth: *Take it from me—he'll be a millionaire before he's 30.* **take it on/upon yourself to do sth** to decide to do sth without asking permission or advice **take it or 'leave it** used to say that you do not care if sb accepts or rejects your offer **take it/a lot 'out of sb** to make sb physically or mentally tired: *Taking care of small children takes it out of you.* **take some/a lot of 'doing** (*informal*) to need a lot of effort or time; to be very difficult to do

PHRV ,**take sb a'back** [usually passive] to shock or surprise sb very much

,**take 'after sb** [no passive] **1** (not used in the progressive tenses) to look or behave like an older member of your family, especially your mother or father: *Your daughter doesn't take after you at all.* **2** (*AmE, informal*) to follow sb quickly: *I was afraid that if I started running the man would take after me.*

,**take a'gainst sb/sth** [no passive] (*old-fashioned, BrE*) to start not liking sb/sth for no clear reason

,**take sb/sth ↔ a'part** (*informal*) **1** to defeat sb easily in a game or competition: *We were simply taken apart by the other team.* **2** to criticize sb/sth severely: *In his speech he took the opposition apart.* ,**take sth ↔ a'part** to separate a machine or piece of equipment into the different parts that it is made of **SYN** DISMANTLE

,**take sth ↔ a'way 1** to make a feeling, pain, etc. disappear: *I was given some pills to take away the pain.* **2** (*BrE*) (*AmE* ,**take sth ↔ 'out**) to buy cooked food at a restaurant and carry it away to eat, for example at home: *Two burgers to take away, please.*—related noun TAKEAWAY, TAKEOUT ,**take a'way from sth** [no passive] to make the effort or value of sth seem less: *I don't want to take away*

from his achievements, but he couldn't have done it without my help.

,**take sb ↔ 'back** to allow sb, such as your husband, wife or partner, to come home after they have left because of a problem ,**take sb 'back (to ...)** to make sb remember sth: *The smell of the sea took him back to his childhood.* ◊ *That song takes me back 30 years.* ,**take sth ↔ 'back 1** if you **take sth back** to a shop/store, or a shop/store **takes sth back**, you return sth that you have bought there, for example because it is the wrong size or does not work **2** to admit that sth you said was wrong or that you should not have said it: *OK, I take it all back!*

,**take sth ↔ 'down 1** to remove a structure, especially by separating it into pieces: *to take down a tent/fence* ◊ *Workmen arrived to take down the scaffolding.* **2** to pull down a piece of clothing worn below the waist without completely removing it: *to take down your trousers/pants* **3** to write sth down: *Reporters took down every word of his speech.*

,**take sb ↔ 'in 1** to allow sb to stay in your home: *to take in lodgers* ◊ *He was homeless, so we took him in.* **2** [often passive] to make sb believe sth that is not true **SYN** DECEIVE: *She took me in completely with her story.* ◊ *Don't be taken in by his charm—he's ruthless.* ,**take sth ↔ 'in 1** to absorb sth into the body, for example by breathing or swallowing: *Fish take in oxygen through their gills.*—related noun INTAKE **2** to make a piece of clothing narrower or tighter: *This dress needs to be taken in at the waist.* **OPP** LET OUT **3** [no passive] to include or cover sth: *The tour takes in six European capitals.* **4** [no passive] to go to see or visit sth such as a film/movie: *I generally take in a show when I'm in New York on business.* **5** to take notice of sth with your eyes: *He took in every detail of her appearance.* ◊ *She took in the scene at a glance.* **6** to understand or remember sth that you hear or read: *Halfway through the chapter I realized I hadn't taken anything in.*

,**take 'off 1** (of an aircraft, etc.) to leave the ground and begin to fly: *The plane took off an hour late.*—related noun TAKE-OFF **OPP** LAND **2** (*informal*) to leave a place, especially in a hurry: *When he saw me coming he took off in the opposite direction.* **3** (of an idea, a product, etc.) to become successful or popular very quickly or suddenly: *The new magazine has really taken off.* ◊ *Her singing career took off after her TV appearance.* ,**take sb ↔ 'off 1** to copy sb's voice, actions or manner in an amusing way **2** (in sports, entertainment, etc.) to make sb stop playing, acting, etc. and leave the field or the stage: *He was taken off after twenty minutes.* ,**take sth ↔ 'off 1** to remove sth, especially a piece of clothing from your/sb's body: *to take off your coat/hat/skirt/glasses* ◊ *He took off my wet boots and made me sit by the fire.* **OPP** PUT ON **2** to have a period of time as a break from work: *I've decided to take a few days off next week.* **3** [often passive] to stop a public service, television programme, performances of a show, etc: *The show was taken off because of poor audience figures.* **4** to remove some of sb's hair, part of sb's body, etc: *The hairdresser asked me how much she should take off.* ◊ *The explosion nearly took his arm off.* ,**take yourself/sb 'off (to ...)** (*informal*) to leave a place; to make sb leave a place **take sb off sth** [often passive] to remove sb from sth such as a job, position, piece of equipment, etc: *The officer leading the investigation has been taken off the case.* ◊ *After three days she was taken off the ventilator.* ,**take sth 'off sth 1** to remove an amount of money or a number of marks, points, etc. in order to reduce the total: *The manager took $10 off the bill.* ◊ *That experience took ten years off my life* (= made me feel ten years older). **2** [often passive] to stop sth from being sold: *Doctors recommended that the slimming pills should be taken off the market.*

,**take sb ↔ 'on 1** to employ sb: *to take on new staff* ◊ *She was taken on as a trainee.* ⇨ note at EMPLOY **2** [no passive] to play against sb in a game or contest; to fight against sb: *to take somebody on at snooker/tennis/chess* ◊ *The rebels took on the entire Roman army.* ,**take sth ↔ 'on** [no passive] to begin to have a particular quality, appearance, etc: *The chameleon can take on the colours of its*

æ	ɑː	e	ɜː	ə	ɪ	iː	i	ɒ	ɔː	ʌ	ʊ	u	uː
cat	father	ten	bird	about	sit	see	many	got	saw	cup	put	actual	too
								(BrE)					

background. ◊ *His voice took on a more serious tone.* **,take sth/sb↔'on 1** to decide to do sth; to agree to be responsible for sb/sth: *I can't take on any extra work.* ◊ *We're not taking on any new clients at present.* **2** (of a bus, plane or ship) to allow sb/sth to enter: *The bus stopped to take on more passengers.* ◊ *The ship took on more fuel at Freetown.* **,take sb↔'out** to go to a restaurant, theatre, club, etc. with sb you have invited **,take sb/sth↔'out** (*informal*) to kill sb or destroy sth: *They took out two enemy bombers.* **,take sth↔'out 1** to remove sth from inside sb's body, especially a part of it: *How many teeth did the dentist take out?* **2** to obtain an official document or service: *to take out an insurance policy/a mortgage/a loan* ◊ *to take out an ad in a newspaper* **3** (*AmE*) = TAKE STH AWAY (2) **,take sth↔'out (against sb)** to start legal action against sb by means of an official document: *The police have taken out a summons against the driver of the car.* **,take sth↔'out (of sth)** to obtain money by removing it from your bank account **,take sth 'out of sth** to remove an amount of money from a larger amount, especially as a payment: *The fine will be taken out of your wages.* **,take it/sth 'out on sb** to behave in an unpleasant way towards sb because you feel angry, disappointed, etc., although it is not their fault: *OK, so you had a bad day. Don't take it out on me.* ◊ *She tended to take her frustrations out on her family.* **,take sb 'out of themselves** to make sb forget their worries and become less concerned with their own thoughts and situation

,take 'over (from sth) to become bigger or more important than sth else; to replace sth: *Try not to let negative thoughts take over.* ◊ *It has been suggested that mammals took over from dinosaurs 65 million years ago.* **,take 'over (from sb)|,take sth↔'over (from sb) 1** to begin to have control of or responsibility for sth, especially in place of sb else **2** to gain control of a political party, a country, etc: *The army is threatening to take over if civil unrest continues.* **,take sth↔'over** to gain control of a business, a company, etc., especially by buying shares: *CBS Records was taken over by Sony.*—related noun TAKEOVER **,take sb 'through sth** to help sb learn or become familiar with sth, for example by reading or talking about each part in turn: *The director took us through the play scene by scene.*

'take to sth [no passive] **1** to go away to a place, especially to escape from danger: *The rebels took to the hills.* **2** to begin to do sth as a habit: [+ -ing] *I've taken to waking up very early.* **3** to develop an ability for sth: *She took to tennis as if she'd been playing all her life.* **'take to sb/sth** [no passive] to start liking sb/sth: *I took to my new boss immediately.* ◊ *He hasn't taken to his new school.* **,take 'up** to continue, especially starting after sb/sth else has finished: *The band's new album takes up where their last one left off.* **,take 'up sth** to fill or use an amount of space or time: *The table takes up too much room.* ◊ *I won't take up any more of your time.* ◊ *Her time is fully taken up with writing.* **,take sth↔'up 1** to make sth such as a piece of clothing shorter: *This skirt needs taking up.* OPP LET DOWN **2** to learn or start to do sth, especially for pleasure: *They've taken up golf.* ◊ *She has taken up (= started to learn to play) the oboe.* **3** to start or begin sth such as a job: *He takes up his duties next week.* **4** to join in singing or saying sth: *to take up the chorus/song/cry* ◊ *Their protests were later taken up by other groups.* **5** to continue sth that sb else has not finished, or that has not been mentioned for some time: *She took up the story where Tim had left off.* ◊ *I'd like to take up the point you raised earlier.* **6** to move into a particular position: *I took up my position by the door.* **7** to accept sth that is offered or available: *to take up a challenge* ◊ *She took up his offer of a drink.* **,take 'up with sb** (*informal*) to begin to be friendly with sb, especially sb with a bad reputation **,take sb 'up on sth 1** to question sb about sth, because you do not agree with them: *I must take you up on that point.* **2** (*informal*) to accept an offer, a bet, etc. from sb: *Thanks for the invitation—we'll take you up on it some time.* **,take sth 'up with sb** to speak or write to sb about sth that they may be able to deal with or help you with: *They decided to take the matter up with their MP.* **be**

,taken 'up with sth/sb to be giving all your time and energy to sth/sb: *She's completely taken up with preparing for her exams.* **be 'taken with sb/sth** to find sb/sth attractive or interesting: *We were all very taken with his girlfriend.* ◊ *I think he's quite taken with the idea.*

■ **noun 1** a scene or part of a film/movie that is filmed at one time without stopping the camera: *We managed to get it right in just two takes.* **2** [usually sing.] (*informal*) an amount of money that sb receives, especially the money that is earned by a business during a particular period of time SYN TAKINGS: *How much is my share of the take?* **3 ~ on sth** (*informal*) the particular opinion or idea that sb has about sth: *What's his take on the plan?* ◊ *Branagh's new take on the Romeo and Juliet story* (= his way of presenting it)—see also DOUBLE TAKE IDM **be on the 'take** (*informal*) to accept money from sb for helping them in a dishonest or illegal way

take·away /'teɪkəweɪ/ (*BrE*) (*AmE* **'take-out**) (also **'carry-out** *AmE, ScotE*) *noun* **1** a restaurant that cooks and sells food that you take away and eat somewhere else: *We can get something to eat from the Chinese takeaway.* **2** a meal that you buy at this type of restaurant: *Let's have a takeaway tonight.*

'take-home pay *noun* [U] the amount of money that you earn after you have paid tax, etc.

'take-off *noun* **1** [U, C] the moment at which an aircraft leaves the ground and starts to fly: *The plane is ready for take-off.* ◊ *take-off speed* ◊ (*figurative*) *The local economy is poised for take-off.* OPP LANDING **2** [C, U] the moment when your feet leave the ground when you jump **3** [C] if you do a take-off of sb, you copy the way they speak or behave, in a humorous way to entertain people

take·over /'teɪkəʊvə(r); *AmE* -oʊ-/ *noun* [C, U] **1** an act of taking control of a company by buying most of its shares: *They made a takeover bid for the company.* **2** an act of taking control of a country, an area or a political organization by force: *a military takeover of the government*

taker /'teɪkə(r)/ *noun* **1** [usually pl.] a person who is willing to accept sth that is being offered: *They won't find many takers for the house at that price.* **2** (often in compounds) a person who takes sth: *drug/hostage/risk takers* ◊ *It is better to be a giver than a taker.*

'take-up *noun* [U, sing.] the rate at which people accept sth that is offered or made available to them: *a high/low take-up of government benefits*

tak·ings /'teɪkɪŋz/ *noun* [pl.] the amount of money that a shop/store, theatre, etc. receives from selling goods or tickets over a particular period of time: *The box office takings are up on last week.*

tal·cum pow·der /'tælkəm paʊdə(r)/ (also *informal* **talc** /tælk/) *noun* [U] a fine soft powder, usually with a pleasant smell, that you put on your skin to make it feel smooth and dry

tale /teɪl/ *noun* **1** an imaginative story, especially one that is full of action and adventure: *Dickens' 'A Tale of Two Cities'* ◊ *a fairy/moral/romantic tale*—see also FOLK TALE **2** an exciting spoken description of an event, which may not be completely true: *I love listening to his tales of life at sea.* ◊ *I've heard tales of people seeing ghosts in that house.* ◊ *The team's tale of woe continued on Saturday* (= they lost another match). ◊ *Her experiences provide a cautionary tale* (= a warning) *for us all.*—see also TELL-TALE IDM see OLD, TELL

tal·ent /'tælənt/ *noun* **1** [C, U] **~ (for sth)** a natural ability to do sth well: *to have great artistic talent* ◊ *a man/ woman of many talents* ◊ *She showed considerable talent for getting what she wanted.* ◊ *a talent competition/ contest/show* (= in which people perform, to show how well they can sing, dance, etc.) **2** [U, C] people or a person with a natural ability to do sth well: *There is a wealth of young talent in British theatre.* ◊ *He is a great talent.* **3** [U] (*BrE, slang*) people who are sexually attractive: *He likes to spend his time chatting up the local talent.*

tal·ent·ed /'tæləntɪd/ *adj.* having a natural ability to do sth well: *talented players/artists/youngsters*

aɪ	aʊ	eɪ	əʊ	oʊ	ɔɪ	ɪə	eə	ʊə	j	w
my	now	say	go	go	boy	near	hair	pure	yes	wet
			(BrE)	(AmE)						

'talent scout (also **scout**, **'talent spotter**) *noun* a person whose job is to find people who are good at singing, acting, sport, etc. in order to give them work

tal·is·man /'tælɪzmən/ *noun* an object that is thought to have magic powers and to bring good luck

talk /tɔːk/ *verb*, *noun*

■ *verb*

SPEAK TO SB | **1** ~ **(to/with sb) (about sb/sth)** | ~ **of/on sth** to say things; to speak in order to give information or to express feelings, ideas, etc: [V] *Stop talking and listen!* ◇ *We talked on the phone for over an hour.* ◇ *Who were you talking to just now?* ◇ *We looked around the school and talked with the principal.* ◇ *Ann and Joe aren't talking to each other right now* (= they refuse to speak to each other because they have argued). ◇ *When they get together, all they talk about is football.* ◇ *What are you talking about?* (= used when you are surprised, annoyed and/or worried by sth that sb has just said) ◇ *Mary is talking of looking for another job.* ◇ [VN-ADJ] *We talked ourselves hoarse, catching up on all the news.* ⇨ note at SPEAK

DISCUSS | **2** ~ **(to/with sb) (about sth)** to discuss sth, usually sth serious or important: [V] *This situation can't go on. We need to talk.* ◇ *The two sides in the dispute say they are ready to talk.* ◇ *Talk to your doctor if you're still worried.* ◇ [VN] *to talk business/politics*

SAY WORDS | **3** to say words in a language: [V] *The baby is just starting to talk.* ◇ *We couldn't understand them because they were talking in Chinese.* ◇ [VN] *Are they talking Swedish or Danish?*

SENSE/NONSENSE | **4** [VN] to say things that are/are not sensible: *She talks a lot of sense.* ◇ *(BrE) You're talking rubbish!* ◇ *See if you can talk some sense into him* (= persuade him to be sensible).

FOR EMPHASIS | **5** [VN] **(be talking sth)** *(informal)* used to emphasize an amount of money, how serious sth is, etc: *We're talking £500 for three hours' work.*

ABOUT PRIVATE LIFE | **6** [V] to talk about a person's private life SYN GOSSIP: *Don't phone me at work—people will talk.*

GIVE INFORMATION | **7** [V] to give information to sb, especially unwillingly: *The police questioned him but he refused to talk.*

IDM **look who's 'talking** | **'you can/can't talk** | **you're a 'fine one to talk** *(spoken)* used to tell sb that they should not criticize sb else for sth because they do the same things too: *'George is so careless with money.' 'Look who's talking!'* **now you're 'talking** *(spoken)* used when you like what sb has suggested very much **'talk about . . .** *(spoken)* used to emphasize sth: *Talk about mean! She didn't even buy me a card.* **talk 'dirty** *(informal)* to talk to sb about sex in order to make them sexually excited **talk the hind leg off a 'donkey** *(informal)* to talk too much, especially about boring or unimportant things **talking of sb/sth** *(spoken, especially BrE)* used when you are going to say more about a subject that has already been mentioned: *Talking of Sue, I met her new boyfriend last week.* **talk 'shop** *(usually disapproving)* to talk about your work with the people you work with, especially when you are also with other people who are not connected with or interested in it **talk through your 'hat** *(old-fashioned, informal)* to say silly things while you are talking about a subject you do not understand **talk 'tough (on sth)** *(informal, especially AmE)* to tell people very strongly what you want **talk 'turkey** *(informal, especially AmE)* to talk about sth seriously **talk your way out of sth/of doing sth** to make excuses and give reasons for not doing sth; to manage to get yourself out of a difficult situation: *I managed to talk my way out of having to give a speech.* ◇ *His wife's found out about everything! I'd like to see him talk his way out of this one!* **you can/can't talk** *(spoken)* = LOOK WHO'S TALKING **you're a 'fine one to talk** *(spoken)* = LOOK WHO'S TALKING—more at DEVIL, KNOW *v.*, LANGUAGE, MONEY, SENSE *n.*, TURN *n.*

PHRV **talk a'round/'round sth** to talk about sth in a general way without dealing with the most important parts of it **'talk at sb** to speak to sb without listening to what they say in reply **talk 'back (to sb)** to answer sb rudely, especially sb in authority—related noun BACK TALK **talk sb/sth↔'down** to help a pilot of a plane to land by giving instructions from the ground **talk sth↔'down** to make sth seem less important or successful than it really is: *You shouldn't talk down your own achievements.* **talk 'down to sb** to speak to sb as if they were less important or intelligent than you **talk sb 'into/ 'out of sth** to persuade sb to do/not to do sth: *I didn't want to move abroad but Bill talked me into it.* ◇ [+-ing] *She tried to talk him out of leaving.* **talk sth↔'out** to discuss sth thoroughly in order to make a decision, solve a problem, etc. **talk sth↔'over (with sb)** to discuss sth thoroughly, especially in order to reach an agreement or make a decision: *You'll find it helpful to talk things over with a friend.* **talk sb 'round (to sth)** *(BrE)* to persuade sb to accept sth or agree to sth: *We finally managed to talk them round to our way of thinking.* **talk sth↔'through** to discuss sth thoroughly until you are sure you understand it **talk sb/sth 'up** to describe sb/sth in a way that makes them sound better than they really are

■ *noun*

CONVERSATION | **1** [C] ~ **(with sb) (about sth)** a conversation or discussion: *I had a long talk with my boss about my career prospects.* ◇ *We need to have a serious talk about money matters.*

FORMAL DISCUSSIONS | **2 (talks)** [pl.] formal discussions between governments or organizations: *arms/pay/peace talks* ◇ *to hold talks*

SPEECH | **3** [C] ~ **(on sth)** a speech or LECTURE on a particular subject: *She gave an interesting talk on her visit to China.*

WORDS WITHOUT ACTIONS | **4** [U] *(informal)* words that are spoken, but without the necessary facts or actions to support them: *It's just talk. He'd never carry out his threats.* ◇ *Don't pay any attention to her—she's all talk.*

STORIES/RUMOURS | **5** [U] ~ **(of sth/of doing sth)** | ~ **(that . . .)** stories that suggest a particular thing might happen in the future: *There was talk in Washington of sending in troops.*

TOPIC/WAY OF SPEAKING | **6** [U] *(often in compounds)* a topic of conversation or a way of speaking: *girl/sales talk* ◇ *It was tough talk, coming from a man who had begun the year in a hospital bed.*—see also SMALL TALK, SWEET TALK

IDM **the talk of sth** the person or thing that everyone is talking about in a particular place: *Overnight, she became the talk of the town* (= very famous).—more at FIGHT *v.*

talka·tive /'tɔːkətɪv/ *adj.* liking to talk a lot: *He's not very talkative, except on the subject of his plants.* ◇ *She was in a talkative mood.*

talk·er /'tɔːkə(r)/ *noun* a person who talks in a particular way or who talks a lot: *a brilliant/persuasive/good talker* ◇ *She's a (great) talker* (= she talks a lot). ◇ *He's more a talker than a doer* (= he talks instead of doing things). IDM see FAST *adj.*

talkie /'tɔːki/ *noun* [usually pl.] *(old-fashioned, especially AmE)* a film/movie that has sounds and not just pictures—see also WALKIE-TALKIE

'talking point *noun* **1** *(BrE)* a subject that is talked about or discussed by many people: *The judge's decision became a legal talking point.* **2** *(AmE)* an item that sb will speak about at a meeting, often one that supports a particular argument

'talking-to *noun* [sing.] *(informal)* a serious talk with sb who has done sth wrong: *to give sb a good talking-to*

'talk show *noun (especially AmE)* = CHAT SHOW: *a talk-show host*

tall /tɔːl/ *adj.* **(tall·er, tall·est) 1** (of a person, building, tree, etc.) having a greater than average height: *She's tall and thin with light brown hair.* ◇ *tall chimneys/towers* ◇ *the tallest building in the world* ◇ *a tall glass of iced tea* OPP SHORT **2** used to describe or ask about the height of sb/sth: *How tall are you?* ◇ *He's six feet tall and weighs 200 pounds.* ⇨ note at HIGH ▶ **tall·ness** *noun* [U] IDM **stand 'tall** *(especially AmE)* to show that you are proud and able to deal with anything **be a ,tall 'order** *(informal)* to be very difficult to do—more at WALK *v.*

b	d	f	g	h	k	l	m	n	p	r
bad	did	fall	get	hat	cat	leg	man	now	pen	red

tall·boy /'tɔːlbɔɪ/ (*BrE*) (*AmE* **high·boy**) *noun* a tall piece of furniture with drawers, used for storing clothes in

tal·low /'tæləʊ; *AmE* -loʊ/ *noun* [U] animal fat used for making candles, soap, etc.

tall 'story (*especially BrE*) (*AmE usually* **tall 'tale**) *noun* a story that is difficult to believe because what it describes seems exaggerated and not likely to be true

tally /'tæli/ *noun, verb*
■ *noun* (*pl.* **-ies**) a record of the number or amount of sth, especially one that you can keep adding to: *He hopes to improve on his tally of three goals in the past nine games.* ◊ *Keep a tally of how much you spend while you're away.*
■ *verb* (**tal·lies, tally·ing, tal·lied, tal·lied**) **1** [V] ~ (**with sth**) to be the same as or to match another person's account of sth, another set of figures, etc. **SYN** MATCH UP: *Her report of what happened tallied exactly with the story of another witness.* **2** [VN] ~ **sth** (**up**) to calculate the total number, cost, etc. of sth

Tal·mud /'tælmʊd; *AmE* also 'tɑːl-/ (**the Talmud**) *noun* [sing.] a collection of ancient writings on Jewish law and traditions ▶ **Tal·mud·ic** /ˌtælˈmʊdɪk; *AmE* also ˌtɑːl-/ *adj.*

talon /'tælən/ *noun* a long sharp curved nail on the feet of some birds, especially BIRDS OF PREY (= birds that kill other creatures for food)—picture on page A6

tam·ar·ind /'tæmərɪnd/ *noun* a tropical tree that produces fruit, also called **tamarinds**, that are often preserved and used in Asian cooking

tam·bour·ine /ˌtæmbə'riːn/ *noun* a musical instrument that has a circular wooden frame covered with plastic or skin, with metal discs around the edge. To play it you shake it or hit it with your hand.—picture on page 841

tame /teɪm/ *adj., verb*
■ *adj.* (**tamer, tam·est**) **1** (of animals, birds, etc.) not afraid of people, and used to living with them **OPP** WILD **2** (*informal*) not interesting or exciting: *You'll find life here pretty tame after New York.* **3** (*informal*) (of a person) willing to do what other people ask: *I have a tame doctor who'll always give me a sick note when I want a day off.* ▶ **tame·ly** *adv.* **tame·ness** *noun* [U]
■ *verb* [VN] to make sth tame or easy to control: *Lions can never be completely tamed.* ◊ *She made strenuous efforts to tame her anger.*

tamer /'teɪmə(r)/ *noun* (usually in compounds) a person who trains wild animals: *a lion-tamer*

Tamil /'tæmɪl/ *noun* **1** [C] a member of a race of people living in parts of S India and Sri Lanka **2** [U] the language of the Tamils ▶ **Tamil** *adj.*

tamp /tæmp/ *verb* [VN] ~ **sth** (**down**) to press sth down firmly, especially into a closed space: *He tamped down the tobacco in his pipe with his thumb.*

tam·per /'tæmpə(r)/ *verb* **PHRV** 'tamper with sth to make changes to sth without permission, especially in order to damage it: *Someone had obviously tampered with the brakes of my car.*

tam·pon /'tæmpɒn; *AmE* -pɑːn/ *noun* a specially shaped piece of cotton material that a woman puts inside her VAGINA to absorb blood during her PERIOD—compare SANITARY TOWEL

tan /tæn/ *verb, noun, adj., abbr.*
■ *verb* (**-nn-**) **1** if a person or their skin **tans** or is **tanned**, they become brown as a result of spending time in the sun: [V] *My skin tans really easily.* [also VN] **2** [VN] to make animal skin into leather by treating it with chemicals **IDM** see HIDE *n.*
■ *noun* **1** [U] a yellowish-brown colour **2** (also **sun·tan**) [C] the brown colour that sb with pale skin goes when they have been in the sun: *to get a tan* ◊ *My tan's fading already.*
■ *adj.* yellowish brown in colour
■ *abbr.* (*mathematics*) TANGENT

tan·dem /'tændəm/ *noun* a bicycle for two riders, one behind the other **IDM** in 'tandem (with sb/sth) a thing that works or happens in tandem with sth else works together with it or happens at the same time as it

tan·doori /tæn'dʊəri; *AmE* -'dʊri/ *noun* [U] (often used as an adjective) an Indian method of cooking meat on a

metal rod (called a SPIT) in a clay oven: *tandoori chicken* ◊ *a tandoori restaurant*

tang /tæŋ/ *noun* [usually sing.] a strong sharp taste or smell: *the tang of lemons* ▶ **tangy** /'tæŋi/ *adj.*: *a refreshing tangy lemon flavour* ◊ *She breathed in the crisp, tangy air and realized that it was almost autumn.*

tan·gent /'tændʒənt/ *noun* **1** (*geometry*) a straight line that touches the outside of a curve but does not cross it—picture at CIRCLE **2** (*abbr.* **tan**) (*mathematics*) the RATIO of the length of the side opposite an angle in a RIGHT-ANGLED triangle to the length of the side next to it—compare COSINE, SINE **IDM** fly/go off at a 'tangent (*BrE*) (*AmE* go off on a 'tangent) (*informal*) to suddenly start saying or doing sth that does not seem to be connected to what has gone before

tan·gen·tial /tæn'dʒenʃl/ *adj.* **1** (*formal*) having only a slight or indirect connection with sth: *a tangential argument* **2** (*geometry*) of or along a tangent ▶ **tan·gen·tial·ly** *adv.*

tan·ger·ine /ˌtændʒə'riːn; *AmE* 'tændʒəriːn/ *noun* **1** [C] a type of small sweet orange with loose skin that comes off easily **2** [U] a deep orange-yellow colour ▶ **tan·ger·ine** *adj.*: *a tangerine evening gown*

tan·gible /'tændʒəbl/ *adj.* **1** [usually before noun] that can be clearly seen to exist: *tangible benefits/improvements/results* ◊ *We cannot accept his findings without tangible evidence.* ◊ *tangible assets* (= a company's buildings, machinery, etc.) **2** that you can touch and feel: *The tension between them was almost tangible.* ◊ (*formal*) *the tangible world* **OPP** INTANGIBLE ▶ **tan·gibly** /'tændʒəbli/ *adv.*

tan·gle /'tæŋgl/ *noun, verb*
■ *noun* **1** a twisted mass of threads, hair, etc. that cannot be easily separated: *a tangle of branches* ◊ *Her hair was a mass of tangles.* **2** a state of confusion or disorder: *His financial affairs are in a tangle.* **3** (*informal*) a disagreement or fight
■ *verb* ~ (**sth**) **up** to twist sth into an untidy mass; to become twisted in this way: [VN] *She had tangled up the sheets on the bed as she lay tossing and turning.* [also V] **PHRV** 'tangle with sb/sth to become involved in an argument or a fight with sb/sth: *Last time I tangled with him, he won!*

tan·gled /'tæŋgld/ *adj.* **1** twisted together in an untidy way: *tangled hair/bed clothes* **2** complicated, and not easy to understand: *tangled financial affairs*

tango /'tæŋgəʊ; *AmE* -goʊ/ *noun, verb*
■ *noun* (*pl.* **-os** /-gəʊz; *AmE* -goʊz/) a fast S American dance with a strong beat, in which two people hold each other closely; a piece of music for this dance
■ *verb* (**tango·ing, tan·goed, tan·goed**) [V] to dance the tango

tank /tæŋk/ *noun* **1** a large container for holding liquid or gas: *a hot water tank* ◊ *a fuel/petrol/fish tank*—see also SEPTIC TANK, THINK TANK—picture at SNORKELLING **2** (also **tank·ful** /-fʊl/) the contents of a tank or the amount it will hold: *We drove there and back on one tank of petrol.* **3** a military vehicle covered with strong metal and armed with guns. It can travel over very rough ground using wheels that move inside metal belts.

tank·ard /'tæŋkəd; *AmE* -ərd/ *noun* a large, usually metal, cup with a handle, that is used for drinking beer from

tanked 'up (*BrE*) (*AmE* **tanked**) *adj.* (*informal*) very drunk

tank·er /'tæŋkə(r)/ *noun* a ship or lorry/truck that carries oil, gas or petrol/gas in large quantities: *an oil tanker* ◊ *a tanker driver*—see also SUPERTANKER

'tank top *noun* **1** (*BrE*) a sweater without sleeves **2** (*AmE*) a piece of clothing like a T-SHIRT without sleeves

tanned /tænd/ (also **sun·tanned**) *adj.* having a brown skin colour as a result of being in the sun: *He had a tanned face and clear eyes.*

tan·ner /'tænə(r)/ *noun* a person whose job is to TAN animal skins to make leather

tan·nery /'tænəri/ *noun* (*pl.* **-ies**) a place where animal skins are TANNED and made into leather

s	t	v	z	ʃ	ʒ	tʃ	dʒ	θ	ð	ŋ
see	tea	van	zoo	shoe	vision	chain	jam	thin	this	sing

tan·nin /'tænɪn/ *noun* [U] a yellowish or brownish substance found in the bark of some trees and the fruit of many plants, used especially in making leather, ink and wine ▶ **tan·nic** /'tænɪk/ *adj.*

Tan·noy™ /'tænɔɪ/ *noun* (*BrE*) a system with LOUDSPEAKERS used for giving information in a public place: *to make an announcement over the Tannoy*

tan·tal·ize (*BrE* also **-ise**) /'tæntəlaɪz/ *verb* [VN] to make a person or an animal want sth that they cannot have or do ▶ **tan·tal·iz·ing, -is·ing** *adj.*: *The tantalizing aroma of fresh coffee wafted towards them.* ◇ *a tantalizing glimpse of the future* **tan·tal·iz·ing·ly, -is·ing·ly** *adv.*: *The branch was tantalizingly out of reach.*

tan·ta·mount /'tæntəmaʊnt/ *adj.* **~ to sth** (*written*) having the same bad effect as sth else: *If he resigned it would be tantamount to admitting that he was guilty.*

tan·trum /'tæntrəm/ *noun* a sudden short period of angry, unreasonable behaviour, especially in a child: *to have / throw a tantrum*

Taoi·seach /'tiːʃəx/ *noun* the Prime Minister of the Irish Republic

tap /tæp/ *verb, noun*

■ *verb* (**-pp-**) **1** to hit sb/sth quickly and lightly: [V] *Someone tapped at the door.* ◇ *He was busy tapping away at his computer.* ◇ [VN] *Ralph tapped me on the shoulder.* **2** if you **tap** your fingers, feet, etc. or they **tap**, you hit them gently against a table, the floor, etc., for example to the rhythm of music: [VN] *He kept tapping his fingers on the table.* ◇ [V] *The music set everyone's feet tapping.* **3 ~ (into) sth** to make use of a source of energy, knowledge, etc. that already exists: [VN] *We need to tap the expertise and skill of the people we already have.* ◇ [V] *The movie seems to tap into a general sentimentality about animals.* **4** [VN] (also **wire-tap** especially in *AmE*) to fit a device to a telephone so that sb's calls can be listened to secretly: *He was convinced his phone was being tapped.* **5** [VN] to cut into a tree in order to get liquid from it PHRV **tap sb for sth** (*BrE, informal*) to persuade sb to give you sth, especially money: *He tried to tap me for a loan.* ,**tap sth↩'in/ 'out** to put information, numbers, letters, etc. into a machine by pressing buttons: *Tap in your PIN number.* ,**tap sth↩'out** to hit a surface gently to the rhythm of music: *She tapped out the beat on the table.*

■ *noun* **1** (*especially BrE*) (*AmE* usually **fau·cet**) [C] a device for controlling the flow of liquid or gas from a pipe or container: *bath taps* ◇ *the hot / cold tap* (= the tap that hot / cold water comes out of) ◇ *a gas tap* ◇ *Turn the tap on / off.* ◇ *Don't leave the tap running.* ◇ *the sound of a dripping tap*—see also TAP WATER—picture at PLUG **2** [C] a light hit with your hand or fingers: *a tap at / on the door* ◇ *He felt a tap on his shoulder and turned round.* **3** [C] an act of fitting a device to a telephone so that sb's telephone calls can be listened to secretly: *a phone tap* **4** [U] = TAP-DANCING IDM **on 'tap 1** available to be used at any time: *We have this sort of information on tap.* **2** beer that is **on tap** is in a BARREL with a tap on it

'**tap dance** *noun* [U, C] a style of dancing in which you tap the rhythm of the music with your feet, wearing special shoes with pieces of metal on the heels and toes ▶ '**tap dancer** *noun* '**tap-dancing** (also **tap**) *noun* [U]

tape /teɪp/ *noun, verb*

■ *noun* **1** [U] a long narrow strip of MAGNETIC material that is used for recording sounds, pictures or information: *His albums are available on tape and CD.*—see also MAGNETIC TAPE, VIDEOTAPE **2** [C] a cassette that contains sounds, or sounds and pictures, that have been recorded: *a blank tape* (= a tape that has nothing recorded on it) ◇ *I lent her my Bob Marley tapes.* ◇ *Police seized various books and tapes.* **3** [U] a long narrow strip of material with a sticky substance on one side that is used for sticking things together: *adhesive / sticky tape*—see also INSULATING TAPE, MASKING TAPE, SCOTCH TAPE, SELLOTAPE **4** [C, U] a narrow strip of material that is used for tying things together or as a label: *The papers were in a pile, tied together with a tape.*—see also RED TAPE, TICKER TAPE **5** [C] a long narrow strip of material that is stretched across the place where a race will finish: *the finishing tape* **6** [C] = TAPE MEASURE

■ *verb* [VN] **1** to record sb/sth on MAGNETIC tape using a special machine: *Will you tape 'Friends' for me tonight?* ◇ *Private conversations between the two had been taped and sent to a newspaper.* ◇ *a taped announcement* **2 ~ sth (up)** to fasten sth by sticking or tying it with tape: *Put it in a box and tape it up securely.* **3** [+adv. / prep.] to stick sth onto sth else using sticky tape: *Someone had taped a message on the door.* **4** (*AmE*) **~ sth (up)** to tie a BANDAGE firmly around an injury or a wound: *That's a nasty cut—come on, we'll get it all taped up.* IDM **have (got) sb/sth 'taped** (*BrE, informal*) to understand sb/sth completely and to have learned how to deal with them/it successfully: *He can't fool me—I've got him taped.*

'**tape measure** (also **tape**, '**measuring tape**) *noun* a long narrow strip of plastic, fabric or FLEXIBLE metal that has measurements marked on it and is used for measuring the length of sth—picture at SEW

taper /'teɪpə(r)/ *verb, noun*

■ *verb* to become gradually narrower; to make sth become gradually narrower: [V] *The tail tapered to a rounded tip.* ◇ [VN] *The pots are wide at the base and tapered at the top.* PHRV ,**taper 'off** to become gradually less in number, amount, degree, etc: *The number of applicants for teaching posts has tapered off.* ,**taper sth↩'off** to make sth become gradually less in number, amount, degree, etc: *They are gradually tapering off production of the older models.*

■ *noun* **1** a long thin piece of wood, paper, etc. that is used for lighting fires or lamps **2** a long thin candle **3** [usually sing.] the way that sth gradually decreases in shape or size

'**tape-record** *verb* [VN] to record sth on tape: *a tape-recorded interview*

'**tape recorder** *noun* a machine that is used for recording and playing sounds on tape

'**tape recording** *noun* something that has been recorded on tape: *a tape recording of the interview*

tap·es·try /'tæpəstri/ *noun* [C, U] (*pl.* **-ies**) a picture or pattern that is made by weaving coloured wool on to heavy fabric; the art of doing this: *medieval tapestries* ◇ *tapestry cushions* ◇ *crafts such as embroidery and tapestry* ▶ **tap·es·tried** *adj.*: *tapestried walls*

tape·worm /'teɪpwɜːm; *AmE* -wɜːrm/ *noun* a long flat worm that lives in the INTESTINES of humans and animals

tapi·oca /ˌtæpi'əʊkə; *AmE* -'oʊkə/ *noun* [U] hard white grains obtained from the CASSAVA plant, often cooked with milk to make a DESSERT (= a sweet dish)

tapir /'teɪpə(r)/ *noun* an animal like a pig with a long nose, that lives in Central and S America and SE Asia

tap·root /'tæpruːt/ *noun* the main root of a plant that grows straight downwards and produces smaller side roots

'**tap water** *noun* [U] water supplied through pipes to taps/faucets in a building: *Is the tap water safe to drink?*

tar /tɑː(r)/ *noun, verb*

■ *noun* [U] **1** a thick black sticky liquid that becomes hard when cold. Tar is obtained from coal and is used especially in making roads. **2** a substance similar to tar that is formed by burning tobacco: *low-tar cigarettes*

■ *verb* (**-rr-**) [VN] to cover sth with tar: *a tarred road / roof* IDM **tar and 'feather sb** to put tar on sb then cover them with feathers, as a punishment **be tarred with the same 'brush (as sb)** to be thought to have the same faults, etc. as sb else

tara·ma·sa·lata /ˌtærəməsə'lɑːtə/ *noun* [U] (*BrE*) a type of Greek food made from fish eggs, eaten on bread, etc.

ta·ran·tula /tə'ræntʃələ/ *noun* a large hairy spider that lives in hot countries. Some types of tarantula have a poisonous bite.

tardy /'tɑːdi; *AmE* 'tɑːrdi/ *adj.* **~ (in doing sth)** (*formal*) slow to act, move or happen; late in happening or arriving: *The law is often tardy in reacting to changing attitudes.* ◇ *people who are tardy in paying their bills* ◇ (*AmE*) *to be tardy for school* ▶ **tar·dily** /'tɑːdɪli; *AmE* 'tɑːrd-/ *adv.* **tar·di·ness** *noun* [U]

tar·get /'tɑːgɪt; *AmE* 'tɑːrgɪt/ *noun, verb*

T

æ	ɑː	e	ɜː	ə	ɪ	iː	i	ɒ	ɔː	ʌ	ʊ	u	uː
cat	father	ten	bird	about	sit	see	many	got	saw	cup	put	actual	too
								(BrE)					

T

■ *noun* **1** a result that you try to achieve: *business goals and targets* ◊ *attainment targets* ◊ *Set yourself targets that you can reasonably hope to achieve.* ◊ *to meet a target date of April 2001* ◊ *The university will reach its target of 5000 students next September.* ◊ *The new sports complex is on target to open in June.* ◊ *a target area/audience/company/group* (= the particular area, audience, etc. that a product, programme, etc. is aimed at) **2** ~ **(for sb/sth)** | ~ **(of sth)** an object, a person or a place that people aim at when attacking: *They bombed military and civilian targets.* ◊ *Doors and windows are an **easy target** for burglars.* ◊ *It's a **prime target** (= an obvious target) for terrorist attacks.* ◊ *(figurative)* He's become the target for a lot of criticism recently.* **3** an object that people practise shooting at, especially a round board with circles on it: *to aim at a target* ◊ *to hit/miss the target* ◊ *target practice*
■ *verb* (**tar·get·ing, tar·get·ed, tar·get·ed**) [VN] [usually passive] **1** to aim an attack or a criticism at sb/sth: *The missiles were mainly targeted at the United States.* ◊ *The company has been targeted by animal rights groups for its use of dogs in drugs trials.* **2** to try to have an effect on a particular group of people: *The campaign is clearly targeted on the young.* ◊ *a new magazine that targets single men*

tar·iff /'tærɪf/ *noun* **1** a tax that is paid on goods coming into or going out of a country **2** a list of fixed prices that are charged by a hotel or restaurant for rooms, meals, etc., or by a company for a particular service **3** (*law*) a level of punishment for sb who has been found guilty of a crime

Tar·mac™ /'tɑːmæk; *AmE* 'tɑːrmæk/ *noun* [U] **1** (also *less frequent* **tar·mac·adam** /ˌtɑːmə'kædəm; *AmE* ˌtɑːrm-/) (*AmE also* **black·top**) a black material used for making road surfaces, that consists of small stones mixed with TAR **2** (**the tarmac**) an area with a Tarmac surface, especially at an airport: *Three planes were standing on the tarmac, waiting to take off.*

tar·mac /'tɑːmæk; *AmE* 'tɑːrmæk/ *verb* (**-ck-**) [VN] (*AmE also* **blacktop**) to cover a surface with Tarmac: *tarmacked roads*

tarn /tɑːn; *AmE* tɑːrn/ *noun* a small lake among mountains

tar·nish /'tɑːnɪʃ; *AmE* 'tɑːrnɪʃ/ *verb, noun*
■ *verb* **1** if metal **tarnishes** or sth **tarnishes** it, it no longer looks bright and shiny: [V] *The mirrors had tarnished with age.* ◊ [VN] *The silver candlesticks were tarnished and dusty.* **2** [VN] to spoil the good opinion people have of sb/sth: *He hopes to improve the newspaper's somewhat tarnished public image.*
■ *noun* [sing., U] a thin layer on the surface of a metal that makes it look dull and not bright

tarot /'tærəʊ; *AmE* -roʊ/ *noun* [sing., U] a set of special cards with pictures on them, used for telling sb what will happen to them in the future

tar·paulin /tɑː'pɔːlɪn; *AmE* tɑːr'p-/ (also *AmE informal* **tarp**) *noun* [C, U] a large sheet made of heavy WATERPROOF material, used to cover things to keep rain off

tar·ra·gon /'tærəgən/ *noun* [U] a plant with leaves that have a strong taste and are used in cooking as a herb and to add flavour to VINEGAR

tarry /'tæri/ *verb* (**tar·ries, tarry·ing, tar·ried, tar·ried**) [V] (*old use* or *literary*) to stay in a place, especially when you ought to leave; to delay coming to or going from a place [SYN] LINGER

tart /tɑːt; *AmE* tɑːrt/ *noun, adj., verb*
■ *noun* **1** [C, U] an open pie filled with sweet food such as fruit: *a strawberry tart*—compare FLAN, QUICHE—picture on page A1 **2** [C] (*BrE, informal, disapproving*) a woman who you think behaves or dresses in a way that is immoral and is intended to make men sexually excited **3** [C] (*slang*) a prostitute
■ *adj.* **1** having an unpleasant sour taste: *tart apples* **2** [usually before noun] (of remarks, etc.) quick and unkind: *a tart reply/comment* ▶ **tart·ly** *adv.*: *'Too late!' said my mother tartly.* **tart·ness** *noun* [U]
■ *verb* PHRV ˌtart yourself 'up (*BrE, informal*) (especially of a woman) to make yourself more attractive by putting

on nice clothes, jewellery, make-up, etc. ˌtart sth↔'up (*BrE, informal*) to decorate or improve the appearance of sth, often in a way that other people do not think is attractive

tar·tan /'tɑːtn; *AmE* 'tɑːrtn/ *noun* **1** [U, C] a pattern of squares and lines of different colours and widths that cross each other at an angle of 90°, used especially on fabric, and originally from Scotland: *a tartan shirt/kilt/rug* **2** [C] a tartan pattern connected with a particular group of families (= a CLAN) in Scotland: *the MacLeod tartan* **3** [U] fabric, especially of wool, that is woven with a tartan pattern—compare PLAID—picture on page A5

tar·tar /'tɑːtə(r); *AmE* 'tɑːrt-/ *noun* **1** [U] a hard substance that forms on teeth **2** [C] (*old-fashioned*) a person in a position of authority who has a very bad temper

tar·tare sauce /ˌtɑːtə(r) 'sɔːs; *AmE* ˌtɑːrt-/ *noun* [U] a thick cold white sauce made from MAYONNAISE, chopped onions and CAPERS, usually eaten with fish

tarty /'tɑːti; *AmE* 'tɑːrti/ *adj.* (*disapproving*) (of a woman) dressing or behaving in a way that is intended to attract sexual attention

task /tɑːsk; *AmE* tæsk/ *noun, verb*
■ *noun* a piece of work that sb has to do, especially a hard or unpleasant one: *to perform/carry out/complete/undertake a task* ◊ *a daunting/an impossible/a formidable/an unenviable task* ◊ *a thankless task* (= an unpleasant one that nobody wants to do and nobody thanks you for doing) ◊ *Our first task is to set up a communications system.* ◊ *Detectives are now faced with the task of identifying the body.* ◊ *Getting hold of this information was no easy task* (= was difficult). IDM take sb to 'task (for/over sth) to criticize sb strongly for sth they have done
■ *verb* [VN] [usually passive] ~ sb (with sth) (*formal*) to give sb a task to do

'task force *noun* **1** a military force that is brought together and sent to a particular place **2** a group of people who are brought together to deal with a particular problem

task·mas·ter /'tɑːskmɑːstə(r); *AmE* -mæs-/ *noun* a person who gives other people work to do, often work that is difficult: *She was a hard taskmaster.*

tas·sel /'tæsl/ *noun* a bunch of threads that are tied together at one end and hang from cushions, curtains, clothes, etc. as a decoration

tas·selled (*BrE*) (*AmE* **tas·seled**) /'tæsld/ *adj.* decorated with tassels

taste /teɪst/ *noun, verb*
■ *noun*
FLAVOUR | **1** [C, U] the particular quality that different foods and drinks have that allows you to recognize them when you put them in your mouth: *a salty/bitter/sweet taste* ◊ *I don't like the taste of olives.* ◊ *This dish has an unusual combination of tastes and textures.* ◊ *The soup has very little taste.*
SENSE | **2** [U] the sense you have that allows you to recognize different foods and drinks when you put them in your mouth: *I've lost my sense of taste.*
SMALL QUANTITY | **3** [C, usually sing.] a small quantity of food or drink that you try in order to see what it is like: *Just have a taste of this cheese.*
SHORT EXPERIENCE | **4** [sing.] a short experience of sth: *This was my first taste of live theatre.* ◊ *Although we didn't know it, this incident was a taste of things to come.*
ABILITY TO CHOOSE WELL | **5** [U] a person's ability to choose things that people recognize as being of good quality or appropriate: *He has very good taste in music.* ◊ *They've got more money than taste.* ◊ *The room was furnished with taste.*

cord
braid
tassel

aɪ	aʊ	eɪ	əʊ	oʊ	ɔɪ	ɪə	eə	ʊə	j	w
my	now	say	go	go	boy	near	hair	pure	yes	wet
			(BrE)	(AmE)						

WHAT YOU LIKE | **6** [C, U] ~ **(for sth)** what a person likes or prefers: *That trip gave me a taste for foreign travel.* ◊ *She has very expensive tastes in clothes.* ◊ *The colour and style is a matter of personal taste.* ◊ *Modern art is not to everyone's taste.* ◊ *There are trips to suit all tastes.*

IDM **be in bad, poor, the worst possible, etc. 'taste** to be offensive and not at all appropriate: *Most of his jokes were in very poor taste.* **be in good, the best possible, etc. 'taste** to be appropriate and not at all offensive **leave a bad/nasty 'taste in the mouth** (of events or experiences) to make you feel disgusted or ashamed afterwards **to 'taste** in the quantity that is needed to make sth taste the way you prefer: *Add salt and pepper to taste.*—more at ACCOUNT *v.*, ACQUIRE, MEDICINE

■ *verb* (not used in the progressive tenses)
HAVE FLAVOUR | **1** *linking verb* ~ **(of sth)** to have a particular flavour: [V-ADJ] *It tastes sweet.* ◊ [V] *The ice tasted of mint.* ◊ *This drink tastes like sherry.* **2** (-*tasting*) (in adjectives) having a particular flavour: *foul-tasting medicine*

RECOGNIZE FLAVOUR | **3** [VN] (often used with *can* or *could*) to be able to recognize flavours in food and drink: *You can taste the garlic in this stew.*

TEST FLAVOUR | **4** [VN] to test the flavour of sth by eating or drinking a small amount of it: *Taste it and see if you think there's enough salt in it.*

EAT/DRINK | **5** [VN] to eat or drink food or liquid: *I've never tasted anything like it.*

HAVE SHORT EXPERIENCE | **6** [VN] to have a short experience of sth, especially sth that you want more of: *He had tasted freedom only to lose it again.*

'taste bud *noun* [usually pl.] one of the small cells on the tongue that allow you to recognize the flavours of food and drink

taste·ful /'teɪstfl/ *adj.* (especially of clothes, furniture, decorations, etc.) attractive and of good quality and showing that the person who chose them can recognize good things: *tasteful furniture* ▶ **taste·ful·ly** /-fəli/ *adv.*: *The bedroom was tastefully furnished.*

taste·less /'teɪstləs/ *adj.* **1** having little or no flavour: *tasteless soup* **2** offensive and not appropriate: *tasteless jokes/remarks* **3** showing a lack of the ability to choose things that people recognize as attractive and of good quality: *a tasteless brown suit* ▶ **taste·less·ly** *adv.*

taster /'teɪstə(r)/ *noun* **1** a person whose job is to judge the quality of wine, tea, etc. by tasting it **2** (*informal, especially BrE*) a small example of sth for you to try in order to see if you would like more of it

tast·ing /'teɪstɪŋ/ *noun* an event at which people can try different kinds of food and drink, especially wine, in small quantities: *a wine tasting*

tasty /'teɪsti/ *adj.* (**tasti·er**, **tasti·est**) **1** (*approving*) having a strong and pleasant flavour: *a tasty dish/meal* ◊ *something tasty to eat* **2** (*BrE, informal, sometimes offensive*) a word that some men use about women that they think are sexually attractive

tat /tæt/ *noun* [U] (*BrE, informal*) goods that are cheap and of low quality—see also TIT FOR TAT

ta-ta /ˌtæ ˈtɑː/ *exclamation* (*BrE, informal*) goodbye: *Ta-ta for now!*

tater /'teɪtə(r)/ *noun* [usually pl.] (*slang*) a potato

tat·tered /'tætəd; *AmE* -tərd/ *adj.* old and torn; in bad condition: *tattered clothes* ◊ (*figurative*) *tattered relationships* ◊ (*figurative*) *the hotel's tattered reputation*

tat·ters /'tætəz; *AmE* -tərz/ *noun* [pl.] clothes or pieces of fabric that are badly torn: *a beggar dressed in tatters* **IDM** **in tatters 1** torn in many places: *His clothes were in tatters.* **2** ruined or badly damaged: *Her reputation was in tatters.* ◊ *The government's education policy lies in tatters.*

tat·tie /'tæti/ *noun* (*ScotE, informal*) a potato

tat·tle /'tætl/ *verb* [V] ~ **(on sb)** **(to sb)** (*informal, disapproving, especially AmE*) to tell sb, especially sb in authority, about sth bad that sb else has done **SYN** TELL ON SB

tat·tle·tale /'tætlteɪl/ *noun* (*AmE*) = TELLTALE

tat·too /tə'tuː; *AmE* tæ'tuː/ *noun, verb*

■ *noun* (*pl.* **tat·toos**) **1** a picture or design that is marked permanently on a person's skin by making small holes in the skin with a needle and filling them with coloured ink: *His arms were covered in tattoos.* **2** (*especially BrE*) an outdoor show by members of the armed forces that includes marching, music and military exercises: *the Edinburgh military tattoo* **3** [usually sing.] a rapid and continuous series of taps or hits, especially on a drum as a military signal: *The drummers beat a tattoo each morning.* ◊ *Her fingers tapped a light tattoo on the table.*

■ *verb* [VN] ~ **A on B** | ~ **B (with A)** to mark sb's skin with a tattoo: *He had a heart tattooed on his shoulder.* ◊ *His shoulder was tattooed with a heart.*

tatty /'tæti/ *adj.* (*informal, especially BrE*) in a bad condition because it has been used a lot or has not been cared for well **SYN** SHABBY: *a tatty carpet/office*

taught *pt, pp* of TEACH

taunt /tɔːnt/ *verb, noun*

■ *verb* [VN] ~ **sb (with sth)** to try to make sb angry or upset by saying unkind things about them, laughing at their failures, etc: *The other kids continually taunted him about his size.*

■ *noun* an insulting or unkind remark that is intended to make sb angry or upset: *Black players often had to endure racist taunts.*

taupe /təʊp; *AmE* toʊp/ *noun* [U] a brownish-grey colour ▶ **taupe** *adj.*

Taurus /'tɔːrəs/ *noun* **1** [U] the second sign of the ZODIAC, the BULL **2** [sing.] a person born under the influence of this sign, that is between 21 April and 21 May ▶ **Taurean** /'tɔːriən/ *noun, adj.*

taut /tɔːt/ *adj.* **1** stretched tightly: *taut violin strings* ◊ *Keep the rope taut.* **2** showing that you are anxious or tense: *a voice taut with anger* ◊ *Her face was taut and pale.* **3** (of a person or their body) with firm muscles; not fat: *His body was solid and taut.* **4** (of a piece of writing, etc.) tightly controlled, with no unnecessary parts in it: *a taut thriller* ▶ **taut·ly** *adv.* **taut·ness** *noun* [U]

taut·en /'tɔːtn/ *verb* [V, VN] to become taut; to make sth taut

tau·tol·ogy /tɔː'tɒlədʒi; *AmE* -'tɑːl-/ *noun* [U, C] a statement in which you say the same thing twice in different words, when this is unnecessary, for example 'They spoke in turn, one after the other.' ▶ **tauto·logic·al** /ˌtɔːtə'lɒdʒɪkl; *AmE* -'lɑːdʒ-/ **tau·tolo·gous** /tɔː'tɒləgəs; *AmE* -'tɑːl-/ *adj.*

tav·ern /'tævən; *AmE* -vərn/ *noun* (*old use* or *literary*) a pub or an INN

taw·dry /'tɔːdri/ *adj.* (*disapproving*) **1** intended to be bright and attractive but cheap and of low quality: *tawdry jewellery* **2** involving low moral standards; extremely unpleasant or offensive: *a tawdry affair/scandal*

tawny /'tɔːni/ *adj.* brownish-yellow in colour: *the lion's tawny mane*

'tawny owl *noun* a reddish-brown or grey European BIRD OF PREY (= a bird that kills other creatures for food) of the OWL family

tax /tæks/ *noun, verb*

■ *noun* [C, U] ~ **(on sth)** money that you have to pay to the government so that it can pay for public services. People pay tax according to their income and businesses pay tax according to their profits. Tax is also often paid on goods and services: *to raise/cut taxes* ◊ *tax increases/cuts* ◊ *changes in tax rates* ◊ *to pay over £1000 in tax* ◊ *profits before/after tax* ◊ *a tax on cigarettes/alcohol*—see also CORPORATION TAX, COUNCIL TAX, INHERITANCE TAX, POLL TAX, ROAD TAX, SALES TAX, VALUE ADDED TAX, WITHHOLDING TAX

■ *verb* [VN] **1** to put a tax on sb/sth; to make sb pay tax: *Any interest payments are taxed as part of your income.* ◊ *His declared aim was to tax the rich.* **2** (*BrE*) to pay tax on a vehicle so that you may use it on the roads: *The car is taxed until July.* **3** to need a great amount of physical or mental effort: *The questions did not tax me.* ◊ *The problem is currently taxing the brains of the nation's experts* (= making them think very hard). **PHRV** **'tax sb with sth**

T

(*formal*) to accuse sb of doing sth wrong: *I taxed him with avoiding his responsibility as a parent.*

tax·able /'tæksəbl/ *adj.* (of money) that you have to pay tax on: *taxable income/profits/earnings*

tax·ation /tæk'seɪʃn/ *noun* [U] **1** money that has to be paid as taxes: *to reduce/increase taxation* **2** the system of collecting money by taxes: *changes in the taxation structure*

'tax avoidance *noun* [U] ways of paying only the smallest amount of tax that you legally have to—compare TAX EVASION

'tax bracket *noun* a range of different incomes on which the same rate of tax must be paid: *There are now only two tax brackets—22% and 40%.*

'tax break *noun* (*especially AmE*) a special advantage or reduction in taxes that the government gives to particular people or organizations: *a. tax break for low income families with young children*

'tax collector *noun* a person whose job is collecting the tax that people must pay on the money they earn

,tax-de'ductible *adj.* (of costs) that can be taken off your income before the amount of tax that you have to pay is calculated

'tax disc *noun* (in Britain) a small paper disc that is displayed on the window of a vehicle or on a motorcycle to show that the owner has paid the tax that allows them to use the vehicle on public roads

'tax dodge *noun* (*informal*) a way of paying less tax, legally or illegally ▶ **'tax dodger** *noun*: *Police have begun a campaign against car tax dodgers.*

'tax evasion *noun* [U] the crime of deliberately not paying all the taxes that you should pay—compare TAX AVOIDANCE

,tax-e'xempt *adj.* that is not taxed: *tax-exempt savings*

'tax exile *noun* a rich person who has left their own country and gone to live in a place where the taxes are lower

,tax-'free *adj.* (of money, goods, etc.) that you do not have to pay tax on: *a tax-free allowance*

'tax haven *noun* a place where taxes are low and where people choose to live or officially REGISTER their companies because taxes are higher in their own countries

taxi /'tæksi/ *noun, verb*
■ *noun* (also **cab, taxi·cab**) a car with a driver that you pay to take you somewhere. Taxis usually have METERS which show how much money you have to pay: *a taxi driver/ride* ◇ *We'd better take a taxi.* ◇ *I came home by taxi.* ◇ *to order/hail/call a taxi*
■ *verb* (**taxi·ing, tax·ied, tax·ied**) [V] (of a plane) to move slowly along the ground before taking off or after landing

taxi·der·mist /'tæksɪdɜːmɪst; *AmE* -dɜːrm-/ *noun* a person whose job is taxidermy

taxi·dermy /'tæksɪdɜːmi; *AmE* -dɜːrmi/ *noun* [U] the art of STUFFING dead animals, birds and fish with a special material so that they look like living ones and can be displayed

tax·ing /'tæksɪŋ/ *adj.* needing a great amount of physical or mental effort SYN DEMANDING: *a taxing job* ◇ *This shouldn't be too taxing for you.*

'tax inspector *noun* (*BrE*) = INSPECTOR OF TAXES

'taxi rank (*BrE*) (also **'taxi stand** *AmE, BrE*) *noun* a place where taxis park while they are waiting for passengers

taxi·way /'tæksiweɪ/ *noun* the hard path that a plane uses as it moves to and from the RUNWAY (= the hard surface where planes take off and land)

tax·man /'tæksmæn/ *noun* (*pl.* **-men** /-men/) **1** (**the taxman**) [sing.] (*informal*) a way of referring to the government department that is responsible for collecting taxes: *He had been cheating the taxman for years.* **2** [C] a person whose job is to collect taxes

tax·ono·mist /tæk'sɒnəmɪst; *AmE* -'saːnə-/ *noun* a person who studies or is skilled in taxonomy

tax·onomy /tæk'sɒnəmi; *AmE* -'saːnə-/ *noun* **1** [U] the scientific process of CLASSIFYING things (= arranging them

into groups): *plant taxonomy* **2** [C] a particular system of CLASSIFYING things ▶ **taxo·nom·ic** /ˌtæksə'nɒmɪk; *AmE* -'naːmɪk/ *adj.*

tax·pay·er /'tækspeɪə(r)/ *noun* a person who pays tax to the government, especially on the money that they earn

'tax relief (also **relief**) *noun* [U] a reduction in the amount of tax you have to pay, especially when you are using the money for a particular purpose such as buying property

'tax return *noun* an official document in which you give details of the amount of money that you have earned so that the government can calculate how much tax you have to pay

'tax shelter *noun* a way of using or investing money so that you can legally avoid paying tax on it

TB /ˌtiː 'biː/ *noun* [U] a serious infectious disease in which swellings appear on the lungs and other parts of the body (abbreviation for 'tuberculosis'): *an increase in the number of TB cases*

t.b.a. /ˌtiː biː 'eɪ/ *abbr.* (used in notices about events) to be announced: *party with live band (t.b.a.)*

'T-bone steak *noun* a thick slice of beef containing a bone in the shape of a T

tbsp (also **tbs**) *abbr.* (*pl.* **tbsp** or **tbsps**) TABLESPOONFUL: *Add 3 tbsp sugar.*

TD /ˌtiː 'diː/ *noun* a member of the Irish parliament (abbreviation for 'Teachta Dála', 'Member of the Dáil')

te (*BrE*) (*AmE* **ti**) /tiː/ *noun* (*music*) the 7th note of a MAJOR scale

tea /tiː/ *noun* **1** [U] the dried leaves, (called **tea leaves**), of the tea bush—see also GREEN TEA **2** [U] a hot drink made by pouring boiling water onto tea leaves. It may be drunk with milk or lemon and/or sugar added: *a cup/mug/pot of tea* ◇ *China/lemon/iced tea* ◇ *Would you like tea or coffee?* ◇ *Do you take sugar in your tea?* **3** [C] a cup of tea: *Two teas, please.* **4** [U, C] a hot drink made by pouring boiling water onto the leaves of other plants: *chamomile/ mint/herb tea* **5** [U, C] the name used by some people in Britain for the cooked meal eaten in the evening, especially when it is eaten early in the evening: *You can have your tea as soon as you come home from school.*—compare DINNER, SUPPER **6** [U, C] (*BrE*) a light meal eaten in the afternoon or early evening, usually with sandwiches and/or biscuits and cakes and with tea to drink: *Would you like to come to tea on Sunday?*—see also CREAM TEA, HIGH TEA ⇨ note at MEAL **IDM** **not for all the tea in 'China** not even for a great reward: *I wouldn't do your job. Not for all the tea in China!*—more at CUP *n.*

'tea bag *noun* a small thin paper bag containing tea leaves, which you pour boiling water onto in order to make tea

'tea break *noun* (*BrE*) a short period of time when people stop working and drink tea, coffee, etc.

'tea caddy (also **caddy**) *noun* (*especially BrE*) a small box with a lid that you keep tea in

tea·cake /'tiːkeɪk/ *noun* (*BrE*) a small flat round cake made of a bread-like mixture, usually containing dried fruit: *toasted teacakes*

tea·cart /'tiːkaːt; *AmE* -kaːrt/ *noun* (*AmE*) = TEA TROLLEY

teach /tiːtʃ/ *verb* (**taught, taught** /tɔːt/) **1** to give lessons to students in a school, college, university, etc.; to help sb learn sth by giving information about it: [V] *She teaches at our local school.* ◇ *He taught for several years before becoming a writer.* ◇ [VN] *I'll be teaching history and sociology next term.* ◇ (*AmE*) *to teach school* (= teach in a school) ◇ [VN, VNN] *He teaches English to advanced students.* ◇ *He teaches them English.* **2** to show sb how to do sth so that they will be able to do it themselves: [VN to inf] *Could you teach me to do that?* ◇ [VN wh-] *My father taught me how to ride a bike.* [also VN] to make sb feel or think in a different way: [VN to inf] *She taught me to be less critical of other people.* ◇ [VN that] *My parents taught me that honesty was always the best policy.* ◇ [VNN] *Our experience as refugees taught us many valuable lessons.* [also V that] **4** [no passive] (*informal*) to persuade sb not to do sth again by making them suffer so much that they

s	t	v	z	ʃ	ʒ	tʃ	dʒ	θ	ð	ŋ
see	tea	van	zoo	shoe	vision	chain	jam	thin	this	sing

are afraid to do it: [VN **to** inf] *Lost all your money? That'll teach you to gamble.* ◊ *I'll teach you to call* (= punish you for calling) *me a liar!* ◊ [VNN] *The accident **taught me a lesson** I'll never forget.* **IDM teach your grandmother to suck 'eggs** (*BrE, informal*) to tell or show sb how to do sth that they can already do well, and probably better than you can **(you can't) teach an old dog new 'tricks** (*saying*) (you cannot) successfully make old people change their ideas, methods of work, etc.

VOCABULARY BUILDING
words meaning **'teach'** and **'teacher'**

Verbs

teach *John teaches French at the local school.* ◊ *My mother taught me how to drive.*

educate *Our priority is to educate people about the dangers of drugs.*

instruct *Members of staff should be instructed in the use of fire equipment.*

train *She's a trained midwife.* ◊ *He's training the British Olympic swimming team.*

coach *He's the best football player I've ever coached.* ◊ *She coaches some of the local children in maths.* (*BrE*)

tutor *She tutors some of the local children in math.* (*AmE*)

Nouns

teacher *school/college teachers*

instructor *a swimming/science instructor*

trainer *a horse trainer* ◊ *Do you have a personal trainer?*

coach *a football coach*

tutor *tutors working with migrant children*

---

teach·er /ˈtiːtʃə(r)/ *noun* a person whose job is teaching, especially in a school: *a language/history/science teacher* ◊ *primary school teachers* ◊ *There is a growing need for qualified teachers of Business English.* ⇨ note at TEACH

teacher 'training *noun* [U] the process of teaching or learning the skills you need to be a teacher in a school ► **teacher 'trainer** *noun*: *experienced teachers and teacher trainers*

tea chest *noun* (*BrE*) a large light wooden box lined with metal in which tea is transported. Tea chests are sometimes used for transporting personal possessions, for example, when moving to another home.

teach-in *noun* an informal LECTURE and discussion on a subject of public interest

teach·ing /ˈtiːtʃɪŋ/ *noun* **1** [U] the work of a teacher: *She wants to go into teaching* (= make it a career). ◊ *the teaching profession* **2** [C, usually pl., U] the ideas of a particular person or group, especially about politics, religion or society, that are taught to other people: *the teachings of Lenin* ◊ *views that go against traditional Christian teaching*

teaching assistant *noun* **1** a person who is not a qualified teacher who helps a teacher in a school **2** (*abbr.* TA) (*AmE*) (also **'teaching fellow** *AmE, BrE*) a GRADUATE student who teaches UNDERGRADUATE classes at a university or college, takes discussion or practical classes, marks written work, etc.

tea cloth *noun* (*BrE*) = TEA TOWEL

tea cosy *noun* a cover placed over a TEAPOT in order to keep the tea warm

tea·cup /ˈtiːkʌp/ *noun* a cup in which tea is served **IDM** see STORM *n.*

teak /tiːk/ *noun* [U] the strong hard wood of a tall Asian tree, used especially for making furniture

teal /tiːl/ *noun* **1** [C] (*pl.* **teal**) a small wild duck **2** [U] (*especially AmE*) a bluish-green colour

team /tiːm/ *noun, verb*
■ *noun* [C+sing./pl. *v.*] **1** a group of people who play a particular game or sport against another group of people: *a football/cricket/rugby team* ◊ *a team event* (= one played by groups of people rather than individual players) ◊ (*BrE*) *Whose team are you in?* ◊ (*AmE*) *Whose team*

are you on?* ◊ *The team is/are not playing very well this season.* **2** a group of people who work together at a particular job: *the design/sales team* ◊ *a team leader/member* ◊ *a team player* (= a person who works well with others) ◊ *A team of experts has/have been called in to investigate.* **3** two or more animals that are used together to pull a carriage, CART, etc.
■ *verb* [VN] [usually passive] to combine or match two or more things or people: *This production of 'Macbeth' teams two of our finest actors.* ◊ *He was teamed with his brother in the doubles.* **PHRV team 'up (with sb)** to join with another person or group in order to do sth together

'team handball *noun* [U] (*AmE*) = HANDBALL

team·mate /ˈtiːmmeɪt/ *noun* a member of the same team or group as yourself

team 'spirit *noun* [U] (*approving*) the desire and willingness of people to work together and help each other as part of a team

team·ster /ˈtiːmstə(r)/ *noun* (*AmE*) a person whose job is driving a truck

team·work /ˈtiːmwɜːk; *AmE* -wɜːrk/ *noun* [U] the activity of working well together as a team: *She stressed the importance of good teamwork.*

'tea party *noun* a social event at which people eat cake, drink tea, etc. in the afternoon

tea·pot /ˈtiːpɒt; *AmE* -pɑːt/ *noun* a container with a SPOUT, a handle and a lid, used for making and serving tea—picture at POT **IDM** see TEMPEST

tear¹ /teə(r); *AmE* ter/ *verb, noun*—see also TEAR²
■ *verb* (**tore** /tɔː(r)/ **torn** /tɔːn; *AmE* tɔːrn/)
DAMAGE | **1** to damage sth by pulling it apart or into pieces or by cutting it on sth sharp; to become damaged in this way: [VN] *I tore my jeans on the fence.* ◊ *I tore a hole in my jeans.* ◊ *He tore the letter in two.* ◊ *a torn handkerchief* ◊ [VN-ADJ] *I tore the package open.* ◊ [V] *Careful—the fabric tears very easily.* **2** [VN] ~ **sth in sth** to make a hole in sth by force: *The blast tore a hole in the wall.*
REMOVE FROM STH/SB | **3** [VN+adv./prep.] to remove sth from sth else by pulling it roughly or violently: *The storm nearly tore the roof off.* ◊ *I tore another sheet from the pad.* ◊ *He tore his clothes off* (= took them off quickly and carelessly) *and dived into the lake.* **4** ~ **yourself/sb (from sb/sth)** to pull yourself/sb away by force from sb/sth that is holding you or them: [VN] *She tore herself from his grasp.* ◊ [VN-ADJ] *He tore himself free.*
INJURE MUSCLE | **5** [VN] to injure a muscle, etc. by stretching it too much: *a torn ligament*
MOVE QUICKLY | **6** [V+adv./prep.] to move somewhere very quickly or in an excited way: *He tore off down the street.* ◊ *A truck tore past the gates.*
-TORN | **7** (in adjectives) very badly affected or damaged by sth: *to bring peace to a strife-torn country* ◊ *a strike-torn industry*—see also WAR-TORN
IDM tear sb/sth a'part, to 'shreds, to 'bits, etc. to destroy or defeat sb/sth completely or criticize them or it severely: *We tore the other team apart in the second half.* ◊ *The critics tore his last movie to shreds.* **tear at your 'heart | tear your 'heart out** (*formal*) to strongly affect you in an emotional way **tear your 'hair (out)** (*informal*) to show that you are very angry or anxious about sth: *She's keeping very calm—anyone else would be tearing their hair out.* **(be in) a tearing 'hurry/'rush** (*especially BrE*) (to be) in a very great hurry **tear sb 'off a strip | tear a 'strip off sb** (*BrE, informal*) to speak angrily to sb who has done sth wrong **,that's 'torn it** (*BrE, informal*) used to say that sth has happened to spoil your plans—more at HEART, LIMB, LOOSE *adj.*
PHRV tear sth↔a'part 1 to destroy sth violently, especially by pulling it to pieces: *The dogs tore the fox apart.* ◊ *They tore the room apart, looking for money.* **2** to make people in a country, an organization or other place fight or argue with each other: *Racial strife is tearing our country apart.* **3** to make sb feel very unhappy or worried: *His distress tore me apart.* **tear at sth** to pull or cut sth violently so that it tears: *He tore at the meat with his bare hands.* **,tear yourself a'way (from sth)| ,tear sth a'way (from sth)** to leave somewhere even though you

æ ɑː e ɜː ə ɪ iː i ɒ ɔː ʌ ʊ u uː
cat father ten bird about sit see many got saw cup put actual too
(BrE)

would prefer to stay there; **to take sth away from some-where**: *Dinner's ready, if you can tear yourself away from the TV.* ◊ *She was unable to tear her eyes away from him* (= could not stop looking at him). **be torn between A and B** to be unable to decide or choose between two things or feelings: *I was torn between my parents and my friend.* ,**tear sth↔'down** to pull or knock down a building, wall, etc. [SYN] DEMOLISH ,**tear 'into sb/sth 1** to attack sb/sth physically or with words **2** to start doing sth with a lot of energy: *They tore into their food as if they were starving.* ,**tear sth↔'up** to destroy a document, etc. by tearing it into pieces: *She tore up all the letters he had sent her.* ◊ *(figurative) He accused the leader of tearing up the party's manifesto* (= of ignoring it).

■ *noun* a hole that has been made in sth by tearing: *This sheet has a tear in it.* [IDM] see WEAR *n.*

tear² /tɪə(r); *AmE* tɪr/ *noun* [usually pl.]—see also TEAR¹ a drop of liquid that comes out of your eye when you cry: *A tear rolled down his face.* ◊ *She left the room **in tears** (= crying).* ◊ *He suddenly **burst into tears** (= began to cry).* ◊ *As he listened to the music, his eyes filled with tears.* ◊ *Their story will **move you to tears** (= make you cry).* ◊ *They reduced her to tears (= made her cry, especially by being cruel or unkind).* ◊ *Ann wiped a tear from her eye.* ◊ *The memory **brought a tear to her eye** (= made her cry).* ◊ *Most of the audience was **on the verge of tears**.* ◊ *I was **close to tears** as I told them the news.* ◊ *Desperately she **fought back the tears** (= tried not to cry).* ◊ *to **shed tears** of pain/frustration/happiness* [IDM] see BLOOD *n.*, BORED, CROCODILE, END *v.*

tear·away /'teərəweɪ; *AmE* 'ter-/ *noun* (*informal*) a young person who is difficult to control and often does stupid, dangerous and/or illegal things

tear·drop /'tɪədrɒp; *AmE* 'tɪrdrɑːp/ *noun* a single tear that comes from your eye

tear·ful /'tɪəfl; *AmE* 'tɪrfl/ *adj.* **1** (of a person) crying, or about to cry: *She suddenly became very tearful.* **2** (of an event, etc.) at which people feel emotional and cry: *a tearful farewell* ▶ **tear·ful·ly** /-fəli/ *adv.* **tear·ful·ness** *noun* [U]

tear gas /'tɪə gæs; *AmE* 'tɪr/ *noun* [U] a gas that makes your eyes sting and fill with tears, used by the police or army to control crowds

tear jerker /'tɪə dʒɜːkə(r); *AmE* 'tɪr dʒɜːrkər/ *noun* (*informal*) a film/movie, story, etc. that is designed to make people feel sad

'**tea room** (also '**tea shop**) *noun* (*BrE*) a cafe in which tea, coffee, cakes and sandwiches are served

tease /tiːz/ *verb, noun*

■ *verb* **1** to laugh at sb and make jokes about them either in a friendly way or in order to annoy or embarrass them: [V] *Don't get upset—I was only teasing.* ◊ [VN] *I used to get teased about my name.* [also V speech, VN speech] **2** [VN] to annoy an animal, especially by touching it, pulling its tail, etc. **3** [V, VN] (*disapproving*) to make sb sexually excited, especially when you do not intend to have sex with them **4** [VN] to pull sth gently apart into separate pieces: *to tease wool into strands* **5** [VN] (*AmE*) = BACK-COMB [PHRV] ,**tease sth↔'out 1** to remove knots from hair, wool, etc. by gently pulling or brushing it **2** to spend time trying to find out information or the meaning of sth, especially when this is complicated or difficult: *The teacher helped them tease out the meaning of the poem.*

■ *noun* [usually sing.] **1** a person who likes to play tricks and jokes on other people, especially by telling them sth that is not true or by not telling them sth that they want to know **2** an act that is intended as a trick or joke **3** (*disapproving*) a person who pretends to be attracted to sb, makes them sexually excited and then refuses to have sex with them

tea·sel (also **tea·zle**) /'tiːzl/ *noun* a plant with large prickly flowers, used in the past for brushing woollen or woven fabric to give it a smooth surface

teaser /'tiːzə(r)/ *noun* (*informal*) a difficult problem or question—see also BRAIN-TEASER

'**tea set** (*BrE*) (also '**tea service** *AmE*, *BrE*) *noun* a set consisting of a TEAPOT, sugar bowl, cups, plates, etc., used for serving tea

'**tea shop** *noun* (*BrE*) = TEA ROOM

teas·ing·ly /'tiːzɪŋli/ *adv.* **1** in a way that is intended to make sb feel embarrassed, annoyed, etc. **2** in a way that suggests sth and makes sb want to know more **3** in a way that is intended to make sb sexually excited

tea·spoon /'tiːspuːn/ *noun* **1** a small spoon for putting sugar into tea and other drinks—picture at CUTLERY **2** (also **tea·spoon·ful** /-fʊl/) (*abbr.* **tsp**) the amount a teaspoon can hold: *Add two teaspoons of salt.* ◊ *a teaspoonful of sugar*

teat /tiːt/ *noun* **1** (*BrE*) (*AmE* **nip·ple**) the rubber part at the end of a baby's bottle that the baby sucks in order to get milk, etc. from the bottle **2** one of the parts of a female animal's body that the young suck in order to get milk

tea·time /'tiːtaɪm/ *noun* [U] (*BrE*) the time during the afternoon or early evening when people have the meal called tea

'**tea towel** (also '**tea cloth**) (both *BrE*) (*AmE* **dish·towel**) *noun* a small towel used for drying cups, plates, knives. etc. after they have been washed

'**tea tree** *noun* a small Australian tree. The oil from its leaves can be used to treat wounds and skin problems.

'**tea trolley** (*BrE*) (*AmE* '**tea wagon**, '**tea·cart**) *noun* a small table on wheels that is used for serving tea, coffee, etc.

tea·zle *noun* = TEASEL

tech /tek/ *noun* (*BrE*, *informal*) = TECHNICAL COLLEGE— see also HIGH-TECH, LOW-TECH

tech·nical /'teknɪkl/ *adj.* **1** [usually before noun] connected with the practical use of machinery, methods, etc. in science and industry: *We offer free technical support for those buying our software.* ◊ *a technical education* ◊ *technical drawing* (= especially taught as a school subject) **2** [usually before noun] connected with the skills needed for a particular job, sport, art, etc: *Skaters score extra points for technical complexity.* **3** connected with a particular subject and therefore difficult to understand if you do not know about that subject: *The article is full of technical terms.* ◊ *The guide is too technical for a non-specialist.* **4** [only before noun] connected with the details of a law or set of rules: *Their lawyers spent days arguing over technical details.*

'**technical college** (also *BrE informal* **tech**) *noun* a college where students can study mainly practical subjects

,**technical 'hitch** *noun* a temporary problem or difficulty, especially one caused by a piece of machinery or equipment

tech·ni·cal·ity /ˌteknɪ'kæləti/ *noun* (*pl.* **-ies**) **1** (**technicalities**) [pl.] the small details of how to do sth or how sth works **2** a small detail in a law or set of rules, especially one that does not seem fair: *She was released **on a technicality*** (= because of a small detail in the law).

tech·nic·al·ly /'teknɪkli/ *adv.* **1** according to the exact meaning, facts etc: *Technically (speaking), the two countries are still at war.* ◊ *It is still **technically possible** for them to win* (= but it seems unlikely). **2** in a way that is connected with the skills needed for a particular job, sport, art, etc: *As a musician, she is technically accomplished.* **3** in a way that is connected with the practical use of machinery, methods, etc. in science and industry: *a technically advanced society* ◊ *In those days recording sound was not **technically possible**.*

tech·ni·cian /tek'nɪʃn/ *noun* **1** a person whose job is keeping a particular type of equipment or machinery in good condition: *laboratory/aircraft technicians* **2** a person who is very skilled at the technical aspects of an art, a sport, etc: *As a pianist, she's a brilliant technician, but she lacks passion.*

Tech·ni·color™ /'teknɪkʌlə(r)/ *noun* [U] a process of producing colour film, as used in cinema films/movies

tech·ni·col·our (*BrE*) (*AmE* **tech·ni·color**) /'teknɪkʌlə(r)/ *noun* [U] (*informal*) the state of having many bright colours: *The rooms were painted in glorious technicolour.*

tech·nique /tek'niːk/ *noun* **1** [C] a particular way of

aɪ	aʊ	eɪ	əʊ	oʊ	ɔɪ	ɪə	eə	ʊə	j	w
my	now	say	go (BrE)	go (AmE)	boy	near	hair	pure	yes	wet

technique doing sth, especially one in which you have to learn special skills: *The artist combines different techniques in the same painting.* ◊ *management/marketing techniques* **2** [U, sing.] the skill with which sb is able to do sth practical: *Her technique has improved a lot over the past season.*

techno /'teknəʊ; *AmE* -noʊ/ *noun* [U] a style of modern popular music with a regular rhythm for dancing, that makes use of technology to produce the sound

techno- /'teknəʊ; *AmE* -noʊ/ *combining form* (in nouns, adjectives and adverbs) connected with technology: *technocracy* ◊ *technophobe* (= a person who is afraid of technology)

tech·no·cracy /tek'nɒkrəsi; *AmE* -'nɑːk-/ *noun* [U, C] (*pl.* **-ies**) a social or political system in which people with scientific knowledge have a lot of power

tech·no·crat /'teknəkræt/ *noun* an expert in science, engineering, etc. who has a lot of power in politics and/or industry ▶ **tech·no·crat·ic** /ˌteknə'krætɪk/ *adj.* [usually before noun]

tech·nolo·gist /tek'nɒlədʒɪst; *AmE* -'nɑːl-/ *noun* an expert in technology

tech·nol·ogy /tek'nɒlədʒi; *AmE* -'nɑːl-/ *noun* (*pl.* **-ies**) **1** [U, C] scientific knowledge used in practical ways in industry, for example in designing new machines: *science and technology* ◊ *recent advances in medical technology* ◊ *to make use of the most modern technologies*—see also HIGH TECHNOLOGY, INFORMATION TECHNOLOGY **2** [U] machinery or equipment designed using technology: *The company has invested in the latest technology.* ▶ **tech·no·log·ic·al** /ˌteknə'lɒdʒɪkl; *AmE* -'lɑːdʒ-/ *adj.*: *technological advances/developments* ◊ *technological change/progress* ◊ *a major technological breakthrough* **tech·no·log·ic·al·ly** /-kli/ *adv.*: *technologically advanced*

tec·ton·ic /tek'tɒnɪk; *AmE* -'tɑːnɪk/ *adj.* [only before noun] (*geology*) connected with the structure of the earth's surface—see also PLATE TECTONICS

teddy bear /'tedi beə(r); *AmE* ber/ (*BrE also* **teddy** *pl.* **-ies**) *noun* a soft toy bear—picture on page A8

'**Teddy boy** (*also informal* **ted** /ted/) *noun* (in Britain in the 1950s) a member of a group of young men who liked ROCK AND ROLL music and who had their own style of dressing (usually wearing narrow trousers/pants, long jackets and pointed shoes)

te·di·ous /'tiːdiəs/ *adj.* lasting or taking too long and not interesting [SYN] BORING: *The journey soon became tedious.* ◊ *We had to listen to all the tedious details of his operation.* ▶ **te·di·ous·ly** *adv.* **te·di·ous·ness** *noun* [U]

te·dium /'tiːdiəm/ *noun* [U] (*written*) the quality of being boring [SYN] BOREDOM: *She longed for something to relieve the tedium of everyday life.*

tee /tiː/ *noun, verb*
■ *noun* **1** a flat area on a golf course from which players hit the ball: *to drive off from the first tee* ◊ *a tee shot* **2** a small piece of plastic or wood that you stick in the ground to support a golf ball before you hit it—picture at GOLF [IDM] see T
■ *verb* (**teed, teed**) [PHRV] ,**tee** '**off** to hit a golf ball from a tee, especially at the start of a match ,**tee sb** ↔ '**off** (*AmE, informal*) to make sb angry or annoyed: *It really teed me off when she was late again.* ,**tee sth** ↔ '**up** | ,**tee** '**up** to prepare to hit a golf ball by placing it on a tee

teem /tiːm/ *verb* [V] (usually be '**teeming**) (of rain) to fall heavily: *The rain was teeming down.* ◊ *It was teeming with rain.* [PHRV] '**teem with sth** (usually be '**teeming with sth**) to be full of people, animals, etc. moving around: *The streets were teeming with tourists.* ◊ *a river teeming with fish*

teem·ing /'tiːmɪŋ/ *adj.* present in large numbers; full of people, animals, etc. that are moving around: *teeming insects* ◊ *the teeming streets of the city*

teen·age /'tiːneɪdʒ/ (*also informal* **teen** *especially in AmE*) *adj.* [usually before noun] between 13 and 19 years old; connected with people of this age: *teenage girls/boys* ◊ *teenage problems/rebellion* ◊ *teen magazines*

teen·aged /'tiːneɪdʒd/ *adj.* between 13 and 19 years old: *They have two teenaged daughters.*

teen·ager /'tiːneɪdʒə(r)/ (*also informal* **teen** especially in *AmE*) *noun* a person who is between 13 and 19 years old: *a magazine aimed at teenagers*

teens /tiːnz/ *noun* [pl.] the years of a person's life when they are between 13 and 19 years old: *She began writing poetry in her teens.* ◊ *to be in your early/late teens*

teeny /'tiːni/ *adj.* (*informal*) (**teen·ier, teeni·est**) **1** (*also* **teeny-weeny** /ˌtiːni 'wiːni/ **teensy** /'tiːnzi/ **teensy-weensy** /ˌtiːnzi 'wiːnzi/) very small **2** connected with people between 13 and 19 years old: *teeny magazines*

teeny-bopper /'tiːni bɒpə(r); *AmE* baːp-/ *noun* (*old-fashioned, informal*) a young girl between the ages of about 10 and 13, who is very interested in pop music, fashionable clothes, etc.

tee·pee *noun* = TEPEE

tee·ter /'tiːtə(r)/ *verb* [V] to stand or move in an unsteady way so that you look as if you are going to fall: *She teetered after him in her high-heeled shoes.* [IDM] **teeter on the** '**brink**/'**edge of sth** to be very close to a very unpleasant or dangerous situation: *The country is teetering on the brink of civil war.*

'**teeter-totter** *noun* (*AmE*) = SEE-SAW

teeth *pl.* of TOOTH

teethe /tiːð/ *verb* [V] when a baby is **teething**, its first teeth are starting to grow

'**teething troubles** (*also* '**teething problems**) *noun* [pl.] small problems that a company, product, system, etc. has at the beginning

tee·total /ˌtiː'təʊtl; *AmE* -'toʊtl/ *adj.* never drinking alcohol: *He's strictly teetotal.* ▶ **tee·total·ism** *noun* [U]

tee·total·ler (*BrE*) (*AmE* **tee·total·er**) /ˌtiː'təʊtlə(r); *AmE* -'toʊ-/ *noun* a person who does not drink alcohol

TEFL /'tiː i: ef 'el; 'tefl/ *abbr.* (*BrE*) teaching English as a foreign language

Tef·lon™ /'teflɒn; *AmE* -laːn/ *noun* [U] a substance used especially to cover the inside of cooking pans, that stops food from sticking to them

tel. (*also* **Tel.**) *abbr.* telephone number: *tel. 01865 556767*

tele- /'teli/ *combining form* (in nouns, verbs, adjectives and adverbs) **1** over a long distance; far: *telepathy* ◊ *telescopic* **2** connected with television: *teletext* **3** done using a telephone: *telesales*

tele·cast /'telikɑːst; *AmE* -kæst/ *noun* (*especially AmE*) a broadcast on television ▶ **tele·cast** *verb* (**tele·cast, tele·cast**) [VN] [usually passive]: *The event will be telecast simultaneously to nearly 150 cities.* **tele·cast·er** *noun*

tele·com·mu·ni·ca·tions /ˌtelikəˌmjuːnɪ'keɪʃnz/ (*also informal* **tele·coms** /'telikɒmz; *AmE* -kaːmz/) *noun* [pl.] the technology of sending signals, images and messages over long distances by radio, telephone, television, SATELLITE, etc: *technological developments in telecommunications* ◊ *telecommunications links/networks/operators*

tele·con·fer·ence /'telikɒnfərəns; *AmE* -kaːn-/ *noun* a CONFERENCE or discussion at which members are in different places and speak to each other using telephone and video connections

tele·gen·ic /ˌtelɪ'dʒenɪk/ *adj.* a **telegenic** person looks good on television

tele·gram /'telɪɡræm/ *noun* a message sent by TELEGRAPH and then printed and given to sb

tele·graph /'telɪɡrɑːf; *AmE* -ɡræf/ *noun, verb*
■ *noun* [U] a method of sending messages over long distances, using wires that carry electrical signals
■ *verb* **1** [V, VN] to send a message by telegraph **2** [VN] to make it clear to people what you are going to do, often without intending to

tele·graph·ic /ˌtelɪ'ɡræfɪk/ *adj.* connected with sending messages by telegraph: *You will need to arrange a telegraphic transfer from your bank to ours.*

'**telegraph pole** (*BrE*) (*AmE* '**telephone pole**) *noun* a tall wooden pole used for carrying telephone or telegraph wires high above the ground

tel·eg·raphy /tə'leɡrəfi/ *noun* [U] the process of sending messages by telegraph

tele·mar·ket·ing /'telimaːkɪtɪŋ; *AmE* -maːrk-/ *noun* [U] = TELESALES

tel·em·etry /tə'lemətri/ *noun* [U] (*technical*) the process of using special equipment to take scientific measurements and send them over long distances, usually by radio

tele·ology /ˌtiːli'ɒlədʒi; *AmE* -'ɑːlə-/ *noun* [U, sing.] (*philosophy*) the theory that events and developments are meant to achieve a purpose and happen because of that ▶ **teleo·logic·al** /ˌtiːliə'lɒdʒɪkl; *AmE* -'lɑːdʒ-/ *adj.*

tele·path·ic /ˌtelɪ'pæθɪk/ *adj.* **1** using telepathy: *telepathic communication* **2** (of a person) able to communicate by telepathy: *How do I know what he's thinking? I'm not telepathic!* ▶ **tele·path·ic·al·ly** /-kli/ *adv.*

tel·ep·athy /tə'lepəθi/ *noun* [U] the direct communication of thoughts or feelings from one person to another without using speech, writing, or any other normal method

tele·phone /'telɪfəʊn; *AmE* -foʊn/ (also **phone**) *noun, verb*
■ *noun* **1** [C, U] a system for talking to sb else over long distances, using wires or radio; a machine used for this: *The telephone rang and Pat answered it.* ◊ *You can reserve seats over the telephone.* ◊ *I need to make a telephone call.* ◊ *telephone lines/networks/services* **2** [C] the part of the telephone that you hold in your hand and speak into [SYN] RECEIVER, HANDSET [IDM] **be on the 'telephone 1** to be using the telephone: *He's on the telephone at the moment.* ◊ *You're wanted* (= sb wants to speak to you) *on the telephone.* **2** (*BrE*) to have a telephone in your home or place of work: *We're not on the telephone at the cottage.*
■ *verb* (*formal, especially BrE*) to speak to sb by telephone [SYN] PHONE, CALL: [V] *Please write or telephone for details.* ◊ *He telephoned to say he'd be late.* ◊ [VN] *You can telephone your order 24 hours a day.* ◊ *I was about to telephone the police.* ⇨ note at PHONE

'telephone booth *noun* = PHONE BOOTH

'telephone box *noun* (*BrE*) = PHONE BOX

'telephone directory (also **'phone book, 'telephone book**) *noun* a book that lists the names, addresses and telephone numbers of people in a particular area: *to look up a number in the telephone directory*

'telephone exchange (also **exchange**) *noun* a place where telephone calls are connected so that people can speak to each other

'telephone kiosk *noun* (*BrE*) = PHONE BOX

'telephone number (also **'phone number**) *noun* the number of a particular telephone, that you use when you make a call to it ⇨ Appendix 3

'telephone pole *noun* (*AmE*) = TELEGRAPH POLE

'telephone tapping (also **'phone tapping**) *noun* [U] the practice of connecting a piece of equipment to a telephone in order to listen secretly to other people's telephone conversations

tel·eph·on·ist /tə'lefənɪst/ *noun* (*BrE*) = OPERATOR

tel·eph·ony /tə'lefəni/ *noun* [U] the process of sending messages and signals by telephone

tele·photo lens /ˌtelɪfəʊtəʊ 'lenz; *AmE* -foʊtoʊ/ *noun* a camera LENS that produces a large image of an object that is far away and allows you to take photographs of it

tele·print·er /'telɪprɪntə(r)/ (*AmE* also **tele·type·writer**) *noun* a machine that prints out TELEX messages that have been typed in another place and sent by telephone lines

tele·prompt·er /'telɪprɒmptə(r); *AmE* -prɑːm-/ *noun* (especially *AmE*) = AUTOCUE

tele·sales /'telɪseɪlz/ (*BrE*) (also **tele·mar·ket·ing** *AmE, BrE*) *noun* [U] a method of selling things and taking orders for sales by telephone

tele·scope /'telɪskəʊp; *AmE* -skoʊp/ *noun, verb*
■ *noun* a piece of equipment shaped like a tube, containing LENSES, that you look through to make objects that are far away appear larger and nearer: *to look at the stars through a telescope*—see also RADIO TELESCOPE
■ *verb* **1** [V, VN] to become shorter, or make sth shorter, by sliding sections inside one another **2** [VN] ~ **sth** (**into sth**) to reduce sth so that it happens in less time: *Three episodes have been telescoped into a single programme.*

tele·scop·ic /ˌtelɪ'skɒpɪk; *AmE* -'skɑːpɪk/ *adj.* **1** connected with or using a telescope; making things look larger as a telescope does: *telescopic observations/lenses* ◊ *a rifle with a telescopic sight* **2** made of sections that can slide into each other to make the object longer or shorter: *a telescopic aerial/umbrella* ▶ **tele·scop·ic·al·ly** /-kli/ *adv.*

tele·text /'telɪtekst/ *noun* [U] a service providing written news and information using television: *See if the results are on teletext.*

tele·thon /'teləθɒn; *AmE* -θɑːn/ *noun* a very long television show, broadcast to raise money for charity

tele·type·writer /ˌtelɪ'taɪpraɪtə(r)/ *noun* (*AmE*) = TELE-PRINTER

tele·van·gel·ist /ˌtelɪ'vændʒəlɪst/ *noun* (especially in the US) a person who appears regularly on television to try to persuade people to become Christians and to give money ▶ **tele·van·gel·ism** *noun* [U]

tele·vise /'telɪvaɪz/ *verb* [VN] [usually passive] to broadcast sth on television: *a televised debate* ◊ *to televise a novel* ◊ *The speech will be televised live.*

tele·vi·sion /'telɪvɪʒn/ (*abbr.* TV) *noun* **1** (also **'television set**) (also *BrE informal* **telly**) [C] a piece of electrical equipment with a screen on which you can watch programmes with moving pictures and sounds: *a colour television* ◊ *to turn the television on/off* **2** (also *BrE informal* **telly**) [U] the programmes broadcast on television: *We don't do much in the evenings except watch television.* **3** [U] the system, process or business of broadcasting television programmes: *satellite/terrestrial/digital television* ◊ *the television news* ◊ *a television series/documentary* ◊ *a television company/presenter* ◊ *I'd like to work in television* (= for a television company).—see also CABLE TELEVISION, CLOSED-CIRCUIT TELEVISION [IDM] **on (the) 'television** (also *informal* **on TV**) (also *BrE informal* **on the 'telly**) being broadcast by television; appearing in a television programme: *What's on television tonight?* ◊ *Is there anything good on the telly tonight?* ◊ *It was on TV yesterday.* ◊ *I recognize you. Aren't you on television?*

tele·work·ing /'teliwɜːkɪŋ; *AmE* -wɜːrk-/ *noun* [U] (*BrE*) the practice of working from home, communicating with your office, customers and others by telephone, computer, etc. ▶ **tele·worker** *noun*

telex /'teleks/ *noun, verb*
■ *noun* **1** [U] an international system of communication in which messages are typed on a special machine and sent by the telephone system **2** [C] a message sent or received by telex: *Several telexes arrived this morning.* **3** [C] (*informal*) a machine for sending and receiving messages by telex
■ *verb* [V, VN] to send a message by telex

tell /tel/ *verb* (**told, told** /təʊld; *AmE* toʊld/)
GIVE INFORMATION | **1** ~ **sb** (**sth**) | ~ **sth to sb** (of a person) to give information to sb by speaking or writing: [VN, VNN] *He told the news to everybody he saw.* ◊ *He told everybody he saw the news.* ◊ [VN] *Why wasn't I told about the accident?* ◊ [VNN] *Did she tell you her name?* ◊ [VN (**that**)] *They've told us (that) they're not coming.* ◊ *Are you telling me you didn't have any help with this?* (= I don't believe what you have said) ◊ [VN wh-] *Tell me where you live.* ◊ [VN speech] *'I'm ready to go now,' he told her.* ⇨ note at SAY **2** (of some writing, an instrument, a sign, etc.) to give information about sth: [VNN] *The advertisement told us very little about the product.* ◊ [VN wh-] *This gauge tells you how much fuel you have left.* ◊ [VN (**that**)] *The sound of his breathing told her (that) he was asleep.*
EXPRESS IN WORDS | **3** to express sth in words: [VN] *to tell stories/jokes/lies* ◊ *Are you telling the truth?* ◊ [VN wh-] *I can't tell you how happy I am.*
SECRET | **4** [V] to let sb know a secret: *Promise you won't tell.* ◊ *'Who are you going out with tonight?' 'That would be telling!'* (= it's a secret)
ORDER | **5** to order or advise sb to do sth: [VN to inf] *He was told to sit down and wait.* ◊ *There was a sign telling motorists to slow down.* ◊ *I kept telling myself to keep calm.* ◊ [VNN] *Do what I tell you.* ◊ [VN] *Children must do as they're told.* ◊ [VN wh-] *Don't tell me what to do!* ◊ [VN (**that**)]

The doctor told me (that) I should eat less fat. ⟶ note at ORDER, SAY

KNOW/JUDGE | **6** (not used in the progressive tenses) to know, see or judge sth correctly: [V] *I think he's happy. It's hard to tell.* ◊ *As far as I can tell, she's enjoying the course.* ◊ [V(that)] *I could tell (that) he was angry from his expression.* ◊ [Vwh-] *'That's not an original.' 'How can you tell?'* ◊ *The only way to tell if you like something is by trying it.*

DISTINGUISH | **7 ~ A from B** (not used in the progressive tenses or in the passive) to distinguish one thing or person from another: [VN] *It was hard to tell the difference between the two versions.* ◊ *Can you tell Tom from his twin brother?* ◊ *It's difficult to tell them apart.* ◊ [Vwh-] *The kittens looked exactly alike—how could you tell which was which?*

HAVE EFFECT | **8** [V] **~ (on sb)** to have an effect on sb/sth, especially a bad one: *The strain was beginning to tell on the rescue team.*

IDM **all 'told** with all people, etc. counted and included: *There are 52 people coming, all told.* **don't 'tell me** (*spoken, informal*) used to say that you know or can guess what sb is going to say, especially because it is typical of them: *Don't tell me you were late again!* **I/I'll 'tell you 'what** (*spoken*) used to introduce a suggestion: *I'll tell you what—let's stay in instead.* **I 'tell you | I can 'tell you | I'm 'telling you** (*spoken*) used to emphasize what you are saying, especially when it is surprising or difficult to believe: *It isn't cheap, I can tell you!* ◊ *I'm telling you, that's exactly what she said.* **I 'told you (so)** (*spoken*) used when sth bad has happened, to remind sb that you warned them about it and they did not listen to you **,live, etc. to ,tell the 'tale** to survive a difficult or dangerous experience so that you can tell others what really happened **tell a 'different story/tale** to give some information that is different from what you expect or have been told **tell its own tale/story** to explain itself, without needing any further explanation or comment: *Her face told its own story.* **'tell me** (*spoken*) used to introduce a question: *Tell me, have you had lunch yet?* **'tell me about it** (*spoken*) used to say that you understand what sb is talking about and have had the same experience: *'I get so annoyed with Steve!' 'Tell me about it. He drives me crazy.'* **tell me a'nother!** (*spoken*) used to tell sb that you do not believe what they have said **tell 'tales (about sth/on sb)** (*BrE*) to tell sb about sth that another person has done wrong—related noun TELLTALE **tell the 'time** (*BrE*) (*AmE* **tell 'time**) to read the time from a clock, etc: *She's only five—she hasn't learnt to tell the time yet.* **tell sb where to get 'off/where they get 'off** (*BrE, informal*) to make it clear to sb that you will no longer accept their bad behaviour **tell sb where to 'put/'stick sth | tell sb what they can 'do with sth** (*informal*) to make it clear to sb that you are angry and are rejecting what they are offering you **there's no 'telling** used to say that it is impossible to know what happened or will happen: *There's no telling how they'll react.* **to tell (you) the 'truth** used when admitting sth: *To tell the truth, I fell asleep in the middle of her talk.* **you can never 'tell | you never can 'tell** you can never be sure, for example because things are not always what they appear to be **you're telling 'me!** (*spoken, informal*) I completely agree with you—more at HEAR, KISS *v.*, LITTLE *adj.*, THING, TIME *n.*, TRUTH

PHRV **,tell a'gainst sb** (*BrE, formal*) to be a disadvantage to sb: *Her lack of experience told against her.* **'tell of sth** (*formal* or *literary*) to make sth known; to give an account of sth: *notices telling of the proposed job cuts* **,tell sb↔'off (for sth/for doing sth)** (*informal*) to speak angrily to sb for doing sth wrong SYN SCOLD: *I told the boys off for making so much noise.* ◊ *Did you get told off?*—related noun TELLING-OFF **'tell on sb** (*informal*) to tell a person in authority about sth bad that sb has done: *Promise not to tell on me!*

tell·er /'telə(r)/ *noun* **1** a person whose job is to receive and pay out money in a bank **2** a machine that does this automatically: *automatic teller machines* **3** a person whose job is to count votes, especially in a parliament

4 (usually in compounds) a person who tells stories, etc: *a foul-mouthed teller of lies.*—see also FORTUNE TELLER, STORYTELLER

tell·ing /'telɪŋ/ *adj.* **1** having a strong or important effect; effective: *a telling argument/criticism* **2** showing effectively what sb/sth is really like, but often without intending to: *The number of homeless people is a telling comment on the state of society.* ▶ **tell·ing·ly** *adv.*

,telling-'off *noun* [usually sing.] (*pl.* **,tellings-'off**) (*BrE, informal*) the act of speaking angrily to sb, especially a child, because they have done sth bad

tell·tale /'telteɪl/ *adj., noun*
■ *adj.* [only before noun] showing that sth exists or has happened: *telltale clues/marks/signs/sounds* ◊ *The telltale smell of cigarettes told her that he had been in the room.*
■ *noun* (*BrE*) (*AmE* **tat·tle·tale**) (*informal, disapproving*) a child who tells an adult what another child has done wrong

telly /'teli/ *noun* (*pl.* **-ies**) (*BrE, informal*) **1** [C] a television set: *He spends most evenings just sitting in front of the telly.* **2** [U] the programmes broadcast on television: *daytime telly* ◊ *Is there anything good on telly?*

tem·er·ity /tə'merəti/ *noun* [U] (*formal*) extremely confident behaviour that people are likely to consider rude: *He had the temerity to call me a liar!*

temp /temp/ *noun, verb, abbr.*
■ *noun* a temporary employee in an office, especially a secretary
■ *verb* [V] (*informal*) to do a temporary job or a series of temporary jobs: *I've been temping for an employment agency.*
■ *abbr.* (also **temp.** especially in *AmE*) temperature: *Max temp 17°C*

tem·per /'tempə(r)/ *noun, verb*
■ *noun* **1** [C usually sing., U] if sb has a **temper**, they become angry very easily: *a violent/quick temper* ◊ *He must learn to control his temper.* ◊ *She broke the plates in a fit of temper.* ◊ *After an hour of waiting, tempers began to fray* (= people began to get angry). **2** [C, usually sing.] a short period of feeling very angry: *to fly into a temper* ◊ *She says awful things when she's in a temper.* **3** [C] the way that you are feeling at a particular time SYN MOOD: *Come back when you're in a better temper.* ◊ *to be in a bad/filthy/foul temper* **4** (**-tempered**) (in adjectives) having a particular type of temper: *good-/bad-tempered* ◊ *a sweet-tempered child* HELP You will find other compounds ending in **-tempered** at their place in the alphabet. IDM **lose/keep your 'temper (with sb)** to fail/manage to control your anger: *She lost her temper with a customer and shouted at him.* ◊ *I struggle to keep my temper with the kids when they misbehave.*— more at QUICK *adj.*
■ *verb* [VN] **1 ~ sth (with sth)** (*formal*) to make sth less severe by adding sth that has the opposite effect: *Justice must be tempered with mercy.* **2** (*technical*) to make metal as hard as it needs to be by heating and then cooling it

tem·pera /'tempərə/ *noun* [U] a kind of paint in which the colour is mixed with egg and water; a method of painting that uses this kind of paint

tem·pera·ment /'temprəmənt/ *noun* **1** [C, U] a person's or an animal's nature as shown in the way they behave or react to situations or people: *to have an artistic/a nervous/a fiery temperament* ◊ *a horse with an excellent temperament* ◊ *She's a dreamer and a romantic by temperament.* **2** [U] the tendency to get emotional and excited very easily and behave in an unreasonable way: *an actor given to displays of temperament*

tem·pera·men·tal /,temprə'mentl/ *adj.* **1** (usually *disapproving*) having a tendency to become angry, excited or upset easily, and to behave in an unreasonable way: *You never know what to expect with her. She's so temperamental.* ◊ (*figurative*) *The printer's being temperamental this morning.* **2** connected with sb's nature and personality: *They are firm friends in spite of temperamental differences.* ▶ **tem·pera·men·tal·ly** /-təli/ *adv.*: *I'm temperamentally unsuited to this job.*

T

æ	ɑː	e	ɜː	ə	ɪ	iː	i	ɒ	ɔː	ʌ	ʊ	u	uː
cat	father	ten	bird	about	sit	see	many	got	saw	cup	put	actual	too
								(BrE)					

tem·per·ance /'tempərəns/ *noun* [U] **1** (*old-fashioned*) the practice of not drinking alcohol because of your moral or religious beliefs **2** (*formal*) the practice of controlling your behaviour, the amount you eat, etc., so that it is always reasonable [SYN] MODERATION

tem·per·ate /'tempərət/ *adj.* **1** [usually before noun] (*technical*) (of a climate or region) having a mild temperature without extremes of heat or cold: *temperate zones/ forests/latitudes* **2** (*formal*) behaving in a calm and controlled way [OPP] of sense 2 INTEMPERATE ► **tem·per·ate·ly** *adv.*

tem·pera·ture /'temprətʃə(r); *AmE also* -tʃur/ *noun* [C, U] (*abbr.* **temp**) **1** the measurement in degrees of how hot or cold a thing or place is: *high/low temperatures* ◊ *a sudden fall/drop in temperature* ◊ *The temperature has risen (by) five degrees.* ◊ *Heat the oven to a temperature of 200°C* (= degrees centigrade). ◊ *Some places have had temperatures in the 40s* (= over 40° centigrade). ◊ *Keep the wine at room temperature.* **2** the measurement of how hot sb's body is: *to take sb's temperature* (= measure the temperature of sb's body using a special instrument) ◊ *Does he have a temperature* (= is it higher than normal, because of illness)? ◊ *She's running a temperature* (= it is higher than normal). ◊ *He's in bed with a temperature of 40°.*—compare FEVER ➪ Appendix 3 [IDM] **raise/lower the 'temperature** to increase/decrease the amount of excitement, emotion, etc. in a situation: *His angry refusal to agree raised the temperature of the meeting.* ◊ *The government tried to lower the political temperature by agreeing to some of the demands.*

tem·pest /'tempɪst/ *noun* (*formal* or *literary*) a violent storm [IDM] **a tempest in a 'teapot** (*AmE*) = A STORM IN A TEACUP at STORM *n.*

tem·pes·tu·ous /tem'pestʃuəs/ *adj.* **1** (*written*) full of extreme emotions and excitement: *a tempestuous relationship/love affair* **2** (*formal* or *literary*) caused by or affected by a violent storm: *tempestuous seas*

tem·plate /'templeɪt/ *noun* **1** a shape cut out of a hard material, used as a model for producing exactly the same shape many times in another material **2** a thing that is used as a model for producing other similar examples: *If you need to write a lot of similar letters, set up a template on your computer.*

tem·ple /'templ/ *noun* **1** a building used for the worship of a god or gods, especially in religions other than Christianity: *the Temple of Diana at Ephesus* ◊ *a Buddhist/ Hindu/Sikh temple* ◊ (*AmE*) *to go to temple* (= to a service in a SYNAGOGUE, *where Jews worship*) **2** each of the flat parts at the sides of the forehead: *She had black hair, greying at the temples.*—picture at BODY

tempo /'tempəʊ; *AmE* -poʊ/ *noun* (*pl.* **-os** or, in sense 1, *technical* **tempi** /'tempi:/) **1** the speed or rhythm of a piece of music: *a slow/fast tempo* ◊ *It's a difficult piece, with numerous changes of tempo.* **2** the speed of any movement or activity [SYN] PACE: *the increasing tempo of life in Western society* ◊ *Don't let the other team dictate the tempo of the game.*

tem·por·al /'tempərəl/ *adj.* **1** (*formal*) connected with the real physical world, not spiritual matters: *Although spiritual leader of millions of people, the Pope has no temporal power.* **2** (*formal*) connected with or limited by time: *a universe which has spatial and temporal dimensions* **3** (*anatomy*) near the TEMPLE(S) at the side of the head: *the left/right temporal lobe of the brain*

tem·por·ary /'temprəri; *AmE* -pəreri/ *adj.* lasting or intended to last only for a short time; not permanent: *temporary relief from pain* ◊ *temporary work/accommodation* ◊ *a temporary measure/solution/arrangement* ◊ *More than half the staff are temporary.* [OPP] PERMANENT ► **tem·por·ar·ily** /'temprərəli; *AmE* ˌtempə'rerəli/ *adv.*: *We regret this service is temporarily unavailable.* **tem·por·ari·ness** *noun* [U]

tem·por·ize (*BrE also* **-ise**) /'tempəraɪz/ *verb* [V] (*formal*) to delay making a decision or giving a definite answer, in order to gain time

tempt /tempt/ *verb* **~ sb (into sth/into doing sth) 1** to attract sb or make sb want to do or have sth, even if they know it is wrong: [VN] *I was tempted by the dessert menu.* ◊ *Don't tempt thieves by leaving valuables clearly visible.* ◊ [VN to inf] *I was tempted to take the day off.* **2** to persuade or try to persuade sb to do sth that you want them to do, for example by offering them sth: [VN] *How can we tempt young people into engineering?* ◊ [VN to inf] *Nothing would tempt me to live here.* [IDM] **tempt 'fate/'providence** to do sth too confidently in a way that might mean that your good luck will come to an end: *She felt it would be tempting fate to try the difficult climb a second time.*

temp·ta·tion /temp'teɪʃn/ *noun* **1** [C, U] the desire to do or have sth that you know is bad or wrong: *the temptation of easy profits* ◊ *to give way to/yield to temptation* ◊ *I couldn't resist the temptation to open the letter.* ◊ *Don't put temptation in her way by offering her a cigarette.* **2** [C] a thing that makes sb want to do or have sth that they know is bad or wrong: *An expensive bicycle is a temptation to thieves.*

tempt·er /'temptə(r)/ *noun* a person who tries to persuade sb to do sth, especially sth bad or wrong

tempt·ing /'temptɪŋ/ *adj.* something that is **tempting** is attractive, and makes people want to have it, do it, etc: *It was a tempting offer.* ◊ *That cake looks very tempting.* ◊ *It's tempting to speculate about what might have happened.* ► **tempt·ing·ly** *adv.*

temp·tress /'temptrəs/ *noun* (*old-fashioned* or *humorous*) a woman who TEMPTS sb, especially one who deliberately makes a man want to have sex with her

ten /ten/ *number* 10 [HELP] There are examples of how to use numbers at the entry for **five**. [IDM] **ˌten out of 'ten (for sth)** (*BrE*, often *ironic*) used to say that sb has guessed sth correctly or done sth very well: *Not brilliant, Robyn, but I'll give you ten out of ten for effort.* **ˌten to 'one** very probably: *Ten to one he'll be late.*

ten·able /'tenəbl/ *adj.* **1** (of a theory, an opinion, etc.) easy to defend against attack or criticism: *a tenable position* ◊ *The old idea that this type of work was not suitable for women was no longer tenable.* [OPP] UNTENABLE **2** [not before noun] (of a job, position, etc., especially in a university) that can be held for a particular period of time: *The lectureship is tenable for a period of three years.*

ten·acious /tə'neɪʃəs/ *adj.* (*written*) **1** that does not stop holding sth or give up sth easily; determined: *a tenacious grip* ◊ *The party has kept its tenacious hold on power for more than twenty years.* **2** continuing to exist, have influence, etc. for longer than you might expect [SYN] PERSISTENT: *tenacious traditions/beliefs* ◊ *a tenacious illness* ► **ten·acious·ly** *adv.*: *Though seriously ill, he still clings tenaciously to life.* **ten·acity** /tə'næsəti/ *noun* [U]: *They competed with skill and tenacity.*

ten·ancy /'tenənsi/ *noun* (*pl.* **-ies**) **1** [C] a period of time that you rent a house, land, etc. for: *a three-month tenancy* ◊ *a tenancy agreement* **2** [C, U] the right to live or work in a building or on land that you rent: *They had taken over the tenancy of the farm.*

ten·ant /'tenənt/ *noun, verb*
■ *noun* a person who pays rent for the use of a room, building, land, etc. to the person who owns it: *They had evicted their tenants for non-payment of rent.* ◊ *The decorating was done by a previous tenant.* ◊ *tenant farmers* (= ones who do not own their own farms)
■ *verb* [VN] [usually passive] to live or work in a place as a tenant: *a tenanted farm*

tench /tentʃ/ *noun* (*pl.* **tench**) a European FRESHWATER fish

tend /tend/ *verb* **1** [V to inf] to be likely to do sth or to happen in a particular way because this is what often or usually happens: *Women tend to live longer than men.* ◊ *When I'm tired, I tend to make mistakes.* ◊ *It tends to get very cold here in the winter.* ◊ *People tend to think that the problem will never affect them.* **2** [V] **~ (to/towards sth)** to take a particular direction or often have a particular quality: *His views tend towards the extreme.* ◊ *Prices have tended downwards over recent years.* **3** **~ (to) sb/sth** to care for sb/sth: [VN] *a shepherd tending his sheep* ◊ *Doctors and nurses tended the injured.* ◊ *well-tended gardens* ◊ [V] *Ambulance crews were tending to the injured.* **4** [VN]

(*AmE*) to serve customers in a store, bar, etc: *He had a job **tending bar** in San Francisco.*

ten·den·cy /ˈtendənsi/ *noun* (*pl.* -**ies**) **1** [C] ~ (**for sb/sth**) (**to do sth**)| ~ (**to/towards sth**) if sb/sth has a particular **tendency**, they are likely to behave or act in a particular way: *to display artistic/musical/criminal tendencies* ◊ *I have a tendency to talk too much when I'm nervous.* ◊ *There is a tendency for this disease to run in families.* ◊ *She has a strong natural tendency towards caution.* **2** [C] ~ (**for sb/sth**) (**to do sth**)| ~ (**to/towards sth**) a new custom that is starting to develop [SYN] TREND: *There is a growing tendency among employers to hire casual staff.* **3** [C+sing./pl. *v.*] (*BrE*) a group within a larger political group, whose views are more extreme than those of the rest of the group: *the militant tendency*

ten·den·tious /tenˈdenʃəs/ *adj.* (*formal*, usually *disapproving*) (of a speech, piece of writing, theory, etc.) expressing a very strong opinion that people are likely to disagree with: *tendentious political memoirs* ▶ **ten·den·tious·ly** *adv.* **ten·den·tious·ness** *noun* [U]

ten·der /ˈtendə(r)/ *adj.*, *noun*, *verb*
■ *adj.* (**ten·derer**, **ten·derest**) [HELP] more **tender** and most **tender** are also common **1** kind, gentle and loving: *tender words/looks/kisses* ◊ *What he needs now is a lot of tender loving care* (= sympathetic treatment). **2** (of food) easy to bite through and cut: *This meat is extremely tender.* ◊ *Boil the beans until they are tender.* [OPP] TOUGH **3** (of part of the body) painful when you touch it [SYN] SORE: *My leg is still very tender where I banged it.* **4** easily hurt or damaged [SYN] DELICATE: *tender young plants* ▶ **ten·der·ly** *adv.* **ten·der·ness** *noun* [U] [IDM] **at a ˌtender ˈage | at the tender age of …** used in connection with sb who is still young and does not have much experience: *He left home at the tender age of 15.* ◊ *She shouldn't be having to deal with problems like this **at such a tender age**.*
■ *noun* **1** a formal offer to supply goods or carry out work at a stated price [SYN] BID: *Cleaning and laundry services have been **put out to tender** (= companies have been asked to make offers to supply these services).* ◊ *a competitive tender* **2** a truck attached to a steam engine, carrying fuel and water **3** a small boat, used for carrying people or goods between a larger boat and the shore
■ *verb* **1** [V] ~ (**for sth**) to make a formal offer to supply goods or carry out work at a stated price: *Local firms were invited to tender for the building contract.* ◊ *competitive tendering* **2** [VN] ~ **sth** (**to sb**) (*formal*) to offer or give sth to sb: *He has **tendered his resignation** to the Prime Minister.*

tend·er·foot /ˈtendəfʊt; *AmE* -dərf-/ *noun* (*pl.* **tend·er·feet** or **tend·er·foots**) (*AmE, informal*) a person who is new to sth and not experienced

ˌtender-ˈhearted *adj.* having a kind and gentle nature

ten·der·ize (*BrE* also **-ise**) /ˈtendəraɪz/ *verb* [VN] to make meat softer and easier to cut and eat by preparing it in a particular way

ten·der·loin /ˈtendəlɔɪn; *AmE* -dərl-/ *noun* [U] good quality meat from the back or side of a cow or pig

ten·don /ˈtendən/ *noun* a strong band of tissue in the body that joins a muscle to a bone

ten·dril /ˈtendrəl/ *noun* **1** a thin curling stem that grows from a climbing plant. A plant uses tendrils to attach itself to a wall or other support. **2** (*literary*) a thin curling piece of sth such as hair: *Her hair hung in tendrils about her face.*

tene·ment /ˈtenəmənt/ *noun* a large building divided into flats/apartments, especially in a poor area of a city: *a tenement block/building* ◊ *They lived in a crumbling Glasgow tenement.*

tenet /ˈtenɪt/ *noun* (*formal*) one of the principles or beliefs that a theory or larger set of beliefs is based on: *one of the basic/central tenets of Christianity*

ten·fold /ˈtenfəʊld; *AmE* -foʊld/ *adj.*, *adv.* ⇨ -FOLD

ten·ner /ˈtenə(r)/ *noun* (*BrE, informal*) £10 or a ten-pound note: *You can have it for a tenner.*

ten·nis /ˈtenɪs/ (also *formal* ˌlawn ˈtennis) *noun* [U] a game in which two or four players use RACKETS to hit a ball backwards and forwards across a net on a specially marked court: *a tennis player/tournament/club/court*—picture on page 1250

ˈtennis racket (also **ˈtennis racˌquet**) *noun* the RACKET that you use when you play tennis

ˈtennis shoe (*AmE* also **athˈletic shoe**) *noun* a sports shoe that is made of strong cotton fabric or leather—picture at SHOE

tenon /ˈtenən/ *noun* (*technical*) an end of a piece of wood that has been cut to fit into a MORTISE so that the two are held together

tenor /ˈtenə(r)/ *noun*, *adj.*
■ *noun* **1** [C] a man's singing voice with a range just below the lowest woman's voice; a man with a tenor voice—compare ALTO, BARITONE, BASS **2** [sing.] a musical part written for tenor voice **3** [sing.] **the ~ of sth** (*formal*) the general character or meaning of sth: *I was encouraged by the general tenor of his remarks.*
■ *adj.* [only before noun] (of a musical instrument) with a range of notes similar to that of a tenor voice: *a tenor saxophone/trombone*—compare ALTO, SOPRANO

ˌten ˈpence (also **ˌten pence ˈpiece, 10p** /ˌten ˈpiː/) *noun* a British coin worth ten pence: *Have you got a ten pence piece?*

ten·pin /ˈtenpɪn/ *noun* **1** [C] any of the ten bottle-shaped objects that players try to knock over in the game of TENPIN BOWLING **2** (**ten·pins**) [U] (*AmE*) = TENPIN BOWLING

ˌtenpin ˈbowling (*AmE* also **ten·pins**) *noun* [U] a game in which players try to knock over tenpins by rolling a heavy ball at them, played indoors, especially in a BOWL-ING ALLEY

tense /tens/ *adj.*, *noun*, *verb*
■ *adj.* **1** (of a person) nervous or worried, and unable to relax: *He's a very tense person.* ◊ *She sounded tense and angry.* **2** (of a situation, an event, a period of time, etc.) in which people have strong feelings such as worry, anger, etc. that often cannot be expressed openly: *I spent a tense few weeks waiting for the results of the tests.* ◊ *The atmosphere in the meeting was getting more and more tense.* **3** (of a muscle or other part of the body) tight rather than relaxed: *tense shoulders/hands* ◊ *A massage will relax those tense muscles.* **4** (of wire, etc.) stretched tightly ▶ **tense·ly** *adv.* **tense·ness** *noun* [U]
■ *noun* (*grammar*) any of the forms of a verb that may be used to show the time of the action or state expressed by the verb: *the past/present/future tense*
■ *verb* ~ (**sth**) (**up**) to make your muscles tight and stiff, especially because you are not relaxed: [V] *She tensed, hearing the strange noise again.* ◊ [VN] *He tensed himself, listening to see if anyone had followed him.* [IDM] **be/get tensed ˈup** to become or feel nervous or worried so that you cannot relax

ten·sile /ˈtensaɪl; *AmE* ˈtensl/ *adj.* (*technical*) **1** [only before noun] used to describe the extent to which sth can stretch without breaking: *the tensile strength of wire/rope* **2** that can be drawn out or stretched: *tensile cable*

ten·sion /ˈtenʃn/ *noun*, *verb*
■ *noun* **1** [U, C, usually pl.] ~ (**between A and B**) a situation in which people do not trust each other, or feel unfriendly towards each other, and which may cause them to attack each other: *There is mounting tension along the border.* ◊ *international/racial/political tensions* ◊ *Family tensions and conflicts may lead to violence.* **2** [C, U] ~ (**between A and B**) a situation in which the fact that there are different needs or interests causes difficulties: *There is often a tension between the aims of the company and the wishes of the employees.* **3** [U] a feeling of anxiety and stress that makes it impossible to relax: *nervous tension* ◊ *We laughed and that helped ease the tension.* **4** [U] the feeling of fear and excitement that is created by a writer or a film/movie DIRECTOR: *dramatic tension* ◊ *As the movie progresses the tension builds.* **5** [U] the state of being stretched tight; the extent to which sth is stretched tight: *muscular tension* ◊ *Adjust the string tension of your tennis racket to suit your style of playing.*—see also SURFACE TENSION
■ *verb* [VN] (*technical*) to make a wire, sail, etc. tight and stretched

b	d	f	g	h	k	l	m	n	p	r
bad	did	fall	get	hat	cat	leg	man	now	pen	red

tent /tent/ *noun* a shelter made of a large sheet of CANVAS, NYLON, etc. that is supported by poles and ropes fixed to the ground, and is used especially for camping: *to put up/ take down a tent ◊ to pitch* (= put up) *a tent*

ten·ta·cle /'tentəkl/ *noun* **1** [C] a long thin part of the body of some creatures, such as an OCTOPUS, used for feeling or holding things, for moving or for getting food: *(figurative) Tentacles of fear closed around her body.*— picture on page A7 **2 (tentacles)** [pl.] (usually *disapproving*) the influence that a large place, organization or system has and that is hard to avoid: *The tentacles of satellite television are spreading even wider.*

ten·ta·tive /'tentətɪv/ *adj.* **1** (of an arrangement, agreement, etc.) not definite or certain because you may want to change it later: *We made a tentative arrangement to meet again next Friday. ◊ He reached some tentative conclusions about the possible cause of the accident.* **2** not behaving or done with confidence SYN HESITANT: *a tentative smile/nod/greeting ◊ Her English is correct but tentative.* ▶ **ten·ta·tive·ly** *adv.* **ten·ta·tive·ness** *noun* [U]

tent·ed /'tentɪd/ *adj.* consisting of tents; like a tent: *a tented village/camp*

ten·ter·hooks /'tentəhʊks; *AmE* -tərh-/ *noun* [pl.] IDM **(be) on 'tenterhooks** (*AmE* also **be on ˌpins and 'needles**) (to be) very anxious or excited while you are waiting to find out sth or see what will happen: *I've been on tenterhooks all week waiting for the results.* ORIGIN From **tenterhook**, a hook which in the past was used to keep material stretched on a drying frame during manufacture.

tenth /tenθ/ *ordinal number, noun*
■ *ordinal number* 10th HELP There are examples of how to use ordinal numbers at the entry for **fifth**.
■ *noun* each of ten equal parts of sth

'tent peg *noun* = PEG

tenu·ous /'tenjuəs/ *adj.* **1** so weak or uncertain that it hardly exists: *a tenuous hold on life ◊ His links with the organization turned out to be, at best, tenuous.* **2** extremely thin and easily broken: *the tenuous threads of a spider's web* ▶ **tenu·ous·ly** *adv.*

ten·ure /'tenjə(r)/ *noun* [U] **1** the period of time when sb holds an important job, especially a political one; the act of holding an important job: *his four-year tenure as President ◊ She knew that tenure of high political office was beyond her.* **2** the right to stay permanently in your job, especially as a teacher at a university: *It's still extremely difficult to get tenure.* **3** the legal right to live in a house or use a piece of land: *When you rent a house here, you don't have security of tenure.*

ten·ured /'tenjəd; *AmE* -jərd/ *adj.* [usually before noun] **1** (of an official job) that you can keep permanently: *a tenured appointment/post* **2** (of a person, especially a teacher at a university) having the right to keep their job permanently: *a tenured professor*

tepee (also **tee·pee**) /'ti:pi:/ *noun* a type of tall ˌtent shaped like a CONE, used by Native Americans in the past—see also WIGWAM

tepid /'tepɪd/ *adj.* **1** slightly warm, sometimes in a way that is not pleasant SYN LUKEWARM: *tepid tea ◊ a tepid bath/shower* **2** not enthusiastic SYN LUKEWARM: *The play was greeted with tepid applause.*

te·quila /tə'ki:lə/ *noun* **1** [U] a strong alcoholic drink made in Mexico from a tropical plant **2** [C] a glass of tequila

ter·cen·ten·ary /ˌtɜːsen'ti:nəri; *AmE* ˌtɜːrsen'tenəri/ *noun* (*pl.* -ies) the 300th anniversary of sth: *the tercentenary of the school's foundation ◊ tercentenary celebrations*

term /tɜːm; *AmE* tɜːrm/ *noun, verb*
■ *noun*—see also TERMS **1** [C] a word or phrase used as the name of sth, especially one connected with a particular type of language: *technical/legal/scientific terms ◊ a term of abuse ◊ 'Register' is the term commonly used to describe different levels of formality in language.* **2** (*AmE* also **tri·mes·ter**) [C, U] (especially in Britain) one of the three periods in the year during which classes are held in schools, universities, etc: *the spring/summer/autumn/ fall term ◊ (BrE) It's nearly the end of term. ◊ (AmE) the*

end of the term ◊ during term (*time*)—see also SEMESTER, TERMLY, TERM-TIME **3** [C] a period of time for which sth lasts; a fixed or limited time: *during the president's first term of/in office ◊ He faces a maximum prison/jail term of 25 years. ◊ a long term of imprisonment* **4** [sing.] (*formal*) the end of a particular period of time, especially one for which an agreement, etc. lasts: *His life had reached its natural term. ◊ (medical) The pregnancy went to full term* (= lasted the normal length of time). **5** [C] (*mathematics*) each of the various parts in a series, an EQUATION etc. IDM **in the 'long/'short/'medium term** used to describe what will happen a long, short, etc. time in the future: *Such a development seems unlikely, at least in the short term* (= it will not happen for quite a long time).—see also LONG-TERM, MEDIUM-TERM, SHORT-TERM
■ *verb* [often passive] (*formal*) to use a particular name or word to describe sb/sth: [VN-N] *At his age, he can hardly be termed a young man. ◊ REM sleep is termed 'active' sleep.* [also VN-ADJ]

ter·min·al /'tɜːmɪnl; *AmE* 'tɜːrm-/ *noun, adj.*
■ *noun* **1** a building or set of buildings at an airport where air passengers arrive and leave: *A second terminal was opened in 1998.* **2** a place, building or set of buildings where journeys by train, bus or boat begin or end: *a railway/bus/ferry terminal* **3** (*computing*) a piece of equipment, usually consisting of a keyboard and a screen that joins the user to a central computer system **4** (*technical*) a point at which connections can be made in an electric CIRCUIT: *a positive/negative terminal*
■ *adj.* **1** (of an illness or a disease) that cannot be cured and will lead to death, often slowly: *He has terminal lung cancer. ◊ The illness is usually terminal. ◊ (figurative) She's suffering from terminal* (= very great) *boredom.* **2** (of a person) suffering from an illness that cannot be cured and will lead to death: *a terminal case/patient* **3** certain to get worse and come to an end: *The industry is in terminal decline.* **4** [only before noun] (*formal* or *technical*) at the end of sth: *a terminal branch of a tree ◊ terminal examinations* (= at the end of a course, etc.) ▶ **ter·min·al·ly** /-nəli/ *adv.*: *a hospice for the terminally ill ◊ a terminally dull film*

ter·min·ate /'tɜːmɪneɪt; *AmE* 'tɜːrm-/ *verb* (*formal*) **1** to end; to make sth end: [V] *Your contract of employment terminates in December.* ◊ [VN] *The agreement was terminated immediately. ◊ to terminate a pregnancy* (= to have an ABORTION) **2** [V] (of a bus or train) to end a journey/trip: *This train terminates at London Victoria.*

ter·min·ation /ˌtɜːmɪ'neɪʃn; *AmE* ˌtɜːrm-/ *noun* **1** [U, C] (*formal*) the act of ending sth; the end of sth: *Failure to comply with these conditions will result in termination of the contract.* **2** [C] (*medical*) a medical operation to end a pregnancy at an early stage SYN ABORTION

ter·min·ology /ˌtɜːmɪ'nɒlədʒi; *AmE* ˌtɜːrmə'nɑːl-/ *noun* (*pl.* -ies) **1** [U, C] the set of technical words or expressions used in a particular subject: *medical terminology* **2** [U] words used with particular meanings: *The disagreement arose over a different use of terminology.* ▶ **ter·mino·logic·al** /ˌtɜːmɪnə'lɒdʒɪkl; *AmE* ˌtɜːrmənə'lɑːdʒ-/ *adj.*

ter·minus /'tɜːmɪnəs; *AmE* 'tɜːrm-/ *noun* (*pl.* **ter·mini** /'tɜːmɪnaɪ; *AmE* 'tɜːrm-/) the last station at the end of a railway/railroad line or the last stop on a bus route

ter·mite /'tɜːmaɪt; *AmE* 'tɜːrm-/ *noun* an insect that lives in organized groups, mainly in hot countries. Termites do a lot of damage by eating the wood of trees and buildings: *a termite colony*

term·ly /'tɜːmli; *AmE* 'tɜːrm-/ *adj.* (*BrE*) happening in each of the periods that the school or college year is divided into: *termly reports/examinations ◊ to pay fees in termly instalments*

'term paper *noun* (in an American school or college) a long piece of written work that a student does on a subject that is part of a course of study

terms /tɜːmz; *AmE* tɜːrmz/ *noun* [pl.] **1** the conditions that people offer, demand or accept when they make an agreement, an arrangement or a contract: *peace terms ◊ Under the terms of the agreement, their funding of the project will continue until 2005. ◊ They failed to agree on*

s	t	v	z	ʃ	ʒ	tʃ	dʒ	θ	ð	ŋ
see	tea	van	zoo	shoe	vision	chain	jam	thin	this	sing

the terms of a settlement. ◊ These are the **terms and conditions** of your employment. **2** conditions that you agree to when you buy, sell, or pay for sth; a price or cost: to buy sth on easy terms (= paying for it over a long period) ◊ My terms are £20 a lesson. **3** a way of expressing yourself or of saying sth: We wish to protest in the **strongest possible terms** (= to say we are very angry). ◊ I'll try to explain in simple terms. ◊ The letter was brief, and couched in very polite terms. **IDM** **be on good, friendly, bad, etc. 'terms (with sb)** to have a good, friendly, etc. relationship with sb: I had no idea that you and he were on such intimate terms (= were such close friends). ◊ He is still on excellent terms with his ex-wife. ◊ I'm on **first-name terms** with my boss now (= we call each other by our first names). **come to 'terms (with sb)** to reach an agreement with sb; to find a way of living or working together **come to 'terms with sth** to accept sth unpleasant by learning to deal with it: She is still coming to terms with her son's death. **in terms of 'sth | in …terms** used to show what aspect of a subject you are talking about or how you are thinking about it: The job is great in terms of salary, but it has its disadvantages. ◊ The decision was disastrous in political terms. ◊ He's talking in terms of starting a completely new career. **on your own 'terms | on sb's 'terms** according to the conditions that you or sb else decides: I'll only take the job on my own terms. ◊ I'm not doing it on your terms.—more at CONTRADICTION, EQUAL, SPEAK, UNCERTAIN

ˌterms of 'reference noun [pl.] the limits that are set on what an official committee or report has been asked to do: The matter, they decided, lay outside the commission's terms of reference.

'term-time noun [U] (BrE) the period of time when classes are held at a school, college, or university, as opposed to the holidays/vacations: I never went out in the evenings during term-time. ▶ 'term-time adj. [only before noun]: Please state your home and term-time addresses.

tern /tɜːn; AmE tɜːrn/ noun a seabird with long pointed wings and a tail with two points

ter·race /'terəs/ noun **1** [C] (BrE) (often in the names of streets) a continuous row of similar houses that are joined together in one block: 12 Albert Terrace **2** [C] a flat, hard area, especially outside a house or restaurant, where you can sit, eat and enjoy the sun: a sun terrace ◊ a roof terrace ◊ All rooms have a balcony or terrace.—see also PATIO **3** (terraces) [pl.] (BrE) the wide steps at a football ground where people can stand to watch the game **4** [C] one of a series of flat areas of ground that are cut into the side of a hill like steps so that crops can be grown there

ter·raced /'terəst/ adj. **1** (BrE) used to describe houses that form part of a terrace, or streets with houses in terraces: a terraced cottage ◊ terraced housing ◊ terraced streets **2** (of a slope or the side of a hill) having a series of flat areas of ground like steps cut into it: a terraced garden ◊ a terraced hillside

ˌterraced 'house (also less frequent ˌterrace 'house) (both BrE) (AmE 'row house, 'town·house) noun a house that is one of a row of houses that are joined together on each side

ter·ra·cing /'terəsɪŋ/ noun [U] **1** (BrE) an area with wide steps at a football ground where people can stand to watch the game: Many clubs want to keep terracing at their grounds. **2** a slope or the side of a hill that has had flat areas like steps cut into it

terra·cotta /ˌterəˈkɒtə; AmE -ˈkɑːtə/ noun [U] **1** reddish-brown clay that has been baked but not GLAZED, used for making pots, etc: terracotta pots/tiles/roofs **2** a reddish-brown colour

terra firma /ˌterə ˈfɜːmə; AmE ˈfɜːrmə/ noun [U] (from Latin, usually humorous) safe dry land, as contrasted with water or air: After two days at sea, it was good to be back on terra firma again.

ter·rain /təˈreɪn/ noun [C, U] (written) used to refer to an area of land when you are mentioning its natural features, for example, if it is rough, flat, etc: difficult/rough/mountainous terrain

terra·pin /'terəpɪn/ noun a small TURTLE (= a reptile with a hard round shell), that lives in warm rivers and lakes in N America—compare TORTOISE

ter·res·trial /təˈrestriəl/ adj. **1** (technical) (of animals and plants) living on the land or on the ground, rather than in water, in trees or in the air **2** connected with the planet Earth: terrestrial life—compare CELESTIAL, EXTRA-TERRESTRIAL **3** (of television and broadcasting systems) operating on earth rather than from a SATELLITE

ter·rible /'terəbl/ adj. **1** very unpleasant; making you feel very unhappy, upset or frightened: a terrible shock/experience/nightmare ◊ What terrible news! ◊ I've just had a terrible thought. **2** causing great harm or injury; very serious: a terrible storm/murder/accident ◊ He had suffered terrible injuries. **3** [not before noun] unhappy or ill: I feel terrible—I think I'll go to bed. **4** (informal) of very bad quality; very bad: a terrible meal/book/hotel ◊ I have a terrible memory for names. ◊ Your driving is terrible! **5** [only before noun] used to show the great extent or degree of sth bad: a terrible mistake ◊ to be in terrible pain ◊ The room was in a terrible mess. ◊ (informal) I had a terrible job (= it was very difficult) to persuade her to come!

ter·ribly /'terəbli/ adv. **1** (especially BrE) very: I'm terribly sorry—did I hurt you? ◊ It's terribly important for parents to be consistent. **2** very much; very badly: I miss him terribly. ◊ They suffered terribly when their son was killed. ◊ The experiment went terribly wrong.

ter·rier /'teriə(r)/ noun a small active dog. There are many types of terrier.—see also BULL TERRIER, JACK RUSSELL, PIT BULL TERRIER, YORKSHIRE TERRIER

ter·rif·ic /təˈrɪfɪk/ adj. **1** (informal) excellent; wonderful: I feel absolutely terrific today! ◊ She's doing a terrific job. **2** very large; very great: We drove along at a terrific speed. ◊ I've got a terrific amount of work to do.

ter·rif·ic·al·ly /təˈrɪfɪkli/ adv. (informal) extremely (usually used about positive qualities): terrifically exciting/talented

ter·ri·fied /'terɪfaɪd/ adj. ~ (of sb/sth) | ~ (of doing sth) | ~ (that…) very frightened: to be terrified of heights/spiders ◊ I'm terrified of losing you. ◊ He was terrified (that) he would fall. ◊ She was terrified at the thought of being alone. **IDM** see WIT

ter·rify /'terɪfaɪ/ verb (ter·ri·fies, ter·ri·fy·ing, ter·ri·fied, ter·ri·fied) [VN] to make sb feel extremely frightened: Flying terrifies her. ▶ ter·ri·fy·ing adj.: It was a terrifying experience. ter·ri·fy·ing·ly adv.

ter·rine /teˈriːn/ noun [U, C] a soft mixture of finely chopped meat, fish, etc. pressed into a container and served cold, especially in slices as the first course of a meal: chicken/vegetable terrine

Ter·ri·tor·ial /ˌterəˈtɔːriəl/ noun (in Britain) a member of the Territorial Army

ter·ri·tor·ial /ˌterəˈtɔːriəl/ adj. **1** connected with the land or sea that is owned by a particular country: territorial gains/disputes ◊ Both countries feel they have territorial claims to (= have a right to own) the islands. **2** (technical) (of animals, birds, etc.) guarding and defending an area of land that they believe to be their own: territorial instincts ◊ Cats are very territorial. ▶ ter·ri·tori·al·ity /ˌterətɔːriˈæləti/ noun [U]: the instinctive territoriality of some animals ter·ri·tori·al·ly adv.: The country was trying to expand territorially.

the ˌTerritorial 'Army noun [sing.+ sing./pl. v.] (abbr. TA) (in Britain) a military force of people who are not professional soldiers but who train as soldiers in their free time

ˌterritorial 'waters noun [pl.] the parts of a sea or an ocean which are near a country's coast and are legally under its control

ter·ri·tory /'terətri; AmE -tɔːri/ noun (pl. -ies) **1** [C, U] land that is under the control of a particular country or ruler: enemy/disputed/foreign territory ◊ occupied territories ◊ They have refused to allow UN troops to be stationed in their territory. **2** [C, U] an area that one person, group, animal, etc. considers as their own and defends against others who try to enter it: Mating blackbirds will

æ	ɑː	e	ɜː	ə	ɪ	iː	i	ɒ	ɔː	ʌ	ʊ	u	uː
cat	father	ten	bird	about	sit	see	many	got	saw	cup	put	actual	too

(BrE)

defend their territory against intruders. ◊ *(figurative) This type of work is **uncharted territory** for us.* ◊ *(figurative) Legal problems are Andy's territory* (= he deals with them). **3** [C, U] an area of a town, country, etc. that sb has responsibility for in their work or another activity: *Our representatives cover a very large territory.* **4** [U] a particular type of land: *unexplored territory* **5** (also **Territory**) [C] a country or an area that is part of the US, Australia or Canada but is not a state or PROVINCE: *Guam and American Samoa are US territories.* **IDM** ,**come/**,**go with the** '**territory** to be a normal and accepted part of a particular job, situation, etc.—more at NEUTRAL *adj.*

ter·ror /'terə(r)/ *noun* **1** [U, sing.] a feeling of extreme fear: *a feeling of sheer/pure terror* ◊ *Her eyes were wild with terror.* ◊ *People fled from the explosion in terror.* ◊ *She lives in terror of* (= is constantly afraid of) *losing her job.* ◊ *Some women have a terror of losing control in the birth process.* ◊ *(literary) The very name of the enemy struck terror into their hearts.* **2** [C] a person, situation or thing that makes you very afraid: *These street gangs have become the terror of the neighbourhood.* ◊ *Death holds no terrors for* (= does not frighten or worry) *me.* ◊ *The terrors of the night were past.* **3** [U] violent action or the threat of violent action that is intended to cause fear, usually for political purposes **SYN** TERRORISM: *a campaign of terror* ◊ *terror tactics*—see also REIGN OF TERROR **4** [C] *(informal)* a person (usually a child) or an animal that causes you trouble or is difficult to control: *Their kids are real little terrors.*

ter·ror·ism /'terərɪzəm/ *noun* [U] the use of violent action in order to achieve political aims or to force a government to act: *an act of terrorism*

ter·ror·ist /'terərɪst/ *noun* a person who takes part in terrorism: *The terrorists are threatening to blow up the plane.* ◊ *a terrorist attack/bomb/group*—compare FREEDOM FIGHTER

ter·ror·ize (*BrE* also **-ise**) /'terəraɪz/ *verb* [VN] ~ **sb** **(into doing sth)** to frighten and threaten people so that they will not oppose sth or will do as they are told: *drug dealers terrorizing the neighbourhood* ◊ *Thousands of people were terrorized into leaving their homes.*

'**terror-stricken** *adj.* extremely frightened

terry /'teri/ *noun* [U] a soft cotton fabric that absorbs liquids and has a surface covered with raised LOOPS of thread, used especially for making towels

terse /tɜːs; *AmE* tɜːrs/ *adj.* using few words and often not seeming polite or friendly: *a terse voice/style* ◊ *The President issued a terse statement denying the charges.*
▶ **terse·ly** *adv.* **terse·ness** *noun* [U]

ter·tiary /'tɜːʃəri; *AmE* 'tɜːrʃieri; -ʃəri/ *adj.* third in order, rank or importance: *the tertiary sector* (= the area of industry that deals with services rather than materials or goods) ◊ *(BrE) tertiary education* (= at university or college level)—compare PRIMARY, SECONDARY

'**tertiary college** *noun* (in Britain) a college that provides education for people aged 16 and older, but that is not a university

Tery·lene™ /'terəliːn/ *noun* [U] *(BrE)* a light strong artificial fabric, used for making clothes, etc.

TESL /'tesl/ *abbr.* teaching English as a second language

TESOL /'tiːsɒl; 'tesɒl; *AmE* -sɑːl/ *abbr.* **1** teaching English to speakers of other languages **2** *(AmE)* teachers of English to speakers of other languages (an organization of teachers)

test /test/ *noun, verb*
■ *noun*
OF KNOWLEDGE/ABILITY | **1** ~ **(on sth)** an examination of sb's knowledge or ability, consisting of questions for them to answer or activities for them to carry out: *an IQ/intelligence/aptitude test* ◊ *to take a test* ◊ *(BrE) to do a test* ◊ *a test on irregular verbs* ◊ *to pass/fail a test* ◊ *(BrE) a good mark in the test* ◊ *(AmE) a good grade on the test* **HELP** Use *take/do/sit a test* not *write a test.*—see also DRIVING TEST ⇨ note at EXAM
OF HEALTH | **2** a medical examination to discover what is wrong with you or to check the condition of your health:

a test for Aids ◊ *an eye test* ◊ *a pregnancy test* ◊ *When can I get my test results?*—see also BLOOD TEST, BREATH TEST
OF MACHINE/PRODUCT, etc. | **3** an experiment to discover whether or how well sth works, or to find out more information about it: *laboratory tests* ◊ *a nuclear test* ◊ *Tests have shown high levels of pollutants in the water.*—see also ACID TEST, FIELD TEST, MEANS TEST, ROAD TEST
OF STRENGTH, etc. | **4** a situation or an event that shows how good, strong, etc. sb/sth is: *The local elections will be a good test of the government's popularity.* ◊ *The match with Dundee is a real test of character for us.*
IN CRICKET, etc. | **5** = TEST MATCH
IDM **put sb/sth to the** '**test** to put sb/sth in a situation which will show what their true qualities are: *His theories have never really been put to the test.* **stand the test of** '**time** to prove to be good, popular, etc. over a long period of time: *Her poetry will stand the test of time.*
■ *verb*
KNOWLEDGE/ABILITY | **1** to examine sb's knowledge or ability by asking them questions or giving them activities to carry out: [VN] *We test your English before deciding which class to put you in.* ◊ *Children are tested on core subjects at ages 7, 11 and 14.* ◊ [V] *Schools use various methods of testing.*
HEALTH | **2** ~ **sb/sth (for sth)** to examine the blood, a part of the body, etc. to find out what is wrong with a person, or to check the condition of their health: [VN] *to test sb's eyesight/hearing* ◊ *The doctor tested him for hepatitis.* ◊ [V-ADJ] *to test positive/negative* ◊ *Two athletes tested positive for steroids.*
MACHINE/PRODUCT, etc. | **3** [VN] ~ **sth (on sth/for sth)** to use a machine, product or substance to find out how well it works or to find out more information about it: *You should test your brakes regularly.* ◊ *Our beauty products are not tested on animals.* ◊ *The water is regularly tested for purity.*
STRENGTH, etc. | **4** [VN] to be difficult and therefore need all your strength, ability, etc: *The long climb tested our fitness and stamina.*—see also TESTING
IDM **test the** '**waters** to find out what the situation is before doing sth or making a decision—more at TRIED
PHRV '**test for sth**|**test sth for sth** to examine sth to see if a particular substance, etc. is present: *testing for oil* ◊ *The software has been tested for viruses.*

test·able /'testəbl/ *adj.* that can be tested: *testable predictions/hypotheses*

tes·ta·ment /'testəmənt/ *noun* *(formal)* **1** [C usually sing, U] ~ **(to sth)** a thing that shows that sth else exists or is true **SYN** TESTIMONY: *The new model is a testament to the skill and dedication of the workforce.* **2** [C] = WILL: *This is the last will and testament of…*—see also NEW TESTAMENT, OLD TESTAMENT

'**test ban** *noun* an agreement between countries to stop testing nuclear weapons: *a test ban treaty*

'**test case** *noun* a legal case or other situation whose result will be used as an example when decisions are being made on similar cases in the future

'**test drive** *noun* an occasion when you drive a vehicle that you are thinking of buying so that you can see how well it works and if you like it ▶ '**test-drive** *verb*: [VN] *Why not test-drive the new BMW?*

test·er /'testə(r)/ *noun* **1** a person or thing that tests sth: *a battery tester* ◊ *testers of new software* **2** a small container of a product, such as PERFUME, that you can try in a shop/store to see if you like it

tes·tes *pl.* of TESTIS

tes·ticle /'testɪkl/ *noun* either of the two organs that produce SPERM, enclosed in a bag of skin below the PENIS ▶ **tes·ticu·lar** /te'stɪkjələ(r)/ *adj.* [only before noun]: *testicular cancer*

test·ify /'testɪfaɪ/ *verb* (**testi·fies**, **testi·fy·ing**, **testi·fied**, **testi·fied**) **1** ~ **(against/for sb)** | ~ **(to/about sth)** to make a statement that sth happened or that sth is true, especially as a WITNESS in a court of law: [V] *She refused to testify against her husband.* ◊ *There are several witnesses who will testify for the defence.* ◊ *He was summoned to*

aɪ	aʊ	eɪ	əʊ	oʊ	ɔɪ	ɪə	eə	ʊə	j	w
my	now	say	go	go	boy	near	hair	pure	yes	wet
			(BrE)	(AmE)						

testify before a grand jury. ◊ [V(that)] *He testified (that) he was at the theatre at the time of the murder.* [also V **speech**] **2** [V](that)] to say that you believe sth is true because you have evidence of it: *Too many young people are unable to write or spell well, as employers will testify.* **3** [V] (*especially AmE*) to express your belief in God publicly **PHRV** '**testify to sth** (*formal*) to show or be evidence that sth is true **SYN** EVIDENCE: *The film testifies to the courage of ordinary people during the war.*

tes·ti·mo·nial /ˌtestɪˈməʊniəl; *AmE* -ˈmoʊ-/ *noun* **1** a formal written statement, often by a former employer, about sb's abilities, qualities and character; a formal written statement about the quality of sth: *a glowing testimonial* ◊ *The catalogue is full of testimonials from satisfied customers.* **2** a thing that is given or done to show admiration for sb or to thank sb: *a testimonial game* (= to raise money for a particular player)

tes·ti·mony /ˈtestɪməni; *AmE* -moʊni/ *noun* (*pl.* **-ies**) **1** [U, sing.] **~** (**to sth**) a thing that shows that sth else exists or is true **SYN** TESTAMENT: *This increase in imports bears testimony to the successes of industry.* ◊ *The pyramids are an eloquent testimony to the ancient Egyptians' engineering skills.* **2** [C, U] a formal written or spoken statement saying what you know to be true, usually in a court of law: *a sworn testimony* ◊ *Her claim was supported by the testimony of several witnesses.* ◊ *Can I refuse to give testimony?*

test·ing /ˈtestɪŋ/ *noun, adj.*
■ *noun* [U] the activity of testing sb/sth in order to find sth out, see if it works, etc: *nuclear testing* ◊ *testing and assessment in education*
■ *adj.* (of a problem or situation) difficult to deal with and needing particular strength or abilities: *This has been a testing time for us all.*

'**testing ground** *noun* **1** a place or situation used for testing new ideas and methods to see if they work: *Eastern Europe has been a testing ground for rapid economic reform.* **2** a place used for testing machines, vehicles, etc. to see if they work correctly: *a piece of land in use as a tank testing ground*

tes·tis /ˈtestɪs/ *noun* (*pl.* **tes·tes** /-tiːz/) (*anatomy*) a TESTICLE

'**test match** (also **test**) *noun* a cricket or rugby match played between the teams of two different countries, usually as part of a series of matches on a tour

tes·tos·ter·one /teˈstɒstərəʊn; *AmE* teˈstɑːstəroʊn/ *noun* a HORMONE produced in men's TESTICLES that causes them to develop the physical and sexual features that are characteristic of the male body—compare OESTROGEN, PROGESTERONE

'**test pilot** *noun* a pilot whose job is to fly aircraft in order to test their performance

ˌtest '**run** *noun* = TRIAL RUN

'**test tube** *noun* a small glass tube, closed at one end, that is used in scientific experiments—picture at LABORATORY

'**test-tube baby** *noun* a baby that grows from an egg that is FERTILIZED outside the mother's body and then put back inside to continue developing normally—see also IN VITRO

testy /ˈtesti/ *adj.* (*written*) easily annoyed or irritated **SYN** IRRITABLE: *The old man sounded testy.* ▶ **test·ily** /-ɪli/ *adv.*: '*Leave me alone,' she said testily.*

tet·anus /ˈtetənəs/ *noun* [U] a disease in which the muscles, especially the jaw muscles, become stiff, caused by bacteria entering the body through cuts or wounds

tetchy /ˈtetʃi/ *adj.* bad-tempered; likely to get angry easily or without good reason ▶ **tetch·ily** /-ɪli/ *adv.*

tête-à-tête /ˌteɪt ɑː ˈteɪt/ *noun* (from *French*) a private conversation between two people

tether /ˈteðə(r)/ *verb, noun*
■ *verb* [VN] **~ sth** (**to sth**) to tie an animal to a post so that it cannot move very far
■ *noun* a rope or chain used to tie an animal to sth, allowing it to move around in a small area **IDM** see END *n.*

Teut·on·ic /tjuːˈtɒnɪk; *AmE* tuːˈtɑːnɪk/ *adj.* [usually before noun] (*informal*, often *disapproving*) showing qualities considered typical of German people: *The preparations were made with Teutonic thoroughness.*

Tex-Mex /ˌteks ˈmeks/ *adj.* [only before noun] connected with the variety of Mexican cooking, music, etc. that is found in Texas and the SW part of the US: *a Tex-Mex restaurant*

text /tekst/ *noun* **1** [U] the main printed part of a book or magazine, not the notes, pictures, etc: *My job is to lay out the text and graphics on the page.* **2** [U] any form of written material: *a computer that can process text* ◊ *printed text* **3** [C] the written form of a speech, a play, an article, etc: *The newspaper had printed the full text of the president's speech.* ◊ *Can you act out this scene without referring to the text?* **4** [C] a book, play, etc., especially one studied for an exam: *a literary text* ◊ (*BrE*) *'Macbeth' is a set text this year.* **5** [C] a piece of writing that you have to answer questions about in an exam or a lesson **SYN** PASSAGE: *Read the text carefully and then answer the questions.* **6** [C] (*AmE*) = TEXTBOOK: *medical texts* **7** [C] a sentence or short passage from the Bible that is read out and discussed by sb, especially during a religious service

text·book /ˈtekstbʊk/ *noun, adj.*
■ *noun* (*AmE* also **text**) a book that teaches a particular subject and that is used especially in schools and colleges: *a school/medical/history textbook*
■ *adj.* [only before noun] used to describe sth that is done exactly as it should be done, in the best possible way: *It was a textbook example of how the game should be played.*

tex·tile /ˈtekstaɪl/ *noun* **1** [C, U] any type of fabric made by weaving or knitting: *a factory producing a range of textiles* ◊ *the textile industry* ◊ *a textile mill/designer* **2** (**textiles**) [pl.] the industry that makes fabric

text·ual /ˈtekstʃuəl/ *adj.* [usually before noun] (*written*) connected with or contained in a text: *textual criticism/analysis* ◊ *textual errors*

tex·tural /ˈtekstʃərəl/ *adj.* (*technical*) relating to texture: *the textural characteristics of the rocks*

tex·ture /ˈtekstʃə(r)/ *noun* [C, U] **1** the way a surface, substance or fabric feels when you touch it, for example, how rough, smooth, hard or soft it is: *the soft texture of velvet* ◊ *She uses a variety of different colours, shapes and textures in her wall hangings.* **2** the way food or drink tastes or feels in your mouth, for example, whether it is rough, smooth, light, heavy, etc: *The two cheeses were very different in both taste and texture.* **3** the way that different parts of a piece of music or literature are combined to create a final impression: *the rich texture of the symphony*

tex·tured /ˈtekstʃəd; *AmE* -tʃərd/ *adj.* with a surface that is not smooth, but has a particular texture: *textured wallpaper* ◊ *a coarse-textured surface*

-th *suffix* **1** (in ordinal numbers): *sixth* ◊ *fifteenth* ◊ *hundredth* **2** (in nouns) the action or process of: *growth*

thal·ido·mide /θəˈlɪdəmaɪd/ *noun* [U] a SEDATIVE drug which was given to pregnant women until, in the 1960s, it was found to have prevented some babies from developing normal arms and legs

than /ðən; *rare strong form* ðæn/ *prep., conj.* **1** used to introduce the second part of a comparison: *I'm older than her.* ◊ *There was more whisky in it than soda.* ◊ *He loves me more than you do.* ◊ *It was much better than I'd expected.* ◊ *You should know better than to behave like that.* ◊ *I'd rather e-mail than phone, if that's OK by you.* **2** more/less/fewer, etc. **~** used for comparing amounts, numbers, distances, etc: *It never takes more than an hour.* ◊ *It's less than a mile to the beach.* ◊ *There were fewer than twenty people there.* **3** used in expressions showing that one thing happens straight after another: *No sooner had I sat down than there was a loud knock on the door.* ◊ *Hardly had we arrived than the problems started.* **IDM** see OTHER *adj.*

thank /θæŋk/ *verb* [VN] **~ sb** (**for sth/for doing sth**) to tell sb that you are grateful for sth: *I must write and thank Mary for the present.* ◊ *There's no need to thank me—I enjoyed doing it.* ◊ *In his speech, he thanked everyone for all their hard work.* ◊ *She said goodbye and thanked us* *for coming.* **IDM** **have sb to thank (for sth)** used when you are saying who is responsible for sth: *I have my parents to thank for my success.* **I'll thank you for sth/to do sth** *(formal, spoken)* used to tell sb that you are annoyed and do not want them to do sth: *I'll thank you to mind your own business.* **thank 'God/ 'goodness/ 'heaven(s) (for sth)** used to say that you are pleased about sth: *Thank God you're safe!* ◇ *'Thank goodness for that!' she said with a sigh of relief.* **HELP** Some people find the phrase **thank God** offensive. **thank your lucky 'stars** to feel very grateful and lucky about sth **sb won't 'thank you for sth** used to say that sb will not be pleased or will be annoyed about sth: *John won't thank you for interfering.*

thank·ful /ˈθæŋkfl/ *adj.* [not usually before noun] ~ (for sth)| ~ (to do sth)| ~ (that …) pleased about sth good that has happened, or sth bad that has not happened: *I was thankful to see they'd all arrived safely.* ◇ *He wasn't badly hurt—that's something to be thankful for.* ◇ *I was thankful that they hadn't asked for more.* **IDM** see SMALL *adj.*

thank·ful·ly /ˈθæŋkfəli/ *adv.* **1** used to show that you are pleased and relieved that sth good has happened or that sth bad has been avoided **SYN** FORTUNATELY: *There was a fire in the building, but thankfully no one was hurt.* ◇ *Thankfully, the house was empty when I got home.* **2** in a pleased or grateful way: *At the end of a busy day, I just sink thankfully into bed.* ◇ *I accepted the invitation thankfully.*

thank·less /ˈθæŋkləs/ *adj.* unpleasant or difficult to do and unlikely to bring you any rewards or thanks from anyone: *Sometimes being a mother and a housewife felt like a thankless task.*

thanks /θæŋks/ *exclamation, noun*
■ *exclamation*—see also THANK YOU **1** ~ (for sth/doing sth) used to show that you are grateful to sb for sth they have done: *Thanks a lot for lending me the money.* ◇ **Many thanks** *for your support.* ◇ *'How are you?' 'Fine, thanks.'* (= thanks for asking) **2** a polite way of accepting sth that sb has offered you: *'Would you like a coffee?' 'Oh, thanks.'* ◇ *'Here's the change.' **Thanks very much**.'* **3** (no thanks) a polite way of refusing sth that sb has offered you: *'Would you like some more?' 'No thanks.'*
■ *noun* [pl.] ~ (to sb) (for sth) words or actions that show that you are grateful to sb for sth **SYN** GRATITUDE: *How can I ever express my thanks to you for all you've done?* ◇ *Thanks are due to all those who worked so hard for so many months.* ◇ *She murmured her thanks.*—see also VOTE OF THANKS **IDM** **no thanks to sb/sth** in spite of sb/sth; with no help from sb/sth: *We managed to get it finished in the end—no thanks to him* (= he didn't help). **thanks to sb/sth** (sometimes *ironic*) used to say that sth has happened because of sb/sth: *It was all a great success—thanks to a lot of hard work.* ◇ *Everyone knows about it now, thanks to you!*

thanks·giv·ing /ˌθæŋksˈɡɪvɪŋ/ *noun* **1** Thanks'giving (Day) [U, C] a public holiday in the US (on the fourth Thursday in November) and in Canada (on the second Monday in October), originally to give thanks to God for the HARVEST and for health—compare HARVEST FESTIVAL **2** [U] *(formal)* the expression of thanks to God

'thank you *exclamation, noun*
■ *exclamation*—see also THANKS **1** ~ (for sth/for doing sth) used to show that you are grateful to sb for sth they have done: *Thank you for your letter.* ◇ **Thank you very much** *for sending the photos.* **2** a polite way of accepting sth that sb has offered you: *'Would you like some help with that?' 'Oh, thank you.'* **3** (no thank you) a polite way of refusing sth that sb has offered you: *'Would you like some more cake?' 'No thank you.'* **4** used at the end of a sentence to tell sb firmly that you do not need their help or advice: *'Shall I do that?' 'I can do it myself, thank you.'*
■ *noun* [usually sing.] ~ (to sb) (for sth) an act, a gift, a comment, etc. intended to thank sb for sth they have done: *The actor sent a big thank you to all his fans for their letters of support.* ◇ *She took the money without so much as a thank you.* ◇ *a thank-you letter*

that *det., pron., conj., adv.*

■ *det.* /ðæt/ *(pl. those /ðəʊz; AmE ðoʊz/)* **1** used for referring to a person or thing that is not near the speaker or as near to the speaker as another: *Look at that man over there.* ◇ *How much are those apples at the back?* **2** used for referring to sb/sth that has already been mentioned or is already known about: *I was living with my parents at that time.* ◇ *That incident changed their lives.* ◇ *Have you forgotten about that money I lent you last week?* ◇ *That dress of hers is too short.*
■ *pron.* /ðæt/ *(pl. those /ðəʊz; AmE ðoʊz/)* **1** used for referring to a person or thing that is not near the speaker, or not as near to the speaker as another: *Who's that?* ◇ *That's Peter over there.* ◇ *Hello. Is that Jo?* ◇ *That's a nice dress.* ◇ *Those look riper than these.* **2** used for referring to sb/sth that has already been mentioned, or is already known about: *What can I do about that?* ◇ *Do you remember when we went to Norway? That was a good trip.* ◇ *That's exactly what I think.* **3** *(formal)* used for referring to people or things of a particular type: *Those present were in favour of change.* ◇ *There are those who say* (= some people say) *she should not have got the job.* ◇ *Salaries are higher here than those in my country.* **4** /ðət/ rare strong form ðæt/ *(pl. that)* used as a relative pronoun to introduce a part of a sentence which refers to the person, thing or time you have been talking about: *Where's the letter that came yesterday?* ◇ *Who was it that won the US Open?* ◇ *The watch (that) you gave me keeps perfect time.* ◇ *The people (that) I spoke to were very helpful.* ◇ *It's the best novel (that) I've ever read.* ◇ *We moved here the year (that) my mother died.* **HELP** In spoken and informal written English **that** is nearly always left out when it is the object of the verb or is used with a preposition. **IDM** **and (all) 'that** *(BrE, informal)* and everything else connected with an activity, a situation, etc. **SYN** AND SO ON: *Did you bring the contract and (all) that?* **that is (to say)** used to say what sth means or to give more information: *He's a local government administrator, that is to say a civil servant.* ◇ *You'll find her very helpful—if she's not too busy, that is.* **,that's 'that** used to say that your decision cannot be changed: *Well I'm not going, and that's that.*
■ *conj.* /ðət; rare strong form ðæt/ **1** used after some verbs, adjectives and nouns to introduce a new part of the sentence: *She said (that) the story was true.* ◇ *It's possible (that) he has not received the letter.* ◇ *The fact (that) he's older than me is not relevant.* **HELP** In spoken and informal written English **that** is usually left out after reporting verbs and adjectives. It is less often left out after nouns. **2 so…that …** used to express a result: *She was so tired (that) she couldn't think straight.* **HELP** In informal English **that** is often left out. **3** *(literary)* used for expressing a hope or a wish: *Oh that I could see him again!*
■ *adv.* /ðæt/ **1** used when saying how much or showing how long, big, etc. sth is with your hands: *I can't walk that far* (= as far as that). ◇ *It's about that long.* **2 not (all)** ~ not very, or not as much as has been said: *It isn't all that cold.* ◇ *There aren't that many people here.* **3** *(BrE, informal)* used to emphasize how much: *I was that scared I didn't know what to do.*

thatch /θætʃ/ *noun, verb*
■ *noun* **1** [U, C] dried STRAW, REEDS, etc. used for making a roof; a roof made of this material: *a roof made of thatch* ◇ *The thatch was badly damaged in the storm.* **2** [sing.] ~ of hair *(informal)* thick hair on sb's head
■ *verb* [VN] to cover the roof of a building with thatch
▶ **thatched** *adj.*: *They live in a thatched cottage.*

thatch
dormer window
porch
thatched cottage

thatch·er /ˈθætʃə(r)/ *noun* a person whose job is thatching roofs

thaw /θɔː/ *verb, noun*
■ *verb* **1** [V] ~ (out) (of ice and snow) to turn back into water after being frozen: *The snow started to thaw as the temperature kept up.* **OPP** FREEZE **2** [V] when **it thaws** or

s	t	v	z	ʃ	ʒ	tʃ	dʒ	θ	ð	ŋ
see	tea	van	zoo	shoe	vision	chain	jam	thin	this	sing

is **thawing**, the weather becomes warm enough to melt snow and ice: *It's starting to thaw.* **3 ~ (sth) (out)** to become, or to let frozen food become, soft or liquid ready for cooking—compare DEFROST, DE-ICE, UNFREEZE: [V] *Leave the meat to thaw completely before cooking.* [often VN] **4 ~ (sth) (out)** to become, or make sth become, a normal temperature after being very cold: [V] *I could feel my ears and toes start to thaw out.* [also VN] **5** [V] **~ (out)** to become more friendly and less formal: *Relations between the two countries thawed a little after the talks.*
■ *noun* **1** [C, usually sing.] a period of warmer weather following one of cold weather, causing snow and ice to melt: *The river doubles in size during the spring thaw.* **2** [sing.] **~ (in sth)** a situation in which the relations between two enemy countries become more friendly

the /ðə; ði; *strong form* ðiː/ *definite article* **1** used to refer to sb/sth that has already been mentioned or is easily understood: *There were three questions. The first two were relatively easy but the third one was hard.* ◊ *There was an accident here yesterday. A car hit a tree and the driver was killed.* ◊ *The heat was getting to be too much for me.* ◊ *The nights are getting longer.* **2** used to refer to sb/sth that is the only, normal or obvious one of their kind: *the Mona Lisa* ◊ *the Nile* ◊ *the Queen* ◊ *What's the matter?* ◊ *The phone rang.* ◊ *I patted her on the back.* ◊ *How's the (= your) baby?* **3** used when explaining which person or thing you mean: *the house at the end of the street* ◊ *The people I met there were very friendly.* ◊ *It was the best day of my life.* ◊ *You're the third person to ask me that.* ◊ *Friday the thirteenth* ◊ *Alexander the Great* **4** used to refer to a thing in general rather than a particular example: *He taught himself to play the violin.* ◊ *The dolphin is an intelligent animal.* ◊ *They placed the African elephant on their endangered list.* ◊ *I heard it on the radio.* ◊ *I'm usually out during the day.* **5** used with adjectives to refer to a thing or a group of people described by the adjective: *With him, you should always expect the unexpected.* ◊ *the unemployed/the elderly/the French* **6** used before the plural of sb's last name to refer to a whole family or a married couple: *Don't forget to invite the Jordans.* **7** enough of sth for a particular purpose: *I wanted it but I didn't have the money.* **8** used with a unit of measurement to mean 'every': *My car does forty miles to the gallon.* ◊ *You get paid by the hour.* **9** used with a unit of time to mean 'the present': *Why not have the dish of the day?* ◊ *She's flavour of the month with him.* **10** /ðiː/ (*spoken*) used, stressing *the*, to show that the person or thing referred to is famous or important: *Sheryl Crow? Not 'the Sheryl Crow?* ◊ *At that time London was 'the place to be.* **IDM** **the more, less, etc. ..., the more, less, etc. ...** used to show that two things change to the same degree: *The more she thought about it, the more depressed she became.* ◊ *The less said about the whole thing, the happier I'll be.*

theatre (*BrE*) (*AmE* **theater**) /'θɪətə(r); *AmE* 'θiːətər/ *noun* **1** [C] a building or an outdoor area where plays and similar types of entertainment are performed: *West End/Broadway theatres* ◊ *an open-air theatre* ◊ *How often do you go to the theatre?*—see also LECTURE THEATRE **2** [C] (*AmE*) = CINEMA **3** [U] plays considered as entertainment: *an evening of live music and theatre* ◊ (*BrE*) *I like music, theatre and cinema.* ◊ *current ideas about what makes good theatre (= what makes good entertainment when performed)* **4** [U] (also **the theatre** [sing.]) the work of writing, producing and acting in plays: *I want to work in theatre.* ◊ *He was essentially a man of the theatre.* **5** [C, U] (*BrE*) = OPERATING THEATRE: *a theatre sister (= a nurse who helps during operations)* ◊ *He's still in theatre.* **6** [C, usually sing.] **~ (of war, etc.)** (*formal*) the place in which a war or fighting takes place: *an intelligence officer in the Pacific theatre*

theatre·goer (*BrE*) (*AmE* **theater·goer**) /'θɪətəgəʊə(r); *AmE* 'θiːətərgoʊər/ *noun* a person who goes regularly to the theatre ▶ **theatre·going** (*BrE*) (*AmE* **theater·going**) *adj.*: *the theatregoing public*

the·at·ri·cal /θi'ætrɪkl/ *adj.* **1** [only before noun] connected with the theatre: *a theatrical agent/career* **2** (often *disapproving*) (of behaviour) exaggerated in order to

attract attention or create a particular effect: *a theatrical gesture/sigh* ▶ **the·at·ri·cal·ly** /-kli/ *adv.*

the·at·ri·cal·ity /θi,ætrɪ'kæləti/ *noun* [U] the exaggerated quality of sth that is intended to attract attention or create a particular effect

the·at·ri·cals /θi'ætrɪklz/ *noun* [pl.] **1** performances of plays: *amateur theatricals* **2** (also **the·at·rics** especially in *AmE*) behaviour that is exaggerated and emotional in order to attract attention

thee /ðiː/ *pron.* (*old use* or *dialect*) a word meaning 'you', used when talking to only one person who is the object of the verb: *We beseech thee, O Lord.*—compare THOU

theft /θeft/ *noun* [U, C] **~ (of sth)** the crime of stealing sth from a person or place: *car theft* ◊ *Police are investigating the theft of computers from the company's offices.* ◊ *A number of thefts have been reported recently.*—compare BURGLARY, ROBBERY—see also THIEF

their /ðeə(r); *AmE* ðer/ *det.* (the possessive form of *they*) **1** of or belonging to them: *Their parties are always fun.* ◊ *Which is their house?* **2** used instead of *his* or *her* to refer to a person whose sex is not mentioned or not known: *If anyone calls, ask for their number so I can call them back.*

theirs /ðeəz; *AmE* ðerz/ *pron.* (the possessive form of *they*) of or belonging to them: *Theirs are the children with very fair hair.* ◊ *It's a favourite game of theirs.*

the·ism /'θiːɪzəm/ *noun* [U] belief in the existence of God or gods **OPP** ATHEISM

them /ðəm; *strong form* ðem/ *pron.* (the object form of *they*) **1** used when referring to people, animals or things as the object of a verb or preposition: *Tell them the news.* ◊ *What are you doing with those matches? Give them to me.* ◊ *Did you eat all of them?* **2** used instead of *him* or *her* to refer to a person whose sex is not mentioned or not known: *If anyone comes in before I get back, ask them to wait.*

the·mat·ic /θɪ'mætɪk; θiː-/ *adj.* [usually before noun] connected with the theme or themes of sth: *the thematic structure of a text* ▶ **the·mat·ic·al·ly** /-kli/ *adv.*: *The books have been grouped thematically.*

theme /θiːm/ *noun* **1** the subject or main idea in a talk, piece of writing or work of art: *North American literature is the main theme of this year's festival.* ◊ *The President stressed a favourite campaign theme—greater emphasis on education.* ◊ *The naked male figure was always the central theme of Greek art.* ◊ *The stories are all variations on the theme of unhappy marriage.* **2** (*music*) a short tune that is repeated or developed in a piece of music **3** = THEME MUSIC: *the theme from 'The Godfather'* **4** (*old-fashioned*, *AmE*) a short piece of writing on a particular subject, done for school

themed /θiːmd/ *adj.* [usually before noun] (*BrE*) (of an event or a place of entertainment) designed to reflect a particular subject or period of history: *a themed restaurant*

'theme music *noun* [U] (also **theme**, **'theme song**, **'theme tune** [C]) music that is played at the beginning and end and/or is often repeated in a film/movie, television programme, etc: *theme music for the hit TV series, 'Harry's Game'*—compare SIGNATURE TUNE

'theme park *noun* a large park where people go to enjoy themselves, for example by riding on large machines such as ROLLER COASTERS, and where much of the entertainment is connected with one subject or idea: *a western-style theme park*

them·selves /ðəm'selvz/ *pron.* **1** (the reflexive form of *they*) used when people or animals performing an action are also affected by it: *They seemed to be enjoying themselves.* ◊ *The children were arguing amongst themselves.* ◊ *They've bought themselves a new VCR.* **2** used to emphasize *they* or a plural subject: *They themselves had had a similar experience.* ◊ *Don and Julie paid for it themselves.* **3** used instead of *himself* or *herself* to refer to a person whose sex is not mentioned or not known: *There wasn't anyone who hadn't enjoyed themselves.* **IDM** **(all) by them'selves 1** alone; without anyone else: *They wanted to spend the evening by themselves.* **2** without help: *They*

T

æ	ɑː	e	ɜː	ə	ɪ	iː	i	ɒ	ɔː	ʌ	ʊ	u	uː
cat	father	ten	bird	about	sit	see	many	got	saw	cup	put	actual	too
								(BrE)					

did the cooking by themselves. **(all) to them'selves** for them alone; not shared with anyone

then /ðen/ *adv., adj.*

■ *adv.* **1** used to refer to a particular time in the past or future: *Life was harder then because neither of us had a job.* ◇ *Things were very different back then.* ◇ *She grew up in Zimbabwe, or Rhodesia as it then was.* ◇ *I saw them at Christmas but haven't heard a thing since then.* ◇ *I've been invited too, so I'll see you then.* ◇ *There's a room free in Bob's house next week but you can stay with us until then.* ◇ *Call again next week. They should have reached a decision by then.* ◇ *Just then* (= at that moment) *there was a knock at the door.* ◇ *She left in 1984 and from then on he lived alone.* ◇ *I took one look at the car and offered to buy it there and then / then and there* (= immediately). **2** used to introduce the next item in a series of actions, events, instructions, etc: *He drank a glass of whisky, then another and then another.* ◇ *First cook the onions, then add the mushrooms.* ◇ *We lived in France and then Italy before coming back to England.* **3** used to show the logical result of a particular statement or situation: *If you miss that train then you'll have to get a taxi.* ◇ *'My wife's got a job in Glasgow.' 'I take it you'll be moving, then.'* ◇ *'You haven't done anything to upset me.' 'So what's wrong, then?'* ◇ *Why don't you hire a car? Then you'll be able to visit more of the area.* **4** used to introduce additional information: *She's been very busy at work and then there was all that trouble with her son.* **5** (*formal*) used to introduce a summary of sth that has just been said: *These, then, are the main areas of concern.* **6** used to show the beginning or end of a conversation, statement, etc: *Right then, where do you want the table to go?* ◇ *'I really have to go.' 'OK. Bye, then.'* ◇ *OK then, I think we've just about covered everything on the agenda.* **IDM** **...and 'then some** (*spoken*) used to emphasize the large amount or number of sth, and to say that you have not mentioned everything: *There are Indian, Chinese, Mexican, Thai restaurants...and then some!* **but 'then | then a'gain | but then a'gain** (*spoken*) used to introduce additional information or information that contrasts with sth that has just been said: *She was early, but then again, she always is.* ◇ *'So you might accept their offer?' 'Yes, then again I might not.'*—more at NOW *adv.*

■ *adj.* [only before noun] used to describe sb who had a particular title, job, etc. at the time in the past that is being discussed: *That decision was taken by the then president.*

thence /ðens/ *adv.* (*old use* or *formal*) from that place; following that: *They made their way from Spain to France and thence to England.* ◇ *He was promoted to manager, thence to a partnership in the firm.*

thence·forth /ˌðensˈfɔːθ; *AmE* -ˈfɔːrθ/ (also **thence·for·ward** /ˌðensˈfɔːwəd; *AmE* -ˈfɔːrwərd/) *adv.* (*old use* or *formal*) starting from that time: *Thenceforth he became known as the Lord Protector.*

theo- /ˈθiːəʊ; *AmE* ˈθiːoʊ/ *combining form* (in nouns, adjectives and adverbs) connected with God or a god: *theology*

the·oc·ra·cy /θiˈɒkrəsi; *AmE* θiˈɑːk-/ *noun* (*pl.* **-ies**) **1** [U] government of a country by religious leaders **2** [C] a country that is governed by religious leaders ▶ **theo·crat·ic** /ˌθiːəˈkrætɪk/ *adj.*: *theocratic rule*

the·odo·lite /θiˈɒdəlaɪt; *AmE* θiˈɑːd-/ *noun* a piece of equipment used by SURVEYORS for measuring angles

theo·lo·gian /ˌθiːəˈləʊdʒən; *AmE* -ˈloʊ-/ *noun* a person who studies theology

the·ology /θiˈɒlədʒi; *AmE* -ˈɑːlə-/ *noun* (*pl.* **-ies**) **1** [U] the study of religion and beliefs: *a degree in Theology* ◇ *a theology student* **2** [C] a set of religious beliefs: *the theologies of the East* ▶ **theo·logic·al** /ˌθiːəˈlɒdʒɪkl; *AmE* -ˈlɑːdʒ-/ *adj.*: (*BrE*) *a theological college* ◇ (*AmE*) *a theological seminary* **theo·logic·al·ly** /-kli/ *adv.*

the·orem /ˈθɪərəm; *AmE* ˈθiːə-; ˈθɪr-/ *noun* (*technical*) a rule or principle, especially in mathematics, that can be proved to be true

the·or·et·ical /ˌθɪəˈretɪkl; *AmE* ˌθiːə-/ *adj.* [usually before noun] **1** concerned with the ideas and principles on which a particular subject is based, rather than with

practice and experiment: *a theoretical analysis / approach / debate / model* ◇ *theoretical physics* OPP EXPERIMENTAL, PRACTICAL **2** that could possibly exist, happen or be true, although this is unlikely: *It's a theoretical possibility.* ▶ **the·or·et·ic·al·ly** /-kli/ *adv.*: *theoretically sound conclusions* ◇ *It is theoretically possible for him to overrule their decision, but highly unlikely.*

the·or·ist /ˈθɪərɪst; *AmE* ˈθiːə-; ˈθɪr-/ (also **the·or·et·ician** /ˌθɪərəˈtɪʃn; *AmE* ˌθiːə-; ˌθɪr-/) *noun* a person who develops ideas and principles about a particular subject in order to explain why things happen or exist

the·or·ize (*BrE* also **-ise**) /ˈθɪəraɪz; *AmE* ˈθiːə-/ *verb* ~ **(about/on sth)** to suggest facts and ideas to explain sth; to form a theory or theories about sth: [V] *The study theorizes about the role of dreams in peoples' lives.* [also VN, V that] ▶ **the·or·iz·ing, -is·ing** *noun* [U]

the·ory /ˈθɪəri; *AmE* ˈθiːri; ˈθɪəri/ *noun* (*pl.* **-ies**) **1** [C, U] a formal set of ideas that is intended to explain why sth happens or exists: *According to the theory of relativity, nothing can travel faster than light.* **2** [U] the principles on which a particular subject is based: *the theory and practice of language teaching* **3** [C] ~ (that) an opinion or idea that sb believes is true but that is not proved: *I have this theory that most people prefer being at work to being at home.* **IDM** **in 'theory** used to say that a particular statement is supposed to be true but may in fact be wrong: *In theory, these machines should last for ten years or more.* ◇ *That sounds fine in theory, but have you really thought it through?*

thera·peut·ic /ˌθerəˈpjuːtɪk/ *adj.* **1** [usually before noun] designed to help treat an illness: *the therapeutic properties of herbs* **2** helping you to relax: *Painting can be very therapeutic.* ▶ **thera·peut·ic·al·ly** /-kli/ *adv.*

thera·peut·ics /ˌθerəˈpjuːtɪks/ *noun* [U] the branch of medicine concerned with the treatment of diseases

ther·ap·ist /ˈθerəpɪst/ *noun* **1** (especially in compounds) a specialist who treats a particular type of illness or problem, or who uses a particular type of treatment: *a speech therapist* ◇ *a beauty therapist*—see also OCCUPATIONAL THERAPIST, PHYSIOTHERAPIST **2** = PSYCHOTHERAPIST

ther·apy /ˈθerəpi/ *noun* (*pl.* **-ies**) **1** [U, C] the treatment of a physical problem or an illness: *Most patients undergo some sort of drug therapy* (= treatment using drugs) *for leukaemia.* ◇ *alternative / complementary / natural therapies* (= treatments that do not use traditional drugs) ◇ (*figurative*) *The next stage in the economic shock therapy will be freeing energy prices.* **2** [U] = PSYCHOTHERAPY: *a therapy group / session* ◇ *She's in therapy.*—see also CHEMOTHERAPY, GROUP THERAPY, HORMONE REPLACEMENT THERAPY, OCCUPATIONAL THERAPY, PHYSIOTHERAPY, RADIO-THERAPY, SPEECH THERAPY

there /ðeə(r); *AmE* ðer/ *adv., exclamation*

■ *adv.* **1** (**there is, are, was, were**, etc.) used to show that sth exists or happens: *There's a restaurant around the corner.* ◇ *There are two people waiting outside.* ◇ *Has there been an accident?* ◇ *I don't want there to be any misunderstanding.* ◇ *There seemed to be no doubt about it.* ◇ *There comes a point where you give up.* ◇ *There remains the problem of finance.* ◇ *Suddenly there was a loud bang.* ◇ (*informal*) *There's only four days left.* ◇ (*literary*) *There once was a poor farmer who had four sons.* **2** in, at or to that place or position: *We went on to Paris and stayed there eleven days.* ◇ *I hope we get there in time.* ◇ *It's there, right in front of you!* ◇ *There it is*—*just behind the chair.* ◇ *'Have you seen my pen?' 'Yes, it's over there.'* ◇ *There are a lot of people back there* (= behind) *waiting to get in.* ◇ *I'm not going in there—it's freezing!* ◇ *We're almost there* (= we have almost arrived). ◇ *Can I get there and back in a day?* ◇ *I left in 1990 and I haven't been back there since.* ◇ *Hello, is Bob there please* (= used when calling sb on the phone)? ◇ *I took one look at the car and offered to buy it there and then / then and there* (= immediately). **3** existing or available: *I went to see if my old school was still there.* ◇ *The money's there if you need it.* **4** at that point (in a story, an argument, etc.): *'I feel ...' There she stopped.* ◇ *I don't agree with you there.* **5** (especially *spoken*) used to attract sb's attention: *Hello, there!* ◇ *You there! Come back!* ◇ *There you are! I've been looking for you every-*

where. **6** (especially *spoken*) used to attract sb's attention to a particular person, thing or fact: *There's the statue I was telling you about.* ◊ *That woman there is the boss's wife.* ◊ **There goes** the last bus (= we've just missed it). ◊ **There goes** the phone (= it's ringing). ◊ (*humorous*) **There goes** my career! (= my career is ruined) ◊ *So,* **there you have it**: *that's how it all started.* **7 ~ to do sth** used to show the role of a person or thing in a situation: *The fact is, they're there to make money.* **IDM** ˌbeen ˈthere, ˌdone ˈthat (*informal*) used to show that you think a place or an activity is not very interesting or impressive because you have already experienced it: *Not Spain again! Been there, done that, got the T-shirt.* **be ˈthere for sb** to be available if sb wants to talk to you or if they need help: *You know I'll always be there for you.* **have been there beˈfore** (*informal*) to know all about a situation because you have experienced it **not all ˈthere** (*spoken*) not very intelligent, especially because of mental illness ˌthere it ˈis (*spoken*) that is the situation: *It's crazy, I know, but there it is.* ˈthere's a good boy, girl, dog, etc. (*spoken*) used to praise or encourage small children or animals: *Finish your lunch, there's a good boy.* ˌthere's ˈsth for you (*spoken*) used to say that sth is a very good example of sth: *She visited him every day he was in the hospital. There's devotion for you.* ◊ (*ironic*) *He didn't even say thank you. There's gratitude for you!* ˌthere you ˈare (also ˌthere you ˈgo) (*spoken*) **1** used when giving sb a thing they want or have asked for: *There you are—that'll be £3.80, please.* ◊ *OK, there you go.* **2** used when explaining or showing sth to sb: *You switch on, push in the disk and there you are!* ◊ *There you are! I told you it was easy!* **3** used when you are talking about sth that happens in a typical way or about a situation that cannot be changed: *There you go—that's what they're like.* ◊ *I know it's not ideal but there you go …* ˌthere you go aˈgain used to criticize sb when they behave in a way that is typical of them: *There you go again—jumping to conclusions.*—more at HERE *adv.*
■ *exclamation* used to express satisfaction that you were right about sth; used to show that sth annoys you: *There now! What did I tell you?* (= you can see that I was right.) ◊ *There! That didn't hurt too much, did it?* ◊ *There! You've gone and woken the baby!* **IDM** ˌso ˈthere! used to show that you are determined not to change your attitude or opinion: *Well, you can't have it, so there!* ˌthere, ˈthere! used to persuade a small child to stop crying or being upset: *There, there! Never mind, you'll soon feel better.*

there·abouts /ˌðeərəˈbaʊts; *AmE* ˌðerə-/ *adv.* (usually used after *or*) **1** near the place mentioned: *He comes from Leeds or thereabouts.* **2** used to say that a particular number, quantity, time, etc. is not exact: *They paid $100000 or thereabouts for the house.*

there·after /ˌðeərˈɑːftə(r); *AmE* ˌðerˈæf-/ *adv.* (*formal*) after the time or event mentioned: *She married at 17 and gave birth to her first child shortly thereafter.*—compare HEREAFTER

there·by /ˌðeəˈbaɪ; *AmE* ˌðerˈbaɪ/ *adv.* (*formal*) used to introduce the result of the action or situation mentioned: *Regular exercise strengthens the heart, thereby reducing the risk of heart attack.*

there·fore /ˈðeəfɔː(r); *AmE* ˈðerf-/ *adv.* used to introduce the logical result of sth that has just been mentioned: *He's only 17 and therefore not eligible to vote.* ◊ *There is still much to discuss. We shall, therefore, return to this item at our next meeting.*

there·from /ˌðeəˈfrɒm; *AmE* ˌðerˈfrɑːm/ *adv.* (*formal* or *law*) from the thing mentioned: *The committee will examine the contents of the agreement and any problems arising therefrom.*

there·in /ˌðeərˈɪn; *AmE* ˌðer-/ *adv.* (*formal* or *law*) in the place, object, document, etc. mentioned: *The insurance policy covers the building and any fixtures contained therein.* **IDM** ˌtherein lies … used to emphasize the result or CONSEQUENCE of a particular situation: *He works extremely hard and therein lies the key to his success.*

there·of /ˌðeərˈɒv; *AmE* ˌðerˈɑːv/ *adv.* (*formal* or *law*) of the thing mentioned: *Is the property or any part thereof used for commercial activity?*

there·on /ˌðeərˈɒn; *AmE* ˌðerˈɑːn; -ˈɔːn/ *adv.* (*formal* or *law*) on the thing mentioned: *a meeting to discuss the annual accounts and the auditors' report thereon*

there's /ðeəz; *AmE* ðerz/ *short form* **1** there is **2** there has

there·to /ˌðeəˈtuː; *AmE* ˌðerˈtuː/ *adv.* (*formal* or *law*) to the thing mentioned: *The lease entitles the holder to use the buildings and any land attached thereto.*

there·upon /ˌðeərəˈpɒn; *AmE* ˌðerəˈpɑːn/ *adv.* (*formal*) **1** immediately after the situation mentioned; as a direct result of the situation mentioned: *The audience thereupon rose cheering to their feet.* **2** on the thing mentioned: *a large notice with black letters printed thereupon*

therm /θɜːm; *AmE* θɜːrm/ *noun* a unit of heat, used in Britain for measuring a gas supply

ther·mal /ˈθɜːml; *AmE* ˈθɜːrml/ *adj., noun*
■ *adj.* [only before noun] **1** (*technical*) connected with heat: *thermal energy/insulation* **2** (of clothing) designed to keep you warm by preventing heat from escaping from the body: *thermal underwear* **3** (of streams, lakes, etc.) in which the water has been naturally heated by the earth: *thermal springs* ▶ **ther·mal·ly** *adv.*
■ *noun* **1** [C] a rising current of warm air used, for example, by a GLIDER to gain height **2** (**thermals**) [pl.] (*especially BrE*) warm underwear that prevents heat from escaping from the body

thermo- /ˈθɜːməʊ; *AmE* -moʊ/ *combining form* (in nouns, adjectives and adverbs) connected with heat: *thermonuclear* ◊ *thermometer*

thermo·dynam·ics /ˌθɜːməʊdaɪˈnæmɪks; *AmE* ˌθɜːrmoʊ-/ *noun* [U] the science that deals with the relations between heat and other forms of energy: *the laws of thermodynamics* ▶ **thermo·dynam·ic** *adj.*

therm·om·eter /θəˈmɒmɪtə(r); *AmE* θərˈmɑːm-/ *noun* an instrument used for measuring the temperature of the air, a person's body, etc: *a thermometer reading*—picture on page 599

thermo·nuclear /ˌθɜːməʊˈnjuːkliə(r); *AmE* ˌθɜːrmoʊ-ˈnuːk-/ *adj.* connected with nuclear reactions that only happen at very high temperatures

Ther·mos™ /ˈθɜːməs; *AmE* ˈθɜːrməs/ (*BrE* also **ˈTher·mos flask**) (*AmE* also **ˈThermos bottle**) *noun* a particular kind of VACUUM FLASK (= a container like a bottle with double walls with a VACUUM between them, used for keeping liquids hot or cold)—compare FLASK

thermo·stat /ˈθɜːməstæt; *AmE* ˈθɜːrm-/ *noun* a device that measures and controls the temperature of a machine or room, by switching the heating or cooling system on and off as necessary ▶ **thermo·stat·ic** /ˌθɜːməˈstætɪk; *AmE* ˌθɜːrm-/ *adj.* [only before noun] **thermo·stat·ic·al·ly** /-kli/ *adv.*

the·saurus /θɪˈsɔːrəs/ *noun* (*pl.* **the·sauri** /θɪˈsɔːraɪ/ or **the·saur·uses** /-rəsɪz/) a book that is like a dictionary, but in which the words are arranged in groups that have similar meanings

these ⇨ THIS

thesis /ˈθiːsɪs/ *noun* (*pl.* **theses** /ˈθiːsiːz/) **1 ~ (on sth)** a long piece of writing completed by a student as part of a university degree, based on their own research: (*BrE*) *a doctoral/PhD thesis* ◊ (*AmE*) *a thesis for a master's degree* **2** a statement or an opinion that is discussed in a logical way and presented with evidence in order to prove that it is true: *These latest findings support the thesis that sexuality is determined by nature rather than choice.*

thes·pian /ˈθespiən/ *noun* (often *humorous*) an actor ▶ **thes·pian** *adj.*

they /ðeɪ/ *pron.* (used as the subject of a verb) **1** people, animals or things that have already been mentioned or are easily identified: *'Where are John and Liz?' 'They went for a walk.'* ◊ *They* (= the things you are carrying) *go on the bottom shelf.* **2** used instead of *he* or *she* to refer to a person whose sex is not mentioned or not known: *If anyone arrives late they'll have to wait outside.* **3** people in general: *The rest, as they say, is history.* **4** people in authority or experts: *They cut my water off.* ◊ *They now say that red wine is good for you.*

they'd /ðeɪd/ *short form* **1** they had **2** they would

they'll /ðeɪl/ *short form* they will

they're /ðeə(r); *AmE* ðer; *AmE weak form* ðər/ *short form* they are

they've /ðeɪv/ *short form* they have

thick /θɪk/ *adj., noun, adv.*

■ *adj.* (**thick·er, thick·est**)

• DISTANCE BETWEEN SIDES | **1** having a larger distance between opposite sides or surfaces than other similar objects or than normal: *a thick carpet/slice of bread* ◇ *a thick book* (= one that has a lot of pages) ◇ *a thick coat* (= one made of heavy fabric) ◇ *thick fingers* ◇ *Everything was covered with a thick layer of dust.* **2** used to ask about or state the distance between opposite sides or surfaces: *How thick are the walls?* ◇ *They're two feet thick.*

• HAIR/FUR/TREES | **3** growing closely together in large numbers: *thick dark hair* ◇ *a thick forest* ◇ *a thick bush* (= with a lot of leaves)

• LIQUID | **4** not flowing very easily: *thick cream/soup* ◇ *The effect will be ruined if the paint is too thick.*

• FOG/SMOKE/AIR | **5** ~ (**with sth**) difficult to see through; difficult to breathe in: *The plane crashed in thick fog.* ◇ *thick smoke* ◇ *The air was thick with dust.* ◇ (*figurative*) *The atmosphere was thick with tension.*

• WITH LARGE NUMBER/AMOUNT | **6** ~ **with sb/sth** having a large number of people or a large amount of sth in one place: *The beach was thick with sunbathers.*

• STUPID | **7** (*BrE, informal*) (of a person) slow to learn or understand things: *Are you thick, or what?*

• ACCENT | **8** (sometimes *disapproving*) easily recognized as being from a particular country or area: *a thick Brooklyn accent*

• VOICE | **9** ~ (**with sth**) deep and not as clear as normal, especially because of illness or emotion: *His voice was thick with emotion.*

• FRIENDLY WITH SB | **10** ~ (**with sb**) (*informal*) very friendly with sb, especially in a way that makes other people suspicious: *You seem to be very thick with the boss!*
—see also THICKLY, THICKNESS

IDM **give sb/get a thick ˈear** (*BrE, informal*) to hit sb/be hit on the head as a punishment **lay it on ˈthick** (*informal*) to talk about sb/sth in a way that makes them or it seem much better or much worse than they really are; to exaggerate sth: *Praise them when necessary, but don't lay it on too thick.* **(as) thick as ˈthieves** (*informal*) (of two or more people) very friendly, especially in a way that makes other people suspicious **(as) thick as two short ˈplanks** (*BrE, informal*) (of a person) very stupid **a thick ˈhead** (*informal*) a physical condition in which your head is painful or you cannot think clearly as a result of an illness or of drinking too much alcohol **sb's thick ˈhead** (*informal*) used to show that you are annoyed that sb does not understand sth: *When will you get it into your thick head that I don't want to see you again!* **a ˌthick ˈskin** the ability to accept criticism, insults, etc. without becoming upset **OPP** A THIN SKIN—see also THICK-SKINNED—more at BLOOD *n.*, GROUND *n.*

■ *noun* [U]

IDM **in the ˈthick of sth** involved in the busiest or most active part of sth: *As a player, he's always in the thick of the action.* **through ˌthick and ˈthin** even when there are problems or difficulties: *He's supported the team for over ten years through thick and thin.*

■ *adv.* (*comparative* **thick·er**, no *superlative*) in a way that produces a wide piece or deep layer of sth: *Make sure you cut the bread nice and thick.*

IDM **thick and ˈfast** quickly and in large quantities: *Questions were coming at them thick and fast.*

thick·en /ˈθɪkən/ *verb* to become thicker; to make sth thicker: [V] *Keep stirring until the sauce has thickened.* ◇ *It was a dangerous journey through thickening fog.* ◇ [VN] *You can thicken the stew with flour.* **IDM** see PLOT *n.*

thicket /ˈθɪkɪt/ *noun* **1** a group of bushes or small trees growing closely together: *a dense thicket of bamboo* **2** a large number of things that are not easy to understand or separate: *He spent the morning trying to work his way through a thicket of statistics.*

thick·ly /ˈθɪkli/ *adv.* **1** in a way that produces a wide piece or deep layer of sth: *thickly sliced/buttered bread* ◇ *thickly carpeted stairs* ◇ *Apply the paint thickly in even strokes.* **2** ~ wooded, populated, etc. having a lot of trees, people, etc. close together **3** in a deep voice that is not as clear as normal, especially because of illness or emotion: *'Just leave me alone,' he said thickly.*

thick·ness /ˈθɪknəs/ *noun* **1** [U, C] the size of sth between opposite surfaces or sides **SYN** WIDTH: *Use wood of at least 12 mm thickness.* ◇ *The board is available in four thicknesses.* **2** [C] ~ (**of sth**) a layer of sth: *The jacket was lined with a double thickness* (= two layers) *of fabric.*

thick·set /ˌθɪkˈset/ *adj.* (especially of a man) having a strong heavy body: *He has the same thickset build as his father.*

ˌthick-ˈskinned *adj.* **1** (of a person) not easily upset by criticism or unkind comments: *You have to be pretty thick-skinned to do this job.* **2** (of fruit) having a thick skin: *a thick-skinned variety of grape* **OPP** THIN-SKINNED

thief /θiːf/ *noun* (*pl.* **thieves** /θiːvz/) a person who steals sth from another person or place: *a car/jewel thief*—see also THEFT ⇨ note at STEAL **IDM** see HONOUR *n.*, THICK *adj.*

thiev·ing /ˈθiːvɪŋ/ *noun* [U] (*informal*) the act of stealing things ▶ **thiev·ing** *adj.* (*informal*): *You've no right to take that, you thieving swine!*

thigh /θaɪ/ *noun* **1** the top part of the leg between the knee and the hip—picture at BODY **2** the top part of the leg of a chicken, etc., cooked and eaten

ˈthigh bone *noun* the large thick bone in the top part of the leg between the hip and the knee **SYN** FEMUR—picture at BODY

thim·ble /ˈθɪmbl/ *noun* a small metal or plastic object that you wear on the end of your finger to protect it when sewing—picture at SEW

thin /θɪn/ *adj., adv., verb*

■ *adj.* (**thin·ner, thin·nest**)

• NOT THICK | **1** having a smaller distance between opposite sides or surfaces than other similar objects or than normal: *Cut the vegetables into thin strips.* ◇ *A number of thin cracks appeared in the wall.* ◇ *The body was hidden beneath a thin layer of soil.* ◇ *a thin blouse* (= of light fabric)—see also PAPER-THIN ⇨ note at NARROW

• NOT FAT | **2** (of a person or part of the body) (sometimes *disapproving*) not covered with much flesh: *He was tall and thin, with dark hair.* ◇ *She was looking pale and thin.* ◇ *He is as thin as a rake* (= very thin). ◇ *thin arms/legs/lips*

• HAIR | **3** not growing closely together or in large amounts: *thin grey hair*

• LIQUID | **4** containing more liquid than is normal or expected **SYN** RUNNY: *The sauce was thin and tasteless.*

• SMOKE | **5** fairly easy to see through: *They fought their way through where the smoke was thinner.*

• AIR | **6** containing less OXYGEN than normal

• SOUND | **7** (*disapproving*) high and weak: *Her thin voice trailed off into silence.*

• SMILE | **8** not sincere or enthusiastic: *He gave a thin smile.*

• LIGHT | **9** not very bright: *the thin grey light of dawn*

• POOR QUALITY | **10** of poor quality; lacking an important quality: *a thin excuse* (= one that people are not likely to believe) ◇ *Their arguments all sound a little thin to me.*

▶ **thin·ness** /ˈθɪnnəs/ *noun* [U]—see also THINLY

IDM **be skating/walking on thin ˈice** to be taking a risk **disappear, vanish, etc. into thin ˈair** to disappear suddenly in a mysterious way **have a thin ˈtime (of it)** (*BrE, informal*) to have many problems or difficulties to deal with; to not be successful **out of thin ˈair** from nowhere or nothing, as if by magic: *Unfortunately, I can't just conjure up the money out of thin air!* **the thin end of the ˈwedge** (*especially BrE*) an event or action that is the beginning of sth more serious and/or unpleasant **thin on ˈtop** (*informal*) without much hair on the head: *He's starting to get a little thin on top* (= he's losing his hair). **a ˌthin ˈskin** the lack of ability to accept criticism, insults, etc. without becoming upset: *You shouldn't be in politics if you have such a thin skin.* **OPP** A THICK SKIN—see also THIN-SKINNED—more at GROUND *n.*, LINE *n.*, THICK *adj.*, WEAR *v.*

■ *adv.* **(thin·ner, thin·nest)** in a way that produces a thin piece or layer of sth: *Don't spread it too thin.* ◊ *I like my bread sliced thin.*

■ *verb* **(-nn-)**

LIQUID | **1** [VN] **~ sth (down) (with sth)** to make a liquid less thick or strong by adding water or another substance: *Thin the paint with water.*

OF HAIR | **2** to become less thick: *a middle-aged man with thinning hair*

BECOME LESS THICK | **3 ~ sth (out)** to become less thick or fewer in number; to make sth less thick or fewer, for example by removing some things or people: [V] *The clouds thinned and the moon shone through.* ◊ *The crowd had thinned out and only a few people were left.* ◊ [VN] *Thin out the seedlings to about 10cm apart.*

VOCABULARY BUILDING
saying that someone is **thin**

Thin is the most usual word: *Steve is tall and thin and has brown hair.* It is sometimes used with a negative meaning: *Mother looked thin and tired after her long illness.*

The following words all express praise or admiration:

Slim means pleasantly thin. It is often used to describe women who have controlled their weight by diet or exercise: *She has a beautifully slim figure.*

A **slender** girl or woman is thin and graceful.

A **lean** man is thin and fit.

Willowy describes a woman who is attractively tall and thin.

The following words are more negative in their meaning:

Skinny means very thin, often in a way that is not attractive: *a skinny little kid.*

Bony describes parts of the body when they are so thin that the bones can be seen: *the old man's bony hands.*

Scrawny suggests that a person is thin, weak and not attractive: *a scrawny old woman.*

Gaunt describes a person who is a little too thin and looks sad or ill.

Underweight is used in medical contexts to describe people who are too thin because they are ill or have not had enough food: *Women who smoke risk giving birth to underweight babies.*

Emaciated describes a serious condition resulting from illness or lack of food.

Anorexic is a medical term, but is now also used informally to describe a girl or woman who is so thin that you are worried about them.

It is more acceptable to talk to somebody about how thin or slim they are than about how fat they are.

⇨ note at FAT

---

thine /ðaɪn/ *pron., det.* (*old use*)

■ *pron.* a word meaning 'yours', used when talking to only one person

■ *det.* the form of *thy* that is used before a vowel or 'h', meaning 'your'

thing /θɪŋ/ *noun*

OBJECT | **1** [C] an object whose name you do not use because you do not need to or want to, or because you do not know it: *Can you pass me that thing over there?* ◊ *She's very fond of sweet things* (= sweet foods). ◊ *He's just bought one of those exercise things.* ◊ *Turn that thing off while I'm talking to you!* **2** [C] an object that is not alive in the way that people and plants are: *Don't treat her like that—she's a person, not a thing!* ◊ *He's good at making things with his hands.* ◊ *She took no interest in the people and things around her.*

POSSESSIONS / EQUIPMENT | **3** (**things**) [pl.] objects, clothing or tools that belong to sb or are used for a particular purpose: *Shall I help you pack your things?* ◊ *Bring your swimming things with you.* ◊ *I'll just clear away the*

breakfast things. ◊ *Put your things* (= coat, etc.) *on and let's go.*

ANYTHING | **4** (**a thing**) [sing.] used with negatives to mean 'anything' in order to emphasize what you are saying: *I haven't got a thing to wear!* ◊ *She hasn't had a thing to eat all day.* ◊ *There wasn't a thing we could do to help.* ◊ *Ignore what he said—it doesn't mean a thing.*

FACT / EVENT / SITUATION / ACTION | **5** [C] a fact, an event, a situation or an action; what sb says or thinks: *There are a lot of things she doesn't know about me.* ◊ *There's another thing I'd like to ask you.* ◊ *A terrible thing happened last night.* ◊ *He found the whole thing very boring.* ◊ *I've got loads of things to do today.* ◊ *The main thing to remember is to switch off the burglar alarm.* ◊ *I like camping, climbing and that sort of thing.* ◊ *She said the first thing that came into her head.* ◊ *'Why did you tell her our secret?' 'I did no such thing!'* ◊ *Let's forget the whole thing* (= everything). **6** (**things**) [pl.] the general situation, as it affects sb: *Things haven't gone entirely to plan.* ◊ (*spoken*) *Hi, Jane! How are things?* ◊ *Think things over before you decide.* ◊ *As things stand at present, he seems certain to win.* ◊ *All things considered* (= considering all the difficulties or problems), *she's done very well.* ◊ *Why do you make things so difficult for yourself?*

WHAT IS NEEDED / RIGHT | **7** [C, usually sing.] what is needed or socially acceptable: *You need something to cheer you up—I know just the thing!* ◊ *to do / say the right / wrong thing* ◊ *The best thing to do is to apologize.*

THINGS OF PARTICULAR TYPE | **8** (**things**) [pl.] (*formal*) (followed by an adjective) all that can be described in a particular way: *She loves all things Japanese.*

CREATURE | **9** [C] (used with an adjective) a living creature: *All living things are composed of cells.*

PERSON / ANIMAL | **10** [C] (with an adjective) (*spoken*) used to talk to or about a person or an animal, to show how you feel about them: *You silly thing!* ◊ *You must be starving, you poor things.* ◊ *The cat's very ill, poor old thing.*

IDM **A is 'one thing, B is a'nother** | **it's 'one thing to do A, it's a'nother thing to do B** is very different from A, for example it is more difficult, serious or important: *Romance is one thing, marriage is quite another.* ◊ *It's one thing to tease your sister, but it's another to hit her.* **,all / ,other things being 'equal** if the conditions stay the same; if other conditions are the same: *All things being equal, we should finish the job tomorrow.* **and 'things (like 'that)** (*spoken, informal*) used when you do not want to complete a list: *She likes nice clothes and things like that.* ◊ *I've been busy shopping and things.* **be all things to all 'men / 'people 1** (of people) to please everyone by changing your attitudes or opinions to suit different people **2** (of things) to be understood or used in different ways by different people **come to / be the same 'thing** to have the same result or meaning **be a 'good thing (that) ...** to be lucky that ...: *It's a good thing we got here early.* **be no bad 'thing (that) ...** used to say that although sth seems to be bad, it could have good results: *We didn't want the press to get hold of the story, but it might be no bad thing.* **be onto a good 'thing** to have found a job, situation or style of life that is pleasant or easy **the best thing since sliced 'bread** (*spoken, informal*) if you say that sth is the best thing since sliced bread, you think it is extremely good, interesting, etc. **'do things to sb** (*informal*) to have a powerful emotional effect on sb: *That song just does things to me.* **do your own 'thing** (*informal*) to do what you want to do or what interests you, without thinking about other people; to be independent **,first / ,last 'thing ...** early in the morning / late in the evening: *I need the report on my desk first thing Monday morning.* **,first things 'first** (often *humorous*) the most important matters must be dealt with first: *We have a lot to discuss, but, first things first, let's have a cup of coffee!* **for 'one thing** used to introduce one of two or more reasons for doing sth: *'Why don't you get a car?' 'Well, for one thing, I can't drive!'* **have a 'thing about sb / sth** (*informal*) to have a strong like or dislike of sb / sth in a way that seems strange or unreasonable: *She has a thing about men with beards.* **it isn't my, his, etc. 'thing** it isn't sth that you really enjoy or are interested in**

T

æ	ɑː	e	ɜː	ə	ɪ	iː	i	ɒ	ɔː	ʌ	ʊ	u	uː
cat	father	ten	bird	about	sit	see	many	got	saw	cup	put	actual	too

(BrE)

Instead of using the word **thing**, try to use more precise and interesting words, especially in formal written English.

aspect *That was the most puzzling aspect of the situation. (...the most puzzling thing about...)*

attribute *Curiosity is an essential attribute for a journalist to have.) (...an essential thing for a journalist to have.)*

characteristic *This bird has several interesting characteristics. (There are several interesting things about this bird.)*

detail *I want to know every detail of what happened. (...everything about...)*

feature *Noise is a familiar feature of city life. (...a familiar thing in city life.)*

issue *She has campaigned on many controversial issues. (...many controversial things.)*

matter *We have several important matters to deal with at this meeting. (...several important things...)*

point *That's a very interesting point you made. (...a very interesting thing you said.)*

subject *The book covers a number of subjects. (...a number of things.)*

topic *We discussed a wide range of topics. (...a wide range of things.)*

trait *Her generosity is one of her most attractive traits. (...one of the most attractive things about her.)*

Don't use **thing** after an adjective when the adjective can be used on its own: *Having your own computer is very useful.* ◊ ~~Having your own computer is a very useful thing.~~

It is often more natural to use words like **something**, **anything**, etc. instead of **thing**: *I have something important to tell you.* ◊ ~~I have an important thing to tell you.~~ ◊ *Do you want anything else?* ◊ ~~Do you want any other thing?~~

It is more natural to use **a lot, a great deal, much**, etc. rather than **many things**: *I have so much to tell you.* ◊ ~~I have so many things to tell you.~~ ◊ *She knows a lot about basketball.* ◊ ~~She knows many things about basketball.~~

it's a ...thing (*informal*) it is sth that only a particular group understands: *You wouldn't know what it means—it's a girl thing.* **know/tell sb a 'thing or two (about sb/sth)** (*informal*) to know/tell sb some useful, interesting or surprising information about sb/sth: *She's been married five times, so she knows a thing or two about men!* **make a (big) 'thing of/about sth** (*informal*) to make sth seem more important than it really is **not know, etc. the first 'thing about sth/sb** to know nothing at all about sth/sb: *We've lived next to him for years, but we still don't know the first thing about him.* **not ,quite the 'thing 1** not considered socially acceptable: *It wouldn't be quite the thing to turn up in running gear.* **2** (*old-fashioned*) not healthy or normal **(just) ,one of those 'things** used to say that you do not want to discuss or think about sth bad or unpleasant that has happened, but just accept it: *It wasn't your fault. It was just one of those things.* **,one (damned/damn) thing after a'nother** (*spoken*) used to complain that a lot of unpleasant things keep happening to you **,one thing leads to a'nother** used to suggest that the way one event or action leads to others is so obvious that it does not need to be stated: *He offered me a ride home one night, and, well, one thing led to another and now we're married!* **'seeing/'hearing things** (*informal*) to imagine that you can see or hear sth that is in fact not there: (*humorous*) *Tom's washing the dishes—I must be seeing things!* **there's only ,one thing 'for it** there is only one possible course of action **the ,thing 'is** (*spoken*) used to introduce an important fact, reason or explanation: *I'm sorry my assignment isn't finished. The thing is, I've had a lot of other work this week.* **the ,thing (about/with sth/sb) 'is** used to introduce a problem about sth/sb: *The thing with Karl is, he's always late.* **the (whole) ...thing**

(*informal*) a situation or an activity of the type mentioned: *She really didn't want to be involved in the whole family thing.* **,things that go ,bump in the 'night** (*informal, humorous*) used to refer to ghosts and other SUPERNATURAL things that cannot be explained: *There are mysterious lights in the sky and things that go bump in the night.* **too 'much of a good thing** used to say that, although sth is pleasant, you do not want to have too much of it **(what) with ,one thing and a'nother** (*informal*) because you have been busy with various problems, events or things you had to do: *I completely forgot her birthday, what with one thing and another.*—more at CHANCE *n.*, CLOSE² *adj.*, CLOSE² *adv.*, DAY, DECENT, DONE, EASY *adv.*, NATURE, NEAR *adj.*, ONLY *adj.*, OVERDO, PUSH *v.*, REAL, SCHEME *n.*, SHAPE *n.*, SURE *adj.*, TURN *v.*, WAY *n.*, WORK *v.*

thing·ummy /ˈθɪŋəmi/ *noun* (*pl.* **-ies**) (also **thing·uma·bob** /ˈθɪŋəməbɒb/; *AmE* -bɑːb/ **thing·uma·jig** /ˈθɪŋəmədʒɪɡ/) (*informal, spoken*) used to refer to a person or thing whose name you do not know or have forgotten, or which you do not want to mention: *It's one of those thingummies for keeping papers together.* ◊ *Is thingummy going to be there? You know, that woman from the Sales Department?*

thingy /ˈθɪŋi/ *noun* (*pl.* **-ies**) = THINGUMMY

think /θɪŋk/ *verb, noun*
■ *verb* (**thought, thought** /θɔːt/)

HAVE OPINION/BELIEF | **1** ~ **(about sth)** (not used in the progressive tenses) to have a particular idea or opinion about sth/sb; to believe sth: [V(that)] *Do you think (that) they'll come?* ◊ *I thought I heard a scream.* ◊ *I didn't think you liked sports.* ◊ *Am I right in thinking that you used to live here?* ◊ *I think this is their house, but I'm not sure.* ◊ *He ought to resign, I think.* ◊ *We'll need about 20 chairs, I should think.* ◊ [VN(that)] *It was once thought that the sun travelled around the earth.* ◊ [VN] *What did you think about the idea?* ◊ *Well, I like it. What do you think?* ◊ [V] *'Will we make it in time?' 'I think so.'* ◊ *'Is he any good?' 'I don't think so.'* ◊ [VN-ADJ] *I think it highly unlikely that I'll get the job.* ◊ *She thought him kind and generous.* ◊ [VN to inf] *He's thought to be one of the richest men in Europe.* **HELP** This pattern is not usually used unless **think** is in the passive.

USE MIND | **2** ~ **(about sth)** to use your mind to consider sth, to form connected ideas, to try to solve problems, etc: [V] *Are animals able to think?* ◊ *Let me think (= give me time before I answer).* ◊ *I can't tell you now—I'll have to think about it.* ◊ *She had thought very deeply about this problem.* ◊ *All he ever thinks about is money.* ◊ *I'm sorry, I wasn't thinking (= said when you have upset or offended sb accidentally).* ◊ [V wh-] *He was trying to think what to do.* **3** (usually used in the progressive tenses) to have ideas, words or images in your mind: [VN] *You're very quiet. What are you thinking?* ◊ [V wh-] *I was just thinking what a long way it is.* ◊ [V speech] *'I must be crazy,' she thought.*

IMAGINE | **4** [no passive] to form an idea of sth; to imagine sth: [V wh-] *We couldn't think where you'd gone.* ◊ *Just think how nice it would be to see them again.* ◊ [V(that)] *I can't think (that) he would be so stupid.* ◊ [V] *Just think—we'll be lying on the beach this time tomorrow.* ◊ [VN] *If I'm late home, my mother always thinks the worst.* ◊ *Try to think yourself into the role.*

EXPECT | **5** to expect sth: [V(that)] *I never thought (that) I'd see her again.* ◊ *The job took longer than we thought.* ◊ *You'd think she'd have been grateful for my help (= but she wasn't).* ◊ [V to inf] (*formal*) *Who would have thought to find you here?*

IN A PARTICULAR WAY | **6** (*informal*) [no passive] to think in a particular way or on a particular subject: [V-ADJ] *Let's think positive.* ◊ *You need to think big (= aim to achieve a lot).* ◊ [VN] *If you want to make money, you've got to think money.*

SHOWING ANGER/SURPRISE | **7** [V(that)] (*spoken*) used in questions to show that you are angry or surprised: *What do you think you're doing?*

BEING LESS DEFINITE/MORE POLITE | **8** (*spoken*) used to make

aɪ	aʊ	eɪ	əʊ	oʊ	ɔɪ	ɪə	eə	ʊə	j	w
my	now	say	go	go	boy	near	hair	pure	yes	wet
			(BrE)	(AmE)						

sth you say sound less definite or more polite: [V(**that**)] *I thought we could go out tonight.* ◊ *Twenty guests are enough, I would have thought.* ◊ *Do you **think** you could open the window?* ◊ [V] *'You've made a mistake.' 'I don't think so/I think not.'*

INTEND | **9** to intend sth; to have a plan about sth: [V(**that**)] *I think I'll go for a swim.* ◊ [V] *I'm thinking in terms of about 70 guests at the wedding.*

REMEMBER | **10** to remember sth; to have sth come into your mind: [Vto**inf**] *I didn't think* (= it did not OCCUR *to me*) *to tell her.* ◊ [Vwh-] *I can't think where I put the keys.* [IDM] **come to 'think of it** used when you suddenly remember sth or realize that it might be important: *Come to think of it, he did mention seeing you.* **I ,don't 'think so** (*spoken*) used to say very strongly that you do not agree with sth, or that sth is not possible: *Me? Fail? I don't think so.* **if/when you 'think about it** used to draw attention to a fact that is not obvious or has not previously been mentioned: *They do have a big house, when you think about it.* **I 'thought as much** that is what I expected or suspected: *'He said he'd forgotten.' 'I thought as much.'* ,**think a'gain** to consider a situation again and perhaps change your idea or intention **think a'loud** to say what your thoughts are as you have them **think 'better of it/of doing sth** to decide not to do sth after thinking further about it: *Rosie was about to protest but thought better of it.* **think (the) 'better of sb** to have a higher opinion of sb: *She has behaved appallingly—I must say I thought better of her.* **think 'nothing of it** (*formal*) used as a polite response when sb has said sorry to you or thanked you **think 'nothing of sth/of doing sth** to consider an activity to be normal and not particularly unusual or difficult: *She thinks nothing of walking thirty miles a day.* **think on your 'feet** to be able to think and react to things very quickly and effectively without any preparation **'think straight** to think in a clear or logical way **think 'twice about sth/about doing sth** to think carefully before deciding to do sth: *You should think twice about employing someone you've never met.* **think the world, highly, a lot, not much, poorly, little, etc. of sb/sth** to have a very good, poor, etc. opinion of sb/sth: *He thinks the world of his daughter.* ◊ *I don't think much of her idea.* **to think (that ...)** used to show that you are surprised or shocked by something: *To think that my mother wrote all those books and I never knew!*—more at FIT *adj.,* ILL *adv.,* LET *v.,* LIKE *v.,* OWN *v.*

[PHR V] **'think about/of sb/sth 1** to consider sb/sth when you are doing or planning sth: *Don't you ever think about other people?* **2** to consider doing sth [SYN] CONTEMPLATE[+-ing]: *She's thinking of changing her job.* ,**think a'head (to sth)** to think about a future event or situation and plan for it ,**think 'back (to sth)** to think about sth that happened in the past: *I keep thinking back to the day I arrived here.* ,**think for your'self** to form your own opinions and make decisions without depending on others **'think of sth/sb 1** to have an image or idea of sth/sb in your mind: *When I said that I wasn't thinking of anyone in particular.* **2** to create an idea in your imagination: *Can anybody think of a way to raise money?* ◊ *'What shall we do now?' 'I'll think of something.'* ◊ *Have you thought of a name for the baby yet?* **3** [no passive] (used especially with *can*) to remember sth/sb: *I can think of at least three occasions when he arrived late.* ◊ *I can't think of her name at the moment.* **'think of sb/sth as sb/sth** to consider sb/sth in a particular way: *I think of this place as my home.* ◊ *She is thought of as a possible future director.*—see also WELL THOUGHT OF **'think of sth** to imagine an actual or a possible situation: *Just think of the expense!* ◊[+-ing] *I couldn't think of letting you take the blame* (= I would not allow that to happen). ,**think sth↔'out** to consider or plan sth carefully: *It's a very well thought out plan.* ,**think sth↔'over** to consider sth carefully, especially before reaching a decision: *He'd like more time to think things over.* ◊ *I've been thinking over what you said.* ,**think sth↔'through** to consider a problem or a possible course of action fully ,**think sth↔'up** (*informal*) to create sth in your mind [SYN] INVENT, DEVISE: *Can't you think up a better excuse than that?*

■ *noun* [sing.] [IDM] **have a 'think (about sth)** (*informal*) to think carefully about sth in order to make a decision about it: *I'll have a think and let you know tomorrow.* **you've got another think 'coming** (*informal*) used to tell sb that they are wrong about sth and must change their plans or opinions

think·able /'θɪŋkəbl/ *adj.* [not before noun] that you can imagine as a possibility: *Such an idea was scarcely thinkable ten years ago.* [OPP] UNTHINKABLE

think·er /'θɪŋkə(r)/ *noun* **1** a person who thinks seriously, and often writes about important things, such as philosophy or science **2** a person who thinks in a particular way: *a clear/quick/creative thinker*

think·ing /'θɪŋkɪŋ/ *noun, adj.*
■ *noun* [U] **1** the process of thinking about sth: *I had to do some quick thinking.*—see also LATERAL THINKING, WISHFUL THINKING **2** ideas or opinions about sth: *What is the current thinking on this question?* ◊ *She explained the thinking behind the campaign.* [IDM] see WAY *n.*
■ *adj.* [only before noun] intelligent and able to think seriously about things: *the thinking woman's magazine*

'thinking cap *noun* [IDM] **put your 'thinking cap on** (*informal*) to try to solve a problem by thinking about it

'think tank *noun* a group of experts who provide advice and ideas on political, social or economic issues

thin·ly /'θɪnli/ *adv.* **1** in a way that produces a thin piece or layer of sth: *Slice the potatoes thinly.* **2** with very few things or people close together in one place: *a thinly populated area* ◊ *For best results, sow the seeds thinly in early March.* **3** in a way that is not sincere or enthusiastic: *She smiled thinly.* **4** in a way that does not hide the truth very well: *The novel is a thinly disguised autobiography.* ◊ *thinly veiled contempt*

thin·ner /'θɪnə(r)/ *noun* [U, C] a substance that is added to paint, VARNISH, etc. to make it less thick

,**thin-'skinned** *adj.* **1** easily upset by criticism or insults **2** (of fruit) having a thin skin [OPP] THICK-SKINNED

third /θɜːd; *AmE* θɜːrd/ *ordinal number, noun*
■ *ordinal number* 3rd [HELP] There are examples of how to use ordinal numbers at the entry for *fifth.* [IDM] **third time 'lucky** (*AmE* also **third time is the 'charm**) used when you have failed to do sth twice and hope that you will succeed the third time
■ *noun* **1** each of three equal parts of sth **2** ~ (**in sth**) a level of university degree at British universities, that is lower than average—compare FIRST *n.* (4), SECOND *n.* (7)

,**third 'class** *noun* **1** [U, sing.] (especially in the past) the cheapest and least comfortable part of a train, ship, etc. **2** [U] (in the US) the class of mail used for sending advertisements, etc. **3** [U, sing.] the lowest standard of degree given by a British university

'third-class *adj.* **1** (especially in the past) connected with the cheapest and least comfortable way of travelling on a train, ship, etc. **2** (in the US) connected with the class of mail used to send advertisements, etc. **3** [only before noun] used to describe the lowest standard of degree given by a British university **4** (*disapproving*) (of people) less important than other people: *They are treated as third-class citizens.* ▶ ,**third-'class** *adv.*: *to travel third-class*

,**third de'gree** *noun* [sing.] [IDM] **give sb the ,third de'gree** (*informal*) to question sb for a long time and in a thorough way; to use threats or violence to get information from sb

,**third-'degree** *adj.* **1** ~ **burns** burns of the most serious kind, affecting tissue below the skin **2** (*AmE*) ~ **murder, assault, robbery, etc.** murder, etc. of the least serious of three kinds—compare FIRST-DEGREE, SECOND-DEGREE

third·ly /'θɜːdli; *AmE* 'θɜːrd-/ *adv.* used to introduce the third of a list of points you want to make in a speech or piece of writing: *Thirdly, I would like to say that ...*

,**third 'party** *noun* (*formal* or *law*) a person who is involved in a situation in addition to the two main people involved

,**third party in'surance** *noun* [U] insurance that COVERS (= protects) you if you injure sb or damage sb's property

the ,third 'person *noun* [sing.] **1** (*grammar*) a set of pronouns and verb forms used by a speaker to refer to other people and things: *'They are' is the third person plural of the verb 'to be'.* **2** a way of writing a novel, etc. as the experience of sb else, using third person forms: *a book written in the third person*—compare THE FIRST PERSON, THE SECOND PERSON

,third-'rate *adj.* of very poor quality: *a third-rate actor*

the ,Third 'World *noun* [sing.] a way of referring to the poor or developing countries of Africa, Asia and Latin America, which is sometimes considered offensive: *the causes of poverty and injustice in the Third World* ◇ *third-world debt*—compare FIRST WORLD

thirst /θɜːst; *AmE* θɜːrst/ *noun, verb*
■ *noun* **1** [U, sing.] the feeling of needing or wanting a drink: *He quenched his thirst with a long drink of cold water.* ◇ *She woke up with a raging thirst and a pounding headache.* **2** [U] the state of not having enough water to drink: *Thousands are dying of thirst.* **3** [sing.] ~ (for sth) a strong desire for sth: *a thirst for knowledge*
■ *verb* [V] (*old use*) to be thirsty **PHRV** **'thirst for sth** (*literary*) to feel a strong desire for sth: *She thirsted for power.*

thirsty /'θɜːsti; *AmE* 'θɜːrsti/ *adj.* (**thirst·ier, thirsti·est**) **1** needing or wanting to drink: *We were hungry and thirsty.* ◇ *Digging is* ***thirsty work*** (= makes you thirsty). **2** ~ **for sth** having a strong desire for sth: *He is thirsty for power.* **3** (of plants, fields, etc.) dry; in need of water ▶ **thirst·ily** /-ɪli/ *adv.*: *Paul drank thirstily.*

thir·teen /ˌθɜːˈtiːn; *AmE* ˌθɜːrˈt-/ *number* 13 ▶ **thir·teenth** /ˌθɜːˈtiːnθ; *AmE* ˌθɜːrˈt-/ *ordinal number*

thirty /'θɜːti; *AmE* 'θɜːrti/ *number* 1 30 **2** (**the thirties**) [pl.] numbers, years or temperatures from 30 to 39 ▶ **thir·ti·eth** /'θɜːtiəθ; *AmE* 'θɜːrt-/ *ordinal number* **IDM** **in your 'thirties** between the ages of 30 and 39

this /ðɪs/ *det., pron., adv.*
■ *det., pron.* (*pl.* **these** /ðiːz/) **1** used to refer to a particular person, thing or event that is close to you, especially compared with another: *How long have you been living in this country?* ◇ *Well, make up your mind. Which do you want? This one or that one?* ◇ *I think you'll find these more comfortable than those.* ◇ *Is this your bag?* **2** used to refer to sth/sb that has already been mentioned: *There was a court case resulting from this incident.* ◇ *The boy was afraid and the dog had sensed this.* ◇ *What's this I hear about you getting married?* **3** used for introducing sb or showing sth to sb: *Hello, this is Maria Diaz* (= on the telephone). ◇ *Jo, this is Kate* (= when you are introducing them). ◇ *This is the captain speaking.* ◇ *Listen to this.* ◇ *Do it like this* (= in the way I am showing you). **4** used with periods of time related to the present: *this week/month/year* ◇ *I saw her this morning* (= today in the morning). ◇ *Do you want me to come this Tuesday* (= Tuesday of this week) *or next Tuesday?* ◇ *Do it* ***this minute*** (= now). ◇ *He never comes to see me* ***these days*** (= now, as compared with the past). **5** ~ **sth of sb's** (*informal*) used to refer to sb/sth that is connected with a person, especially when you have a particular attitude towards it or them: *These new friends of hers are supposed to be very rich.* **6** (*informal*) used when you are telling a story or telling sb about sth: *There was this strange man sitting next to me on the plane.* ◇ *I've been getting these pains in my chest.* **IDM** **,this and 'that | ,this, ,that and the 'other** (*spoken*) various things or activities: *'What did you talk about?' 'Oh, this and that.'*
■ *adv.* to this degree; so: *It's about this high* (= as high as I am showing you with my hands). ◇ *I didn't think we'd get this far.*

this·tle /'θɪsl/ *noun* a wild plant with prickly leaves and purple, yellow or white flowers made up of a mass of narrow PETALS pointing upwards. The thistle is the national symbol of Scotland.

thistle·down /'θɪsldaʊn/ *noun* [U] a very light soft substance that contains THISTLE seeds and is blown from THISTLES by the wind

thither /'ðɪðə(r)/ *adv.* (*old use*) to or towards that place **IDM** see HITHER

tho' *adv.* an informal spelling of 'though'

thong /θɒŋ; *AmE* θɔːŋ/ *noun* **1** a narrow strip of leather that is used to fasten sth or as a whip **2** a pair of women's KNICKERS or men's UNDERPANTS that has only a very narrow strip of fabric, like a string, at the back **3** (*AmE*) = FLIP-FLOP

thorax /'θɔːræks/ *noun* (*pl.* **thor·axes** or **thor·aces** /'θɔːrəsiːz/) **1** (*anatomy*) the part of the body that is enclosed by the RIBS, between the neck and the waist **2** the middle section of an insect's body, to which the legs and wings are attached—picture on page A7 ▶ **thor·acic** /θɔːˈræsɪk/ *adj.* [only before noun]

thorn /θɔːn; *AmE* θɔːrn/ *noun* **1** [C] a small sharp pointed part on the stem of some plants, such as roses—picture at PLANT **2** [C, U] a tree or bush that has thorns: *an old hedge of thorns* ◇ *a thorn tree*—see also BLACKTHORN, HAWTHORN **IDM** **a thorn in sb's 'flesh/'side** a person or thing that repeatedly annoys sb or stops them from doing sth

thorny /'θɔːni; *AmE* 'θɔːrni/ *adj.* (**thorn·ier, thorni·est**) **1** [usually before noun] causing difficulty or disagreement: *a thorny question/issue/problem* **2** having thorns: *a thorny bush*

thor·ough /'θʌrə; *AmE* 'θɜːroʊ/ *adj.* **1** done completely; with great attention to detail: *a thorough knowledge of the subject* ◇ *The police carried out a thorough investigation.* **2** [not usually before noun] (of a person) doing things very carefully and with great attention to detail: *She's very thorough and conscientious.* ◇ *He was determined to be thorough in his research.* **3** (*BrE, informal*) used to emphasize how bad or annoying sb/sth is: *Everything was in a thorough mess.* ▶ **thor·ough·ness** *noun* [U]: *I was impressed by the thoroughness of the report.* ◇ *I admire his thoroughness.*

thor·ough·bred /'θʌrəbred; *AmE* 'θɜːroʊb-/ *noun* an animal, especially a horse, of high quality, that has parents that are both of the same breed ▶ **thor·ough·bred** *adj.*: *a thoroughbred mare*

thor·ough·fare /'θʌrəfeə(r); *AmE* 'θɜːroʊfer/ *noun* a public road or street used by traffic, especially a main road in a city or town: *We walked down Patrick Street, Cork's main thoroughfare.*

thor·ough·going /ˌθʌrəˈgəʊɪŋ; *AmE* ˌθɜːroʊˈgoʊɪŋ/ *adj.* [only before noun] (*written*) **1** very thorough; looking at every detail: *a thoroughgoing revision of the text* **2** complete: *a thoroughgoing commitment to change*

thor·ough·ly /'θʌrəli; *AmE* 'θɜːr-/ *adv.* **1** very much; completely: *We thoroughly enjoyed ourselves.* ◇ *I'm thoroughly confused.* ◇ *a thoroughly professional performance* **2** completely and with great attention to detail: *Wash the fruit thoroughly before use.* ◇ *The work had not been done very thoroughly.*

those ⇨ THAT

thou /ðaʊ/ *pron.* (*old use* or *dialect*) a word meaning 'you', used when talking to only one person who is the subject of the verb: *Thou art indeed just, Lord.*—compare THEE

though /ðəʊ; *AmE* ðoʊ/ *conj., adv.*
■ *conj.* **1** in spite of the fact that **SYN** ALTHOUGH: *Anne was fond of Tim, though he often annoyed her.* ◇ *Though she gave no sign, I was sure she had seen me.* ◇ *His clothes, though old and worn, looked clean and of good quality.* ◇ *Strange though it may sound, I was pleased it was over.* **2** used to add a fact or an opinion that makes the previous statement less strong or less important: *They're very different, though they did seem to get on well when they met.* ◇ *He'll probably say no, though it's worth asking.* ⇨ note at ALTHOUGH **IDM** see AS *conj.*, EVEN *adv.*
■ *adv.* (especially *spoken*) used especially at the end of a sentence to add a fact or an opinion that makes the previous statement less strong or less important: *Our team lost. It was a good game though.* ◇ *'Have you ever been to Australia?' 'No. I'd like to, though.'* ⇨ note at ALTHOUGH

thought /θɔːt/ *noun*
STH YOU THINK ▶ **1** [C] ~ (of sth/of doing sth) | ~ (that …) something that you think of or remember: *I don't like the thought of you walking home alone.* ◇ *She was struck by the sudden thought that he might already have left.* ◇ *The*

T

s	t	v	z	ʃ	ʒ	tʃ	dʒ	θ	ð	ŋ
see	tea	van	zoo	shoe	vision	chain	jam	thin	this	sing

very thought of it makes me feel sick. ◊ I've just **had a thought** (= an idea). ◊ Would Mark be able to help? It's **just a thought**. ◊ 'Why don't you try the other key?' 'That's a thought!' ◊ All kinds of thoughts raced through my mind. ◊ I'd like to hear your thoughts on the subject. MIND/IDEAS | **2 (thoughts)** [pl.] a person's mind and all the ideas that they have in it when they are thinking: My thoughts turned to home. PROCESS/ACT OF THINKING | **3** [U] the power or process of thinking: A good teacher encourages independence of thought. ◊ She was lost in thought (= concentrating so much on her thoughts that she was not aware of her surroundings). **4** [U] the act of thinking seriously and carefully about sth: I've given the matter careful thought. ◊ Not enough thought has gone into this essay. CARE/WORRY | **5** [C] ~ **(for sb/sth)** a feeling of care or worry: Spare a thought for those without enough to eat this winter. ◊ **Don't give it another thought** (= to tell sb not to worry after they have said they are sorry). ◊ It's **the thought that counts** (= used to say that sb has been very kind even if they have only done sth small or unimportant). INTENTION | **6** [U, C] ~ **(of sth/of doing sth)** an intention or a hope of doing sth: She had given up all thought of changing her job. ◊ He acted with no thoughts of personal gain. IN POLITICS/SCIENCE, etc. | **7** [U] ideas in politics, science, etc. connected with a particular person, group or period of history: feminist/twentieth century thought —see also THINK v. **IDM** have ˌsecond ˈthoughts to change your opinion after thinking about sth again on ˈsecond thoughts (BrE) (AmE on ˈsecond thought) used to say that you have changed your opinion: I'll wait here. No, on second thoughts, I'll come with you. **without a second ˈthought** immediately; without stopping to think about sth further: He dived in after her without a second thought.—more at COLLECT v., FOOD, PAUSE n., PENNY, PERISH, SCHOOL n., TRAIN n.

thought·ful /ˈθɔːtfl/ adj. **1** quiet, because you are thinking: He looked thoughtful. ◊ They sat in thoughtful silence. **2** (approving) showing that you think about and care for other people: It was very thoughtful of you to send the flowers. **3** showing signs of careful thought: a player who has a thoughtful approach to the game ▶ **thought·ful·ly** /-fəli/ adv.: Martin looked at her thoughtfully. ◊ She wrote down a few ideas on the paper thoughtfully provided by her host. **thought·ful·ness** noun [U]

thought·less /ˈθɔːtləs/ adj. (disapproving) not caring about the possible effects of your words or actions on other people: a thoughtless remark ▶ **thought·less·ly** adv. **thought·less·ness** noun [U]

ˈ**thought-provoking** adj. making people think seriously about a particular subject or issue

thou·sand /ˈθaʊznd/ number (plural verb) (abbr. K) **1** 1000 **HELP** You say **a, one, two,** etc. **thousand** without a final 's' on 'thousand'. **Thousands (of …)** can be used if there is no number or quantity before it. Always use a plural verb with **thousand** or **thousands**. **2 a thousand** or **thousands (of …)** (usually informal) a large number: There were thousands of people there. **3 (the thousands)** the numbers from 1000 to 9999: The cost ran into the thousands. ⇨ Appendix 3 **HELP** There are more examples of how to use numbers at the entry for **hundred**. **IDM** see BAT v.

thou·sandth /ˈθaʊznθ/ ordinal number, noun
■ ordinal number 1000th: the city's thousandth anniversary
■ noun each of one thousand parts of sth: a/one thousandth of a second

thrall /θrɔːl/ noun **IDM** in (sb's/sth's) ˈthrall | in ˈthrall to sb/sth (literary) controlled or strongly influenced by sb/sth

thrash /θræʃ/ verb, noun
■ verb **1** [VN] to hit a person or an animal many times with a stick, etc. as a punishment **SYN** BEAT **2** ~ **(sth) (about/ around)** to move or make sth move in a violent or uncontrolled way: [V] Someone was thrashing around in the

water, obviously in trouble. ◊ [VN] A whale was thrashing the water with its tail. ◊ She thrashed her head from side to side. **3** [VN] (informal, especially BrE) to defeat sb very easily in a game: Scotland thrashed England 5–1. **PHR V** ˌthrash sth↔ˈout to discuss a situation or problem thoroughly in order to decide sth: The details have not been thrashed out yet.
■ noun **1** [U] a type of loud ROCK music **2** [C] (old-fashioned, informal) a party with music and dancing

thrash·ing /ˈθræʃɪŋ/ noun **1** an act of hitting sb very hard, especially with a stick: to give sb/get a thrashing **2** (informal) a severe defeat in a game

thread /θred/ noun, verb
■ noun **1** [U, C] a thin string of cotton, wool, silk, etc. used for sewing or making fabric: a needle and thread ◊ a robe embroidered with gold thread ◊ the delicate threads of a spider's web—picture at ROPE **2** [C] an idea or a feature that is part of sth greater; an idea that connects the different parts of sth: A common thread runs through these discussions. ◊ The author skilfully draws together the different threads of the plot. ◊ I lost the thread of the argument (= I could no longer follow it). **3** [C] ~ **(of sth)** a long thin line of sth: A thread of light emerged from the keyhole. **4** [C] the raised line that runs around the length of a screw and that allows it to be fixed in place by twisting **5 (threads)** [pl.] (old-fashioned, AmE, slang) clothes **IDM** see HANG v., PICK v.
■ verb **1** [VN] [usually +adv./prep.] to pass sth long and thin, especially thread, through a narrow opening or hole: to thread a needle (with cotton) ◊ to thread cotton through a needle ◊ A tiny wire is threaded through a vein to the heart. **2** [+adv./prep.] to move or make sth move through a narrow space, avoiding things that are in the way: [V] The waiters threaded between the crowded tables. ◊ [VN] It took me a long time to thread my way through the crowd. **3** [VN] to join two or more objects together by passing sth long and thin through them: to thread beads (onto a string) **4** [VN] to pass film, tape, string, through parts of a piece of equipment so that it is ready to use **5** [VN] [usually passive] to sew or weave a particular type of thread into sth: a robe threaded with gold and silver

thread·bare /ˈθredbeə(r); AmE -ber/ adj. **1** (of fabric, clothing, etc.) old and thin because it has been used a lot: a threadbare carpet/coat **2** (of an argument, excuse, etc.) that does not have much effect, especially because it has been used too much: an explanation that is becoming increasingly threadbare

thread·worm /ˈθredwɜːm; AmE -wɜːrm/ noun a small thin worm that lives in the INTESTINES of humans and animals

threat /θret/ noun **1** [C, U] ~ **(to do sth)** a statement in which you tell sb that you will punish or harm them, especially if they do not do what you want: to make threats against sb ◊ She is prepared to **carry out her threat** to resign. ◊ He received death threats from right-wing groups. ◊ crimes involving violence or the threat of violence **2** [U, C, usually sing.] the possibility of trouble, danger or disaster: These ancient woodlands are **under threat** from new road developments. ◊ There is a real threat of war. **3** [C, usually sing.] ~ **(to sth)** a person or thing that is likely to cause trouble, danger, etc: He is unlikely to be a threat to the Spanish player in the final. ◊ Drug abuse **poses** a major **threat** to the fabric of our society.

threat·en /ˈθretn/ verb **1** ~ **sb (with sth)** to say that you will cause trouble, hurt sb, etc. if you do not get what you want: [VN] They broke my windows and threatened me. ◊ The attacker threatened them with a gun. ◊ He was threatened with dismissal if he continued to turn up late for work. ◊ The threatened strike has been called off. ◊ [V to inf] The hijackers threatened to kill one passenger every hour if their demands were not met. [also V that] **2** to seem likely to happen or cause sth unpleasant: [V] A storm was threatening. ◊ [V to inf] This dispute threatens to split the party. ◊ [VN] The clouds threatened rain. **3** [VN] to be a danger to sth: Pollution along the coastline is threatening marine life.

threat·en·ing /ˈθretnɪŋ/ adj. **1** expressing a threat of

æ	ɑː	e	ɜː	ə	ɪ	iː	i	ɒ	ɔː	ʌ	ʊ	u	uː
cat	father	ten	bird	about	sit	see	many	got	saw	cup	put	actual	too
													(BrE)

harm or violence: *threatening letters* ◊ *threatening behaviour* ◊ *The house seemed less threatening in the cold light of day.* **2** (of the sky, clouds, etc.) showing that bad weather is likely: *The sky was dark and threatening.* ▶ **threat·en·ing·ly** *adv.*: *He glared at her threateningly.*

three /θriː/ *noun* 3 `HELP` There are examples of how to use numbers at the entry for **five**. `IDM` **the three 'Rs** (*old-fashioned*) reading, writing and ARITHMETIC, thought to be the most important parts of a child's education—more at TWO

three-'cornered *adj.* [usually before noun] **1** having three corners: *a three-cornered hat* **2** involving three people or groups: *a three-cornered contest*

three-'D (also **3-D**) *noun* [U] the quality of having, or appearing to have, length, width and depth (= three DIMENSIONS): *These glasses allow you to see the film in three-D.* ◊ *a three-D image*

three-day e'venting *noun* = EVENTING

three-di'mensional *adj.* having, or appearing to have, length, width and depth: *three-dimensional objects/ forms/graphics*

three·fold /'θriːfəʊld; *AmE* -foʊld/ *adj., adv.* ⟹ -FOLD

three 'fourths *noun* [pl.] (*AmE*) = THREE QUARTERS

three-legged race /ˌθriː ˈlegɪd reɪs/ *noun* a race in which competitors run in pairs, the right leg of one runner being tied to the left leg of the other

three-line 'whip *noun* (in Britain) a written notice to Members of Parliament from their party leaders telling them that they must be present at a particular vote and must vote in a particular way

three·pence /ˌθriːˈpens; *formerly* ˈθrepəns/ *noun* [U] (*BrE*) the sum of three old pence

three·penny bit /ˌθrepəni ˈbɪt/ (also **three·penny 'piece** /-ˈpiːs/) *noun* a British coin in use until 1971, worth three old pence

'three-piece *adj.* [only before noun] consisting of three separate parts or pieces: *a three-piece suit* (= a set of clothes consisting of trousers/pants, a jacket and a WAISTCOAT/VEST) ◊ (*BrE*) *a three-piece suite* (= a set of three pieces of furniture, usually a SOFA *and two* ARMCHAIRS)

'three-ply *adj.* (of wood, wool, etc.) having three layers or threads

three-point 'turn *noun* a method of turning a car in a small space by driving forwards, then backwards, then forwards again, in a series of curves

three-'quarter *adj.* [only before noun] used to describe sth which is three quarters of the usual size: *a three-quarter length coat*

three 'quarters (*AmE also* **three 'fourths**) *noun* ~ (of sth) three of the four equal parts into which sth may be divided: *three quarters of an hour*

three-ring 'circus *noun* [sing.] (*AmE, informal*) a place or situation with a lot of confusing or amusing activity

three·some /'θriːsəm/ *noun* a group of three people

three-'way *adj.* [only before noun] happening or working in three ways or directions, or between three people: *a three-way switch* ◊ *a three-way discussion*

thresh /θreʃ/ *verb* **1** [VN] to separate grains of corn, rice, etc. from the rest of the plant using a machine or, especially in the past, by hitting it with a special tool [V, VN] to make, or cause sth to make, uncontrolled movements `SYN` THRASH ▶ **thresh·ing** *noun* [U]: *a threshing machine*

thresh·old /'θreʃhəʊld; *AmE* -hoʊld/ *noun* **1** the floor or ground at the bottom of a DOORWAY, considered as the entrance to a building or room: *She stood hesitating on the threshold.* ◊ *He stepped across the threshold.* **2** the level at which sth starts to happen: *He has a low boredom threshold* (= he gets bored easily). ◊ *I have a high pain threshold* (= I can suffer a lot of pain before I start to react). **3** [usually sing.] the point just before a new situation, period of life, etc. begins: *She felt as though she was on the threshold of a new life.*

threw *pt* of THROW

thrice /θraɪs/ *adv.* (*old use* or *formal*) three times

thrift /θrɪft/ *noun* [U] **1** (*approving*) the habit of saving money and spending it carefully so that none is wasted—see also SPENDTHRIFT **2** a wild plant with bright pink flowers that grows by the sea/ocean

thrifty /'θrɪfti/ *adj.* (*approving*) careful about spending money and not wasting things

thrill /θrɪl/ *noun, verb*
- *noun* **1** ~ (to do sth)| ~ (of doing sth) a strong feeling of excitement or pleasure; an experience that gives you this feeling: *It gave me a big thrill to meet my favourite author in person.* ◊ *the thrill of catching a really big fish* ◊ *She gets an obvious thrill out of performing.* **2** a sudden strong feeling that produces a physical effect: *A thrill of alarm ran through him.* `IDM` **(the) thrills and 'spills** (*informal*) the excitement that is involved in dangerous activities, especially sports
- *verb* [VN] to excite or please sb very much: *This band has thrilled audiences all over the world.* ◊ *I was thrilled by your news.* `PHRV` **'thrill to sth** (*formal*) to feel very excited at sth: *Audiences still thrill to the sound of The Rolling Stones.*

thrilled /θrɪld/ *adj.* ~ (about/at/with sth)| ~ (to do sth)| ~ (that…) very excited and pleased: *He was thrilled at the prospect of seeing them again.* ◊ *I was thrilled to be invited.* ◊ (*BrE*) *She was thrilled to bits* (= extremely pleased) *that he'd been offered the job.* ◊ 'Are you pleased?' 'I'm thrilled.'

thrill·er /'θrɪlə(r)/ *noun* a book, play or film/movie with an exciting story, especially one about crime or SPYING

thrill·ing /'θrɪlɪŋ/ *adj.* exciting and enjoyable: *a thrilling experience/finish/victory* ▶ **thrill·ing·ly** *adv.*

thrive /θraɪv/ *verb* [V] to become, and continue to be, successful, strong, healthy, etc: *New businesses thrive in this area.* ◊ *These animals rarely thrive in captivity.* ▶ **thriv·ing** *adj.*: *a thriving industry/city/garden* `PHRV` **'thrive on sth** to enjoy sth or be successful at sth, especially sth that other people would not like: *He thrives on hard work.*

throat /θrəʊt; *AmE* θroʊt/ *noun* **1** the tube in the neck that takes food and air into the body; the front part of the neck: *a sore throat* ◊ *A sob caught in his throat.* ◊ *He held the knife to her throat.* ◊ *Their throats had been cut.* **2** (**-throated**) (in adjectives) having the type of throat mentioned: *a deep-throated roar* ◊ *a red-throated diver*—see also CUTTHROAT `IDM` **be at each other's 'throats** (of two or more people, groups, etc.) to be fighting or arguing with each other **cut your own 'throat** to do sth that is likely to harm you, especially when you are angry and trying to harm sb else **force/thrust/ram sth down sb's 'throat** (*informal*) to try to force sb to listen to and accept your opinions in a way that they find annoying—more at CLEAR *v.*, FROG, JUMP *v.*, LUMP *n.*, STICK *v.*

throaty /'θrəʊti; *AmE* 'θroʊti/ *adj.* sounding low and rough: *a throaty growl/laugh/voice* ◊ *the throaty roar of the engines* ▶ **throat·ily** /-ɪli/ *adv.*

throb /θrɒb; *AmE* θrɑːb/ *verb, noun*
- *verb* (**-bb-**) [V] ~ (with sth) **1** (of a part of the body) to feel a series of regular painful movements: *His head throbbed painfully.* ◊ *My feet were throbbing after the long walk home.* **2** to beat or sound with a strong, regular rhythm: *The ship's engines throbbed quietly.* ◊ *a throbbing pain/ drumbeat* ◊ *The blood was throbbing in my veins.* ◊ (*figurative*) *His voice was throbbing with emotion.*
- *noun* (also **throb·bing**) [sing.] a strong regular beat; a feeling of pain that you experience as a series of strong beats: *the throb of the machines* ◊ *My headache faded to a dull throbbing.*—see also HEART-THROB

throes /θrəʊz; *AmE* θroʊz/ *noun* [pl.] violent pains, especially at the moment of death: *The creature went into its death throes.* `IDM` **in the throes of sth/of doing sth** in the middle of an activity, especially a difficult or complicated one: *The country was in the throes of revolutionary change.*

throm·bosis /θrɒmˈbəʊsɪs; *AmE* θrɑːmˈboʊ-/ *noun* [C, U] (*pl.* **throm·boses** /-siːz/) (*medical*) a serious condition caused by a blood CLOT (= a thick mass of blood) forming

aɪ	aʊ	eɪ	əʊ	oʊ	ɔɪ	ɪə	eə	ʊə	j	w
my	now	say	go (BrE)	go (AmE)	boy	near	hair	pure	yes	wet

in a blood VESSEL (= tube) or in the heart—see also CORONARY THROMBOSIS

throne /θrəʊn; AmE θroʊn/ noun **1** [C] a special chair used by a king or queen to sit on at ceremonies **2** (**the throne**) [sing.] the position of being a king or queen: *Queen Elizabeth came/succeeded to the throne in 1952.* ◊ *when Henry VIII was on the throne* (= was king) IDM see POWER *n.*

throng /θrɒŋ; AmE θrɔːŋ; θrɑːŋ/ noun, verb
- noun (*written*) a crowd of people: *We pushed our way through the throng.* ◊ *He was met by a throng of journalists and photographers.*
- verb (*written*) to go somewhere or be present somewhere in large numbers: [V+adv./prep.] *The children thronged into the hall.* ◊ [VtoInf] *People are thronging to see his new play.* ◊ [VN] *Crowds thronged the stores.* PHRV **'throng with sb/sth; be 'thronged with sb/sth** to be full of people, cars, etc: *The cafes were thronging with students.* ◊ *The streets were thronged with people.*

throt·tle /'θrɒtl; AmE 'θrɑːtl/ verb, noun
- verb [VN] to attack or kill sb by squeezing their throat in order to stop them from breathing [SYN] STRANGLE: *He throttled the guard with his bare hands.* ◊ (*humorous*) *I like her, although I could cheerfully throttle her at times* (= because she is annoying). ◊ (*figurative*) *The city is being throttled by traffic.* PHRV **,throttle (sth) 'back/'down/'up** to control the supply of fuel or power to an engine in order to reduce/increase the speed of a vehicle: *I throttled back as we approached the runway.*
- noun a device that controls the amount of fuel that goes into the engine of a vehicle, for example the ACCELERATOR in a car: *He drove along at full throttle* (= as fast as possible).

through /θruː/ prep., adv., adj.
- prep. HELP For the special uses of **through** in phrasal verbs, look at the entries for the verbs. For example **get through sth** is in the phrasal verb section at **get**. **1** from one end or side of sth/sb to the other: *The burglar got in through the window.* ◊ *The bullet went straight through him.* ◊ *Her knees had gone through* (= made holes in) *her jeans.* ◊ *The sand ran through* (= between) *my fingers.* ◊ *The path led through the trees to the river.* ◊ *The doctor pushed his way through the crowd.* ◊ *The Charles River flows through Boston.* **2** see, hear, etc. **~** sth to see, hear, etc. sth from the other side of an object or a substance: *I couldn't hear their conversation through the wall.* ◊ *He could just make out three people through the mist.* **3** from the beginning to the end of an activity, a situation or a period of time: *The children are too young to sit through a concert.* ◊ *He will not live through the night.* ◊ *I'm halfway through* (= reading) *her second novel.* **4** past a barrier, stage or test: *Go through this gate, and you'll see the house on your left.* ◊ *He drove through a red light* (= passed it when he should have stopped). ◊ *First I have to get through the exams.* ◊ *The bill had a difficult passage through Parliament.* ◊ *I'd never have got through it all* (= a difficult situation) *without you.* **5** (also *informal* **thru**) (both *AmE*) until, and including: *We'll be in New York Tuesday through Friday.* ⇨ note at INCLUSIVE **6** by means of; because of: *You can only achieve success through hard work.* ◊ *It was through him* (= as a result of his help) *that I got the job.* ◊ *The accident happened through no fault of mine.*
- adv. HELP For the special uses of **through** in phrasal verbs, look at the entries for the verbs. For example **carry sth through** is in the phrasal verb section at **carry**. **1** from one end or side of sth to the other: *Put the coffee in the filter and let the water run through.* ◊ *The tyre's flat—the nail has gone right through.* ◊ *The onlookers stood aside to let the paramedics through.* ◊ *The flood was too deep to drive through.* **2** from the beginning to the end of a thing or period of time: *Don't tell me how it ends—I haven't read it all the way through yet.* ◊ *I expect I'll struggle through until pay day.* **3** past a barrier, stage or test: *The lights were red but he drove straight through.* ◊ *Our team is through to* (= has reached) *the semi-finals.* **4** travelling through a place without stopping or without people having to get off one train and onto another: '*Did*

you stop in Oxford on the way?' 'No, we drove straight through.' ◊ *This train goes straight through to York.* **5** connected by telephone: *Ask to be put through to me personally.* ◊ *I tried to call you but I couldn't get through.* **6** used after an adjective to mean 'completely': *We got wet through.* IDM **,through and 'through** completely; in every way: *He's British through and through.*
- adj. **1** [only before noun] **through** traffic travels from one side of a place to the other without stopping **2** [only before noun] a **through** train takes you to the final place you want to get to and you do not have to get off and get on another train **3** [only before noun] a **through** road or route is open at both ends and allows traffic to travel from one end to the other: *The village lies on a busy through road.* ◊ *No through road* (= the road is closed at one end). **4** [not before noun] **~** (**with sth/sb**) (*especially AmE*) used to show that you have finished using sth or have ended a relationship with sb: *Are you through with that newspaper?* ◊ *Todd and I are through.*

through·out /θruː'aʊt/ prep. **1** in or into every part of sth: *They export their products to markets throughout the world.* **2** during the whole period of time of sth: *The museum is open daily throughout the year.* ▶ **through·out** adv.: *The house was painted white throughout.* ◊ *The ceremony lasted two hours and we had to stand throughout.*

through·put /'θruːpʊt/ noun [U, C, usually sing.] (*technical*) the amount of work that is done, or the number of people that are dealt with, in a particular period of time: *high/low rates of throughput* ◊ *The centre has a weekly throughput of 200000 shoppers.*

throw /θrəʊ; AmE θroʊ/ verb, noun
- verb (threw /θruː/, thrown /θrəʊn; AmE θroʊn/)
- WITH HAND **1** to send sth from your hand through the air by moving your hand or arm quickly: [VN] *Stop throwing stones at the window!* ◊ *She threw the ball up and caught it again.* ◊ *Don't throw it to him, give it to him!* ◊ [VNN] *Can you throw me that towel?* ◊ [V] *They had a competition to see who could throw the furthest.*
- PUT CARELESSLY **2** [VN+adv./prep.] to put sth in a particular place quickly and carelessly: *Just throw your bag down over there.* ◊ *Don't throw litter on the ground.*
- MOVE WITH FORCE **3** [+adv./prep.] to move sth suddenly and forcefully: [VN] *The boat was thrown onto the rocks.* ◊ *The sea threw up all sorts of debris on the beach.* ◊ [VN-ADJ] *I threw open the windows to let the smoke out.*
- PART OF BODY **4** [VN] to move your body or part of it quickly or suddenly: *He threw back his head and roared with laughter.* ◊ *I ran up and threw my arms around him.* ◊ *Jenny threw herself onto the bed.*
- MAKE SB FALL **5** [VN] to make sb fall quickly or violently to the ground: *Two riders were thrown* (= off their horses) *in the second race.*
- INTO PARTICULAR STATE **6** [VN+adv./prep.] [usually passive] to make sb/sth be in a particular state: *Hundreds were thrown out of work.* ◊ *We were thrown into confusion by the news.* ◊ *The problem was suddenly thrown into sharp focus.*
- DIRECT STH AT SB/STH **7** [VN] to direct sth at sb/sth: *to throw doubt on the verdict* ◊ *to throw the blame on someone* ◊ *to throw threats/insults/accusations at someone* ◊ *He threw the question back at me* (= expected me to answer it myself).
- UPSET **8** [VN] **~** sb (off) (*informal*) to make sb feel upset, confused, or surprised: *The news of her death really threw me.* ◊ *The speaker was completely thrown off by the interruption.*
- DICE **9** [VN] to roll a DICE or let it fall after shaking it; to obtain a particular number in this way: *Throw the dice!* ◊ *He threw three sixes in a row.*
- CLAY POT **10** [VN] (*technical*) to make a clay pot, dish, etc. on a POTTER's wheel: *a hand-thrown vase.*
- LIGHT/SHADE **11** [VN] (*written*) to send light or shade onto sth: *The trees threw long shadows across the lawn.*
- YOUR VOICE **12** [VN] **~** your voice to make your voice sound as if it is coming from another person or place
- A PUNCH **13** [VN] **~** a punch to hit sb with your FIST

b	d	f	g	h	k	l	m	n	p	r
bad	did	fall	get	hat	cat	leg	man	now	pen	red

T

T

SWITCH/HANDLE | **14** [VN] to move a switch, handle, etc. to operate sth

BAD TEMPER | **15** [VN] to have a sudden period of bad temper, violent emotion, etc: *She'll throw a fit if she finds out.* ◊ *Children often throw tantrums at this age.*

A PARTY | **16** [VN] ~ **a party** (*informal*) to give a party

IN SPORTS/COMPETITIONS | **17** [VN] (*informal*) to deliberately lose a game or contest that you should have won: *He was accused of having thrown the game.*

IDM Idioms containing **throw** are at the entries for the nouns and adjectives in the idioms, for example **throw your hat into the ring** is at **hat**.

PHRV ,**throw sth**↔**a'side** to reject sth such as an attitude, a way of life, etc. ,**throw yourself at sth/sb 1** to rush violently at sth/sb **2** (*informal, disapproving*) (usually of a woman) to be too enthusiastic in trying to attract a sexual partner ,**throw sth**↔**a'way 1** (*also* ,**throw sth**↔**'out**) to get rid of sth that you no longer want: *I don't need that—you can throw it away.* ◊ *That old chair should be thrown away.* **2** to fail to make use of sth; to waste sth: *to throw away an opportunity/advantage* ◊ *You must take the exam—you can't throw away all that work!*—see also THROWAWAY ,**throw sth 'back at sb** to remind sb of sth they have said or done in the past, especially to upset or annoy them ,**throw sb 'back on sth** [usually passive] to force sb to rely on sth because nothing else is available: *There was no TV so we were thrown back on our own resources* (= had to entertain ourselves). ,**throw sth**↔**'in 1** to include sth with what you are selling or offering, without increasing the price: *You can have the piano for $200, and I'll throw in the stool as well.* **2** to add a remark to a conversation: *Jack threw in the odd encouraging comment.* ,**throw yourself/sth 'into sth** to begin to do sth with energy and enthusiasm ,**throw sth/sb**↔**'off 1** to manage to get rid of sth/sb that is making you suffer, annoying you, etc: *to throw off a cold/your worries/your pursuers* **2** to take off a piece of clothing quickly and carelessly: *She entered the room and threw off her wet coat.* ,**throw sth**↔**'on** to put on a piece of clothing quickly and carelessly: *She just threw on the first skirt she found.* ,**throw sth**↔**'open (to sb) 1** to allow people to enter or visit a place where they could not go before **2** to allow people to discuss sth, take part in a competition, etc: *The debate will be thrown open to the audience.* ◊ *The organizers are throwing the contest open to under 21s for the first time.* ,**throw sb**↔**'out (of ...)** to force sb to leave a place: *You'll be thrown out if you don't pay the rent.* ,**throw sth**↔**'out 1** to say sth in a way that suggests you have not given it a lot of thought: *to throw out a hint/a suggestion/an idea* **2** to decide not to accept a proposal, an idea, etc. **3** = THROW STH AWAY **4** to produce smoke, light, heat, etc: *a small fire that threw out a lot of heat* ,**throw sb 'over** (*old-fashioned*) to stop being friends with sb or having a romantic relationship with them ,**throw sb**↔**to'gether** [often passive] to bring people into contact with each other, often unexpectedly: *Fate had thrown them together.* ,**throw sth**↔**to'gether** to make or produce sth in a hurry: *I threw together a quick meal.* ,**throw 'up** to VOMIT: *The smell made me want to throw up.* ,**throw sth**↔**'up 1** to VOMIT food: *The baby's thrown up her dinner.* **2** to make people notice sth: *Her research has thrown up some interesting facts.* **3** to build sth suddenly or in a hurry: *They're throwing up new housing estates all over the place.* **4** to leave your job: *to throw up your job/career*

■ *noun* **1** the act of throwing sth, especially a ball or DICE: *a well-aimed throw* ◊ *It's your throw* (= it's your turn to throw the dice). ◊ *He threw me to the ground with a judo throw.* **2** the distance which sth is thrown: *a javelin throw of 57 metres* **3** a loose fabric cover that can be thrown over a SOFA, etc.
IDM $100, £50, etc. a 'throw (*informal*) used to say how much items cost each: *The tickets for the dinner were £50 a throw.*—more at STONE *n.*

throw·away /'θrəʊəweɪ; *AmE* 'θroʊ-/ *adj.* [only before noun] **1** ~ **line/remark/comment** something you say quickly without careful thought, sometimes in order to be funny: *She was very upset at what to him was just a*

throwaway remark. **2** (of goods, etc.) produced cheaply and intended to be thrown away after use: *throwaway products* ◊ *We live in a throwaway society* (= a society in which things are not made to last a long time).

throw·back /'θrəʊbæk; *AmE* 'θroʊ-/ *noun* [usually sing.] ~ **(to sth)** a person or thing that is similar to sb/sth that existed in the past: *The car's design is a throwback to the 1960s.*

throw·er /'θrəʊə(r); *AmE* 'θroʊ-/ *noun* a person who throws sth: *a discus thrower*—see also FLAME-THROWER

'**throw-in** *noun* (in football and rugby) the act of throwing the ball back onto the playing field after it has gone outside the area

thru (*AmE, informal*) = THROUGH *prep.* (5)

thrush /θrʌʃ/ *noun* **1** [C] a bird with a brown back and brown spots on its chest: *a song thrush* **2** [U] an infectious disease that affects the mouth and throat **3** [U] (*BrE*) (*AmE* '**yeast infection**) an infectious disease that affects the VAGINA

thrust /θrʌst/ *verb, noun*
■ *verb* (**thrust, thrust**) **1** [usually +*adv./prep.*] to push sth/sb suddenly or violently in a particular direction; to move quickly and suddenly in a particular direction: [VN] *He thrust the baby into my arms and ran off.* ◊ *She thrust her hands deep into her pockets.* ◊ (*figurative*) *He tends to thrust himself forward too much.* ◊ [V] *She thrust past him angrily and left.* **2** ~ **(at sb) (with sth)** | ~ **(sth at sb)** to make a sudden strong forward movement at sb with a weapon, etc: [V] *He thrust at me with a knife.* ◊ *a thrusting movement* [also VN] **IDM** see THROAT **PHRV** ,**thrust sth**↔**a'side** to refuse to listen to sb's complaints, comments, etc: *All our objections were thrust aside.* '**thrust sth/sb on/upon sb** to force sb to accept or deal with sth/sb that they do not want: *She was annoyed at having three extra guests suddenly thrust on her.* ◊ *Children of famous people have fame thrust upon them.*
■ *noun* **1** (**the thrust**) [sing.] the main point of an argument, a policy, etc: *The thrust of his argument was that change was needed.* **2** [C] a sudden strong movement that pushes sth/sb forward: *He killed her with a thrust of the knife.* **3** [U] (*technical*) the force that is produced by an engine to push a plane, rocket, etc. forward **IDM** see CUT *v.*

thru·way /'θruːweɪ/ *noun* (*AmE*) used in the names of some FREEWAYS (= important roads across or between states): *the New York State Thruway*

thud /θʌd/ *noun, verb*
■ *noun* a sound like the one which is made when a heavy object hits sth else: *His head hit the floor with a dull thud.*
■ *verb* (-**dd**-) **1** to fall or hit sth with a low dull sound: [V, +*adv./prep.*] *His arrow thudded into the target.* ◊ *We heard him thudding up the stairs.* [also VN] **2** [V] (*literary*) (especially of the heart) to beat strongly

thug /θʌg/ *noun* a violent person, especially a criminal: *a gang of thugs* ▶ **thug·gish** /'θʌgɪʃ/ *adj.*: *thuggish brutality*

thug·gery /'θʌgəri/ *noun* [U] (*written*) violent, usually criminal, behaviour

thumb /θʌm/ *noun, verb*
■ *noun* **1** the short thick finger at the side of the hand, slightly apart from the other four: *She still sucks her thumb when she's worried.*—see also GREEN THUMB—picture at BODY **2** the part of a glove that covers the thumb: *There's a hole in the thumb.* **IDM be all** (,**fingers and**) '**thumbs** to be awkward with your hands so that you drop things or are unable to do sth **thumbs 'up/ 'down** used to show that sth has been accepted/rejected or that it is/is not a success: *Their proposals were given the thumbs down.* ◊ *It looks like it's thumbs up for their latest album.* **under sb's 'thumb** (of a person) completely controlled by sb—more at RULE *n.*, SORE *adj.*, TWIDDLE *v.*

Thumbing a lift (*BrE*)/ **ride** (*AmE*).

■ *verb* **1** to make a signal with your thumb to passing drivers to ask them to stop and take you somewhere: [V, +*adv. / prep.*] *He had thumbed all across Europe.* ◊ [VN] *We managed to* **thumb a lift / ride** *with a truck driver.* **2** [VN] [often +*adv. / prep.*] to touch or move sth with your thumb: *She thumbed off the safety catch of her pistol.*—see also WELL THUMBED **IDM** **thumb your ˈnose at sb/sth** to make a rude sign with your thumb on your nose; to show that you have no respect for sb/sth: *The company just thumbs its nose at the legislation on pollution.* **PHR V** **ˈthumb through sth** to turn the pages of a book quickly in order to get a general idea of what is in it

ˈthumb index *noun* a series of cuts in the edge of a book, with letters of the alphabet on them, to help you to find the section that you want more easily

thumb·nail /ˈθʌmneɪl/ *noun* the nail on the thumb

ˌthumbnail ˈsketch *noun* a short description of sth, giving only the main details

thumb·screw /ˈθʌmskruː/ *noun* an instrument that was used in the past for TORTURING people by crushing their thumbs

thumb·tack /ˈθʌmtæk/ *noun* (*AmE*) = DRAWING PIN

thump /θʌmp/ *verb, noun*
■ *verb* **1** [usually +*adv. / prep.*] to hit sb/sth hard, especially with your closed hand: [VN] *He thumped the table angrily.* ◊ *She couldn't get her breath and had to be thumped on the back.* ◊ (*informal*) *I'll thump you if you say that again.* ◊ (*figurative*) *He thumped out a tune* (= played it very loudly) *on the piano.* [also V] **2** [+*adv. / prep.*] to fall on or hit a surface hard, with a loud dull sound; to make sth do this: [V] *A bird thumped against the window.* ◊ [VN] *He thumped the report down on my desk.* **3** [V] to beat strongly: *My heart was thumping with excitement.*—see also TUB-THUMPING
■ *noun* **1** the sound of sth heavy hitting the ground or another object: *There was a thump as the truck hit the bank.* **2** (*BrE, informal*) an act of hitting sb/sth hard: *She gave him a thump on the back.*

thump·ing /ˈθʌmpɪŋ/ *adj.* [only before noun] (*informal*) very big: *a thumping defeat / majority* ▶ **thump·ing** *adv.* (*BrE*): *He told us a thumping great lie.*

thun·der /ˈθʌndə(r)/ *noun, verb*
■ *noun* [U] **1** the loud noise that you hear after a flash of LIGHTNING, during a storm: *the rumble of distant thunder* ◊ *a clap / crash / roll of thunder* ◊ *Thunder crashed in the sky.* **2** a loud noise like thunder: *the thunder of gunfire / hooves* **IDM** see FACE *n.*, STEAL *v.*
■ *verb* **1** [V] when **it thunders**, there is a loud noise in the sky during a storm: *It was thundering all night but there was no rain.* **2** [V] to make a very loud deep noise: *A voice thundered in my ear.* ◊ *thundering traffic / hooves / machinery* **3** [V+*adv. / prep.*] to move very fast and with a loud deep noise: *Heavy trucks kept thundering past.* **4** [VN+*adv. / prep.*] (*informal*) to make sth move somewhere very fast: *Owen thundered the ball past the goalie.* **5** (*written*) to shout, complain, etc. very loudly and angrily: [V] *He thundered against the evils of television.* ◊ [V speech] *'Sit still!' she thundered.* [also VN]

thun·der·bolt /ˈθʌndəbəʊlt; *AmE* ˈθʌndərboʊlt/ *noun* (*written*) a flash of LIGHTNING that comes at the same time as the noise of THUNDER and that hits sth: *The news hit them like a thunderbolt* (= was very shocking).

thun·der·clap /ˈθʌndəklæp; *AmE* -dərk-/ *noun* a loud crash made by THUNDER

thun·der·cloud /ˈθʌndəklaʊd; *AmE* -dərk-/ *noun* a large dark cloud that produces THUNDER and LIGHTNING during a storm

thun·der·ous /ˈθʌndərəs/ *adj.* (*written*) **1** very loud: *thunderous applause* **2** looking very angry: *his thunderous expression* ▶ **thun·der·ous·ly** *adv.*

thun·der·storm /ˈθʌndəstɔːm; *AmE* ˈθʌndərstɔːrm/ *noun* a storm with THUNDER and LIGHTNING and usually very heavy rain

thun·der·struck /ˈθʌndəstrʌk; *AmE* -dərs-/ *adj.* [not usually before noun] (*written*) extremely surprised and shocked

thun·dery /ˈθʌndəri/ *adj.* (of weather) with THUNDER;

suggesting that THUNDER is likely: *thundery rain* ◊ *a thundery sky*

Thurs·day /ˈθɜːzdeɪ; -di; *AmE* ˈθɜːrz-/ *noun* [C, U] (*abbr.* Thur., Thurs.) the day of the week after Wednesday and before Friday **HELP** To see how **Thursday** is used, look at the examples at **Monday**. **ORIGIN** From the Old English for 'day of thunder', translated from Latin *Jovis dies* 'Jupiter's day'. Jupiter was the god associated with thunder.

thus /ðʌs/ *adv.* (*formal*) **1** in this way; like this: *Many scholars have argued thus.* ◊ *The universities have expanded, thus allowing many more people the chance of higher education.* **2** as a result of sth just mentioned **SYN** THEREFORE, HENCE: *He is the eldest son and thus heir to the title.* ◊ *We do not own the building. Thus, it would be impossible for us to make any major changes to it.* **IDM** see FAR *adv.*

thwack /θwæk/ *verb* [VN] to hit sb/sth hard, making a short loud sound ▶ **thwack** *noun*: *the thwack of bat on ball*

thwart /θwɔːt; *AmE* θwɔːrt/ *verb* [VN] [often passive] **~ sth | ~ sb** (in sth) to prevent sb from doing what they want to do: *to thwart sb's plans / ambitions / efforts* ◊ *She was thwarted in her attempt to take control of the party.*

thy /ðaɪ/ (also **thine** /ðaɪn/ before a vowel) *det.* (*old use*) a word meaning 'your', used when talking to only one person: *Honour thy father and thy mother.*

thyme /taɪm/ *noun* [U] a plant with small leaves that have a sweet smell and are used in cooking as a herb

thy·roid /ˈθaɪrɔɪd/ (also **ˈthyroid gland**) *noun* a small organ at the front of the neck that produces HORMONES that control the way in which the body grows and functions

thy·self /ðaɪˈself/ *pron.* (*old use* or *dialect*) a word meaning 'yourself', used when talking to only one person: *Thou shalt love thy neighbour as thyself.*

ti /tiː/ (*AmE*) = TE

tiara /tiˈɑːrə/ *noun* a piece of jewellery like a small CROWN decorated with precious stones, worn by a woman, for example a princess, on formal occasions

tibia /ˈtɪbiə/ *noun* (*pl.* **tib·iae** /-biiː/) (*anatomy*) the SHIN BONE—see also FIBULA—picture at BODY

tic /tɪk/ *noun* a sudden quick movement of a muscle, especially in your face or head, that you cannot control

tick /tɪk/ *verb, noun*
■ *verb* **1** [V] **~ (away)** (of a clock, etc.) to make short, light, regular repeated sounds to mark time passing: *In the silence we could hear the clock ticking.* ◊ *While we waited the taxi's meter kept ticking away.* ◊ *a ticking clock / bomb* **2** [VN] (*BrE*) (*AmE* **check**) to put a mark (✓) next to an item on a list, an answer, etc: *Please tick the appropriate box.* ◊ *Tick 'yes' or 'no' to each question.* ◊ *I've ticked the names of the people who have paid.* **IDM** **what makes sb ˈtick** what makes sb behave in the way that they do: *I've never really understood what makes her tick.* **PHR V** **ˌtick aˈway/ˈby/ˈpast** (of time) to pass: *I had to get to the airport by two, and the minutes were ticking away.* **ˌtick sth↔aˈway** (of a clock, etc.) to mark the time as it passes: *The clock ticked away the minutes.* **ˌtick sb↔ˈoff** **1** (*BrE, informal*) to speak angrily to sb, especially a child, because they have done sth wrong—related noun TICKING OFF **2** (*AmE, informal*) to make sb angry or annoyed **ˌtick sb/sth ˈoff** (*BrE*) (*AmE* **ˌcheck sb/sth ˈoff**) to put a mark (✓) beside a name or an item on a list to show that sth has been dealt with **ˌtick ˈover** (*BrE*) (usually used in the progressive tenses) **1** (of an engine) to run slowly while the vehicle is not moving **2** (of a business, a system, an activity, etc.) to keep working slowly without producing or achieving much: *Just keep things ticking over while I'm away.*
■ *noun* **1** [C] (*BrE*) (*AmE* **ˈcheck mark**, **check**) a mark (✓) put beside a sum or an item on a list, usually to show that it has been checked or done or is correct: *Put a tick in the appropriate box if you would like further information about any of our products.*—compare CROSS, X (4) **2** [C] a small insect that bites humans and animals and sucks their blood. There are several types of tick, some of

æ	ɑː	e	ɜː	ə	ɪ	iː	i	ɒ	ɔː	ʌ	ʊ	u	uː
cat	father	ten	bird	about	sit	see	many	got	saw	cup	put	actual	too
								(BrE)					

which can carry diseases: *a tick bite*—picture on page A7 **3** (also **tick·ing**) [U] a short, light, regularly repeated sound, especially that of a clock or watch: *The only sound was the soft tick of the clock.* **4** [C] (*BrE, informal*) a moment: *Hang on a tick!* ◇ *I'll be with you in two ticks.* **5** [U] (*old-fashioned, BrE, informal*) permission to delay paying for sth that you have bought SYN CREDIT: *Can I have these on tick?*

tick·er /ˈtɪkə(r)/ *noun* (*old-fashioned, informal*) a person's heart

ˈticker tape *noun* [U] (*especially AmE*) long narrow strips of paper with information, for example STOCK MARKET prices, printed on them by a special TELEGRAPH machine: *a ticker-tape parade in the streets of New York* (= an occasion when people throw pieces of paper as part of a celebration, for example in honour of a famous person)

ticket /ˈtɪkɪt/ *noun, verb*
■ *noun* **1** ~ (**for/to sth**) a printed piece of paper that gives you the right to travel on a particular bus, train, etc. or to go into a theatre, etc.: *a bus/theatre/plane ticket* ◇ *free tickets to the show* ◇ *Tickets are available from the Arts Centre at £2.50.* ◇ *a ticket office/machine/collector* ◇ (*figurative*) *She hoped that getting this job would finally be her ticket to success.*—see also MEAL TICKET, RETURN TICKET, SEASON TICKET **2** a label that is attached to sth in a shop/store giving details of its price, size, etc. **3** an official notice that orders you to pay a FINE because you have done sth illegal while driving or parking your car: *a parking/speeding ticket* **4** [usually sing.] (*especially AmE*) a list of candidates that are supported by a particular political party in an election: *She ran for office on the Democratic ticket.*—see also DREAM TICKET IDM **just the ˈticket** = JUST THE JOB at JOB **ˈthat's the ticket** (*old-fashioned, BrE, informal*) used to say that sth is just what is needed or that everything is just right—more at SPLIT *v.*
■ *verb* [VN] **1** (*technical*) to produce and sell tickets for an event, a trip, etc.; to give sb a ticket: *The museum holds both free and ticketed exhibitions.* ◇ *Passengers can now be ticketed electronically.* **2** [usually passive] (*especially AmE*) to give sb an official notice that orders them to pay a FINE because they have done sth illegal while driving or parking a car: *Park illegally, and you're likely to be ticketed.* PHRV **be ˈticketed for sth** (*especially AmE*) to be intended for a particular purpose

ticket·ing /ˈtɪkɪtɪŋ/ *noun* [U] the process of producing and selling tickets: *ticketing systems*

ˈticket tout *noun* (*BrE*) = TOUT

tick·ing /ˈtɪkɪŋ/ *noun* [U] a strong cotton fabric that is often STRIPED, used especially for making MATTRESS and PILLOW covers

ˌticking ˈoff *noun* [sing.] (*old-fashioned, BrE, informal*) the act of telling sb that they have done sth to make you angry

tickle /ˈtɪkl/ *verb, noun*
■ *verb* **1** to move your fingers on a sensitive part of sb's body in a way that makes them laugh: [VN] *The bigger girls used to chase me and tickle me.* ◇ [V] *Stop tickling!* **2** to produce a slightly uncomfortable feeling in a sensitive part of the body; to have a feeling like this: [VN] *His beard was tickling her cheek.* ◇ [V] *My throat tickles.* ◇ *a tickling cough* **3** to amuse and interest sb: [VN] *to tickle sb's imagination/curiosity/sense of humour* ◇ [VN to inf] *I was tickled to discover that we'd both done the same thing.* IDM **be tickled ˈpink** (*informal*) to be very pleased or amused **tickle sb's ˈfancy** (*informal*) to please or amuse sb: *See if any of these tickle your fancy.*
■ *noun* [usually sing.] **1** an act of tickling sb: *She gave the child a little tickle.* **2** a slightly uncomfortable feeling in a part of your body: *to have a tickle in your throat* (= that makes you want to cough) IDM see SLAP *n.*

tick·lish /ˈtɪklɪʃ/ *adj.* **1** (of a person) sensitive to being tickled: *Are you ticklish?* **2** (*informal*) (of a situation or problem) difficult to deal with, and possibly embarrassing **3** (of a cough) that irritates your throat: *a dry ticklish cough*

tick-tock /ˌtɪk ˈtɒk; *AmE* ˈtɑːk/ *noun* [usually sing.] used to describe the sound of a large clock TICKING

ticky-tacky /ˌtɪki ˈtæki/ *noun* [U] (*AmE, informal*) building material that is cheap and of low quality
▶ **ticky-tacky** *adj.*

tic-tac-toe (also **tick-tack-toe**) /ˌtɪk tæk ˈtəʊ; *AmE* ˈtoʊ/ *noun* [U] (*AmE*) = NOUGHTS AND CROSSES

tidal /ˈtaɪdl/ *adj.* connected with TIDES (= the regular rise and fall of the sea): *tidal forces* ◇ *a tidal river*

ˌtidal ˈwave *noun* **1** a very large ocean wave that is caused by a storm or an earthquake, and that destroys things when it reaches the land **2** ~ (**of sth**) a sudden increase in a particular feeling, activity or type of behaviour: *a tidal wave of crime/change/emotion*

tid·bit /ˈtɪdbɪt/ *noun* (*AmE*) = TITBIT

tid·dler /ˈtɪdlə(r)/ *noun* (*BrE, informal*) a very small fish

tid·dly /ˈtɪdli/ *adj.* (*BrE, informal*) **1** slightly drunk: *I feel a bit tiddly.* **2** very small: *All I got to eat was a tiddly little biscuit.*

tiddly·winks /ˈtɪdliwɪŋks/ *noun* [U] a game in which players try to make small plastic discs jump into a cup by pressing them on the edge with a larger disc

tide /taɪd/ *noun, verb*
■ *noun* **1** [C, U] a regular rise and fall in the level of the sea, caused by the pull of the moon and sun; the flow of water that happens as the sea rises and falls: *the ebb and flow of the tide* ◇ *The tide is in/out.* ◇ *Is the tide coming in or going out?* ◇ *The body was washed up on the beach by the tide.*—see also HIGH TIDE, LOW TIDE, NEAP TIDE, SPRING TIDE **2** [C, usually sing.] the direction in which the opinion of a large number of people seems to be moving: *It takes courage to speak out against the tide of opinion.* **3** [C, usually sing.] a large amount of sth unpleasant that is increasing and is difficult to control: *There is anxiety about the rising tide of crime.* **4** [sing.] ~ **of sth** a feeling that you suddenly have that gets stronger and stronger: *A tide of rage surged through her.* **5** [sing.] (*old use*) (in compounds) a time or season of the year: *Christmastide* IDM **go, swim, etc. with/against the ˈtide** to agree with/oppose the attitudes or opinions that most other people have **the ˈtide turned | turn the ˈtide** used to say that there is a change in sb's luck or in how successful they are being
■ *verb* PHRV **ˌtide sb ˈover (sth)** [no passive] to help sb during a difficult period by providing what they need: *Can you lend me some money to tide me over until I get paid?*

tide·mark /ˈtaɪdmɑːk; *AmE* -mɑːrk/ *noun* **1** a line that is made by the sea on a beach at the highest point that the sea reaches **2** (*BrE, informal*) a line that is left around the inside of a bath by dirty water

ˈtide pool *noun* (*AmE*) = ROCK POOL

tide·water /ˈtaɪdwɔːtə(r)/ *noun* **1** [C] (*AmE*) an area of land at or near the coast **2** [U, C] water that is brought by the TIDE

tid·ings /ˈtaɪdɪŋz/ *noun* [pl.] (*old-fashioned* or *humorous*) news: *I am the bearer of good tidings.* ◇ *He brought glad tidings.*

tidy /ˈtaɪdi/ *adj., verb, noun*
■ *adj.* (**tidi·er, tidi·est**) **1** (*especially BrE*) arranged neatly and with everything in order: *a tidy room/desk* ◇ *She keeps her flat very tidy.* ◇ *I like everything to be neat and tidy.* OPP UNTIDY **2** (*especially BrE*) keeping things neat and in order: *I'm a tidy person.* ◇ *tidy habits* OPP UNTIDY **3** [only before noun] (*informal*) a **tidy** amount of money is fairly large: *It must have cost a tidy sum.* ◇ *a tidy profit* ▶ **tidi·ly** *adv.*: *The room was very tidily arranged.* **tidi·ness** *noun* [U]
■ *verb* (**tidies, tidy·ing, tidied, tidied**) ~ (**sth**) (**up**) (*especially BrE*) to make sth look neat by putting things in the place where they belong: [V] *I spent all morning cleaning and tidying.* ◇ *When you cook, could you please tidy up after yourself.* ◇ [VN] *to tidy (up) a room/a cupboard/papers/your hair* PHRV **ˌtidy sth↔aˈway** (*BrE*) to put things in the place where they belong, especially where they cannot be seen, so that a room appears tidy: *Can you tidy away your clothes, please?* **ˌtidy sth↔ˈup** to arrange or

aɪ	aʊ	eɪ	əʊ	oʊ	ɔɪ	ɪə	eə	ʊə	j	w
my	now	say	go	go	boy	near	hair	pure	yes	wet
			(BrE)	(AmE)						

deal with sth so that it is well or correctly finished: *I tidied up the report before handing it in.*

▪ *noun* (*pl.* **-ies**) (*BrE*) (especially in compounds) a container for putting small objects in, in order to keep a place tidy: *a desk tidy*

tie /taɪ/ *verb, noun*

▪ *verb* (**ties, tying, tied, tied**)

FASTEN WITH STRING/ROPE | **1** [VN] [usually +*adv. / prep.*] to attach or hold two or more things together using string, rope, etc.; to fasten sb/sth with string, rope, etc: *She tied the newspapers in a bundle.* ◊ *He had to tie her hands together.* ◊ *They tied him to a chair with cable.* ◊ *Shall I tie the package or tape it?* ◊ *I tie back my hair when I'm cooking.* **2** [VN+*adv. / prep.*] to fasten sth to or around sth else: *She tied a label on to the suitcase.* ◊ *He tied an apron on and got down to work.* **3** [VN] to make a knot in a piece of string, rope, etc: *to tie a ribbon / tie* ◊ *Tie up your shoelaces!* ◊ *She tied her hair in a knot at the back of her head.* ◊ *I tied a knot in the rope.* **4** [V] [usually +*adv. / prep.*] to be closed or fastened with a knot, etc: *The skirt ties at the waist.*

CONNECT/LINK | **5** [VN] [usually passive] **~ sb/sth (to sth/sb)** to connect or link sb/sth closely with sb/sth else: *Pay increases are tied to inflation.* ◊ *The house is tied to the job, so we'll have to move when I retire.*

RESTRICT | **6** [VN] [usually passive] **~ sb (to sth/to doing sth)** to restrict sb and make them unable to do everything they want to: *to be tied by a contract / promise* ◊ *I want to work but I'm tied to the house with the baby.* ◊ *I don't want to be tied to coming home at a particular time.*

IN GAME/COMPETITION | **7** (of two teams, etc.) to have the same number of points: [V] *England tied 2–2 with Germany in the first round.* ◊ *They tied for second place.* ◊ [VN] *The scores are tied at 3–3.* ◊ *Last night's vote was tied.*

MUSIC | **8** to join notes with a tie

—see also TONGUE-TIED

IDM **tie sb/yourself (up) in 'knots** to become or make sb very confused **,tie one 'on** (*old-fashioned, AmE, slang*) to get very drunk **,tie the 'knot** (*informal*) to get married—more at APRON, HAND *n.*

PHRV **,tie sb 'down (to sth/to doing sth)** to restrict sb's freedom, for example by making them accept particular conditions or by keeping them busy: *Kids tie you down, don't they?* ◊ *I don't want to tie myself down to coming back on a particular date.* **,tie 'in (with sth)** to match or agree with sth: *This evidence ties in closely with what we already know.* **,tie 'in (with sth)| ,tie sth↔'in (with sth)** to link sth or be linked to sth; to happen, or arrange for sth to happen, at the same time as sth else: *The concert will tie in with the festival of dance taking place the same weekend.*—related noun TIE-IN **,tie sth↔'off** to put a knot in the end of sth; to close sth with string, thread, etc: *to tie off a rope* ◊ *to tie off an artery* **,tie 'up| ,tie sth↔'up 1** to attach a boat to a fixed object with a rope: *We tied up alongside the quay.* ◊ *We tied the boat up.* **2** to close sth with a knot; to be closed or fastened with a knot: *to tie up a garbage bag* ◊ *I'm so fat my bathrobe won't tie up!* **,tie sb↔'up 1** to tie sb's arms and legs tightly so that they cannot move or escape: *The gang tied up a security guard.* **2** [usually passive] to keep sb busy so that they have no time for other things: *I'm tied up in a meeting until 3.* **,tie sth↔'up 1** to attach an animal to sth with a rope, chain, etc: *He left his dog tied up to a tree.* **2** [usually passive] to connect or link sth to sth else: *Her behaviour is tied up with her feelings of guilt.*—related noun TIE-UP **3** [often passive] to invest money so that it is not easily available for use: *Most of the capital is tied up in property.* **4** to deal with all the remaining details of sth: *We are hoping to tie up the deal by tomorrow.* ◊ *I went into the office for an hour to **tie up any loose ends** (= finish remaining small jobs).*

▪ *noun*

CLOTHES | **1** (*AmE also* **neck·tie**) a long narrow piece of fabric worn around the neck, especially by men, with a knot in front: *a collar and tie* ◊ *a striped silk tie*—see also BLACK TIE, BOW TIE, OLD SCHOOL TIE, WHITE TIE—picture on page A4

FOR FASTENING | **2** a piece of string or wire used for fastening or tying sth: *ties for closing plastic bags*

CONNECTION | **3** [usually pl.] a strong connection between people or organizations: *family ties* ◊ *the ties of friendship* ◊ *economic / diplomatic ties* ◊ *The firm has close ties with an American corporation.*

RESTRICTION | **4** a thing that limits sb's freedom of action: *He was still a young man and he did not want any ties.*

IN GAME/COMPETITION | **5** a situation in a game or competition when two or more players have the same score: *The match ended in a tie.*—compare DRAW *n.* (2) **6** (*BrE*) a sports match, especially a football match, that is part of a larger competition: *the first leg of the Cup tie between Leeds and Roma*

MUSIC | **7** a curved line written over two notes of the same PITCH (how high or low a note is) to show that they are to be played or sung as one note—picture at MUSIC

ON RAILWAY | **8** (*AmE*) = SLEEPER (5)

tie·break /'taɪbreɪk/ (*BrE*) (*AmE* **tie·break·er**) *noun* (in tennis) a period of extra play to decide who is the winner of a SET when both players have won six games

tie·breaker /'taɪbreɪkə(r)/ *noun* **1** (*AmE*) = TIEBREAK **2** an extra question in a competition to decide who is the winner when two or more competitors have equal scores

tied /taɪd/ *adj.* [only before noun] (*BrE*) (of a house) rented to sb on the condition that they work for the owner: *a tied cottage on a farm*

,tied 'house *noun* (*BrE*) a pub that is owned by a particular BREWERY (= a company that produces beer) and that sells only the beer which that brewery produces—compare FREE HOUSE

'tie-dye *verb* [VN] to make patterns on fabric by tying knots in it or tying string around it before you put it in a DYE, so that some parts receive more colour than others

'tie-in *noun* a product such as a book or toy that is connected with a new film/movie, television programme, etc.

tie·pin /'taɪpɪn/ (*AmE also* **'tie tack**) *noun* a small decorative pin that is worn on a tie to keep it in place

tier /tɪə(r); *AmE* tɪr/ *noun* **1** a row or layer of sth that has several rows or layers placed one above the other: *a wedding cake with three tiers* ◊ *The seating is arranged in tiers.*—picture on page A1 **2** one of several levels in an organization or a system: *We have introduced an extra tier of administration.* ◊ *a two-tier system of management*

tiered /tɪəd; *AmE* tɪrd/ *adj.* **1** arranged in tiers: *tiered seating* **2** (-tiered) (in compounds) having the number of tiers mentioned: *a two-tiered system*

'tie-up *noun* **1 ~ (with sb/sth)** (*BrE*) an agreement between two companies to join together: *They're negotiating a tie-up with Ford.* **2 ~ (between A and B)** (*BrE*) a connection between two or more things: *a tie-up between politics and economics* **3** (*especially AmE*) a situation in which sth stops working or moving forward: *a traffic tie-up*

tiff /tɪf/ *noun* a slight argument between close friends or lovers: *to have a tiff with sb*

tig /tɪg/ *noun* [U] (*BrE*) = TAG (5)

tiger /'taɪgə(r)/ *noun* a large wild animal of the cat family, that has yellowish fur with black lines (= STRIPES) and lives in parts of Asia: *She **fought like a tiger** to be able to keep her children.*—compare TIGRESS—see also PAPER TIGER

tight /taɪt/ *adj., adv.*

▪ *adj.* (**tight·er, tight·est**)

FIXED FIRMLY | **1** held or fixed in position firmly; difficult to move or undo: *He kept **a tight grip** on her arm.* ◊ *She twisted her hair into a tight knot.* ◊ *The screw was so tight that it wouldn't move.*

CLOTHES | **2** fitting closely to your body and sometimes uncomfortable: *She was wearing a tight pair of jeans.* ◊ *These shoes are much too tight.* ◊ *The new sweater was a **tight fit.*** OPP LOOSE—see also SKINTIGHT

CONTROL | **3** very strict and firm: *to **exercise / keep tight control** over sb/sth* ◊ *We need tighter security at the airport.*

b	d	f	g	h	k	l	m	n	p	r
bad	**did**	**fall**	**get**	**hat**	**cat**	**leg**	**man**	**now**	**pen**	**red**

STRETCHED | **4** stretched or pulled so that it cannot stretch much further: *The rope was stretched tight.*

CLOSE TOGETHER | **5** [usually before noun] with things or people packed closely together, leaving little space between them: *There was a tight group of people around the speaker.* ◊ *With six of us in the car it was a tight squeeze.*

MONEY/TIME | **6** difficult to manage with because there is not enough: *We have a very tight budget.* ◊ *The president has a tight schedule today.*

EXPRESSION/VOICE | **7** looking or sounding anxious, upset, angry, etc: *'I'm sorry,' she said, with a tight smile.*—see also UPTIGHT

PART OF BODY | **8** feeling painful or uncomfortable because of illness or emotion: *He complained of having a tight chest.* ◊ *Her throat felt tight, just looking at her face.*

RELATIONSHIP | **9** having a close relationship with sb else or with other people: *It was a tight community and new-comers were not welcome.*—see also TIGHT-KNIT

BEND/CURVE | **10** curving suddenly rather than gradually: *The driver slowed down at a tight bend in the road.* ◊ *The plane flew around in a tight circle.*

CONTEST/RACE | **11** with competitors or teams that seem to be equally good [SYN] CLOSE: *a tight race/game*

NOT GENEROUS | **12** (*BrE*, *informal*, *disapproving*) not wanting to spend much money; not generous: *He's very tight with his money.*

DRUNK | **13** [not usually before noun] (*old-fashioned*, *BrE*, *informal*) drunk

-TIGHT | **14** (in compounds) not allowing the substance mentioned to enter: *measures to make your home wea-thertight*—see also AIRTIGHT, WATERTIGHT

▶ **tight·ness** *noun* [U]

IDM **to keep a tight 'rein on sb/sth** to control sb/sth carefully or strictly: *It's essential to keep a tight rein on public spending.* **run a tight 'ship** to organize sth in a very efficient way, controlling other people very closely **a tight 'spot/'corner** a very difficult or dangerous situation: *She'll always help if you're in a tight spot.*

■ *adv.* (**tight·er**, **tight·est**) closely and firmly; tightly: *Hold tight!* ◊ *My suitcase was packed tight.* ◊ *His fists were clenched tight.* IDM see SIT, SLEEP *v.*

WHICH WORD?
tight / tightly ?

Tight and tightly are both adverbs that come from the adjective **tight**. They have the same meaning, but **tight** is often used instead of **tightly** after a verb, especially in informal language, and in compounds: *packed tight* ◊ *a tight-fitting lid.* Before a past participle **tightly** is used: *clusters of tightly packed flowers.*

---

tight·en /'taɪtn/ *verb* ~ (**sth**) (**up**) **1** to become or make sth become tight or tighter: [V] *The rope holding the boat suddenly tightened and broke.* ◊ *His mouth tightened into a thin line.* ◊ [VN] *to tighten a lid/screw/rope/knot* ◊ *The nuts weren't properly tightened and the wheel came off.* ◊ *She tightened her grip on his arm.* **2** [VN] to make sth become stricter: *to tighten security/regulations/rules* [OPP] LOOSEN IDM **tighten your 'belt** to spend less money because there is less available PHRV **,tighten 'up (on sth)** to become stricter or more careful: *Laws on gambling have tightened up recently.* ◊ *The police are tightening up on under-age drinking.*

,tight-'fisted *adj.* not willing to spend or give much money [SYN] MEAN, STINGY

,tight-'fitting *adj.* that fits very tightly or closely: *a tight-fitting skirt*

,tight-'knit (also **,tightly-'knit**) *adj.* (of a family or community) with all the members having strong friendly relationships with one another: *a tight-knit mining community*

,tight-'lipped *adj.* **1** not willing to talk about sth **2** keeping your lips pressed firmly together, especially because you are angry about sth

tight·ly /'taɪtli/ *adv.* closely and firmly; in a tight manner: *Her eyes were tightly closed.* ◊ *He held on tightly to her arm.* ◊ *a tightly packed crowd of tourists* ⇨ note at TIGHT

tight·rope /'taɪtrəʊp; *AmE* -roʊp/ *noun* a rope or wire that is stretched tightly high above the ground and that performers walk along, especially in a CIRCUS: *a tightrope walker* IDM **tread/walk a 'tightrope** to be in a difficult situation in which you do not have much freedom of action and need to be extremely careful about what you do

tights /taɪts/ *noun* [pl.] **1** (*BrE*) (*AmE* **panty·hose**) a piece of clothing made of very thin fabric that fits closely over a woman's hips, legs and feet: *a pair of tights*—compare STOCKING **2** a piece of clothing similar to tights but made of thicker fabric, worn especially by dancers

tight·wad /'taɪtwɒd; *AmE* -wɑːd/ *noun* (*AmE*, *informal*) a person who hates to spend or give money

tig·ress /'taɪgrəs/ *noun* a female TIGER

tike *noun* = TYKE

til, **'til** ⇨ UNTIL

tilde /'tɪldə/ *noun* **1** the mark (~) placed over letters in some languages and some vowels in the International Phonetic Alphabet to show how they should be pronounced, as in *España*, *São Paulo* and *penchant* /'pɒ̃ʃɒ̃/ —compare ACUTE ACCENT, CIRCUMFLEX, GRAVE², UMLAUT **2** the mark (~) used in this dictionary in some parts of an entry to represent the word in dark type at the top of the entry

tile /taɪl/ *noun*, *verb*
■ *noun* **1** a flat, usually square, piece of baked clay, carpet or other material that is used in rows for covering walls and floors: *ceramic floor tiles* ◊ *carpet tiles* **2** a piece of baked clay that is used in rows for covering roofs **3** any of the small flat pieces that are used in particular board games IDM see NIGHT
■ *verb* [VN] **1** to cover a surface with tiles: *a tiled bathroom/roof* **2** (*computing*) to arrange several windows on a computer screen so that they fill the screen but do not cover each other

til·ing /'taɪlɪŋ/ *noun* [U] **1** an area covered with tiles **2** the work of covering a floor, wall, etc. with tiles

till /tɪl/ *conj.*, *prep.*, *noun*, *verb*
■ *conj.*, *prep.* = UNTIL: *We're open till 6 o'clock.* ◊ *Can't you wait till we get home?* ◊ *Just wait till you see it. It's great.* HELP Till is generally felt to be more informal than until and is used much less often in writing. At the beginning of a sentence, until is usually used.
■ *noun* **1** (*BrE*) = CASH REGISTER **2** (*BrE*, *informal*) the place where you pay for goods in a large shop/store: *Please pay at the till.* ◊ *a long queue at the till* **3** (*especially AmE*) the drawer where the money is put in a CASH REGISTER IDM see FINGER *n.*
■ *verb* [VN] (*old use*) to prepare and use land for growing crops

till·er /'tɪlə(r)/ *noun* a bar that is used to turn the RUDDER of a small boat in order to steer it—compare HELM

tilt /tɪlt/ *verb*, *noun*
■ *verb* **1** [usually +*adv.*/*prep.*] to move, or make sth move, into a position with one side or end higher than the other: [V] *Suddenly the boat tilted to one side* ◊ *The seat tilts forward, when you press this lever.* ◊ [VN] *His hat was tilted slightly at an angle.* ◊ *She tilted her head back and looked up at me with a smile.* **2** to make sth/sb change slightly so that one particular opinion, person, etc. is preferred or more likely to succeed than another; to change in this way: [VN] *The hot conditions may tilt the balance in favour of the Kenyan runners.* ◊ [V] *Popular opinion has tilted in favour of the socialists.* IDM **tilt at 'windmills** to waste your energy attacking imaginary enemies ORIGIN From Cervantes' *Don Quixote*, in which the hero thought that the windmills he saw were giants and tried to fight them. PHRV **'tilt at sb/sth** (*BrE*) to attack sb/sth in speech or writing: *a satirical magazine tilting at public figures* **'tilt at sth** (*BrE*) to try to win sth: *He was tilting at the top prize.*
■ *noun* **1** a position in which one end or side of sth is higher than the other; an act of tilting sth to one side:

The table is at a slight tilt. ◊ *He answered with a tilt of his head.* **2** an attempt to win sth or defeat sb: *She aims to have a tilt at the world championship next year.* **IDM** **(at) full 'tilt/'pelt** as fast as possible

tim·ber /'tɪmbə(r)/ *noun* **1** [U] trees that are grown to be used in building or for making things: *the timber industry* **2** [U] (*especially BrE*) (*AmE* usually **lum·ber**) wood that is prepared for use in building, etc: *houses built of timber* **3** [C, usually pl.] a wooden beam used in building a house or ship: *roof timbers*

tim·bered /'tɪmbəd; *AmE* -bərd/ *adj.* built of wooden beams; with a FRAMEWORK of wooden beams—see also HALF-TIMBERED

timbre /'tæmbə(r)/ *noun* (*formal*) the quality of sound that is produced by a particular voice or musical instrument

time /taɪm/ *noun, verb*

■ *noun*—see also TIMES

MINUTES/HOURS/YEARS, etc. | **1** [U] what is measured in minutes, hours, days, etc: *The changing seasons mark the passing of time.* ◊ *A visit to the museum will take you back in time to the 1930s.* ◊ *time and space* ◊ *As time went by we saw less and less of each other.* ◊ *Perceptions change over time* (= as time passes). **2** [U] the time shown on a clock in minutes and hours: *What time is it/What's the time?* ◊ (*BrE*) *What time do you make it?* ◊ (*AmE*) *What time do you have?* ◊ *Do you have the time?* ◊ *The time is now half past ten.* ◊ (*BrE*) *Can she tell the time yet* (= say what time it is by looking at a clock)? ◊ (*AmE*) *Can she tell time yet?* ◊ *My watch keeps perfect time* (= always shows the correct time). ◊ *Look at the time! We'll be late.* ◊ *This time tomorrow I'll be in Canada.* ⇨ Appendix 3 **3** [U] the time measured in a particular part of the world: *Greenwich Mean Time* ◊ *6 o'clock local time*—see also STANDARD TIME, SUMMER TIME **4** [U, C] **~ (to do sth)** the time when sth happens or when sth should happen: *What time do you finish work?* ◊ *The baby loves bath time.* ◊ *I think it's time to go to bed.* ◊ *It's time the kids were in bed.* ◊ *It's time for lunch.* ◊ *A computer screen shows arrival and departure times.* ◊ *The train arrived right on time* (= at exactly the correct time). ◊ *By the time you get there the meeting will be over.* ◊ *You'll feel differently about it when the time comes* (= when it happens).—see also ANY TIME, CLOSING TIME, NIGHT-TIME, OPENING TIME

PERIOD | **5** [U] **~ to do sth** an amount of time; the amount of time available to work, rest, etc: *Allow plenty of time to get to the airport.* ◊ *He spends most of his time working.* ◊ *She doesn't have much free/spare time.* ◊ *I can probably make the time to see them.* ◊ *What a waste of time!* ◊ *We have no time to lose* (= we must hurry). ◊ *It takes time to make changes in the law.* ◊ *I didn't finish the test—I ran out of time.* ◊ *Time's up*—*have you worked out the answer yet?* ◊ *He never takes any time off* (= time spent not working). ◊ *Jane's worked here for some time* (= for a fairly long period of time). ◊ *Do it now please—not in three hours' time* (= three hours from now). ◊ *The journey time is two hours.* **6 (a time)** [sing.] a period of time, either long or short, during which you do sth or sth happens: *His injuries will take a long time to heal.* ◊ *I lived in Egypt for a time.* ◊ *The early morning is the best time of day.* ◊ *Her parents died a long time ago.* ◊ *At one time* (= at a period of time in the past) *Emily was my best friend.* ◊ *Mr Curtis was the manager in my time* (= when I was working there). **7** [U, pl.] a period of history connected with particular events or experiences in people's lives: *The movie is set at the time of the Russian revolution.* ◊ *in ancient/Victorian times* ◊ *the violent times we live in* (= the present period of history) ◊ *Times are hard for the unemployed.* ◊ *Times have changed since Grandma was young.* ◊ *At some time in the future there will be a cure for Aids.*—see also OLD-TIME

OCCASION/EVENT | **8** [C] an occasion when you do sth or when sth happens: *Every time I hear that song I feel happy.* ◊ *Next time you're here let's have lunch together.* ◊ *He failed his driving test three times.* ◊ *He's determined to pass this time.* ◊ *When was the last time you saw her?* ◊ (*spoken*) *How many times* (= how often) *do I have to tell you not to do that?* ◊ (*especially AmE*) *I remember one time*

(= once) *we had to abandon our car in the snow.* ◊ (*formal*) *At no time did I give my consent to the plan.* **HELP** To talk about the first or the last time you do sth, use the **first/ last time (that) I ...**: *This is the first time (that) I've been to London.* ◊ ~~*This is the first time for me to go to London.*~~ ◊ *That was the last time (that) I saw her.* **9** [C] an event or occasion that you experience in a particular way: *Did you have a good time in Spain?* ◊ *I had an awful time in the hospital.*

FOR RACE | **10** [C, U] how long sb takes to run a race or complete an event: *The winner's time was 11.6 seconds.* ◊ *She completed the 500 metres in record time* (= faster than any previous runner). ◊ *one of the fastest times this year*

IN MUSIC | **11** [U] the number of BEATS in a BAR of music: *This piece is in four-four time.* ◊ *a slow waltz time* ◊ *The conductor beat time with a baton.* **12** [U] the correct speed and rhythm of a piece of music: *Try and dance in time to the music* (= with the same speed and rhythm). ◊ *Clap your hands to keep time* (= sing or play with the correct speed and rhythm). ◊ *to play in/out of time* (= follow/not follow the correct speed and rhythm) ◊ *He always plays in perfect time.*—see also BIG TIME, SMALL-TIME

IDM **(and) about 'time ('too)** | **(and) not before 'time** (*spoken*) used to say that sth should have happened before now **against 'time** if you do sth against time, you do it as fast as you can because you do not have much time: *They're working against time to try and get people out of the rubble alive.* **ahead of/behind 'time** earlier/ later than was expected: *We finished 15 minutes ahead of time.* **ahead of your 'time** having advanced or new ideas that other people use or copy later **all the 'time | the whole 'time 1** during the whole of a particular period of time: *The letter was in my pocket all the time* (= while I was looking for it). **2** very often; repeatedly: *She leaves the lights on all the time.* **at all 'times** always: *Our representatives are ready to help you at all times.* **at the 'best of times** even when the circumstances are very good: *He's never very happy at the best of times—he'll be much worse now!* **at the same 'time 1** at one time; together: *She was laughing and crying at the same time.* **2** used to introduce a contrasting fact, etc. that must be considered: *You have to be firm, but at the same time you should try and be sympathetic.* **at a 'time** separately or in groups of two, three, etc. on each occasion: *We had to go and see the principal one at a time.* ◊ *She ran up the stairs two at a time.* **at 'my, 'your, 'his, etc. time of life** at the age you are (especially when you are not young): *Eyesight doesn't get any better at my time of life.* **at 'times** sometimes: *He can be really bad-tempered at times.* **before my, your, his, etc. 'time 1** happening before you were born or can remember or before you lived, worked, etc. somewhere: *'Were you taught by Professor Pascal?' 'No, he was before my time.'* **2** before the usual time in sb's life when sth happens: *She got old before her time.* **behind the 'times** old-fashioned in your ideas, methods, etc. **do 'time** (*informal*) to spend time in prison **every 'time** whenever there is a choice: *I don't really like cities—give me the countryside every time.* **for the time 'being** for a short period of time but not permanently: *You can leave your suitcase here for the time being.* **from ˌtime to 'time** occasionally but not regularly: *She has to work at weekends from time to time.* **have a lot of time for sb/sth** (*informal, especially BrE*) to like and be interested in sb/sth **have no time for sb/sth | not have much time for sb/sth** (*informal*) to dislike sb/sth: *I have no time for lazy people like Steve.* **have the ˌtime of your 'life** (*informal*) to enjoy yourself very much **have time on your 'hands | have time to 'kill** (*informal*) to have nothing to do or not be busy **in good 'time** early; with enough time so that you are not in a hurry **(all) in good 'time** (*spoken*) used to say that sth will be done or will happen at the appropriate time and not before: *Be patient, Emily! All in good time.* **in (less than/next to) 'no time** so soon or so quickly that it is surprising: *The kids will be leaving home in no time.* **in 'time** after a period of time when a situation has changed: *They learned to accept their stepmother in time.* **in time (for sth/to do sth)** not late; with

---

æ	ɑː	e	ɜː	ə	ɪ	iː	i	ɒ	ɔː	ʌ	ʊ	u	uː
cat	father	ten	bird	about	sit	see	many	got	saw	cup	put	actual	too

(BrE)

enough time to be able to do sth: *Will we be in time for the six o'clock train?* ◊ *The ambulance got there just in time* (= to save sb's life). **in your own (good) 'time** (*informal*) when you are ready and not sooner: *Don't hassle him! He'll do it in his own good time.* **in your own time** in your free time and not when you usually work or study **it's a,bout/,high 'time** (*spoken*) used to say that you think sb should do sth soon: *It's about time you cleaned your room!* **keep up/move with the 'times** to change and develop your ideas, way of working, etc. so that you do what is modern and what is expected **make good, etc. 'time** to complete a journey quickly: *We made excellent time and arrived in Spain in two days.* **'many a time | 'many's the time (that) …** (*old-fashioned*) many times; frequently **,nine times out of 'ten | ,ninety-,nine times out of a 'hundred** used to say that sth is usually true or almost always happens: *Nine times out of ten she gives the right answer.* **(and) not before 'time** = (AND) ABOUT TIME (TOO) **(there is) no time like the 'present** (*saying*) now is the best time to do sth, not in the future **of all 'time** that has ever existed: *Many rated him the best singer of all time.—* see also ALL-TIME **take your 'time (over sth) | take your 'time to do sth/doing sth 1** to use as much time as you need without hurrying: *There's no rush—take your time.* **2** used to say you think sb is late or is too slow in doing sth: *You certainly took your time getting here!* **,time after 'time | ,time and (,time) a'gain** often; on many or all occasions: *You will get a perfect result time after time if you follow these instructions.* **time and a 'half** one and a half times the usual rate of pay—see also DOUBLE TIME **time is on your 'side** used to say that sb can wait for sth to happen or can wait before doing sth **(the) next, first, second, etc. time 'round** on the next, first, etc. occasion that the same thing happens: *He repeated none of the errors he'd made first time round.* ◊ *This time round it was not so easy.* **time 'was (when) …** (*old-fashioned*) used to say that sth used to happen in the past: *Time was when you could go for a walk in the country and not see another person for miles.* **time (alone) will 'tell | only time will 'tell** used to say that you will have to wait for some time to find out the result of a situation: *Only time will tell if the treatment has been successful.* **the whole 'time** = ALL THE TIME—more at BEAT *v.*, BIDE, BORROW, BUY *v.*, CALL *v.*, COURSE *n.*, DAY, DEVIL, EASY *adj.*, FORTH, FULLNESS, GAIN *v.*, GIVE *v.*, HARD *adj.*, HIGH *adj.*, KILL *v.*, LONG *adj.*, LOST *adj.*, LUCK *n.*, MARK *v.*, MATTER *n.*, MOVE *v.*, NICK *n.*, OLD, ONCE *adv.*, PASS *v.*, RACE *n.*, SIGN *n.*, STITCH *n.*, SWEET *adj.*, THIN *adj.*, THIRD, WHALE

■ *verb*

ARRANGE TIME **1** [often passive] to arrange to do sth or arrange for sth to happen at a particular time: [VN] *She timed her arrival for shortly after 3.* ◊ *Their request was badly timed* (= it was made at the wrong time). ◊ *'I hope we're not too early.' 'You couldn't have timed it better!'* ◊ [VN to inf] *Publication of his biography was timed to coincide with his 70th birthday celebrations.*

MEASURE TIME **2** to measure how long it takes for sth to happen or for sb to do sth: [VN] *The winner was timed at 20.4 seconds.* ◊ [V wh-] *Time how long it takes you to answer the questions.*

IN SPORT **3** [VN] to hit or kick a ball at a particular moment in a sports game: *She timed the pass perfectly.* ◊ *a beautifully timed shot*

—see also ILL-TIMED, MISTIME, TIMING, WELL TIMED

,time-and-'motion study *noun* a study to find out how efficient a company's working methods are

'time bomb *noun* **1** a bomb that can be set to explode at a particular time **2** a situation that is likely to cause serious problems in the future: *Rising unemployment is a political time bomb for the government.*

'time capsule *noun* a container that is filled with objects that people think are typical of the time they are living in. It is buried so that it can be discovered by people in the future.

'time card *noun* (*especially AmE*) a piece of card on which the number of hours that sb has worked are recorded, usually by a machine

'time clock *noun* a special clock that records the exact time that sb starts and finishes work

'time-consuming *adj.* taking or needing a lot of time: *a difficult and time-consuming process*

'time frame *noun* the length of time that is used or available for sth: *We expect to complete the project within a fairly short time frame.*

'time-honoured (*BrE*) (*AmE* **-honored**) *adj.* (*written*) respected because it has been used or done for a long time: *They showed their approval in the time-honoured way* (= by cheering, for example).

time·keep·er /'taɪmkiːpə(r)/ *noun* a person who records the time that is spent doing sth, for example at work or at a sports event **IDM be a good/bad 'time-keeper** to be regularly on time/late for work

time·keep·ing /'taɪmkiːpɪŋ/ *noun* **1** a person's ability to arrive in time for things, especially work **2** the activity of recording the time sth takes

'time lag (also **lag**, **'time lapse**) *noun* the period of time between two connected events: *There is a long time lag between when I do the work and when I get paid.*

time·less /'taɪmləs/ *adj.* (*formal* or *written*) **1** not appearing to be affected by the passing of time or by changes in fashion: *her timeless beauty* ◊ *His work has a timeless quality.* **2** existing or continuing for ever: *timeless eternity* ▶ **time·less·ly** *adv.* **time·less·ness** *noun* [U]

'time limit *noun* the length of time within which you must do or complete sth: *We have to set a time limit for the work.* ◊ *The work must be completed within a certain time limit.*

time·ly /'taɪmli/ *adj.* happening at exactly the right time: *A nasty incident was prevented by the timely arrival of the police.* ◊ *This has been a timely reminder to us all.* **OPP** UNTIMELY ▶ **time·li·ness** *noun* [U]

'time machine *noun* (in SCIENCE FICTION stories) a machine that enables you to travel in time to the past or the future

time·out /taɪm'aʊt/ *noun* (*AmE*) a short period of rest during a sports game

time·piece /'taɪmpiːs/ *noun* (*formal*) a clock or watch

timer /'taɪmə(r)/ *noun* (often in compounds) a device that is used to measure the time that sth takes; a device that starts or stops a machine working at a particular time: *an oven timer*—see also EGG TIMER, OLD-TIMER

times /taɪmz/ **1** *prep.* (*informal*) multiplied by: *Five times two is/equals ten* (= 5 × 2 = 10). **2** *noun* [pl.] used in comparisons to show how much more, better, etc. sth is than sth else: *three times as long as sth* ◊ *three times longer than sth* ◊ *three times the length of sth*

'time-saving *adj.* [usually before noun] that reduces the amount of time it takes to do sth: *time-saving devices*

time·scale /'taɪmskeɪl/ *noun* the period of time that it takes for sth to happen or be completed: *What's the timescale for the project?* ◊ *We hope the negotiations will be completed within a six-month timescale.*

'time-server *noun* (*disapproving*) a person who does as little work as possible in their job because they are just waiting until they leave for another job or RETIRE (= finish work completely) ▶ **'time-serving** *adj.*, *noun*: *time-serving bureaucrats*

time·share /'taɪmʃeə(r)/; *AmE* -ʃer/ *noun* **1** (also **'time-sharing**) [U] an arrangement in which several people own a holiday/vacation home together and each uses it at a different time of the year: *timeshare apartments* **2** [C] a holiday/vacation home that you own in this way: *They have a timeshare in Spain.*

'time sheet *noun* a piece of paper on which the number of hours that sb has worked are recorded

'time signature *noun* (*music*) a sign at the start of a piece of music, usually in the form of numbers, showing the number of beats in each BAR/MEASURE—picture at MUSIC

'time span *noun* a period of time: *These changes have occurred over a long time span.*

aɪ	aʊ	eɪ	əʊ	oʊ	ɔɪ	ɪə	eə	ʊə	j	w
my	now	say	go	go	boy	near	hair	pure	yes	wet
			(BrE)	(AmE)						

'time switch *noun* a switch that can be set to start and stop working automatically at a particular time: *The heating is on a time switch.*

time·table /'taɪmteɪbl/ *noun, verb*

■ *noun* **1** (*especially BrE*) (*AmE* usually **sched·ule**) a list showing the times at which particular events will happen: *a bus/train timetable* (= when they arrive and leave) ◊ *We have a new timetable each term* (= showing the times of each class in school). ◊ *Sport is no longer so important in the school timetable* (= all the subjects that are taught at schools). **2** a plan of when you expect or hope particular events to happen $\boxed{\text{SYN}}$ SCHEDULE: *I have a busy timetable this week* (= I have planned to do many things). ◊ *The government has set out its timetable for the peace talks.* ⇨ note at AGENDA

■ *verb* [VN] [usually passive] (*especially BrE*) to arrange for sth to take place at a particular time $\boxed{\text{SYN}}$ SCHEDULE: *A series of discussion groups have been timetabled for the afternoons.* ▶ **time·tab·ling** *noun* [U]

'time warp *noun* an imaginary situation, described, for example, in SCIENCE FICTION, in which it is possible for people or things from the past or the future to move to the present $\boxed{\text{IDM}}$ **be (stuck) in a 'time warp** not having changed at all from a time in the past although everything else has: *Her whole house seems to be stuck in a time warp. It's like something out of the 1950s.*

'time-worn *adj.* old and used a lot, and therefore damaged, or no longer useful or interesting

'time zone *noun* one of the 24 areas that the world is divided into, each with its own time that is one hour earlier than that of the time zone immediately to the east

timid /'tɪmɪd/ *adj.* shy and nervous; not brave: *He stopped in the doorway, too timid to go in.* ◊ *They've been rather timid in the changes they've made* (= they've been afraid to make any big changes). ◊ *'May I come in?' she asked in a timid voice.* ▶ **tim·id·ity** /tɪ'mɪdəti/ *noun* [U] **tim·id·ly** *adv.*

tim·ing /'taɪmɪŋ/ *noun* **1** [U, C] the act of choosing when sth happens; a particular point or period of time when sth happens or is planned: *The timing of the decision was a complete surprise.* ◊ (*written*) *Please check your flight timings carefully.* **2** [U] the skill of doing sth at exactly the right time: *an actor with a great sense of comic timing* ◊ *Your timing is perfect. I was just about to call you.* **3** [U] the repeated rhythm of sth; the skill of producing this: *She played the piano confidently but her timing was not good.* **4** [U] (*technical*) the rate at which an electric SPARK is produced in a vehicle's engine in order to make it work

tim·or·ous /'tɪmərəs/ *adj.* (*formal or literary*) nervous and easily frightened: *'Who's that?' asked a timorous voice.* ▶ **tim·or·ous·ly** *adv.*

tim·pani /'tɪmpəni/ *noun* [pl.] a set of large metal drums (also called KETTLEDRUMS) in an orchestra—picture on page 841 ▶ **tim·pan·ist** *noun*

tin /tɪn/ *noun* **1** [U] (*symb* **Sn**) a chemical element. Tin is a soft silver-white metal that is often mixed with other metals or used to cover them to prevent them from RUSTING: *a tin mine* ◊ *a tin box* **2** [C] (also **,tin 'can**) (both *BrE*) (also **can** *AmE, BrE*) ~ (**of sth**) a metal container in which food and drink is sold; the contents of one of these containers: *a tin of beans/soup* ◊ *Next, add two tins of tomatoes.*—picture at PACKAGING **3** [C] (*BrE*) (also **can** *AmE, BrE*) ~ (**of sth**) a metal container with circular ends, straight sides and a lid in which paint, glue, etc. is sold and stored; the contents of one of these containers: *a tin of varnish* ◊ *The bedroom needed three tins of paint* (= in order to paint it). **4** [C] a metal container with a lid used for keeping food in: *a biscuit/cake/cookie tin* **5** [C] (*BrE*) (*AmE* **pan**) a metal container used for cooking food in: *a roasting/cake tin*

,tin 'can *noun* = TIN

tinc·ture /'tɪŋktʃə(r)/ *noun* [C, U] (*technical*) a substance dissolved in alcohol for use as a medicine

tin·der /'tɪndə(r)/ *noun* [U] dry material, especially wood or grass, that burns easily and can be used to light a fire

tin·der·box /'tɪndəbɒks; *AmE* 'tɪndərbɑːks/ *noun* **1** a box containing dry material, used in the past for lighting a fire **2** (*written*) a situation that is likely to become dangerous

tine /taɪn/ *noun* (*technical*) any of the points or sharp parts of, for example, a fork or a deer's ANTLERS

tin·foil /'tɪnfɔɪl/ *noun* [U] metal made into very thin sheets, that is used for wrapping food, etc.

tinge /tɪndʒ/ *verb, noun*

■ *verb* [VN] [usually passive] ~ **sth (with sth) 1** to add a small amount of colour to sth: *white petals tinged with blue* **2** to add a small amount of a particular emotion or quality to sth: *a look of surprise tinged with disapproval*

■ *noun* [usually sing.] a small amount of a colour, feeling or quality: *to feel a tinge of envy/regret/sadness* ◊ *There was a faint pink tinge to the sky.*

tin·gle /'tɪŋgl/ *verb, noun*

■ *verb* [V] **1** (of a part of your body) to feel as if a lot of small sharp points are pushing into it: *The cold air made her face tingle.* ◊ *a tingling sensation* **2** ~ **with sth** to feel an emotion strongly: *She was still tingling with excitement.*

■ *noun* [usually sing.] **1** a slight stinging or uncomfortable feeling in a part of your body **2** an exciting or uncomfortable feeling of emotion: *to feel a tingle of anticipation/excitement/fear*

tin·ker /'tɪŋkə(r)/ *noun, verb*

■ *noun* (in the past) a person who travelled from place to place, selling or repairing things

■ *verb* [V] ~ (**with sth**) to make small changes to sth in order to repair or improve it, especially in a way that may not be helpful: *He's in the garage tinkering with his bike.*

tin·kle /'tɪŋkl/ *noun, verb*

■ *noun* [usually sing.] **1** (also **tink·ling** [sing., U]) a light high ringing sound: *the tinkle of glass breaking* **2** (*old-fashioned, BrE, informal*) a telephone call **3** (*BrE, informal*) an act of URINATING: *to have a tinkle*

■ *verb* to make a series of light high ringing sounds; to make sth produce this sound: [V] *A bell tinkled as the door opened.* ◊ *tinkling laughter* [also VN]

tinned /tɪnd/ (*BrE*) (also **canned** *AmE, BrE*) *adj.* [usually before noun] (of food) preserved in a can: *tinned fruit/soup*

tin·ni·tus /'tɪnɪtəs/ *noun* [U] (*medical*) an unpleasant condition in which sb hears ringing in their ears

tinny /'tɪni/ *adj.* (*disapproving, especially BrE*) having a high thin sound like small pieces of metal hitting each other: *tinny music* ◊ *a tinny voice/radio*

'tin-opener (*BrE*) (also **'can-opener** *AmE, BrE*) *noun* a kitchen UTENSIL (= a tool) for opening tins of food—picture at KITCHEN

tin·plate /'tɪnpleɪt/ *noun* [U] a metal material made from iron and steel and covered with a layer of tin

tin·pot /'tɪnpɒt; *AmE* -pɑːt/ *adj.* [only before noun] (*BrE, disapproving*) (especially of a leader or government) not important and of little worth or use: *a tinpot dictator*

tin·sel /'tɪnsl/ *noun* [U] strips of shiny material like metal, used as decorations, especially at Christmas

tint /tɪnt/ *noun, verb*

■ *noun* **1** a shade or small amount of a particular colour; a faint colour covering a surface: *leaves with red and gold autumn tints* ◊ *the brownish tint of an old photo* **2** an artificial colour used to change the colour of your hair; the act of COLOURING the hair with a tint: *a blond tint* ◊ *to have a tint*

■ *verb* [VN] [usually passive] ~ **sth (with sth)** to add a small amount of colour to sth: *She's had her eyelashes tinted.* ▶ **tint·ed** *adj.* [usually before noun]: *tinted glasses/lenses*

,tin 'whistle (also **,penny 'whistle**) *noun* a simple musical instrument like a short pipe with six holes, that you play by blowing

tiny /'taɪni/ *adj.* (**tini·er, tini·est**) very small in size or amount: *a tiny baby* ◊ *Only a tiny minority hold such extreme views.* $\boxed{\text{IDM}}$ see PATTER *n.*

-tion ⇨ -ION

tip /tɪp/ *noun, verb*

■ *noun*

END OF STH **1** the thin pointed end of sth: *the tips of your*

b	d	f	g	h	k	l	m	n	p	r
bad	did	fall	get	hat	cat	leg	man	now	pen	red

fingers/toes ◊ *the tip of your nose* ◊ *the northern tip of the island*—see also FINGERTIP **2** a small part that fits on or over the end of sth: *a walking stick with a rubber tip*—see also FELT-TIP PEN, FILTER TIP

ADVICE | **3 ~ (on/for sth)| ~ (on/for doing sth)** a small piece of advice about sth practical: *handy tips for buying a computer* ◊ *useful tips on how to save money* **4** (*informal*) a secret or expert piece of advice about what the result of a competition, etc. is likely to be, especially about which horse is likely to win a race: *a hot tip for the big race*

EXTRA MONEY | **5** a small amount of extra money that you give to sb, for example sb who serves you in a restaurant: *to leave a tip* ◊ *He gave the waiter a generous tip.*

FOR RUBBISH | **6** (*BrE*) a place where you can take rubbish/garbage and leave it

UNTIDY PLACE | **7** (*BrE, informal, disapproving*) an untidy place: *Their flat is a tip!*

IDM **on the tip of your 'tongue** if a word or name is **on the tip of your tongue**, you are sure that you know it but you cannot remember it **the tip of the 'iceberg** only a small part of a much larger problem

■ *verb* (-pp-)

LEAN/POUR/PUSH AT AN ANGLE | **1** [usually +*adv./prep.*] to move so that one end or side is higher than the other; to move sth into this position: [V] *The boat tipped to one side.* ◊ *The seat tips forward to allow passengers into the back.* ◊ [VN] *She tipped her head back and laughed loudly.* ◊ *His hat was tipped over his forehead.* **2** [VN+*adv./prep.*] to make sth/sb come out of a container or its/their position by holding or lifting it/them at an angle: *She tipped the dirty water down the drain.* ◊ *The bus stopped abruptly, nearly tipping me out of my seat.* **3** [VN+*adv./prep.*] to touch sth lightly so that it moves in a particular direction: *The goalkeeper just managed to tip the ball over the crossbar.*

LEAVE RUBBISH | **4** (*BrE*) to leave rubbish/garbage somewhere outdoors in order to get rid of it: [V] *'No tipping.'* (= for example, on a notice) [also VN]

GIVE EXTRA MONEY | **5** to give sb an extra amount of money to thank them for sth they have done for you as part of their job: [V] *Americans were always welcome because they tended to tip heavily.* ◊ [VN] *Did you remember to tip the waiter?* ◊ [VNN] *She tipped the porter a pound.*

PREDICT SUCCESS | **6 ~ sb/sth (as/for sth)** to say in advance that sb/sth will be successful: [VN] *The band is being tipped for the top.* ◊ *The senator has been tipped by many as a future president.* ◊ [VN to inf] *The actor is tipped to win an Oscar for his performance.*

COVER END | **7** [VN] [usually passive] **~ sth (with sth)** to cover the end or edge of sth with a colour, a substance, etc: *The wings are tipped with yellow.*

IDM **it is/was 'tipping (it) down** (*BrE, informal*) it is/ was raining heavily **tip the 'balance/'scales** (also **swing the 'balance**) to affect the result of sth in one way rather than another: *In an interview, smart presentation can tip the scales in your favour.* **tip your 'hand** (*AmE*) = SHOW YOUR HAND/CARDS at SHOW *v.* **tip the scales at sth** to weigh a particular amount: *He tipped the scales at just over 80 kilos.* **tip sb the 'wink | tip the 'wink to sb** (*BrE, informal*) to give sb secret information that they can use to gain an advantage for themselves—more at HAT *n.*

PHRV **,tip sb↔'off (about sth)** (*informal*) to warn sb about sth that is going to happen, especially sth illegal: *Three men were arrested after police were tipped off about the raid.* ◊ [+that] *They were tipped off that he might be living in Wales.*—related noun TIP-OFF **,tip 'up/'over| ,tip sth↔'up/'over** to fall or turn over; to make sth do this: *The mug tipped over, spilling hot coffee everywhere.* ◊ *We'll have to tip the sofa up to get it through the door.*

'tip-off *noun* (*informal*) secret information that sb gives, for example to the police, to warn them about an illegal activity that is going to happen: *The man was arrested after an anonymous tip-off.*

Tipp-Ex™ /'tɪpeks/ *noun* [U] (*BrE*) a liquid, usually white, that you use to cover mistakes that you make when you are writing or typing, and that you can write

on top of; a type of CORRECTION FLUID **SYN** WITEOUT ▶ **tippex** *verb* [VN] **~ sth (out)**: *I tippexed out the mistakes.*

tip·ple /'tɪpl/ *noun, verb*
■ *noun* [usually sing.] (*informal, especially BrE*) an alcoholic drink: *His favourite tipple was rum and lemon.*
■ *verb* [V, VN] (*informal, especially BrE*) to drink alcohol ▶ **tip·pler** /'tɪplə(r)/ *noun*

tip·ster /'tɪpstə(r)/ *noun* **1** a person who tells you, often in exchange for money, which horse is likely to win a race, so that you can bet on it and win money **2** (*especially AmE*) a person who gives information to the police about a crime or criminal

tipsy /'tɪpsi/ *adj.* (*informal*) slightly drunk

tip·toe /'tɪptəʊ; *AmE* -toʊ/ *noun, verb*
■ *noun* **IDM** **on 'tiptoe/'tiptoes** standing or walking on the front part of your foot, with your heels off the ground, in order to make yourself taller or to move very quietly or lightly: *She had to stand on tiptoe to reach the top shelf.* ◊ *We crept around on tiptoes so as not to disturb him.*
■ *verb* [V] [usually +*adv./prep.*] to walk using the front parts of your feet only, so that other people cannot hear you: *I tiptoed over to the window.*

,tip-'top *adj.* [usually before noun] (*informal*) excellent: *The house is in tip-top condition.*

tir·ade /taɪ'reɪd; *AmE* 'taɪreɪd/ *noun* **~ (against sb/sth)** a long angry speech criticizing sb/sth or accusing sb of sth: *She launched into a tirade of abuse against politicians.*

tire /'taɪə(r)/ *verb, noun*
■ *verb* to become tired and feel as if you want to sleep or rest; to make sb feel this way: [V] *Her legs were beginning to tire.* ◊ *He has made a good recovery but still tires easily.* [also VN] **IDM** **never tire of doing sth** to do sth a lot, especially in a way that annoys people: *He went to Harvard—as he never tires of reminding us.* **PHRV** **'tire of sth/sb** to become bored with sth/sb or begin to enjoy it/them less: *They soon tired of the beach and went for a walk.* ◊ *There are plenty of restaurants for those who tire of shopping.* **,tire sb/yourself 'out** to make sb/yourself feel very tired—see also TIRED
■ *noun* (*AmE*) = TYRE

tired /'taɪəd; *AmE* 'taɪərd/ *adj.* **1** feeling that you would like to sleep or rest; needing rest: *to be/look/feel tired* ◊ *I'm too tired even to think.* ◊ *They were cold, hungry and tired out* (= very tired). ◊ *tired eyes/feet/muscles* **2 ~ of sb/sth| ~ of doing sth** feeling that you have had enough of sb/sth because you no longer find it/them interesting or because they make you angry or unhappy: *I'm sick and tired of all the arguments.* ◊ *She was tired of hearing about their trip to India.* **3** boring because it is too familiar or has been used too much: *He always comes out with the same tired old jokes.* ▶ **tired·ly** *adv.*: *He shook his head tiredly.* **tired·ness** *noun* [U]—see also DOG-TIRED

'tire iron *noun* (*AmE*) a metal tool for taking tyres off wheels

tire·less /'taɪələs; *AmE* 'taɪərləs/ *adj.* (*approving*) putting a lot of hard work and energy into sth over a long period of time: *a tireless campaigner for human rights* ◊ *to have tireless energy* ◊ *She was tireless in her efforts on our behalf.* ▶ **tire·less·ly** *adv.*

tire·some /'taɪəsəm; *AmE* 'taɪərsəm/ *adj.* making you feel annoyed: *Buying a house can be a very tiresome business.* ◊ *The children were being very tiresome.* ▶ **tire·some·ly** *adv.*

tir·ing /'taɪərɪŋ/ *adj.* making you feel the need to sleep or rest: *It had been a long tiring day.*

'tis /tɪz/ *short form* (*old use*) it is

tis·sue /'tɪʃuː; *BrE* also 'tɪsjuː/ *noun* **1** [U] (also **tis·sues** [pl.]) a mass of cells that form the different parts of humans, animals and plants: *muscle/brain/nerve/scar tissue* **2** [C] a piece of soft paper that absorbs liquids, used especially as a HANDKERCHIEF: *a box of tissues* **3** (also **'tissue paper**) [U] very thin paper used for wrapping and packing things that break easily **IDM** **a ,tissue of 'lies** (*literary*) a story, an excuse, etc. that is full of lies

tit /tɪt/ *noun* **1** [usually pl.] (also **titty**) (⚠, *slang*) a woman's breast or NIPPLE **2** (*BrE, slang*) a stupid person **3** a small European bird that eats insects and seeds.

s	t	v	z	ʃ	ʒ	tʃ	dʒ	θ	ð	ŋ
see	tea	van	zoo	shoe	vision	chain	jam	thin	this	sing

There are several types of tit: *a great tit*—see also BLUE TIT

Titan (also **titan**) /'taɪtn/ *noun* (*written*) a person who is very large, strong, intelligent or important ORIGIN From the **Titans**, who in Greek myth were the older gods who were defeated in a battle with Zeus.

ti·tan·ic /taɪ'tænɪk/ *adj.* (*written*) very large, important, strong or difficult: *a titanic struggle between good and evil*

ti·tan·ium /tɪ'teɪniəm/ *noun* [U] (*symb* **Ti**) a chemical element. Titanium is a silver-white metal used in making various strong light materials.

tit·bit /'tɪtbɪt/ (*BrE*) (*AmE* **tid·bit**) *noun* **1** a small special piece of food: *She had saved a few titbits for her cat.* **2** a small but interesting piece of news: *titbits of gossip/information/news*

titch /tɪtʃ/ *noun* (*BrE, informal* often *humorous*) used as a way of talking about or addressing a very small person

titchy /'tɪtʃi/ *adj.* (*BrE, informal*) very small

,tit for 'tat *noun* [U] a situation in which you do sth bad to sb because they have done the same to you: *the routine tit for tat when countries expel each other's envoys* ◊ *tit-for-tat assassinations by rival gangs*

tithe /taɪð/ *noun* (especially in the past) a TENTH or other fixed part of the goods that sb produces or the money that they earn, that they give regularly to help support the Church

tit·il·late /'tɪtɪleɪt/ *verb* (often *disapproving*) to interest or excite sb, especially in a sexual way: [V] *titillating details/pictures* ◊ [VN] *a story intended to titillate the imagination of the public* ▶ **tit·il·la·tion** /,tɪtɪ'leɪʃn/ *noun* [U]

title /'taɪtl/ *noun, verb*
■ *noun* **1** [C] the name of a book, poem, painting, piece of music, etc: *His poems were published under the title of 'Love and Reason'.* ◊ *the title track from their latest CD* (= the song with the same title as the disc) ◊ *She has sung the title role in 'Carmen'* (= the role of Carmen in that opera). **2** [C] a particular book or magazine: *The company publishes twenty new titles a year.* **3** [C] a word in front of a person's name to show their rank or profession, whether or not they are married, etc: *The present duke inherited the title from his father.* ◊ *Give your name and title* (= Mr, Miss, Ms, Dr, etc.). ➪ note at NAME **4** [C] a name that describes a job: *The official title of the job is 'Administrative Assistant'.* **5** [C] the position of being the winner of a competition, especially a sports competition: *the world heavyweight title* ◊ *She has three world titles.* **6** [U, C] ~ (**to sth/to do sth**) (*law*) the legal right to own sth, especially land or property; the document that shows you have this right: *He claims he has title to the land.*
■ *verb* [VN-N] [usually passive] to give a book, piece of music, etc. a particular name: *Their first album was titled 'Ocean Drive'.*

titled /'taɪtld/ *adj.* having a title such as LORD, LADY, etc.

'title deed *noun* [usually pl.] a legal document proving that sb is the owner of a particular house, etc.

'title-holder *noun* **1** a person or team that has defeated all the other competitors in an important competition: *the current Olympic title-holder* **2** (*AmE, technical*) the legal owner of sth

'title page *noun* a page at the front of a book that has the title and the author's name on it

tit·ter /'tɪtə(r)/ *verb* [V] to laugh quietly, especially in a nervous or embarrassed way SYN GIGGLE: *There was an embarrassing pause on stage and the audience began to titter.* ▶ **tit·ter** *noun*

tittle-tattle /'tɪtl tætl/ *noun* [U] (*informal, disapproving*) unimportant talk, usually not true, about other people and their lives SYN GOSSIP

titty /'tɪti/ *noun* (*pl.* **-ies**) (*slang*) = TIT (1)

titu·lar /'tɪtjulə(r); *AmE* -tʃə-/ *adj.* [only before noun] (*formal*) having a particular title or status but no real power or authority SYN NOMINAL: *the titular head of state*

tizzy /'tɪzi/ (also **tizz** /tɪz/) *noun* [sing.] (*informal*) a state

of nervous excitement or confusion: *She was in a real tizzy before the meeting.*

'T-junction *noun* (*BrE*) a place where one road joins another but does not cross it, so that the roads form the shape of the letter T

TLC /,ti: el 'si:/ *noun* [U] the abbreviation for 'tender loving care' (care that you give sb to make them feel better): *What he needs now is just rest and a lot of TLC.*

TM /,ti: 'em/ *abbr., noun*
■ *abbr.* TRADEMARK
■ *noun* (*BrE*) (*AmE* **T.M.**) [U] the abbreviation for TRAN-SCENDENTAL MEDITATION

TNT /,ti: en 'ti:/ *noun* [U] a powerful explosive

to /*before consonants* tə; *before vowels* tu; *strong form* tu:/ *prep., infinitive marker, adv.*
■ *prep.* HELP For the special uses of **to** in phrasal verbs, look at the entries for the verbs. For example **see to sth** is in the phrasal verb section at **see**. **1** in the direction of sth; towards sth: *I walked to the office.* ◊ *It fell to the ground.* ◊ *It was on the way to the station.* ◊ *He's going to Paris.* ◊ *my first visit to Africa* ◊ *He pointed to something on the opposite bank.* ◊ *Her childhood was spent travelling from place to place.* **2** ~ **the sth** (**of sth**) situated in the direction mentioned from sth: *Place the cursor to the left of the first word.* ◊ *There are mountains to the north.* **3** as far as sth: *The meadows lead down to the river.* ◊ *Her hair fell to her waist.* **4** reaching a particular state: *The vegetables were cooked to perfection.* ◊ *He tore the letter to pieces.* ◊ *She sang the baby to sleep.* ◊ *The letter reduced her to tears* (= made her cry). ◊ *His expression changed from amazement to joy.* **5** used to show the end or limit of a range or period of time: *a drop in profits from $105 million to around $75 million* ◊ *I'd say he was 25 to 30 years old* (= approximately 25 or 30 years old). ◊ *I like all kinds of music from opera to reggae.* ◊ *We only work from Monday to Friday.* ◊ *I watched the programme from beginning to end.* **6** before the start of sth: *How long is it to lunch?* ◊ (*especially BrE*) *It's five to ten* (= five minutes before ten o'clock). **7** used to show the person or thing that receives sth: *He gave it to his sister.* ◊ *I'll explain to you where everything goes.* ◊ *I am deeply grateful to my parents.* ◊ *Who did she address the letter to?* ◊ (*formal*) *To whom did she address the letter?* **8** used to show the person or thing that is affected by an action: *She is devoted to her family.* ◊ *What have you done to your hair?* **9** used to show that two things are attached or connected: *Attach this rope to the front of the car.* **10** used to show a relationship between one person or thing and another: *She's married to an Italian.* ◊ *the Japanese ambassador to France* ◊ *the key to the door* ◊ *the solution to this problem* **11** directed towards; concerning: *It was a threat to world peace.* ◊ *She made a reference to her recent book.* **12** used to introduce the second part of a comparison or RATIO: *I prefer walking to climbing.* ◊ *The industry today is nothing to what it once was.* ◊ *We won by six goals to three.* **13** used to show a quantity or rate: *There are 2.54 centimetres to an inch.* ◊ *This car does 30 miles to the gallon.*—compare PER **14** in honour of sb/sth: *a monument to the soldiers who died in the war* ◊ *Let's drink to Julia and her new job.* **15** while sth else is happening or being done: *He left the stage to prolonged applause.* **16** used after verbs of movement to mean 'with the intention of giving sth': *People rushed to her rescue and picked her up.* **17** used to show sb's attitude or reaction to sth: *His music isn't really to my taste.* ◊ *To her astonishment, he smiled.* **18** used to show what sb's opinion or feeling about sth is: *It sounded like crying to me.*
■ *infinitive marker* HELP **To** is often used before the base form of a verb to show that the verb is in the infinitive. The infinitive is used after many verbs and also after many nouns and adjectives. **1** used to show purpose or intention: *I set out to buy food.* ◊ *I am going to tell you a story.* ◊ *She was determined to do well.* ◊ *His aim was to become president.* ◊ *To be honest with you, I don't remember what he said.* **2** used to show the result of sth: *She managed to escape.* ◊ *It was too hot to go out.* ◊ *He couldn't get close enough to see.* **3** used to show the cause of sth: *I'm sorry to hear that.* **4** used to show an action that you

T

æ	ɑ:	e	ɜ:	ə	ɪ	i:	i	ɒ	ɔ:	ʌ	ʊ	u	u:
cat	father	ten	bird	about	sit	see	many	got	saw	cup	put	actual	too
								(BrE)					

T

want or are advised to do: *I'd love to go to France this summer.* ◇ *The leaflet explains how to apply for a place.* ◇ *I don't know what to say.* **HELP To** can also be used without a verb following when the missing verb is easy to understand: *He asked her to come but she said she didn't want to.* **5** used to show sth that is known or reported about a particular person or thing: *The house was said to be haunted.* **6** used to show that one action immediately follows another: *I reached the station only to find that my train had already left.* **7 am, is, are, was, were ~** used to show that you must or should do sth: *You are not to talk during the exam.* ◇ *She was to be here at 8.30 but she didn't arrive.*
■ *adv.* (usually of a door) in or into a closed position: *Push the door to.*—see also **TOING** **IDM** **,to and 'fro** backwards and forwards: *She rocked the baby to and fro.* **HELP** For the special uses of **to** in phrasal verbs, look at the entries for the verbs. For example **set to** is in the phrasal verb section at **set.**

toad /təʊd; *AmE* toʊd/ *noun* **1** a small animal like a FROG but with a drier and less smooth skin, that lives on land but breeds in water (= is an AMPHIBIAN)—picture on page A7 **2** (*informal, disapproving*) an unpleasant person: *You repulsive little toad!*

,toad-in-the-'hole *noun* [U] a British dish of sausages cooked in BATTER

toad-stool /'təʊdstuːl; *AmE* 'toʊd-/ *noun* a FUNGUS with a round flat or curved head and a short stem. Many types of toadstool are poisonous.—compare MUSHROOM

toady /'təʊdi; *AmE* 'toʊdi/ *noun, verb*
■ *noun* (*pl.* **-ies**) (*disapproving*) a person who treats sb more important with special kindness or respect in order to gain their favour or help
■ *verb* (**toad·ies, toady·ing, toad·ied, toad·ied**) [V] **~ (to sb)** (*disapproving*) to treat sb more important with special kindness or respect in order to gain their favour or help

toast /təʊst; *AmE* toʊst/ *noun, verb*
■ *noun* **1** [U] slices of bread that have been made brown and crisp by heating them on both sides in a toaster or under a GRILL: *cheese on toast* ◇ *a piece of toast* ◇ *two slices/rounds of toast* **2** [C] **~ (to sb/sth)** the act of a group of people wishing sb happiness, success, etc. by drinking a glass of sth, especially alcohol, at the same time: *I'd like to propose a toast to the bride and groom.* ◇ *The committee drank a toast to the new project.* **3** [sing.] **the ~ of ...** a person who is praised by a lot of people in a particular place because of sth that they have done well: *The performance made her the toast of the festival.*
■ *verb* **1** [VN] to lift a glass of wine, etc. in the air and drink it at the same time as other people in order to wish sb/sth success, happiness, etc: *The happy couple were toasted in champagne.* ◇ *We toasted the success of the new company.* **2** to make sth, especially bread, turn brown by heating it in a toaster or close to heat; to turn brown in this way: [VN] *The buns should be served lightly toasted.* ◇ *a toasted sandwich* ◇ [V] *Place under a hot grill until the nuts have toasted.* **3** [VN] to warm a part of your body by placing it near a fire: *He sat toasting his feet in front of the fire.*

toast·er /'təʊstə(r); *AmE* 'toʊ-/ *noun* an electrical machine that you put slices of bread in to make toast—picture on page 275

toast·mas·ter /'təʊstmɑːstə(r); *AmE* 'toʊstmæstər/ *noun* a person who introduces the speakers at a formal dinner and calls for people to drink sth together in honour of a particular person (= proposes the toast)

toasty /'təʊsti; *AmE* 'toʊ-/ *adj.* (*AmE*) warm and comfortable

to·bacco /tə'bækəʊ; *AmE* -koʊ/ *noun* (*U, C*) (*pl.* **-os**) the dried leaves of the tobacco plant that are used for making cigarettes, smoking in a pipe or chewing: *The government imposed a ban on tobacco advertising* (= the advertising of cigarettes and all other forms of tobacco).

to·bac·con·ist /tə'bækənɪst/ *noun* **1** a person who owns, manages or works in a shop/store selling cigarettes, tobacco for pipes, etc. **2** (**to·bac·con·ist's**) (*pl.*

to·bac·con·ists) a shop/store that sells cigarettes, tobacco, etc: *There's a tobacconist's on the corner.*

to·bog·gan /tə'bɒgən; *AmE* -'baːg-/ *noun, verb*
■ *noun* a long light narrow SLEDGE (= a vehicle that slides over snow) sometimes curved up in front, used for sliding down slopes
■ *verb* [V] to travel down a slope on snow or ice using a toboggan ▶ **to·bog·gan·ing** *noun* [U]

toc·cata /tə'kɑːtə/ *noun* a piece of music for ORGAN or HARPSICHORD which includes difficult passages designed to show the player's skill

tod /tɒd; *AmE* tɑːd/ *noun* **IDM** **on your 'tod** (*old-fashioned, BrE, informal*) on your own; alone

today /tə'deɪ/ *adv., noun*
■ *adv.* **1** on this day: *I've got a piano lesson later today.* ◇ *The exams start a week today/today week* (= one week from now). **2** at the present period **SYN** NOWADAYS: *Young people today face a very difficult future at work.*
■ *noun* [U] **1** this day: *Today is her tenth birthday.* ◇ *The review is in today's paper.* ◇ *I'm leaving a week from today.* **2** the present period of time: *today's young people*

tod·dle /'tɒdl; *AmE* 'tɑːdl/ *verb* [V] **1** when a young child who has just learnt to walk **toddles**, it walks with short, unsteady steps: *I have to watch him all the time now that he's toddling.* **2** [+adv./prep.] (*informal*) to walk or go somewhere: *She toddles down to the park most afternoons.*

tod·dler /'tɒdlə(r); *AmE* 'tɑːd-/ *noun* a child who has only recently learnt to walk

toddy /'tɒdi; *AmE* 'tɑːdi/ *noun* [C, U] (*pl.* **-ies**) a drink made with strong alcohol, sugar, hot water and sometimes spices

to-do /tə'duː/ *noun* [sing.] (*informal, becoming old-fashioned*) unnecessary excitement or anger about sth **SYN** FUSS: *What a to-do!*

toe /təʊ; *AmE* toʊ/ *noun, verb*
■ *noun* **1** one of the five small parts that stick out from the foot: *the big/little toe* (= the largest/smallest toe) ◇ *I stubbed my toe on the step.* ◇ *Can you touch your toes?* (= by bending over while keeping your legs straight)—picture at BODY **2** the part of a sock, shoe, etc. that covers the toes—picture at SHOE **3** (**-toed**) (*in adjectives*) having the type or number of toes mentioned: *open-toed sandals* ◇ *a three-toed sloth*—see also PIGEON-TOED **IDM** **keep sb on their 'toes** to make sure that sb is ready to deal with anything that might happen by doing things that they are not expecting: *Regular surprise visits help to keep the staff on their toes.* **make sb's 'toes curl** to make sb feel embarrassed or uncomfortable about sth—more at DIG *v.*, DIP *v.*, HEAD *n.*, STEP *v.*, TOP *n.*, TREAD *v.*
■ *verb* **IDM** **toe the 'line** (*AmE* also **toe the 'mark**) to say or do what sb in authority tells you to say or do, even if you do not share the same opinions, etc: *One or two of them refused to toe the line.* ◇ *to toe the company/party line*

toe·cap /'təʊkæp; *AmE* 'toʊ-/ *noun* a piece of metal or leather that covers the front part of a shoe or boot to make it stronger

TOEFL /'təʊfl; *AmE* 'toʊfl/ *abbr.* Test of English as a Foreign Language (a test of a person's level of English that is taken in order to go to a university in the US)

toe·hold /'təʊhəʊld; *AmE* 'toʊhoʊld/ *noun* **1** a position in a place or an activity from which you hope will lead to more power or success: *The firm is anxious to gain a toehold in the North American market.* **2** a very small hole or space on a cliff, just big enough to put your foot in when you are climbing

toe·nail /'təʊneɪl; *AmE* 'toʊ-/ *noun* the nail on a toe—picture at BODY

toe·rag /'təʊræg/ *noun* (*BrE, slang*) used as a rude and offensive way of addressing sb you do not like or that you are angry with

toff /tɒf; *AmE* tɑːf/ *noun* (*BrE, informal*) a disapproving way of referring to sb from a high social class

tof·fee /'tɒfi; *AmE* 'tɔːfi; 'tɑːfi/ *noun* [U, C] a hard sticky sweet/candy made by heating sugar, butter and water together and allowing it to cool **IDM** **can't do sth for 'toffee** (*old-fashioned, BrE, informal*) if sb can't do sth

aɪ	aʊ	eɪ	əʊ	oʊ	ɔɪ	ɪə	eə	ʊə	j	w
my	now	say	go	go	boy	near	hair	pure	yes	wet
			(BrE)	(AmE)						

for toffee, they are very bad at doing it: *He can't dance for toffee!*

'toffee apple (*BrE*) (*AmE* **'candy apple**) *noun* an apple covered with a thin layer of hard toffee and fixed on a stick

'toffee-nosed *adj.* (*BrE, informal,* becoming *old-fashioned*) behaving as if you are better than other people, especially those of a lower social class SYN SNOBBISH

tofu /'təʊfuː; *AmE* 'toʊfuː/ (also **'bean curd**) *noun* [U] a soft white substance like cheese, made from SOYA and used in cooking, often instead of meat

tog /tɒg; *AmE* tɑːg; tɔːg/ *noun, verb*
- *noun* (*BrE*) **1** (**togs**) [pl.] (*informal,* becoming *old-fashioned*) clothes, especially ones that you wear for a particular purpose: *tennis/swimming/running togs* **2** a unit for measuring the warmth of DUVETS, etc.
- *verb* (**-gg-**) IDM **be ,togged 'out/'up (in sth)** (*informal*) to be wearing clothes for a particular activity or occasion: *They were all togged up in their skiing gear.*

to·geth·er /tə'geðə(r)/ *adv., adj.*
- *adv.* HELP For the special uses of **together** in phrasal verbs, look at the entries for the verbs. For example **pull yourself together** is in the phrasal verb section at **pull**. **1** with or near to sb/sth else; with each other: *We grew up together.* ◇ *Together they climbed the dark stairs.* ◇ *Get all the ingredients together before you start cooking.* ◇ *Stay close together—I don't want anyone to get lost.* **2** so that two or more things touch or are joined to or combined with each other: *He rubbed his hands together in satisfaction.* ◇ *She nailed the two boards together.* ◇ *Mix the sand and cement together.* ◇ *Taken together*, these factors are highly significant. ◇ *He has more money than the rest of us put together.* **3** (of two people) in a close relationship, for example a marriage: *They split up after ten years together.* **4** in or into agreement: *After the meeting the two sides in the dispute were no closer together.* **5** at the same time: *They both spoke together.* ◇ (*spoken*) *All together now: 'Happy birthday to you ...'* **6 for hours, days, etc.** ~ (*written*) for hours, days, etc. without stopping: *She sat for hours together just staring into space.* IDM **together with 1** including: *Together with the Johnsons, there were 12 of us in the villa.* **2** in addition to; as well as: *I sent them my order, together with a cheque for £40.*
- *adj.* (*informal, approving*) (of a person) well organized and confident: *He's incredibly together for someone so young.*

to·geth·er·ness /tə'geðənəs; *AmE* -ðərn-/ *noun* [U] the happy feeling you have when you are with people you like, especially family and friends

tog·gle /'tɒgl; *AmE* 'tɑːgl/ *noun, verb*
- *noun* **1** a short piece of wood, plastic, etc. that is put through a LOOP of thread to fasten sth, such as a coat or bag, instead of a button—picture at FASTENER **2** (also **'toggle switch**) (*computing*) a key on a computer that you press to change from one style or operation to another, and back again
- *verb* (*computing*) to press a key or set of keys on a computer keyboard in order to turn a feature on or off, or to move from one program, etc. to another: [V] *He toggled between the two windows.* ◇ [VN] *This key toggles various views of the data.*

'toggle switch *noun* **1** an electrical switch which you move up and down or backwards and forwards **2** (*computing*) = TOGGLE

toil /tɔɪl/ *verb, noun*
- *verb* [V] (*formal*) **1** ~ **(away) (at/over sth)** to work very hard and/or for a long time: *Hundreds of men toiled for years at building the pyramid.* **2** [+*adv. / prep.*] to move slowly and with difficulty: *They toiled up the hill in the blazing sun.* ▶ **toil·er** *noun*
- *noun* [U] (*formal or literary*) hard unpleasant work that makes you very tired: *a life of hardship and toil*

toi·let /'tɔɪlət/ *noun* **1** [C] a large bowl attached to a pipe that you sit on or stand over when you get rid of waste matter from your body: *Have you flushed the toilet?* ◇ (*BrE*) *I need to go to the toilet* (= use the toilet). ◇ *a toilet seat* ◇ *toilet facilities* **2** (*BrE*) (*AmE* **bath·room**) [C] a room

containing a toilet: *Every flat has its own bathroom and toilet.* ◇ *Who's in the toilet?* **3** (*BrE*) [C] (also **toi·lets** [pl.]) a room or small building containing several toilets, each in a separate smaller room: *public toilets* ◇ *Could you tell me where the ladies' toilet is, please?* **4** [U] (*old-fashioned*) the process of washing and dressing yourself, arranging your hair, etc.

BRITISH / AMERICAN
toilet / bathroom

In *BrE*, but not in *AmE*, the room that has a toilet in it is usually referred to as a **toilet**. This room in people's houses can also be called the **lavatory**, or informally, the **loo**. An extra downstairs toilet in a house can be called the **cloakroom**. In public places, especially on signs, the words **toilets**, **Gents** (for men's toilets) or **Ladies** (for women's toilets) are used for a room or small building containing several toilets. You might also see **WC** or **Public Conveniences** on some signs.
In *AmE* the room that contains a toilet is usually called the **bathroom**, never the **toilet**. A room with a toilet in a public place can also be called a **restroom**, **ladies' room**, **women's room** or **men's room**. **Washroom** is an old-fashioned word.

'toilet bag *noun* (*BrE*) = SPONGE BAG

'toilet paper (also **'toilet tissue**) *noun* [U] thin soft paper used for cleaning your bottom after you have used the toilet: *a roll of toilet paper*

toi·let·ries /'tɔɪlətriz/ *noun* [pl.] things such as soap or TOOTHPASTE that you use for washing, cleaning your teeth, etc.

'toilet roll *noun* (*BrE*) a roll of toilet paper

'toilet soap *noun* [U, C] soap that you use for washing yourself

'toilet-train *verb* [VN] [usually passive] to teach a small child to use the toilet ▶ **'toilet-trained** *adj.* **'toilet-train·ing** *noun* [U]

'toilet water *noun* [U, C] a kind of PERFUME (= a pleasant smelling liquid for the skin) that has water added to it and is not very expensive

toils /tɔɪlz/ *noun* [pl.] (*formal or literary*) if you are caught in the **toils** of an unpleasant feeling or situation, you cannot escape from it SYN SNARE

toing /'tuːɪŋ/ *noun* IDM **,toing and 'froing 1** movement or travel backwards and forwards between two or more places: *All this toing and froing between London and New York takes it out of him.* **2** a lot of unnecessary or repeated activity or discussion: *After a great deal of toing and froing, I decided not to change jobs after all.*

token /'təʊkən; *AmE* 'toʊ-/ *noun, adj.*
- *noun* **1** a round piece of metal or plastic used instead of money to operate some machines or as a form of payment: *a parking token* **2** (*BrE*) a piece of paper that you pay for and that sb can exchange for sth in a shop/store: *a £20 book/record/gift token* ⇨ note at VOUCHER **3** a piece of paper that you can collect when you buy a particular product and then exchange for sth: *Collect six tokens for a free T-shirt.* **4** something that is a symbol of a feeling, a fact, an event, etc: *Please accept this small gift as a token of our gratitude.* IDM **by the same 'token** for the same reasons: *The penalty for failure will be high. But, by the same token, the rewards for success will be great.*
- *adj.* [only before noun] **1** involving very little effort or feeling and intended only as a way of showing other people that you think sb/sth is important, when really you are not sincere: *The government has only made a token gesture towards helping the unemployed.* ◇ *There was one token woman on the committee* (= a woman who is included on the group to make it look as if women are always included, although that is not true). **2** done as a symbol to show that you are serious about sth and will keep a promise or an agreement or do more later: *The government agreed to send a small token force to the area.* ◇ *a one-day token strike* **3** (of a small amount of money) that you pay or charge sb only as a symbol, because a

payment is expected: *We charge only a token fee for use of the facilities.*

token·ism /ˈtəʊkənɪzəm; *AmE* ˈtoʊ-/ *noun* [U] (*disapproving*) the fact of doing sth only in order to do what the law requires or to satisfy a particular group of people, but not in a way that is really sincere: *Appointing one woman to the otherwise all-male staff could look like tokenism.*

Tok Pisin /ˌtɒk ˈpɪzɪn; -sən; *AmE* ˌtɑːk/ (also **pidgin**) *noun* [U] a CREOLE language based on English, used in Papua New Guinea

told *pt, pp* of TELL

tol·er·able /ˈtɒlərəbl; *AmE* ˈtɑːl-/ *adj.* (*written*) **1** fairly good, but not of the best quality [SYN] REASONABLE: *We have had a tolerable degree of success in recruiting good staff.* **2** that you can accept or bear, although unpleasant or painful: *At times, the heat was barely tolerable.* [OPP] INTOLERABLE ▶ **tol·er·ably** /ˈtɒlərəbli; *AmE* ˈtɑːl-/ *adv.*: *He plays the piano tolerably (well).*

tol·er·ance /ˈtɒlərəns; *AmE* ˈtɑːl-/ *noun* **1** [U] ~ (of/for sb/sth) the willingness to accept or TOLERATE sb/sth, especially opinions or behaviour that you may not agree with, or people who are not like you: *She had no tolerance for jokes of any kind.* ◊ *religious/racial tolerance* ◊ *a reputation for tolerance towards refugees*—see also ZERO TOLERANCE [OPP] INTOLERANCE **2** [C, U] ~ (to sth) the ability to suffer sth, especially pain, difficult conditions, etc. without being harmed: *tolerance to antibiotics/cold* ◊ *Tolerance to alcohol decreases with age.* **3** [C, U] (*technical*) the amount by which the measurement of a value can vary without causing problems: *They were working to a tolerance of 0.0001 of a centimetre.*

tol·er·ant /ˈtɒlərənt; *AmE* ˈtɑːl-/ *adj.* **1** ~ (of/towards sb/sth) able to accept what other people say or do even if you do not agree with it: *He has a very tolerant attitude towards other religions.* **2** ~ (of sth) (of plants, animals or machines) able to survive or operate in difficult conditions: *The plants are tolerant of frost.* [OPP] INTOLERANT ▶ **tol·er·ant·ly** *adv.*

tol·er·ate /ˈtɒləreɪt; *AmE* ˈtɑːl-/ *verb* **1** to allow sb to do sth that you do not agree with or like [SYN] PUT UP WITH: [VN] *Their relationship was tolerated but not encouraged.* ◊ *This sort of behaviour will not be tolerated.* ◊ [V-ing] *She refused to tolerate being called a liar.* [also VN-ing] **2** [VN] to accept sb/sth that is annoying, unpleasant, etc. without complaining [SYN] PUT UP WITH: *There is a limit to what one person can tolerate.* ◊ *I don't know how you tolerate that noise!* **3** [VN] to be able to be affected by a drug, difficult conditions, etc. without being harmed: *She tolerated the chemotherapy well.* ◊ *Few plants will tolerate sudden changes in temperature.*

tol·er·ation /ˌtɒləˈreɪʃn; *AmE* ˌtɑːl-/ *noun* [U] a willingness to allow sth that you do not like or agree with to happen or continue: *religious toleration*

toll /təʊl; *AmE* toʊl/ *noun, verb*
■ *noun* **1** [C] money that you pay to use a particular road or bridge: *motorway tolls* ◊ *a toll road/bridge* **2** [C, usually sing.] the amount of damage or the number of deaths and injuries that are caused in a particular war, disaster, etc: *The official death toll has now reached 7000.* ◊ *the war's growing casualty toll* **3** [sing.] the sound of a bell ringing with slow regular strokes **4** [C] (*AmE*) a charge for a telephone call that is calculated at a higher rate than a local call [IDM] **take a heavy ˈtoll (on sb/sth) | take its ˈtoll (on sb/sth)** to have a bad effect on sb/sth; to cause a lot of damage, deaths, suffering, etc: *Illness had taken a heavy toll on her.* ◊ *The recession is taking its toll on the housing markets.*
■ *verb* when a bell **tolls** or sb **tolls** it, it is rung slowly many times, especially as a sign that sb has died: [V] *The Abbey bell tolled for those killed in the war.* ◊ [VN] *The bell tolled the hour.* ◊ (*figurative*) *The revolution tolled the death knell* (= signalled the end) *for the Russian monarchy.*

toll·booth /ˈtəʊlbuːð; *AmE* ˈtoʊlbuːθ/ *noun* a small building by the side of a road where you pay to drive on a road, go over a bridge, etc.

toll-ˈfree *adj.* (*AmE*) (of a telephone call to an organization or a service) that you do not have to pay for: *a toll-free number*—see also FREEPHONE

Tom /tɒm; *AmE* tɑːm/ *noun* [IDM] **any/every ˌTom, ˌDick and ˈHarry** (usually *disapproving*) any ordinary person rather than the people you know or people who have special skills or qualities: *We don't want any Tom, Dick, or Harry using the club bar.*

tom /tɒm; *AmE* tɑːm/ *noun* = TOMCAT

toma·hawk /ˈtɒməhɔːk; *AmE* ˈtɑːm-/ *noun* a light AXE used by Native Americans

to·mato /təˈmɑːtəʊ; *AmE* təˈmeɪtoʊ/ *noun* [C, U] (*pl.* -oes) a soft fruit with a lot of juice and shiny red skin that is eaten as a vegetable either raw or cooked: *a bacon, lettuce and tomato sandwich* ◊ *sliced tomatoes* ◊ *tomato plants*—picture on page A3

tomb /tuːm/ *noun* a large grave, especially one built of stone above or below the ground: *the tombs of the Pharaohs*

tom·bola /tɒmˈbəʊlə; *AmE* tɑːmˈboʊlə/ *noun* [U, C] (*BrE*) a game in which you buy tickets with numbers on them. If the number on your ticket is the same as the number on one of the prizes, you win the prize.

tom·boy /ˈtɒmbɔɪ; *AmE* ˈtɑːm-/ *noun* a young girl who enjoys activities and games that are traditionally considered to be for boys

tomb·stone /ˈtuːmstəʊn; *AmE* -stoʊn/ *noun* a large, flat stone that lies over a grave or stands at one end, that shows the name, age, etc. of the person buried there—compare HEADSTONE, GRAVESTONE

tom·cat /ˈtɒmkæt; *AmE* ˈtɑːm-/ (also **tom**) *noun* a male cat

tome /təʊm; *AmE* toʊm/ *noun* (*formal*) a large heavy book, especially one dealing with a serious topic

tom·fool·ery /tɒmˈfuːləri; *AmE* tɑːm-/ *noun* [U] (*old-fashioned*) silly behaviour

tommy gun /ˈtɒmi ɡʌn; *AmE* ˈtɑːmi/ *noun* a type of SUB-MACHINE GUN

to·mor·row /təˈmɒrəʊ; *AmE* təˈmɑːroʊ; -ˈmɔːr-/ *adv., noun*
■ *adv.* on or during the day after today: *I'm off now. See you tomorrow.* ◊ *She's leaving tomorrow.* [IDM] see JAM *n.*
■ *noun* [U] **1** the day after today: *Today is Tuesday, so tomorrow is Wednesday.* ◊ *tomorrow afternoon/morning/night/evening* ◊ *I'll see you the day after tomorrow.* ◊ *The announcement will appear in tomorrow's newspapers.* ◊ *I want it done by tomorrow.* **2** the future: *Who knows what changes tomorrow may bring?* ◊ *Tomorrow's workers will have to be more adaptable.* [IDM] **do sth as if/like there's no toˈmorrow** to do sth a lot or as though you do not care what effects it will have: *I ate as if there was no tomorrow.* ◊ *She was spending money like there's no tomorrow.*

ˈtom-tom *noun* a tall narrow drum that you play with your hands

ton /tʌn/ *noun* **1** [C] (*pl.* **tons** or **ton**) a unit for measuring weight, in Britain 2240 pounds (**long ton**) and in the US 2000 pounds (**short ton**): (*informal*) *What have you got in this bag? It weighs a ton!*—compare TONNE **2** [C] a unit for measuring the size of a ship. 1 ton is equal to 100 CUBIC feet. **3** (**tons**) [pl.] (*informal*) a lot: *They've got tons of money.* ◊ *I've still got tons to do.* **4** (**a/the ton**) (*BrE, informal*) 100, especially when connected with a speed of 100 miles per hour: *He was caught doing a ton.* [IDM] **like a ton of ˈbricks** (*informal*) very heavily; very severely: *Disappointment hit her like a ton of bricks.* ◊ *They came down on him like a ton of bricks* (= criticized him very severely).

tonal /ˈtəʊnl; *AmE* ˈtoʊnl/ *adj.* **1** (*technical*) relating to tones of sound or colour **2** (*music*) having a particular KEY [OPP] ATONAL ▶ **tonal·ly** *adv.*

ton·al·ity /təʊˈnæləti; *AmE* toʊ-/ *noun* [U, C] (*pl.* -ies) (*music*) the quality of a piece of music that depends on the KEY in which it is written

tone /təʊn; *AmE* toʊn/ *noun, verb*

■ *noun*

OF VOICE | **1** [C] the quality of sb's voice, especially expressing a particular emotion: *speaking in hushed/ low/clipped/measured tones* ◊ *a light/dry/sharp/conversational tone* ◊ *a tone of bitterness/command/surprise* ◊ *Don't speak to me in that tone of voice* (= in that unpleasant or critical way). ◊ *There's no need to take that tone with me—it's not my fault we're late.*

CHARACTER/ATMOSPHERE | **2** [sing.] the general character and attitude of sth such as a piece of writing, or the atmosphere of an event: *The overall tone of the book is gently nostalgic.* ◊ *She set the tone for the meeting with a firm statement of company policy.* ◊ *Trust you to lower the tone of the conversation* (= for example by telling a rude joke). ◊ *The article was moderate in tone and presented both sides of the case.*

OF SOUND | **3** [C] the quality of a sound, especially the sound of a musical instrument or one produced by electronic equipment: *the full, rich, tone of the trumpet* ◊ *the volume and tone controls on a car stereo*

COLOUR | **4** [C] a shade of a colour: *a carpet in warm tones of brown and orange*

OF MUSCLES/SKIN | **5** [U] how strong and firm your muscles or skin are: *how to improve your muscle/skin tone*

ON TELEPHONE | **6** [C] a sound heard on a telephone line: *(BrE) the dialling tone* ◊ *(AmE) the dial tone* ◊ *Please speak after the tone* (= for example as an instruction on an answering machine).

IN MUSIC | **7** *(BrE)* [C] *(AmE* **'whole step***)* [C] one of the five longer INTERVALS in a musical scale, for example the INTERVAL between C and D or between E and F♯—compare SEMITONE, STEP *n.* (10)

PHONETICS | **8** [C] the PITCH (= how high or low a sound is) of a syllable in speaking: *a rising/falling tone*

-TONED | **9** (in adjectives) having the type of tone mentioned: *a bright-toned soprano* ◊ *olive-toned skin*

■ *verb*

MUSCLES/SKIN | **1** [VN] ~ sth (up) to make your muscles, skin, etc. firmer and stronger: *Massage will help to tone up loose skin under the chin.* ◊ *a beautifully toned body*

COLOUR | **2** [V] ~ (in) (with sth) *(BrE)* to match the colour of sth: *The beige of his jacket toned (in) with the cream shirt.*

PHRV **,tone sth↔'down 1** to make a speech, an opinion, etc. less extreme or offensive: *The language of the article will have to be toned down for the mass market.* **2** to make a colour less bright

,tone-'deaf *adj.* unable to hear the difference between musical notes

tone-less /'təʊnləs; *AmE* 'toʊn-/ *adj.* (of a voice, etc.) dull or flat; not expressing any emotion or interest ▶ **tone-less·ly** *adv.*

toner /'təʊnə(r); *AmE* 'toʊ-/ *noun* [U, C] **1** a type of ink used in machines that print or PHOTOCOPY **2** a liquid or cream used for making the skin on your face firm and smooth

tongs /tɒŋz; *AmE* tɑːŋz; tɔːŋz/ *noun* [pl.] **1** a tool with two long parts that are joined at one end, used for picking up and holding things: *a pair of tongs*—picture at SCISSORS, LABORATORY **2** a tool that is heated and used for curling hair IDM see HAMMER *n.*

tongue /tʌŋ/ *noun, verb*

■ *noun* **1** [C] the soft part in the mouth that moves around, used for tasting, swallowing, speaking, etc: *He clicked his tongue to attract their attention.* ◊ *She ran her tongue over her lips.* ◊ *It's very rude to stick your tongue out at people.*—picture at BODY **2** [U, C] the tongue of some animals, cooked and eaten: *a slice of ox tongue* **3** [C] *(formal or literary)* a language: *None of the tribes speak the same tongue.* ◊ *I tried speaking to her in her native tongue.*—see also MOTHER TONGUE **4** [sing.] a particular way of speaking: *He has a sharp tongue.* ◊ *(formal) I'll thank you to keep a civil tongue in your head* (= speak politely). **5** (-tongued) (in adjectives) speaking in the way mentioned: *sharp-tongued* **6** [C] a long narrow piece of leather under the LACES on a shoe—picture at SHOE **7** [C] ~ (of sth) *(literary)* something that is long and narrow and shaped like a tongue: *a tongue of flame/land* IDM **get your 'tongue around/round sth** to pronounce a difficult

word correctly: *He was having trouble getting his tongue around my name.* **,hold your 'tongue/'peace** *(old-fashioned)* to remain silent although you would like to give your opinion **roll/slip/trip off the 'tongue** to be easy to say or pronounce: *It's not a name that exactly trips off the tongue, is it?* **set 'tongues wagging** *(informal)* to cause people to start talking about sb's private affairs **with your tongue in your 'cheek | with tongue in 'cheek** if you say sth **with your tongue in your cheek**, you are not being serious and mean it as a joke—more at BITE *v.*, FIND *v.*, LOOSE *adj.*, LOOSEN *v.*, SLIP *n.*, TIP *n.*, WATCH *v.*

■ *verb* [VN] **1** to stop the flow of air into a wind instrument with your tongue in order to make a note **2** to LICK sth with your tongue

tongue depressor /'tʌŋ dɪpresə(r)/ *noun* *(AmE)* = SPATULA (3)

,tongue-in-'cheek *adj.* not intended seriously; done or said as a joke: *a tongue-in-cheek remark* ▶ **,tongue-in-'cheek** *adv.*: *The offer was made almost tongue-in-cheek.*

'tongue-tied *adj.* not able to speak because you are shy or nervous

'tongue-twister *noun* a word or phrase that is difficult to say quickly or correctly, such as 'She sells sea shells on the sea shore.'

tonic /'tɒnɪk; *AmE* 'tɑːn-/ *noun* **1** (also **'tonic water**) [U, C] a clear FIZZY drink (= with bubbles in it) with a slightly bitter taste, that is often mixed with a strong alcoholic drink, especially GIN or VODKA: *a gin and tonic* **2** [C] a medicine that makes you feel stronger and healthier, taken especially when you feel tired: *herbal tonics* **3** [C, U] a liquid that you put on your hair or skin in order to make it healthier: *hair/skin tonic* **4** [C, usually sing.] *(old-fashioned)* anything that makes people feel healthier or happier: *The weekend break was just the tonic I needed.* **5** [C] *(music)* the first note of a SCALE of eight notes

to·night /tə'naɪt/ *adv., noun*

■ *adv.* on or during the evening or night of today: *Will you have dinner with me tonight?* ◊ *It's cold tonight.*

■ *noun* [U] the evening or night of today: *Here are tonight's football results.* ◊ *Tonight will be cloudy.*

ton·nage /'tʌnɪdʒ/ *noun* [U, C] **1** the size of a ship or the amount it can carry, expressed in TONS **2** the total amount that sth weighs

tonne /tʌn/ *(pl.* **tonnes** or **tonne***)* *noun* = METRIC TON: *a record grain harvest of 236m tonnes* ◊ *a 17-tonne truck*—compare TON

ton·sil /'tɒnsl; *AmE* 'tɑːnsl/ *noun* either of the two small organs at the sides of the throat, near the base of the tongue: *I've had my tonsils out* (= removed).—picture at BODY

ton·sil·litis /,tɒnsə'laɪtɪs; *AmE* ,tɑːn-/ *noun* [U] an infection of the tonsils in which they become swollen and sore

ton·sure /'tɒnʃə(r); *AmE* 'tɑːn-/ *noun* the part of a MONK's or priest's head that has been shaved

tony /'təʊni; *AmE* 'toʊni/ *adj.* *(AmE, informal, becoming old-fashioned)* fashionable and expensive

too /tuː/ *adv.* **1** used before adjectives and adverbs to say that sth is more than is good, necessary, possible, etc: *He's far too young to go on his own.* ◊ *This is too large a helping for me/This helping is too large for me.* ◊ *Is it too much to ask for a little quiet?* ◊ *The dress was too tight for me.* ◊ *It's too late to do anything about it now.* ◊ *Accidents like this happen all too* (= much too) *often.* **2** (usually placed at the end of a clause) also; as well: *Can I come too?* ◊ *When I've finished painting the bathroom, I'm going to do the kitchen too.* ⇨ note at ALSO **3** used to comment on sth that makes a situation worse: *She broke her leg last week—and on her birthday too!* ◊ *Very: I'm not too sure if this is right.* ◊ *I'm just going out—I won't be too long.* ◊ *She's none too* (= not very) *clever.* **5** used to emphasize sth, especially your anger, surprise or agreement with sth: *'He did apologize eventually.' 'I should think so too!' 'She gave me the money.' 'About time too!'* IDM **be too 'much (for sb)** to need more skill or strength than you have; to be more difficult, annoying, etc. than you can bear

took *pt* of TAKE

tool /tuːl/ *noun, verb*

tools
claw
hammer
nail
mallet
file
screwdriver
screw
chisel
nut
washer
bolt
adjustable spanner (*BrE*)/
monkey wrench (*AmE*)
wrench (*BrE*)/pliers (*AmE*)
spanner (*BrE*)/
wrench (*AmE*)
bit   chuck
pliers
drill
handsaw
plane

■ *noun* **1** an instrument such as a hammer, SCREWDRIVER, SAW, etc. that you hold in your hand and use for making things, repairing things, etc: *garden tools* ◇ *a cutting tool* ◇ *a tool kit* (= a set of tools in a box or bag) ◇ *power tools* (= using electricity) ◇ *Always select the right tool for the job.* **2** a thing that helps you to do your job or to achieve sth: *research tools like questionnaires* ◇ *The computer is now an invaluable tool for the family doctor.* ◇ *Some of them carried the guns which were the tools of their trade* (= the things they needed to do their job). **3** a person who is used or controlled by another person or group: *The prime minister was an unwitting tool of the president.* **4** (⚠, *slang*) a PENIS **IDM** see DOWN *v.*
■ *verb* [V+adv. / prep.] (*AmE, informal*) to drive around in a vehicle **PHRV** ,tool ˈup| ,tool sb/sth↔ˈup (*BrE, technical*) to get or provide sb/sth with the equipment, etc. that is necessary to do or produce sth: *The factory is not tooled up to produce this type of engine.*

toot /tuːt/ *noun, verb*
■ *noun* a short high sound made by a car horn or a whistle: *She gave a sharp toot on her horn.*
■ *verb* (*especially BrE*) when a car horn **toots** or you **toot** it, it makes a short high sound: [V] *the sound of horns tooting* ◇ [VN] *Toot your horn to let them know we're here.* **IDM** see HORN

tooth /tuːθ/ *noun* (*pl.* **teeth** /tiːθ/) **1** any of the hard white objects in the mouth used for biting and chewing food: *I've just had a tooth out at the dentist's.* ◇ *to brush/clean your teeth* ◇ *tooth decay* ◇ *false teeth* ◇ *She answered through clenched teeth* (= opening her mouth only a little because of anger). ◇ *The cat sank its teeth into his finger.*—see also BUCK-TEETH, MILK TOOTH, WISDOM TOOTH—picture at BODY **2** a narrow pointed part that sticks out of an object: *the teeth on a saw*—see also FINE-TOOTH COMB **IDM** cut your ˈteeth on sth to do sth that gives you your first experience of a particular type of work: *She cut her teeth on local radio.* cut a ˈtooth (of a baby) to grow a new tooth get your ˈteeth into sth (*informal*) to put a lot of effort and enthusiasm into sth that is difficult enough

to keep you interested: *Choose an essay topic that you can really get your teeth into.* have ˈteeth (*BrE, informal*) (of an organization, a law, etc.) to be powerful and effective in the teeth of sth **1** in spite of problems, opposition, etc: *The new policy was adopted in the teeth of fierce criticism.* **2** in the direction that a strong wind is coming from: *They crossed the bay in the teeth of a howling gale.* set sb's ˈteeth on edge (of a sound or taste) to make sb feel physically uncomfortable: *Just the sound of her voice sets my teeth on edge.*—more at ARM *v.*, BARE *v.*, BIT, EYE *n.*, EYE TEETH, FIGHT *v.*, GNASH, GRIT *v.*, HELL, KICK *v.*, KICK *n.*, LIE²*v.*, LONG *adj.*, RED *adj.*, SKIN *n.*, SWEET *adj.*

tooth·ache /ˈtuːθeɪk/ *noun* [U, C, usually sing.] a pain in your teeth or in one tooth: (*BrE*) *I've got toothache.* ◇ (*AmE, BrE*) *I've got a toothache.*

tooth·brush /ˈtuːθbrʌʃ/ *noun* a small brush for cleaning your teeth

toothed /tuːθt; tuːðd/ *adj.* [only before noun] **1** (*technical*) having teeth: *a toothed whale* **2** (**-toothed**) (in compounds) having the type of teeth mentioned: *a saw-toothed wheel* ◇ *His face broke into a gap-toothed smile.*

tooth·less /ˈtuːθləs/ *adj.* **1** having no teeth: *a toothless old man* ◇ *She gave us a toothless grin.* **2** (*written*) having no power or authority

tooth·paste /ˈtuːθpeɪst/ *noun* [U] a substance that you put on a brush and use to clean your teeth

tooth·pick /ˈtuːθpɪk/ *noun* a short pointed piece of wood or plastic used for removing bits of food from between the teeth

toothy /ˈtuːθi/ *adj.* a **toothy** smile shows a lot of teeth

too·tle /ˈtuːtl/ *verb* (*BrE, informal*) **1** [V+adv. / prep.] to walk, drive, etc. somewhere without hurrying **2** [V, VN] to produce a series of notes by blowing into a musical instrument

top /tɒp; *AmE* tɑːp/ *noun, adj., verb*
■ *noun*
HIGHEST POINT | **1** [C] the highest part or point of sth: *She was standing at the top of the stairs.* ◇ *Write your name at the top.* ◇ *He filled my glass to the top.* ◇ *Snow was falling on the mountain tops.* ◇ (*BrE*) *the top of the milk* (= the cream that rises to the top of a bottle of milk) ◇ *The wind was blowing in the tops of the trees.*—see also ROOFTOP, TREETOP
UPPER SURFACE | **2** [C] the upper flat surface of sth: *Can you polish the top of the table?* ◇ *a desk/bench top*—see also HARDTOP, ROLL-TOP DESK, TABLE TOP
HIGHEST RANK | **3** [sing.] the highest or most important rank or position: *He's at the top of his profession.* ◇ *She is determined to make it to the top* (= achieve fame or success). ◇ *They finished the season at the top of the league.* ◇ *We have a lot of things to do, but packing is at the top of the list.* ◇ *This printer is a top of the range model* (= the best it is possible to buy). ◇ *This decision came right from the top.*
FARTHEST POINT | **4** [sing.] the ~ of sth the end of a street, table, etc. that is farthest away from you or from where you usually come to it: *I'll meet you at the top of Thorpe Street.*
OF PEN/BOTTLE | **5** [C] a thing that you put on the end of sth to close it: *Where's the top of this pen?* ◇ *a bottle with a screw top*
CLOTHING | **6** [C] a piece of clothing worn on the upper part of the body: *I need a top to go with this skirt.* ◇ *a tracksuit/pyjama/bikini top*—see also CROP TOP
LEAVES OF PLANT | **7** [C, usually pl.] the leaves of a plant that is grown mainly for its root: *Remove the green tops from the carrots.*
AMOUNT OF MONEY | **8** (**tops**) [pl.] (*BrE, spoken*) used after an amount of money to show that it is the highest possible: *It couldn't have cost more than £50, tops.*
BEST | **9** (**tops**) [pl.] (*old-fashioned, informal*) a person or thing of the best quality: *Among sports superstars she's (the) tops.* ◇ *In the survey the Brits came out tops for humour.*
TOY | **10** [C] a child's toy that spins on a point when it is

aɪ	aʊ	eɪ	əʊ	oʊ	ɔɪ	ɪə	eə	ʊə	j	w
my	now	say	go	go	boy	near	hair	pure	yes	wet
			(BrE)	(AmE)						

turned round very quickly by hand or by a string: *She was so confused—her mind was **spinning like a top***.
—see also BIG TOP

IDM **at the top of the 'tree** in the highest position or rank in a profession or career* **at the top of your 'voice** as loudly as possible: *She was screaming at the top of her voice*. **come out on 'top** to win a contest or an argument: *In most boardroom disputes he tends to come out on top*. **from ˌtop to 'bottom** going to every part of a place in a very thorough way: *We cleaned the house from top to bottom*. **from ˌtop to 'toe** completely; all over: *She was dressed in green from top to toe*. **get on 'top of sb** to be too much for sb to manage or deal with: *All this extra work is getting on top of him*. **get on 'top of sth** to manage to control or deal with sth: *How will I ever get on top of all this work?* **off the ˌtop of your 'head** (*informal*) just guessing or using your memory, without taking time to think carefully or check the facts: *I can't remember the name off the top of my head, but I can look it up for you*. **on 'top 1** on the highest point or surface: *a cake with cream on top* ◊ *Stand on top and look down*. ◊ *He's going bald on top* (= on the top of his head). **2** in a leading position or in control: *She remained on top for the rest of the match*. **3** in addition: *Look, here's 30 dollars, and I'll buy you lunch on top*. **on top of sth/sb 1** on, over or covering sth/sb: *Books were piled on top of one another*. ◊ *Many people were crushed when the building collapsed on top of them*. **2** in addition to sth: *He gets commission on top of his salary*. ◊ *On top of everything else, my car's been stolen*. **3** very close to sth/sb: *We were all living on top of each other in that tiny apartment*. **4** in control of a situation: *Do you think he's really on top of his job?* **on ˌtop of the 'world** very happy or proud ˌover the 'top (*abbr.* OTT) (*informal, especially BrE*) done to an exaggerated degree and with too much effort: *His performance in the movie is completely over the top*. **ˌtake sth from the 'top** (*informal*) to go back to the beginning of a song, piece of music, speech, etc. and repeat it: *OK, everybody, let's take it from the top*. **up 'top** (*BrE, informal*) used to talk about a person's intelligence: *He hasn't got much up top* (= He isn't very intelligent).—more at BLOW *v*., HEAP *n*., PILE *n*., THIN *adj*.

■ *adj.* [usually before noun] highest in position, rank or degree: *He lives on the top floor*. ◊ *She kept his passport in the top drawer*. ◊ *He's one of the top players in the country*. ◊ *She got the top job*. ◊ *He finished top in the exam*. ◊ *She got top marks for her essay*. ◊ *They're top of the league*. ◊ *The athletes are all on top form* (= performing their best). ◊ *Welfare reform is a top priority for the government*. ◊ *The car was travelling at top speed*.

■ *verb* (**-pp-**) [VN]
BE MORE | **1** to be higher than a particular amount: *Worldwide sales look set to top $1 billion*.
BE THE BEST | **2** to be in the highest position on a list because you are the most successful, important, etc: *The band topped the charts for five weeks with their first single*.
PUT ON TOP | **3** [usually passive] **~ sth (with sth)** to put sth on the top of sth else: *fruit salad topped with cream*
SAY/DO STH BETTER | **4** to say or do sth that is better, funnier, more impressive, etc. than sth that sb else has said or done in the past: *I'm afraid the other company has topped your offer* (= offered more money).
KILL YOURSELF | **5 ~ yourself** (*BrE, informal*) to kill yourself deliberately
CLIMB HILL | **6** (*literary*) to reach the highest point of a hill, etc.
IDM **to top/cap it 'all** (*spoken*) used to introduce the final piece of information that is worse than the other bad things that you have just mentioned ˌtop and 'tail sth (*BrE*) to cut the top and bottom parts off fruit and vegetables to prepare them to be cooked or eaten
PHRV **ˌtop sth ↔ 'off (with sth)** to complete sth successfully by doing or adding one final thing ˌtop 'out (at sth) if sth **tops out** at a particular price, speed, etc. it does not rise any higher: *Inflation topped out at 12%*. ˌtop sth ↔ 'up (*especially BrE*) **1** to fill a container that already has some liquid in it with more liquid: *I want to top the car up with oil before we set off*. ◊ *I want to top the*

oil up before we set off. **2** to increase the amount of sth to the level you want or need: *She relies on tips to top up her wages*.—related noun TOP-UP ˌtop sb 'up (*especially BrE*) to fill sb's glass or cup with sth more to drink: *Can I top you up?*—related noun TOP-UP

topaz /'təʊpæz; *AmE* 'toʊ-/ *noun* [C, U] a clear yellow precious stone: *a topaz ring*

ˌtop 'brass (*BrE*) (also **brass** *AmE, BrE*) *noun* [sing.+ sing./pl. *v*.] (*informal*) the people who are in the most important positions in a company, an organization, etc: *All the top brass was/were at the ceremony*.

ˌtop-'class *adj.* of the highest quality or standard: *a top-class player/performance*

top-coat /'tɒpkəʊt; *AmE* 'tɑːpkoʊt/ *noun* **1** the last layer of paint put on a surface—compare UNDERCOAT **2** (*old-fashioned*) an OVERCOAT

ˌtop 'dog *noun* [usually sing.] (*informal*) a person, group or country that is better than all the others, especially in a situation that involves competition

ˌtop-'down *adj.* (of a plan, project, etc.) starting from a general idea to which details are added later

ˌtop 'drawer *noun* [sing.] if sb/sth is out of **the top drawer**, they are of the highest social class or of the highest quality ▶ **ˌtop-'drawer** *adj.*

topee = TOPI

ˌtop-'flight *adj.* of the highest quality; the best or most successful

ˌtop 'gear *noun* [U] (*BrE*) the highest GEAR in a motor vehicle: *They cruised along **in top gear**.* ◊ (*figurative*) *Her career is moving into top gear*.

ˌtop-'grossing *adj.* [only before noun] earning more money than other similar things or people: *the top-grossing movie of 1999*

ˌtop 'hat (also *informal* **top-per**) *noun* a man's tall black or grey hat, worn with formal clothes on very formal occasions—picture at HAT

ˌtop-'heavy *adj.* **1** too heavy at the top and therefore likely to fall **2** (of an organization) having too many senior staff or managers compared to the number of workers

topi (also **topee**) /'təʊpi; *AmE* 'toʊpi; toʊ'piː/ *noun* a light hard hat worn to give protection from the sun in very hot countries

topi·ary /'təʊpiəri; *AmE* 'toʊpieri/ *noun* [U] the art of cutting bushes into shapes such as birds or animals

topic /'tɒpɪk; *AmE* 'tɑːp-/ *noun* a subject that you talk, write or learn about: *The main topic of conversation was Tom's new girlfriend*. ◊ *The article covered a wide range of topics*.

top·ic·al /'tɒpɪkl; *AmE* 'tɑːp-/ *adj.* connected with sth that is happening or of interest at the present time: *a topical joke/reference* ◊ *topical crimes/events* ▶ **top·ic·al·ity** /ˌtɒpɪ'kæləti; *AmE* ˌtɑːp-/ *noun* [U, sing.]

top-knot /'tɒpnɒt; *AmE* 'tɑːpnɑːt/ *noun* a way of arranging your hair in which it is tied up on the top of your head

top-less /'tɒpləs; *AmE* 'tɑːp-/ *adj.* (of a woman) not wearing any clothes on the upper part of the body so that her breasts are not covered: *a topless model* ◊ *a topless bar* (= where the female staff are topless) ▶ **top-less** *adv.*: *to sunbathe/go topless*

ˌtop-'level *adj.* [only before noun] involving the most important or best people in a company, an organization or a sport: *a top-level meeting* ◊ *top-level tennis*

top·most /'tɒpməʊst; *AmE* 'tɑːpmoʊst/ *adj.* [only before noun] (*written*) highest: *A bird was singing in the topmost branches of the tree*.

ˌtop-'notch *adj.* (*informal*) excellent; of the highest quality

ˌtop-of-the-'range *adj.* [usually before noun] used to describe the most expensive of a group of similar products: *Let me show you our top-of-the-range model*.

top·og·raphy /tə'pɒgrəfi; *AmE* tə'pɑːg-/ *noun* [U] (*technical*) the physical features of an area of land, especially the position of its rivers, mountains, etc.; the study of

T

b	d	f	g	h	k	l	m	n	p	r
bad	did	fall	get	hat	cat	leg	**man**	now	pen	red

these features: *a map showing the topography of the island* ▶ **topo·graph·ic·al** /ˌtɒpəˈɡræfɪkl; *AmE* ˌtɑːpə-/ *adj.*: *a topographical map/feature* **topo·graph·ic·al·ly** /-kli/ *adv.*

top·per /ˈtɒpə(r); *AmE* ˈtɑːp-/ *noun* (*informal*) = TOP HAT

top·ping /ˈtɒpɪŋ; *AmE* ˈtɑːp-/ *noun* [C, U] a layer of food that you put on top of a dish, cake, etc. to add flavour or to make it look nice: *baked vegetables with a cheese topping*—picture on page A1

top·ple /ˈtɒpl; *AmE* ˈtɑːpl/ *verb* **1** [+*adv. / prep.*] to become unsteady and fall down; to make sth do this: [V] *The pile of books toppled over.* ◇ [VN] *He brushed past, toppling her from her stool.* **2** [VN] to make sb lose their position of power or authority [SYN] OVERTHROW: *a plot to topple the President*

top-'ranking *adj.* [only before noun] of the highest rank, status or importance in an organization, a sport, etc: *top-ranking officials / players*

top-'rated *adj.* [only before noun] most popular with the public: *a top-rated TV show*

top 'secret *adj.* that must be kept completely secret, especially from other governments: *This information has been classified top secret.* ◇ *top-secret documents*

top·soil /ˈtɒpsɔɪl; *AmE* ˈtɑːp-/ *noun* [U] the layer of soil nearest the surface of the ground—compare SUBSOIL

top·spin /ˈtɒpspɪn; *AmE* ˈtɑːp-/ *noun* [U] (*sport*) the fast forward spinning movement that a player can give to a ball by hitting or throwing it in a special way

topsy-turvy /ˌtɒpsi ˈtɜːvi; *AmE* ˌtɑːpsi ˈtɜːrvi/ *adj.* (*informal*) in a state of great confusion: *Everything's topsy-turvy in my life at the moment.*

top 'table (*BrE*) (*AmE* **head 'table**) *noun* the table at which the most important guests sit at a formal dinner

the top 'ten *noun* [pl.] the ten pop records that have sold the most copies in a particular week

'top-up *noun* (*BrE*) **1** a sum of money that is added to what you already have in order to increase it to the amount that you need **2** an amount of a drink that you add to a cup or glass in order to fill it again: *Can I give anyone a top-up?*

tor /tɔː(r)/ *noun* a small hill with rocks at the top, especially in parts of SW England

Torah /ˈtɔːrɑː; tɔːˈrɑː/ *noun* (usually **the Torah**) (in Judaism) the law of God as given to Moses and recorded in the first five books of the Bible

torch /tɔːtʃ; *AmE* tɔːrtʃ/ *noun, verb*

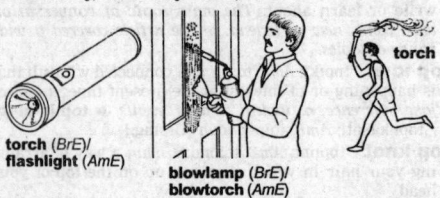

torch (*BrE*) / flashlight (*AmE*)

blowlamp (*BrE*) / blowtorch (*AmE*)

torch

■ *noun* **1** (*BrE*) (also **flash·light** *AmE, BrE*) a small electric lamp that uses batteries and that you can hold in your hand: *Shine the torch on the lock while I try to get the key in.* **2** (*AmE*) = BLOWLAMP **3** a long piece of wood that has material at one end that is set on fire and that people carry to give light: *a flaming torch* ◇ *the Olympic torch* ◇ (*figurative*) *They struggled to keep the torch of idealism and hope alive.* [IDM] **put sth to the 'torch** (*literary*) to set fire to sth deliberately—more at CARRY
■ *verb* [VN] to set fire to a building or vehicle deliberately in order to destroy it

torch·light /ˈtɔːtʃlaɪt; *AmE* ˈtɔːrtʃ-/ *noun* [U] the light that is produced by an electric torch or by burning torches

tore *pt* of TEAR

torea·dor /ˈtɒriədɔː(r); *AmE* ˈtɔːr-; ˈtɑːr-/ *noun* a man, especially one riding a horse, who fights BULLS to entertain people, for example in Spain

tor·ment *noun, verb*

■ *noun* /ˈtɔːment; *AmE* ˈtɔːrm-/ [U, C] (*written*) extreme suffering, especially mental suffering; a person or thing that causes this: *the cries of a man in torment* ◇ *She suffered years of mental torment after her son's death.* ◇ *The flies were a terrible torment.* ·
■ *verb* /tɔːˈment; *AmE* tɔːrˈm-/ [VN] **1** (*written*) to make sb suffer very much: *He was tormented by feelings of insecurity.* **2** to annoy a person or an animal in a cruel way because you think it is amusing

tor·ment·or /tɔːˈmentə(r); *AmE* tɔːrˈm-/ *noun* (*written*) a person who causes sb to suffer: *The dog suddenly turned on its tormentors.*

torn *pp* of TEAR

tor·nado /tɔːˈneɪdəʊ; *AmE* tɔːrˈneɪdoʊ/ *noun* (*pl.* **-oes** or **-os**) a violent storm with very strong winds which move in a circle. There is often also a long cloud which is narrower at the bottom than the top

tor·pedo /tɔːˈpiːdəʊ; *AmE* tɔːrˈpiːdoʊ/ *noun, verb*

■ *noun* (*pl.* **-oes**) a long narrow bomb that is fired under the water from a ship or SUBMARINE and that explodes when it hits a ship, etc.
■ *verb* (**tor·pe·does**, **tor·pe·do·ing**, **tor·pe·doed**, **tor·pe·doed**) [VN] **1** to attack a ship or make it sink using a torpedo **2** to completely destroy the possibility that sth could succeed: *Her comments had torpedoed the deal.*

tor·pid /ˈtɔːpɪd; *AmE* ˈtɔːrpɪd/ *adj.* (*formal*) not active; with no energy or enthusiasm [SYN] LETHARGIC

tor·por /ˈtɔːpə(r); *AmE* ˈtɔːrp-/ *noun* [U, sing.] (*formal*) the state of not being active and having no energy or enthusiasm: *In the heat they sank into a state of torpor.*

torque /tɔːk; *AmE* tɔːrk/ *noun* [U] (*technical*) a twisting force that causes machinery, etc. to ROTATE (= turn round): *The more torque an engine has, the bigger the load it can pull in the same gear.*

tor·rent /ˈtɒrənt; *AmE* ˈtɔːr-; ˈtɑːr-/ *noun* **1** a large amount of water moving very quickly: *After the winter rains, the stream becomes a raging torrent.* ◇ *The rain was coming down in torrents.* **2** a large amount of sth that comes suddenly and violently: *a torrent of abuse / criticism / words*

tor·ren·tial /təˈrenʃl/ *adj.* (of rain) falling in large amounts

tor·rid /ˈtɒrɪd; *AmE* ˈtɔːr-; ˈtɑːr-/ *adj.* [usually before noun] **1** full of strong emotions, especially connected with sex and love: *a torrid love affair* **2** (*formal*) (of a climate or country) very hot or dry: *a torrid summer* **3** (*BrE*) very difficult: *They face a torrid time in tonight's game.*

tor·sion /ˈtɔːʃn; *AmE* ˈtɔːrʃn/ *noun* [U] (*technical*) twisting, especially of one end of sth while the other end is held fixed

torso /ˈtɔːsəʊ; *AmE* ˈtɔːrsoʊ/ *noun* (*pl.* **-os**) **1** the main part of the body, not including the head, arms or legs [SYN] TRUNK **2** a statue of a torso

tort /tɔːt; *AmE* tɔːrt/ *noun* [C, U] (*law*) something wrong that sb does to sb else that is not criminal, but that can lead to action in a CIVIL court of law

tor·tilla /tɔːˈtiːə; *AmE* tɔːrˈt-/ *noun* (from *Spanish*) a thin Mexican PANCAKE made with eggs and corn flour, usually eaten hot and filled with meat, cheese, etc.

tor·toise /ˈtɔːtəs; *AmE* ˈtɔːrtəs/ *noun* a reptile with a hard round shell, that lives on land and moves very slowly. It can pull its head and legs into its shell.—compare TERRAPIN, TURTLE—picture on page A7

tor·toise·shell /ˈtɔːtəʃel; ˈtɔːtəʃl; *AmE* ˈtɔːrt-/ *noun* **1** [U] the hard shell of a TURTLE, especially the type with orange and brown marks, used for making combs and small ornaments **2** (*AmE* also **'calico cat**) [C] a cat with black, brown, orange and white fur **3** [C] a BUTTERFLY with orange and brown marks on its wings

tor·tu·ous /ˈtɔːtʃuəs; *AmE* ˈtɔːrtʃ-/ *adj.* [usually before noun] (*written*) **1** (usually *disapproving*) not simple and direct; long, complicated and difficult to understand: *tortuous language / laws* ◇ *the long, tortuous process of negotiating peace* **2** (of a road, path, etc.) full of bends: *a tortuous mountain track* ▶ **tor·tu·ous·ly** *adv.*

tor·ture /ˈtɔːtʃə(r); *AmE* ˈtɔːrtʃ-/ *noun, verb*

s	t	v	z	ʃ	ʒ	tʃ	dʒ	θ	ð	ŋ
see	tea	van	zoo	shoe	vision	chain	jam	thin	this	sing

■ *noun* [U, C] **1** the act of causing sb severe pain in order to punish them or make them say or do sth: *Many of the refugees have suffered torture.* ◊ *the use of torture* ◊ *terrible instruments of torture* ◊ *His confessions were made **under** torture.* ◊ *I heard stories of gruesome tortures in prisons.* **2** (*informal*) mental or physical suffering; sth that causes this: *The interview was sheer torture from start to finish.*

■ *verb* [VN] [often passive] **1** to hurt sb physically or mentally in order to punish them or make them tell you sth: *Many of the rebels were captured and tortured by secret police.* ◊ *He was tortured into giving them the information.* **2** to make sb feel extremely unhappy or anxious SYN TORMENT: *He spent his life tortured by the memories of his childhood.* ▶ **tor·tur·er** /ˈtɔːtʃərə(r); *AmE* ˈtɔːrtʃ-/ *noun*

tor·tured /ˈtɔːtʃəd; *AmE* ˈtɔːrtʃərd/ *adj.* [only before noun] suffering severely; involving a lot of suffering and difficulty: *a tortured mind*

Tory /ˈtɔːri/ *noun*, (*pl.* **-ies**) (*informal*) a member of the British Conservative party: *The Tories* (= the Tory party) *lost the election.* ▶ **Tory** *adj.* [usually before noun]: *the Tory party* ◊ *Tory policies* **Tory·ism** *noun* [U]

tosh /tɒʃ; *AmE* tɑːʃ/ *noun* [U] (*old-fashioned, BrE, slang*) nonsense

toss /tɒs; *AmE* tɔːs/ *verb, noun*
■ *verb*
THROW | **1** to throw sth lightly or carelessly:[VN, +*adv.*/ *prep.*] *I tossed the book aside and got up.* ◊ [VN+*adv.*/*prep.*, VNN] *He tossed the ball to Anna.* ◊ *He tossed Anna the ball.*
YOUR HEAD | **2** [VN] to move your head suddenly upwards, especially to show that you are annoyed or impatient: *She just tossed her head and walked off.*
SIDE TO SIDE/UP AND DOWN | **3** to move or make sb/sth move from side to side or up and down: [V] *Branches were tossing in the wind.* ◊ *I couldn't sleep but kept **tossing and turning** in bed all night.* ◊ [VN] *Our boat was being tossed by the huge waves.*
IN COOKING | **4** [VN] to shake or turn food in order to cover it with oil, butter, etc: *Drain the pasta and toss it in melted butter.* **5** [VN] **~ a pancake** (*BrE*) to throw a PANCAKE upwards so that it turns over in the air and you can fry the other side
COIN | **6 ~** (**sb**) **for sth** (*especially BrE*) (*BrE also* **toss up (for sth**)) to throw a coin in the air in order to decide sth, especially by guessing which side is facing upwards when it lands SYN FLIP: [VN] *There's one ticket left— I'll toss you for it.* ◊ *Let's toss a coin.* ◊ [V] *We tossed up to see who went first.* ◊ (*figurative*) *He had to toss up between* (= decide between) *paying the rent or buying food.*—related noun TOSS-UP
PHRV ,**toss 'off** | ,**toss sb/yourself 'off** (*BrE*, ⚠, *slang*) to give yourself sexual pleasure by rubbing your sex organs; to give sb sexual pleasure by rubbing their sex organs SYN MASTURBATE ,**toss sth↔'off** (*BrE*) to produce sth quickly and without much thought or effort: *I tossed off my article in half an hour.*
■ *noun* [usually sing.]
OF COIN | **1** an act of throwing a coin in the air to decide sth: *The final result was decided on/by the toss of a coin.* ◊ *to win/lose the toss* (= to guess correctly/wrongly which side of a coin will face upwards when it lands on the ground after it has been thrown in the air)
OF HEAD | (*slang*) **2 ~ of your head** an act of moving your head suddenly upwards, especially to show that you are annoyed or impatient: *She dismissed the question with a toss of her head.*
THROW | **3** an act of throwing sth, especially in a competition or game: *a toss of 10 metres*
IDM **not give a 'toss (about sb/sth)** (*BrE, slang*) to not care at all about sb/sth—more at ARGUE

toss·er /ˈtɒsə(r); *AmE* ˈtɔːs-/ *noun* (*BrE, slang*) a stupid or unpleasant person

ˈtoss-up *noun* [sing.] (*informal*) a situation in which either of two choices, results, etc. is equally possible: *'Have you decided on the colour yet?' 'It's a toss-up between the blue and the green.'*

tot /tɒt; *AmE* tɑːt/ *noun, verb*

■ *noun* **1** (*informal*) a very young child: *TV programmes for tiny tots* **2** (*especially BrE*) a small amount of a strong alcoholic drink in a glass: *a tot of whisky*
■ *verb* (**-tt-**) PHRV ,**tot sth↔'up** (*informal, especially BrE*) to add together several numbers or amounts in order to calculate the total: *The trip isn't really that cheap when you tot everything up.*

total /ˈtəʊtl; *AmE* ˈtoʊtl/ *adj., noun, verb*
■ *adj.* [usually before noun] **1** being the amount or number after everyone or everything is counted or added together: *the total profit* ◊ *This brought the total number of accidents so far this year to 113.* ◊ *The club has a total membership of about 300.* **2** complete; including everything: *The room was in total darkness.* ◊ *They demanded a total ban on handguns.* ◊ *The evening was a total disaster!* ◊ *I can't believe you'd tell a total stranger about it!*
■ *noun* the amount you get when you add several numbers or amounts together; the final number of people or things when they have all been counted: *You got 47 points on the written examination and 18 on the oral, making a total of 65.* ◊ *His businesses are worth a combined total of $3 billion.* ◊ *Out of a total of 15 games, they only won 2.* ◊ *The repairs came to over £500 **in total*** (= including everything).—see also GRAND TOTAL, RUNNING TOTAL, SUM TOTAL
■ *verb* (**-ll-**, *AmE also* **-l-**) **1** [V-N] to reach a particular total: *Imports totalled $1.5 billion last year.* **2** [VN] **~ sth/sb up** to add up the numbers of sth/sb and get a total: *Each student's points were totalled and entered in a list.* **3** [VN] (*informal, especially AmE*) to damage a car very badly, so that is not worth repairing it—see also WRITE STH OFF

to·tali·tar·ian /təʊˌtæləˈteəriən; *AmE* toʊˌtæləˈter-/ *adj.* (*disapproving*) (of a country or system of government) in which there is only one political party that has complete power and control over the people: *a totalitarian state/ regime* ▶ **to·tali·tar·ian·ism** /-ɪzəm/ *noun* [U]

to·tal·ity /təʊˈtæləti; *AmE* toʊ-/ *noun* [C, U] (*formal*) the state of being complete or whole; the whole number or amount: *The seriousness of the situation is difficult to appreciate **in its totality**.*

tot·al·ly /ˈtəʊtəli; *AmE* ˈtoʊ-/ *adv.* completely: *They come from totally different cultures.* ◊ *I'm still not totally convinced that he knows what he's doing.* ◊ *This behaviour is totally unacceptable.* ◊ (*AmE, spoken*) *'She's so cute!' 'Totally!'* (= I agree) ◊ (*AmE, spoken*) *It's a totally awesome experience.*

tote /təʊt; *AmE* toʊt/ *noun, verb*
■ *noun* **1** (also **the Tote**) [sing.] a system of betting on horses in which the total amount of money that is bet on each race is divided among the people who bet on the winners **2** (also **'tote bag**) [C] (*AmE*) a large bag for carrying things with you
■ *verb* [VN] (*informal, especially AmE*) **1** to carry sth, especially sth heavy: *We arrived, toting our bags and suitcases.* **2** (**-toting**) (in adjectives) carrying the thing mentioned: *gun-toting soldiers*

totem /ˈtəʊtəm; *AmE* ˈtoʊ-/ *noun* an animal or other natural object that is chosen and respected as a special symbol of a tribe or family, especially among Native Americans; an image of this animal, etc. ▶ **to·tem·ic** /təʊˈtemɪk; *AmE* toʊ-/ *adj.*: *totemic animals* ◊ *a totemic culture/religion*

ˈtotem pole *noun* **1** a tall wooden pole that has symbols and pictures (called TOTEMS) carved or painted on it, traditionally made by Native Americans **2** (*AmE, informal*) a range of different levels or ranks in an organization, etc: *I didn't want to be **low man on the totem pole** for ever.*

t'other /ˈtʌðə(r)/ *adj., pron.* (*BrE, dialect*) the other: *I saw it t'other day.* ◊ *They were talking of this, that and t'other.*

toto ⇨ IN TOTO

tot·ter /ˈtɒtə(r); *AmE* ˈtɑːt-/ *verb* [V] **1** [usually +*adv.*/ *prep.*] to walk or move with weak unsteady steps, especially because you are drunk or ill/sick: *She managed to totter back to her seat.* **2** to be weak and seem likely to fall: *the tottering walls of the castle* ◊ (*figurative*) *a failed attempt to salvage a tottering dictatorship*

totty /ˈtɒti; *AmE* ˈtɑːti/ *noun* [U] (*BrE, slang*) sexually

T

æ	ɑː	e	ɜː	ə	ɪ	iː	i	ɒ	ɔː	ʌ	ʊ	u	uː
cat	father	ten	bird	about	sit	see	many	got	saw	cup	put	actual	too
								(BrE)					

attractive women (an expression used by men, and usually offensive to women)

tou·can /ˈtuːkæn/ *noun* a tropical American bird with bright feathers and a very large beak

touch /tʌtʃ/ *verb, noun*

■ *verb*

WITH HANDS/FINGERS | **1** [VN] to put your hands or fingers onto sb/sth: *Don't touch that plate—it's hot!* ◊ *Can you touch your toes (= bend and reach them with your hands)?* ◊ *I touched him lightly on the arm.* ◊ *(figurative) I must do some more work on that article—I haven't touched it all week.*

NO SPACE BETWEEN | **2** (of two or more things, surfaces, etc.) to be or come so close together that there is no space between: [V] *Make sure the wires don't touch.* ◊ [VN] *Don't let your coat touch the wet paint.* ◊ *His coat was so long it was almost touching the floor.*

MOVE STH/HIT SB | **3** [VN] (often in negative sentences) to move sth, especially in such a way that you damage it; to hit or harm sb: *I told you not to touch my things.* ◊ *He said I kicked him, but I never touched him!*

EAT/DRINK/USE | **4** [VN] (usually in negative sentences) to eat, drink or use sth: *You've hardly touched your food.* ◊ *He hasn't touched the money his aunt left him.*

AFFECT SB/STH | **5** to make sb feel upset or sympathetic: [VN] *Her story touched us all deeply.* ◊ *What he said really touched my heart.* [also VN to inf] **6** [VN] (*old-fashioned* or *formal*) to affect or concern sb/sth: *These are issues that touch us all.*

EQUAL SB | **7** [VN] (usually in negative sentences) to be as good as sb in skill, quality, etc: *No one can touch him when it comes to interior design.*

REACH LEVEL | **8** [VN] to reach a particular level, etc: *The speedometer was touching 90.*

BE INVOLVED WITH | **9** [VN] to become connected with or work with a situation or person: *Everything she touches turns to disaster.* ◊ *His last two movies have been complete flops and now no studio will touch him.*

OF SMILE | **10** [VN] to be seen on sb's face for a short time: *A smile touched the corners of his mouth.*

IDM **be touched with sth** to have a small amount of a particular quality: *His hair was touched with grey.* ◊ *Some of her poems are touched with real genius.* **not touch sb/sth with a ˈbargepole** (*BrE*) (*AmE* **not touch sb/sth with a ˈten-foot pole**) (*informal*) to refuse to get involved with sb/sth or in a particular situation **touch ˈbase (with sb)** (*informal*) to make contact with sb again **touch ˈbottom 1** to reach the ground at the bottom of an area of water **2** (*BrE*) to reach the worst possible state or condition: *Her career really touched bottom with that movie.* **ˌtouch ˈwood** (*BrE*) (*AmE* ˌknock on ˈwood) (*saying*) used when you have just mentioned some way in which you have been lucky in the past, to avoid bringing bad luck: *I've been driving for over 20 years and never had an accident—touch wood!*—more at CHORD, FORELOCK, HAIR, NERVE *n.*, RAW *n.*

PHRV **ˌtouch ˈdown 1** (of a plane, spacecraft, etc.) to land—related noun TOUCHDOWN **2** (in rugby) to score a TRY by putting the ball on the ground behind the other team's goal line—related noun TOUCHDOWN **ˌtouch sb for sth** (*informal*) to persuade sb to give or lend you sth, especially money **ˌtouch sth↔ˈoff** to make sth begin, especially a difficult or violent situation: *The blaze was touched off by lightning.* ◊ *Her comments touched off a wave of protests.* **ˈtouch on/upon sth** to mention or deal with a subject in only a few words, without going into detail: *In his speech he was only able to touch on a few aspects of the problem.* **ˌtouch sb↔ˈup** (*BrE, informal*) to touch sb sexually, usually in a way that is not expected or welcome **ˌtouch sth↔ˈup** to improve sth by changing or adding to it slightly: *She was busy touching up her make-up in the mirror.*

■ *noun*

SENSE | **1** [U] the sense that enables you to be aware of things and what they are like when you put your hands and fingers on them: *the sense of touch* ◊ *to read Braille by touch*

WITH HANDS/FINGERS | **2** [C, usually sing.] an act of putting your hands and fingers onto sb/sth: *The gentle touch of his hand on her shoulder made her jump.* ◊ *All this information is readily available at the touch of a button (= by simply pressing a button).* ◊ *This type of engraving requires a delicate touch.*

WAY STH FEELS | **3** [sing.] the way that sth feels when you put your hand or fingers on it or when it comes into contact with your body: *The body was cold to the touch.* ◊ *material with a smooth silky touch* ◊ *He could not bear the touch of clothing on his sunburnt skin.*

SMALL DETAIL | **4** [C] a small detail that is added to sth in order to improve it or make it complete: *I spent the morning putting the finishing touches to the report.* ◊ *Meeting them at the airport was a nice touch.*

WAY OF DOING STH | **5** [sing.] a way or style of doing sth: *She prefers to answer any fan mail herself for a more personal touch.* ◊ *Computer graphics will give your presentation the professional touch.* ◊ *He couldn't find his magic touch with the ball today (= he didn't play well).* ◊ *This meal is awful. I think I'm losing my touch (= my ability to do sth).*

SMALL AMOUNT | **6** [C, often sing.] **~ of sth** a very small amount SYN TRACE: *There was a touch of sarcasm in her voice.* ◊ *There could be a touch of frost tonight.*

SLIGHTLY | **7** (**a touch**) [sing.] slightly; a little: *The music was a touch too loud for my liking.*

IN FOOTBALL/RUGBY | **8** [U] the area outside the lines that mark the sides of the playing field: *He kicked the ball into touch.*

IDM **be, get, keep, etc. in ˈtouch (with sb)** to communicate with sb, especially by writing to them or telephoning them: *Are you still in touch with your friends from college?* ◊ *Thanks for showing us your products—we'll be in touch.* ◊ *I'm trying to get in touch with Jane. Do you have her number?* ◊ *Let's keep in touch.* ◊ *I'll put you in touch with someone in your area.* **be, keep, etc. in ˈtouch (with sth)** to know what is happening in a particular subject or area: *It is important to keep in touch with the latest research.* **be out of ˈtouch (with sb)** to no longer communicate with sb, so that you no longer know what is happening to them **be, become, etc. out of ˈtouch (with sth)** to not know or understand what is happening in a particular subject or area: *Unfortunately, the people making the decisions are out of touch with the real world.* **an easy/a soft ˈtouch** (*informal*) a person that you can easily persuade to do sth, especially to give you money: *Unfortunately, my father is no soft touch.* **lose ˈtouch (with sb/sth) 1** to no longer have any contact with sb/sth: *I've lost touch with all my old friends.* **2** to no longer understand sth, especially how ordinary people feel—more at COMMON *adj.*, LIGHT *adj.*

ˌtouch-and-ˈgo *adj.* [not usually before noun] (*informal*) used to say that the result of a situation is uncertain and that there is a possibility that sth bad or unpleasant will happen: *She's fine now, but it was touch-and-go for a while (= there was a possibility that she might die).*

touch·down /ˈtʌtʃdaʊn/ *noun* **1** [C, U] the moment when a plane or spacecraft lands SYN LANDING **2** [C] (in rugby) an act of scoring points by putting the ball down on the area of ground behind the other team's GOAL LINE **3** [C] (in American football) an act of scoring points by crossing the other team's GOAL LINE while carrying the ball, or receiving the ball when you are over the other team's GOAL LINE

tou·ché /ˈtuːʃeɪ; *AmE* tuːˈʃeɪ/ *exclamation* (from *French*) used during an argument or a discussion to show that you accept that sb has answered your comment in a clever way and has gained an advantage by making a good point

touched /tʌtʃt/ *adj.* [not before noun] **1 ~ (by sth)** | **~ (that …)** feeling happy and grateful because of sth kind that sb has done; feeling emotional about sth: *She was touched by their warm welcome.* ◊ *I was touched that he still remembered me.* ◊ *She was touched by the plight of the refugees.* **2** (*old-fashioned, informal*) slightly crazy

,touch 'football *noun* [U] (*AmE*) a type of American football in which touching is used instead of TACKLING—compare FLAG FOOTBALL

touch·ing /'tʌtʃɪŋ/ *adj.* causing feelings of pity or sympathy; making you feel emotional: *It was a touching story that moved many of us to tears.* ◊ *I find his devotion to her rather touching.* ▶ **touch·ing·ly** *adv.*

touch·line /'tʌtʃlaɪn/ *noun* a line that marks the side of the playing field in football, rugby, etc.

touch·stone /'tʌtʃstəʊn; *AmE* -stoʊn/ *noun* [usually sing.] ~ (of/for sth) (*written*) something that provides a standard against which other things are compared and/or judged: *the touchstone for quality*

'Touch-Tone™ *adj.* (of a telephone or telephone system) producing different sounds when different numbers are pushed

'touch-type *verb* [V] to type without having to look at the keys of a TYPEWRITER or KEYBOARD

touchy /'tʌtʃi/ *adj.* (**touch·ier, touchi·est**) **1** [not usually before noun] ~ (about sth) (of a person) easily upset or offended [SYN] SENSITIVE: *He's a little touchy about his weight.* **2** [usually before noun] (of a subject) that may upset or offend people and should therefore be dealt with carefully [SYN] DELICATE, SENSITIVE ▶ **touchi·ness** *noun* [U]

,touchy-'feely *adj.* (*informal*, usually *disapproving*) expressing emotions too openly, especially through physical contact

tough /tʌf/ *adj., noun, verb*
■ *adj.* (**tough·er, tough·est**)
DIFFICULT | **1** having or causing problems or difficulties: *a tough childhood/match* ◊ *It was a tough decision to make.* ◊ *She's been having a tough time of it* (= a lot of problems) *lately.* ◊ *He faces the toughest test of his leadership so far.*
STRICT/FIRM | **2** ~ (on/with sb/sth) demanding that particular rules be obeyed and showing a lack of sympathy for any problems or suffering that this may cause: *Don't be too tough on him—he was only trying to help.* ◊ *It's about time teachers started to get tough with bullies.* ◊ *The school takes a tough line on* (= punishes severely) *cheating.* [OPP] SOFT
STRONG | **3** strong enough to deal successfully with difficult conditions or situations: *a tough breed of cattle* ◊ *He's not tough enough for a career in sales.* ◊ *She's a tough cookie/customer* (= sb who knows what they want and is not easily influenced by other people). **4** (of a person) physically strong and likely to be violent: *You think you're so tough, don't you?* ◊ *He plays the tough guy in the movie.*
MEAT | **5** difficult to cut or chew [OPP] TENDER
NOT EASILY DAMAGED | **6** not easily cut, broken, torn, etc: *a tough pair of shoes* ◊ *The reptile's skin is tough and scaly.*
UNFORTUNATE | **7** ~ (on sb) (*informal*) unfortunate for sb in a way that seems unfair: *It was tough on her being dropped from the team like that.* ◊ (*ironic*) *'I can't get it finished in time.' 'Tough!'* (= I don't feel sorry about it.)
▶ **tough·ly** *adv.* **tough·ness** *noun* [U]
[IDM] **(as) tough as old 'boots | (as) tough as 'nails** (*informal*) **1** very strong and able to deal successfully with difficult conditions or situations: *She's almost 90 but she's still as tough as old boots.* **2** not feeling or showing any emotion **tough 'luck** (*informal*) **1** (*BrE*) used to show sympathy for sth unfortunate that has happened to sb: *'I failed by one point.' 'That's tough luck.'* **2** (*ironic*) used to show that you do not feel sorry for sb who has a problem: *'If you take the car, I won't be able to go out.' 'Tough luck!'*—more at GOING *n.*, HANG *v.*, NUT *n.*, TALK *v.*
■ *noun* (*old-fashioned, informal*) a person who regularly uses violence against other people
■ *verb*
[PHRV] **,tough sth↔'out** to stay firm and determined in a difficult situation: *You're just going to have to tough it out.*

tough·en /'tʌfn/ *verb* ~ (sth/sb) (up) **1** to become or make sth stronger, so that it is not easily cut, broken, etc: [VN] *toughened glass* [also V] **2** [VN] to make sth such as laws or rules stricter: *The government is considering* toughening up the law on censorship. **3** [VN] to make sb stronger and more able to deal with difficult situations: *His parents sent him away to school to toughen him up.*

tou·pee /'tu:peɪ; *AmE* tu:'peɪ/ *noun* a small section of artificial hair, worn by a man to cover an area of his head where hair no longer grows

tour /tʊə(r); tɔ:(r); *AmE* tʊr/ *noun, verb*
■ *noun* **1** ~ (of/round/around sth) a journey made for pleasure during which several different towns, countries, etc. are visited: *a walking/sightseeing tour* ◊ *a coach tour of/around Northern France* ◊ *a tour operator* (= a person or company that organizes tours)—see also PACKAGE TOUR, WHISTLE-STOP **2** an act of walking around a town, building, etc. in order to visit it: *We were given a guided tour* (= by sb who knows about the place) *of the palace.* ◊ *a tour guide* ◊ *a tour of inspection* (= an official visit of a factory, classroom, etc. made by sb whose job is to check that everything is working as expected) **3** an official series of visits made to different places by a sports team, an orchestra, an important person, etc: *The band is currently on a nine-day tour of France.* ◊ *The band is on tour in France.* ◊ *a concert/cricket tour* ◊ *The Prince will visit Boston on the last leg* (= part) *of his American tour.* ◊ *The soldiers all do a six-month tour of duty in Northern Ireland.*
■ *verb* to travel around a place, for example to perform, to advertise sth, etc: [VN] *He toured America with his one-man show.* ◊ *She toured the country promoting her book.* ◊ [V] *We spent four weeks touring around Europe.*

tour de force /,tʊə də 'fɔ:s; *AmE* ,tʊr də 'fɔ:rs/ *noun* (*pl.* **tours de force** /,tʊə də 'fɔ:s; *AmE* ,tʊr də 'fɔ:rs/) (from French) an extremely skilful performance or achievement: *a literary/cinematic tour de force*

tour·ism /'tʊərɪzəm; 'tɔ:r-; *AmE* 'tʊr-/ *noun* [U] the business activity connected with providing accommodation, services and entertainment for people who are visiting a place for pleasure: *We hope that this investment will lead to increased tourism in the area.*

tour·ist /'tʊərɪst; 'tɔ:r-; *AmE* 'tʊr-/ *noun* **1** a person who is travelling or visiting a place for pleasure: *busloads of foreign tourists* ◊ *a popular tourist attraction/destination/resort* ◊ *the tourist industry/sector* ◊ *Further information is available from the local tourist office.* **2** (*BrE*) a member of a sports team that is playing a series of official games in a foreign country

'tourist class *noun* [U] the cheapest type of ticket or accommodation that is available on a plane or ship or in a hotel

'tourist trap *noun* (*informal, disapproving*) a place that attracts a lot of tourists and where food, drink, entertainment, etc. is more expensive than normal

tour·isty /'tʊəristi; 'tɔ:r-; *AmE* 'tʊr-/ *adj.* (*informal, disapproving*) attracting or designed to attract a lot of tourists: *Bali is the most touristy of the islands.* ◊ *a shop full of touristy souvenirs*

tour·na·ment /'tʊənəmənt; 'tɔ:n-; 'tɜ:n-; *AmE* 'tʊrn-; 'tɜ:rn-/ *noun* **1** (*AmE less frequent* **tour·ney**) a sports competition involving a number of teams or players who take part in different games and must leave the competition if they lose. The competition continues until there is only the winner left: *a golf/squash/tennis tournament* **2** a competition in the Middle Ages between soldiers on HORSEBACK fighting to show courage and skill: *a medieval jousting tournament*

tour·ney /'tʊəni; 'tɜ:ni; *AmE* 'tʊrni; 'tɜ:rni/ *noun* (*AmE*) = TOURNAMENT (1)

tour·ni·quet /'tʊənɪkeɪ; *AmE* 'tɜ:rnəkət/ *noun* a piece of fabric, etc. that is tied tightly around an arm or a leg to stop a wound from bleeding

tou·sle /'taʊzl/ *verb* [VN] [usually passive] to make sb's hair untidy ▶ **tou·sled** *adj.*: *a boy with blue eyes and tousled hair*

tout /taʊt/ *verb, noun*
■ *verb* **1** [VN] ~ sb/sth (as sth) to try to persuade people that sb/sth is important or valuable by praising them/it: *She's being touted as the next leader of the party.* **2** ~ (for sth) (*especially BrE*) to try to persuade people to buy your

goods or services, especially by going to them and asking them directly: [V] *the problem of unlicensed taxi drivers touting for business at airports* ◇ [VN] *He's busy touting his client's latest book around London's literary agents.* **3** [V, VN] (*BrE*) (*AmE* **scalp**) to sell tickets that you have bought at one price at a higher price, especially outside a theatre, STADIUM, etc.

■ *noun* (also **'ticket tout**) (both *BrE*) (*AmE* **scalp·er**) a person who buys tickets for concerts, sports events, etc. and then sells them to other people at a higher price

tow /təʊ; *AmE* toʊ/ *verb, noun*
■ *verb* [VN] to pull a car or boat behind another vehicle, using a rope or chain: *Our car was towed away by the police.*—see also TOW BAR, TOW ROPE
■ *noun* [sing.] an act of one vehicle pulling another vehicle using a rope or chain: *The car broke down and we had to get somebody to give us a tow.* ◇ *a tow truck* **IDM** **in tow 1** (*informal*) if you have sb **in tow**, they are with you and following closely behind: *She turned up with her mother in tow.* **2** if a ship is taken **in tow**, it is pulled by another ship

to·wards /təˈwɔːdz; *AmE* tɔːrdz/ (also **to·ward** /təˈwɔːd; *AmE* tɔːrd/ especially in *AmE*) *prep.* **1** in the direction of sb/sth: *They were heading towards the German border.* ◇ *She had her back towards me.* **2** getting closer to achieving sth: *This is a first step towards political union.* **3** close or closer to a point in time: *towards the end of April* **4** in relation to sb/sth: *He was warm and tender towards her.* ◇ *our attitude towards death* **5** with the aim of obtaining sth, or helping sb to obtain sth: *The money will go towards a new school building* (= will help pay for it).

'tow bar *noun* a bar fixed to the back of a vehicle for TOWING (= pulling) another vehicle

towel /ˈtaʊəl/ *noun, verb*
■ *noun* a piece of fabric or paper used for drying things, especially your body: *Help yourself to a clean towel.* ◇ *a hand/bath towel* (= a small/large towel) ◇ *a beach towel* (= a large towel used for lying on in the sun) ◇ *a kitchen towel* (= a piece of paper from a roll that you use to wipe up liquid, etc. in the kitchen)—see also PAPER TOWEL, SANITARY TOWEL, TEA TOWEL **IDM** **throw in the 'towel** (*informal*) to admit that you have been defeated and stop trying
■ *verb* (-ll-, *AmE* also -l-) [VN] **~ yourself/sb/sth (down)** to dry yourself/sb/sth with a towel

tow·el·ling (*BrE*) (*AmE* **tow·el·ing**) /ˈtaʊəlɪŋ/ *noun* [U] a thick soft cotton fabric that absorbs liquids, used especially for making towels: *a towelling bathrobe*—picture on page A5

'towel rail (*BrE*) (*AmE* **'towel rack**) *noun* a bar or frame for hanging towels on in a bathroom

tower /ˈtaʊə(r)/ *noun, verb*
■ *noun* **1** a tall narrow building or part of a building, especially of a church or castle: *a clock/bell tower* ◇ *the Tower of London* ◇ *the Eiffel Tower*—picture at STEEPLE **2** (often in compounds) a tall structure used for sending television or radio signals: *a television tower* **3** (usually in compounds) a tall piece of furniture used for storing things: *a CD tower*—see also CONTROL TOWER, COOLING TOWER, IVORY TOWER, WATCHTOWER, WATER TOWER **IDM** **a ,tower of 'strength** a person that you can rely on to help, protect and comfort you when you are in trouble
■ *verb* **PHRV** **,tower 'over/a'bove sb/sth 1** to be much higher or taller than the people or things that are near: *The cliffs towered above them.* ◇ *He towered over all his classmates.* **2** to be much better than others in ability, quality, fame, etc: *She towers over other dancers of her generation.*

'tower block *noun* (*BrE*) a very tall block of flats/ apartments or offices

tower·ing /ˈtaʊərɪŋ/ *adj.* [only before noun] **1** extremely tall or high and therefore impressive: *towering cliffs* **2** of extremely high quality: *a towering performance* **3** (of emotions) extremely strong: *to be in a towering rage*

town /taʊn/ *noun* **1** [C, U] a place with many houses, shops/stores, etc. where people live and work. It is larger than a village but smaller than a city: *a university town* ◇

They live in a rough part of town. ◇ *The nearest town is ten miles away.* ◇ *We spent a month in the French town of Le Puy.* ◇ *When she retired, she moved back to her home town* (= to the town where she was born and spent her childhood).—see also SMALL-TOWN **HELP** You will find other compounds ending in **town** at their place in the alphabet. **2** (**the town**) [sing.] the people who live in a particular town: *I suppose the whole town is talking about it.* **3** [U] the area of a town where most of the shops/stores and businesses are: *Can you give me a lift into town?*—see also DOWNTOWN, MIDTOWN, OUT-OF-TOWN, UPTOWN **4** [U] (*especially AmE*) a particular town where sb lives and works or one that has just been referred to: *I'll be in town next week if you want to meet for a drink.* ◇ *He married a girl from out of town.*—see also OUT-OF-TOWN **5** [sing., U] life in towns or cities as opposed to life in the country: *Pollution is just one of the disadvantages of living in the town.* **IDM** **go to 'town (on sth)** (*informal*) to do sth with a lot of energy, enthusiasm, etc., especially by spending a lot of money **(out) on the 'town** (*informal*) visiting restaurants, clubs, theatres, etc. for entertainment, especially at night: *a night on the town* ◇ *How about going out on the town tonight?*—more at MAN *n.*, PAINT *v.*

,town 'centre *noun* (*BrE*) the main part of a town, where the shops/stores are—compare DOWNTOWN

,town 'crier (also **crier**) *noun* (in the past) a person whose job was to walk through a town shouting news, official ANNOUNCEMENTS, etc.

townee *noun* = TOWNIE

,town 'hall *noun* a building containing local government offices and, in Britain, usually a hall for public meetings, concerts, etc.

'town house *noun* **1** (*BrE*) a house in a town owned by sb who also has a house in the country: *the Earl of Derby's town house* **2** (*BrE*) a tall narrow house in a town that is part of a row of similar houses: *an elegant Georgian town house* **3** (usually **'townhouse**) (*AmE*) = TERRACED HOUSE

townie (also **townee**) /ˈtaʊni/ *noun* (*disapproving*) **1** a person who lives in or comes from a town or city, especially sb who does not know much about life in the countryside **2** (*AmE*) a person who lives in a town with a college or university but does not attend or work at it

,town 'planner *noun* = PLANNER

,town 'planning (also **plan·ning**) *noun* [U] the control of the growth and development of towns and their buildings, roads, etc. so that they can be pleasant and convenient places for people to live in; the subject that studies this

town·scape /ˈtaʊnskeɪp/ *noun* **1** what you see when you look at a town, for example from a distance: *a historical/industrial townscape* **2** (*technical*) a picture of a town—compare LANDSCAPE, SEASCAPE

town·ship /ˈtaʊnʃɪp/ *noun* **1** (in South Africa in the past) a town or part of a town that black people had to live in, and where only black people lived **2** (in the US or Canada) a division of a county that is a unit of local government

towns·people /ˈtaʊnzpiːpl/ (also **towns·folk** /ˈtaʊnsfəʊk; *AmE* -foʊk/) *noun* [pl.] people who live in towns, not in the countryside; the people who live in a particular town

tow·path /ˈtəʊpɑːθ; *AmE* ˈtoʊpæθ/ *noun* a path along the bank of a river or canal, that was used in the past by horses pulling boats (called BARGES)

'tow rope *noun* a rope that is used for pulling sth along, especially a vehicle

'tow truck *noun* (*AmE*) = BREAKDOWN TRUCK

tox·ae·mia (*BrE*) (*AmE* **tox·emia**) /tɒkˈsiːmiə; *AmE* tɑːk-/ *noun* [U] (*medical*) infection of the blood by harmful bacteria **SYN** BLOOD POISONING

toxic /ˈtɒksɪk; *AmE* ˈtɑːk-/ *adj.* containing poison; poisonous: *toxic chemicals/fumes/gases/substances* ◇ *to dispose of toxic waste* ◇ *Many pesticides are highly toxic.*

tox·icity /tɒkˈsɪsəti; *AmE* tɑːk-/ *noun* (*pl.* -ies) (*technical*) **1** [U] the quality of being poisonous; the extent to which sth is poisonous: *substances with high/low levels of tox-icity* **2** [C] the effect that a poisonous substance has: *Minor toxicities of this drug include nausea and vomiting.*

toxi·col·ogy /ˌtɒksɪˈkɒlədʒi; *AmE* ˌtɑːk-/ *noun* [U] the scientific study of poisons ▶ **toxi·colo·gical** /ˌtɒksɪkəˈlɒdʒɪkl; *AmE* ˌtɑːksɪkəˈlɑːdʒɪkl/ *adj.* **toxi·colo·gist** /-dʒɪst/ *noun*

ˌtoxic ˈshock syndrome *noun* [U] a serious illness in women caused by harmful bacteria in the VAGINA, con-nected with the use of TAMPONS

toxin /ˈtɒksɪn; *AmE* ˈtɑːk-/ *noun* a poisonous substance, especially one that is produced by bacteria in plants and animals

toy /tɔɪ/ *noun, adj., verb*
■ *noun* **1** an object for children to play with: *cuddly/soft toys* ◊ *The children were playing happily with their toys.*—picture on page A8 **2** an object that you have for enjoy-ment or pleasure rather than for a serious purpose: *executive toys* ◊ *His latest toy is the electric drill he bought last week.*
■ *adj.* [only before noun] **1** made as a copy of a particular thing and used for playing with: *a toy car/telephone* ◊ *toy soldiers* **2** (of a dog) of a very small breed: *a toy poodle*
■ *verb* PHR V **ˈtoy with sth 1** to consider an idea or a plan, but not very seriously and not for a long time: *I did briefly toy with the idea of living in France.* **2** to play with sth and move it around carelessly or without think-ing: *He kept toying nervously with his pen.* ◊ *She hardly ate a thing, just toyed with a piece of cheese on her plate.*

toy·boy /ˈtɔɪbɔɪ/ *noun* (*BrE, informal, humorous*) a woman's male lover who is much younger than she is

trace /treɪs/ *verb, noun*
■ *verb* [VN] **1** ~ **sb/sth** (**to sth**) to find or discover sb/sth by looking carefully for them/it: *We finally traced him to an address in Chicago.* ◊ *I have been unable to trace the letter you mentioned.* **2** ~ **sth** (**back**) (**to sth**) to find the origin or cause of sth: *She could trace her family tree back to the 16th century.* ◊ *The leak was eventually traced to a broken seal.* ◊ *The police traced the call* (= used special electronic equipment to find out who made the telephone call) *to her ex-husband's number.* **3** to describe a process or the devel-opment of sth: *Her book traces the town's history from Saxon times to the present day.* **4** ~ **sth** (**out**) to draw a line or lines on a surface: *She traced a line in the sand.* **5** to follow the shape or outline of sth: *He traced the route on the map.* ◊ *A tear traced a path down her cheek.* **6** to copy a map, drawing, etc. by drawing on transparent paper (= TRACING PAPER) placed over it
■ *noun* **1** [C, U] a mark, an object or a sign that shows that sb/sth existed or was present: *It's exciting to discover traces of earlier civilizations.* ◊ *Police searched the area but found no trace of the escaped prisoners.* ◊ *Years of living in England had eliminated all trace of her American accent.* ◊ *The ship had vanished without* (*a*) *trace.* **2** [C] ~ **of sth** a very small amount of sth: *The post-mortem revealed traces of poison in his stomach.* ◊ *She spoke without a trace of bitterness.* **3** [C] (*technical*) a line or pattern on paper or a screen that shows information that is found by a machine: *The trace showed a normal heart rhythm.* **4** [C, usually pl.] one of the two long pieces of leather that fasten a carriage or CART to the horse that pulls it IDM see KICK *v.*

trace·able /ˈtreɪsəbl/ *adj.* ~ (**to sb/sth**) if sth is trace-able, you can find out where it came from, where it has gone, when it began or what its cause was: *Most telephone calls are traceable.* ◊ *a tradition that is traceable back to the 15th century*

ˈtrace element *noun* **1** a chemical substance that is found in very small amounts **2** a chemical substance that living things, especially plants, need only in very small amounts to be able to grow well

tracer /ˈtreɪsə(r)/ *noun* **1** a bullet or SHELL (= a kind of bomb) that leaves a line of smoke or flame behind it **2** (*technical*) a RADIOACTIVE substance that can be seen in the human body and is used to find out what is happen-ing inside the body

tra·cery /ˈtreɪsəri/ *noun* (*pl.* **-ies**) **1** [U] (*technical*) a pat-tern of lines and curves in stone on the top part of some church windows **2** [U, C, usually sing.] (*literary*) an attractive pattern of lines and curves

trachea /trəˈkiːə; *AmE* ˈtreɪkiə/ *noun* (*pl.* **trach·eas** or **trach·eae** /-kiːiː/) (*anatomy*) the tube in the throat that carries air to the lungs SYN WINDPIPE—picture at BODY

trache·ot·omy /ˌtrækiˈɒtəmi; *AmE* ˌtreɪkiˈɑːt-/ *noun* (*pl.* **-ies**) (*medical*) a medical operation to cut a hole in sb's trachea so that they can breathe

tra·cing /ˈtreɪsɪŋ/ *noun* a copy of a map, drawing, etc. that you make by drawing on a piece of transparent paper placed on top of it

ˈtracing paper *noun* [U] strong transparent paper that is placed on top of a map, drawing, etc. so that you can follow the lines with a pen or pencil in order to make a copy of it

track /træk/ *noun, verb*
■ *noun*
ROUGH PATH | **1** [C] a rough path or road, usually one that has not been built but that has been made by people walking there: *a muddy track through the forest*—see also CART TRACK
MARKS ON GROUND | **2** [C, usually pl.] marks left by a person, an animal or a moving vehicle: *We followed the bear's tracks in the snow.* ◊ *There were two sets of fresh tyre tracks outside.*
FOR TRAIN | **3** [C, U] rails that a train moves along: *railway/ railroad tracks* ◊ *India has thousands of miles of track.* **4** [C] (*AmE*) a track with a number at a train station that a train arrives at or leaves from: *The train for Chicago is on track 9.* ⇨ note at PLATFORM
FOR RACES | **5** [C] a piece of ground with a special surface for people, cars, etc. to have races on: *a running track* ◊ *a Formula One Grand Prix track* (= for motor racing)—see also DIRT TRACK (2), TRACK AND FIELD
DIRECTION/COURSE | **6** [C] the path or direction that sb/sth is moving in: *Police are on the track of* (= searching for) *the thieves.* ◊ *She is on the fast track to promotion* (= will get it quickly).—see also ONE-TRACK MIND
ON TAPE/CD | **7** [C] a piece of music or song on a record, tape or CD: *a track from their latest album* **8** [C] part of a tape or computer disk that music or information can be recorded on: *a sixteen track recording studio* ◊ *She sang on the backing track.*—see also SOUNDTRACK
FOR CURTAIN | **9** [C] a pole or rail that a curtain moves along
ON LARGE VEHICLE | **10** [C] a continuous belt of metal plates around the wheels of a large vehicle such as a BULLDOZER that allows it to move over the ground
IDM **ˌback on ˈtrack** going in the right direction again after a mistake, failure, etc: *I tried to get my life back on track after my divorce.* **be ˌon ˈtrack** to be doing the right thing in order to achieve a particular result: *Curtis is on track for the gold medal.* **keep/lose track of sb/sth** to have/not have information about what is happening or where sb/sth is: *Bank statements help you keep track of where your money is going.* ◊ *I lost all track of time* (= forgot what time it was). **make ˈtracks** (*spoken*) to leave a place, especially to go home: *It's getting late—I'd better make tracks.* **on the right/wrong ˈtrack** thinking or behaving in the right/wrong way: *We haven't found a cure yet—but we are on the right track.* **stop/halt sb in their ˈtracks | stop/halt/freeze in your ˈtracks** to suddenly make sb stop by frightening or surprising them; to suddenly stop because sth has frightened or surprised you: *The question stopped Alice in her tracks.* ◊ *The horse stopped dead in its tracks and refused to move.*—more at BEAT *v.*, COVER *v.*, HOT *adj.*, WRONG *adj.*
■ *verb*
FOLLOW | **1** to find sb/sth by following the marks, signs, information, etc., that they have left behind them: [VN] *hunters tracking and shooting bears* [also V] **2** to follow the movements of sb/sth, especially by using special electronic equipment: [VN] *We continued tracking the plane on our radar.* [also V wh-] **3** to follow the progress or development of sb/sth: [VN] *The research project involves*

æ	ɑː	e	ɜː	ə	ɪ	iː	i	ɒ	ɔː	ʌ	ʊ	u	uː
cat	father	ten	bird	about	sit	see	many	got	saw	cup	put	actual	too
								(BrE)					

tracking the careers of 400 law school graduates.
[also V wh-]

OF CAMERA | **4** [V+*adv./prep.*] to move in relation to the thing that is being filmed: *The camera eventually tracked away.*

SCHOOL STUDENTS | **5** [VN] (*AmE*) = STREAM (4)

LEAVE MARKS | **6** [VN] (*especially AmE*) to leave dirty marks behind you as you walk: *Don't track mud on my clean floor.*

PHRV ˌtrack sb/sth↔ˈdown to find sb/sth after searching in several different places: *The police have so far failed to track down the attacker.* ◇ *I finally tracked the reference down in a book of quotations.*

ˌtrack and ˈfield *noun* (*AmE*) = ATHLETICS (1)

track·er /ˈtrækə(r)/ *noun* a person who can find people or wild animals by following the marks that they leave on the ground

ˈtracker dog *noun* a dog that has been trained to help the police find people or explosives

ˈtrack event *noun* [usually pl.] a sports event that is a race run on a track, rather than jumping or throwing sth—compare FIELD EVENT—picture on page 1251

ˈtracking station *noun* a place where people follow the movements of aircraft, etc. in the sky by RADAR or radio

ˈtrack·less trol·ley *noun* (*AmE*) = TROLLEYBUS

ˈtrack record *noun* [sing.] all the past achievements, successes or failures of a person or an organization: *He has a proven track record in marketing.*

track·suit /ˈtræksuːt; *BrE* also -sjuːt/ (also **ˈjogging suit**) *noun* (*BrE*) a warm loose pair of trousers/pants and matching jacket worn for sports practice or as informal clothes—compare SHELL SUIT—picture on page A5

tract /trækt/ *noun* **1** (*technical*) a system of organs or tubes in the body that are connected and that have a particular purpose: *the digestive/urinary tract* **2** an area of land, especially a large one: *vast tracts of forest* **3** (sometimes *disapproving*) a short piece of writing, especially on a religious, moral or political subject, that is intended to influence people's ideas

tract·able /ˈtræktəbl/ *adj.* (*formal*) easy to deal with or control: *This approach helps to make the issues more tractable.* OPP INTRACTABLE ▶ **tract·abil·ity** /ˌtræktə-ˈbɪləti/ *noun* [U]

ˈtract house (also **ˈtract home**) *noun* (*AmE*) a modern house built on an area of land where a lot of other similar houses have also been built

trac·tion /ˈtrækʃn/ *noun* [U] **1** the action of pulling sth along a surface; the power that is used for doing this: *diesel/electric/steam traction* **2** a way of treating a broken bone in your body that involves using special equipment to pull the bone gradually back into its correct place: *He spent six weeks in traction after he broke his leg.* **3** the force that stops sth, for example the wheels of a vehicle, from sliding on the ground

ˈtraction engine *noun* a vehicle, driven by steam or DIESEL oil, used in the past for pulling heavy loads

trac·tor /ˈtræktə(r)/ *noun* **1** a powerful motor vehicle with two large and two smaller wheels, used especially for pulling farm machinery **2** (*AmE*) the front part of a tractor-trailer, where the driver sits

ˈtractor-trailer *noun* (*AmE*) a large lorry/truck with two sections, one in front where the driver sits and one behind for carrying goods. The sections are connected by a FLEXIBLE joint so that the tractor-trailer can turn corners more easily.—see also ARTICULATED—picture at TRUCK

trad /træd/ (also *less frequent* **ˈtrad jazz**) (both *BrE*) *noun* [U] traditional jazz in the style of the 1920s, with free playing (= IMPROVISATION) against a background of fixed rhythms and combinations of notes—see also DIXIELAND

trad·able (also **trade·able**) /ˈtreɪdəbl/ *adj.* (*technical*) that you can easily buy and sell or exchange for money or goods SYN MARKETABLE

trade /treɪd/ *noun, verb*

▪ *noun* **1** [U] the activity of buying and selling or of exchanging goods or services between people or countries: *inter-national/foreign trade* ◇ *Trade between the two countries has increased.* ◇ *the international trade in oil* ◇ *the arms trade*—see also BALANCE OF TRADE, FREE TRADE **2** [C] a particular type of business: *the building/food/tourist trade* ◇ *He works in the retail trade* (= selling goods in shops/stores).—see also RAG TRADE **3** **(the trade)** [sing.+ sing./pl. *v.*] a particular area of business and the people or companies that are connected with it: *They offer discounts to the trade* (= to people who are working in the same business). ◇ *a trade magazine/journal*—see also STOCK-IN-TRADE **4** [U, C] the amount of goods or services that you sell: *Trade was very good last month.* **5** [U, C] a job, especially one that involves working with your hands and that requires special training and skills: *He was a carpenter by trade.* IDM see JACK *n.*, PLY *v.*, ROARING, TRICK *n.*

▪ *verb* **1** ~ (in sth) (with sb) to buy and sell things: [V] *The firm openly traded in arms.* ◇ *Early explorers traded directly with the Indians.* ◇ *trading partners* (= countries that you trade with) ◇ [VN] *Our products are now traded worldwide.* **2** [V] ~ (as sb/sth) to exist and operate as a business or company: *The firm has now ceased trading.* ◇ *They traded as 'Walker and Son'.* **3** to be bought and sold, or to buy and sell sth, on a STOCK EXCHANGE: [V] *Shares were trading at under half their usual value.* [also VN] **4** to exchange sth that you have for sth that sb else has: [VN] *to trade secrets/insults/jokes* ◇ *She traded her posters for his CD.* ◇ *I wouldn't mind trading places with her for a day.* [also VNN] PHRV **ˈtrade at sth** (*AmE*) to buy goods or shop at a particular store ˌtrade ˈdown to spend less money on things than you used to: *Shoppers are trading down and looking for bargains.* ˌtrade sth↔ˈin (to sth) to give sth used as part of the payment for sth new: *He traded in his old car for a new Mercedes.*—related noun TRADE-IN ˌtrade sth↔ˈoff (against/for sth) to balance two things or situations that are opposed to each other: *They were attempting to trade off inflation against unemployment.*—related noun TRADE-OFF **ˈtrade on sth** (*disapproving*) to use sth to your own advantage, especially in an unfair way: *They trade on people's insecurity to sell them insurance.* ˌtrade ˈup (for sth) **1** to sell sth in order to buy sth more expensive: *We're going to trade up to a larger house.* **2** to give sth you have used as part of the payment for sth more expensive

ˈtrade balance *noun* = BALANCE OF TRADE

ˈtrade deficit (also **ˈtrade gap**) *noun* [usually sing.] the difference between the value of a country's imports and the value of its exports: *a widening/worsening trade deficit*

ˈtrade fair (also **ˈtrade show**) *noun* an event at which many different companies show and sell their products

ˈtrade-in *noun* a method of buying sth by giving a used item as part of the payment for a new one; the used item itself: *the trade-in value of a car* ◇ *Do you have a trade-in?*—see also PART EXCHANGE

trade·mark /ˈtreɪdmɑːk; *AmE* -mɑːrk/ *noun* (*abbr.* **TM**) **1** a name, symbol or design that a company uses for its products and that cannot be used by anyone else: *'Big Mac' is McDonald's best-known trademark.* **2** a special way of behaving or dressing that is typical of sb and that makes them easily recognized

ˈtrade name *noun* **1** = BRAND NAME: *Coffee is sold under a wide range of trade names.* **2** a name that is taken and used by a company for business purposes

ˈtrade-off *noun* ~ (between sth and sth) the act of balancing two things that you need or want but which are opposed to each other: *There is a trade-off between the benefits of the drug and the risk of side effects.*

trader /ˈtreɪdə(r)/ *noun* a person who buys and sells things as a job: *small/independent/local traders* ◇ *bond/currency traders*

ˈtrade school *noun* (*AmE*) a school where students go to learn a trade

ˌtrade ˈsecret *noun* a piece of information, for example about how a particular product is made, that is known only to the company that makes it

ˈtrade show *noun* = TRADE FAIR

trades·man /ˈtreɪdzmən/ *noun* (*pl.* **-men** /-mən/) **1** a person whose job involves going to people's houses to sell or deliver goods **2** (*especially BrE*) a person who buys and sells goods, especially in a shop/store [SYN] SHOPKEEPER **3** (*especially AmE*) a skilled person, especially one who makes beautiful things by hand

trades·people /ˈtreɪdzpiːpl/ *noun* [pl.] **1** people whose job involves selling goods or services, especially people who own a shop/store **2** people whose job involves training and special skills, for example CARPENTERS

the ˌTrades ˌUnion ˈCongress *noun* [sing.] = TUC

ˌtrade ˈsurplus *noun* a situation in which a country's exports are worth more than its imports

ˌtrade ˈunion (also **ˌtrades ˈunion**) (both *BrE*) (*AmE* **ˈlabor union**) (also **union** *BrE, AmE*) *noun* an organization of workers, usually in a particular industry, that exists to protect their interests, improve conditions of work, etc. ▶ **ˌtrade-ˈunionism** *noun* [U]: *the history of trade unionism*

ˌtrade ˈunionist (also **ˌtrades ˈunionist, union·ist**) *noun* a member of a trade union

ˈtrade wind *noun* a strong wind that blows all the time towards the EQUATOR and then to the west

trad·ing /ˈtreɪdɪŋ/ *noun* [U] the activity of buying and selling things: *new laws on Sunday trading* (= shops being open on Sundays) ◊ *Supermarkets everywhere reported excellent trading in the run-up to Christmas.* ◊ *Shares worth $8 million changed hands during a day of hectic trading.*

ˈtrading estate *noun* (*BrE*) an area of land, often on the edge of a city or town, where there are a number of businesses and small factories—compare INDUSTRIAL ESTATE

ˈtrading post *noun* a small place in an area that is a long way from any town, used as a centre for buying and selling goods (especially in N America in the past)

trad·ition /trəˈdɪʃn/ *noun* [C, U] a belief, custom or way of doing sth that has existed for a long time among a particular group of people; a set of these beliefs or customs: *religious/cultural/literary traditions* ◊ *This region is steeped in folklore and tradition.* ◊ *The company has a long tradition of fine design.* ◊ *The British are said to love tradition* (= to want to do things in the way they have always been done). ◊ *They broke with tradition* (= did things differently) *and got married quietly.* ◊ *By tradition, children play tricks on 1 April.* ◊ *There's a tradition in our family that we have a party on New Year's Eve.* ◊ *He's a politician in the tradition of* (= similar in style to) *Kennedy.*

trad·ition·al /trəˈdɪʃənl/ *adj.* **1** being part of the beliefs, customs or way of life of a particular group of people, that have not changed for a long time: *traditional dress/music* ◊ *It's traditional in America to eat turkey on Thanksgiving Day.* **2** (sometimes *disapproving*) following older methods and ideas rather than modern or different ones [SYN] CONVENTIONAL: *traditional methods of teaching* ◊ *Their marriage is very traditional.* ▶ **trad·ition·al·ly** /-ʃənəli/ *adv.*: *The festival is traditionally held in May.* ◊ *Housework has traditionally been regarded as women's work.*

trad·ition·al·ism /trəˈdɪʃənəlɪzəm/ *noun* [U] the belief that customs and traditions are more important than a society than modern ideas

trad·ition·al·ist /trəˈdɪʃənəlɪst/ *noun* a person who prefers tradition to modern ideas or ways of doing things ▶ **trad·ition·al·ist** *adj.*

ˈtrad jazz *noun* [U] = TRAD

tra·duce /trəˈdjuːs; *AmE* -ˈduːs/ *verb* [VN] (*rare, formal*) to say things about sb that are unpleasant or not true

traf·fic /ˈtræfɪk/ *noun, verb*

■ *noun* [U] **1** the vehicles that are on a road at a particular time: *heavy/rush-hour traffic* ◊ *local/through traffic* ◊ *There's always a lot of traffic at this time of day.* ◊ *They were stuck in traffic and missed their flight.* ◊ *a plan to reduce traffic congestion* ◊ *traffic police* (= who control traffic on a road or stop drivers who are breaking the law) **2** the movement of ships, trains, aircraft, etc. along a

particular route: *transatlantic traffic* ◊ *air traffic control/controllers* **3** the movement of people or goods from one place to another: *commuter/freight/passenger traffic* ◊ *the traffic of goods between one country and another* **4** ~ (**in sth**) illegal trade in sth: *the traffic in drugs/firearms*

■ *verb* (**-ck-**) [PHRV] **ˈtraffic in sth** to buy and sell sth illegally: *to traffic in drugs/arms* ▶ **traf·fick·er** *noun*: *a drugs trafficker* **traf·fick·ing** *noun* [U]: *to be accused of drug trafficking*

ˈtraffic calming *noun* [U] (*BrE*) ways of making roads safer, especially for people who are walking or riding bicycles, by building raised areas, etc. to make cars go more slowly

ˈtraffic circle *noun* (*AmE*) = ROUNDABOUT

ˈtraffic cone *noun* = CONE

ˈtraffic island (also **island, ref·uge**) (all *BrE*) (*AmE* **ˈsafety island**) *noun* **1** an area in the middle of a road where you can stand and wait for cars to go past until it is safe for you to cross **2** (*AmE*) an area of road with a raised surface, for example at a JUNCTION or between two LANES of traffic, that vehicles must not drive on

ˈtraffic jam *noun* a long line of vehicles on a road that cannot move or that can only move very slowly: *We were stuck in a traffic jam.*

ˈtraffic light *noun* [C] (also **ˈtraffic lights** [pl.]) (*AmE* also **stop-lights** [pl.]) a signal that controls the traffic on a road, by means of red, orange and green lights that show when you must stop and when you can go: *Turn left at the traffic lights.*

ˈtraffic warden *noun* (*BrE*) a person whose job is to check that people do not park their cars in the wrong place or for longer than is allowed, and to report on those who do or tell them that they have to pay a FINE

tra·gedian /trəˈdʒiːdiən/ *noun* (*formal*) **1** a person who writes tragedies for the theatre **2** an actor in tragedies

tra·gedy /ˈtrædʒədi/ *noun* [C, U] (*pl.* **-ies**) **1** a very sad event or situation, especially one that involves death: *It's a tragedy that she died so young.* ◊ *Tragedy struck the family when their three-year-old son was hit by a car and killed.* ◊ *The whole affair ended in tragedy.* **2** a serious play with a sad ending, especially one in which the main character dies; plays of this type: *Shakespeare's tragedies* ◊ *Greek tragedy*—compare COMEDY

tra·gic /ˈtrædʒɪk/ *adj.* **1** making you feel very sad, usually because sb has died or suffered a lot: *He was killed in a tragic accident at the age of 24.* ◊ *Cuts in the health service could have tragic consequences for patients.* ◊ *It would be tragic if her talent remained unrecognized.* **2** [only before noun] connected with tragedy (= the style of literature): *a tragic actor/hero* ▶ **tra·gic·al·ly** /-kli/ *adv.*: *Tragically, his wife was killed in a car accident.* ◊ *He died tragically young.*

tragi·com·edy /ˌtrædʒiˈkɒmədi; *AmE* -ˈkɑːm-/ *noun* [C, U] (*pl.* **-ies**) **1** a play that is both funny and sad; plays of this type **2** an event or a situation that is both funny and sad ▶ **tragi·com·ic** /-ˈkɒmɪk; *AmE* -ˈkɑːm-/ *adj.*

trail /treɪl/ *noun, verb*

■ *noun* **1** a long line or series of marks that is left by sth as it moves and that shows where it has been: *a trail of blood/footprints* ◊ *tourists who leave a trail of litter everywhere they go* ◊ *The hurricane left a a trail of destruction behind it.* **2** a track, sign or smell that is left behind and that can be followed, especially in hunting: *The hounds were following the fox's trail.* ◊ *The police are still on the trail of the escaped prisoner.* ◊ *Fortunately the trail was still warm* (= clear and easy to follow). ◊ *The trail had gone cold.* **3** a path through the countryside: *a trail through the forest*—see also NATURE TRAIL **4** a route that is followed for a particular purpose: *a tourist trail* (= of famous buildings) ◊ *politicians on the campaign trail* (= travelling around to attract support) [IDM] SEE BLAZE *v.*, HIT *v.*, HOT *adj.*

■ *verb* **1** to pull sth behind sb/sth, usually along the ground; to be pulled along in this way: [VN] *A jeep trailing a cloud of dust was speeding in my direction.* ◊ [V] [usually +adv./prep.] *The bride's dress trailed behind her.*

b	d	f	g	h	k	l	m	n	p	r
bad	did	fall	get	hat	cat	leg	man	now	pen	red

2 [V+*adv./prep.*] to walk slowly because you are tired or bored, especially behind sb else: *The kids trailed around after us while we shopped for clothes.* **3 ~ (by/in sth)** (used especially in the progressive tenses) to be losing a game or other contest: [V] *United were trailing 2–0 at half-time.* ◊ *We were trailing by five points.* ◊ *This country is still trailing badly in scientific research.* ◊ [VN] *The Conservatives are trailing Labour in the opinion polls.* **4** [VN] to follow sb/sth by looking for signs that show you where they have been: *The police trailed Dale for days.* **5** [V] (especially of plants) to grow or hang downwards over sth or along the ground: *trailing plants* ◊ *Computer wires were trailing all over the floor.* PHRV ,trail a'way/'off (of sb's speech) to become gradually quieter and then stop: *His voice trailed away to nothing.* ◊[+speech] *'I only hope…' She trailed off.*

trail·blazer /ˈtreɪlbleɪzə(r)/ *noun* a person who is the first to do or discover sth and so makes it possible for others to follow—compare BLAZE A TRAIL at BLAZE ▶ **trail·blaz·ing** *adj.* [usually before noun]: *trailblazing scientific research*

trail·er /ˈtreɪlə(r)/ *noun* **1** a truck, or a container with wheels, that is pulled by another vehicle: *a car towing a trailer with a boat on it*—see also TRACTOR-TRAILER **2** (*AmE*) a vehicle without an engine, that can be pulled by a car or truck or used as a home or an office when it is parked: *a trailer park* (= an area where trailers are parked and used as homes) **3** (*especially BrE*) a series of short scenes from a film/movie or television programme, shown in advance to advertise it

train /treɪn/ *noun, verb*
■ *noun* **1** a railway/railroad engine pulling a number of carriages or trucks, taking people and goods from one place to another: *to get on/off a train* ◊ *I like travelling by train.* ◊ *a passenger/commuter/goods/freight train* ◊ *to catch/take/get the next train to London* ◊ *a train journey/driver* ◊ *You have to change trains at Reading.*—see also GRAVY TRAIN **2** a number of people or animals moving in a line: *a camel train* ◊ *a wagon train* **3** [usually sing.] a series of events or actions that are connected: *His death set in motion a train of events that led to the outbreak of war.* **4** the part of a long formal dress that spreads out on the floor behind the person wearing it IDM **bring sth in its 'train** (*written*) to have sth as a result: *Unemployment brings great difficulties in its train.* **in sb's 'train** (*written*) following behind sb: *In the train of the rich and famous came the journalists.* **set sth in 'train** (*formal*) to prepare or start sth: *That telephone call set in train a whole series of events.* **a train of 'thought** the connected series of thoughts that are in your head at a particular time: *The phone ringing interrupted my train of thought.*
■ *verb* **1 ~ (sb) (as/in/for sth)** to teach a person or an animal the skills for a particular job or activity; to be taught in this way: [VN] *well/badly trained staff* ◊ *Steve can't get a job, he's not trained in anything.* ◊ [VN to inf] *They train dogs to sniff out drugs.* ◊ [V] *He trained as a teacher before becoming an actor.* ◊ *All members of the team have trained in first aid.* ◊ [V to inf] *Sue is training to be a doctor.* **2 ~ (sb) (for/in sth)** to prepare yourself/sb for a particular activity, especially a sport, by doing a lot of exercise; to prepare a person or an animal in this way: [V] *athletes training for the Olympics* ◊ [VN] *She trains horses.* ◊ *He trains the Olympic team.* **3** to develop a natural ability or quality so that it improves: [VN] *An expert with a trained eye will spot the difference immediately.* ◊ [VN to inf] *You can train your mind to think positively.* **4** [VN] **~ sth (around/along/up, etc.)** to make a plant grow in a particular direction: *Roses had been trained around the door.* PHRV **'train sth at/on sb/sth** (*written*) to aim a gun, camera, light, etc. at sb/sth: *He carefully trained his gun on the suspect.*

train·ee /ˌtreɪˈniː/ *noun* a person who is being taught how to do a particular job: *a management trainee* ◊ *a trainee salesman/teacher*

train·er /ˈtreɪnə(r)/ *noun* **1** (also **'training shoe**) (both *BrE*) (*AmE* **sneak·er**) [usually pl.] a shoe that you wear for sports or as a piece of informal clothing: *a pair of trainers*—picture at SHOE **2** a person who teaches people

or animals to perform a particular job or skill well, or to do a particular sport: *teacher trainers* ◊ *a racehorse trainer* ◊ *Her trainer had decided she shouldn't run in the race.*

train·ing /ˈtreɪnɪŋ/ *noun* [U] **1 ~ (in sth/in doing sth)** the process of learning the skills that you need to do a job: *staff training* ◊ *Few candidates had received any training in management.* ◊ *a training course* **2** the process of preparing to take part in a sports competition by doing physical exercises: *to be in training for a race*

'training college *noun* (*BrE*) a college that trains people for a job or profession: *a police training college*

'training shoe *noun* (*BrE*) = TRAINER

'training wheels *noun* [pl.] (*AmE*) = STABILIZERS

train·man /ˈtreɪnmən/ *noun* (*pl.* **-men** /-mən/) (*AmE*) a member of the team of people operating a train

'train set *noun* a toy train, together with the track that it runs on, toy station, etc.

train·spot·ter /ˈtreɪnspɒtə(r); *AmE* -spɑːt-/ *noun* (*BrE*) **1** a person who collects the numbers of railway engines as a hobby **2** (*disapproving*) a person who is interested in the details of a subject that other people think are boring ▶ **'train·spot·ting** *noun* [U]

traipse /treɪps/ *verb* [V+*adv./prep.*] (*informal*) to walk somewhere slowly when you are tired and unwilling: *We spent the afternoon traipsing around the town.*

trait /treɪt/ *noun* a particular quality in your personality: *personality traits*

trai·tor /ˈtreɪtə(r)/ *noun* **~ (to sb/sth)** a person who betrays their friends, their country, etc: *He was seen as a traitor to the socialist cause.* ◊ *She denied that she had turned traitor* (= become a traitor).

trai·tor·ous /ˈtreɪtərəs/ *adj.* (*rare, formal*) betraying your friends, your country, etc. ▶ **trai·tor·ous·ly** *adv.*

tra·jec·tory /trəˈdʒektəri/ *noun* (*pl.* **-ies**) (*technical*) the curved path of sth that has been fired, hit or thrown into the air: *a missile's trajectory* ◊ (*figurative, written*) *My career seemed to be on a downward trajectory.*

tram /træm/ (also **tram·car**) (both *BrE*) (*AmE* **street·car**, **trol·ley**) *noun* a vehicle driven by electricity, that runs on rails along the streets of a town and carries passengers: *a tram route/track/service/stop*

tram·lines /ˈtræmlaɪnz/ *noun* [pl.] **1** the rails in the street that trams run on **2** (*BrE*) (*AmE* **alley**) (*informal*) the pair of parallel lines on a tennis or badminton court that mark the extra area that is used when four people are playing

tram·mel /ˈtræml/ *verb* (**-ll-**, *AmE* **-l-**) [VN] [often passive] (*rare, formal*) to restrict or limit sb's freedom of movement or activity: *He felt himself trammelled by convention.*—compare UNTRAMMELLED

tramp /træmp/ *noun, verb*
■ *noun* **1** (also **hobo**) [C] a person with no home or job who travels from place to place, usually asking people in the street for food or money **2** [sing.] **the ~ of sb/sth** the sound of sb's heavy steps: *the tramp of marching feet* **3** [C, usually sing.] a long walk: *We had a long tramp home.* **4** (*old-fashioned, AmE, disapproving*) a woman who has many sexual partners
■ *verb* (also *AmE informal* **tromp**) to walk with heavy or noisy steps, especially for a long time: [V] *We tramped across the wet grass to look at the statue.* ◊ *the sound of tramping feet* ◊ [VN] *She's been tramping the streets looking for a job.*

tram·ple /ˈtræmpl/ *verb* **1 ~ sb/sth (down)** | **~ on/over sth** to step heavily on sb/sth so that you crush or harm them/it with your feet: [VN] *People were trampled underfoot in the rush for the exit.* ◊ *He was trampled to death* (= killed) *by a runaway horse.* ◊ *The campers had trampled the corn down.* ◊ [V] *Don't trample on the flowers!* **2 ~ (on/over) sb/sth** to ignore sb's feelings or rights and treat them as if they are not important: [V] *The government is trampling on the views of ordinary people.* [also VN]

tram·po·line /ˈtræmpəliːn/ *noun, verb*
■ *noun* a piece of equipment that is used in GYMNASTICS for doing jumps in the air. It consists of a sheet of strong material that is attached by springs to a frame.

s	t	v	z	ʃ	ʒ		tʃ	dʒ	θ	ð	ŋ
see	tea	van	zoo	shoe	vision		chain	jam	thin	this	sing

■ *verb* [V] to jump on a trampoline ▶ **tram·po·lin·ing** *noun* [U]

tram·way /ˈtræmweɪ/ *noun* the rails that form the route for a TRAM

trance /trɑːns; *AmE* træns/ *noun* **1** a state in which sb seems to be asleep but is aware of what is said to them, for example if they are HYPNOTIZED: *to go/fall into a trance* **2** a state in which you are thinking so much about sth that you do not notice what is happening around you: *She drove, gripping the wheel in a trance, hardly aware of her surroundings.*

tranche /trɑːnʃ/ *noun* (*BrE, finance*) one of the parts into which an amount of money or a number of SHARES in a company is divided

tran·quil /ˈtræŋkwɪl/ *adj.* (*written*) quiet and peaceful: *a tranquil scene/place* ◊ *the tranquil waters of the lake* ◊ *She lead a tranquil life in the country.* ▶ **tran·quil·lity** (*BrE*) (*AmE* also **tran·quil·ity**) /træŋˈkwɪləti/ *noun* [U] **tran·quil·ly** *adv.*

tran·quil·lize (*BrE* also **-ise**) (*AmE* **tran·quil·ize**) /ˈtræŋkwəlaɪz/ *verb* [VN] to make person or an animal calm or unconscious, especially by giving them a drug (= a TRANQUILLIZER): *a fast-acting tranquillizing drug*

tran·quil·lizer (*BrE* also **-iser**) /ˈtræŋkwəlaɪzə(r)/ *noun* a drug used to reduce anxiety: *She's on* (= is taking) *tranquillizers.*

trans- /trænz; træns/ *prefix* **1** (in adjectives) across; beyond: *transatlantic* ◊ *transcontinental* **2** (in verbs) into another place or state: *transplant* ◊ *transform*

trans·act /trænˈzækt/ *verb* ~ (**sth**) (**with sb**) (*formal*) to do business with a person or an organization: [VN] *buyers and sellers transacting business* [also V]

trans·ac·tion /trænˈzækʃn/ *noun* **1** [C] ~ (**between A and B**) a piece of business that is done between people, especially an act of buying or selling: *financial transactions between companies* ◊ *commercial transactions* **2** [U] ~ **of sth** (*formal*) the process of doing sth: *the transaction of government business*

trans·at·lan·tic /ˌtrænzətˈlæntɪk/ *adj.* [only before noun] **1** crossing the Atlantic Ocean: *a transatlantic flight* **2** connected with countries on both sides of the Atlantic Ocean: *a transatlantic alliance* **3** on or from the other side of the Atlantic Ocean: *to speak with a transatlantic accent* ◊ *transatlantic* (= American) *visitors to Europe*

trans·ceiver /trænˈsiːvə(r)/ *noun* a radio that can both send and receive messages

tran·scend /trænˈsend/ *verb* [VN] (*formal*) to be or go beyond the usual limits of sth

tran·scend·ent /trænˈsendənt/ *adj.* (*formal*) going beyond the usual limits; extremely great: *a writer of transcendent genius* ▶ **tran·scend·ence** /-dəns/ *noun* [U]: *the transcendence of God*

tran·scen·den·tal /ˌtrænsenˈdentl/ *adj.* [usually before noun] going beyond the limits of human knowledge, experience or reason, especially in a religious or spiritual way: *a transcendental experience*

transcen,dental medi'tation (*BrE*) (*AmE* **Transcendental Meditation**™) *noun* [U] (*abbr.* **TM**) a method of making yourself calm by thinking deeply in silence and repeating a special phrase to yourself many times

trans·con·tin·en·tal /ˌtrænzɪˌkɒntɪˈnentl; ˌtræns-; *AmE* -ˌkɑːn-/ *adj.* crossing a continent: *a transcontinental railway/railroad*

tran·scribe /trænˈskraɪb/ *verb* [VN] **1** ~ **sth** (**into sth**) to record thoughts, speech or data in a written form, or in a different written form from the original: *Clerks transcribe everything that is said in court.* ◊ *The interview was recorded and then transcribed.* ◊ *How many official documents have been transcribed into Braille for blind people?* **2** (*technical*) to show the sounds of speech using a special PHONETIC alphabet **3** ~ **sth** (**for sth**) to write a piece of music in a different form so that it can be played by another musical instrument or sung by another voice: *a piano piece transcribed for the guitar*

tran·script /ˈtrænskrɪpt/ *noun* **1** (also **tran·scrip·tion**)

a written or printed copy of words that have been spoken: *a transcript of the interview/speech/trial* **2** (*especially AmE*) an official record of a student's work that shows the courses they have taken and the marks/grades they have achieved

tran·scrip·tion /trænˈskrɪpʃn/ *noun* **1** [U] the act or process of representing sth in a written or printed form: *errors made in transcription* ◊ *phonetic transcription* **2** [C] = TRANSCRIPT: *The full transcription of the interview is attached.* **3** [C] something that is represented in writing: *This dictionary gives phonetic transcriptions of all headwords.* **4** [C] a change in the written form of a piece of music so that it can be played on a different instrument or sung by a different voice

trans·ducer /trænzˈdjuːsə(r); ˈtræns-; *AmE* -ˈduːsər/ *noun* (*technical*) a device for producing an electrical signal from another form of energy such as pressure

trans·ept /ˈtrænsept/ *noun* (*architecture*) either of the two wide parts of a church shaped like a cross, that are built at RIGHT ANGLES to the main central part—compare NAVE

trans·fer *verb, noun*
■ *verb* /trænsˈfɜː(r)/ (**-rr-**)
TO NEW PLACE | **1** ~ (**sth/sb**) (**from …**) (**to …**) to move from one place to another; to move sth/sb from one place to another: [V] *The film studio is transferring to Hollywood.* ◊ [VN] *How can I transfer money from my bank account to his?* ◊ *The patient was transferred to another hospital.* ◊ [VN, V] (*especially AmE*) *I couldn't transfer all my credits from junior college.* ◊ (*especially AmE*) *If I spend a semester in Madrid, will my credits transfer?*

TO NEW JOB/SCHOOL/SITUATION | **2** ~ (**sb**) (**from …**) (**to …**) to move from one job, school, situation, etc. to another; to arrange for sb to do this: [V] *Children usually transfer to secondary school at 11 or 12.* ◊ *He transferred to UCLA after his freshman year.* ◊ [VN] *Ten employees are being transferred from the sales department.*

FEELING/DISEASE/POWER | **3** if you **transfer** a feeling, a disease, or power, etc., or if it **transfers** from one person to another, the second person has it, often instead of the first: [VN] *Joe had already transferred his affections from Lisa to Cleo.* ◊ *This disease is rarely transferred from mother to baby* (= so that the baby has it as well as the mother). [also V]

PROPERTY | **4** [VN] ~ **sth** (**to sb**) to officially arrange for sth to belong to sb else or for sb else to control sth: *He transferred the property to his son.*

IN SPORT | **5** ~ (**sb**) (**from …**) (**to …**) (*especially BrE*) to move, or to move sb, to a different sports team, especially a professional football team: [V] *He transferred to Everton for £6 million.* ◊ [VN] *He was transferred from Spurs to Arsenal for a huge fee.*

TO NEW VEHICLE | **6** ~ (**sb**) (**from …**) (**to …**) to change to a different vehicle during a journey; to arrange for sb to change to a different vehicle during a journey: [V] *I transferred at Bahrain for a flight to Singapore.* ◊ [VN] *Passengers are transferred from the airport to the hotel by taxi.*

INFORMATION/MUSIC, etc. | **7** ~ (**sth**) (**from sth**) (**to sth**) to copy information, music, an idea, etc. from one method of recording or presenting it to another; to be recorded or presented in a different way: [VN] *You can transfer data to a disk in a few seconds.* ◊ [V] *The novel does not transfer well to the movies.*

■ *noun* /ˈtrænsfɜː(r)/
CHANGE OF PLACE/JOB/SITUATION | **1** [U, C] the act of moving sb/sth from one place, group or job to another; an occasion when this happens: *data/information transfer* ◊ *the transfer of currency from one country to another* ◊ *He has asked for a transfer to the company's Paris branch.* ◊ *After the election there was a swift transfer of power.*

IN SPORT | **2** [U, C] the act of moving a sports player from one club or team to another: *It was the first goal he had scored since his transfer from Chelsea.* ◊ *a transfer fee/request* ◊ *to be on the transfer list* (= available to join another club)

æ	ɑː	e	ɜː	ə	ɪ	iː	i	ɒ	ɔː	ʌ	ʊ	u	uː
cat	father	ten	bird	about	sit	see	many	got (BrE)	saw	cup	put	actual	too

CHANGE OF VEHICLE | **3** [U, C] an act of changing to a different place, vehicle or route when you are travelling: *The transfer from the airport to the hotel is included in the price.*

TRAIN/BUS TICKET | **4** [C] (*AmE*) a ticket that allows a passenger to continue their journey on another bus or train

PICTURE | **5** [C] (*especially BrE*) (*AmE usually* **decal**) a picture or design that can be removed from a piece of paper and stuck onto a surface, for example by being pressed or heated

trans·fer·able /træns'fɜːrəbl/ *adj.* that can be moved from one place, person or use to another: *This ticket is not transferable* (= it may only be used by the person who has bought it). ◊ *We aim to provide our students with transferable skills* (= that can be used in different jobs). ► **trans·fer·abil·ity** /ˌtrænsˌfɜːrə'bɪləti/ *noun* [U]

trans·fer·ence /'trænsfərəns; *AmE* træns'fɜːrəns/ *noun* [U] (*technical* or *formal*) the process of moving sth from one place, person or use to another: *the transference of heat from the liquid to the container* ◊ *the transference of ideas/information/wealth*

trans·fig·ure /træns'fɪɡə(r); *AmE* -ɡjər/ *verb* [VN] [often passive] (*literary*) to change the appearance of a person or thing so that they look more beautiful: *Ann's whole face was transfigured by the early morning light.* ► **trans·fig·ur·ation** /ˌtrænsˌfɪɡə'reɪʃn/ *noun* [U]

trans·fix /træns'fɪks/ *verb* [VN] [usually passive] to be unable to move because sth has all your attention, or because you are afraid, surprised, etc: *Luisa stood transfixed with shock.*

trans·form /træns'fɔːm; *AmE* -'fɔːrm/ *verb* [VN] ~ **sth/sb** **(from sth) (into sth)** **1** to change the form of sth SYN CONVERT: *The photochemical reactions transform the light into electrical impulses.* **2** to completely change the appearance or character of sth, especially so that it is better: *A new colour scheme will transform my bedroom.* ◊ *It was an event that would transform my life.* ◊ *The company has been transformed from a family business to a multi-million-pound operation.*

trans·form·ation /ˌtrænsfə'meɪʃn; *AmE* -fər'm-/ *noun* [C, U] ~ **(from sth) (to/into sth)** a complete change in sb/sth: *The way in which we work has undergone a complete transformation in the past decade.* ◊ *the country's transformation from dictatorship to democracy* ◊ *What a transformation! You look great.*

trans·form·er /træns'fɔːmə(r); *AmE* -'fɔːrm-/ *noun* a device for reducing or increasing the VOLTAGE of an electric power supply, usually to allow a particular piece of electrical equipment to be used

trans·fu·sion /træns'fjuːʒn/ *noun* [C, U] **1** = BLOOD TRANSFUSION **2** ~ **of sth** the act of investing extra money in a place or an activity that needs it: *The project badly needs a transfusion of cash.* ► **trans·fuse** *verb*: [VN] *to transfuse blood to/into a patient*

trans·gen·ic /ˌtrænz'dʒenɪk; 'trænz-/ *adj.* (*biology*) (of an animal or a plant) having GENETIC material introduced from another type of animal or plant

trans·gress /trænz'ɡres; træns-/ *verb* [VN] (*formal*) to go beyond the limit of what is morally or legally acceptable: *They have transgressed the bounds of decency.* ► **trans·gres·sion** /trænz'ɡreʃn; træns-/ *noun* [C, U] **trans·gres·sor** *noun*

tran·si·ent /'trænziənt; *AmE* 'trænʃnt/ *adj., noun*
■ *adj.* (*formal*) **1** continuing for only a short time SYN TEMPORARY: *the transient nature of speech* **2** staying or working in a place for only a short time, before moving on: *a city with a large transient population* (= of students, temporary workers, etc.) ► **tran·si·ence** /-əns/ *noun* [U]: *the transience of human life*
■ *noun* (*especially AmE*) a person who stays or works in a place for only a short time, before moving on

tran·sis·tor /træn'zɪstə(r); -'sɪst-/ *noun* **1** a small electronic device used in computers, radios, televisions, etc. for controlling an electric current as it passes along a CIRCUIT **2** (also **tran,sistor 'radio**) a small radio with transistors

tran·sit /'trænzɪt; -sɪt/ *noun* **1** [U] the process of being moved or carried from one place to another: *The cost includes transit.* ◊ *goods damaged or lost in transit* ◊ *transit times* **2** [U, C, usually sing.] the act of going through a place on the way to somewhere else: *the transit lounge at Vienna airport* ◊ *a transit visa* (= one that allows a person to pass through a country but not to stay there)

'transit camp *noun* a camp that provides temporary accommodation for REFUGEES

tran·si·tion /træn'zɪʃn; -'sɪʃn/ *noun* [U, C] ~ **(from sth) (to sth)** | ~ **(between A and B)** the process or a period of changing from one state or condition to another: *the transition from school to full-time work* ◊ *We need to ensure a smooth transition between the old system and the new one.* ◊ *He will remain head of state during the period of transition to democracy.* ◊ *This course is useful for students who are in transition* (= in the process of changing) *from one training programme to another.* ► **tran·si·tion·al** /-ʃənl/ *adj.*: *a transitional period* ◊ *a transitional government*

tran·si·tive /'trænsətɪv/ *adj.* (*grammar*) (of verbs) used with a DIRECT OBJECT: *In 'She wrote a letter', the verb 'wrote' is transitive and the word 'letter' is the direct object.* OPP INTRANSITIVE ► **tran·si·tive·ly** *adv.*: *The verb is being used transitively.*

tran·si·tory /'trænsətri; *AmE* -tɔːri/ *adj.* (*formal*) continuing for only a short time SYN TEMPORARY: *the transitory nature of his happiness* ◊ *These feelings tend to be transitory.*

trans·late /træns'leɪt; trænz-/ *verb* **1** ~ **(sth) (from sth) (into sth)** | ~ **sth (as sth)** to express the meaning of speech or writing in a different language: [VN] *He translated the letter into English.* ◊ *Her books have been translated into 24 languages.* ◊ *'Suisse' had been wrongly translated as 'Sweden'.* ◊ *Can you help me translate this legal jargon into plain English?* ◊ [V] *I don't speak Greek so Dina offered to translate for me.* ◊ *My work involves translating from German.* **2** [V] ~ **(as sth)** to be changed from one language to another: *Most poetry does not translate well.* ◊ *The Welsh name translates as 'Land's End'.* **3** ~ **(sth) (into sth)** to change sth, or to be changed, into a different form: [VN] *It's time to translate words into action.* ◊ [V] *I hope all the hard work will translate into profits.* ◊ *Most attempts to translate Shakespeare to the small screen* (= television) *are not successful.* **4** ~ **sth (as sth)** to understand sth in a particular way or give sth a particular meaning: [VN] *the various words and gestures that we translate as love* [also V]

trans·la·tion /træns'leɪʃn; trænz-/ *noun* **1** [U] ~ **(of sth) (into sth)** | ~ **(from sth) (into sth)** the process of changing sth that is written or spoken into another language: *an error in translation* ◊ *He specializes in translation from Danish into English.* ◊ *The book loses something in translation.* **2** [C, U] a text or work that has been changed from one language to another: *to make/do a translation of a document* ◊ *The usual translation of 'glasnost' is 'openness'.* ◊ *a rough/a literal/an exact translation* ◊ *I have only read Tolstoy in translation.* ◊ *a copy of Dryden's translation of the Aeneid* **3** [U] ~ **(of sth) into sth** the process of changing sth into a different form: *the translation of theory into practice*

trans·la·tor /træns'leɪtə(r); trænz-/ *noun* a person who translates writing or speech into a different language, especially as a job: *She works as a translator of technical texts.*—compare INTERPRETER

trans·lit·er·ate /træns'lɪtəreɪt; trænz-/ *verb* [VN] ~ **sth (into/as sth)** (*formal*) to write words or letters using letters of a different alphabet or language ► **trans·lit·er·ation** /ˌtrænslɪtə'reɪʃn; ˌtrænz-/ *noun* [C, U]

trans·lu·cent /træns'luːsnt; trænz-/ *adj.* (*written*) allowing light to pass through but not transparent: *The sky was a pale translucent blue.* ◊ *His skin was translucent with age.* ► **trans·lu·cence** /-sns/ (also **trans·lu·cency** /-snsi/) *noun* [U]

trans·mi·gra·tion /ˌtrænzmaɪ'ɡreɪʃn; ˌtræns-/ *noun* [U] the passing of a person's soul after their death into another body

aɪ	aʊ	eɪ	əʊ	oʊ	ɔɪ	ɪə	eə	ʊə	j	w
my	now	say	go	go	boy	near	hair	pure	yes	wet
			(BrE)	(AmE)						

T

trans·mis·sion /trænsˈmɪʃn; trænz-/ noun (formal) **1** [U] the act or process of passing sth from one person, place or thing to another: *the transmission of the disease/virus* ◊ *the risk of transmission* **2** [U] the act or process of sending out an electronic signal or message or of broadcasting a radio or television programme: *the transmission of computer data along telephone lines* ◊ *a break in transmission* (= of a radio or television broadcast) *due to a technical fault* **3** [C] a radio or television message or broadcast: *a live transmission from Sydney* **4** [U, C] the system in a motor vehicle by which power is passed from the engine to the wheels

trans·mit /trænsˈmɪt; trænz-/ verb (-tt-) **1** ~ (sth) (from …) (to …) to send an electronic signal, radio or television broadcast, etc: [VN, usually +adv./prep.] *signals transmitted from a satellite* ◊ *The ceremony was transmitted live by satellite to over fifty countries.* ◊ [V] *a short-wave radio that can transmit as well as receive* **2** [VN] to pass sth from one person to another: *sexually transmitted diseases* ◊ *Parents can unwittingly transmit their own fears to their children.* **3** [VN] (technical) to allow heat, light, sound, etc. to pass through

trans·mit·ter /trænsˈmɪtə(r); trænz-/ noun **1** a piece of equipment used for sending electronic signals, especially radio or television signals—compare RECEIVER **2** ~ of sth (formal) a person or thing that transmits sth from one person or thing to another: *Emphasis was placed on the school as a transmitter of moral values.*

trans·mog·rify /trænzˈmɒɡrɪfaɪ; træns-; AmE -ˈmɑːɡ-/ verb (trans·mog·ri·fies, trans·mog·ri·fy·ing, trans·mog·ri·fied, trans·mog·ri·fied) [VN] [often passive] (often humorous) to change sb/sth completely, especially in a surprising way ▶ **trans·mog·ri·fi·ca·tion** /ˌtrænz-ˌmɒɡrɪfɪˈkeɪʃn; træns-; AmE -ˌmɑːɡ-/ noun [U]

trans·mute /trænzˈmjuːt; træns-/ verb ~ (sth) (into sth) (formal) to change, or make sth change, into sth different: [VN, +adv./prep.] *It was once thought that lead could be transmuted into gold.* [also V] ▶ **trans·mu·ta·tion** /ˌtrænzmjuːˈteɪʃn; træns-/ noun [C, U]

trans·na·tion·al /ˌtrænzˈnæʃnəl; træns-/ adj. (especially business) operating in or between many different countries, without being based in any particular one

tran·som /ˈtrænsəm/ noun **1** a bar of wood or stone across the top of a door or window **2** (AmE) = FANLIGHT

trans·par·ency /trænsˈpærənsi/ noun (pl. -ies) **1** [C] a picture printed on a piece of photographic film, usually in a frame, that can be shown on a screen by shining light through the film [SYN] SLIDE: *an overhead transparency* (= used with an OVERHEAD PROJECTOR) **2** [U] the quality of sth, such as glass, that allows you to see through it **3** [U] the quality of sth, such as an excuse or a lie, that allows sb to see the truth easily: *They were shocked by the transparency of his lies.* **4** [U] the quality of sth, such as a situation or an argument, that makes it easy to understand: *a need for greater transparency in legal documents*

trans·par·ent /trænsˈpærənt/ adj. **1** (of glass, plastic, etc.) allowing you to see through it: *The insect's wings are almost transparent.* [OPP] OPAQUE **2** (of an excuse, a lie, etc.) allowing you to see the truth easily [SYN] OBVIOUS: *a man of transparent honesty* ◊ *a transparent attempt to buy votes* ◊ *Am I that transparent* (= are my intentions that obvious)? **3** (of language, information, etc.) easy to understand: *a campaign to make official documents more transparent* [OPP] OPAQUE ▶ **trans·par·ent·ly** adv.: *transparently clear/honest/obvious*

tran·spire /trænˈspaɪə(r)/ verb (formal) **1** [V that] (not usually used in the progressive tenses) if it transpires that sth has happened or is true, it is known or has been shown to be true: *It transpired that the gang had had a contact inside the bank.* ◊ *This story, it later transpired, was untrue.* **2** [V] to happen: *You're meeting him tomorrow? Let me know what transpires.* **3** [V, VN] (biology) when plants or leaves transpire, water passes out from their surface

trans·plant verb, noun

■ verb /trænsˈplɑːnt; trænz-; AmE -ˈplænt/ [VN] **1** ~ sth (from sb/sth) (into sb/sth) to take an organ, skin, etc. from one person, animal, part of the body, etc. and put it into or onto another: *Surgeons have successfully transplanted a liver into a four-year-old boy.* ◊ *Patients often reject transplanted organs.*—compare IMPLANT **2** to move a growing plant and plant it somewhere else **3** (formal) ~ sb/sth (from …) (to …) to move sb/sth to a different place or environment: *Japanese production methods have been transplanted into some British factories.* ▶ **trans·plan·ta·tion** /ˌtrænsplɑːnˈteɪʃn; ˌtrænz-; AmE -plæn-/ noun [U]: *liver transplantation* ◊ *the transplantation of entire communities overseas*

■ noun /ˈtrænsplɑːnt; ˈtrænz-; AmE -plænt/ **1** [C, U] a medical operation in which a damaged organ, etc. is replaced with one from another person: *to have a heart transplant* ◊ *a transplant operation/patient* ◊ *a shortage of suitable kidneys for transplant* **2** [C] an organ, etc. that is used in a transplant operation: *There is always a chance that the body will reject the transplant.*—compare IMPLANT

tran·spon·der /trænsˈpɒndə(r)/ noun (technical) a piece of equipment that receives radio signals and automatically sends out another signal in reply

trans·port noun, verb

■ noun /ˈtrænspɔːt; AmE -spɔːrt/ **1** (especially BrE) (AmE usually **trans·por·ta·tion**) [U] a system for carrying people or goods from one place to another using vehicles, roads, etc: *air/freight/road transport* ◊ *to travel on/by public transport* (= by train, bus, etc.) ◊ *the government's transport policy* **2** (BrE) (AmE **trans·por·ta·tion**) [U] a vehicle or method of travel: *Applicants must have their own transport.* ◊ *Transport to and from the airport is included in the price.* ◊ *His bike is his only means of transport.* **3** [U] (especially BrE) (also **transportation** AmE, BrE) the activity or business of carrying goods from one place to another using lorries/trucks, trains, etc: *The goods were damaged during transport.* ◊ *controls on the transport of nuclear waste* **4** [C] a ship, plane or lorry/truck used for carrying soldiers, supplies, etc. from one place to another: *Several transports were sent to convey them to the camp.* ◊ *a transport helicopter* **5** (transports) [pl.] ~ of sth (literary) strong feelings and emotions: *to be in transports of joy/delight/grief*

■ verb /trænˈspɔːt; AmE -ˈspɔːrt/ [VN] [usually +adv./prep.] **1** to take sth/sb from one place to another in a vehicle: *to transport goods/passengers/cattle* ◊ *Most of our luggage was transported by sea.* **2** to move sth somewhere by means of a natural process: *The seeds are transported by the wind.* ◊ *Blood transports oxygen around the body.* **3** to make sb feel that they are in a different place, time or situation: *The book transports you to another world.* **4** (in the past) to send sb to a far away place as a punishment

trans·port·able /trænˈspɔːtəbl; AmE -ˈspɔːrt-/ adj. [not usually before noun] that can be carried or moved from one place to another, especially by vehicle

trans·por·ta·tion /ˌtrænspɔːˈteɪʃn; AmE -pɔːrˈt-/ noun [U] **1** (especially AmE) = TRANSPORT: *the transportation industry* ◊ *public transportation* ◊ *The city is providing free transportation to the stadium from downtown.* ◊ *the transportation of heavy loads* ◊ *transportation costs* **2** (in the past) the act of sending criminals to a place that is far away as a form of punishment

'transport cafe (BrE) (AmE **'truck stop**) noun a cafe at the side of a main road that serves cheap food and is used mainly by lorry/truck drivers

trans·port·er /trænˈspɔːtə(r); AmE -ˈspɔːrt-/ noun a large vehicle used for carrying heavy objects, for example other vehicles: *a car transporter*

trans·pose /trænˈspəʊz; AmE -ˈspoʊz/ verb [VN] [often passive] **1** (formal) to change the order of two or more things [SYN] REVERSE **2** (formal) to move or change sth to a different place or environment or into a different form [SYN] TRANSFER: *The director transposes Shakespeare's play from 16th century Venice to present-day England.* **3** (music) to write or play a piece of music or a series of notes in a different key ▶ **trans·pos·ition** /ˌtrænspəˈzɪʃn/ noun [C, U]

b	d	f	g	h	k	l	m	n	p	r
bad	did	fall	get	hat	cat	leg	man	now	pen	red

trans·sex·ual /træns'sekʃuəl; træns-/ *noun* a person who feels emotionally that they want to live, dress, etc. as a member of the opposite sex, especially one who has a medical operation to change their sexual organs

tran·sub·stan·ti·ation /ˌtrænsəbˌstænʃi'eɪʃn/ *noun* [U] the belief that the bread and wine of the COMMUNION service become the actual body and blood of Jesus Christ after they have been BLESSED, even though they still look like bread and wine

trans·verse /'trænzvɜːs; 'træns-; *AmE* -vɜːrs/ *adj.* [usually before noun] (*technical*) situated across sth: *A transverse bar joins the two posts.*

trans·vest·ite /trænz'vestaɪt; træns-/ *noun* a person, especially a man, who enjoys dressing as a member of the opposite sex ▶ **trans·vest·ism** /trænz'vestɪzəm; træns-/ *noun* [U]

trap /træp/ *noun, verb*
■ *noun*
FOR ANIMALS 1 a piece of equipment for catching animals: *a fox with its leg in a trap* ◊ *A trap was laid, with fresh bait.*—see also MOUSETRAP
TRICK 2 a clever plan designed to trick sb, either by capturing them or by making them do or say sth that they did not mean to do or say: *She had set a trap for him and he had walked straight into it.*—see also BOOBY TRAP, RADAR TRAP, SAND TRAP, TOURIST TRAP
BAD SITUATION 3 [usually sing.] an unpleasant situation from which it is hard to escape: *the unemployment trap* ◊ *Some women see marriage as a trap.*—see also DEATH TRAP, POVERTY TRAP
CARRIAGE 4 a light carriage with two wheels, pulled by a horse: *a pony and trap*
MOUTH 5 (*slang*) mouth: *Shut your trap!* (= a rude way of telling sb to be quiet) ◊ *to keep your trap shut* (= to not tell a secret)
FOR RACING DOG 6 a cage from which a GREYHOUND (= a type of dog) is let out at the start of a race
IN GOLF 7 (*AmE*) = BUNKER
IDM **to fall into/avoid the trap of doing sth** to do/avoid doing sth that is a mistake but which seems at first to be a good idea: *Parents often fall into the trap of trying to do everything for their children.*—more at SPRING *v.*
■ *verb* (**-pp-**) [VN]
IN DANGEROUS/BAD SITUATION 1 [often passive] to keep sb in a dangerous place or bad situation that they want to get out of but cannot: *Help! I'm trapped!* ◊ *They were trapped in the burning building.* ◊ *We became trapped by the rising flood water.* ◊ *He was trapped in an unhappy marriage.* ◊ *I feel trapped in my job.*
PART OF BODY/CLOTHING 2 [usually +adv. / prep.] to have part of your body, your clothing, etc. held in a place so tightly that you cannot remove it and it may be injured or damaged: *I trapped my coat in the car door.* ◊ *The pain was caused by a trapped nerve.*
CATCH 3 to catch or keep sth in a place and prevent it from escaping, especially so that you can use it: *Solar panels trap energy from the sun.* 4 to force sb/sth into a place or situation that they cannot escape from, especially in order to catch them: *The escaped prisoners were eventually trapped in an underground garage and recaptured.* 5 to catch an animal in a trap: *Raccoons used to be trapped for their fur.*
TRICK 6 ~ sb (into sth/into doing sth) to trick sb into sth: *He felt he had been trapped into accepting the terms of the contract.*

trap·door /'træpdɔː(r)/ *noun* a small door in a floor or ceiling

trap·eze /trə'piːz; *AmE* træ-/ *noun* a wooden or metal bar hanging from two pieces of rope high above the ground, used especially by CIRCUS performers: *a trapeze artist*

tra·pez·ium /trə'piːziəm/ *noun* (pl. **tra·pez·iums** or **tra·pezia** /trə'piːziə/) (geometry) 1 (*BrE*) (*AmE* **trap·ez·oid**) a flat shape with four straight sides, one pair of opposite sides being parallel and the other pair not parallel 2 (*AmE*) = TRAPEZOID

trap·ez·oid /'træpəzɔɪd/ *noun* (geometry) 1 (*BrE*) (*AmE* **tra·pez·ium**) a flat shape with four straight sides, none of which are parallel 2 (*AmE*) = TRAPEZIUM

trapezium (*BrE*)/
trapezoid (*AmE*)

trapezoid (*BrE*)/
trapezium (*AmE*)

trap·per /'træpə(r)/ *noun* a person who traps and kills animals, especially for their fur

trap·pings /'træpɪŋz/ *noun* [pl.] ~ (of sth) (*written*, especially *disapproving*) the possessions, clothes, etc. that are connected with a particular situation, job or social position: *They enjoyed all the trappings of wealth.*

trash /træʃ/ *noun, verb*
■ *noun* [U] 1 (*AmE*) things that you throw away because you no longer want or need them ⇨ note at RUBBISH 2 (*BrE, informal, disapproving*) objects, writing, ideas, etc. that you think are of poor quality: *What's this trash you're watching?* ◊ *He's talking trash* (= nonsense). 3 (*AmE, informal*) an offensive word used to describe people that you do not respect: *white trash* (= poor white people, especially those living in the southern US)
■ *verb* [VN] (*informal*) 1 to damage or destroy sth: *The band was famous for trashing hotel rooms.* 2 to criticize sth/sb very strongly 3 (*AmE*) to throw away sth that you do not want: *I'm leaving my old toys here—if you don't want them, just trash them.*

'trash can *noun* (*AmE*) = DUSTBIN, LITTER BIN

trashy /'træʃi/ *adj.* (*informal*) of poor quality; with no value SYN RUBBISHY: *trashy TV shows*

trauma /'trɔːmə; *AmE* 'traumə/ *noun* 1 [U] (*psychology*) a mental condition caused by severe shock, especially when the harmful effects last for a long time 2 [C, U] an unpleasant experience that makes you feel upset and/or anxious: *She felt exhausted after the traumas of recent weeks.* 3 [U, C] (*medical*) an injury: *The patient suffered severe brain trauma.*

trau·mat·ic /trɔː'mætɪk; *AmE* trau'm-/ *adj.* 1 extremely unpleasant and causing you to feel upset and/or anxious: *a traumatic childhood/experience* 2 [only before noun] (*psychology* or *medical*) connected with or caused by trauma: *traumatic amnesia*—see also POST-TRAUMATIC STRESS DISORDER ▶ **trau·mat·ic·al·ly** /-kli/ *adv.*

trau·ma·tize (*BrE* also **-ise**) /'trɔːmətaɪz; *AmE* 'traum-/ *verb* [VN] [usually passive] to shock and upset sb very much, often making them unable to think or work normally

trav·ail /'træveɪl; trə'veɪl/ *noun* [U, pl.] (*old use* or *literary*) an unpleasant experience or situation that involves a lot of hard work, difficulties and/or suffering: *the travails of life in post-war Britain*

travel /'trævl/ *verb, noun*
■ *verb* (**-ll-**, *AmE* usually **-l-**) 1 to go from one place to another, especially over a long distance: [V] *to travel abroad/across Africa/around the world* ◊ *I go to bed early if I'm travelling the next day.* ◊ *I love travelling by train.* ◊ *We always travel first class.* ◊ *We travelled to California for the wedding.* ◊ *When I finished college I went travelling for six months* (= spent time visiting different places). ◊ [VN] *He travelled the length of the Nile in a canoe.* ◊ *I travel 40 miles to work every day.* ⇨ note at JOURNEY 2 [V] to go or move at a particular speed, in a particular direction, or a particular distance: *to travel at 50 miles an hour/at twice the speed of sound* ◊ *Messages travel along the spine from the nerve endings to the brain.* ◊ *News travels fast these days.* 3 [V] (of food, wine, an object, etc.) to be still in good condition after a long journey: *Some wines do not travel well.* 4 [V] (of a book, an idea, etc.) to be equally successful in another place and not just where it began: *Some writing travels badly in translation.* 5 [V] to go fast: *Their car can really travel!* 6 [V] (in basketball) to move while you are holding the ball, in a way that is not allowed IDM **travel 'light** to take very little with you when you go on a trip
■ *noun* 1 [U] the act or activity of travelling: *air/rail/space travel* ◊ *travel expenses/arrangements* ◊ *The post involves a considerable amount of foreign travel.* ◊ *the travel industry* ◊ *travel sickness* ◊ *a travel bag/clock* (= for use when

travelling) **2 (travels)** [pl.] time spent travelling, especially in foreign countries and for pleasure: *The novel is based on his travels in India. ◊ When are you off on your travels* (= going travelling)*? ⇨* note at JOURNEY

'travel agency *noun* a company that arranges travel and/or accommodation for people going on a holiday/vacation or journey

'travel agent *noun* **1** a person or business whose job is to make arrangements for people wanting to travel, for example, buying tickets or arranging hotel rooms **2 (travel agent's)** (*pl.* **travel agents**) a shop/store where you can go to arrange a holiday/vacation, etc: *He works in a travel agent's.*—see also TRAVEL AGENCY

trav·elled (*especially BrE*) (*AmE usually* **trav·eled**) /'trævld/ *adj.* (usually in compounds) (*written*) **1** (of a person) having travelled the amount mentioned: *a much-travelled man* **2** (of a road, etc.) used the amount mentioned: *The path was steeper and less travelled than the previous one.*

trav·el·ler (*especially BrE*) (*AmE usually* **trav·el·er**) /'trævələ(r)/ *noun* **1** a person who is travelling or who often travels: *She is a frequent traveller to Belgium. ◊ He passed the time chatting with fellow travellers.*—see also COMMERCIAL TRAVELLER **2** (*BrE*) a person who does not live in one place but travels around, especially as part of a group (often used as a word for a GYPSY): *New Age travellers*

'traveller's cheque (*BrE*) (*AmE* **'traveler's check**) *noun* a cheque for a fixed amount, sold by a bank or TRAVEL AGENT, that can be exchanged for cash in foreign countries

trav·el·ling (*especially BrE*) (*AmE usually* **trav·el·ing**) /'trævəlɪŋ/ *noun*
■ *adj.* [only before noun] **1** going from place to place: *a travelling circus/exhibition/performer ◊ the travelling public ◊* (*BrE*) *travelling people* (= people who have no fixed home, especially those living in a community that moves from place to place, also known as 'travellers') **2** used when you travel: *a travelling clock*
■ *noun* [U] the act of travelling: *The job requires a lot of travelling. ◊ travelling expenses ◊ a travelling companion*

travelling 'salesman (*especially BrE*) (*AmE usually* **traveling 'salesman**) *noun* (*old-fashioned*) = SALES REPRESENTATIVE

trav·el·ogue (*AmE also* **trav·elog**) /'trævəlɒg; *AmE* -lɔːg; -lɑːg/ *noun* a film/movie, broadcast or piece of writing about travel

'travel-sick *adj.* feeling sick because you are travelling in a vehicle ▶ **'travel-sickness** *noun* [U]

tra·verse *verb, noun*
■ *verb* /trə'vɜːs; *AmE* -'vɜːrs/ [VN] (*formal* or *technical*) to cross an area of land or water: *skiers traversing the slopes ◊ The region is traversed by several roads.*
■ *noun* /'trævɜːs; *AmE* -vɜːrs/ (in mountain climbing) an act of moving sideways or walking across a steep slope, not climbing up or down it; a place where this is possible or necessary

trav·esty /'trævəsti/ *noun* (*pl.* **-ies**) **~ (of sth)** something that does not have the qualities or values that it should have, and as a result is often shocking or offensive: *The trial was a travesty of justice.*

trawl /trɔːl/ *verb, noun*
■ *verb* **1 ~ (through sth) (for sth/sb)| ~ sth (for sth/sb)** to search through a large amount of information or a large number of people, places, etc. looking for a particular thing or person: [VN] *She trawled the shops for bargains. ◊ Major companies trawl the universities for potential graduate trainees. ◊* [V] *The police are trawling through their files for similar cases.* **2** [V] **~ (for sth)** to fish for sth by pulling a large net with a wide opening through the water
■ *noun* **1** a search through a large amount of information, documents, etc: *A quick trawl through the newspapers yielded five suitable job adverts.* **2** (also **'trawl net**) a large net with a wide opening, that is dragged along the bottom of the sea by a boat in order to catch fish

trawl·er /'trɔːlə(r)/ *noun* a fishing boat that uses large

nets that it drags through the sea behind it—picture at BOAT

tray /treɪ/ *noun* **1** a flat piece of wood, metal or plastic with raised edges, used for carrying or holding things, especially food: *He brought her breakfast in bed on a tray. ◊ She came in with a tray of drinks. ◊ a tea tray* **2** (*especially BrE*) (often in compounds) a shallow plastic box, used for various purposes: *a seed tray* (= for planting seeds in) *◊ a cat's litter tray*—see also BAKING TRAY, IN TRAY, OUT TRAY

treach·er·ous /'tretʃərəs/ *adj.* **1** that cannot be trusted; intending to harm you: *He was weak, cowardly and treacherous. ◊ lying, treacherous words* **2** dangerous, especially when seeming safe: *The ice on the roads made driving conditions treacherous.* ▶ **treach·er·ous·ly** *adv.*

treach·ery /'tretʃəri/ *noun* [U, C] (*pl.* **-ies**) behaviour that involves betraying sb who trusts you; an example of this: *an act of treachery*

trea·cle /'triːkl/ *noun* [U] (*BrE*) **1** (*AmE* **mo·las·ses**) a thick black sweet sticky liquid produced when sugar is REFINED (= made pure), used in cooking **2** = GOLDEN SYRUP: *a treacle tart*

tread /tred/ *verb, noun*
■ *verb* (**trod** /trɒd/; *AmE* **traːd**/ **trod·den** /'trɒdn/; *AmE* **'traːdn**/ or **trod**) **1** [V] **~ (on/in/over sth/sb)** (*especially BrE*) to put your foot down while you are stepping or walking: *Ouch! You trod on my toe! ◊ Careful you don't tread in that puddle.* **2** [VN] [usually +adv. / prep.] to crush or press sth with your feet: *Don't tread ash into the carpet! ◊ The wine is still made by treading grapes in the traditional way.* **3** (*formal* or *literary*) to walk somewhere: [VN] *Few people had trod this path before. ◊* [V] *He was treading quietly and cautiously.* **IDM** **tread 'carefully, 'warily, etc.** to be very careful about what you do or say: *The government will have to tread very carefully in handling this issue.* **tread a difficult, dangerous, solitary, etc. 'path** to choose and follow a particular way of life, way of doing sth, etc: *A restaurant has to tread the tricky path between maintaining quality and keeping prices down.* **tread on sb's 'heels** to follow sb closely **tread on sb's 'toes** (*especially BrE*) (*AmE usually* **step on sb's 'toes**) (*informal*) to offend or annoy sb, especially by getting involved in sth that is their responsibility: *I don't want to tread on anybody's toes so I'll keep quiet.* **tread 'water 1** to keep yourself upright in deep water by moving your arms and legs **2** to make no progress while you are waiting for sth to happen: *I decided to tread water until a better job came along.*—more at LINE *n.*, TIGHTROPE
■ *noun* **1** [sing.] the way that sb walks; the sound that sb makes when they walk: *I heard his heavy tread on the stairs.* **2** [C, U] the raised pattern on the surface of a tyre on a vehicle: *The tyres were worn below the legal limit of 1·6 mm of tread.* **3** [C] the upper surface of a step or STAIR—compare RISER

treadle /'tredl/ *noun* (especially in the past) a device worked by the foot to operate a machine

tread·mill /'tredmɪl/ *noun* **1** [sing.] work or a way of life that is boring or tiring because it involves always doing the same things: *I'd like to escape the office treadmill.* **2** [C] (especially in the past) a large wheel turned by the weight of people or animals walking on steps around its inside edge, and used to operate machinery **3** [C] an exercise machine that has a moving surface that you can walk or run on while remaining in the same place

trea·son /'triːzn/ *noun* (also **high 'treason**) *noun* [U] the crime of doing sth that could cause danger to your country, such as helping its enemies during a war ▶ **treas·on·able** /'triːzənəbl/ *adj.*: *a treasonable act/offence*

treas·ure /'treʒə(r)/ *noun, verb*
■ *noun* **1** [U] a collection of valuable things such as gold, silver and jewellery: *buried treasure ◊ a pirate's treasure chest* **2** [C, usually pl.] a highly valued object: *the priceless art treasures of the Uffizi gallery* **3** [sing.] a person who is much loved or valued
■ *verb* [VN] to have or keep sth that you love and that is extremely valuable to you: *I treasure his friendship. ◊ This ring is my most treasured possession.*

æ	ɑː	e	ɜː	ə	ɪ	iː	i	ɒ	ɔː	ʌ	ʊ	u	uː
cat	father	ten	bird	about	sit	see	many	got	saw	cup	put	actual	too
								(BrE)					

treasure hunt *noun* a game in which players try to find a hidden prize by answering a series of questions that have been left in different places

treas·urer /'treʒərə(r)/ *noun* a person who is responsible for the money and accounts of a club or an organization

treasure trove *noun* **1** [U, C, usually sing.] valuable things that are found hidden and whose owner is unknown **2** [C, usually sing.] a place, book, etc. containing many useful or beautiful things

treas·ury /'treʒəri/ *noun* (*pl.* **-ies**) **1** (**the Treasury**) [sing.+ sing./pl. *v.*] (in Britain, the US and some other countries) the government department that controls public money **2** [C] a place in a castle, etc. where valuable things are stored

treat /triːt/ *verb, noun*
- *verb* [VN]
 BEHAVE TOWARDS SB/STH | **1** ~ sb/sth (with/as/like sth) to behave in a particular way towards sb/sth: *to treat people with respect/consideration/suspicion* ◊ *Treat your keyboard with care and it should last for years.* ◊ *My parents still treat me like a child.* ◊ *He was treated as a hero on his release from prison.*
 CONSIDER | **2** ~ sth as sth to consider sth in a particular way: *I decided to treat his remark as a joke.* **3** to deal with or discuss sth in a particular way: *The question is treated in more detail in the next chapter.*
 ILLNESS/INJURY | **4** to give medical care or attention to a person, an illness, an injury, etc: *She was treated for sunstroke.* ◊ *The condition is usually treated with drugs and a strict diet.* ◊ *The hospital treated forty cases of malaria last year.*
 USE CHEMICAL | **5** ~ sth (with sth) to use a chemical substance or process to clean, protect, preserve, etc. sth: *to treat crops with insecticide* ◊ *wood treated with preservative*
 PAY FOR STH ENJOYABLE | **6** ~ sb/yourself (to sth) to pay for sth that sb/you will enjoy and that you do not usually have or do: *She treated him to lunch.* ◊ *Don't worry about the cost—I'll treat you.* ◊ *I'm going to treat myself to a new pair of shoes.*
 ▶ **treat·able** *adj.*: *a treatable condition/infection*
 IDM **treat sb like 'dirt** (*informal*) to treat sb with no respect at all
 PHRV **'treat sb to sth** to entertain sb with sth special: *The crowd were treated to a superb display of tennis.*
- *noun* something very pleasant and enjoyable, especially sth that you give sb or do for them: *We took the kids to the zoo as a special treat.* ◊ *You've never been to this area before? Then you're in for a real treat.* ◊ *When I was young chocolate was a treat.* ◊ *Let's go out for lunch—my treat* (= I will pay).
 IDM **a 'treat** (*BrE, informal*) extremely well or good: *His idea worked a treat* (= was successful).—more at TRICK *n.*

trea·tise /'triːtɪs, -tɪz/ *noun* ~ (on sth) a long and serious piece of writing on a particular subject

treat·ment /'triːtmənt/ *noun* **1** [U, C] ~ (for sth) something that is done to cure an illness or injury, or to make sb look and feel good: *He is receiving treatment for shock.* ◊ *She is responding well to treatment.* ◊ *to require hospital/medical treatment* ◊ *There are various treatments available for this condition.* ◊ *Guests at the health spa receive a range of beauty and fitness treatments.* **2** [U] a way of behaving towards or dealing with a person or thing: *the brutal treatment of political prisoners* ◊ *Certain city areas have been singled out for special treatment.* **3** [U, C] a way of dealing with or discussing a subject, work of art, etc: *Shakespeare's treatment of madness in 'King Lear'* **4** [U, C] ~ (for sth) a process by which sth is cleaned, or protected against sth: *a sewage/water treatment plant* ◊ *an effective treatment for dry rot*

treaty /'triːti/ *noun* (*pl.* **-ies**) a formal agreement between two or more countries: *the Treaty of Rome* ◊ *a peace treaty* ◊ *to draw up/sign/ratify a treaty* ◊ *Under the terms of the treaty, La Rochelle was ceded to the English.*

treble /'trebl/ *noun, verb, det., adj.*

- *noun* **1** [U] the high tones or part in music or a sound system: *to turn up the treble on the stereo* ◊ *the piping treble of childish voices*—compare BASS **2** [C] a child's high voice; a boy who sings with a treble voice—compare SOPRANO **3** [sing.] a musical part written for a treble voice **4** [sing.] (*BrE*) three successes in a row: *The victory completed a treble for the horse's owner.*
- *verb* to become, or to make sth, three times as much or as many **SYN** TRIPLE: [V] *Cases of food poisoning have trebled in the last two years.* ◊ [VN] *He trebled his earnings in two years.*
- *det.* [usually before noun] three times as much or as many: *Capital expenditure was treble the 1998 level.*
- *adj.* [only before noun] high in tone: *a treble voice* ◊ *the treble clef* (= the symbol in music showing that the notes following it are high)—picture at MUSIC—compare BASS

tree /triː/ *noun* a tall plant that can live a long time. Trees have a thick central wooden stem (the TRUNK) from which branches grow, usually with leaves on them: *an oak/an ash/a pine tree* ◊ *to plant a tree* ◊ *to chop/cut down a tree* ◊ *They followed a path through the trees.*—compare BUSH, SHRUB—see also BAY TREE, CHRISTMAS TREE, FAMILY TREE, GUM TREE, PLANE TREE **IDM** see BARK *v.*, FOREST, GROW, TOP *n.*, WOOD

tree house *noun* a structure built in the branches of a tree, usually for children to play on

tree·less /'triːləs/ *adj.* without trees: *a treeless plain*

tree·line /'triːlaɪn/ *noun* [sing.] a level of land, for example on a mountain, above which trees will not grow

tree surgeon *noun* a person whose job is treating trees that are damaged or have a disease, especially by cutting off branches, to try to preserve them ▶ **tree surgery** *noun* [U]

tree·top /'triːtɒp/ ; *AmE* -tɑːp/ *noun* [usually pl.] the branches at the top of a tree: *birds nesting in the treetops*

tref·oil /'trefɔɪl/ *noun* **1** (*technical*) a plant whose leaves are divided into three similar parts, for example CLOVER **2** an ornament or a design shaped like a trefoil leaf

trek /trek/ *noun, verb*
- *noun* **1** a long, hard walk lasting several days or weeks, especially in the mountains **2** (*informal*) a long walk: *It's a long trek into town.*
- *verb* (**-kk-**) [V] [usually+adv./prep.] **1** (*informal*) to make a long or difficult journey, especially on foot: *I hate having to trek up that hill with all the groceries.* **2** (also **go trekking**) to spend time walking, especially in mountains and for enjoyment and interest: *We went trekking in Nepal.* ◊ *During the expedition, they trekked ten to thirteen hours a day.*—see also PONY-TREKKING

trel·lis /'trelɪs/ *noun* [C, U] a light frame made of long narrow pieces of wood that cross each other, used to support climbing plants—picture at LATTICE

trem·ble /'trembl/ *verb, noun*
- *verb* [V] **1** ~ (with sth) to shake in a way that you cannot control, especially because you are very nervous, excited, frightened, etc: *My legs were trembling with fear.* ◊ *Her voice trembled with excitement.* ◊ *He opened the letter with trembling hands.* **2** to shake slightly: *leaves trembling in the breeze* **3** to be very worried or frightened: *I trembled at the thought of having to make a speech.*
- *noun* [C, usually sing.] (also **trem·bling** [C, U]) a feeling, movement or sound of trembling: *a tremble of excitement/fear* ◊ *She tried to control the trembling in her legs.*

tre·men·dous /trə'mendəs/ *adj.* **1** very great: *a tremendous explosion* ◊ *A tremendous amount of work has gone into the project.* **2** extremely good: *It was a tremendous experience.* ▶ **tre·men·dous·ly** *adv.*: *a tremendously exciting challenge*

trem·olo /'tremələʊ; *AmE* -loʊ/ *noun* (*pl.* **-os**) (*music*) a special effect in singing or playing a musical instrument made by repeating the same note or two notes very quickly

tremor /'tremə(r)/ *noun* **1** a small earthquake in which the ground shakes slightly: *an earth tremor* **2** a slight shaking movement in a part of your body caused, for example, by cold or fear: *There was a slight tremor in his voice.*

aɪ	aʊ	eɪ	əʊ	oʊ	ɔɪ	ɪə	eə	ʊə	j	w
my	now	say	go	go	boy	near	hair	pure	yes	wet
			(BrE)	(AmE)						

tremu·lous /'tremjələs/ adj. (literary) shaking slightly because you are nervous; causing you to shake slightly: a tremulous voice/smile ◇ He was in a state of tremulous excitement. ▶ **tremu·lous·ly** adv.

trench /trentʃ/ noun **1** a long deep hole dug in the ground, for example for carrying away water **2** a long deep hole dug in the ground in which soldiers can be protected from enemy attacks (for example in northern France and Belgium in the First World War): life in the trenches ◇ trench warfare

tren·chant /'trentʃənt/ adj. (written) (of criticism, remarks, etc.) expressed strongly and effectively, in a clear way: His trenchant views on the subject are well known. ▶ **tren·chant·ly** adv.

'trench coat noun a long loose coat, worn especially to keep off rain, with a belt and pockets in the style of a military coat—picture on page A5

trench·er /'trentʃə(r)/ noun a wooden plate used in the past for serving food

trend /trend/ noun ~ a general direction in which a situation is changing or developing: economic/ social/political trends ◇ There is a growing trend towards earlier retirement. ◇ current trends in language teaching ◇ a downward/upward trend in sales ◇ You seem to have set (= started) a new trend. ◇ This trend is being reversed (= is going in the opposite direction).

trend·set·ter /'trendsetə(r)/ noun (often approving) a person who starts a new fashion or makes it popular ▶ **trend·set·ting** adj. [only before noun]: a trendsetting band

trendy /'trendi/ adj., noun
■ adj. (**trend·ier**, **trendi·est**) (informal) very fashionable: trendy clothes/restaurants ▶ **trend·ily** adv. **trendi·ness** noun [U]
■ noun (pl. **-ies**) (BrE, informal, usually disapproving) a trendy person: young trendies from art college

trepi·da·tion /ˌtrepɪ'deɪʃn/ noun [U] (formal) great worry or fear about sth unpleasant that may happen: He knocked on the door with some trepidation.

tres·pass /'trespəs/ verb, noun
■ verb [V] **1** ~ (on sth) to enter land or a building that you do not have permission or the right to enter: He told me I was trespassing on private land. **2** (old use) to do sth wrong PHRV 'trespass on sth (formal) to make unfair use of sb's time, help, etc: I mustn't trespass on your time any longer.
■ noun **1** [U, C] an act of trespassing on land **2** [C] (old use) something that you do that is morally wrong SYN SIN

tres·pass·er /'trespəsə(r)/ noun a person who goes onto sb's land without their permission: The notice read: 'Trespassers will be prosecuted'.

tresses /'tresɪz/ noun [pl.] (literary) a woman's long hair

tres·tle /'tresl/ noun a wooden or metal structure with two pairs of sloping legs. Trestles are used in pairs to support a flat surface, for example the top of a table.

'trestle table noun a table that consists of a wooden top supported by trestles

trews /truːz/ noun [pl.] trousers/pants, especially when they are made of TARTAN

tri- /traɪ/ combining form (in nouns and adjectives) three; having three: tricycle ◇ triangular

triad /'traɪæd/ noun **1** (formal) a group of three related people or things **2** (also **Triad**) a Chinese secret organization involved in criminal activity

tri·age /'triːɑːʒ; AmE triːˈɑːʒ/ noun [U] (in a hospital) the process of deciding how seriously ill/sick or injured a person is, so that the most serious cases can be treated first

trial /'traɪəl/ noun, verb
■ noun
LAW **1** [U, C] a formal examination of evidence in a court of law by a judge and often a JURY, to decide if sb accused of a crime is guilty or not: a murder trial ◇ He's on trial for murder. ◇ She will stand trial/go on trial for fraud. ◇ The men were arrested but not brought to trial. ◇ The case never came to trial. ◇ She is awaiting trial on

corruption charges. ◇ He did not receive a fair trial. ◇ She was detained without trial.
TEST **2** [C, U] the process of testing the ability, quality or performance of sb/sth, especially before you make a final decision about them: The new drug is undergoing clinical trials. ◇ She agreed to employ me for a trial period. ◇ The system was introduced on a trial basis for one month. ◇ a trial separation (= of a couple whose marriage is in difficulties) ◇ We had the machine on trial for a week. ◇ a trial of strength (= a contest to see who is stronger)
IN SPORT **3** [C, usually pl.] (BrE) (AmE 'try-out) a competition or series of tests to find the best players for a sports team or an important event: Olympic trials
FOR ANIMALS **4** [C, usually pl.] an event at which animals compete or perform: sheepdog/horse trials
DIFFICULT EXPERIENCE **5** [C] ~ (to sb) an experience or a person that causes difficulties for sb: the trials and tribulations of married life ◇ She was a sore trial to her family at times.
IDM ˌtrial and 'error the process of solving a problem by trying various methods until you find a method that is successful: Children learn to use computer programs by trial and error.
■ verb (-ll-) [VN, V] (BrE) to test the ability, quality or performance of sth to see if it will be effective or successful

ˌtrial 'run (also ˌtest 'run) noun a test of how well sth new works, so that you can see if any changes are necessary: This year is a trial run for the new service, before it is officially introduced in 2001.

triangle

right-angled triangle (BrE)/
right triangle (AmE)

hypotenuse

equilateral triangle   **isosceles triangle**   right angle

tri·angle /'traɪæŋɡl/ noun **1** a flat shape with three straight sides and three angles; a thing in the shape of a triangle: (BrE) a right-angled triangle ◇ (AmE) a right triangle ◇ Cut the sandwiches into triangles. **2** a simple musical instrument that consists of a metal rod bent into the shape of a triangle, that you hit with another metal rod—picture on page 841 **3** a situation involving three people in a complicated relationship: a love triangle—see also ETERNAL TRIANGLE **4** (AmE) = SET SQUARE

tri·angu·lar /traɪˈæŋɡjələ(r)/ adj. **1** shaped like a triangle **2** involving three people or groups: a triangular contest in an election

tri·angu·la·tion /traɪˌæŋɡjuˈleɪʃn/ noun [U] (technical) a method of finding out distance and position, usually on a map, by measuring the distance between two fixed points and then measuring the angle from each of these to the third point

tri·ath·lon /traɪˈæθlən/ noun a sporting event in which people compete in three different sports, usually swimming, CYCLING and running—compare BIATHLON, DECATHLON, HEPTATHLON, PENTATHLON

tri·bal /'traɪbl/ adj. [usually before noun] connected with a tribe or tribes: tribal art/peoples/leaders

tri·bal·ism /'traɪbəlɪzəm/ noun [U] **1** behaviour, attitudes, etc. that are based on being loyal to a tribe or other social group **2** the state of being organized in a tribe or tribes

tribe /traɪb/ noun **1** (sometimes offensive) (in developing countries) a group of people of the same race, and with the same customs, language, religion, etc., living in a particular area and often led by a CHIEF: tribes living in remote areas of the Amazonian rainforest **2** (usually disapproving) a group or class of people, especially of one profession: He had a sudden outburst against the whole tribe of actors. **3** (biology) a group of related animals or plants: a tribe of cats **4** (informal or humorous) a large number of people: One or two of the grandchildren will be there, but not the whole tribe.

tribes·man /'traɪbzmən/, **tribes·woman** /'traɪbzwʊmən/ *noun* (*pl.* **-men** /-mən/ **-women** /-wɪmɪn/) a member of a tribe

tribu·la·tion /ˌtrɪbjuˈleɪʃn/ *noun* [C, U] (*literary* or *humorous*) great trouble or suffering: *the tribulations of modern life*

tri·bu·nal /traɪˈbjuːnl/ *noun* [sing.+ sing./pl. *v.*] a type of court with the authority to deal with a particular problem or disagreement: *She took her case to a tribunal.* ◊ *a disciplinary tribunal*—see also INDUSTRIAL TRIBUNAL

trib·une /ˈtrɪbjuːn/ *noun* **1** an official elected by the people in ancient Rome to defend their rights; a popular leader **2** a raised area that sb stands on to make a speech in public

tribu·tary /ˈtrɪbjətri; *AmE* -teri/ *noun* (*pl.* **-ies**) a river or stream that flows into a larger river or a lake—picture at COAST ▶ **tribu·tary** *adj.* [only before noun]: *a tributary stream/river*

trib·ute /ˈtrɪbjuːt/ *noun* **1** [U, C] ~ **(to sb)** an act, a statement or a gift that is intended to show your respect or admiration, especially for a dead person: *At her funeral her oldest friend **paid tribute** to her life and work.* ◊ *This book is a fitting tribute to the bravery of the pioneers.* ◊ *floral tributes* (= gifts of flowers at a funeral) **2** [sing.] ~ **to sth/sb** showing the good effects or influence of sth/sb: *His recovery is a tribute to the doctors' skill.* **3** [U, C] (especially in the past) money given by one country or ruler to another, especially in return for protection or for not being attacked

trice /traɪs/ *noun* **IDM** **in a 'trice** very quickly or suddenly: *He was gone in a trice.*

tri·ceps /ˈtraɪseps/ *noun* (*pl.* **tri·ceps**) the large muscle at the back of the top part of the arm—compare BICEPS

trick /trɪk/ *noun, verb*
■ *noun*
STH TO DECEIVE SB | **1** something that you do to deceive sb or to annoy sb as a joke: *They had to think of a trick to get past the guards.* ◊ *The kids are always **playing tricks on** their teacher.* ◊ *It was a **trick question** (= one to which the answer seems easy but actually is not).*—see also CONFIDENCE TRICK, DIRTY TRICK

STH CONFUSING | **2** something that confuses you so that you see, understand, remember, etc. things in the wrong way: *One of the problems of old age is that your memory can start to **play tricks** on you.* ◊ *Was there somebody standing there or was it **a trick of the light**?* ◊ *It's all done using **trick photography** (= photography that uses clever techniques to show things that do not actually exist or are impossible).*

ENTERTAINMENT | **3** a clever action that sb/sb performs as a way of entertaining people: *He amused the kids with conjuring tricks.* ◊ *a card trick*—see also HAT-TRICK

GOOD METHOD | **4** [usually sing.] a way of doing sth that works well; a good method: ***The trick is** to pick the animal up by the back of its neck.* ◊ *He used the old trick of attacking in order to defend himself.*

IN CARD GAMES | **5** the cards that you play or win in a single part of a card game: *I made/won six tricks in a row.*

IDM **a bag/box of 'tricks** (*informal*) a set of methods or equipment that sb can use: *Hotel managers are using a whole new bag of tricks to attract their guests.* **be up to your (old) 'tricks** (*informal, disapproving*) to be behaving in the same dishonest way as before **do the 'trick** (*informal*) to succeed in solving a problem or achieving a particular result: *I don't know what it was that did the trick, but I am definitely feeling much better.* **every trick in the 'book** every available method, whether it is honest or not: *He'll **try every trick in the book** to stop you from winning.* **have a trick, some more 'tricks, etc. up your sleeve** to have an idea, some plans, etc. that you keep ready to use if it becomes necessary **,trick or 'treat** said by children who visit people's houses at Halloween and threaten to play tricks on people who do not give them sweets/candy **the ,tricks of the 'trade** the clever ways of doing things, known and used by people who do a particular job or activity **,turn a 'trick** (*AmE, slang*) to have sex with sb for money—more at MISS *v.*, TEACH

■ *verb* [VN] to deceive sb: *I'd been tricked and I felt stupid.* ◊ *He managed to trick his way past the security guards.*
PHRV **,trick sb 'into sth/into doing sth** to make sb do sth by means of a trick: *He tricked me into lending him £100.* **,trick sb 'out of sth** to get sth from sb by means of a trick: *She was tricked out of her life savings.* **,trick sb/ sth↔'out (in/with sth)** (*literary*) to dress or decorate sb/sth in a way that attracts attention

trick·ery /ˈtrɪkəri/ *noun* [U] (*written*) the use of dishonest methods to trick people in order to achieve what you want

trickle /ˈtrɪkl/ *verb, noun*
■ *verb* **1** [usually +adv./prep.] to flow, or to make sth flow, slowly in a thin stream: [V] *Tears were trickling down her cheeks.* ◊ [VN] *Trickle some oil over the salad.* **2** [+adv./ prep.] to go, or to make sth go, somewhere slowly or gradually: [V] *People began trickling into the hall.* ◊ *News is starting to trickle out.* [also VN] **PHRV** **,trickle 'down** (especially of money) to spread from rich to poor people through the economic system of a country
■ *noun* **1** a small amount of liquid, flowing slowly **2** [usually sing.] ~ **(of sth)** a small amount or number of sth, coming or going slowly: *a steady trickle of visitors*

trick·ster /ˈtrɪkstə(r)/ *noun* a person who deceives or cheats people

tricky /ˈtrɪki/ *adj.* (**trick·ier, tricki·est**) **1** difficult to do or deal with: *a tricky question/situation* ◊ *Getting it to fit exactly is a tricky business.* ◊ *The equipment can be tricky to install.* **2** (of people) clever but likely to deceive you **SYN** CRAFTY

tri·col·our (*BrE*) (*AmE* **tri·color**) /ˈtrɪkələ(r); *AmE* ˈtraɪkʌlər/ *noun* [C] a flag which has three bands of different colours, especially the French and Irish national flags

tri·cycle /ˈtraɪsɪkl/ (also *informal* **trike**) *noun* a vehicle similar to a bicycle, but with one wheel at the front and two at the back

tri·dent /ˈtraɪdnt/ *noun* a weapon used in the past that looks like a long fork with three points

tried /traɪd/ *adj.*—see also TRY, *v.* **IDM** **,tried and 'tested/ 'trusted** (*BrE*) (*AmE* **,tried and 'true**) that you have used or relied on in the past successfully: *a tried and tested method for solving the problem*

tri·en·nial /traɪˈeniəl/ *adj.* happening every three years

trier /ˈtraɪə(r)/ *noun* a person who tries very hard at what they are doing and does their best: *He's a real trier. He gets tired but he never gives up.*

trifle /ˈtraɪfl/ *noun, verb*
■ *noun* **1** (**a trifle**) [sing.] (*formal*) slightly: *She seemed a trifle anxious.* **2** [C] something that is not valuable or important: *There's no point worrying over such trifles.* ◊ *$1000 is a mere trifle to her.* **3** [C, U] (*BrE*) a cold DESSERT (= a sweet dish) made from cake and fruit soaked in wine and/or jelly, covered with CUSTARD and cream—picture on page A1
■ *verb* **PHRV** **'trifle with sb/sth** (*formal*) (used especially in negative sentences) to treat sb/sth without genuine respect: *He is not a person to be trifled with.*

trif·ling /ˈtraɪflɪŋ/ *adj.* (*formal*) small and not important **SYN** TRIVIAL: *trifling details/matters*

trig·ger /ˈtrɪgə(r)/ *noun, verb*
■ *noun* **1** the part of a gun that you press in order to fire it: *to pull/squeeze the trigger* ◊ *He kept his finger on the trigger.* **2** ~ **(for sth)** | ~ **(to sth/to do sth)** something that is the cause of a particular reaction or development, especially a bad one: *The trigger for the strike was the closure of yet another factory.* **3** the part of a bomb that causes it to explode: *nuclear triggers*
■ *verb* [VN] **1** ~ **sth (off)** to make sth happen suddenly: *Nuts can trigger off a violent allergic reaction.* **2** to cause a device to start functioning: *to trigger an alarm/a switch*

'trigger-happy *adj.* (*informal, disapproving*) too willing and quick to use violence, especially with guns

trig·onom·etry /ˌtrɪgəˈnɒmətri; *AmE* -ˈnɑːm-/ *noun* [U] the type of mathematics that deals with the relationship between the sides and angles of triangles ▶ **trig·ono-**

s	t	v	z	ʃ	ʒ	tʃ	dʒ	θ	ð	ŋ
see	tea	van	zoo	shoe	vision	chain	jam	thin	this	sing

met·ric /ˈmɪtrɪɡənəˈmetrɪk/ *adj*. **trig·ono·met·ric·al** /-kl/ *adj*.

trike /traɪk/ *noun* (*informal*) = TRICYCLE

trilby /ˈtrɪlbi/ *noun* (*pl*. **-ies**) (*especially BrE*) a man's soft hat with a narrow BRIM and the top part pushed in from front to back—picture at HAT

trill /trɪl/ *noun*, *verb*

■ *noun* **1** a repeated short high sound made, for example, by sb's voice or by a bird **2** (*music*) the sound made when two notes next to each other in the musical scale are played or sung quickly several times one after the other

■ *verb* **1** [V] to make repeated short high sounds: *A phone trilled on the desk*. ◊ *The canary was trilling away happily*. **2** [V speech] to say sth in a high cheerful voice: *'How wonderful!' she trilled*. **3** [VN] (*phonetics*) to pronounce the letter 'r' by VIBRATING the tongue against the top of the mouth

tril·lion /ˈtrɪljən/ *number* (*plural verb*) **1** 1 000 000 000 000; one million million HELP You say **a**, **one**, **two**, **several**, etc. **trillion** without a final 's' on 'trillion'. **Trillions** (**of** …) can be used if there is no number or quantity before it. Always use a plural verb with **trillion** or **trillions**. **2** (**a trillion** or **trillions**) (*informal*) a very large amount HELP There are more examples of how to use numbers at the entry for **hundred**. **3** (*old-fashioned, BrE*) 1 000 000 000 000 000 000; one million million million

tril·ogy /ˈtrɪlədʒi/ *noun* (*pl*. **-ies**) a group of three books, films/movies, etc. that have the same subject or characters

trim /trɪm/ *verb*, *noun*, *adj*.

■ *verb* (**-mm-**) [VN] **1** to make sth neater, smaller, better, etc., by cutting parts from it: *to trim your hair* ◊ *to trim a hedge* (*back*) ◊ (*figurative*) *The training budget had been trimmed by £10000*. **2 ~ sth** (**off sth**) | **~ sth** (**off/away**) to cut away unnecessary parts from sth: *Trim any excess fat off the meat*. ◊ *I trimmed two centimetres off the hem of the skirt*. **3** [usually passive] **~ sth** (**with sth**) to decorate sth, especially around its edges: *gloves trimmed with fur* IDM **,trim your 'sails 1** to arrange the sails of a boat to suit the wind so that the boat moves faster **2** to reduce your costs PHRV **,trim 'down** | **,trim sth↔'down** to become smaller in size; to make sth smaller: *By a combination of diet and exercise he's trimmed down from 90 kilos to 70*.

■ *noun* **1** [C, usually sing.] an act of cutting a small amount off sth, especially hair: *How much is it for a wash and trim?* ◊ *The hedge needs a trim*. **2** [U, sing.] material that is used to decorate clothes, furniture, cars, etc., especially along the edges, by being a different colour, etc: *The car is available with black or red trim* (= the colour of the seats). ◊ *a blue jacket with a white trim* IDM **in** (**good, etc.**) **'trim** (*BrE, informal*) in good condition or order: *He keeps in trim by running every day*. ◊ *The team need to get in trim for the coming season*.

■ *adj*. **1** (of a person) looking thin, healthy and attractive: *She has kept very trim*. ◊ *a trim figure* **2** neat and well cared for: *a trim garden*

tri·maran /ˈtraɪməræn/ *noun* a fast sailing boat like a CATAMARAN, but with three HULLS instead of two

tri·mes·ter /traɪˈmestə(r)/ *noun* **1** (*medical*) a period of three months when a woman is pregnant: *the first/second/third trimester of pregnancy* **2** (*AmE*) = TERM: *The school year is divided into three trimesters*.—compare SEMESTER

trim·mer /ˈtrɪmə(r)/ *noun* a machine for cutting the edges of bushes, grass and HEDGES: *a hedge trimmer*

trim·ming /ˈtrɪmɪŋ/ *noun* **1** (*AmE* also **fix·ings**) [pl.] the extra things that it is traditional to have for a special meal or occasion: *a splendid feast of turkey with all the trimmings* **2** (**trimmings**) [pl.] the small pieces of sth that are left when you have cut sth: *hedge trimmings* **3** [U, C, usually pl.] material that is used to decorate sth, for example along its edges: *a white blouse with navy-blue trimming*

trin·ity /ˈtrɪnəti/ *noun* [sing.] **1** (**the Trinity**) (in Christianity) the union of Father, Son and HOLY SPIRIT as one God **2** (*formal*) a group of three people or things

trin·ket /ˈtrɪŋkɪt/ *noun* a piece of jewellery or small ornament that is not worth much money

trio /ˈtriːəʊ; *AmE* ˈtriːoʊ/ *noun* (*pl*. **-os**) **1** [C+sing./pl. *v*.] a group of three people or things: *A trio of English runners featured in the women's 1500 metres*.—compare DUO **2** [C+sing./pl. *v*.] a group of three musicians or singers who play or sing together **3** [C] a piece of music for three musicians or singers: *a trio for piano, oboe and bassoon*—compare DUET

trip /trɪp/ *noun*, *verb*

■ *noun* **1** a journey to a place and back again, especially a short one for pleasure or a particular purpose: *Did you have a good trip?* ◊ *We went on a trip to the mountains*. ◊ *a day trip* (= lasting a day) ◊ *a boat/coach trip* ◊ *a business/school/shopping trip* ◊ *They took a trip down the river*. ◊ *We had to make several trips to bring all the equipment over*.—see also EGO TRIP, FIELD TRIP, ROUND TRIP ⇨ note at JOURNEY **2** (*slang*) the experience that sb has if they take a powerful drug that affects the mind and makes them imagine things: *an acid* (= LSD) *trip* **3** an act of falling or nearly falling down, because you hit your foot against sth IDM see GUILT

■ *verb* (**-pp-**) **1** [V] [often +*adv./prep*.] **~** (**over/up**) | **~** (**over/on sth**) to catch your foot on sth and fall or almost fall: *She tripped and fell*. ◊ *Someone will trip over that cable*. ◊ *Be careful you don't trip up on the step*. **2** [VN] (*BrE* also **trip sb up**) to catch sb's foot and make them fall or almost fall: *As I passed, he stuck out a leg and tried to trip me up*. **3** [V+*adv./prep*.] (*literary*) to walk, run or dance with quick light steps: *She said goodbye and tripped off along the road*. **4** [VN] to release a switch, etc. or to operate sth by doing so: *to trip a switch* ◊ *Any intruders will trip the alarm*. **5** [V] (*informal*) to be under the influence of a drug that makes you HALLUCINATE IDM see MEMORY LANE, TONGUE *n*. PHRV **,trip 'up** | **,trip sb↔'up** to make a mistake; to deliberately make sb do this: *Read the questions carefully, because the examiners sometimes try to trip you up*.

tri·par·tite /traɪˈpɑːtaɪt; *AmE* -ˈpɑːrt-/ *adj*. [usually before noun] (*formal*) having three parts or involving three people, groups, etc.

tripe /traɪp/ *noun* [U] **1** the LINING of a cow's or pig's stomach, eaten as food: *tripe and onions* **2** (*informal*) something that sb says or writes that you think is nonsense or not of good quality: *What a load of tripe!* ◊ *I don't read that tripe!*

triple /ˈtrɪpl/ *adj*., *verb*

■ *adj*. [only before noun] **1** having three parts or involving three people or groups: *a triple heart bypass operation* ◊ *a triple alliance/partnership* ◊ *They're showing a triple bill of horror movies* (= three horror movies one after the other). **2** three times as much or as many as sth: *The amount of alcohol in his blood was triple the legal maximum*. ◊ *Its population is about triple that of Venice*. ◊ *a triple murderer* (= one who has killed three people) ▶ **triply** /ˈtrɪpli/ *adv*.

■ *verb* to become, or to make sth, three times as much or as many SYN TREBLE: [V] *Output should triple by next year*. [also VN]

the 'triple jump *noun* [sing.] a sporting event in which people try to jump as far forward as possible with three jumps. The first jump lands on one foot, the second on the other, and the third on both feet.

trip·let /ˈtrɪplət/ *noun* **1** one of three children born at the same time to the same mother **2** (*music*) a group of three equal notes to be played or sung in the time usually taken to play or sing two of the same kind

trip·li·cate /ˈtrɪplɪkət/ *noun* IDM **in 'triplicate 1** done three times: *Each sample was tested in triplicate*. **2** (of a document) copied twice, so that there are three copies in total—compare DUPLICATE

tri·pod /ˈtraɪpɒd; *AmE* -pɑːd/ *noun* a support with three legs for a camera, TELESCOPE, etc.—picture at LABORATORY

trip·per /ˈtrɪpə(r)/ *noun* (*BrE*) a person who is visiting a place for a short time for pleasure: *a day tripper*

trip·tych /ˈtrɪptɪk/ *noun* (*technical*) a picture or carved

æ	ɑː	e	ɜː	ə	ɪ	iː	i	ɒ	ɔː	ʌ	ʊ	u	uː
cat	father	ten	bird	about	sit	see	many	got	saw	cup	put	actual	too

(BrE)

design on three pieces of wood placed side by side, especially one over an ALTAR in a church

trip·wire /ˈtrɪpwaɪə(r)/ *noun* a wire that is stretched close to the ground as part of a device for catching sb/sth if they touch it

trite /traɪt/ *adj.* (of a remark, an opinion, etc.) dull and boring because it has been expressed so many times before; not original ▶ **trite·ly** *adv.* **trite·ness** *noun* [U]

tri·umph /ˈtraɪʌmf/ *noun, verb*
■ *noun* **1** [C, U] ~ (over sb/sth) a great success, achievement or victory: *one of the greatest triumphs of modern science* ◇ *It was a personal triumph over her old rival.* **2** [U] the feeling of great satisfaction or joy that you get from a great success or victory: *a cry/glance/smile of triumph* ◇ *The winning team returned home in triumph.* **3** [sing.] **a ~ (of sth)** an excellent example of how successful sth can be: *Her arrest was a triumph of international cooperation.*
■ *verb* [V] ~ (over sb/sth) to defeat sb/sth; to be successful: *As is usual in this kind of movie, good triumphs over evil in the end.* ◇ *France triumphed 3–0 in the final.*

tri·umph·al /traɪˈʌmfl/ *adj.* [usually before noun] done or made in order to celebrate a great success or victory

tri·umph·al·ism /traɪˈʌmfəlɪzəm/ *noun* [U] (*disapproving*) behaviour that celebrates a victory or success in a way that is too proud and intended to upset the people you have defeated ▶ **tri·umph·al·ist** *adj.*

tri·umph·ant /traɪˈʌmfənt/ *adj.* **1** very successful in a way that causes great satisfaction: *They emerged triumphant in the September election.* **2** showing great satisfaction or joy about a victory or success: *a triumphant expression/smile* ▶ **tri·umph·ant·ly** *adv.*

tri·um·vir·ate /traɪˈʌmvərət/ *noun* (*formal*) a group of three powerful people or groups who control sth together

trivet /ˈtrɪvɪt/ *noun* a metal stand that you can put a hot dish, etc. on

trivia /ˈtrɪviə/ *noun* [U] **1** unimportant matters, details or information: *We spent the whole evening discussing domestic trivia.* **2** (usually in compounds) facts about many subjects that are used in a game to test people's knowledge: *a trivia quiz*

triv·ial /ˈtrɪviəl/ *adj.* not important or serious; not worth considering: *a trivial detail/matter/problem* ◇ *I know it sounds trivial, but I'm worried about it.* ◇ *I'll try to fix it—but it's not trivial* (= it may be difficult to fix). ▶ **trivi·al·ly** /-iəli/ *adv.*

triv·ial·ity /ˌtrɪviˈæləti/ *noun* (*pl.* **-ies**) (*disapproving*) **1** [C] a matter that is not important: *I don't want to waste time on trivialities.* **2** [U] the state of being unimportant or dealing with unimportant things: *His speech was one of great triviality.*

trivi·al·ize (*BrE* also **-ise**) /ˈtrɪviəlaɪz/ *verb* [VN] (usually *disapproving*) to make sth seem less important, serious, difficult, etc. than it really is: *It is important not to trivialize children's worries.* ▶ **trivi·al·iza·tion, -isa·tion** /ˌtrɪviəlaɪˈzeɪʃn; *AmE* -ləˈz-/ *noun* [U]

trod *pt of* TREAD

trod·den *pp of* TREAD

trog·lo·dyte /ˈtrɒglədaɪt; *AmE* ˈtrɑːg-/ *noun* a person living in a CAVE, especially in PREHISTORIC times

troika /ˈtrɔɪkə/ *noun* (*formal*) a group of three politicians or countries working together

Tro·jan /ˈtrəʊdʒən; *AmE* ˈtroʊ-/ *noun, adj.* a person from the ancient city of Troy in Asia Minor IDM **work like a 'Trojan** (*old-fashioned*) to work very hard

Trojan 'horse *noun* a person or thing that is used to deceive an enemy in order to achieve a secret purpose ORIGIN From the myth in which the Greeks hid inside a hollow wooden statue of a horse in order to enter the city of their enemies, Troy.

troll /trəʊl; *AmE* troʊl/ *noun, verb*
■ *noun* (in Scandinavian stories) a creature that looks like an ugly person. Some trolls are very large and evil, others are small and friendly but like to trick people.
■ *verb* [V] ~ (for sth) (*especially AmE*) to catch fish by pulling a line with BAIT on it through the water behind a boat: (*figurative*) *to troll for votes*

trol·ley /ˈtrɒli; *AmE* ˈtrɑːli/ *noun* **1** (*BrE*) (*AmE* **cart**) a small vehicle with wheels that can be pushed or pulled along and is used for carrying things: *a shopping/supermarket/luggage trolley* **2** (*BrE*) (*AmE* **cart, wagon**) a small table on very small wheels, used for carrying or serving food or drink: *a drinks trolley* ◇ *a tea trolley* **3** (*AmE*) = TRAM IDM **off your 'trolley** (*BrE, informal*) crazy; stupid

shopping trolley (*BrE*)/ shopping cart (*AmE*)

drinks trolley (*BrE*)/ drinks cart (*AmE*)

trol·ley·bus /ˈtrɒlibʌs; *AmE* ˈtrɑːl-/ (*BrE*) (*AmE* **trackless trolley**) *noun* a bus driven by electricity from a cable above the street

trol·lop /ˈtrɒləp; *AmE* ˈtrɑːləp/ *noun* (*old-fashioned, offensive*) **1** a woman who is very untidy **2** a woman who has many sexual partners

trom·bone /trɒmˈbəʊn; *AmE* trɑːmˈboʊn/ *noun* a large BRASS musical instrument that you blow into, with a sliding tube used to change the note—picture on page 840

trom·bon·ist /trɒmˈbəʊnɪst; *AmE* trɑːmˈboʊ-/ *noun* a person who plays the trombone

tromp /trɒmp; *AmE* trɑːmp; trɔːmp/ *verb* [V, VN] (*AmE, informal*) = TRAMP

troop /truːp/ *noun, verb*
■ *noun* **1** (**troops**) [pl.] soldiers, especially in large groups: *They announced the withdrawal of 12 000 troops from the area.* ◇ *American/French/Russian troops* **2** [C] one group of soldiers, especially in TANKS or on horses: (*figurative*) *A troop of guests was mooning towards the house.* **3** [C] a local group of SCOUTS ▶ **troop** *adj.* [only before noun]: *troop movements/numbers/reductions* (= of soldiers)
■ *verb* [V+*adv./prep.*] (used with a plural subject) to walk somewhere together as a group: *After lunch we all trooped down to the beach.*

troop·er /ˈtruːpə(r)/ *noun* **1** a soldier of low rank in the part of an army that uses TANKS or horses **2** (*AmE*) a member of a State police force IDM see SWEAR

troop·ship /ˈtruːpʃɪp/ *noun* a ship used for transporting soldiers

trop ⇨ DE TROP

trope /trəʊp; *AmE* troʊp/ *noun* (*technical*) a word or phrase that is used in a way that is different from its usual meaning in order to create a particular mental image or effect. METAPHORS and SIMILES are tropes.

trophy /ˈtrəʊfi; *AmE* ˈtroʊfi/ *noun* (*pl.* **-ies**) **1** an object such as a silver cup that is given as a prize for winning a competition **2** (**Trophy**) used in the names of some competitions and races in which a trophy is given to the winner **3** an object that you keep to show that you were successful in sth, especially hunting or war

trop·ic /ˈtrɒpɪk; *AmE* ˈtrɑːpɪk/ *noun* **1** [C, usually sing.] one of the two imaginary lines drawn around the world 23° 7′ north (**the Tropic of Cancer**) or south (**the Tropic of Capricorn**) of the EQUATOR **2** (**the tropics**) [pl.] the area between the two tropics, which is the hottest part of the world

trop·ic·al /ˈtrɒpɪkl; *AmE* ˈtrɑː-/ *adj.* coming from, found in or typical of the tropics: *tropical fish/birds/plants* ◇ *tropical Africa/rainforests* ◇ *a tropical island/paradise*

trot /trɒt; *AmE* trɑːt/ *verb, noun*
■ *verb* (**-tt-**) **1** [V] (of a horse or its rider) to move forward at a speed that is faster than a walk and slower than a CANTER **2** [VN] to ride a horse in this way: *She trotted her pony around the field.* **3** [V+*adv./prep.*] (of a person or an animal) to run or walk fast, taking short quick steps: *The children trotted into the room.* **4** [V+*adv./prep.*] (*informal*)

to walk or go somewhere: *The guide led the way and we trotted along behind him.* PHRV **'trot sth↔'out** (*informal, disapproving*) to give the same excuses, facts, explanations, etc. for sth that have often been used before: *They trotted out the same old excuses for the lack of jobs in the area.*
■ *noun* **1** [sing.] a trotting speed, taking short quick steps: *The horse slowed to a trot.* ◊ *The girl **broke into a trot** and disappeared around the corner.* **2** [C] a period of trotting IDM **on the 'trot** (*BrE, informal*) **1** one after the other: *They've now won 3 games on the trot.* **2** busy all the time: *I've been on the trot all day.*

troth /trəʊθ; *AmE* trɑːθ/ *noun* IDM see PLIGHT *v.*

Trot·sky·ist /'trɒtskiɪst; *AmE* 'trɑːt-/ (also **Trot·sky·ite** /'trɒtskiaɪt; *AmE* 'trɑːt-/) *noun* a supporter of the political ideas of Leon Trotsky, especially that SOCIALISM should be introduced all over the world by means of revolution
▶ **Trot·sky·ist** (also **Trot·sky·ite**) *adj.*

trot·ter /'trɒtə(r); *AmE* 'trɑːt-/ *noun* **1** a pig's foot, especially when cooked and eaten as food **2** a horse that has been trained to TROT fast in races

trou·ba·dour /'truːbədɔː(r)/ *noun* (*literary*) a writer and performer of songs or poetry (after the French travelling performers of the 11th-13th centuries)

trouble /'trʌbl/ *noun, verb*
■ *noun*
PROBLEM/WORRY | **1** [U, C] **~ (with sb/sth)** a problem, worry, difficulty, etc. or a situation causing this: *We've been having trouble getting staff.* ◊ *He could **make trouble** for me if he wanted to.* ◊ *The trouble with you is you don't really want to work.* ◊ *Her trouble is she's incapable of making a decision.* ◊ *The trouble is* (= what is difficult is) *there aren't any trains at that time.* ◊ *The only trouble is we won't be here then.* ◊ *No, I don't know his number—I have quite enough trouble remembering my own.* ◊ *We've never had much trouble with vandals around here.* ◊ *financial troubles* ◊ *She was on the phone for an hour telling me her troubles.* ◊ *Our troubles aren't over yet.*—see also TEETHING TROUBLES
ILLNESS/PAIN | **2** [U] illness or pain: *back/eye/heart trouble* ◊ *I've been having trouble with my knee.*
WITH MACHINE | **3** [U] something that is wrong with a machine, vehicle, etc: *mechanical trouble*
DIFFICULT/VIOLENT SITUATION | **4** [U] a situation that is difficult or dangerous; a situation in which you can be criticized or punished: *The company **ran into trouble** early on, when a major order was cancelled.* ◊ *I've never been one to run away from trouble.* ◊ *A yachtsman **got into trouble** off the coast and had to be rescued.* ◊ *If I don't get this finished in time, I'll **be in trouble**.* ◊ *He's **in trouble with** the police.* ◊ *My brother was always **getting me into trouble** with my parents.* **5** [C, U] an angry or violent situation: *The police were expecting trouble after the match.* ◊ *If you're not in by midnight, there'll be trouble* (= I'll be very angry). ◊ *the troubles in Northern Ireland* ◊ *He had to throw out a few drunks who were causing trouble in the bar.*
EXTRA EFFORT | **6** [U] **~ (to sb)** extra effort or work SYN BOTHER: *I don't want to **put you to a lot of trouble**.* ◊ *I'll get it if you like, that will **save you the trouble of** going out.* ◊ *Making your own yogurt is **more trouble than it's worth**.* ◊ *She went to a lot of trouble to find the book for me.* ◊ *He thanked me for my trouble and left.* ◊ *Nothing is ever **too much trouble** for her* (= she's always ready to help). ◊ *I can call back later—it's **no trouble*** (= I don't mind). ◊ *I hope the children weren't too much trouble.*
IDM **get sb into 'trouble** (*old-fashioned*) to make a woman who is not married pregnant **give (sb) (some, no, any, etc.) 'trouble** to cause problems or difficulties: *My back's been giving me a lot of trouble lately.* ◊ *The children didn't give me any trouble at all when we were out.* **look for 'trouble** to behave in a way that is likely to cause an argument, violence, etc: *Drunken youths hang around outside looking for trouble.* **take trouble over/ with sth | take trouble doing/to do sth** to try hard to do sth well: *They take a lot of trouble to find the right person for the right job.* **take the trouble to do sth** to do

sth even though it involves effort or difficulty: *She didn't even take the trouble to find out how to spell my name.*—more at ASK
■ *verb*
MAKE SB WORRIED | **1** [VN] to make sb worried or upset: *What is it that's troubling you?* ◊ *He was deeply troubled by the allegations.*
DISTURB | **2** (*often used in polite requests*) to disturb sb because you want to ask them sth SYN BOTHER: [VN] *Sorry to trouble you, but could you tell me the time?* ◊ *I don't want to trouble the doctor with such a small problem.* ◊ (*formal*) [VN to inf] *Could I trouble you to open the window, please?*
MAKE EFFORT | **3** [V to inf] (*BrE, formal*) (*usually used in negative sentences*) to make an effort to do sth SYN BOTHER: *He rushed into the room without troubling to knock.*
CAUSE PAIN | **4** [VN] (of a medical problem) to cause pain: *My back's been troubling me again.*
IDM see POUR

troubled /'trʌbld/ *adj.* **1** (of a person) worried and anxious: *She looked into his **troubled** face.* **2** (of a place, situation or time) having a lot of problems: *a **troubled** marriage* ◊ *We live in **troubled** times.*

trouble·maker /'trʌblmeɪkə(r)/ *noun* a person who often causes trouble, especially by involving others in arguments or encouraging them to complain about people in authority

trouble·shoot·er /'trʌblʃuːtə(r)/ *noun* a person who helps to solve problems in a company or an organization
▶ **trouble·shoot·ing** *noun* [U]

trouble·some /'trʌblsəm/ *adj.* causing trouble, pain, etc. over a long period of time: *a **troublesome** cough/ child/problem*

'trouble spot *noun* a place or country where trouble often happens, especially violence or war

trough /trɒf; *AmE* trɔːf/ *noun* **1** [C] a long narrow open container for animals to eat or drink from: *a water trough* **2** (**the trough**) [sing.] (*informal*) if you say that people have their noses **in the trough**, you mean that they are trying to get a lot of money for themselves **3** [C] (*technical*) a long narrow region of low air pressure between two regions of higher pressure—compare RIDGE **4** [C] a period of time when the level of sth is low, especially a time when a business or the economy is not growing: *There have been **peaks and troughs** in the long-term trend of unemployment.* **5** [C] a low area between two waves in the sea, or two hills

trounce /traʊns/ *verb* [VN] (*written*) to defeat sb completely: *Brazil trounced Italy 5–1 in the final.*

troupe /truːp/ *noun* a group of actors, singers, etc. who work together—compare TROOP

trouper /'truːpə(r)/ *noun* (*informal*) an actor or other person who has a lot of experience and who you can depend on

trou·sers /'traʊzəz; *AmE* -zərz/ (*especially BrE*) (*AmE* usually **pants**) *noun* [pl.] a piece of clothing that covers the body from the waist down and is divided into two parts to cover each leg separately: *a pair of grey trousers* ◊ *I was still **in short trousers*** (= still only a boy) *at the time.* ◊ *He dropped his trousers.*—picture on page A4
▶ **trou·ser** *adj.* [only before noun]: *trouser buttons/legs/ pockets* IDM see CATCH *v.*, WEAR *v.*

'trouser suit (*BrE*) (*AmE* **pant·suit**) *noun* a woman's suit of jacket and trousers/pants

trous·seau /'truːsəʊ; *AmE* -soʊ/ *noun* (*pl.* **trous·seaus** or **trous·seaux** /-səʊz; *AmE* -soʊz/) (*old-fashioned*) the clothes and other possessions collected by a woman who is soon going to get married, to begin her married life with

trout /traʊt/ *noun* **1** [C, U] (*pl.* **trout**) a common FRESH-WATER fish that is used for food. There are several types of trout: *rainbow/brown trout* ◊ *trout fishing* ◊ *Shall we have trout for dinner?*—picture on page A7 **2** [C, usually sing.] (usually **old trout**) (*informal, disapproving*) a bad-tempered or annoying old woman

b	d	f	g	h	k	l	m	n	p	r
bad	**did**	**fall**	**get**	**hat**	**cat**	**leg**	**man**	**now**	**pen**	**red**

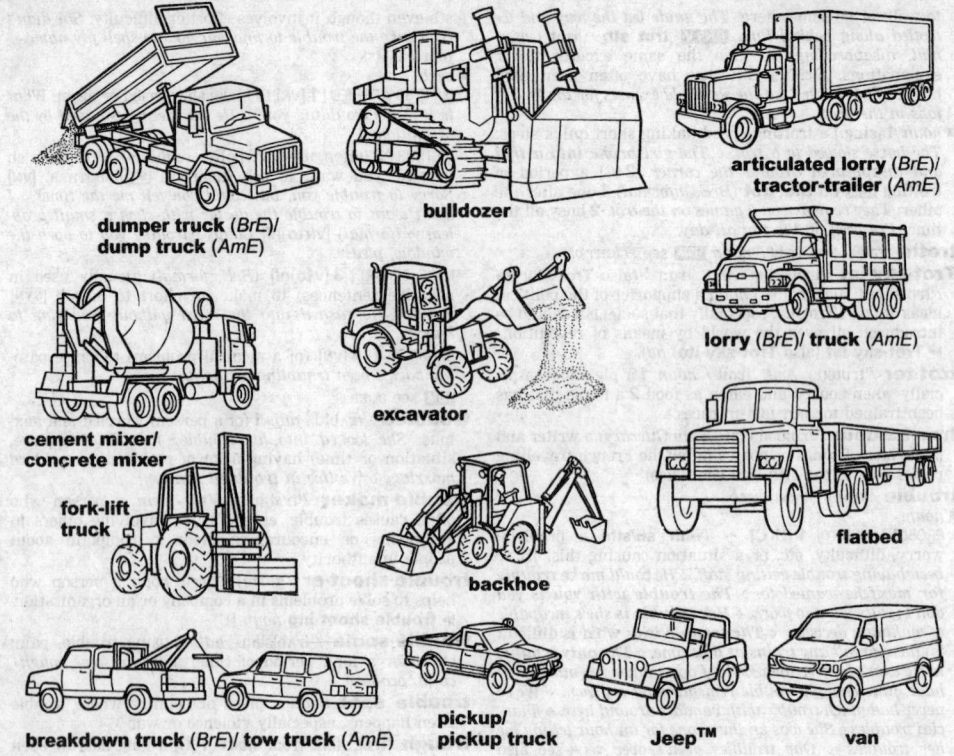

dumper truck (*BrE*)/ **dump truck** (*AmE*)

bulldozer

articulated lorry (*BrE*)/ **tractor-trailer** (*AmE*)

lorry (*BrE*)/ **truck** (*AmE*)

cement mixer/ concrete mixer

excavator

fork-lift truck

backhoe

flatbed

breakdown truck (*BrE*)/ **tow truck** (*AmE*)

pickup/ pickup truck

Jeep™

van

trove /trəʊv; *AmE* troʊv/ *noun* ⇨ TREASURE TROVE

trowel /ˈtraʊəl/ *noun* **1** a small garden tool with a curved blade for lifting plants and digging holes—picture at GARDEN **2** a small tool with a flat blade, used in building for spreading CEMENT or PLASTER **IDM** **lay it on with a** **ˈtrowel** (*informal*) to talk about sb/sth in a way that makes them or it seem much better or much worse than they really are; to exaggerate sth: *He was laying the flattery on with a trowel.*

tru·ancy /ˈtruːənsi/ *noun* [U] the practice of staying away from school without permission: *Truancy rates at the school are very high.*

tru·ant /ˈtruːənt/ *noun* a child who stays away from school without permission ▸ **tru·ant** *verb*: [V] *A number of pupils have been truanting regularly.* **IDM** **play ˈtruant** (*BrE*) (*AmE* informal **play ˈhooky**) (*old-fashioned*) to stay away from school without permission—see also BUNK OFF, SKIVE

truce /truːs/ *noun* an agreement between enemies or opponents to stop fighting for an agreed period of time; the period of time that this lasts: *to call/ break a truce*

truck /trʌk/ *noun, verb*
■ *noun* **1** [C] (*especially AmE*) = LORRY: *a truck driver* **2** [C] (*BrE*) (*AmE* **car**) an open railway vehicle for carrying goods or animals: *a cattle truck* **3** [C] a vehicle that is open at the back, used for carrying goods, soldiers, animals, etc: *a farm/ an army truck* **4** [C] a vehicle for carrying things, that is pulled or pushed by hand—see also FORK-LIFT TRUCK, PICKUP TRUCK, SALT TRUCK **IDM** **have/want no truck with sb/sth** (*BrE*) to refuse to deal with sb; to refuse to accept or consider sth: *We in this party will have no truck with illegal organizations.*
■ *verb* [VN] (*especially AmE*) to take sth somewhere by truck: *Water had to be trucked in to the town.* ▸ **truck·ing** *noun* [U]: *trucking companies*

truck·er /ˈtrʌkə(r)/ *noun* (*especially AmE*) a person whose job is driving a truck

ˈtruck farm *noun* (*AmE*) = MARKET GARDEN ▸ **ˈtruck farmer** *noun* **ˈtruck farming** *noun* [U]

truck·load /ˈtrʌkləʊd; *AmE* -loʊd/ *noun* ~ (of sb/sth) the amount of sb/sth that fills a truck (often used to express the fact that an amount is large)

ˈtruck stop *noun* (*AmE*) = TRANSPORT CAFE

trucu·lent /ˈtrʌkjələnt/ *adj.* (*written, disapproving*) tending to argue or be bad-tempered; slightly aggressive ▸ **trucu·lence** /-ləns/ *noun* [U] **trucu·lent·ly** *adv.*

trudge /trʌdʒ/ *verb, noun*
■ *verb* to walk slowly or with heavy steps, because you are tired or carrying sth heavy: [VN] *He trudged the last two miles to the town.* ◊ [V+*adv./prep.*] *The men trudged up the hill, laden with supplies.*
■ *noun* [sing.] a long tiring walk

true /truː/ *adj., adv., noun*
■ *adj.* (**truer, tru·est**)
CORRECT | **1** connected with facts rather than things that have been invented or guessed: *Indicate whether the following statements are true or false.* ◊ *Is it true she's leaving?* ◊ *All the rumours turned out to be true.* ◊ *That's not strictly (= completely) true.* ◊ *The novel is based on **a true story**.* ◊ *His excuse just doesn't **ring** (= sound) **true**.* ◊ *Unfortunately, these findings do not **hold true** (= are not valid) for women and children.* ◊ *The music is dull and uninspiring, and **the same is true of** the acting.* ◊ *You never spoke a **truer word** (= used to emphasize that you agree with what sb has just said).* **OPP** UNTRUE

REAL | **2** real or exact, especially when this is different from how sth seems: *the true face of socialism (= what socialism is really like rather than what people think it is like)* ◊ *The true cost of these experiments to the environment will not be known for years to come.* ◊ *He reveals his true character to very few people.* **3** [usually before noun]

> **WORD FAMILY**
> **true** *adj.* (≠ untrue)
> **truth** *n.* (≠ untruth)
> **truthful** *adj.* (≠ untruthful)
> **truly** *adv.*
> **truism** *n.*

having the qualities or characteristics of the thing mentioned: *It was true love between them.* ◇ *He's a true gentleman.* ◇ *She is not the true owner of this house.* ◇ *The painting is a masterpiece in the truest sense of the word.* ◇ *He is credited with inventing the first true helicopter.*
ADMITTING FACT | **4** used to admit that a particular fact or statement is true, although you think that sth else is more important: *It's true that he could do the job, but would he fit in with the rest of the team?* ◇ *'We could get it cheaper.' 'True, but would it be as good?'*
LOYAL | **5 ~ (to sb/sth)** showing respect and support for a particular person or belief in a way that does not change, even in different situations: *a true friend* ◇ *She has always been true to herself* (= done what she thought was good, honourable, etc.). ◇ *He was true to his word* (= did what he promised to do).
ACCURATE | **6 ~ (to sth)** being an accurate version or copy of sth: *The movie is not true to the book.* **7** [not usually before noun] *(old-fashioned* or *literary)* straight and accurate: *His aim was true* (= he hit the target).
⇨ note at REAL
IDM **come 'true** (of a hope, wish, etc.) to become reality: *Winning the medal was like a dream come true.* **too ˌgood to be 'true** used to say that you cannot believe that sth is as good as it seems: *'I'm afraid you were quoted the wrong price.' 'I thought it was too good to be true.'* **your true 'colours** (often *disapproving*) your real character, rather than the one that you usually allow other people to see **true to 'form** used to say that sb is behaving in the way that you expect them to behave, especially when this is annoying **true to 'life** (of a book, film/movie, etc.) seeming real rather than invented: *I don't think the characters are very true to life.*—more at RING² *v.,* TRIED
■ *adv.* *(old-fashioned* or *literary)*
STRAIGHT | **1** in a direct line: *The arrow flew straight and true to the target.*
CORRECTLY | **2 speak ~** to tell the truth: *He had spoken truer than he knew.*
■ *noun*
IDM **ˌout of 'true** if an object is **out of true**, it is not straight or in the correct position
ˌtrue-'blue *adj.* **1** *(BrE)* strongly supporting the British Conservative Party: *true-blue Tory voters* **2** *(especially AmE)* being a loyal supporter of a particular person, group, principle, etc.; being a typical example of sth: *a true-blue Californian*
ˌtrue-'life *adj.* [only before noun] a **true-life** story is one that actually happened rather than one that has been invented
ˌtrue 'north *noun* [U] north according to the earth's AXIS (= the imaginary line through the earth's centre from north to south)—compare MAGNETIC NORTH
truf·fle /ˈtrʌfl/ *noun* **1** an expensive type of FUNGUS that grows underground, used in cooking **2** a soft round sweet/candy made of chocolate
trug /trʌg/ *noun* a shallow basket used for carrying garden tools, plants, etc.
tru·ism /ˈtruːɪzəm/ *noun* a statement that is clearly true and does not therefore add anything interesting or important to a discussion
truly /ˈtruːli/ *adv.* **1** used to emphasize that a particular statement, feeling, etc. is sincere or genuine: *I'm truly sorry that things had to end like this.* **2** used to emphasize a particular quality: *a truly memorable occasion* **3** used to emphasize that a particular description is accurate or correct: *a truly democratic system of government* ◇ *(spoken)* *Well, really and truly, things weren't quite how she described them.* **IDM** **Yours Truly** *(AmE, formal, written)* used at the end of a formal letter before you sign your name ⇨ Study page B14—more at WELL *adv.*
trump /trʌmp/ *noun, verb*
■ *noun* **1** (also **'trump card**) [C] (in some card games) a card that belongs to the SUIT (= one of the four sets in a pack/deck of cards) that has been chosen for a particular game to have a higher value than the other three suits: *I played a trump and won the trick.* **2** (**trumps**) [U+sing./pl.

v.] (in some card games) the SUIT that has been chosen for a particular game to have a higher value than the other three suits: *What's trumps?* ◇ *Clubs are trumps.* **IDM** **ˌcome up/ˌturn up 'trumps** to do what is necessary to make a particular situation successful, especially when this is sudden or unexpected: *I didn't honestly think he'd pass the exam but he came up trumps on the day.*
■ *verb* [VN] **1 ~ sth (with sth)** (in some card games) to play a trump card that beats sb else's card **2** to beat sth that sb says or does by saying or doing sth even better: *They were trumped by another firm that made a lower bid.* **PHRV** **ˌtrump sth↔'up** to make up a false story about sb/sth, especially accusing them of doing sth wrong: *She was arrested on a trumped-up charge.*
'trump card *noun* **1** = TRUMP **2** something that gives you an advantage over other people, especially when they do not know what it is and you are able to use it to surprise them
trum·pet /ˈtrʌmpɪt/ *noun, verb*
■ *noun* **1** a BRASS musical instrument made of a curved metal tube that you blow into, with three VALVES for changing the note: *a trumpet blast/call*—picture on page 840 **2** a thing shaped like a trumpet, especially the open flower of a DAFFODIL **IDM** see BLOW *v.*
■ *verb* **1 ~ sth (as sth)** to talk about sth publicly in a proud or enthusiastic way: [VN] *to trumpet sb's achievements* ◇ *Their marriage was trumpeted as the society wedding of the year.* [also V speech] **2** [V] (especially of an elephant) to make a loud noise
trum·pet·er /ˈtrʌmpɪtə(r)/ *noun* a person who plays a trumpet
trun·cate /trʌŋˈkeɪt; AmE ˈtrʌŋkeɪt/ *verb* [VN] [usually passive] *(formal)* to make sth shorter, especially by cutting off the top or end: *My article was published in truncated form.* ◇ *a truncated pyramid* ◇ *Further discussion was truncated by the arrival of tea.* ▶ **trun·ca·tion** *noun* [U, C]
trun·cheon /ˈtrʌntʃən/ (also **baton**) (both *especially BrE*) *(AmE* usually **night-stick**) *noun* a short thick stick that police officers carry as a weapon
trun·dle /ˈtrʌndl/ *verb* [+adv. / prep.] **1** to move or roll somewhere slowly and noisily; to move sth slowly and noisily, especially sth heavy, with wheels: [V] *A train trundled across the bridge.* [also VN] **2** [V] (of a person) to walk slowly with heavy steps **PHRV** **ˌtrundle sth↔'out** *(disapproving, especially BrE)* to mention or do sth that you have often mentioned or done before: *A long list of reasons was trundled out to justify their demands.*
trunk /trʌŋk/ *noun* **1** [C] the thick main stem of a tree, that the branches grow from **2** [C] (*AmE*) = BOOT (2) **3** [C] the long nose of an elephant—picture on page A6 **4** (**trunks**) [pl.] = SWIMMING TRUNKS **5** [C] a large strong box with a lid used for storing or transporting clothes, books, etc. **6** [C, usually sing.] the main part of the human body apart from the head, arms and legs—see also TORSO
'trunk road *noun* (*BrE*) an important main road
truss /trʌs/ *noun, verb*
■ *noun* **1** a special belt with a thick piece of material, worn by sb suffering from a HERNIA in order to support the muscles **2** a frame made of pieces of wood or metal used to support a roof, bridge, etc.
■ *verb* [VN] **1 ~ sb/sth (up)** to tie up sb's arms and legs so that they cannot move: *The guard had been gagged and trussed up.* **2** to tie the legs and wings of a chicken, etc. before it is cooked
trust /trʌst/ *noun, verb*
■ *noun* **1** [U] **~ (in sb/sth)** the belief that sb/sth is good, sincere, honest, etc. and will not try to harm or deceive you: *Her trust in him was unfounded.* ◇ *a partnership based on trust* ◇ *It has taken years to earn their trust.* ◇ *If you put your trust in me, I will not let you down.* ◇ *She will not betray your trust* (= do sth that you have asked her not to do). ◇ *He was appointed to a position of trust* (= a job involving a lot of responsibility, because people trust him). **2** [C, U] *(law)* an arrangement by which an organization or a group of people has legal control of money or property that has been given to sb, usually

æ	ɑː	e	ɜː	ə	ɪ	iː	i	ɒ	ɔː	ʌ	ʊ	u	uː
cat	father	ten	bird	about	sit	see	many	got (BrE)	saw	cup	put	actual	too

until that person reaches a particular age; an amount of money or property that is controlled in this way: *He set up a trust for his children.* ◊ *The money will be held in trust until she is 18.* ◊ *Our fees depend on the value of the trust.*—see also UNIT TRUST **3** [C] (*law*) an organization or a group of people that invests money that is given or lent to it and uses the profits to help a charity: *a charitable trust* **4** [C] (*business*) (*especially AmE*) a group of companies that work together illegally to reduce competition, control prices, etc: *anti-trust laws* **IDM** **in sb's 'trust | in the trust of sb** being looked after by sb: *The family pet was left in the trust of a neighbour.* **take sth on 'trust** to believe what sb says even though you do not have any proof or evidence to show that it is true

■ *verb* **1** to have confidence in sb; to believe that sb is good, sincere, honest, etc: [VN] *She trusts Alan implicitly.* ◊ [VNto inf] *Can they be trusted to take care of the business while we are away?* ◊ *You can trust me not to tell anyone.* **2** [VN] to believe that sth is true or correct or that you can rely on it: *He trusted her judgement.* ◊ *Don't trust what the newspapers say!* **3** [V(that)] (*formal*) to hope and expect that sth is true: *I trust (that) you have no objections to our proposals?* **IDM** **not trust sb an 'inch** to not trust sb at all: *He says he just wants to help you but I wouldn't trust him an inch if I were you.* **trust 'you, 'him, 'her, etc. (to do sth)** (*spoken, informal*) used when sb does or says sth that you think is typical of them: *Trust John to forget Sue's birthday!*—more at TRIED **PHRV** **'trust in sb/sth** (*formal*) to have confidence in sb/sth; to believe that sb/sth is good and can be relied on: *She needs to trust more in her own abilities.* **'trust to sth** [no passive] to put your confidence in sth such as luck, chance, etc. because there is nothing else to help you: *I stumbled along in the dark, trusting to luck to find the right door.* **'trust sb with sth/sb** to give sth/sb to a person to take care of because you believe they would be very careful with it/them: *I'd trust her with my life.*

trust·ee /trʌˈstiː/ *noun* **1** a person or an organization that has control of money or property that has been put into a TRUST for sb: *The bank will act as trustees for the estate until the child is 18.* **2** a member of a group of people that controls the financial affairs of a charity or other organization

trustee·ship /trʌˈstiːʃɪp/ *noun* [U, C] **1** the job of being a trustee **2** the responsibility for governing a particular region, given to a country by the United Nations Organization; a region that is governed by another country in this way

'trust fund *noun* money that is controlled for sb by an organization or a group of people: *She set up a trust fund for her children.*

trust·ing /ˈtrʌstɪŋ/ *adj.* tending to believe that other people are good, sincere, honest, etc: *If you're too trusting, other people will take advantage of you.*

'trust territory *noun* a region governed by the United Nations Organization or by another country that has been chosen by the United Nations Organization

trust·worthy /ˈtrʌstwɜːði; AmE -wɜːrði/ *adj.* that you can rely on to be good, honest, sincere, etc. **SYN** RELIABLE ▶ **trust·worthi·ness** *noun* [U]

trusty /ˈtrʌsti/ *adj., noun*
■ *adj.* [only before noun] (*old use* or *humorous*) that you have had a long time and have always been able to rely on **SYN** RELIABLE: *a trusty friend* ◊ *She spent years touring Europe with her trusty old camera.*
■ *noun* (*pl.* **-ies**) a prisoner who is given special privileges because of good behaviour

truth /truːθ/ *noun* (*pl.* **truths** /truːðz/) **1** (**the truth**) [sing.] the true facts about sth, rather than the things that have been invented or guessed: *Do you think she's telling the truth?* ◊ *We are determined to get at (= discover) the truth.* ◊ *The truth (of the matter) is we can't afford to keep all the staff on.* ◊ *I don't think you are telling me the whole truth about what happened.* **2** [U] the quality or state of being based on fact: *There is no truth in the rumours.* ◊ *There is not a grain of truth in what she says.* **OPP** FALSITY **3** [C] a fact that is believed by most people to be

true: *universal truths* ◊ *She was forced to face up to a few unwelcome truths about her family.*—see also HALF-TRUTH, HOME TRUTH—compare UNTRUTH **IDM** **if (the) ,truth be 'known/'told** used to tell sb the true facts about a situation, especially when these are not known by other people **in 'truth** (*written*) used to emphasize the true facts about a situation: *She laughed and chatted but was, in truth, not having much fun.* **,nothing could be ,further from the 'truth** used to say that a fact or comment is completely false **,truth is stranger than 'fiction** (*saying*) used to say that things that actually happen are often more surprising than stories that are invented **(the) ,truth will 'out** (*saying*) used to say that people will find out the true facts about a situation even if you try to keep them secret—more at BEND *v.*, ECONOMICAL, MOMENT

truth·ful /ˈtruːθfl/ *adj.* **1** ~ (about sth) (of a person) saying only what is true: *They were less than truthful about their part in the crime.* ◊ *Are you being completely truthful with me?* **2** (of a statement) giving the true facts about sth: *a truthful answer* **OPP** UNTRUTHFUL ▶ **truth·ful·ly** /-fəli/ *adv.*: *She answered all their questions truthfully.* **truth·ful·ness** *noun* [U]

try /traɪ/ *verb, noun*
■ *verb* (**tries, try·ing, tried, tried**) **1** to make an attempt or effort to do or get sth: [V] *I don't know if I can come but I'll try.* ◊ [V to inf] *What are you trying to do?* ◊ *I tried hard not to laugh.* ◊ [VN to inf] *She tried her best to solve the problem.* ◊ [VN] *Just try your hardest.* **HELP** In spoken English **try** can be used with **and** plus another verb, instead of with **to** and the infinitive: *I'll try and get you a new one tomorrow.* ◊ *Try and finish quickly.* In this structure, **try** can only be used in the infinitive, or to tell somebody what to do. **2** to use, do or test sth in order to see if it is good, suitable, etc: [VN] *Have you tried this new coffee? It's very good.* ◊ *Would you like to try some raw fish?' 'Why not? I'll try anything once!'* ◊ *Have you ever tried windsurfing?* ◊ *Try these shoes for size—they should fit you.* ◊ *She tried the door, but it was locked.* ◊ [V-ing] *John isn't here. Try phoning his home number.* **HELP** Notice the difference between **try to do sth** and **try doing sth**: *You should try to eat more fruit.* means 'You should make an effort to eat more fruit.'; *You should try eating more fruit.* means 'You should see if eating more fruit will help you' (to feel better, for example). **3** [VN] ~ sb (for sth) | ~ sth to examine evidence in a court of law and decide whether sb is innocent or guilty: *He was tried for murder.* ◊ *The case was tried before a jury.* **IDM** **,not for want/lack of 'trying** used to say that although sb has not succeeded in sth, they have tried very hard: *They haven't won a game yet, but it isn't for want of trying.* **try your 'hand (at sth)** to do sth such as an activity or a sport for the first time **,try it 'on (with sb)** (*BrE, informal, disapproving*) **1** to behave badly towards sb or try to get sth from them, even though you know this will make them angry: *Children often try it on with new teachers.* **2** to try to start a sexual relationship with sb **try your 'luck (at sth)** to do sth that involves risk or luck, hoping to succeed: *My grandparents emigrated to Canada to try their luck there.* **try sb's 'patience** to make sb feel impatient—more at DAMNEDEST, LEVEL *adj.* **PHRV** **'try for sth** to make an attempt to get or win sth **,try sth↔'on** to put on a piece of clothing to see if it fits and how it looks: *Try the shoes on before you buy them.* **,try 'out for sth** (*especially AmE*) to compete for a position or place in sth, or to be a member of a team: *She's trying out for the school play.*—related noun TRY-OUT **,try sb/sth↔'out (on sb)** to test or use sb/sth in order to see how good or effective they are: *They're trying out a new presenter for the show.*—related noun TRY-OUT
■ *noun* (*pl.* **tries**) **1** [usually sing.] ~ (at sth/at doing sth) an act of trying to do sth: *I doubt they'll be able to help but it's worth a try (= worth asking them).* ◊ *Why don't you have a try at convincing him?* ◊ *I don't think I'll be any good at tennis, but I'll give it a try.* ◊ (*spoken*) *'What's that behind you?' ' Nice try (= at making me turn round), but you'll have to do better than that!'* ◊ (*AmE*) *The US negotiators decided to make another try at reaching a settlement.* **2** (in rugby) an act of scoring

aɪ	aʊ	eɪ	əʊ	oʊ	ɔɪ	ɪə	eə	ʊə	j	w
my	now	say	go	go	boy	near	hair	pure	yes	wet
			(BrE)	(AmE)						

points by touching the ground behind your opponents' GOAL LINE with the ball: *to score a try*

try·ing /ˈtraɪɪŋ/ *adj.* annoying or difficult to deal with: *She can be very trying at times.* ◊ *These are trying times for all of us.*

ˈtry-out *noun* **1** an act of testing how good or effective sb/sth is before deciding whether to use them in the future **2** (*AmE*) = TRIAL (3)

tryst /trɪst/ *noun* (*literary* or *humorous*) a secret meeting between lovers

tsar (also **tzar, czar**) /zɑː(r)/ *noun* the title of the EMPEROR of Russia in the past: *Tsar Nicholas II*

tsar·ina (also **tzar·ina, czar·ina**) /zɑːˈriːnə/ *noun* the title of the EMPRESS of Russia in the past

tsar·ism (also **tzar·ism, czar·ism**) /ˈzɑːrɪzəm/ *noun* [U] the Russian system of government by a tsar, which existed before 1917 ▶ **tsar·ist** (also **tzar·ist, czar·ist**) *noun, adj.*

tsetse fly /ˈtsetsi flaɪ/ *noun* [C, U] an African fly that bites humans and animals and sucks their blood and can spread a disease called SLEEPING SICKNESS

ˈT-shirt *noun* an informal shirt with short sleeves and no buttons, or just a few buttons at the top

tsp *abbr.* (*pl.* **tsp** or **tsps**) TEASPOONFUL: *1 tsp chilli powder*

ˈT-square *noun* a plastic or metal instrument in the shape of a T for drawing or measuring RIGHT ANGLES (= of 90°)

tsu·nami /tsuːˈnɑːmi/ *noun* (from *Japanese*) an extremely large wave in the sea caused, for example, by an earthquake [SYN] TIDAL WAVE

tub /tʌb/ *noun* **1** a large round container without a lid, used for washing clothes, growing plants in, etc: *There were tubs of flowers on the balcony.* **2** a small wide, usually round, plastic or paper container with a lid, used for food, etc: *a tub of margarine*—picture at PACKAGING **3** (*especially AmE*) = BATH, BATHTUB: *They found her lying in the tub.*—see also HOT TUB

tuba /ˈtjuːbə; *AmE* ˈtuːbə/ *noun* a large BRASS musical instrument that you play by blowing, and that produces low notes—picture on page 840

tubby /ˈtʌbi/ *adj.* (*informal*) (of a person) short and slightly fat

tube /tjuːb; *AmE* tuːb/ *noun*

PIPE | **1** [C] a long hollow pipe made of metal, plastic, rubber, etc., through which liquids or gases move from one place to another—see also CATHODE RAY TUBE, INNER TUBE, TEST TUBE **2** [C] a hollow object in the shape of a pipe or tube: *a bike's inner tube* ◊ *the cardboard tube from the centre of a toilet roll*

CONTAINER | **3** [C] ~ (**of sth**) a long narrow container made of soft metal or plastic, with a lid, used for holding thick liquids that can be squeezed out of it: *a tube of tooth-paste*—picture at PACKAGING

PART OF BODY | **4** [C] a part inside the body that is shaped like a tube and through which air, liquid, etc. passes: *bronchial tubes*—see also FALLOPIAN TUBES

UNDERGROUND RAILWAY | **5** (**the tube**) [sing.] (*BrE*) the underground railway system in London: *a tube station/train* ▷ *We came by tube.* ⇨ note at UNDERGROUND

TELEVISION | **6** (**the tube**) [sing.] (*AmE, informal*) the television

IN EAR | **7** [C] (*AmE*) = GROMMET

[IDM] **go down the ˈtube/ˈtubes** (*informal*) (of a plan, company, situation, etc.) to fail: *The education system is going down the tubes.*

tuber /ˈtjuːbə(r); *AmE* ˈtuː-/ *noun* the short thick round part of an underground stem or root of some plants, such as potatoes, which stores food and from which new plants grow ▶ **tu·ber·ous** /ˈtjuːbərəs; *AmE* ˈtuː-/ *adj.*

tu·ber·cu·losis /tjuːˌbɜːkjuˈləʊsɪs; *AmE* tuːˌbɜːrkjəˈləʊsɪs/ *noun* [U] (*abbr.* **TB**) a serious infectious disease in which swellings appear on the lungs and other parts of the body ▶ **tu·ber·cu·lar** /tjuːˈbɜːkjələ(r); *AmE* tuːˈbɜːrk-/ *adj.*: *a tubercular infection/lung*

ˈtube top *noun* (*AmE*) = BOOB TUBE

tub·ing /ˈtjuːbɪŋ; *AmE* ˈtuːbɪŋ/ *noun* [U] metal, plastic, etc. in the shape of a tube: *a piece/length of copper tubing*—picture at LABORATORY

ˈtub-thumping *noun* [U] (*BrE, disapproving*) the act of giving your opinions about sth in a loud and aggressive way ▶ **ˈtub-thumping** *adj.*

tu·bu·lar /ˈtjuːbjələ(r); *AmE* ˈtuː-/ *adj.* **1** made of tubes or of parts that are shaped like tubes: *a tubular metal chair* **2** shaped like a tube

TUC /ˌtiː juː ˈsiː/ *abbr.* Trades Union Congress. The TUC is an organization to which many British trade unions belong.

tuck /tʌk/ *verb, noun*

■ *verb* [VN +*adv./prep.*] **1** to push, fold or turn the ends or edges of clothes, paper, etc. so that they are held in place or look neat: *She tucked up her skirt and waded into the river.* ◊ *The sheets should be tucked in neatly* (= around the bed). ◊ *Tuck the flap of the envelope in.* **2** to put sth into a small space, especially to hide it or keep it safe or comfortable: *She tucked her hair* (*up*) *under her cap.* ◊ *He sat with his legs tucked up under him.* ◊ *The letter had been tucked under a pile of papers.* **3** to cover sb with sth so that they are warm and comfortable: *She tucked a blanket around his legs.* [PHR V] **ˌtuck sth↔aˈway 1** (**be tucked away**) to be situated in a quiet place, where not many people go: *The shop is tucked away down a backstreet.* **2** to hide sth somewhere or keep it in a safe place: *She kept his letters tucked away in a drawer.* ◊ *They have thousands of pounds tucked away in a savings account.* **3** (*BrE, informal*) to eat a lot of food. **ˌtuck sb ˈin/ˈup** to make sb feel comfortable in bed by pulling the covers up around them: *I tucked the children in and said good night.* **ˌtuck ˈin/ˌtuck ˈinto sth** (*BrE*, especially *spoken*) to eat a lot of food, especially when it is done quickly and with enthusiasm: *Come on, tuck in everyone!* ◊ *He was tucking into a huge plateful of pasta.*

■ *noun* **1** [C] a fold that is sewn into a piece of clothing or fabric, either for decoration or to change the shape of it **2** [C] (*informal*) a medical operation in which skin and/or fat is removed to make sb look younger or thinner **3** [U] (*old-fashioned, BrE, informal*) food, especially sweets, etc. eaten by children at school

tuck·er /ˈtʌkə(r)/ *noun* [IDM] see BIB

Tues·day /ˈtjuːzdeɪ; -di; *AmE* ˈtuː-/ *noun* [C, U] (*abbr.* **Tue., Tues.**) the day of the week after Monday and before Wednesday [HELP] To see how **Tuesday** is used, look at the examples at **Monday**. [ORIGIN] Originally translated from the Latin for 'day of Mars' *dies Marti* and named after the Germanic god *Tiw*.

tuft /tʌft/ *noun* ~ (**of sth**) a number of pieces of hair, grass, etc. growing or held closely together at the base

tuft·ed /ˈtʌftɪd/ *adj.* [usually before noun] having a tuft or tufts; growing in tufts: *a tufted carpet* ◊ *a tufted duck* ◊ *tufted grass*

tug /tʌg/ *verb, noun*

■ *verb* (**-gg-**) **1** ~ (**at/on**) **sth** to pull sth hard, often several times: [V] *She tugged at his sleeve to get his attention.* ◊ (*figurative*) *a sad story that tugs at your heartstrings* (= makes you feel sad) ◊ [VN] *The baby was tugging her hair.* ◊ [VN-ADJ] *He tugged the door open.* **2** [VN +*adv./prep.*] to pull sth in a particular direction: *He tugged the hat down over his head.* [IDM] see FORELOCK

■ *noun* **1** (also **tug-boat** /ˈtʌgbəʊt; *AmE* -boʊt/) a small powerful boat for pulling ships, especially into harbour or up river—picture at BOAT **2** a sudden hard pull: *I felt a tug at my sleeve.* ◊ *She gave her sister's hair a sharp tug.* **3** [usually sing.] a sudden strong emotional feeling: *a tug of attraction/jealousy/sympathy*

ˌtug of ˈlove *noun* [sing.] (*BrE, informal*) a situation in which a child's parents are divorced or no longer living together and are fighting over who the child should live with

ˌtug of ˈwar *noun* [sing., U] **1** a sporting event in which two teams pull at opposite ends of a rope until one team drags the other over a line on the ground **2** a situation in which two people or groups try very hard to get or keep

T

b	d	f	g	h	k	l	m	n	p	r
bad	did	fall	get	hat	cat	leg	man	now	pen	red

the same thing: *After the divorce they became involved in an emotional tug of war over the children.*

tu·ition /tjuˈɪʃn; *AmE* tuˈ-/ *noun* [U] **1** ~ **(in sth)** (*formal*) the act of teaching sth, especially to one person or to people in small groups: *She received private tuition in French.* **2** (also **tu'ition fees** [pl.]) the money that you pay to be taught, especially in a college or university

tulip /ˈtjuːlɪp; *AmE* ˈtuː-/ *noun* a large, brightly coloured spring flower, shaped like a cup, on a tall stem

tulle /tjuːl; *AmE* tuːl/ *noun* [U] a soft fine fabric made of silk, NYLON, etc. and full of very small holes, used especially for making VEILS and dresses

tum /tʌm/ *noun* (*BrE, informal*) a person's stomach or the area around the stomach: *I'd like to lose some weight from my tum.*

tum·ble /ˈtʌmbl/ *verb, noun*
- *verb* **1** [+adv. / prep.] to fall downwards, often hitting the ground several times, but usually without serious injury; to make sb/sth fall in this way: [V] *He slipped and tumbled down the stairs.* [also VN] **2** [V] ~ **(down)** to fall suddenly and in a dramatic way: *The scaffolding came tumbling down.* ◊ (*figurative*) *World records tumbled at the last Olympics.*—see also TUMBLEDOWN **3** [V] to fall rapidly in value or amount: *The price of oil is still tumbling.* **4** [V+adv. / prep.] to move or fall somewhere in a relaxed, UNCONTROLLED, or noisy way: *I undressed and tumbled into bed.* ◊ *A group of noisy children tumbled out of the bus.* ◊ *The water tumbled over the rocks.* ◊ *Thick golden curls tumbled down over her shoulders.* PHRV **'tumble to sth/sb** (*BrE, informal*) to suddenly understand sth or be aware of sth
- *noun* **1** [C, usually sing.] a sudden fall: *The jockey took a nasty tumble at the third fence.* ◊ *Share prices took a sharp tumble following news of the merger.*—see also ROUGH AND TUMBLE **2** [sing.] ~ **(of sth)** an untidy group of things: *a tumble of blond curls*

tumble·down /ˈtʌmbldaʊn/ *adj.* [usually before noun] (of a building) old and in a poor condition so that it looks as if it is falling down

tumble-'dryer (also **tumble-'drier**) (both *BrE*) *noun* a machine that uses hot air to dry clothes after they have been washed—compare SPIN DRYER

tum·bler /ˈtʌmblə(r)/ *noun* **1** a glass for drinking out of, with a flat bottom, straight sides and no handle or stem—picture at GLASS **2** (also **tum·bler·ful** /-fʊl/) the amount held by a tumbler **3** (*old-fashioned*) an ACROBAT who performs SOMERSAULTS (= a jump in which you turn over completely in the air)

tumble·weed /ˈtʌmblwiːd/ *noun* [U] a plant that grows like a bush in the desert areas of N America and Australia. In the autumn/fall, it breaks off just above the ground and is blown around like a ball by the wind.

tum·bril /ˈtʌmbrəl/ *noun* an open vehicle used for taking people to their deaths at the GUILLOTINE during the French Revolution

tu·mes·cent /tjuːˈmesnt; *AmE* tuː-/ *adj.* (*formal*) (especially of parts of the body) larger than normal, especially as a result of sexual excitement SYN SWOLLEN ▶ **tu·mes·cence** /-sns/ *noun* [U]

tummy /ˈtʌmi/ *noun* (*pl.* -ies) (*informal*) (used especially by children or when speaking to children) the stomach or the area around the stomach: *Mum, my tummy hurts.* ◊ *to have (a) tummy ache* ◊ *a tummy bug/upset* (= an illness when you feel sick or vomit)

tu·mour (*BrE*) (*AmE* **tu·mor**) /ˈtjuːmə(r); *AmE* ˈtuː-/ *noun* a mass of cells growing in or on a part of the body where they should not, usually causing medical problems: *a brain tumour* ◊ *a benign/malignant* (= harmless/harmful) *tumour*

tu·mult /ˈtjuːmʌlt; *AmE* ˈtuː-/ *noun* [U, C, usually sing.] (*formal*) **1** a confused situation in which there is usually a lot of noise and excitement, often involving large numbers of people: *the tumult of war* ◊ *A tumult of shouting and screaming came from within the house.* **2** a state in which your thoughts or feelings are confused

tu·mul·tu·ous /tjuːˈmʌltʃuəs; *AmE* tuː-/ *adj.* [usually before noun] **1** very loud; involving strong feelings, especially feelings of approval: *tumultuous applause* ◊ *a tumultuous reception/welcome* **2** involving a lot of change and confusion and/or violence: *the tumultuous years of the English Civil War* ◊ *It was a tumultuous time in her life.*

tu·mu·lus /ˈtjuːmjələs; *AmE* ˈtuː-/ *noun* (*pl.* **tu·muli** /-laɪ/) (*technical*) a large pile of earth built over the grave of an important person in ancient times

tuna /ˈtjuːnə; *AmE* ˈtuːnə/ *noun* [C, U] (*pl.* **tuna** or **tunas**) (also **'tuna fish**) (*BrE* also *less frequent* **tunny**) a large sea fish that is used for food: *fishing for tuna* ◊ *tuna steaks* ◊ *a tin/can of tuna in vegetable oil*

tun·dra /ˈtʌndrə/ *noun* [U] the large flat Arctic regions of northern Europe, Asia and N America where no trees grow and where the soil below the surface of the ground is always frozen

tune /tjuːn; *AmE* tuːn/ *noun, verb*
- *noun* [C] a series of musical notes that are sung or played in a particular order to form a piece of music: *He was humming a familiar tune.* ◊ *I don't know the title but I recognize the tune.* ◊ *It was a catchy tune* (= song). ◊ *a football song sung to the tune of* (= using the tune of) *'When the saints go marching in'*—see also SIGNATURE TUNE, THEME TUNE IDM **be ,in/,out of 'tune (with sb/sth)** to be/not be in agreement with sb/sth; to have/not have the same opinions, feelings, interests, etc. as sb/sth: *These proposals are perfectly in tune with our own thoughts on the subject.* ◊ *The President is out of tune with public opinion.* **,in/,out of 'tune** to be/not be singing or playing the correct musical notes to sound pleasant: *None of them could sing in tune.* ◊ *The piano is out of tune.* **to the tune of sth** (*informal*) used to emphasize how much money sth has cost: *The hotel has been refurbished to the tune of a million dollars.*—more at CALL v., CHANGE v., DANCE v., PAY v., SING
- *verb* [VN] **1** to adjust a musical instrument so that it plays at the correct PITCH: *to tune a guitar/piano* **2** to adjust an engine so that it runs smoothly and as well as possible **3** [usually passive] ~ **sth (in) (to sth)** to adjust the controls on a radio or television so that you can receive a particular programme or channel: *The radio was tuned (in) to the BBC World Service.* ◊ (*spoken*) *Stay tuned for the news and weather coming up next.* **4** ~ **sth (to sth)** to prepare or adjust sth so that it is suitable for a particular situation: *His speech was tuned to what the audience wanted to hear.* PHRV **,tune 'in (to sth)** to listen to a radio programme or watch a television programme **,tune 'in to sb/sth** to become aware of other people's thoughts and feelings, etc. **,tune 'out| ,tune sb/sth↔'out** to stop listening to sth: *When she started talking about her job, he just tuned out.* **,tune 'up| ,tune sth↔'up** to adjust musical instruments so that they can play together: *The orchestra was tuning up as we entered the hall.*

,tuned 'in *adj.* [not before noun] ~ **(to sth)** aware of what is happening in a particular situation: *The resort is tuned in to the tastes of young and old alike.*

tune·ful /ˈtjuːnfl; *AmE* ˈtuːnfl/ *adj.* having a pleasant tune SYN MELODIOUS: *a tuneful song/melody* ◊ *a tuneful voice* (= that has a musical quality) ▶ **tune·ful·ly** /-fəli/ *adv.* **tune·ful·ness** *noun* [U]

tune·less /ˈtjuːnləs; *AmE* ˈtuːn-/ *adj.* not having a pleasant tune: *tuneless singing* ▶ **tune·less·ly** *adv.*: *He was humming tunelessly.*

tuner /ˈtjuːnə(r); *AmE* ˈtuː-/ *noun* **1** (especially in compounds) a person who tunes musical instruments, especially pianos **2** the part of a radio, television, etc. that you move in order to change the signal and receive the radio or television station that you want **3** an electronic device that receives a radio signal and sends it to an AMPLIFIER so that it can be heard

tung·sten /ˈtʌŋstən/ *noun* [U] (*symb* W) a chemical element. Tungsten is a very hard silver-grey metal, used especially in making steel and in FILAMENTS for LIGHT BULBS.

tunic /ˈtjuːnɪk; *AmE* ˈtuː-/ *noun* **1** a loose piece of clothing covering the body down to the knees, usually without sleeves, as worn in ancient Greece and Rome **2** a piece of women's clothing like a tunic, that reaches to the hips and is worn over trousers/pants or a skirt **3** (*BrE*) a tightly fitting jacket worn as part of a uniform by police officers, soldiers, etc.

'tuning fork *noun* a small metal instrument with two long parts joined together at one end, that produces a particular musical note when you hit it and is used in TUNING musical instruments

'tuning peg *noun* = PEG

tun·nel /'tʌnl/ *noun, verb*
- *noun* **1** a passage built underground, for example to allow a road or railway/railroad to go through a hill, under a river, etc: *a railway/railroad tunnel* ◊ *the Channel Tunnel*—see also WIND TUNNEL **2** an underground passage made by an animal IDM see LIGHT *n.*
- *verb* (**-ll-**, *AmE* also **-l-**) [+*adv./prep.*] to dig a tunnel under or through the ground: [V] *The engineers had to tunnel through solid rock.* ◊ [VN] *The rescuers tunnelled their way in to the trapped miners.*

tunnel 'vision *noun* [U] **1** (*medical*) a condition in which sb cannot see well things that are not straight ahead of them **2** (*disapproving*) an inability to see or understand all the aspects of a situation, an argument, etc. instead of just one part of it

tunny /'tʌni/ *noun* (*pl.* **tunny**) (*BrE*) = TUNA

tup·pence /'tʌpəns/ *noun* [U] (*BrE, informal*) the sum of two pence IDM **not care/give 'tuppence for sb/sth** to think that sb/sth is not important or that they have no value

tup·penny /'tʌpəni/ *adj.* [only before noun] (*BrE, informal*) = TWOPENNY

tur·ban /'tɜːbən; *AmE* 'tɜːrbən/ *noun* **1** a long piece of fabric wound tightly around the head, worn especially by Sikh, Muslim and Hindu men **2** a woman's hat that looks like a turban ▶ **tur·baned** /'tɜːbənd; *AmE* 'tɜːrb-/ *adj.*: *turbaned Sikhs*

tur·bid /'tɜːbɪd; *AmE* 'tɜːrbɪd/ *adj.* (*rare, formal*) (of liquid) full of mud, dirt, etc. so that you cannot see through it ▶ **tur·bid·ity** /tɜː'bɪdəti; *AmE* tɜːr'b-/ *noun* [U]

tur·bine /'tɜːbaɪn; *AmE* 'tɜːrb-/ *noun* a machine or an engine that receives its power from a wheel that is turned by the pressure of water, air or gas

turbo·char·ger /'tɜːbəʊtʃɑːdʒə(r); *AmE* 'tɜːrbəʊtʃɑːrdʒər/ (also **turbo** *pl.* **-os**) *noun* a system driven by a turbine that gets its power from an engine's EXHAUST gases. It sends the mixture of petrol/gas and air into the engine at high pressure, making it more powerful. ▶ **turbo·charge** *verb*: [VN] *turbocharged engines*

turbo·jet /'tɜːbəʊdʒet; *AmE* 'tɜːrbəʊ-/ *noun* **1** a TURBINE engine that produces forward movement by forcing out a stream of hot air and gas behind it **2** a plane that gets its power from this type of engine

turbo·prop /'tɜːbəʊprɒp; *AmE* 'tɜːrbəʊprɑːp/ *noun* **1** a TURBINE engine that produces forward movement by turning a PROPELLOR (= a set of spinning blades) **2** a plane that gets its power from this type of engine

tur·bot /'tɜːbət; *AmE* 'tɜːrbət/ *noun* [C, U] (*pl.* **tur·bot** or **tur·bots**) a large flat European sea fish that is used for food

tur·bu·lence /'tɜːbjələns; *AmE* 'tɜːrb-/ *noun* [U] **1** a situation in which there is a lot of sudden change, confusion, disagreement and sometimes violence **2** a series of sudden and violent changes in the direction that air or water is moving in: *We experienced severe turbulence during the flight.*

tur·bu·lent /'tɜːbjələnt; *AmE* 'tɜːrb-/ *adj.* [usually before noun] **1** in which there is a lot of sudden change, confusion, disagreement and sometimes violence: *a short and turbulent career in politics* ◊ *a turbulent part of the world* **2** (of air or water) changing direction suddenly and violently: *The aircraft is designed to withstand turbulent conditions.* ◊ *a turbulent sea/storm* (= caused by turbulent water/air) **3** (of people) noisy and/or difficult to control: *a turbulent crowd*

turd /tɜːd; *AmE* tɜːrd/ *noun* (⚠, *slang*) **1** a lump of solid waste from the bowels: *dog turds* **2** an offensive word for an unpleasant person

tur·een /tjʊ'riːn; tə'riːn/ *noun* a large deep dish with a lid, used for serving vegetables or soup

turf /tɜːf; *AmE* tɜːrf/ *noun, verb*
- *noun* (*pl.* **turfs** or **turves** /tɜːvz; *AmE* tɜːrvz/) **1** [U, C] short grass and the surface layer of soil that is held together by its roots; a piece of this that has been cut from the ground and is used especially for making LAWNS (= the area of grass in a garden/yard): *newly laid turf* ◊ (*especially BrE*) *the hallowed turf of Wembley, etc.* (= the grass used for playing a sport on) **2** [U, C] PEAT that is cut to be used as fuel; a piece of this **3** (**the turf**) [sing.] the sport of horse racing **4** [U] sb's ~ (*informal, especially AmE*) the place where sb lives and/or works, especially when they think of it as their own: *He feels more confident on home turf.*
- *verb* [VN] to cover an area of ground with turf PHRV **turf sb 'out (of sth)**| **turf sb 'off (sth)** (*BrE, informal*) to make sb leave a place, an organization, etc: *He was turfed out of the party.* ◊ *The boys were turfed off the bus.*

'turf accountant *noun* (*BrE, formal*) = BOOKMAKER

tur·gid /'tɜːdʒɪd; *AmE* 'tɜːrdʒɪd/ *adj.* (*written*) **1** (of language, writing, etc.) boring, complicated and difficult to understand: *turgid prose* **2** swollen; containing more water than usual: *the turgid waters of the Thames*

tur·key /'tɜːki; *AmE* 'tɜːrki/ *noun* (*pl.* **-eys**) **1** [C] a large bird that is often kept for its meat, eaten especially at Christmas in Britain and at Thanksgiving in the US—picture on page A6 **2** [U] meat from a turkey: *roast turkey* **3** [C] (*AmE, informal*) a failure: *His latest movie is a real turkey.* **4** [C] (*AmE, informal*) a stupid or useless person—see also COLD TURKEY IDM see TALK *v.*

Turkish bath /ˌtɜːkɪʃ 'bɑːθ; *AmE* ˌtɜːrkɪʃ 'bæθ/ *noun* a type of bath in which you sit in a room full of hot steam, have a MASSAGE and then a cold shower or bath; a building where this treatment takes place

Turkish 'coffee *noun* very strong, usually very sweet, black coffee

Turkish de'light *noun* [U, C] a sweet/candy made from a substance like jelly that is flavoured with fruit and covered with fine white sugar

tur·meric /'tɜːmərɪk; *AmE* 'tɜːrm-/ *noun* [U] a yellow powder made from the root of an E Indian plant, used in cooking as a spice, especially in CURRY

tur·moil /'tɜːmɔɪl; *AmE* 'tɜːrm-/ *noun* [U, sing.] a state of great anxiety, confusion and uncertainty: *emotional/mental/political turmoil* ◊ *His statement threw the court into turmoil.* ◊ *Her mind was in (a) turmoil.*

turn /tɜːn; *AmE* tɜːrn/ *verb, noun*
- *verb*
  MOVE ROUND | **1** to move or make sth move around a central point: [V] *The wheels of the car began to turn.* ◊ *I can't get the screw to turn.* ◊ [VN] *He turned the key in the lock.* ◊ *She turned the wheel sharply to the left.*
  CHANGE POSITION/ DIRECTION | **2** [usually +*adv./prep.*] to move your body or part of your body so as to face or start moving in a different direction: [V] *We turned and headed for home.* ◊ *She turned to look at me.* ◊ *He turned back to his work.* ◊ *I turned away and looked out of the window.* ◊ [VN] *He turned his back to the wall.* ◊ *She turned her head away.*—see also TURN OVER **3** [VN +*adv./prep.*] to move sth so that it is in a different position or facing a different direction: [VN] *She turned the chair on its side to repair it.* ◊ *Turn the sweater inside out before you wash it.*—see also TURN OVER **4** to change the direction you are moving or travelling in; to make sth change the direction it is moving in: [V] *He turned into a narrow street.* ◊ [VN] *The man turned the corner and disappeared.* ◊ *I turned the car into the car park.* **5** [V] [usually +*adv./prep.*] (of a road or river) to curve in a particular direction: *The road turns to the left after the church.* ◊ *The river turns north at this point.*
  AIM/POINT | **6** to aim or point sth in a particular direction: [VN] *Police turned water cannon on the rioters.* ◊ *He turned the gun on himself.* ◊ *Don't turn your anger on the children.* ◊ *She looked at him then turned her attention back to me.* ◊ [V] *His thoughts turned to his dead wife.*
  OF TIDE | **7** [V] to start to come in or go out: *The tide is turning—we'd better get back.*

æ	ɑː	e	ɜː	ə	ɪ	iː	i	ɒ	ɔː	ʌ	ʊ	u	uː
cat	father	ten	bird	about	sit	see	many	got	saw	cup	put	actual	too

(BrE)

LET SB/STH GO | 8 to make or let sb/sth go into a particular place or state: [VN] *They turned the horse into the field.* ◊ [VN-ADJ] *to turn the dogs loose*

FOLD | 9 [VN] to fold sth in a particular way: *She turned down the blankets and climbed into bed.* ◊ *He turned up the collar of his coat and hurried out into the rain.*

CARTWHEEL/SOMERSAULT | 10 [VN] [no passive] to perform a movement by moving your body in a circle: *to turn cartwheels/somersaults*

PAGE | 11 if you **turn** a page of a book or magazine, you move it so that you can read the next page: [VN] *He sat turning the pages idly.* ◊ [V] *Turn to p.23.*

GAME | 12 [V, VN] ~ (sth) (around) if a game **turns** or sb **turns** it, it changes the way it is developing so that a different person or team starts to win

BECOME | 13 to change into a particular state or condition; to make sth do this: [V-ADJ] *The leaves were already turning brown.* ◊ *The weather has turned cold and windy.* ◊ *He turned nasty when we refused to give him the money.* ◊ *He has decided to **turn professional**.* ◊ [VN-ADJ] *The heat turned the milk sour.* ◊ [V-N] *She turned a deathly shade of white when she heard the news.* ◊ *He's a lawyer turned politician* (= he used to be a lawyer but is now a politician). ⇨ note at BECOME

AGE/TIME | 14 [V-N] (not used in the progressive tenses) to reach or pass a particular age or time: *She turns 21 in June.* ◊ *It's turned midnight.*

STOMACH | 15 [V, VN] when your stomach **turns** or sth **turns** your stomach, you feel as though you will VOMIT

WOOD | 16 [VN] to shape sth on a LATHE: *to turn a chair leg* ◊ *turned boxes and bowls*

IDM Most idioms containing **turn** are at the entries for the nouns and adjectives in the idioms, for example **not turn a hair** is at **hair**. **as it/things turned 'out** as was shown or proved by later events: *I didn't need my umbrella, as it turned out* (= because it didn't rain). **be well, badly, etc. turned 'out** to be well, badly, etc. dressed **turn round/around and do sth** (*informal*) used to report what sb says or does, when this is surprising or annoying: *How could she turn round and say that, after all I've done for her.*

PHR V ,**turn a'gainst sb | ,turn sb a'gainst sb** to stop or make sb stop being friendly towards sb: *She turned against her old friend.* ◊ *After the divorce he tried to turn the children against their mother.*

,**turn a'round/'round | ,turn sb/sth a'round/'round** to change position or direction so as to face the other way; to make sb/sth do this: *Turn around and let me look at your back.* ◊ *I turned my chair round to face the fire.* ,**turn a'round/'round | ,turn sth↔a'round/'round** if a business, economy, etc. **turns around** or sb **turns** it **around**, it starts being successful after it has been unsuccessful for a time—related noun TURNAROUND

,**turn sb↔a'way (from sth)** to refuse to allow sb to enter a place: *Hundreds of people were turned away from the stadium* (= because it was full). ◊ *They had nowhere to stay so I couldn't turn them away.*

,**turn 'back | ,turn sb/sth↔'back** to return the way you have come; to make sb/sth do this: *The weather became so bad that they had to turn back.* ◊ (*figurative*) *We said we would do it—there can be no turning back.* ◊ *Our car was turned back at the border.*

,**turn sb/sth↔'down** to reject or refuse to consider an offer, a proposal, etc. or the person who makes it: *Why did she turn down your invitation?* ◊ *He has been turned down for ten jobs so far.* ◊ *He asked her to marry him but she turned him down.* ,**turn sth↔'down** to reduce the noise, heat, etc. produced by a piece of equipment by moving its controls: *Please turn the volume down.* ◊ [+ADJ] *He turned the lights down low.*

,**turn 'in 1** to face or curve inwards: *Her feet turn in.* **2** (*old-fashioned*) to go to bed: *It's late—I think I'll turn in.* ,**turn sb↔'in** (*informal*) to take sb to the police or sb in authority because they have committed a crime: *She threatened to turn him in to the police.* ◊ *He decided to turn himself in.* ,**turn sth↔'in 1** to give back sth that you no longer need: *You must turn in your pass when you leave the building.* **2** (*especially AmE*) to give sth to sb in authority: *They turned in a petition with 80 000 signatures.* ◊ *Only a few guns have been turned in so far.* ◊ *I haven't even turned in Monday's work yet.* **3** to achieve a score, performance, profit, etc: *The champion turned in a superb performance to retain her title.* ,**turn 'in on yourself** to become too concerned with your own problems and stop communicating with others

,**turn 'off | ,turn 'off sth** [no passive] to leave a road in order to travel on another: *Is this where we turn off?* ◊ *The jet began to turn off the main runway.* ,**turn 'off** (*informal*) to stop listening to or thinking about sb/sth: *I couldn't understand the lecture so I just turned off.* ,**turn 'off | ,turn sb↔'off 1** to make sb feel bored or not interested: *People had been turned off by both candidates in the election.* **2** to stop sb feeling sexually attracted; to make sb have a feeling of disgust—related noun TURN-OFF ,**turn sth↔'off** to stop the flow of electricity, gas, water, etc. by moving a switch, button, etc: *to turn off the light/oven* ◊ *They've turned off the water while they repair a burst pipe.* ◊ *Please turn the television off before you go to bed.*

'**turn on sb** to attack sb suddenly and unexpectedly: *The dogs suddenly turned on each other.* ◊ *Why are you all turning on me* (= criticizing or blaming me)? '**turn on sth** [no passive] **1** (*BrE*) to depend on sth: *Much turns on the outcome of the current peace talks.* **2** [no passive] to have sth as its main topic: *The discussion turned on the need to raise standards.* ,**turn sb↔'on** (*informal*) to make sb excited or interested, especially sexually: *Jazz has never really turned me on.* ◊ *She gets turned on by men in uniform.*—related noun TURN-ON ,**turn sb 'on (to sth)** (*informal*) to make sb become interested in sth or to use sth for the first time: *He turned her on to jazz.* ,**turn sth↔'on** to start the flow of electricity, gas, water, etc. by moving a switch, button, etc: *to turn on the light/ heating* ◊ *I'll turn the television on.* ◊ (*figurative*) *He really knows how to turn on the charm* (= suddenly become pleasant and attractive).

,**turn 'out 1** to be present at an event: *A vast crowd turned out to watch the procession.*—related noun TURNOUT **2** (used with an adverb or adjective, or in questions with *how*) to happen in a particular way; to develop or end in a particular way: *Despite our worries everything turned out well.* ◊ *You never know how your children will turn out!* ◊ [+ADJ] *If the day turns out wet, we may have to change our plans.* **3** to point outwards: *Her toes turn out.* **4** to be discovered to be; to prove to be: [+ that] *It turned out that she was a friend of my sister.* ◊ [+ to inf] *The job turned out to be harder than we thought.* ◊ *The house they had offered us turned out to be a tiny apartment.* ,**turn sb/sth↔'out** to produce sb/sth: *The factory turns out 900 cars a week.* ,**turn sb 'out (of/from sth)** to force sb to leave a place ,**turn sth↔'out 1** to switch a light or a source of heat off: *Remember to turn out the lights when you go to bed.* **2** (*BrE*) to clean sth thoroughly by removing the contents and organizing them again: *to turn out the attic/a drawer* **3** to empty sth, especially your pockets **4** to make sth point outwards: *She turned her toes out.*

,**turn 'over 1** to change position so that the other side is facing outwards or upwards: *If you turn over you might find it easier to get to sleep.* ◊ *The car skidded and turned over.* ◊ (*figurative*) *The smell made my stomach turn over* (= made me feel sick). **2** (of an engine) to start or to continue to run **3** to change to another channel when you are watching television ,**turn 'over sth** to do business worth a particular amount of money in a particular period of time: *The company turns over £3.5 million a year.*—related noun TURNOVER ,**turn sth↔'over 1** to make sth change position so that the other side is facing outwards or upwards: *Brown the meat on one side, then turn it over and brown the other side.* **2** to think about sth carefully: *She kept turning over the events of the day in her mind.* **3** (of a shop/store) to sell goods and replace them: *A supermarket will turn over its stock very rapidly.*—related noun TURNOVER **4** (*informal*) to rob a place: *Burglars had turned the house over.* **5** to make an engine start running, **turn sb↔'over to sb** to deliver sb to the control or care of sb else, especially sb in authority: *Customs* officials *turned* the man *over* to the police. ,turn sth↔'over **to sb** to give the control of sth to sb: *He turned the business over to his daughter.* ,turn sth↔'over **to sth** to change the use or function of sth: *The factory was turned over to the manufacture of aircraft parts.*

'turn **to sb/sth** to go to sb/sth for help, advice, etc: *She has nobody she can turn to.*

,turn 'up **1** to be found, especially by chance, after being lost: *Don't worry about the letter—I'm sure it'll turn up.* **2** (of a person) to arrive: *We arranged to meet at 7.30, but she never turned up.* **3** (of an opportunity) to happen, especially by chance: *He's still hoping something* (= for example, a job or a piece of luck) *will turn up.*—related noun TURN-UP ,turn sth↔'up **1** to increase the sound, heat, etc. of a piece of equipment: *Could you turn the TV up?* ◇[+ADJ] *The music was turned up loud.* **2** (*BrE*) to make a piece of clothing shorter by folding and sewing it up at the bottom [OPP] LET DOWN—related noun TURN-UP **3** to find sth: *Our efforts to trace him turned up nothing.*

■ *noun* [C]

MOVEMENT | **1** an act of turning sb/sth around: *Give the handle a few turns.*

OF ROAD/VEHICLE | **2** a change in direction in a vehicle: *Make a left/right turn into West street.*—see also THREE-POINT TURN, U-TURN **3** (*especially AmE*) = TURNING **4** a bend or corner in a road: *a lane full of twists and turns*

TIME | **5** the time when sb in a group of people should or is allowed to do sth: *When it's your turn, take another card.* ◇ *Please wait your turn.* ◇ *Whose turn is it to cook?* ◇ *Steve took a turn driving while I slept.*

CHANGE | **6** an unusual or unexpected change in what is happening: *a surprising turn of events* ◇ *His health has taken a turn for the worse* (= suddenly got worse). ◇ *Events took a dramatic turn in the weeks that followed.* ◇ *The book is, by turns, funny and very sad.*—see also ABOUT-TURN

PERFORMANCE | **7** a short performance or piece of entertainment such as a song, etc: *Everyone got up on stage to do a turn.*—see also STAR TURN

WALK | **8** (*old-fashioned*) a short walk: *We took a turn around the park.*

ILLNESS | **9** (*old-fashioned*) a feeling of illness: *a funny turn* (= a feeling that you may faint)

[IDM] **at every turn** everywhere or every time you try and do sth: *At every turn I met with disappointment.* **(do sb) a good 'turn** (to do) sth that helps sb: *Well, that's my good turn for the day.* **done to a 'turn** (*BrE*) cooked for exactly the right amount of time **give sb a 'turn** (*old-fashioned*) to frighten or shock sb **in 'turn 1** one after the other in a particular order: *The children called out their names in turn.* **2** as a result of sth in a series of events: *Increased production will, in turn, lead to increased profits.* ,one good ,turn deserves a'nother (*saying*) you should help sb who has helped you **on the 'turn** (*especially BrE*) going to change soon: *His luck is on the turn.* **speak/talk ,out of 'turn** to say sth that you should not because it is the wrong situation or because it offends sb **take 'turns (in sth/to do sth)** (*BrE also* **take it in 'turns**) if people take turns or take it in turns to do sth, they do it one after the other to make sure it is done fairly: *The male and female birds take turns in sitting on the eggs.* ◇ *We take it in turns to do the housework.* **the ,turn of the 'century/ 'year** the time when a new century/year starts: *It was built at the turn of the century.* **a ,turn of 'mind** a particular way of thinking about things **a ,turn of 'phrase** a particular way of describing sth **a ,turn of the 'screw** an extra amount of pressure, CRUELTY, etc. added to a situation that is already difficult to bear or understand **a ,turn of 'speed** a sudden increase in your speed or rate of progress; the ability to suddenly increase your speed: *He put on an impressive turn of speed in the last lap.*—more at HAND *n.*, SERVE *v.*

turn·about /'tɜːnəbaʊt; *AmE* 'tɜːrn-/ *noun* [sing.] **~ (in sth)** a sudden and complete change in sb/sth: *a dramatic turnabout in overseas policy*

turn·around /'tɜːnəraʊnd; *AmE* 'tɜːrn-/ (*BrE also* **turn-round**) *noun* [usually sing.] **1** the amount of time it takes

to unload a ship or plane at the end of one journey and load it again for the next one **2** the amount of time it takes to do a piece of work that you have been given and return it **3** a situation in which sth changes from bad to good: *a turnaround in the economy* **4** a complete change in sb's opinion, behaviour, etc.

turn·coat /'tɜːnkəʊt; *AmE* 'tɜːrnkoʊt/ *noun* (*disapproving*) a person who leaves one political party, religious group, etc. to join one that has very different views

turn·ing /'tɜːnɪŋ; *AmE* 'tɜːrnɪŋ/ (*BrE*) (*also* **turn** *AmE*, *BrE*) *noun* a place where a road leads away from the one you are travelling on: *Take the first turning on the right.* ◇ *I think we must have taken a wrong turning somewhere.*

'turning circle *noun* the smallest circle that a vehicle can turn around in

'turning point *noun* **~ (in sth)** the time when an important change takes place, usually with the result that a situation improves: *The promotion marked a turning point in her career.* ◇ *That game was a turning point for the team.*

tur·nip /'tɜːnɪp; *AmE* 'tɜːrnɪp/ *noun* [C, U] **1** a round white, or white and purple, root vegetable—picture on page A3 **2** (*ScotE*) = SWEDE

turn·key /'tɜːnkiː; *AmE* 'tɜːrn-/ *adj.* (especially of computer systems) complete and ready to use immediately

'turn-off *noun* **1** a place where a road leads away from another larger or more important road: *We missed the turn-off for/to the airport.* **2** [usually sing.] (*informal*) a person or thing that people do not find interesting, attractive or sexually exciting: *The city's crime rate is a serious turn-off to potential investors.* ◇ *I find beards a real turn-off.*

'turn-on *noun* [usually sing.] (*informal*) a person or thing that people find sexually exciting

turn·out /'tɜːnaʊt; *AmE* 'tɜːrn-/ *noun* [C usually sing, U] **1** the number of people who attend a particular event: *This year's festival attracted a record turnout.* **2** the number of people who vote in a particular election: *a high/ low/poor turnout* ◇ *a 60% turnout of voters*

turn·over /'tɜːnəʊvə(r); *AmE* 'tɜːrnoʊ-/ *noun* **1** [C usually sing, U] **~ (of sth)** the total amount of goods or services sold by a company during a particular period of time: *The firm has an annual turnover of $75 million.* ◇ *a rise/ fall in turnover* **2** [sing.] **~ (of sb)** the rate at which employees leave a company and are replaced by other people: *The factory has a high turnover of staff.* **3** [sing.] **~ (of sth)** the rate at which goods are sold in a shop/store and replaced by others: *Special offers help to ensure a fast turnover of stock.* **4** [C] a small pie in the shape of a triangle or half a circle, filled with fruit or jam: *an apple turnover*

turn·pike /'tɜːnpaɪk; *AmE* 'tɜːrn-/ (*also* **pike**) (*both AmE*) *noun* a road that drivers must pay a TOLL to use

turn·round /'tɜːnraʊnd; *AmE* 'tɜːrn-/ *noun* (*BrE*) = TURN-AROUND

'turn signal *noun* (*AmE*) = INDICATOR (3)

turn·stile /'tɜːnstaɪl; *AmE* 'tɜːrn-/ *noun* a gate at the entrance to a public building, STADIUM, etc. that turns in a circle when pushed, allowing one person to go through at a time—picture at STILE

turn·table /'tɜːnteɪbl; *AmE* 'tɜːrn-/ *noun* **1** the round surface on a RECORD PLAYER that you place the record on to be played **2** a large round surface that is able to move in a circle and onto which a railway/railroad engine is driven in order to turn it to go in the opposite direction

'turn-up *noun* (*BrE*) **1** (*AmE* **cuff**) [C] the bottom of the leg of a pair of trousers/pants that has been folded over on the outside—picture on page A4 **2** (*informal*) something surprising or unexpected that happens: *He actually offered to help? That's a turn-up for the books!*

tur·pen·tine /'tɜːpəntaɪn; *AmE* 'tɜːrp-/ (*also informal* **turps** /tɜːps; *AmE* tɜːrps/) *noun* [U] a colourless liquid with a strong smell, used especially for making paint thinner and for cleaning paint from brushes and clothes

tur·pi·tude /'tɜːpɪtjuːd; *AmE* 'tɜːrpətuːd/ *noun* [U] (*rare, formal*) very immoral behaviour [SYN] WICKEDNESS

tur·quoise /ˈtɜːkwɔɪz; AmE ˈtɜːrk-/ noun **1** [C, U] a blue or greenish-blue precious stone: *a turquoise brooch* **2** [U] a greenish-blue colour ▶ **tur·quoise** adj.: *a turquoise dress*

tur·ret /ˈtʌrət; AmE ˈtɜːrət/ noun **1** a small tower on top of a wall or building, especially a castle **2** a small metal tower on a ship, plane or TANK that can usually turn around and from which guns are fired

tur·ret·ed /ˈtʌrətɪd; AmE ˈtɜːr-/ adj. [usually before noun] having one or more turrets

tur·tle /ˈtɜːtl; AmE ˈtɜːrtl/ noun **1** (AmE also **'sea turtle**) a large reptile with a hard round shell, that lives in the sea **2** (AmE, informal) any reptile with a large shell, for example a TORTOISE or TERRAPIN—picture on page A7 [IDM] **turn 'turtle** (of a boat) to turn over completely while sailing

'turtle dove noun a wild DOVE (= a type of bird) with a pleasant soft call, thought to be a very loving bird

turtle·neck /ˈtɜːtlnek; AmE ˈtɜːrtl-/ noun **1** (also **,turtle-neck 'sweater**) a sweater with a high part fitting closely around the neck **2** (AmE) = POLO NECK—picture on page A5

turves pl. of TURF

tusk /tʌsk/ noun either of the long curved teeth that stick out of the mouth of elephants and some other animals—see also IVORY—picture on page A6

tus·sle /ˈtʌsl/ noun, verb
■ noun ~ (for/over sth) a short struggle, fight or argument especially in order to get sth: *He was injured during a tussle for the ball.*
■ verb [V] to fight or compete with sb/sth, especially in order to get sth: *The children were tussling with one another for the ball.*

tus·sock /ˈtʌsək/ noun a small area of grass that is longer and thicker than the grass around it ▶ **tus·socky** adj.: *tussocky grass*

tut /tʌt/ (also **,tut-'tut**) exclamation, noun used as the written or spoken way of showing the sound that people make when they disapprove of sth (made by putting the tongue behind the teeth and sucking in air): *Tut-tut, I expected better of you.* ◊ *tut-tuts of disapproval* ▶ **tut** (also **,tut-'tut**) verb (**-tt-**): [V] *He tut-tutted under his breath.*

tu·tel·age /ˈtjuːtəlɪdʒ; AmE ˈtuː-/ noun [U] (formal) **1** the teaching and instruction that one person gives to another **2** the state of being protected or controlled by another person, organization or country: *parental tutelage*

tutor /ˈtjuːtə(r); AmE ˈtuː-/ noun, verb
■ noun **1** a private teacher, especially one who teaches an individual student or a very small group **2** (especially BrE) a teacher whose job is to pay special attention to the studies or health, etc. of a student or a group of students: *a history/German tutor* ◊ *He was my personal tutor at university.* ◊ *She's your course tutor in anthropology.* ◊ *She's in my tutor group at school.* **3** (BrE) a teacher, especially one who teaches adults or who has a special role in a school or college: *a part-time adult education tutor* **4** (AmE) an assistant LECTURER in a college **5** a book of instruction in a particular subject, especially music: *a violin tutor*
■ verb **1** [VN] ~ sb (in sth) to be a tutor to a an individual student or a small group; to teach sb, especially privately: *He tutors students in mathematics.* **2** [V] to work as a tutor: *Her work was divided between tutoring and research.*

tu·tor·ial /tjuːˈtɔːriəl; AmE tuː-/ noun, adj.
■ noun **1** a period of teaching in a university that involves discussion between an individual student or a small group of students and a tutor **2** a short book or computer program that gives information on a particular subject or explains how sth is done: *An online tutorial is provided.*
■ adj. connected with the work of a tutor: *tutorial staff* ◊ (BrE) *a tutorial college* (= a private school that prepares students for exams)

tutti-frutti /ˌtuːti ˈfruːti/ noun [U] a type of ice cream that contains pieces of fruit of various kinds

tutu /ˈtuːtuː/ noun a ballet dancer's skirt made of many layers of material. Tutus may be either short and stiff, sticking out from the waist, or long and bell-shaped.

tu-whit, tu-whoo /təˌwɪt təˈwuː/ noun used to represent the sound that an OWL makes

tux·edo /tʌkˈsiːdəʊ; AmE -doʊ/ noun (pl. **-os**) (also informal **tux** /tʌks/) (AmE) = DINNER SUIT—compare DINNER JACKET [ORIGIN] From Tuxedo Park in New York, where it was first worn.

TV /ˌtiː ˈviː/ noun [C, U] television: *What's on TV tonight?* ◊ *We're buying a new TV with the money.* ◊ *Almost all homes have at least one TV set.* ◊ *All rooms have a bathroom and colour TV.* ◊ *a TV series/show/programme* ◊ *satellite/cable TV* ◊ *She's a highly paid TV presenter.*

twad·dle /ˈtwɒdl; AmE ˈtwɑːdl/ noun [U] (old-fashioned, informal) something that has been said or written that you think is stupid and not true [SYN] NONSENSE

twain /tweɪn/ number (old use) two [IDM] **never the ,twain shall 'meet** (saying) used to say that two things are so different that they cannot exist together

twang /twæŋ/ noun, verb
■ noun [usually sing.] **1** used to describe a way of speaking, usually one that is typical of a particular area and especially one in which the sounds are produced through the nose as well as the mouth **2** a sound that is made when a tight string, especially on a musical instrument, is pulled and released
■ verb to make a sound like a tight wire or string being pulled and released; to make sth do this: [V] *The bed springs twanged.* ◊ [VN] *Someone was twanging a guitar in the next room.*

twat /twæt; twɒt; AmE twɑːt/ noun (⚠ slang, especially BrE) **1** an offensive word for an unpleasant or stupid person **2** an offensive word for the outer female sex organs

tweak /twiːk/ verb, noun
■ verb [VN] **1** to pull or twist sth suddenly: *She tweaked his ear playfully.* **2** to make slight changes to a machine, system, etc. to improve it: *I think you'll have to tweak these figures a little before you show them to the boss.*
■ noun **1** a sharp pull or twist: *She gave his ear a tweak.* **2** a slight change that you make to a machine, system, etc. to improve it

twee /twiː/ adj. (BrE, informal, disapproving) very pretty, in a way that you find unpleasant and silly; appearing SENTIMENTAL: *The room was decorated with twee little pictures of animals.*

tweed /twiːd/ noun **1** [U] a thick rough woollen fabric that has small spots of different coloured thread in it: *a tweed jacket/skirt/suit*—picture on page A4 **2** (**tweeds**) [pl.] clothes made of tweed

tweedy /ˈtwiːdi/ adj. **1** made of or looking like tweed: *a tweedy jacket* **2** (BrE, informal, often disapproving) used to describe the sort of person who often wears tweeds and therefore shows that they belong to the social class of rich people who live in the country

tweet /twiːt/ noun the short high sound made by a small bird

tweet·er /ˈtwiːtə(r)/ noun a LOUDSPEAKER for reproducing the high notes from a STEREO—compare WOOFER

tweez·ers /ˈtwiːzəz; AmE -ərz/ noun [pl.] a small tool with two long thin parts joined together at one end, used for picking up small things or for pulling out hairs: *a pair of tweezers*

tweezers

twelve /twelv/ number 12 ▶ **twelfth** /twelfθ/ ordinal number

twenty /ˈtwenti/ number **1** 20 **2** (**the twenties**) [pl.] numbers, years or temperatures from 20 to 29 [IDM] **in your 'twenties** between the ages of 20 and 29

,twenty-'first noun [sing.] (informal, especially BrE) a person's 21st birthday and the celebrations for this occasion

,twenty 'pence (also **,twenty pence 'piece, 20p** /ˌtwenti ˈpiː/) noun a British coin worth 20 pence: *You need two 20ps for the machine.*

,twenty-,twenty 'vision (also **20/20 vision**) noun [U] the ability to see perfectly

twerp /twɜːp; *AmE* twɜːrp/ *noun* (*old-fashioned, informal*) a stupid or annoying person

twice /twaɪs/ *adv.* **1** two times; on two occasions: *I don't know him well; I've only met him twice.* ◊ *They go there twice a week/month/year.* ◊ *a twice-monthly/yearly newsletter* **2** double in quantity, rate, etc: *an area twice the size of Wales* ◊ *Cats sleep twice as much as people.* ◊ *At 56 he's twice her age.* **IDM** **twice 'over** not just once but twice: *There was enough of the drug in her stomach to kill her twice over.*—more at LIGHTNING *n.*, ONCE *adv.*, THINK *v.*

twid·dle /ˈtwɪdl/ *verb, noun*
■ *verb* (*BrE*) ~ (**with**) **sth** to twist or turn sth with your fingers often because you are nervous or bored: [V] *He twiddled with the radio knob until he found the right programme.* ◊ [VN] *She was twiddling the ring on her finger.* **IDM** **twiddle your thumbs 1** to move your thumbs around each other with your fingers joined together, because you are bored or waiting for sth **2** to do nothing while you are waiting for sth to happen
■ *noun* **1** (*BrE*) a twist or turn: *a twiddle of the knob* **2** a decorative twist in a pattern, piece of music, etc: *twiddles on the clarinet*

twid·dly /ˈtwɪdli/ *adj.* (*BrE, informal*) detailed or complicated

twig /twɪg/ *noun, verb*
■ *noun* a small very thin branch that grows out of a larger branch on a bush or tree: *Use dry sticks and twigs to start a fire.*
■ *verb* (**-gg-**) (*BrE, informal*) to suddenly understand or realize sth: [V] *Haven't you twigged yet?* ◊ [V wh-] *I finally twigged what he meant.* [also VN, V(that)]

twi·light /ˈtwaɪlaɪt/ *noun, adj.*
■ *noun* [U] **1** the faint light or the period of time at the end of the day after the sun has gone down: *It was hard to see him clearly in the twilight.* ◊ *We went for a walk along the beach at twilight.* **2** the ~ (**of sth**) (*written*) the final stage of sth when it becomes weaker or less important than it was: *the twilight years* (= the last years of your life)
■ *adj.* [only before noun] **1** (*written*) used to describe a state in which things are strange and mysterious, or where things are kept secret and do not seem to be part of the real world: *the twilight world of the occult* ◊ *They lived in the twilight zone on the fringes of society.* **2** used to describe a situation or area of thought that is not clearly defined

twi·lit /ˈtwaɪlɪt/ *adj.* (*literary*) lit by twilight

twill /twɪl/ *noun* [U] a strong fabric that is woven in a particular way to produce a surface of raised DIAGONAL lines: *a cotton twill skirt*

twin /twɪn/ *noun, verb, adj.*
■ *noun* **1** one of two children born at the same time to the same mother: *She's expecting twins.*—see also IDENTICAL TWIN, SIAMESE TWIN **2** one of two similar things that make a pair
■ *verb* (**-nn-**) [VN] ~ **sth** (**with sth**) **1** [usually passive] (especially in Britain) to make a close relationship between two towns or areas: *Oxford is twinned with Bonn in Germany.* **2** to join two people or things closely together: *The opera twins the themes of love and death.*
■ *adj.* [only before noun] **1** used to describe one of a pair of children who are twins: *twin boys/girls* ◊ *a twin brother/sister* **2** used to describe two things that are used as a pair: *a ship with twin propellers* **3** used to describe two things that are connected, or present or happening at the same time: *The prison service has the twin goals of punishment and rehabilitation.*

twin 'bed *noun* **1** [usually pl.] one of a pair of single beds in a room: *Would you prefer twin beds or a double?* **2** (*AmE*) a bed big enough for one person: *sheets to fit a twin bed*

twin-'bedded *adj.* (of a room) having two single beds in it

twin 'bedroom *noun* a room in a hotel, etc. that has two single beds

twine /twaɪn/ *noun, verb*

■ *noun* [U] strong string that has two or more STRANDS (= single thin pieces of thread or string) twisted together
■ *verb* [+adv./prep.] ~ (**sth**) **around/round/through/in sth** to wind or twist around sth; to make sth do this: [V] *ivy twining around a tree trunk* ◊ [VN] *She twined her arms around my neck.*

twin-'engined *adj.* (of an aircraft) having two engines

twinge /twɪndʒ/ *noun* **1** a sudden short feeling of pain: *He felt a twinge in his knee as he jumped over the wall.* **2** ~ (**of sth**) a sudden short feeling of an unpleasant emotion: *a twinge of disappointment/envy/guilt/jealousy/regret*

twin·kle /ˈtwɪŋkl/ *verb, noun*
■ *verb* [V] **1** to shine with a light that keeps changing from bright to faint to bright again: *Stars twinkled in the sky.* ◊ *twinkling lights in the distance* **2** ~ (**with sth**) ~ (**at sb**) if your eyes **twinkle**, you have a bright expression because you are happy or excited: *twinkling blue eyes* ◊ *Her eyes twinkled with merriment.*
■ *noun* [sing.] **1** an expression in your eyes that shows you are happy or amused about sth: *He looked at me with a twinkle in his eye.* **2** a small light that keeps changing from bright to faint to bright again: *the twinkle of stars* ◊ *We could see the twinkle of the harbour lights in the distance.*

twink·ling /ˈtwɪŋklɪŋ/ *noun* [sing.] (*old-fashioned, informal*) a very short time **IDM** **in the ,twinkling of an 'eye** very quickly: *Suddenly, in the twinkling of an eye, her whole life had been turned upside down.*

twin·set /ˈtwɪnset/ *noun* (*BrE*) a woman's matching sweater and CARDIGAN that are designed to be worn together

twin 'town *noun* one of two towns in different countries that have a special relationship with each other: *a visit to Lyon, Birmingham's twin town in France*

twirl /twɜːl; *AmE* twɜːrl/ *verb, noun*
■ *verb* **1** ~ (**sb**) (**around/round**) to move or dance round and round; to make sb do this: [V] *She twirled around in front of the mirror.* ◊ [VN] *He held her hand and twirled her around.* **2** [VN] ~ **sth** (**around/about**) to make sth turn quickly and lightly round and round **SYN** SPIN: *He twirled his hat in his hand.* ◊ *She sat twirling the stem of the glass in her fingers.* **3** [VN] to twist or curl sth with your fingers: *He kept twirling his moustache.*
■ *noun* the action of a person spinning around once: *Kate did a twirl in her new dress.*

twist /twɪst/ *verb, noun*
■ *verb*
BEND INTO SHAPE | **1** [VN] to bend or turn sth into a particular shape: *Twist the wire to form a circle.* ◊ *Her hair was twisted into a knot on top of her head.* **2** [often +adv./prep.] to bend or turn sth into a shape or position that is not normal or natural; to be bent or turned in this way: [VN] *The bike was just a heap of twisted metal.* ◊ *He grabbed me and twisted my arm behind my back.* ◊ [V] *Her face twisted in anger.*
TURN BODY | **3** to turn part of your body around while the rest stays still: [VN] *He twisted his head around to look at her.* ◊ [V] *She twisted in her chair when I called her name.* **4** [usually +adv./prep.] to turn your body with quick sharp movements and change direction often: [V] *I twisted and turned to avoid being caught.* ◊ *She tried unsuccessfully to twist free.* [VN] ◊ *He managed to twist himself round in the restricted space.*
TURN WITH HAND | **5** [VN] to turn sth around in a circle with your hand: *Twist the knob to the left to open the door.* ◊ *Nervously I twisted the ring on my finger.*
OF ROADS/RIVERS | **6** [V] to bend and change direction often: *The road twists and turns along the coast.* ◊ *narrow twisting streets* ◊ *a twisting staircase*
ANKLE/WRIST/KNEE | **7** [VN] to injure part of your body, especially your ankle, wrist or knee, bending it in an awkward way: *She fell and twisted her ankle.*
WIND AROUND | **8** [VN +adv./prep.] to wind sth around or through an object: *She twisted a scarf around her head.* ◊ *The telephone cable has got twisted* (= wound around itself). **9** [V] ~ (**round/around sth**) to move or grow by

æ	ɑː	e	ɜː	ə	ɪ	iː	i	ɒ	ɔː	ʌ	ʊ	uː
cat	father	ten	bird	about	sit	see	many	got	saw	cup	put	actual	too
								(BrE)				

winding around sth: *A snake was twisting around his arm.*

FACTS | **10** [VN] to deliberately change the meaning of what sb has said, or to present facts in a particular way, in order to benefit yourself or harm sb else: *You always twist everything I say.* ◊ *The newspaper was accused of twisting the facts.*

THREADS | **11** [VN] ~ **sth** (**into sth**) to turn or wind threads, etc. together to make sth longer or thicker: *They had twisted the sheets into a rope and escaped by climbing down it.*

IDM **twist sb's 'arm** (*informal*) to persuade or force sb to do sth—more at KNIFE *n.*, LITTLE FINGER

PHRV **twist sth↔'off** to turn and pull sth with your hand to remove it from sth: *I twisted off the lid and looked inside.* ◊ *a twist-off cap/top*

▪ *noun*

ACTION OF TURNING | **1** [C] the action of turning sth with your hand, or of turning a part of your body: *She gave the lid another twist and it came off.* ◊ *He gave a shy smile and a little twist of his head.*

UNEXPECTED CHANGE | **2** [C] an unexpected change or development in a story or situation: *the twists and turns of his political career* ◊ *The story has taken another twist.* ◊ *The disappearance of a vital witness added a **new twist** to the case.* ◊ *By a curious **twist of fate** we met again only a week or so later.*

IN ROAD/RIVER | **3** [C] a sharp bend in a road or river: *The car followed the **twists and turns** of the mountain road.*

SHAPE | **4** [C] a thing that has been twisted into a particular shape: *a twist of tobacco/paper* ◊ *mineral water with a twist of lemon*

DANCE | **5** (**the twist**) [sing.] a fast dance that was popular in the 1960s in which you twist from side to side

IDM **round the bend/twist** (*informal, especially BrE*) crazy: *She's gone completely round the twist.*—more at KNICKERS

twist·ed /'twɪstɪd/ *adj.* **1** bent or turned so that the original shape is lost: *After the crash the car was a mass of twisted metal.* ◊ *a twisted ankle/knee* (= injured by being turned suddenly) ◊ *She gave a small twisted smile.*—picture at CURL **2** (of a person's mind or behaviour) not normal; strange in an unpleasant way **SYN** PERVERTED

twist·er /'twɪstə(r)/ *noun* (*AmE, informal*) a violent storm that is caused by a powerful spinning column of air **SYN** TORNADO

twisty /'twɪsti/ *adj.* (especially of a road) having many bends or turns

twit /twɪt/ *noun* (*informal, especially BrE*) a silly or annoying person

twitch /twɪtʃ/ *verb, noun*

▪ *verb* **1** if a part of your body **twitches**, or if you **twitch** it, it makes a sudden movement, sometimes one that you cannot control: [V] *Her lips twitched with amusement.* ◊ *The cats watched each other, their tails twitching.* [also VN] **2** to give sth a short sharp pull; to be pulled in this way: [VN] *He twitched the package out of my hands.* ◊ [V] *The curtains twitched as she rang the bell.*

▪ *noun* **1** a sudden quick movement that you cannot control in one of your muscles: *She has a twitch in her left eye.* ◊ *a nervous twitch* **2** a sudden quick movement or feeling: *He greeted us with a mere twitch of his head.* ◊ *At that moment she felt the first twitch of anxiety.*

twitchy /'twɪtʃi/ *adj.* (*informal*) **1** nervous or anxious about sth **SYN** JITTERY **2** making sudden quick movements

twit·ter /'twɪtə(r)/ *verb, noun*

▪ *verb* **1** [V] when birds **twitter**, they make a series of short high sounds: *starlings twittering in the trees* **2** [V, V speech] ~ (**on**) (**about sth**) (*especially BrE*) to talk quickly in a high excited voice, especially about sth that is not very important

▪ *noun* [sing.] **1** (also **twit·ter·ing**) a series of short high sounds that birds make: *the twitter of starlings* **2** (*informal*) a state of nervous excitement

twixt /twɪkst/ *prep.* (*old use*) between

two /tuː/ *number* **2** **HELP** There are examples of how to

use numbers at the entry for five. **IDM** **a 'day, 'moment, 'pound, etc. or two** one or a few days, moments, pounds, etc: *May I borrow it for a day or two?* **fall between 'two 'stools** (*BrE*) to fail to be or to get either of two choices, both of which would have been satisfactory **in 'two** in or into two pieces or halves: *He broke the bar of chocolate in two and gave me half.* **in ,twos and 'threes** two or three at a time; in small numbers: *People arrived in twos and threes.* **it 'takes two to do sth** (*saying*) one person cannot be completely responsible for sth: *You can't put all the blame on him. It takes two to make a marriage.* **not have two beans, brain cells, etc. to rub to'gether** (*informal*) to have no money; to be very stupid, etc. **put ,two and ,two to'gether** to guess the truth from what you see, hear, etc: *He's inclined to put two and two together and make five* (= make an incorrect guess from what he sees, hears, etc.). **that makes 'two of us** (*informal*) I am in the same position or I agree with you: *'I'm tired!' 'That makes two of us!'* **two ,sides of the same 'coin** used to talk about two ways of looking at the same situation—more at MIND *n.*, SHAKE *n.*

'two-bit *adj.* [only before noun] (*informal, especially AmE*) not good or important: *She wanted to be more than just a two-bit secretary.*

two 'bits *noun* [pl.] (*old-fashioned, AmE, informal*) 25 cents

two-di'mensional *adj.* flat; having no depth; appearing to have only two DIMENSIONS: *a two-dimensional drawing* ◊ (*figurative*) *The novel was criticized for its two-dimensional characters* (= that did not seem like real people).

two-'edged *adj.* **1** (of a blade, knife, etc.) having two sharp edges for cutting **2** having two possible meanings or results, one good and one bad: *Fame can be a two-edged sword.* ◊ *a two-edged remark*

two-'faced *adj.* (*informal, disapproving*) not sincere; not acting in a way that supports what you say that you believe; saying different things to different people about a particular subject **SYN** HYPOCRITICAL

two 'fingers *noun* [pl.] (*BrE, informal*) a sign that you make by holding up your hand with the inside part facing towards you and making a V-shape with your first and second fingers (used as a way of being rude to other people): *I gave him the two fingers.*—compare V-SIGN

two·fold /'tuːfəʊld; *AmE* -foʊld/ *adj.* (*written*) **1** consisting of two parts: *The problem was twofold.* **2** twice as much or as many: *a twofold increase in demand* ▶ **twofold** *adv.*: *Her original investment has increased twofold.*

two-'handed *adj.* using or needing both hands: *a two-handed backhand* (= in tennis) ◊ *a two-handed catch*

two 'pence (also **,two pence 'piece, 2p** /ˌtuː 'piː/) *noun* a British coin worth two pence

two-pence /'tʌpəns; *AmE* 'tuː pens/ *noun* (*BrE*) = TUPPENCE

two·penny (also *informal* **tupp·enny**) /'tʌpəni; *AmE* also 'tuː peni/ *adj.* (*BrE*) costing or worth two old pence: *a twopenny stamp*

two-'piece *noun* a set of clothes consisting of two matching pieces of clothing, for example a skirt and jacket or trousers/pants and a jacket ▶ **,two-'piece** *adj.*: *a two-piece suit*

'two-ply *adj.* (of wool, wood or other material) with two threads or thicknesses

two-'seater *noun* a vehicle, an aircraft or a piece of furniture with seats for two people—picture at CHAIR

two·some /'tuːsəm/ *noun* a group of two people who do sth together **SYN** PAIR

'two-time *verb* [VN] (*informal*) to deceive a person you have a relationship with, especially a sexual one, by having a secret relationship with sb else at the same time: *Are you sure he's not two-timing you?* ▶ **'two-timer** *noun*

'two-tone *adj.* [only before noun] having two different colours or sounds

two-'way *adj.* [usually before noun] **1** moving in two different directions; allowing sth to move in two different

aɪ	aʊ	eɪ	əʊ	oʊ	ɔɪ	ɪə	eə	ʊə	j	w
my	now	say	go	go	boy	near	hair	pure	yes	wet
			(BrE)	(AmE)						

directions: *two-way traffic* ◊ *two-way trade* ◊ *a two-way switch* (= that allows electric current to be turned on or off from either of two points) **2** (of communication between people) needing equal effort from both people or groups involved: *Friendship is a two-way process.* **3** (of radio equipment, etc.) used both for sending and receiving signals

,two-way 'mirror *noun* a piece of glass that is a mirror on one side, but that you can see through from the other

ty·coon /taɪˈkuːn/ *noun* a person who is successful in business or industry and has become rich and powerful: *a business/property/media tycoon*

tyke (also **tike**) /taɪk/ *noun* (*informal*) **1** a small child, especially one who behaves badly **2** (*BrE*) a person from Yorkshire

type /taɪp/ *noun, verb*
■ *noun* **1** [C] ~ (**of sth**) a class or group of people or things that share particular qualities or features and are part of a larger group; a kind or sort: *different racial types* ◊ *a rare blood type* ◊ *There are three main types of contract(s).* ◊ *Bungalows are a type of house.* ◊ *She mixes with all types of people.* ◊ *She mixes with people of all types.* ◊ *I love this type of book.* ◊ *I love these types of books.* ◊ (*informal*) *I love these type of books.* ◊ *What do you charge for this type of work?* ◊ *What do you charge for work of this type?* ◊ *It is the first car of its type to have this design feature.* **2** [sing.] (*informal*) a person of a particular character, with particular features, etc: *She's the artistic type.* ◊ *He's not the type to be unfaithful.* ◊ *She's **not my type*** (= not the kind of person I am usually attracted to). **3** (**-type**) (in adjectives) having the qualities or features of the group, person or thing mentioned: *a police-type badge* ◊ *a continental-type cafe* **4** [U] letters that are printed or typed: *The type was too small for me to read.* ◊ *The important words are in bold type.* **5** [U] (*technical*) the small metal blocks used for printing letters and numbers
■ *verb* **1** to write sth using a WORD PROCESSOR or TYPEWRITER: [V] *How fast can you type?* ◊ *typing errors/courses* ◊ [VN] *This letter will need to be typed* (*out*) *again.* ◊ *Type* (*in*) *the file name, then press 'Return'.* ◊ *Has that report been **typed up** yet?* **2** [VN] (*technical*) to find out the group or class that a person or thing belongs to: *Blood samples were taken from patients for typing.*

type·cast /ˈtaɪpkɑːst; *AmE* -kæst/ *verb* (**type-cast, type-cast**) [VN] [usually passive] ~ **sb** (**as sth**) if an actor is **typecast**, he or she is always given the same kind of character to play: *She didn't want to be typecast as a dumb blonde.*

type·face /ˈtaɪpfeɪs/ *noun* a set of letters, numbers, etc. of a particular design, used in printing: *I'd like the heading to be in a different typeface from the text.*

type·script /ˈtaɪpskrɪpt/ *noun* [C, U] a copy of a text or document that has been typed

type·set·ter /ˈtaɪpsetə(r)/ *noun* a person, machine or company that prepares a book, etc. for printing ▶ **type·set** *verb* (**type-set-ting, type-set, type-set**): [VN] *Pages can now be typeset on-screen.* **type·set·ting** *noun* [U]: *computerized typesetting*

type·writer /ˈtaɪpraɪtə(r)/ *noun* a machine that produces writing similar to print. It has keys that you press to make metal letters or signs hit a piece of paper through a strip of fabric covered with ink.—see also TYPIST

type·writ·ing /ˈtaɪpraɪtɪŋ/ *noun* = TYPING

type·writ·ten /ˈtaɪprɪtn/ *adj.* written using a typewriter or WORD PROCESSOR

ty·phoid /ˈtaɪfɔɪd/ (also *less frequent* **,typhoid 'fever**) *noun* [U] a serious infectious disease that causes fever, red spots on the chest and severe pain in the bowels, and sometimes causes death: *a typhoid epidemic*

ty·phoon /taɪˈfuːn/ *noun* a violent tropical storm with very strong winds—compare CYCLONE, HURRICANE

ty·phus /ˈtaɪfəs/ *noun* [U] a serious infectious disease that causes fever, HEADACHES, purple marks on the body and often death

typ·ical /ˈtɪpɪkl/ *adj.* **1** ~ (**of sb/sth**) having the usual qualities or features of a particular type of person, thing or group [SYN] REPRESENTATIVE: *a typical Italian cafe* ◊

This is a typical example of Roman pottery. ◊ *This meal is typical of local cookery.* ◊ *The weather at the moment is not typical for July.* [OPP] ATYPICAL **2** happening in the usual way; showing what sth is usually like [SYN] NORMAL: *A typical working day for me begins at 7·30.* ◊ *On a typical day, we receive about 50 letters.* [OPP] UNTYPICAL **3** ~ (**of sb/sth**) (often *disapproving*) behaving in the way that you expect: *It was typical of her to forget.* ◊ *He spoke with typical enthusiasm.* ◊ (*informal*) *She's late again—typical!*

typ·ic·al·ly /ˈtɪpɪkli/ *adv.* **1** used to say that sth usually happens in the way that you are stating: *The factory typically produces 500 chairs a week.* ◊ *A typically-priced meal will be around $10.* **2** in a way that shows the usual qualities or features of a particular type of person, thing or group: *typically American hospitality* ◊ *Mothers typically worry about their children.* **3** in the way that you expect sb/sth to behave: *Typically, she couldn't find her keys.* ◊ *He was typically modest about his achievements.*

typ·ify /ˈtɪpɪfaɪ/ *verb* (**typi·fies, typi·fy·ing, typi·fied, typi·fied**) [VN] (not usually used in the progressive tenses) **1** to be a typical example of sth: *clothes that typify the 1960s* ◊ *the new style of politician, typified by the Prime Minister* **2** to be a typical feature of sth: *the haunting guitar melodies that typify the band's music*

typ·ing /ˈtaɪpɪŋ/ (also *less frequent* **type·writ·ing**) *noun* [U] **1** the activity or job of using a TYPEWRITER or WORD PROCESSOR to write sth: *to do the typing* ◊ *typing errors* ◊ *a **typing pool*** (= a group of people who share a company's typing work) **2** writing that has been done on a TYPEWRITER or WORD PROCESSOR

typ·ist /ˈtaɪpɪst/ *noun* **1** a person who works in an office typing letters, etc. **2** a person who uses a TYPEWRITER or computer keyboard: *I'm quite a fast typist.*

typo /ˈtaɪpəʊ; *AmE* -poʊ/ *noun* (*pl.* **-os**) (*informal*) a small mistake in a typed or printed text

typ·og·raph·er /taɪˈpɒɡrəfə(r); *AmE* -ˈpɑːɡ-/ *noun* a person who is skilled in typography

typ·og·raphy /taɪˈpɒɡrəfi; *AmE* -ˈpɑːɡ-/ *noun* [U] the art or work of preparing books, etc. for printing, especially of designing how text will appear when it is printed ▶ **typo·graph·ic·al** /ˌtaɪpəˈɡræfɪkl/ (also **typo·graph·ic** /ˌtaɪpəˈɡræfɪk/) *adj.*: *a typographical error* ◊ *typographic style/design* **typo·graph·ic·al·ly** /-kli/ *adv.*

typ·ology /taɪˈpɒlədʒi; *AmE* -ˈpɑːl-/ *noun* (*pl.* **-ies**) (*technical*) a system of dividing things into different types

tyr·an·nical /tɪˈrænɪkl/ (also *formal* **tyr·an·nous** /ˈtɪrənəs/) *adj.* using power or authority over people in an unfair and cruel way: *tyrannical power* ◊ *a tyrannical government*

tyr·an·nize (*BrE* also **-ise**) /ˈtɪrənaɪz/ *verb* ~ (**over**) **sb/sth** (*written*) to use your power to treat sb in a cruel or unfair way: [VN] *a father tyrannizing his children* ◊ [V] *a political leader who tyrannizes over his people*—see also TYRANT

tyr·anny /ˈtɪrəni/ *noun* [U, C] (*pl.* **-ies**) **1** unfair or cruel use of power or authority: *a victim of oppression and tyranny* ◊ *The children had no protection against the tyranny of their father.* ◊ *the tyrannies of Nazi rule* ◊ (*figurative*) *These days it seems we must all submit to the tyranny of the motor car.* **2** the rule of a tyrant; a country under this rule: *a protest against tyranny* ◊ *Any political system refusing to allow dissent becomes a tyranny.*

tyr·ant /ˈtaɪrənt/ *noun* a person who has complete power in a country and uses it in a cruel and unfair way: *The country was ruled by a succession of tyrants.* ◊ (*figurative*) *His boss is a complete tyrant.*

tyre (*BrE*) (*AmE* **tire**) /ˈtaɪə(r)/ *noun* a thick rubber ring that fits around the edge of a wheel of a car, bicycle, etc: *a front tyre* ◊ *a back/rear tyre* ◊ *to pump up a tyre* ◊ *a flat/burst/punctured tyre* ◊ *bald/worn tyres*—see also SPARE TYRE—picture at BICYCLE, CAR

tyro /ˈtaɪrəʊ; *AmE* -roʊ/ *noun* (*pl.* **-os**) a person who has little or no experience of sth or is beginning to learn sth

tzar, tzar·ina, tzar·ism, tzar·ist = TSAR, TSARINA, TSARISM, TSARIST

b	d	f	g	h	k	l	m	n	p	r
bad	**did**	**fall**	**get**	**hat**	**cat**	**leg**	**man**	**now**	**pen**	**red**

Uu

U /ju:/ noun, abbr.
- noun (also **u**) [C, U] (pl. **U's**, **u's** /ju:z/) the 21st letter of the English alphabet: *'Under' begins with (a) U/'U'.*—see also U-BOAT, U-TURN
- abbr. (BrE) universal (the label of a film that is suitable for anyone including children): *Aladdin, certificate U*

ubi·qui·tous /ju:'bɪkwɪtəs/ adj. [usually before noun] (formal or humorous) seeming to be everywhere or in several places at the same time; very common: *the ubiquitous bicycles of university towns ◊ the ubiquitous movie star, Tom Hanks* ▶ **ubi·qui·tous·ly** adv. **ubi·quity** /ju:'bɪkwəti/ noun [U]: *the ubiquity of the mass media*

'U-boat noun a German SUBMARINE (= a ship that can travel underwater)

UCAS /'ju:kæs/ abbr. (in Britain) Universities and Colleges Admissions Service (an official organization that deals with APPLICATIONS to study at universities)

UDA /ju: di: 'eɪ/ abbr. Ulster Defence Association (an illegal military organization in Northern Ireland that wants Northern Ireland to remain part of the UK)

udder /'ʌdə(r)/ noun an organ shaped like a bag that produces milk and hangs underneath the body of a cow, goat, etc.

UDR /ˌju: di: 'ɑ:(r)/ abbr. Ulster Defence Regiment (a branch of the British army in Northern Ireland, now forming part of the Royal Irish Regiment)

UEFA /ju'eɪfə/ abbr. Union of European Football Associations

UFO (also **ufo**) /ju: ef 'əʊ; 'ju:fəʊ; AmE ju: ef 'oʊ; 'ju:foʊ/ noun (pl. **UFOs**) a strange object that some people claim to have seen in the sky and believe is a spacecraft from another planet (abbreviation for 'Unidentified Flying Object')—compare FLYING SAUCER

ugh exclamation the way of writing the sound (/ɜ:; ʊx/) that people make when they think that sth is disgusting or unpleasant: *Ugh! How can you eat that stuff?*

Ugli™ /'ʌgli/ (also **'Ugli fruit**) noun a large CITRUS fruit with a rough, yellowish-orange skin and sweet flesh with a lot of juice

ugly /'ʌgli/ adj. (**ug·lier**, **ugli·est**) **1** unpleasant to look at SYN UNATTRACTIVE: *an ugly face/building* **2** (of an event, a situation, etc.) unpleasant or dangerous; involving threats or violence: *an ugly incident ◊ There were ugly scenes in the streets last night as rioting continued.* ▶ **ugli·ness** noun [U] IDM see REAR v., SIN n.

,ugly 'duckling noun a person or thing that at first does not seem attractive or likely to succeed but that later becomes successful or much admired

uh exclamation the way of writing the sound /ʌ; ɜ:/ that people make when they are not sure about sth, when they do not hear or understand sth you have said, or when they want you to agree with what they have said: *Uh, yeah, I guess so. ◊ 'Are you ready yet?' 'Uh? Oh. Yes.' ◊ We can discuss this another time, uh?*

UHF /ˌju: eɪtʃ 'ef/ abbr. ultra-high frequency (a range of radio waves used for high-quality radio and television broadcasting)

uh-huh exclamation the way of writing the sound /'ʌ hʌ/ that people make when they understand or agree with what you have said, when they want you to continue or when they are answering 'Yes': *'Did you read my note?' 'Uh-huh.'*

uh-oh exclamation the way of writing the sound /'ʌ əʊ; AmE oʊ/ that people make when they want to say that they have done sth wrong or that they think there will be trouble: *Uh-oh. I forgot to write that letter. ◊ Uh-oh! Turn the TV off. Here comes Dad!*

UHT /ˌju: eɪtʃ 'ti:/ abbr. (BrE) ultra heat treated. UHT milk has been heated to a very high temperature in order to make it last for a long time.

uh-uh exclamation the way of writing the sound /'ʌ ʌ/ that people make when they are answering 'No' to a question

UK (also **U.K.** especially in AmE) /ju: 'keɪ/ abbr. United Kingdom (Great Britain and Northern Ireland)

uku·lele /ˌju:kə'leɪli/ noun a musical instrument with four strings, like a small guitar

ulcer /'ʌlsə(r)/ noun a sore area on the outside of the body or on the surface of an organ inside the body which is painful and may bleed or produce a poisonous substance: *a stomach ulcer*—see also MOUTH ULCER

ul·cer·ate /'ʌlsəreɪt/ verb [V, VN] [usually passive] (medical) to become, or make sth become, covered with ulcers ▶ **ul·cer·ation** /ˌʌlsə'reɪʃn/ noun [U, C]

ulna /'ʌlnə/ noun (pl. **ulnae** /-ni:/) (anatomy) the longer bone of the two bones in the lower part of the arm between the elbow and the wrist, on the side opposite the thumb—see also RADIUS (3)—picture at BODY

ul·ter·ior /ʌl'tɪəriə(r); AmE 'tɪr-/ adj. [only before noun] (of a reason for doing sth) that sb keeps hidden and does not admit: *She must have some **ulterior motive** for being nice to me—what does she really want?*

ul·tim·ate /'ʌltɪmət/ adj., noun
- adj. [only before noun] **1** happening at the end of a long process SYN FINAL: *our ultimate goal/aim/objective/target ◊ We will accept ultimate responsibility for whatever happens. ◊ The ultimate decision lies with the parents.* **2** most extreme; best, worst, greatest, most important, etc: *This race will be the ultimate test of your skill. ◊ Silk sheets are the ultimate luxury.* **3** from which sth originally comes; basic SYN FUNDAMENTAL: *the ultimate truths of philosophy and science*
- noun [sing.] **the ~ in sth** (informal) the best, most advanced, greatest, etc. of its kind: *the ultimate in modern design*

ul·tim·ate·ly /'ʌltɪmətli/ adv. **1** in the end; finally: *Ultimately, you'll have to make the decision yourself. ◊ A poor diet will ultimately lead to illness.* **2** at the most basic and important level: *All life depends ultimately on oxygen.*

ul·ti·matum /ˌʌltɪ'meɪtəm/ noun (pl. **ul·ti·matums** or **ul·ti·ma·ta**) a final warning to a person or country that if they do not do what you ask, you will use force or take action against them: *to issue an ultimatum*

ultra- /'ʌltrə/ prefix (in adjectives and nouns) extremely; beyond a particular limit: *ultra-modern ◊ ultraviolet*—compare INFRA-

ultra·mar·ine /ˌʌltrəmə'ri:n/ noun [U] a bright blue colour

ultra·son·ic /ˌʌltrə'sɒnɪk; AmE 'sɑ:n-/ adj. [usually before noun] (of sounds) higher than human beings can hear: *ultrasonic frequencies/waves/signals*

ultra·sound /'ʌltrəsaʊnd/ noun **1** [U] sound that is higher than human beings can hear **2** [U, C] a medical process that produces an image of what is inside your body: *Ultrasound showed she was expecting twins.*

ultra·vio·let /ˌʌltrə'vaɪələt/ adj. [usually before noun] (physics) of or using ELECTROMAGNETIC waves that are just shorter than those of VIOLET light in the SPECTRUM and that cannot be seen: *ultraviolet rays* (= that cause the skin to go darker) ◊ *an ultraviolet lamp*—compare INFRARED

ulu·late /'ju:ljuleɪt/ verb [V] (rare, literary) to give a long cry ▶ **ulu·la·tion** /-'leɪʃn/ noun [U, C]

um exclamation the way of writing the sound /ʌm; əm/

s	t	v	z	ʃ	ʒ	tʃ	dʒ	θ	ð	ŋ
see	tea	van	zoo	shoe	vision	chain	jam	thin	this	sing

that people make when they hesitate, or do not know what to say next: *Um, I'm not sure how to ask you this ....*

umber /ˈʌmbə(r)/ *noun* [U] a dark brown or yellowish-brown colour used in paints: *burnt/raw umber*

um·bil·ical cord /ˌʌmˌbɪlɪkl ˈkɔːd; *AmE* ˈkɔːrd/ *noun* a long tube of tissue that connects a baby to its mother before it is born and is cut at the moment of birth

um·brage /ˈʌmbrɪdʒ/ *noun* **IDM** **take ˈumbrage (at sth)** (*formal* or *humorous*) to feel offended, insulted or upset by sth, often without a good reason

um·brella /ʌmˈbrelə/ *noun* **1** (also *BrE informal* **brolly**) an object with a folding circular frame of metal rods covered with material, that you use to protect yourself from the rain or from hot sun: *I put up my umbrella.* ◊ *colourful beach umbrellas*—compare PARASOL, SUNSHADE **2** a thing that contains or includes many different parts or elements: *Many previously separate groups are now operating under the umbrella of a single authority.* ◊ *an umbrella organization/group/fund* ◊ *'Contact sports' is an umbrella term for a variety of different sports.* **3** (*written*) a country or system that protects people: *For decades the United States with its nuclear weapons was the umbrella for the western world.*

um·laut /ˈʊmlaʊt/ *noun* the mark placed over a vowel in some languages to show how it should be pronounced, as over the *u* in the German word *für*—compare ACUTE ACCENT, CIRCUMFLEX, GRAVE², TILDE

um·pire /ˈʌmpaɪə(r)/ *noun, verb*
■ *noun* (also *AmE informal* **ump**) (in sports such as tennis and baseball) a person whose job is to watch a game and make sure that rules are not broken—compare REFEREE
■ *verb* to act as the umpire in a game or competition: [V] *We need someone to umpire.* ◊ [VN] *to umpire a game of baseball/cricket*

ump·teen /ˌʌmpˈtiːn/ *det.* (*informal*) very many: *I've told this story umpteen times.* ► **ump·teen** *pron.*: *Umpteen of them all arrived at once.* **ump·teenth** /ˌʌmpˈtiːnθ/ *det.*: *'This is crazy,' she told herself for the umpteenth time* (= she had done it many times before).

UN (also **U.N.** especially in *AmE*) /ˌjuː ˈen/ *abbr.* United Nations. The UN is an association of many countries that aims to help economic and social conditions improve and to solve political problems in the world in a peaceful way: *the UN Security Council* ◊ *a UN peacekeeping plan*

un- /ʌn/ *prefix* **1** (in adjectives, adverbs and nouns) not; the opposite of: *unable* ◊ *unconsciously* ◊ *untruth* ◊ *un-American concepts such as subsidized medical treatment and free education* (= not typical of the US) ◊ *un-American activities* (= against the interests of the US) **2** (in verbs that describe the opposite of a process): *unlock* ◊ *undo* ◊ *unfold*

'un /ən/ *pron.* (*BrE, informal*) a way of saying or writing 'one': *That was a good 'un.* ◊ *The little 'uns* (= the small children) *couldn't keep up.*

un·abashed /ˌʌnəˈbæʃt/ *adj.* (*written*) not ashamed, embarrassed or affected by people's disapproval, when other people would be **OPP** ABASHED ► **un·abashed·ly** /-ʃɪdli/ *adv.*

un·abated /ˌʌnəˈbeɪtɪd/ *adj.* [not usually before noun] (*written*) without becoming any less strong: *The rain continued unabated.*

un·able /ʌnˈeɪbl/ *adj.* [not before noun] **~ to do sth** (rather *formal*) not having the skill, strength, time, knowledge, etc. to do sth: *He lay there, unable to move.* ◊ *I tried to contact him but was unable to.* **OPP** ABLE

un·abridged /ˌʌnəˈbrɪdʒd/ *adj.* (of a novel, play, speech, etc.) complete, without being made shorter in any way **OPP** ABRIDGED

un·accept·able /ˌʌnəkˈseptəbl/ *adj.* that you cannot accept, allow or approve of: *Such behaviour is totally unacceptable in a civilized society.* ◊ *Noise from the factory has reached an unacceptable level.* **OPP** ACCEPTABLE ► **un·accept·ably** /-bli/ *adv.*: *unacceptably high levels of unemployment*

un·accom·pan·ied /ˌʌnəˈkʌmpənid/ *adj.* **1** (*formal*) without a person going together with sb/sth: *No unaccompanied children allowed.* ◊ *unaccompanied lug-*

gage/baggage (= travelling separately from its owner) **2** (*music*) performed without anyone else playing or singing at the same time: *a sonata for unaccompanied violin* **3** (*formal*) **~ by sth** not together with a particular thing: *Mere words, unaccompanied by any violence, cannot amount to an assault.*

un·account·able /ˌʌnəˈkaʊntəbl/ *adj.* (*written*) **1** impossible to understand or explain **SYN** INEXPLICABLE: *There has been an unaccountable increase in cases of the disease.* ◊ *For some unaccountable reason, the letter never arrived.* **2 ~ (to sb/sth)** not having to explain or give reasons for your actions to anyone: *Too many government departments are unaccountable to the general public.* **OPP** ACCOUNTABLE

un·account·ably /ˌʌnəˈkaʊntəbli/ *adv.* (*written*) in a way that is very difficult to explain; without any obvious reason: *He has been unaccountably delayed.*

un·account·ed for /ˌʌnəˈkaʊntɪd fɔː(r)/ *adj.* [not before noun] **1** a person or thing that is **unaccounted for** cannot be found and people do not know what has happened to them or it: *At least 300 civilians are unaccounted for after the bombing raids.* **2** not explained: *In the story he gave the police, half an hour was left unaccounted for.*

un·accus·tomed /ˌʌnəˈkʌstəmd/ *adj.* (*formal*) **1 ~ to sth/to doing sth** not in the habit of doing sth; not used to sth: *He was unaccustomed to hard work.* ◊ *I am unaccustomed to being told what to do.* **2** [usually before noun] not usual, normal or familiar: *The unaccustomed heat made him weary.* **OPP** ACCUSTOMED

un·achiev·able /ˌʌnəˈtʃiːvəbl/ *adj.* that you cannot manage to reach or obtain: *unachievable goals/ambitions/profits* **OPP** ACHIEVABLE

un·acknow·ledged /ˌʌnəkˈnɒlɪdʒd; *AmE* -ˈnɑːl-/ *adj.* **1** not receiving the thanks or praise that is deserved: *Her contribution to the research went largely unacknowledged.* **2** that people do not admit as existing or true; that people are not aware of: *unacknowledged feelings* **3** not publicly or officially recognized: *the unacknowledged leader of the group*

un·acquaint·ed /ˌʌnəˈkweɪntɪd/ *adj.* **~ (with sth/sb)** (*written*) not familiar with sth/sb; having no experience of sth: *visitors unacquainted with local customs* **OPP** ACQUAINTED

un·adorned /ˌʌnəˈdɔːnd; *AmE* -ˈdɔːrnd/ *adj.* (*written*) without any decoration; simple: *The walls were plain and unadorned.*

un·adul·ter·ated /ˌʌnəˈdʌltəreɪtɪd/ *adj.* **1** [usually before noun] you use **unadulterated** to emphasize that sth is complete or total: *For me, the holiday was sheer unadulterated pleasure.* **2** not mixed with other substances; pure; not ADULTERATED: *unadulterated, unprocessed foods*

un·ad·ven·tur·ous /ˌʌnədˈventʃərəs/ *adj.* not willing to take risks or try new and exciting things **OPP** ADVENTUROUS

un·affect·ed /ˌʌnəˈfektɪd/ *adj.* **1 ~ (by sth)** not changed or influenced by sth; not affected by sth: *People's rights are unaffected by the new law.* ◊ *His attitudes have remained largely unaffected by changes in fashion.* ◊ *Some members of the family may remain unaffected by the disease.* **2** (*approving*) (of a person or their behaviour) natural and sincere: *She had a warm smile and an unaffected manner.* **OPP** AFFECTED

un·affili·ated /ˌʌnəˈfɪlieɪtɪd/ *adj.* **~ (with sth)** not belonging to or connected with a political party or a large organization **SYN** INDEPENDENT **OPP** AFFILIATED

un·afraid /ˌʌnəˈfreɪd/ *adj.* [not before noun] **~ (of sth)** | **~ (to do sth)** (*written*) not afraid or nervous; not worried about what might happen: *He felt calm and unafraid.* ◊ *She was unafraid of conflict.* ◊ *He's unafraid to speak his mind.*

un·aid·ed /ʌnˈeɪdɪd/ *adj.* without help from anyone or anything: *Did she produce this work unaided?* ◊ *He can now walk unaided.*

un·alloyed /ˌʌnəˈlɔɪd/ *adj.* (*formal*) not mixed with anything else, such as negative feelings **SYN** PURE: *unalloyed joy/delight*

æ	ɑː	e	ɜː	ə	ɪ	iː	i	ɒ	ɔː	ʌ	ʊ	u	uː
cat	father	ten	bird	about	sit	see	many	got	saw	cup	put	actual	too
								(BrE)					

un·alter·able /ʌnˈɔːltərəbl/ *adj.* (*formal*) that cannot be changed: *the unalterable laws of the universe*

un·altered /ʌnˈɔːltəd; *AmE* -tərd/ *adj.* (*written*) that has not changed or been changed: *This practice has remained unaltered for centuries.*

un·am·bigu·ous /ˌʌnæmˈbɪgjuəs/ *adj.* clear in meaning; that can only be understood in one way: *an unambiguous statement/definition* ◊ *The message was clear and unambiguous—'Get out!'* OPP AMBIGUOUS ▶ **un·am·bigu·ous·ly** *adv.*

un·am·bi·tious /ˌʌnæmˈbɪʃəs/ *adj.* (*written*) **1** (of a person) not interested in becoming successful, rich, powerful, etc. **2** not involving a lot of effort, time, money, etc. or anything new: *an unambitious plan/novel* OPP AMBITIOUS

unan·im·ity /ˌjuːnəˈnɪməti/ *noun* [U] (*written*) complete agreement about sth among a group of people

unani·mous /juˈnænɪməs/ *adj.* **1** if a decision or an opinion is **unanimous**, it is agreed or shared by everyone in a group: *a unanimous vote* ◊ *unanimous condemnation/support* ◊ *The decision was not unanimous.* **2 ~ (in sth)** if a group of people are **unanimous**, they all agree about sth: *Local people are unanimous in their opposition to the proposed new road.* ▶ **unani·mous·ly** *adv.*: *The motion was passed unanimously.*

un·announced /ˌʌnəˈnaʊnst/ *adj.* happening without anyone being told or warned in advance: *She just turned up unannounced on my doorstep.* ◊ *an unannounced increase in bus fares*

un·answer·able /ʌnˈɑːnsərəbl; *AmE* ʌnˈæn-/ *adj.* **1** an **unanswerable** argument, etc. is one that nobody can question or disagree with: *They presented an unanswerable case for more investment.* **2** an **unanswerable** question is one that has no answer or that you cannot answer

un·answered /ʌnˈɑːnsəd; *AmE* -sərd/ *adj.* (*written*) **1** (of a question, problem, etc.) that has not been answered: *Many questions about the crime remain unanswered.* **2** (of a letter, telephone call, etc.) that has not been replied to: *unanswered letters* ◊ *Their cries for help went unanswered.*

un·antici·pated /ˌʌnænˈtɪsɪpeɪtɪd/ *adj.* (*written*) that you have not expected or predicted; that you have not ANTICIPATED: *unanticipated events/consequences/costs*

un·apolo·get·ic /ˌʌnəˌpɒləˈdʒetɪk; *AmE* -ˌpɑːl-/ *adj.* (*written*) not saying that you are sorry about sth, even in situations in which other people might expect you to OPP APOLOGETIC ▶ **un·apolo·get·ic·al·ly** /-kli/ *adv.*

un·appeal·ing /ˌʌnəˈpiːlɪŋ/ *adj.* not attractive or pleasant: *The room was painted in an unappealing shade of brown.* ◊ *The prospect of studying for another five years was distinctly unappealing.* OPP APPEALING

un·appe·tiz·ing (*BrE* also **-ising**) /ʌnˈæpɪtaɪzɪŋ/ *adj.* (of food) unpleasant to eat; looking as if it will be unpleasant to eat OPP APPETIZING

un·appre·ci·ated /ˌʌnəˈpriːʃieɪtɪd/ *adj.* [not usually before noun] (*written*) not having your work or your qualities recognized and enjoyed by other people; not APPRECIATED: *He was in a job where he felt unappreciated and undervalued.*

un·approach·able /ˌʌnəˈprəʊtʃəbl; *AmE* -ˈproʊ-/ *adj.* (of a person) unfriendly and not easy to talk to OPP APPROACHABLE

un·argu·able /ʌnˈɑːgjuəbl; *AmE* -ˈɑːrg-/ *adj.* (*formal*) that nobody can disagree with: *unarguable proof/logic*—compare ARGUABLE ▶ **un·argu·ably** *adv.*: *She is unarguably one of the country's finest athletes.*

un·armed /ʌnˈɑːmd; *AmE* ʌnˈɑːrmd/ *adj.* **1** not carrying a weapon: *unarmed civilians/planes* ◊ *He walked into the camp alone and unarmed.* **2** not involving the use of weapons: *The soldiers were trained in unarmed combat.* OPP ARMED

un·ashamed /ˌʌnəˈʃeɪmd/ *adj.* feeling no shame or embarrassment about sth or about sth you have done, especially when people might expect you to: *There were unashamed tears in his eyes.*—compare ASHAMED ▶ **un·ashamed·ly** /ˌʌnəˈʃeɪmɪdli/ *adv.*: *She wept unashamedly.* ◊ *an unashamedly sentimental song*

un·asked /ʌnˈɑːskt; *AmE* ʌnˈæskt/ *adj.* **1** an **unasked** question is one that you have not asked even though you would like to know the answer **2** without being invited or asked: *He came to the party unasked.* ◊ *She brought him, unasked, the relevant file.*

un·assail·able /ˌʌnəˈseɪləbl/ *adj.* (*written*) that cannot be destroyed, defeated or questioned: *The party now has an unassailable lead.* ◊ *Their ten-point lead puts the team in an almost unassailable position.* ◊ *She replied with what she thought was unassailable logic...*

un·assist·ed /ˌʌnəˈsɪstɪd/ *adj.* not helped by anyone or anything: *She could not move unassisted.*

un·assum·ing /ˌʌnəˈsjuːmɪŋ; *AmE* ˌʌnəˈsuː-/ *adj.* (*approving*) not wanting to draw attention to yourself or to your abilities or status

un·attached /ˌʌnəˈtætʃt/ *adj.* **1** not married or involved in a romantic relationship: *He was still unattached at the age of 34.* **2** not connected with or belonging to a particular group or organization—compare ATTACHED

un·attain·able /ˌʌnəˈteɪnəbl/ *adj.* (*written*) impossible to achieve or reach: *an unattainable dream/goal* OPP ATTAINABLE

un·attend·ed /ˌʌnəˈtendɪd/ *adj.* without the owner present; not being watched or cared for: *unattended luggage/vehicles* ◊ *She was reprimanded for leaving the children unattended.*

un·attract·ive /ˌʌnəˈtræktɪv/ *adj.* **1** not attractive or pleasant to look at: *an unattractive brown colour* **2** not good, interesting or pleasant: *one of the unattractive aspects of the free market economy* OPP ATTRACTIVE ▶ **un·attract·ive·ly** *adv.*

un·author·ized (*BrE* also **-ised**) /ʌnˈɔːθəraɪzd/ *adj.* (*written*) without official permission: *No access for unauthorized personnel.* OPP AUTHORIZED

un·avail·able /ˌʌnəˈveɪləbl/ *adj.* [not usually before noun] **~ (to sb/sth) 1** that cannot be obtained: *Such luxury items were unavailable to ordinary people.* **2** not able or not willing to see, meet or talk to sb: *The minister was unavailable for comment.* OPP AVAILABLE ▶ **un·avail·abil·ity** *noun* [U]

un·avail·ing /ˌʌnəˈveɪlɪŋ/ *adj.* (*formal*) without success SYN UNSUCCESSFUL: *Their efforts were unavailing.*

un·avoid·able /ˌʌnəˈvɔɪdəbl/ *adj.* impossible to avoid or prevent: *unavoidable delays* OPP AVOIDABLE ▶ **un·avoid·ably** /-əbli/ *adv.*: *I was unavoidably delayed.*

un·aware /ˌʌnəˈweə(r); *AmE* -ˈwer/ *adj.* [not before noun] **~ of sth | ~ that...** not knowing or realizing that sth is happening or that sth exists: *He was completely unaware of the whole affair.* ◊ *She was unaware that I could see her.* OPP AWARE ▶ **un·aware·ness** *noun* [U]

un·awares /ˌʌnəˈweəz; *AmE* -ˈwerz/ *adv.* **1** when not expected: *The camera had caught her unawares.* ◊ *The announcement took me unawares.* ◊ *She came upon him unawares when he was searching her room.* **2** (*formal*) without noticing or realizing: *He slipped unawares into sleep.*

un·bal·ance /ʌnˈbæləns/ *verb* [VN] **1** to make sth no longer balanced, for example by giving too much importance to one part of it **2** to make sb/sth unsteady so that they are likely to fall down **3** to make sb slightly crazy or mentally ill

un·bal·anced /ʌnˈbælənst/ *adj.* **1** [not usually before noun] (of a person) slightly crazy; mentally ill **2** [usually before noun] giving too much or too little importance to one part or aspect of sth: *an unbalanced article* ◊ *an unbalanced diet*

unban /ʌnˈbæn/ *verb* (**-nn-**) [VN] to allow sth that was forbidden before

un·bear·able /ʌnˈbeərəbl; *AmE* -ˈber-/ *adj.* too painful, annoying or unpleasant to deal with or accept SYN INTOLERABLE: *The heat was becoming unbearable.* ◊ *unbearable pain/loneliness* ◊ *He's been unbearable since he won that prize.* OPP BEARABLE ▶ **un·bear·ably** /-əbli/ *adv.*: *unbearably hot/arrogant/painful*

un·beat·able /ʌnˈbiːtəbl/ *adj.* **1** (of a team, player, etc.) impossible to defeat **2** (of prices, value, etc.) impossible to improve: *unbeatable discounts/offers*

aɪ	aʊ	eɪ	əʊ	oʊ	ɔɪ	ɪə	eə	ʊə	j	w
my	now	say	go	go	boy	near	hair	pure	yes	wet
			(BrE)	(AmE)						

un·beat·en /ʌnˈbiːtn/ adj. (sport) not having been defeated: *The team are unbeaten in their last four games.* ◊ *They will be putting their **unbeaten record** to the test next Saturday.*

un·be·com·ing /ˌʌnbɪˈkʌmɪŋ/ adj. (formal) **1** not suiting a particular person: *She was wearing an unbecoming shade of purple.* **2 ~ (to/of sb)** not appropriate or acceptable: *He was accused of conduct unbecoming to an officer.* OPP BECOMING

un·be·known /ˌʌnbɪˈnəʊn/; AmE -ˈnoʊn/ (also less frequent **un·be·knownst** /ˌʌnbɪˈnəʊnst/; AmE -ˈnoʊnst/) adj. **~ to sb** (written) without the person mentioned knowing: *Unbeknown to her they had organized a surprise birthday party.*

un·belief /ˌʌnbɪˈliːf/ noun [U] (formal) lack of belief, or the state of not believing, especially in God, a religion, etc.—compare BELIEF, DISBELIEF

un·believ·able /ˌʌnbɪˈliːvəbl/ adj. **1** used to emphasize how good, bad or extreme sth is SYN INCREDIBLE: *We had an unbelievable* (= very good) *time in Paris.* ◊ *Conditions in the prison camp were unbelievable* (= very bad). ◊ *We get through an unbelievable amount of food each week.* ◊ *The cold was unbelievable* (= it was extremely cold). ◊ *It's unbelievable that* (= very shocking) *they have permitted this trial to go ahead.* **2** very difficult to believe and unlikely to be true SYN INCREDIBLE: *I found the whole story bizarre, not to say unbelievable.* OPP BELIEVABLE for sense 2 ▶ **un·believ·ably**: *unbelievably good/hot/painful/stupid* ◊ *Unbelievably it actually works.*

un·believer /ˌʌnbɪˈliːvə(r)/ noun (formal) a person who does not believe in God, a religion, etc. OPP BELIEVER

un·believ·ing /ˌʌnbɪˈliːvɪŋ/ adj. (written) feeling or showing that you do not believe sb/sth: *She stared at us with unbelieving eyes.* ◊ *He gazed at the letter, unbelieving.*

un·bend /ˌʌnˈbend/ verb (**un·bent, un·bent** /ˌʌnˈbent/) **1** [V] to relax and become less strict or formal in your behaviour or attitude: *He could be fun if he'd unbend a little.* **2** [VN, V] to make sth that was bent become straight; to become straight

un·bend·ing /ˌʌnˈbendɪŋ/ adj. (often disapproving) unwilling to change your opinions, decisions, etc.

un·biased (also **un·biassed**) /ʌnˈbaɪəst/ adj. fair and not influenced by your own or sb else's opinions, desires, etc. SYN IMPARTIAL: *unbiased advice/reporting/information* ◊ *an unbiased judge/observer* OPP BIASED

un·bid·den /ʌnˈbɪdn/ adj. (literary) (usually used after the verb) without being asked, invited or expected: *He walked into the room unbidden.*

un·bleached /ʌnˈbliːtʃt/ adj. not made whiter by the use of chemicals; not bleached: *unbleached paper/flour*

un·blem·ished /ʌnˈblemɪʃt/ adj. (written) not spoiled, damaged or marked in any way: *He had an unblemished reputation.* ◊ *her pale unblemished skin*

un·blink·ing /ʌnˈblɪŋkɪŋ/ adj. (written) if sb has an unblinking stare or looks with unblinking eyes, they look very steadily at sth and do not BLINK ▶ **un·blink·ing·ly** adv.

un·block /ˌʌnˈblɒk; AmE -ˈblɑːk/ verb [VN] to clean sth, for example a pipe, by removing sth that is blocking it

un·born /ˌʌnˈbɔːn; AmE -ˈbɔːrn/ adj. [usually before noun] not yet born: *her unborn baby/child*

un·bound·ed /ʌnˈbaʊndɪd/ adj. (formal) having, or seeming to have, no limits SYN BOUNDLESS: *her unbounded energy/enthusiasm*

un·bowed /ˌʌnˈbaʊd/ adj. (literary) not defeated or not ready to accept defeat: *The losing team left the field bloody but unbowed.*

un·break·able /ʌnˈbreɪkəbl/ adj. impossible to break: *This new material is virtually unbreakable.* ◊ *the unbreakable bond between parent and child* OPP BREAKABLE

un·bridge·able /ʌnˈbrɪdʒəbl/ adj. an **unbridgeable** GAP or difference between two people or groups or their opinions is one that cannot be closed or made less wide

un·bridled /ʌnˈbraɪdld/ adj. [usually before noun] (formal) not controlled and therefore extreme: *unbridled enthusiasm/lust/passion*

un·broken /ʌnˈbrəʊkən; AmE -ˈbroʊ-/ adj. **1** not interrupted or disturbed in any way: *a single unbroken line* ◊ *30 years of virtually unbroken peace* ◊ *Last night was my first night of unbroken sleep since the baby was born.* **2** (of a record in a sport, etc.) that has not been improved on

un·buckle /ˌʌnˈbʌkl/ verb [VN] to undo the BUCKLE of a belt, shoe, etc.

un·bur·den /ˌʌnˈbɜːdn; AmE -ˈbɜːrdn/ verb [VN] **1 ~ yourself/sth (of sth) (to sb)** (formal) to talk to sb about your problems or sth you have been worrying about, so that you feel less anxious: *She needed to unburden herself to somebody.* **2 ~ sb/sth (of sth)** to take sth that causes a lot of work or worry away from sb/sth OPP BURDEN

un·but·ton /ˌʌnˈbʌtn/ verb [VN] to undo the buttons on a piece of clothing: *He unbuttoned his shirt.* OPP BUTTON (UP)

un'called for adj. (of behaviour or remarks) not fair or appropriate: *His comments were uncalled for.* ◊ *uncalled-for comments*

un·canny /ʌnˈkæni/ adj. strange and difficult to explain: *I had an uncanny feeling I was being watched.* ◊ *It was uncanny really, almost as if she knew what I was thinking.* ▶ **un·can·nily** /-ɪli/ adv.: *He looked uncannily like someone I knew.*

un'cared for adj. not looked after SYN NEGLECTED: *The garden looked uncared for.* ◊ *an uncared-for garden*

un·car·ing /ʌnˈkeərɪŋ; AmE -ˈker-/ adj. (disapproving) not sympathetic about the problems or suffering of other people: *He was selfish and uncaring.* ◊ *We live in an uncaring society.* OPP CARING

un·ceas·ing /ʌnˈsiːsɪŋ/ adj. (written) continuing all the time SYN INCESSANT: *unceasing efforts* ◊ *Planes passed overhead with unceasing regularity.* ▶ **un·ceas·ing·ly** adv.: *Snow fell unceasingly.*

un·cen·sored /ʌnˈsensəd; AmE -sərd/ adj. (of a report, film/movie, etc.) not CENSORED (= having had parts removed that are not considered suitable for the public): *an uncensored newspaper article*

un·cere·mo·ni·ous /ˌʌnˌserəˈməʊniəs; AmE -ˈmoʊ-/ adj. (written) done roughly and rudely: *He was bundled out of the room with unceremonious haste.*—compare CEREMONIOUS

un·cere·mo·ni·ous·ly /ˌʌnˌserəˈməʊniəsli; AmE -ˈmoʊ-/ adv. (written) in a rough or rude way, without caring about a person's feelings: *They dumped his belongings unceremoniously on the floor.*

un·cer·tain /ʌnˈsɜːtn; AmE ʌnˈsɜːrtn/ adj. **1** [usually after noun] **~ (about/of sth)** feeling doubt about sth; not sure: *They're both uncertain about what to do.* ◊ *I'm still uncertain of my feelings for him.* OPP CERTAIN **2** likely to change, especially in a negative or unpleasant way: *Our future looks uncertain.* ◊ *a man of uncertain temper* **3** not definite or decided: *It is uncertain what his role in the company will be.* **4** not confident SYN HESITANT: *The baby took its first uncertain steps.* IDM **in ˌno unˌcertain ˈterms** clearly and strongly: *I told him what I thought of him in no uncertain terms.*

un·cer·tain·ly /ʌnˈsɜːtnli; AmE -ˈsɜːrtn-/ adv. without confidence SYN HESITANTLY: *They smiled uncertainly at one another.*

un·cer·tainty /ʌnˈsɜːtnti; AmE -ˈsɜːrtn-/ noun (pl. -ies) **1** [U] the state of being uncertain: *There is considerable uncertainty about the company's future.* ◊ *He had an air of uncertainty about him.* **2** [C] something that you cannot be sure about; a situation that causes you to be or feel uncertain: *life's uncertainties* ◊ *the uncertainties of war*

un·chal·lenge·able /ʌnˈtʃælɪndʒəbl/ adj. that cannot be questioned or argued with; that cannot be CHALLENGED: *unchallengeable power/evidence/truth* ◊ *The committee's decision is unchallengeable.*

un·chal·lenged /ʌnˈtʃælɪndʒd/ adj. **1** not doubted; accepted without question; not CHALLENGED: *She could not allow such a claim to go unchallenged.* **2** (of a ruler or leader, or their position) not opposed by anyone: *He is in*

U

a position of unchallenged authority. **3** without being stopped and asked to explain who you are, what you are doing, etc: *I walked into the building unchallenged.*

un·change·able /ʌn'tʃeɪndʒəbl/ *adj.* that cannot be changed: *unchangeable laws/circumstances*—compare CHANGEABLE

un·changed /ʌn'tʃeɪndʒd/ *adj.* [not usually before noun] that has stayed the same and not changed: *My opinion remains unchanged.*

un·chan·ging /ʌn'tʃeɪndʒɪŋ/ *adj.* that always stays the same and does not change: *unchanging customs/principles/truths* ◊ *The days went by, unchanging.*

un·char·ac·ter·is·tic /ˌʌn,kærəktə'rɪstɪk/ *adj.* ~ **(of sb)** not typical of sb; not the way sb usually behaves: *The remark was quite uncharacteristic of her.* OPP CHARACTERISTIC ▶ **un·char·ac·ter·is·tic·al·ly** /-kli/ *adv.*: *The children had been uncharacteristically quiet.*

un·char·it·able /ʌn'tʃærɪtəbl/ *adj.* unkind and unfair in the way that you judge people; not sympathetic: *uncharitable thoughts/remarks* ◊ *I don't want to be uncharitable, but he isn't very intelligent, is he?* OPP CHARITABLE

un·chart·ed /ˌʌn'tʃɑːtɪd; AmE -'tʃɑːrt-/ *adj.* [usually before noun] **1** that has not been visited or investigated before; not familiar: *They set off into the country's uncharted interior.* ◊ *(figurative) The party is sailing in uncharted waters* (= a situation it has not been in before). ◊ *(figurative) I was moving into uncharted territory* (= a completely new experience) *with this relationship.* **2** not marked on a map: *The ship hit an uncharted rock.*

un·checked /ˌʌn'tʃekt/ *adj.* if sth harmful is unchecked, it is not controlled or stopped from getting worse: *The fire was allowed to burn unchecked.* ◊ *The rise in violent crime must not go unchecked.* ◊ *The plant will soon choke ponds and waterways if **left unchecked.***

un·civil /ˌʌn'sɪvl/ *adj.* (rare, formal) not polite OPP CIVIL—see also INCIVILITY

un·civ·il·ized (BrE also **-ised**) /ʌn'sɪvəlaɪzd/ *adj.* (disapproving) **1** (of people or their behaviour) not behaving in a way that is acceptable according to social or moral standards **2** (of people or places) not having developed a modern culture and way of life: *I have worked in the wildest and most uncivilized parts of the world.* OPP CIVILIZED

un·claimed /ˌʌn'kleɪmd/ *adj.* that nobody has claimed as belonging to them or being owed to them

un·clas·si·fied /ʌn'klæsɪfaɪd/ *adj.* **1** (of documents, information, etc.) not officially secret; available to everyone OPP CLASSIFIED **2** (technical) that has not been CLASSIFIED as being the member of a particular group: (BrE) *A high proportion of candidates get low or unclassified grades* (= their work is not good enough to receive a grade). **3** (BrE) (of a road) not large or important enough to be given a number

uncle /'ʌŋkl/ *noun* **1** the brother of your mother or father; the husband of your aunt: *Uncle Ian* ◊ *I'm going to visit my uncle.* ◊ *I've just become an uncle* (= because your brother/sister has had a baby). **2** used by children, with a first name, to address a man who is a close friend of their parents IDM see BOB

un·clean /ˌʌn'kliːn/ *adj.* **1** (formal) dirty and therefore likely to cause disease: *unclean water* ◊ *unclean premises/hands* OPP CLEAN **2** considered to be bad, immoral or not pure in a religious way, and therefore not to be touched, eaten, etc: *unclean thoughts* ◊ *unclean food/animals*

un·clear /ˌʌn'klɪə(r); AmE -'klɪr/ *adj.* **1** not clear or definite; difficult to understand or be sure about: *His motives are unclear.* ◊ *Our plans are unclear at the moment.* ◊ *It is unclear whether there is any damage.* ◊ *Some of your diagrams are unclear.* **2** ~ **(about sth)** ~ **(as to sth)** not fully understanding sth; uncertain about sth: *I'm unclear about what you want me to do.*

Uncle 'Sam *noun* (informal) a way of referring to the United States of America or the US government (sometimes shown as a tall man with a white BEARD and a tall hat): *He owed $20 000 in tax to Uncle Sam.*

Uncle 'Tom *noun* (informal, ⚠) (offensive) sometimes used in the past to refer to a black man who wants to please or serve white people

un·clothed /ˌʌn'kləʊðd; AmE -kloʊðd/ *adj.* (formal) not wearing any clothes SYN NAKED

un·clut·tered /ˌʌn'klʌtəd; AmE -tərd/ *adj.* (approving) not containing too many objects, details or unnecessary items SYN TIDY: *an uncluttered surface/room* OPP CLUTTERED

un·coil /ˌʌn'kɔɪl/ *verb* to become or make sth straight after it has been wound or twisted round in a circle: [V] *The snake slowly uncoiled.* ◊ [VN] *to uncoil a rope*

un·col·oured (BrE) (AmE **un·col·ored**) /ˌʌn'kʌləd; AmE -ərd/ *adj.* with no colour; with no colour added: *plain, uncoloured glass*

un·com·fort·able /ˌʌn'kʌmftəbl; BrE also -fət-; AmE also -fərt-/ *adj.* **1** (of clothes, furniture, etc.) not letting you feel physically comfortable; unpleasant to wear, sit on, etc: *uncomfortable shoes* ◊ *I couldn't sleep because the bed was so uncomfortable.* OPP COMFORTABLE **2** not feeling physically relaxed, warm, etc: *I was sitting in an extremely uncomfortable position.* ◊ *She still finds it uncomfortable to stand without support.* OPP COMFORTABLE **3** anxious, embarrassed or afraid and unable to relax; making you feel like this: *He looked distinctly uncomfortable when the subject was mentioned.* ◊ *There was an uncomfortable silence.* OPP COMFORTABLE **4** unpleasant or difficult to deal with: *an uncomfortable truth/fact* ◊ *I had the uncomfortable feeling that it was my fault.*

un·com·fort·ably /ˌʌn'kʌmftəbli; BrE also -fət-; AmE also -fərt-/ *adv.* **1** in a way that makes you feel anxious or embarrassed; in a way that shows you are anxious or embarrassed: *I became uncomfortably aware that no one else was laughing.* ◊ *Her comment was uncomfortably close to the truth.* ◊ *He shifted uncomfortably in his seat when I mentioned money.* **2** in a way that is not physically comfortable: *I was feeling uncomfortably hot.* ◊ *She perched uncomfortably on the edge of the table.*

un·com·mit·ted /ˌʌnkə'mɪtɪd/ *adj.* ~ **(to sb/sth)** not having given or promised support to a particular person, group, belief, action, etc: *The party needs to canvass the uncommitted voters.*—compare COMMITTED

un·com·mon /ʌn'kɒmən; AmE -'kɑːm-/ *adj.* **1** not existing in large numbers or in many places SYN UNUSUAL, RARE: *an uncommon occurrence/experience* ◊ *Side effects from the drug are uncommon.* ◊ *It is not uncommon for college students to live at home.* ◊ *Red squirrels are uncommon in England.* OPP COMMON **2** (formal or literary) unusually large in degree or amount; great: *She showed uncommon pleasure at his arrival.*

un·com·mon·ly /ʌn'kɒmənli; AmE -'kɑːm-/ *adv.* (formal) **1** to an unusual degree; extremely: *an uncommonly gifted child* **2** not often; not usually: *Not uncommonly, there is a great deal of rain in August.*

un·com·mu·ni·ca·tive /ˌʌnkə'mjuːnɪkətɪv/ *adj.* (disapproving) (of a person) not willing to talk to other people or give opinions OPP COMMUNICATIVE

un·com·peti·tive /ˌʌnkəm'petətɪv/ *adj.* (business) not cheaper or better than others and therefore not able to compete equally: *an uncompetitive industry* ◊ *uncompetitive prices* OPP COMPETITIVE

un·com·plain·ing /ˌʌnkəm'pleɪnɪŋ/ *adj.* (approving) not saying that you are unhappy about a difficult or unpleasant situation; not saying that you are in pain ▶ **un·com·plain·ing·ly** *adv.*

un·com·pleted /ˌʌnkəm'pliːtɪd/ *adj.* that has not been finished: *an uncompleted building/project/investigation*

un·com·pli·cated /ʌn'kɒmplɪkeɪtɪd; AmE -'kɑːm-/ *adj.* simple; without any difficulty or confusion SYN STRAIGHTFORWARD: *an easygoing, uncomplicated young man* ◊ *Why can't I have an uncomplicated life?* OPP COMPLICATED

un·com·pli·men·tary /ʌn,kɒmplɪ'mentri; AmE -,kɑːm-/ *adj.* rude or insulting: *uncomplimentary remarks*—compare COMPLIMENTARY

un·com·pre·hend·ing /ʌn,kɒmprɪ'hendɪŋ; AmE

-ˌkɑːm-/ *adj.* (*written*) (of a person) not understanding a situation or what is happening ▶ **un·com·pre·hend·ing·ly** *adv.*: *She looked at him uncomprehendingly*

un·com·prom·is·ing /ʌnˈkɒmprəmaɪzɪŋ; *AmE* -ˈkɑːm-/ *adj.* unwilling to change your opinions or behaviour: *an uncompromising attitude* ◊ *He has a reputation for being tough and uncompromising.* ▶ **un·com·prom·is·ing·ly** *adv.*

un·con·cealed /ˌʌnkənˈsiːld/ *adj.* [usually before noun] (of an emotion, etc.) that you do not try to hide $\boxed{\text{SYN}}$ OBVIOUS: *unconcealed anxiety/curiosity*

un·con·cern /ˌʌnkənˈsɜːn; *AmE* -ˈsɜːrn/ *noun* [U] (*written*) a lack of care, interest or worry about sth that other people would care about: *She received the news with apparent unconcern.*—compare CONCERN

un·con·cerned /ˌʌnkənˈsɜːnd; *AmE* -ˈsɜːrnd/ *adj.* **1 ~ (about/by sth)** not worried or anxious about sth because you feel it does not affect you or is not important: *He drove on, apparently unconcerned about the noise the engine was making.* **2 ~ (with sb/sth)** not interested in sth: *Young people are often quite unconcerned with political issues.* $\boxed{\text{OPP}}$ CONCERNED ▶ **un·con·cern·ed·ly** /ˌʌnkənˈsɜːnɪdli/ *adv.*

un·con·di·tion·al /ˌʌnkənˈdɪʃənl/ *adj.* without any conditions or limits: *the unconditional surrender/withdrawal of military forces* ◊ *unconditional love* $\boxed{\text{OPP}}$ CONDITIONAL ▶ **un·con·di·tion·al·ly** /-ʃənəli/ *adv.*

un·con·di·tioned /ˌʌnkənˈdɪʃnd/ *adj.* (*psychology*) (of behaviour) not trained or influenced by experience; natural: *an unconditioned response/stimulus*

un·con·firmed /ˌʌnkənˈfɜːmd; *AmE* -ˈfɜːrmd/ *adj.* that has not yet been proved to be true or CONFIRMED: *unconfirmed rumours* ◊ *Unconfirmed reports said that at least six people had been killed.*

un·con·gen·ial /ˌʌnkənˈdʒiːniəl/ *adj.* (*formal*) **1** (of a person) not pleasant or friendly; not like yourself: *uncongenial company* **2 ~ (to sb)** (of a place, job, etc.) not pleasant; not making you feel relaxed; not suitable for your personality: *an uncongenial atmosphere* ◊ *A career in commerce proved uncongenial for him.* **3 ~ (to sth)** not suitable for sth; not encouraging sth: *The religious climate at the time was uncongenial to new ideas.* $\boxed{\text{OPP}}$ CONGENIAL

un·con·nect·ed /ˌʌnkəˈnektɪd/ *adj.* **~ (with/to sth)** not related or connected in any way: *The two crimes are apparently unconnected.* ◊ *My resignation was totally unconnected with recent events.*

un·con·scion·able /ʌnˈkɒnʃənəbl; *AmE* -ˈkɑːn-/ *adj.* [usually before noun] (*formal*) **1** (of an action, etc.) so bad, immoral, etc. that it should make you feel ashamed: *It would be unconscionable for her to keep the money.* **2** (often *humorous*) too great, large, long, etc. $\boxed{\text{SYN}}$ EXCESSIVE: *You take an unconscionable amount of time getting dressed!*

the un·con·scious /ʌnˈkɒnʃəs; *AmE* -ˈkɑːn-/ *noun* [sing.] (*psychology*) the part of a person's mind with thoughts, feelings, etc. that they are not aware of and cannot control but which can sometimes be understood by studying their behaviour or dreams—compare SUB-CONSCIOUS

un·con·scious /ʌnˈkɒnʃəs; *AmE* -ˈkɑːn-/ *adj.* **1** in a state like sleep because of an injury or illness, and not able to use your senses: *She was knocked unconscious.* ◊ *They found him lying unconscious on the floor.* **2** (of feelings, thoughts, etc.) existing or happening without you realizing or being aware; not deliberate or controlled: *unconscious desires/feelings/impulses* ◊ *The brochure is full of unconscious humour.*—compare SUBCONSCIOUS **3 ~ of sb/sth** not aware of sb/sth; not noticing sth; not conscious $\boxed{\text{SYN}}$ OBLIVIOUS: *She is unconscious of the effect she has on people.* ◊ *He was quite unconscious of the danger.* $\boxed{\text{OPP}}$ CONSCIOUS

un·con·scious·ly /ʌnˈkɒnʃəsli; *AmE* -ˈkɑːn-/ *adv.* without being aware: *Perhaps, unconsciously, I've done something to offend her.* $\boxed{\text{OPP}}$ CONSCIOUSLY

un·con·scious·ness /ʌnˈkɒnʃəsnəs; *AmE* -ˈkɑːn-/ *noun* [U] a state like sleep caused by injury or illness, when

you are unable to use your senses: *He had lapsed into unconsciousness.*

un·con·sid·ered /ˌʌnkənˈsɪdəd; *AmE* -ərd/ *adj.* (*written*) not thought about, or not thought about with enough care: *I came to regret my unconsidered remarks.*

un·con·sti·tu·tion·al /ˌʌnˌkɒnstɪˈtjuːʃənl; *AmE* -kɑːn-stəˈtuː-/ *adj.* not allowed by the CONSTITUTION of a country, a political system or an organization $\boxed{\text{OPP}}$ CONSTITUTIONAL ▶ **un·con·sti·tu·tion·al·ly** *adv.*

un·con·tam·in·ated /ˌʌnkənˈtæmɪneɪtɪd/ *adj.* not harmed or spoilt by sth (for example, dangerous substances): *uncontaminated water/food* $\boxed{\text{OPP}}$ CONTAMINATED

un·con·ten·tious /ˌʌnkənˈtenʃəs/ *adj.* (*formal*) not likely to cause disagreement between people: *The proposal is relatively uncontentious.* $\boxed{\text{OPP}}$ CONTENTIOUS

un·con·test·ed /ˌʌnkənˈtestɪd/ *adj.* without any opposition or argument: *an uncontested election/divorce* ◊ *These claims have not gone uncontested.*

un·con·trol·lable /ˌʌnkənˈtrəʊləbl; *AmE* -ˈtroʊ-/ *adj.* that you cannot control or prevent: *an uncontrollable temper* ◊ *uncontrollable bleeding* ◊ *I had an uncontrollable urge to laugh.* ◊ *The ball was uncontrollable.* ◊ *He's an uncontrollable child* (= he behaves very badly and cannot be controlled). ▶ **un·con·trol·lably** *adv.*: *She began shaking uncontrollably.*

un·con·trolled /ˌʌnkənˈtrəʊld; *AmE* -ˈtroʊld/ *adj.* **1** (of emotions, behaviour, etc.) that sb cannot control or stop: *uncontrolled anger/fear* ◊ *The thoughts rushed into my mind uncontrolled.* **2** that is not limited or managed by law or rules: *the uncontrolled growth of cities* ◊ *uncontrolled dumping of toxic wastes*—compare CONTROLLED

un·con·tro·ver·sial /ˌʌnˌkɒntrəˈvɜːʃl; *AmE* ˌʌnkɑːn-trəˈvɜːrʃl/ *adj.* not causing, or not likely to cause, any disagreement: *an uncontroversial policy/opinion* $\boxed{\text{OPP}}$ CONTROVERSIAL—compare NON-CONTROVERSIAL

un·con·ven·tion·al /ˌʌnkənˈvenʃənl/ *adj.* (often *approving*) not following what is done or considered normal or acceptable by most people; different and interesting: *an unconventional artist/teacher* ◊ *She is known for her unconventional views.* $\boxed{\text{OPP}}$ CONVENTIONAL ▶ **un·con·ven·tion·al·ity** /ˌʌnkənvenʃəˈnæləti/ *noun* [U] **un·con·ven·tion·al·ly** *adv.*

un·con·vinced /ˌʌnkənˈvɪnst/ *adj.* **~ (of sth)| ~ (by sth)| ~ (that…)** not believing or not certain about sth in spite of what you have been told: *I remain unconvinced of the need for change.* ◊ *She seemed unconvinced by their promises.* ◊ *The jury were unconvinced that he was innocent.* $\boxed{\text{OPP}}$ CONVINCED

un·con·vin·cing /ˌʌnkənˈvɪnsɪŋ/ *adj.* not seeming true or real; not making you believe that sth is true: *I find the characters in the book very unconvincing.* ◊ *His explanation was unconvincing.* ◊ *She managed a weak, unconvincing smile.* $\boxed{\text{OPP}}$ CONVINCING ▶ **un·con·vin·cing·ly** *adv.*: *He laughed unconvincingly.*

un·cooked /ˌʌnˈkʊkt/ *adj.* not cooked $\boxed{\text{SYN}}$ RAW: *Eat plenty of uncooked fruit and vegetables.* ◊ *The steak was uncooked in the middle.*

un·cool /ˌʌnˈkuːl/ *adj.* (*informal*) not considered acceptable by fashionable young people $\boxed{\text{OPP}}$ COOL

un·co·opera·tive /ˌʌnkəʊˈɒpərətɪv; *AmE* -koʊˈɑːp-/ *adj.* not willing to be helpful to other people or do what they ask: *The witness was extremely uncooperative.* $\boxed{\text{OPP}}$ COOPERATIVE

un·co·or·din·ated /ˌʌnkəʊˈɔːdɪneɪtɪd; *AmE* -koʊˈɔːrd-/ *adj.* **1** if a person is **uncoordinated**, they are not able to control their movements well, and therefore not very skilful at some sports and physical activities **2** (of movements or parts of the body) not controlled; not moving smoothly or together: *uncoordinated limbs/movements* **3** (of plans, projects, etc.) not well organized; with no thought for how the different parts work together

un·cork /ˌʌnˈkɔːk; *AmE* -ˈkɔːrk/ *verb* [VN] to open a bottle by removing the CORK from the top $\boxed{\text{OPP}}$ CORK

un·cor·rob·or·ated /ˌʌnkəˈrɒbəreɪtɪd; *AmE* -ˈrɑːb-/ *adj.* (of a statement or claim) not supported by any other evidence; not having been CORROBORATED

æ	ɑː	e	ɜː	ə	ɪ	iː	i	ɒ	ɔː	ʌ	ʊ	u	uː
cat	father	ten	bird	about	sit	see	many	got	saw	cup	put	actual	too
								(BrE)					

un·count·able /ʌnˈkaʊntəbl/ *adj.* (*grammar*) a noun that is **uncountable** cannot be made plural or used with *a* or *an*, for example *water*, *bread* and *information*—compare COUNTABLE, COUNTLESS

un·couple /ˌʌnˈkʌpl/ *verb* [VN] ~ **sth (from sth)** to remove the connection between two vehicles, two parts of a train, etc.

un·couth /ʌnˈkuːθ/ *adj.* (of a person or their behaviour) rude or socially unacceptable [SYN] COARSE: *uncouth laughter* ▸ *an uncouth young man*

un·cover /ʌnˈkʌvə(r)/ *verb* [VN] **1** to remove sth that is covering sth: *Uncover the pan and let the soup simmer.* **2** to discover sth that was previously hidden or secret: *Police have uncovered a plot to kidnap the President's son.*

un·covered /ʌnˈkʌvəd; AmE -ərd/ *adj.* not covered by anything: *His head was uncovered.*

un·crit·ic·al /ʌnˈkrɪtɪkl/ *adj.* (usually *disapproving*) not willing to criticize sb/sth or to judge whether sb/sth is right or wrong: *an uncritical attitude/view* ▸ *Her uncritical acceptance of everything I said began to irritate me.* [OPP] CRITICAL ▸ **un·crit·ic·al·ly** /-ɪkli/ *adv.*

un·crowd·ed /ʌnˈkraʊdɪd/ *adj.* not full of people: *Did you manage to find an uncrowded beach?* [OPP] CROWDED

un·crowned /ʌnˈkraʊnd/ *adj.* (of a king or queen) not yet CROWNED [IDM] **the ˌuncrowned ˈking/ˈqueen (of sth)** the person considered to be the best, most famous or successful in a particular place or area of activity

unc·tu·ous /ˈʌŋktjuəs; AmE -tʃuəs/ *adj.* (*formal, disapproving*) friendly or giving praise in a way that is not sincere and which is therefore unpleasant: *an unctuous host* ▸ **unc·tu·ous·ly** *adv.*

un·culti·vated /ʌnˈkʌltɪveɪtɪd/ *adj.* (of land) not used for growing crops [OPP] CULTIVATED

un·curl /ˌʌnˈkɜːl; AmE -ˈkɜːrl/ *verb* ~ **(sth/yourself)** to become straight, or to make sth become straight, after being in a curled position: [VN] *The cat uncurled itself and jumped off the wall.* ◇ [V] *The snake slowly uncurled.* [OPP] CURL UP

uncut /ˌʌnˈkʌt/ *adj.* **1** left to grow; not cut short: *The uncut grass came up to her waist.* **2** (of a book, film/ movie, etc.) left in its complete form; without any parts removed; not CENSORED: *the original uncut version* **3** (of a precious stone) not shaped by cutting: *uncut diamonds* **4** not cut into separate pieces: *an uncut loaf of bread*

un·dam·aged /ʌnˈdæmɪdʒd/ *adj.* not damaged or spoilt: *There was a slight collision but my car was undamaged.* ◇ *He emerged from the court case with his reputation undamaged.*

un·dated /ˌʌnˈdeɪtɪd/ *adj.* **1** without a date written or printed on it: *an undated letter* **2** of which the date is not known: *undated archaeological remains*—compare DATED

un·daunt·ed /ʌnˈdɔːntɪd/ *adj.* [not usually before noun] (*written*) still enthusiastic and determined, in spite of difficulties or disappointment [SYN] UNDETERRED: *He seemed undaunted by all the opposition to his idea.*

un·decided /ˌʌndɪˈsaɪdɪd/ *adj.* [not usually before noun] **1** ~ **(about sb/sth)** | ~ **(as to sth)** not having made a decision about sb/sth: *I'm still undecided (about) who to vote for.* **2** not having been decided: *The venue for the World Cup remains undecided.*—compare DECIDED

un·declared /ˌʌndɪˈkleəd; AmE -ˈklerd/ *adj.* not admitted to; not stated in an open way; not having been DECLARED: *No income should remain undeclared.* ◇ *Undeclared goods* (= that the customs are not told about) *may be confiscated.*

un·defeat·ed /ˌʌndɪˈfiːtɪd/ *adj.* (especially in sport) not having lost or been defeated: *They are undefeated in 13 games.* ◇ *the undefeated world champion*

un·defend·ed /ˌʌndɪˈfendɪd/ *adj.* **1** not protected or guarded: *undefended frontiers* **2** if a case in a court of law is **undefended**, no defence is made against it

un·defined /ˌʌndɪˈfaɪnd/ *adj.* not made clear or definite: *The money was lent for an undefined period of time.* ◇ *His power is undefined, and therefore unlimited.*

un·demand·ing /ˌʌndɪˈmɑːndɪŋ/ *adj.* **1** not needing a lot of effort or thought: *an undemanding job* **2** (of a

person) not asking for a lot of attention or action from other people: *She was a pleasant and undemanding companion.* [OPP] DEMANDING

un·demo·crat·ic /ˌʌndeməˈkrætɪk/ *adj.* against or not acting according to the principles of DEMOCRACY: *undemocratic decisions* ◇ *an undemocratic regime* [OPP] DEMOCRATIC

un·demon·stra·tive /ˌʌndɪˈmɒnstrətɪv; AmE -ˈmɑːn-/ *adj.* not showing feelings openly, especially feelings of affection [OPP] DEMONSTRATIVE

un·deni·able /ˌʌndɪˈnaɪəbl/ *adj.* true or certain; that cannot be DENIED [SYN] INDISPUTABLE: *undeniable achievements/charm/attractions* ◇ *It is an undeniable fact that drug-related crime is increasing.* ▸ **un·deni·ably** /-əbli/ *adv.*: *undeniably beautiful/impressive*

under /ˈʌndə(r)/ *prep., adv., adj.*

■ *prep.* **1** in, to or through a position that is below sth: *Have you looked under the bed?* ◇ *She placed the ladder under* (= just lower than) *the window.* ◇ *The dog squeezed under the gate and ran into the road.* **2** below the surface of sth; covered by sth: *The boat lay under several feet of water.* **3** less than; younger than: *an annual income of under £10000* ◇ *It took us under an hour.* ◇ *Nobody under 18 is allowed to buy alcohol.* **4** used to say who or what controls, governs or manages sb/sth: *The country is now under martial law.* ◇ *The coinage was reformed under Elizabeth I* (= when she was queen). ◇ *She has a staff of 19 working under her.* ◇ *Under its new conductor, the orchestra has established an international reputation.* **5** according to an agreement, a law or a system: *Six suspects are being held under the Prevention of Terrorism Act.* ◇ *Under the terms of the lease you had no right to sublet the property.* ◇ *Is the television still under guarantee?* **6** experiencing a particular process: *The hotel is still under construction.* ◇ *The matter is under investigation.* **7** affected by sth: *The wall collapsed under the strain.* ◇ *I've been feeling under stress lately.* ◇ *I'm under no illusions about what hard work this will be.* ◇ *You'll be under anaesthetic, so you won't feel a thing.* **8** using a particular name: *She also writes under the pseudonym of Barbara Vine.* **9** found in a particular part of a book, list, etc: *If it's not under 'sports', try looking under 'games'.*

■ *adv.* **1** below sth: *He pulled up the covers and crawled under.* **2** below the surface of water: *She took a deep breath and stayed under for more than a minute.* ◇ *The boat was going under fast.* **3** less; younger: *prices of ten dollars and under* ◇ *children aged 12 and under* **4** in or into an unconscious state: *He felt himself going under.*

■ *adj.* [only before noun] lower; underneath: *the under layer* ◇ *the under surface of a leaf*

WHICH WORD? (?)

under / below / underneath / beneath

You use **under** to say that one thing is directly under another thing: *The cat is asleep under the table.* ◇ *I think your letter is under that book.* **Underneath** can also be used when you want to emphasize that something is being covered or hidden by another thing: *Have you looked underneath the sofa as well as behind it?* You can also use **beneath** in this sense, but it is a very formal or literary word.

Below is usually preferred to say that one thing is in a lower position than another when they are both in the same building, on the same hill, on the same part of the body, etc: *They live in the apartment below us.* ◇ *Can you see those trees below the summit?* ◇ *It hurts here — just below the knee.*

Below is used for measurements or position on a scale: *The temperature was below zero last night.* **Under** is used to mean 'less than': *All our goods are under £20.* You use **under** (not **below**) to talk about movement from one side of something to the other side: *We swam under the bridge.*

---

under- /ˈʌndə(r)/ *prefix* **1** (in nouns and adjectives) below; BENEATH: *undergrowth* ◇ *undercover* **2** (in nouns) lower in age or rank: *the under-fives* ◇ *an undergraduate*

aɪ	aʊ	eɪ	əʊ	oʊ	ɔɪ	ɪə	eə	ʊə	j	w
my	now	say	go	go	boy	near	hair	pure	yes	wet
			(BrE)	(AmE)						

3 (in adjectives and verbs) not enough: *underripe* ◊ *under-cooked*

under·achieve /ˌʌndərə'tʃiːv/ *verb* [V] to do less well than you could do, especially in school work ▶ **under·achieve·ment** *noun* [U] **under·achiever** *noun*

,under 'age *adj.* ⇨ AGE: *under-age drinking*

under·arm /'ʌndərɑːm; *AmE* -ɑːrm/ *adj., adv.*
■ *adj.* **1** [only before noun] connected with a person's ARM-PIT: *underarm hair/deodorant/sweating* **2** an **underarm** throw of a ball is done with the hand kept below the level of the shoulder—compare OVERARM
■ *adv.* if you throw, etc. **underarm**, you throw keeping your hand below the level of your shoulder—compare OVERARM

under·belly /'ʌndəbeli; *AmE* -dərb-/ *noun* [sing.] **1** the weakest part of sth that is most easily attacked: *The trade deficit remains the soft underbelly of the US economy.* **2** the underneath part of an animal: *(figurative) He became familiar with the dark underbelly of life in the city* (= the parts that are usually hidden).

under·bid /ˌʌndə'bɪd; *AmE* -dər'b-/ *verb* (**under·bid·ding, under·bid, under·bid**) [VN] to make a lower BID than sb else, for example when trying to win a contract

under·brush /'ʌndəbrʌʃ; *AmE* -dərb-/ *noun* [U] (*AmE*) = UNDERGROWTH

under·car·riage /'ʌndəkærɪdʒ; *AmE* -dərk-/ (also '**landing gear**) *noun* the part of an aircraft, including the wheels, that supports it when it is landing and taking off—picture at PLANE

under·charge /ˌʌndə'tʃɑːdʒ; *AmE* ˌʌndər'tʃɑːrdʒ/ *verb* [V, VN] **~ (sb) (for sth)** to charge too little for sth, usually by mistake OPP OVERCHARGE

under·class /'ʌndəklɑːs; *AmE* 'ʌndərklæs/ *noun* [sing.] a social class that is very poor and has no status: *The long-term unemployed are becoming a new underclass.*

under·class·man /ˌʌndə'klɑːsmən; *AmE* -dər'klæs-/, **under·class·woman** /ˌʌndə'klɑːswʊmən; *AmE* -dər'klæs-/ *noun* (*pl.* -**men** /-men/) (*pl.* -**women** /-wʊmən/) (*AmE*) a student in the first or second year of high school or college—compare UPPERCLASSMAN

under·clothes /'ʌndəkləʊðz; *AmE* 'ʌndərkloʊðz/ *noun* [pl.] (also **under·cloth·ing** /-kləʊðɪŋ; *AmE* -kloʊ-/ [U]) (*formal*) = UNDERWEAR

under·coat /'ʌndəkəʊt; *AmE* 'ʌndərkoʊt/ *noun* [C, U] a layer of paint under the final layer; the paint used for making this: *Apply the undercoat first.*—compare TOPCOAT

under·cover /ˌʌndə'kʌvə(r); *AmE* -dər'k-/ *adj.* [usually before noun] working or done secretly in order to find out information for the police, a government, etc: *an undercover agent/officer* ◊ *an undercover operation/investigation* ▶ **under·cover** *adv.*: *The illegal payments were discovered by a journalist working undercover.*

under·cur·rent /'ʌndəkʌrənt; *AmE* -dərkɜːr-/ *noun* **~ (of sth)** a feeling, especially a negative one, that is hidden but whose effects are felt: *I detect an undercurrent of resentment towards the new proposals.* ◊ *Racial hatred has been a powerful undercurrent in the country's history.*

under·cut *verb, noun*
■ *verb* /ˌʌndə'kʌt; *AmE* ˌʌndər'kʌt/ (**under·cut·ting, under·cut, under·cut**) [VN] **1** to sell goods or services at a lower price than your competitors: *to undercut sb's prices* ◊ *We were able to undercut our European rivals by 5%.* **2** to make sth weaker or less likely to be effective SYN UNDERMINE: *Some members of the board were trying to undercut the chairman's authority.*
■ *noun* /'ʌndəkʌt; *AmE* 'ʌndərkʌt/ a way of cutting sb's hair in which the hair is left quite long on top but the hair on the lower part of the head is cut much shorter—picture at HAIR

under·devel·oped /ˌʌndədɪ'veləpt; *AmE* -dərdɪ-/ *adj.* (of a country, society, etc.) having few industries and a low standard of living—compare DEVELOPED, DEVELOPING, UNDEVELOPED HELP 'A **developing** country' is now the usual expression used. ▶ **under·devel·op·ment** *noun* [U]

under·dog /'ʌndədɒg; *AmE* 'ʌndərdɔːg/ *noun* a person, team, country, etc. that is thought to be in a weaker

position than others and therefore not likely to be successful, win a competition, etc: *Before the game we were definitely the underdogs.* ◊ *In politics, he was a champion of the underdog* (= always fought for the rights of weaker people).

under·done /ˌʌndə'dʌn; *AmE* -dər'd-/ *adj.* not completely cooked—compare WELL DONE, OVERDONE

under·employed /ˌʌndərɪm'plɔɪd/ *adj.* not having enough work to do; not having work that makes full use of your skills and abilities

under·esti·mate *verb, noun*
■ *verb* /ˌʌndər'estɪmeɪt/ **1** to think or guess that the amount, cost or size of sth is smaller than it really is: [VN] *to underestimate the cost/difficulty/danger of the expedition* ◊ *We underestimated the time it would take to get there.* [also V wh-] **2** [VN] to not realize how good, strong, determined, etc. sb really is: *Never underestimate your opponent.* OPP OVERESTIMATE—compare UNDERRATE
■ *noun* /ˌʌndər'estɪmət/ (also **under·esti·ma·tion** /ˌʌndərˌestɪ'meɪʃn/ [C, U]) an estimate about the size, cost, etc. of sth that is too low: *My guess of 400 proved to be a serious underestimate.* OPP OVERESTIMATE

under·expose /ˌʌndərɪk'spəʊz; *AmE* -'spoʊz/ *verb* [VN] [usually passive] to allow too little light to reach the film when you take a photograph OPP OVEREXPOSE

under·fed /ˌʌndə'fed; *AmE* -dər'f-/ *adj.* having had too little food to eat: *underfed children/animals* OPP OVERFED

under·floor /ˌʌndə'flɔː(r); *AmE* -dər'f-/ *adj.* [only before noun] situated underneath the floor: *underfloor heating*

under·foot /ˌʌndə'fʊt; *AmE* -dər'f-/ *adv.* under your feet; on the ground where you are walking: *The ground was dry and firm underfoot.* ◊ *I was nearly trampled underfoot by the crowd of people rushing for the door.*

under·fund·ed /ˌʌndə'fʌndɪd; *AmE* -dər'f-/ *adj.* (of an organization, a project, etc.) not having enough money to spend, with the result that it cannot function well: *seriously/chronically underfunded*

under·gar·ment /'ʌndəgɑːmənt; *AmE* -dərgɑːrm-/ *noun* (*old-fashioned* or *formal*) a piece of underwear

under·go /ˌʌndə'gəʊ; *AmE* ˌʌndər'goʊ/ *verb* (**under·went** /-'went/ **under·gone** /-'gɒn; *AmE* -'gɔːn; -'gɑːn/) [VN] to experience sth, especially a change or sth unpleasant: *to undergo tests/trials/repairs* ◊ *My mother underwent major surgery last year.* ◊ *Some children undergo a complete transformation when they become teenagers.*

under·gradu·ate /ˌʌndə'grædʒuət; *AmE* -dər'g-/ *noun* a university or college student who is studying for their first degree: *a first-year undergraduate* ◊ *an undergraduate course/student/degree* ⇨ note at STUDENT

BRITISH / AMERICAN
underground / subway / metro / tube

A city's underground railway / railroad system is usually called the **underground** (often the **Underground**) in *BrE* and the **subway** in *AmE*. Speakers of *BrE* also use **subway** for systems in American cities and **metro** for systems in other European countries. **The Metro** is the name for the systems in Paris and Washington, D.C. London's system is often called **the Tube**.

---

under·ground *adj., adv., noun*
■ *adj.* /'ʌndəgraʊnd; *AmE* -dərg-/ [only before noun] **1** under the surface of the ground: *underground passages/caves/streams* ◊ *underground cables*—compare OVERGROUND **2** operating secretly and often illegally, especially against a government: *an underground resistance movement*
■ *adv.* /ˌʌndə'graʊnd; *AmE* -dər'g-/ **1** under the surface of the ground: *Rescuers found victims trapped several feet underground.* ◊ *toxic waste buried deep underground* **2** in or into a secret place in order to hide from the police, the government, etc: *He went underground to avoid arrest.*
■ *noun* /'ʌndəgraʊnd; *AmE* -dərg-/ **1** (often the **Underground**) (*BrE*) (*AmE* **sub·way**) [sing.] an underground railway/railroad system in a city: *underground stations* ◊ *the London Underground* ◊ *I always travel by under-*

ground.—compare METRO, TUBE **2 (the underground)**
[sing.+ sing./pl. v.] a secret political organization, usually working against the government of a country

under·growth /ˈʌndəɡrəʊθ; AmE ˈʌndərɡroʊθ/ (BrE)
(AmE **under·brush**) noun [U] a mass of bushes and
plants that grow close together under trees in woods and
forests: They used their knives to clear a path through the
dense undergrowth. ◊ The murder weapon was found concealed in undergrowth.

under·hand /ˌʌndəˈhænd; AmE -dərˈh-/ (also less frequent **under·hand·ed** /-ˈhændɪd/) adj. (disapproving)
secret and dishonest: I would never have expected her to
behave in such an underhand way.

under·lay /ˈʌndəleɪ; AmE ˈʌndərleɪ/ noun [U, C] a layer of
thick material placed under a carpet to protect it

under·lie /ˌʌndəˈlaɪ; AmE ˌʌndərˈlaɪ/ verb (**under·lying**,
under·lay /-ˈleɪ/ **under·lain** /-ˈleɪn/) [VN] [no passive]
(formal) to be the basis or cause of sth: These ideas
underlie much of his work. ◊ It is a principle that underlies
all the party's policies.—see also UNDERLYING

under·line /ˌʌndəˈlaɪn; AmE -dərˈl-/ (also **under·score**
especially in AmE) verb **1** [VN] to draw a line under a
word, sentence, etc. **2** to emphasize or show that sth is
important or true: [VN] The report underlines the importance of pre-school education. ◊ [Vwh-] Her question under-
lined how little she understood him [also Vthat]

under·ling /ˈʌndəlɪŋ; AmE ˈʌndərlɪŋ/ noun (disapproving) a person with a lower rank or status [SYN] MINION: He
dishes out orders to his underlings.

under·lying /ˌʌndəˈlaɪɪŋ; AmE -dərˈl-/ adj. [only before
noun] **1** important in a situation but not always easily
noticed or stated clearly: The underlying assumption is
that the amount of money available is limited. ◊ Unemployment may be an underlying cause of the rising crime rate.
2 existing under the surface of sth else: the underlying
rock formation—see also UNDERLIE

under·manned /ˌʌndəˈmænd; AmE -dərˈm-/ adj. (of a
hospital, factory, etc.) not having enough people working
in order to be able to function well [SYN] UNDERSTAFFED
[OPP] OVERMANNED

under·mine /ˌʌndəˈmaɪn; AmE -dərˈm-/ verb [VN] **1** to
make sth, especially sb's confidence or authority, gradually weaker or less effective: Our confidence in the team
has been seriously undermined by their recent defeats. ◊
This crisis has undermined his position. **2** to make sth
weaker at the base, for example by digging under it

under·neath /ˌʌndəˈniːθ; AmE -dərˈn-/ prep., adv., noun
■ prep., adv. **1** under or below sth else, especially when it is
hidden or covered by the thing on top: The coin rolled
underneath the piano. ◊ This jacket's too big, even with a
sweater underneath. **2** used to talk about sb's real feelings
or character, as opposed to the way they seem to be:
Underneath her cool exterior she was really very frightened. ◊ He seems bad-tempered, but he's very soft-hearted
underneath. ⇨ note at UNDER
■ noun **(the underneath)** [sing.] the lower surface or part of
sth: She pulled the drawer out and examined the underneath carefully.

under·nour·ished /ˌʌndəˈnʌrɪʃt; AmE -dərˈnɜːr-/ adj. in
bad health because of a lack of food or a lack of the right
type of food [SYN] MALNOURISHED: severely undernourished
children ► **under·nour·ish·ment** /-ˈnʌrɪʃmənt; AmE
-ˈnɜːr-/ noun [U]

under·paid /ˌʌndəˈpeɪd; AmE -dərˈp-/ adj. not paid
enough for the work you do

under·pants /ˈʌndəpænts; AmE -dərp-/ noun [pl.] **1** (also
informal **pants**) (BrE) a piece of men's underwear worn
under their trousers/pants **2** (AmE) a piece of underwear
worn by men or women under trousers/pants, a skirt,
etc.

under·pass /ˈʌndəpɑːs; AmE ˈʌndərpæs/ noun a road or
path that goes under another road or railway/railroad
track—compare OVERPASS

under·pay /ˌʌndəˈpeɪ; AmE -dərˈp-/ verb (**under·paid**,
under·paid /-peɪd/) [VN] [usually passive] to pay sb too

little money, especially for their work: Nurses complain
of being **overworked and underpaid**. [OPP] OVERPAY

under·pin /ˌʌndəˈpɪn; AmE -dərˈp-/ verb (-nn-) [VN]
1 (written) to support or form the basis of an argument, a
claim, etc: The report is underpinned by extensive
research. ◊ Certain qualities and values underpin good
journalism. **2** (technical) to support a wall by putting
metal, CONCRETE, etc. under it ► **under·pin·ning** noun
[C, U]

under·play /ˌʌndəˈpleɪ; AmE -dərˈp-/ verb [VN] (written,
especially BrE) to make sth seem less important than it
really is [SYN] PLAY DOWN, DOWNPLAY [OPP] OVERPLAY

under·priv·il·eged /ˌʌndəˈprɪvəlɪdʒd; AmE -dərˈp-/ adj.
1 [usually before noun] having less money and fewer
opportunities than most people in society [SYN] DISADVAN-
TAGED: underprivileged sections of the community ◊ educa-
tionally/socially underprivileged groups—compare
PRIVILEGED **2 (the underprivileged)** noun [pl.] people who
are underprivileged

under·rate /ˌʌndəˈreɪt/ verb [VN] to not recognize how
good, important, etc. sb/sth really is: He's seriously underrated as a writer. ◊ an underrated movie—compare OVER-
RATE, UNDERESTIMATE

under·score /ˌʌndəˈskɔː(r); AmE -dərˈs-/ verb (especially
AmE) = UNDERLINE

under·sea /ˈʌndəsiː; AmE ˈʌndərsi:/ adj. [only before
noun] found, used or happening below the surface of the
sea: undersea cables/earthquakes

under·sec·re·tary /ˌʌndəˈsekrətri; AmE ˌʌndər-
ˈsekrəteri/ noun (pl. **-ies**) **1** (in Britain) a senior CIVIL
SERVANT in charge of one part of a government department—compare PERMANENT UNDERSECRETARY **2** (in Britain) a junior minister who reports to the minister in
charge of a government department **3** (in the US) an
official of high rank in a government department, directly below a member of a CABINET: an undersecretary of
State for inter-American affairs

under·sell /ˌʌndəˈsel; AmE ˌʌndərˈsel/ verb (**un·der·sold**,
un·der·sold /-ˈsəʊld; AmE -ˈsoʊld/) [VN] **1** to sell goods or
services at a lower price than your competitors **2** to sell
sth at a price lower than its real value **3** to make people
think that sth is not as good or as interesting as it really
is: Don't undersell yourself at the interview.

under·shirt /ˈʌndəʃɜːt; AmE ˈʌndərʃɜːrt/ noun (AmE) =
VEST (1)

under·side /ˈʌndəsaɪd; AmE -dərs-/ noun the side or
surface of sth that is underneath [SYN] BOTTOM

the under·signed /ˌʌndəˈsaɪnd; AmE -dərˈs-/ noun (pl.
the under·signed) (formal) the person who has signed
that particular document: We, the undersigned, agree to ...

under·sized /ˌʌndəˈsaɪzd; AmE -dərˈs-/ adj. not as big as
normal

under·sold pt, pp of UNDERSELL

under·staffed /ˌʌndəˈstɑːft; AmE ˌʌndərˈstæft/ adj. [not
usually before noun] not having enough people working
and therefore not able to function well [SYN] UNDER-
MANNED [OPP] OVERSTAFFED

under·stand /ˌʌndəˈstænd; AmE -dərˈs-/ verb (**under·
stood, under·stood** /-ˈstʊd/) (not used in the progressive
tenses)

MEANING | **1** to know or realize the meaning of words, a
language, what sb says, etc: [VN] Can you understand
French? ◊ Do you understand the instructions? ◊ She didn't
understand the form she was signing. ◊ [V] I'm not sure
that I understand. Go over it again. ◊ (figurative) I don't
want you doing that again. Do you understand? ◊ [Vwh-] I
don't understand what he's saying.

HOW STH WORKS/HAPPENS | **2** to know or realize how or why
sth happens, how it works or why it is important: [VN]
Doctors still don't understand much about the disease. ◊ No
one is answering the phone—I can't understand it. ◊
[Vwh-] I could never understand why she was fired. ◊
[VN-ing] I just can't understand him taking the money. ◊
(formal) I just can't understand his taking the money.
[also Vthat, V]

KNOW SB | **3** to know sb's character, how they feel and why they behave in the way they do: [VN] *Nobody understands me.* ◊ *He doesn't understand women at all.* ◊ [Vwh-] *They understand what I have been through.* ◊ [Vthat] *I quite understand that you need some time alone.* ◊ [VN-ing] *I quite understand you needing some time alone.* ◊ [V] *If you want to leave early, I'm sure he'll understand.*

THINK/BELIEVE **4** (*formal*) to think or believe that sth is true because you have been told that it is: [V(that)] *I understand (that) you wish to see the manager.* ◊ *Am I to understand that you refuse?* ◊ [VNtoinf] *The Prime Minister is understood to have been extremely angry about the report.* ◊ [VNthat] *It is understood that the band are working on their next album.*

BE AGREED **5** [VN(that)] [usually passive] to agree sth with sb without it needing to be said: *I thought it was understood that my expenses would be paid.*

MISSING WORD **6** [VN] [usually passive] to realize that a word in a phrase or sentence is not expressed and to supply it in your mind: *In the sentence 'I can't drive', the object 'a car' is understood.*

IDM **,make yourself under'stood** to make your meaning clear, especially in another language: *He doesn't speak much Japanese but he can make himself understood.*— more at GIVE *v.*

under·stand·able /ˌʌndəˈstændəbl; *AmE* -dərs-/ *adj.* **1** (of behaviour, feelings, reactions, etc.) seeming normal and reasonable in a particular situation SYN NATURAL: *an understandable concern/fear/temptation* ◊ *Their attitude is perfectly understandable.* ◊ *It was an understandable mistake to make.* **2** (of language, documents, etc.) easy to understand SYN COMPREHENSIBLE: *Warning notices must be readily understandable.*

under·stand·ably /ˌʌndəˈstændəbli; *AmE* -dərs-/ *adv.* in a way that seems normal and reasonable in a particular situation: *They were understandably disappointed with the result.*

under·stand·ing /ˌʌndəˈstændɪŋ; *AmE* -dərs-/ *noun, adj.*
- *noun* **1** [U, sing.] ~ (of sth) the knowledge that sb has about a particular subject or situation: *The committee has little or no understanding of the problem.* ◊ *The existence of God is beyond human understanding* (= humans cannot know whether God exists or not). **2** [C, usually sing.] an informal agreement: *We finally came to an understanding about what hours we would work.* ◊ *We have this understanding that nobody talks about work over lunch.* **3** [U, sing.] the ability to understand why people behave in a particular way and the willingness to forgive them when they do sth wrong: *We must tackle the problem with sympathy and understanding.* ◊ *We are looking for a better understanding between the two nations.* **4** [U, C] ~ (of sth) the particular way in which sb understands sth SYN INTERPRETATION: *My understanding of the situation is ...* ◊ *The statement is open to various understandings.* IDM **on the understanding that ...** (*formal*) used to introduce a condition that must be agreed before sth else can happen: *They agreed to the changes on the understanding that they would be introduced gradually.*
- *adj.* showing sympathy for other people's problems and being willing to forgive them when they do sth wrong SYN SYMPATHETIC: *She has very understanding parents.*

under·state /ˌʌndəˈsteɪt; *AmE* -dərs-/ *verb* [VN] to state that sth is smaller, less important or less serious than it really is: *It would be a mistake to understate the seriousness of the problem.* ◊ *The figures probably understate the real unemployment rate.* OPP OVERSTATE

under·stated /ˌʌndəˈsteɪtɪd; *AmE* -dərs-/ *adj.* (*approving*) if a style, colour, etc. is **understated**, it is pleasing and elegant in a way that is not too obvious SYN SUBTLE

under·state·ment /ˈʌndəsteɪtmənt; *AmE* -dərs-/ *noun* **1** [C] a statement that makes sth seem less important, impressive, serious, etc. than it really is: *To say we were pleased is an understatement* (= we were extremely pleased). ◊ *'These figures are a bit disappointing.' 'That's got to be the understatement of the year.'* **2** [U] the practice of making things seem less impressive, important, serious, etc. than they really are: *typical English*

understatement ◊ *He always goes for subtlety and understatement in his movies.* OPP OVERSTATEMENT

under·study /ˈʌndəstʌdi; *AmE* -dərs-/ *noun, verb*
- *noun* (*pl.* **-ies**) ~ (to sb) an actor who learns the part of another actor in a play so that they can play that part if necessary
- *verb* (**under·stud·ies, under·study·ing, under·stud·ied, under·stud·ied**) [VN] to learn a part in a play as an understudy; to act as an understudy to sb

under·take /ˌʌndəˈteɪk; *AmE* -dərˈt-/ *verb* (**under·took** /-ˈtʊk/ **under·taken** /-ˈteɪkən/) (*formal*) **1** [VN] to make yourself responsible for sth and start doing it: *to undertake a task/project* ◊ *University professors both teach and undertake research.* ◊ *The company has announced that it will undertake a full investigation into the accident.* **2** to agree or promise that you will do sth: [Vtoinf] *He undertook to finish the job by Friday.* [alsoVthat]

under·taker /ˈʌndəteɪkə(r); *AmE* -dərt-/ (also **'funeral director**) (*AmE* also **mor·ti·cian**) *noun* a person whose job is to prepare dead people to be buried or CREMATED, and to arrange funerals

under·tak·ing /ˌʌndəˈteɪkɪŋ; *AmE* -dərt-/ *noun* **1** [C] a task or project, especially one that is important and/or difficult SYN VENTURE: *He is interested in buying the club as a commercial undertaking.* ◊ *In those days, the trip across country was a dangerous undertaking.* **2** [C] ~ (to do sth) | ~ (that ...) (*formal*) an agreement or a promise to do sth: *a government undertaking to spend more on education* ◊ *The landlord gave a written undertaking that repairs would be carried out before the end of the month.* **3** /ˈʌndəteɪkɪŋ; *AmE* -dərt-/ [U] the business of an undertaker

,under-the-'counter *adj.* (*informal*) illegal: *under-the-counter payments/deals*

under·tone /ˈʌndətəʊn; *AmE* ˈʌndərtoʊn/ *noun* ~ (of sth) a feeling, quality or meaning that is not expressed directly but is still noticeable from what sb says or does: *His soft words contained an undertone of warning.* ◊ *The play does not have the political undertones of the novel.*— compare OVERTONE IDM **in an 'undertone** | **in 'under·tones** in a quiet voice: *'I must leave now,' he said in an undertone.*

under·tow /ˈʌndətəʊ; *AmE* ˈʌndərtoʊ/ *noun* [usually sing.] **1** a current in the sea or ocean that moves in the opposite direction to the water near the surface: *The children were carried out to sea by the strong undertow.* **2** ~ (of sth) a feeling or quality that influences people in a particular situation even though they are not really aware of it

under·used /ˌʌndəˈjuːzd; *AmE* -dərˈj-/ (also *formal* **under·util·ized**) *adj.* not used as much as it could or should be: *The airport is currently grossly underused.* ▶ **under·use** /ˌʌndəˈjuːs; *AmE* -dərˈj-/ (also *formal* **under·util·iza·tion**) *noun* [U]

under·util·ized (*BrE* also **-ised**) /ˌʌndəˈjuːtəlaɪzd; *AmE* -dərˈj-/ *adj.* (*formal*) = UNDERUSED ▶ **under·util·iza·tion, -isa·tion** /ˌʌndəjuːtəlaɪzˈeɪʃn; *AmE* -dərjuːtələˈz-/ *noun* [U] = UNDERUSE

under·value /ˌʌndəˈvæljuː; *AmE* -dərˈv-/ *verb* [VN] [usually passive] to not recognize how good, valuable or important sb/sth really is: *Education is currently undervalued in this country.* ◊ *He believes his house has been undervalued.* OPP OVERVALUE

under·water /ˌʌndəˈwɔːtə(r); *AmE* -dərˈw-/ *adj.* [only before noun] found, used or happening below the surface of water: *underwater creatures* ◊ *an underwater camera* ◊ *police underwater divers* ▶ **under·water** *adv.*: *Take a deep breath and see how long you can stay underwater.*

under·way /ˌʌndəˈweɪ; *AmE* -dərˈw-/ *adj.* [not before noun] IDM **be underway** = BE UNDER WAY at WAY

under·wear /ˈʌndəweə(r); *AmE* -dərwer/ *noun* [U] (also *formal* **under·clothes** [pl.] **under·cloth·ing** [U]) clothes that you wear under other clothes and next to the skin: *She packed one change of underwear.*

under·weight /ˌʌndəˈweɪt; *AmE* -dərˈw-/ *adj.* (especially of a person) weighing less than the normal or expected weight: *The baby was dangerously underweight at birth.* ◊

U

She is a few pounds underweight for (= in relation to) *her height.* OPP OVERWEIGHT

under·went *pt* of UNDERGO

under·whelmed /ˌʌndəˈwelmd; *AmE* -dərˈw-/ *adj.* (*informal, humorous*) not impressed with or excited about sth at all: *We were distinctly underwhelmed by the director's speech.*—compare OVERWHELMED

under·whelm·ing /ˌʌndəˈwelmɪŋ; *AmE* -dərˈw-/ *adj.* (*informal, humorous*) not impressing or exciting you at all: *the contrast between his overwhelming guitar-playing and his underwhelming singing*

under·world /ˈʌndəwɜːld; *AmE* ˈʌndərwɜːrld/ *noun* [sing.] **1** the people and activities involved in crime in a particular place: *the criminal underworld* ◊ *the Glasgow underworld* **2** (**the underworld**) (in myths and legends, for example those of Ancient Greece) the place under the earth where people are believed to go when they die

under·write /ˌʌndəˈraɪt/ *verb* (**under·wrote** /-ˈrəʊt; *AmE* -ˈroʊt/ **under·writ·ten** /-ˈrɪtn/) [VN] (*technical*) **1** to accept financial responsibility for an activity so that you will pay for special costs or for losses it may make **2** to accept responsibility for an insurance policy so that you will pay money in case loss or damage happens **3** to agree to buy shares that are not bought by the public when new shares are offered for sale

under·writer /ˈʌndəraɪtə(r)/ *noun* **1** a person or organization that underwrites insurance policies, especially for ships **2** a person whose job is to estimate the risks involved in a particular activity and decide how much sb must pay for insurance

un·deserved /ˌʌndɪˈzɜːvd; *AmE* -ˈzɜːrvd/ *adj.* that sb does not deserve and therefore unfair: *The criticism was totally undeserved.* ◊ *an undeserved success/victory* ▶ **un·deserv·ed·ly** /-dɪˈzɜːvɪdli; *AmE* -ˈzɜːrv-/ *adv.*

un·deserv·ing /ˌʌndɪˈzɜːvɪŋ; *AmE* -ˈzɜːrv-/ *adj.* ~ (**of sth**) (*formal*) not deserving to have or receive sth: *He was undeserving of her affections.* ◊ *the undeserving victim of a conspiracy* OPP DESERVING

un·desir·able /ˌʌndɪˈzaɪərəbl/ *adj., noun*
- *adj.* not wanted or approved of; likely to cause trouble or problems: *undesirable behaviour/consequences/effects* ◊ *It would be highly undesirable to increase class sizes further.* OPP DESIRABLE ▶ **un·desir·ably** /-əbli/ *adv.*
- *noun* [usually pl.] a person who is not wanted in a particular place, especially because they are considered dangerous or criminal: *He's been mixing with drug addicts and other undesirables.*

un·detect·able /ˌʌndɪˈtektəbl/ *adj.* impossible to see or find: *The sound is virtually undetectable to the human ear.* OPP DETECTABLE

un·detect·ed /ˌʌndɪˈtektɪd/ *adj.* not noticed by anyone: *How could anyone break into the palace undetected?* ◊ *The disease often remains undetected for many years.*

un·deterred /ˌʌndɪˈtɜːd; *AmE* -ˈtɜːrd/ *adj.* if sb is undeterred by sth, they do not allow it to stop them from doing sth

un·devel·oped /ˌʌndɪˈveləpt/ *adj.* **1** (of land) not used for farming, industry, building, etc. **2** (of a country) not having modern industries, and with a low standard of living **3** not grown to full size: *undeveloped buds/limbs*—compare UNDERDEVELOPED

un·did *pt* of UNDO

un·dies /ˈʌndiz/ *noun* [pl.] (*informal*) underwear

un·dif·fer·en·ti·ated /ˌʌndɪfəˈrenʃieɪtɪd/ *adj.* having parts that you cannot distinguish between; not split into different parts or sections: *an undifferentiated whole* ◊ *an undifferentiated target audience*

un·dig·ni·fied /ʌnˈdɪɡnɪfaɪd/ *adj.* causing you to look silly and to lose the respect of other people: *There was an undignified scramble for the best seats.* OPP DIGNIFIED

un·diluted /ˌʌndaɪˈluːtɪd; *BrE* also -ˈljuːtɪd/ *adj.* **1** (of a liquid) not made weaker by having water added to it; not having been DILUTED **2** (of a feeling or quality) not mixed or combined with anything and therefore very strong: *I looked back on that time with undiluted pleasure.*

un·dimin·ished /ˌʌndɪˈmɪnɪʃt/ *adj.* that has not become

smaller or weaker: *They continued with undiminished enthusiasm.* ◊ *Her influence in the company remained undiminished.*

un·dis·charged /ˌʌndɪsˈtʃɑːdʒd; *AmE* -ˈtʃɑːrdʒd/ *adj.* (*law*) an **undischarged** BANKRUPT is a person who has been officially stated to be bankrupt by a court of law but who still has to pay his or her debts

un·dis·cip·lined /ʌnˈdɪsəplɪnd/ *adj.* lacking control and organization; behaving badly OPP DISCIPLINED

un·dis·closed /ˌʌndɪsˈkləʊzd; *AmE* -ˈkloʊzd/ *adj.* not made known or told to anyone; not having been DISCLOSED: *He was paid an undisclosed sum.*

un·dis·cov·ered /ˌʌndɪsˈkʌvəd; *AmE* -ərd/ *adj.* that has not been found or noticed; that has not been DISCOVERED: *a previously undiscovered talent*

un·dis·guised /ˌʌndɪsˈɡaɪzd/ *adj.* (especially of a feeling) that you do not try to hide from other people; not DISGUISED: *a look of undisguised admiration*

un·dis·mayed /ˌʌndɪsˈmeɪd/ *adj.* [not before noun] (*formal*) not worried or frightened by sth unpleasant or unexpected SYN UNDAUNTED

un·dis·puted /ˌʌndɪˈspjuːtɪd/ *adj.* **1** that cannot be questioned or proved to be false; that cannot be DISPUTED SYN IRREFUTABLE: *undisputed facts/evidence* **2** that everyone accepts or recognizes: *the undisputed champion of the world*

un·dis·tin·guished /ˌʌndɪˈstɪŋɡwɪʃt/ *adj.* not very interesting, successful or attractive: *an undistinguished career* OPP DISTINGUISHED

un·dis·turbed /ˌʌndɪˈstɜːbd; *AmE* -ˈstɜːrbd/ *adj.* **1** [not usually before noun] not moved or touched by anyone or anything SYN UNTOUCHED: *The treasure had lain undisturbed for centuries.* **2** not interrupted by anyone SYN UNINTERRUPTED: *She succeeded in working undisturbed for a few hours.* **3** [not usually before noun] ~ (**by sth**) not affected or upset by sth SYN UNCONCERNED: *He seemed undisturbed by the news of her death.*—compare DISTURBED

un·div·ided /ˌʌndɪˈvaɪdɪd/ *adj.* **1** not split into smaller parts; not divided: *an undivided Church* **2** [usually before noun] total; complete; not divided: *undivided love/loyalty/concentration* ◊ *You must be prepared to give the job your undivided attention.*

undo /ʌnˈduː/ *verb* (**un·does** /ʌnˈdʌz/ **un·did** /ʌnˈdɪd/ **un·done** /ʌnˈdʌn/) [VN] **1** to open sth that is fastened, tied or wrapped: *to undo a button/knot/zip* ◊ *to undo a jacket/shirt/bag* ◊ *I undid the package and took out the books.* OPP DO UP **2** to cancel the effect of sth: *He undid most of the good work of the previous manager.* ◊ *It's not too late to try and undo some of the damage.* ◊ *UNDO* (= an editing command on a computer that cancels the previous action) **3** [usually passive] (*formal*) to make sb/sth fail: *The team was undone by the speed and strength of their opponents.*

un·do·ing /ʌnˈduːɪŋ/ *noun* [sing.] the reason why sb fails at sth or is unsuccessful in life SYN DOWNFALL: *That one mistake was his undoing.*

un·done /ʌnˈdʌn/ *adj.* [not usually before noun] **1** (especially of clothing) not fastened or tied: *Her blouse had come undone.* **2** (especially of work) not finished: *Most of the work had been left undone.* **3** (*old use*) (of a person) defeated and without any hope for the future

un·doubt·ed /ʌnˈdaʊtɪd/ *adj.* [usually before noun] used to emphasize that sth exists or is definitely true: *undoubted difficulties/problems* ◊ *She has an undoubted talent as an organizer.* ▶ **un·doubt·ed·ly** *adv.*: *There is undoubtedly a great deal of truth in what he says.*

undreamed-of /ʌnˈdriːmd ɒv; *AmE* ʌv/ (also **undreamt-of** /ʌnˈdremt ɒv; *AmE* ʌv/ especially in *BrE*) *adj.* much more or much better than you thought was possible: *undreamed-of happiness/success*

un·dress /ʌnˈdres/ *verb, noun*
- *verb* to take off your clothes; to remove sb else's clothes: [V] *She undressed and got into bed.* ◊ *He got undressed in a small cubicle next to the pool.* ◊ [VN] *to undress a child/doll* OPP DRESS

■ *noun* [U] (*formal*) the fact of sb wearing no, or few, clothes: *He appeared at the window in a **state of undress**.*

un·dressed /ʌnˈdrest/ *adj.* [not usually before noun] not wearing any clothes: *She began to **get undressed** (= remove her clothes).* OPP DRESSED

undue /ˌʌnˈdjuː; *AmE* ˌʌnˈduː/ *adj.* [only before noun] (*formal*) more than you think is reasonable or necessary SYN EXCESSIVE: *They are taking undue advantage of the situation. ◊ The work should be carried out without undue delay. ◊ We did not want to put any undue pressure on them.*—compare DUE *adj.* (6)

un·du·late /ˈʌndjuleɪt; *AmE* -dʒə-/ *verb* [V] (*written*) to go or move gently up and down like waves: *The countryside undulates pleasantly.*

un·du·la·tion /ˌʌndjuˈleɪʃn; *AmE* -dʒə-/ *noun* [C, U] a smooth curving shape or movement like a series of waves

un·duly /ʌnˈdjuːli; *AmE* -ˈduːli/ *adv.* (*formal*) more than you think is reasonable or necessary SYN EXCESSIVELY: *He did not sound unduly worried at the prospect. ◊ The levels of pollution in this area are unduly high. ◊ The thought did not disturb her unduly.*—compare DULY

un·dy·ing /ʌnˈdaɪɪŋ/ *adj.* [only before noun] lasting for ever: *undying love/support/gratitude*

un·earned /ʌnˈɜːnd; *AmE* ʌnˈɜːrnd/ *adj.* [U] used to describe money that you receive but do not earn by working: *Declare all unearned income.*

un·earth /ʌnˈɜːθ; *AmE* ʌnˈɜːrθ/ *verb* [VN] **1** to find sth in the ground by digging SYN DIG UP: *to unearth buried treasures* **2** to find or discover sth by chance or after searching for it SYN DIG UP: *I unearthed my old diaries when we moved house. ◊ The newspaper has unearthed some disturbing facts.*

un·earth·ly /ʌnˈɜːθli; *AmE* -ˈɜːrθ-/ *adj.* [usually before noun] very strange; not natural and therefore frightening: *an unearthly cry/yell ◊ an unearthly light/sight* IDM **at an unearthly ʹhour** (*informal*) very early, especially when this is annoying: *The job involved getting up at some unearthly hour to catch the first train.*

un·ease /ʌnˈiːz/ (also **un·easi·ness** /ʌnˈiːzinəs/) *noun* [U, sing.] the feeling of being worried or unhappy about sth: *a deep feeling/sense of unease ◊ There was a growing unease about their involvement in the war. ◊ He was unable to hide his unease at the way the situation was developing.*

un·easy /ʌnˈiːzi/ *adj.* **1** ~ (**about sth/about doing sth**) feeling worried or unhappy about a particular situation, especially because you think that sth bad or unpleasant may happen or because you are not sure that what you are doing is right: *an uneasy laugh/smile ◊ He was beginning to feel distinctly uneasy about their visit. ◊ She felt uneasy about leaving the children with them.* OPP EASY **2** not certain to last; not safe or settled: *an uneasy alliance/truce/peace/relationship ◊ The two sides eventually reached an uneasy compromise.* **3** that does not enable you to relax or feel comfortable: *She woke from an uneasy sleep to find the house empty.* **4** used to describe a mixture of two things, feelings, etc. that do not go well together: *an uneasy mix of humour and violence ◊ Old farmhouses and new villas stood together in uneasy proximity.* ▶ **un·eas·ily** /ʌnˈiːzɪli/ *adv.*: *I wondered uneasily what he was thinking. ◊ She shifted uneasily in her chair. ◊ His socialist views sit uneasily with his huge fortune.*

un·eat·able /ʌnˈiːtəbl/ *adj.* (of food) not good enough to be eaten—see also INEDIBLE

un·eat·en /ʌnˈiːtn/ *adj.* (*written*) not eaten: *Bill put the uneaten food away.*

un·eco·nom·ic /ˌʌniːkəˈnɒmɪk; ˌʌneˌk-; *AmE* -ˈnɑːm-/ *adj.* **1** (of a business, factory, etc.) not making a profit SYN UNPROFITABLE: *uneconomic farms/industries* OPP ECONOMIC **2** = UNECONOMICAL

un·eco·nom·ic·al /ˌʌniˌkəˈnɒmɪkl; ˌʌneˌk-; *AmE* -ˈnɑːm-/ (also **un·eco·nom·ic**) *adj.* ~ (**to do sth**) using too much time or money, or too many materials, and therefore not likely to make a profit: *It soon proved uneconomical to stay open 24 hours a day.* OPP ECONOMICAL

un·edify·ing /ʌnˈedɪfaɪɪŋ/ *adj.* (*formal, especially BrE*) unpleasant in a way that makes you feel disapproval: *the*

unedifying sight of the two party leaders screeching at each other—compare EDIFYING

un·edu·cated /ʌnˈedʒukeɪtɪd/ *adj.* having had little or no formal education at a school; showing a lack of education: *an uneducated workforce ◊ an uneducated point of view*—compare EDUCATED

un·emo·tion·al /ˌʌnɪˈməʊʃənl; *AmE* -ˈmoʊ-/ *adj.* not showing your feelings: *an unemotional speech/voice ◊ She seemed very cool and unemotional.* OPP EMOTIONAL ▶ **un·emo·tion·al·ly** *adv.*

un·employ·able /ˌʌnɪmˈplɔɪəbl/ *adj.* lacking the skills or qualities that you need to get a job OPP EMPLOYABLE

un·employed /ˌʌnɪmˈplɔɪd/ *adj.* without a job although able to work: *How long have you been unemployed? ◊ an unemployed builder/teacher* ▶ **the un·employed** *noun* [pl.]: *a programme to get the long-term unemployed back to work ◊ I've joined the ranks of the unemployed (= I've lost my job).*

un·employ·ment /ˌʌnɪmˈplɔɪmənt/ *noun* [U] **1** the fact of a number of people not having a job; the number of people without a job: *an area of high unemployment ◊ rising/falling rates of unemployment ◊ measures to help reduce/tackle unemployment* **2** the state of not having a job: *Thousands of young people are facing long-term unemployment.*—compare EMPLOYMENT

unemʹployment benefit (*BrE*) (*AmE* **unemˌploy·ment compenˈsation**) *noun* [U] (also **unemʹployment benefits** [pl.]) money paid by the government to sb who is unemployed: *people on (= receiving) unemployment benefit ◊ Applications for unemployment benefits dropped last month.*

un·end·ing /ʌnˈendɪŋ/ *adj.* seeming to last for ever: *a seemingly unending supply of money*

un·en·dur·able /ˌʌnɪnˈdjʊərəbl; *AmE* -ˈdʊr-/ *adj.* (*formal*) too bad, unpleasant, etc. to bear: *unendurable heat/noise/pain*

un·envi·able /ʌnˈenviəbl/ *adj.* [usually before noun] difficult or unpleasant; that you would not want to have: *She was given the **unenviable task** of informing the losers.* OPP ENVIABLE

un·equal /ʌnˈiːkwəl/ *adj.* **1** [usually before noun] in which people are treated differently or have different advantages in a way that seems unfair: *an unequal distribution of power/wealth ◊ an unequal contest/relationship* **2** ~ (**in sth**) different in size, amount, etc: *The sleeves are unequal in length. ◊ The rooms upstairs are of unequal size.* **3** ~ **to sth** (*formal*) not capable of doing sth: *She suddenly felt unequal to the task she had set herself.* OPP EQUAL ▶ **un·equal·ly** /-kwəli/ *adv.*

un·equalled (*BrE*) (*AmE* **un·equaled**) /ʌnˈiːkwəld/ *adj.* better than all others SYN UNPARALLELED: *an unequalled record of success*

un·equivo·cal /ˌʌnɪˈkwɪvəkl/ *adj.* (*formal*) expressing your opinion or intention very clearly and firmly: *an unequivocal answer/rejection/warning ◊ The answer was an unequivocal 'no'.* OPP EQUIVOCAL ▶ **un·equivo·cal·ly** /-kəli/ *adv.*

un·err·ing /ʌnˈɜːrɪŋ/ *adj.* always right or accurate: *She had an unerring instinct for a good business deal.* ▶ **un·err·ing·ly** *adv.*

UNESCO (also **Unesco**) /juːˈneskəʊ; *AmE* -koʊ/ *abbr.* United Nations Educational, Scientific and Cultural Organization

un·eth·ic·al /ʌnˈeθɪkl/ *adj.* not morally acceptable: *unethical behaviour/conduct* OPP ETHICAL ▶ **un·eth·ic·al·ly** /-kli/ *adv.*

un·even /ʌnˈiːvn/ *adj.* **1** not level, smooth or flat: *an uneven path/wall ◊ The floor felt uneven under his feet.* OPP EVEN **2** not following a regular pattern; not having a regular size and shape SYN IRREGULAR: *Her breathing was quick and uneven. ◊ uneven teeth* OPP EVEN **3** not having the same quality in all parts: *an uneven performance (= with some good parts and some bad parts)* **4** (of a contest or match) in which one group, team or player is much better than the other SYN UNEQUAL OPP EVEN **5** organized in a way that is not regular and/or fair SYN

UNEQUAL: *an uneven distribution of resources* OPP EVEN ▶ **un·even·ly** *adv.* **un·even·ness** *noun* [U]

un·event·ful /ˌʌnɪˈventfl/ *adj.* in which nothing interesting, unusual or exciting happens: *an uneventful career/life/weekend* OPP EVENTFUL ▶ **un·event·ful·ly** /-fəli/ *adv.*: *The day passed uneventfully.*

un·ex·cep·tion·able /ˌʌnɪkˈsepʃənəbl/ *adj.* **1** (*formal*) not giving any reason for criticism: *a man of unexceptionable character* **2** (*informal*) not very new or exciting

un·ex·cep·tion·al /ˌʌnɪkˈsepʃənl/ *adj.* not interesting or unusual SYN UNREMARKABLE—compare EXCEPTIONAL

un·ex·cit·ing /ˌʌnɪkˈsaɪtɪŋ/ *adj.* dull; boring OPP EXCITING

un·ex·pect·ed /ˌʌnɪkˈspektɪd/ *adj.* if sth is unexpected, it surprises you because you were not expecting it: *an unexpected development/result/visitor* ◊ *The announcement was not entirely unexpected.* ▶ **the unexpected** *noun* [sing.]: *Police officers must be prepared for the unexpected.* **un·ex·pect·ed·ly** *adv.*: *They had arrived unexpectedly.* ◊ *an unexpectedly large bill* ◊ *The plane was unexpectedly delayed.* **un·ex·pect·ed·ness** *noun* [U] —compare EXPECT

un·ex·pired /ˌʌnɪkˈspaɪəd; AmE -ˈspaɪərd/ *adj.* [usually before noun] (of an agreement or a period of time) still valid; not yet having come to an end or EXPIRED

un·ex·plained /ˌʌnɪkˈspleɪnd/ *adj.* for which the reason or cause is not known; that has not been explained: *an unexplained mystery* ◊ *He died in unexplained circumstances.*

un·ex·ploded /ˌʌnɪkˈspləʊdɪd; AmE -ˈsploʊ-/ *adj.* [only before noun] (of a bomb, etc.) that has not yet exploded

un·ex·plored /ˌʌnɪkˈsplɔːd; AmE -ˈsplɔːrd/ *adj.* **1** (of a country or an area of land) that nobody has investigated or put on a map; that has not been EXPLORED **2** (of an idea, a theory, etc.) that has not yet been examined or discussed thoroughly

un·ex·pressed /ˌʌnɪkˈsprest/ *adj.* (of a thought, a feeling or an idea) not shown or made known in words, looks or actions; not expressed

un·fail·ing /ʌnˈfeɪlɪŋ/ *adj.* that you can rely on to always be there and always be the same SYN UNERRING: *unfailing devotion/support* ◊ *She fought the disease with unfailing good humour.* ▶ **un·fail·ing·ly** *adv.*: *unfailingly loyal/polite*

un·fair /ˌʌnˈfeə(r); AmE -ˈfer/ *adj.* ~ (on/to sb) not right or fair according to a set of rules or principles; not treating people equally SYN UNJUST: *unfair criticism/treatment* ◊ *It seems unfair on him to make him pay for everything.* ◊ *It would be unfair not to let you have a choice.* ◊ *They had been given an unfair advantage.* ◊ **unfair dismissal** (= a situation in which sb is illegally dismissed from their job) ◊ *measures to prevent unfair competition between member countries* ◊ *Life seems so unfair sometimes.* ◊ *It's so unfair!* OPP FAIR ▶ **un·fair·ly** *adv.*: *She claims to have been unfairly dismissed.* ◊ *The tests discriminate unfairly against older people.* **un·fair·ness** *noun* [U]

un·faith·ful /ʌnˈfeɪθfl/ *adj.* ~ (to sb) having sex with sb who is not your husband, wife or usual partner: *Have you ever been unfaithful to him?* OPP FAITHFUL ▶ **un·faith·ful·ness** *noun* [U]

un·famil·iar /ˌʌnfəˈmɪliə(r)/ *adj.* **1** ~ (to sb) that you do not know or recognize: *an unfamiliar feeling/place/sound* ◊ *Please highlight any terms that are unfamiliar to you.* **2** ~ with sth not having any knowledge or experience of sth: *an introductory course for students who are unfamiliar with computers* OPP FAMILIAR ▶ **un·famil·iar·ity** /ˌʌnfəˌmɪliˈærəti/ *noun* [U]

un·fash·ion·able /ʌnˈfæʃnəbl/ *adj.* not popular or fashionable at a particular time: *They live in an unfashionable part of London.* ◊ *unfashionable ideas/attitudes* OPP FASHIONABLE ▶ **un·fash·ion·ably** *adv.*: *a man with unfashionably long hair*

un·fas·ten /ʌnˈfɑːsn; AmE ʌnˈfæsn/ *verb* [VN] to undo sth that is fastened: *to unfasten a belt/button/chain/lock* OPP FASTEN

un·fath·om·able /ʌnˈfæðəməbl/ *adj.* (*formal*) **1** too

strange or difficult to be understood: *an unfathomable mystery* **2** if sb has an **unfathomable** expression, it is impossible to know what they are thinking

un·favour·able (*BrE*) (*AmE* **un·favor·able**) /ʌnˈfeɪvərəbl/ *adj.* **1** ~ (of conditions, situations, etc.) not good and likely to cause problems or make sth more difficult: *The conditions were unfavourable for intensive agricultural production.* ◊ *an unfavourable exchange rate* **2** showing that you do not approve of or like sb/sth: *an unfavourable attitude/comment* ◊ *The documentary presents him in a very unfavourable light.* ◊ *an unfavourable comparison* (= one that makes one thing seem much worse than another) OPP FAVOURABLE ▶ **un·favour·ably** (*BrE*) (*AmE* **un·favor·ably**) *adv.*: *In this respect, Britain compares unfavourably with other European countries.*

un·fazed /ʌnˈfeɪzd/ *adj.* (*informal*) not worried or surprised by sth unexpected that happens: *She was totally unfazed by the news.* OPP FAZED

un·feas·ible /ʌnˈfiːzəbl/ *adj.* not possible to do or achieve: *The teachers' demands were economically unfeasible.* OPP FEASIBLE

un·feel·ing /ʌnˈfiːlɪŋ/ *adj.* not showing care or sympathy for other people

un·feigned /ʌnˈfeɪnd/ *adj.* (*written*) real and sincere SYN GENUINE: *He looked at her with unfeigned admiration.*

un·fenced /ʌnˈfenst/ *adj.* (of a road or piece of land) without fences beside or around it

un·fet·tered /ʌnˈfetəd; AmE -tərd/ *adj.* (*formal*) not controlled or restricted: *an unfettered free market* ◊ *unfettered by regulations/restrictions*

un·filled /ʌnˈfɪld/ *adj.* **1** if a job or position is **unfilled**, nobody has been chosen for it **2** if a pause in a conversation is **unfilled**, nobody speaks **3** an **unfilled** cake has nothing inside it **4** (*especially AmE*) if an order for goods is **unfilled**, the goods have not been supplied

un·fin·ished /ʌnˈfɪnɪʃt/ *adj.* not complete; not finished: *We have some unfinished business to settle.* ◊ *an unfinished drink/game/book*

unfit /ʌnˈfɪt/ *adj.* **1** ~ (for sth)| ~ (to eat, drink, live in, etc.)| ~ (to do sth) not of an acceptable standard; not suitable: *unfit for human consumption/habitation* ◊ *This water is unfit to drink.* ◊ *Most of the buildings are unfit to live in.* ◊ *They described him as unfit to govern.* ◊ (*technical*) *Many of the houses were condemned as unfit.* ◊ (*technical*) *The court claims she is an unfit mother.* **2** ~ for sth| ~ to do sth not capable of doing sth, for example because of illness: *He's still unfit for work.* ◊ *The company's doctor found that she was unfit to carry out her normal work.* **3** (*especially BrE*) (of a person) not in good physical condition; not fit, because you have not taken exercise: *The captain is still unfit and will miss tonight's game.* OPP FIT ▶ **un·fit·ness** *noun* [U]

un·fit·ted /ʌnˈfɪtɪd/ *adj.* ~ for sth| ~ to do sth (*formal*) not suitable for sth: *She felt herself unfitted for marriage.*

un·flag·ging /ˌʌnˈflægɪŋ/ *adj.* [usually before noun] remaining strong; not becoming weak or tired: *unflagging effort/energy* ◊ *She had shown unflagging support for the cause.*

un·flap·pable /ˌʌnˈflæpəbl/ *adj.* (*informal*) able to stay calm in a difficult situation

un·flat·ter·ing /ʌnˈflætərɪŋ/ *adj.* making sb/sth seem worse or less attractive than they really are: *an unflattering dress/portrait* ◊ *Short hair can be very unflattering.* ◊ *unflattering comments* OPP FLATTERING

un·flinch·ing /ʌnˈflɪntʃɪŋ/ *adj.* remaining strong and determined, even in a difficult or dangerous situation: *unflinching determination/loyalty/pride* ◊ *an unflinching gaze/stare* ▶ **un·flinch·ing·ly** *adv.*—see also FLINCH

un·focused (also **un·focussed**) /ʌnˈfəʊkəst; AmE -ˈfoʊ-/ *adj.* **1** (especially of eyes) not looking at a particular thing or person; not having been FOCUSED: *an unfocused glance/look* **2** (of plans, work, etc.) not having a clear aim or purpose; not well organized or clear: *The research is too unfocused to have any significant impact.* ◊ *unfocused questions/longings*

					ʃ		ʒ	tʃ	dʒ	θ	ð	ŋ
s	t	v	z		shoe		vision	chain	jam	thin	this	sing
see	tea	van	zoo									

un·fold /ʌnˈfəʊld; AmE ʌnˈfoʊld/ verb **1** to spread open or flat sth that has previously been folded; to become open and flat: [VN] *to unfold a map/tablecloth/letter* ◊ *She unfolded her arms.* [also V] OPP FOLD **2** to be gradually made known; to gradually make sth known to other people: [V] *The audience watched the story unfold before their eyes.* ◊ [VN] *She unfolded her tale to us.*

un·forced /ʌnˈfɔːst; AmE ʌnˈfɔːrst/ adj. **1** (especially in sports) an unforced ERROR (= mistake) is one that you make by playing badly, not because your opponent has caused you to make a mistake by their skilful play **2** natural; done without effort: *unforced humour/style*

un·fore·see·able /ˌʌnfɔːˈsiːəbl; AmE -fɔːrˈs-/ adj. that you cannot predict or FORESEE: *Building a dam here could have unforeseeable consequences for the environment.* OPP FORESEEABLE

un·fore·seen /ˌʌnfɔːˈsiːn; AmE -fɔːrˈs-/ adj. that you did not expect to happen SYN UNEXPECTED: *unforeseen delays/problems* ◊ *The project was running late owing to unforeseen circumstances.*—compare FORESEE

un·for·get·table /ˌʌnfəˈɡetəbl; AmE -fərˈɡ-/ adj. if sth is unforgettable, you cannot forget it, usually because it is so beautiful, interesting, enjoyable, etc. SYN MEMORABLE—compare FORGETTABLE

un·for·giv·able /ˌʌnfəˈɡɪvəbl; AmE -fərˈɡ-/ adj. if sb's behaviour is unforgivable, it is so bad or unacceptable that you cannot forgive the person SYN INEXCUSABLE OPP FORGIVABLE ▶ **un·for·giv·ably** adv.

un·for·giv·ing /ˌʌnfəˈɡɪvɪŋ; AmE -fərˈɡ-/ adj. (written) **1** (of a person) unwilling to forgive other people when they have done sth wrong OPP FORGIVING **2** (of a place, situation, etc.) unpleasant and causing difficulties for people

un·formed /ˌʌnˈfɔːmd; AmE ˌʌnˈfɔːrmd/ adj. (formal) not fully developed: *unformed ideas*

un·forth·com·ing /ˌʌnfɔːˈθkʌmɪŋ; AmE -fɔːrˈθ-/ adj. not wanting to help or give information about sth: *He was very unforthcoming about what had happened.* OPP FORTHCOMING

un·for·tu·nate /ʌnˈfɔːtʃənət; AmE -ˈfɔːrtʃ-/ adj., noun
■ adj. **1** having bad luck; caused by bad luck SYN UNLUCKY: *He was unfortunate to lose in the final round.* ◊ *It was an unfortunate accident.* OPP FORTUNATE **2** (formal) if you say that a situation is unfortunate, you wish that it had not happened or that it had happened differently SYN REGRETTABLE: *She described the decision as 'unfortunate'.* ◊ *It was unfortunate that he couldn't speak English.* ◊ *You're putting me in a most unfortunate position.* **3** embarrassing and/or offensive: *It was an unfortunate choice of words.*
■ noun (literary) a person who does not have much luck, money, etc: *one of life's unfortunates*

un·for·tu·nate·ly /ʌnˈfɔːtʃənətli; AmE -ˈfɔːrtʃ-/ adv. used to say that a particular situation or fact makes you sad or disappointed, or gets you into a difficult position SYN REGRETTABLY: *Unfortunately, I won't be able to attend the meeting.* ◊ *I can't make it, unfortunately.* ◊ *Unfortunately for him, the police had been informed and were waiting outside.* ◊ *It won't be finished for a few weeks. Unfortunately!* OPP FORTUNATELY

un·found·ed /ʌnˈfaʊndɪd/ adj. (written) not based on reason or fact: *unfounded allegations/fears/optimism* ◊ *Speculation about a divorce proved totally unfounded.*

un·freeze /ˌʌnˈfriːz/ verb (un·froze /-ˈfrəʊz; AmE -ˈfroʊz/ un·frozen /-ˈfrəʊzn; AmE -ˈfroʊzn/) **1** [VN, V] if you unfreeze sth that has been frozen or very cold, or it unfreezes, it melts or warms until it reaches a normal temperature—compare DEFROST, DE-ICE, THAW **2** [VN] to remove official controls on money or an economy: *The party plans to unfreeze some of the cash held by local government.* OPP FREEZE

un·friend·ly /ʌnˈfrendli/ adj. ~ (to/towards sb) not kind or pleasant to sb: *unfriendly eyes/people* ◊ *an unfriendly atmosphere* ◊ *There's no need to be so unfriendly towards them.* ◊ *the use of environmentally unfriendly products* (= that harm the environment) OPP FRIENDLY ▶ **un·friend·li·ness** noun [U]

un·ful·filled /ˌʌnfʊlˈfɪld/ adj. **1** (of a need, wish, etc.) that has not been satisfied or achieved: *unfulfilled ambitions/hopes/promises* **2** if a person feels unfulfilled, they feel that they could achieve more in their life or work OPP FULFILLED

un·funny /ʌnˈfʌni/ adj. not funny or amusing, especially when sth is supposed to be funny: *The show was deeply unfunny.*

un·furl /ˌʌnˈfɜːl; AmE ˌʌnˈfɜːrl/ verb to open, or to make sth open, that is curled or rolled up: *The leaves slowly unfurled.* ◊ [VN] *to unfurl a flag/sail/banner*

un·fur·nished /ʌnˈfɜːnɪʃt; AmE -ˈfɜːrn-/ adj. without furniture: *We rented an unfurnished apartment.* OPP FURNISHED

un·gain·ly /ʌnˈɡeɪnli/ adj. moving in a way that is not graceful SYN AWKWARD: *He was a tall, ungainly boy of 18.*

un·gentle·man·ly /ʌnˈdʒentlmənli/ adj. (of a man's behaviour) not polite or pleasant; not acceptable OPP GENTLEMANLY

un·glam·or·ous /ʌnˈɡlæmərəs/ adj. not attractive or exciting; dull: *an unglamorous job* ◊ *Lunch was a decidedly unglamorous affair.* OPP GLAMOROUS

un·glued /ʌnˈɡluːd/ adj. IDM **come un·glued** (AmE, informal) **1** to become very upset **2** if a plan, etc. comes unglued, it does not work successfully

un·god·ly /ʌnˈɡɒdli; AmE -ˈɡɑːd-/ adj. (old-fashioned) not showing respect for God; wicked OPP GODLY IDM **at an ungodly 'hour** very early or very late and therefore annoying

un·gov·ern·able /ʌnˈɡʌvənəbl; AmE -ˈɡʌvərn-/ adj. **1** (written) (of a country, region, etc.) impossible to govern or control **2** (formal) (of a person's feelings) impossible to control: *ungovernable rage*

un·gra·cious /ʌnˈɡreɪʃəs/ adj. (formal) not polite or friendly, especially towards sb who is being kind to you OPP GRACIOUS ▶ **un·gra·cious·ly** adv.

un·gram·mat·ical /ˌʌnɡrəˈmætɪkl/ adj. not following the rules of grammar OPP GRAMMATICAL

un·grate·ful /ʌnˈɡreɪtfl/ adj. not showing or expressing thanks for sth that sb has done for you or given to you OPP GRATEFUL ▶ **un·grate·ful·ly** /-fəli/ adv.

un·guard·ed /ʌnˈɡɑːdɪd; AmE -ˈɡɑːrd-/ adj. **1** not protected or watched: *The museum was unguarded at night.* ◊ *an unguarded fire* (= that has nothing to stop people from burning themselves on it) **2** (of a remark, look, etc.) said or done carelessly, at a time when you are not thinking about the effects of your words or are not paying attention: *an unguarded response/remark* ◊ *It was something I'd let out in an unguarded moment.*—compare GUARDED

un·hap·pily /ʌnˈhæpɪli/ adv. **1** in an unhappy way: *He sighed unhappily.* **2** (written) used to say that a particular situation or fact makes you sad or disappointed SYN UNFORTUNATELY: *Unhappily, such good luck is rare.* ◊ *His wife, unhappily, died five years ago.* OPP HAPPILY

un·happy /ʌnˈhæpi/ adj. (un·hap·pier, un·happi·est) HELP more unhappy and most unhappy are also common **1** not happy; sad: *to look/seem/sound unhappy* ◊ *an unhappy childhood/marriage* **2** ~ (about/at/with sth) not pleased or satisfied with sth: *They were unhappy with their accommodation.* ◊ *He was unhappy at being left out of the team.* **3** (formal) unfortunate or not suitable: *an unhappy coincidence* ◊ *It was an unhappy choice of words.* ▶ **un·hap·pi·ness** noun [U]

un·harmed /ʌnˈhɑːmd; AmE ʌnˈhɑːrmd/ adj. not injured or damaged; NOT HARMED

un·healthy /ʌnˈhelθi/ adj. **1** not having good health; showing a lack of good health: *They looked poor and unhealthy.* ◊ *unhealthy hair/skin* **2** harmful to your health; likely to make you ill: *unhealthy living conditions* ◊ *an unhealthy diet/lifestyle* **3** not normal and likely to be harmful: *He had an unhealthy interest in disease and death.* OPP HEALTHY ▶ **un·health·ily** /-ɪli/ adv.

un·heard /ʌnˈhɜːd; AmE ʌnˈhɜːrd/ adj. **1** that nobody pays attention to: *Their protests went unheard.* **2** not listened to or heard: *a previously unheard tape of their conversations*

æ	ɑː	e	ɜː	ə	ɪ	iː	i	ɒ	ɔː	ʌ	ʊ	u	uː
cat	father	ten	bird	about	sit	see	many	got	saw	cup	put	actual	too
								(BrE)					

unheard-of /ʌnˈhɜːd ɒv; AmE ʌnˈhɜːrd ʌv/ adj. that has never been known or done; very unusual: *He'd dyed his hair, which was almost unheard-of in the 1960s.* ◊ *Home computers are now used on a scale unheard-of a few years ago.* ◊ *It is almost unheard-of for a new band to be offered such a deal.*

un·heat·ed /ʌnˈhiːtɪd/ adj. having no form of heating: *an unheated bathroom* OPP HEATED

un·heed·ed /ʌnˈhiːdɪd/ adj. (formal) that is heard, seen or noticed but then ignored: *Her warning went unheeded.*—compare HEED

un·help·ful /ʌnˈhelpfl/ adj. not helpful or useful; not willing to help sb: *an unhelpful response/reply* OPP HELPFUL ► **un·help·ful·ly** /-fəli/ adv.

un·her·ald·ed /ʌnˈherəldɪd/ adj. (formal) not previously mentioned; happening without any warning

un·hesi·tat·ing /ʌnˈhezɪteɪtɪŋ/ adj. done or given immediately and confidently: *an unhesitating reply/answer* ► **un·hesi·tat·ing·ly** adv.

un·hin·dered /ʌnˈhɪndəd; AmE -dərd/ adj. without anything stopping or preventing the progress of sb/sth: *She had unhindered access to the files.* ◊ *He was able to pass unhindered through several military checkpoints.*—see also HINDER

un·hinge /ʌnˈhɪndʒ/ verb [VN] [usually passive] to make sb mentally ill: *Her mind was unhinged by the death of her child and she never recovered.*

un·hitch /ʌnˈhɪtʃ/ verb [VN] to undo sth that is tied to sth else: *to unhitch a horse/trailer*—see also HITCH

un·holy /ʌnˈhəʊli; AmE -ˈhoʊ-/ adj. **1** dangerous; likely to be harmful: *an unholy alliance between the medical profession and the pharmaceutical industry* **2** not respecting the laws of a religion: *(figurative) He took an unholy delight in her discomfort.* OPP HOLY **3** [only before noun] (informal) used to emphasize how bad sth is: *She wondered how she had got into this unholy mess.*

un·hook /ʌnˈhʊk/ verb [VN] **~ sth (from sth)** to remove sth from a hook; to undo the hooks on clothes, etc: *He unhooked his coat from the door.* ◊ *She unhooked her bra.*

un·hur·ried /ʌnˈhʌrid; AmE -ˈhɜːr-/ adj. (written) relaxed and calm; not done too quickly: *His conversation was relaxed and unhurried.* OPP HURRIED ► **un·hur·ried·ly** adv.: *Lynn walked unhurriedly into the kitchen.*

un·hurt /ʌnˈhɜːt; AmE ʌnˈhɜːrt/ adj. [not before noun] not injured or harmed SYN UNHARMED: *He escaped from the crash unhurt.* OPP HURT

un·hygien·ic /ˌʌnhaɪˈdʒiːnɪk/ adj. not clean and therefore likely to cause disease or infection OPP HYGIENIC

uni /ˈjuːni/ noun (BrE, spoken) university: *friends from uni*

uni- /ˈjuːni/ combining form (in nouns, adjectives and adverbs) one; having one: *uniform* ◊ *unilaterally*

uni·cam·eral /ˌjuːnɪˈkæmərəl/ adj. (technical) (of a parliament) that has only one main governing body

UNICEF /ˈjuːnɪsef/ abbr. United Nations Children's Fund (an organization within the United Nations that helps to look after the health and education of children all over the world)

uni·corn /ˈjuːnɪkɔːn; AmE -kɔːrn/ noun (in stories) an animal like a white horse with a long straight horn on its forehead

uni·cycle /ˈjuːnɪsaɪkl/ noun a vehicle that is similar to a bicycle but that has only one wheel

un·iden·ti·fi·able /ˌʌnaɪˈdentɪfaɪəbl/ adj. impossible to identify: *He had an unidentifiable accent.* ◊ *Many of the bodies were unidentifiable except by dental records.* OPP IDENTIFIABLE

un·iden·ti·fied /-ˌʌnaɪˈdentɪfaɪd/ adj. not recognized or known; not IDENTIFIED: *an unidentified virus* ◊ *He was shot and killed by an unidentified gunman.* ◊ *The painting was sold to an unidentified American dealer* (= his or her name was not given).

uni·form /ˈjuːnɪfɔːm; AmE -fɔːrm/ noun, adj.
■ noun [C, U] the special set of clothes worn by all members of an organization or a group at work, or by children at school: *a military/police/nurse's uniform* ◊ *soldiers/sailors in uniform* ◊ *The hat is part of the school uniform.*
■ adj. not varying; the same in all parts and at all times: *uniform rates of pay* ◊ *The walls were a uniform grey.* ◊ *Growth has not been uniform across the country.* ◊ *uniform lines of terraced houses* (= they all looked the same) ► **uni·form·ity** /ˌjuːnɪˈfɔːməti/ noun [U, sing.]: *They tried to ensure uniformity across the different departments.* ◊ *the drab uniformity of the houses* **uni·form·ly** adv.: *The principles were applied uniformly across all the departments.* ◊ *The quality is uniformly high.* ◊ *Pressure must be uniformly distributed over the whole surface.*

uni·formed /ˈjuːnɪfɔːmd; AmE -fɔːrmd/ adj. wearing a uniform: *a uniformed chauffeur*

unify /ˈjuːnɪfaɪ/ verb (uni·fies, uni·fy·ing, uni·fied, uni·fied) [VN] to join people, things, parts of a country, etc. together so that they form a single unit: *The new leader hopes to unify the country.* ◊ *the task of unifying Europe* ◊ *a unified transport system* ► **uni·fi·ca·tion** /ˌjuːnɪfɪˈkeɪʃn/ noun [U]: *the unification of Germany*

uni·lat·eral /ˌjuːnɪˈlætrəl/ adj. done by one member of a group or an organization without the agreement of the other members: *a unilateral decision* ◊ *a unilateral declaration of independence* ◊ *They were forced to take unilateral action.* ◊ *They had campaigned vigorously for* **unilateral nuclear disarmament** (= when one country gets rid of its nuclear weapons without waiting for other countries to do the same).—compare BILATERAL, MULTILATERAL ► **uni·lat·eral·ly** /-rəli/ adv.

un·imagin·able /ˌʌnɪˈmædʒɪnəbl/ adj. (written) impossible to think of or to believe exists; impossible to imagine: *unimaginable wealth/possibilities* ◊ *This level of success would have been unimaginable just last year.* OPP IMAGINABLE ► **un·imagin·ably** adv.

un·imagina·tive /ˌʌnɪˈmædʒɪnətɪv/ adj. lacking in original or new ideas: *an unimaginative solution to a problem* ◊ *The food was adequate but unimaginative.* ◊ *a boring unimaginative man* OPP IMAGINATIVE

un·im·paired /ˌʌnɪmˈpeəd; AmE -ˈperd/ adj. (written) not damaged or spoiled: *Although he's ninety, his mental faculties remain unimpaired.* OPP IMPAIRED

un·im·peach·able /ˌʌnɪmˈpiːtʃəbl/ adj. (formal, approving) that you cannot doubt or question: *evidence from an unimpeachable source/witness*

un·im·peded /ˌʌnɪmˈpiːdɪd/ adj. (written) with nothing blocking or stopping sb/sth: *an unimpeded view of the bay* ◊ *free and unimpeded trade*

un·im·port·ant /ˌʌnɪmˈpɔːtnt; AmE -ˈpɔːrtnt/ adj. not important: *unimportant details* ◊ *relatively/comparatively unimportant* ◊ *They dismissed the problem as unimportant.* ◊ *This consideration was not unimportant.* ◊ *I was just a young girl from a small town and I felt very unimportant.* ► **un·im·port·ance** noun [U]

un·im·pressed /ˌʌnɪmˈprest/ adj. **~ (by/with sb/sth)** not thinking that sb/sth is particularly good, interesting, etc.; not IMPRESSED by sb/sth

un·im·pres·sive /ˌʌnɪmˈpresɪv/ adj. ordinary; not special in any way: *His academic record was unimpressive.* OPP IMPRESSIVE

un·in·forma·tive /ˌʌnɪnˈfɔːmətɪv; AmE -ˈfɔːrm-/ adj. not giving enough information: *The TV reports of the explosion were brief and uninformative.* OPP INFORMATIVE

un·in·formed /ˌʌnɪnˈfɔːmd; AmE -ˈfɔːrmd/ adj. having or showing a lack of knowledge or information about sth: *an uninformed comment/criticism* ◊ *The public is generally uninformed about these diseases.* OPP INFORMED

un·in·hab·it·able /ˌʌnɪnˈhæbɪtəbl/ adj. not fit to live in; impossible to live in: *The building was totally uninhabitable.* OPP HABITABLE

un·in·hab·it·ed /ˌʌnɪnˈhæbɪtɪd/ adj. with no people living there; not INHABITED: *an uninhabited island*

un·in·hib·it·ed /ˌʌnɪnˈhɪbɪtɪd/ adj. behaving or expressing yourself freely without worrying about what other people think: *uninhibited dancing/fun/passion* OPP INHIBITED

un·initi·ated /ˌʌnɪˈnɪʃieɪtɪd/ **(the uninitiated)** noun [pl.]

U

people who have no special knowledge or experience of sth: *To the uninitiated the system seems extremely complicated.* ▶ **un·ini·ti·ated** *adj.*

un·in·jured /ʌnˈɪndʒəd; *AmE* -dʒərd/ *adj.* [not usually before noun] not hurt or injured in any way [SYN] UNHURT: *They escaped from the crash uninjured.*

un·in·spired /ˌʌnɪnˈspaɪəd; *AmE* -ˈspaɪərd/ *adj.* not original or exciting [SYN] DULL [OPP] INSPIRED

un·in·spir·ing /ˌʌnɪnˈspaɪərɪŋ/ *adj.* not making people interested or excited: *The view from the window was uninspiring.* [OPP] INSPIRING

un·in·tel·li·gent /ˌʌnɪnˈtelɪdʒənt/ *adj.* not intelligent: *a good-natured but unintelligent boy*

un·in·tel·li·gible /ˌʌnɪnˈtelɪdʒəbl/ *adj.* ~ (**to sb**) impossible to understand: *unintelligible noises/shouts* ◊ *She turned away and muttered something unintelligible.* ◊ *A lot of the jargon they use is unintelligible to outsiders.* [OPP] INTELLIGIBLE ▶ **un·in·tel·li·gib·ly** /-əbli/ *adv.*

un·in·tend·ed /ˌʌnɪnˈtendɪd/ *adj.* an **unintended** effect, result or meaning is one that you did not plan or intend to happen: *In law you are considered responsible for the unintended consequences of your actions.*

un·in·ten·tion·al /ˌʌnɪnˈtenʃənl/ *adj.* not done deliberately, but happening by accident: *Perhaps I misled you, but it was quite unintentional* (= I did not mean to). [OPP] INTENTIONAL ▶ **un·in·ten·tion·al·ly** /-ʃənəli/ *adv.* They had unintentionally provided wrong information.

un·inter·est·ed /ʌnˈɪntrəstɪd; -trest-/ *adj.* ~ (**in sb/sth**) not interested; not wanting to know about sb/sth: *He was totally uninterested in sport.* ◊ *She seemed cold and uninterested.* ⇨ note at INTERESTED

un·inter·est·ing /ʌnˈɪntrəstɪŋ; -trest-/ *adj.* not attracting your attention or interest; not interesting ⇨ note at INTERESTED

un·inter·rupt·ed /ˌʌnˌɪntəˈrʌptɪd/ *adj.* not stopped or blocked by anything; continuous and not interrupted: *We had an uninterrupted view of the stage.* ◊ *eight hours of uninterrupted sleep* ◊ *We managed to eat our meal uninterrupted by phone calls.*

un·in·vited /ˌʌnɪnˈvaɪtɪd/ *adj.* doing sth or going somewhere when you have not been asked or invited to, especially when sb does not want you to: *uninvited guests at a party* ◊ *He turned up uninvited.*

un·in·vit·ing /ˌʌnɪnˈvaɪtɪŋ/ *adj.* not attractive or pleasant: *The water looked cold and uninviting.* [OPP] INVITING

union /ˈjuːniən/ *noun* **1** [C] = TRADE UNION **2** [C] an association or a club for people or organizations with the same interest: *the Scottish Rugby Union*—see also STUDENTS' UNION (2) **3** [C] a group of states or countries that have the same central government or that agree to work together: *the former Soviet Union* ◊ *the European Union* **4** (**Union**) [sing.] the US (used especially at the time of the Civil War): *the Union and the Confederacy* ◊ *the State of the Union address by the President* **5** [U, sing.] the act of joining two or more things together; the state of being joined together; the act of two people joining together: *a summit to discuss economic and monetary union* ◊ *Northern Ireland's union with Britain* ◊ *sexual/physical union* **6** [C] (*old-fashioned*) a marriage: *Their union was blessed with six children.*

union·ist /ˈjuːniənɪst/ *noun* **1** = TRADE UNIONIST **2** (**Unionist**) a person who believes that Northern Ireland should stay part of the United Kingdom **3** (**Union·ist**) a supporter of the Union during the Civil War in the US ▶ **union·ism** /ˈjuːniənɪzəm/ *noun* [U]

union·ize (*BrE* also **-ise**) /ˈjuːniənaɪz/ *verb* to organize people to become members of a trade union: [VN] *a unionized workforce/industry* [also V] ▶ **union·iza·tion, -isa·tion** /ˌjuːniənaɪˈzeɪʃn; *AmE* -nəˈz-/ *noun* [U]

the ˌUnion ˈJack *noun* [sing.] the name for the national flag of the United Kingdom

unique /juˈniːk/ *adj.* **1** being the only one of its kind: *Everyone's fingerprints are unique.* [HELP] You can use **absolutely**, **totally** or **almost** with **unique** in this meaning. **2** very special or unusual: *a unique talent* ◊ *The preview offers a unique opportunity to see the show without*

the crowds. ◊ *The deal will put the company in a unique position to export goods to Eastern Europe.* [HELP] You can use **more**, **very**, etc. with **unique** in this meaning. **3** ~ (**to sb/sth**) belonging to or connected with one particular person, place or thing: *an atmosphere that is unique to New York* ◊ *The koala is unique to Australia.* ▶ **unique·ly** *adv.*: *Her past experience made her uniquely suited to lead the campaign.* ◊ *The UK, uniquely, has not had to face the problem of mass unemployment.* ◊ *He was a uniquely gifted teacher.* **unique·ness** *noun* [U]: *The author stresses the uniqueness of the individual.*

uni·sex /ˈjuːniseks/ *adj.* intended for or used by both men and women: *a unisex hair salon* ◊ *unisex jeans*

uni·son /ˈjuːnɪsn/ *noun* [IDM] **in ˈunison (with sb/sth) 1** if people do or say sth **in unison**, they all do it at the same time **2** if people or organizations are working **in unison**, they are working together, because they agree with each other

unit /ˈjuːnɪt/ *noun*

SINGLE THING **1** a single thing, person or group that is complete by itself but can also form part of sth larger: *The cell is the unit of which all living organisms are composed.* ◊ *The basic unit of society is the family.* **2** (*business*) a single item of the type of product that a company sells: *The game's selling price was $15 per unit.* ◊ *What's the unit cost?*

GROUP OF PEOPLE **3** a group of people who work or live together, especially for a particular purpose: *army/military/police units* ◊ *Medical units were operating in the disaster area.*

IN HOSPITAL **4** a department, especially in a hospital, that provides a particular type of care or treatment: *the intensive care unit* ◊ *a maternity/psychiatric unit*

MEASUREMENT **5** ~ (**of sth**) a fixed quantity, etc. that is used as a standard measurement: *a unit of time/length/weight* ◊ *a unit of currency, such as the euro or the dollar* ◊ *Women are advised not to drink more than fourteen units of alcohol per week.*

FURNITURE **6** a piece of furniture, especially a cupboard, that fits with and matches others of the same type: *a fitted kitchen with white units* ◊ *floor/wall units* ◊ *bedroom/kitchen/storage units*

SMALL MACHINE **7** a small machine that has a particular purpose or is part of a larger machine: *a waste disposal unit* ◊ *the central processing unit of a computer*

IN TEXTBOOK **8** one of the parts into which a TEXTBOOK or a series of lessons is divided: *The present perfect is covered in Unit 8.*

FLAT/APARTMENT **9** a single flat/apartment in a building that contains a number of them

NUMBER **10** any whole number from 0 to 9: *a column for the tens and a column for the units*

Uni·tar·ian /ˌjuːnɪˈteəriən; *AmE* -ˈter-/ *noun* a member of a Christian Church that does not believe in the TRINITY and has no formal teachings ▶ **Uni·tar·ian** *adj.* **Uni·tar·ian·ism** /-ɪzəm/ *noun* [U]

uni·tary /ˈjuːnətri; *AmE* -teri/ *adj.* **1** (*technical*) (of a country or an organization) consisting of a number of areas or groups that are joined together and are controlled by one government or group: *a single unitary state* ◊ (*BrE*) a **unitary authority** (= a type of local council, introduced in some areas from 1995 to replace existing local governments which consisted of county and district councils) **2** (*formal*) single; forming one unit

unite /juˈnaɪt/ *verb* **1** [V] ~ (**in sth/in doing sth**)| ~ (**behind/against sb/sth**) to join together with other people in order to do sth as a group: *Local resident groups have united in opposition to the plan.* ◊ *We will unite in fighting crime.* ◊ *Will they unite behind the new leader?* ◊ *Nationalist parties united to oppose the government's plans.* **2** ~ (**sb/sth**) (**with sb/sth**) to make people or things join together to form a unit; to join together: [VN] *A special bond unites our two countries.* ◊ *His aim was to unite Italy.* ◊ *She unites keen business skills with a charming personality.* ◊ [V] *The two countries united in 1887.*

united /juˈnaɪtɪd/ *adj.* **1** (of countries) joined together politically or by shared aims: *the United States of America*

◇ *efforts to build a united Europe* **2** (of people or groups) in agreement and working together: *We need to become a more united team.* ◇ *They are united in their opposition to the plan.* ◇ *We should present **a united front** (= an appearance of being in agreement with each other).* **3** used in the names of some teams and companies: *Manchester United* ◇ *United Distillers*

the U·nited 'Kingdom *noun* [sing.] (*abbr.* (**the**) **UK**) England, Scotland, Wales and Northern Ireland

the U·nited 'Nations *noun* [sing.+ sing./pl. *v.*] (*abbr.* (**the**) **UN**) an association of many countries which aims to improve economic and social conditions and to solve political problems in the world in a peaceful way

the U·nited 'States (of A'merica) *noun* [sing.+ sing./pl. *v.*] (*abbr.* (**the**) **US, USA**) a large country in N America consisting of 50 states and the District of Columbia ⇨ note at AMERICAN

unit 'trust (*BrE*) (*AmE* **'mutual fund**) *noun* a company that offers a service to people by investing their money in various different businesses

unity /'juːnəti/ *noun* (*pl.* **-ies**) **1** [U, sing.] the state of being in agreement and working together; the state of being joined together to form one unit: *European unity* ◇ *a plea for unity within the party* ◇ *unity of interest/purpose* OPP DISUNITY **2** [U] (in art, etc.) the state of looking or being complete in a natural and pleasing way: *The design lacks unity.* **3** [C] (in literature and theatre) any of the principles of CLASSICAL or NEOCLASSICAL theatre that restrict the action of a play to a single story, day and place: *the unities of action, time and place* **4** [sing.] (*formal*) a single thing that may consist of a number of different parts: *If society is to exist as a unity, its members must have shared values.*

Univ. *abbr.* (in writing) University

uni·ver·sal /ˌjuːnɪ'vɜːsl; *AmE* -'vɜːrsl/ *adj.* **1** done by or involving all the people in the world or in a particular group: *Such problems are a universal feature of old age.* ◇ *Agreement on this issue is almost universal.* ◇ *universal suffrage* (= the right of all the people in a country to vote) **2** true or right at all times and in all places: *universal facts about human nature* ► **uni·ver·sal·ity** /ˌjuːnɪvɜː'sæləti; *AmE* -vɜːr's-/ *noun*: *the universality of religious experience*

uni·ver·sal·ly /ˌjuːnɪ'vɜːsəli; *AmE* -'vɜːrs-/ *adv.* **1** by everyone: *to be universally accepted/condemned/known/recognized* **2** everywhere or in every situation: *This treatment is not universally available.* ◇ *The theory does not apply universally.*

uni·verse /'juːnɪvɜːs; *AmE* -vɜːrs/ *noun* **1** (**the universe**) [sing.] the whole of space and everything in it, including the earth, the planets and the stars: *theories of how the universe began* **2** [C] a system of stars, planets, etc. in space outside our own: *The idea of a parallel universe is hard to grasp.* ◇ *He lives in a little universe of his own.* **3** [sing.] a set of experiences of a particular type: *the moral universe*

uni·ver·sity /ˌjuːnɪ'vɜːsəti; *AmE* -'vɜːrs-/ *noun* [C, U] (*pl.* **-ies**) (*abbr.* **Univ.**) an institution at the highest level of education where you can study for a degree or do research: *Is there a university in this town?* ◇ *the University of York* ◇ *York University* ◇ (*BrE*) *Both their children are at university.* ◇ (*BrE*) *He's hoping to go to university next year.* ◇ *a university course/degree/lecturer* ⇨ note at COLLEGE

un·just /ˌʌn'dʒʌst/ *adj.* not deserved or fair: *an unjust accusation/law/punishment* ◇ *The system is corrupt and unjust.* OPP JUST ► **un·just·ly** *adv.*: *She felt that she had been unjustly treated.*

un·jus·ti·fi·able /ˌʌn'dʒʌstɪfaɪəbl/ *adj.* (of an action) impossible to excuse or accept because there is no good reason for it: *an unjustifiable delay/expense/remark* OPP JUSTIFIABLE ► **un·jus·ti·fi·ably** /-əbli/ *adv.*

un·jus·ti·fied /ˌʌn'dʒʌstɪfaɪd/ *adj.* not fair or necessary: *The criticism was wholly unjustified.* OPP JUSTIFIED

un·kempt /ˌʌn'kempt/ *adj.* (especially of sb's hair or general appearance) not well cared for; not neat or tidy: *greasy, unkempt hair*

un·kind /ˌʌn'kaɪnd/ *adj.* ~ (**to sb/sth**) (**to do sth**) unpleasant or unfriendly; slightly cruel: *an unkind person/remark* ◇ *He was never actually unkind to them.* ◇ *It would be unkind to go without him.* OPP KIND ► **un·kind·ly** *adv.*: *'That's your problem,' she remarked unkindly.* **un·kind·ness** *noun* [U]

un·know·able /ˌʌn'nəʊəbl; *AmE* -'noʊ-/ *adj.* (*formal*) that cannot be known: *a distant, unknowable divine power*

un·know·ing /ˌʌn'nəʊɪŋ; *AmE* -'noʊ-/ *adj.* [usually before noun] (*formal*) not aware of what you are doing or what is happening: *He was the unknowing cause of all the misunderstanding.*—compare KNOWING ► **un·know·ing·ly** *adv.*: *She had unknowingly broken the rules.*

un·known /ˌʌn'nəʊn; *AmE* -'noʊn/ *adj., noun*
■ *adj.* **1** ~ (**to sb**) not known or identified: *a species of insect previously unknown to science* ◇ *He was trying, for some unknown reason, to count the stars.* ◇ *The man's identity remains unknown.* **2** (of people) not famous or well known: *an unknown actor/artist/writer* ◇ *The author is virtually unknown outside Poland.* **3** never happening or existing: *The disease is as yet unknown in Europe* (= there have been no cases there). ◇ *It was **not unknown for** people to have to wait several hours* (= it happened sometimes). IDM **an ˌunknown 'quantity** a person or thing whose qualities or abilities are not yet known **unknown to sb** without the person mentioned being aware of it: *Unknown to me, he had already signed the agreement.*
■ *noun* **1** (**the unknown**) [sing.] places or things that are not known about: *a journey into the unknown* ◇ *a fear of the unknown* **2** [C] a person who is not well known: *A young unknown played the leading role.* **3** [C] a fact or an influence that is not known: *There are so many unknowns in the proposal.* **4** [C] (*mathematics*) a quantity that does not have a known value: *X and Y in the equation are both unknowns.*

un·lace /ˌʌn'leɪs/ *verb* [VN] to undo the LACES of shoes, clothes, etc.

un·laden /ˌʌn'leɪdn/ *adj.* (*technical*) (of a vehicle) not loaded: *a vehicle with an unladen weight of 3000 kg*—compare LADEN

un·law·ful /ˌʌn'lɔːfl/ *adj.* (*formal*) not allowed by the law SYN ILLEGAL OPP LAWFUL ► **un·law·ful·ly** /-fəli/ *adv.*

un·lead·ed /ˌʌn'ledɪd/ *adj.* (of petrol/gas) not containing LEAD and therefore less harmful to the environment OPP LEADED ► **un·lead·ed** *noun* [U]: *Unleaded is cheaper than diesel.*

un·learn /ˌʌn'lɜːn; *AmE* ˌʌn'lɜːrn/ *verb* [VN] to deliberately forget sth that you have learned, especially sth bad or wrong: *You'll have to unlearn all the bad habits you learned with your last piano teacher.*

un·leash /ˌʌn'liːʃ/ *verb* [VN] ~ **sth (on/upon sb/sth)** to suddenly let a strong force, emotion, etc. be felt or have an effect: *The government's proposals unleashed a storm of protest in the press.*

un·leav·ened /ˌʌn'levnd/ *adj.* (of bread) made without any YEAST and therefore flat and heavy—see also LEAVEN

un·less /ən'les/ *conj.* **1** used to say that sth can only happen or be true in a particular situation: *You won't get paid for time off unless you have a doctor's note.* ◇ *I won't tell them—not unless you say I can.* ◇ *Unless I'm mistaken, she was back at work yesterday.* ◇ *He hasn't got any hobbies—unless you call watching TV a hobby.* **2** used to give the only situation in which sth will not happen or be true: *I sleep with the window open unless it's really cold.* ◇ *Unless something unexpected happens, I'll see you tomorrow.* ◇ *Have a cup of tea—unless you'd prefer a cold drink?* HELP **Unless** is used to talk about a situation that could happen, or something that could be true, in the future. If you know that something has not happened or that sth is not true, use **if…not**: *If you weren't always in such a hurry* (= but you are), *your work would be much better.* ◇ ~~Your work would be much better unless you were always in such a hurry.~~

un·licensed /ˌʌn'laɪsnst/ *adj.* without a LICENCE (= an official document that gives you permission to do or own sth): *an unlicensed pistol/vehicle* OPP LICENSED

un·like /ˌʌn'laɪk/ *prep., adj.*

■ *prep.* **1** different from a particular person or thing: *Music is quite unlike any other art form.* ◊ (*written*) *The sound was not unlike that of birds singing.* **2** used to contrast sb/sth with another person or thing: *Unlike most systems, this one is very easy to install.* **3** not typical of sb/sth: *It's very unlike him to be so late.* OPP LIKE

■ *adj.* [not before noun] (*written*) (of two people or things) different from each other: *They are both teachers. Otherwise they are quite unlike.*—compare ALIKE, LIKE

un·like·ly /ʌnˈlaɪkli/ *adj.* (**un·like·li·er**, **un·likeli·est**) HELP more unlikely and most unlikely are the usual forms **1** ~ (**to do sth**)| ~ (**that…**) not likely to happen; not probable: *The project seemed unlikely to succeed.* ◊ *It's most* (= very) *unlikely that she'll arrive before seven.* ◊ *In the unlikely event of a problem arising, please contact the hotel manager.* **2** [only before noun] not the person, thing or place that you would normally think of or expect: *He seems a most unlikely candidate for the job.* ◊ *They have built hotels in the most unlikely places.* **3** [only before noun] difficult to believe: *She gave me an unlikely explanation for her behaviour.* OPP LIKELY ► **un·like·li·hood** /ʌnˈlaɪklihʊd/, **un·like·li·ness** /-nəs/ *noun* [U]

un·lim·it·ed /ʌnˈlɪmɪtɪd/ *adj.* as much or as many as is possible; not limited in any way: *The ticket gives you unlimited travel for seven days.* ◊ *The court has the power to impose an unlimited fine for this offence.* ◊ *You will be allowed unlimited access to the files.*

un·lined /ʌnˈlaɪnd/ *adj.* **1** not marked with lines: *unlined paper/skin* **2** (of a piece of clothing, etc.) made without an extra layer of fabric on the inside: *an unlined skirt* OPP LINED

un·list·ed /ʌnˈlɪstɪd/ *adj.* **1** not on a published list, especially of STOCK EXCHANGE prices: *an unlisted company* **2** (of a telephone number) not listed in the public telephone book, at the request of the owner of the telephone. The telephone company will not give unlisted numbers to people who ask for them.—see also EX-DIRECTORY

unlit /ʌnˈlɪt/ *adj.* **1** dark because there are no lights or the lights are not switched on: *an unlit passage* **2** not yet burning: *an unlit cigarette* OPP LIGHTED

un·load /ʌnˈləʊd; *AmE* ʌnˈloʊd/ *verb* **1** ~ **sth (from sth)** to remove things from a vehicle or ship after it has taken them somewhere: [VN] *Everyone helped to unload the luggage from the car.* ◊ *This isn't a suitable place to unload the van.* ◊ [V] *The truck driver was waiting to unload.* OPP LOAD **2** [VN] to remove the contents of sth after you have finished using it, especially the bullets from a gun or the film from a camera OPP LOAD **3** [VN] ~ **sth/sb (on/onto sb)** (*informal*) to pass the responsibility for sb/sth to sb else: *It's his problem, not something he should unload onto you.* **4** [VN] ~ **sth (on/onto sb/sth)** (*informal*) to get rid of or sell sth, especially sth illegal or of bad quality: *They want to unload their shares at the right price.*

un·lock /ʌnˈlɒk; *AmE* ʌnˈlɑːk/ *verb* [VN] **1** to undo the lock of a door, window, etc., using a key: *to unlock the front door* OPP LOCK **2** to discover sth and let it come out: *The divers hoped to unlock some of the secrets of the sea bed.*

un·locked /ʌnˈlɒkt; *AmE* ʌnˈlɑːkt/ *adj.* not locked: *Don't leave your desk unlocked.*

unlooked-for /ʌnˈlʊkt ˌfɔː(r)/ *adj.* (*formal*) not expected: *unlooked-for developments/happiness*

un·loose /ʌnˈluːs/ (also **un·loosen** /ʌnˈluːsn/) *verb* [VN] (*old-fashioned* or *formal*) to make sth loose: *He unloosed his tie.*

un·loved /ʌnˈlʌvd/ *adj.* (*formal*) not loved by anyone: *unloved children*

un·love·ly /ʌnˈlʌvli/ *adj.* (*written*) not attractive: *an unlovely building*

un·luck·ily /ʌnˈlʌkɪli/ *adv.* unfortunately; as a result of bad luck: *He was injured in the first game and unluckily missed the final.* OPP LUCKILY

un·lucky /ʌnˈlʌki/ *adj.* (**un·luck·ier**, **un·lucki·est**) HELP You can also use more unlucky and most unlucky. **1** ~ (**to do sth**) having bad luck or happening because of bad luck; not lucky: *He was very unlucky not to win.* ◊ *By some unlucky chance, her name was left off the list.* **2** ~ (**to do sth**) causing bad luck: *Some people think it's unlucky to*

walk under a ladder. ◊ *Thirteen is often considered an unlucky number.* OPP LUCKY

un·made /ˌʌnˈmeɪd/ *adj.* **1** an **unmade** bed is not ready for sleeping in because the sheets, etc. have not been arranged neatly **2** (*BrE*) an **unmade** road does not have a hard smooth surface

un·man·age·able /ʌnˈmænɪdʒəbl/ *adj.* difficult or impossible to control or deal with: *The costs involved had become unmanageable.* OPP MANAGEABLE

un·man·ly /ʌnˈmænli/ *adj.* (*rare, formal*) not having the qualities that are admired or expected in a man OPP MANLY

un·manned /ˌʌnˈmænd/ *adj.* if a machine, vehicle or place is **unmanned**, it does not have or need a person to control or operate it: *an unmanned spacecraft/station*

un·marked /ʌnˈmɑːkt; *AmE* ʌnˈmɑːrkt/ *adj.* without a sign or words to show what or where sth is: *an unmarked police car* ◊ *He was buried in an unmarked grave.*—compare MARKED

un·mar·ried /ˌʌnˈmærid/ *adj.* not married SYN SINGLE: *an unmarried mother* ◊ *He remained unmarried all his life.*

un·mask /ʌnˈmɑːsk; *AmE* ʌnˈmæsk/ *verb* [VN] to show the true character of sb, or a hidden truth about sth SYN EXPOSE: *to unmask a killer/spy*

un·matched /ʌnˈmætʃt/ *adj.* ~ (**by sb/sth**) (*written*) better than all others: *He had a talent unmatched by any other politician of this century.*

un·mem·or·able /ʌnˈmemərəbl/ *adj.* that cannot be remembered because it was not special OPP MEMORABLE

un·men·tion·able /ʌnˈmenʃənəbl/ *adj.* [usually before noun] too shocking or embarrassing to be mentioned or spoken about: *an unmentionable disease/subject*

unmet /ˌʌnˈmet/ *adj.* (*written*) (of needs, etc.) not satisfied: *a report on the unmet needs of elderly people*

un·mind·ful /ʌnˈmaɪndfl/ *adj.* ~ **of sb/sth** (*rare, formal*) not giving thought or attention to sb/sth OPP MINDFUL

un·miss·able /ʌnˈmɪsəbl/ *adj.* that you must not miss because it is so good: *an unmissable opportunity*

un·mis·tak·able (also *less frequent* **un·mis·take·able**) /ˌʌnmɪˈsteɪkəbl/ *adj.* that cannot be MISTAKEN for sb/sth else: *Her accent was unmistakable.* ◊ *the unmistakable sound of gunfire* ► **un·mis·tak·ably** (also *less frequent* **un·mis·take·ably**) /-əbli/ *adv.*: *His accent was unmistakably British.*

un·miti·gated /ʌnˈmɪtɪɡeɪtɪd/ *adj.* [only before noun] used to mean 'complete', usually when describing sth bad: *The evening was an unmitigated disaster.*—see also MITIGATE

un·mol·est·ed /ˌʌnməˈlestɪd/ *adj.* [not usually before noun] (*written*) not disturbed or attacked by sb; not prevented from doing sth: *They allowed him to leave unmolested.*

un·moved /ʌnˈmuːvd/ *adj.* ~ (**by sth**) not feeling pity or sympathy, especially in a situation where it would be normal to do so: *Alice seemed totally unmoved by the whole experience.* ◊ *She pleaded with him but he remained unmoved.*

un·mov·ing /ʌnˈmuːvɪŋ/ *adj.* (*written*) not moving: *He stood, unmoving, in the shadows.*

un·music·al /ˌʌnˈmjuːzɪkl/ *adj.* **1** (of a sound) unpleasant to listen to: *His voice was harsh and unmusical.* **2** (of a person) unable to play or enjoy music OPP MUSICAL

un·named /ˌʌnˈneɪmd/ *adj.* whose name is not given or not known: *information from an unnamed source* ◊ *Two casualties, as yet unnamed, were still in the local hospital last night.*

un·nat·ural /ʌnˈnætʃrəl/ *adj.* **1** different from what is normal or expected, or from what is generally accepted as being right: *It seems unnatural for a child to spend so much time alone.* ◊ *There was an unnatural silence and then a scream.* ◊ *unnatural sexual practices* ◊ *He gave an unnatural smile* (= that did not seem genuine). **2** different from anything in nature: *Her leg was bent at an unnatural angle.* ◊ *an unnatural death* (= one not from natural causes) OPP NATURAL ► **un·nat·ur·al·ly** /-rəli/ *adv.*: *She*

æ	ɑː	e	ɜː	ə	ɪ	iː	i	ɒ	ɔː	ʌ	ʊ	u	uː
cat	father	ten	bird	about	sit	see	many	got	saw	cup	put	actual	too
								(BrE)					

*was, not **unnaturally**, very surprised at the news.* ◊ *His eyes were unnaturally bright.*

un·neces·sary /ʌnˈnesəsəri; *AmE* -seri/ *adj.* **1** not needed; more than is needed: *unnecessary expense/risks/delays* ◊ *They were found guilty of causing unnecessary suffering to animals.* ◊ *All this fuss is totally unnecessary.* OPP NECESSARY **2** (of remarks, etc.) not necessary in the situation and likely to be offensive: *That last comment was a little unnecessary, wasn't it?* ► **un·neces·sar·ily** /ʌnˈnesəsərəli; *AmE* ˌʌnˌnesəˈserəli/ *adv.*: *There's no point worrying him unnecessarily.* ◊ *unnecessarily complicated instructions*

un·nerve /ʌnˈnɜːv; *AmE* ʌnˈnɜːrv/ *verb* [VN] to make sb feel nervous or frightened or lose confidence: *His silence unnerved us.* ► **un·nerv·ing** *adj.*: *an unnerving experience* **un·nerv·ing·ly** *adv.*

un·noticed /ʌnˈnəʊtɪst; *AmE* -ˈnoʊ-/ *adj.* [not before noun] not seen or noticed: *His kindness did not go unnoticed by his staff.* ◊ *Her death passed almost unnoticed.*

un·num·bered /ʌnˈnʌmbəd; *AmE* -bərd/ *adj.* not marked with a number; not NUMBERED: *unnumbered seats*

un·ob·jec·tion·able /ˌʌnəbˈdʒekʃənəbl/ *adj.* (formal) (of an idea, etc.) that you can accept

un·ob·served /ˌʌnəbˈzɜːvd; *AmE* -ˈzɜːrvd/ *adj.* without being seen: *It's not easy for somebody to get into the building unobserved.*

un·ob·tain·able /ˌʌnəbˈteɪnəbl/ *adj.* [not usually before noun] that cannot be obtained OPP OBTAINABLE

un·ob·tru·sive /ˌʌnəbˈtruːsɪv/ *adj.* (formal, often approving) not attracting unnecessary attention: *The service at the hotel is efficient and unobtrusive.* OPP OBTRUSIVE ► **un·ob·tru·sive·ly** *adv.*: *Dora slipped unobtrusively in through the back door.*

un·occu·pied /ˌʌnˈɒkjupaɪd; *AmE* -ˈɑːk-/ *adj.* **1** empty, with nobody living there or using it: *an unoccupied house* ◊ *I sat down at the nearest unoccupied table.* **2** (of a region or country) not controlled by foreign soldiers: *unoccupied territory* OPP OCCUPIED

un·offi·cial /ˌʌnəˈfɪʃl/ *adj.* **1** that does not have permission or approval from sb in authority: *an unofficial agreement/strike* ◊ *Unofficial estimates put the figure at over 2 million.* **2** that is not part of sb's official business: *The former president paid an unofficial visit to China.* OPP OFFICIAL ► **un·offi·cial·ly** /-ʃəli/ *adv.*

un·opposed /ˌʌnəˈpəʊzd; *AmE* -ˈpoʊzd/ *adj.* [not usually before noun] not opposed or stopped by anyone: *The party leader was re-elected unopposed.*

un·organ·ized (*BrE* also **-ised**) /ʌnˈɔːɡənaɪzd; *AmE* -ˈɔːrɡ-/ *adj.* **1** (of workers) without a trade union or other organization to represent or support them **2** (rare) = DISORGANIZED **3** not having been organized: *unorganized data*—compare ORGANIZED

un·ortho·dox /ʌnˈɔːθədɒks; *AmE* ʌnˈɔːrθədɑːks/ *adj.* different from what is usual or accepted: *unorthodox behaviour/methods* OPP ORTHODOX—compare HETERODOX

un·pack /ʌnˈpæk/ *verb* **1** to take things out of a suitcase, bag, etc: [VN] *I unpacked my bags as soon as I arrived.* ◊ *She unpacked all the clothes she needed and left the rest in the case.* ◊ [V] *She went to her room to unpack.* OPP PACK **2** [VN] to separate sth into parts so that it is easier to understand: *to unpack a theory/proposition/problem*

un·paid /ʌnˈpeɪd/ *adj.* **1** not yet paid: *unpaid bills/debts/fees/rent* **2** done or taken without payment: *unpaid domestic work* ◊ *to take unpaid leave* OPP PAID **3** (of people) not receiving payment for work that they do: *unpaid volunteers* OPP PAID

un·pal·at·able /ʌnˈpælətəbl/ *adj.* ~ (to sb) **1** (of facts, ideas, etc.) unpleasant and not easy to accept: *Only then did I learn the unpalatable truth.* **2** not pleasant to taste: *unpalatable food* OPP PALATABLE

un·par·al·leled /ʌnˈpærəleld/ *adj.* (formal) used to emphasize that sth is bigger, better or worse than anything else like it: *It was an unparalleled opportunity to develop her career.* ◊ *The book has enjoyed a success unparalleled in recent publishing history.*—compare PARALLEL *v.*

un·par·don·able /ʌnˈpɑːdnəbl; *AmE* -ˈpɑːrd-/ *adj.* (written) that cannot be forgiven or excused SYN UNFORGIVABLE, INEXCUSABLE OPP PARDONABLE

un·par·lia·men·tary /ˌʌnˌpɑːləˈmentri; *AmE* -ˌpɑːrl-/ *adj.* against the accepted rules of behaviour in a parliament: *unparliamentary language*

un·pat·ri·ot·ic /ˌʌnˌpætriˈɒtɪk; *AmE* -ˌpeɪtriˈɑːt-/ *adj.* not supporting your own country OPP PATRIOTIC

un·per·turbed /ˌʌnpəˈtɜːbd; *AmE* ˌʌnpərˈtɜːrbd/ *adj.* not worried or anxious: *She seemed unperturbed by the news.* OPP PERTURBED

un·pick /ˌʌnˈpɪk/ *verb* [VN] to take out stitches from a piece of sewing or knitting

un·placed /ˌʌnˈpleɪst/ *adj.* (BrE) not one of the first three to finish in a race or competition

un·planned /ˌʌnˈplænd/ *adj.* not planned in advance: *an unplanned pregnancy*

un·play·able /ˌʌnˈpleɪəbl/ *adj.* (especially BrE) not able to be played; impossible to play on or with: *The ball was unplayable* (= it was hit so well that it was impossible to hit it back).—compare PLAYABLE

un·pleas·ant /ʌnˈpleznt/ *adj.* **1** not pleasant or comfortable: *an unpleasant atmosphere/experience/feeling/smell* ◊ *The minerals in the water made it unpleasant to drink.* **2** ~ (to sb) not kind, friendly or polite: *He was very unpleasant to me.* ◊ *She said some very unpleasant things about you.* OPP PLEASANT ► **un·pleas·ant·ly** *adv.*: *The drink is very sweet, but not unpleasantly so.* ◊ *He laughed unpleasantly.*

un·pleas·ant·ness /ʌnˈplezntnəs/ *noun* [U] bad feeling or arguments between people

un·plug /ˌʌnˈplʌɡ/ *verb* (-gg-) [VN] to remove the PLUG of a piece of electrical equipment from the electricity supply: *If I'm very busy, I unplug the phone.* OPP PLUG STH IN

un·pol·luted /ˌʌnpəˈluːtɪd/ *adj.* that has not been POLLUTED (= made dirty by harmful substances)

un·popu·lar /ʌnˈpɒpjələ(r); *AmE* -ˈpɑːp-/ *adj.* ~ (with/among sb) not liked or enjoyed by a person, a group or people in general: *an unpopular choice/decision/leader/government* ◊ *The proposed increase in income tax proved deeply unpopular with the electorate.* OPP POPULAR ► **un·popu·lar·ity** /ˌʌnˌpɒpjuˈlærəti; *AmE* -ˌpɑːp-/ *noun* [U]: *the growing unpopularity of the military regime*

un·pre·ced·ent·ed /ʌnˈpresɪdentɪd/ *adj.* that has never happened, been done or been known before: *unprecedented levels of unemployment* ◊ *The situation is unprecedented in modern times.* ► **un·pre·ced·ent·ed·ly** *adv.*: *a period of unprecedentedly high food prices*

un·pre·dict·able /ˌʌnprɪˈdɪktəbl/ *adj.* **1** that cannot be predicted because it changes a lot or depends on too many different things: *unpredictable weather* ◊ *The result is entirely unpredictable.* **2** if a person is unpredictable, you cannot predict how they will behave in a particular situation OPP PREDICTABLE ► **un·pre·dict·abil·ity** /ˌʌnprɪˌdɪktəˈbɪləti/ *noun* [U]: *the unpredictability of the English weather* **un·pre·dict·ably** *adv.*

un·pre·ju·diced /ʌnˈpredʒədɪst/ *adj.* not influenced by an unreasonable fear or dislike of sth/sb; willing to consider different ideas and opinions OPP PREJUDICED

un·pre·medi·tated /ˌʌnpriːˈmedɪteɪtɪd/ *adj.* (written) (of a crime or bad action) not planned in advance OPP PREMEDITATED

un·pre·pared /ˌʌnprɪˈpeəd; *AmE* -ˈperd/ *adj.* **1** ~ (for sth) not ready or not expecting sth: *She was totally unprepared for his response.* **2** ~ (to do sth) (formal) not willing to do sth: *She was unprepared to accept that her marriage was over.* OPP PREPARED

un·pre·pos·sess·ing /ˌʌnˌpriːpəˈzesɪŋ/ *adj.* (formal) not attractive; not making a good or strong impression—compare PREPOSSESSING

un·pre·ten·tious /ˌʌnprɪˈtenʃəs/ *adj.* (approving) not trying to appear more special, intelligent, important, etc. than you really are OPP PRETENTIOUS

un·prin·cipled /ʌnˈprɪnsəpld/ *adj.* without moral principles SYN DISHONEST OPP PRINCIPLED

un·print·able /ʌnˈprɪntəbl/ *adj.* (of words or comments) too offensive or shocking to be printed and read by people OPP PRINTABLE

un·prob·lem·at·ic /ˌʌnˌprɒbləˈmætɪk; *AmE* -ˌprɑ:b-/ (also *less frequent* **un·prob·lem·at·ic·al** /-ɪkl/) *adj.* not having or causing problems OPP PROBLEMATIC ▶ **un·prob·lem·at·ic·al·ly** /-kli/ *adv.*

un·pro·duct·ive /ˌʌnprəˈdʌktɪv/ *adj.* not producing very much; not producing good results: *an unproductive discussion/meeting ◊ I've had a very unproductive day.* OPP PRODUCTIVE ▶ **un·pro·duct·ive·ly** *adv.*

un·pro·fes·sion·al /ˌʌnprəˈfeʃənl/ *adj.* not reaching the standard expected in a particular profession: *She was found guilty of unprofessional conduct.* OPP PROFESSIONAL—compare NON-PROFESSIONAL ▶ **un·pro·fes·sion·al·ly** /-ʃənəli/ *adv.*

un·prof·it·able /ʌnˈprɒfɪtəbl/ *AmE* -ˈprɑ:f-/ *adj.* **1** not making enough financial profit: *unprofitable companies/products/services* **2** (*formal*) not bringing any advantage OPP PROFITABLE ▶ **un·prof·it·ably** /-əbli/ *adv.*

un·prom·is·ing /ʌnˈprɒmɪsɪŋ/ *AmE* -ˈprɑ:m-/ *adj.* not likely to be successful or show good results: *The first attempt was unpromising.* OPP PROMISING

un·prompt·ed /ʌnˈprɒmptɪd/ *AmE* -ˈprɑ:m-/ *adj.* said or done without sb asking you to say or do it: *Quite unprompted, Sam started telling us exactly what had happened that night.*—see also PROMPT

un·pro·nounce·able /ˌʌnprəˈnaʊnsəbl/ *adj.* (of a word, especially a name) too difficult to pronounce OPP PRONOUNCEABLE

un·pro·tect·ed /ˌʌnprəˈtektɪd/ *adj.* **1** not protected against being hurt or damaged **2** not covered to prevent it from causing damage or injury: *Machinery was often unprotected and accidents were frequent.* **3** (of sex) done without using a CONDOM

un·proven /ʌnˈpru:vn/ *adj.* not proved or tested: *unproven theories*—compare PROVEN

un·pro·voked /ˌʌnprəˈvəʊkt/ *AmE* -ˈvoʊkt/ *adj.* (especially of an attack) not caused by anything the person being attacked has said or done: *an act of unprovoked aggression ◊ Her angry outburst was totally unprovoked.*—see also PROVOKE

un·pub·lished /ʌnˈpʌblɪʃt/ *adj.* not published: *unpublished data/material*

un·pun·ished /ʌnˈpʌnɪʃt/ *adj.* (*written*) not punished: *He promised that the murder would not go unpunished.*

un·quali·fied /ʌnˈkwɒlɪfaɪd/ *AmE* -ˈkwɑ:l-/ *adj.* **1** ~ (**to do sth**)| ~ (**for sth**) not having the right knowledge, experience or qualifications to do sth: *an unqualified instructor ◊ I feel unqualified to comment on the subject. ◊ He was totally unqualified for his job as a senior manager.* **2** /ʌnˈkwɒlɪfaɪd/ [usually before noun] complete; not limited by any negative qualities: *The event was not an unqualified success. ◊ I gave her my unqualified support.* OPP QUALIFIED

un·quench·able /ʌnˈkwentʃəbl/ *adj.* (*formal*) that cannot be satisfied—see also QUENCH

un·ques·tion·able /ʌnˈkwestʃənəbl/ *adj.* that cannot be doubted: *a man of unquestionable honesty and integrity* OPP QUESTIONABLE ▶ **un·ques·tion·ably** /-əbli/ *adv.*: *It was unquestionably a step in the right direction.*

un·ques·tioned /ʌnˈkwestʃənd/ *adj.* (*formal*) **1** so obvious that it cannot be doubted: *His courage remains unquestioned.* **2** accepted as right or true without really being considered: *an unquestioned assumption*

un·ques·tion·ing /ʌnˈkwestʃənɪŋ/ *adj.* (*formal*) done or given without asking questions, expressing doubt, etc: *unquestioning acceptance/obedience/support* ▶ **un·ques·tion·ing·ly** *adv.*

un·quiet /ʌnˈkwaɪət/ *adj.* [usually before noun] (*literary*) not calm; anxious or RESTLESS

un·quote /ˈʌnkwəʊt; *AmE* ˈʌnkwoʊt/ *noun* IDM see QUOTE

un·ravel /ʌnˈrævl/ *verb* (-**ll-**, *AmE* -**l-**) **1** if you **unravel** threads that are twisted, woven or knitted, or if they **unravel**, they become separated into loose threads: [VN] *I unravelled the string and wound it into a ball.* [also V] **2** [V] (of a system, plan, relationship, etc.) to start to fail or no

longer stay together as a whole: *When did communism begin to unravel in Eastern Europe?* **3** to explain sth that is difficult to understand or is mysterious; to become clearer or easier to understand: [VN] *The discovery will help scientists unravel the mystery of the Ice Age.* [also V]

un·read /ˌʌnˈred/ *adj.* (of a book, etc.) that has not been read: *a pile of unread newspapers*

un·read·able /ʌnˈri:dəbl/ *adj.* **1** (of a book, etc.) too dull or difficult to be worth reading **2** = ILLEGIBLE **3** if sb's face or expression is **unreadable**, you cannot tell what they are thinking or feeling

un·real /ˌʌnˈrɪəl; *AmE* ˌʌnˈri:əl/ *adj.* **1** so strange that it is more like a dream than reality: *The party began to take on an unreal, almost nightmarish quality.* **2** not related to reality: *Many people have unreal expectations of what marriage will be like.* **3** (*spoken*) used to say that you like sth very much or that sth surprises you: *'That's unreal!' she laughed.* ▶ **un·real·ity** /ˌʌnriˈæləti/ *noun* [U]

un·real·is·tic /ˌʌnrɪəˈlɪstɪk/ *AmE* -riːə-/ *adj.* not showing or accepting things as they are: *unrealistic expectations ◊ It is unrealistic to expect them to be able to solve the problem immediately.* OPP REALISTIC ▶ **un·real·is·tic·al·ly** *adv.*: *These prices are unrealistically high.*

un·rea·son·able /ʌnˈri:znəbl/ *adj.* not fair; expecting too much: *The job was beginning to make unreasonable demands on his free time. ◊ The fees they charge are not unreasonable. ◊ It would be unreasonable to expect somebody to come at such short notice. ◊ He was being totally unreasonable about it.* OPP REASONABLE ▶ **un·rea·son·able·ness** *noun* [U] **un·rea·son·ably** /-əbli/ *adv.*

un·rea·son·ing /ʌnˈri:zənɪŋ/ *adj.* [usually before noun] (*formal*) not based on facts or reason: *unreasoning fear/hatred*

un·rec·og·niz·able (*BrE* also **-is·able**) /ˌʌnrekəɡˈnaɪzəbl/ *adj.* (of a person or thing) so changed or damaged that you do not recognize them or it: *He was unrecognizable without his beard.* OPP RECOGNIZABLE

un·rec·og·nized (*BrE* also **-ised**) /ʌnˈrekəɡnaɪzd/ *adj.* **1** that people are not aware of or do not realize is important: *The problem of ageism in the workplace often goes unrecognized.* **2** (of a person) not having received the admiration they deserve for sth that they have done or achieved

un·re·con·struct·ed /ˌʌnri:kənˈstrʌktɪd/ *adj.* [only before noun] (*disapproving*) (of people and their beliefs) not having changed, although the situation they are in has changed

un·re·cord·ed /ˌʌnrɪˈkɔ:dɪd; *AmE* -ˈkɔ:rd-/ *adj.* not written down or recorded: *Many crimes go unrecorded.*

un·re·fined /ˌʌnrɪˈfaɪnd/ *adj.* **1** (of a substance) not separated from the other substances that it is combined with in its natural form: *unrefined sugar/oil* **2** (of a person or their behaviour) not polite or educated OPP REFINED

un·re·lated /ˌʌnrɪˈleɪtɪd/ *adj.* **1** not connected; not related to sth else: *The two events were totally unrelated.* **2** (of people, animals, etc.) not belonging to the same family; not related OPP RELATED

un·re·lent·ing /ˌʌnrɪˈlentɪŋ/ *adj.* (*written*) **1** (of an unpleasant situation) not stopping or becoming less severe SYN RELENTLESS: *unrelenting criticism/pressure ◊ The heat was unrelenting.* **2** if a person is **unrelenting**, they continue with sth without considering the feelings of other people SYN RELENTLESS: *He was unrelenting in his search for the truth about his father.* ▶ **un·re·lent·ing·ly** *adv.*

un·re·li·able /ˌʌnrɪˈlaɪəbl/ *adj.* that cannot be trusted or depended on: *The trains are notoriously unreliable. ◊ He's totally unreliable as a source of information.* OPP RELIABLE ▶ **un·re·li·abil·ity** /ˌʌnrɪˌlaɪəˈbɪləti/ *noun* [U]: *the unreliability of some statistics*

un·re·lieved /ˌʌnrɪˈliːvd/ *adj.* (*written*) (of an unpleasant situation) continuing without changing: *unrelieved gloom*

un·re·mark·able /ˌʌnrɪˈmɑːkəbl; *AmE* -ˈmɑːrk-/ *adj.* ordinary; not special or REMARKABLE in any way: *an unremarkable life/building*

un·re·marked /ˌʌnrɪˈmɑːkt; AmE -ˈmɑːrkt/ adj. [not usually before noun] (formal) not noticed: *His absence went unremarked.*

un·re·mit·ting /ˌʌnrɪˈmɪtɪŋ/ adj. (formal) never stopping: *unremitting hostility* ▶ **un·re·mit·ting·ly** adv.: *unremittingly gloomy weather*

un·re·peat·able /ˌʌnrɪˈpiːtəbl/ adj. **1** too offensive or shocking to be repeated **2** that cannot be repeated or done again: *an unrepeatable experience/event* OPP REPEATABLE

un·re·pent·ant /ˌʌnrɪˈpentənt/ adj. showing no shame about your actions or beliefs OPP REPENTANT ▶ **un·re·pent·ant·ly** adv.

un·rep·re·sen·ta·tive /ˌʌnˌreprɪˈzentətɪv/ adj. ~ (of sb/sth) not typical of a group of people or things and therefore not useful as a source of information about that group: *an unrepresentative sample* OPP REPRESENTATIVE

un·re·quit·ed /ˌʌnrɪˈkwaɪtɪd/ adj. (formal) (of love) not returned by the person that you love—compare REQUITE

un·re·served /ˌʌnrɪˈzɜːvd; AmE -ˈzɜːrvd/ adj. **1** (of seats in a theatre, etc.) not paid for in advance; not kept for the use of a particular person **2** (formal) complete and without any doubts: *He offered us his unreserved apologies.*

un·re·served·ly /ˌʌnrɪˈzɜːvɪdli; AmE -ˈzɜːrv-/ adv. completely; without hesitating or having any doubts: *We apologize unreservedly for any offence caused by his remarks.*

un·re·solved /ˌʌnrɪˈzɒlvd; AmE -ˈzɑːlvd/ adj. (formal) (of a problem or question) not yet solved or answered; not having been RESOLVED

un·re·spon·sive /ˌʌnrɪˈspɒnsɪv; AmE -ˈspɑːn-/ adj. ~ (to sth) (formal) not reacting to sb/sth; not giving the response that you would expect or hope for: *a politician who is unresponsive to the mood of the country* OPP RESPONSIVE

un·rest /ʌnˈrest/ noun [U] a political situation in which people are angry and likely to protest or fight: *industrial/civil/social/political/popular unrest* ◇ *There is growing unrest in the south of the country.*

un·re·strained /ˌʌnrɪˈstreɪnd/ adj. (written) not controlled; not having been RESTRAINED: *unrestrained aggression/delight*

un·re·strict·ed /ˌʌnrɪˈstrɪktɪd/ adj. not controlled or limited in any way SYN UNLIMITED: *We have unrestricted access to all the facilities.* OPP RESTRICTED

un·re·ward·ed /ˌʌnrɪˈwɔːdɪd; AmE -ˈwɔːrd-/ adj. not receiving the success that you are trying to achieve: *Real talent often goes unrewarded.*

un·re·ward·ing /ˌʌnrɪˈwɔːdɪŋ; AmE -ˈwɔːrd-/ adj. (of an activity, etc.) not bringing feelings of satisfaction or achievement OPP REWARDING

un·ripe /ˌʌnˈraɪp/ adj. not yet ripe: *unripe fruit* OPP RIPE

un·rivalled (especially BrE) (AmE usually **un·rivaled**) /ʌnˈraɪvld/ adj. (formal) better or greater than any other SYN UNSURPASSED

un·roll /ʌnˈrəʊl; AmE ʌnˈroʊl/ verb **1** if you **unroll** paper, fabric, etc. that was in a roll or if it **unrolls**, it opens and becomes flat: [VN] *We unrolled our sleeping bags.* [also V] —compare ROLL **2** [V] (of events) to happen one after another in a series: *We watched the events unroll before the cameras.*

un·ruf·fled /ʌnˈrʌfld/ adj. (of a person) calm SYN UNPERTURBED: *He remained unruffled by their accusations.*

un·ruly /ʌnˈruːli/ adj. difficult to control or manage: *an unruly crowd/child* ◇ *unruly behaviour* ◇ *unruly hair* (= difficult to keep looking neat) ▶ **un·ru·li·ness** noun [U]

un·sad·dle /ʌnˈsædl/ verb **1** [VN, V] to take the saddle off a horse **2** [VN] to throw a rider off SYN UNSEAT

un·safe /ʌnˈseɪf/ adj. **1** (of a thing, a place or an activity) not safe; dangerous: *The roof was declared unsafe.* ◇ *It was considered unsafe to release the prisoners.* ◇ *unsafe sex* (= for example, sex without a CONDOM) **2** (of people) in danger of being harmed: *He felt unsafe and alone.* **3** (law) (of a decision in a court of law) based on evidence that may be false or is not good enough: *Their convictions were declared unsafe.* OPP SAFE

un·said /ʌnˈsed/ adj. [not before noun] thought but not spoken: *Some things are better left unsaid.*

un·sale·able (also **un·sal·able**) /ʌnˈseɪləbl/ adj. that cannot be sold, because it is not good enough or because nobody wants to buy it OPP SALEABLE

un·sani·tary /ʌnˈsænətri; AmE -teri/ adj. (especially AmE) = INSANITARY

un·sat·is·fac·tory /ˌʌnˌsætɪsˈfæktəri/ adj. not satisfactory; not good enough SYN INADEQUATE, UNACCEPTABLE ▶ **un·sat·is·fac·tor·ily** /-tərəli/ adv.

un·sat·is·fied /ʌnˈsætɪsfaɪd/ adj. **1** (of a need, demand, etc.) not dealt with in a satisfactory way **2** (of a person) not having got what you hoped; not having had enough of sth: *The novel had interested him, but left him unsatisfied.*—compare DISSATISFIED, SATISFIED

un·sat·ur·ated /ʌnˈsætʃəreɪtɪd/ adj. (chemistry) unsaturated fats are easily dealt with by the body when eaten, because of the way their chemical structure is arranged: *soft spread with a high percentage of unsaturated fats*—compare POLYUNSATURATED, SATURATED

un·savoury (BrE) (AmE **un·savory**) /ʌnˈseɪvəri/ adj. unpleasant or offensive; not considered morally acceptable: *an unsavoury incident/reputation* ◇ *Her friends are all pretty unsavoury characters.*

un·scathed /ʌnˈskeɪðd/ adj. [not before noun] not hurt SYN UNHARMED: *The hostages emerged from their ordeal unscathed.*

un·sched·uled /ʌnˈʃedjuːld; AmE ʌnˈskedʒuːld/ adj. that was not planned in advance: *an unscheduled stop/visit*

un·sci·en·tif·ic /ˌʌnˌsaɪənˈtɪfɪk/ adj. (often disapproving) not scientific; not done in a careful, logical way: *an unscientific approach to a problem*—compare NON-SCIENTIFIC

un·scram·ble /ˌʌnˈskræmbl/ verb [VN] **1** to change a word, message, television signal, etc. that has been sent in a CODE (= a secret form) so that it can be read or understood OPP SCRAMBLE **2** to arrange sth that is confused or in the wrong order in a clear, correct way

un·screw /ˌʌnˈskruː/ verb [VN] **1** to undo sth by twisting or turning it; to become undone in this way: [VN] *I can't unscrew the lid of this jar.* [also V] OPP SCREW STH UP **2** to take the screws out of sth: *You'll have to unscrew the handles to paint the door.*

un·script·ed /ʌnˈskrɪptɪd/ adj. (of a speech, broadcast, etc.) not written or prepared in detail in advance OPP SCRIPTED

un·scru·pu·lous /ʌnˈskruːpjələs/ adj. without moral principles; not honest or fair SYN UNPRINCIPLED: *unscrupulous methods/treatment* OPP SCRUPULOUS ▶ **un·scru·pu·lous·ly** adv. **un·scru·pu·lous·ness** noun [U]

un·sea·son·able /ʌnˈsiːznəbl/ adj. unusual for the time of year: *unseasonable weather* OPP SEASONABLE ▶ **un·sea·son·ably** /-əbli/ adv.: *unseasonably warm*

un·sea·son·al /ʌnˈsiːzənl/ adj. not typical of or not suitable for the time of year: *unseasonal weather* OPP SEASONAL

un·seat /ˌʌnˈsiːt/ verb [VN] **1** to remove sb from a position of power **2** to make sb fall off a horse or bicycle: *The horse unseated its rider at the first fence.*

un·seed·ed /ʌnˈsiːdɪd/ adj. not chosen as a SEED in a sports competition, especially in tennis: *unseeded players* OPP SEEDED

un·see·ing /ˌʌnˈsiːɪŋ/ adj. (literary) not noticing or really looking at anything although your eyes are open ▶ **un·see·ing·ly** adv.: *They stared unseeingly at the wreckage.*

un·seem·ly /ʌnˈsiːmli/ adj. (old-fashioned or formal) (of behaviour, etc.) not polite or suitable for a particular situation SYN IMPROPER OPP SEEMLY

un·seen /ˌʌnˈsiːn/ adj. **1** that cannot be seen: *unseen forces/powers* ◇ *He was killed by a single shot from an unseen soldier.* ◇ *I managed to slip out the room unseen.* **2** not previously seen: *unseen dangers/difficulties* ◇ *The exam consists of an essay and an unseen translation.* IDM see SIGHT n.

un·self·con·scious /ˌʌnselfˈkɒnʃəs; AmE -ˈkɑːn-/ adj. not worried about or aware of what other people think of you OPP SELF-CONSCIOUS ▶ **un·self·con·scious·ly** adv.

	s	t	v	z	ʃ	ʒ	tʃ	dʒ	θ	ð	ŋ
	see	tea	van	zoo	shoe	vision	chain	jam	thin	this	sing

un·self·ish /ʌnˈselfɪʃ/ adj. giving more time or importance to other people's needs, wishes, etc. than to your own SYN SELFLESS: *unselfish motives* OPP SELFISH ▶ **un·self·ish·ly** adv. **un·self·ish·ness** noun [U]

un·sen·ti·men·tal /ˌʌnsentɪˈmentl/ adj. not having or expressing emotions such as love or pity; not allowing such emotions to influence what you do: *an unsentimental approach to life* OPP SENTIMENTAL

un·ser·vice·able /ʌnˈsɜːvɪsəbl; AmE -ˈsɜːrv-/ adj. not suitable to be used OPP SERVICEABLE

un·set·tle /ˌʌnˈsetl/ verb [VN] to make sb feel upset or worried, especially because a situation has changed: *Changing schools might unsettle the kids.*

un·set·tled /ˌʌnˈsetld/ adj. **1** (of a situation) that may change; making people uncertain about what might happen: *These were difficult and unsettled times.* ◊ *The weather has been very unsettled* (= it has changed a lot). **2** not calm or relaxed: *They all felt restless and unsettled.* **3** (of an argument, etc.) that continues without any agreement being reached SYN UNRESOLVED **4** (of a bill, etc.) not yet paid

un·set·tling /ʌnˈsetlɪŋ/ adj. making you feel upset, nervous or worried

un·shake·able (BrE) (also **un·shak·able** AmE, BrE) /ʌnˈʃeɪkəbl/ adj. (of a feeling or an attitude) that cannot be changed or destroyed

un·shaken /ˌʌnˈʃeɪkən/ adj. ~ (in sth) not having changed a particular feeling or attitude: *They remain unshaken in their loyalty.*

un·shaven /ˌʌnˈʃeɪvn/ adj. not having shaved or been shaved recently: *He looked pale and unshaven.* ◊ *his unshaven face*—compare SHAVEN

un·sight·ly /ʌnˈsaɪtli/ adj. not pleasant to look at SYN UGLY

un·skilled /ˌʌnˈskɪld/ adj. not having or needing special skills or training: *unskilled manual workers* ◊ *unskilled work* OPP SKILLED

un·smil·ing /ʌnˈsmaɪlɪŋ/ adj. (written) not smiling; looking unfriendly: *His eyes were hard and unsmiling.* ▶ **un·smil·ing·ly** adv.

un·soci·able /ʌnˈsəʊʃəbl; AmE -ˈsoʊ-/ adj. **1** not enjoying the company of other people; not friendly OPP SOCIABLE **2** = UNSOCIAL

WHICH WORD?

unsociable / antisocial / unsocial

An **unsociable** person does not enjoy being with other people.

Such a person can also be described as **antisocial** in *BrE*, but this word is more often used to talk about a person or behaviour that harms or annoys other people.

Unsocial hours (*BrE*) are those that are outside the normal working day.

---

un·social /ʌnˈsəʊʃl; AmE ˌʌnˈsoʊʃl/ (also less frequent **un·soci·able** (BrE)) adj. outside the normal times of working: *I work long and unsocial hours, so I don't get out much.*

un·sold /ˌʌnˈsəʊld; AmE ˌʌnˈsoʊld/ adj. not bought by anyone: *Many of the houses remain unsold.*

un·soli·cit·ed /ˌʌnsəˈlɪsɪtɪd/ adj. not asked for and sometimes not wanted: *unsolicited comments/criticism/advice* ◊ *The record company receives dozens of unsolicited demo tapes each week.*

un·solved /ˌʌnˈsɒlvd; AmE ˌʌnˈsɑːlvd/ adj. not having been solved: *an unsolved murder/mystery/problem*

un·sophis·ti·cated /ˌʌnsəˈfɪstɪkeɪtɪd/ adj. **1** not having or showing much experience of the world and social situations: *unsophisticated tastes/people* **2** simple and basic; not complicated SYN CRUDE: *unsophisticated equipment/methods* OPP SOPHISTICATED

un·sound /ˌʌnˈsaʊnd/ adj. **1** not acceptable; not holding acceptable views: *politically/ideologically unsound* ◊ *The use of disposable products is considered ecologically unsound.* **2** containing mistakes; that you cannot rely on:

The methods used were unsound. **3** (of a building, etc.) in poor condition; weak and likely to fall down OPP SOUND ▶ **un·sound·ness** noun [U] IDM **of ˌunsound ˈmind** (law) not responsible for your actions because of a mental illness or condition

un·spar·ing /ʌnˈspeərɪŋ; AmE -ˈsper-/ adj. (formal) **1** ~ (in sth) | ~ (of sb/sth) severe; not caring about people's feelings: *She is unsparing in her criticism.* **2** giving generously: *He is unsparing of his own peace and comfort.*—compare SPARING ▶ **un·spar·ing·ly** adv.

un·speak·able /ʌnˈspiːkəbl/ adj. (literary, usually disapproving) that cannot be described in words, usually because it is so bad ▶ **un·speak·ably** /-əbli/ adv.

un·speci·fied /ˌʌnˈspesɪfaɪd/ adj. not stated clearly or definitely; not having been SPECIFIED: *The story takes place at an unspecified date.*

un·spec·tacu·lar /ˌʌnspekˈtækjələ(r)/ adj. ordinary; not exciting or special: *He had a steady but unspectacular career.*

un·spoiled /ˌʌnˈspɔɪld/ (BrE also **un·spoilt** /ˌʌnˈspɔɪlt/) adj. (approving) **1** (of a place) beautiful because it has not been changed or built on **2** (of a person) not made unpleasant, bad-tempered, etc. by being praised too much OPP SPOILT

un·spoken /ˌʌnˈspəʊkən/ adj. (formal) not stated; not said in words but understood or agreed between people SYN UNSTATED: *an unspoken assumption* ◊ *Something unspoken hung in the air between them.*

un·sport·ing /ˌʌnˈspɔːtɪŋ; AmE -ˈspɔːrt-/ adj. (disapproving) not fair or generous in your behaviour or treatment of others, especially of an opponent in a game OPP SPORTING

un·stable /ʌnˈsteɪbl/ adj. **1** likely to change suddenly: *unstable share prices* ◊ *The political situation remains highly unstable.* **2** if people are **unstable**, their behaviour and emotions change often and suddenly because their minds are upset: *emotionally/mentally unstable* **3** likely to move or fall **4** (technical) (of a substance) not staying in the same chemical or ATOMIC state: *chemically unstable* OPP STABLE—see also INSTABILITY

un·stated /ʌnˈsteɪtɪd/ adj. (formal) not stated; not said in words but understood or agreed between people SYN UNSPOKEN: *Their reasoning was based on a set of unstated assumptions.*

un·steady /ʌnˈstedi/ adj. **1** not completely in control of your movements so that you might fall: *She is still a little unsteady on her feet after the operation.* **2** shaking or moving in a way that is not controlled: *an unsteady hand/voice/step* OPP STEADY ▶ **un·stead·ily** /-ɪli/ adv. **un·steadi·ness** noun [U]

un·stint·ing /ʌnˈstɪntɪŋ/ adj. ~ (in sth) (written) given or giving generously: *unstinting support* ◊ *They were unstinting in their praise.* ▶ **un·stint·ing·ly** adv.

un·stop·pable /ʌnˈstɒpəbl; AmE -ˈstɑːp-/ adj. that cannot be stopped or prevented: *an unstoppable rise in prices* ◊ *On form, the team was simply unstoppable.*

un·stressed /ˌʌnˈstrest/ adj. (phonetics) (of a syllable) pronounced without emphasis OPP STRESSED

un·struc·tured /ʌnˈstrʌktʃəd; AmE -tʃərd/ adj. (written) without structure or organization: *an unstructured interview*

un·stuck /ˌʌnˈstʌk/ adj. IDM **ˌcome unˈstuck 1** to become separated from sth it was stuck or fastened to: *The flap of the envelope had come unstuck.* **2** (BrE, informal) (of a person, plan, etc.) to fail completely, with bad results

un·sub·stan·ti·ated /ˌʌnsəbˈstænʃieɪtɪd/ adj. (formal) not proved to be true by evidence SYN UNSUPPORTED: *an unsubstantiated claim/rumour*

un·suc·cess·ful /ˌʌnsəkˈsesfl/ adj. not successful; not achieving what you wanted to: *His efforts to get a job proved unsuccessful.* ◊ *They were unsuccessful in meeting their objectives for the year.* ◊ *She made several unsuccessful attempts to see him.* ▶ **un·suc·cess·ful·ly** adv.

un·suit·able /ʌnˈsuːtəbl; BrE also -ˈsjuː-/ adj. ~ (for sb/sth) not right or appropriate for a particular person, purpose or occasion: *He was wearing shoes that were*

U

æ	ɑː	e	ɜː	ə	ɪ	iː	i	ɒ	ɔː	ʌ	ʊ	u	uː
cat	father	ten	bird	about	sit	see	many	got	saw	cup	put	actual	too
								(BrE)					

totally unsuitable for climbing. OPP SUITABLE ▶ **un·suit·abil·ity** *noun* [U] **un·suit·ably** *adv.*: *They were unsuitably dressed for the occasion.*

un·suit·ed /ˌʌnˈsuːtɪd; *BrE* also -ˈsjuː-/ *adj.* **1** ~ (to/for sth)| ~ (to do sth) not having the right or necessary qualities for sth: *He is unsuited to academic work.* ◇ *She was totally unsuited for the job.* **2** if two people are **unsuited** to each other they do not have the same interests, etc. and are therefore not likely to make a good couple OPP SUITED

un·sul·lied /ˌʌnˈsʌlid/ *adj.* (*literary*) not spoiled by anything; still pure or in the original state

un·sung /ˌʌnˈsʌŋ/ *adj.* [usually before noun] (*formal*) not praised or famous but deserving to be: *the unsung heroes of the war*

un·sup·port·ed /ˌʌnsəˈpɔːtɪd; *AmE* -ˈpɔːrt-/ *adj.* **1** (of a statement, etc.) not proved to be true by evidence SYN UNSUBSTANTIATED: *Their claims are unsupported by research findings.* **2** not helped or supported financially by sb/sth else: *She has brought up three children unsupported.* **3** not physically supported: *Sections of the structure have been left unsupported.*

un·sure /ˌʌnˈʃʊə(r); -ˈʃɔː(r); *AmE* -ˈʃʊr/ *adj.* [not before noun] **1** ~ about/of sth| ~ (as to) whether, how, what, etc. not certain of sth; having doubts: *There were a lot of things I was unsure about.* ◇ *He was unsure of what to do next.* ◇ *I was unsure how to reply to this question.* ◇ *They were unsure as to what the next move should be.* **2** ~ (of yourself) lacking confidence in yourself: *Like many women, deep down she was unsure of herself.* OPP SURE

un·sur·passed /ˌʌnsəˈpɑːst; *AmE* ˌʌnsərˈpæst/ *adj.* (*formal*) better or greater than any other SYN UNRIVALLED

un·sur·prised /ˌʌnsəˈpraɪzd; *AmE* -sərˈp-/ *adj.* [not usually before noun] not surprised: *She appeared totally unsurprised at the news.*

un·sur·pris·ing /ˌʌnsəˈpraɪzɪŋ; *AmE* -sərˈp-/ *adj.* not causing surprise OPP SURPRISING ▶ **un·sur·pris·ing·ly** *adv.*: *Unsurprisingly, the plan failed.*

un·sus·pect·ed /ˌʌnsəˈspektɪd/ *adj.* (*written*) not predicted or known; that you were not previously aware of

un·sus·pect·ing /ˌʌnsəˈspektɪŋ/ *adj.* [usually before noun] (*written*) feeling no suspicion; not aware of danger or of sth bad: *He had crept up on his unsuspecting victim from behind.*

un·sus·tain·able /ˌʌnsəˈsteɪnəbl/ *adj.* (*written*) that cannot be continued at the same level, rate, etc: *unsustainable growth/demands* OPP SUSTAINABLE

un·sweet·ened /ˌʌnˈswiːtnd/ *adj.* (of food or drinks) without sugar or a similar substance having been added

un·swerv·ing /ˌʌnˈswɜːvɪŋ; *AmE* -ˈswɜːrv-/ *adj.* (*written*) strong and not changing or becoming weaker: *unswerving loyalty/support*

un·sym·pa·thet·ic /ˌʌnˌsɪmpəˈθetɪk/ *adj.* **1** ~ (to/towards sb) not feeling or showing any sympathy: *I told him about the problem but he was totally unsympathetic.* **2** ~ (to/towards sth) not in agreement with sth; not supporting an idea, aim, etc: *How can you trust a government that is unsympathetic to public opinion?* **3** (of a person) not easy to like; unpleasant: *All the characters in the novel are as unsympathetic as each other.* OPP SYMPATHETIC ▶ **un·sym·pa·thet·ic·al·ly** *adv.*: *'You've only got yourself to blame,' she said unsympathetically.*

un·sys·tem·at·ic /ˌʌnˌsɪstəˈmætɪk/ *adj.* not organized into a clear system OPP SYSTEMATIC ▶ **un·sys·tem·at·ic·al·ly** *adv.*

un·taint·ed /ˌʌnˈteɪntɪd/ *adj.* ~ (by sth) (*formal*) not damaged or spoiled by sth unpleasant; not TAINTED by sth

un·tamed /ˌʌnˈteɪmd/ *adj.* (*written*) allowed to remain in a wild state; not changed, controlled or influenced by anyone; not TAMED

un·tan·gle /ˌʌnˈtæŋgl/ *verb* [VN] **1** to undo string, hair, wire, etc. that has become twisted or has knots in it: *Can you untangle all those cables on the floor?* **2** to make sth that is complicated or confusing easier to deal with or understand: *It will not be easy to untangle his financial affairs.*

un·tapped /ˌʌnˈtæpt/ *adj.* (*written*) available but not yet used: *untapped reserves of oil*

un·ten·able /ˌʌnˈtenəbl/ *adj.* (*formal*) (of a theory, position, etc.) that cannot be defended against attack or criticism: *His position had become untenable and he was forced to resign.* OPP TENABLE

un·test·ed /ˌʌnˈtestɪd/ *adj.* not tested; of unknown quality or value

un·think·able /ˌʌnˈθɪŋkəbl/ *adj.* ~ (for sb) (to do sth)| ~ (that ...) impossible to imagine or accept SYN INCONCEIVABLE: *It was unthinkable that she could be dead.* OPP THINKABLE ▶ **the un·think·able** *noun* [sing.]: *Suddenly the unthinkable happened and he drew out a gun.* ◇ *The time has come to think the unthinkable* (= consider possibilities that used to be unacceptable).

un·think·ing /ˌʌnˈθɪŋkɪŋ/ *adj.* (*written*) not thinking about the effects of what you do or say; not thinking much about serious things ▶ **un·think·ing·ly** *adv.*

un·tidy /ˌʌnˈtaɪdi/ *adj.* **1** not neat or well arranged; in a state of disorder: *an untidy desk/room* ◇ *untidy hair/writing* **2** (of a person) not keeping things neat or well organized OPP TIDY ▶ **un·tidi·ly** /-ɪli/ *adv.* **un·tidi·ness** *noun* [U]

untie /ˌʌnˈtaɪ/ *verb* [VN] to undo a knot in sth; to undo sth that is tied: *to untie a knot* ◇ *I quickly untied the package and peeped inside.* ◇ *He untied the rope and pushed the boat into the water.*

until /ənˈtɪl/ *conj., prep.* (also *informal* **till, til, 'til.** HELP These short forms are not usually used at the beginning of a sentence.) up to the point in time or the event mentioned: *Let's wait until the rain stops.* ◇ *Until she spoke I hadn't realized she wasn't English.* ◇ *You're not going out until you've finished this.* ◇ *Until now I have always lived alone.* ◇ *They moved here in 1990. Until then they'd always been in the London area.* ◇ *He continued working up until his death.* ◇ *The street is full of traffic from morning till night.* ◇ *You can stay on the bus until London* (= until you reach London).

un·time·ly /ʌnˈtaɪmli/ *adj.* (*formal*) **1** happening too soon or sooner than is normal or expected SYN PREMATURE: *She met a tragic and untimely death at 25.* **2** happening at a time or in a situation that is not suitable SYN ILL-TIMED: *His interruption was untimely.* OPP TIMELY

un·tir·ing /ʌnˈtaɪərɪŋ/ *adj.* (*approving*) continuing to do sth for a long period of time with a lot of effort and/or enthusiasm SYN TIRELESS

un·titled /ˌʌnˈtaɪtld/ *adj.* (of a work of art) without a title

unto /ˈʌntə; *before vowels* ˈʌntu/ *prep.* (*old use*) **1** to or towards sb/sth: *The angel appeared unto him in a dream.* **2** until a particular time or event: *The knights swore loyalty unto death.*

un·told /ˌʌnˈtəʊld; *AmE* ˌʌnˈtoʊld/ *adj.* **1** [only before noun] used to emphasize how large, great, unpleasant, etc. sth is: *untold misery/wealth* ◇ *These gases cause untold damage to the environment.* **2** (of a story) not told to anyone

un·touch·able /ˌʌnˈtʌtʃəbl/ *adj., noun*

■ *adj.* **1** a person who is **untouchable** is in a position where they are unlikely to be punished or criticized: *Given his political connections, he thought he was untouchable.* **2** that cannot be touched or changed by other people: *She looked delicate and untouchable, dressed in white.* ◇ *The department's budget is untouchable.* **3** (in India) belonging to or connected with the Hindu social class (or CASTE) that is considered by other classes as the lowest

■ *noun* (often **Untouchable**) a member of a Hindu social class (or CASTE) that is considered by other classes to be the lowest

un·touched /ˌʌnˈtʌtʃt/ *adj.* [not usually before noun] **1** ~ (by sth) not affected by sth, especially sth bad or unpleasant; not damaged: *The area has remained relatively untouched by commercial development.* ◇ *Some buildings had remained untouched by the explosion.* **2** (of food or drink) not eaten or drunk: *She left her meal untouched.* **3** not changed in any way: *The final clause in the contract will be left untouched.*

aɪ	aʊ	eɪ	əʊ	oʊ	ɔɪ	ɪə	eə	ʊə	j	w
my	now	say	go (BrE)	go (AmE)	boy	near	hair	pure	yes	wet

un·to·ward /ˌʌntəˈwɔːd; *AmE* ʌnˈtɔːrd/ *adj.* unusual and unexpected, and usually unpleasant: *That's the plan—unless anything untoward happens.* ◊ *He had noticed nothing untoward.*

un·trained /ˌʌnˈtreɪnd/ *adj.* ~ **(in sth)** not trained to perform a particular job or skill; without formal training in sth: *untrained in keyboard skills* ◊ *untrained teachers* ◊ *To the untrained eye, the two products look remarkably similar.*

un·tram·melled (*BrE*) (*AmE* **un·tram·meled**) /ʌnˈtræmld/ *adj.* ~ **(by sth)** (*formal*) not restricted or limited by sth—compare TRAMMEL

un·treat·ed /ˌʌnˈtriːtɪd/ *adj.* **1** not receiving medical treatment: *If untreated, the illness can become severe.* **2** (of substances) not made safe by chemical or other treatment: *untreated sewage* **3** (of wood) not treated with substances to preserve it

un·tried /ˌʌnˈtraɪd/ *adj.* (*written*) **1** without experience of doing a particular job: *She chose two untried actors for the leading roles.* **2** not yet tried or tested to discover if it works or is successful: *This is a new and relatively untried procedure.*

un·true /ʌnˈtruː/ *adj.* **1** not true; not based on facts: *These accusations are totally untrue.* ◊ *an untrue claim/ statement* ◊ *It would be untrue to say that something like this could never happen again.* **2** ~ **(to sb/sth)** (*literary*) not loyal to sb/sth SYN UNFAITHFUL: *If he agreed to their demands, he would have to be untrue to his own principles.* OPP TRUE

un·trust·worthy /ʌnˈtrʌstwɜːði; *AmE* -wɜːrði/ *adj.* that cannot be trusted OPP TRUSTWORTHY

un·truth /ʌnˈtruːθ/ *noun* (*pl.* **un·truths** /ʌnˈtruːðz; -ˈtruːθs/) **1** [C] (*formal*) a lie. People often say 'untruth' to avoid saying 'lie'.—compare TRUTH **2** [U] the state of being false

un·truth·ful /ʌnˈtruːθfl/ *adj.* saying things that you know are not true OPP TRUTHFUL ▶ **un·truth·ful·ly** /-fəli/ *adv.*

un·turned /ˌʌnˈtɜːnd; *AmE* ʌnˈtɜːrnd/ *adj.* IDM see STONE *n.*

un·tutored /ˌʌnˈtjuːtəd; *AmE* ˌʌnˈtuːtərd/ *adj.* (*formal*) not having been formally taught about sth

un·typ·ical /ʌnˈtɪpɪkl/ *adj.* ~ **(of sb/sth)** not typical: *an untypical example* ◊ *Schools in this area are quite untypical of schools in the rest of the country.* ◊ *All in all, it had been a not untypical day* (= it had been very like other days). OPP TYPICAL—compare ATYPICAL ▶ **un·typ·ic·al·ly** *adv.*

un·usable /ˌʌnˈjuːzəbl/ *adj.* in such a bad condition or of such low quality that it cannot be used OPP USABLE

un·used¹ /ˌʌnˈjuːzd/ *adj.* not being used at the moment; never having been used—compare DISUSED

un·used² /ʌnˈjuːst/ *adj.* ~ **to sth/to doing sth** not having much experience of sth and therefore not knowing how to deal with it; not used to sth: *This is an easy routine, designed for anyone who is unused to exercise.* ◊ *She was unused to talking about herself.*

un·usual /ʌnˈjuːʒuəl; -ʒəl/ *adj.* **1** different from what is usual or normal SYN STRANGE: *It's unusual for the trees to flower so early.* ◊ *She has a very unusual name.* ◊ *It's not unusual for young doctors to work a 70-hour week* (= it happens often). **2** different from other similar things and therefore interesting and attractive: *an unusual colour/ feature/hobby*

un·usual·ly /ʌnˈjuːʒuəli; -ʒəli/ *adv.* **1** used before adjectives to emphasize that a particular quality is greater than normal: *unusually high levels of radiation* ◊ *an unusually cold winter* **2** used to say that a particular situation is not normal or expected: *Unusually for him, he wore a tie.*

un·utter·able /ʌnˈʌtərəbl/ *adj.* [only before noun] (*formal*) used to emphasize how great a particular emotion or quality is: *unutterable loneliness/sadness/pleasure* ▶ **un·utter·ably** /-əbli/ *adv.*

un·var·nished /ʌnˈvɑːnɪʃt; *AmE* -ˈvɑːrn-/ *adj.* **1** [only before noun] (*written*) with nothing added: *It was the plain unvarnished truth.* **2** (of wood, etc.) not covered with VARNISH

un·vary·ing /ʌnˈveəriŋ; *AmE* -ˈveri-; -ˈværi-/ *adj.* (*written*) never changing: *an unvarying routine*

un·veil /ˌʌnˈveɪl/ *verb* [VN] **1** to remove a cover or curtain from a painting, statue, etc. so that it can be seen in public for the first time: *The Queen unveiled a plaque to mark the official opening of the hospital.* **2** to show or introduce a new plan, product, etc. to the public for the first time: *They will be unveiling their new models at the Motor Show.*

un·voiced /ˌʌnˈvɔɪst/ *adj.* **1** thought about but not expressed in words—compare VOICE *v.* **2** (*phonetics*) (of consonants) produced without VIBRATION of the VOCAL CORDS; not VOICED SYN VOICELESS: *unvoiced consonants such as 'p' and 't'*

un·waged /ˌʌnˈweɪdʒd/ *adj.* (*BrE, written*) **1** (of a person) not earning money by working OPP WAGED **2** (of work) for which you are not paid SYN UNPAID **3** **(the unwaged)** *noun* [pl.] people who are unwaged

un·want·ed /ˌʌnˈwɒntɪd; *AmE* -ˈwɑːnt-/ *adj.* that you do not want: *unwanted advice/attention* ◊ *unwanted pregnancies* ◊ *It is very sad when children feel unwanted* (= feel that other people do not care about them).

un·war·rant·ed /ʌnˈwɒrəntɪd; *AmE* -ˈwɔːr-; -ˈwɑːr-/ *adj.* (*formal*) not reasonable or necessary; not appropriate SYN UNJUSTIFIED: *Much of the criticism was totally unwarranted.* ◊ *They condemned the new law as an unwarranted intrusion into people's private lives.*

un·wary /ʌnˈweəri; *AmE* -ˈweri/ *adj.* **1** [only before noun] not aware of the possible dangers or problems of a situation and therefore likely to be harmed in some way—compare WARY **2** **(the unwary)** *noun* [pl.] people who are unwary: *The stock market is full of traps for the unwary.*

un·washed /ˌʌnˈwɒʃt; *AmE* ˌʌnˈwɑːʃt; -ˈwɔːʃt/ *adj.* not washed; dirty: *a pile of unwashed dishes* ◊ *Their clothes were dirty and their hair unwashed.*

un·waver·ing /ʌnˈweɪvərɪŋ/ *adj.* (*formal*) not changing or becoming weaker in any way: *unwavering support/ determination* ▶ **un·waver·ing·ly** *adv.*

un·wel·come /ʌnˈwelkəm/ *adj.* not wanted: *an unwelcome visitor* ◊ *To avoid attracting unwelcome attention he kept his voice down.* OPP WELCOME

un·wel·com·ing /ʌnˈwelkəmɪŋ/ *adj.* **1** (of a person) not friendly towards sb who is visiting or arriving **2** (of a place) not attractive and looking uncomfortable to be in: *She went back to her cold unwelcoming house.* OPP WELCOMING

un·well /ʌnˈwel/ *adj.* [not before noun] (rather *formal*) ill/sick: *She said she was feeling unwell and went home.* OPP WELL

un·whole·some /ˌʌnˈhəʊlsəm; *AmE* -ˈhoʊl-/ *adj.* (*written*) **1** harmful to health; not looking healthy **2** that you consider unpleasant or not natural OPP WHOLESOME

un·wieldy /ʌnˈwiːldi/ *adj.* **1** (of an object) difficult to move or control because of its size, shape or weight SYN CUMBERSOME **2** (of a system or group of people) difficult to control or organize because it is very large or complicated

un·will·ing /ʌnˈwɪlɪŋ/ *adj.* **1** [not usually before noun] ~ **(to do sth)** not wanting to do sth and refusing to do it: *They are unwilling to invest any more money in the project.* ◊ *She was unable, or unwilling, to give me any further details.* **2** [only before noun] not wanting to do sth, but forced to by other people SYN RELUCTANT: *an unwilling hero* ◊ *He became the unwilling object of her attention.* OPP WILLING ▶ **un·will·ing·ly** *adv.* **un·will·ing·ness** *noun* [U]

un·wind /ˌʌnˈwaɪnd/ *verb* (**un·wound**, **un·wound** /ˌʌnˈwaʊnd/) **1** to undo sth that has been wrapped into a ball or around sth: [VN] *to unwind a ball of string* ◊ *He unwound his scarf from his neck.* ◊ [V] *The bandage gradually unwound and fell off.* **2** [V] to stop worrying or thinking about problems and start to relax SYN WIND DOWN: *Listening to music helps me unwind after a busy day.*

un·wise /ˌʌnˈwaɪz/ *adj.* ~ **(to do sth)** showing a lack of good judgement SYN FOOLISH: *It would be unwise to comment on the situation without knowing all the facts.* ◊ *an*

U

b	d	f	g	h	k	l	m	n	p	r
bad	did	fall	get	hat	cat	leg	man	now	pen	red

unwise decision/investment OPP WISE ▶ un·wise·ly adv.: Perhaps unwisely, I agreed to help.

un·wit·ting /ʌnˈwɪtɪŋ/ adj. [only before noun] (written) not aware of what you are doing or of the situation you are involved in: He became an unwitting accomplice in the crime. ◇ She was the unwitting cause of the argument.

un·wit·ting·ly /ʌnˈwɪtɪŋli/ adv. without being aware of what you are doing or the situation that you are involved in: She had broken the law unwittingly, but still she had broken it. OPP WITTINGLY

un·wont·ed /ʌnˈwəʊntɪd; AmE -ˈwoʊn-/ adj. (formal) not usual or expected: He spoke with unwonted enthusiasm.

un·work·able /ʌnˈwɜːkəbl; AmE -ˈwɜːrk-/ adj. not practical or possible to do successfully: an unworkable plan/ proposal OPP WORKABLE

un·world·ly /ʌnˈwɜːldli; AmE -ˈwɜːrld-/ adj. **1** not interested in money or the things that it buys **2** lacking experience of life SYN NAIVE OPP WORLDLY **3** having qualities that do not seem to belong to this world: The landscape had a stark, unworldly beauty.

un·wor·ried /ʌnˈwʌrid; AmE -ˈwɜːr-/ adj. [not usually before noun] (written) not worried; calm; relaxed: She appeared unworried by criticism.

un·worthy /ʌnˈwɜːði; AmE -ˈwɜːrði/ adj. (formal) **1** ~ (of sth) not having the necessary qualities to deserve sth, especially respect: an unworthy opponent ◇ He considered himself unworthy of the honour they had bestowed on him. OPP WORTHY **2** ~ (of sth) not acceptable from sb, especially sb who has an important job or high social position: Such opinions are unworthy of educated people. ▶ un·worthi·ness noun [U]: feelings of unworthiness

un·wound pt, pp of UNWIND

un·wrap /ʌnˈræp/ verb (-pp-) [VN] to take off the paper, etc. that covers or protects sth: Don't unwrap your present until your birthday. OPP WRAP UP

un·writ·ten /ˌʌnˈrɪtn/ adj. **1** ~ law, rule, agreement, etc. a law, etc. that everyone knows about and accepts even though it has not been made official: We have an unwritten understanding that nobody leaves before five o'clock. **2** (of a book, etc.) not yet written: The photographs were to be included in his as yet unwritten autobiography.

un·yield·ing /ʌnˈjiːldɪŋ/ adj. (written) **1** if a person is unyielding, they are not easily influenced and they are unlikely to change their mind: severe unyielding parents **2** an unyielding substance or object does not bend or break when pressure is put on it

unzip /ˌʌnˈzɪp/ verb (-pp-) [VN, V] if you unzip a piece of clothing, a bag, etc., or if it unzips, you open it by undoing the ZIP that fastens it OPP ZIP UP

up /ʌp/ adv., prep., adj., verb, noun
■ adv. HELP For the special uses of **up** in phrasal verbs, look at the entries for the verbs. For example **break up** is in the phrasal verb section at **break**. **1** towards or in a higher position: He jumped up from his chair. ◇ The sun was already up (= had risen) when they set off. ◇ They live up in the mountains. ◇ It didn't take long to put the tent up. ◇ I pinned the notice up on the wall. ◇ Lay the cards face up (= facing upwards) on the table. ◇ You look nice with your hair up (= arranged on top of or at the back of your head). ◇ (spoken) Up you come! (= said when lifting a child). **2** to or at a higher level: She turned the volume up. ◇ Prices are still going up (= rising). ◇ United were 3–1 up at half time. ◇ The wind is getting up (= blowing more strongly). ◇ Sales are well up on last year. **3** to the place where sb/sth is: A car drove up and he got in. ◇ She went straight up to the door and knocked loudly. **4** to or at an important place, especially a large city: We're going up to New York for the day. ◇ (BrE, formal) His son's up at Oxford (= Oxford University). **5** to a place in the north of a country: They've moved up north. ◇ We drove up to Inverness to see my father. **6** into pieces or parts: She tore the paper up. ◇ They've had the road up (= with the surface broken or removed) to lay some pipes. ◇ How shall we divide up the work? **7** completely: We ate all the food up. ◇ The stream has dried up. **8** so as to be formed or brought together: The government agreed to set up a committee of inquiry. ◇ She gathered up her belong ings. **9** so as to be finished or closed: I have some paperwork to finish up. ◇ Do your coat up; it's cold. **10** (of a period of time) finished; over: Time's up. Stop writing and hand in your papers. **11** out of bed: I stayed up late (= did not go to bed until late) last night. ◇ (BrE) He's up and about again after his illness. **12** (spoken) used to say that sth is happening, especially sth unusual or unpleasant: I could tell something was up by the looks on their faces. ◇ What's up? (= What is the matter?) ◇ What's up with him? He looks furious. ◇ Is anything up? You can tell me. HELP In AmE What's up? can just mean 'What's new?' or 'What's happening?' There may not be anything wrong. IDM be up to sb to be sb's duty or responsibility; to be for sb to decide: It's not up to you to tell me how to do my job. ◇ Shall we eat out or stay in? It's up to you. not be 'up to much (BrE) to be of poor quality; to not be very good: His work isn't up to much. up against sth (informal) facing problems or opposition: Teachers are up against some major problems these days. ◇ She's really up against it (= in a difficult situation). ˌup and 'down **1** moving upwards and downwards: The boat bobbed up and down on the water. **2** in one direction and then in the opposite direction: She was pacing up and down in front of her desk. **3** sometimes good and sometimes bad: My relationship with him was up and down. ˌup and 'running (of a system, for example a computer system) working; being used: By that time the new system should be up and running. up before sb/sth appearing in front of sb in authority for a judgement to be made about sth that you have done: He came up before the local magistrate for speeding. up for sth **1** on offer for sth: The house is up for sale. **2** being considered for sth, especially as a candidate: Two candidates are up for election. **3** willing to take part in a particular activity: We're going clubbing tonight. Are you up for it? up to sth **1** as far as a particular number, level, etc: I can take up to four people (= but no more than four) in my car. ◇ The temperature went up to 35°C. **2** (also up until sth) not further or later than sth; until sth: Read up to page 100. ◇ Up to now he's been very quiet. **3** as high or as good as sth: Her latest book isn't up to her usual standard. **4** (also up to doing sth) physically or mentally capable of sth: He's not up to the job. ◇ I don't feel up to going to work today. **5** (spoken) doing sth, especially sth bad: What's she up to? ◇ What've you been up to? ◇ I'm sure he's up to no good (= doing sth bad).
■ prep. **1** to or in a higher position somewhere: She climbed up the flight of steps. ◇ The village is further up the valley. **2** along or further along a road or street: We live just up the road, past the post office. **3** towards the place where a river starts: a cruise up the Rhine IDM up and down sth in one direction and then in the opposite direction along sth: I looked up and down the corridor. ˌup 'yours! (△, slang) an offensive way of being rude to sb, for example because they have said sth that makes you angry
■ adj. **1** [only before noun] directed or moving upwards: an up stroke ◇ the up escalator **2** [not before noun] (informal) cheerful; happy or excited: The mood here is resolutely up. **3** [not before noun] (of a computer system) working: Our system should be up by this afternoon.
■ verb (-pp-) **1** [V] (up and…) (informal or humorous) to suddenly move or do sth unexpected: He upped and left without telling anyone. **2** [VN] to increase the price or amount of sth SYN RAISE: The buyers upped their offer by £1000. IDM ˌup 'sticks (BrE, informal) to suddenly move from your house and go to live somewhere else: He upped sticks and went back to France.—more at ANTE
■ noun IDM on the 'up increasing or improving: Business confidence is on the up. on the ˌup and 'up (informal) **1** (BrE) becoming more and more successful: The club has been on the up and up since the beginning of the season. **2** (AmE) = ON THE LEVEL at LEVEL n.: The offer seems to be on the up and up. ˌups and 'downs the mixture of good and bad things in life or in a particular situation or relationship: Every business has its ups and downs.

up- /ʌp/ prefix (in adjectives, verbs and related nouns) higher; upwards; towards the top of sth: upland ◇ upturned ◇ upgrade ◇ uphill

s	t	v	z	ʃ	ʒ	tʃ	dʒ	θ	ð	ŋ
see	tea	van	zoo	shoe	vision	chain	jam	thin	this	sing

up-and-'coming adj. [only before noun] (informal) likely to be successful and popular in the future: up-and-coming young actors

up·beat /'ʌpbiːt/ adj. (informal) positive and enthusiastic; making you feel that the future will be good: The tone of the speech was upbeat. ◊ The presentation ended on an upbeat note. **OPP** DOWNBEAT

up·braid /ʌp'breɪd/ verb [VN] ~ sb (for sth/for doing sth) (formal) to criticize sb or speak angrily to them because you do not approve of sth that they have said or done

up·bring·ing /'ʌpbrɪŋɪŋ/ noun (sing., U) the way in which a child is cared for and taught how to behave while it is growing up: to have a sheltered/religious/strict upbringing ◊ He was a Catholic by upbringing.

UPC /ˌjuː piː 'siː/ abbr. (AmE, technical) Universal Product Code: The Universal Product Code symbol, also known as the 'bar code', is printed on products for sale and contains information that a computer can read.

up·com·ing /'ʌpkʌmɪŋ/ adj. [only before noun] (especially AmE) going to happen soon: the upcoming presidential election ◊ a single from the band's upcoming album

up-'country adj. [only before noun] connected with an area of a country that is situated away from large towns ► up-'country adv.

up·date /ˌʌp'deɪt/ verb [VN] **1** to make sth more modern by adding new parts, etc: It's about time we updated our software. **2** ~ sb (on sth)|~ sth to give sb the most recent information about sth; to add the most recent information to sth: I called the office to update them on the day's developments. ◊ Our records are regularly updated. ► up-date /'ʌpdeɪt/ noun ~ (on sth): a news update ◊ The newsletter gives an update on current activities.

up·end /ʌp'end/ verb [VN] to turn sb/sth upside down: The bicycle lay upended in a ditch.

up·field /ʌp'fiːld/ adv. (sport) towards your opponent's end of the playing field

up·front /ˌʌp'frʌnt/ adj. **1** ~ (about sth) not trying to hide what you think or do **SYN** HONEST, FRANK: He's been upfront about his intentions since the beginning. **2** [only before noun] paid in advance, before other payments are made: There will be an upfront fee of 4%.—see also UP FRONT at FRONT

up·grade /ˌʌp'greɪd/ verb [VN] [often passive] **1** to make a piece of machinery, computer system, etc. more powerful and efficient **2** ~ sb (to sth) to give sb a more important job **SYN** PROMOTE **3** ~ sb (to sth) to give sb a better seat on a plane, room in a hotel, etc. than the one that they have paid for **4** to improve the condition of a building, etc. in order to provide a better service: The money will enable us to upgrade the town's leisure facilities.—compare DOWNGRADE ► up·grade /'ʌpgreɪd/ noun

up·heav·al /ʌp'hiːvl/ noun [C, U] a big change that causes a lot of confusion, worry and problems: the latest upheavals in the education system ◊ I can't face the upheaval of moving house again. ◊ a period of emotional upheaval

up·hill /ˌʌp'hɪl/ adj., adv.
■ adj. **1** sloping upwards: an uphill climb/slope ◊ The last part of the race is all uphill. **OPP** DOWNHILL **2** ~ battle, struggle, task, etc. an argument or a struggle that is difficult to win and takes a lot of effort over a long period of time
■ adv. towards the top of a hill or slope: We cycled uphill for over an hour. ◊ The path slopes steeply uphill. **OPP** DOWN-HILL

up·hold /ʌp'həʊld/ verb (up·held, up·held /-'held/) [VN] **1** to support sth that you think is right, fair, etc. and make sure that it continues to exist: We have a duty to uphold the law. **2** (especially of a court of law) to agree that a previous decision was correct or that a request is reasonable: to uphold a conviction/an appeal/a complaint ► up·hold·er noun: an upholder of traditional values

up·hol·ster /ʌp'həʊlstə(r); AmE -'hoʊl-/ verb [VN] [usually passive] ~ sth (in sth) to cover a chair, etc. with soft material (= PADDING) and fabric

up·hol·ster·er /ʌp'həʊlstərə(r); AmE -'hoʊl-/ noun a person whose job is to upholster furniture

up·hol·stery /ʌp'həʊlstəri; AmE -'hoʊl-/ noun [U] **1** soft covering on furniture such as ARMCHAIRS and SOFAS **2** the process or trade of UPHOLSTERING

up·keep /'ʌpkiːp/ noun [U] **1** ~ (of sth) the cost or process of keeping sth in good condition **SYN** MAINTENANCE: Tenants are responsible for the upkeep of rented property. **2** ~ (of sb/sth) the cost or process of giving a child or an animal the things that they need: He makes regular payments to his ex-wife for the upkeep of their children.

up·land /'ʌplənd/ noun [usually pl.] an area of high land that is situated away from the coast ► up·land adj. [only before noun]: upland agriculture

up·lift noun, verb
■ noun /'ʌplɪft/ [U, sing.] **1** the fact of sth being raised or of sth increasing: an uplift in sales ◊ an uplift bra (= that raises the breasts) **2** a feeling of hope and happiness: The news gave them a much needed uplift. **3** (geology) the process or result of land being moved to a higher level by movements inside the earth
■ verb /ʌp'lɪft/ [VN] (formal) to make sb feel happier or more hopeful

up·lift·ed /ʌp'lɪftɪd/ adj. **1** [not before noun] feeling happy and full of hope: Everyone left the meeting feeling uplifted. **2** (literary) lifted upwards: a sea of uplifted faces

up·lift·ing /ʌp'lɪftɪŋ/ adj. making you feel happier or more hopeful: an uplifting experience/speech

up·mar·ket /ˌʌp'mɑːkɪt; AmE -'mɑːrk-/ (BrE) (AmE up·scale) adj. [usually before noun] designed for or used by people who belong to a high social class: an upmarket brand/restaurant/store **OPP** DOWNMARKET ► ˌup·'mar·ket (BrE) (AmE ˌup·'scale) adv.: The company has been forced to move more upmarket.

upon /ə'pɒn; AmE ə'pɑːn/ prep. (formal, especially BrE) = ON: The decision was based upon two considerations. **IDM** (almost) u'pon you if sth in the future is almost upon you, it is going to arrive or happen very soon: The summer season was almost upon them again.—more at ONCE adv.

upper /'ʌpə(r)/ adj., noun
■ adj. [only before noun] **1** situated above sth else, especially sth of the same type or the other of a pair: the upper jaw/lip ◊ the upper deck/floor/storey **2** at or near the top of sth: the upper arm/body ◊ the upper slopes of the mountain ◊ a member of the upper middle class ◊ salaries at the upper end of the pay scale ◊ There is an upper limit of £20000 spent on any one project. **3** (of a place) situated away from the coast, on high ground or towards the north of an area: the upper reaches of the Thames **OPP** LOWER **IDM** gain, get, have, etc. the ,upper 'hand to get an advantage over sb so that you are in control of a particular situation—more at STIFF adj.
■ noun [usually pl.] **1** the top part of a shoe that is attached to the sole: shoes with leather uppers **2** (informal) a drug that makes you feel excited and full of energy—compare DOWNER **IDM** on your 'uppers (BrE, informal) having very little money

upper 'case noun [U] capital letters (= the large form of letters, for example A, B, C rather than a, b, c): Headings should be in upper case.—compare LOWER CASE ► ,upper 'case adj.: upper-case letters

the ,upper 'class noun [sing.] (also the ,upper 'classes [pl.]) the groups of people that are considered to have the highest social status and that have more money and/or power than other people in society: a member of the upper class/upper classes ► ,upper 'class adj.: Her family is very upper class. ◊ an upper-class accent—compare LOWER CLASS, MIDDLE CLASS, WORKING CLASS

upper·class·man /ˌʌpə'klɑːsmən; AmE ˌʌpər'klæs-/, **upper·class·woman** /ˌʌpə'klɑːswʊmən; AmE ˌʌpər'klæs-/ noun (pl. -men /-men/ -women /-wɪmɪn/) (AmE) a student in the last two years of high school or college—compare UNDERCLASSMAN

the ,upper 'crust noun [sing.+ sing./pl. v.] (informal) the people who belong to the highest social class ► ,upper-'crust adj. [only before noun]

upper·cut /'ʌpəkʌt; AmE 'ʌpərkʌt/ noun (in boxing) a

way of hitting sb on the chin, in which you bend your arm and move your hand upwards

ˌupper ˈhouse (also **ˌupper ˈchamber**) (also **ˌsecond ˈchamber** especially in *BrE*) *noun* [sing.] one of the parts of a parliament in countries which have a parliament that is divided into two parts. In Britain it is the House of Lords and in the US it is the Senate.—compare LOWER HOUSE

upper·most /ˈʌpəməʊst; *AmE* ˈʌpərmoʊst/ *adj., adv.*
■ *adj.* **1** [usually before noun] (*written*) higher or nearer the top than other things: *the uppermost branches of the tree* **2** [not usually before noun] more important than other things in a particular situation: *These thoughts were **uppermost in my mind**.* ◊ *Defence is no longer uppermost in their priorities.*
■ *adv.* (*written*) in the highest position; facing upwards: *Place the material on a flat surface, shiny side uppermost.*

ˈupper school *noun* (*BrE*) a school, or the classes in a school, for older students, usually between the ages of 14 and 18—compare LOWER SCHOOL, MIDDLE SCHOOL

up·pity /ˈʌpəti/ *adj.* (*old-fashioned, informal*) behaving as if you are more important than you really are, especially when this means that you refuse to obey orders

up·raised /ˌʌpˈreɪzd/ *adj.* lifted upwards: *She strode towards them, her fist upraised.*

up·right /ˈʌpraɪt/ *adj., noun*
■ *adj.* **1** (of a person) not lying down, and with the back straight rather than bent: *She sat upright in bed.* ◊ *He managed to pull himself upright.* ◊ *an upright posture/stance* ◊ *Gradually raise your body into an upright position.* **2** placed in a vertical position: *Keep the bottle upright.* ◊ *an upright bar* ◊ *an upright freezer* (= one that is taller than it is wide) ◊ *an upright chair* (= one with a high straight back) **3** (of a person) behaving in a moral and honest way: *an upright citizen* **IDM** see BOLT *adv.*
■ *noun* **1** a long piece of wood, metal or plastic that is placed in a vertical position, especially in order to support sth **2** = UPRIGHT PIANO

ˌupright piˈano (also **up·right**) *noun* a piano in which the strings are vertical—compare GRAND PIANO, SPINET—picture at PIANO

up·ris·ing /ˈʌpraɪzɪŋ/ *noun* ~ (**against sth**) a situation in which a group of people join together in order to fight against the people who are in power **SYN** REBELLION, REVOLT: *an armed uprising against the government* ◊ *a popular uprising* (= by the ordinary people of the country) ◊ *to crush/suppress an uprising*

up·river /ˌʌpˈrɪvə(r)/ *adv.* = UPSTREAM

up·roar /ˈʌprɔː(r)/ *noun* [U, sing.] **1** a situation in which people shout and make a lot of noise because they are angry or upset about sth: *The room was in (an) uproar.* ◊ *Her comments provoked (an) uproar from the audience.* **2** a situation in which there is a lot of public criticism and angry argument about sth that sb has said or done: *The article caused (an) uproar when it was published.*

up·roari·ous /ʌpˈrɔːriəs/ *adj.* [not usually before noun] (*written*) **1** in which there is a lot of noise and people laugh or shout a lot: *an uproarious party* **2** extremely funny: *an uproarious story* ▶ **up·roari·ous·ly** *adv.*: *The audience laughed uproariously.* ◊ *uproariously funny*

up·root /ˌʌpˈruːt/ *verb* [VN] **1** to pull a tree, plant, etc. out of the ground **2** ~ **yourself/sb** to leave a place where you have lived for a long time; to make sb do this: *If I accept the job, it will mean uprooting my family and moving to Italy.*

up·scale /ˌʌpˈskeɪl/ *adj., adv.* (*AmE*) = UPMARKET

upset *verb, adj., noun*
■ *verb* /ʌpˈset/ (**up·set·ting, upset, upset**) **1** to make sb/ yourself feel unhappy, anxious or annoyed **SYN** DISTRESS: [VN] *This decision is likely to upset a lot of people.* ◊ *Don't upset yourself about it—let's just forget it ever happened.* [VN that] *It upset him that nobody had bothered to tell him about it.* ◊ [VN to inf] *It upsets me to think of her all alone in that big house.* **2** [VN] to make a plan, situation, etc. go wrong: *He arrived an hour late and upset all our arrangements.* **3** [VN] ~ **sb's stomach** to make sb feel sick after they have eaten or drunk sth **4** [VN] to make sth fall over

by hitting it accidentally: *She stood up suddenly, upsetting a glass of wine.* **IDM** **upset the ˈapple cart** to cause problems for sb or spoil their plans, arrangements, etc.
■ *adj.* /ʌpˈset/ **1** [not before noun] ~ (**about sth**)| ~ (**that ...**) unhappy or disappointed because of sth unpleasant that has happened: *There's no point getting upset about it.* ◊ *I understand how upset you must be feeling.* ◊ *She was upset that he had left without saying goodbye.* **2** an ˌupset ˈstomach an illness in the stomach that makes you feel sick or have DIARRHOEA
■ *noun* /ˈʌpset/ **1** [C] a situation in which there are problems or difficulties, especially when these are unexpected: *The company has survived the recent upset in share prices.* ◊ *His health has not been improved by all the upset at home.* **2** [C] (in a competition) a situation in which a person or team beats the person or team that was expected to win **3** [C] an illness in the stomach that makes you feel sick or have DIARRHOEA: *a stomach upset* **4** [U, C] feelings of unhappiness and disappointment caused by sth unpleasant that has happened: *It had been the cause of much emotional upset.*

up·set·ting /ʌpˈsetɪŋ/ *adj.* making you feel unhappy, anxious or annoyed: *an upsetting experience* ◊ *She finds the divorce too upsetting to talk about.*

up·shot /ˈʌpʃɒt; *AmE* -ʃɑːt/ *noun* (**the upshot**) [sing.] the final result of a particular series of events: *The upshot of it all was that he left college and got a job.*

up·side /ˈʌpsaɪd/ *noun* [sing.] the more positive aspect of a situation that is generally bad **OPP** DOWNSIDE

ˌupside ˈdown *adv.* in or into a position in which the top of sth is where the bottom is normally found and the bottom is where the top is normally found: *The canoe floated upside down on the lake.* ◊ *Turn the cake upside down and cover it with cream.* **OPP** RIGHT SIDE UP ▶ **ˌupside ˈdown** *adj.* [not usually before noun]: *The painting looks like it's upside down to me.* **IDM** **turn sth ˌupside ˈdown** **1** to make a place untidy when looking for sth: *The police turned the whole house upside down looking for clues.* **2** to cause large changes and confusion in a person's life: *His sudden death turned her world upside down.*

it's upsidedown!

upside down

up·stage /ˌʌpˈsteɪdʒ/ *adv., adj., verb*
■ *adv.* at or towards the back of the stage in a theatre ▶ **up·stage** *adj.* [only before noun]
■ *verb* [VN] to say or do sth that makes people notice you more than the person that they should be interested in: *She was furious at being upstaged by her younger sister.*

up·stairs /ˌʌpˈsteəz; *AmE* -ˈsterz/ *adv., adj., noun*
■ *adv.* up the stairs; on or to a floor of a house or other building higher than the one that you are on: *The cat belongs to the people who live upstairs.* ◊ *I carried her bags upstairs.* ◊ *She went upstairs to get dressed.* **OPP** DOWNSTAIRS ▶ **up·stairs** *adj.* [only before noun]: *an upstairs room/window* **IDM** see KICK *v.*
■ *noun* [sing.] the floor or floors in a building that are above the ground floor: *We've converted the upstairs into an office.* **OPP** DOWNSTAIRS

up·stand·ing /ˌʌpˈstændɪŋ/ *adj.* [usually before noun] (*formal*) behaving in a moral and honest way **SYN** UPRIGHT: *an upstanding member of the community*

up·start /ˈʌpstɑːt; *AmE* -stɑːrt/ *noun* (*disapproving*) a person who has just started in a new position or job but who behaves as if they are more important than other people, in a way that is annoying

up·state /ˌʌpˈsteɪt/ *adv.* (*AmE*) in or to the northern part of a state that is far from its main cities: *They retired and went to live upstate.* ▶ **up·state** *adj.* [only before noun]: *upstate New York*

up·stream /ˌʌpˈstriːm/ (also *less frequent* **up·river**) *adv.* ~ (**of/from sth**) along a river, in the opposite direction to

aɪ	aʊ	eɪ	əʊ	oʊ	ɔɪ	ɪə	eə	ʊə	j	w
my	now	say	go (BrE)	go (AmE)	boy	near	hair	pure	yes	wet

the way in which the water flows: *The nearest town is about ten miles upstream.* ◊ *upstream of/from the bridge* **OPP** DOWNSTREAM

up·surge /ˈʌpsɜːdʒ; *AmE* -sɜːrdʒ/ *noun* [usually sing.] ~ **(in/of sth)** (*written*) a sudden large increase in sth: *an upsurge in violent crime* ◊ *a recent upsurge of interest in his movies*

up·swing /ˈʌpswɪŋ/ *noun* [usually sing.] ~ **(in sth)** (*written*) a situation in which sth improves or increases over a period of time **SYN** UPTURN: *an upswing in economic activity* ◊ *an upswing in the team's fortunes*

up·take /ˈʌpteɪk/ *noun* [U, sing.] ~ **(of sth)** (*technical*) the process by which sth is taken into a body or system; the rate at which this happens: *the uptake of oxygen by muscles* **IDM** **be ˌquick/ˌslow on the ˈuptake** to be quick/slow to understand sth: (*informal*) *Is he always this slow on the uptake?*

up·tempo /ˈʌptempəʊ; *AmE* -poʊ/ *adj.* (especially of music) fast: *uptempo dance tunes*

up·tight /ˌʌpˈtaɪt/ *adj.* ~ **(about sth)** (*informal*) **1** anxious and/or angry about sth: *Relax! You're getting too uptight about it.* **2** (*especially AmE*) nervous about showing your feelings: *I remember him when he was an uptight teenager.*

ˌup to ˈdate *adj.* **1** modern; fashionable: *This technology is bang up to date* (= completely modern). ◊ *up-to-date clothes* ◊ *up-to-date equipment/methods* **2** having or including the most recent information: *We are keeping up to date with the latest developments.* ◊ *up-to-date information/records*—see also OUT OF DATE

ˌup-to-the-ˈminute *adj.* [usually before noun] **1** having or including the most recent information: *up-to-the-minute news/information* **2** modern; fashionable: *up-to-the-minute designs/styles*—see also UP TO THE MINUTE at MINUTE *n.*

up·town /ˌʌpˈtaʊn/ *adv.* (*AmE*) in or to the parts of a town or city that are away from the centre: *They live in an apartment uptown.* ◊ *We walked uptown a couple of blocks until we found a cab.*—compare DOWNTOWN, MIDTOWN ► **up·town** *adj.* [only before noun]: *an uptown district/train*

up·trend /ˈʌptrend/ *noun* [sing.] (*AmE*) a situation in which business activity or performance increases or improves over a period of time **OPP** DOWNTREND

up·turn /ˈʌptɜːn; *AmE* -tɜːrn/ *noun* [usually sing.] ~ **(in sth)** a situation in which sth improves or increases over a period of time **SYN** UPSWING: *There are signs of an upturn in the economy.* ◊ *The restaurant trade is on the upturn.* **OPP** DOWNTURN

up·turned /ˌʌpˈtɜːnd; *AmE* ˌʌpˈtɜːrnd/ *adj.* [usually before noun] **1** pointing or facing upwards: *an upturned nose* (= that curves upwards at the end) ◊ *She looked down at the sea of upturned faces.* **2** turned upside down: *She sat on an upturned box.*

up·ward /ˈʌpwəd; *AmE* -wərd/ *adj.* [only before noun] **1** pointing towards or facing a higher place: *an upward gaze/look* ◊ *an upward curve* **2** increasing in amount or price: *a sharp upward movement in property prices* **OPP** DOWNWARD

ˌupwardly ˈmobile *adj.* moving towards a higher social position, usually in which you become richer: *upwardly mobile immigrant groups* ◊ *an upwardly mobile lifestyle* ► **ˌupward moˈbility** *noun* [U]

up·wards /ˈʌpwədz; *AmE* -wərdz/ (*especially BrE*) (also **up·ward** especially in *AmE*) *adv.* **1** towards a higher, place or position: *A flight of steps led upwards to the front door.* ◊ *Place your hands on the table with the palms facing upwards.* **OPP** DOWNWARDS **2** towards a higher amount or price: *Bad weather forced the price of fruit upwards.* ◊ *The budget has been revised upwards.* **OPP** DOWNWARDS **3 ~ of sth** more than the amount or number mentioned: *You should expect to pay upwards of £50 for a hotel room.*

up·wind /ˌʌpˈwɪnd/ *adv.* in the opposite direction to the way in which the wind is blowing: *to sail upwind* ◊ *The house was upwind of the factory and its smells* (= the wind did not blow the smells towards the house). **OPP** DOWNWIND ► **up·wind** *adj.*

ur·an·ium /juˈreɪniəm/ *noun* [U] (*symb* **U**) a chemical element. Uranium is a heavy, silver-white, RADIOACTIVE metal, used mainly in producing nuclear energy.

Ura·nus /ˈjʊərənəs; jʊˈreɪnəs; *AmE* ˈjʊr-; jʊˈr-/ *noun* the planet in the SOLAR SYSTEM that is 7th in order of distance from the sun

urban /ˈɜːbən; *AmE* ˈɜːrbən/ *adj.* [only before noun] connected with a town or city: *damage to both urban and rural environments* ◊ *urban areas/centres/populations* ◊ *urban life/unrest* ◊ *urban development* (= the process of building towns and cities or making them larger) ◊ *urban renewal/regeneration* (= the process of improving the buildings, etc. in the poor parts of a town or city) ◊ *efforts to control urban sprawl* (= the spread of city buildings into the countryside)—compare RURAL

ur·bane /ɜːˈbeɪn; *AmE* ɜːrˈb-/ *adj.* (*written*) (especially of a man) good at knowing what to say and how to behave in social situations; appearing relaxed and confident: *He was charming and urbane, full of witty conversation.* ► **ur·bane·ly** *adv.* **ur·ban·ity** /ɜːˈbænəti; *AmE* ɜːrˈb-/ *noun* [U]

ur·ban·ized (*BrE* also **-ised**) /ˈɜːbənaɪzd; *AmE* ˈɜːrb-/ *adj.* **1** (of an area, a country, etc.) having a lot of towns, streets, factories, etc. rather than countryside **2** (of people) living and working in towns and cities rather than in the country: *an increasingly urbanized society* ► **ur·ban·iza·tion**, **-isa·tion** (*BrE*) /ˌɜːbənaɪˈzeɪʃn; *AmE* ˌɜːrbənəˈz-/ *noun* [U]

ur·chin /ˈɜːtʃɪn; *AmE* ˈɜːrtʃɪn/ *noun* **1** (*old-fashioned*) a young child who is poor and dirty, often one who has no home: *a dirty little street urchin* **2** = SEA URCHIN

Urdu /ˈʊəduː; ˈɜːduː; *AmE* ˈʊrduː; ˈɜːrduː/ *noun* [U] the official language of Pakistan, also widely used in India

-ure *suffix* (in nouns) the action, process or result of: *closure* ◊ *failure*

urea /juˈriːə/ *noun* [U] (*technical*) a colourless substance containing NITROGEN that is found especially in URINE

ur·ethra /juˈriːθrə/ *noun* (*anatomy*) the tube that carries liquid waste out of the body. In men and male animals SPERM also flows along this tube. ► **ur·eth·ral** *adj.* [only before noun]

urge /ɜːdʒ; *AmE* ɜːrdʒ/ *verb, noun*

■ *verb* **1** to advise or try hard to persuade sb to do sth: [VN to inf] *She urged him to stay.* ◊ [V that] *The report urged that all children be taught to swim.* [also V speech, VN speech] **2** [VN] ~ **sth (on/upon sb)** to recommend sth strongly: *The situation is dangerous, but the UN is urging caution.* **3** [VN + adv./prep.] (*written*) to make a person or an animal move more quickly and/or in a particular direction, especially by pushing or forcing them: *He urged his horse forward.* **PHRV** **ˌurge sb↔ˈon** to encourage sb to do sth or support them so that they do it better: *She could hear him urging her on as she ran past.*

■ *noun* ~ **(to do sth)** a strong desire to do sth: *sexual/creative urges* ◊ *I had a sudden urge to hit him.*

ur·gent /ˈɜːdʒənt; *AmE* ˈɜːrdʒ-/ *adj.* **1** that needs to be dealt with immediately: *an urgent appeal for information* ◊ *a problem that requires urgent attention* ◊ *'Can I see you for a moment?' 'Is it urgent?'* ◊ *Mark the message 'urgent', please.* ◊ *The law is in urgent need of reform.* **2** (*written*) showing that you think that sth needs to be dealt with immediately: *an urgent look/whisper* ► **ur·gen·cy** /-dʒənsi/ *noun* [U, sing.]: *This is a matter of some urgency.* ◊ *The attack added a new urgency to the peace talks.* **ur·gent·ly** *adv.*: *New equipment is urgently needed.* ◊ *I need to speak to her urgently.* ◊ *'We must find him,' she said urgently.*

ur·inal /juəˈraɪnl; ˈjʊərɪnl; *AmE* ˈjʊrənl/ *noun* a type of toilet for men that is attached to the wall; a room or building containing urinals

urin·ary /ˈjʊərɪnəri; *AmE* ˈjʊrəneri/ *adj.* [usually before noun] (*medical*) connected with URINE or the parts of the body through which it passes

urin·ate /ˈjʊərɪneɪt; *AmE* ˈjʊrən-/ *verb* [V] (*formal or technical*) to get rid of URINE from the body ► **urin·ation** /ˌjʊərɪˈneɪʃn; *AmE* ˌjʊrəˈn-/ *noun* [U]

b	d	f	g	h	k	l	m	n	p	r
bad	did	fall	get	hat	cat	leg	man	now	pen	red

urine /ˈjʊərɪn; -raɪn; *AmE* ˈjʊrən/ (also *spoken* **wee** especially in *BrE*) *noun* [U] the waste liquid that collects in the BLADDER and that you pass from your body

URL /ˌjuː ɑː(r) ˈel/ *abbr.* (*computing*) uniform/universal resource locator (the address of a WORLD WIDE WEB page)

urn /ɜːn; *AmE* ɜːrn/ *noun* **1** a tall decorated container, especially one used for holding the ashes of a dead person **2** a large metal container with a tap, used for making and/or serving tea or coffee: *a tea urn*

ur·ology /jʊəˈrɒlədʒi; *AmE* jʊˈrɑːl-/ *noun* [U] (*medical*) the scientific study of the URINARY system ▶ **uro·logic·al** /ˌjʊərəˈlɒdʒɪkl; *AmE* /ˌjʊrəˈlɑːdʒ-/ *adj.* **ur·olo·gist** /-dʒɪst/ *noun*

US (also **U.S.** especially in *AmE*) /ˌjuː ˈes/ *abbr.* United States (of America): *She became a US citizen.* ◇ *the US dollar*

us /əs; *strong form* ʌs/ *pron.* (the object form of *we*) **1** used when the speaker or writer and another or others are the object of a verb or preposition: *She gave us a picture as a wedding present.* ◇ *We'll take the dog with us.* ◇ *Hello, it's us back again.* **2** (*BrE, spoken, informal*) me: *Give us the newspaper, will you?*

us·able /ˈjuːzəbl/ *adj.* that can be used; in good enough condition to be used: *The bike is rusty but usable.* ◇ *How can we display this data in a usable form?* OPP UNUSABLE

USA (also **U.S.A.** especially in *AmE*) /ˌjuː es ˈeɪ/ *abbr.* United States of America: *Do you need a visa for the USA?*

USAF /ˌjuː es eɪ ˈef/ *abbr.* United States Air Force

usage /ˈjuːsɪdʒ; ˈjuːz-/ *noun* **1** [U, C] the way in which words are used in a language: *current English usage* ◇ *It's not a word in common usage.* **2** [U] the fact of sth being used; how much sth is used: *land usage* ◇ *Car usage is predicted to increase.*

use *verb, noun*
■ *verb* /juːz/ (**used, used** /juːzd/) **1** [VN] ~ **sth (for sth/for doing sth)** | ~ **sth (as sth)** to do sth with a machine, a method, an object, etc. for a particular purpose: *Can I use your phone?* ◇ *Have you ever used this software before?* ◇ *How often do you use* (= travel by) *the bus?* ◇ *They were able to achieve a settlement without using military force.* ◇ *Police used tear gas to disperse the crowds.* ◇ *The blue files are used for storing old invoices.* ◇ *The building is currently being used as a warehouse.* ◇ *You can't keep using your bad back as an excuse.* ◇ *I have some information you may be able to use* (= to get an advantage from). **2** [VN] to take a particular amount of a liquid, substance, etc. in order to achieve or make sth: *This type of heater uses a lot of electricity.* ◇ *I hope you haven't used all the milk.* **3** [VN] (*disapproving*) to be kind, friendly, etc. to sb with the intention of getting an advantage for yourself from them; *Can't you see he's just using you for his own ends?* ◇ *I felt used.* **4** to take illegal drugs: [VN] *Most of the inmates have used drugs at some point in their lives.* ◇ [V] (*slang*) *She's been using since she was 13.* IDM **I, you, etc. could use sth** (*spoken*) used to say that you would like to have sth very much: *I think we could all use a drink after that!* **use your ˈhead** (*BrE* also **use your ˈloaf**) (*informal*) used to tell sb to think about sth, especially when they have asked for your opinion or said sth stupid: *'Why don't you want to see him again?' 'Oh, use your head!'* ORIGIN From rhyming slang, in which **loaf of bread** stands for 'head'. PHR V **use sth↔ˈup** to use sth so that there is none left: *Making soup is a good way of using up leftover vegetables.*
■ *noun* /juːs/ **1** [U, sing.] the act of using sth; the state of being used: *A ban was imposed on the use of chemical weapons.* ◇ *The software is designed for use in schools.* ◇ *I'm not sure that this is the most valuable use of my time.* ◇ *The chapel was built in the 12th century and is still in use today.* ◇ *The bar is for the use of members only.* **2** [C, U] a purpose for which sth is used; a way in which sth is or can be used: *I'm sure you'll think of a use for it.* ◇ *This chemical has a wide range of industrial uses.* **3** [U] ~ **(of sth)** the right or opportunity to use sth, for example sth that belongs to sb else: *I have the use of the car this week.* **4** [U] the ability to use your mind or body: *He lost the use of his legs* (= became unable to walk) *in an accident.* IDM **be no ˈuse (to sb)** (also *formal* **be of no ˈuse**) to be

useless: *You can throw those away—they're no use to anyone.* **be of ˈuse (to sb)** (*formal*) to be useful: *Can I be of any use* (= can I help)*?* **come into/go out of ˈuse** to start/stop being used: *These pesticides are gradually being phased out of use.* ◇ *When did this word come into common use?* **have its/their/your ˈuses** (*informal*, often *humorous*) to be useful sometimes: *I know you don't like him, but he has his uses.* **have no ˈuse for sb** to dislike sb: *I've no use for people who don't make an effort.* **have no ˈuse for sth** to not need sth **it's no ˈuse (doing sth)** | **What's the ˈuse (of doing sth)?** used to say that there is no point in doing sth because it will not be successful or have a good result: *What's the use of worrying about it?* ◇ *It's no use—I can't persuade her.* **make ˈuse of sth/sb** to use sth/sb, especially in order to get an advantage: *We could make better use of our resources.* ◇ *You should make use of your contacts.* **put sth to good ˈuse** to be able to use sth for a purpose, and get an advantage from doing so: *She'll be able to put her languages to good use in her new job.*

used¹ /juːst/ *adj.* ~ **to sth/to doing sth** familiar with sth because you do it or experience it often: *I'm not used to eating so much at lunchtime.* ◇ *I found the job tiring at first but I soon got used to it.* ⇨ note at USED TO

used² /juːzd/ *adj.* [usually before noun] that has belonged to or been used by sb else before SYN SECOND-HAND: *used cars*

WHICH WORD?
used to / be used to

Do not confuse **used to do sth** with **be used to sth**.

You use **used to do sth** to talk about something that happened regularly or was the case in the past, but is not now: *I used to smoke, but I gave up a couple of years ago.*

You use **be used to sth/to doing sth** to talk about something that you are familiar with so that it no longer seems new or strange to you: *We're used to the noise from the traffic now.* ◇ *I'm used to getting up early.* You can also use **get used to sth**: *Don't worry — you'll soon get used to his sense of humour.* ◇ *I didn't think I could ever get used to living in a big city after living in the country.*

---

used to /ˈjuːst tə; *before vowels and finally* ˈjuːst tu/ *modal verb* (*negative* **didn't use to** /-juːs/, *BrE also, old-fashioned or formal* **used not to** *short form* **usedn't to** /ˈjuːsnt tə; *before vowels and finally* ˈjuːsnt tu/) used to say that sth happened continuously or frequently during a period in the past: *I used to live in London.* ◇ *We used to go sailing on the lake in summer.* ◇ *I didn't use to like him much when we were at school.* ◇ *You used to see a lot of her, didn't you?* ⇨ note at MODAL

GRAMMAR POINT
used to

Except in negatives and questions, the correct form is **used to**: *I used to go there every Saturday.* ◇ *I use to go there every Saturday.*

To form questions, use **did**: *Did she use to have long hair?* Note that the correct spelling is **use to**, not 'used to'.

The negative form is usually **didn't use to**, but in *BrE* this is quite informal and is not usually used in writing.

The negative form **used not to** (rather formal) and the question form **used you to...?** (old-fashioned and very formal) are only used in *BrE*, usually in writing.

---

use·ful /ˈjuːsfl/ *adj.* **1** ~ **(to do sth)** | ~ **(to sb)** | ~ **(for sth/for doing sth)** that can help you to do or achieve what you want: *a useful gadget/book* ◇ *It can be useful to write a short summary of your argument first.* ◇ *He might be useful to us.* ◇ *These plants are particularly useful for brightening up shady areas.* ◇ *Don't just sit watching television—make yourself useful!* ◇ *This information* *could* **prove** *useful.* ◊ *Your knowledge of German may* **come in useful** (= be useful in a particular situation). ◊ *Some products can be recycled at the end of their useful life.* **2** (*BrE, informal*) good; satisfactory: *He's a very useful player.* ▶ **use·ful·ly** /-fəli/ *adv.*: *The money could be more usefully spent on new equipment.*

use·ful·ness /ˈjuːsfʊlnəs/ *noun* [U] the fact of being useful or possible to use: *There are doubts about the usefulness of these tests.* ◊ *The building has outlived its usefulness.*

use·less /ˈjuːsləs/ *adj.* **1** ~ **(to do sth)** | ~ **(doing sth)** not useful; not doing or achieving what is wanted or wanted: *This pen is useless.* ◊ *He knew it was useless to protest.* ◊ *It's useless worrying about it.* ◊ *She tried to work, but it was useless* (= she wasn't able to). **2** ~ **(at doing sth)** (*informal*) not very good at sth; not able to do things well: *I'm useless at French.* ◊ *Don't ask her to help. She's useless.* ▶ **use·less·ly** *adv.* **use·less·ness** *noun* [U]

user /ˈjuːzə(r)/ *noun* **1** a person or thing that uses sth: *road users* ◊ *computer software users* ◊ *Please enter your* **user name.** **2** (*slang*) a person who is ADDICTED TO drugs

'user fee *noun* (*AmE*) a tax on a service that is provided for the public

,user-'friendly *adj.* easy for people who are not experts to use or understand: *Computer programs have become more user-friendly.* ▶ **,user-'friendli·ness** *noun* [U]

usher /ˈʌʃə(r)/ *noun, verb*
■ *noun* **1** a person who shows people where to sit in a church, public hall, etc. **2** an official who has special responsibilities in a court of law, for example allowing people in and out of the court **3** a friend of the BRIDEGROOM at a wedding, who has special duties
■ *verb* [VN+*adv.*/*prep.*] to take or show sb where they should go: *The secretary ushered me into his office.* PHRV **,usher sth ↔ 'in** (*formal*) to be the beginning of sth new or to make sth new begin: *The change of management ushered in fresh ideas and policies.*

ush·er·ette /ˌʌʃəˈret/ *noun* (*especially BrE*) a woman whose job is to lead people to their seats in a theatre or cinema/movie theater

USN /ˌjuː es ˈen/ *abbr.* United States Navy

USS /ˌjuː es ˈes/ *abbr.* United States Ship: *USS Oklahoma*

USSR /ˌjuː es es ˈɑː(r)/ *abbr.* (the former) Union of Soviet Socialist Republics

usual /ˈjuːʒuəl; -ʒəl/ *adj.* **1** ~ **(for sb/sth) (to do sth)** that happens or is done most of the time or in most cases: *She made all the usual excuses.* ◊ *He came home later than usual.* ◊ *She sat in her usual seat at the back.* ◊ **It is usual to** start a speech by thanking everybody for coming. ◊ *He didn't sound like his usual happy self.* ⇨ note at NORMAL—compare UNUSUAL **2** (**the usual**) *noun* [sing.] (*spoken*) what usually happens; what you usually have, especially the drink that you usually have **IDM as usual** in the same way as what happens most of the time or in most cases: *Steve, as usual, was the last to arrive.* ◊ *As usual at that hour, the place was deserted.* ◊ *Despite her problems, she carried on working as usual.*—more at BUSINESS, PER

usu·al·ly /ˈjuːʒuəli; -ʒəli/ *adv.* in the way that is usual or normal; most often: *I'm usually home by 6 o'clock.* ◊ *We usually go by car.* ◊ *How long does the journey usually take?*

us·urer /ˈjuːʒərə(r)/ *noun* (*old-fashioned, disapproving*) a person who lends money to people at unfairly high rates of interest

usurp /juːˈzɜːp; *AmE* -ˈzɜːrp/ *verb* [VN] (*formal*) to take sb's position and/or power without having the right to do this: *He attempted to usurp the principal's authority.* ▶ **usurp·ation** /ˌjuːzɜːˈpeɪʃn; *AmE* -zɜːrˈp-/ *noun* [U, C] **usurp·er** *noun*

usury /ˈjuːʒəri/ *noun* [U] (*old-fashioned, disapproving*) the practice of lending money to people at unfairly high rates of interest

uten·sil /juːˈtensl/ *noun* a tool that is used in the house: *cooking/kitchen utensils*

uterus /ˈjuːtərəs/ *noun* (*anatomy*) the organ in women and female animals in which babies develop before they are born SYN WOMB ▶ **uter·ine** /ˈjuːtəraɪn/ *adj.* [only before noun] —see also INTRAUTERINE DEVICE

utili·tar·ian /ˌjuːtɪlɪˈteəriən; *AmE* -ˈter-/ *adj.* **1** (*formal*) designed to be useful and practical rather than attractive: *a utilitarian building* **2** (*philosophy*) based on or supporting the idea of utilitarianism

utili·tar·ian·ism /ˌjuːtɪlɪˈteəriənɪzəm; *AmE* -ˈter-/ *noun* [U] (*philosophy*) the belief that the right course of action is the one that will produce the greatest happiness of the greatest number of people

util·ity /juːˈtɪləti/ *noun, adj.*
■ *noun* (*pl.* **-ies**) **1** [C] (*especially AmE*) a service provided for the public, for example an electricity, water or gas supply: *the administration of public utilities* **2** [U] (*formal*) the quality of being useful **3** [C] (*computing*) a piece of computer SOFTWARE that performs a particular task
■ *adj.* [only before noun] that can be used for several different purposes: *a utility vehicle*

u'tility room *noun* a room, especially in a private house, that contains large pieces of equipment such as a washing machine, FREEZER, etc.

util·ize (*BrE also* **-ise**) /ˈjuːtəlaɪz/ *verb* [VN] ~ **sth** (**as sth**) (*formal*) to use sth, especially for a practical purpose: *The Romans were the first to utilize concrete as a building material.* ◊ *The resources at our disposal could have been better utilized.* ▶ **util·iza·tion, -isa·tion** /ˌjuːtəlaɪˈzeɪʃn; *AmE* -ləˈz-/ *noun* [U]

ut·most /ˈʌtməʊst; *AmE* -moʊst/ *adj., noun*
■ *adj.* (*also less frequent* **ut·ter·most**) [only before noun] greatest; most extreme: *This is a matter of the utmost importance.* ◊ *You should study this document with the utmost care.*
■ *noun* [sing.] the greatest amount possible: *Our resources are strained to the utmost.* ◊ *He* **did his utmost** (= tried as hard as possible) *to persuade me not to go.*

Uto·pia /juːˈtəʊpiə; *AmE* -ˈtoʊ-/ *noun* [C, U] an imaginary place or state in which everything is perfect: *a Socialist Utopia* ▶ **Uto·pian** /juːˈtəʊpiən; *AmE* -ˈtoʊ-/ *adj.*: *Utopian ideals* **Uto·pian·ism** *noun* [U]

utter /ˈʌtə(r)/ *adj., verb*
■ *adj.* [only before noun] used to emphasize how complete sth is: *That's complete and utter nonsense!* ◊ *To my utter amazement she agreed.* ◊ *He felt an utter fool!* ▶ **ut·ter·ly** *adv.*: *We're so utterly different from each other.* ◊ *She utterly failed to convince them.*
■ *verb* [VN] (*formal*) to make a sound with your voice; to say sth: *to utter a cry/groan/moan/sigh* ◊ *She did not* **utter a word** *during lunch* (= said nothing).

ut·ter·ance /ˈʌtərəns/ *noun* (*formal*) **1** [U] the act of expressing sth in words: *to give utterance to your thoughts* **2** [C] something that you say: *one of her few recorded public utterances*

ut·ter·most /ˈʌtəməʊst/ = UTMOST

'U-turn *noun* **1** a turn of 180° that a vehicle makes so that it can move forwards in the opposite direction: *to do/make a U-turn* **2** (*informal*) a complete change in policy or behaviour, usually one that is embarrassing

uvula /ˈjuːvjələ/ *noun* (*pl.* **uvu·lae** /-liː/) (*anatomy*) a small piece of flesh that hangs from the top of the inside of the mouth just above the throat—picture at BODY

U

æ	ɑː	e	ɜː	ə	ɪ	iː	i	ɒ	ɔː	ʌ	ʊ	u	uː
cat	father	ten	bird	about	sit	see	many	got	saw	cup	put	actual	too
								(BrE)					

Vv

V /viː/ *noun, abbr., symbol*

■ *noun* (also **v**) (*pl.* **V's, v's** /viːz/) [C, U] the 22nd letter of the English alphabet: *'Violin' begins with (a) V/'V'.* **2 a** thing shaped like a V: *Ahead was the deep V of a gorge with water pouring down it.*—see also V-NECK, V-SIGN
■ *abbr.* (in writing) VOLT(S): *a 1.5 V battery*
■ *symbol* (also **v**) the number 5 in ROMAN NUMERALS

v *abbr.* **1** (also **vs** especially in *AmE*) (in sport or in a legal case) versus (= against): *England v West Indies ◇ the State vs Kramer* (= a case in a court of law) **2** (*BrE, informal, written*) very: *I was v pleased to get your letter.*

vac /væk/ *noun* (*BrE, informal*) a university VACATION

va·cancy /'veɪkənsi/ *noun* (*pl.* **-ies**) **1** [C] ~ **(for sb/sth)** a job that is available for sb to do: *a casual/temporary vacancy ◇ vacancies for bar staff ◇ to fill a vacancy* **2** [C] a room that is available in a hotel, etc: *I'm sorry, we have no vacancies.* **3** [U] (*written*) lack of interest or ideas SYN EMPTINESS: *the vacancy of her expression*

va·cant /'veɪkənt/ *adj.* **1** (of a seat, hotel room, house, etc.) empty; not being used: *vacant properties ◇ The seat next to him was vacant. ◇* (*especially AmE*) *a vacant lot* (= a piece of land in a city that is not being used)—compare ENGAGED, OCCUPIED **2** (*formal*) if a job in a company is **vacant**, nobody is doing it and it is available for sb to take: *When the post finally fell* (= became) *vacant, they offered it to Fiona. ◇* (*BrE*) *Situations Vacant* (= a section in a newspaper where jobs are advertised) **3** (*written*) (of a look, an expression, etc.) showing no sign that the person is thinking of anything: *a vacant look/stare* ▶ **va·cant·ly** *adv.*: *to look/smile/stare vacantly*

vacant pos'session *noun* [U] (*BrE, technical*) the fact of owning a house that is empty because the people who lived there have moved out

vac·ate /və'keɪt; veɪ'k-; *AmE* also 'veɪkeɪt/ *verb* [VN] (*formal*) **1** to leave a building, seat, etc., especially so that sb else can use it: *Guests are requested to vacate their rooms by noon on the day of departure.* **2** to leave a job, position of authority, etc. so that it is available for sb else: *She has taken over the role vacated by her boss.*

vac·ation /və'keɪʃn; veɪ'k-/ *noun, verb*

■ *noun* **1** (in Britain) one of the periods of time when universities or courts of law are closed; (in the US) one of the periods of time when schools, colleges, universities or courts of law are closed: *the Christmas/Easter/summer vacation ◇* (*BrE*) *the long vacation* (= the summer vacation)—see also VAC **2** [U, C] (*AmE*) = HOLIDAY: *They're on vacation in Hawaii right now. ◇ You look tired—you should take a vacation. ◇ The job includes two weeks' paid vacation. ◇ a vacation home* ➪ note at HOLIDAY
■ *verb* [V] (*AmE*) = HOLIDAY: *They are currently vacationing in Florida.*

vac·ation·er /və'keɪʃnə(r); veɪ'k-/ *noun* (*AmE*) = HOLIDAYMAKER

vac·cin·ate /'væksɪneɪt/ *verb* [VN] [often passive] ~ **sb** **(against sth)** to give a person or an animal a vaccine, especially by INJECTING it, in order to protect them against a disease: *Have you been vaccinated against polio?*—compare IMMUNIZE, INOCULATE ▶ **vac·cin·ation** /,væksɪ'neɪʃn/ *noun* [C, U]: *Make sure your vaccinations are up to date. ◇ vaccination against hepatitis B*

vac·cine /'væksiːn; *AmE* væk'siːn/ *noun* [C, U] a substance that is put into the blood and that protects the body from a disease: *a polio/measles vaccine ◇ There is no vaccine against HIV infection*—picture on page 599

vacil·late /'væsəleɪt/ *verb* [V] (*formal*) to keep changing your opinion or thoughts about sth, especially in a way that annoys other people SYN WAVER: *The country's lead-*

ers are still vacillating between confrontation and compromise. ▶ **va·cil·la·tion** /,væsə'leɪʃn/ *noun* [U, C]

vacu·ity /və'kjuːəti/ *noun* [U] (*formal*) lack of serious thought or purpose SYN EMPTINESS

vacu·ous /'vækjuəs/ *adj.* (*formal*) showing no sign of intelligence or sensitive feelings: *a vacuous look/expression/smile* ▶ **vacu·ous·ly** *adv.* **vacu·ous·ness** *noun* [U]

vac·uum /'vækjuəm/ *noun, verb*

■ *noun* **1** a space that is completely empty of all substances, including all air or other gas: *a vacuum pump* (= one that creates a vacuum in an enclosed space) *◇ vacuum-packed foods* (= in a package from which most of the air has been removed) **2** [usually sing.] a situation in which sb/sth is missing or lacking: *His resignation has created a vacuum which cannot easily be filled.* **3** [usually sing.] the act of cleaning sth with a vacuum cleaner: *to give a room a quick vacuum* IDM **in a 'vacuum** existing separately from other people, events, etc. when there should be a connection: *This kind of decision cannot ever be made in a vacuum.*
■ *verb* to clean sth using a vacuum cleaner SYN HOOVER [VN] *Have you vacuumed the stairs?* [also V]

'vacuum cleaner (*BrE* also **Hoover**™) *noun* an electrical machine that cleans floors, carpets, etc. by sucking up dirt and dust

'vacuum flask (also **flask**) (both *BrE*) (*AmE* **'vacuum bottle**) *noun* a container like a bottle with double walls with a vacuum between them, used for keeping liquids hot or cold—compare THERMOS

vaga·bond /'vægəbɒnd; *AmE* -bɑːnd/ *noun* (*old-fashioned, disapproving*) a person who has no home or job and who travels from place to place

va·gar·ies /'veɪgəriz/ *noun* [pl.] changes in sb/sth that are difficult to predict or control

va·gina /və'dʒaɪnə/ *noun* the passage in the body of a woman or female animal between the outer sex organs and the WOMB ▶ **va·ginal** /və'dʒaɪnl/ *adj.* [only before noun]

va·grancy /'veɪgrənsi/ *noun* [U] (*law*) the crime of living on the streets and BEGGING (= asking for money) from people

va·grant /'veɪgrənt/ *noun* (*formal or law*) a person who has no home or job, especially one who BEGS (= asks for money) from people ▶ **va·grant** *adj.*

vague /veɪg/ *adj.* (**vaguer, vaguest**) **1** not clear in a person's mind: *to have a vague impression/memory/recollection of sth ◇ They had only a vague idea where the place was.* **2** ~ **(about sth)** not having or giving enough information or details about sth: *She's a little vague about her plans for next year. ◇ The politicians made vague promises about tax cuts. ◇ He was accused of being deliberately vague. ◇ We had only a vague description of the attacker.* **3** (of a person's behaviour) suggesting a lack of clear thought or attention: *a vague expression/look ◇ His vague manner concealed a brilliant mind.* **4** not having a clear shape SYN INDISTINCT: *In the darkness they could see the vague outline of a church.* ▶ **vague·ness** *noun* [U]

vague·ly /'veɪgli/ *adv.* **1** in a way that is not detailed or exact: *a vaguely worded statement ◇ I can vaguely remember my first day at school.* **2** slightly: *There was something vaguely familiar about her face. ◇ He was vaguely aware of footsteps behind him.* **3** in a way that shows that you are not paying attention or thinking clearly: *He smiled vaguely, ignoring her questions.*

vain /veɪn/ *adj.* **1** that does not produce the result you want SYN USELESS: *She closed her eyes tightly in a vain attempt to hold back the tears. ◇ I knocked loudly in the*

aɪ	aʊ	eɪ	əʊ	oʊ	ɔɪ	ɪə	eə	ʊə	j	w
my	now	say	go	go	boy	near	hair	pure	yes	wet
			(BrE)	(AmE)						

vain hope that someone might answer. **2** (*disapproving*) too proud of your own appearance, abilities or achievements SYN CONCEITED: *She's too vain to wear glasses.*—see also VANITY IDM **in 'vain** without success: *They tried in vain to persuade her to go.* ◇ *All our efforts were in vain.*—more at NAME *n.*

vain·glori·ous /ˌveɪnˈɡlɔːriəs/ *adj.* (*literary, disapproving*) too proud of your own abilities or achievements ▶ **vainglory** /ˌveɪnˈɡlɔːri/ *noun* [U]

vain·ly /ˈveɪnli/ *adv.* without success: *He shouted after them, vainly trying to attract their attention.*

val·ance /ˈvæləns/ *noun* **1** a narrow piece of fabric like a short curtain that hangs around the frame of a bed, under a shelf, etc. **2** (*especially AmE*) = PELMET

vale /veɪl/ *noun* (*old use or literary*) (also used in modern place names) a valley: *a wooded vale* ◇ *the Vale* of the White Horse

val·edic·tion /ˌvælɪˈdɪkʃn/ *noun* [C, U] (*formal*) the act of saying goodbye, especially in a formal speech

val·edic·tor·ian /ˌvælɪdɪkˈtɔːriən/ *noun* (*AmE*) the student who has the highest marks/grades in a particular group of students and who gives the valedictory speech at a GRADUATION ceremony

val·edic·tory /ˌvælɪˈdɪktəri/ *adj.* [usually before noun] (*formal*) connected with saying goodbye, especially at a formal occasion: *a valedictory speech*

va·lency /ˈveɪlənsi/ *noun* [C, U] (*pl.* **-ies**) (also **va·lence** /ˈveɪləns/ especially in *AmE*) **1** (*chemistry*) a measurement of the power of an atom to combine with others, by the number of HYDROGEN atoms it can combine with or DISPLACE: *Carbon has a valency of 4.* **2** (*linguistics*) the number of GRAMMATICAL elements that a word, especially a verb, combines with in a sentence

val·en·tine /ˈvæləntaɪn/ *noun* **1** (also **'valentine card**) a card that you send to sb that you love on St Valentine's Day (14 February), often without putting your name on it **2** a person that you send a valentine to

valet *noun, verb*
■ *noun* /ˈvæleɪ; ˈvælɪt; AmE* also *væˈleɪ/* **1** a man's personal servant who takes care of his clothes, serves his meals, etc. **2** (*BrE*) a hotel employee whose job is to clean the clothes of hotel guests **3** (*AmE*) a person who parks your car for you at a hotel or restaurant
■ *verb* /ˈvælɪt/ **1** [VN] (*BrE*) to clean a person's car thoroughly, especially on the inside: *a car valeting service* **2** [V] to perform the duties of a valet

vali·ant /ˈvæliənt/ *adj.* (especially *literary*) very brave or determined: *valiant warriors/efforts* ◇ *She made a valiant attempt not to laugh.* ▶ **vali·ant·ly** *adv.*

valid /ˈvælɪd/ *adj.* **1** that is legally or officially acceptable: *a valid passport* ◇ *a bus pass valid for 1 month* ◇ *They have a valid claim to compensation.* **2** based on what is logical or true: *She had valid reasons for not supporting the proposals.* ◇ *The point you make is perfectly valid.* **3** (*computing*) that is accepted by the system: *a valid password* OPP INVALID ▶ **val·id·ly** *adv.*: *The contract had been validly drawn up.*

val·id·ate /ˈvælɪdeɪt/ *verb* [VN] (*formal*) **1** to prove that sth is true: *to validate a claim/theory* OPP INVALIDATE **2** to make sth legally valid: *to validate a contract* OPP INVALIDATE **3** to state officially that sth is useful and of an acceptable standard: *Check that their courses have been validated by a reputable organization.* ▶ **val·id·ation** /ˌvælɪˈdeɪʃn/ *noun* [U, C]

val·id·ity /vəˈlɪdəti/ *noun* [U] **1** the state of being legally or officially acceptable: *The period of validity of the agreement has expired.* **2** the state of being logical and true: *We had doubts about the validity of their argument.*

val·ise /vəˈliːz; AmE vəˈliːs/ *noun* (*old-fashioned*) a small bag for carrying clothes, used when you are travelling

Val·ium ™ /ˈvæliəm/ *noun* [U] a drug used to reduce anxiety: *The doctor prescribed Valium.*

val·ley /ˈvæli/ *noun* an area of low land between hills or mountains, often with a river flowing through it; the land that a river flows through: *a small town set in a valley* ◇ *the Loire Valley*—picture at MOUNTAIN

val·our (*BrE*) (*AmE* **valor**) /ˈvælə(r)/ *noun* [U] (*literary*) great courage, especially in war: *acts of valour* ▶ **val·or·ous** /ˈvælərəs/ *adj.* IDM see DISCRETION

valu·able /ˈvæljuəbl/ *adj.* **1 ~ (to sb/sth)** very useful or important: *a valuable experience/resource/tool/insight* ◇ *The book provides valuable information on recent trends.* ◇ *This advice was to prove valuable.* **2** worth a lot of money: *valuable antiques/jewellery* OPP VALUELESS, WORTHLESS—compare INVALUABLE, PRICELESS

valu·ables /ˈvæljuəblz/ *noun* [pl.] things that are worth a lot of money, especially small personal things such as jewellery, cameras, etc.

valu·ation /ˌvæljuˈeɪʃn/ *noun* [C, U] **1** a professional judgement about how much money sth is worth; its estimated value: *land valuation* ◇ *Surveyors carried out a valuation of the property.* ◇ *Experts set a high valuation on the painting.* **2** (*formal*) a judgement about how useful or important sth is; its estimated importance: *She puts a high valuation on trust between colleagues.*

value /ˈvæljuː/ *noun, verb*
■ *noun*
HOW MUCH STH IS WORTH | **1** [U, C] how much sth is worth in money or other goods for which it can be exchanged: *to go up/rise/increase in value* ◇ *to go down/fall/drop in value* ◇ *rising property values* ◇ *The winner will receive a prize to the value of £1000.* ◇ *The winner will receive a prize* **to the value of** £1000.* ◇ *The winner will receive a prize* to the value well.—see also MARKET VALUE, STREET VALUE **2** [U] (*especially BrE*) how much sth is worth compared with its price: *to be good/excellent value* (= worth the money it costs) ◇ *to be bad/poor value* (= not worth the money it costs) ◇ *Charter flights give the best* **value for money.**

BEING USEFUL/IMPORTANT | **3** [U] the quality of being useful or important: *The value of regular exercise should not be underestimated.* ◇ *The arrival of canals was* **of great value** *to many industries.* ◇ *to be of little/no value to sb* ◇ *food with a high nutritional/energy value* ◇ *The story has very little news value.* ◇ *This ring has great* **sentimental value** *for me.* ◇ *I suppose it has a certain* **novelty value** (= it's interesting because it's new) *but you'll soon get bored of it.*

BELIEFS | **4** (**values**) [pl.] beliefs about what is right and wrong and what is important in life: *cultural/social/moral values* ◇ *a return to traditional values in education, such as firm discipline* ◇ *The young have a completely different set of values and expectations.*

MATHEMATICS | **5** [C] the amount represented by a letter or symbol: *Let y have the value 33.*
■ *verb* [VN]
CONSIDER IMPORTANT | **1** (not used in the progressive tenses) **~ sb/sth (as sth)** | **~ sb/sth (for sth)** to think that sb/sth is important: *I really value him as a friend.* ◇ *The area is valued for its vineyards.* ◇ *a valued member of staff*

DECIDE WORTH | **2** [usually passive] **~ sth (at sth)** to decide that sth is worth a particular amount of money: *The property has been valued at over $2 million.*

value 'added tax *noun* [U] = VAT

'value judgement (also **'value judgment** especially in *AmE*) *noun* [C, U] (sometimes *disapproving*) a judgement about how good or important sth is, based on personal opinions rather than facts

value·less /ˈvæljuːləs/ *adj.* (*formal*) without value or worth SYN WORTHLESS OPP VALUABLE

valuer /ˈvæljuːə(r)/ *noun* a person whose job is to estimate how much property, land, etc. is worth

valve /vælv/ *noun* **1** a device for controlling the flow of a liquid or gas, letting it move in one direction only—picture at BICYCLE **2** a structure in the heart or in a VEIN that lets blood flow in one direction only **3** a device in some BRASS musical instruments for changing the note

vamp /væmp/ *noun* (*old-fashioned, disapproving*) a sexually attractive woman who uses this power to control men

vam·pire /ˈvæmpaɪə(r)/ *noun* (in stories) a dead person who leaves his or her grave at night to suck the blood of living people

'vampire bat *noun* a S American BAT (= an animal like a mouse with wings) that sucks the blood of other animals

van /væn/ *noun* **1** a covered vehicle with no side windows in its back half, usually smaller than a lorry/truck, used for carrying goods or people: *a furniture/removal van* ◇ *a police van* (= for carrying police officers or prisoners) ◇ *a delivery van* ◇ *a van driver*—picture at TRUCK **2** (*AmE*) a covered vehicle with side windows, usually smaller than a lorry/truck, that can carry about twelve passengers **3** (*BrE*) a closed railway carriage for carrying bags, cases, etc. or mail: *a mail/luggage van* **IDM** **in the 'van** (*BrE, formal*) at the front or in the leading position

van·adium /vəˈneɪdiəm/ *noun* [U] (*symb* V) a chemical element. Vanadium is a soft poisonous silver-grey metal that is added to some types of steel to make it stronger.

'van conversion *noun* (*AmE*) = CONVERSION VAN

van·dal /ˈvændl/ *noun* a person who commits acts of vandalism

van·dal·ism /ˈvændəlɪzəm/ *noun* [U] the crime of destroying or damaging sth, especially public property, deliberately and for no good reason: *an act of vandalism*

van·dal·ize (*BrE* also **-ise**) /ˈvændəlaɪz/ *verb* [VN] [usually passive] to damage sth, especially public property, deliberately and for no good reason: *The pay phone had been vandalized and wasn't working.*

vane /veɪn/ *noun* a flat blade that is moved by wind or water and is part of the machinery in a WINDMILL, etc.—see also WEATHERVANE

van·guard /ˈvænɡɑːd; *AmE* -ɡɑːrd/ *noun* (usually **the vanguard**) [sing.] **1** the leaders of a movement in society, for example in politics, art, industry, etc: *The company is proud to be in the vanguard of scientific progress.* **2** the part of an army, etc. that is at the front when moving forward to attack the enemy **OPP** REARGUARD

van·illa /vəˈnɪlə/ *noun, adj.*
▪ *noun* [U] a substance obtained from the beans of the tropical **vanilla** plant, used to give flavour to sweet foods, for example ice cream: (*BrE*) *vanilla essence* ◇ (*AmE*) *vanilla extract* ◇ (*BrE*) *a vanilla pod* ◇ (*AmE*) *a vanilla bean*
▪ *adj.* **1** flavoured with vanilla: *vanilla ice cream* **2** (*informal, especially AmE*) plain and ordinary: *The city is pretty much plain vanilla.*

van·ish /ˈvænɪʃ/ *verb* [V] **1** to disappear suddenly and/or in a way that you cannot explain: *The magician vanished in a puff of smoke.* ◇ *My glasses seem to have vanished.* ◇ *He seems to have vanished without trace.* **2** to stop existing: *the vanishing woodlands of northern Europe* ◇ *All hopes of a peaceful settlement had now vanished.* **IDM** see ACT *n.*, FACE *n.*

'vanishing point *noun* [usually sing.] (*technical*) the point in the distance at which parallel lines appear to meet

van·ity /ˈvænəti/ *noun* (*pl.* **-ies**) **1** [U] (*disapproving*) too much pride in your own appearance, abilities or achievements: *She had no personal vanity* (= about her appearance).—see also VAIN **2** [U] (*literary*) the quality of being unimportant, especially compared with other things that are important: *the vanity of human ambition in the face of death* **3** (**vanities**) [pl.] behaviour or attitudes that show people's vanity: *Politics is too often concerned only with the personal vanities of politicians.* **4** [C] (*AmE*) = DRESSING TABLE

van·quish /ˈvæŋkwɪʃ/ *verb* [VN] (*literary*) to defeat sb completely in a competition, war, etc. **SYN** CONQUER: *a vanquished enemy/opponent*

the van·quished /ˈvæŋkwɪʃt/ *noun* [pl.] (*literary*) people who have been completely defeated in a competition, war, etc.

'vant·age point /ˈvɑːntɪdʒ pɔɪnt/ (*also formal* **vant·age**) *noun* a position from which you watch sth; a point in time or a situation from which you consider sth, especially the past: *The cafe was a good vantage point for watching the world go by.* ◇ *From the vantage point of the late 20th century, the war seems to have achieved nothing.*

vapid /ˈvæpɪd/ *adj.* (*rare, formal*) lacking interest or intelligence ▶ **vap·id·ity** /væˈpɪdəti/ *noun* [U]

vapor (*AmE*) = VAPOUR

va·por·ize (*BrE* also **-ise**) /ˈveɪpəraɪz/ *verb* [VN] (*technical*) to turn into gas; to make sth turn into gas ▶ **va·por·iza·tion, -isa·tion** /ˌveɪpəraɪˈzeɪʃn; *AmE* -rəˈz-/ *noun* [U]

va·por·ous /ˈveɪpərəs/ *adj.* (*rare, formal*) full of vapour; like vapour: *clouds of vaporous air*

va·pour (*BrE*) (*AmE* **vapor**) /ˈveɪpə(r)/ *noun* [C, U] a mass of very small drops of liquid in the air, for example steam: *water vapour*

'vapour trail (*BrE*) (*AmE* **'va·por trail**) *noun* the white line that is left in the sky by a plane

vari·abil·ity /ˌveəriəˈbɪləti; *AmE* ˌver-; ˌvær-/ *noun* [U] (*written*) the fact of sth being likely to vary: *climatic variability* ◇ *a degree of variability in the exchange rate*

vari·able /ˈveəriəbl; *AmE* ˈver-; ˈvær-/ *adj., noun*
▪ *adj.* **1** often changing; likely to change: *variable rainfall/temperature* ◇ *The acting is of variable quality* (= some of it is good and some of it is bad).—compare INVARIABLE **2** able to be changed: *The drill has variable speed control.* ◇ *variable lighting* ▶ **vari·ably** /-iəbli/ *adv.*
▪ *noun* a situation, number or quantity that can vary or be varied: *With so many variables to consider, it is difficult to calculate the cost.* ◇ *The temperature remained constant while pressure was a variable in the experiment.* **OPP** CONSTANT

vari·ance /ˈveəriəns; *AmE* ˈver-; ˈvær-/ *noun* [U, C] (*formal*) the amount by which sth changes or is different from sth else: *variance in temperature/pay* ◇ *a note with subtle variances of pitch* **IDM** **at 'variance (with sb/sth)** (*formal*) disagreeing with or opposing sb/sth: *These conclusions are totally at variance with the evidence.*

vari·ant /ˈveəriənt; *AmE* ˈver-; ˈvær-/ *noun* **~ (of/on sth)** a thing that is a slightly different form or type of sth else: *This game is a variant of/on baseball.* ▶ **vari·ant** *adj.*: *variant forms of spelling* ◇ *a variant form of oxygen known as ozone*

vari·ation /ˌveəriˈeɪʃn; *AmE* ˌver-/ *noun* **1** [C, U] **~ (in/of sth)** a change, especially in the amount or level of sth: *The dial records very slight variations in pressure.* ◇ *Currency exchange rates are always subject to variation.* ◇ *regional/seasonal variation* (= depending on the region or time of year) **2** [C] **~ (on sth)** a thing that is different from other things in the same general group: *This soup is a spicy variation on a traditional favourite.* **3** [C] (*music*) any of a set of short pieces of music based on a simple tune repeated in a different and more complicated form: *a set of variations on a theme by Mozart* ◇ (*figurative*) *His numerous complaints are all variations on a theme* (= all about the same thing).

vari·cose vein /ˌværɪkəʊs ˈveɪn; *AmE* -koʊs/ *noun* a VEIN, especially one in the leg, which has become swollen and painful

var·ied /ˈveərid; *AmE* ˈverid; ˈvær-/ *adj.* (usually *approving*) **1** of many different types: *varied opinions/cultures/menus* ◇ *a wide and varied selection of cheeses* **2** not staying the same, but changing often: *He led a full and varied life.*

varie·gated /ˈveəriəɡeɪtɪd; ˈveərɪɡ-; *AmE* ˈver-/ *adj.* **1** (*technical*) having differently coloured spots or marks: *a plant with variegated leaves* **2** (*rare, written*) consisting of many different types of thing or person

var·iety /vəˈraɪəti/ *noun* (*pl.* **-ies**) **1** [sing.] **~ (of sth)** several different sorts of the same thing: *There is a wide variety of patterns to choose from.* ◇ *He resigned for a variety of reasons.* ◇ *This tool can be used in a variety of ways.* ◇ *I was impressed by the variety of dishes on offer.* **2** [U] the quality of not being the same or not doing the same thing all the time: *We all need variety in our diet.* ◇ *We want more variety in our work.* **3** [C] **~ (of sth)** a type of a thing, for example a plant or a language, that is different from the others in the same general group: *Apples come in a great many varieties.* ◇ *a rare variety of orchid* ◇ *different varieties of English* ◇ (*spoken*) *My cooking is of the 'quick and simple' variety.* **4** (*AmE* also **vaude·ville**) [U] a form of theatre or television entertainment that consists of a series of short performances, such

V

as singing, dancing and funny acts: *a variety show/ theatre* **IDM** **variety is the spice of ʹlife** (*saying*) new and exciting experiences make life more interesting

vaʹriety store *noun* (*old-fashioned, AmE*) a shop/store that sells a wide range of goods at low prices

vari·ous /ˈveəriəs; *AmE* ˈver-; ˈvær-/ *adj.* **1** several different: *Tents come in various shapes and sizes.* ◊ *She took the job for various reasons.* ◊ *There are various ways of doing this.* **2** (*formal*) having many different features: *a large and various country*

vari·ous·ly /ˈveəriəsli; *AmE* ˈver-; ˈvær-/ *adv.* (*written*) in several different ways, usually by several different people: *He has been **variously described** as a hero, a genius and a bully.* ◊ *The cost has been variously estimated at between £10 million and £20 million.*

var·nish /ˈvɑːnɪʃ; *AmE* ˈvɑːrnɪʃ/ *noun, verb*
■ *noun* [U, C] a liquid that is painted onto wood, metal, etc. and that forms a hard shiny transparent surface when it is dry—see also NAIL VARNISH
■ *verb* to put varnish on the surface of sth: [VN] *The doors are then stained and varnished.* ◊ (*BrE*) *Josie was sitting at her desk, varnishing her nails.* ◊ [VN-N] *Her nails were varnished a brilliant shade of red.*

var·sity /ˈvɑːsəti; *AmE* ˈvɑːrs-/ *noun, adj.*
■ *noun* (*pl.* **-ies**) (*AmE*) the main team that represents a college or high school, especially in sports competitions
■ *adj.* [only before noun] (*old-fashioned, BrE, informal*) used when describing activities connected with the universities of Oxford and Cambridge, especially sports competitions: *the varsity match*

vary /ˈveəri; *AmE* ˈveri; ˈværi/ *verb* (**vary·ing, var·ied, var·ied**) **1** [V] ~ **(in sth)** (of a group of similar things) to be different from each other in size, shape, etc. **SYN** DIFFER: *The students' work varies considerably in quality.* ◊ *The quality of the students' work varies considerably.* ◊ *New techniques were introduced with **varying degrees** of success.* **2** [V] ~ **(with sth)** | ~ **(from sth to sth)** | ~ **(between A and B)** to change or be different according to the situation: *The menu varies with the season.* ◊ *Prices vary according to the type of room you require.* ◊ *Class numbers vary between 25 and 30.* ◊ *'What time do you start work?' 'It varies.'* **3** [VN] to make changes to sth to make it slightly different: *The job enables me to vary the hours I work.*—see also VARIED ⇨ note at CHANGE

vas·cu·lar /ˈvæskjələ(r)/ *adj.* [usually before noun] (*technical*) of or containing VEINS (= the tubes that carry liquids around the bodies of animals and plants)

vase /vɑːz; *AmE* veɪs; veɪz/ *noun* a container made of glass, etc., used for holding cut flowers or as an ornament: *a vase of flowers*

vas·ec·tomy /vəˈsektəmi/ *noun* (*pl.* **-ies**) (*medical*) a medical operation to remove part of each of the tubes in a man's body that carry SPERM, after which he is not able to make a woman pregnant

Vas·el·ine™ /ˈvæsəliːn/ *noun* [U] a thick soft clear substance that is used on skin to heal or protect it, or as a LUBRICANT to stop surfaces from sticking together

vas·sal /ˈvæsl/ *noun* **1** a man in the Middle Ages who promised to fight for and be loyal to a king or other powerful owner of land, in return for being given land to live on **2** a country that is dependent on and controlled by another country

vast /vɑːst; *AmE* væst/ *adj.* extremely large in area, size, amount, etc. **SYN** HUGE: *a vast area of forest* ◊ *a vast crowd* ◊ *a vast amount of information* ◊ *At dusk bats appear in vast numbers.* ◊ *His business empire was vast.* ◊ *In the **vast majority** of cases, this should not be a problem.* ▶ **vast·ness** (*written*) *noun* [U, C]: *the vastness of space*

vast·ly /ˈvɑːstli; *AmE* ˈvæstli/ *adv.* very much: *I'm a vastly different person now.* ◊ *The quality of the training has vastly improved.*

VAT /ˌviː eɪ ˈtiː; væt/ *noun* [U] (*BrE*) a tax that is added to the price of goods and services (abbreviation for 'value added tax'): *Prices include VAT.* ◊ *£27.50 + VAT*

vat /væt/ *noun* a large container for holding liquids,

especially in industrial processes: *distilling/fermenting vats* ◊ *a vat of whisky*

Vati·can /ˈvætɪkən/ *noun* (**the Vatican**) **1** [sing.] the group of buildings in Rome where the POPE lives and works **2** [sing.+ sing./pl. v.] the centre of government of the Roman Catholic Church

vaude·ville /ˈvɔːdəvɪl/ *noun* [U] **1** (*AmE*) = VARIETY **2** = MUSIC HALL (1)

ʹvaudeville theater *noun* (*AmE*) = MUSIC HALL (2)

vault /vɔːlt/ *noun, verb*
■ *noun* **1** a room with thick walls and a strong door, especially in a bank, used for keeping valuable things safe: *Most of her jewellery is stored in bank vaults.* **2** a room under a church or in a CEMETERY, used for burying people: *She is to be buried in the family vault.* **3** a roof or ceiling in the form of an arch or a series of arches **4** a jump made by vaulting—see also POLE VAULT
■ *verb* ~ **(over)** sth to jump over an object in a single movement, using your hands or a pole to push you: [V] *She vaulted over the gate and ran up the path.* ◊ [VN] *There's no way he could have vaulted the fence with that injury.*—see also POLE VAULT

vault·ed /ˈvɔːltɪd/ *adj.* (*architecture*) made in the shape of an arch or a series of arches; having a ceiling or roof of this shape: *a vaulted ceiling/cellar*

vault·ing /ˈvɔːltɪŋ/ *noun* [U] (*architecture*) a pattern of arches in a ceiling or roof

ʹvaulting horse (also **horse**) *noun* a large object with legs, and sometimes handles, that GYMNASTS use to vault over

vaunt·ed /ˈvɔːntɪd/ *adj.* [usually before noun] (*formal*) proudly talked about or praised as being very good, especially when this is not deserved: *Their much vaunted reforms did not materialize.*

VC /ˌviː ˈsiː/ *noun* [sing.] a medal for special courage that is given to members of the British and Commonwealth armed forces (abbreviation for 'Victoria Cross'): *He was awarded the VC.* ◊ *Col James Blunt VC*

VCR /ˌviː siː ˈɑː(r)/ *noun* (*especially AmE*) a machine which is used to play videos or to record programmes from a television (abbreviation for 'video cassette recorder'): *Don't forget to program the VCR.*

VD /ˌviː ˈdiː/ *abbr.* VENEREAL DISEASE

VDU /ˌviː diː ˈjuː/ (*BrE*) (*AmE* **VDT** /ˌviː diː ˈtiː/) *noun* a machine with a screen like a television that displays information from a computer (abbreviation for 'visual display unit/video display terminal')

veal /viːl/ *noun* [U] meat from a CALF (= a young cow)

vec·tor /ˈvektə(r)/ *noun* **1** (*mathematics*) a quantity that has both size and direction: *Acceleration and velocity are both vectors.*—compare SCALAR **2** (*biology*) an insect, etc. that carries a particular disease from one living thing to another **3** (*technical*) a course taken by an aircraft

veep /viːp/ *noun* (*AmE, informal*) VICE-PRESIDENT

veer /vɪə(r); *AmE* vɪr/ *verb* [V+adv./prep.] **1** (especially of a vehicle) to change direction suddenly **SYN** SWERVE: *The bus veered onto the wrong side of the road.* ◊ *It is still not clear why the missile veered off course.* **2** (of a conversation or way of behaving or thinking) to change in the way it develops: *The debate veered away from the main topic of discussion.* ◊ *His emotions veered between fear and anger.* **3** (*technical*) (of the wind) to change direction: *The wind slowly veered around to the west.*

veg /vedʒ/ *noun, verb*
■ *noun* [U, C] (*pl.* **veg**) (*BrE, informal*) a vegetable or vegetables: *a fruit and veg stall* ◊ *He likes the traditional meat and two veg for his main meal.*
■ *verb* (**-gg-**) **PHRV** ˌveg ˈout (*informal*) to relax by doing sth that needs very little effort, for example watching television

vegan /ˈviːgən/ *noun* a person who does not eat any animal products such as meat, milk or eggs. Some vegans do not use animal products such as silk or leather.

Vege·bur·ger™ /ˈvedʒɪbɜːgə(r); *AmE* -bɜːrg-/ *noun* = VEGGIE BURGER

vege·table /ˈvedʒtəbl/ *noun* **1** (also *informal* **veg·gie**

æ	ɑː	e	ɜː	ə	ɪ	iː	i	ɒ	ɔː	ʌ	ʊ	u	uː
cat	father	ten	bird	about	sit	see	many	got	saw	cup	put	actual	too
								(BrE)					

especially in *AmE*) a plant or part of a plant that is eaten as food. Potatoes, beans and onions are all vegetables: *green vegetables* (for example CABBAGE) ◇ *root vegetables* (for example CARROTS) ◇ *a salad of raw vegetables* ◇ *a vegetable garden/patch/plot* ◇ *vegetable oils* ◇ *vegetable matter* (= plants in general)—compare ANIMAL, FRUIT, MINERAL—picture on page A3 **2** (*BrE* also **cab·bage**) a person who is physically alive but not capable of much mental or physical activity, for example because of an accident or illness: *Severe brain damage turned him into a vegetable.* **3** a person who has a boring life: *Since losing my job I've felt like a vegetable.*

vege·tar·ian /ˌvedʒəˈteəriən; *AmE* -ˈter-/ (also *BrE informal* **veg·gie**) *noun* a person who does not eat meat or fish: *Is she a vegetarian?*—compare HERBIVORE ▶ **vege·tar·ian** *adj.: Are you vegetarian?* ◇ *a vegetarian diet* (= with no meat or fish in it) ◇ *a vegetarian restaurant* (= that serves no meat or fish) **vege·tar·ian·ism** /-ɪzəm/ *noun* [U]

vege·tate /ˈvedʒəteɪt/ *verb* [V] (of a person) to spend time doing very little and feeling bored

vege·tated /ˈvedʒəteɪtɪd/ *adj.* having the amount of plant life mentioned: *a densely/sparsely vegetated area*

vege·ta·tion /ˌvedʒəˈteɪʃn/ *noun* [U] (*written*) plants in general, especially the plants that are found in a particular area or environment: *The hills are covered in lush green vegetation.*

vege·ta·tive /ˈvedʒɪtətɪv; *AmE* -teɪtɪv/ *adj.* **1** relating to plant life **2** (*medical*) (of a person) alive but showing no sign of brain activity—see also PERSISTENT VEGETATIVE STATE

veg·gie /ˈvedʒi/ *noun* **1** (*BrE, informal*) = VEGETARIAN: *He's turned veggie* (= become a vegetarian). **2** (*especially AmE*) = VEGETABLE ▶ **veg·gie** *adj.*

'veggie burger (also **Vege·bur·ger**™) *noun* a BURGER made with vegetables, especially beans, instead of meat

vehe·ment /ˈviːəmənt/ *adj.* (*written*) showing very strong feelings, especially anger: *a vehement denial/attack/protest* ◇ *He had been vehement in his opposition to the idea.* ▶ **vehe·mence** /-məns/ *noun* [U] **vehe·ment·ly** *adv.: The charge was vehemently denied.*

ve·hicle /ˈviːəkl; *AmE* also ˈviːhɪkl/ *noun* **1** (rather *formal*) a thing that is used for transporting people or goods from one place to another, such as a car or lorry/truck: *motor vehicles* (= cars, buses, lorries/trucks, etc.) ◇ *Are you the driver of this vehicle?* ◇ *rows of parked vehicles* **2** ~ (for sth) something that can be used to express your ideas or feelings or as a way of achieving sth: *Art may be used as a vehicle for propaganda.* ◇ *The play is an ideal vehicle for her talents.*

ve·hicu·lar /vəˈhɪkjələ(r); *AmE* viːˈh-/ *adj.* (*formal*) intended for vehicles or consisting of vehicles: *vehicular access* ◇ *The road is closed to vehicular traffic.*

veil /veɪl/ *noun, verb*
■ *noun* **1** a covering of very thin transparent material worn, especially by women, to protect or hide the face, or as part of a hat, etc: *a bridal veil* **2** a piece of fabric worn by NUNS over the head and shoulders **3** [sing.] (*written*) something that stops you from learning the truth about a situation: *Their work is carried out behind a veil of secrecy.* ◇ *It would be better to draw a veil over what happened next* (= not talk about it). **4** [sing.] (*written*) a thin layer that stops you from seeing sth: *The mountain tops were hidden beneath a veil of mist.* **IDM** **take the 'veil** (*old-fashioned*) to become a NUN
■ *verb* [VN] **1** to cover your face with a veil **2** (*literary*) to cover sth with sth that hides it partly or completely: *A fine drizzle began to veil the hills.* ◇ *eyes veiled with tears*

veiled /veɪld/ *adj.* **1** not expressed directly or clearly because you do not want your meaning to be obvious: *a thinly veiled threat/attack/warning/criticism* **2** wearing a veil: *a mysterious veiled woman*

vein /veɪn/ *noun* **1** [C] any of the tubes that carry blood from all parts of the body to the heart: *the jugular vein*—compare ARTERY—see also VARICOSE VEIN **2** [C] any of the very thin tubes that form the frame of a leaf or an insect's wing **3** [C] a narrow strip of a different colour in some types of stone, wood and cheese **4** [C] a thin layer of minerals or metal contained in rock: *a vein of gold* **SYN** SEAM **5** [sing.] ~ (of sth) an amount of a particular quality or feature in sth: *They had tapped a rich vein of information in his secretary.* **6** [sing., U] a particular style or manner: *A number of other people commented in a similar vein.* ◇ *'And that's not all,' he continued in angry vein.*

veined /veɪnd/ *adj.* having or marked with veins or thin lines: *thin blue-veined hands* ◇ *veined marble*

velar /ˈviːlə(r)/ *noun* (*phonetics*) a speech sound, such as /k/ or /g/, made by placing the back of the tongue against or near the back part of the mouth ▶ **velar** *adj.*

Vel·cro™ /ˈvelkrəʊ; *AmE* -kroʊ/ *noun* [U] a material for fastening clothes, etc. consisting of two strips of fabric, one rough and one smooth, that stick to each other when they are pressed together—picture at FASTENER

veld /velt/ *noun* [U] (in S Africa) flat open land with grass and no trees—compare PAMPAS, PRAIRIE, SAVANNAH, STEPPE

vel·lum /ˈveləm/ *noun* [U] **1** material made from the skin of a sheep, goat or CALF, used for making book covers and, in the past, for writing on **2** smooth cream-coloured paper used for writing on

vel·ocity /vəˈlɒsəti; *AmE* -ˈlɑːs-/ *noun* [U, C] (*pl.* **-ies**) **1** (*technical*) the speed of sth in a particular direction: *the velocity of light* ◇ *to gain/lose velocity* ◇ *a high-velocity rifle/bullet* **2** (*formal*) high speed: *Jaguars can move with an astonishing velocity.*

velo·drome /ˈvelədrəʊm; *AmE* -droʊm/ *noun* a track or building used for CYCLE RACING

vel·our /vəˈlʊə(r); *AmE* vəˈlʊr/ *noun* [U] a silk or cotton fabric with a thick soft surface like VELVET

vel·vet /ˈvelvɪt/ *noun* [U] a fabric woven from silk, cotton or NYLON, with a thick soft surface made of a mass of threads: *a velvet dress* ◇ *velvet curtains/drapes* **IDM** see IRON *adj.*

vel·vet·een /ˌvelvəˈtiːn/ *noun* [U] a cotton fabric that looks like VELVET but is less expensive

vel·vety /ˈvelvəti/ *adj.* pleasantly smooth and soft: *velvety skin* ◇ *a velvety red wine*

venal /ˈviːnl/ *adj.* (*formal*) prepared to do dishonest or immoral things in return for money: *venal politicians/journalists* ▶ **ve·nal·ity** /viːˈnæləti/ *noun* [U] (*rare*)

ven·detta /venˈdetə/ *noun* **1** a long and violent dispute between two families, in which people are murdered in return for previous murders **2** ~ (against sb) a long argument or disagreement in which one person or group does or says things to harm another: *He has accused the British media of pursuing a vendetta against him.* ◇ *She conducted a personal vendetta against me.*

vending machine /ˈvendɪŋ məʃiːn/ *noun* a machine from which you can buy cigarettes, drinks, etc. by putting coins into it

vend·or /ˈvendə(r)/ *noun* **1** a person who sells things, for example food or newspapers, usually outside on the street: *street vendors* **2** (*law*) a person who is selling a house or other property—compare SELLER

ven·eer /vəˈnɪə(r); *AmE* vəˈnɪr/ *noun, verb*
■ *noun* **1** [C, U] a thin layer of wood or plastic that is glued to the surface of cheaper wood, especially on a piece of furniture **2** [sing.] ~ (of sth) (*formal*) an outer appearance of a particular quality that hides the true nature of sb/sth: *For the first time her veneer of politeness began to crack.*
■ *verb* [VN] ~ sth (with/in sth) to cover the surface of sth with a veneer of wood, etc.

ven·er·able /ˈvenərəbl/ *adj.* **1** (*formal*) venerable people or things deserve respect because they are old, important, wise, etc: *a venerable old man* ◇ *a venerable institution/tradition* **2** (the Venerable ...) [only before noun] (in the Anglican Church), a title of respect used when talking about an ARCHDEACON: *the Venerable Martin Roberts* **3** (the Venerable ...) [only before noun] (in the Roman Catholic Church), a title given to a dead person who is very holy but who has not yet been made a saint

aɪ	aʊ	eɪ	əʊ	oʊ	ɔɪ	ɪə	eə	ʊə	j	w
my	now	say	go	go	boy	near	hair	pure	yes	wet
			(BrE)	(AmE)						

ven·er·ate /ˈvenəreɪt/ *verb* [VN] ~ **sb/sth (as sth)** (*formal*) to have and show a lot of respect for sb/sth, especially sb/sth that is considered to be holy or very important [SYN] REVERE ▶ **ven·er·ation** /ˌvenəˈreɪʃn/ *noun* [U]: *The relics were objects of veneration.*

ven·ereal /vəˈnɪəriəl; *AmE* -ˈnɪr-/ *adj.* [only before noun] relating to diseases spread by sexual contact: *a venereal infection/complaint*

ve,nereal di'sease *noun* [C, U] (*abbr.* **VD**) any disease caught by having sex with an infected person

ven·etian blind /vəˌniːʃn ˈblaɪnd/ *noun* a BLIND for a window that has flat horizontal plastic or metal strips going across it that you can turn to let in as much light as you want—picture at BLIND

ven·geance /ˈvendʒəns/ *noun* [U] ~ **(on/upon sb)** (*formal*) the act of punishing or harming sb in return for what they have done to you, your family or friends [SYN] REVENGE: *a desire for vengeance ◊ to take vengeance on sb ◊ He swore vengeance on his child's killer.* [IDM] **with a 'vengeance** (*informal*) to a greater degree than is expected or usual: *She set to work with a vengeance. ◊ After two days the infection came back with a vengeance.*

venge·ful /ˈvendʒfl/ *adj.* (*formal*) showing a desire to punish sb who has harmed you ▶ **vengeful·ly** /-fəli/ *adv.*

ve·nial /ˈviːniəl/ *adj.* [usually before noun] (*formal*) (of a SIN or mistake) not very serious and therefore able to be forgiven

ven·ison /ˈvenɪsn; -zn/ *noun* [U] meat from a deer

venom /ˈvenəm/ *noun* [U] **1** the poisonous liquid that some snakes, spiders, etc. produce when they bite or sting you **2** (*written*) strong bitter feeling; hatred and a desire to hurt sb: *His voice was full of venom. ◊ a look of pure venom* [IDM] see SPIT *v.*

ven·om·ous /ˈvenəməs/ *adj.* **1** (of a snake, etc.) producing venom **2** (*written*) full of bitter feeling or hatred: *a venomous look ◊ a venomous attack on his political enemies* ▶ **ven·om·ous·ly** *adv.*

ven·ous /ˈviːnəs/ *adj.* (*technical*) of or contained in VEINS (= the tubes that carry liquids around the bodies of animals and plants): *venous blood*

vent /vent/ *noun, verb*

■ *noun* **1** an opening that allows air, gas or liquid to pass out of or into a room, building, container, etc: *air/heating vents*—picture at CAR—compare REGISTER **2** (*technical*) the opening in the body of a bird, fish, reptile or other small animal, though which waste matter is passed out **3** a long thin opening at the bottom of the back or side of a coat or jacket [IDM] **give (full) vent to sth** (*formal*) to express a feeling, especially anger: *Children give vent to their anger in various ways. ◊ She gave full vent to her feelings in a violent outburst.*

■ *verb* [VN] ~ **sth (on sb)** (*written*) to express feelings, especially anger, strongly: *He vented his anger on the referee.*

ven·ti·late /ˈventɪleɪt/ *verb* [VN] **1** to allow fresh air to enter and move around a room, building, etc: *a well-ventilated room ◊ The bathroom is ventilated by means of an extractor fan.* **2** (*formal*) to express your feelings or opinions publicly [SYN] AIR ▶ **ven·ti·lation** /ˌventɪˈleɪʃn/ *noun* [U]: *a ventilation shaft/opening/system ◊ Make sure that there is adequate ventilation in the room before using the paint.*

ven·ti·la·tor /ˈventɪleɪtə(r)/ *noun* **1** a device or an opening for letting fresh air come into a room, etc. **2** a piece of equipment that helps sb to breathe by pumping air in and out of their lungs: *He was put on a ventilator.*

ven·tricle /ˈventrɪkl/ *noun* (*anatomy*) **1** either of the two lower spaces in the heart that pump blood around the body—compare AURICLE **2** any hollow space in the body, especially one of four main hollow spaces in the brain

ven·trilo·quism /venˈtrɪləkwɪzəm/ *noun* [U] the art of speaking without moving your lips and of making it look as if your voice is coming from another person ▶ **ven·trilo·quist** /venˈtrɪləkwɪst/ *noun*: *Entertainment included a hypnotist and a ventriloquist. ◊ a ventriloquist's dummy*

ven·ture /ˈventʃə(r)/ *noun, verb*

■ *noun* a business project or activity, especially one that involves taking risks: *The project is a joint venture between the public and private sectors. ◊ A disastrous business venture lost him thousands of dollars.*

■ *verb* **1** [V+*adv.*/*prep.*] to go somewhere even though you know that it might be dangerous or unpleasant: *They ventured nervously into the water. ◊ He's never ventured abroad in his life.* **2** (*formal*) to say or do sth in a careful way, especially because it might upset or offend sb: [VN] *She hardly dared to venture an opinion. ◊* [V to inf] *I ventured to suggest that she might have made a mistake. ◊* [V speech] *'And if I say no?' she ventured.* [also V that] **3** [VN] ~ **sth (on sth)** to risk losing sth valuable or important if you are not successful at sth: *It was wrong to venture his financial security on such a risky deal.* [IDM] **nothing 'ventured, nothing 'gained** (*saying*) used to say that you have to take risks if you want to achieve things and be successful [PHRV] **'venture into/on sth** to do sth, even though it involves risks: *This is the first time the company has ventured into movie production.*

'venture capital *noun* [U] (*business*) money that is lent to sb to buy buildings, equipment, etc. when they start a business—compare WORKING CAPITAL

ven·ture·some /ˈventʃəsəm; *AmE* -tʃərs-/ *adj.* (*formal* or *literary*) willing to take risks [SYN] DARING

venue /ˈvenjuː/ *noun* a place where people meet for an organized event, for example a concert, sporting event or CONFERENCE: *The band will be playing at twenty different venues on their UK tour. ◊ Please note the change of venue for this event.*

Venus /ˈviːnəs/ *noun* the planet in the SOLAR SYSTEM that is second in order of distance from the sun, between Mercury and the earth

ver·acity /vəˈræsəti/ *noun* [U] (*formal*) the quality of being true; the habit of telling the truth [SYN] TRUTHFULNESS: *Some people questioned the veracity of her story.*

ver·anda (also **ver·an·dah**) /vəˈrændə/ (*especially BrE*) (*AmE* usually **porch**) *noun* a platform with an open front and a roof, built onto the side of a house on the ground floor: *After dinner, we sat talking on the veranda.*

verb /vɜːb; *AmE* vɜːrb/ *noun* (*grammar*) a word or group of words that expresses an action (such as *eat*), an event (such as *happen*) or a state (such as *exist*): *regular/irregular verbs ◊ transitive/intransitive verbs*—see also PHRASAL VERB

ver·bal /ˈvɜːbl; *AmE* ˈvɜːrbl/ *adj.* **1** relating to words: *The job applicant must have good verbal skills. ◊ non-verbal communication* (= gestures, expressions of the face, etc.) **2** spoken, not written: *a verbal agreement/warning ◊ verbal instructions*—compare ORAL **3** (*grammar*) relating to verbs: *a verbal noun*

ver·bal·ize (*BrE* also **-ise**) /ˈvɜːbəlaɪz; *AmE* ˈvɜːrb-/ *verb* (*formal*) to express your feelings or ideas in words: [VN] *He's a real genius but he has difficulty verbalizing his ideas.* [also V]

ver·bal·ly /ˈvɜːbəli; *AmE* ˈvɜːrb-/ *adv.* in spoken words and not in writing or actions: *The company had received complaints both verbally and in writing.*

ver·ba·tim /vɜːˈbeɪtɪm; *AmE* vɜːrˈb-/ *adj., adv.* exactly as spoken or written; word for word: *a verbatim report ◊ He reported the speech verbatim.*

ver·bi·age /ˈvɜːbiːdʒ; *AmE* ˈvɜːrb-/ *noun* [U] (*formal, disapproving*) the use of too many words, or of more difficult words than are needed, to express an idea, etc.

ver·bose /vɜːˈbəus; *AmE* vɜːrˈbous/ *adj.* (*formal, disapproving*) using or containing more words than are needed: *a verbose speaker/speech/style* ▶ **ver·bos·ity** /vɜːˈbɒsəti; *AmE* vɜːrˈbɑːs-/ *noun* [U]

ver·dant /ˈvɜːdnt; *AmE* ˈvɜːrdnt/ *adj.* (*literary*) (of grass, plants, fields, etc.) fresh and green

ver·dict /ˈvɜːdɪkt; *AmE* ˈvɜːrd-/ *noun* **1** a decision that is made by a JURY in a court of law, stating if sb is considered guilty of a crime or not: *Has the jury reached a verdict? ◊ The jury returned a verdict* (= gave a verdict) *of guilty/not guilty.*—see also MAJORITY VERDICT, OPEN VERDICT **2** ~ **(on sth/sb)** a decision that you make or an opinion that you give about sth, after you have tested it

V

b	d	f	g	h	k	l	m	n	p	r
bad	did	fall	get	hat	cat	leg	man	now	pen	red

or considered it carefully: *The coroner **recorded a verdict** of accidental death.* ◊ *The panel will give their verdict on the latest video releases.*

verge /vɜːdʒ; *AmE* vɜːrdʒ/ *noun, verb*
- *noun* (*BrE*) (*AmE* ˌsoft 'shoulder) a piece of grass at the edge of a path, road, etc: *a grass verge* **IDM** **on/to the verge of sth/of doing sth** very near to the moment when sb does sth or sth happens: *He was on the verge of tears.* ◊ *They are on the verge of signing a new contract for a further two years' work.* ◊ *These events left her on the verge of having a nervous breakdown.*
- *verb* **PHRV** **'verge on sth** to be very close to an extreme state or condition **SYN** BORDER ON STH: *Some of his suggestions verged on the outrageous.* ◊ *a dislike verging on contempt*

ver·ger /ˈvɜːdʒə(r); *AmE* ˈvɜːrdʒ-/ *noun* (*especially BrE*) a Church of England official whose job is to look after the inside of a church and to perform some simple duties during church services

ver·ify /ˈverɪfaɪ/ *verb* (**veri·fies, veri·fy·ing, veri·fied, verified**) **1** to check that sth is true or accurate: [VN] *We have no way of verifying his story.* ◊ [V that] *Please verify that there is sufficient memory available before loading the program.* ◊ [V wh-] *I'll leave you to verify whether these claims are true.* **2** to show or say that sth is true or accurate **SYN** CONFIRM: [VN] *Her version of events was verified by neighbours.* [also V that] ▶ **veri·fi·able** /ˈverɪfaɪəbl/ *adj.*: *a verifiable fact/statement* **veri·fi·ca·tion** /ˌverɪfɪˈkeɪʃn; *AmE* ˌverɪfɪ-/ *noun* [U]: *the verification of hypotheses*

verily /ˈverɪli/ *adv.* (*old use*) really; TRULY

veri·sim·ili·tude /ˌverɪsɪˈmɪlɪtjuːd; *AmE* -tuːd/ *noun* [U] (*formal*) the quality of seeming to be true or real **SYN** AUTHENTICITY: *To add verisimilitude, the stage is covered with sand for the desert scenes.*

ver·it·able /ˈverɪtəbl/ *adj.* [only before noun] (*formal or humorous*) a word used to emphasize that sb/sth can be compared to sb/sth else that is more exciting, more impressive, etc. **SYN** POSITIVE: *The meal that followed was a veritable banquet.*

ver·ity /ˈverəti/ *noun* (*pl.* **-ies**) **1** [usually pl.] (*formal*) a belief or principle about life, the world, etc. that is accepted as true: *the eternal verities of life* **2** [U] (*old use*) truth

ver·mil·ion /vəˈmɪliən; *AmE* vərˈm-/ *adj.* bright red in colour ▶ **ver·mil·ion** *noun* [U]

ver·min /ˈvɜːmɪn; *AmE* ˈvɜːrmɪn/ *noun* [pl.] **1** wild animals or birds that destroy plants or food, or attack farm animals and birds: *On farms the fox is considered vermin and treated as such.* **2** insects that live on the bodies of animals and sometimes human beings: *The room was crawling with vermin.* **3** (*disapproving*) people who are very unpleasant or dangerous to society

ver·min·ous /ˈvɜːmɪnəs; *AmE* ˈvɜːrm-/ *adj.* (*written*) covered with vermin

ver·mouth /ˈvɜːməθ; *AmE* vərˈmuːθ/ *noun* [U] a strong wine, flavoured with herbs and spices, often mixed with other drinks as a COCKTAIL

ver·nacu·lar /vəˈnækjələ(r); *AmE* vərˈn-/ *noun* **1** (usually **the vernacular**) [sing.] the language spoken in a particular area or by a particular group, especially one that is not the official or written language **2** [U] (*technical*) a style of architecture concerned with ordinary houses rather than large public buildings ▶ **ver·nacu·lar** *adj.*: *vernacular languages/architecture*

ver·nal /ˈvɜːnl; *AmE* ˈvɜːrnl/ *adj.* [only before noun] (*formal or literary*) connected with the season of spring: *the vernal equinox*

ver·ruca /vəˈruːkə/ *noun* (*pl.* **ver·rucas** or, in medical use, **ver·ru·cae** /-kiː/) (*BrE*) (*AmE* ˈplantar wart) a small hard infectious growth like a WART, on the bottom of the foot

ver·sa·tile /ˈvɜːsətaɪl; *AmE* ˈvɜːrsətl/ *adj.* (*approving*) **1** (of a person) able to do many different things: *He's a versatile actor who has played a wide variety of parts.* **2** (of food, a building, etc.) having many different uses: *Eggs are easy to cook and can be an extremely versatile food.* ▶ **ver·sa·til·ity** /ˌvɜːsəˈtɪləti; *AmE* ˌvɜːrs-/ *noun* [U]: *She is a designer of extraordinary versatility.*

verse /vɜːs; *AmE* vɜːrs/ *noun* **1** [U] writing that is arranged in lines, often with a regular rhythm or pattern of RHYME **SYN** POETRY: *Most of the play is written in verse, but some of it is in prose.*—see also BLANK VERSE, FREE VERSE **2** [C] a group of lines that form a unit in a poem or song: *a hymn with six verses* **3** (**verses**) [pl.] (*old-fashioned*) poetry: *a book of comic verses* **4** [C] any one of the short NUMBERED divisions of a CHAPTER in the Bible **IDM** see CHAPTER

versed /vɜːst; *AmE* vɜːrst/ *adj.* **~ in sth** having a lot of knowledge about sth, or skill at sth: *He had become **well versed in** employment law.*

ver·si·fi·ca·tion /ˌvɜːsɪfɪˈkeɪʃn; *AmE* ˌvɜːrs-/ *noun* [U] (*formal*) the art of writing poetry in a particular pattern; the pattern in which poetry is written

ver·sion /ˈvɜːʃn; -ʒn; *AmE* ˈvɜːrʒn/ *noun* **1** a copy of sth that is slightly different from the original thing: *the latest version of the Volkswagen Golf* ◊ *the de luxe/luxury version* ◊ *The English version of the novel is due for publication next year.* **2** a description of an event from the point of view of a particular person or group of people: *She gave us her version of what had happened that day.* ◊ *Their versions of how the accident happened conflict.* **3** a film/movie, play, piece of music, etc. that is slightly different from the original film, etc. on which it is based: *the film version of 'War and Peace'* ◊ *the latest version of the software package*—see also THE AUTHORIZED VERSION, COVER VERSION

verso /ˈvɜːsəʊ; *AmE* ˈvɜːrsoʊ/ *noun* (*pl.* **-os**) (*technical*) the page on the left side of an open book **OPP** RECTO

ver·sus /ˈvɜːsəs; *AmE* ˈvɜːrsəs/ *prep.* (*abbr.* **v, vs**) **1** (especially *sport* or *law*) used to show that two teams or sides are against each other: *It is France versus Brazil in the final.* ◊ *in the case of the State versus Ford* **2** used to compare two different ideas, choices, etc: *It was the promise of better job opportunities versus the inconvenience of moving away and leaving her friends.*

ver·tebra /ˈvɜːtɪbrə; *AmE* ˈvɜːrt-/ *noun* (*pl.* **ver·te·brae** /-reɪ; -riː/) any of the small bones that are connected together to form the SPINE—picture at BODY ▶ **ver·te·bral** *adj.* [only before noun]

ver·te·brate /ˈvɜːtɪbrət; *AmE* ˈvɜːrt-/ *noun* (*technical*) any animal with a BACKBONE, including all MAMMALS, birds, fish, reptiles and AMPHIBIANS—compare INVERTEBRATE ▶ **ver·te·brate** *adj.*

ver·tex /ˈvɜːteks; *AmE* ˈvɜːrt-/ *noun* (*pl.* **ver·ti·ces** /-tɪsiːz/ or **ver·texes**) **1** (*geometry*) a point where two lines meet to form an angle, especially the point of a triangle or CONE opposite the base **2** (*technical*) the highest point or top of sth

ver·ti·cal /ˈvɜːtɪkl; *AmE* ˈvɜːrt-/ *adj., noun*
- *adj.* **1** (of a line, pole, etc.) going straight up or down from a level surface or from top to bottom in a picture, etc: *the vertical axis of the graph* ◊ *The cliff was almost vertical.* ◊ *There was a vertical drop to the ocean.*—compare HORIZONTAL **2** having a structure in which there are top, middle and bottom levels: *a vertical flow of communication* ▶ **ver·ti·cal·ly** /-kli/ *adv.*
- *noun* (usually **the vertical**) a vertical line or position **SYN** PERPENDICULAR: *The wall is several degrees off the vertical.*

ver·tigin·ous /vɜːˈtɪdʒɪnəs; *AmE* vɜːrˈt-/ *adj.* (*formal*) causing a feeling of vertigo: *From the top of the mountain there was a vertiginous drop to the valley below.*

ver·tigo /ˈvɜːtɪɡəʊ; *AmE* ˈvɜːrtɪɡoʊ/ *noun* [U] the feeling of DIZZINESS and fear, and of losing your balance, that is caused in some people when they look down from a very high place

verve /vɜːv; *AmE* vɜːrv/ *noun* [U, sing.] (*written*) energy, excitement or enthusiasm **SYN** GUSTO: *It was a performance of verve and vitality.*

very /ˈveri/ *adv., adj.*
- *adv.* (*abbr.* **v**) **1** used before adjectives, adverbs and DETERMINERS to mean 'in a high degree' or 'extremely': *very small/hot/useful* ◊ *very quickly/soon/far* ◊ *Very few people know that.* ◊ *Thanks very much.* ◊ *'Do you like it?' 'Yeah, I do. **Very much**.'* ◊ *'Is it what you expected?' 'Oh*

s	t	v	z	ʃ	ʒ	tʃ	dʒ	θ	ð	ŋ
see	tea	van	zoo	shoe	vision	chain	jam	thin	this	sing

yes, *very much so.'* ◊ *'Are you busy?' 'Not very.'* ◊ *The new building has been very much admired.* ◊ *I'm **not very** (=* not at all) *impressed.* **2** used to emphasize a superlative adjective or before *own: They wanted the very best quality.* ◊ *Be there by six at the very latest.* ◊ *At last he had his very own car* (= belonging to him and to nobody else). **3 the ~ same** exactly the same: *Mario said the very same thing.*
■ *adj.* [only before noun] **1** used to emphasize that you are talking about a particular thing or person and not about another SYN ACTUAL: *Those were her very words.* ◊ *He might be phoning her at this very moment.* ◊ *That's the very thing I need.* **2** extreme: *It happens at the very beginning of the book.* **3** used to emphasize a noun MERE: *The very thought of drink made him feel sick.* ◊ *'I can't do that!' she gasped, appalled at the very idea.* IDM see EYE *n.*, IMAGE

GRAMMAR POINT
very / very much

Very is used with adjectives, past participles used as adjectives, and adverbs: *I am very hungry.* ◊ *I was very pleased to get your letter.* ◊ *You played very well.* But notice: *I'm very much afraid that your son may be involved in the crime.*

Very is not used with past participles that have a passive meaning. **Much, very much** or **greatly** (formal) are usually used instead: *Your help was very much appreciated.* ◊ *He was much loved by everyone.* ◊ *She was greatly admired.*

Very is used to emphasize superlative adjectives: *my very best work* ◊ *the very youngest children* . However, with comparative adjectives **much, very much, a lot,** etc. are used: *Your work is very much better.* ◊ *much younger children.*

Very is not used with adjectives and adverbs that already have an extreme meaning. You are more likely to use an adverb such as *absolutely, completely,* etc.: *She was absolutely furious.* ◊ *I'm completely exhausted.* ◊ *You played really brilliantly.*

Very is not used with verbs. Use **very much** instead: *We enjoyed staying with you very much.*

ˌvery high ˈfrequency *noun* [U] = VHF

ves·icle /ˈvesɪkl/ *noun* **1** (*biology*) a small bag or hollow structure in the body of a plant or an animal **2** (*medical*) a small swelling filled with liquid under the skin SYN BLISTER

ves·pers /ˈvespəz; *AmE* -pərz/ *noun* [U] the service of evening prayer in some Christian Churches—compare EVENSONG, MATINS

ves·sel /ˈvesl/ *noun* **1** (*formal*) a large ship or boat: *ocean-going vessels* **2** (*old use* or *technical*) a container used for holding liquids, such as a bowl, cup, etc: *a Bronze Age drinking vessel* **3** a tube that carries blood through the body of a person or an animal, or liquid through the parts of a plant—see also BLOOD VESSEL

vest /vest/ *noun, verb*
■ *noun* **1** (*BrE*) (*AmE* **under·shirt**) a piece of underwear worn under a shirt, etc. next to the skin: *a cotton/string/thermal vest*—compare SINGLET—picture on page A4 **2** a special piece of clothing that covers the upper part of the body: *a bullet-proof vest* ◊ *a running vest* **3** (*AmE*) = WAISTCOAT
■ *verb* PHRV ˈvest in sb/sth (*law*) (of power, property, etc.) to belong to sb/sth legally **vest sth in sb/sth | vest sb with sth** [often passive] (*formal*) **1** to give sb the legal right or power to do sth: *Overall authority is vested in the Supreme Council.* ◊ *The Supreme Council is vested with overall authority.* **2** to make sb the legal owner of land or property

ˌvested ˈinterest *noun* ~ (**in sth**) a personal reason for wanting sth to happen, especially because you get some advantage from it: *They have a vested interest in keeping their club as exclusive as possible.* ◊ *Powerful vested interests* (= people with a vested interest) *are opposing the plan.*

ves·ti·bule /ˈvestɪbjuːl/ *noun* **1** (*formal*) an entrance hall, for example where hats and coats can be left: *the vestibule of a church/theatre/hotel* **2** (*technical*) an enclosed space at the end of a carriage on a train that connects it with the next carriage

ves·tige /ˈvestɪdʒ/ *noun* (*formal*) **1** a small part of sth that still exists after the rest of it has stopped existing: *the last vestiges of the old colonial regime* **2** usually used in negative sentences, to say that not even a small amount of sth exists: *There's not a vestige of truth in the rumour.*

ves·tigial /veˈstɪdʒiəl/ *adj.* [usually before noun] (*formal* or *technical*) remaining as the last small part of sth that used to exist: *vestigial traces of an earlier culture* ◊ *It is often possible to see the vestigial remains of rear limbs on some snakes.*

vest·ment /ˈvestmənt/ *noun* [usually pl.] a piece of clothing worn by a priest during church services

ves·try /ˈvestri/ *noun* (*pl.* **-ies**) a room in a church where a priest prepares for a service by putting on special clothes and where various objects used in worship are kept SYN SACRISTY

vet /vet/ *noun, verb*
■ *noun* **1** (*especially BrE*) (*AmE* usually **vet·er·in·ar·ian**) (*also BrE formal* **'veterinary surgeon**) a person who has been trained in the science of animal medicine, whose job is to treat animals who are ill or injured **2** (*vet's*) (*pl.* **vets**) the place where a vet works: *I've got to take the dog to the vet's tomorrow.* **3** (*AmE, informal*) = VETERAN: *a Vietnam vet*
■ *verb* (**-tt-**) [VN] (*BrE*) **1** to find out about a person's past life and career in order to decide if they are suitable for a particular job SYN SCREEN: *All candidates are carefully vetted for security reasons.*—see also POSITIVE VETTING **2** to check the contents, quality, etc. of sth carefully SYN SCREEN: *All reports are vetted before publication.*

vetch /vetʃ/ *noun* [U, C] a plant of the pea family. There are several types of vetch, one of which is used as food for farm animals.

vet·eran /ˈvetərən/ *noun* **1** a person who has a lot of experience in a particular area or activity: *the veteran British actor and producer, Sir Richard Attenborough* **2** (*also AmE informal* **vet**) a person who has been a soldier, sailor, etc. in a war: *war veterans* ◊ *a veteran of the Spanish Civil War* ◊ *a Vietnam vet*

ˌveteran ˈcar *noun* (*BrE*) a car made before 1916—compare VINTAGE

ˈVeterans Day *noun* [U, C] a holiday in the US on 11 November, in honour of members of the armed forces and others who have died in war—see also MEMORIAL DAY, REMEMBRANCE SUNDAY

vet·er·in·ar·ian /ˌvetərɪˈneəriən; *AmE* -ˈner-/ *noun* (*AmE*) = VET

vet·er·in·ary /ˈvetnri; ˈvetrənəri; *AmE* ˈvetərəneri/ *adj.* [only before noun] connected with caring for the health of animals: *veterinary medicine/science*

ˈveterinary surgeon *noun* (*BrE, formal*) = VET

veto /ˈviːtəʊ; *AmE* -toʊ/ *noun, verb*
■ *noun* (*pl.* **-oes**) **1** [C, U] the right to refuse to allow sth to be done, especially the right to stop a law from being passed or a decision from being taken: *The British government used its veto to block the proposal.* ◊ *to have the power/right of veto* ◊ *the use of the presidential veto* **2** [C] **~ (on sth)** an occasion when sb refuses to allow sth to be done: *For months there was a veto on employing new staff.*
■ *verb* (**ve·toes, veto·ing, ve·toed, ve·toed**) [VN] **1** to stop sth from happening or being done by using your official authority (= by using your veto): *Plans for the dam have been vetoed by the Environmental Protection Agency.* **2** to refuse to accept or do what sb has suggested: *I wanted to go camping but the others quickly vetoed that idea.*

vex /veks/ *verb* [VN] (*old-fashioned* or *formal*) to annoy or worry sb: *The memory of their conversation still vexed him.* ▶ **vex·ing** *adj.*: *a vexing problem/question*

vex·ation /vekˈseɪʃn/ *noun* (*old-fashioned* or *formal*) **1** [U] the state of feeling upset or annoyed: *She sat down*

æ	ɑː	e	ɜː	ə	ɪ	iː	i	ɒ	ɔː	ʌ	ʊ	u	uː
cat	father	ten	bird	about	sit	see	many	got	saw	cup	put	actual	too
								(BrE)					

and cried in vexation. **2** [C] a thing that upsets or annoys you

vex·atious /vek'seɪʃəs/ *adj.* (*old-fashioned* or *formal*) making you feel upset or annoyed

vexed /vekst/ *adj.* **1** ~ **question/issue** a problem that is difficult to deal with [SYN] THORNY: *The conference spent much of its time discussing the vexed question of border controls.* **2** ~ (**at/with sb/sth**) (*old-fashioned*) upset or annoyed

VHF /ˌviː eɪtʃ 'ef/ *abbr.* very high frequency (a range of radio waves used for high-quality broadcasting): *a VHF transmitter*

via /'vaɪə; 'viːə/ *prep.* **1** through a place: *We flew home via Dubai.* **2** by means of a particular person, system, etc: *I heard about the sale via Jane.* ◊ *The news programme came to us via satellite.*

vi·able /'vaɪəbl/ *adj.* **1** that can be done; that will be successful: *a viable option/proposition* ◊ *There is no viable alternative.* ◊ *to be commercially/politically/financially/economically viable* ◊ *If there was any delay then the rescue plan would cease to be viable.* **2** (*biology*) capable of developing and surviving independently: *viable organisms* ▶ **via·bil·ity** /ˌvaɪə'bɪləti/ *noun* [U]: *commercial/economic/financial viability*

via·duct /'vaɪədʌkt/ *noun* a long high bridge, usually with arches, that carries a road or railway/railroad across a river or valley

Viagra™ /vaɪ'ægrə/ *noun* [U] a drug used to treat IMPOTENCE in men

vial /'vaɪəl/ *noun* (*especially AmE*) = PHIAL

vibes /vaɪbz/ *noun* [pl.] **1** (also *formal* **vi·bra·tions**) (also **vibe** [sing.]) (*informal*) a mood or an atmosphere produced by a particular person, thing or place: *good/bad vibes* ◊ *The vibes weren't right.* **2** = VIBRAPHONE: *a jazzy vibes backing*

vi·brant /'vaɪbrənt/ *adj.* (*written*) **1** full of life and energy [SYN] EXCITING: *a vibrant city/personality* ◊ *Thailand is at its most vibrant during the New Year celebrations.* **2** (of colours) very bright and strong [SYN] BRILLIANT: *The room was decorated in vibrant reds and yellows.* **3** (of music, sounds, etc.) loud and powerful: *vibrant rhythms/tunes* ▶ **vi·brancy** /-brənsi/ *noun* [U]

vi·bra·phone /'vaɪbrəfəʊn; *AmE* -foʊn/ *noun* [C] (also *informal* **vibes** [pl.]) a musical instrument used especially in jazz, that has two rows of metal bars that you hit, and a motor that makes them vibrate

vi·brate /vaɪ'breɪt; *AmE* usually 'vaɪbreɪt/ *verb* to move or make sth move from side to side very quickly and with small movements: [V] *Every time a train went past the walls vibrated.* ◊ *The atmosphere seemed to vibrate with tension.* [also VN]

vi·bra·tion /vaɪ'breɪʃn/ *noun* **1** [C, U] a continuous shaking movement or feeling: *We could feel the vibrations from the trucks passing outside.* ◊ *a reduction in the level of vibration in the engine* **2** (**vibrations**) [pl.] (*formal*) = VIBES

vi·brato /vɪ'brɑːtəʊ; *AmE* -toʊ/ *noun* [U, C] (*pl.* **-os**) (*music*) a shaking effect in singing or playing a musical instrument, made by rapid slight changes in PITCH (= how high or low a sound is)

vi·bra·tor /vaɪ'breɪtə(r)/ *noun* an electrical device that produces a continuous shaking movement, used in MASSAGE or for sexual pleasure

vicar /'vɪkə(r)/ *noun* (*especially BrE*) an Anglican priest who is in charge of a church and the area around it (called a PARISH)—compare CURATE, MINISTER, PRIEST, RECTOR

vic·ar·age /'vɪkərɪdʒ/ *noun* (*BrE*) a vicar's house

vic·ar·ious /vɪ'keəriəs; *AmE* vaɪ'ker-/ *adj.* [only before noun] felt or experienced by watching or reading about sb else doing sth, rather than by doing it yourself: *He got a vicarious thrill out of watching his son score the winning goal.* ▶ **vic·ari·ous·ly** *adv.*

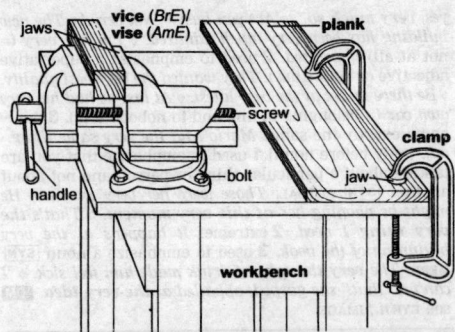

vice (*BrE*)/
vise (*AmE*)
jaws — plank — screw — clamp — bolt — jaw — handle — workbench

vice /vaɪs/ *noun* **1** [U] criminal activities that involve sex or drugs: *plain-clothes detectives from the vice squad* **2** [U, C] evil or immoral behaviour; an evil or immoral quality in sb's character: *The film ended most satisfactorily: vice punished and virtue rewarded.* ◊ *Greed is a terrible vice.* ◊ (*humorous*) *Cigarettes are my only vice.* **3** (*BrE*) (*AmE* **vise**) [C] a tool with two metal blocks that can be moved together by turning a screw. The vice is used to hold an object firmly while work is done on it: *He held my arm in a vice-like* (= very firm) *grip.*

vice- /vaɪs/ *combining form* (in nouns and related adjectives) next in rank to sb and able to represent them or act for them: *vice-captain*

vice 'chancellor *noun* the head of a university in Britain, who is in charge of the work of running the university. (Compare the CHANCELLOR, who is the official head of a university but only has duties at various ceremonies.)

vice-'president *noun* (*abbr.* **VP**) **1** the person below the president of a country in rank, who takes control of the country if the president is not able to **2** (*AmE*) a person in charge of a particular part of a business company: *the vice-president of sales*

vice·roy /'vaɪsrɔɪ/ *noun* (often used as a title) a person who is sent by a king or queen to govern a COLONY

vice versa /ˌvaɪs 'vɜːsə; *AmE* 'vɜːrsə ˌvaɪsɪ-/ *adv.* used to say that the opposite of what you have just said is also true: *You can cruise from Cairo to Aswan or vice versa* (= also from Aswan to Cairo).

vicin·ity /və'sɪnəti/ *noun* (**the vicinity**) [sing.] the area around a particular place: *Crowds gathered in the vicinity of Trafalgar Square.* ◊ *There is no hospital in the immediate vicinity.*

vi·cious /'vɪʃəs/ *adj.* **1** violent and cruel [SYN] BRUTAL: *a vicious assault/attack/murder* ◊ *a vicious criminal/gang* ◊ *She has a vicious temper.* **2** (of animals) fierce and dangerous: *a vicious dog* **3** (of an attack, criticism, etc.) full of hatred and anger: *She wrote me a vicious letter after the incident.* **4** (*informal*) very bad or severe: *a vicious headache* ◊ *a vicious spiral of rising prices* ▶ **vi·cious·ly** *adv.* **vi·cious·ness** *noun* [U]: *Police were shocked by the viciousness of the assault.*

vicious 'circle *noun* [sing.] a situation in which one problem causes another problem which then makes the first problem worse

vi·cis·si·tude /vɪ'sɪsɪtjuːd; *AmE* -tuːd/ *noun* [usually pl.] (*formal*) one of the many changes and problems in a situation or in your life, that you have to deal with: *the vicissitudes of family life*

vic·tim /'vɪktɪm/ *noun* **1** a person who has been attacked, injured or killed as the result of a crime, a disease, an accident, etc: *murder/rape victims* ◊ *accident/earthquake/famine victims* ◊ *Aids/cancer/stroke victims* ◊ *victims of crime* ◊ *She was the innocent victim of an arson attack.* ◊ *Schools are the latest victims of cuts in public spending.* **2** a person who has been tricked: *They were the victims of a cruel hoax.* ◊ *She's a fashion victim* (= wears the newest fashions even if they do not suit her). **3** an animal or a person that is killed and offered as a SACRIFICE: *a sacrificial victim* [IDM] **fall 'victim (to sth)** (*writ-*

ten) to be injured, damaged or killed by sth: *Many plants have fallen victim to the sudden frost.*

vic·tim·ize (*BrE* also **-ise**) /ˈvɪktɪmaɪz/ *verb* [VN] [often passive] to make sb suffer unfairly because you do not like them, their opinions, or sth that they have done: *For years the family had been victimized by racist neighbours.* ◊ *The union claimed that some of its members had been victimized for taking part in the strike.* ▶ **vic·tim·iza·tion**, **-isa·tion** /ˌvɪktɪmaɪˈzeɪʃn; *AmE* -məˈz-/ *noun* [U]

vic·tor /ˈvɪktə(r)/ *noun* (*literary*) the winner of a battle, competition, game, etc.

Vic·tor·ian /vɪkˈtɔːriən/ *adj., noun*
■ *adj.* **1** connected with the period from 1837 to 1901 when Queen Victoria ruled Britain: *Victorian architecture/novels/England* ◊ *the Victorian age/era/period* **2** having the attitudes that were typical of society during Queen Victoria's REIGN: *Victorian attitudes to sex* (= being easily shocked by sexual matters) ◊ *She advocated a return to Victorian values* (= hard work, pride in your country, etc.).
■ *noun* a British person who was alive during the period from 1837 to 1901, when Queen Victoria ruled

vic·tori·ous /vɪkˈtɔːriəs/ *adj.* ~ (**in sth**) having won a victory; that ends in victory: *the victorious army/team* ◊ *a victorious battle/campaign* ◊ *He emerged victorious in the elections.* ▶ **vic·tori·ous·ly** *adv.*

vic·tory /ˈvɪktəri/ *noun* (*pl.* **-ies**) [C, U] ~ (**over/against sb/sth**) success in a game, an election, a war, etc: *the team's 3–2 victory over/against Poland* ◊ *to win a decisive/narrow/stunning victory* ◊ *an election/a military victory* ◊ *She is confident of victory in Saturday's final.* ◊ *victory celebrations/parades*—see also MORAL VICTORY **IDM** **roar, romp, sweep, etc. to victory** to win sth easily: *He swept to victory in the final of the championship.*

vict·uals /ˈvɪtlz/ *noun* [pl.] (*old-fashioned*) food and drink

video /ˈvɪdiəʊ; *AmE* -oʊ-/ *noun, verb*
■ *noun* (*pl.* **-os**) **1** (also **video·tape**) [U, C] a type of MAGNETIC tape used for recording television pictures and sound; a box containing this tape, also called a **video cassette**: *The movie will be released on video in June.* ◊ *Do we have any blank videos?* **2** [C] a copy of a film/movie, programme, etc. that is recorded on VIDEOTAPE: *a video of 'ET'* ◊ *The school made a short promotional video.* ◊ *a home video* (= not a professional one) ◊ *a video shop/store* **3** [C] (*BrE*) = VIDEO CASSETTE RECORDER: *to programme the video to record a movie* **4** [U] the process of recording and showing films/movies and programmes using a special camera and a television set: *A wedding is the perfect subject for video.* ◊ *the use of video in schools* ◊ *video equipment/material*
■ *verb* (also *formal* **video·tape**) [VN] (*especially BrE*) to record a television programme using a VIDEO RECORDER; to film sb/sth using a video camera: *Did you remember to video that programme?* ◊ *Videoing students can be a useful teaching exercise.*

ˈvideo arcade *noun* a place where you can play video games on machines that you use coins to operate

ˈvideo camera *noun* a special camera for making video films—see also CAMCORDER

ˌvideo caˈssette recorder *noun* (*abbr.* **VCR**) (also **video**, **ˌvideo caˈssette player**, **ˈvideo recorder**) a piece of equipment that you use to record and play films/movies and TV programmes on video

video·con·fer·en·cing /ˈvɪdiəʊkɒnfərənsɪŋ; *AmE* ˈvɪdioʊkɑːn-/ *noun* [U] a system that enables people in different parts of the world to have a meeting by watching and listening to each other using video screens

video·disc /ˈvɪdiəʊdɪsk; *AmE* -oʊ-/ *noun* [U, C] a plastic disc that you can record films/movies and programmes on, for showing on a television screen—see also DVD

ˈvideo game *noun* a game in which you press buttons to control and move images on a screen—picture on page A8

ˌvideo ˈnasty *noun* (*BrE, informal*) a video film/movie that shows offensive scenes of sex and violence

video·phone /ˈvɪdiəʊfəʊn; *AmE* -oʊfoʊn/ *noun* a type of telephone with a screen that enables you to see the person you are talking to

video·tape /ˈvɪdiəʊteɪp; *AmE* -oʊ-/ *noun, verb*
■ *noun* [U, C] = VIDEO
■ *verb* [VN] (*formal*) = VIDEO: *a videotaped interview*

video·tex /ˈvɪdiəʊteks; *AmE* -oʊ-/ *noun* [U] (*AmE*) = VIEWDATA

vie /vaɪ/ *verb* (**vying** /ˈvaɪɪŋ/ **vied, vied**) ~ (**with sb**) (**for sth**) (*formal*) to compete strongly with sb in order to obtain or achieve sth: [V] *She was surrounded by men all vying for her attention.* ◊ *a row of restaurants vying with each other for business* ◊ [V to inf] *Screaming fans vied to get closer to their idol.*

view /vjuː/ *noun, verb*
■ *noun*
OPINION | **1** [C, often *pl.*] ~ (**about/on sth**) a personal opinion about sth; an attitude towards sth: *to have different/conflicting/opposing views* ◊ *to have strong political views* ◊ *His views on the subject were well known.* ◊ *This evidence supports the view that there is too much violence on television.* ◊ *We take the view that it would be wrong to interfere.* ◊ *In my view it was a waste of time.*—see also POINT OF VIEW
WAY OF UNDERSTANDING | **2** [sing.] ~ (**of sth**) a way of understanding or thinking about sth: *He has an optimistic view of life.* ◊ *the Christian view of the world/the Christian world view* ◊ *The traditional view was that marriage was meant to last.*
WHAT YOU CAN SEE | **3** [U, sing.] used when you are talking about whether you can see sth or whether sth can be seen in a particular situation: *The lake soon came into view.* ◊ *The sun disappeared from view.* ◊ *There was nobody in view.* ◊ *Sit down—you're blocking my view.* ◊ *I didn't have a good view of the stage.* **4** [C] what you can see from a particular place or position, especially beautiful natural scenery: *There were magnificent views of the surrounding countryside.* ◊ *The view from the top of the tower was spectacular.* ◊ *a sea/mountain view* ◊ *I'd like a room with a view.* ⇨ note at SIGHT
PHOTOGRAPH/PICTURE | **5** [C] a photograph or picture that shows an interesting place or scene: *a book with views of Paris*
CHANCE TO SEE STH | **6** (also **view·ing**) [C] a special chance to see or admire sth: *a private view* (for example, of an art exhibition)
IDM **have, etc. sth in ˈview** (*formal*) to have a particular aim, plan, etc. in your mind: *He wanted to make money and went abroad with this end in view.* **in full ˈview (of sb/sth)** completely visible, directly in front of sb/sth: *He was shot in full view of a large crowd.* **in view of sth** considering sth: *In view of the weather, the event will now be held indoors.* **on ˈview** being shown in a public place so that people can look at it **with a view to sth/to doing sth** (*formal*) with the intention or hope of doing sth: *He's painting the house with a view to selling it.*—more at BIRD, DIM *adj.*, HEAVE *v.*, LONG *adj.*
■ *verb* [VN]
THINK ABOUT STH | **1** ~ **sb/sth as sth** | ~ **sb/sth with sth** to think about sb/sth in a particular way [SYN] REGARD: *When the car was first built, the design was viewed as highly original.* ◊ *How do you view your position within the company?* ◊ *She has always viewed him with suspicion.*
LOOK AT STH | **2** to look at sth, especially when you look carefully: *People came from all over the world to view her work.* ◊ *A viewing platform gave stunning views over the valley.* **3** to visit a house, etc. with the intention of buying or renting it: *The property can only be viewed by appointment.*
WATCH TV, FILM/MOVIE | **4** (*formal*) to watch television, a film/movie, etc: *The show has a viewing audience of six million* (= six million people watch it). ◊ *an opportunity to view the movie before it goes on general release*

view·data /ˈvjuːdeɪtə; *AmE* also -dætə/ (*AmE* also **video·tex**) *noun* [U] an information system in which computer data is sent along telephone lines and shown on a television screen: *viewdata services/systems*

view·er /ˈvjuːə(r)/ *noun* **1** a person watching television: *The programme attracted millions of viewers.* **2** a person

V

who looks at or considers sth: *Some of her art is intended to shock the viewer.* ◊ *viewers of the current political scene* **3** a device like a small box with a light in it, that is used for looking at SLIDES (= photographs on special film)

view·find·er /'vjuːfaɪndə(r)/ *noun* the part of a camera that you look through to see the area that you are photographing

view·point /'vjuːpɔɪnt/ *noun* **1** ~ **(on sth)** a way of thinking about a subject: *Try looking at things from a different viewpoint.* ◊ *She will have her own viewpoint on the matter.* ◊ *From a practical viewpoint, I'd advise you not to go.* **2** a direction or place from which you look at sth: *The artist has painted the scene from various viewpoints.*—see also POINT OF VIEW

vigil /'vɪdʒɪl/ *noun* [C, U] a period of time when people stay awake, especially at night, in order to watch a sick person, say prayers, protest, etc: *His parents kept a round-the-clock vigil at his bedside.*

vigi·lant /'vɪdʒɪlənt/ *adj.* (*formal*) very careful to notice any signs of danger or trouble: *A pilot must remain vigilant at all times.* ▶ **vigi·lance** /-əns/ *noun* [U]: *She stressed the need for constant vigilance.* **vigi·lant·ly** *adv.*

vigi·lante /ˌvɪdʒɪ'lænti/ *noun* (sometimes *disapproving*) a member of a group of people who try to prevent crime or punish criminals in their community, especially because they think the police are not doing this ▶ **vigi·lant·ism** /ˌvɪdʒɪ'læntɪzəm/ *noun* [U]

vi·gnette /vɪn'jet/ *noun* (*formal*) **1** a short piece of writing or acting that clearly shows what a particular person, situation, etc. is like **2** a small picture or drawing, especially on the first page of a book

vig·or·ous /'vɪgərəs/ *adj.* **1** very active, determined or full of energy: *a vigorous campaign against tax fraud* ◊ *a vigorous opponent/supporter of the government* ◊ *Take vigorous exercise for several hours a week.* **2** strong and healthy: *a vigorous young man* ◊ *This plant is a vigorous grower.* ▶ **vig·or·ous·ly** *adv.*

vig·our (*BrE*) (*AmE* **vigor**) /'vɪgə(r)/ *noun* [U] energy, force or enthusiasm: *He worked with renewed vigour and determination.*

Vi·king /'vaɪkɪŋ/ *noun* a member of a race of Scandinavian people who attacked and sometimes settled in parts of NW Europe, including Britain, in the 8th to the 11th centuries: *Viking invaders/ships*

vile /vaɪl/ *adj.* (**viler**, **vil·est**) **1** (*informal*) extremely unpleasant or bad: *a vile smell/taste* ◊ *The weather was really vile most of the time.* ◊ *He was in a vile mood.* **2** (*formal*) wicked; completely unacceptable: *the vile practice of taking hostages* ▶ **vile·ly** /'vaɪlli/ *adv.* **vile·ness** *noun* [U]

vil·ify /'vɪlɪfaɪ/ *verb* (**vili·fies**, **vili·fy·ing**, **vili·fied**, **vili·fied**) [VN] ~ **sb/sth (as sth)** | ~ **sb/sth (for sth/for doing sth)** (*formal*) to say or write unpleasant things about sb/sth so that other people will have a low opinion of them SYN MALIGN: *They were vilified by the press as 'international terrorists'.* ▶ **vili·fi·ca·tion** /ˌvɪlɪfɪ'keɪʃn/ *noun* [U]: *the vilification of single parents by right-wing politicians*

villa /'vɪlə/ *noun* **1** (*BrE*) a house where people stay on holiday/vacation: *We rented a holiday villa in Spain.* **2** a house in the country with a large garden, especially in southern Europe **3** (in Roman times) a country house or farm with land attached to it

vil·lage /'vɪlɪdʒ/ *noun* **1** [C] a very small town situated in a country area: *We visited towns and villages all over Spain.* ◊ *a fishing/mountain/seaside village* ◊ (*especially BrE*) *the village hall/shop* ◊ *Her books are about village life.* **2** (**the village**) [sing.] (*especially BrE*) the people who live in a village: *The whole village was invited to the party.* **HELP** Do not use **village** to talk about small towns in the US. In *AmE* **village** is used for a small place in another country that seems more old-fashioned than a town in the US.

vil·la·ger /'vɪlɪdʒə(r)/ *noun* a person who lives in a village

vil·lain /'vɪlən/ *noun* **1** the main bad character in a story, play, etc: *He often plays the part of the villain.* **2** a wicked person: *the heroes and villains of the 20th century* **3** (*BrE,*

informal) a criminal **IDM** **the 'villain of the piece** (especially *humorous*) the person or thing that is responsible for all the trouble in a situation

vil·lain·ous /'vɪlənəs/ *adj.* [usually before noun] (*written*) very wicked; very unpleasant

vil·lainy /'vɪləni/ *noun* [U] (*formal*) wicked behaviour

vil·lein /'vɪleɪn/ *noun* (in the Middle Ages) a poor man who had to work for a richer man in return for a small piece of land to grow food on

vim /vɪm/ *noun* [U] (*old-fashioned, informal*) energy

vin·ai·grette /ˌvɪnɪ'gret/ *noun* [U] a mixture of oil, VINEGAR and various herbs, etc., used to add flavour to a salad SYN FRENCH DRESSING

vin·di·cate /'vɪndɪkeɪt/ *verb* [VN] (*formal*) **1** to prove that sth is true or that you were right to do sth, especially when other people thought differently SYN JUSTIFY: *Our fears of conflict were partially vindicated by today's events.* ◊ *I have every confidence that this decision will be fully vindicated.* **2** to prove that sb is not guilty when they have been accused of doing sth wrong or illegal: *New evidence emerged, vindicating him completely.* ▶ **vin·di·ca·tion** /ˌvɪndɪ'keɪʃn/ *noun* [U, sing.]: *Anti-nuclear protesters regarded the Chernobyl accident as a clear vindication of their campaign.*

vin·dic·tive /vɪn'dɪktɪv/ *adj.* trying to harm or upset sb, or showing that you want to, because you think that they have harmed you: *He accused her of being vindictive.* ◊ *a vindictive comment/person* ▶ **vin·dic·tive·ly** *adv.* **vin·dic·tive·ness** *noun* [U]

vine /vaɪn/ *noun* **1** a climbing plant that produces grapes: *grapes on the vine* ◊ *vine leaves*—see also GRAPEVINE **2** any climbing plant with long thin stems; one of these stems

vin·egar /'vɪnɪgə(r)/ *noun* [U] a liquid with a bitter taste made from MALT (= a type of grain) or wine, used to add flavour to food or to preserve it: *malt/wine vinegar* ◊ *onions pickled in vinegar*

vin·egary /'vɪnɪgəri/ *adj.* having a taste or smell that is typical of vinegar: *a vinegary wine*

vine·yard /'vɪnjəd; *AmE* -jɑrd/ *noun* a piece of land where grapes are grown in order to produce wine

vino /'viːnəʊ; *AmE* -noʊ/ *noun* [U] (*informal, humorous*) wine

vin·tage /'vɪntɪdʒ/ *noun, adj.*

■ *noun* **1** the wine that was produced in a particular year or place; the year in which it was produced **2** [usually sing.] the period or season of gathering grapes for making wine: *The vintage was later than usual.*

■ *adj.* [only before noun] **1** vintage wine is of very good quality and has been stored for several years **2** (*BrE*) (of a vehicle) made between 1917 and 1930 and admired for its style and interest—compare VETERAN CAR **3** typical of a period in the past and of high quality; the best work of the particular person: *a collection of vintage designs* ◊ *vintage TV drama* ◊ *The opera is vintage Rossini.* **4** ~ **year** a particularly good and successful year: *1999 was not a vintage year for the movies.*

vint·ner /'vɪntnə(r)/ *noun* (*old-fashioned, formal*) a person whose business is buying and selling wines or a person who grows grapes and makes wine

vinyl /'vaɪnl/ *noun* [U, C] a strong plastic that can bend easily, used for making wall, floor and furniture coverings, book covers, and, especially in the past, records: *a vinyl sofa*

viol /'vaɪəl/ *noun* an early type of musical instrument with strings, in the violin family

viola /vi'əʊlə; *AmE* -'oʊ-/ *noun* a musical instrument with strings, that you hold under your chin and play with a BOW. A viola is larger than a violin and plays lower notes: *a viola player*—picture on page 840

vio·late /'vaɪəleɪt/ *verb* [VN] **1** (*formal*) to go against or refuse to obey a law, an agreement, etc: *to violate human rights/international law* **2** (*formal*) to disturb or not respect sb's peace, PRIVACY, etc: *She accused the press photographers of violating her privacy.* **3** to damage or destroy a holy or special place SYN DESECRATE: *to violate a grave/shrine/tomb* **4** (*literary* or *old-fashioned*) to force sb to have sex SYN RAPE ▶ **vio·la·tion** /ˌvaɪə'leɪʃn/ *noun*

s	t	v	z	ʃ	ʒ	tʃ	dʒ	θ	ð	ŋ
see	tea	van	zoo	shoe	vision	chain	jam	thin	this	sing

[U, C]: *They were in open violation of the treaty.* ◊ *gross violations of human rights* **vio·la·tor** *noun*

vio·lence /ˈvaɪələns/ *noun* [U] **1** ~ (**against sb**) violent behaviour that is intended to hurt or kill sb: *crimes/acts/ threats of violence* ◊ *He condemned the protesters' use of violence against the police.* ◊ **domestic violence** (= between family members) ◊ *Is there too much sex and violence on TV?* **2** physical or emotional force and energy: *The violence of her feelings surprised him.*

vio·lent /ˈvaɪələnt/ *adj.* **1** involving or caused by physical force that is intended to hurt or kill sb: *violent crime* ◊ *Students were involved in violent clashes with the police.* ◊ *to die/meet with a violent death* (for example, to be murdered) ◊ *Her husband was a violent man.* ◊ *Children should not be allowed to watch violent movies* (= that show a lot of violence). **2** showing or caused by very strong emotion: *There was a violent reaction from the public.* **3** very strong and sudden: *I took a violent dislike to him.* ◊ *a violent explosion/storm* ◊ *a violent change/upheaval* ◊ *a violent headache* **4** (of a colour) extremely bright: *Her dress was a violent pink.*

vio·lent·ly /ˈvaɪələntli/ *adv.* **1** with great energy or strong movement, especially caused by a strong emotion such as fear or hatred: *She shook her head violently.* ◊ *to shiver/tremble/shudder violently* **2** very strongly or severely: *He was violently sick.* ◊ *They are violently opposed to the idea.* **3** in a way that involves physical violence: *The crowd reacted violently.*

vio·let /ˈvaɪələt/ *noun* **1** [C] a small wild or garden plant with purple or white flowers with a sweet smell that appear in spring **2** [U] a bluish-purple colour: *dressed in violet* ▶ **vio·let** *adj.*: *violet eyes* **IDM** see SHRINK *v.*

vio·lin /ˌvaɪəˈlɪn/ *noun* a musical instrument with strings, that you hold under your chin and play with a BOW: *Brahms' violin concerto*—compare VIOLA—see also FIDDLE—picture on page 840

vio·lin·ist /ˌvaɪəˈlɪnɪst/ *noun* a person who plays the violin

VIP /ˌviː aɪ ˈpiː/ *noun* a famous or important person who is treated in a special way (abbreviation for 'Very Important Person'): *the VIP lounge* ◊ *to get/give sb the VIP treatment*

viper /ˈvaɪpə(r)/ *noun* **1** a small poisonous snake **2** (*written*) a person who harms other people

vir·ago /vɪˈrɑːɡəʊ; *AmE* -ɡoʊ/ *noun* (*pl.* **-os**) (*literary, disapproving*) a fierce aggressive woman

viral /ˈvaɪrəl/ *adj.* like or caused by a VIRUS: *a viral infection*

vir·gin /ˈvɜːdʒɪn; *AmE* ˈvɜːrdʒ-/ *noun, adj.*
■ *noun* **1** [C] a person who has never had sex **2** (**the (Blessed) Virgin**) [sing.] the Virgin Mary, mother of Jesus Christ
■ *adj.* **1** [usually before noun] in its original pure or natural condition and not changed, touched or spoiled: *virgin forest/land/territory* ◊ *virgin snow* (= fresh and not marked) **2** [only before noun] with no sexual experience: *a virgin bride/saint* ◊ *the virgin birth* (= the belief that Mary was a virgin before and after giving birth to Jesus)

vir·gin·al /ˈvɜːdʒɪnl; *AmE* ˈvɜːrdʒ-/ *adj.* of or like a virgin; pure and innocent: *She was dressed in virginal white.*

Vir·ginia creep·er /vəˌdʒɪniə ˈkriːpə(r); *AmE* vərˈdʒ-/ *noun* [U, C] a climbing plant, often grown on walls, with large leaves that turn red in the autumn/fall

vir·gin·ity /vəˈdʒɪnəti; *AmE* vərˈdʒ-/ *noun* [U] the state of being a virgin: *He lost his virginity* (= had sex for the first time) *when he was 18.*

virgin 'olive oil *noun* [U] good quality oil obtained the first time that OLIVES are pressed: *extra virgin olive oil* (= the best quality oil)

Virgo /ˈvɜːɡəʊ; *AmE* ˈvɜːrɡoʊ/ *noun* **1** [U] the 6th sign of the ZODIAC, the VIRGIN **2** [C] (*pl.* **-os**) a person born under the influence of this sign, that is between 23 August and 23 September, approximately

vir·ile /ˈvɪraɪl; *AmE* ˈvɪrəl/ *adj.* (usually *approving*) **1** (of men) strong and full of energy, especially sexual energy **2** having or showing the strength and energy that is considered typical of men: *a virile performance* ◊ *virile athleticism*

vir·il·ity /vəˈrɪləti/ *noun* [U] **1** sexual power in men: *displays of male virility* ◊ *a need to prove his virility* **2** strength or energy: *political/economic virility*

vir·ology /vaɪˈrɒlədʒi; *AmE* -ˈrɑː-/ *noun* [U] the scientific study of VIRUSES and the diseases caused by them ▶ **vir·olo·gist** /vaɪˈrɒlədʒɪst; *AmE* -ˈrɑː-/ *noun*

vir·tual /ˈvɜːtʃuəl; *AmE* ˈvɜːrtʃ-/ *adj.* [only before noun] **1** almost or very nearly the thing described, so that any slight difference is not important: *The country was sliding into a state of virtual civil war.* ◊ *The company has a virtual monopoly in this area of trade.* ◊ *He married a virtual stranger.* ◊ *When her husband had a stroke, she was given virtual control of the business.* **2** made to appear to exist by the use of computer SOFTWARE: *virtual memory/space* ◊ *New technology has enabled development of an online 'virtual library'.*

vir·tu·al·ly /ˈvɜːtʃuəli; *AmE* ˈvɜːrtʃ-/ *adv.* **1** almost, or very nearly, so that any slight difference is not important: *to be virtually impossible/unknown/identical/certain* ◊ *Virtually all students will be exempt from the tax.* ◊ *He virtually admitted he was guilty.* **2** (*computing*) by the use of computer SOFTWARE that makes sth appear to exist; using VIRTUAL REALITY technology

virtual re'ality *noun* [U] images created by a computer that appear to surround the person looking at them and seem almost real

vir·tue /ˈvɜːtʃuː; *AmE* ˈvɜːrtʃuː/ *noun* **1** [U] (*formal*) behaviour or attitudes that show high moral standards: *He led a life of virtue.* ◊ *She was certainly no paragon of virtue!* **2** [C] a particular good quality or habit: *Patience is not one of her virtues, I'm afraid.* **3** [C, U] an attractive or useful quality **SYN** ADVANTAGE: *The plan has the virtue of simplicity.* ◊ *He was extolling the virtues of the Internet.* ◊ *They could see no virtue in discussing it further.* **IDM** **by/in virtue of sth** (*formal*) by means of or because of sth: *She got the job by virtue of her greater experience.* **make a virtue of ne'cessity** to manage to gain an advantage from sth that you have to do and cannot avoid—more at EASY *adj.*

vir·tu·os·ity /ˌvɜːtʃuˈɒsəti; *AmE* ˌvɜːrtʃuˈɑːs-/ *noun* [U] (*formal*) a very high degree of skill in performing or playing: *orchestral/technical virtuosity* ◊ *a performance of breathtaking virtuosity*

vir·tu·oso /ˌvɜːtʃuˈəʊsəʊ; -ˈəʊzəʊ; *AmE* ˌvɜːrtʃuˈoʊsoʊ; -ˈoʊzoʊ/ *noun, adj.*
■ *noun* (*pl.* **vir·tu·osos** or **vir·tu·osi** /-siː; -ziː/) a person who is extremely skilful at doing sth, especially playing a musical instrument: *a piano virtuoso* ◊ *a virtuoso pianist*
■ *adj.* [only before noun] showing extremely great skill: *a virtuoso display/performance*

vir·tu·ous /ˈvɜːtʃuəs; *AmE* ˈvɜːrtʃ-/ *adj.* **1** (*formal*) behaving in a very good and moral way: *a wise and virtuous man* ◊ *She lived an entirely virtuous life.* **2** (*disapproving* or *humorous*) claiming to behave better or have better morals than other people: *He was feeling virtuous because he had finished and they hadn't.* ▶ **vir·tu·ous·ly** *adv.*

viru·lent /ˈvɪrələnt; -rjəl-/ *adj.* **1** (of a disease or poison) extremely dangerous or harmful and quick to have an effect **2** (*formal*) showing strong negative and bitter feelings: *virulent nationalism/hatred/criticism* ▶ **viru·lence** /-ləns/ *noun* [U] **viru·lent·ly** *adv.*

virus /ˈvaɪrəs/ *noun* **1** a living thing, too small to be seen without a MICROSCOPE, that causes infectious disease in people, animals and plants: *the flu virus* ◊ *a virus infection* **2** (*informal*) a disease caused by a virus: *There's a virus going around the office.* **3** instructions that are hidden within a computer program and are designed to cause faults or destroy data—see also VIRAL

visa /ˈviːzə/ *noun* a stamp or mark put in your PASSPORT by officials of a foreign country that gives you permission to enter, pass through or leave their country: *entry/tourist/transit/exit visas*

vis·age /ˈvɪzɪdʒ/ *noun* (*literary*) a person's face

vis-à-vis /ˌviːz ɑː ˈviː/ *prep.* (from French, *written*) **1** in relation to: *Britain's role vis-à-vis the United States* **2** in

V

æ	ɑː	e	ɜː	ə	ɪ	iː	i	ɒ	ɔː	ʌ	ʊ	u	uː
cat	father	ten	bird	about	sit	see	many	got	saw	cup	put	actual	too

(BrE)

comparison with: *It was felt that the company had an unfair advantage vis-à-vis smaller companies elsewhere.*

vis·cera /ˈvɪsərə/ *noun* [pl.] (*anatomy*) the large organs inside the body, such as the heart, lungs and stomach

vis·ceral /ˈvɪsərəl/ *adj.* **1** (*literary*) resulting from strong feelings rather than careful thought **2** (*technical*) relating to the viscera

vis·cose /ˈvɪskəʊz; -kəʊs; *AmE* -koʊs; -koʊz/ *noun* [U] (*especially BrE*) a smooth fabric made from CELLULOSE, used for making clothes

vis·count /ˈvaɪkaʊnt/ *noun* (in Britain) a NOBLEMAN of a rank below an EARL and above a BARON

vis·count·cy /ˈvaɪkaʊntsi/ *noun* the rank or position of a viscount

vis·count·ess /ˈvaɪkaʊntəs/ *noun* **1** a woman who has the rank of a VISCOUNT **2** the wife of a VISCOUNT

vis·cous /ˈvɪskəs/ *adj.* (*technical*) (of a liquid) thick and sticky; not flowing freely ▶ **vis·cos·ity** /vɪˈskɒsəti; *AmE* -ˈskɑːs-/ *noun* [U]

vise /vaɪs/ *noun* (*AmE*) = VICE

visi·bil·ity /ˌvɪzəˈbɪləti/ *noun* [U] **1** how far or well you can see, especially as affected by the light or the weather: *poor/bad/zero visibility* ◊ *Visibility was down to about 100 metres in the fog.* ◊ *The car has excellent all-round visibility* (= you can see what is around you very easily from it). **2** the fact or state of being easy to see: *high visibility equipment for cyclists* ◊ *The advertisements were intended to increase the company's visibility in the marketplace* (= to make people more aware of their products and services).

vis·ible /ˈvɪzəbl/ *adj.* **1** that can be seen: *The house is clearly visible from the beach.* ◊ *Most stars are not visible to the naked eye.* **2** that is obvious enough to be noticed: *visible benefits/changes* ◊ *a visible police presence* ◊ *He showed no visible sign of emotion.* ◊ *She made a visible effort to control her anger.*

vis·ibly /ˈvɪzəbli/ *adv.* in a way that is easily noticeable: *He was visibly shocked.* ◊ *She paled visibly at the news.*

vi·sion /ˈvɪʒn/ *noun* **1** [U] the ability to see; the area that you can see from a particular position: *to have good/perfect/poor/blurred/normal vision* ◊ *20–20 vision* (= the ability to see perfectly) ◊ *Cats have good night vision.* ◊ *The couple moved outside her field of vision.* ◊ *He glimpsed something on the edge of his vision.*—see also TUNNEL VISION **2** [C] an idea or a picture in your imagination: *He had a vision of a world in which there would be no wars.* ◊ *I had visions of us getting hopelessly lost.* **3** [C] a dream or similar experience, especially of a religious kind: *The idea came to her in a vision.* **4** [U] the ability to think about or plan the future with great imagination and intelligence: *a leader of vision* **5** [C] **a ~ (of sth)** (*literary*) a person of great beauty or who shows the quality mentioned: *She was a vision in white lace.* ◊ *a vision of loveliness/beauty/health* **6** [U] the picture on a television or cinema/movie theater screen: *We apologize for the temporary loss of vision.*

vi·sion·ary /ˈvɪʒənri; *AmE* -ʒəneri/ *adj.*, *noun*
■ *adj.* **1** (*approving*) original and showing the ability to think about or plan the future with great imagination and intelligence: *a visionary leader* ◊ *visionary leadership/speeches* **2** relating to dreams or strange experiences, especially of a religious kind: *visionary experiences*
■ *noun* (*pl.* **-ies**) (usually *approving*) a person who has the ability to think about or plan the future in an intelligent, imaginative way: *She was a true visionary.* ◊ *The company needs visionaries to see opportunities.*

visit /ˈvɪzɪt/ *verb*, *noun*
■ *verb* **1** [VN] to go to see a person or a place for a period of time: *She went to visit relatives in Wales.* ◊ *The Prime Minister is visiting Japan at the moment.* ◊ *You should visit your dentist at least twice a year.* **2** to stay somewhere for a short time: [V] *We don't live here. We're just visiting.* ◊ [VN] *The lake is also visited by seals in the summer.* **3** [VN] to make an official visit to sb, for example to carry out checks or give advice: *government inspectors visiting schools/prisons/factories* PHRV **'visit sth on/upon sb/sth** (*old use*) to punish sb/sth: *The sins of the*

fathers are visited upon the children (= children are blamed or suffer for what their parents have done). **'visit with sb** (*AmE*) to spend time with sb, especially talking socially: *Come and visit with me some time.*
■ *noun* **1 ~ (to sb/sth) (from sb)** an occasion or a period of time when sb goes to see a place or person and spends time there: *It's my first visit to New York.* ◊ *They're on an exchange visit to France.* ◊ *If you have time, pay a visit to the local museum.* ◊ *We had a visit from the police last night.* ◊ *Is this a social visit, or is it business?* ◊ *a visit to the doctor/dentist* ◊ (*BrE*) *a home visit* (= when your doctor visits you)—see also FLYING VISIT **2 ~ (with sb)** (*AmE*, *informal*) an occasion when two or more people, especially important people, meet to talk in an informal way: *He had a visit with the President.*

vis·it·ation /ˌvɪzɪˈteɪʃn/ *noun* **1** [U] (*AmE*) the right of a parent who is divorced or separated from his or her partner to visit a child who is living with the partner: *She is seeking more liberal visitation with her daughter.* ◊ *visitation rights*—compare ACCESS *n.* (3) **2** [C, U] **~ (of/from sb/sth)** (*formal*) an official visit, especially to to check that rules are being obeyed and everything is satisfactory **3** [C] **~ (of/from sb/sth)** (*formal*) an unexpected appearance of sth, for example a ghost **4** [C] **~ (of sth)** (*formal*) a disaster that is believed to be a punishment from God: *a visitation of plague*

vis·it·ing /ˈvɪzɪtɪŋ/ *adj.* [only before noun] a **visiting** professor or lecturer is one who is teaching for a fixed period at a particular university or college, but who normally teaches at another one

'visiting card (*BrE*) (*AmE* **'calling card**) (also **card** *BrE*, *AmE*) *noun* a small card with your name on it which you leave with sb after, or instead of, a formal visit—compare BUSINESS CARD

vis·it·or /ˈvɪzɪtə(r)/ *noun* **~ (to …)** a person who visits a person or place: *We've got visitors coming this weekend.* ◊ *Do you get many visitors?* ◊ *She's a frequent visitor to the US.* ◊ *The theme park attracts 2.5 million visitors a year.*—see also HEALTH VISITOR

'visitors' book *noun* a book in which visitors write their names, addresses and sometimes comments, for example, at a hotel or place of public interest

visor /ˈvaɪzə(r)/ *noun* **1** a part of a helmet that can be pulled down to protect the eyes and face—picture at HAT **2** a curved piece of plastic, etc. worn on the head above the eyes to protect them from the sun **3** a small piece of plastic, etc. inside the front window of a car that can be pulled down to protect the driver's eyes from the sun **4** (*AmE*) = PEAK (4)

vista /ˈvɪstə/ *noun* **1** (*literary*) a beautiful view, for example, of the countryside, a city, etc. **2** (*written*) a range of things that might happen in the future: *This new job could open up whole new vistas for her.*

vis·ual /ˈvɪʒuəl/ *adj.*, *noun*
■ *adj.* of or connected with seeing or sight: *I have a very good visual memory.* ◊ *the visual arts* ◊ *The building makes a tremendous visual impact.* ▶ **visu·al·ly** *adv.*: *visually handicapped/impaired* ◊ *visually exciting/dull*
■ *noun* a picture, map, piece of film, etc. used to make an article or a talk easier to understand or more interesting: *He used striking visuals to get his point across.*

,visual 'aid *noun* [usually pl.] a picture, video, etc. used in teaching to help people to learn or understand sth

,visual di'splay unit *noun* (*computing*) = VDU

,visual 'field *noun* (*technical*) = FIELD OF VISION

visu·al·ize (*BrE* also **-ise**) /ˈvɪʒuəlaɪz/ *verb* **~ sth (as sth)** to form a picture of sb/sth in your mind SYN IMAGINE: [VN] *Try to visualize him as an old man.* ▶ [Vwh-] *I can't visualize what this room looked like before it was decorated.* ◊ [VN-ing] *It can help to visualize yourself making your speech clearly and confidently.* ◊ [V-ing] *She couldn't visualize climbing the mountain.* ▶ **visu·al·iza·tion, -isa·tion** /ˌvɪʒuəlaɪˈzeɪʃn; *AmE* -ləˈz-/ *noun* [U, C]

vital /ˈvaɪtl/ *adj.* **1 ~ (for/to sth)** necessary or essential in order for sth to succeed or exist: *the vitamins that are vital for health* ◊ *Good financial accounts are vital to the success of any enterprise.* ◊ *It is vital that you keep* accurate records when you are self-employed. ◊ *Reading is of vital importance in language learning.* ◊ *The police play a vital role in our society.* ◊ *It was vital to show that he was not afraid.* **2** [only before noun] connected with or necessary for staying alive: *the vital organs* (= the brain, heart, lungs, etc.) **3** (*written*) (of a person) full of energy and enthusiasm

vi·tal·ity /vaɪˈtæləti/ *noun* [U] energy and enthusiasm [SYN] VIGOUR: *She is bursting with vitality and new ideas.* ◊ *The music has a wonderful freshness and vitality.*

vi·tal·ly /ˈvaɪtəli/ *adv.* extremely; in an essential way: *Education is vitally important for the country's future.*

the vitals /ˈvaɪtlz/ *noun* [pl.] (*old-fashioned* or *humorous*) the organs of the body that are essential for staying alive, for example the brain, heart, lungs, etc.

ˌvital staˈtistics *noun* [pl.] **1** figures that show the number of births and deaths in a country **2** (*BrE, informal*) the measurements of a woman's chest, waist and hips

vita·min /ˈvɪtəmɪn; *AmE* ˈvaɪt-/ *noun* a natural substance found in food that is an essential part of what humans and animals eat to help them grow and stay healthy. There are many different vitamins: *Oranges are rich in vitamin C.* ◊ *breakfast cereals enriched with vitamins* ◊ *vitamin deficiency* ◊ *vitamin pills*

viti·ate /ˈvɪʃieɪt/ *verb* [VN] [usually passive] (*rare, formal*) to spoil or reduce the effect of sth: *The 'yes' vote was vitiated by the low turnout in the election.*

viti·cul·ture /ˈvɪtɪkʌltʃə(r); ˈvaɪt-/ *noun* [U] (*technical*) the science or practice of growing grapes to make wine

vit·re·ous /ˈvɪtriəs/ *adj.* (*technical*) hard, shiny and transparent like glass: *vitreous enamel/china*

vit·riol /ˈvɪtriɒl; *AmE* -aːl/ *noun* [U] (*formal*) very cruel and bitter comments or criticism

vit·ri·ol·ic /ˌvɪtriˈɒlɪk; *AmE* -ˈɑːlɪk/ *adj.* (*formal*) (of language or comments) full of anger and hatred: *The newspaper launched a vitriolic attack on the president.*

vitro ⇨ IN VITRO

vi·tu·per·ation /vɪˌtjuːpəˈreɪʃn; *AmE* vaɪˌtuː-/ *noun* [U] (*rare, formal*) cruel and angry criticism ► **vi·tu·pera·tive** /vɪˈtjuːpərətɪv; *AmE* vaɪˈtuːpəreɪtɪv/ *adj.*: *a vituperative article/attack/commentary*

viv·acious /vɪˈveɪʃəs; *AmE* also vaɪˈv-/ *adj.* (*approving*) (especially of a woman) having a lively, attractive personality: *a vivacious manner* ◊ *He had three pretty, vivacious daughters.* ► **viv·acious·ly** *adv.* **viv·acity** /vɪˈvæsəti; *AmE* also vaɪˈv-/ *noun* [U]: *He was charmed by her beauty and vivacity.*

viva voce /ˌvaɪvə ˈvəʊtʃi; *AmE* ˈvoʊtʃi/ (*BrE* also **viva**) *noun* (from *Latin*) a spoken exam, especially in a British university

vivid /ˈvɪvɪd/ *adj.* **1** (of memories, a description, etc.) producing very clear pictures in your mind: *vivid memories/dreams* ◊ *He gave a vivid account of his life as a fighter pilot.* **2** (of light, colours, etc.) very bright: *vivid blue eyes* **3** (of sb's imagination) able to form pictures of ideas, situations, etc. easily in the mind ► **viv·id·ly** *adv.*: *I vividly remember the day we first met.* **viv·id·ness** *noun* [U]: *the frightening vividness of my dream*

vivi·sec·tion /ˌvɪvɪˈsekʃn/ *noun* [U] the practice of doing experiments on live animals for medical or scientific research

vivo ⇨ IN VIVO

vixen /ˈvɪksn/ *noun* **1** a female FOX (= a wild animal of the dog family) **2** (*old-fashioned*) an unpleasant and bad-tempered woman

viz. /vɪz/ *adv.* (*formal written, especially BrE*) used to introduce a list of things that explain sth more clearly or are given as examples [SYN] NAMELY: *four major colleges of surgery, viz. London, Glasgow, Edinburgh and Dublin*

vizier /vɪˈzɪə(r); *AmE* vɪˈzɪr/ *noun* an important official in some Muslim countries in the past

ˈV-neck *noun* an opening for the neck in a piece of clothing shaped like the letter V; a piece of clothing with a V-neck: *a V-neck sweater* ◊ *I went out and bought a navy V-neck.* ► **ˈV-necked** *adj.*: *a V-necked sweater*—picture on page A5

vo·cabu·lary /vəˈkæbjələri; *AmE* -leri/ *noun* (*pl.* **-ies**) **1** [C, U] all the words that a person knows or uses: *to have a wide/limited vocabulary* ◊ *your active vocabulary* (= the words that you use) ◊ *your passive vocabulary* (= the words that you understand but don't use) ◊ *Reading will increase your vocabulary.* ◊ *The word 'failure' is not in his vocabulary* (= for him, failure does not exist). **2** [C] all the words in a particular language: *When did the word 'bungalow' first enter the vocabulary?* **3** [C, U] the words that people use when they are talking about a particular subject: *The word has become part of advertising vocabulary.* **4** (also *informal* **vocab** /ˈvəʊkæb/) [C, U] a list of words with their meanings, especially in a book for learning a foreign language

vocal /ˈvəʊkl; *AmE* ˈvoʊkl/ *adj., noun*

■ *adj.* **1** [only before noun] connected with the voice: *vocal music* ◊ *the vocal organs* (= the tongue, lips, etc.) **2** telling people your opinions or protesting about sth loudly and with confidence: *He has been very vocal in his criticism of the government's policy.* ◊ *The protesters are a small but vocal minority.*

■ *noun* [usually pl.] the part of a piece of music that is sung, rather than played on a musical instrument: *backing vocals* ◊ *In this recording Armstrong himself is on vocals.*

ˌvocal ˈcords *noun* [pl.] the thin strips of muscle in the throat that move to produce the voice

vo·cal·ist /ˈvəʊkəlɪst; *AmE* ˈvoʊ-/ *noun* a singer, especially in a pop or jazz band: *a lead/guest/backing vocalist*—compare INSTRUMENTALIST

vo·cal·iza·tion (*BrE* also **-isa·tion**) /ˌvəʊkəlaɪˈzeɪʃn; *AmE* ˌvoʊkələˈzeɪʃn/ *noun* (*formal*) **1** [C] a word or sound that is produced by the voice: *the vocalizations of animals* **2** [U] the process of producing a word or sound with the voice

vo·cal·ize (*BrE* also **-ise**) /ˈvəʊkəlaɪz; *AmE* ˈvoʊ-/ *verb* (*formal*) **1** [VN] to use words to express sth: *Showing children pictures sometimes helps them to vocalize their ideas.* **2** to say or sing sounds or words: [V] *Your baby will begin to vocalize long before she can talk.* [also VN]

vo·cal·ly /ˈvəʊkəli; *AmE* ˈvoʊ-/ *adv.* **1** in a way that uses the voice: *to communicate vocally* **2** by speaking in a loud and confident way: *They protested vocally.*

vo·ca·tion /vəʊˈkeɪʃn; *AmE* voʊ-/ *noun* **1** [C] a type of work or way of life that you believe is especially suitable for you [SYN] CALLING: *Nursing is not just a job—it's a vocation.* ◊ *She believes that she has found her true vocation in life.* ◊ *You missed your vocation—you should have been an actor.* **2** [C, U] ~ (for sth) a belief that a particular type of work or way of life is especially suitable for you: *He has a vocation for teaching.* ◊ *She is a doctor with a strong sense of vocation.* **3** [C, U] a belief that you have been chosen by God to be a priest or NUN: *a vocation to the priesthood*

vo·ca·tion·al /vəʊˈkeɪʃənl; *AmE* voʊ-/ *adj.* connected with the skills, knowledge, etc. that you need to have in order to do a particular job: *vocational education/qualifications/training*

voca·tive /ˈvɒkətɪv; *AmE* ˈvɑːk-/ *noun* (*grammar*) (in some languages) the form of a noun, a pronoun or an adjective used when addressing a person or thing—compare ACCUSATIVE, DATIVE, GENITIVE, NOMINATIVE ► **voca·tive** *adj.*: *the vocative case*

vo·cif·er·ous /vəˈsɪfərəs; *AmE* voʊˈs-/ *adj.* (*formal*) expressing your opinions or feelings in a loud and confident way [SYN] STRIDENT: *vociferous complaints/protests/demands* ◊ *He is a vociferous critic of the president's stance on abortion.* ► **vo·cif·er·ous·ly** *adv.*: *to complain/protest vociferously*

vodka /ˈvɒdkə; *AmE* ˈvɑːdkə/ *noun* **1** [U] a strong clear alcoholic drink, made from grain, originally from Russia **2** [C] a glass of vodka: *I'll have a vodka and lime.*

vogue /vəʊɡ; *AmE* voʊɡ/ *noun* [C usually sing, U] ~ (for sth) a fashion for sth: *the vogue for child-centred education* ◊ *Black is in vogue again.*

voice /vɔɪs/ *noun, verb*

■ *noun*

SOUND FROM MOUTH | **1** [C, U] the sound or sounds produced

V

through the mouth by a person speaking or singing: *I could hear voices in the next room.* ◊ *to speak in a deep/ soft/loud/husky voice* ◊ *to raise/lower your voice* (= to speak louder/more quietly) ◊ *Keep your voice down* (= speak quietly). ◊ *Don't take that tone of voice with me!* ◊ *Her voice shook with emotion.* ◊ *'There you are,' said a voice behind me.* ◊ *When did his voice break* (= become deep like a man's)? ◊ *He was suffering from flu and had lost his voice* (= could not speak). ◊ *She has a good singing voice.* ◊ *She was in good voice* (= singing well) *at the concert tonight.*

-VOICED | **2** (in adjectives) having a voice of the type mentioned: *low-voiced* ◊ *squeaky-voiced*

OPINION | **3** [sing.] ~ **(in sth)** the right to express your opinion and influence decisions: *Employees should have a voice in the decision-making process.* **4** [C] a particular attitude, opinion or feeling that is expressed; a feeling or an opinion that you become aware of inside yourself: *He pledged that his party would listen to the voice of the people.* ◊ *Very few dissenting voices were heard on the right of the party.* ◊ *the voice of reason/sanity/conscience* ◊ *'Coward!' a tiny inner voice insisted.*

GRAMMAR | **5** [sing.] **the active/passive** ~ the form of a verb that shows whether the subject of a sentence performs the action (*the active voice*) or is affected by it (*the passive voice*)

PHONETICS | **6** [U] a sound produced by movement of the VOCAL CORDS used in the pronunciation of vowels and some consonants (/b, d, g, dʒ, v, ð, z, ʒ, m, n, ŋ, w, r, l, j/)

IDM **give voice to sth** to express your feelings, worries, etc. **make your ˈvoice heard** to express your feelings, opinions, etc. in a way that makes people notice and consider them **with ˌone ˈvoice** as a group; with everyone agreeing: *The various opposition parties speak with one voice on this issue.*—more at FIND *v.*, SOUND *n.*, TOP *n.*

■ *verb* [VN]
GIVE OPINION | **1** to tell people your feelings or opinions about sth: *to voice complaints/criticisms/doubts/objections* ◊ *A number of parents have voiced concern about their children's safety.*

PHONETICS | **2** to produce a sound with a movement of your VOCAL CORDS as well as your breath: *voiced consonants*—compare UNVOICED, VOICELESS

ˈvoice box *noun* the area at the top of the throat that contains the VOCAL CORDS **SYN** LARYNX

voice·less /ˈvɔɪsləs/ *adj.* (*phonetics*) (of consonants) produced without VIBRATION of the VOCAL CORDS. The consonants /p, t, k, tʃ, f, θ, s, ʃ, h/ are voiceless. **SYN** UNVOICED **OPP** VOICED

voice·mail /ˈvɔɪsmeɪl/ *noun* [U] an electronic system which can store telephone messages, so that sb can listen to them later

ˈvoice-over *noun* information or comments in a film/ movie, television programme, etc. that are given by a person who is not seen on the screen: *She earns a lot of money doing voice-overs for TV commercials.*

void /vɔɪd/ *noun, adj., verb*
■ *noun* [usually sing.] (*formal* or *literary*) a large empty space: *Below him was nothing but a black void.* ◊ (*figurative*) *The void left by his mother's death was never filled.*
■ *adj.* **1** ~ **of sth** (*formal*) completely lacking sth **SYN** DEVOID: *The sky was void of stars.* **2** (*law*) (of a contract, an agreement etc.) not valid or legal: *The agreement was declared void.* **3** (*formal*) empty: *void spaces* **IDM** see NULL
■ *verb* [VN] **1** (*law*) to state officially that sth is no longer valid **SYN** NULLIFY **2** (*formal*) to empty waste matter from the BLADDER or bowels

voile /vɔɪl/ *noun* [U] a cotton, woollen or silk fabric that is almost transparent, used for making clothes

vol. *abbr.* VOLUME *n.*: *the Complete Works of Byron Vol. 2*

vola·tile /ˈvɒlətaɪl; *AmE* ˈvɑːlətl/ *adj.* **1** (often *disapproving*) (of a person or their moods) changing easily from one mood to another: *a highly volatile personality* **2** (of a situation) likely to change suddenly; easily becoming dangerous: *a highly volatile situation from which riots might develop* ◊ *a volatile exchange rate* **3** (*technical*) (of a

substance) that changes quickly into a gas: *Petrol is a volatile substance.* ▶ **vola·til·ity** /ˌvɒləˈtɪləti; *AmE* ˌvɑːl-/ *noun* [U]

vol-au-vent /ˈvɒl ə vɒ̃; *AmE* ˌvɔːl oʊ ˈvɑː/ *noun* (*BrE*, from *French*) a small round case of light pastry filled with meat, fish, etc. in a cream sauce, often eaten with your fingers at parties

vol·can·ic /vɒlˈkænɪk; *AmE* vɑːl-/ *adj.* caused or produced by a volcano: *volcanic rocks/eruptions/ash* ◊ *volcanic activity*

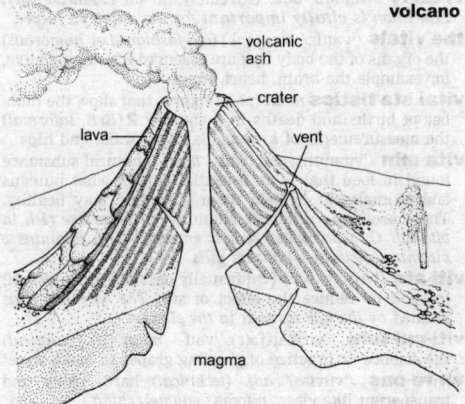

volcano

volcanic ash
crater
lava
vent
magma

vol·cano /vɒlˈkeɪnəʊ; *AmE* vɑːlˈkeɪnoʊ/ *noun* (*pl.* **-oes** or **-os**) a mountain with a large opening at the top through which gases and LAVA (= hot liquid rock) are forced out into the air, or have been in the past: *An active volcano may erupt at any time.* ◊ *a dormant volcano* (= one that is not active at present) ◊ *an extinct volcano* (= one that is no longer active)

vole /vəʊl; *AmE* voʊl/ *noun* a small animal like a mouse or rat that lives in fields or near rivers—see also WATER VOLE

vol·ition /vəˈlɪʃn; *AmE* also voʊˈl-/ *noun* [U] (*formal*) the power to choose sth freely or to make your own decisions: *They left entirely of their own volition* (= because they wanted to).

vol·ley /ˈvɒli; *AmE* ˈvɑːli/ *noun, verb*
■ *noun* **1** (in some sports, for example tennis or football) a hit or kick of the ball before it touches the ground: *She hit a forehand volley into the net.* **2** a lot of bullets, stones, etc. that are fired or thrown at the same time: *A volley of shots rang out.* ◊ *Police fired a volley over the heads of the crowd.* **3** a lot of questions, comments, insults, etc. that are directed at sb quickly one after the other: *She faced a volley of angry questions from her mother.*
■ *verb* (in some sports, for example tennis or football) to hit or kick the ball before it touches the ground: [VN] *He volleyed the ball into the back of the net.* [also V]

vol·ley·ball ·/ˈvɒlibɔːl; *AmE* ˈvɑːl-/ *noun* [U] a game in which two teams of six players use their hands to hit a large ball backwards and forwards over a high net while trying not to let the ball touch the ground on their own side

volt /vəʊlt; vɒlt; *AmE* voʊlt/ *noun* (*abbr.* **V**) a unit for measuring the force of an electric current: *a high security fence with 5000 volts passing through it*

volt·age /ˈvəʊltɪdʒ; *AmE* ˈvoʊlt-/ *noun* [U, C] electrical force measured in volts: *high/low voltage*

volte-face /ˌvɒlt ˈfɑːs; *AmE* ˌvɔːlt-/ *noun* [sing.] (*formal*) a complete change of opinion or plan **SYN** ABOUT-TURN: *This represents a volte-face in government thinking.*

volt·meter /ˈvəʊltmiːtə(r); *AmE* ˈvoʊlt-/ *noun* an instrument for measuring VOLTAGE

vol·ubie /ˈvɒljʊbl; *AmE* ˈvɑːljə-/ *adj.* (*formal*) **1** talking a lot, and with enthusiasm, about a subject: *Evelyn was very voluble on the subject of women's rights.* **2** expressed in many words and spoken quickly: *voluble protests* ▶ **vol·ubly** /ˈvɒljʊbli; *AmE* ˈvɑːljə-/ *adv.*

vol·ume /ˈvɒljuːm; *AmE* ˈvɑːl-; -jəm/ *noun* **1** [U, C] the amount of space that an object or a substance fills; the amount of space that a container has: *How do you measure the volume of a gas?* ◊ *jars of different volumes* **2** [C, U] the amount of sth: *the **sheer volume** (= large amount) of business* ◊ *This work has grown in volume recently.* ◊ *New roads are being built to cope with the increased volume of traffic.* ◊ *Sales volumes fell 0.2% in June.* **3** [U] the amount of sound that is produced by a television, radio, etc: *to turn the volume up/down* ◊ *the volume control on the television* **4** [C] (*abbr.* **vol.**) a book, especially one that is part of a series of books: *an encyclopedia in 20 volumes* **5** [C] (*formal*) a book: *a library of over 50000 volumes* ◊ *a slim volume of poetry* **6** [C] (*abbr.* **vol.**) a series of different ISSUES of the same magazine, especially all the ISSUES for one year: *'New Scientist' volume 142, number 3* **IDM** see SPEAK

vo·lu·min·ous /vəˈluːmɪnəs/ *adj.* (*formal*) **1** (of clothing) very large; having a lot of fabric: *a voluminous cloak/skirt* **2** (of a piece of writing, a book, etc.) very long and detailed **3** (of a container, piece of furniture, etc.) very large: *I sank down into a voluminous armchair.* ▶ **vo·lu·min·ous·ly** *adv.*

vol·un·tar·ily /ˈvɒləntrəli; *AmE* ˌvɑːlənˈterəli/ *adv.* **1** willingly; without being forced: *He was not asked to leave—he went voluntarily.* **2** without payment; free of charge: *The fund is voluntarily administered.*

vol·un·tary /ˈvɒləntri; *AmE* ˈvɑːlənteri/ *adj., noun*
■ *adj.* **1** done willingly, not because you are forced: *a voluntary agreement/arrangement* ◊ *Attendance on the course is purely voluntary.* ◊ *to pay **voluntary contributions** into a pension fund* ◊ (*BrE*) *He took **voluntary redundancy**.* **OPP** COMPULSORY **2** [usually before noun] (of work) done by people who choose to do it without being paid: *I do some voluntary work at the local hospital.* ◊ *She works there on a **voluntary basis**.* ◊ *voluntary services/bodies/agencies/organizations* (= organized, controlled or supported by people who choose to do this and are usually not paid) ◊ *the **voluntary sector*** (= organizations which are set up to help people and which do not make a profit, for example charities) **3** [only before noun] (of a person) doing a job without wanting to be paid for it: *a voluntary worker* **4** (*technical*) (of movements of the body) that you can control **OPP** INVOLUNTARY
■ *noun* (*pl.* **-ies**) a piece of music played before, during or after a church service, usually on an ORGAN

vol·un·teer /ˌvɒlənˈtɪə(r); *AmE* ˌvɑːlənˈtɪr/ *noun, verb*
■ *noun* **1** a person who does a job without being paid for it: *volunteer carers/helpers* ◊ *Schools need volunteers to help children to read.* **2** a person who offers to do sth without being forced to do it: *Are there any volunteers to help clear up?* ◊ *No volunteers came forward.* **3** a person who chooses to join the armed forces without being forced to join—compare CONSCRIPT
■ *verb* **1** ~ (sth) (for/as sth) to offer to do sth without being forced to do it or without getting paid for it: [V to inf] *Jill volunteered to organize a petition.* ◊ [V] *Several staff members volunteered for early retirement.* ◊ [VN] *He volunteered his services as a driver.* **2** to suggest sth or tell sb sth without being asked: [VN] *to volunteer advice/information* [also V speech] **3** ~ (for sth) to join the army, etc. without being forced to: [V] *to volunteer for military service* [also V to inf] **4** ~ sb (for/as sth) to suggest sb for a job or an activity, even though they may not want to do it: [VN] *They volunteered me for the job of interpreter.* [also VN to inf]

vo·lup·tu·ous /vəˈlʌptʃuəs/ *adj.* **1** (*written*) (of a woman) attractive in a sexual way with large breasts and hips: *a voluptuous woman* ◊ *a voluptuous body/mouth* **2** (*literary*) giving you physical pleasure: *voluptuous perfume* ◊ *voluptuous soft velvet* ▶ **vo·lup·tu·ous·ly** *adv.* **vo·lup·tu·ous·ness** *noun* [U]

vomit /ˈvɒmɪt; *AmE* ˈvɑːm-/ *verb, noun*
■ *verb* (also *informal* ˌ**throw** ˈ**up**) ~ (sth up) | ~ sth to bring food from the stomach back out through the mouth **SYN** BE SICK: [V] *The smell made her want to vomit.* ◊ [VN] *He*

had vomited up his supper. ◊ *The injured man was vomiting blood.*—see also SICK
■ *noun* [U] food from the stomach brought back out through the mouth

voo·doo /ˈvuːduː/ *noun* [U] a religion that is practised especially in Haiti and involves magic and WITCHCRAFT

vor·acious /vəˈreɪʃəs/ *adj.* (*written*) **1** eating or wanting large amounts of food: *a voracious eater* ◊ *to have a **voracious appetite*** **2** wanting a lot of new information and knowledge: *a voracious reader* ◊ *a boy with a voracious and undiscriminating appetite for facts* ▶ **vor·acious·ly** *adv.* **vor·acity** /vəˈræsəti/ *noun* [C, U] (*formal*)

vor·tex /ˈvɔːteks; *AmE* ˈvɔːrt-/ *noun* (*pl.* **vor·texes** or **vor·ti·ces** /-tɪsiːz/) **1** (*technical*) a mass of air, water, etc. that spins around very fast and pulls things into its centre **2** (*literary*) a very powerful feeling, force or situation that you cannot avoid or escape from: *They were both caught up in a whirling vortex of emotion.*

vote /vəʊt; *AmE* voʊt/ *noun, verb*
■ *noun* **1** [C] ~ (for/against sb/sth) a formal choice that you make in an election or at a meeting in order to choose sb or decide sth: *There were 21 votes for and 17 against the motion, with 2 abstentions.* ◊ *The motion was passed by 6 votes to 3.* ◊ *The chairperson has the **casting/deciding vote**.* ◊ *The Green candidate won over 3000 of the 14000 votes cast.* **2** [C] ~ (on sth) an occasion when a group of people vote on sth: *to have/take a vote on an issue* ◊ *The issue was **put to the vote**.* ◊ *The vote was unanimous.* **3** (**the vote**) [sing.] the total number of votes in an election: *She obtained 40% of the vote.* ◊ *The party increased their share of the vote.* **4** (**the vote**) [sing.] the vote given by a particular group of people, or for a particular party, etc: *the popular/student/working class vote* ◊ *the Labour/Conservative vote* **5** (**the vote**) [sing.] the right to vote, especially in political elections: *In Britain and the US, people get the vote at 18.*—see also BLOCK VOTE
■ *verb* **1** ~ (for/against sb/sth) | ~ (on sth) to show formally by marking a paper or raising your hand which person you want to win an election, or which plan or idea you support: [V, usually + *adv./prep.*] *Did you vote for or against her?* ◊ *How did you vote at the last election?* ◊ *We'll listen to the arguments on both sides and then vote on it.* ◊ *Over 60% of members voted **in favour of** (= for) the motion.* ◊ *Only about half of the electorate bothered to vote.* ◊ [VN] *We voted Democrat in the last election.* ◊ [V to inf] *Parliament voted to set up an independent inquiry into the matter.* **2** [VN-N] [usually passive] to choose sb/sth for a position or an award by voting: *He was voted most promising new director.* **3** [VN-N] [usually passive] to say that sth is good or bad: *The event was voted a great success.* **4** [VNN] to agree to give sb/yourself sth by voting: *The directors have just voted themselves a huge pay increase.* **5** [V (that)] to suggest sth or support a suggestion that sb has made: *I vote (that) we go out to eat.* **IDM** ˌ**vote with your 'feet** to show what you think about sth by going or not going somewhere: *Shoppers voted with their feet and avoided the store.* **PHRV** ˌ**vote sb/sth** ↔ ˈ**down** to reject or defeat sb/sth by voting for sb/sth else | ˌ**vote sb 'in** | ˌ**vote sb 'into/'onto sth** to choose sb for a position by voting: *He was voted in as treasurer.* ◊ *She was voted onto the board of governors.* | ˌ**vote sb 'out** | ˌ**vote sb 'out of/'off sth** to dismiss sb from a position by voting: *He was voted out of office.* | ˌ**vote sth** ↔ ˈ**through** to bring a plan, etc. into effect by voting for it: *A proposal to merge the two companies was voted through yesterday.*

ˌ**vote of 'confidence** *noun* [usually sing.] a formal vote to show that people support a leader, a political party, an idea, etc.

ˌ**vote of ˌno 'confidence** *noun* [usually sing.] a formal vote to show that people do not support a leader, a political party, an idea, etc.

ˌ**vote of 'thanks** *noun* [usually sing.] a short formal speech in which you thank sb for sth and ask other people to join you in thanking them

voter /ˈvəʊtə(r); *AmE* ˈvoʊ-/ *noun* a person who votes or has the right to vote, especially in a political election: *A*

æ	ɑː	e	ɜː	ə	ɪ	iː	i	ɒ	ɔː	ʌ	ʊ	u	uː
cat	father	ten	bird	about	sit	see	many	got	saw	cup	put	actual	too
								(BrE)					

clear majority of *voters* were in favour of the motion. ◊
Only 60% of eligible *voters* actually used their *vote.*—see
also FLOATING VOTER

vot·ing /ˈvəʊtɪŋ; *AmE* ˈvoʊ-/ *noun* [U] the action of choosing sb/sth in an election or at a meeting: *He was eliminated in the first round of voting.* ◊ *Voting will take place on
May 1.* ◊ *tactical voting* ◊ *to be of voting age*

ˈvoting booth *noun* (*especially AmE*) = POLLING BOOTH

vo·tive /ˈvəʊtɪv; *AmE* ˈvoʊ-/ *adj.* [usually before noun]
(*technical*) presented to a god as a sign of thanks: *votive
offerings*

vouch /vaʊtʃ/ *verb* PHRV ˈvouch for sb/sth to say that
you believe that sb will behave well and that you will be
responsible for their actions: *Are you willing to vouch for
him?* ◊ *I can vouch for her ability to work hard.* ˈvouch for
sth to say that you believe that sth is true or good
because you have evidence for it: *I was in bed with the
flu. My wife can vouch for that.*

vouch·er /ˈvaʊtʃə(r)/ *noun* (*BrE*) a printed piece of paper
that can be used instead of money to pay for sth, or that
allows you to pay less than the usual price of sth: *a
voucher for a free meal* ◊ *a food/travel voucher* ◊ *This
discount voucher entitles you to 10% off your next purchase.*—see also LUNCHEON VOUCHER

WHICH WORD? ⓘ
voucher / coupon / token

These words all have a meaning that refers to
something you can use instead of money and
exchange for goods.

A **voucher** or **token** is a piece of paper with an
amount of money printed on it that you can exchange for particular goods or use in a particular
store: a £10 *book/record token* ◊ a *Marks and
Spencer's gift voucher/token* (*AmE* gift certificate).

A **coupon** or **voucher** is a printed piece of paper that
can be used to pay for something or that allows you
to pay less than the usual price: a *money-off coupon.*

Tokens or **coupons** are also small pieces of paper
that you can collect and then exchange for a
particular item.

---

vouch·safe /ˌvaʊtʃˈseɪf/ *verb* ~ sth (to sb) (*old-fashioned* or *formal*) to give, offer or tell sth to sb, especially
as a privilege: [VN] *He vouchsafed to me certain family
secrets.* [also Vthat, VNN, Vspeech]

vow /vaʊ/ *noun, verb*
■ *noun* a formal and serious promise, especially a religious
one, to do sth: *to make/take a vow* ◊ *to break/keep a vow* ◊
*to break your **marriage** vows* ◊ *Nuns take a vow of
chastity.*
■ *verb* to make a formal and serious promise to do sth or a
formal statement that is true: [Vtoinf] *She vowed never to
speak to him again.* ◊ [V(that)] *He vowed (that) he had not
hurt her.* ◊ [VN] *They vowed eternal friendship.*
[also Vspeech]

vowel /ˈvaʊəl/ *noun* (*phonetics*) **1** a speech sound in
which the mouth is open and the tongue is not touching
the top of the mouth, the teeth, etc., for example /ɑː, e,
ɔː/: *vowel sounds* ◊ *Each language has a different vowel
system.* **2** a letter that represents a vowel sound. In English the vowels are a, e, i, o, and u.—compare CONSON-
ANT—see also DIPHTHONG

vox pop /ˌvɒks ˈpɒp; *AmE* ˌvɑːks ˈpɑːp/ *noun* [C, U] (*BrE,
informal*) the opinion of members of the public, especially when it is broadcast or published

voy·age /ˈvɔɪɪdʒ/ *noun, verb*

■ *noun* (*especially written*) a long journey, especially by sea
or in space: *an around-the-world voyage* ◊ *a voyage in
space* ◊ *The Titanic sank on its **maiden** voyage* (= first
journey). ◊ (*figurative*) *Going to college can be a voyage of
self-discovery.*
■ *verb* [V+adv./prep.] (*literary*) to travel, especially in a
ship and over a long distance

voy·ager /ˈvɔɪɪdʒə(r)/ *noun* (*old-fashioned* or *literary*) a
person who goes on a long journey, especially by ship to
unknown parts of the world

voy·eur /vwaɪˈɜː(r); vɔɪˈɜː(r)/ *noun* (*disapproving*) **1** a person who gets pleasure from secretly watching other
people have sex **2** a person who enjoys watching the
problems and private lives of others: *Most writers are
voyeurs of a kind.* ► **voy·eur·ism** /vwaɪˈɜːrɪzəm; vɔɪˈɜː-/
noun [U] **voy·eur·is·tic** /ˌvwaɪɜːˈrɪstɪk; ˌvɔɪəˈr-/ *adj.*: *a
voyeuristic interest in other people's lives*

VP /ˌviː ˈpiː/ *abbr.* VICE-PRESIDENT

vs *abbr.* (*especially AmE*) VERSUS

ˈ**V-sign** *noun* a sign that you make by holding up your
hand and making a V-shape with your first and second
fingers. When the PALM (= inside part) of your hand is
facing away from you, the sign means 'victory'; when the
palm is facing towards you the sign is used as a way of
being rude to other people.—compare TWO FINGERS

vul·can·ized (*BrE* also **-ised**) /ˈvʌlkənaɪzd/ *adj.* (*technical*) (of rubber) treated with SULPHUR at great heat to
make it stronger

vul·gar /ˈvʌlɡə(r)/ *adj.* **1** not having or showing good
taste; not polite, elegant or well behaved: *a vulgar man/
woman* ◊ *vulgar decorations/furnishings* ◊ *She found their
laughter and noisy games coarse and rather vulgar.*
2 rude and likely to offend: *vulgar jokes/language* ► **vul-
gar·ly** *adv.* (*rare*): *He eyed her vulgarly.*

ˌ**vulgar ˈfraction** *noun* (*BrE*) a FRACTION (= a number
less than one) that is shown as numbers above and below
a line: ¾ *and* ⅝ *are vulgar fractions.*—compare DECIMAL
FRACTION

vul·gar·ity /vʌlˈɡærəti/ *noun* [U, C] the fact of being rude
or not having good taste; a rude object, picture, etc: *the
vulgarity of mass tourism* ◊ *She was offended by the vulgarity of their jokes.* ◊ *a pornographic magazine full of
vulgarities*

vul·gar·ize (*BrE* also **-ise**) /ˈvʌlɡəraɪz/ *verb* [VN]
(*formal, disapproving*) to spoil sth by changing it so that
it is more ordinary than before and not of such a high
standard ► **vul·gar·iza·tion, -isa·tion** /ˌvʌlɡəraɪˈzeɪʃn;
AmE -rəˈz-/ *noun* [U]

vul·ner·able /ˈvʌlnərəbl/ *adj.* ~ (to sb/sth) weak and
easily hurt physically or emotionally: *to be vulnerable to
abuse/attack/illness* ◊ *She looked very vulnerable standing there on her own.* ◊ *In cases of food poisoning, young
children are especially vulnerable.* ◊ *The sudden resignation of the financial director put the company in a very
vulnerable position.* ► **vul·ner·abil·ity** /ˌvʌlnərəˈbɪləti/
noun [U] ~ (of sb/sth) (to sth): *financial/political vulnerability* ◊ *the vulnerability of newborn babies to disease* **vul-
ner·ably** /-əbli/ *adv.*

vul·pine /ˈvʌlpaɪn/ *adj.* (*formal*) of or like a FOX

vul·ture /ˈvʌltʃə(r)/ *noun* **1** a large bird, usually without
feathers on its head or neck, that eats the flesh of animals
that are already dead: *vultures circling/wheeling overhead*—picture on page A6 **2** a person who hopes to gain
from the troubles or sufferings of other people

vulva /ˈvʌlvə/ *noun* (*anatomy*) the outer opening of the
female sex organs

vying *pres part* of VIE

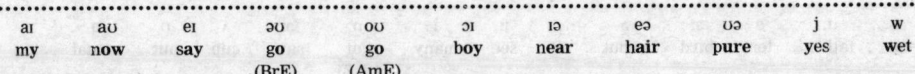

aɪ	aʊ	eɪ	əʊ	oʊ	ɔɪ	ɪə	eə	ʊə	j	w
my	now	say	go	go	boy	near	hair	pure	yes	wet
			(BrE)	(AmE)						

Ww

W /ˈdʌblju:/ *noun, abbr.*

■ *noun* (also **w**) [C, U] (*pl.* **W's, w's** /ˈdʌblju:z/) the 23rd letter of the English alphabet: *'Water' begins with (a) W/ 'W'.*

■ *abbr.* **1** west; western **2** WATT: *a 100W light bulb*

wacko /ˈwækəʊ; *AmE* -koʊ/ *adj.* (*informal, disapproving*) crazy: *wacko opinions*

wacky (also **whacky**) /ˈwæki/ *adj.* (**wack·ier, wacki·est**) (*informal*) funny or amusing in a slightly crazy way: *wacky humour/ideas*

wad /wɒd; *AmE* wɑ:d/ *noun, verb*

■ *noun* **1** a thick pile of pieces of paper, paper money, etc. folded or rolled together: *He pulled a thick wad of £10 notes out of his pocket.* ◇ (*BrE, slang*) *They had a wad/ wads of money* (= a large amount). **2** a mass of soft material, used for blocking sth or keeping sth in place: *The nurse used a wad of cotton wool to stop the bleeding.*

■ *verb* (**-dd-**) [VN] **1** ~ **sth** (**up**) (*especially AmE*) to fold or press sth into a tight wad **2** to fill sth with soft material for warmth or protection

wad·ding /ˈwɒdɪŋ; *AmE* ˈwɑ:d-/ *noun* [U] soft material that you wrap around things to protect them

wad·dle /ˈwɒdl; *AmE* ˈwɑ:dl/ *verb* [V] [usually +*adv./ prep.*] to walk with short steps, swinging from side to side, like a duck: *A short plump man came waddling towards me.* ▶ **wad·dle** *noun* [sing.]: *She walked with a waddle.*

wade /weɪd/ *verb* **1** [usually +*adv./prep.*] to walk with an effort through sth, especially water or mud: [V] *He waded into the water to push the boat out.* ◇ *Sometimes they had to wade waist-deep through mud.* ◇ *They waded the river at a shallow point.* **2** [V] (*AmE*) = PADDLE **PHRV** ˌwade ˈin| ˌwade ˈinto sth (*informal*) to enter a fight, a discussion or an argument in a forceful or not very sensitive way: *The police waded into the crowd with batons.* ◇ *You shouldn't have waded in with all those unpleasant accusations.* ˌwade ˈinto sb (*informal*) to attack sb with words in a forceful angry way: *She waded into him as soon as he got home.* ˌwade ˈthrough sth [no passive] to deal with or read sth that is boring and takes a lot of time: *I spent the whole day wading through the paperwork on my desk.*

wader /ˈweɪdə(r)/ *noun* **1** (also **ˈwading bird**) [C] any of several different types of bird with long legs that feed in shallow water **2** (**waders**) [pl.] long rubber boots that reach up to your THIGH, that you wear for standing in water, especially when fishing: *a pair of waders*

wadi /ˈwɒdi; *AmE* ˈwɑ:di/ *noun* (in the Middle East and North Africa) a valley or channel that is dry except when it rains

ˈwading pool *noun* (*AmE*) = PADDLING POOL

wafer /ˈweɪfə(r)/ *noun* **1** a thin crisp light biscuit/cookie, often eaten with ice cream: *The sundae was topped with chocolate and a wafer.* ◇ *chocolate/vanilla wafers* (= biscuits/cookies made of two wafers with chocolate/vanilla inside) **2** a very thin round piece of special bread given by the priest during COMMUNION **3** ~ (**of sth**) a very thin piece of sth

ˌwafer-ˈthin *adj.* very thin—compare PAPER-THIN

waf·fle /ˈwɒfl; *AmE* ˈwɑ:fl/ *noun, verb*

■ *noun* **1** [C] a crisp flat cake with a pattern of squares on both sides, often eaten with sweet sauce, cream, etc. on top: *a waffle iron* (= for making waffles with)—picture on page A1 **2** [U] (*BrE, informal*) language that uses a lot of words but does not say anything important or interesting: *The report is just full of waffle.*

■ *verb* [V] **1** ~ (**on**) (**about sth**) (*BrE, informal, disapproving*) to talk or write using a lot of words but without saying anything interesting or important: *The principal waffled on about exam results but no one was listening.* **2** ~ (**on/over sth**) (*AmE, informal*) to be unable to decide what to do about sth or what you think about sth: *The senator was accused of waffling on major issues.*

waft /wɒft; *AmE* wɑ:ft; wæft/ *verb, noun*

■ *verb* [+*adv./prep.*] to move, or make sth move, gently through the air: [V] *The sound of their voices wafted across the lake.* ◇ *Delicious smells wafted up from the kitchen.* ◇ [VN] *The scent of the flowers was wafted along by the breeze.*

■ *noun* (*written*) a smell or a line of smoke carried through the air: *wafts of perfume/smoke*

wag /wæg/ *verb, noun*

■ *verb* (**-gg-**) **1** [V, VN] if a dog **wags** its tail, or its tail **wags**, its tail moves from side to side several times **2** [VN] to shake your finger or your head from side to side or up and down, often as a sign of disapproval **IDM** see TAIL *n.*, TONGUE *n.*

■ *noun* **1** (*old-fashioned, especially BrE*) a person who enjoys making jokes **SYN** JOKER **2** a wagging movement

wage /weɪdʒ/ *noun, verb*

■ *noun* [sing.] (also **wages** [pl.]) a regular amount of money that you earn, usually every week, for work or services: *wages of £200 a week* ◇ *a weekly wage of £200* ◇ *wage reductions/cuts* ◇ (*BrE*) *a wage rise of 3%* ◇ *a wage increase of 3%* ◇ *wage demands/claims/settlements* ◇ *Wages are paid on Fridays.* ◇ *There are extra benefits for people on low wages.*—see also LIVING WAGE, MINIMUM WAGE—compare SALARY

■ *verb* [VN] ~ **sth** (**against/on sb/sth**) to begin and continue a war, a battle, etc: *The rebels have waged a guerrilla war since 1995.* ◇ *He alleged that a press campaign was being waged against him.*

waged /weɪdʒd/ *adj.* **1** (of a person) having regular paid work: *waged workers* **2** (of work) for which you are paid: *waged work/employment* **3** (**the waged**) *noun* [pl.] people who are **waged** **OPP** UNWAGED

ˈwage earner *noun* a person who earns money, especially a person who works for wages: *We have two wage earners in the family.*

ˈwage packet *noun* (*BrE*) = PAY PACKET

wager /ˈweɪdʒə(r)/ *noun, verb*

■ *noun* (*old-fashioned or formal*) an arrangement to risk money on the result of a particular event **SYN** BET

■ *verb* (*old-fashioned or formal*) **1** ~ (**sth**) (**on sth**)| ~ **sth/sb that…** | ~ **sth/sb** to bet money: [V] *She always wagered on an outsider.* ◇ [VN] *to wager £50 on a horse* ◇ [VN that] *I had wagered a great deal of money that I would beat him.* **2** [V (that)] (*spoken*) used to say that you are so confident that sth is true or will happen that you would be willing to bet money on it: *I'll wager that she knows more about it than she's saying.*

wag·gle /ˈwægl/ *verb* (*informal*) to make sth move with short movements from side to side or up and down; to move in this way: [VN] *Can you waggle your ears?* [alsoV] ▶ **wag·gle** *noun*

wagon /ˈwægən/ *noun* **1** (*BrE*) (*AmE* **ˈfreight car**) a railway/railroad truck for carrying goods **2** (*BrE* also **wag-gon**) a vehicle with four wheels, pulled by horses or OXEN and used for carrying heavy loads **3** (*AmE*) = TROLLEY—see also BANDWAGON, STATION WAGON **IDM** be/go on the ˈwagon (*informal*) to not drink alcohol, either for a short time or permanently

ˈwagon train *noun* a long line of WAGONS and horses, used by people travelling west in N America in the 19th century

b	d	f	g	h	k	l	m	n	p	r
bad	**did**	**fall**	**get**	**hat**	**cat**	**leg**	**man**	**now**	**pen**	**red**

wag·tail /ˈwægteɪl/ *noun* a small bird with a long tail that moves up and down when the bird is walking

wah-wah /ˈwɑː wɑː/ *noun* [U] (*music*) a special effect made on electric musical instruments, especially the guitar, which varies the quality of the sound

waif /weɪf/ *noun* a small thin person, usually a child, who looks as if they do not have enough to eat: *the waifs and strays of our society* (= people with no home) ▶ **ˈwaif-like** *adj.*: *waif-like young girls*

wail /weɪl/ *verb, noun*
■ *verb* **1** [V] to make a long loud high cry, especially because you are sad or in pain: *The little girl was wailing miserably.* ◊ *women wailing and weeping* ◊ *The cat was wailing to be let out.* **2** to cry or complain about sth in a loud high voice: [V speech] *'It's broken,' she wailed.* ◊ [V] *There's no point wailing about something that happened so long ago.* **3** [V] (of things) to make a long high sound: *Ambulances raced by with sirens wailing.* ▶ **wail·ing** *noun* [sing., U]: *We heard a high-pitched wailing.*
■ *noun* a long loud high cry, especially one expressing pain or sadness; a sound similar to this: *a wail of anguish/ despair/distress* ◊ *the distant wail of sirens*

wains·cot /ˈweɪnskət/ *noun* (*old use*) = SKIRTING BOARD

waist /weɪst/ *noun* **1** the area around the middle of the body between the RIBS and the hips, often narrower than the areas above and below: *He put his arm around her waist.* ◊ *She was paralysed from the waist down* (= in the area below her waist). ◊ *The workmen were stripped to the waist* (= wearing no clothes on the top half of their bodies).—picture at BODY **2** the part of a piece of clothing that covers the waist: *It's much too tight at the waist.* **3** (-waisted) (in adjectives) having the type of waist mentioned: *a high-waisted dress*

waist·band /ˈweɪstbænd/ *noun* the strip of fabric that forms the waist of a piece of clothing, especially at the top of a skirt or trousers/pants: *an elasticated waistband*—picture on page A4

waist·coat /ˈweɪskəʊt; *AmE* usually ˈweskət/ (*BrE*) (*AmE* **vest**) *noun* a short piece of clothing with buttons down the front but no sleeves, usually worn over a shirt and under a jacket, often forming part of a man's suit—picture on page A4

ˌwaist-ˈdeep *adj., adv.* up to the waist: *The water was waist-deep.* ◊ *We waded waist-deep into the muddy water.*

ˌwaist-ˈhigh *adj., adv.* high enough to reach the waist: *waist-high grass* ◊ *The grass had grown waist-high.*

waist·line /ˈweɪstlaɪn/ *noun* **1** the amount that a person measures around the waist, used to talk about how fat or thin they are: *an expanding waistline* **2** the place on a piece of clothing where your waist is [SYN] WAIST

wait /weɪt/ *verb, noun*
■ *verb* **1** ~ (**for sb/sth**) to stay where you are or delay doing sth until sb/sth comes or sth happens: [V] *She rang the bell and waited.* ◊ *Have you been waiting long?* ◊ *I've been waiting (for) twenty minutes.* ◊ *Wait for me!* ◊ *We're waiting for the rain to stop before we go out.* ◊ *I'll wait outside until the meeting's over.* ◊ *No waiting* (= on a sign at the side of the road, telling vehicles that they must not stop there). ◊ [V to inf] *Hurry up! We're waiting to go.* ◊ [VN] *You'll just have to wait your turn* (= wait until your turn comes).* ⇨ note at EXPECT **2** ~ (**for sth**) to hope or wait for sth to happen, especially for a long time: [V] *Leeds United had waited for success for eighteen years.* ◊ *This is just the opportunity I've been waiting for.* ◊ *He's waiting for me to make a mistake.* ◊ [VN] *I waited my chance and slipped out when no one was looking.* **3** (**be waiting**) (of things) to be ready for sb to have or use: [V] *There's a letter waiting for you at home.* ◊ [V to inf] *The hotel had a taxi waiting to collect us.* **4** [V] to be left to be dealt with at a later time because it is not urgent: *I've got some calls to make but they can wait until tomorrow.* [IDM] **an ˌacci-dent/a diˌsaster waiting to ˈhappen** a thing or person that is very likely to cause danger or a problem in the future because of the condition it is in or the way they behave **I, they, etc. can't ˈwait/can hardly ˈwait** used when you are emphasizing that sb is very excited about sth or keen to do it: *The children can't wait for Christ-*

mas to come. ◊ *I can hardly wait to see him again.* **keep sb ˈwaiting** to make sb have to wait or be delayed, especially because you arrive late: *I'm sorry to have kept you wait-ing.* **ˌwait and ˈsee** used to tell sb that they must be patient and wait to find out about sth later: *We'll just have to wait and see—there's nothing we can do at the moment.* ◊ *a wait-and-see policy/attitude* ◊ *'Where are we going?' 'Wait and see!'* **wait at ˈtable** (*formal*) to serve food to people, for example at a formal meal **ˈwait for it** (*spoken, especially BrE*) **1** used to say that you are about to tell sb sth that is surprising or amusing: *They're off on a trip, to—wait for it—the Maldives!* **2** used to tell sb not to start doing sth yet, but to wait until you tell them **wait a minute/moment/second 1** to wait for a short time: *Can you wait a second while I make a call?* **2** used when you have just noticed or remembered sth, or had a sudden idea: *Wait a minute—this isn't the right key.* **wait on sb hand and ˈfoot** (*disapproving*) to take care of sb's needs so well that they do not have to do anything for themselves **wait ˈtables** (*AmE*) to work serving food to people in a restaurant **ˈwait till/until ...** (*spoken*) used to show that you are very excited about telling or showing sth to sb: *Wait till you see what I've found!* **what are we ˈwaiting for?** (*spoken*) used to suggest that you should all start doing what you have been discussing **what are you ˈwaiting for?** (*spoken*) used to tell sb to do sth now rather than later: *If the car needs cleaning, what are you waiting for?* (**just**) **you ˈwait** used to emphasize a threat, warning or promise: *I'll be famous one day, just you wait!*—more at WING *n.* [PHRV] **ˌwait aˈbout/aˈround** to stay in a place, with nothing particular to do, for example because you are expecting sth to happen or sb to arrive **ˌwait beˈhind** (*especially BrE*) to stay after other people have gone, especially to speak to sb privately **ˌwait ˈin** (*BrE*) to stay at home because you are expecting sb to come, telephone, etc. **ˈwait on sb** to act as a servant to sb, especially by serving food to them **ˈwait on sth/sb** (*informal, especially AmE*) to wait for sth to happen before you do or decide sth: *She is waiting on the result of a blood test.* **ˌwait sth↔ˈout** to wait until an unpleasant event has finished: *We sheltered in a doorway to wait out the storm.* **ˌwait ˈup** (*AmE*) used to ask sb to stop or go more slowly so that you can join them **ˌwait ˈup (for sb)** to wait for sb to come home at night before you go to bed
■ *noun* [usually sing.] ~ (**for sb/sth**) an act of waiting; an amount of time waited: *We had a long wait for the bus.* [IDM] see LIE *v.*

wait·er /ˈweɪtə(r)/ (*feminine* **wait·ress** /ˈweɪtrəs/) *noun* a person whose job is to serve customers at their tables in a restaurant, etc: *I'll ask the waitress for the bill.* ◊ *Waiter, could you bring me some water?*—see also DUMB WAITER, SERVER ⇨ note at GENDER

ˈwaiting game *noun* [sing.] a policy of waiting to see how a situation develops before you decide how to act

ˈwaiting list *noun* a list of people who are waiting for sth such as a service or medical treatment that is not yet available: *There are no places available right now but I'll put you on a waiting list.* ◊ *There's a waiting list to join the golf club.* ◊ (*BrE*) *The government has promised to cut hospital waiting lists.*

ˈwaiting room *noun* a room where people can sit while they are waiting, for example for a bus or train, or to see a doctor or dentist

waive /weɪv/ *verb* [VN] to choose not to demand sth in a particular case, even though you have a legal or official right to do so

waiver /ˈweɪvə(r)/ *noun* (*law*) a situation in which sb gives up a legal right or claim; an official document stating this

wake /weɪk/ *verb, noun*
■ *verb* (**woke** /wəʊk/ **woken** /ˈwəʊkən/) **1** [usually +adv. / prep.] ~ (**sb**) (**up**) to stop sleeping; to make sb stop sleeping: [V] *What time do you usually wake up in the morning?* ◊ *I always wake early in the summer.* ◊ *Wake up! It's eight o'clock.* ◊ (*written*) *They woke to a clear blue sky.* ◊ (*written*) *She had just woken from a deep sleep.* ◊ [V to inf] *He woke up to find himself alone in the house.* ◊ [VN] *Try not to wake the baby up.* ◊ *I was woken by the*

sound of someone moving around. ⇨ note at AWAKE **2** [VN] (*literary* or *formal*) to make sb remember sth or feel sth again: *The incident woke memories of his past sufferings.* **PHR V** ,**wake 'up** to become more lively and interested: *Wake up and listen!*—see also WAKE (1) ,**wake sb ↔ 'up** to make sb feel more lively: *A cold shower will soon wake you up.* ◊ *The class needs waking up.*—see also WAKE (1) ,**wake 'up to sth** to become aware of sth; to realize sth: *He hasn't yet woken up to the seriousness of the situation.*

■ *noun* **1** an occasion before a funeral when people gather to remember the dead person, traditionally held at night to watch over the body before it is buried **2** the track that a boat or ship leaves behind on the surface of the water **IDM in the wake of sb/sth** coming after or following sb/sth: *There have been demonstrations on the streets in the wake of the recent bomb attack.* ◊ *A group of reporters followed in her wake.* ◊ *The storm left a trail of destruction in its wake.*

wake·ful /ˈweɪkfl/ *adj.* (*written*) **1** not sleeping; unable to sleep: *He lay wakeful all night.* **2** (of a period at night) spent with little or no sleep: *She had spent many wakeful nights worrying about him.* ▶ **wake·ful·ness** *noun* [U]

waken /ˈweɪkən/ *verb* (*written*) **1 ~ (sb) (up)** to wake, or make sb wake, from sleep: [V] *The child had just wakened.* ◊ [VN] *I was wakened by a knock at the door.* **2** [VN] to make sb remember sth or feel sth again: *The dream wakened a forgotten memory.* ⇨ note at AWAKE

wakey-wakey /ˌweɪki ˈweɪki/ *exclamation* (*BrE, informal, humorous*) used to tell sb to wake up

wak·ing /ˈweɪkɪŋ/ *adj.* [only before noun] (*written*) used to describe time when you are awake: *She spends all her waking hours caring for her mother.* ▶ **wak·ing** *noun* [U]: *the dreamlike state between waking and sleeping*

walk /wɔːk/ *verb, noun*

■ *verb* **1** [usually +*adv.*/*prep.*] to move or go somewhere by putting one foot in front of the other on the ground, but without running: [V] *The baby is just learning to walk.* ◊ *'How did you get here?' 'I walked.'* ◊ *He walked slowly away from her.* ◊ *The door opened and Jo walked in.* ◊ *She missed the bus and had to walk home.* ◊ *The school is within easy walking distance of the train station.* ◊ [VN] *Children here walk several miles to school.* **2** (also **go walking**) (both *especially BrE*) to spend time walking for pleasure: [V] *We're going walking in the mountains this summer.* ◊ *I walked across Scotland with a friend.* ◊ [VN] *They love walking the moors.* **3** [VN+*adv.*/*prep.*] to go somewhere with sb on foot, especially in order to make sure they get there safely: *He always walked her home.* **4** [VN] to take an animal for a walk; to make an animal walk somewhere: *They walk their dogs every day.* **5** [V] (*informal*) to disappear; to be taken away: *Lock up any valuables. Things tend to walk here* (= be stolen). **6** [V] (*literary*) (of a ghost) to appear **IDM** ,**run before you can 'walk** to do things that are difficult, without learning the basic skills first **walk the 'beat** (of police officers) to walk around the area that they are responsible for **walk 'free** to be allowed to leave a court of law, etc., without receiving any punishment '**walk it** (*spoken*) **1** to go somewhere on foot instead of in a vehicle, etc. **2** to easily achieve sth that you want: *It's not a difficult exam. You'll walk it!* **walk sb off their 'feet** (*informal*) to make sb walk so far or so fast that they are very tired **walk off the 'job** (*AmE*) to stop working in order to go on strike **walk the 'plank** (in the past) to walk along a board placed over the side of a ship and fall into the sea, as a punishment **walk the 'streets** to walk around the streets of a town or city: *Is it safe to walk the streets alone at night?* **walk 'tall** to feel proud and confident—more at AIR *n.*, AISLE, LINE *n.*, MEMORY LANE, THIN *adj.*, TIGHTROPE **PHR V** ,**walk a'way (from sb/sth)** to leave a difficult situation or relationship, etc. instead of staying and trying to deal with it ,**walk a'way with sth** (*informal*) to win or obtain sth easily: *She walked away with the gold medal.* ,**walk 'in on sb/sth** to enter a room when sb in there is doing sth private and does not expect you ,**walk 'into sth** (*informal*) **1** to become involved in an unpleasant situation, especially because you were not sensible enough to avoid it: *I realized I'd walked into a trap.* **2** to

succeed in getting a job very easily ,**walk 'into sth/sb** to crash into sth/sb while you are walking, for example because you do not see them ,**walk 'off** to leave a person or place suddenly because you are angry or upset ,**walk sth ↔ 'off** to go for a walk after a meal so that you feel less full: *We walked off a heavy Sunday lunch.* ,**walk 'off with sth** (*informal*) **1** to win sth easily **2** to take sth that is not yours; to steal sth ,**walk 'out** (*informal*) (of workers) to stop working in order to go on strike—related noun WALKOUT ,**walk 'out (of sth)** to leave a meeting, performance, etc. suddenly, especially in order to show your disapproval ,**walk 'out (on sb)** (*informal*) to suddenly leave sb that you are having a relationship with and that you have a responsibility for: *How could she walk out on her kids?* ,**walk 'out (on sth)** (*informal*) to stop doing sth that you have agreed to do before it is completed: *I never walk out on a job half done.* ,**walk (all) 'over sb** (*informal*) **1** to treat sb badly, without considering them or their needs: *She'll always let him walk all over her.* **2** to defeat sb easily—related noun WALKOVER ,**walk 'up (to sb/sth)** to walk towards sb/sth, especially in a confident way

■ *noun* **1** [C] a journey on foot, usually for pleasure or exercise: *Let's go for a walk.* ◊ *I like to have a walk in the evenings.* ◊ *She's taken the dog for a walk.* ◊ *He set out on the long walk home.* ◊ *The office is ten minutes' walk from here.* ◊ *a ten-minute walk* ◊ *It's only a short walk to the beach.* **2** [C] a path or route for walking, usually for pleasure; an organized event when people walk for pleasure: *a circular walk* ◊ *There are some interesting walks in the area.* ◊ *a guided walk around the farm* **3** [sing.] a way or style of walking; the act or speed of walking rather than running: *I recognized him by his walk.* ◊ *The horse slowed to a walk.* **4** [C] (*AmE*) a SIDEWALK or path **IDM a walk of 'life** a person's job or position in society **SYN** BACKGROUND: *She has friends from all walks of life.*

> **VOCABULARY BUILDING**
> ways of **walking**
>
> **creep** *He could hear someone creeping around down-stairs.*
>
> **limp** *One player limped off the field with a twisted ankle.*
>
> **pace** *I found him in the corridor nervously pacing up and down.*
>
> **pad** *She spent the morning padding about the house in her slippers.*
>
> **plod** *They wearily plodded home through the rain.*
>
> **shuffle** *The queue gradually shuffled forward.*
>
> **stagger** *They staggered out of the pub, completely drunk.*
>
> **stomp** *She stomped out of the room, slamming the door behind her.*
>
> **stroll** *Families were strolling around the park.*
>
> **tiptoe** *They tiptoed upstairs so they wouldn't wake the baby.*
>
> **trudge** *We trudged up the hill.*

walk·about /ˈwɔːkəbaʊt/ *noun* (*BrE*) an occasion when an important person walks among ordinary people to meet and talk to them

walk·er /ˈwɔːkə(r)/ *noun* **1** (*especially BrE*) a person who walks, usually for pleasure or exercise: *The coastal path is a popular route for walkers.* **2** a fast, slow, etc. ~ a person who walks fast, slow, etc. **3** (*AmE*) = ZIMMER FRAME: *He now needs a walker to get around.* **4** (*AmE*) = BABY WALKER

walkie-talkie /ˌwɔːki ˈtɔːki/ *noun* (*informal*) a small radio that you can carry with you and use to send or receive messages

'**walk-in** *adj.* [only before noun] **1** large enough to walk into: *a walk-in closet* **2** not arranged in advance; where you do not need to arrange a time in advance: *a walk-in interview* ◊ *a walk-in clinic*

walk·ing /ˈwɔːkɪŋ/ *noun, adj.*

W

■ *noun* [U] **1** (*especially BrE*) the activity of going for walks in the countryside for exercise or pleasure: *to go walking* ◇ *walking boots* ◇ *a walking holiday in Scotland* **2** the sport of walking a long distance as fast as possible without running

■ *adj.* [only before noun] (*informal*) used to describe a human or living example of the thing mentioned: *She's a walking dictionary* (= she knows a lot of words).

'walking papers *noun* [pl.] (*AmE, informal*) the letter or notice dismissing sb from a job

'walking stick (also **stick** especially in *BrE*) *noun* a stick that you carry and use as a support when you are walking

Walk·man™ /'wɔːkmən/ *noun* (*pl.* **-mans** /-mənz/) (also ,**personal 'stereo**) a small cassette player with HEAD-PHONES that you carry with you and use while you are moving around

'walk-on *adj.* ~ **part/role** used to describe a very small part in a play or film/movie, without any words to say

walk·out /'wɔːkaʊt/ *noun* **1** a sudden strike by workers **2** the act of suddenly leaving a meeting as a protest against sth

walk·over /'wɔːkəʊvə(r)/ *noun* an easy victory in a game or competition

'walk-up *noun* (*AmE*) a tall building with stairs but no lift/elevator; an office or a flat/apartment in such a building

walk·way /'wɔːkweɪ/ *noun* a passage or path for walking along, often outside and raised above the ground

wall /wɔːl/ *noun, verb*

■ *noun* **1** a long upright solid structure, made of stone, brick or CONCRETE, that surrounds, divides or protects an area of land: *The fields were divided by stone walls.* ◇ *He sat on the wall and watched the others playing.*—see also SEA WALL **2** any of the upright sides of a building or room: *I'm going to paint the walls white and the ceiling pink.* ◇ *Hang the picture **on the wall** opposite the window.* ◇ *She leaned against the wall.* **3** something that forms a barrier or stops you from making progress: *The boat struck a solid wall of water.* ◇ *The investigators were confronted by a wall of silence.* **4** the outer layer of sth hollow such as an organ of the body or a cell of an animal or a plant: *the abdominal wall* ◇ *The knife had just ruptured the wall of an artery.* **IDM go to the 'wall** (*informal*) (of a company or an organization) to fail because of lack of money **off the 'wall** (*informal*) unusual and amusing; slightly crazy: *Some of his ideas are really off the wall.* ◇ *off-the-wall ideas* **up the 'wall** (*informal*) crazy or angry: *That noise is driving me up the wall.* ◇ *I mustn't be late or Dad will go up the wall.* ,**walls have 'ears** (*saying*) used to warn people to be careful what they say because other people may be listening—more at BACK *n.*, BRICK *n.*, FLY *n.*, FOUR, HANDWRITING, HEAD *n.*, WRITING

■ *verb* [VN] [usually passive] to surround an area, a town, etc. with a wall or walls: *a walled city/garden* **PHRV** ,**wall sth↔'in** [usually passive] to surround sth/sb with a wall or barrier ,**wall sth↔'off** [usually passive] to separate one place or area from another with a wall ,**wall sb↔'up** [usually passive] to keep sb as a prisoner behind walls ,**wall sth↔'up** [usually passive] so that you can no longer use it

wal·laby /'wɒləbi/ *AmE* /'wɑːl-/ *noun* (*pl.* **-ies**) an Australian animal like a small KANGAROO, that moves by jumping on its strong back legs and keeps its young in a POUCH (= a pocket of skin) on the front of the mother's body

wal·lah /'wɒlə/ *AmE* /'wɑːlə/ *noun* (in India) a person connected with a particular job: *office wallahs*

wal·let /'wɒlɪt/ *AmE* /'wɑːl-/ /'wɔːl-/ *noun* **1** (*AmE* also **bill-fold**) a small flat folding case made of leather or plastic used for keeping paper money and CREDIT CARDS in ⇨ note at PURSE—picture at MONEY **2** a flat leather, plastic or cardboard case for carrying documents in: *a document wallet*

wall·flower /'wɔːlflaʊə(r)/ *noun* **1** a garden plant with yellow, orange or red flowers with a sweet smell that appear in late spring **2** (*informal*) a person who does not

dance at a party because they do not have sb to dance with or because they are too shy

wall·ing /'wɔːlɪŋ/ *noun* [U] **1** material from which a wall is built: *stone/concrete walling* **2** the act or skill of building a wall or walls: *a firm that does paving and walling*

,**wall-'mounted** *adj.* fixed onto a wall: *wall-mounted lights*

wal·lop /'wɒləp/ *AmE* /'wɑːl-/ *noun, verb*

■ *noun* [sing.] (*informal*) a heavy powerful hit

■ *verb* [VN] (*informal*) **1** to hit sb/sth very hard: *My father used to wallop me if I told lies.* **2** to defeat sb completely in a contest, match, etc: *We walloped them 6–0.*

wal·low /'wɒləʊ/ *AmE* /'wɑːloʊ/ *verb, noun*

■ *verb* [V] ~ **(in sth) 1** (of large animals or people) to lie and roll about in water or mud, to keep cool or for pleasure: *hippos wallowing in the river* ◇ *He loves to wallow in a hot bath after a game.* **2** (often *disapproving*) to enjoy sth that causes you pleasure: *She wallowed in the luxury of the hotel.* ◇ *to wallow in despair/self-pity* (= to think about your unhappy feelings all the time and seem to be enjoying them)

■ *noun* [sing.] an act of wallowing: *pigs having a wallow in the mud*

'wall painting *noun* a picture painted straight onto the surface of a wall

wall·paper /'wɔːlpeɪpə(r)/ *noun, verb*

■ *noun* [U] thick paper, often with a pattern on it, used for covering the walls and ceiling of a room: *wallpaper paste* ◇ *a roll of wallpaper* ◇ *to hang wallpaper*

■ *verb* (also **paper**) [VN, V] to put wallpaper onto the walls of a room

'Wall Street *noun* [U] the US financial centre and STOCK EXCHANGE in New York City (used to refer to the business that is carried out there): *Share prices fell on Wall Street today.* ◇ *Wall Street responded quickly to the news.*

,**wall-to-'wall** *adj.* [only before noun] **1** covering the floor of a room completely: *wall-to-wall carpets/carpeting* **2** (*informal*) continuous; happening or existing all the time or everywhere: *wall-to-wall TV sports coverage*

wally /'wɒli/ *AmE* /'wɑːli/ *noun* (*pl.* **-ies**) (*BrE, informal*) a stupid person

wal·nut /'wɔːlnʌt/ *noun* **1** [C] the light brown nut of the walnut tree that has a rough surface and a hard round shell in two halves—picture at NUT **2** (also **'walnut tree**) [C] the tree on which walnuts grow **3** [U] the brown wood of the walnut tree, used in making furniture: *a walnut writing desk*

wal·rus /'wɔːlrəs/ *noun* an animal like a large SEAL (= a sea animal with thick fur, that eats fish and lives around coasts), that has two long outer teeth called TUSKS and lives in Arctic regions

waltz /wɔːls/ *AmE* /wɔːlts/ *noun, verb*

■ *noun* a graceful dance in which two people dance together to a regular rhythm; a piece of music for this dance: *to dance a/the waltz* ◇ *a Strauss waltz*

■ *verb* **1** [often +*adv./prep.*] to dance a waltz: [V] *I watched them waltzing across the floor.* ◇ [VN] *He waltzed her around the room.* **2** [V+*adv./prep.*] (*informal*) to walk or go somewhere in a very confident way: *I don't like him waltzing into the house as if he owned it.* **3** [V] ~ **(through sth)** to complete or achieve sth without any difficulty: *The recruits have waltzed through their training.* **PHRV** ,**waltz 'off (with sth/sb)** (*informal*) to leave a place or person in a way that is very annoying, often taking sth that is not yours: *He just waltzed off with my car!*

WAN /wæn/ *noun* (*pl.* **WANs**) (*computing*) the abbreviation for 'wide area network' (a system in which computers in different places are connected, usually over a large area)—compare LAN

wan /wɒn/ *AmE* /wɑːn/ *adj.* (*written*) looking pale and weak: *his grey, wan face* ◇ *She gave me a wan smile* (= showing no energy or enthusiasm). ▶ **wanly** *adv.*: *He smiled wanly.*

wand /wɒnd/ *AmE* /wɑːnd/ *noun* **1** (also ,**magic 'wand**) a straight thin stick that is held by sb when performing magic or magic tricks: *The fairy waved her wand and the table disappeared.* ◇ *You can't expect me to just wave a*

aɪ	aʊ	eɪ	əʊ	oʊ	ɔɪ	ɪə	eə	ʊə	j	w
my	now	say	go	go	boy	near	hair	pure	yes	wet
			(BrE)	(AmE)						

(*magic*) *wand and make everything all right again.* **2** any object in the shape of a straight thin stick: *a mascara wand*

wan·der /ˈwɒndə(r); *AmE* ˈwɑːn-/ *verb, noun*
- *verb* **1** to walk slowly around or to a place, often without any particular sense of purpose or direction: [V, +*adv. / prep.*] *She wandered aimlessly around the streets.* ◊ *We wandered back towards the car.* ◊ [VN] *The child was found wandering the streets alone.* **2** [V] ~ **(away/off)|** ~ **(from/off sth)** to move away from the place where you ought to be or the people you are with [SYN] STRAY: *The child wandered off and got lost.* ◊ *They had wandered from the path into the woods.* **3** [V] ~ **(away, back, to, etc. sth)** (of a person's mind or thoughts) to stop being directed on sth and to move without much control to other ideas, subjects, etc: *It's easy to be distracted and **let your attention wander**.* ◊ *Try not to **let your mind wander**.* ◊ *Her thoughts wandered back to her youth.* ◊ *Don't wander off the subject—keep to the point.* **4** [V] [usually +*adv. / prep.*] (of a person's eyes) to move slowly from looking at one thing to looking at another thing or in other directions: *His eyes wandered towards the photographs on the wall.* ◊ *She **let her gaze wander**.* **5** [V] [usually +*adv. / prep.*] (of a road or river) to curve instead of following a straight course: *The road wanders along through the hills.*
- *noun* [sing.] a short walk in or around a place, usually with no special purpose: *I went to the park and had a wander around.*

wan·der·er /ˈwɒndərə(r); *AmE* ˈwɑːn-/ *noun* (*written*) a person who keeps travelling from place to place with no permanent home

wan·der·ings /ˈwɒndərɪŋz; *AmE* ˈwɑːn-/ *noun* [pl.] (*written*) journeys from place to place, usually with no special purpose: *His wanderings took him first to India.*

wan·der·lust /ˈwɒndəlʌst; *AmE* ˈwɑːndərl-/ *noun* [U] (from *German*) a strong desire to travel

wane /weɪn/ *verb, noun*
- *verb* [V] **1** (*written*) to become gradually weaker or less important: *Her enthusiasm for the whole idea was waning rapidly.* ◊ *Their popularity waned during that period.* **2** (of the moon) to appear slightly smaller each day after being round and full [OPP] *see sense 2* WAX [IDM] see WAX *v.*
- *noun* [sing.] [IDM] **on the wane** (*written*) becoming smaller, less important or less common: *Her popularity has been on the wane for some time.*

wan·gle /ˈwæŋgl/ *verb* ~ **sth (from/out of sb)** (*informal*) to get sth that you or another person wants by persuading sb or by a clever plan: [VN] *She had wangled an invitation to the opening night.* ◊ *I'll try to wangle some money out of my parents.* ◊ *We should be able to **wangle it** so that you can start tomorrow.* ◊ *He managed to **wangle his way onto the course**.* ◊ [VNN] *He had wangled her a seat on the plane.*

wank /wæŋk/ *verb, noun*
- *verb* [V] (*BrE*, △, *slang*) to MASTURBATE
- *noun* [usually sing.] (*BrE*, △, *slang*) an act of MASTURBATION

wank·er /ˈwæŋkə(r)/ *noun* (*BrE*, △, *slang*) an offensive word used to insult sb, especially a man, and to show anger or dislike: *a bunch of wankers*

wanna /ˈwɒnə; *AmE* ˈwɑːnə; ˈwɔːnə; ˈwʌnə/ (*informal, non-standard*) the written form of the word some people use to mean 'want to' or 'want a', which is not considered to be correct: *I wanna go.* ◊ *Wanna drink?* (= Do you want …) [HELP] You should not write this form, unless you are copying somebody's speech.

wan·nabe /ˈwɒnəbi; *AmE* ˈwɑːn-; ˈwɔːn-; ˈwʌn-/ *noun* (*informal, disapproving*) a person who behaves, dresses, etc. like sb famous because they want to be like them

want /wɒnt; *AmE* wɑːnt; wɔːnt/ *verb, noun*
- *verb* (not usually used in the progressive tenses)
  - WISH | **1** to have a desire or a wish for sth: [VN] *Do you want some more tea?* ◊ *She's always wanted a large family.* ◊ *All I want is the truth.* ◊ *Thanks for the present—it's just what I wanted.* ◊ (*informal*) *I can do whatever I want.* ◊ *The last thing I wanted was to upset you.* ◊ *The party wants her as leader.* ◊ [V to inf] *What do you want to do*

tomorrow? ◊ *'It's time you did your homework.' 'I don't want to!'* ◊ *There are two points which I wanted to make.* ◊ [VN to inf] *Do you want me to help?* ◊ *We didn't want this to happen.* ◊ *I want it (to be) done as quickly as possible.* [HELP] Notice that you cannot say 'want that …': *I want that you do it quickly.* When the infinitive is used after **want**, it must have *to*: *I want study in America.* [VN -ing] *I don't want you coming home so late.* ◊ [VN-ADJ] *Do you want your coffee black or white?* ◊ [V] (*spoken, informal*) *You can come too, if you want.*

NEED | **2** (*informal*) to need sth: [VN] *We'll want more furniture for the new office.* ◊ *What this house wants is a good clean.* ◊ [V -ing, V to inf] *The plants want watering daily.* ◊ *The plants want to be watered daily.* **3** [VN] [usually passive] to need sb to be present in the place or for the purpose mentioned: *She's wanted immediately in the director's office.* ◊ *Excuse me, you're wanted on the phone.*—see also WANTED

SHOULD/OUGHT TO | **4** [V to inf] (*informal*) used to give advice to sb, meaning 'should' or 'ought to': *If possible, you want to avoid alcohol.* ◊ *He wants to be more careful.*

FEEL SEXUAL DESIRE | **5** [VN] to feel sexual desire for sb

LACK | **6** [VN] (*formal*) to lack sth: *He doesn't want courage.*

[IDM] **not want to ˈknow (about sth)** (*informal*) to take no interest in sth because you do not care about it or it is too much trouble: *I've tried to ask her advice, but she doesn't want to know* (= about my problems). **want ˈrid of sb/sth** (*BrE, spoken, informal*) to want to be free of sb/sth that has been annoying you or that you do not want: *Are you trying to say you want rid of me?* **what do you ˈwant?** used to ask sb in a rude or angry way why they are there or what they want you to do—more at NONE *pron.*, PART *n.*, TRUCK *n.*, WASTE *v.*, WAY *n.*

[PHRV] **ˈwant for sth** (especially in negative sentences) (*formal*) to lack sth that you really need: *He's ensured that his children will want for nothing* (= will have everything they need). **want sth from/out of sth/sb** to hope to get sth from a particular experience or person: *I had to discover what I really wanted out of life.* ◊ *What do you want from me?* **ˌwant ˈin/ˈout** (*informal, especially AmE*) to want to come in or out of a place: *The dog wants in.* **ˌwant ˈin| ˌwant ˈin/ˈinto sth** (*informal*) to want to be involved in sth: *He wants in on the deal.* **ˌwant ˈout| ˌwant ˈout of sth** (*informal*) to want to stop being involved in sth: *Jenny was fed up. She wanted out.*
- *noun* (*formal*)
  - STH YOU NEED | **1** [C, usually pl.] something that you need or want: *human / bodily wants* ◊ *She spent her life pandering to the wants of her children.*
  - LACK | **2** [U, sing.] ~ **of sth** (*formal*) a situation in which there is not enough of sth; a lack of sth: *a want of adequate medical facilities*
  - BEING POOR | **3** [U] (*formal*) the state of being poor, not having food, etc: *Visitors to the slums were clearly shocked to see so many families living in want.*

[IDM] **for (the) want of sth** because of a lack of sth; because sth is not available: *The project failed for want of financial backing.* ◊ *We call our music 'postmodern' for the want of a better word.* **in want of sth** (*formal*) needing sth: *The present system is in want of a total review.* **not for (the) want of doing sth** used to say that if sth is not successful, it is not because of a lack of effort: *If he doesn't manage to convince them, it won't be for want of trying* (= he has tried hard).

b	d	f	g	h	k	l	m	n	p	r
bad	did	fall	get	hat	cat	leg	man	now	pen	red

'want ads *noun* [pl.] (*AmE*) = CLASSIFIED ADVERTISEMENTS

want·ed /'wɒntɪd; *AmE* 'wɑːn-; 'wɔːn-/ *adj.* being searched for by the police, in connection with a crime: *He is wanted by the police in connection with the deaths of two people.* ◊ *Italy's most wanted man*

want·ing /'wɒntɪŋ; *AmE* 'wɑːn-; 'wɔːn-/ *adj.* [not before noun] **~ (in sth)** (*formal*) **1** not having enough of sth [SYN] LACKING: *The students were certainly not wanting in enthusiasm.* **2** not good enough: *This explanation is wanting in many respects.* ◊ *The new system was tried and found wanting.*

wan·ton /'wɒntən; *AmE* 'wɑːn-; 'wɔːn-/ *adj.* (*formal*) **1** [usually before noun] causing harm or damage deliberately and for no acceptable reason: *wanton destruction/ vandalism* ◊ *a wanton disregard for human life* **2** (*old-fashioned, disapproving*) (usually of a woman) behaving in a very immoral way; having many sexual partners ▶ **wan·ton·ly** *adv.* **wan·ton·ness** *noun* [U]

wap·iti /'wɒpɪti; *AmE* 'wɑːp-/ *noun* (*pl.* **wap·iti**) (*AmE also* **elk**) a very large N American deer

war /wɔː(r)/ *noun* **1** [U, C] a situation in which two or more countries or groups of people fight against each other over a period of time: *the Second World War* ◊ *the threat of (a) nuclear war* ◊ *to win/lose a/the war* ◊ *the war between England and Scotland* ◊ *England's war with/ against Scotland* ◊ *It was the year Britain declared war on Germany.* ◊ *Social and political problems led to the outbreak* (= the beginning) *of war.* ◊ *Where were you living when war broke out?* ◊ *The government does not want to go to war* (= start a war) *unless all other alternatives have failed.* ◊ *How long have they been at war?* ◊ *a war widow/hero* ◊ (*formal*) *In the Middle Ages England waged war on France.*—see also WARRING, CIVIL WAR, COLD WAR, COUNCIL OF WAR, PHONEY WAR, POST-WAR, PRISONER OF WAR, WORLD WAR **2** [C, U] a situation in which there is aggressive competition between groups, companies, countries, etc: *the class war* ◊ *a trade war*—see also PRICE WAR **3** [U, sing.] **~ (against/on sb/sth)** a fight or an effort over a long period of time to get rid of or stop sth unpleasant: *The government has declared war on drug dealers.* ◊ *We seem to be winning the war against crime.* [IDM] **have been in the 'wars** (*spoken*) to have been injured in a fight or an accident: *You look like you've been in the wars—who gave you that black eye?* **a ,war of 'nerves** an attempt to defeat your opponents by putting pressure on them so that they lose courage or confidence **a ,war of 'words** a fierce argument or disagreement over a period of time between two or more people or groups: *the political war of words over tax*—more at FAIR *adj.*

war·ble /'wɔːbl; *AmE* 'wɔːrbl/ *verb* **1** (*humorous*) to sing, especially in a high voice that is not very steady: [VN] *He warbled his way through the song.* [also V, V speech] **2** [V, VN] (of a bird) to sing with rapidly changing notes ▶ **war·ble** *noun*: *I heard the faint warble of Laura's voice.*

warb·ler /'wɔːblə(r); *AmE* 'wɔːrb-/ *noun* a small bird. There are many types of warbler, some of which have a musical call.

'war chest *noun* an amount of money that a government or an organization has available to spend on a particular plan, project, etc.

'war crime *noun* a cruel act that is committed during a war and is against the international rules of war

'war criminal *noun* a person who has committed war crimes

'war cry *noun* a word or phrase that is shouted by people fighting in a battle in order to give themselves courage and to frighten the enemy

ward /wɔːd; *AmE* wɔːrd/ *noun, verb*
■ *noun* **1** a separate room or area in a hospital for people with the same type of medical condition: *a maternity/ surgical/psychiatric/children's ward* **2** (in Britain) one of the areas into which a city is divided and which elects and is represented by a member of the local council **3** (especially *law*) a person, especially a child, who is under the legal protection of a court of law or another person (called a GUARDIAN): *The child was made a ward of court.*

■ *verb* [PHRV] **,ward sb/sth↔'off** to protect or defend yourself against danger, illness, attack, etc: *to ward off criticism/intruders* ◊ *She put up her hands to ward him off.*

-ward (*also less frequent* **-wards**) *suffix* (in adjectives) in the direction of: *backward* ◊ *eastward* ◊ *homeward* ▶ **-wards** (*also* **-ward** especially in *AmE*) (in adverbs): *onwards* ◊ *forwards*

'war dance *noun* a dance that is performed by the members of a tribe, for example before battle or to celebrate a victory

war·den /'wɔːdn; *AmE* 'wɔːrdn/ *noun* **1** a person who is responsible for taking care of a particular place and making sure that the rules are obeyed: *a wildlife/forest warden* ◊ (*BrE*) *the warden of a youth hostel*—see also CHURCHWARDEN, GAME WARDEN, TRAFFIC WARDEN **2** (in Britain), a title given to the head of some colleges and institutions: *the Warden of Wadham College, Oxford* **3** (*especially AmE*) the person in charge of a prison **4** a person who guards prisoners in a prison

war·der /'wɔːdə(r); *AmE* 'wɔːrd-/ (*feminine* **ward·ress** /'wɔːdrəs; *AmE* 'wɔːrd-/) *noun* (*BrE*) a person who guards prisoners in a prison—compare GUARD *n.* (1)

ward·robe /'wɔːdrəʊb; *AmE* 'wɔːrdroʊb/ *noun* **1** a large cupboard for hanging clothes in which is either a piece of furniture or (in British English) built into the wall: *a fitted wardrobe*—compare CLOSET **2** [usually sing.] the clothes that a person has: *everything you need for your winter/summer wardrobe* **3** [usually sing.] the department in a theatre or television company that takes care of the clothes that actors wear

'wardrobe mistress *noun* a woman whose job is to take care of the clothes that the actors in a theatre company, etc. wear on stage

ward·room /'wɔːdruːm; -rʊm; *AmE* 'wɔːrd-/ *noun* a room in a ship, especially a WARSHIP, where the officers live and eat

-wards ⇨ -WARD

ward·ship /'wɔːdʃɪp; *AmE* 'wɔːrd-/ *noun* [U] (*law*) the fact of a child being cared for by a GUARDIAN (= a person who is not his or her parent) or of being protected by a court of law—see also WARD *n.* (3)

ware /weə(r); *AmE* wer/ *noun* **1** [U] (in compounds) objects made of the material or in the way or place mentioned: *ceramic ware* ◊ *a collection of local ware*—see also EARTHENWARE, FLATWARE, GLASSWARE, SILVERWARE **2** [U] (in compounds) objects used for the purpose or in the room mentioned: *bathroom ware* ◊ *ornamental ware*—see also KITCHENWARE, TABLEWARE **3** (**wares**) [pl.] (*old-fashioned*) things that sb is selling, especially in the street or at a market: *He travelled from town to town selling his wares.*

ware·house /'weəhaʊs; *AmE* 'werh-/ *noun* a building where large quantities of goods are stored, especially before they are sent to shops/stores to be sold

ware·hous·ing /'weəhaʊzɪŋ; *AmE* 'werh-/ *noun* [U] the practice or business of storing things in a warehouse

war·fare /'wɔːfeə(r); *AmE* 'wɔːrfer/ *noun* [U] **1** the activity of fighting a war, especially using particular weapons or methods: *air/naval/guerrilla warfare* ◊ *countries engaged in warfare*—see also BIOLOGICAL WARFARE, CHEMICAL WARFARE, GERM WARFARE **2** the activity of competing in an aggressive way with another group, company, etc: *class/gang warfare*—see also PSYCHOLOGICAL WARFARE

'war game *noun* **1** a practice battle that is used to test military plans and equipment **2** a game in which models representing soldiers, ships, etc. are moved around on maps

war·head /'wɔːhed; *AmE* 'wɔːrhed/ *noun* the explosive part of a MISSILE: *nuclear warheads*

war·horse /'wɔːhɔːs; *AmE* 'wɔːrhɔːrs/ *noun* **1** (in the past) a large horse used in battle **2** (*informal*) an old soldier or politician who has a lot of experience

wari·ly, **wari·ness** ⇨ WARY

war·like /'wɔːlaɪk; *AmE* 'wɔːrl-/ *adj.* (*formal*) **1** aggressive and wanting to fight: *a warlike nation* **2** connected with fighting wars: *warlike preparations*

war·lock /'wɔːlɒk; AmE 'wɔːrlɑːk/ noun a man who is believed to have magic powers, especially evil ones

war·lord /'wɔːlɔːd; AmE 'wɔːrlɔːrd/ noun (disapproving) the leader of a military group that is not official and that fights against other groups within a country or an area: rival/local warlords

warm /wɔːm; AmE wɔːrm/ adj., verb, noun, adv.

■ adj. (warm·er, warm·est)

AT PLEASANT TEMPERATURE | **1** at a fairly high temperature in a way that is pleasant, rather than being hot or cold: a warm breeze/climate ◊ Wash the blouse in warm soapy water. ◊ It's nice and warm in here. ◊ Are you warm enough? ◊ The children jumped up and down to **keep warm**. ◊ You'll be as **warm as toast** in here.

CLOTHES/BUILDINGS | **2** keeping you warm or staying warm in cold weather: a warm pair of socks ◊ This sleeping bag is very warm. ◊ a warm house

FRIENDLY | **3** showing enthusiasm and/or affection; friendly: His smile was warm and friendly. ◊ The speaker was given **a warm welcome/reception**. ◊ Please send her my warmest congratulations.

COLOURS/SOUNDS | **4** creating a pleasant, comfortable and relaxed feeling or atmosphere: The room was decorated in warm shades of red and orange.

IN GAME | **5** [not before noun] used to say that sb has almost guessed the answer to sth or that they have almost found sb/sth that has been hidden: Keep guessing—you're getting warmer.

▶ **warm·ly** adv.: They were warmly dressed in coats and scarves.— ◊ The play was warmly received by the critics.— see also WARMTH

■ verb

MAKE/BECOME WARM | **1** ~ (sth/sb) (up) to make sth/sb warm or warmer; to become warm or warmer: [VN] I'll warm up some milk. ◊ Come in and warm yourself by the fire. ◊ The alcohol warmed and relaxed him. ◊ [V] As the climate warms (up) the ice caps will melt.

BECOME FRIENDLY | **2** [V, VN] to become more friendly, loving, etc.; to make sb feel or become more friendly, loving, etc.

—see also GLOBAL WARMING, HOUSE-WARMING

IDM **warm the 'cockles (of sb's 'heart)** (BrE) to make sb feel happy or sympathetic—more at DEATH
PHRV **'warm to/towards sb** to begin to like sb: I warmed to her immediately. **'warm to/towards sth** to become more interested in or enthusiastic about sth: The speaker was now warming to her theme. ,**warm 'up 1** to prepare for physical exercise or a performance by doing gentle exercises or practice—related noun WARM-UP **2** (of a machine, an engine, etc.) to run for a short time in order to reach the temperature at which it will operate well ,**warm 'up| ,warm sb/sth↔'up** to become more lively or enthusiastic; to make sb/sth more lively or enthusiastic: The party soon warmed up. ,**warm sth↔'up** to heat previously cooked food again for eating

■ noun

PLACE (**the warm**) [sing.] a place where the temperature is warm: Come inside into the warm.

■ adv. (comparative warm·er, no superlative) (informal) in a way that makes you feel warm SYN WARMLY: **Wrap up warm** before you go outside!

,**warm-'blooded** adj. (of animals) having a warm blood temperature that does not change if the temperature around them changes—compare COLD-BLOODED, HOT-BLOODED

warm·er /'wɔːmə(r); AmE 'wɔːrm-/ noun (especially in compounds) a piece of clothing, a device, etc. that warms sb/sth: leg warmers ◊ a plate warmer

,**warm-'hearted** adj. (of a person) kind, friendly and sympathetic—compare COLD-HEARTED

warm·ing /'wɔːmɪŋ; AmE 'wɔːrmɪŋ/ noun [U] the process of making sth, or of becoming, warm or warmer: atmospheric warming ◊ the seasonal warming of the Pacific—see also GLOBAL WARMING ▶ **warm·ing** adj.: the warming rays of the sun ◊ a warming drink

war·mon·ger /'wɔːmʌŋgə(r); AmE 'wɔːrm-/ noun (formal, disapproving) a person, especially a politician or

leader, who wants to start a war or encourages people to start a war ▶ **war·mon·ger·ing** noun [U] **war·mon·ger·ing** adj. [only before noun]

warmth /wɔːmθ; AmE wɔːrmθ/ noun [U] **1** the state or quality of being warm, rather than hot or cold: She felt the warmth of his arms around her. ◊ The animals huddled together for warmth. ◊ He led the child into the warmth and safety of the house. **2** the state or quality of being enthusiastic and/or friendly: They were touched by the warmth of the welcome.

'**warm-up** noun [usually sing.] **1** a short practice or a series of gentle exercises that you do to prepare yourself for doing a particular sport or activity: He swam ten lengths of the pool as a warm-up. ◊ warm-up exercises **2** a short performance of music, COMEDY, etc. that is intended to prepare the audience for the main show: a warm-up act

warn /wɔːn; AmE wɔːrn/ verb **1** ~ (sb) (of sth)| ~ (sb) (**about/against sb/sth**) to tell sb about sth, especially sth dangerous or unpleasant that is likely to happen, so that they can avoid it: [VN] I tried to warn him, but he wouldn't listen. ◊ If you're thinking of getting a dog, **be warned**— they take a lot of time and money. ◊ He warned us against pickpockets. ◊ [VNthat] She was warned that if she did it again she would lose her job. ◊ [VNwh-] I had been warned what to expect. ◊ [V] Police have warned of possible delays. [also Vthat, Vspeech, VNspeech] **2** ~ (sb) (**against/about sth**) to strongly advise sb to do or not to do sth in order to avoid danger or punishment: [V] The guidebook warns against walking alone at night. ◊ [VNtoinf] He warned Billy to keep away from his daughter. [also VN] **3** [VN] (in sport, etc.) to give sb an official warning after they have broken a rule: The referee warned Ince for dangerous play. **PHRV** ,**warn sb 'off (sth) 1** to tell sb to leave or stay away from a place or person, especially in a threatening way: The farmer warned us off his land when we tried to camp there. **2** to advise sb not to do sth or to stop doing sth: [+ -ing] We were warned off buying the house.

warn·ing /'wɔːnɪŋ; AmE 'wɔːrn-/ noun **1** [C, U] a statement, an event, etc. telling sb that sth bad or unpleasant may happen in the future so that they can try to avoid it: Doctors issued a **warning against** eating any fish caught in the river. ◊ to give sb fair/advance/adequate warning of sth ◊ The bridge collapsed **without (any) warning**. ◊ Let me give you **a word of warning**. ◊ a government health warning—see also EARLY WARNING **2** [C] a statement telling sb that they will be punished if they continue to behave in a particular way: to give sb a verbal/written/final warning ▶ **warn·ing** adj. [only before noun]: She had ignored the **warning signs** of trouble ahead. ◊ Police fired a number of **warning shots**. ◊ Warning bells began to ring (= it was a sign that sth was wrong) when her letters were returned unopened.

warp /wɔːp; AmE wɔːrp/ verb, noun

■ verb [usually passive] **1** to become, or make sth become, twisted or bent out of its natural shape, for example because it has become too hot, too damp, etc: [V] The window frames had begun to warp. [also VN] **2** [VN] to influence sb so that they begin to behave in an unacceptable or shocking way: His judgement was warped by prejudice.

■ noun (**the warp**) [sing.] (technical) the threads on a LOOM (= a machine used for weaving) that other threads are passed over and under in order to make fabric—compare WEFT—see also TIME WARP

war·paint /'wɔːpeɪnt; AmE 'wɔːrp-/ noun [U] **1** paint that some tribes, for example Native American tribes, put on their bodies and faces before fighting a battle **2** (informal, humorous) MAKE-UP, especially when it is thick or bright

war·path /'wɔːpɑːθ; AmE 'wɔːrpæθ/ noun **IDM** (**be/go**) **on the 'warpath** (informal) (to be) angry and wanting to fight or punish sb

warped /wɔːpt; AmE wɔːrpt/ adj. **1** (disapproving) (of a person) having ideas that most people think are strange or unpleasant: a warped mind ◊ a warped sense of humour **2** bent or twisted and not in the normal shape

war·rant /'wɒrənt; AmE 'wɔːr-; 'wɑːr-/ noun, verb

W

■ *noun* **1** [C] ~ **(for sth)** | ~ **(to do sth)** a legal document that is signed by a judge and gives the police authority to do sth: *They issued a warrant for her arrest.* ◊ *an arrest warrant* ◊ *They had a warrant to search the house.*—see also DEATH WARRANT, SEARCH WARRANT **2** [C] ~ **(for sth)** a document that gives you the right to receive money, services, etc: *the issue of warrants for equity shares* **3** [U] ~ **(for sth/for doing sth)** (*formal*) (usually in negative sentences) an acceptable reason for doing sth: *There is no warrant for such criticism.*

■ *verb* (*formal*) to make sth necessary or appropriate in a particular situation: [VN] *Further investigation is clearly warranted.* ◊ [VN-ing] *The situation scarcely warrants their/them being dismissed.* [also V-ing]—see also UNWAR-RANTED **IDM** **I/I'll warrant (you)** (*old-fashioned*) used to tell sb that you are sure of sth and that they can be sure of it too

'**warrant officer** *noun* a member of one of the middle ranks in the army, the British air force and the US navy: *Warrant Officer Gary Owen*

war·ranty /ˈwɒrənti; *AmE* ˈwɔːr-; ˈwɑːr-/ *noun* (*pl.* **-ies**) [C, U] a written agreement in which a company selling sth promises to repair or replace it if there is a problem within a particular period of time [SYN] GUARANTEE: *The television comes with a full two-year warranty.* ◊ *Is the car still under warranty?*

war·ren /ˈwɒrən; *AmE* ˈwɔːr-; ˈwɑːr-/ *noun* = RABBIT WAR-REN: (*figurative*) *The offices were a warren of small rooms and passages.*

war·ring /ˈwɔːrɪŋ/ *adj.* [only before noun] involved in a war: *A ceasefire has been agreed by the country's three warring factions.*

war·rior /ˈwɒriə(r); *AmE* ˈwɔːr-; ˈwɑːr-/ *noun* (*formal*) (especially in the past) a person who fights in a battle or war: *a warrior nation* (= whose people are skilled in fighting) ◊ *a Zulu warrior*

war·ship /ˈwɔːʃɪp; *AmE* ˈwɔːrʃɪp/ *noun* a ship used in war

wart /wɔːt; *AmE* wɔːrt/ *noun* **1** a small hard lump that grows on your skin and that is caused by a VIRUS **2** (*AmE*) = VERRUCA **IDM** **,warts and 'all** (*informal*) including all the bad or unpleasant features of sb/sth: *She still loves him, warts and all.*

wart·hog /ˈwɔːthɒg; *AmE* ˈwɔːrthɔːg; -hɑːg/ *noun* an African wild pig with two large outer teeth called TUSKS and lumps like warts on its face

war·time /ˈwɔːtaɪm; *AmE* ˈwɔːrt-/ *noun* [U] the period during which a country is fighting a war: *Different rules applied in wartime.* ▶ **war·time** *adj.* [only before noun]: *Fruit was a luxury in wartime Britain.*—compare PEACE-TIME

'**war-torn** *adj.* [only before noun] (*written*) a **war-torn** country or area is severely affected by the fighting that is taking place there

warty /ˈwɔːti; *AmE* ˈwɔːrti/ *adj.* covered with WARTS

wary /ˈweəri; *AmE* ˈweri/ *adj.* (*comparative* **wari·er**, no superlative*) ~ **(of sb/sth)** | ~ **(of doing sth)** careful when dealing with sb/sth because you think that there may be a danger or problem [SYN] CAUTIOUS: *Be wary of strangers who offer you a ride.* ◊ *She was wary of getting involved with him.* ◊ *He gave her a wary look.* ◊ *The police will need to keep a wary eye on this area of town* (= watch it carefully, in case there is trouble).—compare UNWARY ▶ **wari·ly** /-rəli/ *adv.*: *The cat eyed him warily.* **wari-ness** *noun* [U]: *feelings of wariness* ◊ *There was a wari-ness in her tone.*

was /wəz; *strong form* wɒz; *AmE* wʌz *AmE also* wʌz/ ⇨ BE

wash /wɒʃ; *AmE* wɑːʃ; wɔːʃ/ *verb, noun*

■ *verb* **1** to make sth/sb clean using water and usually soap: [VN] *These jeans need washing.* ◊ *to wash the car/floor/dishes* ◊ *to wash your hands/face/hair* ◊ *Wash the fruit thoroughly before eating.* ◊ *She washed the blood from his face.* ◊ [VN-ADJ] *The beach had been washed clean by the tide.* **2** ~ **(yourself)** (*especially BrE*) to make your-self clean using water and usually soap: [V] *I washed and changed before going out.* ◊ [VN] *She was no longer able to wash herself.* **3** [V] (of clothes, fabrics, etc.) to be able to be washed without losing colour or being damaged: *This sweater washes well.* **4** [usually +*adv./prep.*] (of water) to flow or carry sth/sb in a particular direction: [V] *Water washed over the deck.* ◊ [VN] *Pieces of the wreckage were washed ashore.* ◊ *He was washed overboard by a huge wave.* **IDM** **wash your dirty linen in 'public** (*BrE, disap-proving*) to discuss your personal affairs in public, espe-cially sth embarrassing **wash your 'hands of sb/sth** to refuse to be responsible for or involved with sb/sth: *When her son was arrested again she washed her hands of him.* **sth won't/doesn't 'wash (with sb)** used to say that sb's explanation, excuse, etc. is not valid or that you/sb else will not accept it: *That excuse simply won't wash with me.* **PHRV** **,wash sb/sth↔a'way** (of water) to remove or carry sb/sth away to another place: *Part of the path had been washed away by the sea.* **,wash sth↔'down (with sth) 1** to clean sth large or a surface with a lot of water: *Wash down the walls before painting them.* **2** to drink sth after, or at the same time as, eating sth: *For lunch we had bread and cheese, washed down with beer.* **,wash 'off** to be removed from the surface of sth or from a fabric by washing: *Those grease stains won't wash off.* **,wash sth↔'off (sth)** to remove sth from the surface of sth or from a fabric by washing: *Wash that mud off your boots before you come in.* **,wash 'out** (of a dirty mark) to be removed from a fabric by washing: *These ink stains won't wash out.* **,wash sth↔'out 1** to wash the inside of sth to remove dirt, etc: *to wash out empty bottles* **2** to remove a substance from sth by washing: *Wash the dye out with shampoo.* **3** (of rain) to make a game, an event, etc. end early or prevent it from starting: *The game was com-pletely washed out.*—related noun WASHOUT **,wash 'over sb 1** (also ,wash ,through sb) (*written*) (of a feeling) to suddenly affect sb strongly, so that they are not aware of anything else: *Waves of nausea washed over him.* **2** to happen to or around sb without affecting them: *She man-ages to let criticism just wash over her.* **,wash 'up 1** (*BrE*) (also **do the dishes** *AmE, BrE*) to wash plates, glasses, etc. after a meal—see also WASHING-UP **2** (*AmE*) to wash your face and hands: *Go and get washed up.* **,wash sth↔'up 1** (*BrE*) to wash dishes after a meal: *I didn't wash up the pans.* **2** (of water) to carry sth onto the shore: *The body was found washed up on a beach.*

■ *noun* **1** [C, usually sing.] (*especially BrE*) an act of clean-ing sb/sth using water and usually soap: *These towels are ready for a wash.* ◊ *I'll just* **have a** *quick* **wash** *before dinner.* ◊ *The curtains could do with a good* (= thorough) *wash.* ◊ *I'm doing a dark wash* (= washing all the dark clothes together). ◊ *Your shirt's in the wash* (= being washed or waiting to be washed). ◊ *My sweater shrank in the wash.* ◊ *That blouse shouldn't look like that after only two washes.*—see also CAR WASH **2 (the wash)** [sing.] an area of water that has waves and is moving a lot, espe-cially after a boat has moved through it; the sound made by this: *The dinghy was rocked by the wash of a passing ferry.* ◊ *They listened to the wash of waves on the beach.* **3** [C] a thin layer of a liquid, especially paint, that is put on a surface: *The walls were covered with a pale yellow wash.*—see also WHITEWASH **4** [C, U] a liquid containing soap, used for cleaning your skin: *an antiseptic skin wash*—see also MOUTHWASH **IDM** **it will (all) come out in the 'wash** (*spoken*) **1** used to say that the truth about a situation will be made known at some time in the future **2** used to make sb less anxious by telling them that any problems or difficulties will be solved in the future

wash·able /ˈwɒʃəbl; *AmE* ˈwɑːʃ-; ˈwɔːʃ-/ *adj.* that can be washed without being damaged: *machine washable* (= that can be washed in a washing machine)

wash·bag /ˈwɒʃbæg; *AmE* ˈwɑːʃ-; ˈwɔːʃ-/ *noun* (*BrE*) SPONGE BAG

wash·basin /ˈwɒʃbeɪsn; *AmE* ˈwɑːʃ-; ˈwɔːʃ-/ (also **basin**) (both *especially BrE*) (also **sink** *AmE, BrE*) (*AmE also* **wash·bowl**) *noun* a large bowl that has taps/faucets and is fixed to the wall in a bathroom, used for washing your hands and face in

wash·board /ˈwɒʃbɔːd; *AmE* ˈwɑːʃbɔːrd; ˈwɔːʃ-/ *noun* a board with a surface with RIDGES on it, used in the past for rubbing clothes on when washing them; a similar board played as a musical instrument

wash·cloth /'wɒʃklɒθ; *AmE* 'wɑːʃklɔːθ; 'wɔːʃ-/ *noun* (*AmE*) = FLANNEL (2)

washed 'out *adj.* **1** (of fabric, clothes or colours) no longer brightly coloured, often as a result of frequent washing: *She didn't like jeans that looked too washed out.* ◊ *a pair of washed-out old jeans* ◊ *The walls were a washed-out blue colour.* **2** (of a person) pale and tired: *He always looks washed out at the end of the week.*

washed 'up *adj.* (*informal*) no longer successful and unlikely to succeed again in the future: *Her singing career was all washed up by the time she was 27.*

wash·er /'wɒʃə(r); *AmE* 'wɑːʃ-; 'wɔːʃ-/ *noun* **1** a small flat ring made of rubber, metal or plastic placed between two surfaces, for example under a NUT (2) to make a connection tight—picture at TOOL **2** (*informal*) a WASHING MACHINE—see also DISHWASHER

wash·ing /'wɒʃɪŋ; *AmE* 'wɑːʃ-; 'wɔːʃ-/ *noun* [U] **1** the act of cleaning sth using water and usually soap: *a gentle shampoo for frequent washing* ◊ *I do the washing* (= wash the clothes) *in our house.*—see also BRAINWASHING **2** (*BrE*) clothes, sheets, etc. that are waiting to be washed, being washed or have just been washed: *a pile of dirty washing* ◊ *Would you hang the washing out* (= hang it outside to dry)*?*

washing line *noun* (*BrE*) = CLOTHES LINE

washing machine *noun* an electric machine for washing clothes

washing powder *noun* [U] (*BrE*) soap or DETERGENT in the form of powder for washing clothes

washing soda *noun* [U] = SODIUM CARBONATE

washing-'up (*BrE*) *noun* [U] **1** the act of washing plates, glasses, pans, etc. after a meal: *If you cook, I'll do the washing-up.* ◊ *a washing-up bowl* **2** the dirty plates, glasses, pans, etc. that have to be washed after a meal: *The sink was still full of last night's washing-up.*

washing-'up liquid *noun* [U] (*BrE*) liquid soap for washing dishes, pans, etc.

wash·out /'wɒʃaʊt; *AmE* 'wɑːʃ-; 'wɔːʃ-/ *noun* (*informal*) an event, etc. that is a complete failure, especially because of rain

wash·room /'wɒʃruːm; -rʊm; *AmE* 'wɑːʃ-; 'wɔːʃ-/ *noun* (*old-fashioned, AmE*) a toilet, especially one that is in a public building

wash·stand /'wɒʃstænd; *AmE* 'wɑːʃ-; 'wɔːʃ-/ *noun* (especially in the past) a special table in a bedroom that holds a BASIN for washing yourself in

wasn't /'wɒznt; *AmE* also 'wʌznt/ ⇨ BE

Wasp (also **WASP**) /wɒsp; *AmE* wɑːsp; wɔːsp/ *noun* (especially *AmE*, usually *disapproving*) the abbreviation for 'White Anglo-Saxon Protestant' (a white American whose family originally came from northern Europe and is therefore thought to be from the most powerful section of society): *a privileged Wasp background*

wasp /wɒsp; *AmE* wɑːsp; wɔːsp/ *noun* a black and yellow flying insect that can sting: *a wasp sting* ◊ *a wasps' nest*—picture on page A7

wasp·ish /'wɒspɪʃ; *AmE* 'wɑːs-; 'wɔːs-/ *adj.* (*written*) bad-tempered and unpleasant: *a waspish look/remark/voice* ▶ **wasp·ish·ly** *adv.*

wast·age /'weɪstɪdʒ/ *noun* **1** [U, sing.] ~ (of sth) the fact of losing or destroying sth, especially because it has been used or dealt with carelessly: *It was a new production technique aimed at minimizing wastage.* ◊ *This lack of jobs has resulted in a huge wastage of talent.* **2** [U] the amount of sth that is wasted: *There is little wastage from a lean cut of meat.* **3** [U] (*BrE*) the loss of employees because they stop working or move to other jobs; the number of students who do not finish a particular course of study: *Half of the posts will be lost through natural wastage.* ◊ *student wastage rates*

waste /weɪst/ *verb, noun, adj.*
■ *verb* [VN]
NOT USE WELL | **1** ~ sth (on sth) | ~ sth (in) doing sth to use more of sth than is necessary or useful: *to waste time/food/energy* ◊ *Why waste money on clothes you don't need?* ◊ *She wasted no time in rejecting the offer* (= she rejected it immediately). ◊ *You're wasting your time trying to explain it to him* (= because he will not understand). **2** ~ sth (on sb/sth) to give, say, use, etc. sth good where it is not valued or used in the way that it should be: *Don't waste your sympathy on him—he got what he deserved.* ◊ *Her comments were not wasted on Chris* (= he understood what she meant). **3** [usually passive] to not make good or full use of sb/sth: *It was a wasted opportunity.* ◊ *You're wasted as a sales manager—you should have been an actor.*

KILL SB | **4** (*informal, especially AmE*) to get rid of sb, usually by killing them

DEFEAT SB | **5** (*AmE, informal*) to defeat sb very badly in a game or competition

IDM **waste your 'breath** to say sth that nobody takes any notice of **,waste not, 'want not** (*saying*) if you never waste anything, especially food or money, you will always have it when you need it

PHR V **,waste a'way** (of a person) to become thin and weak, especially because of illness
■ *noun*
NOT GOOD USE | **1** [U, sing.] ~ (of sth) the act of using sth in a careless or unnecessary way, causing it to be lost or destroyed: *I hate unnecessary waste.* ◊ *It seems such a waste to throw good food away.* ◊ *I hate to see good food go to waste* (= be thrown away). ◊ *The report is critical of the department's waste of resources.* ◊ *What a waste of paper!* **2** [sing.] a situation in which it is not worth spending time, money, etc. on sth: *These meetings are a complete waste of time.* ◊ *They believe the statue is a waste of taxpayers' money.*

MATERIALS | **3** [U] (also **wastes** [pl.]) materials that are no longer needed and are thrown away: *household/industrial waste* ◊ *toxic/radioactive wastes* ◊ *waste pipes* (= that carry waste away from a building) ◊ *waste disposal* (= the process of getting rid of waste)

LAND | **4** (**wastes**) [pl.] (*formal*) a large area of land where there are very few people, animals or plants: *the frozen wastes of Siberia*

IDM **a waste of 'space** (*spoken*) a person who is useless or no good at anything
■ *adj.* [usually before noun]
LAND | **1** not suitable for building or growing things on and is therefore not used: *The car was found on a piece of waste ground.*

MATERIALS | **2** no longer needed for a particular process and therefore thrown away: *Waste water is pumped from the factory into a nearby river.*

IDM **lay sth 'waste | lay 'waste (to) sth** (*formal*) to destroy a place completely

waste·bas·ket /'weɪstbɑːskɪt; *AmE* -bæs-/ *noun* (*AmE*) = WASTE-PAPER BASKET

wasted /'weɪstɪd/ *adj.* **1** [only before noun] (of an action) unsuccessful because it does not produce the result you wanted: *We had a wasted trip—they weren't in.* **2** too thin, especially because of illness: *thin wasted legs* **3** (*slang*) strongly affected by alcohol or drugs: *He went to a party and came home wasted.*

waste-disposal unit (also **'waste disposer**) *noun* (both *BrE*) (*AmE* **dis·posal**) a machine connected to the waste pipe of a kitchen SINK, for cutting food waste into small pieces

waste·ful /'weɪstfl/ *adj.* ~ (of sth) using more of sth than is necessary; not saving or keeping sth that could be used: *The whole process is wasteful and inefficient.* ◊ *a wasteful use of resources* ◊ *an engine that is wasteful of fuel* ▶ **waste·ful·ly** /-fəli/ *adv.* **waste·ful·ness** *noun* [U]

waste·land /'weɪstlænd/ *noun* [C, U] an area of land that cannot be used or that is no longer used for building or growing things on: *industrial/urban wasteland* ◊ *the desert wastelands of Arizona* ◊ (*figurative*) *The mid 1970s are seen as a cultural wasteland for rock music.*

waste paper *noun* [U] paper that is not wanted and is thrown away

waste-'paper basket (*BrE*) (*AmE* **waste·basket**) *noun* a basket or other container for waste paper, etc.

W

b	d	f	g	h	k	l	m	n	p	r
bad	did	fall	get	hat	cat	leg	man	now	pen	red

'waste product *noun* a useless material or substance produced while making sth else

waster /'weɪstə(r)/ *noun* **1** (often in compounds) a person or thing that uses too much of sth in an unnecessary way: *He's a time waster.* **2** (*spoken, disapproving*) a person who is useless or no good at anything

wast·ing /'weɪstɪŋ/ *adj.* a **wasting** disease or illness is one that causes sb to gradually become weaker and thinner

wast·rel /'weɪstrəl/ *noun* (*literary*) a lazy person who spends their time and/or money in a careless and stupid way

watch /wɒtʃ; *AmE* wɑːtʃ; wɔːtʃ/ *verb, noun*
■ *verb* **1** to look at sb/sth for a time, paying attention to what happens: [VN] *to watch television/a football game* ◇ [VN, V] *He watched the house for signs of activity.* ◇ *He watched for signs of activity in the house.* ◇ [V] *'Would you like to play?' 'No thanks—I'll just watch.'* ◇ *We watched to see what would happen next.* ◇ [V wh-] *Watch what I do, then you try.* ◇ [V-ing] *She watched the kids playing in the yard.* ◇ [VNinf] *They watched the bus disappear into the distance.* **2** [VN] to take care of sb/sth for a short time: *Could you watch my bags for me while I buy a paper?* **3** (*BrE* also **mind**) (*informal*) to be careful about sth: [VN] *Watch yourself* (= be careful, because you're in a dangerous situation)*!* ◇ *Watch your bag—there are thieves around.* ◇ *I have to watch every penny* (= be careful what I spend)*.* ◇ *Watch your head on the low ceiling.* ◇ [V wh-] *Hey, watch where you're going!* **IDM** **watch the 'clock** (*disapproving*) to be careful not to work longer than the required time; to think more about when your work will finish than about the work itself **'watch it** (*informal*) used as a warning to sb to be careful **watch your 'mouth/'tongue** to be careful what you say in order not to offend sb or make them angry **watch this 'space** (*informal*) used in orders, to tell sb to wait for more news about sth to be announced: *I can't tell you any more right now, but watch this space.* **watch the 'world go by** to relax and watch people in a public place: *We sat outside a cafe, watching the world go by.*—more at LANGUAGE, STEP *n.* **PHRV** **'watch for sb/sth** to look and wait for sb/sth to appear or for sth to happen: *The cat was on the wall, watching for birds.* **watch 'out** (*spoken*) used to warn sb about sth dangerous: *Watch out! There's a car coming!* **watch 'out for sb/sth 1** to make an effort to be aware of what is happening, so that you will notice if anything bad or unusual happens: *The cashiers were asked to watch out for forged banknotes.* **2** to be careful of sth: *Watch out for the stairs—they're steep.* **watch 'over sb/sth** (*formal*) to take care of sb/sth; to guard and protect sb/sth
■ *noun* **1** [C] a type of small clock that you wear on your wrist, or (in the past) carried in your pocket: *She kept looking anxiously at her watch.* ◇ *My watch is fast/slow.*—see also STOPWATCH, WRISTWATCH—picture at JEWELLERY **2** [sing., U] the act of watching sb/sth carefully in case of possible danger or problems: *The police have mounted a watch outside the hotel.* ◇ *I'll keep watch while you go through his papers* (= watch and warn you if somebody is coming)*.* ◇ *The government is keeping a close watch on how the situation develops.*—see also NEIGHBOURHOOD WATCH **3** [C, U] a fixed period of time, usually while other people are asleep, during which sb watches for any danger so that they can warn others, for example on a ship; the person or people who do this: *I'm on first watch.* ◇ *I go on watch in an hour.*—see also NIGHTWATCHMAN **IDM** **be on the 'watch (for sb/sth)** to be looking carefully for sb/sth that you expect to see, especially in order to avoid possible danger: *Be on the watch for thieves.*—more at CLOSE² *adj.*

watch·able /'wɒtʃəbl; *AmE* 'wɑːtʃ-; 'wɔːtʃ-/ *adj.* (*informal*) entertaining or pleasant to watch

watch·band /'wɒtʃbænd; *AmE* wɑːtʃ-; wɔːtʃ-/ *noun* (*AmE*) = WATCH STRAP

watch·dog /'wɒtʃdɒg; *AmE* 'wɑːtʃdɔːg; wɔːtʃ-/ *noun* a person or group of people whose job is to check that companies are not doing anything illegal or ignoring people's rights: *a consumer watchdog*—compare GUARD DOG

watch·er /'wɒtʃə(r); *AmE* 'wɑːtʃ-; 'wɔːtʃ-/ *noun* (often in compounds) a person who watches and studies sb/sth regularly: *an industry/a market watcher*—see also BIRD-WATCHER, CLOCK-WATCHER

watch·ful /'wɒtʃfl; *AmE* 'wɑːtʃ-; 'wɔːtʃ-/ *adj.* paying attention to what is happening in case of danger, accidents, etc: *Her expression was watchful and alert.* ◇ *His mother kept a watchful eye on him.* ◇ *The children played under the watchful eye of their teacher.* ▶ **watch·ful·ly** /-fəli/ *adv.* **watch·ful·ness** *noun* [U]

watching 'brief *noun* [sing.] the task of watching a group, especially a political organization, to make sure that it is doing everything it should and nothing wrong or illegal

watch·maker /'wɒtʃmeɪkə(r); *AmE* 'wɑːtʃ-; 'wɔːtʃ-/ *noun* a person who makes and repairs watches and clocks as a job

watch·man /'wɒtʃmən; *AmE* 'wɑːtʃ-; 'wɔːtʃ-/ *noun* (*pl.* -men /-mən/) (*old-fashioned*) a man whose job is to guard a building, for example a bank, an office building or a factory, especially at night—see also NIGHTWATCHMAN

'watch strap (*BrE*) (*AmE* **'watch·band**) *noun* a thin leather, etc. strap for fastening your watch around your wrist—picture at JEWELLERY

watch·tower /'wɒtʃtaʊə(r); *AmE* 'wɑːtʃ-; 'wɔːtʃ-/ *noun* a tall tower from which soldiers, etc. watch when they are guarding a place

watch·word /'wɒtʃwɜːd; *AmE* 'wɑːtʃwɜːrd; 'wɔːtʃ-/ *noun* a word or phrase that expresses sb's beliefs or attitudes, or that explains what sb should do in a particular situation: *Quality is our watchword.*

water /'wɔːtə(r); *AmE* also 'wɑːt-/ *noun, verb*
■ *noun* **1** [U] a liquid without colour, smell or taste that falls as rain, is in lakes, rivers and seas, and is used for drinking, washing, etc: *a glass of water* ◇ *drinking water* ◇ *water pollution* ◇ *clean/dirty water* ◇ *water shortages* ◇ *There is hot and cold running water in all the bedrooms.*—see also BATHWATER **2** [U] an area of water, especially a lake, river, sea or ocean: *We walked down to the water's edge.* ◇ *She fell into the water.* ◇ *shallow/deep water* ◇ *In the lagoon the water was calm.*—see also BACKWATER, BREAKWATER **3** (**waters**) [pl.] the water in a particular lake, river, sea or ocean: *the grey waters of the River Clyde* ◇ *This species is found in coastal waters around the Indian Ocean.* **4** [U] the surface of a mass of water: *She dived under the water.* ◇ *The leaves floated on the water.*—see also UNDERWATER **5** (**waters**) [pl.] an area of sea or ocean belonging to a particular country: *We were still in British waters.* ◇ *fishing in international waters*—see also TERRITORIAL WATERS **HELP** There are many other compounds ending in **water**. You will find them at their place in the alphabet. **IDM** **by water** (*formal*) using a boat or ship **it's (all) water under the 'bridge** (*spoken*) used to say that sth happened in the past and is now forgotten or no longer important **like 'water** (*informal*) in large quantities: *He spends money like water.* **(be in/get into) murky/uncharted 'waters** to get into a difficult or dangerous situation that you do not know anything about **not hold 'water** (*informal*) if an argument, an excuse, a theory, etc. does not **hold water**, you cannot believe it **sb's 'waters break** when a pregnant woman's **waters break**, the liquid in her WOMB passes out of her body just before the baby is born **(like) water off a ˌduck's 'back** (*informal*) used to say that sth, especially criticism, has no effect on sb/sth: *I can't tell my son what to do; it's water off a duck's back with him.*—more at BLOOD, COLD *adj.*, DEAD *adj.*, DEEP *adj.*, DIP *v.*, DUCK *n.*, FISH *n.*, HEAD *n.*, HELL, HOT *adj.*, PASS *v.*, POUR, STILL *adj.*, TEST *v.*, TREAD *adj.*
■ *verb* **1** [VN] to pour water on plants, etc: *to water the plants/garden* **2** [V] (of the eyes) to become full of tears: *The smoke made my eyes water.* **3** [V] (of the mouth) to produce SALIVA: *The smells from the kitchen made our mouths water.* **4** [VN] to give water to an animal to drink: *to water the horses* ◇ (*humorous*) *After a tour of the grounds, the guests were fed and watered.* **5** [VN] [usually passive] (*technical*) (of a river, etc.) to provide an area of land with water: *The valley is watered by a stream.* **6** [VN]

to add water to an alcoholic drink: *watered wine* PHRV ,water sth↔'down 1 to make a liquid weaker by adding water SYN DILUTE 2 [usually passive] to change a speech, a piece of writing, etc. in order to make it less offensive or forceful SYN DILUTE

water·bed /'wɔːtəbed; AmE 'wɔːtərb-; 'wɑːt-/ noun a bed with a rubber or plastic MATTRESS that is filled with water

water·bird /'wɔːtəbɜːd; AmE 'wɔːtərbɜːrd; 'wɑːt-/ noun a bird that lives near and walks or swims in water, especially rivers or lakes

'**water-borne** adj. spread or carried by water: *cholera and other water-borne diseases* ◊ *water-borne goods*—compare AIRBORNE

'**water buffalo** noun a large Indian animal of the cow family, used for pulling vehicles and farm equipment in Asia

'**water butt** noun a large BARREL for collecting rain as it flows off a roof

'**water cannon** noun a machine that produces a powerful flow of water, used by the police against crowds of people who are causing trouble

'**water chestnut** noun the thick round white root of a tropical plant that grows in water, often used in Chinese cooking

'**water closet** noun (abbr. WC) (old-fashioned) a toilet

water·col·our (BrE) (AmE **water·color**) /'wɔːtəkʌlə(r); AmE 'wɔːtərk-; 'wɑːt-/ noun 1 (**watercolours**) [pl.] paints that you mix with water, not oil, and use for painting pictures 2 [C] a picture painted with these paints

'**water cooler** noun a machine, for example in an office, that cools water and supplies it for drinking

water·course /'wɔːtəkɔːs; AmE 'wɔːtərkɔːrs; 'wɑːt-/ noun (technical) a stream or an artificial channel for water

water·cress /'wɔːtəkres; AmE 'wɔːtərk-; 'wɑːt-/ noun [U] a water plant with small round green leaves and thin stems. It has a strong taste and is often eaten raw in salads.

water·fall /'wɔːtəfɔːl; AmE 'wɔːtərf-; 'wɑːt-/ noun a place where a stream or river falls from a high place, for example over a cliff or rock—picture at MOUNTAIN

'**water fountain** noun (AmE) = DRINKING FOUNTAIN

water·fowl /'wɔːtəfaʊl; AmE 'wɔːtərf-; 'wɑːt-/ noun [usually pl.] (pl. **water·fowl**) a bird that can swim and lives near water, especially a duck or GOOSE

water·front /'wɔːtəfrʌnt; AmE 'wɔːtərf-; 'wɑːt-/ noun [usually sing.] a part of a town or an area that is next to water, for example in a harbour: *a waterfront apartment*

'**water gun** noun (AmE) = WATER PISTOL—picture on page A8

water·hole /'wɔːtəhəʊl; AmE 'wɔːtərhoʊl; 'wɑːt-/ (also '**watering hole**) noun a place in a hot country, where animals go to drink

'**water ice** noun [U, C] (BrE) = SORBET

'**watering can** noun a metal or plastic container with a handle and a long SPOUT, used for pouring water on plants—picture at GARDEN

'**watering hole** noun 1 = WATERHOLE 2 (informal, humorous) a bar or place where people go to drink

'**watering place** noun (old-fashioned) a town with a natural supply of MINERAL WATER where people go for their health SYN SPA

'**water jump** noun an area of water that horses or runners have to jump over in a race or competition

'**water level** noun [U, C] the height that the surface of a mass of water rises or falls to, or is at

'**water lily** noun a plant that floats on the surface of water, with large round flat leaves and white, yellow or pink flowers

water·line /'wɔːtəlaɪn; AmE 'wɔːtərl-; 'wɑːt-/ noun (**the waterline**) [sing.] the level that the water reaches along the side of a ship

water·logged /'wɔːtəlɒgd; AmE 'wɔːtərlɔːgd; 'wɑːt-; -lɑːgd/ adj. 1 (of soil, a field, etc.) so full of water that it cannot hold any more and becomes flooded: *They couldn't*

play because the pitch was waterlogged. **2** (of a boat, etc.) so full of water that it can no longer float

Water·loo /,wɔːtə'luː; AmE ,wɔːtər'luː; 'wɑːt-/ noun [sing.] **sb's ~** a final defeat for sb: *This was the point at which he was to* **meet his Waterloo.** ORIGIN From the battle of Waterloo in 1815, in which the British (under the Duke of Wellington) and the Prussians finally defeated Napoleon.

'**water main** noun a large underground pipe that supplies water to buildings, etc.

water·mark /'wɔːtəmɑːk; AmE 'wɔːtərmɑːrk; 'wɑːt-/ noun a symbol or design in some types of paper, which can be seen when the paper is held against the light—see also HIGH-WATER MARK, LOW-WATER MARK

'**water meadow** noun [usually pl.] a field near a river that is often flooded

water·melon /'wɔːtəmelən; AmE 'wɔːtərm-; 'wɑːt-/ noun [C, U] a type of large MELON with hard, dark green skin, red flesh and black seeds—picture on page A2

water·mill /'wɔːtəmɪl; AmE 'wɔːtərm-; 'wɑːt-/ noun a MILL next to a river in which the machinery for GRINDING grain into flour is driven by the power of the water turning a wheel

'**water pistol** (BrE) (AmE '**water gun**) noun a toy gun that shoots water—picture on page A8

'**water polo** noun [U] a game played by two teams of people swimming in a swimming pool. Players try to throw a ball into the other team's goal.

'**water power** noun [U] power produced by the movement of water, used to drive machinery or produce electricity

water·proof /'wɔːtəpruːf; AmE 'wɔːtərp-; 'wɑːt-/ adj., noun, verb
■ adj. that does not let water through: *waterproof clothing*
■ noun [usually pl.] a piece of clothing made from material that does not let water through: *You'll need waterproofs* (= a waterproof jacket and trousers/pants).
■ verb [VN] to make sth waterproof

'**water rat** noun = WATER VOLE

'**water-repellent** adj. a material, etc. that is **water-repellent** is specially treated so that water runs off it rather than going into it: *a water-repellent coating*

'**water-resistant** adj. that does not let water through easily: *a water-resistant jacket*

water·shed /'wɔːtəʃed; AmE 'wɔːtərʃed; 'wɑːt-/ noun **1** [C] **~ (in sth)** an event or a period of time that marks an important change: *The middle decades of the 19th century marked a watershed in Russia's history.* **2** [C] a line of high land where streams on one side flow into one river, and streams on the other side flow into a different river **3** (**the watershed**) [sing.] (in Britain) the time before which programmes that are not considered suitable for children may not be shown on television: *Scenes like this should only be shown after the 9 o'clock watershed.*

water·side /'wɔːtəsaɪd; AmE 'wɔːtərs-; 'wɑːt-/ noun [sing.] the area at the edge of a river, lake, etc: *They strolled down to the waterside.* ◊ *a waterside cafe* ◊ *waterside plants*

water·ski /'wɔːtəskiː; AmE 'wɔːtərs-; 'wɑːt-/ verb, noun
■ verb [VN] to ski on water while being pulled by a fast boat
▶ **water·ski·ing** noun [U]: *We snorkelled and did some waterskiing.*
■ noun either of the pair of long flat boards on which a person stands in order to waterski

'**water softener** noun [U, C] a device or substance that removes particular minerals, especially chalk, from water

water·spout /'wɔːtəspaʊt; AmE 'wɔːtərs-; 'wɑːt-/ noun a column of water that is pulled up from the sea during a storm by a rapidly spinning column of air

'**water supply** noun [C, U] the water provided for a town, an area or a building; the act of or system for supplying water to a town, etc: *a clean/contaminated water supply* ◊ *plans to improve the water supply to rural villages*

W

æ	ɑː	e	ɜː	ə	ɪ	iː	i	ɒ	ɔː	ʌ	ʊ	u	uː
cat	father	ten	bird	about	sit	see	many	got	saw	cup	put	actual	too
								(BrE)					

'water table *noun* [usually sing.] (*technical*) the level at and below which water is found in the ground

water·tight /ˈwɔːtətaɪt; *AmE* ˈwɔːtərt-; ˈwɑːt-/ *adj.* **1** that does not allow water to get in or out: *a watertight container/seal* **2** (of an excuse, a plan, an argument, etc.) carefully prepared so that it contains no mistakes, faults or weaknesses: *a watertight alibi* ◊ *The case has to be made watertight.*

'water tower *noun* a tall structure with a TANK (= large container) of water at the top from which water is supplied to buildings in the area around it

'water vole (also **'water rat**) *noun* an animal like a rat that swims and lives in a hole beside a river or lake

water·way /ˈwɔːtəweɪ; *AmE* ˈwɔːtərw-; ˈwɑːt-/ *noun* a river, canal, etc. along which boats can travel: *inland waterways* ◊ *a navigable waterway*

water·wheel /ˈwɔːtəwiːl; *AmE* ˈwɔːtərw-; ˈwɑːt-/ *noun* a wheel turned by the movement of water, used, especially in the past, to drive machinery

water·works /ˈwɔːtəwɜːks; *AmE* ˈwɔːtərwɜːrks; ˈwɑːt-/ *noun* (*pl.* **water·works**) **1** [C+sing./pl. *v.*] a building with pumping machinery for supplying water to an area **2** [pl.] (*informal* or *humorous*) the organs of the body through which URINE (= waste water) is passed **IDM turn on the 'waterworks** (*informal, disapproving*) to start crying, especially in order to get sympathy or attention

watery /ˈwɔːtəri; *AmE* ˈwɑːt-/ *adj.* **1** of or like water; containing a lot of water: *a watery fluid* ◊ *His eyes were red and watery.* ◊ (*literary*) *She was rescued from a watery grave* (= saved from drowning). **2** weak and/or pale: *a watery sun* ◊ *His eyes were a watery blue.* ◊ *a watery smile* (= weak and without much feeling) **3** (of food, drink, etc.) containing too much water; thin and having no taste: *The vegetables were watery and tasteless.* ◊ *watery soup*

watt /wɒt; *AmE* wɑːt/ *noun* (*abbr.* **W**) a unit for measuring electrical power: *a 60-watt light bulb*

watt·age /ˈwɒtɪdʒ; *AmE* ˈwɑːt-/ *noun* [U] (*technical*) an amount of electrical power expressed in watts

wat·tle /ˈwɒtl; *AmE* ˈwɑːtl/ *noun* **1** [U] sticks woven together as a material for making fences, walls, etc: *walls made of wattle and daub* **2** [C] a piece of red skin that hangs down from the throat of a bird such as a TURKEY

wave /weɪv/ *noun, verb*
■ *noun*
OF WATER | **1** [C] a raised line of water that moves across the surface of the sea, ocean, etc: *Huge waves were breaking on the shore.* ◊ *The wind made little waves on the pond.* ◊ *The pool has a wave machine* (= for making waves).— see also TIDAL WAVE—picture at COAST
OF ACTIVITY/FEELING | **2** [C] a sudden increase in a particular activity or feeling: *a wave of opposition/protest/violence* ◊ *a crime wave* ◊ *A wave of fear swept over him.* ◊ *Guilt and horror flooded her in waves.* ◊ *A wave of panic spread through the crowd.*—see also BRAINWAVE, HEAT-WAVE
LARGE NUMBER | **3** [C] a large number of people or things suddenly moving or appearing somewhere: *Wave after wave of aircraft passed overhead.*—see also NEW WAVE
MOVEMENT OF ARM/HAND/BODY | **4** [C] a movement of your arm and hand from side to side: *She declined the offer with a wave of her hand.* ◊ *He gave us a wave as the bus drove off.* **5** (**the wave**) [sing.] (*AmE*) = MEXICAN WAVE
OF HEAT/SOUND/LIGHT | **6** [C] the form that some types of energy such as heat, sound, light, etc. take as they move: *radio/sound/ultrasonic waves*—see also AIRWAVES, LONG WAVE, MEDIUM WAVE, MICROWAVE, SHOCK WAVE, SHORT WAVE, SOUND WAVE
IN HAIR | **7** [C] if a person's hair has **a wave** or **waves**, it is not straight but curls slightly—see also PERMANENT WAVE
SEA | **8** (**the waves**) [pl.] (*literary*) the sea
—see also WAVY
IDM make 'waves (*informal*) to be very active in a way that makes people notice you, and that may sometimes cause problems—more at CREST *n.*, RIDE *v.*
■ *verb*
MOVE HAND/ARM | **1** ~ (**at/to sb**) | ~ **sth** (**at sb**) | ~ **sth**

(**about/around**) to move your hand or arm from side to side in the air in order to attract attention, as a greeting, etc: [V] *The people on the bus waved and we waved back.* ◊ *Why did you wave at him?* ◊ [VN] *A man in the water was shouting and waving his arms around frantically.* ◊ [VNN, VN] *My mother was crying as I **waved her goodbye**.* ◊ *My mother was crying as I **waved goodbye** to her.* **2** [+adv./prep.] to show where sth is, show sb where to go, etc. by moving your hand in a particular direction: [V] *She waved vaguely in the direction of the house.* ◊ [VN] *'He's over there,' said Ali, waving a hand towards some trees.* ◊ *I showed my pass to the security guard and he waved me through.* **3** [VN] [usually +adv./prep.] to hold sth in your hand and move it from side to side: *Crowds lined the route, waving flags and cheering.* ◊ *'I'm rich!' she exclaimed, waving the money under his nose.*
MOVE FREELY | **4** [V] to move freely and gently, for example in the wind, while one end or side is held in position: *The flag waved in the breeze.*
HAIR | **5** [V] to curl slightly: *His hair waves naturally.* **6** [VN] to make sb's hair curl slightly: *She's had her hair waved.*
IDM see FLAG *n.*
PHR V ,wave sth↔a'side/a'way to not accept sth because you do not think it is necessary or important **SYN** DISMISS: *My objections to the plan were waved aside.* **,wave sth/sb↔'down** to signal to a vehicle or its driver to stop by waving your hand **,wave sb↔'off** to wave goodbye to sb as they are leaving

wave·band /ˈweɪvbænd/ *noun* = BAND: *a radio set with medium and short wavebands*

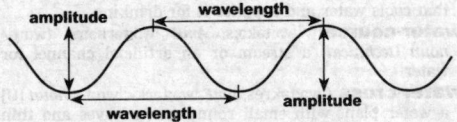

wave·length /ˈweɪvleŋθ/ *noun* **1** the distance between two similar points on a wave of energy, such as light or sound **2** the size of a radio wave that is used by a particular radio station, etc. for sending signals or broadcasting programmes **IDM on the same 'wavelength | be on sb's 'wavelength** (*informal*) to have the same way of thinking or the same ideas or feelings as sb else: *We work together but we aren't really on the same wavelength.*

wave·let /ˈweɪvlət/ *noun* (*literary*) a small wave on the surface of a lake, the sea or the ocean

waver /ˈweɪvə(r)/ *verb* [V] **1** to be or become weak or unsteady: *His voice wavered with emotion.* ◊ *Her determination never wavered.* ◊ *She never wavered in her determination to succeed.* **2** ~ (**between A and B**) | ~ (**on/over sth**) to hesitate and be unable to make a decision or choice: *She's wavering between buying a house in the city or moving away.* **3** (especially of light) to move in an unsteady way: *wavering flames/shadows* ▶ **waver·er** /ˈweɪvərə(r)/ *noun*: *The strength of his argument convinced the waverers.*

wavy /ˈweɪvi/ *adj.* having curves; not straight: *brown wavy hair* ◊ *a pattern of wavy lines*—picture at CURL

wax /wæks/ *noun, verb*
■ *noun* [U] **1** a solid substance that is made from BEESWAX or from various fats and oils and used for making candles, polish, models, etc. It becomes soft when it is heated: *styling wax for the hair* ◊ *floor wax* ◊ *wax crayons* ◊ *wax polish*—see also SEALING WAX **2** a soft sticky yellowish substance that is found in your ears
■ *verb* **1** [VN] to polish sth with wax **2** [VN] [usually passive] to cover sth with wax: *waxed paper* ◊ *a waxed jacket* **3** [VN] [often passive] to remove hair from a part of the body using wax: *to wax your legs/to have your legs waxed* **4** [V] (of the moon) to seem to get gradually bigger until its full form is visible **OPP** WANE **5** [V-ADJ] ~ **lyrical, eloquent, sentimental, etc.** (*written*) to become LYRICAL, etc. when speaking or writing: *He waxed lyrical on the food at the new restaurant.* **IDM ,wax and 'wane** (*literary*) to increase then decrease in strength, importance, etc. over a period of time

aɪ	aʊ	eɪ	əʊ	oʊ	ɔɪ	ɪə	eə	ʊə	j	w
my	now	say	go	go	boy	near	hair	pure	yes	wet
			(BrE)	(AmE)						

W

'wax bean *noun* (*AmE*) a type of bean that is a long thin yellow POD, cooked and eaten whole as a vegetable

'waxed paper (*AmE* also **'wax paper**) *noun* [U] paper covered with a thin layer of wax, used to wrap food or when cooking

waxen /'wæksn/ *adj.* **1** (*formal*) made of wax: *waxen images/figures* **2** (*literary*) pale and looking ill/sick: *The old man's waxen face was cold.*

'wax paper *noun* (*AmE*) = GREASEPROOF PAPER, WAXED PAPER

wax·work /'wækswɜːk; *AmE* -wɜːrk/ *noun* **1** a model of a person that is made of wax (**wax·works**) (*pl.* **wax·works**) (*especially BrE*) (*AmE usually* **'wax museum**) a museum where you can see wax models of famous people

waxy /'wæksi/ *adj.* made of wax; looking or feeling like wax

way /weɪ/ *noun, adv.*

■ *noun*

METHOD/STYLE | **1** [C] ~ (**to do sth**)| ~ (**of doing sth**) a method, style or manner of doing sth: *I'm not happy with this way of working.* ◇ *That's not the right way to hold a pair of scissors.* ◇ *I hate the way she always criticizes me.* ◇ *I told you we should have done it my way!* ◇ *Infectious diseases can be acquired in several ways.* ◇ *I generally get what I want one way or another* (= by some means). ◇ (*spoken, disapproving*) *That's no way to speak to your mother!* ◇ *It's not what you say, it's the way that you say it.*

BEHAVIOUR | **2** [C] a particular manner or style of behaviour: *They grinned at her in a friendly way.* ◇ *It was not his way to admit that he had made a mistake.* ◇ *Don't worry, if she seems quiet—it's just her way.* ◇ *He was showing off, as is the way with adolescent boys.* **3** (**ways**) [pl.] the typical way of behaving and living of a particular group of people: *After ten years I'm used to the strange British ways.*

ROUTE/ROAD | **4** [C, usually sing.] ~ (**from …**) (**to …**) a route or road that you take in order to reach a place: *the best/quickest/shortest way from A to B* ◇ *Can you tell me the way to Leicester Square?* ◇ *to ask/tell sb the way* ◇ *We went the long way round.* **5** [C, usually sing.] the route along which sb/sth is moving; the route that sb/sth would take if there was nothing stopping them/it: *Get out of my way! I'm in a hurry.* ◇ *Riot police with shields were blocking the demonstrators' way.* ◇ *We fought our way through the dense vegetation.* ◇ *Unfortunately they ran into a snowstorm along the way.*—see also RIGHT OF WAY **6** [C] a road, path or street for travelling along: *There's a way across the fields.*—see also FREEWAY, HIGHWAY, MOTORWAY, RAILWAY, WATERWAY **7** (**Way**) used in the names of streets: *106 Headley Way*

DIRECTION | **8** [C, usually sing.] **which, this, that,** etc. ~ a particular direction; in a particular direction: *Which way did they go?* ◇ *We just missed a car coming the other way.* ◇ *Look both ways* (= look left and right) *before crossing the road.* ◇ *Make sure that sign's the right way up.* ◇ *Kids were running this way and that* (= in all directions). ◇ *They decided to split the money four ways* (= between four different people). ◇ (*figurative*) *Which way* (= for which party) *are you going to vote?*—see also EACH WAY, ONE-WAY, THREE-WAY, TWO-WAY

FOR ENTERING/LEAVING | **9** [C, usually sing.] a means of going into or leaving a place, such as a door or gate: *the way in/out* ◇ *They escaped out the back way.*—see also COMPANIONWAY

DISTANCE/TIME | **10** [sing.] (also *AmE informal* **ways**) a distance or period of time between two points: *A little way up on the left hand-side is the Museum of Modern Art.* ◇ *September was a long way off.* ◇ (*figurative*) *The area's wine industry still has a way to go to full maturity.* ◇ *You came all this way to see us?* ◇ (*AmE, informal*) *We still have a ways to go.*

AREA | **11** [sing.] (*informal*) an area, a part of a country, etc: *I think he lives somewhere over London way.* ◇ *I'll stop by and see you next time I'm down your way.*

ASPECT | **12** [C] a particular aspect of sth SYN RESPECT: *I have changed in every way.* ◇ *It's been quite a day, one way and another* (= for several reasons).

CONDITION/STATE | **13** [sing.] a particular condition or state: *The economy's in a bad way.* ◇ *I don't know how we're going to manage, the way things are.*

IDM **across the 'way** (*BrE* also **over the 'way**) on the other side of the street, etc: *Music blared from the open window of the house across the way.* **all the 'way 1** (also **the ,whole 'way**) during the whole journey/period of time: *She didn't speak a word to me all the way back home.* **2** completely; as much as it takes to achieve what you want: *I'm fighting him all the way.* ◇ *You can feel that the audience is with her all the way.* **(that's/it's) always the 'way** (*spoken*) used to say that things often happen in a particular way, especially when it is not convenient **any way you 'slice it** (*AmE, informal*) however you choose to look at a situation **be/be 'born/be 'made that way** (of a person) to behave or do things in a particular manner because it is part of your character: *It's not his fault he's so pompous—he was born that way.* **be ,set in your 'ways** to have habits or opinions that you have had for a long time and that you do not want to change **by the 'way** (*spoken*) used to introduce a comment or question that is not directly related to what you have been talking about: *By the way, I found that book you were looking for.* ◇ *What's the time, by the way?* ◇ *Oh by the way, if you see Jackie, tell her I'll call her this evening.* **by way of sth** by a route that includes the place mentioned SYN VIA: *The artist recently arrived in Paris from Bulgaria by way of Vienna.* ◇ *She came to TV by way of drama school.* **by way of/in the way of sth** as a form of sth; for sth; as a means of sth: *He recovered £600 by way of compensation from the company.* ◇ *She rolled her eyes by way of an answer and left.* **come your 'way** to happen to you by chance, or when you were not expecting it: *He took whatever came his way.* **cut both/two 'ways** (of an action, argument, etc.) to have two opposite effects or results **either way | one way or the other** used to say that it does not matter which one of two possibilities happens, is chosen or is true: *Was it his fault or not? Either way, an explanation is due.* ◇ *We could meet today or tomorrow—I don't mind one way or the other.* **every 'which way** (*informal*) in all directions: *Her hair tumbled every which way.* **get into/out of the way of (doing) sth** to become used to doing sth/to lose the habit of doing sth: *The women had got into the way of going up on the deck every evening.* **get in the way of** to prevent sb from doing sth; to prevent sth from happening: *He wouldn't allow emotions to get in the way of him doing his job.* **get/have your own 'way** to get or do what you want, especially when sb has tried to stop you: *She always gets her own way in the end.* **give 'way** to break or fall down: *The pillars gave way and a section of the roof collapsed.* ◇ *Her numb leg gave way beneath her and she stumbled clumsily.* **give 'way (to sb/sth) 1** to stop resisting sb/sth; to agree to do sth that you do not want to do: *He refused to give way on any of the points.* **2** (*BrE*) to allow sb/sth to be or go first: *Give way to traffic already on the roundabout.* **give way to sth 1** to allow yourself to be very strongly affected by sth, especially an emotion: *Flinging herself on the bed, she gave way to helpless misery.* **2** to be replaced by sth: *The storm gave way to bright sunshine.* **go all the 'way (with sb)** (*informal*) to have full sexual INTERCOURSE with sb **go a long/some way towards doing sth** to help very much/a little in achieving sth: *The new law goes a long way towards solving the problem.* **go out of your 'way (to do sth)** to make a special effort to do sth: *He would always go out of his way to be friendly towards her.* **go your own 'way** to do as you choose, especially when sb has advised you against it: *It's best to let her go her own way if you don't want a fight.* **go sb's way 1** to travel in the same direction as sb: *I'm going your way—I'll walk with you.* **2** (of events) to go well for you; to be in your favour: *By the third round he knew the fight was going his way.* **go the way of all 'flesh** (*saying*) to die **have it your 'own way!** (*spoken*) used to say in an angry way that although you are not happy about sth that sb has said, you are not going to argue: *Oh OK, then. Have it your own way.* **have it/things/everything your 'own way** to have what you want, especially by opposing other people **have a way of**

b	d	f	g	h	k	l	m	n	p	r
bad	**did**	**fall**	**get**	**hat**	**cat**	**leg**	**man**	**now**	**pen**	**red**

doing sth used to say that sth often happens in a particular way, especially when it is out of your control: *First love affairs have a way of not working out.* **have a way with sb/sth** to be good at dealing with sb/sth: *He has a way with small children.* ◊ *She has a way with words* (= is very good at expressing herself). **have/want it 'both ways** to have or want to have the advantages of two different situations or ways of behaving that are impossible to combine: *You can't have it both ways. If you can afford to go out all the time, you can afford to pay off some of your debts.* **have your (wicked) way with sb** (*old-fashioned, humorous*) to persuade sb to have sex with you **in a big/small way** on a large/small scale: *The new delivery service has taken off in a big way.* ◊ *Many people are investing in a small way in the stock market.* **in ˌmore ways than 'one** used to show that a statement has more than one meaning: *With the first goal he used his head in more ways than one.* **in her, his, its, etc. (own) 'way** in a manner that is appropriate to or typical of a person or thing but that may seem unusual to other people: *I expect she does love you in her own way.* **in a 'way | in 'one way | in 'some ways** to some extent; not completely: *In a way it was one of our biggest mistakes.* **in the/sb's 'way** stopping sb from moving or doing sth: *You'll have to move—you're in my way.* ◊ *I left them alone, as I felt I was in the way.* **in the way of sth** used in questions and negative sentences to talk about the types of sth that are available: *There isn't much in the way of entertainment in this place.* **keep/stay out of sb's 'way** to avoid sb **look the other 'way** to deliberately avoid seeing sb/sth: *Prison officers know what's going on, but look the other way.* **lose your 'way 1** to become lost: *We lost our way in the dark.* **2** to forget or move away from the purpose or reason for sth: *I feel that the project has lost its way.* **make your 'way (to/towards sth)** to move or get somewhere; to make progress: *Will you be able to make your own way to the airport* (= get there without help, a ride, etc.)? ◊ *Is this your plan for making your way in the world?* **make 'way (for sb/sth)** to allow sb/sth to pass; to allow sb/sth to take the place of sb/sth: *Make way for the Lord Mayor!* ◊ *Tropical forest is felled to make way for grassland.* **(there are) no two ways a'bout it** (*saying*) used to show that you are certain about sth: *It was the wrong decision—there are no two ways about it.* **(there is) ˌno 'way** (*informal*) used to say that there is no possibility that you will do sth or that sth will happen: *'Do you want to help?' 'No way!'* ◊ *No way am I going to drive them there.* ◊ *There's no way we could afford that sort of money.* **on your/the/its 'way 1** going or coming: *I'd better be on my way* (= I must leave) *soon.* ◊ *The letter should be on its way to you.* **2** during the journey: *He stopped for breakfast on the way.* ◊ *She grabbed her camera and bag on her way out.* **3** (of a baby) not yet born: *They've got three kids and one on the way.* **on the way 'out 1** as you are leaving **2** going out of fashion: *The Saturday rave craze seems to be on the way out.* **the ˌother way 'round 1** in the opposite position, direction or order: *I think it should go on the other way round.* **2** the opposite situation: *I didn't leave you. It was the other way round* (= you left me). **ˌout of the 'way 1** no longer stopping sb from moving or doing sth: *I moved my legs out of the way so that she could get past.* ◊ *I didn't say anything until Dad was out of the way.* **2** finished; dealt with: *Our region is poised for growth once the election is out of the way.* **3** far from a town or city: *a little out-of-the-way place on the coast* **4** used in negative sentences to mean 'unusual': *She had obviously noticed nothing out of the way.* **ˌout of your 'way** not on the route that you planned to take: *I'd love a ride home—if it's not out of your way.* **see your 'way ('clear) to doing sth/to do sth** to find that it is possible or convenient to do sth: *Small builders cannot see their way clear to take on many trainees.* **see which way the 'wind is blowing** to get an idea of what is likely to happen before doing sth **(not) stand in sb's 'way** to (not) prevent sb from doing sth: *If you believe you can make her happy, I won't stand in your way.* **that's the way the cookie 'crumbles** (*informal*) that is the situation and we cannot change it, so we must accept it **to 'my way of**

thinking in my opinion **under 'way** (also **under·way**) having started: *Preparations are well under way for a week of special events in May.* **a/the/sb's way of 'life** the typical pattern of behaviour of a person or group: *the British/rural/traditional way of life* **the ˌway of the 'world** the way that most people behave; the way that things happen, which you cannot change: *The rich and powerful make the decisions—that's the way of the world.* **ˌways and 'means** the methods and materials available for doing sth: *ways and means of raising money* **the way to sb's 'heart** the way to make sb like or love you: *The way to a man's heart is through his stomach* (= by giving him good food). **way to 'go!** (*AmE, informal, spoken*) used to tell sb that you are pleased about sth they have done: *Good work, guys! Way to go!* **ˌwork your 'way through college, round the world, etc.** to have a job or series of jobs while studying, travelling, etc. in order to pay for your education, etc. **ˌwork your way 'through sth** to do sth from beginning to end, especially when it takes a lot of time or effort: *She worked her way through the pile of documents.* **ˌwork your way 'up** to move regularly to a more senior position in a company: *He worked his way up from messenger boy to account executive.*—more at CHANGE *v.*, CLAW *v.*, CLEAR *v.*, DOWNHILL, EASY *adj.*, ERROR, FAMILY *n.*, FAR *adv.*, FEEL *v.*, FIND *v.*, HARD *adj.*, HARM *n.*, HEAD *n.*, KNOW *v.*, LAUGH *v.*, LIE *v.*, LONG *adj.*, MEND *v.*, MIDDLE *adj.*, OPEN *v.*, ORDINARY, PARTING *n.*, PAVE, PAY *v.*, PICK *v.*, RUB *v.*, SEPARATE *adj.*, SHAPE *n.*, SHOW *v.*, SMOOTH *v.*, SWEET *adj.*, SWING *v.*, TALK *v.*, WELL *adv.*, WILL *n.*, WRONG *adj.*

■ *adv.* (used with a preposition or an adverb) very far; by a large amount: *She finished the race way ahead of the other runners.* ◊ *I must be going home; it's way past my bedtime.* ◊ *The price is way above what we can afford.* ◊ *They live way out in the suburbs.* ◊ *This skirt is way* (= a lot) *too short.*
IDM **'way back (in …)** a long time ago: *I first met him way back in the 60s.*

way·far·er /ˈweɪfeərə(r); *AmE* -fer-/ *noun* (*old-fashioned* or *literary*) a person who travels from one place to another, usually on foot

way·lay /ˌweɪˈleɪ/ *verb* (**way·laid**, **way·laid** /-ˈleɪd/) [VN] to stop sb who is going somewhere, especially in order to talk to them or attack them: *I got waylaid on my way here.*

ˌway-'out *adj.* (*old-fashioned, informal*) unusual or strange [SYN] WEIRD: *way-out ideas/music*

-ways *suffix* (in adjectives and adverbs) in the direction of: *lengthways* ◊ *sideways*

way·side /ˈweɪsaɪd/ *noun* [sing.] the area at the side of a road or path: *a wayside hotel/inn/shrine* ◊ *wild flowers growing by the wayside* [IDM] **fall by the 'wayside** to fail or be unable to make progress in sth: *Many clubs fall by the wayside for financial reasons.*

'way station *noun* (*especially AmE*) a place where people stop to eat or rest during a long journey

way·ward /ˈweɪwəd; *AmE* -wərd/ *adj.* (*written*) difficult to control: *a wayward child/animal* ◊ *wayward emotions/thoughts* ▶ **way·ward·ness** *noun* [U]

WC /ˌdʌblju: ˈsi:/ *noun* (*BrE*) (on signs and doors in public places) toilet (abbreviation for 'water closet')

we /wi; *strong form* wi:/ *pron.* (used as the subject of a verb) **1** I and another person or other people; I and you: *We've moved to Atlanta.* ◊ *We'd* (= the company would) *like to offer you the job.* ◊ *Why don't we go and see it together?* **2** people in general: *We should take more care of our historic buildings.*—see also THE ROYAL 'WE at ROYAL

weak /wi:k/ *adj.* (**weaker**, **weakest**)
NOT PHYSICALLY STRONG | **1** not physically strong: *She is still weak after her illness.* ◊ *His legs felt weak.* ◊ *She suffered from a weak heart.*
LIKELY TO BREAK | **2** that cannot support a lot of weight; likely to break: *That bridge is too weak to carry heavy traffic.*
WITHOUT POWER | **3** easy to influence; not having much power: *a weak and cowardly man* ◊ *In a weak moment* (= when I was easily persuaded) *I said she could borrow the*

s	t	v	z	ʃ	ʒ	tʃ	dʒ	θ	ð	ŋ
see	tea	van	zoo	shoe	vision	chain	jam	thin	this	sing

car. ◊ *a weak leader/country* ◊ *The unions have always been weak in this industry.*

POOR/SICK PEOPLE | **4 (the weak)** *noun* [pl.] people who are poor, sick or without power

CURRENCY/ECONOMY | **5** not financially strong or successful: *a weak currency/economy/market*

NOT GOOD AT STH | **6 ~ (in sth)** not good at sth: *a weak team* ◊ *I was always weak in the science subjects.*

NOT CONVINCING | **7** that people are not likely to believe or be persuaded by: *weak arguments/evidence* ◊ *I enjoyed the movie but I thought the ending was very weak.*

HARD TO SEE/HEAR | **8** not easily seen or heard: *a weak light/signal/sound*

WITHOUT ENTHUSIASM | **9** done without enthusiasm or energy: *a weak smile* ◊ *He made a weak attempt to look cheerful.*

LIQUID | **10** a weak liquid contains a lot of water: *weak tea*

POINT/SPOT | **11 ~ point/spot** the part of a person's character, an argument, etc. that is easy to attack or criticize: *The team's weak points are in defence.* ◊ *He knew her weak spot where Steve was concerned.*

GRAMMAR | **12** a **weak** verb forms the past tense, etc. by adding -*d*, -*ed* or -*t* (for example *walk*, *walked*) and not by changing a vowel (for example *run*, *ran*)

PHONETICS | **13** (of the pronunciation of some words) used when there is no stress on the word. For example, the weak form of *and* is /ən/ or /n/ as in *bread and butter* /ˌbred n ˈbʌtə(r)/.

OPP STRONG

IDM **ˌweak at the ˈknees** (*informal*) hardly able to stand because of emotion, fear, illness, etc: *His sudden smile made her go weak at the knees.* **the weak link (in the ˈchain)** the point at which a system or an organization is most likely to fail: *She went straight for the one weak link in the chain of his argument.*

weak·en /ˈwiːkən/ *verb* **1** to make sb/sth less strong or powerful; to become less strong or powerful: [VN] *The team has been weakened by injury.* ◊ *The new evidence weakens the case against her.* ◊ [V] *His authority is steadily weakening.* OPP STRENGTHEN **2** to make sb less physically strong; to become less physically strong: [VN] *The explosion had weakened the building's foundations.* ◊ [V] *She felt her legs weaken.* **3** to become or make sb become less determined or certain about sth: [VN] *Nothing could weaken his resolve to continue.* ◊ [V] *You must not agree to do it. Don't weaken.*

ˌweak-ˈkneed *adj.* (*informal*) lacking courage or strength

weak·ling /ˈwiːklɪŋ/ *noun* (*disapproving*) a person who is not physically strong

weak·ly /ˈwiːkli/ *adv.* in a weak way: *She smiled weakly at them.* ◊ *'I'm not sure about it,' he said weakly.*

weak·ness /ˈwiːknəs/ *noun* **1** [U] lack of strength, power or determination: *The sudden weakness in her legs made her stumble.* ◊ *the weakness of the dollar against the pound* ◊ *He thought that crying was a sign of weakness.* **2** [C] a weak point in a system, sb's character, etc: *It's important to know your own strengths and weaknesses.* ◊ *Can you spot the weakness in her argument?* **3** [C, usually sing.] **~ (for sth/sb)** difficulty in resisting sth/sb that you like very much: *He has a weakness for chocolate.*

weal /wiːl/ *noun* a sore red mark on sb's skin where they have been hit

wealth /welθ/ *noun* **1** [U] a large amount of money, property, etc. that a person or country owns: *a person of wealth and influence* ◊ *His personal wealth is estimated at around $100 million.* ◊ *the distribution of wealth in Britain* **2** [U] the state of being rich: *The purpose of industry is to create wealth.* ◊ *Good education often depends on wealth.* **3** [sing.] **~ of sth** a large amount of sth: *a wealth of information/talent/detail* ◊ *The new manager brings a great wealth of experience to the job.*—compare RICHNESS

wealthy /ˈwelθi/ *adj.* (**wealth·ier, wealthi·est**) **1** rich; having a lot of money, possessions, etc: *a wealthy businessman/family/nation* ◊ *The couple are said to be fabu-*

lously wealthy. ◊ *They live in a wealthy suburb of Chicago.* **2 (the wealthy)** *noun* [pl.] people who are rich

wean /wiːn/ *verb* [VN] **~ sb/sth (off/from sth)** to gradually stop feeding a baby or young animal with its mother's milk and start feeding it with solid food PHRV **ˈwean sb off/from sth** to make sb gradually stop doing or using sth: *The doctor tried to wean her off sleeping pills.* **ˈwean sb on sth** [usually passive] to make sb experience sth regularly, especially from an early age: *He was weaned on a diet of rigid discipline and duty.*

weapon /ˈwepən/ *noun* **1** an object such as a knife, gun, bomb, etc. that is used for fighting or attacking sb: *nuclear/chemical weapons* ◊ *a lethal/deadly weapon* ◊ *The police still haven't found the **murder weapon**.* ◊ *He was charged with carrying an **offensive weapon**.* **2** something such as knowledge, words, actions, etc. that can be used to attack or fight against sb/sth: *Education is the only weapon to fight the spread of the disease.* ◊ *Guilt is the **secret weapon** for the control of children.* IDM see DOUBLE-EDGED

weap·on·ry /ˈwepənri/ *noun* [U] (*written*) all the weapons of a particular type or belonging to a particular country or group: *high-tech weaponry* ◊ *US weaponry*

wear /weə(r); AmE wer/ *verb, noun*
■ *verb* (**wore** /wɔː(r)/ **worn** /wɔːn; AmE wɔːrn/)

CLOTHING/ORNAMENT | **1** [VN] to have sth on your body as a piece of clothing, an ornament, etc: *Do I have to wear a tie?* ◊ *to wear a coat/hat/ring/badge/watch* ◊ *Was she wearing a seat belt?* ◊ *He wore glasses.* ◊ *She always wears black* (= black clothes).

HAIR | **2** to have your hair in a particular style; to have a BEARD or MOUSTACHE: [VN-ADJ] *She wears her hair long.* ◊ [VN] *to wear a beard/moustache*

EXPRESSION ON FACE | **3** [VN] to have a particular expression on your face: *He wore a puzzled look on his face.* ◊ *His face wore a puzzled look.*

DAMAGE WITH USE | **4** to become, or make sth become thinner, smoother or weaker through continuous use or rubbing: [V] *The carpets are starting to wear.* ◊ [V-ADJ] *The sheets have worn thin.* ◊ [VN-ADJ] *The stones have been worn smooth by the constant flow of water.* **5** [VN+adv./prep.] to make a hole, path, etc. in sth by continuous use or rubbing: *I've worn holes in all my socks.*

STAY IN GOOD CONDITION | **6** [V] **~ well** to stay in good condition after being used for a long time: *That carpet is wearing well, isn't it?* ◊ (*figurative, humorous*) *You're wearing well—only a few grey hairs!*

ACCEPT/ALLOW | **7** [VN] (usually used in questions and negative sentences) (*BrE, informal*) to accept or allow sth, especially sth that you do not approve of

IDM **wear your ˌheart on your ˈsleeve** to allow your feelings to be seen by other people **wear ˈthin** to begin to become weaker or less acceptable: *These excuses are wearing a little thin* (= because we've heard them so many times before). **wear the ˈtrousers** (*BrE*) (*AmE* **wear the ˈpants**) (often *disapproving*) (especially of a woman) to be the person in a marriage or other relationship who makes most of the decisions—more at CAP *n*. PHRV **ˌwear aˈway|, ˌwear sth↔aˈway** to become, or make sth become, gradually thinner or smoother by continuously using or rubbing it: *The inscription on the coin had worn away.* ◊ *The steps had been worn away by the feet of thousands of pilgrims.* **ˌwear ˈdown|, ˌwear sth↔ˈdown** to become, or make sth become, gradually smaller or smoother by continuously using or rubbing it: *Notice how the tread on this tyre has worn down.* **ˌwear sb/sth↔ˈdown** to make sb/sth weaker or less determined, especially by continuously attacking or putting pressure on it or them over a period of time: *Her persistence paid off and she eventually wore me down.* **ˌwear ˈoff** to gradually disappear or stop: *The effects of the drug will soon wear off.* **ˌwear ˈon** (*written*) (of time) to pass, especially in a way that seems slow: *As the evening wore on, she became more and more nervous.* **ˌwear ˈout|, ˌwear sth↔ˈout** to become, or make sth become, thin or no longer able to be used, usually because it has been used too much: *He wore out two pairs of shoes last year.* **ˌwear**

W

æ	ɑː	e	ɜː	ə	ɪ	iː	i	ɒ	ɔː	ʌ	ʊ	u	uː
cat	father	ten	bird	about	sit	see	many	got	saw	cup	put	actual	too
								(BrE)					

yourself/sb 'out to make yourself/sb feel very tired: *The kids have totally worn me out.* ◇ *You'll wear yourself out if you carry on working so hard.*

■ *noun* [U]

<u>CLOTHING</u> **1** (usually in compounds) used especially in shops/stores to describe clothes for a particular purpose or occasion: *casual/evening wear* ◇ *children's/ladies' wear* ◇ *sportswear*—see also FOOTWEAR, UNDERWEAR **2** the fact of wearing sth: *casual clothes for everyday wear* ◇ *These woollen suits are not designed for wear in hot climates.*

<u>USE</u> **3** the amount or type of use that sth has over a period of time: *You should get years of wear out of that carpet.*

<u>DAMAGE</u> **4** the damage or loss of quality that is caused when sth has been used a lot: *His shoes were beginning to show signs of wear.* ◇ *The machines have to be checked regularly for wear.*

IDM ,**wear and 'tear** the damage to objects, furniture, property, etc. that is the result of normal use: *The insurance policy does not cover damage caused by normal wear and tear.*—more at WORSE *n.*

> ### WHICH WORD?
> **wear / carry / have on**
>
> You **wear** clothes, including gloves, scarves, belts, watches and glasses, and also perfume on your skin: *Do you have to wear a suit for work?* ◇ *I've been wearing glasses for ten years.* You can also say you **have** something **on**: *She had on some very unusual earrings.* ◇ *He ran outside without any shoes on.*
> You **carry** objects with you when you go somewhere, especially in your hands or arms: *He wasn't wearing his raincoat, he was carrying it over his arm.* ◇ *She always carries an umbrella in her briefcase.*

wear·able /ˈweərəbl; *AmE* ˈwer-/ *adj.* (of clothes, etc.) pleasant and comfortable to wear; suitable to be worn

wear·er /ˈweərə(r); *AmE* ˈwer-/ *noun* the person who is wearing sth; a person who usually wears the thing mentioned: *The straps can be adjusted to suit the wearer.* ◇ *contact lens wearers*

wear·ing /ˈweərɪŋ; *AmE* ˈwer-/ *adj.* that makes you feel very tired mentally or physically **SYN** EXHAUSTING

weari·some /ˈwɪərɪsəm; *AmE* ˈwɪr-/ *adj.* (*formal*) that makes you feel very bored and tired

weary /ˈwɪəri; *AmE* ˈwɪri/ *adj.*, *verb*

■ *adj.* (**weari·er**, **weari·est**) **1** very tired, especially after you have been working hard or doing sth for a long time: *a weary traveller* ◇ *She suddenly felt old and weary.* ◇ *a weary sigh/smile* **2** (*literary*) making you feel tired or bored: *a weary journey* ◇ *weary hours spent in negotiation* **3** ~ **of sth/of doing sth** (*formal*) no longer interested in or enthusiastic about sth: *Students soon grow weary of listening to a parade of historical facts.* ▶ **wear·ily** /ˈwɪərəli; *AmE* ˈwɪr-/ *adv.*: *He closed his eyes wearily.* **weari·ness** *noun* [U]

■ *verb* (**wear·ies**, **weary·ing**, **wear·ied**, **wear·ied**) **1** [VN] (*formal*) to make sb feel tired **SYN** TIRE: *a wearying tour around the museums and art galleries* **2** [V] ~ **of sth/of doing sth** to lose your interest in or enthusiasm for sth **SYN** TIRE: *She soon wearied of his stories.*

weasel /ˈwiːzl/ *noun*, *verb*

■ *noun* a small wild animal with reddish-brown fur, a long thin body and short legs. Weasels eat smaller animals.

■ *verb* (**-ll-**, *AmE* **-l-**) **PHRV** ,**weasel 'out (of sth)** (*informal disapproving, especially AmE*) to avoid doing sth that you ought to do or have promised to do: *He's now trying to weasel out of our agreement.*

'weasel word *noun* [usually pl.] (*informal, disapproving*) a word that has little meaning, or more than one meaning, that you use when you want to avoid saying sth in a clear or direct way

wea·ther /ˈweðə(r)/ *noun*, *verb*

■ *noun* [U] **1** the condition of the atmosphere at a particular place and time, such as the temperature, and if there is wind, rain, sun, etc: *hot/cold/wet/fine/summer/windy*

weather ◇ *Did you have good weather on your trip?* ◇ *I'm not going out in this weather!* ◇ *There's going to be a change in the weather.* ◇ *if the weather holds/breaks* (= if the good weather continues/changes) ◇ *The weather is very changeable at the moment.* ◇ *'Are you going to the beach tomorrow?' 'It depends on the weather.'* ◇ *We'll have the party outside,* **weather permitting** (= if it doesn't rain). ◇ *a weather map/chart* ◇ *a weather report* **2 (the weather)** (*informal*) a report of what the weather will be like, that is on the radio or television, or in the newspapers: *to listen to the weather* **IDM** **in** ,**all 'weathers** (*BrE*) in all kinds of weather, good and bad: *She goes out jogging in all weathers.* **keep a 'weather eye on sb/sth** to watch sb/sth carefully in case you need to take action **under the 'weather** (*informal*) if you are or feel **under the weather**, you feel slightly ill/sick and not as well as usual—more at BRASS, HEAVY

■ *verb* **1** to change, or make sth change, colour or shape because of the effect of the sun, rain or wind: [V] *This brick weathers to a warm pinkish-brown colour.* ◇ [VN] *Her face was weathered by the sun.* **2** [VN] to come safely through a difficult period or experience: *The company just managed to weather the recession.* ◇ *She refuses to resign, intending to* **weather the storm** (= wait until the situation improves again).

> ### VOCABULARY BUILDING
> **types of weather**
>
> **Rain**
>
> **Drizzle** is fine light rain.
> A **shower** is a short period of rain.
> A **downpour** or a **cloudburst** is a heavy fall of rain that often starts suddenly.
> When it is raining very hard you can say that it is **pouring**. In informal *BrE* you can also say that it is **bucketing down** or **chucking it down**. You can also say: **The heavens opened.**
>
> **Storms**
>
> A **cyclone** and a **typhoon** are types of violent tropical storms with very strong winds.
> A **hurricane** has very strong winds and is usually at sea.
> A **monsoon** is a period of very heavy rain in particular countries, or the wind that brings this rain.
> A **squall** is a sudden strong, violent wind, usually in a rain or snow storm.
> A **tornado** (or **twister** *informal*) has very strong winds which move in a circle, often with a long narrow cloud.
> A **whirlwind** moves very fast in a spinning movement and causes a lot of damage.
> A **blizzard** is a snow storm with very strong winds.
> **Tempest** is used mainly in literary language to describe a violent storm.

'weather-beaten *adj.* [usually before noun] (especially of a person or their skin) rough and damaged because the person spends a lot of time outside

wea·ther·board /ˈweðəbɔːd; *AmE* ˈweðərbɔːrd/ (also **clap·board** especially in *AmE*) *noun* one of a series of long, narrow, horizontal pieces of wood, each with one edge thicker than the other. They are fixed to the outside walls of a house with the bottom of one over the top of the one below, to cover the wall and protect it from rain and wind: *a weatherboard house* ▶ **'wea·ther·boarded** *adj.* **'wea·ther·board·ing** *noun* [U]

wea·ther·cock /ˈweðəkɒk; *AmE* ˈweðərkɑːk/ *noun* a WEATHERVANE in the shape of a male chicken (called a COCK or ROOSTER)

'weather forecast (also **fore·cast**) *noun* a description, for example on the radio or television, of what the weather will be like tomorrow or for the next few days

wea·ther·ize /ˈweðəraɪz/ *verb* [VN] (*AmE*) to protect a building against the effects of cold weather, for example by providing INSULATION

aɪ	aʊ	eɪ	əʊ	oʊ	ɔɪ	ɪə	eə	ʊə	j	w
my	now	say	go	go	boy	near	hair	pure	yes	wet
			(BrE)	(AmE)						

W

wea·ther·man /ˈweðəmæn; AmE -ðərm-/ (pl. **-men** /-men/) **wea·ther·girl** /ˈweðəgɜːl; AmE -ðərgɜːrl/ noun (informal) a person on radio or television whose job is describing the weather and telling people what it is going to be like

wea·ther·proof /ˈweðəpruːf; AmE -ðərp-/ adj. that is not affected by weather; that protects sb/sth from wind and rain: *The finished roof should be weatherproof for years.* ◇ *a weatherproof jacket*

ˈ**weather station** noun a place where weather conditions are studied and recorded

ˈ**weather strip** noun (AmE) = DRAUGHT EXCLUDER

wea·ther·vane /ˈweðəveɪn; AmE -ðərv-/ noun a metal object on the roof of a building that turns easily in the wind and shows which direction the wind is blowing from—see also WEATHERCOCK

weave /wiːv/ verb, noun
■ verb (**wove** /wəʊv; AmE woʊv/ **woven** /ˈwəʊvn; AmE ˈwoʊvn/ **HELP** In sense 4 **weaved** is used for the past tense and past participle.) **1** ~ **A (from B)** | ~ **B (into A)** | ~ **sth (together)** to make fabric, a carpet, a basket, etc. by crossing threads or strips across, over and under each other by hand or on a machine called a LOOM: [VN] *The baskets are woven from strips of willow.* ◇ *The strips of willow are woven into baskets.* ◇ *Most spiders weave webs that are almost invisible.* ◇ *threads woven together* ◇ [V] *She is skilled at spinning and weaving.* **2** [VN] ~ **A (out of/from B)** | ~ **B (into A)** to make sth by twisting flowers, pieces of wood, etc. together: *She deftly wove the flowers into a garland.* **3** [VN] ~ **sth (into sth)** | ~ **sth (together)** to put facts, events, details, etc. together to make a story or a closely connected whole: *to weave a story/narrative* ◇ *The biography weaves together the various strands of Einstein's life.* **4** (**weaved**, **weaved**) [+adv./prep.] to move along by running and changing direction continuously to avoid things that are in your way: [V] *She was weaving in and out of the traffic.* ◇ *The road weaves through a range of hills.* ◇ [VN] *He had to weave his way through the milling crowds.* **IDM** **weave your ˈmagic** | **weave a ˈspell (over sb)** (especially BrE) to perform or behave in a way that attracts and interests sb very much or makes them react in a particular way: *Will Owen be able to weave his magic against Scotland on Wednesday?*
■ noun the way in which threads are arranged in a piece of fabric that has been woven; the pattern that the threads make

weaver /ˈwiːvə(r)/ noun a person whose job is weaving fabric

web /web/ noun **1** [C] = SPIDER'S WEB: *A spider had spun a perfect web outside the window.*—picture on page A7 **2** [C] a complicated pattern of things that are closely connected to each other: *a web of streets* ◇ *We were caught in a tangled web of relationships.* ◇ *She discovered a web of intrigue in the company.* **3** [C] a piece of skin that joins the toes of some birds and animals that swim, for example ducks and FROGS **4** (**the Web**) [sing.] = WORLD WIDE WEB: *Web pages* ◇ *a website* (= where a company, etc. has information about itself on the Web) ⇨ see page 250

web·bed /webd/ adj. [only before noun] a bird or an animal (such as a duck or FROG) that has **webbed feet** has pieces of skin between the toes—picture on page A6

web·bing /ˈwebɪŋ/ noun [U] strong strips of woven material that are used to make belts or straps, and to support the seats of chairs, etc.

web·master /ˈwebmɑːstə(r); AmE -mæs-/ noun (computing) a person who is responsible for particular pages of information on the World Wide Web

wed /wed/ verb (**wed·ded**, **wed·ded** or **wed**, **wed**) (not used in the progressive tenses) (old-fashioned or used in newspapers) to marry: [V] *The couple plan to wed next summer.* ◇ [VN] *Rock star to wed top model* (= in a newspaper headline).

we'd /wiːd; wid/ short form **1** we had **2** we would

wed·ded /ˈwedɪd/ adj. **1** ~ **to sth** (formal) if you are **wedded** to sth, you like or support it so much that you are not willing to give it up: *She's wedded to her job.*

2 [usually before noun] ~ **(to sb)** (old-fashioned or formal) legally married: *your lawfully wedded husband/wife* ◇ *to live together in wedded bliss* **3** [not before noun] ~ **(to sth)** (formal or literary) combined or united with sth

wed·ding /ˈwedɪŋ/ noun a marriage ceremony, and the meal or party that usually follows it: *a wedding present/dress* ◇ *a wedding ceremony/reception* ◇ *Have you been invited to their wedding?* ◇ *She looked beautiful on her wedding day.* ◇ *Today is our wedding anniversary.* ◇ *All her friends could hear wedding bells* (= they thought she would soon get married).—see also SHOTGUN WEDDING, WHITE WEDDING

ˈ**wedding band** noun a wedding ring in the form of a plain band, usually of gold—picture at JEWELLERY

ˈ**wedding breakfast** noun (BrE, formal) a special meal after a marriage ceremony

ˈ**wedding cake** noun [C, U] a cake covered with ICING, and usually with several layers, eaten at a wedding party—picture on page A1

ˈ**wedding ring** noun a ring that is given during a marriage ceremony and worn afterwards to show that you are married—picture at JEWELLERY

wedge /wedʒ/ noun, verb
■ noun **1** a piece of wood, rubber, metal, etc. with one thick end and one thin pointed end that you use to keep a door open, to keep two things apart, or to split wood or rock: *He hammered the wedge into the crack in the stone.* ◇ *(figurative)* *A wedge had been tapped into their friendship.* ◇ *I don't want to drive a wedge between the two of*

wedge

wedge

wedge of lemon

you (= to make you start disliking each other). **2** something that is shaped like a wedge or that is used like a wedge: *a wedge of lemon/cake/cheese* **3** a golf CLUB that has the part that you hit the ball with shaped like a wedge **IDM** see THIN adj.
■ verb **1** [VN+adv./prep.] to put or squeeze sth tightly into a narrow space, so that it cannot move easily: *The boat was now wedged between the rocks.* ◇ *She wedged herself into the passenger seat.* **2** to make sth stay in a particular position, especially open or shut, by placing sth against it: [VN-ADJ] *to wedge the door open/shut* [also VN]

wed·lock /ˈwedlɒk; AmE -lɑːk/ noun [U] (old-fashioned or law) the state of being married: *children born in/out of wedlock* (= whose parents are/are not married)

Wed·nes·day /ˈwenzdeɪ; -di/ noun [C, U] (abbr. **Wed.**, **Weds.**) the day of the week after Tuesday and before Thursday **HELP** To see how **Wednesday** is used, look at the examples at **Monday**. **ORIGIN** Originally translated from the Latin for 'day of Mercury' *Mercurii dies* and named after the Germanic god *Odin*.

wee /wiː/ adj., noun, verb
■ adj. (informal) **1** (especially ScotE) very small in size: *a wee girl* **2** small in amount; little: *Just a wee drop of milk for me.* ◇ *I felt a wee bit guilty about it.* **IDM** **the wee small ˈhours** (ScotE) (AmE **the wee ˈhours**) = THE SMALL/EARLY HOURS at HOUR
■ noun (also ˈ**wee-wee**) (spoken, especially BrE) (often used by young children or when you are talking to them) **1** [sing.] an act of passing liquid waste (called URINE) from your body: *to do/have a wee* **2** [U] = URINE
■ verb [V] (also ˈ**wee-wee**) (informal, especially BrE) (often used by young children or when you are talking to them) to pass liquid waste (called URINE) from the body: *Do you need to wee?*

weed /wiːd/ noun, verb
■ noun **1** [C] a wild plant growing where it is not wanted, especially among crops or garden plants: *The yard was overgrown with weeds.* **2** [U] any wild plant without flowers that grows in water and forms a green floating mass **3** (**the weed**) [sing.] (humorous) tobacco or cigarettes: *I wish I could give up the weed* (= stop smoking).

W

4 [U] (*informal*) the drug CANNABIS **5** [C] (*BrE, informal, disapproving*) a person with a weak character or body: *Don't be such a weed!*
■ *verb* to take out weeds from the ground:[VN] *I've been weeding the flower beds.* [alsoV] PHRV **,weed sth/sb↔'out** to remove or get rid of people or things from a group because they are not wanted or are less good than the rest

weed·kill·er /'wiːdkɪlə(r)/ *noun* [U, C] a substance that is used to destroy weeds

weedy /'wiːdi/ *adj.* (**weed·ier, weedi·est**) **1** (*BrE, informal, disapproving*) having a thin weak body: *a weedy little man* **2** full of or covered with weeds

week /wiːk/ *noun* **1** a period of seven days, either from Monday to Sunday or from Sunday to Saturday: *last/this/next week* ◊ *It rained all week.* ◊ *What day of the week is it?* ◊ *He comes to see us once a week.* **2** any period of seven days: *a two-week holiday/vacation* ◊ *The course lasts five weeks.* ◊ *a week ago today* (= seven days ago) ◊ *She'll be back in a week.* **3** the five days other than Saturday and Sunday: *They live in town during the week and go to the country for the weekend.* ◊ (*BrE*) *I never have the time to go out in the week.* **4** the part of the week when you go to work: *a 35-hour week* ◊ *The firm is introducing a shorter working week.* IDM **today, tomorrow, Monday, etc. 'week** (*BrE*) (also **a ,week from to'day, etc.** *AmE, BrE*) seven days after the day that you mention: *I'll see you Thursday week.* **,week after 'week** (*informal*) continuously for many weeks: *Week after week the drought continued.* **,week by 'week** as the weeks pass: *Week by week he grew a little stronger.* **week ,in, week 'out** happening every week: *Every Sunday, week in, week out, she goes to her parents for lunch.* **a ,week next/on/this 'Monday, etc. | a ,week to'morrow, etc.** (*BrE*) (also **a ,week from 'Monday, etc.** *AmE, BrE*) seven days after the day that you mention: *It's my birthday a week on Tuesday.* **a ,week 'yesterday, last 'Monday, etc.** (*especially BrE*) seven days before the day that you mention: *She started work a week yesterday.*—more at OTHER *adj.*

week·day /'wiːkdeɪ/ *noun* any day except Saturday and Sunday: *The centre is open from 9 a.m. to 6 p.m. on weekdays.* ► **week·days** *adv.*: *open weekdays from 9 a.m. to 6 p.m.*

week·end /ˌwiːk'end; AmE 'wiːkend/ *noun, verb*
■ *noun* **1** Saturday and Sunday: *Are you doing anything over the weekend?* ◊ *Have a good weekend!* ◊ *It happened on the weekend of 24 and 25 April.* ◊ (*BrE*) *The office is closed at the weekend.* ◊ (*especially AmE*) *The office is closed on the weekend.* ◊ (*BrE, informal*) *I like to go out on a weekend.* ◊ *We go skiing most weekends in winter.*—see also DIRTY WEEKEND, LONG WEEKEND **2** Saturday and Sunday, or a slightly longer period, as a holiday/vacation: *He won a weekend for two in Rome.* ◊ *a weekend break*
■ *verb* [V+adv. / prep.] to spend the weekend somewhere: *They're weekending in Paris.*

week·end·er /ˌwiːk'endə(r)/ *noun* a person who visits or lives in a place only on Saturdays and Sundays

'week-long *adj.* (*written*) lasting for a week: *a week-long visit to Rome* ◊ *week-long seminars/courses*

week·ly /'wiːkli/ *adj., noun*
■ *adj.* happening, done or published once a week or every week: *weekly payments/meetings* ◊ *a weekly magazine/newspaper* ► **week·ly** *adv.*: *Employees are paid weekly.* ◊ *The newspaper is published twice weekly.*
■ *noun* (*pl.* **-ies**) a newspaper or magazine that is published every week

week·night /'wiːknaɪt/ *noun* any night except those on Saturday and Sunday: *I have to stay in on weeknights.*

weenie /'wiːni/ *noun* (*AmE, informal*) **1** (*disapproving*) a person who is not strong, brave or confident SYN WIMP: *Don't be such a weenie!* **2** = FRANKFURTER

weeny /'wiːni/ *adj.* (*informal*) extremely small SYN TINY: *Weren't you just a weeny bit scared?*—see also TEENY

weep /wiːp/ *verb, noun*
■ *verb* (**wept, wept** /wept/) **1** ~ (**for/with sth**)| ~ (**at/over sth**) (*formal* or *literary*) to cry, usually because you are

sad: [V] *She started to weep uncontrollably.* ◊ *He wept for joy.* ◊ *I do not weep over his death.* ◊ *I could have wept thinking about what I'd missed.* ◊ [VN] *She wept bitter tears of disappointment.* ◊ [Vto inf] *I wept to see him looking so sick.* [alsoV **speech**] **2** [V] (usually used in the progressive tenses) (of a wound) to produce liquid: *His legs were covered with weeping sores* (= sores which had not healed).
■ *noun* [sing.] an act of crying: *Sometimes you feel better for a good weep.*

weep·ing /'wiːpɪŋ/ *adj.* [only before noun] (of some trees) with branches that hang downwards: *a weeping willow/fig/birch*

weepy /'wiːpi/ *adj., noun*
■ *adj.* (*informal*) sad and tending to cry easily: *She was feeling tired and weepy.*
■ *noun* (also **weepie**) (*pl.* **-ies**) (*informal*) a sad film/movie or play that makes you want to cry

wee·vil /'wiːvl/ *noun* a small insect with a hard shell, that eats grain, nuts and other seeds and destroys crops

weft /weft/ (also *less frequent* **woof**) *noun* (**the weft**) [sing.] the threads that are woven under and over the threads that are held on a LOOM (= a frame or machine for weaving fabric)—compare WARP

weigh /weɪ/ *verb* **1** *linking verb* to have a particular weight: [V] *How much do you weigh* (= how heavy are you)? ◊ [V-N] *She weighs 60 kilos.* ◊ *These cases weigh a ton* (= are very heavy). **2** [VN] to measure how heavy sth is, usually by using SCALES/A SCALE: *He weighed himself on the bathroom scales.* ◊ *She weighed the stone in her hand* (= estimated how heavy it was by holding it). **3** [VN] ~ **sth (up)**| ~ (**up**) **sth** (**against sth**) to consider sth carefully before making a decision: *You must weigh up the pros and cons* (= consider the advantages and disadvantages of sth). ◊ *I weighed the benefits of the plan against the risks involved.* ◊ *She weighed up all the evidence.* **4** [V] ~ (**with sb**) (**against sb/sth**) to have an influence on sb's opinion or the result of sth: *His past record weighs heavily against him.* **5** [VN] ~ **anchor** to lift an ANCHOR out of the water and into a boat before sailing away IDM **weigh your 'words** to choose your words carefully so that you say exactly what you mean PHRV **,weigh sb↔'down** to make sb feel worried or anxious SYN BURDEN: *The responsibilities of the job are weighing her down.* ◊ *He is weighed down with guilt.* **,weigh sb/sth↔'down** to make sth/sb heavier so that they are not able to move easily: *I was weighed down with baggage.* **,weigh 'in (at sth)** to have your weight measured, especially before a contest, race, etc: *Both boxers weighed in at several pounds below the limit.*—related noun WEIGH-IN **,weigh 'in (with sth)** (*informal*) to join in a discussion, an argument, an activity, etc. by saying sth important, persuading sb, or doing sth to help: *We all weighed in with our suggestions.* ◊ *Finally the government weighed in with financial aid.* **'weigh on sb/sth** to make sb anxious or worried: *The responsibilities weigh heavily on him.* ◊ *Something was weighing on her mind.* **,weigh sth↔'out** to measure an amount of sth by weight: *She weighed out a kilo of flour.* **,weigh sb↔'up** to form an opinion of sb by watching or talking to them: *It was obvious that she was cautiously weighing me up.*

weigh·bridge /'weɪbrɪdʒ/ *noun* a machine for weighing vehicles and their loads, usually with a platform onto which the vehicle is driven

'weigh-in *noun* the occasion when the weight of a boxer, JOCKEY, etc. is checked just before a fight, race, etc.

'weighing machine *noun* a machine for weighing large objects or for weighing people in a public place

weight /weɪt/ *noun, verb*
■ *noun*
BEING HEAVY **1** [U, C] how heavy sb/sth is, which can be measured in, for example, kilograms or pounds: *It is about 76 kilos in weight.* ◊ *Bananas are sold by weight.* ◊ *In the wild, this fish can reach a weight of 5lbs.* ◊ *She is trying to lose weight* (= become less heavy and less fat). ◊ *He's put on/gained weight* (= become heavier and fatter) *since he gave up smoking.* ◊ *Sam has a weight problem*

s	t	v	z	ʃ	ʒ	tʃ	dʒ	θ	ð	ŋ
see	tea	van	zoo	shoe	vision	chain	jam	thin	this	sing

(= is too fat). ◊ *No more for me. I have to* **watch my weight**.—see also OVERWEIGHT, UNDERWEIGHT **2** [U] the fact of being heavy: *He staggered a little* **under the weight** *of his backpack.* ◊ *I just hoped the branch would* **take my weight**. ◊ *The pillars have to support the weight of the roof.* ◊ *Don't put any weight on that ankle for at least a week.*—see also DEADWEIGHT

HEAVY OBJECT | **3** [C] an object that is heavy: *The doctor said he should not lift heavy weights.* **4** [C] an object used to keep sth in position or as part of a mechanism: *He used weights to keep the tablecloth in place.* ◊ *weights on a fishing line*—picture at GRANDFATHER CLOCK—see also PAPERWEIGHT

RESPONSIBILITY/WORRY | **5** [sing.] **~ (of sth)** a great responsibility or worry: *The full weight of responsibility falls on her.* ◊ *The news was certainly a* **weight off my mind** (= I did not have to worry about it any more). ◊ *Finally telling the truth was* **a great weight off my shoulders**.

INFLUENCE/ STRENGTH | **6** [U] importance, influence or strength: *The many letters of support* **added weight** *to the campaign.* ◊ *The President has now offered to* **lend his weight** *to the project.* ◊ *Your opinion* **carries weight** *with the boss.* ◊ *How can you ignore the sheer weight of medical opinion?* ◊ *The weight of evidence against her is overwhelming.*

FOR MEASURING/LIFTING | **7** [C, U] a unit or system of units by which weight is measured: *tables of weights and measures* ◊ *imperial/metric weight* **8** [C] a piece of metal that is known to weigh a particular amount and is used to measure the weight of sth, or lifted by people to improve their strength and as a sport: *a set of weights* ◊ *She lifts weights as part of her training.* ◊ *weight training*

IDM **take the weight off your feet** (*informal*) to sit down and rest, especially when you are tired: *Come and sit down and take the weight off your feet for a while.* **throw your 'weight about/ around** (*informal*) to use your position of authority or power in an aggressive way in order to achieve what you want: *She was a good manager, who didn't find it necessary to throw her weight around.* **throw/put your weight behind sth** to use all your influence and power to support sth **weight of 'numbers** the combined power, strength or influence of a group: *They won the argument by sheer weight of numbers.*—more at GROAN *v.*, PULL *v.*, WORTH *adj.*

■ *verb* [VN]
ATTACH HEAVY OBJECT | **1 ~ sth (down) (with sth)** to attach a weight to sth in order to keep it in the right position or make it heavier: *The fishing nets are weighted with lead.* ◊ *The body had been weighted down with stones.*

GIVE IMPORTANCE | **2** [usually passive] to give different values to things to show how important you think each of them is compared with the others: *The results of the survey were weighted to allow for variations in the sample.* ◊ *a weighted vote* (= one that is worth more than a single vote) ◊ (*AmE*) *a weighted grade* (= given at school for a course that is more advanced or harder and so has a higher value)

weight·ed /ˈweɪtɪd/ *adj.* [not before noun] **~ towards/ against sb/sth| ~ in favour of sb/sth** arranged in such a way that a particular person or thing has an advantage or a disadvantage: *The proposal is weighted towards smaller businesses.* ◊ *Everything seemed weighted against them.* ◊ *The course is heavily weighted in favour of engineering.*

weight·ing /ˈweɪtɪŋ/ *noun* **1** [U] (*BrE*) extra money that you get paid for working in a particular area because it is expensive to live there: *a weighting allowance for London* **2** [C, U] a value that you give to each of a number of things to show how important it is compared with the others: *Each of the factors is given a weighting on a scale of 1 to 10.* ◊ *Each question in the exam has equal weighting.*

weight·less /ˈweɪtləs/ *adj.* having no weight or appearing to have no weight, for example because there is no GRAVITY: *Astronauts work in weightless conditions.* ▶ **weight·less·ness** *noun* [U]

weight·lift·ing /ˈweɪtlɪftɪŋ/ *noun* [U] the sport or activity of lifting heavy weights ▶ **weight·lift·er** *noun*

weighty /ˈweɪti/ *adj.* (**weight·ier**, **weighti·est**) (*formal*) **1** important and serious: *weighty issues/questions/matters* **2** heavy: *a weighty volume/tome* ▶ **weight·ily** /-ɪli/ *adv.* **weighti·ness** *noun* [U]

weir /wɪə(r); *AmE* wɪr/ *noun* a low wall or barrier built across a river in order to control the flow of water or change its direction

weird /wɪəd; *AmE* wɪrd/ *adj.* (**weird·er**, **weird·est**) **1** unusual or different; not normal: *a weird dream* ◊ *She's a really weird girl.* ◊ *He's got some weird ideas.* ◊ *It's really weird seeing yourself on television.* ◊ *the weird and wonderful creatures that live beneath the sea* **2** (*written*) strange, mysterious or frightening: *She began to make weird inhuman sounds.* ▶ **weird·ly** *adv.*: *The town was weirdly familiar.* **weird·ness** *noun* [U]

weirdo /ˈwɪədəʊ; *AmE* ˈwɪrdoʊ/ *noun* (*pl.* **-os** /-əʊz/) (*informal, disapproving*) a person who looks strange and/or behaves in a strange way

welch /weltʃ; welʃ/ *verb* = WELSH

wel·come /ˈwelkəm/ *verb, adj., noun, exclamation*
■ *verb* **1 ~ sb (to sth)** to greet sb in a friendly way when they arrive somewhere: [VN] *They were at the door to welcome us.* ◊ *It is a pleasure to welcome you to our home.* ◊ [V] *a welcoming smile* **2** [VN] to be pleased that sb has come or has joined an organization, activity, etc: *They welcomed the new volunteers* **with open arms** (= with enthusiasm). **3** [VN] to be pleased to receive or accept sth: *I'd welcome any suggestions.* ◊ *I warmly welcome this decision.* ◊ *In general, the changes they had made were to be welcomed.*

■ *adj.* **1** that you are pleased to have, receive, etc: *a welcome opportunity/relief/sight* ◊ *Your letter was very welcome.* ◊ *The fine weather* **made a welcome change**. **2** (of people) accepted or wanted somewhere: *Children are always welcome at the hotel.* ◊ *Our neighbours* **made us welcome** *as soon as we arrived.* ◊ *I had the feeling we were not welcome at the meeting.* **3 ~ to do sth** (especially *spoken*) used to say that you are happy for sb to do sth if they want to: *They're welcome to stay here as long as they like.* **4 ~ to sth** (especially *spoken*) used to say that you are very happy for sb to have sth because you definitely do not want it: *It's an awful job. If you want it, you're welcome to it!* **IDM** **you're 'welcome** (especially *AmE*) used as a polite reply when sb thanks you for sth: *'Thanks for your help.' 'You're welcome.'*

■ *noun* **1** [C, U] a greeting that is given to sb when they arrive, especially a friendly one: *Thank you for your* **warm welcome**. ◊ *The winners were* **given an** *enthusiastic welcome when they arrived home.* ◊ *a speech/smile of welcome* ◊ *to receive a hero's welcome* **2** [C] the way that people react to sth, which shows their opinion of it: *This new comedy deserves a* **warm welcome**. ◊ *The proposals were given a cautious welcome by the trade unions.* **IDM** **outstay/overstay your 'welcome** to stay somewhere as a guest longer than you are wanted

■ *exclamation* used as a greeting to a person who is arriving: *Welcome home!* ◊ *Welcome to Oxford!*

'welcome mat *noun* **IDM** **lay, put, roll, etc. out the 'welcome mat (for sb)** (especially *AmE*) to make sb feel welcome; to try to attract visitors, etc: *The county has put out the welcome mat for international investors.*

wel·com·ing /ˈwelkəmɪŋ/ *adj.* **1** (of a person) friendly towards sb who is visiting or arriving **2** (of a place) attractive and looking comfortable to be in: *His room was quiet, warm and welcoming.* **OPP** UNWELCOMING

weld /weld/ *verb, noun*
■ *verb* **1 ~ A and B (together)| ~ A (on) to B** to join pieces of metal together by heating their edges and pressing them together: [VN] *to weld a broken axle* ◊ *The car has had a new wing welded on.* ◊ *All the parts of the sculpture have to be welded together.* [also V] **2** [VN] **~ sb/sth into sth| ~ sth together** to unite people or things into a strong and effective group: *They had welded a bunch of untrained recruits into an efficient fighting force.* ◊ *The crisis helped to weld the party together.*
■ *noun* a joint made by welding

weld·er /ˈweldə(r)/ *noun* a person whose job is welding metal

W

æ	ɑː	e	ɜː	ə	ɪ	iː	i	ɒ	ɔː	ʌ	ʊ	u	uː
cat	father	ten	bird	about	sit	see	many	got	saw	cup	put	actual	too
								(BrE)					

wel·fare /ˈwelfeə(r); *AmE* -fer/ *noun* [U] **1** the general health, happiness and safety of a person, an animal or a group SYN WELL-BEING: *We are concerned about the child's welfare.* **2** practical or financial help that is provided, often by the government, for people or animals that need it: *The state is still the main provider of welfare.* ◊ *animal/ child welfare* ◊ *a social welfare programme* ◊ *welfare provision/services/work* **3** (*especially AmE*) = SOCIAL SECURITY: *They would rather work than live on welfare.*

welfare ˈstate *noun* **1** (often **the Welfare State**) [usually sing.] a system by which the government provides a range of free services to people who need them, for example medical care, money for people without work, care for old people, etc. **2** [C] a country that has such a system

well /wel/ *adv., adj., exclamation, noun, verb*

■ *adv.* (**bet·ter** /ˈbetə(r)/ **best** /best/) **1** in a good, right or satisfactory way: *The kids all behaved well.* ◊ *The conference was very well organized.* ◊ (*spoken*) **Well done!** (= expressing admiration for what sb has done) ◊ *His campaign was not going well.* ◊ *These animals make very good pets if treated well* (= with kindness). ◊ *People* **spoke well of** (= spoke with approval of) *him.* ◊ *She took it very well* (= did not react too badly), *all things considered.* ◊ *They lived well* (= in comfort and spending a lot of money) *and were generous with their money.* ◊ *She was determined to marry well* (= marry sb rich and/or with a high social position). **2** thoroughly and completely: *Add the lemon juice and mix well.* ◊ *The surface must be well prepared before you start to paint.* ◊ *How well do you know Carla?* ◊ *He's well able to take care of himself.* ◊ (*BrE, spoken, informal*) *I was well annoyed, I can tell you.* **3** to a great extent or degree: *He was driving at well over the speed limit.* ◊ *a well-loved tale* ◊ *The castle is well worth a visit.* ◊ *He liked her well enough* (= to a reasonable degree) *but he wasn't going to make a close friend of her.* **4** can/could ~ easily: *She could well afford to pay for it herself.* **5** can/could/may/might ~ probably: *You may well be right.* ◊ *It may well be that the train is delayed.* **6** can/could/may/might ~ with good reason: *I can't very well leave now.* ◊ *I couldn't very well refuse to help them, could I?* ◊ *'What are we doing here?' 'You may well ask* (= I don't really know either).*'* IDM **as well (as sb/sth)** in addition to sb/sth; too: *Are they coming as well?* ◊ *They sell books as well as newspapers.* ◊ *She is a talented musician as well as being a photographer.* ⇨ note at ALSO **be doing ˈwell** to be getting healthier after an illness; to be in good health after a birth: *Mother and baby are doing well.* **be well on the way to sth/doing sth** to have nearly achieved sth and be going to achieve it soon: *She is well on the way to recovery.* ◊ *He is well on the way to establishing himself among the top ten players in the world.* **be ˌwell ˈout of sth** (*BrE, informal*) to be lucky that you are not involved in sth **be ˌwell ˈup in sth** to know a lot about sth: *He's well up in all the latest developments.* **do ˈwell** to be successful: *Jack is doing very well at school.* **do ˈwell by sb** to treat sb generously **do ˈwell for yourself** to become successful or rich **do ˈwell out of sb/sth** to make a profit or get money from sb/sth **do ˈwell to do sth** to be sensible or wise to do sth: *He would do well to concentrate more on his work.* ◊ *You did well to sell when the price was high.* **leave/let well aˈlone** (*BrE*) (*AmE* **let well enough aˈlone**) to not get involved in sth that does not concern you: *When it comes to other people's arguments, it's better to leave well alone.* **may/might (just) as well do sth** to do sth because it seems best in the situation that you are in, although you may not really want to do it: *If no one else wants it, we might as well give it to him.* **ˌwell and ˈtruly** (*informal*) completely: *By that time we were well and truly lost.* **ˈwell away** (*BrE, informal*) **1** having made good progress: *If we got Terry to do that, we'd be well away.* **2** drunk or fast asleep **ˌwell ˈin (with sb)** (*informal*) to be good friends with sb, especially sb important: *She seems to be well in with all the right people.* **ˌwell ˈoff for 1** having a lot of money; rich: *His family is not very well off.* ◊ *The less well-off pensioners are finding it hard to survive on what they get.* **2** in a good situation: *Some people don't know when they're well off* (=

do not realize how lucky they are). **ˌwell ˈoff for sth** having plenty of sth: *We're well off for storage space in the new offices.*—more at BLOODY¹, FUCKING, JOLLY *adv.*, KNOW *v.*, MEAN *v.*, PRETTY *adv.*

■ *adj.* (**bet·ter** /ˈbetə(r)/ **best** /best/) **1** [not usually before noun] in good health: *I don't feel very well.* ◊ *Is she well enough to travel?* ◊ *Get well soon!* (for example, on a card) ◊ *I'm better now, thank you.* ◊ (*informal*) *He's not a well man.* ⇨ note at HEALTHY **2** [not before noun] in a satisfactory state or position: *It seems that all is not well at home.* ◊ *All's well that ends well* (= used when sth has ended happily, even though you thought it might not). **3** [not before noun] (**as**) ~ (**to do sth**) sensible; a good idea: *It would be just as well to call and say we might be late.* ◊ (*formal*) *It would be well to start early.* IDM **ˌall very ˈwell (for sb) (to do sth)** (*informal*) used to criticize or reject a remark that sb has made, especially when they were trying to make you feel happier about sth: *It's all very well for you to say it doesn't matter, but I've put a lot of work into this and I want it to be a success.* **ˌall well and ˈgood** (*informal*) good but not completely satisfactory: *That's all well and good, but why didn't he call her to say so?*

■ *exclamation* **1** used to express surprise, anger or RELIEF: *Well, well—I would never have guessed it!* ◊ *Well, really! What a thing to say!* ◊ *Well, thank goodness that's over!* **2** used to show that you accept that sth cannot be changed: *Well, it can't be helped.* ◊ *'We lost.' 'Oh, well. Better luck next time.'* **3** used to agree to sth, rather unwillingly: *Well, I suppose I could fit you in at 3.45.* ◊ *Oh, very well, then, if you insist.* **4** used when continuing a conversation after a pause: *Well, as I was saying …* **5** used to express uncertainty: *'Do you want to come?' 'Well, I'm not sure.'* **6** used to show that you are waiting for sb to say sth: *Well? Are you going to tell us or not?* **7** used to mark the end of a conversation: *Well, I'd better be going now.* **8** used when you are pausing to consider your next words: *I think it happened, well, towards the end of last summer.* **9** used when you want to correct or change sth that you have just said: *There were thousands of people there—well, hundreds, anyway.* IDM **well I ˈnever (ˈdid)!** (*old-fashioned*) used to express surprise—more at SAY *v.*

■ *noun* **1** a deep hole in the ground from which people obtain water. The sides of wells are usually covered with brick or stone and there is usually some covering or a small wall at the top of the well. **2** = OIL WELL **3** a narrow space in a building that drops down from a high to a low level and usually contains a staircase or lift/elevator—see also STAIRWELL **4** (*BrE*) the space in front of the judge in a court of law, where the lawyers sit

■ *verb* [V] ~ (**up**) **1** (of a liquid) to rise to the surface of sth and start to flow: *Tears were welling up in her eyes.* **2** (*literary*) (of an emotion) to become stronger: *Hate welled up inside him as he thought of the two of them together.*

we'll /wiːl; wɪl/ *short form* **1** we will **2** we shall

GRAMMAR POINT

well

Compound adjectives beginning with **well** are generally written with no hyphen when they are used alone after a verb, but with a hyphen when they come before a noun: *She is well dressed.* ◊ *a well-dressed woman.* The forms without hyphens are given here, but forms with hyphens can be seen in some examples.

The comparative and superlative forms of these are usually formed with **better** and **best**: *better-known poets* ◊ *the best-dressed person in the room.*

ˌwell adˈjusted *adj.* (of a person) able to deal with people, problems and life in general in a normal, sensible way—compare MALADJUSTED

ˌwell adˈvised *adj.* [not before noun] ~ (**to do sth**) acting in the most sensible way: *You would be well advised to tackle this problem urgently.*—compare ILL-ADVISED

aɪ	aʊ	eɪ	əʊ	oʊ	ɔɪ	ɪə	eə	ʊə	j	w
my	now	say	go	go	boy	near	hair	pure	yes	wet
			(BrE)	(AmE)						

,well ap'pointed *adj.* (*formal*) having all the necessary equipment; having comfortable and attractive furniture, etc.

,well at'tended *adj.* attended by a lot of people: *a well-attended conference*

,well 'balanced *adj.* **1** containing a sensible variety of the sort of things or people that are needed: *a well-balanced diet/meal* ◊ *The team was not well balanced.* **2** (of a person or their behaviour) sensible and emotionally in control: *His response was well balanced.*

,well be'haved *adj.* behaving in a way that other people think is polite or correct: *a well-behaved child/dog* ◊ *The audience was surprisingly well behaved.*

'well-being *noun* [U] general health and happiness: *emotional/physical/psychological well-being* ◊ *to have a sense of well-being*

,well 'born *adj.* (*formal*) from a rich family or a family of high social class

,well 'bred *adj.* (*old-fashioned, formal*) having or showing good manners; typical of a high social class: *a well-bred young lady* ◊ *She was too well bred to show her disappointment.* OPP ILL-BRED

,well 'built *adj.* **1** (of a person) with a solid, strong body **2** (of a building or machine) strongly made

,well con'nected *adj.* (*formal*) (of a person) having important or rich friends or relatives

,well 'cut *adj.* (of clothes) made well and therefore probably expensive

,well de'fined *adj.* easy to see or understand: *well-defined laws/patterns/rules* ◊ *These categories are not well defined.* OPP ILL-DEFINED

,well de'veloped *adj.* fully developed; fully grown: *He had a well-developed sense of his own superiority.*

,well dis'posed *adj.* ~ (towards/to sb/sth) having friendly feelings towards sb or a positive attitude towards sth: *It's a country that is well disposed to the West.* OPP ILL-DISPOSED

,well 'documented *adj.* having a lot of written evidence to prove, support or explain it: *The problem is well documented.* ◊ *well-documented facts/cases*

,well 'done *adj.* (of food, especially meat) cooked thoroughly or for a long time: *He prefers his steak well done.*—compare RARE, UNDERDONE

,well 'dressed *adj.* wearing fashionable or expensive clothes: *This is what today's well-dressed man is wearing.*

,well 'earned *adj.* much deserved: *a well-earned rest*

,well en'dowed *adj.* **1** (*informal, humorous*) (of a woman) having large breasts **2** (*informal, humorous*) (of a man) having large GENITALS **3** (of an organization) having a lot of money: *well-endowed colleges*

,well e'stablished *adj.* having a respected position, because of being successful, etc. over a long period: *a well-established firm/reputation/tradition* ◊ *He is now well established in his career.*

,well 'fed *adj.* having plenty of good food to eat regularly: *well-fed family pets* ◊ *The animals all looked well fed and cared for.*

,well 'founded (also *less frequent* ,well 'grounded) *adj.* having good reasons or evidence to cause or support it: *well-founded suspicions* ◊ *His fear turned out to be well founded.* OPP ILL-FOUNDED

,well-'groomed *adj.* (of a person) looking clean, neat and carefully dressed

,well 'grounded *adj.* **1** ~ in sth having a good training in a subject or skill **2** = WELL FOUNDED

,well 'heeled *adj.* (*informal*) having a lot of money; rich

,well in'formed *adj.* having or showing knowledge or information about many subjects or about one particular subject: *a well-informed decision* OPP ILL-INFORMED

wel·ling·ton /'welɪŋtən/ (also ,wellington 'boot, *informal* welly) (all *BrE*) (*AmE* ,rubber 'boot) *noun* one of a pair of long rubber boots, usually reaching almost up to the knee, that you wear to stop your feet getting wet: *a pair of wellingtons*—picture at SHOE

,well in'tentioned *adj.* intending to be helpful or useful but not always succeeding very well

,well 'kept *adj.* **1** kept neat and in good condition: *well-kept gardens* **2** (of a secret) known only to a few people

,well 'known *adj.* **1** known about by a lot of people SYN FAMOUS: *a well-known actor* ◊ *His books are not well known.* **2** (of a fact) generally known and accepted: *It is a well-known fact that caffeine is a stimulant.*

,well 'mannered *adj.* (*formal*) having good manners SYN POLITE OPP ILL-MANNERED

,well 'matched *adj.* able to live together, play or fight each other, etc. because they are similar in character, ability, etc: *a well-matched couple* ◊ *The two teams were well matched.*

,well 'meaning *adj.* intending to do what is right and helpful but often not succeeding: *her well-meaning but anxious family and friends* ◊ *a well-meaning attempt to be helpful* ◊ *He's very well meaning.*

,well 'meant *adj.* done, said, etc. in order to be helpful but often not succeeding: *well-meant comments* ◊ *His offer was well meant.*

well·ness /'welnəs/ *noun* [U] (*especially AmE*) the state of being healthy

well-'nigh *adv.* (*formal*) almost: *Defence was well-nigh impossible against such opponents.*

,well 'oiled *adj.* (*written*) operating smoothly and well: *The system ran like a well-oiled machine.*

,well pre'served *adj.* not showing many signs of age; kept in good condition

,well 'read *adj.* having read many books and therefore having gained a lot of knowledge

,well 'rounded *adj.* **1** having a variety of experiences and abilities and a fully developed personality: *well-rounded individuals* **2** providing or showing a variety of experience, ability, etc: *a well-rounded education* **3** (of a person's body) pleasantly round in shape

,well 'run *adj.* managed smoothly and well: *a well-run hotel*

,well 'spoken *adj.* having a way of speaking that is considered correct or elegant

well·spring /'welsprɪŋ/ *noun* (*literary*) a supply or source of a particular quality, especially one that never ends

,well 'thought of *adj.* respected, admired and liked: *Their family has always been well thought of around here.*

,well thought 'out *adj.* carefully planned

,well 'thumbed *adj.* a well-thumbed book has been read many times

,well 'timed *adj.* done or happening at the right time or at an appropriate time SYN TIMELY: *a well-timed intervention* ◊ *Your remarks were certainly well timed.* OPP ILL-TIMED

,well-to-'do *adj.* having a lot of money; rich: *a well-to-do family* ◊ *They're very well-to-do.*

,well 'tried *adj.* used many times before and known to be successful: *a well-tried method*

,well 'trodden *adj.* (*formal*) (of a road or path) much used

,well 'turned *adj.* (*formal*) expressed in an elegant way: *a well-turned phrase*

'well-wisher *noun* a person who wants to show that they support sb and want them to be happy, successful, etc.

,well 'worn *adj.* **1** worn or used a lot or for a long time: *a well-worn jacket* ◊ *Most British visitors beat a well-worn path to the same tourist areas of the US.* **2** (of a phrase, story, etc.) heard so often that it does not sound interesting any more SYN HACKNEYED

welly /'weli/ *noun* (*pl.* -ies) (*BrE, informal*) = WELLINGTON: *a pair of green wellies*

Welsh /welʃ/ *noun, adj.*

■ *noun* **1** [U] the Celtic language of Wales: *Do you speak Welsh?* **2** (the Welsh) [pl.] the people of Wales

■ *adj.* of or connected with Wales, its people or its language: *Welsh mountains/poetry*

welsh /welʃ/ (also welch /welʃ/) *verb* [V] ~ (on sb/sth) (*disapproving, informal*) to not do sth that you have promised to do, for example to not pay money that you owe a

b	d	f	g	h	k	l	m	n	p	r
bad	did	fall	get	hat	cat	leg	man	now	pen	red

person: *'I'm not in the habit of welshing on deals,'* said Don.

Welsh 'dresser *noun* (*BrE*) = DRESSER

Welsh 'rarebit (also **rare·bit**) *noun* [U] (*BrE*) a hot dish of cheese melted on toast

welt /welt/ *noun* a raised mark on the skin where sth has hit or rubbed you SYN WEAL

wel·ter /'weltə(r)/ *noun* [sing.] (*formal*) ~ **of sth** a large and confusing amount of sth: *a welter of criticism/enquiries/information*

wel·ter·weight /'weltəweɪt; *AmE* -tərw-/ *noun* a boxer weighing between 61 and 67 kilograms, heavier than a LIGHTWEIGHT: *a welterweight champion*

wench /wentʃ/ *noun* (*old use* or *humorous*) a young woman

wend /wend/ *verb* (*old use* or *literary*) to move or travel slowly somewhere: [VN] *Leo* **wended his way** *home through the wet streets.* [also V]

Wendy house /'wendi haʊs/ *noun* (*BrE*) = PLAYHOUSE

went *pt* of GO

wept *pt*, *pp* of WEEP

were /wə(r); *strong form* wɜː(r)/ ⇨ BE

we're /wɪə(r); *AmE* wɪr/ *short form* we are

weren't /wɜːnt/ *short form* were not

were·wolf /'weəwʊlf; *AmE* 'werw-/ *noun* (*pl.* **-wolves** /-wʊlvz/) (in stories) a person who sometimes changes into a WOLF, especially at the time of the full moon

west /west/ *noun*, *adj.*, *adv.*
- *noun* [U, sing.] (*abbr.* **W**) **1** (usually **the west**) the direction that you look towards to see the sun set; one of the four main points of the COMPASS: *Which way is west?* ◇ *Rain is spreading from the west.* ◇ *He lives* **to the west of** (= further west than) *the town.*—compare EAST, NORTH, SOUTH—picture at COMPASS **2** (**the West**) Europe, N America and Canada, contrasted with eastern countries: *I was born in Japan, but I've lived in the West for some years now.* **3** (**the West**) (*AmE*) the western side of the US: *the history of the American West*—see also THE MIDWEST, THE WILD WEST **4** (**the West**) (in the past) western Europe and N America, when contrasted with the Communist countries of Eastern Europe: *East-West relations*
- *adj.* [only before noun] (*abbr.* **W**) **1** in or towards the west: *West Africa* ◇ *the west coast of Scotland* **2** a west wind blows from the west—compare WESTERLY
- *adv.* towards the west: *This room faces west.*

west·bound /'westbaʊnd/ *adj.* travelling or leading towards the west: *westbound traffic* ◇ *the westbound carriageway of the motorway*

west·er·ly /'westəli; *AmE* -ərli/ *adj.*, *noun*
- *adj.* **1** [only before noun] in or towards the west: *travelling in a westerly direction* **2** [usually before noun] (of winds) blowing from the west: *westerly gales*—compare WEST
- *noun* (*pl.* **-ies**) a wind that blows from the west: *light westerlies*

west·ern /'westən; *AmE* -ərn/ *adj.*, *noun*
- *adj.* **1** [only before noun] (*abbr.* **W**) (also **Western**) situated in the west or facing west: *western Spain* ◇ *Western Europe* ◇ *the western slopes of the mountain* **2** (usually **Western**) connected with the west part of the world, especially Europe and N America: *Western art*—see also COUNTRY AND WESTERN
- *noun* a film/movie or book about life in the western US in the 19th century, usually involving COWBOYS

west·ern·er /'westənə(r); *AmE* -ərn-/ *noun* a person who comes from or lives in the western part of the world, especially western Europe or N America

west·ern·iza·tion (*BrE* also **-isa·tion**) /ˌwestənaɪ-ˈzeɪʃn; *AmE* -ərnəˈz-/ *noun* [U] the process of becoming westernized

west·ern·ize (*BrE* also **-ise**) /'westənaɪz; *AmE* -ərn-/ *verb* [VN] [usually passive] to bring ideas or ways of life that are typical of western Europe and N America to other countries: *The islands have been westernized by the growth of tourism.* ▶ **west·ern·ized, -ised** *adj.*: *a westernized society*

west·ern·most /'westənməʊst; *AmE* -ərnmoʊst/ *adj.* (*written*) situated furthest west: *the westernmost tip of the island*

west·wards /'westwədz; *AmE* -wərdz/ (also **west·ward**) *adv.* towards the west: *to go/look/turn westwards* ▶ **west·ward** *adj.*: *in a westward direction*

wet /wet/ *adj.*, *verb*, *noun*
- *adj.* (**wet·ter**, **wet·test**) **1** covered or soaked with liquid, especially water: *wet clothes/grass/hair/roads* ◇ *You'll get wet* (= in the rain) *if you go out now.* ◇ *Try not to get your shoes wet.* ◇ *His face was wet with tears.* ◇ *We were all* **soaking wet** (= extremely wet). ◇ *Her hair was still* **dripping wet.** ◇ *My shirt was* **wet through** (= completely wet). **2** (of weather, etc.) with rain: *a wet day* ◇ *a wet climate* ◇ *It's wet outside.* ◇ *It's going to be wet tomorrow.* ◇ *It was the wettest October for many years.* **3** (of paint, ink, etc.) not yet dry: *Keep off! Wet paint.* **4** if a child or its NAPPY/DIAPER is **wet**, its NAPPY/DIAPER is soaked with URINE **5** (*BrE*) (of a person) (*informal, disapproving*) lacking a strong character: *'Don't be so wet,' she laughed.* ▶ **wetly** *adv.* **wet·ness** *noun* [U] IDM **(still) ,wet behind the 'ears** (*informal, disapproving*) young and without much experience SYN NAIVE
- *verb* (**wet·ting**, **wet**, **wet**) or (**wet·ting**, **wet·ted**, **wet·ted**) [VN] to make sth wet: *Wet the brush slightly before putting it in the paint.* IDM **wet the/your 'bed** [no passive] to accidentally URINATE in your bed: *It is quite common for small children to wet their beds.* **'wet yourself | wet your 'pants/'knickers** [no passive] to accidentally URINATE in your underwear
- *noun* **1** (**the wet**) [sing.] wet weather; rain: *Come in out of the wet.* **2** [U] liquid, especially water: *The dog shook the wet from its coat.* **3** [C] (*BrE, disapproving*) a CONSERVATIVE politician who supports MODERATE policies rather than extreme ones: *Tory wets* **4** [C] (*BrE, informal, disapproving*) a person who lacks a strong character: *Don't be such a wet!*

wet·back /'wetbæk/ *noun* (*AmE*, ⚠, *slang*) an offensive word for a Mexican person, especially one who enters the US illegally

,wet 'blanket *noun* (*informal, disapproving*) a person who is not enthusiastic about anything and who stops other people from enjoying themselves

,wet 'dream *noun* a sexually exciting dream that a man has that results in an ORGASM

wet·land /'wetlənd/ *noun* [C, U] (also **wet·lands** [pl.]) an area of wet land: *The wetlands are home to a large variety of wildlife.* ▶ **wet·land** *adj.* [only before noun]: *wetland birds/plants/habitats*

'wet nurse *noun* (usually in the past) a woman employed to feed another woman's baby with her own breast milk

'wet suit *noun* a piece of clothing made of rubber that fits the whole body closely, worn by people swimming underwater or sailing—picture at SNORKELLING

we've /wiːv; wiv/ *short form* we have

whack /wæk/ *verb*, *noun*
- *verb* [VN] **1** (*informal*) to hit sb/sth very hard: *She whacked him with her handbag.* ◇ *James whacked the ball over the net.* **2** [+adv./prep.] (*spoken*) to put sth somewhere without much care: *Just whack your bags in the corner.*
- *noun* [usually sing.] (*informal*) **1** the act of hitting sb/sth hard; the sound made by this: *He gave the ball a good whack.* ◇ *I heard the whack of the bullet hitting the wood.* **2** (*BrE*) a share of sth; an amount of sth: *Don't leave all the work to her. Everyone should do their fair whack.* ◇ *You have to pay the full whack. There are no reductions.* ◇ *He charges top whack* (= the highest amount possible). IDM **out of 'whack** (*AmE, informal*) (of a system or machine) not working as it should because its different parts are not working together correctly

whacked /wækt/ (also ,**whacked 'out**) *adj.* [not usually before noun] (*BrE, informal*) very tired: *I'm whacked!*

whack·ing /'wækɪŋ/ (also **'whacking great**) *adj.* (*BrE, informal*) used to emphasize how big or how much sth is SYN WHOPPING: *a whacking great hole in the roof* ◇ *They were fined a whacking £100000.*

s	t	v	z	ʃ	ʒ	tʃ	dʒ	θ	ð	ŋ
see	tea	van	zoo	shoe	vision	chain	jam	thin	this	sing

W

whacky = WACKY

whale /weɪl/ *noun* a very large animal that lives in the sea and looks like a very large fish. There are several types of whale, some of which are hunted: *whale meat*—see also BLUE WHALE, KILLER WHALE, PILOT WHALE, SPERM WHALE **IDM** **have a ˈwhale of a time** (*informal*) to enjoy yourself very much; to have a very good time

whale·bone /ˈweɪlbəʊn; *AmE* -boʊn/ *noun* [U] a thin hard substance found in the upper jaw of some types of whale, used in the past to make some clothes stiffer

whaler /ˈweɪlə(r)/ *noun* 1 a ship used for hunting whales 2 a person who hunts whales

whal·ing /ˈweɪlɪŋ/ *noun* [U] the activity or business of hunting and killing WHALES

wham /wæm/ *exclamation* (*informal*) 1 used to represent the sound of a sudden, loud hit: *The bombs went down—wham!—right on target.* 2 used to show that sth that is unexpected has suddenly happened: *I saw him yesterday and—wham!—I realized I was still in love with him.*

whammy /ˈwæmi/ *noun* (*pl.* -ies) (*informal*) an unpleasant situation or event that causes problems for sb/sth: *With this government we've had a **double whammy** of tax increases and benefit cuts.* **ORIGIN** From the 1950s American cartoon *Li'l Abner*, in which one of the characters could **shoot a whammy** (put a curse on sb) by pointing a finger with one eye open, or a **double whammy** with both eyes open.

wharf /wɔːf; *AmE* wɔːrf/ *noun* (*pl.* **wharves** /wɔːvz; *AmE* wɔːrvz/ or **wharfs**) a flat structure built beside the sea or a river where boats can be tied up and goods unloaded

what /wɒt; *AmE* wɑːt; wʌt/ *pron., det.* 1 used in questions to ask for particular information about sb/sth: *What is your name?* ◊ *What* (= what job) *does he do?* ◊ *What time is it?* ◊ *What kind of music do you like?*—compare WHICH 2 the thing or things that; whatever: *What you need is a good meal.* ◊ *Nobody knows what will happen next.* ◊ *I spent what little time I had with my family.* 3 used to say that you think that sth is especially good, bad, etc: *What awful weather!* ◊ *What a beautiful house!* **IDM** **and ˈwhat not | and what ˈhave you** (*spoken*) and other things of the same type: *It's full of old toys, books and what not.* **get/give sb what ˈfor** (*BrE, spoken*) to be punished/punish sb severely: *I'll give her what for if she does that again.* **or ˈwhat** (*spoken*) 1 used to emphasize your opinion: *Is he stupid or what?* 2 used when you are not sure about sth: *I don't know if he's a teacher or what.* ◊ *Are we going now or what?* **what?** (*spoken, informal*) 1 used when you have not heard or have not understood sth: *What? I can't hear you.* 2 used to show that you have heard sb and to ask what they want: *'Mummy!' 'What?' 'I'm thirsty.'* 3 used to express surprise or anger: *'It will cost $500.' 'What?'* ◊ *'I asked her to marry me.' 'You what?'* **ˈWhat about ...?** (*spoken*) 1 used to make a suggestion: *What about a trip to France?* 2 used to introduce sb/sth into the conversation: *What about you, Joe? Do you like football?* **ˈwhat-d'you-call-him/-her/-it/-them | ˈwhat's-his/-her/-its/-their-name** used instead of a name that you cannot remember: *She's just gone out with old what-d'you-call-him.* **what for?** for what purpose or reason?: *What is this tool for?* ◊ *What did you do that for* (= why did you do that)? ◊ *'I need to see a doctor.' 'What for?'* **what if ...?** what would happen if?: *What if the train is late?* ◊ *What if she forgets to bring it?* **what ˈof it?** (*spoken*) used when admitting that sth is true, to ask why it should be considered important: *Yes, I wrote the article. What of it?* **what's ˈwhat** (*spoken*) what things are useful, important, etc: *She certainly knows what's what.* **what's ˈwith sb** (*AmE, spoken*) used to ask why sb is behaving in a strange way: *What's with you? You haven't said a word all morning.* **what's ˈwith sth** (*AmE, spoken*) used to ask the reason for sth: *What's with all this walking? Can't we take a cab?* **what with sth** used to list the various reasons for sth: *What with the cold weather and my bad leg, I haven't been out for weeks.*

whatch·am·acall·it /ˈwɒtʃəməkɔːlɪt; *AmE* ˈwɑːt-; ˈwʌt-/ *noun* (*spoken*) used when you cannot think of the name of sth: *Have you got a whatchamacallit? You know ...a screwdriver?*

what·ever /wɒtˈevə(r); *AmE* wət-; wɑːt-/ *det., pron., adv.*

■ *det., pron.* 1 any or every; anything or everything: *Take whatever action is needed.* ◊ *Do whatever you like.* 2 used when you are saying that it does not matter what sb does or what happens, because the result will be the same: *Whatever decision he made I would support it.* ◊ *You have our support, whatever you decide.* 3 (*especially BrE*) used in questions to express surprise or confusion: *Whatever do you mean?* ◊ *Chocolate-flavoured carrots! Whatever next?* 4 (*spoken, ironic*) used as a reply to tell sb that you do not care what happens or that you are not interested in what they are talking about: *'You should try a herbal remedy.' 'Yeah, whatever.'* 5 (*spoken, especially AmE*) used to say that you do not mind what you do, have, etc. and that anything is acceptable: *'What would you like to do today?' 'Whatever.'* **IDM** **or what'ever** (*spoken*) or something of a similar type: *It's the same in any situation: in a prison, hospital or whatever.* **what'ever you do** used to warn sb not to do sth under any circumstances: *Don't tell Paul, whatever you do!*

■ *adv.* 1 (*also* **what·so·ever**) no, nothing, none. ~ not at all; not of any kind: *They received no help whatever.* ◊ *'Is there any doubt about it?' 'None whatsoever.'* 2 (*informal*) used to say that it does not matter what sb does, or what happens, because the result will be the same: *We told him we'd back him whatever.*

what·not /ˈwɒtnɒt; *AmE* ˈwɑːtnɑːt/ *noun* [U] **and ~** (*informal*) used when you are referring to sth, but are not being exact and do not mention its name: *It's a new firm. They make toys and whatnot.*

whats·it /ˈwɒtsɪt; *AmE* ˈwɑːt-; ˈwʌt-/ *noun* (*spoken, especially BrE*) used when you cannot think of the word or name you want, or do not want to use a particular word: *I've got to make a whatsit for the party. That's it—a flan.*

wheat /wiːt/ *noun* [U] a plant grown for its grain that is used to produce the flour for bread, cakes, PASTA, etc.; the grain of this plant: *wheat flour*—picture at CEREAL **IDM** **sort out/separate the ˌwheat from the ˈchaff** to distinguish useful or valuable people or things from ones that are not useful or have no value

wheat·germ /ˈwiːtdʒɜːm; *AmE* -dʒɜːrm/ *noun* [U] the centre of the wheat grain, which is especially good for your health

whee /wiː/ *exclamation* used to express excitement

whee·dle /ˈwiːdl/ *verb* ~ sth (out of sb) | ~ sb into doing sth (*disapproving*) to persuade sb to give you sth or do sth by saying nice things that you do not mean: [VN] *The kids can always wheedle money out of their father.* ◊ *She wheedled me into lending her my new coat.* [also V speech]

wheel /wiːl/ *noun, verb*

■ *noun*

ON/IN VEHICLES | 1 [C] one of the circular objects under a car, bicycle, bus, etc. that turns when it moves: *He braked suddenly, causing the front wheels to skid.* ◊ *One of the boys was pushing the other along in a little box on wheels.* 2 [C, usually sing.] the circular object used to steer a car, etc. or ship: *This is the first time I've sat behind the wheel since the accident.* ◊ *A car swept past with Laura at the wheel.* ◊ *Do you want to take the wheel* (= drive) *now?*—see also HELM, STEERING WHEEL 3 (**wheels**) [pl.] (*informal*) a car: *At last he had his own wheels.*

IN MACHINE | 4 [C] a flat circular part in a machine: *gear wheels*—see also CARTWHEEL, CATHERINE WHEEL, FERRIS WHEEL, MILL WHEEL, SPINNING WHEEL, WATERWHEEL

ORGANIZATION/SYSTEM | 5 (**wheels**) [pl.] ~ (**of sth**) an organization or a system that seems to work like a complicated machine that is difficult to understand: *the wheels of bureaucracy/commerce/government* ◊ *It was Rob's idea. I merely set the wheels in motion* (= started the process).

-WHEELED | 6 (in adjectives) having the number or type of wheels mentioned: *a sixteen-wheeled lorry*

-WHEELER | 7 (in nouns) a car, bicycle, etc. with the number of wheels mentioned: *a three-wheeler*

IDM **ˌwheels within ˈwheels** a situation which is difficult to understand because it involves complicated or

W

æ	ɑː	e	ɜː	ə	ɪ	iː	i	ɒ	ɔː	ʌ	ʊ	u	uː
cat	father	ten	bird	about	sit	see	many	got	saw	cup	put	actual	too
								(BrE)					

W

secret processes and decisions: *There are wheels within wheels in this organization—you never really know what is going on.*—more at COG, GREASE *v.*, OIL *v.*, REINVENT, SHOULDER *n.*, SPOKE
■ *verb* [usually +*adv.* / *prep.*]
MOVE STH WITH WHEELS | **1** [VN] to push or pull sth that has wheels: *She wheeled her bicycle across the road.* **2** [VN] to move sb/sth that is in or on sth that has wheels: *The nurse wheeled him along the corridor.*
MOVE IN CIRCLE | **3** [V] to move or fly in a circle: *Birds wheeled above us in the sky.*
TURN QUICKLY | **4** to turn quickly or suddenly and face the opposite direction; to make sb/sth do this: [V] *She wheeled around and started running.* ◊ [VN] *He wheeled his horse back to the gate.*
IDM **,wheel and 'deal** (usually used in the progressive tenses) to do a lot of complicated DEALS in business or politics, often in a dishonest way
PHRV **,wheel sth↔'out** to show or use sth to help you do sth, even when it has often been seen or heard before: *They wheeled out the same old arguments we'd heard so many times before.*
wheel·bar·row /'wi:lbærəʊ; *AmE* -roʊ/ (also **bar·row**) *noun* a large open container with a wheel and two handles that you use outside to carry things—picture at GARDEN
wheel·base /'wi:lbeɪs/ *noun* [sing.] (*technical*) the distance between the front and back wheels of a car or other motor vehicle
wheel·chair /'wi:ltʃeə(r); *AmE* -tʃer/ *noun* a special chair with wheels, used by people who cannot walk because of illness, an accident, etc: *Does the hotel have wheelchair access?* ◊ *He's been confined to a wheelchair since the accident.* ◊ *wheelchair users*—picture at CHAIR
'wheel clamp *noun* (*BrE*) = CLAMP
wheeler-dealer /,wi:lə 'di:lə(r)/ *noun* (*informal*) a person who does a lot of complicated DEALS in business or politics, often in a dishonest way
wheel·house /'wi:lhaʊs/ *noun* a small enclosed CABIN on a ship where the person steering stands at the wheel
wheelie /'wi:li/ *noun* (*informal*) a trick that you can do on a bicycle by balancing on the back wheel, with the front wheel off the ground: *to do a wheelie*
'wheelie bin *noun* (*BrE*, *informal*) a large container with a lid and wheels, that you keep outside your house and use for putting rubbish in
wheel·wright /'wi:lraɪt/ *noun* a person whose job is making and repairing wheels, especially wooden ones
wheeze /wi:z/ *verb*, *noun*
■ *verb* to breathe noisily and with difficulty: [V] *He was coughing and wheezing all night.* ◊ [V speech] *'I have a chest infection,' she wheezed.*
■ *noun* [usually sing.] **1** the high whistling sound that your chest makes when you cannot breathe easily **2** (*old-fashioned*, *BrE*, *informal*) a clever trick or plan
wheezy /'wi:zi/ *adj.* making the high whistling sound that your chest makes when you cannot breathe easily: *a wheezy chest / cough / laugh* ▶ **wheez·ily** /-ɪli/ *adv.* **wheezi·ness** *noun* [U]
whelk /welk/ *noun* a small shellfish that can be eaten
whelp /welp/ *noun*, *verb*
■ *noun* (*technical*) a young animal of the dog family; a PUPPY or CUB
■ *verb* [V, VN] (*formal*) (of a female dog) to give birth to a PUPPY or PUPPIES
when /wen/ *adv.*, *pron.*, *conj.*
■ *adv.* **1** (used in questions) at what time; on what occasion: *When did you last see him?* ◊ *When can I see you?* ◊ *When* (= in what circumstances) *would such a solution be possible?* **2** used after an expression of time to mean 'at which' or 'on which': *Sunday is the only day when I can relax.* ◊ *There are times when I wonder why I do this job.* **3** at which time; on which occasion: *The last time I went to Scotland was in May, when the weather was beautiful.*
■ *pron.* what/which time: *Until when can you stay?* ◊ *'I've got a new job.' 'Since when?'*

■ *conj.* **1** at or during the time that: *I loved history when I was at school.* **2** after: *Call me when you've finished.* **3** at any time that; whenever: *Can you spare five minutes when it's convenient?* **4** just after which: *He had just drifted off to sleep when the phone rang.* **5** considering that: *How can they expect to learn anything when they never listen?* **6** although: *She claimed to be 18, when I know she's only 16.* **IDM** see AS *conj.*
whence /wens/ *adv.* (*old use*) from where: *They returned whence they had come.*
when·ever /wen'evə(r)/ *conj.*, *adv.*
■ *conj.* **1** at any time that; on any occasion that: *You can ask for help whenever you need it.* **2** every time that: *Whenever she comes, she brings a friend.* ◊ *The roof leaks whenever it rains.* ◊ *We try to help whenever possible.* **3** used when the time when sth happens is not important: *'When do you need it by?' 'Saturday or Sunday. Whenever.'* ◊ *It's not urgent—we can do it next week or whenever.*
■ *adv.* used in questions to mean 'when', expressing surprise: *Whenever did you find time to do all that cooking?*
where /weə(r); *AmE* wer/ *adv.*, *conj.*
■ *adv.* **1** in or to what place or situation: *Where do you live?* ◊ *I wonder where they will take us to.* ◊ *Where* (= at what point) *did I go wrong in my calculations?* ◊ *Where* (= in what book, newspaper, etc.) *did you read that?* ◊ *Just where* (= to what situation or final argument) *is all this leading us?* **2** used after words or phrases that refer to a place or situation to mean 'at, in or to which': *It's one of the few countries where people drive on the left.* **3** the place or situation in which: *We then moved to Paris, where we lived for six years.*
■ *conj.* (in) the place or situation in which: *This is where I live.* ◊ *Sit where I can see you.* ◊ *Where people were concerned, his threshold of boredom was low.* ◊ *That's where* (= the point in the argument at which) *you're wrong.*
where·abouts *noun*, *adv.*
■ *noun* /'weərəbaʊts; *AmE* 'wer-/ [U+sing./pl. *v.*] the place where sb/sth is: *His whereabouts are / is still unknown.*
■ *adv.* /,weərə'baʊts; *AmE* ,wer-/ used to ask the general area where sb/sth is: *Whereabouts did you find it?*
where·as /,weər'æz; *AmE* ,wer-/ *conj.* **1** used to compare or contrast two facts: *Some of the studies show positive results, whereas others do not.* **2** (*law*) used at the beginning of a sentence in an official document to mean 'because of the fact that ...'
where·by /weə'baɪ; *AmE* wer-/ *adv.* (*formal*) by which; because of which: *They have introduced a new system whereby all employees must undergo regular training.*
where·fore /'weəfɔ:(r); *AmE* 'werf-/ *noun* **IDM** see WHY *n.*
where·in /weər'ɪn; *AmE* wer-/ *adv.*, *conj.* (*formal*) in which place, situation or thing; in what way: *an organization wherein each employee is valued and respected* ◊ *Wherein lies the difference between conservatism and liberalism?*
where·of /weər'ɒv; *AmE* -'ʌv/ *conj.* (*old use* or *humorous*) of what or which: *I know whereof I speak* (= I know a lot about what I am talking about).
where·upon /,weərə'pɒn; *AmE* ,werə'pɑ:n; -'pɔ:n; 'werəpɑ:n/ *conj.* (*written*) and then; as a result of this: *He told her she was a liar, whereupon she walked out.*
wher·ever /weər'evə(r); *AmE* wer-/ *conj.*, *adv.*
■ *conj.* **1** in any place: *Sit wherever you like.* ◊ *He comes from Boula, wherever that may be* (= I don't know where it is). **2** in all places that [SYN] EVERYWHERE: *Wherever she goes, there are crowds of people waiting to see her.* **3** in all cases that [SYN] WHENEVER: *Use wholegrain breakfast cereals wherever possible.* **IDM** **or wher'ever** (*informal*) or any other place: *tourists from Spain, France or wherever*
■ *adv.* used in questions to mean 'where', expressing surprise: *Wherever can he have gone to?*
where·withal /'weəwɪðɔ:l; *AmE* 'werw-/ *noun* (**the wherewithal**) [sing.] **~ (to do sth)** the money, things or skill that you need in order to be able to do sth: *They lacked the wherewithal to pay for the repairs.*
whet /wet/ *verb* (**-tt-**) [VN] to increase your desire for or interest in sth: *The book will whet your appetite for more of her work.*

whether /'weðə(r)/ *conj.* **1** used to express a doubt or choice between two possibilities: *He seemed undecided* **whether** *to go* **or** *stay.* ◊ *It remains to be seen* **whether** *or* **not** *this idea can be put into practice.* ◊ *I asked him* **whether** *he had done it all himself* **or** **whether** *someone had helped him.* ◊ *I'll see* **whether** *she's at home* (= or not at home). ◊ *It's doubtful* **whether** *there'll be any seats left.* ⇨ note at IF **2** used to show that sth is true in either of two cases: *You are entitled to a free gift* **whether** *you accept our offer of insurance or not.* ◊ *I'm going* **whether** *you like it* **or** **not.** ◊ **Whether** *or* **not** *we're successful, we can be sure that we did our best.*

whet·stone /'wetstəʊn/ *AmE* -stoʊn/ *noun* a stone that is used to make cutting tools and weapons sharp

whew /hwju:; fju:/ *exclamation* a sound that people make to show that they are surprised or RELIEVED about sth or that they are very hot or tired: *Whew—and I thought it was serious!* ◊ *Ten grand? Whew!*—compare PHEW

whey /weɪ/ *noun* [U] the thin liquid that is left from sour milk after the solid part (called CURDS) has been removed

which /wɪtʃ/ *pron., det.* **1** used in questions to ask sb to be exact about one or more people or things from a limited number: *Which is better exercise—swimming or tennis?* ◊ *Which of the applicants has got the job?* ◊ *Which of the patients have recovered?* ◊ *Which way is the wind blowing?*—compare WHAT **2** used to be exact about the thing or things that you mean: *Houses which overlook the lake cost more.* ◊ *It was a crisis for which she was totally unprepared.* **HELP** *That* can be used instead of *which* in this meaning, but it is not used immediately after a preposition: *It was a crisis that she was totally unprepared for.* **3** used to give more information about sth: *His best movie, which won several awards, was about the life of Gandhi.* ◊ *Your claim ought to succeed, in which case the damages will be substantial.* **HELP** *That* cannot be used instead of *which* in this meaning. **IDM** **,which is 'which** used to talk about distinguishing one person or thing from another: *The twins are so alike I can't tell which is which.*

which·ever /wɪtʃ'evə(r)/ *det., pron.* **1** used to say what feature or quality is important in deciding sth: *Choose* **whichever** *brand you prefer.* ◊ *Pensions should be increased annually in line with earnings or prices, whichever is the higher.* ◊ *Whichever of you gets here first will get the prize.* **2** used to say that it does not matter which, as the result will be the same: *It takes three hours, whichever route you take.* ◊ *The situation is an awkward one,* **whichever** *way you look at it.* ◊ *Whichever they choose, we must accept their decision.*

whiff /wɪf/ *noun* [usually sing.] **1** ~ (of sth) a smell, especially one that you only smell for a short time: *a whiff of cigar smoke* ◊ *He caught a whiff of perfume as he leaned towards her.* **2** ~ (of sth) a slight sign or feeling of sth: *a whiff of danger/fear/success*

while /waɪl/ *conj., noun, verb*
■ *conj.* (also *formal* **whilst** /waɪlst/ especially in *BrE*) **1** during the time that sth is happening **SYN** WHEN: *We must have been burgled while we were asleep.* ◊ *Her parents died while she was still at school.* ◊ *While I was waiting at the bus stop, three buses went by in the opposite direction.* **2** at the same time as sth else is happening: *You can go swimming while I'm having lunch.* ◊ *shoes mended while you wait* **3** used to contrast two things: *While Tom's very good at science, his brother is absolutely hopeless.* **4** (used at the beginning of a sentence) although; in spite of the fact that …: *While I am willing to help, I do not have much time available.*
■ *noun* [sing.] a period of time: *They chatted* **for a while.** ◊ *I'll be back* **in a little while** (= a short time). ◊ *I haven't seen him for* **quite a while** (= a fairly long time). ◊ *They walked back together, talking* **all the while** (= all the time). **IDM** see ONCE *adv.*, WORTH *adj.*
■ *verb* **PHRV** **,while sth↔a'way** to spend time in a pleasant lazy way: *We whiled away the time reading and playing cards.*

whim /wɪm/ *noun* [C, U] a sudden wish to do or have sth,

especially when it is sth unusual or unnecessary: *He was forced to pander to* **her every whim.** ◊ *We bought the house* **on a whim.** ◊ *My duties seem to change daily* **at the whim** *of the boss.* ◊ *the whims of fashion* ◊ *She hires and fires people* **at whim.**

whim·per /'wɪmpə(r)/ *verb, noun*
■ *verb* to make low, weak crying noises; to speak in this way: [V] *The child was lost and began to whimper.* ◊ [V speech] *'Don't leave me alone,' he whimpered.*
■ *noun* a low weak cry that a person or an animal makes when they are hurt, frightened or sad

whim·si·cal /'wɪmzɪkl/ *adj.* (*written*) unusual and not serious in a way that is either amusing or annoying: *to have a whimsical sense of humour* ◊ *Much of his writing has a whimsical quality.* ▶ **whim·si·cal·ly** /-kli/ *adv.*

whimsy /'wɪmzi/ *noun* [U] a way of thinking or behaving, or a style of doing sth that is unusual and not serious, in a way that is either amusing or annoying: *All her drawings have a touch of whimsy.*

whine /waɪn/ *verb, noun*
■ *verb* **1** to complain in an annoying, crying voice: [V] *Stop whining!* ◊ [V speech] *'I want to go home,' whined Toby.* [also V that] **2** [V] to make a long high unpleasant sound because you are in pain or unhappy: *The dog whined and scratched at the door.* **3** [V] (of a machine) to make a long high unpleasant sound
■ *noun* [usually sing.] **1** a long high sound that is usually unpleasant or annoying: *the steady whine of the engine* **2** a long high cry that a child or dog makes when it is hurt or wants sth **3** a high tone of voice that you use when you complain about sth

whinge /wɪndʒ/ *verb* (*pres.part.* **whinge·ing** or **whing·ing**) [V] (*BrE, informal, disapproving*) ~ (about sb/sth) to complain in an annoying way: *She's always whingeing about how unfair everything is.* ▶ **whinge** *noun* **whin·ger** *noun*

whinny /'wɪni/ *verb* (**whin·nies, whinny·ing, whin·nied, whin·nied**) [V] (of a horse) to make a quiet NEIGH ▶ **whinny** *noun* (*pl.* **-ies**)

whip /wɪp/ *noun, verb*
■ *noun* **1** [C] a long thin piece of rope or leather, attached to a handle, used for making animals move or punishing people: *He cracked his whip and the horse leapt forward.* **2** [C] (in Britain and the US) an official in a political party who is responsible for making sure that party members attend and vote in important government debates: *the chief whip* **3** [C] (in Britain and the US) a written instruction telling members of a political party how to vote on a particular issue—see also THREE-LINE WHIP **4** [U, C] a sweet dish made from cream, eggs, sugar and fruit mixed together **IDM** **have/hold, etc. the 'whip hand (over sb/sth)** to be in a position where you have power or control over sb/sth—more at FAIR *adj.*
■ *verb* (**-pp-**) **1** [VN] to hit a person or an animal hard with a whip, as a punishment or to make them go faster or work harder **2** to move, or make sth move, quickly and suddenly or violently in a particular direction: [V, +*adv./prep.*] *A branch whipped across the car window.* ◊ *Her hair whipped around her face in the wind.* ◊ [VN] *The waves were being whipped by 50 mile an hour winds.* **3** [VN+*adv./prep.*] to remove or pull sth quickly and suddenly: *She whipped the mask off her face.* ◊ *The man whipped out a knife.* **4** [VN] ~ **sth (up)** to stir cream, etc. very quickly until it becomes stiff: *Serve the pie with whipped cream.* ◊ *Whip the egg whites up into stiff peaks.* **5** [VN] (*BrE, informal*) to steal sth **PHRV** **,whip 'through sth** (*informal*) to do or finish sth very quickly: *We whipped through customs in ten minutes.* **,whip sb/sth↔'up 1** to deliberately try and make people excited or feel strongly about sth **SYN** ROUSE: *The advertisements were designed to whip up public opinion.* ◊ *He was a speaker who could really whip up a crowd.* **2** to quickly make a meal or sth to eat: *She whipped up a delicious lunch for us in 15 minutes.*

whip·lash /'wɪplæʃ/ *noun* **1** [C, usually sing.] a hit with a whip **2** [U] = WHIPLASH INJURY: *He was very bruised and suffering from whiplash.*

b	d	f	g	h	k	l	m	n	p	r
bad	**did**	**fall**	**get**	**hat**	**cat**	**leg**	**man**	**now**	**pen**	**red**

W

'whiplash injury noun [C, U] (also **whip·lash** [U]) a neck injury caused when your head moves forward and back suddenly, especially in a car accident

whip·per·snap·per /'wɪpəsnæpə(r); AmE 'wɪpərs-/ noun (old-fashioned, informal, disapproving) a young and unimportant person who behaves in a way that others think is too confident and rude

whip·pet /'wɪpɪt/ noun a small thin dog, similar to a GREYHOUND, that can run very fast and is often used for racing

whip·ping /'wɪpɪŋ/ noun [usually sing.] an act of hitting sb with a whip, as a punishment

'whipping boy noun a person who is often blamed or punished for things other people have done

'whipping cream noun [U] cream that becomes thicker when it is stirred quickly (= WHIPPED)

whip·poor·will /'wɪpəwɪl; AmE -pərw-/ noun a brown N American bird with a cry that sounds like its name

'whip-round noun (BrE, informal) if a group of people have a **whip-round**, they all give money so they can buy sth for sb

whir (especially AmE) = WHIRR

whirl /wɜːl; AmE wɜːrl/ verb, noun
■ verb 1 [usually+adv./prep.] to move, or make sb/sth move, around quickly in a circle or in a particular direction: [V] Leaves whirled in the wind. ◊ She whirled around to face him. ◊ the whirling blades of the helicopter ◊ [VN] Tom whirled her across the dance floor. 2 [V] if your mind, thoughts, etc. **whirl**, you feel confused and excited and cannot think clearly: I couldn't sleep—my mind was whirling from all that had happened. ◊ So many thoughts whirled around in her mind.
■ noun [sing.] 1 a movement of sth spinning round and round: a whirl of dust ◊ (figurative) Her mind was in a **whirl** (= in a state of confusion or excitement). 2 a number of activities or events happening one after the other: Her life was one long whirl of parties. ◊ It's easy to get caught up in the social whirl. IDM give sth a **'whirl** (informal) to try sth to see if you like it or can do it

whirli·gig /'wɜːlɪgɪg; AmE 'wɜːrl-/ noun 1 something that is very active and always changing: the whirligig of fashion 2 (old-fashioned) a MERRY-GO-ROUND at a FAIRGROUND for children to ride on

whirl·pool /'wɜːlpuːl; AmE 'wɜːrl-/ noun 1 a place in a river or the sea where currents of water spin round very fast: (figurative) She felt she was being dragged into a whirlpool of emotion. 2 (also ,whirlpool **'bath**) a special bath or swimming pool for relaxing in, in which the water moves in circles—see also JACUZZI

whirl·wind /'wɜːlwɪnd; AmE 'wɜːrl-/ noun, adj.
■ noun 1 a very strong wind that moves very fast in a spinning movement and causes a lot of damage 2 a situation or series of events where a lot of things happen very quickly: To recover from the divorce, I threw myself into a whirlwind of activities.
■ adj. [only before noun] happening very fast: a whirlwind romance ◊ a whirlwind tour of America

whirr (especially BrE) (AmE usually **whir**) /wɜː(r)/ verb, noun
■ verb (-rr-) [V] to make a continuous low sound like the parts of a machine moving: The clock began to whirr before striking the hour.
■ noun (also **whir·ring**) [usually sing.] a continuous low sound, for example the sound made by the regular movement of a machine or the wings of a bird: the whirr of a motor ◊ There was a whirring of machinery.

whisk /wɪsk/ verb, noun
■ verb [VN] 1 to mix liquids, eggs, etc. into a stiff light mass, using a fork or special tool: Whisk the egg whites until stiff. 2 [+adv./prep.] to take sb/sth somewhere very quickly and suddenly: Jamie whisked her off to Paris for the weekend. ◊ The waiter whisked away the plates before we had finished.
■ noun a kitchen UTENSIL (= a tool) for stirring eggs, etc. very fast: an electric whisk—picture at KITCHEN

whis·ker /'wɪskə(r)/ noun 1 [C] any of the long stiff hairs that grow near the mouth of a cat, rat, etc. 2 (whiskers)

[pl.] (old-fashioned or humorous) the hair growing on a man's face, especially on his cheeks and chin IDM **be, come, etc. within a whisker of sth/doing sth** (BrE) to almost do sth: They came within a whisker of being killed. **by a 'whisker** by a very small amount—more at CAT—picture on page A6

whis·kered /'wɪskəd; AmE -kərd/ (also **whis·kery** /'wɪskəri/) adj. having whiskers

whisky (BrE) (AmE, IrishE **whis·key**) /'wɪski/ noun (pl. **whis·kies, whis·keys**) 1 [U, C] a strong alcoholic drink made from MALTED grain. It is sometimes drunk with water and/or ice: a barrel/bottle of whisky ◊ Scotch whisky ◊ highland whiskies 2 [C] a glass of whisky: a whisky and soda ◊ Two whiskies, please.—see also SCOTCH

whis·per /'wɪspə(r)/ verb, noun
■ verb 1 to speak very quietly to sb so that other people cannot hear what you are saying: [V] Don't you know it's rude to whisper? ◊ What are you two whispering about? ◊ [V speech] 'Can you meet me tonight?' he whispered. ◊ [VN] She leaned over and whispered something in his ear. ◊ [V that] He whispered to me that he was afraid. 2 [often passive] to say or suggest sth about sb/sth in a private or secret way: [VN that] It was whispered that he would soon die and he did. [also V that] 3 [V] (written) (of leaves, the wind, etc.) to make a soft, quiet sound: A warm breeze whispered through the trees.
■ noun 1 a low quiet voice or the sound it makes: They spoke **in whispers**. ◊ Her voice dropped to a whisper.—see also STAGE WHISPER 2 (also **whis·per·ing**) (written) a soft sound: I could hear the whispering of the sea. 3 a piece of news that is spread by being talked about but may not be true SYN RUMOUR: I've heard whispers that he's leaving.

'whispering campaign noun an attempt to damage sb's reputation by saying unpleasant things about them and passing this information from person to person

whist /wɪst/ noun [U] a card game for two pairs of players in which each pair tries to win the most cards

whis·tle /'wɪsl/ noun, verb
■ noun 1 a small metal or plastic tube that you blow to make a loud high sound, used to attract attention or as a signal: The referee blew the whistle to stop the game.—see also TIN WHISTLE 2 the sound made by blowing a whistle: He scored the winning goal just seconds before the final whistle. 3 the sound that you make by forcing your breath out when your lips are closed: a shrill whistle—see also WOLF WHISTLE 4 the high loud sound produced by air or steam being forced through a small opening, or by sth moving quickly through the air IDM see BLOW v., CLEAN adj.
■ verb 1 to make a high sound or a musical tune by forcing your breath out when your lips are closed: [VN] to whistle a tune [V] He whistled in amazement. ◊ The crowd booed and whistled as the player came onto the field. ◊ She whistled to the dog to come back. 2 [V] to make a high sound by blowing into a whistle: The referee whistled for a foul. 3 [V] (of a KETTLE or other machine) to make a high sound: The kettle began to whistle. ◊ The microphone was making a strange whistling sound. 4 [V+adv./prep.] to move quickly, making a high sound: The wind whistled down the chimney. ◊ A bullet whistled past his ear. 5 [V] (of a bird) to make a high sound IDM **sb can 'whistle for sth** (BrE, spoken) used to say that you are not going to give sb sth that they have asked for: If he wants his money he can whistle for it—I'm broke!

'whistle-blower noun (used especially in newspapers) a person who informs people in authority or the public that the company they work for is doing sth wrong or illegal

'whistle-stop adj. [only before noun] visiting a lot of different places in a very short time: to go on a **whistle-stop tour** of Europe ◊ politicians on a whistle-stop election campaign

Whit /wɪt/ adj. connected with Whitsun: Whit Monday

whit /wɪt/ noun [sing.] (old-fashioned) (usually in negative sentences) a very small amount IDM **not a 'whit | not one 'whit** not at all; not the smallest amount

white /waɪt/ adj., noun

s	t	v	z	ʃ	ʒ	tʃ	dʒ	θ	ð	ŋ
see	tea	van	zoo	shoe	vision	chain	jam	thin	this	sing

■ *adj.* (**whiter**, **whit·est**) **1** having the colour of fresh snow or milk: *a crisp white shirt* ◊ *white bread* ◊ *a set of perfect white teeth* ◊ *His hair was as white as snow.* ◊ *The horse was almost pure white in colour.* **2** belonging to, or connected with a race of people who have pale skin: *white middle-class families* ◊ *She writes about her experiences as a black girl in a predominantly white city.* **3** (of the skin) pale because of emotion or illness: *white with anger/shock/fear* ◊ *She went white as a sheet when she heard the news.* **4** (*BrE*) (of tea or coffee) with milk added: *Two white coffees, please.* ◊ *Do you take your coffee black or white?*—compare BLACK ▶ **white·ness** *noun* [U, sing.]

■ *noun* **1** [U] the colour of fresh snow or milk: *the pure white of the newly painted walls* ◊ *She was dressed all in white.* **2** [C, usually pl.] a member of a race or people who have pale skin **3** [U, C] white wine: *Would you like red or white?* ◊ *a very dry white* **4** [C, U] the part of an egg that surrounds the YOLK (= the yellow part): *Use the whites of two eggs.* **5** [C, usually pl.] the white part of the eye: *The whites of her eyes were bloodshot.* **6** (**whites**) [pl.] white clothes, sheets, etc. when they are separated from coloured ones to be washed: (*BrE*) *Don't wash whites and coloureds together.* ◊ (*AmE*) *Don't wash whites and colors together.* **7** (**whites**) [pl.] white clothes worn for playing some sports: *cricket/tennis whites* IDM see BLACK *n.*

white·bait /ˈwaɪtbeɪt/ *noun* [pl.] very small young fish of several types that are fried and eaten whole

white-board /ˈwaɪtbɔːd; *AmE* -bɔːrd/ *noun* a large board with a smooth white surface that teachers, etc. write on with special pens—compare BLACKBOARD

white-bread *adj.* [only before noun] (*AmE, informal*) ordinary and traditional: *a white-bread town*

white·caps /ˈwaɪtkæps/ *noun* [pl.] (*AmE*) = WHITE HORSES

white-ˈcollar *adj.* [usually before noun] working in an office, rather than in a factory, etc.; connected with work in offices: *white-collar workers* ◊ *a white-collar job* ◊ *white-collar crime* (= in which office workers steal from their company, etc.)—compare BLUE-COLLAR

white ˈdwarf *noun* (*astronomy*) a small star that is near the end of its life and is very DENSE (= solid and heavy)

white ˈelephant *noun* [usually sing.] a thing that is useless and no longer needed, although it may have cost a lot of money: *The new office block has become an expensive white elephant.* ORIGIN From the story that in Siam (now Thailand), the king would give a white elephant as a present to somebody that he did not like. That person would have to spend all their money on looking after the rare animal.

white ˈflag *noun* [usually sing.] a sign that you accept defeat and wish to stop fighting: *to raise/show/wave the white flag*

white goods *noun* [pl.] (*BrE*) large pieces of electrical equipment in the house, such as WASHING MACHINES, etc.

White·hall /ˈwaɪthɔːl/ *noun* [U] **1** [U] a street in London where there are many government offices **2** [sing.+ sing./pl. *v.*] a way of referring to the British Government: *Whitehall are/is refusing to comment.*

white ˈheat *noun* [U] the very high temperature at which metal looks white

white ˈhope *noun* [sing.] (*informal*) a person who is expected to bring success to a team, an organization, etc: *He was once the great white hope of British boxing.*

white ˈhorses (*BrE*) (*AmE* **white·caps**) *noun* [pl.] waves in the sea or ocean with white tops on them

white-ˈhot *adj.* **1** (of metal or sth burning) so hot that it looks white **2** very strong and INTENSE

the ˈWhite House *noun* [sing.] **1** the official home of the President of the US in Washington, DC **2** the US President and his or her officials: *The White House has issued a statement.* ◊ *White House advisers/aides*

white ˈknight *noun* a person or an organization that rescues a company from being bought by another company at too low a price

white-ˈknuckle ride *noun* a ride at a FAIRGROUND that makes you feel very excited and frightened at the same time

white ˈlie *noun* a harmless or small lie, especially one that you tell to avoid hurting sb

white ˈlight *noun* [U] ordinary light that is colourless

white ˈmeat *noun* [U] **1** meat that is pale in colour when it has been cooked, such as chicken, PORK and VEAL—compare RED MEAT **2** pale meat from the breast of a chicken or other bird that has been cooked

whiten /ˈwaɪtn/ *verb* to become white or whiter; to make sth white or whiter: [V] *He gripped the wheel until his knuckles whitened.* ◊ [VN] *Snow had whitened the tops of the trees.*

white ˈnoise *noun* [U] unpleasant noise, like the noise that comes from a television or radio that is turned on but not TUNED IN

white-out *noun* weather conditions in which there is so much snow or cloud that it is impossible to see anything—see also WITEOUT

White ˈPaper *noun* (in Britain) a government report that gives information about sth and explains government plans before a new law is introduced—compare GREEN PAPER

white ˈsauce *noun* [U] a thick sauce made from butter, flour and milk

white ˈspirit *noun* [U] (*BrE*) a colourless liquid made from petrol/gas, used as a cleaning substance or to make paint thinner

white ˈtie *noun* a man's white BOW TIE, also used to mean very formal evening dress for men: *dressed in white tie and tails*

white-ˈtie *adj.* (of social occasions) very formal, when men are expected to wear white BOW TIES and jackets with TAILS: *Is it a white-tie affair?*

white·wash /ˈwaɪtwɒʃ; *AmE* -wɑːʃ; -wɔːʃ/ *noun, verb*

■ *noun* **1** [U] a mixture of chalk or LIME and water, used for painting houses and walls white **2** [U, sing.] (*disapproving*) an attempt to hide unpleasant facts about sb/sth SYN COVER-UP: *The opposition claimed the report was a whitewash.* **3** [C, usually sing.] (*informal*) a complete defeat in a sports game: *a 7-0 whitewash* ◊ *a whitewash victory*

■ *verb* [VN] **1** to cover sth such as a wall with whitewash **2** (*disapproving*) to try to hide unpleasant facts about sb/sth; to try to make sth seem better than it is: *His wife had wanted to whitewash his reputation after he died.* **3** (*especially BrE*) (in sport) to defeat an opponent easily

white ˈwater *noun* [U] **1** a part of a river that looks white because the water is moving very fast over rocks: *a stretch of white water* ◊ *white-water rafting* **2** a part of the sea or ocean that looks white because it is very rough and the waves are high

white ˈwedding *noun* a traditional wedding, especially in a church, at which the BRIDE wears a white dress

white ˈwine *noun* **1** [U, C] pale yellow wine: *a bottle of dry/sweet white wine* ◊ *chilled white wine* **2** [C] a glass of white wine—compare RED WINE, ROSÉ

whither /ˈwɪðə(r)/ *adv., conj.* **1** (*old use*) where; to which: *Whither should they go?* ◊ *They did not know whither they should go.* ◊ *the place whither they were sent* **2** (*formal*) used to ask what is likely to happen to sth in the future: *Whither modern architecture?*

whit·ing /ˈwaɪtɪŋ/ *noun* [C, U] (*pl.* **whit·ing**) a small sea fish with white flesh that is used for food

whit·ish /ˈwaɪtɪʃ/ *adj.* fairly white in colour: *a bird with a whitish throat*

Whit·sun /ˈwɪtsn/ *noun* [U, C] the 7th Sunday after Easter and the days close to it

Whit ˈSunday *noun* [U, C] (*BrE*) = PENTECOST

whit·tle /ˈwɪtl/ *verb* [VN] **~ A (from B)** | **~ B (into A)** to form a piece of wood, etc. into a particular shape by cutting small pieces from it: *He whittled a simple toy from the piece of wood.* ◊ *He whittled the piece of wood into a simple toy.* PHRV **whittle sth ↔ aˈway** to make sth gradually decrease in value or amount: *Inflation has steadily whittled away their savings.* **whittle sth ↔ ˈdown** to reduce the size or number of sth: *I finally managed to whittle down the names on the list to only five.*

W

æ	ɑː	e	ɜː	ə	ɪ	iː	i	ɒ	ɔː	ʌ	ʊ	u	uː
cat	father	ten	bird	about	sit	see	many	got	saw	cup	put	actual	too
								(BrE)					

whizz (*especially BrE*) (also **whiz** especially in *AmE*) /wɪz/ *verb, noun*

■ *verb* [V+adv. / prep.] **1** to move very quickly, making a high continuous sound: *A bullet whizzed past my ear.* ◊ *He whizzed down the road on his motorbike.* **2** to do sth very quickly: *She whizzed through the work and was finished before lunch.*

■ *noun* (*informal*) a person who is very good at sth: *She's a whizz at crosswords.*

'whizz-kid (*especially BrE*) (*AmE* usually **'whiz-kid**) *noun* (*informal*) a person who is very good and successful at sth, especially at a young age: *financial whizz-kids*

who /hu:/ *pron.* **1** used in questions to ask about the name, identity or function of one or more people: *Who is that woman?* ◊ *I wonder who that letter was from.* ◊ *Who are you phoning?* ◊ *Who's the money for?* **2** used to show which person or people you mean: *The people who called yesterday want to buy the house.* ◊ *The people (who) we met in France have sent us a card.* **3** used to give more information about sb: *Mrs Smith, who has a lot of teaching experience at junior level, will be joining the school in September.* ◊ *And then Mary, who we had been talking about earlier, walked in.*—compare WHOM **IDM** **who am 'I, who are 'you, etc. to do sth?** used to ask what right or authority sb has to do sth: *Who are you to tell me I can't park here?* **who's** 'who people's names, jobs, status, etc: *You'll soon find out who's who in the office.*

WHO /ˌdʌbljuː eɪtʃ ˈəʊ; *AmE* ˈoʊ/ *abbr.* World Health Organization (an international organization that aims to fight and control disease)

whoa /wəʊ; *AmE* woʊ/ *exclamation* used as a command to a horse, etc. to make it stop or stand still

who'd /hu:d/ *short form* **1** who had **2** who would

who·dun·nit (*BrE*) (also **who·dun·it** *AmE, BrE*) /ˌhuːˈdʌnɪt/ *noun* (*informal*) a story, play, etc. about a murder in which you do not know who did the murder until the end

who·ever /huːˈevə(r)/ *pron.* **1** the person or people who; any person who: *Whoever says that is a liar.* ◊ *Send it to whoever is in charge of sales.* **2** used to say that it does not matter who, since the result will be the same: *Come out of there, whoever you are.* ◊ *I don't want to see them, whoever they are.* **3** used in questions to mean 'who', expressing surprise: *Whoever heard of such a thing!*

whole /həʊl; *AmE* hoʊl/ *adj., noun*

■ *adj.* **1** [only before noun] full; complete: *He spent the whole day writing.* ◊ *We drank a whole bottle each.* ◊ *The whole country* (= all the people in it) *mourned her death.* ◊ *Let's forget the* **whole thing.** ◊ *She wasn't telling the* **whole truth.** **2** [only before noun] used to emphasize how large or important sth is: *We offer a whole variety of weekend breaks.* ◊ *I can't afford it—that's* **the whole point.** **3** not broken or damaged: *Owls usually swallow their prey whole* (= without chewing it). ⇨ note at HALF ▶ **whole·ness** *noun* [U]—see also WHOLLY **IDM** Most idioms containing **whole** are at the entries for the nouns and verbs in the idioms, for example **go the whole hog** is at **hog.** **a 'whole lot** (*informal*) very much; a lot: *I'm feeling a whole lot better.* **a 'whole lot (of sth)** (*informal*) a large number or amount: *There were a whole lot of people I didn't know.* ◊ *I lost a whole lot of money.* **the ˌwhole 'lot** everything; all of sth: *I've sold the whole lot.*

■ *noun* **1** [C] a thing that is complete in itself: *Four quarters make a whole.* ◊ *The subjects of the curriculum form a coherent whole.* **2** [sing.] **the ~ of sth** all that there is of sth: *The effects will last for the whole of his life.* ⇨ note at HALF **IDM** **as a 'whole** as one thing or piece and not as separate parts: *The festival will be great for our city and for the country as a whole.* **on the whole** considering everything; in general: *On the whole, I'm in favour of the idea.*

whole·food /ˈhəʊlfuːd; *AmE* ˈhoʊl-/ *noun* [U] (also **whole·foods** [pl.]) food that is considered healthy because it is in a simple form, has not been REFINED, and does not contain artificial substances

whole·grain /ˈhəʊlɡreɪn; *AmE* ˈhoʊl-/ *adj.* made with or containing whole grains, for example of wheat: *wholegrain mustard*

whole·heart·ed /ˌhəʊlˈhɑːtɪd; *AmE* ˌhoʊlˈhɑːrtəd/ *adj.* (*approving*) complete and enthusiastic: *The plan was given wholehearted support.* ▶ **whole·heart·ed·ly** *adv.*: *to agree wholeheartedly*

whole·meal /ˈhəʊlmiːl; *AmE* ˈhoʊl-/ (also **whole·wheat**) *adj.* containing whole grains of wheat, etc. including the HUSK: *wholemeal bread / flour*

'whole note *noun* (*AmE, music*) = SEMIBREVE

ˌwhole 'number *noun* (*mathematics*) a number that consists of one or more units, with no FRACTIONS (= parts of a number less than one)

whole·sale /ˈhəʊlseɪl; *AmE* ˈhoʊl-/ *adj.* [only before noun] **1** connected with goods that are bought and sold in large quantities, especially so they can be sold again to make a profit: *wholesale goods / prices*—compare RETAIL **2** (especially of sth bad) happening or done to a very large number of people or things: *the wholesale slaughter of innocent people* ▶ **whole·sale** *adv.*: *We buy the building materials wholesale.* ◊ *These young people die wholesale from heroin overdoses.*

whole·sal·ing /ˈhəʊlseɪlɪŋ; *AmE* ˈhoʊl-/ *noun* [U] the business of buying and selling goods in large quantities, especially so they can be sold again to make a profit—compare RETAILING ▶ **whole·saler** *noun*: *fruit and vegetable wholesalers*

whole·some /ˈhəʊlsəm; *AmE* ˈhoʊl-/ *adj.* **1** good for your health: *fresh, wholesome food* **2** morally good; having a good moral influence: *It was clean wholesome fun.* **OPP** UNWHOLESOME ▶ **whole·some·ness** *noun* [U]

'whole step *noun* (*AmE, music*) = TONE (7)

whole·wheat /ˈhəʊlwiːt; *AmE* ˈhoʊl-/ *adj.* = WHOLEMEAL

who'll /hu:l/ *short form* who will

whol·ly /ˈhəʊlli; *AmE* ˈhoʊlli/ *adv.* (*formal*) completely; TOTALLY: *wholly inappropriate behaviour* ◊ *The government is not wholly to blame for the recession.* ◊ *The company is a wholly-owned subsidiary of a large multinational.*

whom /hu:m/ *pron.* (*formal*) used instead of 'who' as the object of a verb or preposition: *Whom did they invite?* ◊ *To whom should I write?* ◊ *The author whom you criticized in your review has written a reply.* ◊ *Her mother, in whom she confided, said she would support her unconditionally.*

GRAMMAR POINT

whom

Whom is not used very often in spoken English. **Who** is usually used as the object pronoun, especially in questions: *Who did you invite to the party?*

The use of **whom** as the pronoun after prepositions is very formal: *To whom should I address the letter?* ◊ *He asked me with whom I had discussed it.* In spoken English it is much more natural to use **who** and put the preposition at the end of the sentence: *Who should I address the letter to?* ◊ *He asked me who I had discussed it with.*

In defining relative clauses the object pronoun **whom** is not often used. You can either use **who** or **that**, or leave out the pronoun completely: *The family (who / that / whom) I met at the airport were very kind.*

In non-defining relative clauses **who** or, more formally, **whom** (but not **that**) is used and the pronoun cannot be left out: *Our doctor, who / whom we all liked very much, retired last week.* This pattern is not used very much in spoken English.

---

whom·ever /ˌhuːmˈevə(r)/, **whom·so·ever** /ˌhuːmsəʊˈevə(r); *AmE* -soʊ-/ *pron.* (*literary*) used instead of 'whoever' as the object of a verb or preposition: *He was free to marry whomever he chose.*

whoop /wu:p; hu:p/ *noun, verb*

■ *noun* a loud cry expressing joy, excitement, etc: *whoops of delight / laughter*

■ *verb* [V] to shout loudly because you are happy or excited **IDM** ,whoop it 'up /wu:p; *AmE* wʊp/ (*informal*) **1** to enjoy yourself very much with a noisy group of people **2** (*AmE*) to make people excited or enthusiastic about sth

whoo·pee /wʊˈpiː/ *exclamation, noun*
■ *exclamation* used to express happiness: *Whoopee, we've won!*
■ *noun* [U] **IDM** **make 'whoopee** (*old-fashioned, informal*) to celebrate in a noisy way

whoop·ing cough /ˈhuːpɪŋ kɒf; *AmE* kɔːf/ *noun* [U] an infectious disease, especially of children, that makes them cough and have difficulty breathing

whoops /wʊps/ *exclamation* **1** used when sb has almost had an accident, broken sth, etc: *Whoops! Careful, you almost spilt coffee everywhere.* **2** used when you have done sth embarrassing, said sth rude by accident, told a secret, etc: *Whoops, you weren't supposed to hear that.*

whoosh /wʊʃ; wuːʃ/ *noun, verb*
■ *noun* [usually sing.] (*informal*) the sudden movement and sound of air or water rushing past: *a whoosh of water/air* ◊ *There was a whoosh as everything went up in flames.*
■ *verb* [V+adv./prep.] (*informal*) to move very quickly with the sound of air or water rushing

whop·per /ˈwɒpə(r); *AmE* ˈwɑːp-/ *noun* (*informal*) **1** something that is very big for its type: *Pete has caught a whopper* (= a large fish). **2** a lie: *She's told some whoppers about her past.*

whop·ping /ˈwɒpɪŋ; *AmE* ˈwɑːp-/ (also **'whopping great**) *adj.* [only before noun] (*informal*) very big: *The company made a whopping 75 million dollar loss.*

whore /hɔː(r)/ *noun* **1** (*old-fashioned*) a female prostitute (= a woman who has sex with men for money) **2** (⚠) an offensive word to refer to a woman who has sex with a lot of men

who're /ˈhuːə(r)/ *short form* who are

whore·house /ˈhɔːhaʊs; *AmE* ˈhɔːrh-/ *noun* (*old-fashioned*) a BROTHEL (= a place where people pay to have sex)

whor·ing /ˈhɔːrɪŋ/ *noun* [U] (*old-fashioned*) the activity of having sex with a prostitute

whorl /wɜːl; *AmE* wɜːrl/ *noun* **1** a pattern made by a curved line that forms a rough circle, with smaller circles inside bigger ones: *the whorls on your fingertips* **2** (*technical*) a ring of leaves, flowers, etc. around the stem of a plant

who's /huːz/ *short form* **1** who is **2** who has

whose /huːz/ *det., pron.* **1** used in questions to ask who sth belongs to: *Whose house is that?* ◊ *I wonder whose this is.* **2** used to say which person or thing you mean: *He's a man whose opinion I respect.* ◊ *It's the house whose door's painted red.* **3** used to give more information about a person or thing: *Isobel, whose brother he was, had heard the joke before.*

who·so·ever /ˌhuːsəʊˈevə(r); *AmE* -soʊ-/ *pron.* (*old use*) = WHOEVER

who've /huːv/ *short form* who have

whup /wʌp/ *verb* [VN] (*informal, especially AmE*) to defeat sb easily in a game, a fight, an election, etc.

why /waɪ/ *adv., exclamation, noun*
■ *adv.* **1** used in questions to ask the reason for or purpose of sth: *Why were you late?* ◊ *Tell me why you did it.* ◊ *'I would like you to go.' 'Why me?'* ◊ (*spoken*) *Why oh why do people keep leaving the door open?* **2** used in questions to suggest that it is not necessary to do sth: *Why get upset just because you got one bad grade?* ◊ *Why bother to write? We'll see him tomorrow.* **3** used to give or talk about a reason: *That's why I left so early.* ◊ *I know you did it—I just want to know why.* ◊ *The reason why the injection needs repeating every year is that the virus changes.* **IDM** **why 'ever** used in questions to mean 'why', expressing surprise: *Why ever didn't you tell us before?* ,**why 'not?** used to make or agree to a suggestion: *Why not write to her?* ◊ *'Let's eat out.' 'Why not?'* ◊ *Why don't we go together?*
■ *exclamation* (*old-fashioned* or *AmE*) used to express surprise, lack of patience, etc: *Why Jane, it's you!* ◊ *Why, it's easy—a child could do it!*

■ *noun* **IDM** **the ,whys and (the) 'wherefores** the reasons for sth: *I had no intention of going into the whys and the wherefores of the situation.*

WI *abbr.* **1** West Indies **2** /ˌdʌbljuː ˈaɪ/ Women's Institute. The WI is a British women's organization in which groups of women meet regularly to take part in various activities.

wick /wɪk/ *noun* **1** the piece of string in the centre of a candle which you light so that the candle burns **2** the piece of woven material in an oil lamp which soaks up the oil and which you light so that the lamp burns **IDM** **get on sb's 'wick** (*BrE, informal*) to annoy sb

wicked /ˈwɪkɪd/ *adj., noun*
■ *adj.* (**wick·ed·er, wick·ed·est**) **HELP** You can also use **more wicked** and **most wicked**. **1** morally bad **SYN** EVIL: *a wicked man/deed* ◊ *stories about a wicked witch* **2** (*informal*) slightly bad but in a way that is amusing and/or attractive **SYN** MISCHIEVOUS: *a wicked grin* ◊ *Jane has a wicked sense of humour.* **3** dangerous, harmful or powerful: *He has a wicked punch.* ◊ *a wicked-looking knife* ◊ *The rejection was a wicked blow to her pride.* **4** (*slang*) very good: *This song's wicked.* ► **wick·ed·ly** *adv.*: *Martin grinned wickedly.* ◊ *a wickedly funny comedy* ◊ *a wickedly sharp blade* **wick·ed·ness** *noun* [U]
■ *noun* (**the wicked**) [pl.] people who are wicked **IDM** (**there's**) **no peace/rest for the 'wicked** (*usually humorous*) used when sb is complaining that they have a lot of work to do

wicker /ˈwɪkə(r)/ *noun* [U] thin sticks of wood woven together to make baskets, furniture, etc: *a wicker chair*

wick·er·work /ˈwɪkəwɜːk; *AmE* ˈwɪkərwɜːrk/ *noun* [U] baskets, furniture, etc. made from wicker

wicket /ˈwɪkɪt/ *noun* (in cricket) **1** either of the two sets of three upright sticks (called STUMPS) with pieces of wood (called BAILS) lying across the top. The BOWLER tries to hit the wicket with the ball.—picture on page 1250 **2** the area of ground between the two wickets **IDM** **keep 'wicket** to act as a WICKETKEEPER—more at STICKY *adv.*

'wicket gate *noun* a small gate, especially one at the side of a larger one

wicket·keep·er /ˈwɪkɪtkiːpə(r)/ (also *BrE informal* **keep·er**) *noun* (in cricket) a player who stands behind the WICKET in order to stop or catch the ball—picture on page 1250

wide /waɪd/ *adj., adv., noun*
■ *adj.* (**wider, wid·est**)
> FROM ONE SIDE TO THE OTHER | **1** measuring a lot from one side to the other: *a wide river/road* ◊ *Sam has a wide mouth.* ◊ *a jacket with wide lapels* ◊ *Her face broke into a wide grin.* **OPP** NARROW—see also WIDTH **2** measuring a particular distance from one side to the other: *How wide is that stream?* ◊ *It's about 2 metres wide.* ◊ *The road was just wide enough for two vehicles to pass.*
> LARGE NUMBER/AMOUNT | **3** including a large number or variety of different people or things; covering a large area: *a wide range/choice/variety of goods* ◊ *Her music appeals to a wide audience.* ◊ *Jenny has a wide circle of friends.* ◊ *a manager with experience of industry* ◊ *It's the best job in the whole wide world.* ◊ *The incident has received wide coverage in the press.* ◊ *The festival attracts people from a wide area.*
> DIFFERENCE/GAP | **4** very big: *There are wide variations in prices.*
> GENERAL | **5** (only used in the comparative and superlative) general; not only looking at details: *wider issues/aims/problems* ◊ *We are talking about education in its widest sense.* ◊ *We need to consider the problem of vandalism within a wider context.*
> EYES | **6** fully open: *She stared at him with wide eyes.*
> NOT CLOSE | **7** ~ (of sth) far from the point aimed at: *Her shot was wide (of the target).*
> -WIDE | **8** (in adjectives and adverbs) happening or existing in the whole of a country, etc: *a nationwide search* ◊ *We need to act on a Europe-wide scale.*
> **IDM** **give sb/sth a wide 'berth** to not go too near sb/sth; to avoid sb/sth: *He gave the dog a wide berth.* **wide of the**

'mark not accurate: *Their predictions turned out to be wide of the mark.*

■ *adv.* (comparative **wider**, no *superlative*) as far or fully as possible: *The door was **wide** open.* ◇ *He stood with his legs wide apart.* ◇ *In a few seconds she was **wide awake**.* ◇ *Open your mouth wide.* **IDM** see CAST *v.*, FAR *adv.*

■ *noun* (*sport*) a ball that has been BOWLED (= thrown) where the BATSMAN or BATTER cannot reach it

---

WHICH WORD?
wide / broad　(?)

These adjectives are frequently used with the following nouns:

wide ~	**broad ~**
street	shoulders
river	back
area	smile
range	range
variety	agreement
choice	outline

Wide is the word most commonly used to talk about something that measures a long distance from one side to the other. **Broad** is more often used to talk about parts of the body. It is used in more formal or written language to describe the features of the countryside, etc.: *a broad river* ◇ *a broad stretch of meadowland*.
Both **wide** and **broad** can be used to describe something that includes a large variety of different people or things: *a wide/broad range of products.* **Broad**, but not **wide**, can be used to mean 'general' or 'not detailed': *All of us are in broad agreement on this matter.*

,wide-angle 'lens *noun* a camera LENS that can give a wider view than a normal lens

'wide boy *noun* (*BrE, informal, disapproving*) a man who makes money in dishonest ways

,wide-'eyed *adj.* (*written*) **1** with your eyes fully open because of fear, surprise, etc: *She stared at him in wide-eyed amazement.* **2** having little experience and therefore very willing to believe, trust or accept sb/sth **SYN** NAIVE: *wide-eyed innocence*

wide·ly /'waɪdli/ *adv.* **1** by a lot of people; in or to many places: *a widely held belief* ◇ *The idea is now widely accepted.* ◇ *He has travelled widely in Asia.* ◇ *Her books are widely read* (= a lot of people read them). ◇ *He's an educated, widely-read man* (= he has read a lot of books). **2** to a large degree; a lot: *Standards vary widely.*

widen /'waɪdn/ *verb* **1** to become wider; to make sth wider: [V] *Her eyes widened in surprise.* ◇ *Here the stream widens into a river.* ◇ [VN] *They may have to widen the road to cope with the increase in traffic.* **2** to become larger in degree or range; to make sth larger in degree or range: [V] *the widening gap between rich and poor* ◇ [VN] *We plan to widen the scope of our existing activities by offering more language courses.* ◇ *The legislation will be widened to include all firearms.*

,wide-'ranging *adj.* (*written*) including or dealing with a large number of different subjects or areas: *The commission has been given wide-ranging powers.* ◇ *a wide-ranging discussion*

wide·spread /'waɪdspred/ *adj.* existing or happening over a large area or among many people: *widespread damage/confusion* ◇ *The plan received widespread support throughout the country.*

widget /'wɪdʒɪt/ *noun* (*informal*) used to refer to any small device that you do not know the name of

widow /'wɪdəʊ; *AmE* 'wɪdoʊ/ *noun, verb*
■ *noun* a woman whose husband has died and who has not married again: *She gets a widow's pension.*
■ *verb* [VN] (**be widowed**) if sb **is widowed**, their husband or wife has died: *She was widowed when she was 35.*
▶ **widowed** *adj.*: *his widowed father*

wid·ow·er /'wɪdəʊə(r); *AmE* 'wɪdoʊ-/ *noun* a man whose wife has died and who has not married again

widow·hood /'wɪdəʊhʊd; *AmE* 'wɪdoʊ-/ *noun* [U] the state or period of being a widow or widower

width /wɪdθ; wɪtθ/ *noun* **1** [U,C] the measurement from one side of sth to the other; how wide sth is: *It's about 10 metres **in width**.* ◇ *The terrace runs **the full width** of the house.* ◇ *The carpet is available in different widths.* **2** [C] a piece of material of a particular width: *You'll need two widths of fabric for each curtain.* **3** [C] the distance between the two long sides of a swimming pool: *How many widths can you swim?*—compare LENGTH

width·ways /'wɪdθweɪz; 'wɪtθ-/ *adv.* along the width and not the length: *Cut the cake in half widthways.*—compare LENGTHWAYS

wield /wiːld/ *verb* [VN] **1** to have and use power, authority, etc: *She wields enormous power within the party.* **2** to hold sth, ready to use it as a weapon or tool **SYN** BRANDISH: *He was wielding a large knife.*

wie·ner /'wiːnə(r)/ *noun* (*AmE*) = FRANKFURTER

wife /waɪf/ *noun* (*pl.* **wives** /waɪvz/) the woman that a man is married to; a married woman: *the doctor's wife* ◇ *She's his second wife.* ◇ *an increase in the number of working wives*—see also FISHWIFE, HOUSEWIFE, MIDWIFE **IDM** see HUSBAND *n.*, OLD, WORLD

wife·ly /'waɪfli/ *adj.* (*old-fashioned or humorous*) typical or expected of a wife: *wifely duties/loyalty*

wig /wɪg/ *noun* a piece of artificial hair that is worn on the head, for example to hide the fact that a person is BALD, to cover sb's own hair, or by a judge and some other lawyers in some courts of law

wig·gle /'wɪgl/ *verb, noun*
■ *verb* (*informal*) to move from side to side or up and down in short quick movements; to make sth move in this way: [V] *Her bottom wiggled as she walked past.* ◇ [VN] *He removed his shoes and wiggled his toes.*
■ *noun* a small movement from side to side or up and down

wig·gly /'wɪgli/ *adj.* (*informal*) (of a line) having many curves in it; **SYN** WAVY

wig·wam /'wɪgwæm; *AmE* -wɑːm/ *noun* a type of tent, shaped like a DOME or CONE, used by Native Americans in the past—see also TEPEE

wild /waɪld/ *adj., noun*
■ *adj.* (**wild·er, wild·est**)
‣ ANIMALS/PLANTS **1** living or growing in natural conditions; not kept in a house or on a farm: *wild animals/flowers* ◇ *a wild rabbit* ◇ *wild strawberries* ◇ *The plants **grow wild** along the banks of rivers.*
‣ SCENERY/LAND **2** in its natural state; not changed by people: *wild moorland/mountains* ◇ *The island is a wild and lonely place.*
‣ OUT OF CONTROL **3** lacking discipline or control: *The boy is wild and completely out of control.* ◇ *He had a wild look in his eyes.*
‣ FEELINGS **4** full of very strong feeling: *wild laughter/applause/cheers* ◇ *a wild and romantic love affair* ◇ *The crowd **went wild**.* ◇ *It makes me wild* (= very angry) *to see such waste.*
‣ NOT SENSIBLE **5** not carefully planned; not sensible or accurate: *He made a wild guess at the answer.* ◇ *wild accusations/rumours*
‣ EXCITING **6** (*informal*) very good, enjoyable or exciting: *We had a wild time in New York.*
‣ ENTHUSIASTIC **7** ~ **about sb/sth** (*informal*) very enthusiastic about sb/sth: *She's totally wild about him.* ◇ *I'm not wild about the idea.*
‣ WEATHER/SEA **8** affected by storms and strong winds: *a wild night* ◇ *The sea was wild.*
▶ **wild·ness** *noun* [U]—see also WILDLY
IDM **beyond your wildest 'dreams** far more, better, etc. than you could ever have imagined or hoped for **run 'wild 1** to grow or develop freely without any control: *The ivy has run wild.* ◇ *Let your **imagination run wild** and be creative.* **2** if children or animals **run wild**, they behave as they like because nobody is controlling them: *Those boys have been allowed to run wild.* **wild 'horses**

W

would not drag, make, etc. sb (do sth) used to say that nothing would prevent sb from doing sth or make them do sth they do not want to do—more at sow *v.*

■ *noun* **1 (the wild)** [sing.] a natural environment that is not controlled by people: *The bird is too tame now to survive in the wild.* **2 (the wilds)** [pl.] areas of a country far from towns or cities, where few people live: *the wilds of Alaska* ◇ *(humorous) They live on a farm somewhere out in the wilds.*

ˌwild ˈboar *noun* = BOAR

ˈwild card *noun* **1** (in card games) a card that has no value of its own and takes the value of any card that the player chooses **2** *(sport)* an opportunity for sb to play in a competition when they have not qualified in the usual way; a player who enters a competition in this way **3** *(computing)* a symbol that has no meaning of its own and can represent any letter **4** a person or thing whose behaviour or effect is difficult to predict

wild·cat /ˈwaɪldkæt/ *adj., verb*

■ *adj.* [only before noun] **1** a **wildcat strike** happens suddenly and without the official support of a trade union **2** (of a business or project) that has not been carefully planned and that will probably not be successful; that does not follow normal standards and methods

■ *verb* [V] *(AmE)* to look for oil in a place where nobody has found any yet ▶ **wild·cat·ter** *noun*

wilde·beest /ˈwɪldəbiːst/ *noun (pl.* **wilde·beest)** (also **gnu**) a large ANTELOPE (= an African animal like a. deer) with curved horns: *a herd of wildebeest*

wil·der·ness /ˈwɪldənəs; *AmE* -dərn-/ *noun* [usually sing.] **1** a large area of land that has never been developed or used for growing crops because it is difficult to live there: *The Antarctic is the world's last great wilderness.* ◇ *(AmE) a wilderness area* (= one where it is not permitted to build houses or roads) ◇ *(figurative) the barren wilderness of modern life* **2** a place that people do not take care of or control: *Their garden is a wilderness of grass and weeds.* **IDM** **in the ˈwilderness** no longer in an important position, especially in politics: *After three years in the wilderness she was given a government post.*

wild·fire /ˈwaɪldfaɪə(r)/ *noun* [U] **IDM** see SPREAD *v.*

wild·fowl /ˈwaɪldfaʊl/ *noun* [pl.] birds that people hunt for sport or food, especially birds that live near water such as ducks and GEESE

ˌwild ˈgoose chase *noun* a search for sth that is impossible for you to find or that does not exist, that makes you waste a lot of time

wild·life /ˈwaɪldlaɪf/ *noun* [U] animals, birds, insects, etc. that are wild and live in a natural environment: *Development of the area would endanger wildlife.* ◇ *a wildlife habitat/sanctuary*

wild·ly /ˈwaɪldli/ *adv.* **1** in a way that is not controlled: *She looked wildly around for an escape.* ◇ *His heart was beating wildly.* **2** extremely; very: *The story had been wildly exaggerated.* ◇ *It is not a wildly funny play.*

the ˌWild ˈWest *noun* [sing.] the western states of the US during the years when the first Europeans were settling there, used especially when you are referring to the fact that there was not much respect for the law there

wiles /waɪlz/ *noun* [pl.] *(written)* clever tricks that sb uses in order to get what they want or to make sb behave in a particular way

wil·ful *(especially BrE) (AmE* usually **will·ful)** /ˈwɪlfl/ *adj.* *(disapproving)* **1** [usually before noun] (of a bad or harmful action) done deliberately, although the person doing it knows that it is wrong: *wilful damage/neglect* **2** determined to do what you want; not caring about what other people want: *a wilful child* ▶ **wil·ful·ly** /-fəli/ *adv.* **wil·ful·ness** *noun* [U]

will /wɪl/ *modal verb, verb, verb, noun*

■ *modal verb (short form* **'ll** /l/, *negative* **will not,** *short form* **won't** /wəʊnt/, *pt* **would** /wəd/; *strong form* wʊd/, *short form* **'d** /d/, *negative* **would not,** *short form* **wouldn't** /ˈwʊdnt/) **1** used for talking about or predicting the future: *You'll be in time if you hurry.* ◇ *How long will you be staying in Paris?* ◇ *Fred said he'd be leaving soon.* ◇ *By next year all the money will have been spent.* **2** used for

showing that sb is willing to do sth: *I'll check this letter for you, if you want.* ◇ *They won't lend us any more money.* ◇ *He wouldn't come—he said he was too busy.* ◇ *We said we would keep them.* **3** used for asking sb to do sth: *Will you send this letter for me, please?* ◇ *You'll water the plants while I'm away, won't you?* ◇ *I asked him if he wouldn't mind calling later.* **4** used for ordering sb to do sth: *You'll do it this minute!* ◇ *Will you be quiet!* **5** used for stating what you think is probably true: *That'll be the doctor now.* ◇ *You'll have had dinner already, I suppose.* **6** used for stating what is generally true: *If it's made of wood it will float.* ◇ *Engines won't run without lubricants.* **7** used for stating what is true or possible in a particular case: *This jar will hold a kilo.* ◇ *The door won't open!* **8** used for talking about habits: *She'll listen to music, alone in her room, for hours.* ◇ *He would spend hours on the telephone.* **HELP** If you put extra stress on the word **will** or **would** in this meaning, it shows that the habit annoys you: *He 'will comb his hair at the table, even though he knows I don't like it.* ⇨ note at MODAL, SHALL

■ *verb* [V wh-] *(third person sing. pres. t.* **will)** (only used in the simple present tense) *(old-fashioned* or *formal)* to want or like: *Call it what you will, it's still a problem.*

■ *verb* **1** to use the power of your mind to do sth or to make sth happen: [VN] *As a child he had thought he could fly, if he willed it enough.* ◇ [VN to inf] *She willed her eyes to stay open.* ◇ *He willed himself not to panic.* **2** *(old use)* to intend or want sth to happen: [VN] *They thought they had been victorious in battle because God had willed it.* [also V that] **3 ~ sth (to sb)| ~ sth sb** to formally give your property or possessions to sb after you have died, by means of a will: [VNN, VN] *Joe had willed them everything he possessed.* ◇ *Joe had willed everything he possessed to them.*

■ *noun* **1** [C, U] the ability to control your thoughts and actions in order to achieve what you want to do; a feeling of strong determination to do sth that you want to do: *to have a strong will* ◇ *to have an iron will/a will of iron* ◇ *Her decision to continue shows great strength of will.* ◇ *In spite of what happened, he never lost the will to live.* ◇ *The meeting turned out to be a clash of wills.* ◇ *She always wants to impose her will on other people* (= to get what she wants).—see also FREE WILL, WILL POWER **2** [sing.] what sb wants to happen in a particular situation: *I don't want to go against your will.* ◇ *(formal) It is God's will.* **3** (also **tes·ta·ment)** [C] a legal document that says what is to happen to sb's money and property after they die: *I ought to make a will.* ◇ *My father left me the house in his will.*—see also LIVING WILL **4** (in adjectives) having the type of will mentioned: *a strong-willed young woman* ◇ *weak-willed greedy people* **IDM** **against your ˈwill** when you do not want to: *I was forced to sign the agreement against my will.* **at ˈwill** whenever or wherever you like: *They were able to come and go at will.* **where there's a ˌwill there's a ˈway** *(saying)* if you really want to do sth then you will find a way of doing it **with a ˈwill** *(written)* in a willing and enthusiastic way **with the ˌbest will in the ˈworld** used to say that you cannot do sth, even though you really want to: *With the best will in the world I could not describe him as a good father.*

will·ful *(AmE)* = WILFUL

wil·lie *noun* = WILLY

wil·lies /ˈwɪliz/ *noun* **(the willies)** [pl.] *(informal)* if sth gives you the willies you are frightened by it or find it unpleasant

will·ing /ˈwɪlɪŋ/ *adj.* **1** [not usually before noun] **~ (to do sth)** not objecting to doing sth; having no reason for not doing sth: *They keep a list of people (who are) willing to work nights.* ◇ *I'm perfectly willing to discuss the problem.* **2** [usually before noun] ready or pleased to help and not needing to be persuaded; done or given in an enthusiastic way: *willing helpers/volunteers* ◇ *willing support/consent* ◇ *She's very willing.* **OPP** UNWILLING ▶ **will·ing·ly** *adv.*: *People would willingly pay more for better services.* ◇ *I would never willingly upset you.* ◇ *'Will you help me?' 'Willingly.'* **will·ing·ness** *noun* [U, sing.] **IDM** see GOD, SHOW *v.*, SPIRIT

will-o'-the-wisp /ˌwɪl ə ðə ˈwɪsp/ *noun* [usually sing.]

W

æ	ɑː	e	ɜː	ə	ɪ	iː	i	ɒ	ɔː	ʌ	ʊ	u	uː
cat	father	ten	bird	about	sit	see	many	got	saw	cup	put	actual	too

(BrE)

1 a thing that is impossible to obtain; a person that you cannot depend on **2** a blue light that is sometimes seen at night on soft wet ground and is caused by natural gases burning

wil·low /ˈwɪləʊ; *AmE* ˈwɪloʊ/ *noun* **1** [C] a tree with long thin branches and long thin leaves, that often grows near water—see also PUSSY WILLOW **2** [U] the wood of the willow tree, used especially for making cricket bats

wil·lowy /ˈwɪləʊi; *AmE* ˈwɪloʊi/ *adj.* (*approving*) (of a person, especially a woman) tall, thin and graceful

ˈwill power *noun* [U] the ability to control your thoughts and actions in order to achieve what you want to do: *He's intelligent but he's got no will power.*

willy (also **wil·lie**) /ˈwɪli/ *noun* (*pl.* **-ies**) (*BrE, informal*) a word for a PENIS, used especially by children or when speaking to children

willy-nilly /ˌwɪli ˈnɪli/ *adv.* (*informal*) **1** whether you want to or not: *She was forced willy-nilly to accept the company's proposals.* **2** in a careless way without planning: *Don't use your credit card willy-nilly.*

wilt /wɪlt/ *verb* [V, VN] if a plant or flower **wilts**, or sth **wilts**, it, it bends towards the ground because of the heat or a lack of water **2** [V] (*informal*) to become weak or tired or less confident: *The spectators were wilting visibly in the hot sun.* ◊ *He was wilting under the pressure of work.* **3** (**thou wilt**) (*old use*) used to mean 'you will', when talking to one person

wily /ˈwaɪli/ *adj.* (**wili·er**, **wili·est**) clever at getting what you want, and willing to trick people [SYN] CUNNING: *The boss is a wily old fox.* ◊ *He was outwitted by his wily opponent.*

wimp /wɪmp/ *noun, verb*
- *noun* (*informal, disapproving*) a person who is not strong, brave or confident ▶ **wimp·ish** (also **wimpy**) *adj.*: *wimpish behaviour*
- *verb* [PHRV] ˌwimp **'out (of sth)** (*informal, disapproving*) to not do sth that you intended to do because you are too frightened or not confident enough to do it

wim·ple /ˈwɪmpl/ *noun* a head covering made of fabric folded around the head and neck, worn by women in the Middle Ages and now by some NUNS

win /wɪn/ *verb, noun*
- *verb* (**win·ning**, **won**, **won** /wʌn/) **1** to be the most successful in a competition, race, battle, etc: [V] *to win at cards/chess* ◊ *Which team won?* ◊ [VN] *to win an election/a game/a war* ◊ *She loves to win an argument.* **2** ~ **sth (from sb)** to get sth as the result of a competition, race, election, etc: [VN] *Britain won five gold medals.* ◊ *He won £3000 in the lottery.* ◊ *How many states did the Republicans win?* ◊ *The Conservatives won the seat from Labour in the last election.* ◊ [VNN] *You've won yourself a trip to New York.* **3** [VN] to achieve or get sth that you want, especially by your own efforts: *They are trying to win support for their proposals.* ◊ *The company has won a contract to supply books and materials to schools.* ◊ *She won the admiration of many people in her battle against cancer.*—see also WINNER, WINNING [IDM] **you, he, etc. ˌcan't 'win** (*spoken*) used to say that there is no satisfactory way of dealing with a particular situation: *I can't win. If I agree with her, she says I have no mind of my own; if I don't, she says I'm being difficult.* **you can't win them 'all | you 'win some, you 'lose some** (*spoken*) used to express sympathy for sb who has been disappointed about sth **'you win** (*spoken*) used to agree to what sb wants after you have failed to persuade them to do or let you do sth else: *OK, you win, I'll admit I was wrong.* **win (sth) ˌhands 'down** (*informal*) to win sth very easily **win sb's 'heart** to make sb love you **ˌwin or 'lose** whether you succeed or fail: *Win or lose, we'll know we've done our best.*—more at DAY, SPUR *n.* [PHRV] ˌwin sb↔aˈround/ˈover/ˈround **(to sth)** to get sb's support or approval by persuading them that you are right: *She's against the idea but I'm sure I can win her over.* ˌwin sth/sb↔'back to get or have again sth/sb that you had before: *The party is struggling to win back voters who have been alienated by recent scandals.* ˌwin 'out/ 'through (*informal*) to be successful in spite of difficul-

ties: *It's not going to be easy but we'll win through in the end.*
- *noun* a victory in a game, contest, etc: *two wins and three defeats* ◊ *They have not had a win so far this season.* ◊ *France swept to a 6–2 win over Denmark.*—see also NO-WIN

wince /wɪns/ *verb* [V] ~ **(at sth)** to suddenly make an expression with your face that shows that you are feeling pain or embarrassment: *He winced as a sharp pain shot through his left leg.* ◊ *I still wince when I think about that stupid thing I said.* ▶ **wince** *noun* [usually sing.]: *a wince of pain*

winch /wɪntʃ/ *noun, verb*
- *noun* a machine for lifting or pulling heavy objects using a rope or chain
- *verb* [VN+adv./prep.] to lift sb/sth up into the air using a winch

wind¹ /wɪnd/ *noun, verb*—see also WIND²
- *noun* **1** [C, U] (also **the wind**) air that moves quickly as a result of natural forces: *strong/high winds* ◊ *gale-force winds* ◊ *a light wind* ◊ *a north/south/east/west wind* ◊ *a chill/cold/biting north wind* ◊ *The wind is blowing from the south.* ◊ *The trees were swaying in the wind.* ◊ *A gust of wind blew my hat off.* ◊ *The weather was hot, without a breath of wind.* ◊ *The wall gives some protection from the prevailing wind.* ◊ *The wind is getting up* (= starting to blow strongly). ◊ *The wind has dropped* (= stopped blowing strongly). ◊ *wind speed/direction*—see also CROSSWIND, DOWNWIND, HEADWIND, TAILWIND, TRADE WIND, WINDY **2** (*BrE*) (*AmE* **gas**) [U] air that you swallow with food or drink; gas that is produced in your stomach or INTESTINES that makes you feel uncomfortable: *I can't eat beans—they give me wind.* ◊ *Try to bring the baby's wind up.* **3** [U] breath that you need when you do exercise or blow into a musical instrument: *I need time to get my wind back after that run.* ◊ *He kicked Gomez in the stomach, knocking the wind out of him.*—see also SECOND WIND **4** [U+sing./pl. *v.*] the group of musical instruments in an orchestra that produce sounds when you blow into them; the musicians who play these instruments: *music for wind and strings* ◊ *the wind section* ◊ *The wind played beautifully.*—compare WOODWIND [IDM] **break 'wind** to release gas from your bowels through your ANUS **get 'wind of sth** (*informal*) to hear about sth secret or private **get/have the 'wind up (about sth)** (*informal*) to become/be frightened about sth **in the 'wind** about to happen soon, although you do not know exactly how or when: *Once again, changes are in the wind.* **like the 'wind** very quickly **put the 'wind up sb** (*BrE, informal*) to make sb frightened **take the 'wind out of sb's 'sails** (*informal*) to make sb suddenly less confident or angry, especially when you do or say sth that they do not expect **a wind/the winds of 'change** (used especially by journalists) an event or a series of events that has started to happen and will cause important changes or results: *A wind of change was blowing through the banking world.*—more at CAUTION *n.*, FOLLOWING, ILL *adj.*, SAIL *v.*, STRAW, WAY *n.*
- *verb* [VN] **1** [usually passive] to make sb unable to breathe easily for a short time: *He was momentarily winded by the blow to his stomach.* **2** (*BrE*) to gently hit or rub a baby's back to make it BURP (= release gas from its stomach through its mouth) [SYN] BURP—see also LONG-WINDED

wind² /waɪnd/ *verb*—see also WIND¹ (**wound, wound** /waʊnd/) **1** [+adv./prep.] (of a road, river, etc.) to have many bends and twists: [V] *The path wound down to the beach.* ◊ [VN] *The river winds its way between two meadows.*—see also WINDING **2** [VN+adv./prep.] to wrap or twist sth around itself or sth else: *He wound the wool into a ball.* ◊ *Wind the bandage around your finger.* **3** ~ **(sth) (up)** to make a clock or other mechanism work by turning a KNOB, handle, etc. several times; to be able to be made to work in this way: [VN] *He had forgotten to wind his watch.* ◊ [V] *It was one of those old-fashioned gramophones that winds up.*—see also WIND-UP **4** ~ **(sth) forward/back** to operate a tape, film, etc. so that it moves nearer to its ending or starting position: [VN] *He wound the tape back to the beginning.* ◊ [V] *Wind forward to the bit where they discover the body.* **5** [VN] to turn a handle several times: *You operate the trapdoor by winding this*

aɪ	aʊ	eɪ	əʊ	oʊ	ɔɪ	ɪə	eə	ʊə	j	w
my	now	say	go	go	boy	near	hair	pure	yes	wet
			(BrE)	(AmE)						

W

handle. **IDM** see LITTLE FINGER ▶ **wind** *noun*: *Give the handle another couple of winds.* **PHRV** ,**wind** '**down 1** (of a person) to rest or relax after a period of activity or excitement **SYN** UNWIND **2** (of a piece of machinery) to go slowly and then stop ,**wind sth**‹›'**down 1** to bring a business, an activity, etc. to an end gradually over a period of time: *The government is winding down its nuclear programme.* **2** to make sth such as the window of a car move downwards by turning a handle, pressing a button, etc: *Can I wind my window down?* ,**wind** '**up** (*informal*) (of a person) to find yourself in a particular place or situation: *I always said he would wind up in prison.* ◊[+-ing] *We eventually wound up staying in a little hotel a few miles from town.* ◊[+ADJ] *If you take risks like that you'll wind up dead.* ,**wind** '**up**| ,**wind sth**‹›'**up** to bring sth such as a speech or meeting to an end: *The speaker was just winding up when the door was flung open.* ◊ *If we all agree, let's wind up the discussion.* ,**wind sb**‹›'**up** (*BrE, informal*) to deliberately say or do sth in order to annoy sb: *Calm down! Can't you see he's only winding you up?* ◊ *That can't be true! You're winding me up.*—related noun WIND-UP ,**wind sth**‹›'**up 1** to stop running a company, business, etc. and close it completely **2** to make sth such as the window of a car move upwards by turning a handle, pressing a button, etc: *Are all the windows wound up?*

wind·bag /'wɪndbæɡ/ *noun* (*informal, disapproving*) a person who talks too much, and does not say anything important or interesting

wind-blown /'wɪnd bləʊn; *AmE* bloʊn/ *adj.* **1** carried from one place to another by the wind **2** made untidy by the wind: *wind-blown hair*

wind·break /'wɪndbreɪk/ *noun* a row of trees, a fence, etc. that provides protection from the wind

wind·cheat·er /'wɪndtʃiːtə(r)/ (*old-fashioned, BrE*) (*AmE* **wind·break·er** /'wɪndbreɪkə(r)/) *noun* a jacket designed to protect you from the wind

wind chill /'wɪnd tʃɪl/ *noun* [U] the effect of low temperature combined with wind on sb/sth: *Take the wind-chill factor into account.*

wind·fall /'wɪndfɔːl/ *noun* **1** an amount of money that sb/sth wins or receives unexpectedly: *The hospital got a sudden windfall of £300000.* ◊ *windfall gains/profits* ◊ *The government imposed a windfall tax* (= a tax on profits to be paid once only, not every year) *on some industries.* **2** a fruit, especially an apple, that the wind has blown down from a tree

wind farm /'wɪnd fɑːm; *AmE* fɑːrm/ *noun* an area of land on which there are a lot of WINDMILLS for producing electricity

wind·ing /'waɪndɪŋ/ *adj.* having a curving and twisting shape: *a long and winding road*

winding sheet /'waɪndɪŋ ʃiːt/ *noun* (especially in the past) a piece of fabric that a dead person's body was wrapped in before it was buried

wind instrument /'wɪnd ɪnstrəmənt/ *noun* any musical instrument that you play by blowing—compare BRASS, WOODWIND

wind·lass /'wɪndləs/ *noun* a type of WINCH (= a machine for lifting or pulling heavy objects)

wind·less /'wɪndləs/ *adj.* (*written*) without wind: *a windless day* **OPP** WINDY

wind·mill /'wɪndmɪl/ *noun* **1** a building with machinery for GRINDING grain into flour that is driven by the power of the wind turning long arms (called SAILS) **2** a tall thin structure with parts that turn round, used to change the power of the wind into electricity **IDM** see TILT *v.*

win·dow /'wɪndəʊ; *AmE* 'wɪndoʊ/ *noun* **1** an opening in the wall or roof of a building, car, etc., usually covered with glass, that allows light and air to come in and people to see out; the glass in a window: *She looked out of the window.* ◊ *Do you mind if I open the window?* ◊ *the bedroom/car/kitchen window* ◊ *a broken window*—see also BAY WINDOW, DORMER WINDOW, FRENCH WINDOW, PIC-TURE WINDOW, ROSE WINDOW, SASH WINDOW **2** the glass at the front of a shop/store and the area behind it where goods are shown to the public: *I saw the dress I wanted in*

the window. ◊ *a window display* **3** an area within a frame on a computer screen, in which a particular program is operating or in which information of a particular type is shown: *to create/open a window*—picture on page 251 **4** a small area of sth that you can see through, for example to talk to sb or read sth on the other side: *There was a long line of people at the box-office window.* ◊ *The address must be clearly visible through the window of the envelope.* **5** [sing.] **~ on/into sth** a way of seeing and learning about sth: *Television is a sort of window on the world.* ◊ *It gave me an intriguing window into the way people live.* **6** a time when there is an opportunity to do sth, although it may not last long: *We now have a small window of opportunity in which to make our views known.* **IDM** **fly/go out (of) the** '**window** (*informal*) to stop existing; to disappear completely: *As soon as the kids arrived, order went out of the window.*

'**window box** *noun* a long narrow box outside a window, in which plants are grown—picture at HOUSE

'**window dressing** *noun* [U] **1** the art of arranging goods in shop/store windows in an attractive way **2** (*disapproving*) the fact of doing or saying sth in a way that creates a good impression but does not show the real facts: *The reforms have been interpreted as window dress-ing.*

win·dow·less /'wɪndəʊləs; *AmE* -doʊ-/ *adj.* without win-dows: *a tiny, windowless cell*

win·dow·pane /'wɪndəʊpeɪn; *AmE* -doʊ-/ *noun* a piece of glass in a window

'**window shade** *noun* (*AmE*) = BLIND

'**window-shopping** *noun* [U] the activity of looking at the goods in shop/store windows, usually without intend-ing to buy anything: *to go window-shopping*

'**window sill** (also **sill**, '**window ledge**) *noun* a narrow shelf below a window, either inside or outside: *Place the plants on a sunny window sill.*—picture at HOUSE

wind·pipe /'wɪndpaɪp/ *noun* the tube in the throat that carries air to the lungs **SYN** TRACHEA—picture at BODY

wind·screen /'wɪndskriːn/ (*BrE*) (*AmE* **wind·shield**) *noun* the window across the front of a motor vehicle—picture at CAR

'**windscreen wiper** (*BrE*) (*AmE* '**windshield wiper**) (also **wiper** *BrE, AmE*) *noun* a blade with a rubber edge that moves across a windscreen to make it clear of rain, snow, etc.—picture at CAR

wind·shield /'wɪndʃiːld/ *noun* **1** (*AmE*) = WINDSCREEN **2** a glass or plastic screen that provides protection from the wind, for example at the front of a motorcycle

wind·sock /'wɪndsɒk; *AmE* -sɑːk/ *noun* a fabric tube, open at both ends, that hangs at the top of a pole, for example on an AIRFIELD, to show the direction of the wind

wind·surf·er /'wɪndsɜːfə(r); *AmE* -sɜːrf-/ *noun* **1** (*AmE* also **Wind·surf·er™**) (also **sail·board** *BrE, AmE*) a long narrow board with a sail, that you stand on and sail across water on **2** a person on a windsurfer

wind·surf·ing /'wɪndsɜːfɪŋ; *AmE* -sɜːrf-/ *noun* [U] the sport of sailing on water standing on a windsurfer: *to go windsurfing* ▶ **wind·surf** *verb*: [V] *Most visitors come to sail or windsurf.*

wind·swept /'wɪndswept/ *adj.* **1** (of a place) having strong winds and little protection from them: *the wind-swept Atlantic coast* **2** looking as though you have been in a strong wind: *windswept hair*

wind tunnel /'wɪnd tʌnl/ *noun* a large tunnel where aircraft, etc. are tested by forcing air past them

wind-up /'waɪnd ʌp/ *adj., noun*
■ *adj.* [only before noun] **1** that you operate by turning a key or handle: *an old-fashioned wind-up gramophone* **2** intended to bring sth to an end: *a wind-up speech*
■ *noun* (*BrE, informal*) something that sb says or does in order to be deliberately annoying, especially as a joke

wind·ward /'wɪndwəd; *AmE* -wərd/ *adj., noun*
■ *adj.* on the side of sth from which the wind is blowing: *the windward side of the boat* **OPP** LEEWARD—see also LEE ▶ **wind·ward** *adv.* **OPP** LEEWARD
■ *noun* [U] the side or direction from which the wind is blowing: *to sail to windward*—compare LEEWARD

b	d	f	g	h	k	i	m	n	p	r
bad	did	fall	get	hat	cat	leg	man	now	pen	red

windy /'wɪndi/ adj. (wind·ier, windi·est) **1** (of weather, etc.) with a lot of wind: *a windy day* ◊ *It's too windy to go out in the boat.* OPP WINDLESS **2** (of a place) getting a lot of wind: *windy hills/moors* **3** (*informal, disapproving*) (of speech) involving speaking for longer than necessary and in a way that is complicated and not clear

wine /waɪn/ noun, verb
■ noun **1** [U, C] an alcoholic drink made from the juice of grapes that has been left to FERMENT. There are many different kinds of wine: *a bottle of wine* ◊ *a glass of dry/sweet wine* ◊ *red/rosé/white wine* ◊ *dessert/sparkling wine* **2** [U, C] an alcoholic drink made from plants or fruits other than grapes: *elderberry/rice wine* **3** [U] (also **wine 'red**) a dark red colour: *a wine velvet jacket*
■ verb IDM ˌwine and 'dine (sb) to go to restaurants, etc. and enjoy good food and drink; to entertain sb by buying them good food and drink: *The town offers many opportunities for wining and dining.* ◊ *The firm spent thousands wining and dining potential clients.*

'wine bar noun a bar or small restaurant where wine is the main drink available

'wine cellar (also **cel·lar**) noun an underground room where wine is stored; the wine stored in this room

ˌwine 'cooler noun **1** (*AmE*) a drink made with wine, fruit juice, ice and SODA WATER **2** **'wine cooler** a container for putting a bottle of wine in to cool it

'wine glass noun a glass for drinking wine from

win·ery /'waɪnəri/ noun (pl. **-ies**) (*especially AmE*) a place where wine is made SYN VINEYARD

wing /wɪŋ/ noun, verb
■ noun
OF BIRD/INSECT ▸ **1** [C] one of the parts of the body of a bird, insect or BAT that it uses for flying: *The swan flapped its wings noisily.* ◊ *wing feathers*—picture on pages A6–7
OF PLANE ▸ **2** [C] one of the large flat parts that stick out from the side of a plane and help to keep it in the air when it is flying—picture at PLANE
OF BUILDING ▸ **3** [C] one of the parts of a large building that sticks out from the main part: *the east/west wing* ◊ *the new wing of the hospital*
OF CAR ▸ **4** (*BrE*) (*AmE* **fend·er**) [C] a part of a car that is above a wheel: *There was a dent in the nearside wing.* ◊ *a wing mirror* (= fixed to the side of a car)—picture at CAR
OF ORGANIZATION ▸ **5** [C] one section of an organization that has a particular function or whose members share the same opinions SYN ARM: *the radical wing of the party* ◊ *the political wing of the National Resistance Army*—see also LEFT WING, RIGHT WING
IN FOOTBALL/HOCKEY ▸ **6** [C] = WINGER—see also LEFT WING, RIGHT WING **7** [C] the far left or right side of the sports field: *He plays on the wing.*
IN THEATRE ▸ **8** (the wings) [pl.] the area at either side of the stage that cannot be seen by the audience: *She watched every performance from the wings.*
IDM **get your 'wings** to pass the exams that mean you are allowed to fly a plane **(waiting) in the 'wings** ready to take over a particular job or be used in a particular situation when needed **on a ˌwing and a 'prayer** with only a very slight chance of success **on the 'wing** (*literary*) (of a bird, insect, etc.) flying **take sb under your 'wing** to take care of and help sb who has less experience of sth than you **take 'wing** (*literary*) (of a bird, insect, etc.) to fly away: (*figurative*) *Her imagination took wing.*—more at CLIP *v.*, SPREAD *v.*
■ verb
FLY ▸ **1** [+adv. / prep.] (*literary*) to fly somewhere: [VN] *A solitary seagull winged its way across the bay.* [also V]
GO QUICKLY ▸ **2** [VN+adv. / prep.] to be sent somewhere very quickly: *An application form will be winging its way to you soon.*
IDM **'wing it** (*informal*) to do sth without planning or preparing it first SYN IMPROVISE: *I didn't know I'd have to make a speech—I just had to wing it.*

ˌwing 'collar noun a high stiff shirt collar for men, worn with formal clothes

'wing commander noun an officer of high rank in the British air force: *Wing Commander Brian Moore*

winged /wɪŋd/ adj. **1** having wings: *winged creatures/insects* OPP WINGLESS **2** (**- winged**) (in adjectives) having the number or type of wings mentioned: *a long-winged bird*

wing·er /'wɪŋə(r)/ noun (also **wing**) (*sport*) either of the attacking players who play towards the side of the playing area in sports such as football or hockey

wing·less /'wɪŋləs/ adj. (especially of insects) without wings OPP WINGED

'wing nut noun a NUT (2) for holding things in place, which has parts that stick out at the sides so that you can turn it easily

wing·span /'wɪŋspæn/ noun the distance between the end of one wing and the end of the other when the wings are fully stretched: *a bird with a two-foot wingspan* ◊ *the wingspan of a glider*

wing·tips /'wɪŋtɪps/ noun [pl.] (*AmE*) strong leather shoes that fasten with LACES and have an extra piece of leather with small holes in it over the toe

wink /wɪŋk/ verb, noun
■ verb **1** ~ (**at sb**) [V] to close one eye and open it again quickly, especially as a private signal to sb, or to show sth is a joke: *He winked at her and she knew he was thinking the same thing that she was.*—compare BLINK **2** [V] (*written*) to shine with an unsteady light; to flash on and off SYN BLINK: *We could see the lights of the ship winking in the distance.* PHRV **'wink at sth** to pretend that you have not noticed sth, especially sth bad or illegal
■ noun an act of winking, especially as a signal to sb: *He gave her a knowing wink.*—see also FORTY WINKS IDM **not get/have a 'wink of sleep | not sleep a 'wink** to not be able to sleep: *I didn't get a wink of sleep last night.* ◊ *I hardly slept a wink.*—more at NOD *n.*, NUDGE *n.*, TIP *v.*

win·kle /'wɪŋkl/ noun, verb
■ noun (*BrE*) (also **peri·win·kle** *AmE, BrE*) a small shellfish, like a SNAIL, that can be eaten
■ verb (*BrE, informal*) PHRV **ˌwinkle sth/sb↔'out (of sth)** to get sb/sth out of a place or position, especially when they do not want to leave **ˌwinkle sth 'out of sb** to get information from sb, especially with difficulty: *She always manages to winkle secrets out of people.*

win·ner /'wɪnə(r)/ noun **1** a person, a team, an animal, etc. that wins sth: *The winners of the competition will be announced next month.* ◊ *There are no winners in a divorce* (= everyone suffers). **2** [usually sing.] (*informal*) a thing or person that is successful or likely to be successful: *I think your idea is a winner.* ◊ *The design is very good. We could be onto a winner* (= we may do or produce sth successful). **3** [sing.] (*sport*) a goal or point that causes a team or a person to win a game: *Owen scored the winner after 20 minutes*—compare LOSER IDM see PICK *v.*

win·ning /'wɪnɪŋ/ adj. **1** [only before noun] that wins or has won sth, for example a race or competition: *the winning horse/goal/ticket* **2** [usually before noun] attractive in a way that makes other people like you: *a winning smile* IDM see CARD *n.*

'winning post noun (*especially BrE*) a post that shows where the end of a race is: *to be first past the winning post*

win·nings /'wɪnɪŋz/ noun [pl.] money that sb wins in a competition or game or by gambling

win·now /'wɪnəʊ; *AmE* -noʊ/ verb [VN] to blow a current of air through grain in order to remove its outer covering (called the CHAFF) PHRV **ˌwinnow sb/sth 'out (of sth)** (*written*) to remove people or things from a group so that only the best ones are left

wino /'waɪnəʊ; *AmE* -noʊ/ noun (pl. **-os**) (*informal*) a person who drinks a lot of cheap alcohol and who has no home

win·some /'wɪnsəm/ adj. (*formal*) (of people or their manner) pleasant and attractive: *She gave him a winsome smile.* ▶ **win·some·ly** adv.

win·ter /'wɪntə(r)/ noun, verb
■ noun [U, C] the coldest season of the year, between autumn/fall and spring: *a mild/severe/hard winter* ◊ *Our house can be very cold in* (the) *winter.* ◊ *They worked on the building all through the winter.* ◊ *We went to New*

s	t	v	z	ʃ	ʒ	tʃ	dʒ	θ	ð	ŋ
see	tea	van	zoo	shoe	vision	chain	jam	thin	this	sing

Zealand last winter. ◊ *the winter months* ◊ *a winter coat* **IDM** see DEAD *n.*
■ *verb* [V] [usually +*adv./prep.*] to spend the winter somewhere: *Many British birds winter in Africa.*—compare OVERWINTER

ˌwinter ˈsports *noun* [pl.] sports that people do on snow or ice

win·ter·time /ˈwɪntətaɪm; *AmE* -tərt-/ *noun* [U] the period of time when it is winter: *The days are shorter in (the) wintertime.*

win·try /ˈwɪntri/ *adj.* **1** typical of winter; cold: *wintry weather/showers* ◊ *a wintry landscape* **2** (*written*) not friendly: *a wintry smile*

wipe /waɪp/ *verb, noun*
■ *verb* **1** ~ sth (on/with sth) to rub a surface with a cloth, etc. in order to clean it; to rub sth against a surface, in order to remove dirt or liquid from it: [VN] *She was sniffing and wiping her eyes with a tissue.* ◊ *Please wipe your feet on the mat.* ◊ *He wiped his hands on a clean towel.* ◊ [VN-ADJ] *He wiped his plate clean with a piece of bread.* **2** [VN] ~ sth (from/off sth)| ~ sth ˈ(away/off/up) to remove dirt, liquid, etc. from sth by using a cloth, your hand, etc: *He wiped the sweat from his forehead.* ◊ *She wiped off her make-up.* ◊ *Use that cloth to wipe up the mess.* ◊ (*figurative*) *Wipe that stupid smile off your face.* **3** [VN] ~ sth (off/off sth) to remove information, sound, images, etc. from a computer, tape or video: *You must have wiped off that programme I recorded.* ◊ *Somebody had wiped all the tapes.* **4** [VN] ~ sth from sth| ~ sth out to deliberately forget an experience because it was unpleasant or embarrassing: *I tried to wipe the whole episode from my mind.* ◊ *You can never wipe out the past.* **IDM** wipe the ˈfloor with sb (*informal*) to defeat sb completely in an argument or a competition wipe sb/sth off the ˌface of the ˈearth | wipe sth off the ˈmap to destroy or remove sb/sth completely wipe the slate ˈclean to agree to forget about past mistakes or arguments and start again with a relationship **PHRV** ˌwipe sth↔ˈdown to clean a surface completely, using a wet cloth: *She took a cloth and wiped down the kitchen table.* wipe sth off sth to remove sth from sth: *Billions of pounds were wiped off share prices as the pound slumped again.* ˌwipe ˈout (*informal*) to fall over, especially when you are doing a sport such as skiing or SURFING: *She wiped out at the third gate in the slalom race.* ˌwipe sb/sth↔ˈout [often passive] to destroy or remove sb/sth completely: *Whole villages were wiped out by the earthquake.* ◊ *Last year's profits were virtually wiped out.* ◊ *a campaign to wipe out malaria*
■ *noun* **1** an act of cleaning sth using a cloth: *Can you give the table a quick wipe?* **2** a special piece of thin fabric or soft paper that is soaked in a liquid and that you use to clean away dirt and bacteria: *Remember to take nappies and baby wipes.*

wiper /ˈwaɪpə(r)/ *noun* = WINDSCREEN WIPER

wire /ˈwaɪə(r)/ *noun, verb*
■ *noun* **1** [U, C] metal in the form of thin thread; a piece of this: *a coil of copper wire* ◊ *a wire rack/basket* ◊ *The box was fastened with a rusty wire.*—see also BARBED WIRE, HIGH WIRE, TRIPWIRE—picture at ROPE **2** [C, U] a piece of wire that is used to carry an electric current or signal: *overhead wires* ◊ *fuse wire* ◊ *The telephone wires had been cut.*—see also HOT-WIRE **3** (the wire) [sing.] a wire fence: *Three prisoners escaped by crawling under the wire.* **4** [C] (*informal, especially AmE*) = TELEGRAM: *We sent a wire asking him to join us.*—see also WIRY **IDM** get your ˈwires crossed (*informal*) to become confused about what sb has said to you so that you think they meant sth else go, come, etc. (right) down to the ˈwire (*informal*) if you say that a situation goes down to the wire, you mean that the result will not be decided or known until the very end—more at LIVE², PULL *v.*
■ *verb* **1** [VN] ~ sth (up) to connect a building, piece of equipment, etc. to an electricity supply using wires: *Make sure the plug is wired up correctly.* **2** [VN] ~ sb/sth up (to sth)| ~ sb/sth to sth to connect sb/sth to a piece of equipment, especially a TAPE RECORDER or computer system: *He was wired up to a police tape recorder.* **3** [VN] ~ sth (for sth) to put a special device somewhere in order

to listen secretly to other people's conversations [SYN] BUG: *The room had been wired for sound.* **4** ~ (sth) (to sb)| ~ sb (sth) (*especially AmE*) to send sb a message by TELEGRAM: [VN, VNN] *He wired the news to us.* ◊ *He wired us the news.* **5** ~ sth (to sb)| ~ sb sth to send money from one bank to another using an electronic system: [VN, VNN] *The bank wired the money to her.* ◊ *The bank wired her the money.* **6** [VN] to join things together using wire

ˈwire-cutters *noun* [pl.] a tool for cutting wire: *a pair of wire-cutters*

wired /ˈwaɪəd; *AmE* ˈwaɪərd/ *adj.* **1** connected to a system of computers: *Many colleges now have high-tech libraries and wired dormitories.* **2** (of glass, material, etc.) containing wires that make it strong or stiff **3** (*informal*) excited or nervous; not relaxed **4** (*informal, especially AmE*) under the influence of alcohol or an illegal drug

wire·less /ˈwaɪələs; *AmE* ˈwaɪərləs/ *noun* (*old-fashioned*) **1** [C] (*especially BrE*) a radio **2** [U] a system of sending and receiving signals: *a message sent by wireless*

ˌwire ˈnetting *noun* [U] wire that is woven into a net, used especially for fences

wire·tap·ping /ˈwaɪətæpɪŋ; *AmE* ˈwaɪərt-/ *noun* [U] the act of secretly listening to other people's telephone conversations by attaching a device to the telephone line ▶ wire·tap *verb* (-pp-) [VN] wire·tap *noun*: *the use of illegal wiretaps*—see also TAP

ˌwire ˈwool *noun* [U] (*BrE*) = STEEL WOOL

wir·ing /ˈwaɪərɪŋ/ *noun* [U] the system of wires that is used for supplying electricity to a building or machine: *to check the wiring* ◊ *a wiring diagram*

wiry /ˈwaɪəri/ *adj.* **1** (of a person) thin but strong: *a wiry little man* **2** (of hair, plants, etc.) stiff and strong; like wire

wis·dom /ˈwɪzdəm/ *noun* [U] **1** the ability to make sensible decisions and give good advice because of the experience and knowledge that you have: *a woman of great wisdom* ◊ *words of wisdom* **2** ~ of sth/of doing sth how sensible sth is: *I question the wisdom of giving a child so much money.* **3** the knowledge that a society or culture has gained over a long period of time: *the collective wisdom of the Native American people* **IDM** conventional/received ˈwisdom the view or belief that most people hold: *Conventional wisdom has it that riots only ever happen in cities.* in his/her/its, etc. (infinite) ˈwisdom used when you are saying that you do not understand why sb has done sth: *The government in its wisdom has decided to support the ban.*—more at PEARL

ˈwisdom tooth *noun* any of the four large teeth at the back of the mouth that do not grow until you are an adult

wise /waɪz/ *adj., verb*
■ *adj.* (**wiser, wis·est**) **1** (of people) able to make sensible decisions and give good advice because of the experience and knowledge that you have: *a wise old man* ◊ *I'm older and wiser after ten years in the business.* **2** (of actions and behaviour) sensible; based on good judgement: *a wise decision/precaution* ◊ *It was very wise to leave when you did.* ◊ *The wisest course of action is just to say nothing.* ◊ *I was grateful for her wise counsel.* ▶ wise·ly *adv.*: *She nodded wisely.* ◊ *He wisely decided to tell the truth.* **IDM** be none the ˈwiser | not be any the ˈwiser **1** to not understand sth, even after it has been explained to you: *I've read the instructions, but I'm still none the wiser.* **2** to not know or find out about sth bad that sb has done: *If you put the money back, no one will be any the wiser.* be ˌwise after the eˈvent (often *disapproving*) to understand sth, or realize what you should have done, only after sth has happened be/get ˈwise to sb/sth (*informal*) to become aware that sb is being dishonest: *He thought he could fool me but I got wise to him.* put sb ˈwise (to sth) (*informal*) to inform sb about sth
■ *verb* **PHRV** ˌwise ˈup (to sth) (*informal*) to become aware of the unpleasant truth about a situation

-wise *suffix* (in adjectives and adverbs) **1** in the manner or direction of: *likewise* ◊ *clockwise* ◊ *lengthwise* **2** (*informal*) concerning: *Things aren't too good businesswise.*

wise·crack /ˈwaɪzkræk/ *noun* (*informal*) a clever

æ	ɑː	e	ɜː	ə	ɪ	iː	i	ɒ	ɔː	ʌ	ʊ	u	uː
cat	father	ten	bird	about	sit	see	many	got	saw	cup	put	actual	too
								(BrE)					

W

remark or joke ► **wise·crack** *verb*: [V] *He plays a wise-cracking detective.* [also V **speech**]

'wise guy *noun* (*informal disapproving, especially AmE*) a person who speaks or behaves as if they know more than other people

wish /wɪʃ/ *verb, noun*

■ *verb* **1** (not usually used in the present progressive tense) to want sth to happen or to be true even though it is unlikely or impossible: [V(that)] *I wish I were taller.* ◊ (*BrE* also) *I wish I was taller.* ◊ *I wish I hadn't eaten so much.* ◊ *'Where is he now?' ' I only wish I knew!'* ◊ *I wish you wouldn't leave your clothes all over the floor.* **HELP** 'That' is nearly always left out, especially in speech. [VN-ADJ] *He's dead and it's no use wishing him alive again.* ◊ [VN+*adv./prep.*] *She wished herself a million miles away.* **2** (*especially BrE, formal*) to want to do sth; to want sth to happen: [V] *You may stay until morning, **if you wish.*** ◊ *'I'd rather not talk now.' ' (Just) as you wish.'* ◊ [V to inf] *This course is designed for people wishing to update their computer skills.* ◊ *I wish to speak to the manager.* ◊ *I don't wish* (= I don't mean) *to be rude, but could you be a little quieter?* ◊ [VNN] *She could not believe that he wished her harm.* ◊ [VN to inf] *He was not sure whether he wished her to stay or go.* **3** [V] *~ (for sth)* to think very hard that you want sth, especially sth that can only be achieved by good luck or magic: *She shut her eyes and wished for him to get better.* ◊ *If you wish really hard, maybe you'll get what you want.* ◊ *It's no use wishing for the impossible.* ◊ *He has everything he could possibly wish for.* **4** to say that you hope that sb will be happy, lucky, etc: [VNN] *I wished her a happy birthday.* ◊ *Wish me luck!* ◊ [VN] *We **wish them** both **well** in their retirement.* **IDM** **I 'wish!** (*spoken*) used to say that sth is impossible or very unlikely, although you wish it were possible **SYN** IF ONLY: *'You'll have finished by tomorrow.' 'I wish!'* **PHRV** **,wish sth a'way** to try to get rid of sth by wishing it did not exist **'wish sb/sth on sb** (*informal*) (used in negative sentences) to want sb to have sth unpleasant: *I wouldn't wish something like that on my worst enemy.*

■ *noun* **1** [C] *~ (to do sth)* | *~ (for sth)* a desire or a feeling that you want to do sth or have sth: *She expressed a wish to be alone.* ◊ *He had no wish to start a fight.* ◊ *I can understand her wish for secrecy.* ◊ *His dearest wish* (= what he wants most of all) *is to see his grandchildren again.* **2** [C] a thing that you want to have or to happen: *to carry out sb's wishes* ◊ *I'm sure that you will get your wish.* ◊ *She married against her parents' wishes.*—see also DEATH WISH **3** [C] an attempt to make sth happen by thinking hard about it, especially in stories when it often happens by magic: *Throw some money in the fountain and make a wish.* ◊ *The genie granted him three wishes.* ◊ *The prince's wish came true.* **4** (**wishes**) [pl.] *~ (for sth)* especially in a letter or card to say that you hope that sb will be happy, well or successful: *We all send our best wishes for the future.* ◊ *Give my good wishes to the family.* ◊ *With best wishes* (= for example, at the end of a letter) **IDM** **your wish is my com'mand** (*humorous*) used to say that you are ready to do whatever sb asks you to do—see also DEATH WISH

> **GRAMMAR POINT**
> **wish**
>
> After the verb **wish** in sense 1, a past tense is always used in a *that* clause: *Do you wish you had a better job?* In more formal English, especially in *AmE*, many people use *were* after *I, he, she, it* instead of *was*: *I wish he were here tonight.*

wish·bone /'wɪʃbəʊn; *AmE* -boʊn/ *noun* a V-shaped bone between the neck and breast of a chicken, duck, etc. When the bird is eaten, this bone is sometimes pulled apart by two people, and the person who gets the larger part can make a wish.

,wishful 'thinking *noun* [U] the belief that sth that you want to happen is happening or will happen, although this is actually not true or very unlikely: *I've got a feeling that Alex likes me, but that might just be wishful thinking.*

'wish list *noun* (*informal*) all the things that you would like to have, or that you would like to happen

wishy-washy /'wɪʃi wɒʃi; *AmE* -wɔːʃi; -wɑːʃi/ *adj.* (*informal, disapproving*) **1** not having clear or firm ideas or beliefs: *a wishy-washy liberal* **2** not bright in colour: *a wishy-washy blue*

wisp /wɪsp/ *noun* *~ (of sth)* **1** a small, thin piece of hair, grass, etc. **2** a long thin line of smoke or cloud

wispy /'wɪspi/ *adj.* consisting of small, thin pieces; not thick: *wispy hair/clouds* ◊ *a wispy beard*

wis·teria /wɪ'stɪəriə; *AmE* -'stɪr-/ (also **wis·taria** /wɪ'steəriə; *AmE* -'ster-/) *noun* [U] a climbing plant with bunches of pale purple or white flowers that hang down

wist·ful /'wɪstfl/ *adj.* thinking sadly about sth that you would like to have, especially sth in the past that you can no longer have: *a wistful smile/tone/look* ► **wist·ful·ly** /-fəli/ *adv.*: *She sighed wistfully.* ◊ *'If only I had known you then,' he said wistfully.* **wist·ful·ness** *noun* [U]

wit /wɪt/ *noun* **1** [U, sing.] the ability to say or write things that are both clever and amusing: *to have a quick/ sharp/ dry/ ready wit* ◊ *a woman of wit and intelligence* ◊ *a book full of the wit and wisdom of his 30 years in politics* **2** [C] a person who has the ability to say or write things that are both clever and amusing: *a well-known wit and raconteur* **3** (**wits**) [pl.] your ability to think quickly and clearly and to make good decisions: *He needed all his wits to find his way out.* ◊ *The game was a long battle of wits.* ◊ *Kate paused and **gathered her wits**.* ◊ *a chance to **pit your wits against*** (= compete with, using your intelligence) *our quiz champion* **4** (**-witted**) (in adjectives) having the type of intelligence mentioned: *a quick-witted group of students* **5** [U] *~ to do sth* the intelligence or good sense to know what is the right thing to do: *At least you had the wit to ask for help.* ◊ *It should not be beyond the wit of man to resolve this dispute.*—see also WITLESS **IDM** **be at your wits' end** to be so worried by a problem that you do not know what to do next **be frightened/scared/terrified out of your 'wits** to be very frightened **have/keep your 'wits about you** to be aware of what is happening around you and ready to think and act quickly **to 'wit** (*old-fashioned, formal*) you use *to wit* when you are about to be more exact about sth that you have just referred to: *Pilot error, to wit failure to follow procedures, was the cause of the accident.*—more at LIVE[1]

> **WORD FAMILY**
> **wit** *n.*
> **witty** *adj.*
> **witticism** *n.*
> **outwit** *v.*

witch /wɪtʃ/ *noun* **1** a woman who is believed to have magic powers, especially to do evil things. In stories, she usually wears a black pointed hat and flies on a BROOM-STICK. **2** (*disapproving*) an ugly unpleasant old woman **IDM** see BREW *n.*

witch·craft /'wɪtʃkrɑːft; *AmE* -kræft/ *noun* [U] the use of magic powers, especially evil ones

'witch doctor *noun* (especially in Africa) a person who is believed to have special magic powers that can be used to heal people—compare MEDICINE MAN

'witch hazel *noun* [U] a liquid that is used for treating injuries on the skin

'witch-hunt *noun* (usually *disapproving*) an attempt to find and punish people who hold opinions that are thought to be unacceptable or dangerous to society

the 'witching hour *noun* [sing.] the time, late at night, when it is thought that magic things can happen

Wite-out™ /'waɪtaʊt/ *noun* [U] (*AmE*) a white liquid that you use to cover mistakes that you make when you are writing or typing, and that you can write on top of; a type of CORRECTION FLUID **SYN** TIPP-EX—see also WHITE-OUT

with /wɪð; wɪθ/ *prep.* **HELP** For the special uses of **with** in phrasal verbs, look at the entries for the verbs. For example **bear with sb/sth** is in the phrasal verb section at **bear**. **1** in the company or presence of sb/sth: *She lives with her parents.* ◊ *I have a client with me right now.* ◊ *a nice steak with a bottle of red wine* **2** having or carrying sth: *a girl with* (= who has) *red hair* ◊ *a jacket with a hood* ◊ *He looked at her with a hurt expression.* ◊ *They're both in*

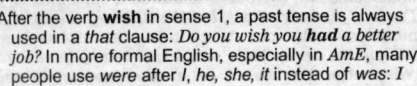

aɪ	aʊ	eɪ	əʊ	oʊ	ɔɪ	ɪə	eə	ʊə	j	w
my	now	say	go	go	boy	near	hair	pure	yes •	wet
			(BrE)	(AmE)						

bed with flu. ◊ *a man with a suitcase* **3** using sth: *Cut it with a knife.* ◊ *It is treated with acid before being analysed.* **4** used to say what fills, covers, etc. sth: *The bag was stuffed with dirty clothes.* ◊ *Sprinkle the dish with salt.* **5** in opposition to sb/sth; against sb/sth: *to fight/argue/ quarrel with sb* ◊ *to play tennis with sb* ◊ *at war with a neighbouring country* ◊ *I had an argument with my boss.* **6** concerning; in the case of: *Be careful with the glasses.* ◊ *Are you pleased with the result?* ◊ *Don't be angry with her.* ◊ *With these students it's pronunciation that's the problem.* **7** used when considering one fact in relation to another: *She won't be able to help us with all the family commitments she has.* ◊ *It's much easier compared with last time.* **8** including: *The meal with wine came to $20 each.* ◊ *With all the lesson preparation I have to do I work 12 hours a day.* **9** used to show the way in which sb does sth: *He behaved with great dignity.* ◊ *She sleeps with the window open.* ◊ *Don't stand with your hands in your pockets.* **10** because of; as a result of: *She blushed with embarrassment.* ◊ *His fingers were numb with cold.* **11** because of sth and as it happens: *The shadows lengthened with the approach of sunset.* ◊ *Skill comes with practice.* **12** in the same direction as sth: *Marine mammals generally swim with the current.* **13** used to show who has possession of or responsibility for sth: *The keys are with reception.* ◊ *Leave it with me.* **14** employed by; using the services of: *She acted with a touring company for three years.* ◊ *I bank with HSBC.* **15** showing separation from sth/sb: *I could never part with this ring.* ◊ *Can we dispense with the formalities?* **16** in spite of sth: *With all her faults I still love her.* **17** used in exclamations: *Off to bed with you!* ◊ *Down with school!* **IDM** **be ᶦwith me/you** (*informal*) to be able to understand what sb is talking about: *Are you with me?* ◊ *I'm afraid I'm not quite with you.* **be ᶦwith sb (on sth)** to support sb and agree with what they say: *We're all with you on this one.* **ᶦwith it** (*informal*) **1** knowing about current fashions and ideas **SYN** TRENDY: *Don't you have anything more with it to wear?* **2** understanding what is happening around you **SYN** ALERT: *You don't seem very with it today.* **with ᶦthat** (*written*) straight after that; then: *He muttered a few words of apology and with that he left.*

with·draw /wɪðˈdrɔː; wɪθˈd-/ *verb* (**with·drew** /-ˈdruː/ **with·drawn** /-ˈdrɔːn/) **1 ~ (sb/sth) (from sth)** to move back or away from a place or situation; to make sb/sth do this **SYN** PULL OUT: [V] *Government troops were forced to withdraw.* ◊ [VN] *Both powers withdrew their forces from the region.* ◊ *She withdrew her hand from his.* **2** [VN] **~ sth (from sth)** to stop giving or offering sth to sb: *Workers have threatened to withdraw their labour* (= go on strike). ◊ *The drug was **withdrawn from sale** after a number of people suffered serious side effects.* ◊ *He withdrew his support for our campaign.* **3 ~ (sb/sth) (from sth)** to stop taking part in an activity or being a member of an organization; to stop sb/sth from doing these things: [V] *There have been calls for Britain to withdraw from the EU.* ◊ [VN] *The horse had been withdrawn from the race.* **4** [VN] to take money out of a bank account: *I'd like to withdraw £250 please.* **5** [VN] (*formal*) to say that you no longer believe that sth you previously said is true **SYN** RETRACT: *The newspaper withdrew the allegations the next day.* **6** [V] **~ (from sth) (into sth)** to become quieter and spend less time with other people: *She's beginning to withdraw into herself.*

with·draw·al /wɪðˈdrɔːəl; wɪθˈd-/ *noun* **1** [U, C] the act of moving or taking sth away or back: *the withdrawal of support/troops* ◊ *the withdrawal of a product from the market* ◊ *US withdrawal from Vietnam* **2** [U] the act of no longer taking part in sth or being a member of an organization: *his withdrawal from the election* ◊ *a campaign for Britain's withdrawal from the EU* **3** [C] the act of taking an amount of money out of your bank account: *You can make withdrawals of up to $250 a day.* **4** [U] the period of time when sb is getting used to not taking a drug that they have become dependent on, and the unpleasant effects of doing this: *I got **withdrawal symptoms** after giving up smoking.* **5** [C usually sing, U] the act of saying that you no longer believe that sth you have previously said is true: *The newspaper published a withdrawal the*

next day. **SYN** RETRACTION **6** [U] (*psychology*) the behaviour of sb who wants to be alone and does not want to communicate with other people: *She is showing signs of withdrawal and depression.*

with·drawn /wɪðˈdrɔːn/ *adj.* not wanting to talk to other people; extremely quiet and shy

wither /ˈwɪðə(r)/ *verb* **1** if a plant **withers** or sth **withers** it, it dries up and dies: [V] *The grass had withered in the warm sun.* [also VN] **2** [V] **~ (away)** to become less or weaker, especially before disappearing completely: *All our hopes just withered away.*

withered /ˈwɪðəd; AmE -ərd/ *adj.* [usually before noun] **1** (of plants) dried up and dead: *withered leaves* **2** (of people) looking old because they are thin and weak and have very dry skin **3** (of parts of the body) thin and weak and not fully developed because of disease: *withered limbs*

wither·ing /ˈwɪðərɪŋ/ *adj.* (of a look, remark, etc.) intended to make sb feel silly or ashamed: *withering scorn/contempt* ◊ *She gave him a withering look.* ▶ **wither·ing·ly** *adv.*

with·ers /ˈwɪðəz; AmE -ərz/ *noun* [pl.] the highest part of a horse's back, between its shoulders

with·hold /wɪðˈhəʊld; wɪθ-; AmE -ˈhoʊld/ *verb* (**with·held, with·held** /-ˈheld/) [VN] **~ sth (from sb/sth)** (*formal*) to refuse to give sth to sb: *She was accused of withholding information from the police.*

with·holding tax *noun* [C, U] (in the US) an amount of money that an employer takes out of sb's income as tax and pays directly to the government—compare PAY AS YOU EARN

with·in /wɪˈðɪn/ *prep., adv.*
- *prep.* **1** before a particular period of time has passed; during a particular period of time: *You should receive a reply within seven days.* ◊ *The ambulance arrived **within minutes** of the call being made.* ◊ *Two elections were held **within the space** of a year.* **2** not further than a particular distance from sth: *a house within a mile of the station* ◊ *Is it **within walking distance**?* **3** inside the range or limits of sth: *That question is not within the scope of this talk.* ◊ *We are now within range of enemy fire.* ◊ *He finds it hard to live within his income* (= without spending more than he earns). **OPP** OUTSIDE **4** (*formal*) inside sth/sb: *The noise seems to be coming from within the building.* ◊ *There is discontent within the farming industry.*
- *adv.* (*formal*) inside: *Cleaner required. Apply within.* (= on a sign)

with·out /wɪˈðaʊt/ *prep., adv.*
- *prep.* **1** not having, experiencing or showing sth: *They had gone two days without food.* ◊ *He found the place without difficulty.* ◊ *She spoke without much enthusiasm.* **2** not in the company of sb: *Don't go without me.* **3** not using or taking sth: *Can you see without your glasses?* ◊ *Don't go out without your coat.* **4 ~ (sb) doing sth** not doing the action mentioned: *He left without saying goodbye.* ◊ *The party was organized without her knowing anything about it.* ◊ *You can't make an omelette without breaking eggs.* ◊ ***Without wanting** to criticize, I think you could have done better.* (= used before you make a critical comment)
- *adv.* not having or showing sth: *Do you want a room with a bath or one without?* ◊ *If there's none left we'll have to **do without**.* ◊ *I'm sure we'll **manage without**.*

with·stand /wɪðˈstænd; wɪθˈs-/ *verb* (**with·stood, with·stood** /-ˈstʊd/) [VN] (*formal*) to be strong enough not to be hurt or damaged by extreme conditions, the use of force, etc. **SYN** RESIST, STAND UP TO: *The materials used have to be able to withstand high temperatures.* ◊ *They had withstood siege, hunger and deprivation.*

wit·less /ˈwɪtləs/ *adj.* (*rare*) silly or stupid; not sensible: *a witless child/remark* **IDM** **be scared/bored ᶦwitless** (*informal*) to be extremely frightened or bored

wit·ness /ˈwɪtnəs/ *noun, verb*
- *noun*
<u>PERSON WHO SEES STH</u> **1** (also **eye·wit·ness**) [C] a person who sees sth happen and is able to describe it to other

people: *Police have appealed for witnesses to the accident.* ◇ *We have a witness to the killing.*

IN COURT OF LAW | **2** [C] a person who gives evidence in a court of law: *a defence/prosecution witness* ◇ *to appear as* (a) *witness for the defence/prosecution*

OF SIGNATURE | **3** [C] a person who is present when an official document is signed and who also signs it to prove that they saw this happen

OF RELIGIOUS BELIEFS | **4** [U] evidence of a person's strong religious beliefs, that they show by what they say and do in public

—see also JEHOVAH'S WITNESS

IDM **be (a) 'witness to sth 1** (*formal*) to see sth take place: *He has been witness to a terrible murder.* **2** (*written*) to show that sth is true; to provide evidence for sth: *His good health is a witness to the success of the treatment.* **bear/give 'witness (to sth)** to provide evidence of the truth of sth

■ *verb*

SEE STH | **1** [VN] to see sth happen because you are there when it happens: *She was shocked by the violent scenes she had witnessed.* ◇ *Police have appealed for anyone who witnessed the incident to contact them.* ◇ *We are now witnessing an unprecedented increase in violent crime.*

OF TIME/PLACE | **2** [VN] to be the place, period, organization, etc. in which particular events take place: *Recent years have witnessed a growing social mobility.* ◇ *The retail trade is witnessing a sharp fall in sales.*

SIGNATURE | **3** [VN] to be present when an official document is signed and sign it yourself to prove that you saw this happen: *to witness a signature*

BE SIGN/PROOF | **4** [VN] [usually passive] to be a sign or proof of sth: *There has been increasing interest in her life and work, as witnessed by the publication of two new biographies.* **5** [VN] (*formal*) used in orders when giving an example that proves sth you have just said: *Authentic Italian cooking is very healthy—witness the low incidence of heart disease in Italy.*

IN COURT OF LAW | **6** [V] **~ (to sth)** (*law* or *formal*) to give evidence about sth in a court of law

TO RELIGIOUS BELIEFS | **7** [V] **~ (to sth)** (*especially AmE*) to speak to people about your strong religious beliefs

'witness box (*BrE*) (*AmE* **'witness stand**) (also **stand** *BrE, AmE*) *noun* the place in a court of law where people stand to give evidence

wit·ter /ˈwɪtə(r)/ *verb* [V] **~ (on) (about sth)** (*BrE, informal*, usually *disapproving*) to talk about sth unimportant and boring for a long time: *What's he wittering on about?*

wit·ti·cism /ˈwɪtɪsɪzəm/ *noun* a clever and amusing remark

wit·ting·ly /ˈwɪtɪŋli/ *adv.* (*formal*) in a way that shows that you are aware of what you are doing: *It was clear that, wittingly or unwittingly, he had offended her.*—see also UNWITTING

witty /ˈwɪti/ *adj.* (**wit·tier, wit·ti·est**) able to say or write clever, amusing things: *a witty speaker/writer* ◇ *a witty remark* ▶ **wit·tily** /-ɪli/ *adv.*

wives *pl.* of WIFE

wiz·ard /ˈwɪzəd; *AmE* -ərd/ *noun* **1** a man who is believed to have magic powers **2** a person who is especially good at sth: *a computer/financial wizard*

wiz·ard·ry /ˈwɪzədri; *AmE* -ərd-/ *noun* [U] a very impressive and clever achievement; great skill: *financial/computing/electronic wizardry* ◇ *The second goal was sheer wizardry.*

wiz·ened /ˈwɪznd/ *adj.* (*written*) looking smaller and having many folds and lines in the skin, because of being old: *a wizened little man* ◇ *wizened apples*

woad /wəʊd; *AmE* woʊd/ *noun* [U] a blue substance that people used to paint their bodies and faces in ancient times

wob·ble /ˈwɒbl; *AmE* ˈwɑːbl/ *verb* **1** to move from side to side in an unsteady way; to make sth do this: [V] *This chair wobbles.* ◇ (*figurative*) *Her voice wobbled with emotion.* ◇ [VN] *Don't wobble the table—I'm trying to write.* **2** [V+adv./prep.] to go in a particular direction while

moving from side to side in an unsteady way: *He wobbled off on his bike.* ▶ **wob·ble** *noun* [usually sing.]: *The handlebars developed a wobble.*

wob·bly /ˈwɒbli; *AmE* ˈwɑːbli/ *adj., noun*

■ *adj.* (*informal*) **1** moving in an unsteady way from side to side: *a chair with a wobbly leg* ◇ *a wobbly tooth* ◇ *He's still a bit wobbly after the operation* (= not able to stand firmly). **2** not firm or confident **SYN** SHAKY: *the wobbly singing of the choir* ◇ *The evening got off to a wobbly start.*

■ *noun* **IDM** **throw a 'wobbly** (*BrE, informal*) to suddenly become very angry or upset

wodge /wɒdʒ; *AmE* wɑːdʒ/ *noun* **~ (of sth)** (*BrE, informal*) a large piece or amount of sth: *a thick wodge of ten-pound notes*

woe /wəʊ; *AmE* woʊ/ *noun* (*old-fashioned* or *humorous*) **1** (**woes**) [pl.] the troubles and problems that sb has: *financial/economic woes* ◇ *Thanks for listening to my woes.* **2** [U] great unhappiness: *a tale of woe* **IDM** **woe be'tide sb** | **'woe to sb** (*formal* or *humorous*) a phrase that is used to warn sb that there will be trouble for them if they do sth or do not do sth: *Woe betide anyone who gets in her way!* **woe is 'me!** *exclamation* (*old use* or *humorous*) a phrase that is used to say that you are very unhappy

woe·be·gone /ˈwəʊbɪɡɒn; *AmE* ˈwoʊbɪɡɔːn; -ɡɑːn/ *adj.* (*written*) looking very sad: *a woebegone face/expression*

woe·ful /ˈwəʊfl; *AmE* ˈwoʊfl/ *adj.* **1** [usually before noun] very bad or serious; that you disapprove of **SYN** DEPLORABLE: *She displayed a woeful ignorance of the rules.* **2** (*literary* or *formal*) very sad: *a woeful face* ◇ *woeful tales of broken romances* ▶ **woe·ful·ly** /-fəli/ *adv.*

wog /wɒg; *AmE* wɑːg/ *noun* (*BrE,* △, *slang*) a very offensive word for a person who does not have white skin

wok /wɒk; *AmE* wɑːk/ *noun* a large pan shaped like a bowl, used for cooking food, especially Chinese food—picture at PAN

woke *pt* of WAKE

woken *pp* of WAKE

wolds /wəʊldz; *AmE* woʊldz/ *noun* [pl.] used in the names of places in Britain for an area of high open land: *the Yorkshire Wolds*

wolf /wʊlf/ *noun, verb*

■ *noun* (*pl.* **wolves** /wʊlvz/) a large wild animal of the dog family, that lives and hunts in groups: *a pack of wolves* **IDM** **keep the 'wolf from the door** (*informal*) to have enough money to avoid going hungry; to stop sb feeling hungry **throw sb to the 'wolves** to leave sb to be roughly treated or criticized without trying to help or defend them **a wolf in sheep's 'clothing** a person who seems to be friendly or harmless but is really an enemy—more at CRY *v.*, LONE

■ *verb* [VN] **~ sth (down)** (*informal*) to eat food very quickly, especially by putting a lot of it in your mouth at once **SYN** GOBBLE

wolf·hound /ˈwʊlfhaʊnd/ *noun* a very large tall dog with long hair and long legs, originally used for hunting wolves: *an Irish wolfhound*

wolf·ish /ˈwʊlfɪʃ/ *adj.* (*written*) like a wolf: *wolfish yellow eyes* ◇ (*figurative*) *a wolfish grin* (= showing sexual interest in sb)

'wolf whistle *noun* a whistle with a short rising note and a long falling note, that a man uses to show that he finds a woman attractive, especially one passing in the street. Many women find this offensive. ▶ **'wolf-whistle** *verb* [V, VN]

wolves *pl.* of WOLF

woman /ˈwʊmən/ *noun* (*pl.* **women** /ˈwɪmɪn/) **1** [C] an adult female human being: *men, women and children* ◇ *a 24-year-old woman* ◇ *I prefer to see a woman doctor.* **2** [U] female human beings in general: (*informal*) *She's all woman!* (= has qualities that are typical of women) **3** [C] (in compounds) a woman who comes from the place mentioned or whose job or interest is connected with the thing mentioned: *an Englishwoman* ◇ *a businesswoman* ◇ *a Congresswoman* ◇ *a horsewoman* ▷ note at GENDER **4** [C] a female worker, especially one who works with her hands: *We used to have a woman to do the cleaning.*

5 [sing.] (*old-fashioned, spoken*) a rude way of addressing a female person in an angry or important way: *Be quiet, woman!* **6** [C] (sometimes *disapproving*) a wife or sexual partner: *He's got a new woman in his life.*—see also FALLEN WOMAN, KEPT WOMAN, OTHER WOMAN **IDM be your own 'man/'woman** to act or think independently, not following others or being ordered: *Working for herself meant that she could be her own woman.*—more at HEART, HELL, HONEST, MAN *n.*, PART *n.*, POSSESSED, SUBSTANCE, WORLD

woman·hood /ˈwʊmənhʊd/ *noun* [U] (*formal*) **1** the state of being a woman, rather than a girl: *He watched his daughters grow to womanhood.* **2** women in general: *the womanhood of this country*—compare MANHOOD

woman·iz·ing (*BrE* also **-is·ing**) /ˈwʊmənaɪzɪŋ/ *noun* [U] (*disapproving*) the fact of having sexual relationships with many different women **SYN** PHILANDERING ▶ **woman·izer, -iser** *noun*

woman·kind /ˈwʊmənkaɪnd/ *noun* [U] (*old-fashioned, formal*) women in general—compare MANKIND

woman·ly /ˈwʊmənli/ *adj.* (*approving*) behaving, dressing, etc. in a way that people think is typical of or very suitable for a woman **SYN** FEMININE: *womanly qualities/wiles* ◊ *She has a soft womanly figure.* ▶ **woman·li·ness** *noun* [U]

womb /wuːm/ *noun* the organ in women and female animals in which babies develop before they are born **SYN** UTERUS

wom·bat /ˈwɒmbæt; *AmE* ˈwɑːm-/ *noun* an Australian animal like a small bear, that carries its young in a POUCH (= a pocket of skin) on the front of the mother's body

women·folk /ˈwɪmɪnfəʊk; *AmE* -foʊk/ *noun* [pl.] (*formal* or *humorous*) all the women in a community or family, especially one that is led by men: *The male hunters brought back the food for their womenfolk to cook.*—compare MENFOLK

,women's libe'ration *noun* [U] (*old-fashioned*) (also *informal* **,women's 'lib** /lɪb/) **1** the freedom of women to have the same social and economic rights as men **2** (**Women's Liberation**) (also *informal* **Women's Lib**) the movement that aimed to achieve equal social and economic rights for women

'women's studies *noun* [pl.] the study of women and their role in history, literature and society: *to major in women's studies.*

won *pt, pp* of WIN

won·der /ˈwʌndə(r)/ *verb, noun*

■ *verb* **1 ~ (about sth)** to think about sth and try to decide what is true, what will happen, what you should do, etc: [V wh-] *I wonder who she is.* ◊ *I was just beginning to wonder where you were.* ◊ [V] *'Why do you want to know?' 'No particular reason. I was just wondering.'* ◊ *We were wondering about next April for the wedding.* ◊ [V speech] *'What should I do now?' she wondered.* **2** [V wh-] used as a polite way of asking a question or asking sb to do sth: *I wonder if you can help me.* ◊ *I was wondering whether you'd like to come to a party.* **3 ~ (at sth)** to be very surprised by sth: [V] *She wondered at her own stupidity.* ◊ (*BrE, spoken*) *He's gone and left us to do all the work,* **I shouldn't wonder** (= I wouldn't be surprised if he had). ◊ [V (that)] *I wonder (that) he didn't hurt himself jumping over that wall.* ◊ *I don't wonder you're tired. You've had a busy day.*

■ *noun* **1** [U] a feeling of surprise and admiration that you have when you see or experience sth beautiful, unusual or unexpected **SYN** AWE: *He retained a childlike sense of wonder.* ◊ *She gazed down in wonder at the city spread below her.* **2** [C] something or a quality in sth that fills you with surprise and admiration: *The Grand Canyon is one of the natural wonders of the world.* ◊ *the wonders of modern technology* ◊ *That's the wonder of poetry—you're always discovering something new.* **3** [sing.] (*informal*) a person who is very clever at doing sth; a person or thing that seems very good or effective: *Geoff, you're a wonder! I would never have thought of doing that.* ◊ *Have you seen the boy wonder play yet?* ◊ *a new wonder drug* **IDM do 'wonders (for sb/sth)** to have a very good effect on

sb/sth: *The news has done wonders for our morale.* **(it's) no/little/small 'wonder (that) …** it is not surprising: *It is little wonder (that) she was so upset.* ◊ (*informal*) *No wonder you're tired, you've been walking for hours.* **it's a 'wonder (that) …** (especially *spoken*) it is surprising or strange: *It's a wonder (that) more people weren't hurt.* **wonders will never 'cease** (*spoken, usually ironic*) a phrase used to express surprise and pleasure at sth: *'I've cleaned my room.' 'Wonders will never cease!'* **work 'wonders** to achieve very good results: *Her new diet and exercise programme has worked wonders for her.*—more at NINE

won·der·ful /ˈwʌndəfl; *AmE* -dərfl/ *adj.* **1** very good, pleasant or enjoyable: *a wonderful view/opportunity/person/surprise/day* ◊ *We had a wonderful time last night.* ◊ *You've all been absolutely wonderful!* ◊ *It's wonderful to see you!* **2** making you feel surprise or admiration **SYN** REMARKABLE: *It's wonderful what you can do when you have to.*

won·der·ful·ly /ˈwʌndəfəli; *AmE* -dərf-/ *adv.* (*formal*) **1** very; very well: *The hotel is wonderfully comfortable.* ◊ *Things have worked out wonderfully (well).* **2** unusually; in a surprising way: *He's wonderfully fit for his age.*

won·der·ing·ly /ˈwʌndrɪŋli/ *adv.* (*written*) in a way that shows surprise and/or admiration: *She gazed at him wonderingly.*

won·der·land /ˈwʌndəlænd; *AmE* -dərl-/ *noun* [usually sing.] **1** an imaginary place in children's stories **2** a place that is exciting and full of beautiful and interesting things

won·der·ment /ˈwʌndəmənt; *AmE* -dərm-/ *noun* [U] (*formal*) a feeling of pleasant surprise or WONDER

won·drous /ˈwʌndrəs/ *adj.* (*literary*) strange, beautiful and impressive: *It was a wondrous thing to see the sea for the first time.* ▶ **won·drous·ly** *adv.*

wonk /wɒŋk; *AmE* wɑːŋk/ *noun* (*AmE, informal, disapproving*) **1** a person who works too hard and is considered boring **2** a person who takes too much interest in the less important details of political policy: *the President's chief economic* **policy wonk**

wonky /ˈwɒŋki; *AmE* ˈwɑːŋki/ *adj.* (*BrE, informal*) not steady; not straight: *a wonky chair*

wont /wəʊnt; *AmE* wɔːnt/ *adj., noun*

■ *adj.* [not before noun] **~ (to do sth)** (*old-fashioned, formal*) in the habit of doing sth: *He was wont to fall asleep after supper.*

■ *noun* [sing.] (*old-fashioned, formal*) something a person often does **SYN** HABIT: *She got up early, as was her wont.*

won't /wəʊnt; *AmE* woʊnt/ *short form* will not

woo /wuː/ *verb* [VN] **1** to try to get the support of sb: *Voters are being wooed with promises of lower taxes.* **2** (*old-fashioned*) (of a man) to try to persuade a woman to love him and marry him **SYN** COURT

wood /wʊd/ *noun* **1** [U, C] the hard material that the TRUNK and branches of a tree are made of; this material when it is used to build or make things with, or as a fuel: *He chopped some wood for the fire.* ◊ *a plank of wood* ◊ *All the furniture was made of wood.* ◊ *a wood floor* ◊ *furniture made of a variety of different woods*—see also DEAD WOOD, HARDWOOD, SOFTWOOD, WOODEN, WOODY **2** [C] (also **woods** [pl.]) an area of trees, smaller than a forest: *a large wood* ◊ *a walk in the woods*—see also WOODED **3** [C] a heavy wooden ball used in the game of BOWLS **4** [C] a GOLF CLUB with a large head, that was usually made of wood in the past—compare IRON **IDM not see the ,wood for the 'trees** (*BrE*) (*AmE* **not see the ,forest for the 'trees**) to not see or understand the main point about sth, because you are paying too much attention to small details **not ,out of the 'woods** (*informal*) not yet free from difficulties or problems: *We're not out of the woods yet, you know.*—more at KNOCK *v.*, NECK *n.*, TOUCH *v.*

wood·block /ˈwʊdblɒk; *AmE* -blɑːk/ *noun* **1** each of the small flat pieces of wood that are fitted together to cover a floor: *a woodblock floor*—compare PARQUET **2** a piece of wood with a pattern cut into it, used for printing

wood·carv·ing /ˈwʊdkɑːvɪŋ; *AmE* -kɑːrv-/ *noun* [U, C] the process of shaping a piece of wood with a sharp tool;

æ	ɑː	e	ɜː	ə	ɪ	iː	i	ɒ	ɔː	ʌ	ʊ	u	uː
cat	father	ten	bird	about	sit	see	many	got	saw	cup	put	actual	too
								(BrE)					

a decorative object made in this way ▶ **wood·carver** *noun*

wood·chuck /ˈwʊdtʃʌk/ (also **ground·hog**) *noun* a small N American animal of the SQUIRREL family

wood·cock /ˈwʊdkɒk; *AmE* -kɑːk/ *noun* (*pl.* **wood·cock** or **wood·cocks**) a brown bird with a long straight beak, short legs and a short tail, hunted for food or sport

wood·cut /ˈwʊdkʌt/ *noun* a print that is made from a pattern cut in a piece of wood

wood·cut·ter /ˈwʊdkʌtə(r)/ *noun* (*old-fashioned*) a person whose job is cutting down trees

wood·ed /ˈwʊdɪd/ *adj.* (of land) covered with trees

wood·en /ˈwʊdn/ *adj.* **1** [usually before noun] made of wood: *a wooden box* **2** not showing enough natural expression, emotion or movement: *The actor playing the father was too wooden.* ▶ **wood·en·ly** *adv.*: *She speaks her lines very woodenly.* **wood·en·ness** *noun* [U]

ˌ**wooden ˈspoon** *noun* a spoon made of wood, used in cooking for stirring and mixing—picture at KITCHEN **IDM** **get, win, take, etc. the ˌwooden ˈspoon** (*BrE, informal*) to come last in a race or competition

wood·land /ˈwʊdlənd/ *noun* [U, C] (also **wood·lands** [pl.]) an area of land that is covered with trees: *ancient/dense/mixed woodland* ◊ *The house is fringed by fields and woodlands.* ◊ *woodland walks/scenery*

wood·louse /ˈwʊdlaʊs/ *noun* (*pl.* **wood·lice** /ˈwʊdlaɪs/) a small grey creature like an insect, with a hard shell, that lives in decaying wood or damp soil—picture on page A7

wood·man /ˈwʊdmən/ *noun* (*pl.* **-men** /-mən/) (also **woods·man**) a person who works or lives in a forest, taking care of and sometimes cutting down trees, etc.

wood·peck·er /ˈwʊdpekə(r)/ *noun* a bird with a long beak that it uses to make holes in trees when it is looking for insects to eat

ˈ**wood pigeon** *noun* a bird of the PIGEON family, that lives in woods and fields rather than in cities

ˈ**wood pulp** *noun* [U] wood that has been broken into small pieces and crushed until it is soft. It is used for making paper.

wood·shed /ˈwʊdʃed/ *noun* a small building for storing wood in, especially for fuel

woods·man /ˈwʊdzmən/ *noun* (*pl.* **-men** /-men/) = WOODMAN

woodsy /ˈwʊdzi/ *adj.* (*informal, especially AmE*) covered with trees; connected with WOODS

wood·wind /ˈwʊdwɪnd/ *noun* [C+sing./pl. *v.*] (also **wood·winds** [pl.] especially in *AmE*) the group of musical instruments in an orchestra that are mostly made of wood or metal and are played by blowing. FLUTES, CLARINETS and BASSOONS are all woodwind instruments: *the woodwind section of the orchestra*—compare BRASS, PERCUSSION, STRINGS, WIND *n.* (4), WIND INSTRUMENT

wood·work /ˈwʊdwɜːk; *AmE* -wɜːrk/ *noun* [U] **1** things made of wood in a building or room, such as doors and stairs: *The woodwork needs painting.* ◊ *He hit the woodwork* (= the wooden frame of the goal) *twice before scoring.* **2** (*BrE*) (also ˈ**wood·work·ing** *AmE, BrE*) the activity or skill of making things from wood **IDM** **blend/fade into the ˈwoodwork** to behave in a way that does not attract any attention; to disappear or hide **come/crawl out of the ˈwoodwork** (*informal, disapproving*) if you say that sb **comes/crawls out of the woodwork**, you mean that they have suddenly appeared in order to express an opinion or to take advantage of a situation: *When he won the lottery, all sorts of distant relatives came out of the woodwork.*

wood·worm /ˈwʊdwɜːm; *AmE* -wɜːrm/ *noun* **1** [C] a small worm that eats wood, making a lot of small holes in it **2** [U] the damage caused by woodworms: *The beams are riddled with woodworm.*

woody /ˈwʊdi/ *adj.* **1** (of plants) having a thick, hard stem like wood **2** covered with trees: *a woody valley* **3** having a smell like wood: *This new fragrance has woody notes.*

woof /wʊf/ *exclamation, verb, noun*

■ *exclamation* (*informal*) a word used to describe the loud noise that a dog makes: *'Woof! Woof!' he barked.* ▶ **woof** *verb* [V]

■ *noun* = WEFT

woof·er /ˈwuːfə(r)/ *noun* a LOUDSPEAKER for reproducing the low notes from a STEREO—compare TWEETER

wool /wʊl/ *noun* [U] **1** the soft fine hair that covers the body of sheep, goats and some other animals **2** long thick thread made from animal's wool, used for knitting: *a ball of wool*—picture at SEW **3** fabric made from animal's wool, used for making clothes, etc: *This scarf is 100% wool.* ◊ *pure new wool* ◊ *a wool coat/blanket*—see also COTTON WOOL, DYED IN THE WOOL, LAMBSWOOL, STEEL WOOL, WIRE WOOL **IDM** see PULL *v.*

wool·len (*BrE*) (*AmE* **wool·en**) /ˈwʊlən/ *adj.* **1** [usually before noun] made of wool: *a woollen blanket/coat* ◊ *woollen cloth/gloves* **2** [only before noun] involved in making fabric from wool: *a woollen mill* ◊ *the woollen industry*

wool·lens (*BrE*) (*AmE* **wool·ens**) /ˈwʊlənz/ *noun* [pl.] clothes made of wool, especially knitted clothes

wool·ly /ˈwʊli/ *adj., noun*

■ *adj.* (*AmE* also **wooly**) **1** covered with wool or with hair like wool: *woolly monkeys* **2** (*informal, especially BrE*) made of wool; like wool **SYN** WOOLLEN: *a woolly hat/jumper* **3** (of people or their ideas, etc.) not thinking clearly; confused; not clearly expressed: *woolly arguments/concepts* ▶ **wool·li·ness** *noun* [U]

■ *noun* (*pl.* **-ies**) (*BrE, informal, becoming old-fashioned*) a piece of clothing made of wool, especially one that has been knitted

woozy /ˈwuːzi/ *adj.* (*informal*) **1** feeling unsteady, confused and unable to think clearly **2** (*especially AmE*) feeling as though you might VOMIT

wop /wɒp; *AmE* wɑːp/ *noun* (⚠, *slang*) a very offensive word for a person from southern Europe, especially an Italian

word /wɜːd; *AmE* wɜːrd/ *noun, verb*

■ *noun*

UNIT OF LANGUAGE **1** [C] a single unit of language which means sth and can be spoken or written: *Do not write more than 200 words.* ◊ *Do you know the words to this song?* ◊ *What's the Spanish word for 'table'?* ◊ *He was a true friend in all senses of the word.* ◊ *Tell me what happened in your own words.* ◊ *I could hear every word they were saying.* ◊ *He couldn't find the words to thank her enough.* ◊ *Words fail me* (= I cannot express how I feel). ◊ *There are no words to say how sorry we are.* ◊ *I can't remember her exact words.* ◊ *Angry is not the word for it*—I was furious.—see also BUZZWORD, FOUR-LETTER WORD, HOUSEHOLD WORD, SWEAR WORD

STH YOU SAY **2** [C] a thing that you say; a remark or statement: *Have a word with Pat and see what she thinks.* ◊ *Could I have a quick word with you* (= speak to you quickly)*?* ◊ *A word of warning: read the instructions very carefully.* ◊ *words of love* ◊ *She left without a word* (= without saying anything). ◊ *I don't believe a word of his story* (= I don't believe any of it). ◊ *a man/woman of few words* (= who doesn't talk very much) ◊ *I'd like to say a few words about future plans.* ◊ *Remember—not a word to* (= don't tell) *Peter about any of this.* ◊ *He never breathed a word of this to me.*

PROMISE **3** [sing.] a promise or GUARANTEE that you will do sth or that sth will happen or is true: *I give you my word that this won't happen again.* ◊ *I give you my word of honour* (= my sincere promise) ... ◊ *We never doubted her word.* ◊ *We only have his word for it that the cheque is in the post.* ◊ *to keep your word* (= do what you promised) ◊ *He promised to help and was as good as his word* (= did what he promised). ◊ *He's a man of his word* (= he does what he promises). ◊ *I trusted her not to go back on her word* (= break her promise). ◊ *I can't prove it—you'll have to take my word for it* (= believe me).

INFORMATION/NEWS **4** [sing.] a piece of information or news: *There's been no word from them since before Christmas.* ◊ *She sent word that she would be late.* ◊ *If word gets out about the affair, he will have to resign.* ◊ *Word* *has it that* she's leaving. ◊ *The word is they've split up.* ◊ *He likes to* **spread the word** *about the importance of healthy eating.*

BIBLE | **5** (**the Word**) (also **the ˌWord of ˈGod**) [sing.] the Bible and its teachings

IDM **by ˌword of ˈmouth** because people tell each other and not because they read about it: *The news spread by word of mouth.* (**right**) **from the word ˈgo** (*informal*) from the very beginning **(not) get a word in ˈedgeways** (*BrE*) (*AmE* (**not**) **get a word in ˈedgewise**) (not) to be able to say anything because sb else is speaking too much: *When Mary starts talking, no one else can get a word in edgeways.* **have a word in sb's ˈear** (*BrE*) to speak to sb privately about sth **have/exchange ˈwords (with sb) (about sth)** (*especially BrE*) to argue or quarrel with sb: *We've had words.* ◊ *Words were exchanged.* **in ˈother words** used to introduce an explanation of sth: *They asked him to leave—in other words he was fired.* (**not**) **in so/as many ˈwords** (not) in exactly the same words as sb says were used: *'Did she say she was sorry?' 'Not in so many words.'* ◊ *He didn't approve of the plan and said so in as many words.* **in a ˈword** (*spoken*) used for giving a very short, usually negative, answer or comment: *'Would you like to help us?' 'In a word, no.'* **in words of one ˈsyllable** using very simple language: *Could you say that again in words of one syllable?* **the last/final word (on sth)** the last comment or decision about sth: *He always has to* **have the last word** *in any argument.* (**upon**) **my ˈword** (*old-fashioned*) used to show that you are surprised about sth **not have a good word to ˈsay for sb/sth** (*informal*) to never say anything good about sb/sth: *Nobody had a good word to say about him.* **put in a (good) ˈword for sb** to praise sb to sb else in order to help them get a job, etc. **put ˈwords into sb's mouth** to suggest that sb has said sth when in fact they have not **say/give the ˈword** to give an order; to make a request: *Just say the word, and I'll go.* **take sb at their ˈword** to believe exactly what sb says or promises **take the ˈwords right out of sb's mouth** to say what sb else was going to say **too funny, silly, ridiculous, etc. for ˈwords** extremely funny, silly, ridiculous, etc. ˌword for ˈword in exactly the same words or (when translated) exactly EQUIVALENT words: *She repeated their conversation word for word to me.* ◊ *a word-for-word translation* **sb's word is their ˈbond** sb's promise can be relied on completely—more at ACTION *n.*, BANDY *v.*, DIRTY *adj.*, EAT, HANG *v.*, LAST *det.*, LOST *adj.*, MINCE *v.*, MUM *adj.*, OPERATIVE *adj.*, PLAY *n.*, PRINT *v.*, WAR *n.*, WEIGH, WRITTEN

■ *verb* [VN] [often passive] to write or say sth using particular words: *How was the letter worded (= what did it say exactly)?* ▶ **word·ed** *adj.*: *a carefully worded speech* ◊ *a strongly worded letter of protest*

ˈword break (also **ˈword division**) *noun* a point at which a word is split between two lines of text

word·ing /ˈwɜːdɪŋ; *AmE* ˈwɜːrd-/ *noun* [U, C, usually sing.] the words that are used in a piece of writing or speech, especially when they have been carefully chosen: *The wording was deliberately ambiguous.*

word·less /ˈwɜːdləs; *AmE* ˈwɜːrd-/ *adj.* (*formal* or *literary*) **1** [usually before noun] without any words; silent: *a wordless cry/prayer* **2** (of people) not saying anything ▶ **word·less·ly** *adv.*

ˌword-ˈperfect (*BrE*) (*AmE* ˌletter-ˈperfect) *adj.* able to remember and repeat sth exactly without making any mistakes

word·play /ˈwɜːdpleɪ; *AmE* ˈwɜːrd-/ *noun* [U] making jokes by using words in a clever or amusing way, especially by using a word that has two meanings, or different words that sound the same—compare PUN

ˈword processing *noun* [U] the use of a computer to create, store and print a piece of text, usually typed in from a keyboard: *We've got a computer but I only use it for word processing.*

ˈword processor *noun* a computer that runs a WORD PROCESSING program and is usually used for writing letters, reports, etc.

wordy /ˈwɜːdi; *AmE* ˈwɜːrdi/ *adj.* (usually *disapproving*)

using too many words, especially formal ones **SYN** VERBOSE: *a wordy and repetitive essay* ▶ **wordi·ness** *noun* [U]

wore *pt* of WEAR

work /wɜːk; *AmE* wɜːrk/ *verb, noun*

■ *verb*

DO JOB/TASK | **1** ~ (**at/on sth**) to do sth that involves physical or mental effort, especially as part of a job: [V] *I can't work if I'm cold.* ◊ *I've been working at my assignment all day.* ◊ *He is working on a new novel.* ◊ *She's outside, working on the car.* ◊ *Doctors often work very long hours.* **2** [V] ~ (**for sb/sth**) | ~ (**as sth**) to have a job: *Both my parents work.* ◊ *She works for an engineering company.* ◊ *I've always worked in education.* ◊ *Do you enjoy working with children?* ◊ *My son is working as a science teacher.*

MAKE EFFORT | **3** [VN] to make yourself/sb work, especially very hard: *She works herself too hard.* **4** ~ (**for sth**) to make efforts to achieve sth: [V] *She dedicated her life to working for peace.* ◊ [Vto inf] *The committee is working to get the prisoners freed.*

MANAGE | **5** [VN] to manage or operate sth to gain benefit from it: *to work the land (= grow crops on it, etc.)* ◊ *He works a large area (= selling a company's goods, etc.).* ◊ (*figurative*) *She was a skilful speaker who knew how to work a crowd (= to excite them or make them feel sth strongly).*

MACHINE/DEVICE | **6** [V] to function; to operate: *The phone isn't working.* ◊ *It works by electricity.* ◊ *Are they any closer to understanding how the brain works?* **7** [VN] to make a machine, device, etc. operate: *Do you know how to work the coffee machine?* ◊ *The machine is worked by wind power.*

HAVE RESULT/EFFECT | **8** [V] ~ (**on sb/sth**) to have the result or effect that you want: *The pills the doctor gave me aren't working.* ◊ *My plan worked, and I got them to agree.* ◊ *His charm doesn't work on me (= does not affect or impress me).* **9** [V+adv./prep.] to have a particular effect: *Your age can work against you in this job.* ◊ *Speaking Italian should work in his favour.* **10** [VN] to cause or produce sth as a result of effort: *You can work miracles with very little money if you follow our home decoration tips.*

USE MATERIAL | **11** [VN] ~ **sth** (**into sth**) to make a material into a particular shape or form by pressing, stretching, hitting it, etc: *to work clay/dough* ◊ *to work gold/iron* ◊ *to work the mixture into a paste* **12** [V] ~ (**in/with sth**) (of an artist, etc.) to use a particular material to produce a picture or other item: *an artist working in oils* ◊ *a craftsman working with wool*

OF PART OF FACE/BODY | **13** [V] (*written*) to move violently: *He stared at me in horror, his mouth working.*

MOVE GRADUALLY | **14** to move or pass to a particular place or state, usually gradually: [V] *It will take a while for the drug to work out of your system.* ◊ [VN] (*figurative*) *He worked his way to the top of his profession.* ◊ [VN-ADJ] *I was tied up, but managed to work myself free.* ◊ [V-ADJ] *The screw had worked loose.*

IDM Most idioms containing **work** are at the entries for the nouns and adjectives in the idioms, for example **work your fingers to the bone** is at **finger**.   **ˈwork it/ things** (*informal*) to arrange sth in a particular way, especially by being clever: *Can you work it so that we get free tickets?*

PHRV ˌwork aˈround/ˈround to sth/sb to gradually turn a conversation towards a particular topic, subject, etc: *It was some time before he worked around to what he really wanted to say.* ˌwork sth ˈin | work sth into sth **1** to try to include sth: *Can't you work a few more jokes into your speech?* **2** to add one substance to another and mix them together: *Gradually work in the butter.* ˌwork sth↔ˈoff **1** to get rid of sth, especially a strong feeling, by using physical effort: *She worked off her anger by going for a walk.* **2** to earn money in order to be able to pay a debt: *They had a large bank loan to work off.* ˌwork ˈout **1** to train the body by physical exercise: *I work out regularly to keep fit.*—related noun WORKOUT **2** to develop in a successful way: *My first job didn't work out.* ◊ *Things have worked out quite well for us.* ˌwork ˈout (at sth) if sth

b	d	f	g	h	k	l	m	n	p	r
bad	did	fall	get	hat	cat	leg	man	now	pen	red

W

works out at sth, you calculate that it will be a particular amount: [+ADJ] *It'll work out cheaper to travel by bus.* ,**work sb**↔'**out** to understand sb's character: *I've never been able to work her out.* ,**work sth**↔'**out 1** to calculate sth: *to work out the answer* **2** to find the answer to sth; to solve sth: *to work out a problem/puzzle/code* ◊ [+wh-] *Can you work out what these squiggles mean?* ◊ *I couldn't work out where the music was coming from.* **3** to plan or think of sth: *I've worked out a new way of doing it.* **4** [usually passive] to remove all the coal, minerals, etc. from a mine over a period of time: *a worked-out silver mine* ,**work sb**↔'**over** (*slang*) to attack sb and hit them, for example to make them give you information '**work to sth** to follow a plan, TIMETABLE, etc: *to work to a budget* ◊ *We're working to a very tight deadline* (= we have little time in which to do the work). '**work towards sth** to try to reach or achieve a goal ,**work sth**↔'**up** to develop or improve sth with some effort: *I can't work up any enthusiasm for his idea.* ◊ *She went for a long walk to work up an appetite.* ,**work sb/yourself** '**up (into sth)** to make sb/yourself reach a state of great excitement, anger, etc: *Don't work yourself up into a state about it. It isn't worth it.* ◊ *I can't get worked up about cars.* ◊ *What are you so worked up about?* ,**work sth** '**up into sth** to bring sth to a more complete or more satisfactory state: *I'm working my notes up into a dissertation.* ,**work** '**up to sth** to develop or move gradually towards sth, usually sth more exciting or extreme: *The music worked up to a rousing finale.* ◊ *I began by jogging in the park and worked up to running 5 miles a day.*

■ *noun*

JOB/TASK | **1** [U] the job that a person does especially in order to earn money SYN EMPLOYMENT: (*BrE*) *They are in work* (= have a job). ◊ (*BrE, AmE*) *She had been out of work* (= without a job) *for a year.* ◊ *He started work as a security guard.* ◊ *It is difficult to find work in the present economic climate.* ◊ *I'm still looking for work.* ◊ *She's planning to return to work once the children start school.* ◊ *What line of work are you in* (= what type of work do you do)? ◊ *before/after work* (= in the morning/evening each day) ◊ *full-time/part-time/unpaid/voluntary work* **2** [U] the duties that you have and the activities that you do as part of your job: *Police work is mainly routine.* ◊ *The accountant described his work to the sales staff.* ◊ *Students do work experience in local firms.*—see also PIECEWORK, SOCIAL WORK **3** [U] tasks that need to be done: *There is plenty of work to be done in the garden.* ◊ *I have some work for you to do.* ◊ *Stop talking and get on with your work.*—see also HOMEWORK **4** [U] materials needed or used for doing work, especially books, papers, etc: *She often brings work* (= for example, files and documents) *home with her from the office.* ◊ *His work was spread all over the floor.*—see also PAPERWORK

PLACE OF JOB | **5** [U] (used without *the*) the place where you do your job: *I go to work at 8 o'clock.* ◊ *When do you leave for work?* ◊ *The new legislation concerns health and safety at work.* ◊ *I have to leave work early today.* ◊ *Her friends from work came to see her in the hospital.*

EFFORT | **6** [U] the use of physical strength or mental power in order to do or make sth: *She earned her grades through sheer hard work.* ◊ *We started work on the project in 1998.* ◊ *Work continues on renovating the hotel.* ◊ *The work of building the bridge took six months.* ◊ *The art collection was his life's work.* ◊ *She set them to work painting the fence.* ◊ *They carried out pioneering work on the treatment of cancer.*—see also DONKEY WORK, FIELD-WORK

PRODUCT OF WORK | **7** [U] a thing or things that are produced as a result of work: *She's an artist whose work I really admire.* ◊ *Is this all your own work* (= did you do it without help from others)? ◊ *The book is a detailed and thorough piece of work covering all aspects of the subject.*

RESULT OF ACTION | **8** [U] the result of an action; what is done by sb: *The damage is clearly the work of vandals.*

BOOK/MUSIC/ART | **9** [C] a book, piece of music, painting, etc: *the collected/complete works of Tolstoy* ◊ *works of fiction/literature* ◊ *Beethoven's piano works*—see also WORK OF ART—compare OPUS

BUILDING/REPAIRING | **10** (**works**) [pl.] (often in compounds) activities involving building or repairing sth: *roadworks* ◊ *They expanded the shipyards and started engineering works.*—see also PUBLIC WORKS

FACTORY | **11** (**works**) [C+sing./pl. *v.*] (often in compounds) a place where things are made or industrial processes are carried out: *an engineering works* ◊ *a brickworks*

PARTS OF MACHINE | **12** (**the works**) [pl.] the moving parts of a machine, etc. SYN MECHANISM

EVERYTHING | **13** (**the works**) [pl.] (*informal*) everything: *We went to the chip shop and had the works: fish, chips, gherkins, mushy peas.*

PHYSICS | **14** [U] the use of force to produce movement—see also JOULE

IDM at '**work 1** having an effect on sth: *She suspected that secret influences were at·work.* **2** ~ (**on sth**) busy doing sth: *He is still at work on the painting.* ◊ *Danger—men at work.* **get (down) to/set to** '**work** to begin; to make a start: *We set to work on the outside of the house* (= for example, painting it). **give sb the** '**works** (*informal*) to give or tell sb everything ,**good** '**works** kind acts to help others **go/set about your** '**work** to do/start to do your work: *She went cheerfully about her work.* **have your** '**work cut out** (*informal*) to be likely to have difficulty doing sth: *You'll have your work cut out to get there by nine o'clock.* **in the** '**works** something that is in the works is being discussed, planned or prepared and will happen or exist soon **the work of a** '**moment,** '**second, etc.** (*written*) a thing that takes a very short time to do—more at DAY, DIRTY *adj.*, HAND *n.*, HARD *adj.*, JOB, LIGHT *adj.*, NASTY, NICE, SHORT *adj.*, SPANNER

VOCABULARY BUILDING
a day's work

work [U] *Looking after children all day is hard work.*
job [C] *I have a few jobs to do in the house this morning.* ◊ *Writing this report is going to be a long job.* ◊ *I've been given the enjoyable job of presenting the prizes.*
task [C] *We'll soon have robots performing simple everyday tasks.* ◊ *The police face a very difficult task dealing with the increase in violent crime.*
chore [C] *the household chores* ◊ *Don't turn reading into a chore for your kids.*
assignment [C] *I have three assignments to do by the end of term.*
project [C] *My next project is painting the living room.*
labour [U] *I was trained as a builder so I'm used to manual labour.*
toil [U] (*formal* or *literary*) *A lifetime of hard toil on the farm had made him look old and tired.*
⇨ note at JOB

---

work·able /'wɜːkəbl; *AmE* 'wɜːrk-/ *adj.* **1** (of a system, an idea, etc.) that can be used successfully and effectively SYN PRACTICAL: *a workable plan/solution* **2** that you can shape, spread, dig, etc: *Add more water until the dough is workable.*

work·aday /'wɜːkədeɪ; *AmE* 'wɜːrk-/ *adj.* [usually before noun] (*written*) ordinary; not very interesting SYN EVERYDAY: *This was a far cry from her normal workaday world.*

work·ahol·ic /ˌwɜːkə'hɒlɪk; *AmE* ˌwɜːrkə'hɔːlɪk; -'hɑːl-/ *noun* (*informal*, usually *disapproving*) a person who works very hard and finds it difficult to stop working and do other things

work·bench /'wɜːkbentʃ; *AmE* 'wɜːrk-/ (also **bench**) *noun* a long heavy table used for doing practical jobs, working with tools, etc.—picture at VICE

work·book /'wɜːkbʊk; *AmE* 'wɜːrk-/ (*BrE*) (*AmE* '**exercise book**) *noun* a book with exercises in it, often with spaces for students to write answers in, to help them practise what they have learnt

work·day /'wɜːkdeɪ; *AmE* 'wɜːrk-/ *noun* **1** (*AmE*) = WORKING DAY (1): *an 8-hour workday* **2** = WORKING DAY (2): *workday traffic*

---

s	t	v	z	ʃ	ʒ	tʃ	dʒ	θ	ð	ŋ
see	tea	van	zoo	shoe	vision	chain	jam	thin	this	sing

W

worked 'up *adj.* [not before noun] ~ **(about sth)** (*informal*) very excited or upset about sth: *There's no point in getting worked up about it.*

work·er /ˈwɜːkə(r); *AmE* ˈwɜːrk-/ *noun* **1** (often in compounds) a person who works, especially one who does a particular kind of work: *farm/factory/office workers* ◊ *rescue/aid/research workers* ◊ *temporary/part-time/casual workers* ◊ *manual/skilled/unskilled workers*—see also GUEST WORKER, SOCIAL WORKER **2** a person who is employed to do physical work rather than organizing things or managing people: *Conflict between employers and workers intensified and the number of strikes rose.* ◊ *talks between workers and management* ◊ *profit-sharing and worker participation in decision-making* **3** (usually after an adjective) a person who works hard or who works in a particular way: *a hard/fast/quick worker* **4** a female bee that helps do the work of the group of bees but does not reproduce—compare DRONE, QUEEN BEE **IDM** see FAST *adj.*

'work experience *noun* [U] **1** the work or jobs that you have done in your life so far: *The opportunities available will depend on your previous work experience and qualifications.* **2** (*BrE*) a period of time that a young person, especially a student, spends working in a company as a form of training—compare INTERNSHIP

work·fare /ˈwɜːkfeə(r); *AmE* ˈwɜːrkfer/ *noun* [U] a system in which unemployed people have to work in order to get money for food, rent, etc. from the government

work·force /ˈwɜːkfɔːs; *AmE* ˈwɜːrkfɔːrs/ *noun* [C+sing./pl. *v.*] **1** all the people who work for a particular company, organization, etc. **SYN** STAFF: *The factory will have to lose half of its 1000-strong workforce.* ◊ *Two thirds of the workforce is/are women.* **2** all the people in a country or an area who are available for work: *A quarter of the local workforce is/are unemployed.*

work·horse /ˈwɜːkhɔːs; *AmE* ˈwɜːrkhɔːrs/ *noun* a person or machine that you can rely on to do hard and/or boring work

work·house /ˈwɜːkhaʊs; *AmE* ˈwɜːrk-/ (*BrE*) (also **poor·house** *AmE, BrE*) *noun* (in Britain in the past) a building where very poor people were sent to live and given work to do

work·ing /ˈwɜːkɪŋ; *AmE* ˈwɜːrk-/ *adj., noun*

■ *adj.* [only before noun] **1** having a job for which you are paid **SYN** EMPLOYED: *the working population* ◊ *a working wife/mother*—see also HARD-WORKING **2** having a job that involves manual physical work rather than office work, studying, etc: *a working man* ◊ *a working men's club* **3** connected with your job and the time you spend doing it: *long working hours* ◊ *poor working conditions* ◊ *I have a good working relationship with my boss.* ◊ *She spent most of her working life as a teacher.* ◊ *recent changes in working practices* **4** a working breakfast or lunch is one at which you discuss business **5** used as a basis for work, discussion, etc. but likely to be changed or improved in the future: *a working hypothesis/theory* ◊ *Have you decided on a working title for your thesis yet?* **6** if you have a working knowledge of sth, you can use it at a basic level **7** the working parts of a machine are the parts that move in order to make it function **8** a working MAJORITY is a small MAJORITY that is enough to enable a government to win votes in parliament and make new laws **IDM** see ORDER *n.*

■ *noun* [usually pl.] **1** ~ **(of sth)** the way in which a machine, a system, an organization, etc. works: *an introduction to the workings of Congress* ◊ *the workings of the human mind* ◊ *the machine's inner workings* **2** the parts of a mine or QUARRY where coal, metal, stone, etc. is or has been dug from the ground

working 'capital *noun* [U] (*business*) the money that is needed to run a business rather than the money that is used to buy buildings and equipment when starting the business—compare VENTURE CAPITAL

the working 'class *noun* [sing.+ sing./pl. *v.*] (also **the working 'classes** [pl.]) the social class whose members do not have much money or power and are usually employed to do MANUAL work (= physical work using

their hands): *the political party of the working class* ◊ *The working class has/have rejected them in the elections.*—compare MIDDLE CLASS, UPPER CLASS ▶ **working-'class** *adj.*: *a working-class background/community/family*

working 'day *noun* (*BrE*) **1** (*AmE* **work-day**) the part of a day during which you work: *I spend most of my working day sitting at a desk.* ◊ *Their working day can last anything up to 15 hours.* **2** (also *less frequent* **work-day**) a day on which you usually work or on which most people usually work: *Sunday is a normal working day for me.* ◊ *Thousands of working days were lost through strikes last year.* ◊ *Allow two working days (= not Saturday or Sunday) for delivery.*

'working girl *noun* (*informal*) **1** (becoming *old-fashioned*) a prostitute. People say 'working girl' to avoid saying 'prostitute'. **2** (sometimes *offensive*) a woman who has a paid job

'working paper *noun* **1** [C] a report written by a group of people chosen to study an aspect of law, education, health, etc. **2** (**working papers**) [pl.] (in the US) an official document that enables sb under 16 years old or born outside the US to have a job

'working party (*BrE*) (also **'working group** *AmE, BrE*) *noun* [C+sing./pl. *v.*] ~ **(on sth)** a group of people chosen to study a particular problem or situation in order to suggest ways of dealing with it

working 'week (*BrE*) (*AmE* **work-week**) *noun* the total amount of time that you spend at work during the week: *a 40-hour working week*

work·load /ˈwɜːkləʊd; *AmE* ˈwɜːrkloʊd/ *noun* the amount of work that has to be done by a particular person or organization: *a heavy workload* ◊ *We have taken on extra staff to cope with the increased workload.*

work·man /ˈwɜːkmən; *AmE* ˈwɜːrk-/ *noun* (*pl.* **-men** /-mən/) **1** a man who is employed to do physical work **2** (with an adjective) a person who works in the way mentioned: *a good/bad workman*

work·man·like /ˈwɜːkmənlaɪk; *AmE* ˈwɜːrk-/ *adj.* done, made, etc. in a skilful and thorough way but not usually very original or exciting: *They've done a workmanlike job.* ◊ *It was a workmanlike performance from the local team.*

work·man·ship /ˈwɜːkmənʃɪp; *AmE* ˈwɜːrk-/ *noun* [U] the skill with which sb makes sth, especially when this affects the way it looks or works: *Our buyers insist on high standards of workmanship and materials.*

work·mate /ˈwɜːkmeɪt; *AmE* ˈwɜːrk-/ *noun* (*especially BrE*) a person that you work with, often doing the same job, in an office, a factory, etc.

work of 'art *noun* (*pl.* **works of 'art**) **1** a painting, statue, etc: *A number of priceless works of art were stolen from the gallery.* **2** something that is attractive and skilfully made: *The bride's dress was a work of art.*

work·out /ˈwɜːkaʊt; *AmE* ˈwɜːrk-/ *noun* a period of physical exercise that you do to keep fit: *She does a 20-minute workout every morning.*

work·place /ˈwɜːkpleɪs; *AmE* ˈwɜːrk-/ *noun* (often **the workplace**) [sing.] the office, factory, etc. where people work: *the introduction of new technology into the workplace*

'work release *noun* (*AmE*) a system that allows prisoners to leave prison during the day to go to work

work·room /ˈwɜːkruːm; -rʊm; *AmE* ˈwɜːrk-/ *noun* a room in which work is done, especially work that involves making things: *The jeweller has a workroom at the back of his shop.*

works *noun* ⇨ WORK

works 'council *noun* (*especially BrE*) a group of employees who represent all the employees at a factory, etc. in discussion with their employers over conditions of work

work·sheet /ˈwɜːkʃiːt; *AmE* ˈwɜːrk-/ *noun* **1** a piece of paper on which there is a series of questions and exercises to be done by a student **2** a piece of paper on which work that has been done or has to be done is recorded

work·shop /ˈwɜːkʃɒp; *AmE* ˈwɜːrkʃɑːp/ *noun* **1** a room or

æ	ɑː	e	ɜː	ə	ɪ	iː	i	ɒ	ɔː	ʌ	ʊ	u	uː
cat	father	ten	bird	about	sit	see	many	got	saw	cup	put	actual	too

(BrE)

building in which things are made or repaired using tools or machinery **2** a period of discussion and practical work on a particular subject, in which a group of people share their knowledge and experience: *a drama workshop* ◊ *a poetry workshop*

'work-shy *adj.* (*BrE, disapproving*) unwilling to work **SYN** LAZY

work·sta·tion /'wɜːksteɪʃn; *AmE* 'wɜːrk-/ *noun* the desk and computer at which a person works; one computer that is part of a NETWORKED computer system—picture on page 250

work·top /'wɜːktɒp; *AmE* 'wɜːrktɑːp/ (*BrE*) (also **work surface** especially in *BrE*) (also **counter** *AmE, BrE*) *noun* a flat surface in a kitchen for preparing food on

,work-to-'rule *noun* [usually sing.] a situation in which workers refuse to do any work that is not in their contracts, in order to protest about sth—compare GO-SLOW

work·week /'wɜːkwiːk; *AmE* 'wɜːrk-/ *noun* (*AmE*) = WORKING WEEK

world /wɜːld; *AmE* wɜːrld/ *noun*

THE EARTH/ITS PEOPLE | **1 (the world)** [sing.] the earth, with all its countries, peoples and natural features: *to sail around the world* ◊ *travelling (all over) the world* ◊ *a map of the world* ◊ *French is spoken in many parts of the world.* ◊ *Which is the largest city in the world?* ◊ *He's the world's highest paid entertainer.* ◊ *a meeting of world leaders* ◊ *campaigning for world peace* **2** [C, usually sing.] a particular part of the earth; a particular group of countries or people; a particular period of history and the people of that period: *the Arab world* ◊ *the English-speaking world* ◊ *the industrialized and developing worlds* ◊ *the ancient/ modern world*—see also THE FIRST WORLD, THE NEW WORLD, THE OLD WORLD, THE THIRD WORLD

ANOTHER PLANET | **3** [C] a planet like the earth: *There may be other worlds out there.*

TYPE OF LIFE | **4** [C] the people or things belonging to a particular group or connected with a particular interest, job, etc: *the animal/plant/insect world* ◊ *the world of fashion* ◊ *stars from the sporting and artistic worlds* **5** [usually sing.] (usually used with an adjective) everything that exists of a particular kind; a particular kind of life or existence: *the natural world* (= animals, plants, minerals, etc.) ◊ *the dream world of travel brochures* ◊ *They are a couple in **the real world** as well as in the movie.* ◊ *The island is a world of brilliant colours and dramatic sunsets.* ◊ *They had little contact with the **outside world*** (= people and places that were not part of their normal life).

PERSON'S LIFE | **6** [sing.] a person's environment, experiences, friends and family, etc: *Parents are the most important people in a child's world.* ◊ *When his wife died, his entire world was turned upside down.*

SOCIETY | **7** [sing.] our society and the way people live and behave; the people in the world: *We live in a rapidly changing world.* ◊ *He's too young to understand the **ways of the world**.* ◊ *The whole world was waiting for news of the astronauts.* ◊ *She felt that the world was against her.* ◊ *The eyes of the world are on the President.* **8 (the world)** [sing.] a way of life where possessions and physical pleasures are important, rather than spiritual values: *monks and nuns renouncing the world*—see also OLDE WORLDE, OLD-WORLD

HUMAN EXISTENCE | **9** [sing.] the state of human existence: *this world and the next* (= life on earth and existence after death)

IDM be ,all the 'world to sb to be loved by and very important to sb **the best of 'both/'all possible worlds** the benefits of two or more completely different situations that you can enjoy at the same time: *If you enjoy the coast and the country, you'll get the best of both worlds on this walk.* **be 'worlds apart** to be completely different in attitudes, opinions, etc. **come/go 'down/'up in the world** to become less/more important or successful in society **come into the 'world** (*literary*) to be born **do sb/sth the 'world of good** to make sb feel much better; to improve sth: *A change of job would do you the world of good.* **for all the world as if/though ... | for all the**

world like sb/sth (*written*) exactly as if...; exactly like sb/sth: *She behaved for all the world as if nothing unusual had happened.* ◊ *He looked for all the world like a schoolboy caught stealing apples.* **have the world at your 'feet** to be very successful and admired **how, why, etc. in the 'world** (*informal*) used to emphasize sth and to show that you are surprised or annoyed: *What in the world did they think they were doing?* **in an ideal/a perfect 'world** used to say that sth is what you would like to happen or what should happen, but you know it cannot: *In an ideal world we would be recycling and reusing everything.* **in the 'world** used to emphasize what you are saying: *There's nothing in the world I'd like more than to visit New York.* ◊ *Don't rush—we've got all the time in the world!* ◊ *You look as if you haven't got a care in the world!* **(be/live) in a world of your 'own** if you are in a world of your own, you are so concerned with your own thoughts that you do not notice what is happening around you **a man/woman of the 'world** a person with a lot of experience of life, who is not easily surprised or shocked **not for (all) the 'world** used to say that you would never do sth: *I wouldn't hurt you for the world.* **the ...of this world** (*informal*) used to refer to people of a particular type: *We all envy the Bill Gateses of this world* (= the people who are as rich and successful as Bill Gates). **,out of this 'world** (*informal*) used to emphasize how good, beautiful, etc. sth is: *The meal was out of this world.* **see the 'world** to travel widely and gain wide experience **set/put the world to 'rights** to talk about how the world could be changed to be a better place: *We stayed up all night, setting the world to rights.* **set the 'world on fire** (*BrE*) (also **set the 'world alight**) (*informal*) (usually used in negative sentences) to be very successful and gain the admiration of other people: *He's never going to set the world on fire with his paintings.* **what is the world 'coming to?** used to express disapproval, surprise or shock, especially at changes in people's attitudes or behaviour: *When I listen to the news these days, I sometimes wonder what the world is coming to.* **(all) the ,world and his 'wife** (*BrE, informal, humorous*) everyone; a large number of people **a 'world away (from sth)** used to emphasize how different two things are: *His new luxury mansion was a world away from the tiny house where he was born.* **the ,world is your 'oyster** there is no limit to the opportunities open to you: *With talent like that, the world is her oyster.* **a/the 'world of difference** (*informal*) used to emphasize how much difference there is between two things: *There's a world of difference between liking someone and loving them.* **the (whole) world 'over** everywhere in the world: *People are basically the same the world over.*—more at BRAVE *adj.*, DEAD *adj.*, END *n.*, LOST, PROMISE *v.*, SMALL *adj.*, TOP *n.*, WATCH *v.*, WAY *n.*, WILL *n.*, WORST *n.*

'world-beater *noun* a person or thing that is better than all others ▶ **'world-beating** *adj.*: *world-beating achievements*

,world-'class *adj.* as good as the best in the world: *a world-class athlete/violinist*

,world-'famous *adj.* known all over the world: *a world-famous scientist* ◊ *His books are world-famous.*

world·ly /'wɜːldli; *AmE* 'wɜːrld-/ *adj.* (*written*) **1** [only before noun] connected with the world in which we live rather than with spiritual things: *worldly concerns/interests/success* ◊ *your worldly goods* (= the things that you own) **2** having a lot of experience of life and therefore not easily shocked: *At 15, he was more worldly than his older cousins who lived in the country.* **OPP** UNWORLDLY ▶ **world·li·ness** *noun* [U]

,worldly-'wise *adj.* having a lot of experience of life and therefore not easily shocked: *She's not as worldly-wise as she would have you believe.*

'world music *noun* [U] a type of pop music that includes influences from different parts of the world, especially Africa and Asia

,world 'power *noun* a powerful country that has a lot of influence in international politics

aɪ	aʊ	eɪ	əʊ	oʊ	ɔɪ	ɪə	eə	ʊə	j	w
my	now	say	go (BrE)	go (AmE)	boy	near	hair	pure	yes	wet

,**world** '**war** *noun* [C, U] a war that involves many countries: *the First/Second World War*

'**world-weary** *adj.* (*written*) no longer excited by life;
showing this SYN JADED: *a world-weary look/smile/voice*
▶ '**world-weariness** *noun* [U]

world-wide /'wɜːldwaɪd; *AmE* 'wɜːrld-/ *adj.* [usually
before noun] affecting all parts of the world: *an increase
in worldwide sales ◇ The story has attracted worldwide
attention.* ▶ ,**world**-'**wide** *adv.*: *We have 2000 members
worldwide. ◇ In her new job she travels worldwide as a
consultant.*

the ,**World Wide** '**Web** (also **the Web**) (*abbr.* **WWW**)
noun a MULTIMEDIA system of sound, pictures and video
for finding information on the Internet: *to browse a site
on the World Wide Web*

worm /wɜːm; *AmE* wɜːrm/ *noun, verb*
▪ *noun* **1** [C] a long thin creature with no bones or legs,
that lives in soil: *birds looking for worms*—see also
EARTHWORM, LUGWORM **2** (**worms**) [pl.] long thin creatures
that live inside the bodies of humans or animals and can
cause illness: *The dog has worms.*—see also HOOKWORM,
TAPEWORM **3** [C] the young form of an insect when it looks
like a short worm: *This apple is full of worms.*—see also
GLOW-WORM, SILKWORM, WOODWORM **4** [C, usually sing.]
(*informal, disapproving*) a person you do not like or
respect, especially because they have a weak character
and do not behave well towards other people IDM **the
,worm will** '**turn** a person who is normally quiet and
does not complain will protest when the situation
becomes too hard to bear—more at CAN² *n.*
▪ *verb* [VN] **1** [+*adv./prep.*] **~ your way ...** to use a twisting
and turning movement, especially to move through a
narrow or crowded place: *She wormed her way through
the crowd to the reception desk.* **2** to give an animal medicine that makes worms pass out of its body in the FAECES
PHRV ,**worm your way/yourself** '**into sth** (*disapproving*) to make sb like you or trust you, in order to gain
some advantage for yourself: *He managed to worm his
way into her life.* ,**worm sth** '**out of sb** (*informal*) to make
sb tell you sth, by asking them questions in a clever way
for a long period of time: *We eventually wormed the secret
out of her.*

'**worm-eaten** *adj.* full of holes made by worms or WOOD-
WORMS

worm·wood /'wɜːmwʊd; *AmE* 'wɜːrm-/ *noun* [U] a plant
with a bitter flavour, used in making alcoholic drinks
and medicines

worn /wɔːn; *AmE* wɔːrn/ *adj.* **1** [usually before noun] (of a
thing) damaged or thinner than normal because it is old
and has been used a lot: *an old pair of worn jeans ◇ The
stone steps were worn and broken. ◇ The tapestry is still
valuable in spite of its worn condition.*—see also WELL
WORN **2** (of a person) looking very tired: *She came out of
the ordeal looking thin and worn.*—see also WEAR *v.*

,**worn** '**out** *adj.* **1** (of a thing) badly damaged and/or no
longer useful because it has been used a lot: *These shoes
are worn out. ◇ the gradual replacement of worn-out equipment ◇ a speech full of worn-out old clichés* **2** [not usually
before noun] (of a person) looking or feeling very tired,
especially as a result of hard work or physical exercise:
Can we sit down? I'm worn out.—compare OUTWORN

wor·ried /'wʌrid; *AmE* 'wɜːr-/ *adj.* **~** (**about sb/sth**)| **~**
(**by sth**)| **~** (**that ...**) thinking about unpleasant things
that have happened or that might happen and therefore
feeling unhappy and afraid: *Don't look so worried! ◇ I'm
not worried about her—she can take care of herself. ◇
Doctors are worried about the possible spread of the disease. ◇ We're not too worried by these results. ◇ The police
are worried that the man may be armed. ◇ Where have you
been? I've been worried sick (= extremely worried). ◇ I
was worried you wouldn't come. ◇ Try not to get worried.
◇ She gave me a worried look.* ▶ **wor·ried·ly** *adv.*: *He
glanced worriedly at his father.* IDM **you had me** '**worried** (*spoken*) used to tell sb that you were worried
because you had not understood what they had said
correctly: *You had me worried for a moment—I thought
you were going to resign!*

wor·rier /'wʌriə(r); *AmE* 'wɜːr-/ *noun* a person who worries a lot about unpleasant things that have happened or
that might happen

wor·ri·some /'wʌrisəm; *AmE* 'wɜːr-/ *adj.* (*especially
AmE*) that makes you worry

worry /'wʌri; *AmE* 'wɜːri/ *verb, noun*
▪ *verb* (**wor·ries, worry·ing, wor·ried, wor·ried**) **1 ~** (**about/
over sb/sth**) to keep thinking about unpleasant things
that might happen or about problems that you have: [V]
*Don't worry. We have plenty of time. ◇ Don't worry about
me. I'll be all right. ◇ He's always worrying about his
weight. ◇ There's no point in worrying over things you
can't change. ◇* [V(**that**)] *I worry that I won't get into
college.* **2 ~** **sb/yourself** (**about sb/sth**) to make sb/your-
self anxious about sb/sth: [VN] *What worries me is how I
am going to get another job. ◇* [VN-ADJ] *He's worried
himself sick* (= become extremely anxious) *about his
daughter. ◇* [VN**that**] *It worries me that he hasn't come
home yet.* [also VN to inf] **3** [VN] **~ sb** (**with sth**) to annoy or
disturb sb: *The noise never seems to worry her. ◇ Don't
keep worrying him with a lot of silly questions.* **4** [VN] (of a
dog) to attack animals, especially sheep, by chasing
and/or biting them IDM ,**not to** '**worry** (*informal, especially BrE*) it is not important; it does not matter: *Not to
worry—I can soon fix it. ◇ Not to worry—no harm done.*
PHRV '**worry at sth 1** to bite sth and shake or pull it:
*Rebecca worried at her lip. ◇ He began to worry at the knot
in the cord.* **2** to think about a problem a lot and try and
find a solution
▪ *noun* (*pl.* -**ies**) **1** [U] the state of worrying about sth SYN
ANXIETY: *The threat of losing their jobs is a constant source
of worry to them. ◇ to be frantic/sick with worry* **2** [C] **~**
(**about/over sth**)| **~** (**for/to sb**) something that worries
you: *family/financial worries ◇ Mugging is a real worry
for many old people. ◇ My only worry is that ...*

'**worry beads** *noun* [pl.] small BEADS on a string that you
move and turn in order to keep calm

worry·ing /'wʌriɪŋ; *AmE* 'wɜːr-/ *adj.* that makes you
worry: *a worrying development/trend/sign ◇ It must be
worrying for you not to know where he is. ◇ It is particularly worrying that nobody seems to be in charge. ◇ It's
been a worrying time for us all.* ▶ **worry·ing·ly** *adv.*:

W

b	d	f	g	h	k	l	m	n	p	r
bad	**did**	**fall**	**get**	**hat**	**cat**	**leg**	**man**	**now**	**pen**	**red**

worryingly high levels of radiation ◊ *Worryingly, the plan contains few details on how spending will be cut.*

worry·wart /ˈwʌriwɔːt; *AmE* ˈwɜːriwɔːrt/ *noun* (*AmE, informal*) a person who worries about unimportant things

worse /wɜːs; *AmE* wɜːrs/ *adj., adv., noun*

▪ *adj.* (comparative of *bad*) ~ (**than sth/doing sth**) **1** of poorer quality or lower standard; less good or more unpleasant: *The rooms were awful and the food was worse.* ◊ *The weather got worse during the day.* ◊ *The interview was much worse than he had expected.* ◊ *I've been to far worse places.* ◊ *There's nothing worse than going out in the cold with wet hair.* **2** more serious or severe: *They were trying to prevent an even worse tragedy.* ◊ *The crisis was getting worse and worse.* ◊ *Don't tell her that—you'll only make things worse.* ◊ *Never mind—it could be worse* (= although the situation is bad, it is not as bad as it might have been). **3** [not before noun] more ill/sick or unhappy: *If he gets any worse we'll call the doctor.* ◊ *He told her she'd let them down and she felt worse than ever.* **IDM** come off **worse** to lose a fight, competition, etc. or suffer more compared with others **go from ˌbad to ˈworse** (of a bad condition, situation, etc.) to get even worse ˌworse ˈluck! (*BrE, spoken*) used to show that you are disappointed about sth: *I shall have to miss the party, worse luck!*—more at BARK *n.*, FATE *n.*

▪ *adv.* (comparative of *badly*) ~ (**than sth**) **1** less well: *I didn't do it very well, but, if anything, he did it worse than I did.* **2** more seriously or severely: *It's raining worse than ever.* **3** used to introduce a statement about sth that is more serious or unpleasant than things already mentioned: *She'd lost her job. Even worse, she'd lost her house and her children, too.* **IDM** be ˌworse ˈoff to be poorer, unhappier, etc. than before or than sb else: *The increase in taxes means that we'll be £30 a month worse off than before.* **you can/could do worse than do sth** used to say that you think sth is a good idea: *If you want a safe investment, you could do a lot worse than put your money in a building society.*

▪ *noun* [U] more problems or bad news: *I'm afraid there is worse to come.* **IDM** be none the ˈworse (for sth) to not be harmed by sth: *The kids were none the worse for their adventure.* the ˌworse for ˈwear (*informal*) **1** in a poor condition because of being used a lot **2** drunk—more at BETTER *n.*, CHANGE *n.*

worsen /ˈwɜːsn; *AmE* ˈwɜːrsn/ *verb* to become or make sth worse than it was before: [V] *The political situation is steadily worsening.* ◊ *Her health has worsened considerably since we last saw her.* ◊ [VN] *Staff shortages were worsened by the flu epidemic.* ▸ **worsen·ing** *noun* [sing.]: *The result could be a worsening of the international debt crisis.* **worsen·ing** *adj.*: *worsening weather conditions*

wor·ship /ˈwɜːʃɪp; *AmE* ˈwɜːrʃɪp/ *noun, verb*

▪ *noun* **1** [U] the practice of showing respect for God or a god, by saying prayers, singing with others, etc.; a ceremony for this: *an act/a place of worship* ◊ *devil/ancestor worship* ◊ *morning/evening worship* (= a church service in the morning/evening) **2** [U] a strong feeling of love and respect for sb/sth: *What she feels for him is akin to worship.*—see also HERO WORSHIP **3** (**His, Your, etc. Worship**) [C] (*BrE, formal*) a polite way of addressing or referring to a MAGISTRATE or MAYOR

▪ *verb* (**-pp-**, *AmE* also **-p-**) **1** [VN] to show respect for God or a god, especially by saying prayers, singing, etc. with other people in a church, etc. **2** [V] to go to a church service: *We worship at St Mary's.* **3** [VN] to love and admire sb very much, especially so much that you cannot see their faults: *She worships her children.* ◊ *He worshipped her from afar* (= he loved her but did not tell her his feelings). ◊ *She worships the ground he walks on.*

wor·ship·ful /ˈwɜːʃɪpfl; *AmE* ˈwɜːrʃ-/ *adj.* [only before noun] **1** (*formal*) showing or feeling respect and admiration for sb/sth **2** (**Worshipful**) (in Britain), used in the titles of some MAYORS and some groups of CRAFTSMEN: *the Worshipful Company of Goldsmiths*

wor·ship·per (*AmE* also **wor·ship·er**) /ˈwɜːʃɪpə(r); *AmE* ˈwɜːrʃ-/ *noun* a person who worships God or a god:

regular worshippers at St Andrew's Church ◊ (*figurative*) *sun worshippers lying on the beach*

worst /wɜːst; *AmE* wɜːrst/ *adj., adv., noun, verb*

▪ *adj.* (superlative of *bad*) of the poorest quality or lowest standard; worse than any other person or thing of a similar kind: *It was by far the worst speech he had ever made.* ◊ *What's the worst thing that could happen?* ◊ *What she said confirmed my worst fears* (= proved they were right). **IDM** be your ˌown worst ˈenemy to be the cause of your own problems: *Her indecisiveness makes her her own worst enemy.* **come off ˈworst** to lose a fight, competition, etc. or suffer more compared with others

▪ *adv.* (superlative of *badly*) most badly or seriously: *He was voted the worst dressed celebrity.* ◊ *Manufacturing industry was worst affected by the fuel shortage.* ◊ *Worst of all, I lost the watch my father had given me.*

▪ *noun* (**the worst**) [sing.] the most serious or unpleasant thing that could happen; the part, situation, possibility, etc. that is worse than any other: *The worst of the storm was over.* ◊ *When they did not hear from her, they feared the worst.* ◊ *The worst of it is that I can't even be sure if they received my letter.* ◊ *He was always optimistic, even when things were at their worst.* **IDM** at (the) ˈworst used for saying what is the worst thing that can happen: *At the very worst, he'll have to pay a fine.* **bring out the ˈworst in sb** to make sb show their worst qualities: *Pressure can bring out the worst in people.* **do your ˈworst** (of a person) to do as much damage or be as unpleasant as possible: *Let them do their worst—we'll fight them every inch of the way.* **get the ˈworst of it** to be defeated: *He'd been in a fight and had obviously got the worst of it.* **if the ˌworst comes to the ˈworst** (*AmE* also **if ˌworst comes to ˈworst**) if the situation becomes too difficult or dangerous: *If the worst comes to the worst, we'll just have to sell the house.* **the worst of ˈall (possible) worlds** all the disadvantages of every situation

▪ *verb* [VN] (*old-fashioned* or *formal*) [usually passive] to defeat sb in a fight, a contest or an argument

ˈworst-case *adj.* [only before noun] involving the worst situation that could happen: *In the worst-case scenario more than ten thousand people might be affected.*

worst·ed /ˈwʊstɪd/ *noun* [U] a tightly woven woollen fabric with a smooth surface, used for making clothes: *a grey worsted suit*

worth /wɜːθ; *AmE* wɜːrθ/ *adj., noun*

▪ *adj.* [not before noun] (usually used like a preposition) **1** having a value in money, etc: *Our house is worth about £100000.* ◊ *How much is this painting worth?* ◊ *to be worth a bomb/packet/fortune* (= a lot of money) ◊ *It isn't worth much.* ◊ *If you answer this question correctly, it's worth five points.* **2** ~ sth/doing sth used to recommend the action mentioned because you think it may be useful, enjoyable, etc: *The museum is certainly worth a visit.* ◊ *This idea is well worth considering.* ◊ *It's worth making an appointment before you go.* **3** ~ sth/doing sth important, good or enjoyable enough to make sb feel satisfied, especially when difficulty or effort is involved: *to be worth the effort/expense/fuss* ◊ *The new house really wasn't worth all the expense involved.* ◊ *The job involves a lot of hard work but it's worth it.* ◊ *The trip was expensive but it was worth every penny.*—see also WORTHWHILE **4** (of a person) having money and possessions of a particular value: *He's worth about £10 million.* **IDM** for ˌall sb/it is ˈworth **1** with great energy, effort and determination: *He was rowing for all he was worth.* **2** in order to get as much as you can from sb/sth: *She is milking her success for all it's worth.* **for ˌwhat it's ˈworth** (*spoken*) used to emphasize that what you are saying is only your own opinion or suggestion and may not be very helpful: *I prefer this colour, for what it's worth.* **(the game is) not worth the ˈcandle** (*old-fashioned, saying*) the advantages to be gained from doing sth are not great enough, considering the effort or cost involved **not worth the paper it's ˈwritten/ˈprinted on** (of an agreement or official document) having no value, especially legally, or because one of the people involved has no intention of doing what they said they would **ˌworth your/its ˈsalt** deserving respect, especially because you do your job well: *Any*

W

teacher worth her salt knows that. ˌ**worth your/its** ˌ**weight in** ˈ**gold** very useful or valuable: *A good mechanic is worth his weight in gold.* ˌ**worth your** ˈ**while** interesting or useful for sb to do: *It will be worth your while to come to the meeting.* ◊ *He'll do the job if you make it worth his while* (= pay him well).—more at BIRD, JOB

■ *noun* [U] **1 ten dollars', £40, etc. ~ of sth** an amount of sth that has the value mentioned: *The winner will receive ten pounds' worth of books.* ◊ *a dollar's worth of change* **2 a week's, month's, etc. ~ of sth** an amount of sth that lasts a week, etc. **3** the financial, practical or moral value of sb/sth: *Their contribution was of great worth.* ◊ *The activities help children to develop a sense of their own worth.* ◊ *A good interview enables candidates to prove their worth* (= show how good they are). ◊ *a personal net worth of $10 million* **IDM** see MONEY

worth·less /ˈwɜːθləs; *AmE* ˈwɜːrθ-/ *adj.* **1** having no practical or financial value: *Critics say his paintings are worthless.* **OPP** VALUABLE **2** (of a person) having no good qualities or useful skills: *a worthless individual* ◊ *Constant rejections made him feel worthless.* ▶ **worth·less·ness** *noun* [U]: *a sense/feeling of worthlessness*

worth·while /ˌwɜːθˈwaɪl; *AmE* ˌwɜːrθ-/ *adj.* **~ (to do sth)|** **~ (doing sth)** important, enjoyable, interesting, etc.; worth spending time, money or effort on: *a worthwhile cause/discussion/job* ◊ *The smile on her face made it all worthwhile.* ◊ *High prices in the UK make it worthwhile for buyers to look abroad.* ◊ *It is worthwhile to include really high-quality illustrations.* ◊ *It didn't seem worthwhile writing it all out again.* **HELP** This word can be written **worth while**, except when it is used before a noun: *Did you feel the meeting was worth while?*

worthy /ˈwɜːði; *AmE* ˈwɜːrði/ *adj., noun*
■ *adj.* (**wor·thier, wor·thi·est**) **1 ~ (of sb/sth)** (*formal*) having the qualities that deserve sb/sth: *to be worthy of attention/consideration/mention* ◊ *A number of the report's findings are worthy of note.* ◊ *No composer was considered worthy of the name until he had written an opera.* ◊ *a worthy champion/winner* (= one who deserved to win) ◊ *He felt he was not worthy of her.* **2** [usually before noun] having qualities that deserve your respect, attention or admiration: *The money we raise will be going to a very worthy cause.* ◊ *a worthy member of the team* ◊ *He's a very worthy man, I suppose, but he's very dull.* **3 ~ (of sb/sth)** typical of what a particular person or thing might do, give, etc: *He gave a speech that was worthy of Martin Luther King.* **4** (**-worthy**) (in compounds) deserving, or suitable for, the thing mentioned: *trustworthy* ◊ *roadworthy* **OPP** UNWORTHY ▶ **wor·thily** /-ɪli/ *adv.* **wor·thi·ness** *noun* [U]
■ *noun* (*pl.* **-ies**) (often *humorous*) an important person: *a meeting attended by local worthies*

wot (*BrE, non-standard,* often *humorous*) a way of writing 'what', used to show that sb is speaking very informal English: *"Ere, wot's going on?" he shouted.*

would / *strong form* wʊd; *weak form* wəd; əd/ *modal verb* (*short form* **'d** /d/, *negative* **would not**, *short form* **wouldn't** /ˈwʊdnt/) **1** used as the past form of *will* when reporting what sb has said or thought: *He said he would be here at eight o'clock* (= He said: 'I will be there at 8 o'clock.'). ◊ *She asked if I would help.* ◊ *They told me that they probably wouldn't come.* **2** used for talking about the result of an event that you imagine: *She'd look better with shorter hair.* ◊ *If you went to see him, he would be delighted.* ◊ *Hurry up! It would be a shame to miss the beginning of the play.* ◊ *She'd be a fool to accept it* (= if she accepted). **3** used for describing an action or event that would have happened if sth else had happened first: *If I had seen the advertisement in time I would have applied for the job.* ◊ *They would never have met if she hadn't gone to Emma's party.* **4 so that/in order that sb/sth ~** used for saying why sb does sth: *She burned the letters so that her husband would never read them.* **5 wish (that) sb/sth ~** used for saying what you want to happen: *I wish you'd be quiet for a minute.* **6** used to show that sb/sth was not willing or refused to do sth: *She wouldn't change it, even though she knew it was wrong.* ◊ *My car wouldn't start this morning.* **7** used to ask sb politely to do sth: *Would*

you mind leaving us alone for a few minutes? ◊ *Would you open the door for me, please?* **8** used in polite offers or invitations: *Would you like a sandwich?* ◊ *Would you have dinner with me on Friday?* **9 ~ like, love, hate, prefer, etc. sth/(sb) to do sth |~ rather do sth/sb did sth** used to say what you like, love, hate, etc: *I'd love a coffee.* ◊ *I'd be only too glad to help.* ◊ *I'd hate you to think I was criticizing you.* ◊ *I'd rather come with you.* ◊ *I'd rather you came with us.* **10 ~ imagine, say, think, etc. (that)** ... used to give opinions that you are not certain about: *I would imagine the job will take about two days.* ◊ *I'd say he was about fifty.* **11 (I would ...)** used to give advice: *I wouldn't have any more to drink, if I were you.* **12** used for talking about things that often happened in the past **SYN** USED TO: *When my parents were away, my grandmother would take care of me.* ◊ *He'd always be the first to offer to help.* **13** (usually *disapproving*) used for talking about behaviour that you think is typical: *'She said it was your fault.' 'Well, she would say that, wouldn't she?' She's never liked me.'* **14 ~ that ...** (*literary*) used to express a strong wish: *Would that he had lived to see it.* ⇨ note at MODAL, SHOULD

ˈ**would-be** *adj.* [only before noun] used to describe sb who is hoping to become the type of person mentioned: *a would-be actor* ◊ *advice for would-be parents*

wound¹ /wuːnd/ *noun, verb*—see also WOUND²
■ *noun* **1** an injury to part of the body, especially one in which a hole is made in the skin using a weapon: *a leg/head wound* ◊ *a knife/bullet wound* ◊ *a stab/gunshot wound* ◊ *an old war wound* ◊ *The nurse cleaned the wound.* ◊ *The wound healed slowly.* ◊ *He died from the wounds he had received to his chest.*—see also FLESH WOUND **2** (*written*) mental or emotional pain caused by sth unpleasant that has been said or done to you: *After a serious argument, it can take some time for the wounds to heal.* ◊ *Seeing him again opened up old wounds.* **IDM** see LICK *v.*, REOPEN, RUB *v.*
■ *verb* [VN] [often passive] **1** to injure part of the body, especially by making a hole in the skin using a weapon: *He was wounded in the arm.* ◊ *About 50 people were seriously wounded in the attack.* **2** to hurt sb's feelings: *She felt deeply wounded by his cruel remarks.*

wound² /waʊnd/ *pt, pp* of WIND²—see also WOUND¹

wound·ed /ˈwuːndɪd/ *adj.* **1** injured by a weapon, for example in a war: *wounded soldiers* ◊ *There were 79 killed and 230 wounded.* **2** feeling emotional pain because of sth unpleasant that sb has said or done: *wounded pride* **3 (the wounded)** *noun* [pl.] people who are wounded, for example in a war

wound·ing /ˈwuːndɪŋ/ *adj.* that hurts sb's feelings: *He found her remarks deeply wounding.*

wove *pt* of WEAVE

woven *pp* of WEAVE

wow /waʊ/ *exclamation, verb, noun*
■ *exclamation* (also **wowee** /ˌwaʊˈiː/) (*informal*) used to express great surprise or admiration: *Wow! You look terrific!*
■ *verb* [VN] **~ sb (with sth)** (*informal*) to impress sb very much, especially with a performance: *He wowed audiences around the country with his new show.*
■ *noun* **1** [sing.] (*informal*) a great success: *Don't worry. You'll be a wow.* **2** [U] (*technical*) changes in the PITCH of sound played on a record or tape

WPC /ˌdʌbljuː piː ˈsiː/ *noun* (*BrE*) the abbreviation for 'woman police constable' (a woman police officer of the lowest rank): *WPC (Linda) Green*

wpm *abbr.* words per minute: *to type at 60 wpm*

WRAC /ræk; ˌdʌbljuː ɑːr eɪ ˈsiː/ *abbr.* (in Britain) Women's Royal Army Corps

wrack (*rare*) = RACK

WRAF /ræf; ˌdʌbljuː ɑːr eɪ ˈef/ *abbr.* (in Britain) Women's Royal Air Force

wraith /reɪθ/ *noun* the ghost of a person that is seen a short time before or after that person dies: *a wraith-like figure* (= a very thin, pale person)

æ	ɑː	e	ɜː	ə	ɪ	iː	i	ɒ	ɔː	ʌ	ʊ	u	uː
cat	father	ten	bird	about	sit	see	many	got	saw	cup	put	actual	too
								(BrE)					

W

wran·gle /ˈræŋgl/ *noun, verb*

■ *noun* ~ **(with sb)(over sth)**| ~ **(between A and B)** an argument that is complicated and continues over a long period of time: *a legal wrangle between the company and their suppliers* ▶ **wran·gling** *noun* [U, C]

■ *verb* [V] ~ **(with sb)** **(over/about sth)** to argue angrily and usually for a long time about sth. *They're still wrangling over the financial details.*

wrap /ræp/ *verb, noun*

■ *verb* (-pp-) [VN] **1** ~ **sth (up) (in sth)** to cover sth completely in paper or other material, for example when you are giving it as a present: *He spent the evening wrapping up the Christmas presents.* ◇ *individually wrapped chocolates*—see also GIFT-WRAP **2** ~ **A (up) in B**| ~ **B round/around A** to cover sth/sb in material, for example in order to protect it/them: *I wrapped the baby (up) in a blanket.* ◇ *I wrapped a blanket around the baby.* ◇ *Wrap the meat in foil before you cook it.* ◇ *He tossed her a towel. 'Wrap yourself in that.'*—see also SHRINK-WRAPPED **3** ~ **sth around/round sth/sb** to put sth firmly around sth/sb: *A scarf was wrapped around his neck.* ◇ *His arms were wrapped around her waist.*—compare UNWRAP **IDM** be **ˌwrapped ˈup in sb/sth** to be so involved with sb/sth that you do not pay enough attention to other people or things—more at LITTLE FINGER **PHRV** **ˌwrap ˈup**| **ˌwrap it ˈup** (*slang*) usually used as an order to tell sb to stop talking or causing trouble, etc. **ˌwrap ˈup**| **ˌwrap sb/yourself ˈup** to put warm clothes on sb/yourself: *She told them to wrap up warm/warmly.* **ˌwrap sth↔ˈup** (*informal*) to complete sth such as an agreement or a meeting in a satisfactory way: *That just about wraps it up for today.*

■ *noun* **1** [C] a piece of fabric that a woman wears around her shoulders for decoration or to keep warm **2** [U] paper, plastic, etc. that is used for wrapping things in: *We stock a wide range of cards and gift wrap.*—see also PLASTIC WRAP **3** [sing.] used when making a film/movie to say that filming has finished: *Cut! That's a wrap.* **IDM** under **ˈwraps** (*informal*) being kept secret until some time in the future: *Next year's collection is still being kept under wraps.*

wrap·per /ˈræpə(r)/ *noun* a piece of paper, plastic, etc. that is wrapped around sth, especially food, when you buy it in order to protect it and keep it clean: (*BrE*) *sweet wrappers* ◇ (*AmE*) *candy wrappers*

wrap·ping /ˈræpɪŋ/ *noun* [U] (also **wrap·pings** [pl.]) paper, plastic, etc. used for covering sth in order to protect it: *She tore the cellophane wrapping off the box.* ◇ *shrink wrapping* (= plastic designed to SHRINK around objects so that it fits them tightly) ◇ *The painting was still in its wrappings.*

ˈwrapping paper *noun* [U] coloured paper used for wrapping presents: *a piece/sheet/roll of wrapping paper*

wrath /rɒθ; *AmE* ræθ/ *noun* [U] (*old-fashioned* or *formal*) extreme anger: *the wrath of God* ▶ **wrath·ful** /-fl/ *adj.* **wrath·ful·ly** *adv.*

wreak /riːk/ *verb* [VN] ~ **sth (on sb)** (*formal*) to do great damage or harm to sb/sth: *Their policies would wreak havoc on the economy.* ◇ *He was determined to wreak vengeance on those who had betrayed him.*—see also WROUGHT

wreath *pl.* /riːθ/ *noun* (*pl.* **wreaths** /riːðz/) **1** an arrangement of flowers and leaves, especially in the shape of a circle, placed on graves, etc. as a sign of respect for sb who has died: *The Queen laid a wreath at the war memorial.* **2** an arrangement of flowers and/or leaves in the shape of a circle, traditionally hung on doors as a decoration at Christmas: *a holly wreath* **3** a circle of flowers or leaves worn on the head, and used in the past as a sign of honour: *a laurel wreath* **4** (*literary*) a circle of smoke, cloud, etc: *wreaths of mist*

holly wreath

wreathe /riːð/ *verb* (*written*) **1** [VN] [usually passive] ~ **sth (in/with sth)** to surround or cover sth: *The mountain tops were wreathed in mist.* ◇ (*figurative*) *Her face was wreathed in smiles* (= she was smiling a lot). **2** [V+adv./prep.] to move slowly and lightly, especially in circles: *smoke wreathing upwards into the sky*

wreck /rek/ *noun, verb*

■ *noun* **1** a ship that has sunk or that has been very badly damaged—see also SHIPWRECK **2** a car, plane, etc. that has been very badly damaged in an accident: *Two passengers are still trapped in the wreck.* **3** [usually sing.] (*informal*) a person who is in a bad physical or mental condition: *Physically, I was a total wreck.* ◇ *The interview reduced him to a nervous wreck.* **4** (*informal*) a vehicle, building, etc. that is in very bad condition: *The house was a wreck when we bought it.* ◇ (*figurative*) *They still hoped to salvage something from the wreck of their marriage.* **5** (*AmE*) = CRASH: *a car/train wreck*

■ *verb* [VN] **1** to damage or destroy sth: *The building had been wrecked by the explosion.* ◇ *The road was littered with wrecked cars.* **2** ~ **sth (for sb)** to spoil sth completely: *The weather wrecked all our plans.* ◇ *A serious injury nearly wrecked his career.* **3** [usually passive] to damage a ship so much that it sinks or can no longer sail: *The ship was wrecked off the coast of France.*—see also SHIPWRECK

wreck·age /ˈrekɪdʒ/ *noun* [U] the parts of a vehicle, building, etc. that remain after it has been badly damaged or destroyed: *A few survivors were pulled from the wreckage.* ◇ *Pieces of wreckage were found ten miles away from the scene of the explosion.* ◇ (*figurative*) *Could nothing be rescued from the wreckage of her dreams?*

wrecked /rekt/ *adj.* **1** [only before noun] having been wrecked: *a wrecked ship/marriage* **2** [not before noun] (*BrE, slang*) very drunk

wreck·er /ˈrekə(r)/ *noun* **1** a person who ruins another person's plans, relationship, etc. **2** (*AmE*) a vehicle used for moving other vehicles that have been damaged in an accident

wren /ren/ *noun* a very small brown bird

wrench /rentʃ/ *verb, noun*

■ *verb* **1** to pull or twist sth/sb/yourself suddenly and violently: [VN, usually+adv./prep.] *The bag was wrenched from her grasp.* ◇ *He grabbed Ben, wrenching him away from his mother.* ◇ (*figurative*) *Guy wrenched his mind back to the present.* ◇ [VN-ADJ] *They wrenched the door open.* ◇ *She managed to wrench herself free.* [also V] **2** [VN] to twist and injure a part of your body, especially your ankle or shoulder: *She wrenched her knee when she fell.* **3** ~ **sth (from sb)**| ~ **(at) sth** (*formal*) to make sb feel great pain or unhappiness, especially so that they make a sound or cry: [VN] *His words wrenched a sob from her.* ◇ [V] *Her words wrenched at my heart.* ◇ *a wrenching experience*

■ *noun* **1** (*especially AmE*) (*BrE* usually **span·ner**) [C] a metal tool with a specially shaped end for holding and turning things, including one which can be adjusted to fit objects of different sizes, also called a MONKEY WRENCH or an ADJUSTABLE SPANNER—picture at TOOL **2** [sing.] pain or unhappiness that you feel when you have to leave a person or place that you love: *Leaving home was a terrible wrench for me.* **3** [C, usually sing.] a sudden and violent twist or pull: *She stumbled and gave her ankle a painful wrench.*

wrest /rest/ *verb* **PHRV** **ˈwrest sth from sb/sth** (*formal*) **1** to take sth such as power or control from sb/sth with great effort: *They attempted to wrest control of the town from government forces.* **2** to take sth from sb that they do not want to give, suddenly or violently: *He wrested the gun from my grasp.*

wres·tle /ˈresl/ *verb* **1** ~ **(with sb)** to fight sb by holding them and trying to throw or force them to the ground, sometimes as a sport: [V] *As a boy he had boxed and wrestled.* ◇ *Armed guards wrestled with the intruder.* ◇ [VN] *Shoppers wrestled the raider to the ground.* **2** ~ **(with sth)** to struggle to deal with sth that is difficult: [V] *She had spent the whole weekend wrestling with the problem.* ◇ *He wrestled with the controls as the plane plunged.* ◇ [V to inf] *She wrestled to look serious.* [also VN]

aɪ	aʊ	eɪ	əʊ	oʊ	ɔɪ	ɪə	eə	ʊə	j	w
my	now	say	go (BrE)	go (AmE)	boy	near	hair	pure	yes	wet

wrest·ler /ˈreslə(r)/ *noun* a person who takes part in the sport of wrestling

wrest·ling /ˈreslɪŋ/ *noun* [U] a sport in which two people fight by holding each other and trying to throw or force the other one to the ground

wretch /retʃ/ *noun* **1** a person that you feel sympathy or pity for: *a poor/a miserable/an unfortunate wretch* **2** (often *humorous*) an evil, unpleasant or annoying person

wretch·ed /ˈretʃɪd/ *adj.* **1** (of a person) feeling ill/sick or unhappy: *You look wretched—what's wrong?* ◇ *I felt wretched about the way things had turned out.* **2** extremely bad or unpleasant: *She had a wretched time of it at school.* ◇ *The animals are kept in the most wretched conditions.* **3** making you feel sympathy or pity: *She finally agreed to have the wretched animal put down.* **4** [only before noun] used to show that you think that sb/sth is extremely annoying: *Is it that wretched woman again?* ▶ **wretch·ed·ly** *adv.* **wretch·ed·ness** *noun* [U]

wrig·gle /ˈrɪɡl/ *verb, noun*
■ *verb* **1** ~ (about/around) to twist and turn your body or part of it with quick short movements: [V] *The baby was wriggling around on my lap.* ◇ [VN] *She wriggled her toes.* **2** [usually +adv./prep.] to move somewhere by twisting and turning your body or part of it: [V] *The fish wriggled out of my fingers.* ◇ [V-ADJ] *She managed to wriggle free.* ◇ [VN] *They wriggled their way through the tunnel.* PHRV **wriggle out of sth/out of doing sth** (*informal, disapproving*) to avoid doing sth that you should do, especially by thinking of clever excuses: *He tried desperately to wriggle out of giving a clear answer.*
■ *noun* [usually sing.] an act of wriggling

wring /rɪŋ/ *verb* (**wrung**, **wrung** /rʌŋ/) [VN] **1** ~ sth (**out**) to twist and squeeze clothes, etc. in order to get the water out of them **2** if you **wring** a bird's neck, you twist it in order to kill the bird IDM **wring sb's hand** to squeeze sb's hand very tightly when you shake hands **wring your hands** to hold your hands together, and twist and squeeze them in a way that shows you are anxious or upset, especially when you cannot change the situation **wring sb's 'neck** (*spoken, informal*) when you say that you will **wring sb's neck**, you mean that you are very angry or annoyed with them PHRV **wring sth from/out of sb** to obtain sth from sb with difficulty, especially by putting pressure on them

She wrung out her clothes.

wring·er /ˈrɪŋə(r)/ *noun* = MANGLE IDM **go through the 'wringer** (*informal*) to have a difficult or unpleasant experience, or a series of them

wringing 'wet *adj.* (especially of clothes) very wet

wrin·kle /ˈrɪŋkl/ *noun, verb*
■ *noun* **1** a line or small fold in your skin, especially on your face, that forms as you get older: *There were fine wrinkles around her eyes.* **2** [usually pl.] a small fold that you do not want in a piece of fabric or paper

He wrinkled his forehead.

■ *verb* **1** ~ (sth) (**up**) to make the skin on your face tighten into lines or folds; to form lines or folds in this way: [VN] *She wrinkled up her nose in distaste.* ◇ *He wrinkled his brow in concentration.* ◇ [V] *His face wrinkled in a grin.* **2** to form raised folds or lines in an untidy way; to make sth do this: [V] *Her stockings were wrinkling at the knees.* [also VN]

wrin·kled /ˈrɪŋkld/ *adj.* (of skin, clothing, etc.) having wrinkles

wrink·ling /ˈrɪŋklɪŋ/ *noun* [U] the process by which WRINKLES form in the skin

wrin·kly /ˈrɪŋkli/ *adj., noun*
■ *adj.* (*informal*) (of skin, clothing, etc.) having WRINKLES
■ *noun* (*pl.* **-ies**) (*BrE, informal*) an offensive word for an old person, used by younger people

wrist /rɪst/ *noun* the joint between the hand and the arm: *She's broken her wrist.* ◇ *He wore a copper bracelet on his wrist.*—picture at BODY IDM see SLAP *n.*

wrist·watch /ˈrɪstwɒtʃ; *AmE* -wɑːtʃ; -wɔːtʃ/ *noun* a watch that you wear on your wrist

writ /rɪt/ *noun, verb*
■ *noun* ~ (**for sth**) (**against sb**) a legal document from a court of law telling sb to do or not to do sth: *The company has been served with a writ for breach of contract.* ◇ *We fully intend to issue a writ against the newspaper.*
■ *verb* (*old use*) *pp* of WRITE IDM **writ 'large** (*literary*) **1** easy to see or understand: *Mistrust was writ large on her face.* **2** (used after a noun) being a larger or more obvious version of the thing mentioned: *The party's new philosophies are little more than their old beliefs writ large.*

write /raɪt/ *verb* (**wrote** /rəʊt/ **writ·ten** /ˈrɪtn/)
LETTERS/NUMBERS | **1** ~ (**in/on/with sth**) to make letters or numbers on a surface, especially using a pen or a pencil: [V] *In some countries children don't start learning to read and write until they are six.* ◇ *Please write in pen on both sides of the paper.* ◇ *I haven't got anything to write with.* ◇ [VN] *Write your name at the top of the paper.* ◇ *The teacher wrote the answers on the board.* ◇ *The 'b' had been wrongly written as a 'd'.*
BOOK/MUSIC/PROGRAM | **2** ~ (**sth**) (**about/on sth**) to produce sth in written form so that people can read, perform or use it, etc: [VN] *to write a novel/a song/an essay/a computer program* ◇ *He hopes to write a book about his experiences one day.* ◇ *She had to write a report on the project.* ◇ *Who was 'London Fields' written by?* ◇ *Which opera did Verdi write first?* ◇ [V] *I wanted to travel and then write about it.* ◇ *He writes for the 'New Yorker' (= works as a writer).* ◇ *No decision has been made at the time of writing.* ◇ [VNN] *She wrote him several poems.*
A LETTER | **3** ~ (**sth**) (**to sb**) to put information, greetings, etc. in a letter and send it to sb: [V] *Bye! Don't forget to write.* ◇ *She wrote to him in France.* ◇ *Can you write and confirm your booking?* ◇ *I'm writing to enquire about language courses.* ◇ [VN, VNN] *I wrote a letter to the Publicity Department.* ◇ *I wrote the Publicity Department a letter.* ◇ [Vthat] *She wrote that they were all fine.* ◇ [VN] (*AmE*) *Write me while you're away.* ◇ [VNthat] (*AmE*) *He wrote me that he would be arriving Monday.* ◇ [V-ing] *They wrote thanking us for the present.*
STATE IN WRITING | **4** to state the information or the words mentioned: [Vthat] *In his latest book he writes that the theory has since been disproved.* ◇ [V] *Ancient historians wrote of a lost continent beneath the ocean.* [also V speech]
CHEQUE/FORM | **5** ~ **sth** (**out**) to put information in the appropriate places on a cheque or other form: [VN] *to write out a cheque* ◇ [VNN] *I'll write you a receipt.*
COMPUTING | **6** ~ (**sth**) **to/onto sth** to record data in the memory of a computer: [VN] *An error was reported when he tried to write data to the file for the first time.* [also V]
OF PEN/PENCIL | **7** [V] to work correctly or in the way mentioned: *This pen won't write.*
IDM **be written all over sb's 'face** (of a feeling) to be very obvious to other people from the expression on sb's face: *Guilt was written all over his face.* **have sth/sb written all 'over it/sb** (*informal*) to show clearly the quality mentioned or the influence of the person mentioned: *It was performance with star quality written all over it.* ◇ *This essay has got Mike written all over it.* **nothing (much) to write 'home about** (*informal*) not especially good; ordinary—more at WORTH *adj.*
PHRV **write a'way** = WRITE OFF/AWAY **write 'back (to sb)** to write sb a letter replying to their letter: *I'm afraid I never wrote back.* ◇ *She wrote back saying that she couldn't come.* **write sth↔'down 1** to write sth on paper, especially in order to remember or record it: *Write down*

W

the address before you forget it. **2** (*business*) to reduce the value of ASSETS when stating it in a company's accounts—related noun WRITE-DOWN ,**write** '**in** (**to sb/sth**) (**for sth**) to write a letter to an organization or a company, for example to ask about sth or to express an opinion: *I'll write in for more information.* ◊ *She wrote in to the BBC to complain.* ,**write sb/sth**↔'**in** (*AmE, politics*) to add an extra name to your voting paper in an election in order to be able to vote for them—related noun WRITE-IN ,**write sth** '**into sth** to include a rule or condition in a contract or an agreement when it is made ,**write** '**off/a'way** (**to sb/sth**) (**for sth**) to write to an organization or a company, usually in order to ask them to send you sth: *I've written off for the catalogue.* ,**write sth**↔'**off 1** (*business*) to cancel a debt; to recognize that sth is a failure, has no value, etc: *to write off a debt/an investment* **2** (*BrE*) to damage sth, especially a vehicle, so badly that it cannot be repaired: *He's written off two cars this year.*—related noun WRITE-OFF—see also TOTAL ,**write sb/sth**↔'**off** (**as sth**) to decide that sb/sth is a failure or not worth paying any attention to ,**write sth**↔'**out** to write sth on paper, including all the details, especially a piece of work or an account of sth—see also WRITE (5) ,**write sb**↔'**out** (**of sth**) to remove a character from a regular series on television or radio: *She was written out after 20 years in the role.* ,**write sth**↔'**up** to record sth in writing in a full and complete form, often using notes that you made earlier: *to write up your notes/the minutes of a meeting* ◊ *They had to do a survey of the island and write up their findings.*—related noun WRITE-UP

'**write-down** *noun* (*business*) a reduction in the value of ASSETS, etc.

'**write-in** *noun* (*AmE*) a vote for sb who is not an official candidate in an election, in which you write their name on your BALLOT PAPER

'**write-off** *noun* **1** (*BrE*) a vehicle that has been so badly damaged in an accident that it is not worth spending money to repair it **2** [sing.] (*informal*) a period of time during which you do not achieve anything: *With meetings and phone calls, yesterday was a complete write-off.* **3** ~ (**of sth**) (*business*) an act of cancelling a debt and accepting that it will never be paid

writer /'raɪtə(r)/ *noun* **1** a person whose job is writing books, stories, articles, etc: *writers of poetry* ◊ *a travel/science/cookery writer* **2** a person who has written a particular thing: *the writer of this letter/article/computer program* **3** (with an adjective) a person who forms letters in a particular way when they are writing: *a neat/messy writer*

,**writer's** '**cramp** *noun* [U] a pain or stiff feeling in the hand caused by writing for a long time

'**write-up** *noun* an article in a newspaper or magazine in which sb writes what they think about a new book, play, product, etc.

writhe /raɪð/ *verb* [V] ~ (**about/around**) (**in/with sth**) to twist or move your body without stopping, often because you are in great pain: *She was writhing around on the floor in agony.* ◊ *The snake writhed and hissed.* ◊ (*figurative*) *He was writhing* (= suffering a lot) *with embarrassment.*

writ·ing /'raɪtɪŋ/ *noun* **1** [U] the activity of writing, in contrast to reading, speaking, etc: *Our son's having problems with his reading and writing* (= at school) ◊ *a writing case/desk* **2** [U] the activity of writing books, articles, etc., especially as a job: *Only later did she discover a talent for writing.* ◊ *He is leaving the band to concentrate on his writing.* ◊ *creative/essay/letter writing*—see also SONGWRITING **3** [U] books, articles, etc. in general: *The review is a brilliant piece of writing.* ◊ *feminist/travel writing* **4** (**writings**) [pl.] a group of pieces of writing, especially by a particular person or on a particular subject: *His experiences in India influenced his later writings.* ◊ *the writings of Hegel* **5** [U] words that have been written or painted on sth: *There was writing all over the desk.* **6** [U] the particular way in which sb forms letters when they write SYN HANDWRITING: *Who's this from? I don't recognize the writing.* IDM **in** '**writing** in the form of a

letter, document, etc. (that gives proof of sth): *All telephone reservations must be confirmed in writing.* ◊ *You must get his agreement in writing.* **the** ,**writing is on the** '**wall | see the** ,**writing on the** '**wall** (*AmE* **the** ,**handwriting on the** '**wall**) (*saying*) used when you are describing a situation in which there are signs that sth is going to have problems or that it is going to be a failure: *It is amazing that not one of them saw the writing on the wall.* ORIGIN From the Bible story in which strange writing appeared on a wall during a feast given by King Belshazzar, foretelling Belshazzar's death and the end of his kingdom.

'**writing paper** *noun* [U] = NOTEPAPER

writ·ten /'rɪtn/ *adj.* **1** [usually before noun] expressed in writing rather than in speech: *written instructions/language* **2** [usually before noun] (of an exam, a piece of work, etc.) involving writing rather than speaking or practical skills: *a written test* ◊ *written communication skills* **3** [only before noun] in the form of a letter, document, etc. and therefore official: *a written apology/statement* ◊ *a written contract*—see also WRITE *v.* IDM **the** ,**written** '**word** language expressed in writing rather than in speech: *the permanence of the written word*

wrong /rɒŋ; *AmE* rɔːŋ/ *adj., adv., noun, verb*

■ *adj.*

NOT CORRECT | **1** not right or correct: *I got all the answers wrong.* ◊ *He was driving on the wrong side of the road.* ◊ *Sorry, I must have dialled the wrong number.* ◊ *You're holding the camera the wrong way up!* ◊ *That picture is the wrong way round.* **2** [not before noun] ~ (**about sth/sb**) | ~ (**to do sth**) (of a person) not right about sth/sb SYN MISTAKEN: *I think she lives at number 44, but I could be wrong.* ◊ *You were wrong about Tom; he's not married after all.* ◊ *We were wrong to assume that she'd agree.* ◊ *She would prove him wrong* (= prove that he was wrong) *whatever happened.* ◊ (*spoken*) *You think you've beaten me but that's where you're wrong.* ◊ (*spoken*) *Correct me if I'm wrong* (= I may be wrong) *but didn't you say you two knew each other?*

CAUSING PROBLEMS | **3** [not before noun] ~ (**with sb/sth**) causing problems or difficulties; not as it should be: *Is anything wrong? You look worried.* ◊ '*What's wrong?*' '*Oh, nothing.*' ◊ *There's something wrong with the printer.* ◊ *The doctor could find nothing wrong with him.* ◊ *I have something wrong with my foot.*

NOT SUITABLE | **4** [usually before noun] ~ (**sth**) (**for sth**) | ~ (**sth to do**) not suitable, right or what you need: *He's the wrong person for the job.* ◊ *I realized that it was the wrong thing to say.* ◊ *We don't want this document falling into the wrong hands.* ◊ *It was his bad luck to be in the wrong place at the wrong time* (= so that he got involved in trouble without intending to).

NOT MORALLY RIGHT | **5** [not usually before noun] ~ (**of/for sb**) (**to do sth**) not morally right or honest: *This man has done nothing wrong.* ◊ *She acknowledged that she'd done wrong.* ◊ *It is wrong to tell lies.* ◊ *It was wrong of me to get so angry.* ◊ *What's wrong with eating meat?*

▶ **wrong·ness** *noun* [U] (*rare, formal*)

IDM **from/on the** ,**wrong side of the** '**tracks** from or living in a poor area or part of town **get (hold of) the** ,**wrong end of the** '**stick** (*BrE, informal*) to understand sth in the wrong way **on the** ,**wrong side of the** '**law** in trouble with the police **take sth the wrong** '**way** to be offended by a remark that was not intended to be offensive—more at BACK *v.*, BARK *v.*, BED *n.*, FAR *adv.*, FOOT *n.*, NOTE *n.*, RUB *v.*, SIDE *n.*, TRACK *n.*

■ *adv.* (used after verbs) in a way that produces a result that is not correct or that you do not want: *My name is spelt wrong.* ◊ *The program won't load. What am I doing wrong?* ◊ *I was trying to apologize but it came out wrong* (= what I said sounded wrong). ◊ '*I thought you were going out.*' '*Well you must have thought wrong, then!*' OPP RIGHT

IDM **get sb** '**wrong** (*spoken*) to not understand correctly what sb means: *Don't get me wrong* (= do not be offended by what I am going to say), *I think he's doing a good job, but...* **get sth** '**wrong** (*spoken*) **1** to not understand a situation correctly: *No, you've got it all wrong.*

s	t	v	z	ʃ	ʒ	tʃ	dʒ	θ	ð	ŋ
see	tea	van	zoo	shoe	vision	chain	jam	thin	this	sing

She's his wife. **2** to make a mistake with sth: *I must have got the figures wrong.* **go ˈwrong 1** to make a mistake: *If you do what she tells you, you won't go far wrong.* ◊ *Where did we go wrong with those kids* (= what mistakes did we make for them to behave so badly)*?* **2** (of a machine) to stop working correctly: *My watch keeps going wrong.* **3** to experience problems or difficulties: *The relationship started to go wrong when they moved abroad.* ◊ *What else can go wrong* (= what other problems are we going to have)*?* **you can't go ˈwrong (with sth)** (*spoken*) used to say that sth will always be acceptable in a particular situation: *For a quick lunch you can't go wrong with pasta.*—more at FOOT *n.*

▪ *noun* **1** [U] behaviour that is not honest or morally acceptable: *Children must be taught the difference between right and wrong.* ◊ *Her son can* **do no wrong** *in her eyes.* **2** [C] (*formal*) an act that is not legal, honest or morally acceptable: *It is time to forgive past wrongs if progress is to be made.* OPP RIGHT

IDM **in the ˈwrong** responsible for an accident, a mistake, an argument, etc: *The motorcyclist was clearly in the wrong.* **two ˌwrongs don't make a ˈright** (*saying*) used to say that if sb does sth bad to you, the situation will not be improved by doing sth bad to them—more at RIGHT *v.*

▪ *verb* [VN] [usually passive] (*formal*) to treat sb badly or in an unfair way: *He felt deeply wronged by the allegations.*

WHICH WORD?

wrong / wrongly / wrongfully

In informal language **wrong** can be used as an adverb instead of **wrongly**, when it means 'incorrectly' and comes after a verb or its object: *My name was spelled wrong.* ◊ *I'm afraid you guessed wrong.* **Wrongly** is used before a past participle or a *that* clause: *My name was wrongly spelt.* ◊ *She guessed wrongly that he was a teacher.*

Wrongfully is usually used in a formal legal situation with words like *convicted, dismissed* and *imprisoned*.

---

wrong·doer /ˈrɒŋduːə(r); *AmE* ˈrɔːŋ-/ *noun* (*formal*) a person who does sth dishonest or illegal

wrong·doing /ˈrɒŋduːɪŋ; *AmE* ˈrɔːŋ-/ *noun* [U, C] (*formal*) illegal or dishonest behaviour: *The company denies any wrongdoing.*

ˌwrong-ˈfoot *verb* [VN] (*BrE*) to put sb in a difficult or embarrassing situation by doing sth that they do not expect: *It was an attempt to wrong-foot the opposition.*

wrong·ful /ˈrɒŋfl; *AmE* ˈrɔːŋ-/ *adj.* [usually before noun] (especially *law*) not fair, morally right or legal: *She decided to sue her employer for wrongful dismissal.* ▸ **wrong·ful·ly** /-fəli/ *adv.*: *to be wrongfully convicted/ dismissed* ⇨ note at WRONG

ˌwrong-ˈheaded *adj.* (*written*) having or showing bad judgement: *wrong-headed beliefs/ideas*

wrong·ly /ˈrɒŋli; *AmE* ˈrɔːŋ-/ *adv.* in a way that is unfair, immoral or not correct: *She was wrongly accused of stealing.* ◊ *He assumed, wrongly, that she did not care.* ◊ *The sentence had been wrongly translated.* ◊ *They knew they had acted wrongly.* ◊ *Rightly or wrongly, they felt they should have been better informed* (= I do not know whether they were right to feel this way)*.* ⇨ note at WRONG

wrote *pt* of WRITE

wrought /rɔːt/ *verb* [VN] (*formal* or *literary*) (used only in the past tense) caused sth to happen, especially a change: *This century wrought major changes in our society.* ◊ *The storm wrought havoc in the south.*—see also WREAK **HELP** **Wrought** is an old form of the past tense of **work**.

ˌwrought ˈiron *noun* [U] a form of iron used to make decorative fences, gates, etc: *The gates were made of wrought iron.* ◊ *wrought-iron gates*—compare CAST IRON

wrung *pt, pp* of WRING

wry /raɪ/ *adj.* [usually before noun] (*written*) **1** showing that you are both amused and disappointed or annoyed: *'At least we got one vote,' she said with a wry smile.* ◊ *He pulled a wry face when I asked him how it had gone.* **2** amusing in an IRONIC way: *a wry comedy about family life* ◊ *a wry comment* ◊ *wry humour* ▸ **wryly** *adv.*: *to grin/ smile wryly* **wry·ness** *noun* [U]

WTO /ˌdʌbljuː tiː ˈəʊ; *AmE* ˈoʊ/ *abbr.* World Trade Organization (an international organization that encourages international trade and economic development, especially by reducing restrictions on trade)

wun·der·kind /ˈwʊndəkɪnd; *AmE* -dɜːrk-/ *noun* (*pl.* **wun·der·kind·er** /ˈwʊndəkɪndə(r); *AmE* -dɜːrk-/) (from *German*, sometimes *disapproving*) a person who is very successful at a young age

wuss /wʊs/ *noun* (*slang*) a stupid person

WWW /ˌdʌbljuː dʌbljuː ˈdʌbljuː/ *abbr.* = WORLD WIDE WEB: *several useful WWW addresses*

WYSIWYG /ˈwɪziwɪg/ *abbr.* (*computing*) what you see is what you get (what you see on the computer screen is exactly the same as will be printed)

W

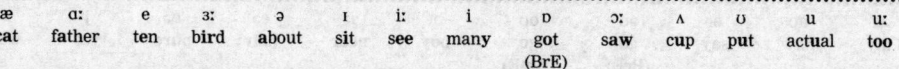

æ	ɑː	e	ɜː	ə	ɪ	iː	i	ɒ	ɔː	ʌ	ʊ	u	uː
cat	father	ten	bird	about	sit	see	many	got	saw	cup	put	actual	too
								(BrE)					

Xx

X (also **x**) /eks/ *noun, symbol*

■ *noun* (pl. **X's**, **x's** /'eksɪz/) **1** [C, U] the 24th letter of the English alphabet: *'Xylophone' begins with (an) X/'X'.* **2** [U] (*mathematics*) used to represent a number whose value is not mentioned: *The equation is impossible for any value of x greater than 2.* **3** [U] a person, a number, an influence, etc. that is not known or not named: *Let's suppose X knows what Y is doing.*—see also X CHROMOSOME, X-RATED, X-RAY

■ *symbol* **1** the number 10 in ROMAN NUMERALS **2** used to represent a kiss at the end of a letter, etc: *Love from Kathy XXX.* **3** used to show a vote for sb in an election: *Write X beside the candidate of your choice.* **4** used to show that a written answer is wrong—compare TICK *n.* (1) **5** used to show position, for example on a map: *X marks the spot.*

'X chromosome *noun* (*biology*) a SEX CHROMOSOME that exists in pairs in female cells and that exists by itself in male cells—compare Y CHROMOSOME

xeno·pho·bia /ˌzenə'fəʊbiə; *AmE* -'foʊ-/ *noun* [U] (*disapproving*) a strong feeling of dislike or fear of people from other countries: *a campaign against racism and xenophobia* ▶ **xeno·pho·bic** /-'fəʊbɪk; *AmE* -'foʊ-/ *adj.*

Xerox™ /'zɪərɒks; *AmE* 'zɪrɑːks/ *noun* a process for producing copies of letters, documents, etc. using a special machine; a copy made using this process: *a Xerox machine*

xerox /'zɪərɒks; *AmE* 'zɪrɑːks/ *verb* [VN] to make a copy of a letter, document, etc. by using Xerox or a similar process [SYN] PHOTOCOPY: *Could you xerox this letter, please?*

-xion ⇨ -ION

XL /ˌeks 'el/ *abbr.* extra large (used for sizes of things, especially clothes): *an XL T-shirt*

Xmas /'krɪsməs; 'eksməs/ *noun* [C, U] (*informal, written*) used as a short way of writing 'Christmas': *A merry Xmas to all our readers!*

'X-rated *adj.* (especially of a film/movie) that people under 18 are not allowed to see because it contains sex and/or violence

X-ray /'eks reɪ/ *noun, verb*

■ *noun* **1** [usually pl.] a type of RADIATION that can pass through objects that are not transparent and make it possible to see inside them: *an X-ray machine* (= one that produces X-rays) **2** a photograph made by X-rays, especially one showing bones or organs in the body: *a chest X-ray* ◊ *The doctor studied the X-rays of her lungs.* ◊ *to take an X-ray* **3** a medical examination using X-rays: *I had to go for an X-ray.*

■ *verb* [VN] to photograph and examine bones and organs inside the body, using X-rays: *He had to have his chest X-rayed.*

xylo·phone /'zaɪləfəʊn; *AmE* -foʊn/ *noun* a musical instrument made of two rows of wooden bars of different lengths that you hit with two small sticks—compare GLOCKENSPIEL—picture on page 841

Yy

Y /waɪ/ *noun, abbr.*

■ *noun* (also **y**) (pl. **Y's**, **y's** /waɪz/) **1** [C, U] the 25th letter of the English alphabet: *'Year' begins with (a) Y/'Y'.* **2** [U] (*mathematics*) used to represent a number whose value is not mentioned: *Can the value of y be predicted from the value of x?* **3** [U] a person, a number, an influence, etc. that is not known or not named: *Let's suppose X knows what Y is doing.*—see also Y CHROMOSOME, Y-FRONTS

■ *abbr.* (**the Y**) (*AmE, informal*) YMCA, YWCA

-y *suffix* **1** (also **-ey**) (in adjectives) full of; having the quality of: *dusty* ◊ *clayey* **2** (in adjectives) tending to: *runny* ◊ *sticky* **3** (in nouns) the action or process of: *inquiry* **4** (also **-ie**) (in nouns, showing affection): *doggy* ◊ *daddy*

yacht /jɒt; *AmE* jɑːt/ (*AmE* also **sail·boat**) *noun* a large sailing boat, often also with an engine and a place to sleep on board, used for pleasure trips and racing: *a yacht club/race* ◊ *a motor yacht* ◊ *a luxury yacht*—compare DINGHY

yacht·ing /'jɒtɪŋ; *AmE* 'jɑːt-/ *noun* [U] the sport or activity of sailing or racing yachts

yachts·man /'jɒtsmən; *AmE* 'jɑːt-/, **yachts·wo·man** /-wʊmən/ *noun* (pl. **-men** /-mən/, **-women** /-wɪmɪn/) a person who sails a yacht for pleasure or as a sport: *a round-the-world yachtsman*

Yah·weh /'jɑːweɪ/ *noun* = JEHOVAH

yak /jæk/ *noun, verb*

■ *noun* an animal of the cow family, with long horns and long hair, that lives in central Asia

■ *verb* (also **yack**) (**-kk-**) [V] (*informal, often disapproving*) to talk continuously about things that are not very serious or important: *She just kept yakking on.*

y'all /jɔːl/ *pron.* = YOU-ALL

yam /jæm/ *noun* [C, U] the large root of a tropical plant that is cooked as a vegetable—picture on page A3

yang /jæŋ/ *noun* [U] (in Chinese philosophy) the bright active male principle of the universe—compare YIN

Yank /jæŋk/ (also **Yan·kee**) *noun* (*BrE, informal, often disapproving*) a person from the US; an American

yank /jæŋk/ *verb* [usually +adv./prep.] (*informal*) to pull sth/sb hard, quickly and suddenly: [VN] *He yanked her to her feet.* ◊ [VN-ADJ] *I yanked the door open/yanked open the door.* ◊ [V] *Liz yanked at my arm.* ▶ **yank** *noun*: *She gave the rope a yank.*

Yan·kee /'jæŋki/ *noun* **1** (*AmE*) a person who comes from or lives in any of the northern states of the US, especially New England **2** a soldier who fought for the Union (= the northern states) in the American Civil War **3** (*BrE, informal*) = YANK

yap /jæp/ *verb* (**-pp-**) [V] **1** ~ (at sb/sth) (especially of small dogs) to BARK a lot, making a high, sharp and usually irritating sound: *The dogs yapped at his heels.* ◊ *yapping dogs* **2** (*informal*) to talk in a silly, noisy and usually irritating way ▶ **yap** *noun*

aɪ	aʊ	eɪ	əʊ	oʊ	ɔɪ	ɪə	eə	ʊə	j	w
my	now	say	go (BrE)	go (AmE)	boy	near	hair	pure	yes	wet

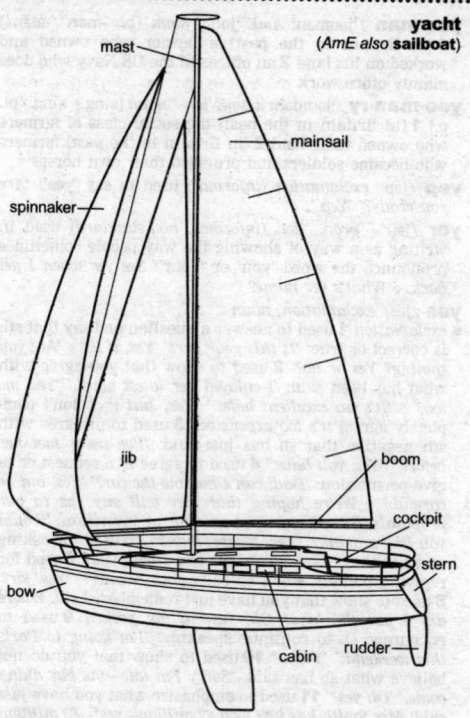

yacht
(*AmE also* **sailboat**)

mast

mainsail

spinnaker

jib

boom

cockpit

stern

bow

cabin rudder

yard /jɑːd; *AmE* jɑːrd/ *noun* **1** (*BrE*) an area outside a building, usually with a hard surface and a surrounding wall: *the prison yard* ◇ *The children were playing in the yard at the front of the school.*—see also BACKYARD **2** (*AmE*) = GARDEN *n.* (1)—see also BACKYARD—picture at HOUSE **3** (usually in compounds) an area of land used for a special purpose or business: *a boat yard* **HELP** You will find other compounds ending in **yard** at their place in the alphabet. **4** (*abbr.* **yd**) a unit for measuring length, equal to 3 feet (36 INCHES) or 0.9144 of a metre **5** (*technical*) a long piece of wood fastened to a MAST that supports a sail on a boat or ship **IDM** see INCH *n.*

yard·age /ˈjɑːdɪdʒ; *AmE* ˈjɑːrd-/ *noun* [C, U] (*technical*) **1** size measured in yards or square yards **2** (in American football) the number of yards that a team or player has moved forward

yard·arm /ˈjɑːdɑːm; *AmE* ˈjɑːrdɑːrm/ *noun* (*technical*) either end of the long piece of wood fastened to a ship's MAST that supports a sail

yard sale *noun* (*AmE*) a sale of things from sb's house, held in their yard—see also GARAGE SALE

yard·stick /ˈjɑːdstɪk; *AmE* ˈjɑːrd-/ *noun* **1** (*especially AmE*) a RULER for measuring one YARD **2** a standard used for judging how good or successful sth is: *a yardstick by/ against which to measure sth* ◇ *Exam results are not the only yardstick of a school's performance.*

yar·mulke (also **yar·mulka**) /ˈjɑːmʊlkə; *AmE* ˈjɑːrm-/ *noun* a small round cap worn on top of the head by Jewish men; a type of SKULLCAP

yarn /jɑːn; *AmE* jɑːrn/ *noun* **1** [U] thread that has been spun, used for knitting, weaving, etc.—picture at SEW **2** [C] (*informal*) a long story, especially one that is exaggerated or invented: *He used to spin yarns* (= tell stories) *about his time in the Army.* **IDM** see PITCH *v.*

yash·mak /ˈjæʃmæk/ *noun* a piece of fabric covering most of the face, worn by some Muslim women

yaw /jɔː/ *verb* [V] (*technical*) (of a ship or plane) to turn to one side, away from a straight course, in an unsteady way ► **yaw** *noun* [C, U]

yawn /jɔːn/ *verb, noun*

■ *verb* [V] **1** to open your mouth wide and breathe in deeply through it, usually because you are tired or bored: *He stood up, stretched and yawned.* **2** (of a large hole or an empty space) to be very wide and often frightening and difficult to get across: *A crevasse yawned at their feet.* ◇ (*figurative*) *There's a **yawning gap** between rich and poor.*

■ *noun* **1** an act of yawning: *She stifled another yawn and tried hard to look interested.* **2** [usually sing.] (*informal*) a boring event, idea, etc: *The meeting was one big yawn from start to finish.*

yaws /jɔːz/ *noun* [U] a tropical skin disease that causes large red swellings

'Y chromosome *noun* (*biology*) a SEX CHROMOSOME that exists by itself and only in male cells—compare X CHROMOSOME

yd *abbr.* (*pl.* **yds**) YARD: *12 yds of silk*

ye *pron., det.*

■ *pron.* /jiː; *weak form* ji/ (*old use* or *dialect*) a word meaning 'you', used when talking to more than one person: *Gather ye rosebuds while ye may.*

■ *det.* /jiː/ a word meaning 'the', used in the names of pubs, shops, etc. to make them seem old: *Ye Olde Starre Inn*

yea /jeɪ/ *adv., noun* (*old use*) yes—compare NAY

yeah /jeə/ *adv.* used in writing to show the way 'yes' is pronounced in informal speech **IDM** ,**oh 'yeah?** used when you are commenting on what sb has just said: *'We're off to France soon.' 'Oh yeah? When's that?'* ◇ *'I'm going to be rich one day.' 'Oh yeah?'* (= I don't believe you.)

year /jɪə(r); jɜː(r); *AmE* jɪr/ *noun* (*abbr.* **yr**) **1** (also ,**calendar 'year**) [C] the period from 1 January to 31 December, that is 365 or 366 days, divided into 12 months: *in the year 1865* ◇ *I lost my job earlier this year.* ◇ *Elections take place every year.* ◇ *The museum is open all (the) year round* (= during the whole year).—see also LEAP YEAR, NEW YEAR **2** [C] a period of 12 months, measured from any particular time: *It's exactly a year since I started working here.* ◇ *She gave up teaching three years ago.* ◇ *in the first year of their marriage* ◇ *the pre-war/war/post-war years* (= the period before/during/after the war) ◇ *I have happy memories of my years in Poland* (= the time I spent there).—see also LIGHT YEAR **3** [C] a period of 12 months connected with a particular activity: *the academic/school year* ◇ *the tax year*—see also FINANCIAL YEAR **4** [C] (*especially BrE*) (at a school, etc.) a level that you stay in for one year; a student at a particular level: *We started German in year seven.* ◇ *a year-seven pupil* ◇ *The first years do French.* ◇ *She was in my year at school.* **5** [C, usually pl.] age; time of life: *He was 14 years old when it happened.* ◇ *She looks young for her years.* ◇ *They were both only 20 years of age.* ◇ *a twenty-year-old man* ◇ *He died in his sixtieth year.* ◇ *She's getting on in years* (= is no longer young). **6** (**years**) [pl.] (*informal*) a long time: *It's years since we last met.* ◇ *They haven't seen each other for years.* ◇ *That's the best movie I've seen in years.* **IDM** ,**man, woman, car, etc. of the 'year** a person or thing that people decide is the best in a particular field in a particular year **not/ never in a hundred, etc. 'years** (*spoken*) used to emphasize that you will/would never do sth: *I'd never have thought of that in a million years.* **put 'years on sb** to make sb feel or look older **take 'years off sb** to make sb feel or look younger ,**year after 'year** every year for many years ,**year by 'year** as the years pass; each year: *Year by year their affection for each other grew stronger.* **the year 'dot** (*BrE*) (*AmE* **the year 'one**) (*informal*) a very long time ago: *I've been going there every summer since the year dot.* **year 'in, year 'out** every year ,**year of 'grace | ,year of our 'Lord** (*formal*) any particular year after the birth of Christ ,**year on 'year** (used especially when talking about figures, prices, etc.) each year, compared with the last year: *Spending has increased year on year.* ◇ *a year-on-year increase in spending*—more at ADVANCED, DECLINE *v.*, DONKEY, TURN *n.*

year·book /ˈjɪəbʊk; *AmE* ˈjɪrbʊk/ *noun* **1** a book published once a year, giving details of events, etc. of the previous year, especially those connected with a particular area of activity **2** (*especially AmE*) a book that is

Y

æ	ɑː	e	ɜː	ə	ɪ	iː	i	ɒ	ɔː	ʌ	ʊ	u	uː
cat	father	ten	bird	about	sit	see	many	got (BrE)	saw	cup	put	actual	too

produced by the senior class in a school or college, containing photographs of students and details of school activities

year·ling /ˈjɪəlɪŋ; *AmE* ˈjɪrlɪŋ/ *noun* an animal, especially a horse, between one and two years old

‚year·ˈlong *adj.* [only before noun] continuing for a whole year: *a year-long dispute/investigation*

year·ly /ˈjɪəli; ˈjɜːli; *AmE* ˈjɪrli/ *adj.* **1** happening once a year or every year: *Pay is reviewed on a yearly basis.* **2** paid, valid or calculated for one year: *yearly income/interest* ► **year·ly** *adv.*: *The magazine is issued twice yearly* (= twice every year).

yearn /jɜːn; *AmE* jɜːrn/ *verb* ~ **(for sth/sb)** (*literary*) to want sth very much, especially when it is very difficult to get: [V] *The people yearned for peace.* ◊ *There was a yearning look in his eyes.* ◊ [V to inf] *She yearned to escape from her office job.*

yearn·ing /ˈjɜːnɪŋ; *AmE* ˈjɜːrnɪŋ/ *noun* [C, U] ~ **(for sb/ sth)**| ~ **(to do sth)** (*written*) a strong and emotional desire: *a yearning for a quiet life* ◊ *She had no great yearning to go back.* ► **yearn·ing·ly** *adv.*

‚year-ˈround *adj.* all through the year: *an island with year-round sunshine*

yeast /jiːst/ *noun* [U, C] a FUNGUS used in making beer and wine, or to make bread rise ► **yeasty** *adj.*: *a yeasty smell*

ˈyeast extract *noun* [U] a black substance made from yeast, spread on bread, etc.—see also MARMITE

ˈyeast infection *noun* (*AmE*) = THRUSH

yell /jel/ *verb*, *noun*
■ *verb* ~ **(out) (sth)**|~ **(sth) (at sb/sth)** to shout loudly, for example because you are angry, excited, frightened or in pain: [V] *He yelled at the other driver.* ◊ *They yelled with excitement.* ◊ *She yelled out in pain.* ◊ *She yelled at the child to get down from the wall.* ◊ [V speech] '*Be careful!*' *he yelled.* ◊ [VN] *The crowd yelled encouragement at the players.* ⇨ note at SHOUT
■ *noun* a loud cry of pain, excitement, etc.: *to let out/give a yell* ◊ *a yell of delight/surprise*

yel·low /ˈjeləʊ; *AmE* ˈjeloʊ/ *adj.*, *noun*, *verb*
■ *adj.* (**yel·low·er**, **yel·low·est**) **1** having the colour of lemons or butter: *pale yellow flowers* ◊ *a bright yellow waterproof jacket* **2** an offensive word used to describe the light brown skin of people from some E Asian countries **3** (*informal, disapproving*) easily frightened [SYN] COWARDLY ► **yel·low·ness** *noun* [U, sing.]
■ *noun* [U, C] the colour of lemons or butter: *She was dressed in yellow.* ◊ *the reds and yellows of the trees*
■ *verb* [V, VN] to become yellow; to make sth become yellow

‚yellow ˈcard *noun* (*BrE*) (in football) a card shown by the REFEREE to a player as a warning about bad behaviour—compare RED CARD

‚yellow ˈfever *noun* [U] an infectious tropical disease that makes the skin turn yellow and often causes death

yel·low·ham·mer /ˈjeləʊhæmə(r); *AmE* -loʊ-/ *noun* a small bird, the male of which has a yellow head, neck and breast

yel·low·ish /ˈjeləʊɪʃ; *AmE* -loʊ-/ (also *less frequent* **yel·lowy** /ˈjeləʊi; *AmE* -loʊ-/) *adj.* fairly yellow in colour: *The paper had a yellowish tinge because it was so old.*

‚yellow ˈline *noun* (in Britain) a yellow line painted at the side of a road to show that you can only park your car there at particular times or for a short time: *double yellow lines* (= two lines that mean you cannot park there at all)

‚Yellow ˈPages™ (*BrE*) (*AmE* **‚yellow ˈpages**) *noun* [pl.] a book with yellow pages that gives a list of companies and organizations and their telephone numbers, arranged according to the type of services they offer

yelp /jelp/ *verb* [V, V speech] to give a sudden short cry, usually of pain ► **yelp** *noun*

yen /jen/ *noun* **1** (*pl.* **yen**) [C] the unit of money in Japan **2** (**the yen**) [sing.] (*finance*) the value of the yen compared with the value of the money of other countries **3** [C, usually sing.] ~ **(for sth/to do sth)** a strong desire: *I've always had a yen to travel around the world.*

yeo·man /ˈjəʊmən; *AmE* ˈjoʊ-/ *noun* (*pl.* **-men** /-mən/) **1** (in Britain in the past) a farmer who owned and worked on his land **2** an officer in the US Navy who does mainly office work

yeo·man·ry /ˈjəʊmənri; *AmE* ˈjoʊ-/ *noun* [sing.+ sing./pl. v.] **1** (in Britain in the past) the social class of farmers who owned their land **2** (in Britain in the past) farmers who became soldiers and provided their own horses

yep /jep/ *exclamation* (*informal*) used to say 'yes': *Are you ready?' 'Yep.'*

yer /jə(r)/ *pron.*, *det.* (*informal, non-standard*) used in writing as a way of showing the way people sometimes pronounce the word 'you' or 'your': *See yer when I get back.* ◊ *What's yer name?*

yes /jes/ *exclamation, noun*
■ *exclamation* **1** used to answer a question and say that sth is correct or true: *'Is this your car?' 'Yes, it is.'* ◊ *'Are you coming? Yes or no?'* **2** used to show that you agree with what has been said: *'I enjoyed her latest novel.' 'Yes, me too.'* ◊ *'It's an excellent hotel.' 'Yes, but* (= I don't completely agree) *it's too expensive.'* **3** used to disagree with sth negative that sb has just said: *'I've never met her before.' 'Yes, you have.'* **4** used to agree to a request or to give permission: *'Dad, can I borrow the car?' 'Yes, but be careful.'* ◊ *We're hoping that they will **say yes** to our proposals.* **5** used to accept an offer or invitation: *'Would you like a drink?' 'Yes, please/thanks.'* **6** used for asking sb what they want: *Yes? How can I help you?* **7** used for replying politely when sb calls you: *'Waiter!' 'Yes, sir?'* **8** used to show that you have just remembered sth: *Where did I put the keys? Oh, yes—in my pocket!* **9** used to encourage sb to continue speaking: *'I'm going to Paris this weekend.' 'Yes …'* **10** used to show that you do not believe what sb has said: *'Sorry I'm late—the bus didn't come.' 'Oh yes?'* **11** used to emphasize what you have just said: *Mrs Smith has just won £2 million—yes!—£2 million!* **12** used to show that you are excited or extremely pleased about sth that you have done or sth that has happened: *'They've scored another goal.' 'Yes!!'* **13** (**yes, yes**) used to show that you are impatient or irritated about sth: *'Hurry up—it's late.' 'Yes, yes—I'm coming.'* [IDM] **‚yes and ˈno** used when you cannot give a clear answer to a question: *'Are you enjoying it?' 'Yes and no.'*
■ *noun* (*pl.* **yes·ses** or **yeses** /ˈjesɪz/) an answer that shows that you agree with an idea, a statement, etc.; a person who says 'yes': *I need a simple yes or no to my questions.* ◊ *There will be two ballot boxes—one for yesses and one for noes.* ◊ *I'll put you down as a yes.*

ˈyes-man *noun* (*pl.* **-men** /-men/) (*disapproving*) a person who always agrees with people in authority in order to gain their approval

yes·ter·day /ˈjestədeɪ; ˈjestədi; *AmE* -tərd-/ *adv.*, *noun*
■ *adv.* on the day before today: *They arrived yesterday.* ◊ *I can remember our wedding as if it were yesterday.* ◊ *Where were you yesterday morning?* ◊ *To think I was lying on a beach only the **day before yesterday**.* [IDM] see BORN v.
■ *noun* [U] **1** the day before today: *Yesterday was Sunday.* ◊ *What happened at yesterday's meeting?* **2** (also **yes·ter·days** [pl.]) the recent past: *Yesterday's students are today's employees.* ◊ *All her yesterdays had vanished without a trace.*

yes·ter·year /ˈjestəjɪə(r); *AmE* ˈjestərjɪr/ *noun* [U] (*old-fashioned* or *literary*) the past, especially a time when attitudes and ideas were different

yet /jet/ *adv.*, *conj.*
■ *adv.* **1** used in negative sentences and questions to talk about sth that has not happened but that you expect to happen: (*BrE*) *I haven't received a letter from him yet.* ◊ (*AmE*) *I didn't receive a letter from him yet.* ◊ *'Are you ready?' 'No, not yet.'* ◊ *We **have yet to** decide what action to take* (= We have not decided what action to take). ⇨ note at ALREADY **2** (used in negative sentences) now; as soon as this: *Don't go yet.* ◊ *We don't need to start yet.* **3** from now until the period of time mentioned has passed: *He'll be busy for ages yet.* ◊ *They won't arrive for at least two hours yet.* **4** **could, might, may, etc. do sth** ~ used to say that sth could, might, etc. happen in the future, even though it

seems unlikely: *We may win yet.* ◇ (*formal*) *She could yet surprise us all.* **5 the best, longest, etc. sth ~** (**done**) the best, longest, etc. thing of its kind made, produced, written, etc. until now/then: *the most comprehensive study yet of his music* ◇ *It was the highest building yet constructed.* **6 ~ another/more … | ~ again** used to emphasize an increase in number or amount or the number of times sth happens: *snow, snow and yet more snow* ◇ *yet another diet book* ◇ *Prices were cut yet again* (= once more, after many other times). **7 ~ worse, more importantly, etc.** used to emphasize an increase in the degree of sth (= how bad, important, etc. it is) SYN EVEN, STILL: *a recent and yet more improbable theory* IDM **as 'yet** until now or until a particular time in the past: *an as yet unpublished report* ◇ *As yet little was known of the causes of the disease.*
■ *conj.* in spite of what has just been said SYN NEVERTHELESS: *It's a small car, yet it's surprisingly spacious.* ◇ *He has a good job, and yet he never seems to have any money.*

yeti /ˈjeti/ (also A,bominable 'Snowman) *noun* a large hairy creature like a man or a bear, that some people believe lives in the Himalayan mountains

yew /juː/ *noun* **1** [C, U] (also 'yew tree) a small tree with dark green leaves and small red berries. Yews are often planted near churches. **2** [U] the wood of the yew tree

'Y-fronts™ *noun* [pl.] (*BrE*) men's UNDERPANTS, with an opening in the front sewn in the shape of a Y upside-down: *a pair of Y-fronts*

YHA /ˌwaɪ eɪtʃ ˈeɪ/ *abbr.* Youth Hostels Association (an organization that exists in many countries and provides cheap simple accommodation)

yid /jɪd/ *noun* (⚠, *slang*) a very offensive word for a Jewish person

Yid·dish /ˈjɪdɪʃ/ *noun* [U] a Jewish language, originally used in central and eastern Europe, based on a form of German with words from Hebrew and several modern languages—compare HEBREW ▶ **Yid·dish** *adj.*

yield /jiːld/ *verb, noun*
■ *verb* **1** [VN] to produce or provide sth, for example a profit, result or crop: *Higher-rate deposit accounts yield good returns.* ◇ *The research has yielded useful information.* ◇ *trees that no longer yield fruit* **2** [V] **~ (to sth/sb)** to stop resisting sth/sb; to agree to sth that you do not want to do: *After a long siege, the town was forced to yield.* ◇ *He reluctantly yielded to their demands.* ◇ *I yielded to temptation and had a chocolate bar.* **3** [VN] **~ sth/sb (up) (to sb)** (*formal*) to allow sb to win, have or take control of sth that has been yours until now: *He refused to yield up his gun.* ◇ (*figurative*) *The universe is slowly yielding up its secrets.* **4** [V] to move, bend or break because of pressure: *Despite our attempts to break it, the lock would not yield.* **5** [V] **~ (to sb/sth)** (*AmE, IrishE*) to allow vehicles on a bigger road to go first SYN GIVE WAY: *Yield to oncoming traffic.* ◇ *a yield sign* PHRV **'yield to sth** (*formal*) to be replaced by sth: *Barges yielded to road vehicles for transporting goods.*
■ *noun* [C, U] the total amount of crops, profits, etc. that are produced: *a high crop yield* ◇ *a reduction in milk yield* ◇ *This will give a yield of 10% on your investment.*

yield·ing /ˈjiːldɪŋ/ *adj.* (*written*) **1** (of a substance) soft and easy to bend or move when you press it **2** (of a person) willing to do what other people want **3** (used with an adverb) giving the amount of crops, profits, etc. mentioned: *high/low yielding crops*

yikes /jaɪks/ *exclamation* (*informal*) used to show that you are surprised or suddenly afraid

yin /jɪn/ *noun* [U] (in Chinese philosophy) the dark, not active, female principle of the universe—compare YANG

yip·pee /jɪˈpiː; *AmE* ˈjɪpi/ *exclamation* (*old-fashioned, informal*) used to show you are pleased or excited

YMCA /ˌwaɪ em es ˈiː/ (also *AmE informal* **the Y**) *abbr.* Young Men's Christian Association (an organization that exists in many countries and provides accommodation and social and sports activities): *We stayed at the YMCA.*

yo /jəʊ; *AmE* joʊ/ *exclamation* (*slang*) used as a greeting by young people

yob /jɒb; *AmE* jɑːb/ (also **yobbo** /ˈjɒbəʊ; *AmE* ˈjɑːboʊ/ *pl.*

-os) *noun* (*BrE, informal*) a rude, noisy and sometimes aggressive and violent boy or young man SYN LOUT

yodel /ˈjəʊdl; *AmE* ˈjoʊdl/ *verb, noun*
■ *verb* (**-ll-**, *AmE* **-l-**) [V, VN] to sing or call in the traditional Swiss way, changing your voice frequently between its normal level and a very high level
■ *noun* a song or musical call in which sb yodels

yoga /ˈjəʊɡə; *AmE* ˈjoʊɡə/ *noun* [U] **1** a Hindu philosophy that teaches you how to control your body and mind in the belief that you can become united with the spirit of the universe in this way **2** a system of exercises for your body and for controlling your breathing, used by people who want to become fitter or to relax ▶ **yogic** /ˈjəʊɡɪk; *AmE* ˈjoʊ-/ *adj.*: *yogic teachings/techniques*

yogi /ˈjəʊɡi; *AmE* ˈjoʊɡi/ *noun* (*pl.* **yogis**) an expert in, or teacher of, the philosophy of yoga

yog·urt (also **yog·hurt**, **yog·hourt**) /ˈjɒɡət; *AmE* ˈjoʊɡərt/ *noun* [U, C] a thick white liquid food, made by adding bacteria to milk, served cold and often flavoured with fruit; an amount of this sold in a small pot: *Greek/natural yogurt* ◇ *There's a yogurt left if you're still hungry.* ◇ *a lemon yogurt*

yoke /jəʊk; *AmE* joʊk/ *noun, verb*
■ *noun* **1** [C] a long piece of wood that is fastened across the necks of two animals, especially OXEN, so that they can pull heavy loads **2** [sing.] (*literary or formal*) harsh treatment or sth that restricts your freedom and makes your life very difficult to bear: *the yoke of imperialism* ◇ *Young people often chafe under the yoke of parental control.* **3** [C] a piece of wood that is shaped to fit across a person's shoulders so that they can carry two equal loads **4** [C] a part of a dress, skirt, etc. that fits around the shoulders or hips and from which the rest of the fabric hangs
■ *verb* [VN] **1** to join two animals together with a yoke: *A pair of oxen, yoked together, was used.* ◇ *an ox yoked to a plough* **2** [usually passive] (*formal*) to bring two people, countries, ideas, etc. together so that they are forced into a close relationship: *The Hong Kong dollar was yoked to the American dollar for many years.*

yokel /ˈjəʊkl; *AmE* ˈjoʊkl/ *noun* (often *humorous*) if you call a person a **yokel**, you are saying that they do not have much education or understanding of modern life, because they come from the countryside

yolk /jəʊk; *AmE* joʊk/ *noun* [C, U] the round yellow part in the middle of an egg: *Separate the whites from the yolks.*

Yom Kip·pur /ˌjɒm ˈkɪpə(r); kɪˈpʊə(r); *AmE* ˌjɑːm kɪˈpʊr; ˌjoʊm/ *noun* [U] a Jewish religious holiday in September or October when people eat nothing all day and say prayers of PENITENCE in the SYNAGOGUE, also known as the Day of Atonement

yon /jɒn; *AmE* jɑːn/ *det., adv.*
■ *det.* (*old use* or *dialect*) that: *There's an old farm over yon hill.*
■ *adv.* IDM see HITHER

yon·der /ˈjɒndə(r); *AmE* ˈjɑːn-/ *det.* (*old use* or *dialect*) that is over there; that you can see over there: *Let's rest under yonder tree.* ▶ **yon·der** *adv.*: *Whose is that farm over yonder?*

yonks /jɒŋks; *AmE* jɑːŋks/ *noun* [U] (*BrE, informal, becoming old-fashioned*) a long time: *I haven't seen you for yonks!*

yoo-hoo /ˈjuː huː/ *exclamation* (*informal, becoming old-fashioned*) used to attract sb's attention, especially when they are some distance away

yore /jɔː(r)/ *noun* IDM **of 'yore** (*old use* or *literary*) long ago: *in days of yore*

York·shire pud·ding /ˌjɔːkʃə ˈpʊdɪŋ; *AmE* ˌjɔːrkʃər/ *noun* [U, C] a type of British food made from BATTER that is baked until it rises, traditionally eaten with ROAST beef

Yorkshire terrier /ˌjɔːkʃə ˈteriə(r); *AmE* ˌjɔːrkʃər/ *noun* a very small dog with long brown and grey hair

you /ju; *AmE* jə; *strong form* juː/ *pron.* **1** used as the subject or object of a verb or after a preposition to refer to the person or people being spoken or written to: *You said you knew the way.* ◇ *I thought she told you.* ◇ *Can I sit next to you?* ◇ *I don't think that hairstyle is you* (= it doesn't suit your appearance or personality). **2** used with nouns and

Y

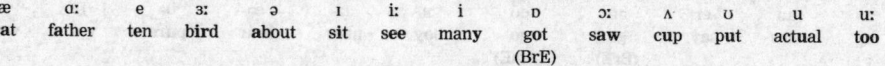

æ	ɑː	e	ɜː	ə	ɪ	iː	i	ɒ	ɔː	ʌ	ʊ	u	uː
cat	father	ten	bird	about	sit	see	many	got	saw	cup	put	actual	too
								(BrE)					

adjectives to speak to sb directly: *You girls, stop talking!* ◊ *You stupid idiot!* **3** used for referring to people in general: *You learn a language better if you visit the country where it is spoken.* ◊ *It's a friendly place—people come up to you in the street and start talking.*

you-all /ˈjuː ˈɔːl/ (also **y'all**) *pron.* (*informal*) used especially in the southern US to mean *you* when talking to more than one person: *Have you-all brought swimsuits?*

you'd /juːd/ *short form* **1** you had **2** you would

you'll /juːl/ *short form* you will

young /jʌŋ/ *adj., noun*
■ *adj.* (**young·er** /ˈjʌŋɡə(r)/ **young·est** /ˈjʌŋɡɪst/) **1** having lived or existed for only a short time; not fully developed: *young babies / children / animals* ◊ *a young country / company* ◊ *Caterpillars eat the young leaves of this plant.* ◊ *a young wine* ◊ (*humorous*) *The night is still young* (= it has only just started). OPP OLD **2** not yet old; not as old as others: *young people* ◊ *talented young football players* ◊ *I am the youngest of four sisters.* ◊ *In his younger days he played rugby for Wales.* ◊ *I met the young Bill Clinton at Oxford.* ◊ *Her grandchildren keep her young.* ◊ *My son's thirteen but he's young for his age* (= not as developed as other boys of the same age). ◊ *They married young* (= at an early age). ◊ *My mother died young.* OPP OLD **3** suitable or appropriate for young people: *young fashion / ideas* ◊ *The clothes she wears are much too young for her.* **4** consisting of young people or young children; with a low average age: *They have a young family.* ◊ *a young audience* **5** ~ **man/lady/woman** used to show that you are angry or annoyed with a particular young person: *I think you owe me an apology, young lady!* **6** (**the younger**) used before or after a person's name to distinguish them from an older relative: *the younger Kennedy* ◊ (*BrE, formal*) *William Pitt the younger*—compare THE ELDER at ELDER *adj.*, JUNIOR *adj.* (3) IDM **be getting 'younger** (*spoken*) used to say that people seem to be doing sth at a younger age than they used to, or that they seem younger because you are now older: *The band's fans are getting younger.* ◊ *Why do police officers seem to be getting younger?* **not be getting any 'younger** (*spoken*) used when you are commenting that time is passing and that you, or sb else, is growing older ,**young at 'heart** thinking and behaving like a young person even when you are old—more at OLD, ONLY *adv.*
■ *noun* [pl.] **1** (**the young**) young people considered as a group: *It's a movie that will appeal to the young.* ◊ *It's a book for young and old alike.* **2** young animals of a particular type or that belong to a particular mother: *a mother bird feeding her young*

young·ish /ˈjʌŋɪʃ/ *adj.* fairly young: *a youngish president*

,**young of'fender** *noun* (*BrE*) a criminal who, according to the law, is not yet an adult but no longer a child: *a young offenders' institution*

young·ster /ˈjʌŋstə(r)/ *noun* (*informal*) a young person or a child: *The camp is for youngsters aged 8 to 14.*

,**young 'thing** *noun* (*informal*) a young adult: *bright young things working in the computer business*

your /jɔː(r); *AmE* jʊr *weak form* jə(r)/ *det.* (the possessive form of *you*) **1** of or belonging to the person or people being spoken to or written to: *I like your dress.* ◊ *Excuse me, is this your seat?* ◊ *The bank is on your right.* **2** of or belonging to people in general: *Dentists advise you to have your teeth checked every six months.* ◊ *In Japan you are taught great respect for your elders.* **3** (*informal*) used to show that sb/sth is well known or often talked about: *This is your typical English pub.* ◊ (*ironic, disapproving*) *You and your bright ideas!* **4** (**Your**) used in some titles, especially those of royal people: *Your Majesty* ◊ *Your Excellency*

you're /jʊə(r); jɔː(r); *AmE* jʊr; *AmE weak form* jər/ *short form* you are

yours /jɔːz; *AmE* jɜːrz; jɔːrz; jʊrz/ *pron.* **1** of or belonging to you: *Is that book yours?* ◊ *Is she a friend of yours?* ◊ *My hair is very fine. Yours is much thicker.* **2** (usually **Yours**) used at the end of a letter before signing your name:

(*BrE*) *Yours sincerely / faithfully* ◊ (*AmE*) *Sincerely Yours* ◊ (*AmE*) *Yours Truly* ⊏> Study pages B13–14

your·self /jɔːˈself; *weak form* jə-; *AmE* jər-; jɔːr-; jʊr-/ (*pl.* **your·selves** /-ˈselvz/) *pron.* **1** (the reflexive form of *you*) used when the person or people being spoken to both cause and are affected by an action: *Have you hurt yourself?* ◊ *You don't seem quite yourself today* (= you do not seem well or do not seem as happy as usual). ◊ *Enjoy yourselves!* **2** used to emphasize the fact that the person who is being spoken to is doing sth: *Do it yourself—I don't have time.* ◊ *You can try it out for yourselves.* ◊ *You yourself are one of the chief offenders.* **3** you: *We sell a lot of these to people like yourself.* ◊ *'And yourself,' he replied, 'How are you?'* IDM **(all) by your'self/your'selves 1** alone; without anyone else: *How long were you by yourself in the house?* **2** without help: *Are you sure you did this exercise by yourself?* **(all) to your'self/your'selves** for only you to have, use, etc: *I'm going to be away next week so you'll have the office to yourself.* **be your'self** to act naturally: *Don't act sophisticated—just be yourself.*

youth /juːθ/ *noun* (*pl.* **youths** /juːðz/) **1** [U] the time of life when a person is young, especially the time before a child becomes an adult: *He had been a talented musician in his youth.* **2** [U] the quality or state of being young: *She brings to the job a rare combination of youth and experience.* **3** [C] (*often disapproving*) a young man: *The fight was started by a gang of youths.* **4** (also **the youth**) [pl.] young people considered as a group: *the nation's youth* ◊ *the youth of today* ◊ *youth culture* ◊ *youth unemployment*

'**youth club** *noun* (in Britain) a club where young people can meet each other and take part in various activities

,**youth 'custody** *noun* [U] (*BrE*) a period of time when a young criminal is kept in a type of prison as a punishment: *He was sentenced to two years' youth custody.* ◊ *a youth custody centre*

youth·ful /ˈjuːθfl/ *adj.* **1** typical of young people: *youthful enthusiasm / energy / inexperience* **2** young or seeming younger than you are: *She's a very youthful 65.* ▶ **youth·ful·ly** /-fəli/ *adv.* **youth·ful·ness** *noun* [U]

'**youth hostel** *noun* a building that provides cheap and simple accommodation and meals, especially to young people who are travelling

'**youth hostelling** *noun* [U] (*BrE*) the activity of staying in different youth hostels and walking, etc. between them: *to go youth hostelling*

you've /juːv/ *short form* you have

yowl /jaʊl/ *verb* [V] to make a long loud cry that sounds unhappy ▶ **yowl** *noun*

'**Yo Yo**™ (also **'yo-yo**) *noun* (*pl.* **Yo Yos, yo-yos**) a toy that consists of two round pieces of plastic or wood joined together, with a piece of string wound between them. You put the string around your finger and make the yo-yo go up and down it: *He kept bouncing up and down like a yo-yo.*—picture on page A8

yr (also **yr.** especially in *AmE*) *abbr.* **1** (*pl.* **yrs**) year(s): *children aged 4–11 yrs* **2** your

yuan /juˈɑːn/ *noun* (*pl.* **yuan**) the unit of money in China

yucca /ˈjʌkə/ *noun* a tropical plant with long stiff pointed leaves on a thick straight stem, often grown indoors

yuck (*BrE* also **yuk**) /jʌk/ *exclamation* (*informal*) used to show that you think sth is disgusting or unpleasant

yucky (*BrE* also **yukky**) /ˈjʌki/ *adj.* (*informal*) disgusting or very unpleasant: *yucky food*

Yule /juːl/ *noun* [C, U] (*old use* or *literary*) the festival of Christmas

Yule·tide /ˈjuːltaɪd/ *noun* [U, C] (*old use* or *literary*) the period around Christmas Day: *Yuletide food and drink*

yum /jʌm/ (also ,**yum-'yum**) *exclamation* (*informal*) used to show that you think sth tastes or smells very nice

yummy /ˈjʌmi/ *adj.* (*informal*) very good to eat SYN DELICIOUS: *a yummy cake*

yup·pie (also **yuppy**) /ˈjʌpi/ *noun* (*pl.* **-ies**) (*informal, often disapproving*) a young professional person who

Y

lives in a city and earns a lot of money that they spend on expensive and fashionable things `ORIGIN` Formed from the first letters of the words 'young urban professional'.

YWCA /ˌwaɪ dʌbljuː siː ˈeɪ/ (also *AmE informal* **the Y**) *abbr.* Young Women's Christian Association (an organization that exists in many countries and provides accommodation and social and sports activities): *members of the YWCA*

Zz

Z (also **z**) /zed; *AmE* ziː/ *noun* (*pl.* **Z's, z's** /zedz; *AmE* ziːz/) **1** [C, U] the 26th and last letter of the English alphabet: *'Zebra' begins with (a) 'Z'/'Z'.* **2** (**Z's**) [pl.] (*AmE, informal, humorous*) sleep: *I need to catch some Z's.* `IDM` see A *n.*

zany /ˈzeɪni/ *adj.* (**zani·er, zani·est**) (*informal*) strange or unusual in an amusing way: *zany humour*

zap /zæp/ *verb* (**-pp-**) (*informal*) **1** [VN] **~ sb/sth (with sth)** to destroy, kill or hit sb/sth suddenly and with force: *The monster got zapped by a flying saucer* (= in a computer game). ◊ *It's vital to zap stress fast.* ◊ *He jumped like a man who'd been zapped with 1 000 volts.* **2** [V+adv./prep.] to do sth very fast: *I'm zapping through* (= reading very fast) *some modern novels at the moment.* **3** [V, VN] to use the REMOTE CONTROL to change television channels quickly **4** [+adv./prep.] to move, or make sb/sth move, very fast in the direction mentioned `SYN` ZIP: [V] *The racing cars zapped past us.* [also VN]

zap·per /ˈzæpə(r)/ *noun* (*informal*) **1** = REMOTE CONTROL **2** a device or weapon that attacks or destroys sth quickly: *a bug zapper*

zeal /ziːl/ *noun* [U, C] **~ (for/in sth)** (*written*) great energy or enthusiasm connected with sth that you feel strongly about: *her missionary/reforming/religious/political zeal*

zealot /ˈzelət/ *noun* (often *disapproving*) a person who is extremely enthusiastic about sth, especially religion or politics

zeal·ot·ry /ˈzelətri/ *noun* [U] (often *disapproving*) the attitude or behaviour of a zealot: *religious zealotry*

zeal·ous /ˈzeləs/ *adj.* (*written*) showing great energy and enthusiasm for sth, especially because you feel strongly about it: *a zealous reformer/preacher* ▶ **zeal·ous·ly** *adv.*

zebra /ˈzebrə, ˈziːbrə/ *noun* (*pl.* **zebra** or **zebras**) an African wild animal like a horse with black and white lines (= STRIPES) on its body

zebra 'crossing *noun* (*BrE*) an area of road marked with broad black and white lines where vehicles must stop for people to walk across—see also PEDESTRIAN CROSSING, PELICAN CROSSING

Zeit·geist /ˈzaɪtɡaɪst/ *noun* [sing.] (from *German, formal*) the general mood or quality of a particular period of history, as shown by the ideas, beliefs, etc. common at the time

Zen /zen/ *noun* [U] a Japanese form of Buddhism

zen·ith /ˈzenɪθ/ *noun* **1** the highest point that the sun or moon reaches in the sky, directly above you: *The sun rose towards its zenith.* **2** (*formal*) the time when sth is strongest and most successful `SYN` PEAK `OPP` NADIR

zephyr /ˈzefə(r)/ *noun* (*old-fashioned* or *literary*) a soft gentle wind

Zep·pelin /ˈzepəlɪn/ *noun* a German type of large AIRSHIP

zero /ˈzɪərəʊ; *AmE* ˈzɪroʊ, ˈziː-/ *number, verb*
- *number* **1** (*especially AmE*) (*BrE* also **nought**) 0: *Five, four, three, two, zero…We have lift-off.* **2** a temperature, pressure, etc. that is equal to zero on a scale: *It was ten degrees below zero last night* (= −10°C or −10°F). ◊ *The thermometer had fallen to zero.* ➪ Appendix 3 **3** the lowest possible amount or level; nothing at all: *I rated my chances as zero.* ◊ *zero inflation/growth/profit*
- *verb* (**zer·oes, zero·ing, zer·oed, zer·oed**) [VN] to turn an instrument, control, etc. to zero `PHRV` ,**zero 'in on sb/sth 1** to fix all your attention on the person or thing mentioned: *They zeroed in on the key issues.* **2** to aim guns, etc. at the person or thing mentioned

,**zero 'hour** *noun* [U] the time when an important event, an attack, etc. is planned to start

,**zero-'rated** *adj.* (*BrE, technical*) (of goods, services, etc.) that you do not need to pay VAT (= value added tax) on

,**zero-'sum game** *noun* a situation in which what is gained by one person or group is lost by another person or group

,**zero 'tolerance** *noun* [U] the policy of applying laws very strictly so that people are punished even for offences that are not very serious: *Howard County has a zero tolerance policy on alcohol use by teenagers.*

zest /zest/ *noun* **1** [sing., U] **~ (for sth)** enjoyment and enthusiasm: *He had a great zest for life.* ◊ *She danced with the zest of a twenty-year-old.* **2** [U, sing.] the quality of being exciting, interesting and enjoyable: *The slight risk added zest to the experience.* **3** [U] the outer skin of an orange, a lemon, etc., when it is used to give flavour in cooking—compare PEEL, RIND, SKIN ▶ **zest·ful** /-fl/ *adj.*

zig·zag /ˈzɪɡzæɡ/ *noun, verb*
- *noun* a line or pattern that looks like a series of letter W's as it bends to the left and then to the right again: *The path descended the hill in a series of zigzags.* ▶ **zig·zag** *adj.* [only before noun]: *a zigzag line/path/pattern*
- *verb* (**-gg-**) [V, usually +adv./prep.] to move forward by making sharp sudden turns first to the left and then to the right: *The narrow path zigzags up the cliff.*

The road zigzagged into the distance.

zilch /zɪltʃ/ *noun* [U] (*informal*) nothing: *I arrived in this country with zilch.*

zil·lion /ˈzɪljən/ *noun* (*informal, especially AmE*) a very large number: *There was a bunch of kids waiting and zillions of reporters.*

Zim·mer frame™ /ˈzɪmə freɪm; *AmE* ˈzɪmər/ (also *informal* **Zim·mer** /ˈzɪmə(r)/) (both *BrE*) (*AmE* **walk·er**) *noun* a metal frame that people use to help them to walk, for example people who are old or who have sth wrong with their legs

zinc /zɪŋk/ *noun* [U] (*symb* Zn) a chemical element. Zinc is a bluish-white metal that is mixed with COPPER to produce BRASS and is often used to cover other metals to prevent them from RUSTING.

zing /zɪŋ/ *verb, noun*
- *verb* (*informal*) **1** to move or to make sth move very quickly, often with a high whistling sound: [V] *electrical pulses zinging down a wire* [also VN] **2** [VN] **~ sb/sth (for/on sth)** (*AmE*) to criticize sb strongly
- *noun* [U] (*informal*) interest or excitement

Zion·ism /ˈzaɪənɪzəm/ *noun* [U] a political movement that was originally concerned with establishing an independent state for Jewish people, and is now concerned with developing the state of Israel ▶ **Zion·ist** /ˈzaɪənɪst/ *noun, adj.*

zip /zɪp/ *noun, verb*

■ *noun* **1** (also ˌ**zip ˈfastener**) (both *BrE*) (also **zip·per** *AmE*, *BrE*) [C] a thing that you use to fasten clothes, bags, etc. It consists of two rows of metal or plastic teeth that you can pull together to close sth or pull apart to open it: *to do up/undo/open/close a zip* ◊ *My zip's stuck.*—picture at FASTENER **2** [U] (*informal*) energy or speed **3** [sing.] (*informal*) nothing: *We won four zip* (= 4–0). ◊ *He said zip all evening.*

■ *verb* (-pp-) **1** to fasten clothes, bags, etc. with a zip/zipper: [VN] *I zipped and buttoned my jacket.* ◊ *The children were safely zipped into their sleeping bags.* ◊ [VN-ADJ] *He zipped his case shut.*—compare UNZIP **2** [V] to be fastened with a zip/zipper: *The sleeping bags can zip together.* **3** [+adv./prep.] (*informal*) to move very quickly or to make sth move very quickly in the direction mentioned: [V] *I'm just zipping into town to buy some food.* ◊ *A sports car zipped past us.* [also VN] PHRV ˌ**zip ˈup**; ˌ**zip sb/sth ˈup** to be fastened with a zip/zipper; to fasten sth with a zip/zipper: *This jacket zips up right to the neck.* ◊ *Shall I zip you up* (= fasten your dress, etc.)?

ˈ**ZIP code** (also ˈ**Zip code**) *noun* (*AmE*) = POSTCODE

zip·per /ˈzɪpə(r)/ *noun* (*especially AmE*) = ZIP

zit /zɪt/ *noun* (*informal*) a spot on the skin, especially on the face SYN PIMPLE—compare SPOT

zith·er /ˈzɪðə(r)/ *noun* a musical instrument with a lot of metal strings stretched over a flat wooden box, that you play with your fingers or a PLECTRUM/PICK

zo·diac /ˈzəʊdiæk; *AmE* ˈzoʊ-/ *noun* **1** (**the zodiac**) [sing.] the imaginary area in the sky in which the sun, moon and planets appear to lie, and which has been divided into twelve equal parts each with a special name and symbol: *the signs of the zodiac* **2** [C] a diagram of these twelve parts, and signs that some people believe can be used to predict how the planets will influence our lives ▶ **zo·di·ac·al** /zəʊˈdaɪəkl; *AmE* zoʊ-/ *adj.*

zom·bie /ˈzɒmbi; *AmE* ˈzɑːmbi/ *noun* **1** (*informal*) a person who seems only partly alive, without any feeling or interest in what is happening **2** (in some African and Caribbean religions and in horror stories) a dead body that has been made alive again by magic

zonal /ˈzəʊnl; *AmE* ˈzoʊnl/ *adj.* (*technical*) connected with zones; arranged in zones

zone /zəʊn; *AmE* zoʊn/ *noun, verb*

■ *noun* **1** an area or a region with a particular feature or use: *a war/security/demilitarized zone* ◊ *an earthquake/danger zone* ◊ *a pedestrian zone* (= where vehicles may not go)—see also NO-FLY ZONE, TIME ZONE, TWILIGHT **2** one of the areas that a larger area is divided into for the purpose of organization: *postal charges to countries in zone 2* **3** an area or a part of an object, especially one that is different from its surroundings: *When the needle enters the red zone the engine is too hot.* ◊ *the erogenous zones of the body* **4** one of the five parts that the earth's surface is divided into by imaginary lines that are parallel to the EQUATOR: *the northern/southern temperate zone*

■ *verb* [VN] [usually passive] **1** ~ sth (for sth) to keep an area of land to be used for a particular purpose: *The town centre was zoned for office development.* **2** to divide an area of land into smaller areas ▶ **zon·ing** *noun* [U]

zonked /zɒŋkt; *AmE* zɑːŋkt/ *adj.* [not before noun] ~ (out) (*slang*) extremely tired or suffering from the effects of alcohol or drugs

zoo /zuː/ *noun* (*pl.* **zoos**) (also *formal* ˌ**zoological ˈgarden(s)**) a place where many kinds of wild animals are kept for the public to see and where they are studied, bred and protected

zoo·keep·er /ˈzuːkiːpə(r)/ *noun* a person who works in a zoo, taking care of the animals

zoo·logic·al /ˌzəʊəˈlɒdʒɪkl; ˌzuː-l-; *AmE* ˌzoʊəˈlɑːdʒ-/ *adj.* connected with the science of ZOOLOGY

ˌ**zoological ˈgarden** *noun* (also ˌ**zoological ˈgardens** [pl.]) (*formal*) = ZOO

zo·olo·gist /zəʊˈɒlədʒɪst; zuˈɒl-; *AmE* zoʊˈɑːl-/ *noun* a scientist who studies zoology

zo·ology /zəʊˈɒlədʒi; zuˈɒl-; *AmE* zoʊˈɑːl-/ *noun* [U] the scientific study of animals and their behaviour—compare BIOLOGY, BOTANY

zoom /zuːm/ *noun, verb*

■ *verb* **1** [V+adv./prep.] to move or go somewhere very fast: *Traffic zoomed past us.* ◊ *For five weeks they zoomed around Europe.* **2** [V] ~ (up) (to …) (of prices, costs, etc.) to increase a lot quickly and suddenly: *House prices have zoomed up this year.* PHRV ˌ**zoom ˈin/ˈout** (of a camera) to show the object that is being photographed from closer/further away, with the use of a ZOOM LENS: *The camera zoomed in on the actor's face.*

■ *noun* **1** [C] = ZOOM LENS: *a zoom shot* **2** [sing.] the sound of a vehicle moving very fast

ˈ**zoom lens** (also **zoom**) *noun* a camera LENS that you use to make the thing that you are photographing appear nearer to you or further away from you than it really is

Zoro·ast·rian·ism /ˌzɒrəʊˈæstriənɪzəm; *AmE* ˌzɔːroʊ-/ *noun* [U] a religion started in ancient Persia by Zoroaster, that teaches that there is one God and a continuing struggle in the world between forces of light and darkness ▶ **Zoro·ast·rian** *noun*—see also PARSEE **Zoro·ast·rian** *adj.*

zuc·chini /zuˈkiːni/ *noun* (*pl.* **zuc·chini** or **zuc·chi·nis**) (*AmE*) = COURGETTE

Zulu /ˈzuːluː/ *noun* **1** [C] a member of a race of black people who live in S Africa **2** [U] the language spoken by Zulus and many other black south Africans ▶ **Zulu** *adj.*

zy·deco /ˈzaɪdɪkəʊ; *AmE* -koʊ/ *noun* [U] a type of dance music, originally played by black Americans in Louisiana

s	t	v	z	ʃ	ʒ	tʃ	dʒ	θ	ð	ŋ
see	tea	van	zoo	shoe	vision	chain	jam	thin	this	sing

Appendix 1
Irregular verbs

This appendix lists all the verbs with irregular forms that are included in the dictionary, except for those formed with a hyphenated prefix (e.g. pre-set, re-lay) and the modal verbs (e.g. can, must). Irregular forms that are only used in certain senses are marked with an asterisk (e.g. *abode). Full information on usage, pronunciation, etc. is given at the entry.

Infinitive	Past tense	Past participle	Infinitive	Past tense	Past participle
abide	abided,*abode	abided, *abode	fight	fought	fought
arise	arose	arisen	find	found	found
awake	awoke	awoken	fit	fitted; (AmE usually fit)	fitted; (AmE usually fit)
baa	baaed, baa'd	baaed, baa'd	flee	fled	fled
babysit	babysat	babysat	fling	flung	flung
bear	bore	borne	floodlight	floodlit	floodlit
beat	beat	beaten	fly	flew, *flied	flown, *flied
become	became	become	forbear	forbore	forborne
befall	befell	befallen	forbid	forbade	forbidden
beget	begot, *begat	begot, *begotten	forecast	forecast, forecasted	forecast, forecasted
begin	began	begun	foresee	foresaw	foreseen
behold	beheld	beheld	foretell	foretold	foretold
bend	bent	bent	forget	forgot	forgotten
beseech	beseeched, besought	beseeched, besought	forgive	forgave	forgiven
beset	beset	beset	forgo	forwent	forgone
bet	bet	bet	forsake	forsook	forsaken
bid¹	bid	bid	forswear	forswore	forsworn
bid²	bade, bid	bidden, bid	freeze	froze	frozen
bind	bound	bound	gainsay	gainsaid	gainsaid
bite	bit	bitten	get	got	got; (AmE, spoken) gotten
bleed	bled	bled	give	gave	given
bless	blessed	blessed	go	went	gone, *been
blow	blew	blown, *blowed	grind	ground	ground
breastfeed	breastfed	breastfed	grow	grew	grown
break	broke	broken	hamstring	hamstrung	hamstrung
breed	bred	bred	hang	hung, *hanged	hung, *hanged
bring	brought	brought	hear	heard	heard
broadcast	broadcast	broadcast	heave	heaved, *hove	heaved, *hove
browbeat	browbeat	browbeaten	hew	hewed	hewed, hewn
build	built	built	hide	hid	hidden
burn	burnt, burned	burnt, burned	hit	hit	hit
burst	burst	burst	hold	held	held
bust	bust, busted	bust, busted	hurt	hurt	hurt
buy	bought	bought	inlay	inlaid	inlaid
cast	cast	cast	input	input, inputted	input, inputted
catch	caught	caught	inset	inset	inset
choose	chose	chosen	interweave	interwove	interwoven
cleave	cleaved, *cleft, *clove	cleaved, *cleft	keep	kept	kept
cling	clung	clung	kneel	knelt; (AmE also kneeled)	knelt; (AmE also kneeled)
come	came	come	knit	knitted, *knit	knitted, *knit
cost	cost, *costed	cost, *costed	know	knew	known
creep	crept	crept	lay	laid	laid
cut	cut	cut	lead	led	led
deal	dealt	dealt	lean	leaned; (BrE also leant)	leaned; (BrE also leant)
dig	dug	dug	leap	leapt, leaped	leapt, leaped
dive	dived; (AmE also dove)	dived	learn	learnt, learned	learnt, learned
draw	drew	drawn	leave	left	left
dream	dreamt, dreamed	dreamt, dreamed	lend	lent	lent
drink	drank	drunk	let	let	let
drive	drove	driven	lie¹	lay	lain
dwell	dwelt, dwelled	dwelt, dwelled	light	lit, *lighted	lit, *lighted
eat	ate	eaten	lose	lost	lost
fall	fell	fallen	make	made	made
feed	fed	fed	mean	meant	meant
feel	felt	felt			

Infinitive	Past tense	Past participle	Infinitive	Past tense	Past participle
meet	met	met	rewind	rewound	rewound
miscast	miscast	miscast	rewrite	rewrote	rewritten
mishear	misheard	misheard	rid	rid	rid
mishit	mishit	mishit	ride	rode	ridden
mislay	mislaid	mislaid	ring²	rang	rung
mislead	misled	misled	rise	rose	risen
/ˌmɪsˈliːd/	/ˌmɪsˈled/	/ˌmɪsˈled/	run	ran	run
misread	misread	misread	saw	sawed	sawn; (AmE also
/ˌmɪsˈriːd/	/ˌmɪsˈred/	/ˌmɪsˈred/			sawed)
misspell	misspelled,	misspelled,	say	said	said
	misspelt	misspelt	see	saw	seen
misspend	misspent	misspent	seek	sought	sought
mistake	mistook	mistaken	sell	sold	sold
misunder-stand	misunderstood	misunderstood	send	sent	sent
			set	set	set
mow	mowed	mown, mowed	sew	sewed	sewn, sewed
offset	offset	offset	shake	shook	shaken
outbid	outbid	outbid	shear	sheared	shorn, sheared
outdo	outdid	outdone	shed	shed	shed
outfight	outfought	outfought	shine	shone, *shined	shone, *shined
outgrow	outgrew	outgrown	shit	shit, shat; (BrE	shit, shat; (BrE
output	output	output		also shitted)	also shitted)
outrun	outran	outrun	shoe	shod	shod
outsell	outsold	outsold	shoot	shot	shot
outshine	outshone	outshone	show	showed	shown, *showed
overcome	overcame	overcome	shrink	shrank, shrunk	shrunk
overdo	overdid	overdone	shut	shut	shut
overdraw	overdrew	overdrawn	simulcast	simulcast	simulcast
overeat	overate	overeaten	sing	sang	sung
overfly	overflew	overflown	sink	sank, *sunk	sunk
overhang	overhung	overhung	sit	sat	sat
overhear	overheard	overheard	slay	slew	slain
overlay	overlaid	overlaid	sleep	slept	slept
overpay	overpaid	overpaid	slide	slid	slid
override	overrode	overridden	sling	slung	slung
overrun	overran	overrun	slink	slunk	slunk
oversee	oversaw	overseen	slit	slit	slit
overshoot	overshot	overshot	smell	smelled; (BrE	smelled; (BrE
oversleep	overslept	overslept		also smelt)	also smelt)
overspend	overspent	overspent	smite	smote	smitten
overtake	overtook	overtaken	sow	sowed	sown, sowed
overthrow	overthrew	overthrown	speak	spoke	spoken
overwrite	overwrote	overwritten	speed	speeded, *sped	speeded, *sped
partake	partook	partaken	spell	spelt, spelled	spelt, spelled
pay	paid	paid	spend	spent	spent
plead	pleaded; (AmE also pled)	pleaded; (AmE also pled)	spill	spilled; (BrE also spilt)	spilled; (BrE also spilt)
			spin	spun	spun
preset	preset	preset	spit	spat; (also spit	spat; (also spit
proofread	proofread	proofread		especially in	especially in AmE)
/ˈpruːfriːd/	/ˈpruːfred/	/ˈpruːfred/		AmE)	
prove	proved	proved; (also proven especially in AmE)	split	split	split
put	put	put	spoil	spoiled; (BrE also spoilt)	spoiled; (BrE also spoilt)
quit	quit; (BrE also quitted)	quit; (BrE also quitted)	spotlight	spotlit, *spotlighted	spotlit, *spotlighted
read /riːd/	read /red/	read /red/	spread	spread	spread
rebuild	rebuilt	rebuilt	spring	sprang; (AmE	sprung
recast	recast	recast		also sprung)	
redo	redid	redone	stand	stood	stood
redraw	redrew	redrawn	stave	staved, *stove	staved, *stove
rehear	reheard	reheard	steal	stole	stolen
remake	remade	remade	stick	stuck	stuck
rend	rent	rent	sting	stung	stung
rerun	reran	rerun	stink	stank, stunk	stunk
resell	resold	resold	strew	strewed	strewed, strewn
reset	reset	reset	stride	strode	—
resit	resat	resat	strike	struck	struck; (AmE also stricken)
retake	retook	retaken			
retell	retold	retold	string	strung	strung
rethink	rethought	rethought			

Infinitive	Past tense	Past participle
strive	strove, *strived	striven, *strived
sublet	sublet	sublet
swear	swore	sworn
sweep	swept	swept
swell	swelled	swollen, swelled
swim	swam	swum
swing	swung	swung
take	took	taken
teach	taught	taught
tear	tore	torn
telecast	telecast	telecast
tell	told	told
think	thought	thought
throw	threw	thrown
thrust	thrust	thrust
tread	trod	trodden, trod
typecast	typecast	typecast
unbend	unbent	unbent
underbid	underbid	underbid
undercut	undercut	undercut
undergo	underwent	undergone
underlie	underlay	underlain
underpay	underpaid	underpaid
undersell	undersold	undersold
understand	understood	understood
undertake	undertook	undertaken
underwrite	underwrote	underwritten
undo	undid	undone
unfreeze	unfroze	unfrozen
unwind	unwound	unwound
uphold	upheld	upheld
upset	upset	upset
wake	woke	woken
waylay	waylaid	waylaid
wear	wore	worn
weave	wove, *weaved	woven, *weaved
wed	wedded, wed	wedded, wed
weep	wept	wept
wet	wet, wetted	wet, wetted
win	won	won
wind² /waɪnd/	wound /waʊnd/	wound /waʊnd/
withdraw	withdrew	withdrawn
withhold	withheld	withheld
withstand	withstood	withstood
wring	wrung	wrung
write	wrote	written

Full forms	Short forms	Negative short forms
be present tense		
I am	I'm	I'm not
you are	you're	you aren't/you're not
he is	he's	he isn't/he's not
she is	she's	she isn't/she's not
it is	it's	it isn't/it's not
we are	we're	we aren't/ we're not
you are	you're	you aren't/ you're not
they are	they're	they aren't/ they're not
be past tense		
I was	—	I wasn't
you were	—	you weren't
he was	—	he wasn't
she was	—	she wasn't
it was	—	it wasn't
we were	—	we weren't
you were	—	you weren't
they were	—	they weren't
have present tense		
I have	I've	I haven't/I've not
you have	you've	you haven't/you've not
he has	he's	he hasn't/he's not
she has	she's	she hasn't/she's not
it has	it's	it hasn't/it's not
we have	we've	we haven't/we've not
you have	you've	you haven't/you've not
they have	they've	they haven't/they've not
have past tense (all persons)		
had	I'd you'd etc.	hadn't
do present tense		
I do	—	I don't
you do	—	you don't
he does	—	he doesn't
she does	—	she doesn't
it does	—	it doesn't
we do	—	we don't
you do	—	you don't
they do	—	they don't
do past tense (all persons)		
did	—	didn't

	be	do	have
present participle	being	doing	having
past participle	been	done	had

be, do, have

The negative full forms are formed by adding **not**

Questions in the present and past are formed by placing the verb before the subject:
am I? • isn't he? • was I? • weren't we? • do I? • don't you? • did I? • didn't I? • have I? • hadn't they? etc.

Questions using the negative full form are more formal: *has he not? • do you not?* etc.

The short negative question form for **I am** is aren't: *aren't I?*

When **do** or **have** is used as a main verb, questions and negative statements can be formed with **do/does/doesn't** and **did/didn't**: *How did you do it? • I don't do any teaching now • Do you have any money on you? • We didn't have much time.*

The short forms *'ve*, *'s* and *'d* are not usually used when **have** is a main verb:
I have a shower every morning • I've a shower every morning.

The short forms of **be**, *'s* and *'re* can be added to other subjects: *Sally's ill. • The boys're late.*

The **other tenses** of **be**, **do** and **have** are formed in the same way as those of other verbs: *will be, would be, has been; will do, would do, has done; will have, would have, have had;* etc.

The **pronunciation** of each form of **be**, **do** and **have** is given at its entry in the dictionary.

Appendix 2
Geographical names

These lists show the spelling and pronunciation of geographical names.

If a country has different words for the country, adjective and person, all are given, (eg **Denmark; Danish, Dane**). To make the plural of a word for a person from a particular country, add **–s**, except for **Swiss** and for words ending in **-ese** (eg **Japanese**), which stay the same, and for words that end in **-man** or **-woman**, which change to **-men** or **-women**.

(Inclusion in this list does not imply status as a sovereign state.)

Afghanistan /æfˈgænɪstɑːn; AmE -stæn/; Afghan /ˈæfgæn/, Afghani /æfˈgɑːni; AmE æfˈgæni/, Afghanistani /æf,gænɪˈstɑːni; AmE -ˈstæni/
Africa /ˈæfrɪkə/; African /ˈæfrɪkən/
Albania /ælˈbeɪniə/; Albanian /ælˈbeɪniən/
Algeria /ælˈdʒɪəriə; AmE -ˈdʒɪr-/; Algerian /ælˈdʒɪəriən; AmE -ˈdʒɪr-/
America /əˈmerɪkə/; American /əˈmerɪkən/
Andorra /ænˈdɔːrə/; Andorran /ænˈdɔːrən/
Angola /æŋˈgəʊlə; AmE -ˈgoʊ-/; Angolan /æŋˈgəʊlən; AmE -ˈgoʊ-/
Antarctica /ænˈtɑːktɪkə; AmE -ˈtɑːrk-/; Antarctic /ænˈtɑːktɪk; AmE -ˈtɑːrk-/
Antigua and Barbuda /æn,tiːgə ən bɑːˈbjuːdə; AmE bɑːrˈb-/; Antiguan /ænˈtiːgən/, Barbudan /bɑːˈbjuːdən; AmE bɑːrˈb-/
(the) Arctic Ocean /ɑːktɪk ˈəʊʃn; AmE ,ɑːrktɪk ˈoʊʃn/; Arctic /ˈɑːktɪk; AmE ˈɑːrk-/
Argentina /,ɑːdʒənˈtiːnə; AmE ,ɑːrdʒ-/, the Argentine /ˈɑːdʒəntaɪn; AmE ˈɑːrdʒ-/; Argentinian /,ɑːdʒənˈtɪniən; AmE ,ɑːrdʒ-/, Argentine /ˈɑːdʒəntaɪn; AmE ˈɑːrdʒ-/
Armenia /ɑːˈmiːniə; AmE ɑːrˈm-/; Armenian /ɑːˈmiːniən; AmE ɑːrˈm-/
Asia /ˈeɪʃə, ˈeɪʒə/; Asian /ˈeɪʃn, ˈeɪʒn/
(the) Atlantic Ocean /ət,læntɪk ˈəʊʃn; AmE ˈoʊʃn/
Australasia /,ɒstrəˈleɪʃə, -ʒə; AmE ,ɔːstrə-/; Australasian /,ɒstrəˈleɪʃn, -ʒn; AmE ,ɔːstrə-/
Australia /ɒˈstreɪliə; AmE ɔːˈs-/; Australian /ɒˈstreɪliən; AmE ɔːˈs-/
Austria /ˈɒstriə; AmE ˈɔːs-/; Austrian /ˈɒstriən; AmE ˈɔːs-/
Azerbaijan /,æzəbaɪˈdʒɑːn; AmE -zərb-/; Azerbaijani /,æzəbaɪˈdʒɑːni; AmE -zərb-/, Azeri /əˈzeəri; AmE əˈzeri/
(the) Bahamas /bəˈhɑːməz/; Bahamian /bəˈheɪmiən/
Bahrain, Bahrein /bɑːˈreɪn/; Bahraini, Bahreini /bɑːˈreɪni/
Bangladesh /,bæŋgləˈdeʃ/; Bangladeshi /,bæŋgləˈdeʃi/
Barbados /bɑːˈbeɪdɒs; AmE bɑːrˈbeɪdoʊs/; Barbadian /bɑːˈbeɪdiən; AmE bɑːrˈb-/
Belarus /bi,eləˈruːs/; Belorussian /bi,eləˈrʌʃn/
Belgium /ˈbeldʒəm/; Belgian /ˈbeldʒən/
Belize /bəˈliːz/; Belizean /bəˈliːziən/
Benin /beˈniːn/; Beninese /,benɪˈniːz/
Bhutan /buːˈtɑːn/; Bhutani /buːˈtɑːni/, Bhutanese /,buːtəˈniːz/
Bolivia /bəˈlɪviə/; Bolivian /bəˈlɪviən/
Bosnia-Herzegovina /,bɒzniə ,hɜːtsəgəˈviːnə; AmE ,bɑːzniə ,hɜːrts-, ,bɔːz-/; Bosnian /ˈbɒzniən; AmE ˈbɑːz-, ˈbɔːz-/
Botswana /bɒtˈswɑːnə; AmE bɑːt-/; Botswanan /bɒtˈswɑːnən; AmE bɑːt-/, (person: Motswana /mɒtˈswɑːnə; AmE ˈmɑːt-/, people: Batswana /bætˈswɑːnə/)
Brazil /brəˈzɪl/; Brazilian /brəˈzɪliən/

Brunei Darussalam /,bruːnaɪ dæˈruːsæləm/; Brunei, Bruneian /bruːˈnaɪən/
Bulgaria /bʌlˈgeəriə; AmE -ˈger-/; Bulgarian /bʌlˈgeəriən; AmE -ˈger-/
Burkina /bɜːˈkiːnə; AmE bɜːrˈk-/; Burkinese /,bɜːkɪˈniːz; AmE ,bɜːrk-/
Burma /ˈbɜːmə; AmE ˈbɜːrmə/; Burmese /bɜːˈmiːz; AmE bɜːrˈm-/ —see also Myanmar
Burundi /bʊˈrʊndi/; Burundian /bʊˈrʊndiən/
Cambodia /kæmˈbəʊdiə; AmE -ˈboʊ-/; Cambodian /kæmˈbəʊdiən; AmE -ˈboʊ-/
Cameroon /ˌkæməˈruːn/; Cameroonian /ˌkæməˈruːniən/
Canada /ˈkænədə/; Canadian /kəˈneɪdiən/
Cape Verde /ˌkeɪp ˈvɜːd; AmE ˈvɜːrd/; Cape Verdean /ˌkeɪp ˈvɜːdiən; AmE ˈvɜːrd-/
(the) Caribbean Sea /ˌkærəbiːən ˈsiː, kəˈrɪbiən/; Caribbean /ˌkærəˈbiːən, kəˈrɪbiən/
Central African Republic /ˌsentrəl ˌæfrɪkən rɪˈpʌblɪk/
Chad /tʃæd/; Chadian /ˈtʃædiən/
Chile /ˈtʃɪli/; Chilean /ˈtʃɪliən/
China /ˈtʃaɪnə/; Chinese /ˌtʃaɪˈniːz/
Colombia /kəˈlʌmbiə/; Colombian /kəˈlʌmbiən/
Comoros /ˈkɒmərəʊz; AmE ˈkɑːməroʊz/; Comoran /kəˈmɔːrən/
Congo /ˈkɒŋgəʊ; AmE ˈkɑːŋgoʊ/; Congolese /ˌkɒŋgəˈliːz; AmE ˌkɑːŋ-/
the Democratic Republic of the Congo /ˌdeməkrætɪk rɪˌpʌblɪk əv ðə ˈkɒŋgəʊ; AmE ˈkɑːŋgoʊ/
Costa Rica /ˌkɒstə ˈriːkə; AmE ˌkɑːstə, ˌkoʊstə/; Costa Rican /ˌkɒstə ˈriːkən; AmE ˌkɑːstə, ˌkoʊstə/
Côte d'Ivoire /ˌkəʊt diːˈvwɑː; AmE ˌkoʊt diːˈvwɑːr/
Croatia /krəʊˈeɪʃə; AmE kroʊ-/; Croatian /krəʊˈeɪʃn; AmE kroʊ-/
Cuba /ˈkjuːbə/; Cuban /ˈkjuːbən/
Cyprus /ˈsaɪprəs/; Cypriot /ˈsɪpriət/
(the) Czech Republic /ˌtʃek rɪˈpʌblɪk/; Czech /tʃek/
Denmark /ˈdenmɑːk; AmE -mɑːrk/; Danish /ˈdeɪnɪʃ/, Dane /deɪn/
Djibouti /dʒɪˈbuːti/; Djiboutian /dʒɪˈbuːtiən/
Dominica /ˌdɒmɪˈniːkə; AmE ˌdɑːmə-/; Dominican /ˌdɒmɪˈniːkən; AmE ˌdɑːmə-/
(the) Dominican Republic /də,mɪnɪkən rɪˈpʌblɪk/; Dominican /dəˈmɪnɪkən/
Ecuador /ˈekwədɔː(r)/; Ecuadorian /ˌekwəˈdɔːriən/
Egypt /ˈiːdʒɪpt/; Egyptian /iˈdʒɪpʃn/
El Salvador /ˌel ˈsælvədɔː(r)/; Salvadorean /ˌsælvəˈdɔːriən/
Equatorial Guinea /ˌekwətɔːriəl ˈgɪni/; Equatorial Guinean /ˌekwətɔːriəl ˈgɪniən/
Eritrea /ˌerɪˈtreɪə; AmE -ˈtriːə/; Eritrean /ˌerɪˈtreɪən; AmE -ˈtriːən/
Estonia /eˈstəʊniə; AmE eˈstoʊ-/; Estonian /eˈstəʊniən; AmE eˈstoʊ-/

Ethiopia /ˌiːθiˈəʊpiə; *AmE* -ˈoʊ-/; Ethiopian /ˌiːθiˈəʊpiən; *AmE* -ˈoʊ-/

Europe /ˈjʊərəp; *AmE* ˈjʊrəp/; European /ˌjʊərəˈpiːən; *AmE* ˌjʊrə-/

(the) Federated States of Micronesia /ˌfedəreɪtɪd sterts əv ˌmaɪkrəˈniːziə; *AmE* -ʒə/; Micronesian /ˌmaɪkrəˈniːziən; *AmE* -ʒn/

Fiji /ˈfiːdʒiː/; Fijian /ˌfiːˈdʒiːən, ˈfiːdʒiən/

Finland /ˈfɪnlənd/; Finnish /ˈfɪnɪʃ/, Finn /fɪn/

(the) Former Yugoslav Republic of Macedonia /ˌfɔːmə ˌjuːgəslɑːv rɪˌpʌblɪk əv ˌmæsɪˈdəʊniə; *AmE* ˌfɔːrmər, ˌmæsɪˈdoʊniə/; Macedonian /ˌmæsɪˈdəʊniən; *AmE* ˌmæsɪˈdoʊniən/

France /frɑːns; *AmE* fræns/; French /frentʃ/, Frenchman /ˈfrentʃmən/, Frenchwoman /ˈfrentʃwʊmən/

Gabon /gæˈbɒn; *AmE* gæˈboʊn/; Gabonese /ˌgæbəˈniːz/

(the) Gambia /ˈgæmbiə/; Gambian /ˈgæmbiən/

Georgia /ˈdʒɔːdʒə; *AmE* ˈdʒɔːrdʒə/; Georgian /ˈdʒɔːdʒən; *AmE* ˈdʒɔːrdʒən/

Germany /ˈdʒɜːməni; *AmE* ˈdʒɜːrm-/; German /ˈdʒɜːmən; *AmE* ˈdʒɜːrmən/

Ghana /ˈgɑːnə/; Ghanaian /gɑːˈneɪən/

Greece /griːs/; Greek /griːk/

Grenada /grəˈneɪdə/; Grenadian /grəˈneɪdiən/

Guatemala /ˌgwɑːtəˈmɑːlə/; Guatemalan /ˌgwɑːtəˈmɑːlən/

Guinea /ˈgɪni/; Guinean /ˈgɪniən/

Guinea-Bissau /ˌgɪni bɪˈsaʊ/

Guyana /gaɪˈænə/; Guyanese /ˌgaɪəˈniːz/

Haiti /ˈheɪti/; Haitian /ˈheɪʃn/

Honduras /hɒnˈdjʊərəs; *AmE* hɑːnˈdʊrəs/; Honduran /hɒnˈdjʊərən; *AmE* hɑːnˈdʊrən/

Hungary /ˈhʌŋgəri/; Hungarian /hʌŋˈgeəriən; *AmE* -ˈger-/

Iceland /ˈaɪslənd/; Icelandic /aɪsˈlændɪk/, Icelander /ˈaɪsləndə/

India /ˈmdiə/; Indian /ˈmdiən/

(the) Indian Ocean /ˌɪndiən ˈəʊʃn; *AmE* ˈoʊʃn/

Indonesia /ˌmdəˈniːʒə; *BrE also* -ziə/; Indonesian /ˌmdəˈniːʒn; *BrE also* -ziən/

Iran /ɪˈrɑːn, ɪˈræn/; Iranian /ɪˈremiən/

Iraq /ɪˈrɑːk, ɪˈræk/; Iraqi /ɪˈrɑːki, ɪˈræki/

Israel /ˈɪzreɪl/; Israeli /ɪzˈreɪli/

Italy /ˈɪtəli/; Italian /ɪˈtæliən/

Jamaica /dʒəˈmeɪkə/; Jamaican /dʒəˈmeɪkən/

Japan /dʒəˈpæn/; Japanese /ˌdʒæpəˈniːz/

Jordan /ˈdʒɔːdn; *AmE* ˈdʒɔːrdn/; Jordanian /dʒɔːˈdemiən; *AmE* dʒɔːrˈd-/

Kazakhstan /ˌkæzækˈstɑːn; *AmE* -stæn/; Kazakh /kəˈzæk/

Kenya /ˈkenjə, ˈkiːnjə/; Kenyan /ˈkenjən, ˈkiːnjən/

Kirgyzstan /ˌkɜːgɪzˈstɑːn; *AmE* ˌkɜːrgɪzˈstæn/; Kirgyz /ˈkɜːgɪz; *AmE* ˈkɜːrgɪz/

Kiribati /ˈkɪrəbæs/

Korea /kəˈriə/; North Korea, South Korea; North Korean /ˌnɔːθ kəˈriən; *AmE* ˌnɔːrθ/, South Korean /ˌsaʊθ kəˈriən/

Kuwait /kuˈweɪt/; Kuwaiti /kuˈweɪti/

Laos /laʊs/; Laotian /ˈlaʊʃn; *AmE also* leɪˈoʊʃn/

Latvia /ˈlætviə/; Latvian /ˈlætviən/

Lebanon /ˈlebənən; *AmE also* -nɑːn/; Lebanese /ˌlebəˈniːz/

Lesotho /ləˈsuːtuː/; Sotho /ˈsuːtuː/, (person: Mosotho /məˈsuːtuː/, people: Basotho /bəˈsuːtuː/

Liberia /laɪˈbɪəriə; *AmE* -ˈbɪr-/; Liberian /laɪˈbɪəriən; *AmE* -ˈbɪr-/

Libya /ˈlɪbiə/; Libyan /ˈlɪbiən/

Liechtenstein /ˈlɪktənstaɪn, ˈlɪxt-/; Liechtenstein, Liechtensteiner /ˈlɪktənstaɪnə(r), ˈlɪxt-/

Lithuania /ˌlɪθjuˈeɪniə/; Lithuanian /ˌlɪθjuˈeɪniən/

Luxembourg /ˈlʌksəmbɜːg; *AmE* -bɜːrg/; Luxembourg, Luxembourger /ˈlʌksəmbɜːgə(r); *AmE* -bɜːrgər/

Madagascar /ˌmædəˈgæskə(r)/; Madagascan /ˌmædəˈgæskən/, Malagasy /ˌmæləˈgæsi/

Malawi /məˈlɑːwi/; Malawian /məˈlɑːwiən/

Malaysia /məˈleɪʒə; *BrE also* -ziə/; Malaysian /məˈleɪʒn; *BrE also* -ziən/

(the) Maldives /ˈmɔːldiːvz/; Maldivian /mɔːlˈdɪviən/

Mali /ˈmɑːli/; Malian /ˈmɑːliən/

Malta /ˈmɔːltə/; Maltese /ˌmɔːlˈtiːz/

(the) Marshall Islands /ˈmɑːʃl aɪləndz; *AmE* ˈmɑːrʃl/

Mauritania /ˌmɒrɪˈteɪniə; *AmE* ˌmɔːr-/; Mauritanian /ˌmɒrɪˈteɪniən; *AmE* ˌmɔːr-/

Mauritius /məˈrɪʃəs; *AmE* mɔːˈr-/; Mauritian /məˈrɪʃn; *AmE* mɔːˈr-/

Mexico /ˈmeksɪkəʊ; *AmE* -koʊ/; Mexican /ˈmeksɪkən/

Moldova /mɒlˈdəʊvə; *AmE* mɑːlˈdoʊvə, mɔːl-/; Moldovan /mɒlˈdəʊvn; *AmE* mɑːlˈdoʊvn, mɔːl-/

Monaco /ˈmɒnəkəʊ; *AmE* ˈmɑːnəkoʊ/; Monacan /ˈmɒnəkən; *AmE* ˈmɑːn-/, Monégasque /ˌmɒniˈgæsk; *AmE* ˌmɑːn-/

Mongolia /mɒŋˈgəʊliə; *AmE* mɑːŋˈgoʊ-/; Mongolian /mɒŋˈgəʊliən; *AmE* mɑːŋˈgoʊ-/, Mongol /ˈmɒŋgl; *AmE* ˈmɑːŋ-/

Morocco /məˈrɒkəʊ; *AmE* məˈrɑːkoʊ/; Moroccan /məˈrɒkən; *AmE* məˈrɑːkən/

Mozambique /ˌməʊzæmˈbiːk; *AmE* ˌmoʊ-/; Mozambican /ˌməʊzæmˈbiːkən; *AmE* ˌmoʊ-/

Myanmar /miˌænˈmɑː(r)/ —see also Burma

Namibia /nəˈmɪbiə/; Namibian /nəˈmɪbiən/

Nauru /ˈnaʊruː/; Nauruan /naʊˈruːən/

Nepal /nəˈpɔːl/; Nepalese /ˌnepəˈliːz/

(the) Netherlands /ˈneðələndz; *AmE* -ðərl-/; Dutch /dʌtʃ/, Dutchman /ˈdʌtʃmən/, Dutchwoman /ˈdʌtʃwʊmən/

New Zealand /ˌnjuː ˈziːlənd; *AmE* ˌnuː/; New Zealand, New Zealander /ˌnjuː ˈziːləndə(r); *AmE* ˌnuː/

Nicaragua /ˌnɪkəˈrægjuə; *AmE* -ˈrægwə/; Nicaraguan /ˌnɪkəˈrægjuən; *AmE* -ˈrægwən/

Niger /ˈnaɪdʒə(r)/; Nigerien /naɪˈdʒɪəriən; *AmE* -dʒɪr-/

Nigeria /naɪˈdʒɪəriə; *AmE* -ˈdʒɪr-/ Nigerian /naɪˈdʒɪəriən; *AmE* -ˈdʒɪr-/

Norway /ˈnɔːweɪ; *AmE* ˈnɔːrweɪ/; Norwegian /nɔːˈwiːdʒən; *AmE* nɔːrˈw-/

Oman /əʊˈmɑːn, -mæn; *AmE* oʊ-/; Omani /əʊˈmɑːni, -mæni; *AmE* oʊ-/

(the) Pacific Ocean /pəˌsɪfɪk ˈəʊʃn; *AmE* ˈoʊʃn/

Pakistan /ˌpɑːkɪˈstɑːn; *AmE* ˌpækɪˈstæn/; Pakistani /ˌpɑːkɪˈstɑːni; *AmE* ˌpækɪˈstæni/

Panama /ˈpænəmɑː/; Panamanian /ˌpænəˈmeɪniən/

Papua New Guinea /ˌpæpuə njuː ˈgɪni; *AmE* nuː/; Papuan /ˈpæpuən/

Paraguay /ˈpærəgwaɪ/; Paraguayan /ˌpærəˈgwaɪən/

Peru /pəˈruː/; Peruvian /pəˈruːviən/

(the) Philippines /ˈfɪlɪpiːnz/; Philippine /ˈfɪlɪpiːn/, Filipino /ˌfɪlɪˈpiːnəʊ; *AmE* -noʊ/

Poland /ˈpəʊlənd; *AmE* ˈpoʊ-/; Polish /ˈpəʊlɪʃ; *AmE* ˈpoʊ-/, Pole /pəʊl; *AmE* poʊl/

Portugal /ˈpɔːtʃʊgl; *AmE* ˈpɔːrt-/; Portuguese /ˌpɔːtʃʊˈgiːz; *AmE* ˌpɔːrt-/

Qatar /ˈkʌtɑː(r)/; Qatari /kʌˈtɑːri/

Romania /ruˈmeɪniə/; Romanian /ruˈmeɪniən/

Russia /ˈrʌʃə/; Russian /ˈrʌʃn/

Rwanda /ruˈændə/; Rwandan /ruˈændən/

Samoa /səˈməʊə; *AmE* səˈmoʊə/; Samoan /səˈməʊən; *AmE* səˈmoʊən/

San Marino /ˌsæn məˈriːnəʊ; *AmE* -noʊ/; San

Marinese /ˌsæn mærɪˈniːz/
São Tomé and Principe /ˌsaʊ təˌmeɪ ən ˈprɪnsɪpeɪ/
Saudi Arabia /ˌsaʊdi əˈreɪbiə/; Saudi /ˈsaʊdi/, Saudi Arabian /ˌsaʊdi əˈreɪbiən/
Senegal /ˌsenɪˈɡɔːl/; Senegalese /ˌsenɪɡəˈliːz/
(the) Seychelles /seɪˈʃelz/; Seychellois /ˌseɪʃelˈwɑ/
Sierra Leone /siˌerə liˈəʊn; AmE liˈoʊn/; Sierra Leonean /siˌerə liˈəʊniən; AmE -ˈoʊn-/
Singapore /ˌsɪŋəˈpɔː(r), ˌsɪŋɡə-; AmE usually ˈsɪŋə-/; Singaporean /ˌsɪŋəˈpɔːriən, ˌsɪŋɡə-/
Slovakia /sləˈvækiə; AmE sloʊ-/; Slovak /ˈsləʊvæk; AmE ˈsloʊ-/
Slovenia /sləˈviːniə; AmE sloʊ-/; Slovene /ˈsləʊviːn; AmE ˈsloʊ-/, Slovenian /sləʊˈviːniən; AmE sloʊ-/
(the) Solomon Islands /ˈsɒləmən aɪləndz; AmE ˈsɑːl-/
Somalia /səˈmɑːliə/; Somali /səˈmɑːli/
(the Republic of) South Africa /ˌsaʊθ ˈæfrɪkə/; South African /ˌsaʊθ ˈæfrɪkən/
(the) Southern Ocean /ˌsʌðərn ˈəʊʃn; AmE ˌsʌðərn ˈoʊʃn/
Spain /speɪn/; Spanish /ˈspænɪʃ/, Spaniard /ˈspænɪəd; AmE -njərd/
Sri Lanka /ˌsri ˈlæŋkə; AmE also ˈlɑːŋkə/; Sri Lankan /ˌsri ˈlæŋkən; AmE also ˈlɑːŋ-/
St Kitts-Nevis /snt ˌkɪts ən ˈniːvɪs; AmE also seɪnt/
St Lucia /ˌsnt ˈluːʃə; AmE also ˌseɪnt/
St Vincent and the Grenadines /snt ˌvɪnsnt ən ðə ˈɡrenədiːnz; AmE also seɪnt/
Sudan /suˈdɑːn; AmE also suˈdæn/; Sudanese /ˌsuːdəˈniːz/
Suriname /ˌsʊərɪˈnɑːm; AmE ˌsʊr-/; Surinamese /ˌsʊərɪnæˈmiːz; AmE ˌsʊr-/
Swaziland /ˈswɑːzilænd/; Swazi /ˈswɑːzi/
Sweden /ˈswiːdn/; Swedish /ˈswiːdɪʃ/, Swede /swiːd/
Switzerland /ˈswɪtsələnd; AmE -ərl-/; Swiss /swɪs/
Syria /ˈsɪriə/; Syrian /ˈsɪriən/
Taiwan /taɪˈwɑːn/; Taiwanese /ˌtaɪwəˈniːz/
Tajikistan /tæˌdʒiːkɪˈstɑːn; AmE -ˈstæn/; Tajik /tæˈdʒiːk/
Tanzania /ˌtænzəˈniːə/; Tanzanian /ˌtænzəˈniːən/
Thailand /ˈtaɪlænd/; Thai /taɪ/
Togo /ˈtəʊɡəʊ; AmE ˈtoʊɡoʊ/; Togolese /ˌtəʊɡəˈliːz; AmE ˌtoʊ-/
Tonga /ˈtɒŋə, ˈtɒŋɡə; AmE ˈtɑːŋ-/; Tongan /ˈtɒŋən, ˈtɒŋɡən; AmE ˈtɑːŋ-/
Trinidad and Tobago /ˌtrɪnɪdæd ən təˈbeɪɡəʊ; AmE -ɡoʊ/; Trinidadian /ˌtrɪnɪˈdædiən/, Tobagan /təˈbeɪɡən/, Tobagonian /ˌtəʊbəˈɡəʊniən; AmE ˌtoʊbəˈɡoʊ-/
Tunisia /tjuˈnɪziə; AmE usually tuˈniːʒə/; Tunisian /tjuˈnɪziən; AmE usually tuˈniːʒn/
Turkey /ˈtɜːki; AmE ˈtɜːrki/; Turkish /ˈtɜːkɪʃ; AmE ˈtɜːrkɪʃ/, Turk /tɜːk; AmE tɜːrk/
Turkmenistan /tɜːkˌmenɪˈstɑːn; AmE tɜːrkˌmenɪˈstæn/; Turkmen /ˈtɜːkmen; AmE ˈtɜːrk-/
Tuvalu /tuːˈvɑːluː/; Tuvaluan /ˌtuːvɑːˈluːən/
Uganda /juːˈɡændə/; Ugandan /juːˈɡændən/
Ukraine /juːˈkreɪn/; Ukrainian /juːˈkreɪniən/
(the) United Arab Emirates /juˌnaɪtɪd ˌærəb ˈemɪrəts/
(the) United States of America /juˌnaɪtɪd ˌsteɪts əv əˈmerɪkə/; American /əˈmerɪkən/
Uruguay /ˈjʊərəɡwaɪ; AmE ˈjʊr-/; Uruguayan /ˌjʊərəˈɡwaɪən; AmE ˌjʊr-/
Uzbekistan /ʊzˌbekɪˈstɑːn; AmE -ˈstæn/; Uzbek /ˈʊzbek/
Vanuatu /ˌvænuˈɑːtuː/
(the) Vatican City /ˌvætɪkən ˈsɪti/

Venezuela /ˌvenəˈzweɪlə/; Venezuelan /ˌvenəˈzweɪlən/
Vietnam /ˌvietˈnæm, -ˈnɑːm/; Vietnamese /viˌetnəˈmiːz/
Yemen Republic /ˌjemən rɪˈpʌblɪk/; Yemeni /ˈjeməni/
Yugoslavia /ˌjuːɡəʊˈslɑːviə; AmE ˈjuːɡoʊ-/; Yugoslavian /ˌjuːɡəʊˈslɑːviən; AmE ˈjuːɡoʊ-/, Yugoslav /ˈjuːɡəʊslɑːv; AmE ˈjuːɡoʊ-/
Zambia /ˈzæmbiə/; Zambian /ˈzæmbiən/
Zimbabwe /zɪmˈbɑːbwi, -bweɪ/; Zimbabwean /zɪmˈbɑːbwiən/

The British Isles /ðə ˌbrɪtɪʃ ˈaɪlz/

(the) United Kingdom /juˌnaɪtɪd ˈkɪŋdəm/
Great Britain /ˌɡreɪt ˈbrɪtn/
England /ˈɪŋɡlənd/
Scotland /ˈskɒtlənd; AmE ˈskɑːt-/
Wales /weɪlz/
Northern Ireland /ˌnɔː ðən ˈaɪələnd; AmE ˌnɔːrðərn ˈaɪərlənd/
(the) Republic of Ireland /rɪˌpʌblɪk əv ˈaɪələnd; AmE ˈaɪərlənd/

Towns and cities in the British Isles

Aberdeen /ˌæbəˈdiːn; AmE ˌæbərˈdiːn/
Ayr /eə(r); AmE er/
Bath /bɑːθ; AmE bæθ/
Belfast /ˌbelˈfɑːst; ˈbelfɑːst/
Berwick-upon-Tweed /ˌberɪk əpɒn ˈtwiːd; AmE əpɑːn/
Birmingham /ˈbɜːmɪŋəm; AmE ˈbɜːrmɪŋhæm/
Blackpool /ˈblækpuːl/
Bournemouth /ˈbɔːnməθ; AmE ˈbɔːrn-/
Bradford /ˈbrædfəd; AmE -fərd/
Brighton /ˈbraɪtn/
Bristol /ˈbrɪstl/
Caernarfon /kəˈnɑːvn; AmE kɑːrˈnɑːrvn, kə(r)-/
Cambridge /ˈkeɪmbrɪdʒ/
Canterbury /ˈkæntəbəri; AmE also -tərberi/
Cardiff /ˈkɑːdɪf; AmE ˈkɑːrdɪf/
Carlisle /kɑːˈlaɪl; AmE ˈkɑːrl-/
Chester /ˈtʃestə(r)/
Colchester /ˈkəʊltʃɪstə(r); AmE ˈkoʊltʃestər/
Cork /ˈkɔːk; AmE kɔːrk/
Coventry /ˈkɒvəntri; AmE ˈkɑːv-/
Derby /ˈdɑːbi; AmE ˈdɑːrbi, ˈdɜːrbi/
Douglas /ˈdʌɡləs/
Dover /ˈdəʊvə(r); AmE ˈdoʊ-/
Dublin /ˈdʌblɪn/
Dundee /dʌnˈdiː/
Durham /ˈdʌrəm; AmE also ˈdɜːr-/
Eastbourne /ˈiːstbɔːn; AmE -bɔːrn/
Edinburgh /ˈedɪnbrə, -bərə/
Ely /ˈiːli/
Exeter /ˈeksɪtə(r)/
Galway /ˈɡɔːlweɪ/
Glasgow /ˈɡlɑːzɡəʊ; AmE ˈɡlæzɡoʊ/
Gloucester /ˈɡlɒstə(r); AmE ˈɡlɑːs-, ˈɡlɔːs-/
Hastings /ˈheɪstɪŋz/
Hereford /ˈherɪfəd; AmE -fərd/
Holyhead /ˈhɒlihed; AmE ˈhɑːl-/
Inverness /ˌɪnvəˈnes; AmE -vərˈn-/
Ipswich /ˈɪpswɪtʃ/
John o'Groats /ˌdʒɒn ə ˈɡrəʊts; AmE ˌdʒɑːn ə ˈɡroʊts/
Keswick /ˈkezɪk/
Kingston upon Hull /ˌkɪŋstən əpɒn ˈhʌl; AmE əpɑːn/
Leeds /liːdz/
Leicester /ˈlestə(r)/

Limerick /ˈlɪmərɪk/
Lincoln /ˈlɪŋkən/
Liverpool /ˈlɪvəpu:l; *AmE* -vərp-/
London /ˈlʌndən/
Londonderry /ˈlʌndəndəri/
Luton /ˈlu:tn/
Manchester /ˈmæntʃɪstə(r)/
Middlesbrough /ˈmɪdlzbrə/
Newcastle upon Tyne /ˌnju:kɑ:sl əpɒn ˈtaɪn; *AmE* ˌnu:kæsl əpɑ:n/
Northampton /nɔ:θˈhæmptən; *AmE* nɔ:rθ-/
Norwich /ˈnɒrɪdʒ; *AmE* ˈnɑ:r-/
Nottingham /ˈnɒtɪŋəm; *AmE* ˈnɑ:tɪŋəm, -hæm/
Oxford /ˈɒksfəd; *AmE* ˈɑ:ksfərd/
Plymouth /ˈplɪməθ/
Poole /pu:l/
Portsmouth /ˈpɔ:tsməθ; *AmE* ˈpɔ:rts-/
Ramsgate /ˈræmzgeɪt/
Reading /ˈredɪŋ/
Salisbury /ˈsɔ:lzbəri; *AmE also* -beri/
Sheffield /ˈʃefi:ld/
Shrewsbury /ˈʃrəʊzbəri; *AmE* ˈʃrəʊz-, -beri/
Southampton /saʊˈθæmptən/
St. Andrews /ˌsnt ˈændru:z; *AmE also* semt/
St. David's /ˌsnt ˈdeɪvɪdz; *AmE also* ˌseɪnt/
Stirling /ˈstɜːlɪŋ; *AmE* ˈstɜːrlɪŋ/
Stoke-on-Trent /ˌstəʊk ɒn ˈtrent; *AmE* ˌstoʊk ɑːn/
Stratford-upon-Avon /ˌstrætfəd əpɒn ˈeɪvn; *AmE* -fərd əpɑ:n/
Swansea /ˈswɒnzi; *AmE* ˈswɑ:nzi/
Taunton /ˈtɔ:ntən/
Warwick /ˈwɒrɪk; *AmE* ˈwɑ:rɪk, ˈwɔ:r-/
Worcester /ˈwʊstə(r)/
York /jɔ:k; *AmE* jɔ:rk/

The United States of America and Canada

The states of the United States of America

Alabama /ˌæləˈbæmə/
Alaska /əˈlæskə/
Arizona /ˌærɪˈzəʊnə; *AmE* -ˈzoʊ-/
Arkansas /ˈɑːkənsɔː; *AmE* ˈɑːrk-/
California /ˌkælɪˈfɔːniə; *AmE* -ˈfɔːrn-/
Colorado /ˌkɒləˈrɑːdəʊ; *AmE* ˌkɑːləˈrædoʊ/
Connecticut /kəˈnetɪkət/
Delaware /ˈdeləweə(r); *AmE* -wer/
Florida /ˈflɒrɪdə; *AmE* ˈflɔːr-/
Georgia /ˈdʒɔːdʒə; *AmE* ˈdʒɔːrdʒə/
Hawaii /həˈwaɪi/
Idaho /ˈaɪdəhəʊ; *AmE* -hoʊ/
Illinois /ˌɪləˈnɔɪ/
Indiana /ˌɪndiˈænə/
Iowa /ˈaɪəwə/
Kansas /ˈkænzəs/
Kentucky /kenˈtʌki/
Louisiana /luˌiːziˈænə/
Maine /meɪn/
Maryland /ˈmeərɪlənd; *AmE* ˈmerə-/
Massachusetts /ˌmæsəˈtʃuːsɪts/
Michigan /ˈmɪʃɪɡən/
Minnesota /ˌmɪnɪˈsəʊtə; *AmE* -ˈsoʊtə/
Mississippi /ˌmɪsɪˈsɪpi/
Missouri /mɪˈzʊəri; *AmE* məˈzʊri/
Montana /mɒnˈtænə; *AmE* mɑ:n-/
Nebraska /nəˈbræskə/
Nevada /nəˈvɑːdə; *AmE* nəˈvædə/
New Hampshire /ˌnju: ˈhæmpʃə(r); *AmE* ˌnu:/
New Jersey /ˌnju: ˈdʒɜːzi; *AmE* ˌnu: ˈdʒɜːrzi/
New Mexico /ˌnju: ˈmeksɪkəʊ; *AmE* ˌnu: ˈmeksɪkoʊ/

New York /ˌnju: ˈjɔːk; *AmE* ˌnu: ˈjɔːrk/
North Carolina /ˌnɔːθ kærəˈlaɪnə; *AmE* ˌnɔːrθ/
North Dakota /ˌnɔːθ dəˈkəʊtə; *AmE* ˌnɔːrθ dəˈkoʊtə/
Ohio /əʊˈhaɪəʊ; *AmE* oʊˈhaɪoʊ/
Oklahoma /ˌəʊkləˈhəʊmə; *AmE* ˌoʊkləˈhoʊmə/
Oregon /ˈɒrɪgən; *AmE* ˈɔːrəgən, ˈɑːr-/
Pennsylvania /ˌpenslˈveɪniə/
Rhode Island /ˌrəʊd ˈaɪlənd; *AmE* ˌroʊd/
South Carolina /ˌsaʊθ kærəˈlaɪnə/
South Dakota /ˌsaʊθ dəˈkəʊtə; *AmE* dəˈkoʊtə/
Tennessee /ˌtenəˈsi:/
Texas /ˈteksəs/
Utah /ˈjuːtɑː/
Vermont /vəˈmɒnt; *AmE* vərˈmɑːnt/
Virginia /vəˈdʒɪniə; *AmE* vərˈdʒ-/
Washington /ˈwɒʃɪŋtən; *AmE* ˈwɑːʃ-, ˈwɔːʃ-/
West Virginia /ˌwest vəˈdʒɪniə; *AmE* vərˈdʒ-/
Wisconsin /wɪsˈkɒnsɪn; *AmE* -ˈkɑːn-/
Wyoming /waɪˈəʊmɪŋ; *AmE* -ˈoʊmɪŋ/

Towns and cities in the United States

Albany /ˈɔːlbəni/
Albuquerque /ˈælbəkɜːki; *AmE* -kɜːrki/
Amarillo /ˌæməˈrɪləʊ; *AmE* -loʊ/
Anchorage /ˈæŋkərɪdʒ/
Atlanta /ətˈlæntə; *AmE* æt-/
Augusta /ɔːˈgʌstə/
Austin /ˈɒstɪn; *AmE* ˈɔːstɪn/
Baltimore /ˈbɔːltɪmɔː(r)/
Baton Rouge /ˌbætn ˈruːʒ/
Berkeley /ˈbɜːkli; *AmE* ˈbɜːrkli/
Billings /ˈbɪlɪŋz/
Birmingham /ˈbɜːmɪŋəm; *AmE* ˈbɜːrmɪŋhæm/
Bismarck /ˈbɪzmɑːk; *AmE* -mɑːrk/
Boise /ˈbɔɪsi/
Boston /ˈbɒstən; *AmE* ˈbɔːs-/
Buffalo /ˈbʌfələʊ; *AmE* -loʊ/
Burlington /ˈbɜːlɪŋtən; *AmE* ˈbɜːrl-/
Charleston /ˈtʃɑːlstən; *AmE* ˈtʃɑːrl-/
Charlotte /ˈʃɑːlət; *AmE* ˈʃɑːrlət/
Cheyenne /ʃaɪˈæn/
Chicago /ʃɪˈkɑːgəʊ; *AmE* -goʊ/
Cincinnati /ˌsɪnsɪˈnæti/
Cleveland /ˈkliːvlənd/
Colorado Springs /ˌkɒlərɑːdəʊ ˈsprɪŋz; *AmE* ˌkɑːlərædoʊ/
Columbia /kəˈlʌmbiə/
Columbus /kəˈlʌmbəs/
Dallas /ˈdæləs/
Dayton /ˈdeɪtn/
Denver /ˈdenvə(r)/
Des Moines /dɪ ˈmɔɪn/
Detroit /dɪˈtrɔɪt/
Dover /ˈdəʊvə(r); *AmE* ˈdoʊ-/
Duluth /dəˈluːθ/
El Paso /el ˈpæsəʊ; *AmE* -soʊ/
Eugene /juːˈdʒiːn/
Fort Worth /ˌfɔːt ˈwɜːθ; *AmE* ˌfɔːrt ˈwɜːrθ/
Grand Forks /ˌgrænd ˈfɔːks; *AmE* ˈfɔːrks/
Great Falls /ˌgreɪt ˈfɔːlz/
Green Bay /ˌgriːn ˈbeɪ/
Hartford /ˈhɑːtfəd; *AmE* ˈhɑːrtfərd/
Hollywood /ˈhɒliwʊd; *AmE* ˈhɑːli-/
Honolulu /ˌhɒnəˈluːluː; *AmE* ˌhɑːnə-/
Houston /ˈhjuːstən/
Idaho Falls /ˌaɪdəhəʊ ˈfɔːlz; *AmE* -hoʊ/
Indianapolis /ˌɪndiəˈnæpəlɪs/
Jackson /ˈdʒæksən/
Jacksonville /ˈdʒæksənvɪl/
Juneau /ˈdʒuːnəʊ; *AmE* -noʊ/
Kansas City /ˌkænzəs ˈsɪti/
Knoxville /ˈnɒksvɪl; *AmE* ˈnɑːks-/

Laramie /'lærəmi/
Las Vegas /ˌlæs 'veɪgəs/
Lincoln /'lɪŋkən/
Little Rock /'lɪtl rɒk; *AmE* rɑːk/
Los Angeles /ˌlɒs 'ændʒəliːz; *AmE* ˌlɔːs 'ændʒələs/
Louisville /'luːivɪl/
Madison /'mædɪsən/
Manchester /'mæntʃestə(r)/
Memphis /'memfɪs/
Miami /maɪ'æmi/
Milwaukee /mɪl'wɔːki/
Minneapolis /ˌmɪni'æpəlɪs/
Mobile /məʊ'biːl; *AmE* moʊ-/
Montgomery /mɒnt'gʌməri; *AmE* mənt'gɑːm-/
Nashville /'næʃvɪl/
New Haven /ˌnjuː 'heɪvən; *AmE* ˌnuː/
New Orleans /ˌnjuː ɔː'liːənz; *AmE* ˌnuː 'ɔːrliənz/
New York /ˌnjuː 'jɔːk; *AmE* ˌnuː 'jɔːrk/
Newark /'njuːək; *AmE* 'nuːərk/
Norfolk /'nɔːfək; *AmE* 'nɔːrfək/
Oklahoma City /ˌəʊkləhəʊmə 'siti; *AmE* ˌoʊkləhoʊmə/
Omaha /'əʊməhɑː; *AmE* 'oʊ-/
Orlando /ɔː'lændəʊ; *AmE* ɔːr'lændoʊ/
Philadelphia /ˌfɪlə'delfiə/
Phoenix /'fiːnɪks/
Pierre /pi'eə(r); *AmE* pɪr/
Pittsburgh /'pɪtsbɜːg; *AmE* -bɜːrg/
Portland /'pɔːtlənd; *AmE* 'pɔːrt-/
Princeton /'prɪnstən/
Providence /'prɒvɪdəns; *AmE* 'prɑːv-/
Raleigh /'rɑːli; *AmE also* 'rɔːli/
Reno /'riːnəʊ; *AmE* 'riːnoʊ/
Richmond /'rɪtʃmənd/
Rochester /'rɒtʃɪstə(r); *AmE* 'rɑːtʃəs-/
Sacramento /ˌsækrə'mentəʊ; *AmE* -toʊ/
Salt Lake City /ˌsɔːlt leɪk 'sɪti/
San Antonio /ˌsæn æn'təʊniəʊ; *AmE* æn'toʊnioʊ/
San Diego /ˌsæn di'eɪgəʊ; *AmE* -goʊ/
San Francisco /ˌsæn frən'sɪskəʊ; *AmE* -koʊ/
San Jose /ˌsæn həʊ'zeɪ; *AmE* hoʊ-/
Santa Fe /ˌsæntə 'feɪ/
Savannah /sə'vænə/
Scranton /'skræntən/
Seattle /si'ætl/
Sioux City /ˌsuː 'sɪti/
Sioux Falls /ˌsuː 'fɔːlz/
Springfield /'sprɪŋfiːld/
St Paul /ˌsnt 'pɔːl; *AmE also* ˌseɪnt/
St. Louis /ˌsnt 'luːɪs; *AmE also* ˌseɪnt/
Syracuse /'sɪrəkjuːs/
Tallahassee /ˌtælə'hæsi/
Tampa /'tæmpə/
Toledo /tə'liːdəʊ; *AmE* -doʊ/
Topeka /tə'piːkə/
Tucson /'tuːsɒn; *AmE* -sɑːn/
Tulsa /'tʌlsə/
Twin Falls /ˌtwɪn 'fɔːlz/
Washington D.C. /ˌwɒʃɪŋtən diː 'siː; *AmE* ˌwɑːʃ-, ˌwɔːʃ-/
Wichita /'wɪtʃɪtɔː/

The provinces and territories of Canada

Alberta /æl'bɜːtə; *AmE* æl'bɜːrtə/
British Columbia /ˌbrɪtɪʃ kə'lʌmbiə/
Manitoba /ˌmænɪ'təʊbə; *AmE* -toʊ-/
New Brunswick /ˌnjuː 'brʌnzwɪk; *AmE* ˌnuː/
Newfoundland /'njuːfəndlənd; *AmE* 'nuː-/
Northwest Territories /ˌnɔːθwest 'terətriz; *AmE* ˌnɔːrθwest 'terətɔːriz/
Nova Scotia /ˌnəʊvə 'skəʊʃə; *AmE* ˌnoʊvə 'skoʊʃə/
Nunavut /'nʊnəvʊt/

Ontario /ɒn'teəriəʊ; *AmE* ɑːn'teerioʊ/
Prince Edward Island /ˌprɪns 'edwəd aɪlənd; *AmE* 'edwərd/
Québec /kwɪ'bek/
Saskatchewan /sə'skætʃəwən/
Yukon Territory /'juːkɒn terətri; *AmE* 'juːkɑːn terətɔːri/

Towns and cities in Canada

Calgary /'kælgəri/
Chicoutimi-Jonquière /ʃɪˌkuːtəmi ʒɒ̃'kjeə(r); *AmE* ʒɔː'kjer/
Edmonton /'edməntən/
Fredericton /'fredrɪktən/
Halifax /'hælɪfæks/
Hamilton /'hæmɪltən/
Iqaluit /ɪ'kæluːɪt/
London /'lʌndən/
Moncton /'mʌŋktən/
Montréal /ˌmɒntri'ɔːl; *AmE* ˌmɑːn-/
Niagara Falls /naɪˌægrə 'fɔːlz/
Ottawa /'ɒtəwə; *AmE* 'ɑːt-/
Québec /kwɪ'bek/
Regina /rɪ'dʒaɪnə/
Saint John /ˌseɪnt 'dʒɒn; *AmE* 'dʒɑːn/
Saskatoon /ˌsæskə'tuːn/
Sault Sainte Marie /ˌsuː seɪnt mə'riː/
St John's /ˌsnt 'dʒɒnz; *AmE* ˌseɪnt 'dʒɑːnz/
Sudbury /'sʌdbəri; *AmE* -beri/
Sydney /'sɪdni/
Thunder Bay /ˌθʌndə 'beɪ; *AmE* -dər/
Toronto /tə'rɒntəʊ; *AmE* tə'rɑːntoʊ/
Vancouver /væn'kuːvə(r)/
Victoria /vɪk'tɔːriə/
Whitehorse /'waɪthɔːs; *AmE* -hɔːrs/
Windsor /'wɪnzə(r)/
Winnipeg /'wɪnɪpeg/
Yellowknife /'jeləʊnaɪf; *AmE* -loʊ-/

Australia and New Zealand

The states of Australia

Australian Capital Territory (ACT) /ɒˌstreɪliən kæpɪtl 'terətri; *AmE* ɔː'streɪliən, 'terətɔːri/
New South Wales /ˌnjuː saʊθ 'weɪlz; *AmE* ˌnuː/
Northern Territory /ˌnɔːðən 'terətri; *AmE* ˌnɔːrðərn 'terətɔːri/
Queensland /'kwiːnzlənd/
South Australia /ˌsaʊθ ɒ'streɪliə; *AmE* ɔː'str-/
Tasmania /tæz'meɪniə/
Victoria /vɪk'tɔːriə/
Western Australia /ˌwestən ɒ'streɪliə; *AmE* ˌwestərn ɔː'streɪliə/

Towns and cities in Australia and New Zealand

Adelaide /'ædəleɪd/
Auckland /'ɔːklənd/
Brisbane /'brɪzbən/
Canberra /'kænbərə; *AmE also* -berə/
Christchurch /'kraɪstʃɜːtʃ; *AmE* -tʃɜːrtʃ/
Darwin /'dɑːwɪn; *AmE* 'dɑːrwɪn/
Dunedin /dʌ'niːdɪn/
Geelong /dʒɪ'lɒŋ; *AmE* dʒə'lɔːŋ/
Hamilton /'hæmɪltən/
Hobart /'həʊbɑːt; *AmE* 'hoʊbɑːrt/
Melbourne /'melbən; *AmE* -bərn/
Newcastle /'njuːkɑːsl; *AmE* 'nukæsl/
Perth /pɜːθ; *AmE* pɜːrθ/
Sydney /'sɪdni/
Townsville /'taʊnsvɪl/
Wellington /'welɪŋtən/

Appendix 3
Numbers

Writing and saying numbers

Numbers over 20

- are written with a hyphen:
  35 *thirty-five*
  67 *sixty-seven*

- When writing a cheque we often use words for the pounds or dollars and figures for the pence or cents:
  £22.45 *twenty-two pounds (and) 45 pence*
  $79.30 *seventy-nine dollars (and)* ³⁰/₁₀₀

Numbers over 100

329 *three hundred and twenty nine*

- The **and** is pronounced /n/ and the stress is on the final number.

- In *AmE* the **and** is sometimes left out.

Numbers over 1000

1100 *one thousand one hundred*
     (also *informal*) *eleven hundred*

2500 *two thousand five hundred*
     (also *informal, especially in AmE*)
     twenty-five hundred

- These informal forms are most common for whole hundreds between 1100 and 1900.

- A comma or (in *BrE*) a space is often used to divide large numbers into groups of 3 figures:
  33,423 or *33 423* (*thirty three thousand four hundred and twenty three*)

  2,768,941 or *2 768 941* (*two million seven hundred and sixty-eight thousand nine hundred and forty-one*)

A or one?

130   *a / one hundred and thirty*
1 000 000 *a / one million*

- **one** is more formal and more precise and can be used for emphasis:
  The total cost was one hundred and sixty three pounds exactly.
  It cost about a hundred and fifty quid.

- **a** can only be used at the beginning of a number:
  1000 *a / one thousand*
  2100 *two thousand one hundred*
       ~~two thousand a hundred~~

- **a** is not usually used between 1100 and 1999:
  1099 *a / one thousand and ninety-nine*
  1100 *one thousand one hundred*
  1340 *one thousand three hundred and forty*
       ~~a thousand three hundred and forty~~

Ordinal numbers

1st	*first*
2nd	*second*
3rd	*third*
4th	*fourth*
5th	*fifth*
9th	*ninth*
12th	*twelfth*
21st	*twenty-first*
etc.	

Fractions

½	*a / one half*
⅓	*a / one third*
¼	*a / one quarter* (*AmE* also *a / one fourth*)

(for emphasis use **one** instead of **a**)

¹/₁₂	*one twelfth*
¹/₁₆	*one sixteenth*
⅔	*two thirds*
¾	*three quarters* (*AmE* also *three fourths*)
⁹/₁₀	*nine tenths*

More complex fractions

- use **over**
  ¹⁹/₅₆ *nineteen over fifty-six*
  ³¹/₁₄₄ *thirty-one over one four four*

Whole numbers and fractions

- link with **and**
  2½ *two and a half*
  5⅔ *five and two thirds*

Fractions/percentages and noun phrases

- use **of**:
  a fifth of the women questioned
  three quarters of the population
  75% of the population

- with **half** do not use **a**, and **of** can sometimes be omitted:
  Half (of) the work is already finished.

- do not use **of** in expressions of measurement or quantity:
  How much is half a pint of milk?
  It takes me half an hour by bus.

- use **of** before pronouns
  We can't start- only half of us are here.

Fractions/percentages and verbs

- If a fraction/percentage is used with an uncountable or a singular noun the verb is generally singular:

Fifty per cent of the land is cultivated.
Half (of) the land is cultivated.

- If the noun is singular but represents a group of people, the verb is singular in *AmE* but in *BrE* it may be singular or plural:
Three quarters/75% of the workforce is/are against the strike.

- If the noun is plural, the verb is plural:
Two thirds/65% of children play computer games.

Decimals

- write and say with a point (.) (not a comma)
- say each figure after the point separately

79.3	*seventy-nine point three*
3.142	*three point one four two*
0.67	*(zero) point six seven*
	(BrE also) *nought point six seven*

Mathematical expressions

+	plus
−	minus
×	times/multiplied by
÷	divided by
=	equals/is
%	per cent (*AmE* usually percent)
3^2	three squared
5^3	five cubed
6^{10}	six to the power of ten
√	square root of

The figure '0'

The figure 0 has several different names in English, although in American English *zero* is commonly used in all cases:

Zero

- used in precise scientific, medical and economic contexts and to talk about temperature:
It was ten degrees below zero last night.
zero inflation/growth/profit

Nought

- used in British English to talk about a number, age, etc.:
A million is written with six noughts.
The car goes from nought to sixty in ten seconds.
clothes for children aged nought to six

'o' /əʊ/ *AmE* /oʊ/

- used when saying a bank account number, telephone number, etc.

Nil

- used to talk about the score in a team game, for example in football:
The final score was one nil. (1–0)

- used to mean 'nothing at all':
The doctors rated her chances as nil.

Telephone numbers

- All numbers are said separately. 0 is pronounced /əʊ/ *(BrE)* or /oʊ/ *(AmE)*
(01865) 556767 *o one eight six five, five five six seven six seven* (or *double five six seven six seven*)

Temperature

- The Celsius or Centigrade (°C) scale is officially used in Britain and for scientific purposes in the US.
a high of thirty-five degrees Celsius
The normal temperature of the human body is 37°C.

- The Fahrenheit (°F) scale is used in all other contexts in the US and is also still commonly used in Britain. The words 'degrees Fahrenheit/Centigrade/Celsius' are often omitted.
Temperatures soared to over a hundred. (100°F)
She's ill in bed with a temperature of a hundred and two. (102°F)

Money

In Britain

100 pence/p = 1 British pound (£1)
It costs 90p/90 pence return on the bus.

- when talking about an individual coin:
a twenty pence piece/a twenty p piece

- when talking about pounds and pence people often only say the numbers:
It only cost five ninety nine. (£5.99)

- in informal British English

£1	*a quid*
£5	*five quid* or *a fiver*
£10	*ten quid* or *a tenner*

In the US

1c	one cent	a penny
5c	five cents	a nickel
10c	ten cents	a dime
25c	twenty-five cents	a quarter
$1.00	one dollar	a dollar bill

- in informal American English dollars are called **bucks**
This shirt cost fifty bucks.

Writing and saying dates

British English
14 October 1998 or *14th October 1998*
(14/10/98)
Her birthday is on **the ninth of** December.
Her birthday is on December **the ninth**.

American English
October 14, 1998 (10/14/98)
Her birthday is December 9th.

Years
1999	*nineteen ninety-nine*
1608	*sixteen o eight* (or, less commonly, *nineteen <u>hundred</u> and ninety-nine* and *sixteen <u>hundred</u> and eight*)
1700	*seventeen hundred*
2000	*(the year) two thousand*
2002	*two thousand and two*
2015	*twenty fifteen*

AD 76 *AD seventy-six*
76 CE *seventy-six CE*
(Both these expressions mean '76 years after the beginning of the Christian calendar'.)

1000 BC *one thousand BC*
1000 BCE *one thousand BCE*
(Both these expressions mean '1000 years before the beginning of the Christian calendar'.)

Age

- when saying a person's age use only numbers:
  Sue is ten and Tom is six.
  She left home at sixteen.

- a man/woman/boy/girl, etc. of ...
  They've got a girl of three and a boy of five.
  a young woman of nineteen

- in writing, in descriptions or to emphasize sb's age use **... years old**:
  She was thirty-one years old and a barrister by profession.
  He is described as white, 5ft 10 ins tall and about 50 years old.
  You're forty years old – stop behaving like a teenager!

- **... years old** is also used for things:
  The monument is 120 years old.

- You can also say **a ... year-old/month-old/ week-old**, etc.
  Youth training is available to all sixteen year-olds.
  a ten week-old baby
  a remarkable 1000 year-old tomb

- Use **... years of age** in formal or written contexts:

Not applicable to persons under eighteen years of age.

- Use **the ... age group** to talk about people between certain ages:
  He took first prize in the 10–16 age group.

- To give the approximate age of a person:
13–19	*in his/her teens*
21–29	*in his/her twenties*
31–33	*in his/her early thirties*
34–36	*in his/her mid thirties*
37–39	*in his/her late thirties*

- To refer to a particular event you can use **at/by/before, etc. the age of ...**
  Most smokers start smoking cigarettes before the age of sixteen.

Numbers in time

There is often more than one way of telling the time:

Half hours
6:30	*six thirty*
	half past six (BrE)
	half six (BrE informal)

Other times
5:45	*five forty-five*	*(a) quarter to six (BrE)*
		(a) quarter to/of six (AmE)
2:15	*two fifteen*	*(a) quarter past two (BrE)*
		(a) quarter after two (AmE)
1:10	*one ten*	*ten past one (BrE)*
		ten after one (AmE)
3:05	*three o five*	*five past three (BrE)*
		five after three (AmE)
1:55	*one fifty-five*	*five to two (BrE)*
		five to/of two (AmE)

- with 5, 10, 20 and 25 the word **minutes** is not necessary, but it is used with other numbers:
  10.25 *twenty-five past/after ten*
  10.17 *seventeen **minutes** past/after ten*

- use **o'clock** only for whole hours:
  It's three o'clock.

- If it is necessary to specify the time of day use **in the morning, in the afternoon, in the evening** or **at night.**

- in more formal contexts use:
  a.m. = in the morning or after midnight
  p.m. = in the afternoon, in the evening or before midnight
  He gets up at 4 a.m. to deliver the mail.
  Do not use **o'clock** with **a.m.** or **p.m.**:
  ~~He gets up at 4 o'clock a.m.~~
  He gets up at 4 o'clock in the morning.
  ~~I'll see you at 6 o'clock p.m.~~
  I'll see you at 6 o'clock this evening.

Twenty-four hour clock

- used for military purposes and in some other particular contexts, for example on train timetables in Britain:
  13:52 *thirteen fifty-two* (1:52 p.m.)
  22:30 *twenty-two thirty* (10:30 p.m.)

- for military purposes whole hours are said as **hundred hours**:
  0400 *(o) four hundred hours* (4 a.m.)
  2400 *twenty four hundred hours* (midnight)

Expressing time

When referring to days, weeks, etc. in the past, present and future the following expressions are used, speaking from a point of view in the present:

	past	present	future
morning	*yesterday morning*	*this morning*	*tomorrow morning*
afternoon	*yesterday afternoon*	*this afternoon*	*tomorrow afternoon*
evening	*yesterday evening*	*this evening*	*tomorrow evening*
night	*last night*	*tonight*	*tomorrow night*
day	*yesterday*	*today*	*tomorrow*
week	*last week*	*this week*	*next week*
month	*last month*	*this month*	*next month*
year	*last year*	*this year*	*next year*

To talk about a time further back in the past or further forward in the future use:

past	future
the day before yesterday	*the day after tomorrow*
the week/month/year before last	*the week/month/year after next*
two days/weeks, etc. ago	*in two days/weeks, etc. time*

To talk about sth that happens regularly use expressions with **'every'**
*He has to work **every third** weekend.*
*I wash my hair **every other** day* (= every second day).

Prepositions of time

in *(the)*
parts of the day
(not night)   *in the morning(s), in the evening(s), etc.*
months   *in February*
seasons   *in (the) summer*
years   *in 1995*
decades   *in the 1920s*
centuries   *in the 20th century*

at *(the)*
clock time   *at 5 o'clock*
                at 7.45 pm
night   *at night*
holiday periods *at Christmas*
                at the weekend (BrE)

on *(the)*
day of the week   *on Saturdays*
dates   *on (the) 20th (of) May*
                  (AmE also on May 20th)
particular days   *on Good Friday*
                  on New Year's Day
                  on my birthday
                  on the following day

Numbers in measurement in Britain and America

item being measured	unit of measurement	examples
length of time	hours (hrs) / minutes (mins) / seconds (secs)	*Cover the pan and simmer gently for one hour.* *He took just two minutes to knock out his opponent.* *The fastest time was 12 mins 26 secs.*
person's height	feet and inches metres and centimetres (UK)	*She's 1.63 metres tall.* *He's only five feet four (inches).* *He's only five foot four.*
distance by road	miles	*It is 42 miles to Liverpool.* *The signpost said: 'Liverpool 42'.*
speed	miles per hour (mph) kilometres per hour (kph) kilometres per second, etc. miles an hour (*informal*)	*She was driving at 75 miles an hour.* *a speed limit of 50kph* *Light travels at 299 792 kilometres per second.* *a hundred-mile-an-hour police chase*
distance in sport	metres yards / miles (US)	*the women's 800 metres freestyle* *a six-mile run*
area of land (for example farmland)	acres / hectares	*a house with 10 acres of grounds* *a 2 000-hectare farm*
regions or areas of a country	square miles square kilometres (UK)	*Dartmoor covers an area of more than 350 square miles.* *Population density is only 24 people per square kilometre.*
area of a room/ garden, etc.	square yards / feet square metres (UK) ... by ... (... × ...)	*5 000 square feet of office space* *15 square metres of carpet (5m × 3m)* *a carpet fifteen metres square (15m × 15m)* *a room sixteen feet by twelve (16ft × 12ft)*
weight of food	pounds and ounces kilograms and grams (UK) cups (US, in cooking)	*Fold in 6 ounces of flour.* *250 grams of Brie please* *Add half a cup of sugar.*
weight of a person	stones and pounds (UK) pounds only (US)	*She weighs 8st 10lb.* *My brother weighs 183 pounds.*
weight of a baby	pounds and ounces kilograms (UK)	*The baby weighed 6lb 4oz at birth.*
heavy items/ large amounts	tons / tonnes pounds kilograms (UK)	*The price of copper fell by £11 a tonne* *a car packed with 140 pounds of explosive* *a 40kg sack of gravel* *Our baggage allowance is only 20 kilos.*
milk	pints / half pints (UK) pints / quarts / gallons (US)	*a one-pint carton of milk* *a quart of milk*
beer	pints / half pints (UK)	*a half of lager please* (= half a pint) (*informal*)
wine, bottled drinks	litres / centilitres	*a litre of juice*
other liquids	litres (UK) fluid ounces / gallons (US) millilitres (scientific context)	*half a litre of cooking oil* *5 litres of paint; 2 gallons of paint* *100 ml sulphuric acid*
liquid in cooking	fluid ounces millilitres (UK)	*Add 8 fl oz milk and beat thoroughly.*
petrol (*BrE*) (*AmE* gasoline) /diesel	gallons (US) litres (UK)	*My new car does over 50 miles to the gallon.*

As the table shows, both metric and non-metric systems of measurement can be used in many cases, especially in the UK. Often the choice depends on the speaker or the situation. In the UK the metric system must now be used on packaging and for displaying prices by weight or measurement in shops. The metric system is always used in a scientific context. In the US the metric system is much less widely used.

Metric measures

(with approximate non-metric equivalents)

	Metric		Non-metric
Length	10 millimetres (mm)	= 1 centimetre (cm)	= 0.394 inch
	100 centimetres	= 1 metre (m)	= 39.4 inches/1.094 yards
	1000 metres	= 1 kilometre (km)	= 0.6214 mile
Area	100 square metres (m²)	= 1 are (a)	= 0.025 acre
	100 ares	= 1 hectare (ha)	= 2.471 acres
	100 hectares	= 1 square kilometre (km²)	= 0.386 square mile
Weight	1000 milligrams (mg)	= 1 gram (g)	= 15.43 grains
	1000 grams	= 1 kilogram (kg)	= 2.205 pounds
	1000 kilograms	= 1 tonne	= 19.688 hundredweight
Capacity	10 millilitres (ml)	= 1 centilitre	= 0.018 pint (0.021 US pint)
	100 centilitres (cl)	= 1 litre (l)	= 1.76 pints (2.1 US pints) ·
	10 litres	= 1 decalitre (dal)	= 2.2 gallons (2.63 US gallons)

Non-metric measures

(with approximate metric equivalents)

	Non-metric		Metric
Length	1 inch (in)		= 25.4 millimetres
	12 inches	= 1 foot (ft)	= 30.48 centimetres
	3 feet	= 1 yard (yd)	= 0.914 metre
	220 yards	= 1 furlong	= 201.17 metres
	8 furlongs	= 1 mile	= 1.609 kilometres
	1760 yards	= 1 mile	= 1.609 kilometres
Area	1 square (sq) inch		= 6.452 sq centimetres (cm²)
	144 sq inches	= 1 sq foot	= 929.03 sq centimetres
	9 sq feet	= 1 sq yard	= 0.836 sq metre
	4840 sq yards	= 1 acre	= 0.405 hectare
	640 acres	= 1 sq mile	= 259 hectares/ 2.59 sq kilometres
Weight	437 grains	= 1 ounce (oz)	= 28.35 grams
	16 ounces	= 1 pound (lb)	= 0.454 kilogram
	14 pounds	= 1 stone (st)	= 6.356 kilograms
	8 stone	= 1 hundredweight (cwt)	= 50.8 kilograms
	20 hundredweight	= 1 ton	= 1016.04 kilograms
British capacity	20 fluid ounces (fl oz)	= 1 pint (pt)	= 0.568 litre
	2 pints	= 1 quart (qt)	= 1.136 litres
	8 pints	= 1 gallon (gal)	= 4.546 litres
American capacity	16 US fluid ounces	= 1 US pint	= 0.473 litre
	2 US pints	= 1 US quart	= 0.946 litre
	4 US quarts	= 1 US gallon	= 3.785 litres

Appendix 4
Punctuation

full stop (BrE) period (AmE)

- at the end of a sentence that is not a question or an exclamation:
  I knocked at the door. There was no reply. I knocked again.

- sometimes in abbreviations:
  Jan. e.g. a.m.

- in internet and e-mail addresses (said 'dot')
  http://www.oup.co.uk

comma ,

- to separate words in a list, though they are often omitted before *and*:
  a bouquet of red, pink and white roses
  tea, coffee, milk or hot chocolate

- to separate phrases or clauses:
  If you keep calm, take your time, concentrate and think ahead, then you're likely to pass your test.
  Worn out after all the excitement of the party, the children soon fell asleep.

- before and after a clause or phrase that gives additional, but not essential, information about the noun it follows:
  The Pennine Hills, which are very popular with walkers, are situated between Lancashire and Yorkshire.

  (do not use commas before and after a clause that **defines** the noun it follows)
  The hills that separate Lancashire from Yorkshire are called the Pennines.

- to separate main clauses, especially long ones, linked by a conjunction such as *and, as, but, for, or*:
  We had been looking forward to our holiday all year, but unfortunately it rained every day.

- to separate an introductory word or phrase, or an adverb or adverbial phrase that applies to the whole sentence, from the rest of the sentence:
  Oh, so that's where it was.
  As it happens, however, I never saw her again.
  By the way, did you hear about Sue's car?

- to separate a tag question from the rest of the sentence:
  It's quite expensive, isn't it?
  You live in Bristol, right?

- before or after 'he said', etc. when writing down conversation:
  'Come back soon,' she said.

- before a short quotation:
  Disraeli said, 'Little things affect little minds'.

colon :

- to introduce a list of items:
  These are our options: we go by train and leave before the end of the show; or we take the car and see it all.

- in formal writing, before a clause or phrase that gives more information about the main clause. (You can use a semicolon or a full stop, but not a comma, instead of a colon here.)
  The garden had been neglected for a long time: it was overgrown and full of weeds.

- to introduce a quotation, which may be indented:
  As Kenneth Morgan writes:
    The truth was, perhaps, that Britain in the years from 1914 to 1983 had not changed all that fundamentally.
  Others, however, have challenged this view...

semicolon ;

- instead of a comma to separate parts of a sentence that already contain commas:
  She was determined to succeed whatever the cost; she would achieve her aim, whoever might suffer on the way.

- in formal writing, to separate two main clauses, especially those not joined by a conjunction:
  The sun was already low in the sky; it would soon be dark.

question mark ?

- at the end of a direct question:
  Where's the car?
  You're leaving already?

  Do not use a question mark at the end of an indirect question:
  He asked if I was leaving.

- especially with a date, to express doubt:
  John Marston (?1575–1634)

exclamation mark (BrE) / exclamation point (AmE)

- at the end of a sentence expressing surprise, joy, anger, shock or another strong emotion:
  That's marvellous!
  'Never!' she cried.

- in informal written English, you can use more than one exclamation mark, or an exclamation mark and a question mark:
  'Your wife's just given birth to triplets.'
  'Triplets!?'

apostrophe   '

- with *s* to indicate that a thing or person belongs to somebody:
  my friend's brother
  the waitress's apron
  King James's crown / King James' crown
  the students' books
  the women's coats

- in short forms, to indicate that letters or figures have been omitted:
  I'm (I am)
  they'd (they had / they would)
  the summer of '89 (1989)

- sometimes, with s to form the plural of a letter, a figure or an abbreviation:
  roll your r's
  during the 1990's

hyphen   -

- to form a compound from two or more other words:
  hard-hearted
  fork-lift truck
  mother-to-be

- to form a compound from a prefix and a proper name:
  pre-Raphaelite
  pro-European

- when writing compound numbers between 21 and 99 in words:
  seventy-three
  thirty-one

- sometimes, in British English, to separate a prefix ending in a vowel from a word beginning with the same vowel:
  co-operate
  pre-eminent

- after the first section of a word that is divided between one line and the next:
  decide what to do in order to avoid mis-takes of this kind in the future

dash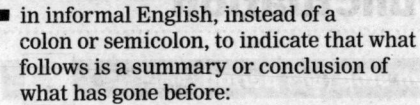

- in informal English, instead of a colon or semicolon, to indicate that what follows is a summary or conclusion of what has gone before:
  Men were shouting, women were screaming, children were crying—it was chaos.
  You've admitted that you lied to me—how can I trust you again?

- singly or in pairs to separate a comment or an afterthought from the rest of the sentence:
  He knew nothing at all about it—or so he said.

dots / ellipsis

- to indicate that words have been omitted, especially from a quotation or at the end of a conversation:
  … challenging the view that Britain … had not changed all that fundamentally.

slash / oblique

- to separate alternative words or phrases:
  have a pudding and / or cheese
  single / married / widowed / divorced

- in internet and e-mail addresses to separate the different elements (often said 'forward slash')
  http://www.oup.co.uk/elt/

quotation marks

- to enclose words and punctuation in direct speech:
  'Why on earth did you do that?' he asked.
  'I'll fetch it,' she replied.

- to draw attention to a word that is unusual for the context, for example a slang expression, or to a word that is being used for special effect, such as irony:
  He told me in no uncertain terms to 'get lost'.
  Thousands were imprisoned in the name of 'national security'

- around the titles of articles, books, poems, plays, etc:
  Keats's 'Ode to Autumn'
  I was watching 'Match of the Day'.

- around short quotations or sayings:
  Do you know the origin of the saying: 'A little learning is a dangerous thing'?

- in American English, double quotation marks are used:
  "Help! I'm drowning!"

brackets/parentheses

- to separate extra information or a comment from the rest of a sentence:
  Mount Robson (12 972 feet) is the highest mountain in the Canadian Rockies.
  He thinks that modern music (i.e. anything written after 1900) is rubbish.

- to enclose cross-references:
  This moral ambiguity is a feature of Shakespeare's later works (see Chapter Eight).

- around numbers or letters in text:
  Our objectives are (1) to increase output, (2) to improve quality and (3) to maximize profits.

square brackets

- around words inserted to make a quotation grammatically correct:
  Britain in [these] years was without ...

italics

In handwritten or typed text, and in the examples that follow, italics are indicated by underlining.

- to show emphasis:
  I'm not going to do it – <u>you</u> are.
  ... proposals which we cannot accept <u>under any circumstances</u>

- to indicate the titles of books, plays, etc:
  Joyce's <u>Ulysses</u>
  the title role in Puccini's <u>Tosca</u>
  a letter in <u>The Times</u>

- for foreign words or phrases:
  the English oak (<u>Quercus robur</u>)
  I had to renew my <u>permesso di soggiorno</u> (residence permit).

Quoting conversation

When you write down a conversation, you normally begin a new paragraph for each new speaker.

Quotation marks enclose the words spoken:
  'You're sure of this?' I asked.
  He nodded grimly.
  'I'm certain.'

Verbs used to indicate direct speech, for example *he said, she complained*, are separated by commas from the words spoken, unless a question mark or an exclamation mark is used:
  'That's all I know,' said Nick.
  Nick said, 'That's all I know.'
  'Why?' asked Nick.

When *he said* or *said Nick* follows the words spoken, the comma is placed inside the quotation marks, as in the first example above. If, however, the writer puts the words *said Nick* within the actual words Nick speaks, the comma is outside the quotation marks:
  'That', said Nick, 'is all I know.'

Double quotation marks are used to indicate direct speech being quoted by somebody else within direct speech:
  'But you said you loved me! "I'll never leave you, Sue, as long as I live." That's what you said, isn't it?'

Appendix 5
The language of literary criticism

Figurative language

Imagery is language that produces pictures in the mind. The term can be used to discuss the various stylistic devices listed below, especially **figures of speech** (= ways of using language to convey or suggest a meaning beyond the literal meaning of the words).

Metaphor is the imaginative use of a word or phrase to describe something else, to show that the two have the same qualities:

All the world's a stage
And all the men and women merely players.
(William Shakespeare, *As You Like It*)

In **simile** the comparison between the two things is made explicit by the use of the words 'as' or 'like':

I wandered lonely as a cloud
(William Wordsworth, *Daffodils*)

Like as the waves make towards the
pebbled shore,
So do our minutes hasten to their end.
(Shakespeare, Sonnet 60)

Metonymy is the fact of referring to something by the name of something else closely connected with it, used especially as a form of shorthand for something familiar or obvious, as in 'I've been reading Shakespeare' instead of 'I've been reading the plays of Shakespeare'.

Allegory is a style of writing in which each character or event is a symbol representing a particular quality. In John Bunyan's *Pilgrim's Progress* Christian escapes from the City of Destruction, travels through the Slough of Despond, visits Vanity Fair and finally arrives at the Celestial City. He meets characters such as the Giant Despair and Mr Worldly Wiseman and is accompanied by Faithful and Hopeful.

Personification is the act of representing objects or qualities as human beings:

Love bade me welcome: yet my soul drew
back,
Guilty of dust and sin.
(George Herbert, *Love*)

Pathetic fallacy is the effect produced when animals and things are shown as having human feelings. For example, in John Milton's poem, *Lycidas*, the flowers are shown as weeping for the dead shepherd, Lycidas.

Patterns of sound

Alliteration is the use of the same letter or sound at the beginning of words that are close together. It was used systematically in Old English poetry but in modern English poetry is generally only used for a particular effect:

On the bald street breaks the blank day.
(Alfred, Lord Tennyson, *In Memoriam*)

Assonance is the effect created when two syllables in words that are close together have the same vowel sound but different consonants, or the same consonants but different vowels:

It seemed that out of battle I escaped
Down some profound dull tunnel long since
scooped ...
(Wilfred Owen, *Strange Meeting*)

Onomatopoeia is the effect produced when the words used contain similar sounds to the noises they describe:

murmuring of innumerable bees
(Tennyson, *The Princess*)

Other stylistic effects

Irony is the use of words that say the opposite of what you really mean, often in order to make a critical comment.

Hyperbole is the use of exaggeration:

An hundred years should go to praise
Thine eyes and on thy forehead gaze
(Andrew Marvell, *To His Coy Mistress*)

An **oxymoron** is a phrase that combines two words that seem to be the opposite of each other:

Parting is such sweet sorrow
(Shakespeare, *Romeo and Juliet*)

A **paradox** is a statement that contains two opposite ideas or seems to be impossible:

The Child is father of the Man.
(Wordsworth, 'My heart leaps up ...')

Poetry

Lyric poetry is usually fairly short and expresses thoughts and feelings. Examples are Wordsworth's *Daffodils* and Dylan Thomas's *Fern Hill*.

Epic poetry can be much longer and deals with the actions of great men and women or the history of nations. Examples are Homer's *Iliad* and Virgil's *Aeneid*.

Narrative poetry tells a story, like Chaucer's *Canterbury Tales*, or Coleridge's *Rime of the Ancient Mariner*.

Dramatic poetry takes the form of a play, and includes the plays of Shakespeare (which also contain scenes in **prose**).

A **ballad** is a traditional type of narrative poem with short **verses** or **stanzas** and a simple **rhyme scheme** (= pattern of rhymes).

An **elegy** is a type of lyric poem that expresses sadness for someone who has died. Thomas Gray's *Elegy Written in a Country Churchyard* mourns all who lived and died quietly and never had the chance to be great.

An **ode** is a lyric poem that addresses a person or thing or celebrates an event. John Keats wrote five great odes, including *Ode to a Nightingale*, *Ode on a Grecian Urn* and *To Autumn*.

Metre is the rhythm of poetry determined by the arrangement of stressed and unstressed, or long and short, syllables in each line of the poem.

Prosody is the theory and study of metre.

Iambic pentameter is the most common metre in English poetry. Each line consists of five **feet** (pentameter), each containing an unstressed syllable followed by a stressed syllable (iambic):

The curfew tolls the knell of parting day
(Gray's Elegy)

Most lines of iambic pentameter, however, are not absolutely regular in their pattern of stresses:

Shall I compare thee to a summer's day?
(Shakespeare, Sonnet 18)

A **couplet** is a pair of lines of poetry with the same metre, especially ones that rhyme:
For never was a story of more woe
Than this of Juliet and her Romeo.
(Shakespeare, Romeo and Juliet)

A **sonnet** is a poem of 14 lines, in English written in iambic pentameter, and with a fixed pattern of rhyme, often ending with a rhyming couplet.

Blank verse is poetry written in iambic pentameters that do not rhyme. A lot of Shakespeare's dramatic verse is in blank verse, as is Milton's epic *Paradise Lost*.

Free verse is poetry without a regular metre or rhyme scheme. Much twentieth century poetry is written in free verse, for example T. S. Eliot's *The Waste Land*.

Drama

The different **genres** of drama include **comedy**, **tragedy** and **farce**.

Catharsis is the process of releasing and providing relief from strong emotions such as pity and fear by watching the same emotions being played out on stage.

A **deus ex machina** is an unexpected power or event that suddenly appears to resolve a situation that seems hopeless. It is often used to talk about a character in a play or story who only appears at the end.

Dramatic irony is when a character's words carry an extra meaning, especially because of what is going to happen that the character does not know about. For example, King Duncan in Shakespeare's *Macbeth* is pleased to accept Macbeth's hospitality, not knowing that Macbeth is going to murder him that night.

Hubris is too much pride or self-confidence, especially when shown by a tragic hero or heroine who tries to defy the gods or fate.

Nemesis is what happens when the hero or heroine's past mistakes or sins finally cause his or her downfall and death.

A **soliloquy** is a speech in a play for one character who is alone on the stage and speaks his or her thoughts aloud. The most famous soliloquy in English drama is Hamlet's beginning 'To be or not to be …'

Narrative

A **novel** is a **narrative** (= a story) long enough to fill a complete book. The story may be told by a **first-person narrator**, who is a character in the story and relates what happens to himself or herself, or there may be an **omniscient narrator** who relates what happens to all the characters in the third person.

A **short story** is a story that is short enough to be read from beginning to end without stopping.

The **denouement** is the end of a book or play in which everything is explained or settled. It is often used to talk about mystery or detective stories.

Stream of consciousness is a style of writing used in novels that shows the continuous flow of a character's thoughts and feelings without using the usual methods of description or conversation. It was used particularly in the twentieth century by writers such as James Joyce and Virginia Woolf.

Appendix 6
Notes on usage

In the dictionary you will find many notes on various aspects of usage in English. These notes are listed below according to the type of note.

Which word?

These notes show the differences between pairs of words that are often confused or groups of words with similar meanings. The word in **bold** shows you the entry where you can find the note.

above / over
actual / current / present
affect / effect
afraid / frightened / scared
agenda / diary / schedule / timetable / itinerary
allow / let / permit
almost / nearly / practically
alone / lonely / lone
also / as well / too
although / even though / though / however
altogether / all together
answer / reply
around / round / about
as / like
ashamed / embarrassed
awake / awaken / wake up / waken
back – at the back / at the rear / behind
baggage / luggage
bath / bathe / swim / sunbathe
become / get / go / turn
begin / start
beside / besides
besides / apart from / except
big / large / great
blind / blindly
borrow / lend
break / recess / interval / intermission / interlude / pause
British / English / Briton / Brit
calm / calmness
can / may
care – take care of / look after / care for
cause / reason / purpose
cautious / careful
change / alter / modify / vary
citizen / subject / national
classic / classical
close / shut
clothes / clothing
coast / shore / beach / seaside
compliment / complement
comprise / compose / consist of / constitute / make up / include
condition / state
continuous / continual

country / state
court / law court / court of law
customer / client
deep / deeply
degree / certificate / diploma
disabled / handicapped
discover / invent / find out / learn / know
distrust / mistrust
double / dual
earth / floor / ground / soil / land
economic / economical
electric / electrical
employ / take on
enough / adequate / sufficient / satisfactory / acceptable / will do
entrance / entry / admission
especially / specially
event / occurrence / incident / happening
exam / examination / test / quiz
expect / wait for / hope / look forward to
farther / further / farthest / furthest
fast / quick / rapid
firstly / first of all / at first
front – in front of / in the front of
good / goodness
happen / occur / take place
hard / hardly
hardly / scarcely / barely / no sooner
hate / hatred
healthy / well
help / aid / assist / attend / be present / participate
high / tall
historic / historical
infer / imply
interested / interesting / uninterested / disinterested / uninteresting
journey / travel / trip
landscape / scenery / countryside
last / take
lastly / at last
lawful / legal
lawyer / barrister / advocate / attorney / solicitor
light / lighting
long – (for) long / (for) a long time
loud / loudly / aloud
many / a lot of / lots of
much / a lot of / lots of
naked / bare
narrow / thin
near / close
next / nearest
noise / sound

normal / usual / ordinary
old – older / elder
order / tell / instruct / command
partly / partially
peace / peacefulness
persuade / convince
place / space / room
price / cost / charge
possibility / occasion / opportunity / chance
quick / quickly / fast
quite / fairly / rather / pretty
real / true
reason / explanation / excuse / pretext /
  grounds
regretfully / regrettably
right / rightly
rise / raise
say / tell
Scottish / Scots / Scotch / Scot
sensible / sensitive
sensual / sensuous / sensory
shade / shadow
shout / cry / scream
sight / eyesight
sight / view
sign / signal
slow / slowly
small / little
soon / early / quickly
speak / talk
steal / rob / burgle / thief / robber / burglar
storey / floor
strength / force / power
student / pupil / undergraduate / graduate /
  postgraduate
sure / certain
surely / certainly
tight / tightly
under / below / underneath / beneath
unsociable / antisocial / unsocial
used to / be used to
voucher / coupon / token
want / like / care (for sth/to do sth)
wear / carry / have on
wide / broad
worried / concerned / anxious / nervous /
  excited
wrong / wrongly / wrongfully

Vocabulary building

These notes help you to choose
more interesting and varied words to use
and so increase your vocabulary. The word
in **bold** gives you the general area of
meaning of the note and shows you where to
find it.

about – ways of saying 'approximately'
bad and very bad
a bar of chocolate

body – actions expressing emotions
break – verbs for ways of breaking things
cry – verbs for ways of crying
do – household jobs: do or make?
face – expressions on your face
fat
good and very good
hand – verbs for ways of using your hands
jobs and employment – nouns
laugh – verbs for ways of laughing
learn – verbs for learning
look – verbs for ways of looking
nice and very nice
object – nouns you can use for objects
piece – words for pieces of things
see – verbs for ways of seeing
smell – adjectives and nouns
teach and teachers – verbs and nouns
thin
thing – other words you can use
walk – verbs for ways of walking
weather – nouns for types of weather
work – nouns

Grammar point

These notes help make clear points of
grammar that often cause problems.
The word in **bold** shows you the entry
where you can find the note.

avenge / revenge
can / could / be able to / manage
dare
depend on
each / every
enjoy
half / whole / quarter
if / whether
kind / sort
late / lately
likely
modal verbs
must / have (got) to / don't have to / must
  not
need
neither / either
none of
one / ones
per cent – expressing percentages
proportion
school
shall / will
should / ought / had better
should / would
sit
staff
used to
very / very much
well
whom
wish

British/American

These notes explain differences between British and American usage. The word in **bold** shows you the entry where you can find the note.

already / just / yet
bit – a bit / a little
college / university
course / program
different from / to / than
floor
have – have you got? / do you have?
holiday / vacation
hospital
inclusive / through
phone / call / ring
platform / track
post / mail
presently
purse / handbag / wallet
rent / hire / let
rubbish / garbage / trash / refuse
school – in/at school
sea / ocean
toilet / bathroom
underground / subway / metro / tube

More about

These notes give you more information about an aspect of life or language in Britain and America and show you the correct words to use. The word in **bold** shows you the topic of the note and the entry where you can find it.

America
course – ways of saying 'of course'
gender – ways of talking about men and women
hello – greetings
meals
names and titles
roads

Appendix 7
Defining vocabulary

In order to make the dictionary definitions easy to understand, we have written them using only the words in the following list of just under 3 000 words. The words in the list were carefully chosen according to their frequency in the language and their value to students as a 'core vocabulary' of English. Other forms of the words listed (for example plural forms of nouns or **-ing** forms of verbs) are also used, but not words with suffixes added. (For example **technical** is used, but not **technically**. **Careful** and **carefully** are both used and so they are each listed separately.)

Occasionally it has been necessary to use in a definition a word that is not in this list. When such a word is used it is shown in SMALL CAPITAL LETTERS. If you do not know the meaning of this word, look it up at its alphabetical place in the dictionary.

The only exceptions to the list (= words which are not in the list but which are not marked in a special way when they are used in definitions) are proper names (beginning with a capital letter) of people, places, religions, institutions, etc., such as **Jesus**, **America**, **Islam**.

a *indefinite article*
abbreviation *n.*
ability *n.*
able *adj.*
about *adv., prep.*
above *adv., prep.*
absorb *v.*
academic *adj.*
accept *v.*
acceptable *adj.*
accident *n.*
accidentally *adv.*
accommodation *n.*
according to *prep.*
account *n.*
accurate *adj.*
accurately *adv.*
accuse *v.*
achieve *v.*
achievement *n.*
acid *n., adj.*
across *adv., prep.*
act *n., v.*
action *n.*
active *adj.*
activity *n.*
actor *n.*
actual *adj.*
actually *adv.*
adapt *v.*
add *v.*
in addition (to sb/sth)
address *n., v.*
adjective *n.*
adjust *v.*
administrative *adj.*
admiration *n.*
admire *v.*
admit *v.*
adult *n., adj.*
in advance
advanced *adj.*
advantage *n.*
adventure *n.*
adverb *n.*

advertise *v.*
advertisement *n.*
advertising *n.*
advice *n.*
advise *v.*
affair *n.*
affect *v.*
affection *n.*
afford *v.*
afraid *adj.*
after *prep., conj., adv.*
afternoon *n.*
afterwards *adv.*
again *adv.*
against *prep.*
age *n.*
aged *adj.*
aggressive *adj.*
ago *adv.*
agree *v.*
agreement *n.*
ahead *adv.*
aim *n., v.*
air *n.*
air force *n.*
aircraft *n.*
airport *n.*
alcohol *n.*
alcoholic *adj.*
alive *adj.*
all *det., pron., adv.*
allow *v.*
almost *adv.*
alone *adj., adv.*
along *prep., adv.*
aloud *adv.*
alphabet *n.*
alphabetical *adj.*
already *adv.*
also *adv.*
although *conj.*
always *adv.*
American football *n.*
among *prep.*
amount *n.*

amuse *v.*
amusement *n.*
amusing *adj.*
an *indefinite article*
analyse *v.*
ancestor *n.*
ancient *adj.*
and *conj.*
anger *n.*
angle *n.*
angrily *adv.*
angry *adj.*
animal *n.*
ankle *n.*
anniversary *n.*
announce *v.*
annoy *v.*
annoying *adj.*
another *det., pron.*
answer *n., v.*
anxiety *n.*
anxious *adj.*
any *det., pron., adv.*
anyone *pron.*
anything *pron.*
anywhere *adv.*
apart *adv.*
apart from *prep.*
apartment *n.*
appear *v.*
appearance *n.*
apple *n.*
apply *v.*
appropriate *adj.*
approval *n.*
approve of *v.*
approximately *adv.*
arch *n.*
architecture *n.*
area *n.*
argue *v.*
argument *n.*
arm *n.*
armed *adj.*

army *n.*
around *adv., prep.*
arrange *v.*
arrangement *n.*
arrest *v.*
arrive *v.*
arrow *n.*
art *n.*
article *n.*
artificial *adj.*
artificially *adv.*
artist *n.*
artistic *adj.*
as *prep., adv., conj.*
ash *n.*
ashamed *adj.*
ask *v.*
asleep *adj.*
aspect *n.*
assistant *n.*
association *n.*
associated with *adj.*
at *prep.*
atmosphere *n.*
atom *n.*
attach *v.*
attack *v., n.*
attempt *v., n.*
attend *v.*
attention *n.*
attitude *n.*
attract *v.*
attraction *n.*
attractive *adj.*
audience *n.*
aunt *n.*
author *n.*
authority *n.*
automatically *adv.*
autumn/fall *n.*
available *adj.*
average *adj., n.*
avoid *v.*
awake *adj.*
award *n.*
aware *adj.*

away *adv.*
awkward *adj.*

baby *n.*
back *n., adj., adv.*
background *n.*
backwards *adv.*
bacteria *n.*
bad *adj.*
  go bad
badly *adv.*
bad-tempered *adj.*
bag *n.*
bake *v.*
balance *n., v.*
ball *n.*
ballet *n.*
band *n.*
bank *n.*
bar *n.*
bare *adj.*
bark *n.*
barrier *n.*
base *n.*
base on *v.*
baseball *n.*
basic *adj.*
basis *n.*
basket *n.*
basketball *n.*
bat *n.*
bath *n.*
bathroom *n.*
battery *n.*
battle *n.*
be *v., auxiliary v.*
beach *n.*
beak *n.*
beam *n.*
bean *n.*
bear *v., n.*
beat *n., v.*
beautiful *adj.*
beauty *n.*
because *conj.*
because of *prep.*
become *v.*

bed *n.*
bedroom *n.*
bee *n.*
beef *n.*
beer *n.*
before *prep., conj., adv.*
begin *v.*
beginning *n.*
on behalf of/on sb's behalf
behave *v.*
behaviour *n.*
behind *prep., adv.*
being *n.*
belief *n.*
believe *v.*
bell *n.*
belong *v.*
below *prep., adv.*
belt *n.*
bend *v., n.*
benefit *v., n.*
bent *adj.*
berry *n.*
beside *prep.*
best *adj., adv.*
bet *n., v.*
betray *v.*
better *adj., adv.*
between *prep., adv.*
beyond *prep., adv.*
bicycle *n.*
big *adj.*
bill *n.*
biology *n.*
bird *n.*
birth *n.*
  give birth (to sb/sth)
birthday *n.*
biscuit/cookie *n.*
bit *n.*
bite *v.*
bitter *adj.*
black *adj., n.*
blade *n.*
blame *n., v.*
bleed *v.*
blind *adj.*
block *n., v.*
blood *n.*
blow *n., v.*
blue *adj., n.*
bluish *adj.*
board *n.*
boat *n.*
body *n.*
boil *v.*
bomb *n.*
bone *n.*
book *n.*
boot *n.*
border *n.*
bored *adj.*
boring *adj.*
be born *v.*
borrow *v.*
both *det., pron.*

bottle *n.*
bottom *n., adj.*
bounce *v.*
bowels *n.*
bowl *n.*
box *n.*
boxer *n.*
boxing *n.*
boy *n.*
boyfriend *n.*
brain *n.*
branch *n.*
brave *adj.*
bread *n.*
break *v.*
breakfast *n.*
breast *n.*
breath *n.*
breathe *v.*
breathing *n.*
breed *v., n.*
brick *n.*
bridge *n.*
bright *adj.*
brightly *adv.*
bring *v.*
  bring back
broad *adj.*
broadcast *n., v.*
broken *adj.*
brother *n.*
brown *adj.*
brownish *adj.*
brush *n., v.*
bubble *n.*
build *v.*
building *n.*
bullet *n.*
bunch *n.*
burn *v.*
burnt *adj.*
burst *v.*
bury *v.*
bus *n.*
bush *n.*
business *n.*
busy *adj.*
but *conj., prep., adv.*
butter *n.*
button *n.*
buy *v.*
by *prep., adv.*

cable *n.*
cafe *n.*
cage *n.*
cake *n.*
calculate *v.*
calculation *n.*
call *v., n.*
  be called
calm *adj.*
calmly *adv.*
camera *n.*
camp *n., v.*
can *n.*
can *modal v.*
canal *n.*
cancel *v.*

candidate *n.*
candle *n.*
candy *n. (in sweet/candy)*
cap *n.*
capable of *adj.*
capital city *n.*
capital letter *n.*
captain *n.*
capture *v.*
car *n.*
card *n.*
cardboard *n.*
card game *n.*
care *n.*
  care about
  care for
career *n.*
careful *adj.*
carefully *adv.*
careless *adj.*
carelessly *adv.*
carpet *n.*
carriage *n.*
carry *v.*
  carry out
carve *v.*
case *n.*
  in case (of)
cash *n.*
cassette *n.*
castle *n.*
cat *n.*
catch *v.*
  catch fire
cause *v., n.*
CD *n.*
ceiling *n.*
celebrate *v.*
celebration *n.*
cell *n.*
cent *n.*
centimetre *n.*
central *adj.*
centre *n.*
century *n.*
ceremony *n.*
certain *adj.*
certainly *adv.*
chain *n.*
chair *n.*
chalk *n.*
chance *n.*
change *n., v.*
channel *n.*
character *n.*
characteristic *n.*
charge *v.*
  in charge of
charity *n.*
chase *v.*
cheap *adj.*
cheaply *adv.*
cheat *v.*
check *n., v.*
cheek *n.*
cheerful *adj.*
cheese *n.*
chemical *n., adj.*

chemical element *n.*
chemistry *n.*
cheque *n.*
chest *n.*
chew *v.*
chicken *n.*
chief *n.*
child *n.*
chimney *n.*
chin *n.*
chocolate *n.*
choice *n.*
choose *v.*
chop *v.*
church *n.*
cigarette *n.*
cinema/movie theater *n.*
circle *n.*
circular *adj.*
circumstances *n.*
citizen *n.*
city *n.*
claim *v., n.*
class *n.*
classical music *n.*
classroom *n.*
clause *n.*
clay *n.*
clean *adj., v.*
clear *adj., v.*
clearly *adv.*
clever *adj.*
cliff *n.*
climb *v.*
clock *n.*
close/s/ *adj., adv.*
close /z/ *v.*
closely *adv.*
closet *n. (in cupboard/closet)*
cloth *n.*
clothes *n.*
clothing *n.*
cloud *n.*
club *n.*
coal *n.*
coast *n.*
coat *n.*
coffee *n.*
coin *n.*
cold *adj., n.*
collar *n.*
collect *v.*
collection *n.*
college *n.*
colour *n.*
coloured *adj.*
  -coloured
colourful *adj.*
colourless *adj.*
column *n.*
comb *n., v.*
combination *n.*
combine *v.*
come *v.*
comfort *n., v.*
comfortable *adj.*
command *v.*

comment *n.*
commercial *adj.*
commit *v.*
committee *n.*
common *adj.*
  in common
communicate *v.*
communication *n.*
community *n.*
company *n.*
comparative *n.*
compare *v.*
comparison *n.*
compete *v.*
competition *n.*
competitor *n.*
complain *v.*
complaint *n.*
complete *adj., v.*
completely *adv.*
complicated *adj.*
compound *n.*
computer *n.*
concern *v.*
concerning *prep.*
concert *n.*
condition *n.*
confidence *n.*
confident *adj.*
confidently *adv.*
confuse *v.*
confused *adj.*
confusion *n.*
connect *v.*
connection *n.*
conscious *adj.*
consciousness *n.*
consider *v.*
consist of *v.*
consonant *n.*
contact *n.*
contain *v.*
container *n.*
contents *n.*
contest *n.*
continent *n.*
continue *v.*
continuous *adj.*
continuously *adv.*
contract *n.*
contrast *n., v.*
control *n., v.*
  in control of
  under control
convenient *adj.*
conversation *n.*
cook *v., n.*
cooker/stove *n.*
cookie *n. (in biscuit/cookie)*
cooking *n.*
cool *adj., v.*
copy *v., n.*
corn *n.*
corner *n.*
correct *adj., v.*
correctly *adv.*
cost *v., n.*
cotton *n.*
cough *v., n.*

could *modal v.*
council *n.*
count *v.*
countable *adj.*
country *n.*
countryside *n.*
county *n.*
couple *n.*
courage *n.*
course *n.*
  of course
court *n.*
  court of law
cover *v., n.*
covering *n.*
cow *n.*
cowboy *n.*
crack *n., v.*
crash *n., v.*
crazy *adj.*
cream *n., adj.*
create *v.*
creature *n.*
cricket *n.*
crime *n.*
criminal *n.*
crisp *adj.*
critical *adj.*
criticism *n.*
criticize *v.*
crop *n.*
cross *n., v.*
crowd *n.*
crowded *adj.*
cruel *adj.*
crush *v.*
cry *v., n.*
cultural *adj.*
culture *n.*
cup *n.*
cupboard/closet
  n.
cure *v.*
curl *n., v.*
curly *adj.*
current *n.*
curtain *n.*
curve *n., v.*
curved *adj.*
cushion *n.*
custom *n.*
customer *n.*
cut *v., n.*

damage *v., n.*
damp *adj.*
dance *n., v.*
dancer *n.*
danger *n.*
dangerous *adj.*
dark *adj., n.*
darkness *n.*
data *n.*
date *n.*
daughter *n.*
day *n.*
dead *adj.*
deal with *v.*
death *n.*
debate *n.*

debt *n.*
decay *v., n.*
deceive *v.*
decide *v.*
decision *n.*
deck *n.* (in
  pack/deck)
decorate *v.*
decoration *n.*
decorative *adj.*
decrease *v., n.*
deep *adj., adv.*
deeply *adv.*
deer *n.*
defeat *v., n.*
defence *n.*
defend *v.*
define *v.*
definite *adj.*
definitely *adv.*
degree *n.*
delay *n., v.*
deliberate *adj.*
deliberately *adv.*
delicate *adj.*
deliver *v.*
demand *v., n.*
dentist *n.*
department *n.*
depend on *v.*
dependent on *adj.*
depressed *adj.*
depressing *adj.*
depth *n.*
descended from
describe *v.*
description *n.*
desert *n.*
deserve *v.*
design *n., v.*
desire *n.*
desk *n.*
destroy *v.*
destruction *n.*
detail *n.*
  in detail
detailed *adj.*
determination *n.*
determined *adj.*
develop *v.*
development *n.*
device *n.*
devil *n.*
diagram *n.*
diamond *n.*
dictionary *n.*
die *v.*
difference *n.*
different *adj.*
differently *adv.*
difficult *adj.*
difficulty *n.*
dig *v.*
dinner *n.*
direct *adj., v.*
direction *n.*
directly *adv.*
dirt *n.*
dirty *adj.*
disadvantage *n.*

disagree *v.*
disagreement *n.*
disappear *v.*
disappointed *adj.*
disappointing *adj.*
disappointment *n.*
disapproval *n.*
disapprove *v.*
disapproving *adj.*
disaster *n.*
disc *n.*
discipline *n.*
discover *v.*
discovery *n.*
discuss *v.*
discussion *n.*
disease *n.*
disgust *n.*
disgusted *adj.*
disgusting *adj.*
dish *n.*
dishonest *adj.*
dishonestly *adv.*
disk *n.*
dislike *n., v.*
dismiss *v.*
disorder *n.*
display *n., v.*
dispute *n.*
dissolve *v.*
distance *n.*
distinguish *v.*
district *n.*
disturb *v.*
divide *v.*
division *n.*
divorced *adj.*
do *v.*
doctor *n.*
document *n.*
dog *n.*
dollar *n.*
door *n.*
dot *n.*
double *adj.*
doubt *n., v.*
down *adv., prep.*
downward *adj.*
downwards *adv.*
drag *v.*
dramatic *adj.*
draw *v.*
drawer *n.*
drawing *n.*
dream *n., v.*
dress *n., v.*
dressed *adj.*
drink *n., v.*
drive *v.*
driver *n.*
drop *v., n.*
drug *n.*
drum *n.*
drunk *adj.*
dry *adj.*
duck *n.*
dull *adj.*
during *prep.*
dust *n.*
duty *n.*

each *det., pron.*
ear *n.*
early *adj., adv.*
earn *v.*
earth *n.*
earthquake *n.*
easily *adv.*
east *n., adj., adv.*
eastern *adj.*
easy *adj.*
eat *v.*
economic *adj.*
economy *n.*
edge *n.*
educate *v.*
education *n.*
effect *n.*
effective *adj.*
effectively *adv.*
efficient *adj.*
efficiently *adv.*
effort *n.*
egg *n.*
eight *number*
either *det., pron.,*
  adv.
elastic *adj.*
elbow *n.*
eldest *adj.*
elect *v.*
election *n.*
electric *adj.*
electrical *adj.*
electricity *n.*
electronic *adj.*
elegant *adj.*
elephant *n.*
elevator *n.* (in
  lift/elevator)
eleven *number*
else *adv.*
e-mail *n., v.*
embarrass *v.*
embarrassed *adj.*
embarrassing *adj.*
embarrassment *n.*
emergency *n.*
emotion *n.*
emotional *adj.*
emotionally *adv.*
emphasis *n.*
emphasize *v.*
empire *n.*
employ *v.*
employee *n.*
employer *n.*
employment *n.*
empty *adj., v.*
enable *v.*
enclose *v.*
enclosed *adj.*
encourage *v.*
encouragement *n.*
end *v., n.*
  in the end
ending *n.*
enemy *n.*
energy *n.*
engine *n.*
engineer *n.*

engineering *n.*
enjoy *v.*
enjoyable *adj.*
enjoyment *n.*
enough *det., pron.,*
  adv.
enter *v.*
entertain *v.*
entertainer *n.*
entertainment *n.*
enthusiasm *n.*
enthusiastic *adj.*
entrance *n.*
entry *n.*
envelope *n.*
environment *n.*
equal *adj.*
equally *adv.*
equipment *n.*
escape *v., n.*
especially *adv.*
essential *adj.*
establish *v.*
estimate *v., n.*
euro *n.*
even *adj., adv.*
  even if
  even though
evening *n.*
evenly *adv.*
event *n.*
ever *adv.*
every *det.*
everyone *pron.*
everything *pron.*
everywhere *adv.*
evidence *n.*
evil *adj.*
exact *adj.*
exactly *adv.*
exaggerate *v.*
exam *n.*
examination *n.*
examine *v.*
example *n.*
excellent *adj.*
except *prep., conj.*
exchange *v., n.*
  in exchange (for
  sth)
excite *v.*
excited *adj.*
excitement *n.*
exciting *adj.*
exclamation *n.*
excuse *n., v.*
exercise *n.*
exist *v.*
existence *n.*
expect *v.*
expensive *adj.*
experience *n., v.*
experiment *n.*
expert *n.*
explain *v.*
explanation *n.*
explode *v.*
explosion *n.*
explosive *adj., n.*
export *n., v.*

express v.
expression n.
extent n.
extra adj.
extreme adj., n.
extremely adv.
eye n.

fabric n.
face n., v.
fact n.
factory n.
fail v.
failure n.
faint adj.
fair adj.
fairly adv.
faith n.
faithful adj.
fall v., n.
  fall asleep
false adj.
fame n.
familiar adj.
family n.
famous adj.
far adv., adj.
farm n.
farmer n.
farming n.
fashion n.
fashionable adj.
fast adj., adv.
fasten v.
fat adj., n.
fate n.
father n.
faucet n. (in
  tap/faucet)
fault n.
favour n.
  in favour (of
  sb/sth)
favourite adj., n.
fear n.
feather n.
feature n.
feed v.
feel v.
feeling n.
female adj., n.
fence n.
festival n.
fever n.
few det., adj.,
  pron.
field n.
fierce adj.
fifth ordinal
  number
fight v., n.
figure n.
file n.
fill v.
film n., v.
film/movie n.
final adj.
finally adv.
financial adj.
financially adv.

find v.
  find out
fine adj.
finely adv.
finger n.
fingernail n.
finish v., n.
fire n., v.
firm adj.
firmly adv.
first det., ordinal
  number, adv.
  at first
fish n., v.
fit adj., v.
five number
fix v.
fixed adj.
flag n.
flame n.
flash n., v.
flat adj.
flat/apartment n.
flavour n., v.
flesh n.
flight n.
float v.
flood n., v.
floor n.
flour n.
flow v., n.
flower n.
fly v., n.
fold v., n.
follow v.
food n.
foot n.
football n.
for prep.
forbid v.
force v., n.
forceful adj.
forcefully adv.
forehead n.
foreign adj.
forest n.
forget v.
forgive v.
fork n.
form n., v.
formal adj.
formally adv.
former adj.
forward adj., adv.
forwards adv.
four number
fourth ordinal
  number
frame n.
free adj., v., adv.
  free of charge
freedom n.
freely adv.
freeway n. (in
  motorway/
  freeway)
freeze v.
frequent adj.
frequently adv.
fresh adj.

friend n.
friendly adj.
friendship n.
frighten v.
frightened adj.
frightening adj.
from prep.
front adj., n.
  in front of
frozen adj.
fruit n.
fry v.
fuel n.
full adj.
full stop n.
fully adv.
fun n.
  make fun of
function n., v.
funeral n.
funny adj.
fur n.
furniture n.
further adj., adv.
furthest adj.
future n.

gain v.
gamble v.
game n.
garbage n. (in
  rubbish/
  garbage)
garden n.
gas n. (see also
  petrol)
gate n.
gather v.
general adj.
  in general
generally adv.
generous adj.
generously adv.
gentle adj.
gently adv.
genuine adj.
geography n.
get v.
ghost n.
gift n.
girl n.
girlfriend n.
give v.
  give away
  give out
  give up
glass adj., n.
glove n.
glue n.
go v.
  be going to
  go up
goal n.
goat n.
god n.
gold n., adj.
golf n.
good adj.
  good at
  good for

goodbye
  exclamation, n.
goods n.
govern v.
government n.
graceful adj.
grade n. (in
  mark/grade)
gradual adj.
gradually adv.
grain n.
gram n.
grammar n.
grand adj.
granddaughter n.
grandfather n.
grandmother n.
grandparent n.
grandson n.
grape n.
grass n.
grateful adj.
grave n.
great adj.
green adj., n.
greenish adj.
greet v.
greeting n.
grey adj., n.
greyish adj.
ground n.
group n.
grow v.
growth n.
guard v.
guess v., n.
guest n.
guide n., v.
guilt n.
guilty adj.
guitar n.
gun n.

habit n.
hair n.
hairstyle n.
hairy adj.
half n., det., pron.,
  adv.
halfway adv.
hall n.
hamburger n.
hammer n.
hand n.
handbag n.
handle n.
hang v.
happen v.
happily adv.
happiness n.
happy adj.
harbour n.
hard adj., adv.
hardly adv.
harm v., n.
harmful adj.
harmless adj.
harsh adj.
harshly adv.
hat n.

hate v.
hatred n.
have v., auxiliary
  v.
have to modal v.
he pron.
head n.
heal v.
health n.
healthy adj.
hear v.
hearing n.
heart n.
heat n., v.
heaven n.
heavily adv.
heavy adj.
heel n.
height n.
hello exclamation
help v., n.
helpful adj.
her pron., det.
herb n.
here adv.
hers pron.
herself pron.
hesitate v.
hide v.
high adj., adv.
high school n.
highly adv.
hill n.
him pron.
himself pron.
hip n.
hire v.
his det.
historical adj.
history n.
hit v., n.
hobby n.
hockey n.
hold v., n.
hole n.
holiday n.
hollow adj.
holy adj.
home adv., n.
honest adj.
honestly adv.
honour n.
hook n.
hope v., n.
hopeful adj.
horizontal adj.
horn n.
horror n.
horse n.
horse racing n.
hospital n.
hot adj.
hotel n.
hour n.
house n.
how adv.
however adv.
human n., adj.
human being n.
humorous adj.

humour *n.*
hundred *number*
hunger *n.*
hungry *adj.*
hunt *v.*
hurry *n., v.*
  in a hurry
hurt *v.*
husband *n.*
hut *n.*

I *pron.*
ice *n.*
ice cream *n.*
ice hockey *n.*
idea *n.*
identify *v.*
identity *n.*
if *conj.*
ignore *v.*
ill *adj.*
illegal *adj.*
illegally *adv.*
illness *n.*
image *n.*
imaginary *adj.*
imagination *n.*
imaginative *adj.*
imagine *v.*
immediate *adj.*
immediately *adv.*
immoral *adj.*
impatient *adj.*
import *v., n.*
importance *n.*
important *adj.*
impossible *adj.*
impress *v.*
impression *n.*
impressive *adj.*
improve *v.*
improvement *n.*
in *adv., prep.*
inability *n.*
include *v.*
income *n.*
increase *v., n.*
independent *adj.*
independently
  adv.
indirect *adj.*
indirectly *adv.*
individual *adj.*
indoors *adv.*
industrial *adj.*
industry *n.*
infect *v.*
infection *n.*
infectious *adj.*
influence *n., v.*
inform *v.*
informal *adj.*
information *n.*
injure *v.*
injured *adj.*
injury *n.*
ink *n.*
inner *adj.*
innocent *adj.*
insect *n.*

inside *prep., adv.,*
  n., adj.
instead *adv.*
instead of *prep.*
institution *n.*
instruction *n.*
instrument *n.*
insult *n., v.*
insurance *n.*
intelligence *n.*
intelligent *adj.*
intend *v.*
intention *n.*
interest *n., v.*
interested *adj.*
interesting *adj.*
international *adj.*
Internet *n.*
interrupt *v.*
interruption *n.*
interval *n.*
into *prep.*
introduce *v.*
introduction *n.*
invent *v.*
invention *n.*
invest *v.*
investigate *v.*
investigation *n.*
invitation *n.*
invite *v.*
involve *v.*
involved in
inwards *adv.*
iron *n.*
irritate *v.*
irritating *adj.*
island *n.*
issue *n.*
it *pron.*
item *n.*
its *det.*
itself *pron.*

jacket *n.*
jam *n.*
jaw *n.*
jazz *n.*
jealous *adj.*
jelly *n.*
jewel *n.*
jewellery *n.*
job *n.*
join *v.*
joint *n.*
joke *n., v.*
journalist *n.*
journey *n.*
joy *n.*
judge *v., n.*
judgement *n.*
juice *n.*
jump *v., n.*
junior *adj.*
just *adv.*
justice *n.*

keep *v.*
key *n.*
keyboard *n.*

kick *v., n.*
kill *v.*
killing *n.*
kilogram *n.*
kilometre *n.*
kind *adj., n.*
kindness *n.*
king *n.*
kiss *n., v.*
kitchen *n.*
knee *n.*
kneel *v.*
knife *n.*
knit *v.*
knitted *adj.*
knock *n., v.*
knot *n.*
know *v.*
knowledge *n.*

label *n.*
lack *v., n.*
ladder *n.*
lake *n.*
lamp *n.*
land *n., v.*
language *n.*
large *adj.*
last *det., adv., n., v.*
late *adj.*
laugh *v., n.*
laughter *n.*
law *n.*
lawyer *n.*
lay *v.*
layer *n.*
lazy *adj.*
lead *v.*
leader *n.*
leaf *n.*
lean *v.*
learn *v.*
least *det., pron.,*
  adv.
  at least
leather *n.*
leave *v.*
  leave out
left *adj., adv., n.*
leg *n.*
legal *adj.*
legally *adv.*
lemon *n.*
lend *v.*
length *n.*
less *det., pron.,*
  adv.
lesson *n.*
let *v.*
letter *n.*
level *adj., n.*
library *n.*
lid *n.*
lie *v., n.*
life *n.*
lift *v., n.*
lift/elevator *n.*
light *adj., n., v.*
lightly *adv.*
like *prep., v.*

likely *adj.*
limb *n.*
limit *n., v.*
limited *adj.*
line *n.*
link *n., v.*
lion *n.*
lip *n.*
liquid *n.*
list *n.*
listen *v.*
literature *n.*
litre *n.*
little *adj., det.,*
  pron., adv.
live /lɪv/ *v.*
live /laɪv/ *adj.*
lively *adj.*
load *v., n.*
local *adj.*
lock *v., n.*
logical *adj.*
lonely *adj.*
long *adj., adv.*
look *n., v.*
  look after
  look for
  look forward to
  look up
loose *adj.*
loosely *adv.*
lorry/truck *n.*
lose *v.*
loss *n.*
lost *adj.*
a lot *det., adv.*
loud *adj.*
loudly *adv.*
love *n., v.*
lover *n.*
low *adj., adv.*
lower *v.*
loyal *adj.*
luck *n.*
lucky *adj.*
lump *n.*
lunch *n.*
lung *n.*

machine *n.*
machinery *n.*
magazine *n.*
magic *adj., n.*
mail *n.*
main *adj.*
mainly *adv.*
make *v.*
  make sth up
male *adj., n.*
man *n.*
manage *v.*
manager *n.*
manner *n.*
many *det., pron.*
map *n.*
march *v., n.*
mark *v., n.*
mark/grade *n.*
market *n.*
marriage *n.*

married *adj.*
marry *v.*
mass *n.*
match *n., v.*
material *n.*
mathematics *n.*
matter *n., v.*
may *modal v.*
me *pron.*
meal *n.*
mean *v.*
meaning *n.*
means *n.*
  by means of
measure *v.*
measurement *n.*
meat *n.*
mechanism *n.*
medal *n.*
medical *adj.*
medicine *n.*
medium *adj.*
meet *v.*
meeting *n.*
melt *v.*
member *n.*
memory *n.*
  in memory of
mend *v.*
mental *adj.*
mentally *adv.*
mention *v.*
message *n.*
messenger *n.*
metal *n.*
method *n.*
metre *n.*
metric *adj.*
midday *n.*
middle *n.*
midnight *n.*
might *modal v.*
mild *adj.*
mile *n.*
military *adj.*
milk *n.*
million *number*
mind *n., v.*
mine *pron., n.*
mineral *n.*
minister *n.*
minute *n.*
mirror *n.*
miss *v.*
mistake *n.*
mix *v.*
mixture *n.*
model *n.*
modern *adj.*
moment *n.*
money *n.*
monkey *n.*
month *n.*
mood *n.*
moon *n.*
moral *adj.*
morals *n.*
morally *adv.*
more *det., pron.,*
  adv.

morning *n.*
most *det., pron., adv.*
mostly *adv.*
mother *n.*
motor *n.*
motor boat *n.*
motor vehicle *n.*
motorcycle *n.*
motorway/ freeway *n.*
mountain *n.*
mouse *n.*
mouth *n.*
move *v., n.*
movement *n.*
movie *n.*
movie theater *n.* (*in* cinema/ movie theater)
much *det., pron., adv.*
mud *n.*
multiply *v.*
murder *v., n.*
muscle *n.*
museum *n.*
music *n.*
musical *adj.*
musician *n.*
must *modal v.*
my *det.*
myself *pron.*
mysterious *adj.*

nail *n.*
naked *adj.*
name *n., v.*
narrow *adj.*
nation *n.*
national *adj.*
native *adj.*
natural *adj.*
naturally *adv.*
nature *n.*
navy *n.*
near *adj., adv., prep.*
nearly *adv.*
neat *adj.*
neatly *adv.*
necessary *adj.*
neck *n.*
need *v., n.*
needle *n.*
negative *adj.*
neither *det., pron., adv.*
nerve *n.*
nervous *adj.*
nest *n.*
net *n.*
never *adv.*
new *adj.*
news *n.*
newspaper *n.*
next *adj., adv., n.*
next to *prep.*
nice *adj.*
night *n.*

nine *number*
no *exclamation, det.*
nobody *pron.*
noise *n.*
noisily *adv.*
noisy *adj.*
none *pron.*
nonsense *n.*
nor *conj., adv.*
normal *adj.*
normally *adv.*
north *n., adj., adv.*
north-east *n., adj., adv.*
north-eastern *adj.*
northern *adj.*
north-west *n., adj., adv.*
north-western *adj.*
nose *n.*
not *adv.*
note *n.*
nothing *pron.*
notice *n., v.*
take notice of
noticeable *adj.*
noun *n.*
novel *n.*
now *adv.*
nowhere *adv.*
nuclear *adj.*
number *n.*
nurse *n.*
nut *n.*

obey *v.*
object *n., v.*
obtain *v.*
obvious *adj.*
occasion *n.*
occasionally *adv.*
ocean *n.*
o'clock *adv.*
of *prep.*
off *adv., prep.*
offence *n.*
offend *v.*
offensive *adj.*
offer *v., n.*
office *n.*
officer *n.*
official *adj.*
officially *adv.*
often *adv.*
oil *n.*
old *adj.*
old age *n.*
old-fashioned *adj.*
on *prep., adv.*
once *adv., conj.*
one *number, det. pron.*
one after another
onion *n.*
only *adj., adv.*
onto *prep.*
open *adj., v.*
open air

opening *n.*
openly *adv.*
opera *n.*
operate *v.*
operation *n.*
opinion *n.*
opponent *n.*
opportunity *n.*
oppose *v.*
opposed to
opposite *adj., n., prep.*
opposition *n.*
or *conj.*
orange *n., adj.*
orchestra *n.*
order *n., v.*
in order to
ordinary *adj.*
organ *n.*
organization *n.*
organize *v.*
origin *n.*
original *adj.*
originally *adv.*
ornament *n.*
other *adj., pron.*
ought to *modal v.*
our *det.*
ours *pron.*
ourselves *pron.*
out (of) *adv., prep.*
outdoor *adj.*
outdoors *adv.*
outer *adj.*
outline *n.*
outside *n., adj., prep., adv.*
outwards *adv.*
oven *n.*
over *adv., prep.*
owe *v.*
own *v., adj.*
owner *n.*

pack *v.*
pack/deck *n.*
package *n.*
packet *n.*
page *n.*
pain *n.*
painful *adj.*
paint *v., n.*
painter *n.*
painting *n.*
pair *n.*
pale *adj.*
pan *n.*
pants *n.* (*in* trousers/pants)
paper *n.*
parallel *adj.*
parcel/package *n.*
parent *n.*
park *n., v.*
parliament *n.*
part *n.*
participle *n.*
particular *adj.*
particularly *adv.*

partly *adv.*
partner *n.*
party *n.*
pass *v.*
passage *n.*
passenger *n.*
passive *adj., n..*
past *adj., n., prep., adv.*
pastry *n.*
path *n.*
patience *n.*
patient *adj.*
pattern *n.*
pause *n.*
pay *v.*
pay attention
payment *n.*
pea *n.*
peace *n.*
peaceful *adj.*
pen *n.*
pence *n.*
pencil *n.*
people *n.*
pepper *n.*
per *prep.*
perfect *adj.*
perfectly *adv.*
perform *v.*
performance *n.*
performer *n.*
perhaps *adv.*
period *n.*
permanent *adj.*
permanently *adv.*
permission *n.*
person *n.*
personal *adj.*
personality *n.*
persuade *v.*
pet *n.*
petrol/gas *n.*
philosophy *n.*
photograph *n.*
photographer *n.*
photographic *adj.*
photography *n.*
phrase *n.*
physical *adj.*
physically *adv.*
physics *n.*
piano *n.*
pick *v.*
pick up
picture *n.*
pie *n.*
piece *n.*
pile *n., v.*
pilot *n.*
pin *n.*
pink *adj.*
pinkish *adj.*
pipe *n.*
pit *n.* (*in* stone/pit)
pity *n.*
place *n., v.*
plain *adj.*
plan *n., v.*

plane *n.*
planet *n.*
plant *n., v.*
plastic *n., adj.*
plate *n.*
platform *n.*
play *v., n.*
player *n.*
playing card *n.*
pleasant *adj.*
pleasantly *adv.*
please *exclamation, v.*
pleased *adj.*
pleasing *adj.*
pleasure *n.*
plenty *pron., adv., n.*
plural *n., adj.*
pocket *n.*
poem *n.*
poetry *n.*
point *n., v.*
point of view
pointed *adj.*
poison *n.*
poisonous *adj.*
pole *n.*
police *n.*
policy *n.*
polish *v., n.*
polite *adj.*
politely *adv.*
political *adj.*
politically *adv.*
politician *n.*
politics *n.*
poor *adj.*
pop *n.*
pop music *n.*
popular *adj.*
population *n.*
port *n.*
position *n.*
positive *adj.*
possession(s) *n.*
possibility *n.*
possible *adj.*
possibly *adv.*
post *n., v.*
post office *n.*
pot *n.*
potato *n.*
pound *n.*
pour *v.*
powder *n.*
power *n.*
powerful *adj.*
practical *adj.*
practice *n.*
practise *v.*
praise *v., n.*
prayer *n.*
precious metal *n.*
precious stone *n.*
predict *v.*
prefer *v.*
pregnancy *n.*
pregnant *adj.*
preparation *n.*

prepare v.
prepared adj.
preposition n.
presence n.
present n., adj., v.
preserve v.
president n.
press v., n.
pressure n.
pretend v.
pretty adj.
prevent v.
previous adj.
previously adv.
price n.
prickly adj.
pride n.
priest n.
prince n.
princess n.
principle n.
print v., n.
printer n.
printing n.
prison n.
prisoner n.
private adj.
privately adv.
privilege n.
prize n.
probable adj.
probably adv.
problem n.
process n., v.
produce v.
product n.
production n.
profession n.
professional adj.
profit n.
program n.
programme n.
progress n.
progressive adj.
project n.
promise n., v.
pronoun n.
pronounce v.
pronunciation n.
proof n.
property n.
proposal n.
prostitute n.
protect v.
protection n.
protective adj.
protest v., n.
proud adj.
proudly adv.
prove v.
provide v.
pub n.
public n., adj.
publicly adv.
publish v.
pull v., n.
pump v., n.
punish v.
punishment n.
pure adj.

purple adj., n.
purplish adj.
purpose n.
    on purpose
push v., n.
put v.
    put on
    put out

qualification n.
qualified adj.
quality n.
quantity n.
quarrel v., n.
quarter n.
queen n.
question n., v.
quick adj.
quickly adv.
quiet adj.
quietly adv.
quite adv.

rabbit n.
race n., v.
racing n.
radio n.
rail n.
railroad n.
railway n.
rain v., n.
raise v.
range n.
rank n.
rapid adj.
rapidly adv.
rare adj.
rarely adv.
rat n.
rate n.
rather adv.
    rather than
raw adj.
ray n.
reach v.
react v.
reaction n.
read v.
reader n.
reading n.
ready adj.
real adj.
realistic adj.
reality n.
realize v.
really adv.
reason n.
reasonable adj.
receive v.
recent adj.
recently adv.
recognize v.
recommend v.
record v., n.
recording n.
red adj., n.
reddish adj.
reduce v.
reduction n.
refer to v.

reflect v.
refusal n.
refuse v.
region n.
regular adj.
regularly adv.
reject v.
relate to v.
related adj.
relation n.
relationship n.
relative adj., n.
relatively adv.
relax v.
relaxed adj.
release v.
religion n.
religious adj.
rely on v.
remain v.
remark n.
remember v.
remind v.
removal n.
remove v.
rent v., n.
repair v., n.
repeat v.
repeatedly adv.
replace v.
reply v., n.
report n., v.
represent v.
representative n.
reproduce v.
reptile n.
republic n.
reputation n.
request n., v.
require v.
rescue v.
research n.
resist v.
respect v., n.
response n.
responsibility n.
responsible adj.
rest n., v.
    the rest
restaurant n.
restrict v.
restriction n.
result n., v.
return n., v.
review v.
revolution n.
reward n.
rhythm n.
rice n.
rich adj.
rid v. (in get rid of)
ride v., n.
rider n.
ridiculous adj.
right adj., adv., n.
ring n., v.
ripe adj.
rise v., n.
risk v., n.
river n.

road n.
rob v.
rock n.
rocket n.
rod n.
role n.
roll v., n.
romantic adj.
roof n.
room n.
root n.
rope n.
rose n.
rough adj.
roughly adv.
round adj., adv.,
    prep.
route n.
row /rəʊ, AmE
    roʊ/ n., v.
royal adj.
rub v.
rubber n.
rubbish/garbage
    n.
rude adj.
rudely adv.
rugby n.
ruin v.
rule n., v.
ruler n.
run v.
runner n.
rush v., n.

sad adj.
sadly adv.
sadness n.
safe adj.
safely adv.
safety n.
sail v., n.
sailor n.
saint n.
salad n.
sale n.
salt n.
salty adj.
same adj., pron.
sand n.
sandwich n.
satisfaction n.
satisfactory adj.
satisfied adj.
satisfy v.
sauce n.
sausage n.
save v.
say v.
sb = somebody
scale n.
scene n.
scenery n.
school n.
science n.
scientific adj.
scientist n.
scissors n.
score v., n.
scratch v.

screen n.
screw v., n.
sea n.
sea fish n.
seabird n.
search v., n.
season n.
seat n.
second det.,
    ordinal number,
    adv., n.
secondary adj.
secret n., adj.
secretary n.
secretly adv.
section n.
see v.
seed n.
seem v.
sell v.
send v.
    send out
senior adj.
sense n.
sensible adj.
sensitive adj.
sentence n.
separate adj.
separately adv.
separation n.
series n.
serious adj.
seriously adv.
servant n.
serve v.
service n.
set n., v.
    set fire to sth
settle v.
seven number
several det., pron.
severe adj.
severely adv.
sew v.
sex n.
sexual adj.
sexually adv.
shade n.
shadow n.
shake v.
shallow adj.
shame n.
shape n., v.
shaped adj.
share v., n.
sharp adj.
shave v.
she pron.
sheep n.
sheet n.
shelf n.
shell n.
shellfish n.
shelter n., v.
shine v.
shiny adj.
ship n.
shirt n.
shock n., v.
shocking adj.

shoe *n.*
shoot *v.*
shop *v.*
shop/store *n.*
shopping *n.*
shore *n.*
short *adj.*
shot *n.*
should *modal v.*
shoulder *n.*
shout *v.*
show *v., n.*
shower *n.*
shut *v., adj.*
shy *adj.*
sick *adj.*
  be sick
  feel sick
side *n.*
sideways *adv.*
sight *n.*
sign *n., v.*
signal *n., v.*
signature *n.*
silence *n.*
silent *adj.*
silk *n.*
silly *adj.*
silver *n., adj.*
similar *adj.*
simple *adj.*
simply *adv.*
since *conj., prep.*
sincere *adj.*
sing *v.*
singer *n.*
singing *n.*
single *adj.*
singular *adj.*
sink *v.*
sister *n.*
sit *v.*
situated *adj.*
situation *n.*
six *number*
size *n.*
ski *v., n.*
skiing *n.*
skilful *adj.*
skilfully *adv.*
skill *n.*
skilled *adj.*
skin *n.*
skirt *n.*
sky *n.*
slave *n.*
sleep *v.*
sleeve *n.*
slice *n.*
slide *v.*
slight *adj.*
slightly *adv.*
slip *v.*
slope *n.*
slow *adj.*
  slow down
slowly *adv.*
small *adj.*
smart *adj.*

smell *v., n.*
smile *v., n.*
smoke *n., v.*
smooth *adj.*
smoothly *adv.*
snake *n.*
snow *n., v.*
so *adv., conj.*
  so that
soak *v.*
soap *n.*
soccer *n.*
social *adj.*
socially *adv.*
society *n.*
sock *n.*
soft *adj.*
soften *v.*
soil *n.*
soldier *n.*
sole *n.*
solid *adj., n.*
solution *n.*
solve *v.*
some *det., pron.*
somebody *pron.*
something *pron.*
sometimes *adv.*
somewhere *adv.*
son *n.*
song *n.*
soon *adv.*
  as soon as
sore *adj.*
sorry *adj.*
sort *n.*
soul *n.*
sound *n., v.*
soup *n.*
sour *adj.*
source *n.*
south *n., adj., adv.*
south-east *n., adj.,*
  adv.
south-eastern *adj.*
southern *adj.*
south-west *n.,*
  adj., adv.
south-western *adj.*
space *n.*
spacecraft *n.*
speak *v.*
speaker *n.*
special *adj.*
specialist *n.*
specially *adv.*
speech *n.*
speed *n.*
spell *v.*
spelling *n.*
spend *v.*
spice *n.*
spicy *adj.*
spider *n.*
spin *v.*
spirit *n.*
spiritual *adj.*
spite *n.* (*in* in spite
  of)

split *v.*
spoil *v.*
spoon *n.*
sport *n.*
spot *n.*
spray *v., n.*
spread *v.*
spring *n.*
square *adj., n.*
squeeze *v.*
staff *n.*
stage *n.*
stairs *n.*
staircase *n.*
stamp *n., v.*
stand *v., n.*
standard *n., adj.*
star *n.*
stare *v.*
start *v., n.*
state *n., v.*
statement *n.*
station *n.*
statue *n.*
status *n.*
stay *v.*
steadily *adv.*
steady *adj.*
steal *v.*
steam *n.*
steel *n.*
steep *adj.*
steeply *adv.*
steer *v.*
stem *n.*
step *v., n.*
sth = something
stick *v., n.*
  stick out
sticky *adj.*
stiff *adj.*
still *adj., adv.*
sting *v., n.*
stir *v.*
stitch *n.*
stomach *n.*
stone *n.*
stop *v., n.*
store *v.*
store *n.* (*in*
  shop/store)
storm *n.*
story *n.*
stove *n.* (*in*
  cooker/stove)
straight *adj., adv.*
strange *adj.*
strap *n.*
stream *n.*
street *n.*
strength *n.*
strengthen *v.*
stress *v., n.*
stretch *v.*
strict *adj.*
strictly *adv.*
strike *n.*
string *n.*
strip *n.*

stroke *n.*
strong *adj.*
strongly *adv.*
structure *n.*
struggle *v., n.*
student *n.*
study *v., n.*
stupid *adj.*
style *n.*
subject *n.*
substance *n.*
succeed *v.*
success *n.*
successful *adj.*
successfully *adv.*
such *det., pron.*
  such as
suck *v.*
sudden *adj.*
suddenly *adv.*
suffer *v.*
suffering *n.*
sugar *n.*
suggest *v.*
suggestion *n.*
suit *n., v.*
suitable *adj.*
suitcase *n.*
suited *adj.*
sum *n.*
summary *n.*
summer *n.*
sun *n.*
sunlight *n.*
superlative *n.,*
  adj.
supermarket *n.*
supply *v., n.*
support *v., n.*
supporter *n.*
suppose *v.*
sure *adj.*
  make sure
surface *n.*
surprise *v., n.*
surprised *adj.*
surprising *adj.*
surround *v.*
surroundings *n.*
survive *v.*
suspect *v.*
suspicion *n.*
suspicious *adj.*
swallow *v.*
swear *v.*
sweat *n.*
sweater *n.*
sweet *adj.*
sweet/candy *n.*
swell *v.*
swelling *n.*
swim *v.*
swimming pool *n.*
swing *v.*
switch *n.*
switch on/off *v.*
syllable *n.*
symbol *n.*
sympathetic *adj.*

sympathy *n.*
system *n.*

table *n.*
tail *n.*
take *v.*
  take off (*plane*)
  take over
  take part (in)
  take place
talk *v.*
tall *adj.*
tap/faucet *n.*
tape *n.*
task *n.*
taste *v., n.*
tax *n., v.*
taxi *n.*
tea *n.*
teach *v.*
teacher *n.*
teaching *n.*
team *n.*
tear /teə(r),
  AmE ter/ *v.*
tear /tɪə(r),
  AmE tɪr/ *n.*
technical *adj.*
technology *n.*
telephone *n.*
television *n.*
tell *v.*
temper *n.*
temperature *n.*
temporarily *adv.*
temporary *adj.*
ten *number*
tend *v.*
tendency *n.*
tennis *n.*
tense *n.*
tent *n.*
terrible *adj.*
test *n., v.*
text *n.*
than *prep., conj.*
thank *v.*
thank you
  exclamation, n.
thanks *n.*
that *det., pron.,*
  conj.
the *definite article*
theatre *n.*
their *det.*
theirs *pron.*
them *pron.*
themselves *pron.*
then *adv.*
theory *n.*
there *adv.*
therefore *adv.*
these *det., pron.*
they *pron.*
thick *adj.*
thickly *adv.*
thickness *n.*
thief *n.*
thin *adj.*

thing *n.*
think *v.*
third *ordinal*
  number
thirsty *adj.*
this *det., pron.*
thorough *adj.*
thoroughly *adv.*
those *det., pron.*
though *conj., adv.*
thought *n.*
thousand *number*
thread *n.*
threat *n.*
threaten *v.*
three *number*
throat *n.*
through *prep., adv.*
throw *v.*
  throw away
thumb *n.*
ticket *n.*
tidy *adj.*
tie *v., n.*
tight *adj.*
tighten *v.*
tightly *adv.*
time *n.*
tin *n.*
tip *n.*
tired *adj.*
tiring *adj.*
title *n.*
to *prep., infinitive*
  marker
toast *n.*
tobacco *n.*
today *adv.*
toe *n.*
together *adv.*
toilet *n.*
tomato *n.*
tomorrow *adv.*
tone *n.*
tongue *n.*
too *adv.*
tool *n.*
tooth *n.*
top *adj., n.*
topic *n.*
total *adj., n.*
touch *v., n.*
tour *n.*
tourist *n.*
towards *adv.*
towel *n.*
tower *n.*
town *n.*
toy *n.*
track *n.*
trade *n., v.*
trade union *n.*
tradition *n.*
traditional *adj.*
traditionally *adv.*
traffic *n.*
train *n., v.*
training *n.*
translate *v.*

transparent *adj.*
transport *n., v.*
trap *n., v.*
travel *v.*
traveller *n.*
treat *v.*
treatment *n.*
tree *n.*
trial *n.*
triangle *n.*
tribe *n.*
trick *n., v.*
trip *n.*
tropical *adj.*
trouble *n.*
trousers/pants *n.*
truck *n.*
true *adj.*
trust *v., n.*
truth *n.*
try *v.*
tube *n.*
tune *n.*
tunnel *n.*
turn *v., n.*
twelve *number*
twice *adv.*
twist *v., n.*
two *number*
type *n., v.*
typical *adj.*
tyre *n.*

ugly *adj.*
umbrella *n.*
unable *adj.*
unacceptable *adj.*
uncertain *adj.*
uncertainty *n.*
uncle *n.*
uncomfortable
  adj.
unconscious *adj.*
uncontrolled *adj.*
uncountable *adj.*
under *prep.*
underground *adj.,*
  adv.
underneath *prep.,*
  adv.
understand *v.*
understanding *n.*
underwater *adj.,*
  adv.
underwear *n.*
undo *v.*
unemployed *adj.*
unexpected *adj.*
unexpectedly *adv.*
unfair *adj.*
unfairly *adv.*
unfortunate *adj.*
unfortunately
  adv.
unfriendly *adj.*
unhappiness *n.*
unhappy *adj.*
uniform *n.*
unimportant *adj.*

union *n.*
unit *n.*
unite *v.*
united *adj.*
universe *n.*
university *n.*
unkind *adj.*
unknown *adj.*
unless *conj.*
unlikely *adj.*
unload *v.*
unnecessary *adj.*
unpleasant *adj.*
unreasonable *adj.*
unsteady *adj.*
unsuccessful *adj.*
untidy *adj.*
until *conj., prep.*
unusual *adj.*
unusually *adv.*
unwilling *adj.*
unwillingly *adv.*
up *adv., prep.*
upper *adj.*
upright *adj.*
upset *v., adj.*
upside down *adv.*
upstairs *adj., adv.,*
  n.
upward *adj.*
upwards *adv.*
urgent *adj.*
us *pron.*
use *v., n.*
  used to
  be/get used to
useful *adj.*
useless *adj.*
user *n.*
usual *adj.*
usually *adv.*

vacation *n. (in*
  holiday/
  vacation)
valid *adj.*
valley *n.*
valuable *adj.*
value *n., v.*
van *n.*
variety *n.*
various *adj.*
vary *v.*
vegetable *n.*
vehicle *n.*
verb *n.*
verse *n.*
version *n.*
vertical *adj.*
very *adv.*
victory *n.*
video *n.*
view *n.*
village *n.*
violence *n.*
violent *adj.*
violently *adv.*
violin *n.*
visible *adj.*

visit *n., v.*
visitor *n.*
voice *n.*
volume *n.*
vote *v., n.*
vowel *n.*

wage *n.*
waist *n.*
wait *v.*
wake (up) *v.*
walk *v., n.*
wall *n.*
want *v.*
war *n.*
warm *adj., v.*
warmth *n.*
warn *v.*
warning *n.*
wash *v., n.*
waste *v., n.*
watch *v., n.*
water *n.*
waterbird *n.*
wave *v., n.*
way *n.*
we *pron.*
weak *adj.*
weakness *n.*
wealth *n.*
weapon *n.*
wear *v.*
weather *n.*
weave *v.*
wedding *n.*
week *n.*
weigh *v.*
weight *n.*
welcome *v., adj.,*
  n.
well *adj., adv.*
  as well (as
  sb/sth)
well known *adj.*
west *n., adj., adv.*
western *adj.*
wet *adj.*
what *pron., det.*
whatever *det.,*
  pron.
wheat *n.*
wheel *n.*
when *adv., conj.*
whenever *conj.*
where *adv., conj.*
wherever *conj.*
whether *conj.*
which *pron., det.*
while *conj.*
whip *n., v.*
whisky *n.*
whistle *n., v.*
white *adj., n.*
whitish *adj.*
who *pron.*
whoever *pron.*
whole *adj., n.*
whom *pron.*
whose *det., pron.*

why *adv.*
wicked *adj.*
wide *adj., adv.*
widely *adv.*
width *n.*
wife *n.*
wild *adj.*
will *modal v.*
willing *adj.*
willingly *adv.*
willingness *n.*
win *v., n.*
wind /wind/ *n.*
wind /waind/ *v.*
  wind up
window *n.*
wine *n.*
wing *n.*
winner *n.*
winter *n.*
wire *n.*
wise *adj.*
wish *v., n.*
with *prep.*
within *prep.*
without *prep.*
woman *n.*
wonderful *adj.*
wood *n.*
wooden *adj.*
wool *n.*
woollen *adj.*
word *n.*
work *v., n.*
worker *n.*
world *n.*
worm *n.*
worry *v., n.*
worse *adj., adv.*
worship *v., n.*
worst *adj., n.*
worth *v., n.*
would *modal v.*
wound *n., v.*
wrap *v.*
wrist *n.*
write *v.*
writer *n.*
writing *n.*
wrong *adj., n.*
  go wrong
wrongly *adv.*

yard *n. (in*
  garden/yard)
year *n.*
yellow *adj., n.*
yellowish *adj.*
yes *exclamation,*
  n.
yesterday *adv.*
yet *adv.*
you *pron.*
young *adj.*
your *det.*
yours *pron.*
yourself *pron.*

zero *number*

Pronunciation and phonetic symbols

The British pronunciations given are those of younger speakers of General British. This includes RP (Received Pronunciation) and a range of similar accents which are not strongly regional. The American pronunciations chosen are also as far as possible the most general (not associated with any particular region). If there is a difference between British and American pronunciations of a word, the British one is given first, with *AmE* before the American pronunciation.

Consonants

p	pen	/pen/
b	bad	/bæd/
t	tea	/tiː/
d	did	/dɪd/
k	cat	/kæt/
g	get	/get/
tʃ	chain	/tʃeɪn/
dʒ	jam	/dʒæm/
f	fall	/fɔːl/
v	van	/væn/
θ	thin	/θɪn/
ð	this	/ðɪs/

s	see	/siː/
z	zoo	/zuː/
ʃ	shoe	/ʃuː/
ʒ	vision	/ˈvɪʒn/
h	hat	/hæt/
m	man	/mæn/
n	now	/naʊ/
ŋ	sing	/sɪŋ/
l	leg	/leg/
r	red	/red/
j	yes	/jes/
w	wet	/wet/

The symbol (r) indicates that British pronunciation will have /r/ only if a vowel sound follows directly at the beginning of the next word, as in **far away**; otherwise the /r/ is omitted. For American English, all the /r/ sounds should be pronounced.

/x/ represents a fricative sound as in /lɒx/ for Scottish **loch**, Irish **lough**.

Vowels and diphthongs

iː	see	/siː/	
i	happy	/ˈhæpi/	
ɪ	sit	/sɪt/	
e	ten	/ten/	
æ	cat	/kæt/	
ɑː	father	/ˈfɑːðə(r)/	
ɒ	got	/gɒt/	(British English)
ɔː	saw	/sɔː/	
ʊ	put	/pʊt/	
u	actual	/ˈæktʃuəl/	
uː	too	/tuː/	
ʌ	cup	/kʌp/	
ɜː	fur	/fɜː(r)/	
ə	about	/əˈbaʊt/	
eɪ	say	/seɪ/	
əʊ	go	/gəʊ/	(British English)
oʊ	go	/goʊ/	(American English)
aɪ	my	/maɪ/	
ɔɪ	boy	/bɔɪ/	
aʊ	now	/naʊ/	
ɪə	near	/nɪə(r)/	(British English)
eə	hair	/heə(r)/	(British English)
ʊə	pure	/pjʊə(r)/	(British English)

Many British speakers use /ɔː/ instead of the diphthong /ʊə/, especially in common words, so that **sure** becomes /ʃɔː(r)/, etc.

The sound /ɒ/ does not occur in American English, and words which have this vowel in British pronunciation will instead have /ɑː/ or /ɔː/ in American English. For instance, **got** is /gɒt/ in British English, but /gɑːt/ in American English, while **dog** is British /dɒg/, American /dɔːg/.

The three diphthongs /ɪə eə ʊə/ are found only in British English. In corresponding places, American English has a simple vowel followed by /r/, so **near** is /nɪr/, **hair** is /her/, and **pure** is /pjʊr/.

Nasalized vowels, marked with /˜/, may be retained in certain words taken from French, as in **penchant** /ˈpɒ̃ʃɒ̃/, **coq au vin** /ˌkɒk əʊ ˈvæ̃/.

Syllabic consonants

The sounds /l/ and /n/ can often be 'syllabic' – that is, they can form a syllable by themselves without a vowel. There is a syllabic /l/ in the usual pronunciation of **middle** /ˈmɪdl/, and a syllabic /n/ in **sudden** /ˈsʌdn/.

Weak vowels /i/ and /u/

The sounds represented by /iː/ and /ɪ/ must always be made different, as in **heat** /hiːt/ compared with **hit** /hɪt/. The symbol /i/ represents a vowel that can be sounded as either /iː/ or /ɪ/, or as a sound which is a compromise between them. In a word such as **happy** /ˈhæpi/, younger speakers use a quality more like /iː/, but short in duration. When /i/ is followed by /ə/ the sequence can also be pronounced /jə/. So the word **dubious** can be /ˈdjuːbiəs/ or /ˈdjuːbjəs/.

In the same way, the two vowels represented /uː/ and /ʊ/ must be kept distinct but /u/ represents a weak vowel that varies between them. If /u/ is followed directly by a consonant sound, it can also be pronounced as /ə/. So **stimulate** can be /ˈstɪmjuleɪt/ or /ˈstɪmjəleɪt/.